2025
STANDARD POSTAGE STAMP CATALOGUE

ONE HUNDRED AND EIGHTY-FIRST EDITION IN SIX VOLUMES

Volume 2B
Cyp-F

EDITOR-IN-CHIEF	Jay Bigalke
EDITOR-AT-LARGE	Donna Houseman
CONTRIBUTING EDITOR	Charles Snee
EDITOR EMERITUS	James E. Kloetzel
SENIOR EDITOR /NEW ISSUES AND VALUING	Martin J. Frankevicz
ASSOCIATE EDITOR	David Hartwig
CATALOGUE COORDINATOR	Eric Wiessinger
SENIOR GRAPHIC DESIGNER	Cinda McAlexander
SALES DIRECTOR	David Pistello
SALES DIRECTOR	Eric Roth
SALES DIRECTOR	Brenda Wyen
SALES REPRESENTATIVE	Julie Dahlstrom

Released May 2024
Includes New Stamp Listings through the March 2024 *Scott Stamp Monthly* Catalogue Update

Copyright© 2024 by
AMOS MEDIA

1660 Campbell Road, Suite A, Sidney, OH 45365
Publishers of *Linn's Stamp News, Scott Stamp Monthly, Coin World* and *Coin World Monthly.*

Scott catalog editorial team contact information
scottstamp.com | scottcatalogueeditorial@amosmedia.com

Scott catalog customer service contact information
amosadvantage.com | cuserv@amosmedia.com | 800-572-6885 | Monday-Thursday 9 a.m. to 5 p.m.; Friday 9 a.m. to noon, Eastern Standard Time

Table of contents

Letter from the editor	Vol. 2A, 3A
Acknowledgments	Vol. 2A, 4A
Information on philatelic societies	Vol. 2A, 5A
Expertizing services	Vol. 2A, 8A
Information on catalogue values, grade and condition	Vol. 2A, 9A
Grading illustrations	Vol. 2A, 10A
Gum chart	Vol. 2A, 12A
Catalogue listing policy	Vol. 2A, 13A
Understanding the listings	Vol. 2A, 14A
Special notices	Vol. 2A, 16A
Abbreviations	Vol. 2A, 16A
Basic stamp information	Vol. 2A, 18A
Terminology	Vol. 2A, 25A
The British Commonwealth of Nations	Vol. 2A, 50A
Colonies, former colonies, offices, territories controlled by parent states	Vol. 2A, 52A
Dies of British Colonial stamps referred to in the catalogue	Vol. 2A, 53A
British Colonial and Crown Agents watermarks	Vol. 2A, 54A
Countries of the World C-Cur	1
Index and Identifier	**878**
Currency conversion	884
Pronunciation Symbols	885
2025 Volume 2A-2B catalogue number additions, deletions and changes	886
Index to advertisers	892
Dealer directory yellow pages	892

See the following volumes for other country listings:
Volume 1A: United States, United Nations, Abu Dhabi-Australia; Volume 1B: Austria-B
Volume 2A: C-Cur
Volume 3A: G; Volume 3B: H-I
Volume 4A: J-L; Volume 4B: M
Volume 5A: N-Phil; Volume 5B: Pit-Sam
Volume 6A: San-Tete; Volume 6B: Thai-Z

Scott Catalogue Mission Statement

The Scott Catalogue Team exists to serve the recreational, educational and commercial hobby needs of stamp collectors and dealers.
We strive to set the industry standard for philatelic information and products by developing and providing goods that help collectors identify, value, organize and present their collections.
Quality customer service is, and will continue to be, our highest priority.
We aspire toward achieving total customer satisfaction.

Copyright Notice

The contents of this book are owned exclusively by Amos Media Co. and all rights thereto are reserved under the Pan American and Universal Copyright Conventions.

Copyright ©2024 by Amos Media Co., Sidney, Ohio. Printed in U.S.A.

COPYRIGHT NOTE
Permission is hereby given for the use of material in this book and covered by copyright if:
  (a) The material is used in advertising matter, circulars or price lists for the purpose of offering stamps for sale or purchase at the prices listed therein; and
  (b) Such use is incidental to the business of buying and selling stamps and is limited in scope and length, i.e., it does not cover a substantial portion of the total number of stamps issued by any country or of any special category of stamps of any country; and
  (c) Such material is not used as part of any catalogue, stamp album or computerized or other system based upon the Scott catalogue numbers, or in any updated valuations of stamps not offered for sale or purchase; and
  (d) Such use is not competitive with the business of the copyright owner; and
  (e) Such use is for editorial purposes in publications in the form of articles or commentary, except for computer software or the serialization of books in such publications, for which separate written permission is required.
Any use of the material in this book which does not satisfy all the foregoing conditions is forbidden in any form unless permission in each instance is given in writing by the copyright owner.

Trademark Notice

The terms SCOTT, SCOTT'S, SCOTT CATALOGUE NUMBERING SYSTEM, SCOTT CATALOGUE NUMBER, SCOTT NUMBER and abbreviations thereof, are trademarks of Amos Media Co., used to identify its publications and its copyrighted system for identifying and classifying postage stamps for dealers and collectors. These trademarks are to be used only with the prior consent of Amos Media Co.
  No part of this work may be reproduced in any form or by any means, electronic or mechanical, including photocopying, without permission in writing from Amos Media Co., P.O. Box 4129, Sidney, OH 45365-4129.

ISBN 978-0-89487-723-0

Library of Congress Card No. 2-3301

CYPRUS

ˈsī-prəs

LOCATION — An island in the Mediterranean Sea off the coast of Turkey
GOVT. — Republic
AREA — 3,572 sq. mi.
POP. — 1,210,000 (2020 est.)
CAPITAL — Nicosia

The British Crown Colony of Cyprus became a republic in 1960.
Turkey invaded Cyprus in 1974 resulting in the the northern 40% of the island becoming the Turkish Republic of Northern Cyprus. No other country recognizes this division of the island.
See Turkey in Volume 6.

12 Pence = 1 Shilling
40 Paras = 1 Piaster
9 Piasters = 1 Shilling
20 Shillings = 1 Pound
1000 Milliemes = 1 Pound (1955)
100 Cents = 1 Cyprus Pound (1983)
100 Cents = 1 Euro (2008)

Catalogue values for unused stamps in this country are for Never Hinged items, beginning with Scott 156 in the regular postage section and Scott RA1 in the postal tax section.

Values for unused stamps are for examples with original gum as defined in the catalogue introduction. Very fine examples of Nos. 1, 2 and 7-10 will have perforations touching the design on at least one or more sides due to the narrow spacing of the stamps on the plates and to imperfect perforation methods. Stamps with perfs clear on all four sides are scarce and will command higher prices.

Watermark

Wmk. 344 — Map of Cyprus and KC/K Delta

 Queen Victoria — A1

 A2   A3

 A4   A5

A6   A7

Various Watermarks as in Great Britain (#20, 23, 25, 27 & 29)

1880   Typo.   Perf. 14
1 A1 ½p rose (P 15)   125.00   115.00
   Plate 12   240.00   300.00
   Plate 19   5,750.   950.00

b. Double overprint (P 15)   45,000.
2 A2 1p red (P 216)   24.00   55.00
   Plate 217   24.00   60.00
   Plate 174   1,500.   1,500.
   Plate 181   525.00   210.00
   Plate 184   22,000.   3,500.
   Plate 193   840.00
   Plate 196   725.00
   Plate 201   27.50   57.50
   Plate 205   90.00   57.50
   Plate 208   135.00   65.00
   Plate 215   24.00   57.50
   Plate 218   32.50   65.00
   Plate 220   550.00   475.00
b. Double overprint (P 218)   5,400.
   Double overprint (P 208)   27,500.
c. Pair, one without ovpt. (P 208)   27,500.
3 A3 2½p claret (P 14)   4.50   19.00
   (P 16)   8.00   50.00
4 A4 4p lt ol grn   150.00   240.00
5 A5 6p ol gray (P 16)   575.00   750.00
6 A6 1sh green (P 13)   900.00   525.00

Black Surcharge

7 A7 30 paras on 1p red (P 216)   150.00   95.00
   Plate 201   180.00   110.00
   Plate 217   210.00   210.00
   Plate 220   175.00   190.00
b. Dbl. surch., one invtd. (P 220)   2,000.   1,500.
   Dbl. surch., one invtd. (P 216)   7,750.

No. 2 Surcharged

18mm Long

1881
8 A2 ½p on 1p (205, 216)   82.50   100.00
   Plate 174   250.00   400.00
   Plate 181   225.00   260.00
   Plate 201   115.00   140.00
   Plate 205   85.00   100.00
   Plate 208   225.00   375.00
   Plate 215   840.00   1,000.
   Plate 217   1,000.   900.00
   Plate 218   550.00   675.00
   Plate 220   325.00   450.00
b. Double surcharge (P 220)   2,750.

16mm or 16½mm Long

9 A2 ½p on 1p (P 201)   140.00   190.00
   Plate 216   400.00   460.00
a. Double surcharge (P 201, 216)   3,750.   3,000.

17mm Long

9B A2 ½p on 1p (P 201)   —   800.00
    Plate 216   —   1,200.
No. 9, Plate 218, previously listed, is believed to be a forgery.

13mm Long

10 A2 ½p on 1p red (P 215)   52.50   75.00
    Plate 205   425.00
    Plate 217   175.00   110.00
    Plate 218   90.00   125.00
c. Double surcharge (P 215)   550.00   700.00
   Double surcharge (P 205)   875.00
e. Triple surcharge (P 215)   875.00
   Triple surcharge (P 205)   4,750.
   Triple surcharge (P 217)
   Triple surcharge (P 218)   4,750.
h. Quadruple surch. (P 205, 215)   7,500.
j. "CYPRUS" double (P 218)   6,000.

A8

1881, July   Typo.   Wmk. 1
11 A8 ½pi emer grn   210.00   52.50
12 A8 1pi rose   425.00   37.50
13 A8 2pi ultramarine   525.00   37.50
14 A8 4pi olive green   1,050.   375.00
15 A8 6pi olive gray   1,900.   500.00

Postage and revenue stamps of Cyprus with "J.A.B." (the initials of Postmaster J.A. Bulmer) in manuscript, or with "POSTAL SURCHARGE" (with or without "J. A. B."), were not Postage Due stamps but were employed for accounting purposes between the chief PO at Larnaca and the sub-offices.
See Nos. 19-25, 28-37. For surcharges see Nos. 16-18, 26-27.

Nos. 1881-1894 Surcharged in Black

1882   Wmk. 1
16 A8 ½pi on ½pi grn   750.00   92.50
17 A8 30pa on 1pi rose   1,750.   140.00
a. Double surcharge, one inverted   1,400.   850.00

1884   Wmk. 2
18 A8 ½pi on ½pi grn   190.00   10.00
a. Double surcharge   3,200.
See Nos. 26, 27.

1882-94   Die B

For description of Dies A and B see "Dies of British Colonial Stamps" in Table of Contents.

19 A8 ½pi green   16.00   2.50
20 A8 30pa violet   12.50   14.00
21 A8 1pi rose   15.50   11.00
22 A8 2pi blue   15.50   2.10
23 A8 4pi pale ol grn   20.00   42.50
24a A8 6pi   275.00   800.00
25a A8 12pi   190.00   450.00
Nos. 19-25a (7)   544.50   1,322.

Die A

10a A0 ½pi   25.00   3.25
b. ½pi emerald   6,000.   525.00
20a A8 30pa lilac   85.00   30.00
21a A8 1pi   110.00   4.50
22a A8 2pi   170.00   4.00
23a A8 4pi   375.00   40.00
24 A8 6pi olive gray   75.00   21.00
25 A8 12pi brown org   225.00   45.00
Nos. 19a-25 (7)   1,065.   147.75

Nos. 1881-1894 Surcharged in Black

Type I — Figures "½" 8mm apart.
Type II — Figures "½" 6mm apart.
The space between the fraction bars varies from 5½ to 8½mm but is usually 6 or 8mm.

Black Surcharge Type I

1886   Wmk. 2
26 A8 ½pi on ½pi grn   525.00   17.50
a. Type II   325.00   100.00

Wmk. 1
27 A8 ½pi on ½pi grn   8,750.   500.00
a. Type II   24,000.
No. 27a probably is a proof.

1894-96   Wmk. 2
28 A8 ½pi grn & car rose   5.25   1.75
29 A8 30pa violet & green   5.75   6.00
30 A8 1pi rose & ultra   8.50   1.75
31 A8 2pi ultra & mar   19.00   1.75

32 A8 4pi ol green & vio   22.50   17.50
33 A8 6pi ol gray & grn   22.50   40.00
34 A8 9pi brown & rose   29.00   40.00
35 A8 12pi brn org & blk   25.00   72.50
36 A8 18pi slate & brown   60.00   62.50
37 A8 45pi dk vio & ultra   125.00   165.00
Nos. 28-37 (10)   322.50   408.75

 King Edward VII — A12

1903   Typo.
38 A12 ½pi grn & car rose   16.00   1.40
39 A12 30pa violet & green   26.00   5.50
40 A12 1pi car rose & ultra   42.50   7.50
41 A12 2pi ultra & mar   90.00   18.00
42 A12 4pi ol grn & vio   62.50   27.50
43 A12 6pi ol brn & grn   52.50   145.00
44 A12 9pi brn & car rose   125.00   275.00
45 A12 12pi org brn & blk   37.50   87.50
46 A12 18pi blk & brn   100.00   175.00
47 A12 45pi dk vio & ultra   250.00   600.00
Nos. 38-47 (10)   802.00   1,342.

1904-07   Wmk. 3
48 A12 5pa bis & blk ('07)   1.25   2.00
49 A12 10pa org & grn ('07)   6.00   1.90
50 A12 ½pi grn & car rose   12.00   1.60
51 A12 30pa redsh vio & grn   21.50   2.75
52 A12 1pi car rose & ultra   17.50   1.10
53 A12 2pi ultra & mar   20.00   2.00
54 A12 4pi ol grn & red vio   32.50   20.00
55 A12 6pi ol brn & grn   32.50   17.00
56 A12 9pi brn & car rose   52.50   9.75
57 A12 12pi org brn & blk   40.00   67.50
58 A12 18pi blk & brn   55.00   15.00
59 A12 45pi dk vio & ultra   120.00   175.00
Nos. 48-59 (12)   410.75   315.60

CYPRUS

King George V — A13

1912

61a	A13	10pa org yel & br grn ('15)	2.75	1.60
62	A13	½pi grn & car rose	2.90	.35
63	A13	30pa vio & grn	3.25	2.40
64	A13	1pi car & ultra	5.75	1.90
65	A13	2pi ultra & mar	8.50	2.25
66	A13	4pi ol grn & red vio	5.50	5.25
67	A13	6pi ol brn & grn	6.00	11.50
68	A13	9pi brn & car rose	42.50	28.00
69	A13	12pi org brn & blk	25.00	57.50
70	A13	18pi blk & brn	50.00	50.00
71	A13	45pi dl vio & ultra	130.00	170.00
		Nos. 61a-71 (11)	282.15	330.75

1921-23   **Wmk. 4**

72	A13	10pa org & grn	16.00	13.50
73	A13	10pa gray & yel	16.00	9.50
74	A13	30pa violet & grn	3.75	2.00
75	A13	30pa green	9.00	1.75
76	A13	1pi rose & ultra	26.00	45.00
77	A13	1pi violet & car	4.00	5.00
78	A13	1½pi org & blk	12.50	7.25
79	A13	2pi ultra & red vio	35.00	25.00
80	A13	2pi rose & ultra	16.00	27.50
81	A13	2¾pi ultra & red vio	11.00	12.00
82	A13	4pi ol grn & red vio	19.00	26.00
83	A13	6pi ol brn & grn	37.50	80.00
84	A13	9pi brn & car	47.50	95.00
85	A13	18pi black & brn	90.00	175.00
86	A13	45pi dl vio & ultra	275.00	325.00
		Nos. 72-86 (15)	618.25	849.50

Wmk. 3

87	A13	10sh grn & red, yel	425.00	900.00
88	A13	£1 vio & blk, red		1,400. 3,250.

Years of issue: Nos. 73, 75, 77-78, 80-81, 87-88, 1923; others, 1921.

A14

1924-28   **Chalky Paper**   **Wmk. 4**

89	A14	¼pi gray & brn org	2.10	.55
90	A14	½pi gray blk & blk	6.25	14.50
91	A14	½pi grn & dp grn ('25)	2.50	1.10
92	A14	¾pi grn & dp grn	4.25	1.10
93	A14	¾pi gray blk & blk ('25)	4.50	1.10
94	A14	1pi brn vio & org brn	2.40	2.10
95	A14	1½pi org & blk	3.50	14.50
96	A14	1½pi car ('25)	5.25	1.60
97	A14	2pi car & grn	4.25	21.00
98	A14	2pi org & blk ('25)	15.00	4.25
99	A14	2½pi ultra ('25)	9.00	1.90
100	A14	2¾pi ultra & dl vio	3.75	5.00
101	A14	4pi ap grn & vio	5.25	5.25
102	A14	4½pi blk & yel, emer	4.00	5.25
103	A14	6pi grn ol & grn	5.25	9.00
104	A14	9pi brn & dk vio	9.00	5.75
105	A14	12pi org brn & blk	14.50	65.00
106	A14	18pi blk & org	29.00	5.75
		Revenue cancel		1.00
107	A14	45pi gray vio & ultra	65.00	45.00
		Revenue cancel		1.50
108	A14	90pi grn & red, yel	125.00	270.00
		Revenue cancel		3.75
109	A14	£5 blk, yel ('28)	3,750.	8,000.
		On cover (overfranked)		275.00

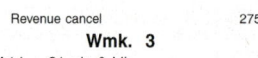

		Revenue cancel		275.00

Wmk. 3

110	A14	£1 vio & blk, red	350.00	900.00
		Revenue cancel		12.50
		Nos. 89-108 (20)	319.75	479.70

Nos. 96 and 99 are on ordinary paper.

Silver Coin of Amathus
A15

Philosopher Zeno
A16

Map of Cyprus
A17

Discovery of Body of St. Barnabas
A18

Cloisters of Bella Paise Monastery
A19

Badge of the Colony
A20

Hospice of Umm Haram at Larnaca
A21

Statue of Richard Coeur de Lion, London
A22

St. Nicholas Cathedral, Famagusta
A23

King George V
A24

Perf. 12

1928, Feb. 1   **Engr.**   **Wmk. 4**

114	A15	¾pi dark violet	3.75	1.60
115	A16	1pi Prus bl & blk	4.00	2.00
116	A17	1½pi red	7.50	2.25
117	A18	2½pi ultramarine	4.75	2.75
118	A19	4pi dp red brown	9.50	9.50
119	A20	6pi dark blue	14.00	32.50
120	A21	9pi violet brown	11.00	17.50
121	A22	18pi dk brn & blk	30.00	35.00
122	A23	45pi dp blue & vio	52.50	62.50
123	A24	£1 brn & dp blue	275.00	400.00
		Nos. 114-123 (10)	412.00	565.60

50th year of Cyprus as a British colony.

Ruins of Vouni Palace — A25

Columns at Salamis — A26

Silver Jubilee Issue
Common Design Type

1935, May 6   **Perf. 11x12**

136	CD301	¾pi gray blk & ultra	4.25	1.50
137	CD301	1½pi car & dk bl	6.25	3.00
138	CD301	2½pi ultra & brn	5.25	1.90
139	CD301	9pi brn vio & ind	24.00	28.00
		Nos. 136-139 (4)	39.75	34.40
		Set, never hinged	60.00	

Peristerona Church — A27

Soli Theater — A28

Kyrenia Castle and Harbor — A29

Kolossi Castle — A30

St. Sophia Cathedral
A31

Bairakdar Mosque
A32

Queen's Window, St. Hilarion Castle — A33

Buyuk Khan, Nicosia — A34

Forest Scene — A35

1934, Dec. 1   **Engr.**   **Perf. 12½**

125	A25	¼pi yel brn & ultra	1.40	1.10
		Never hinged	2.10	
a.		Vert. pair, imperf. between	52,500.	35,000.
126	A26	½pi green	1.90	1.25
		Never hinged	2.10	
a.		Vert. pair, imperf. between	18,000.	20,000.
127	A27	¾pi vio & blk	3.50	.45
		Never hinged	4.50	
a.		Vert. pair, imperf. between	52,500.	
128	A28	1pi brn & blk	3.00	2.50
		Never hinged	4.50	
a.		Vert. pair, imperf. between	26,000.	26,000.
b.		Horiz. pair, imperf. btwn.	19,000.	
129	A29	1½pi rose red	4.00	2.10
		Never hinged	6.00	
130	A30	2½pi dk ultra	5.25	2.40
		Never hinged	7.75	
131	A31	4½pi dk car & blk	5.25	5.00
		Never hinged	14.00	
132	A32	6pi blue & blk	12.50	20.00
		Never hinged	26.00	
133	A33	9pi dl vio & blk brn	20.00	8.50
		Never hinged	32.50	
134	A34	18pi ol grn & blk	55.00	50.00
		Never hinged	120.00	
135	A35	45pi blk & emer	120.00	85.00
		Never hinged	225.00	
		Nos. 125-135 (11)	231.80	178.30
		Set, never hinged	405.00	

Common Design Types pictured following the introduction.

Coronation Issue
Common Design Type

1937, May 12   **Perf. 11x11⅛**

140	CD302	¾pi dark gray	1.00	1.00
141	CD302	1½pi dark car	1.25	2.50
142	CD302	2½pi deep ultra	1.50	3.00
		Nos. 140-142 (3)	3.75	6.50
		Set, never hinged	7.75	

Ruins of Vouni Palace — A36

Columns at Salamis — A37

Peristerona Church — A38

Soli Theater — A39

Kyrenia Castle and Harbor — A40

Kolossi Castle — A41

Map of Cyprus
A42

Bairakdar Mosque
A43

Citadel, Famagusta
A44

Buyuk Khan
A45

Forest Scene
A46

King George VI
A47

1938-44   **Wmk. 4**   **Perf. 12½**

143	A36	¼pi yel brn & ultra	.60	.60
144	A37	½pi green	.80	.50
145	A38	¾pi violet & blk	7.25	1.75
146	A39	1pi orange	.90	.40
a.		Perf. 13½x12½ ('44)	375.00	30.00
		Never hinged	575.00	
147	A40	1½pi rose car	3.25	2.00
147A	A40	1½pi lt vio ('43)	.90	.75
147B	A38	2pi car & blk ('42)	.90	.45
c.		Perf. 12½x13½ ('44)	2.00	12.50
		Never hinged	3.25	
148	A41	2½pi ultramarine	15.00	4.50
148A	A41	3pi dp ultra ('42)	1.25	.60
149	A42	4½pi gray	.90	.40
150	A43	6pi blue & blk	1.25	1.10
151	A44	9pi dk vio & blk	1.00	.80
152	A45	18pi ol grn & blk	5.00	1.75
153	A46	45pi blk & emer	16.00	5.00
154	A47	90pi blk & brt vio	21.00	8.00
155	A47	£1 ind & dl red	45.00	32.50
		Nos. 143-155 (16)	121.00	61.10
		Set, never hinged	275.00	

See Nos. 164-166.

Catalogue values for unused stamps in this section, from this point to the end of the section, are for Never Hinged items.

CYPRUS

Peace Issue
Common Design Type
1946, Oct. 21 Engr. Perf. 13½x14
156 CD303 1½pi purple .45 .25
157 CD303 3pi deep blue .45 .45

Silver Wedding Issue
Common Design Types
1948, Dec. 20 Photo. Perf. 14x14½
158 CD304 1½pi purple 1.00 .55

Engr.; Name Typo.
Perf. 11½x11
159 CD305 £1 dark blue 57.50 77.50

UPU Issue
Common Design Types
Perf. 13½, 11x11½
1949, Oct. 10 Engr. Wmk. 4
160 CD306 1½pi violet .65 1.60
161 CD307 2pi deep carmine 1.75 1.60
162 CD308 3pi indigo 1.10 1.50
163 CD309 9pi rose violet 1.10 6.00
Nos. 160-163 (4) 4.60 10.70

Types of 1938-43
Perf. 12½
1951, July 2 Engr.
164 A37 ½pi purple 3.75 .75
165 A40 1½pi deep green 6.25 1.25
166 A41 4pi deep ultra 6.75 1.40
Nos. 164-166 (3) 16.75 3.40

Coronation Issue
Common Design Type
1953, June 2 Perf. 13½x13
167 CD312 1½pi brt grn & black 2.75 .25

Carobs — A48

Copper Pyrites Mine — A49

Coin of Paphos — A49a

St. Hilarion Castle — A50

Queen Elizabeth II and Cyprian Coin Devices — A51

Designs: 3m, Grapes. 5m, Oranges. 15m, Troodos forest. 20m, Aphrodite beach. 30m, Kyrenia. 35m. Harvest in Mesaoria. 40m, Famagusta harbor. 100m, Hala Sultan Tekke. 250m, Kanakaria church. £1, Queen Elizabeth II and devices of Byzantium, Lusignan, Ottoman Empire and Venice.

Perf. 11½
1955, Aug. 1 Engr. Wmk. 4
168 A48 2m chocolate .30 .50
169 A48 3m violet blue .30 .25
170 A48 5m orange 1.15 .25
171 A49 10m gray grn & chocolate 1.40 .25
172 A49 15m indigo & olive 4.00 .50
173 A49 20m ultra & brown 1.40 .25
174 A49a 25m aquamarine 3.65 .25
175 A49 30m carmine & blk 3.40 .25
176 A49 35m aqua & org brn 1.40 .50
177 A49 40m brn & dk grn 2.25 .75

Perf. 13½
178 A50 50m red brn & aqua 2.35 .30
179 A50 100m bl green & mag 14.75 .60
180 A50 250m vio brn & dk blue gray 18.00 13.00

Perf. 11x11½
181 A51 500m lilac rose & grnsh gray 42.50 15.00
182 A51 £1 grnsh gray & brn red 34.00 52.50
  Revenue cancel 1.00
Nos. 168-182 (15) 130.85 85.60

Republic

Nos. 168-182 Overprinted in Dark Blue

1960, Aug. 16 Ovpt. 10x6½mm
183 A48 2m chocolate .30 .75
184 A48 3m violet blue .30 .25
185 A48 5m orange 2.25 .25

Overprint 12½x11mm
186 A49 10m gray grn & choc 1.00 .25
187 A49 15m indigo & ol 3.25 .30
188 A49 20m ultra & brn 1.75 1.50
  a. Double overprint 12,000.
189 A49 25m aquamarine 1.75 1.75
190 A49 30m car & black 1.75 .30
  a. Double overprint 45,000.
191 A49 35m aqua & org 1.75 .70
192 A49 40m choc & dk grn 2.00 2.50

2-line overprint 2½mm apart
193 A50 50m red brown & aqua 2.00 .75
194 A50 100m bl grn & mag 9.00 2.50
195 A50 250m vio brn & dk blue gray 30.00 5.50

2-line overprint 22mm apart

196 A51 500m lil rose & grnsh gray 45.00 27.00
197 A51 £1 grnsh gray & brn red 50.00 62.50
Nos. 183-197 (15) 152.10 106.80

The overprint, in Greek and Turkish, reads "Republic of Cyprus."

Map of Cyprus — A52

Wmk. 314
1960, Aug. 16 Engr. Perf. 11½
198 A52 10m brown & green .30 .25
199 A52 30m blue & brown .60 .50
200 A52 100m purple & black 1.75 1.50
Nos. 198-200 (3) 2.65 2.25

Independence of Republic of Cyprus.

Europa Issue

Nineteen Doves Flying as One — CD4

Perf. 14x13½
1962, Mar. 19 Litho. Unwmk.
201 CD4 10m lilac .30 .25
202 CD4 40m deep ultra .30 .25
203 CD4 100m emerald .30 .25
Nos. 201-203 (3) .90 .75

Admission of Cyprus to Council of Europe.

Malaria Eradication Emblem — A54

1962, May 14 Perf. 14x13½
204 A54 10m gray green & black .30 .25
205 A54 30m red brown & black .35 .25

WHO drive to eradicate malaria.

Iron Age Jug — A55

St. Barnabas Church, Salamis — A56

Designs: 5m, Grapes. 10m, Head of Apollo. 15m, St. Sophia Church, Nicosia. 30m, Temple of Apollo. 35m, Head of Aphrodite. 40m, Skiing on Mt. Troodos. 50m, Ruins of Gymnasium, Salamis. 100m, Hala Sultan Tekke (sheep, Salt Lake Larnaca and tomb). 250m, Bella Paise Monastery. 500m, Cyprus mouflon. £1, St. Hilarion Castle.

Perf. 13½x14, 14x13½
1962, Sept. 17 Wmk. 344
206 A55 3m dk brn & sal .30 .30
207 A55 5m dull green & red lilac .30 .25
208 A55 10m dk slate grn & yel green .30 .25
209 A55 15m dk brn & rose vio .35 .25
210 A56 25m salmon & brn .40 .25
211 A55 30m lt bl & dk bl .30 .25
212 A55 35m dk bl & pale grn .40 .25
213 A56 40m vio bl & dk bl 1.30 1.75
214 A56 50m olive bis & dk grn .50 .25
215 A55 100m brn & yel brn 3.75 .30
216 A55 250m tan & black 9.75 2.40
217 A55 500m brown & olive 18.50 9.00
218 A56 £1 gray & green 19.75 30.00
Nos. 206-218 (13) 55.90 45.50

Wmk. 344 is found in two positions: normal or inverted on vertical stamps, and reading up or down on horizontal stamps.
For overprints see Nos. 232-236, 265-268.
For surcharge see No. 273.

Europa Issue, 1962
Common Design Type
Perf. 14x13½
1963, Jan. 28 Wmk. 344
219 CD5 10m ultra & black 1.35 .25
220 CD5 40m red & black 4.50 1.50
221 CD5 150m green & black 15.50 5.00
Nos. 219-221 (3) 21.35 6.75

Cypriot Farm Girl — A57

75m, Statue of Demeter, goddess of agriculture.

1963, Mar. 21 Perf. 13½x14
222 A57 25m blk, ultra & ocher 1.10 .30
223 A57 75m dk car, gray & blk 3.00 2.75

FAO "Freedom from Hunger" campaign.

Cub Scout and Tents — A58

20m, Sea Scout. 150m, Boy Scout & mouflon.

1963, Aug. 21 Wmk. 344
224 A58 3m multicolored .30 .25
225 A58 20m multicolored .40 .25
226 A58 150m multicolored 1.10 2.50
  a. Souvenir sheet of 3 120.00 200.00
Nos. 224-226 (3) 1.80 3.00

Boy Scout movement in Cyprus, 50th anniv. No. 226a contains 3 imperf. stamps similar to Nos. 224-226 with simulated perforations. Sold for 250m.

Red Cross Nurse — A59

Children's Home, Kyrenia — A60

Perf. 13½x14, 14x13½
1963, Sept. 9 Litho. Wmk. 344
227 A59 10m multicolored .55 .25
228 A60 100m multicolored 4.00 5.25

Intl. Red Cross, cent.

Europa Issue

Stylized Links, Symbolizing Unity — CD6

1963, Nov. 4 Perf. 14x13½
229 CD6 20m multicolored 1.65 .45
230 CD6 30m multicolored 1.65 .45
231 CD6 150m multicolored 15.00 7.75
Nos. 229-231 (3) 18.30 8.65

Nos. 208, 211, 213-215 Overprinted in Ultramarine

1964, May 5 Perf. 13½x14, 14x13½
232 A55 10m dk sl grn & yel grn .30 .25
233 A55 30m lt blue & dk blue .30 .25
234 A55 40m vio bl & dull bl .30 .25
235 A55 50m ol bis & dk grn .30 .25
236 A55 100m brn & yel brown .30 .55
Nos. 232-236 (5) 1.50 1.60

Decision by the UN and its Security Council to help restore the country to normality and to seek a solution of its problems.

Clay Mask and Soli Theater — A62

Designs: 35m, Curium theater. 50m, Salamis theater. 100m, Performance of "Othello" in front of Othello Tower.

1964, June 15 Perf. 13½x14
237 A62 15m multicolored .95 .25
238 A62 35m multicolored .95 .25
239 A62 50m multicolored .95 .25
240 A62 100m multicolored 1.65 2.25
Nos. 237-240 (4) 4.50 3.00

400th anniversary of Shakespeare's birth.

Boxers — A63

14th century B.C. art: 10m, Runners, vert. 75m, Chariot.

1964, July 6 Perf. 13½x14, 14x13½
241 A63 10m brn, bis & blk .30 .25
242 A63 25m gray bl, bl & brn .30 .25
243 A63 75m brick red, blk & brn .40 .70
  a. Souvenir sheet of 3 5.15 20.00
Nos. 241-243 (3) 1.00 1.20

18th Olympic Games, Tokyo, Oct. 10-25, 1964. No. 243a contains three imperf. stamps similar to Nos. 241-243 with gray marginal inscription. Sheet sold for 250m; the difference between face value and selling price went for the promotion of classical athletics in Cyprus.

Europa Issue

Symbolic Daisy — CD7

Perf. 13½x14
1964, Sept. 14   Litho.   Wmk. 344
244 CD7 20m bis brn & red brn   1.10   .25
245 CD7 30m lt blue & dk blue   1.10   .25
246 CD7 150m grn & ol grn   8.75   4.50
   Nos. 244-246 (3)   10.95   5.00

CEPT, 5th anniv. The 22 petals of the flower symbolize the 22 members of the organization.

 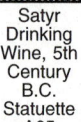

Satyr Drinking Wine, 5th Century B.C. Statuette A65

Modern Winery A66

Cypriot Wine Industry: 10m, Dionysus and Acme drinking wine, 3rd century mosaic. 50m, Commandaria wine, Knight Templar and Kolossi Castle.

Perf. 14x13½, 13½x14
1964, Oct. 26   Wmk. 344
247 A66 10m multicolored   .30   .25
248 A65 40m multicolored   .60   .80
249 A65 50m multicolored   .80   .25
250 A66 100m multicolored   1.20   1.65
   Nos. 247-250 (4)   2.90   2.95

Pres. John F. Kennedy (1917-1963) A67

Perf. 14x13½
1965, Feb. 15   Litho.   Wmk. 344
251 A67 10m violet blue   .30   .25
252 A67 40m green   .30   .35
253 A67 100m rose claret   .30   .40
   a. Souvenir sheet of 3   2.25   13.00
   Nos. 251-253 (3)   .90   1.00

No. 253a contains 3 imperf. stamps similar to Nos. 251-253 with simulated perforations. Sold for 250m, 100m going to charitable organizations in Cyprus.

Old Couple A68

Mother and Children by A. Diamantis A69

45m, Man with broken leg (accident insurance).

1965, Apr. 12   Perf. 13½x14
254 A68 30m dull green & tan   .30   .25
255 A68 45m dk vio bl, bl & gray   .30   .25

Perf. 13½x12½
256 A69 75m buff & red brown   1.25   1.75
   Nos. 254-256 (3)   1.85   2.25

Introduction of Social Insurance Law.

ITU Emblem, Old and New Communication Equipment — A70

1965, May 17   Litho.   Perf. 14x13½
257 A70 15m brn, yel & blk   .80   .25
258 A70 60m grn, lt grn & blk   7.00   3.50
259 A70 75m dk & lt bl & blk   8.25   5.00
   Nos. 257-259 (3)   16.05   8.75

ITU, cent.

ICY Emblem — A71

1965, May 17   Wmk. 344
260 A71 50m multicolored   .80   .25
261 A71 100m multicolored   1.30   .55

International Cooperation Year.

Europa Issue

Leaves and Fruit — CD8

Perf. 14x13½
1965, Sept. 27   Litho.   Wmk. 344
262 CD8 5m org, org brn & black   .55   .25
263 CD8 45m lt grn, org brn & black   3.25   2.20
264 CD8 150m gray, org brn & black   7.00   5.00
   Nos. 262-264 (3)   10.80   7.45

Nos. 206, 208, 211 and 216 Overprinted in Dark Blue

1966, Jan. 31   Perf. 13½x14, 14x13½
265 A55 3m dk brn & salmon   .30   .55
266 A55 10m dk sl grn & yel green   .30   .25
267 A56 30m lt bl & dk blue   .30   .25
268 A56 250m tan & black   .90   2.25
   Nos. 265-268 (4)   1.80   3.30

UN General Assembly's resolution to mediate the dispute between Greeks and Turks on Cyprus, Dec. 18, 1965.

St. Barnabas, Ancient Icon — A73

Chapel over Tomb of St. Barnabas — A74

Bishop Anthemios of Constantine Dreaming of St. Barnabas, Discovering Tomb, etc. — A75

Design: 15m, Discovery of body of St. Barnabas (scene as in type A18).

Perf. 13x14, 14x13
1966, Apr. 25   Litho.   Wmk. 344
269 A73 15m multicolored   .30   .25
270 A74 25m multicolored   .30   .25
271 A73 100m multicolored   .50   2.00

Size: 110x91mm
Imperf
272 A75 250m multicolored   2.25   15.50
   Nos. 269-272 (4)   3.35   18.00

1900th anniv. of the death of St. Barnabas.

No. 206 Surcharged with New Value and Three Bars

Perf. 13½x14
1966, May 30   Litho.   Wmk. 344
273 A55 5m on 3m dk brn & sal   .30   .25

Gen. K. S. Thimayya — A76

1966, June 6   Perf. 14x13½
274 A76 50m tan & black   .35   .25

In memory of Gen. Kodendera Subayya Thimayya (1906-1965), commander of the UN Peace-keeping Force on Cyprus.

Europa Issue

Symbolic Sailboat — CD9

Perf. 13½x14
1966, Sept. 26   Litho.   Wmk. 344
275 CD9 20m multicolored   .35   .25
276 CD9 30m multicolored   .35   .25
277 CD9 150m multicolored   2.40   2.75
   Nos. 275-277 (3)   3.10   3.25

Stavrovouni Monastery A78

St. Nicholas Cathedral, Famagusta A79

Ingot Bearer, Bronze Age — A80

Designs: 5m, St. James' Church, Tricomo, vert. 10m, Zeno of Citium, marble bust, vert. 15m, Ship from 7th cent. BC vase, horiz. 20m, Silver coin, 4th cent. BC (head of Hercules with lion skin). 25m, Sleeping Eros (1st cent. marble statue; horiz.). 35m, Hawks on 11th cent. gold and enamel scepter from Curium. 40m, Marriage of David (7th cent. silver disc). 50m, Silver coin of Alexander the Great showing Hercules and Zeus, horiz. 100m, Bird catching fish on 7th cent. BC jug. 500m, The Rape of Ganymede (3rd cent. mosaic). £1, Aphrodite (1st cent. marble statue).

Perf. 12x12½, 12½x12
1966, Nov. 21   Litho.   Wmk. 344
278 A78 3m bl, dl yel, grn & black   .40   .25
279 A78 5m bk bl, ol & blk   .30   .25
280 A78 10m olive & black   .30   .25

Perf. 14x13½, 13½x14
281 A79 15m org brn, blk & red brn   .30   .25
282 A79 20m red brn & blk   1.25   1.55
283 A79 25m red brn, gray & black   .40   .25
284 A79 30m aqua, tan & blk   .60   .30
285 A79 35m dk car, yel & blk   .60   .45
286 A79 40m brt bl, gray & blk   .80   .45
287 A79 50m org brn, gray & blk   1.10   .25
288 A79 100m gray, buff, blk & red   4.00   .25

Perf. 13x14
289 A80 250m dull yel, grn & blk   1.10   .50
290 A80 500m multicolored   3.00   .90
291 A80 £1 gray, lt gray & black   2.50   7.75
   Nos. 278-291 (14)   16.65   13.65

Electric Power Station, Limassol — A81

Arghaka-Maghounda Dam — A82

Designs: 35m, Troodos Highway. 50m, Cyprus Hilton Hotel. 100m, Ships in Famagusta Harbor.

Perf. 14x13½, 13½x14
1967, Apr. 10   Litho.   Wmk. 344
292 A81 10m lt brn, dark brn & yellow   .30   .25
293 A82 15m lt bl, bl & grn   .30   .25
294 A82 35m dark gray, indigo & dark grn   .30   .25
295 A82 50m gray, olive & blue   .30   .25
296 A82 100m gray, ind & bl   .35   1.20
   Nos. 292-296 (5)   1.55   2.20

1st development program, 1962-66, completion.

Europa Issue, 1967
Common Design Type

1967, May 2   Perf. 13x14
Size: 21x37mm
297 CD10 20m yel grn & olive   .30   .25
298 CD10 30m rose vio & pur   .30   .25
299 CD10 150m pale brn & brn   1.95   2.40
   Nos. 297-299 (3)   2.55   2.90

Javelin Thrower, Map of Eastern Mediterranean and "Victory" — A83

Map of Eastern Mediterranean, Victory Statue and: 35m, Runner. 100m, High jumper. 250m, Amphora, map of Eastern Mediterranean and Victory statue.

Perf. 13½x13
1967, Sept. 4   Litho.   Wmk. 344
300 A83 15m multicolored   .30   .25
301 A83 35m multicolored   .30   .30
302 A83 100m multicolored   .35   1.00

Size: 97x77mm
Imperf
303 A83 250m multicolored   1.35   11.00
   Nos. 300-303 (4)   2.30   12.55

Cyprus-Crete-Salonika Athletic Games.

A84

ITY Emblem and: 10m, Marble Forum at Salamis, Church of St. Barnabas and Bellapais Abbey. 40m, Famagusta Beach. 50m, Plane and Nicosia International Airport. 100m, Youth Hostel and skiing on Mt. Troodos.

Perf. 13½x13
1967, Oct. 16   Litho.   Wmk. 344
304 A84 10m multicolored   .30   .25
305 A84 40m multicolored   .30   1.00
306 A84 50m multicolored   .30   .25
307 A84 100m multicolored   .30   1.00
   Nos. 304-307 (4)   1.20   2.50

Intl. Tourist Year, 1967.

CYPRUS

St. Andrew, 6th Century Mosaic A85

Crucifixion, 15th Century A86

The Three Kings, 15th Century Fresco — A87

1967, Nov. 8   Perf. 13x13½
308	A85	25m multicolored	.30	.25
309	A86	50m multicolored	.30	.25
310	A87	75m multicolored	.30	.25
		Nos. 308-310 (3)	.90	.75

St. Andrew's Monastery, cent. (25m); Exhibition of Art of Cyprus, Paris, Nov. 7, 1967-Jan. 3, 1968 (50m); 20th anniv. of UNESCO (75m).

Human Rights Flame and Stars — A88

Designs: 90m, Human Rights flame and UN emblem. 250m, Scroll showing Article One of the Declaration of Human Rights.

1968, Mar. 18   Perf. 13½x14   Wmk. 344
| 311 | A88 | 50m multicolored | .30 | .25 |
| 312 | A88 | 90m multicolored | .30 | .70 |

Size: 110x90mm   Imperf
| 313 | A88 | 250m multicolored | .65 | 9.50 |
| | | Nos. 311-313 (3) | 1.25 | 10.45 |

Intl. Human Rights Year.

Europa Issue, 1968
Common Design Type
1968, Apr. 29   Perf. 14x13½
314	CD11	20m multicolored	.30	.25
315	CD11	30m dk car rose, gray brn & blk	.30	.25
316	CD11	150m multicolored	1.10	2.40
		Nos. 314-316 (3)	1.70	2.90

Boy Holding Milk, UNICEF Emblem A89

Aesculapius and WHO Emblem A90

Perf. 14x13½, 13½x14
1968, Sept. 2   Wmk. 344
| 317 | A89 | 35m dk red, lt brn & blk | .30 | .25 |
| 318 | A90 | 50m gray ol, blk & grn | .30 | .25 |

21st anniv. of UNICEF (No. 317), 20th anniv. of the WHO (No. 318).

Discus Thrower — A91

25m, Runners. 100m, Stadium, Mexico City.

Perf. 13½x14, 14x13½
1968, Oct. 24   Litho.
319	A91	10m multicolored	.30	.25
320	A91	25m vio blue & multi	.30	.25
321	A91	100m blue & multi, horiz.	.30	1.25
		Nos. 319-321 (3)	.90	1.75

19th Olympic Games, Mexico City, 10/12-27.

ILO Emblem — A92

Perf. 12x13½
1969, Mar. 3   Wmk. 344
| 322 | A92 | 50m bl, vio bl & org brn | .30 | .25 |
| 323 | A92 | 90m gray, blk & org brn | .30 | .55 |

ILO, 50th anniv.

Ancient Map of Cyprus — A93

Design: 50m, Medieval map of Cyprus.

Perf. 13½x13
1969, Apr. 7   Wmk. 344
| 324 | A93 | 35m multicolored | .30 | .30 |
| 325 | A93 | 50m olive & multi | .30 | .25 |

1st Intl. Congress of Cypriot Studies.

Europa Issue

"EUROPA" and "CEPT" — CD12

1969, Apr. 28   Litho.   Perf. 14x13½
326	CD12	20m bl, blk & gray	.30	.25
327	CD12	30m cop red, blk & ocher	.30	.25
328	CD12	150m grn, blk & yel	1.00	2.20
		Nos. 326-328 (3)	1.60	2.70

CEPT, 10th anniv.

European Roller — A95

Birds: 15m, Audouin's gull. 20m, Cyprus warbler. 30m, Eurasian jay, vert. 40m, Hoopoe, vert. 90m, Eleonora's falcon, vert.

Perf. 13½x12, 12x13½
1969, July 7   Wmk. 344
329	A95	5m multicolored	.30	.25
330	A95	15m multicolored	.35	.25
331	A95	20m multicolored	.35	.25
332	A95	30m multicolored	.35	.25
333	A95	40m multicolored	.40	.30
334	A95	90m multicolored	1.05	4.00
		Nos. 329-334 (6)	2.80	5.30

Nativity, Mural, 1192 — A96

Christmas: 45m, Nativity, mural in Church of Ayios Nicolaos tis Steghis, 14th century. 250m, Virgin and Child between Archangels Michael and Gabriel, mosaic in Church of Panayia Angeloktistos, 6th-7th centuries. Design of 20m is a mural in Church of Panayia tou Arakos, Lagoudhera.

1969, Nov. 24   Litho.   Perf. 13½x13
| 335 | A96 | 20m multicolored | .30 | .25 |
| 336 | A96 | 45m multicolored | .30 | .25 |

Size: 109x89mm   Imperf
| 337 | A96 | 250m dk blue & multi | 3.50 | 16.50 |
| | | Nos. 335-337 (3) | 4.10 | 17.00 |

Mahatma Gandhi — A97

1970, Jan. 26   Perf. 14x13½
| 338 | A97 | 25m multicolored | .55 | .25 |
| 339 | A97 | 75m multicolored | .80 | .75 |

Birth cent. of Mohandas K. Gandhi (1869-1948), leader in India's struggle for independence.

Europa Issue

Interwoven Threads — CD13

1970, May 4   Litho.   Wmk. 344
340	CD13	20m brn, yel & org	.30	.25
341	CD13	30m brt bl, yel & org	.30	.25
342	CD13	150m brt rose lil, yel & orange	1.10	2.25
		Nos. 340-342 (3)	1.70	2.75

Landscape with Flowers — A99

Designs: Various landscapes with flowers.

Perf. 13x14
1970, Aug. 3   Litho.   Wmk. 344
343	A99	10m multicolored	.30	.25
344	A99	50m multicolored	.30	.25
345	A99	90m multicolored	.55	1.40
		Nos. 343-345 (3)	1.15	1.90

European Nature Conservation Year.

Education Year Emblem A100

Grapes and Partridge (Mosaic) A101

UN Emblem, Dove, Globe and Wheat — A102

Perf. 13x14, 14x13
1970, Sept. 7   Litho.   Wmk. 344
346	A100	5m tan, blk & brn	.30	.25
347	A101	15m multicolored	.30	.25
348	A102	75m multicolored	.30	.75
		Nos. 346-348 (3)	.90	1.25

Intl. Education Year (No. 346); 50th General Assembly of the Intl. Vine and Wine Office (No. 347); 25th anniv. of the UN (No. 348).

Virgin and Child, Mural from Podhithou Church, 16th Century A103

Perf. 14x14½
1970, Nov. 23   Photo.   Unwmk.
349	A103	Strip of three	.45	.70
a.		25m Left angel	.30	.25
b.		25m Virgin and Child	.30	.25
c.		25m Right angel	.30	.25
350	A103	75m multicolored	.30	.35

Christmas. Design of No. 349 is same as No. 350, but divided by perforation into 3 stamps with 25m denomination each. Size of No. 349: 71x46mm; size of No. 350: 42x31mm.

Cotton Napkin A104

Festive Costume A105

Drinking Cup, 7th Cent. B.C. — A106

Mouflon from Mosaic Pavement, 3rd Century — A107

Cypriot Art: 5m, St. George, bas-relief on pine board, 19th cent. 20m, kneeling donors, painting, Church of St. Mamas, 1465. 25m, Mosaic head, 5th cent. A.D. 30m, Athena mounting horse-drawn chariot, terracotta figurine, 5th cent. B.C. 40m, Shepherd playing pipe, 14th cent. fresco. 50m, Woman's head, limestone, 3rd cent. B.C. 75m, Angel, mosaic, 6th cent. 90m, Mycenaean silver bowl, 14th cent. B.C. 500m, Woman and tree, decoration from amphora, 7th-6th cent. B.C. £1, God statue (horned helmet), from Enkomi, 12th cent. B.C., vert.

Perf. 12½x13½ (A104), 13x14 (A105), 14x13 (A106), 13½x13, 13x13½ (A107)
1971, Feb. 22   Wmk. 344
351	A104	3m blk, red & brn	.35	.35
352	A104	5m citron, red brn & black	.30	.25
353	A105	10m multicolored	.30	.25
354	A106	15m bister brn, blk & slate	.30	.25
355	A105	20m slate, red brn & black	.40	.35
356	A105	25m multicolored	.30	.25
357	A106	30m multicolored	.30	.25
358	A105	40m gray & multi	1.10	.75
359	A105	50m bl, bio & blk	.90	.25
360	A105	75m cit & multi	2.00	.85
361	A106	90m multicolored	2.25	1.65
362	A107	250m lt red brn, brn & black	1.75	.25
363	A107	500m tan & multi	.90	.35
364	A107	£1 multicolored	1.75	.50
		Nos. 351-364 (14)	12.90	6.55

For surcharges & overprints see Nos. 403, 424-427, 444, RA1.

Europa Issue

"Fraternity, Cooperation, Common Effort" — CD14

1971, May 3   Litho.   Perf. 14x13½
Size: 36½x23½mm
365	CD14	20m lt bl, vio bl & blk	.30	.25
366	CD14	30m brt yel grn, yel & blk	.30	.25
367	CD14	150m yel, grn & blk	1.20	2.25
		Nos. 365-367 (3)	1.80	2.75

CYPRUS

Archbishop Kyprianos, 1821 — A109

Paintings: 30m, Young Greek Taking Oath, horiz. 100m, Bishop Germanòs of Patras Declaring Greek Independence.

Perf. 13x13½, 13½x13
1971, July 9   **Wmk. 344**
368	A109	15m multicolored	.30	.25
369	A109	30m multicolored	.30	.25
370	A109	100m multicolored	.30	.50
		Nos. 368-370 (3)	.90	1.00

150th anniversary of Greek independence.

Arch and Castle — A110

Tourist Publicity: 25m, Decorated gourd and sun over shore, vert. 60m, Mountain road, vert. 100m, Village church.

Perf. 13½x13, 13x13½
1971, Sept. 20
371	A110	15m vio bl & multi	.30	.25
372	A110	25m ocher & multi	.30	.25
373	A110	60m green & multi	.30	.60
374	A110	100m blue & multi	.30	.60
		Nos. 371-374 (4)	1.20	1.70

Virgin and Child — A111

1971, Nov. 22   **Perf. 13½x14**
375	A111	10m shown	.30	.25
376	A111	50m The Three Kings	.30	.35
377	A111	100m Shepherds	.30	.35
a.		Strip of 3, Nos. 375-377	.40	.75

Christmas.

Heart and Electrocardiogram A112

1972, Apr. 11   **Perf. 13½x12½**
| 378 | A112 | 15m bister & multi | .30 | .25 |
| 379 | A112 | 50m brown & multi | .30 | .45 |

"Your heart is your health," World Health Day.

Europa Issue

Sparkles, Symbolic of Communications CD15

1972, May 22   **Perf. 12½x13½**
380	CD15	20m brn, org & fawn	.35	.25
381	CD15	30m pur, org & lilac	.35	.25
382	CD15	150m dk ol, org & brt green	1.75	2.75
		Nos. 380-382 (3)	2.45	3.25

Archery, Olympic and Motion Emblems — A114

1972, July 24   **Perf. 14x13½**
383	A114	10m shown	.30	.25
384	A114	40m Wrestling	.35	.25
385	A114	100m Soccer	.55	1.65
		Nos. 383-385 (3)	1.20	2.15

20th Olympic Games, Munich, 8/26-9/11.

Apollo, Silver Stater, Marion, 5th Century B.C. — A115

Silver Staters of Cyprus: 30m, Eagle's head, Paphos, c. 460 B.C. 40m, Pallas Athena, Lapithos, 388-387 B.C. 100m, Sphinx (obverse) and lotus flower (reverse), Idalion, c. 460 B.C.

1972, Sept. 25   **Litho.**   **Wmk. 344**
Coins in Silver
386	A115	20m lt grnsh bl & blk	.30	.25
387	A115	20m pale bl & silver	.30	.25
388	A115	40m ol bister & black	.30	.25
389	A115	100m pale brn & blk	.65	1.10
		Nos. 386-389 (4)	1.55	1.85

Bathing the Christ Child — A116

Christmas: 20m, The Three Kings. 100m, Nativity. 250m, The Nativity, 1466, mural in Church of the Holy Cross, Platanistasa. The designs of the 10m, 20m, 100m, show details from mural shown entirely on 250m.

1972, Nov. 20   **Litho.**   **Perf. 13½x14**
390	A116	10m multicolored	.30	.25
391	A116	20m multicolored	.30	.25
392	A116	100m multicolored	.30	.35

Size: 110x90mm
Imperf
| 393 | A116 | 250m multicolored | 1.20 | 5.00 |
| | | Nos. 390-393 (4) | 2.10 | 5.85 |

Landscape, Troodos Mountains A117

100m, FIS Congress emblem and map of Cyprus.

Perf. 14x13½
1973, Mar. 13   **Wmk. 344**
| 394 | A117 | 20m blue & multi | .30 | .25 |
| 395 | A117 | 100m blue & multi | .30 | .40 |

29th Meeting of the Intl. Ski Fed. (FIS), Nicosia, June 1973.

Europa Issue

Post Horn of Arrows — CD16

1973, May 7   **Size: 37x21mm**
396	CD16	20m dl bl & multi	.30	.25
397	CD16	30m multicolored	.30	.25
398	CD16	150m multicolored	1.20	1.90
		Nos. 396-398 (3)	1.80	2.40

Archbishop's Palace, Nicosia — A119

Traditional Architecture: 30m, Konak, Nicosia, 18th century, vert. 50m, House, Gourri, 1850, vert. 100m, House, Rizokarpaso, 1772.

1973, July 23   **Perf. 14x13, 13x14**
399	A119	20m multicolored	.30	.25
400	A119	50m multicolored	.30	.25
401	A119	50m multicolored	.30	.25
402	A119	100m multicolored	.45	.85
		Nos. 399-402 (4)	1.35	1.60

No. 354 Surcharged

1973, Sept. 24   **Perf. 14x13**
| 403 | A106 | 20m on 15m multi | .30 | .25 |

Cyprus Scout Emblem A120

EEC Emblem A121

FAO Emblem — A121a

Cyprus Airways Emblem — A122

Interpol Emblem — A122a

1973, Sept. 24   **Perf. 13x14, 14x13**
404	A120	10m brn ol, ol & buff	.30	.25
405	A121	25m pur, bl & plum	.30	.25
406	A121a	35m grn, gray grn & citron	.30	.25
407	A122	50m black & blue	.30	.25
408	A122a	100m brown & fawn	.55	.80
		Nos. 404-408 (5)	1.75	1.80

60th anniv. of Cyprus Boy Scout Organization; association of Cyprus with EEC; 10th anniv. of FAO; 25th anniv. of Cyprus Airways; 50th anniv. of Intl. Criminal Police Organization.

Archangel Gabriel A123

Virgin and Child A124

Christmas: 100m, Panaya tou Araka Church, horiz. Designs of 10m, 20m are from wall paintings in Arakas Church.

1973, Nov. 26   **Wmk. 344**
409	A123	10m multicolored	.30	.25
410	A123	20m multicolored	.30	.25
411	A124	100m multicolored	.45	.75
		Nos. 409-411 (3)	1.05	1.25

Grapes — A125

1974, Mar. 18   **Litho.**   **Perf. 13x14**
412	A125	25m shown	.30	.25
413	A125	50m Grapefruit	.30	.55
414	A125	50m Oranges	.30	.55
415	A125	50m Lemons	.30	.55
a.		Strip of 3, #413-415	.60	2.20
		Nos. 412-415 (4)	1.20	1.90

Europa Issue

Rape of Europa — A126

Design shows a silver stater of Marion, second half of 5th century B.C.

1974, Apr. 29
416	A126	10m org brn & multi	.30	.25
417	A126	40m multicolored	.45	.35
418	A126	150m dk car & multi	1.20	3.00
		Nos. 416-418 (3)	1.95	3.60

Solon, 3rd Century Mosaic — A127

Designs: 10m, Front page of "History of Cyprus," by Archimandrite Kyprianos, 1788, vert. 100m, St. Neophytos, mural. 250m, Maps of Cyprus and Greek Islands, by Abraham Ortelius, 1584.

Perf. 13x14, 14x13
1974, July 22   **Litho.**   **Wmk. 344**
419	A127	10m multicolored	.30	.25
420	A127	25m multicolored	.30	.25
421	A127	100m multicolored	.65	.85

Size: 110x90mm
Imperf
| 422 | A127 | 250m multicolored | 1.40 | 6.50 |
| | | Nos. 419-422 (4) | 2.65 | 7.85 |

2nd Intl. Congress of Cypriot Studies, Nicosia, Sept. 15-21. No. 422 has simulated perforations.

Nos. 353, 358-359, 362 Overprinted

Perf. 13x14, 13½x13
1974, Oct. 14   **Litho.**
424	A105	10m multicolored	.30	.25
425	A105	40m multicolored	.30	.95
426	A105	50m multicolored	.30	.25
427	A107	250m multicolored	.65	2.50
		Nos. 424-427 (4)	1.55	3.95

UN Security Council Resolution No. 353 to end hostilities on Cyprus. Overprint is in 3 lines on No. 427.

Virgin and Child, 1466 A129

Adoration of the Kings, c. 1500 A130

Christmas: 100m, Flight into Egypt, mural, Monastery Church of Ayios Neophytos, c. 1500. (50m is from same church). Mural on 10m is in Church of Stavros tou Agiasmati.

Perf. 14x13, 13x14
1974, Dec. 2   **Wmk. 344**
429	A129	10m multicolored	.30	.25
430	A130	50m multicolored	.30	.25
431	A129	100m multicolored	.30	.45
		Nos. 429-431 (3)	.90	.95

CYPRUS

Disabled Persons, Emblem A131

Council of Europe Flag A132

1975, Feb. 17   Unwmk.   Perf. 14½
| 432 | A131 | 30m ocher & ultra | .30 | .25 |
| 433 | A132 | 100m multicolored | .55 | .65 |

8th European Meeting of the Intl. Society for the Rehabilitation of Disabled Persons (30m; design shows society's emblem); 25th anniv. of Council of Europe (100m).

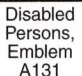
First Mail Coach in Cyprus — A133

1975, Feb. 17
| 434 | A133 | 20m multicolored | .30 | .25 |
| 435 | A133 | 50m ultra & multi | .30 | .25 |

Centenary (in 1974) of UPU.

The Distaff, by Michael Kashalos — A134

Europa (Paintings): 30m, Still Life, by Christotoros Savva. 150m, Virgin and Child of Liopetri, by Georghios P. Georghiou.

Perf. 13½x14½

1975, Apr. 28   Photo.
436	A134	20m multicolored	.30	.45
437	A134	30m multicolored	.30	.70
438	A134	150m multicolored	.45	.60
a.	Strip of 3, #436-438		.90	1.60

Red Cross Flag over Cyprus A135

Nurse and Nurses Emblem A136

Steatite Female Figure, c. 3000 B.C. — A137

Perf. 12½x13½, 13½x12½

1975, Aug. 4   Litho.   Wmk. 344
439	A135	25m blue green & red	.30	.25
440	A136	30m dp blue & lt grn	.30	.25
441	A137	75m multicolored	.60	1.00
Nos. 439-441 (3)			.90	1.50

Cyprus Red Cross, 25th anniv.; Intl. Nurses' Day 1975; IWY.

Submarine Cable A138

International Telephone A139

Perf. 12½x13½, 13½x12½

1975, Oct. 13   Litho.
| 442 | A138 | 50m multicolored | .35 | .25 |
| 443 | A139 | 100m purple & org | .40 | 1.00 |

Telecommunications achievements.

No. 351 Surcharged

1976, Jan. 5   Perf. 12½x13½
| 444 | A104 | 10m on 3m multi | .30 | 1.10 |

Vessel in Shape of Woman, 19th Century A140

Composite Vessel, 2100-2000 B.C. A141

Europa: 100m, Byzantine goblet, 15th cent.

Perf. 13x14

1976, May 3   Litho.   Wmk. 344
445	A140	20m violet & multi	.30	.25
446	A141	60m gray & multi	.55	.90
447	A140	100m brown & multi	1.00	1.90
Nos. 445-447 (3)			1.85	3.05

Self-help Housing — A142

Cyprus Airways Jet — A143

Designs: 25m, Women sewing in front of tents. 30m, Aforestation.

1976, May 3   Perf. 14x13
448	A142	10m multicolored	.30	.25
449	A142	25m multicolored	.30	.25
450	A142	30m multicolored	.30	.25
451	A143	60m multicolored	.30	.55
Nos. 448-451 (4)			1.20	1.30

Re-activation of the economy.

Terracotta Statue, 7th-6th Centuries B.C. A144

Bronze Plate with Inscription, Idalion, 5th Century B.C. A145

Designs: 10m, Limestone head of bearded man, 5th cent. B.C. 20m, Gold necklace, Lamboussa, 6th cent. A.D. 25m, Terracotta warrior on horseback, 7th cent. B.C. 30m, Limestone figure, priest of Aphrodite, 5th cent. B.C. 50m, Mycenaean crater, 13th cent. B.C. 60m, Limestone sarcophagus, Amathus, 550-500 B.C. 100m, Gold bracelet, Lamboussa, 6th cent. A.D. 250m, Silver dish, Lamboussa, 6th cent. A.D. 500m, Bronze stand, 10th cent. B.C. £1, Marble statue of Artemis, Larnaca, 4th cent. B.C.

Perf. 12x13½

1976, June 7   Wmk. 344
Size: 22x33mm
| 452 | A144 | 5m brn & multi | .30 | .90 |
| 453 | A144 | 10m gray & multi | .30 | .65 |

Size: 24x37mm, 37x24mm
Perf. 13x14, 14x13
454	A144	20m red & multi	.30	.25
455	A144	25m lt brn & blk	.30	.25
456	A144	30m green & multi	.30	.25
457	A145	40m bis gray & blk	.30	.60
458	A145	50m brn & multi	.30	.25
459	A145	60m dk brn & multi	.30	.25
460	A145	£1 crim & multi	.40	.45

Size: 28x40mm
Perf. 13x12½
461	A144	250m dk bl & multi	.50	1.55
462	A144	500m yel & multi	.65	1.65
463	A144	£1 slate & multi	1.10	1.90
Nos. 452-463 (12)			5.05	8.95

George Washington — A146

1976, July 5   Perf. 13x13½
| 464 | A146 | 100m multicolored | .45 | .35 |

American Bicentennial.

Montreal Olympic Games Emblem A147

Various Sports A148

100m, like 60m, with different sports.

1976, July 5   Unwmk.   Perf. 14
465	A147	20m yel, blk & dk car	.30	.25
466	A148	60m ultra & multi	.30	.30
467	A148	100m lilac & multi	.35	.40
Nos. 465-467 (3)			.95	.95

21st Olympic Games, Montreal, Canada, July 17-Aug. 1.

Children in Library A149

Low-cost Housing Development A150

Hands Shielding Eye — A151

Perf. 13½x14, 13x13½

1976, Sept. 27   Litho.   Wmk. 344
468	A149	40m black & multi	.30	.25
469	A150	50m multicolored	.30	.25
470	A151	80m ultra & multi	.35	.65
Nos. 468-470 (3)			.95	1.15

Books for Children (40m); Habitat, UN Conference on Human Settlements, Vancouver, Canada, May 31-June 11 (50m); World Health Day: Foresight prevents blindness (80m).

Archangel Michael — A152

Christmas: 15m, Archangel Gabriel. 150m, Nativity. Icons in Ayios Neophytos Monastery, 16th century.

1976, Nov. 15   Unwmk.   Perf. 12½
471	A152	10m multicolored	.25	.25
472	A152	15m multicolored	.25	.25
473	A152	150m multicolored	.30	.80
Nos. 471-473 (3)			.80	1.30

Landscape, by A. Diamantis A154

Europa (Paintings): 60m, Trees and Meadow, by T. Kanthos. 120m, Harbor, by V. Ioannides.

Perf. 13½x13

1977, May 2   Litho.   Unwmk.
475	A154	20m multicolored	.30	.25
476	A154	60m multicolored	.30	.60
477	A154	65m multicolored	.65	1.90
Nos. 475-477 (3)			1.25	2.75

Cyprus No. 196 — A155

Perf. 13x13½

1977, June 13   Litho.   Wmk. 344
| 478 | A155 | 120m multicolored | .35 | .35 |

25th anniv. of reign of Queen Elizabeth II.

Silver Tetradrachm of Demetrios Poliorcetes A156

Ancient Coins of Cyprus: 10m, Bronze coin of Emperor Trajan. 60m, Silver Tetradrachm of Ptolemy VIII. 100m, Gold octadrachm of Arsinoe II.

1977, June 13   Unwmk.   Perf. 14
479	A156	10m multicolored	.30	.25
480	A156	40m multicolored	.30	.25
481	A156	60m multicolored	.40	.40
482	A156	100m multicolored	.55	1.05
Nos. 479-482 (4)			1.55	1.95

Archbishop Makarios (1913-1977), Pres. of Cyprus — A157

20m, Archbishop in full vestments. 250m, Head.

Perf. 13x14

1977, Sept. 10   Litho.   Unwmk.
483	A157	20m multicolored	.30	.25
484	A157	60m multicolored	.30	.25
485	A157	250m multicolored	.55	1.20
Nos. 483-485 (3)			1.15	1.70

Handicrafts A158

Sputnik over Earth A159

Designs: 40m, Map of the Mediterranean Sea. 60m, Gold medals and sports emblems.

Perf. 13½x12

1977, Oct. 17   Wmk. 344
486	A158	20m multicolored	.30	.25
487	A158	40m multicolored	.30	.25
488	A158	60m multicolored	.30	.25
489	A159	80m multicolored	.30	.95
Nos. 486-489 (4)			1.20	1.70

Revitalization of handicrafts (20m); Man and the biosphere (40m); Gold medals won by secondary school students in France for long jump and 200 meter race (60m); 60th anniv. of Bolshevik Revolution (80m).

Nativity — A160

Christmas (Children's Drawings): 10m, Three Kings following the star. 150m, Flight into Egypt.

Perf. 14x13½
1977, Nov. 21   Litho.   Unwmk.
490	A160	10m multicolored	.30	.25
491	A160	40m multicolored	.30	.25
492	A160	150m multicolored	.30	.85
	Nos. 490-492 (3)		.90	1.35

Demetrios Lipertis (1866-1937) A161

150m, Vasilis Michaelides (1849-1917).

1978, Mar. 6   Wmk. 344   Perf. 14x13
| 493 | A161 | 40m bister & olive | .30 | .25 |
| 494 | A161 | 150m gray, ver & blk | .35 | .55 |

Cypriot poets.

Chrysorrhogiatissa Monastery — A162

Europa: 75m, Kolossi Castle. 125m, Municipal Library, Paphos.

Perf. 14½x13
1978, Apr. 24   Litho.   Unwmk.
495	A162	25m multicolored	.30	.25
496	A162	75m multicolored	.30	.40
497	A162	125m multicolored	.50	1.40
	Nos. 495-497 (3)		1.10	2.05

Makarios as Archbishop 1950-1977 — A163

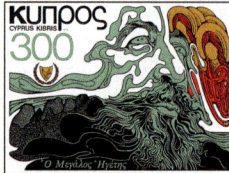
"The Great Leader" A164

Archbishop Makarios: 25m, Exiled, Seychelles, 1956-1957. 50m, President of Cyprus, 1960-1977. 75m, Soldier of Christ. 100m, Freedom fighter.

Perf. 14x14½
1978, Aug. 3   Unwmk.
498	A163	15m multicolored	.30	.25
499	A163	25m multicolored	.30	.25
500	A163	50m multicolored	.30	.25
501	A163	75m multicolored	.30	.35
502	A163	100m multicolored	.30	.35
a.	Strip of 5, #498-502		1.05	2.75

Size: 110x80mm
Imperf
| 503 | A164 | 300m multicolored | 1.10 | 2.75 |
| | Nos. 498-503 (6) | | 2.60 | 4.20 |

Archbishop Makarios, President of Cyprus.

Blood Cells with Low Hemoglobin A165

Bust of Aristotle A166

Heads and Human Rights Emblem — A167

Wilbur and Orville Wright, Flyer I — A168

Perf. 13x14, 14x13
1978, Oct. 23   Unwmk.   Litho.
504	A165	15m multicolored	.30	.25
505	A166	35m multicolored	.30	.25
506	A167	75m black	.30	.35
507	A168	125m multicolored	.35	.85
	Nos. 504-507 (4)		1.25	1.70

Anemia prevention (15m); 2300th death anniv. of Aristotle (35m); 30th anniv. of Universal Declaration of Human Rights (75m); 75th anniv. of first powered flight (125m).

Kiti Icon Stand — A169

Christmas: 35m, Athienou icon stand. 150m, Omodhos icon stand.

1978, Dec. 4   Perf. 14x14½
508	A169	15m multicolored	.30	.25
509	A169	35m multicolored	.30	.25
510	A169	150m multicolored	.40	.70
	Nos. 508-510 (3)		1.00	1.20

Venus Statue from Soli — A170

125m, Birth of Venus, by Botticelli (detail).

1979, Mar. 12   Litho.   Perf. 14x13½
| 511 | A170 | 75m multicolored | .30 | .25 |
| 512 | A170 | 125m multicolored | .40 | .30 |

Mail Coach, Envelope and Truck — A171

Europa: 75m, Old telephone, dish antenna and satellite. 125m, Steamship, jet and envelopes.

1979, Apr. 30   Litho.   Perf. 14x13½
513	A171	25m multicolored	.30	.25
514	A171	75m multicolored	.35	.25
515	A171	125m multicolored	.95	1.10
	Nos. 513-515 (3)		1.60	1.60

Peacock Wrasse — A172

Designs: 50m, Black partridge, vert. 75m, Cyprus cedar, vert. 125m, Mule.

Perf. 13½x12½, 12½x13½
1979, June 25   Litho.
516	A172	25m multicolored	.30	.25
517	A172	50m multicolored	.75	.65
518	A172	75m multicolored	.50	.35
519	A172	125m multicolored	.55	1.00
	Nos. 516-519 (4)		2.10	2.25

Children Holding Globe, UNESCO Emblem A173

Dove, Magnifying Glass, Album A174

Lord Kitchener, Map of Cyprus — A175

Smiling Child, IYC Emblem — A176

Soccer A177

Rotary Emblem A178

1979, Oct. 1   Litho.   Perf. 12½
520	A173	15m multicolored	.30	.25
521	A174	25m multicolored	.30	.25
522	A175	50m multicolored	.30	.25
523	A176	75m multicolored	.30	.25
524	A177	100m multicolored	.30	.25
525	A178	125m multicolored	.30	.85
	Nos. 520-525 (6)		1.80	2.10

Intl. Bureau of Education, Geneva, 50th anniv.; Cyprus Philatelic Society, 20th anniv.; Horatio Herbert Kitchener's survey of Cyprus, cent.; IYC; European Soccer Assoc., 25th anniv.; Rotary Club of Cyprus, 75th anniv.

Jesus, Icon, 12th Century — A179

Christmas (Icons): 35m, Nativity, 16th cent. 150m, Virgin and Child, 12th cent.

Perf. 13½x14, 13x14
1979, Nov. 5   Litho.
Sizes: 24x37mm; 27x40mm (35m)
526	A179	15m multicolored	.30	.25
527	A179	35m multicolored	.30	.25
528	A179	150m multicolored	.40	.45
	Nos. 526-528 (3)		.90	.95

Cyprus No. 1, Nicosia Cancel — A180

Cyprus Stamp Centenary: 125m, #3, Kyrenia cancel. 175m, #6, Larnaca cancel. 500m, #1-6.

1980, Mar. 17   Litho.   Perf. 14x13
529	A180	40m multicolored	.30	.25
530	A180	125m multicolored	.30	.25
531	A180	175m multicolored	.30	.30

Size: 105x85mm
Imperf
| 532 | A180 | 500m multicolored | .85 | 1.65 |
| | Nos. 529-532 (4) | | 1.75 | 2.45 |

Holy Cross, St. Barnabas Church, Agiasmati — A181

Europa: 125m, Zeno of Citium, Ny Carsberg Glyptothek, Copenhagen.

1980, Apr. 28   Perf. 12½
| 533 | A181 | 40m multicolored | .30 | .25 |
| 534 | A181 | 125m multicolored | .35 | .25 |

Sailing, Moscow '80 Emblem — A182

1980, June 23   Litho.   Perf. 14x13
535	A182	40m shown	.30	.25
536	A182	125m Swimming	.30	.25
537	A182	200m Gymnast	.30	.25
	Nos. 535-537 (3)		.90	.75

22nd Summer Olympic Games, Moscow, July 19-Aug. 3.

Gold Necklace A183

Clay Amphora A184

Archaeological finds on Cyprus, 12th cent. B.C. to 3rd cent. A.D. 15m, 40m, 150m, 500m, horiz.

Perf. 13½x14, 14x13½
1980, Sept. 15   Litho.   Wmk. 344
538	A183	10m shown	.30	.90
539	A184	15m Bronze cow	.30	.90
540	A184	25m shown	.30	.30
541	A184	40m Lion, gold ring	.40	.65
542	A184	50m Bronze cauldron	.40	.25
543	A184	75m Stele	1.10	1.40
544	A184	100m Clay jug	.80	.25
545	A184	125m Warrior, terracotta bust	.80	.90
546	A184	150m Lions attacking bull	1.25	.25
547	A184	175m Faience and enamel vase	.90	1.25
548	A184	200m Warrior god, bronze	.90	.40
549	A184	500m Stone bowl	.90	1.50
550	A183	£1 Ivory plaque	1.10	1.25
551	A183	£2 Leda and the swan, mosaic	1.90	2.25
	Nos. 538-551 (14)		11.35	12.45

For surcharges see Nos. 584, 600-611.

Cyprus Flag A185

Archbishop Makarios A187

Treaty Signing Establishing Republic, 20th Anniversary A186

CYPRUS

1980, Oct. 1   Perf. 13½x14, 14x13
552 A185 40m multicolored   .30 .25
553 A186 125m multicolored   .30 .25
554 A187 175m multicolored   .40 .30
      Nos. 552-554 (3)   1.00 .80

Dove and Woman — A188

Perf. 14x13
1980, Nov. 29   Litho.   Wmk. 344
555 A188 40m shown   .30 .30
556 A188 125m Dove and man   .40 .40
  a. Pair, #555-556   .60 .90
    Intl. Palestinian Solidarity Day.

Pulpit, Ayios Lazaros Church, Larnaca — A189

Christmas: 25m, Pulpit, Tripiotis Church, Nicosia. 100m, Iconostatis (Holy Door), Panayia Church, Paralimni.

1980, Nov. 29   Perf. 13½x14
557 A189 25m multicolored   .30 .25
      Size: 24x37mm
558 A189 100m multicolored   .30 .25
      Size: 21x37mm
559 A189 125m multicolored   .30 .25
      Nos. 557-559 (3)   .90 .75

Europa Issue

Folk Dance — A190

1981, May 4   Photo.   Perf. 14
560 A190 40m shown   .30 .25
561 A190 175m Dance, diff.   .65 .50

Self-portrait, by Leonardo Da Vinci — A191

The Last Supper, by Da Vinci — A192

Perf. 13½x14, 12½x13½
1981, June 15   Wmk. 344   Litho.
562 A191 50m shown   .35 .25
563 A192 125m shown   .75 .45
564 A191 175m Lace pattern, Milan Cathedral   .90 .65
      Nos. 562-564 (3)   2.00 1.35
    Da Vinci's visit to Cyprus, 500th anniv.

Ophrys Kotschyi — A193

Orchids: 50m, Orchis puntulata. 75m, Ophrys argolica elegantis. 150m, Epipactis veratrifolia.

1981, July 6   Perf. 13½x14
565 A193 25m shown   .45 .65
566 A193 50m multi   .55 .75
567 A193 75m multi   .60 .85

568 A193 150m multi   .70 1.00
  a. Block of 4, #565-568   2.10 3.00
      Nos. 565-568 (4)   2.30 3.25

Prince Charles and Lady Diana, St. Paul's Cathedral A194

Perf. 14x13
1981, Sept. 28   Wmk. 344
569 A194 200m multicolored   .70 .80
    Royal wedding.

Heinrich von Stephan (1831-1897), UPU Founder A195

World Food Day (Oct. 16) — A196

Intl. Year of the Disabled A197

European Campaign for Urban Renaissance A198

1981, Sept. 28
570 A195 25m multicolored   .30 .25
571 A196 40m multicolored   .30 .25
572 A197 125m multicolored   .30 .30
573 A198 150m multicolored   .35 .35
      Nos. 570-573 (4)   1.25 1.15

Our Lady of the Angels, Transfiguration Church, Palekhori — A199

Christmas (Frescoes): 100m, Christ, Madonna of Arakas Church, Lagoudera, 25m: wine, 250m) to the 125m, Baptism of Christ, Our Lady of Assinou Church, Nikitari.

1981, Nov. 16   Perf. 12½
574 A199 25m multicolored   .30 .25
575 A199 100m multicolored   .65 .25
576 A199 125m multicolored   .75 .35
      Nos. 574-576 (3)   1.70 .85

Bathing Aphrodite, Sculpture, Soloi, 250 B.C. — A200

Design: 175m, Aphrodite Emerging from the Water, by Titian, 16th cent.

Perf. 13½x14
1982, Apr. 12   Litho.   Wmk. 344
577 A200 125m multicolored   .60 .50
578 A200 175m multicolored   .80 .70

Europa Issue

Liberation by Emperor Nicephorus II Phocas, 965 A.D. — A201

175m, Conversion of Sergius Paulus, 45 A.D.

Perf. 12½
1982, May 3   Photo.   Unwmk.
579 A201 40m shown   .65 .25
580 A201 175m multi   .80 1.10

Mosaic Chrismon — A202

Cultural Heritage: 125m, King of Palaepaphos (High Priest of Aphrodite), sculpture, vert. 225m, Theseus Struggling with the Minotaur, mosaic.

1982, July 5   Litho.   Wmk. 344
581 A202 50m multicolored   .30 .25
582 A202 125m multicolored   .45 .30
583 A202 175m multicolored   .65 1.00
      Nos. 581-583 (3)   1.40 1.55

No. 543 Surcharged

1982, Sept. 6   Litho.   Perf. 13½x14
584 A184 100m on 75m multi   .55 .55

Scouting Year — A203

Perf. 13½x12½, 12½x13½
1982, Nov. 8   Wmk. 344
585 A203 100m Emblem, horiz. .40 .25
586 A203 125m Baden-Powell   .45 .45
587 A203 175m Camp site, horiz. .45 1.00
      Nos. 585-587 (3)   1.30 1.70

A203a

Christmas — A204

Designs: 25m, 250m, Christ Giving Holy Communion (bread, 25m: wine, 250m) to the Apostles, St. Neophytos Monastery Church, Paphos. 100m, Chalice, Church of St. Savvas, Nicosia.

Perf. 12½, 13½x14 (100m)
1982, Dec. 6
588 A203a 25m multicolored   .30 .25
589 A204   100m multicolored   .65 .25
590 A203a 250m multicolored   .75 1.10
      Nos. 588-590 (3)   1.40 1.60

A204a

50m, Cyprus Forest Industries, Ltd. 125m, Mosaic, 3rd cent. 150m, Dancers. 175m, Royal Exhibition Building, Melbourne.

1983, Mar. 14   Perf. 14x13½
591 A204a 50m multi   .30 .25
592 A204a 125m multi   .30 .25
593 A204a 150m multi   .30 .35
594 A204a 175m multi   .30 .45
      Nos. 591-594 (4)   1.20 1.30
    Commonwealth Day.

Europa — A205

50m, Cyprosyllabic script funerary stele, 6th cent. B.C. 200m, Copper ore, Enkomi ingot, 1400-1250 BC, bronze jug, 2nd cent.

1983, May 3   Photo.   Perf. 14½x14
595 A205 50m multicolored   .35 .25
596 A205 200m multicolored   .90 1.75

Local Butterflies — A206

60m, Pararge aegeria. 130m, Aricia medon. 250m, Glaucopsyche paphos.

Wmk. 344
1983, June 28   Litho.   Perf. 12½
597 A206 60m multi   .30 .25
598 A206 130m multi   .50 .25
599 A206 250m multi   .95 1.65
      Nos. 597-599 (3)   1.75 2.15

Nos. 538-549 Surcharged
Perf. 13½x14, 14x13½
1983, Oct. 3   Litho.   Wmk. 344
600 A183 1c on 10m multi   .30 .90
601 A184 2c on 15m multi   .30 1.10
602 A184 3c on 25m multi   .30 .90
603 A184 4c on 40m multi   .30 .90
604 A184 5c on 50m multi   .55 .40
605 A184 6c on 75m multi   .55 .90
606 A184 10c on 100m multi   .55 .50
607 A184 13c on 125m multi   .55 .60
608 A184 15c on 150m multi   .55 .70
609 A184 20c on 200m multi   .55 .80
610 A184 25c on 175m multi   .60 1.25
611 A184 50c on 500m multi   .85 2.25
      Nos. 600-611 (12)   5.95 11.20

Electricity Authority of Cyprus, 30th Anniv. A207

World Communications Year A208

Intl. Maritime Org., 25th Anniv. A209

Nicos Kazantzakis, 100th Birth Anniv. A211

Universal Declaration of Human Rights, 35th Anniv. A210

Archbishop Makarios III, 70th Birth Anniv. A212

1983, Oct. 27   Litho.   Perf. 13½x14
612 A207 3c multicolored   .30 .25
613 A208 6c multicolored   .30 .25
614 A209 13c multicolored   .30 .25
615 A210 15c multicolored   .30 .25
616 A211 20c multicolored   .30 .75
617 A212 25c multicolored   .30 .80
      Nos. 612-617 (6)   1.80 2.55

Christmas — A213

Designs: 4c, Belfry, St. Lazaros Church, Larnaca. 13c, Belfry, St. Varvara Church,

CYPRUS

Kaimakli, Nicosia. 20c, Belfry, St. Ioannis Church, Larnaca.

1983, Dec. 12   *Perf. 12½x14*
618	A213	4c multicolored	.30 .25
619	A213	13c multicolored	.45 .40
620	A213	20c multicolored	.75 1.40
		Nos. 618-620 (3)	1.50 2.05

Waterside Cafe at the Marina, Larnaca — A214

19th Century engravings. Size of 6c: 41x27mm; 75c, 110x85mm.

Perf. 14½x14 (6c), 14, Imperf. (75c)
1984, Mar. 6
621	A214	6c shown	.30 .25
622	A214	20c Bazaar, Larnaca	.45 .95
623	A214	30c East Gate, Nicosia	.70 1.65
624	A214	75c St. Lazarus Church Interior, Larnaca	1.65 2.45
		Nos. 621-624 (4)	3.10 5.30

Europa (1959-1984) A215

1984, Apr. 30   *Wmk. 344*   *Perf. 12½*
625	A215	6c multicolored	.45 .25
626	A215	15c multicolored	.75 1.40

1984 Summer Olympics A216

1984, June 18   *Litho.*   *Perf. 14*
627	A216	3c Running	.30 .25
628	A216	4c Olympic column	.30 .25
629	A216	13c Swimming	.40 .75
630	A216	20c Gymnastics	.50 1.65
		Nos. 627-630 (4)	1.50 2.90

Turkish Invasion, 10th Anniv. — A217

15c, Prisoners, barbed wire. 20c, Map.

1984, July 20   *Litho.*   *Perf. 14x13½*
631	A217	15c multicolored	.45 .45
632	A217	20c multicolored	.60 .60

Cyprus Philatelic Society, 25th Anniv. A218

Cyprus Soccer Assoc., 50th Anniv. A219

George Papanicolaou (1883-1962), Cancer Researcher A220

Medieval Map A221

1984, Oct. 15   *Wmk. 344*   *Perf. 12½*
633	A218	6c multicolored	.30 .25
634	A219	10c multicolored	.40 .35
635	A220	15c multicolored	.70 .55
636	A221	25c multicolored	1.25 2.20
		Nos. 633-636 (4)	2.65 3.35

Intl. Symposium of Cyprus Cartography and First Intl. Symposium on Medieval Paleography (25c).

Christmas — A222

4c, St. Mark. 13c, Gospel page (St. Mark). 20c, St. Luke.

1984, Nov. 26   *Litho.*   *Perf. 12½*
637	A222	4c multicolored	.30 .25
638	A222	13c multicolored	.50 .55
639	A222	20c multicolored	.80 2.20
		Nos. 637-639 (3)	1.60 3.00

Landscapes A223

1c, Autumn at Platania. 2c, Ayia Napa Monastery. 3c, Phine Village. 4c, Kykko Monastery. 5c, Beach at Makronissos. 6c, Village Street, Omodhos, vert. 10c, Sea view. 13c, Water sports. 15c, Beach at Protaras. 20c, Forestry, vert. 25c, Sunrise at Protaras, vert. 30c, Village houses, Pera Orinis. 50c, Apollo Hylates Sanctuary. £1, Troodos Mountain, vert. £5, Personification of Autumn, Dionyssos House, vert.

Perf. 15x14, 14x15
1985, Mar. 18   *Litho.*
640	A223	1c multicolored	.30 .65
641	A223	2c multicolored	.30 .65
642	A223	3c multicolored	.30 .65
643	A223	4c multicolored	.30 .35
644	A223	5c multicolored	.30 .25
645	A223	6c multicolored	.30 .25
646	A223	10c multicolored	.50 .35
647	A223	13c multicolored	.60 .30
648	A223	15c multicolored	.80 .25
649	A223	20c multicolored	1.10 .25
650	A223	25c multicolored	1.35 1.10
651	A223	30c multicolored	1.65 1.35
652	A223	50c multicolored	2.75 .85
653	A223	£1 multicolored	4.40 3.30
654	A223	£5 multicolored	15.50 16.50
		Nos. 640-654 (15)	30.45 27.05

For surcharges see Nos. 684-685, 712.

Europa — A224

6c, Ceramic figures playing the double flute, lyre and tambourine, 7th-6th cent. B.C. 15c, Cypriot violin, lute, flute, the Fourth Women's Dance from the Cyprus Suite.

1985, May 6   *Litho.*   *Perf. 12½*
655	A224	6c multicolored	.55 .40
656	A224	15c multicolored	1.00 1.65

Republic of Cyprus, 25th Anniv. A225

Natl. Liberation Movement, 30th Anniv. — A226

Intl. Youth Year — A227

Solon Michaelides (1905-1979), Conductor, European Music Year — A228

Perf. 14½ (#657), 14½x14, 15 (#661)
1985, Sept. 23   *Litho.*
657	A225	4c multicolored	.30 .25
658	A226	6c multicolored	.30 .25
659	A227	13c multicolored	.30 1.10
660	A228	15c multicolored	1.10 1.10
661	A229	20c multicolored	.35 1.10
		Nos. 657-661 (5)	2.35 3.80

Christmas — A230

Murals of the St. Ioannis Lampadistis Monastery, Kalopanyiotis: 4c, Virgin Mary's Visit to Elizabeth. 13c, The Nativity. 20c, The Candlemas, Church of Our Lady of Assinous, Nikitari.

1985, Nov. 18   *Litho.*   *Perf. 12½*
662	A230	4c multicolored	.30 .25
663	A230	13c multicolored	.50 .50
664	A230	20c multicolored	.85 1.65
		Nos. 662-664 (3)	1.65 2.40

Hellenistic Platinum Spoon — A231

Designs: 20c, Ionian helmet, foot of a sculpture. 25c, Union of Eros and Intellect personified, abstract. 30c, Statue profile.

1986, Feb. 17   *Perf. 15x14*
665	A231	15c multicolored	.35 .40
666	A231	20c multicolored	.45 .65
667	A231	25c multicolored	.50 .90
668	A231	30c multicolored	.55 1.05
a.		Souv. sheet of 4, #665-668	12.00 16.50
		Nos. 665-668 (4)	1.85 3.00

Construction of the New Archaeological Museum, Nicosia. Department of Antiquities, 50th anniv. No. 668a sold for £1.

Europa Issue

Mouflon, Cedar Trees — A232

17c, Flamingos, Larnaca Salt Lake.

1986, Apr. 28   *Litho.*   *Perf. 14x13*
669	A232	7c shown	.40 .35
670	A232	17c multicolored	1.50 3.00

Seashells — A233

1986, July 1   *Perf. 14x13½*
671	A233	5c Chlamys pesfelis	.35 .25
672	A233	7c Charonia variegata	.40 .25
673	A233	18c Murex brandaris	.65 .80
674	A233	25c Cypraea spurca	1.10 2.20
		Nos. 671-674 (4)	2.50 3.50

Overseas Cypriots Year — A234

Halley's Comet A235

Designs: No. 676, Halley's Comet. No. 677, Comet tail, Edmond Halley.

1986, Oct. 13   *Litho.*   *Wmk. 344*
Perf. 13½x13
675	A234	15c multicolored	1.10 .50
676		18c multicolored	1.40 2.20
677		18c multicolored	1.40 2.20
a.	A235	Pair, #676-677	2.75 4.50
		Nos. 675-677 (3)	3.90 4.90

No. 677a has continuous design.

Road Safety — A236

5c, Pedestrian crossing. 7c, Helmet, motorcycle controls. 18c, Seatbelt, rearview mirror.

1986, Nov. 10   *Perf. 14x13*
678	A236	5c multicolored	.70 .35
679	A236	7c multicolored	.75 .35
680	A236	18c multicolored	1.65 2.75
		Nos. 678-680 (3)	3.10 3.45

Intl. Peace Year, Christmas — A237

Nativity frescoes (details): 5c, Church of Panayia tou Araka. 15c, Church of Panayia tou Moutoulla. 17c, Church of St. Nicholaos tis Steyis.

1986, Nov. 24   *Perf. 13½x14*
681	A237	5c multicolored	.40 .25
682	A237	15c multicolored	.95 .35
683	A237	17c multicolored	1.10 2.20
		Nos. 681-683 (3)	2.45 2.80

Nos. 645 and 647 Surcharged
Perf. 14x15, 15x14
1986, Oct. 13   *Litho.*   *Wmk. 344*
684	A223	7c on 6c multi	.65 .35
685	A223	18c on 13c multi	1.55 .80

Miniature Sheet

Troodos Churches on UNESCO World Heritage List — A238

Churches and frescoes: a, Assinou, Nikitari. b, Moutoulla, Moutoullas. c, Podithou, Galata. d, Ayios Ioannis Lampadistis, Kalopanayiotis. e, Timios Stavros, Pelentri. f, Stavros Ayiasmati, Platanistasa. g, Archangelos Pedoula, Pedoulas. h, Ayios Nicolaos tis Steyis, Kakopetria. i, Araka, Lagoudera.

Perf. 12½
1987, Apr. 22   *Photo.*   *Unwmk.*
686	A238	Sheet of 9	6.00 12.00
a.-i.		15c any single	.80 .90

CYPRUS

Europa Issue

Modern Architecture A239

7c, Central Bank of Cyprus. 18c, Cyprus Communications Authority.

Perf. 14x13½
1987, May 11   Litho.   Wmk. 344
| 687 | A239 | 7c multicolored | .45 | .35 |
| 688 | A239 | 18c multicolored | .95 | 1.65 |

Ships Named Kyrenia — A240

2c, The Kyrenia, Kyrenia Castle. 3c, Kyrenia II, Perama Shipyard. 5c, Kyrenia II, Paphos. 17c, Kyrenia II, NY Harbor.

1987, Oct. 3
689	A240	2c multicolored	.40	.25
690	A240	3c multicolored	.50	1.00
691	A240	5c multicolored	.85	.25
692	A240	17c multicolored	1.95	1.00
		Nos. 689-692 (4)	3.70	2.50

Blood Donation Coordinating Committee, 10th Anniv. — A241

European Campaign for Countryside A242

TROODOS '87 — A243

Perf. 14x13½
1987, Nov. 2   Litho.   Wmk. 344
693	A241	7c multicolored	.55	.30
694	A242	15c multicolored	1.20	.45
695	A243	20c multicolored	1.55	3.30
		Nos. 693-695 (3)	3.30	4.05

Christmas A244

1987, Nov. 30   Perf. 14
696	A244	5c Babe in a manger	.40	.25
697	A244	15c Ornament	1.25	.25
698	A244	17c Fruit bowl	1.40	2.20
		Nos. 696-698 (3)	3.05	2.85

Cyprus Customs Union in Cooperation with the EEC — A245

15c, Natl. and EEC flags. 18c, Maps.

Perf. 13x13½
1988, Jan. 11   Wmk. 344
| 699 | A245 | 15c multicolored | 1.10 | 1.95 |
| 700 | A245 | 18c multicolored | 1.10 | .90 |

A246

Europa (Communication and transportation): No. 701, Electronic mail (Intelpost). No. 702, Cellular telephone system. No. 703, Cyprus Airways, technology vs. ecology (jet, 3 flamingos). No. 704, Cyprus Airways (jet, 4 flamingos).

1988, May 9   Perf. 14x14½
701	A246	7c multicolored	.85	1.40
702	A246	7c multicolored	.85	1.40
a.		Pair, #701-702	1.65	2.75
703	A246	18c multicolored	3.30	3.30
704	A246	18c multicolored	3.30	3.30
a.		Pair, #703-704	6.75	6.75
		Nos. 701-704 (4)	8.30	9.40

1988 Summer Olympics, Seoul — A247

Unwmk.
1988, June 27   Photo.   Perf. 12   Granite Paper
705	A247	5c Sailing	.35	.25
706	A247	7c Track	.40	.45
707	A247	10c Marksmanship	.45	.80
708	A247	20c Judo	1.00	1.65
		Nos. 705-708 (4)	2.20	3.15

Non-Aligned Foreign Minister's Conference A248

Designs: 10c, Natl. coat of arms. 50c, Jawaharlal Nehru, Tito, Gamal Abdel Nasser and Makarios III (1913-77).

Perf. 14x13½
1988, Sept. 5   Litho.   Wmk. 344
709	A248	1c shown	.30	.25
710	A248	10c multicolored	.50	.80
711	A248	50c multicolored	3.85	2.75
		Nos. 709-711 (3)	4.65	3.80

No. 643 Srchd.

1988, Oct. 3   Litho.   Perf. 15x14
| 712 | A223 | 15c on 4c multi | 2.50 | 1.40 |

Christmas — A249

5c, Candlemas. 15c, Madonna and child. 17c, Adoration of the Magi.

Perf. 13½x14
1988, Nov. 28   Litho.   Wmk. 344
713	A249	5c multicolored	.30	.25
714	A249	15c multicolored	.80	.30
715	A249	17c multicolored	.90	1.90
		Nos. 713-715 (3)	2.00	2.45

A250

1988, Dec. 10
| 716 | A250 | 25c lt ultra & int blue | 1.10 | 1.40 |

UN Declaration of Human Rights, 40th anniv.

3rd Games of Small European States, Nicosia — A251

Perf. 13½
1989, Apr. 10   Litho.   Unwmk.
717	A251	1c Discus	.55	.25
718	A251	5c Javelin	.35	.25
719	A251	15c Wrestling	.70	.25
720	A251	18c Running	.95	1.10

Size: 110x80mm
Imperf
| 721 | A251 | £1 Nike, laurel, bird | 6.75 | 8.25 |
| | | Nos. 717-721 (5) | 9.30 | 10.10 |

Various Children's Games — A252

Perf. 13x13½
1989, May 8   Litho.   Unwmk.
722	A252	7c multi (5 boys)	1.20	1.65
723	A252	7c multi (6 boys)	1.20	1.65
a.		Pair, #722-723	2.30	3.30
724	A252	18c multi (6 boys)	1.40	1.75
725	A252	18c multi (5 boys)	1.40	1.75
a.		Pair, #724-725	2.75	3.50
		Nos. 722-725 (4)	5.20	6.80

Europa.

French Revolution, Bicent. A253

Perf. 11½
1989, July 7   Granite Paper   Unwmk.
| 726 | A253 | 10c multicolored | 1.10 | .05 |

A254   A255

1989, Sept. 4   Perf. 13½
| 727 | A254 | 15c multicolored | .70 | .45 |
| 728 | A255 | 30c multicolored | 1.20 | 1.20 |

15c for Interparliamentary Union, cent. 30c for 9th Non-Aligned Summit Conf., Belgrade.

Apiculture — A256

3c, Honeycomb and bees. 10c, Gathering nectar on pink flower. 15c, Gathering nectar on white flower. 18c, Queen, worker bees.

1989, Oct. 15   Perf. 13½x14
729	A256	3c multicolored	.35	.25
730	A256	10c multicolored	.75	.55
731	A256	15c multicolored	1.05	.55
732	A256	18c multicolored	1.20	1.90
		Nos. 729-732 (4)	3.35	3.25

Annivs. & Events — A257

Designs: 3c, Armenian earthquake. 5c, Cyprus Philatelic Society. 7c, European Cancer Year. 17c, World Food Day.

1989, Nov. 13
733	A257	3c multicolored	.35	1.40
734	A257	5c multicolored	.50	.25
735	A257	7c multicolored	.85	1.55
736	A257	17c multicolored	1.20	1.55
		Nos. 733-736 (4)	2.90	4.75

A258   A259

Mosaics, 3rd-5th Cent. — A260

Details: 1c, Winter, from *The Four Seasons*, House of Dionysos. 2c, Personification of Crete, from *Theseus Slaying the Minotaur*, Villa of Theseus. 3c, Centaur and Maenad, from *The Dionysiac Procession*, House of Aion, vert. 4c, *Poseidon and Amymone*, House of Dionysos. 5c, Leda, from *Leda and the Swan*, House of Aion. 7c, Apollon, from *Apollo and Marsyas*, House of Aion. 10c, Hermes and Dionysos, from *Hermes Presenting Dionysos to Tropheus*, House of Aion, vert. 15c, Cassiopeia, from *Cassiopeia and the Nereids*, House of Aion. 18c, *Orpheus Playing the Lyre*, House of Orpheus. 20c, Nymphs preparing bath, from *Hermes Presenting Dionysos to Tropheus*, vert. 25c, Amazon holding double ax and reins, House of Orpheus, vert. 40c, Doris, one of 3 Nereids in *Cassiopeia and the Nereids*. 50c, Hercules and the lion, from *The First Labor of Hercules*, House of Orpheus. £1, *Apollon and Daphne*, House of Dionysos. £3, Cupid hunting, Villa of Theseus.

Perf. 13, 13x13½ (2c, 4c, 18c, 40c), 13½x13 (3c, 10c, 20c, 25c)
1989, Dec. 29
737	A258	1c multicolored	.50	1.50
738	A259	2c multicolored	.50	1.50
739	A259	3c multicolored	.65	1.50
740	A259	4c multicolored	.85	1.50
741	A258	5c multicolored	.85	.30
742	A258	7c multicolored	1.10	.35
743	A259	10c multicolored	1.30	.40
744	A258	15c multicolored	2.10	.65
745	A259	18c multicolored	2.10	.70
746	A259	20c multicolored	2.50	.90
747	A259	25c multicolored	2.50	.90
748	A259	40c multicolored	3.75	2.00

Perf. 13½x14
749	A260	50c multicolored	2.75	2.00
750	A260	£1 multicolored	6.25	3.75
751	A260	£3 multicolored	13.00	14.00
		Nos. 737-751 (15)	40.70	31.95

UNESCO World Literacy Year — A261   83rd Interparliamentary Conference, Nicosia — A262

Lions Europa Forum — A263

CYPRUS

Anniversaries & events.

1990, Apr. 3			Perf. 14x13½	
752	A261	15c multicolored	.70	.55
753	A262	17c multicolored	.90	1.00
754	A263	18c multicolored	1.00	1.00
		Nos. 752-754 (3)	2.60	2.55

Europa — A264

Post Offices: 7c, Paphos. 18c, Limassol City Center.

1990, May 10		Litho.	Perf. 13x13½	
755	A264	7c multicolored	1.20	.25
756	A264	18c multicolored	1.55	2.75

European Year of Tourism — A265

Designs: 5c, Hotel and Catering Institute, 25th anniv. 7c, Holy Church of St. Lazarus, 1100th anniv. 15c, Female silhouette, butterflies. 18c, Male silhouette, birds.

1990, July 9			Perf. 14	
757	A265	5c multicolored	.30	.25
758	A265	7c multicolored	.35	.25
759	A265	15c multicolored	2.50	.50
760	A265	18c multicolored	2.75	4.75
		Nos. 757-760 (4)	5.90	5.75

Republic of Cyprus, 30th Anniv. — A266

1990, Sept. 29		Photo.	Perf. 11½	
761	A266	15c Sun	.70	.50
762	A266	17c shown	.85	.65
763	A266	18c Fish	.95	.80
764	A266	40c Birds, flowers	3.00	6.00

Size: 90x90mm
Imperf

765	A266	£1 Stylized bird	3.60	8.25
		Nos. 761-765 (5)	9.10	16.20

Flowers — A267

2c, Chionodoxa lochiae. 3c, Pancrayium maritimum. 5c, Paeonia mascula. 7c, Cyclamen cyprium. 15c, Tulipa cypria. 18c, Crocus cyprius.

1990, Nov. 5		Litho.	Perf. 13½x13	
766	A267	2c multicolored	.65	1.75
767	A267	3c multicolored	.65	1.75
768	A267	5c multicolored	.95	.25
769	A267	7c multicolored	1.00	.25
770	A267	15c multicolored	1.90	.35
771	A267	18c multicolored	2.10	4.25
		Nos. 766-771 (6)	7.25	8.60

Christmas — A268

1990, Dec. 3			Perf. 13½x14	
772	A268	5c Nativity	.65	.25
773	A268	15c Virgin and Child	1.65	.35
774	A268	17c Nativity, diff.	1.90	2.75
		Nos. 772-774 (3)	4.20	3.35

Mosaics From Kanakaria Church — A269

1991, Mar. 28		Photo.	Perf. 12	
		Granite Paper		
775	A269	5c Archangel	.30	.25
776	A269	15c Christ Child	.85	.25
777	A269	17c St. James	1.65	1.90
778	A269	18c St. Matthew	1.90	2.50
		Nos. 775-778 (4)	4.70	4.90

Europa — A270

1991, May 6		Litho.	Perf. 13x13½	
779	A270	7c Spacecraft Ulysses	1.00	.25
780	A270	18c Spacecraft Giotto	1.75	2.75

Oenanthe Cypriaca (Cyprus Wheatear) — A271

1991, July 4		Litho.	Perf. 13½	
781	A271	5c Juvenile bird	1.10	.50
782	A271	7c Autumn plumage	1.25	.50
783	A271	15c Male bird	1.50	.75
784	A271	30c Female bird	2.40	3.75
		Nos. 781-784 (4)	6.25	5.50

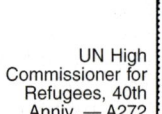

UN High Commissioner for Refugees, 40th Anniv. — A272

1991, Oct. 7		Litho.	Perf. 14x13½	
785	A272	5c shown	.30	.25
786	A272	15c Legs	1.00	.75
787	A272	18c Faces	1.20	2.75
		Nos. 785-787 (3)	2.50	3.75

Christmas — A273

1991, Nov. 25		Litho.	Perf. 13½	
788	A273	5c Nativity scene	.45	.25
789	A273	15c St. Basil	.90	.45
790	A273	17c Baptism of Jesus	1.20	2.20
a.		Strip of 3, #788-790	3.00	3.00

Strips of 3 are from sheets of 9.

A274

1992, Apr. 3		Litho.	Perf. 12	
		Granite Paper		
791	A274	10c Swimming	.65	.40
792	A274	20c Long jump	1.10	.75
793	A274	30c Running	1.55	1.55
794	A274	35c Discus	1.75	2.75
		Nos. 791-794 (4)	5.05	5.45

1992 Summer Olympics, Barcelona.

Expo '92, Seville — A275

10th Youth Under 16 European Soccer Tournament A276

Opening of University of Cyprus — A277

1992, Apr. 20		Litho.	Perf. 14	
795	A275	20c multicolored	1.75	.90
796	A276	25c multicolored	1.95	1.20
797	A277	30c multicolored	1.95	3.30
		Nos. 795-797 (3)	5.65	5.40

Discovery of America, 500th Anniv. — A278

No. 798, Map. No. 799, Embarkation at Palos. No. 800, Three ships. No. 801, Columbus.

1992, May 29		Litho.	Perf. 13x13½	
798	A278	10c multicolored	1.20	.90
799	A278	10c multicolored	1.20	.90
a.		Pair, #798-799	2.30	2.25
800	A278	30c multicolored	1.65	1.25
801	A278	30c multicolored	1.65	1.25
a.		Pair, #800-801	3.25	3.25
		Nos. 798-801 (4)	5.70	4.30

Europa.

Reptiles — A279

Designs: 7c, Chamaeleo chamaeleon. 10c, Lacerta laevis troodica. 15c, Mauremys caspica. 20c, Coluber cypriensis.

1992, Sept. 14		Litho.	Perf. 14x13½	
802	A279	7c multicolored	.95	.35
803	A279	10c multicolored	1.40	.50
804	A279	15c multicolored	1.55	.90
805	A279	20c multicolored	1.75	3.00
		Nos. 802-805 (4)	5.65	4.75

Intl. Maritime and Shipping Conference A280

1992, Nov. 9		Unwmk. Litho.	Perf. 14	
806	A280	50c multicolored	3.30	3.30

Christmas — A281

Church wall paintings: 7c, "Virgin Mary Greeting Elizabeth," Church of Timios Stavros, Pelendri. 15c, "The Virgin and Child," Church of Panayia tou Araka. 20c, "Holy Mother Odigitria," Church of Ayios Nicolaos tis Steyis.

1992, Nov. 9			Perf. 13½x14	
807	A281	7c multicolored	.55	.25
808	A281	15c multicolored	.95	.50
809	A281	20c multicolored	1.40	2.75
		Nos. 807-809 (3)	2.90	3.50

A282

1993, Feb. 15		Litho.	Perf. 14	
810	A282	10c multicolored	.85	.65

Pancyprian Gymnasium, cent.

A283

Europa: 10c, Bronze sculpture, Motherhood, by N. Dymiotis (1930-1990). 30c, Applique, Motherhood, by Savva (1924-1968), horiz.

1993, Apr. 3			Perf. 13½x14, 14x13½	
811	A283	10c multicolored	.85	.55
812	A283	30c multicolored	1.65	2.50

13th European Cup for Women Athletes A284

Scouting in Cyprus, 80th Anniv. A285

Water Skiing Mouflon Encouragement Cup — A286

Archbishop Makarios III, 80th Anniv. of Birth — A287

Perf. 13½x14, 14x13½

1993, May 24			Litho.	
813	A284	7c multicolored	.45	.35
814	A285	10c multicolored	.60	.45
815	A286	20c multicolored	1.10	1.10
a.		Inscribed "MUFFLON"	17.50	17.50
816	A287	25c multicolored	1.55	2.25
		Nos. 813-816 (4)	3.70	4.15

Fish — A288

1993, Sept. 6		Litho.	Perf. 14x13½	
817	A288	7c Holocentrus ruber	.55	.25
818	A288	15c Scorpaena scrofa	.85	.60
819	A288	20c Serranus scriba	.95	.95
820	A288	30c Balistes capriscus	1.75	2.75
		Nos. 817-820 (4)	4.10	4.55

Maritime Cyprus — A289

1993, Oct. 4			Perf. 14	
821	A289	25c multicolored	1.90	1.90

CYPRUS

12th Commonwealth Summit Conference A290

1993, Oct. 4   Perf. 14x13½
822 A290 35c red brown & tan   1.75   2.10
823 A290 40c olive brown & tan   2.10   2.65

Christmas — A291

7c, Carved wooden cross, Stavrovouni Monastery. 20c, Crucifixion, cross from Lefkara Church. 25c, Nativity, cross from Pedoulas Church.

1993, Nov. 22   Litho.   Perf. 13½x14
824 A291 7c multicolored   .45   .25
825 A291 20c multicolored   1.10   .65
    Perf. 14x13½
826 A291 25c multi, horiz.   1.40   2.75
    Nos. 824-826 (3)   2.95   3.65

Copper Industry — A292

Europa: 10c, Early smelting of copper. 30c, Map, boat, copper ingot.

1994, Mar. 1   Litho.   Perf. 13x13½
827 A292 10c multicolored   .55   .40
828 A292 30c multicolored   1.65   2.20

Persons with Special Needs A293   Intl. Olympic Committee, Cent. A294

World Gymnasiade, Nicosia A295   Intl. Year of the Family A296

1994, May 9   Litho.   Perf. 13
829 A293 7c multicolored   .65   .25
830 A294 15c multicolored   .95   .60
831 A295 20c multicolored   1.10   .90
832 A296 25c multicolored   1.40   2.50
    Nos. 829-832 (4)   4.10   4.25

Turkish Invasion and Occupation of Cyprus, 20th Anniv. — A297

1994, June 27   Litho.   Perf. 14
833 A297 10c Human rights   .65   .45
834 A297 50c Cultural heritage   2.65   3.60

Trees — A298

7c, Pinus nigra. 15c, Cedrus libani. 20c, Quercus alnifolia. 30c, Arbutus andrachne.

1994, Oct. 10   Litho.   Perf. 13½
835 A298 7c multicolored   .55   .25
836 A298 15c multicolored   .85   .60
837 A298 20c multicolored   1.00   .90
838 A298 30c multicolored   1.55   2.75
    Nos. 835-838 (4)   3.95   4.50

ICAO, 50th Anniv. — A299

1994, Nov. 21   Litho.   Perf. 14
839 A299 30c multicolored   2.50   2.25

Christmas — A300

Designs: 7c, Virgin Mary (Vlahernitissa). 20c, Nativity. 25c, Archangel Michael.

1994, Nov. 21   Perf. 13½
840 A300 7c multicolored   .65   .25
841 A300 20c multicolored   1.55   .65
842 A300 25c multicolored   1.75   3.00
    Nos. 840-842 (3)   3.95   3.90

Traditional Costumes — A301

Costumes: 1c, Female, Phapos. 2c, Bridal, Karpess. 3c, Female, Phapos, diff. 5c, Female, Messaoria. 7c, Bridegroom's. 10c, Shepherd's, Messaoria. 15c, Festive female, Nicosia. 20c, Festive female, Karpass. 25c, Female, Mountain-Pitsillia. 30c, Festive female, Karpass, diff. 35c, Rural male. 40c, Plain festive male, Messaoria. 50c, Urban male. £1, Urban festive male, Sarka.

1994, Dec. 27   Litho.   Perf. 13½x13
843 A301 1c multicolored   .40   2.20
844 A301 2c multicolored   .60   2.20
845 A301 3c multicolored   .65   2.20
846 A301 5c multicolored   .80   2.20
847 A301 7c multicolored   .85   .25
848 A301 10c multicolored   1.25   .45
849 A301 15c multicolored   2.10   .45
850 A301 20c multicolored   2.10   .55
851 A301 25c multicolored   2.40   .65
852 A301 30c multicolored   2.40   .75
853 A301 35c multicolored   2.40   1.65
854 A301 40c multicolored   2.75   2.20
855 A301 50c multicolored   3.50   2.75
856 A301 £1 multicolored   6.00   5.00
   a. Inscribed "1998"   6.00   5.00
    Nos. 843-856 (14)   £0.20   £0.50

Third Intl. Congress of Cypriot Studies — A302

Excavations: 20c, Hearth room, Ashlar building, Paliotaverna. 30c, Hall, Agios Demetrios area, Kalavasos. £1, Old Nicosia Archbishopric building, 18th cent.

1995, Feb. 27   Litho.   Perf. 14
859 A302 20c multicolored   .85   .85
860 A302 30c multicolored   1.10   1.90
    Size: 107x71mm
    Imperf
861 A302 £1 multicolored   3.85   6.60
    Nos. 859-861 (3)   5.80   9.35

A303

Liberation Monument, Nicosia: a, People walking left. b, Statue of Liberty, prisoners leaving prison. c, People walking right.

1995, Mar. 31   Litho.   Perf. 13x14
862   Strip of 3   3.50   4.25
  a.-c. A303 20c any single   1.20   1.10

No. 862 is a continuous design. Formation of EOKA (Natl. Organization of Cypriot Struggle), 40th anniv.

Europa — A304

10c, Concentration camp prisoners, dove, rainbow, map of Europe. 30c, Prisoner, dove.

1995, May 8   Litho.   Perf. 13½
863 A304 10c multicolored   1.10   .55
864 A304 30c multicolored   2.50   3.60

Liberation of the concentration camps, 50th anniv.

Health — A305

7c, Proper nutrition, exercise. 10c, Fight against AIDS. 15c, Fight against illegal drugs. 20c, Stop smoking campaign.

1995, June 26   Litho.   Perf. 13½
865 A305 7c multi, vert.   .35   .25
866 A305 10c multi   .75   .65
867 A305 15c multi   .80   .65
868 A305 20c multi, vert.   1.10   1.65
    Nos. 865-868 (4)   3.00   3.20

European Cultural Month — A306

25c, Map of Europe, building.

1995, Sept. 18   Litho.   Perf. 13x13½
869 A306 20c shown   .60   .65
870 A306 25c multicolored   .75   1.40

    Souvenir Sheet

Europhilex '95 — A307

Designs: a, Dove carrying letter, stars. b, Stars, exhibition emblem.

1995, Sept. 18   Litho.   Perf. 14
871 A307 Sheet of 2   5.50   10.00
  a.-b. 50c any single   2.75   5.00

A limited number were surcharged £5 on each stamp and sold at "Europhilex '95" on Oct. 27 and 28, 1995. Value $200.

UN, 50th Anniv. — A308   Volleyball, Cent. — A309

European Conservation Year — A310

World Clay Target Shooting Championships A311

   Perf. 13x13½, 13½x13

1995, Oct. 24   Litho.
872 A308 10c multicolored   .50   .40
873 A309 15c multicolored   1.05   .55
874 A310 20c multicolored   1.20   .90
875 A311 25c multicolored   1.40   2.50
    Nos. 872-875 (4)   4.15   4.35

Christmas — A312

Various reliquaries, Kykko Monastery.

1995, Nov. 27   Litho.   Perf. 13½x13
876 A312 7c multicolored   .50   .25
877 A312 20c multicolored   1.20   .50
878 A312 25c multicolored   1.55   2.50
    Nos. 876-878 (3)   3.25   3.25

A313   A314

A315

Anniversaries and Events — A316

1996, Jan. 4   Litho.   Perf. 13½x13
879 A313 10c multicolored   .55   .40
880 A314 20c multicolored   1.40   .80
881 A315 35c multicolored   1.90   1.90
882 A316 40c multicolored   1.90   3.00
    Nos. 879-882 (4)   5.75   6.10

Pancyprian Organization of Large Families, 25th anniv. (No. 879). Motion pictures, cent. (NO. 880). UNICEF, 50th anniv. (No. 881). 13th Conf. of Commonwealth Speakers and Presiding Officers (No. 882).

CYPRUS

Portraits of Women
A317   A318

1996, Apr. 8   Litho.   Perf. 14
883 A317 10c multicolored   1.10 .35
884 A318 30c multicolored   2.20 2.90
Europa.

1996 Summer Olympics, Atlanta — A319

1996, June 10   Litho.   Perf. 13
885 A319 10c High jump   .80 .35
886 A319 20c Javelin   1.40 .70
887 A319 25c Wrestling   1.55 1.20
888 A319 30c Swimming   1.75 2.75
   Nos. 885-888 (4)   5.50 5.00

Mills of Cyprus — A320

1996, Sept. 23   Litho.   Perf. 13
889 A320 10c Watermill   .75 .45
890 A320 15c Olivemill   .95 .55
891 A320 20c Windmill   1.10 1.00
892 A320 25c Handmill   1.20 2.20
   Nos. 889-892 (4)   4.00 4.20

Icons, Religious Landmarks — A321

Designs: No. 893, Icon of Our Lady of Iberia, Moscow. No. 894, Holy Monastery of Stavrovouni, Cyprus. No. 895, Icon of St. Nicholas, Cyprus. No. 896, Iveron Mother of God Resurrection Gate, Moscow.

1996, Nov. 13   Litho.   Perf. 11½
893 A321 30c multicolored   1.95 1.65
894 A321 30c multicolored   1.95 1.65
895 A321 30c multicolored   1.95 1.65
896 A321 30c multicolored   1.95 1.65
   a. Block of 4, #893-896   7.00 7.75
See Russia No. 6356.

Christmas A322

Paintings from Church of the Virgin of Asinou: 7c, Detail from Nativity. 20c, Virgin Mary between Archangels Gabriel and Michael. 25c, Christ bestowing blessings, vert.

1996, Dec. 2   Perf. 13x13½, 13½x13
897 A322 7c multicolored   .65 .25
898 A322 20c multicolored   1.65 .60
899 A322 25c multicolored   2.10 3.00
   Nos. 897-899 (3)   4.40 3.75

Easter — A323

1997, Mar. 24   Litho.   Perf. 13x13½
900 A323 15c The Last Supper   1.10 .55
901 A323 25c The Crucifixion   1.40 1.65

A324

1997, Mar. 24   Perf. 13½x13
902 A324 30c multicolored   2.50 2.25
European Men's Clubs Basketball Cup finals.

A325

Europa (Stories and Legends): 30c, Man in red cape fighting Death, eagle above.

1997, May 5   Litho.   Perf. 13½x13
903 A325 15c shown   1.10 .50
904 A325 30c multicolored   1.40 1.65

Insects — A326

10c, Oedipoda miniata. 15c, Acherontia atropos. 25c, Daphnis nerii. 35c, Ascalaphus macaronius.

1997, June 30   Litho.   Perf. 13x13½
905 A326 10c multicolored   .70 .40
906 A326 15c multicolored   1.05 .60
907 A326 25c multicolored   2.20 1.25
908 A326 35c multicolored   2.20 2.50
   Nos. 905-908 (4)   6.15 4.75

Archbishop Makarios III (1913-77), 1st Pres. of Cyprus Republic — A327

1997, Aug. 1   Litho.   Perf. 13x13½
909 A327 15c multicolored   1.75 .55

Christmas — A328

Frescoes from Church of Ayios Ioannis Lambadestis: 10c, Nativity. 25c, Magi on way to Bethlehem. 30c, Flight into Egypt.

1997, Nov. 17   Litho.   Perf. 13½x13
910 A328 10c multicolored   .65 .25
911 A328 25c multicolored   1.90 .65
912 A328 30c multicolored   2.10 3.00
   Nos. 910-912 (3)   4.65 3.90

Minerals — A329

1998, Mar. 9   Litho.   Perf. 13x13½
913 A329 10c Green jasper   .55 .35
914 A329 15c Iron pyrite   .80 .65
915 A329 25c Gypsum   1.30 1.40
916 A329 30c Chalcedony   1.60 3.60
   Nos. 913-916 (4)   4.25 6.00

1998 World Cup Soccer Championships, France — A330

1998, May 4   Litho.   Perf. 14
917 A330 35c multicolored   1.90 1.55

Europa — A331

Festivals, holidays: 15c, "Kataklysmos" Larnaca. 30c, People watching proclamation of independence, 1960.

1998, May 4
918 A331 15c multicolored   1.40 2.45
919 A331 30c multicolored   1.90 2.75

Ovis Gmelini Ophion — A332

World Wildlife Fund: No. 920, Male, female, calf. No. 921, Group running. No. 922, Male up close. No. 923, Male with front legs up on rock, one grazing.

1998, June 22   Litho.   Perf. 13x13½
920 A332 25c multicolored   1.65 2.10
921 A332 25c multicolored   1.65 2.10
922 A332 25c multicolored   1.65 2.10
923 A332 25c multicolored   1.65 2.10
   a. Block of 4, #920-923   6.00 7.75
Issued in sheets of 16.

World Stamp Day — A333

1998, Oct. 9   Litho.   Perf. 14
924 A333 30c multicolored   1.75 1.75
   a. Booklet pane of 8   17.50
   Complete booklet, #924a   18.00

A334

1998, Oct. 9
925 A334 50c multicolored   1.40 1.75
Universal Declaration of Human Rights, 50th anniv.

A335

Christmas (Scenes from paintings in the Church of the Virgin of Théosképasti, Kalopanayiotis): 10c, The Annunciation. 25c, The Nativity. 30c, Baptism of Christ.

1998, Nov. 16   Litho.   Perf. 14
926 A335 10c multicolored   .85 .25
927 A335 25c multicolored   1.90 .85
928 A335 30c multicolored   1.90 3.60
   a. Souvenir sheet, #926-928   4.50 4.50
   Nos. 926-928 (3)   4.65 4.70

Mushrooms — A336

10c, Pleurotus eryngii. 15c, Lactarius deliciosus. 25c, Sparassis crispa. 30c, Morchella elata.

1999, Mar. 4   Litho.   Perf. 13½x13
929 A336 10c multicolored   .60 .35
930 A336 15c multicolored   .95 .55
931 A336 25c multicolored   2.20 1.10
932 A336 30c multicolored   2.75 3.30
   Nos. 929-932 (4)   6.50 5.30

Natl. Parks and Nature Preserves A337

1999, May 6   Litho.   Perf. 14
933 A337 15c Tripylos Reserve   1.10 .85
934 A337 30c Lara Reserve   2.20 2.75
   a. Booklet pane, 4 each #933-934   14.50
   Complete booklet, #934a   15.50
Europa.

Council of Europe, 50th Anniv. — A338

1999, May 6
935 A338 30c multicolored   2.10 2.10

4000 Years of Hellenism — A339

a, Sanctuary of Apollo Hylates, Kourion. b, Mycenaean "Krater of the Warriors," Athens. c, Mycenaean amphoral krater, Cyprus Museum. d, Sanctuary of Apollo Epikourios, Delphi.

1999, June 28   Litho.   Perf. 13½x13
936 A339 25c Block of 4, #a.-d.   6.00 9.00
See Greece No. 1938.

UPU, 125th Anniv. — A340

1999, Sept. 30   Litho.   Perf. 14
937 A340 15c shown   1.10 .55
938 A340 35c "125"   1.90 2.50

Souvenir Sheet

Maritime Cyprus Shipping Conference — A341

CYPRUS

Cyprus flag and: a, Container ship. b, Binoculars, chart, cap. c, Ship with yellow stripe on tower. d, Tanker.

1999, Sept. 30
939 A341 25c Sheet of 4, #a.-d.   5.00 5.50

Souvenir Sheet

Turkish Invasion of Cyprus, 25th Anniv. — A342

1999, Nov. 11   Litho.   Imperf.
940 A342 30c multicolored   3.85 4.50

A343

1999, Nov. 11   Perf. 14
941 A343 10c Angel   .80 .25
942 A343 25c Magi   1.65 .80
943 A343 30c Madonna and child   1.75 3.30
  Nos. 941-943 (3)   4.20 4.35

Christmas.

Souvenir Sheet

A344

Miss Universe 2000: a, 15c, Woman, stars. b, 35c, Armless nude statue of woman.

2000, Mar. 30   Litho.   Perf. 13¼x13
944 A344 Sheet of 2, #a.-b.   3.50 4.00

Jewelry — A345

Various pieces of jewelry. Nos. 945-952 vert.

2000, Mar. 30   Litho.   Perf. 14
945 A345 10c multi   .60 1.10
946 A345 15c multi   .80 1.10
947 A345 20c multi   .95 .65
948 A345 25c multi   .95 .65
949 A345 30c multi   1.20 .85
950 A345 35c multi   1.40 1.10
951 A345 40c multi   1.90 1.10
952 A345 50c multi   2.25 1.40
953 A345 75c multi   3.00 1.90
954 A345 £1 multi   5.50 3.60
955 A345 £2 multi   10.00 9.00
956 A345 £3 multi   15.50 14.25
  Nos. 945-956 (12)   44.05 37.80

Cyprus Red Cross, 50th Anniv. — A346

2000, May 9   Litho.   Perf. 13½x13¼
957 A346 15c multi   2.25 1.65

Memorial to Heroes of 1955-59 Independence Struggle — A347

2000, May 9   Perf. 13¼x13
958 A347 15c multi   2.40 1.65

Europa, 2000
Common Design Type

2000, May 9   Perf. 14
959 CD17 30c multi   2.10 1.40

World Meteorological Org., 50th Anniv. — A348

2000, May 9
960 A348 30c multi   2.25 2.25

European Convention of Human Rights, 50th Anniv. — A349

2000, June 29   Litho.   Perf. 13x13¼
961 A349 30c multi   2.25 2.25

Churches Damaged Under Turkish Occupation A350

Designs: 10c, Monastery of Antifonitis, Kalograia, vert. 15c, Church of St. Themonianos, Lysi, vert. 25c, Church of Panagia Kanakaria, Lytrhagkomi. 30c, Avgasida Monastery Church, Milia.

Perf. 13¼x13, 13x13¼
2000, June 29
962 A350 10c multi   .75 .25
963 A350 15c multi   1.10 .50
964 A350 25c multi   1.55 1.20
965 A350 30c multi   1.65 2.75
  Nos. 962-965 (4)   5.05 4.70

2000 Summer Olympics, Sydney — A351

Designs: 10c, Archery. 15c, Pommel horse. 25c, Diving. 35c, Trampoline.

2000, Sept. 14   Litho.   Perf. 13x13½
966-969 A351 Set of 4   4.75 4.75

Christmas — A352

Gospel covers: 10c, Annunciation. 25c, Nativity. 30c, Baptism of Jesus.

2000, Nov. 2   Perf. 13½x13
970-972 A352 Set of 3   4.50 4.50

Pavlos Liasides (1901-85), Poet — A353

2001, Mar. 12   Litho.   Perf. 13¼x13
973 A353 13c multi   1.25 .65

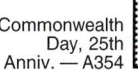

Commonwealth Day, 25th Anniv. — A354

2001, Mar. 12   Perf. 13x13¼
974 A354 30c multi   1.95 2.20

UN High Commissioner for Refugees, 50th Anniv. — A355

2001, Mar. 12
975 A355 30c multi   2.50 2.20

Europa — A356

Designs: 20c, Bridge over Diarizos River. 30c, Akaki River.

2001, May 3
976-977 A356 Set of 2   3.50 3.75
  977a Booklet pane, 4 each
    #976-977   14.50
  Booklet, #977a   15.00

Crabs — A357

Designs: 13c, Parthenope massena. 20c, Calappa granulata. 25c, Ocypode cursor. 30c, Pagurus bernhardus.

2001, June 7
978-981 A357 Set of 4   6.75 5.50

Loukis Akritas (1909-65), Writer — A358

2001, Oct. 25   Litho.   Perf. 13½x13
982 A358 20c multi   1.90 1.65

Christmas — A359

Holy Monastery of Macheras, 800th anniv.: 13c, Icon of Madonna. 25c, Monastery building. 30c, Crucifix.

2001, Oct. 25
983-985 A359 Set of 3   4.25 4.25

Cats A360

No. 986, 20c: a, Red brown panel. b, Green panel.
No. 987, 25c: a, Dark brown panel. b, Orange brown panel.

2002, Mar. 21   Litho.   Perf. 13x13½
Horiz. Pairs, #a-b
986-987 A360 Set of 2   7.00 9.00

Europa — A361

Designs: 20c, Equestrian act. 30c, Tightrope walker.

2002, May 9   Perf. 13½x13
988-989 A361 Set of 2   3.50 3.75
  a. Booklet pane, 4 each #988-989   14.50
  Booklet, #989a   15.50

Medicinal Plants — A362

Designs: 13c, Myrtus communis. 20c, Lavandula stoechas. 25c, Capparis spinosa. 30c, Ocimum basilicum.

2002, June 13   Perf. 13x13½
990-993 A362 Set of 4   7.00 6.50

Mother Teresa (1910-97) — A363

2002, Sept. 12   Litho.   Perf. 13½x13
994 A363 40c multi   3.00 3.00

Intl. Teachers' Day — A364

No. 995: a, 13c, Blackboard and teachers. b, 30c, Computer and teachers.

2002, Sept. 12   Perf. 13½
995 A364 Horiz. pair, #a-b   3.25 3.50

Cyprus-Europhilex 02 Philatelic Exhibition — A365

No. 996: a, Seal, 490-470 B.C. (red brown background). b, Silver coin of Timoharis, 5th-4th cent. B.C. (blue background) c, Silver coin of Stasioikos, 449 B.C. (yellow background).
No. 997: a, Clay oil lamp, 2nd cent. A.D. (olive green background). b, Clay statue of Europa on a bull, 7th-6th cent. B.C. (yellow background). c, Clay oil lamp, 1st cent. B.C. (lilac background).
No. 998: a, 15th cent. map of eastern Crete and western Cyprus, and statue of Aphrodite, 1st cent. B.C. b, Map of eastern Cyprus, and Abduction of Europe, by Francesco di Giorgio.

2002, Sept. 22
996   Horiz. strip of 3   3.75 4.50
  a.-c. A365 20c Any single   1.40 1.50
997   Horiz. strip of 3   4.50 5.50
  a.-c. A365 30c Any single   1.65 1.90

Souvenir Sheet
998   Sheet of 2, #a-b   7.75 11.00
  a.-b. A365 50c Any single   3.75 5.25

Christmas — A366

Wall painting in Church of Metamorphosis Sotiros, Palechori: 13c, Nativity, detail. 25c, Angels, detail. 30c, Entire painting (37x37mm).

Perf. 13x13½, 13¾ (30c)
2002, Nov. 21
999-1001 A366 Set of 3   5.50 5.00

CYPRUS

Antique Automobiles — A367

No. 1002: a, 20c, 1946 Triumph Roadster 1800. b, 25c, 1917 Ford Model T. c, 30c, 1932 Baby Ford.

2003, Mar. 20   Litho.   *Perf. 13x13½*
1002   A367   Vert. strip of 3, #a-c   6.25   7.25

Europa — A368

2003, May 5   *Perf. 13½x13*
Color of Triangles
1003   A368   20c yellow   1.00   .55
  a.   Perf. 13½x13¾ on 3 sides   1.10   1.65
1004   A368   30c red   1.60   2.20
  a.   Perf. 13½x13¾ on 3 sides   1.60   2.45
  b.   Booklet pane, 4 each
     #1003a-1004a   17.50
     Complete booklet, #1004b   18.00

European Ministers of Education, 7th Conference — A369

2003, June 12   Litho.   *Perf. 13½x13*
1005   A369   30c multi   2.25   2.40

Worldwide Fund for Nature (WWF) — A370

Mediterranean horseshoe bat: a, In flight. b, Close-up. c, Hanging from rock. d, With open mouth.

2003, June 12   *Perf. 13x13½*
1006   A370   25c Block of 4, #a-b   7.00   9.75

Birds of Prey — A371

No. 1007, 20c: a, Eleonora's falcon. b, Eleonora's falcons in flight.
No. 1008, 25c: a, Head of Imperial eagle. b, Imperial eagles in flight.
No. 1009, 30c: a, Owl on branch. b, Owl in flight, eggs.

2003, Sept. 25   Litho.   *Perf. 14*
Horiz. pairs, #a-b
1007-1009   A371   Set of 3   10.50   15.00

Famous Men — A372

Designs: No. 1010, 5c, Constantinos Spyridakis (1903-76), Education minister. No. 1011, 5c, Tefkros Anthias (1903-68), poet (23x31mm).

Perf. 13x13¼, 13¼x13
2003, Nov. 13
1010-1011   A372   Set of 2   1.45   2.20

Christmas — A373

Details of Nativity icon from church in Kourdali: 13c, Angels. 30c, Three Magi on horses. 40c, Entire icon (37x60mm).

Perf. 13¾x13¼, 13¾x14 (40c)
2003, Nov. 13
1012-1014   A373   Set of 3   5.50   5.00

FIFA (Fédération Internationale de Football Association), Cent. — A374

Perf. 13¼x13¾
2004, Mar. 11   Litho.
1015   A374   30c multi   2.45   2.25

UEFA (European Soccer Union), 50th Anniv. — A375

2004, Mar. 11   *Perf. 13¼x13*
1016   A375   30c multi   2.45   2.25

Yiannos Kranidiotis (1947-99), Politician — A376

2004, May 1   *Perf. 13¼x13½*
1017   A376   20c multi   1.65   1.10

Admission to European Union — A377

2004, May 1   *Perf. 14¼x14*
1018   A377   30c multi   1.90   2.25

Europa — A378

Cliff and: 20c, Amphitheater, ship. 30c, Family at seashore, sculpture.

2004, May 1   *Perf. 13¾x13¼*
1019   A378   20c multi   1.10   1.10
  a.   Perf. 13¾ on 3 sides   1.50   .70
1020   A378   30c multi   1.90   2.75
  a.   Perf. 13¾ on 3 sides   2.00   1.10
  b.   Booklet pane, 4 each #1019a, 1020a   12.25   —
     Complete booklet, #1020b   13.50

2004 Summer Olympics, Athens — A379

Designs: 13c, Equestrian. 20c, Runners. 30c, Swimmers. 40c, Athletes, man in robe.

2004, June 10   Litho.   *Perf. 13¼x13*
1021-1024   A379   Set of 4   5.50   5.75

Mammals — A380

No. 1025, 20c — Tursiops truncatus: a, Blue background. b, White background.
No. 1026, 30c — Vulpes vulpes indutus: a, Green background. b, White background.
No. 1027, 40c, Lepus europaeus cyprium: a, Orange brown background. b, White background.

2004, Sept. 9   Litho.   *Perf. 13¾x13½*
Horiz. Pairs, #a-b
1025-1027   A380   Set of 3   13.50   16.50

Georgios Philippou Pierides (1904-99), Writer A381

Emilios Chourmouzios (1904-73), Writer A382

2004, Nov. 11   *Perf. 13¼x13*
1028   A381   5c multi   .70   1.10
1029   A382   5c multi   .70   1.10

Christmas — A383

Details from icon depicting the birth of Christ, Monastery of Chrysoroyiatissa: 13c, Angels. 30c, Magi on horseback. 40c, Annunciation, vert. (37x60mm). £1, Adoration of the Shepherds.

Perf. 13¾x13¼, 13¾x14 (40c)
2004, Nov. 11
1030-1032   A383   Set of 3   5.50   5.00

Souvenir Sheet
Perf. 13¾ on 3 Sides
1033   A383   £1 multi   7.50   10.00
No. 1033 contains one 37x38mm stamp.

Carolina Pelendritou, Swimming Gold Medalist at 2004 Paralympics — A384

2005, Mar. 3   Litho.   *Perf. 13¼x13¾*
1034   A384   20c multi   2.20   1.10

Rotary International, Cent. — A385

2005, Mar. 3
1035   A385   40c multi   2.20   1.10

Natl. Organization of Cypriot Struggle (EOKA), 50th Anniv. — A386

2005, Mar. 3
1036   A386   50c multi   2.20   2.75

Europa — A387

Table with food and: 20c, Purple grapes, sailboat. 30c, Green grapes, steamship.

2005, May 5   *Perf. 13½x13*
White Frame All Around
1037   A387   20c multi   1.10   .55
1038   A387   30c multi   1.65   2.20

Booklet Stamps
White Frame on 3 Sides
Perf. 13½ on 3 Sides
1039   A387   20c multi   1.10   1.65
1040   A387   30c multi   1.65   2.50
  a.   Horiz. pair, #1039-1040   3.25   2.25
  b.   Booklet pane, 4 #1040a   13.50
     Complete booklet, #1040b   15.00
     Nos. 1037-1040 (4)   5.50   6.90

Dogs — A388

Designs: 13c, German shepherd. 20c, Hungarian vizsla. 30c, Labrador retriever. 40c, Dalmatian.

2005, June 16   Litho.   *Perf. 13¼*
1041-1044   A388   Set of 4   8.50   5.50
1044a   Booklet pane, #1041-1044   8.50
     Complete booklet, #1044a   8.75

Christmas — A389

Icons: 13c, Annunciation to the Shepherds. 30c, Adoration of the Magi. 40c, Madonna and Child, vert. (38x60mm).

Perf. 13¼, 13¾x14 (40c)
2005, Nov. 10   Litho.
1045-1047   A389   Set of 3   5.50   5.00

Souvenir Sheet

Europa Stamps, 50th Anniv. A390

No. 1048: a, Cyprus #246. b, Cyprus #202. c, Cyprus #220. d, Cyprus #231.

2006, Feb. 23   Litho.   *Perf. 13¾*
1048   A390   30c Sheet of 4, #a-d   4.50   5.00

CYPRUS

Postal Museum, 25th Anniv. — A391

2006, Mar. 30   Perf. 13¾x13¼
1049 A391 25c multi   2.00 1.40

Rembrandt (1606-69), Painter — A392

2006, Mar. 30
1050 A392 40c multi   3.00 3.00

2006 World Cup Soccer Championships, Germany — A393

2006, Mar. 30   Perf. 13¼x13¾
1051 A393 50c multi   2.50 3.00

Souvenir Sheet

Folk Dances A394

No. 1052 — Folk dancers from: a, Cyprus. b, India.

2006, Apr. 12   Perf. 13x13½
1052 A394 40c Sheet of 2, #a-b   4.50 5.50
See India No. 2151.

Europa — A395

2006, May 4   Perf. 13½x13
1053 A395 30c grn & multi   1.95   .55
   a. Perf. 13½x13¾ on 3 sides   1.95 2.50
1054 A395 40c red & multi   2.20 3.00
   a. Perf. 13½x13¾ on 3 sides   2.50 3.30
   b. Booklet pane, 4 each
       #1053a-1054a   17.50   —
       Complete booklet, #1054b   17.50

Organ Transplantation A396

2006, June 15   Litho.   Perf. 13¼
1055 A396 13c multi   1.10   .65

Fruit — A397

Designs: 20c, Elaeagnus angustifolia. 25c, Mespilus germanica, horiz. 60c, Opuntia ficus barbarica.

Perf. 13¼x13½, 13½x13¼
2006, June 15
1056-1058 A397 Set of 3   8.00 6.75

Fire Trucks — A398

Designs: 13c, Bedford water carrier. 20c, Hino pump water tender. 50c, Bedford ladder truck.

2006, Sept. 14   Perf. 13¾x13¼
1059-1061 A398 Set of 3   9.00 7.25

Nicos Nicolaides (1884-1956), Writer — A399

2006, Nov. 16   Litho.   Perf. 13½x13
1062 A399 5c multi   .70   .80

Christmas — A400

Items from Agiou Eleftheriou Church: 13c, Carved wood iconostasis. 30c, Cross. 40c, Bas-relief of cross, spear and sponge.

2006, Nov. 16   Perf. 13¼x13¾
1063-1065 A400 Set of 3   5.25 5.00

St. Xenon, the Postman A401

Litho. & Embossed
2007, Feb. 8   Imperf.
1066 A401 £1 multi   8.00 11.00

Echinodorma A402

No. 1067: a, Antedon mediterranea. b, Centrostephanus longispinus. c, Astropecten jonstoni. d, Ophioderma longicadum.

2007, Feb. 8   Litho.   Perf. 13¾x13¼
1067   Horiz. strip of 4   7.75 8.75
   a.-d. A402 25c Any single   1.95 2.20

Motorcycles A403

Designs: 13c, 1972 Triumph Daytona. 20c, 1941 Matchless. 40c, 1940 BSA. 60c, 1939 Ariel Red Hunter.

2007, Mar. 15
1068-1071 A403 Set of 4   7.25 6.75

Treaty of Rome, 50th Anniv. — A404

2007, May 3   Perf. 13¼x13¾
1072 A404 30c multi   1.60 1.95

Europa — A405

Scouting emblem in gold, knot in: 30c, Light blue. 40c, Buff.

Litho. & Embossed With Foil Application
2007, May 3
1073-1074 A405 Set of 2   4.50 5.25
1074a   Booklet pane, 4 each
           #1073-1074, perf. on 3
           sides   15.50   —
           Complete booklet, #1074a 16.50

Scouting, cont.

Social Insurance, 50th Anniv. — A406

No. 1075: a, Text in Greek. b, Text in English.

2007, June 14   Litho.   Perf. 13¼
1075 A406 40c Horiz. pair, #a-b 3.30 4.40

Miniature Sheet

Cyprus Throughout the Ages — A407

No. 1076: a, Skeleton of pygmy hippopotamus, 10,000 B.C. b, Stone vessel, 7000 B.C. c, Choirokoitia Settlement, 7000 B.C. d, Female terracotta figurine, 3000 B.C. e, Terracotta vessel, 2000 B.C. f, Greek inscriptions on bronze skewer, 1000 B.C. g, Bird-shaped vessel, 800 B.C. h, Map of ancient kingdoms of Cyprus.

2007, Oct. 2   Perf. 13¾
1076 A407 25c Sheet of 8, #a-h   12.00 15.50
See Nos. 1101, 1116, 1138.

Neoclassical Buildings — A408

Designs: 13c, Limassol District Administration Building. 15c, National Bank of Greece Building, Nicosia. 20c, Archaeological Research Unit Building, Nicosia. 30c, National Art Gallery, Nicosia. 40c, Paphos Municipal Library. 50c, A. G. Leventis Foundation Office Building, Nicosia. £1, Limassol Municipal Library. £3, Phaneromeni Gymnasium, Nicosia.

2007, Oct. 2   Perf. 13¾x13½
1077 A408 13c multi   .90   .85
1078 A408 15c multi   1.00   .90
1079 A408 20c multi   1.20 1.05
1080 A408 30c multi   1.40 1.10
1081 A408 40c multi   1.55 1.55
1082 A408 50c multi   1.95 2.20
1083 A408 £1 multi   4.15 3.30
1084 A408 £3 multi   9.50 10.00
      Nos. 1077-1084 (8)   21.65 20.95

Christmas — A409

Murals from Chapel of St. Themonianus, Lysi: 13c, Virgin Mary. 30c, Archangel Gabriel. 40c, Christ Pantocrator (35x45mm).

Perf. 14x13¾, 13¾ (40c)
2007, Nov. 15
1085-1087 A409 Set of 3   4.00 4.15

100 Cents = 1 Euro
Souvenir Sheet

Introduction of Euro Currency — A410

No. 1088: a, Statue of Aphrodite, map of Cyprus. b, Sleeping Lady statue.

2008, Jan. 1   Litho.   Perf. 13¾
1088 A410 €1 Sheet of 2, #a-b   8.00 10.00
See Malta No. 1329.

Anemone Flowers — A411

Variously colored Anemone coronaria flowers with background colors of: 26c, Blue. 34c, Red. 51c, Green. 68c, Yellow orange.

2008, Mar. 6   Perf. 13¼x13¾
1089-1092 A411 Set of 4   6.50 7.25

Europa — A412

Designs: 51c, Closed and open envelopes. 68c, Envelopes and mail boxes.

2008, May 2   Litho.   Perf. 13¼x13¾
1093-1094 A412 Set of 2   4.50 5.25
1094a   Booklet pane, 4 each
           #1093-1094, perf.
           13¼x13¾ on 3 sides   17.00   —
           Complete booklet, #1094a 17.50

Souvenir Sheet

Fourth Intl. Congress of Cypriot Studies, Nicosia — A413

2008, May 2   Perf. 13¾ on 3 Sides
1095 A413 85c multi   5.00 6.00

CYPRUS

12th Francophone Summit, Quebec — A414

2008, June 5 Litho. Perf. 13¾
1096 A414 85c multi 2.75 3.25

2008 Summer Olympics, Beijing — A415

Designs: 22c, Sailboarding. 34c, High jump. 43c, Tennis. 51c, Shooting.

2008, June 5 Perf. 13x13¼
1097-1100 A415 Set of 4 6.50 6.50

Cyprus Throughout the Years Type of 2007
Miniature Sheet

No. 1101: a, Coin from Archaic period, 750 B.C.-480 B.C. b, Ship from Archaic period. c, Bust of Kimon the Athenian and ship, Classical period, 480 B.C.-310 B.C. d, Tomb of the Kings, Hellenistic period, 310 B.C.-30 B.C. e, Coin from Hellenistic period. f, Painting of St. Paul from Roman period, 30 B.C.-A.D. 324. g, Bust of Septimus Severus from Roman period. h, Granting of church privileges from Early Byzantine period, 324-841.

2008, Oct. 2 Litho. Perf. 13¾
1101 A407 43c Sheet of 8, #a-h 11.00 14.50

Christmas — A416

Icons from church, Pelendri: 22c, Archangel Gabriel. 51c, Archangel Michael. 68c, Madonna and Child.

2008, Nov. 13 Perf. 13¼x13
1102-1104 A416 Set of 3 5.50 6.00

Cooperative Movement, Cent. — A417

2009, Mar. 12 Litho. Perf. 13¾
1105 A417 26c multi .85 .60

Louis Braille (1809-52), Educator of the Blind — A418

2009, Mar. 12 Litho. & Embossed
1106 A418 68c multi 2.50 3.00

Introduction of the Euro, 10th Anniv. — A419

Reverse of Cyprus: 51c, Cent coin. 68c, 2-euro coin.

2009, Mar. 12 Litho.
1107-1108 A419 Set of 2 3.30 4.75

Intl. Year of Planet Earth A420

No. 1109: a, Western Hemisphere. b, Eastern Hemisphere.

2009, May 4 Litho. Perf. 13x13¼
1109 A420 51c Horiz. pair, #a-b 4.50 4.75

Europa — A421

Constellations: 51c, Cassiopeia. 68c, Andromeda.

2009, May 4 Perf. 13¼x13¾
1110-1111 A421 Set of 2 4.50 5.00
1111a Booklet pane of 8, 4 each #1110-1111, perf. 13¼x13¾ on 3 sides 15.00 —
Complete booklet, #1111a 15.00

Intl. Year of Astronomy.

18th Games of the Small States of Europe, Cyprus — A422

Designs: 22c, Tennis. 34c, Sailing. 43c, Cycling.

2009, June 1 Litho. Perf. 13¼x13¾
1112-1114 A422 Set of 3 3.50 3.75

Souvenir Sheet

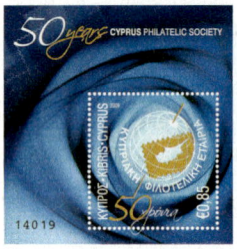

Cyprus Philatelic Society, 50th Anniv. A423

Litho. & Embossed With Foil Application
2009, June 1 Perf. 13¾
1115 A423 85c multi 3.50 3.75

Cyprus Throughout the Years Type of 2007
Miniature Sheet

No. 1116: a, St. Paraskevi Church, 9th cent. b, Monastery of St. John Chrysostom, 1090-1100. c, Lusignan coat of arms, 1192-1489. d, Chronicle of Leontios Macharias, 15th cent. e, Queen Caterina Cornaro cedes Cyprus to Venice, 1489. f, Venetian Walls, Nicosia, 1567-70. g, Ottoman siege of Nicosia, 1570. h, Larnaca Aqueduct, 18th cent.

2009, Sept. 10 Litho. Perf. 13¾
1116 A407 43c Sheet of 8, #a-h 13.50 15.50

Domesticated Birds — A424

Designs: 22c, Pigeon. 34c, Turkey. 43c, Rooster. 51c, Duck.

2009, Sept. 10 Perf. 13¾x13¼
1117-1120 A424 Set of 4 5.25 6.00

European Court of Human Rights, 50th Anniv. — A425

2009, Nov. 12 Litho. Perf. 13x13¼
1121 A425 51c multi 1.65 2.20

A426

Christmas — A427

Perf. 13¼x13¾
2009, Nov. 12 Litho.
1122 A426 22c shown .75 .35

Litho. & Embossed With Foil Application
Perf. 13¾
1123 A427 51c shown 1.95 1.65
1124 A427 68c Solid silver star 2.75 4.00
Nos. 1122-1124 (3) 5.45 6.00

Republic of Cyprus, 50th Anniv. — A428

Denomination color: 68c, Bister. 85c, Blue.

Litho. & Embossed With Foil Application
2010, Jan. 27 Perf. 13¾x13¼
1125-1126 A428 Set of 2 5.25 6.60

Expo 2010, Shanghai — A429

2010, Mar. 17 Litho. Perf. 13x13¼
1127 A429 51c multi 2.20 2.20

2010 World Cup Soccer Championships, South Africa — A430

2010, Mar. 17 Perf. 13¾
1128 A430 €1.71 multi 6.50 7.00

Barnyard Animals — A431

Designs: 22c, Pig. 26c, Sheep. 34c, Goat. 43c, Cow. €1.71, Rabbit.

2010, Mar. 17 Perf. 13¾x13¼
1129-1133 A431 Set of 5 10.00 11.00

Europa A432

No. 1134 — Stack of books and: a, Sun, flowers, tree, snails, bees. b, Tree, bees.

2010, May 5 Perf. 13¼x13¾
1134 A432 51c Horiz. pair, #a-b 3.85 4.50
c. Booklet pane of 8, 4 each #1134a-1134b, perf. 13¼x13¾ on 3 sides 13.00
Complete booklet, #1134c 13.00

Visit of Pope Benedict XVI — A433

2010, June 4 Perf. 13¾x14¼
1135 A433 51c multi 1.60 1.60

Cyprus Railway A434

No. 1136 — Locomotive with denomination in: a, Black. b, White.
85c, Train, map of stations.

2010, June 4 Perf. 13¾x13¼
1136 A434 43c Pair, #a-b 4.40 5.00

Souvenir Sheet
1137 A434 85c multi 3.60 4.10

Cyprus Through the Ages Type of 2007
Miniature Sheet

No. 1138: a, Treaties of Sevres, 1920, and Lausanne, 1923. b, Burnt Government House, 1931. c, Imprisoned graves, 1955-59. d, Statue of Gregoris Afxentiou (1928-57), anti-colonialist leader. e, Presidential Palace, 1960. f, Black Summer 1974, painting by Telemachos Kanthos. g, Pres. Tassos Papadopoulos signing Treaty of Accession to the European Union, 2004. h, Flag of Cyprus.

2010, Oct. 1 Litho. Perf. 13¾
1138 A407 43c Sheet of 8, #a-h 13.75 16.00

Souvenir Sheet

Viticulture — A435

No. 1139: a, Wine barrels, wine glass. b, Grapes, pitcher.

Perf. 14 on 3 Sides
2010, Nov. 10 Litho.
1139 A435 51c Sheet of 2, #a-b 6.00 6.50
See Romania Nos. 5216-5217.

Nativity A436   Christmas Ornament A437

Perf. 13¼x13¾
2010, Nov. 10 Litho.
1140 A436 22c shown .70 .35

Litho. & Embossed With Foil Application
Perf. 13¾
1141 A437 51c shown 1.50 1.20
1142 A437 68c Ornament, diff. 2.10 3.30
Nos. 1140-1142 (3) 4.15 4.40

CYPRUS

Anorthosis Ammochostos Soccer Team, Cent. — A438

2011, Jan. 28   Litho.   *Perf. 13¾*
1143   A438   34c multi   1.20   1.40

Composers A439

No. 1144: a, Johann Sebastian Bach (1685-1750). b, Wolfgang Amadeus Mozart (1756-91). c, Ludwig van Beethoven (1770-1827).

2011, Jan. 28   *Perf. 13¾x14¼*
1144   Horiz. strip of 3   6.00   6.50
a.-c.   A439 51c Any single   1.95   2.20

Lace — A440

Lace with: 26c, Floral pattern. 43c, Diamonds and squares pattern.

2011, Mar. 23   *Perf. 13¾x14*
1145-1146   A440   Set of 2   2.20   2.25

Rosa Damascena A441

2011, Mar. 23   *Perf. 13¾*
1147   A441   34c shown   1.10   1.40

Souvenir Sheet
1148   A441   85c Roses, diff.   3.85   4.40

Nos. 1147-1148 are impregnated with a rose scent.

Europa — A442

2011, May 4   *Perf. 14*
1149   A442   51c Blue forest   2.75   2.20
   a.   Perf. 13x13½ on 3 sides   2.75
1150   A442   68c Green forest   3.60   4.40
   a.   Perf. 13x13½ on 3 sides   3.60   3.90
   b.   Booklet pane of 8, 4 each #1149a-1150a   22.00
   Complete booklet, #1150b   24.00

Intl. Year of Forests.

Lighthouses — A443

Map and: 34c, Paphos Lighthouse. 43c, Cape Greco Lighthouse. €1.71 Cape Kiti Lighthouse.

2011, May 4   *Perf. 14*
1151-1152   A443   Set of 2   5.50   4.15

Souvenir Sheet
Perf. 13½x13¼
1153   A443   €1.71 multi   8.00   8.00

Booklet Stamp
Self-Adhesive
Die Cut Perf. 13¼x13
1153A   A443   43c multi (RA28Ab)   2.50   2.75

No. 1153 contains one 27x35mm stamp.

Christopher A. Pissarides, 2010 Nobel Laureate in Economics A444

2011, June 8   *Perf. 14x14¼*
1154   A444   €1.71 multi   5.00   5.00

Tall Ships — A445

Designs: 22c, Galleon. 43c, Caravel. 85c, Brig.

2011, June 8   *Perf. 13¾*
1155-1157   A445   Set of 3   4.25   4.25

The Hare and the Tortoise A446

No. 1158: a, Hare. b, Tortoise. c, Tortoise passing sleeping hare, horiz. d, Hare running. e, Tortoise crossing finish line.

Die Cut Perf. 11½x12, 12x11½
2011, Oct. 5   Litho.
Self-Adhesive
1158   A446   34c Booklet pane of 5, #a-e   7.00   8.25

Nativity A447

Christmas Ornament A448

Perf. 13¼x13¾
2011, Nov. 11   Litho.
1159   A447   22c shown   .85   .35

Litho. & Embossed With Foil Application
Perf. 13¾
1160   A448   51c shown   1.90   1.40
1161   A448   68c Ornament, diff.   2.75   4.40
   Nos. 1159-1161 (3)   5.50   6.15

Horses — A449

Various horses: 26c, 34c, 51c, 85c.

2012, Jan. 31   Litho.   *Perf. 13¾x13¼*
1162-1165   A449   Set of 4   7.25   7.25

2012 Summer Olympics, London — A450

Designs: 22c, Men's gymnastics. 26c, Men's tennis. 34c, Men's high jump. 43c, Shooting.

Litho. With Foil Application
2012, Mar. 21   *Perf. 14*
1166-1169   A450   Set of 4   4.75   5.00

Souvenir Sheet

Soccer A451

2012, Mar. 21   Litho.   *Perf.*
1170   A451   €1.71 multi   6.25   6.25

Jasminum Grandiflorum A452

2012, May 2   *Perf. 13¾*
1171   A452   34c shown   1.40   1.55

Souvenir Sheet
1172   A452   85c Flowers, diff.   3.30   3.85

Nos. 1171-1172 are impregnated with a jasmine scent.

Europa — A453

Various Cyprus tourist attractions and silhouette of: 51c, Family. 68c, Man and woman with bicycles.

2012, May 2   *Perf. 13¾x13½*
1173-1174   A453   Set of 2   5.25   4.95
   1174a   Booklet pane of 8, 4 each #1173-1174, perf. 13¾x13½ on 3 sides   18.75
   Complete booklet, #1174a   19.00

Cyprus Presidency of European Union Council — A454

Litho. With Foil Application
2012, July 1   *Perf. 13¾*
1175   A454   51c multi   1.55   1.90

Souvenir Sheet
1176   A454   €10 multi   23.50   26.50

The Cricket and the Ant — A455

No. 1177: a, Cricket with fiddle, sun. b, Ant with seeds. c, Ant carrying seeds. d, Cricket fiddling under tree. e, Cricket outside in winter, ant at door.

2012, Oct. 3   *Die Cut Perf. 11¼x12*
Self-Adhesive
1177   A455   34c Booklet pane of 5, #a-e   6.50   6.50

Pavlos Kontides, Silver Medalist in Sailing at 2012 Summer Olympics — A456

Litho. With Foil Application
2012, Nov. 14   *Perf. 14*
1178   A456   34c multi   1.40   1.55

Christmas — A457

Icons from: 22c, Madonna and Child, Christ Antiphonitis Church. 51c, Madonna and Child, Panayia Church, Lysi. 68c, Madonna and Child Enthroned Between St. George and St. Nicholas, St. George's Church, Vatyli.

Perf. 13¼x13¾
2012, Nov. 12   Litho.
1179   A457   22c multi   .90   .35
1180   A457   51c multi   1.75   1.55

Size: 65x65mm
Imperf
1181   A457   68c multi   2.75   3.85

Admission of Cyprus Red Cross to International Red Cross, 1st Anniv. — A458

2013, Jan. 30   *Perf. 14¼x13¾*
1182   A458   22c multi   1.40   1.10

Cyprus Scouts Association, Cent. — A459

2013, Jan. 30   *Perf. 13¾*
1183   A459   43c multi   1.95   1.95

Archbishop Makarios (1913-77), President of Cyprus — A460

2013, Jan. 30   *Perf. 14*
1184   A460   85c multi   3.00   3.30

Easter — A461

Icons depicting: 26c, Christ's entry into Jerusalem. 34c, Crucifixion. €1.71, Resurrection (27x40mm).

2013, Apr. 3   *Perf. 14x14¼*
1185-1187   A461   Set of 3   7.25   7.25

Origanum Dubium — A462

2013, May 2   *Perf. 13¾*
1188   A462   22c shown   1.40   1.10

Souvenir Sheet
1189   A462   85c Flowers, diff.   3.25   3.75

Nos. 1188-1189 are impregnated with an oregano scent.

Europa — A463

CYPRUS

Mailbox and postal vehicles: 34c, Automobile, van and airplane. 51c, Automobile.

2013, May 2			Perf. 14	
1190-1191	A463	Set of 2	4.15	4.40
1191a	Booklet pane of 8, 4 each #1190-1191, perf. 14 on 3 sides		14.50	—
	Complete booklet, #1191a		15.00	

Marine Life — A464

Designs: 34c, Seahorse. 43c, Sea anemone. €1.71, Sea fan coral.

2013, June 5			Perf. 13¾	
1192-1194	A464	Set of 3	7.50	7.50

For surcharge, see No. 1225.

Cypriot Folk Tale "Spanos and the Forty Dragons" A465

No. 1195: a, Spanos in cloud near dragon. b, Boar chasing Spanos up a tree, vert. c, Spanos, river, woman holding flowers. d, Spanos sitting near dragon. e, Spanos pouring water on dragon.

Die Cut Perf. 13x13½, 13½x13

2013, Nov. 13		Litho.		
		Self-Adhesive		
1195	A465	34c Booklet pane of 5, #a-e	6.50	6.50

Christmas A466

Winning art in children's stamp design contest: 22c, Santa Claus and Christmas tree. 34c, Snowman, Christmas trees and houses. 85c, Christmas tree and gifts, vert.

Perf. 14¼x14, 14x14¼

2013, Nov. 13			Litho.	
1196-1198	A466	Set of 3	5.25	5.25

Olive Production A467

Designs: 34c, Olive tree and grove.
No. 1200: a, Olives. b, Olives, container of olive oil.

2014, Jan. 30		Litho.	Perf. 14	
1199	A467	34c multi	1.65	.45
1200	A467	51c Horiz. pair, #a-b	4.40	6.60

Four Seasons — A468

Designs: 22c, Child under umbrella (winter). 43c, Girl wearing butterfly costume standing in flowers (spring). 85c, Girl with balloons, fish and dolphins (summer). €1.71, Child holding fallen leaf in front of face (autumn).

2014, Mar. 12		Litho.	Perf. 13¾	
1201-1204	A468	Set of 4	10.00	10.00

For surcharges, see Nos. 1212-1214.

Europa — A469

Musicians with instruments: 34c, Cyprus flute. 51c, Lute.

2014, May 2		Litho.	Perf. 14	
1205-1206	A469	Set of 2	3.30	3.30
1206a	Booklet pane of 8, 4 each #1205-1206, perf. 14 on 3 sides		12.00	—
	Complete booklet, #1206a		12.50	

Famous Men — A470

Designs: 41c, El Greco (1541-1614), painter. 50c, Michelangelo (1475-1564), painter and sculptor. 64c, Galileo Galilei (1564-1642), astronomer. 75c, Henri de Toulouse-Lautrec (1864-1901), painter.

2014, June 30		Litho.	Perf. 14	
1207-1210	A470	Set of 4	8.75	7.25

Euromed Postal Emblem and Mediterranean Sea — A471

2014, July 9		Litho.	Perf. 14	
1211	A471	60c multi	1.90	1.90

Nos. 1201, 1202 and 1204 Surcharged

Methods and Perfs. As Before

2014, Aug. 1				
1212	A468	4c on 22c #1201	.45	.75
1213	A468	€1 on 43c #1202	3.00	3.00
1214	A468	€1.88 on €1.71 #1204	6.00	7.25
	Nos. 1212-1214 (3)		9.45	11.00

Famous People A472

No. 1215: a, Theodoulos Kallinikos (1904-2004), cantor and musicologist. b, Stylianos Hourmouzios (1850-1937), cantor and journalist.
No. 1216: a, Sozos Tombolis (1914-2002), cantor and music professor. b, Achilleas Lymbourides (1917-2008), composer.
No. 1217: a, Telemachos Kanthos (1910-93), painter. b, Loukia Nicolaidou (1909-94), painter.
No. 1218: a, George Pol Georgiou (1901-72), painter. b, Michael Kashalos (1885-1974), painter.
No. 1219: a, Kypros Chrysanthis (1915-98), writer. b, Antis Pernaris (1903-80), writer.
No. 1220: a, Glafkos Alithersis (1897-1965), writer. b, Costas Montis (1914-2004), writer.

2014, Oct. 10		Litho.	Perf. 14	
1215	A472	Horiz. pair	.45	.65
a.-b.		4c Either single	.30	.35
1216	A472	Horiz. pair	1.55	1.55
a.-b.		34c Either single	.80	.80
1217	A472	Horiz. pair	2.00	2.00
a.-b.		41c Either single	1.00	1.00
1218	A472	Horiz. pair	2.30	2.30
a.-b.		50c Either single	1.20	1.20
1219	A472	Horiz. pair	2.75	2.75
a.-b.		64c Either single	1.35	1.35
1220	A472	Horiz. pair	4.40	3.30
a.-b.		85c Either single	1.65	1.65
	Nos. 1215-1220 (6)		13.45	12.55

See Nos. 1226-1231.

Cypriot Folk Tale "The Prince of Venice" A473

No. 1221: a, Prince carried by angel. b, Angel carrying sword, vert. c, Woman with veil, vert. d, Angel and woman, vert. e, Ship at sea.

Die Cut Perf. 13½

2014, Nov. 24		Litho.		
		Self-Adhesive		
1221	A473	Booklet pane of 5	7.50	
a.-e.		41c Any single	1.65	1.75

Christmas — A474

Icons depicting: 41c, Nativity. 64c, Madonna and Child. 75c, Nativity, diff.

2014, Nov. 24		Litho.	Perf. 14	
1222-1224	A474	Set of 3	5.25	4.75

No. 1193 Surcharged

Method and Perf. As Before

2015, Feb. 4				
1225	A464	34c on 43c #1193	.75	.75

Famous People Type of 2014

No. 1226: a, Adamantios Diamantis (1900-94), painter. b, Theodosis Pierides (1908-68), poet.
No. 1227: a, Maria Rousia (1894-1957), writer. b, Melis Nicolaides (1892-1979), writer.
No. 1228: a, Kyriakos Hadjioannou (1909-97), folklorist. b, Polyxeni Loizia (1855-1942), educator.
No. 1229: a, Loizos Philippou (1895-1950), newspaper editor. b, Persefoni Papadopoulou (1888-1948), educator.
No. 1230: a, Georgios Frangoudes (1869-1939), politician. b, Porfyrios Dikaios (1904-71), archaeologist.
No. 1231: a, Nicos Pantelides (1906-84), actor. b, Pavlos Xioutas (1908-91), folklorist.

2015, Feb. 4		Litho.	Perf. 14	
1226	A472	Horiz. pair	.45	.65
a.-b.		4c Either single	.30	.35
1227	A472	Horiz. pair	2.30	2.30
a.-b.		50c Either single	1.20	1.20
1228	A472	Horiz. pair	2.80	2.80
a.-b.		60c Either single	1.40	1.40
1229	A472	Horiz. pair	3.00	3.00
a.-b.		75c Either single	1.50	1.50
1230	A472	Horiz. pair	5.50	4.50
a.-b.		€1 Either single	2.25	2.25
1231	A472	Horiz. pair	6.50	6.00
a.-b.		€1.50 Either single	3.00	3.00
	Nos. 1226-1231 (6)		20.55	19.25

Melkonian Orphanage A475

2015, Apr. 2		Litho.	Perf. 13¾x14¼	
1232	A475	64c multi	2.50	2.50

See Armenia No. 1034.

Preserved Fruit — A476

Designs: 34c, Bitter orange. 41c, Bitter orange, diff. €1.88, Cherry.

2015, Apr. 2		Litho.	Perf. 13¾	
1233-1235	A476	Set of 3	6.00	6.00

Souvenir Sheet

Independence Struggle of National Organization of Cypriot Fighters, 60th Anniv. — A477

Litho., Sheet Margin Litho. With Foil Application

2015, Apr. 2			Perf. 13¾	
1236	A477	€2 multi	5.50	5.50

Europa — A478

Children and: 34c, Top. 64c, Marbles.

2015, May 5		Litho.	Perf. 14	
1237-1238	A478	Set of 2	2.75	3.00
1238a	Booklet pane of 8, 4 each #1237-1238, perf. 14 on 3 sides		12.00	—
	Complete booklet, #1238a		12.50	

Map of Mediterranean Sea and Cypriot Boats — A479

2015, July 9		Litho.	Perf. 14	
1239	A479	75c multi	3.00	3.00

Akamas Peninsula A480

Avakas Gorge A481

2015, July 9		Litho.	Perf. 14	
1240	A480	34c multi	1.40	.55
1241	A481	64c multi	2.75	3.00

International Telecommunication Union, 150th Anniv. — A482

2015, Sept. 14		Litho.	Perf. 14	
1242	A482	64c multi	2.75	2.50

Castles — A483

Designs: 4c, Buffavento Castle. 34c, Kantara Castle. 41c, Agios Ilarionos (St. Hilarion) Castle. 75c, Kyrenia Castle.

CYPRUS

	Perf. 13¾x13½	
2015, Sept. 14	Litho.	
1243-1246 A483 Set of 4		6.00 5.00

Handicrafts — A484

No. 1247: a, Carved wooden chair. b, Decorated gourds.
No. 1248: a, Silver merrecha. b, Clay vessels.

2015, Sept. 14	Litho.	Perf. 14
1247 A484 Pair		2.75 2.75
a.-b. 34c Either single		1.40 1.40
1248 A484 Pair		5.00 5.00
a.-b. 64c Either single		2.50 2.50

A485   A486

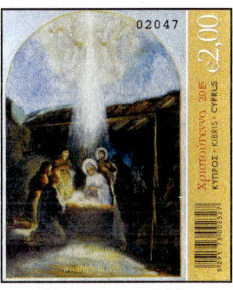

Christmas — A487

Designs: 34c, Girl burning olive leaves. 41c, Madonna and Child icon. 64c, Child mailing letter to Santa Claus. €2, Nativity.

2015, Nov. 19	Litho.	Perf. 14
1249 A485 34c multi		1.10 .25
1250 A486 41c multi		1.65 .40
1251 A485 64c multi		3.00 4.40
Nos. 1249-1251 (3)		5.75 5.05
	Imperf	
1252 A487 €2 multi		7.75 8.25

Traditional Crafts — A488

Designs: 41c, Basket weaving. 64c, Wood carving.

2016, Mar. 10	Litho.	Perf. 14
1253-1254 A488 Set of 2		3.75 4.00

2016 Summer Olympics, Rio de Janeiro A489

Designs: 34c, Taekwondo. 41c, Tennis. 64c, High jump. 75c, Sprinter.

2016, Apr. 11	Litho.	Perf. 13¾
1255-1258 A489 Set of 4		7.75 7.75

No. 1258 is a square stamp.

A490

Europa — A491

2016, May 9	Litho.	Perf. 14
1259 A490 34c multi		.80 .80
1260 A491 64c multi		1.50 1.50
a. Booklet pane of 8, 4 each #1259-1260, perf. 14 on 3 sides		11.00 —

Think Green Issue.
No. 1260a was sold with but unattached to a booklet cover.

A492

Winning Art in "Principles and Values of the European Union" Children's Stamp Design Contest
A493   A494

2016, May 9	Litho.	Perf. 14
1261 A492 34c multi		.85 .45
1262 A493 41c multi		1.10 .60
1263 A494 64c multi		1.65 2.50
Nos. 1261-1263 (3)		3.60 3.55

Montage of Fish of the Mediterranean Sea — A495

2016, July 8	Litho.	Perf. 14
1264 A495 €1.88 multi		4.40 4.95

Fountains — A496

Designs: 34c, Children at Panayla Fountain, Paphos. 41c, Woman carrying water jug, Pegeia Fountain, Pegia.

2016, July 8	Litho.	Perf. 14
1265-1266 A496 Set of 2		1.75 1.75

Stelios Joannou (1915-99), Businessman and Philanthropist A497

Georgios Paraskevaides (1916-2007), Businessman and Philanthropist A498

Anastasios Georgios Leventis (1902-78), Businessman and Philanthropist — A499

Cyprus Chairmanship of the Council of Europe — A500

2016, Oct. 17	Litho.	Perf. 14
1267 A497 34c multi		.75 .75
1268 A498 34c multi		.75 .75
1269 A499 34c multi		.75 .75
Nos. 1267-1269 (3)		2.25 2.25

2016, Nov. 17	Litho.	Perf. 13¾
1270 A500 €1 multi		3.00 2.75

A501   Christmas — A502

Designs: 34c, String of Christmas lights. 41c, Christmas tree. 64c, Adoration of the Magi icon.

2016, Nov. 17	Litho.	Perf. 14
1271 A501 34c multi		.75 .30
1272 A501 41c multi		1.10 .40
1273 A502 64c multi		1.65 2.50
Nos. 1271-1273 (3)		3.50 3.20

Flowers — A503

Designs: 34c, Crocus hartmannianus. 41c, Carlina pygmaea. 64c, Centaurea akamantis. €1, Tulipa cypria.

2017, Feb. 16	Litho.	Perf. 14
1274-1277 A503 Set of 4		6.75 6.50

Television Broadcasting in Cyprus, 60th Anniv. — A504

2017, Mar. 24	Litho.	Perf. 14
1278 A504 34c multi		.75 .45

Cyprus Medical Association, 50th Anniv. — A505

2017, Mar. 24	Litho.	Perf. 14
1279 A505 41c multi		1.10 .65

Lions Clubs International, Cent. — A506

2017, Mar. 24	Litho.	Perf. 14
1280 A506 64c multi		2.25 2.25

Paphos, 2017 European Capital of Culture — A507

No. 1281: a, Aphrodite's Rock. b, Emblem. c, Pillars of House of Theseus.

2017, Mar. 24	Litho.	Perf. 14
1281 Horiz. strip of 3		5.25 6.00
a.-c. A507 64c Any single		1.90 2.20

International Year of Sustainable Tourism for Development A508

2017, May 4	Litho.	Perf. 14
1282 A508 64c multi		1.50 1.50

Europa — A509

Designs: 41c, Larnaka Castle. 64c, Paphos Castle.

2017, May 4	Litho.	Perf. 14
1283-1284 A509 Set of 2		2.40 2.40
1284a Booklet pane of 8, 4 each #1283-1284, perf. 14 on 3 sides		9.75 —
Complete booklet, #1284a		9.75

Stylized Tree — A510

2017, July 10	Litho.	Perf. 14
1285 A510 64c multi		2.20 2.20

Triptych From Church of Our Lady Chryseleousa Strovolos — A511

Children Opening Gift A512

Boy Writing Letter to Santa Claus — A513

No. 1286: a, St. Minas the Egyptian (carmine panel at left). b, Madonna and Child, ship (carmine panel at bottom). c, St. Spyridon (carmine panel at right).
No. 1287: a, Child in red and white striped shirt, Santa Claus and reindeer. b, Child in green shirt.

2017, Nov. 24	Litho.	Perf. 14
1286 A511 34c Horiz. strip of 3, #a-c		3.25 3.25
1287 A512 41c Horiz. pair, #a-b		2.75 2.75
1288 A513 64c multi		1.75 1.75
Nos. 1286-1288 (3)		7.75 7.75

Christmas.

Souvenir Sheet

St. Andrew the Apostle Monastery, Rizokarpaso, 150th Anniv. — A514

CYPRUS

Litho. With Foil Application
2017, Nov. 30   *Perf. 13¼x13*
1289   A514   €10 sil & multi   30.00   30.00

Flowers — A515

Designs: 34c, Allium sphaerocephalon. 41c, Anthemis tricolor. 64c, Onobrychis venosa. €1.88, Tragopogon porrifolius.

Perf. 13¼x13½
2018, Feb. 12   *Litho.*
1290-1293   A515   Set of 4   8.00   8.00

Halloumi Cheese — A516

2018, Mar. 28   *Litho.*   *Perf. 14*
1294   A516   41c multi   1.00   1.00

2018 World Cup Soccer Championships, Russia — A517

2018, Mar. 28   *Litho.*   *Perf. 14*
1295   A517   64c multi   1.60   1.60

Marios Tokas (1954-2008), Composer — A518

2018, Apr. 27   *Litho.*   *Perf. 13¾x14¼*
1296   A518   64c multi   1.60   1.60

Europa — A519

Designs: 34c, Kelefos Bridge. 64c, Akapnou Bridge.

2018, May 2   *Litho.*   *Perf. 14*
1297-1298   A519   Set of 2   2.40   2.40
1298a   Booklet pane of 8, 4 each #1297-1298, perf. 14 on 3 sides   9.75   —
Complete booklet, #1298a   9.75

Houses, Lefkosa — A520

2018, July 9   *Litho.*   *Perf. 14*
1299   A520   64c multi   1.50   1.50

Interparliamentary Assembly on Orthodoxy, 25th Anniv. — A521

2018, July 9   *Litho.*   *Perf. 13¾x14¼*
1300   A521   64c multi   1.50   1.50

Birds — A522

Designs: 34c, Carduelis carduelis. 64c, Chloris chloris. €1, Fringilla coelebs.

2018, Sept. 27   *Litho.*   *Perf. 14*
1301-1303   A522   Set of 3   4.75   4.75

Children and Snowman A523

Nativity Icon, Panagia Odigitria Church, Galata A524

Children Singing Carols A525

No. 1306: a, Girl with triangle at left. b, Boy with drum at left.

Perf. 14¼x14, 14 (41c)
2018, Nov. 8   *Litho.*
1304   A523   34c multi   .80   .80
1305   A524   41c multi   .95   .95
1306   A525   64c Horiz. pair, #a-b   3.00   3.00
   Nos. 1304-1306 (3)   4.75   4.75

Carnival — A526

Carnival revelers wearing: 41c, Clown and Native American costumes. 50c, Pirate and witch costumes.

Perf. 13¾x13½
2019, Feb. 20   *Litho.*
1307-1308   A526   Set of 2   2.10   2.10

Old Trees — A527

Designs: 34c, 800-year old Platanus orientalis. 41c, 700-year old Cupressus sempervirens. 64c, 1500-year old Pistacia atlantica.

2019, Mar. 28   *Litho.*   *Perf. 13¾x14*
1309-1311   A527   Set of 3   3.25   3.25

Pres. Glafcos Clerides (1919-2013) — A528

2019, Apr. 20   *Litho.*   *Perf. 13¼*
1312   A528   €1 multi   2.25   2.25

Europa — A529

Birds: 41c, Gyps fulvus. 64c, Aquila fasciata.

Traditional Costumes of Men and Women of Cyprus — A530

2019, May 2   *Litho.*   *Perf. 13½*
1313-1314   A529   Set of 2   2.40   2.40
1314a   Booklet pane of 8, 4 each #1313-1314, perf. 13½ on 3 sides   9.75   —
Complete booklet, #1314a   9.75

2019, July 9   *Litho.*   *Perf. 13¼x13¾*
1315   A530   €1.88 multi   4.25   4.25

Miniature Sheet

Athletic Associations — A531

No. 1316 — Organization and year of establishment: a, Olympia Athletic Association, 1892. b, Pancypria Athletic Association, 1894. c, Zenon Athletic Association, 1896. d, Korivos Athletic Association, 1898. e, Evagoras Athletic Association of Ammochostos, 1903. f, Praxandros Athletic Association, 1919.

2019, July 9   *Litho.*   *Perf. 13¾x13¼*
1316   A531   34c Sheet of 6, #a-f   4.50   4.50

Council of Europe, 70th Anniv. — A532

Perf. 13¾x13¼
2019, Sept. 10
1317   A532   34c multi   .75   .75

International Civil Aviation Organization, 75th Anniv. — A533

Perf. 13¾x13¼
2019, Sept. 10   *Litho.*
1318   A533   41c multi   .90   .90

Express Mail Service, 20th Anniv. — A534

Perf. 13¾x13¼
2019, Sept. 10   *Litho.*
1319   A534   64c multi   1.40   1.40

Mohandas K. Gandhi (1869-1948), Indian Nationalist Leader — A535

2019, Sept. 10   *Litho.*   *Perf. 13½*
1320   A535   75c multi   1.75   1.75

Angel — A536

Snowman A537

Painting of Our Lady of Araka A538

Perf. 13¾x13¼
2019, Nov. 14   *Litho.*
1321   A536   34c multi   .75   .75
1322   A537   41c multi   .90   .90
Perf. 13¼x13¾
1323   A538   64c multi   1.40   1.40
   Nos. 1321-1323 (3)   3.05   3.05
Christmas.

Dams — A539

Designs: 50c, Asprokremmos Dam. €1, Kouris Dam.

Perf. 13¼x13½
2020, Feb. 12   *Litho.*
1324-1325   A539   Set of 2   3.50   3.50

Butterflies A540

Designs: 34c, Aporia crataegi. 41c, Papilio machaon. 64c, Cigaritis acamas cypriaca.

Perf. 13¼x13½
2020, Feb. 12   *Litho.*
1326-1328   A540   Set of 3   3.25   3.25

Stelios Kyriakides (1910-87), Marathon Runner and Humanitarian — A541

No. 1329 — Kyriakides: a, Wearing victory wreath on head. b, Running.

2020, Mar. 19   *Litho.*   *Perf. 13¼*
1329   A541   34c Pair, #a-b   1.50   1.50

2020 Olympic Games, Tokyo — A542

Designs: 34c, Gymnastics. 41c, Discus. 64c, High jump. 75c, Runner crossing finish line.

Perf. 13½x13¼
2020, Mar. 19   *Litho.*
1330-1333   A542   Set of 4   4.75   4.75
The 2020 Summer Olympics was postponed because of the coronavirus pandemic.

Florence Nightingale (1820-1910), Nurse — A543

2020, May 4   *Litho.*   *Perf. 13¾x13¼*
1334   A543   34c multi   .75   .75
International Year of the Nurse and Midwife.

CYPRUS

Europa — A544

Map of Cyprus postal routes with background color of: 34c, Olive green. 64c, Blue.

2020, May 4   Litho.   Perf. 13¾x13¼
1335-1336 A544 Set of 2   2.25 2.25
1336a   Booklet pane of 8, 4 each
         #1335-1336, perf.
         13¾x13¼ on 3 sides   9.00   —
         Complete booklet, #1336a 9.00

National Organization of Cypriot Fighters, 65th Anniv. — A545

2020, July 9   Litho.   Perf. 13¾x14
1337 A545 34c multi   .80   .80

National Organization of Cypriot Fighters House, 25th Anniv. — A546

2020, July 9   Litho.   Perf. 13¾x14
1338 A546 41c multi   1.00 1.00

Employers and Industrialists Federation, 60th Anniv. — A547

2020, July 9   Litho.   Perf. 13¾x13¼
1339 A547 41c multi   1.00 1.00

Kolokasi (Taro Stew) — A548

2020, July 9   Litho.   Perf. 13¼x13¾
1340 A548 64c multi   1.50 1.50

Famous People — A549

Designs: No. 1341, 34c, Nearchos Clerides (1892-1969), writer. No. 1342, 34c, Stella Soulioti (1920-2012), Attorney General. No. 1343, 34c, Vassos Lyssaridis, physician and politician.

Perf. 13¾x13¼
2020, Sept. 17   Litho.
1341-1343 A549 Set of 3   2.40 2.40
100th birthday of Lyssaridis.

Wreath of Christmas Cookies — A550

Christmas Cookies and Cakes — A551

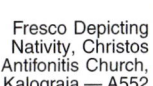

Fresco Depicting Nativity, Christos Antifonitis Church, Kalograia — A552

2020, Nov. 19   Litho.   Perf. 13½x13¼
1344 A550 34c multi   .85   .85
1345 A551 41c multi   1.00 1.00
Perf. 13¼x13¾
1346 A552 64c multi   1.60 1.60
         Nos. 1344-1346 (3)   3.45 3.45

Famous Airplanes A553

Designs: 34c, Wright Flyer, 1903. 75c, Spirit of St. Louis, 1927. €1, Bell X-1, 1947.

Perf. 13¾x13¼
2021, Feb. 18   Litho.
1347-1349 A553 Set of 3   5.00 5.00

Cyprus Cancer Association, 50th Anniv. — A554

Perf. 13¾x13¼
2021, Mar. 24   Litho.
1350 A554 34c multi   .80   .80

Cyprus Telecommunications Authority, 60th Anniv. — A555

Perf. 13¾x13¼
2021, Mar. 24   Litho.
1351 A555 41c multi   1.00 1.00

A556

Greek Revolution, 200th Anniv. — A557

Designs: 34c, Monument of Cypriot Fighters, Missolonghi, and Greek flag. 64c, Mausoleum of the Cypriot Martyrs of July 9, 1821, Nicosia, and Greek flag.
€1, The Bishop of Old Patras Germanos Blesses the Flag of Revolution, painting by Theodoros Vryzakis (1819-78).

Perf. 13¼x13¾
2021, Mar. 24   Litho.
1352-1353 A556 Set of 2   2.40 2.40
Souvenir Sheet
Litho. Sheet Margin Litho. With Foil Application
1354 A557 €1 multi   2.40 2.40

Efrosini Proestou (1903-93), Midwife Who Fed and Protected Soldiers Trapped in Cave — A558

2021, May 6   Litho.   Perf. 13¾x13¼
1355 A558 34c multi   .85   .85

Endangered Animals — A559

Designs: 34c, Apis mellifera cypria. 64c, Monachus monachus.

2021, May 6   Litho.   Perf. 13¾
1356-1357 A559 Set of 2   2.40 2.40
1357a   Booklet pane of 8, 4 each
         #1356-1357, perf. 13¾ on
         3 sides   9.75   —
         Complete booklet, #1357a 9.75
Europa.

14th-13th Cent. B.C. Gold Pendant — A560

2021, July 8   Litho.   Perf. 13¾x13¼
1358 A560 64c multi   1.60 1.60

Miniature Sheet

Natura 2000 Network of Protected Natural Areas — A561

No. 1359: a, Flamingos at Oroklini Lake. b, Mouflon in forest near Paphos. c, Snow crane on Akamas Peninsula. d, Caretta caretta and posidonia oceanica underwater.

2021, July 8   Litho.   Perf. 13½
1359 A561 34c Sheet of 4, #a-d 3.25 3.25

Cyprus Theater Organization, 50th Anniv. — A562

Perf. 13¼x13¾
2021, Sept. 17   Litho.
1360 A562 34c multi   .80   .80

Confucius (c. 551-479 B.C.) and Zenon of Citium (c. 334-262 B.C.), Philosophers A563

Perf. 13¼x13¾
2021, Sept. 17   Litho.
1361 A563 75c multi   1.75 1.75
Diplomatic relations between Cyprus and People's Republic of China, 50th anniv.

Cats — A564

Cat: 34c, Facing forward. 41c, Sleeping. 50c, Facing left. 64c, Licking its paw.

Perf. 13¾x13¼
2021, Sept. 17   Litho.
1362-1365 A564 Set of 4   4.50 4.50

A565

Embroidered Christmas Ornaments A566

Nativity A567

Perf. 13¾x13¼
2021, Nov. 18   Litho.
1366 A565 34c multi   .80   .80
1367 A566 41c multi   .95   .95
Perf. 13¼x13¾
1368 A567 64c multi   1.50 1.50
         Nos. 1366-1368 (3)   3.25 3.25
Christmas.

Human Rights Commission, 30th Anniv. — A568

Perf. 13¼x13½
2021, Dec. 10   Litho.
1369 A568 34c multi   .80   .80

Owls — A569

Designs: 34c, Tyto alba. 64c, Otus cyprius.

2022, Feb. 18   Litho.   Perf. 13¼
1370-1371 A569 Set of 2   2.25 2.25

Pancyprian Organization of Large Families, 50th Anniv. — A570

Perf. 13½x13¼
2022, Mar. 23   Litho.
1372 A570 34c multi   .75   .75

World Autism Awareness Day — A571

CYPRUS

2022, Mar. 23   **Perf. 13½x13¼**   Litho.
1373   A571   41c multi   .90   .90

Limassol Chamber of Commerce and Industry, 60th Anniv. — A572

2022, Mar. 23   **Perf. 13½x13¼**   Litho.
1374   A572   50c multi   1.10   1.10

Europa — A573

Designs: 34c, Legend of the Secret Treasure of Regina. 64c, Legend of Digenis Akritas.

2022, May 6   Litho.   **Perf. 13¼x13¾**
1375-1376   A573   Set of 2   2.10   2.10
   1376a   Booklet pane of 8, 4 each #1375-1376, perf. 13¼x13¾ on 3 sides   8.50   —
   Complete booklet, #1376a   8.50

Office of the Commissioner for Electronic Communications and Postal Regulation, 20th Anniv. — A574

Perf. 13¼x13¾
2022, June 17   Litho.
1377   A574   64c multi   1.40   1.40

Maritime Link Between Cyprus and Greece — A575

Perf. 13¾x13¼
2022, June 17   Litho.
1378   A575   64c multi   1.40   1.40

7th Century B.C. Stone Vase From Acropolis of Amathunta A576

2022, July 11   Litho.   **Perf. 13¾x13¼**
1379   A576   64c multi   1.30   1.30

Zeus — A577

Hera — A578

Apollo — A579

Athena — A580

Aries — A581

Artemis — A582

Hephaestus A583

Aphrodite A584

Hermes — A585

Hestia — A586

Poseidon A587

Demeter — A588

2022, Sept. 16   **Perf. 13¾x13¼**   Litho.
1380   Sheet of 12   8.50   8.50
  a.   A577 34c multi   .70   .70
  b.   A578 34c multi   .70   .70
  c.   A579 34c multi   .70   .70
  d.   A580 34c multi   .70   .70
  e.   A581 34c multi   .70   .70
  f.   A582 34c multi   .70   .70
  g.   A583 34c multi   .70   .70
  h.   A584 34c multi   .70   .70
  i.   A585 34c multi   .70   .70
  j.   A586 34c multi   .70   .70
  k.   A587 34c multi   .70   .70
  l.   A588 34c multi   .70   .70

Greek gods.

Souvenir Sheet

Great Fire of Smyrna, Cent. A589

Litho., Sheet Margin Litho. With Foil Application
2022, Sept. 16   **Perf. 13¼x13¾**
1381   A589   €1 multi   2.00   2.00

2022 World Cup Soccer Championships, Qatar — A590

2022, Nov. 18   Litho.   **Perf. 13½**
1382   A590   34c multi   .70   .70

A591

A592

Christmas — A593

No. 1383: a, Gifts in sled. b, Reindeer.
No. 1384: a, Stocking cap. b, Santa Claus and "Ho Ho Ho."
64c, Icon from Holy Church of St. Savvas.

2022, Nov. 18   Litho.   **Perf. 13¼**
1383   A591   34c Horiz. pair, #a-b   1.40   1.40
1384   A592   41c Vert. pair, #a-b   1.75   1.75

Perf. 13¼x13¾
1385   A593   64c multi   1.40   1.40
   Nos. 1383-1385 (3)   4.55   4.55

Dragonflies — A594

Designs: 75c, Orthetrum sabina. €1, Epallage fatime.

2023, Feb. 23   **Perf. 13¼x13¾**   Litho.
1386-1387   A594   Set of 2   4.00   4.00

Cyprus Thalassemia Foundation, 50th Anniv. — A595

2023, Apr. 4   Litho.   **Perf. 13¾x13¼**
1388   A595   34c multi   .75   .75

Pancyprian Greek Teachers Association, 70th Anniv. — A596

2023, Apr. 4   Litho.   **Perf. 13¾x13¼**
1389   A596   41c multi   .90   .90

Cyprus Ports Authority, 50th Anniv. — A597

2023, Apr. 4   Litho.   **Perf. 13¼x13¾**
1390   A597   50c multi   1.10   1.10

Aerial Firefighting Cyprus - Israel
Air Tanker Fighting Fire — A598

2023, Apr. 4   Litho.   **Perf. 13¼**
1391   A598   75c multi   1.75   1.75

See Israel No. 2348.

Child, Doves and Rainbow — A599   Interlocking Hands — A600

2023, May 9   Litho.   **Perf. 13½**
1392   A599   34c multi   .75   .75
1393   A600   64c multi   1.40   1.40
  a.   Booklet pane of 8, 4 each #1392-1393, perf. 13½ on 3 sides   8.75   —
   Complete booklet, #1393a   8.75

Europa.

Rose Festival, Agros — A601

2023, July 10   Litho.   **Perf. 13¾x13¼**
1394   A601   75c multi   1.75   1.75

POSTAL TAX STAMPS

    Catalogue values for unused stamps in this section are for Never Hinged items.

    Unless otherwise stated, Cyprus postal tax stamps are for the Refugee Fund.

No. 352 Surcharged

Perf. 12x12½
1974, Dec. 2   **Wmk. 344**
RA1   A104   10m on 5m multi   .30   .25

Old Woman and Child — PT1

1974, Oct. 1   **Perf. 12½x13½**
RA2   PT1   10m gray & black   .30   .25

CYPRUS — CYRENAICA

Child and Barbed Wire — PT2

Perf. 13x12½
1977, Jan. 10   Litho.   Wmk. 344
RA3   PT2   10m black   .30   .25

Inscribed 1984
1984, June 18   Perf. 13x12½
RA4   PT2   1c black   .30   .25
There are two types of No. RA4.

Inscribed 1988 — PT3

1988-2007   Perf. 13x12½
Design Size 22x28mm
RA5   PT3   1c black & pale gray   .40   .25

Perf. 11½x12
RA6   PT3   1c Inscribed 1989   .65   .55
RA7   PT3   1c Inscribed 1990   .65   .55

Unwmk.
Perf. 13
RA8   PT3   1c Inscribed 1991   .35   .25
RA9   PT3   1c Inscribed 1992   .35   .25
RA10 PT3   1c Inscribed 1993   .35   .25
RA11 PT3   1c Inscribed 1994   .35   .25

Perf. 14½x13¾
Design Size 21x24.5mm
RA12 PT3   1c Inscribed 1995   .35   .25
RA13 PT3   1c Inscribed 1996   .35   .25
RA14 PT3   1c Inscribed 1997   .35   .25
RA15 PT3   1c Inscribed 1998   .35   .25
RA16 PT3   1c Inscribed 1999   .35   .25
RA17 PT3   1c Inscribed 2000   .35   .25
RA18 PT3   1c Inscribed 2001   .35   .25

Size: 22x27mm
Perf. 12¾
RA19 PT3   1c Inscribed 2002   .35   .25
RA20 PT3   1c Inscribed 2003   .35   .25

Perf. 12¾x13
RA21 PT3   1c Inscribed 2004   .35   .25
RA22 PT3   1c Inscribed 2005   .35   .25
RA23 PT3   1c Inscribed 2006   .35   .25

Perf. 13½x14
RA24 PT3   1c Inscribed 2007   .35   .25
Nos. RA5-RA24 (20)   7.65   5.60

Issued: No. RA5, 9/12/88; No. RA6, 9/4/89; No. RA7, 9/29/90; No. RA8, 10/7/91; No. RA9, 11/9/92; No. RA10, 1993; No. RA11, 11/21/94; No. RA12, 10/24/95; No. RA13, 6/10/96; No. RA14, 6/30/97; No. RA15, 1998; No. RA16, 1999; No. RA17, 2000; No. RA18, 2001; No. RA19, 2002. No. RA19, 2003. No. RA20, 2003. No. RA21, 11/11/04, No. RA22, 6/16/05 No. RA23, 5/4/06. No. RA24, 3/15/07.

Child and Barbed Wire With Denomination in Euro Currency — PT4

2008-21   Litho.   Perf. 13½x14
RA25 PT4   2c dk gray & gray   .35   .25

Inscribed "2009"
RA26 PT4   2c blk & lilac gray   .35   .25

Inscribed "2010"
RA27 PT4   2c blk & tan   .30   .25

Inscribed "2011"
RA28 PT4   2c blk & lt green   .30   .25

Booklet Stamp
Self-Adhesive
Die Cut Perf. 13½x14¼
RA28A PT4   2c blk & lt grn   .50   1.40
  b. Booklet pane of 12, 6 each #1153A, RA28A   18.00

Inscribed "2012"
Perf. 13½
RA29 PT4   2c blk & lt blue   .30   .25

Inscribed "2013"
RA30 PT4   2c blk & dull org   .30   .25

Inscribed "2014"
RA31 PT4   2c blk & gray   .30   .25

Inscribed "2015"
RA32 PT4   2c blk & bl gray   .30   .25

Inscribed "2016"
RA33 PT4   2c ol gray & lt brnish gray   .30   .25

Inscribed "2017"
Perf. 13½x14
RA34 PT4   2c blk & bl gray   .35   .25

Inscribed "2018"
Perf. 13½
RA35 PT4   2c blk & grnsh gray   .30   .25

Inscribed "2019"
Perf. 13x13¼
RA36 PT4   2c blk & olive grn   .35   .25

Inscribed "2020"
Perf. 12¾x13¼
RA37 PT4   2c blk & gray   .35   .35

Inscribed "2021"
RA38 PT4   2c black & buff   .35   .35

Inscribed "2022"
RA39 PT4   2c black & light green   .35   .35

Inscribed "2023"
RA40 PT4   2c blk & lt yellow   .30   .30

Issued: Nos. RA28, RA28A, 5/4/11; No. RA29, 1/31/12; No. RA30, 1/30/13; No. RA31, 3/12/14; No. RA32, 4/2/15; No. RA33, 3/10/16; No. RA34, 2/16/17; No. RA35, 2/12/18; No. RA36, 2/20/19; No. RA37, 2/12/20; No. RA38, 2/18/21; No. RA39, 2/16/22; No. RA40, 2/23/23.

CYRENAICA

ˌsir-ə-ˈnā-ə-kə

LOCATION — In northern Africa bordering on the Mediterranean Sea
GOVT. — Italian colony
AREA — 75,340 sq. ml.
POP. — 225,000 (approx. 1934)
CAPITAL — Bengasi (Benghazi)

Cyrenaica was an Italian Colony. In 1949 Great Britain granted the Amir of Cyrenaica autonomy in internal affairs. Cyrenaica was incorporated into the kingdom of Libya in 1951.

100 Centesimi = 1 Lira
1000 Milliemes = 1 Pound (1950)

Catalogue values for unused stamps in this country are for Never Hinged items, beginning with Scott 65 in the regular postage section, Scott J1 in the postage due section.

Used values in italics are for postally used stamps. CTO's sell for about the same as unused, hinged stamps.

Watermark

Wmk. 140 — Crown

Propaganda of the Faith Issue
Italy Nos. 143-146 Overprinted

1923, Oct. 24   Wmk. 140   Perf. 14
1   A68   20c ol grn & brn org   8.00   35.00
2   A68   30c claret & brn org   8.00   35.00
3   A68   50c violet & brn org   5.00   40.00
4   A68   1 l blue & brn org   10.00   60.00
    Nos. 1-4 (4)   31.00   170.00
    Set, never hinged   65.00

Fascisti Issue

Italy Nos. 159-164 Overprinted in Red or Black

1923, Oct. 29   Unwmk.   Perf. 14
5   A69   10c dk grn (R)   9.00   13.00
6   A69   30c dk vio (R)   9.00   13.00
7   A69   50c brn car   9.00   17.50

Wmk. 140
8   A70   1 l blue   9.00   32.50
9   A70   2 l brown   9.00   37.50
10 A71   5 l blk & bl (R)   9.00   60.00
    Nos. 5-10 (6)   54.00   173.50
    Set, never hinged   112.50

Manzoni Issue

Italy Nos. 165-170 Ovptd. in Red

1924, Apr. 1   Perf. 14
11 A72   10c brn red & blk   9.00   45.00
12 A72   15c bl grn & blk   9.00   45.00
13 A72   30c blk & slate   9.00   45.00
14 A72   50c org brn & blk   9.00   45.00
15 A72   1 l bl & blk   55.00   275.00
  a. Double overprint   825.00
      Never hinged   1,250.
16 A72   5 l vio & blk   350.00   2,250.
    Nos. 11-16 (6)   441.00   2,705.
    Set, never hinged   930.00

Vertical overprints on Nos. 11-14 are essays. On Nos. 15-16 the overprint is vertical at the left.
All examples of No. 15a are poorly centered.

Victor Emmanuel Issue

Italy Nos. 175-177 Overprinted

1925-26   Unwmk.   Perf. 11
17 A78   60c brn car   1.35   7.25
18 A/8   1 l dark brown   1.35   7.25
19 A78   1.25 l dk bl ('26)   3.75   10.00
  a. Perf. 13½   360.00   1,000.
      Never hinged   900.00
    Nos. 17-19 (3)   6.45   24.50
    Set, never hinged   16.00

Issue dates: Nov. 1925, July 1926.

Saint Francis of Assisi Issue

Italian Stamps of 1926 Ovptd.

1926, Apr. 12   Wmk. 140   Perf. 14
20 A79   20c gray green   2.00   8.50
21 A80   40c dark violet   2.00   8.50
22 A81   60c red brown   2.00   15.00

Ovptd. in Red

Unwmk.
23 A82   1.25 l dk bl, perf. 11   2.00   20.00
24 A83   5 l + 2.50 l ol grn   4.50   42.50
    Nos. 20-24 (5)   12.50   94.50
    Set, never hinged   31.50

Volta Issue

Type of Italy 1927, Overprinted

1927, Oct. 10   Wmk. 140   Perf. 14
25 A84   20c purple   4.50   23.00
26 A84   50c dp org   5.50   16.00
27 A84   1.25 l brt bl   9.50   37.50
    Nos. 25-27 (3)   19.50   76.50
    Set, never hinged   35.00

Monte Cassino Issue

Types of 1929 Issue of Italy, Ovptd. in Red or Blue

1929, Oct. 14
28 A96   20c dk grn (R)   4.50   12.75
29 A96   25c red org (Bl)   4.50   12.75
30 A98   50c + 10c crim (Bl)   4.50   13.50
31 A98   75c + 15c ol brn (Π)   4.50   13.50
32 A96   1.25 l + 25c dk vio (R)   9.00   25.00
33 A98   5 l + 1 l saph (R)   9.00   27.50

Overprinted in Red

Unwmk.
34 A100 10 l + 2 l gray brn   9.00   40.00
    Nos. 28-34 (7)   45.00   145.00
    Set, never hinged   114.00

Royal Wedding Issue

Type of Italian Stamps of 1930 Overprinted

1930, Mar. 17   Wmk. 140
35 A101 20c yel grn   2.25   5.50
36 A101 50c + 10c dp org   1.60   7.25
37 A101 1.25 l + 25c rose red   1.60   11.00
    Nos. 35-37 (3)   5.45   23.75
    Set, never hinged   13.75

Ferrucci Issue

Types of Italian Stamps of 1930, Ovptd. in Red or Blue

1930, July 26
38 A102 20c violet (R)   5.50   4.50
39 A103 25c dk grn (R)   5.50   4.50
40 A103 50c black (H)   5.50   10.00
41 A103 1.25 l dp bl (R)   5.50   16.00
42 A104 5 l + 2 l dp car   12.00   35.00
    Nos. 38-42 (5)   34.00   70.00
    Set, never hinged   84.00

Virgil Issue

Italian Stamps of 1930 Ovptd. in Red or Blue

1930, Dec. 4
43 A106 15c vio blk   .75   7.00
44 A106 20c org brn (Bl)   .75   2.75
45 A106 25c dk grn   .75   2.75
46 A106 30c lt brn (Bl)   .75   2.75
47 A106 50c dl vio   .75   2.75
48 A106 75c rose red (Bl)   .75   5.50
49 A106 1.25 l gray bl   .75   6.75

CYRENAICA

Unwmk.
50	A106	5 l + 1.50 l dk vio	2.75	27.50
51	A106	10 l + 2.50 l ol brn (Bl)	2.75	42.50
	Nos. 43-51 (9)		10.75	100.25
	Set, never hinged		26.00	

Saint Anthony of Padua Issue

Italian Stamps of 1931 Ovptd. in Blue or Red

1931, May 7 — Wmk. 140
52	A116	20c brown (Bl)	1.10	13.75
53	A116	25c green (R)	1.10	5.50
54	A118	30c gray brn (Bl)	1.10	5.50
55	A118	50c dl vio (Bl)	1.10	5.50
56	A120	1.25 l slate bl (R)	1.10	13.75

Overprinted like Nos. 23-24 in Red or Black
Unwmk.
57	A121	75c black (R)	1.10	25.00
58	A122	5 l + 2.50 l dk brn	8.25	50.00
	Nos. 52-58 (7)		14.85	119.00
	Set, never hinged		37.50	

Carabineer — A1

1934, Oct. 16 — Photo. — Wmk. 140
59	A1	5c dk ol grn & brn	4.00	12.75
60	A1	10c brn & blk	4.00	12.75
61	A1	20c scar & indigo	4.00	11.50
62	A1	50c pur & brn	4.00	11.50
63	A1	60c org brn & ind	4.00	16.00
64	A1	1.25 l dk bl & grn	4.00	27.50
	Nos. 59-64 (6)		24.00	92.00
	Set, never hinged		60.00	

2nd Colonial Art Exhibition held at Naples. See Nos. C24-C29.

> **Catalogue values for unused stamps in this section, from this point to the end of the section, are for Never Hinged items.**

Autonomous State

Senussi Warrior
A2   A3

Perf. 12½
1950, Jan. 16 — Unwmk. — Engr.
65	A2	1m dark brown	.65	2.25
66	A2	2m rose car	.85	2.00
67	A2	3m orange	.85	2.00
68	A2	4m dark green	4.25	3.25
69	A2	5m gray	1.10	1.25
70	A2	8m red orange	1.25	1.50
71	A2	10m purple	1.25	1.50
72	A2	12m red	1.25	1.50
73	A2	20m deep blue	1.25	1.50
74	A3	50m choc & ultra	6.75	8.50
75	A3	100m bl blk & car rose	21.00	42.50
76	A3	200m vio & pur	25.00	67.50
77	A3	500m dk grn & org	110.00	135.00
	Nos. 65-77 (13)		175.45	270.25

SEMI-POSTAL STAMPS

Many issues of Italy and Italian Colonies include one or more semipostal denominations. To avoid splitting sets, these issues are generally listed as regular postage unless all values carry a surtax.

Holy Year Issue
Italian Semi-Postal Stamps of 1924 Overprinted in Black or Red

1925, June 1 — Wmk. 140 — Perf. 12
B1	SP4	20c + 10c dk grn & brn	2.25	14.00
B2	SP4	30c + 15c dk brn & brn	2.25	15.00
B3	SP4	50c + 25c vio & brn	2.25	14.00
B4	SP4	60c + 30c dp rose & brn	2.25	18.00
B5	SP8	1 l + 50c dp bl & vio (R)	2.25	22.50
B6	SP8	5 l + 2.50 l org brn & vio (R)	2.25	35.00
	Nos. B1-B6 (6)		13.50	118.50
	Set, never hinged		34.50	

Colonial Institute Issue

"Peace" Substituting Spade for Sword — SP1

1926, June 1 — Typo. — Perf. 14
B7	SP1	5c + 5c brown	.75	5.50
B8	SP1	10c + 5c olive grn	.75	5.50
B9	SP1	20c + 5c blue grn	.75	5.50
B10	SP1	40c + 5c brown red	.75	5.50
B11	SP1	60c + 5c orange	.75	5.50
B12	SP1	1 l + 5c blue	.75	11.50
	Nos. B7-B12 (6)		4.50	39.00
	Set, never hinged		10.50	

Surtax for Italian Colonial Institute.

Types of Italian Semi-Postal Stamps of 1926 Overprinted like Nos. 17-19
1927, Apr. 21 — Unwmk. — Perf. 11
B13	SP10	40c + 20c dk brn & blk	2.20	25.00
B14	SP10	60c + 30c brn red & ol brn	2.20	25.00
B15	SP10	1.25 l + 60c dp bl & blk	2.20	37.50
a.		Double overprint	1,450.	
		Never hinged	2,200.	
B16	SP10	5 l + 2.50 l dk grn & blk	3.75	57.50
	Nos. B13-B16 (4)		10.35	145.00
	Set, never hinged		21.00	

The surtax on these stamps was for the charitable work of the Voluntary Militia for Italian National Defense.

Allegory of Fascism and Victory — SP2

1928, Oct. 15 — Wmk. 140 — Perf. 14
B17	SP2	20c + 5c bl grn	2.25	8.25
B18	SP2	30c + 5c red	2.25	8.25
B19	SP2	50c + 10c orange	2.25	14.00
B20	SP2	1.25 l + 20c dk bl	2.75	18.00
	Nos. B17-B20 (4)		9.50	48.50
	Set, never hinged		24.50	

46th anniv. of the Societa Africana d'Italia. The surtax aided that society.

1926 Italian Semi-Postal Types Overprinted in Red or Black

1929, Mar. 4 — Unwmk. — Perf. 11
B21	SP10	30c + 10c red & blk (Bk)	2.75	16.00
B22	SP10	50c + 20c vio & blk	2.75	17.50
B23	SP10	1.25 l + 50c brn & bl	4.25	30.00
B24	SP10	5 l + 2 l ol grn & blk	4.25	60.00
	Nos. B21-B24 (4)		14.00	123.50
	Set, never hinged		35.50	

Surtax for the charitable work of the Voluntary Militia for Italian Natl. Defense.

Types of Italian Semi-Postal Stamps of 1926 Overprinted in Black or Red like Nos. 52-56
1930, Oct. 20 — Perf. 14
B25	SP10	30c + 10c dk grn & bl (Bk)	25.00	55.00
B26	SP10	50c + 10c dk grn & vio	25.00	80.00
B27	SP10	1.25 l + 30c ol brn & red	25.00	80.00
B28	SP10	5 l + 1.50 l ind & grn	100.00	215.00
	Nos. B25-B28 (4)		175.00	430.00
	Set, never hinged		438.00	

Surtax for the charitable work of the Voluntary Militia for Italian Natl. Defense.

Sower — SP3

1930, Nov. 27 — Photo. — Wmk. 140
B29	SP3	50c + 20c ol brn	2.75	16.00
B30	SP3	1.25 l + 20c dp bl	2.75	16.00
B31	SP3	1.75 l + 20c green	2.75	18.00
B32	SP3	2.55 l + 50c purple	8.25	27.50
B33	SP3	5 l + 1 l dp car	8.25	42.50
	Nos. B29-B33 (5)		24.75	120.00
	Set, never hinged		67.00	

25th anniv. of the Italian Colonial Agricultural Institute. The surtax was for the aid of that institution.

AIR POST STAMPS

Air Post Stamps of Tripolitania, 1931, Overprinted in Blue like Nos. 38-42
1932, Jan. 7 — Wmk. 140 — Perf. 14
C1	AP1	50c rose car	1.00	.25
C2	AP1	60c dp org	4.00	9.00
C3	AP1	80c dl vio	4.00	14.00
	Nos. C1-C3 (3)		9.00	23.25
	Set, never hinged		22.50	

Air Post Stamps of Tripolitania, 1931, Overprinted in Blue

1932, May 12
C4	AP1	50c rose car	1.00	1.20
C5	AP1	80c dull violet	4.50	17.50
	Set, never hinged		14.00	

This overprint was also applied to the 60c, Tripolitania No. C9. The overprinted stamp was never used in Cyrenaica, but was sold at Rome in 1943 by the Postmaster General for the Italian Colonies. Value $10.

Arab on Camel AP2

Airplane in Flight AP3

1932, Aug. 8 — Photo.
C6	AP2	50c purple	11.00	.25
C7	AP2	75c brn rose	11.00	10.00
C8	AP2	80c deep blue	11.00	19.00
C9	AP3	1 l black	4.50	.25
C10	AP3	2 l green	4.50	11.50
C11	AP3	5 l deep car	7.70	22.50
	Nos. C6-C11 (6)		49.70	63.50
	Set, never hinged		124.50	

For surcharges and overprint see Nos. C20-C23.

Graf Zeppelin Issue

Zeppelin and Clouds forming Pegasus — AP4

Zeppelin and Ancient Galley — AP5

Zeppelin and Giant Bowman — AP6

1933, Apr. 15
C12	AP4	3 l dk brn	10.00	72.50
C13	AP5	5 l purple	10.00	72.50
C14	AP6	10 l dp grn	10.00	135.00
C15	AP5	12 l deep blue	10.00	150.00
C16	AP4	15 l carmine	10.00	150.00
C17	AP6	20 l black	10.00	200.00
	Nos. C12-C17 (6)		60.00	780.00
	Set, never hinged		150.00	

North Atlantic Crossing Issue

Airplane Squadron and Constellations AP7

1933, June 1
C18	AP7	19.75 l grn & dp bl	13.75	375.00
C19	AP7	44.75 l red & indigo	14.00	375.00
	Set, never hinged		70.00	

Type of 1932 Ovptd. and Srchd.

1934, Jan. 20
C20	AP3	2 l on 5 l org brn	3.25	55.00
C21	AP3	3 l on 5 l yel grn	3.25	55.00
C22	AP3	5 l ocher	3.25	65.00
C23	AP3	10 l on 5 l rose	4.50	65.00
	Nos. C20-C23 (4)		14.25	240.00
	Set, never hinged		35.50	

For use on mail to be carried on a special flight from Rome to Buenos Aires.

Transport Plane — AP8

Venus of Cyrene — AP9

1934, Oct. 9
C24	AP8	25c sl bl & org red	4.00	13.00
C25	AP8	50c dk grn & ind	4.00	11.50
C26	AP8	75c dk brn & org red	4.00	11.50
a.		Imperf.	3,000.	
		Never hinged	4,500.	
C27	AP9	80c org brn & ol grn	4.00	12.50

CYRENAICA — CZECHOSLOVAKIA

C28	AP9	1 l scar & ol grn	4.00	16.00	
C29	AP9	2 l dk bl & brn	4.00	27.50	
	Nos. C24-C29 (6)		24.00	92.00	
	Set, never hinged			60.00	

2nd Colonial Arts Exhib. held at Naples.

AIR POST SEMI-POSTAL STAMPS

King Victor Emmanuel III — SPAP1

Wmk. 104

1934, Nov. 5   Photo.   Perf. 14

CB1	SPAP1	25c + 10c gray grn	9.00	16.00
CB2	SPAP1	50c + 10c brn	9.00	16.00
CB3	SPAP1	75c + 15c rose red	9.00	16.00
CB4	SPAP1	80c + 15c brn blk	9.00	16.00
CB5	SPAP1	1 l + 20c red brn	9.00	16.00
CB6	SPAP1	2 l + 20c brt bl	9.00	16.00
CB7	SPAP1	3 l + 25c pur	22.50	72.50
CB8	SPAP1	5 l + 25c org	22.50	72.50
CB9	SPAP1	10 l + 30c dp vio	22.50	72.50
CB10	SPAP1	25 l + 2 l dp grn	22.50	72.50
	Nos. CB1-CB10 (10)		144.00	386.00
	Set, never hinged			365.00

65th birthday of King Victor Emmanuel III and the non-stop flight, Rome-Mogadiscio.

AIR POST SEMI-POSTAL OFFICIAL STAMP

Type of Air Post Semi-Postal Stamps, 1934, Overprinted Crown and "SERVIZIO DI STATO" in Black

1934, Nov. 5   Wmk. 140   Perf. 14

CBO1	SPAP1	25 l + 2 l cop red	1,500.

POSTAGE DUE STAMPS

Catalogue values for unused stamps in this section are for Never Hinged items.

D1

Perf. 13½

1950, July 1   Unwmk.   Engr.

J1	D1	2m dark brown	77.50	110.00
J2	D1	4m deep green	77.50	110.00
J3	D1	8m scarlet	77.50	110.00
J4	D1	10m vermilion	77.50	120.00
J5	D1	20m orange yel	77.50	120.00
J6	D1	40m deep blue	77.50	160.00
J7	D1	100m dark gray	77.50	250.00
	Nos. J1-J7 (7)		542.50	980.00

CZECHOSLOVAKIA

,che-kə-slō-'vä-kē-ə

LOCATION — Central Europe
GOVT. — Republic
AREA — 49,355 sq. mi.
POP. — 10,710,000 (2020 est.)

CAPITAL — Prague

The Czechoslovakian Republic consists of Bohemia, Moravia and Silesia, Slovakia and Ruthenia (Carpatho-Ukraine). In March 1939, a German protectorate was established over Bohemia and Moravia, as well as over Slovakia which had meanwhile declared its independence. Ruthenia was incorporated in the territory of Hungary. These territories were returned to the Czechoslovak Republic in 1945, except for Ruthenia, which was ceded to Russia. Czechoslovakia became a federal state on Jan. 2, 1969. On Jan. 1, 1993 Czechoslovakia separated into Slovakia and the Czech Republic. See Volume 5 for the stamps of Slovakia.

100 Haleru = 1 Koruna

Catalogue values for unused stamps in this country are for Never Hinged items, beginning with Scott 142 in the regular postage section, B144 in the semi-postal section, Scott C19 in the air post section, Scott EX1 in the personal delivery section, and Scott J58 in the postage due section, Scott O1 in the officials section, and Scott P14 in the newspaper section.

Watermarks

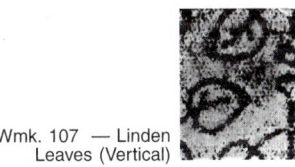

Wmk. 107 — Linden Leaves (Vertical)

Wmk. 135 — Crown in Oval or Circle, Sideways

Wmk. 136

Wmk. 136a

Wmk. 341 — Striped Ovals

Stamps of Austria overprinted "Ceskoslovenska Republika," lion and "Cesko Slovensky Stat," "Provisorni Ceskoslovenska Vlada" and Arms, and "Ceskoslovenska Statni Posta" and Arms were made privately. A few of them were passed through the post but all have been pronounced unofficial and unauthorized by the Postmaster General.

During the occupation of part of Northern Hungary by the Czechoslovak forces, stamps of Hungary were overprinted "Cesko Slovenska Posta," "Ceskoslovenska Statni Posta" and Arms, and "Slovenska Posta" and Arms. These stamps were never officially issued though examples have passed the post.

Hradcany at Prague — A1

1918-19   Unwmk.   Typo.   Imperf.

1	A1	3h red violet	.25	.25
2	A1	5h yellow green	.25	.25
3	A1	10h rose	.25	.25
4	A1	20h bluish green	.25	.25
5	A1	25h deep blue	.25	.25
6	A1	30h bister	.35	.25
7	A1	40h red orange	.35	.25
8	A1	100h brown	.75	.25
9	A1	200h ultra	1.50	.25
10	A1	400h purple	3.00	.25

On the 3h-40h "Posta Ceskoslovenska" is in white on a colored background; on the higher values the words are in color on a white background.

No. 5c was not valid for postage.
Nos. 1-6 exist as tete-beche gutter pairs.
See Nos. 368, 1554, 1600. For surcharges see Nos. B130, C1, C4, J15, J19-J20, J22-J23, J30.

Perf. 11½, 13½

13	A1	5h yellow green	.60	.25
a.	Perf. 11½x10¾		3.00	.45
14	A1	10h rose	.35	.25
15	A1	20h bluish green	.35	.25
a.	Perf. 11½		.35	.25
16	A1	25h deep blue	.75	.35
a.	Perf. 11½		1.50	.35
20	A1	200h ultra	6.00	.25
	Nos. 1-10,13-16,20 (15)		15.25	3.85

All values of this issue exist with various private perforations and examples have been used on letters.

The 3h, 30h, 40h, 100h and 400h formerly listed are now known to have been privately perforated.

For overprints see Eastern Silesia Nos. 2, 5, 7-8, 14, 16, 18, 30.

A2

Type II

Type III

Type IV

Type II — Sun behind cathedral. Colorless foliage in foreground.
Type III — Without sun. Shaded foliage in foreground.
Type IV — No foliage in foreground. Positions of buildings changed. Letters redrawn.

1919   Imperf.

23	A2	1h dark brown (II)	.25	.25
25	A2	5h blue green (IV)	.35	.25
27	A2	15h red (IV)	.35	.25
29	A2	25h dull violet (IV)	.65	.25
30	A2	50h dull violet (I)	.40	.25
31	A2	50h dark blue (IV)	.35	.25
32	A2	60h orange (III)	1.50	.25
33	A2	75h slate (IV)	1.10	.25
34	A2	80h olive grn (III)	.75	.25
36	A2	120h gray black (IV)	2.25	.25
38	A2	300h dark green (III)	7.00	.35
39	A2	500h red brown (IV)	7.00	.25
40	A2	1000h violet (III)	15.00	1.10
a.	1000h bluish violet		35.00	4.25
	Nos. 23-40 (13)		36.95	4.20

For overprints see Eastern Silesia Nos. 1, 3-4, 6, 9-13, 15, 17, 20-21.

1919-20   Perf. 11½, 13¾, 13¾x11½

41	A2	1h dk brown (II)	.25	.25
42	A2	5h blue grn (IV), perf. 13½	.60	.25
a.	Perf. 11½		25.00	5.00
43	A2	10h yellow grn (IV)	.35	.25
a.	Imperf.		17.50	14.00
b.	Perf. 11¾		10.00	1.00
44	A2	15h brick red (IV)	.35	.25
a.	Perf. 11½x10¾		27.50	5.00
b.	Perf. 11½x13¾		75.00	22.50
c.	Perf. 13¾x10¾		100.00	22.50
45	A2	20h rose (IV)	.60	.25
a.	Imperf.		90.00	85.00
46	A2	25h dull vio (IV), perf. 11½	.65	.25
a.	Perf. 11½x10¾		4.50	1.10
b.	Perf. 13¾x10¾		150.00	37.50
47	A2	30h red violet (IV)	.35	.25
a.	Imperf.		150.00	175.00
b.	Perf. 13¾x13½		450.00	175.00
c.	30h deep violet		.60	.25
d.	As "c," perf. 13¾x13½		525.00	190.00
e.	As "c," imperf.		150.00	160.00
50	A2	60h orange (III)	.40	.25
a.	Perf. 13¾x13½		16.00	4.50
53	A2	120h gray black (IV)	4.00	1.00
	Nos. 41-53 (9)		7.55	3.00

CZECHOSLOVAKIA

Nos. 43a, 45a, 47a and 47e were imperforate by accident and not issued in quantities as were Nos. 23 to 40.

Rouletted stamps of the preceding issues are said to have been made by a postmaster in a branch post office at Prague, or by private firms, but without authority from the Post Office Department.

The 50, 75, 80, 300, 500 and 1000h have been privately perforated.

Unlisted color varieties of types A1 and A2 were not officially released, and some are printer's waste.

For surcharges and overprints see Nos. B131, C2-C3, C5-C6, J16-J18, J21, J24-J29, J31, J42-J43, Eastern Silesia 22-29.

Pres. Thomas Garrigue Masaryk — A4

1920 — *Perf. 13½*
61	A4	125h gray blue	1.50	.25
a.		125h ultramarine	20.00	19.00
62	A4	500h slate, *grysh*	2.50	1.50
63	A4	1000h blk brn, *brnsh*	6.50	3.00
		Nos. 61-63 (3)	10.50	4.75

Nos. 61, 61a, 63 imperf. were not regularly issued. Values: unused singles, No. 61 $30; No. 61a $150; No. 63 $40.

For surcharge and overprints, see Nos. B131, Eastern Silesia 31-32.

Carrier Pigeon with Letter — A5

Czechoslovakia Breaking Chains to Freedom — A6

Hussite Priest A7 — Agriculture and Science A8

Type I — Type II

Two types of 40h:
Type I: 9 leaves by woman's hip.
Type II: 10 leaves by woman's hip.

1920 — *Perf. 14*
65	A5	5h dark blue	.25	.25
		Perf. 13¾	275.00	150.00
66	A5	10h blue green	.25	.25
		Perf. 13¾	125.00	110.00
67	A5	15h red brown	.25	.25
68	A6	20h rose	.25	.25
69	A6	25h lilac brown	.25	.25
70	A6	30h red violet	.25	.25
71	A6	40h red brown (I)	.50	.25
a.		As "b," tête bêche pair	2.50	1.50
b.		*Perf. 13½*	.60	.25
c.		Type II	.25	.25
72	A6	50h carmine	.35	.25
73	A6	60h dark blue	.35	.25
a.		As "b," tête bêche pair	3.50	3.50
b.		*Perf. 13½*	.35	1.50

Photo.
74	A7	80h purple	.25	.25
75	A7	90h black brown	.30	.25

Typo. Perf. 13¾
76	A8	100h dark green	.50	.25
77	A8	200h violet	.75	.25
78	A8	300h vermilion	1.50	.25
a.		*Perf. 13¾x13½*	.45	.35
79	A8	400h brown	3.50	.45
80	A8	500h deep green	3.50	.45
a.		*Perf. 13¾x13½*	40.00	5.50
81	A8	600h deep violet	4.50	.45
a.		*Perf. 13¾x13½*	125.00	7.00
		Nos. 65-81 (17)	17.50	4.85

No. 69 has background of horizontal lines.
Imperfs. were not regularly issued.

Nos. 71 and 73 exist as tete-beche gutter pairs.
For surcharges and overprint see Nos. C7-C9, J44-J56.

Type I — Type II

Two types of 20h:
Type I: Base of 2 is long, interior of 0 is angular.
Type II: Base of 2 is short, interior of 0 is an oval.

Type I — Type II

Two types of 25h:
Type I: Top of 2 curves up.
Type II: Top of 2 curves down.

1920-25 — *Perf. 14*
82	A5	5h violet	.25	.25
a.		As "b," tête bêche pair	2.00	1.00
b.		*Perf. 13½*	1.00	.35
83	A5	10h olive bister	.25	.25
a.		As "b," tête bêche pair	2.00	1.50
b.		*Perf. 13½*	.60	.35
84	A5	20h deep orange (II)	.25	.25
a.		As "b," tête bêche pair	14.00	15.00
b.		*Perf. 13½*	3.50	.60
c.		Type I		
85	A5	25h blue green (I)	.25	.25
a.		Type II	.25	.25
86	A5	30h deep violet ('25)	3.00	.25
87	A6	50h yellow green	.60	.25
a.		As "b," tête bêche pair	27.50	27.50
b.		*Perf. 13½*	7.50	2.00
88	A6	100h dark brown	1.00	.25
a.		*Perf. 13½*	15.00	.30
89	A6	150h rose	2.00	.50
a.		*Perf. 13½*	35.00	2.00
90	A6	185h orange	1.50	.30
91	A6	250h dark green	2.25	.50
		Nos. 82-91 (10)	11.35	3.05

Imperfs. were not regularly issued.
Nos. 82-84, 87 exist as tete-beche gutter pairs.

Type of 1920 Issue Redrawn

Type I — Type II — Type III

Type I — Rib of leaf below "O" of POSTA is straight and extends to tip. White triangle above book is entirely at left of twig. "P" has a stubby, abnormal appendage.
Type II — Rib is extremely bent; does not reach tip. Triangle extends at right of twig. "P" like Type I.
Type III — Rib of top left leaf is broken in two. Triangle like Type II. "P" has no appendage.

1923 — *Perf. 13¾, 13¾x13½*
92	A8	100h red, *yellow*, III, perf. 14x13½	.75	.50
a.		Type I, perf. 13¾	1.00	.25
b.		Type II, perf. 13¾x13½	.75	.25
c.		Type II, perf. 13¾	1.25	.25
d.		Type II, perf. 13¾x13½	1.10	.25
e.		Type III, perf. 13¾	7.50	.25
93	A8	200h blue, *yellow*, II, perf. 13¾	10.00	.30
a.		Type I, perf. 13¾x13½	10.00	.30
b.		Type III, perf. 13¾	6.50	.30
c.		Type III, perf. 13¾x13½	45.00	.50
94	A8	300h violet, *yellow*, I, perf. 13¾	4.50	.25
a.		Type II, perf. 13¾	35.00	.35
b.		Type II, perf. 13¾x13½	50.00	.50
c.		Type III, perf. 13¾x13½	6.00	.30
d.		Type III, perf. 13¾	27.50	.35
		Nos. 92-94 (3)	15.25	1.05

President Masaryk
A9 — A10

Perf. 13¾x13½, 13¾
1925 — *Photo. Wmk. 107*
Size: 19½x23mm
95	A9	40h brown orange	.75	.25
96	A9	50h olive green	1.50	.25
97	A9	60h red violet	1.75	.25
		Nos. 95-97 (3)	4.00	.75

Distinctive Marks of the Engravings.
I, II, III — Background of horizontal lines in top and bottom tablets. Inscriptions in Roman letters with serifs.
IV — Crossed horizontal and vertical lines in the tablets. Inscriptions in Antique letters without serifs.
I, II, IV — Shading of crossed diagonal lines on the shoulder at the right.
III — Shading of single lines only.
I — "T" of "Posta" over middle of "V" of "Ceskoslovenska." Three short horizontal lines in lower part of "A" of "Ceskoslovenska."
II — "T" over right arm of "V." One short line in "A."
III — "T" as in II. Blank space in lower part of "A."
IV — "T" over left arm of "V."

Wmk. Horizontally (107)
Engr.
I. First Engraving
Size: 19¾x22½mm
98	A10	1k carmine	.85	.25
99	A10	2k deep blue	1.75	.35
100	A10	3k brown	3.75	.65
101	A10	5k blue green	1.25	.35
		Nos. 98-101 (4)	7.60	1.60

Wmk. Vertically (107)
Size: 19¼x23mm
101A	A10	1k carmine	60.00	3.50
101B	A10	2k deep blue	60.00	12.50
101C	A10	3k brown	150.00	12.50
101D	A10	5k blue green	3.50	.60
		Nos. 101A-101D (4)	273.50	29.10

II. Second Engraving
Wmk. Horizontally (107)
Size: 19x21½mm
102	A10	1k carmine	35.00	.60
103	A10	2k deep blue	3.50	.30
104	A10	3k brown	4.50	.35
		Nos. 102-104 (3)	43.00	1.25

III. Third Engraving
Size: 19-19½x21½-22mm
Perf. 10
105	A10	1k carmine rose	.75	.25
a.		Perf. 14	6.00	.25

IV. Fourth Engraving
Size: 19x22mm
1926 — *Perf. 10*
106	A10	1k carmine rose	1.00	.25

Perf. 14
108	A10	3k brown	4.50	.25

There is a 2nd type of No. 106: with long mustache. Same values. See No. 130, design SP3.

Karlstein Castle — A11

1926, June 1 — *Engr. Perf. 10*
109	A11	1.20k red violet	.50	.25
110	A11	1.50k car rose	.35	.25
111	A11	2.50k dark blue	3.25	.35
		Nos. 109-111 (3)	4.10	.90

See Nos. 133, 135.

Karlstein Castle A12 — Pernstein Castle A13

Orava Castle A14 — Masaryk A15

Strahov Monastery A16 — Hradcany at Prague A17

Great Tatra — A18

Short Mustache — Long, Wavy Mustache

1926-27 — *Engr. Wmk. 107*
114	A13	30h gray green	1.25	.25
115	A14	40h red brown	.50	.25
116	A15	50h deep green	.50	.25
117	A15	60h red vio, *lil*	.85	.25
118	A16	1.20k red violet	4.00	1.50

Perf. 13½
119	A17	2k blue	1.00	.25
a.		2k ultramarine	6.00	.75
120	A17	3k dep grnd	1.25	.25
121	A18	4k brn vio ('27)	4.50	.60
122	A18	5k dk grn ('27)	14.00	3.00
		Nos. 114-122 (9)	27.85	6.60

No. 116 exists in two types. The one with short, straight mustache at left sells for several times as much as that with longer wavy mustache.
See Nos. 137-140.

Coil Stamps
Perf. 10 Vertically
123	A12	20h brick red	.50	.40
a.		Vert. pair, imperf. horiz.	100.00	
124	A13	30h gray green	.35	.25
a.		Vert. pair, imperf. horiz.	100.00	
125	A15	50h deep green	.25	.25
		Nos. 123-125 (3)	1.10	.90

See No. 141.

Short Mustache — Long, Wavy Mustache

1927-31 — *Unwmk. Perf. 10*
126	A13	30h gray green	.25	.25
127	A14	40h deep brown	.70	.25
128	A15	50h deep green	.25	.25
129	A15	60h red violet	.70	.25
130	A10	1k carmine rose	1.10	.25
131	A15	1k deep red	.75	.25
132	A16	1.20k red violet	.40	.25
133	A11	1.50k carmine ('29)	.55	.25
134	A13	2k dp grn ('29)	.50	.25
135	A11	2.50k dark blue	5.50	.30
136	A14	3k red brown ('31)	.60	.25
		Nos. 126-136 (11)	11.30	2.80

No. 130 exists in two types. The one with longer mustache at right sells for several times as much as that with the short mustache.

1927-28 — *Perf. 13½*
137	A17	2k ultra	.85	.25
138	A17	3k deep red ('28)	1.90	.65
139	A18	4k brown violet ('28)	6.00	1.00
140	A18	5k dark green ('28)	6.25	.50
		Nos. 137-140 (4)	15.00	2.40

Coil Stamp
1927 — *Perf. 10 Vertically*
141	A12	20h brick red	.50	.25

Catalogue values for unused stamps in this section, from this point to the end of the section, are for Never Hinged items.

CZECHOSLOVAKIA

Hradec Castle
A19

Brno Cathedral
A25

Masaryk — A27

10th anniv. of Czech. independence: 40h, Town Hall, Levoca. 50h, Telephone exchange, Prague. 60h, Town of Jasina. 1k, Hluboka Castle. 1.20k, Pilgrims' House, Velehrad. 2.50k, Great Tatra. 5k, Old City Square, Prague.

1928, Oct. 22 — Perf. 13½

142	A19	30h black	.25	.25
143	A19	40h red brown	.25	.25
144	A19	50h dark green	.25	.25
145	A19	60h orange red	.25	.25
146	A19	1k carmine	.30	.25
147	A19	1.20k brown vio	1.00	.45
148	A25	2k ultra	1.00	.75
149	A19	2.50k dark blue	3.00	2.50
150	A27	3k dark brown	1.50	1.25
151	A25	5k deep violet	3.00	3.00
		Nos. 142-151 (10)	10.80	9.20

From one to three sheets each of Nos. 142-148, perf 12½, appeared on the market in the early 1950's.

Coat of Arms — A29

1929-37 — Perf. 10

152	A29	5h dark ultra ('31)	.25	.25
153	A29	10h bister brn ('31)	.25	.25
154	A29	20h red	.25	.25
155	A29	25h green	.25	.25
156	A29	30h red violet	.25	.25
157	A29	40h dk brown ('37)	1.60	.25
a.		40h red brown ('29)	.80	.25
		Nos. 152-157 (6)	2.85	1.50

Coil Stamp
Perf. 10 Vertically

| 158 | A29 | 20h red | .25 | .25 |

For overprints, see Bohemia and Moravia Nos. 1-5, Slovakia Nos. 2-6.

St. Wenceslas
A30

Founding St. Vitus' Cathedral
A31

Design: 3k, 5k, St. Wenceslas martyred.

1929, May 14 — Perf. 13½

159	A30	50h gray green	.30	.25
160	A30	60h slate violet	.45	.25
161	A31	2k dull blue	1.10	.25
162	A30	3k brown	1.00	.55
163	A30	5k brown violet	5.50	3.50
		Nos. 159-163 (5)	8.85	4.65

Millenary of the death of St. Wenceslas.

Statue of St. Wenceslas and National Museum, Prague — A33

1929 — Perf. 10

| 164 | A33 | 2.50k deep blue | 2.00 | .25 |

Brno Cathedral
A34

Tatra Mountain Scene
A35

Design: 5k, Old City Square, Prague.

1929, Oct. 15 — Perf. 13½

165	A34	3k red brown	3.00	.25
166	A35	4k indigo	6.75	.25
167	A35	5k gray green	12.00	.30
		Nos. 165-167 (3)	21.75	.80

See No. 183.

A37

Type I

Type II

Two types of 50h:
I — A white space exists across the bottom of the vignette between the coat, shirt and tie and the "HALERU" frame panel.
II — An extra frame line has been added just above the "HALERU" panel which finishes off the coat and tie shading evenly.

1930, Jan. 2 — Perf. 10

168	A37	50h myrtle green (II)	.25	.25
a.		Type I	1.10	.25
169	A37	60h brown violet	1.00	.25
170	A37	1k brown red	.40	.25
		Nos. 168-170 (3)	1.65	.75

See No. 234.

Coil Stamp
1931 — Perf. 10 Vertically

| 171 | A37 | 1k brown red | 1.50 | .60 |

President Masaryk — A38

1930, Mar. 1 — Perf. 13½

175	A38	2k gray green	1.50	.35
176	A38	3k red brown	2.25	.35
177	A38	5k slate blue	6.00	1.50
178	A38	10k gray black	16.00	3.50
		Nos. 175-178 (4)	25.75	5.70

Eightieth birthday of President Masaryk. Nos. 175-178 were each issued in sheets with ornamental tabs at the bottom. Value, set with tabs $65.50.

St. Nicholas' Church, Prague — A39

1931, May 15

| 183 | A39 | 10k black violet | 11.00 | 1.10 |

Krivoklat Castle
A40

Krumlov Castle
A42

Design: 4k, Orlik Castle.

1932, Jan. 2 — Perf. 10

184	A40	3.50k violet	5.00	1.10
185	A40	4k deep blue	4.00	.60
186	A42	5k gray green	7.00	.60
		Nos. 184-186 (3)	16.00	2.30

A43

A44

1932, Mar. 16

187	A43	50h yellow green	.35	.25
188	A43	1k brown carmine	1.10	.25
189	A44	2k dark blue	9.00	.35
190	A44	3k red brown	19.00	.35
		Nos. 187-190 (4)	29.45	1.20

Miroslav Tyrs — A45

1933, Feb. 1

| 191 | A45 | 60h dull violet | .00 | .25 |

Miroslav Tyrs (1832-84), founder of the Sokol movement; and the 9th Sokol Congress (Nos. 187-190).

First Christian Church at Nitra
A46   A47

1933, June 20

192	A46	50h yellow green	.75	.25
193	A47	1k carmine rose	7.00	.25

Prince Pribina who introduced Christianity into Slovakia and founded there the 1st Christian church in A.D. 833.
All gutter pairs are vertical. Values unused: No. 192 $300; No. 193 $15,000.

Bedrich Smetana, Czech Composer and Pianist, 50th Death Anniv. — A48

1934, Mar. 26 — Engr. — Perf. 10

| 194 | A48 | 50h yellow green | .60 | .25 |

Consecration of Legion Colors at Kiev, Sept. 21, 1914 — A49

Ensign Heyduk with Colors
A51

Legionnaires
A52

1k, Legion receiving battle flag at Bayonne.

1934, Aug. 15 — Perf. 10

195	A49	50h green	.35	.25
196	A49	1k rose lake	.50	.25
197	A51	2k deep blue	2.75	.25
198	A52	3k red brown	4.50	.45
		Nos. 195-198 (4)	8.10	1.20

20th anniv. of the Czechoslovakian Legion which fought in WWI.

Antonin Dvorák, (1841-1904), Composer — A53

1934, Nov. 22

| 199 | A53 | 50h green | .60 | .25 |

Pastoral Scene — A54

1934, Dec. 17 — Perf. 10

200	A54	1k claret	.60	.25
a.		Souv. sheet of 15, perf. 13½	160.00	250.00
b.		As "a," single stamp	10.00	12.50
201	A54	2k blue	1.75	.45
a.		Souv. sheet of 15, perf. 13½	850.00	900.00
b.		As "a," single stamp	50.00	27.50

Centenary of the National Anthem.
Nos. 200-201 were each issued in sheets of 100 stamps and 12 blank labels. Value, set with attached labels: mint $21; used $7.
Nos. 200a & 201a have thick paper, darker shades, no gum. Forgeries exist.

CZECHOSLOVAKIA

A55

President Masaryk — A56

1935, Mar. 1
202	A55	50h green, buff	.35	.25
203	A55	1k claret, buff	.35	.25
204	A56	2k gray blue, buff	.50	.60
205	A56	3k brown, buff	3.00	.50
		Nos. 202-205 (4)	4.20	1.60

85th birthday of President Masaryk.
Nos. 204-205 were each issued in sheets of 100 stamps and 12 blank labels. Value, set with attached labels: mint $30; used $30.
See No. 235.

Monument to Czech Heroes at Arras, France — A57

1935, May 4
| 206 | A57 | 1k rose | .35 | .25 |
| 207 | A57 | 2k dull blue | 1.50 | .45 |

20th anniversary of the Battle of Arras.
Nos. 206-207 were each issued in sheets of 100 stamps and 12 blank labels. Value, set with attached labels: mint $8; used $8.

Gen. Milan Stefánik — A58

1935, May 18
| 208 | A58 | 50h green | .25 | .25 |

Sts. Cyril and Methodius — A59

1935, June 22
209	A59	50h green	.25	.25
210	A59	1k claret	.45	.25
211	A59	2k deep blue	1.50	.25
		Nos. 209-211 (3)	2.20	.75

Millenary of the arrival in Moravia of the Apostles Cyril and Methodius.

Masaryk — A60

1935, Oct. 20 Perf. 12½
| 212 | A60 | 1k rose lake | .25 | .25 |

No. 212 exists imperforate. See Bohemia and Moravia No. 1A. For overprints see Bohemia and Moravia Nos. 9-10, Slovakia 12.

Statue of Macha, Prague — A61

1936, Apr. 30
| 213 | A61 | 50h deep green | .25 | .25 |
| 214 | A61 | 1k rose lake | .40 | .25 |

Karel Hynek Macha (1810-1836), Bohemian poet.
Nos. 213-214 were each issued in sheets of 100 stamps and 12 blank labels. Value, set with attached labels: mint $1; used 75c.

Jan Amos Komensky (Comenius) — A61a

Pres. Eduard Benes A62

Gen. Milan Stefánik A63

1936
215	A61a	40h dark blue	.25	.25
216	A62	50h dull green	.25	.25
217	A63	60h dull violet	.25	.25
		Nos. 215-217 (3)	.75	.75

See no. 252, Slovakia 23A. For overprints see Bohemia and Moravia Nos. 6, 8, Slovakia 7, 9-11.

Castle Palanok near Mukacevo A64

Town of Banska Bystrica A65

Castle at Zvikov A66

Ruins of Castle at Strecno A67

Castle at Cesky Raj A68

Palace at Slavkov (Austerlitz) A69

Statue of King George of Podebrad A70

Town Square at Olomouc A71

Castle Ruins at Bratislava — A72

1936, Aug. 1
218	A64	1.20k rose lilac	.25	.25
219	A65	1.50k carmine	.25	.25
220	A66	2k dark blue green	.25	.25
221	A67	2.50k dark blue	.25	.25
222	A68	3k brown	.25	.25
223	A69	3.50k dark violet	1.50	.25
224	A70	4k dark violet	.60	.25
225	A71	5k green	.60	.25
226	A72	10k blue	1.00	.25
		Nos. 218-226 (9)	4.95	2.25

Nos. 224-226 were each issued in sheets of 100 stamps and 12 blank labels. Value, set with attached labels: mint $6; used $6.

For overprints and surcharge see Nos. 237-238, 254A, Bohemia and Moravia 11-12, 14-19, Slovakia 13-14, 16-23.

President Benes — A73

1937, Apr. 26 Unwmk. Perf. 12½
| 227 | A73 | 50h deep green | .25 | .25 |

For overprints see Nos. 236, Slovakia 8.

Soldiers of the Czech Legion — A74

1937, June 15
| 228 | A74 | 50h deep green | .25 | .25 |
| 229 | A74 | 1k rose lake | .30 | .25 |

20th anniv. of the Battle of Zborov.
Nos. 228-229 were each issued in sheets of 100 stamps and 12 blank labels. Value, set with attached labels: mint $2; used $1.50.

Cathedral at Prague — A75

1937, July 1
| 230 | A75 | 2k green | .90 | .25 |
| 231 | A75 | 2.50k blue | 1.40 | .30 |

Founding of the "Little Entente," 16th anniv.
Nos. 230-231 were each issued in sheets of 100 stamps and 12 blank labels. Value, set with attached labels: mint $17.50; used $9.

Jan Evangelista Purkyne — A76

1937, Sept. 2
| 232 | A76 | 50h slate green | .25 | .25 |
| 233 | A76 | 1k dull rose | .30 | .25 |

150th anniv. of the birth of Purkyne, Czech physiologist.
Nos. 232-233 were printed in sheets of 100 with 12 decorated labels. Value, set with labels, $2.50.

Masaryk Types of 1930-35
1937, Sept. Perf. 12½
| 234 | A37 | 50h black | .25 | .25 |

With date "14.IX. 1937" in design
| 235 | A56 | 2k black | .30 | .25 |

Death of former President Thomas G. Masaryk on Sept. 14, 1937.
No. 235 was issued in sheets of 100 stamps and 12 inscribed labels. Value, with attached label: mint $3.50; used $3.50.

International Labor Bureau Issue

Stamps of 1936-37 Overprinted in Violet or Black

1937, Oct. 6 Perf. 12½
236	A73	50h dp green (Bk)	.35	.35
237	A65	1.50k carmine (V)	.35	.35
238	A66	2k dp green (V)	.70	.35
		Nos. 236-238 (3)	1.40	1.05

Bratislava Philatelic Exhibition Issue
Souvenir Sheet

A77

1937, Oct. 24 Perf. 12½
239	A77	Sheet of 2	2.50	2.75
a.		50h dark blue	.80	1.20
b.		1k brown carmine	.80	1.20

The stamps show a view of Poprad Lake (50h) and the tomb of General Milan Stefanik (1k).
No. 239 overprinted with the Czechoslovak arms and "Czecho-Slovak Participation New York World's Fair 1939 and 1940, Czecho-Slovak Pavilion" were privately produced to finance Czechoslovak participation in the exhibition. The overprint exists in black, green, red, blue, gold and silver.
No. 239 overprinted "Liberation de la Tchechoslovaquie, 28-X-1945" etc., was sold at a philatelic exhibition in Brussels, Belgium.

St. Barbara's Church, Kutna Hora — A79

1937, Dec. 4
| 240 | A79 | 1.60h olive green | .25 | .25 |

For overprints see Bohemia and Moravia No. 13, Slovakia 15.

Peregrine Falcon, Sokol Emblem — A80

1938, Jan. 21
| 241 | A80 | 50h deep green | .25 | .25 |
| 242 | A80 | 1k rose lake | .25 | .25 |

10th Intl. Sokol Games.
Nos. 241-242 were each issued in sheets of 100 stamps and 12 inscribed labels. Value, set with attached labels: mint $1.50; used $2.50.
Imperf. examples of No. 242 are essays.

Legionnaires
A81   A82

Legionnaire — A83

1938
243	A81	50h deep green	.25	.25
244	A82	50h deep green	.25	.25
245	A83	50h deep green	.25	.25
		Nos. 243-245 (3)	.75	.75

20th anniv. of the Battle of Bachmac, Vouziers and Doss Alto.
Nos. 243-245 were each issued in sheets of 100 stamps and 12 inscribed labels. Value, set with attached labels $2, mint or used.

Jindrich Fügner, Co-Founder of Sokol Movement — A84

1938, June 18 Perf. 12½
246	A84	50h deep green	.25	.25
247	A84	1k rose lake	.25	.25
248	A84	2k slate blue	.40	.25
		Nos. 246-248 (3)	.90	.75

10th Sokol Summer Games.
Nos. 246-248 were each issued in sheets of 100 stamps and 12 inscribed labels. Value, set with attached labels: mint $2.50; used $2.

CZECHOSLOVAKIA

View of Pilsen — A85

1938, June 24
249 A85 50h deep green .25 .25

Provincial Economic Council meeting, Pilsen.
No. 249 was issued in sheets of 150 stamps and 10 labels depicting a flower within a cogwheel. Value, with attached label $1, mint or used.
For overprint see Bohemia & Moravia No. 7.

Cathedral of Kosice — A86

1938, July 15   Perf. 12½
250 A86 50h deep green .25 .25

Kosice Cultural Exhibition.
No. 250 was issued in sheets of 150 stamps and 10 labels depicting grapes. Value, with attached label $1, $7.50 mint, $4.50 used.

Prague Philatelic Exhibition Issue
Souvenir Sheet

Vysehrad Castle — Hradcany — A87

1938, June 26   Perf. 12½
251 A87 Sheet of 2 5.00 5.00
 a.   50h dark blue 1.50 1.50
 b.   1k deep carmine 1.50 1.50
See No. 3036.

Stefánik Type of 1936
1938, Nov. 21
252 A63 50h deep green .25 .25

Allegory of the Republic — A89

1938, Dec. 19   Unwmk.
253 A89 2k lt ultra .30 .25
254 A09 3k pale brown .50 .40

20th anniv. of Independence.
Nos. 253-254 were each issued in sheets of 100 stamps and 12 blank labels. Value, set with attached labels $2, mint or used.
See No. B153.

"Wir sind frei!"
Stamps of Czechoslovakia, 1918-37, overprinted with a swastika in black or red and "Wir sind frei!" were issued locally and unofficially in 1938 as Czech authorities were evacuating and German authorities arriving. They appeared in the towns of Asch, Karlsbad, Reichenberg-Maffersdorf, Rumburg, etc.
The overprint, sometimes including a surcharge or the town name (as in Karlsbad), exists on many values of postage, air post, semi-postal, postage due and newspaper stamps.

No. 226 Surcharged in Orange Red

1939, Jan. 18   Unwmk.   Perf. 12½
254A A72 300h on 10k blue 1.25 1.75
Opening of the Slovakian Parliament.

No. 254A was issued in sheets of 100 stamps with 12 blank labels. Value with attached labels, mint $4.

The stamp formerly listed as No. 254B is now listed as Carpatho-Ukraine No. 1 in Vol. 2 of the *Scott Standard Postage Stamp Catalogue*.
The stamps formerly listed as Czechoslovakia Nos. 255, 256 and C18 are now listed with Bohemia and Moravia and Slovakia. No. 255 is now Slovakia No. 23A. No. 256 and C18 are now listed as Bohemia and Moravia 1A and C1, respectively.

Linden Leaves and Buds — A90

Closed Buds

Open Buds

1945   Photo.   Perf. 14
256A A90 10h black .25 .25
257   A90 30h yellow brown .25 .25
258   A90 50h dark green .25 .25
258A A90 60h dark blue .25 .25

Engr.
(Buds Open)
Perf. 12½
259   A90 60h blue .25 .25
259A A90 80h orange ver .25 .25
260   A90 1.20k rose .25 .25
261   A90 3k violet brown .25 .25
262   A90 5k green .25 .25
Nos. 256A-262 (9) 2.25 2.25

Compare with Bohemia-Moravia type A1.

Thomas G. Masaryk — A91

1945-46   Photo.   Perf. 12
262A A91 5h dull violet ('46) .25 .25
262B A91 10h orange yel ('46) .25 .25
262C A91 20h dk brown ('46) .25 .25
263   A91 50h brt green .25 .25
264   A91 1k orange red .25 .25
265   A91 2k chalky blue .25 .25
Nos. 262A-265 (6) 1.50 1.50

Coat of Arms — A92

1945   Imperf.
266 A92 50h olive gray .25 .25
267 A92 1k brt red vio .25 .25
268 A92 1.50k dk carmine .25 .25
269 A92 2k deep blue .25 .25

269A A92 2.40k henna brn .25 .25
270   A92 3k brown .25 .25
270A A92 4k dk slate grn .25 .25
271   A92 6k violet blue .25 .25
271A A92 10k sepia .25 .25
Nos. 266-271A (9) 2.25 2.25

Nos. 266, 268, 269, 270 and 271 exist in 2 printings. Stamps of the 1st printing have a coarse impression and are on thin, hard paper in sheets of 100; all values exist in the 2nd printing, with fine impressions on thick, soft wove paper in sheets of 200. Values are the same.

Staff Capt. Ridky (British Army) A93

Dr. Miroslav Novak (French Army) A94

Capt. Otakar Jaros (Russian Army) A95

Staff Capt. Stanislav Zimprich (Foreign Legion) A96

2nd Lt. Jiri Kral (French Air Force) A97

Josef Gabcik (Parachutist) A98

Staff Capt. Alois Vasatko (Royal Air Force) A99

Private Frantisek Adamek (British Colonial Service) A100

1945, Aug. 18   Engr.   Perf. 11½x12½
272 A93 5h intense blue .25 .25
273 A94 10h dark brown .25 .25
274 A95 20h brick red .25 .25
275 A96 25h rose red .25 .25
276 A97 30h purple .25 .25
277 A98 40h sepia .25 .25
278 A99 50h dark olive .25 .25
279 A100 60h violet .25 .25
280 A93 1k carmine .25 .25
281 A94 1.50k lake .25 .25
282 A96 2k ultra .25 .25
283 A95 2.50k deep violet .25 .25
284 A97 3k sepia .25 .25
285 A98 4k rose lilac .25 .25
286 A99 5k myrtle green .25 .25
287 A100 10k brt ultra .65 .65
Nos. 272-287 (16) 4.40 4.00

Flags of Russia, Great Britain, US and Czechoslovakia A101

View of Banská Bystrica A102

Patriot Welcoming Russian Soldier, Turciansky A103

Ruins of Castle at Sklabina A104

Czech Patriot, Strecno — A105

1945, Aug. 29   Photo.   Perf. 10
288 A101 1.50k brt carmine .25 .25
289 A102 2k brt blue .25 .25
290 A103 4k dark brown .25 .25
291 A104 4.50k purple .25 .30
292 A105 5k deep green .50 .50
Nos. 288-292 (5) 1.50 1.55

National uprising against the Germans.
A card contains one each of Nos. 288-292 on thin cardboard, ungummed. Size: 148x210mm. Sold for 50k. Value, $20 unused, $120 used. Forged cancellations exist.

Stefánik A106

Benes A107

Masaryk — A108

1945-47   Engr.   Perf. 12, 12½
293   A106 30h rose violet .25 .25
294   A107 60h blue .25 .25
294A A106 1k red org ('47) .25 .25
295   A106 1k car rose .25 .25
295A A108 1.20(k) rose lil ('46) .25 .25
296   A106 2.40(k) rose .25 .25
297   A107 3k red violet .25 .25
297A A108 4k dark blue ('46) .25 .25
298   A108 5k Prus green .25 .25
299   A107 7k gray .25 .25
300   A106 10k gray blue .30 .25
300A A108 20k sepia ('46) .30 .25
Nos. 293-300A (12) 3.10 3.00

1945   Photo.   Perf. 14
301 A108 50h brown .25 .25
302 A106 80h dark green .25 .25
303 A107 1.60(k) olive green .25 .25
304 A108 15k red violet .30 .25
Nos. 301-304 (4) 1.05 1.00

Statue of Kozina and Chod Castle, Domazlice — A109

1945, Nov. 28   Engr.   Perf. 12½
305 A109 2.40k rose carmine .25 .25
306 A109 4k blue .25 .25

250th anniv. of the death of Jan Sladky Kozina, peasant leader.
Nos. 305-306 were issued in sheets of 100 stamps with 12 blank labels. Value, set with attached labels, mint $6.

Red Army Soldier — A110

CZECHOSLOVAKIA

1945, Mar. 26   Litho.   *Imperf.*
307 A110 2k crimson rose .40 .40
308 A110 5k slate black 1.10 1.10
309 A110 6k ultramarine 1.10 1.10
    Nos. 307-309 (3) 2.60 2.60

Souvenir Sheet
1945, July 16   *Gray Burelage*
310   Sheet of 3 4.00 4.00
   a. A110 2k crimson rose .75 .75
   b. A110 5k slate black .75 .75
   c. A110 6k ultramarine .75 .75
    Return of Pres. Benes, Apr., 1945.

Clasped Hands — A112

1945   *Rouletted 12½*
311 A112 1.50k brown red 1.50 1.50
312 A112   9k red orange .35 .35
313 A112 13k orange brown .65 .65
314 A112 20k blue 1.50 1.50
    Nos. 311-314 (4) 4.00 4.00

Karel Havlíček Borovsky — A113

1946, July 5   Engr.   *Perf. 12½*
315 A113 1.20k gray black .25 .25
    Borovsky (1821-56), editor and writer.
    Issued in sheets of 100 stamps and 12 inscribed labels. Value with attached label: $1.25.

Old Town Hall, Brno A114

Hodonin Square A115

Perf. 12½x12, 12x12½
1946, Aug. 3   Engr.   *Unwmk.*
316 A114 2.40k deep rose .25 .25
317 A115 7.40k dull violet .25 .25
    See No. B159.

President Eduard Benes — A116

1946, Oct. 28
318 A116 60h indigo .25 .25
319 A116 1.60k dull green .25 .25
320 A116 3k red lilac .25 .25
321 A116 8k sepia .25 .25
    Nos. 318-321 (4) 1.00 1.00

Flag, Symbols — A117

1947, Jan. 1   *Perf. 12½*
322 A117 1.20k Prus green .25 .25
323 A117 2.40k deep rose .25 .25
324 A117 4k deep blue .45 .45
    Nos. 322-324 (3) .95 .75
    Czechoslovakia's two-year reconstruction and rehabilitation program.
    Nos. 322-324 each issued in sheets of 100 stamps and 12 inscribed labels. Value, set with attached labels, $3.

Saint Adalbert — A118

1947, Apr. 23
326 A118 1.60k gray .75 .60
327 A118 2.40k rose carmine .90 .60
328 A118 5k blue green 1.10 .45
    Nos. 326-328 (3) 2.75 1.65
    950th anniv. of the death of Saint Adalbert, Bishop of Prague.
    Nos. 326-328 each issued in sheets of 100 stamps and 12 monogrammed labels. Value, set with attached labels, $35.

Grief A119

Allegorical Figure A120

1947, June 10   *Engr.*
329 A119 1.20k black .40 .25
330 A119 1.60k slate black .45 .45
331 A120 2.40k brown violet .45 .45
    Nos. 329-331 (3) 1.30 1.15
    Destruction of Lidice, 5th anniversary.
    Nos. 329-331 each issued in sheets of 100 stamps and 12 inscribed labels. Value, set with attached labels, $15.

World Federation of Youth Symbol — A121

1947, July 20
332 A121 1.20k violet brown .50 .35
333 A121 4k slate .50 .35
    World Youth Festival held in Prague, July 20-Aug. 17.

Thomas G. Masaryk — A122

1947, Sept. 14
334 A122 1.20k gray blk, *buff* .25 .25
335 A122 4k blue blk, *cream* .30 .25
    Death of Masaryk, 10th anniv.
    Nos. 334-335 each issued in sheets of 100 stamps and 12 inscribed labels. Value, set with attached labels, $5.

Msgr. Stefan Moyses — A123

1947, Oct. 19
336 A123 1.20k rose violet .25 .25
337 A123 4k deep blue .25 .25
    150th anniversary of the birth of Stefan Moyses, first Slovakian chairman of the Slavic movement.
    Each issued in sheets of 100 stamps and 12 labels with "MOYSES" and floral decoration. Value, set with attached labels, $7.50.

"Freedom from Social Oppression" — A124

1947, Oct. 26   Photo.   *Perf. 14*
338 A124 2.40k brt carmine .40 .30
339 A124 4k brt ultra .50 .25
    Russian revolution of Oct., 1917, 30th anniv.

Benes — A125

1948, Feb. 15   *Photo.*
Size: 17½x21½mm
340 A125 1.50k brown .25 .25
Size: 19x23mm
341 A125 2k deep plum .25 .25
342 A125 5k brt ultra .25 .25
    Nos. 340-342 (3) .75 .75

"Czechoslovakia" Greeting Sokol Marchers — A126

1948, Mar. 7   Engr.   *Perf. 12½*
343 A126 1.50k brown .25 .25
344 A126 3k rose carmine .25 .25
345 A126 5k blue .50 .25
    Nos. 343-345 (3) 1.00 .75
    The 11th Sokol Congress.
    Nos. 343-345 each issued in sheets of 100 stamps and 12 labels depicting dates and bouquet. Values, set with attached labels: mint $4.50; used $3.75.

King Charles IV — A127

St. Wenceslas, King Charles IV — A128

1948, Apr. 7
346 A127 1.50k black brown .25 .25
347 A128 2k dark brown .25 .25
348 A128 3k brown red .25 .25
349 A127 5k dark blue .25 .25
    Nos. 346-349 (4) 1.00 1.00
    600th anniv. of the foundation of Charles University, Prague.
    Nos. 346-349 each issued in sheets of 100 stamps and 12 inscribed labels. Value, set with attached labels, $4.50.

Czech Peasants in Revolt — A129

    Unwmk.
1948, May 14   Photo.   *Perf. 14*
350 A129 1.50k dk olive brown .25 .25
    Centenary of abolition of serfdom.

Jindrich Vanicek — A130

    Designs: 1.50k, 2k, Josef Scheiner.
1948, June 10   Engr.   *Perf. 12½*
351 A130 1k dark green .25 .25
352 A130 1.50k sepia .25 .25
353 A130 2k gray blue .25 .25
354 A130 3k claret .25 .25
    Nos. 351-354 (4) 1.00 1.00
    11th Sokol Congress, Prague, 1948.
    Nos. 351-354 each issued in sheets of 100 stamps and 12 labels depicting a sunflower. Values, set with attached labels: $3.75 mint; $3 used.

Frantisek Palacky & F. L. Rieger — A131

1948, June 20   *Unwmk.*
355 A131 1.50k gray .25 .25
356 A131 3k brown carmine .25 .25
    Constituent Assembly at Kromeriz, cent.
    Nos. 355-356 each issued in sheets of 100 stamps and 12 labels depicting a wreath. Value, set with attached labels, $1.50.

Miloslav Josef Hurban — A132

    3k, Ludovit Stur. 5k, Michael M. Hodza.
1948, Aug. 27   *Perf. 12½*
357 A132 1.50k dark brown .25 .25
358 A132 3k carmine lake .25 .25
359 A132 5k indigo .25 .25
    Nos. 357-359 (3) .75 .75
    Cent. of 1848 insurrection against Hungary.
    Nos. 357-359 each issued in sheets of 100 stamps and 12 labels depicting signatures. Values, set with attached labels: mint $5; used $3.50.

Eduard Benes — A133

1948, Sept. 28
360 A133 8k black .25 .25
    President Eduard Benes, 1884-1948.

Czechoslovak Family — A134

1948, Oct. 28   *Perf. 12½x12*
361 A134 1.50k deep blue .25 .25
362 A134 3k rose carmine .25 .25
    Czechoslovakia's Independence, 30th anniv.
    Nos. 361-362 each issued in sheets of 100 stamps and 12 labels depicting dates, leaves. Value, set with attached labels, $2.

Pres. Klement Gottwald — A135

1948-49   *Perf. 12½*
Size: 18½x23½mm
363 A135 1.50k dk brown .25 .25
364 A135 3k car rose .30 .25
   a. 3k rose brown 1.00 1.00
365 A135 5k gray blue .25 .25
Size: 23½x29mm
366 A135 20k purple .90 .25
    Nos. 363-366 (4) 1.70 1.00
    No. 366 was issued in sheets of 100 stamps and 12 monogrammed labels. Value, with attached label, $3.50.
    See Nos. 373, 564, 600-604.

Souvenir Sheet
1948, Nov. 23   Unwmk.   *Imperf.*
367 A135 30k rose brown 4.25 3.00
    52nd birthday of Pres. Klement Gottwald (1896-1953).

Hradcany Castle Type of 1918
Souvenir Sheet
1948, Dec. 18
368 A1 10k dk blue violet 3.00 2.40
    1st Czech postage stamp, 30th anniv.

CZECHOSLOVAKIA

Czechoslovak and Russian Workmen Shaking Hands — A138

1948, Dec. 12   Perf. 12½
369 A138 3k rose carmine   .25   .25

5th anniv. of the treaty of alliance between Czechoslovakia and Russia.
No. 369 issued in sheets of 100 stamps and 12 labels depicting Czech and Soviet flags. Value with attached label 60c.

Lenin — A139

1949, Jan. 21   Engr.   Perf. 12½
370 A139 1.50k violet brown   .30   .25
371 A139 5k deep blue   .30   .30

25th anniversary of the death of Lenin.
Nos. 370-371 each issued in sheets of 100 stamps and 12 labels depicting torch. Value, set with attached labels: mint $1.75; used $1.50.

Gottwald Type of 1948 Inscribed: "UNOR 1948" and

Gottwald Addressing Meeting — A140

1949, Feb. 25   Photo.   Perf. 14
372 A140 3k red brown   .25   .25

     Perf. 12½
     Engr.
     Size: 23½x29mm
373 A135 10k deep green   .40   .25

1st anniv. of Gottwald's speech announcing the appointment of a new government. No. 372 exists in a souvenir sheet of 1. It was not sold to the public.
No. 373 issued in sheets of 100 stamps and 12 inscribed labels. Values with attached label: mint $2.50; used $1.50.

A141

Writers: 50h, P. O. Hviezdoslav. 80h, V. Vancura. 1k, J. Sverma. 2k, Julius Fucik. 4k, Jiri Wolker. 8k, Alois Jirasek.

1949   Photo.   Perf. 14
374 A141 50h violet brown   .25   .25
375 A141 80h scarlet   .25   .25
376 A141 1k dk olive green   .25   .25
377 A141 2k brt blue   .40   .25

     Perf. 12½
     Engr.
378 A141 4k violet brown   .40   .25
379 A141 8k brown black   .50   .25
     Nos. 374-379 (6)   2.05 1.50

A142

3k, Stagecoach and Train. 5k, Postrider and post bus. 13k, Sailing ship and plane.

1949, May 20
380 A142 3k brown carmine   1.50 1.50
381 A142 5k deep blue   1.00   .45
382 A142 13k deep green   1.50 1.00
     Nos. 380-382 (3)   4.00 2.95

75th anniv. of the UPU.

Reaping A143

Communist Emblem and Workers A144

Workman, Symbol of Industry — A145

     Perf. 12½x12, 12x12½
1949, May 24   Unwmk.
383 A143 1.50k deep green   .50   .45
384 A144 3k brown carmine   .50   .45
385 A145 5k deep blue   .50   .45
     Nos. 383-385 (3)   1.50 1.35

No. 384 for the 9th meeting of the Communist Party of Czechoslovakia, 5/25/49.
Nos. 383-385 each issued in sheets of 100 stamps and 12 inscribed labels. Value, set with attached labels, $12.

Bedrich Smetana and Natl. Theater, Prague — A146

1949, June 4   Perf. 12½x12
386 A146 1.50k dull green   .25   .25
387 A146 5k deep blue   .75   .25

Birth of Bedrich Smetana, composer, 125th anniv.

Aleksander Pushkin — A147

1949, June 6   Perf. 12x12½
388 A147 2k olive gray   .25   .25

Birth of Aleksander S. Pushkin, 150th anniv.

Frederic Chopin and Conservatory, Warsaw — A148

1949, June 24   Perf. 12½x12
389 A148 3k dark red   .40   .25
390 A148 8k violet brown   .75   .50

Cent. of the death of Frederic F. Chopin.

Globe and Ribbon — A149

1949, Aug. 20   Perf. 12½x12
391 A149 1.50k violet brown   .35   .35
392 A149 5k ultra   .90   .90

50th Prague Sample Fair, Sept. 11-20, 1949.

Starting in October, 1949, some commemorative sets included one "blocked" value, which could be obtained only by purchasing the complete set. These restricted values were printed in smaller quantities than other stamps in the set and were typically sold for more than face value.

Zvolen Castle — A150

1949, Aug. 28   Perf. 12½
393 A150 10k rose lake   .75   .25

Early Miners A151

Miner of Today A152

Design: 5k, Mining Machine.

1949, Sept. 11   Perf. 12½
394 A151 1.50k sepia   .70   .50
395 A152 3k carmine rose   5.50 2.00
396 A151 5k deep blue   4.00 1.50
     Nos. 394-396 (3)   10.20 4.00

700th anniv. of the Czechoslovak mining industry; 150th anniv. of the miner's laws.

Construction Workers — A153

1949, Dec. 11   Perf. 12½
397 A153 1k shown   3.00 1.40
398 A153 2k Machinist   2.00   .70

2nd Trade Union Congress, Prague, 1949.

Joseph V. Stalin — A154

Design: 3k, Stalin facing left.

Cream Paper

1949, Dec. 21   Unwmk.
399 A154 1.50k greenish gray   .75   .35
400 A154 3k claret   4.50 1.75

70th birthday of Joseph V. Stalin.

Skier A155

Efficiency Badge A156

     Engr., Photo. (3k)
1950, Feb. 15   Perf. 12½, 13½
401 A155 1.50k gray blue   2.75 1.50
402 A156 3k vio brn, pale org   2.75 1.50
403 A155 5k ultramarine   2.00 1.10
     Nos. 401-403 (3)   7.50 4.10

51st Ski Championship for the Tatra cup, Feb. 15-26, 1950.

Vladimir V. Mayakovsky, Poet, 20th Death Anniv. — A157

1950, Apr. 14   Engr.   Perf. 12½
404 A157 1.50k dark brown   2.25 1.10
405 A157 3k brown red   2.25 1.10

See Nos. 414-417, 422-423, 432-433, 464-465, 477-478.

Soviet Tank Soldier and Hradcany A158

2k, Hero of Labor medal. 3k, Two workers (militiamen) and Town Hall, Prague. 5k, Text of government program and heraldic lion.

1950, May 5
406 A158 1.50k gray green   .35   .25
407 A158 2k dark brown   1.00 1.00
408 A158 3k brown red   .25   .25
409 A158 5k dark blue   .50   .25
     Nos. 406-409 (4)   2.10 1.75

5th anniv. of the Czechoslovak People's Democratic Republic.

Factory and Young Couple with Tools — A159

Designs: 2k, Steam shovel. 3k, Farmer and farm scene. 5k, Three workers leaving factory.

1950, May 9   Engr.
410 A159 1.50k dark green   1.75   .85
411 A159 2k dark brown   1.75   .85
412 A159 3k rose red   1.00   .35
413 A159 5k deep blue   1.00   .35
     Nos. 410-413 (4)   5.50 2.40

Canceled to Order

The government philatelic department started about 1950 to sell canceled sets of new issues. Values in the second ("used") column are for these canceled-to-order stamps. Postally used stamps are worth more.

Portrait Type of 1950

Design: S. K. Neumann.

1950, June 5   Unwmk.   Perf. 12½
414 A157 1.50k deep blue   .35   .25
415 A157 3k violet brown   1.10 1.00

Stanislav Kostka Neumann (1875-1947), journalist and poet.

1950, June 21

Design: Bozena Nemcova.

416 A157 1.50k deep blue   1.25   .75
417 A157 7k dark brown   .30   .25

Bozena Nemcova (1820-1862), writer.

Liberation of Colonies — A160

Designs: 2k, Allegory, Fight for Peace. 3k, Group of Students. 5k, Marching Students with flags.

1950, Aug. 14
418 A160 1.50k dark green   .25   .25
419 A160 2k sepia   .25   .25
420 A160 3k rose carmine   .25   .25
421 A160 5k ultra   .60   .45
     Nos. 418-421 (4)   1.35 1.20

2nd International Students World Congress, Prague, Aug. 12-24, 1950.

Portrait Type of 1950

Design: Zdenek Fibich.

1950, Oct. 15
422 A157 3k rose brown   .90   .55
423 A157 8k gray green   .35   .25

Zdenek Fibich, musician, birth centenary.

Miner, Soldier and Farmer — A161

CZECHOSLOVAKIA

Czech and Soviet Soldiers — A162

1950, Oct. 6
424 A161 1.50k slate .35 .35
425 A162 3k carmine rose .35 .35
Issued to publicize Czech Army Day.

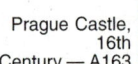

Prague Castle, 16th Century — A163

Prague, 1493 — A164

3k, Prague, 1606. 5k, Prague, 1794.

1950, Oct. 21 Perf. 14
426 A163 1.50k black 4.50 2.25
427 A164 2k chocolate 4.50 2.25
428 A164 3k brown car 4.50 2.25
429 A164 5k gray 4.50 2.25
 a. Block of 4, #426-429 25.00 15.00
See Nos. 434-435.

Communications Symbols — A165

1950, Oct. 25 Perf. 12½
430 A165 1.50k chocolate .35 .35
431 A165 3k brown carmine .75 .60
1st anniv. of the foundation of the Intl. League of P.T.T. Employees.

Portrait Type of 1950
Design: J. Gregor Tajovsky.

1950, Oct. 26
432 A157 1.50k brown 1.00 .75
433 A157 5k deep blue 1.00 .75
10th anniversary of the death of J. Gregor Tajovsky (1874-1940), Slovakian writer.

Scenic Type of 1950
Design: Prague, 1950.

1950, Oct. 28
434 A164 1.50k indigo .35 .25
 a. Souvenir sheet of 4, imperf. 30.00 11.00
435 A164 3k brown car .90 .50

Czech and Soviet Steel Workers — A166

1950, Nov. 4 Unwmk.
436 A166 1.50k chocolate .45 .30
437 A166 5k deep blue .90 .60
Issued to publicize the 2nd meeting of the Union of Czechoslovak-Soviet Friendship.

Dove by Picasso — A167

1951, Jan. 20 Photo. Perf. 14
438 A167 2k deep blue 6.00 4.50
439 A167 3k rose brown 4.00 1.50
1st Czechoslovak Congress of Fighters for Peace, held in Prague.

Julius Fucik — A168

1951, Feb. 17 Engr. Perf. 12½
440 A168 1.50k gray .75 .75
441 A168 5k gray blue 1.50 1.50
No. 441 exists in a sheet of 12. Value, $500.

Drop Hammer A169

Installing Gear A170

1951, Feb. 24
442 A169 1.50k gray blk .25 .25
443 A170 3k violet brn .25 .25
444 A169 4k gray blue .60 .50
Nos. 442-444 (3) 1.10 1.00

Women Machinists — A171

Designs: 3k, Woman tractor operator. 5k, Women of different races.

1951, Mar. 8 Photo. Perf. 14
445 A171 1.50k olive brown .40 .30
446 A171 3k brown car 1.40 1.00
447 A171 5k blue .70 .40
Nos. 445-447 (3) 2.50 1.70
International Women's Day, Mar. 8.

Apprentice Miners — A172

1951, Apr. 12 Engr. Perf. 12½
448 A172 1.50k gray .55 .50
449 A172 3k red brown .25 .25

Plowing A173

Collective Cattle Breeding A174

1951, Apr. 28 Photo. Perf. 14
450 A173 1.50k brown .70 .70
451 A174 2k dk green 1.40 1.40

Tatra Mountain Recreation Center — A175

Mountain Recreation Centers: 2k, Beskydy (Beskids). 3k, Krkonose (Carpathians).

1951, May 5 Engr. Perf. 12½
452 A175 1.50k deep green .25 .25
453 A175 2k dark brown 1.00 .75
454 A175 3k rose brown .25 .25
Nos. 452-454 (3) 1.50 1.25
Issued to publicize the summer opening of trade union recreation centers.

Klement Gottwald and Joseph Stalin A176

Factory Militiaman A177

Red Army Soldier and Partisan A178

Marx, Engels, Lenin and Stalin A179

1951 Unwmk. Perf. 12½
455 A176 1.50k olive gray .75 .25
456 A177 2k red brown .35 .25
457 A178 3k rose brown .35 .25
458 A178 5k deep blue 1.40 1.00
459 A179 8k gray .70 .25
Nos. 455-459 (5) 3.55 2.00
30th anniv. of the founding of the Czechoslovak Communist Party.

A180

Design: 1k, 2k, Antonin Dvorák. 1.50k, 3k, Bedrich Smetana.

1951, May 30
460 A180 1k redsh brown .35 .25
461 A180 1.50k olive gray 1.40 .70
462 A180 2k dk redsh brn 1.40 .70
463 A180 3k rose brown .35 .25
Nos. 460-463 (4) 3.50 1.90
International Music Festival, Prague. Nos. 461 and 462 were each issued in sheets of 10 stamps. Value, $700 for 461, $600 for 462.

Portrait Type of 1950
Portrait: Bohumir Smeral (facing right).

1951, June 21
464 A157 1.50k dark gray .75 .50
465 A157 3k rose brown .35 .25
10th anniv. of the death of Bohumir Smeral, political leader.

A181

1951, June 21
466 A181 1k shown .75 .35
467 A181 1.50k Discus .75 .35
468 A181 3k Soccer 1.50 .35
469 A181 5k Skier 3.50 1.50
Nos. 466-469 (4) 6.50 2.55
Issued to honor the 9th Congress of the Czechoslovak Sokol Federation.

Scene from "Fall of Berlin" — A182

Scene from "The Great Citizen" — A183

1951, July 14
470 A182 80h rose brown .35 .35
471 A183 1.50k dark gray .35 .35
472 A182 4k gray blue 1.40 1.10
Nos. 470-472 (3) 2.10 1.80
Intl. Film Festival, Karlovy Vary, July 14-29.

Alois Jirásek A184

"Fables and Fate" A185

Design: 4k, Scene from "Reign of Tabor."

1951, Aug. 23 Engr. Perf. 12½
473 A184 1.50k gray .35 .25
474 A184 5k dark blue 2.10 .80
 Photo.
 Perf. 14
475 A185 3k dark red .50 .25
476 A185 4k dark brown .50 .25
Nos. 473-476 (4) 3.45 1.55
Cent. of the birth of Alois Jirásek, author. No. 474 was issued in a sheet of 10 stamps. Value: mint $1,000.

Portrait Type of 1950
Design: Josef Hybes (1850-1921), co-founder of Czech Communist Party.

1951, July 21 Engr.
477 A157 1.50k chocolate .35 .25
478 A157 2k rose brown .75 .40

"Ostrava Region" A186

Mining Iron Ore A187

1951, Sept. 9
479 A186 1.50k dk brown .25 .25
480 A187 3k rose brown .25 .25
481 A186 5k deep blue 1.00 .65
Nos. 479-481 (3) 1.50 1.15
Miner's Day, Sept. 9, 1951.

Soldiers on Parade — A188

1k, Gunner and field gun. 1.50k, Klement Gottwald. 3k, Tankman and tank. 5k, Aviators.

 Photo. (80h, 5k), Engr.
1951, Oct. 6 Perf. 14 (80h, 5k), 12½
Inscribed: "Den CS Armady 1951"
482 A188 80h olive brown .35 .30
483 A188 1k dk olive grn .35 .30
484 A188 1.50k sepia .35 .30
485 A188 3k claret .75 .35
486 A188 5k blue 1.75 .75
Nos. 482-486 (5) 3.55 2.00
Issued to publicize Army Day, Oct. 6, 1951.

Stalin and Gottwald A189

Lenin, Stalin and Soldiers A190

CZECHOSLOVAKIA

1951, Nov. 3   Engr.   Perf. 12½
487 A189 1.50k sepia   .25   .25
488 A190 3k red brown   .25   .25
489 A189 4k deep blue   1.00   .45
       Nos. 487-489 (3)   1.50   .95

Issued to publicize the month of Czechoslovak-Soviet friendship, 1951.

Peter Jilemnicky — A191

1951, Dec. 5   Unwmk.
491 A191 1.50k redsh brown   .25   .25
492 A191 2k dull blue   .80   .30

Peter Jilemnicky (1901-1949), writer.

Ladislav Zapotocky — A192

1952, Jan. 12   Perf. 11½
493 A192 1.50k brown red   .25   .25
494 A192 4k gray   1.00   .45

Centenary of the birth of Ladislav Zapotocky, Bohemian socialist pioneer.

Jan Kollar — A193

1952, Jan. 30   Unwmk.   Perf. 11½
495 A193 3k dark carmine   .25   .25
496 A193 5k violet blue   1.10   .60

Jan Kollar (1793-1852), poet.

Lenin and Lenin Hall — A194

1952, Jan. 30   Perf. 12½
497 A194 1.50k rose carmine   .30   .25
498 A194 5k deep blue   1.10   .75

6th All-Russian Party Conf., 40th anniv.

Emil Holub and African — A195

1952, Feb. 21   Perf. 11½
499 A195 3k red brown   .35   .25
500 A195 5k gray   1.50   .90

Death of Emil Holub, explorer, 50th anniv.

Gottwald Metallurgical Plant — A196

Designs: 2k, Foundry. 3k, Chemical plant.

1952, Feb. 25   Photo.   Perf. 14
501 A196 1.50k sepia   .25   .25
502 A196 2k red brown   1.50   .60
503 A196 3k scarlet   .25   .25
       Nos. 501-503 (3)   2.00 1.10

Student, Soldier and Miner A197

Youths of Three Races A198

1952, Mar. 21   Unwmk.   Perf. 14
504 A197 1.50k blue   .25   .25
505 A198 2k olive black   .25   .25
506 A197 3k lake   1.00   .50
       Nos. 504-506 (3)   1.50 1.00

International Youth Day, Mar. 25, 1952.

Similar to Type of 1951
Portrait: Otakar Sevcik.

1952, Mar. 22   Engr.   Perf. 12½
507 A184 2k choc, cr   .80   .35
508 A184 3k rose brn, cr   .25   .25

Otakar Sevcik, violinist, birth cent.

Jan A. Komensky — A199

1952, Mar. 28
509 A199 1.50k dk brown, cr   1.50   .65
510 A199 11k dk blue, cr   .35   .25

360th anniv. of the birth of Jan Amos Komensky (Comenius), teacher and philosopher.

Industrial and Farm Women — A200

1952, Mar. 8
511 A200 1.50k dp blue, cr   1.20   .50

International Women's Day Mar. 8, 1952.

Woman and Children — A201

1952, Apr. 12
512 A201 2k chocolate, cr   1.60 1.00
513 A201 3k dp claret, cr   .25   .25

Intl. Conf. for the Protection of Children, Vienna, Apr. 12-16, 1952.

Antifascist — A202

1952, Apr. 11   Photo.   Perf. 14
514 A202 1.50k red brown   .25   .25
515 A202 2k ultra   1.10   .60

Day of International Solidarity of Fighters against Fascism, Apr. 11, 1952.

Harvester — A203

Design: 3k, Tractor and Seeders.

1952, Apr. 30
516 A203 1.50k deep blue   2.10 1.20
517 A203 2k brown   .30   .30
518 A203 3k brown red   .30   .30
       Nos. 516-518 (3)   2.70 1.80

Youths Carrying Flags — A204

1952, May 1
519 A204 3k brown red   .35   .25
520 A204 4k dk red brown   1.40 1.25

Issued to publicize Labor Day, May 1, 1952.

Crowd Cheering Soviet Soldiers A205

1952, May 9
521 A205 1.50k dark red   .55   .45
522 A205 5k deep blue   2.25 1.25

Liberation of Czechoslovakia from German occupation, 7th anniversary.

Children — A206

Design: 3k, "Pioneer" teaching children.

1952, May 31   Engr.   Perf. 12½
523 A206 1.50k dk brn, cr   .25   .25
524 A206 2k Prus grn, cr   1.50   .60
525 A206 3k rose brn, cr   .25   .25
       Nos. 523-525 (3)   2.00 1.10

International Children's Day May 31, 1952.

J. V. Myslbek — A207

Design: 8k, Allegory, "Music."

1952, June 2
526 A207 1.50k red brown   .30   .25
527 A207 2k dark brown   1.25   .90
528 A207 8k gray green   .25   .25
       Nos. 526-528 (3)   1.80 1.40

Joseph V. Myslbek (1848-1922), sculptor.

Beethoven A208

House of Artists A209

1952, June 7   Unwmk.   Perf. 11½
529 A208 1.50k sepia   .35   .25
530 A209 3k red brown   .35   .25
531 A208 5k indigo   1.40 1.10
       Nos. 529-531 (3)   2.10 1.60

International Music Festival, Prague, 1952.

Lidice, Symbol of a New Life — A210

1952, June 10   Perf. 12½
532 A210 1.50k dk violet brn   .25   .25
533 A210 5k dark blue   1.00   .60

Destruction of Lidice, 10th anniversary.

Jan Hus A211

Bethlehem Chapel A212

1952, July 5
534 A211 1.50k brown   .25   .25
535 A212 3k red brown   .25   .25
536 A211 5k black   1.10   .65
       Nos. 534-536 (3)   1.60 1.15

550th anniv. of the installation of Jan Hus as pastor of Bethlehem Chapel, Prague.

Doctor Examining Patient — A213

2k, Doctor, Nurse, Mother and child.

1952, July 31
537 A213 1.50k dark brown   1.40   .80
538 A213 2k blue violet   .35   .25
539 A213 3k rose brown   .35   .25
       Nos. 537-539 (3)   2.10 1.30

Czechoslovakia's Unified Health Service.

A214   United Physical Education Program — A214a

1952, Aug. 2   Perf. 11½
540 A214   1.50k Relay race   .95   .60
541 A214a 2k Canoeing   2.50 1.10
542 A214a 3k Cycling   .60   .55
543 A214a 4k Hockey   3.25 3.00
       Nos. 540-543 (4)   7.30 5.25

Issued to publicize Czechoslovakia's Unified Physical Education program.

F. L. Celakovski — A215

1952, Aug. 5   Perf. 12½
544 A215 1.50k dark brown   .25   .25
545 A215 2k dark green   1.40   .90

Centenary of the death of Frantisek L. Celakovski, poet and writer.

Mikulas Ales — A216

Perf. 11x11½
1952, Aug. 30   Engr.   Unwmk.
546 A216 1.50k dk gray grn   .45   .35
547 A216 6k red brown   3.00 2.25

Birth centenary of Mikulas Ales, painter.

17th Century Mining Towers — A217

Designs: 1.50k, Coal Excavator. 2k, Peter Bezruc mine. 3k, Automatic coaling crane.

CZECHOSLOVAKIA

1952, Sept. 14   **Perf. 12½**
548 A217 1k sepia   1.25 .45
549 A217 1.50k dark blue   .25 .25
550 A217 2k olive gray   .25 .25
551 A217 3k violet brown   .25 .25
Nos. 548-551 (4)   2.00 1.20

Miners' Day, Sept. 14, 1952. No. 550 also for the 85th anniv. of the birth of Peter Bezruc (Vladimir Vasek), poet.

Jan Zizka — A218

Designs: 2k, Fraternization with Russians. 3k, Marching with flag.

Inscribed: ".... Armady 1952,"

1952, Oct. 5   **Engr.**   **Perf. 11½**
552 A218 1.50k rose lake   .25 .25
553 A218 2k olive bister   .25 .25
554 A218 3k dk car rose   .25 .25
555 A218 4k gray   1.50 .45
Nos. 552-555 (4)   2.25 1.20

Issued to publicize Army Day, Oct. 5, 1952.

Souvenir Sheet

Statues to Bulgarian Partisans and to Soviet Army — A219

1952, Oct. 18   **Unwmk.**   **Perf. 12½**
556 A219 Sheet of 2   85.00 16.00
   a. 2k deep carmine   35.00 7.50
   b. 3k ultramarine   35.00 7.50

National Philatelic Exhibition, Bratislava, Oct. 18-Nov. 2, 1952.

Danube River, Bratislava — A220

1952, Oct. 18
557 A220 1.50k dark brown   .25 .25

National Philatelic Exhibition, Bratislava.

Conference with Lenin and Stalin — A221

1952, Nov. 7
558 A221 2k brown black   1.40 .95
559 A221 3k carmine   .25 .25

35th anniv. of the Russian Revolution and to publicize Czechoslovak-Soviet friendship.

Worker and Nurse Holding Dove and Olive Branch — A222

1952, Nov. 15   **Photo.**   **Perf. 14**
560 A222 2k brown   1.40 .80
561 A222 3k red   .25 .25

Issued to publicize the first State Congress of the Czechoslovak Red Cross.

Matej Louda, Hussite Leader, Painted by Mikulas Ales — A223

3k, Dragon-killer Trutnov, painted by Ales.

1952, Nov. 18   **Engr.**   **Perf. 11½**
562 A223 2k red brown   .35 .25
563 A223 3k grnsh gray   .75 .25

Mikulas Ales, painter, birth cent.

Gottwald Type of 1948-49
1952, June 2   **Unwmk.**   **Perf. 12½**
Size: 19x24mm
564 A135 1k dark green   .60 .25

"Peace" Flags — A224

1952, Dec. 12   **Photo.**   **Perf. 14**
565 A224 3k red brown   .35 .25
566 A224 4k deep blue   .75 1.00

Issued to publicize the Congress of Nations for Peace, Vienna, Dec. 12-19, 1952.

Dove by Picasso — A225

Design: 4k, Czech Family.

1953, Jan. 17
567 A225 1.50k dark brown   .25 .25
568 A225 4k slate blue   .65 .30

2nd Czechoslovak Peace Congress.

Smetana Museum — A226

Design: 4k, Jirásek Museum.

1953, Feb. 10   **Engr.**   **Perf. 11½**
569 A226 1.50k dk violet brn   .25 .25
570 A226 4k dark gray   1.50 .75

Prof. Zdenek Nejedly, 75th birth anniv.

Martin Kukucin A227

Jaroslav Vrchlicky A228

Designs: 2k, Karel Jaromir Erben. 3k, Vaclav Matej Kramerius. 5k, Josef Dobrovsky.

1953, Feb. 28
571 A227 1k gray   .25 .25
572 A228 1.50k olive   .25 .25
573 A228 2k rose lake   .25 .25
574 A228 3k lt brown   .50 .25
575 A228 5k slate blue   1.50 .75
Nos. 571-575 (5)   2.75 1.75

Issued to honor Czech writers and poets: 1k, 25th anniv. of death of Kukucin. 1.50k, birth cent. of Vrchlicky. 2k, cent. of completion of "Kytice" by Erben. 3k, birth bicent. of Kramerius. 5k, birth bicent. of Dobrovsky.

Militia A229

Gottwald A230

Design: 8k, Portraits of Stalin and Gottwald and Peoples Assembly.

Perf. 13½x14
1953, Feb. 25   **Photo.**   **Unwmk.**
576 A229 1.50k deep blue   .25 .25
577 A230 3k red   .25 .25
578 A229 8k dark brown   2.10 .75
Nos. 576-578 (3)   2.60 1.25

5th anniv. of the defeat of the attempt to reinstate capitalism.

Book and Torch — A231

Design: 3k, Bedrich Vaclavek.

1953, Mar. 5   **Engr.**   **Perf. 11½**
579 A231 1k sepia   1.50 .60
580 A231 3k orange brown   .25 .25

Bedrich Vaclavek (1897-1943), socialist writer.

Stalin Type of 1949
Inscribed "21 XII 1879-5 III 1953"
1953, Mar. 12
581 A154 1.50k black   .35 .25

Death of Joseph Stalin, Mar. 5, 1953.

Mother and Child A232

Girl Revolutionist A233

1953, Mar. 8
582 A232 1.50k ultra   .25 .25
583 A233 2k brown red   1.25 .60

International Women's Day.

Klement Gottwald — A234

1953, Mar. 19
584 A234 1.50k black   .25 .25
585 A234 3k black   .25 .25

Souvenir Sheet
Imperf
586 A234 5k black   5.00 4.00

Death of Pres. Klement Gottwald, 3/14/53.

Josef Pecka, Ladislav Zapotocky and Josef Hybes — A236

1953, Apr. 7   **Unwmk.**   **Perf. 11½**
587 A236 2k lt violet brn   .25 .25

75th anniversary of the first congress of the Czech Social Democratic Party.

Cyclists — A237

1953, Apr. 29
588 A237 3k deep blue   .75 .35

6th International Peace Bicycle Race, Prague-Berlin-Warsaw.

Medal of "May 1, 1890" — A238

Designs: 1.50k, Lenin and Stalin. 3k, May Day Parade. 8k, Marx and Engels.

Engraved and Photogravure
1953, Apr. 30   **Perf. 11½x11, 14**
589 A238 1k chocolate   1.40 .35
590 A238 1.50k dark gray   .25 .25
591 A238 3k carmine lake   .25 .25
592 A238 8k dk gray green   .30 .25
Nos. 589-592 (4)   2.20 1.10

Issued to publicize Labor Day, May 1, 1953.

Sowing Grain — A239

1953, May 8   **Photo.**   **Perf. 14**
593 A239 1.50k shown   .35 .25
594 A239 7k Reaper   1.60 1.40

Socialization of the village.

Dam A240

Welder A241

Design: 3k, Iron works.

1953, May 8   **Perf. 11½**
595 A240 1.50k gray   1.10 .30
596 A241 2k blue gray   .25 .25
597 A240 3k red brown   .25 .25
Nos. 595-597 (3)   1.60 .80

Josef Slavik A242

Leos Janacek A243

1953, June 19   **Photo.**
598 A242 75h dp gray blue   .75 .25
599 A243 1.60k dark brown   1.00 .25

Issued on the occasion of the International Music Festival, Prague, 1953.

Gottwald Type of 1948-49
Perf. 12½ (15h, 1k), 11½ (20h, 3k)
1953
600 A135 15h yellow green   .35 .25
601 A135 20h dk violet brn   .45 .25
602 A135 1k purple   1.10 .25
603 A135 3k brown car   .25 .25
604 A135 3k gray   .75 .25
Nos. 600-604 (5)   2.90 1.25

Nos. 600-604 vary slightly in size.

Pres. Antonin Zapotocky — A244

1953, June 19   **Perf. 14**
605 A244 30h violet blue   .75 .25
606 A244 60h cerise   1.00 .25

CZECHOSLOVAKIA 37

Julius
Fucik
A245

Book and
Carnation
A246

1953, Sept. 8   Engr.   Perf. 12½
607 A245 40h dk violet brn   .30   .25
608 A246 60h pink   .50   .30

10th anniv. of the death of Julius Fucik, Communist leader executed by the Nazis.

Miner and
Flag — A247

Design: 60h, Oil field and workers.

1953, Sept. 10   Perf. 11½
609 A247 30h gray   .30   .25
610 A247 60h brown vio   1.25   .50

Miner's Day, Sept. 10, 1953.

Volleyball
Game
A248

Motorcyclist
A249

Design: 60h, Woman throwing javelin.

1953, Sept. 15
611 A248 30h brown red   4.50 1.50
612 A249 40h dk violet brn   2.75   .85
613 A248 60h rose violet   2.50   .85
     Nos. 611-613 (3)   9.75 3.20

Hussite Warrior — A250

Designs: 60h, Soldier presenting arms. 1k, Red army soldiers.

1953, Oct. 8
614 A250 30h brown   .30   .25
615 A250 60h rose lake   .35   .25
616 A250   1k brown red   1.50 1.25
     Nos. 614-616 (3)   2.15 1.75

Issued to publicize Army Day, Oct. 3, 1953.

Pres. Antonin
Zapotocky — A251

1953   Unwmk.   Perf. 11½, 12½
617 A251 30h violet blue   .50   .25
618 A251 60h carmine rose   .80   .25

No. 617 is perf. 11½ & measures 19x23mm, No. 618 perf. 12½ & 18½x23½mm. See No. 780.

Charles Bridge and
Prague
Castle — A252

1953, Aug. 15   Engr.   Perf. 11½
619 A252 5k gray   4.00   .25

Korean and Czech
Girls — A253

1953, Oct. 11   Perf. 11x11½
620 A253 30h dark brown   2.40 1.50

Czechoslovakia's friendship with Korea.

Flags,
Hradcany
Castle and
Kremlin
A254

Designs: 60h, Lomonosov University, Moscow. 1.20k, Lenin Ship Canal.

1953, Nov. 7
621 A254 30h dark gray   .75   .50
622 A254 60h dark brown   1.10   .85
623 A254 1.20k ultra   3.00 1.90
     Nos. 621-623 (3)   4.85 3.25

Czechoslovak-Soviet friendship month.

Emmy
Destinn,
Opera Singer
A255

National
Theater,
Prague
A256

Portrait: 2k, Eduard Vojan, actor.

1953, Nov. 18   Perf. 14
624 A255 30h blue black   1.10   .75
625 A256 60h brown   .35   .35
626 A255   2k sepia   2.75 1.10
     Nos. 624-626 (3)   4.20 2.20

Natl. Theater founding, 70th anniv.
Nos. 624 and 626 each were issued in sheets of 10. Values: No. 624, $100; No. 626, $75.

Josef Manes — A257

1953, Nov. 28   Perf 11x11½
627 A257 60h brown carmine   .35   .25
628 A257 1.20k deep blue   1.50   .90

Issued to honor Josef Manes, painter.

Vaclav Hollar — A258

Portrait: 1.20k, Head framed, facing right.

1953, Dec. 5
629 A258 30h brown black   .35   .25
630 A258 1.20k dark brown   1.50   .65

Vaclav Hollar, artist and etcher.

Leo N. Tolstoy — A259

1953, Dec. 29   Unwmk.
631 A259 60h dark green   .35   .25
632 A259   1k chocolate   1.50   .50

Leo N. Tolstoy, 125th birth anniv.

Locomotive
A260

Design: 1k, Plane loading mail.

**Engraved, Center Photogravure
1953, Dec. 29   Perf. 11½x11**
633 A260 60h brn org & gray vio 1.50 .45
634 A260   1k org brn & brt bl 3.50 1.10

Lenin — A261

Lenin
Museum,
Prague
A262

1954, Jan. 21   Engr.   Perf. 11½
635 A261 30h dark brown   .45   .25
636 A262 1.40k chocolate   1.50   .65

30th anniversary of the death of Lenin.

Klement
Gottwald — A263

Design: 2.40k, Revolutionist with flag.

1954, Feb. 18   Perf. 11x11½, 14x13½
637 A263 60h dark brown   .30   .25
638 A263 2.40k rose lake   3.50 1.50

25th anniversary of the fifth congress of the Communist Party in Czechoslovakia.
No. 638 was issued in a sheet of 10 stamps. Value, $90.

Gottwald   Gottwald and
Mausoleum,   Stalin — A265
Prague — A264

1.20k, Lenin & Stalin mausoleum, Moscow.

1954, Mar. 5   Perf. 11½, 14x13½
639 A264 30h olive brown   .35   .25
640 A264 60h deep ultra   .35   .25
641 A264 1.20k rose brown   2.25 1.00
     Nos. 639-641 (3)   2.95 1.50

1st anniv. of the deaths of Stalin and Gottwald.
No. 641 was issued in a sheet of 10 stamps. Value, $120.

Two
Runners
A266

Group of Hikers
A267

Design: 1k, Woman swimmer.

1954, Apr. 24   Perf. 11¼, 13¾ (#643)
642 A266 30h dark brown   2.10 1.10
643 A267 80h dark green   7.00 3.50
644 A266   1k dk violet blue   1.75   .75
     Nos. 642-644 (3)   10.85 5.35

No. 643 was issued in a sheet of 10 stamps. Value, $350.

Nurse — A268

Designs: 15h, Construction worker. 40h, Postwoman. 45h, Ironworker. 50h, Soldier. 75h, Lathe operator. 80h, Textile worker. 1k, Farm woman. 1.20k, Scientist and microscope. 1.60k, Miner. 2k, Physician and baby. 2.40k, Engineer. 3k, Chemist.

1954   Perf. 12½x12, 11½x11
645 A268   15h dark green   .35   .25
646 A268   20h lt violet   .40   .25
647 A268   40h dark brown   .50   .25
648 A268   45h dk gray blue   .40   .25
649 A268   50h dk gray green   .50   .25
650 A268   75h deep blue   .50   .25
651 A268   80h violet brown   .50   .25
652 A268   1k green   .80   .25
653 A268 1.20k dk violet blue .50   .25
654 A268 1.60k brown blk   1.20   .25
655 A268   2k orange brown   1.60   .25
656 A268 2.40k violet blue   1.60   .25
657 A268   3k carmine   1.60   .25
     Nos. 645-657 (13)   10.45 3.25

Antonin Dvorák — A269

40h, Leos Janacek. 60h, Bedrich Smetana.

1954, May 22   Perf. 11x11½
658 A269 30h violet brown   2.25   .25
659 A269 40h brick red   3.00   .35
660 A269 60h dark blue   .90   .25
     Nos. 658-660 (3)   6.15   .85

"Year of Czech Music," 1954.

Prokop Divis — A270

1954, June 15
661 A270 30h gray   .35   .25
662 A270 75h violet brown   1.40   .50

200th anniv. of the invention of a lightning conductor by Prokop Divis.

Slovak
Insurrectionist — A271

Design: 1.20k, Partisan woman.

1954, Aug. 28   Perf. 11½
663 A271 30h brown orange   .25   .25
664 A271 1.20k dark blue   .85   .50

Slovak national uprising, 10th anniv.

Anton P.
Chekhov — A272

1954, Sept. 24
665 A272 30h dull gray grn   .30   .25
666 A272 45h dull gray brn   1.10   .50

50th anniv. of the death of Chekhov, writer.

Soviet Representative Giving
Agricultural Instruction
A273

Designs: 60h, Soviet industrial instruction. 2k, Dancers (cultural collaboration).

CZECHOSLOVAKIA

1954, Nov. 6   *Perf. 11½x11*
667 A273 30h yellow brown   .25   .25
668 A273 60h dark blue   .25   .25
669 A273 2k vermilion   1.40   .90
    Nos. 667-669 (3)   1.90   1.40
Czechoslovak-Soviet friendship month.

Jan Neruda — A274

60h, Janko Jesensky. 1.60k, Jiri Wolker.

1954, Nov. 25   *Perf. 11x11½*
670 A274 30h dark blue   .85   .25
671 A274 60h dull red   1.40   .50
672 A274 1.60k sepia   .35   .25
    Nos. 670-672 (3)   2.60   1.00
Issued to honor Czechoslovak poets.

View of Telc — A275

Views: 60h, Levoca. 3k, Ceske Budejovice.

1954, Dec. 10   *Engr. & Photo.*
673 A275 30h black & bis   .70   .25
674 A275 60h brown & bis   .80   .25
675 A275 3k black & bis   2.50   1.25
    Nos. 673-675 (3)   4.00   1.75

Pres. Antonin Zapotocky — A276

1954, Dec. 18   *Engr.*   *Perf. 11½*
676 A276 30h black brown   .50   .25
677 A276 60h dark brown   .55   .25

Souvenir Sheet
Imperf
678 A276 2k deep claret   15.00   6.00

70th birthday of Pres. Antonin Zapotocky. See Nos. 829-831.

Attacking Soldiers — A278

Design: 2k, Soldier holding child.

1954, Oct. 3   *Perf. 11½*
679 A278 60h dark green   .30   .25
680 A278 2k dark brown   1.40   1.25

Army Day, Oct. 6, 1954.

Woman Holding Torch — A279

Design: 45h, Ski jumper.

1955, Jan. 20   *Engr.*
681 A279 30h red   2.10   .50

Engraved and Photogravure
682 A279 45h black & blue   3.50   .45

First National Spartacist Games, 1955.

Comenius University Building — A280

Design: 75h, Jan A. Komensky medal.

1955, Jan. 28   *Engr.*   *Perf. 11½*
683 A280 60h deep green   .30   .25
684 A280 75h chocolate   1.40   .65

35th anniversary of the founding of Comenius University, Bratislava.

Czechoslovak Automobile — A281

60h, Textile worker. 75h, Lathe operator.

1955, Mar. 15   *Unwmk.*
685 A281 45h dull green   1.40   .30
686 A281 60h dk violet blue   .60   .25
687 A281 75h sepia   .90   .25
    Nos. 685-687 (3)   2.90   .80

Woman Decorating Soviet Soldier A282

Stalin Memorial, Prague A283

Designs: 35h, Tankman with flowers. 60h, Children greeting soldier.

1955, May 5   *Engr.*   *Perf. 11½*
688 A282 30h blue   .35   .25
689 A282 35h dark brown   1.50   .30
690 A282 60h cerise   .35   .25

Photo.
691 A283 60h sepia   .35   .25
    Nos. 688-691 (4)   2.55   1.05

10th anniv. of Czechoslovakia's liberation.

Music and Spring — A284

Design: 1k, Woman with lyre.

1955, May 12   *Engr. & Photo.*
692 A284 30h black & pale blue   .35   .25
693 A284 1k black & pale rose   1.40   1.20

International Music Festival, Prague, 1955.

Foundry Worker — A285

Design: 45h, Farm workers.

1955, May 12   *Engr.*
694 A285 30h violet   .25   .25
695 A285 45h green   1.20   .60

Issued to publicize the third congress of the Trade Union Revolutionary Movement.

Woman Athlete — A286

60h, Dancing couple. 1.60k, Athlete.

1955, June 21
696 A286 20h violet blue   1.00   .40
697 A286 60h green   .35   .25
698 A286 1.60k red   .75   .25
    Nos. 696-698 (3)   2.10   .90

Issued to publicize the first National Spartacist Games, Prague, June-July, 1955.

Jakub Arbes — A287

Portraits: 30h, Jan Stursa. 40h, Elena Marothy-Soltesova. 60h, Josef Vaclav Sladek. 75h, Alexander Stepanovic Popov. 1.40k, Jan Holly. 1.60k, Pavel Josef Safarik.

1955
699 A287 20h brown   .25   .25
700 A287 30h black   .25   .25
701 A287 40h gray green   .60   .25
702 A287 60h black   .50   .25
703 A287 75h claret   1.75   .25
704 A287 1.40k black, *cr*   .50   .25
705 A287 1.60k dark blue   .50   .25
    Nos. 699-705 (7)   4.35   1.75

Various anniversaries of prominent Slavs.

Girl and Boy of Two Races — A288

1955, July 20
706 A288 60h violet blue   .75   .25

5th World Festival of Youth in Warsaw, July 31-Aug. 14.

Costume of Ocova, Slovakia — A289

Regional Costumes: 75h, Detva man, Slovakia. 1.60k, Chodsko man, Bohemia. 2k, Hana woman, Moravia.

1955, July 25
Frame and Outlines in Brown
707 A289 60h orange & rose   10.00   7.00
708 A289 75h orange & lilac   4.00   4.00
709 A289 1.60k blue & orange   11.50   7.00
710 A289 2k yellow & rose   11.50   7.00
    Nos. 707-710 (4)   37.00   25.00

Nos. 707-710 were each issued in sheets of 10 stamps. Value, $450.

Carp — A290

Designs: 30h, Beetle. 35h, Gray Partridge. 1.40k, Butterfly. 1.50k, Hare.

1955, Aug. 8   *Engr. & Photo.*
711 A290 20h sepia & lt bl   2.25   .35
712 A290 30h sepia & pink   1.50   .30
713 A290 35h sepia & buff   1.50   .75
714 A290 1.40k sepia & cream   7.50   4.50
715 A290 1.50k sepia & lt grn   2.75   1.10
    Nos. 711-715 (5)   15.50   7.00

Tabor — A291

45h, Prachatice. 60h, Jindrichuv Hradec.

1955, Aug. 26   *Engr.*
716 A291 30h violet brown   .50   .25
717 A291 45h rose carmine   2.00   .45
718 A291 60h sage green   1.00   .25
    Nos. 716-718 (3)   3.50   .95

Issued to publicize the architectural beauty of the towns of Southern Bohemia.

Souvenir Sheet
Various Views of Prague A292

1955, Sept. 10   *Engr.*   *Perf. 14x13½*
719 A292 Sheet of 5   27.50   27.50
  a.   30h gray black   4.75   5.25
  b.   45h gray black   4.75   5.25
  c.   60h rose lake   4.75   5.25
  d.   75h rose lake   4.75   5.25
  e.   1.60k gray black   4.75   5.25

International Philatelic Exhibition, Prague, Sept. 10-25, 1955. Size: 145x110mm. Exists imperf., value $47.50.

Motorcyclists — A293

1955, Aug. 28
720 A293 60h violet brown   3.00   .75

30th International Motorcycle Races at Gottwaldov, Sept. 13-18, 1955.

Workers, Soldier and Pioneer — A294

Army Day: 60h, Tanks and planes.

1955, Oct. 6   *Unwmk.*   *Perf. 11½*
721 A294 30h violet brown   .35   .25
722 A294 60h slate   1.75   .75

Hans Christian Andersen — A295

Portraits: 40h, Friedrich von Schiller. 60h, Adam Mickiewicz. 75h, Walt Whitman.

1955, Oct. 27
723 A295 30h brown red   .35   .25
724 A295 40h dark blue   2.25   1.00
725 A295 60h deep claret   .35   .25
726 A295 75h greenish black   .75   .35
    Nos. 723-726 (4)   3.70   1.85

Issued in honor of these four poets and to mark the 100th anniversary of the publication of Walt Whitman's "Leaves of Grass."

Railroad Bridge — A296

30h, Train crossing bridge. 60h, Train approaching tunnel. 1.60k, Miners' housing project.

Inscribed: "Stavba Socialismu"
1955, Dec. 15
727 A296 20h dull green   .75   .25
728 A296 30h violet brown   .75   .25
729 A296 60h slate   .75   .25
730 A296 1.60k carmine rose   .75   .25
    Nos. 727-730 (4)   3.00   1.00

Issued to publicize socialist public works.

Hydroelectric Plant — A297

CZECHOSLOVAKIA

2nd Five Year Plan: 10h, Miner with drill. 25h, Building construction. 30h, Harvester. 60h, Metallurgical plant.

Inscribed: "Druhy Petilety Plan 1956-1960."

1956, Feb. 20 *Perf. 11½x11*
731	A297	5h violet brown	.30	.25
732	A297	10h gray black	.30	.25
733	A297	25h dk car rose	.45	.25
734	A297	30h green	.30	.25
735	A297	60h violet blue	.30	.25
		Nos. 731-735 (5)	1.65	1.25

Jewelry — A298

1956, Mar. 17 *Perf. 11x11½*
736	A298	30h shown	.45	.25
737	A298	45h Glassware	3.50	1.60
738	A298	60h Ceramics	.45	.25
739	A298	75h Textiles	.45	.30
		Nos. 736-739 (4)	4.85	2.40

Products of Czechoslovakian industries.

Karlovy Vary (Karlsbad) — A299

Various Spas: 45h, Marianske Lazne (Marienbad). 75h, Piestany. 1.20k, Tatry Vysne Ruzbachy (Tatra Mountains).

1956, Mar. 17
740	A299	30h olive green	1.50	.30
741	A299	45h brown	1.10	.30
742	A299	75h claret	6.00	3.00
743	A299	1.20k ultra	.75	.30
		Nos. 740-743 (4)	9.35	3.90

Issued to publicize Czechoslovakian spas.

"We Serve our People" — A300

Designs: 60h, Russian War Memorial, Berlin. 1k, Tank crewman with standard.

1956, Apr. 9 *Photo.* *Perf. 11x11½*
744	A300	30h olive brown	.75	.25
745	A300	60h carmine rose	.75	.25
746	A300	1k ultra	4.50	2.75
		Nos. 744-746 (3)	6.00	3.25

Exhibition: "The Construction and Defense of our Country," Prague, Apr., 1956.

Cyclists A301 — Girl Basketball Players A302

Athletes and Olympic Rings A303

Engraved and Photogravure

1956, Apr. 25 *Unwmk.* *Perf. 11½*
747	A301	30h green & lt blue	3.50	.35
748	A302	45h dk blue & car	1.40	.35
749	A303	75h brown & lemon	1.10	.70
		Nos. 747-749 (3)	6.00	1.40

9th Intl. Peace Cycling Race, Warsaw-Berlin-Prague, May 1-15, 1956 (No. 747). 5th European Womens' Basketball Championship (No. 748). Summer Olympics, Melbourne, Nov. 22-Dec. 8, 1956 (No. 749). See No. 765.

Mozart — A304

45h, Josef Myslivecek. 60h, Jiri Benda. 1k, Bertramka House, Prague. 1.20k, Xaver Dusek (1731-99) and wife Josepha. 1.60k, Nostic Theater, Prague.

1956, May 12 *Engr.*
Design in Gray Black
750	A304	30h bister	1.50	.35
751	A304	45h gray green	8.50	6.00
752	A304	60h pale rose lilac	1.50	.35
753	A304	1k salmon	1.50	.35
754	A304	1.40k lt blue	4.50	.75
755	A304	1.60k lemon	3.00	.35
		Nos. 750-755 (6)	20.50	8.15

200th anniv. of the birth of Wolfgang Amadeus Mozart and to publicize the International Music Festival in Prague.

Home Guard — A305

1956, May 25
| 756 | A305 | 60h violet blue | .75 | .25 |

Issued to commemorate the first meeting of the Home Guard, Prague, May 25-27, 1956.

Josef Kajetan Tyl — A306

Portraits: 20h, Ludovit Stur. 30h, Frana Sramek. 1.40k, Karel Havlicek Borovsky.

1956, June 23
757	A306	20h dull purple	.75	.25
758	A306	30h blue	.45	.25
759	A306	60h black	.45	.25
760	A306	1.40k claret	3.00	1.75
		Nos. 757-760 (4)	4.65	2.50

Issued to honor various Czechoslovakian writers. See Nos. 781-784, 873-876.

River Patrol — A307

Design: 60h, Guard and dog.

1956, July 8 *Perf. 11x11½*
761	A307	30h ultra	.75	.25
762	A307	60h green	.60	.25

Issued to honor men of Frontier Guard.

Type of 1956 and

Steeplechase A308

1956, Sept. 8 *Unwmk.* *Perf. 11½*
763	A308	60h indigo & bister	3.00	.75
764	A308	80h brown vio & vio	1.50	.35
765	A303	1.20k slate & orange	3.00	1.50
		Nos. 763-765 (3)	7.50	2.60

Steeplechase, Pardubice, 1956 (No. 763). Marathon race, Kosice, 1956 (No. 764). Olympic Games, Melbourne, Nov. 22-Dec. 8 (No. 765).

Woman Gathering Grapes A309 — Fishermen A310

35h, Women gathering hops. 95h, Logging.

1956, Sept. 20 *Engr.*
766	A309	30h brown lake	.35	.25
767	A309	35h gray green	.35	.25
768	A310	80h dark blue	.75	.25
769	A310	95h chocolate	2.25	1.00
		Nos. 766-769 (4)	3.70	1.75

Issued to publicize natural resources.

European Timetable Conf., Prague, Nov. 9-13 — A311
A312

Locomotives: 10h, 1846. 30h, 1855. 40h, 1945. 45h, 1952. 60h, 1955. 1k, 1954.

1956, Nov. 9 *Unwmk.* *Perf. 11½*
770	A311	10h brown	2.50	.35
771	A312	30h gray	2.50	.35
772	A312	40h green	5.00	.35
773	A312	45h brown car	8.50	5.00
774	A312	60h indigo	2.50	.35
775	A312	1k ultra	6.00	.35
		Nos. 770-775 (6)	27.00	6.75

Costume of Moravia — A313

Regional Costumes (women): 1.20k, Blata, Bohemia. 1.40k, Cicmany, Slovakia. 1.60k, Novohradsko, Slovakia.

1956, Dec. 15 *Perf. 13½*
776	A313	30h brn, ultra & car	1.75	1.75
777	A313	1.20k brn, car & ultra	2.75	.40
778	A313	1.40k brn, ocher & vel	10.00	3.25
779	A313	1.60k brn, car & grn	3.50	.80
		Nos. 776-779 (4)	18.00	6.20

See Nos. 832-835.

Nos. 776-779 each were issued in sheets of 10 stamps. Value, $160.

Zapotocky Type of 1953

1956, Oct. 7 *Unwmk.* *Perf. 12½*
| 780 | A251 | 30h blue | .75 | .25 |

Portrait Type of 1956

15h, Ivan Olbracht. 20h, Karel Toman. 30h, F. X. Salda. 1.60k, Terezia Vansova.

1957, Jan. 18 *Engr.* *Perf. 11½*
781	A306	15h dk red brn, cr	.30	.25
782	A306	20h dk green, cr	.30	.25
783	A306	30h dk brown, cr	.30	.25
784	A306	1.60k dk blue, cr	.60	.25
		Nos. 781-784 (4)	1.50	1.00

Issued in honor of Czechoslovakian writers.

Kolin Cathedral A315

Views: No. 786, Banska Stiavnica. No. 787, Uherske Hradiste. No. 788, Karlstein. No. 789, Charles Bridge, Prague. 1.25k, Moravska Trebova.

1957, Feb. 23
785	A315	30h dk blue gray	.40	.25
786	A315	30h rose violet	.50	.25
787	A315	60h deep rose	.50	.25
788	A315	60h gray green	.50	.25
789	A315	60h brown	.75	.25
790	A315	1.25k gray	3.00	1.25
		Nos. 785-790 (6)	5.65	2.50

Anniversaries of various towns and landmarks.

Komensky Mausoleum, Naarden A316 — Jan A. Komensky A317

Old Prints: 40h, Komensky teaching. 1k, Sun, moon, stars and earth.

Perf. 11½x11, 14 (A317)

1957, Mar. 28 *Engr.* *Unwmk.*
791	A316	30h pale brown	.45	.25
792	A316	40h dark green	.45	.25
793	A317	60h chocolate	3.00	.75
794	A316	1k carmine rose	.60	.25
		Nos. 791-794 (4)	4.50	1.50

300th anniv. of the publication of "Didactica Opera Omnia" by J. A. Komensky (Comenius). No. 793 issued in sheets of four. Value, $24.

Farm Woman — A318

1957, Mar. 22 *Perf. 11½*
| 795 | A318 | 30h lt blue green | .75 | .25 |

3rd Cong. of Agricultural Cooperatives.

Cyclists — A319

Woman Archer A320 — Boxers A321

Rescue Team — A322

1957, Apr. 30 *Perf. 11½x11, 11x11½*
796	A319	30h sepia & ultra	.60	.25
797	A319	60h dull grn & bis	2.25	1.25
798	A320	60h gray & emer	.45	.25

CZECHOSLOVAKIA

799	A321	60h sepia & org	.45	.25
800	A322	60h violet & choc	.75	.25
		Nos. 796-800 (5)	4.50	2.25

10th Intl. Peace Cycling Race, Prague-Berlin-Warsaw (Nos. 796-797). Intl. Archery Championships (No. 798). European Boxing Championships, Prague (No. 799). Mountain Climbing Rescue Service (No. 800).

Jan V. Stamic — A323

Musicians: No. 802, Ferdinand Laub. No. 803, Frantisek Ondricek. No. 804, Josef B. Foerster. No. 805, Vitezslav Novak. No. 806, Josef Suk.

1957, May 12   Perf. 11½
801	A323	60h purple	.35	.25
802	A323	60h black	.35	.25
803	A323	60h slate blue	.35	.25
804	A323	60h brown	.35	.25
805	A323	60h dull red brn	.90	.35
806	A323	60h blue green	.35	.25
		Nos. 801-806 (6)	2.65	1.50

Spring Music Festival, Prague.

Josef Bozek A324   School of Engineering A325

60h, F. J. Gerstner. 1k, R. Skuhersky.

1957, May 25
807	A324	30h bluish black	.25	.25
808	A324	60h gray brown	.30	.25
809	A324	1k rose lake	.30	.25
810	A325	1.40k blue violet	.65	.25
		Nos. 807-810 (4)	1.50	1.00

School of Engineering in Prague, 250th anniv.

Pioneer and Philatelic Symbols — A326

Design: 60h, Girl and carrier pigeon.

Engraved and Photogravure
1957, June 8   Perf. 11½
| 811 | A326 | 30h olive grn & org | .45 | .25 |

     Engr.   Perf. 13½
| 812 | A326 | 60h brn & vio bl | 3.00 | 2.25 |

Youth Philatelic Exhibition, Pardubice. No. 812 was printed in miniature sheets of 4. Value $12.

"Grief" — A327

Design: 60h, Rose, symbol of new life.

1957, June 10
| 813 | A327 | 30h black | .35 | .25 |
| 814 | A327 | 60h blk & rose red | 1.25 | .35 |

Destruction of Lidice, 15th anniversary. No. 814 was issued in a sheet of 10 stamps. Value, $28.

Motorcyclists — A328

1957, July 5   Perf. 11½
| 815 | A328 | 60h dk gray & blue | 1.50 | .30 |

32nd International Motorcycle Race.

Karel Klic A329   Josef Ressel A330

1957, July 5
| 816 | A329 | 30h gray black | .60 | .25 |
| 817 | A330 | 60h violet blue | .60 | .25 |

Klic, inventor of photogravure, and Ressel, inventor of the ship screw.

Chamois A331   Gentian A332

Designs: 30h, Brown bear. 60h, Edelweiss. 1.25k, Tatra Mountains.

1957, Aug. 28   Engr.   Perf. 11½
818	A331	20h emer & brnsh gray	1.00	.25
819	A331	30h lt blue & brn	1.00	.25
820	A332	40h gldn brn & vio	1.60	.30
821	A332	60h yellow & grn	1.00	.25

   Size: 48x28½mm
| 822 | A332 | 1.25k ol grn & bis | 1.60 | .80 |
| | | Nos. 818-822 (5) | 6.20 | 1.85 |

Tatra Mountains National Park.

"Marycka Magdonova" — A333

Engraved and Photogravure
1957, Sept. 15   Unwmk.   Perf. 11½
| 823 | A333 | 60h black & dull red | .45 | .25 |

90th birthday of Petr Bezruc, poet and author of "Marycka Magdonova."

Man Holding Banner of Trade Union Cong. — A334

1957, Sept. 28   Engr.
| 824 | A334 | 75h rose red | .45 | .25 |

4th Intl. Trade Union Cong., Leipzig, 10/4-15.

Television Transmitter and Antennas — A335

Design: 60h, Family watching television.

1957, Oct. 19   Engr.   Perf. 11½
| 825 | A335 | 40h dk blue & car | .30 | .25 |
| 826 | A335 | 60h redsh brown & emer | .45 | .25 |

Issued to publicize the television industry.

Worker, Globe and Lenin — A336

60h, Worker, factory, hammer and sickle.

1957, Nov. 7   Perf. 12x11½
| 827 | A336 | 30h claret | .25 | .25 |
| 828 | A336 | 60h gray blue | .25 | .25 |

Russian Revolution, 40th anniversary.

Zapotocky Type of 1954 dated: 19 XII 1884-13 XI 1957
1957, Nov. 18   Unwmk.   Perf. 11½
| 829 | A276 | 30h black | .25 | .25 |
| 830 | A276 | 60h black | .25 | .25 |

Souvenir Sheet
Imperf
| 831 | A276 | 2k black | 5.00 | 1.25 |

Death of Pres. Antonin Zapotocky.

Costume Type of 1956
Regional Costumes: 45h, Pilsen woman, Bohemia. 75h, Slovacko man, Moravia. 1.25k, Hana woman, Moravia. 1.95k, Teshinsko woman, Silesia.

1957, Dec. 18   Engr.   Perf. 13½
832	A313	45h brn, bl & dk red	4.25	1.50
833	A313	75h dk brn, red & grn	3.00	.80
834	A313	1.25k dk brn, scar & ocher	5.25	1.50
835	A313	1.95k sepia, bl & ver	6.00	3.75
		Nos. 832-835 (4)	18.50	7.55

Nos. 832-835 each was issued in sheets of 10 stamps. Value, set $200.

A337   A338

Designs: 30h, Radio telescope and observatory. 45h, Meteorological station in High Tatra. 75h, Sputnik 2 over Earth.

1957, Dec. 20   Perf. 11½
836	A337	30h violet brn & yel	1.60	.50
837	A338	45h sepia & lt bl	.65	.30
838	A337	75h claret & blue	2.00	.85
		Nos. 836-838 (3)	4.25	1.65

IGY, 1957-58. No. 838 also for the launching of Sputnik 2, Nov. 3, 1957.

Girl Skater — A339

Designs: 40h, Canoeing. 60h, Volleyball. 80h, Parachutist. 1.60k, Soccer.

1958, Jan. 25   Engr.   Perf. 11½x12
839	A339	30h rose violet	1.75	.25
840	A339	40h blue	.35	.25
841	A339	60h redsh brown	.35	.25
842	A339	80h violet blue	1.50	.45
843	A339	1.60k brt green	.65	.25
		Nos. 839-843 (5)	4.60	1.45

Issued to publicize various sports championship events in 1958.

Litomysl Castle — A340

Design: 60h, Bethlehem Chapel.

1958, Feb. 10   Perf. 11½
| 844 | A340 | 30h green | .30 | .25 |
| 845 | A340 | 60h redsh brown | .30 | .25 |

80th anniversary of the birth of Zdenek Nejedly, restorer of Bethlehem Chapel.

Giant Excavator — A341

Peace Dove and: 60h, Soldiers, flame and banner, horiz. 1.60k, Harvester and rainbow, horiz.

1958, Feb. 25
846	A341	30h gray violet & yel	.25	.25
847	A341	60h gray brown & car	.25	.25
848	A341	1.60k green & dull yel	.45	.25
		Nos. 846-848 (3)	.95	.75

10th anniv. of the "Victorious February."

Jewelry — A342

Designs: 45h, Dolls. 60h, Textiles. 75h, Kaplan turbine. 1.20k, Glass.

Engraved and Photogravure
1958   Unwmk.   Perf. 11½
849	A342	30h rose car & blue	.40	.25
850	A342	45h rose red & pale lil	.40	.25
851	A342	60h violet & aqua	.60	.25
852	A342	75h ultra & salmon	1.50	.75
853	A342	1.20k blue grn & pink	.60	.25
		Nos. 849-853 (5)	3.50	1.75

Issued for the Universal and International Exposition at Brussels.

King George of Podebrad A343

Design: 60h, View of Prague, 1628.

1958, May 19   Engr.
| 854 | A343 | 30h carmine rose | .50 | .25 |
| 855 | A343 | 60h violet blue | .30 | .25 |

Issued to publicize the National Archives Exhibition, Prague, May 15-Aug. 15.

"Towards the Stars" A344   Women of Three Races A345

Boy, Girl and Globes — A346

1958, May 26
856	A344	30h carmine rose	.45	.25
857	A345	45h rose violet	.45	.25
858	A346	60h blue	.45	.25
		Nos. 856-858 (3)	1.35	.75

The Soc. for Dissemination of Political and Cultural Knowledge (No. 856). 4th Cong. of the Intl. Democratic Women's Fed. (No. 857).

CZECHOSLOVAKIA

1st World Trade Union Conf. of Working Youths, Prague, July 14-20 (No. 858).

 Grain, Hammer and Sickle — A347

 Atomic Reactor — A348

45h, Map of Czechoslovakia, hammer & sickle.

1958, May 26
859	A347	30h dull red	.25	.25
860	A347	45h green	.30	.25
861	A348	60h dark blue	.30	.25
		Nos. 859-861 (3)	.85	.75

11th Congress of the Czech Communist Party and the 15th anniv. of the Russo-Czechoslovakian Treaty.

 Karlovy Vary — A349

Various Spas: 40h, Podebrady. 60h, Marianske Lazne. 80h, Luhacovice. 1.20k, Strbske Pleso. 1.60k, Trencianske Teplice.

1958, June 25
862	A349	30h rose claret	.45	.25
863	A349	40h redsh brown	.45	.25
864	A349	60h gray green	.30	.25
865	A349	80h sepia	.45	.25
866	A349	1.20k violet blue	.60	.25
867	A349	1.60k lt violet	1.20	.75
		Nos. 862-867 (6)	3.45	2.00

 Telephone Operator — A350

Design: 45h, Radio transmitter.

1958, June 20
868	A350	30h black & brn org	.40	.25
869	A350	45h black & lt grn	.40	.25

Conference of Postal Ministers of Communist Countries, Prague, June 30-July 9.

 Pres. Novotny — A351

1958-59 Perf. 12½
870	A351	30h brt violet blue	.65	.25
b.		Perf. 11½	.50	.25
870A	A351	30h violet ('59)	4.00	1.75
871	A351	60h carmine rose	.45	.25

Perf. 11½
Redrawn
871A	A351	60h rose red	.50	.25
		Nos. 870-871A (4)	5.60	2.50

On No. 871 the top of the "6" turns down; on No. 871A it is open.

 Czechoslovak Pavilion, Brussels — A352

1958, July 15 Engr. & Photo.
872	A352	1.95k lt blue & bis brn	.90	.25

Czechoslovakia Week at the Universal and International Exhibition at Brussels.

Portrait Type of 1956
30h, Julius Fucik. 45h, G. K. Zechenter 60h, Karel Capek. 1.40k, Svatopluk Cech.

1958, Aug. 20 Engr. Perf. 11½
873	A306	30h rose red	.30	.25
874	A306	45h violet	1.50	.25
875	A306	60h dk blue gray	.60	.25
876	A306	1.40k gray	.60	.25
		Nos. 873-876 (4)	3.00	1.00

Death anniversaries of four famous Czechs.

 The Artist and the Muse — A353

1958, Aug. 20 Perf. 14
877	A353	1.60k black	3.50	1.10

85th birthday of Max Svabinsky, artist and engraver.
No. 877 was printed in miniature sheets of 4. Value $24.

 Children's Hospital, Brno — A354

Designs: 60h, New Town Hall, Brno. 1k, St. Thomas Church. 1.60k, View of Brno.

1958, Sept. 6 Unwmk. Perf. 11½
Size: 40x23mm
878	A354	30h violet	.25	.25
879	A354	60h rose red	.25	.25
880	A354	1k brown	.35	.25

Perf. 14
Size: 50x28mm
881	A354	1.60k dk slate grn	1.75	1.25
		Nos. 878-881 (4)	2.60	2.00

Natl. Phil. Exhib., Brno, Sept. 9.
No. 881 sold for 3.10k, including entrance ticket to exhibition. Issued in sheets of four. Value, $10.

 Lepiota Procera — A355

Mushrooms: 40h, Boletus edulis. 60h, Krombholzia rufoscens. 1.40k, Amanita muscaria L. 1.60k, Armillariella mellea.

1958, Oct. 6 Perf. 14
882	A355	30h dk brn, grn & buff	1.60	.35
883	A355	40h vio brn & brn org	1.60	.35
884	A355	60h black, red & buff	2.40	.35
885	A355	1.40k brown, scar & grn	4.00	1.60
886	A355	1.60k blk, red brn & ol	8.00	4.50
		Nos. 882-886 (5)	17.60	7.15

Nos. 882-886 were each issued in a miniature sheet of 10 stamps. Value, set $275.

 Children on Beach — A356

1958, Oct. 24 Unwmk. Perf. 14
887	A356	30h blue, yel & red	.35	.25
888	A356	45h ultra & carmine	1.40	.60
889	A356	60h brown, blue & yel	.35	.25
		Nos. 887-889 (3)	2.10	1.10

UNESCO Headquarters in Paris opening, Nov. 3. Nos. 887-889 each were issued in sheets of 10. Value, set $75.

 Bozek's Steam Car of 1815 — A357

Designs: 45h, "Präsident" car of 1897. 60h, "Skoda" sports car. 80h, "Tatra" sedan. 1k, "Autocar Skoda" bus. 1.25k, Trucks.

Engraved and Photogravure
1958, Dec. 1 Perf. 11½x11
890	A357	30h vio blk & buff	.70	.25
891	A357	45h ol & lt grn	.70	.25
892	A357	60h ol gray & sal	1.75	.25
893	A357	80h claret & bl grn	1.10	.25
894	A357	1k brn & lt yel grn	1.40	.30
895	A357	1.25k green & buff	2.10	.45
		Nos. 890-895 (6)	7.75	1.75

Issued to honor the automobile industry.

 Stamp of 1918 and Allegory — A358

1958, Dec. 18 Engr. Perf. 11x11½
896	A358	60h dark blue gray	.85	.30

1st Czechoslovakian postage stamp, 40th anniv.

 Ice Hockey — A359

30h, Girl throwing javelin. 60h, Ice hockey 1k, Hurdling. 1.60k, Rowing. 2k, High jump

1959, Feb. 14 Perf. 11½x11
897	A359	20h dk brown & gray	.50	.25
898	A359	30h red brn & org brn	.40	.25
899	A359	60h dk bl & pale grn	.65	.25
900	A359	1k maroon & citron	.50	.25
901	A359	1.60k dull vio & lt bl	.80	.25
902	A359	2k red brn & lt bl	1.75	.25
		Nos. 897-902 (6)	4.60	1.50

 Congress Emblem — A360

60h, Industrial & agricultural workers, emblem.

1959, Feb. 27 Perf. 11½
903	A360	30h maroon & lt blue	.45	.25
904	A360	60h dk blue & yellow	.45	.25

4th Agricultural Cooperative Cong. in Prague.

 "Equality of All Races" — A361

Designs: 1k, "Peace." 2k, Mother and Child: "Freedom for Colonial People."

1959, Mar. 23
905	A361	60h gray green	.30	.25
906	A361	1k gray	.45	.25
907	A361	2k dk gray blue	1.50	.50
		Nos. 905-907 (3)	2.25	1.00

10th anniversary of the signing of the Universal Declaration of Human Rights.

 Girl Holding Puppet — A362

40h, Pioneer studying map. 60h, Pioneer with radio. 80h, Girl pioneer planting tree.

1959, Mar. 28 Engr. & Photo.
908	A362	30h violet bl & yel	.35	.25
909	A362	40h indigo & ultra	.45	.25
910	A362	60h black & lilac	.35	.25
911	A362	80h brown & lt green	.65	.25
		Nos. 908-911 (4)	1.80	1.00

10th anniv. of the Pioneer organization.

 Frederic Joliot Curie — A363

1959, Apr. 17 Engr.
912	A363	60h sepia	1.40	.30

Frederic Joliot Curie and the 10th anniversary of the World Peace Movement

 "Reaching for the Moon" — A364

1959, Apr. 17
913	A364	30h violet blue	1.10	.30

2nd Cong. of the Czechoslovak Assoc. for the Propagation of Political and Cultural knowledge.

 Town Hall Pilsen — A365

Designs: 60h, Part of steam condenser turbine. 1k, St. Bartholomew's Church, Pilsen. 1.60k, Part of lathe.

1959, May 2
914	A365	30h lt brown	.30	.25
915	A365	60h violet & lt grn	.30	.25
916	A365	1k violet blue	.40	.25
917	A365	1.60k black & yellow	1.10	.50
		Nos. 914-917 (4)	2.10	1.25

2nd Pilsen Stamp Exhib. in connection with the centenary of the Skoda (Lenin) armament works.

CZECHOSLOVAKIA

Factory and Emblem — A366

Inscribed: "IV Vseodborovy sjezd, 1959"

1959, May 13
918 A366 30h shown .45 .25
919 A366 60h Dam .30 .25

4th Trade Union Congress.

Zvolen Castle — A367

1959, June 13
920 A367 60h gray olive & yel .60 .25

Regional Stamp Exhibition, Zvolen, 1959.

Frantisek Benda A368 — Aurel Stodola A369

30h, Vaclav Kliment Klicpera. 60h, Karel V. Rais. 80h, Antonin Slavicek. 1k, Peter Bezruc.

1959, June 22 Perf. 11½x11
921 A368 15h violet blue .25 .25
922 A368 30h orange brown .25 .25
923 A369 40h dull green .25 .25
924 A369 60h dull red brn .35 .25
925 A369 80h dull violet .55 .25
926 A368 1k dark brown .55 .25
Nos. 921-926 (6) 2.20 1.50

View of the Fair Grounds A370

Designs: 60h, Fair emblem and world map. 1.60k, Pavilion "Z".

Inscribed: "Mezinarodni Veletrh Brne 6.-20.IX. 1959"

Engraved and Photogravure
1959, July 20 Unwmk. Perf. 11½
927 A370 30h lilac & yellow .25 .25
928 A370 60h dull blue .25 .25
929 A370 1.60k dk blue & bister .75 .25
Nos. 927-929 (3) 1.25 .75

International Fair at Brno, Sept. 6-20.

Revolutionist and Flag A371 — Slovakian Fighter A372

1.60k, Linden leaves, sun and factory.

Perf. 11½
1959, Aug. 29 Unwmk. Engr.
930 A371 30h black & rose .25 .25
931 A372 60h carmine rose .25 .25
932 A371 1.60k dk blue & yel .45 .25
Nos. 930-932 (3) .95 .75

Natl. Slovakian revolution, 15th anniv. and Slovakian Soviet Republic, 40th anniv.

Alpine Marmots A373

1959, Sept. 25 Engr. & Photo.
933 A373 30h shown 1.25 .25
934 A373 40h Bison 1.00 .40
935 A373 60h Lynx, vert. 2.60 .30
936 A373 1k Wolf 2.60 1.00
937 A373 1.60k Red deer 2.25 .55
Nos. 933-937 (5) 9.70 2.50

Tatra National Park, 10th anniv.

Lunik 2 Hitting Moon and Russian Flag — A374

1959, Sept. 23 Perf. 11½
938 A374 60h dk red & lt ultra 1.50 .30

Issued to commemorate the landing of the Soviet rocket on the moon, Sept. 13, 1959.

Stamp Printing Works, Peking — A375

1959, Oct. 1
939 A375 30h pale green & red .40 .25

10 years of Czechoslovakian-Chinese friendship.

Haydn — A376

Design: 3k, Charles Darwin.

1959, Oct. 16 Engr. Perf. 11½
940 A376 60h violet black .50 .25
941 A376 3k dark red brown 1.25 .65

150th death anniv. of Franz Joseph Haydn, Austrian composer, and 150th birth anniv. of Charles Darwin, English naturalist.

Great Spotted Woodpecker — A377

Birds: 30h, Blue tits. 40h, Nuthatch. 60th, Golden oriole. 80h, Goldfinch. 1k, Bullfinch. 1.20k, European kingfisher.

1959, Nov. 16 Perf. 14
942 A377 20h multicolored 1.50 .60
943 A377 30h multicolored 1.50 .60
944 A377 40h multicolored 4.50 1.50
945 A377 60h multicolored 1.50 .60
946 A377 80h multicolored 2.25 .75
947 A377 1k multicolored 2.25 .75
948 A377 1.20k multicolored 3.00 .75
Nos. 942-948 (7) 16.50 5.55

Nos. 942-948 were each issued in miniature sheets of 10. Value, set $275.

Nikola Tesla — A378

Designs: 30h, Alexander S. Popov. 35h, Edouard Branly. 60h, Guglielmo Marconi. 1k, Heinrich Hertz. 2k, Edwin Howard Armstrong and research tower, Alpine, N. J.

Engraved and Photogravure
1959, Dec. 7 Perf. 11½
949 A378 25h black & pink 1.00 .25
950 A378 30h black & orange .25 .25
951 A378 35h black & lt vio .25 .25
952 A378 60h black & blue .25 .25
953 A378 1k black & lt grn .25 .25
954 A378 2k black & bister 1.25 .25
Nos. 949-954 (6) 3.25 1.50

Issued to honor inventors in the fields of telegraphy and radio.

Gymnast — A379

2nd Winter Spartacist Games: 60h, Skier. 1.60k, Basketball players.

1960, Jan. 20 Perf. 11½
955 A379 30h salmon pink & brn 1.00 .25
956 A379 60h lt blue & blk 1.00 .25
957 A379 1.60k bister & brn .85 .25
Nos. 955-957 (3) 2.85 .75

1960, June 15 Unwmk.

Designs: 30h, Two girls in "Red Ball" drill. 60h, Gymnast with stick. 1k, Three girls with hoops.

958 A379 30h lt grn & rose claret .65 .25
959 A379 60h pink & black .50 .25
960 A379 1k ocher & vio bl .85 .25
Nos. 958-960 (3) 2.00 .75

2nd Summer Spartacist Games, Prague, June 23-July 3.

River Dredge Boat — A380

Ships: 60h, River tug. 1k, Tourist steamer. 1.20k, Cargo ship "Lidice."

1960, Feb. 22 Perf. 11½
961 A380 30h slate grn & sal 2.75 .30
962 A380 60h mar & pale bl 1.40 .30
963 A380 1k dk violet & yel 2.50 .30
964 A380 1.20k lilac & pale grn 3.50 .90
Nos. 961-964 (4) 10.15 1.80

Ice Hockey Players A381

Design: 1.80k, Figure skaters.

1960, Feb. 27
965 A381 60h sepia & lt blue 2.00 .40
966 A381 1.80k black & lt green 6.00 1.75

8th Olympic Winter Games, Squaw Valley, Calif., Feb. 18-29, 1960.

1960, June 15 Unwmk.

Designs: 1k, Running. 1.80k, Women's gymnastics. 2k, Rowing.

967 A381 1k black & orange .85 .30
968 A381 1.80k black & sal pink 1.40 .40
969 A381 2k black & blue 2.50 .75
Nos. 967-969 (3) 4.75 1.45

17th Olympic Games, Rome, 8/25-9/11.

Trencin Castle — A382

Castles: 10h, Bezdez. 20h, Kost. 30h, Pernstein. 40h, Kremnica. 50h, Krivoklát castle. 60h, Karlstein. 1k, Smolenice. 1.60k, Kokorin.

1960-63 Engr. Perf. 11½
970 A382 5h gray violet .30 .25
971 A382 10h black .30 .25
972 A382 20h brown org .35 .25
973 A382 30h green .30 .25
974 A382 40h brown .35 .25
974A A382 50h black ('63) 3.50 .25
975 A382 60h rose red .45 .25
976 A382 1k lilac .45 .25
977 A382 1.60k dark blue .75 .25
Nos. 970-977 (9) 6.75 2.25

1961, Oct. Wmk. 341
977A A382 30h green 3.00 .40

Lenin — A383

1960, Apr. 22 Unwmk.
978 A383 60h gray olive 1.40 .25

90th anniversary of the birth of Lenin.

Soldier Holding Child — A384

Designs: No. 980, Child eating pie. No. 981, Soldier helping concentration camp victim. No. 982, Welder and factory, horiz. No. 983, Tractor driver and farm, horiz.

1960, May 5 Engr. & Photo.
979 A384 30h maroon & lt blue .35 .25
980 A384 30h dull red .35 .25
981 A384 30h green & dull blue .40 .25
982 A384 30h dk blue & buff .35 .25
983 A384 60h redsh brn & yel grn .40 .25
Nos. 979-983 (5) 1.85 1.25

15th anniversary of liberation.

Steelworker A385

Design: 60h, Farm woman and child.

1960, May 24
984 A385 30h maroon & gray .30 .25
985 A385 60h green & pale blue .30 .25

1960 parliamentary elections.

Red Cross Nurse Holding Dove — A386

Fire Fighters A387

1960, May 26 Unwmk.
986 A386 30h brown car & bl .30 .25
987 A387 60h dk blue & pink .45 .25

3rd Congress of the Czechoslovakian Red Cross (No. 986), and the 2nd Fire Fighters' Congress (No. 987).

Hand of Philatelist with Tongs and Two Stamps — A388

Design: 1k, Globe and 1937 Bratislava stamp (shown in miniature on 60h).

1960, July 11 Perf. 11½
988 A388 60h black & dull yel .75 .25
989 A388 1k black & blue .90 .25

Issued to publicize the National Stamp Exhibition, Bratislava, Sept. 24-Oct. 9. See Nos. C49-C50.

CZECHOSLOVAKIA

Stalin Mine, Ostrava-Hermanovice A390

Designs: 20h, Power station, Hodonin. 30h, Gottwald iron works, Kuncice. 40h, Harvester. 60h, Oil refinery.

1960, July 25

				Engr.	
992	A390	10h black & pale grn		.30	.25
993	A390	20h maroon & lt bl		.30	.25
994	A390	30h indigo & pink		.30	.25
995	A390	40h green & pale lilac		.30	.25
996	A390	60h dk blue & yel		.30	.25
		Nos. 992-996 (5)		1.50	1.25

Issued to publicize the new five-year plan.

Viktorin Cornelius, Lawyer — A391

Portraits: 20h, Karel Matej Capek-Chod, writer. 30h, Hana Kvapilova, actress. 40h, Oskar Nedbal, composer. 60h, Otakar Ostrcil, composer.

1960, Aug. 23 Engr.

997	A391	10h black	.30	.25
998	A391	20h red brown	.45	.25
999	A391	30h rose red	.55	.25
1000	A391	40h dull green	1.40	.60
1001	A391	60h gray violet	.45	.25
		Nos. 997-1001 (5)	3.15	1.60

See Nos. 1037-1041.

Skoda Sports Plane Flying Upside Down — A392

1960, Aug. 28 Engr. & Photo.
1002 A392 60h violet blue & blue 1.40 .30

1st aerobatic world championships, Bratislava.

Constitution and "Czechoslovakia" — A393

1960, Sept. 10
1003 A393 30h violet bl & pink .40 .25

Proclamation of the new socialist constitution.

Workers Reading Newspaper A394

Man Holding Newspaper A395

1960, Sept. 18
1004	A394	30h slate & ver	.25	.25
1005	A395	60h black & rose	.25	.25

Day of the Czechoslovak Press, Sept. 21, 1960, and 40th anniv. of the Rudé Právo paper.

Globes and Laurel — A396

1960, Sept. 18 Engr.
1006 A396 30h dk blue & bister .40 .25

World Federation of Trade Unions, 15th anniv.

Black-crowned Night Heron — A397

Birds: 30h, Great crested grebe. 40h, Lapwing. 60h, Gray heron. 1k, Graylag goose, horiz. 1.60k, Mallard, horiz.

Engraved and Photogravure
1960, Oct. 24 Unwmk. Perf. 11½
Designs in Black

1007	A397	25h pale vio blue	.90	.25
1008	A397	30h pale citron	.80	.25
1009	A397	40h pale blue	.90	.30
1010	A397	60h pink	.60	.25
1011	A397	1k pale yellow	1.75	.25
1012	A397	1.60k lt violet	4.50	1.25
		Nos. 1007-1012 (6)	9.45	2.55

Doronicum Clusii (Thistle) — A398

Flowers: 30h, Cyclamen. 40h, Primrose. 60h, Hen-and-chickens. 1k, Gentian. 2k, Pasqueflower.

1960, Nov. 21 Engr. Perf. 14
1013	A398	20h black, yel & grn	.80	.40
1014	A398	30h black, car rose & grn	.80	.40
1015	A398	40h black, yel & grn	.80	.40
1016	A398	60h black, pink & grn	.80	.40
1017	A398	1k black, bl, vio & grn	2.00	.40
1018	A398	2k black, lil, yel & grn	2.75	1.40
		Nos. 1013-1018 (6)	7.95	3.60

Nos. 1013-1018 were each issued in sheets of 10. Value, set $100.

Alfons Mucha — A399

1960, Dec. 18 Engr. Perf. 11½x12
1019 A399 60h dk blue gray 3.00 .25

Day of the Czechoslovak Postage Stamp and birth cent. of Alfons Mucha, designer of the 1st Czechoslovakian stamp (Type A1).

Rolling-mill Control Bridge — A400

Designs: 30h, Turbo generator. 60h, Ditch-digging machine.

1961, Jan. 20 Unwmk. Perf. 11½
1020	A400	20h blue	.30	.25
1021	A400	30h rose	.30	.25
1022	A400	60h brt green	.30	.25
		Nos. 1020-1022 (3)	.90	.75

Third Five-Year Plan.

Athletes with Flags — A401

Designs: No. 1024, Motorcycle race, horiz. 40h, Sculling, horiz. 60h, Ice skater. 1k, Rugby. 1.20k, Soccer. 1.60k, Long-distance runners.

Perf. 11x11½, 11½x11
1961, Feb. 20 Engr. & Photo.
1023	A401	30h rose red & bl	.30	.25
1024	A401	30h dk blue & car	.30	.25
1025	A401	40h dk gray & car	.45	.25
1026	A401	60h lilac & blue	.45	.25
1027	A401	1k ultra & yel	.45	.25
1028	A401	1.20k green & buff	1.10	.25
1029	A401	1.60k sepia & salmon	1.50	.30
		Nos. 1023-1029 (7)	4.55	1.80

Various sports events.

Exhibition Emblem — A402

1961, Mar. 6 Engr. Perf. 11½
1030 A402 2k dk blue & red 2.25 .25

"Praga 1962" International Stamp Exhibition, Prague, Sept. 1962.

Rocket Launching — A403

30h, Sputnik III, horiz. 40h, As 20h, but inscribed "Start Kosmicke Rakety k Venusi — 12.II.1961". 60h, Luna I, horiz. 1.60k, Interplanetary station, horiz. 2k, Similar to type A404, without commemorative inscription.

1961, Mar. 6 Engr. & Photo.
1031	A403	20h violet & pink	.30	.25
1032	A403	30h dk green & buff	.65	.25
1033	A403	40h dk red & yel grn	.65	.30
1034	A403	60h violet & buff	.80	.25
1035	A403	1.60k dk bl & pale grn	.55	.25
1036	A403	2k mar & palo bl	1.25	.75
		Nos. 1031-1036 (6)	4.20	2.05

Issued to publicize Soviet space research.

Portrait Type of 1960

No. 1037, Jindrich Mosna. No. 1038, Pavol Orszagh Hviezdoslav. No. 1039, Alois Mrstik. No. 1040, Joza Uprka. No. 1041, Josef Hora.

1961, Mar. 27 Perf. 11½
1037	A391	60h green	.30	.25
1038	A391	60h dark blue	.60	.25
a.		"ORSZACH" instead of "ORSZAGH"	175.00	25.00
1039	A391	60h dull claret	.70	.25
1040	A391	60h gray	.55	.25
1041	A391	60h sepia	.30	.25
		Nos. 1037-1041 (5)	2.50	1.25

Man Flying into Space — A404

1961, Apr. 13
1042	A404	60h car & pale bl	.65	.25
1043	A404	3k ultra & yel	2.00	.60

1st man in space, Yuri A. Gagarin, Apr. 12, 1961. See No. 1036.

Flute Player — A405

1961, Apr. 24 Engr.
1044	A405	30h shown	.45	.25
1045	A405	30h Dancer	.45	.25
1046	A405	60h Lyre player	.65	.25
		Nos. 1044-1046 (3)	1.55	.75

Prague Conservatory of Music, 150th anniv.

Blast Furnace and Mine, Kladno — A406

1961, Apr. 24
1047 A406 3k dull red .65 .25

City of Kladno, 400th anniv.

Marching Workers A407

Woman with Hammer and Sickle A408

Klement Gottwald Museum A409

Designs: No. 1050, Lenin Museum. No. 1051, Crowd with flags. No. 1053, Man saluting Red Star.

1961, May 10
1048	A407	30h dull violet	.30	.25
1049	A409	30h dark blue	.30	.25
1050	A409	30h redsh brown	.30	.25
1051	A407	60h vermilion	.30	.25
1052	A408	60h dark green	.30	.25
1053	A408	60h carmine	.30	.25
		Nos. 1048-1053 (6)	1.80	1.50

Czech Communist Party, 40th anniversary.

Puppet — A410

Designs: Various Puppets.

Engraved and Photogravure
1961, June 20 Unwmk. Perf. 11½
1054	A410	30h ver & yel	.30	.25
1055	A410	40h sepia & bluish grn	.30	.25
1056	A410	60h vio bl & sal	.30	.25
1057	A410	1k green & lt blue	.30	.25
1058	A410	1.60k mar & pale vio	.95	.25
		Nos. 1054-1058 (5)	2.15	1.25

Woman, Map of Africa and Flag of Czechoslovakia A411

1961, June 26
1059 A411 60h red & blue .35 .25

Issued to publicize the friendship between the people of Africa and Czechoslovakia.

CZECHOSLOVAKIA

Map of Europe and Fair Emblem — A412

Fair emblem and: 60h Horizontal boring machine, vert. 1k, Scientists' meeting and nuclear physics emblem.

1961, Aug. 14   Perf. 11½
1060	A412	30h dk bl & pale grn	.30	.25
1061	A412	60h green & pink	.30	.25
1062	A412	1k vio brn & lt bl	.60	.25
		Nos. 1060-1062 (3)	1.20	.75

International Trade Fair, Brno, Sept. 10-24.

Sugar Beet, Cup of Coffee and Bags of Sugar — A413

1961, Sept. 18   Unwmk.   Perf. 11½
1063	A413	20h shown	.25	.25
1064	A413	30h Clover	.25	.25
1065	A413	40h Wheat	.25	.25
1066	A413	60h Hops	.25	.25
1067	A413	1.40k Corn	.30	.25
1068	A413	2k Potatoes	2.00	.35
		Nos. 1063-1068 (6)	3.30	1.60

Charles Bridge, St. Nicholas Church and Hradcany — A414

1961, Sept. 25
1069	A414	60h violet bl & car	1.20	.25

26th session of the Governor's Council of the Red Cross Societies League, Prague.

Orlik Dam and Kaplan Turbine — A415

Designs: 30h, View of Prague, flags and stamps. 40h, Hluboká Castle, river and fish. 60h, Karlovy Vary and cup. 1k, Pilsen and beer bottle. 1.20k, North Bohemia landscape and vase. 1.60k, Tatra mountains, boots, ice pick and rope. 2k, Ironworks, Ostrava Kuncice and pulley. 3k, Brno and ball bearing. 4k, Bratislava and grapes. 5k, Prague and flags.

1961   Unwmk.   Perf. 11½
Size: 41x23mm
1070	A415	20h gray & blue	1.50	.45
1071	A415	30h vio blue & red	1.50	.75
1072	A415	40h dk blue & lt grn	1.60	.75
1073	A415	60h dk blue & yel	1.10	.75
1074	A415	1k mar & grn	1.60	.75
1075	A415	1.20k green & pink	1.60	1.10
1076	A415	1.60k brn & vio bl	1.90	1.10
1077	A415	2k blk & ocher	1.90	.45
1078	A415	3k ultra & yel	2.00	.55
1079	A415	4k purple & sal	2.40	1.10

Perf. 13½
Engr.
Size: 50x29mm
1080	A415	5k multicolored	20.00	20.00
		Nos. 1070-1080 (11)	37.00	27.75

"PRAGA 1962 World Exhib. of Postage Stamps," Aug. 18-Sept. 2, 1962.
No. 1080 was printed in sheet of 4. Value $120.

Globe — A416

Engraved and Photogravure
1961, Nov. 27   Perf. 11½
1081	A416	60h red & ultra	.50	.25

Issued to publicize the Fifth World Congress of Trade Unions, Moscow, Dec. 4-16.

Orange Tip Butterfly — A417

Designs (butterflies): 20h, Zerynthia hypsipyle Sch. 30h, Apollo. 40h, Swallowtail. 60h, Peacock. 80h, Mourning cloak (Camberwell beauty). 1k, Underwing (moth). 1.60k, Red admiral. 2k, Brimstone (sulphur).

1961, Nov. 27   Engr.
1082	A417	15h multicolored	.80	.30
1083	A417	20h multicolored	.80	.30
1084	A417	30h multicolored	.80	.30
1085	A417	40h multicolored	.80	.30
1086	A417	60h multicolored	.80	.30
1087	A417	80h multicolored	2.40	.90
1088	A417	1k multicolored	2.40	.90
1089	A417	1.60k multicolored	2.40	.90
1090	A417	2k multicolored	6.50	3.00
		Nos. 1082-1090 (9)	17.70	7.20

Nos.1082-1090 were each issued in sheets of 10. Value, set $400.

Bicyclists — A418

Sports: 40h, Woman gymnast. 60h, Figure skaters. 1k, Woman bowler. 1.20k, Goalkeeper, soccer. 1.60k, Discus thrower.

Engraved and Photogravure
1962, Feb. 5   Unwmk.   Perf. 11½
1091	A418	30h black & vio bl	.25	.25
1092	A418	40h black & yel	.25	.25
1093	A418	60h slate & grnsh bl	.35	.25
1094	A418	1k black & pink	.35	.25
1095	A418	1.20k black & green	.35	.25
1096	A418	1.60k blk & dull grn	1.50	.45
		Nos. 1091-1096 (6)	3.05	1.70

Various 1962 sports events.
No. 1095 does not have the commemorative inscription.

Karel Kovarovic A419   Frantisek Zaviska and Karel Petr A420

20h, Frantisek Skroup. 30h, Bozena Nemcova. 60h, View of Prague & staff of Aesculapius. 1.60k, Ladislav Celakovsky. 1.80k, Miloslav Valouch & Juraj Hronec.

1962, Feb. 26   Engr.
1097	A419	10h red brown	.25	.25
1098	A419	20h violet blue	.25	.25
1099	A419	30h brown	.25	.25
1100	A420	40h claret	.50	.25
1101	A419	60h black	.25	.25
1102	A419	1.60k slate green	.25	.25
1103	A420	1.80k dark blue	.60	.25
		Nos. 1097-1103 (7)	2.35	1.75

Various cultural personalities and events.

Miner and Flag — A421

1962, Mar. 19   Engr. & Photo.
1104	A421	60h indigo & rose	.25	.25

30th anniv. of the miners' strike at Most.

"Man Conquering Space" — A422

Soviet Spaceship Vostok 2 — A423

40h, Launching of Soviet space rocket. 80h, Multi-stage automatic rocket. 1k, Automatic station on moon. 1.60k, Television satellite.

1962, Mar. 26
1105	A422	30h dk red & lt blue	.35	.25
1106	A422	40h dk blue & sal	.35	.25
1107	A423	60h dk blue & pink	.35	.25
1108	A423	80h rose vio & lt grn	.35	.25
1109	A422	1k indigo & citron	.35	.25
1110	A423	1.60k green & buff	1.90	1.50
		Nos. 1105-1110 (6)	3.65	1.50

Issued to publicize space research.

Polar Bear — A424

Zoo Animals: 30h, Chimpanzee. 60h, Camel. 1k, African and Indian elephants, horiz. 1.40k, Leopard, horiz. 1.60k, Przewalski horse, horiz.

1962, Apr. 24   Unwmk.   Perf. 11½
Design and Inscriptions in Black
1111	A424	20h grnsh blue	.75	.25
1112	A424	30h violet	.75	.25
1113	A424	60h orange	.75	.25
1114	A424	1k green	.75	.25
1115	A424	1.40k carmine rose	.75	.25
1116	A424	1.60k lt brown	1.90	1.25
		Nos. 1111-1116 (6)	5.65	2.50

Child and Grieving Mother — A425

60h, Flowers growing from ruins of Lezáky.

1962, June 9   Engr. & Photo.
1118	A425	30h black & red	.45	.25
1119	A425	60h black & dull bl	.75	.25

20th anniversary of the destruction of Lidice and Lezáky by the Nazis.

Klary's Fountain, Teplice — A426

1962, June 9
1120	A426	60h dull grn & yel	.40	.25

1,200th anniversary of the discovery of the medicinal springs of Teplice.

Malaria Eradication Emblem, Cross and Dove — A427

3k, Dove and malaria eradication emblem.

1962, June 18
1121	A427	60h black & crimson	.45	.25
1122	A427	3k dk blue & yel	1.10	.35

WHO drive to eradicate malaria.

Soccer Goalkeeper — A428

1962, June 20   Unwmk.   Perf. 11½
1123	A428	1.60k green & yellow	1.50	.25

Czechoslovakia's participation in the World Cup Soccer Championship, Chile, May 30-June 17. See No. 1095.

Soldier in Swimming Relay Race — A429

Designs: 40h, Soldier hurdling. 60h, Soccer player. 1k, Soldier with rifle in relay race.

1962, July 20
1124	A429	30h green & lt ultra	.25	.25
1125	A429	40h dk purple & yel	.25	.25
1126	A429	60h brown & green	.25	.25
1127	A429	1k dk blue & sal pink	.25	.25
		Nos. 1124-1127 (4)	1.00	1.00

2nd Summer Spartacist Games of Friendly Armies, Prague, Sept., 1962.

"Agriculture" — A430

Designs: 60h, Astronaut in capsule. 80h, Boy with flute, horiz. 1k, Workers of three races, horiz. 1.40k, Children dancing around tree. 1.60k, Flying bird, horiz. 5k, View of Prague, horiz.

1962   Engr.   Perf. 13½
1128	A430	30h multicolored	1.20	.60
1129	A430	60h multicolored	.60	.30
a.		Miniature sheet of 8	20.00	20.00
1130	A430	80h multicolored	1.75	1.25
1131	A430	1k multicolored	1.75	1.25
1132	A430	1.40k multicolored	1.75	1.25
1133	A430	1.60k multicolored	2.10	2.10
		Nos. 1128-1133 (6)	10.05	6.75

Souvenir Sheet
1134		5k multicolored	13.00	10.00
a.		Imperf.	40.00	35.00

"PRAGA 1962 World Exhib. of Postage Stamps," 8/18-9/2/62. No. 1133 also for FIP Day, Sept. 1. Printed in sheets of 10. Value: Nos. 1128-1133 $150; No. 1134 $80.
No. 1129a contains 4 each of Nos. 1128-1129 and 2 labels arranged in 2 rows of 2 setenant pairs of Nos. 1128-1129 with label between. Sold for 5k, only with ticket.
No. 1134 contains one 51x30mm stamp. Sold only with ticket.

Children in Day Nursery and Factory A431

Sailboat and Trade Union Rest Home, Zinkovy A432

CZECHOSLOVAKIA

Engraved and Photogravure
1962, Oct. 29   Unwmk.   Perf. 11½
| 1135 | A431 | 30h black & lt blue | .25 | .25 |
| 1136 | A432 | 60h brown & yellow | .25 | .25 |

Cruiser "Aurora" — A433

1962, Nov. 7
| 1137 | A433 | 30h black & gray bl | .25 | .25 |
| 1138 | A433 | 60h black & pink | .25 | .25 |

Russian October revolution, 45th anniv.

Cosmonaut and Worker A434 — Lenin A435

1962, Nov. 7
| 1139 | A434 | 30h dark red & blue | .25 | .25 |
| 1140 | A435 | 60h black & dp rose | .25 | .25 |

40th anniversary of the USSR.

Symbolic Crane A436

40h, Agricultural products, vert. 60h, Factories.

1962, Dec. 4
1141	A436	30h dk red & yel	.25	.25
1142	A436	40h gray blue & yel	.25	.25
1143	A436	60h black & dp rose	.30	.25
		Nos. 1141-1143 (3)	.80	.75

Communist Party of Czechoslovakia, 12th cong.

Ground Beetle — A437

Beetles: 30h, Cardinal beetle. 60h, Stag beetle, vert. 1k, Great water beetle. 1.60k, Alpine longicorn, vert. 2k, Ground beetle, vert.

1962, Dec. 15   Engr.   Perf. 14
1144	A437	20h multicolored	.80	.40
1145	A437	30h multicolored	.80	.40
1146	A437	80h multicolored	.80	.40
1147	A437	1k multicolored	1.60	.60
1148	A437	1.60k multicolored	3.25	.60
1149	A437	2k multicolored	4.50	2.00
		Nos. 1144-1149 (6)	11.75	4.40

Nos. 1144-1149 were each printed in sheets of 10. Value, set $225.

Table Tennis — A438

Sports: 60h, Bicyclist. 80h, Skier. 1k, Motorcyclist. 1.20k, Weight lifter. 1.60k, Hurdler.

Engraved and Photogravure
1963, Jan.   Perf. 11½
1150	A438	30h black & dp grn	.25	.25
1151	A438	60h black & orange	.25	.25
1152	A438	80h black & ultra	.25	.25
1153	A438	1k black & violet	.40	.25
1154	A438	1.20k blk & pale brn	.40	.25
1155	A438	1.60k blk & car	.85	.25
		Nos. 1150-1155 (6)	2.40	1.50

Various 1963 sports events.

Industrial Plant, Laurel and Star A439 — Symbol of Pioneer Summer Camp A440

Industrial Plant and Symbol of Growth — A441

1963, Feb. 25   Unwmk.   Perf. 11½
1156	A439	30h carmine & lt bl	.25	.25
1157	A440	60h black & car	.25	.25
1158	A441	60h black & red	.25	.25
		Nos. 1156-1158 (3)	.75	.75

15th anniv. of the "Victorious February" and 5th Trade Union Cong.

Artists' Guild Emblem A442 — Juraj Jánosik A443

Eduard Urx — A444 — National Theater, Prague — A445

Engr. & Photo.; Engr. (A444)
1963, Mar. 25   Unwmk.   Perf. 11½
1159	A442	20h black & Prus bl	.25	.25
1160	A443	30h car & lt bl	.25	.25
1161	A444	30h carmine	.25	.25
1162	A445	60h dl red brn & lt bl	.25	.25
1163	A444	60h green	.25	.25
1164	A444	60h black	.25	.25
1165	A444	1.60k brown	.50	.25
		Nos. 1159-1165 (7)	2.00	1.75

Various cultural personalities and events.

No. 1163, Woman reading to children. No. 1164, Juraj Pálkovic. 1.60k, Max Svabinsky.

Boy and Girl with Flag — A446

Engraved and Photogravure
1963, Apr. 18   Perf. 11½
| 1166 | A446 | 30h slate & rose red | .35 | .25 |

The 4th Congress of Czechoslovak Youth.

Television Transmitter — A447

40h, Television camera, mast and set, horiz.

1963, Apr. 25
| 1167 | A447 | 40h buff & slate | .40 | .25 |
| 1168 | A447 | 60h dk red & lt blue | .40 | .25 |

Czechoslovak television, 10th anniversary.

Rocket to the Sun — A448

50h, Rockets & Sputniks leaving Earth. 60h, Spacecraft to & from Moon. 1k, 3k, Interplanetary station & Mars 1. 1.60k, Atomic rocket & Jupiter. 2k, Rocket returning from Saturn.

1963, Apr. 25
1169	A448	30h red brn & buff	.45	.25
1170	A448	50h slate & bluish grn	.45	.25
1171	A448	60h dk green & yel	.40	.25
1172	A448	1k dk gray & sal	.65	.25
1173	A448	1.60k gray brn & lt grn	.65	.25
1174	A448	2k dk purple & yel	1.25	.75
		Nos. 1169-1174 (6)	3.85	2.00

Souvenir Sheet
Imperf
| 1175 | A448 | 3k Prus grn & org red | 10.00 | 5.00 |

No. 1175 issued for 1st Space Research Exhib., Prague, Apr. 1963.

Studio and Radio — A449

1k, Globe inscribed "Peace" & aerial mast, vert.

1963, May 18   Unwmk.   Perf. 11½
| 1176 | A449 | 30h choc & pale grn | .40 | .25 |
| 1177 | A449 | 1k bluish grn & lilac | .40 | .25 |

40th anniversary of Czechoslovak radio.

Tupolev Tu-104B Turbojet — A450

Design: 1.80k, Ilyushin Il-18 Moskva.

1963, May 25
| 1178 | A450 | 80h violet & lt bl | 1.00 | .35 |
| 1179 | A450 | 1.80k dk blue & lt grn | 1.50 | .35 |

40th anniversary of Czechoslovak airlines.

9th Cent. Ring, Map of Moravian Settlements — A451

1.60k, Falconer, 9th cent. silver disk.

1963, May 25
| 1180 | A451 | 30h lt green & blk | .25 | .25 |
| 1181 | A451 | 1.60k dull yel & blk | .75 | .25 |

1100th anniv. of Moravian empire.

Woman Singing — A452

1963, May 25   Engr.
| 1182 | A452 | 30h bright red | .55 | .25 |

60th anniversary of the founding of the Moravian Teachers' Singing Club.

Kromeriz Castle and Barley — A453

Engraved and Photogravure
1963, June 20   Unwmk.   Perf. 11½
| 1183 | A453 | 30h slate grn & yel | .55 | .25 |

Natl. Agricultural Exhib. and 700th anniv. of Kromeriz.

Centenary Emblem, Nurse and Playing Child — A454

1963, June 20
| 1184 | A454 | 30h dk gray & car | .50 | .25 |

Centenary of the International Red Cross.

Bee, Honeycomb and Emblem — A455

1963, June 20
| 1185 | A455 | 1k brown & yellow | .75 | .25 |

19th Intl. Beekeepers Cong., Apimondia, 1963.

Liberec Fair Emblem — A456

1963, July 13
| 1186 | A456 | 30h black & dp rose | .40 | .25 |

Liberec Consumer Goods Fair.

Town Hall, Brno — A457

Design: 60h, Town Hall tower, Brno.

1963, July 29
| 1187 | A457 | 30h lt blue & maroon | .35 | .25 |
| 1188 | A457 | 60h pink & dk blue | .35 | .25 |

International Trade Fair, Brno.

Cave, Moravian Karst — A458

No. 1190, Trout, Hornad Valley. 60h, Great Hawk Gorge. 80h, Macocha mountains.

1963, July 29
1189	A458	30h brown & lt bl	.80	.25
1190	A458	30h dk bl & dull grn	.95	.25
1191	A458	60h green & blue	1.00	.25
1192	A458	80h sepia & pink	.80	.25
		Nos. 1189-1192 (4)	3.35	1.00

Blast Furnace — A459

1963, Aug. 15   Unwmk.   Perf. 11½
| 1193 | A459 | 60h blk & bluish grn | .40 | .25 |

30th Intl. Cong. of Iron Founders, Prague.

CZECHOSLOVAKIA

White Mouse — A460

1963, Aug. 15
1194 A460 1k black & carmine .60 .25
2nd Intl. Pharmacological Cong., Prague.

Farm Machinery for Underfed Nations — A461

1963, Aug. 15 Engr.
1195 A461 1.60k black .50 .25
FAO "Freedom from Hunger" campaign.

Wooden Toys — A462

Folk Art (Inscribed "UNESCO"): 80h, Cock and flowers. 1k, Flowers in vase. 1.20k, Janosik, Slovak hero. 1.60k, Stag. 2k, Postilion.

1963, Sept. 2 Engr. Perf. 13½
1196 A462 60h red & vio bl .65 .30
1197 A462 80h multi .65 .30
1198 A462 1k multi .65 .30
1199 A462 1.20k multi .65 .30
1200 A462 1.60k multi .65 .30
1201 A462 2k multi 2.75 1.75
Nos. 1196-1201 (6) 6.00 3.25

Nos. 1196-1201 were printed in sheets of 10. Value, set $100.

Canoeing — A463

Sports: 40h, Volleyball. 60h, Wrestling. 80h, Basketball. 1k, Boxing. 1.60k, Gymnastics.

Engraved and Photogravure
1963, Oct. 26 Perf. 11½
1202 A463 30h indigo & grn .30 .25
1203 A463 40h red brn & lt bl .30 .25
1204 A463 60h brn red & yel .35 .25
1205 A463 80h dk pur & dp org .45 .25
1206 A463 1k ultra & dp rose .60 .35
1207 A463 1.60k vio bl & ultra 2.00 1.00
Nos. 1202-1207 (6) 4.00 2.35

1964 Olympic Games, Tokyo.

Tree and Star — A464

1963, Dec. 11 Unwmk. Perf. 11½
1208 A464 30h bis brn & lt bl .30 .25
1209 A464 60h carmine & gray .30 .25
Russo-Czechoslovakian Treaty, 20th anniv.

Atom Diagrams Surrounding Head — A465

1963, Dec. 12 Engr.
1210 A465 60h dark purple .40 .25
3rd Congress of the Association for the Propagation of Scientific Knowledge.

Chamois — A466

40h, Alpine ibex. 60h, Mouflon. 1.20k, Roe deer. 1.60k, Fallow deer. 2k, Red deer.

1963, Dec. 14 Perf. 14
1211 A466 30h multi 1.25 .35
1212 A466 40h multi 1.25 .35
1213 A466 60h brn, yel & grn 1.25 .35
1214 A466 1.20k multi 2.00 1.00
1215 A466 1.60k multi 2.50 1.25
1216 A466 2k multi 5.00 2.50
Nos. 1211-1216 (6) 13.25 5.80

Nos. 1211-1216 were each issued in sheets of 10 stamps. Value, set $400.

Figure Skating — A467

80h, Skiing, horiz. 1k, Field ball player.

Engraved and Photogravure
1964, Jan. 20 Unwmk. Perf. 11½
1217 A467 30h violet bl & yel .30 .25
1218 A467 80h dk blue & org .45 .25
1219 A467 1k brown & lilac .75 .25
Nos. 1217-1219 (3) 1.50 .75

Intl. University Games (30h, 80h) and the World Field Ball Championships (1k).

Ice Hockey — A468

1964, Jan. 20
1220 A468 1k shown 1.10 .45
1221 A468 1.80k Toboggan 1.20 .60
1222 A468 2k Ski jump 2.25 1.00
Nos. 1220-1222 (3) 4.55 2.05

9th Winter Olympic Games, Innsbruck, Jan. 29-Feb. 9, 1964.

Magura Rest Home, High Tatra — A469

Design: 80h, Slovak National Insurrection Rest Home, Low Tatra.

1964, Feb. 19 Unwmk. Perf. 11½
1223 A469 60h green & yellow .30 .25
1224 A469 80h violet bl & pink .30 .25

Tourism — A470

30h, Skiers at Belianske Tatras mountains. 60h, Automobile camp, Telc. 1k, Fishing, Spis Castle. 1.80k, Lake & boats, Cesky Krumlov.

1964, Feb. 19 Engr. & Photo.
1225 A470 30h dk vio brn & bl .40 .25
1226 A470 60h slate & car .45 .25
1227 A470 1k red brn & olive .80 .25
1228 A470 1.80k slate grn & org 1.10 .35
Nos. 1225-1228 (4) 2.75 1.10

Moses, Day and Night by Michelangelo A471

Designs: 60h, "A Midsummer Night's Dream," by Shakespeare. 1k, Man, telescope and heaven, vert. 1.60k, King George of Podebrad (1420-71).

1964, Mar. 20
1229 A471 40h black & yel grn .35 .25
1230 A471 60h grnsh blk & cerise .35 .25
1231 A471 1k black & lt blue 1.25 .25
1232 A471 1.60k black & yellow 1.25 .25
a. Souvenir sheet of 4, imperf. ('88) 9.50 6.50
Nos. 1229-1232 (4) 3.20 1.00

UNESCO issue. 400th anniv. of the death of Michelangelo (40h); 400th anniv. of the birth of Shakespeare (60h); 400th anniv. of the birth of Galileo (1k); 500th anniv. of the pacifist efforts of King George of Podebrad (1.60k).
No. 1232a for PRAGA '88.

Yuri A. Gagarin A472

Astronauts: 60h, Gherman Titov. 80h, John H. Glenn, Jr. 1k, Scott M. Carpenter, vert. 1.20k, Pavel R. Popovich and Andrian G. Nikolayev. 1.40k, Walter M. Schirra, vert. 1.60k, Gordon L. Cooper, vert. 2k, Valentina Tereshkova and Valeri Bykovski, vert.

1964, Apr. 27 Unwmk. Perf. 11½
Yellow Paper
1233 A472 30h black & vio bl .50 .25
1234 A472 60h dk grn & dk car .50 .25
1235 A472 80h dk car & vio .55 .25
1236 A472 1k ultra & rose vio .75 .25
1237 A472 1.20k ver & ol gray .60 .25
1238 A472 1.40k black & dl grn 1.00 .45
1239 A472 1.60k pale pur & Prus grn 2.25 1.50
1240 A472 2k dk blue & red .75 .40
Nos. 1233-1240 (8) 6.90 3.65

World's first 10 astronauts.

Creeping Bellflower — A473

Flowers: 80h, Musk thistle. 1k, Chicory. 1.20k, Yellow iris. 1.60k, Gentian. 2k, Corn poppy.

1964, June 15 Engr. Perf. 14
1241 A473 60h dk grn, lil & org .75 .25
1242 A473 80h blk, grn & red lil 1.10 .25
1243 A473 1k vio bl, grn & pink 1.10 .45
1244 A473 1.20k black, yel & grn 1.10 .30
1245 A473 1.60k violet & grn 1.10 .40
1246 A473 2k vio, red & grn 4.50 1.50
Nos. 1241-1246 (6) 9.65 3.15

Nos. 1241-1246 were each issued in sheets of 10. Value, set $250.

Film "Flower" and Karlovy Vary Colonnade — A474

Engraved and Photogravure
1964, June 20 Unwmk. Perf. 13½
1247 A474 60h black, blue & car 2.00 .50
14th Intl. Film Festival at Karlovy Vary, July 4-19.
Issued in sheets of 10. Value, $80.

Silesian Coat of Arms — A475

1964, June 20 Perf. 11½
1248 A475 30h black & yel .30 .25
150th anniv. of the Silesian Museum, Opava.

Young Miner of 1764 — A476

1964, June 20
1249 A476 60h sepia & lt grn .30 .25
Mining School at Banska Stiavnica, bicent.

Skoda Fire Engine — A477

1964, June 20
1250 A477 60h car rose & lt bl 1.00 .25
Voluntary fire brigades in Bohemia, cent.

Gulls, Hradcany Castle, Red Cross — A478

1964, July 10
1251 A478 60h car & bluish gray .55 .25
4th Czechoslovak Red Cross Congress at Prague.

Human Heart — A479

1964, July 10
1252 A479 1.60k ultra & car 1.10 .25
4th European Cardiological Cong. at Prague.

Partisans, Girl and Factories A480 / Battle Scene, 1944 A481

Design: No. 1254, Partisans and flame.

Engraved and Photogravure
1964, Aug. 17 Unwmk. Perf. 11½
1253 A480 30h brown & red .25 .25
1254 A480 60h dk blue & red .25 .25
1255 A481 60h black & red .25 .25
Nos. 1253-1255 (3) .75 .75

20th anniv. of the Slovak Natl. Uprising; No. 1255, 20th anniv. of the Battles of Dukla Pass.

CZECHOSLOVAKIA

Hradcany at Prague — A482

Design: 5k, Charles Bridge and Hradcany.

1964, Aug. 30   Perf. 11½x12
1256 A482 60h black & red .65 .25

Souvenir Sheet
     Engr.   Imperf.
1257 A482 5k deep claret 3.50 2.50

Millenium of the Hradcany, Prague. No. 1257 stamp size: 30x50mm.

Discus Thrower and Pole Vaulter — A483

Designs: 60h, Bicycling, horiz. 1k, Soccer. 1.20k, Rowing. 1.60k, Swimming, horiz. 2.80k, Weight lifting, horiz.

Engraved and Photogravure
1964, Sept. 2   Perf. 13½
1258 A483 60h multi .80 .30
1259 A483 80h multi .80 .30
1260 A483 1k multi .80 .30
1261 A483 1.20k multi .80 .30
1262 A483 1.60k multi .80 .30
1263 A483 2.80k multi 4.00 2.00
Nos. 1258-1263 (6) 8.00 3.50

Issued to commemorate the 18th Olympic Games, Tokyo, Oct. 10-25.
Nos. 1258-1263 were issued in sheets of 10. Value, set $125.

Miniature Sheet

Space Ship Voskhod I, Astronauts and Globe — A484

1964, Nov. 12   Unwmk.   Perf. 11½
1264 A484 3k dk bl & dl lil, buff 5.00 3.50

Russian 3-man space flight of Vladimir M. Komarov, Boris B. Yegorov and Konstantin Feoktistov, Oct. 12-13.

Steam Engine and Atomic Power Plant — A485   Diesel Engine "CKD Praha" — A486

1964, Nov. 16   Engr.
1265 A485 30h dull red brown .25 .25

Engraved and Photogravure
1266 A486 60h green & salmon 1.00 .25

Traditions and development of engineering; No. 1265 for 150th anniv. of the First Brno Engineering Works, No. 1266 for the engineering concern CKD Praha.

European Redstart — A487

Birds: 60h, Green woodpecker. 80h, Hawfinch. 1k, Black woodpecker. 1.20k, European robin. 1.60k, European roller.

1964, Nov. 16   Litho.   Perf. 10½
1267 A487 30h multicolored 1.10 .30
1268 A487 60h black & multi 1.10 .30
1269 A487 80h multicolored 1.40 .35
1270 A487 1k multicolored 1.75 .40
1271 A487 1.20k lt vio bl & blk 1.75 .40
1272 A487 1.60k yellow & blk 3.50 1.00
Nos. 1267-1272 (6) 10.60 2.75

Dancer A488   "In the Sun" Pre-school Children A489

Designs: 60h, "Over the Obstacles," teenagers. 1k, "Movement and Beauty," woman flag twirler. 1.60k, Runners at start.

Engraved and Photogravure
1965   Unwmk.   Perf. 11½
1273 A488 30h red & lt blue .25 .25
     Perf. 11½x12
1274 A489 30h vio bl & car .25 .25
1275 A489 60h brown & ultra .25 .25
1276 A489 1k black & yellow .25 .25
1277 A489 1.00k maroon & gray .60 .25
Nos. 1273-1277 (5) 1.60 1.25

3rd Natl. Spartacist Games. Issue dates: No. 1273, Jan. 3; Nos. 1274-1277, May 24.

Mountain Rescue Service — A490

Designs: No. 1279, Woman gymnast. No. 1280, Bicyclists. No. 1281, Women hurdlers.

1965, Jan. 15   Unwmk.   Perf. 11½
1278 A490 60h violet & blue .30 .25
1279 A490 60h maroon & ocher .30 .25
1280 A490 60h black & carmine .30 .25
1281 A490 60h green & yellow .30 .25
Nos. 1278-1281 (4) 1.20 1.00

Mountain Rescue Service (No. 1278); 1st World Championship in Artistic Gymnastics, Prague, Dec. 1965 (No. 1279); World Championship in Indoor Bicycling, Prague, Oct. 1965 (No. 1280); "Universiada 1965," Brno (No. 1281).

Arms and View, Beroun — A491

Designs: No. 1283, Town Square, Domazlice. No. 1284, Old and new buildings, Frydek-Mystek. No. 1285, Arms and view, Lipnik. No. 1286, Fortified wall, City Hall and Arms, Policka. No. 1287, View and hops, Zatek. No. 1288, Small fortress and rose, Terezin.

1965, Feb. 15
1282 A491 30h vio bl & lt bl .30 .25
1283 A491 30h dull pur & yel .30 .25
1284 A491 30h slate & gray .30 .25
1285 A491 30h green & bis .30 .25
1286 A491 30h brown & tan .30 .25
1287 A491 30h dk blue & cit .30 .25
1288 A491 30h black & rose .30 .25
Nos. 1282-1288 (7) 2.10 1.75

Nos. 1282-1287 for 700th anniv. of the founding of various Bohemian towns; No. 1288 the 20th anniv. of the liberation of the Theresienstadt (Terezin) concentration camp.

Sun's Corona — A492

Space Research: 30h, Sun. 60h, Exploration of the Moon. 1k, Twin space craft, vert. 1.40k, Space station. 1.60k, Exploration of Mars, vert. 2k, USSR and US Meteorological collaboration.

1965, Mar. 15   Perf. 12x11½, 11½x12
1289 A492 20h rose & red lilac .25 .25
1290 A492 30h rose red & yel .25 .25
1291 A492 60h bluish blk & yel .25 .25
1292 A492 1k pur & pale bl .25 .25
1293 A492 1.40k black & salmon .35 .25
1294 A492 1.60k black & pink .50 .25
1295 A492 2k bluish blk & lt bl 1.50 1.00
Nos. 1289-1295 (7) 3.35 2.50

Space research; Nos. 1289-1290 also for the Intl. Quiet Sun Year, 1964-65.

Frantisek Ventura, Equestrian; Amsterdam, 1928 — A493

Czechoslovakian Olympic Victories: 30h, Discus, Paris, 1900. 60h, Running, Helsinki, 1952. 1k, Weight lifting, Berlin, 1936. 1.60k, Double sculling, Rome, 1960. 2k, Women's gymnastics, Tokyo, 1964.

1965, Apr. 16   Perf. 11½x12
1296 A493 20h choc & gold .25 .25
1297 A493 30h indigo & emer .25 .25
1298 A493 60h ultra & gold .25 .25
1299 A493 1k red brn & gold .25 .25
1300 A493 1.40k dk sl grn & gold 1.10 .45
1301 A493 1.60k black & gold 1.10 .45
1302 A493 2k maroon & gold .55 .30
Nos. 1296-1302 (7) 3.75 2.20

Astronauts Virgil Grissom and John Young A494

Designs: No. 1304, Alexei Leonov floating in space. No. 1305, Launching pad at Cape Kennedy. No. 1306, Leonov leaving space ship.

1965, Apr. 17   Perf. 11x11½
1303 A494 60h slate bl & lil rose .45 .25
1304 A494 60h vio blk & blue .45 .25
1305 A494 3k slate bl & lil rose 1.60 1.00
   a. Pair, #1303, 1305 3.50 1.50
1306 A494 3k vio blk & blue 1.60 1.00
   a. Pair, #1304, 1306 3.50 1.50
Nos. 1303-1306 (4) 4.10 2.50

Issued to honor American and Soviet astronauts. Printed in sheets of 25; one sheet contains 20 No. 1303 and 5 No. 1305, the other sheet contains 20 No. 1304 and 5 No. 1306. Value, $125 each.

Russian Soldier, View of Prague and Guerrilla Fighters — A495

Designs: No. 1308, Blast furnace, workers and tank. 60h, Worker and factory. 1k, Worker and new constructions. 1.60k, Woman farmer, new farm buildings and machinery.

1965, May 5   Engr.   Perf. 13½
1307 A495 30h dk red, blk & ol .35 .25
1308 A495 30h multicolored .35 .25
1309 A495 60h vio bl, red & blk .35 .25
1310 A495 1k dp org, blk & brn .50 .25
1311 A495 1.60k yel, red & blk 1.00 .50
Nos. 1307-1311 (5) 2.10 1.25

20th anniv. of liberation from the Nazis. Nos. 1307-1311 were each printed in sheets of 10. Value, set $120.

Slovakian Kopov Dog — A496

Dogs: 40h, German shepherd. 60h, Czech hunting dog with pheasant. 1k, Poodle. 1.60k, Czech terrier. 2k, Afghan hound.

1965, June 10   Perf. 12x11½
1312 A496 30h black & red org .45 .25
1313 A496 40h black & yellow .45 .25
1314 A496 60h black & ver .70 .25
1315 A496 1k black & dk car rose 1.00 .25
1316 A496 1.60k black & orange 1.25 .25
1317 A496 2k black & orange 2.00 1.25
Nos. 1312-1317 (6) 5.85 2.50

World Dog Show at Brno and the International Dog Breeders Congress, Prague.

UN Headquarters Building, NY — A497

Emblems: 60h, UN & inscription. 1.60k, ICY.

1965, June 24   Perf. 12x11½
1318 A497 60h dk red brn & yel .25 .25
1319 A497 1k ultra & lt blue .65 .25
1320 A497 1.60k gold & dk red .55 .25
Nos. 1318-1320 (3) 1.45 .75

20th anniv. of the UN and the ICY, 1965.

Trade Union Emblem A498

1965, June 24   Engr.
1321 A498 60h dk red & ultra .40 .25

Intl. Trade Union Federation, 20th anniv.

Women and Globe — A499

1965, June 24   Perf. 11½x12
1322 A499 60h violet blue .40 .25

20th anniv. of the Intl. Women's Federation.

Children's House (Burgraves' Palace), Hradcany A500   Matthias Tower A501

1965, June 25   Perf. 11½
1323 A500 30h slate green .30 .25
1324 A501 60h dark brown .30 .25

Issued to publicize the Hradcany, Prague.

Marx and Lenin — A502

1965, July 1   Engr. & Photo.
1325 A502 60h car rose & gold .40 .25

6th conf. of Postal Ministers of Communist Countries, Peking, June 21-July 15.

Joseph Navratil A503   Jan Hus A504

47

CZECHOSLOVAKIA

Gregor Johann Mendel
A505

Costume Jewelry A506

Bohuslav Martinu A507

Seated Woman and University of Bratislava A508

ITU Emblem and Communication Symbols A509 / Macromolecular Symposium Emblem A510

Design: No. 1327, Ludovit Stur (diff. frame).

1965		Unwmk.	Perf. 11½
1326	A503	30h black & fawn	.25 .25
1327	A503	30h black & dull grn	.25 .25
1328	A504	60h black & crimson	.25 .25
1329	A505	60h vio bl & red	.25 .25
1330	A506	60h purple & gold	.25 .25
1331	A507	60h black & orange	.25 .25
1332	A508	60h brn, yel	.25 .25
1333	A509	1k orange & blue	.35 .25
1334	A510	1k black & dp org	.35 .25
	Nos. 1326-1334 (9)		2.45 2.25

No. 1326, Navratil (1798-1865), painter; No. 1327, Stur (1815-56), Slovak author and historian; No. 1328, the 550th anniv. of the death of Hus, religious reformer;

No. 1329, cent. of publication of Mendel's laws of inheritance; No. 1330 publicizes the "Jablonec 1965" costume jewelry exhib.; No. 1331, Martinu (1890-1959), composer; No. 1332, 500th anniv. of the founding of the University of Bratislava as Academia Istropolitana; No. 1333, cent. of the ITU; No. 1334, Intl. Symposium on Macromolecular Chemistry, Prague, Sept. 1-8.
Issued: No. 1333, 7/10.

Miniature Sheet

"Young Woman at her Toilette," by Titian A512

1965, Aug. 12
1336 A512 5k multicolored   6.00 4.00
Hradcany Art Gallery. No. 1336 contains one stamp.

Help for Flood Victims A513

Rescue of Flood Victims A514

1965, Sept. 6   Engr.
1337 A513 30h violet blue   .25 .25
Engraved and Photogravure
1338 A514 2k dk ol grn & ol   .65 .45
Help for Danube flood victims in Slovakia.

Dotterel A515

Mountain Birds: 60h, Wall creeper, vert. 1.20k, Lesser redpoll. 1.40k, Golden eagle, vert. 1.60k, Ring ouzel. 2k, Eurasian nutcracker, vert.

1965, Sept. 20   Litho.   Perf. 11
1339 A515 30h multi   .80 .25
1340 A515 60h multi   .80 .25
1341 A515 1.20k multi   .80 .25
1342 A515 1.40k multi   1.50 .25
1343 A515 1.60k multi   1.00 .45
1344 A515 2k multi   4.00 1.75
Nos. 1339-1344 (6)   8.90 3.20

Levoca — A516

Views of Towns: 10h, Jindrichuv Hradec. 20h, Nitra. 30h, Kosice. 40h, Hradec Králové. 50h, Telc. 60h, Ostrava. 1k, Olomouc. 1.20k, Ceske Budejovice. 1.60k, Cheb. 2k, Brno. 3k, Bratislava. 5k, Prague.

Engraved and Photogravure
1965-66   Perf. 11½x12
Size: 23x19mm
1345 A516 5h black & yel   .25 .25
1346 A516 10h ultra & ol bis   .80 .25
1347 A516 20h black & lt bl   .25 .25
1348 A516 30h vio bl & lt grn   .25 .25
1348A A516 40h dk brn & lt bl ('66)   .25 .25
1348B A516 50h black & ocher ('66)   .50 .25
1348C A516 60h red & gray ('66)   1.00 .25
1348D A516 1k pur & pale grn ('66)   1.00 .25

Perf. 11½x11
Size: 30x23mm
1349 A516 1.20k slate & lt bl   .75 .25
1350 A516 1.60k indigo & yel   .75 .25
1351 A516 2k sl grn & pale yel   .75 .25
1352 A516 3k brn & yel   1.25 .25
1353 A516 5k black & pink   1.75 .25
Nos. 1345-1353 (13)   9.55 3.25

Medicinal Plants — A517

1965, Dec. 3   Engr.   Perf. 14
1354 A517 30h Coltsfoot   .35 .25
1355 A517 60h Meadow saffron   .35 .25
1356 A517 80h Corn poppy   1.00 .25
1357 A517 1k Foxglove   1.00 .40
1358 A517 1.20k Arnica   1.40 .60
1359 A517 1.60k Cornflower   1.40 .45
1360 A517 2k Dog rose   3.50 1.50
Nos. 1354-1360 (7)   9.00 3.70

Nos. 1354-1360 were each printed in sheets of 10. Value, set $225.

Strip of "Stamps" A518

Engraved and Photogravure
1965, Dec. 18   Perf. 11½
1361 A518 1k dark red & gold   3.50 2.00
Issued for Stamp Day, 1965.

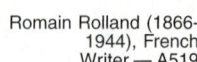
Romain Rolland (1866-1944), French Writer — A519

Portraits: No. 1362, Stanislav Sucharda (1866-1916), sculptor. No. 1363, Ignac Josef Pesina (1766-1808), veterinarian. No. 1365, Donatello (1386-1466), Italian sculptor.

1966, Feb. 14   Engr.   Perf. 11½
1362 A519 30h deep green   .25 .25
1363 A519 30h violet blue   .25 .25
1364 A519 60h rose lake   .25 .25
1365 A519 60h brown   .25 .25
Nos. 1362-1365 (4)   1.00 1.00

Symbolic Musical Instruments & Names of Composers — A520

1966, Jan. 15   Engr. & Photo.
1366 A520 30h black & gold   .55 .25
Czech Philharmonic Orchestra, 70th anniv.

Figure Skating Pair — A521

No. 1368, Man skater. No. 1369, Volleyball player, spiking, vert. 1k, Volleyball player, saving, vert. 1.60k, Woman skater. 2k, Figure skating pair.

1966, Feb. 17
1367 A521 30h dk car rose   .30 .25
1368 A521 60h green   .30 .25
1369 A521 60h carmine & buff   .30 .25
1370 A521 1k vio & lt bl   .40 .25
1371 A521 1.60k brown & yellow   .50 .25
1372 A521 2k blue & grnsh bl   2.40 .40
Nos. 1367-1372 (6)   4.20 1.65

Nos. 1367-1368, 1371-1372 for the European Figure Skating Championships, Bratislava; Nos. 1369-1370 for the World Volleyball Championships.

Souvenir Sheet

Girl Dancing A522

1966, Mar. 21   Engr.   Imperf.
1373 A522 3k slate bl, red & bl   3.50 1.50
Cent. of the opera "The Bartered Bride" by Bedrich Smetana.

"Ajax" 1841 — A523

Locomotives: 30h, "Karlstejn" 1865. 60h, Steam engine, 1946. 1k, Steam engine with tender, 1946. 1.60k, Electric locomotive, 1964. 2k, Diesel locomotive, 1964.

1966, Mar. 21   Perf. 11½x11
Buff Paper
1374 A523 20h sepia   1.10 .25
1375 A523 30h dull violet   1.60 .25
1376 A523 60h dull purple   1.10 .25
1377 A523 1k dark blue   1.25 .50
1378 A523 1.60k dk blue grn   1.75 .40
1379 A523 2k dark red   3.25 2.10
Nos. 1374-1379 (6)   10.05 3.75

European Perch — A524

30h, Brown trout, vert. 1k, Carp. 1.20k, Northern pike. 1.40k, Grayling. 1.60k, Eel.

Perf. 13x13½, 13½x13
1966, Apr. 22   Litho.   Unwmk.
1380 A524 30h multi   .60 .25
1381 A524 60h multi   .60 .25
1382 A524 1k multi   1.25 .25
1383 A524 1.20k multi   .60 .25
1384 A524 1.40k multi   1.10 .50
1385 A524 1.60k multi   2.50 1.00
Nos. 1380-1385 (6)   6.65 2.50

Intl. Fishing Championships, Svit, Sept. 3-5.

WHO Headquarters, Geneva — A525

Engraved and Photogravure
1966, Apr. 25   Perf. 12x11½
1386 A525 1k dk blue & lt blue   .35 .25
Opening of the WHO Headquarters, Geneva.

Symbolic Handshake and UNESCO Emblem — A526

1966, Apr. 25   Perf. 11½
1387 A526 60h bister & olive gray   .45 .25
20th anniv. of UNESCO.

Prague Castle Issue

Belvedere Palace and St. Vitus' Cathedral — A527

Crown of St. Wenceslas, 1346 — A528

Design: 60h, Madonna, altarpiece from St. George's Church.

1966, May 9   Engr.   Perf. 11½
1388 A527 30h dark blue   .50 .25
Engraved and Photogravure
1389 A527 60h blk & yel bis   .75 .25

Souvenir Sheet
Engr.
1390 A528 5k multi   5.00 2.50
See Nos. 1537-1539.

Tiger Swallowtail A529

CZECHOSLOVAKIA

Butterflies and Moths: 60h, Clouded sulphur. 80h, European purple emperor. 1k, Apollo. 1.20k, Burnet moth. 2k, Tiger moth.

1966, May 23	Engr.	Perf. 14
1391 A529 30h multi	.90	.25
1392 A529 60h multi	.90	.25
1393 A529 80h multi	1.25	.40
1394 A529 1k multi	1.90	.60
1395 A529 1.20k multi	1.90	.50
1396 A529 2k multi	5.50	2.00
Nos. 1391-1396 (6)	12.35	4.00

Nos. 1391-1396 were issued in sheets of 10. Value, set $250.

Flags of Russia and Czechoslovakia — A530

Designs: 60h, Rays surrounding hammer and sickle "sun." 1.60k, Girl's head and stars.

Engraved and Photogravure
1966, May 31		Perf. 11½
1397 A530 30h dk bl & crim	.25	.25
1398 A530 60h bl & red	.25	.25
1399 A530 1.60k red & dk bl	.30	.25
Nos. 1397-1399 (3)	.80	.75

13th Congress of the Communist Party of Czechoslovakia.

Dakota Chief — A531

Designs: 20h, Indians, canoe and tepee, horiz. 30h, Tomahawk. 40h, Haida totem poles. 60h, Kachina, good spirit of the Hopis. 1k, Indian on horseback hunting buffalo, horiz. 1.20k, Calumet, Dakota peace pipe.

1966, June 20		Size: 23x40mm
1400 A531 20h vio bl & dp org	.25	.25
1401 A531 30h blk & dl org	.25	.25
1402 A531 40h blk & lt bl	.25	.25
1403 A531 60h grn & yel	.25	.25
1404 A531 1k pur & emer	.40	.25
1405 A531 1.20k vio bl & rose lil	.65	.30

	Perf. 14
	Engr.
	Size: 23x37mm
1406 A531 1.40k multi	1.60 .90
Nos. 1400-1406 (7)	3.65 2.45

Cent. of the Náprstek Ethnographic Museum, Prague, and "The Indians of North America" exhibition.
No. 1406 was issued in sheets of 10. Value, $500.

Model of Molecule — A532

Engraved and Photogravure
1966, July 4	Unwmk.	Perf. 11½
1407 A532 60h blk & lt bl	.50	.25

Czechoslovak Chemical Society, cent.

"Guernica" by Pablo Picasso — A533

1966, July 5		Size: 75x30mm
1408 A533 60h blk & pale bl	2.75	1.40

30th anniversary of International Brigade in Spanish Civil War.
Sheets of 15 stamps and 5 labels inscribed "Picasso-Guernica 1937." Values: with tab attached, $6; sheet $75.

Pantheon, Bratislava — A534

Designs: No. 1410, Devin Castle and Ludovit Stur. No. 1411, View of Nachod. No. 1412, State Science Library, Olomouc.

1966, July 25		Engr.
1409 A534 30h dl pur	.30	.25
1410 A534 60h dk bl	.35	.25
1411 A534 60h green	.35	.25
1412 A534 60h sepia	.30	.25
Nos. 1409-1412 (4)	1.30	1.00

No. 1409, Russian War Memorial, Bratislava; No. 1410, the 9th cent. Devin Castle as symbol of Slovak nationalism; No. 1411, 700th anniv. of the founding of Nachod; No. 1412, the 400th anniv. of the State Science Library, Olomouc.

Atom Symbol and Sun — A535

Engraved and Photogravure
1966, Aug. 29		Perf. 11½
1413 A535 60h blk & red	.40	.25

Issued to publicize Jachymov (Joachimsthal), where pitchblende was first discovered, "cradle of the atomic age."

Brno Fair Emblem — A536

1966, Aug. 29		
1414 A536 60h blk & red	.40	.25

8th International Trade Fair, Brno.

Olympia Coin and Olympic Rings — A537

Design: 1k, Olympic flame, Czechoslovak flag and Olympic rings.

1966, Aug. 29		
1415 A537 60h blk & gold	.30	.25
1416 A537 1k dk bl & red	1.10	.30

70th anniv. of the Olympic Committee.

Missile Carrier, Tank and Jet Plane — A538

1966, Aug. 31		
1417 A538 60h blk & apple grn	.40	.25

Issued to commemorate the maneuvers of the armies of the Warsaw Pact countries.

Mercury A539

30h, Moravian silver thaler, 1620, reverse & obverse, vert. 1.60k, Old & new buildings of Brno State Theater. 5k, Intl. Trade Fair Administration Tower & postmark, vert.

1966, Sept. 10		
1418 A539 30h dk red & blk	.45	.25
1419 A539 60h org & blk	.45	.25
1420 A539 1.60k blk & brt grn	.75	.25
Nos. 1418-1420 (3)	1.65	.75

Souvenir Sheet
| 1421 A539 5k multi | 3.00 | 3.00 |

Brno Philatelic Exhibition, Sept. 11-25. No. 1421 contains one 30x40mm stamp.

First Meeting in Orbit A540

30h, Photograph of far side of Moon & Russian satellite. 60h, Photograph of Mars & Mariner 4. 80h, Soft landing on Moon. 1k, Satellite, laser beam & binary code. 1.20k, Telstar over Earth & receiving station.

1966, Sept. 26		Perf. 11½
1422 A540 20h vio & lt grn	.25	.25
1423 A540 30h blk & sal pink	.25	.25
1424 A540 60h slate & lilac	.35	.25
1425 A540 80h dk pur & lt bl	.35	.25
1426 A540 1k blk & vio	.40	.25
1427 A540 1.20k red & bl	1.75	.25
Nos. 1422-1427 (6)	3.35	1.50

Issued to publicize American and Russian achievements in space research.

Badger — A541

Game Animals: 40h, Red deer, vert. 60h, Lynx. 80h, Hare. 1k, Red fox. 1.20k, Brown bear, vert. 2k, Wild boar.

1966, Nov. 28	Litho.	Perf. 13½
1428 A541 30h multi	.60	.25
1429 A541 40h multi	.60	.25
1430 A541 60h multi	.50	.25
1431 A541 80h multi (europaens)	1.25	.25
a. 80h multi (europaeus)	6.00	3.50
1432 A541 1k multi	.90	.30
1433 A541 1.20k multi	1.25	.50
1434 A541 2k multi	3.00	1.25
Nos. 1428-1434 (7)	8.10	3.05

The sheet of 50 of the 80h contains 40 with misspelling "europaens" and 10 with "europaeus."

"Spring" by Václav Hollar, 1607-77 — A542

Paintings: No. 1436, Portrait of Mrs. F. Wussin, by Jan Kupecky (1667-1740). No. 1437, Snow Owl by Karel Purkyne (1834-1868). No. 1438, Tulips by Václav Spála (1885-1964). No. 1439, Recruit by Ludovit Fulla (1902-1980).

1966, Dec. 8	Engr.	Perf. 14
1435 A542 1k black	3.75	2.50
1436 A542 1k multicolored	5.25	1.90
1437 A542 1k multicolored	2.40	1.90
1438 A542 1k multicolored	2.40	1.90
1439 A542 1k multicolored	19.00	18.00
Nos. 1435-1439 (5)	32.80	25.20

Printed in sheets of 4 stamps and 2 labels. The labels in sheet of No. 1435 are inscribed "Václav Hollar 1607-1677" in fancy frame. Other labels are blank. Value, set $135. See No. 1484.

Symbolic Bird A543

Engraved and Photogravure
1966, Dec. 17		Perf. 11½
1440 A543 1k dp blue & yel	1.25	.80

Issued for Stamp Day.

Youth — A544

1967, Jan. 16		Perf. 11½
1441 A544 30h ver & lt bl	.30	.25

5th Cong. of the Czechoslovak Youth Org.

Symbolic Flower and Machinery — A545

1967, Jan. 16		
1442 A545 30h carmine & yel	.30	.25

6th Trade Union Congress, Prague.

Parents with Dead Child — A545a

1967, Jan. 16		Perf. 11½
1442A A545a 60h blk & sal	.30	.25

"Peace and Freedom in Viet Nam."

View of Jihlava and Tourist Year Emblem A546

Views and Tourist Year Emblem: 40h, Spielberg Castle and churches, Brno. 1.20k, Danube, castle and churches, Bratislava. 1.60k, Vltava River bridges, Hradcany and churches, Prague.

1967, Feb. 13	Engr.	Perf. 11½
	Size: 40x23mm	
1443 A546 30h brown violet	.25	.25
1444 A546 40h maroon	.25	.25
	Size: 75x30mm	
1445 A546 1.20k violet blue	.60	.25
1446 A546 1.60k black	2.00	.80
Nos. 1443-1446 (4)	3.10	1.55

International Tourist Year, 1967.

Black-tailed Godwit — A547

Birds: 40h, Shoveler, horiz. 60h, Purple heron. 80h, Penduline tit. 1k, Avocet. 1.40k, Black stork. 1.60k, Tufted duck, horiz.

1967, Feb. 20	Litho.	Perf. 13½
1447 A547 30h multi	.75	.30
1448 A547 40h multi	.75	.30
1449 A547 60h multi	.75	.30
1450 A547 80h multi	.75	.30
1451 A547 1k multi	.75	.20
1452 A547 1.40k multi	1.40	.60
1453 A547 1.60k multi	2.75	1.20
Nos. 1447-1453 (7)	7.90	3.30

Solar Research and Satellite A548

Space Research: 40h, Space craft, rocket and construction of station. 60h, Man on moon and orientation system. 1k, Exploration of solar system and rocket. 1.20k, Lunar satellites and moon photograph. 1.60k, Planned lunar architecture and moon landing.

CZECHOSLOVAKIA

Engraved and Photogravure
1967, Mar. 24   Perf. 11½
1454	A548	30h yel & dk red	.30	.25
1455	A548	40h vio bl & blk	.45	.25
1456	A548	60h lilac & grn	.45	.25
1457	A548	1k brt pink & sl	.45	.25
1458	A548	1.20k lt violet & blk	.70	.25
1459	A548	1.60k brn lake & blk	2.10	.60

Nos. 1454-1459 (6)   4.45   1.85

Gothic Painting, by Master Theodoric — A549

Designs: 40h, "Burning of Master Hus," from Litomerice Hymnal. 60h, Modern glass sculpture. 80h, "The Shepherdess and the Chimney Sweep," Andersen fairy tale, painting by J. Trnka. 1k, Section of pressure vessel from atomic power station. 1.20k, Three ceramic figurines, by P. Rada. 3k, Montreal skyline and EXPO '67 emblem.

1967, Apr. 10   Engr.   Perf. 14
Size: 37x23mm
1460	A549	30h multi	.25	.25
1461	A549	40h multi	.25	.25
1462	A549	60h multi	.25	.25
1463	A549	80h multi	.25	.25
1464	A549	1k multi	1.00	.25
1465	A549	1.20k multi	1.25	.25

Nos. 1460-1465 (6)   3.25   1.85

Souvenir Sheet
Perf. 11½
Size: 40x30mm
| 1466 | A549 | 3k multi | 3.00 | 2.50 |

EXPO '67, International Exhibition, Montreal, Apr. 28-Oct. 27, 1967.
Nos. 1460-1465 were each issued in a miniature sheet of 10 stamps. Value, set $50.
Examples of No. 1466 imperf. were not issued.

Canoe Race A550   Women Playing Basketball A551

No. 1468, Wheels, dove & emblems of Warsaw, Berlin, Prague. 1.60k, Canoe slalom.

Perf. 12x11½, 11½x12
1967, Apr. 17   Engr. & Photo.
1467	A550	60h black & brt bl	.25	.25
1468	A550	60h black & salmon	.25	.25
1469	A551	60h blk & grnsh bl	.25	.25
1470	A551	1.60k black & brt vio	1.10	.55

Nos. 1467-1470 (4)   1.85   1.30

No. 1467, 5th Intl. Wild-Water Canoeing Championships; No. 1468, 20th Warsaw-Berlin-Prague Bicycle Race: No. 1469, Women's Basketball Championships; No. 1470, 10th Intl. Water Slalom Championships.

"Golden Street" — A552

Designs: 60h, Interior of Hall of King Wenceslas. 5k, St. Matthew, from illuminated manuscript, 11th century.

1967, May 9   Perf. 11½x11
| 1471 | A552 | 30h rose claret | .25 | .25 |
| 1472 | A552 | 60h bluish black | .50 | .25 |

Souvenir Sheet
Perf. 11½
| 1473 | A552 | 5k multicolored | 2.60 | 2.40 |

Issued to publicize the Castle of Prague.

Stylized Lyre with Flowers — A553

1967, May 10   Perf. 11½
| 1474 | A553 | 60h dull pur & brt grn | .30 | .25 |

Prague Music Festival.

Old-New Synagogue, Prague — A554

30h, Detail from Torah curtain, 1593. 60h, Prague Printer's emblem, 1530. 1k, Mikulov jug, 1804. 1.40k, Memorial for Concentration Camp Victims 1939-45, Pincas Synagogue (menorah & tablet). 1.60k, Tombstone of David Gans, 1613.

1967, May 22   Perf. 11½
1475	A554	30h dull red & lt bl	.30	.25
1476	A554	60h blk & lt grn	.25	.25
1477	A554	1k dk bl & rose lil	.25	.25
1478	A554	1.20k dk brn & mar	.65	.25
1479	A554	1.40k black & yellow	.55	.25
1480	A554	1.60k green & yel	4.50	2.75

Nos. 1475-1480 (6)   6.60   4.00

Issued to show Jewish relics. The items shown on the 30h, 60h and 1k are from the State Jewish Museum, Prague.

"Lidice" — A555

1967, June 9   Unwmk.   Perf. 11½
| 1481 | A555 | 30h black & brt rose | .30 | .25 |

Destruction of Lidice by the Nazis, 25th anniv.

Prague Architecture — A556

1967, June 10   Engr. & Photo.
| 1482 | A556 | 1k black & gold | .35 | .25 |

Issued to publicize the 9th Congress of the International Union of Architects, Prague.

Peter Bezruc — A557

1967, June 21
| 1483 | A557 | 60h dull rose & blk | .30 | .25 |

Peter Bezruc, poet & writer, birth cent.

Painting Type of 1966

2k, Henri Rousseau (1844-1910), self-portrait.

1967, June 22   Engr.   Perf. 11½
| 1484 | A542 | 2k multicolored | 2.00 | 1.60 |

Praga 68, World Stamp Exhibition, Prague, June 22-July 7, 1968.
Printed in sheets of 4 stamps (2x2), separated by horizontal gutter with inscription and picture of Natl. Gallery, site of Praga 68. Value, $10.

View of Skalitz — A558

No. 1486, Mining tower & church steeple, Pribram. No. 1487, Hands holding book & view of Presov.

1967, Aug. 21   Engr.   Perf. 11½
1485	A558	30h violet blue	.25	.25
1486	A558	30h slate green	.25	.25
1487	A558	30h claret	.25	.25

Nos. 1485-1487 (3)   .75   .75

Towns of Skalitz, Pribram, Presov, annivs.

Colonnade and Spring, Karlovy Vary and Communications Emblem — A559

1967, Aug. 21   Engr. & Photo.
| 1488 | A559 | 30h violet bl & gold | .30 | .25 |

5th Sports & Cultural Festival of the Employees of the Ministry of Communications, Karlovy Vary.

Ondrejov Observatory and Galaxy — A560

1967, Aug. 22   Engr.
| 1489 | A560 | 60h vio bl, rose lil & sil | 1.50 | .25 |

13th Cong. of the Intl. Astronomical Union. No. 1489 was issued in a sheet of 10 stamps. Value, set $60.

Orchid — A561

Flowers from the Botanical Gardens: 30h, Cobaea scandens. 40h, Lycaste deppei. 60h, Glottiphyllum davisii. 1k, Anthurium. 1.20k, Rhodocactus. 1.40k, Moth orchid.

1967, Aug. 30   Litho.   Perf. 12½
1490	A561	20h multicolored	.30	.25
1491	A561	30h pink & multi	.30	.25
1492	A561	40h multicolored	.45	.25
1493	A561	60h lt blue & multi	.45	.25
1494	A561	1k multicolored	.60	.25
1495	A561	1.20k lt yellow & multi	.65	.30
1496	A561	1.40k multicolored	1.75	.70

Nos. 1490-1496 (7)   4.50   2.25

Red Squirrel — A562

Animals from the Tatra National Park: 60h, Wild cat. 1k, Ermine. 1.20k, Dormouse. 1.40k, Hedgehog. 1.60k, Pine marten.

Engraved and Photogravure
1967, Sept. 25   Perf. 11½
1497	A562	30h black, yel & org	.35	.25
1498	A562	60h black & buff	.35	.25
1499	A562	1k black & lt blue	.40	.25
1500	A562	1.20k brn, pale grn & yel	.50	.25
1501	A562	1.40k blk, pink & yel	.55	.25
1502	A562	1.60k black, org & yel	2.75	1.25

Nos. 1497-1502 (6)   4.90   2.50

Rockets and Weapons — A563

1967, Oct. 6   Engr.   Perf. 11½
| 1503 | A563 | 30h slate green | .30 | .25 |

Day of the Czechoslovak People's Army.

Cruiser "Aurora" Firing at Winter Palace — A564

Designs: 60h, Hammer and sickle emblems and Red Star, vert. 1k, Hands reaching for hammer and sickle, vert.

1967, Nov. 7   Engr. & Photo.
1504	A564	30h black & dk car	.25	.25
1505	A564	60h black & dk car	.25	.25
1506	A564	1k black & dk car	.25	.25

Nos. 1504-1506 (3)   .75   .75

Russian October Revolution, 50th anniv.

The Conjurer, by Frantisek Tichy — A565

Paintings: 80h, Don Quixote, by Cyprian Majernik. 1k, Promenade in the Park, by Norbert Grund. 1.20k, Self-portrait, by Peter J. Brandl. 1.60k, Saints from Jan of Jeren Epitaph, by Czech Master of 1395.

1967, Nov. 13   Engr.   Perf. 11½
1507	A565	60h multi	.35	.25
1508	A565	80h multi	.50	.30
1509	A565	1k multi	.75	.50
1510	A565	1.20k multi	.75	.50
1511	A565	1.60k multi	3.25	2.75

Nos. 1507-1511 (5)   5.60   4.30

Nos. 1507-1511 were issued in sheets of 4. Value, set $24.

See Nos. 1589-1593, 1658-1662, 1711-1715, 1779-1783, 1847-1851, 1908-1913, 2043-2047, 2090-2093, 2147-2151, 2265-2269, 2335-2339, 2386-2390, 2437-2441, 2534-2538, 2586-2590, 2634-2638, 2810-2813, 2843-2847, 2872-2874, 2908-2910, 2936-2938, 2973-2975, 2995, 3001-3002, 3028-3030, 3054-3055, 3075-3076, 3105-3107, 3133-3135, 3160-3162, 3188-3190, 3224-3226, 3233, 3255-3257, 3287-3289, 3323-3325, 3359-3361, 3401-3402, 3435-3436, 3478-3480, 3518-3520, 3552-3553, 3591-3593, 3616, 3618, 3656-3658, 3680, 3690-3692, 3726-3727, 3729, 3774-3776, 3794-3795, 3810-3811, 3828-3830, 3851-3852, 3881-3883, 3917-3918, 3927.

Pres. Antonin Novotny — A566

1967, Dec. 9   Engr.   Perf. 11½
| 1512 | A566 | 2k blue gray | 1.40 | .25 |
| 1513 | A566 | 3k brown | 1.40 | .25 |

Czechoslovakia Nos. 65, 71 and 81 of 1920 — A567

1967, Dec. 18
| 1514 | A567 | 1k maroon & silver | 1.60 | 1.10 |

Issued for Stamp Day.

CZECHOSLOVAKIA 51

Symbolic Flag and Dates — A568

1968, Jan. 15   Engr.   Perf. 11½
1515 A568 30h red, dk bl & ultra   .75   .25

50th anniversary of Czechoslovakia.
No. 1515 was issued in a sheet of 10. Value, $30.

Figure Skating and Olympic Rings A569

Olympic Rings and: 1k, Ski course. 1.60k, Toboggan chute. 2k, Ice hockey.

1968, Jan. 29   Engr. & Photo.
1516 A569 60h blk, yel & ocher   .30   .25
1517 A569 1k ol grn, lt bl & lem   .55   .25
1518 A569 1.60k blk, lil & bl grn   .70   .25
1519 A569 2k blk, ap grn & lt bl   1.10   .25
    Nos. 1516-1519 (4)   2.65 1.00

10th Winter Olympic Games, Grenoble, France, Feb. 6-18.

Factories and Rising Sun — A570

Design: 60h, Workers and banner.

1968, Feb. 25   Perf. 11½x12
1520 A570 30h car & dk bl   .25   .25
1521 A570 60h car & dk bl   .25   .25

20th anniversary of February Revolution.

Map of Battle of Sokolovo A571

Human Rights Flame A572

1968, Mar. 8   Perf. 11½
1522 A571 30h blk, brt bl & car   .40   .25
   Engr.
1523 A572 1k rose carmine   1.10   .40

25th anniv. of the Battle of Sokolovo, Mar. 8, 1943, against the German Army, No. 1522; Intl. Human Rights Year, No. 1523.

Janko Kral and Liptovsky Mikulas — A573

Karl Marx A574

Girl's Head A575

Arms and Allegory A576

Head A577

1968, Mar. 25   Engr.
1524 A573 30h green   .30   .25
1525 A574 30h claret   .25   .25
   Engraved and Photogravure
1526 A575 30h dk red & gold   .25   .25
1527 A576 30h dk blue & dp org   .25   .25
1528 A577 1k multicolored   .50   .25
   Nos. 1524-1528 (5)   1.55 1.25

The writer Janko Kral and the Slovak town Liptovsky Mikulas (No. 1524); 150th anniv. of the birth of Karl Marx (No. 1525); cent. of the cornerstone laying of the Prague Natl. Theater (No. 1526); 150th anniv. of the Prague Natl. Museum (No. 1527); 20th anniv. of WHO (1k).

Symbolic Radio Waves — A578

No. 1530, Symbolic television screens.

1968, Apr. 29   Perf. 11½
1529 A578 30h blk, car & vio bl   .25   .25
1530 A578 30h blk, car & vio bl   .25   .25

45th anniv. of Czechoslovak broadcasting (No. 1529), 15th anniv. of television (No. 1530).

Olympic Rings, Mexican Sculpture and Diver — A579

Olympic Rings and: 40h, Runner and "The Sanctification of Quetzalcoatl." 60h, Volleyball and Mexican ornaments. 1k, Czechoslovak and Mexican Olympic emblems and carved altar. 1.60k, Soccer and ornaments. 2k, View of Hradcany, weather vane and key.

1968, Apr. 30
1531 A579 30h black, bl & car   .25   .25
1532 A579 40h multi   .25   .25
1533 A579 60h multi   .25   .25
1534 A579 1k multi   .35   .25
1535 A579 1.60k multi   .35   .25
1536 A579 2k black & multi   1.75   .40
   Nos. 1531-1536 (6)   3.20 1.65

19th Olympic Games, Mexico City, 10/12-27.

Prague Castle Types of 1966

Designs: 30h, Tombstone of Bretislav I. 60h, Romanesque door knocker, St. Wenceslas Chapel. 5k, Head of St. Peter, mosaic from Golden Gate of St. Vitus Cathedral.

1968, May 9   Perf. 11½
1537 A527 30h multicolored   .40   .25
1538 A527 60h black, red & cit   .40   .25
   Souvenir Sheet
   Engr.
1539 A528 5k multicolored   2.75 2.75

Pres. Ludvik Svoboda — A580

1968-70   Engr.   Perf. 11½
1540 A580 30h ultramarine   .25   .25
1540A A580 50h green ('70)   .25   .25
1541 A580 60h maroon   .25   .25
1541A A580 1k rose car ('70)   .25   .25
   Nos. 1540-1541A (4)   1.05 1.00

Shades exist of No. 1541A.

"Business," Sculpture by Otto Gutfreund A581

Cabaret Performer, by Frantisek Kupka A582

Designs (The New Prague): 40h, Broadcasting Corporation Building. 60h, New Parliament. 1.40k, Tapestry by Jan Bauch "Prague 1787." 3k, Presidential standard.

Engr. & Photo.; Engr. (2k)
1968, June 5
1542 A581 30h black & multi   .25   .25
1543 A581 40h black & multi   .25   .25
1544 A581 60h dk brn & multi   .25   .25
1545 A581 1.40k dk brn & multi   .40   .25
1546 A582 2k indigo & multi   .85   .70
1547 A581 3k black & multi   .85   .30
   Nos. 1542-1547 (6)   2.85 2.00

Designs (The Old Prague): 30h, St. George's Basilica. 60h, Renaissance fountain. 1k, Villa America-Dvorak Museum, 18th cent. building. 1.60k, Emblem from the House of Three Violins, 18th cent. 2k, Josefina, by Josef Manes. 3k, Emblem of Prague, 1475.

1968, June 21   Perf. 11½
1548 A581 30h grn, gray & yel   .25   .25
1549 A581 60h dk vio, ap grn & gold   .25   .25
1550 A581 1k blk, lt blu & pink   .30   .25
1551 A581 1.60k slate grn & multi   .55   .25
1552 A582 2k brown & multi   1.25   .60
1553 A581 3k blk, yel, bl & pink   1.25   .60
   Nos. 1548-1553 (6)   3.85 2.20

Nos. 1542-1553 publicized the Praga 68 Philatelic Exhibition. Nos. 1542-1545, 1547-1551, 1553 issued in sheets of 15 + 15 labels with Praga 68 emblem and inscription.
Nos. 1546, 1552 issued in sheets of 4 (2x2) with one horizontal label between top and bottom rows showing Praga 68 emblem. Values for sheets of 4, each $8.

Souvenir Sheet

View of Prague and Emblems — A583

Engraved and Photogravure
1968, June 22   Imperf.
1554 A583 10k multicolored   3.25 2.50

Praga 68 and 50th anniv. of Czechoslovak postage stamps. Sold only together with a 5k admission ticket to the Praga 68 philatelic Exhibition. Value $20.

Madonna with the Rose Garlands, by Dürer — A584

1968, July 6   Perf. 11½
1555 A584 5k multicolored   3.75 2.75

FIP Day, July 6. Issued in sheets of 4 (2x2) with one horizontal label between, showing Praga 68 emblem. Value, $20.

Stagecoach on Rails — A585

Design: 1k, Steam and electric locomotives.

1968, Aug. 6
1556 A585 60h multicolored   .45   .25
1557 A585 1k multicolored   1.60   .60

No. 1556: 140th anniv. of the horse-drawn railroad Ceské Budejovice to Linz; No. 1557: cent. of the Ceské Budejovice to Plzen railroad.

6th Intl. Slavonic Cong. in Prague — A586

1968, Aug. 7   Perf. 11½
1558 A586 30h vio blue & car   .40   .25

Ardspach Rocks and Ammonite A587

60h, Basalt formation & frog skeleton fossil. 80h, Rocks, basalt veins & polished agate. 1k, Pelecypoda (fossil shell) & Belanske Tatra mountains. 1.60k, Trilobite & Barrande rock formation.

1968, Aug. 8
1559 A587 30h black & citron   .25   .25
1560 A587 60h black & rose cl   .25   .25
1561 A587 80h blk, lt vio & pink   .30   .25
1562 A587 1k black & lt blue   .40   .25
1563 A587 1.60k black & bister   1.40   .65
   Nos. 1559-1563 (5)   2.60 1.65

Issued to publicize the 23rd International Geological Congress, Prague, Aug. 8-Sept. 3.

Raising Slovak Flag A588

60h, Slovak partisans, and mountain.

1968, Sept. 9   Engr.   Perf. 11½
1564 A588 30h ultra   .25   .25
1565 A588 60h red   .25   .25

No. 1564 for the Slovak Natl. Council, No. 1565 the 120th anniv. of the Slovak national uprising.

Flowerpot, by Jiri Schlessinger (age 10) — A589

Drawings by Children in Terezin Concentration Camp: 30h, Jew and Guard, by Jiri Beutler (age 10). 60h, Butterflies, by Kitty Brunnerova (age 11).

CZECHOSLOVAKIA

Engraved and Photogravure
1968, Sept. 30   **Perf. 11½**
Size: 30x23mm
| 1566 | A589 | 30h blk, buff & rose lil | .30 | .25 |
| 1567 | A589 | 60h black & multi | .30 | .25 |

Perf. 12x11½
Size: 41x23mm
| 1568 | A589 | 1k black & multi | .80 | .25 |

Nos. 1566-1568 (3)   1.40   .75

30th anniversary of Munich Pact.

Arms of Regional Capitals A590

Arms of Prague A591

1968, Oct. 21   **Perf. 11½**
1569	A590	60h Banská Bystrica	.25	.25
1570	A590	60h Bratislava	.25	.25
1571	A590	60h Brno	.25	.25
1572	A590	60h Ceské Budejovice	.25	.25
1573	A590	60h Hradec Králové	.25	.25
1574	A590	60h Kosice	.25	.25
1575	A590	60h Ostrava (horse)	.25	.25
1576	A590	60h Plzen	.25	.25
1577	A590	60h Ustí nad Labem	.25	.25

Perf. 11½x16
| 1578 | A591 | 1k shown | .25 | .25 |

Nos. 1569-1578 (10)   2.50   2.50

No. 1578 issued in sheets of 10. Value, $40.
See Nos. 1652-1657, 1742-1747, 1886-1888, 2000-2001.

Flag and Linden Leaves — A592

Bohemian Lion Breaking Chains (Type SP1 of 1919) — A593

Design: 60h, Map of Czechoslovakia, linden leaves, Hradcany in Prague and Castle in Bratislava.

1968, Oct. 28   **Perf. 12x11½**
| 1579 | A592 | 30h dp blue & mag | .30 | .25 |
| 1580 | A592 | 60h blk, gold, red & ultra | .30 | .25 |

Souvenir Sheet
Engr.
Perf. 11½x12
| 1581 | A593 | 5k red | 3.50 | 2.75 |

Founding of Czechoslovakia, 50th anniv.

Ernest Hemingway — A594

Caricatures: 30h, Karel Capek (1890-1938), writer. 40h, George Bernard Shaw. 60h, Maxim Gorki. 1k, Pablo Picasso. 1.20k, Taikan Yokoyama (1868-1958), painter. 1.40k, Charlie Chaplin.

Engraved and Photogravure
1968, Nov. 18   **Perf. 11½x12**
1582	A594	20h black, org & red	.25	.25
1583	A594	30h black & multi	.25	.25
1584	A594	40h blk, lic & car	.30	.25
1585	A594	60h black, sky bl & grn	.25	.25
1586	A594	1k black, brn & yel	.45	.25
1587	A594	1.20k black, dp car & vio	.45	.25
1588	A594	1.40k black, brn & dp org	1.75	.40

Nos. 1582-1588 (7)   3.75   1.90

Cultural personalities of the 20th cent. and UNESCO. See Nos. 1628-1633.

Painting Type of 1967
Czechoslovakian Art: 60h, Cleopatra II, by Jan Zrzavy (1890-1977). 80h, Black Lake (man and horse), by Jan Preisler (1872-1918). 1.20k, Giovanni Francisci as a Volunteer, by Peter Michal Bohun (1822-1879). 1.60k, Princess Hyacinth, by Alfons Mucha (1860-1939). 3k, Madonna and Child, woodcarving, 1518, by Master Paul of Levoca.

1968, Nov. 29   **Engr.**   **Perf. 11½**
1589	A565	60h multi	.75	.35
1590	A565	80h multi	.75	.35
1591	A565	1.20k multi	.75	.35
1592	A565	1.60k multi	.75	.35
1593	A565	3k multi	2.50	2.50

Nos. 1589-1593 (5)   5.50   3.90

Nos. 1589-1593 were issued in sheets of 4. Value, set $25.

Cinderlad — A595

Slovak Fairy Tales: 60h, The Proud Lady. 80h, The Ruling Knight. 1k, Good Day, Little Bench. 1.20k, The Spellbound Castle. 1.80k, The Miraculous Hunter. The designs are from illustrations by Ludovit Fulla for "Slovak Stories."

1968, Dec. 18   **Engr. & Photo.**
1594	A595	30h multi	.25	.25
1595	A595	60h multi	.25	.25
1596	A595	80h multi	.40	.25
1597	A595	1k multi	.55	.25
1598	A595	1.20k multi	.55	.25
1599	A595	1.80k multi	1.50	.65

Nos. 1594-1599 (6)   3.50   1.90

Czechoslovakia Nos. 2 and 3 — A596

1968, Dec. 18
| 1600 | A596 | 1k violet bl & gold | .95 | .65 |

50th anniv. of Czechoslovakian postage stamps.

Crescent, Cross and Lion and Sun Emblems — A597

60h, 12 crosses in circles forming large cross.

1969, Jan. 31   **Perf. 11½**
| 1601 | A597 | 60h black, red & gold | .25 | .25 |
| 1602 | A597 | 1k black, ultra & red | .35 | .25 |

No. 1601: 50th anniv. of the Czechoslovak Red Cross. No. 1602: 50th anniv. of the League of Red Cross Societies.

ILO Emblem — A598

1969, Jan. 31
| 1603 | A598 | 1k black & gray | .30 | .25 |

50th anniv. of the ILO.

Cheb Pistol — A599

Historical Firearms: 40h, Italian pistol with Dutch decorations, c. 1600. 60h, Wheellock rifle from Matej Kubik workshop c. 1720. 1k, Flintlock pistol, Devieuxe workshop, Liege, c. 1760. 1.40k, Duelling pistols, from Lebeda workshop, Prague, c. 1835. 1.60k, Derringer pistols, US, c. 1865.

1969, Feb. 18
1604	A599	30h black & multi	.25	.25
1605	A599	40h black & multi	.25	.25
1606	A599	60h black & multi	.25	.25
1607	A599	1k black & multi	.25	.25
1608	A599	1.40k black & multi	.35	.25
1609	A599	1.60k black & multi	1.40	.25

Nos. 1604-1609 (6)   2.75   1.50

Bratislava Castle, Muse and Book A600

No. 1611, Science symbols & emblem (Brno University). No. 1612, Harp, laurel & musicians' names. No. 1613, Theatrical scene. No. 1614, Arms of Slovakia, banner & blossoms. No. 1615, School, outstretched hands & woman with linden leaves.

1969, Mar. 24   **Engr.**   **Perf. 11½**
| 1610 | A600 | 60h violet blue | .25 | .25 |

Engraved and Photogravure
1611	A600	60h blk, gold & slate	.25	.25
1612	A600	60h gold, blue, blk & red	.25	.25
1613	A600	60h black & rose red	.25	.25
1614	A600	60h rose red, sil & bl	.25	.25
1615	A600	60h black & gold	.25	.25

Nos. 1610-1615 (6)   1.50   1.50

50th anniv. of: Komensky University in Bratislava (No. 1610); Brno University (No. 1611); Brno Conservatory of Music (No. 1612); Slovak Natl. Theater (No. 1613); Slovak Soviet Republic (No. 1614); cent. of the Zniev Gymnasium (academic high school) (No. 1615).

Baldachin-top Car and Four-seat Coupé of 1900-1905 — A601

Designs: 1.60k, Laurin & Klement Voiturette, 1907, and L & K touring car with American top, 1907. 1.80k, First Prague bus, 1907, and sectionalized Skoda bus, 1967.

1969, Mar. 25   **Engr. & Photo.**
1616	A601	30h blk, lil & lt grn	.60	.25
1617	A601	1.60k blk, org brn & lt bl	.75	.25
1618	A601	1.80k multi	1.40	.60

Nos. 1616-1618 (3)   2.75   1.10

Peace, by Ladislav Guderna A602

1969, Apr. 21   **Perf. 11**
| 1619 | A602 | 1.60k multi | .50 | .35 |

20th anniv. of the Peace Movement. Issued in sheets of 15 stamps and 5 tabs. Stamp with tab $2.50.

Horse and Rider, by Vaclav Hollar — A603

Old Engravings of Horses: 30h, Prancing Stallion, by Hendrik Goltzius, horiz. 80h, Groom Leading Horse, by Matthäus Merian, horiz. 1.80k, Horse and Soldier, by Albrecht Dürer. 2.40k, Groom and Horse, by Johann E. Ridinger.

1969, Apr. 24   **Perf. 11x11½, 11½x11**
Yellowish Paper
1620	A603	30h dark brown	.25	.25
1621	A603	80h violet brown	.25	.25
1622	A603	1.80k slate	.45	.25
1623	A603	1.80k sepia	.50	.25
1624	A603	2.40k multi	2.40	.60

Nos. 1620-1624 (5)   3.85   1.60

M. R. Stefánik as Astronomy Professor and French General A604

1969, May 4   **Engr.**   **Perf. 11½**
| 1625 | A604 | 60h rose claret | .40 | .25 |

Gen. Milan R. Stefánik, 50th death anniv.

St. Wenceslas Pressing Wine, Mural by the Master of Litomerice A605

Design: No. 1627, Coronation banner of the Estates, 1723, with St. Wenceslas and coats of arms of Bohemia and Czech Crown lands.

1969, May 9   **Engr.**   **Perf. 11½**
| 1626 | A605 | 3k multicolored | 2.00 | 1.40 |
| 1627 | A605 | 3k multicolored | 2.00 | 1.40 |

Issued to publicize the art treasures of the Castle of Prague.
Issued in sheets of 4. Value, set $20.
See Nos. 1689-1690.

Caricature Type of 1968
Caricatures: 30h, Pavol Orszagh Hviezdoslav (1849-1921), Slovak writer. 40h, Gilbert K. Chesterton (1874-1936), English writer. 60h, Vladimir Mayakovski (1893-1930), Russian poet. 1k, Henri Matisse (1869-1954), French painter. 1.80k, Ales Hrdlicka (1869-1943), Czech-born American anthropologist. 2k, Franz Kafka (1883-1924), Austrian writer.

Engraved and Photogravure
1969, June 17   **Perf. 11½x12**
1628	A594	30h blk, red & bl	.25	.25
1629	A594	40h blk, bl & lt vio	.25	.25
1630	A594	60h blk, rose & yel	.25	.25
1631	A594	1k black & multi	.25	.25
1632	A594	1.80k blk, ultra & ocher	.25	.25
1633	A594	2k blk, yel & brt grn	1.50	.50

Nos. 1628-1633 (6)   2.75   1.75

Issued to honor cultural personalities of the 20th century and UNESCO.

"Music," by Alfons Mucha — A606

Paintings by Mucha: 60h, "Painting." 1k, "Dance." 2.40k, "Ruby" and "Amethyst."

CZECHOSLOVAKIA

1969, July 14   **Perf. 11½x11**
     Size: 30x49mm
1634	A606	30h black & multi	.80	.25
1635	A606	60h black & multi	.80	.25
1636	A606	1k black & multi	1.00	.25

     Size: 39x51mm
| 1637 | A606 | 2.40k black & multi | 2.00 | 1.25 |
| | | Nos. 1634-1637 (4) | 4.60 | 2.00 |

Alfons Mucha (1860-1930), painter and stamp designer (Type A1).
No. 1637 was issued in sheets of 4. Value $12.50.

Pres. Svoboda and Partisans — A607

No. 1639, Slovak fighters and mourners.

1969, Aug. 29   **Perf. 11**
| 1638 | A607 | 30h ol grn & red, yel | .25 | .25 |
| 1639 | A607 | 30h vio bl & red, yel | .25 | .25 |

25th anniversary of the Slovak uprising and of the Battle of Dukla.

Tatra Mountain Stream and Gentians — A608

Designs: 60h, Various views in Tatra Mountains. No. 1644, Mountain pass and gentians. No. 1645, Houses, Krivan Mountain and autumn crocuses.

1969, Sept. 8   **Engr.**   **Perf. 11**
     Size: 71x33mm
1640	A608	60h gray	.25	.25
1641	A608	60h dark blue	.25	.25
1642	A608	60h dull gray vio	.25	.25

     Perf. 11½
     Size: 40x23mm
1643	A608	1.60k multi	.55	.25
1644	A608	1.60k multi	1.25	.50
1645	A608	1.60k multi	.55	.25
		Nos. 1640-1645 (6)	3.10	1.75

20th anniv. of the creation of the Tatra Mountains Natl. Park.
Nos. 1640-1642 are printed in sheets of 15 (3x5) with 5 labels showing mountain plants. Value, set with tabs $2.50.
Nos. 1643-1645 were issued in sheets of 10. Value, $70.

Bronze Belt Ornaments — A609

Archaeological Treasures from Bohemia and Moravia: 30h, Gilt ornament with 6 masks. 1.60k, Jeweled earrings. 1.80k, Front and back of lead cross with Greek inscription. 2k, Gilt strap ornament with human figure.

Engraved and Photogravure
1969, Sept. 30   **Perf. 11½x11**
1646	A609	20h gold & multi	.25	.25
1647	A609	30h gold & multi	.25	.25
1648	A609	1k red & multi	.25	.25
1649	A609	1.80k dull org & multi	.45	.25
1650	A609	2k gold & multi	1.75	.25
		Nos. 1646-1650 (5)	2.95	1.25

"Mail Circling the World" — A610

1969, Oct. 1   **Engr.**   **Perf. 12**
| 1651 | A610 | 3.20k multi | .95 | .60 |

16th UPU Cong., Tokyo, Oct. 1-Nov. 14. Issued in sheets of 4. Value $9.

Coat of Arms Type of 1968
Engraved and Photogravure
1969, Oct. 25   **Perf. 11½**
1652	A590	50h Bardejov	.25	.25
1653	A590	50h Hranice	.25	.25
1654	A590	50h Kezmarok	.25	.25
1655	A590	50h Krnov	.25	.25
1656	A590	50h Litomerice	.25	.25
1657	A590	50h Manetin	.25	.25
		Nos. 1652-1657 (6)	1.50	1.50

Painting Type of 1967

Designs: 60h, Requiem, 1944, by Frantisek Muzika. 1k, Resurrection, 1380, by the Master of the Trebon Altar. 1.60k, Crucifixion, 1950, by Vincent Hloznik. 1.80k, Girl with Doll, 1863, by Julius Bencur. 2.20k, St. Jerome, 1357-67, by Master Theodorik.

1969, Nov. 25   **Perf. 11½**
1658	A565	60h multi	.75	.25
1659	A565	1k multi	.75	.25
1660	A565	1.60k multi	.75	.40
1661	A565	1.80k multi	.75	.40
1662	A565	2.20k multi	3.00	2.00
		Nos. 1658-1662 (5)	6.00	3.30

Nos. 1658-1662 were each issued in sheets of 4. Value, set $30.

Symbolic Sheet of Stamps A611

1969, Dec. 18   **Perf. 11½x12**
| 1663 | A611 | 1k dk brn, ultra & gold | .30 | .30 |

Issued for Stamp Day 1969.

Ski Jump A612

Designs: 60h, Long distance skier. 1k, Ski jump and slope. 1.60k, Woman skier.

1970, Jan. 6   **Perf. 11½**
1664	A612	50h multi	.25	.25
1665	A612	60h multi	.25	.25
1666	A612	1k multi	.25	.25
1667	A612	1.60k multi	.60	.30
		Nos. 1664-1667 (4)	1.35	1.05

Intl. Ski Championships "Tatra 1970."

Ludwig van Beethoven — A613

Portraits: No. 1669, Friedrich Engels (1820-95), German socialist. No. 1670, Maximilian Hell (1720-92), Slovakian Jesuit and astronomer. No. 1671, Lenin, Russian Communist leader. No. 1672, Josef Manes (1820-71), Czech painter. No. 1673, Comenius (1592-1670), theologian and educator.

1970, Feb. 17   **Engr.**   **Perf. 11x11½**
1668	A613	40h black	.25	.25
1669	A613	40h dull red	.25	.25
1670	A613	40h yellow brn	.25	.25
1671	A613	40h dull red	.25	.25
1672	A613	40h brown	.25	.25
1673	A613	40h black	.25	.25
		Nos. 1668-1673 (6)	1.50	1.50

Anniversaries of birth of Beethoven, Engels, Hell, Lenin and Manes, 300th anniv. of the death of Comenius, and to honor UNESCO.

Bells — A614

80h, Machine tools & lathe. 1k, Folklore masks. 1.60k, Angel & Three Wise Men, 17th cent. icon from Koniec. 2k, View of Orlik Castle, 1787, by F. K. Wolf. 3k, "Passing through Koshu down to Mishima" from Hokusai's 36 Views of Fuji.

Engraved and Photogravure
1970, Mar. 13   **Perf. 11½x11**
     Size: 40x23mm
1674	A614	50h multi	.25	.25
1675	A614	80h multi	.25	.25
1676	A614	1k multi	.25	.25

     Size: 50x40mm
     Perf. 11½
1677	A614	1.60k multi	.35	.30
1678	A614	2k multi	.45	.25
1679	A614	3k multi	2.10	.70
		Nos. 1674-1679 (6)	3.65	2.00

EXPO '70 Intl. Exhib., Osaka, Japan, Mar. 15-Sept. 13, 1970.
Nos. 1674-1676 issued in sheets of 50, Nos. 1677-1679 in sheets of 4. Value, set of 3 sheets, $18.

Kosice Townhall, Laurel and Czechoslovak Arms — A615

1970, Apr. 5   **Perf. 11**
| 1680 | A615 | 60h slate, vor & gold | .40 | .25 |

Government's Kosice Program, 25th anniv.

"The Remarkable Horse" by Josef Lada — A616

Paintings by Josef Lada: 60h, Autumn, 1955, horiz. 1.80k, "The Water Sprite." 2.40k, Children in Winter, 1943, horiz.

1970, Apr. 21   **Perf. 11½**
1681	A616	60h black & multi	.30	.25
1682	A616	1k black & multi	.45	.25
1683	A616	1.80k black & multi	.75	.25
1684	A616	2.40k black & multi	1.50	.25
		Nos. 1681-1684 (4)	3.00	1.00

Lenin A617

Design: 60h, Lenin without cap, facing left.

1970, Apr. 22
| 1685 | A617 | 30h dk red & gold | .25 | .25 |
| 1686 | A617 | 60h black & gold | .25 | .25 |

Lenin (1870-1924), Russian communist leader.

Fighters on the Barricades A618

No. 1688, Lilac, Russian tank and castle.

1970, May 5   **Perf. 11x11½**
| 1687 | A618 | 30h dull pur, gold & bl | .25 | .25 |
| 1688 | A618 | 30h dull grn, gold & red | .25 | .25 |

No. 1687: 25th anniv. of the Prague uprising. No. 1688: 25th anniv. of the liberation of Czechoslovakia from the Germans.

Prague Castle Art Type of 1969

No. 1689, Bust of St. Vitus, 1486. No. 1690, Hermes and Athena, by Bartholomy Spranger (1546-1611), mural from White Tower.

1970, May 7   **Engr.**   **Perf. 11½**
| 1689 | A605 | 3k maroon & multi | 1.90 | 1.25 |
| 1690 | A605 | 3k lt blue & multi | 1.75 | 1.00 |

Nos. 1689-1690 were issued in sheets of 4. Value, set of 2 sheets, $18.

Compass Rose, UN Headquarters and Famous Buildings of the World — A619

Engraved and Photogravure
1970, June 26   **Perf. 11**
| 1691 | A619 | 1k black & multi | .40 | .25 |

25th anniv. of the UN. Issued in sheets of 15 (3x5) and 5 labels showing UN emblem. Value of single with tab attached: unused $1; used 75c.

Cannon from 30 Years' War and Baron Munchhausen — A620

Historical Cannons: 60h, Cannon from Hussite war and St. Barbara. 1.20k, Cannon from Prussian-Austrian war, and legendary cannoneer Javurek. 1.80k, Early 20th century cannon and spaceship "La Colombiad" (Jules Verne). 2.40k, World War I cannon and "Good Soldier Schweik."

1970, Aug. 31   **Perf. 11½**
1692	A620	30h black & multi	.25	.25
1693	A620	60h black & multi	.25	.25
1694	A620	1.20k black & multi	.25	.25
1695	A620	1.80k black & multi	.25	.25
1696	A620	2.40k black & multi	1.25	.25
		Nos. 1692-1696 (5)	2.25	1.25

"Rude Pravo" (Red Truth) — A621

1970, Sept. 21   **Perf. 11½x11**
| 1697 | A621 | 60h car, gold & blk | .25 | .25 |

50th anniv. of the Rude Pravo newspaper.

"Great Sun" House Sign and Old Town Tower Bridge, Prague — A622

60h, "Blue Lion" & Town Hall Tower, Brno. 1k, Gothic corner stone & Town Hall Tower, Bratislava. 1.40k, Coat of Arms & Gothic Tower, Bratislava, & medallion. 1.60k, Moravian Eagle & Gothic Town Hall Tower, Brno. 1.80k, "Black Sun" & "Green Frog" house signs & New Town Hall, Prague.

1970, Sept. 23   **Perf. 11x11½**
1698	A622	40h black & multi	.25	.25
1699	A622	60h black & multi	.25	.25
1700	A622	1k black & multi	.25	.25
1701	A622	1.40k black & multi	1.40	.25
1702	A622	1.60k black & multi	.90	.25
1703	A622	1.80k black & multi	.80	.25
		Nos. 1698-1703 (6)	3.25	1.50

Germany-Uruguay Semifinal Soccer Match — A623

Designs: 20h, Sundisk Games' emblem and flags of participating nations. 60h, England-Czechoslovakia match and coats of arms. 1k, Romania-Czechoslovakia match and coats of arms. 1.20k, Brazil-Italy, final match and emblems. 1.80k, Brazil-Czechoslovakia match and emblems.

CZECHOSLOVAKIA

1970, Oct. 29		Perf. 11½
1704	A623 20h blk & multi	.25 .25
1705	A623 40h blk & multi	.25 .25
1706	A623 60h blk & multi	.30 .25
1707	A623 1k blk & multi	.45 .25
1708	A623 1.20k blk & multi	.45 .25
1709	A623 1.80k blk & multi	1.50 .25
	Nos. 1704-1709 (6)	3.20 1.50

9th World Soccer Championships for the Jules Rimet Cup, Mexico City, 5/30-6/21.

Congress Emblem — A624

1970, Nov. 9	Engr. & Photo.
1710	A624 30h blk, gold, ultra & red .25 .25

Congress of the Czechoslovak Socialist Youth Federation.

Painting Type of 1967

Paintings: 1k, Seated Mother, by Mikulas Galanda. 1.20k, Bridesmaid, by Karel Svolinsky. 1.40k, Walk by Night, 1944, by Frantisek Hudecek. 1.80k, Banska Bystrica Market, by Dominik Skutecky. 2.40k, Adoration of the Kings, from the Vysehrad Codex, 1085.

1970, Nov. 27	Engr.	Perf. 11½
1711	A565 1k multi	.35 .25
1712	A565 1.20k multi	.70 .30
1713	A565 1.40k multi	.35 .30
1714	A565 1.80k multi	.70 .30
1715	A565 2.40k multi	3.00 2.00
	Nos. 1711-1715 (5)	5.10 3.15

Nos. 1711-1715 were each issued in sheets of 4. Value, set $20.

Radar — A625

Designs: 40h, Interkosmos 3, geophysical satellite. 60h, Kosmos meteorological satellite. 1k, Astronaut and Vostok satellite. No. 1720, Interkosmos 4, solar research satellite. No. 1720A, Space satellite (Sputnik) over city. 1.60k, Two-stage rocket on launching pad.

1970-71	Engr. & Photo.	Perf. 11
1716	A625 20h black & multi	.25 .25
1717	A625 40h black & multi	.25 .25
1718	A625 60h black & multi	.25 .25
1719	A625 1k black & multi	.25 .25
1720	A625 1.20k black & multi	.25 .25
1720A	A625 1.20k black & multi ('71)	.25 .25
1721	A625 1.60k black & multi	.90 .25
	Nos. 1716-1721 (7)	2.40 1.75

"Interkosmos," the collaboration of communist countries in various phases of space research.
Issued: No. 1720A, 11/15/71; others, 11/30/70.

Face of Christ on Veronica's Veil A626

Slovak Ikons, 16th-18th Centuries: 60h, Adam and Eve in the Garden, vert. 2k, St. George and the Dragon. 2.80k, St. Michael, vert.

1970, Dec. 17	Engr.	Perf. 11½
	Cream Paper	
1722	A626 60h multi	.70 .35
1723	A626 1k multi	1.00 .35
1724	A626 2k multi	1.00 .70
1725	A626 2.80k multi	2.10 1.40
	Nos. 1722-1725 (4)	4.80 2.80

Nos. 1722-1725 were each issued in sheets of 4. Value, set $22.50.

Carrier Pigeon Type of 1920

Engraved and Photogravure

1970, Dec. 18		Perf. 11x11½
1726	A627 1k red, blk & yel grn	.40 .30

Stamp Day.

Song of the Barricades, 1938, by Karel Stika — A628

Czech and Slovak Graphic Art: 50h, Fruit Grower's Barge, 1941, by Cyril Bouda. 60h, Moon (woman) Searching for Lilies of the Valley, 1913, by Jan Zrzavy. 1k, At the Edge of Town (working man and woman), 1931, by Koloman Sokol. 1.60k, Summer, 1641, by Vaclav Hollar. 2k, Gamekeeper and Shepherd of Orava Castle, 1847, by Peter M. Bohun.

	Engr. & Photo.; Engr. (40h, 60h, 1k)	
1971, Jan. 28		Perf. 11½
1727	A628 40h brown	.25 .25
1728	A628 50h black & multi	.25 .25
1729	A628 60h slate	.25 .25
1730	A628 1k black	.30 .25
1731	A628 1.60k black & buff	.30 .25
1732	A628 2k black & multi	1.25 .25
	Nos. 1727-1732 (6)	2.60 1.50

Church of St. Bartholomew, Chrudim A629

Bell Tower, Hronsek A630

Designs: 1k, Roofs and folk art, Horácko. 1.60k, Saris Church. 2.40k, House, Jicin. 3k, House and folk art, Melnik. 5k, Watch Tower, Nachod. 5.40k, Baroque house, Posumavi. 6k, Cottage, Orava. 9k, Cottage, Turnov. 10k, Old houses, Liptov. 14k, House and wayside bell stand. 20k, Houses, Cicmany.

Engraved and Photogravure

1971-72	Perf. 11½x11, 11x11½
1733	A630 1k multi .25 .25
1734	A629 1.60k multi 1.50 .25
1735	A630 2k multi 2.10 .25
1736	A629 2.40k multi 1.10 .25
1736A	A630 3k multi ('72) 2.10 .25
1737	A629 3.60k multi 1.40 .25
1737A	A630 5k multi ('72) 2.10 .25
1738	A629 5.40k multi .75 .25
1739	A630 6k multi 3.50 .25
1740	A630 9k multi 1.40 .25
1740A	A629 10k multi ('72) 2.10 .25
1741	A629 14k multi 2.25 .25
1741A	A629 20k multi ('72) 2.10 .25
	Nos. 1733-1741A (13) 22.65 3.30

Nos. 1736A, 1738, 1740 are horizontal.
See No. 2870.

Coat of Arms Type of 1968

1971, Mar. 26		Perf. 11½
1742	A590 60h Zilina	.25 .25
1743	A590 60h Levoca	.25 .25
1744	A590 60h Ceska Trebova	.25 .25
1745	A590 60h Uhersky Brod	.25 .25
1746	A590 60h Trutnov	.25 .25
1747	A590 60h Karlovy Vary	.25 .25
	Nos. 1742-1747 (6)	1.50 1.50

"Fight of the Communards and Rise of the International" — A631

Design: No. 1749, World fight against racial discrimination, and "UNESCO."

1971, Mar. 18		Perf. 11
1748	A631 1k multicolored	.30 .25
1749	A631 1k multicolored	.30 .25

No. 1748 for cent. of the Paris Commune. No. 1749 for the Year against Racial Discrimination. Issued in sheets of 15 stamps and 5 labels. Value for single with attached tab, each $1.

A632

Edelweiss, mountaineering map & equipment.

1971, Apr. 27		Perf. 11½x11
1750	A632 30h multicolored	.25 .25

50th anniversary of Slovak Alpine Club.

A633

1971, Apr. 27		Perf. 11
1751	A633 30h Singer	.25 .25

50th anniversary of Slovak Teachers' Choir.

Abbess' Crosier, 16th Century A634

No. 1753, Allegory of Music, 16th cent. mural.

1971, May 9		
1752	A634 3k gold & multi	1.90 1.40
1753	A634 3k blk, dk brn & buff	1.90 1.40

Nos. 1752-1753 were each issued in sheets of 4. Value, set $15.
See Nos. 1817-1818, 1884-1885, 1937-1938, 2040-2041, 2081-2082, 2114-2115, 2176-2177, 2238-2239, 2329-2330, 2384-2385, 2420-2421.

Lenin — A635

40h, Hammer & sickle allegory. 60h, Raised fists. 1k, Star, hammer & sickle.

1971, May 14		Perf. 11
1754	A635 30h blk, red & gold	.25 .25
1755	A635 40h blk, ultra, red & gold	.25 .25
1756	A635 60h blk, ultra, red & gold	.25 .25
1757	A635 1k blk, ultra, red & gold	.30 .25
	Nos. 1754-1757 (4)	1.05 1.00

Czechoslovak Communist Party, 50th anniv.

Star, Hammer-Sickle Emblems A636

60h, Hammer-sickle emblem, fist & people, vert.

	Perf. 11½x11, 11x11½
1971, May 24	Engr. & Photo.
1758	A636 30h blk, red, gold & yel .25 .25
1759	A636 60h blk, red, gold & bl .25 .25

14th Congress of Communist Party of Czechoslovakia.

Ring-necked Pheasant A637

Designs: 60h, Rainbow trout. 80h, Mouflon. 1k, Chamois. 2k, Stag. 2.60k, Wild boar.

1971, Aug. 17		Perf. 11½x11
1760	A637 20h orange & multi	.25 .25
1761	A637 60h lt blue & multi	.25 .25
1762	A637 80h yellow & multi	.25 .25
1763	A637 1k lt green & multi	.30 .25
1764	A637 2k lilac & multi	.40 .25
1765	A637 2.60k bister & multi	2.25 .65
	Nos. 1760-1765 (6)	3.70 1.90

World Hunting Exhib., Budapest, Aug. 27-30.

Diesel Locomotive — A638

1971, Sept. 2		Perf. 11x11½
1766	A638 30h lt bl, blk & red	.40 .25

Cent. of CKD, Prague Machine Foundry.

Gymnasts and Banners — A639

1971, Sept. 2		Perf. 11½x11
1767	A639 30h red brn, gold & ultra	.25 .25

50th anniversary of Workers' Physical Exercise Federation.

Road Intersections and Bridge — A640

1971, Sept. 2		Engr. & Photo.
1768	A640 1k blk, gold, red & bl	.30 .25

14th World Highways and Bridges Congress. Sheets of 25 stamps and 25 labels printed se-tenant with continuous design. Value, single with attached tab, unused 60c; used 30c.

Chinese Fairytale, by Eva Bednarova — A641

Designs: 1k, Tiger and other animals, by Mirko Hanak. 1.60k, The Miraculous Bamboo Shoot, by Yasuo Segawa, horiz.

	Perf. 11½x11, 11x11½
1971, Sept. 10	
1769	A641 60h multi .25 .25
1770	A641 1k multi .30 .25
1771	A641 1.60k multi .45 .25
	Nos. 1769-1771 (3) 1.00 .75

Bratislava BIB 71 biennial exhibition of illustrations for children's books.

Apothecary Jars and Coltsfoot A642

CZECHOSLOVAKIA 55

Intl. Pharmaceutical Cong.: 60h, Jars and dog rose. 1k, Scales and adonis vernalis. 1.20k, Mortars and valerian. 1.80k, Retorts and chicory. 2.40k, Mill, mortar and henbane.

1971, Sept. 20   *Perf. 11½x11*
Yellow Paper

1772	A642	30h multi	.25	.25
1773	A642	60h multi	.25	.25
1774	A642	1k multi	.25	.25
1775	A642	1.20k multi	.25	.25
1776	A642	1.80k multi	.25	.25
1777	A642	2.40k multi	1.25	.25
		Nos. 1772-1777 (6)	2.50	1.50

Painting Type of 1967

Paintings: 1k, "Waiting" (woman's head), 1967, by Imro Weiner-Král. 1.20k, Resurrection, by Master of Vyssi Brod, 14th century. 1.40k, Woman with Pitcher, by Milos Bazovsky. 1.80k, Veruna Cudova (in folk costume), by Josef Mánes. 2.40k, Detail from "Feast of the Rose Garlands," by Albrecht Dürer.

1971, Nov. 27   *Perf. 11½*

1779	A565	1k multi	.30	.30
1780	A565	1.20k multi	.75	.45
1781	A565	1.40k multi	.60	.30
1782	A565	1.80k multi	1.10	.50
1783	A565	2.40k multi	1.75	.75
		Nos. 1779-1783 (5)	4.50	2.30

Nos. 1779-1783 were each issued in sheets of 4. Value, set $25.

Workers Revolt in Krompachy, by Julius Nemcik — A643

1971, Nov. 28   *Perf. 11x11½*
1784   A643   60h multi   .30   .25

History of the Czechoslovak Communist Party.

Wooden Dolls and Birds — A644

Folk Art and UNICEF Emblem: 80h, Jug handles, carved. 1k, Horseback rider. 1.60k, Shepherd carrying lamb. 2k, Easter eggs and rattle. 3k, "Zbojnik," folk hero.

1971, Dec. 11   *Perf. 11½*

1785	A644	60h multi	.40	.25
1786	A644	80h multi	.80	.25
1787	A644	1k multi	.40	.25
1788	A644	1.60k multi	.40	.25
1789	A644	2k multi	.40	.30
1790	A644	3k multi	2.00	.60
		Nos. 1785-1790 (6)	4.40	1.90

25th anniv. of UNICEF.
Nos. 1785-1790 were each issued in sheets of 10. Value, set $45.

Runners, Parthenon, Czechoslovak Olympic Emblem — A645

Designs: 40h, Women's high jump, Olympic emblem and plan for Prague Stadium. 1.60k, Cross-country skiers, Sapporo '72 emblem and ski jump in High Tatras. 2.60k, Discus thrower, Discobolus and St. Vitus Cathedral.

1971, Dec. 16   *Engr. & Photo.*

1791	A645	30h multi	.25	.25
1792	A645	40h multi	.25	.25
1793	A645	1.60k multi	.25	.25
1794	A645	2.60k multi	1.50	.75
		Nos. 1791-1794 (4)	2.25	1.50

75th anniversary of Czechoslovak Olympic Committee (30h, 2.60k); 20th Summer Olympic Games, Munich, Aug. 26-Sept. 10, 1972 (40h); 11th Winter Olympic Games, Sapporo, Japan, Feb. 3-13, 1972 (1.60k).

Post Horns and Lion — A646

1971, Dec. 17   *Perf. 11x11½*
1795   A646   1k blk, gold, car & bl   .30   .25

Stamp Day.

Figure Skating — A647

Olympic Emblems and: 50h, Ski jump. 1k, Ice hockey. 1.60k, Sledding, women's.

1972, Jan. 13   *Perf. 11½*

1796	A647	40h pur, org & red	.25	.25
1797	A647	50h dk bl, org & red	.25	.25
1798	A647	1k mag, org & red	.30	.25
1799	A647	1.60k bl grn, org & red	1.25	.25
		Nos. 1796-1799 (4)	2.05	1.00

11th Winter Olympic Games, Sapporo, Japan, Feb. 3-13.

"Lezáky" — A648

No. 1801, Boy's head behind barbed wire, horiz. No. 1802, Hand rising from ruins. No. 1803, Soldier and banner, horiz.

1972, Feb. 16

1800	A648	30h blk, dl org & red	.25	.25
1801	A648	30h blk & brn org	.25	.25
1802	A648	60h blk, yel & red	.25	.25
1803	A648	60h sl grn & multi	.25	.25
		Nos. 1800-1803 (4)	1.00	1.00

30th anniv. of: destruction of Lezáky (No. 1800) and Lidice (No. 1802); Terezin concentration camp (No. 1801); Czechoslovak Army unit in Russia (No. 1803).

Book Year Emblem — A649

1972, Mar. 17   *Perf. 11½x11*
1804   A649   1k blk & org brn   .30   .25

International Book Year 1972.

Steam and Diesel Locomotives — A650

1972, Mar. 17   *Perf. 11½x11*
1805   A650   30h multi   .75   .25

Centenary of the Kosice-Bohumin railroad.

"Pasture," by Vojtech Sedlacek — A651

Designs: 50h, Dressage, by Frantisek Tichy. 60h, Otakar Kubin, by Vaclav Fiala. 1k, The Three Kings, by Ernest Zmetak. 1.60k, Woman Dressing, by Ludovit Fulla.

1972, Mar. 27   *Perf. 11½x11*

1806	A651	40h multi	.25	.25
1807	A651	50h multi	.25	.25
1808	A651	60h multi	.25	.25
1809	A651	1k multi	.25	.25
1810	A651	1.60k multi	1.25	.90
		Nos. 1806-1810 (5)	2.25	1.90

Czech and Slovak graphic art. 1.60k issued in sheets of 4. Value $9. See Nos. 1859-1862, 1921-1924.

Ice Hockey — A652

Design: 1k, Two players.

1972, Apr. 7   *Perf. 11*
| 1811 | A652 | 60h blk & multi | .25 | .25 |
| 1812 | A652 | 1k blk & multi | .40 | .25 |

World and European Ice Hockey Championships, Prague.
For overprint see Nos. 1845-1846.

Bicycling, Olympic Rings and Emblem — A653

1972, Apr. 7

1813	A653	50h shown	.25	.25
1814	A653	1.60k Diving	.35	.25
1815	A653	1.80k Canoeing	.55	.25
1816	A653	2k Gymnast	1.10	.25
		Nos. 1813-1816 (4)	2.25	1.00

20th Olympic Games, Munich, 8/26-9/11.

Prague Castle Art Type of 1971

Designs: No. 1817, Adam and Eve, column capital, St. Vitus Cathedral. No. 1818, Czech coat of arms (lion); c. 1500.

1972, May 9   *Perf. 11½*
| 1817 | A634 | 3k blk & multi | 2.10 | 1.40 |
| 1818 | A634 | 3k blk, red, sil & gold | 1.40 | .85 |

Nos. 1817-1818 were each issued in sheets of 4. Value, set $15.

Andrej Sladkovic (1820-1872), Poet — A654

No. 1820, Janko Kral (1822-1876), poet. No. 1821, Ludmilla Podjavorinska (1872-1951), writer. No. 1822, Antonin Hudecek (1872-1941), painter. No. 1823, Frantisek Bilek (1872-1941), sculptor. No. 1824, Jan Preisler (1872-1918), painter.

1972, June 14   *Perf. 11*

1819	A654	40h pur, ol & bl	.25	.25
1820	A654	40h dk grn, bl & yel	.25	.25
1821	A654	40h blk & multi	.25	.25
1822	A654	40h brn, lt grn	.25	.25
1823	A654	40h choc, grn & org	.25	.25
1824	A654	40h grn & org brn	.25	.25
		Nos. 1819-1824 (6)	1.50	1.50

Men with Banners — A655

1972, June 14   *Perf. 11x11½*
1825   A655   30h dk vio bl, red & yel   .25   .25

8th Trade Union Congress, Prague.

Art Forms of Wire — A656

Ornamental Wirework: 60h, Plane and rosette. 80h, Four-headed dragon and ornament. 1k, Locomotive and loops. 2.60k, Tray and owl.

1972, Aug. 28   *Perf. 11½x11*

1826	A656	20h sal & multi	.25	.25
1827	A656	60h multi	.25	.25
1828	A656	80h pink & multi	.25	.25
1829	A656	1k multi	.25	.25
1830	A656	2.60k rose & multi	1.40	.25
		Nos. 1826-1830 (5)	2.40	1.25

"Jiskra" — A657

Engr. & Photo.
1972, Sept. 27   *Perf. 11½x11*
Size: 40x22mm
Multicolored Design on Blue Paper

1831	A657	50h shown	.25	.25
1832	A657	60h "Mir"	.25	.25
1833	A657	80h "Republika"	.25	.25

Size: 48x29mm   *Perf. 11x11½*

1834	A657	1k "Kosice"	.30	.25
1835	A657	1.60k "Dukla"	.45	.25
1836	A657	2k "Kladno"	1.40	.55
		Nos. 1831-1836 (6)	2.90	1.80

Czechoslovak sea-going vessels.

Hussar, 18th Century Tile — A658

60h, Janissary. 80h, St. Martin. 1.60k, St. George. 1.80k, Nobleman's guard. 2.20k, Slovakian horseman.

1972, Oct. 24   *Perf. 11½x11*

1837	A658	30h shown	.25	.25
1838	A658	60h multicolored	.25	.25
1839	A658	80h multicolored	.25	.25
1840	A658	1.60k multicolored	.45	.25
1841	A658	1.80k multicolored	.70	.25
1842	A658	2.20k multicolored	1.25	.25
		Nos. 1837-1842 (6)	3.15	1.50

Horsemen from 18th-19th century tiles or enamel paintings on glass.

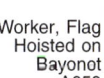

Worker, Flag Hoisted on Bayonet A659

Star, Hammer and Sickle — A660

1972, Nov. 7   *Perf. 11x11½*
| 1843 | A659 | 30h gold & multi | .25 | .25 |
| 1844 | A660 | 60h rose car & gold | .25 | .25 |

55th anniv. of the Russian October Revolution (30h); 50th anniv. of the Soviet Union (60h).

Nos. 1811-1812 Overprinted in Violet Blue or Black

CZECHOSLOVAKIA

1972		Perf. 11	
1845	A652 60h multi (Vbl)	7.00	6.50
1846	A652 1k multi (Bk)	7.00	6.50

Czechoslovakia's victorious ice hockey team. The overprint on the 60h (shown) is in Czech and reads CSSR/MISTREM/SVETA; the overprint on the 1k is in Slovak.

Painting Type of 1967

Designs: 1k, "Nosegay" (nudes and flowers), by Max Svabinsky. 1.20k, Struggle of St. Ladislas with Kuman nomad, anonymous, 14th century. 1.40k, Lady with Fur Hat, by Vaclav Hollar. 1.80k, Midsummer Night's Dream, 1962, by Josef Liesler. 2.40k, Pablo Picasso, self-portrait.

1972, Nov. 27		Engr. & Photo.	
1847	A565 1k multi	.85	.40
1848	A565 1.20k multi	.85	.40
1849	A565 1.40k blk & cream	1.10	.40
1850	A565 1.80k multi	.85	.40
1851	A565 2.40k multi	2.10	1.40
Nos. 1847-1851 (5)		5.75	3.10

Nos. 1847-1851 were each issued in sheets of 4. Value, set $24.

Goldfinch — A661

Songbirds: 60h, Warbler feeding young cuckoo. 80h, Cuckoo. 1k, Black-billed magpie. 1.60k, Bullfinch. 3k, Song thrush.

1972, Dec. 15		Size: 30x48½mm	
1852	A661 60h yel & multi	.25	.25
1853	A661 80h multi	.25	.25
1854	A661 1k lt bl & multi	.25	.25

| | Engr. | | |
	Size: 30x23mm		
1855	A661 1.60k multi	1.50	.70
1856	A661 2k multi	1.50	.70
1857	A661 3k multi	1.50	.70
Nos. 1852-1857 (6)		5.25	2.85

Nos. 1855-1857 were each issued in a sheet of 10. Value, set $55.

Post Horn and Allegory A662

1972, Dec. 18		Engr. & Photo.	
1858	A662 1k blk, red lil & gold	.30	.30

Stamp Day.

Art Type of 1972

Designs: 30h, Flowers in Window, by Jaroslav Grus. 60h, Quest for Happiness, by Josef Balaz. 1.60k, Balloon, by Kamil Lhotak. 1.80k, Woman with Viola, by Richard Wiesner.

1973, Jan. 25		Perf. 11½x11	
1859	A651 30h multi	.25	.25
1860	A651 60h multi	.25	.25
1861	A651 1.60k multi	.30	.25
1862	A651 1.80k multi	.25	.35
Nos. 1859-1862 (4)		1.05	1.10

Czech and Slovak graphic art.

Tennis Player A663 — Figure Skater A664

Torch and Star — A665

1973, Feb. 22		Perf. 11	
1863	A663 30h vio & multi	.25	.25
1864	A664 60h blk & multi	.25	.25
1865	A665 1k multi	.30	.25
Nos. 1863-1865 (3)		.80	.75

80th anniversary of the tennis organization in Czechoslovakia (30h); World figure skating championships, Bratislava (60h); 3rd summer army Spartakiad of socialist countries (1k).

Star and Factories A666 — Workers' Militia, Emblem and Flag A667

1973, Feb. 23			
1866	A666 30h multi	.25	.25
1867	A667 60h multi	.25	.25

25th anniversary of the Communist revolution in Czechoslovakia and of the Militia.

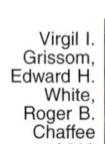

A668

Torch &: 30h, Capt. Jan Nalepka, Major Antonin Sochor and Laurel. 40h, Evzen Rosicky, Mirko Nespor & ivy leaves. 60h, Vlado Clementis, Karol Smidke & linden leaves. 80h, Jan Osoha, Josef Molak & oak leaves. 1k, Marie Kuderikova, Jozka Jaburkova & rose. 1.60k, Vaclav Sinkule, Eduard Urx & palm leaf.

| 1973, Mar. 20 | | Perf. 11½x11 | |
	Yellow Paper		
1868	A668 30h blk, ver & gold	.30	.25
1869	A668 40h blk, ver & grn	.30	.25
1870	A668 60h blk, ver & gold	.30	.25
1871	A668 80h blk, ver & gold	.30	.25
1872	A668 1k blk, ver & grn	.30	.25
1873	A668 1.60k blk, ver & sil	.75	.25
Nos. 1868-1873 (6)		2.25	1.50

Fighters against and victims of Fascism and Nazism during German Occupation.

Virgil I. Grissom, Edward H. White, Roger B. Chaffee A669

Designs: 20h, Soviet planetary station "Venera." 30h, "Intercosmos" station. 40h, Lunokhod on moon. 3.60k, Vladimir M. Komarov, Georgi T. Dobrovolsky, Vladislav N. Volkov, Victor I. Patsayev. 5k, Yuri A. Gagarin. Two types of 3.60k: type I, Cosmonaut on background of cross-hatched lines; type 2, Cosmonaut on background of parallel diagonal lines.

| 1973, Apr. 12 | | Perf. 11½x11 | |
	Size: 40x22mm		
1874	A669 20h multi	.25	.25
1875	A669 30h multi	.25	.25
1876	A669 40h multi	.25	.25

| | Engr. | | |
| | Perf. 11½ | | |
	Size: 49x30mm		
1877	A669 3k multi	1.00	.50
1878	A669 3.60k multi, type 1	1.00	.75
a.	Type 2	20.00	7.50
1879	A669 5k multi	2.50	2.00
Nos. 1874-1879 (6)		5.25	4.00

In memory of American and Russian astronauts.
Nos. 1877-1879 were each issued in sheets of 4. Values: set (with No. 1878) $30; mset (with No. 1878a) $90.

Radio A670 — Telephone and Map of Czechoslovakia A671

Television — A672

1973, May 1		Perf. 11½x11	
1880	A670 30h blk & multi	.25	.25
1881	A671 30h lt bl, pink & blk	.25	.25
1882	A672 30h dp bl & multi	.25	.25
Nos. 1880-1882 (3)		.75	.75

Czechoslovak anniversaries: 50 years of broadcasting (No. 1880); 20 years of telephone service to all communities (No. 1881); 20 years of television (No. 1882).

Coat of Arms and Linden Branch — A673

1973, May 9		Perf. 11x11½	
1883	A673 60h red & multi	.25	.25

25th anniv. of the Constitution of May 9.

Prague Castle Art Type of 1971

No. 1884, Royal Legate, 14th century. No. 1885, Seal of King Charles IV, 1351.

1973, May 9		Perf. 11½	
1884	A634 3k blue & multi	1.25	.75
1885	A634 3k gold, grn & dk brn	1.75	1.50

Nos. 1884-1885 were each issued in sheets of 4. Value, set $13.

Coat of Arms Type of 1968

1973, June 20			
1886	A590 60h Mikulov	.25	.25
1887	A590 60h Zlutice	.30	.25
1888	A590 60h Smolenice	.35	.25
Nos. 1886-1888 (3)		.90	.75

Coats of arms of Czechoslovakian cities.

Heraldic Colors of Olomouc and Moravia — A674

1973, Aug. 23		Engr. & Photo.	
1889	A674 30h multi	.25	.25

University of Olomouc, 400th anniv.

Flower Show — A675

60h, Tulips (30x50mm). 1k, Rose (30x50mm). 1.60k, Anthurium (23x39mm). 1.80k, Iris (23x39mm). 2k, Chrysanthemum (30x50mm). 3.60k, Cymbidium (23x39mm).

1973, Aug. 23		Perf. 11½	
1890	A675 60h multi	.75	.35
1891	A675 1k multi	.75	.35
1892	A675 1.60k shown	.40	.35
1893	A675 1.80k multi	.40	.35
1894	A675 2k multi	1.90	1.00
1895	A675 3.60k multi	.75	.35
Nos. 1890-1895 (6)		4.95	2.75

Olomouc, Aug. 18-Sept. 2. 60h, 1k, 2k issued in sheets of 4, others in sheets of 10. Value, set $50.

Hunting Dogs — A676

1973, Sept. 5			
1896	A676 20h Irish setter	.45	.25
1897	A676 30h Czech terrier	.45	.25
1898	A676 40h Bavarian hunting dog	.55	.25
1899	A676 60h German pointer	.55	.25
1900	A676 1k Cocker spaniel	.85	.25
1901	A676 1.60k Dachshund	2.10	.50
Nos. 1896-1901 (6)		4.95	1.75

Czechoslovak United Hunting Org., 50th anniv.

St. John, the Baptist, by Svabinsky — A677

Works by Max Svabinsky: 60h, "August Noon" (woman). 80h, "Marriage of True Minds" (artist and muse). 1k, "Paradise Sonata I" (Adam dreaming of Eve). 2.60k, Last Judgment, stained glass window, St. Vitus Cathedral.

1973, Sept. 17		Litho. & Engr.	
1902	A677 20h blk & pale grn	.25	.25
1903	A677 60h black & buff	.25	.25

	Engr.		
1904	A677 80h black	.75	.25
1905	A677 1k slate green	.75	.25
1906	A677 2.60k multi	1.90	1.25
Nos. 1902-1906 (5)		3.90	2.25

Centenary of the birth of Max Svabinsky (1873-1962), artist and stamp designer. 20h and 60h issued in sheets of 25; 80h and 1k se-tenant in sheets of 4 checkerwise (value $4); 2.60k in sheets of 4 (value $10).

Trade Union Emblem — A678

1973, Oct. 15		Engr. & Photo.	
1907	A678 1k red, bl & yel	.25	.25

8t (valueh Congress of the World Federation of Trade Unions, Varna, Bulgaria.

Painting Type of 1967

1k, Boy from Martinique, by Antonin Pelc. 1.20k, "Fortitude" (mountaineer), by Martin Benka. 1.80k, Rembrandt, self-portrait. 2k, Pierrot, by Bohumil Kubista. 2.40k, Ilona Kubinyiova, by Peter M. Bohun. 3.60k, Virgin and Child (Veveri Madonna), c. 1350.

1973, Nov. 27		Perf. 11½	
1908	A565 1k multi, vio bl inscriptions	2.50	1.25
a.	1k multi, black inscriptions	9.00	9.00
1909	A565 1.20k multi	2.50	1.25
1910	A565 1.80k multi	.80	.80
1911	A565 2k multi	.80	.80
1912	A565 2.40k multi	.80	.80
1913	A565 3.60k multi	.80	.80
Nos. 1908-1913 (6)		8.20	5.70

Nos. 1908-1909 were each issued in sheets of 4. Nos. 1910-1913 were printed se-tenant with gold and black inscription on gutter. Value, sheet $35. No. 1908a in sheet of 4, value $45.
The central backgroundis light bluish green on No. 1908; grayish blue on No. 1908a.

Postilion A679

1973, Dec. 18			
1914	A679 1k gold & multi	.30	.25

Stamp Day 1974 and 55th anniversary of Czechoslovak postage stamps. Printed with 2 labels showing telephone and telegraph. Value of single with two labels, $1.75.

CZECHOSLOVAKIA

"CSSR" — A680

1974, Jan. 1
1915 A680 30h red, gold & ultra .25 .25

5th anniversary of Federal Government in the Czechoslovak Socialist Republic.

Bedrich Smetana A681 — Pablo Neruda, Chilean Flag A682

1974, Jan. 4 — Perf. 11x11½
1916 A681 60h shown .25 .25
1917 A681 60h Josef Suk .25 .25
1918 A682 60h shown .25 .25
 Nos. 1916-1918 (3) .75 .75

Smetana (1824-84), composer; Suk (1874-1935), composer, and Pablo Neruda (Neftali Ricardo Reyes, 1904-73), Chilean poet.

Comecon Building, Moscow — A683

1974, Jan. 23
1919 A683 1k gold, red & vio bl .25 .25

25th anniversary of the Council of Mutual Economic Assistance (COMECON).

Symbols of Postal Service A684

1974, Feb. 20 — Perf. 11½
1920 A684 3.60k multi .85 .45

BRNO '74 National Stamp Exhibition, Brno, June 8-23.

No. 1920 was issue both in normal sheets of 25 stamps and in sheets containing 16 stamps se-tenant with 9 labels depicting Brno. Values: single stamp with attached tab unused $2.50; used $2.50; full sheet of 16 stamps and 9 labels $35.

Art Type of 1972

Designs: 60h, Tulips 1973, by Josef Broz. 1k, Structures 1961 (poppy and building), by Orest Dubay. 1.60k, Bird and flowers (Golden Sun-Glowing Day), by Adolf Zabransky. 1.80k, Artificial flowers, by Frantisek Gross.

1974, Feb. 21 — Perf. 11½x11
1921 A651 60h multi .25 .25
1922 A651 1k multi .30 .25
1923 A651 1.60k multi .40 .25
1924 A651 1.80k multi 1.10 .50
 Nos. 1921-1924 (4) 2.05 1.05

Czech and Slovak graphic art.

Oskar Bonoo and Vaclav Prochazka A685

40h, Milos Uher, Anton Sedlacek. 60h, Jan Hajecek, Marie Sedlackova. 80h, Jan Sverma, Albin Grznar. 1k, Jaroslav Neliba, Alois Hovorka. 1.60k, Ladislav Exnar, Ludovit Kukorelli.

1974, Mar. 21 — Perf. 11½x11
1925 A685 30h indigo & multi .25 .25
1926 A685 40h indigo & multi .25 .25
1927 A685 60h indigo & multi .25 .25
1928 A685 80h indigo & multi .25 .25
1929 A685 1k indigo & multi .30 .25
1930 A685 1.60k indigo & multi .85 .25
 Nos. 1925-1930 (6) 2.15 1.50

Partisan commanders and fighters.

"Water, the Source of Energy" — A686

1974, Apr. 25 Engr. Perf. 11½
1931 A686 60h multi .55 .25
1932 A686 1k multi .55 .25
1933 A686 1.20k multi 1.10 .45
1934 A686 1.60k multi 1.10 .45
1935 A686 2k multi 2.10 1.40
 Nos. 1931-1935 (5) 5.40 2.80

Hydrological Decade (UNESCO), 1965-1974. Nos. 1931-1935 were each issued in sheets of 4. Value $25.

Allegory Holding "Molniya," and Ground Station — A687

1974, Apr. 30 Engr. & Photo.
1936 A687 30h vio bl & multi .25 .25

"Intersputnik," first satellite communications ground station in Czechoslovakia.

Prague Castle Art Type of 1971

No. 1937, Golden Cock, 17th century locket. No. 1938, Glass monstrance, 1840.

1974, May 9 Engr. Perf. 11½
1937 A634 3k gold & multi 1.50 1.10
1938 A634 3k blk & multi 2.25 1.50

Nos. 1937-1938 were each issued in sheets of 4. Value, set $15.

Sousaphone — A688

30h, Bagpipe. 40h, Violin, by Martin Benka. 1k, Pyramid piano. 1.60k, Tenor quinton, 1754.

Engraved and Photogravure
1974, May 12 Perf. 11x11½
1939 A688 20h shown .25 .25
1940 A688 30h multi .25 .25
1941 A688 40h multi .55 .25
1942 A688 1k multi .25 .25
1943 A688 1.60k multi .80 .25
 Nos. 1939-1943 (5) 1.80 1.25

Prague and Bratislava Music Festivals. The 1.60k also commemorates 25th anniversary of Slovak Philharmonic Orchestra.

Child — A689

1974, June 1 Perf. 11½
1944 A689 60h multi .25 .25

Children's Day. Design is from illustration for children's book by Adolf Zabransky.

Globe, People and Exhibition Emblems A690

Design: 6k, Rays and emblems symbolizing "Oneness and Mutuality."

1974, June 1
1945 A690 30h multi .25 .25
1946 A690 6k multi 1.50 .75

BRNO 74 Natl. Stamp Exhib., Brno, June 8-23.

Nos. 2171-2172 were each issued both in sheet of 50 stamps and in sheets of 16 stamps and 14 labels. Values: stamps with attached labels, $1.75; 2 sheets of 16 stamps and 14 labels $35.

Resistance Fighter — A691

1974, Aug. 29 Perf. 11½
1947 A691 30h multi .25 .25

Slovak National Uprising, 30th anniversary.

Actress Holding Tragedy and Comedy Masks — A692

1974, Aug. 29
1948 A692 30h red, sil & blk .25 .25

Bratislava Academy of Music and Drama, 25th anniversary.

Slovak Girl with Flower — A693

1974, Aug. 29
1949 A693 30h multi .25 .25

SLUK, Slovak folksong and dance ensemble, 25th anniversary.

Hero and Leander A694

Design: 2.40k, Hero watching Leander swim the Hellespont. No. 1952, Leander reaching shore. No. 1953, Hero mourning over Leander's body. No. 1954, Hermione, Leander's sister. No. 1955, Mourning Cupid. Designs are from 17th century English tapestries in Bratislava Council Palace.

1974-76
1950 A694 2k multi 1.25 1.10
1951 A694 2.40k multi 1.50 1.25
1952 A694 3k multi 1.00 .45
1953 A694 3k multi 1.75 1.75
1954 A694 3.60k multi 2.50 1.10
1955 A694 3.60k multi .85 .60
 Nos. 1950-1955 (6) 8.85 6.25

Issued: Nos. 1950-1951, 9/25/74; Nos. 1952, 1954, 8/29/75; Nos. 1953, 1955, 5/9/76. Nos. 1950-1951 were each issued in sheets of 4, with 2 blank labels; Nos. 1952-1955 were issued in sheets of 4. Value, set $50.

Soldier Standing Guard, Target, 1840 — A695

Painted Folk-art Targets: 60h, Landscape with Pierrot and flags, 1828. 1k, Diana crowning champion marksman, 1832. 1.60k, Still life with guitar, 1839. 2.40k, Salvo and stag in flight, 1834. 3k, Turk and giraffe, 1831.

1974, Sept. 26 Perf. 11½
Size: 30x50mm
1956 A695 30h black & multi .25 .25
1957 A695 60h black & multi .25 .25
1958 A695 1k black & multi .30 .25

Engr.
Perf. 12
Size: 40x50mm
1959 A695 1.60k green & multi .50 .45
1960 A695 2.40k sepia & multi .90 .75
1961 A695 3k multi 3.00 3.00
 Nos. 1956-1961 (6) 5.20 4.95

Nos. 1959-1961 were each issued in sheets of 4. Value, set $17.50.

UPU Emblem and Postilion A696

UPU Cent. (UPU Emblem and): 40h, Mail coach. 60h, Railroad mail coach, 1851. 80h, Early mail truck. 1k, Czechoslovak Airlines mail plane. 1.60k, Radar.

Engraved and Photogravure
1974, Oct. 9 Perf. 11½
1962 A696 30h multi .25 .25
1963 A696 40h multi .25 .25
1964 A696 60h multi .25 .25
1965 A696 80h multi .25 .25
1966 A696 1k multi .40 .25
1967 A696 1.60k multi 1.25 .25
 Nos. 1962-1967 (6) 2.65 1.50

Sealed Letter A697 — Post Rider A698

20h, Post Horn, Old Town Bridge Tower. No. 1971, Carrier pigeon.

1974, Oct. 31 Perf. 11½x11
1968 A698 20h multi .25 .25
1969 A697 30h brn, bl & red .25 .25
1970 A698 40h multi .25 .25
1971 A697 60h bl, yel & red .25 .25
 Nos. 1968-1971 (4) 1.00 1.00

Nos. 1968-1971 were reissued in 1979, printed on fluorescent paper. Value, set $15. See No. 2675.

Stylized Bird — A699

No. 1977, Same design as No. 1976. No. 1979, Map of Czechoslovakia with postal code numbers.

Coil Stamps
1975 Photo. Perf. 14
1976 A699 30h brt bl .25 .25
1977 A699 60h carmine .25 .25

Postal Code Symbol — A699a

CZECHOSLOVAKIA

1976   Perf. 11½
| 1978 | A699a | 30h emer | .25 | .25 |
| 1979 | A699a | 60h scar | .25 | .25 |

Nos. 1976-1979 have black control number on back of every fifth stamp.

Ludvik Kuba, Self-portrait, 1941 — A700

Paintings: 1.20k, Violinist Frantisek Ondricek, by Vaclav Brozik. 1.60k, Vase with Flowers, by Otakar Kubin. 1.80k, Woman with Pitcher, by Janko Alexy. 2.40k, Bacchanalia, c. 1635, by Karel Skreta.

1974, Nov. 27   Engr.   Perf. 11½
1980	A700	1k multi	.50	.30
1981	A700	1.20k multi	.80	.40
1982	A700	1.60k multi	.80	.60
1983	A700	1.80k multi	1.00	.40
1984	A700	2.40k multi	2.50	1.75
	Nos. 1980-1984 (5)		5.60	3.45

Czech and Slovak art.
Nos. 1980-1984 were each issued in sheets of 4. Value, set $25.
See Nos. 2209-2211, 2678-2682, 2721-2723, 2743, 2766-2768.

Post Horn A701

Engraved and Photogravure
1974, Dec. 18   Perf. 11x11½
| 1985 | A701 | 1k multicolored | .30 | .25 |

Stamp Day.

Still-life with Hare, by Hollar — A702

Designs: 1k, The Lion and the Mouse, by Vaclav Hollar. 1.60k, Deer Hunt, by Philip Galle. 1.80k, Grand Hunt, by Jacques Callot.

1975, Feb. 26   Perf. 11½x11
1988	A702	60h blk & buff	.25	.25
1989	A702	1k blk & buff	.25	.25
1990	A702	1.60k blk & yel	.25	.25
1991	A702	1.80k blk & buff	1.25	.65
	Nos. 1988-1991 (4)		2.00	1.40

Hunting scenes from old engravings.

Guns Pointing at Family — A703

Designs: 1k, Women and building on fire. 1.20k, People and roses. All designs include names of destroyed villages.

1975, Feb. 26   Perf. 11
1992	A703	60h multi	.25	.25
1993	A703	1k multi	.25	.25
1994	A703	1.20k multi	.30	.25
	Nos. 1992-1994 (3)		.80	.75

Destruction of 14 villages by the Nazis, 30th anniversary.

Young Woman and Globe — A704

1975, Mar. 7   Perf. 11½x11
| 1995 | A704 | 30h red & multi | .25 | .25 |

International Women's Year 1975.

Little Queens, Moravian Folk Custom — A705

Folk Customs: 1k, Straw masks (animal heads and blackened faces), Slovak. 1.40k, The Tale of Maid Dorothea (executioner, girl, king and devil). 2k, Drowning of Morena, symbol of death and winter.

1975, Mar. 26   Engr.   Perf. 11½
1996	A705	60h blk & multi	.45	.25
1997	A705	1k blk & multi	.70	.45
1998	A705	1.40k blk & multi	.85	.60
1999	A705	2k blk & multi	1.00	.75
	Nos. 1996-1999 (4)		3.00	2.05

Nos. 1996-1999 were each issued in sheets of four. Value $12.50.

Coat of Arms Type of 1968
Engraved and Photogravure
1975, Apr. 17   Perf. 11½
| 2000 | A590 | 60h Nymburk | .25 | .25 |
| 2001 | A590 | 60h Znojmo | .25 | .25 |

Coats of arms of Czechoslovakian cities.

Czech May Uprising A706

Liberation by Soviet Army — A707

Czechoslovak-Russian Friendship — A708

Engr. & Photo.; Engr. (A707)
1975, May 9
2002	A706	1k multi	.25	.25
2003	A707	1k multi	.25	.25
2004	A708	1k multi	.25	.25
	Nos. 2002-2004 (3)		.75	.75

30th anniv. of the May uprising of the Czech people and of liberation by the Soviet Army; 5th anniv. of the Czechoslovak-Soviet Treaty of Friendship, Cooperation and Mutual Aid.

Adolescents' Exercises A709

Designs: 60h, Children's exercises. 1k, Men's and women's exercises.

Engraved and Photogravure
1975, June 15   Perf. 12x11½
2005	A709	30h lil & multi	.25	.25
2006	A709	60h multi	.25	.25
2007	A709	1k vio & multi	.25	.25
	Nos. 2005-2007 (3)		.75	.75

Spartakiad 1975, Prague, June 26-29. Nos. 2005-2007 each issued in sheets of 30 stamps and 40 labels, showing different Spartakiad emblems. Value, set with tabs, $1.

Datrioides Microlepis and Sea Horse A710

Tropical Fish (Aquarium): 1k, Beta splendens regan and Pterophyllum scalare. 1.20k, Carassius auratus. 1.60k, Amphiprion percula and Chaetodon sp. 2k, Pomacanthodes semicirculatus, Pomacanthus maculosus and Paracanthurus hepatus.

1975, June 27   Perf. 11½
2008	A710	60h multi	.25	.25
2009	A710	1k multi	.35	.25
2010	A710	1.20k multi	.40	.25
2011	A710	1.60k multi	.55	.25
2012	A710	2k multi	1.75	.50
	Nos. 2008-2012 (5)		3.30	1.50

Pelicans, by Nikita Charushin — A711

Book Illustrations: 30h, The Dreamer, by Lieselotte Schwarz. 40h, Hero on horseback, by Val Munteanau. 60h, Peacock, by Klaus Ensikat. 80h, Woman on horseback, by Robert Dubravec.

1975, Sept. 5
2013	A711	20h multi	.25	.25
2014	A711	30h multi	.25	.25
2015	A711	40h multi	.30	.25
2016	A711	60h multi	.30	.25
2017	A711	80h multi	.60	.25
	Nos. 2013-2017 (5)		1.70	1.25

Bratislava BIB 75 biennial exhibition of illustrations for children's books.
Nos. 2013-2017 issued in sheets of 25 stamps and 15 labels with designs and inscriptions in various languages. Value, set with attached labels, $2.

Strakonice, 1951 — A712

Designs: Motorcycles.

1975, Sept. 29   Perf. 11½
2018	A712	20h shown	.25	.25
2019	A712	40h Jawa 250, 1945	.25	.25
2020	A712	60h Jawa 175, 1935	.25	.25
2021	A712	1k ITAR, 1921	.25	.25
2022	A712	1.20k ORION, 1903	.25	.25
2023	A712	1.80k Laurin & Klement, 1898	1.40	.40
	Nos. 2018-2023 (6)		2.65	1.65

Study of Shortwave Solar Radiation A713

Soyuz-Apollo Link-up in Space — A714

60h, Study of aurora borealis & Oréol satellite. 1k, Study of ionosphere & cosmic radiation. 2k, Copernicus, radio map of the sun & satellite.

1975, Sept. 30
2024	A713	30h multi	.25	.25
2025	A713	60h yel, rose red & vio	.25	.25
2026	A713	1k bl, yel & vio	.25	.25
2027	A713	2k red, vio & yel	.35	.25

Engr.
| 2028 | A714 | 5k vio & multi | 2.00 | 1.50 |
| | Nos. 2024-2028 (5) | | 3.10 | 2.50 |

International cooperation in space research.
No. 2028 issued in sheets of 4. Value $15.
The design of No. 2026 appears to be inverted.

Slovnaft, Petrochemical Plant — A715

Designs: 60h, Atomic power station. 1k, Construction of Prague subway. 1.20k, Construction of Friendship pipeline. 1.40k, Combine harvesters. 1.60k, Apartment house construction.

Engraved and Photogravure
1975, Oct. 28
2029	A715	30h multi	.25	.25
2030	A715	60h multi	.25	.25
2031	A715	1k multi	.25	.25
2032	A715	1.20k multi	.25	.25
2033	A715	1.40k multi	.25	.25
2034	A715	1.60k multi	.75	.30
	Nos. 2029-2034 (6)		2.00	1.55

Socialist construction, 30th anniversary. Nos. 2029-2034 printed se-tenant with labels. Value, set with attached labels, $2.50.

Pres. Gustav Husak — A716

1975, Oct. 28   Engr.
| 2035 | A716 | 30h ultra | .25 | .25 |
| 2036 | A716 | 60h rose red | .25 | .25 |

Prague Castle Art Type of 1971

3k, Gold earring, 9th cent. 3.60k, Arms of Premysl Dynasty & Bohemia from lid of leather case containing Bohemian crown, 14th cent.

1975, Oct. 29
| 2040 | A634 | 3k blk, grn, pur & gold | .95 | .50 |
| 2041 | A634 | 3.60k red & multi | 2.00 | 1.60 |

Nos. 2040-2041 each issued in sheets of 4. Value, set $12.50.

Miniature Sheet

Ludvik Svoboda, Map of Journey from Buzuluk to Prague, Carnations — A717

1975, Nov. 25
| 2042 | A717 | 10k multi | 9.00 | 7.00 |

Pres. Ludvik Svoboda, 80th birthday. Exists imperf. Value, $40 unused, $25 used.

Painting Type of 1967

Paintings: 1k, "May 1975" (Woman and doves for 30th anniv. of peace), by Zdenek Sklenar. 1.40k, Woman in national costume, by Eugen Nevan. 1.80k, "Liberation of Prague," by Alena Cermakova, horiz. 2.40k, "Fire 1938" (woman raising fist), by Josef Capek. 3.40k, Old Prague, 1828, by Vincenc Morstadt.

CZECHOSLOVAKIA

1975, Nov. 27   Engr.   Perf. 11½
2043	A565	1k blk, buff & brn	.30	.25
2044	A565	1.40k multi	.55	.25
2045	A565	1.80k multi	.55	.30
2046	A565	2.40k multi	1.50	.75
2047	A565	3.40k multi	1.50	1.25
		Nos. 2043-2047 (5)	4.40	2.80

Nos. 2043-2047 were each issued in sheets of 4. Value, set $20.

Carrier Pigeon A718

Engraved and Photogravure
1975, Dec. 18   Perf. 11½
2048   A718   1k red & multi   .30   .25
Stamp Day 1975.

 Frantisek Halas A719

 Wilhelm Pieck A720

 Frantisek Lexa A721

Jindrich Jindrich A722

 Ivan Krasko — A723

1976, Feb. 25   Perf. 11½
2049	A719	60h multi	.25	.25
2050	A720	60h multi	.25	.25
2051	A721	60h multi	.25	.25
2052	A722	60h multi	.25	.25
2053	A723	60h multi	.25	.25
		Nos. 2049-2053 (5)	1.25	1.25

Halas (1901-49), poet; Pieck (1876-1960), pres. of German Democratic Republic; Lexa (1876-1960), professor of Egyptology; Jindrich (1876-1967), composer and writer; Krasko (1876-1958), Slovak poet.
No. 2051 printed in sheets of 10, others in sheets of 50. Value, No. 2051 sheet, $4.

Ski Jump, Olympic Emblem A724

1976, Mar. 22   Perf. 12x11½
2054	A724	1k gold & multi	.25	.25
2055	A724	1.40k gold & multi	.25	.25
2056	A724	1.60k gold & multi	1.00	.50
		Nos. 2054-2056 (3)	1.50	.80

12th Winter Olympic Games, Innsbruck, Austria, Feb. 4-15.

Javelin and Olympic Rings A725

1976, Mar. 22   Perf. 11½
2057	A725	2k shown	.30	.25
2058	A725	3k Relay race	.45	.25
2059	A725	3.60k Shot put	1.40	.90
		Nos. 2057-2059 (3)	2.15	1.40

21st Olympic Games, Montreal, Canada, July 17-Aug. 1.

Table Tennis — A726

1976, Mar. 22   Perf. 11x12
2060   A726   1k multi   .30   .25
European Table Tennis Championship, Prague, Mar. 26-Apr. 4.

Symbolic of Communist Party A727

Worker, Derrick, Emblem A728

1976, Apr. 12   Perf. 11x12
2061	A727	30h gold & multi	.25	.25
2062	A728	60h gold & multi	.25	.25

15th Congress of the Communist Party of Czechoslovakia.

Radio Prague Orchestra A729

Dancer, Violin, Tragic Mask A730

Actors A731

Folk Dancers A732

Film Festival — A733

1976, Apr. 26   Perf. 11½
2063	A729	20h gold & multi	.25	.25
2064	A730	20h pink & multi	.25	.25
2065	A731	20h lt bl & multi	.25	.25
2066	A732	30h blk & multi	.25	.25
2067	A733	30h vio bl, rose & grn	.25	.25
		Nos. 2063-2067 (5)	1.25	1.25

Czechoslovak Radio Symphony Orchestra, Prague, 50th anniv. (No. 2063); Academy of Music and Dramatic Art, Prague, 50th anniv. (No. 2064); Nova Scena Theater Co., Bratislava, 30th anniv. (No. 2065); Intl. Folk Song and Dance Festival, Straznice, 30th anniv. (No. 2066); 20th Intl. Film Festival, Karlovy Vary (No. 2067).

Hammer and Sickle
A734   A735

Design: 6k, Hammer and sickle, horiz.

1976, May 14
2068   A734   30h gold, red & dk bl   .25   .25

2069   A735   60h gold, red & dp car   .25   .25

Souvenir Sheet
2070   A735   6k red & multi   2.00   2.00
Czechoslovak Communist Party, 55th anniv. No. 2070 contains a 50x30mm stamp.

Ships in Storm, by Frans Huys (1522-1562) — A736

Old Engravings of Ships: 60h, by Václav Hollar (1607-77). 1k, by Regnier Nooms Zeeman (1623-68). 2k, by Francois Chereau (1680-1729).

Engraved and Photogravure
1976, July 21   Perf. 11x11½
2071	A736	40h buff & blk	.25	.25
2072	A736	60h gray, buff & blk	.25	.25
2073	A736	1k lt grn, buff & blk	.25	.25
2074	A736	2k lt bl, buff & blk	1.40	.25
		Nos. 2071-2074 (4)	2.15	1.00

"UNESCO" — A737

1976, July 30   Perf. 11½
2075   A737   2k gray & multi   .35   .30
30th anniversary of UNESCO. Issued in sheets of 10. Value $5.

Souvenir Sheet

Hands Holding Infant, Globe and Dove — A738

1976, July 30
2076   A738   Sheet of 2   4.00   3.50
   a.   6k multi   2.50   2.00
European Security and Cooperation Conference, Helsinki, Finland, 2nd anniv.

Morino Ram — A739

1976, Aug. 28   Perf. 11½x12
2077	A739	30h multi	.25	.25
2078	A739	40h multi	.25	.25
2079	A739	1.60k multi	.35	.25
		Nos. 2077-2079 (3)	.85	.75

Bountiful Earth Exhibition, Ceske Budejovice, Aug. 28-Sept. 12.

Couple Smoking, WHO Emblem and Skull — A740

1976, Sept. 7   Perf. 12x11½
2080   A740   2k multi   .60   .30
Fight against smoking, WHO drive against drug addiction.
Printed in sheets of 10 (2x5) with WHO emblems and inscription in margin. Value $10.

Prague Castle Art Type of 1971
Designs: 3k, View of Prague Castle, by F. Hoogenberghe, 1572. 3.60k, Faun and Satyr, sculptured panel, 16th century.

1976, Oct. 22   Engr.   Perf. 11½
2081	A634	3k multi	2.50	2.10
2082	A634	3.60k multi	.90	.60

Nos. 2081-2082 were each issued in sheets of 4. Value $15.

Guernica 1937, by Imro Weiner-Král — A741

1976, Oct. 22
2083   A741   5k multi   .80   .40
40th anniv. of the Intl. Brigade in Spain.

Zebras — A742

20h, Elephants. 30h, Cheetah. 40h, Giraffes. 60h, Rhinoceros. 3k, Bongos.

Engraved and Photogravure
1976, Nov. 3   Perf. 11½x11, 11x11½
2084	A742	10h multi	.25	.25
2085	A742	20h multi, vert.	.25	.25
2086	A742	30h multi	.30	.25
2087	A742	40h multi, vert.	.45	.25
2088	A742	60h multi	.45	.25
2089	A742	3k multi, vert.	2.00	.25
		Nos. 2084-2089 (6)	3.70	1.50

African animals in Dvur Kralove Zoo.

Painting Type of 1967
Paintings of Flowers: 1k, by Peter Matejka. 1.40k, by Cyril Bouda. 2k, by Jan Brueghel. 3.60k, J. Rudolf Bys.

1976, Nov. 27   Engr.   Perf. 11½
2090	A565	1k multi	.75	.50
2091	A565	1.40k multi	1.50	.90
2092	A565	2k multi	1.20	.90
2093	A565	3.60k multi	.80	.40
		Nos. 2090-2093 (4)	4.25	2.70

Nos. 2090-2093 were each issued in sheets of 4, with emblem and name of Praga 1978 on horizontal gutter. Value, set $17.50.

Postrider, 17th Century, and Satellites A743

1976, Dec. 18   Engr. & Photo.
2094   A743   1k multi   .25   .25
Stamp Day 1976.

Ice Hockey — A744

1977, Feb. 11 — Perf. 11½

2095	A744	60h shown	.25	.25
2096	A744	1k Biathlon	.25	.25
2097	A744	1.60k Ski jump	.85	.25
2098	A744	2k Downhill skiing	.25	.25
	Nos. 2095-2098 (4)		1.60	1.00

6th Winter Spartakiad of Socialist Countries' Armies.

Arms of Vranov — A745

Coats of Arms of Czechoslovak towns.

1977, Feb. 20

2099	A745	60h shown	.25	.25
2100	A745	60h Kralupy nad Vltavou	.25	.25
2101	A745	60h Jicin	.25	.25
2102	A745	60h Valasske Mezirici	.25	.25
	Nos. 2099-2102 (4)		1.00	1.00

See Nos. 2297-2300.

Window, Michna Palace — A746

Prague Renaissance Windows: 30h, Michna Palace. 40h, Thun Palace. 60h, Archbishop's Palace, Hradcany. 5k, St. Nicholas Church.

1977, Mar. 10

2103	A746	20h multi	.25	.25
2104	A746	30h multi	.25	.25
2105	A746	40h multi	.25	.25
2106	A746	60h multi	.25	.25
2107	A746	5k multi	1.50	1.00
	Nos. 2103-2107 (5)		2.50	1.25

PRAGA 1978 International Philatelic Exhibition, Prague, Sept. 8-17, 1978.

Children, Auxiliary Police — A747

1977, Apr. 21 — Perf. 11½

2108	A747	60h multi	.25	.25

Auxiliary Police, 25th anniversary.

Warsaw, Polish Flag, Bicyclists — A748

Designs: 60h, Berlin, DDR flag, bicyclists. 1k, Prague, Czechoslovakian flag, victorious bicyclist. 1.40k, Bicyclists on highways, modern views of Berlin, Prague and Warsaw.

1977, May 7

2109	A748	30h multi	.25	.25
2110	A748	60h multi	.25	.25
2111	A748	1k multi	.60	.25
2112	A748	1.40k multi	.40	.25
	Nos. 2109-2112 (4)		1.50	1.00

30th International Bicycle Peace Race Warsaw-Prague-Berlin.

Congress Emblem — A749

1977, May 25 — Perf. 11½

2113	A749	30h car, red & gold	.25	.25

9th Trade Union Congress, Prague 1977.

Prague Castle Art Type of 1971

Designs: 3k, Onyx footed bowl, 1350. 3.60k, Bronze horse, 1619.

1977, June 7 — Engr.

2114	A634	3k multi	1.25	1.10
2115	A634	3.60k multi	1.10	1.10

Nos. 2114-2115 were each issued in sheets of 4. Value, set $11.

French Postrider, 19th Century, PRAGA '78 Emblem A750

Postal Uniforms: 1k, Austrian, 1838. 2k, Austrian, late 18th century. 3.60k, Germany, early 18th century.

1977, June 8 — Engr. & Photo.

2116	A750	60h multi	.25	.25
2117	A750	1k multi	.25	.25
2118	A750	2k multi	.40	.25
2119	A750	3.60k multi	1.50	.35
	Nos. 2116-2119 (4)		2.40	1.10

PRAGA 1978 International Philatelic Exhibition, Prague, Sept. 8-17, 1978.
Nos. 2116-2119 were each issued both in sheets of 50 and in sheets of 4 stamps with 4 inscribed labels and 2 blank labels. Value, set of sheets of 4, $10.

Coffeepots, Porcelain Mark — A751

Czechoslovak Porcelain and Porcelain Marks: 30h, Urn. 40h, Vase. 60h, Cup and saucer, jugs. 1k, Candlestick and plate. 3k, Cup and saucer, coffeepot.

1977, June 15

2120	A751	20h multi	.25	.25
2121	A751	30h multi	.25	.25
2122	A751	40h multi	.25	.25
2123	A751	60h multi	.25	.25
2124	A751	1k multi	.25	.25
2125	A751	3k multi	1.10	.35
	Nos. 2120-2125 (6)		2.35	1.60

Mlada Boleslav Costume — A752

PRAGA Emblem and Folk Costumes from: 1.60k, Vazek. 3.60k, Zavadka. 5k, Belkovice.

1977, Aug. 31 — Engr. Perf. 11½

2126	A752	1k multi	1.25	.95
2127	A752	1.60k multi	1.25	.95
2128	A752	3.60k multi	1.25	.95
2129	A752	5k multi	1.25	.95
	Nos. 2126-2129 (4)		5.00	3.80

Issued in sheets of 10 and in sheets of 8 plus 2 labels showing PRAGA '78 emblem. Value, set: sheets of 10 $50; sheets of 8 $40.

Old Woman, Devil and Spinner, by Viera Bombova A753

Book Illustrations: 60h, Bear and tiger, by Genadij Pavlisin. 1k, Coach drawn by 4 horses (Hans Christian Andersen), by Ulf Lovgren. 2k, Bear and flamingos (Lewis Carroll), by Nicole Claveloux. 3k, King with keys, and toys, by Jiri Trnka.

1977, Sept. 9 — Engr. & Photo.

2130	A753	40h multi	.25	.25
2131	A753	60h multi	.25	.25
2132	A753	1k multi	.25	.25
2133	A753	2k multi	.25	.25
2134	A753	3k multi	1.00	.35
	Nos. 2130-2134 (5)		2.00	1.35

Prize-winning designs, 6th biennial exhibition of illustrations for children's books, Bratislava.

Globe, Violin, Doves, View of Prague — A754

1977, Sept. 28 — Perf. 11½

2135	A754	60h multi	.25	.25

Congress of International Music Council of UNESCO, Prague and Bratislava.

Souvenir Sheets

"For a Europe of Peace" — A755

1.60k, "For a Europe of Cooperation." 2.40k, "For a Europe of Social Progress."

1977, Oct. 3

2136	A755	Sheet of 2	.50	.50
a.		60h multi	.25	.25
2137	A755	Sheet of 2	1.00	1.00
a.		1.60k multi	.25	.25
2138	A755	Sheet of 2	2.00	1.75
a.		2.40k multi	.50	.50

2nd European Security and Cooperation Conference, Belgrade. Nos. 2136-2138 each contain 2 stamps and 2 blue on buff inscriptions and ornaments.
Nos. 2136-2138 were issued imperforate in sheets of 2. Value, $30.
For overprint of No. 2137, see No. 2334.

S. P. Korolev, Sputnik I Emblem — A756

30h, Yuri A. Gagarin & Vostok I. 40h, Alexei Leonov. 1k, Neil A. Armstrong & footprint on moon. 1.60k, Construction of orbital space station.

1977, Oct. 4

2139	A756	20h multi	.25	.25
2140	A756	30h multi	.25	.25
2141	A756	40h multi	.25	.25
2142	A756	1k multi	.25	.25
2143	A756	1.60k multi	.60	.25
	Nos. 2139-2143 (5)		1.60	1.25

Space research, 20th anniv. of 1st earth satellite.

Sailors, Cruiser Aurora — A757

1977, Nov. 7

2144	A757	30h multi	.25	.25

60th anniv. of Russian October Revolution.

"Russia," Arms of USSR, Kremlin — A758

1977, Nov. 7

2145	A758	30h multi	.25	.25

55th anniversary of the USSR.

"Science" — A759

1977, Nov. 17

2146	A759	3k multi	.50	.25

Czechoslovak Academy of Science, 25th anniversary.

Painting Type of 1967

Paintings: 2k, "Fear" (woman), by Jan Mudroch. 2.40k, Jan Francisci, portrait by Peter M. Bohun. 2.60k, Vaclav Hollar, self-portrait, 1647. 3k, Young Woman, 1528, by Lucas Cranach. 5k, Cleopatra, by Rubens.

1977, Nov. 27 — Engr. Perf. 11½

2147	A565	2k multi	.75	.45
2148	A565	2.40k multi	1.20	.90
2149	A565	2.60k multi	1.20	.90
2150	A565	3k multi	.75	.60
2151	A565	5k multi	1.50	1.50
	Nos. 2147-2151 (5)		5.40	4.35

Nos. 2147-2151 were each issued in sheets of 4. Value, set $25.

View of Bratislava, by Georg Hoefnagel A760

Design: 3.60k, Arms of Bratislava, 1436.

1977, Dec. 6

2152	A760	3k multi	1.90	1.60
2153	A760	3.60k multi	.80	.50

Nos. 2152-21531 were each issued in sheets of 4. Value, set $12.50.
See Nos. 2174-2175, 2270-2271, 2331-2332, 2364-2365, 2422-2423, 2478-2479, 2514-2515, 2570-2571, 2618-2619.

Stamp Pattern and Post Horn A761

1977, Dec. 18 — Engr. & Photo.

2154	A761	1k multi	.25	.25

Stamp Day.

CZECHOSLOVAKIA

Zdenek Nejedly
A762

Karl Marx
A763

1978, Feb. 10 — Perf. 11½
2155 A762 30h multi .25 .25
2156 A763 40h multi .25 .25

Zdenek Nejedly (1878-1962), musicologist and historian; Karl Marx (1818-1883), political philosopher.

Civilians Greeting Guardsmen
A764

Intellectual, Farm Woman and Steel Worker, Flag — A765

1978, Feb. 25
2157 A764 1k gold & multi .25 .25
2158 A765 1k gold & multi .25 .25

30th anniv. of "Victorious February" (No. 2157), and Natl. Front (No. 2158). An imperforate sheet of four of No. 2157 was sold with an admission ticket to PRAGA 78 international philatelic exhibition. Value, $4. See note after 2190.

Yuri A. Gagarin, Vostok I — A766

Design: 30h, 3.60k, like No. 2140.

Engraved; Overprint Photogravure
(Blue and carmine on 30h, green and lilac rose on 3.60k)
1978, Mar. 2 — Perf. 11½x12
2159 A766 30h dk red .25 .25
2160 A766 3.60k vio bl 2.40 2.40

Capt. V. Remek, 1st Czechoslovakian cosmonaut on Russian spaceship Soyuz 28, Mar. 2-9.

10k Coin, 1964, and 25k Coin, 1965 — A767

40h, Medal for Culture, 1972. 1.40k, Charles University medal, 1948. 3k, Ferdinand I medal, 1568. 5k, Gold florin, 1335.

1978, Mar. 14 — Engr. & Photo.
2161 A767 20h sil & multi .25 .25
2162 A767 40h sil & multi .25 .25
2163 A767 1.40k gold & multi 1.00 .25
2164 A767 3k gold & multi .35 .25
2165 A767 5k gold & multi .95 .85
Nos. 2161-2165 (5) 2.20 1.25

650th anniversary of Kremnica Mint.

Tire Tracks and Ball — A768

1978, Mar. 15
2166 A768 60h multi .25 .25

Road safety.

Congress Emblem — A769

1978, Apr. 16 — Perf. 11½
2167 A769 1k multi .25 .25

9th World Trade Union Cong., Prague 1978.

Shot Put and Praha '78 Emblem — A770

1k, Pole vault. 3.60k, Women runners.

1978, Apr. 26
2168 A770 40h multi .30 .30
2169 A770 1k multi .40 .32
2170 A770 3.60k multi .90 .50
Nos. 2168-2170 (3) 1.60 1.10

5th European Athletic Championships, Prague 1978.

Ice Hockey A771

Designs: 30h, Hockey. 2k, Ice hockey play.

1978, Apr. 26
2171 A771 30h multi .25 .25
2172 A771 60h multi .35 .25
2173 A771 2k multi .35 .25
Nos. 2171-2173 (3) .95 .75

5th European Ice Hockey Championships and 70th anniversary of Bandy hockey.

Bratislava Type of 1977

Designs: 3k, Bratislava, 1955, by Orest Dubay. 3.60k, Fishpound Square, Bratislava, 1955, by Imro Weiner-Kral.

1978, May 9 — Engr. — Perf. 11½
2174 A760 3k multi .95 .80
2175 A760 3.60k multi 1.25 .80
Nos. 2174-2175 were each issued in sheets of 4. Value, set $10.

Prague Castle Art Type of 1971

3k, King Ottokar II, detail from tomb. 3.60k, Charles IV, detail from votive panel by Jan Ocko.

1978, May 9
2176 A634 3k multi .75 .60
2177 A634 3.60k multi 3.50 2.40

Nos. 2176-2177 were each issued in sheets of 4. Value, set $18.

Ministry of Post, Prague — A772

Engraved and Photogravure
1978, May 29 — Perf. 12x11½
2178 A772 60h multi .25 .25

14th session of permanent COMECOM Commission (Ministers of Post and Telecommunications of Socialist Countries).

Palacky Bridge — A773

Prague Bridges and PRAGA '78 Emblem: 40h, Railroad bridge. 1k, Bridge of May 1. 2k, Manes Bridge. 3k, Svatopluk Cech Bridge. 5.40k, Charles Bridge.

1978, May 30
2179 A773 20h blk & multi .25 .25
2180 A773 40h blk & multi .25 .25
2181 A773 1k blk & multi .25 .25
2182 A773 2k blk & multi .25 .25
2183 A773 3k blk & multi .30 .25
2184 A773 5.40k blk & multi 1.40 .25
Nos. 2179-2184 (6) 2.70 1.50

PRAGA 1978 International Philatelic Exhibition, Prague, Sept. 8-17.

St. Peter and Apostles, Clock Tower, and Emblem — A774

Town Hall Clock, Prague, by Josef Manes, and PRAGA '78 Emblem: 1k, Astronomical clock. 2k, Prague's coat of arms. 3k, Grape harvest (September). 3.60k, Libra. 10k, Arms surrounded by zodiac signs and scenes symbolic of 12 months, horiz. 2k, 3k, 3.60k show details from design of 10k.

1978, June 20 — Perf. 11½x11
2185 A774 40h multi .25 .25
2186 A774 1k multi .25 .25
2187 A774 2k multi .25 .25
2188 A774 3k multi 1.50 .35
2189 A774 3.60k multi .55 .25
Nos. 2185-2189 (5) 2.80 1.35

Souvenir Sheet
Perf. 12x12
2190 A774 10k multi 10.00 7.50

PRAGA '78 Intl. Philatelic Exhibition, Prague, Sept. 8-17. No. 2190 contains one 50x40mm stamp. Sheet exists imperf. Value $27.50.
A non-valid souvenir sheet contains 4 imperf. examples of No. 2157. Sold only with PRAGA ticket.

Folk Dancers — A775

1978, July 7 — Perf. 11½x12
2191 A775 30h multi .25 .25

25th Folklore Festival, Vychodna.

Overpass and PRAGA Emblem A776

1k, 2k, Modern office buildings, diff. 6k, Old & new Prague. 20k, Charles Bridge & Old Town, by Vincent Morstadt, 1828.

1978 — Perf. 12x11½
2192 A776 60h blk & multi .25 .25
2193 A776 1k blk & multi .25 .25
2194 A776 2k blk & multi .25 .25
2195 A776 6k blk & multi 1.50 .99
Nos. 2192-2195 (4) 2.25 1.50

Souvenir Sheet
Engr.
2196 A776 20k multi 9.50 7.50

PRAGA 1978 Intl. Phil. Exhib., Prague, Sept. 8-17. No. 2196 also for 60th anniv. of Czechoslovak postage stamps. No. 2196 contains one 61x45mm stamp.
Issued: Nos. 2192-2195, 9/8; No. 2196, 9/10.

Souvenir Sheet

Titian (1488-1576), Venetian painter — A777

No. 2197a, Apollo's Companion, by Titian. No. 2197b, King Midas. Stamps show details from "Apollo Flaying Marsya" by Titian.

1978, Sept. 12 — Perf. 11½
2197 A777 Sheet of 2 11.00 8.75
 a. 10k multi 5.00 4.25
 b. 10k multi 5.00 4.25

No. 2197 with dark blue marginal inscription "FIP" was sold only with entrance ticket to PRAGA Philatelic Exhibition. Value $25.

Exhibition Hall — A778

Engraved and Photogravure
1978, Sept. 13 — Perf. 11½x11
2198 A778 30h multi .25 .25

22nd International Engineering Fair, Brno.

Postal Newspaper Service — A779

TV Screen, Headquarters and Logo — A780

Newspaper, Microphone — A781

1978, Sept. 21 — Perf. 11½
2199 A779 30h multi .25 .25
2200 A780 30h multi .25 .25
2201 A781 30h multi .25 .25
Nos. 2199-2201 (3) .75 .75

Postal News Service, 25th anniv.; Czechoslovakian television, 25th anniv.; Press, Broadcasting and Television Day.

Sulky Race — A782

Pardubice Steeplechase: 10h, Falling horses and jockeys at fence. 30h, Race. 40h, Horses passing post. 1.60k, Hurdling. 4.40k, Winner.

1978, Oct. 6 — Perf. 12x11½
2202 A782 10h multi .25 .25
2203 A782 20h multi .25 .25
2204 A782 30h multi .25 .25
2205 A782 40h multi .25 .25

CZECHOSLOVAKIA

| 2206 | A782 | 1.60k multi | .25 | .25 |
| 2207 | A782 | 4.40k multi | 1.25 | .25 |

Nos. 2202-2207 (6)   2.50 1.50

Woman Holding Arms of Czechoslovakia — A783

1978, Oct. 28   Perf. 11½
2208   A783   60h multi   .25 .25

60th anniversary of independence.

Art Type of 1974

2.40k, Flowers, by Jakub Bohdan (1660-1724). 3k, The Dream of Salas, by Ludovit Fulla, horiz. 3.60k, Apostle with Censer, Master of the Spissko Capitals (c. 1480-90).

1978, Nov. 27   Engr.
2209	A700	2.40k multi	.90	.45
2210	A700	3k multi	1.00	.75
2211	A700	3.60k multi	2.75	2.25

Nos. 2209-2211 (3)   4.65 3.45

Slovak National Gallery, 30th anniversary. Nos. 2209-2211 were each issued in sheets of 4. Value, set $20.

Musicians, by Jan Könyves — A784

Slovak Ceramics: 30h, Janosik on Horseback, by Jozef Franko. 40h, Woman in Folk Costume by Michal Polasko. 1k, Three Girls Singing, by Ignac Bizmayer. 1.60k, Janosik Dancing, by Ferdis Kostka.

Engraved and Photogravure
1978, Dec. 5   Perf. 11½x12
2212	A784	20h multi	.25	.25
2213	A784	30h multi	.25	.25
2214	A784	40h multi	.25	.25
2215	A784	1k multi	.25	.25
2216	A784	1.60k multi	.60	.25

Nos. 2212-2216 (5)   1.60 1.25

Alfons Mucha and his Design for 1918 Issue A785

1978, Dec. 18   Perf. 11½
2217   A785   1k multi   .25 .25

60th Stamp Day.

COMECON Building, Moscow — A786

1979, Jan. 1   Perf. 11½
2218   A786   1k multi   .25 .25

Council for Mutual Economic Aid (COMECON), 30th anniversary.

Woman's Head and Grain — A787   Woman, Workers, Child, Doves — A788

1979, Jan. 1
| 2219 | A787 | 30h multi | .25 | .25 |
| 2220 | A788 | 60h multi | .25 | .25 |

United Agricultural Production Assoc., 30th anniv. (30h); Czechoslovakian Federation, 10th anniv. (60h).

Soyuz 28, Rockets and Capsule A789

60h, Astronauts Aleksei Gubarev and Vladimir Remek on launching pad, vert. 1.60k, Soviet astronauts J. Romanenko and G. Grecko, Salyut 6 and recovery ship. 2k, Salyut-Soyuz orbital complex, post office in space and Czechoslovakia No. 2153. 4k, Soyuz 28, crew after landing and trajectory map, vert. 10k, Gubarev and Remek, Intercosmos emblem, arms of Czechoslovakia and USSR.

1979, Mar. 2
2221	A789	30h multi	.25	.25
2222	A789	60h multi	.25	.25
2223	A789	1.60k multi	.25	.25
2224	A789	2k multi	1.40	.25
2225	A789	4k multi	.60	.25

Nos. 2221-2225 (5)   2.75 1.25

Souvenir Sheet
2226   A789   10k multi   4.50 2.75

1st anniv. of joint Czechoslovak-Soviet space flight. Size of No. 2226: 76x93mm (stamp 39x55mm). No. 2226 has Cyrillic inscription, No. 2455a does not.
No. 2226 exists imperf. Value, $30.

Alpine Bellflowers — A790

Mountain Flowers: 20h, Crocus. 30h, Pinks. 40h, Alpine hawkweed. 3k, Larkspur.

1979, Mar. 23   Perf. 11½
2227	A790	10h multi	.25	.25
2228	A790	20h multi	.25	.25
2229	A790	30h multi	.25	.25
2230	A790	40h multi	.25	.25

Perf. 14
2231   A790   3k multi   1.10 .25

Nos. 2227-2231 (5)   2.10 1.25

Mountain Rescue Service, 25th anniversary.
The 3k exists perf. 11½. Value, $20 unused, $10 used.
The 3k was issued in sheets of 10. Values: perf 14 (No. 2231), $25; perf 11½, $180.

Stylized Satellite, Dial, Tape — A791

1979, Apr. 2
2232   A791   10h multi   .25 .25

Telecommunications research, 30th anniv.

Artist and Model, Dove, Bratislava Castle A792

Cog Wheels, Transformer and Student A793

Musical Instruments, Bratislava Castle — A794

Pioneer Scarf, IYC Emblem A795

Red Star, Man, Child and Doves A796

1979, Apr. 2
2233	A792	20h multi	.25	.25
2234	A793	20h multi	.25	.25
2235	A794	30h multi	.25	.25
2236	A795	30h multi	.25	.25
2237	A796	60h multi	.25	.25

Nos. 2233-2237 (5)   1.25 1.25

Fine Arts Academy, Bratislava, 30th anniv.; Slovak Technical University, 40th anniv.; Radio Symphony Orchestra, Bratislava, 30th anniv.; Young Pioneers, 30th anniv. and IYC; Peace Movement, 30th anniversary.

Prague Castle Art Type of 1971

3k, Burial crown of King Ottokar II. 3.60k, Portrait of Mrs. Reitmayer, by Karel Purkyne.

1979, May 9   Perf. 11½
| 2238 | A634 | 3k multi | 1.75 | 1.10 |
| 2239 | A634 | 3.60k multi | 1.75 | .80 |

Nos. 2238-2239 were each issued in sheets of 4. Value, set $13.50.

Arms of Vlachovo Brezi, 1538 — A797

Animals in Heraldry: 60h, Jesenik, 1509 (bear and eagle). 1.20k, Vysoke Myto, 1471 (St. George slaying dragon). 1.80k, Martin, 1854 (St. Martin giving coat to beggar). 2k, Zebrak, 1674 (mythological beast).

1979, May 25   Perf. 11½x12
2240	A797	30h multi	.25	.25
2241	A797	60h multi	.25	.25
2242	A797	1.20k multi	.25	.25
2243	A797	1.80k multi	1.00	.25
2244	A797	2k multi	.60	.25

Nos. 2240-2244 (5)   2.35 1.25

Forest, Thriving and Destroyed — A798

Designs: 1.80k, Water. 3.60k, City. 4k, Cattle. All designs show good and bad environment, separated by exclamation point; Man and Biosphere emblem.

1979, June 22   Engr.   Perf. 11½
2245	A798	60h multi	.25	.25
2246	A798	1.80k multi	.25	.25
2247	A798	3.60k multi	1.60	.60
2248	A798	4k multi	1.10	.25

Nos. 2245-2248 (4)   3.20 1.35

Man and Biosphere Program of UNESCO.
Nos. 2245-2248 were each issued in sheets of 10. Value, set $32.50.

Refinery, Smokestacks — A799

Engraved and Photogravure
1979, Aug. 29   Perf. 11x11½
2249   A799   30h multi   .25 .25

Slovak National Uprising, 35th anniversary.

Frog and Goat — A800

Book Illustrations (IYC Emblem and): 40h, Knight on horseback. 60h, Maidens. 1k, Boy with sled following rooster. 3k, King riding flying beast.

1979, Apr. 2   Perf. 11½x11
2250	A800	20h multi	.25	.25
2251	A800	40h multi	.25	.25
2252	A800	60h multi	.25	.25
2253	A800	1k multi	.25	.25
2254	A800	3k multi	1.10	.25

Nos. 2250-2254 (5)   2.10 1.25

Prize-winning designs, 7th biennial exhibition of illustrations for children's books, Bratislava; International Year of the Child.
Printed with labels showing story characters. Value, set with attached labels, $2.75.

"Bone Shaker" Bicycles, 1870 — A801

Bicycles from: 20h, 1978. 40h, 1910. 60h, 1886. 3.60k, 1820.

1979, Sept. 14   Perf. 12x11½
2255	A801	20h multi	.25	.25
2256	A801	40h multi	.25	.25
2257	A801	60h multi	.25	.25
2258	A801	2k multi	.25	.25
2259	A801	3.60k multi	1.50	.30

Nos. 2255-2259 (5)   2.50 1.30

Bracket Clock, 18th Century — A802

Designs: 18th century clocks.

1979, Oct. 1   Perf. 11½
2260	A802	40h multi	.25	.25
2261	A802	60h multi	.25	.25
2262	A802	80h multi	1.25	.25
2263	A802	1k multi	.25	.25
2264	A802	2k multi	.35	.25

Nos. 2260-2264 (5)   2.35 1.25

Painting Type of 1967

Paintings: 1.60k, Sunday by the River, by Alois Moravec. 2k, Self-portrait, by Gustav Mally. 3k, Self-portrait, by Ilia Yefimovic Repin. 3.60k, Horseback Rider, by Jan Bauch. 5k, Dancing Peasants, by Albrecht Dürer.

1979, Nov. 27   Engr.   Perf. 12
2265	A565	1.60k multi	.40	.35
2266	A565	2k multi	.60	.50
2267	A565	3k multi	.60	.50
2268	A565	3.60k multi	2.00	1.75
2269	A565	5k multi	1.60	1.25

Nos. 2265-2269 (5)   5.20 4.35

Nos. 2265-2269 were each issued in sheets of 4. Value, set $20.

Bratislava Type of 1977

Designs: 3k, Bratislava Castle on the Danube, by L. Janscha, 1787. 3.60k, Bratislava Castle, stone engraving by Wolf, 1815.

1979, Dec. 5
| 2270 | A760 | 3k multi | 1.00 | .80 |
| 2271 | A760 | 3.60k multi | 1.75 | 1.50 |

Nos. 2270-2272 were each issued in sheets of 4. Value, set $12.50.

Stamp Day A803

Engraved and Photogravure
1979, Dec. 18   Perf. 11½x12
2272   A803   1k multi   .25 .25

CZECHOSLOVAKIA

Electronic Circuits — A804

Designs: 50h, Satellite dish. 2k, Airplane. 3k, Computer punch tape.

1979-80   Photo.   *Perf. 11½x12*
Coil Stamps
2273	A804	50h red	.25	.25
2274	A804	1k brown	.25	.25
2275	A804	2k green ('80)	.30	.25
2276	A804	3k lake ('80)	.45	.25
Nos. 2273-2276 (4)			1.25	1.00

The 1k comes in two shades.

Runners and Dove — A805

Engraved and Photogravure
1980, Jan. 29   *Perf. 12x11½*
2289	A805	50h multi	.25	.25

50th Intl. Peace Marathon, Kosice, Oct. 4.

Downhill Skiing — A806

1980, Jan. 29   *Perf. 11½x12*
2290	A806	1k shown	.30	.25
2291	A806	2k Speed skating	.95	.35
2292	A806	3k Four-man bobsled	.80	.35
Nos. 2290-2292 (3)			2.05	.95

13th Winter Olympic Games, Lake Placid, NY, Feb. 12-24.

Basketball A807

1980, Jan. 29   *Perf. 11½*
2293	A807	40h shown	.25	.25
2294	A807	1k Swimming	.25	.25
2295	A807	2k Hurdles	1.50	.35
2296	A807	3.60k Fencing	1.10	.30
Nos. 2293-2296 (4)			3.10	1.15

22nd Olympic Games, Moscow, 7/19-8/3.

Arms Type of 1977

No. 2297, Bystrice Nad Pernstejnem. No. 2298, Kunstat. No. 2299, Rozmital Pod Tremsinem. No. 2300, Zlata Idka.

1980, Feb. 20   *Perf. 11½*
2297	A745	50h multi	.25	.25
2298	A745	50h multi	.25	.25
2299	A745	50h multi	.25	.25
2300	A745	50h multi	.25	.25
Nos. 2297-2300 (4)			1.00	1.00

Theatrical Mask A808   Slovak National Theater, Actors A809

1980, Mar. 1
2301	A808	50h multi	.25	.25
2302	A809	1k multi	.25	.25

50th Jiraskuv Hronov Theatrical Ensemble Review; Slovak National Theater, Bratislava, 60th anniversary.

Mouse in Space, Satellite — A810

Intercosmos: 1k, Weather map, satellite. 1.60k, Intersputnik television transmission. 4k, Camera, satellite. 5k, Czech satellite station, 1978, horiz. 10k, Intercosmos emblem, horiz.

1980, Apr. 12   *Perf. 11½x12, 12x11½*
2303	A810	50h multi	.25	.25
2304	A810	1k multi	.25	.25
2305	A810	1.60k multi	1.40	.25
2306	A810	4k multi	1.00	.25
2307	A810	5k multi	1.40	.25
Nos. 2303-2307 (5)			4.30	1.25

Souvenir Sheet
2308	A810	10k multi	3.50	2.50

Intercosmos cooperative space program. No. 2305 was issued in a sheet of 10. Value, $25.

No. 2308 exists imperf. Value, $30.

Police Corps Banner, Emblem — A811

1980, Apr. 17   *Perf. 11½*
2309	A811	50h multi	.25	.25

National Police Corps, 35th anniversary.

Lenin's 110th Birth Anniversary — A812

Design: No. 2311, Engels's 160th birth anniv.

1980, Apr. 22
2310	A812	1k tan & brn	.25	.25
2311	A812	1k lt grn & brn	.25	.25

Old and Modern Prague, Czech Flag, Bouquet A813

Boy Writing "Peace" — A814

Pact Members' Flags, Dove — A815

Czech and Soviet Arms, Prague and Moscow Views — A816

1980, May 6   *Perf. 12x11½*
2312	A813	50h multi	.25	.25
2313	A814	1k multi	.25	.25
2314	A815	1k multi	.25	.25
2315	A816	1k multi	.25	.25
Nos. 2312-2315 (4)			1.00	1.00

Liberation by Soviet army, 35th anniv.; Soviet victory in WWII, 35th anniv.; Signing of Warsaw Pact (Bulgaria, Czechoslovakia, German Democratic Rep., Hungary, Poland, Romania, USSR), 25th anniv.; Czechoslovak-Soviet Treaty of Friendship, Cooperation and Mutual Aid, 10th anniv.

Souvenir Sheet

UN, 35th Anniv. — A817

1980, June 3   *Engr.*   *Perf. 12*
2316	A817	Sheet of 2	3.25	2.50
a.		4k multicolored	1.25	1.25

Athletes Parading Banners in Strahov Stadium, Prague, Spartakiad Emblem — A818

Engraved and Photogravure
1980, June 3   *Perf. 12x11½*
2317	A818	50h shown	.25	.25
2318	A818	1k Gymnast, vert.	.25	.25

Spartakiad 1980, Prague, June 26-29.

Aechmea Fasciata — A819

Flowers: 50ch, Gerbera Jamesonii. 1k, Aechmea fasciata. 2k, Strelitzia reginae. 4k, Paphiopedilum.

1980, Aug. 13   *Perf. 12*
2319	A819	50h multicolored	.45	.25
2320	A819	1k multicolored	2.10	.65
2321	A819	2k multicolored	.55	.25
2322	A819	4k multicolored	2.25	.25
Nos. 2319-2322 (4)			5.35	1.40

Olomouc and Bratislava Flower Shows. Nos. 2319-2322 were each issued in sheets of 10. Values, set: unused, $65; used, $30.

A820

Designs: Folktale character embroideries.

1980, Sept. 24   *Perf. 11½x12*
2323	A820	50h Ohad girl	.25	.25
2324	A820	1k Punch and dog	.25	.25
2325	A820	2k Dandy and Posy	.35	.25
2326	A820	4k Lion and moon	1.30	.75
2327	A820	5k Wallachian dance	.65	.25
Nos. 2323-2327 (5)			2.80	1.75

National Census — A821

1980, Sept. 24   *Perf. 12x11½*
2328	A821	1k multi	.25	.25

Prague Castle Type of 1971

Designs: 3k, Old Palace gateway. 4k, Armorial lion, 16th century.

1980, Oct. 28   *Perf. 12*
2329	A634	3k multi	1.60	1.25
2330	A634	4k multi	1.10	.65

Nos. 2329-2330 were each issued in sheets of 4. Value, set: unused, $12; used, $9.

Bratislava Type of 1977

3k, View across the Danube, by J. Eder, 1810. 4k, The Old Royal Bridge, by J.A. Lantz, 1820.

1980, Oct. 28
2331	A760	3k multi	1.60	1.40
2332	A760	4k multi	1.25	.80

Nos. 2331-2332 were each issued in sheets of 4. Value, set $16.

10th Anniversary of Socialist Youth Federation — A822

1980, Nov. 9   *Perf. 12x11½*
2333	A822	50h multi	.25	.25

No. 2137 Overprinted 3. / MEZINARODNI VELETRH ZNAMEK / ESSEN '80 in Red

1980, Nov. 18
2334	A755	1.60k multi	18.00	10.00

Czechoslovak Day/ ESSEN '80, 3rd International Stamp Exhibition, No. 2334 has overprinted red marginal inscription.

Painting Type of 1967

Designs: 1k, Pavel Jozef Safarik, by Jozef B. Klemens. 2k, Peasant Revolt mosaic, Anna Podzemna. 3k, St. Lucia, 14th century statue. 4k, Waste Heaps, by Jan Zrzavy, horiz. 5k, Labor, sculpture by Jan Stursa.

1980, Nov. 27   *Engr.*   *Perf. 12*
2335	A565	1k multi	1.25	1.10
2336	A565	2k multi	1.25	1.10
2337	A565	3k multi	.65	.45
2338	A565	4k multi	.75	.55
2339	A565	5k multi	.75	.55
Nos. 2335-2339 (5)			4.65	3.75

Nos. 2335-2339 were each issued in sheets of 4. Value, set $27.

Stamp Day — A823

Engraved and Photogravure
1980, Dec. 18   *Perf. 11½x12*
2340	A823	1k multi	.25	.25

7th Five-year Plan, 1981-1985 — A824

1981, Jan. 1   *Perf. 11½*
2341	A824	50h multi	.25	.25

International Year of the Disabled — A825

1981, Feb. 24
2342	A825	1k multi	.25	.25

Landau, 1800 — A826

1k, Mail coach, 1830. 3.60k, Mail sled, 1840. 5k, 4-horse mail coach, 1860. 7k, Open carriage, 1840.

1981, Feb. 25   *Perf. 12x11½*
2343	A826	50h shown	.25	.25
2344	A826	1k multi	.25	.25
2345	A826	3.60k multi	1.00	.35
2346	A826	5k multi	.75	.25

CZECHOSLOVAKIA

2347	A826	7k multi	1.10	.75
a.		Sheet of 4	15.00	10.00
		Nos. 2343-2347 (5)	3.35	1.85

WIPA '81 Intl. Philatelic Exhibition, Vienna, Austria, May 22-31. No. 2347a issued May 10.

Wolfgang Amadeus Mozart — A827

Famous Men: No. 2348, Josef Hlavka (1831-1908). No. 2349, Juraj Hronec (1881-1959). No. 2350, Jan Sverma (1901-44). No. 2351, Mikulas Schneider-Trnavsky (1881-1958). No. 2352, B. Bolzano (1781-1848). No. 2353, Dimitri Shostakovich, composer. No. 2354, George Bernard Shaw, playwright. No. 2355, Wolfgang Amadeus Mozart.

1981, Mar. 10   Perf. 11½
2348	A827	50h multi	.25	.25
2349	A827	50h multi	.25	.25
2350	A827	50h multi	.25	.25
2351	A827	50h multi	.25	.25
2352	A827	1k multi	.45	.25
2353	A827	1k multi	.25	.25
2354	A827	1k multi	.25	.25
2355	A827	1k multi	.25	.25
		Nos. 2348-2355 (8)	2.20	2.00

Souvenir Sheet

Yuri Gagarin — A828

1981, Apr. 5   Perf. 12
2356	A828	Sheet of 2	4.50	4.00
a.		6k multicolored	2.00	1.60

20th anniv. of 1st manned space flight.

Workers and Banner — A829

1k, Hands holding banner. 4k, Worker holding banner, vert.

1981, Apr. 6   Perf. 12x11½
2357	A829	50h shown	.25	.25
2358	A829	1k multi	.25	.25
2359	A829	4k multi	.35	.25
		Nos. 2357-2359 (3)	.85	.75

Czechoslovakian Communist Party, 60th anniv.

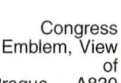

Congress Emblem, View of Prague — A830

1981, Apr. 6
2360	A830	50h shown	.25	.25
2361	A830	1k Bratislava	.25	.25

16th Communist Party Congress.

Agriculture Museum, 90th Anniv. — A831

1981, May 14   Perf. 11½x12
| 2362 | A831 | 1k multi | .25 | .25 |

Natl. Assembly Elections — A832

1981, June 1
| 2363 | A832 | 50h multi | .25 | .25 |

Bratislava Type of 1977

Designs: 3k, Bratislava Castle, by G.B. Probst, 1760. 4k, Grassalkovic Palace, by C. Bschor, 1815.

1981, June 10   Perf. 12
2364	A760	3k multi	1.40	1.25
2365	A760	4k multi	1.00	.75

Nos. 2364-2365 were each issued in sheets of 4. Value, set: unused, $12; used, $9.

Uran and Red October (Health) Resorts — A833

Successes of Socialist Achievements Exhibition: 1k, Brno-Bratislava Highway, Jihlava. 2k, Nuclear power station, Jaslovske Bohunice.

1981, June 10   Perf. 12x11½
2366	A833	80h multi	.25	.25
2367	A833	1k multi	.25	.25
2368	A833	2k multi	.25	.25
		Nos. 2366-2368 (3)	.75	.75

Border Defense Units, 30th Anniv. A834   Civil Defense, 30th Anniv. A835

Union for Cooperation with the Army (SVAZARM), 30th Anniv. — A836   Intl. Youth Character Building Contest, Rysy Mtn., 25th Anniv. — A837

Engraved and Photogravure

1981, July 11   Perf. 11½
2369	A834	40h multi	.25	.25
2370	A835	50h multi	.25	.25
2371	A836	1k multi	.25	.25
2372	A837	3.60k multi	.75	.30
		Nos. 2369-2372 (4)	1.50	1.05

30th Natl. Festival of Amateur Puppet Ensembles — A838

1981, July 2   Perf. 11½
| 2373 | A838 | 2k Punch and Devil | .50 | .25 |

Souvenir Sheet

Guernica, by Pablo Picasso — A839

1981, July 2   Engr.   Perf. 11½x12
| 2374 | A839 | 10k multi | 3.50 | 2.50 |

Picasso's birth centenary; 45th anniv. of Intl. Brigades in Spain.

Cat Holding Flower, by Etienne Delessert — A840

8th Biennial Exhibition of Children's Book Illustrations (Designs by): 50h, Albin Brunovsky, vert. 1k, Adolf Born. 2k, Vive Tolli. 10k, Suekichi Akaba.

Engraved and Photogravure
1981, Sept. 5   Perf. 11½
2375	A840	50h multi	.25	.25
2376	A840	1k multi	.25	.25
2377	A840	2k multi	.25	.25
2378	A840	4k multi	.55	.25
2379	A840	10k multi	1.50	.25
		Nos. 2375-2379 (5)	2.80	1.25

Prague Zoo, 50th Anniv. A841

1981, Sept. 28   Perf. 11½x12
2380	A841	50h Gorillas	.45	.25
2381	A841	1k Lions	.80	.25
2382	A841	7k Przewalski's horses	2.25	.80
		Nos. 2380-2382 (3)	3.50	1.30

Anti-smoking Campaign — A842

1981, Oct. 27   Perf. 12
| 2383 | A842 | 4k multi | .85 | .45 |

No. 2383 was issued in sheets of 10, containing 8 stamps and 2 labels. Values: single with label attached, $1.25; sheet, $9.

Prague Castle Art Type of 1971

Designs: 3k, Carved dragon, Palais Lobkovitz, 16th cent. 4k, St. Vitus Cathedral, by J. Sember and G. Dobler, 19th cent.

1981, Oct. 28
2384	A634	3k multi	.75	.45
2385	A634	4k multi	1.75	1.40

Nos. 2384-2385 were each issued in sheets of 4. Value, set $12.

Painting Type of 1967

Designs: 1k, View of Prague, by Vaclav Hollar (1607-1677). 2k, Czechoslovak Academy medallion, engraved by Otakar Spaniel (1881-1955). 3k, Jihoceska Vysivka, by Zdenek Sklenar (b. 1910). 4k, Still Life, by A.M. Gerasimov (1881-1963). 5k, Standing Woman, by Pablo Picasso (1881-1973).

1981, Nov. 27   Engr.   Perf. 12
2386	A565	1k multi	2.10	1.40
2387	A565	2k multi	.55	.30
2388	A565	3k multi	.70	.45
2389	A565	4k multi	.85	.45
2390	A565	5k multi	1.40	1.10
		Nos. 2386-2390 (5)	5.60	3.70

Nos. 2386-2390 were each issued in sheets of 4. Value, set $27.50.
Sheets of No. 2390 exist with center gutter inscribed with Philexfrance 82 and FIP emblems. Value, $10.

Stamp Day A843

Engraved and Photogravure
1981, Dec. 18   Perf. 11½x12
| 2391 | A843 | 1k Engraver Edward Karel | .25 | .25 |

Russian Workers' Party, Prague Congress, 70th Anniv. — A844

1982, Jan. 18   Perf. 12
2392	A844	2k Lenin	.50	.25
a.		Sheet of 4	4.50	4.00

No. 2392 issued in sheet of 8. Value $10.

1982 World Cup Soccer — A845

Designs: Various soccer players.

1982, Jan. 29   Perf. 12x11½
2393	A845	1k multi	.25	.25
2394	A845	3.60k multi	.70	.30
2395	A845	4k multi	1.40	.50
		Nos. 2393-2395 (3)	2.35	1.05

10th World Trade Union Congress, Havana — A846

1982, Feb. 10   Perf. 11½
| 2396 | A846 | 1k multi | .25 | .25 |

Arms of Hrob — A847

Arms of various cities: No. 2398, Nove Mesto Nad Metuji. No. 2399, Trencin. No. 2400, Mlada Boleslav.

1982, Feb. 10   Perf. 12x11½
2397	A847	50h shown	.25	.25
2398	A847	50h multicolored	.25	.25
2399	A847	50h multicolored	.25	.25
2400	A847	50h multicolored	.25	.25
		Nos. 2397-2400 (4)	1.00	1.00

See Nos. 2499-2502, 2542-2544, 2595-2597, 2783-2786.

50th Anniv. of the Great Strike at Most — A848

1982, Mar. 23   Perf. 11½
| 2401 | A848 | 1k multi | .25 | .25 |

60th Intl. Railway Union Congress A849

6k, Steam locomotive, 1922, electric, 1982.

1982, Mar. 23   Perf. 12x11½
| 2402 | A849 | 6k multicolored | 3.25 | .95 |

10th Workers' Congress, Prague — A850

1982, Apr. 15
| 2403 | A850 | 1k multi | .25 | .25 |

CZECHOSLOVAKIA

George Dimitrov — A851

1982, May 1
2404 A851 50h multi .25 .25

A852

Engravings: 40h, The Muse Euterpe Playing a Flute, by Crispin de Passe (1565-1637). 50h, The Lute Player, by Jacob de Gheyn (1565-1629). 1k, Woman Flautist, by Adriaen Collaert (1560-1618). 2k, Musicians in a Hostel, by Rembrandt (1606-1669). 3k, Hurdy-gurdy Player, by Jacques Callot (1594-1635).

1982, May 18   *Perf. 11½x12*
2405 A852 40h multi .25 .25
2406 A852 50h multi .25 .25
2407 A852 1k multi .25 .25
2408 A852 2k multi .30 .25
2409 A852 3k multi 1.10 .60
    Nos. 2405-2409 (5) 2.15 1.60

10th Lidice Intl. Children's Drawing Contest — A853

1982, May 18
2410 A853 2k multi 1.25 .90
Issued in sheets of 6 with 3 labels. Value $9.

40th Anniv. of Destruction of Lidice and Lezaky — A854

1982, June 4   *Perf. 11½*
2411 A854 1k Girl, rose .45 .25
2412 A854 1k Hands, barbed wire .45 .25

Souvenir Sheet

UN Disarmament Conference — A855

1982, June 4   *Perf. 12*
2413 A855 Sheet of 2 9.00 7.00
   a. 6k Woman holding doves 4.00 3.00

Souvenir Sheet

2nd UN Conference on Peaceful Uses of Outer Space, Vienna, Aug. 9-21 — A856

1982, Aug. 9   *Engr. & Photo.*
2414 A856 Sheet of 2 12.50 9.00
   a. 5k multi 4.50 3.50

Krivoklat Castle — A857

1k, Statues (Krivoklat). 2k, Nitra Castle. 3k, Pottery, lock (Nitra).

1982, Aug. 31   *Perf. 12x11½*
2415 A857 50h shown .25 .25
2416 A857 1k multi .25 .25
2417 A857 2k multi .30 .25
2418 A857 3k multi .40 .35
   a. Souv. sheet of 4, #2415-2418 2.00 1.60
    Nos. 2415-2418 (4) 1.20 1.10

50th Anniv. of Zizkov Hill Natl. Monument — A858

1982, Sept. 16
2419 A858 1k multi .25 .25

Prague Castle Art Type of 1971

Designs: 3k, St. George and the Dragon, 1373. 4k, Tomb of King Vratislav I, 10th cent.

1982, Sept. 28   *Perf. 12*
2420 A634 3k multi 1.60 1.25
2421 A634 4k multi .85 .85

Nos. 2420-2421 were each issued in sheets of 4. Value, set: unused, $11; used, $10.

Bratislava Type of 1977

Designs: 3k, Paddle steamer, Parnik, 1818. 4k, View from Bridge, 19th cent.

1982, Sept. 29
2422 A760 3k multi 1.40 1.00
2423 A760 4k multi 1.40 1.00

Nos. 2422-2423 were each issued in sheets of 4. Value, set $15.

European Danube Commission A859

3k, Steamer, Bratislava Bridge. 3.60k, Ferry, Budapest.

1982, Sept. 29   *Perf. 11½x12*
2424 A859 3k multi .65 .25
   a. Souvenir sheet of 4 4.00 3.00
2425 A859 3.60k multi .85 .25
   a. Souvenir sheet of 4 6.00 5.00

16th Communist Party Congress A860

1982, Oct. 28   *Perf. 12x11½*
2426 A860 20h Agriculture .25 .25
2427 A860 1k Industry .25 .25
2428 A860 3k Engineering .25 .25
    Nos. 2426-2428 (3) .75 .75

30th Anniv. of Academy of Sciences — A861

1982, Oct. 29   *Perf. 12*
2429 A861 6k Emblem .90 .35

65th Anniv. of October Revolution A862

Design: 1k, 60th anniv. of USSR.

1982, Nov. 7   *Perf. 12x11½*
2430 A862 50h multi .25 .25
2431 A862 1k multi .25 .25

Jaroslav Hasek, Writer, Sculpture by Josef Malejovsky — A863

Sculptures: 2k, Jan Zrzavy, painter and graphic artist, by Jan Simota. 4.40k, Leos Janacek, composer, by Milos Axman. 6k, Martin Kukucin, freedom fighter, by Jan Kulich. 7k, Peaceful Work, by Rudolf Pribis.

Engraved and Photogravure

1982, Nov. 26   *Perf. 11½x12*
2432 A863 1k multi .25 .25
2433 A863 2k multi .25 .25
2434 A863 4.40k multi .75 .25
2435 A863 6k multi .80 .25
2436 A863 7k multi 1.20 .50
    Nos. 2432-2436 (5) 3.25 1.50

Nos. 2432-2436 were each issued in sheets of 4. Value, set $20.

Painting Type of 1967

1k, Revolution in Spain, by Josef Sima (1891-1971). 2k, Woman Dressing, by Rudolf Kremlicka (1886-1932). 3k, The Girl Bride, by Dezider Milly (1906-1971). 4k, Performers, by Jan Zelibsky (b. 1907). 5k, The Complaint of the Birds, by Emil Filla (1882-1953).

1982, Nov. 27   *Perf. 12*
2437 A565 1k multi .70 .45
2438 A565 2k multi 1.40 1.00
2439 A565 3k multi .70 .45
2440 A565 4k multi .70 .45
2441 A565 5k multi 1.40 1.00
    Nos. 2437-2441 (5) 4.90 3.35

Nos. 2437-2441 were each issued in sheets of 4. Value, set $20.

Stamp Day — A864

1k, Engraver Jaroslav Goldschmied (1890-1977).

1982, Dec. 8   *Perf. 11½*
2442 A864 1k multicolored .25 .25

A865

1983, Jan. 10   *Engr. Perf. 12x11½*
2443 A865 50h dark blue .25 .25

Pres. Gustav Husak, 70th birthday. See No. 2686.

A866

Designs: 50h, Jaroslav Hasek (1882-1923), writer. 1k, Julius Fucik (1903-1943), antifascist martyr. 2k, Martin Luther (1483-1546). 5k, Johannes Brahms (1833-1897), composer.

1983, Feb. 24   *Engr. & Photo.*
2444 A866 50h multi .25 .25
2445 A866 1k multi .25 .25
2446 A866 2k multi .25 .25
   a. Souvenir sheet of 4 24.00 12.50
2447 A866 5k multi .65 .25
    Nos. 2444-2447 (4) 1.40 1.00

Nordposta '83 Intl. Stamp Exhibition, Hamburg. No. 2446a issued Nov. 1.

Workers Marching A867

Family A868

1983, Feb. 25   *Perf. 11½*
2448 A867 50h multi .25 .25
2449 A868 1k multi .25 .25

35th anniv. of "Victorious February" (50h), and Natl. Front (1k).

World Communications Year — A869

Perf. 11½, 12x11½ (2k)

1983, Mar. 16
2450 A869 40h multi .25 .25
2451 A869 1k multi .25 .25
2452 A869 2k multi .25 .25
2453 A869 3.60k multi .40 .25
    Nos. 2450-2453 (4) 1.15 1.00

Various wave patterns. 2k, 40x23mm; 3.60k, 49x19mm.

7th World Ski-jumping Championships A870

1983, Mar. 16   *Perf. 11½*
2454 A870 1k multi .25 .25

Souvenir Sheet

5th Anniv. of Czechoslovak-USSR Intercosmos Cooperative Space Program — A871

1983, Apr. 12   *Perf. 12*
2455 A871 Sheet of 2 11.00 7.50
   a. 10k multi 3.50 3.50

See No. 2226.

Protected Species A872

50h, Butterfly, violets. 1k, Water lilies, frog. 2k, Pine cones, crossbill. 3.60k, Herons. 5k, Gentians, lynx. 7k, Stag.

1983, Apr. 28   *Perf. 12x11½*
2456 A872 50h multi .30 .25
2457 A872 1k multi .65 .25
2458 A872 2k multi .65 .30
2459 A872 3.60k multi .80 .35
2460 A872 5k multi 1.10 .45
2461 A872 7k multi 2.50 1.00
    Nos. 2456-2461 (6) 6.00 2.60

Soviet Marshals — A873

50h, Ivan S. Konev. 1k, Andrei I. Yeremenko. 2k, Rodion J. Malinovsky.

1983, May 5   *Perf. 11½*
2462 A873 50h multi .25 .25
2463 A873 1k multi .25 .25
2464 A873 2k multi .25 .25
    Nos. 2462-2464 (3) .75 .75

30th anniv. of Czechoslovak-Soviet defense treaty.

66 CZECHOSLOVAKIA

A874

1983, July 13 Perf. 12
2465 A874 2k multi .35 .25
  a. Souvenir sheet of 4 6.50 5.50

World Peace and Life Congress, Prague. No. 2465 issued in sheets of 8. Value $4.50.

Emperor Rudolf II by Adrian De Vries (1560-1626) — A875

Art treasures of the Prague Castle: 5k, Kinetic relief, Timepiece, Rudolf Svoboda.

1983, Aug. 25 Perf. 11½
2466 A875 4k multi .80 .60
2467 A875 5k multi .80 .60

Nos. 2466-2467 were each issued in sheets of 6. Value, set $12.
See Nos. 2518-2519, 2610-2611, 2654-2655, 2717-2718, 2744-2745, 2792-2793.

9th Biennial of Illustrations for Children and Youth — A876

Illustrators: 50h, Oleg K. Zotov, USSR. 1k, Zbigniew Rychlicki, Poland. 4k, Lisbeth Zwerger, Austria. 7k, Antonio Domingues, Angola.

1983, Sept. 9 Engr. & Photo.
2468 A876 50h multi .25 .25
2469 A876 1k multi .25 .25
2470 A876 4k multi .25 .25
2471 A876 7k multi .50 .25
  a. Souv. sheet of 4, #2468-2471 5.00 3.00
    Nos. 2468-2471 (4) 1.25 1.00

World Communications Year — A877

Emblems and aircraft.

1983, Sept. 30 Perf. 11½
2472 A877 50h red & black .25 .25
2473 A877 1k red & black, vert. .25 .25
2474 A877 4k red & black .75 .25
    Nos. 2472-2474 (3) 1.25 .75

60th anniv. of the Czechoslovak Airlines.

16th Party Congress Achievements A878

1983, Oct. 20 Perf. 12x11½
2475 A878 50h Civil engineering construction .25 .25
2476 A878 1k Chemical industry .25 .25
2477 A878 3k Health services .40 .25
    Nos. 2475-2477 (3) .90 .75

Bratislava Type of 1977

Designs: 3k, Two sculptures, Viktor Tilgner (1844-96). 4k, Mirbachov Palace, 1939, by Julius Schubert (1888-1947).

1983, Oct. 28 Perf. 12
2478 A760 3k multi 1.50 1.25
2479 A760 4k multi 1.25 1.00

Nos. 2478-2479 were each issued in sheets of 4 stamps. Value, set $12.

Natl. Theater, Prague, Centenary — A879

50h, Natl. Theater building. 2k, State Theater, Natl. Theater.

1983, Nov. 8 Engr. Perf. 11½
2480 A879 50h brown .25 .25
2481 A879 2k green .30 .25

Messenger of Mourning, by Mikolas Ales — A880

Designs: 2k, Genius, theater curtain by Vojtech Hynais (1854-1925). 3k, Music, Lyric drawings by Frantisek Zenisek (1849-1916). 4k, Symbolic figure of Prague, by Vaclav Brozik (1851-1901). 5k, Hradcany Castle, by Julius Marak (1832-1899).

1983, Nov. 18 Engr.
2482 A880 1k multi 1.20 .75
2483 A880 2k multi 1.50 1.10
2484 A880 3k multi .90 .45
2485 A880 4k multi 1.40 .45
2486 A880 5k multi 1.10 .60
    Nos. 2482-2486 (5) 6.10 3.35

Nos. 2482-2486 were each issued in sheets of 4 stamps. Value, set $30.

Warrior with Sword and Shield, Engraving, 17th Cent. — A881

Engravings of Costumes: 50h, Bodyguard of Rudolf II, by Jacob de Gheyn (1565-1629). 1k, Lady with Lace Collar, by Jacques Callot (1592-1635). 4k, Lady, by Vaclav Hollar (1607-77). 5k, Man, by Antoine Watteau (1684-1721).

Engraved and Photogravure

1983, Dec. 2 Perf. 11½x12
2487 A881 40h multi .25 .25
2488 A881 50h multi .25 .25
2489 A881 1k multi .25 .25
2490 A881 4k multi .55 .25
2491 A881 5k multi 1.25 .75
    Nos. 2487-2491 (5) 2.55 1.75

Stamp Day A882

1k, Karl Seizinger (1889-1978), #114.

1983, Dec. 18
2492 A882 1k multicolored .25 .25

Czechoslovak Federation, 15th Anniv. — A883

50h, Bratislava, Prague Castles.

1984, Jan. 1 Perf. 11½
2493 A883 50h multicolored .25 .25

35th Anniv. of COMECON — A884

1k, Headquarters, Moscow.

1984, Jan. 23
2494 A884 1k dark blue & red brown .25 .25

1984 Winter Olympics A885

1984, Feb. 7 Perf. 12x11½
2495 A885 2k Cross-country skiing .40 .25
2496 A885 3k Hockey .50 .25
  a. Souvenir sheet of 4 5.00 4.00
2497 A885 5k Biathlon 1.25 .35
    Nos. 2495-2497 (3) 2.15 .85

Intl. Olympic Committee, 90th Anniv. — A886

1984, Feb. 7 Perf. 11½x12
2498 A886 7k Rings, runners, torch 1.25 .35

City Arms Type of 1982

1984, Mar. 1 Perf. 12x11½
2499 A847 50h Kutna Hora .25 .25
2500 A847 50h Turnov .25 .25
2501 A847 1k Martin .25 .25
2502 A847 1k Milevsko .25 .25
    Nos. 2499-2502 (4) 1.00 1.00

Intercosmos Space Program — A887

Various satellites. Nos. 2503-2507 se-tenant with labels showing flags.

1984, Apr. 12 Perf. 11½x12
2503 A887 50h multi .30 .25
2504 A887 1k multi .45 .25
2505 A887 2k multi .45 .25
2506 A887 4k multi .75 .25
2507 A887 5k multi .75 .25
    Nos. 2503-2507 (5) 2.70 1.25

Resistance Heroes — A888

Designs: 50h, Vendelin Opatrny (1908-44). 1k, Ladislav Novomesky (1904-76). 2k, Rudolf Jasiok (1919-44). 4k, Jan Nalepka (1912-43).

1984, May 9 Perf. 11x11½
2508 A888 50h multi .25 .25
2509 A888 1k multi .25 .25
2510 A888 2k multi .25 .25
2511 A888 4k multi .25 .25
    Nos. 2508-2511 (4) 1.00 1.00

Music Year — A889

1984, May 11 Perf. 11½
2512 A889 50h Instruments .25 .25
2513 A889 1k Organ pipes, vert. .25 .25

Bratislava Type of 1977

Designs: 3k, Vintners' Guild arms, 19th cent. 4k, View of Bratislava (painting commemorating shooting competition, 1827).

1984, June 1 Perf. 12
2514 A760 3k multi 1.10 .85
2515 A760 4k multi 1.60 1.10

Nos. 2514-2515 were each issued in sheets of 4 stamps. Value, set $12.

Central Telecommunications Building, Bratislava — A890

1984, June 1 Perf. 11½
2516 A890 2k multi .25 .25

A891

1984, June 12 Perf. 12
2517 A891 5k UPU emblem, dove, globe 2.50 2.50

1984 UPU Congress. Issued in sheet of 4 with and without Philatelic Salon text. Values, $30 with text, $12 without text.

Prague Castle Type of 1983

Designs: 3k, Crowing rooster, St. Vitus Cathedral, 19th cent. 4k, King David from the Roundnice, Book of Psalms illuminated manuscript, Bohemia, 15th cent.

1984, Aug. 9 Engr. & Photo.
2518 A875 3k multi .75 .60
2519 A875 4k multi 1.00 .75

Nos. 2518-2519 were each issued in sheets of 6 stamps. Value, set $10.

Playing Cards — A893

50h, Jack of Spades, 16th cent. 1k, Queen of spades, 17th cent. 2k, 9 of hearts, 18th cent. 3k, Jack of clubs, 18th cent. 5k, King of hearts, 19th cent.

1984, Aug. 28 Perf. 11½x12
2520 A893 50h multi .25 .25
2521 A893 1k multi .25 .25
2522 A893 2k multi .25 .25
2523 A893 3k multi .35 .25
2524 A893 5k multi 1.00 .25
    Nos. 2520-2524 (5) 2.10 1.25

Slovak Natl. Uprising, 40th Anniv. — A894

1984, Aug. 29 Perf. 12x11½
2525 A894 50h Family, factories, flowers .25 .25

Battle of Dukla Pass (Carpathians), 40th Anniv. — A895

1984, Sept. 8 Perf. 11½x12
2526 A895 2k Soldiers, flag .40 .25

1984 Summer Olympics A896

1984, Sept. 9 Perf. 12x11½
2527 A896 1k Pole vault .25 .25
2528 A896 2k Bicycling .40 .25
2529 A896 3k Rowing .60 .35
2530 A896 5k Weight lifting 1.00 .45
  a. Souv. sheet of 4, #2527-2530 4.00 3.25
    Nos. 2527-2530 (4) 2.25 1.30

CZECHOSLOVAKIA

16th Party Congress Goals and Projects — A897

1984, Oct. 28   *Perf. 12x11½*
2531	A897	1k Communications	.25	.25
2532	A897	2k Transportation	.25	.25
2533	A897	3k Transgas pipeline	.35	.25
a.		Souvenir sheet of 3	2.00	1.60
		Nos. 2531-2533 (3)	.85	.75

Painting Type of 1967

1k, The Milevsky River, by Karel Stehlik (b. 1912). 2k, Under the Trees, by Viktor Barvitius (1834-1902). 3k, Landscape with Flowers, by Zolo Palugyay (1898-1935). 4k, King in Palace, Visehrad Codex miniature, 1085. 5k, View of Kokorin Castles, by Antonin Manes. Nos. 2534-2537 horiz.; issued in sheets of 4.

1984, Nov. 16   *Perf. 11½*
2534	A565	1k multi	1.75	.90
2535	A565	2k multi	1.75	.90
2536	A565	3k multi	1.75	.90
2537	A565	4k multi	2.75	.90
2538	A565	5k multi	3.25	.90
		Nos. 2534-2538 (5)	11.25	4.50

Nos. 2534-2538 were each issued in sheets of 4 stamps. Value, set $45.

Students' Intl. 45th Anniv. — A898

1984, Nov. 17
2539	A898	1k Head, dove	.25	.25

Birth Cent., Antonin Zapotocky — A899

Engr. & Photo.
1984, Dec. 18   *Perf. 11½*
2540	A899	50h multi	.25	.25

Stamp Day — A900

1k, Engraver Bohumil Heinz (1894-1940).

1984, Dec. 18   *Perf. 11½x12*
2541	A900	1k multi	.25	.25

City Arms Type of 1982

1985, Feb. 6   *Perf. 12x11½*
2542	A847	50h Kamyk nad Vltavou	.25	.25
2543	A847	50h Havirov	.25	.25
2544	A847	50h Trnava	.25	.25
		Nos. 2542-2544 (3)	.75	.75

University of Applied Arts, Prague, Centenary — A901

1985, Feb. 6   *Perf. 11½x12*
2545	A901	3k Art and Pleasure, sculpture	.40	.25

Trnava University, 350th Anniv. A902

1985, Feb. 6   *Perf. 11½x12*
2546	A902	2k Town of Trnava	.40	.25

Military Museum Exposition — A903

50h, Armor, crossbow, vert. 1k, Medals, vert. 2k, Biplane, spacecraft.

1985, Feb. 7   *Perf. 11½x12, 12x11½*
2547	A903	50h multi	.25	.25
2548	A903	1k multi	.25	.25
2549	A903	2k multi	.40	.25
		Nos. 2547-2549 (3)	.90	.75

Vladimir I. Lenin (1870-1924), 1st Chairman of Russia — A904

1985, Mar. 15   *Engr.*   *Perf. 12*
2550	A904	2k multi	.80	.40

No. 2550 printed in sheets of 6 stamps. Value $5.

UN 40th Anniv., Peace Year 1986 — A905

1985, Mar. 15
2551	A905	6k UN, Peace Year emblems	2.75	2.40

Issued in sheets of 4 stamps. Value $12.

Natl. Arms, Twig, Crowd — A906

Engraved and Photogravure
1985, Apr. 5   *Perf. 11½*
2552	A906	4k multicolored	.60	.25

Kosice govt. plan, Apr. 5, 1945.

Natl. Arms, Flag, Soldiers — A907

1985, Apr. 5
2553	A907	50h multicolored	.25	.25

Natl. Security Forces, 40th anniv.

Halley's Comet, INTERCOSMOS Project Vega — A908

Design: Emblem, space platform, interstellar map, intercept data.

1985, Apr. 12   *Perf. 12x11½*
2554		Sheet of 2	9.00	9.00
a.		A908 5k multicolored	4.00	3.25

Project Vega, a joint effort of the USSR, France, German Democratic Republic, Austria, Poland, Bulgaria and CSSR, was for the geophysical study of Halley's Comet, Dec. 1984-Mar. 1986.

European Ice Hockey Championships, Prague, Apr. 17-May 3 — A909

1985, Apr. 13
2555	A909	1k Hockey players, emblem	.25	.25

No. 2555 Ovptd. "CSSR MISTREM SVETA" in Violet Blue

1985, May 31   *Perf. 12x11½*
2556	A909	1k multi	2.00	2.00

Natl. Chess Org., 80th Anniv. — A910

1985, Apr. 13   *Perf. 11½*
2557	A910	6k Emblem, game board, chessmen	1.25	.50

Anniversaries — A911

No. 2558, May Uprising, 1945. No. 2559, Soviet Army in CSSR, 1945. No. 2560, Warsaw Treaty, 1950. No. 2561, Czech-Soviet Treaty, 1970.

1985, May 5   *Perf. 11½x12*
2558	A911	1k multicolored	.25	.25
2559	A911	1k multicolored	.25	.25
2560	A911	1k multicolored	.25	.25
2561	A911	1k multicolored	.25	.25
		Nos. 2558-2561 (4)	1.00	1.00

Spartakiad '85, Strahov Stadium, Prague, June 27 — A912

Designs: 50h, Gymnasts warming up with rackets and balls. 1k, Rhythmic gymnastics floor exercise, Prague Castle.

1985, June 3   *Perf. 11½, 11½x12*
2562	A912	50h multi	.25	.25

Size: 53x22mm
2563	A912	1k multi	.25	.25

WWII Anti-Fascist Political Art — A913

Drawings and caricatures: 50h, Fire, and From the Concentration Camp, by Joseph Capek (1887-1945). 2k, The Conference on Disarmament in Geneva, 1927 and The Prophecy of Three Parrots, 1933, by Frantisek Bidlo (1895-1945). 4k, The Unknown Warrior to Order, 1936, and The Almost Peaceful Dove, 1937, by Antonin Pelc (1895-1967).

1985, June 4   *Perf. 12x11½*
2564	A913	50h multi	.25	.25
2565	A913	2k multi	.25	.25
2566	A913	4k multi	.90	.25
		Nos. 2564-2566 (3)	1.40	.75

Helsinki Conference on European Security and Cooperation, 10th Anniv. — A914

1985, July 1   *Engr. & Photo.*
2567	A914	7k multi	2.25	1.50
a.		Souvenir sheet of 4	7.00	

An imperf. souv. sheet similar to No. 2567a was issued June 1, 1988 for FINLANDIA '88 and PRAGA '88. Value $35.

12th World Youth Festival, Moscow A915

1985, July 2
2568	A915	1k Kremlin, youths	.25	.25

A916

1985, Sept. 3   *Perf. 11½*
2569	A916	50h multi	.25	.25

Federation of World Trade Unions, 40th anniv.

Bratislava Type of 1977

Designs: 3k, Castle and river, lace embroidery by Elena Holeczyova (1906-1983). 4k, Pottery cups and mugs, 1600-1500 B.C.

1985, Sept. 4   *Engr.*   *Perf. 12*
2570	A760	3k multi	1.60	.45
2571	A760	4k multi	2.10	.60

Nos. 2570-2571 were each issued in sheets of 4 stamps. Value, set $14.

A918

Children's book illustrations: 1k, Rocking Horse, by Kveta Pacovska, USSR. 2k, Fairies, by Gennadij Spirin, USSR. 3k, Butterfly and Girl, by Kaarina Kaila, Finland. 4k, Boy and Animals, by Erick Ingraham, US.

Engraved and Photogravure
1985, Sept. 5   *Perf. 11½*
2572	A918	1k multi	.25	.25
2573	A918	2k multi	.25	.25
2574	A918	3k multi	.70	.25
2575	A918	4k multi	.70	.30
a.		Souv. sheet of 4, #2572-2575	4.50	3.00
		Nos. 2572-2575 (4)	1.90	1.05

10th biennial of illustrations.

5-Year Development Plan — A919

50h, Construction machinery. 1k, Prague subway, map. 2k, Modern textile spinning.

1985, Oct. 28   *Perf. 12x11½*
2576	A919	50h multicolored	.25	.25
2577	A919	1k multicolored	.25	.25
2578	A919	2k multicolored	.25	.25
		Nos. 2576-2578 (3)	.75	.75

16th Communist Party Congress goals.

Prague Castle — A920

2k, Presidential Palace Gate, 1768. 3k, St. Vitus' Cathedral.

Engr., Engr. & Photo. (3k)
1985, Oct. 28   *Perf. 12*
2579	A920	2k multicolored	.40	.40
2580	A920	3k multicolored	.50	.50

Nos. 2579-2580 were each issued in sheets of 6 stamps. Value, set $9.

A921

Glassware: 50h, Pitcher, Near East, 4th cent. 1k, Venetian pitcher, 16th cent. 2k, Bohemian goblet, c. 1720. 4k, Harrachov

68 CZECHOSLOVAKIA

Bohemian vase, 18th cent. 6k, Jablonec Bohemian vase, c. 1900.

Engraved and Photogravure
1985, Nov. 23   *Perf. 11½x12*
2581	A921	50h multi	.25 .25
2582	A921	1k multi	.25 .25
2583	A921	2k multi	.30 .25
2584	A921	4k multi	.50 .25
2585	A921	6k multi	1.00 .35
Nos. 2581-2585 (5)			2.30 1.35

Arts and Crafts Museum, Prague, cent.

Painting Type of 1967
Designs: 1k, Young Woman in a Blue Gown, by Jozef Ginovsky (1800-1857). 2k, Lenin on the Charles Bridge, Prague, 1952, by Martin Sladky (b. 1920). 3k, Avenue of Poplars, 1935, by Vaclav Rabas (1885-1954). 4k, The Martyrom of St. Dorothea, 1516, by Hans Baldung Grien (c. 1484-1545). 5k, Portrait of Jasper Schade van Westrum, 1645, by Frans Hals (c. 1581-1666).

1985, Nov. 27   *Engr.*   *Perf. 12*
2586	A565	1k multi	1.60 .80
2587	A565	2k multi	1.10 .35
2588	A565	3k multi	1.50 .35
2589	A565	4k multi	.90 .50
2590	A565	5k multi	.90 .50
Nos. 2586-2590 (5)			6.00 2.50

Nos. 2586-2590 were each issued in sheets of 4 stamps with punched out holes by denomination. Value, set $30.

Bohdan Roule (1921-1960), Engraver — A922

Engraved and Photogravure
1985, Dec. 18   *Perf. 11½x12*
| 2591 | A922 | 1k multicolored | .25 .25 |

Stamp Day 1985.

Intl. Peace Year A923

1986, Jan. 2
| 2592 | A923 | 1k multi | .25 .25 |

Philharmonic Orchestra, 90th Anniv. — A924

1986, Jan. 2   *Perf. 11½*
| 2593 | A924 | 1k Victory Statue, Prague | .25 .25 |

EXPO '86, Vancouver — A925

Design: Z 50 LS monoplane, Cenyerth Prague-Kladno locomotive, Sahara Desert rock drawing, 5th-6th cent. B.C.

1986, Jan. 23   *Perf. 11½*
| 2594 | A925 | 4k multicolored | .85 .25 |

City Arms Type of 1982
1986, Feb. 10   *Perf. 12x11½*
Size: 42x54mm
2595	A847	50h Myjava	.25 .25
2596	A847	50h Vodnany	.25 .25
2597	A847	50h Zamberk	.25 .25
Nos. 2595-2597 (3)			.75 .75

17th Natl. Communist Party Congress, Prague, Mar. 24 — A926

1986, Mar. 20   *Perf. 11½*
| 2598 | A926 | 50h shown | .25 .25 |
| 2599 | A926 | 1k Industry | .25 .25 |

Natl. Communist Party, 65th Anniv. — A927

50h, Star, man, woman. 1k, Hammer, sickle, laborers.

1986, Mar. 20   *Perf. 12x11½*
| 2600 | A927 | 50h multi | .25 .25 |
| 2601 | A927 | 1k multi | .25 .25 |

Natl. Front Election Program A928

1986, Mar. 28
| 2602 | A928 | 50h multi | .25 .25 |

Karlovy Vary Intl. Film Festival, 25th Anniv. — A929

1986, Apr. 3   *Perf. 11½*
| 2603 | A929 | 1k multi | .25 .25 |

A930

1986, Apr. 8   *Engr. & Photo.*
| 2604 | A930 | 1k multi | .25 .25 |

Spring of Prague Music Festival.

A931

1986, Apr. 25
| 2605 | A931 | 50h multi | .40 .25 |

Prague-Moscow air service, 50th anniv.

Intl. Olympic Committee, 90th Anniv. — A932

1986, May 12   *Perf. 11½x12*
| 2606 | A932 | 2k multi | .30 .25 |

1986 World Cup Soccer Championships, Mexico — A933

1986, May 15   *Perf. 12x11½*
| 2607 | A933 | 4k multi | .80 .40 |

Women's World Volleyball Championships, Prague — A934

1986, May 19
| 2608 | A934 | 1k multi | .25 .25 |

Souvenir Sheet

Intl. Philatelic Federation, FIP, 60th Anniv. — A935

1986, June 3   *Engr.*   *Perf. 12*
| 2609 | A935 | 20k multi | 6.50 5.00 |

Exists imperf and with perforations between stamps omitted. Values, $15 and $27.50, respectively.

Prague Castle Type of 1983
Designs: 2k, Jewelled funerary pendant, 9th cent. 3k, Allegory of Blossoms, sculpture by Jaroslav Horejc (1886-1983), St. Vitus' Cathedral.

1986, June 6   *Engr.*   *Perf. 12*
| 2610 | A875 | 2k multi | .40 .30 |
| 2611 | A875 | 3k multi | .70 .45 |

Nos. 2610-2611 were each issued in sheets of 6 stamps. Value, set $8.

UN Child Survival Campaign — A937

Toys.

Engraved and Photogravure
1986, Sept. 1   *Perf. 11½*
2612	A937	10h Rooster	.25 .25
2613	A937	20h Horse and rider	.25 .25
2614	A937	1k Doll	.25 .25
2615	A937	2k Doll, diff.	.50 .25
2616	A937	3k Tin omnibus, c. 1910	.65 .30
Nos. 2612-2616 (5)			1.90 1.30

UNICEF, 40th anniv.

Registration, Cent. — A938

1986, Sept. 2   *Perf. 11½x12*
| 2617 | A938 | 4k Label, mail coach | .45 .25 |

Bratislava Type of 1977
1986, Sept. 11   *Engr.*   *Perf. 12*
| 2618 | A760 | 3k Sigismund Gate | 1.25 .80 |
| 2619 | A760 | 4k St. Margaret, bas-relief | 1.25 .65 |

Nos. 2618-2619 were each issued in sheets of 4 stamps. Value, set $12.

Owls — A939

Engraved and Photogravure
1986, Sept. 18   *Perf. 11½*
2620	A939	50h Bubo bubo	.70 .25
2621	A939	2k Asio otus	.85 .25
2622	A939	3k Strix aluco	1.40 .30
2623	A939	4k Tyto alba	1.40 .45
2624	A939	5k Asio flammeus	2.10 .60
Nos. 2620-2624 (5)			6.45 1.85

Souvenir Sheet

Intl. Brigades in Spain — A940

Theater curtain: Woman Savaged by Horses, 1936, by Vladimir Sychra (1903-1963), Natl Gallery, Prague.

1986, Oct. 1   *Engr.*   *Perf. 12*
| 2625 | A940 | Sheet of 2 | 4.50 3.50 |
| a. | | 5k multi | 2.00 1.25 |

Locomotives and Streetcars A941

Engraved and Photogravure
1986, Oct. 6   *Perf. 12x11½*
2626	A941	50h KT-8	.25 .25
2627	A941	1k E458.1	.25 .25
2628	A941	3k T466.2	.75 .30
2629	A941	5k M152.0	.80 .25
Nos. 2626-2629 (4)			2.05 1.05

Paintings in the Prague and Bratislava Natl. Galleries A942

Designs: 1k, The Circus Rider, 1980, by Jan Bauch (b. 1898). 2k, The Ventriloquist, 1954, by Frantisek Tichy (1896-1961). 3k, In the Circus, 1946, by Vincent Hloznik (b. 1919). 6k, Clown, 1985, by Karel Svolinsky (1896-1986).

1986, Oct. 13   *Engr.*   *Perf. 12*
2630	A942	1k multi	1.25 .65
2631	A942	2k multi	1.60 .85
2632	A942	3k multi	1.60 .85
2633	A942	6k multi	1.10 .95
Nos. 2630-2633 (4)			5.55 3.30

Nos. 2630-2633 were each issued in sheets of 4 stamps. Value, set $25.

Painting Type of 1967
1k, The Czech Lion, May 1918, by Vratislav H. Brunner (1886-1928). 2k, Boy with Mandolin, 1945, by Jozef Sturdik (b. 1920). 3k, Metra Building, 1984, by Frantisek Gross (1909-1985). 4k, Portrait of Maria Maximiliana at Sternberk, 1665, by Karel Skreta (1610-1674). 5k, Adam & Eve, 1538, by Lucas Cranach (1472-1553).

1986, Nov. 3   *Engr.*   *Perf. 12*
2634	A565	1k multi	3.00 2.25
2635	A565	2k multi	3.00 2.25
2636	A565	3k multi	3.00 2.25
2637	A565	4k multi	3.00 2.25
2638	A565	5k multi	3.00 2.25
Nos. 2634-2638 (5)			15.00 11.25

Nos. 2634-2638 were each issued in sheets of 4 stamps. Value, set $75.

Stamp Day A943

Design: V.H. Brunner (1886-1928), stamp designer, and No. 88.

Photo. & Engr.
1986, Dec. 18   *Perf. 11½x12*
| 2639 | A943 | 1k multicolored | .25 .25 |

World Cyclocross Championships, Jan. 24-25, Central Bohemia A944

1987, Jan. 22   *Perf. 11½*
| 2640 | A944 | 6k multi | .80 .25 |

CZECHOSLOVAKIA

Czechoslovakian Bowling Union, 50th Anniv. — A945

1987, Jan. 22		Perf. 11½
2641 A945 2k multi	.35	.25

State Decorations A946

Designs: 50h, Gold Stars of Socialist Labor and Czechoslovakia. 2k, Order of Klement Gottwald. 3k, Order of the Republic. 4k, Order of Victorious February. 5k, Order of Labor.

1987, Feb. 4		Perf. 12x11½
2642 A946 50h multi	.25	.25
2643 A946 2k multi	.25	.25
2644 A946 3k multi	.30	.25
2645 A946 4k multi	.45	.25
2646 A946 5k multi	.60	.40
Nos. 2642-2646 (5)	1.85	1.40

Butterflies A947

1k, Limenitis populi. 2k, Smerinthus ocellatus. 3k, Pericallia matronula. 4k, Saturnia pyri.

1987, Mar. 4		
2647 A947 1k multi	.65	.25
2648 A947 2k multi	1.00	.25
2649 A947 3k multi	1.25	.35
2650 A947 4k multi	1.60	.35
Nos. 2647-2650 (4)	4.50	1.20

Natl. Nuclear Power Industry A948

1987, Apr. 6		
2651 A948 5k multi	.60	.25

11th Revolutionary Trade Union Movement Congress, Apr. 14-17, Prague — A949

1987, Apr. 7		Perf. 11½
2652 A949 1k multi	.25	.25

Souvenir Sheet

INTERCOSMOS, 20th Anniv. — A950

Cosmonauts Alexei Gubarev of the USSR & Vladimir Remek of Czechoslovakia, rocket & emblem.

1987, Apr. 12	Engr.	Perf. 12
2653 A950 Sheet of 2	6.00	5.00
a. 10k multi	2.75	1.75
b. Souv. sheet of 4, litho. & engr., imperf.	9.00	7.00

No. 2653b issued Nov. 15, 1987, and exists in two formats with either exhibition emblem or "Dni Nametove Filatelie" at top.

Prague Castle Type of 1983

Designs: 2k, Three Saints, stained-glass window detail, c. 1870, St. Vitus Cathedral, by Frantisek Sequens (1830-1896). 3k, Coat of Arms, New Land Rolls Hall, 1605.

1987, May 9		Perf. 11½
2654 A875 2k multi	.40	.30
2655 A875 3k dk red, slate gray & yel org	.60	.45

Nos. 2634-2638 were each issued in sheets of 6 stamps. Value, set $6.

PRAGA '88 — A951

1987, May 12	Photo. & Engr.	Perf. 12x11½
2656 A951 3k Telephone, 1894	.75	.25
2657 A951 3k Postal van, 1924	.75	.30
2658 A951 4k Tender locomotive, 1907	.75	.30
2659 A951 4k Tram, 1900	.75	.30
2660 A951 5k Steam roller, 1936	.75	.30
Nos. 2656-2660 (5)	3.75	1.45

Printed in sheets of 8 + 2 labels picturing telephone or vehicles. Value $25.

Nos. 2657-2658 were also printed in sheets of 4 + label picturing vehicles. Value, $30 for both sheets.

Destruction of Lidice and Lezaky, 45th Anniv. — A952

Drawings: No. 2661, When the Fighting Ended, 1945, by Pavel Simon. No. 2662, The End of the game, 1945, by Ludmila Jirincova.

1987, June		Perf. 11½
2661 A952 1k blk, cerise & vio	.25	.25
2662 A952 1k blk, gold, pale lil & cerise	.25	.25

Union of Czechoslovakian Mathematicians and Physicists, 125th Anniv. — A953

Designs: No. 2663, Prague Town Hall mathematical clock, Theory of Functions diagram. No. 2664, J.M. Petzval (1807-1891), C. Strouhal (1850-1922) and V. Jarnik (1897-1970). No. 2665, Geographical measurement from A.M. Malletta's book, 1672, earth fold and Brownian motion diagrams.

1987, July 6		Perf. 11½x12
2663 A953 50h multi	.25	.25
2664 A953 50h multi	.25	.25
2665 A953 50h multi	.25	.25
Nos. 2663-2665 (3)	.75	.75

11th Biennial of Children's Book Illustration — A954

Award-winning illustrations: 50h, Asun Balzola, Spain. 1k, Frederic Clement, France. 2k, Elzbieta Gaudasinska, Poland. 4k, Marija Lucija Stupica, Yugoslavia.

1987, Sept. 3		Perf. 11½
2666 A954 50h multi	.25	.25
2667 A954 1k multi	.25	.25
2668 A954 2k multi	.25	.25
a. Souv. sheet of 2 + label	2.00	1.50
2669 A954 4k multi	.55	.35
Nos. 2666-2669 (4)	1.30	1.10

Sept. 11-Oct. 30, Bratislava.

Eternal Flame, Flower — A955

1987, Sept. 23		
2670 A955 50h multicolored	.25	.25

Theresienstadt Memorial for the victims from 23 European countries who died in the Small Fortress, Terezin, a Nazi concentration camp.

Socialist Communications Organization, 30th Anniv. — A956

1987, Sept. 23		
2671 A956 4k Emblem, satellite, dish receiver	.40	.25

Jan Evangelista Purkyne (1787-1869), Physiologist — A957

1987, Sept. 30		
2672 A957 7k multicolored	.80	.25

Views of Bratislava A958

Designs: 3k, Male and female figures supporting an oriel, Arkier Palace, c. 1552. 4k, View of Bratislava from Ware Conterfactur de Stadt Presburg, from an engraving by Hans Mayer, 1563.

1987, Oct. 1	Engr.	Perf. 12
2673 A958 3k multicolored	.50	.35
2674 A958 4k multicolored	.70	.45

Each printed in sheets of 4 with Bratislava Castle (from Mayer's engraving) between. Value, set $5.

See Nos. 2719-2720, 2763-2764, 2800-2801.

Type of 1974

1987, Nov. 1	Photo. & Engr.	Perf. 11½
2675 A699 1k Post rider	.25	.25

PRAGA '88, Aug. 26-Sept. 4, 1988. No. 2675 printed se-tenant with label picturing exhibition emblem. Value for single with attached label 40c.

October Revolution, Russia, 70th Anniv. — A959

Establishment of the Union of Soviet Socialist Republics, 65th Anniv. — A960

1987, Nov. 6		Perf. 12x11½
2676 A959 50h multicolored	.25	.25
2677 A960 50h multicolored	.25	.25

Art Type of 1974

Paintings in national galleries: 1k, Enclosure of Dreams, by Kamil Lhotak (b. 1912). 2k, Tulips, by Ester Simerova-Martincekova (b. 1909). 3k, Triptych with Bohemian Landscape, by Josef Lada (1887-1957). 4k, Accordion Player, by Josef Capek (1887-1945). 5k, Self-portrait, by Jiri Trnka (1912-1969).

1987, Nov. 18	Engr.	Perf. 12
2678 A700 1k multi	3.00	.95
2679 A700 2k multi	3.00	1.60
2680 A700 3k multi	3.00	1.10
2681 A700 4k multi	3.00	.80
2682 A700 5k multi	3.00	1.25
Nos. 2678-2682 (5)	15.00	5.50

Czech and Slovak art. Nos. 2678-2682 were each issued in sheets of 4. Value, set $65.

69th Stamp Day A961

Portrait of Jacob Obrovsky (1882-1949), stamp designer, Bohemian Lion (Type SP1), sketch of a lion and PRAGA '88 emblem.

1987, Dec. 18	Photo. & Engr.	Perf. 11½x12
2683 A961 1k multicolored	.25	.25

No. 2683 printed in sheet of four with eight labels se-tenant with stamps, inscribed "100 Years of the National Philatelic Movement in Czechoslovakia" in Czech. The four labels between the "blocks of six" are blank. Value, sheet $3.

Czechoslovak Republic, 70th Anniv. — A962

1k, Woman, natl. arms, linden branch.

1988, Jan. 1		Perf. 12x11½
2684 A962 1k multicolored	.25	.25

Natl. Front, 40th Anniv. — A963

1988, Feb. 25		Perf. 11½
2685 A963 50h multicolored	.25	.25

Husak Type of 1983

1988, Jan. 10	Photo. & Engr.	Perf. 12x11½
2686 A865 1k brt rose & dk carmine	.25	.25

Olympics A965

50h, Ski jumping, ice hockey. 1k, Basketball, soccer. 6k, Discus, weight lifting.

1988, Feb. 1		Perf. 11½x12
2687 A965 50h multicolored	.25	.25
2688 A965 1k multicolored	.25	.25
2689 A965 6k multicolored	.70	.25
Nos. 2687-2689 (3)	1.20	.75

Exist in souv. sheets of 2, imperf. between and in souv. sheets of 2, imperf. Value, each set, $16.

Victorious February, 40th Anniv. — A966

Statue of Klement Gottwald by Rudolf Svoboda.

1988, Feb. 25		Perf. 11½
2690 A966 50h multicolored	.25	.25

No. 2690 exists in a souvenir sheet of two No. 2690 and two postally invalid imperf impressions of No. 637. Value $5. Sheet exists imperf. Value $9.

Classic Automobiles A967

50h, 1914 Laurin & Klement. 1k, 1902 Tatra NW Type B. 2k, 1905 Tatra NW Type E. 3k, 1929 Tatra 12 Normandie. 4k, 1899 Meteor.

1988, Mar. 1		Perf. 11½x12
2691 A967 50h multi	.25	.25
2692 A967 1k multi	.25	.25
2693 A967 2k multi	.25	.25
2694 A967 3k multi	.45	.25
2695 A967 4k multi	.75	.25
a. Bklt. pane, 2 3k, 3 4k + label	4.00	
Complete booklet, #2695a	5.00	
Nos. 2691-2695 (5)	1.95	1.25

70 CZECHOSLOVAKIA

Postal Museum, 70th Anniv. — A968

Praga '88 emblem and: 50h, Postman, Malostranske Namesti Square p.o., Prague, c. 1742, and Velka Javorina television transmitter, 1979. 1k, Telecommunications Center, Mlada Boleslav, 1986, and Carmelite Street p.o., Prague, c. 1792. 2k, Prague 1 (1873) and Bratislava 56 (1984) post offices. 4k, Communications Center, Prachatice (1982), postman and Maltetske Nameski Square p.o., Prague, c. 1622.

1988, Mar. 10
2696	A968	50h multi	.25	.25
2697	A968	1k multi	.25	.25
2698	A968	2k multi	.25	.25
2699	A968	4k multi	.30	.25
a.		Souv. sheet, 2 ea #2698-2699	2.25	1.25
		Nos. 2696-2699 (4)	1.05	1.00

In No. 2699a the top pair of Nos. 2698-2699 is imperf. at top and sides.

A969

1988, Mar. 29   **Perf. 11½**
2700   A969   50h multicolored   .25   .25

Matice Slovenska Cultural Assoc., 125th anniv.

A970

PRAGA '88. (Exhibition emblem and aspects of the Museum of Natl. Literature, Prague): 1k, Gate and distant view of museum. 2k, Celestial globe, illuminated manuscript, bookshelves and ornately decorated ceiling. 5k, Illuminated "B" and decorated binder of a medieval Bible. 7k, Celestial globe, illuminated manuscript, Zodiacal signs (Aries and Leo), view of museum.

1988, May 12   **Photo. & Engr.**
2701	A970	1k multicolored	.30	.25
a.		Souvenir sheet of 4	1.50	1.25
2702	A970	2k multicolored	.55	.25
a.		Souvenir sheet of 4	3.25	2.00
2703	A970	5k multicolored	.80	.30
a.		Souvenir sheet of 4	5.75	4.75
2704	A970	7k multicolored	1.75	.65
a.		Souvenir sheet of 4	11.00	9.00
b.		Souv. sheet of 4, imperf., #2701-2704	3.75	3.00
		Nos. 2701-2704 (4)	3.40	1.45

PRAGA '88 — A971

Exhibition emblem and fountains, Prague.

1988, June 1   **Perf. 11½x12**
2705	A971	1k Waldstein Palace	.30	.25
2706	A971	2k Old town square	.30	.25
2707	A971	3k Charles University	.45	.25
2708	A971	4k Prague Castle	.75	.30
a.		Souv. sheet of 4, #2705-2708	4.00	2.00
		Nos. 2705-2708 (4)	1.80	1.05

Souvenir Sheet

Soviet-US Summit Conference on Arms Reduction, Moscow — A972

Design: The Capitol, Washington, and the Kremlin, Moscow.

1988, June 1   **Perf. 12x11½**
2709   A972   4k blue blk, dark red & gold   2.50   1.50
Exists imperf. Value $7.

PRAGA '88 — A973

Exhibition emblem and modern architecture, Prague: 50h, Trade Unions Central Recreation Center. 1k, Koospol foreign trade company. 2k, Motol Teaching Hospital. 4k, Culture Palace.

1988, July 1   **Perf. 12x11½**
2710	A973	50h multicolored	.25	.25
2711	A973	1k blk, lt blue & bister	.25	.25
2712	A973	2k multicolored	.25	.25
a.		Souv. sheet of 2 1k, 2 2k + 4 labels, imperf.	2.00	1.50
2713	A973	4k multicolored	.25	.25
a.		Souv. sheet, 2 50h, 2 4k + 4 labels, imperf.	2.00	1.50
		Nos. 2710-2713 (4)	1.00	1.00

Souvenir Sheet

PRAGA '88 — A974

Design: Exhibition emblem and Alfons Mucha (1860-1939), designer of first Czech postage stamp.

1988, Aug. 18   **Engr.**   **Perf. 12**
2714   A974   Sheet of 2   5.50   3.25
a.   5k multicolored   2.40   1.25

Czech postage stamps, 70th anniv.

Souvenir Sheets

PRAGA '88 — A975

5k, Turin, Monte Superga, by Josef Navratil (1798-1865), Postal Museum, Prague. Details of Bacchus and Ariadne, by Sebastiano Ricci (1659-1734), Natl. Gallery, Prague: No. 2716a, Ariadne. No. 2716b, Bacchus and creatures.

1988
2715	A975	Sheet of 2	5.00	4.00
a.		5k multi	2.50	1.80
2716	A975	Sheet of 2	9.00	6.00
a.-b.		10k any single	4.00	2.40

No. 2716 exists with emblem and inscription "DEN F.I.P. JOURNEE DE LA FEDERATION INTERNATIONALE DE PHILATELIE." Value $12.
Issue dates: 5k, Aug. 19; 10k, Aug. 26.

Prague Castle Type of 1983

2k, Pottery jug, 17th cent. 3k, St. Catherine with Angel, 1580, by Paolo Veronese.

1988, Sept. 28   **Engr.**   **Perf. 12**
2717	A875	2k shown	.40	.40
2718	A875	3k multi	.45	.45

Nos. 2717-2718 were each issued in sheets of 6. Value, set $6.

Bratislava Views Type of 1987

3k, Hlavne Square, circa 1840 an etching by R. Alt-Sandman, 1840. 4k, Ferdinand House, circa 1850, a pen-and-ink drawing by V. Reim.

1988, Oct. 19
2719	A958	3k multicolored	.50	.50
2720	A958	4k multicolored	.65	.65

Nos. 2719-2720 were each issued in sheets of 4. Value, set $4.50.

Art Type of 1974

Paintings in natl. galleries: 2k, With Bundles, 1931, by Martin Benka (1888-1971). 6k, Blue Bird, 1903, by Vojtech Preissig (1873-1944). 7k, A Jaguar Attacking a Rider, c. 1850, by Eugene Delacroix (1798-1863).

1988, Nov. 17   **Engr.**   **Perf. 12**
2721	A700	2k multicolored	2.00	1.00
2722	A700	6k multicolored	3.50	1.50
2723	A700	7k multicolored	3.50	1.50
		Nos. 2721-2723 (3)	9.00	4.00

Czech and Slovak art.

Nos. 2721-2723 were each issued in sheets of 4. Value, set $40.

Stamp Day A978

Design: 1k, Jaroslav Benda (1882-1970), illustrator and stamp designer.

1988, Dec. 18   **Photo. & Engr.**   **Perf. 11½x12**
2724   A978   1k multicolored   .25   .25

Paris-Dakar Rally — A979

Trucks: 50h, Earth, Motokov Liaz. 1k, Liaz, globe. 2k, Earth, Motokov Tatra. No. 607. 4k, Map of racecourse, turban, Tatra.

1989, Jan. 2   **Perf. 12x11½**
2725	A979	50h multicolored	.35	.25
2726	A979	1k multicolored	.35	.25
2727	A979	2k multicolored	.45	.25
2728	A979	4k multicolored	.75	.25
		Nos. 2725-2728 (4)	1.90	1.00

Czechoslovakian Federation, 20th Anniv. — A980

1989, Jan. 1
2729   A980   50h multicolored   .25   .25

Jan Botto (1829-1881) A981

Taras Grigorievich Shevchenko (1814-1861) A982

Jean Cocteau (1889-1963) A983

Charlie Chaplin (1889-1977) A984

Jawaharlal Nehru (1889-1964) and "UNESCO" — A985

Famous men: No. 2732, Modest Petrovich Musorgsky (1839-1881).

Photo. & Engr.
1989, Mar. 9   **Perf. 12x11½**
2730	A981	50h brn blk & lt blue green	.25	.25
2731	A982	50h shown	.25	.25
2732	A982	50h multicolored	.25	.25
2733	A983	50h red brn, grnh blk & org brn	.25	.25
2734	A984	50h blk, int blue & dark red	.25	.25
2735	A985	50h brn blk & lt yel green	.25	.25
		Nos. 2730-2735 (6)	1.50	1.50

Shipping Industry — A986

1989, Mar. 27
2736	A986	50h Republika	.25	.25
2737	A986	1k Pionyr, flags	.25	.25
2738	A986	2k Brno, flags	.25	.25
2739	A986	3k Trinec	.35	.25
2740	A986	4k Flags, mast, Orlik	.75	.25
2741	A986	5k Vltava, communication hardware	1.00	.30
		Nos. 2736-2741 (6)	2.85	1.55

Pioneer Organization, 40th Anniv. — A987

Photo. & Engr.
1989, Apr. 20   **Perf. 11½**
2742   A987   50h multi   .25   .25

Art Type of 1974

Details of Feast of Rose Garlands, 1506, by Albrecht Durer, Natl. Gallery, Prague: a, Virgin and Child. b, Angel playing mandolin.

1989, Apr. 21   **Engr.**   **Perf. 12**
Miniature Sheet
2743   Sheet of 2   7.50   4.00
a.-b. A700 10k any single   3.50   2.00

Prague Castle Art Type of 1983

2k, Bas-relief picturing Kaiser Karl IV, from Kralovske tomb by Alexander Colin (c. 1527-1612). 3k, Self-portrait, by V.V. Reiner (1689-1743).

1989, May 9   **Photo. & Engr.**
2744	A875	2k dark red, sepia & buff	.35	.30
2745	A875	3k multi	.50	.40

Nos. 2744-2745 were each issued in sheets of 6. Value, set $6.

Souvenir Sheet

PHILEXFRANCE '89, French Revolution Bicent. — A988

1989, July 14   **Engr.**   **Perf. 12**
2746   A988   5k brt blue, blk & dk red   2.00   1.50

CZECHOSLOVAKIA

Haliaeetus albicilla — A989

Photo. & Engr.

1989, July 17			Perf. 12x11½
2747	A989	1k multicolored	.50 .25

World Wildlife Fund A990

Toads and newts.

1989, July 18			Perf. 11½x12
2748	A990	2k Bombina bombina	.65 .30
2749	A990	3k Bombina variegata	1.00 .45
2750	A990	4k Triturus alpestris	1.40 .60
2751	A990	5k Triturus montandoni	1.60 .70
		Nos. 2748-2751 (4)	4.65 2.05

Slovak Folk Art Collective, 40th Anniv. — A991

1989, Aug. 29			Perf. 12x11½
2752	A991	50h multicolored	.25 .25

Slovak Uprising, 45th Anniv. A992

Photo. & Engr.

1989, Aug. 29			Perf. 11½x12
2753	A992	1k multicolored	.25 .25

A993

Award-winning illustrations: 50h, Hannu Taina, Finland. 1k, Aleksander Aleksov, Bulgaria. 2k, Jurgen Spohn, West Berlin. 4k, Robert Brun, Czechoslovakia.

1989, Sept. 4			Perf. 11½
2754	A993	50h multicolored	.25 .25
2755	A993	1k multicolored	.25 .25
2756	A993	2k multicolored	.25 .25
2757	A993	4k multicolored	.60 .25
a.		Souvenir sheet of 2	2.00 .80
		Nos. 2754-2757 (4)	1.35 1.00

12th Biennial of Children's Book Illustration, Bratislava.

A994

Poisonous mushrooms: 50h, Nolanea verna. 1k, Amanita phalloides. 2k, Amanita virosa. 3k, Cortinarius orellanus. 5k, Galerina marginata.

1989, Sept. 5	Engr.		Perf. 11½x12
2758	A994	50h multicolored	.30 .25
2759	A994	1k multicolored	.40 .25
2760	A994	2k multicolored	.55 .25
2761	A994	3k multicolored	.90 .25
2762	A994	5k multicolored	1.00 .25
		Nos. 2758-2762 (5)	3.15 1.25

Nos. 2758-2762 were each issued in sheets of 10. Value, set $40.

Bratislava Views Type of 1987

Views of Devin, a Slavic castle above the Danube, Bratislava.

1989, Oct. 16	Engr.		Perf. 12
2763	A958	3k Castle, flower	.60 .60
2764	A958	4k Castle, urn	.80 .80

Nos. 2763-2764 were each issued in sheets of 4. Value, set $6.

Jan Opletal (1915-39) — A996

Photo. & Engr.

1989, Nov. 17			Perf. 12x11½
2765	A996	1k multicolored	.25 .25

Intl. Student's Day. Funeral of Opletal, a Nazi victim, on Nov. 15, 1939, sparked student demonstrations that resulted in the closing of all universities in occupied Bohemia and Moravia.

Art Type of 1974

Paintings in Natl. Galleries: 2k, *Nirvana*, c. 1920, by Anton Jasusch (1882-1965). 4k, *Winter Evening in Town*, c. 1907, by Jakub Schikaneder (1855-1924), horiz. 5k, *The Bakers*, 1926, by Pravoslav Kotik (1889-1970), horiz.

1989, Nov. 27	Engr.		Perf. 12
2766	A700	2k multicolored	.80 .60
2767	A700	4k multicolored	1.40 1.10
2768	A700	5k multicolored	1.40 1.10
		Nos. 2766-2768 (3)	3.60 2.80

Nos. 2766-2768 were each issued in sheets of 4. Value, set $15.

Stamp Day A997

Design: Portrait of Cyril Bouda, stamp designer, art tools and falcon.

Photo. & Engr.

1989, Dec. 18			Perf. 11½x12
2769	A997	1k multicolored	.25 .25

A998

Photo. & Engr.

1990, Jan. 8			Perf. 11½x12
2770	A998	1k multicolored	.60 .25

UNESCO World Literacy Year. Printed setenant with inscribed label picturing UN and UNESCO emblems. Value, single with label attached 75c.

A999

Famous men: No. 2771, Karel Capek, writer. No. 2772, Thomas G. Masaryk. 1k, Lenin. 2k, Emile Zola, French writer. 3k, Jaroslav Heyrovsky (1890-1987), chemical physicist. 10k, Bohuslav Martinu (1890-1959), composer.

1990, Jan. 9			Perf. 11½
2771	A999	50h multicolored	.25 .25
2772	A999	50h multicolored	.25 .25
2773	A999	1k multicolored	.25 .25
2774	A999	2k multicolored	.30 .25
2775	A999	3k multicolored	.50 .30
2776	A999	10k multicolored	1.60 .90
		Nos. 2771-2776 (6)	3.15 2.20

Nos. 2771, 2775-2776 inscribed "UNESCO."

Pres. Vaclav Havel — A1000

1990, Jan. 9			Perf. 12x11½
2777	A1000	50h red, brt vio & bl	.30 .25

See Nos. 2879, 2948.

Handball Players — A1001

1990, Feb. 1			Perf. 11½
2778	A1001	50h multicolored	.25 .25

1990 Men's World Handball Championships, Czechoslovakia.

Flora — A1002

Flowers: 50h, Antirrhinum majus. 1k, Zinnia elegans. 3k, Tigridia pavonia. 5k, Lilium candidum.

Photo. & Engr.

1990, Mar. 1			Perf. 11½
2779	A1002	50h multicolored	.55 .25
2780	A1002	1k multicolored	.80 .25
2781	A1002	3k multicolored	1.00 .25
			Perf. 12x12½
2782	A1002	5k multicolored	1.40 .60
		Nos. 2779-2782 (4)	3.75 1.35

No. 2782 was issued in a sheet of 10. Value, $12.50.

City Arms Type of 1982

Photo. & Engr.

1990, Mar. 28			Perf. 12x11½
2783	A847	50h Prostejov	.25 .25
2784	A847	50h Bytca	.25 .25
2785	A847	50h Sobeslav	.25 .25
2786	A847	50h Podebrady	.25 .25
		Nos. 2783-2786 (4)	1.00 1.00

A1003

1990, Apr. 16			Perf. 11½x12
2787	A1003	1k brn vio, rose & buff	.60 .25

Visit of Pope John Paul II.

World War II Liberation — A1004

Photo. & Engr.

1990, May 5			Perf. 11½
2788	A1004	1k multicolored	.25 .25

Souvenir Sheet

150th Anniv. of the Postage Stamp A1005

1990, May 6	Engr.		Perf. 12
2789	A1005	7k multicolored	4.00 1.50

Stamp World London 90.

A1006

Photo. & Engr.

1990, May 8			Perf. 11½
2790	A1006	1k multicolored	.60 .25

World Cup Soccer Championships, Italy.

Free Elections — A1007

1990, June 1			
2791	A1007	1k multicolored	.60 .25

Prague Castle Type of 1983

2k, Gold and jeweled hand. 3k, King Otakar II's Seal.

1990, June 6, 1990			Engr.
2792	A875	2k multicolored	.55 .30
2793	A875	3k multicolored	.80 .40

Art treasures of Prague Castle.

Nos. 2792-2793 were each issued in sheets of 6. Value, set $9.

Helsinki Conference, 15th Anniv. — A1008

Photo & Engr.

1990, June 21			Perf. 12x11½
2794	A1008	7k multicolored	.90 .40

Dr. Milada Horakova A1009

1990, June 25			Perf. 12x11½
2795	A1009	1k multicolored	.30 .25

Intercanis Dog Show, Brno — A1010

Designs: 50h, Poodles. 1k, Afghan hound, Irish wolfhound, greyhound. 4k, Czech terrier, bloodhound, Hannoverian hound. 7k, Cavalier King Charles Spaniel, cocker spaniel, American cocker spaniel.

1990, July 2			
2796	A1010	50h multicolored	.50 .25
2797	A1010	1k multicolored	.75 .25
2798	A1010	4k multicolored	1.25 .30
2799	A1010	7k multicolored	1.75 .65
		Nos. 2796-2799 (4)	4.25 1.45

Bratislava Art Type of 1987

1990		Engr.	Perf. 12
2800	A958	3k Ancient Celtic coin	.65 .40
2801	A958	4k Gen. Milan Stefanik	.65 .45

Issue dates: 3k, Sept. 29. 4k, July 21.
Nos. 2800-2801 were each issued in sheets of 4. Value, set $6.

Grand Pardubice Steeplechase, Cent. — A1011

Photo. & Engr.

1990, Sept. 7			Perf. 12x11½
2802	A1011	50h multicolored	.25 .25
2803	A1011	4k multi, diff.	.50 .25

CZECHOSLOVAKIA

Protected Animals — A1012

Litho. & Engr.
1990, Oct. 1 Perf. 12x11
2804 A1012 50h Marmota marmota 1.00 .25
2805 A1012 1k Felis silvestris 1.00 .25
2806 A1012 4k Castor fiber 1.75 .30
2807 A1012 5k Plecotus auritus 1.75 .75
Nos. 2804-2807 (4) 5.50 1.55

Conf. of Civic Associations, Helsinki — A1013

Litho. & Engr.
1990, Oct. 15 Perf. 12x11½
2808 A1013 3k blue, gold & yel .50 .30

Christmas — A1014

Photo. & Engr.
1990, Nov. 15 Perf. 11½x12
2809 A1014 50h multicolored .25 .25

Painting Type of 1967
Works of art: 2k, Krucemburk by Jan Zrzavy (1890-1977), horiz. 3k, St. Agnes of Bohemia from the St. Wenceslas Monument, Prague by Josef V. Myslbek (1848-1922). 4k, The Slavs in their Homeland by Alfons Mucha (1860-1939). 5k, St. John the Baptist by Auguste Rodin (1840-1917).

1990, Nov. 27 Engr. Perf. 11½
2810 A565 2k multicolored 1.25 .50
2811 A565 3k multicolored 1.25 .60
2812 A565 4k multicolored 2.10 .60
2813 A565 5k multicolored 2.10 .60
Nos. 2810-2813 (4) 6.70 2.30
Nos. 2810-2813 were each issued in sheets of 4. Value, set $30.

Karel Svolinsky (1896-1986), Vignette from No. 1182 — A1016

1990, Dec. 18 Photo. & Engr.
2814 A1016 1k multicolored .25 .25
Stamp Day.

A1017

1991, Jan. 10 Perf. 11½
2815 A1017 1k multicolored .30 .25
European Judo Championships, Prague.

A1018

Design: A. B. Svojsik (1876-1938), Czech Scouting Founder.
1991, Jan. 10
2816 A1018 3k multicolored .75 .30
Scouting in Czechoslovakia, 80th Anniv.

Bethlehem Chapel, Prague, 600th Anniv. — A1019

1991, Feb. 4 Perf. 12x11½
2817 A1019 50h multicolored .25 .25

Wolfgang Amadeus Mozart (1756-1791), Old Theatre A1020

1991, Feb. 4
2818 A1020 1k multicolored .25 .25

Steamship Bohemia, 150th Anniv. A1021

1991, Feb. 4 Perf. 11½x12
2819 A1021 5k multicolored .85 .30

Famous Men — A1022

Designs: No. 2820, Antonin Dvorak (1841-1904), composer. No. 2821, Andrej Kmet (1841-1908), botanist. No. 2822, Jaroslav Seifert (1901-1986), poet, Nobel laureate for Literature. No. 2823, Jan Masaryk (1886-1948), diplomat. No. 2824, Alois Senefelder (1771-1834), lithographer.

1991, Feb. 18 Perf. 12x11½
2820 A1022 1k multicolored .25 .25
2821 A1022 1k multicolored .25 .25
2822 A1022 1k multicolored .25 .25
2823 A1022 1k multicolored .25 .25
2824 A1022 1k multicolored .25 .25
Nos. 2820-2824 (5) 1.25 1.25
Nos. 2820-2824 printed with se-tenant labels. See No. 2831.

Europa — A1023

Photo. & Engr.
1991, May 6 Perf. 11½x12
2825 A1023 6k blk, bl & red 2.00 .60

A1024

Photo. & Engr.
1991, May 10 Perf. 11½x12
2826 A1024 1k multicolored .25 .25
General Exhibition in Prague, cent.

Antarctic Treaty, 30th Anniv. — A1025

1991, May 20 Perf. 12x11½
2827 A1025 8k multicolored 1.75 .60

Castles — A1026

1991, June 3 Perf. 11½
2828 A1026 50h Blatna .25 .25
2829 A1026 1k Bouzov .40 .25
2830 A1026 3k Kezmarok .60 .25
Nos. 2828-2830 (3) 1.25 .75

Famous Men Type
Design: Jan Palach (1948-1969), Student.
Photo. & Engr.
1991, Aug. 9 Perf. 12x11½
2831 A1022 4k black 2.00 .30
Printed se-tenant with label.

Scenic Views — A1027

Photo. & Engr.
1991, Aug. 28 Perf. 11½
2832 A1027 4k Krivan mountains 1.00 .60
2833 A1027 4k Rip mountain 1.00 .60

A1028

Illustrations by: 1k, Binette Schroeder, Germany. 2k, Stasys Eidrigevicius, Poland.

Photo. & Engr.
1991, Sept. 2 Perf. 11½
2834 A1028 1k multicolored .25 .25
2835 A1028 2k multicolored .35 .25
13th Biennial Exhibition of Children's Book Illustrators, Bratislava.

A1029

Design: Father Andrej Hlinka (1864-1938), Slovak nationalist.

1991, Sept. 27 Engr. Perf. 11½
2836 A1029 10k blue black 1.40 .30

Art of Prague and Bratislava — A1030

Designs: No. 2837, Holy Infant of Prague. No. 2838, Blue Church of Bratislava.
1991, Sept. 30
2837 A1030 3k multicolored 1.25 .50
2838 A1030 3k multicolored 1.25 .50
Nos. 2837-2838 were each issued in sheets of 8. Value, set $15.

Flowers — A1031

1k, Gagea bohemica. 2k, Aster alpinus. 5k, Fritillaria meleagris. 11k, Daphne cneorum.

Photo. & Engr.
1991, Nov. 3 Perf. 12x11½
2839 A1031 1k multicolored .60 .25
2840 A1031 2k multicolored .85 .25
2841 A1031 5k multicolored 1.25 .30
2842 A1031 11k multicolored 2.50 .45
Nos. 2839-2842 (4) 5.20 1.25

Painting Type of 1967
Paintings: 2k, Everyday Homelife by Max Ernst. 3k, Lovers by Auguste Renoir. 4k, Head of Christ by El Greco. 5k, Coincidence by Ladislav Guderna. 7k, Two Maidens by Utamaro.

1991, Nov. 3 Engr. Perf. 11½
2843 A565 2k multicolored 1.25 .60
2844 A565 3k multicolored 1.25 .60
2845 A565 4k multicolored 1.25 .75
2846 A565 4k multicolored 1.75 1.25
2847 A565 7k multicolored 1.75 1.25
Nos. 2843-2847 (5) 7.25 4.45
Nos. 2843-2847 were each issued in sheets of 4. Value, set $30.

Christmas — A1033

1991, Nov. 19
2848 A1033 50h multicolored .30 .25

 Stamp Day A1034

Martin Benka (1888-1971), stamp engraver.

Photo. & Engr.
1991, Dec. 18 Perf. 11½x12
2849 A1034 2k multicolored .45 .25

1992 Winter Olympics, Albertville — A1035

1992, Jan. 6 Perf. 11½
2850 A1035 1k Biathlon .25 .25

Photo. & Engr.
2851 A1035 2k Tennis .30 .25
1992 Summer Olympics, Barcelona.

Souvenir Sheet

Jan Amos Komensky (Comenius), Educator — A1036

1992, Mar. 5 Engr.
2852 A1036 10k multicolored 4.00 3.50

World Ice Hockey Championships, Prague and Bratislava — A1037

1992, Mar. 31 Photo. & Engr.
2853 A1037 3k multicolored .75 .25

CZECHOSLOVAKIA

Traffic Safety — A1038

1992, Apr. 2
2854 A1038 2k multicolored .50 .25

Expo '92, Seville — A1039

1992, Apr. 2
2855 A1039 4k multicolored .75 .25

Discovery of America, 500th Anniv. — A1040

1992, May 5 Engr.
2856 A1040 22k multicolored 2.00 2.00
Europa. Printed in sheets of 8. Value $18.

Czechoslovak Military Actions in WWII — A1041

Designs: 1k, J. Kubis and J. Gabcik, assassins of Reinhard Heydrich, 1942. 2k, Pilots flying for France and Great Britain. 3k, Defense of Tobruk. 6k, Capture of Dunkirk, 1944-45.

1992, May 21 Engr. Perf. 12x11½
2857 A1041 1k multicolored .50 .25
2858 A1041 2k multicolored .60 .25
2859 A1041 3k multicolored .75 .25
2860 A1041 6k multicolored 1.60 .35
 Nos. 2857-2860 (4) 3.45 1.10

A1042

Photo. & Engr.
1992, June 10 Perf. 11½
2861 A1042 2k multicolored .30 .25
Czechoslovakian Red Cross.

A1043

1992, June 30
2862 A1043 1k multicolored .30 .25
Junior European Table Tennis Championships, Topolcany.

Beetles — A1044

1992, July 15
2863 A1044 1k Polyphylla fullo .65 .25
2864 A1044 2k Ergates faber .90 .25
2865 A1044 3k Meloe violaceus 1.90 .45
2866 A1044 4k Dytiscus latissimus 1.90 .45
 Nos. 2863-2866 (4) 5.35 1.40
The 1k exists with denomination omitted.

Troja Castle A1045

1992, Aug. 28 Engr. Perf. 11½
2867 A1045 6k shown 2.60 1.00
2868 A1045 7k Statue of St. Martin, vert. 3.00 1.10
2869 A1045 8k Lednice Castle 3.50 1.25
 Nos. 2867-2869 (3) 9.10 3.35
Nos. 2867-2869 were each issued in sheets of 8. Value, set $75.

Chrudim Church Type of 1971
Photo. & Engr.
1992, Aug. 28 Perf. 11½x11
2870 A629 50h multicolored .75 .25

Postal Bank — A1045a

Photo. & Engr.
1992, Aug. 28 Perf. 11½x12
2870A A1045a 20k multicolored 2.00 .75

Antonius Bernolak, Georgius Fandly — A1046

Photo. & Engr.
1992, Oct. 6 Perf. 12x11½
2871 A1046 5k multicolored .75 .30
Slovakian Educational Society, bicent.

Cesky Krumlov — A1046a

Photo. & Engr.
1992, Oct. 19 Perf. 11½x12
2871A A1046a 3k brick red & brn .75 .25
See No. 2890.

Painting Type of 1967
6k Old Man on a Raft, by Koloman Sokol. 7k, Still Life of Grapes and Raisins, by Georges Braque, horiz. 8k, Abandoned Corset, by Toyen.

Perf. 11½x12, 12x11½
1992, Nov. 2 Engr.
2872 A565 6k multicolored 2.00 .95
2873 A565 7k multicolored 3.25 1.10
2874 A565 8k multicolored 3.25 1.25
 Nos. 2872-2874 (3) 8.50 3.30
Nos. 2872-2874 were each issued in sheets of 4. Value, set $37.50.

Christmas — A1047

Photo. & Engr.
1992, Nov. 9 Perf. 12x11½
2875 A1047 2k multicolored .75 .25

Jindra Schmidt (1897-1984), Graphic Artist and Engraver — A1048

Photo. & Engr.
1992, Dec. 18 Perf. 11½x12
2876 A1048 2k multicolored .75 .25
Stamp Day.

On January 1, 1993, Czechoslovakia split into Czech Republic and Slovakia. Czech Republic listings continue here. Slovakia can be found in Volume 5.

CZECH REPUBLIC
AREA — 30,449 sq. mi.
POP. — 10,280,513 (1999 est.)

Natl. Arms — A1049

Photo. & Engr.
1993, Jan. 20 Perf. 11
2877 A1049 3k multicolored .40 .25

1993 World Figure Skating Championships, Prague — A1050

1993, Feb. 25 Perf. 11½x11
2878 A1050 2k multicolored .30 .25

Havel Type of 1990 Inscribed "Ceska Republika"
Photo. & Engr.
1993, Mar. 2 Perf. 12x11½
2879 A1000 2k vio, vio brn & blue .30 .25

St. John Nepomuk, Patron Saint of Czechs, 600th Death Anniv. — A1051

1993, Mar. 11
2880 A1051 8k multicolored 1.00 .35
See Germany No. 1776; Slovakia No. 158.

Holy Hunger, by Mikulas Medek — A1052

1993, Mar. 11 Perf. 11½
2881 A1052 14k multicolored 3.75 2.00
Europa.
Issued in sheets of 4. Value, $18.

Sacred Heart Church, Prague A1053

1993, Mar. 30 Engr. Perf. 11½
2882 A1053 5k multicolored 1.00 .50
Issued in sheets of 8. Value, $10.

Brevnov Monastery, 1000th Anniv. — A1054

Litho. & Engr.
1993, Apr. 12 Perf. 12x11½
2883 A1054 4k multicolored .55 .25

1993 Intl. Junior Weight Lifting Championships, Cheb — A1055

Photo. & Engr.
1993, May 12 Perf. 11½
2884 A1055 6k multicolored 1.00 .35

Clock Tower and Church, Brno — A1056

1993, June 16 Engr. Perf. 12x11½
2885 A1056 8k multicolored 1.50 1.50
Brno, 750th anniv.
Issued in sheets of 8. Value, $12.

Arrival of St. Cyril and St. Methodius, 1130th Anniv. — A1057

1993, June 22 Photo. & Engr.
2886 A1057 8k multicolored 1.00 .50
See Slovakia No. 167.

Souvenir Sheet

State Arms — A1058

1993, June 22 Perf. 11½
2887 A1058 8k Sheet of 2 2.60 2.60

Architecture Type of 1992 Inscribed "Ceska Republika" and

A1059

Cities: 1k, Ceske Budejovice. 2k, Usti Nad Labem. No. 2890, like #2871A. No. 2891, Brno. 5k, Pizen. 6k, Slany. 7k, Ostrava. 8k, Olomouc. 10k, Hradec Kralove. 20k, Prague. 50k, Opava.

Perf. 12x11½, 11½x12
1993-94 Photo. & Engr.
2888 A1059 1k dp cl & org .25 .25
2889 A1059 2k red vio & bl .25 .25
2890 A1046a 3k gray bl & red .25
 Complete booklet, 5 #2890 4.50
2891 A1059 3k dk bl & red .25 .25
 Complete booklet, 5 #2891 3.75
2892 A1059 5k bluish green & brn .25 .25
2893 A1059 6k grn & org yel 1.00 .30
2894 A1059 7k blk brn & grn 1.00 .30
2895 A1059 8k dp vio & yel .80 .30
2896 A1059 10k olive gray & red .90 .40
2897 A1059 20k red & blue 2.50 .75
2898 A1059 50k brn & grn 4.75 1.75
 Nos. 2888-2898 (11) 12.20 5.05
Issued: No. 2891, 3/30/94; 6k, 10/1/94; 7k, 11/23/94; others, 7/1/93.

World Rowing Championships, Racice — A1060

CZECHOSLOVAKIA

Photo. & Engr.
1993, Aug. 18 — *Perf. 11½*
2901 A1060 3k multicolored .40 .25

A1061

Famous men: 2k, August Sedlacek (1843-1926), historian. 3k, Eduard Cech (1893-1960), mathematician.

1993, Aug. 26 — *Perf. 12x11½*
2902 A1061 2k multicolored .40 .25
2903 A1061 3k multicolored .55 .25

Trees — A1062

1993, Oct. 26 — *Perf. 11½*
2904 A1062 5k Quercus robur .60 .30
2905 A1062 7k Carpinus betulus .80 .40
2906 A1062 9k Pinus silvestris 1.25 .50
  Nos. 2904-2906 (3) 2.65 1.20

See Slovakia Nos. 160-162.

Christmas — A1063

Photo. & Engr.
1993, Nov. 8 — *Perf. 11½*
2907 A1063 2k multicolored .30 .25

Painting Type of 1967 Inscribed "ČESKA REPUBLIKA"

Paintings: 9k, Strahovska Madonna, by "Bohemian Master" in the year 1350. 11k, Composition, by Miro, horiz. 14k, Field of Green, by Van Gogh, horiz.

1993 — *Engr.* *Perf. 11½x12*
2908 A565 9k multicolored 2.00 2.00
  Perf. 12x11½
2909 A565 11k multicolored 2.25 2.25
2910 A565 14k multicolored 3.25 3.25
  Nos. 2908-2910 (3) 7.50 7.50

Issued: 11k, 14k, Nov. 8; 9k, Dec. 15. Nos. 2908-2910 were each issued in sheets of 4. Value, set $30.

Intl. Year of the Family — A1064

Photo. & Engr.
1994, Jan. 19 — *Perf. 11½*
2911 A1064 2k multicolored .30 .25

Jan Kubelik (1880-1940), Composer — A1065

Photo. & Engr.
1994, Jan. 19 — *Perf. 11½*
2912 A1065 3k multicolored .40 .25

UNESCO A1065a

Designs: 2k, Voltaire (1694-1778), philosopher. 6k, Georgius Agricola (1494-1555), mineralogist, humanist.

1994, Feb. 2 — *Perf. 12x11½*
2913 A1065a 2k multicolored .25 .25
2914 A1065a 6k multicolored .80 .35

1994 Winter Olympics, Lillehammer — A1066

Photo. & Engr.
1994, Feb. 2 — *Perf. 11½*
2915 A1066 5k multicolored .70 .35

A1067

Europa (Marco Polo &): No. 2916, Stylized animals, Chinese woman. No. 2917, Stylized animals.

Photo. & Engr.
1994, May 4 — *Perf. 11½*
2916 A1067 14k multicolored 1.75 1.75
2917 A1067 14k multicolored 1.75 1.75
  a. Pair, #2916-2917 3.50 3.50

Nos. 2916-2917 were issued in sheets of 2 + 2 labels. Value, $8.

Eduard Benes — A1068

1994, May 18
2918 A1068 5k violet & brt purple .60 .25

Architectural Sights — A1069

UNESCO: 8k, Houses at the square, Telc. 9k, Cubist house designed by Chochol, Prague.

1994, May 18
2919 A1069 8k multicolored 1.25 .75
2920 A1069 9k multicolored 1.25 .75

Issued in sheets of 8. Value, pair of sheets $20.

Children's Day — A1070

Photo. & Engr.
1994, June 1 — *Perf. 11½*
2921 A1070 2k multicolored .40 .25

Dinosaurs A1071

Perf. 11½x11, 11x11½ *Litho.*
1994, June 1
2922 A1071 2k Stegosaurus .30 .25
2923 A1071 4k Apatosaurus .50 .25
2924 A1071 5k Tarbosaurus, vert. .70 .35
  Nos. 2922-2924 (3) 1.50 .85

A1072

Photo. & Engr.
1994, June 1 — *Perf. 11½x11*
2925 A1072 8k multicolored 1.00 .50

1994 World Cup Soccer Championships, US.

A1073

1994, June 15 — *Perf. 11x11½*
2926 A1073 2k multicolored .35 .25

12th Pan-Sokol Rally, Prague.

Intl. Olympic Committee, Cent. — A1074

1994, June 15
2927 A1074 7k multicolored 1.00 .50

UPU, 120th Anniv. — A1075

1994, Aug. 3 — *Engr.* *Perf. 11½*
2928 A1075 11k multicolored 1.40 1.00

Songbirds — A1076

Designs: 3k, Saxicola torquata. 5k, Carpodacus erythrinus. 14k, Luscinia svecica.

1994, Aug. 24 — *Perf. 11x11½*
2929 A1076 3k multicolored .40 .25
2930 A1076 5k multicolored .60 .30
2931 A1076 14k multicolored 1.50 .80
  Nos. 2929-2931 (3) 2.50 1.35

Historic Race Cars — A1077

Photo. & Engr.
1994, Oct. 5 — *Perf. 11½*
2932 A1077 2k 1900 NW .25 .25
  Complete booklet, 10 #2932 3.00
2933 A1077 3k 1908 L&K .45 .25
  Complete booklet, 5 #2933 2.75
2934 A1077 9k 1912 Praga 1.10 .50
  Nos. 2932-2934 (3) 1.80 1.00

Christmas — A1078

Photo. & Engr.
1994, Nov. 9 — *Perf. 11½*
2935 A1078 2k multicolored .45 .25

Painting Type of 1967 Inscribed "ČESKA REPUBLIKA"

Engraving or paintings: 7k, Stary Posetilec A Zena, by Lucas Van Leyden. 10k, Moulin Rouge, by Henri de Toulouse-Lautrec. 14k, St. Vitus Madonna, St. Vitus Cathedral, Prague.

1994, Nov. 9 — *Engr.* *Perf. 12*
2936 A565 7k multicolored .95 .95
2937 A565 10k multicolored 1.40 1.40
2938 A565 14k multicolored 2.00 2.00
  Nos. 2936-2938 (3) 4.35 4.35

Nos. 2936-2938 were each printed in sheets of 4. Value, set $17.

World Tourism Organization, 20th Anniv. — A1079

Photo. & Engr.
1995, Jan. 2 — *Perf. 11x12*
2939 A1079 8k green blue & red .95 .50

Czech Stamp Production — A1080

1995, Jan. 20
2940 A1080 3k Design N1 .60 .25

Czech Republic & European Union Association Agreement — A1081

1995, Jan. 20 — *Litho.* *Perf. 13½x12½*
2941 A1081 8k multicolored 1.20 .65

Famous Men — A1082

Designs: 2k, Johannes Marcus Marci (1595-1667). 5k, Ferdinand Peroutka (1895-1978). 7k, Premysl Pitter (1895-1976).

Photo. & Engr.
1995, Feb. 1 — *Perf. 12x11*
2942 A1082 2k multicolored .30 .25
2943 A1082 5k multicolored .30 .25
2944 A1082 7k multicolored .90 .35
  Nos. 2942-2944 (3) 1.50 .85

Theater Personalities — A1083

Designs: No. 2945, Jiri Voskovec (1905-81). No. 2946, Jan Werich (1905-80). No. 2947, Jaroslav Jezek (1906-42). 22k, Caricatures of Voskovec, Werich, and Jezek with piano.

1995 — *Photo. & Engr.* *Perf. 12x11*
2945 A1083 3k multicolored .35 .25
  Complete booklet, 3 #2945 6.00
2946 A1083 3k multicolored .35 .25
  Complete booklet, 3 #2946 6.00
2947 A1083 3k multicolored .35 .25
  Complete booklet, 3 #2947 6.00
  a. Strip of 3, #2945-2947 1.10 1.10
  Complete booklet, 2 #2947a 9.00
  Nos. 2945-2947 (3) 1.05 .75

Souvenir Sheet
Photo.
Perf. 12
2947B A1083 22k yellow & black 2.50 2.50

Issued: 3k, 3/15; 22k, 9/20.

Havel Type of 1990 Inscribed "Ceska Republika"

Photo. & Engr.
1995, Mar. 22 — *Perf. 12x11½*
2948 A1000 3.60k bl, vio & mag .45 .25
  Complete booklet, 5 #2948 4.00

CZECHOSLOVAKIA

75

Rural Architecture — A1084

1995, Mar. 22   *Perf. 11½*
2949 A1084 40h shown .25 .25
2950 A1084 60h Homes, diff. .25 .25

European Nature Conservation Year — A1085

1995, Apr. 12
2951 A1085 3k Bombus terrestris .55 .30
    Complete booklet, 5 #2951 4.00
2952 A1085 5k Mantis religiosa .70 .30
    Complete booklet, 5 #2952 4.50
2953 A1085 6k Calopteryx splendens .80 .30
    Complete booklet, 5 #2953 5.00
    Nos. 2951-2953 (3) 2.05 .90

Peace & Freedom A1086

Photo. & Engr.
1995, May 3   *Perf. 11½*
2954 A1086 9k Rose, profiles 1.00 .35
2955 A1086 14k Butterfly, profiles 1.50 .75
    Europa.

Natural Beauties in Czech Republic A1087

Designs: 8k, "Stone Organ" scenic mountain. 9k, Largest sandstone bridge in Europe.

Photo. & Engr.
1995, May 3   *Perf. 11½*
2956 A1087 8k multicolored .95 .95
2957 A1087 9k multicolored 1.00 1.00
    Nos. 2956-2957 were each issued in sheets of 8. Value, set $16.

Children's Day — A1088

Photo. & Engr.
1995, June 1   *Perf. 11½*
2958 A1088 3.60k multicolored .60 .25

First Train from Vienna to Prague, 150th Anniv. — A1089

3k, Chocen Tunnel. 9.60k, Entering Prague.

1995, June 21
2959 A1089 3k multicolored .35 .25
    Complete booklet, 5 #2959 4.00
2960 A1089 9.60k multicolored 1.15 .50

World Wrestling Championships, Prague — A1090

Photo. & Engr.
1995, Sept. 6   *Perf. 11½*
2961 A1090 3k multicolored .75 .25

Cartoon Characters — A1091

Designs: 3k, Man playing violin, woman washing, by Vladimir Rencin. 3.60k, Angel, naked man, by Vladimir Jiranek. 5k, Circus trainer holding ring for champagne cork to pop through, by Jiri Sliva.

1995, Sept. 6
2962 A1091 3k multicolored .35 .25
    Complete booklet, 5 #2962 3.50
2963 A1091 3.60k multicolored .35 .25
    Complete booklet, 5 #2963 3.50
2964 A1091 5k multicolored .35 .30
    Complete booklet, 5 #2964 3.50
    Nos. 2962-2964 (3) 1.05 .80

A1092

1995, Sept. 20   Litho.   *Perf. 13½x13*
2965 A1092 3k multicolored .35 .25
    SOS Children's Villages, 25th anniv.

A1093

Designs: 2.40k, Gothic. 3k, Secession. 3.60k, Romance. 4k, Classic portal; 4.60k, Rococo. 9.60k, Renaissance Portal. 12.60k, Cubist. 14k, Baroque.

Photo. & Engr.
1995-97   *Perf. 12x11½*
2966 A1093 2.40k red & green .30 .25
2967 A1093 3k grn & bl .35 .25
2967A A1093 3.60k pur & grn .45 .25
2968 A1093 4k blue & red .50 .25
    Complete booklet, 5 #2967A 3.00
2968A A1093 4.60k multicolored .55 .25
2969 A1093 9.60k blue & red 1.10 .45
2969A A1093 12.60k red brn & bl 1.50 .45
2970 A1093 14k grn & pur 1.60 .60
    Nos. 2966-2970 (8) 6.35 2.75

Issued: 9.60k, 9/27; 2.40k, 14k, 10/11; 3k, 3.60k, 10/25; 4k, 6/12/96; 4.60k, 3/26/97; 12.60k, 6/25/97.

UN, 50th Anniv. — A1094

1995, Oct. 11   Litho.   *Perf. 12x11½*
2971 A1094 14k multicolored 1.60 .80

Wilhelm Röntgen (1845-1923), Discovery of the X-Ray, Cent. — A1095

1995, Oct. 11   **Photo. & Engr.**
2972 A1095 6k blk, buff & bl vio .75 .35

Painting Type of 1967 Inscribed "CESKA REPUBLIKA"

Designs: 6k, Parisiene, by Ludek Marold. 9k, Vase of Flowers, by J.K. Hirschely. 14k, Portrait of J. Malinsky, by Antonín Machek.

1995, Nov. 8   *Perf. 12*
2973 A565 6k multicolored .95 .45
2974 A565 9k multicolored 1.25 .65
2975 A565 14k multicolored 2.00 1.00
    Nos. 2973-2975 (3) 4.20 2.10

Nos. 2973-2975 were each printed in sheets of 4. Value, set $13.50.

Christmas — A1096

1995, Nov. 8   *Perf. 11½*
2976 A1096 3k multicolored .50 .25
    Complete booklet, 5 #2976 3.00

Czech Philharmonic Orchestra, Cent. — A1097

Photo. & Engr.
1996, Jan. 2   *Perf. 12x11½*
2977 A1097 3.60k multicolored .55 .25

Tradition of Czech Stamp Production — A1098

Photo. & Engr.
1996, Jan. 20   *Perf. 11½x12*
2978 A1098 3.60k Design A5 of 1920 .55 .25

Vera Mencikova (1906-44), Chess Player — A1099

Photo. & Engr.
1996, Feb. 14   *Perf. 12x11½*
2979 A1099 6k multicolored .75 .35

Easter — A1100

1996, Mar. 13   *Perf. 11½x12*
2980 A1100 3k multicolored .45 .25
    Complete booklet, 5 #2980 2.00

Josef Sudek (1896-1976), Photographer A1101

Photo. & Engr.
1996, Mar. 13   *Perf. 11*
2981 A1101 9.60k multicolored 1.10 .60

Rulers from House of Luxembourg — A1102

Designs: a, John of Luxembourg (1296-1346). b, Charles IV (1316-78). c, Wenceslas IV. (1361-1419). d, Sigismund (1368-1437).

1996, Mar. 27   Engr.   *Perf. 11½*
2982 A1102 14k Sheet of 4, #a.-d. + label 6.00 6.00

Jiri Guth-Jarkovsky, Participant in First Modern Olympic Games, Athens — A1103

Photo. & Engr.
1996, Mar. 27   *Perf. 11½*
2983 A1103 9.60k multicolored 1.25 .60
    Modern Olympic Games, cent.

World Wildlife Fund A1104

Designs: a, 3.60k, Eliomys quercinus. b, 5k, Dryomys nitedula. c, 6k, Spermophilus citellus. d, 8k, Sicista betulina.

Photo. & Engr.
1996, Apr. 24   *Perf. 11½x12*
2984 A1104 Block of 4, #a.-d. 2.50 2.50
    Issued in sheets of 8 stamps. Value $5.

Ema Destinnova (1878-1930), Singer — A1105

1996, May 2   *Perf. 11½*
2985 A1105 8k multicolored .85 .35
    Europa.
    No. 2985 was issued in sheets of 10. Value $8.50.

A1106

Photo. & Engr.
1996, May 15   *Perf. 11x11½*
2986 A1106 12k multicolored 1.20 .65
    Jean Gaspart Deburau (1796-1846), mime.

1996, May 29
2987 A1107 3k multicolored .35 .25
    1996 Summer Olympic Games, Atlanta.

Intl. Children's Day — A1108

Photo. & Engr.
1996, May 29   *Perf. 11½*
2988 A1108 3k multicolored .35 .25

CZECHOSLOVAKIA

Architectural Sites — A1109

UNESCO: 8k, St. Nepomuk Church, Zelena Hora. 9k, Loreta Tower, Prague.

1996, June 26		Engr.	Perf. 11½
2989	A1109	8k multicolored	1.00 1.00
2990	A1109	9k multicolored	1.10 1.10

Nos. 2989-2990 were each issued in sheets of 8. Value, set $16.
See Nos. 3056-3057.

UNICEF, 50th Anniv. — A1110

	Photo. & Engr.	
1996, Sept. 11		Perf. 12x11
2991	A1110 3k multicolored	.35 .25

Horses
A1111 A1112

	Photo. & Engr.	
1996, Sept. 25		Perf. 11x11½
2992	A1111 3k multicolored	.50 .25
2993	A1112 3k multicolored	.50 .25
a.	Pair, #2992-2993	1.00 .75
	Complete booklet, 3 #2992, 2 #2993	3.00
	Complete booklet, 2 #2992, 3 #2993	3.00

Souvenir Sheet

Vaclav Havel, 60th Birthday A1113

1996, Oct. 5			
2994	A1113	Sheet of 2	1.25 1.25
a.	6k red & blue		.60 .50

Painting Type of 1967 Inscribed "CESKA REPUBLIKA"

The Baroque Chair, by Endre Nemes (1909-85).

1996, Oct. 5		Engr.	Perf. 11½
2995	A565	20k multicolored	2.00 2.00

No. 2995 was issued in sheets of 4. Value $8.
See Slovakia No. 255; Sweden No. 2199.

Tycho Brahe (1546-1601), Astronomer A1114

	Photo. & Engr.	
1996, Oct. 9		Perf. 11½x11
2996	A1114 5k multicolored	.85 .30

Biplanes — A1115

1996, Oct. 9			
2997	A1115	7k Letov S1 (1920)	.70 .40
2998	A1115	8k Aero A11 (1925)	.90 .40
2999	A1115	10k Avia BH21 (1925)	1.00 .50
	Nos. 2997-2999 (3)		2.60 1.30

Christmas — A1116

	Photo. & Engr.	
1996, Nov. 13		Perf. 11½
3000	A1116 3k multicolored	.45 .25
	Complete booklet, 5 #3000	3.50

Painting Type of 1967 Inscribed "CESKA REPUBLIKA"

Designs: 9k, Garden of Eden, by Josef Váchal (1884-1969), horiz. 11k, Breakfast, by Georg Flegel (1566-1638).

1996, Nov. 13		Engr.	Perf. 11½
3001	A565	9k multicolored	1.00 1.00
3002	A565	11k multicolored	1.25 1.25

Nos. 3001-3002 were each issued in sheets of 4. Value, set $10.

Czech Stamp Production — A1117

	Photo. & Engr.	
1997, Jan. 20		Perf. 11½x12
3003	A1117 3.60k #68, bl & red	.75 .25

Easter — A1118

	Photo. & Engr.	
1997, Mar. 12		Perf. 11½
3004	A1118 3k multicolored	.75 .25
	Complete booklet, 5 #3004	4.00

Flowers — A1119

3.60k, Erythronium dens-canis. 4k, Calla palustris. 5k, Cypripedium calceolus. 8k, Iris pumila.

1997, Mar. 12			Perf. 11x11½
3005	A1119	3.60k multicolored	.30 .25
	Complete booklet, 5 #3005		2.50
3006	A1119	4k multicolored	.30 .25
	Complete booklet, 5 #3006		2.50
3007	A1119	5k multicolored	.50 .30
	Complete booklet, 5 #3007		3.50
3008	A1119	8k multicolored	.60 .45
	Complete booklet, 5 #3008		5.00
	Nos. 3005-3008 (4)		1.70 1.25

A1120

Jewish Monuments in Prague: 8k, Altneuschul Synagogue. 10k, Tombstone of Rabbi Judah Loew MaHaRal.

1997, Apr. 30			Perf. 11½
3009	A1120	8k multicolored	.75 .45
3010	A1120	10k multicolored	.90 .55
a.	Sheet, 4 each #3009-3010		7.00 4.00

See Israel Nos. 1302-1303.

Greetings Stamp — A1121

1997, Mar. 26		Litho.	Perf. 13x13½
3011	A1121 4k Girl with cats		.50 .25

A1122

1997, Apr. 23		Engr.	Perf. 11½
3012	A1122 7k deep violet		.95 .40

St. Adalbert (956-97). See Germany No. 1964, Hungary No. 3569, Poland No. 3337, Vatican City No. 1040.
No. 3012 was issued in sheets of 4 + 4 labels. Value, $7.

A1123

Europa (Stories and Legends): No. 3013, Queen, knight with sword, lion, snakes. No. 3014, Man riding in chariot drawn by chickens, King looking through window.

	Photo. & Engr.		
1997, Apr. 30			Perf. 11½x12
3013	A1123	8k multicolored	1.00 .60
3014	A1123	8k multicolored	1.00 .60

Nos. 3013-3014 were each issued in sheets of 8. Value, set $16.

Souvenir Sheet

Collections of Rudolf II (1522-1612), Prague Exhibition — A1124

Designs: a, 6k, Musical instruments, flowers, face of bearded man. b, 8k, Rudolf II wearing laurel wreath, holding rose, Muses. c, 10k, Rudolf II, skull, moth's wings, tree, flowers, leaves, fruit.

1997, May 14		Engr.	Perf. 12
3015	A1124	Sheet of 3, #a.-c.	2.25 2.25

Intl. Children's Day — A1125

	Photo. & Engr.	
1997, May 28		Perf. 11½
3016	A1125 4.60k multicolored	.75 .25

Frantisek Krizik (1847-1941), Electrical Engineer, Inventor of Arc Lamp — A1126

	Photo. & Engr.	
1997, June 25		Perf. 12x11½
3017	A1126 6k multicolored	.85 .25

European Swimming & Diving Championships, Prague A1127

	Photo. & Engr.	
1997, Aug. 27		Perf. 11½
3018	A1127 11k multicolored	1.00 .40

"The Good Soldier Schweik," by Jaroslav Hasek, 110th Anniv. — A1128

4k, Mrs. Müller, Schweik in wheelchair. 4.60k, Lt. Lukás, Col. Kraus von Zillergut, dog. 6k, Schweik smoking pipe, winter scene.

	Photo. & Engr.		
1997, Sept. 10			Perf. 12x11½
3019	A1128	4k multicolored	.50 .25
a.	Booklet pane of 8 + 4 labels		4.50
	Complete booklet, #3019a		4.50
3020	A1128	4.60k multicolored	.50 .25
a.	Booklet pane of 8 + 4 labels		5.00
	Complete booklet, #3020a		5.00
3021	A1128	6k multicolored	.50 .30
a.	Booklet pane of 8 + 4 labels		6.00
	Complete booklet, #3021a		6.00
	Nos. 3019-3021 (3)		1.50 .80

Praga 1998, Intl. Stamp Exhibition A1129

No. 3022, Lesser Town, Prague Castle. No. 3023, Old Town, bridges over Vltava River.

	Photo. & Engr.		
1997, Sept. 24			Perf. 11½
3022	A1129	15k multicolored	1.40 .60
3023	A1129	15k multicolored	1.40 .60
a.	Souvenir sheet, #3022-3023 + 2 labels		3.75 3.00

Historic Service Vehicles A1130

Designs: 4k, Postal bus, Prague. 4.60k, Sentinel truck, Skoda. 8k, Fire truck, Tatra.

	Photo. & Engr.		
1997, Oct. 8			Perf. 12x11½
3024	A1130	4k multicolored	.30 .25
	Complete booklet, 5 #3024		2.50
3025	A1130	4.60k multicolored	.30 .25
	Complete booklet, 5 #3025		3.50
3026	A1130	8k multicolored	.60 .40
	Complete booklet, 5 #3026		5.00
	Nos. 3024-3026 (3)		1.20 .90

A1131

	Photo. & Engr.	
1997, Nov. 12		Perf. 11½
3027	A1131 4k multicolored	.50 .25
	Complete booklet, 5 #3027	2.75

Christmas

CZECHOSLOVAKIA 77

Painting Type of 1967 Inscribed "CESKA REPUBLIKA"

7k, Landscape with Chateau in Chantilly, by Antonín Chittussi (1847-91). 12k, The Prophets Came Out of the Desert, by Frantisek Bílek (1872-1941). 1.6k, Parisian Antiquarians, by T. F. Simon (1877-1942).

1997, Nov. 12   Engr.   Perf. 12
3028	A565	7k multi, horiz.	.50	.50
3029	A565	12k multi	1.00	1.00
3030	A565	16k multi	1.50	1.50
		Nos. 3028-3030 (3)	3.00	3.00

Nos. 3028-3030 were each issued in sheets of 4. Value, set $12.

A1132

1998, Jan. 20   Litho.   Perf. 11½x12
3031	A1132	7k multicolored	.85	.30

1998 Winter Olympic Games, Nagano.

Tradition of Czech Stamp Production — A1133

Photo. & Engr.
1998, Jan. 20   Perf. 12x11½
3032	A1133	12.60k Type A8	1.25	.55
a.		Booklet pane of 8 + 4 labels		12.50
		Complete booklet, #3032a		12.50

Pres. Václav Havel — A1134

1998, Jan. 22
3033	A1134	4.60k dark grn & red	.85	.25

See No. 3114.

Love — A1135

1998, Feb. 4   Perf. 11½
3034	A1135	4k multicolored	.50	.25
		Complete booklet, 5 #3034		2.50

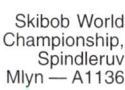

Skibob World Championship, Spindleruv Mlyn — A1136

1998, Feb. 25
3035	A1136	8k multicolored	.85	.35

Prague Philatelic Exhibition Type of 1938
Souvenir Sheet
1998, Feb. 25   Engr.   Perf. 12x11½
3036	A87	Sheet of 2	5.00	5.00
a.		30k like #251a		2.50	2.00

Prague '98, Intl. Philatelic Exhibition.

Easter — A1137

Photo. & Engr.
1998, Mar. 25   Perf. 11x11½
3037	A1137	4k multicolored	.55	.25
		Complete booklet, 5 #3037		2.75

Ondrejov Observatory, Cent. — A1138

1998, Mar. 25   Perf. 12x11½
3038	A1138	4.60k multicolored	.85	.25

Czech Ice Hockey Team, Gold Medalists at Nagano Winter Olympic Games — A1139

1998, Apr. 1   Litho.   Perf. 11½x12
3039	A1139	23k Dominik Hasek	1.50	1.50

No. 3039 was issued in a sheet with two labels. Value, $2.

Charles University and New Town, Prague, 650th Anniv. — A1140

Designs: a, 15k, Hands forming arch, University seal. b, 22k, Charles IV (1316-78), Holy Roman Emperor, King of Bohemia. c, 23k, Groin vault, St. Vitus Cathedral, Prague.

1998, Apr. 1   Engr.   Perf. 12
3040	A1140	Sheet of 3, #a.-c.	5.50	5.50

World Book and Copyright Day — A1141

1998, Apr. 23   Litho.   Perf. 12x11½
3041	A1141	10k multicolored	1.00	.45

Nature Conservation — A1142

1998, Apr. 23   Perf. 13x13½
3042	A1142	4.60k Perdix perdix	.45	.25
3043	A1142	4.60k Lyrurus tetrix	.45	.25
a.		Pair, #3042-3043	1.10	.60
3044	A1142	8k Cervus elaphus	.65	.30
3045	A1142	8k Alces alces	.65	.30
a.		Pair, #3044-3045	1.50	1.10
		Nos. 3042-3045 (4)	2.20	1.10

Natl. Festivals and Holidays A1143

Europa: 11k, King's Ride. 15k, Wearing masks for Carnival.

Litho. & Engr.
1998, May 5   Perf. 11½
3046	A1143	11k multicolored	.90	.55
3047	A1143	15k multicolored	1.40	.75

Intl. Children's Day — A1144

Designs: 4k, Two satyr musicians. 4.60k, Character riding on fish.

Photo. & Engr.
1998, May 27   Perf. 11½
3048	A1144	4k multicolored	.60	.25
a.		Booklet of 6 +4 labels		4.00
		Complete booklet, #3048a		4.00
3049	A1144	4.60k multicolored	.60	.25
a.		Booklet of 6 + 4 labels		4.50
		Complete booklet, #3049a		4.50

Famous Men — A1145

Designs: 4k, Frantisek Kmoch (1848-1912), bandleader, composer. 4.60k, Frantisek Palacky (1798-1876), historian, politician. 6k, Rafael Kubelík (1914-96), composer, conductor.

1998, May 27   Perf. 11½x12
3050	A1145	4k multicolored	.35	.25
3051	A1145	4.60k multicolored	.45	.25
3052	A1145	6k multicolored	.55	.25
		Nos. 3050-3052 (3)	1.35	.75

Revolt of 1848, 150th Anniv. — A1146

1998, May 27   Perf. 12x11½
3053	A1146	15k multicolored	1.60	.75

Painting Type of 1967 Inscribed "CESKA REPUBLIKA"

Praga 1998 Intl. Stamp Exhibition, works of art: 22k, Amorfa Dvoubarevna Fuga, by Frantisek Kupka (1871-1957), horiz. 23k, Escape, by Paul Gauguin (1848-1903), horiz.

1998, June 12   Engr.   Perf. 12
3054	A565	22k multicolored	1.75	1.75
3055	A565	23k multicolored	2.25	1.75

Nos. 3054-3055 were each issued in sheets of 4. Value, set $16.

UNESCO World Heritage Sites Type of 1996

8k, St. Barbara Cathedral, Kutná Hora, horiz. 11k, The Chateau of Valtice, horiz.

1998, Oct. 7   Engr.   Perf. 11½x12
3056	A1109	8k multicolored	.70	.40
3057	A1109	11k multicolored	1.00	.60

Nos. 3056-3057 were each issued in sheets of 8. Value, set $15.

Czechoslovak Republic, 80th Anniv. — A1147

Designs based on World War I recruitment posters by Vojtech Preissig (1873-1944): 4.60k, Soldiers holding flags, guns. 5k, Three soldiers marching. 12.60k, Flags waving from city buildings.

Perf. 11½x11¾
1998, Oct. 28   Litho. & Engr.
3058	A1147	4.60k multicolored	.50	.30
3059	A1147	5k multicolored	.70	.30
3060	A1147	12.60k multicolored	1.25	.90
		Nos. 3058-3060 (3)	2.45	1.50

No. 3060 was issued in sheets of 6+2 labels. Value $25.

Christmas — A1148

Designs: 4k, People following star. 6k, Angel blowing trumpet over town, vert.

Photo. & Engr.
1998, Nov. 18   Perf. 11½
3061	A1148	4k multicolored	.45	.25
		Complete booklet, 5 #3061		2.50
3062	A1148	6k multicolored	.70	.25
		Complete booklet, 5 #3062		4.00

Signs of the Zodiac — A1149

1998-2003   Perf. 11¾x11½
3063	A1149	1k Capricorn	.25	.25
3064	A1149	10k Aquarius	.75	.25
3065	A1149	9k Libra	.75	.25
3066	A1149	8k Cancer	.65	.25
3067	A1149	20k Sagittarius	1.60	.45
3068	A1149	5k Taurus	.55	.25
		Booklet, 5 #3068		2.75
3069	A1149	5.40k Scorpio	.60	.25
		Booklet, 5 #3069		3.00
3070	A1149	2k Virgo	.25	.25
3071	A1149	40h Pisces	.65	.25
3072	A1149	12k Leo	1.00	.30
3073	A1149	17k Gemini	1.60	.65
3074	A1149	26k Aries	2.40	.95
		Nos. 3063-3074 (12)	11.05	4.35

Issued: 1k, 10k, 11/18; 9k, 5/5/99; 8k, 20k, 9/8/99; 5k, 5.40k, 12/8/99; 2k, 5/9/00. 40h, 1/20/01. 12k, 2/21/01 17k, 9/1/02. 26k, 2/12/03.

Painting Type of 1967 Inscribed "CESKA REPUBLIKA"

15k, Painting from the Greater Cycle, 1902, by Jan Preisler (1872-1918), horiz. 16k, Spinner, by Josef Navrátil (1798-1865).

1998, Dec. 9   Perf. 12
3075	A565	15k multicolored	1.40	1.00
3076	A565	16k multicolored	1.40	1.00

Nos. 3075-3076 were each issued in sheets of 4. Value, set $11.

A1150

Photo. & Engr.
1999, Jan. 20   Perf. 11½x11¾
3077	A1150	4.60k #164	.85	.25
a.		Booklet pane of 8 + 4 labels		5.00
		Complete booklet, #3077a		5.50

Tradition of Czech stamp production.

Domestic Cats — A1151

Photo. & Engr.
1999, Feb. 17   Perf. 11½
3078	A1151	4.60k shown	.55	.25
		Complete booklet, 5 #3078		3.60
3079	A1151	5k Adult, kitten	.55	.25
		Complete booklet, 5 #3079		3.50
3080	A1151	7k Two cats	.80	.30
		Complete booklet, 5 #3080		3.50
		Nos. 3078-3080 (3)	1.90	.80

Easter — A1152

Photo. & Engr.
1999, Mar. 10   Perf. 11¼x11½
3081	A1152	3k multicolored	.35	.25

Protected Birds — A1153

No. 3082, Merops apiaster. No. 3083, Upupa epops. Protected butterflies: No. 3084, Catocala electa. No. 3085, Euphydryas maturna.

Perf. 12¾x13¼
1999, Mar. 10   **Litho.**
3082	A1153	4.60k multicolored	.45	.25
3083	A1153	4.60k multicolored	.45	.25
a.		Pair, #3082-3083	.95	.60
		Complete booklet, 3 #3082, 2 #3083	5.00	
3084	A1153	5k multicolored	.45	.25
3085	A1153	5k multicolored	.45	.25
a.		Pair, #3084-3085	.95	.60
		Complete booklet, 3 #3084, 2 #3085	5.00	

Nature conservation.

Czech Republic's Entry Into NATO — A1154

Photo. & Engr.
1999, Mar. 12   **Perf. 12x11½**
| 3086 | A1154 | 4.60k multicolored | .45 | .25 |

Council of Europe, 50th Anniv. — A1155

Photo. & Engr.
1999, Apr. 14   **Perf. 11¾x11¼**
| 3087 | A1155 | 7k multicolored | 1.20 | .40 |

Natl. Olympic Committee, Cent. — A1156

Design: Josef Rössler-Orovsky (1869-1933), founder of Czech Olympic Committee.

1999, Apr. 14   **Perf. 11¼x11¾**
| 3088 | A1156 | 9k multicolored | 1.20 | .35 |

Europa A1157

Natl. Parks: 11k, Sumava. 17k, Podyji.

1999, May 5   **Perf. 11¾x11¼**
| 3089 | A1157 | 11k multicolored | .90 | .40 |
| 3090 | A1157 | 17k multicolored | 1.40 | .65 |

Nos. 3089-3090 were each issued in sheets of 8. Value, set $27.

Ferda the Ant, Pytlik the Beetle and Ladybird — A1158

Photo. & Engr.
1999, May 26   **Perf. 11½x11¼**
| 3091 | A1158 | 4.60k multicolored | .75 | .25 |
| | | Complete booklet, 8 #3091 | 6.00 | |

Bridges A1159

1999, May 26   **Engr.**   **Perf. 11¾**
| 3092 | A1159 | 8k Stádlec, vert. | .60 | .40 |
| 3093 | A1159 | 11k Cernvír | 1.00 | .60 |

Nos. 3092-3094 were each issued in sheets of 8. Value, set $13.

Souvenir Sheet

Paleontologist Joachim Barrande (1799-1883) and Trilobite Fossils — A1160

a, 13k, Barrande, fossils. b, 31k, Delphon forbesi, Ophioceras simplex, Carolicrinus barrandei.

1999, June 23   **Engr.**   **Perf. 11¾**
| 3094 | A1160 | Sheet of 2, #a.-b. + 2 labels | 4.00 | 4.00 |

Jihlava Mining Rights, 750th Anniv. — A1161

Photo. & Engr.
1999, June 23   **Perf. 11¾x11¼**
3095	A1161	8k multicolored	.95	.35
a.		Bklt. pane of 8 + 4 labels	8.00	
		Complete booklet, #3095a	8.00	

UPU, 125th Anniv. — A1162

Litho. & Engr.
1999, June 23   **Perf. 11¾**
| 3096 | A1162 | 9k multicolored | 1.00 | .40 |

No. 3096 was issued in sheets of 5 + 10 labels. Value, $6.

Vincenc Preissnitz (1799-1851), Hydrotherapy Advocate — A1163

Photo. & Engr.
1999, Sept. 8   **Perf. 11¼**
| 3097 | A1163 | 4.60k multicolored | .50 | .25 |

UNESCO.

Carved Beehives — A1164

Designs: 4.60k, Woman. 5k, St. Joseph and Infant Jesus. 7k, Chimney sweep.

Photo. & Engr.
1999, Sept. 29   **Perf. 11¼x11½**
3098	A1164	4.60k multi	.55	.25
		Complete booklet, 5 #3098	2.75	
3099	A1164	5k multi	.60	.25
		Complete booklet, 5 #3099	3.00	
3100	A1164	7k multi	.80	.30
		Complete booklet, 5 #3100	4.00	
		Nos. 3098-3100 (3)	1.95	.80

Cartoons by Miroslav Bartak — A1165

Designs: 4.60k, Doctor in clown mask, infant. 5k, Dog with pipe. 7k, Night seeping through window sill.

1999, Oct. 20
3101	A1165	4.60k multi	.45	.25
3102	A1165	5k multi	.55	.25
3103	A1165	7k multi	.70	.30
		Nos. 3101-3103 (3)	1.70	.80

Souvenir Sheet

Beuron Art School A1166

Designs: a, 11k, Mater Dei, 1898. b, 13k, Pantocrator, 1911.

Litho. & Engr.
1999, Oct. 20   **Perf. 11¾**
| 3104 | A1166 | Sheet of 2, #a.-b. | 2.25 | 2.25 |

Painting Type of 1967 Inscribed "CESKA REPUBLIKA"

Designs: 13k, Red Orchid, by Jindrich Styrsky (1899-1942). 17k, Landscape with Marsh, by Julius Marák (1832-99). 26k, Monument, by Frantisek Hudecek (1909-90).

1999, Nov. 10   **Engr.**   **Perf. 11¾**
3105	A565	13k multi	1.00	1.00
3106	A565	17k multi	1.50	1.50
3107	A565	26k multi	2.50	2.00
		Nos. 3105-3107 (3)	5.00	4.50

Nos. 3105-3107 were each issued in sheets of 4. Value, set $20.

Christmas — A1167

Photo. & Engr.
1999, Nov. 10   **Perf. 11¼x11½**
| 3108 | A1167 | 3k multi | .35 | .25 |

A1168

Photo. & Engr.
2000, Jan. 20   **Perf. 11¼x11¾**
3109	A1168	5.40k #B151	.75	.25
a.		Bklt. pane of 8 + 4 labels	6.00	
		Booklet, #3109a	6.00	

Tradition of Czech stamp production.

Brno 2000 Philatelic Exhibition A1169

Designs: 5k, 1593 view of Brno. 50k, St. James's Church, vert.

2000, Jan. 20   **Perf. 11¾x11¼**
| 3110 | A1169 | 5k multi | .60 | .25 |

Souvenir Sheet
Perf. 11¼x11¾
| 3111 | A1169 | 50k multi | 5.00 | 4.25 |

No. 3110 printed in sheets of 35 stamps and 30 labels.

Kutna Hora Royal Mining Law, 700th Anniv. — A1170

2000, Mar. 1   **Perf. 11¼x11¾**
3112	A1170	5k multi	.60	.25
a.		Booklet pane of 8 + 4 labels	5.00	
		Booklet, #3112a	5.00	

Souvenir Sheet

Pres. Thomas Garrigue Masaryk (1850-1937) — A1171

2000, Mar. 1   **Engr.**   **Perf. 11¾**
| 3113 | A1171 | 17k multi | 1.75 | 1.50 |

Pres. Havel Type of 1998
Photo. & Engr.
2000, Mar. 1   **Perf. 11¾x11¼**
| 3114 | A1134 | 5.40k Prus bl & org brn | .60 | .25 |

Easter — A1172

Photo. & Engr.
2000, Apr. 5   **Perf. 11¼x11¾**
| 3115 | A1172 | 5k multi | .60 | .25 |

Souvenir Sheet

Prague, 2000 European City of Culture — A1173

No. 3116: a, 9k, Statue of man. b, 11k, Statue of harpist. c, 17k, Statue of King Charles IV.

Litho. & Engr.
2000, Apr. 5   **Perf. 11¾**
| 3116 | A1173 | Sheet of 3, #a-c + 3 labels | 4.00 | 4.00 |

CZECHOSLOVAKIA

Souvenir Sheet

Trains
A1174

No. 3117: a, 8k, Train from 1900. b, 15k, Train from 2000.

Litho. & Engr.
2000, May 5   Perf. 11¾
3117   A1174   Sheet of 2, #a-b, +3 labels   3.00   3.00

Czech Personalities — A1175

5k, Vítězslav Nezval (1900-58), writer. 8k, Gustav Mahler (1860-1911), composer.

Photo. & Engr.
2000, May 5   Perf. 11¼x11¾
3118-3119   A1175   Set of 2   1.40   .50

Europa, 2000
Common Design Type

2000, May 5   Litho.   Perf. 12¾x13¼
3120   CD17   9k multi   1.20   .40

Intl. Children's Year — A1176

Photo. & Engr.
2000, May 31   Perf. 11½x11¼
3121   A1176   5.40k multi   .75   .25
   a.   Booklet pane of 8 + 2 labels   6.00
     Booklet, #3121a   6.00

1995 Proof of Fermat's Last Theorem by Andrew Wiles — A1177

2000, May 31   Perf. 11⅞x11¼
3122   A1177   7k multi   .80   .25
Intl. Mathematics Year.

Prague Landmarks
A1178

Designs: 9k, Charles Bridge tower. 11k, St. Nicholas Church. 13k, Town Hall.

2000, June 28   Engr.   Perf. 11¾
3123-3125   A1178   Set of 3   3.00   1.10
Issued in sheets of 8. Value, set $24.

Mushrooms
A1179

No. 3126, 5k: a, Geastrum pouzarii. b, Boletus satanoides.
No. 3127, 5.40k: a, Morchella pragensis. b, Verpa bohemica.

Photo. & Engr.
2000, June 28   Perf. 11¼x11½
Pairs, #a-b
3126-3127   A1179   Set of 2   2.40   .70
     Booklet, 3 #3126a, 2 #3126b   3.50
     Booklet, 3 #3127b, 2 #3127a   3.50

Meeting of Intl. Monetary Fund and World Bank Group, Prague
A1180

2000, Aug. 30   Perf. 11¾x11¼
3128   A1180   7k multi   .95   .25

Ancient Olympics
A1181

2000, Aug. 30
3129   A1181   9k multi   1.00   .35

2000 Summer Olympics, Sydney
A1182

2000, Aug. 30
3130   A1182   13k multi   1.25   .45

No. 3130 was issued in sheets of 35 + 25 labels. Values: stamp + 1 label, $1.50; stamp + 2 labels, $1.75.

Hunting
A1183

No. 3131: a, 5k, Falconry. b, 5k, Deer at feed trough.
No. 3132: a, 5.40k, Ducks and blind. b, 5.40k, Deer and blind.

Photo. & Engr.
2000, Oct. 4   Perf. 11¼x11¾
Horiz. Pairs, #a-b
3131-3132   A1183   Set of 2   2.40   .55
     Booklet, 3 #3131a, 2 #3131b   3.50
     Booklet, 3 #3132a, 2 #3132b   3.50

Painting Type of 1967 Inscribed "CESKA REPUBLIKA"

Designs: 13k, St. Luke the Evangelist, by Master Theodoricus. 17k, Simeon With Infant Jesus, by Petr Jan Brandl. 26k, Brunette, by Alfons Mucha.

2000, Nov. 15   Engr.   Perf. 11¾
3133-3135   A565   Set of 3   5.00   4.50
Nos. 3133-3135 were each issued in sheets of 4. Value, set $20.

Christmas — A1184

Photo. & Engr.
2000, Nov. 15   Perf. 11¼x11½
3136   A1184   5k multi   .60   .25

End of Millennium — A1185

2000, Nov. 22
3137   A1185   9k multi   1.20   .35

Advent of New Millennium — A1186

2001, Jan. 2
3138   A1186   9k multi   1.20   .35

Tradition of Czech Stamp Production — A1187

2001, Jan. 20   Perf. 11¼x11¾
3139   A1187   5.40k #474   .75   .25
   a.   Booklet pane of 8 + 4 labels   6.00
     Booklet, #3139a   6.00

Jan Amos Komensky (Comenius, 1592-1670), Theologian — A1188

Photo. & Engr.
2001, Mar. 14   Perf. 11¼x11½
3140   A1188   9k red & black   1.10   .35

Souvenir Sheet

Architecture — A1189

No. 3141: a, 13k, Church and decorations, Jakub. b, 17k, Arcade decorations, Bucovice Castle. c, 31k, Dance Hall, Prague.

2001, Mar. 28   Engr.   Perf. 11¾x11½
3141   A1189   Sheet of 3, #a-c   6.00   4.50

Easter — A1190

Photo. & Engr.
2001, Mar. 28   Perf. 11¼x11½
3142   A1190   5.40k multi   .75   .25

Souvenir Sheet

Allegory of Art, by Vaclav Vavrinec Reiner
A1191

Litho. & Engr.
2001, Apr. 18   Perf. 11¾
3143   A1191   50k multi   5.00   4.25

Europa — A1192

Photo. & Engr.
2001, May 9   Perf. 11¾x11¼
3144   A1192   9k pur & lilac   1.20   .35

European Men's Volleyball Championships, Ostrova — A1193

Photo. & Engr.
2001, May 9   Perf. 11¼x11½
3145   A1193   12k multi   1.25   .50

Intl. Children's Day — A1194

Photo. & Engr.
2001, May 30   Perf. 11¼x11½
3146   A1194   5.40k multi   .60   .25
   a.   Booklet pane of 8 + 2 labels   5.00
     Booklet, #3146a   5.00

Famous Men — A1195

Designs: 5.40k, Frantisek Skroup (1801-62), composer. 16k, Frantisek Halas (1901-49), writer.

2001, May 30
3147-3148   A1195   Set of 2   2.50   .80

Congratulations
A1196

2001, June 20
3149   A1196   5.40k multi   .75   .25
     Booklet, 5 #3149   4.00

Dogs — A1197

No. 3150: a, West Highland terrier. b, Beagle.
No. 3151: a, German shepherd. b, Golden retriever.

Photo. & Engr.
2001, June 20   Perf. 11½x11¼
3150   Pair   1.25   1.00
   a.-b.   A1197 5.40k Any single   .60   .25
     Booklet, 3 #3150a, 2 #3150b   3.25
     Booklet, 3 #3150b, 2 #3150a   3.25
3151   Pair   1.25   1.00
   a.-b.   A1197 5.40k Any single   .60   .25
     Booklet, 3 #3151a, 2 #3151b   3.25

Zoo Animals
A1198

No. 3152: a, Pongo pygmaeus. b, Panthera tigris altaica.
No. 3153: a, Ailurus fulgens. b, Fennecus zerda.

Photo. & Engr.
2001, Sept. 5   Perf. 11¾x11¼
3152   A1198   Pair   1.00   1.00
   a.-b.   5.40k Any single   .50   .25
     Booklet, 3 #3152b, 2 #3152a   3.25
3153   A1198   Pair   1.00   1.00
   a.-b.   5.40k Any single   .50   .25
     Booklet, 3 #3153b, 2 #3153a   3.25

UNESCO World Heritage Sites — A1199

CZECHOSLOVAKIA

Designs: 12k, Kormeríz Castle and Gardens. 14k, Holasovice Historical Village Restoration.

2001, Oct. 9		Engr.	Perf. 11½x11¾
3154-3155	A1199	Set of 2	2.00 1.25

See Nos. 3177-3178, 3267-3268.

Year of Dialogue Among Civilizations — A1200

Photo. & Engr.
2001, Oct. 9			Perf. 11¼x11½
3156	A1200	9k multi	.85 .35

Mills — A1201

Designs: 9k, Windmill. 14.40k, Water mill.

2001, Oct. 9			
3157-3158	A1201	Set of 2	2.25 1.00

Christmas — A1202

Photo. & Engr.
2001, Nov. 14			Perf. 11¼x11½
3159	A1202	5.40k multi	.60 .30

Painting Type of 1967 Inscribed "CESKA REPUBLIKA"

Designs: 12k, The Annunciation of the Virgin Mary, by Michael J. Rentz. 17k, The Sans Souci Bar in Nimes, by Cyril Bouda. 26k, The Goose Keeper, by Vaclav Brozík.

2001, Nov. 14		Engr.	Perf. 11¾
3160-3162	A565	Set of 3	4.50 4.25

Nos. 3160-3162 were each issued in sheets of 4. Value, set $18.

Tradition of Czech Stamp Production — A1203

Photo. & Engr.
2002, Jan. 20			Perf. 11¼x11¾
3163	A1203	5.40k Type A89	.75 .25
a.		Booklet pane of 8 + 4 labels	5.00 —
		Booklet, #3163a	5.00

2002 Winter Olympics, Salt Lake City — A1204

2002, Jan. 30			Perf. 11¼
3164	A1204	12k multi	1.25 .45

For overprint, see No. 3168.

2002 Winter Paralympics, Salt Lake City — A1205

2002, Jan. 30			Perf. 11¼x11½
3165	A1205	5.40k multi	.85 .25

Composers Jaromír Vejvoda (1902-88), Josef Poncar (1902-86) and Karel Vacek (1902-82) A1206

2002, Mar. 6			Perf. 11¾x11¼
3166	A1206	9k multi	1.10 .35

Easter — A1207

2002, Mar. 6			Perf. 11¼x11½
3167	A1207	5.40k multi	.85 .25

No. 3164 Overprinted in Blue

Photo. & Engr.
2002, Mar. 8			Perf. 11¼
3168	A1204	12k multi	1.25 .65

Divan, by Vlaho Bukovac (1855-1922) — A1208

Litho. & Engr.
2002, Apr. 23			Perf. 11¾
3169	A1208	17k multi	2.00 1.40

Printed in sheets of 4 + 2 labels. Value $8. See Croatia No. 487.

Europa — A1209

Photo. & Engr.
2002, May 7			Perf. 11¾x11¼
3170	A1209	9k multi	1.20 .35

Souvenir Sheet

Czech Culture and France A1210

No. 3171: a, 23k, Klávesy Piana-Jezero, by Frantisek Kupka. b, 31k, Man with Broken Nose, sculpture by Auguste Rodin.

Perf. 11¾x11½
2002, May 7		Litho. & Engr.	
3171	A1210	Sheet of 2, #a-b	5.25 4.00

Intl. Children's Day — A1211

Photo. & Engr.
2002, May 29			Perf. 11¼x11¾
3172	A1211	5.40k multi	.60 .25
a.		Booklet pane of 8 + 2 labels	5.00 —
		Complete booklet, #3172a	5.00

Margaritifera Margaritifera — A1212

2002, June 6			
3173	A1212	9k multi	1.00 .35

Jan Hus (1372-1415), Religious Leader — A1213

2002, June 19			
3174	A1213	9k multi + label	1.00 .35

Souvenir Sheet

Worldwide Fund for Nature (WWF) — A1214

Butterflies: a, 5.40k, Maculinea nausithous. b, 5.40k, Maculinea alcon. c, 9k, Maculinea teleius. d, 9k, Maculinea arion.

Litho. & Engr.
2002, June 19			Perf. 11¾
3175	A1214	Sheet of 4, #a-d + 4 labels	3.50 2.75

Pansy — A1215

Photo. & Engr.
2002, Sept. 1			Perf. 11¾x11¼
3176	A1215	6.40k multi	.85 .25

See Nos. 3220-3221, 3262-3263, 3293-3294, 3340, 3345-3347, 3363-3366, 3467-3469, 3500, 3756, 3789.

World Heritage Sites Type of 2001

Designs: 12k, Litomysl Castle. 14k, Holy Trinity Column, Olomouc, vert.

Perf. 11½x11¾, 11¾x11¼
2002, Sept. 11			Engr.
3177-3178	A1199	Set of 2	2.75 2.00

Nos. 3177-3178 were each issued in sheets of 8. Value, set $25.

Emil Zátopek (1922-2000), Olympic Long Distance Runner — A1216

Photo. & Engr.
2002, Sept. 11			Perf. 11¼x11¾
3179	A1216	9k multi	1.10 .35

Pres. Havel Type of 1998
Photo. & Engr.
2002, Nov. 6			Perf. 11¾x11¼
3180	A1134	6.40k pur & blue	.85 .25

St. Nicholas' Day — A1217

2002, Nov. 6			Perf. 11¼x11½
3181	A1217	6.40k multi	.85 .25
a.		Booklet pane of 8 + 2 labels	6.00 —
		Complete booklet, #3181a	6.00

Christmas — A1218

2002, Nov. 13			
3182	A1218	6.40k multi	.85 .25

NATO Summit, Prague — A1219

2002, Nov. 14			Perf. 11¼x11¾
3183	A1219	9k multi	1.00 .30

Furniture — A1220

Designs: 6.40k, Armchair, 17th cent. 9k, Sewing table with hemispheric cover, 1820. 12k, Dressing table with mirror, 1860. 17k, Art deco amchair, 1923.

2002, Dec. 11			
3184-3187	A1220	Set of 4	4.50 2.25

Painting Type of 1967 Inscribed "CESKA REPUBLIKA"

Designs: 12k, The Abandoned, by Jaroslav Panuska, horiz. 20k, St. Wenceslas, by Mikolás Ales. 26k, Portrait of a Young Man with a Lute, by Jan Petr Molitor.

2002, Dec. 11		Engr.	Perf. 11¾
3188-3190	A565	Set of 3	5.75 3.75

Nos. 3188-3190 were each issued in sheets of 4. Value, set $23.

Souvenir Sheet

Czech Republic, 10th Anniv. A1221

CZECHOSLOVAKIA

Litho. & Engr.
2003, Jan. 1 — Perf. 11¾
3191 A1221 25k multi — 2.75 1.60

Tradition of Czech Stamp Production — A1222

Photo. & Engr.
2003, Jan. 20 — Perf. 11¼x11¾
3192 A1222 6.40k Type A75 — .95 .25
a. Booklet pane of 8 + 2 labels — 7.50 —
   Complete booklet, #3192a — 7.50

Famous Men — A1223

Designs: 6.40k, Jaroslav Vrchlicky (1853-1912), poet. 8k, Josef Thomayer (1853-1927), physician and writer.

2003, Feb. 12 — Perf. 11½x11¼
3193-3194 A1223 Set of 2 — 1.75 .50

Easter — A1224

2003, Mar. 26 — Perf. 11¼x11½
3195 A1224 6.40k multi — .95 .25

Roses Above Prague A1225

— Perf. 12¾x13¼
2003, Mar. 26 — Litho.
3196 A1225 6.40k multi + label — .75 .35
Labels could be personalized.
Issued in sheets of 9 stamps and 12 labels. Value $9.
See No. 3517.

Lace — A1226

Designs: 6.40k, Netted lace. 9k, Bobbin lace.

Photo. & Engr.
2003, Mar. 26 — Perf. 11¼
3197 A1226 6.40k bl, dk bl & red — .75 .25
a. Booklet pane of 6 + 4 labels — 4.50 —
   Complete booklet, #3197a — 4.50
3198 A1226 9k dk bl & red — 1.00 .35
a. Booklet pane of 6 + 4 labels — 6.00 —
   Complete booklet, #3198a — 6.00

Europa — A1227

Litho. & Engr.
2003, May 7 — Perf. 11¾
3199 A1227 9k multi — 1.20 .65

Geologic Attractions A1228

Designs: 12k, Sandstone towers, Hrubá Skála Region. 14k, Punkva Caves, Moravian karst area.

2003, May 7 — Engr. Perf. 11½x11¾
3200-3201 A1228 Set of 2 — 3.00 2.00
Nos. 3200-3201 were each issued in sheets of 8. Value, set $25.

Mach and Sebestova, Children's Television Show Characters — A1229

Photo. & Engr.
2003, May 28 — Perf. 11¼x11½
3202 A1229 6.40k multi — .95 .35
a. Booklet pane of 8 + 2 labels — 7.50 —
   Complete booklet, #3202a — 7.50

First Electric Railway, Tábor — Bechyne, Cent. — A1230

2003, May 28 — Perf. 11¾x11¼
3203 A1230 10k multi — 1.25 .50

A1231

Observation towers: No. 3204, 6.40k, Klet. No. 3205, 6.40k, Slovanka.

2003, May 28 — Perf. 11¼x11½
3204-3205 A1231 Set of 2 — 1.50 .50

A1232

2003, June 25 — Perf. 11¾x11¼
3206 A1232 9k multi — 1.25 .35
European Shooting Championships, Plzen and Brno.

A1233

2003, June 25 — Perf. 11¼x11½
3207 A1233 9k multi — 1.20 .35
Josef Dobrovsky (1753-1829), linguist.

Pres. Vaclav Klaus — A1234

Photo. & Engr.
2003 — Perf. 11¾x11¼
3208 A1234 6.40k buff, red & vio bl — .95 .35
3209 A1234 6.50k Prus bl & pur — .95 .35
Issued 6.40k, 7/30; 6.50k, 11/5.
See No. 3264.

Souvenir Sheet

Tropical Fish A1235

No. 3210: a, 12k, Betta splendens (27x44mm). b, 14k, Pterophyllum scalare (27x44mm). c, 16k, Carassius auratus (54x44mm). d, 20k, Symphysodon aequifasciatus (54x44mm).

Litho. & Engr.
2003, Sept. 10 — Perf. 11¾
3210 A1235 Sheet of 4, #a-d — 6.00 5.00
No. 3210 exists in six different varieties, which may be distinguished by the number of horizontal lines in the stone in the bottom sheet margin below the 14k stamp. Values given are for sheets with 1, 2 or 5 lines in the stone; value for sheet with no lines or 3 lines in the stone, $21; value for sheet with 4 lines in the stone, $72.50.

Oriental Carpets A1236

Designs: 9k, Turkish prayer carpet, 19th cent. 12k, Turkish carpet, 18th cent.

2003, Oct. 1 — Engr. Perf. 11¾
3211-3212 A1236 Set of 2 — 2.50 1.75
Nos. 3211-3212 were each issued in sheets of 4. Value, set $10.

Tympanum, Porta Coeli Monastery, Predkláster̆í A1237

Photo. & Engr.
2003, Oct. 15 — Perf. 11¾x11½
3213 A1237 6.50k multi — .95 .45
a. Booklet pane of 8 + 4 labels — 7.50 —
   Complete booklet, #3213a — 7.50

Birds of Prey — A1238

Designs: 6.50k, Milvus milvus. 8k, Falco peregrinus. 9k, Hieraaetus pennatus.

2003, Oct. 15 — Perf. 11¼x11½
3214 A1238 6.50k multi — .75 .35
   Booklet, 5 #3214 — 3.75
3215 A1238 8k multi — .90 .30
   Booklet, 5 #3215 — 4.50
3216 A1238 9k multi — 1.00 .30
   Booklet, 5 #3216 — 5.00
   Nos. 3214-3216 (3) — 2.65 .85

Czech Fire Fighters, 140th Anniv. — A1239

Fire engines: 6.50k, Wooden fire engine, 1822. 9k, Motorized fire engine, 1933. 12k, CAS 8/Avia Daewoo fire truck, 2002.

2003, Oct. 15 — Perf. 11¾x11¼
3217-3219 A1239 Set of 3 — 3.00 1.50

Flower Type of 2002

Designs: 50h, Cornflower (chrpa). 6.50k, Dahlia (jirina).

2003, Oct. 22
3220 A1215 50h multi — .25 .25
3221 A1215 6.50k multi — .75 .25

Roses Over Prague Type of 2003 and

Prague Castle Lantern A1240

2003, Oct. 22 — Litho. Perf. 12¾x13¼
3222 A1225 6.50k multi + label — .75 .25
3223 A1240 9k multi + label — 1.00 .30
Labels could be personalized.
Nos. 3222-3223 were each issued in sheets of 9 stamps and 12 labels. Value, set $17.50.

Painting Type of 1967 Inscribed "ČESKÁ REPUBLIKA"

Designs: 17k, Poor Countryside, by Max Svabinsky, horiz. 20k, Autumn in Veltrusy, by Antonín Slavíček. 26k, Eleanora de Toledo, by Agnolo Bronzino.

2003, Nov. 5 — Engr. Perf. 11¾
3224-3226 A505 Set of 3 — 6.50 4.00
Nos. 3224-3226 were each issued in sheets of 4. Value, set $26.

Christmas — A1241

Photo. & Engr.
2003, Nov. 5 — Perf. 11¼x11½
3227 A1241 6.50k multi — .75 .35

Tradition of Czech Stamp Production — A1242

Photo. & Engr.
2004, Jan. 20 — Perf. 11¼x11¾
3228 A1242 6.20k Vignette of #1703 — .95 .35
a. Booklet pane of 8 + 4 labels — 7.50 —
   Complete booklet, #3228a — 7.50

Church of the Assumption of the Virgin Mary, Brno A1243

2004, Feb. 18 — Engr. Perf. 11¾
3229 A1243 17k multi — 1.90 1.00
Brno 2005 Philatelic Exhibition.
No. 3229 was issued in sheets of 4. Value $8.

Industrial Building Historical Preservation A1244

Designs: 6.50k, Busek's Water Forging Hammer, Lniste. 17k, Iron Furnace, Stará Hut u Adamova.

Photo. & Engr.
2004, Feb. 18 — Perf. 11½x11¼
3230-3231 A1244 Set of 2 — 2.40 .90

CZECHOSLOVAKIA

Easter — A1245

2004, Mar. 17
3232 A1245 6.50k multi .95 .25

Painting Type of 1967 Inscribed "ČESKÁ REPUBLIKA"

Design: Prometheus, by Antonín Procházka.

2004, Mar. 17 Engr. Perf. 11¾
3233 A565 26k multi 2.60 1.60

Brno 2005 Philatelic Exhibition. No. 3233 was issued in sheets of 4. Value $11.

World Ice Hockey Championships, Prague and Ostrava — A1246

Photo. & Engr.
2004, Apr. 14 Perf. 11¼x11¾
3234 A1246 12k multi 1.50 .50

Admission to European Union — A1247

Photo. & Engr.
2004, May 1 Perf. 11¼
3235 A1247 9k multi 1.20 .35

Admission to the European Union — A1248

2004, May 1 Litho. Perf. 11¾x11¼
3236 A1248 9k multi 1.10 .35

No. 3236 was issued in sheets of 10. Value $11.

Europa — A1249

2004, May 5 Perf. 11¼
3237 A1249 9k multi 1.10 .35

Composers of Czech Operas — A1250

Designs: 6.50k, Dalibor, by Bedrich Smetana (1824-84). 8k, Jakobín, by Antonín Dvořák (1841-1904). 10k, Její Pastorkyna, by Leos Janáček (1854-1928).

Photo. & Engr.
2004, May 5 Perf. 11¼x11¾
3238-3240 A1250 Set of 3 2.60 1.10

For Children — A1251

Photo. & Engr.
2004, May 26 Perf. 11½x11¼
3241 A1251 6.50k multi .85 .25
a. Booklet pane of 8 + 2 labels 7.00 —
 Complete booklet, #3241a 7.00

Statue of Radegast, by Albín Polášek — A1252

2004, May 26 Perf. 11¼x11½
3242 A1252 6.50k multi .85 .25

Brno 2005 Philatelic Exhibition.

Tourist Attractions A1253

Designs: 12k, Holy Mountain, Přibram. 14k, Holy Shrine, Bystrice pod Hostýnem.

2004, May 26 Engr. Perf. 11½x11¾
3243-3244 A1253 Set of 2 2.60 1.50

Nos. 3243-3244 were each issued in sheets of 8. Value, set $24.

A1254

Photo. & Engr.
2004, June 23 Perf. 11¼x11¾
3245 A1254 6.50k multi 1.20 .25

2004 Paralympics, Athens.

A1255

2004, June 23
3246 A1255 9k multi 1.00 .35

2004 Summer Olympics, Athens.

Petrarch (1304-74), Poet — A1256

2004, June 23 Perf. 11¾x11¼
3247 A1256 14k multi 1.40 .60

Famous Trees — A1257

Designs: 6.50k, Singing lime tree, Telecí. 8k, Jan Zizka oak tree, Podhradí.

Photo. & Engr.
2004, Sept. 8 Perf. 11¼x11½
3248 A1257 6.50k multi .75 .25
 Complete booklet, 5 #3248 3.75
3249 A1257 8k multi .90 .30
 Complete booklet, 5 #3249 4.50

Miniature Sheet

Parrots A1258

No. 3250: a, 12k, Melopsittacus undulatus. b, 14k, Agapornis personata. c, 16k, Psittacula krameri. d, 20k, Ara chloroptera.

Litho. & Engr.
2004, Sept. 8 Perf. 11¾
3250 A1258 Sheet of 4, #a-d, + 4 labels 6.00 4.50

Compulsory School Attendance, 230th Anniv. — A1259

Photo. & Engr.
2004, Sept. 29 Perf. 11¼x11¼
3251 A1259 6.50k multi .85 .25

Baby Carriages — A1260

Carriages made about: 12k, 1880. 14k, 1890. 16k, 1900.

2004, Oct. 20
3252-3254 A1260 Set of 3 4.00 2.00

Painting Type of 1967 Inscribed "ČESKÁ REPUBLIKA"

Designs: 20k, On the Outskirts of the Cesky Ráj Region, by Alois Bubák, horiz. 22k, The Long, the Broad and the Sharpsight, by Hanus Schwaiger. 26k, The Spring, by Vojtěch Hynais.

2004, Nov. 10 Engr. Perf. 11¾
3255-3257 A565 Set of 3 6.50 4.25

Nos. 3255-3257 were each issued in sheets of 4. Value, set $32.

Christmas — A1261

Photo. & Engr.
2004, Nov. 10 Perf. 11¼x11½
3258 A1261 6.50k multi .75 .25

Tradition of Czech Stamp Production — A1262

Photo. & Engr.
2005, Jan. 18 Perf. 11¼x11¾
3259 A1262 6.50k Design of #975 .95 .30
a. Booklet pane of 8 + 4 labels 7.50
 Complete booklet, #3259a 7.50

Peacock and Bugler Portal Decoration A1263

2005, Jan. 18 Litho. Perf. 12¾x13¼
3260 A1263 7.50k multi + label .95 .30

Labels could be personalized for an additional fee.
Issued in sheets of 9 stamps and 12 labels. Value $9.
See Nos. 3372, 3516.

Souvenir Sheet

Moonscape, by Petr Ginz — A1264

Perf. 11¾x11½
2005, Jan. 18 Litho. & Engr.
3261 A1264 31k multi 3.00 2.00

Flower Type of 2002

Designs: 7.50k, Lily (lilie). 19k, Fuchsia (fuchsie).

Photo. & Engr.
2005 Perf. 11¾x11¼
3262 A1215 7.50k multi .85 .30
3263 A1215 19k multi 2.25 .85

Issued: 7.50k, 1/20; 19k, 3/2.

Pres. Vaclav Klaus Type of 2003
2005, Feb. 9
3264 A1234 7.50k claret & red .85 .30

Granny, by Božena Nemcová, 150th Anniv. of Publication — A1265

2005, Feb. 9 Perf. 11¼x11¾
3265 A1265 7.50k multi .85 .30

Easter — A1266

Photo. & Engr.
2005, Mar. 2 Perf. 11¼x11½
3266 A1266 7.50k multi .85 .30

UNESCO World Heritage Sites Type of 2001

Designs: 14k, St. Prokop's Basilica, Trebic, vert. 16k, Villa Tugendhat, Brno.

CZECHOSLOVAKIA 83

Perf. 11¾x11½, 11½x11¾
2005, Mar. 23 Engr.
3267-3268 A1199 Set of 2 3.25 1.90
Nos. 3267-32682 were each issued in sheets of 8. Value, set $26.

Famous Men — A1267

Designs: 7.50k, Bohuslav Brauner (1855-1935), chemist. 12k, Adalbert Stifter (1805-68), writer, painter. 19k, Mikuláš Dacicky of Heslov (1555-1626), poet.

Photo. & Engr.
2005, Apr. 13 **Perf. 11¼x11¾**
3269-3271 A1267 Set of 3 3.75 1.60

Europa — A1268

2005, May 4 Litho. **Perf. 11¼**
3272 A1268 9k multi 1.20 .35
Issued in sheets of 6. Value, $7.50.

Battle of Austerlitz, Dicent. A1269

Napoleon Before the Battle of Austerlitz, by Louis-François Lejeune — A1270

Photo. & Engr.
2005, May 4 **Perf. 11¾x11¼**
3273 A1269 19k multi 2.25 .00

Souvenir Sheet
Litho. & Engr.
Perf. 11¾
3274 A1270 30k multi 3.50 2.25
Brno 2005 Stamp Exhibition (No. 3274). No. 3273 was issued in sheets of 40 + 20 labels. Value, one stamp + label $3.25. See France No. 3115.

Kremílek and Vochomurka, by Václav Čtvrtek — A1271

Photo. & Engr.
2005, May 25 **Perf. 11¼x11½**
3275 A1271 7.50k multi .85 .30
  a. Booklet pane of 8 + 2 labels 7.00 —
  Complete booklet, #3275a 7.00

Intl. Year of Physics A1272

2005, May 25 **Perf. 11¼x11¾**
3276 A1272 12k multi 1.40 .75

2005 European Baseball Championships A1273

2005, June 22
3277 A1273 9k multi 1.10 .50

Souvenir Sheet

Protected Flora and Fauna of the Krkonose Mountains — A1274

No. 3278: a, 12k, Viola lutea sudetica, Hedysarum hedysaroides (44x28mm). b, 14k, Cinclus cinclus, Leucojum vernum (44x28mm). c, 15k, Sorex alpinus, Salamandra salamandra, Primula minima (44x54mm). d, 22k, Mt. Snezka, Luscinia svecica svecica, Aeschna coerulea, Pneumonanthe asclepiadea (44x54mm).

Litho. & Engr.
2005, June 22 **Perf. 11¾**
3278 A1274 Sheet of 4, #a-d, + 4 labels 7.00 4.25

Church Bells — A1275

Bells from: 7.50k, Benesov, 1322, Havlíckuv Brod, 1335. 9k, Dobrs, 1561, 1596. 12k, Olomouc, 1827.

Photo. & Engr.
2005, Sept. 7 **Perf. 11½x11¼**
3279 A1275 7.50k multi .80 .30
  Complete booklet, 5 #3279 4.00
3280 A1275 9k multi .90 .40
  Complete booklet, 5 #3280 4.50
3281 A1275 12k multi 1.20 .50
  Complete booklet, 5 #3281 6.00
Nos. 3279-3281 (3) 2.90 1.20

Tractors — A1276

Designs: 7.50k, 1923 John Deere 15/27. 9k, 1921 Lanz Bulldog HL-12, 1596. 18k, 1937 Skoda HT 40.

2005, Sept. 21 **Perf. 11½x11¼**
3282 A1276 7.50k multi .60 .30
  Complete booklet, 5 #3282 3.50
3283 A1276 9k multi .90 .35
  Complete booklet, 5 #3283 5.00
3284 A1276 18k multi 1.90 .75
  Complete booklet, 5 #3284 9.50
Nos. 3282-3284 (3) 3.40 1.40

World Summit on the Information Society, Tunis — A1277

2005, Sept. 21 **Perf. 11¼**
3285 A1277 9k org & violet 1.10 .35

Curling A1278

Photo. & Engr.
2005, Oct. 12 **Perf. 11¾x11¼**
3286 A1278 17k multi 2.00 .70

Painting Type of 1967 Inscribed "ČESKA REPUBLIKA"

Designs: 22k, Summer Landscape, by Adolf Kosárek. 25k, Deinotherium, by Zdeněk Burian. 26k, Osiky Near Velké Nemcice, by Alois Kalvoda.

2005, Nov. 9 Engr. **Perf. 11¾**
3287-3289 A565 Set of 3 8.00 5.25
Nos. 3287-3289 were each issued in sheets of 4. Value, set $32.50.

A1279

Christmas — A1280

Photo. & Engr.
2005, Nov. 9 **Perf. 11¼x11½**
3290 A1279 7.50k multi .85 .30
  Perf. 11½x11¼
3291 A1280 9k multi 1.00 .35

Tradition of Czech Stamp Production — A1281

Photo. & Engr.
2006, Jan. 20 **Perf. 11¼x11¾**
3292 A1281 7.50k Portion of #C59 .95 .30
  a. Booklet pane of 8 + 2 labels 7.50
  Complete booklet, #3292a 7.50

Flower Type of 2002

Designs: 11k, Marshmallow (ibisek). 24k, Daffodil (narcis).

2006 **Perf. 11¾x11¼**
3293 A1215 11k multi 1.25 .45
3294 A1215 24k multi 2.75 1.00
Issued: 11k, 2/1; 24k, 2/22.

Flowers A1282

Flowers, Grapes, Glass of Wine A1283

2006 Litho. **Perf. 12¾x13¼**
3295 A1282 10k multi + label 1.10 .60
3296 A1283 12k multi + label 1.40 .75
Issued: 10k, 2/1; 12k, 2/22. Labels could be personalized for an additional fee.
Nos. 3295-3296 were issued in sheets of 9 stamps and 12 labels. Value, set $22.50. See No. 3373.

Madonna of Zbraslav A1284

2006, Feb. 8 Engr. **Perf. 11¾**
3297 A1284 25k multi 2.50 1.75
Printed in sheets of 4. Value $10.

2006 Winter Paralympics, Turin — A1285

Photo. & Engr.
2006, Feb. 8 **Perf. 11¾x11¼**
3298 A1285 7.60k multi .85 .30

2006 Winter Olympics, Turin — A1286

2006 **Perf. 11¼x11¾**
3299 A1286 9k multi 1.00 .40

With "K. NEUMANNOVA / ZLATA MEDAILE" Overprinted in Red Reading Up

3300 A1286 9k multi 1.10 .40
Issued: No. 3299, 2/8; No. 3300, 3/15.

Famous Men — A1287

Designs: 11k, Frantisek Josef Gerstner (1756-1832), mathematician and educator. 12k, Jaroslav Jezek (1906-42), composer. 19k, Sigmund Freud (1856-1939), psychoanalyst.

2006, Feb. 22 **Perf. 11½x11¼**
3301-3303 A1287 Set of 3 4.00 1.75

Easter — A1288

2006, Mar. 22 **Perf. 11¼x11½**
3304 A1288 7.50k multi 1.20 .30

Osek Monastery A1289

CZECHOSLOVAKIA

Kokorinsko Capstones A1290

2006, Mar. 22   Engr.   Perf. 11½x11¾
3305 A1289 12k multi   1.20   .65
3306 A1290 15k multi   1.40   .85
Nos. 3305-3306 were each issued in sheets of 8. Value, set $22.

Love — A1291

Photo. & Engr.
2006, Apr. 26   Perf. 11¼x11½
3307 A1291 7.50k multi   .95   .35
   Complete booklet, 5 #3307 4.75

Europa A1292

Silhouette of person and: 10k, Horse. 20k, Dog.

2006, May 3   Perf. 11¾x11¼
3308-3309 A1292 Set of 2   3.00 1.40
Issued in sheets of 8. Value, set $24.

Rumcajs, Manka and Cipísek, by V. Ctvrtek — A1293

Photo. & Engr.
2006, May 31   Perf. 11¼x11½
3310 A1293 7.50k multi   .95   .35
   a. Booklet pane of 8 + 2 labels 7.50
      Complete booklet, #3310a   7.50

A1294

2006, June 14   Perf. 11¼x11¾
3311 A1294 19k multi   2.00   .90
Kamenice Pass, Czech Switzerland National Park.

A1295

Jewelry with garnets: 15k, Silver brooch with pearl, 1904. 18k, Gold pendant, 1930.

2006, June 14
3312-3313 A1295 Set of 2   3.00 1.75

Miniature Sheet

Bohemian Kings of Premyslid Dynasty — A1296

No. 3314: a, 12k, Otakar I Premysl (c. 1155-1230). b, 14k, Václav (Wenceslas) I (1205-53). c, 15k, Otakar II Premysl (1230-78). d, 22k, Václav (Wenceslas) II (1271-1305). e, 28k, Václav (Wenceslas) III (1289-1306).

2006, June 14   Engr.   Perf. 11¾
3314 A1296 Sheet of 5, #a-e,   8.25 6.00
              + label

Souvenir Sheet

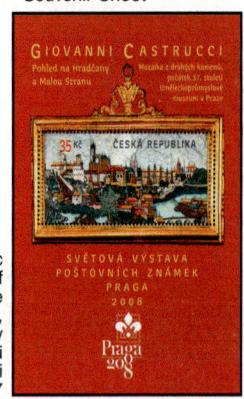

Mosaic of Prague Castle, by Giovanni Castrucci A1297

Litho. & Engr.
2006, Sept. 13   Perf. 11¾
3315 A1297 35k multi   3.50 2.25

Cacti A1298

No. 3316: a, Gymnocalycium denudatum. b, Obregonia denegrii.
No. 3317: a, Astrophytum asterias. b, Cintia knizei.

Perf. 11¼x11¾
2006, Sept. 13   Litho.
3316 A1298 7.50k Pair, #a-b   1.50   .90
   Complete booklet, 2 #3316a, 3
   #3316b   3.50
3317 A1298 10k Pair, #a-b   2.00 1.25
   Complete booklet, 2 #3317a, 3
   #3317b   5.00

Ecology — A1299

2006, Sept. 27   Perf. 11¾x11¼
3318 A1299 7.50k multi   .95   .35

Christmas A1300

2006, Oct. 11   Perf. 12¾x13¼
3319 A1300 7.50k multi + label 1.10   .35
Printed in sheets of 9 stamps + 12 labels. Labels could be personalized. Value, $11.

Vrtbovská Garden, Prague — A1301

Photo. & Engr.
2006, Oct. 11   Perf. 11½x11¾
3320 A1301 7.50k multi   .95   .35
   a. Booklet pane of 8 + 4 labels 7.50
      Complete booklet, #3320a   7.50
Praga 2008 Intl. Philatelic Exhibition, Prague.

Wooden Churches A1302

Designs: 7.50k, Church of the Virgin Mary, Broumov. 19k, Church of St. Andrew, Hodslavice.

Photo. & Engr.
2006, Oct. 11   Perf. 11¾x11¼
3321-3322 A1302 Set of 2   2.60 1.60

Painting Type of 1967 Inscribed "ČESKÁ REPUBLIKA"

Designs: 22k, Still Life with Fruit, by Jan Davidsz de Heem. 25k, Montenegrin Madonna, by Jaroslav Cermák. 28k, Pod Suchym Skalim, by Frantisek Kaván, horiz.

2006, Nov. 8   Engr.   Perf. 11¾
3323-3325 A565 Set of 3   7.00 4.50

Christmas A1303

Photo. & Engr.
2006, Nov. 8   Perf. 11¾x11½
3326 A1303 7.50k multi   .95   .35

Emblem of Praga 2008 Intl. Philatelic Exhibition — A1304

2006, Dec. 1   Litho.
3327 A1304 7.50k multi   .95   .35
See Nos. 3341, 3368.

Czech Technical University, Prague, 300th Anniv. — A1305

Photo. & Engr.
2007, Jan. 10   Perf. 11¾x11½
3328 A1305 9k multi   1.10   .50

Famous Men — A1306

Designs: 7.50k, Frána Šrámek (1877-1952), writer. 19k, Karel Slavoj Amerling (1807-84), educator.

2007, Jan. 10   Perf. 11½x11¼
3329-3330 A1306 Set of 2   2.50 1.40

Tradition of Czech Stamp Production — A1307

2007, Jan. 20   Perf. 11½x11¾
3331 A1307 7.50k Type A242   .85   .35
   a. Booklet pane of 8 + 4 labels 6.75
      Complete booklet, #3331a   6.75

Cancer Prevention — A1308

Photo. & Engr.
2007, Feb. 21   Perf. 11¼x11½
3332 A1308 7.50k multi   .85   .35

Snake — A1309

Perf. 11¼x11¾
2007, Feb. 21   Litho.
3333 A1309 12k multi   1.20   .70

Oriental Art — A1310

Designs: 12k, Girl with a Puppet, by Kunisawa Utagawa. 24k, Siva, Parvati and Ganesa, 19th cent. Indian glass painting.

Litho. & Engr.
2007, Feb. 21   Perf. 11¾
3334-3335 A1310 Set of 2   3.50 2.10

Easter — A1311

Photo. & Engr.
2007, Mar. 14   Perf. 11¼x11½
3336 A1311 7.50k multi   .85   .35

Model of Mala Strana Area of Prague, by Antonín Langweil A1312

2007, Mar. 14   Perf. 11¾x11¼
3337 A1312 7.50k multi   .85   .35
   a. Booklet pane of 8 + 4 labels 7.00
      Complete booklet, #3337a   7.00
Praga 2008 Intl. Philatelic Exhibition, Prague.
No. 3337 was issued in sheets of 8 + 4 labels. Value, $10.

CZECHOSLOVAKIA

Stoclet House, Brussels, Designed by Josef Hoffmann — A1313

Designs: 20k, Building interior. 35k, Building exterior.

2007, Mar. 26   *Perf. 11¼x11¾*
3338-3339 A1313 Set of 2   5.00 3.25
See Belgium Nos. 2228-2229.

Flowers Type of 2002
Perf. 12¾x13¼
2007, Mar. 26   Litho.
3340 A1282 11k multi + label   1.25 .60
Label could be personalized for an additional fee.

Praga 2008 Emblem Type of 2006
2007, Apr. 4   *Perf. 11¾x11½*
3341 A1304 11k blue & multi   1.25 .60

Spas — A1314

Designs: 12k, Jurkovic House, Luhacovice. 15k, Gocár Pavillion, Lázne Bohdanec.

2007, Apr. 4   Engr.   *Perf. 11½x11¾*
3342-3343 A1314 Set of 2   2.50 1.75
Issued in sheets of 8. Value, $20.

Europa — A1315

Photo. & Engr.
2007, May 9   *Perf. 11¼*
3344 A1315 11k multi   1.25 .60
Scouting, cent.

Flowers Type of 2002
Designs: 1k, Cyclamen (bramborik). 15k, Tropaeolum (lichorerisnice), 23k, Geranium (pelargonie).

Photo. & Engr.
2007   *Perf. 11¾x11¼*
3345 A1215 1k multi   .25 .25
3346 A1215 15k multi   1.60 .90
3347 A1215 23k multi   2.00 1.25
Nos. 3345-3347 (3)   3.85 2.40
Issued: 1k, 23k, 5/9. 15k, 9/5.

Fast Arrows, Comic Strip by Jaroslav Foglar — A1316

Photo. & Engr.
2007, May 30   *Perf. 11¾x11¼*
3348 A1316 7.50k multi   .85 .35
   a. Booklet pane of 8 + 4 labels   7.00 —
     Complete booklet, #3348a   7.00

Historic Stoves — A1317

Designs: 7.50k, Gothic era stove, Olomouc, and tile. 12k, Renaissance era stove, Rícany u Prahy and tile.

Photo. & Engr.
2007, June 20   *Perf. 11½x11¾*
3349 A1317 7.50k multi   .70 .35
     Complete booklet, 5 #3349   3.50
3350 A1317 12k multi   1.25 .60
     Complete booklet, 5 #3350   6.25

Souvenir Sheet

Vaclav Hollar (1607-77), Engraver — A1318

Litho. & Engr.
2007, June 20   *Perf. 11¾*
3351 A1318 35k multi + 2 labels   3.00 2.10

Souvenir Sheet

Charles Bridge, Prague, 650th Anniv. — A1319

2007, June 20
3352 A1319 45k multi   4.50 3.00
Praga 2008 World Philatelic Exhibition.

First Movie Theater in Prague, Cent. — A1320

Photo. & Engr.
2007, Sept. 5   *Perf. 11¾x11¼*
3353 A1320 7.50k multi   .75 .35

Didactica Opera Omnia, by Comenius, 350th Anniv. — A1321

2007, Sept. 5
3354 A1321 12k multi   1.25 .75

Miniature Sheet

Flora and Fauna of the White Carpathians — A1322

No. 3355: a, 9k, Ophrys holosericea (27x44mm). b, 10k, Colias myrmidone, Anacamptis pyramidalis (27x44mm). c, 11k, Ophrys apifera (27x44mm). d, 12k, Coracias garrulus, Gymnadenia densiflora (54x44mm).

Litho. & Engr.
2007, Sept. 5   *Perf. 11¾*
3355 A1322 Sheet of 4, #a-d, + 4 labels   4.25 2.75

Emil Holub (1847-1902), Naturalist A1323

Photo. & Engr.
2007, Oct. 3   *Perf. 11¾x11¼*
3356 A1323 11k multi   1.25 .65

Water Towers — A1324

Towers in: 7.50k, Karviná. 18k, Plzen.

2007, Oct. 3   *Perf. 11¼x11¾*
3357-3358 A1324 Set of 2   2.75 1.50

Painting Type of 1967 Inscribed "CESKA REPUBLIKA"

Designs: 22k, Vrbicany Castle, by Amálie Manesova, horiz. 25k, Way to Bechnye Castle, by Otakar Lebeda. 28k, Montmartre, by Sobeslav Hippolyt Pinkas, horiz.

2007, Nov. 7   Engr.   *Perf. 11¾*
3359-3361 A565 Set of 3   7.25 4.50

Christmas — A1325

Photo. & Engr.
2007, Nov. 7   *Perf. 11¼x11½*
3362 A1325 7.50k multi   .85 .40

Flower Type of 2002
Design: 2.50k, Gaillardia (kokarda); 3k, Azalea (azalka); 10k, Rose (ruze); 21k, Gerbera daisy (gerbera).

Photo. & Engr.
2007-08   *Perf. 11¾x11¼*
3363 A1215 2.50k multi   .30 .25
3364 A1215 3k multi   .30 .25
3365 A1215 10k multi   1.10 .60
3366 A1215 21k multi   2.00 1.40
Nos. 3363-3366 (4)   3.70 2.50
Issued: 2.50k, 12/12/07; 3k, 3/19/08; 10k, 1/30/08; 21k, 3/5/08.

Czech Republic's Entry Into Schengen Border-Free Zone — A1326

2007, Dec. 19   Litho.   *Perf. 11¼*
3367 A1326 10k multi   1.10 .55

Praga 2008 Emblem Type of 2006
2007, Dec. 19   *Perf. 11¾x11¼*
3368 A1304 18k blu grn & multi   2.00 1.00

Tradition of Czech Stamp Production — A1327

Photo. & Engr.
2008, Jan. 20   *Perf. 11¼x11¾*
3369 A1327 10k Type A311   .95 .60
   a. Booklet pane of 8 + 4 labels   8.00 —
     Complete booklet, #3369a   8.00

Famous Men — A1328

Designs: 11k, Karel Klostermann (1848-1923), writer. 14k, Josef Kajetán Tyl (1808-56), playwright.

2008, Jan. 20   *Perf. 11¼x11½*
3370-3371 A1328 Set of 2   2.50 1.50

Peacock and Bugler Type of 2005 and Flowers, Grapes and Glass of Wine Type of 2006 Redrawn

2008, Jan. 30   Litho.   *Perf. 12¾x13¼*
3372 A1263 10k multi + label   1.00 .60
3373 A1283 17k multi + label   1.75 1.00
Nos. 3372-3373 were issued in sheets of 9 stamps and 12 labels. Labels could be personalized for an additional fee.

George of Podebrady (1420-71), King of Bohemia — A1329

Photo. & Engr.
2008, Feb. 20   *Perf. 11¼x11¾*
3374 A1329 12k multi   1.25 .75
No. 3374 was issued in sheets of 8 + 1 label. Values: single stamp + label, $4; complete sheet, $10.

Intl. Year of Planet Earth — A1330

2008, Feb. 20   Litho.   *Perf. 11¼*
3375 A1330 18k multi   1.75 1.10

Easter — A1331

Photo. & Engr.
2008, Mar. 5   *Perf. 11½x11¼*
3376 A1331 10k multi   1.25 .60

Bath Servant Zuzana Carrying King Wenceslas IV Over the Vltava River, by J. Navrátil — A1332

2008, Mar. 5   *Perf. 11¾x11¼*
3377 A1332 10k multi   1.10 .60
   a. Booklet pane of 8 + 4 labels   9.00 —
     Complete booklet, #3377a   9.00

Praga 2008 Intl. Philatelic Exhibition, Prague.

Publication of Orbis Pictus, Children's Picture Book, by Comenius, 350th Anniv. — A1333

2008, Mar. 19   *Perf. 11¼x11¾*
3378 A1333 10k multi   1.25 .60

CZECHOSLOVAKIA

 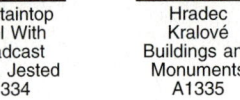

Mountaintop Hotel With Broadcast Tower, Jested — A1334

Hradec Kralové Buildings and Monuments — A1335

2008, Mar. 19 Engr. Perf. 11½
3379 A1334 12k multi 1.10 .75
3380 A1335 15k multi 1.50 .95

Pres. Klaus Type of 2003
Photo. & Engr.
2008, Apr. 2 Perf. 11¾x11¼
3381 A1234 10k multi 1.10 .60

A1336

Items in National Technical Museum: 10k, Reichenbach-Ertel astronomical theodolite, c. 1830. 14k, 1935 Jawa 750 sports car, horiz. 18k, Märky, Bromovsky-Schulz gasoline combustion engine, c. 1889.

Perf. 11¼x11¾, 11¾x11¼
2008, Apr. 16 Photo. & Engr.
3382-3384 A1336 Set of 3 4.25 2.60

National Technical Museum, Prague, cent.

A1337

2008, Apr. 16 Perf. 11¼x11¾
3385 A1337 17k multi 1.75 1.10

Czech Hockey Association, cent.

Europa — A1338

2008, May 7 Litho. Perf. 11¾x11¼
3386 A1338 17k multi 1.75 1.10

The Doggy's and Pussy's Tales, Children's Book by Josef Capek — A1339

Photo. & Engr.
2008, May 28 Perf. 11½x11¼
3387 A1339 10k multi 1.00 .70
  a. Booklet pane of 8 + 2 labels 9.00
      Complete booklet, #3387a 9.00

Souvenir Sheet

Ledeburk Gardens, Prague — A1340

Litho. & Engr.
2008, May 28 Perf. 11¾
3388 A1340 51k multi 5.50 3.25

Praga 2008 World Philatelic Exhibition.

Miniature Sheet

Flora and Fauna of Trebon Basin UNESCO Biosphere Reservation — A1341

No. 3389: a, 10k, Alcedo atthis (28x44mm). b, 12k, Lutra lutra and Spiraea salicifolia (54x44mm). c, 14k, Haliaeetus albicilla (54x44mm). d, 18k, Netta rufina and Nymphaea alba (54x44mm).

2008, May 28
3389 A1341 Sheet of 4, #a-d, + 3 labels 6.25 3.50

2008 Paralympics, Beijing — A1342

Perf. 11¾x11¼
2008, June 18 Litho.
3390 A1342 10k multi 1.10 .70

2008 Summer Olympics, Beijing — A1343

2008, June 18
3391 A1343 18k multi 1.75 1.25

Explorers — A1344

Designs: 12k, Ferdinand Stolicka (1838-74), explorer of Himalayas. 21k, Alois Musil (1868-1944), explorer of Jordanian desert.

2008, June 18 Photo. & Engr.
3392-3393 A1344 Set of 2 3.25 2.25

Children's Book Illustration by Josef Palacek — A1345

2008, Sept. 3 Litho. Perf. 12¾x13¼
3394 A1345 10k multi + label 1.10 .60

Printed in sheets of 9 stamps + 12 labels. Labels could be personalized. Value, $10.

Emmaus Monastery, Prague — A1346

Photo. & Engr.
2008, Sept. 3 Perf. 11¼x11¾
3395 A1346 10k multi 1.00 .60
  Tete-beche pair 2.00 2.00

Praga 2008 World Philatelic Exhibition.

Applied Art Designers' Association, Cent. — A1347

2008, Sept. 3 Perf. 11¾x11¼
3396 A1347 26k multi 2.75 1.60

Karel Plicka (1894-1987), Photographer — A1348

Litho. & Engr.
2008, Sept. 12 Perf. 11¾
3397 A1348 35k multi + 2 labels 4.00 2.10

See Slovakia No. 548.

Souvenir Sheet

Mail Coach — A1349

2008, Sept. 12
3398 A1349 35k multi 4.00 2.10

Praga 2008 Intl. Stamp Exhibition, Prague, and 2008 Vienna Intl. Stamp Exhibition. See Austria No. 2172.

Stoves — A1350

Stove from: 10k, Sternberk Castle. 17k, Archbishop's Palace, Prague.

Photo. & Engr.
2008, Oct. 15 Perf. 11¼x11¾
3399 A1350 10k multi 1.00 .55
  Complete booklet, 5 #3399 5.50
3400 A1350 17k multi 1.75 .95
  Complete booklet, 5 #3400 9.50

Painting Type of 1967 Inscribed "CESKA REPUBLIKA"

Designs: 23k, Vltava River at Klecany, by Zdenka Braunerová, horiz. 26k, Autumn Road, by Otakar Nejedly.

2008, Nov. 5 Engr. Perf. 11¾
3401-3402 A565 Set of 2 5.25 3.00

Issued in sheets of 4. Value, set $21.

Souvenir Sheet

Allegory of Water, by Jan Jakub Hartman — A1351

2008, Nov. 5 Litho. & Engr.
3403 A1351 30k multi 3.25 1.75

Basket With Apples — A1352

Winter Scene — A1353

Mechanical Christmas Display — A1354

Photo. & Engr.
2008, Nov. 5 Perf. 11¼x11½
3404 A1352 10k multi .95 .55

Litho.
Perf. 12¾x13¼
3405 A1353 10k multi + label .95 .55

Souvenir Sheet
Litho. & Engr.
Perf. 11¾
3406 A1354 30k multi 3.25 1.75

Christmas.
No. 3405 was printed in sheets of 9 stamps + 12 labels. Value $10. Labels could be personalized.

Czech Republic Presidency of European Union, January to June 2009 — A1355

Perf. 11¾x11¼
2008, Nov. 25 Litho.
3407 A1355 17k multi + label 1.75 .90

No. 3407 was issued in sheets of 30 stamps + 30 labels.

Louis Braille (1809-52), Educator of the Blind — A1356

Charles Darwin (1809-82), Naturalist — A1357

2009, Jan. 2 Photo. & Engr.
3408 A1356 10k multi .95 .55
3409 A1357 12k multi 1.10 .60

Tradition of Czech Stamp Production — A1358

2009, Jan. 20 Perf. 11¼x11¾
3410 A1358 10k Design of #980 1.00 .50
  a. Booklet pane of 8 + 4 labels 8.25
      Complete booklet, #3410a 8.25

Nordic World Skiing Championships, Liberec — A1359

Perf. 11¾x11¼
2009, Feb. 11 Litho.
3411 A1359 18k multi 1.25 1.25

CZECHOSLOVAKIA

Souvenir Sheet

Preservation of Polar Regions and Glaciers — A1360

Litho. & Engr.
2009, Feb. 11   Perf. 11¾
3412 A1360 35k multi   3.50 1.90

Easter — A1361

Photo. & Engr.
2009, Mar. 18   Perf. 11½x11¼
3413 A1361 10k multi   .95 .55

Lu Tung-pin, by Unknown Chinese Artist — A1362

Mythical Beings, by Unknown Balinese Artist — A1363

Litho. & Engr.
2009, Mar. 18   Perf. 11¾
3414 A1362 18k multi   1.75 1.00
3415 A1363 24k multi   2.25 1.40

Souvenir Sheet

Reliquary of St. Maurus, Becov nad Teplou Castle — A1364

2009, Apr. 8
3416 A1364 51k multi   5.00 3.00

Pardubice to Liberec Rail Line, 150th Anniv. — A1365

Photo. & Engr.
2009, Apr. 22   Perf. 11¾x11¼
3417 A1365 10k multi   1.00 .60

Industry and Trade Ministry Building, 75th Anniv. — A1366

Photo. & Engr.
2009, Apr. 22   Perf. 11¾x11½
3418 A1366 10k multi   1.00 .60

Europa — A1367

2009, May 6   Litho.   Perf. 11¼
3419 A1367 17k multi   1.75 1.00
Intl. Year of Astronomy.

Buildings — A1368

Designs: 12k, Cistercian Monastery, Vyssí Brod. 14k, Horsovsky Castle, Tyn.

2009, May 6   Engr.   Perf. 11¾x11½
3420-3421 A1368 Set of 2   2.50 1.50
Nos. 3420-3421 also were issued in souvenir sheets of 1. Value, set of two sheets $27.

Marionettes Spejbl and Hurvínek — A1369

Photo. & Engr.
2009, May 27   Perf. 11¼x11½
3422 A1369 10k multi   1.10 .60
   a. Booklet pane of 8 + 2 labels   9.00
      Complete booklet, #3422a   9.00

Rabbi Jehuda Löw (c. 1525-1609) — A1370

2009, May 27   Litho.   Perf. 11¼x11¾
3423 A1370 21k multi   2.00 1.25
Printed in sheets of 5 + 4 labels. Value, $10.

Granting of Religious Freedom by Rudolf II, 400th Anniv. — A1371

Photo. & Engr.
2009, June 17   Perf. 11¼
3424 A1371 26k multi   2.50 1.50

Intl. Firefighters' Games, Ostrava — A1372

   Perf. 11¾x11¼
2009, June 17   Litho.
3425 A1372 17k multi   1.75 1.00

Miniature Sheet

Krivoklát UNESCO Biosphere Reservation — A1373

No. 3426: a, 10k, Eudia pavonia (44x27mm). b, 12k, Aglia tau, Cervus elaphus (44x54mm). c, 14k, Bubo bubo, Lunaria rediviva, Ciconia nigra (44x54mm). d, 17k, Tyto alba, Krivoklát Castle (44x54mm).

Litho. & Engr.
2009, Sept. 2   Perf. 11¾
3426 A1373 Sheet of 4, #a-d, + 4 labels   5.50 4.50

Souvenir Sheet

Bohemian-Moravian Highlands — A1374

2009, Sept. 2
3427 A1374 43k multi   4.00 2.50

Windmill, Huprechtov A1375   Water Mill, Hoslovice A1376

Photo. & Engr.
2009, Sept. 23   Perf. 11¼x11½
3428 A1375 10k multi   1.00 .60
   Complete booklet, 5 #3428   5.50
   Perf. 11½x11¼
3429 A1376 12k multi   1.25 .70
   Complete booklet, 5 #3429   7.00

Czech National Anthem, 175th Anniv. — A1377

2009, Oct. 14   Perf. 11¼x11¾
3430 A1377 10k multi   1.00 .60

Barbora Markéta Eliásová (1874-1957), Travel Writer — A1378

2009, Oct. 14   Perf. 11¾x11¼
3431 A1378 18k multi   1.75 1.10

Stoves — A1379

Designs: 10k, Empire stove, Litomysl Castle. 14k, Biedermeier stove, Vyskov Castle.

2009, Oct. 14   Perf. 11¼x11¾
3432 A1379 10k multi   1.00 .60
   Complete booklet, 5 #3432   5.50
3433 A1379 14k multi   1.25 .80
   Complete booklet, 5 #3433   7.50

Protest Rallies of Nov. 17, 1939, and Nov. 17, 1989 — A1380

2009, Nov. 4   Litho.
3434 A1380 14k multi   1.25 .80

Painting Type of 1967 Inscribed "CESKA REPUBLIKA"

Designs: 24k, Canal Lock in Moret, by Alfred Sisley, horiz. 26k, Alley, by Alfred Justitz, horiz.

2009, Nov. 4   Engr.   Perf. 11¾
3435-3436 A565 Set of 2   5.25 3.00

Souvenir Sheet

Oldrich and Bozena, by Frantisek Zenísek A1381

Litho. & Engr.
2009, Nov. 4   Perf. 11¾
3437 A1381 34k multi   3.50 2.00

Christmas — A1382

Photo. & Engr.
2009, Nov. 4   Perf. 11¼x11½
3438 A1382 10k multi   1.10 .60

Tradition of Czech Stamp Production — A1383

2010, Jan. 20   Perf. 11¼x11¾
3439 A1383 10k Vignette of #2121   1.10 .55
   a. Booklet pane of 8 + 4 labels   9.00
      Complete booklet, #3439a   9.00

Magdalena Dobromila Rettigová (1785-1845), Writer — A1384

2010, Jan. 20   Perf. 11¾x11¼
3440 A1384 12k multi   1.25 .65

CZECHOSLOVAKIA

2010 Winter Olympics, Vancouver — A1385

2010, Feb. 10		Perf. 11¼x11¾
3441 A1385	18k multi	1.25 .95

2010 Winter Paralympics, Vancouver — A1386

2010, Feb. 10		
3442 A1386	18k multi	1.25 .95

Souvenir Sheet

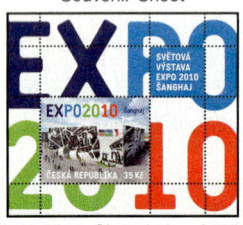

Expo 2010, Shanghai — A1387

2010, Feb. 10		Litho.
3443 A1387	35k multi + 3 labels	3.00 1.90

Easter — A1388

		Photo. & Engr.
2010, Mar. 10		Perf. 11½x11¼
3444 A1388	10k multi	1.10 .55

Martina Sáblíková, Gold Medalist at 2010 Winter Olympic Games — A1389

		Perf. 11¼x11¾
2010, Mar. 24		Litho.
3445 A1389	10k multi	1.10 .55

Souvenir Sheet

Karel Hynek Macha (1810-36), Writer — A1390

		Perf. 11½x11¾
2010, Mar. 10		Litho. & Engr.
3446 A1390	43k multi	4.00 2.40

Enrique Stanko Vráz (1860-1932), Travel Writer — A1391

		Photo. & Engr.
2010, Apr. 14		Perf. 11¾x11¼
3447 A1391	24k multi	2.25 1.25

19th Century Transcaucasian Carpets — A1392

Designs: 21k, Kasim Usak carpet. 24k, Celaberd carpet.

		Litho. & Engr.
2010, Apr. 14		Perf. 11¾
3448-3449 A1392	Set of 2	4.00 2.40

Ctyrlístek Comic Strip Character Fifinka — A1393

Serpentine Die Cut 15x16½

2010, Apr. 28		Litho.
3450 A1393	A multi	1.10 .55
a.	Booklet pane of 10	11.00

No. 3450 sold for 10k on day of issue.

Prague Castle — A1394

2010, May 5		Engr.	Perf. 11¾
3451 A1394	17k brown		1.50 .85

Prague Castle in the Art of the Postage Stamp Exhibition, Prague. Printed in sheets of 4 + label. Value, $6.

Dásenka, Children's Book by Karel Capek — A1395

2010, May 5		Litho.	Perf. 11¼
3452 A1395	17k multi		1.50 .85

Europa.

Children's Book Illustration by Helena Zmatlíková (1923-2005) — A1396

		Photo. & Engr.
2010, May 26		Perf. 11¼x11½
3453 A1396	10k multi	1.10 .50
a.	Booklet pane of 8 + 2 labels	9.00 —
	Complete booklet, #3453a	9.00

Alphonse Mucha (1860-1939), Illustrator — A1397

Designs: E, Gismonda. Z, Zodiac.

Serpentine Die Cut 14¼x14½

2010, May 26		Litho.

Booklet Stamps
Self-Adhesive

3454 A1397	E multi	1.60 .80
a.	Booklet pane of 6	9.75

Size: 43x54mm
Serpentine Die Cut 14½

3455 A1397	Z multi	1.75 .85
a.	Booklet pane of 6	10.50

No. 3454 sold for 17k and No. 3455 sold for 18k on day of issue.

Zd'árské Hills Protected Landscape — A1398

		Photo. & Engr.
2010, June 16		Perf. 11¾x11½
3456 A1398	10k multi	1.10 .50

Marriage of John of Luxembourg and Elizabeth of Bohemia, 700th Anniv. — A1399

		Photo. & Engr.
2010, June 16		Perf. 11¾x11¼
3457 A1399	17k multi	1.50 .85

Accession to the throne of Bohemia by the House of Luxembourg. See Luxembourg No. 1292.
No. 3457 was issued in sheets 5 stamps + 4 labels. Values: single stamp + label, $1.75; complete sheet, $9.

Astronomical Clock, Prague, 600th Anniv. — A1400

2010, June 16		Litho.
3458 A1400	21k multi	2.25 1.10

Towns — A1401

Designs: 12k, Klatovy. 14k, Stramberk.

2010, June 16		Engr.
3459-3460 A1401	Set of 2	2.40 1.25

Czech Republic, Winners of 2010 World Ice Hockey Championships A1402

		Perf. 11¼x11¾
2010, June 23		Litho.
3461 A1402	10k multi	1.10 .50

Ctyrlístek Comic Strip Characters Fifinka, Pind'a, Bobík and Myspulín A1403

2010, Sept. 1	Litho.	Perf. 12¾x13¼
3462 A1403	A multi + label	1.10 .55

No. 3462 was printed in sheets of 9 + 12 labels that could be personalized and had a franking value of 10k on day of issue.

Children With Magnifying Glass and Stamp Album A1404

Boy Examining Stamp A1405

2010, Sept. 1		
3463 A1404	A multi + label	1.10 .55
3464 A1405	E multi + label	2.10 1.10

Nos. 3463-3464 each were printed in sheets of 9 + 12 labels that could be personalized. On day of issue, No. 3463 had a franking value of 10k and No. 3464 had a franking value of 20k.

2010 Women's World Basketball Championships, Czech Republic — A1406

2010, Sept. 1		Perf. 11¼x11¾
3465 A1406	17k multi	1.75 .90

Miniature Sheet

Flora and Fauna of Lower Morava UNESCO Biosphere Reserve — A1407

No. 3466: a, 10k, Tichodroma muraria, Papilio machaon, Aster amellus (45x55mm). b, 12k, Saga pedo, Iris variegata (45x27mm). c, 14k, Lacerta viridis, Pulsatilla grandis (45x27mm). d, 18k, Upupa epops, Arenaria grandiflora (45x55mm).

		Litho. & Engr.
2010, Sept. 1		Perf. 11¾
3466 A1407	Sheet of 4, #a-d, + 3 labels	6.00 3.00

Flowers Type of 2002

Designs: 4k, Anemone (sasanka). 25k, Iris (kosatec). 30k, Tulip (tulipán).

		Photo. & Engr.
2010		Perf. 11¾x11¼
3467 A1215	4k multi	.45 .25
3468 A1215	25k multi	2.00 1.50
3469 A1215	30k multi	2.25 1.75
Nos. 3467-3469 (3)		4.70 3.50

Issued: 4k, 9/29; 25k, 30k, 9/15.

Austrian Empire Post Office Sign, Postal Map, Dwarves with Letters, Handstamp and Posthorn — A1408

2010, Sept. 29	Litho.	Perf. 11¼
3470 A1408	A multi	1.10 .55

Postal Musuem, Prague. No. 3470 sold for 10k on day of issue.

CZECHOSLOVAKIA

Famous Men — A1409

Designs: 10k, Adolf Branald (1910-2008), writer. 12k, Karel Zeman (1910-89), film director and animator.

Photo. & Engr.
2010, Sept. 29   Perf. 11¼x11½
3471-3472 A1409 Set of 2   2.25 1.25

Ctyrlístek Comic Strip Character Myspulín — A1410

Serpentine Die Cut 15x16½
2010, Oct. 20   Litho.
Booklet Stamp
Self-Adhesive
3473 A1410 A multi   1.25 .60
   a. Booklet pane of 10   12.50
No. 3473 sold for 10k on day of issue.

Bridges A1411

Designs: 10k, Mariánsky Bridge, Ústí nad Labem. 12k, Stone Bridge, Písek.

Photo. & Engr.
2010, Oct. 20   Perf. 11¾x11¼
3474 A1411 10k multi   1.00 .60
   Complete booklet, 5 #3474   5.50
3475 A1411 12k multi   1.25 .70
   Complete booklet, 5 #3475   7.00

Stoves — A1412

Designs: 10k, Art Nouveau stove. 20k, Art Deco stove.

2010, Oct. 20   Perf. 11¼x11¾
3476 A1412 10k multi   1.00 .60
   Complete booklet, 5 #3476   6.25
3477 A1412 20k multi   1.75 1.25
   Complete booklet, 5 #3477   12.00

Art Type of 1967 Inscribed "CESKA REPUBLIKA"

Designs: 24k, Paris and Helen, by Karel Skréta. 26k, Sand Bargemen, by Milos Jiránek. 30k, Spring, by Karel Spillar, horiz.

Litho. & Engr. (24k), Engr.
2010, Nov. 10   Perf. 11¾
3478-3480 A565 Set of 3   7.50 4.50

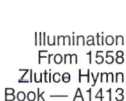

Illumination From 1558 Zlutice Hymn Book — A1413

   Perf. 11¼x11¾
2010, Nov. 10   Litho.
3481 A1413 10k multi   1.10 .55
Christmas.

2011 Census — A1414

2011, Jan. 5
3482 A1414 10k black & green   1.10 .55

Souvenir Sheet

Kaspar Maria von Sternberg (1761-1838), Paleobotanist — A1415

   Perf. 11¾x11½
2011, Jan. 5   Litho. & Engr.
3483 A1415 43k multi   5.00 2.40

Mail Coach on Charles Bridge, 1966 Envelope Indicia by Josef Hercík A1416

Photo. & Engr.
2011, Jan. 20   Perf. 11¾x11¼
3484 A1416 10k multi   1.10 .55
   a. Booklet pane of 8 + 4 labels   9.00
   Complete booklet, #3484a   9.50
Tradition of Czech stamp production.

St. Agnes of Bohemia (1211-82) — A1417

2011, Jan. 20   Perf. 11¼x11¾
3485 A1417 12k multi   1.25 .70

Ctyrlístek Comic Strip Character Pind'a — A1418

Booklet Stamp
Serpentine Die Cut 15x16½
2011, Feb. 9   Litho.   Self-Adhesive
3486 A1418 A multi   1.10 .55
   a. Booklet pane of 10   11.00
No. 3486 sold for 10k on day of issue.

Jirí Melantrich of Aventinum (c. 1511-80), Printer — A1419

Photo. & Engr.
2011, Feb. 9   Perf. 11¼x11¾
3487 A1419 30k multi   3.00 1.75

Cheb, 950th Anniv. — A1420

Black Madonna House, Prague, Cent. — A1421

2011, Feb. 9   Engr.   Perf. 11¾x11½
3488 A1420 12k multi   1.10 .70
   Perf. 11½x11¾
3489 A1421 14k multi   1.40 .80

Visegrád Group, 20th Anniv. — A1422

   Perf. 11¾x11¼
2011, Feb. 11   Litho.
3490 A1422 20k multi   2.00 1.10
See Hungary No. 4183, Poland No. 4001, and Slovakia No. 611.
No. 3490 was issued in sheets of 8 + 8 labels. Values: single stamp + label, $2.25; complete sheet, $18.

Architecture — A1423

Designs: A, House gables from Blatensko region, North Moravia and West Bohemia. E, House gables from North Bohemia and South Bohemia, gable shutter from North Bohemia. E, House gables from North Bohemia and South Bohemia, Wallachian cottage, Central Bohemian gate. Z, Houses from North Bohemia, West Bohemia and Wallachia, vert.

Photo. & Engr.
2011   Perf. 11¼x11¾
3491 A1423 A blk, lt bl & bl   1.00 .60
3492 A1423 E blk, beige & brn   2.25 1.25
   Perf. 11¾x11¼
3493 A1423 Z blk, gray grn & bl grn   2.25 1.25
   Nos. 3491-3493 (3)   5.50 3.10
Issued: Nos. 3491-3492, 2/23; No. 3493, 5/27. On day of issue Nos. 3491-3493 sold for 10k, 20k and 21k, respectively. See No. 3559.

Souvenir Sheet

Petr Vok (1539-1611) and Vilém (1535-92) von Rosenberg, Aristocrats — A1424

2011, Mar. 9   Engr.   Perf. 11¾
3494 A1424 49k multi   4.50 3.00

Easter — A1425

   Perf. 11¼x11¾
2011, Mar. 23   Litho.
3495 A1425 A multi   1.10 .60
No. 3495 sold for 10k on day of issue.

Vlasta Burian (1891-1962), Actor — A1426

Photo. & Engr.
2011, Apr. 6   Perf. 11¾x11¼
3496 A1426 10k multi   1.10 .60

Teaching at Prague Conservatory, Bicent. — A1427

2011, Apr. 6   Perf. 11¼x11¾
3497 A1427 10k multi   1.10 .60

Ctyrlistek Comic Strip Character Bobík — A1428

Booklet Stamp
Serpentine Die Cut 15x16½
2011, May 4   Litho.   Self-Adhesive
3498 A1428 A multi   1.25 .60
   a. Booklet pane of 10   12.50
No. 3498 sold for 10k on day of issue.

Europa — A1429

2011, May 4   Litho.   Perf. 11¼
3499 A1429 20k multi   2.00 1.25
Intl. Year of Forests.

Flower Type of 2003

Design: 2k, Chrysanthemum (chryzantéma).

Photo. & Engr.
2011, May 27   Perf. 11¾x11¼
3500 A1215 2k multi   .25 .25

Souvenir Sheet

Johann Gerstner (1851-1939), Violinist — A1430

Litho. & Engr.
2011, May 27   Perf. 11¾
3501 A1430 34k multi   3.50 2.10
See Slovenia No. 891.

CZECHOSLOVAKIA

The Little Witch and Abraxas, the Raven, Animated Characters by Zdenek Smetana — A1431

	Photo. & Engr.		
2011, June 1		Perf. 11½x11¼	
3502	A1431 10k multi	1.25	.60
a.	Booklet pane of 8 + 2 labels	10.00	
	Complete booklet, #3502a	10.00	

First Public Long-Distance Flight of Jan Kaspar (1883-1927), Cent. — A1432

2011, June 1		Perf. 11¼x11¾	
3503	A1432 21k multi	2.25	1.25

Execution of 27 Protestant Leaders in Prague, 390th Anniv. A1433

	Litho. & Engr.		
2011, June 1		Perf. 11¾	
3504	A1433 26k rose pink & blk	2.50	1.60

Cricetus Cricetus — A1434

		Perf. 11¼x11¾	
2011, June 15		Litho.	
3505	A1434 10k multi	1.10	.60
	Complete booklet, 5 #3505	6.00	

Floral Arrangement — A1435

2011, June 15			
3506	A1435 25k multi	2.50	1.50

Europa Cup, Championships of European Federation of Professional Florist Associations, Havirov.

Men's European Volleyball Championships, Prague and Karlovy Vary — A1436

		Perf. 11¼x11¾	
2011, Aug. 31		Litho.	
3507	A1436 20k multi	2.25	1.10

Wolfgang Amadeus Mozart (1756-91), Composer A1437

Booklet Stamp
Serpentine Die Cut 11½

2011, Aug. 31		Self-Adhesive	
3508	A1437 E multi	2.25	1.10
a.	Booklet pane of 6	13.50	

No. 3508 sold for 20k on day of issue.

Miniature Sheet

Flora and Fauna of Sumava UNESCO Biosphere Reserve — A1438

No. 3509: a, 10k,Turdus torquatus, Erebia euryale, Tetrao urogallus (54x44mm). b, 14k, Dactylorhiza traunsteineri, Colias palaeno (27x44mm). c, 18k, Aeshna juncea, Alces alces, Tetrao tetrix (54x44mm). d, 20, Lynx lynx, Picoides tridactylus (54x44mm).

	Litho. & Engr.		
2011, Aug. 31		Perf. 11¾	
3509	A1438 Sheet of 4, #a-d, + 4 labels	6.00	3.50

Organ, Church of the Assumption of Our Lady, Plasy — A1439

	Perf. 11¼x11¾		
2011, Sept. 14		Litho.	
3510	A1439 10k multi	1.10	.55

Frantisek Alexander Elstner (1902-74), Travel Writer — A1440

	Photo. & Engr.		
2011, Sept. 14		Perf. 11¾x11¼	
3511	A1440 14k multi	1.40	.80

Pat and Mat, Characters From Children's Television Show — A1441

Booklet Stamp
Serpentine Die Cut 15x16½

2011, Oct. 5		Litho. Self-Adhesive	
3512	A1441 A multi	1.10	.55
a.	Booklet pane of 10	11.00	

No. 3512 sold for 10k on day of issue.

World Post Day — A1442

2011, Oct. 5		Perf. 11¼	
3513	A1442 21k multi	2.25	1.25

Film Posters A1443

Poster for: No. 3514, 10k, Une Femme Douce, 1970. No. 3515, 10k, Markéta Lazarová, 1966.

2011, Oct. 5	Litho.	Perf. 11¾x11¼	
3514-3515	A1443 Set of 2	2.25	1.10

Peacock & Bugler Type of 2005 and Roses Above Prague Type of 2003

2011, Oct. 27		Perf. 11¼x11¾	
3516	A1263 A multi + label	1.10	.55
3517	A1225 E multi + label	2.25	1.10

On day of issue, No. 3516 sold for 10k and No. 3517 sold for 20k. Nos. 3516-3517 each were issued in sheets of 9 stamps and 12 labels that could be personalized. Value, $30.

Art Type of 1967 Inscribed "CESKA REPUBLIKA"

Designs: 24k, Lovers, by Jaroslav Vozniak, horiz. 26k, Woman in Corn Field, by Joza Uprka. 30k, Winter Landscape, by August Bedrich Piepenhagen, horiz.

2011, Nov. 9		Engr. Perf. 11¾	
3518-3520	A565 Set of 3	8.00	4.50

Christmas — A1444

2011, Nov. 9	Litho.	Perf. 11¾x11¼	
3521	A1444 A multi	1.10	.55

No. 3521 sold for 10k on day of issue.

House, Vidim — A1445

	Photo. & Engr.		
2012, Jan. 20		Perf. 11¼x11¾	
3522	A1445 6k multi	.65	.30

Josef Liesler (1912-2005), Stamp Designer A1446

2012, Jan. 20		Perf. 11¼x11¾	
3523	A1446 10k multi	1.10	.55
a.	Booklet pane of 8 + 4 labels	9.00	
	Complete booklet, #3523a	9.00	

Tradition of Czech stamp production.

Jirí Trnka (1912-69), Film Animator and Director A1447

2012, Feb. 15			
3524	A1447 10k multi	1.10	.55

Sokol Movement, 150th Anniv. — A1448

	Perf. 11¼x11¾		
2012, Feb. 15		Litho.	
3525	A1448 14k multi	1.50	.75

Union of Czech Mathematicians and Physicists, 150th Anniv. — A1449

2012, Mar. 7		Perf. 11¾x11¼	
3526	A1449 10k multi	1.10	.55

Kuks — A1450

Designs: 14k, Buildings in Kuks. 18k, Statue by Matthias B. Braun, vert.

Perf. 11½x11¾, 11¾x11½

2012, Mar. 7		Engr.	
3527-3528	A1450 Set of 2	3.00	1.75

Hiker at Signpost A1451

	Perf. 11¼x11¾		
2012, Mar. 21		Litho.	
3529	A1451 A multi + label	1.10	.55

No. 3529 was printed in sheets of 9 + 12 labels that could be personalized and had a franking value of 10k on day of issue.

Gregor Mendel (1822-84), Genetics Pioneer A1452

	Photo. & Engr.		
2012, Apr. 4		Perf. 11¾x11¼	
3530	A1452 20k multi	1.90	1.10

First Hebrew Book Printed in Prague, 500th Anniv. — A1453

2012, Apr. 18	Litho.	Perf. 11¼	
3531	A1453 25k multi	2.40	1.40

Prague Tourist Attractions — A1454

	Photo. & Engr.		
2012, May 2		Perf. 11¼x11¾	
3532	A1454 20k multi	2.00	1.10

Europa.

Scouting in Czechoslovakia, Cent. — A1455

2012, May 2	Litho.	Perf. 11¼	
3533	A1455 21k multi	2.00	1.10

Boats on Bat'a Canal — A1456

2012, May 16	Engr.	Perf. 11¾x11¼	

Booklet Stamp

3534	A1456 10k dark blue	1.20	.50
a.	Booklet pane of 8 + 4 labels	9.50	
	Complete booklet, #3534a	9.50	

CZECHOSLOVAKIA

The Whipping of Christ, by Tintoretto
A1457

2012, May 16   Perf. 11¾
3535 A1457 30k multi   3.50   1.50

Art in Prague Castle. See Nos. 3569, 3605, 3642, 3674, 3705, 3755, 3790.

St. Wenceslas (c. 907-35) — A1458

Serpentine Die Cut 11 Syncopated
2012, June 6   Litho.
Self-Adhesive
3536 A1458 A multi   1.00   .50

No. 3536 sold for 10k on day of issue. See No. 3576.

Lezáky Massacre, 70th Anniv. — A1459

2012, June 6   Perf. 11¾x11¼
3537 A1459 10k multi   1.00   .50

Lidice Massacre, 70th Anniv. — A1460

2012, June 6   Photo. & Engr.
3538 A1460 20k multi   2.00   1.00

Coronation of Statue of Our Lady of Hostýn, Cent. — A1461

2012, June 20   Litho. & Engr.   Perf. 11¾
3539 A1461 21k multi   1.90   1.00

No. 3539 was issued in sheets of 8 stamps + 1 label. Values: single stamp + label, $2.50; complete sheet, $16.

A1462   A1463

Personalized Stamps — A1464

Serpentine Die Cut 11 Syncopated
2012, June 20   Litho.
Self-Adhesive
3540 A1462 A multi   .95   .50
3541 A1463 A multi   .95   .50
3542 A1464 E multi   1.90   .95
   Nos. 3540-3542 (3)   3.80   1.85

Nos. 3540-3542 each were printed in sheets of 25. Vignette portions of each stamp could be personalized. The generic vignettes of these stamps are shown. On day of issue, the franking value of Nos. 3540-3541 each were 10k, and of No. 3542, 20k.

2012 Summer Olympics, London — A1465

2012, June 20   Litho. & Engr.   Perf. 11¾
3543 A1465 20k multi   1.90   .95

No. 3543 was issued in sheets of 3 stamps + 2 labels. Values: single stamp + label, $2.25; complete sheet, $6.

Alberto Vojtech Fric (1882-1944), Cactus Collector, Botanist and Ethnographer
A1466

2012, Sept. 5   Litho.   Perf. 11¾x11¼
3544 A1466 10k multi   1.10   .55

Illustrations of Antique Automobiles by Václav Zapadlík — A1467

No. 3545: a, 1933 Duesenberg SJ. b, 1931, Wikov 70. c, 1936 Mercedes-Benz 540. d, 1938 Rolls Royce Phantom III. e, 1934 Bugatti Royale 41. f, 1929 Isotta Fraschini Tipo 8A.

Serpentine Die Cut 11½
2012, Sept. 5
Self-Adhesive
3545   Booklet pane of 6   13.00
   a.-f. A1467 E Any single   2.10   1.10

On day of issue, Nos. 3545a-3545f each sold for 20k. See Nos. 3580-3581, 3610-3611, 3645-3646.

Miniature Sheet

Orchids
A1468

No. 3546: a, 10k, Dendrobium peguanum (44x27mm). b, 14k, Stanhopea tigrina and Coryanthes feildingii (44x54mm). c, 18k, Cattleya aclandiae and Cattleya maxima (44x54mm). d, 20k, Paphiopedilum charlesworthii, Paphiopedilum insigne, and Paphiopedilum hirsutissimum (44x54mm).

Litho. & Engr.
2012, Sept. 5   Perf. 11¾
3546 A1468   Sheet of 4, #a-d, + 4 labels   6.00   3.25

Souvenir Sheet

Golden Bull of Sicily, 800th Anniv.
A1469

2012, Sept. 19   Engr.   Perf. 11¾
3547 A1469 49k multi   4.75   2.60

Paphiopedilum Venustum — A1470

2012, Oct. 3   Litho.   Perf. 11¼x11¾
3548 A1470 A multi + label   1.10   .55

No. 3548 was printed in sheets of 9 + 12 labels that could be personalized. On day of issue, No. 3548 had a franking value of 10k.

Masaryk Circuit Racers — A1471

Designs: 18k, Frantisek St'astny (1927-2000), motorcycle racer. 25k, Louis Chiron (1899-1979), automobile racer.

2012, Oct. 3   Photo. & Engr.
3549-3550 A1471 Set of 2   4.50   2.25

1891 Ericsson Desk Telephone
A1472

2012, Oct. 3   Litho.   Perf. 11¼
3551 A1472 26k multi   2.75   1.40

World Post Day.

Art Type of 1967 Inscribed "CESKA REPUBLIKA" and

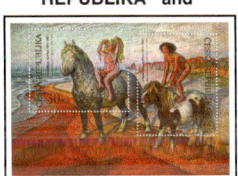

Life's Pleasures, by Frantisek Kupka — A1473

Designs: 26k, A Long-haired Girl, by Kamil Lhoták. 32k, Self-portrait with Family, by Jan Kupecky. No. 3554: a, Blonde nude on horse. b, Brunette nude on pony, vert.

2012, Nov. 7   Engr.   Perf. 11¾
3552-3553 A565 Set of 2   5.50   3.00
Litho. & Engr.
Souvenir Sheet
3554 A1473 30k Sheet of 2, #a-b   6.00   3.00

Christmas
A1474

2012, Nov. 7   Litho.   Perf. 11¼x11¾
3555 A1474 A multi + label   1.00   .50

No. 3555 sold for 10k on day of issue and was printed in sheets of 9 + 12 labels that could be personalized.

Pinda, Bobik, Myspulin and Fifinka Riding Griffin — A1475   Myspulin Taking Picture of Bobik, Fifinka, King Rudolf II, Aurix the Lion and Pinda — A1476

Serpentine Die Cut 16½x15
2012, Nov. 7   Self-Adhesive
Booklet Stamps
3556 A1475 A multi   1.00   .50
3557 A1476 A multi   1.00   .50
   a. Booklet pane of 10, 5 each #3556-3557   10.00

On day of issue, Nos. 3556-3557 each sold for 10k.

Architecture Type of 2011 and

Building, Busanovice, 1847 — A1477

Photo. & Engr.
2012   Perf. 11¼x11¾
3558 A1477 5k multi   .75   .25
3559 A1423 A black & blue   1.25   .50

Issued: No. 3558, 12/19; No. 3559, 11/8. No. 3559 sold for 10k on day of issue. Compare No. 3559 with No. 3491.

Ivan Strnad (1926-2005), Stamp Designer
A1478

2013, Jan. 20   Perf. 11¾x11¼
3560 A1478 10k multi   1.10   .55
   a. Booklet pane of 8 + 4 labels   9.00
   Complete booklet, #3560a   9.00

Tradition of Czech stamp production.

Bertha von Suttner (1843-1914), 1905 Nobel Peace Laureate — A1479

Perf. 11¾x11¼
2013, Feb. 13   Litho.
3561 A1479 18k multi   1.90   .95

Cottage, Novy Hrozenkov — A1480

Photo. & Engr.
2013, Mar. 6   Perf. 11¾x11¼
3562 A1480 14k brn & dk brn   1.50   .75

CZECHOSLOVAKIA

Transportation — A1481

No. 3563: a, Aero HC2 Heli Baby helicopter. b, Pécko-18 tugboat.

2013, Mar. 6   Litho.
3563   A1481   25k Vert. pair, #a-b   4.50   2.60

Zlatá Koruna Monastery, 750th Anniv. — A1482

2013, Apr. 3   Engr.   Perf. 11¾x11½
3564   A1482   14k multi   1.40   .70

George Orwell (1903-50), Writer — A1483

Photo. & Engr.
2013, Apr. 3   Perf. 11¼x11¾
3565   A1483   26k multi   2.60   1.40

Pres. Milos Zeman — A1484

2013, Apr. 24   Perf. 11¾x11¼
3566   A1484   A red & purple   1.00   .50

No. 3566 sold for 10k on day of issue. See No. 3752.

Europa — A1485

2013, May 2   Litho.   Perf. 11¼
3567   A1485   25k multi   2.25   1.40

Fláje Dam — A1486

2013, May 15   Engr.   Perf. 11¾x11¼
3568   A1486   14k green   1.25   .75
   a.   Booklet pane of 8 + 4 labels   10.50   —
      Complete booklet, #3568a   10.50

Art in Prague Castle Type of 2012

Design: 25k, Portrait of Jacob König, Goldsmith and Bookseller, by Paolo Veronese.

2013, May 15   Engr.   Perf. 11¾
3569   A1457   25k multi   2.25   1.40

Cross of Závis of Falkenstejn — A1487

2013, May 29   Perf. 11¾
3570   A1487   26k multi   2.40   1.40

Krtek the Mole — A1488

Serpentine Die Cut 16½x15
2013, May 29   Litho.
Booklet Stamp
Self-Adhesive
3571   A1488   A multi   1.25   .55
   a.   Booklet pane of 10   12.50
   b.   As No. 3571, serpentine die cut 11x11¼ syncopated ('15)   1.50   .55
   c.   Booklet pane of 10 #3571b   15.00

No. 3571 sold for 10k on day of issue. No. 3571b sold for 13k when issued.

Historic Methods of Transportation — A1489

No. 3572: a, Tatra 15/30 automobile. b, Cechie 33 Böhmerland motorcycle.

Perf. 11¾x11¼
2013, June 12   Litho.
3572   A1489   10k Horiz. pair, #a-b   2.40   1.10

Souvenir Sheet

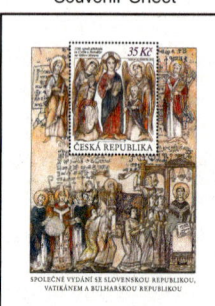

Mission of Sts. Cyril and Methodius to Slavic Lands, 1150th Anniv. — A1490

Litho. & Engr.
2013, June 12   Perf. 11¾
3573   A1490   35k multi   3.75   1.90

See Bulgaria No. 4647, Slovakia No. 666 and Vatican City No. 1536.

Postal Banking Services, 130th Anniv. — A1491

Perf. 11¾x11¼
2013, June 26   Litho.
3574   A1491   20k multi   1.75   1.00

Franz Kafka (1883-1924), Writer — A1492

Serpentine Die Cut 11½
2013, June 26   Litho.
Booklet Stamp
Self-Adhesive
3575   A1492   E multi   2.00   1.00
   a.   Booklet pane of 6   12.00

No. 3575 sold for 20k on day of issue.

St. Wenceslas Type of 2012
2013, July 31   Litho.   Perf. 11¼x11¾
3576   A1458   13k multi   1.40   .70

2013 Canoe Slalom World Championships, Prague — A1493

Photo. & Engr.
2013, Sept. 4   Perf. 11¾x11¼
3577   A1493   10k multi   1.10   .55

Novy Jicín, 700th Anniv. — A1494

2013, Sept. 4   Engr.   Perf. 11¾
3578   A1494   20k multi   1.75   1.75

Miniature Sheet

Flora and Fauna of the Karlstejn Region — A1495

No. 3579: a, 10k, Dracocephalum austriacum, Chorthippus vagans (27x44mm). b, 14k, Oenanthe oenanthe, Velká Amerika Limestone Quarry (27x44mm). c, 18k, Polyommatus coridon, Pulsatilla pratensis, Colias crocea (54x44mm). d, 20k, Rosa gallica, Karlstejn Castle (54x44mm).

Litho. & Engr.
2013, Sept. 4   Perf. 11¾
3579   A1495   Sheet of 4, #a-d, + 4 labels   6.00   3.25

Antique Automobiles Type of 2012

Illustrations by Václav Zapadlík: No. 3580, 1930 Skoda 860. No. 3581, 1932 Skoda 645.

Serpentine Die Cut 11¼ Syncopated
2013, Sept. 4   Litho.
Booklet Stamps
Self-Adhesive
3580   A1467   A multi   1.25   .70
3581   A1467   A multi   1.25   .70
   a.   Booklet pane of 8, 4 each #3580-3581   10.00

Nos. 3580-3581 each sold for 13k on day of issue.

Personalized Stamps — A1497

Serpentine Die Cut 11¼ Syncopated
2013, Sept. 4   Litho.
Booklet Stamps
Self-Adhesive
3582   A1496   A black   1.50   .70
   a.   Booklet pane of 8   12.00
3583   A1497   E black   3.00   1.25
   a.   Booklet pane of 8   24.00

On day of issue, No. 3582 sold for 13k, and No. 3583 sold for 25k. Nos. 3582 and 3583 could have the image portions of the stamp personalized for an additional fee. The horizontal generic vignettes of these stamps are shown. Nos. 3582a and 3583a contain four stamps with these horizontal generic vignettes and four stamps with similar generic vignettes but with a vertical orientation. Values for Nos. 3582 and 3583 are for stamps with images with either a horizontal or vertical orientation.

Josef Bican (1913-2001), Soccer Player — A1498

Photo. & Engr.
2013, Sept. 18   Perf. 11¼x11¾
3584   A1498   13k multi   1.25   .70

Horses From Chlumetz Stud Farm — A1499

Design: 13k, Kinsky horse. 17k, Palomino horse.

Perf. 11¼x11¾
2013, Sept. 18   Litho.
3585-3586   A1499   Set of 2   2.75   1.60

Cottage, Salajna — A1500

2013, Oct. 2   Engr.   Perf. 11¼x11¾
3587   A1500   29k green   2.60   1.60

Souvenir Sheet

Battle of Leipzig, 200th Anniv. A1501

Litho. & Engr.
2013, Oct. 2   Perf. 11¾
3588   A1501   53k multi   5.50   3.00

CZECHOSLOVAKIA

Bible of Kralice, 400th Anniv. — A1502

2013, Oct. 16   Litho.   Perf. 11¼
3589   A1502   17k multi   1.75   .85

Otto Wichterle (1912-98), Inventor of Soft Contact Lenses — A1503

Photo. & Engr.
2013, Oct. 16   Perf. 11¼x11¾
3590   A1503   21k multi   1.90   1.10

Art Type of 1967 Inscribed "CESKA REPUBLIKA"

Designs: 25k, A View of Roman Churches, by Giovanni Battista Piranesi, horiz. 30k, Still Life with the Author, by Bohuslav Reynek. 35k, Round Portrait, by Max Svabinsky.

Engr., Litho & Engr. (30k)
2013, Nov. 27   Perf. 11¾
3591-3593   A565   Set of 3   7.50   4.50

Ladislav Jirka (1914-86), Stamp Engraver A1504

2014, Jan. 20   Litho.   Perf. 11¾x11¼
3594   A1504   13k multi   1.25   .65
  a. Booklet pane of 8 + 4 labels   10.00
    Complete booklet, #3594a   10.00

Tradition of Czech stamp production.

Dog and Four-Leaf Clover A1505

2014, Jan. 20   Litho.   Perf. 11¼x11¾
3595   A1505   A multi + label   1.25   .65

No. 3595 was printed in sheets of 9 + 12 labels that could be personalized. On day of issue, No. 3595 had a franking value of 13k.

2014 Winter Olympics, Sochi, Russia A1506

2014, Feb. 5   Litho.   Perf. 11¾x11¼
3596   A1506   25k multi   2.50   1.35

2014 Winter Paralympics, Sochi, Russia — A1507

2014, Feb. 5   Litho.   Perf. 11¾x11¼
3597   A1507   13k multi   1.25   .70
  a. Tête-bêche pair   2.50   1.40

Czech Firefighters, 150th Anniv. — A1508

2014, Mar. 5   Litho.   Perf. 11¾x11¼
3598   A1508   13k multi   1.25   .70

Transportation — A1509

No. 3599: a, Rapid, 1912 airplane of Eugen Cihák. b, Type R1 Prague Metro train.

2014, Mar. 5   Litho.   Perf. 11¾x11¼
3599   A1509   13k Pair, #a-b   2.25   1.40

Bohumil Hrabal (1914-97), Writer — A1510

Photo. & Engr.
2014, Mar. 26   Perf. 11¼x11¾
3600   A1510   17k blk & brn   1.75   .85

Cervená Lhota Castle — A1511

2014, Mar. 26   Engr.   Perf. 11¾
3601   A1511   17k multi   1.50   .85

Zdenek Kopal (1914-93), Astronomer A1512

Perf. 11¾x11¼
2014, Mar. 26   Litho.
3602   A1512   21k multi   2.10   1.10

Silesian Museum, Opava, 200th Anniv. — A1513

Photo. & Engr.
2014, Apr. 30   Perf. 11¼x11¾
3603   A1513   13k multi   1.25   .70

Bagpipes — A1514

Photo. & Engr.
2014, Apr. 30   Perf. 11¼
3604   A1514   25k multi   2.10   1.25

Europa.

Art in Prague Castle Type of 2012

Design: 37k, Assembly of Olympian Gods, by Peter Paul Rubens.

Litho. & Engr.
2014, May 28   Perf. 11¾
3605   A1457   37k multi   3.75   1.90

No. 3605 was printed in sheets of 2. Value, $7.50.

Paper Mill, Velké Losiny — A1515

Photo. & Engr.
2014, May 28   Perf. 11¾x11¼
3606   A1515   13k multi   1.25   .70

Animated Characters Ju and Hele — A1516

Serpentine Die Cut 11 Syncopated
2014, May 28   Litho.
Booklet Stamp
Self-Adhesive
3607   A1516   A multi   1.25   .70
  a. Booklet pane of 10   12.50

No. 3607 sold for 13k on day of issue.

Historic Methods of Transportation — A1517

No. 3608: a, Paddle steamer Franz Joseph I. b, 1936 Zbrojovka Brno Z4 automobile.

Perf. 11¾x11¼
2014, June 11   Litho.
3608   A1517   25k Horiz. pair, #a-b   4.50   2.50

Souvenir Sheet

World War I, Cent. A1518

No. 3609: a, Soldier carrying rifle, mother holding child. b, Soldiers, people falling into pit.

2014, June 11   Litho.   Perf. 11¾
3609   A1518   29k Sheet of 2, #a-b, + 3 labels   5.00   3.00

Antique Automobiles Type of 2012

Designs: No. 3610, 1938 Skoda Popular Monte Carlo. No. 3611, 1941 Skoda Superb 0000.

Serpentine Die Cut 11¼ Syncopated
2014, Sept. 3   Litho.
Booklet Stamps
Self-Adhesive
3610   A1467   A multi   1.10   .60
3611   A1467   A multi   1.10   .60
  a. Booklet pane of 8, 4 each #3610-3611   9.00

Nos. 3610-3611 each sold for 13k on day of issue.

Karel, Elder of Zierotín (1564-1636), Governor of Moravia A1519

Photo. & Engr.
2014, Sept. 3   Perf. 11¾x11¼
3612   A1519   29k multi   2.50   1.40

Miniature Sheet

Flora and Fauna of the Beskid Mountains — A1520

No. 3613: a, 13k, Meles meles (44x27mm). b, 17k, Felis silvestris (44x27mm). c, 21k, Ursus arctos, Carabus variolosus (44x54mm). d, 25k, Nucifraga caryocatactes, Canis lupus (44x54mm).

Litho. & Engr.
2014, Sept. 3   Perf. 11¾
3613   A1520   Sheet of 4, #a-d, + 3 labels   7.00   3.50

Flower Bouquet in Wine Bottle A1521

2014, Oct. 15   Litho.   Perf. 11¼x11¾
3614   A1521   A multi + label   1.25   .60

No. 3614 was printed in sheets of 9 + 12 labels that could be personalized. On day of issue No. 3614 had a franking value of 13k.

Souvenir Sheet

St. Vitus Cathedral, Prague, 670th Anniv. — A1522

Litho. & Engr.
2014, Oct. 15   Perf. 11¾
3615   A1522   58k multi   5.25   2.60

Art Type of 1967 Inscribed "CESKA REPUBLIKA" and

Solitude and Spectacles, Photograph by Jaromír Funke A1523

Designs: 25k, Street in Winter, by Jakub Schikaneder. 37k, Leda Atomica, by Salvador Dalí.

Engr., Litho. (29k)
2014, Nov. 5   Perf. 11¾
3616   A565   25k multi   2.25   1.10
3617   A1523   29k multi   2.60   1.40
3618   A565   37k multi   3.50   1.75
  Nos. 3616-3618 (3)   8.35   4.25

CZECHOSLOVAKIA

Historical Events of November 17 — A1524

2014, Nov. 5   Litho.   Perf. 11¼x11¾
3619 A1524 13k multi   1.25 .60

Nazi attack on Czech university students, 75th anniv.; start of Velvet Revolution, 25th anniv.

Andreas Vesalius (1514-64), Anatomist — A1525

Photo. & Engr.
2014, Nov. 5   Perf. 11¼x11¾
3620 A1525 25k multi   2.25 1.10

Bethlehem in Winter, by Josef Lada — A1526

2014, Nov. 5   Litho.   Perf. 11¾x11¼
3621 A1526 A multi   1.25 .60

Christmas. No. 3621 sold for 13k on day of issue.

A1527   Personalized Stamps — A1528

Serpentine Die Cut Syncopated
2014, Nov. 26   Litho.
Self-Adhesive
3622 A1527 A multi   1.25 .60
3623 A1528 Z multi   2.75 1.40

Nos. 3622-3623 were each printed in sheets of 25. Vignette portions of each stamp could be personalized. The generic vignettes of these stamps are shown. On day of issue, the franking value of No. 3622 was 13k; No. 3623, 30k.

Oldrich Kulhánek (1940-2013), Stamp Designer A1529

Photo. & Engr.
2015, Jan. 20   Perf. 11¾x11¼
3624 A1529 13k multi   1.20 .55
  a. Booklet pane of 8 + 4 labels 9.50 —
     Complete booklet, #3624a   9.50

Vitezslava Kaprálová (1915-40), Composer A1530

2015, Jan. 20   Litho.   Perf. 11¾x11¼
3625 A1530 17k multi   1.40 .70

Military Aircraft and Vehicles A1531

Designs: No. 3626, Supermarine Spitfire LF Mk IXE. No. 3627, T-34/76.2 tank. No. 3628, Harley-Davidson motorcycle. No. 3629, Jeep-Ford GPW.

Serpentine Die Cut 11¼ Syncopated
2015, Jan. 20   Litho.
Booklet Stamps
Self-Adhesive
3626 A1531 A multi   1.10 .55
3627 A1531 A multi   1.10 .55
3628 A1531 A multi   1.10 .55
3629 A1531 A multi   1.10 .55
  a. Booklet pane of 8, 2 each
     #3626-3629   9.00
     Nos. 3626-3629 (4)   4.40 2.20

On day of issue, Nos. 3626-3629 each sold for 13k.

Cartoon Character Vecerníček, 50th Anniv. — A1532

Serpentine Die Cut 11 Syncopated
2015, Feb. 18   Litho.
Self-Adhesive
3630 A1532 A multi   1.10 .55

No. 3630 sold for 13k on day of issue.

Plzen, 2015 European Capital of Culture — A1533

Photo. & Engr.
2015, Feb. 18   Perf. 11¼
3631 A1533 25k multi   2.00 1.00

Printed in sheets of 3, with 3 labels. Value, $9.50.

Historic Methods of Transportation — A1534

No. 3632: a, Walter 6B automobile. b, Monoplane of Metodej Vlach.

Perf. 11¾x11¼
2015, Feb. 18   Litho.
3632 A1534 13k Horiz. pair, #a-b 2.10 1.10

Easter — A1535

2015, Mar. 4   Litho.   Perf. 11¼x11¾
3633 A1535 A multi   1.10 .55

No. 3633 sold for 13k on day of issue.

Postmen on Geese Above Charles Bridge A1536

2015, Mar. 4   Litho.   Perf. 11¼x11¾
3634 A1536 A multi + label   1.10 .55

No. 3633 has a franking value of 13k on day of issue and was printed in sheets of 9 + 12 labels that could be personalized.

Souvenir Sheet

The Last Supper, by Leonardo da Vinci — A1537

Perf. 11¼x11¾
2015, Mar. 18   Litho.
3635 A1537 25k multi   2.25 1.00

Expo 2015, Milan.

Church of St. Ignatius and Spejchar Gallery, Chomutov — A1538

Photo. & Engr.
2015, Apr. 15   Perf. 11¼x11¾
3636 A1538 25k multi   2.10 2.10
  a. Booklet pane of 8 + 4 labels 17.00 —
     Complete booklet, #3636a   17.00

Sixth Czech and German Philatelic Exhibition, Chomutov.

2015 Men's Ice Hockey World Championships, Czech Republic A1539

2015, Apr. 15   Litho.   Perf. 11¾x11¼
3637 A1539 30k multi   2.50 1.25

Animated Film Characters Bob and Bobek — A1540

Bob and Bobek: No. 3638, Playing ice hockey. No. 3639, Rowing raft.

Serpentine Die Cut 11 Syncopated
2015, Apr. 29   Litho.
Booklet Stamps
Self-Adhesive
3638 A1540 A multi   1.10 .55
3639 A1540 A multi   1.10 .55
  a. Booklet pane of 10, 5 each
     #3638-3639   11.00

Nos. 3638-3639 each sold for 13k on day of issue.

Moldava Railway, 130th Anniv. — A1541

2015, May 6   Engr.   Perf. 11¾x11¼
3640 A1541 13k black   1.10 .55
  a. Booklet pane of 8 + 4 labels 9.00 —
     Complete booklet, #3640a   9.00

Europa — A1542

2015, May 6   Litho.   Perf. 11¼
3641 A1542 25k multi   2.10 2.10

Art in Prague Castle Type of 2012

Design: 34k, Head of a Woman, by Hans von Aachen.

2015, May 27   Engr.   Perf. 11¾
3642 A1457 34k multi   3.00 1.40

Rabí Castle Ruins — A1543

2015, May 27   Engr.   Perf. 11¾
3643 A1543 17k multi   1.50 .70

Jan Hus (c. 1370-1415), Church Reformer — A1544

Perf. 11¼x11¾
2015, June 17   Litho.
3644 A1544 13k multi   1.25 .55

Antique Automobiles Type of 2012

Illustrations by Václav Zapadlik: No. 3645, 1955 Skoda 1201. No. 3646, 1947 Skoda Rapid 1500.

Serpentine Die Cut 11¼ Syncopated
2015, Sept. 2   Litho.
Booklet Stamps
Self-Adhesive
3645 A1467 A multi   1.10 .55
3646 A1467 A multi   1.10 .55
  a. Booklet pane of 8, 4 each
     #3645-3646   9.00

Nos. 3645-3646 each sold for 13k on day of issue.

Sir Nicholas Winton (1909-2015), Rescuer of Jewish Children During World War II — A1545

2015, Sept. 2   Litho.   Perf. 11¾x11¼
3647 A1545 13k multi   1.25 .55

Postcrossing — A1546

Serpentine Die Cut 11¼ Syncopated
2015, Sept. 2   Litho.
Self-Adhesive
3648 A1546 E multi   2.50 1.10

No. 3648 sold for 25k on day of issue.

Miniature Sheet

Owls A1547

No. 3649: a, 13k, Athene noctua (27x44mm). b, 17k, Aegolius funereus (27x44mm). c, 21k, Nyctea scandiaca (27x44mm). d, 25k, Bubo bubo (44x54mm).

Litho. & Engr.
2015, Sept. 2   Perf. 11¾
3649 A1547 Sheet of 4, #a-d, +
       4 labels   6.50 3.25

CZECHOSLOVAKIA

Historic Methods of Transportation — A1548

No. 3650: a, Tatra T3 tram, 1960s. b, Primátor Dittrich paddle steamer.

Perf. 11¾x11¼
2015, Sept. 23 Litho.
3650 A1548 25k Vert. pair, #a-b 4.25 2.10

Flag of Czech Republic — A1549

Serpentine Die Cut 11¼ on 1 Side Syncopated
2015, Oct. 14 Litho.
Self-Adhesive
3651 A1549 A multi 1.25 .55

No. 3651 sold for 13k on day of issue.

Organ and Jakub Jan Ryba (1765-1815), Composer — A1550

Photo. & Engr.
2015, Oct. 14 Perf. 11¼x11¾
3652 A1550 13k multi 1.25 .55

Wedding of Oldrich and Bozena, Painting From Dalimil's Chronicle A1551

2015, Oct. 14 Litho. Perf. 11¾x11¼
3653 A1551 21k multi 2.00 .85

Souvenir Sheet

World War I, Cent. A1552

No. 3654: a, Unveiling of statue of Jan Hus burning at the stake. b, Soldier carrying dying comrade.

2015, Oct. 14 Litho. Perf. 11¾
3654 A1552 27k Sheet of 2, #a-b, + 3 labels 4.50 2.25

Jan Opletal (1915-39), Medical Student Killed in Anti-Nazi Protests — A1553

Photo. & Engr.
2015, Nov. 11 Perf. 11¼x11¾
3655 A1553 13k blue & red 1.25 .55

Art Type of 1967 Inscribed "CESKA REPUBLIKA"

Designs: 27k, The Bride, book illustration by Antonín Strnadel. 30k, Sitting, by Bohumír Matal. 34k, Great Dialogue, sculpture by Karel Nepras, horiz.

Engr., Litho. & Engr. (34k)
2015, Dec. 16 Perf. 11¾
3656-3658 A565 Set of 3 8.00 3.75

Postman With Posthorn A1554

Perf. 11¼x11¾
2015, Dec. 16 Litho.
3659 A1554 Z multi + label 2.60 1.25

No. 3659 was printed in sheets of 9 + 12 labels that could be personalized. On day of issue, No. 3659 had a franking value of 30k.

Karel Svolinsky (1896-1986), Stamp Designer A1555

2016, Jan. 20 Litho. Perf. 11¾x11¼
3660 A1555 13k multi 1.25 .55
a. Booklet pane of 8 + 4 labels 10.00 —
Complete booklet, #3660a 10.00

Tradition of Czech stamp production.

Jerome of Prague (c. 1378-1416), Church Reformer A1556

2016, Jan. 20 Litho. Perf. 11¾x11¼
3661 A1556 17k multi 1.60 .70

Czech Spotted Dogs — A1557

2016, Feb. 3 Litho. Perf. 12
3662 A1557 13k multi 1.25 .55

Transportation A1558

No. 3663: a, Tatra rail coach M290.0. b, Paddle steamer Vysehrad.

Perf. 11¾x11¼
2016, Feb. 17 Litho.
3663 A1558 27k Pair, #a-b 5.00 2.25

Tomás Bat'a (1876-1932), Shoe Manufacturer — A1559

Photo. & Engr.
2016, Mar. 16 Perf. 11¼x11¾
3664 A1559 13k black & red 1.25 .55

Petrín Observation Tower and Funicular, 125th Anniv. — A1560

Photo. & Engr.
2016, Mar. 16 Perf. 11¼x11¾
3665 A1560 13k redsh brn & cream 1.25 .55
a. Booklet pane of 8 + 4 labels 10.00 —
Complete booklet, #3665a 10.00

Joint Institute for Nuclear Research, Dubna, Russia, 00th Anniv. — A1561

Perf. 11¾x11¼
2016, Mar. 16 Litho.
3666 A1561 27k multi 2.50 1.10

Buchlov Castle A1562

2016, Apr. 6 Engr. Perf. 11½x11¾
3667 A1562 17k multi 1.50 .75

Czech and Slovak Philatelic Exhibition, Zd'ár nad Sázavou — A1563

2016, Apr. 27 Litho. Perf. 11¼x11¾
3668 A1563 13k multi 1.25 .55
a. Booklet pane of 8 + 4 labels 10.00 —
Complete booklet, #3668a 10.00

Common Yellow Swallowtail Butterflies and Thistles — A1564

2016, Apr. 27 Litho. Perf. 12
3669 A1564 16k multi 1.50 .70

Europa A1565

2016, May 4 Litho. Perf. 11¾x11¼
3670 A1565 27k multi 2.50 1.10

Think Green Issue.
Printed in sheets of 8. Value, $20.

Souvenir Sheet

Holy Roman Emperor Charles IV (1316-78) — A1566

Litho. & Engr. Perf. 11¾
2016, May 4
3671 A1566 54k multi + 2 labels 8.00 5.00

No. 3671 was issued on May 4 with the incorrectly-spelled Latin inscription "Karolus Quatrus" in the sheet margin. Value, $100. The sheet was withdrawn from sale on May 5, and replaced soon thereafter with sheets bearing the correct inscription "Karolus Quartus."

Animated Cartoon Character Amálka the Fairy — A1567

Serpentine Die Cut 11¼ Syncopated
2016, May 18 Litho.
Booklet Stamp
Self-Adhesive
3672 A1567 A multi 1.50 .70
a. Booklet pane of 10 15.00

No. 3672 sold for 16k on day of issue.

Premiere of *The Bartered Bride*, by Bedrich Smetana, 150th Anniv. — A1567a

2016, May 18 Litho. Perf. 11¼x11¾
3673 A1567a 16k multi 1.50 .70

Art in Prague Castle Type of 2012

Design: 38k, Prague Altarpiece detail depicting St. Barbara, by Lucas Cranach the Elder.

2016, May 18 Engr. Perf. 11¾
3674 A1457 38k multi 3.25 1.60

Flower Arrangement A1568

2016, June 8 Litho. Perf. 11¾x11¼
3675 A1568 A multi + label 1.40 .70

No. 3675 was printed in sheets of 9 + 12 labels that could be personalized. On day of issue, No. 3675 had a franking value of 16k.

CZECHOSLOVAKIA

International Folklore Festival, Stráznice — A1569

Photo. & Engr.
2016, June 22 Perf. 11¼x11¾
3676 A1569 20k multi 1.75 .85

Jan Jessenius (1566-1621), Physician and Professor of Anatomy — A1570

Photo. & Engr.
2016, June 22 Perf. 11¼x11¾
3677 A1570 27k multi + label 2.50 1.10

See Hungary No. 4393, Poland No. 4232, Slovakia No. 743.

2016 Summer Olympics, Rio de Janeiro A1571

Perf. 11¾x11¼
2016, June 22 Litho.
3678 A1571 32k multi 3.00 1.40

2016 Summer Paralympics, Rio de Janeiro A1572

Perf. 11¾x11¼
2016, June 22 Litho.
3679 A1572 16k multi 1.50 .70

Art Type of 1967 Inscribed "CESKA REPUBLIKA"

Design: Young Woman on a Balcony, by Gerrit Dou.

2016, Sept. 7 Engr. Perf. 11¾
3680 A565 27k multi 2.50 1.10

See Liechtenstein No. 1691.

Tree Frog — A1573

2016, Sept. 7 Litho. Perf. 11¾x11¼
3681 A1573 A multi 1.50 .70

No. 3681 sold for 16k on day of issue.

Dr. Antonín Holy (1936-2012), Developer of Antiretroviral Drugs — A1574

2016, Sept. 7 Litho. Perf. 11¼x11¾
3682 A1574 20k multi 2.00 .85

UNESCO World Heritage Sites in Czech Republic A1575

Designs: 16k, Lednice-Valtice Cultural Landscape. 27k, Historic Center of Prague.

2016, Sept. 7 Litho. Perf. 11¼x11¾
3683-3684 A1575 Set of 2 4.00 1.90

See United Nations Nos. 1142, 1144a, 1144e; Offices in Geneva Nos. 626, 627a, 627e; Offices in Vienna Nos. 594a, 594e.

Miniature Sheet

Animals in Czech Republic Zoos A1576

No. 3685: a, 16k, Panthera uncia, Jihlava Zoo. b, 20k, Oryx gazella gazella, Panthera leo leo, Olomouc Zoo. c, 24k, Diceros bicornis, Lycaon pictus, Dvur Králové Zoo. d, 27k, Equus przewalskii, Prague Zoo.

Litho. & Engr.
2016, Sept. 7 Perf. 11¾
3685 A1576 Sheet of 4, #a-d, + 3 labels 8.00 3.75

Historic Methods of Transportation — A1577

No. 3686: a, Tatra 87 automobile. b, Aero Ab-11 biplane.

Perf. 11¾x11¼
2016, Sept. 21 Litho.
3686 A1577 16k Horiz. pair, #a-b 3.00 1.40

Zelezné Hory Protected Landscape Area, 25th Anniv. — A1578

2016, Oct. 12 Litho. Perf. 11¾x11¼
3687 A1578 16k multi 1.50 .70

Bee-eaters — A1579

2016, Oct. 12 Litho. Perf. 11¾x11¼
3688 A1579 20k multi 2.00 .85

Souvenir Sheet

Fight for Czech Statehood — A1580

No. 3689: a, St. Wenceslas, King Ottokar II of Bohemia, Holy Roman Emperor Charles IV, flags, soldiers. b, Grieving widow and children, Austrian imperial eagle.

2016, Oct. 12 Litho. Perf. 11¾
3689 A1580 27k Sheet of 2, #a-b, + 3 labels 5.00 2.25

Art Type of 1967 Inscribed "CESKA REPUBLIKA"

Designs: 27k, Two Women, by Jaroslav Král, horiz. 30k, Girl with Absinthe, sculpture by Bedrich Stefan. 38k, Clown with Monkey, by Frantisek Tichy.

2016, Nov. 9 Litho. Perf. 11¾
3690-3692 A565 Set of 3 8.50 3.75

United Nations Educational, Scientific and Cultural Organization, 70th Anniv. — A1581

2016, Nov. 9 Litho. Perf. 12
3693 A1581 32k multi 2.90 1.40

Oldrich Posmurny (1942-2010), Stamp Designer — A1582

Photo. & Engr.
2017, Jan. 20 Perf. 11¼x11¾
3694 A1582 16k multi 1.50 .70
a. Booklet pane of 8 + 4 labels 12.00
Complete booklet, #3694a 12.00

Tradition of Czech stamp production.

Czech Crown Jewels A1583

Serpentine Die Cut 11½ Syncopated
2017, Jan. 20 Litho.

Booklet Stamp Self-Adhesive

3695 A1583 E multi 2.90 1.40
a. Booklet pane of 8 24.00

No. 3695 sold for 32k on day of issue.

Historic Methods of Transportation — A1584

Designs: No. 3696a, Skoda 606DNd postal bus. No. 3696b, Fk-5-1401 railroad mail car.

No. 3697, Paddle steamer "Prague." 32k, Aero A-14 biplane.

2017 Litho. Perf. 11¾x11¼
3696 A1584 16k Horiz. pair, #a-b 3.00 1.25
3697 A1584 16k multi 1.50 .65
3698 A1584 32k multi 3.00 1.40
Nos. 3696-3698 (3) 7.50 3.30

Issued: No. 3696, 2/15; No. 3697, 3/8; No. 3698, 1/20.

Straka Academy, 120th Anniv. — A1585

2017, Mar. 8 Litho. Perf. 11¾x11¼
3699 A1585 24k multi 2.25 .95

Porta Bohemica River Valley — A1586

2017, Apr. 5 Engr. Perf. 11¾
3700 A1586 20k multi 1.75 .85

Prague Airport, 80th Anniv. — A1587

Photo. & Engr.
2017, Apr. 5 Perf. 11¾x11¼
3701 A1587 32k multi 2.60 1.40

Vera Cáslavská (1942-2016), Gymnast and President of Czech Olympic Committee — A1588

2017, May 3 Litho. Perf. 11¼x11¾
3702 A1588 16k multi 1.40 .70

Frydlant Castle — A1589

Photo. & Engr.
2017, May 3 Perf. 11¼
3703 A1589 32k multi 2.75 1.40

Europa.

Holy Roman Empress Maria Theresa (1717-80) A1590

Photo. & Engr.
2017, May 3 Perf. 11¾
3704 A1590 32k multi 2.75 1.40

Art in Prague Castle Type of 2012

No. 3705 — St. Catherine with Angel, by Paolo Veronese: a, Black image. b, Multicolored image.

2017, May 17 Engr. Perf. 11¾
3705 A1457 32k Horiz. pair, #a-b 5.50 2.75

Printed in sheets containing two each of Nos. 3705a-3705b + central label.

CZECHOSLOVAKIA

Souvenir Sheet

Operation Anthropoid (Assassination of Reinhard Heydrich), 75th Anniv. — A1591

Litho. & Engr.
2017, May 17   Perf. 11¾
3706 A1591 46k multi + 7 labels   4.00   2.00

 Josef Kainar (1917-71), Writer — A1592

Photo. & Engr.
2017, June 7   Perf. 11¼x11¾
3707 A1592 16k multi   1.40   .70

Heliodor Píka (1897-1949), General Executed by Communists — A1593

Photo. & Engr.
2017, June 7   Perf. 11¼x11¾
3708 A1593 37k multi   3.25   1.60

 Joze Plecnik (1872-1957), Architect A1594

   Perf. 11½x11¾
2017, June 7   Litho. & Engr.
3709 A1594 32k multi   2.75   1.40

No. 3709 was printed in sheets of 2 + central label.

Locomotives — A1595

Designs: No. 3710, Steam locomotive No. 7. No. 3711, Cog locomotive "The Austrian."

Serpentine Die Cut 11½ Syncopated
2017, June 7   Litho.
Booklet Stamps
Self-Adhesive
3710 A1595 A multi   1.40   .70
3711 A1595 A multi   1.40   .70
   a. Booklet pane of 8, 4 each #3710-3711   11.50

On day of issue, Nos. 3710-3711 each sold for 16k.

 Prague Pneumatic Mail System — A1596

2017, June 21   **Litho.**   **Perf. 11¼**
3712 A1596 A multi   1.40   .70

No. 3712 sold for 16k on day of issue.

 Church of the Assumption of Our Lady, Most, 500th Anniv. — A1597

Photo. & Engr.
2017, June 21   Perf. 11¼x11¾
3713 A1597 16k multi   1.40   .70

 Moravian Museum, Brno, 200th Anniv. — A1598

Photo. & Engr.
2017, June 21   Perf. 11¾x11¼
3714 A1598 20k multi   1.75   .85

 Gas Street Lighting in Prague, 170th Anniv. — A1599

Photo. & Engr.
2017, Sept. 6   Perf. 11¼x11¾
3715 A1599 16k multi   1.50   .75
   a. Booklet pane of 8 + 4 labels   12.00   —
     Complete booklet, #3715a   12.00

Josef Balabán (1894-1941), Václav Morávek (1904-42), and Josef Masín (1896-1942), Members of "Three Kings" Anti-Nazi Resistance Group — A1600

2017, Sept. 6   Litho.   Perf. 11¼x11¼
3716 A1600 16k multi   1.50   .75

 Mauritius No. 2 — A1601

2017, Sept. 6   Litho.   Perf. 12
3717 A1601 A multi   1.50   .75

No. 3717 sold for 16k on day of issue.

 Worker for Partner Post Office — A1602

2017, Sept. 6   Litho.   Perf. 11¾x11¼
3718 A1602 A multi   1.50   .75
     Complete booklet, 5 #3718   7.50

No. 3718 sold for 16k on day of issue.

Miniature Sheet

 Animals in Czech Republic Zoos A1603

No. 3719: a, 16k, Bison bonasus, Chomutov Zoo. b, 20k, Pan troglodytes, Panthera leo krugeri, Hodonín Zoo. c, 24k, Ursus maritimus, Brno Zoo. d, 30k, Rhinoceros unicornis, Varanus macraei, Plzen Zoo.

Litho. & Engr.
2017, Sept. 6   Perf. 11¾
3719 A1603   Sheet of 4, #a-d, + 4 labels   8.25   4.25

Nature Protection.

 Václav Hollar Association of Czech Graphic Artists, Cent. — A1604

Photo. & Engr.
2017, Sept. 20   Perf. 11¼x11¾
3720 A1604 20k multi   1.90   .95

 Imperial Austrian Letter Boxes, 200th Anniv. — A1605

Photo. & Engr.
2017, Oct. 4   Perf. 11¼x11¾
3721 A1605 16k multi   1.50   .75
   a. Booklet pane of 8 + 4 labels   12.00
     Complete booklet, #3721a   12.00

 Family on Bicycle — A1606

Photo. & Engr.
2017, Oct. 4   Perf. 11½x11¼
3722 A1606 16k blk & red   1.50   .75

 Self-Sculpture of Fictional Character Jára Cimrman, 50th Anniv. — A1607

Serpentine Die Cut 11¼ Syncopated
2017, Oct. 4   Litho.
Booklet Stamp
Self-Adhesive
3723 A1607 A multi   1.50   .75
   a. Booklet pane of 8   12.00

Jára Cimrman, fictional character created for 1967 Czech radio program, selected as "Greatest Czech" in 2005. No. 3723 sold for 16k on day of issue.

Souvenir Sheet

Fight for Czech Statehood — A1608

No. 3724: a, Soldiers, flag, independence leaders Milan R. Stefánik (1880-1919), Tomás G. Masaryk (1850-1937), and Jan Syrový (1880-1970). b, Writers Alois Jirásek (1851-1930), and Jaroslav Kvapil (1868-1950) and Manifesto of Czech Writers.

Litho., Sheet Margin Litho. With Foil Application
2017, Oct. 4   Perf. 11¾
3724 A1608 30k Sheet of 2, #a-b, + 3 labels   5.50   2.75

 Tatra Automobile at Railroad Crossing — A1609

2017, Oct. 18   Litho.   Perf. 11¾x11½
3725 A1609 A multi + label   1.50   .75

No. 3725 was printed in sheets of 9 + 12 labels that could be personalized. On day of issue No. 3725 had a franking value of 16k.

Art Type of 1967 Inscribed "CESKA REPUBLIKA"

Designs: 32k, Cuddled, photograph by Taras Kuscynskyj. 38k, Tempter, painting by Norbert Grund.

Litho. (32k), Engr. (38k)
2017, Nov. 8   Perf. 11¾
3726-3727 A565 Set of 2   6.50   3.25

 Czech Astronomical Society, Cent. — A1610

2017, Nov. 8   Litho.   Perf. 11¼x11¾
3728 A1610 16k multi   1.50   .75

Art Type of 1967 Inscribed "CESKA REPUBLIKA"

Design: Winner, by Jaroslava Pesicová.

2017, Dec. 13   Engr.   Perf. 11¾
3729 A565 30k multi   3.00   1.50

Souvenir Sheet

Postal Officials A1611

No. 3730: a, 32k, Jirí Strítbny (1880-1955), first Czechoslovakian minister of Posts and Telegraphs. b, 37k, Maxmilián Fatka (1868-1962), first director general of Czechoslovak Post.

98   CZECHOSLOVAKIA

	Litho. & Engr.
2017, Dec. 13	**Perf. 11¾**
3730 A1611 Sheet of 2, #a-b	6.50 3.25

Czech Republic, 25th Anniv. — A1612

2018, Jan. 3	**Litho.**	**Perf. 12**
3731 A1612 24k multi		2.40 1.25

No. 3731 was printed in sheets of 2 + central label.

2018 Winter Paralympics, PyeongChang, South Korea — A1613

2018 Winter Olympics, PyeongChang, South Korea — A1614

2018, Jan. 20	**Litho.**	**Perf. 11¾x11¼**
3732 A1613 16k multi		1.60 .80
Perf. 11¼x11¾		
3733 A1614 37k multi		3.75 1.90

Jiří Bouda (1934-2015), Stamp Designer — A1615

Perf. 11¾x11¼		
		Litho. & Engr.
3734 A1615 A multi		1.90 .95
a. Booklet pane of 8 + 4 labels	15.50	—
Complete booklet, #3734a	15.50	

Tradition of Czech stamp production. No. 3734 sold for 19k on day of issue.

Prague Castle — A1616

Perf. 11¾x11¼		
2018, Feb. 21		**Litho.**
3735 A1616 A red & indigo + label		1.90 .95

No. 3735 was printed in sheets of 9 + 12 labels that could be personalized. On day of issue, No. 3735 had a franking value of 19k. See No. 3837.

Person Making Willow Whip — A1617

Perf. 11¾x11¼		
2018, Feb. 21		**Litho.**
3736 A1617 A multi		1.90 .95

Easter. On day of issue, No. 3736 sold for 19k.

Prague Municipal Library — A1618

Perf. 11¼x11¾		
2018, Feb. 21		**Litho.**
3737 A1618 A multi		1.90 .95

On day of issue, No. 3737 sold for 19k.

Silesian Eagle in National Coat of Arms A1619

Moravian Eagle in National Coat of Arms A1620

Presidential Standard A1621

National Seal A1622

Bohemian Lion in National Coat of Arms A1623

National Flag A1624

National Colors A1625

National Anthem A1626

Serpentine Die Cut 11½ Syncopated

2018, Feb. 21		**Litho.**
Booklet Stamps		
Self-Adhesive		
3738 A1619 A multi		1.90 .95
3739 A1620 A multi		1.90 .95
3740 A1621 A multi		1.90 .95
3741 A1622 A multi		1.90 .95
3742 A1623 A multi		1.90 .95
3743 A1624 A multi		1.90 .95
3744 A1625 A multi		1.90 .95
3745 A1626 A multi		1.90 .95
a. Booklet pane of 8, #3738-3745	15.50	
Nos. 3738-3745 (8)	15.20	7.60

On day of issue, Nos. 3738-3745 each sold for 19k.

Dr. Frantisek Hamza (1868-1930), and Hamza Hospital — A1627

2018, Feb. 21	**Photo. & Engr.**	**Perf. 11¼x11¾**
3746 A1627 20k blue & claret		1.90 .95

Paddle Steamer Vltava — A1628

Perf. 11¾x11¼		
2018, Mar. 14		**Litho.**
3747 A1628 A multi		1.90 .95

On day of issue, No. 3747 sold for 19k.

Dlouhé Stráne Hydroelectric Power Plant — A1629

Perf. 11¾x11¼		
2018, Mar. 14		**Litho.**
3748 A1629 23k multi		2.25 1.10

Carriage of Emperor Ferdinand I of Austria A1630

Carriage of Princess Pauline Clémentine von Metternich-Sándor A1631

Postal Coach, Zamberk A1632

Carriage of Johann Adolf II, Prince of Schwarzenberg A1633

Passenger Coach — A1634

Serpentine Die Cut Syncopated

2018, Mar. 14		**Self-Adhesive**
3749 Strip of 5	17.50	8.75
a. A1630 E multi	3.50	1.75
b. A1631 E multi	3.50	1.75
c. A1632 E multi	3.50	1.75
d. A1633 E multi	3.50	1.75
e. A1634 E multi	3.50	1.75

Coaches and carriages from Postal Museum. Praga 2018 International Philatelic Exhibition. Nos. 3749a-3749e each sold for 35k on day of issue. Round stamps for the "E" rate are personalizable.

Eduard Storch (1878-1956), Archaeologist and Writer — A1635

2018, Apr. 4	**Litho.**	**Perf. 11¾x11¼**
3750 A1635 19k multi		1.75 .90

Czech National Library Architectural Design of Jan Kaplicky (1937-2009) A1636

2018, Apr. 4	**Photo. & Engr.**	**Perf. 11¼x11¾**
3751 A1636 E multi		3.25 1.60

No. 3751 sold for 35k on day of issue.

Pres. Zeman Type of 2013

		Photo. & Engr.
2018, Apr. 18		**Perf. 11¾x11¼**
3752 A1484 A red & dk blue		1.75 .90

No. 3752 sold for 19k on day of issue.

Stadlec Bridge and Podolsko Bridge — A1637

2018, May 2	**Litho.**	**Perf. 11**
3753 A1637 E gold & multi		3.25 1.60

Europa. No. 3751 sold for 35k on day of issue.

Czech Jazz Music — A1638

2018, May 2	**Litho.**	**Perf. 11¼x11¾**
3754 A1638 Z multi		3.75 1.90

No. 3754 sold for 41k on day of issue.

Art in Prague Castle Type of 2012

Design: 32k, Sacrifice at the Temple, by Francesco da Ponte, the Younger.

2018, May 23	**Engr.**	**Perf. 11¾**
3755 A1457 32k multi		3.00 1.50

Flowers Type of 2002

Design: 1k, Lily of the valley (konvalinka).

		Perf. 11¾x11¼
2018, June 20		**Litho.**
3756 A1215 1k multi		.25 .25

Bentwood Chairs by Factory Established by Michael Thonet (1796-1871) — A1639

	Perf. 11¼x11¾	
2018, June 20		**Litho.**
3757 A1639 19k multi		1.75 .85
a. Booklet pane of 8 + 4 labels	14.00	
Complete booklet, #3757a	14.00	

Mushrooms — A1640

Designs: No. 3758, Leccinum rufescens. No. 3759, Amanita rubescens.

CZECHOSLOVAKIA

Serpentine Die Cut 11¼ Syncopated
2018, June 20   Litho.
Booklet Stamps
Self-Adhesive
3758	A1640	A multi	1.75	.85
3759	A1640	A multi	1.75	.85
a.	Booklet pane of 10, 5 each #3758-3759		17.50	

Souvenir Sheet

Czechoslovakian Postage Stamps, Cent. — A1641

No. 3760: a, 27k, Czechoslovakia Nos. B125, P3, 244, P27, 575, 152, 329, 1133. b, 44k, Czech Republic Nos. 3040b, 3210b, 3467, 3567, 3615, 3692.

2018, June 20   Litho.   Perf. 11¾
3760	A1641	Sheet of 2, #a-b, + 3 labels	6.50	3.25

Souvenir Sheet

Czech Postal Museum, Cent. A1642

Directors: a, 19k, Václav Dragoun (1865-1950). b, 23k, Jirí Karásek (1871-1951). c, 27k, Pavel Ctvrtnik (1947-2008).

Litho. & Engr., Litho. Sheet Margin
2018, Aug. 8   Perf. 11¾x11½
3761	A1642	Sheet of 3, #a-c	6.25	3.25

Praga 2018 International Philatelic Exhibition, Prague.

Souvenir Sheet

1850 Cover to Bombay, India From Port Louis, Mauritius A1643

2018, Aug. 8   Litho.   Perf. 11¾
3762	A1643	59k multi	5.50	2.75

Sale of Bombay Cover to Czech collector, Praga 2018 International Philatelic Exhibition, Prague.

Locomotives — A1644

Designs: No. 3763, 1939 M260001 locomotive. No. 3764, Steam locomotive 365024, 1923.

Serpentine Die Cut 11½ Syncopated
2018, Sept. 5   Litho.
Booklet Stamps
Self-Adhesive
3763	A1644	A multi	1.75	.85
3764	A1644	A multi	1.75	.85
a.	Booklet pane of 8, 4 each #3763-3764		14.00	

On day of issue, Nos. 3763-3764 each sold for 19k.

Miniature Sheet

Animals in Czech Republic Zoos A1645

No. 3765: a, 19k, Ursus arctos horribilis, Decín Zoo. b, 23k, Pongo pygmaeus, Ústí nad Labem Zoo. c, 27k, Loxodonta africana, Zlín Zoo. d, 33k, Cercopithecus diana, Hippopotamus amphibius, Ostrava Zoo.

Litho. & Engr.
2018, Sept. 5   Perf. 11¾
3765	A1645	Sheet of 4, #a-d, + 4 labels	9.25	4.75

National Agricultural Museum, Prague, Cent. — A1646

Photo. & Engr.
2018, Sept. 19   Perf. 11¾x11¼
3766	A1646	27k multi	2.50	1.25

Souvenir Sheet

Fight for Czech Statehood — A1647

No. 3767 — Flags and: a, Monument to St. Wenceslas, Prague. b, Tomás G. Masaryk (1850-1937), first president of Czechoslovakia.

Litho., Sheet Margin Litho. With Foil Application
2018, Oct. 10   Perf. 11¾
3767	A1647	99h Sheet of 2, #a b, + 3 labels	6.00	3.00

National Museum, Prague, 200th Anniv. — A1648

2018, Oct. 10   Litho.   Perf. 11¼x11¾
3768	A1648	19k multi	1.75	.85

Goose and Wine Bottle — A1649

2018, Oct. 24   Litho.   Perf. 11¼x11¾
3769	A1649	A multi	1.75	.85
a.	Booklet pane of 8 + 4 labels		14.00	
	Complete booklet, #3769a		14.00	
b.	Tete-beche pair		3.50	3.50

St. Martin's Day. No. 3769 sold for 19k on day of issue. No. 3769b is found in No. 3769a.

Miroslav Hornícek (1918-2003), Actor — A1650

Photo. & Engr.
2018, Oct. 24   Perf. 11¼x11¾
3770	A1650	19k multi	1.75	.85

Frantisek Ladislav Rieger (1818-1903), Politician — A1651

Photo. & Engr.
2018, Oct. 24   Perf. 11¼x11¾
3771	A1651	27k multi	2.40	1.25

Miniature Sheet

Czech Orders and Medals, Cent. A1652

No. 3772: a, 19k, Medal of Merit. b, 23k, Order of Thomas Garrigue Masaryk. c, 27k, Order of the White Lion. d, 33k, Medal for Heroism.

2018, Oct. 24   Litho.   Perf. 12
3772	A1652	Sheet of 4, #a-d	9.00	4.50

Christmas — A1653

No. 3773: a, Christmas ornament and apple. b, Christmas ornament and cookie.

2018, Oct. 24   Litho.   Perf. 11¾x11¼
3773	A1653	A Pair, #a-b	3.50	1.75

On day of issue, Nos. 3773a-3773b each sold for 19k.

Art Type of 1967 Inscribed "CESKA REPUBLIKA"

Designs: 27k, The Great Angel's Others I, II, sculpture by Stanislav Libensky. 33k, Birds of Jevis, painting by Vladimir Komárek. 41k, Diego de Guzmán, engraving by Paulus Pontius.

Litho. (27k), Litho. & Engr. (33k), Engr. (41k)
2018, Nov. 14   Perf. 11¾
3774-3776	A565	Set of 3	9.00 4.50

Thomas Garrigue Masaryk (1850-1937), First President of Czechoslovakia A1654

Photo. & Engr.
2018, Nov. 14   Perf. 11¼x11¾
3777	A1654	A multi	1.75	.85
a.	Souvenir sheet of 1		1.75	.85

No. 3777 sold for 19k on day of issue.

Prague Castle Guard, Cent. — A1655

2018, Dec. 5   Litho.   Perf. 11¼x11¾
3778	A1655	A multi	1.75	.85
a.	Booklet pane of 8 + 4 labels		14.00	
	Complete booklet, #3778a		14.00	

No. 3778 sold for 19k on day of issue.

Petr Eben (1929-2007), Composer — A1656

2019, Jan. 20   Litho.   Perf. 11¼x11¾
3779	A1656	19k multi	1.75	.85

Masaryk University, Brno, Cent. — A1657

2019, Jan. 20   Litho.   Perf. 11¼x11¾
3780	A1657	A multi	1.75	.85

No. 3780 sold for 19k on day of issue.

Adolf Born (1930-2016), Illustrator A1658

2019, Jan. 20   Litho.   Perf. 11¾x11¼
3781	A1658	A multi	1.75	.85
a.	Booklet pane of 8 + 4 labels		14.00	
	Complete booklet, #3781a		14.00	

Tradition of Czech stamp production. No. 3781 sold for 19k on day of issue.

Rudolf Tomás Jedlicka (1869-1926), Surgeon and Radiologist A1659

Perf. 11¾x11¼
2019, Feb. 14   Litho.
3782	A1659	19k multi	1.75	.85

100 CZECHOSLOVAKIA

Souvenir Sheet

Jirí Hanzelka (1920-2003) and Miroslav Zikmund, Travel Writers and Film Makers — A1660

No. 3783: a, Zikmund holding camera. b, Hanzelka.

Perf. 11¾x11½
2019, Feb. 14   Litho. & Engr.
3783 A1660 45k Sheet of 2, #a-b + 2 labels   8.00 4.00
100th birthday of Zikmund.

Process of Making Sugar Cubes by Jakub Krystof Rad, 175th Anniv. — A1661

2019, Mar. 6   Litho.   Perf. 11¼x11¾
3784 A1661 19k multi   1.75 .85

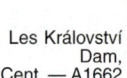

Les Království Dam, Cent. — A1662

2019, Mar. 6   Litho.   Perf. 11¾x11¼
3785 A1662 A multi   1.75 .85
a. Booklet pane of 8 + 4 labels   14.00   —
    Complete booklet, #3785a   14.00

No. 3785 sold for 19k on day of issue.

Maltese Cross and Church of Our Lady Under the Chain, Prague, Headquarters of Grand Priory of Bohemia of the Sovereign Military Order of Malta — A1663

2019, Mar. 6   Litho.   Perf. 11¼x11¾
3786 A1663 45k multi   4.00 2.00

Alois Rasin (1867-1923), Minister of Finance A1664

2019, Apr. 3   Litho.   Perf. 11¾x11¼
3787 A1664 23k multi   2.00 1.00
Czechoslovakian currency, cent.

Alcedo Atthis — A1665

2019, Apr. 24   Litho.   Perf. 11
3788 A1665 E multi   3.50 1.75
Europa. No. 3788 sold for 39k on day of issue.

Flowers Type of 2002
Design: E, Dandelion (pampeliska).

2019, May 22   Litho.   Perf. 11¾x11¼
3789 A1215 E multi   3.50 1.75
No. 3789 sold for 39k on day of issue.

Art in Prague Castle Type of 2012
No. 3790 — Paintings by Adolf Absolon: a, Prague Castle in Summer. b, Prague Castle in Winter.

Litho. & Engr.
2019, May 22   Perf. 11¾
3790 A1457 Horiz. pair   7.00 3.50
a.-b. E Either single   3.50 1.75
Nos. 3790a-3790b each sold for 39k on day of issue.

Gelasius Dobner (1719-90), Historian A1666

2019, May 22   Litho.   Perf. 11¾x11¼
3791 A1666 27k multi   2.40 1.25

A1667   Ctylistek Comic Strip, 50th Anniv. — A1668

Serpentine Die Cut 11 Syncopated
2019, May 22   Litho.
Booklet Stamps
Self-Adhesive
3792 A1667 A blue & multi   1.75 .85
3793 A1668 A red & multi   1.75 .85
a. Booklet pane of 10, 5 each #3792-3793   17.50

Nos. 3792-3793 each sold for 19k on day of issue.

Art Type of 1967 Inscribed "CESKA REPUBLIKA"
Designs: 27k, Line No. 56, by Zdenek Sykora (1920-2011). 45k, Poplars, by Václav Radimsky (1867-1946).

Litho. (27k), Engr. (45k)
2019, June 12   Perf. 11¾
3794-3795 A565 Set of 2   6.50 3.25

First Horse-drawn Tram in Brno, 150th Anniv. — A1669

Perf. 11¾x11¼
2019, June 26   Litho.
3796 A1669 A multi   1.75 .85
No. 3796 sold for 19k on day of issue.

Jan Palach (1948-1969) and Jan Zajic (1950-69), Student Protestors Who Set Themselves Afire — A1670

Perf. 11¾x11¼
2019, June 26   Litho.
3797 A1670 A multi   1.75 .85
No. 3797 sold for 19k on day of issue.

Mohandas K. Gandhi (1869-1948), Indian Nationalist Leader — A1671

Perf. 11¼x11¾
2019, June 26   Litho.
3798 A1671 Z multi   4.00 2.00
No. 3798 sold for 45k on day of issue.

Electra 10A in Flight A1672

Electra 10A at Airport A1673

Serpentine Die Cut 11½ Syncopated
2019, Sept. 4   Litho.
Booklet Stamps
Self-Adhesive
3799 A1672 E multi   3.50 1.75
3800 A1673 E multi   3.50 1.75
a. Booklet pane of 8, 4 each #3799-3800   28.00

Nos. 3799 and 3800 each sold for 39k on day of issue.

Clock and Horseman Lancing Dragon A1674

2019, Sept. 4   Litho.   Perf. 11¼x11¾
3801 A1674 A multi + label   1.60 .80

No. 3801 was printed in sheets of 9 + 12 labels that could be personalized. On day of issue, No. 3801 had a franking value of 19k.

Miniature Sheet

Animals in Czech Republic Zoos A1675

No. 3802: a, 19k, Crocodylus mindorensis, Protivín Zoo (45x27mm). b, 23k, Ovis aries strepsiceros, Vyskov Zoopark (45x27mm). c, 27k, Platalea leucordia, Lutra lutra, Huboká Zoo (45x54mm). e, 33k, Budorcas taxicolor bedfordi, Liberec Zoo (45x54mm).

Litho. & Engr.
2019, Sept. 4   Perf. 11¾
3802 A1675 Sheet of 4, #a-d, + 4 labels   8.75 4.50

Automobile Designed by Václav Král (1936-2005) A1676

2019, Oct. 2   Litho.   Perf. 11¾x11¼
3803 A1676 A multi   1.75 .85
a. Booklet pane of 8 + 4 labels   14.00   —
    Complete booklet, #3803a   14.00
No. 3803 sold for 19k on day of issue.

Souvenir Sheet

Service of Czechoslovakians in Royal Air Force in World War II — A1677

No. 3804: a, Flag of Czechoslovakia, Royal Air Force emblem and emblems of four Czechoslovak squadrons. b, Frantisek Perina (1911-2006), pilot.

2019, Oct. 2   Litho.   Perf. 11¾
3804 A1677 E Sheet of 2, #a-b   7.00 3.50
Nos. 3804a-3804b each sold for 39k on day of issue.

Semafor Theater, Prague, 60th Anniv. — A1678

2019, Oct. 23   Litho.   Perf. 11¾x11¼
3805 A1678 A gold & multi   1.75 .85
No. 3805 sold for 19k on day of issue.

Souvenir Sheet

Actors and Actresses — A1679

No. 3806: a, 23k, Dana Medrická (1920-83). b, 27k, Radovan Lukavsky (1918-2008).

2019, Oct. 23   Litho.   Perf. 11¾
3806 A1679 Sheet of 2, #a-b   4.50 2.25

Ivan Blatny (1919-90), Poet — A1680

Perf. 11¼x11¾
2019, Nov. 13   Litho.
3807 A1680 A multi   1.75 .85
No. 3807 sold for 19k on day of issue.

Czechoslovakian Red Cross, Cent. — A1681

Perf. 11¾x11¼
2019, Nov. 13   Litho.
3808 A1681 19k multi   1.75 .85

CZECHOSLOVAKIA

Souvenir Sheet

Velvet Revolution, 30th Anniv. — A1682

Litho. & Engr.
2019, Nov. 13   *Perf. 11¾*
3809   A1682   44k multi   4.00   2.00

Joint Issue between Czech Republic and Slovakia.
See Slovakia No. 835.

Art Type of 1967 Inscribed "CESKA REPUBLIKA"

Designs: 39k, Touch of Fate II, sculpture by Ladislav Saloun. 45k, Flora, painting by Ota Janecek, horiz.

Litho. (39k), Litho. & Engr. (45k)
2019   *Perf. 11¾*
3810-3811   A565   Set of 2   7.25   7.25

Issued: 39k, 11/27; 45k, 11/13.

Bedrich Housa (1926-2020), Stamp Engraver — A1683

2020, Jan. 20   Litho.   *Perf. 11¾x11¼*
3812   A1683   A multi   1.75   .85
    a.   Booklet pane of 8 + 4 labels   14.00   —
     Complete booklet, #3812a   14.00

No. 3812 sold for 19k on day of issue.

Minting of Thalers at Joachimstal Mint, 500th Anniv. — A1684

2020, Jan. 20   Litho.   *Perf. 11¾*
3813   A1684   A multi   1.75   .85

No. 3813 sold for 19k on day of issue.

The Organ Grinder, by Josef Capek (1887-1945) — A1685

Serpentine Die Cut 11½ Syncopated
2020, Jan. 20   Litho.
Booklet Stamp
Self-Adhesive
3814   A1685   Z multi   4.00   2.00
    a.   Booklet pane of 6   24.00

No. 3814 sold for 45k on day of issue.

Favorit Bicycle — A1686

2020, Feb. 1   Litho.   *Perf. 11¾x11¼*
3815   A1686   B multi   1.75   .85

No. 3815 sold for 19k on day of issue.

Post Rider — A1687

Serpentine Die Cut 11 Syncopated
2020, Feb. 1   Litho.
Booklet Stamp
Self-Adhesive
3816   A1687   B multi   1.75   .85
    a.   Booklet pane of 10   17.50

No. 3816 sold for 19k on day of issue.

Pillars — A1688

Perf. 11¾x11¼
2020, Feb. 26   Litho.
3817   A1688   B multi   1.75   .85

Constitutional judiciary, cent. No. 3817 sold for 19k on day of issue.

Easter — A1689

Perf. 11¼x11¾
2020, Feb. 26   Litho.
3818   A1689   B multi   1.75   .85

No. 3818 sold for 19k on day of issue.

Temptation, by Vladimir Suchanek — A1690

Perf. 11¼x11¾
2020, Feb. 26   Litho.
3819   A1690   B multi + label   1.75   .85

No. 3819 was printed in sheets of 9 + 12 labels that could be personalized. On day of issue, No. 3819 had a franking value of 19k.

Kasperk Castle — A1691

Perf. 11¾x11¼
2020, Mar. 11   Litho.
3820   A1691   27k multi   2.10   1.10

Carduelis Carduelis, Fringilla Coelebs, and Coccothraustes Coccothraustes — A1692

Parus Palustris, Parus Cristatus, Parus Caeruleus, and Parus Major — A1693

Perf. 11¼x11¾
2020, Mar. 11   Litho.
3821   A1692   B multi   1.50   .75
3822   A1693   B multi   1.50   .75

On day of issue, Nos. 3821-3822 each sold for 19k.

Souvenir Sheet

Modern Architecture of Hradec Kralove — A1694

No. 3823: a, J. K. Tyla Gymnasium, statue, Church of Prince Ambrose, designed by Josef Gocár (1880-1945). b, Gocár and map of Hradec Králové.

Perf. 11½x11¾
2020, Mar. 11   Litho.
3823   A1694   Sheet of 2 + label   5.25   2.75
    a.   23k multi   1.75   .90
    b.   45k multi   3.50   1.75

Apis Mellifica and Flowers — A1695

Serpentine Die Cut 11 Syncopated
2020, Mar. 25   Litho.
Self-Adhesive
3824   A1695   B multi   1.50   .75

No. 3824 sold for 19k on day of issue.

Post Wagon — A1696

2020, Apr. 22   Litho.   *Perf. 11*
3825   A1696   E multi   3.25   1.60

Europa. No. 3825 sold for 30k on day of issue.

Amanita Muscaria — A1697

Boletus Satanas — A1698

Serpentine Die Cut 11 Syncopated
2020, Apr. 22   Litho.
Booklet Stamps
Self-Adhesive
3826   A1697   B multi   1.60   .80
3827   A1698   B multi   1.60   .80
    a.   Booklet pane of 10, 5 each #3826-3827   16.00

On day of issue, Nos. 3826-3827 each sold for 19k.

Art Type of 1967 Inscribed "CESKA REPUBLIKA"

Designs: 30k, Portrait of Frantisek Ferdinand Khünburg, Archbishop of Prague, by Petr Brandl (1668-1735). 47k, Chiasmage Object, by Jirí Kolár (1914-2002), horiz.
No. 3830 — Paintings by Josef Liesler (1912-2005): a, How Do You Like it When I Grin?, 1985. b, Variations on an Old Master, Theme I, 1977. c, Variations on an Old Master, Theme II, 1978.

Litho., Litho. & Engr. (47k)
2020   *Perf. 13½x14, 11¾ (47k)*
3828   A565   30k multi   2.50   1.25
3829   A525   47k multi   4.00   2.00

Miniature Sheet
3830   Sheet of 4, #3830b, 3830c, 2 #3830a   10.50   5.25
    a.   A565 B multi   1.60   .80
    b.   A565 E multi   3.25   1.60
    c.   A565 Z multi   3.75   1.90

Issued: Nos. 3828-3829, 5/13; No. 3830, 6/17. On day of issue, No. 3830a sold for 19k; No. 3830b, 39k; No. 3830c, 45k.

Václav Neumann (1920-95), Conductor — A1699

2020, May 13   Litho.   *Perf. 14x13½*
3831   A1699   19k multi   1.60   .80

Pica Pica, Garrulus Glandarius, and Corvus Corax A1700

Eritacus Rubecula, Phoenicurus Phoenicurus, and Turdus Pilaris A1701

Perf. 11¼x11¾
2020, June 17   Litho.
3832   A1700   B multi   1.60   .80
3833   A1701   B multi   1.60   .80

On day of issue, Nos. 3832-3833 each sold for 19k.

Protective Face Masks — A1702

No. 3834 — Various face masks with country name at: a, LL. b, UR.

Perf. 11¾x11¼
2020, June 24   Litho.
3834   A1702   B Pair, #a-b   3.25   1.60

Tribute to workers fighting the coronavirus pandemic. On day of issue, Nos. 3834a-3834b each sold for 19k.

Aero L-39 Albatros — A1703

Serpentine Die Cut 11 Syncopated
2020, Sept 9   Litho.
Self-Adhesive
3835   A1703   B multi   1.75   .85

No. 3835 sold for 19k on day of issue.

CZECHOSLOVAKIA

Jozin Eats Prazák from the Swamps, Painting by Ivan Mládek
A1704

Serpentine Die Cut 11½ Syncopated
2020, Sept 9   Litho.
Booklet Stamp
Self-Adhesive
3836   A1704   B multi   1.75   .85
   a.   Booklet pane of 8   14.00

Ivan Mládek's Banjo Band, 50th anniv. No. 3836 sold for 19k on day of issue.

Prague Castle Type of 2018
2020, Sept. 9   Litho.   Perf. 11¾x11¼
3837   A1616   B grn & brnsh blk + label   1.75   .85

No. 3837 was printed in sheets of 9 + 12 labels that could be personalized. On day of issue, No. 3837 had a franking value of 19k.

Birds
A1705

No. 3838: a, Aegithalos caudatus, Passer montanus, Passer domesticus. b, Emberiza calandra, Emberiza schoeniclus, Emberiza citrinella, Emberiza hortulana.

2020, Sept. 9   Litho.   Perf. 11¼x11¾
3838   A1705   E Horiz. pair, #a-b   6.75   3.50

On day of issue, Nos. 3838a-3838b each sold for 39k.

Souvenir Sheet

Model of MB10 Space Base, by Ondrej Doule, Space Architect
A1706

2020, Sept. 9   Litho.   Perf. 14x13½
3839   A1706   54k multi   4.75   2.40

Czechoslovakia No.
J52a — A1707

Austria No.
P4 — A1708

2020, Sept. 23   Litho.   Perf. 12
3840   A1707   B multi   1.75   .85
3841   A1708   E multi   3.50   1.75

On day of issue, No. 3840 sold for 19k, and No. 3841 sold for 39k.

Personalized Stamp — A1709

Serpentine Die Cut 11 Syncopated
2020, Sept. 23   Litho.
Self-Adhesive
3842   A1709   Z multi   4.00   2.00

No. 3842, a personalized stamp having a franking value of 45k on the day of issue, that has the generic image of Mauritius No. 1 shown, was printed in sheets of 25, of which 12 examples of No. 3842 alternated with 13 examples of No. 3540 showing an image of the not regularly issued 1919 4k Czechoslovakian semi-postal on granite paper.
Starting in 2021, stamps of the same size as No. 3842, bearing the letter "B" (having a franking value of 19k on the day of issue) instead of "Z," were printed in sheets of 25 on the apparatus that creates personalized stamps. The stamps on these sheets sold by the Czech Philatelic Bureau had 25 different vignettes that were chosen by them. Any stamp from these sheets, or any subsequent sheets of 25 different vignettes, bearing the letters "B," "E," or "Z," will be considered to be a variety of No. 3842 (stamps of this size bearing the letter "A" would be varieties of No. 3540).

Butterflies — A1711

Designs: 1k, Belásek (orange tip butterfly). 2k, Modrásek (common blue butterfly). 4k, Zluťásek (clouded yellow butterfly). 23k, Babocka (peacock butterfly).

2020-21   Litho.   Perf. 11¼x11¾
3844   A1711   1k multi   .25   .25
3845   A1711   2k multi   .25   .25
3846   A1711   4k multi   .35   .25
3847   A1711   23k multi   2.10   1.10
   Nos. 3844-3847 (4)   2.95   1.85

Issued: 2k, 4k, 10/7; 23k, 11/25; 1k, 2/15/21.

Souvenir Sheet

Actors
A1712

No. 3848: a, 30k, Jirí Sovák (1920-2000). b, 34k, Vlastimil Brodsky (1920-2002).

Litho. (30k), Litho. With Hologram Affixed (34k)
2020, Oct. 7   Perf. 13½x14
3848   A1712   Sheet of 2, #a-b   5.50   2.25

Aero 750 Sport Coupé — A1713

Serpentine Die Cut 11 Syncopated
2020, Oct. 21   Litho.
Booklet Stamp
Self-Adhesive
3849   A1713   B multi   1.75   .85
   a.   Booklet pane of 10   17.50

No. 3849 sold for 19k on day of issue.

The Holy Night, by Josef Lada (1887-1957) — A1714

2020, Oct. 21   Litho.   Perf. 11¼x11¾
3850   A1714   B multi   1.75   .85

Christmas. No. 3850 sold for 19k on day of issue.

Art Type of 1967 Inscribed "CESKA REPUBLIKA"

Designs: 33k, Jump, painting by Grigorij A. Musatov (1889-1941). 40k, Groping, painting by Josef Vyletal (1940-89).

2020, Nov. 11   Litho.   Perf. 13½x14
3851-3852   A565   Set of 2   6.75   3.50

St. Norbert of Xanten (c. 1075-1134), Founder of Order of Prémontré
A1715

2020, Nov. 25   Litho.   Perf. 12x11½
3853   A1715   B multi   1.75   .85

Order of Prémontré, 900th anniv. No. 3853 sold for 19k on day of issue.

Souvenir Sheet

Prague Castle as Seen From National Theater
A1716

No. 3854 — Color of Prague Castle: a, E, Violet. b, Z, Light brown.

Litho. & Engr. (#3854a), Litho. (#3854b)
2020, Nov. 25   Perf. 11¾
3854   A1716   Sheet of 2, #a-b, + 2 labels   7.75   4.00

On day of issue, No. 3854a sold for 39k, and No. 3854b sold for 45k.

2021 Census — A1717

2021, Jan. 20   Litho.   Perf. 11¾x11¼
3855   A1717   B multi   1.75   .90

No. 3855 sold for 19k on day of issue.

Automobiles and Václav Zapadlík (1943-2018), Stamp Designer
A1718

2021, Jan. 20   Litho.   Perf. 13½
3856   A1718   B multi   1.75   .90
   a.   Booklet pane of 8 + 4 labels   14.00
     Complete booklet, #3856a   14.00

No. 3856 sold for 19k on day of issue.

Carnival Procession
A1719

2021, Jan. 20   Litho.   Perf. 13½
3857   A1719   B multi   1.75   .90
   a.   Booklet pane of 8 + 4 labels   14.00
     Complete booklet, #3857a   14.00

No. 3857 sold for 19k on day of issue.

Josef Masopust (1930-2015), Soccer Player and Coach — A1720

2021, Feb. 9   Litho.   Perf. 13½
3858   A1720   19k multi   1.75   .90

Milotice Chateau
A1721

2021, Feb. 9   Litho.   Perf. 13½
3859   A1721   23k multi   2.25   1.10

Visegrád Group, 30th Anniv. — A1722

2021, Feb. 15   Litho.   Perf. 12
3860   A1722   39k multi   3.75   1.90

See Hungary No. 4582, Poland No. 4528, and Slovakia No. 870.

Negrelli Viaduct
A1723

         Perf. 11¾x11¼
2021, Mar. 24   Litho.
3861   A1723   B multi   1.75   .85
   a.   Booklet pane of 8 + 4 labels   14.00   —
     Complete booklet, #3861a   14.00

No. 3861 sold for 19k on day of issue.

Bohous, Sculpture by Bohumil Zemánek (1942-96) — A1724

2021, Mar. 24   Litho.   Perf. 11¾
3862   A1724   30k multi + label   2.75   1.40

First Soccer Match Between AC Sparta and SK Slavia, 125th Anniv.
A1725

No. 3863 — Half of soccer ball and emblem of: a, AC Sparta (shield). b, SK Slavia (star).

         Perf. 11¼x11¾
2021, Mar. 24   Litho.
3863   A1725   B Horiz. pair, #a-b   3.50   1.75

On day of issue, Nos. 3863a-3863b each sold for 19k.

Dancing House, Prague, Designed by Vlado Milunic and Frank Gehry
A1726

CZECHOSLOVAKIA

Perf. 11¼x11¾
2021, Mar. 24   Litho.
3864   A1726   E multi + label   3.50   1.75

No. 3864 was printed in sheets of 7 + 14 labels that could be personalized and had a franking value of 39k on day of issue.

Mocked-up Hiking Map
A1727

2021, Apr. 21   Litho.   **Perf. 11¼x11½**
3865   A1727   B multi + label   1.75   .90

No. 3865 was printed in sheets of 7 + 14 labels that could be personalized. On day of issue, No. 3865 had a franking value of 19k.

Rock Formation on Czech-Polish Border
A1728

2021, Apr. 21   Litho.   **Perf. 11¾x11¼**
3866   A1728   23k multi   2.25   1.10

Felis Silvestris — A1729

2021, Apr. 21   Litho.   **Perf. 11**
3867   A1729   E multi   3.75   1.90

Europa. No. 3867 sold for 39k on day of issue.

Gustav Brom (1921-95), Jazz Musician and Band Leader
A1730

2021, May 19   Litho.   **Perf. 11¾x11¼**
3868   A1730   27k multi   2.60   1.30

Black Stork in Wetlands
A1731

2021, May 19   Litho.   **Perf. 11¾x11¼**
3869   A1731   Z multi   4.50   2.25

Ramsar Convention on Wetlands, 50th anniv. No. 3869 sold for 45k on day of issue.

Glass Sculpture From Prague Castle, by Borek Šípek (1949-2016) — A1732

2021, June 9   Litho.   **Perf. 14x13½**
3870   A1732   E multi   3.75   1.90

No. 3870 sold for 39k on day of issue.

Souvenir Sheet

Krusnohorí Mining Region UNESCO World Heritage Site — A1733

No. 3871: a, Jezerí Castle. b, Wolf Pit tin mining area.

2021, June 9   Litho.   **Perf. 11½x11¾**
3871   A1733   Sheet of 2   5.00   2.50
   a.   26k multi   2.40   1.25
   b.   27k multi   2.50   1.25

Kyjov Folk Festival
A1734

Perf. 11¾x11¼
2021, June 23   Litho.
3872   A1734   B multi   1.75   .90

No. 3872 sold for 19k on day of issue.

Souvenir Sheet

Mike the Tomcat, Children's Book by Josef Lada (1887-1957) — A1735

Litho. & Engr.
2021, June 23   **Perf. 11¾**
3873   A1735   55k multi   5.25   2.60

Czech Mountain Dog Puppy
A1736

Czech Mountain Dog Puppies
A1737

Serpentine Die Cut 11¼ Syncopated
2021, Sept. 8   Litho.
Booklet Stamps
Self-Adhesive
3874   A1736   B multi   1.75   .85
3875   A1737   B multi   1.75   .85
   a.   Booklet pane of 10, 5 each #3874-3875   17.50

Nos. 3874-3875 each sold for 19k on day of issue.

Miniature Sheet

Flora and Fauna of Milovice Nature Reserve
A1738

No. 3876: a, 23k, Phengaris alcon, Gentiana cruciata (27x45mm). b, 26k, Bison bonasus (54x45mm). c, 27k, Bos primigenius (54x45mm). d, 30k, Exmoor ponies (54x45mm).

Litho. & Engr.
2021, Sept. 8   **Perf. 11¾**
3876   A1738   Sheet of 4, #a-d, + 2 labels   9.75   5.00

Miniature Sheet

Dante Alighieri (c. 1265-1321), Writer — A1739

No. 3877: a, B, Alighieri (45x27mm). b, E, Alighieri, diff. (45x54mm).

2021, Sept. 8   Litho.   **Perf. 13½x14**
3877   A1739   Sheet of 4, 2 each #3877a-3877b, + label   11.00   5.50

On day of issue, Nos. 3877a-3877b sold for 19k and 39k, respectively.

Souvenir Sheet

Expo 2021, Dubai
A1740

Litho. & Silk-Screened, Sheet Margin Litho. With Hologram Affixed
2021, Sept. 8   **Perf. 14x13½**
3878   A1740   Z multi   4.25   2.10

No. 3878 sold for 45k on day of issue.

Wikov 7/28 Roadster — A1741

Serpentine Die Cut 11¼ Syncopated
2021, Oct. 6   Litho.
Self-Adhesive
3879   A1741   B multi   1.75   .85

No. 3879 sold for 19k on day of issue.

Actors
A1742

No. 3880: a, 27k, Bohumil Záhorsky (1906-80). b, 33k, Jirina Sejbalová (1905-81).

2021, Oct. 6   Litho.   **Perf. 14x13½**
3880   A1742   Vert. pair, #a-b   5.50   2.75

No. 3880 was printed in sheets containing two pairs + central label.

Art Type of 1967 Inscribed "CESKA REPUBLIKA"

Designs: 30k, Ecce Homo, by Theodor Pistek. 33k, Nude, by Frantizek Ronovsky (1929-2006), horiz. 34k, The Self-portrait by the Window, by Pistek.

Perf. 13½x14, 14x13½
2021, Oct. 20   Litho.
3881-3883   A565   Set of 3   8.75   4.50

Nos. 3881 and 3883 were printed in sheets containing two of each stamp + central label. No. 3882 was printed in sheets of 4 + central label.

Muriel, Comic Book Character Created by Kája Saudek (1935-2015) — A1743

Perf. 11¼x11¾
2021, Nov. 10   Litho.
3884   A1743   B multi   1.75   .85

No. 3884 sold for 19k on day of issue.

Karel Styblo (1921-98), Epidemiologist, and Tuberculosis Bacilli — A1744

Perf. 11¾x11¼
2021, Nov. 10   Litho.
3885   A1744   26k multi   2.40   1.25

Souvenir Sheet

Jan Kotera (1871-1923), Architect, and Charles University Law Faculty Building, Prague — A1745

Perf. 11½x11¾
2021, Nov. 10   Litho.
3886   A1745   52k multi + 2 labels   4.75   2.40

Souvenir Sheet

St. Ludmila (c. 860-921)
A1746

CZECHOSLOVAKIA

Litho. & Engr.
2021, Nov. 10 *Perf. 11¾*
3887 A1746 60k multi 5.50 2.75

Christmas — A1747

Perf. 11¼x11¾
2021, Nov. 10 *Litho.*
3888 A1747 B multi 1.75 .85
No. 3888 sold for 19k on day of issue and is impregnated with a pine scent.

Infant Jesus of Prague Statue — A1748

Serpentine Die Cut 11¼ Syncopated
2021, Nov. 30 *Litho.*
Self-Adhesive
3889 A1748 E multi 3.50 1.75
No. 3889 sold for 39k on day of issue.

Pres. Tomás G. Masaryk (1850-1937), and Mosaic at Kfar Masaryk Kibbutz, Israel — A1749

2021, Nov. 30 *Litho.* *Perf. 11¾*
3890 A1749 Z multi 4.00 2.00
No. 3890 sold for 45k on day of issue. See Israel No. 2299.

Waite & Saville Flat Plate Printing Press — A1750

2022, Jan. 20 *Engr.* *Perf. 13½x14*
3891 A1750 B olive gray 1.75 .90
a. Booklet pane of 8 + 2 labels 14.00
 Complete booklet, #3891a 14.00
No. 3891 sold for 19k on day of issue.

Molière (1622-73), Playwright and Actor — A1751

2022, Jan. 20 *Litho.* *Perf. 11¾x11¼*
3892 A1751 23k multi 2.25 1.10

Milos Forman (1932-2018), Film Director — A1752

Perf. 11¾x11¼
2022, Feb. 16 *Litho.*
3893 A1752 19k multi 1.75 .85

Souvenir Sheet

Gothic Murals A1753

No. 3894: a, Crucifixion, attributed to Master of the Karlstejn Apocalypse, from Chapel of St. Catherine, Karlstejn Castle. b, Life of St. Margaret, from Velké Meziříčí Castle.

2022, Feb. 16 *Litho.* *Perf. 11¾*
3894 A1753 Sheet of 2 6.50 3.25
a. 34k multi 3.00 1.50
b. 40k multi 3.50 1.75

Fresco by Emil Filla (1882-1953) A1754

The Girl with a Mandolin, Painting by Filla — A1755

2022, Mar. 8 *Litho.* *Perf. 11¼x11¾*
3895 A1754 B multi + label 1.75 .85
Perf. 13½x14
3896 A1755 39k multi 3.50 1.75
No. 3895 was printed in sheets of 7 + 8 labels that could be personalized. On day of issue, No. 3895 had a franking value of 19k.

Souvenir Sheet

Kosice-Bohumín Railway, 150th Anniv. — A1756

Litho. & Engr.
2022, Mar. 18 *Perf. 11¾*
3897 A1756 58k multi + 2 labels 5.25 2.60
Joint issue between Czechoslovakia and Slovakia. See Slovakia No.

Schwarzenberg Canal — A1757

2022, Apr. 6 *Litho.* *Perf. 11¾x11¼*
3898 A1757 B multi 1.75 .85
a. Booklet pane of 8 + 4 labels 14.00
 Complete booklet, #3898a 14.00
No. 3898 sold for 19k on day of issue.

Legend of Libuse and Premysl — A1758

2022, Apr. 6 *Litho.* *Perf. 11¼*
3899 A1758 E multi 3.50 1.75
Europa. No. 3899 sold for 39k on day of issue.

Actors A1759

No. 3900: a, 30k, Jan Werich (1905-80). b, 34k, Stella Zázvorková (1922-2005).

2022, Apr. 6 *Litho.* *Perf. 14x13½*
3900 A1759 Vert. pair, #a-b 5.50 2.75
No. 3900 was printed in sheets containing two pairs + central label.

Philatelic Youth Olympiad, 50th Anniv. — A1760

2022, May 18 *Litho.* *Perf. 11¼x11¾*
3901 A1760 B multi 1.75 .85
a. Booklet pane of 8 + 4 labels 14.00
 Complete booklet, #3901a 14.00
No. 3901 sold for 19k on day of issue.

Czech Beekeepers Association, 150th Anniv. — A1761

Serpentine Die Cut 11 Syncopated
2022, May 18 *Litho.*
Self-Adhesive
3902 A1761 23k multi 2.00 1.00
No. 3903 was printed in sheets of 5.

Personalized Stamp — A1762

Serpentine Die Cut 11 Syncopated
2022, June 15 *Litho.*
Self-Adhesive
3903 A1762 B multi 1.60 .80
Nos. 3903 was printed in sheets of 5. Vignette of each stamp could be personalized. The generic vignette depicting a Brozík & Krizík tram car is shown. On day of issue, the franking value of No. 3903 was 19k.

Bengal Kitten A1763   Persian Kitten A1764

Serpentine Die Cut 11¼ Syncopated
2022, June 15 *Litho.*
Booklet Stamps
Self-Adhesive
3904 A1763 B multi 1.60 .80
3905 A1764 B multi 1.60 .80
a. Booklet pane of 10, 5 each #3904-3905 16.00
On day of issue, Nos. 3904-3905 each sold for 19k.

2022 International Council of Museums General Conference, Prague — A1765

Perf. 11¼x11¾
2022, June 15 *Litho.*
3906 A1765 E multi 3.25 1.60
No. 3906 sold for 39k on day of issue.

Czech Presidency of the Council of the European Union — A1766

Perf. 11¾x11¼
2022, June 15 *Litho.*
3907 A1766 E multi 3.25 1.60
No. 3907 sold for 39k on day of issue.

Chudobín Pine — A1767

2022, Sept. 7 *Litho.* *Perf. 11¼*
3908 A1767 B multi 1.50 .75
No. 3908 sold for 19k on day of issue.

Road and Roses on Gate A1768

2022, Sept. 7 *Litho.* *Perf. 11¼x11¾*
3909 A1768 B multi + label 1.50 .75
No. 3909 was printed in sheets of 7 + 14 labels that could be personalized. On day of issue, No. 3909 had a franking value of 19k.

Jindrich Fügner (1822-65), Co-founder of Sokol Sports Organization A1769

2022, Sept. 7 *Litho.* *Perf. 11¾x11¼*
3910 A1769 27k blue & red 2.25 1.10

Souvenir Sheet

1952 Summer Olympic Gold Medalists — A1770

No. 3911: a, Dana Zátopková (1922-2020), javelin gold medalist. b, Emil Zátopek (1922-2000), long-distance running gold medalist and husband of Zátopková.

CZECHOSLOVAKIA

2022, Sept. 7 Litho. Perf. 11¾
3911 A1770 Sheet of 2   5.00   2.50
   a.   27k multi   2.25   1.10
   b.   33k multi   2.75   1.40

Miniature Sheet

Flora and Fauna of Mácha Lake Region — A1771

No. 3912: a, 23k, Apatura iris, Lilium martagon (27x45mm). b, 26k, Cygnus olor, Trollius altissimus, Pinguicula bohemica (55x45mm). c, 27k, Grus grus, Ledum paluste, Dactylorhiza bohemica, Iris sibirica (55x45mm). d, 30k, Birds over Mácha Lake, sailboat and Bezdez Castle (55x45mm).

2022, Sept. 7 Litho. Perf. 14x13½
3912 A1771 Sheet of 4, #a-d, + 2 labels   8.50   4.25

Tiles From St. Wenceslas Rotunda, Prague — A1772

No. 3913 — Tile depicting: a, Griffin. b, Lion.

2022, Sept. 21 Litho. Perf. 11¼
3913 A1772 B Horiz. pair, #a-b   3.00   1.50
On day of issue, Nos. 3913a-3913b each sold for 19k.

2022 European Stamp Exhibition, Liberec — A1773

No. 3914: a, Penguins carrying letters and stamps. b, Birds in birdhouses carrying stamps.

2022, Oct. 12 Litho. Perf. 11¼x11¾
3914 A1773 E Horiz. pair, #a-b   0.50   0.25
On day of issue, Nos. 3914a-3914b each sold for 39k.

Miniature Sheet

Breeding and Training of Ceremonial Carriage Horses at Kladruby and Labem — A1774

No. 3915: a, 26k, Kladruber mare, foal and stud farm. b, 30k, Foal and stud farm. c, 34k, Coach and two horses. d, 40k, Two horses.

2022, Oct. 12 Litho. Perf. 14x13½
3915 A1774 Sheet of 4, #a-d, + 2 labels   10.50   5.25

Christmas — A1775

Serpentine Die Cut 11¼ Syncopated
2022, Oct. 26 Litho.
Self-Adhesive
3916 A1775 B multi   1.60   .80
No. 3916 sold for 19k on day of issue.

Art Type of 1967 Inscribed "CESKA REPUBLIKA"

Designs: 39k, 45k, Plague, by Jaroslav Panuska (1872-1958).

2022, Nov. 9 Engr. Perf. 11¾
3917 A565 39k black   3.25   1.60
Litho.
3918 A565 45k multi   3.75   1.90
Printed in sheets of 4 containing two each of Nos. 3917 and 3918.

Vladimír Suchánek (1933-2021), Stamp Designer — A1776

2023, Jan. 20 Litho. Perf. 11¾x11¼
3919 A1776 B multi   1.90   .95
No. 3919 sold for 21k on day of issue.

Nicolaus Copernicus (1473-1543), Astronomer — A1777

Perf. 11¼x11¾
2023, Feb. 15 Litho.
3920 A1777 B multi   2.10   1.10
No. 3920 sold for 23k on day of issue.

Zdenek Podskalsky (1923-93), Film Director — A1778

Perf. 11¼x11¾
2023, Feb. 15 Litho.
3921 A1778 B multi   2.10   1.10
No. 3921 sold for 23k on day of issue.

Easter — A1779

Serpentine Die Cut 11 Syncopated
2023, Feb. 15 Litho.
Self-Adhesive
3922 A1779 B multi   2.10   1.10
No. 3922 sold for 23k on day of issue.

Kozel Hunting Lodge, Sťáhlavy — A1780

2023, Feb. 15 Litho. Perf. 11¾
3923 A1780 E multi   3.75   1.90
No. 3923 sold for 39k on day of issue.

Bicycle with Hearts as Wheels — A1781

Perf. 11¾x11¼
2023, Mar. 15 Litho.
3924 A1781 B multi + label   2.25   1.10
No. 3924 was printed in sheets of 7 + 14 labels that could be personalized. On day of issue, No. 3924 had a franking value of 23k.

Jan Jansky (1873-1921), Neurologist and Serologist — A1782

Perf. 11¼x11¾
2023, Mar. 15 Litho.
3925 A1782 27k multi   2.50   1.25

Cesky Sternberk Castle, Cesky Sternberk — A1783

Litho. & Engr.
2023, Mar. 15 Perf. 11¾
3926 A1783 A multi   2.75   1.40
No. 3926 sold for 30k on day of issue.

Art Type of 1967 Inscribed "CESKA REPUBLIKA"

Design: The Soul, photograph by Frantisek Drtikol (1883-1961).

2023, Mar. 15 Litho. Perf. 11¾
3927 A565 34k multi   3.25   1.60

Souvenir Sheet

Buildings Designed by Jan Santini Aichel (1677-1723) — A1784

No. 3928: a, 27k, Chapel of St. Anne, Panenské Brezany. b, 31k, Rychnov nad Kneznou Castle, Rychnov nad Kneznou. c, 37k, Pilgrimage Church of St. John of Nepomuk, Zďár nad Sázavou.

2023, Apr. 5 Litho. Perf. 11¾
3928 A1784 Sheet of 3, #a-c   9.00   4.50

Souvenir Sheet

Dendrological Garden, Pruhonice — A1785

No. 3929: a, 27k, Branch from Blue Emperor variety of Korean fir tree (45x27mm). b, 31k, Doncaster variety of rhododendron (45x55mm). c, 34k, Virgata variety of snake spruce tree (45x55mm).

2023, Apr. 5 Litho. Perf. 13½x14
3929 A1785 Sheet of 3, #a-c   8.75   4.25

Radio Broadcasting in Czechoslovakia, Cent. — A1786

2023, May 9 Litho. Perf. 11¼x11¾
3930 A1786 30k multi   2.75   1.40

Europa — A1787

2023, May 9 Litho. Perf. 11¼
3931 A1787 E multi   3.50   1.75
No. 3931 sold for 39k on day of issue.

Porcelain Coffee Service by Jaroslav Jezek (1923-2002) — A1788

2023, May 17 Litho. Perf. 11¾x11¼
3932 A1788 B multi   2.10   1.10
No. 3932 sold for 23k on day of issue.

Souvenir Sheet

Baroque Murals — A1789

No. 3933: a, 38k, Mural by Carpoforo Tencalla (1623-85) from Kromeríz Castle. b, 44k, Mural by Isaac Godyn (c. 1660-c. 1712) from Troja Castle.

2023, May 17 Litho. Perf. 14x13½
3933 A1789 Sheet of 2, #a-b   7.50   3.75

Miniature Sheet

Pres. Petr Pavel — A1790

No. 3934 — Pavel and background color of: a, Gray. b, Orange. c, Dark red. d, Dark blue. e, Pink. f, Blue gray. g, Buff. h, Yellow. i, Light blue. j, Dark green.

Serpentine Die Cut 11x11¼ Syncopated
2023, June 7 Litho.
Self-Adhesive
3934 A1790 Sheet of 10   21.00
   a.-j.   B Any single   2.10   1.10
On day of issue, Nos. 3934a-3934j each sold for 23k.

CZECHOSLOVAKIA

Josef Jungmann (1773-1847), Lexicographer — A1791

2023, June 14   *Perf. 11¼x11¾*   Litho.
3935   A1791   B multi   2.10   1.10

No. 3935 sold for 23k on day of issue.

Jan Vesely (1923-2003), Cyclist — A1792

2023, June 14   *Perf. 11¼x11¾*   Litho.
3936   A1792   23k multi   2.10   1.10

Blaise Pascal (1623-62), Mathematician — A1793

2023, June 14   *Perf. 11¾x11¼*   Litho.
3937   A1793   27k multi   2.50   1.25

Actors — A1794

No. 3938: a, Libuse Safránková (1953-2021). b, Josef Abrhám (1939-2022).

2023, June 14   Litho.   *Perf. 14x13½*
3938   A1794   34k Vert. pair, #a-b   6.25   3.00

Spa, Frantiskovy Lázně — A1795

2023, Sept. 6   Litho.   *Perf. 11¾x11¼*
3939   A1795   B multi   2.40   1.25

No. 3939 sold for 27k on day of issue.

Myron's Discobolus — A1796

2023, Sept. 6   Litho.   *Perf. 11¼x11¾*
3940   A1796   B multi + label   2.40   1.25

No. 3940 was printed in sheets of 7 + 14 labels that could be personalized. On day of issue, No. 3940 had a franking value of 27k.

Poppy Doll and Emanuel the Butterfly — A1797

Serpentine Die Cut 11¼ Syncopated
2023, Sept. 6   Litho.
Booklet Stamp
Self-Adhesive
3941   A1797   B multi   2.40   1.25
   a.   Booklet pane of 10   24.00

No. 3941 sold for 27k on day of issue.

Miniature Sheet

Flora and Fauna of Podyjí National Park — A1798

No. 3942: a, 27k, Verbascum phoeniceum, Parnassius mnemosyne (27x45mm). b, 31k, Spermophilus citellus (27x45mm). c, 34k, Dictamnus albus, grapes and Sobes Vineyard (55x45mm). d, 38k, Ciconia nigra (55x45mm).

2023, Sept. 6   Litho. & Engr.   *Perf. 11¾*
3942   A1798   Sheet of 4, #a-d, + 4 labels   11.50   5.75

Miniature Sheet

Characters From Plays by William Shakespeare (1564-1616) — A1799

No. 3943: a, E, Queen (40x50mm). b, E, Elf (40x30mm). c, Z, Lute player (40x50mm). d, Z, Jester (40x30mm).

2023, Sept. 6   Litho.   *Perf. 12*
3943   A1799   Sheet of 4, #a-d, + label   16.50   8.25

On day of issue, Nos. 3943a-3493b each sold for 44k, and Nos. 3943c-3943d each sold for 50k.

Souvenir Sheet

Carrier Pigeon With Letter — A1800

2023, Oct. 2   Litho. & Engr.   *Perf. 11¾*
3944   A1800   63k multi + 2 labels   5.75   3.00

Establishment of Czech Post, 30th anniv. See Slovakia No. 942.

Fritillary Butterfly — A1801

2023, Oct. 18   Litho.   *Perf. 11¼x11¾*
3945   A1801   5k multi   .45   .30

Palacky University, Olomouc, 450th Anniv. — A1802

2023, Oct. 18   Litho.   *Perf. 11¾x11¼*
3946   A1802   B multi   2.40   1.25

No. 3946 sold for 27k on day of issue.

Souvenir Sheet

Airship and Frantisek Behounek (1898-1973), Arctic Explorer — A1803

2023, Oct. 18   Litho. & Engr.   *Perf. 11¾*
3947   A1803   72k multi   6.25   3.25

Painting From Venus Series, by Ladislav Sutnar (1897-1976) — A1804

After the Show, Painting by Toyen (1902-80) — A1805

2023, Nov. 8   Litho.   *Perf. 13½x14*
3948   A1804   34k multi   3.00   1.50
3949   A1805   44k multi   4.00   2.00

Mythical Greek Figure and Zdenek Mézl (1934-2016), Stamp Designer — A1806

2024, Jan. 20   Litho.   *Perf. 11¾x11¼*
3950   A1806   B multi   2.40   1.25

No. 3950 sold for 27k on day of issue.

Josef Suk (1874-1935), Composer and Violinist — A1807

2024, Jan. 20   Litho.   *Perf. 11¾x11¼*
3951   A1807   31k multi   2.75   1.40

SEMI-POSTAL STAMPS

Nos. B1-B123 were sold at 1½ times face value at the Philatelists' Window of the Prague P.O. for charity benefit. They were available for ordinary postage.

Almost all stamps between Nos. B1-B123 are known with misplaced or inverted overprints and/or in pairs with one stamp missing the overprint.

The overprints of Nos. B1-B123 have been well forged.

Austrian Stamps of 1916-18 Overprinted in Black or Blue — a

Two sizes of type A40:
Type I: 25x30mm.
Type II: 26x29mm.

1919   *Perf. 12½*

B1	A37	3h brt violet	.25	.25
B2	A37	5h lt green	.25	.25
B3	A37	6h dp orange (Bl)	.50	.70
B4	A37	6h dp orange (Bk)	3,250.	2,500.
B5	A37	10h magenta	1.00	.85
B6	A37	12h lt blue	.70	.70
B7	A42	15h dull red	.35	.35
B8	A42	20h dark green	.35	.35
a.		20h green	55.00	40.00
B9	A42	25h blue	.30	.25
B10	A42	30h dull violet	.30	.25
B11	A39	40h olive grn	.35	.35
B12	A39	50h dk green	.35	.35
B13	A39	60h dp blue	.35	.35
B14	A39	80h orange brn	.35	.35
B15	A39	90h red violet	.70	.70
B16	A39	1k car, *yel* (Bl)	.50	.50
B17	A39	1k car, *yel* (Bk)	52.50	52.50
B18	A40	2k light blue (I)	3.00	3.00
a.		2k dark blue (II)	5,000.	3,500.
B19	A40	3k car rose (I)	32.50	32.50
a.		3k claret (I)	3,750.	1,500.
B20	A40	4k yellow grn (I)	27.50	21.00
a.		4k deep green (I)	55.00	45.00
B21	A40	10k violet	300.00	160.00
a.		10k deep violet	375.00	275.00
b.		10k black violet	450.00	300.00

The used value of No. B18a is for a stamp that has only a Czechoslovakian cancellation. Some examples of Austria No. 160, which were officially overprinted with type "a" and sold by the post office, had previously been used and lightly canceled with Austrian cancellations. These canceled-before-overprinting stamps, which were postally valid, sell for about one-fourth as much.

Granite Paper

B22	A40	2k light blue	3.50	2.50
B23	A40	3k carmine rose	9.00	7.00

The 4k and 10k on granite paper with this overprint were not regularly issued.

Excellent counterfeits of Nos. B1-B23 exist.

Austrian Newspaper Stamps Overprinted — b

Imperf
On Stamp of 1908

B26	N8	10h carmine	3,500.	2,000.

On Stamps of 1916

B27	N9	2h brown	.25	.25
B28	N9	4h green	.35	.35
B29	N9	6h deep blue	.35	.35
B30	N9	10h orange	4.25	4.25
B31	N9	30h claret	1.40	1.40
		Nos. B27-B31 (5)	6.60	6.60

Austrian Special Handling Stamps Overprinted in Blue or Black — c

Perf. 12½
Stamps of 1916 Overprinted

B32	SH1	2h claret, *yel* (Bl)	25.00	25.00
B33	SH1	4h dp grn, *yel* (Bk)	800.00	700.00

Stamps of 1917 Overprinted — d

B34	SH2	2h cl, *yel* (Bl)	.25	.35
a.		Vert. pair, imperf. btwn.	250.00	
B35	SH2	2h cl, *yel* (Bk)	35.00	32.50
B36	SH2	5h grn, *yel* (Bk)	.25	.25

CZECHOSLOVAKIA

Austrian Air Post Stamps, #C1-C3, Overprinted Type "c" Diagonally

B37	A40	1.50k on 2k lil	90.00	70.00
B38	A40	2.50k on 3k ocher	110.00	90.00
B39	A40	4k gray	800.00	650.00

1919
Austrian Postage Due Stamps of 1908-13 Overprinted Type "b"

B40	D3	2h carmine	4,500.	2,750.
B41	D3	4h carmine	17.50	17.50
B42	D3	6h carmine	10.50	9.00
B43	D3	14h carmine	35.00	32.50
B44	D3	25h carmine	30.00	30.00
B45	D3	30h carmine	325.00	250.00
B46	D3	50h carmine	650.00	650.00

Austria Nos. J49-J56 Overprinted Type "b"

B47	D4	5h rose red	.25	.30
B48	D4	10h rose red	.25	.30
B49	D4	15h rose red	.25	.30
B50	D4	20h rose red	1.75	1.75
B51	D4	25h rose red	1.75	1.75
B52	D4	30h rose red	.60	.60
B53	D4	40h rose red	1.75	1.75
B54	D4	50h rose red	300.00	250.00

Austria Nos. J57-J59 Overprinted Type "a"

B55	D5	1k ultra	10.50	9.00
B56	D5	5k ultra	21.00	21.00
B57	D5	10k ultra	225.00	200.00

Austria Nos. J47-J48, J60-J63 Overprinted Type "c" Diagonally

B58	A22	1h gray	20.00	16.00
B59	A23	15h on 2h vio	95.00	90.00
B60	A38	10h on 24h blue	80.00	70.00
B61	A38	15h on 36h vio	.35	.35
B62	A38	20h on 54h org	70.00	65.00
B63	A38	50h on 42h choc	.75	.75

Hungarian Stamps Ovptd. Type "b"
1919 Wmk. 137 Perf. 15
On Stamps of 1913-16

B64	A4	1f slate	2,200.	1,800.
B65	A4	2f yellow	5.25	4.50
B66	A4	3f orange	32.50	25.00
B67	A4	6f olive green	5.00	5.00
B68	A4	50f lake, *bl*	.90	.75
B69	A4	60f grn, *sal*	45.00	35.00
B70	A4	70f red brn, *grn*	2,250.	1,750.

On Stamps of 1916

B71	A8	10f rose	300.00	225.00
B72	A8	15f violet	150.00	100.00

On Stamps of 1916-18

B73	A9	2f brown orange	.25	.25
B74	A9	3f red lilac	.25	.25
B75	A9	5f green	.25	.25
B76	A9	6f grnsh blue	.50	.50
B77	A9	10f rose red	1.40	1.00
B78	A9	15f violet	.25	.25
B79	A9	20f gray brown	12.00	11.00
B80	A9	25f dull blue	.90	.70
B81	A9	35f brown	9.00	9.00
B82	A9	40f olive green	3.00	2.25

Overprinted Type "d"

B83	A10	50f red vio & lil	1.10	1.40
B84	A10	75f brt bl & pale bl	1.10	1.40
B85	A10	80f yel grn & pale grn	1.10	1.40
B86	A10	1k red brn & cl	2.10	2.00
B87	A10	2k ol brn & bls	9.00	9.00
B88	A10	3k dk vio & ind	37.50	35.00
B89	A10	5k dk brn & lt brn	90.00	60.00
B90	A10	10k vio brn & vio	1,300.	800.00

Overprinted Type "b"
On Stamps of 1918

B91	A11	10f scarlet	.25	.25
B92	A11	20f dark brown	.30	.30
B93	A11	25f deep blue	1.10	.75
B94	A12	40f olive grn	3.50	2.75
B95	A12	50f lilac	30.00	22.50

On Stamps of 1919

B96	A13	10f red	9.00	7.00
B97	A13	20f dk brn	6,500.	4,500.

Same Overprint On Hungarian Newspaper Stamp of 1914
Imperf

B98	N5	(2f) orange	.25	.25

Same Overprint On Hungarian Special Delivery Stamp
Perf. 15

B99	SD1	2f gray grn & red	.25	.25

Same Ovpt. On Hungarian Semi-Postal Stamps

B100	SP3	10f + 2f rose red	.70	.70
B101	SP4	15f + 2f violet	1.10	1.10
B102	SP5	40f + 2f brn car	3.50	3.50
		Nos. B98-B102 (5)	5.80	5.80

Hungarian Postage Due Stamps of 1903-18 Overprinted Type "b"
1919 Wmk. 135 Perf. 11½, 12

B103	D1	50f green & black	350.00	300.00

Wmk. Crown (136, 136a)
Perf. 11½x12, 15

B104	D1	1f green & black	1,200.	1,000.
B105	D1	2f green & black	750.00	650.00
B106	D1	12f green & black	4,250.	3,500.
B107	D1	50f green & black	275.	150.

Wmk. Double Cross (137)
Perf. 15
On Stamps of 1914

B110	D1	1f green & black	1,250.	600.
B111	D1	2f green & black	700.	550.
B112	D1	5f green & black	1,325.	900.
B113	D1	12f green & black	5,250.	4,000.
B114	D1	50f green & black	275.	150.

On Stamps of 1915-18

B115	D1	1f green & red	125.00	100.00
B116	D1	2f green & red	.75	.75
B117	D1	5f green & red	12.50	10.00
B118	D1	6f green & red	2.00	2.00
B119	D1	10f green & red	.50	.50
		a. Pair, one without overprint		
B120	D1	12f green & red	2.00	2.00
B121	D1	15f green & red	5.00	4.50
B122	D1	20f green & red	1.25	1.25
B123	D1	30f green & red	40.00	35.00
		Nos. B115-B123 (9)	189.00	156.00

Excellent counterfeits of Nos. B1-B123 exist.

Bohemian Lion Breaking its Chains — SP1

Mother and Child — SP2

Perf. 11½, 13¾ and Compound
1919 Typo. Unwmk.
Pinkish Paper

B124	SP1	15h gray green	.25	.25
		a. 15h light green	32.50	25.00
B125	SP1	25h dark brown	.25	.25
		a. 25h light brown	5.00	4.00
B126	SP1	50h dark blue	.25	.25

Photo.
Yellowish Paper

B127	SP2	75h slate	.25	.25
B128	SP2	100h brn vio	.25	.25
B129	SP2	120h vio, *yel*	.25	.25
		Nos. B124-B129 (6)	1.50	1.50

Values are for perf 13¾. Other perfs are valued higher.
Nos. B124-B126 commemorate the 1st anniv. of Czechoslovak independence. Nos. B127-B129 were sold for the benefit of Legionnaires' orphans. Imperforates exist.
See No. 1581.

Regular Issues of Czechoslovakia Surcharged in Red

a   b

1920 Perf. 13¾

B130	A1(a)	40h + 20h bister	.75	1.00
B131	A2(a)	60h + 20h green	.75	1.00
B132	A4(b)	125h + 25h gray bl	3.25	2.75
		Nos. B130-B132 (3)	4.75	4.75
		Set, never hinged	12.00	

President Masaryk — SP3

Wmk. Linden Leaves (107)
1923 Engr. Perf. 13¾x13¾

B133	SP3	50h gray green	.60	.40
B134	SP3	100h carmine	1.10	.75
B135	SP3	200h blue	3.25	2.50
B136	SP3	300h dark brown	3.25	3.50
		Nos. B133-B136 (4)	8.20	7.15
		Set, never hinged	15.00	

5th anniv. of the Republic.
The gum was applied through a screen and shows the monogram "CSP" (Ceskoslovenska Posta). These stamps were sold at double their face values, the excess being given to the Red Cross and other charitable organizations.

International Olympic Congress Issue

Semi-Postal Stamps of 1923 Overprinted in Blue or Red

1925

B137	SP3	50h gray green	5.50	7.50
B138	SP3	100h carmine	7.00	12.00
B139	SP3	200h blue (R)	35.00	45.00
		Nos. B137-B139 (3)	47.50	64.50
		Set, never hinged	120.00	

These stamps were sold at double their face values, the excess being divided between a fund for post office clerks and the Olympic Games Committee.

Sokol Issue

Semi-Postal Stamps of 1923 Overprinted in Blue or Red

1926

B140	SP3	50h gray green	1.60	4.00
B141	SP3	100h carmine	3.25	4.00
B142	SP3	200h blue (R)	10.00	11.00
		a. Double overprint		
B143	SP3	300h dk brn (R)	20.00	15.00
		Nos. B140-B143 (4)	34.85	34.00
		Set, never hinged	100.00	

These stamps were sold at double their face values, the excess being given to the Congress of Sokols, June, 1926.

Catalogue values for unused stamps in this section, from this point to the end of the section, are for Never Hinged items.

Midwife Presenting Newborn Child to its Father; after a Painting by Josef Manes
SP4   SP5

1936 Unwmk. Engr. Perf. 12½

B144	SP4	50h + 50h green	.50	.35
B145	SP5	1k + 50h claret	1.00	.60
B146	SP4	2k + 50h blue	2.50	1.25
		Nos. B144-B146 (3)	4.00	2.20

Nos. B144-B146 were each issued in sheets of 100 with 12 labels. Value, set $40.

SP6

"Lullaby" by Stanislav Sucharda — SP7

1937 Perf. 12½

B147	SP6	50h + 50h dull green	.50	.25
B148	SP6	1k + 50h rose lake	1.00	.60
B149	SP7	2k + 1k dull blue	2.50	1.25
		Nos. B147-B149 (3)	4.00	2.10

Nos. B147-B149 were each issued in sheets of 100 with 12 labels. Value, set of singles with attached labels hinged mint $5; used $5.

President Masaryk and Little Girl in Native Costume — SP8

1938 Perf. 12½

B150	SP8	50h + 50h deep green	.75	.50
B151	SP8	1k + 50h rose lake	.70	.55

Souvenir Sheet
Imperf

B152	SP8	2k + 3k black	4.25	5.00

88th anniv. of the birth of Masaryk (1850-1937).
Nos. B150-B151 were each issued in sheets of 100 stamps and 12 blank labels. Value, set of singles with attached labels: mint $4; used $3.

Allegory of the Republic Type
Souvenir Sheet
1938 Perf. 12½

B153	A89	2k (+ 8k) dark blue	3.00	3.50

The surtax was devoted to national relief for refugees.

"Republic" and Congress Emblem — SP10

1945 Engr.

B154	SP10	1.50k + 1.50k car rose	.25	.25
B155	SP10	2.50k + 2.50k blue	.25	.25

Students' World Cong., Prague, 11/17/45.

St. George Slaying the Dragon — SP11

1946

B156	SP11	2.40k + 2.60k car rose	.25	.25
B157	SP11	4k + 6k blue	.25	.25

Souvenir Sheet
Imperf

B158	SP11	4k + 6k blue	1.50	1.50

1st anniv. of Czechoslovakia's liberation.
Nos. B156-B157 were each issued in sheets of 100 stamps and 12 inscribed labels. Value for set of singles with attached labels, mint or used $3.50.

Old Town Hall Type of 1946
Souvenir Sheet

1946, Aug. 3 Imperf.

B159	A114	2.40k rose brown	1.10	.75

Brno Natl. Stamp Exhib., Aug., 1946.
The sheet was sold for 10k.

"You Went Away" — SP14

"You Remained Ours" — SP15

CZECHOSLOVAKIA

"You Came Back" — SP16

1946, Oct. 28 Photo. Perf. 14
B160 SP14 1.60k + 1.40k red brn .35 .35
B161 SP15 2.40k + 2.60k scarlet .35 .35
B162 SP16 4k + 4k deep blue .70 .70
  Nos. B160-B162 (3) 1.40 1.40

The surtax was for repatriated Slovaks.

Barefoot Boy — SP17

2k+1k, Mother and child. 3k+1k, Little girl.

Perf. 12½
1948, Dec. 18 Unwmk. Engr.
B163 SP17 1.50k + 1k rose lilac .45 .25
B164 SP17 2k + 1k dp blue .25 .25
B165 SP17 3k + 1k rose car .35 .25
  Nos. B163-B165 (3) 1.05 .75

The surtax was for child welfare.
Nos. B163-B165 were each issued in sheets of 100 stamps and 12 inscribed labels. Value for set of singles with attached labels: mint $3; used $2.

Woman and Child — SP18

Design: 3k+1k, Man lifting child.

1949, Dec. 18 Perf. 12½
B166 SP18 1.50k + 50h gray 4.75 1.90
B167 SP18 3k + 1k claret 7.00 2.75

The surtax was for child welfare.

SP19

Dove Carrying Olive Branch — SP20

1949, Dec. 18
B168 SP19 1.50k + 50h claret 4.50 1.50
B169 SP20 3k + 1k rose red 4.50 1.50

The surtax was for the Red Cross.

AIR POST STAMPS

Nos. 9, 39-40, 20, and Types of 1919 Srchd. in Red, Blue or Green

1920 Unwmk. Imperf.
C1 A1 14k on 200h (R) 15.00 12.00
  a. Inverted surcharge 125.00
C2 A2 24k on 500h (Bl) 40.00 25.00
  a. Inverted surcharge 225.00
C3 A2 28k on 1000h (G) 25.00 20.00
  a. Inverted surcharge 150.00
  b. Double surcharge 200.00
  Nos. C1-C3 (3) 80.00 57.00

Perf. 13¾
C4 A1 14k on 200h (R) 22.50 22.50
  a. Perf. 13¾x13½ 150.00 95.00

C5 A2 24k on 500h (Bl) 45.00 70.00
  a. Perf. 13¾x13½ 150.00 75.00

Perf. 13¾x13½
C6 A2 28k on 1000h (G) 20.00 17.50
  a. Inverted surcharge 400.00 —
  b. Perf. 13¾ 475.00 475.00
  c. As "b," invtd. surcharge 350.00
  Nos. C4-C6 (3) 87.50 110.00
  Nos. C1-C6 (6) 167.50 167.00

Excellent counterfeits of the overprint are known.

Stamps of 1920 Srchd. in Black or Violet

1922, June 15 Perf. 13¾
C7 A8 50h on 100h dl grn 1.75 1.50
  a. Inverted surcharge 150.00
  b. Double surcharge 160.00
C8 A8 100h on 200h vio 3.50 2.25
  a. Inverted surcharge 150.00
C9 A8 250h on 400h brn (V) 5.00 3.50
  a. Inverted surcharge 275.00
  Nos. C7-C9 (3) 10.25 7.25
  Set, never hinged 20.00

Fokker Monoplane AP3

Smolik S 19 AP4

Smolik S 19 — AP5

Fokker over Prague — AP6

1930, Dec. 16 Engr. Perf. 13½
C10 AP3 50h deep green .25 .25
C11 AP3 1k deep red .25 .45
C12 AP4 2k dark green .40 .90
C13 AP4 3k red violet .85 1.10
C14 AP5 4k indigo .75 1.10
C15 AP5 5k red brown 1.75 3.50
C16 AP6 10k vio blue 3.00 3.50
  a. 10k ultra 8.50 10.00
C17 AP6 20k gray violet 3.00 4.50
  Nos. C10-C17 (8) 10.25 15.30
  Set, never hinged 17.50

Two types exist of the 50h, 1k and 2k, and three types of the 3k, differing chiefly in the size of the printed area. A "no hill at left" variety of the 3k exists.
Imperf. examples of Nos. C10-C17 are proofs.
See Bohemia and Moravia No. C1.

Perf. 12
C10a AP3 50h deep green 2.50 4.50
C11a AP3 1k deep red 13.00 22.50
C12a AP4 2k dark green 13.00 22.50
C14a AP5 4k indigo 2.00 3.50
C17a AP6 20k gray violet 3.00 7.00

Perf. 12x13½, 13½x12
C11b AP3 1k deep red 6.50
C12b AP4 2k dark green 10.00 15.00

Perf. 13¾x12¼
C17b AP6 20k gray violet 1,750.

Perf. 12½
C15a AP5 5k red brown 2,000.

> Catalogue values for unused stamps in this section, from this point to the end of the section, are for Never Hinged items.

Capt. Frantisek Novak AP7

Plane over Bratislava Castle AP8

Plane over Charles Bridge, Prague — AP9

1946-47 Perf. 12½
C19 AP7 1.50k rose red .25 .25
C20 AP7 5.50k dk gray bl .50 .25
C21 AP7 9k sepia ('47) .85 .25
C22 AP7 10k dl grn .85 .25
C23 AP7 16k violet 1.50 .60
C24 AP8 20k light blue 1.60 1.10
C25 AP8 24k dk bl, cr 1.00 .65
C26 AP9 24k rose lake 1.75 1.00
C27 AP9 50k dk gray bl 3.25 2.60
  Nos. C19-C27 (9) 11.55 7.05

No. C25 was issued June 12, 1946, for use on the first Prague-New York flight.
Nos. C22, C24-C27 were each issued in sheets of 100 stamps and 12 labels depicting airplane over globe. Values for singles with attached labels (mint/used): C22, $2/$1.50; C24, $4/$3; C25, $7.50/$4; C26, $5.50/$4.50; C27, $9/$7.50.

Nos. C19-C24, C26-C27 Surcharged with New Value and Bars in Various Colors

1949, Sept. 1 Perf. 12½
C28 AP7 1k on 1.50k (Bl) .25 .25
C29 AP7 3k on 5.50k (C) .35 .25
C30 AP7 6k on 9k (Br) .55 .25
C31 AP7 7.50k on 16k (C) .75 .25
C32 AP8 8k on 10k (G) .75 .75
C33 AP8 12.50k on 20k (Bl) 1.10 .55
C34 AP9 15k on 24k rose lake (Bl) 2.75 1.00
C35 AP9 30k on 50k (Bl) 2.00 .90
  Nos. C28-C35 (8) 8.50 4.20

Karlovy Vary (Karlsbad) — AP10

1951, Apr. 2 Engr. Perf. 13½
C36 AP10 6k shown 3.50 1.75
C37 AP10 10k Piestany 3.50 1.75
C38 AP10 15k Marienbad 6.00 1.75
C39 AP10 20k Silac 9.50 4.50
  Nos. C36-C39 (4) 22.50 9.75

Nos. C36-C39 were each issued in a sheet of 10 stamps. Value, set $950.

View of Cesky Krumlov AP11

1955 Cream Paper Perf. 11½
C40 AP11 80h olive green 1.00 .25
C41 AP11 1.55k violet brn 1.40 .45
C42 AP11 2.35k violet blue 1.90 .25
C43 AP11 2.75k rose brown 2.75 .45
C44 AP11 10k indigo 5.50 2.75
  Nos. C40-C44 (5) 12.55 4.15

Issue dates: 10k, Feb. 20. Others, Mar. 28.

Airline: Moscow-Prague-Paris — AP12

2.35k, Airline: Prague-Cairo-Beirut-Damascus.

Engraved and Photogravure
1957, Oct. 15 Unwmk. Perf. 11½
C45 AP12 75h ultra & rose 1.00 .25
C46 AP12 2.35k ultra & org yel 1.00 .30

Planes at First Czech Aviation School, Pardubice AP13

Design: 1.80k, Jan Kaspar and flight of first Czech plane, 1909.

1959, Oct. 15
C47 AP13 1k gray & yel .25 .25
C48 AP13 1.80k blk & pale bl .75 .25

50th anniv. of Jan Kaspar's 1st flight Aug. 25, 1909, at Pardubice.

Mail Coach, Plane and Arms of Bratislava AP14

Design: 2.80k, Helicopter over Bratislava.

1960, Sept. 24 Unwmk. Perf. 11½
C49 AP14 1.60k dk bl & gray 1.50 .75
C50 AP14 2.80k grn & buff 1.75 1.10

Issued to publicize the National Stamp Exhibition, Bratislava, Sept. 24-Oct. 9.

AP15

Designs: 60h, Prague hails Gagarin. 1.80k, Gagarin, rocket and dove.

1961, June 22
C51 AP15 60h gray & car .30 .25
C52 AP15 1.80k gray & blue .45 .25

No. C51 commemorates Maj. Gagarin's visit to Prague, Apr. 28-29; No. C52 commemorates the first man in space, Yuri A. Gagarin, Apr. 12, 1961.

AP16

"PRAGA" emblem and: 80h, Dove & Nest of Eggs. 1.40k, Dove. 2.80k, Symbolic flower with five petals. 4.20k, Five leaves.

1962, May 14 Engr. Perf. 14
C53 AP16 80h multicolored .75 .35
C54 AP16 1.40k blk, dk red & bl 1.50 1.50
C55 AP16 2.80k multicolored 1.50 1.50
C56 AP16 4.20k multicolored 1.50 1.50
  Nos. C53-C56 (4) 5.25 4.85

PRAGA 1962 World Exhibition of Postage Stamps, Aug. 18-Sept. 2, 1962.
Nos. C53-C56 were each issued in sheets of 10. Value, set $85.

Vostok 5 and Lt. Col. Valeri Bykovski AP17

2.80k, Vostok VI & Lt. Valentina Tereshkova.

1963, June 26
C57 AP17 80h slate bl & pink 1.00 .35
C58 AP17 2.80k dl red brn & lt bl 1.75 .35

Space flights of Valeri Bykovski, June 14-19, and Valentina Tereshkova, first woman astronaut, June 16-19, 1963.

CZECHOSLOVAKIA

PRAGA 1962 Emblem, View of Prague and Plane — AP18

Designs: 60h, Istanbul '63 (Hagia Sophia). 1k, Philatec Paris 1964 (Ile de la Cité). 1.40k, WIPA 1965 (Belvedere Palace, Vienna). 1.60k, SIPEX 1966 (Capitol, Washington). 2k, Amphilex '67 (harbor and old town, Amsterdam). 5k, PRAGA 1968 (View of Prague).

Engraved and Photogravure
1967, Oct. 30 — Perf. 11½
Size: 30x50mm

C59	AP18	30h choc, yel & rose	.25	.25
C60	AP18	60h dk grn, yel & lil	.25	.25
C61	AP18	1k blk, brick red & lt bl	.35	.25
C62	AP18	1.40k vio, yel & dp org	.45	.25
C63	AP18	1.60k ind, tan & lil	.45	.25
C64	AP18	2k dk grn, org & red	.45	.25

Size: 40x50mm

C65	AP18	5k multi	2.50	1.60
		Nos. C59-C65 (7)	4.70	3.10

PRAGA 1968 World Stamp Exhibition, Prague, June 22-July 7, 1968. Nos. C59-C64 issued in sheets of 15 stamps and 15 bilingual labels. Values, set of singles with attached labels: mint $6.50; used $4.50. No. C65 issued in sheets of 4 stamps and one center label. Value $15.

Glider L-13 — AP19

Airplanes: 60h, Sports plane L-40. 80h, Aero taxi L-200. 1k, Crop-spraying plane Z-37. 1.60k, Aerobatics trainer Z-526. 2k, Jet trainer L-29.

1967, Dec. 11

C66	AP19	30h multi	.25	.25
C67	AP19	60h multi	.25	.25
C68	AP19	80h multi	.25	.25
C69	AP19	1k multi	.30	.25
C70	AP19	1.60k multi	.50	.25
C71	AP19	2k multi	1.60	.90
		Nos. C66-C71 (6)	3.15	2.15

Charles Bridge, Prague, and Balloon — AP20

Designs: 1k, Belvedere, fountain and early plane. 2k, Hradcany, Prague, and airship.

1968, Feb. 5 — Unwmk. Perf. 11½

C72	AP20	60h multicolored	.30	.25
C73	AP20	1k multicolored	.45	.25
C74	AP20	2k multicolored	.75	.30
		Nos. C72-C74 (3)	1.50	.85

PRAGA 1968 World Stamp Exhibition, Prague, June 22-July 7, 1968. Nos. C72-C74 were each issued in a sheet of 10 stamps. Value, set $24.

Astronaut, Moon and Manhattan — AP21

Design: 3k, Lunar landing module and J. F. Kennedy Airport, New York.

1969, July 21

C75	AP21	60h blk, vio, yel & sil	.40	.25
C76	AP21	3k blk, bl, ocher & sil	1.60	.25

Man's 1st landing on the moon, July 20, 1969, US astronauts Neil A. Armstrong and Col. Edwin E. Aldrin, Jr., with Lieut. Col. Michael Collins piloting Apollo 11.

Nos. C75-C76 printed with label inscribed with names of astronauts and European date of moon landing. Values for pair of singles with attached labels: mint $3; used $1.

TU-104A over Bitov Castle — AP22

Designs: 60h, IL-62 over Bezdez Castle. 1.40k, TU-13A over Orava Castle. 1.90k, IL-18 over Veveri Castle. 2.40k, IL-14 over Pernstejn Castle. 3.60k, TU-154 over Trencin Castle.

1973, Oct. 24 — Engr. Perf. 11½

C77	AP22	30h multi	.25	.25
C78	AP22	60h multi	.25	.25
C79	AP22	1.40k multi	.25	.25
C80	AP22	1.90k multi	.40	.25
C81	AP22	2.40k multi	1.50	.75
C82	AP22	3.60k multi	.70	.25
		Nos. C77-C82 (6)	3.35	2.00

50 years of Czechoslovakian aviation. Nos. C77-C82 were each printed in sheets of 10. Values, set: mint $50; used $25.

Old Water Tower and Manes Hall — AP23

Designs: Praga 1978 Emblem, Plane Silhouette and: 1.60k, Congress Hall. 2k, Powder Tower, vert. 2.40k, Charles Bridge and Old Town Tower. 4k, Old Town Hall on Old Town Square, vert. 6k, Prague Castle and St. Vitus' Cathedral, vert.

Engraved and Photogravure
1976, June 23 — Perf. 11½

C83	AP23	60h ind & multi	.25	.25
C84	AP23	1.60k ind & multi	.25	.25
C85	AP23	2k ind & multi	.35	.25
C86	AP23	2.40k ind & multi	.40	.25
C87	AP23	4k ind & multi	.80	.30
C88	AP23	6k ind & multi	2.00	.80
		Nos. C83-C88 (6)	4.05	2.10

PRAGA 1978 International Philatelic Exhibition, Prague, Sept. 8-17, 1978.

Zeppelin, 1909 and 1928 — AP24

PRAGA '78 Emblem and: 1k, Ader, 1890, L'Eole & Dunn, 1914. 1.60k, Jeffries-Blanchard balloon, 1785. 2k, Otto Lilienthal's glider, 1896. 4.40k, Jan Kaspar's plane, Pardubice, 1911.

1977, Sept. 15 — Perf. 11½

C89	AP24	60h multi	.25	.25
C90	AP24	1k multi	.30	.25
C91	AP24	1.60k multi	.35	.25
C92	AP24	2k multi	.45	.25
C93	AP24	4.40k multi	2.25	.50
		Nos. C89-C93 (5)	3.60	1.50

History of aviation.
Nos. C89-C93 were each issued in sheets of 30 stamps, 15 labels depicting the exhibition emblem, and 5 blank labels. Values for set of singles with attached inscribed labels: mint $5; used $2.50.

SPECIAL DELIVERY STAMPS

Doves — SD1

1919-20 — Unwmk. Typo. Imperf.

E1	SD1	2h red vio, yel	.25	.25
E2	SD1	5h yel grn, yel	.25	.25
E3	SD1	10h red brn, yel ('20)	.75	.75
		Nos. E1-E3 (3)	1.25	1.25

For overprints and surcharge see Nos. P11-P13, Eastern Silesia E1-E2.

1921 — White Paper

E1a	SD1	2h red violet	9.00
E2a	SD1	5h yellow green	6.00
E3a	SD1	10h red brown	140.00
		Nos. E1a-E3a (3)	155.00

It is doubted that Nos. E1a-E3a were regularly issued.

PERSONAL DELIVERY STAMPS

Catalogue values for unused stamps in this section are for Never Hinged items.

PD1

Design: No. EX2, "D" in each corner.

1937 — Unwmk. Photo. Perf. 13½

EX1	PD1	50h blue	.25	.25
EX2	PD1	50h carmine	.25	.25

PD3

1946 — Perf. 13½

EX3	PD3	2k deep blue	.50	.75

POSTAGE DUE STAMPS

D1

1918-20 — Unwmk. Typo. Imperf.

J1	D1	5h deep bister	.25	.25
J2	D1	10h deep bister	.25	.25
J3	D1	15h deep bister	.25	.25
J4	D1	20h deep bister	.30	.25
J5	D1	25h deep bister	.45	.25
J6	D1	30h deep bister	.45	.25
J7	D1	40h deep bister	.60	.25
J8	D1	50h deep bister	.75	.25
J9	D1	100h blk brn	1.50	.25
J10	D1	250h orange	11.00	1.40
J11	D1	400h scarlet	15.00	1.40
J12	D1	500h gray grn	7.50	.25
J13	D1	1000h purple	7.50	.25
J14	D1	2000h dark blue	22.50	.60
		Nos. J1-J14 (14)	68.30	6.15

For surcharges and overprints see Nos. J32-J41, J57, Eastern Silesia J1-J11.

Nos. 1, 33-34, 10 Surcharged in Blue

1922

J15	A1	20h on 3h red vio	.30	.25
J16	A2	50h on 75h slate	1.50	.25
J17	A2	60h on 80h olive grn	.80	.25
J18	A2	100h on 80h olive grn	3.00	.25
J19	A1	200h on 400h purple	4.00	.25
		Nos. J15-J19 (5)	9.60	1.25

Same Surcharge on Nos. 1, 10, 30-31, 33-34, 36, 40 in Violet

1923-26

J20	A1	10h on 3h red vio	.25	.25
J21	A1	20h on 3h red vio	.30	.25
J22	A1	30h on 3h red vio	.25	.25
J23	A1	40h on 3h red vio	.25	.25
J24	A2	50h on 75h slate	.25	.25
J25	A2	60h on 50h dk vio ('26)	4.00	1.25
J26	A2	60h on 50h dk bl ('26)	4.00	1.50
J27	A2	60h on 75h slate	.50	.25
J28	A2	100h on 80h ol grn	27.50	.25
J29	A2	100h on 120h gray blk	1.00	.25
J30	A1	100h on 400h pur ('26)	1.00	.25
J31	A2	100h on 400h dp vio ('26)	1.60	.25
		Nos. J20-J31 (12)	41.90	5.25

Postage Due Stamp of 1918-20 Surcharged in Violet

1924

J32	D1	50h on 400h scar	.90	.25
J33	D1	60h on 400h scar	3.25	.60
J34	D1	100h on 400h scar	2.00	.25
		Nos. J32-J34 (3)	6.15	1.10

Postage Due Stamps of 1918-20 Surcharged with New Values in Violet as in 1924

1925

J35	D1	10h on 5h bister	.25	.25
J36	D1	20h on 5h bister	.25	.25
J37	D1	30h on 15h bister	.25	.25
J38	D1	40h on 15h bister	.25	.25
J39	D1	50h on 250h org	1.10	.25
J40	D1	60h on 250h org	1.50	.60
J41	D1	100h on 250h org	2.25	.25
		Nos. J35-J41 (7)	5.85	2.10

Stamps of 1918-19 Surcharged with New Values in Violet as in 1922

1926 — Perf. 14, 11½

J42	A2	30h on 15h red	.50	.30
J43	A2	40h on 15h red	.50	.30

Surcharged in Violet

1926 — Perf. 14

J44	A8	30h on 100h dk grn	.25	.25
J45	A8	40h on 200h violet	.25	.25
J46	A8	40h on 300h ver	.95	.25
a.		Perf. 14x13½	60.00	
J47	A8	50h on 500h dp grn	.60	.25
a.		Perf. 14x13½	2.75	
J48	A8	60h on 400h brown	1.00	.25
J49	A8	100h on 600h dp vio	2.50	.25
a.		Perf. 14x13½	30.00	1.25
		Nos. J44-J49 (6)	5.45	1.00

Surcharged in Violet

1927

J50	A6	100h dark brown	.55	.25
a.		Perf. 13½	200.00	10.00

Surcharged in Violet

J51	A6	40h on 185h org	.25	.25
J52	A6	50h on 20h car	.25	.25
a.		50h on 50h carmine (error)	55,000.	

CZECHOSLOVAKIA

J53	A6	50h on 150h rose	.25	.25
a.		Perf. 13½	12.50	2.00
J54	A6	60h on 25h brown	.25	.25
J55	A6	60h on 185h orange	.55	.25
J56	A6	100h on 25h brown	.55	.25
		Nos. J50-J56 (7)	2.65	1.75

No. J52a is known only used.

No. J12 Surcharged in Deep Violet

1927 *Imperf.*
J57 D1 200h on 500h gray grn 8.00 2.50

Catalogue values for unused stamps in this section, from this point to the end of the section, are for Never Hinged items.

D5

1928 *Perf. 14x13½*

J58	D5	5h dark red	.25	.25
J59	D5	10h dark red	.25	.25
J60	D5	20h dark red	.25	.25
J61	D5	30h dark red	.25	.25
J62	D5	40h dark red	.25	.25
J63	D5	50h dark red	.25	.25
J64	D5	60h dark red	.25	.25
J65	D5	1k ultra	.25	.25
J66	D5	2k ultra	.50	.25
J67	D5	5k ultra	.75	.25
J68	D5	10k ultra	1.90	.25
J69	D5	20k ultra	3.75	.30
		Nos. J58-J69 (12)	8.90	3.05

D6

1946-48 *Photo.* *Perf. 14*

J70	D6	10h dark blue	.25	.25
J71	D6	20h dark blue	.25	.25
J72	D6	50h dark blue	.25	.25
J73	D6	1k carmine rose	.25	.25
J74	D6	1.20k carmine rose	.25	.25
J75	D6	1.50k carmine rose ('48)	.25	.25
J76	D6	1.60k carmine rose	.25	.25
J77	D6	2k carmine rose ('48)	.25	.25
J78	D6	2.40k carmine rose	.25	.25
J79	D6	3k carmine rose	.25	.25
J80	D6	5k carmine rose	.25	.25
J81	D6	6k carmine rose ('48)	.25	.25
		Nos. J70-J81 (12)	3.00	3.00

D7 D8

1954-55 *Engr.* *Perf. 12½, 11½*

J82	D7	5h gray green ('55)	.25	.25
J83	D7	10h gray green ('55)	.25	.25
J84	D7	30h gray green	.25	.25
J85	D7	50h gray green ('55)	.25	.25
J86	D7	60h gray green ('55)	.25	.25
J87	D7	95h gray green	.35	.25
J88	D8	1k violet	.35	.25
J89	D8	1.20k violet ('55)	.35	.25
J90	D8	1.50k violet	.70	.25
J91	D8	1.60k violet ('55)	.45	.25
J92	D8	2k violet	.85	.25
J93	D8	3k violet	1.10	.25
J94	D8	5k violet ('55)	1.40	.25
		Nos. J82-J94 (13)	6.80	3.25

Perf. 11½ stamps are from a 1963 printing which lacks the 95h, 1.60k, and 2k.

Stylized Flower — D9

Designs: Various stylized flowers.

Engraved and Photogravure
1971-72 *Perf. 11½*

J95	D9	10h vio bl & pink	.25	.25
J96	D9	20h vio & lt bl	.25	.25
J97	D9	30h emer & lil rose	.25	.25
J98	D9	60h pur & emer	.25	.25
J99	D9	80h org & vio bl	.25	.25
J100	D9	1k dk red & emer	.25	.25
J101	D9	1.20k grn & org	.25	.25
J102	D9	2k blue & red	.25	.25
J103	D9	3k blk & yel	.30	.25
J104	D9	4k brn & ultra	.45	.25
J105	D9	5.40k red & lilac	.60	.25
J106	D9	6k brick red & org	.75	.25
		Nos. J95-J106 (12)	4.10	3.00

All except 5.40k issued in 1972.

OFFICIAL STAMPS

Catalogue values for unused stamps in this section are for Never Hinged items.

Coat of Arms — O1

1945 *Unwmk.* *Litho.* *Perf. 10½x10*

O1	O1	50h dp slate grn	.25	.25
O2	O1	1k dp bl vio	.25	.25
O3	O1	1.20k plum	.25	.25
O4	O1	1.50k crimson rose	.25	.25
O5	O1	2.50k bright ultra	.25	.25
O6	O1	5k dk vio brn	.30	.25
O7	O1	8k rose pink	.30	.30
		Nos. O1-O7 (7)	1.85	1.80

Redrawn
1947 *Photo.* *Perf. 14*

O8	O1	60h red	.25	.25
O9	O1	80h dk olive grn	.25	.25
O10	O1	1k lilac gray	.25	.25
O11	O1	1.20k dp plum	.25	.25
O12	O1	2.40k car rose	.25	.25
O13	O1	4k brt ultra	.25	.25
O14	O1	5k dk vio brn	.25	.25
O15	O1	7.40k purple	.25	.25
		Nos. O8-O15 (8)	2.00	2.00

There are many minor changes in design, size of numerals, etc., of the redrawn stamps.

NEWSPAPER STAMPS

Windhover — N1

1918-20 *Unwmk.* *Typo.* *Imperf.*

P1	N1	2h gray green	.25	.25
P2	N1	5h green ('20)	.25	.25
a.		5h dark green	.40	.25
P3	N1	6h red	.30	.25
P4	N1	10h dull violet	.25	.25
P5	N1	20h blue	.25	.25
P6	N1	30h gray brown	.25	.25
P7	N1	50h orange ('20)	.30	.25
P8	N1	100h red brown ('20)	.40	.25
		Nos. P1-P8 (8)	2.25	2.00

Nos. P1-P8 exist privately perforated.
For surcharges and overprints see Nos. P9-P10, P14-P16, Eastern Silesia P1-P5.

Stamps of 1918-20 Surcharged in Violet

1925-26

P9	N1	5h on 2h gray green	.50	.40
P10	N1	5h on 6h red ('26)	.25	.40

Special Delivery Stamps of 1918-20 Overprinted in Violet

1926

P11	SD1	5h apple grn, yel	.25	.25
a.		5h dull green, yellow	.50	.40
P12	SD1	10h red brn, yel	.25	.25

With Additional Surcharge of New Value

P13	SD1	5h on 2h red vio, yel	.35	.35
		Nos. P11-P13 (3)	.85	.85

Catalogue values for unused stamps in this section, from this point to the end of the section, are for Never Hinged items.

Newspaper Stamps of 1918-20 Overprinted in Violet

1934

P14	N1	10h dull violet	.25	.25
P15	N1	20h blue	.25	.25
P16	N1	30h gray brown	.25	.25
		Nos. P14-P16 (3)	.75	.75

Overprinted for use by commercial firms only.

Carrier Pigeon — N2

1937 *Imperf.*

P17	N2	2h bister brown	.25	.25
P18	N2	5h dull blue	.25	.25
P19	N2	7h red orange	.25	.25
P20	N2	9h emerald	.25	.25
P21	N2	10h henna brown	.25	.25
P22	N2	12h ultra	.25	.25
P23	N2	20h dark green	.25	.25
P24	N2	50h dark brown	.25	.25
P25	N2	1k olive gray	.25	.25
		Nos. P17-P25 (9)	2.25	2.25

For overprint see Slovakia Nos. P1-P9.

Bratislava Philatelic Exhibition Issue
Souvenir Sheet

1937 *Imperf.*

P26	N2	10h henna brn, sheet of 25	4.00	4.00

Newspaper Delivery Boy — N4

1945 *Unwmk.* *Typo.* *Imperf.*

P27	N4	5h dull blue	.25	.25
P28	N4	10h red	.25	.25
P29	N4	15h emerald	.25	.25
P30	N4	20h dark slate green	.25	.25
P31	N4	25h bright red vio	.25	.25
P32	N4	30h ocher	.25	.25
P33	N4	40h red orange	.25	.25
P34	N4	50h brown red	.25	.25
P35	N4	1k slate gray	.25	.25
P36	N4	5k deep vio blue	.25	.25
		Nos. P27-P36 (10)	2.50	2.50

CZECHOSLOVAK LEGION POST

The Czechoslovak Legion in Siberia issued these stamps for use on its mail and that of local residents. Forgeries exist.

For more detailed listings of Czechoslovak Legion Post issues, see the *Classic Specialized Catalogue of Stamps and Covers*.

Russia No. 79 Overprinted

1918 *Typo.* *Perf. 14x14½*
A1 A15 10k dark blue 2,500.

No. A1 was sold for a few days in Chelyabinsk. It was withdrawn because of a spelling error ("CZESZKJA," instead of "CZESZKAJA").

This overprint was also applied to Russia Nos. 73-78, 80-81, 83-85, 119-121, 123 and 130-131. These were trial printings, never sold to the public, although favor-cancelled covers exist.

Urn and Cathedral at Irkutsk — A1

Armored Railroad Car — A2

Sentinel — A3

1919-20 *Litho.* *Imperf.*

1	A1	25k carmine	10.50	—
a.		Perf 11½ ('20)	15.00	—
2	A2	50k yellow green	10.50	—
a.		Perf 11½ ('20)	15.00	—
3	A3	1r red brown	19.00	—
a.		Perf 11½ ('20)	22.50	—

Originals of Nos. 1-3 and 1a-3a have a crackled yellow gum. Ungummed remainders, which were given a white gum, exist imperforate and perforated 11½ and 13¼. Value per set, $3.

Lion of Bohemia — A4

Two types: 1 — 6 points on star-like mace head at right of goblet; large saber handle; measures 20x25¼mm. 2 — 5 points on mace head; small saber handle; measures 19½x25mm.

Perce en Arc in Blue
1920 *Embossed*
4 A4 (25k) blue & rose 3.00 —

No. 4 Overprinted

1920
5 A4 (25k) bl & rose 10.00 —

Both types of No. 4 received overprint.

No. 5 Surcharged with New Values in Green

6	A4	2k bl & rose	35.00	
7	A4	3k bl & rose	35.00	
8	A4	5k bl & rose	35.00	
9	A4	10k bl & rose	35.00	
10	A4	15k bl & rose	35.00	
11	A4	25k bl & rose	35.00	
12	A4	35k bl & rose	35.00	
13	A4	50k bl & rose	35.00	
14	A4	1r bl & rose	35.00	
		Nos. 6-14 (9)	315.00	

CZECHOSLOVAKIA — BOHEMIA AND MORAVIA

BOHEMIA AND MORAVIA

Catalogue values for unused stamps in this country are for never hinged items, beginning with Scott 20 in the regular postage section, Scott B1 in the semi-postal section, Scott J1 in the postage due section, and Scott P1 in the newspaper section.

Castle at Zvikov — A2

Karlstein Castle — A3

Samson Fountain, Budweis — A15

Kromeriz — A16

Adolf Hitler — A21

Masaryk Type of Czechoslovakia with hyphen in "Cesko-Slovensko" — A60

1939, Apr. 23
1A A60 1k rose lake .25 .25

Prepared by Czechoslovakia prior to the German occupation March 15, 1939. Subsequently issued for use in Bohemia and Moravia.
See No. C1.

German Protectorate

Stamps of Czechoslovakia, 1928-39, Overprinted in Black

Perf. 10, 12½, 12x12½

1939, July 15 — Unwmk.
1	A29	5h dk ultra	.25	1.25
2	A29	10h brown	.25	1.25
3	A29	20h red	.25	1.25
4	A29	25h green	.25	1.25
5	A29	30h red vio	.25	1.25
6	A61a	40h dk bl	2.50	5.00
7	A85	50h dp grn	.25	1.25
8	A63	60h dl vio	2.50	5.00
9	A60	1k rose lake (#212)	.75	1.75
10	A60	1k rose lake	.30	1.25
11	A64	1.20k rose lilac	3.00	5.00
12	A65	1.50k carmine	3.00	5.75
13	A79	1.60k olive grn	5.00	5.75
a.	"Mähnen"		32.50	75.00
14	A66	2k dk bl grn	1.10	4.00
15	A67	2.50k dk bl	3.00	5.00
16	A68	3k brown	3.00	5.75
17	A70	4k dk vio	9.50	6.50
18	A71	5k green	5.50	10.00
19	A72	10k blue	5.50	5.00
	Nos. 1-19 (19)		46.15	83.25
	Set, never hinged		60.00	

The size of the overprint varies, Nos. 1-10 measure 17½x15½mm, Nos. 11-16 19x18mm, Nos. 17 and 19 28x17½mm and No. 18 23½x23mm.

Nos. 11-13 exist with the period missing after the contraction "u."

Catalogue values for unused stamps in this section, from this point to the end of the section, are for never hinged items.

Linden Leaves and Closed Buds — A1

1939-41 — Photo. — Perf. 14
20	A1	5h dark blue	.25	.25
21	A1	10h blk brn	.25	.40
22	A1	20h crimson	.25	.30
23	A1	25h dk bl grn	.25	.30
24	A1	30h dp plum	.25	.30
24A	A1	30h golden brn ('41)	.25	.30
25	A1	40h orange ('40)	.25	.25
26	A1	50h slate grn ('40)	.25	.35
	Nos. 20-26 (8)		2.00	2.40

See Nos. 49-51.

St. Barbara's Church, Kutna Hora — A4

Cathedral at Prague — A5

Brno Cathedral — A6

Town Square, Olomouc — A7

1939 — Engr. — Perf. 12½
27	A2	40h dark blue	.25	.30
28	A3	50h dk bl grn	.25	.30
29	A4	60h dl vio	.25	.30
30	A5	1k dp rose	.25	.30
31	A6	1.20k rose lilac	.25	.50
32	A6	1.50k rose car	.25	.30
33	A7	2k dk bl grn	.25	.45
34	A7	2.50k dark blue	.25	.30
	Nos. 27-34 (8)		2.00	2.75

No. 31 measures 23½x29½mm, No. 42 measures 18½x23mm.
See #52-53, 53B. For overprints see #60-61.

Zlin — A8

Iron Works at Moravská Ostrava — A9

Prague — A10

1939-40
35	A8	3k dl rose vio	.25	.30
36	A9	4k slate ('40)	.25	.40
37	A10	5k green	.45	.65
38	A10	10k lt ultra	.35	.75
39	A10	20k yel brn	1.00	1.50
	Nos. 35-39 (5)		2.30	3.60

Types of 1939 and

Neuhaus — A11

Pernstein Castle — A12

Pardubice Castle — A13

Lainsitz Bridge near Bechyne — A14

Wallenstein Palace, Prague — A17

1940 — Engr. — Perf. 12½
40	A11	50h dk bl grn	.25	.25
41	A12	80h dp bl	.25	.30
42	A6	1.20k vio brn	.30	.25
43	A13	2k gray grn	.25	.25
44	A14	5k dk bl grn	.25	.25
45	A15	6k brn vio	.25	.50
46	A16	8k slate grn	.25	.25
47	A17	10k blue	.45	.30
48	A10	20k sepia	.75	2.00
	Nos. 40-48 (9)		3.00	4.40

No. 42 measures 18½x23mm; No. 31, 23½x29½mm.

Types of 1939-40

1941
49	A1	60h violet	.25	.25
50	A1	80h red org	.25	.25
51	A1	1k brown	.25	.25
52	A5	1.20k rose red	.25	.25
53	A4	1.50k lil rose	.25	.25
53A	A13	2k light blue	.25	.25
53B	A6	2.50k ultra	.25	.25
53C	A12	3k olive	.25	.25
	Nos. 49-53C (8)		2.00	2.00

Nos. 49-51 show buds open. Nos. 52 and 53B measure 18¾x23½mm and have no inscriptions below design.
For overprints see Nos. 60-61.

Antonin Dvorák — A18

1941, Aug. 25 — Engr. — Perf. 12½
54	A18	60h dull lilac	.40	.50
55	A18	1.20k sepia	.40	.50

Antonin Dvorák (1841-1904), composer. Nos. 54-55 were issued in sheets of 50 stamps and 50 alternating inscribed labels. Value for set of singles with attached labels, unused or used, $1.25.

Farming Scene — A19

Factories — A20

1941, Sept. 7 — Photo. — Perf. 13½
56	A19	30h dk red brn	.25	.30
57	A19	60h dark green	.25	.30
58	A20	1.20k dk plum	.25	.30
59	A20	2.50k sapphire	.25	1.50
	Nos. 56-59 (4)		1.00	2.40

Issued to publicize the Prague Fair.

Nos. 52 and 53B Overprinted in Blue or Red

1942, Mar. 15 — Perf. 12½
60	A5	1.20k rose red (Bl)	.70	1.00
61	A6	2.50k ultra (R)	.70	1.00

3rd anniv. of the Protectorate of Bohemia and Moravia.

1942 — Photo. — Perf. 14
Size: 17½x21½mm
62	A21	10h gray blk	.25	.25
63	A21	30h bister brn	.25	.25
64	A21	40h slate blue	.25	.25
65	A21	50h slate grn	.25	.25
66	A21	60h purple	.25	.25
67	A21	80h org ver	.25	.25

Perf. 12½ — Engr.
Size: 18x21mm
68	A21	1k dl brn	.25	.25
69	A21	1.20k carmine	.25	.30
70	A21	1.50k claret	.25	.30
71	A21	1.60k Prus grn	.25	.30
72	A21	2k light blue	.25	.30
73	A21	2.40k fawn	.25	.30

Size: 18½x24mm
74	A21	2.50k ultra	.25	.30
75	A21	3k olive grn	.25	.30
76	A21	4k brt red vio	.25	.30
77	A21	5k myrtle grn	.25	.30
78	A21	6k claret brn	.25	.40
79	A21	8k indigo	.25	.40

Size: 23½x29¾mm
80	A21	10k dk gray grn	.25	.75
81	A21	20k gray vio	.50	.90
82	A21	30k red	.75	1.50
83	A21	50k deep blue	1.50	2.50
	Nos. 62-83 (22)		7.50	10.90

17th Century Messenger — A22

1943, Jan. 10 — Photo. — Perf. 13½
84	A22	60h dark rose violet	.40	.40

Stamp Day.

Scene from "Die Meistersinger" — A23

Richard Wagner — A24

Scene from "Siegfried" — A25

1943, May 22
85	A23	60h violet	.25	.25
86	A24	1.20k carmine rose	.25	.25
87	A25	2.50k deep ultra	.25	.25
	Nos. 85-87 (3)		.75	.75

Richard Wagner (1813-83).

St. Vitus' Cathedral, Prague — A26

1944, Nov. 21 — Engr. — Perf. 12½
88	A26	1.50k dull rose brn	.25	.25
89	A26	2.50k dull lilac blue	.25	.35

Adolf Hitler — A27

1944
90	A27	4.20k green	.50	.50

CZECHOSLOVAKIA — BOHEMIA AND MORAVIA

SEMI-POSTAL STAMPS

Catalogue values for unused stamps in this section are for never hinged items.

Nurse and Wounded Soldier — SP1

1940, June 29   Photo.   Unwmk.
B1   SP1   60h + 40h indigo   .35   .75
B2   SP1   1.20k + 80h deep plum   .35   .75

Surtax for German Red Cross.
Nos. B1-B2 were issued in sheets of 50 stamps and 50 alternating inscribed labels. Value for set of singles with attached labels: unused $4.50; used $4.

Red Cross Nurse and Patient — SP2

1941, Apr. 20   Perf. 13½
B3   SP2   60h + 40h indigo   .40   .75
B4   SP2   1.20k + 80h dp plum   .40   .75

Surtax for German Red Cross.
Nos. B3-B4 were issued in sheets of 50 stamps and 50 alternating inscribed labels. Value for set of singles with attached labels: unused $3.50; used $4.50.

Old Theater, Prague SP3   Mozart SP4

1941, Oct. 26
B5   SP3   30h + 30h brown   .25   .25
B6   SP3   60h + 60h Prus grn   .25   .25
B7   SP4   1.20k + 1.20k scar   .25   .25
B8   SP4   2.50k + 2.50k dk bl   .45   .45
   Nos. B5-B8 (4)   1.20   1.20

150th anniversary of Mozart's death.
Labels alternate with stamps in sheets of Nos. B5-B8. The labels with Nos. B5-B6 show two bars of Mozart's opera "Don Giovanni." Those with Nos. B7-B8 show Mozart's piano. Value for set of singles with attached labels: unused $2.50; used $3.50.

Adolf Hitler — SP5

1942, Apr. 20   Engr.   Perf. 12½
B9   SP5   30h + 20h dl brn vio   .25   .25
B10   SP5   60h + 40h dl grn   .25   .25
B11   SP5   1.20k + 80h dp claret   .25   .35
B12   SP5   2.50k + 1.50k dl bl   .40   .75
   Nos. B9-B12 (4)   1.15   1.60

Hitler's 53rd birthday.
Nos. B9-B12 were issued in sheets of 100 stamps and 12 blank labels. Value for set of singles with attached labels: unused $3; used $2.25.

Nurse and Soldier — SP6

1942, Sept. 4   Perf. 13½
B13   SP6   60h + 40h deep blue   .25   .25
B14   SP6   1.20(k) + 80(h) dp plum   .25   .25

The surtax aided the German Red Cross.

Emperor Charles IV SP7

Peter Parler SP8

John the Blind, King of Bohemia — SP9

1943, Jan. 29
B15   SP7   60h + 40h violet   .25   .25
B16   SP8   1.20k + 80h carmine   .25   .25
B17   SP9   2.50k + 1.50k vio bl   .25   .25
   Nos. B15-B17 (3)   .75   .75

The surtax was for the benefit of the German wartime winter relief.

Adolf Hitler — SP10

1943, Apr. 20   Engr.   Perf. 12½
B18   SP10   60h + 1.40k dl vio   .25   .45
B19   SP10   1.20k + 3.80k carmine   .25   .45

Hitler's 54th birthday.
Nos. B18-B19 were issued in sheets of 100 stamps and 12 blank labels. Value for set of singles with attached labels: unused $1.10; used $1.

Deathmask of Reinhard Heydrich — SP11

1943, May 28   Photo.   Perf. 13½
B20   SP11   60h + 4.40k black   .75   1.50

No. B20 exists in a souvenir sheet containing a single stamp. It was given to high Nazi officials attending a ceremony one year after Heydrich's assassination. Value $15,000.

Eagle and Red Cross — SP12

1943, Sept. 16   Perf. 13
B21   SP12   1.20k + 8.80k blk & car   .60   .35

The surtax aided the German Red Cross.

Native Costumes SP13

Nazi Emblem, Arms of Bohemia, Moravia SP14

1944, Mar. 15   Perf. 13½
B22   SP13   1.20(k) + 3.80(k) rose lake   .25   .25
B23   SP14   4.20(k) + 10.80(k) golden brn   .25   .25
B24   SP13   10k + 20k saph   .25   .25
   Nos. B22-B24 (3)   .75   .75

Fifth anniversary of protectorate.

Adolf Hitler — SP15

1944, Apr. 20
B25   SP15   60h + 1.40k olive blk   .30   .25
B26   SP15   1.20k + 3.80k slate grn   .30   .25

Bedrich Smetana — SP16

1944, May 12   Engr.   Perf. 12½
B27   SP16   60h + 1.40k dk gray grn   .25   .25
B28   SP16   1.20k + 3.80k brn car   .25   .25

Bedrich Smetana (1824-84), Czech composer and pianist.

AIR POST STAMP

Catalogue values for unused stamps in this section are for never hinged items.

Type of Czechoslovakia 1930 with hyphen in "Cesko-Slovensko"

Fokker Monoplane — AP3

1939, Apr. 22   Perf. 13½
C1   AP3   30h rose lilac   1.60   .25

Prepared by Czechoslovakia prior to the German occupation March 15, 1939. Subsequently issued for use in Bohemia and Moravia. See No. 1A.

PERSONAL DELIVERY STAMPS

PD1

1939-40   Unwmk.   Photo.   Perf. 13½
EX1   PD1   50h indigo & blue ('40)   1.00   2.50
   Never hinged   2.25
EX2   PD1   50h carmine & rose   .60   3.00
   Never hinged   1.60

POSTAGE DUE STAMPS

Catalogue values for unused stamps in this section are for never hinged items.

D1

1939-40   Unwmk.   Typo.   Perf. 14
J1   D1   5h dark carmine   .25   .30
J2   D1   10h dark carmine   .25   .30
J3   D1   20h dark carmine   .25   .30
J4   D1   30h dark carmine   .25   .30
J5   D1   40h dark carmine   .25   .30
J6   D1   50h dark carmine   .25   .30
J7   D1   60h dark carmine   .25   .30
J8   D1   80h dark carmine   .25   .30
J9   D1   1k bright ultra   .25   .30
J10   D1   1.20k brt ultra ('40)   .30   .35
J11   D1   2k bright ultra   .80   1.00
J12   D1   5k bright ultra   1.00   1.40
J13   D1   10k bright ultra   1.75   1.75
J14   D1   20k bright ultra   3.50   3.50
   Nos. J1-J14 (14)   9.60   10.75

OFFICIAL STAMPS

Catalogue values for unused stamps in this section are for never hinged items.

Numeral — O1

1941, Jan. 1   Unwmk.   Typo.   Perf. 14
O1   O1   30h ocher   .25   .25
O2   O1   40h indigo   .25   .25
O3   O1   50h emerald   .25   .25
O4   O1   60h slate grn   .25   .25
O5   O1   80h org red   .65   .25
O6   O1   1k red brn   .35   .25
O7   O1   1.20k carmine   .35   .25
O8   O1   1.50k dp plum   .50   .25
O9   O1   2k brt bl   .50   .25
O10   O1   3k olive   .50   .25
O11   O1   4k red vio   .70   .40
O12   O1   5k org yel   1.60   .90
   Nos. O1-O12 (12)   6.15   3.80

Eagle — O2

1943, Feb. 15
O13   O2   30(h) bister   .25   .25
O14   O2   40(h) indigo   .25   .30
O15   O2   50(h) yel grn   .25   .30
O16   O2   60(h) dp vio   .25   .30
O17   O2   80(h) org red   .25   .30
O18   O2   1k chocolate   .25   .30
O19   O2   1.20(k) carmine   .25   .30
O20   O2   1.50(k) brn red   .25   .30
O21   O2   2k lt bl   .25   .30
O22   O2   3k olive   .25   .30
O23   O2   4k red vio   .25   .40
O24   O2   5k dk grn   .25   .40
   Nos. O13-O24 (12)   3.00   3.80

NEWSPAPER STAMPS

Catalogue values for unused stamps in this section are for never hinged items.

Carrier Pigeon — N1

1939   Unwmk.   Typo.   Imperf.
P1   N1   2h ocher   .25   .30
P2   N1   5h ultra   .25   .30
P3   N1   7h red orange   .25   .30
P4   N1   9h emerald   .25   .30
P5   N1   10h henna brown   .25   .30
P6   N1   12h dark ultra   .25   .30
P7   N1   20h dark green   .25   .30
P8   N1   50h red brown   .25   .30
P9   N1   1k greenish gray   .25   .80
   Nos. P1-P9 (9)   2.25   3.25

No. P5 Overprinted in Black

1940
P10   N1   10h henna brown   .45   .65

Overprinted for use by commercial firms.

N2

CZECHOSLOVAKIA — BOHEMIA AND MORAVIA — DAHOMEY

1943, Feb. 15

P11	N2	2(h) ocher	.25	.25
P12	N2	5(h) light blue	.25	.25
P13	N2	7(h) red orange	.25	.25
P14	N2	9(h) emerald	.25	.25
P15	N2	10(h) henna brown	.25	.25
P16	N2	12(h) dark ultra	.25	.25
P17	N2	20(h) dark green	.25	.25
P18	N2	50(h) red brown	.25	.25
P19	N2	1k slate green	.25	.25
		Nos. P11-P19 (9)	2.25	2.25

DAHOMEY
də-'hō-mē

LOCATION — West coast of Africa
AREA — 43,483 sq. mi.
POP. — 3,030,000 (est. 1974)
CAPITAL — Porto-Novo

Formerly a native kingdom including Benin, Dahomey was annexed by France in 1894. It became part of the colonial administrative unit of French West Africa in 1895. Stamps of French West Africa superseded those of Dahomey in 1945. The Republic of Dahomey was proclaimed Dec. 4, 1958.

The republic changed its name to the People's Republic of Benin on Nov. 30, 1975. See Benin for stamps issued after that date.

100 Centimes = 1 Franc

> Catalog values for unused stamps in this country are for Never Hinged items, beginning with Scott 137 in the regular postage section, Scott B15 in the semi-postal section, Scott C14 in the airpost section, Scott CQ1 in the airpost parcel post section, Scott J29 in the postage due section, and Scott Q1 in the parcel post section.

See French West Africa No. 71 for stamp inscribed "Dahomey" and "Afrique Occidentale Francaise."

Navigation and Commerce — A1

Perf. 14x13½

1899-1905 Typo. Unwmk.
Name of Colony in Blue or Carmine

1	A1	1c black, lil bl ('01)	1.00	.80
2	A1	2c brown, buff ('04)	1.60	.80
3	A1	4c claret, lav ('04)	2.40	2.40
4	A1	5c yellow grn ('04)	6.50	4.00
5	A1	10c red ('01)	6.00	.60
6	A1	15c gray ('01)	4.00	4.00
7	A1	20c red, grn ('04)	20.00	16.00
8	A1	25c black, rose ('99)	24.00	24.00
9	A1	25c blue ('01)	20.00	16.00
10	A1	30c brown, bis ('04)	24.00	12.00
11	A1	40c red, straw ('04)	24.00	16.00
12	A1	50c brn, az (name in red) ('01)	40.00	24.00
12A	A1	50c brn, az (name in bl) ('05)	32.50	24.00
13	A1	75c dp vio, org ('04)	85.00	55.00
14	A1	1fr brn, grn, straw ('04)	40.00	32.50
15	A1	2fr violet, rose ('04)	110.00	72.50
16	A1	5fr red lilac, lav ('04)	135.00	105.00
		Nos. 1-16 (17)	578.60	413.00

Perf. 13½x14 stamps are counterfeits.
For surcharges see Nos. 32-41.

Gen. Louis Faidherbe — A2

Oil Palm — A3

Dr. Noel Eugène Ballay — A4

1906-07   Perf. 13½x14
Name of Colony in Red or Blue

17	A2	1c slate	1.60	.80
18	A2	2c chocolate	2.40	.80
19	A2	4c choc, gray bl	4.00	3.25
20	A2	5c green	8.00	3.25
21	A2	10c carmine (B)	24.00	4.00
22	A3	20c black & red, azure	16.00	12.00
23	A3	25c blue, pnksh	16.00	16.00
24	A3	30c choc, pnksh	16.00	16.00
25	A3	35c black, yellow	87.50	12.00
26	A3	45c choc, grnsh ('07)	24.00	16.00
27	A3	50c dark violet	20.00	20.00
28	A3	75c blue, orange	24.00	24.00
29	A4	1fr black, azure	32.00	24.00
30	A4	2fr blue, pink	110.00	110.00
31	A4	5fr car, straw (B)	110.00	110.00
		Nos. 17-31 (15)	480.50	368.10

Nos. 2-3, 6-7, 9-13 Surcharged in Black or Carmine

Spacing between figures of surcharge 1.5mm (5c), 2mm (10c)

1912   Perf. 14x13½

32		5c on 2c brn, buff	2.00	2.40
33		5c on 4c claret, lav (C)	1.60	2.00
a.		Double surcharge	275.00	
34		5c on 15c gray (C)	2.00	2.40
35		5c on 20c red, grn	2.00	2.40
36		5c on 25c blue (C)	2.00	2.40
a.		Inverted surcharge	240.00	
37		5c on 30c brown, bis (C)	2.00	2.40
38		10c on 40c red, straw	2.00	2.40
a.		Inverted surcharge	325.00	
39		10c on 50c brn, az, name in bl (C)	2.40	2.75
40		10c on 50c brn, az, name in red (C)	1,125.	1,300.
41		10c on 75c violet, org	8.00	8.00
a.		Double surcharge	5,500.	
		Nos. 32-39,41 (9)	24.00	27.15

Two spacings between the surcharged numerals are found on Nos. 32 to 41. For detailed listings, see the Scott Classic Specialized Catalogue of Stamps and Covers.

Man Climbing Oil Palm — A5

1913-39   Perf. 13½x14

42	A5	1c violet & blk	.40	.30
43	A5	2c choc & rose	.40	.40
44	A5	4c black & brn	.40	.40
45	A5	5c yel grn & bl grn	1.20	.55
46	A5	5c vio brn & vio ('22)	.40	.80
47	A5	10c org red & rose	1.60	.80
a.		Half used as 5c on wrapper or printed matter	—	
48	A5	10c yel grn & bl grn ('22)	.80	.80
49	A5	10c red & ol ('25)	.40	.40
50	A5	15c brn org & dk vio ('17)	.80	.80
51	A5	20c gray & red brown	.80	.75
52	A5	20c bluish grn & grn ('26)	.40	.40
53	A5	20c mag & blk ('27)	.40	.40
54	A5	25c ultra & dp blue	2.00	1.60
55	A5	25c vio brn & org ('22)	1.20	.80
56	A5	30c choc & vio	2.75	2.40
57	A5	30c red org & rose ('22)	3.25	3.25
58	A5	30c yellow & vio ('25)	.40	.40
59	A5	30c dl grn & grn ('27)	.40	.40
60	A5	35c brown & blk	.80	.80
61	A5	35c bl grn & grn ('38)	.40	.30
62	A5	40c black & red org	.80	.80
63	A5	45c gray & ultra	.80	.80
64	A5	50c chocolate & brn	6.50	6.00
a.		Half used as 25c on cover		500.00
65	A5	50c ultra & bl ('22)	1.60	1.60
66	A5	50c brn red & bl ('26)	1.20	1.20
67	A5	55c gray grn & choc ('38)	.80	.55
68	A5	60c vio, pnksh ('25)	.40	.40
69	A5	65c yel brn & ol grn ('26)	1.20	1.20
70	A5	75c blue & violet	1.20	1.20
71	A5	80c henna brn & ultra ('38)	.40	.40
72	A5	85c dk bl & ver ('26)	1.60	1.60
73	A5	90c rose & brn red ('30)	.80	.80
74	A5	90c yel bis & red org ('39)	1.20	.80
75	A5	1fr blue grn & blk	1.20	1.20
76	A5	1fr dk bl & ultra ('26)	1.60	1.60
77	A5	1fr yel brn & lt red ('28)	1.60	1.20
78	A5	1fr dk red & red org ('38)	1.05	.95
79	A5	1.10fr vio & bis ('28)	5.50	6.00
80	A5	1.25fr dp bl & dk brn ('33)	17.50	7.25
81	A5	1.50fr dk bl & lt bl ('30)	1.60	.80
82	A5	1.75fr dk brn & dp buff ('33)	4.00	2.00
83	A5	1.75fr ind & ultra ('38)	1.60	.95
84	A5	2fr yel org & choc	1.20	1.60
85	A5	3fr red violet ('30)	2.40	1.75
86	A5	5fr violet & dp bl ('33)	2.40	2.75
		Nos. 42-86 (45)	79.35	62.15

The 1c gray and yellow green and 5c dull red and black are Togo Nos. 193a, 196a.

Nos. 47a and 64a were authorized for use in Paouignan during the last part of November 1921. Other values exist as bisects but were not authorized.

For surcharges see Nos. 87-96, B1, B8-B11.

Type of 1913 Surcharged

1922-25

87	A5	60c on 75c vio, pnksh	1.20	1.20
a.		Double surcharge	200.00	
88	A5	65c on 15c brn org & dk vio ('25)	2.00	2.00
89	A5	85c on 15c brn org & dk vio ('25)	2.00	2.00
		Nos. 87-89 (3)	5.20	5.20

Stamps and Type of 1913-39 Surcharged with New Value and Bars

1924-27

90	A5	25c on 2fr org & choc	1.20	1.20
91	A5	90c on 75c cer & brn red ('27)	2.00	2.00
92	A5	1.25fr on 1fr dk bl & ultra (R) ('26)	1.60	1.60
93	A5	1.50fr on 1fr dk bl & grnsh bl ('27)	2.75	2.75
94	A5	3fr on 5fr olvn & dp org ('27)	10.50	10.50
95	A5	10fr on 5fr bl vio & red brn ('27)	8.00	8.00
96	A5	20fr on 5fr vio & dl org ('27)	8.75	8.75
		Nos. 90-96 (7)	34.80	34.80

Common Design Types pictured following the introduction.

Colonial Exposition Issue
Common Design Types

1931   Engr.   Perf. 12½
Name of Country in Black

97	CD70	40c deep green	6.50	6.50
98	CD71	50c violet	6.50	6.50
99	CD72	90c red orange	6.50	6.50
100	CD73	1.50fr dull blue	6.50	6.50
		Nos. 97-100 (4)	26.00	26.00

Paris International Exposition Issue
Common Design Types

1937   Engr.   Perf. 13

101	CD74	20c deep violet	2.00	2.00
102	CD75	30c dark green	2.00	2.00
103	CD76	40c car rose	2.00	2.00
104	CD77	50c dark brown	1.60	1.60
105	CD78	90c red	1.60	1.60
106	CD79	1.50fr ultra	2.40	2.40
		Nos. 101-106 (6)	11.60	11.60

Souvenir Sheet
Imperf

107	CD77	3fr dp blue & blk	12.00	16.00
a.		Inscription inverted	1,600.	1,600.

Caillié Issue
Common Design Type

1939, Apr. 5   Engr.   Perf. 12½x12

108	CD81	90c org brn & org	.40	1.20
109	CD81	2fr brt violet	.40	1.20
110	CD81	2.25fr ultra & dk blue	.40	1.20
		Nos. 108-110 (3)	1.20	3.60

New York World's Fair Issue
Common Design Type

1939   Engr.

111	CD82	1.25fr car lake	.80	1.60
112	CD82	2.25fr ultra	.80	1.60

Man Poling a Canoe — A7

Pile House — A8

Sailboat on Lake Nokoué A9

Dahomey Warrior A10

1941   Perf. 13

113	A7	2c scarlet	.25	.25
114	A7	3c deep blue	.25	.25
115	A7	5c brown violet	.70	.70
116	A7	10c green	.30	.30
117	A7	15c black	.25	.25
118	A8	20c violet brown	.30	.30
119	A8	30c dk violet	.30	.30
120	A8	40c scarlet	.70	.70
121	A8	50c slate green	.95	.95
122	A8	60c black	.30	.30
123	A8	70c brt red violet	1.20	1.20
124	A8	80c brown black	1.20	1.20
125	A9	1fr violet	1.20	1.20
126	A9	1.30fr brown violet	1.20	1.20
127	A9	1.40fr green	1.20	1.20
128	A9	1.50fr brt rose	1.20	1.20
129	A9	2fr brown orange	1.20	1.20
130	A10	2.50fr dark blue	1.20	1.20
131	A10	3fr scarlet	1.20	1.20
132	A10	5fr slate green	1.20	1.20
133	A10	10fr violet brown	2.00	2.00
134	A10	20fr black	2.40	2.40
		Nos. 113-134 (22)	20.70	20.70

Nos. 101, 122 without "RF," see Nos. 136A-136B.

Pile House and Marshal Pétain — A11

1941   Perf. 12½x12

135	A11	1fr green	.80	—
136	A11	2.50fr blue	.80	—

For surcharges see Nos. B14A-B14B.

113

DAHOMEY

Type of 1941 without "RF"
1944 — **Perf. 13**
136A A8 50c slate green 1.20
136B A8 60c black 1.20

Nos. 136A-136B were issued by the Vichy government in France, but were not placed on sale in Dahomey.

Catalogue values for unused stamps in this section, from this point to the end of the section, are for Never Hinged items.

Republic

Village Ganvié — A12

1960, Mar. 1 — **Engr.** — **Perf. 12**
137 A12 25fr dk blue, brn & red .65 .25

For overprint see No. 152.

Imperforates
Most Dahomey stamps from 1960 onward exist imperforate in issued and trial colors, and also in small presentation sheets in issued colors.

C.C.T.A. Issue
Common Design Type
1960, May 16
138 CD106 5fr rose lilac & ultra .50 .25

Emblem of the Entente — A13

Council of the Entente Issue
1960, May 29 — **Photo.** — **Perf. 13x13½**
139 A13 25fr multicolored .65 .40

1st anniv. of the Council of the Entente (Dahomey, Ivory Coast, Niger and Upper Volta).

Prime Minister Hubert Maga — A14

1960, Aug. — **Engr.** — **Perf. 13**
140 A14 85fr deep claret & blk 1.60 .90

Issued on the occasion of Dahomey's proclamation of independence, Aug. 1, 1960. For surcharge see No. 149.

Weaver — A15

2fr, 10fr, Wood sculptor. 3fr, 15fr, Fisherman and net, horiz. 4fr, 20fr, Potter, horiz.

1961, Feb. 17 — **Engr.** — **Perf. 13**
141 A15 1fr red, org & carmine .25 .25
142 A15 2fr bister brn & choc .25 .25
143 A15 3fr green & orange .25 .25
144 A15 4fr olive bis & dp clar .25 .25
145 A15 6fr rose, lt vio & ver .40 .25
146 A15 10fr blue & green .55 .40
147 A15 15fr red lilac & violet .75 .40
148 A15 20fr bluish vio & Prus bl .90 .55
Nos. 141-148 (8) 3.60 2.60

For surcharges see Benin No. 1374, Dahomey #Q1-Q7.

No. 140 Surcharged in Black

1961, Aug. 1
149 A14 100fr on 85fr dp cl & blk 3.25 3.25

First anniversary of Independence.

Doves, UN Building and Emblem — A16

1961, Sept. 20 — **Unwmk.** — **Perf. 13**
150 A16 5fr multicolored .35 .25
151 A16 60fr multicolored 1.20 .90

1st anniv. of Dahomey's admission to the UN. See No. C16 and souvenir sheet No. C16a.

No. 137 Overprinted in Black

1961, Dec. 24
152 A12 25fr dk blue, brn & red .65 .40

Abidjan Games, Dec 24-31.

Interior of Burned-out Fort Ouidah and Wrecked Car — A17

1962, July 31 — **Photo.** — **Perf. 12½**
153 A17 30fr multicolored .45 .45
154 A17 60fr multicolored .75 .60

Evacuation of Fort Ouidah by the Portuguese, and its occupation by Dahomey. 1st anniv.

African and Malgache Union Issue
Common Design Type
1962, Sept. 8 — **Perf. 12½x12**
155 CD110 30fr red lil, bluish grn, red & gold 1.25 .90

Red Cross Nurses and Map — A18

1962, Oct. 5 — **Engr.** — **Perf. 13**
156 A18 5fr blue, choc & red .30 .25
157 A18 20fr blue, dk grn & red .60 .45
158 A18 25fr blue, brown & red .65 .45
159 A18 30fr blue, black & red .85 .70
Nos. 156-159 (4) 2.40 1.85

Ganvié Woman in Canoe A19

Peuhl Herdsman and Cattle A20

Designs: 3fr, 65fr, Bariba chief of Nikki. 15fr, 50fr, Ouidah witch doctor, rock python. 20fr, 30fr, Nessoukoué women carrying vases on heads, Abomey. 25fr, 40fr, Dahomey girl. 60fr,

Peuhl herdsman and cattle. 85fr, Ganvié woman in canoe.

1963, Feb. 18 — **Unwmk.** — **Perf. 13**
160 A19 2fr grnsh blue & vio .25 .25
161 A19 3fr blue & black .25 .25
162 A20 5fr brown, blk & grn .35 .25
163 A19 15fr brn, bl grn & red brn .35 .25
164 A19 20fr green, blk & car .30 .25
165 A19 25fr dk brn, bl & bl grn .40 .25
166 A19 30fr brn org, choc & mag .60 .40
167 A20 40fr choc, grn & brt bl 1.00 .40
168 A19 50fr blk, grn, brn & red brn 1.60 .55
169 A20 60fr choc, org red & ol 3.50 1.00
170 A19 65fr orange brn & choc 1.75 .65
171 A19 85fr brt blue & choc 2.50 1.00
Nos. 160-171 (12) 12.85 5.50

For surcharges see Nos. 211, 232-233, Benin 655A, 690F, 700, 722, 1375, 1417.

Boxers — A21

Designs: 1fr, 20fr, Soccer goalkeeper, horiz. 2fr, 5fr, Runners.

1963, Apr. 11 — **Engr.**
172 A21 50c green & black .25 .25
173 A21 1fr olive, blk & brn .25 .25
174 A21 2fr olive, blue & brn .25 .25
175 A21 5fr brown, crim & blk .25 .25
176 A21 15fr dk violet & brn .35 .25
177 A21 20fr multicolored .55 .55
Nos. 172-177 (6) 1.90 1.80

Friendship Games, Dakar, Apr. 11-21. For surcharges & overprint see Benin Nos. 697, 704, 716, 1372, 1382, 1384.

President's Palace, Cotonou — A22

1963, Aug. 1 — **Photo.** — **Perf. 12½x12**
178 A22 25fr multicolored .45 .25

Third anniversary of independence.

Gen. Toussaint L'Ouverture — A23

1963, Nov. 18 — **Unwmk.** — **Perf. 12x13**
179 A23 25fr multicolored .55 .25
180 A23 30fr multicolored .70 .25
181 A23 100fr ultra, brn & red 1.60 .80
Nos. 179-181 (3) 2.85 1.30

Pierre Dominique Toussaint L'Ouverture (1743-1803), Haitian gen., statesman and descendant of the kings of Allada (Dahomey). For overprint, see Benin No. 1367. For surcharge, see Benin No. 1466.

UN Emblem, Flame, "15" — A24

1963, Dec. 10 — **Perf. 12**
182 A24 4fr multicolored .25 .25
183 A24 6fr multicolored .25 .25
184 A24 25fr multicolored .45 .25
Nos. 182-184 (3) .95 .75

15th anniversary of the Universal Declaration of Human Rights. For surcharge, see Benin No. 1377.

Somba Dance — A25

Regional Dances: 3fr, Nago dance, Pobe-Ketou, horiz. 10fr, Dance of the baton. 15fr, Nago dance, Ouidah, horiz. 25fr, Dance of the Sakpatassi. 30fr, Dance of the Nessouhouessi, horiz.

1964, Aug. 8 — **Engr.** — **Perf. 13**
185 A25 2fr red, emerald & blk .25 .25
186 A25 3fr dull red, blue & grn .25 .25
187 A25 10fr purple, blk & red .45 .25
188 A25 15fr magenta, blk & grn .45 .25
189 A25 25fr Prus blue, brn & org .90 .30
190 A25 30fr dk red, choc & org 1.15 .40
Nos. 185-190 (6) 3.45 1.70

Runner A26

1964, Oct. 20 — **Photo.** — **Perf. 11**
191 A26 60fr shown 1.60 1.00
192 A26 85fr Bicyclist 2.75 1.40

18th Olympic Games, Tokyo, Oct. 10-25.

Cooperation Issue
Common Design Type
1964, Nov. 7 — **Engr.** — **Perf. 13**
193 CD119 25fr org, vio & dk brn .80 .35

UNICEF Emblem, Mother and Child — A27

25fr, Mother holding child in her arms.

1964, Dec. 11 — **Unwmk.** — **Perf. 13**
194 A27 20fr yel grn, dk red & blk .40 .25
195 A27 25fr blue, dk red & blk .60 .45

18th anniv. of UNICEF. For overprints, see Benin Nos. 691A, and 1368.

IQSY Emblem and Apollo — A28

100fr, IQSY emblem, Nimbus weather satellite.

1964, Dec. 22 — **Photo.** — **Perf. 13x12½**
196 A28 25fr green & lt yellow .55 .25
197 A28 100fr deep plum & yellow 2.00 .95

International Quiet Sun Year, 1964-65.

Abomey Tapestry — A29

Designs (Abomey tapestries): 25fr, Warrior and fight scenes. 50fr, Birds and warriors, horiz. 85fr, Animals, ship and plants, horiz.

DAHOMEY

1965, Apr. 12   Photo.   Perf. 12½
198	A29	20fr multicolored	.80	.25
199	A29	25fr multicolored	.95	.40
200	A29	50fr multicolored	1.50	.80
201	A29	85fr multicolored	3.25	1.10
a.	Min. sheet of 4, #198-201		8.00	8.00
	Nos. 198-201 (4)		6.50	2.55

Issued to publicize the local rug weaving industry.

Baudot Telegraph Distributor and Ader Telephone — A30

1965, May 17   Engr.   Perf. 13
202 A30 100fr lilac, org & blk   1.75 1.60
Cent. of the ITU.

Cotonou Harbor — A31

100fr, Cotonou Harbor, denomination at left.

1965, Aug. 1   Photo.   Perf. 12½
203 25fr multicolored   1.10 .25
204 100fr multicolored   2.50 1.10
a. A31 Pair, #203-204   4.50 2.10

The opening of Cotonou Harbor. No. 204a has a continuous design.
For surcharges see Nos. 219-220.

Cybium Tritor — A32

Fish: 25fr, Dentex filosus. 30fr, Atlantic sailfish. 50fr, Blackish tripletail.

1965, Sept. 20   Engr.   Perf. 13
205 A32 10fr black & brt blue   .75 .25
206 A32 25fr brt blue, org & blk   1.00 .55
207 A32 30fr violet bl & grnsh bl   1.75 .80
208 A32 50fr black, gray bl & org   2.75 1.00
  Nos. 205-208 (4)   6.25 2.60

For surcharge see Benin No. 911.

Independence Monument — A33

1965, Oct. 28   Photo.   Perf. 12x12½
209 A33 25fr gray, black & red   .40 .25
210 A33 30fr lt ultra, black & red   .65 .25

October 28 Revolution, 2nd anniv. For surcharge, see Benin No. 1385.

No. 165 Surcharged

1965, Nov.   Engr.   Perf. 13
211 A20 1fr on 25fr   .30 .25

Porto Novo Cathedral — A34

Designs: 50fr, Ouidah Pro-Cathedral, vert. 70fr, Cotonou Cathedral.

1966, Mar. 21   Engr.   Perf. 13
212 A34 30fr Prus bl, vio brn & grn   .55 .25
213 A34 50fr vio brn, Prus bl & brn   .70 .50
214 A34 70fr grn, Prus bl & vio brn   1.25 .75
  Nos. 212-214 (3)   2.50 1.50

Jewelry — A35

Designs: 30fr, Architecture. 50fr, Musician. 70fr, Crucifixion, sculpture.

1966, Apr. 4   Engr.   Perf. 13
215 A35 15fr dull red brn & blk   .45 .25
216 A35 30fr dk brn, ultra & brn red   .70 .45
217 A35 50fr brt blue & dk brn   1.20 .55
218 A35 70fr red brown & blk   2.50 .85
  Nos. 215-218 (4)   4.85 2.10

International Negro Arts Festival, Dakar, Senegal, Apr. 1-24.

Nos. 203-204 Surcharged

1966, Apr. 24   Photo.   Perf. 12½
219 A31 15fr on 25fr multi   .55 .35
220 A31 15fr on 100fr multi   .55 .35
a. Pair, #219-220   1.50 1.10

Fifth anniversary of the Cooperation Agreement between France and Dahomey.

WHO Headquarters from the East — A36

1966, May 3   Perf. 12½x13   Size: 35x22½mm
221 A36 30fr multicolored   .75 .25

Inauguration of the WHO Headquarters, Geneva. See No. C32.
For surcharge see Benin No. 717.

Boy Scout Signaling — A37

Designs: 10fr, Patrol standard with pennant, vert. 30fr, Campfire and map of Dahomey, vert. 50fr, Scouts building foot bridge.

1966, Oct. 17   Engr.   Perf. 13
222 A37 5fr dk brn, ocher & red   .30 .25
223 A37 10fr black, grn & rose cl   .30 .25
224 A37 30fr org, red brn & pur   .70 .35
225 A37 50fr vio bl, grn & dk brn   1.20 .45
a. Min. sheet of 4, #222-225   3.00 3.00
  Nos. 222-225 (4)   2.50 1.30

Clappertonia Ficifolia — A38

Flowers: 3fr, Hewittia sublobata. 5fr, Butterfly pea. 10fr, Water lily. 15fr, Commelina forskalaei. 30fr, Eremomastax speciosa.

1967, Feb. 20   Photo.   Perf. 12x12½
226 A38 1fr multicolored   .25 .25
227 A38 3fr multicolored   .35 .25
228 A38 5fr multicolored   .55 .25
229 A38 10fr multicolored   .90 .35
230 A38 15fr multicolored   1.10 .55
231 A38 30fr multicolored   2.10 .90
  Nos. 226-231 (6)   5.25 2.55

For surcharges see Benin Nos. 707, 715, 1376, 1390, 1402.

Nos. 170-171 Surcharged

1967, Mar. 1   Engr.   Perf. 13
232 A19 30fr on 65fr   .85 .60
a. Double surcharge   36.00
233 A19 30fr on 85fr   .85 .60
a. Double surcharge   60.00
b. Inverted surcharge   60.00

Lions Emblem, Dancing Children, Bird — A39

1967, Mar. 20
234 A39 100fr dl vio, dp bl & grn   1.50 1.10

50th anniversary of Lions International.

"Man in the City" Pavilion — A40

"The New Africa" Exhibit — A40a

1967, June 12   Engr.   Perf. 13
235 A40 30fr green & choc   .70 .25
236 A40a 70fr green & brn red   1.50 .60

EXPO '67, International Exhibition, Montreal, Apr. 28-Oct. 27, 1967. See No. C57 and miniature sheet No. C57a.
For overprint, see Benin No. 897.

Europafrica Issue

Trade (Blood) Circulation, Map of Europe and Africa — A41

1967, July 20   Photo.   Perf. 12x12½
237 A41 30fr multicolored   .70 .25
238 A41 45fr multicolored   1.10 .45

For surcharge, see Benin No. 1386.

Scouts Climbing Mountain, Jamboree Emblem — A42

70fr, Jamboree emblem, Scouts launching canoe.

1967, Aug. 7   Engr.   Perf. 13
239 A42 30fr brt bl, red brn & sl   .80 .25
240 A42 70fr black, sl grn & dk brn   1.60 .65

12th Boy Scout World Jamboree, Farragut State Park, Idaho, Aug. 1-9. For souvenir sheet see No. C59a.
For surcharges see Benin Nos. 902, 912, 1391.

Rhone River and Olympic Emblems — A43

Designs (Olympic Emblems and): 45fr, View of Grenoble, vert. 100fr, Rhone Bridge, Grenoble, and Pierre de Coubertin.

1967, Sept. 2   Engr.   Perf. 13
241 A43 30fr bis, dp bl & grn   .70 .40
242 A43 45fr ultra, grn & brn   .90 .55
243 A43 100fr choc, grn & brt bl   2.25 1.00
a. Min. sheet of 3, #241-243   4.50 4.50
  Nos. 241-243 (3)   3.85 1.95

10th Winter Olympic Games, Grenoble, Feb. 6-18, 1968.
For surcharges, see Benin Nos. 903, 1054E, 1054F, 1392.

Monetary Union Issue
Common Design Type

1967, Nov. 4   Engr.   Perf. 13
244 CD125 30fr grn, dk car & dk brn   .65 .65

Animals from the Pendjari Reservation A45

Designs: 15fr, Cape Buffalo. 30fr, Lion. 45fr, Buffon's kob. 70fr, African slender-snouted crocodile. 100fr, Hippopotamus.

1968, Mar. 18   Photo.   Perf. 12½x13
245 A45 15fr multicolored   .55 .25
246 A45 30fr purple & multi   .65 .50
247 A45 45fr blue & multi   1.25 .60
248 A45 70fr multicolored   2.25 .75
249 A45 100fr multicolored   4.00 2.25
  Nos. 245-249 (5)   8.70 4.35

See Nos. 252-256.
For surcharges see No. 310, Benin Nos. 655E, 725, 1415, 1420, 1421.

WHO Emblem — A46

1968, Apr. 22   Engr.   Perf. 13
250 A46 30fr multicolored   .60 .25
251 A46 70fr multicolored   1.40 .70

20th anniv. of WHO. For surcharges, see Benin Nos. 1012, 1387, 1465.

Animals from the Pendjari Reservation A47

Animals: 5fr, Warthog. 30fr, Leopard. 60fr, Spotted hyena. 75fr, Anubius baboon. 90fr, Hartebeest.

1969, Feb. 10   Photo.   Perf. 12½x12
252 A47 5fr dark brown & multi   .25 .25
253 A47 30fr deep ultra & multi   .70 .50
254 A47 60fr dark green & multi   1.25 .70
255 A47 75fr dark blue & multi   3.00 1.00
256 A47 90fr dark green & multi   4.00 2.25
  Nos. 252-256 (5)   9.20 4.70

For surcharges, see Benin Nos. 700, 1400.

Heads, Symbols of Agriculture and Science, and Globe — A48

1969, Mar. 10   Engr.   Perf. 13
257 A48 30fr orange & multi   .60 .25
258 A48 70fr maroon & multi   1.50 .70

50th anniv. of the ILO.
For surcharges see Benin Nos. 904, 913.

Arms of Dahomey A49

1969, June 30   Litho.   Perf. 13½x13
259 A49 5fr yellow & multi   .35 .30
260 A49 30fr orange red & multi   1.50 .45

See No. C101.

DAHOMEY

Development Bank Issue

Cornucopia and Bank Emblem — A50

1969, Sept. 10   Photo.   Perf. 13
261 A50 30fr black, grn & ocher   .75   .55

African Development Bank, 5th anniv.
For surcharge see Benin No. 905.

Europafrica Issue

Ambary (Kenaf) Industry, Cotonou — A51

Design: 45fr, Cotton industry, Parakou.

1969, Sept. 22   Litho.   Perf. 14
262 A51 30fr multicolored   1.00   .50
263 A51 45fr multicolored   1.25   .75

See Nos. C105-C105a.
For overprints and surcharges see Benin No. 1054A.

Sakpata Dance and Tourist Year Emblem — A52

Dances and Tourist Year Emblem: 30fr, Guelede dance. 45fr, Sato dance.

1969, Dec. 15   Litho.   Perf. 14
264 A52 10fr multicolored   .75   .30
265 A52 30fr multicolored   1.45   .45
266 A52 45fr multicolored   2.00   .55
   Nos. 264-266 (3)   4.20   1.30

See No. C108. For surcharges see Benin Nos. 690J, 1054B, 1388, 1433.

UN Emblem, Garden and Wall — A53

1970, Apr. 6   Engr.   Perf. 13
267 A53 30fr ultra, red org & slate   .70   .25
268 A53 40fr ultra, brn & sl grn   1.25   .50

25th anniversary of the United Nations.
For surcharge see No. 294. For overprint see Benin 647B.

ASECNA Issue
Common Design Type

1970, June 1   Engr.   Perf. 13
269 CD132 40fr red & purple   .90   .55

For surcharges, see Benin Nos. 906, 1396.

Mt. Fuji, EXPO '70 Emblem, Monorail Train — A54

1970, June 15   Litho.   Perf. 13½x14
270 A54 5fr green, red & vio bl   .40   .25

EXPO '70 International Exhibition, Osaka, Japan, 3/15-9/13/70. See Nos. C124-C125.

Alkemy, King of Ardres — A55

40fr, Sailing ships "La Justice" & "La Concorde," Ardres, 1670. 50fr, Matheo Lopes, ambassador of the King of Ardres & his coat of arms. 200fr, Louis XIV & fleur-de-lis.

1970, July 6   Engr.   Perf. 13
271 A55 40fr brt grn, ultra & brn   .75   .25
272 A55 50fr dk car, choc & emer   1.05   .40
273 A55 70fr gray, lemon & choc   1.60   .65
274 A55 200fr Prus bl, dk car & choc   4.00   1.25
   Nos. 271-274 (4)   7.40   2.55

300th anniv. of the mission from the King of Ardres to the King of France, and of the audience with Louis XIV on Dec. 19, 1670.
For surcharges see Benin Nos. 721, 724, 914.

Star of the Order of Independence — A56

1970, Aug. 1   Photo.   Perf. 12
275 A56 30fr multicolored   .40   .25
276 A56 40fr multicolored   .60   .25

10th anniversary of independence.
For surcharge see Benin Nos. 720, 1464.

Bariba Warrior — A57

Designs: 2fr, 50fr, Two horsemen. 10fr, 70fr, Horseman facing left.

1970, Aug. 24   Perf. 12½x13
277 A57 1fr yellow & multi   .30   .25
278 A57 2fr gray grn & multi   .45   .25
279 A57 10fr blue & multi   .60   .25
280 A57 40fr yellow grn & multi   1.90   .35
281 A57 50fr gold & multi   2.40   .50
282 A57 70fr lilac rose & multi   3.00   .80
   Nos. 277-282 (6)   8.65   2.40

For surcharges see Benin Nos. 350-351, 613, 703, 1373, 1401.

Globe and Heart — A58

Design: 40fr, Hands holding heart, vert.

1971, June 7   Engr.   Perf. 13
283 A58 40fr red, green & dk brn   2.00   .50
284 A58 100fr green, red & blue   4.00   1.25

For surcharges see Benin Nos. 617, 647A, 712, 907, 1429.

Intl. year against racial discrimination.

Ancestral Figures and Lottery Ticket — A59

1971, June 24   Litho.   Perf. 14
285 A59 35fr multicolored   .80   .25
286 A59 40fr multicolored   1.25   .35

4th anniv. of the National Lottery.

For overprint and surcharge, see Benin Nos. 710, 1430.

King Behanzin's Emblem (1889-1894) — A60

Emblems of the Kings of Abomey: 25fr, Agoliagbo (1894-1900). 35fr, Ganyehoussou (1620-45), bird and cup, horiz. 100fr, Guezo (1818-58), bull, tree and birds. 135fr, Ouegbadja (1645-85), horiz. 140fr, Glèle (1858-89), lion and sword, horiz.

   Photo.; Litho. (25fr, 135fr)
1971-72   Perf. 12½
287 A60 25fr multicolored   .55   .25
288 A60 35fr green & multi   .90   .25
289 A60 40fr green & multi   1.25   .55
290 A60 100fr red & multi   2.25   .90
291 A60 135fr multicolored   3.25   1.40
292 A60 140fr brown & multi   3.75   1.90
   Nos. 287-292 (6)   11.95   5.25

Issued: 25fr, 135fr, 7/17/72; others, 8/3/71.
For surcharges and overprint, see Benin Nos. 614, 634B, 708A, 726, 791, 1054D, 1369, 1422, 1431, 1467, 1470.

Kabuki Actor, Long-distance Skiing — A61

1972, Feb.   Engr.   Perf. 13
293 A61 35fr dk car, brn & bl grn   2.50   .75

11th Winter Olympic Games, Sapporo, Japan, Feb. 3-13. See No. C153.

No. 268 Surcharged

1972
294 A53 35fr on 40fr multi   .90   .35

Brahms and "Soir d'été" — A62

Design: 65fr, Brahms, woman at piano & music, horiz.

1972, June 29   Engr.   Perf. 13
295 A62 30fr red brn, blk & lilac   4.00   .80
296 A62 65fr red brn, blk & lilac   6.75   1.50

75th anniversary of the death of Johannes Brahms (1833-1897), German composer.
For surcharges see Benin Nos. 654B, 718, 1389.

The Hare and The Tortoise, by La Fontaine A63

Fables: 35fr, The Fox and The Stork, vert. 40fr, The Cat, The Weasel and Rabbit.

1972, Aug. 28   Engr.   Perf. 13
297 A63 10fr multicolored   2.25   .75
298 A63 35fr dark red & multi   4.25   1.25
299 A63 40fr ultra & multi   5.50   1.75
   Nos. 297-299 (3)   12.00   3.75

Jean de La Fontaine (1621-1695), French fabulist. For surcharges, see Benin Nos. 1380, 1393, 1397.

West African Monetary Union Issue
Common Design Type

1972, Nov. 2   Engr.   Perf. 13
300 CD136 40fr choc, ocher & gray   .65   .25

Dr. Armauer Hansen, Microscope, Bacilli — A65

Design: 85fr, Portrait of Dr. Hansen.

1973, May 14   Engr.   Perf. 13
301 A65 35fr ultra, vio brn & brn   .50   .35
302 A65 85fr yel grn, bis & ver   1.25   .75

Centenary of the discovery by Dr. Armauer G. Hansen of the Hansen bacillus, the cause of leprosy.
For surcharges see Benin Nos. 655G, 1084, 1437.

Arms of Dahomey — A66

1973, June 25   Photo.   Perf. 13
303 A66 5fr ultra & multi   .25   .25
304 A66 35fr ocher & multi   .40   .25
305 A66 red orange & multi   .60   .25
   Nos. 303-305 (3)   1.25   .75

For overprint and surcharge see Benin Nos. 690A, 1403.

INTERPOL Emblem and Spiderweb — A67

Design: 50fr, INTERPOL emblem and communications symbols, vert.

1973, July   Engr.
306 A67 35fr ver, grn & brn   .60   .25
307 A67 50fr green, brn & red   .85   .45

50th anniversary of International Criminal Police Organization (INTERPOL).
For overprints and surcharges, see Benin Nos. 634A, 810, 1011, 1434, 1471.

Education in Hygiene and Nutrition — A68

WHO, 25th Anniv.: 100fr, Prenatal examination and care, WHO emblem.

1973, Aug. 2   Photo.   Perf. 12½x13
308 A68 35fr multicolored   .50   .30
309 A68 100fr multicolored   1.50   .65

For surcharges, see Benin Nos. 655B, 1439.

No. 248 Srchd. and Ovptd. in Red

1973, Aug. 16
310 A45 100fr on 70fr multi   2.50   1.00

African solidarity in drought emergency.

DAHOMEY

African Postal Union Issue
Common Design Type
1973, Sept. 12   Engr.   *Perf. 13*
311 CD137 100fr red, purple & blk   1.25   .55

For surcharges, see Benin Nos. 690I, 1440.

Epinephelus Aeneus A69

Fish: 15fr, Drepane africana. 35fr, Pragus ehrenbergi.

1973, Sept. 18
312 A69 5fr slate blue & indigo   1.00   .30
313 A69 15fr black & brt blue   1.50   .35
314 A69 35fr emerald, ocher & sep   4.00   .60
    Nos. 312-314 (3)   6.50   1.25

For surcharges, see Benin No. 698, 1378, 1383, 1394.

Chameleon A70

40fr, Emblem over map of Dahomey, vert.

1973, Nov. 30   Photo.   *Perf. 13*
315 A70 35fr olive & multi   .55   .30
316 A70 40fr multicolored   1.25   .35

1st anniv. of the Oct. 26 revolution.

The Chameleon in the Tree — A71

Designs: 5fr, The elephant, the hen and the dog, vert. 10fr, The sparrowhawk and the dog, vert. 25fr, The chameleon in the tree. 40fr, The eagle, the viper and the hen.

1974, Feb. 14   Photo.   *Perf. 13*
317 A71 5fr emerald & multi   .75   .25
318 A71 10fr slate blue & multi   .90   .25
319 A71 25fr slate blue & multi   1.75   .30
320 A71 40fr light blue & multi   2.50   .45
    Nos. 317-320 (4)   5.90   1.25

Folktales of Dahomey.
For surcharges and overprint see Benin Nos. 699, 709, 908, 1363, 1370, 1379, 1381, 1432.

German Shepherd A72

1974, Apr. 25   Photo.   *Perf. 13*
321 A72 40fr shown   1.50   .35
322 A72 50fr Boxer   1.75   .35
323 A72 100fr Saluki   3.50   .80
    Nos. 321-323 (3)   6.75   1.50

For surcharges, see Benin No. 1398, 1435, 1441.

Council Issue

Map and Flags of Members — A73

1974, May 29   Photo.   *Perf. 13x12½*
324 A73 40fr blue & multi   .80   .25

15th anniversary of the Council of Accord.

Locomotive 232, 1911 — A74

Designs: Locomotives.

1974, Sept. 2   Photo.   *Perf. 13x12½*
325 A74 35fr shown   1.00   .30
326 A74 40fr Freight, 1877   2.00   .30
327 A74 100fr Crampton, 1849   3.00   1.00
328 A74 200fr Stephenson, 1846   6.00   1.60
    Nos. 325-328 (4)   12.00   3.20

For overprints and surcharges see Benin Nos. 654E, 690D, 690K, 727, 909, 1395, 1399, 1442, 1444.

Globe, Money, People in Bank — A75

1974, Oct. 31   Engr.   *Perf. 13*
329 A75 35fr multicolored   .50   .35

World Savings Day. For surcharge, see Benin No. 1468.

Dompago Dance, Hissi Tribe — A76

Folk Dances: 25fr, Fetish Dance, Vaudou-Tchinan. 40fr, Bamboo Dance, Agbehoun. 100fr, Somba Dance, Sandoua, horiz.

1975, Aug. 4   Litho.   *Perf. 12*
330 A76 10fr yellow & multi   .65   .25
331 A76 25fr dk green & multi   1.25   .25
332 A76 40fr red & multi   1.60   .50
333 A76 100fr multicolored   3.00   .60
    Nos. 330-333 (4)   6.50   1.60

For surcharges and overprints see Benin Nos. 655D, 690C, 713, 1371,1404, 1414, 1443.

Flags of Dahomey and Nigeria over Africa — A77

Design: 100fr, Arrows connecting maps of Dahomey and Nigeria, horiz.

1975, Aug. 11   Photo.   *Perf. 12½x13*
334 A77 65fr multicolored   .75   .25
335 A77 100fr green & multi   1.00   .45

Year of intensified cooperation between Dahomey and Nigeria.
For surcharges & overprint see Benin Nos. 690H, 711, 806, 907, 1416, 1422.

Map, Pylons, Emblem A78

Benin Electric Community Emblem and Pylon — A79

1975, Aug. 18
336 A78 40fr multicolored   .75   .35
337 A79 150fr multicolored   2.00   1.00

Benin Electric Community and Ghana-Togo-Dahomey cooperation.
For surcharges see Benin Nos. 601, 900, 910, 1400, 1405, Q12A, Q12B.

Map of Dahomey, Rising Sun — A80

1975, Aug. 25   Photo.   *Perf. 12½x13*
338 A80 35fr multicolored   .50   .25

Cooperation Year for the creation of a new Dahoman society.
For overprint see Benin No. 690E. For surcharge, see Benin No. 1362.

Albert Schweitzer, Nurse, Patient — A81

1975, Sept. 22   Engr.   *Perf. 13*
339 A81 200fr olive, grn & red brn   6.25   1.50

Birth centenary of Albert Schweitzer (1875-1965), medical missionary and musician.
For surcharges, see Benin Nos. 655F, 1445.

Woman Speaking on Telephone, IWY Emblem — A82

1975, Oct. 20   Engr.   *Perf. 12½x13*
340 A82 50fr Prus blue & lilac   .75   .35
341 A82 150fr emerald, brn & org   2.00   .80

International Women's Year 1975.
For surcharges, see Benin Nos. 655C, 1054C, 1436, 1469.

SEMI-POSTAL STAMPS

Regular Issue of 1913 Surcharged in Red

1915   Unwmk.   *Perf. 14x13½*
B1 A5 10c + 5c orange red & rose   1.60   1.60

Curie Issue
Common Design Type
1938   *Perf. 13*
B2 CD80 1.75fr + 50c brt ultra   9.50   9.50

French Revolution Issue
Common Design Type
1939   Photo.
Name and Value Typo. in Black
B3 CD83 45c + 25c green   9.50   9.50
B4 CD83 70c + 30c brown   9.50   9.50
B5 CD83 90c + 35c red org   9.50   9.50
B6 CD83 1.25fr + 1fr rose pink   9.50   9.50
B7 CD83 2.25fr + 2fr blue   9.50   9.50
    Nos. B3-B7 (5)   47.50   47.50

Postage Stamps of 1913-38 Surcharged in Black

1941   *Perf. 13½x14*
B8 A5 50c + 1fr brn red & bl   3.25   3.25
B9 A5 80c + 2fr hn brn & ultra   7.25   7.25
B10 A5 1.50fr + 2fr dk bl & lt bl   7.25   7.25
B11 A5 2fr + 3fr yel org & choc   7.25   7.25
    Nos. B8-B11 (4)   25.00   25.00

Common Design Type and

Radio Operator SP1   Senegalese Artillerymen SP2

1941   Photo.   *Perf. 13½*
B12 SP1 1fr + 1fr red   1.20
B13 CD86 1.50fr + 3fr claret   1.20
B14 SP2 2.50fr + 1fr blue   1.20
    Nos. B12-B14 (3)   3.60

Surtax for the defense of the colonies. Nos. B12-B14 were issued by the Vichy government in France, but were not placed on sale in Dahomey.

Nos. 135-136 Srchd. in Black or Red

1944   Engr.   *Perf. 12½x12*
B14A 50c + 1.50fr on 2.50fr deep blue (R)   .80
B14B + 2.50fr on 1fr green   .80

Colonial Development Fund.
Nos. B14A-B14D were issued by the Vichy government in France, but were not placed on sale in Dahomey.

Catalogue values for unused stamps in this section, from this point to the end of the section, are for Never Hinged items.

Republic
Anti-Malaria Issue
Common Design Type
1962, Apr. 7   Engr.   *Perf. 12½x12*
B15 CD108 25fr + 5fr orange brn   .75   .75

Freedom from Hunger Issue
Common Design Type
1963, Mar. 21   Unwmk.   *Perf. 13*
B16 CD112 25fr + 5fr ol, brn red & brn   .80   .80

AIR POST STAMPS

Common Design Type
1940   Unwmk.   Engr.   *Perf. 12½*
C1 CD85 1.90fr ultra   .40   .40
C2 CD85 2.90fr dk red   .40   .40
C3 CD85 4.50fr dk gray grn   .80   .80

DAHOMEY

C4	CD85	4.90fr yel bister	.80	.80
C5	CD85	6.90fr deep org	1.60	1.60
		Nos. C1-C5 (5)	4.00	4.00

Common Design Types
1942

C6	CD88	50c car & bl	.30
C7	CD88	1fr brn & blk	.30
C8	CD88	2fr dk grn & red brn	.50
C9	CD88	3fr dk bl & scar	.95
C10	CD88	5fr vio & brn red	1.05

Frame Engr., Center Typo.

C11	CD89	10fr ultra, ind & org	1.05
C12	CD89	20fr rose car, mag & gray blk	1.10
C13	CD89	50fr yel grn, dl grn & dp bl	1.90	3.25
a.		50fr yellow green, dull green & pale blue	2.75	3.75
		Nos. C6-C13 (8)	7.15	

Nos. C6-C12 were issued by the Vichy government in France, but were not placed on sale in Dahomey.

> Catalogue values for unused stamps in this section, from this point to the end of the section, are for Never Hinged items.

Republic

Somba House AP4

Design: 500fr, Royal Court of Abomey.

1960, Apr. 1   Engr.   *Unwmk.*   *Perf. 13*

| C14 | AP4 | 100fr multi | 3.25 | .80 |
| C15 | AP4 | 500fr multi | 13.50 | 4.00 |

For overprint see Benin Nos. C419, C541. For surcharges, see No. CQ5, Benin No. C609.

Type of Regular Issue, 1961
1961, Sept. 20

| C16 | A16 | 200fr multi | 3.50 | 2.25 |
| a. | Souv. sheet of 3, #150-151, C16 | 7.00 | 7.00 |

Air Afrique Issue
Common Design Type

1962, Feb. 17   *Perf. 13*

| C17 | CD107 | 25fr ultra, blk & org brn | .80 | .40 |

Palace of the African and Malgache Union, Cotonou AP5

1963, July 27   Photo.   *Perf. 13x12*

| C18 | AP5 | 250fr multi | 5.00 | 2.75 |

Assembly of chiefs of state of the African and Malgache Union held at Cotonou in July.

African Postal Union Issue
Common Design Type

1963, Sept. 8   *Unwmk.*   *Perf. 12½*

| C19 | CD114 | 25fr brt bl, ocher & red | .75 | .25 |

See note after Cameroun No. C47.

Boeing 707 — AP6

Boeing 707: 200fr, On the ground. 300fr, Over Cotonou airport. 500fr, In the air.

1963, Oct. 25   Engr.   *Perf. 13*

C20	AP6	100fr multi	2.00	.60
C21	AP6	200fr multi	3.00	2.00
C22	AP6	300fr multi	5.00	2.00
C23	AP6	500fr multi	10.00	2.50
	Nos. C20-C23 (4)	20.00	7.10

For surcharges see Nos. CQ1-CQ5, Benin No. C610.

Priests Carrying Funerary Boat, Isis Temple, Philae AP7

1964, Mar. 9   *Unwmk.*   *Perf. 13*

| C24 | AP7 | 25fr vio bl & brn | 2.00 | .95 |

UNESCO world campaign to save historic monuments in Nubia.

Weather Map and Symbols AP8

1965, Mar. 23   Photo.   *Perf. 12½*

| C25 | AP8 | 50fr multi | .80 | .55 |

Fifth World Meteorological Day.

ICY Emblem and Men of Various Races AP9

1965, June 26   Engr.   *Perf. 13*

| C26 | AP9 | 25fr dl pur, mar & grn | .65 | .25 |
| C27 | AP9 | 85fr dp bl, mar & sl grn | 1.25 | .80 |

International Cooperation Year, 1965.

Winston Churchill — AP10

1965, June 15   Photo.   *Perf. 12½*

| C28 | AP10 | 100fr multi | 2.25 | 1.75 |

For surcharges, see Benin Nos. C519, C611.

Abraham Lincoln AP11

1965, July 15   *Perf. 13*

| C29 | AP11 | 100fr multi | 2.00 | 1.00 |

Centenary of death of Lincoln
For surcharge see No. C55.

John F. Kennedy and Arms of Dahomey AP12

1965, Nov. 22   Photo.   *Perf. 12½*

| C30 | AP12 | 100fr dp grn & blk | 2.75 | 1.10 |

President John F. Kennedy (1917-63).
For surcharge see No. C56.

Dr. Albert Schweitzer and Patients AP13

1966, Jan. 17   Photo.   *Perf. 12½*

| C31 | AP13 | 100fr multi | 3.00 | 1.25 |

Dr. Albert Schweitzer (1875-1965), medical missionary, theologian and musician.
For surcharge see Benin No. C435.

WHO Type of Regular Issue
Design: WHO Headquarters from the West.

1966, May 3   *Unwmk.*   *Perf. 13*
Size: 47x28mm

| C32 | A36 | 100fr ultra, yel & blk | 1.75 | 1.50 |

Pygmy Goose AP14   Broad-billed Rollers AP15

Birds: 100fr, Fiery-breasted bush-shrike. 250fr, Emerald cuckoos. 500fr, Emerald starling.

1966-67   *Perf. 12½*

C33	AP14	50fr multi	2.00	.55
C34	AP14	100fr multi	3.00	.85
C35	AP15	200fr multi	10.00	2.25
C36	AP15	250fr multi	10.00	3.00
C37	AP14	500fr multi	15.00	6.00
	Nos. C33-C37 (5)	40.00	12.65

Issued: 50fr, 100fr, 500fr, 6/13/66; others, 1/20/67.

For overprints and surcharges see No. C107, Benin Nos. 1472, C353-C355, C357, C368, C426, C436, C511, C550, C590.

Industrial Symbols — AP16

1966, July 21   Photo.   *Perf. 12x13*

| C38 | AP16 | 100fr multi | 1.75 | .80 |

Agreement between European Economic Community & the African & Malagache Union, 3rd anniv.

Pope Paul VI and St. Peter's, Rome AP17

Pope Paul VI and UN General Assembly AP18

70fr, Pope Paul VI and view of NYC.

1966, Aug. 22   Engr.   *Perf. 13*

C39	AP17	50fr multi	.75	.45
C40	AP17	70fr multi	.95	.55
C41	AP18	100fr multi	1.75	1.00
a.	Min. sheet of 3, #C39-C41	4.50	4.50
	Nos. C39-C41 (3)	3.45	2.00

Pope Paul's appeal for peace before the UN General Assembly, Oct. 4, 1965.

Air Afrique Issue, 1966
Common Design Type

1966, Aug. 31   Photo.   *Perf. 12½*

| C42 | CD123 | 30fr dk vio, blk & gray | .75 | .25 |

"Science" AP20

Designs: 45fr, "Art" (carved female statue), vert. 100fr, "Education" (book and letters).

1966, Nov. 4   Engr.   *Perf. 13*

C43	AP20	30fr mag, ultra & vio brn	.45	.25
C44	AP20	45fr mar & grn	.80	.55
C45	AP20	100fr blk, mar & brt bl	1.90	1.00
a.	Min. sheet of 3, #C43-C45	3.25	3.25
	Nos. C43-C45 (3)	3.15	1.80

20th anniversary of UNESCO.

Madonna by Alessio Baldovinetti AP21

Christmas: 50fr, Nativity after 15th century Beaune tapestry. 100fr, Adoration of the Shepherds, by José Ribera.

1966, Dec. 25   Photo.   *Perf. 12½x12*

C46	AP21	50fr multi	3.25	2.75
C47	AP21	100fr multi	4.50	3.25
C48	AP21	200fr multi	9.00	5.00
	Nos. C46-C48 (3)	16.75	10.50

See Nos. C95-C96, C109-C115. For surcharges, see No. C60, Benin Nos. C427, C520. For overprint, see Benin No. C544.

1967, Apr. 10   *Perf. 12½x12*

Paintings by Ingres: No. C49, Self-portrait, 1804. No. C50, Oedipus and the Sphinx.

| C49 | AP21 | 100fr multi | 3.25 | 1.75 |
| C50 | AP21 | 100fr multi | 3.25 | 1.75 |

Jean Auguste Dominique Ingres (1780-1867), French painter.

Three-master Suzanne — AP22

Windjammers: 45fr, Three-master Esmeralda, vert. 80fr, Schooner Marie Alice, vert. 100fr, Four-master Antonin.

1967, May 8   *Perf. 13*

C51	AP22	30fr multi	1.00	.50
C52	AP22	45fr multi	1.25	.75
C53	AP22	80fr multi	2.50	1.25
C54	AP22	100fr multi	3.25	1.50
	Nos. C51-C54 (4)	8.00	4.00

For overprint and surcharges see Benin Nos. C369, C420, C606, C612.

Nos. C29-C30 Surcharged

1967, May 29   Photo.   *Perf. 13, 12½*

| C55 | AP11 | 125fr on 100fr | 2.75 | 1.25 |
| C56 | AP12 | 125fr on 100fr | 2.75 | 1.25 |

50th anniv. of the birth of Pres. John F. Kennedy.

EXPO '67 "Man In Space" Pavilion — AP23

DAHOMEY

1967, June 12   Engr.   Perf. 13
C57 AP23 100fr dl red & Prus bl   2.00   .75
  a. Min. sheet of 3, #235-236, C57   4.00   4.00

EXPO '67, International Exhibition, Montreal, Apr. 28-Oct. 27, 1967.

Europafrica Issue

Konrad Adenauer, by Oscar Kokoschká — AP24

1967, July 19   Photo.   Perf. 12½x12
C58 AP24 70fr multi   2.00   1.25
  a. Souv. sheet of 4   8.50   8.50

Konrad Adenauer (1876-1967), chancellor of West Germany (1949-1963). For surcharges, see Benin Nos. C428, C572, C602.

Jamboree Emblem, Ropes and World Map — AP25

1967, Aug. 7   Engr.   Perf. 13
C59 AP25 100fr lil, sl grn & dp bl   1.60   .75
  a. Souv. sheet of 3, #239-240, C59   3.50   3.50

12th Boy Scout World Jamboree, Farragut State Park, Idaho, Aug. 1-9.

No. C48 Srchd. in Red

1967, Aug. 12   Photo.   Perf. 12½x12
C60 AP21 150fr on 200fr   3.50   2.75
  a. "150F" omitted   300.00   300.00

Riccione, Italy Stamp Exhibition.

African Postal Union Issue, 1967
Common Design Type

1967, Sept. 9   Engr.   Perf. 13
C61 CD124 100fr red, brt lil & emer   1.75   .95

For surcharge see Benin No. C471.

Charles de Gaulle — AP26

1967, Nov. 21   Photo.   Perf. 12½x13
C62 AP26 100fr multi   3.75   2.50
  a. Souv. sheet of 4   16.00   16.00

Pres. Charles de Gaulle of France on the occasion of Pres. Christophe Soglo's state visit to Paris, Nov. 1967.

Madonna, by Matthias Grunewald — AP27

Paintings: 50fr, Holy Family by the Master of St. Sebastian, horiz. 100fr, Adoration of the Magi by Ulrich Apt the Elder. 200fr, Annunciation, by Matthias Grunewald.

1967, Dec. 11   Photo.   Perf. 12½
C63 AP27 30fr multi   .55   .45
C64 AP27 50fr multi   1.10   .60
C65 AP27 100fr multi   2.00   1.25
C66 AP27 200fr multi   5.00   2.00
  Nos. C63-C66 (4)   8.65   4.30

Christmas 1967.

Venus de Milo and Mariner 5 — AP28

1968, Feb. 17   Photo.   Perf. 13
C67 AP28 70fr grnsh bl & multi   1.75   .75
C68 AP28 70fr dp bl & multi   1.75   .75
  a. Souv. sheet of 2, #C67-C68   4.00   4.00

Explorations of the planet Venus, Oct. 18-19, 1967.

#C68, Venus de Milo and Venera 4 rocket.

For surcharges see Nos. C103-C104, Benin Nos. C573, C587.

Gutenberg Monument, Strasbourg Cathedral — AP29

1968, May 20   Litho.   Perf. 14x13½
C69 AP29 45fr grn & org   1.00   .40
C70 AP29 100fr dk & lt bl   2.00   1.00
  a. Souv. sheet of 2, #C69-C70   3.75   3.75

500th anniv. of the death of Johann Gutenberg, inventor of printing from movable type.

For surcharges see Benin Nos. C512, C516.

Martin Luther King, Jr. — AP30

Designs: 30fr, "We must meet hate with creative love" in French, English and German. 100fr, Full-face portrait.

Perf. 12½, 13½x13
1968, June 17   Photo.
  Size: 26x46mm
C71 AP30 30fr red brn, yel & blk   .60   .35
  Size: 26x37mm
C72 AP30 55fr multi   1.00   .45
C73 AP30 100fr multi   1.50   .90
  a. Min. sheet of 3, #C71-C73   4.00   4.00
  Nos. C71-C73 (3)   3.10   1.70

Martin Luther King, Jr. (1929-68), American civil rights leader.

For surcharges, see Benin Nos. C517, C561, C613.

Robert Schuman — AP31

45fr, Alcide de Gasperi. 70fr, Konrad Adenauer.

1968, July 20   Photo.   Perf. 13
C74 AP31 30fr dp yel, blk & grn   .40   .40
C75 AP31 45fr org, dk brn & ol   .85   .50
C76 AP31 70fr multi   1.40   .50
  Nos. C74-C76 (3)   2.65   1.40

5th anniversary of the economic agreement between the European Economic Community and the African and Malgache Union.

For surcharges, see Benin Nos. C462, C562, C603.

Battle of Montebello, by Henri Philippoteaux — AP32

Paintings: 45fr, 2nd Zouave Regiment at Magenta, by Riballier. 70fr, Battle of Magenta, by Louis Eugène Charpentier. 100fr, Battle of Solferino, by Charpentier.

1968, Aug. 12   Perf. 12½x12
C77 AP32 30fr multi   1.15   .50
C78 AP32 45fr multi   1.60   .65
C79 AP32 70fr multi   3.25   1.25
C80 AP32 100fr multi   4.00   1.00
  Nos. C77-C80 (4)   10.00   3.40

Issued for the Red Cross. For surcharges, see Benin Nos. C574, C594, C614.

Mail Truck in Village — AP33

Designs: 45fr, Mail truck stopping at rural post office. 55fr, Mail truck at river bank. 70fr, Mail truck and train.

1968, Oct. 7   Photo.   Perf. 13x12½
C81 AP33 30fr multi   .90   .50
C82 AP33 45fr multi   1.10   .55
C83 AP33 55fr multi   1.75   .55
C84 AP33 70fr multi   4.25   1.00
  Nos. C81-C84 (4)   8.00   2.60

For surcharges see Benin Nos. C352, C357A, C584.

Aztec Stadium, Mexico City — AP34

45fr, Ball player, Mayan sculpture, vert. 70fr, Wrestler, sculpture from Uxpanapan, vert. 150fr, Olympic Stadium, Mexico City.

1968, Nov. 20   Engr.   Perf. 13
C85 AP34 30fr dp ol & sl grn   .80   .30
C86 AP34 45fr ultra & dk rose brn   1.50   .60
C87 AP34 70fr sl grn & dk brn   2.10   .65
C88 AP34 150fr dk car & dk brn   3.00   1.25
  a. Min. sheet of 4, #C85-C88   7.50   7.50
  Nos. C85-C88 (4)   7.40   2.80

19th Olympic Games, Mexico City, Oct. 12-27. No. C88a is folded down the vertical gutter separating Nos. C85-C86 se-tenant at left and Nos. C87-C88 se-tenant at right.

For overprint and surcharges see Benin Nos. C457, C461, C513.

The Annunciation, by Foujita — AP35

Paintings by Foujita: 30fr, Nativity, horiz. 100fr, The Virgin and Child. 200fr, The Baptism of Christ.

Perf. 12x12½, 12½x12
1968, Nov. 25   Photo.
C89 AP35 30fr multi   .80   .55
C90 AP35 70fr multi   1.60   .80
C91 AP35 100fr multi   1.75   1.25
C92 AP35 200fr multi   4.00   2.75
  Nos. C89-C92 (4)   8.15   5.35

Christmas 1968. For surcharges, see Benin Nos. C531, C563, C575, C615, C648.

PHILEXAFRIQUE Issue

Painting: Diderot, by Louis Michel Vanloo.

1968, Dec. 16   Perf. 12½x12
C93 AP35 100fr multi   3.75   3.75

PHILEXAFRIQUE, Philatelic Exhibition in Abidjan, Feb. 14-23. Printed with alternating label.

For surcharges, see Benin Nos. C522, C629.

2nd PHILEXAFRIQUE Issue
Common Design Type

50fr, Dahomey #119 and aerial view of Cotonou.

1969, Feb. 14   Engr.   Perf. 13
C94 CD128 50fr bl, brn & pur   2.25   2.25

For surcharge see Benin Nos. C467, C651.

Christmas Painting Type

Paintings: No. C95, Virgin of the Rocks, by Leonardo da Vinci. No. C96, Virgin with the Scales, by Cesare da Sesto.

1969, Mar. 17   Photo.   Perf. 12½x12
C95 AP21 100fr vio & multi   2.00   1.00
C96 AP21 100fr grn & multi   2.00   1.00

Leonardo da Vinci (1452-1519).
For surcharge see Benin No. C651B.

General Bonaparte, by Jacques Louis David — AP36

Paintings: 60fr, Napoleon I in 1809, by Robert J. Lefevre. 75fr, Napoleon on the Battlefield of Eylau, by Antoine Jean Gros, horiz. 200fr, Gen. Bonaparte at Arcole, by Gros.

1969, Apr. 14   Photo.   Perf. 12½x12
C97 AP36 30fr multi   1.50   1.25
C98 AP36 60fr multi   2.75   1.75
C99 AP36 75fr multi   3.25   2.50
C100 AP36 200fr multi   7.50   5.50
  Nos. C97-C100 (4)   15.00   11.00

Bicentenary of the birth of Napoleon I. For surcharges, see Benin Nos. C599, C605.

Arms Type of Regular Issue, 1969

1969, June 30   Litho.   Perf. 13½x13
C101 A49 50fr multi   .75   .30

For overprint and surcharge see Benin Nos. C417, C596.

Apollo 8 Trip Around the Moon AP37

DAHOMEY

Embossed on Gold Foil
1969, July **Die-cut Perf. 10½**
C102 AP37 1000fr gold   20.00 20.00

US Apollo 8 mission, which put the 1st men into orbit around the moon, Dec. 21-27, 1968.

Nos. C67-C68 Surcharged

1969, Aug. 1 **Photo.** **Perf. 13**
C103 AP28 125fr on 70fr, #C67   2.50 1.75
C104 AP28 125fr on 70fr, #C68   2.50 1.75

Man's 1st landing on the moon, July 20, 1969; US astronauts Neil A. Armstrong, Col. Edwin E. Aldrin, Jr., with Lieut. Col. Michael Collins piloting Apollo 11.

Europafrica Issue
Type of Regular Issue, 1969

Design: 100fr, Oil palm industry, Cotonou.

1969, Sept. 22 **Litho.** **Perf. 14**
C105 A51 100fr multi   2.25 .35
  a. Souv. sheet of 3, #262-263, C105   4.25 4.25

For surcharge see Benin No. C523.

Dahomey Rotary Emblem — AP38

1969, Sept. 25 **Perf. 14x13½**
C106 AP38 50fr multi   1.00 .75

For surcharge see Benin No. C468.

No. C33 Surcharged

1969, Nov. 15 **Photo.** **Perf. 12½**
C107 AP14 10fr on 50fr multi   .45 .25

Dance Type of Regular Issue
Design: Teke dance and Tourist Year emblem.

1969, Dec. 15 **Litho.** **Perf. 14**
C108 A52 70fr multi   2.50 1.50

For surcharge see Benin No. C398.

Painting Type of 1966
Christmas: 30fr, Annunciation, by Vrancke van der Stockt. 45fr, Nativity, Swabian School, horiz. 110fr, Madonna and Child, by the Master of the Gold Brocade. 200fr, Adoration of the Kings, Antwerp School.

1969, Dec. 20 **Perf. 12½x12, 12x12½**
C109 AP21 30fr multi   .50 .40
C110 AP21 45fr red & multi   .85 .65
C111 AP21 110fr multi   2.10 1.25
C112 AP21 200fr multi   3.75 2.25
  Nos. C109-C112 (4) 7.20 4.55

For surcharges see Benin #C425, C463, C475, C532, C595.

1969, Dec. 27 **Perf. 12½x12**

Paintings: No. C113, The Artist's Studio (detail), by Gustave Courbet. No. C114, Self-portrait with Gold Chain, by Rembrandt. 150fr, Hendrickje Stoffels, by Rembrandt.

C113 AP21 100fr red & multi 2.25 1.25
C114 AP21 100fr grn & multi 2.25 1.25
C115 AP21 150fr multi   3.75 1.75
  Nos. C113-C115 (3)   8.25 4.25

For overprints and surcharges see Benin Nos. C458, C472, C524.

Franklin D. Roosevelt — AP39

1970, Feb. **Photo.** **Perf. 12½**
C116 AP39 100fr ultra, yel grn & blk   1.75 .80

25th anniversary of the death of Pres. Franklin Delano Roosevelt (1882-1945). For surcharges see Benin Nos. C525, C637.

Astronauts, Rocket, US Flag — AP40

Astronauts: 50fr, Riding rocket through space. 70fr, In landing module approaching moon. 110fr, Planting US flag on moon.

1970, Mar. 9 **Photo.** **Perf. 12½**
C117 AP40 30fr multi   .65 .25

Souvenir Sheet
C118 Sheet of 4   8.00 8.00
  a. AP40 50fr violet blue & multi   .75 .75
  b. AP40 70fr violet blue & multi 1.00 1.00
  c. AP40 110fr violet blue & multi 1.25 1.25

See note after No. C104. No. C118 contains Nos. C117, C118a, C118b and C118c. For surcharge see Benin No. C120.

Walt Whitman and Dahoman Huts AP41

1970, Apr. 30 **Engr.** **Perf. 13**
C119 AP41 100fr Prus bl, brn & emer   1.40 .80

Walt Whitman (1818-92), American poet. For surcharge, see Benin No. C510.

No. C117 Surcharged in Silver

1970, May 15 **Photo.** **Perf. 12½**
C120 AP40 40fr on 30fr multi 1.20 .75

The flight of Apollo 13. For surcharge see Benin No. C464.

Soccer Players and Globe AP42

Designs: 50fr, Goalkeeper catching ball. 200fr, Players kicking ball.

1970, May 19
C121 AP42 40fr multi   .75 .40
C122 AP42 50fr multi   .95 .50
C123 AP42 200fr multi   3.50 1.25
  Nos. C121-C123 (3)   5.20 2.15

9th World Soccer Championships for the Jules Rimet Cup, Mexico City, May 30-June 21, 1970.
For surcharges, see No. C126, Benin Nos. C502, C504.

EXPO '70 Type of Regular Issue
EXPO '70 Emblems and: 70fr, Dahomey pavilion. 120fr, Mt. Fuji, temple and torii.

1970, June 15 **Litho.** **Perf. 13½x14**
C124 A54 70fr yel, red & dk vio   1.25 .60
C125 A54 120fr yel, red & grn 2.25 1.00

For surcharges see Benin Nos. C470, C477.

No. C123 Surcharged and Overprinted

1970, July 13 **Photo.** **Perf. 12½**
C126 AP42 100fr on 200fr multi 2.10 1.00

Brazil's victory in the 9th World Soccer Championships, Mexico City.
For surcharge see Benin No. C515.

Mercury, Map of Africa and Europe — AP43

Europafrica Issue, 1970

1970, July 20 **Photo.** **Perf. 12x13**
C127 AP43 40fr multi   .90 .40
C128 AP43 70fr multi   1.50 .60

For surcharges see Benin Nos. C429, C488, C566.

Ludwig van Beethoven — AP44

1970, Sept. 21 **Litho.** **Perf. 14x13½**
C129 AP44 90fr brt bl & vio blk 1.40 .45
C130 AP44 110fr yel grn & dk brn 1.75 .65

Bicentenary of the birth of Ludwig van Beethoven (1770-1827), composer.
For surcharges, see Benin Nos. C476, C608.

Symbols of Learning — AP45

1970, Nov. 6 **Photo.** **Perf. 12½**
C131 AP45 100fr multi   1.40 .75

Laying of the foundation stone for the University at Calavi.
For overprint and surcharges see Benin Nos. C356, C399, C616.

Annunciation, Rhenish School, c.1340 — AP46

Paintings of Rhenish School, circa 1340: 70fr, Nativity. 110fr, Adoration of the Kings. 200fr, Presentation at the Temple.

1970, Nov. 9 **Perf. 12½x12**
C132 AP46 40fr gold & multi   .55 .40
C133 AP46 70fr gold & multi 1.00 .55
C134 AP46 110fr gold & multi 2.40 1.25
C135 AP46 200fr gold & multi 4.00 2.00
  Nos. C132-C135 (4)   7.95 4.20

Christmas 1970.
For surcharges see Benin Nos. C479, C518, C527.

Charles de Gaulle, Arc de Triomphe and Flag — AP47

Design: 500fr, de Gaulle as old man and Notre Dame Cathedral, Paris.

1971, Mar. 15 **Photo.** **Perf. 12½**
C136 AP47 40fr multi   .80 .45
C137 AP47 500fr multi   6.50 3.25

Gen. Charles de Gaulle (1890-1970), President of France.
For surcharges see Benin Nos. C465, C567.

L'Indifférent, by Watteau — AP48

Painting: No. C139, Woman playing stringed instrument, by Watteau.

1971, May 3 **Photo.** **Perf. 13**
C138 AP48 100fr red brn & multi 3.25 1.75
C139 AP48 100fr red brn & multi 3.25 1.75

See Nos. C151-C152. For overprints and surcharges, see Benin Nos. C357D, C372, C456, C526, C617, C638.

1971, May 29 **Photo.** **Perf. 13**

Dürer Paintings: 100fr, Self-portrait, 1498. 200fr, Self-portrait, 1500.

C140 AP48 100fr bl grn & multi 2.25 1.25
C141 AP48 200fr dk grn & multi 4.50 2.25

Albrecht Dürer (1471-1528), German painter and engraver. See Nos. C151-C152, C174-C175. For surcharges and overprints see Benin Nos. C357B, C381, C533, C545, C618.

Johannes Kepler and Diagram AP49

200fr, Kepler, trajectories, satellite and rocket.

1971, July 12 **Engr.** **Perf. 13**
C142 AP49 40fr brt rose lil, blk & vio bl   .90 .55
C143 AP49 200fr red, blk & dk bl 3.25 1.75

Kepler (1571-1630), German astronomer.
For overprint and surcharges see Benin Nos. C342, C348, C466, C480, C568.

DAHOMEY

Europafrica Issue

Jet Plane, Maps of Europe and Africa — AP50

100fr, Ocean liner, maps of Europe and Africa.

1971, July 19   Photo.   Perf. 12½x12
C144 AP50 50fr blk, lt bl & org   1.60 .60
C145 AP50 100fr multi   2.50 1.00
   For surcharges see Benin Nos. C374, C404, C421, C585, C630.

African Postal Union Issue, 1971
Common Design Type

Design: 100fr, Dahomey coat of arms and UAMPT building, Brazzaville, Congo.

1971, Nov. 13   Perf. 13x13½
C146 CD135 100fr bl & multi   1.75 .80
   For overprint and surcharge see Benin Nos. C357E, C619.

Flight into Egypt, by Van Dyck — AP51

Paintings: 40fr, Adoration of the Shepherds, by the Master of the Hausbuch, c. 1500, vert. 70fr, Adoration of the Kings, by Holbein the Elder, vert. 200fr, The Birth of Christ, by Dürer.

1971, Nov. 22   Perf. 13
C147 AP51 40fr gold & multi   .85 .45
C148 AP51 70fr gold & multi   1.40 .55
C149 AP51 100fr gold & multi   2.10 .80
C150 AP51 200fr gold & multi   5.00 1.75
   Nos. C147-C150 (4)   9.35 3.55
   Christmas 1971
   For overprint and surcharges see Benin Nos. C394, C394A, C397, C403, C403A, C405, C481, C503, C546, C581, C630, C631.

Painting Type of 1971 Inscribed: "25e ANNIVERSAIRE DE L'UNICEF"

Paintings: 40fr, Prince Balthazar, by Velasquez. 100fr, Infanta Margarita María, by Velázquez.

1971, Dec. 11
C151 AP48 40fr gold & multi   1.75 .55
C152 AP48 100fr gold & multi   3.00 .85
   25th anniv. of UNICEF.
   For surcharges see Benin Nos. C366, C418, C437, C592, C639.

Olympic Games Type

Design: 150fr, Sapporo '72 emblem, ski jump and stork flying.

1972, Feb.   Engr.   Perf. 13
C153 A61 150fr brn, dp rose lil & bl   3.50 1.25
   11th Winter Olympic Games, Sapporo, Japan, Feb. 3-13.
   For overprint and surcharge see Benin Nos. C347, C433, C645.

Boy Scout and Scout Flag — AP52

Designs: 40fr, Scout playing marimba. 100fr, Scouts doing farm work.

1972, Mar. 19   Photo.   Perf. 13
Size: 26x35mm
C154 AP52 35fr multi   .50 .25
C155 AP52 40fr multi   .85 .40

Size: 26x46mm
C156 AP52 100fr yel & multi   1.75 .85
  a. Souvenir sheet of 3, #C154-C156, perf. 12½   4.25 4.25
   Nos. C154-C156 (3)   3.10 1.50
   World Boy Scout Seminar, Cotonou, Mar. 1972.
   For overprint and surcharges see Benin Nos. C373, C414, C569.

Workers Training Institute and Friedrich Naumann — AP53

Design: 250fr, Workers Training Institute and Pres. Theodor Heuss of Germany.

1972, Mar. 29   Photo.   Perf. 13x12
C157 AP53 100fr brt rose, blk & vio   1.50 .65
C158 AP53 250fr bl, blk & vio   3.50 1.40
   Laying of foundation stone for National Workers Training Institute.
   For surcharges see Benin Nos. C380, C473, C640, C649, Q25A.

Mosaic Floor, St. Mark's, Venice — AP54

12th Century Mosaics from St. Mark's Basilica: 40fr, Roosters carrying fox on a pole. 65fr, Noah sending out dove.

1972, Apr. 10   Perf. 13
C159 AP54 35fr gold & multi   1.35 .75
C160 AP54 40fr gold & multi   1.50 .90
C161 AP54 65fr gold & multi   3.00 1.50
   Nos. C159-C161 (3)   5.85 3.15
   UNESCO campaign to save Venice.
   For surcharges see Benin Nos. 690G, C600.

Neapolitan and Dahoman Dancers — AP55

1972, May 3   Perf. 13½x13
C162 AP55 100fr multi   1.50 .65
   12th Philatelic Exhibition, Naples.
   For overprint and surcharge, see Benin Nos. C395, C620.

Running, German Eagle, Olympic Rings — AP56

85fr, High jump and Glyptothek, Munich. 150fr, Shot put and Propylaeum, Munich.

1972, June 12   Engr.   Perf. 13
C163 AP56 20fr ultra, grn & brn   .40 .25
C164 AP56 85fr brn, gold & ultra   .95 .60
C165 AP56 150fr grn, brn & ultra   2.00 1.00
  a. Min. sheet of 3, #C163-C165   4.00 4.00
   Nos. C163-C165 (3)   3.35 1.85
   20th Olympic Games, Munich, 8/26-9/10.
   For overprints and surcharges see Nos. C170-C172, Benin C343, C346, C370, C404A, C559, C577, C651A.

Louis Blériot and his Plane — AP57

1972, June 26
C166 AP57 100fr vio, cl & brt bl   4.00 1.75
   Birth centenary of Louis Blériot (1872-1936), French aviation pioneer.
   For surcharges see Benin Nos. C386, C621.

Adam, by Lucas Cranach — AP58

Design: 200fr, Eve, by Lucas Cranach.

1972, Oct. 24   Photo.
C167 AP58 150fr multi   2.75 1.25
C168 AP58 200fr multi   4.50 1.75
   Cranach (1472-1553), German painter.
   For surcharges see Benin Nos. C402, C434A, C537, C643.

Pauline Borghese, by Canova — AP59

1972, Nov. 8
C169 AP59 250fr multi   7.00 1.75
   Antonio Canova (1757-1822), Italian sculptor.
   For surcharge, see Benin No. 1366.

Nos. C163-C165 Overprinted

a

b

c

1972, Nov. 13   Engr.   Perf. 13
C170 AP56(a) 20fr multi   .45 .25
C171 AP56(b) 85fr multi   1.25 .60
C172 AP56(c) 150fr multi   2.25 1.25
  a. Miniature sheet of 3   5.25 5.25
   Nos. C170-C172 (3)   3.95 2.10
   Gold medal winners in 20th Olympic Games: Lasse Viren, Finland, 5,000m. and 10,000m. races (20fr); Ulrike Meyfarth, Germany, women's high jump (85fr); Wladyslaw Komar, Poland, shot put (150fr).
   For surcharges, see Benin Nos. C343A, C371, C538, C607.

Louis Pasteur — AP60

1972, Nov. 30
C173 AP60 100fr brt grn, lil & brn   2.50 1.00
   Pasteur (1822-95), chemist and bacteriologist.
   For surcharges see Benin Nos. C344, C622.

Painting Type of 1971

Paintings by Georges de La Tour (1593-1652), French painter: 35fr, Vielle player. 150fr, The Newborn, horiz.

1972, Dec. 11   Photo.
C174 AP48 35fr multi   .80 .40
C175 AP48 150fr multi   2.25 1.25
   For surcharges see Benin Nos. C364, C490, C578.

Annunciation, School of Agnolo Gaddi — AP61

Paintings: 125fr, Nativity, by Simone dei Crocifissi. 140fr, Adoration of the Shepherds, by Giovanni di Pietro. 250fr, Adoration of the Kings, by Giotto.

1972, Dec. 15
C176 AP61 35fr gold & multi   .75 .25
C177 AP61 125fr gold & multi   2.00 .65
C178 AP61 140fr gold & multi   2.75 1.00
C179 AP61 250fr gold & multi   4.50 1.50
   Nos. C176-C179 (4)   10.00 3.40
   Christmas 1972. See Nos. C195-C198, C234, C251, C253-C254. For overprint and surcharges see Benin Nos. C383A, C384, C392, C401, C444, C528, C628, C652.

Statue of St. Teresa, Basilica of Lisieux — AP62

100fr, St. Teresa, roses, and globe, vert.

1973, May 14   Photo.   Perf. 13
C180 AP62 40fr blk, gold & lt ultra   .75 .45
C181 AP62 100fr gold & multi   2.50 1.00
   St. Teresa of Lisieux (Therese Martin, 1873-97), Carmelite nun.
   For surcharges see Benin Nos. C390, C570, C623.

Scouts, African Scout Emblem — AP63

Designs (African Scout Emblem and): 20fr, Lord Baden-Powell, vert. 40fr, Scouts building bridge.

1973, July 2   Engr.   Perf. 13
C182 AP63 15fr bl, grn & choc   .45 .25
C183 AP63 20fr ol & Prus bl   .75 .25
C184 AP63 40fr grn, Prus bl & brn   .90 .35
  a. Souvenir sheet of 3   3.00 3.00
   Nos. C182-C184 (3)   2.10 .85
   24th Boy Scout World Conference, Nairobi, Kenya, July 16-21. No. C184a contains 3 stamps similar to Nos. C182-C184 in changed colors (15fr in ultramarine, slate green and chocolate; 20fr in chocolate, ultramarine and indigo; 40fr in slate green, indigo and chocolate).

DAHOMEY

For surcharges see Nos. C217-C218, Benin C365, C409, C558, C560, C571.

Copernicus, Venera and Mariner Satellites AP64

125fr, Copernicus, sun, earth & moon, vert.

1973, Aug. 20		Engr.		Perf. 13
C185	AP64	65fr blk, dk brn & org	1.50	.55
C186	AP64	125fr bl, slate grn & pur	2.75	1.00

For surcharges and overprints see Benin Nos. C345, C349A, C375, C601, C642.

Head and City Hall, Brussels — AP64a

1973, Sept. 17		Engr.		Perf. 13
C187	AP64a	100fr blk, Prus bl & dk grn	1.10	.60

African Weeks, Brussels, Sept. 15-30, 1973. For surcharge see Benin No. C400.

WMO Emblem, World Weather Map AP65

1973, Sept. 25
C188 AP65 100fr ol grn & lt brn 1.40 .75

Cent. of intl. meteorological cooperation. For surcharges and overprint see Nos. C199, Benin Nos. C382, C624.

Europafrica Issue

AP66

Design: 40fr, similar to 35fr.

1973, Oct. 1		Engr.		Perf. 13
C189	AP66	35fr multi	.55	.35
C190	AP66	40fr bl, sepia & ultra	.70	.40

For overprint and surcharges, see Benin Nos. C411, C564, C593.

John F. Kennedy — AP67

1973, Oct. 18
C191 AP67 200fr bl grn, vio & sl grn 2.75 2.75

Souvenir Sheet
C191A AP67 200fr bl, rd brn, brn 5.00 5.00

For surcharge and overprint see Benin Nos. C377, C441, C547.

Soccer AP68

40fr, 2 soccer players. 100fr, 3 soccer players.

1973, Nov. 19		Engr.		Perf. 13
C192	AP68	35fr multi	.55	.25
C193	AP68	40fr multi	.65	.25
C194	AP68	100fr multi	1.25	.65
		Nos. C192-C194 (3)	2.45	1.15

World Soccer Cup, Munich 1974. For surcharges and overprint see Nos. C219-C220, Benin Nos. C396, C591, C644.

Painting Type of 1972

Christmas: 35fr, Annunciation, by Dirk Bouts. 100fr, Nativity, by Giotto. 150fr, Adoration of the Kings, by Botticelli. 200fr, Adoration of the Shepherds, by Jacopo Bassano, horiz.

1973, Dec. 20		Photo.		Perf. 13
C195	AP61	35fr gold & multi	.80	.40
C196	AP61	100fr gold & multi	1.50	.65
C197	AP61	150fr gold & multi	3.00	1.10
C198	AP61	200fr gold & multi	3.25	1.75
		Nos. C195-C198 (4)	8.55	3.90

For overprints and surcharges see Benin Nos. C378, C388, C410, C434, C438, C442, C487, C565, C646.

No C188 Surcharged in Violet

1974, Feb. 4		Engr.		Perf. 13
C199	AP65	200fr on 100fr multi	2.25	1.25

Skylab US space missions, 1973-74.

Skiers, Snowflake, Olympic Rings AP69

1974, Feb. 25		Engr.		Perf. 13
C200	AP69	100fr vio bl, brn & brt bl	1.75	1.10

50th anniversary of first Winter Olympic Games, Chamonix, France. For surcharges, see Benin Nos. C389, C625.

Marie Curie — AP70

1974, June 7		Engr.		Perf. 13
C201	AP70	50fr Lenin	1.75	.65
C202	AP70	125fr shown	2.25	.90
C203	AP70	150fr Churchill	2.50	1.40
		Nos. C201-C203 (3)	6.50	2.95

50th anniv. of the death of Lenin; 40th anniv. of the death of Marie Sklodowska Curie; cent. of the birth of Winston Churchill.

For overprints and surcharges see Benin Nos. C387A, C391A, C489, C529, C597, C632, C634.

Bishop, Persian, 18th Century — AP71

200fr, Queen, Siamese chess piece, 19th cent.

1974, June 14		Photo.		Perf. 12½x13
C204	AP71	50fr org & multi	2.50	1.00
C205	AP71	200fr brt grn & multi	6.00	2.50

21st Chess Olympiad, Nice, 6/6-30/74. For surcharges and overprint see Benin Nos. C469, C482, C598, C627, Q11.

Frederic Chopin — AP72

Design: No. C207, Ludwig van Beethoven.

1974, June 24		Engr.		Perf. 13
C206	AP72	150fr blk & copper red	4.50	1.40
C207	AP72	150fr blk & copper red	4.50	1.40

Famous musicians: Frederic Chopin and Ludwig van Beethoven. For overprints and surcharges see Benin Nos. C376, C452, C459, C539, C579, C647, C655.

Astronaut on Moon, and Earth — AP73

1974, July 10		Engr.		Perf. 13
C208	AP73	150fr multi	2.75	1.50

5th anniversary of the first moon walk. For surcharges and overprint see Benin Nos. C391, C460, C635.

Litho. & Embossed 'Gold Foil' Stamps

These stamps generally are of a different design format from the rest of the issue. Since there is a commemorative inscription tying them to the issue a separate illustration is not being shown.

World Cup Soccer Championships, Munich — AP74

World Cup trophy and players and flags of: 35fr, West Germany, Chile, Australia, DDR. 40fr, Zaire, Scotland, Brazil, Yugoslavia. 100fr, Sweden, Bulgaria, Uruguay, Netherlands. 200fr, Italy, Haiti, Poland, Argentina. 300fr, Stadium. 500fr, Trophy and flags.

		Perf. 14x13, 13x14		Litho.
1974, July 16				
C209	AP74	35fr multicolored	.40	.25
C210	AP74	40fr multicolored	.55	.25
C211	AP74	100fr multicolored	1.10	.70
C212	AP74	200fr multicolored	2.50	1.25
C213	AP74	300fr multi, horiz.	2.50	1.50

Souvenir Sheet
C215 AP74 500fr multi, horiz. 7.25 7.25

It is uncertain if this issue was valid for postage or recognized by the Dahomey government.

Nos. C182-C183 Srchd. and Ovptd. in Black or Red

1974, July 19				
C217	AP63	100fr on 15fr multi	1.25	.60
C218	AP63	140fr on 20fr multi (R)	1.75	.90

11th Pan-Arab Jamboree, Batrun, Lebanon, Aug. 1974. Overprint includes 2 bars over old denomination; 2-line overprint on No. C217, 3 lines on No. C218.

Nos. C193-C194 Overprinted and Surcharged

1974, July 26		Engr.		Perf. 13
C219	AP68	100fr on 40fr	1.10	.65
C220	AP68	150fr on 100fr	1.60	1.00

World Cup Soccer Championship, 1974, victory of German Federal Republic.

Earth and UPU Emblem AP75

Designs (UPU Emblem and): 65fr, Concorde in flight. 125fr, French railroad car, c. 1860. 200fr, African drummer and Renault mail truck, pre-1939.

1974, Aug. 5		Engr.		Perf. 13
C221	AP75	35fr rose cl & vio	.75	.40
C222	AP75	65fr Prus grn & cl	1.50	.95
C223	AP75	125fr multi	3.50	1.50
C224	AP75	200fr multi	3.50	2.00
		Nos. C221-C224 (4)	9.25	4.85

Centenary of Universal Postal Union. For surcharges, see Benin Nos. C422, C530, C540, C586, C653, C657, Q13B, Q17B.

UPU, Cent. AP76

Communications and transportation: 50fr, Rocket, Indian shooting arrow. 100fr, Airplane, dog sled, vert. 125fr, Rocket launch, balloon. 150fr, Rocket re-entry into Earth's atmosphere, drum. 200fr, Locomotive, Pony Express rider. 500fr, UPU headquarters. No. C230, Train, 1829. No. C232, Astronaut canceling envelope on moon.

1974		Litho.	Perf. 13x14, 14x13	
C225	AP76	50fr multicolored	.50	.30
C226	AP76	100fr multicolored	.75	.60
C227	AP76	125fr multicolored	1.00	.85
C228	AP76	150fr multicolored	1.75	1.00
C229	AP76	200fr multicolored	2.50	1.25

Litho. & Embossed
Perf. 13½
Size: 48x60mm
C230 AP76 1000fr gold & multi 12.00 12.00

Souvenir Sheets
Litho.
Perf. 13x14
C231 AP76 500fr multicolored 4.50 4.50

Litho. & Embossed
Perf. 13½
C232 AP76 1000fr gold & multi 7.25 7.25

Issued: #C230, C232, Oct. 9; others, Aug. 5.

DAHOMEY

It is uncertain if this issue was valid for postage or recognized by the Dahomey government.

Lion of Belfort by Frederic A. Bartholdi AP77

1974, Aug. 20 Engr. Perf. 13
C233 AP77 100fr rose brn 2.50 1.00
For surcharges see Benin Nos. C387, C626.

Paintins Type of 1972
1974, Aug. 20 Engr. Perf. 13
Painting: 250fr, Girl with Falcon, by Philippe de Champaigne.
C234 AP61 250fr multi 4.00 2.40
For surcharges see Benin Nos. C363, C445, C551.

Prehistoric Animals AP78

1974, Sept. 23 Photo.
C235 AP78 35fr Rhamphorhynchus 1.50 .80
C236 AP78 150fr Stegosaurus 5.00 2.25
C237 AP78 200fr Tyrannosaurus 7.00 2.75
Nos. C235-C237 (3) 13.50 5.80
For surcharges and overprint, see Benin Nos. C349, C350, C440, C443, C548, C636.

Conquest of Space — AP79

Various spacecraft and: 50fr, Mercury. 100fr, Venus. 150fr, Mars. 200fr, Jupiter. 400fr, Sun.

1974, Oct. 31 Litho. Perf. 13x14
C238 AP79 50fr multicolored .40 .30
C239 AP79 100fr multicolored 1.00 .50
C240 AP79 150fr multicolored 1.75 .90
C241 AP79 200fr multicolored 2.25 1.25
Nos. C238-C241 (4) 5.40 2.95

Souvenir Sheet
C242 AP79 400fr multicolored 5.25 5.25
It is uncertain if this issue was valid for postage or recognized by the Dahomey government.

West Germany, World Cup Soccer Champions — AP80

Designs: 100fr, Team. 125fr, Paul Breitner. 150fr, Gerd Muller. 300fr, Presentation of trophy. 500fr, German team positioned on field.

1974, Nov. Litho. Perf. 13x14
C243 AP80 100fr multicolored .75 .50
C244 AP80 125fr multicolored 1.00 .75
C245 AP80 150fr multicolored 1.50 1.00
C246 AP80 300fr multicolored 3.25 2.00
Nos. C243-C246 (4) 6.50 4.25

Souvenir Sheet
C248 AP80 500fr multicolored 5.25 5.25
It is uncertain if this issue was valid for postage or recognized by the Dahomey government.

Europafrica Issue

Globe, Cogwheel, Emblem AP81

1974, Dec. 20 Typo. Perf. 13
C250 AP81 250fr red & multi 3.25 2.75
Printed tête bêche in sheets of 10.
For surcharges see Benin Nos. C430, C509, C650.

Christmas Type of 1972 and

Nativity, by Martin Schongauer AP82

Paintings: 35fr, Annunciation, by Schongauer. 100fr, Virgin in Rose Arbor, by Schongauer. 250fr, Virgin and Child, with St. John the Baptist, by Botticelli.

1974, Dec. 23 Photo. Perf. 13
C251 AP61 35fr gold & multi .60 .30
C252 AP82 40fr gold & multi .60 .40
C253 AP61 100fr gold & multi 1.60 .55
C254 AP61 250fr gold & multi 4.25 1.75
Nos. C251-C254 (4) 7.05 3.00
For overprints and surcharges, see Benin Nos. C413, C431, C439, C446, C552, C641.

Apollo and Soyuz Spacecraft AP83

200fr, American and Russian flags, rocket take-off. 500fr, Apollo-Soyuz link-up.

1975, July 16 Litho. Perf. 12½
C255 AP83 35fr multi .50 .30
C256 AP83 200fr vio bl, red & bl 2.40 1.25
C257 AP83 500fr vio bl, ind & red 5.50 3.00
Nos. C255-C257 (3) 8.40 4.55
Apollo Soyuz space test project (Russo-American cooperation); launching July 15; link-up, July 17.
For surcharges and overprints, see Benin Nos. C406, C415-C410, C451, C542-C543, C549, C580.

Nos. C255-C256 Surcharged

No. C258

No. C259

1975, July 17 Litho. Perf. 12½
C258 AP83 100fr on 35fr (S) 1.25 .60
C259 AP83 300fr on 200fr 3.25 1.40
Apollo-Soyuz link-up in space, July 17, 1975.

ARPHILA Emblem, "Stamps" and Head of Ceres AP84

1975, Aug. 22 Engr. Perf. 13
C260 AP84 100fr blk, bl & lilac 1.50 .75
ARPHILA 75, International Philatelic Exhibition, Paris, June 6-16.
For overprint and surcharge, see Benin Nos. C383, C474.

Europafrica Issue

Holy Family, by Michelangelo — AP85

1975, Sept. 29 Litho. Perf. 12
C261 AP85 300fr gold & multi 4.50 1.50
For overprints, see Benin Nos. C447, C554.

Infantry and Stars — AP86

American bicentennial (Stars and): 135fr, Drummers and fifer. 300fr, Artillery with cannon. 500fr, Cavalry.

1975, Nov. 18 Engr. Perf. 13
C262 AP86 75fr grn car & pur 1.00 .45
C263 AP86 135fr bl, mag & sep 1.75 .90
C264 AP86 300fr vio bl, ver & choc 3.25 1.75
C265 AP86 500fr ver, dk grn & brn 5.75 2.50
Nos. C262-C265 (4) 11.75 5.60
For overprints and surcharges see Benin Nos. C247-C249, C385, C412, C429A, C453, C478, C534, C555, C557, C576, C580.

Diving and Olympic Rings — AP87

Design: 250fr, Soccer and Olympic rings.

1975, Nov. 24
C266 AP87 40fr vio, grnsh bl & ol brn .55 .25
C267 AP87 250fr red, emer & brn 2.40 1.25
Pre-Olympic Year 1975.
For surcharges see Benin Nos. C341, C393, C553, C582.

AIR POST SEMI-POSTAL STAMPS

Maternity Hospital, Dakar SPAP1

Dispensary, Mopti SPAP2

Nurse Weighing Baby SPAP3

Perf. 13½x12½, 13 (#CB3)
Photo, Engr. (#CB3)
1942, June 22
CB1 SPAP1 1.50fr + 3.50fr green .80 5.50
CB2 SPAP2 2fr + 6fr brown .80 5.50
CB3 SPAP3 3fr + 9fr car red .80 5.50
Nos. CB1-CB3 (3) 2.40 16.50
Native children's welfare fund.

Colonial Education Fund
Common Design Type
Perf. 12½x13½
1942, June 22 Engr.
CB4 CD86a 1.20fr + 1.80fr blue & red .80 5.50

AIR POST PARCEL POST STAMPS

Catalogue values for unused stamps in this section are for Never Hinged items.

Nos. C20-C23, C14 Surcharged in Black or Red

No. CQ2

No. CQ5

1967-69 Engr. Perf. 13
CQ1 AP6 200fr on 200fr 2.10 2.10
CQ2 AP6 300fr on 100fr 2.40 2.40
CQ3 AP6 500fr on 300fr 4.50 4.50
CQ4 AP6 1000fr on 500fr 9.50 9.50
CQ5 AP4 5000fr on 100fr (R) ('69) 35.00 35.00
Nos. CQ1-CQ5 (5) 53.50 53.50
On No. CQ5, "Colis Postaux" is at top, bar at right.

POSTAGE DUE STAMPS

Dahomey Natives — D1

1906 Unwmk. Typo. Perf. 14x13½
J1 D1 5c grn, grnsh 4.00 4.00
J2 D1 10c red brn 4.00 4.00
J3 D1 15c dark blue 8.00 8.00
J4 D1 20c blk, yellow 8.00 8.00
J5 D1 30c red, straw 12.00 12.00
J6 D1 50c violet 24.00 24.00
J7 D1 60c blk, buff 16.00 16.00
J8 D1 1fr blk, pinkish 52.50 40.00
Nos. J1-J8 (8) 128.50 116.00

D2

DAHOMEY — DALMATIA — DANISH WEST INDIES

1914

J9	D2	5c green	.25	.25
J10	D2	10c rose	.55	.55
J11	D2	15c gray	.55	.55
J12	D2	20c brown	1.10	1.10
J13	D2	30c blue	1.40	1.40
J14	D2	50c black	1.60	1.60
J15	D2	60c orange	2.00	2.00
J16	D2	1fr violet	2.10	2.10
	Nos. J9-J16 (8)		9.55	9.55

Type of 1914 Issue Surcharged

1927

J17	D2	2fr on 1fr lilac rose	5.50	5.50
J18	D2	3fr on 1fr org brn	5.50	5.50

Carved Mask — D3

1941   Engr.   Perf. 14x13

J19	D3	5c black	.25	.25
J20	D3	10c lilac rose	.25	.25
J21	D3	15c dark blue	.25	.25
J22	D3	20c bright yel green	.30	.30
J23	D3	30c orange	.50	.50
J24	D3	50c violet brown	.70	.70
J25	D3	60c slate green	1.10	1.10
J26	D3	1fr rose red	1.40	1.40
J27	D3	2fr yellow	1.50	1.50
J28	D3	3fr dark purple	1.90	1.90
	Nos. J19-J28 (10)		8.15	8.15

Type D3 without "RF"

1944

J28A	D3	10c lilac rose		.50
J28B	D3	15c dark blue		.55
J28C	D3	20c bright yel green		.55
	Nos. J28A-J28C (3)			1.60

Nos. J28A-J28C were issued by the Vichy government in France, but were not placed on sale in Dahomey.

Catalogue values for unused stamps in this section, from this point to the end of the section, are for Never Hinged items.

Republic

Panther and Man — D4

Perf. 14x13½

1963, July 22   Typo.   Unwmk.

J29	D4	1fr green & rose	.25	.25
J30	D4	2fr brn & emerald	.30	.30
J31	D4	5fr org & vio bl	.30	.30
J32	D4	10fr magenta & blk	.65	.65
J33	D4	20fr vio bl & org	1.10	1.10
	Nos. J29-J33 (5)		2.60	2.60

Heliograph — D5

No. J35, Mail boat. No. J36, Morse receiver. No. J37, Mailman on bicycle. No. J38, Early telephone. No. J39, Autorail. No. J40, Mail truck. No. J41, Radio tower. No. J42, DC-8F jet plane. No. J43, Early Bird communications satellite.

1967, Oct. 24   Engr.   Perf. 11

J34	D5	1fr brn, dl pur & bl	.25	.25
J35	D5	1fr dl pur, brn & bl	.25	.25
a.	Pair, #J34-J35		.50	
J36	D5	3fr dk brn, dk grn & org	.25	.25
J37	D5	3fr dk grn, dk brn & org	.25	.25
a.	Pair, #J36-J37		.50	
J38	D5	5fr ol bis, lil & bl	.35	.35
J39	D5	5fr lil, ol bis & bl	.35	.35
a.	Pair, #J38-J39		.75	
J40	D5	10fr brn org, vio & grn	.50	.50
J41	D5	10fr vio, brn org & grn	.50	.50
a.	Pair, #J40-J41		1.10	
J42	D5	30fr Prus bl, mar & vio	1.00	1.00
J43	D5	30fr vio, Prus bl & mar	1.00	1.00
a.	Pair, #J42-J43		2.25	
	Nos. J34-J43 (10)		4.70	4.70

Pairs printed tete beche, se-tenant at the base.

PARCEL POST STAMPS

Catalogue values for unused stamps in this section are for Never Hinged items.

Nos. 141-146 and 148 Surcharged

1967, Jan.   Unwmk.   Engr.   Perf. 13

Q1	A15	5fr on 1fr multi	.25	.25
Q2	A15	10fr on 2fr multi	.35	.35
Q3	A15	20fr on 6fr multi	.60	.60
Q4	A15	25fr on 3fr multi	.90	.90
Q5	A15	30fr on 4fr multi	1.00	1.00
Q6	A15	50fr on 10fr multi	1.40	1.40
a.	"20" instead of "50"		100.00	
Q7	A15	100fr on 20fr multi	2.50	2.50
	Nos. Q1-Q7 (7)		7.00	7.00

The surcharge is arranged to fit the shape of the stamp.

No. Q6a occurred once on the sheet.

DALMATIA

dal-ˈmā-sh(ē-)ə

LOCATION — A promontory in the northwestern part of the Balkan Peninsula, together with several small islands in the Adriatic Sea.

GOVT. — Part of the former Austro-Hungarian crownland of the same name.

AREA — 113 sq. mi.

POP. — 18,719 (1921)

CAPITAL — Zara.

Stamps were issued during Italian occupation. This territory was subsequently annexed by Italy.

100 Centesimi = 1 Corona = 1 Lira

Used values are for postally used stamps.

Issued under Italian Occupation

Italy No. 87 Surcharged

1919, May 1   Wmk. 140   Perf. 14

1	A46	1cor on 1 l brn & grn	3.00	12.00
a.	Pair, one without surcharge		1,050.	1,050.

Italian Stamps of 1906-08 Surcharged — a

1921-22

2	A48	5c on 5c green	4.00	8.00
3	A48	10c on 10c claret	4.00	8.00
a.	Pair, one without surcharge		775.00	
4	A49	25c on 25c blue ('22)	6.00	11.25
5	A49	50c on 50c vio ('22)	6.00	11.00
a.	Double surcharge		300.00	
b.	Pair, one without surcharge		1,000.	

Italian Stamps of 1901-10 Surcharged — b

6	A46	1cor on 1 l brn & grn ('22)	10.00	24.00
7	A46	5cor on 5 l bl & rose ('22)	40.00	110.00
8	A51	10cor on 10 l gray grn & red ('22)	40.00	110.00
	Nos. 2-8 (7)		110.00	282.25

Surcharges similar to these but differing in style or arrangement of type were used in Austria under Italian occupation.

SPECIAL DELIVERY STAMPS

Italian Special Delivery No. E1 Srchd. Type "a"

1921   Wmk. 140   Perf. 14

E1	SD1	25c on 25c rose red	3.00	12.00
a.	Double surcharge		290.00	500.00

Italian Special Delivery Stamp Surcharged

1922

E2	SD2	1.20 l on 1.20 l		195.00

No. E2 was not placed in use.

POSTAGE DUE STAMPS

Italian Postage Due Stamps and Type Surcharged types "a" or "b"

1922   Wmk. 140   Perf. 14

J1	D3 (a)	50c on 50c buff & mag	4.00	9.00
J2	D3 (b)	1cor on 1 l bl & red	9.00	32.50
J3	D3 (b)	2cor on 2 l bl & red	55.00	135.00
J4	D3 (b)	5cor on 5 l bl & red	55.00	135.00
	Nos. J1-J4 (4)		123.00	311.50

DANISH WEST INDIES

ˈdā-nish ˈwest ˈin-dēs

LOCATION — Group of islands in the West Indies, lying east of Puerto Rico

GOVT. — Danish colony

AREA — 132 sq. mi.

POP. — 27,086 (1911)

CAPITAL — Charlotte Amalie

The US bought these islands in 1917 and they became the US Virgin Islands, using US stamps and currency.

100 Cents = 1 Dollar
100 Bit = 1 Franc (1905)

Wmk. 111 — Small Crown

Wmk. 112 — Crown

Wmk. 113 — Crown

Wmk. 114 — Multiple Crosses

Coat of Arms — A1

Yellowish Paper
Yellow Wavy-line Burelage, UL to LR

1856   Typo.   Wmk. 111   Imperf.

1	A1	3c dark carmine, brown gum	210.	235.
a.	3c dark carmine, yellow gum	350.	375.
b.	3c carmine, white gum	3,750.	3,750.

The brown and yellow gums were applied locally.

Reprint: 1981, carmine, back-printed across two stamps ("Reprint by Dansk Post og Telegrafmuseum 1978"), value, pair, $10.

White Paper

1866
Yellow Wavy-line Burelage UR to LL

2	A1	3c rose	42.50	50.

No. 2 reprints, unwatermarked: 1930, carmine, value $100. 1942, rose carmine, back-printed across each row ("Nytryk 1942 G. A. Hagemann Danmark og Dansk Vestindiens Frimaerker Bind 2"), value $50.

1872   Perf. 12½

3	A1	3c rose	130.	320.

1873   Without Burelage

4	A1	4c dull blue	325.	700.
a.	Imperf., pair		775.	
b.	Horiz. pair, imperf. vert.		575.	

The 1930 reprint of No. 4 is ultramarine, unwatermarked and imperf., value $100.

The 1942 4c reprint is blue, unwatermarked, Imperf. and has printing on back (see note below No. 2), value $60.

A2

Normal Frame   Inverted Frame

The arabesques in the corners have a main stem and a branch. When the frame is in normal position, in the upper left corner the branch leaves the main stem half way between two little leaflets. In the lower left corner the branch starts at the foot of the second leaflet. When the frame is inverted the corner designs are, of course, transposed.

Values for inverted frames, covers and blocks are for the cheapest variety.

White Wove Paper
Varying from Thin to Thick

1874-79   Wmk. 112   Perf. 14x13½

5	A2	1c green & brown red	35.00	32.50
a.	1c green & rose lilac, thin paper		160.00	190.00
b.	1c green & red violet, medium paper		50.00	65.00
c.	1c green & claret, thick paper		32.50	26.00
e.	As "c," inverted frame		40.00	26.00
f.	As "a," inverted frame		900.00	1,900.

No. 5 exists with a surcharge similar to the surcharge on No. 15, with 10 CENTS value and 1895 date. This stamp is an essay.

6	A2	3c blue & carmine	35.00	18.00
a.	3c light blue & rose carmine, thin paper		45.00	35.00
b.	3c deep blue & dark carmine, medium paper		45.00	25.00
c.	3c greenish blue & lake, thick paper		29.00	18.00

DANISH WEST INDIES — DANZIG

d.	Imperf., pair	325.00	—
e.	Inverted frame, thick paper	45.00	35.00
f.	As "a," inverted frame	800.00	1,200.
7	A2 4c brown & dull blue	23.00	22.50
b.	4c brown & ultramarine, thin paper	290.00	250.00
c.	Diagonal half used as 2c on cover		165.00
d.	As "b," inverted frame	1,450.	2,400.
8	A2 5c grn & gray ('76)	45.00	29.00
a.	5c yellow green & dark gray, thin paper	85.00	45.00
b.	Inverted frame, thick paper	37.50	26.00
9	A2 7c lilac & orange	40.00	135.00
a.	7c lilac & yellow	120.00	130.00
b.	Inverted frame	65.00	220.00
10	A2 10c blue & brn ('76)	57.50	34.00
a.	10c dark blue & black brown, thin paper	85.00	47.50
b.	Period between "t" & "s" of "cents"	72.50	47.50
c.	Inverted frame	26.00	27.50
11	A2 12c red lil & yel grn ('77)	60.00	170.00
a.	12c lilac & deep green	230.00	240.00
12	A2 14c lilac & green	1,050.	1,750.
a.	Inverted frame	4,000.	4,800.
13	A2 50c vio, thin paper ('79)	260.00	390.00
a.	50c gray violet, thick paper	310.00	525.00
	Nos. 5-13 (9)	1,606.	2,581.

The central element in the fan-shaped scrollwork at the outside of the lower left corner of Nos. 5a and 7b looks like an elongated diamond.
See Nos. 16-20. For surcharges see Nos. 14-15, 23-28, 40.

No. 9 Surcharged in Black

 a

1887

14	A2 (a) 1c on 7c lilac & orange	140.00	275.00
b.	1c on 7c lilac & yellow	190.00	300.00
d.	Inverted frame	175.00	525.00

No. 13 Surcharged in Black

 b

1895

15	A2 (b) 10c on 50c violet, thin paper	45.00	72.50

The "b" surcharge also exists on No. 5, with "10" found in two sizes. These are essays.

Type of 1874-79

1896-1901   **Perf. 13**

16	A2 1c grn & red vio, inverted frame ('98)	26.00	36.50
a.	Normal frame	590.00	735.00
17	A2 3c blue & lake, inverted frame ('98)	15.50	17.00
a.	Normal frame	400.00	600.00
18	A2 4c bister & dull blue ('01)	21.50	13.50
a.	Diagonal half used as 2c on cover		67.50
b.	Inverted frame	85.00	110.00
c.	As "b," diagonal half used as 2c on cover		425.00
19	A2 5c groon & gray, inverted frame	47.50	42.50
a.	Normal frame	1,375.	1,700.
20	A2 10c blue & brn ('01)	110.00	145.00
a.	Inverted frame	1,550.	2,025.
b.	Period between "t" and "s" of "cents"	155.00	180.00
	Nos. 16-20 (5)	220.50	254.50

Arms — A5

1900

21	A5 1c light green	2.60	2.25
22	A5 5c light blue	17.00	25.00

See Nos. 29-30. For surcharges see Nos. 41-42.

Nos. 6, 17, 20 Surcharged

 c

Surcharge "c" in Black

1902   **Perf. 14x13½**

23	A2 2c on 3c blue & carmine, inverted frame	1,075.	1,450.
a.	"2" in date with straight tail	1,200.	1,600.
b.	Normal frame	—	—

Perf. 13

24	A2 2c on 3c blue & lake, inverted frame	11.50	32.00
a.	"2" in date with straight tail	30.00	50.00
b.	Dated "1901"	1,000.	1,000.
c.	Normal frame	320.00	825.00
d.	Dark green surcharge	3,000.	—
e.	As "d" & "a"	—	—
f.	As "d" & "c"	—	—

The overprint on No. 24b exists in two types: with "1901" measuring 2.5 mm or 2.2 mm high.
Only one example of No. 24f can exist.

25	A2 8c on 10c blue & brown	26.00	55.00
a.	"2" with straight tail	35.00	60.00
b.	On No. 20b	55.00	85.00
c.	Inverted frame	300.00	675.00

 d

Surcharge "d" in Black

1902   **Perf. 13**

27	A2 2c on 3c blue & lake, inverted frame	15.75	63.00
a.	Normal frame	415.00	720.00
28	A2 8c on 10c blue & brown	14.00	15.00
a.	On No. 20b	26.00	32.00
b.	Inverted frame	415.00	675.00
	Nos. 23-28 (5)	1,142.	1,615.

1903   **Wmk. 113**

29	A5 2c carmine	9.50	25.00
30	A5 8c brown	36.00	62.00

King Christian IX — A8   St. Thomas Harbor — A9

1905   **Typo.**   **Perf. 13**

31	A8 5b green	4.75	3.00
32	A8 10b red	4.75	3.00
33	A8 20b green & blue	9.50	8.00
34	A8 25b ultramarine	9.50	8.00
35	A8 40b red & gray	9.50	7.00
36	A8 50b yellow & gray	14.00	11.00

Perf. 12

Wmk. Two Crowns (113)
Frame Typographed, Center Engraved

37	A9 1fr green & blue	17.50	50.00
38	A9 2fr orange red & brown	32.50	67.50
39	A9 5fr yellow & brown	85.00	315.00
	Nos. 37-39 (3)	187.00	472.50

Favor cancels exist on Nos. 37-39. Value 25% less.

Nos. 18, 22 and 30 Surcharged in Black

1905   **Wmk. 112**

40	A2 5b on 4c bister & dull blue	17.50	70.00
a.	Inverted frame	110.00	190.00
41	A5 5b on 5c light blue	13.00	64.00

Wmk. 113

42	A5 5b on 8c brown	13.00	75.00
	Nos. 40-42 (3)	43.50	209.00

Favor cancels exist on Nos. 40-42. Value 25% less.

Frederik VIII — A10

Frame Typographed, Center Engraved

1908

43	A10 5b green	2.75	1.90
44	A10 10b red	2.75	1.90
45	A10 15b violet & brown	5.00	5.75
46	A10 20b green & blue	32.50	27.50
47	A10 25b blue & dark blue	2.25	2.50
48	A10 30b claret & slate	67.50	60.00
49	A10 40b vermilion & gray	8.00	11.50
50	A10 50b yellow & brown	8.50	10.00
	Nos. 43-50 (8)	129.25	121.05

Christian X — A11

1915   **Wmk. 114**   **Perf. 14x14½**

51	A11 5b yellow green	5.25	6.25
52	A11 10b red	5.25	110.00
53	A11 15b lilac & red brown	5.25	110.00
54	A11 20b green & blue	5.25	110.00
55	A11 25b blue & dark blue	5.25	16.00
56	A11 30b claret & black	5.25	200.00
57	A11 40b orange & black	5.25	200.00
58	A11 50b yellow & brown	5.25	200.00
	Nos. 51-58 (8)	42.00	952.25

Forged and favor cancellations exist.

POSTAGE DUE STAMPS

Royal Cipher, "Christian 9 Rex" — D1

1902   **Litho. Unwmk.**   **Perf. 11½**

J1	D1 1c dark blue	8.25	45.00
J2	D1 4c dark blue	20.00	45.00
J3	D1 6c dark blue	40.00	87.50
J4	D1 10c dark blue	40.00	87.50
	Nos. J1-J4 (4)	108.25	265.00

There are five types of each value. On the 4c they may be distinguished by differences in the figure "4"; on the other values differences are minute.
Used values of Nos. J1-J8 are for canceled stamps. Uncanceled stamps without gum have probably been used. Value 60% of unused.
Excellent counterfeits of Nos. J1-J4 exist.

Numeral of value — D2

1905-13   **Perf. 13**

J5	D2 5b red & gray	6.50	8.00
J6	D2 20b red & gray	11.50	14.50
J7	D2 30b red & gray	9.50	14.50
J8	D2 50b red & gray	9.00	36.00
a.	Perf. 14x14½ ('13)	75.00	290.00
b.	Perf. 11½	475.00	
	Nos. J5-J8 (4)	36.50	73.00

All values of this issue are known imperforate, but were not regularly issued.
Used values of Nos. J5-J8 are for canceled stamps. Uncanceled examples without gum have probably been used. Value 60% of unused.
No. J8b is valued in the grade of fine.
Counterfeits of Nos. J5-J8 exist.
Danish West Indies stamps were replaced by those of the U.S. in 1917, after the U.S. bought the islands.

DANZIG

ˈdant͡s-sig

LOCATION — In northern Europe bordering on the Baltic Sea
AREA — 754 sq. mi.
POP. — 407,000 (approx. 1939)

CAPITAL — Danzig

Established as a "Free City and State" under the protection of the League of Nations in 1920, Danzig was seized by Germany in 1939. It became a Polish province in 1945.

100 Pfennig = 1 Gulden (1923)
100 Pfennig = 1 Mark

Watermarks

Wmk. 108 — Honeycomb   Wmk. 109 — Webbing

Wmk. 110 — Octagons   Wmk. 125 — Lozenges

Wmk. 237 — Swastikas

Used Values of 1920-23 are for favor-canceled stamps unless otherwise noted. Postally used examples bring much higher prices.

For additional varieties, see the *Scott Classic Catalogue*.

German Stamps of 1906-20 Overprinted in Black

Perf. 14, 14½, 15x14½

1920   **Wmk. 125**

1	A16 5pf green	.30	.50
a.	Pair, one without overprint	100.00	
b.	Double overprint	—	
2	A16 10pf car rose	.30	.30
3	A22 15pf violet brown	.30	.30
4	A16 20pf blue violet	.30	1.10
5	A16 30pf org & blk, buff	.30	.30
a.	Pair, one without overprint	—	—
6	A16 40pf car rose	.30	.30
7	A16 50pf pur & blk, buff	.50	.30
a.	Pair, one without overprint	175.00	
8	A17 1m red	.50	.60
a.	Pair, one without overprint	100.00	
9	A17 1.25m green	.60	.60
10	A17 1.50m yellow brn	.90	1.60
11	A21 2m blue	3.25	7.25
	Double overprint	375.00	
12	A21 2.50m lilac rose	3.00	4.50
c.	Double overprint	1,000.	
13	A19 3m black violet	7.50	10.50
a.	3m blackish slate-violet	67.50	135.00
	Double overprint		
14	A16 4m black & rose	4.75	6.00
15	A20 5m slate & car (25x17 holes)	2.50	3.75
a.	Center & "Danzig" invtd.	15,000.	
b.	Inverted overprint	20,000.	
	Nos. 1-15 (15)	25.20	37.90
	Set, never hinged	122.50	

The 5pf brown, 10pf orange and 40pf lake and black with this overprint were not regularly issued. Value for trio, $450.
For surcharges see Nos. 19-23, C1-C3.

DANZIG

Issued: 40pf, 9/13; 1.50m, 3m 7/20; 4m, 12/21; others 6/14.

Nos. 5, 4 Surcharged in Various Sizes

1920

19	A16	5pf on 30pf (V)	.25	.25
20	A16	10pf on 20pf (R)	.25	.25
	a.	Double surcharge	110.00	
21	A16	25pf on 30pf (G)	.25	.25
	a.	Inverted surcharge	85.00	275.00
22	A16	60pf on 30pf (Br)	.70	1.00
	a.	Double surcharge	85.00	290.00
	b.	Pair, one without surcharge	75.00	
23	A16	80pf on 30pf (V)	.70	1.00

Issued: No. 21, 8/10. No. 20, 8/17. Nos. 19, 22-23, 11/1.

German Stamps Surcharged in Various Styles

 No. 25   No. 27

 No. 30

Burelage With Points Up

Gray Burelage with Points Up

25	A16	1m on 30pf org & blk, buff (Bk)	.85	1.50
	a.	Pair, one without surcharge		
26	A16	1¼m on 3pf brn (H)	1.00	1.50
27	A22	2m on 35pf red brn (Bl)	1.50	1.50
	d.	Surcharge omitted	70.00	—
28	A22	3m on 7½pf org (G)	1.00	1.50
29	A22	5m on 2pf gray (R)	1.00	2.00
30	A22	10m on 7½pf org (Bk)	3.00	7.00
		Nos. 19-30 (11)	10.50	17.75
		Set, never hinged	64.00	

Gray Burelage with Points Down

26a	A16	1¼m on 3pf brown	36.00	42.50
27a	A22	2m on 35pf red brn	400.00	325.00
28a	A22	3m on 7½pf orange	25.00	17.00
29a	A22	5m on 2pf gray	25.00	30.00
30a	A22	10m on 7½pf orange	5.75	11.00
		Nos. 26a-30a (5)	491.75	425.50
		Set, never hinged	2,100.	

Violet Burelage with Points Up

25b	A16	1m on 30pf org & blk, buff	85.00	30.00
26b	A16	1¼m on 3pf brown	4.50	6.50
27b	A22	2m on 35pf red brn	11.50	37.50
28b	A22	3m on 7½pf orange	2.50	2.50
29b	A22	5m on 2pf gray	1.25	2.50
30b	A22	10m on 7½pf orange	1.25	2.50
	h.	Double overprint	70.00	
		Nos. 25b-30b (6)	106.00	81.50
		Set, never hinged	430.00	

Burelage with Points Down

Violet Burelage with Points Down

25c	A16	1m on 30pf org & blk, buff	1.25	2.50
26c	A16	1¼m on 3pf brown	6.50	11.00
	e.	Double overprint	450.00	
27c	A22	2m on 35pf red brn	30.00	50.00
28c	A22	3m on 7½pf orange	40.00	85.00
29c	A22	5m on 2pf gray	6.50	8.50
30c	A22	10m on 7½pf orange	13.50	29.00
		Nos. 25c-30c (6)	97.75	186.00
		Set, never hinged	380.00	

Excellent counterfeits of the surcharges are known.

German Stamps of 1906-20 Overprinted in Blue

1920

31	A22	2pf gray	110.00	200.00
32	A22	2½pf gray	150.00	300.00
33	A16	3pf brown	11.00	17.00
	a.	Double overprint	75.00	
34	A16	5pf green	.60	.70
	a.	Double overprint	85.00	
35	A22	7½pf orange	40.00	57.50
36	A16	10pf carmine	3.75	7.00
	b.	Double overprint	75.00	
37	A22	15pf dk violet	.60	.70
	b.	Double overprint	85.00	
38	A16	20pf blue violet	.60	.70

Overprinted in Carmine or Blue

39	A16	25pf org & blk, yel	.60	.70
40	A16	30pf org & blk, buff	50.00	92.50
42	A16	40pf lake & blk	2.25	2.50
	a.	Inverted overprint	210.00	
	b.	Double overprint	425.00	
43	A16	50pf pur & blk, buff	175.00	300.00
44	A16	60pf mag (Bl)	1,250.	2,100.
45	A16	75pf green & blk	.60	.70
	a.	Double overprint	450.00	
46	A16	80pf lake & blk, rose	2.40	4.25
47	A17	1m carmine	1,200.	2,100.
	a.	Double overprint	4,250.	

Overprinted in Carmine

48	A21	2m gray blue	1,200.	2,100.

Counterfeit overprints of Nos. 31-48 exist.
Nos. 44, 47 and 48 were issued in small quantities and usually affixed directly to the mail by the postal clerk.
For surcharge see No. 62.

A8   Hanseatic Trading Ship — A9

1921, Jan. 31   Typo.   Wmk. 108   Serrate Roulette 13½

49	A8	5pf brown & violet	.25	.25
50	A8	10pf orange & dk vio	.25	.25
51	A8	25pf green & car rose	.50	.65
52	A8	40pf carmine rose	3.75	3.25
53	A8	80pf ultra	.50	.50
54	A9	1m car rose & blk	1.60	2.00
55	A9	2m dk blue & dk grn	5.00	5.00
56	A9	3m blk & grnsh bl	2.00	2.00
57	A9	5m indigo & rose red	2.00	2.00
58	A9	10m dk grn & brn org	2.50	4.50
		Nos. 49-58 (10)	18.35	20.40
		Set, never hinged	82.50	

Issued in honor of the Constitution.
Nos. 49 and 50 with center in red instead of violet and Nos. 49-51, 54-58 with center inverted are probably proofs. All values of this issue exist imperforate but are not known to have been regularly issued in that condition.

1921, Mar. 11   Perf. 14

59	A8	25pf green & car rose	.50	.85
60	A8	40pf carmine rose	.50	.85
61	A8	80pf ultra	5.50	10.00
		Nos. 59-61 (3)	6.50	11.70
		Set, never hinged	34.00	

No. 45 Surcharged in Black

1921, May 6   Wmk. 125

62	A16	60pf on 75pf	.95	.90
		Never hinged	5.50	
	a.	Double surcharge	100.00	110.00

Surcharge on No. 62 normally appears at top of design.

 Arms A11   Coat of Arms A12

Wmk. 108 (Upright or Sideways)
1921-22   Perf. 14

63	A11	5(pf) orange	.25	.25
64	A11	10(pf) dark brown	.25	.25
65	A11	15(pf) green	.25	.25
66	A11	20(pf) slate	.25	.25
67	A11	25(pf) dark green	.25	.25
68	A11	30(pf) blue & car	.25	.25
		Center inverted	75.00	150.00
69	A11	40pf green & car	.25	.25
	a.	Center inverted	75.00	150.00
70	A11	50pf dk grn & car	.25	.25
71	A11	60pf carmine	.45	.45
72	A11	80pf black & car	.35	.35

Paper With Faint Gray Network

73	A11	1m org & car	.50	.40
	a.	Center inverted	75.00	150.00
74	A11	1.20m blue violet	1.25	1.25
75	A11	2m gray & car	3.25	4.25
76	A11	3m violet & car	9.00	10.00

Serrate Roulette 13½
Wmk. 108 Upright

77	A12	5m grn, red & blk	1.25	3.00
78	A12	9m rose, red & org ('22)	3.00	8.50
79	A12	10m ultra, red & blk	1.25	3.00
80	A12	20m red & black	1.25	3.00
		Nos. 63-80 (18)	23.55	36.30
		Set, never hinged	85.00	

In this and succeeding issues the mark values usually have the face of the paper covered with a gray network. This network is often very faint and occasionally is omitted.
Nos. 64-76 exist imperf. Value, each $16-$50 unused, $50-$150 never hinged.
See Nos. 81-93, 99-105. For surcharges and overprints see Nos. 96-98, O1-O33.

Type of 1921 and

 A13   Coat of Arms — A13a

1922   Wmk. 108 Upright   Perf. 14

81	A11	75(pf) deep vio	.25	.25
82	A11	80(pf) green	.25	.25
83	A11	1.25m vio & car	.25	.25
84	A11	1.50m slate gray	.25	.40
85	A11	2m car rose	.25	.25
86	A11	2.40m dk brn & car	1.15	2.00
87	A11	3m car lake	.25	.40
88	A11	4m dark blue	1.15	2.00
89	A11	5m deep grn	.25	.35
90	A11	6m car lake	.25	.35
	a.	6m car rose, wmk. 109 sideways	1,800.	
91	A11	8m light blue	.45	1.60
92	A11	10m orange	.25	.35
93	A11	20m org brn	.25	.35
94	A13	50m gold & car	2.00	6.50
95	A13a	100m metallic grn & red	3.25	6.00
		Nos. 81-95 (15)	10.50	21.30
		Set, never hinged	42.50	

No. 95 has buff instead of gray network.
Nos. 81-83, 85-86, 88 exist imperf. Value, each $12.50.
Nos. 94-95 exist imperf. Value, each $50

Nos. 87, 88 and 91 Surcharged in Black or Carmine

1922

96	A11	6m on 3m car lake	.35	.60
	a.	Double surcharge		
97	A11	8m on 4m dk blue	.35	.85
	a.	Double surcharge	70.00	145.00
	b.	Pair, one without surcharge	150.00	
98	A11	20m on 8m lt bl (C)	.35	.60
		Nos. 96-98 (3)	1.05	2.05
		Set, never hinged	4.00	

Wmk. 109 Sideways
1922-23   Perf. 14

99	A11	4m dark blue	.25	.40
100	A11	5m dark green	.25	.40
102	A11	10m orange	.25	.40
103	A11	20m orange brn	.25	.40

Paper Without Network
Wmk. 109 Upright

104	A11	40m pale blue	.25	.60
105	A11	80m red	.25	.60
		Nos. 99-105 (6)	1.50	2.80
		Set, never hinged	5.40	

Nos. 100, 102 and 103 also exist with watermark vertical. Values slightly higher.

Nos. 104-105 exist imperf. Value, each $12.50 unused, $32.50 never hinged.

 A15   A15a

Coat of Arms — A16

1922-23   Wmk. 109 Upright   Perf. 14
Paper With Gray Network

106	A15	50m pale bl & red	.25	.40
107	A15a	100m dk grn & red	.25	.40
108	A15a	150m violet & red	.25	.40
109	A16	250m violet & red	.40	.40
110	A16	500m gray blk & red	.40	.40
111	A16	1000m brn & red	.40	.40
112	A16	5000m silver & red	1.50	6.00

Paper Without Network

113	A15	50m pale blue	.40	.60
114	A15a	100m deep green	.40	.60
115	A15	200m orange	.40	.60
		Nos. 106-115 (10)	4.65	10.20
		Set, never hinged	19.00	

Nos. 108-112 exist imperf. Value, each $50 unused, $125 never hinged.
Nos. 113-115 exist imperf. Value, each $35 unused, $92.50 never hinged.
See Nos. 123-125. For surcharges and overprints see Nos. 126, 137-140, 143, 156-167, O35-O38.

 A17

1923   Perf. 14
Paper With Gray Network

117	A17	250m violet & red	.25	.55
118	A17	300m bl grn & red	.25	.55
119	A17	500m gray & red	.25	.55
120	A17	1000m brown & red	.25	.55
121	A17	3000m violet & red	.25	.55
123	A16	10,000m orange & red	.60	.60
124	A16	20,000m pale bl & red	.60	1.00
125	A16	50,000m green & red	.60	1.00
		Nos. 117-125 (8)	3.05	5.35
		Set, never hinged	12.50	

Nos. 117, 119-121 exist imperf. Value, each $19 unused, $45 never hinged; Nos. 123-125 also exist imperf. Values each, $25 unused, $85 never hinged.

See Nos. 127-135. For surcharges & overprints see Nos. 141-142, 144-155, O39-O41.

DANZIG

No. 124 Surcharged in Red

1923, Aug. 14
126	A16	100,000m on #124	1.00	6.00
		Never hinged	4.50	

No. 126 exists imperf. Value $50 unused, $125 never hinged.

1923 — **Perf. 14**
Paper Without Network
127	A17	1000m brown	.25	.40
129	A17	5000m rose	.25	.40
131	A17	20,000m pale blue	.25	.40
132	A17	50,000m green	.25	.40

Paper With Gray Network
133	A17	100,000m deep blue	.25	.40
b.		Double impression	80.00	
134	A17	250,000m violet	.25	.40
135	A17	500,000m slate	.25	.40
		Nos. 127-135 (7)	1.75	2.80
		Set, never hinged	5.00	

Abbreviations:
th=(tausend) thousand
mil=million

Nos. 115, 114, 132, and Type of 1923 Surcharged

No. 137-139   No. 140

No. 141   No. 142

1923 — **Perf. 14**
Paper Without Network
137	A15	40th m on 200m	.85	2.00
a.		Double surcharge	85.00	
138	A15	100th m on 200m	.85	2.00
139	A15	250th m on 100m	6.25	13.00
140	A15a	400th m on 100m	.60	.60
141	A17	500th m on #132	.40	.60

On 10,000m
142	A17	1mil m org	3.75	6.25

The surcharges on Nos. 140-142 differ in details from those on Nos. 137-139.

Type of 1923 Surcharged

Paper With Gray Network
On 1,000,000m
143	A16	10mil m org	.40	1.25
		Nos. 137-143 (7)	13.10	25.70
		Set, never hinged	60.00	

Nos. 142-143 exist imperf. Values: No. 142 unused $50, never hinged $125; No. 143 unused $25, never hinged $85.

Type of 1923 Surcharged

Wmk. 109 Upright
Perf. 14
10,000m rose on paper without Network
144	A17	1mil m on 10,000m	.25	.60
145	A17	2mil m on 10,000m	.25	.60
146	A17	3mil m on 10,000m	.25	.60
147	A17	5mil m on 10,000m	.35	.60
b.		Double surcharge	85.00	

10,000m gray lilac on paper without Network
148	A17	10mil m on 10,000m	.40	.75
149	A17	20mil m on 10,000m	.40	.75
150	A17	25mil m on 10,000m	.25	.75
151	A17	40mil m on 10,000m	.25	.75
a.		Double surcharge	52.50	
152	A17	50mil m on 10,000m	.25	.75

Type of 1923 Surcharged in Red

10,000m gray lilac on paper without Network
153	A17	100mil m on 10,000m	.25	.75
154	A17	300mil m on 10,000m	.25	.75
155	A17	500mil m on 10,000m	.25	.75
		Nos. 144-155 (12)	3.40	8.40
		Set, never hinged	15.00	

Nos. 144-147 exist imperf. Value, each $25 unused, $85 never hinged. Nos. 148-155 exist imperf. Value, each $32.50 unused, $85 never hinged.

Types of 1923 Surcharged

1923, Oct. 31   **Wmk. 110**   **Perf. 14**
156	A15	5pf on 50m	.45	.40
157	A15	10pf on 50m	.45	.40
158	A15	20pf on 100m	.45	.40
159	A15	25pf on 50m	3.50	9.00
160	A16	30pf on 50m	3.50	2.00
161	A15a	40pf on 100m	2.25	2.00
162	A15	50pf on 100m	2.25	3.00
163	A15a	75pf on 100m	8.00	16.00

Type of 1923 Surcharged

1923, Nov. 5
164	A16	1g on 1mil m rose	4.50	6.25
165	A16	2g on 1mil m rose	12.00	17.50
166	A16	3g on 1mil m rose	22.00	62.50
167	A16	5g on 1mil m rose	25.00	67.50
		Nos. 156-167 (12)	84.35	186.95
		Set, never hinged	400.00	

Coat of Arms — A19

1924-37   **Wmk. 109**   **Perf. 14**
168	A19	3pf brn, yelsh ('35)	1.25	1.50
a.		3pf dp brn, white ('27)	2.10	1.90
170	A19	5pf org, yelsh	3.25	.55
		White paper	8.50	2.00
c.		Tête bêche pair	375.00	
d.		Syncopated perf. #170	10.50	9.25
e.		Syncopated perf. #170a	25.00	22.50
171	A19	7pf yel grn ('33)	1.60	3.00
172	A19	8pf yel grn ('37)	1.60	6.00
173	A19	10pf grn, yelsh	5.50	.50
a.		White paper	11.50	2.50
c.		10pf blue grn, yellowish	7.75	1.10
d.		Tête bêche pair	325.00	
e.		Syncopated perf. #173	18.00	11.00
f.		Syncopated perf. #173a	27.50	13.00
g.		Syncopated perf. #173c	11.00	14.50
175	A19	15pf gray	3.75	.65
176	A19	15pf red, yelsh		
		('35)	2.10	1.10
a.		White paper ('25)	4.50	1.10
177	A19	20pf carmine & red	15.00	.65
178	A19	20pf gray ('35)	2.25	2.50
179	A19	25pf slate & red	27.00	3.75
180	A19	25pf carmine ('35)	16.00	1.60
181	A19	30pf green & red	14.00	.85
182	A19	30pf dk violet ('35)	2.25	4.25
183	A19	35pf ultra	4.50	1.50
184	A19	40pf dk blue & blue	12.00	1.00
185	A19	40pf yel brn & red	6.50	12.50
186	A19	40pf dk blue ('35)	2.25	3.75
a.		Imperf.	60.00	
187	A19	50pf blue & red	16.00	7.50
a.		Yellowish paper	17.50	32.50
188	A19	55pf plum & scar	5.00	14.50
189	A19	60pf dk grn & red	6.25	17.50
190	A19	70pf yel grn & red ('35)	2.25	7.50
191	A19	75pf violet & red, yellowish	7.50	29.00
a.		White paper	10.00	8.50
192	A19	80pf dk org brn & red ('35)	2.25	7.50
		Nos. 168-192 (23)	160.05	129.15
		Set, never hinged	675.00	

The 5pf and 10pf with syncopated perforations (Netherlands type C) are coils.
See Nos. 225-232. For overprints and surcharges see Nos. 200-209, 211-215, 241-252, B9-B11, O42-O52.

Oliva Castle and Cathedral   St. Mary's Church
A20   A23

Council Chamber on the Langenmarkt — A24

2g, Mottlau River & Krantor. 3g, View of Zoppot.

1924-32   **Engr.**   **Wmk. 125**
193	A20	1g yel grn & blk	21.00	45.00
		Parcel post cancel		20.00
194	A20	1g org & gray blk ('32)	17.00	3.75
		Parcel post cancel		1.00
a.		1g red orange & blk	17.00	11.00
		Parcel post cancel		40.00
195	A20	2g red vio & blk	45.00	110.00
		Parcel post cancel		40.00
196	A20	2g rose & blk	3.75	8.00
		Parcel post cancel		1.75
197	A20	3g dk blue & blk	4.75	5.00
		Parcel post cancel		2.25
198	A23	5g brn red & blk	4.75	8.50
		Parcel post cancel		1.90
199	A24	10g dk brn & blk	21.00	110.00
		Parcel post cancel		18.00
		Nos. 193-199 (7)	117.25	290.25
		Set, never hinged	600.00	

See No. 233. For overprints and surcharges see Nos. 210, 253-254, C31-C35.

Stamps of 1924-25 Overprinted in Black, Violet or Red

1930, Nov. 15   **Typo.**   **Wmk. 109**
200	A19	5pf orange	2.50	3.50
201	A19	10pf yellow grn (V)	3.50	4.25
202	A19	15pf red	6.00	10.00
203	A19	20pf carmine & red	3.00	5.50
204	A19	25pf slate & red	4.25	10.00
205	A19	30pf green & red	8.50	22.50
206	A19	35pf ultra (R)	32.50	90.00
207	A19	40pf dk bl & bl (R)	11.50	35.00
208	A19	50pf dp blue & red	32.50	75.00
209	A19	75pf violet & red	32.50	82.50
		Nos. 200-210 (11)	169.25	413.25
		Set, never hinged	675.00	

Wmk. (125)
210	A20	1g orange & blk (R)	32.50	75.00

10th anniv. of the Free State. Counterfeits exist.

Nos. 171 and 183 Surcharged in Red, Blue or Green

Nos. 211, 213-214   No. 212

No. 215

1934-36
211	A19	6pf on 7pf (R)	1.00	1.50
212	A19	8pf on 7pf (Bl)	2.00	2.25
213	A19	8pf on 7pf (R)	1.15	2.40
214	A19	8pf on 7pf (G)	.75	2.40
215	A19	30pf on 35pf (Bl)	11.00	24.50
		Nos. 211-215 (5)	15.90	33.05
		Set, never hinged	60.00	

Bathing Beach, Brösen — A25

View of Brösen Beach   War Memorial at Brösen
A26   A27

1936, June 23   **Typo.**   **Wmk. 109**
216	A25	10pf deep green	.70	.70
217	A26	25pf rose red	1.25	2.40
218	A27	40pf bright blue	2.25	4.50
		Nos. 216-218 (3)	4.20	7.60
		Set, never hinged	15.00	

Village of Brösen, 125th anniversary. Exist imperf. Value each, $40 unused, $110 never hinged.

Skyline of Danzig — A28

1937, Mar. 27
219	A28	10pf dark blue	.50	1.40
220	A28	15pf violet brown	1.60	2.00
		Set, never hinged	11.25	
		Set of 2, #219-220 on one		
		1st day cover		20.00

Air Defense League.

Danzig Philatelic Exhibition Issue
Souvenir Sheet

St. Mary's Church
A29

1937, June 6   **Wmk. 109**   **Perf. 14**
221	A29	50pf dark opal green	4.00	20.00
		Never hinged	11.00	

Danzig Philatelic Exhib., June 6-8, 1937.

Arthur Schopenhauer
A30   A31

Design: 40pf, Full-face portrait, white hair.

Unwmk.
1938, Feb. 22   **Photo**   **Perf. 14**
222	A30	15pf dull blue	1.35	2.40
223	A31	25pf sepia	3.25	8.00
224	A31	40pf orange ver	1.35	3.25
		Nos. 222-224 (3)	5.95	13.65
		Set, never hinged	20.00	
		Set of 3, #222-224 on one		
		1st day cover		37.50

150th anniv. of the birth of Schopenhauer.

Type of 1924-35

1938-39   **Typo.**   **Wmk. 237**   **Perf. 14**
225	A19	3pf brown	.90	7.25
226	A19	5pf orange	.90	2.00
b.		Syncopated perf.	1.40	7.50
227	A19	8pf yellow grn	4.00	32.50
228	A19	10pf blue green	.90	2.00
b.		Syncopated perf.	3.00	10.00
229	A19	15pf scarlet	1.60	10.00
230	A19	25pf carmine	2.10	7.50

128 DANZIG

| 231 | A19 | 40pf dark blue | 2.10 | 27.50 |
| 232 | A19 | 50pf brt bl & red | 2.10 | 130.00 |

Engr.

233	A20	1g red org & blk	6.75	110.00
		Nos. 225-233 (9)	21.35	328.75
		Set, never hinged		90.00

Sizes: No. 233, 32½x21¼mm; No. 194, 31x21mm.

Nos. 226b and 228b are coils with Netherlands type C perforation.

Knights in Tournament, 1500 — A33

French Leaving Danzig, 1814 — A35

Stamp Day: 10pf, Signing of Danzig-Sweden neutrality treaty, 1630. 25pf, Battle of Weichselmünde, 1577.

1939, Jan. 7   Unwmk.   Photo.   Perf. 14

234	A33	5pf dark green	.40	2.00
235	A33	10pf copper brown	.85	2.25
236	A35	15pf slate black	1.25	3.00
237	A35	25pf brown violet	1.60	3.75
		Nos. 234-237 (4)	4.10	10.75
		Set, never hinged		14.00
		Set of 4, #234-237 on one 1st day cover		30.00

Gregor Mendel — A37

15pf, Dr. Robert Koch. 25pf, Wilhelm Roentgen.

1939, Apr. 29   Photo.   Perf. 13x14

238	A37	10pf copper brown	.65	.85
239	A37	15pf indigo	.65	2.00
240	A37	25pf dark olive green	1.25	2.75
		Nos. 238-240 (3)	2.55	5.60
		Set, never hinged		7.25

Issued in honor of the achievements of Mendel, Koch and Roentgen.

Issued under German Administration
Stamps of Danzig, 1925-39, Surcharged in Black

a   b

c

1939   Wmk. 109   Perf. 14

241	A19(b)	4rpf on 35pf ultra	.75	2.25
242	A19(b)	12rpf on 7pf yel grn	1.50	2.25
243	A19(a)	20rpf gray	3.00	8.50

Wmk. 237

244	A19(a)	3rpf brown	.75	2.40
245	A19(a)	5rpf orange	.65	3.00
246	A19(a)	8rpf yellow grn	1.10	4.25
247	A19(a)	10rpf blue grn	2.25	4.25
248	A19(a)	15rpf scarlet	6.00	11.00
249	A19(a)	25rpf carmine	4.50	10.00
250	A19(a)	30rpf dk violet	2.00	4.50
251	A19(a)	40rpf dk blue	2.75	6.00
252	A19(a)	50rpf brt bl & red	4.00	7.00

Thick Paper

| 253 | A20(c) | 1rm on 1g red org & blk | 14.00 | 57.50 |

Wmk. 125 Thin White Paper

254	A20(c)	2rm on 2g rose & blk	20.00	62.50
		Nos. 241-254 (14)	63.25	185.40
		Set, never hinged		190.00

Nos. 241-254 were valid throughout Germany.

SEMI-POSTAL STAMPS

St. George and Dragon — SP1

1921, Oct. 16   Wmk. 108   Typo.   Perf. 14
Size: 19x22mm

| B1 | SP1 | 30pf + 30pf grn & org | .45 | .95 |
| B2 | SP1 | 60pf + 60pf rose & org | 1.25 | 1.60 |

Size: 25x30mm
Serrate Roulette 13½

B3	SP1	1.20m + 1.20m dk bl & org	2.00	2.25
		Nos. B1-B3 (3)	3.70	4.80
		Set, never hinged		16.00

Nos. B1-B3 exist imperf. Value each, $45 unused, $125 never hinged.

Aged Pensioner SP2

1923, Mar.   Wmk. 109   Perf. 14
Paper With Gray Network

B4	SP2	50m + 20m lake	.25	.60
B5	SP2	100m + 30m red vio	.25	.60
		Set, never hinged		2.50

Nos. B4-B5 exist imperf. Value each, $50 unused, $30 used, $210 never hinged.

Philatelic Exhibition Issue

Neptune Fountain — SP3

Various Frames.

1929, July 7   Engr.   Unwmk.

B6	SP3	10pf yel grn & gray	2.40	1.60
B7	SP3	15pf car & gray	2.40	1.60
B8	SP3	25pf ultra & gray	8.50	13.00
a.		25pf violet blue & black	25.00	80.00
		Nos. B6-B8 (3)	13.30	16.20
		Set, never hinged		45.00
		Set of 3, #B6-B8 on one 1st day cover		200.00

These stamps were sold exclusively at the Danzig Philatelic Exhibition, June 7-14, 1929, at double their face values, the excess being for the aid of the exhibition.

Regular Issue of 1924-25 Surcharged in Black

1934, Jan. 15   Wmk. 109

B9	A19	5pf + 5pf orange	9.50	19.00
B10	A19	10pf + 5pf yel grn	22.50	45.00
B11	A19	15pf + 5pf carmine	13.50	35.00
		Nos. B9-B11 (3)	45.50	99.00
		Set, never hinged		220.00

Surtax for winter welfare. Counterfeits exist.

Stock Tower SP4

George Hall SP6

City Gate, 16th Century — SP5

1935, Dec. 16   Typo.   Perf. 14

B12	SP4	5pf + 5pf orange	.65	1.50
B13	SP5	10pf + 5pf green	1.10	2.25
B14	SP6	15pf + 10pf scarlet	2.75	3.50
		Nos. B12-B14 (3)	4.50	7.25
		Set, never hinged		16.00
		Set of 3, #B12-B14 on one 1st day cover		40.00

Surtax for winter welfare.

Milk Can Tower SP7

Frauentor SP8

Krantor SP9

Langgartor Gate SP10

High Gate — SP11

1936, Nov. 25

B15	SP7	10pf + 5pf dk bl	1.60	4.50
a.		Imperf.	75.00	
B16	SP8	15pf + 5pf dull grn	1.60	5.75
B17	SP9	25pf + 10pf red brn	2.25	9.00
B18	SP10	40pf + 20pf brn & red brn	3.00	10.00
B19	SP11	50pf + 20pf bl & dk bl	5.25	15.00
		Nos. B15-B19 (5)	13.70	44.25
		Set, never hinged		80.00

Surtax for winter welfare.

SP12   SP13

1937, Oct. 30   Wmk. 109 Sideways

| B20 | SP12 | 25pf + 25pf dk car | 2.75 | 5.25 |

Wmk. 109 Upright

B21	SP13	40pf + 40pf blue & red	2.75	5.25
a.		Souvenir sheet of 2, #B20a-B21	60.00	110.00
		Set, never hinged		27.50

Founding of Danzig community at Magdeburg. No. B21a exists imperf. Value, $1,600 unused, $3,250 never hinged.

Madonna SP14

Mercury SP15

Weather Vane, Town Hall SP16

Neptune Fountain SP17

St. George and Dragon — SP18

1937, Dec. 13

B23	SP14	5pf + 5pf brt violet	2.50	7.50
B24	SP15	10pf + 10pf dk brn	2.50	5.75
B25	SP16	15pf + 5pf bl & yel brn	2.50	8.25
B26	SP17	25pf + 10pf bl grn & grn	3.25	11.00
B27	SP18	40pf + 25pf brt car & bl	5.75	15.00
		Nos. B23-B27 (5)	16.50	47.50
		Set, never hinged		65.00
		Set of 5, #B23-B27 on one 1st day cover		100.00

Surtax for winter welfare. Designs are from frieze of the Artushof.

"Peter von Danzig" Yacht Race — SP19

Ships: 10pf+5pf, Dredger Fu Shing. 15pf+10pf, S. S. Columbus. 25pf+10pf, S. S. City of Danzig. 40pf+15pf, Peter von Danzig, 1472.

1938, Nov. 28   Photo.   Unwmk.

B28	SP19	5pf + 5pf dk bl grn	1.40	1.50
B29	SP19	10pf + 5pf gldn brn	1.40	3.00
B30	SP19	15pf + 10pf ol grn	1.60	3.00
B31	SP19	25pf + 10pf indigo	2.50	4.00
B32	SP19	40pf + 15pf vio brn	3.00	6.75
		Nos. B28-B32 (5)	9.90	18.25
		Set, never hinged		50.00
		Set of 5, #B28-B32 on one 1st day cover		60.00

Surtax for winter welfare.

AIR POST STAMPS

No. 6 Surcharged in Blue or Carmine

DANZIG

1920, Sept. 29   Wmk. 125   Perf. 14

C1	A16	40pf on 40pf	1.25	2.60
a.		Double surcharge	160.00	250.00
C2	A16	60pf on 40pf (C)	1.25	2.60
a.		Double surcharge	125.00	250.00
C3	A16	1m on 40pf	1.25	2.60
a.		Double surcharge	125.00	250.00
	Nos. C1-C3 (3)		3.75	7.80
	Set, never hinged		13.50	

Plane faces left on No. C2.

 AP3   Plane over Danzig — AP4

Wmk. (108) Upright
1921-22   Typo.   Perf. 14

C4	AP3	40(pf) blue green	.25	.45
C5	AP3	60(pf) dk violet	.25	.45
C6	AP3	1m carmine	.25	.45
C7	AP3	2m org brn	.25	.45

Serrate Roulette 13½
Size: 34½x23mm

C8	AP4	5m violet blue	1.25	2.25
C9	AP4	10m dp grn	2.00	4.25
	Nos. C4-C9 (6)		4.25	8.30
	Set, never hinged		18.00	

Nos. C4-C9 exist imperf. Value, each $32.50 unused, $125 never hinged.

1923   Wmk. (109) Upright   Perf. 14

C10	AP3	40(pf) blue green	.55	1.90
C11	AP3	60(pf) dk violet	.55	1.90
a.		Double impression		
C12	AP3	1m carmine	.55	1.90
C13	AP3	2m org brown	.55	1.90
C14	AP3	25m pale blue	.40	.70

Serrate Roulette 13½
Size: 34½x23mm

C15	AP4	5m violet blue	.55	1.00
C16	AP4	10m deep green	.55	1.00

Paper With Gray Network

C17	AP4	20m org brn	.55	1.00

Size: 40x23mm

C18	AP4	50m orange	.40	.70
C19	AP4	100m red	.40	.70
C20	AP4	250m dark brown	.60	.70
C21	AP4	500m car rose	.60	.70
	Nos. C10-C21 (12)		6.25	14.10
	Set, never hinged		30.00	

Nos. C11, C12, C14-C21 exist imperf. Value, Nos. C11, C12, C15-C17, each $8.50 unused, $32.50 never hinged. Value, No. C14, C18-C21, each $40 unused, $125 never hinged.

Nos. C18, C19 and C21 exist with wmk. sideways, both perf and imperf. Value each, $60 unused, $160 never hinged.

Post Horn and Airplanes — AP5

1923, Oct. 18   Perf. 14
Paper Without Network

C22	AP5	250,000m scarlet	.35	1.25
C23	AP5	500,000m scarlet	.35	1.25
	Set, never hinged		2.50	

Exist imperf. Value, each; $50 unused; $125 never hinged.

Surcharged

On 100,000m

C24	AP5	2mil m scarlet	.35	1.25

On 50,000m

C25	AP5	5mil m scarlet	.35	1.25
b.	Cliché of 10,000(m) in sheet of 50,000m		32.50	160.00

Exist imperf. Value, each $125 unused, $290 never hinged.

Nos. C24 and C25 were not regularly issued without surcharge, although examples have been passed through the post. Values: C24 unused $8.50, never hinged $32.50; C25 unused $12, never hinged $21.

 AP6

Plane over Danzig — AP7

1924

C26	AP6	10(pf) vermilion	21.00	3.50
C27	AP6	20(pf) carmine rose	2.10	1.50
C28	AP6	40(pf) olive brown	3.00	1.75
C29	AP6	1g deep green	3.00	3.00
C30	AP7	2½g violet brown	17.50	32.50
	Nos. C26-C30 (5)		46.60	42.25
	Set, never hinged		175.00	

Exist imperf. Value Nos. C26, C30, $85 unused, $200 never hinged; others, each $40 unused, $110 never hinged.

Nos. 193, 195, 197-199 Srchd. in Various Colors

1932   Wmk. 125

C31	A20	10pf on 1g (G)	9.00	21.00
C32	A20	15pt on 2g (V)	9.00	21.00
C33	A20	20pf on 3g (Bl)	9.00	21.00
C34	A23	25pf on 5g (R)	9.00	21.00
C35	A24	30pf on 10g (Br)	9.00	21.00
	Nos. C31-C35 (5)		45.00	105.00
	Set, never hinged		200.00	

Intl. Air Post Exhib. of 1932. The surcharges were variously arranged to suit the shapes and designs of the stamps. The stamps were sold at double their surcharged values, the excess being donated to the exhibition funds.

No. C31 exists with inverted surcharge and with double surcharge. Value each, $85 unused, $210 never hinged.

Airplane
AP8   AP9

1935, Oct. 24   Wmk. 109

C36	AP8	10pf scarlet	1.75	.85
C37	AP8	15pf yellow	1.75	1.25
C38	AP8	25pf dark green	1.75	1.50
C39	AP8	50pf gray blue	9.00	9.25
C40	AP9	1g magenta	3.50	13.00
	Nos. C36-C40 (5)		17.75	25.85
	Set, never hinged		65.00	

Nos. C36 and C40 exist imperf. Values: C36 unused $20, never hinged $62.50; C40 unused $20, never hinged $85.

See Nos. C42-C45.

Souvenir Sheet

DAPOSTA 1937
St Mary's Church AP10

1937, June 6   Perf. 14

C41	AP10	50pf dark grayish blue	3.75	16.00

Danzig Phil. Exhib., June 6-8, 1937.

Type of 1935

1938-39   Wmk. 237

C42	AP8	10pf scarlet	1.25	3.75
C43	AP8	15pf yellow ('39)	2.00	12.00
C44	AP8	25pf dark green	1.60	6.50
C45	AP8	50pf gray blue ('39)	4.00	57.50
	Nos. C42-C45 (4)		8.85	79.75
	Set, never hinged		42.50	

POSTAGE DUE STAMPS

Danzig Coat of Arms — D1

1921-22   Typo.   Wmk. (108)   Perf. 14
Paper Without Network

J1	D1	10(pf) deep violet	.35	.45
J2	D1	20(pf) deep violet	.35	.45
J3	D1	40(pf) deep violet	.35	.45
J4	D1	60(pf) deep violet	.35	.45
J5	D1	75(pf) dp violet ('22)	.35	.45
J6	D1	80(pf) deep violet	.35	.45
J7	D1	120(pf) deep violet	.35	.45
J8	D1	200(pf) dp violet ('22)	.95	1.00
J9	D1	240(pf) deep violet	.35	1.00
J10	D1	300(pf) dp violet ('22)	.95	1.00
J11	D1	400(pf) deep violet	.95	1.00
J12	D1	500(pf) deep violet	.95	1.00
J13	D1	800(pf) deep violet ('22)	.95	1.00
J14	D1	20m dp violet ('22)	8.50	10.15
	Nos. J1-J14 (14)		27.50	
	Set, never hinged			

Nos. J1-J14 exist imperf. Value, each $30 unused, $75 never hinged.

1923   Wmk. 109 Sideways

J15	D1	100(pf) deep violet	.60	.75
J16	D1	200(pf) deep violet	2.50	3.75
J17	D1	300(pf) deep violet	.60	.75
J18	D1	400(pf) deep violet	.60	.75
J19	D1	500(pf) deep violet	.60	.75
J20	D1	800(pf) deep violet	1.25	3.75
J21	D1	10m deep violet	.60	1.00
J22	D1	20m deep violet	.60	.75
J23	D1	50m deep violet	.60	.75

Paper With Gray Network

J24	D1	100m deep violet	.60	1.00
J25	D1	800m deep violet	1.25	3.75
	Nos. J15-J25 (11)		9.15	15.00
	Set, never hinged		25.00	

Nos. J15, J17, J22-J25 exist imperf. Value each, $12.50 unused, $40 never hinged.

Nos. J22-J23 and Type of 1923 Surcharged

1923, Oct. 1
Paper without Network

J26	D1	5000m on 50m	.40	.75
J27	D1	10,000m on 20m	.40	.75
J28	D1	50,000m on 500m	.40	.75
J29	D1	100,000m on 20m	.85	1.25
	Nos. J26-J29 (4)		2.05	3.50
	Set, never hinged		8.00	

On No. J26 the numerals of the surcharge are all of the larger size.

A 1000(m) on 100m deep violet was prepared but not issued. Value, $145, never hinged $350.

Nos. J26-J28 exist imperf. Value each, $18 unused, $45 never hinged.

Danzig Coat of Arms — D2

1923-28   Wmk. 110

J30	D2	5(pf) blue & blk	.85	.75
J31	D2	10(pf) blue & blk	.40	.75
J32	D2	15(pf) blue & blk	1.25	1.10
J33	D2	20(pf) blue & blk	1.25	2.00
J34	D2	30(pf) blue & blk	9.00	2.00
J35	D2	40(pf) blue & blk	2.10	3.00
J36	D2	50(pf) blue & blk	2.10	2.25
J37	D2	60(pf) blue & blk	13.00	18.00
J38	D2	100(pf) blue & blk	17.50	9.75
J39	D2	3g blue & blk	10.00	40.00
a.		"Guldeu" instead of "Gulden"	325.00	1,050.
	Nos. J30-J39 (10)		57.45	79.60
	Set, never hinged		225.00	

Used values of Nos. J30-J39 are for postally used stamps.

See Nos. J43-J47.

Postage Due Stamps of 1923 Issue Surcharged in Red

1932, Dec. 20

J40	D2	5pf on 40(pf)	4.25	7.50
J41	D2	10pf on 60(pf)	32.50	9.00
J42	D2	20pf on 100(pf)	2.75	7.50
	Nos. J40-J42 (3)		39.50	24.00
	Set, never hinged		160.00	

Type of 1923

1938-39   Wmk. 237   Perf. 14

J43	D2	10(pf) bl & blk ('39)	1.25	62.50
J44	D2	30(pf) bl & blk	2.25	50.00
J45	D2	40(pf) bl & blk ('39)	6.75	100.00
J46	D2	60(pf) bl & blk ('39)	6.75	100.00
J47	D2	100(pf) bl & blk	11.00	72.50
	Nos. J43-J47 (5)		28.00	385.00
	Set, never hinged		125.00	

OFFICIAL STAMPS

Regular Issues of 1921-22 Overprinted — a

1921-22   Wmk. 108   Perf. 14x14½

O1	A11	5(pf) orange	.25	.25
O2	A11	10(pf) dark brown	.25	.25
a.		Inverted overprint	60.00	
O3	A11	15(pf) green	.25	.25
O4	A11	20(pf) slate	.25	.25
O5	A11	25(pf) dark green	.25	.25
a.		Pair, one without overprint	170.00	
O6	A11	30(pf) blue & car	.60	.60
O7	A11	40(pf) grn & car	.25	.25
O8	A11	50(pf) dk grn & car	.25	.25
O9	A11	60(pf) carmine	.25	.25
O10	A11	75(pf) dp vio	.25	.40
O11	A11	80(pf) black & car	.85	.85
O12	A11	80(pf) green	.25	2.40

Paper With Faint Gray Network

O14	A11	1m org & car	.25	.25
O15	A11	1.20m blue violet	1.25	1.25
O16	A11	1.25m vio & car	.25	.40
O17	A11	1.50m slate gray	.25	.40
O18	A11	2m gray & car	16.00	12.00
a.		Inverted overprint	110.00	
O19	A11	2m car rose	.25	.40
O20	A11	2.40m dk brn & car	1.25	2.40
O21	A11	3m violet & car	8.50	10.00
O22	A11	3m car lake	.25	.40
O23	A11	4m dk blue	1.25	.85
O24	A11	5m dp grn	.25	.40
O25	A11	6m car lake	.25	.40
O26	A11	10m orange	.25	.40
O27	A11	20m org brn	.25	.40
	Nos. O1-O27 (26)		34.45	36.20
	Set, never hinged		175.00	

Double overprints exist on Nos. O1-O2, O5-O7, O10 and O12.

Same Overprint on No. 96

O28	A11	6m on 3m	.35	.75
	Never hinged		1.00	
a.		Inverted overprint	30.00	
	Never hinged		85.00	

No. 77 Overprinted

Serrate Roulette 13½
1922   Wmk. 108 Sideways

O29	A12	5m grn, red & blk	3.75	6.00
	Never hinged		18.00	

Nos. 99-103, 106-107 Overprinted Type "a"

1922-23   Wmk. 109   Perf. 14

O30	A11	4m dark blue	.25	.60
O31	A11	5m dark green	.25	.60
O32	A11	10m orange	.25	.60
O33	A11	20m orange brn	.25	.60
O34	A15	50m pale blue & red	.25	.60

130 DANZIG — DENMARK

O35	A15a	100m dk grn & red	.25	.60

Nos. 113-115, 118-120 Overprinted Type "a"

O36	A15	50m pale blue	.25	.75
a.		Inverted overprint	25.00	
O37	A15	100m dark green	.25	.75
O38	A15	200m orange	.25	.75
a.		Inverted overprint	25.00	

Paper With Gray Network

O39	A17	300m bl grn & red	.25	.60
O40	A17	500m gray & red	.25	.75
O41	A17	1000m brn & red	.25	.75
		Nos. O30-O41 (12)	3.00	7.95
		Set, never hinged		16.80

Regular Issue of 1924-25 Overprinted

1924-25   Perf. 14x14½

O42	A19	5pf red orange	2.10	3.25
O43	A19	10pf green	2.10	9.00
O44	A19	15pf gray	2.10	3.25
O45	A19	15pf red	19.00	10.00
O46	A19	20pf car & red	2.10	2.10
O47	A19	25pf slate & red	19.00	27.50
O48	A19	30pf green & red	3.00	3.75
O49	A19	35pf ultra	60.00	50.00
O50	A19	40pf dk bl & dull bl	7.00	8.50
O51	A19	50pf dp blue & red	21.00	42.50
O52	A19	75pf violet & red	42.50	120.00
		Nos. O42-O52 (11)	179.90	279.85
		Set, never hinged		640.00

Double overprints exist on Nos. O42-O44, O47, O50-O52.

DENMARK

'den-ˌmärk

LOCATION — Northern part of a peninsula which separates the North and Baltic Seas, and includes the surrounding islands
GOVT. — Kingdom
AREA — 16,631 sq. mi.
POP. — 5,790,000 (2020 est.)
CAPITAL — Copenhagen

96 Skilling = 1 Rigsbank Daler
100 Ore = 1 Krone (1875)

> Catalogue values for unused stamps in this country are for Never Hinged items, beginning with Scott 297 in the regular postage section, Scott B15 in the semipostal section, and Scott Q28 in the parcel post section.

Values for unused stamps are for examples with original gum as defined in the catalogue introduction. Very fine examples of Nos. 9-37 and O1-O9 will have perforations clear of the framelines but with the design noticeably off center. Well centered stamps are quite scarce and will command substantial premiums.

Watermarks

Wmk. 111 — Small Crown

Wmk. 112 — Crown

Wmk. 113 — Crown

Wmk. 114 — Multiple Crosses

Royal Emblems — A2

1851   Typo.   Wmk. 111   Imperf.
With Yellow Brown Burelage

1	A1	2rs blue	3,500.	1,000.
a.		First printing	8,250.	2,400.
2	A2	4rs brown	600.00	40.00
a.		First printing	600.00	40.00
b.		4rs yellow brown	875.00	55.00
c.		4rs chestnut (4th printing)	2,400.	250.00

The first printing of Nos. 1 and 2 had the burelage printed from a copper plate, giving a clear impression with the lines in slight relief. The subsequent impressions had the burelage typographed, with the lines fainter and not rising above the surface of the paper.
Nos. 1-2 were reprinted in 1885 and 1901 on heavy yellowish paper, unwatermarked and imperforate, with a brown burelage. No. 1 was also reprinted without burelage, on both yellowish and white paper. Value for least costly reprint of No. 1, $50.
No. 2 was reprinted in 1951 in 10 shades with "Colour Specimen 1951" printed on the back. It was also reprinted in 1961 in 2 shades without burelage and with "Farve Nytryk 1961" printed on the back. Value for least costly reprint of No. 2, $8.50.

Dotting in Spandrels — A3

1854-57

3	A3	2s blue ('55)	75.00	60.00
4	A3	4s brown	325.00	15.00
a.		4s yellow brown	350.00	15.00
5	A3	8s green ('57)	300.00	67.50
a.		8s yellow green	300.00	80.00
6	A3	16s gray lilac ('57)	525.00	190.00
		Nos. 3-6 (4)	1,225.	332.50

See No. 10. For denominations in cents see Danish West Indies Nos. 1-4.

Wavy Lines in Spandrels — A4

1858-62

7	A4	4s yellow brown	65.00	8.50
		4s brown	67.50	
b.		Wmk. 112 ('62)	75.00	12.00
8	A4	8s green	800.00	82.50

Nos. 2 to 8 inclusive are known with unofficial perforation 12 or 13, and Nos. 4, 5, 7 and 8 with unofficial roulette 9½. Certificates of authenticity issued by competent authorities are recommended.
Nos. 3, 6-8 were reprinted in 1885 on heavy yellowish paper, unwatermarked, imperforate and without burelage. Nos. 4-5 were reprinted in 1924 on white paper, unwatermarked, imperforate, gummed and without burelage. Value for No. 3, $15; Nos. 4-5, each $110; No. 6, $20; Nos. 7-8, each $15.

1863   Wmk. 112   Rouletted 11

9	A4	4s brown	100.00	15.00
a.		4s deep brown	100.00	15.00
b.		4s red brown	100.00	15.00
10	A3	16s violet	1,400.	650.00

Royal Emblems — A5

1864-68   Perf. 13x12.75

11	A5	2s blue ('65)	65.00	35.00
12	A5	3s red vio ('65)	80.00	75.00
13	A5	4s red	40.00	8.00
b.		4s carmine ('64)	250.00	.45
14	A5	8s bister ('68)	275.00	95.00
15	A5	16s olive green	475.00	175.00
		Nos. 11-15 (5)	935.00	388.00

Nos. 11-15 were reprinted in 1886 on heavy yellowish paper, unwatermarked, imperforate and without gum. The reprints of all values except the 4s were printed in two vertical rows of six, inverted with respect to each other, so that horizontal pairs are always tête bêche. Value $12 each.
Nos. 13 and 15 were reprinted in 1942 with printing on the back across each horizontal row: "Nytryk 1942. G. A. Hagemann: Danmarks og Vestindiens Frimaerker, Bind 2." Value, $70 each.

Imperf, single

11a	A5	2s blue	95.00	95.00
12a	A5	3s red violet	140.00	
13a	A5	4s red ('66)	110.00	160.00
14a	A5	8s bister	375.00	
15a	A5	16s olive green	450.00	

A1

A6

1870   Perf. 12½

11b	A5	2s blue	275.00	350.00
12b	A5	3s red violet	475.00	650.00
14b	A5	8s bister	475.00	475.00
15b	A5	16s olive green	725.00	1,450.
		Nos. 11b-15b (4)	1,950.	2,925.

Normal Frame   Inverted Frame

The arabesques in the corners have a main stem and a branch. When the frame is in normal position, in the upper left corner the branch leaves the main stem half way between two little leaflets. In the lower right corner the branch starts at the foot of the second leaflet. When the frame is inverted the corner designs are, of course, transposed.

1870-71   Wmk. 112   Perf. 14x13½
Paper Varying from Thin to Thick

16	A6	2s gray & ultra ('71)	27.50	
		2s gray & blue	70.00	27.50
b.		2s gray & Prussian blue	185.00	165.00
17	A6	3s gray & brt lil ('71)	100.00	110.00
18	A6	4s gray & car	40.00	10.00
19	A6	8s gray & brn ('71)	200.00	75.00
20	A6	16s gray & grn ('71)	275.00	175.00

Perf. 12½

21	A6	2s gray & bl ('71)	2,000.	3,250.
22	A6	4s gray & car	150.00	125.00
24	A6	48s brn & lilac	450.00	275.00

Nos. 16-20, 24 were reprinted in 1886 on thin white paper, unwatermarked, imperforate and without gum. These were printed in sheets of 10 in which 1 stamp has the normal frame (value $32.50 each) and 9 the inverted (value $11 each).

Imperf, single

16b	A6	2s		250.
17a	A6	3s		240.
18a	A6	4s		200.
19a	A6	8s		250.
20a	A6	16s		400.
24a	A6	48s		425.

Inverted Frame

16c	A6	2s	1,000.	775.
17b	A6	3s	2,500.	2,000.
18b	A6	4s	775.	87.50
19b	A6	8s	1,750.	900.
20b	A6	16s	2,000.	1,750.
24b	A6	48s	2,750.	1,900.

1875-79   Perf. 14x13½

25	A6	3o gray blue & gray	18.00	15.00
a.		1st "A" of "DANMARK" missing	60.00	150.00
b.		Imperf	750.00	
c.		Inverted frame	24.00	19.00
d.		As "a," inverted frame	18.00	190.00
e.		3o blue & gray	26.00	18.00
f.		As "e," 1st "A" of "DANMARK" missing	80.00	150.00
g.		As "e," inverted frame	30.00	20.00
h.		As "g," 1st "A" of "DANMARK" missing	80.00	150.00
i.		3o ultra & gray	200.00	75.00
j.		As "i," inverted frame	1,000.	475.00
26	A6	4o slate & blue	25.00	.50
a.		4o gray & blue	25.00	1.10
b.		4o slate & ultra	90.00	17.00
c.		4o gray & ultra	75.00	16.00
d.		Imperf	300.00	
e.		As "#26," inverted frame	25.00	.50
f.		As "b," inverted frame	400.00	240.00
27	A6	5o rose & blue ('79)	30.00	72.50
a.		Ball of lower curve of large "5" missing	125.00	300.00
b.		Imperf	1,000.	2,250.
28	A6	8o slate & car	22.50	.50
a.		8o gray & carmine	75.00	5.00
b.		Imperf	225.00	
c.		As "#28," inverted frame	22.50	.50
d.		8o gray & aniline red ('86)	72.50	9.50
e.		As "d," imperf	150.00	
f.		As "d," inverted frame	750.00	190.00
g.		As "a," inverted frame	550.00	275.00
29	A6	12o sl & dull lake	10.00	4.00
a.		12o gray & bright lilac	65.00	8.00
b.		12o gray & dull magenta	72.50	10.00

c.		As "#29," inverted frame	14.00	4.00
d.		As "a," inverted frame	175.00	22.00
30	A6	16o slate & brn	77.50	6.50
a.		16o light gray & brown	77.50	17.00
b.		As "#30," inverted frame	52.50	4.50
c.		As "a," inverted frame	120.00	45.00
31	A6	20o rose & gray	90.00	32.50
a.		20o carmine & gray	90.00	32.50
b.		As "#31," inverted frame	90.00	32.50
c.		As "a," inverted frame	90.00	32.50
32	A6	25o gray & green	65.00	40.00
		Inverted frame	77.50	62.50
33	A6	50o brown & vio	70.00	37.50
a.		50o brown & blue violet	400.00	175.00
b.		As "#33," inverted frame	70.00	32.50
c.		50o lt brown & pale red vio	—	650.00
34	A6	100o brown & org ('77)	110.00	60.00
a.		Imperf, pair	375.00	
c.		100o greenish gray & orange yellow ('87)	130.00	60.00
d.		100o bluish gray & orange yellow ('91)	60.00	60.00
		Nos. 25-34 (10)	518.00	269.00
		Set, never hinged	1,625.	

The stamps of this issue on thin semi-transparent paper are far scarcer than those on thicker paper.
See Nos. 41-42, 44, 46-47, 50-52. For surcharges see Nos. 55, 79-80, 136.
Certificates of authenticity issued by competent authorities are recommended for No. 33c.

Arms — A7

Two types of numerals in corners

Small Numerals

Large Numerals

1882   Small Corner Numerals

35	A7	5o green	240.00	100.00
		Never hinged	725.00	
37	A7	20o blue	190.00	70.00
		Never hinged	650.00	

1884-88   Larger Corner Numerals

38	A7	5o green	15.00	3.50
a.		Imperf	—	
39	A7	10o carmine ('85)	16.00	2.50
a.		Small numerals in corners ('88)	550.00	725.00
b.		Imperf, single	175.00	
c.		Pair, Nos. 39, 39a	600.00	875.00
40	A7	20o blue	30.00	5.00
a.		Pair, Nos. 37, 40	400.00	875.00
b.		Imperf	—	
		Nos. 38-40 (3)	61.00	11.00
		Set, never hinged	285.00	

Stamps with large corner numerals have white line around crown and lower oval touches frame.
The plate for No. 39, was damaged and 3 clichés in the bottom row were replaced by clichés for post cards, which had small numerals in the corners.
Two clichés with small numerals were inserted in the plate of No. 40.
See Nos. 43, 45, 48-49, 53-54. For surcharge see No. 56.

1895-1901   Wmk. 112   Perf. 13

41	A6	3o blue & gray	10.00	7.25
42	A6	4o slate & bl ('96)	4.50	.40
43	A7	5o green	12.00	.75
44	A6	8o slate & red	4.50	.45
45	A7	10o rose car	24.00	.65
46	A6	12o sl & dull lake	7.00	4.00
47	A6	16o slate & brown	19.00	4.50
48	A7	20o blue	30.00	2.40
49	A7	24o brown ('01)	7.00	6.00
50	A6	25o gray & grn ('98)	110.00	19.50
51	A6	50o brown & vio ('97)	60.00	24.00
52	A6	100o slate & org	90.00	35.00
		Nos. 41-52 (12)	378.00	104.90
		Set, never hinged	875.00	

Inverted Frame

41b	A6	3o	12.00	7.00
42a	A6	4o	4.50	.45
44a	A6	8o	4.50	.50
46a	A6	12o	14.00	4.50
47a	A6	16o	30.00	5.00
50a	A6	25o	60.00	27.50
51a	A6	50o	95.00	32.50
52a	A6	100o	90.00	57.50
		Nos. 41b-52a (8)	310.00	134.95
		Set, never hinged	635.00	

DENMARK

1902-04			Wmk. 113	
41c	A6	3ø blue & gray	2.75	3.00
42b	A6	4ø slate & blue	17.00	20.00
43a	A7	5ø green	2.00	.25
44d	A6	8ø slate & red	525.00	425.00
45a	A7	10ø rose carmine	3.00	.25
48a	A7	20ø blue	20.00	4.75
50b	A6	25ø gray & green	10.50	4.50
51b	A6	50ø brown & violet	27.50	20.00
52b	A6	100ø slate & orange	30.00	15.00
	Nos. 41c-52b (9)		637.75	492.75
	Set, never hinged		1,325.	

Inverted Frame

41d	A6	3ø	75.00	130.00
42c	A6	4ø	140.00	190.00
50c	A6	25ø	210.00	60.00
51c	A6	50ø	260.00	240.00
52c	A6	100ø	225.00	240.00
	Nos. 41d-52c (5)		910.00	800.00
	Set, never hinged		2,500.	

1902			Wmk. 113	
53	A7	1ø orange	.75	.65
a.		Imperf.		4,250.
54	A7	15ø lilac	11.00	.75
a.		Imperf, single		4,250.

Nos. 44d, 44, 49 Surcharged

a

b

1904-12			Wmk. 113	
55	A6(a)	4ø on 8ø sl & red	3.50	4.00
a.		Wmk. 112 ('12)	21.00	60.00
		Never hinged	42.50	
b.		As "a," inverted frame	—	6,000.
		Wmk. 112		
56	A7(b)	15ø on 24ø brown	5.75	17.50
a.		Short "15" at right	27.50	105.00
		Never hinged	60.00	
	Set, never hinged		16.00	

A10

1905-17			Wmk. 113	Perf. 13
57	A10	1ø orange ('06)	2.25	.75
58	A10	2ø carmine	4.75	.40
a.		Perf. 14x14½ ('17)	3.75	19.00
59	A10	3ø gray	9.75	.65
60	A10	4ø dull blue	7.00	.60
a.		Perf. 14x14½ ('17)	11.00	37.50
61	A10	5ø dp green ('12)	5.25	.35
62	A10	10ø dp rose ('12)	6.75	.35
63	A10	15ø lilac	25.00	2.25
64	A10	20ø dk blue ('12)	35.00	.90
	Nos. 57-64 (8)		95.75	6.25
	Set, never hinged		310.00	

The three wavy lines in design A10 are symbolical of the three waters which separate the principal Danish islands.
See Nos. 85-96, 1338-1342A, 1468-1473. For surcharges and overprints see Nos. 163, 181, J1, J38, Q1-Q2.

King Christian IX — A11

1904-05				Engr.
65	A11	10ø scarlet	4.00	.65
66	A11	20ø blue	22.50	3.00
67	A11	25ø brown ('05)	27.50	8.00
68	A11	50ø dull vio ('05)	110.00	120.00
69	A11	100ø ocher ('05)	13.00	60.00
	Nos. 65-69 (5)		177.00	191.65
	Set, never hinged		505.00	

1905-06				Re-engraved
70	A11	5ø green	4.50	.35
71	A11	10ø scarlet ('06)	21.00	.60
	Set, never hinged		56.00	

The re-engraved stamps are much clearer than the originals, and the decoration on the king's left breast has been removed.

King Frederik VIII — A12

1907-12				
72	A12	5ø green	1.75	.40
a.		Imperf.		
73	A12	10ø red	4.25	.40
a.		Imperf.		
74	A12	20ø indigo	19.00	.65
a.		20ø bright blue ('11)	40.00	2.75
75	A12	25ø olive brn	35.00	1.25
76	A12	35ø dp org ('12)	6.00	10.00
77	A12	50ø claret	35.00	7.00
78	A12	100ø bister brn	100.00	5.00
	Nos. 72-78 (7)		201.00	24.70
	Set, never hinged		525.00	

Nos. 47, 31 and O9 Surcharged

c

d

Dark Blue Surcharge

1912			Wmk. 112	Perf. 13
79	A6(c)	35ø on 16ø	17.00	50.00
a.		Inverted frame	325.00	625.00
		Perf. 14x13½		
80	A6(c)	35ø on 20ø	30.00	85.00
a.		Inverted frame	130.00	325.00

Black Surcharge

81	O1(d)	35ø on 32ø	42.50	120.00
	Nos. 79-81 (3)		89.50	255.00
	Set, never hinged		185.00	

General Post Office, Copenhagen
A15

1912	Engr.		Wmk. 113	Perf. 13
82	A15	5k dark red	500.00	200.00
		Never hinged	1,500.	

See Nos. 135, 843.

Perf. 14x14½

1913-30	Typo.		Wmk. 114	
85	A10	1ø dp orange ('14)	.40	.45
a.		Bklt. pane, 2 ea #85, 91 + 2 labels	20.00	
86	A10	2ø car ('13)	3.75	.35
a.		Imperf	150.00	300.00
b.		Booklet pane, 4 + 2 labels	27.50	
87	A10	3ø gray ('13)	6.75	.40
88	A10	4ø blue ('13)	8.00	.45
a.		Half used as 2ø on cover		1,250.
89	A10	5ø dk brown ('21)	.75	.35
a.		Imperf	190.00	
b.		Booklet pane, 4 + 2 labels	14.00	
90	A10	5ø lt green ('30)	1.50	.40
a.		Booklet pane, 4 + 2 labels	16.00	
b.		Booklet pane of 50		
91	A10	7ø apple grn ('26)	5.75	7.25
a.		Booklet pane, 4 + 2 labels	20.00	
92	A10	7ø dk violet ('30)	16.00	6.50
93	A10	8ø gray ('21)	7.00	3.25
94	A10	10ø green ('21)	.85	.35
a.		Imperf	225.00	
b.		Booklet pane, 4 + 2 labels	37.50	
95	A10	10ø bister brn ('30)	2.25	.35
a.		Booklet pane, 4 + 2 labels	16.00	
b.		Booklet pane of 50		
96	A10	12ø violet ('26)	25.00	9.75
	Nos. 85-96 (12)		78.00	29.85
	Set, never hinged		200.00	

No. 88a was used with No. 97 in Faroe Islands, Jan. 3-23, 1919.
See surcharge and overprint note following No. 64.

King Christian X — A16

1913-28	Typo.			Perf. 14x14½
97	A16	5ø green	1.40	.35
a.		Bklt. pane of 4, with P#	400.00	
98	A16	7ø orange ('18)	2.25	2.75
99	A16	8ø dk gray ('20)	14.00	6.50
100	A16	10ø red	2.40	.40
a.		Imperf	300.00	
b.		Bklt. pane of 4, with P#	500.00	
101	A16	12ø gray grn ('18)	7.50	10.00
102	A16	15ø violet	3.25	.40
103	A16	15ø dp blue	13.00	.35
104	A16	20ø brown ('21)	1.25	.40
105	A16	20ø red ('26)	13.50	.50
106	A16	20ø dk brown	13.50	.50
107	A16	25ø brn & blk ('20)	85.00	8.75
108	A16	25ø red ('22)	4.25	.95
109	A16	25ø yel grn ('25)	3.00	.50
110	A16	27ø ver & blk ('18)	30.00	50.00
111	A16	30ø green & blk ('18)	35.00	3.25
112	A16	30ø orange ('21)	3.00	2.00
113	A16	30ø dk brown ('25)	1.75	1.00
114	A16	35ø orange	29.00	7.50
115	A16	35ø yel & blk ('19)	9.00	6.50
116	A16	40ø vio & blk ('19)	18.00	4.00
117	A16	40ø gray bl & blk ('20)	37.50	7.50
118	A16	40ø dk blue ('22)	6.00	1.60
119	A16	40ø orange ('25)	1.50	1.50
120	A16	50ø claret	37.50	5.75
121	A16	50ø claret & blk ('19)	75.00	2.50
122	A16	50ø lt gray ('22)	9.25	.40
a.		50ø olive gray ('21)	75.00	8.00
		Never hinged	210.00	
123	A16	60ø brn & bl ('19)	60.00	3.75
a.		60ø brown & ultra ('19)	225.00	12.50
		Never hinged	750.00	
124	A16	60ø brn & bl ('21)	9.00	.75
125	A16	70ø brn & grn ('20)	26.00	2.25
126	A16	80ø bl grn ('15)	50.00	22.50
127	A16	90ø brn & red ('20)	18.00	3.25
128	A16	1k brn & bl ('22)	75.00	3.00
129	A16	2k gray & cl ('25)	67.50	15.00
130	A16	5k vio & brn ('27)	7.00	5.75
131	A16	10k ver & yel grn ('28)	325.00	65.00
	Nos. 97-131 (35)		1,082.	247.00
	Set, never hinged		3,085.	

No. 97 surcharged "2 ORE" is Faroe Islands No. 1. Two of the 14 printings of No. 97a have no P# in the selvage. These sell for more.
Nos. 87 and 98, 89 and 94, 89 and 104, 90 and 95, 97 and 103, 100 and 102 exist setenant in coils for use in vending machines.
For surcharges and overprints see Nos. 161-162, 176-177, 182-184, J2-J8, M1-M2, Q3-Q10.

King Christian X — A17

1913-20				Engr.
132	A17	1k yellow brown	95.00	1.25
133	A17	2k gray	150.00	7.00
134	A17	5k purple ('20)	15.00	10.00
	Nos. 132-134 (3)		260.00	18.25
	Set, never hinged		940.00	

For overprint see No. Q11.

G.P.O. Type of 1912
Perf. 14x14½

1915			Wmk. 114	Engr.
135	A15	5k dark red ('15)	500.00	175.00
		Never hinged	1,500.	

Nos. 46 and O10 Surcharged in Black type "c" and

e

1915			Wmk. 112	Typo. Perf. 13
136	A6 (c)	80ø on 12ø	40.00	100.00
a.		Inverted frame	600.00	1,100.
		Never hinged	825.00	
137	O1 (e)	80ø on 8ø	47.50	140.00
a.		"POSTERIM"	95.00	325.00
		Never hinged	140.00	
	Set, never hinged		155.00	

Newspaper Stamps Surcharged
On Issue of 1907

1918			Wmk. 113	Perf. 13
138	N1	27ø on 1ø olive	105.00	325.00
139	N1	27ø on 5ø blue	105.00	325.00
140	N1	27ø on 7ø car	105.00	325.00
141	N1	27ø on 10ø dp lil	105.00	325.00
142	N1	27ø on 68ø yel brn	7.50	37.50
143	N1	27ø on 5k rose & yel	6.75	26.00
144	N1	27ø on 10k bis & bl	7.50	35.00
	Nos. 138-144 (7)		441.75	1,399.
	Set, never hinged		940.00	

On Issue of 1914-15
Wmk. Multiple Crosses (114)
Perf. 14x14½

145	N1	27ø on 1ø gray	5.00	15.50
146	N1	27ø on 5ø blue	7.50	30.00
147	N1	27ø on 7ø rose	5.00	12.50
148	N1	27ø on 8ø green	7.50	16.00
149	N1	27ø on 10ø dp lil	3.25	17.00
150	N1	27ø on 20ø green	8.00	16.50
151	N1	27ø on 29ø org yel	3.25	14.50
152	N1	27ø on 38ø orange	32.50	110.00
153	N1	27ø on 41ø yel brn	7.50	45.00
154	N1	27ø on 1k bl grn & mar	5.00	14.50
	Nos. 145-154 (10)		84.50	291.50
	Set, never hinged		150.00	

Kronborg Castle
A20

Sonderborg Castle
A21

Roskilde Cathedral — A22

Perf. 14½x14, 14x14½

1920, Oct. 5				Typo.
156	A20	10ø red	7.00	.50
157	A21	20ø slate	5.00	.50
158	A22	40ø dark brown	17.00	4.50
	Nos. 156-158 (3)		29.00	5.50
	Set, never hinged		52.00	

Reunion of Northern Schleswig with Denmark.
See Nos. 159-160. For surcharges see Nos. B1-B2.

1921				
159	A20	10ø green	9.00	.55
160	A22	40ø dark blue	67.50	11.50
	Set, never hinged		174.00	

Stamps of 1918 Surcharged in Blue

1921-22				
161	A16	8ø on 7ø org ('22)	2.25	5.00
162	A16	8ø on 12ø gray grn	2.25	15.00
	Set, never hinged		15.75	

No. 87 Surcharged

1921				
163	A10	8ø on 3ø gray	3.75	5.25
		Never hinged	8.25	

Christian X
A23

Christian IV
A24

A25

A26

1924, Dec. 1				Perf. 14x14½
164	A23	10ø green	7.50	7.00
165	A24	10ø green	7.50	7.00
166	A25	10ø green	7.50	7.00
167	A26	10ø green	7.50	7.00
a.		Block of 4, #164-167	37.50	50.00
168	A23	15ø violet	7.50	7.00
169	A24	15ø violet	7.50	7.00
170	A25	15ø violet	7.50	7.00
171	A26	15ø violet	7.50	7.00
a.		Block of 4, #168-171	37.50	50.00
172	A23	20ø dark brown	7.50	7.00
173	A24	20ø dark brown	7.50	7.00
174	A25	20ø dark brown	7.50	7.00
175	A26	20ø dark brown	7.50	7.00
a.		Block of 4, #172-175	37.50	50.00
	Nos. 164-175 (12)		90.00	84.00
	Set, never hinged		180.00	
#167a, 171a, 175a, never hinged			225.00	

300th anniv. of the Danish postal service.

Stamps of 1921-22 Surcharged

k

l

DENMARK

1926
176	A16 (k)	20o on 30o org	6.75 15.00
177	A16 (l)	20o on 40o dk bl	9.00 18.00
	Set, never hinged		31.00

A27

A28

1926, Mar. 11 — Perf. 14x14½
178	A27	10o dull green	1.50 .45
179	A28	20o dark red	2.00 .45
180	A28	30o dark blue	8.50 1.50
	Nos. 178-180 (3)		12.00 2.40
	Set, never hinged		24.50

75th anniv. of the introduction of postage stamps in Denmark.

Stamps of 1913-26 Surcharged in Blue or Black

No. 181

Nos. 182-184

1926-27 — Perf. 14x14½
181	A10	7o on 8o gray (Bl)	1.50 4.75
182	A16	7o on 27o ver & blk	4.50 17.00
183	A16	7o on 20o red ('27)	.75 2.50
184	A16	12o on 15o violet	2.25 6.00

Surcharged on Official Stamps of 1914-23
185	O1 (e)	7o on 1o org	4.00 16.00
186	O1 (e)	7o on 3o gray	7.50 32.50
187	O1 (e)	7o on 4o blue	3.75 7.75
188	O1 (e)	7o on 5o grn	52.50 150.00
189	O1 (e)	7o on 10o grn	4.50 15.50
190	O1 (e)	7o on 15o vio	4.50 15.50
191	O1 (e)	7o on 20o ind	19.00 77.50
a.	Double surcharge		750.00 975.00
	Nos. 181-191 (11)		104.75 345.00
	Set, never hinged		155.00

Caravel — A30

1927 Typo. — Perf. 14x14½
192	A30	15o red	6.00 .40
193	A30	20o gray	11.00 2.40
194	A30	25o light blue	1.25 .40
195	A30	30o ocher	1.25 .40
196	A30	35o red brown	25.00 1.50
197	A30	40o yel green	25.00 4.00
	Nos. 192-197 (6)		69.50 5.50
	Set, never hinged		200.00

See Nos. 232-238J. For surcharges & overprints see Nos. 244-245, 269-272, Q12-Q14, Q19-Q25.

Christian X — A31

1930, Sept. 26
210	A31	5o apple grn	2.50 .35
a.	Booklet pane, 4 + 2 labels		18.00
211	A31	7o violet	6.75 3.00
212	A31	8o dk gray	22.50 32.50
213	A31	10o yel brn	5.00 .35
a.	Booklet pane, 4 + 2 labels		29.00
214	A31	15o red	10.00 .35
215	A31	20o lt gray	25.00 9.75
216	A31	25o lt blue	8.50 1.25
217	A31	30o yel buff	9.00 1.75
218	A31	35o red brown	12.00 4.50
219	A31	40o dp green	10.00 1.25
	Nos. 210-219 (10)		111.25 55.05
	Set, never hinged		295.00

60th birthday of King Christian X.

Wavy Lines and Numeral of Value — A32

Type A10 Redrawn

1933-40 Unwmk. Engr. — Perf. 13
220	A32	1o gray blk	.60 .30
a.	Fluorescent paper ('69)		.50 .25
221	A32	2o scarlet	.35 .30
222	A32	4o blue	.40 .35
223	A32	5o yel grn	1.00 .35
a.	5o gray green		37.50 60.00
b.	Tête bêche gutter pair		8.00 15.50
c.	Booklet pane of 4		11.00
d.	Bklt. pane, 1 #223a, 3 #B6		37.50 70.00
	Never hinged		60.00
e.	As "b," without gutter		17.50 27.50
224	A32	5o rose lake ('38)	.30 .30
a.	Booklet pane of 4		1.20
b.	Booklet pane of 10		12.00
d.	Fluorescent paper ('80)		.50 .25
224C	A32	6o orange ('40)	.30 .30
225	A32	7o violet	2.00 .35
226	A32	7o yel grn ('38)	1.10 .45
226A	A32	7o lt brown ('40)	.35 .35
227	A32	8o gray	.45 .50
227A	A32	8o yellow grn ('40)	.30 .35
228	A32	10o yellow org	12.50 .35
a.	Tête bêche gutter pair		50.00 55.00
b.	Booklet pane of 4		110.00
c.	As "a," without gutter		60.00 70.00
	Never hinged		100.00
229	A32	10o lt brown ('37)	9.50 .35
a.	Booklet pane of 4, 1 #229, 3 #B7		100.00
			32.50 45.00
230	A32	10o violet ('38)	.75 .35
a.	Booklet pane of 4		2.75
b.	Bklt. pane, 2 #230, 2 #B10		2.50 7.00
	Never hinged		7.00
	Nos. 220-230 (14)		29.90 4.95
	Set, never hinged		75.00

Design A10 was typographed. They had a solid background with groups of small hearts below the heraldic lions in the upper corners and below "DA" and "RK" of "DANMARK." The numerals of value were enclosed in single-lined ovals.

Design A32 is line-engraved and has a background of crossed lines. The hearts have been removed and the numerals of value are now in double-lined ovals. Two types exist of some values.

No. 230 with wide margins is from booklet pane No. 230b.

Surcharges of 20, 50 & 60öre on #220, 224 and 224C are listed as Faroe Islands #2-3, 5-6.

See Nos. 318, 333, 382, 416, 437-437A, 493-498, 629, 631, 688-695, 793-795, 883-886, 1111-1113, 1116. For overprints and surcharges see Nos. 257, 263, 267-268, 355-356, Q15-Q17, Q31, Q43.

Certain tête-bêche pairs of 1938-55 issues which reached the market in 1971, and were not regularly issued, are not listed. This group comprises 24 different major-number vertical pairs of types A32, A47, A61 and SP3 (13 with gutters, 11 without), and pairs of some minor numbers and shades. They were removed from booklet pane sheets.

A32a

Type I

Type II

Type I — Two columns of squares between sail and left frame line.

Type I

1933-34 Engr. — Perf. 13
232	A32a	20o gray	15.00 .35
233	A32a	25o blue	85.00 30.00
234	A32a	25o brown ('34)	30.00 .35
235	A32a	30o orange yel	1.50 1.40
236	A32a	30o blue ('34)	1.50 .40
237	A32a	35o violet	.60 .35
238	A32a	40o yellow grn	6.25 .35
	Nos. 232-238 (7)		139.85 33.20
	Set, never hinged		325.00

A32b

Type II — One column of squares between sail and left frame line.

1933-40 Type II
238A	A32b	15o deep red	3.00 .35
k.	Booklet pane of 4		26.00
l.	Bklt. pane, 1 #238A, 3 #B8		45.00
	Never hinged		115.00
238B	A32b	15o yel grn ('40)	9.00 .40
238C	A32b	20o gray blk ('39)	4.50 .70
238D	A32b	20o red ('40)	.90 .35
238E	A32b	25o dp brown ('39)	.90 .35
238F	A32b	30o blue ('39)	2.25 .70
238G	A32b	30o orange ('40)	.75 .35
238H	A32b	30o violet ('40)	1.00 .35
238I	A32b	40o yel grn ('39)	15.00 .35
238J	A32b	40o blue ('40)	1.40 .35
	Nos. 238A-238J (10)		38.70 4.25
	Set, never hinged		95.00

Nos. 232-238J, engraved, have crosshatched background. Nos. 192-197, typographed, have solid background.

For No. 238A surcharged 20 ore see Denmark No. 271, Faroe Islands No. 4.

See note on surcharges and overprints following No. 197.

King Christian X — A33

1934-41 — Perf. 13
239	A33	50o gray	1.20 .30
240	A33	60o blue grn	2.40 .30
240A	A33	75o dk blue ('41)	.45 .35
241	A33	1k lt brown	3.75 .35
242	A33	2k dull red	6.00 1.00
243	A33	5k violet	9.00 3.50
	Nos. 239-243 (6)		22.80 5.85
	Set, never hinged		75.00

For overprints see Nos. Q26-Q27.

Nos. 233, 236 Surcharged in Black

1934, June 9
244	A30	4o on 25o blue	.50 .50
245	A30	10o on 30o org yel	2.40 3.25
	Set, never hinged		7.50

"The Ugly Duckling" A34

Andersen A35

"The Little Mermaid" — A36

1935, Oct. 1 — Perf. 13
246	A34	5o lt green	3.00 .30
a.	Tête bêche gutter pair		15.00 22.50
b.	Booklet pane of 4		40.00
c.	As "a," without gutter		17.00 21.00
	Never hinged		45.00
247	A35	7o dull vio	2.50 2.50
248	A36	10o orange	4.50 .30
a.	Tête bêche gutter pair		18.00 32.50
b.	Booklet pane of 4		65.00
c.	As "a," without gutter		20.00 40.00
	Never hinged		65.00
249	A35	15o red	11.00 .30
a.	Tête bêche gutter pair		45.00 52.50
b.	Booklet pane of 4		160.00
c.	As "a," without gutter		42.50 75.00
	Never hinged		110.00
250	A35	20o gray	9.50 1.25
251	A35	30o dl bl	3.00 .35
	Nos. 246-251 (6)		33.50 5.00
	Set, never hinged		87.50

Centenary of the publication of the earliest installment of Hans Christian Andersen's "Fairy Tales."

Nikolai Church A37

Hans Tausen A38

Ribe Cathedral — A39

1936 — Perf. 13
252	A37	5o green	1.40 .40
a.	Booklet pane of 4		21.00
253	A37	7o violet	2.00 4.50
254	A38	10o lt brown	2.00 .40
a.	Booklet pane of 4		25.00
255	A38	15o dull rose	3.00 .35
256	A39	30o blue	16.00 1.40
	Nos. 252-256 (5)		24.40 7.00
	Set, never hinged		62.50

Church Reformation in Denmark, 400th anniv.

No. 229 Overprinted in Blue

1937, Sept. 17
257	A32	10o lt brown	1.50 1.60
	Never hinged		2.00

Jubilee Exhib. held by the Copenhagen Phil. Club on their 50th anniv. The stamps were on sale at the Exhib. only, each holder of a ticket of admission (1k) being entitled to purchase 20 stamps at face value; of a season ticket (5k), 100 stamps.

Yacht and Summer Palace, Marselisborg A40

Christian X in Streets of Copenhagen A41

Equestrian Statue of Frederik V and Amalienborg Palace — A42

1937, May 15 — Perf. 13
258	A40	5o green	1.40 .30
a.	Booklet pane of 4		15.00
259	A41	10o brown	1.40 .30
a.	Booklet pane of 4		15.00
260	A41	15o scarlet	1.40 .30
a.	Booklet pane of 4		17.00
261	A41	30o blue	15.00 2.40
	Nos. 258-261 (4)		19.20 3.30
	Set, never hinged		42.50

25th anniv. of the accession to the throne of King Christian X.

Emancipation Column, Copenhagen — A43

1938, June 20 — Perf. 13
262	A43	15o scarlet	.60 .30
	Never hinged		1.40

Abolition of serfdom in Denmark, 150th anniv.

No. 223 Overprinted in Red on Alternate Stamps

DENMARK

1938, Sept. 2
263 A32 5ø yellow grn, pair 3.25 7.00
Never hinged 4.50
10th Danish Philatelic Exhibition.

Bertel Thorvaldsen A44

Statue of Jason A45

1938, Nov. 17   *Engr.*   *Perf. 13*
264 A44 5ø rose lake .45 .30
265 A45 10ø purple .45 .30
266 A44 30ø dark blue 1.50 .60
   Nos. 264-266 (3) 2.40 1.20
   Set, never hinged 5.25

The return to Denmark in 1838 of Bertel Thorvaldsen, Danish sculptor.

Stamps of 1933-39 Surcharged with New Values in Black

a

b

c

1940
267 A32 (a) 6ø on 7ø yel grn .30 .35
268 A32 (a) 6ø on 8ø gray .45 .35
269 A30 (b) 15ø on 40ø #238 .90 6.00
270 A30 (b) 15ø on 40ø #238I .75 .95
271 A30 (c) 20ø on 15ø dp red 1.10 .30
272 A30 (b) 40ø on 30ø #238F .60 .60
   Nos. 267-272 (6) 4.50 8.30
   Set, never hinged 9.25

Stamps previously listed as Denmark No. 273-276 are listed as Faroe Islands Nos. 2-6.

Bering's Ship — A46

1941, Nov. 27   *Engr.*   *Perf. 13*
277 A46 10ø dk violet .35 .30
278 A46 20ø red brown .60 .30
279 A46 40ø dk blue .40 .35
   Nos. 277-279 (3) 1.35 .95
   Set, never hinged 3.00

Death of Vitus Bering, explorer, 200th anniv.

King Christian X — A47

1942-46   *Unwmk.*   *Perf. 13*
280 A47 10ø violet .30 .35
281 A47 15ø yel grn .35 .35
282 A47 20ø red .40 .35
283 A47 25ø brown ('43) .50 .35
284 A47 30ø orange ('43) .45 .35
285 A47 35ø brt red vio ('44) .40 .35
286 A47 40ø blue ('43) .35 .35
286A A47 45ø ol brn ('46) .35 .35
286B A47 50ø gray ('45) .60 .35
287 A47 60ø bluish grn ('44) .55 .35
287A A47 75ø dk blue ('46) .55 .35
   Nos. 280-287A (11) 4.85 3.95
   Set, never hinged 8.00

For overprints see Nos. Q28-Q30.

Round Tower — A48

1942, Nov. 27
288 A48 10ø violet .35 .30
   Never hinged .75

300th anniv. of the Round Tower, Copenhagen.
For surcharge see No. B14.

Condor Plane — A49

1943, Oct. 29
289 A49 20ø red .25 .25
   Never hinged .35

25th anniv. of the Danish Aviation Company (Det Danske Luftfartsselskab).

Ejby Church — A50

15ø, Oesterlars Church. 20ø, Hvidbjerg Church.

1944   *Engr.*   *Perf. 13*
290 A50 10ø violet .30 .25
291 A50 15ø yellow grn .30 .25
292 A50 20ø red .30 .25
   Nos. 290-292 (3) .90 .75
   Set, never hinged 1.75

Ole Roemer — A53

1944, Sept. 25
293 A53 20ø henna brown .35 .30
   Never hinged .65

Birth of Ole Roemer, astronomer, 300th anniv.

Christian X — A54

1945, Sept. 26
294 A54 10ø lilac .25 .25
295 A54 20ø red .25 .25
296 A54 40ø deep blue .25 .25
   Nos. 294-296 (3) .75 .75
   Set, never hinged 1.75

75th birthday of King Christian X.

Catalogue values for unused stamps in this section, from this point to the end of the section, are for Never Hinged items.

Small State Seal — A55

1946-47   *Unwmk.*   *Perf. 13*
297 A55 1k brown 1.00 .25
  a. Fluorescent paper ('68) .80 .25
298 A55 2k red ('47) 2.00 .25
  a. Fluorescent paper ('69) .50 .25
299 A55 5k dull blue 6.00 .25
  a. Fluorescent paper ('68) 1.25 .30
   Nos. 297-299 (3) 9.00 .75

See Nos. 395-400, 441A-444D, 499-506, 643-650, 716-720A, 804-815, 909, 1111-1138, 1304-1313, 1474-1478, 1508. For overprints see Nos. Q35, Q40, Q46-Q48.

Tycho Brahe — A56

1946, Dec. 14   *Engr.*
300 A56 20ø dark red .30 .25

Birth of Tycho Brahe, astronomer, 400th anniv.

First Danish Locomotive A57

Modern Steam Locomotive A58

Diesel Locomotive — A59

1947, June 27
301 A57 15ø steel blue .60 .35
302 A58 20ø red 1.10 .35
303 A59 40ø deep blue 3.50 2.25
   Nos. 301-303 (3) 5.20 2.95

Inauguration of the Danish State Railways, cent.

Jacobsen — A60

1947, Nov. 10   *Perf. 13*
304 A60 20ø dark red .30 .25

60th anniv. of the death of Jacob Christian Jacobsen, founder of the Glyptothek Art Museum, Copenhagen.

Frederik IX — A61

Three types among 15ø, 20ø, 30ø:
I — Background of horizontal lines. No outline at left for cheek and ear. King's uniform textured in strong lines.
II — Background of vertical and horizontal lines. Contour of cheek and ear at left. Uniform same.
III — Background and facial contour lines as in II. Uniform lines double and thinner.

1948-50   *Unwmk.*   *Perf. 13*
306 A61 15(ø) green (II) 2.50 .30
  a. Type III ('49) 1.60 .50
307 A61 20(ø) dk red (I) 1.10 .35
  a. Type III ('49) 1.40 .30
308 A61 25(ø) lt brown 1.40 .25
309 A61 30(ø) org (II) 13.00 .50
  a. Type III ('50) 21.00 .50
310 A61 40(ø) dl blue ('49) 4.75 1.00
311 A61 45(ø) olive ('50) 2.10 .35
312 A61 50(ø) gray ('49) 1.75 .30
313 A61 60(ø) grnsh bl ('50) 2.50 .30
314 A61 75(ø) lil rose ('50) 2.00 .40
   Nos. 306-314 (9) 31.10 3.55

See Nos. 319-326, 334-341, 354, For surcharges see Nos. 357-358, 370, B20, B24 B25, Q32-Q34, Q36-Q39.

Legislative Assembly, 1849 — A62

1949, June 5
315 A62 20ø red brown .35 .25

Adoption of the Danish constitution, cent.

Symbol of UPU — A63

1949, Oct. 9
316 A63 40ø dull blue .65 .35

75th anniv. of the UPU.

Kalundborg Radio Station and Masts — A64

1950, Apr. 1   *Engr.*   *Perf. 13*
317 A64 20ø brown red .50 .25

Radio broadcasting in Denmark, 25th anniv.

Types of 1933-50

1950-51   *Unwmk.*   *Perf. 13*
318 A32 10ø green .30 .25
  a. Fluorescent paper .25 .25
319 A61 15(ø) lilac 1.00 .30
  b. 15(ø) gray lilac 4.00 .25
320 A61 20(ø) lt brown 1.10 .30
321 A61 25(ø) dark red 3.50 .25
322 A61 35(ø) gray grn ('51) .95 .25
323 A61 40(ø) gray .95 .25
324 A61 50(ø) dark blue 3.25 .25
325 A61 55(ø) brown ('51) 32.50 2.75
326 A61 70(ø) deep green 3.00 .30
   Nos. 318-326 (9) 46.55 4.90

Warship of 1701 — A65

1951, Feb. 26   *Engr.*   *Perf. 13*
327 A65 25ø dark red .50 .30
328 A65 50ø deep blue 4.00 .80

250th anniv. of the foundation of the Naval Officers' College.

Oersted — A66

1951, Mar. 9   *Unwmk.*
329 A66 50ø blue 1.40 .60

Cent. of the death of Hans Christian Oersted, physicist.

Post Chaise ("Ball Post") — A67

1951, Apr. 1   *Perf. 13*
330 A67 15ø purple .65 .25
331 A67 25ø henna brown .65 .25

Cent. of Denmark's 1st postage stamp.

Marine Rescue — A68

1952, Mar. 26
332 A68 25ø red brown .45 .35

Cent. of the foundation of the Danish Life-saving Service.

Types of 1933-50

1952-53   *Perf. 13*
333 A32 12ø lt yel grn .30 .25
  a. Fluorescent paper ('62) 2.50 3.50
334 A61 25(ø) lt blue 1.10 .35
335 A61 30(ø) brown red 1.00 .35
336 A61 50(ø) aqua ('53) 1.00 .35
337 A61 60(ø) dp blue ('53) 1.10 .35
338 A61 65(ø) gray ('53) 1.10 .35

DENMARK

339	A61 80(o) orange ('53)	1.10	.35
340	A61 90(o) olive ('53)	3.00	.30
341	A61 95(o) red org ('53)	1.10	.35
	Nos. 333-341 (9)	10.80	2.80

Jelling Runic Stone — A69

Designs: 15o, Vikings' camp, Trelleborg. 20o, Church of Kalundborg. 30o, Nyborg castle. 60o, Goose tower, Vordinborg.

1953-56   *Perf. 13*

342	A69 10o dp green	.30	.25
343	A69 15o lt rose vio	.30	.25
344	A69 20o brown	.30	.25
345	A69 30o red ('54)	.30	.25
346	A69 60o dp blue ('54)	.35	.25

Designs: 10o, Manor house, Spottrup. 15o, Hammershus castle ruins. 20o, Copenhagen stock exchange. 30o, Statue of Frederik V, Amalienborg. 60o, Soldier statue at Fredericia.

347	A69 10o green ('54)	.30	.25
348	A69 15o lilac ('55)	.30	.25
349	A69 20o brown ('55)	.30	.25
350	A69 30o red ('55)	.30	.25
351	A69 60o deep blue ('56)	.60	.25
	Nos. 342-351 (10)	3.35	2.50

1000th anniv. of the Kingdom of Denmark. Each stamp represents a different century.

Telegraph Equipment of 1854 — A70

1954, Feb. 2   *Perf. 13*

352	A70 30o red brown	.40	.25

Cent. of the telegraph in Denmark.

Frederik V — A71

1954, Mar. 31

353	A71 30o dark red	.55	.35

200th anniv. of the founding of the Royal Academy of Fine Arts.

Type of 1948-50

1955, Apr. 27

354	A61 25o lilac	1.00	.30

Nos. 224C and 226A Surcharged with New Value in Black. Nos. 307 and 321 Surcharged with New Value and 4 Bars

1955-56

355	A32 5o on 6o org	.30	.25
356	A32 5o on 7o lt brn	.30	.25
357	A61 30(o) on 20(o) dk red (I)	.80	.30
a.	Type III	1.40	.35
b.	Double surcharge	1,150.	1,150.
c.	Inverted surcharge	650.00	
358	A61 30(o) on 25(o) dk red ('56)	.60	.25
a.	Double surcharge	—	
	Nos. 355-358 (4)	2.00	1.05

A72

1955, Nov. 11   *Unwmk.*

359	A72 30o dark red	.50	.25

100th anniv. of the death of Sören Kierkegaard, philosopher and theologian.

A73

1956, Sept. 12   *Engr.*

360	A73 30o Ellehammer's plane	.50	.25

50th anniv. of the 1st flight made by Jacob Christian Hansen Ellehammer in a heavier-than-air craft.

Northern Countries Issue

Whooper Swans — A74

1956, Oct. 30   *Perf. 13*

361	A74 30o rose red	1.75	.25
362	A74 60o ultramarine	1.60	.80

Issued to emphasize the close bonds among the northern countries: Denmark, Finland, Iceland, Norway and Sweden.

Prince's Palace — A75

Design: 60o, Sun God's Chariot.

1957, May 15   *Unwmk.*

363	A75 30o dull red	.90	.25
364	A75 60o dark blue	.90	.75

150th anniv. of the National Museum.

Harvester — A76

1958, Sept. 4   *Engr.*   *Perf. 13*

365	A76 30o fawn	.30	.25

Centenary of the Royal Veterinary and Agricultural College.

Frederik IX — A77

1959, Mar. 11

366	A77 30o rose red	.40	.25
367	A77 35o rose lilac	.50	.25
368	A77 60o ultra	.50	.25
	Nos. 366-368 (3)	1.40	.75

King Frederik's 60th birthday.

Ballet Dancer — A78

1959, May 16

369	A78 35o rose lilac	.30	.25

Danish Ballet and Music Festival, May 17-31. See Nos. 401, 422.

No. 319 Surcharged

1960, Apr. 7

370	A61 30o on 15o lilac	.30	.25

World Refugee Year, 7/1/59-6/30/60.

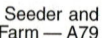

Seeder and Farm — A79

30o, Harvester combine. 60o, Plow.

1960, Apr. 28   *Engr.*   *Perf. 13*

371	A79 12o green	.25	.25
372	A79 30o dull red	.30	.25
373	A79 60o dk blue	.65	.50
	Nos. 371-373 (3)	1.20	1.00

King Frederik IX and Queen Ingrid — A80

1960, May 24   *Unwmk.*

374	A80 30o dull red	.45	.25
375	A80 60o blue	.65	.60

25th anniversary of the marriage of King Frederik IX and Queen Ingrid.

Bascule Light — A81

1960, June 8   *Engr.*

376	A81 30o dull red	.30	.25

400th anniv. of the Lighthouse Service.

Finsen — A82

1960, Aug. 1   *Perf. 13*

377	A82 30o dark red	.30	.25

Centenary of the birth of Dr. Niels R. Finsen, physician and scientist.

Nursing Mother — A83

1960, Aug. 16   *Unwmk.*

378	A83 60o ultra	.55	.50

10th meeting of the regional committee for Europe of WHO, Copenhagen, Aug. 16-20.

Europa Issue, 1960
Common Design Type

1960, Sept. 19   *Perf. 13*
    Size: 28x21mm

379	CD3 60o ultra	.55	.50

DC-8 Airliner — A84

1961, Feb. 24

380	A84 60o ultra	.75	.50
a.	Fluorescent paper	15.00	8.00

10th anniv. of the Scandinavian Airlines System, SAS.

Landscape — A85

1961, Apr. 21   *Perf. 13*

381	A85 30o copper brown	.30	.25

Denmark's Soc. of Nature Lovers, 50th anniv.

Fluorescent Paper

as well as ordinary paper, was used in printing many definitive and commemorative stamps, starting in 1962. These include No. 220, 224; the 15, 20, 25, 30, 35 (Nos. 386 and 387), 50 and 60ö, 1.50k and 25k definitives of following set, and Nos. 297-299, 318, 333, 380, 401-427, 429-435, 438-439, 543, B30.

Only fluorescent paper was used for Nos. 436-437, 437A and 440 onward; in semipostals from B31 onward.

Frederik IX — A86

1961-63   *Engr.*   *Perf. 13*

382	A32 15o green ('63)	.50	.35
a.	Fluorescent paper	.70	.45
383	A86 20o brown	.45	.35
a.	Fluorescent paper ('62)	3.50	4.00
384	A86 25o brown ('63)	.30	.35
a.	Fluorescent paper	.30	.35
385	A86 30o rose red	.65	.75
a.	Fluorescent paper ('62)	1.25	.35
386	A86 35o olive grn	.85	.75
a.	Fluorescent paper ('62)	3.25	3.25
387	A86 35o rose red ('63)	.30	.35
a.	Fluorescent paper	.35	.40
388	A86 40o gray	1.20	.35
389	A86 50o aqua	.55	.30
a.	Fluorescent paper	1.00	.50
390	A86 60o ultra	1.10	.35
a.	Fluorescent paper	1.50	1.00
391	A86 70o green	1.60	.35
392	A86 80o red orange	1.60	.35
393	A86 90o olive bister	4.25	.35
394	A86 95o claret ('63)	1.00	.90
	Nos. 382-394 (13)	14.35	5.45

See Nos. 417-419, 438-441. For overprints see Nos. Q41-Q42, Q44-Q45.

State Seal Type of 1946-47

1962-70

395	A55 1.10k lilac ('65)	5.25	2.00
396	A55 1.20k gray	3.00	.35
397	A55 1.25k orange	3.00	.35
398	A55 1.30k green ('65)	5.50	1.75
399	A55 1.50k red lilac	2.75	.45
a.	Fluorescent paper ('70)	1.60	.35
400	A55 25k yellow grn	35.00	2.00
a.	Fluorescent paper ('69)	7.00	.35
	Nos. 395-400 (6)	54.50	6.80

Dancer Type of 1959 Inscribed "15-31 MAJ"

1962, Apr. 26

401	A78 60o ultra	.30	.25
a.	Fluorescent paper ('70)	1.20	1.00

Issued to publicize the Danish Ballet and Music Festival, May 15-31.

Old Mill — A87

1962, May 10   *Unwmk.*   *Perf. 13*

402	A87 10o red brown	.30	.25
a.	Fluorescent paper	.30	.30

Cent. of the abolition of mill monopolies.

M.S. Selandia — A88

1962, June 14   *Engr.*

403	A88 60o dark blue	1.60	1.50
a.	Fluorescent paper	7.50	7.50

M.S. Selandia, the 1st Diesel ship, 50th anniv.

Violin Scroll, Leaves, Lights and Balloon — A89

DENMARK

1962, Aug. 31
404 A89 35ø rose violet .35 .25
   a. Fluorescent paper .45 .25

150th anniv. of the birth of Georg Carstensen, founder of Tivoli amusement park, Copenhagen.

Cliffs on Moen Island — A90

1962, Nov. 22
405 A90 20ø pale brown .30 .25
   a. Fluorescent paper .65 .40

Issued to publicize preservation of natural treasures and landmarks.

Germinating Wheat — A91

1963, Mar. 21   Engr.
406 A91 35ø fawn .35 .25
   a. Fluorescent paper .45 .30

FAO "Freedom from Hunger" campaign.

Railroad Wheel, Tire Tracks, Waves and Swallow — A92

1963, May 14   Unwmk.   Perf. 13
407 A92 15ø green .60 .40
   a. Fluorescent paper .60 .50

Inauguration of the "Bird Flight Line" railroad link between Denmark and Germany.

Sailing Vessel, Coach, Postilions and Globe — A93

1963, May 27
408 A93 60ø dark blue .40 .40
   a. Fluorescent paper 1.25 1.25

Cent. of the 1st Intl. Postal Conf., Paris, 1863.

Niels Bohr and Atom Diagram — A94

1963, Nov. 21   Engr.
409 A94 35ø red brown .10 .35
   a. Fluorescent paper .40 .35
410 A94 60ø dark blue .65 .35
   a. Fluorescent paper .95 .95

50th anniv. of Prof. Niels Bohr's (1885-1962) atom theory. See Greenland Nos. 66-67.

Early Public School Drawn on Slate — A95

1964, June 19   Unwmk.   Perf. 13
411 A95 35ø red brown .60 .25
   a. Fluorescent paper .75 .30

150th anniversary of the royal decrees for the public school system.

Fish and Chart — A96

1964, Sept. 7   Engr.
412 A96 60ø violet blue .35 .40
   a. Fluorescent paper 1.00 1.00

Conference of the International Council for the Exploration of the Sea, Copenhagen.

Danish Watermarks and Perforations — A97

1964, Oct. 10   Perf. 13
413 A97 35ø pink .30 .25
   a. Fluorescent paper .45 .45

25th anniv. of Stamp Day and to publicize the Odense Stamp Exhibition, Oct. 10-11.

Landscape — A98

1964, Nov. 12   Engr.
414 A98 25ø brown .30 .25
   a. Fluorescent paper .30 .30

Issued to publicize preservation of natural treasures and landmarks.

Calculator, Ledger and Inkwell — A99

1965, Mar. 8   Unwmk.
415 A99 15ø light olive green .30 .25
   a. Fluorescent paper .30 .30

First Business School in Denmark, cent.

Types of 1933 and 1961

1965, May 15   Engr.   Perf. 13
416 A32 25ø apple green 1.00 .35
   a. Fluorescent paper .55 .50
417 A86 40ø brown .45 .35
   a. Fluorescent paper .45 .35
418 A86 50ø rose red .90 .35
   a. Fluorescent paper .75 .65
419 A86 80ø ultra 2.10 .35
   a. Fluorescent paper .75 .65
   Nos. 416-419 (4) 4.45 1.40

For overprints see Nos. Q41-Q42.

ITU Emblem, Telegraph Key, Teletype Paper — A100

1965, May 17
420 A100 80ø dark blue .35 .25
   a. Fluorescent paper .60 .60

Cent. of the ITU.

Carl Nielsen (1865-1931), Composer — A101

1965, June 9   Engr.
421 A101 50ø brown red .40 .25
   a. Fluorescent paper .45 .45

Dancer Type of 1959 Inscribed "15-31 MAJ"

1965, Sept. 23
422 A78 50ø rose red .30 .25
   a. Fluorescent paper .45 .45

Issued to publicize the Danish Ballet and Music Festival, May 15-31.

Bogø Windmill — A102

1965, Nov. 10   Engr.   Perf. 13
423 A102 40ø brown .30 .25
   a. Fluorescent paper .45 .45

Issued to publicize the preservation of natural treasures and landmarks.

Mylius Dalgas Surveying Wasteland — A103

1966, Feb. 24
424 A103 25ø olive green .80 .25
   a. Fluorescent paper .50 .30

Cent. of the Danish Heath Soc. (reclamation of wastelands), founded by Enrico Mylius Dalgas.

Christen Kold (1816-70), Educator — A104

1966, Mar. 29   Perf. 13
425 A104 50ø dull red .80 .25
   a. Fluorescent paper .50 .45

Poorhouse, Copenhagen A105

Holte Allée, Bregentved A106

Dolmen (Grave) in Jutland — A107

1966   Unwmk.
426 A105 50ø dull red .80 .25
   a. Fluorescent paper .55 .45
427 A106 80ø dk blue 1.00 .40
   a. Fluorescent paper 1.20 1.00
428 A107 1.50k dk slate grn 1.40 .25
   a. Fluorescent paper 3.20 .90
   Nos. 426-428 (3)

Publicizing preservation of national treasures and ancient monuments. Issued: 50ø, May 12; 80ø, June 16; 1.50k, Nov. 24.

George Jensen by Ejnar Nielsen — A108

1966, Aug. 31   Engr.   Perf. 13
429 A108 80ø dark blue 1.00 .40
   a. Fluorescent paper 1.00 1.00

George Jensen, silversmith, birth cent.

Music Bar and Instruments — A109

1967, Jan. 9
430 A109 50ø dark red .70 .25
   a. Fluorescent paper .60 .45

Royal Danish Academy of Music, cent.

Cogwheels, and Broken Customs Duty Ribbon — A110

1967, Mar. 2
431 A110 80ø dark blue .70 .25
   a. Fluorescent paper .90 .90

European Free Trade Association. Industrial tariffs were abolished Dec. 31, 1966, among EFTA members: Austria, Denmark, Finland, Great Britain, Norway, Portugal, Sweden and Switzerland.

Windmill and Medieval Fortress — A111

Designs: 40ø, Ship's rigging and baroque house front. 50ø, Old Town Hall. 80ø, New building construction.

1967   Engr.   Perf. 13
432 A111 25ø green .70 .25
   a. Fluorescent paper .60 .60
433 A111 40ø sepia .35 .25
   a. Fluorescent paper .45 .45
434 A111 50ø red brown .35 .40
   a. Fluorescent paper .45 .45
435 A111 80ø dk blue .85 .80
   a. Fluorescent paper 1.25 1.25
   Nos. 432-435 (4) 2.25 1.70

The 800th anniversary of Copenhagen. Issued: Nos. 432-433, 4/6; Nos. 434-435, 5/11.

Princess Margrethe and Prince Henri — A112

1967, June 10
436 A112 50ø red .30 .25

Marriage of Crown Princess Margrethe and Prince Henri de Monpezat.

Types of 1933-1961

1967-71   Engr.   Perf. 13
437 A32 30ø dk green .70 .35
437A A32 40ø orange ('71) .80 .35
438 A86 50ø brown 1.25 .35
   a. Fluorescent paper .85 .35
   Complete booklet, 4 #318, 2 each #437, 438 20.00
439 A86 60ø rose red 1.25 .35
   a. Fluorescent paper 1.25 .35
440 A86 80ø green .85 .35
441 A86 90ø ultra .90 .35
441A A55 1.20k Prus grn ('71) 2.00 .45
442 A55 2.20k orange 3.50 .35
443 A55 2.80k gray 3.00 .35
444 A55 2.90k rose vio 5.25 .35
444A A55 3ø dk sl grn ('69) 1.00 .35
444B A55 3.10k plum ('70) 8.50 .35
444C A55 4k gray ('69) 1.40 .35
444D A55 4.10k olive ('70) 8.50 .35
   Nos. 437-444D (14) 38.90 5.00

Issued: Nos. 437-441, 6/30/67; Nos. 442-443, 7/8/67; No. 444, 4/29/68; Nos. 444A, 444C, 8/28/69; Nos. 444B, 444D, 8/27/70; Nos. 437A, 441A, 6/24/71.

For overprints see Nos. Q44-Q45.

Sonne — A113

1967, Sept. 21
445 A113 60ø red .30 .25

150th anniv. of the birth of Hans Christian Sonne, pioneer of the cooperative movement in Denmark.

Cross-anchor and Porpoise — A114

1967, Nov. 9   Engr.   Perf. 13
446 A114 90ø dk blue .35 .25

Centenary of the Danish Seamen's Church in Foreign Ports.

Esbjerg Harbor — A115

1968, Apr. 24
447 A115 30ø dk yellow grn .30 .25

Centenary of Esbjerg Harbor.

Koldinghus — A116

1968, June 13
448 A116 60ø copper red .65 .25

700th anniversary of Koldinghus Castle.

DENMARK

Shipbuilding Industry — A117

Designs: 50o, Chemical industry. 60o, Electric power. 90o, Engineering.

1968, Oct. 24   Engr.   Perf. 13
449 A117 30o green .25 .25
450 A117 50o brown .25 .25
451 A117 60o red brown .25 .25
452 A117 90o dark blue 1.00 1.00
     Nos. 449-452 (4) 1.75 1.75

Issued to publicize Danish industries.

Sower — A118

1969, Jan. 29
453 A118 30o gray green .30 .25

Royal Agricultural Soc. of Denmark, 200th anniv.

Five Ancient Ships — A119

Nordic Cooperation Issue
1969, Feb. 28   Engr.   Perf. 13
454 A119 60o brown red .80 .25
455 A119 90o blue 1.60 1.60

50th anniv. of the Nordic Soc. and cent. of postal cooperation among the northern countries. The design is taken from a coin found at the site of Birka, an ancient Swedish town. See also Finland No. 481, Iceland Nos. 404-405, Norway Nos. 523-524 and Sweden Nos. 808-810.

Frederik IX — A120

1969, Mar. 11
456 A120 50o sepia .30 .25
457 A120 60o dull red .30 .25

70th birthday of King Frederik IX.

Common Design Types pictured following the introduction.

Europa Issue, 1969
Common Design Type
1969, Apr. 28
     Size: 28x20mm
458 CD12 90o chalky blue .75 .75

Kronborg Castle — A121

1969, May 22   Engr.   Perf. 13
459 A121 50o brown .30 .25

Association of Danes living abroad, 50th anniv.

Danish Flag — A122

1969, June 12
460 A122 60o bluish blk, red & gray .30 .25

750th anniversary of the fall of the Dannebrog (Danish flag) from heaven.

Nexo — A123

1969, Aug. 28
461 A123 80o deep green .30 .25

Centenary of the birth of Martin Andersen Nexo (1869-1954), novelist.

Stensen — A124

1969, Sept. 25
462 A124 1k deep brown .35 .25

300th anniv. of the publication of Niels Stensen's geological work "On Solid Bodies."

Abstract Design — A125

1969, Nov. 10   Engr.   Perf. 13
463 A125 60o rose, red & ultra .30 .25

Symbolic Design — A126

1969, Nov. 20
464 A126 30o olive green .30 .25

Valdemar Poulsen (1869-1942), electrical engineer and inventor.

Post Office Bank — A127

1970, Jan. 15   Engr.   Perf. 13
465 A127 60o dk red & org .30 .25

50th anniv. of post office banking service.

School Safety Patrol — A128

1970, Feb. 19
466 A128 50o brown .30 .25

Issued to publicize road safety.

Candle in Window — A129

1970, May 4   Engr.   Perf. 13
467 A129 50o slate, dull bl & yel .30 .25

25th anniv. of liberation from the Germans.

Deer — A130

1970, May 28
468 A130 60o yel grn, red & brn .30 .25

Tercentenary of Jaegersborg Deer Park.

Elephant Figurehead, 1741 — A131

1970, June 15   Perf. 11½
469 A131 30o multicolored .30 .25

Royal Naval Museum, tercentenary.

"The Homecoming" by Povl Christensen — A132

1970, June 15   Perf. 13
470 A132 60o org, dl vio & ol grn .30 .25

Union of North Schleswig and Denmark, 50th anniv.

Electromagnet A133

1970, Aug. 13   Engr.
471 A133 80o gray green .30 .25

150th anniversary of Hans Christian Oersted's discovery of electromagnetism.

Bronze Age Ship — A134

Ships: 50o, Viking shipbuilding, from Bayeux tapestry. 60o, Thuroe schooner with topgallant. 90o, Tanker.

1970, Sept. 24
472 A134 30o ocher & brown .25 .25
473 A134 50o brn red & rose brn .25 .25
474 A134 60o gray ol & red brn .35 .25
475 A134 90o blue grn & ultra 1.25 1.25
     Nos. 472-475 (4) 2.10 2.00

UN Emblem — A135

1970, Oct. 22   Engr.   Perf. 13
476 A135 90o blue, grn & red 1.00 1.00

25th anniversary of the United Nations.

Bertel Thorvaldsen — A136

1970, Nov. 19
477 A136 2k slate blue .60 .50

Bicentenary of the birth of Bertel Thorvaldsen (1768-1844), sculptor.

Mathide Fibiger — A137

1971, Feb. 25
478 A137 80o olive green .30 .25

Danish Women's Association centenary.

Refugees — A138

1971, Mar. 26   Engr.   Perf. 13
479 A138 50o brown .25 .25
480 A138 60o brown red .35 .25

Joint northern campaign for the benefit of refugees.

Hans Egede — A139

1971, May 27
481 A139 1k brown .35 .25

250th anniversary of arrival of Hans Egede in Greenland and beginning of its colonization.

A140

1971, Oct. 14
482 A140 30o Swimming .25 .25
483 A140 50o Hurdlers .50 .25
484 A140 60o Soccer .75 .25
485 A140 90o Sailing .75 .75
     Nos. 482-485 (4) 2.25 1.50

A141

1971, Nov. 11   Engr.   Perf. 13
486 A141 90o dark blue .35 .35

Centenary of first lectures given by Georg Brandes (1842-1927), writer and literary critic.

A142

1972, Jan. 27
487 A142 80o slate green .35 .25

Centenary of Danish sugar production.

A143

1972, Mar. 11   Engr.   Perf. 13
488 A143 60o red brown .30 .25

Frederik IX (1899-1972).

Abstract Design — A144

1972, Mar. 11
489 A144 1.20k brt rose lil, bl gray & brn .65 .65

Danish Meteorological Institute, cent.

Nikolai F. S. Grundtvig — A145

1972, May 4   Engr.   Perf. 13
490 A145 1k sepia .50 .50

Nikolai Frederik Severin Grundtvig (1783-1872), theologian and poet.

DENMARK

Locomotive, 1847,
Ferry,
Travelers — A146

1972, June 26
491 A146 70o rose red   .30 .25
125th anniversary of Danish State Railways.

Rebild Hills — A147

1972, June 26
492 A147 1k bl, sl grn & mar   .35 .25

Types of 1933-46

1972-78		Engr.	Perf. 13
493	A32	20o slate bl ('74)	.35 .35
494	A32	20o sepia ('74)	.30 .30
a.		Bklt. pane of 12 (4 #318, 4 #493, 4 #494) ('85)	15.00
495	A32	60o apple grn ('76)	1.75 .90
496	A32	60o gray ('78)	.70 .70
497	A32	70o red	1.00 .35
498	A32	70o apple grn ('77)	1.10 .35
499	A55	2.50k orange	1.75 .35
500	A55	2.00k olive ('75)	1.25 .65
501	A55	3.50k lilac	2.00 .35
502	A55	4.50k olive	5.50 .35
503	A55	6k vio blk ('76)	2.00 .35
504	A55	7k red lilac ('78)	2.10 .35
505	A55	9k brown ol ('77)	3.00 .35

With Vertical and Horizontal Engraving Lines

506 A55 10k lemon ('76)   3.00 .35
Nos. 493-506 (14)   25.80 6.05
See footnote after No. 1313.

"Tinker Turned Politician" — A148

1972, Sept. 14
507 A148 70o dark red   .30 .25
250th anniv. of the comedies of Ludvig Holberg (1684-1754) on the Danish stage.

WHO Building, Copenhagen A149

1972, Sept. 14
508 A149 2k bl, blk & lt red brn   .60 .60
Opening of WHO Building, Copenhagen.

Bridge Across Little Belt — A150

Highway engineering (Diagrams): 60o, Hanstholm Harbor. 70o, Lim Fjord Tunnel. 90o, Knudshoved Harbor.

1972, Oct. 10   Engr.   Perf. 13
509 A150 40o dk green   .25 .25
510 A150 60o dk brown   .35 .25
511 A150 70o dk red   .35 .25
512 A150 90o dk blue grn   1.40 .50
Nos. 509-512 (4)   2.35 1.25

Aeroskobing House c. 1740 — A151

Danish Architecture: 60o, East Bornholm farmhouse, 17th century, horiz. 70o, House, Christianshavn, c. 1710. 1.20k, Hvide Sande Farmhouse, c. 1810, horiz.

1972, Nov. 23
Size: 20x28mm, 27x20mm
513 A151 40o red, brn & blk   .35 .25
514 A151 60o blk, vio bl & grn   .35 .25
Size: 18x37mm, 36x20mm
515 A151 70o red, dk red & blk   .45 .30
516 A151 1.20k dk brn, red & grn   1.40 1.00
Nos. 513-516 (4)   2.55 1.80

Jensen — A152

1973, Feb. 22   Engr.   Perf. 13
517 A152 90o green   .35 .25
Centenary of the birth of Johannes Vilhelm Jensen (1873-1950), lyric poet and novelist.

Guard Rails, Cogwheels — A153

1973, Mar. 22
518 A153 50o sepia   .55 .25
Centenary of first Danish Factory Act for labor protection.

Abildgaard — A154

1973, Mar. 22
519 A154 1k dull blue   .70 .35
Bicentenary of Royal Veterinary College, Christianshaven, founded by Prof. P. C. Abildgaard.

Rhododendron — A155

1973, Apr. 26
520 A155 60o brn, grn & vio   .50 .25
521 A155 70o dk red, rose & grn   .50 .25
Centenary of the founding of the Horticultural Society of Denmark.

Nordic Cooperation Issue

Nordic House, Reykjavik — A156

1973, June 26   Engr.   Perf. 13
522 A156 70o multicolored   .50 .25
523 A156 1k multicolored   1.50 1.25
A century of postal cooperation among Denmark, Finland, Iceland, Norway and Sweden, and in connection with the Nordic Postal Conference, Reykjavik.

Sextant, Stella Nova, Cassiopeia — A157

1973, Oct. 18   Engr.   Perf. 13
524 A157 2k dark blue   1.75 .30
400th anniversary of the publication of "De Nova Stella," by Tycho Brahe.

St. Mark, from 11th Cent. Book of Dalby — A158

1973, Oct. 18   Photo.   Perf. 14x14½
525 A158 120o buff & multi   1.10 .65
300th anniversary of Royal Library.

Devil and Gossips, Fanefjord Church, 1480 — A159

Frescoes: No. 527, Queen Esther and King Ahasuerus, Tirsted Church, c.1400. No. 528, Miraculous Harvest, Jetsmark Church, c.1474. No. 529, Jesus carrying cross, and wearing crown of thorns, Biersted Church, c.1400. No. 530, Creation of Eve, Fanefjord Church, c.1480.

1973, Nov. 28   Engr.   Perf. 13
Cream Paper
526 A159 70o dk red, yel & grn   1.40 .30
527 A159 70o dk red, yel & grn   1.40 .30
528 A159 70o dk red, yel & grn   1.40 .30
529 A159 70o dk red, yel & grn   1.40 .30
530 A159 70o dk red, yel & grn   1.40 .30
a. Bklt. pane, 2 each #526-530   35.00
b. Strip of 5, #526-530   6.75

Blood Donors — A160

1974, Jan. 24
531 A160 90o purple & red   1.10 .25
"Blood Saves Lives."

Queen Margrethe — A161

1974-81		Engr.	Perf. 13
532	A161	60o brown	1.00 .50
533	A161	60o orange	.60 .45
534	A161	70o red	1.00 .25
535	A161	70o dk brown	.80 .25
536	A161	80o green	.80 .25
537	A161	80o dp brn ('76)	1.10 .25
538	A161	90o red lilac	1.10 .25
539	A161	90o dull red	1.40 .30
540	A161	90o slate grn ('76)	1.10 .30
541	A161	100o dp ultra	1.10 .25
542	A161	100o gray ('75)	1.10 .25
543	A161	100o red ('76)	1.10 .25
a.		Ordinary paper	1.10
544	A161	100o brown ('77)	1.00 .25
a.		Bklt. pane of 5 (#544, #494, #493, #318), 2 #493, #318)	2.50
		Complete booklet, #544a	2.50
545	A161	110o orange ('78)	1.20 .25
546	A161	120o slate	1.00 .50
547	A161	120o red ('77)	1.40 .25
		Complete booklet, 4 each #318, 493, 544, 547	13.50
548	A161	130o ultra ('75)	1.60 1.40
549	A161	150o vio bl ('78)	1.40 .85
550	A161	100o slate grn ('77)	1.40 .40
551	A161	200o blue ('81)	1.40 1.00
		Nos. 532-551 (20)	22.60 8.55

See Nos. 630, 632-642. For overprint see No. Q10.

Pantomime Theater — A162

1974, May 16
552 A162 100o indigo   .40 .30
Cent. of the Pantomime Theater, Tivoli.

Hverringe — A163

Views: 60o, Norre Lyndelse, Carl Nielsen's childhood home. 70o, Odense, Hans Chr. Andersen's childhood home. 90o, Hesselagergaard, vert. 120o, Hindsholm.

1974, June 20   Engr.   Perf. 13
553 A163 50o brown & multi   .50 .50
554 A163 60o sl grn & multi   .65 .65
555 A163 70o red brn & multi   .50 .50
556 A163 90o dk green & mar   .55 .25
557 A163 120o red org & dk grn   .70 .50
Nos. 553-557 (5)   2.90 2.40

Emblem, Runner with Map — A164

1974, Aug. 22   Engr.   Perf. 13
558 A164 70o shown   .70 .70
559 A164 80o Compass   .25 .25
World Orienteering Championships 1974.

Iris — A165

1974, Sept. 19
560 A165 90o shown   .50 .25
561 A165 120o Purple orchid   .75 .75
Copenhagen Botanical Garden centenary.

Mailman, 1624, and Postilion, 1780 A166

Carrier Pigeon A167

Design: 90o, Balloon and sailing ships.

1974, Oct. 9   Engr.   Perf. 13
562 A166 70o lemon & dk brn   .40 .25
563 A166 90o dull grn & sepia   .40 .25
564 A167 120o dark blue   .65 .65
Nos. 562-564 (3)   1.45 1.15

350th anniv. of Danish PO (70o, 90o) and cent. of UPU (120o).

Souvenir Sheet

Ferslew's Essays, 1849 and 1852 A168

Engraved and Photogravure
1975, Feb. 27   Perf. 13
565 A168 Sheet of 4   7.50 8.50
a. 70o Coat of arms   1.75 2.00
b. 80o King Frederik VII   1.75 2.00
c. 90o King Frederik VII   1.75 2.00
d. 100o Mercury   1.75 2.00

HAFNIA 76 Intl. Stamp Exhib., Copenhagen, Aug. 20-29, 1976. Sold for 5k.
See No. 585.

Early Radio Equipment — A169

1975, Mar. 20   Engr.   Perf. 13
566 A169 90o dull red   .35 .30
Danish broadcasting, 50th anniversary.

137

DENMARK

Flora Danica Plate — A170

Danish China: 90o, Flora Danica tureen. 130o, Vase and tea caddy, blue fluted china.

1975, May 22
567	A170	50o slate grn	.30	.25
568	A170	90o brown red	.65	.65
569	A170	130o violet bl	1.10	1.10
		Nos. 567-569 (3)	2.05	2.00

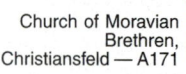
Church of Moravian Brethren, Christiansfeld — A171

120o, Kongsgaard farmhouse, Lejre. 150o, Anna Queenstraede, Helsingor, vert.

1975, June 19
570	A171	70o sepia	.65	.65
571	A171	120o olive green	.80	.80
572	A171	150o violet black	.65	.25
		Nos. 570-572 (3)	2.10	1.70

European Architectural Heritage Year 1975.

Andersen — A172

Designs: 70o, Numbskull Jack, drawing by Vilh. Pedersen. 130o, The Marshking's Daughter, drawing by L. Frohlich.

1975, Aug. 28 — Engr. — Perf. 13
573	A172	70o brown & blk	.60	.60
574	A172	90o brn red & dk brn	.75	.30
575	A172	130o blue blk & sepia	1.75	1.75
		Nos. 573-575 (3)	3.10	2.65

Hans Christian Andersen (1805-75), writer.

Watchman's Square, Abenra — A173

Designs: 90o, Haderslev Cathedral, vert. 100o, Mögeltönder Polder. 120o, Mouth of Vidaaen at Höjer Floodgates.

1975, Sept. 25
576	A173	70o multicolored	.45	.45
577	A173	90o multicolored	.40	.25
578	A173	100o multicolored	.50	.25
579	A173	120o multicolored	.55	.50
		Nos. 576-579 (4)	1.90	1.45

European Kingfisher — A174

1975, Oct. 23 — Engr. — Perf. 13
580	A174	50o shown	.45	.45
581	A174	70o Hedgehog	.45	.45
582	A174	90o Cats	.45	.45
583	A174	130o Avocets	1.25	1.25
584	A174	200o Otter	.65	.25
		Nos. 580-584 (5)	3.25	2.85

Protected animals, and for the centenary of the Danish Society for the Prevention of Cruelty to Animals (90ö).

HAFNIA Type of 1974
Souvenir Sheet

1975, Nov. 20 — Engr. & Photo.
585	A168	Sheet of 4	4.50	6.75
a.		50o buff & brown, No. 2	1.10	1.60
b.		70o buff, brown & blue, No. 1	1.10	1.60
c.		90o buff, blue & brown, No. 11	1.10	1.60
d.		130o olive, brown & buff, No. 19	1.30	1.60

HAFNIA 76 Intl. Stamp Exhib., Copenhagen, Aug. 20-29, 1976. Sold for 5k.

Copenhagen, Center A175 — View from Round Tower A176

Copenhagen, Views: 100o, Central Station, interior. 130o, Harbor.

1976, Mar. 25 — Engr. — Perf. 12½
586	A175	60o multicolored	.45	.45
587	A176	80o multicolored	.45	.45
588	A176	100o multicolored	.45	.25
589	A175	130o multicolored	1.50	1.50
		Nos. 586-589 (4)	2.85	2.65

Postilion, by Otto Bache — A177

1976, June 17 — Engr. — Perf. 12½
590	A177	130o multicolored	1.00	1.25

Souvenir Sheet
591	A177	130o multicolored	10.00	16.00

HAFNIA 76 Intl. Stamp Exhib., Copenhagen, Aug. 20-29. No. 591 contains one stamp similar to No. 590 with design continuous into sheet margin. Sheet shows painting "A String of Horses Outside an Inn" of which No. 590 shows a detail. Sheet sold for 15k including exhibition ticket.

Emil Chr. Hansen, Physiologist, in Laboratory — A178

1976, Sept. 23 — Engr. — Perf. 13
592	A178	100o orange red	.40	.30

Carlsberg Foundation (art and science), centenary.

Glass Blower Molding Glass — A179

Danish Glass Production: 80o, Finished glass removed from pipe. 130o, Glass cut off from foot. 150o, Glass blown up in mold.

1976, Nov. 18 — Engr. — Perf. 13
593	A179	60o slate	.50	.50
594	A179	80o dk brown	.50	.25
595	A179	130o dk blue	1.00	1.00
596	A179	150o red brown	.60	.25
		Nos. 593-596 (4)	2.60	2.00

Five Water Lilies — A180

Photogravure and Engraved

1977, Feb. 2 — Perf. 12½
597	A180	100o brt green & multi	.50	.35
598	A180	130o ultra & multi	2.00	2.00

Nordic countries cooperation for protection of the environment and 25th Session of Nordic Council, Helsinki, Feb. 19.

Road Accident — A181

1977, Mar. 24 — Engr. — Perf. 12½
599	A181	100o brown red	.40	.30

Road Safety Traffic Act, May 1, 1977.

Europa — A182

1977, May 2 — Engr. — Perf. 12½
600	A182	1k Allinge	.60	.30
601	A182	1.30k View, Ringsted	3.00	3.00

Kongeaen — A183

Landscapes, Southern Jutland: 90o, Skallingen. 150o, Torskind. 200o, Jelling.

1977, June 30 — Engr. — Perf. 12½
602	A183	60o multicolored	1.25	1.25
603	A183	90o multicolored	.65	.65
604	A183	150o multicolored	.60	.50
605	A183	200o multicolored	.75	.50
		Nos. 602-605 (4)	3.25	2.90

See Nos. 616-619, 655-658, 666-669.

Hammers and Horseshoes — A184

Designs: 1k, Chisel, square and plane. 1.30k, Trowel, ceiling brush and folding ruler.

1977, Sept. 22 — Engr. — Perf. 12½
606	A184	80o dk brown	.30	.25
607	A184	1k red	.40	.25
608	A184	1.30k violet bl	.75	.60
		Nos. 606-608 (3)	1.45	1.10

Danish crafts.

Globe Flower — A185

Endangered Flora: 1.50k, Cnidium dubium.

1977, Nov. 17 — Engr. — Perf. 12½
609	A185	1k multicolored	.40	.25
610	A185	1.50k multicolored	1.25	1.25

Handball — A186

1978, Jan. 19 — Perf. 12½
611	A186	1.20k red	.40	.30

Men's World Handball Championships.

Christian IV, Frederiksborg Castle A187

Frederiksborg Museum A188

1978, Mar. 16
612	A187	1.20k brown red	.50	.50
613	A188	1.80k black	.60	.30

Frederiksborg Museum, centenary.

Europa Issue

Jens Bang's House, Aalborg A189

Frederiksborg Castle, Ground Plan and Elevation A190

1978, May 11 — Engr. — Perf. 12½
614	A189	1.20k red	.30	.25
615	A190	1.50k dk bl & vio bl	1.25	1.25

Landscape Type of 1977

Landscapes, Central Jutland: 70o, Kongenshus Memorial Park. 120o, Post Office, Old Town in Aarhus. 150o, Lignite fields, Soby. 180o, Church wall, Stadil Church.

1978, June 15 — Engr. — Perf. 12½
616	A183	70o multicolored	.50	.50
617	A183	120o multicolored	.55	.25
		Complete booklet, 10 #617	9.00	
618	A183	150o multicolored	.80	.80
619	A183	180o multicolored	.60	.60
		Nos. 616-619 (4)	2.45	2.15

Boats in Harbor — A191

Danish fishing industry: 1k, Eel traps. 1.80k, Boats in berth. 2.50k, Drying nets.

1978, Sept. 7 — Engr. — Perf. 12½
620	A191	70o olive gray	.50	.50
621	A191	1k redsh brown	.50	.25
622	A191	1.80k slate	.60	.50
623	A191	2.50k sepia	.85	.60
		Nos. 620-623 (4)	2.45	1.85

Edible Morel — A192

Design: 1.20k, Satan's mushroom.

1978, Nov. 16 — Engr. — Perf. 12½
624	A192	1k sepia	.65	.55
625	A192	1.20k dull red	.65	.55

Telephones — A193

1979, Jan. 25 — Engr. — Perf. 12½
626	A193	1.20k dull red	.40	.30

Centenary of Danish telephone.

University Seal A194 — Pentagram: University Faculties A195

1979, Apr. 5 — Engr. — Perf. 12½
627	A194	1.30k vermilion	.40	.25
628	A195	1.60k dk vio blue	.55	.55

University of Copenhagen, 500th anniv.

Types of 1933-1974

1979-82 — Engr. — Perf. 13
629	A32	80o green	.35	.40
630	A161	90o slate	3.00	3.25
631	A32	100o dp green ('81)	.50	.40

DENMARK

632	A161	110o brown	.65	.40
a.	Bklt. pane, #493-494, 632, 2 #318 ('79)		1.50	
	complete booklet, #632a		1.50	
633	A161	130o red	.65	.40
a.	Bklt. pane, 2 ea #494, 629, 632, 4 #633 ('79)		7.50	
	Complete booklet, #633a		8.00	
634	A161	130o brown ('81)	.65	.60
635	A161	140o red org ('80)	2.00	2.50
636	A161	150o red org ('81)	.65	.80
637	A161	160o ultra	1.25	1.25
638	A161	160o red ('81)	.65	.40
a.	Bklt. pane, 2 ea #318, 634, 638, 8 #494)		12.00	
	Complete booklet, #638a		12.00	
639	A161	180o ultra ('80)	1.40	1.40
640	A161	210o gray ('80)	2.00	2.50
641	A161	230o ol grn ('81)	1.00	.65
642	A161	250o blue grn ('81)	1.40	1.00
643	A55	2.80k dull grn	1.40	1.10
644	A55	3.30k brn red ('81)	1.40	.80
645	A55	3.50k grnsh bl ('82)	2.50	3.00
646	A55	4.30k brn red ('80)	4.00	5.25
647	A55	4.70k rose lil ('81)	3.50	5.25
648	A55	8k orange	2.75	.40
649	A55	12k red brn ('81)	5.00	.65
650	A55	14k dk red brn ('82)	5.75	.80
	Nos. 629-650 (22)		42.45	33.20

A196

Europa: 1.30k, Mail cart, 1785. 1.60k, Morse key and amplifier.

1979, May 10   *Perf. 12½*
651	A196	1.30k red	1.00	.25
652	A196	1.60k dark blue	3.00	1.10

A197

Viking Art: 1.10k, Gripping beast pendant. 2k, Key with gripping beast design.

1979, June 14   *Engr.*   *Perf. 13*
| 653 | A197 | 1.10k sepia | .40 | .40 |
| 654 | A197 | 2k grnsh gray | .50 | .40 |

Landscape Type of 1977

Landscapes, Northern Jutland: 80o, Mols Bjerge. 90o, Orslev Kloster. 200o, Trans. 280o, Bovbjerg.

1979, Sept. 6   *Engr.*   *Perf. 12½*
655	A183	80o multicolored	.50	.50
656	A183	90o multicolored	1.60	1.60
657	A183	200o multicolored	.90	.35
658	A183	280o multicolored	1.10	1.10
	Nos. 655-658 (4)		4.10	3.55

Adam Oehlenschläger (1779-1850), Poet and Dramatist — A198

1979, Oct. 4   *Engr.*   *Perf. 13*
| 659 | A198 | 1.30k dk carmine | .40 | .30 |

Sooro, Violin, Dancing Couple A199

Ballerina A200

1979, Nov. 8   *Engr.*   *Perf. 13x12½*
| 660 | A199 | 1.10k brown | .40 | .30 |
| 661 | A200 | 1.60k ultra | .60 | .65 |

Jacob Gade (1879-63), composer; August Bournonville (1805-79), ballet master.

Royal Mail Guards' Office, Copenhagen, 1779 — A201

1980, Feb. 14   *Engr.*   *Perf. 13*
| 662 | A201 | 1.30k brown red | .50 | .35 |

National Postal Service, 200th anniversary.

Symbols of Occupation, Health and Education — A202

1980, May 5   *Engr.*   *Perf. 13*
| 663 | A202 | 1.60k dark blue | .65 | .50 |

World Conference of the UN Decade for Women, Copenhagen, July 14-30.

Karen Blixen (1885-1962), Writer (Pen Name Isak Dinesen) — A203

Europa: 1.60k, August Krogh (1874-1949), physiologist.

1980, May 5
| 664 | A203 | 1.30k red | .65 | .25 |
| 665 | A203 | 1.60k blue | 1.40 | 1.40 |

Landscape Type of 1977

Northern Jutland: 80o, Viking ship burial grounds, Lindholm Hoje. 110o, Lighthouse, Skagen, vert. 200o, Boreglum Monastery. 280o, Fishing boats, Vorupor Beach.

1980, June 19   *Engr.*   *Perf. 13*
666	A183	80o multicolored	.50	.50
667	A183	110o multicolored	.50	.50
668	A183	200o multicolored	.70	.50
669	A183	280o multicolored	2.00	2.00
	Nos. 666-669 (4)		3.70	3.30

Nordic Cooperation Issue

Silver Tankard, by Borchardt Rollufse, 1641 — A204

1.80K, Bishop's bowl, Copenhagen faience, 18th cent.

1980, Sept. 9   *Engr.*   *Perf. 13*
| 670 | A204 | 1.30k shown | .50 | .35 |
| 671 | A204 | 1.80k multicolored | 1.40 | 1.40 |

Frisian Sceat Facsimile, Obverse and Reverse, 9th Century — A205

Coins: 1.40k Silver coin of Valdemar the Great and Absalom, 1157-1182. 1.80k, Gold 12-mark coin of Christian VII, 1781.

1980, Oct. 9   *Engr.*   *Perf. 13*
672	A205	1.30k red & redsh brn	.50	.45
673	A205	1.40k ol gray & sl grn	1.60	1.40
674	A205	1.80k dk bl & sl bl	1.25	1.25
	Nos. 672-674 (3)		3.35	3.10

Tonder Lace Pattern, North Schleswig — A206

Designs: Tonder lace patterns.

1980, Nov. 13   *Engr.*   *Perf. 13*
675	A206	1.10k brown	.65	.65
676	A206	1.30k brown red	.50	.30
677	A206	2k olive gray	.70	.60
	Nos. 675-677 (3)		1.85	1.25

Nyboder Development, Copenhagen, 350th Anniversary — A207

Design: 1.30k, View of Nyboder, diff.

1981, Mar. 19
| 678 | A207 | 1.30k dp org & ocher | .90 | .90 |
| 679 | A207 | 1.60k dp org & ocher | .55 | .55 |

Tilting at a Barrel on Shrovetide — A208

Design: 2k, Midsummer's Eve bonfire.

1981, May 4   *Engr.*   *Perf. 13*
680	A208	1.60k brown red	.40	.25
	Complete booklet, 10 #680		4.00	
681	A208	2k dk blue	1.25	.75

Soro Lake and Academy, Zealand — A209

Designs: Views of Zealand: 150o, Poet N.F.S. Grundtvig's home, Udby. 160o, Kaj Munk's home, Opager. 200o, Gronsund. 230o, Bornholm Island.

1981, June 18   *Engr.*   *Perf. 13*
682	A209	100o shown	.50	.50
683	A209	150o multicolored	.65	.65
684	A209	160o multicolored	.65	.30
685	A209	200o multicolored	.80	.80
686	A209	230o multicolored	1.10	.85
	Nos. 682-686 (5)		3.70	3.10

European Urban Renaissance Year — A210

1981, Sept. 10   *Engr.*   *Perf. 12½x13*
| 687 | A210 | 1.60k dull red | .65 | .35 |

Type of 1933

1981-85   *Engr.*   *Perf. 13*
688	A32	30o orange	.60	.40
a.	Bklt. pane 10 (2 #318, 2 #688, 6 #494)('84)		30.00	
	Complete booklet, #688a, 6 #708		30.00	
689	A32	40o purple	.60	.40
a.	Bklt. pane of 10 (4 #318, 2 #689, 4 #494) ('89)		4.50	
690	A32	80o ol bis ('85)	1.00	.80
691	A32	100o blue ('83)	.85	.40
b.	Bklt. pane of 8 (2 #494, 4 #691, 2 #706) ('80)		£1.00	
	Complete booklet, #691b		21.00	
692	A32	150o dk green ('82)	.85	.40
693	A32	200o green ('83)	1.00	.90
694	A32	230o brt yel grn ('84)	1.50	.60
695	A32	250o brt yel grn ('85)	1.50	.60
	Nos. 688-695 (8)		7.80	4.50

Ellehammer's 18-horsepower Biplane, 1906 — A211

1.30k, R-1 Fokker CV reconnaissance plane, 1926. 1.60k, Bellanca J-300, 1931. 2.30k, DC-7C, 1957.

1981, Oct. 8   *Engr.*   *Perf. 13*
696	A211	1k black & bluish green	.65	.65
697	A211	1.30k brown & lt brown	1.10	1.10
698	A211	1.60k red & orange	.65	.60
699	A211	2.30k dark blue & pale blue	.90	.70
	Nos. 696-699 (4)		3.30	2.75

Arms Type of 1946 and

Queen Margrethe II, 10th Anniv. of Accession — A212

1982-85   *Engr.*   *Perf. 13*
700	A212	1.00k dull red	.65	.40
701	A212	1.60k dk ol grn	2.50	3.00
702	A212	1.80k sepia	.85	.70
703	A212	2k dull red	.90	.30
b.	Bklt. pane, 4 #494, 2 ea #493, 702, 703		20.00	
704	A212	2.20k ol grn ('83)	1.50	2.75
705	A212	2.30k violet	1.00	1.20
706	A212	2.50k org red ('83)	.85	.30
707	A212	2.70k dk blue	1.20	.80
708	A212	2.70k cop red ('84)	1.25	.40
c.	Booklet pane, 3 #688, 2 #494, 3 #708 ('84)		13.00	
709	A212	2.80k cop red ('85)	1.00	.50
	Complete booklet, #494a, 6 #709		13.50	
b.	Booklet pane, 3 #493, 2 #494, 3 #709 ('85)		6.75	
	Complete booklet, #709b		7.00	
710	A212	3k violet ('83)	1.20	.50
711	A212	3.30k bluish blk ('84)	1.75	1.00
712	A212	3.50k blue ('83)	1.50	.65
713	A212	3.50k dk vio ('85)	1.50	.80
714	A212	3.70k dp blue ('84)	1.75	.80
715	A212	3.80k dk blue ('85)	1.40	.60
716	A55	4.30k dk ol grn ('84)	4.50	4.75
717	A55	5.50k dk bl grn ('84)	2.75	1.25
718	A55	16k cop red ('83)	6.00	.90
719	A55	17k cop red ('84)	7.75	1.25
720	A55	18k brn vio ('84)	8.50	1.75
720A	A55	50k dk red ('85)	17.00	3.25
	Nos. 700-720A (22)		67.30	27.35

See Nos. 796-803, 887, 889, 896, 899.

World Figure Skating Championships A213

1982, Feb. 25
| 721 | A213 | 2k dark blue | .80 | .50 |

Revenue Schooner Argus — A214

1982, Feb. 25   *Engr.*   *Perf. 12½*
| 722 | A214 | 1.60k carmine red | .65 | .35 |

Customs Service centenary.

Europa — A215

2k, Abolition of adscription, 1788. 2.70k, Women's voting right, 1915.

1982, May 3   *Engr.*   *Perf. 12½*
723	A215	2k brown lake	.75	.25
	Complete booklet, 10 #723		7.50	
724	A215	2.70k deep blue	1.75	1.00

Butter Churn, Barn, Hjedding — A216

1982, June 10   *Engr.*   *Perf. 13*
| 725 | A216 | 1.80k brown | .80 | .65 |

Cooperative dairy farming centenary.

Records Office, 400th Anniv. — A217

1982, June 10
| 726 | A217 | 2.70k green | 1.20 | .50 |

Steen Steensen Blicher (1782-1848), Poet, by J.V. Gertner — A218

1982, Aug. 26   *Engr.*   *Perf. 13*
| 727 | A218 | 2k brown red | .35 | .30 |

Robert Storm Petersen (1882-1949), Cartoonist — A219

Characters: 1.50k, Three little men and the number man. 2k, Peter and Ping, the penguin, horiz.

1982, Sept. 23   *Engr.*   *Perf. 12½*
| 728 | A219 | 1.50k dk bl & red | .70 | .50 |
| 729 | A219 | 2k red & ol grn | 1.10 | .40 |

Printing in Denmark, 500th Anniv. — A220

DENMARK

1982, Sept. 23
730 A220 1.80k Press, text, ink balls .80 .85

A221

1982, Nov. 4
731 A221 2.70k Library seal 1.20 .50
500th anniv. of University Library.

World Communications Year — A222

1983, Jan. 27 Engr. Perf. 13
732 A222 2k multicolored .80 .35

Amusement Park, 400th Anniv. — A223

1983, Feb. 24
733 A223 2k multicolored .80 .35

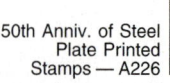
Badminton Championship — A224

1983, Feb. 24
734 A224 2.70k multicolored 1.20 .50

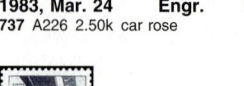
Nordic Cooperation Issue — A225

1983, Mar. 24
735 A225 2.50k Egeskov Castle .90 .40
736 A225 3.50k Troll Church, North Jutland 1.40 .75

50th Anniv. of Steel Plate Printed Stamps — A226

1983, Mar. 24 Engr. Perf. 13
737 A226 2.50k car rose 1.00 .35

Europa 1983 — A227

2.50k, Kildekovshallen Recreation Center, Copenhagen. 3.50k, Salling Sound Bridge.

1983, May 5 Engr. Perf. 13
738 A227 2.50k multicolored 1.10 .25
739 A227 3.50k multicolored 2.00 1.00

Weights and Measures Ordinance, 300th Anniv. — A228

1983, June 16
740 A228 2.50k red 1.00 .35

Christian V Danish Law, 300th Anniv. — A229

1983, Sept. 8 Engr.
741 A229 5k Codex titlepage 2.00 1.00

A230

1k, Car crash, police. 2.50k, Fire, ambulance service. 3.50k, Sea rescue.

1983, Oct. 6 Engr. Perf. 13
742 A230 1k brown .50 .50
743 A230 2.50k red 1.00 .35
744 A230 3.50k blue 1.25 .85
Nos. 742-744 (3) 2.75 1.70
Life saving and salvage services.

Elderly in Society — A231

1983, Oct. 6
745 A231 2k Stages of life .80 .80
746 A231 2.50k Train passengers 1.00 .30

N.F.S. Grundtvig (1783-1872), Poet A232

Street Scene, by C.W. Eckersberg (1783-1853) A233

1983, Nov. 3 Engr.
747 A232 2.50k brown red 1.20 .50
748 A233 2.50k brown red 1.00 .35

Tree Planting Campaign — A234

1984, Jan. 26 Litho. & Engr.
749 A234 2.70k Shovel, sapling 1.20 .35

A235

1984, Jan. 26 Engr.
750 A235 3.70k Game 1.75 .50
1984 Billiards World Championships, Copenhagen, May 10-13.

Hydrographic Dept. Bicentenary A236

Pilotage Service, 300th Anniv. A237

1984, Mar. 22 Engr. Perf. 13
751 A236 2.30k Compass 1.25 .90
752 A237 2.70k Boat 1.25 .50

2nd European Parliament Elections A238

Scouts Around Campfire, Emblems A239

1984, Apr. 12 Litho. & Engr. Perf. 13
753 A238 2.70k org & dk bl 1.75 .35
754 A239 2.70k multi 1.20 .35

Europa (1959-84) — A240

1984, May 3 Engr. Perf. 12½
755 A240 2.70k red 1.75 .25
756 A240 3.70k blue 2.25 1.60

Prince Henrik, 50th Birthday A241

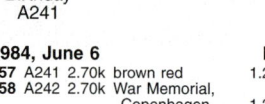
D Day, 40th Anniv. A242

1984, June 6 Engr.
757 A241 2.70k brown red 1.20 .35
758 A242 2.70k War Memorial, Copenhagen 1.20 .35
See Greenland No. 160.

17th Cent. Inn — A243

1984, June 6
759 A243 3k multicolored 1.50 1.40

Fishing and Shipping — A244

1984, Sept. 6 Engr.
760 A244 2.30k Research (Herring) 1.60 1.75
761 A244 2.70k Sea transport 1.10 .60
762 A244 3.30k Deep-sea fishing 1.60 1.75
763 A244 3.70k Deep-sea, diff. 1.60 1.75
Nos. 760-763 (4) 5.90 5.85

A245

1984, Oct. 5 Litho. & Engr.
764 A245 1k Post bird .35 .35

A246

Holberg Meets with an Officer, by Wilhelm Marstrand (1810-73).

1984, Oct. 5
765 A246 2.70k multicolored 1.20 .35
Ludvig Holberg (1684-1754), writer.

Jewish Community in Copenhagen, 300th Anniv. — A247

3.70k, Woman blessing Sabbath candles.

1984, Oct. 5
766 A247 3.70k multicolored 1.75 1.40

Carnival in Rome, by Christoffer W. Eckersberg (1783-1853) A248

Paintings: 10k, Ymer and Odhumble (Nordic mythology figures), by Nicolai A. Abildgaard (1743-1809), vert.

Perf. 12½x13, 13x12½
1984, Nov. 22 Litho. & Engr.
767 A248 5k multicolored 3.25 3.25
768 A248 10k multicolored 5.75 5.75

German and French Reform Church, 300th Anniv. — A249

1985, Jan. 24 Engr. Perf. 13
769 A249 2.80k magenta 1.75 .35

Bonn-Copenhagen Declaration, 30th Anniv. — A250

1985, Feb. 21 Litho. Perf. 14
770 A250 2.80k Map, flags 1.90 .65

Intl. Youth Year — A251

1985, Mar. 14 Perf. 13
771 A251 3.80k multicolored 1.75 .90

Souvenir Sheet

HAFNIA '87 Philatelic Exhibition — A252

Early Postal Ordinances — 1k, Christian IV's Ordinance on Postmen, 1624. 2.50k, Plague Mandate, 1711. 2.80k, Ordinance on Prohibition of Mail by Means other than the Post, 1775. 3.80k, Act on Postal Articles, 1831.

1985, Mar. 14 Litho. & Engr.
772 Sheet of 4 5.50 6.50
 a. A252 1k multi 1.25 1.60
 b. A252 2.50k multi 1.25 1.60
 c. A252 2.80k multi 1.25 1.60
 d. A252 3.80k multi 1.25 1.60
Sold for 15k.

DENMARK

Europa 1985 — A253

1985, May 2
773 A253 2.80k Musical staff 1.50 .50
774 A253 3.80k Musical staff, diff. 1.90 1.25

Arrival of Queen Ingrid in Denmark, 50th Anniv. — A254

2.80k, Queen Mother, chrysanthemums.

1985, May 21
775 A254 2.80k multicolored 1.20 .35

See Greenland No. 163.

Opening of the Faro Bridges — A255

1985, May 21   Litho.   Perf. 13
776 A255 2.80k Faro-Falster Bridge 1.20 .35

St. Cnut's Land Grant to Lund Cathedral, 900th Anniv. — A256

Seal of King Cnut and: 2.80k, Lund Cathedral. 3k, City of Helsingborg, Sweden.

1985, May 21   Engr.
777 A256 2.80k multi 1.10 .45
778 A256 3k multi 2.00 2.00

See Sweden Nos. 1538-1539.

UN Decade for Women — A257

1985, June 27   Litho. & Engr.
779 A257 3.80k Cyclist 1.75 1.00

Sports — A258

1985, June 27
780 A258 2.80k Women's floor exercise 1.25 .30
781 A258 3.80k Canoe & kayak 1.75 .95
782 A258 6k Cycling 2.90 1.75
   Nos. 780-782 (3) 5.90 3.00

Kronborg Castle, Elsinore, 400th Anniv. — A259

1985, Sept. 5
783 A259 2.80k multi 1.75 .35

UN 40th Anniv. — A260

1985, Sept. 5
784 A260 3.80k Dove, emblem 1.75 1.20

Niels Bohr (1885-1962), Physicist A261

1985, Oct. 3   Perf. 13x12½
785 A261 2.80k With wife Margrethe 1.75 1.40

Winner of 1922 Nobel Prize in Physics for theory of atomic structure.

Hand Signing "D" — A262

1985, Nov. 7   Engr.   Perf. 13
786 A262 2.80k multicolored 1.40 .35

Danish Assoc. for the Deaf, 50th anniv.

Boat, by Helge Refn — A263

1985, Nov. 7   Litho.
787 A263 2.80k multicolored 1.40 .35

Abstract Iron Sculpture by Robert Jacobsen A264

Lithographed and Engraved
1985, Nov. 7   Perf. 13x12½
788 A264 3.80k multicolored 3.50 3.75

Painting by Bjørn Wiinblad A265

1986, Jan. 23   Litho.   Perf. 13x12½
789 A265 2.80k multicolored 1.75 1.40

Amnesty Intl., 25th Anniv. — A266

Lithographed and Engraved
1986, Jan. 23   Perf. 13
790 A266 2.80k multicolored 1.20 .35

Miniature Sheet

HAFNIA '87 — A267

1986, Feb. 20
791 A267 Sheet of 4 7.50 11.00
 a. 100ø Holstein carriage, c. 1840 1.75 2.50
 b. 250ø Iceboat, c. 1880 1.75 2.50
 c. 280ø 1st mail van, 1908 1.75 2.50
 d. 380ø Airmail service 1919 1.75 2.50

Sold for 15k.

Changing of the Guard — A268

1986, Mar. 20   Perf. 13
792 A268 2.80k multicolored 1.20 .35

Royal Danish Life Guards barracks and Rosenborg Drilling Ground, bicent.

Types of 1933-85

1986-90   Engr.   Perf. 13
793 A32 5ø brn org ('89) .35 .40
794 A32 270ø brt yel grn 1.90 1.75
 b. Bklt. pane, 6 #318, 2 #691, 2 #794 18.00
795 A32 300ø brt yel grn 1.75 .40
   Complete booklet, #794b, 4 #795 22.50
796 A212 3k cop red 1.20 .60
   Complete booklet, #691, #794, 2 #318, 2 #796 6.00
797 A212 3.20k deep vio 1.00 .80
798 A212 3.20k carmine 1.25 .40
 c. Bklt. pane, 2 #693, 4 #798 9.00
   Complete booklet, #689a, #798c 15.00
   Complete booklet, #693, 2 #798, 2 #318, #689, 2 #494 15.50
799 A212 3.40k dk grn 2.25 3.00
800 A212 3.80k dark vio 1.20 2.90
801 A212 4.10k dark blue 1.40 .60
802 A212 4.20k dk pur 3.50 3.00
803 A212 4.40k dp bl 2.50 .60
804 A55 4.60k gray 5.00 5.50
805 A55 6.50k dp grn 2.50 1.00
806 A55 6.60k green 5.00 5.50
807 A55 7.10k brn vio 3.50 3.50
808 A55 7.30k green 4.75 5.50
809 A55 7.70k dk brn vio 4.50 2.10
810 A55 11k brown 5.50 5.25
811 A55 20k dp ultra 6.75 .80
812 A55 22k henna brn 7.25 2.25
813 A55 23k dark olive grn 10.50 2.25
814 A55 24k dark olive grn 10.50 2.00
815 A55 26k dark olive grn 12.50 2.25
   Nos. 793-815 (23) 96.55 52.35

Issued: 6.50k, 20k, 1/9/86; 22k, 1/3/87; 270ø, 3k, No. 797, 3.80k, 4.10k, 4.60k, 6.60k, 7.10k, 24k, 1/7/88; No. 794b, 1/28/88; 300ø, No. 798, 3.40k, 4.20k, 4.40k, 7.30k, 7.70k, 11k, 26k, 1/26/89; 5ø, 1989; 23k, 1/11/90.

No. 793 issued for use in lieu of currency of the same face value.

Sorø Academy, 400th Anniv. — A269

1986, Apr. 28   Litho. & Engr.
816 A269 2.80k multi 1.40 .50

Intl. Peace Year — A270

1986, Apr. 28
817 A270 3.80k multi 1.60 1.10

A271

1986, May 26   Litho.
818 A271 2.80k multi 1.75 .50

Crown Prince Frederik, 18th birthday.

Nordic Cooperation Issue 1986 — A272

Sister towns.

1986, May 27   Engr.
819 A272 2.80k Aalborg Harbor 1.40 .35
820 A272 3.80k Thisted Church and Town Hall 1.60 1.25

Høje Tåstrup Train Station Opening, May 31 — A273

1986, May 27   Litho.
821 A273 2.80k multi 1.20 .35

Mailbox, Telegraph Lines, Telephone — A274

1986, June 19   Litho.   Perf. 13
822 A274 2.80k multi 1.00 .35

19th European Intl. PTT Congress, Copenhagen, Aug. 12-16.

Natl. Bird Candidates — A275

Finalists: a, Corvus corax. b, Sturnus vulgaris. c, Cygnus olor (winner). d, Vanellus vanellus. e, Alauda arvensis.

1986, June 19   Litho. & Engr.
823   Strip of 5 10.50 24.00
 a.-e. A275 2.80k any single 2.00 1.00
   Complete booklet, 2 #823 21.00

A276

1986, June 19
824 A276 2.80k multi 1.20 .35

Danish Rifle, Gymnastics and Sports Club, 125th anniv.

Souvenir Sheet

HAFNIA '87 — A277

DENEMARK

1986, Sept. 4
825	Sheet of 4		10.00	12.50
a.	A277 100o Mailcoach, c. 1841		2.25	3.00
b.	A277 250o Postmaster, c. 1840		2.25	3.00
c.	A277 280o Postman, c. 1851		2.25	3.00
d.	A277 380o Rural postman, c. 1893		2.25	3.00

Sold for 15k.

Europa 1986 — A278

1986, Sept. 4   *Engr.*
826 A278 2.80k Street sweeper   2.50   .25
827 A278 3.80k Garbage truck   3.50   1.50

Cupid — A279

1986, Oct. 9   *Litho.*
828 A279 3.80k multi   1.50   1.00

Premiere of The Whims of Cupid and the Ballet Master, by Vincenzo Galeotti, bicent.

Refugee — A280

1986, Oct. 9   *Litho. & Engr.*
829 A280 2.80k multi   1.20   .35

Danish Refugee Council Relief Campaign.

A281

Protestant Reformation in Denmark, 450th Anniv.: Sermon, altarpiece detail, 1561, Thorslunde Church, Copenhagen.

1986, Oct. 9   *Litho.*   *Perf. 13*
830 A281 6.50k multi   2.50   1.75

A282

1986, Nov. 6   *Litho. & Engr.*
831 A282 3.80k multi   3.00   3.00

Organization for Economic Cooperation and Development, 25th anniv.

Abstract by Lin Utzon — A283

1987, Jan. 22   *Litho.*   *Perf. 13*
832 A283 2.80k multi   1.00   .35
    Complete booklet, 10 #832   11.00

Art appreciation.

A284

1987, Feb. 26   *Engr.*   *Perf. 13*
833 A284 2.80k lake & black   1.00   .35

Danish Consumer Council, 40th anniv.

A285

Religious art (details) from Ribe Cathedral.

1987, Apr. 9   *Litho.*   *Perf. 13*
834 A285 3k Fresco   1.40   .60
835 A285 3.80k Stained-glass window   2.10   2.10
    Complete booklet, 10 #835   21.00
836 A285 6.50k Mosaic   3.50   3.50
    Nos. 834-836 (3)   7.00   6.20

Ribe Cathedral redecoration, 1982-1987, by Carl-Henning Pedersen.

A286

Europa (Modern architecture): 2.80k, Central Library, Gentofte, 1985. 3.80k, Hoje Tastrup High School, 1985, horiz.

1987, May 4   *Engr.*   *Perf. 13*
837 A286 2.80k rose claret   2.50   .35
838 A286 3.80k bright ultra   3.50   2.25

A287

1987, May 4   *Engr.*
839 A287 2.50k dk red & bl blk   2.00   2.00

Danish Academy of Technical Sciences (ATV), 50th anniv.

8th Gymnaestrada, Herning, July 7-11 — A288

1987, June 18   *Litho. & Engr.*
840 A288 2.80k multi   1.00   .35
    Complete booklet, 10 #840   10.00

A289

1987, June 18
841 A289 3.80k multi   1.60   1.40

Danish Cooperative Bacon Factories, cent.

A290

1987, Aug. 27   *Litho.*
842 A290 3.80k Single-sculler   1.60   1.20

World Rowing Championships, Aug. 23-30.

HAFNIA '87, Bella Center, Copenhagen, Oct. 16-25 — A291

No. 843, Type A15, mail train c. 1912.

Litho. & Engr.
1987, Aug. 27   *Perf. 13x12½*
843 A291 280o multi   1.90   1.50

Souvenir Sheet
843A A291 280o like No. 843   20.00   26.00

Purchase of No. 843A included admission to the exhibition. Sold for 45k.
Due to a color shift, some examples of No. 843A have a green lawn and locomotive.

Abstact by Ejler Bille — A292

1987, Sept. 24   *Litho.*   *Perf. 13*
844 A292 2.80k multi   1.00   .35
    Complete booklet, 10 #844   10.00

Rasmus Rask (1787-1832), Linguist — A293

1987, Oct. 15   *Engr.*   *Perf. 13x12½*
845 A293 2.80k dk hen brn   1.00   .45

A294

Emblem: Miraculous Catch (Luke 5:4-7), New Testament.

1987, Oct. 15   *Perf. 13*
846 A294 3k carmine lake   1.25   .50

Clerical Assoc. for the Home Mission in Denmark, 125th anniv.

A295

Designs: 3k, Two lions from the gate of Rosenburg Castle around the monogram of Christian IV. 4.10k, Portrait of the monarch painted by P. Isaacsz., vert.

Photo. & Engr., Litho. (4.10k)
1988, Feb. 18   *Perf. 13*
847 A295 3k blue gray & gold   1.25   .30
    Complete booklet, 10 #847   12.50
848 A295 4.10k multi   1.60   .75

Accession of Christian IV (1577-1648), King of Denmark and Norway (1588-1648), 400th anniv.

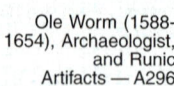
Ole Worm (1588-1654), Archaeologist, and Runic Artifacts — A296

1988, Feb. 18   *Engr.*
849 A296 7.10k chocolate   2.75   2.75

Odense, 1000th Anniv. — A297

Design: St. Cnut's Church and statue of Hans Christian Andersen, Odense.

1988, Mar. 10   *Engr.*
850 A297 3k multi   1.00   .35
    Complete booklet, 10 #850   10.00

A298

1988, Apr. 7   *Litho.*
851 A298 2.70k multi   1.25   1.25

Danish Civil Defense and Emergency Planning Agency, 50th Anniv.

WHO, 40th Anniv. — A299

1988, Apr. 7   *Litho. & Engr.*
852 A299 4.10k multi   1.75   1.00

Abolition of *Stavnsbaand*, 200th Anniv. — A300

Painting: King Christian VII riding past the Liberty Memorial, Copenhagen, by C.W. Eckersberg (1783-1853).

1988, May 5   *Litho.*
853 A300 3.20k multi   1.40   1.00

Stavnsbaand (adscription) provided that all Danish farmers' sons from age 4 to 40 would be bound as villeins to the estates on which they were born, thus providing landowners with free labor.

A301

Europa: Transport and communication — 3k, Postwoman on bicycle. 4.10k, Mobile telephone.

1988, May 5
854 A301 3k multicolored   1.75   .25
855 A301 4.10k multicolored   2.50   1.00

A302

1988, June 16   *Litho.*
856 A302 4.10k multi   1.60   .75

1988 Individual Speedway World Motorcycle Championships, Denmark, Sept. 3.

Federation of Danish Industries, 150th Anniv. — A303

Painting (detail): *The Industrialists*, by P.S. Kroyer.

1988, June 16   *Perf. 13½x13*
857 A303 3k multi   1.00   .50

Danish Metalworkers' Union, Cent. — A304

3k, Glass mosaic by Niels Winkel.

1988, Aug. 18   *Litho.*   *Perf. 13*
858 A304 3k multicolored   1.00   .50

DENMARK

Tonder Teachers' Training College, 200th Anniv. — A305

1988, Aug. 18 Engr. Perf. 13x12½
859 A305 3k lake 1.00 .50

Homage to Leon Degand, Sculpture by Robert Jacobsen — A306

1988, Sept. 22 Perf. 11½x13
860 A306 4.10k blk, lake & gray 3.75 5.00

Danish-French cultural exchange program, 10th anniv. See France No. 2130.

Preservation of Historic Sites — A307

3k, Lumby Windmill, 1818. 7.10k, Vejstrup Water Mill, 1837.

1900, Oct. 13 Engr. Perf. 13x12½
861 A307 3k red & org 1.60 .50
  Complete booklet, 10 #861 16.00
862 A307 7.10k dp blue & bluish grn 4.00 2.75

Paintings in the State Museum of Art, Copenhagen A308

4.10k, *Bathing Boys*, 1902, by Peter Hansen (1868-1928). 10k, *The Hill at Overkaerby*, 1917, by Fritz Syberg (1862-1939).

1988, Nov. 3 Litho. & Engr. Perf. 13
863 A308 4.10k multi 3.25 4.50
864 A308 10k multi 6.50 8.00

See Nos. 881-882, 951-952, 972-973, 1018-1019.

The Little Mermaid, Sculpture by Edvard Eriksen — A309

1989, Feb. 16 Engr.
865 A309 3.20k dark green 1.75 .50
  Complete booklet, 10 #865 17.50

Tourism industry, cent.

Danish Soccer Assoc., Cent. — A310

1989, Mar. 16 Litho.
866 A310 3.20k multi 1.60 .50
  Complete booklet, 10 #866 16.00

NATO Membership, 40th Anniv. — A311

1989, Mar. 16
867 A311 4.40k dk blue, gold & lt blue 2.00 1.25

Nordic Cooperation Issue — A312

Folk costumes.

1989, Apr. 20 Litho. & Engr.
868 A312 3.20k Woman from Valby 1.40 .40
869 A312 4.40k Pork butcher 2.10 1.60

European Parliament 3rd Elections — A313

1989, May 11 Litho.
870 A313 3k blue & yellow 1.60 1.50

Europa 1989 — A314

Children's toys.

1989, May 11 Litho. & Engr.
871 A314 3.20k Lego blocks 1.90 .25
872 A314 4.40k Wooden soldiers, by Kay Bojesen 3.00 .90

Agricultural Museum, Cent. — A315

1989, June 15 Engr. Perf. 13
873 A315 3.20k Tractor, 1889 1.25 .50

Interparliamentary Union, Cent. — A316

1989, June 15 Litho. & Engr.
874 A316 3.40k Folketing Chamber layout 3.50 4.00

Danish Fishery and Marine Research Institute, Cent. — A317

1989, Aug. 24 Litho. & Engr.
875 A317 3.20k multi 1.25 .50

Bernhard Severin Ingemann (1789-1862), Poet and Novelist — A318

1989, Aug. 24 Engr.
876 A318 7.70k dark green 3.00 1.90

A319

Danish Film Office, 50th Anniv.: 3k, Scene from the short feature film *They Reached the Ferry*, 1948. 3.20k, Bodil Ipsen (d. 1964), actress. 4.40k, Carl Th. Dreyer (1889-1968), screenwriter and director.

1989, Sept. 28 Litho.
877 A319 3k multi 1.40 1.40
878 A319 3.20k multi 1.25 .50
879 A319 4.40k multi 1.75 1.00
  Nos. 877-879 (3) 4.40 2.90

Stamp Day, 50th Anniv. — A320

1989, Nov. 10 Litho. & Engr.
880 A320 3.20k multi 1.25 .50

Art Type of 1988

Paintings: 4.40k, *Part of the Northern Gate of the Citadel Bridge*, c. 1837, by Christen Kobke (1810-1848). 10k, *A Little Girl, Elise Kobke, With a Cup in Front of Her*, c. 1850, by Constantin Hansen (1804-1880).

1989, Nov. 10 Perf. 12½x13
881 A308 4.40k multi 3.00 4.00
882 A308 10k multi 6.25 8.50

Types of 1933-82 and

A321 A321a

Queen Margrethe II

1990-98 Engr. Perf. 12¾
883 A32 25o bluish black .55 .40
  a. Bklt. pane, 4 #691, 2 #883 4.75
884 A32 125o carmine lake .95 .40
885 A32 325o lt yel grn 2.10 1.75
886 A32 350o yellow green 2.00 .95
887 A212 3.50k dark red 1.25 .40
  a. Bklt. pane, 2 each #691, 885, 887 8.00
  Complete booklet, #883, #885, #887, 3 #691 16.00
  Complete booklet, #883a, #887a 13.50
888 A321 3.50k henna brown 1.40 .40
  b. Bklt. pane, 4 each #883, #884, #888, 1 #691 ('91) 20.00
  Complete booklet, #888b 20.00
  Complete booklet, 2 each #883, #884, #888 16.00
889 A212 3.75k dark green 2.25 2.40
890 A321 3.75k green 4.00 3.75
891 A321 3.75k red 3.00 .40
  a. Bklt. pane, 4 each #884, #891 17.50
  Complete booklet, #891a 17.50
  b. Booklet pane, 2 each #691, 883, 891 8.75
  Complete booklet, #891b 8.75
892 A321a 3.75k red 2.25 .50
  a. Booklet pane, 2 each #691, 883, 892 14.50
  Complete booklet, #892a 14.50
  b. Booklet pane, 2 #883, 4 #494, 2 #892 12.00
  Complete booklet, #892b 12.00
893 A321 4k brown 2.50 1.20
894 A321a 4k deep bl grn 2.25 .80
895 A321a 4.25k olive brown 2.90 1.90
896 A212 4.50k brown violet 2.75 3.25
897 A321 4.50k violet 2.50 2.40
898 A321a 4.50k deep bl blk 2.60 2.40
899 A212 4.75k dark blue 1.90 .40
900 A321 4.75k blue 2.50 .10
901 A321 4.75k violet 3.50 2.00
902 A321a 4.75k brown 3.50 2.10
903 A321a 5k violet 2.50 1.75
904 A321 5k blue 3.50 .40
905 A321 5.25k black 3.50 1.75
906 A321a 5.25k deep blue 3.25 .80
907 A321 5.50k green 3.25 3.75
908 A321a 5.50k henna brown 3.50 2.75
909 A55 7.50k dark bl grn 3.00 2.75
  Nos. 883-909 (27) 69.15 42.15

Queen Margrethe II's 50th birthday (No. 888).
Issued: No. 888, 4/5; Nos. 890, 897, 900, 1990; No. 888a, 2/14/91; Nos. 886, 891, 891a, 901, 904, 6/10/92; 5.50k, 1/13/94; 4k, 5.25k, 8/27/96; Nos. A321, A329, 1/13/97; Nos. 894, 902, 903, 906, 8/28/97; Nos. 895, 898, 908, 909, 3/26/98; others, 1/11/90.
See Nos. 1114, 1125, 1130.

Museum of Decorative Art, Cent. — A322

Design: Silver coffee pot designed by Axel Johannes Kroyer, Copenhagen, 1726.

1990, Feb. 15 Engr. Perf. 13
911 A322 3.50k dark blue & blk 1.20 .80
  Complete booklet, 10 #911 12.00

A323

Steam engine, 200th anniv.: Steam engine built by Andrew Mitchell, 1790.

1990, Feb. 15
912 A323 8.25k dull red brown 2.75 1.75

Nyholm, 300th Anniv. — A324

1990, Apr. 5 Engr.
913 A324 4.75k black 1.75 .90

Europa 1990 — A325

3.50k, Royal Monogram, Haderslev P.O. 4.75k, Odense P.O.

1990, Apr. 5 Litho.
914 A325 3.50k multi 1.10 .25
915 A325 4.75k multi 1.75 .60

A326

Pieces from the Flora Danica Banquet Service produced for King Christian VII: No. 916, Bell-shaped lid, dish. No. 917, Gravy boat, dish. No. 918, Ice pot, casserole, lid. No. 919, Serving dish.

1990, May 3 Litho.
916 A326 3.50k multicolored 1.25 1.90
917 A326 3.50k multicolored 1.25 1.90
918 A326 3.50k multicolored 1.25 1.90
919 A326 3.50k multicolored 1.25 1.90
  a. Strip of 4, #916-919 5.00 8.50

Flora Danica porcelain, 200th anniv.

A327

Endangered plant species.

1990, June 14
920 A327 3.25k Marshmallow 1.25 1.25
921 A327 3.50k Red helleborine 2.25 .35
  Complete booklet, 10 #921 30.00
922 A327 3.75k Purple orchis 1.50 1.50
923 A327 4.75k Lady's slipper 1.90 .65
  Nos. 920-923 (4) 6.90 3.75

Village Churches, Jutland — A328

Perf. 13x12½, 12½x13
1990, Aug. 30 Engr.
924 A328 3.50k Gjellerup 1.20 .35
  Complete booklet, 10 #924 12.00
925 A328 4.75k Veng 1.60 .75
926 A328 8.25k Bredsten, vert. 3.00 2.00
  Nos. 924-926 (3) 5.80 3.10

Fredericia, "The Town for Everybody" A329

Engr. & Embossed
1990, Oct. 5 Perf. 13
927 A329 3.50k black & red 1.20 .90

DENMARK

Tordenskiold (Peter Wessel, 1690-1720), Admiral — A330

1990, Oct. 5   Litho.   *Perf. 13½x13*
928 A330 3.50k multicolored   1.20 .60
    Complete booklet, 10 #928   12.00

Prevent Bicycle Thefts — A331

Design: 3.50k, Stop drunk driving.

1990, Nov. 8   Litho.   *Perf. 13x12½*
930 A331 3.25k shown   1.10 1.10
931 A331 3.50k Automobile, wine glass   1.10 .30

Locomotives A332

1991, Mar. 14   Engr.   *Perf. 13*
932 A332 3.25k IC3 1990   1.40 1.50
933 A332 3.50k Class A 1882   1.10 .35
    Complete booklet, 10 #933   11.00
934 A332 3.75k Class MY 1954   1.25 1.75
935 A332 4.75k Class P 1907   1.50 1.50
    Nos. 932-935 (4)   5.25 5.10

Europa — A333

Satellite photographs showing temperatures of Danish: 3.50k, Waters. 4.75k, Land.

1991, May 2   Litho.   *Perf. 13*
936 A333 3.50k multicolored   1.75 .25
937 A333 4.75k multicolored   2.10 1.00

Jutland Law, 750th Anniv. — A334

1991, May 2
938 A334 8.25k multicolored   3.00 2.75

Danish Islands — A335

1991, June 6
939 A335 3.50k Fano   1.40 .30
    Complete booklet, 10 #939   18.00
940 A335 4.75k Christianso   1.60 .90

Decorative Art — A336

Designs: 3.25k, Earthenware bowl and jars by Christian Poulsen. 3.50k, Chair by Hans Wegner, vert. 4.75k, Silver cutlery by Kay Bojesen, vert. 8k, Lamp by Poul Henningsen.

1991, Aug. 22   Litho.   *Perf. 13*
941 A336 3.25k multicolored   1.10 1.50
942 A336 3.50k multicolored   1.00 .35
    Complete booklet, 10 #942   10.00
943 A336 4.75k multicolored   1.25 1.75
944 A336 8.25k multicolored   3.00 4.50
    Nos. 941-944 (4)   6.35 8.10

Keep Denmark Clean — A337

Designs: 3.50k, Cleaning up after dog. 4.75k, Picking up litter.

1991, Sept. 19   Engr.   *Perf. 13*
945 A337 3.50k red   2.00 .30
    Complete booklet, 10 #945   20.00
946 A337 4.75k blue   2.00 1.00

Posters from Danish Museum of Decorative Arts — A338

Posters for: 3.50k, Nordic Advertising Congress, by Arne Ungermann (1902-1981). 4.50k, Poster Exhibition at Copenhagen Zoo (baboon), by Valdemar Andersen (1875-1928). 4.75k, Danish Air Lines, by Ib Andersen (1907-1969). 12k, The Sinner, by Sven Brasch (1886-1970).

1991, Sept. 19   Litho.
947 A338 3.50k multicolored   1.00 .30
948 A338 4.50k multicolored   1.75 2.50
949 A338 4.75k multicolored   1.25 1.50
950 A338 12k multicolored   4.00 3.50
    Nos. 947-950 (4)   8.00 7.80

Art Type of 1988

Designs: 4.75k, Lady at her Toilet by Harald Giersing (1881-1927), vert. 14k, Road through a Wood by Edvard Weie (1879-1943), vert.

1991, Nov. 7   Litho. & Engr.   *Perf. 13x12½*
951 A308 4.75k multicolored   1.75 1.75
952 A308 14k multicolored   4.50 4.00

A339

Treasures of Natl. Museum: 3.50k, Earthenware bowl, Skarpsalling. 4.50k, Bronze dancer, Grevensvaenge. 4.75k, Bottom plate of silver cauldron, Gundestrup. 8.25k, Flint knife, Hindsgavl.

1992, Feb. 13   Engr.   *Perf. 13*
953 A339 3.50k dk vio & brown   1.10 .30
    Complete booklet, 10 #953   11.00
954 A339 4.50k dk bl & dk ol green   2.40 2.40
955 A339 4.75k brown & black   1.25 1.10
956 A339 8.25k dk ol grn & vio brown   2.75 2.75
    Nos. 953-956 (4)   7.50 6.55

A340

1992, Mar. 12   *Perf. 13½x13*
957 A340 3.50k rose carmine   1.25 .65

Danish Society of Chemical, Civil, Electrical, and Mechanical Engineers, cent.

Souvenir Sheet
Queen Margaret I (1353-1412) — A341

Litho. & Engr.
1992, Mar. 12   *Perf. 12½*
958 A341   Sheet of 2   6.25 7.25
   a.   3.50k Fresco   3.00 3.50
   b.   4.75k Alabaster bust   3.00 3.50

Nordia '94, Scandinavian Philatelic Exhibition. No. 958 sold for 12k to benefit the exhibition.

Discovery of America, 500th Anniv. — A342

1992, May 7   Engr.   *Perf. 12½*
959 A342 3.50k Potato plant   2.25 .40
    Complete booklet, 10 #959   22.50
960 A342 4.75k Ear of corn   4.25 1.75

Europa.

Protect the Environment A343

3.75k, Hare beside road. 5k, Fish, water pollution. 8.75k, Cut trees, vert.

Litho. & Engr.
1992, June 10   *Perf. 13*
961 A343 3.75k multi   1.25 .30
    Complete booklet, 10 #961   12.50
962 A343 5k multi   1.75 .70
963 A343 8.75k multi   3.50 2.00
    Nos. 961-963 (3)   6.50 3.00

Queen Margrethe II and Prince Henrik, 25th Wedding Anniv. — A344

1992, June 10   Litho.   *Perf. 12½x13*
964 A344 3.75k multicolored   .90 1.60

See Greenland No. 253.

A345

1992, July 16   *Perf. 13*
965 A345 3.75k multicolored   1.75 .75

Denmark, European soccer champions.

Danish Pavilion, Expo '92, Seville — A346

1992, Aug. 27   Engr.   *Perf. 13*
966 A346 3.75k blue   1.50 .75

Single European Market — A347

1992, Oct. 8   Litho. & Engr.   *Perf. 13*
967 A347 3.75k blue & org   1.50 .75

A348

Cartoon characters: 3.50k, A Hug, by Ivar Gjorup. 3.75k, Love Letter, by Phillip Stein Jonsson. 4.75k, Domestic Triangle, by Nikoline Werdelin. 5k, Poet and His Little Wife, by Jorgen Mogensen.

Litho. & Engr.
1992, Oct. 8   *Perf. 12½*
968 A348 3.50k multicolored   1.75 1.00
   Engr.
969 A348 3.75k red & purple   1.40 .30
970 A348 4.75k blk & red brn   2.50 2.50
971 A348 5k blue & red brn   1.75 .70
    Nos. 968-971 (4)   7.40 4.50

Art Type of 1988

5k, Landscape from Vejby, 1843, by John Thomas Lundbye. 10k, Motif from Halleby Brook, 1847, by Peter Christian Skovgaard.

Litho. & Engr.
1992, Nov. 12   *Perf. 12½x13*
972 A308 5k multicolored   2.10 2.00
973 A308 10k multicolored   4.00 3.25

Publication of New Danish Bible — A349

3.75k, Jacob's fight with angel.

1992, Nov. 12   *Perf. 13*
974 A349 3.75k multi   1.75 1.20

A350

Archaeological Treasures. Anthropomorphic gold foil figures found in: 3.75k, Lundeborg, horiz. 5k, Bornholm.

Litho. & Engr.
1993, Feb. 4   *Perf. 13*
975 A350 3.75k multicolored   1.40 .30
976 A350 5k multicolored   1.90 .70

Butterflies — A351

3.75k, Small tortoiseshell. 5k, Large blue. 8.75k, Marsh fritillary. 12k, Red admiral.

DENMARK

1993, Mar. 11 Litho.
977 A351 3.75k multi 1.75 .40
 Complete booklet, 10 #977 17.50
978 A351 5k multi 2.50 .80
979 A351 8.75k multi 5.25 3.50
980 A351 12k multi 5.25 3.50
 Nos. 977-980 (4) 14.75 8.20

Tivoli Gardens, 150th Anniv. — A352

Posters: 3.75k, Pierrot, by Thor Bogelund, 1947, horiz. 5k, Balloons, by Wilhelm Freddie, 1987.

1993, May 6 Litho. Perf. 12½
981 A352 3.75k multicolored 1.75 1.00
 Complete booklet, 10 #981 17.50
982 A352 5k multicolored 1.75 .90

A353

Europa (Contemporary paintings by): 3.75k, Troels Worsel, horiz. 5k, Stig Brogger.

1993, May 6 Perf. 13
983 A353 3.75k multicolored 1.40 1.10
984 A353 5k multicolored 1.90 .90

A354

1993, June 17 Engr. Perf. 13
985 A354 5k dark blue green 4.00 1.00

Danish-Russian relations, 500th anniv. See Russia No. 6154.

Training Ships
A355   A356

Perf. 13, 13½x13 (#987)
1993, June 17 Litho. & Engr.
986 A355 3.75k Danmark 2.00 .30
987 A356 4.75k Jens Krogh 4.00 4.50
988 A355 5k Georg Stage, horiz. 3.00 1.75

Size: 39x28mm
Perf. 13x13½
989 A356 9.50k Marilyn Anne, horiz. 5.50 5.25
 Nos. 986-989 (4) 14.50 11.80

Child's Drawing of Viking Ships
A357   Letter Writing Campaign A358

1993, Aug. 19 Litho. Perf. 13
990 A357 3.75k multicolored 2.25 .65
991 A358 5k lt & dk bl & blk 2.50 1.40

Ethnic Jewelry — A359

1993, Sept. 16 Litho. Perf. 13
992 A359 3.50k Falster 1.75 1.25
993 A359 3.75k Amager 1.75 .30
 Complete booklet, 10 #993 17.50
994 A359 5k Laeso 2.00 .90
995 A359 8.75k Romo 4.50 3.00
 Nos. 992-995 (4) 10.00 5.45

Cubist Paintings A360

5k, Assemblage, by Vilhelm Lundstrom, 1929. 15k, Composition, by Franciska Clausen, 1929.

Litho. & Engr.
1993, Nov. 11 Perf. 12½
996 A360 5k multicolored 2.75 2.25
997 A360 15k multicolored 6.75 5.00
See Nos. 1033-1034, 1080-1081.

Conservation — A361

1994, Jan. 27 Litho. Perf. 13
998 A361 3.75k Save water 3.50 .30
999 A361 5k CO2 4.50 1.10

Castles — A362

Castles: 3.50k, Marselisborg, Aarhus. 3.75k, Amalienborg, Copenhagen. 5k, Fredensborg, North Zealand. 8.75k, Graasten, South Jutland.

Litho. & Engr.
1994, Mar. 17 Perf. 13x12½
1000 A362 3.50k multicolored 1.50 .70
1001 A362 3.75k multicolored 1.75 .30
 Complete booklet, 10 #1001 17.50
1002 A362 5k multicolored 2.25 .30
1003 A362 8.75k multicolored 3.75 3.50
 a. Bklt. pane, #1000-1003 30.00 30.00

No. 1003a printed with 2 different labels. One shows a marching band, the other shows a ship.

Danmark Expedition, 1906-08 — A363

Europa: 3.75k, Expedition ship, Danmark, Alfred Wegener's weather balloon. 5k, Theodolite, Johan Peter Koch, cartographer.

1994, May 5 Engr. Perf. 13
1004 A363 3.75k deep brn vio 1.00 .25
1005 A363 5k dp slate grn 2.60 1.25
 Complete booklet, 10 #1005 35.00

Trams — A364

Designs: 3.75k, Copenhagen tram (Engelhardt). 4.75k, Aarhus car. 5k, Odense tram, vert. 12k, Horse-drawn tram.

Litho. & Engr.
1994, June 9 Perf. 13
1006 A364 3.75k multicolored 1.25 .30
1007 A364 4.75k multicolored 2.25 2.75
1008 A364 5k multicolored 1.75 1.40
Size: 38x21mm
1009 A364 12k multicolored 5.25 5.25
 Nos. 1006-1009 (4) 10.50 9.70

Children's Stamp Competition — A365

1994, Aug. 25 Litho. Perf. 12½
1010 A365 3.75k multicolored 1.50 .70

ILO, 75th Anniv. — A366

1994, Aug. 25 Perf. 13
1011 A366 5k multicolored 2.00 1.00

Wild Animals — A367

Litho. & Engr.
1994, Oct. 20 Perf. 12½
1012 A367 3.75k House sparrows 2.00 .35
1013 A367 4.75k Badger 3.00 2.25
1014 A367 5k Squirrel, vert. 2.60 1.00
1015 A367 9.50k Black grouse 5.00 4.50
Size: 36x26mm
Perf. 13
1016 A367 12k Grass snake 6.00 5.25
 Nos. 1012-1016 (5) 18.60 13.35

A368

1994, Nov. 10 Litho. Perf. 13
1017 A368 3.75k multicolored 1.75 .70

Folk High Schools, 150th anniv.

Painting Type of 1988
Designs: 5k, Study of Italian Woman and Sleeping Child, by Wilhelm Marstrand. 15k, Interior from Amaliegade with the Artist's Brothers, by Wilhelm Bendz.

Litho. & Engr.
1994, Nov. 10 Perf. 12½x13
1018 A308 5k multicolored 2.00 1.40
1019 A308 15k multicolored 6.00 3.25

Aarhus Cathedral School, 800th Anniv. — A369

Litho. & Engr.
1995, Jan. 26 Perf. 13
1020 A369 3.75k multicolored 1.75 .70

UN, 50th Anniv. — A370

Litho. & Engr.
1995, Jan. 26 Perf. 13
1021 A370 5k multicolored 2.50 1.20
 Complete booklet, 10 #1021 35.00

Danish Islands — A371

1995, Mar. 16 Engr. Perf. 13
1022 A371 3.75k Avernako 2.25 .30
 Complete booklet, 10 #1022 22.50
1023 A371 4.75k Fejo 2.75 2.50
1024 A371 5k Fur 3.50 .90
1025 A371 9.50k Endelave 4.50 4.50
 a. Booklet pane, #1022-1025 + 2 labels 15.00
 Complete booklet, 2 #1025a 32.50
 Nos. 1022-1025 (4) 13.00 8.20

No. 1025a printed with four different large labels. Labels with one pane are MF Faaborg II and MF Endelave. The other pane has MF Bukken-bruse and MF Fursund.

Liberation of Denmark, 50th Anniv. — A372

Designs: 3.75k, Gen. Montgomery, Town Hall Square, vert. 5k, White busses returning from concentration camps. 8.75k, Airplane dropping supplies to resistance. 12k, Jews escape across the Sound to Sweden.

1995, May 4 Litho. Perf. 13
1026 A372 3.75k multicolored 2.10 .30
 Complete booklet, 10 #1026 21.00
1027 A372 5k multicolored 2.75 1.00
1028 A372 8.75k multicolored 4.25 4.00
1029 A372 12k multicolored 6.00 6.00
 Nos. 1026-1029 (4) 15.10 11.30

Europa (Nos. 1026-1027).

A373

1995, June 8 Litho. Perf. 13
1030 A373 3.50k multicolored 1.50 .70

Danish Rhymed Chronicle, 500th anniv.

A374

3.75k, Roskilde Festival. 5k, Tonder Festival.

1995, June 8
1031 A374 3.75k multi, horiz. 1.60 .30
 Complete booklet, 10 #1031 16.00
1032 A374 5k multi 2.25 1.00

No. 1031 Roskilde Festival, 25th anniv., No. 1032 Tonder Festival, 21st anniv.
No. 1031 is 28x21mm.

Paintings A375

Designs: 10k, "Sct. Hans Aften, 1955," by Jens Sondergaard. 15k, "Landskab-Gudhjom, 1939," by Niels Lergaard.

Litho. & Engr.
1995, Aug. 24 Perf. 13x12½
1033 A375 10k multicolored 5.00 5.75
1034 A375 15k multicolored 7.50 7.50

Tycho Brahe (1546-1601), Astronomer — A376

3.75k, Uranienborg Observatory. 5.50k, Sextant.

DENMARK

	Litho. & Engr.	
1995, Oct. 27		Perf. 13
1035	A376 3.75k multicolored	2.00 .65
1036	A376 5.50k multicolored	2.75 2.75

See Sweden Nos. 2149-2150.

Toys — A377

Designs: 3.75k, Tekno cars. 5k, Dolls, teddy bear. 8.75k, Model trains. 12k, Glud & Marstrand tin horse-drawn carriage & fire pumper.

1995, Nov. 9		Perf. 13x12½
1037	A377 3.75k multicolored	1.60 .30
	Complete booklet, 10 #1037	16.00
1038	A377 5k multicolored	2.10 1.00
1039	A377 8.75k multicolored	3.25 3.25
1040	A377 12k multicolored	4.25 4.25
	Nos. 1037-1040 (4)	11.20 8.80

A378

Cartoonlike views of Copenhagen: 3.75k, Round Tower as music box. 5k, Christiansborg Castle. 8.75k, Marble Church as top of balloon. 12k, The Little Mermaid statue on stage.

1996, Jan. 25	Litho.	Perf. 13
1041	A378 3.75k multicolored	1.25 .30
	Complete booklet, 10 #1041	13.00
1042	A378 5k multicolored	1.75 .70
1043	A378 8.75k multicolored	3.00 3.00
1044	A378 12k multicolored	4.00 4.50
	Nos. 1041-1044 (4)	10.00 8.50

Copenhagen, 1996 cultural capital of Europe.

A379

1996, Mar. 21	Litho.	Perf. 13
1045	A379 3.75k Sports for disabled	1.25 .30
	Complete booklet, 10 #1045	13.00
1046	A379 4.75k Swimming	1.60 1.60
1047	A379 5k Sailing	1.75 .50
1048	A379 9.50k Cycling	3.25 3.25
a.	Bklt. pane of 4, #1045-1048 + 2 labels	14.00
	Complete booklet, 2 #1048a	28.00

No. 1048a printed with two different large labels. One shows hands and soccer ball, second shows tennis racket and tennis balls.

Danish Federation for Sports for the Disabled (No. 1045). Modern Olympic Games, cent., Sports Confederation of Denmark, cent., 1996 Summer Olympics, Atlanta (Nos. 1046-1048).

A380

1996, May 9	Litho.	Perf. 13
1049	A380 3.75k multicolored	1.50 1.00

Danish Employers' Confederation, cent.

A381

Famous Danish Women (Europa): 3.75k, Karen Blixen (1885-1962), writer. 5k, Asta Nielsen (1881-1972), silent screen actress.

1996, May 9		
1050	A381 3.75k lt brn & dk brn	1.50 .50
1051	A381 5k gray & dk blue	2.00 .75
	Complete booklet, 10 #1051	20.00

A382

Wooden Dinghies: 3.50k, Roskilde Fjord sail boat. 3.75k, Limfjorden skiff. 12.25k, Two-masted smack, South Funen Archipelago.

Perf. 13, 12½ (#1053)

1996, June 13		Engr.
1052	A382 3.50k multicolored	1.25 1.00
1053	A382 3.75k multicolored	1.50 .50
	Complete booklet, 10 #1053	16.00
1054	A382 12.25k multicolored	4.50 5.25
	Nos. 1052-1054 (3)	7.25 6.75

No. 1053 is 20x39mm.

Lighthouses — A383

	Litho. & Engr.	
1996, Sept. 12		Perf. 13x12½
1055	A383 3.75k Fornaes	1.50 .30
	Complete booklet, 10 #1055	16.00
1056	A383 5k Blavandshuk	1.75 .50
a.	Bklt. pane, 8 #1055, 2 #1056	22.00
	Complete booklet, #1056a	22.00
1057	A383 5.25k Bovbjerg	2.00 2.00
1058	A383 8.75k Mon	3.00 3.00
	Nos. 1055-1058 (4)	8.25 5.80

Art Works of Thorvald Bindesboll (1846-1908) — A384

	Litho. & Engr.	
1996, Oct. 10		Perf. 13
1059	A384 3.75k Pitcher	1.50 .30
	Complete booklet, 10 #1059	16.00

	Litho.	
1060	A384 4k Portfolio cover	1.60 1.10

Paintings A385

Designs: 10k, "At Lunch," by P.S. Kroyer, 1893. 15k, "The Girl with Sunflowers," by Michael Ancher, 1889.

1996, Nov. 7		Perf. 13x12½
1061	A385 10k multicolored	4.00 4.00
1062	A385 15k multicolored	5.25 5.25

A386

Queen Margrethe II: 3.50k, With Prince Henrik. 3.75k, With Crown Prince Frederik. 4k, Delivering New Year speech. 5.25k, Waving to crowd.

1997, Jan. 14	Litho.	Perf. 13
1063	A386 3.50k multicolored	1.25 1.25
1064	A386 3.75k multicolored	1.50 .30
	Complete booklet, 10 #1064	16.00
1065	A386 4k multicolored	1.40 .70
1066	A386 5.25k multicolored	2.00 1.50
a.	Sheet of 4, #1063-1066 + 2 labels	6.50 6.50
	Nos. 1063-1066 (4)	6.15 3.75

Queen Margrethe II, 25th anniv. of coronation.

A387

Open Air Museum, Copenhagen, Cent.: 3.50k, Kalstrup post mill. 3.75k, Ellested water mill. 5k, Fjellerup manor barn. 8.75k, Romo farm.

1997, Mar. 13	Engr.	Perf. 13
1067	A387 3.50k multicolored	1.25 1.00
1068	A387 3.75k multicolored	1.50 .30
	Complete booklet, 10 #1068	12.50
1069	A387 5k multicolored	1.75 .75
	Complete booklet, 10 #1069	17.50
1070	A387 8.75k multicolored	3.00 2.50
a.	Booklet pane, #1067-1070 + label	14.00
	Complete booklet, 2 #1070a	28.00
	Nos. 1067-1070 (4)	7.25 4.55

No. 1070a printed with two different large labels. One shows a view of Ellested water mill, the other shows a farm in Ejersted.

Great Belt Railway Link — A388

1997, May 15	Litho.	Perf. 13
1071	A388 3.75k East Tunnel	1.50 .50
	Complete booklet, 10 #1071	15.00
1072	A388 4.75k West Bridge	1.75 1.75

A389

Kalmar Union, 600th Anniv.: No. 1073, Margrete I and Eric of Pomerania. No. 1074, The Three Graces symbolizing Denmark, Norway and Sweden.

1997, June 12	Litho.	Perf. 13
1073	4k multicolored	2.60 2.75
1074	4k multicolored	2.60 2.75
a.	A389 Pair, #1073-1074	5.25 6.50

No. 1074a is a continuous design.

Copenhagen-Roskilde Railway, 150th Anniv. — A390

Designs: 3.75k, Two modern trains under Carlsberg Bridge. 8.75k, Early steam train going under Carlsberg Bridge.

	Litho. & Engr.	
1997, June 12		Perf. 13
1075	A390 3.75k multicolored	2.75 .30
	Complete booklet, 10 #1075	27.50
1076	A390 8.75k multicolored	5.00 2.50

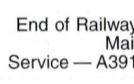

End of Railway Mail Service — A391

1997, June 12		Litho.
1077	A391 5k multicolored	1.75 .70

Stories and Legends — A392

Europa: 3.75k, Large cat on top of treasure chest, from "The Tinder Box." 5.25k, Butterfly, pond, frog, from "Thumbelina."

1997, Aug. 28	Engr.	Perf. 13
1078	A392 3.75k multicolored	1.40 .40
1079	A392 5.25k multicolored	1.75 1.50

Painting Type of 1993

Designs: 9.75k, "Dust Dancing in the Sun," by Vilhelm Hammershoi (1864-1916). 13k, "Woman Mountaineer," by J.F. Willumsen (1863-1958).

	Litho. & Engr.	
1997, Sept. 18		Perf. 13x12½
1080	A360 9.75k multicolored	4.75 5.50
1081	A360 13k multicolored	6.25 7.00

A393

Danish Design: 3.75k, Faaborg chair, vert. 4k, Margrethe bowl, vert. 5k, The Ant (chair). 12.25k, Georg Jensen silver bowl, vert.

1997, Nov. 6	Litho.	Perf. 13
1082	A393 3.75k multicolored	1.25 .30
	Complete booklet, 10 #1082	12.50
1083	A393 4k multicolored	1.25 .75
1084	A393 5k multicolored	2.00 .45
1085	A393 12.25k multicolored	4.50 5.25
	Nos. 1082-1085 (4)	9.00 6.75

Danish Confederation of Trade Unions, Cent. — A394

3.50k, General Workers Union in Denmark (SiD). 3.75k, Danish Confederation of Trade Unions (LO). 4.75k, Danish Nurse's Organization. 5k, Union of Commercial and Clerical Employees in Denmark (HK).

1998, Jan. 22	Litho.	Perf. 13
1086	A394 3.50k multicolored	1.10 .90
1087	A394 3.75k multicolored	1.25 .30
	Complete booklet, 10 #1087	12.50
1088	A394 4.75k multicolored	1.90 2.50
1089	A394 5k multicolored	2.00 .65
	Complete booklet, 10 #1089	20.00
	Nos. 1086-1089 (4)	6.25 4.35

City of Roskilde, 1000th Anniv. — A395

	Litho. & Engr.	
1998, Mar. 26		Perf. 13
1090	A395 3.75k multicolored	1.50 .90
	Complete booklet, 10 #1090	15.00

A396

1998, Mar. 26	Litho.	Perf. 13
1091	A396 5k Ladybug	1.75 .50

Reduce poison.

DENMARK 147

A397

New Post & Tele Museum, Copenhagen: 3.75k, Postman, 1922. 4.50k, Morse code operator, c. 1910. 5.50k, Telephone operator, 1910. 8.75k, Modern postman.

1998, May 28   Litho.   *Perf. 13*
1092	A397	3.75k multicolored	1.25	.30
a.		Booklet pane, 2 each #1087, 1089, 3 ea. 1090, 1092	30.00	
		Complete booklet, #1092a	30.00	
1093	A397	4.50k multicolored	1.50	1.50
1094	A397	5.50k multicolored	2.00	2.00
1095	A397	8.75k multicolored	2.75	2.75
a.		Booklet pane, #1092-1095	14.00	
		Complete booklet, 2 #1095a	28.00	
		Nos. 1092-1095 (4)	7.50	6.55

No. 1095a is printed with two backgrounds. One shows part of King Christian IV's "Order Concerning Postmen," 1624. The other shows part of Copenhagen c. 1923. Complete booklets contain panes with each background.

Bridges over Great Belt — A398

No. 1096, West Bridge. No. 1097, East Bridge (suspension).

1998, May 28   Engr.   *Perf. 13*
1096	A398	5k shown	2.75	.75
1097	A398	5k multi	2.75	.75
a.		Pair, #1096-1097 + label	6.00	1.50

Nordic Stamps — A399

Shipping: No. 1098, Signal flags, harbor master with binoculars. No. 1099, Radar image of entrance to Copenhagen harbor, sextant.

1998, May 28   Litho.   *Perf. 13*
1098	A399	6.50k multicolored	3.50	3.50
1099	A399	6.50k multicolored	3.50	3.50
a.		Pair, #1098-1099	7.25	7.25
b.		Souvenir sheet, #1099a	8.00	10.00

National Festivals A400

Europa: 3.75k, Horse at Danish agricultural show. 4.50k, Theater, tents at Århus Festival Week, Århus.

Litho. & Engr.
1998, Sept. 3   *Perf. 13*
1100	A400	3.75k multicolored	1.50	.60
		Complete booklet, 10 #1100	15.00	
1101	A400	4.50k multicolored	1.75	1.00

Contemporary Art — A401

Paintings: 3.75k, Danish Autumn, by Per Kirkeby. 5k, Alpha, by Mogens Andersen, vert. 8.75k, Imagery, by Ejler Bille, vert. 19k, Celestial Horse, by Carl-Henning Pedersen.

Perf. 12½x13, 13x12½
1998, Oct. 15   Litho. & Engr.
1102	A401	3.75k multicolored	1.25	1.25

Litho.
1103	A401	5k multicolored	2.00	1.50
1104	A401	8.75k multicolored	3.25	3.25
1105	A401	19k multicolored	6.50	7.75
		Nos. 1102-1105 (4)	13.00	13.75

See Nos. 1160-1161, 1190-1191, 1204-1205, 1235-1236, 1255-1256, 1282-1283, 1333-1336.

A402

Fossil, name of Danish geologist: 3.75k, Ammonite, Ole Worm (1588-1654). 4.50k, Shark's teeth, Niels Stensen (1638-86). 5.50k, Sea Urchin, Søren Abildgaard (1718-91). 15k, Slit-shell snail, Erich Pontoppidan (1698-1764).

1998, Nov. 5   Engr.   *Perf. 13*
1106	A402	3.75k multicolored	1.25	.30
		Complete booklet, 10 #1106	12.50	
1107	A402	4.50k multicolored	1.75	1.75
1108	A402	5.50k multicolored	1.75	1.75
1109	A402	15k multicolored	5.00	4.50
a.		Souvenir sheet, #1106-1109	12.00	12.50

Wavy Lines and Queen Types of 1933, 1997 and

Queen Margrethe II — A402a

1999-2004   Engr.   *Perf. 12¾*
1111	A32	150ø purple	.60	.25
1112	A32	375ø green	2.60	.70
1113	A32	400ø green	1.75	.65
1114	A321a	4k red	2.60	.50
a.		Booklet pane, 4 #883, 2 #494, 2 #1114	6.75	
		Complete booklet, #1114a	7.00	
1115	A402a	4k red	1.75	.50
b.		Booklet pane, 4 #883, 2 #494, 2 #1115	5.00	
		Booklet, #1115b	5.00	
c.		Sheet of 8 + label	16.00	
1116	A32	425ø green	2.75	.65
1117	A402a	4.25k blue	2.60	1.00
1118	A402a	4.25k red	1.75	.70
b.		Booklet pane, 6 #883, 2 #1118	5.00	
c.		Sheet of 8 + central label	36.00	—
1119	A402a	4.50k orange	2.00	1.50
a.		Vert. strip of 10 + 10 etiquettes	24.00	
1120	A402a	4.50k red	2.90	1.10
a.		Booklet pane, 2 #494, 2 #1120	6.00	—
		Complete booklet, #1120a	6.00	
b.		Sheet of 8 + central label	26.00	—
1121	A402a	4.75k sepia	3.25	1.75
1122	A402a	5k dk green	2.00	1.00
a.		Sheet of 8 + 8 etiquettes	65.00	—
1123	A402a	5.25k ultra	2.10	1.00
1124	A402a	5.50k violet	2.50	.90
a.		Sheet of 8 + label	24.00	
b.		Sheet of 8 + 8 etiquettes	30.00	
1125	A321a	5.75k blue	2.25	1.25
1126	A402a	5.75k emerald	2.50	1.25
1127	A402a	6k bister	2.50	.75
a.		Sheet of 10 + 10 etiquettes	45.00	—
1128	A402a	6.25k green	4.00	2.00
1129	A402a	6.50k slate grn	2.50	.90
a.		Sheet of 8 + 8 etiquettes	32.00	
b.		Sheet of 8 + central label	42.00	—
1130	A321a	6.75k slate green	4.25	2.75
1131	A402a	6.75k henna brn	3.25	2.50
1132	A402a	7k rose lilac	3.00	2.50
1133	A402a	8.50k bright blue	3.00	3.00
1134	A55	10.50k dk bl gray	4.00	2.50
1135	A55	11.50k dk bl gray	5.75	4.00

With Diagonal Engraving Lines
1136	A55	12.50k gray	6.00	4.50
1137	A55	13k orange	5.50	4.50
1138	A55	15k blue	6.50	5.25
		Nos. 1111-1138 (28)	86.15	49.85

Issued: 375ø, Nos. 1114, 1118, 1130, 1/13/99; No. 1125, 1/3/00; Nos. 1115, 1119, 1119a, 4.25k, 4.50k, 5k, 5.25k, 5.50k, Nos. 1126, 1131, 4/12/00; No. 1119b, 6k, 7k, 5/9/01; Nos. 1119c, 1121a, 1124a, 4/17/01; 150ø, 4.75k, 6.50k, 10.50k, 1/2/02. 400ø, No. 1120, 6.25k, 8.50k, 11.50k, 1/2/03. No. 1120b, 3/12. Nos. 1124b, 1129a, 3/12/03. No. 1128b, 1/2/03; No. 1122a, 4/2/02; 425ø, No. 1120, 12.50k, 13k, 15k, 1/2/04. Nos. 1120b, 1127a, 1/2/04.

Type A55 stamps with diagonal engraving lines have engraver's name of Mörck at lower right. Earlier stamps of type A55 have vertical and horizontal engraving lines. The lettering was also changed slightly in the Mörck engraving.

See Nos. 1295, 1296-1303.

A403

1999, Jan. 13   Litho.   *Perf. 13*
1143	A403	4k Oersted Satellite	1.40	.90

Deciduous Trees — A404

4k, Fagus sylvatica. 5k, Fraxinus excelsior, vert. 5.25k, Tilia cordata, vert. 9.25k, Quercus robur.

1999, Jan. 13   Litho. & Engr.
1144	A404	4k multicolored	1.25	.30
		Complete booklet, 10 #1144	12.50	
1145	A404	5k multicolored	1.75	1.00
1146	A404	5.25k multicolored	1.75	.65
1147	A404	9.25k multicolored	3.00	3.00
		Nos. 1144-1147 (4)	7.75	4.95

50th Anniversaries A405

Litho. & Engr.
1999, Feb. 24   *Perf. 13*
1148	A405	3.75k Home Guard	1.40	.90
1149	A405	4.25k NATO	2.00	1.00

Harbingers of Spring — A406

1999, Feb. 24   Litho.
1150	A406	4k Lapwing in flight	1.60	.30
		Complete booklet, 10 #1150	16.00	
1151	A406	5.25k Geese	1.75	.90
a.		Souvenir sheet, #1150-1151	6.50	5.00

Nature Reserves — A407

Litho. & Engr.
1999, Apr. 28   *Perf. 13*
1152	A407	4.50k Vejlerne	1.75	1.00
1153	A407	5.50k Langli	2.00	1.25

Europa.

Council of Europe, 50th Anniv. — A408

1999, Apr. 28   Engr.
1154	A408	9.75k blue	3.00	3.00

Danish Constitution, 150th Anniv. — A409

1999, June 2   Litho.   *Perf. 13*
1155	A409	4k red & black	1.40	.70

Danish Revue, 150th Anniv. — A410

Performers: 4k, Kjeld Petersen and Dirch Passer, comedians. 4.50k, Osvald Helmuth, singer. 5.25k, Preben Kaas and Jørgen Ryg, comedians, singers. 6.75k, Liva Weel, singer.

1999, June 2   Engr.   *Perf. 13*
1156	A410	4k deep red	1.60	.50
		Complete booklet, 10 #1156	16.00	
1157	A410	4.50k slate	1.75	1.40
1158	A410	5.25k deep blue	1.75	.85
		Complete booklet, 10 #1158	17.50	
1159	A410	6.75k deep claret	2.25	1.60
a.		Bklt. pane, #1156 1160 + 2 labels	14.00	15.00
		Complete booklet, 2 #1159a	28.00	
		Nos. 1156-1159 (4)	7.35	4.35

No. 1159a printed with two different pairs of labels. One version has showgirl label at left, the second version has showgirl label at right. Complete booklets contain one of each pane.

Contemporary Paintings Type

9.25k, Fire Farver, by Thomas Kluge. 16k, Dreng, by Lise Malinovsky.

1999, Aug. 25   Litho.   *Perf. 12¾*
1160	A401	9.25k multi, vert.	3.25	4.00
1161	A401	16k multi, vert.	5.25	5.25

Opening of New Extension of the Royal Library, "The Black Diamond" — A411

1999, Aug. 25   Engr.   *Perf. 13¾*
1162	A411	8.75k black	4.00	3.00

Migratory Birds — A412

Litho. & Engr.
1999, Sept. 29   *Perf. 12¾*
1163	A412	4k Swallows	1.60	.30
		Complete booklet, 10 #1163	16.00	
1164	A412	5.25k Gray-lag geese	1.75	1.00
a.		Souvenir sheet, #1163-1164	5.25	6.50
1165	A412	5.50k Common eider	1.75	.90
1166	A412	12.25k Arctic tern	4.50	5.25
a.		Souvenir sheet, #1165-1166	9.00	10.00
		Nos. 1163-1166 (4)	9.60	7.45

Stamps from Nos. 1164a and 1166a lack white border found on Nos. 1163-1166.

New Year 2000 — A413

1999, Nov. 10   Litho.   *Perf. 13¼*
1167	A413	4k Hearts	1.40	.50
1168	A413	4k Wavy lines	1.40	.50
a.		Bklt. pane, 5 ea #1167-1168	35.00	
		Complete booklet, #1168a	35.00	

The 20th Century — A414

148 DENMARK

4k, Prof. J.H. Deuntzer on front page of newspaper, 1901. 4.50k, Newspaper illustration, 1903. 5.25k, Asta Nielsen and Poul Reumert in the film "The Abyss," 1910. 5.75k, Advertising sticker showing woman on telephone, 1914.
See sheet of 16, #1184a.

2000, Jan. 12   Litho. & Engr.
1169	A414	4k buff & blk	1.40	.50
		Complete booklet, 10 #1169	14.00	
1170	A414	4.50k multicolored	1.75	1.00
1171	A414	5.25k multicolored	1.75	1.00
		Complete booklet, 10 #1171	17.50	
1172	A414	5.75k multicolored	1.75	1.25
		Nos. 1169-1172 (4)	6.65	3.75

2000, May 9

4k, Allegory of women suffrage on front page of newspaper, 1915. 5k, Newspaper caricature of the Kanslergade Agreement, 1933. 5.50k, Film "Long and Short," 1927. 6.75k, Front page of Radio Weekly Review, 1925.

1173	A414	4k multi	1.40	.55
		Booklet, 10 #1173	14.00	
1174	A414	5k multi	1.75	1.00
1175	A414	5.50k multi	2.00	1.60
1176	A414	6.75k multi	2.25	2.50
		Nos. 1173-1176 (4)	7.40	5.65

2000, Aug. 23

4k, Liberation of Denmark on front page of newspaper, 1945. 5.75k, Newspaper caricature of new constitution, 1953. 6.75k, Poster for film "Café Paradise," 1950. 12.25k, Advertisement for Arena television, 1957.

1177	A414	4k multi	1.40	.90
		Booklet, 10 #1177	14.00	
1178	A414	5.75k multi	2.00	1.60
1179	A414	6.75k multi	2.25	2.50
1180	A414	12.25k multi	4.00	4.25
		Nos. 1177-1180 (4)	9.65	9.35

2000, Nov. 8

4k, Entry of Denmark into European Community on front page of newspaper, 1972. 4.50k, Newspaper caricature of youth revolt, 1969. 5.25k, Poster for film "The Olsen Gang," 1968. 5.50k, Denmark Post website on Internet, 1999.

1181	A414	4k multi	1.40	.90
		Booklet, 10 #1181	14.00	
1182	A414	4.50k multi	1.60	1.60
1183	A414	5.25k multi	1.75	1.00
		Booklet, 10 #1183	17.50	
a.		Booklet pane, #1171, 1175, 1179, 1183 + label	8.00	
		Booklet, 2 #1183a	16.00	
1184	A414	5.50k multi	2.00	1.25
a.		Sheet of 16, #1169-1184	47.50	42.50
		Nos. 1181-1184 (4)	6.75	4.75

No. 1183a comes with two different labels. Booklet contains one of each.

60th Birthday of Queen Margrethe II — A415

2000, Apr. 12   Litho.   Perf. 12¾
1185	A415	4k gray & car	1.60	.60
		Complete booklet, 10 #1185	16.00	
1186	A415	5.25k gray & blue	1.75	.90
a.		Souvenir sheet of #1185-1186	4.00	4.25

Oresund Bridge, Sweden-Denmark — A416

Litho. & Engr.
2000, May 9   Perf. 12¾
1187	A416	4.50k shown	2.00	1.90

Litho.
1188	A416	4.50k Map	2.00	1.90
a.		Pair, #1187-1188	4.25	3.75

See Sweden Nos. 2391-2393.

Europa, 2000
Common Design Type

2000, May 9   Litho.   Perf. 13
1189	CD17	9.75k multi	3.50	2.25

Contemporary Art Type of 1998

Designs: 4k, Pegasus, by Kurt Trampedach. 5.25k, Landscape, by Nina Sten-Knudsen.

2000, Sept. 27
1190	A401	4k multi	1.50	1.50
1191	A401	5.25k multi	1.50	1.50

Royal Danish Air Force, 50th Anniv. — A417

2000, Sept. 27   Engr.
1192	A417	9.75k black & red	3.00	2.50
a.		Souvenir sheet of 1	3.00	3.50

Botanical Gardens, Copenhagen A418

Litho. & Engr.
2001, Jan. 24   Perf. 12¾
1193	A418	4k Palm House	1.40	.60
		Booklet, 10 #1193	14.00	

Size: 28x21mm
1194	A418	6k Lake	2.00	.85
1195	A418	12.25k Water lilies	4.00	4.50
		Nos. 1193-1195 (3)	7.40	5.95

"Use the Language" — A419

2001, Mar. 28   Litho.   Perf. 13
1196	A419	4k "A," text	1.40	.55
		Booklet, 10 #1196	14.00	
1197	A419	7k "Z," text	2.75	.90

Danish Postage Stamps, 150th Anniv. — A420

Portion of #2 and: 4k, Engraver Martinus Willam Ferslew. 5.50k, Printer Andreas Thiele. 6k, Head Copenhagen postmaster Frantz Christopher von Jessen. 10.25k, Postmaster General Magrius Otto Spohus Count Danneskjold-Samsoe.

Litho. & Engr.
2001, Apr. 1   Perf. 13¼x13
1198	A420	4k multi	1.50	1.00
1199	A420	5.50k multi	1.90	1.25
		Booklet, 10 #1199	19.00	
1200	A420	6k multi	2.00	1.25
1201	A420	10.25k multi	4.00	2.50
a.		Booklet pane, #1198-1201 + label	20.00	21.00
		Booklet, 2 #1201a	40.00	
		Nos. 1198-1201 (4)	9.40	6.00

No. 1201a printed with two different labels. One version has proof of stamp design, sketch of proposed design and Ferslew's letter to Danneskjold-Samsoe, and other shows two essays and letter from M. T. C. Bartholdy.

Europa — A421

Designs: 4.50k, Hands in water. 9.75k, Woman's head, water.

2001, May 9   Litho.   Perf. 13¼x13
1202	A421	4.50k multi	1.25	.90
a.		Booklet pane of 5 + 5 etiquettes		7.50
		Booklet, 2 #1202a		15.00
1203	A421	9.75k multi	3.00	3.50

Contemporary Paintings Type of 1998

Designs: 18k, Missus, by Jorn Larsen, horiz. 22k, Postbillede, by Henning Damgaard-Sorensen.

Perf. 13x12½, 12½x13
2001, Aug. 22   Litho.
1204	A401	18k multi	6.00	6.50
1205	A401	22k multi	7.25	7.75

Youth Culture — A422

Designs: 4k, Skateboarding. 5.50k, Kissing. 6k, Creating music. 10.25k, Tongue piercing.

2001, Aug. 22   Perf. 13
1206	A422	4k multi	1.60	.60
		Booklet, 10 #1206	16.00	
1207	A422	5.50k multi	1.75	1.10
		Booklet, 10 #1207	17.50	
1208	A422	6k multi	1.90	1.90
1209	A422	10.25k multi	4.00	4.00
a.		Souvenir sheet, #1206-1209	9.00	9.75
		Nos. 1206-1209 (4)	9.25	7.60

Hafnia 01 Philatelic Exhibition, Copenhagen — A423

Monarch and stamps: 4k, Queen Margrethe II, #757, 1000. 4.50k, King Frederik IX, #775, 1003. 5.50k, King Christian X, #1001, B10. 7k, King Christian IX, #1002, 66.

Litho. & Engr.
2001, Oct. 16   Perf. 13x13¼
1210	A423	4k multi	1.60	.75
1211	A423	4.50k multi	1.75	1.75
1212	A423	5.50k multi	1.75	1.75
1213	A423	7k multi	2.50	2.75
a.		Souvenir sheet, #1210-1213	6.50	7.50
b.		Strip, #1210-1213 + central label	10.00	11.50
		Nos. 1210-1213 (4)	7.60	7.00

Island Ferries — A424

Designs: 3.75k, Bukken-Bruse. 4k, Ouro. 4.25k, Hjarno. 6k, Barsofaergen.

2001, Nov. 7   Perf. 12¾
1214	A424	3.75k multi	1.25	1.60
1215	A424	4k multi	1.60	.60
		Booklet, 10 #1215	16.00	
1216	A424	4.25k multi	1.60	1.60
1217	A424	6k multi	2.00	2.25
		Nos. 1214-1217 (4)	6.45	6.05

Comics and Cartoons — A425

Designs: 4k, Rasmus Klump, by Vilhelm Hansen. 5.50k, Valhalla, by Peter Madsen. 6.50k, Jungledyret Hugo, by Flemming Quist Moller. 10.50k, Cirkeline, by Hanne Hastrup.

2002, Jan. 16   Litho.   Perf. 13¼x13
1218	A425	4k multi	1.50	.55
		Booklet, 10 #1218	15.00	
a.		Sheet of 8 + label	50.00	
1219	A425	5.50k multi	1.75	1.00
		Booklet, 10 #1219	17.50	
a.		Sheet of 8 + label	27.50	
1220	A425	6.50k multi	2.10	1.75
1221	A425	10.50k multi	4.00	4.50
a.		Souvenir sheet, #1218-1221	8.00	9.00
		Nos. 1218-1221 (4)	9.35	7.80

The Girls in the Airport, Sculpture by Hanne Varming — A426

Designs: 4k, Rear view. 5k, Front view.

Photo. & Engr.
2002, Mar. 13   Perf. 12¾
1222	A426	4k multi, cream	1.60	.55
		Booklet, 10 #1222	16.00	
1223	A426	5k multi, cream	1.75	1.60

Europa — A427

Winning drawings in children's stamp design contest: 4k, Clown, by Luna Ostergard. 5k, Clown, by Camille Wagner Larsen.

2002, May 15   Litho.   Perf. 13
1224	A427	4k multi	1.50	.90
		Booklet, 10 #1224	15.00	
1225	A427	5k multi	1.75	1.75
a.		Booklet pane of 5 + 5 etiquettes	8.75	—
		Booklet, 2 #1225a	17.50	

Landscapes — A428

2002, May 15   Engr.
1226	A428	4k Bornholm	1.60	.90
1227	A428	6k West Jutland	1.90	1.90
1228	A428	6.50k Langeland	1.75	2.25
1229	A428	12.50k Thy	4.50	4.50
		Nos. 1226-1229 (4)	9.75	9.55

Historic Postal Vehicles — A429

Designs: 4k, 1953 Nimbus motorcycle. 5.50k, 1962 Bedford van. 10k, 1984 Renault 4 van. 19k, 1998 Volvo FH12 tractor trailer.

Litho. & Engr.
2002, Aug. 21   Perf. 13x13¼
1230	A429	4k multi	1.60	.65
a.		Booklet, 10 #1230	16.00	
		Sheet of 8 + central label	36.00	—
1231	A429	5.50k multi	1.90	1.50
		Booklet, 10 #1231	19.00	
1232	A429	10k multi	4.00	4.00
1233	A429	19k multi	7.00	7.00
a.		Booklet pane of 4, #1230-1233	20.00	
		Booklet, 2 #1233a	40.00	
		Nos. 1230-1233 (4)	14.50	13.15

No. 1233a is printed with two different labels. One shows a 1908 Berlíet van and the other a 2002 Peugeot Partner. Both are included in the booklet.

Opening of Copenhagen Metro — A430

2002, Sept. 25   Engr.   Perf. 12¾
1234	A430	5.50k multi, tan	1.50	1.40

Contemporary Paintngs Type of 1998

Designs: 5k, Children's Corner, by Jens Birkemose, vert. 6.50k, Maleren og Modellen, by Frans Kannik, vert.

2002, Sept. 25   Perf. 13x12½
1235	A401	5k red & blue	1.75	1.75
1236	A401	6.50k multi	2.25	2.25

Intl. Council for the Exploration of the Sea, Cent. — A431

Atlantic cod and: 4k, Exploration ship Dana. 10.50k, Hirtshals lighthouse.

Litho. & Engr.
2002, Sept. 25   Perf. 13¼x13
1237	A431	4k multi	1.60	.65
1238	A431	10.50k multi	4.00	4.00
a.		Souvenir sheet, #1237-1238	4.50	5.00

See Faroe Islands No. 426, Greenland Nos. 401-402.

DENMARK

Danish House Architecture A432

Designs: 4k, Dianas Have, Horsholm, by Vandkusten Design Studio, 1992. 4.25k, Blangstedgard, Odense, by Poul Ingemann, 1988. 5.50k, Dansk Folkeferie, Karrebaeksminde, by Stephan Kappel, 1979. 6.50k, Fredensborg Terraces, Fredensborg, by Jorn Utzon, 1963. 9k, Soholm, Klampenborg, by Arne Jacobsen, 1950.

2002, Nov. 8	Litho. & Engr.		Perf. 12¾
1239	A432	4k multi	1.60 1.00
	Booklet, 10 #1239		16.00
1240	A432	4.25k multi	1.60 .70
1241	A432	5.50k multi	1.90 1.50
1242	A432	6.50k multi	2.25 1.75
1243	A432	9k multi	3.00 3.00
Nos. 1239-1243 (5)			10.35 7.95

See Nos. 1257-1261, 1267-1271, 1317-1321.

Youth Sports — A433

2003, Jan. 15	Litho.		Perf. 12¾
1244	A433	4.25k Soccer	1.50 .70
	Booklet, 10 #1244		16.00
a.	Sheet of 8 + central label		13.00 13.00
1245	A433	5.50k Swimming	1.75 1.50
	Booklet, 10 #1245		17.50
1246	A433	8.50k Gymnastics	3.25 3.25
1247	A433	11.50k Handball	4.00 4.00
Nos. 1244-1247 (4)			10.50 9.70

Danish Literary Greenland Expedition, Cent. — A434

Designs: 4.25k, Expedition members Harald Moltke, Knud Rasmussen, Jorgen Bronlund, Ludvig Mylius-Erichsen and Gabriel Olsen. 7k, Campsite.

2003, Mar. 12	Engr.		Perf. 12¾
1248	A434	4.25k blue gray	1.25 .70

Size: 61x22mm

1249	A434	7k multi	2.25 2.25
a.	Souvenir sheet, #1248-1249 + label		5.00 5.00

See Greenland Nos. 407-408.

Europa — A435

Poster art: 4.25k, Poster for Copenhagen International Theater Festival, by Ole Fick, 1985. 5.50k, Poster for Bertel Thorvaldsen Museum, by Ole Woldbye, 1970.

2003, May 14	Litho.		Perf. 12¾
1250	A435	4.25k multi	1.50 .60
	Booklet, 10 #1250		15.00

	Engr.		
1251	A435	5.50k black	1.75 1.40
	Booklet, 10 #1251		17.50
a.	Sheet of 8 + central label		40.00

Insects — A436

Designs: 4.25k, Ephemera danica. 6.50k, Dytiscus latissimus. 12k, Cordulegaster boltoni, vert.

2003, May 14	Litho. & Engr.		
1252	A436	4.25k multi	1.50 .50
a.	Sheet of 8 + central label		25.00
1253	A436	6.50k multi	2.00 2.00
a.	Sheet of 8 + central label		50.00

Size: 21x39mm

1254	A436	12k multi	3.75 3.75
a.	Souvenir sheet, #1252-1254		7.00 7.50
Nos. 1252-1254 (3)			7.25 6.25

Contemporary Art Type of 1998

Designs: 5.50k, Baering, by Sys Hindsbo. 19k, Det Forjaettede Land, by Poul Anker Bech.

2003, Aug. 27	Litho. & Engr.		Perf. 12½x13
1255	A401	5.50k multi	1.75 1.75

	Litho.		
1256	A401	19k multi	6.50 6.50

Danish House Architecture Type of 2002

Designs: 4k, Bellahoj Apartment Complex, Copenhagen, by Tage Nielsen and Mogens Irming, 1944-58. 4.25k, Anchersvej, Klampenborg, by Mogens Lassen, 1935. 5.25k, Gerthasminde, Odense, by Anton Rosen, 1912-35. 9k, Solvang, Vallekilde College, by Andreas Bentsen and Martin Nyrop, 1889. 15k, Stenbrogard, Brorup, by Peter Holdensen, 1868.

2003, Aug. 27	Litho. & Engr.		Perf. 12¾
1257	A432	4k multi	1.60 1.60
1258	A432	4.25k multi	1.60 .90
	Complete booklet, 10 #1258		16.00
1259	A432	5.25k multi	1.75 1.75
1260	A432	9k multi	3.25 3.25
1261	A432	15k multi	4.50 4.50
Nos. 1257-1261 (5)			12.70 12.00

A437

2003, Nov. 7	Engr.		Perf. 12¾
1262	A437	6.50k gray blue	2.00 1.75

Awarding of first Nobel Prize to a Dane (Niels Finsen for Physiology and Medicine), cent.

A438

Artifacts from Royal Jelling World Heritage Site: 4.25k, Queen Thyra's stone. 5.50k, King Gorm's cup. 8.50k, King Harald's stone. 11.50k, Wall paintings, Jelling Church.

2003, Nov. 7	Litho. & Engr.		
1263	A438	4.25k multi	1.50 1.25
	Booklet, 10 #1263		17.50
1264	A438	5.50k multi	1.75 1.50
	Booklet, 10 #1264		22.50
1265	A438	8.50k multi	2.75 2.75
1266	A438	11.50k multi	3.75 3.75
Nos. 1263-1266 (4)			9.75 9.25

A spiral-bound booklet, enclosed in a slip-case, with four booklet panes containing single stamps of Nos. 1263-1266, and a booklet pane containing a strip of Nos. 1263-1266, sold for 99k. Value, $35.

Danish House Architecture Type of 2002

Designs: 4.50k, Spurveskjul, Virum, by Nicolai Abildgaard, 1805. 6k, Liselund, Mon, by Andreas Kirkerup, 1792. 7k, Kampmann's Yard, Varde, by Hans Wolff Ollgaard, Hack Kampmann and Mikkel Stobberup, 1781. 12.50k, Harsdorff's House, Copenhagen, by Caspar Frederik Harsdorff, 1780. 15k, Nyso Manor, Praesto, by Jens Lauridsen.

2004, Jan. 14	Litho. & Engr.		Perf. 12¾
1267	A432	4.50k multi	1.60 1.00
	Booklet, 10 #1267		16.00
1268	A432	6k multi	2.40 1.60
1269	A432	7k multi	2.50 2.50
1270	A432	12.50k multi	4.00 4.00
1271	A432	15k multi	5.25 5.25
Nos. 1267-1271 (5)			15.75 14.35

Academy of Fine Arts, Copenhagen, 250th Anniv. — A439

2004, Mar. 26	Litho. & Engr.		Perf. 13¼x13
1272	A439	5.50k multi	2.10 1.25
	Booklet, 10 #1272		21.00

Norse Gods — A440

Designs: 4.50k, Heimdal guarding Bifrost bridge. 6k, Gefion plowing Sjaelland out of Sweden.

2004, Mar. 26			
1273	A440	4.50k multi	1.75 .85
a.	Sheet of 8 + central label		35.00 35.00
1274	A440	6k multi	2.40 1.10
a.	Souvenir sheet, #1273-1274		8.00 8.00
b.	Sheet of 8 + central label		55.00 55.00

Wedding of Crown Prince Frederik and Mary Donaldson — A441

No. 1275: a, Couple facing right. b, Couple facing left.

2004, May 14	Litho. & Photo.		Perf. 13x13¼
1275	A441	Horiz. pair	3.50 3.50
	Booklet, 5 #1275		20.00
a.-b.	4.50k Either single, denomination 8½ mm wide		1.75 1.25
c.-d.	4.50k Either single, denomination 7½ mm wide		1.75 1.25
e.	Souvenir sheet, #1275c-1275d + central label		4.00 4.00

See Faroe Islands No. 444 and Greenland Nos. 429-430.

Frederiksberg Palace, 300th Anniv. — A442

Designs: 4.25k, Doorway overlooking Sondermarken Park. 4.50k, Gatehouse archway, castle yard. 6.50k, Aerial view.

2004, May 14	Litho. & Engr.		Perf. 13
1276	A442	4.25k multi	1.60 1.60
1277	A442	4.50k multi	1.75 1.00

Size: 55x32mm

1278	A442	6.50k multi	2.50 2.00
a.	Souvenir sheet, #1276-1278		6.00 7.00
Nos. 1276-1278 (3)			5.85 4.60

Prince Henrik, 70th Birthday — A443

2004, June 9	Litho.		Perf. 12¾
1279	A443	4.50k multi	1.60 1.00

Europa — A444

2004, June 9			Perf. 13
1280	A444	6k Cyclists	2.50 1.60
1281	A444	9k Sailboats	3.50 3.00

Contemporary Paintings Type of 1998

Designs: 13k, Senses the Body Landscape, by Lars Ravn, vert. 21k, The Dog Bites, by Lars Norgard, vert.

2004, Aug. 25	Litho. & Engr.		Perf. 13x12½
1282	A401	13k multi	5.00 5.00

	Litho.		
1283	A401	21k multi	7.50 7.50

Viking Ship Museum, Roskilde — A445

Designs: 4.50k, Skuldelev 1 on Roskilde Fjord. 5.50k, Reconstruction of Skuldelev 2. 6.50k, Cross-section of ship. 12.50k, Excavation of archaeological site where ships were found.

2004, Aug. 25	Litho. & Engr.		Perf. 13x13¼
1284	A445	4.50k multi	1.60 1.00
	Complete booklet, 10 #1284		16.00
1285	A445	5.50k multi	2.00 1.60
	Complete booklet, 10 #1285		20.00
1286	A445	6.50k multi	2.40 2.00
1287	A445	12.50k multi	4.50 4.50
Nos. 1284-1287 (4)			10.50 9.10

A spiral-bound booklet, enclosed in a slip-case, with four booklet panes containing single stamps of Nos. 1284-1287 and a booklet pane containing a strip of Nos. 1284-1287, sold for 99k. Value, $40.

Birds of Prey — A446

Designs: 4.50k, Falco tinnunculus. 5.50k, Accipiter nisus. 6k, Buteo buteo. 7k, Circus aeruginosus.

2004, Nov. 5	Litho. & Engr.		Perf. 13
1288	A446	4.50k multi	1.75 .90
	Complete booklet, 10 #1288		17.50
a.	Sheet of 8 + central label		17.50 17.50
1289	A446	5.50k multi	2.10 1.00
a.	Sheet of 8 + central label		22.50 22.50
1290	A446	6k multi	2.40 2.00
1291	A446	7k multi	2.75 2.25
Nos. 1288-1291 (4)			9.00 6.15

Queen and Small State Seal Types of 1946-2000

2005-09	Engr.		Perf. 12¾
1295	A402a	4.75k red	1.90 1.00
a.	Sheet of 8 + central label		17.00 —
1296	A402a	5.50k red	2.25 .50
b.	Sheet of 8 #1296 + central label		20.00 —
1296A	A402a	6.50k blue	2.75 .50
1297	A402a	7.25k blk vio	3.00 2.50
1298	A402a	7.50k blue	3.25 2.50
1299	A402a	7.75k vio blk	3.50 .90
1300	A402a	8k indigo	4.00 2.50
1301	A402a	8.25k Prus blue	2.50 2.50
1302	A402a	8.75k Prus blue	3.75 1.00
1303	A402a	9k blue	3.25 3.25

With Diagonal Engraving Lines

1304	A55	10k olive yellow	3.50 1.25
1304A	A55	10.50k car rose	4.00 3.25
1305	A55	13.50k green	5.00 4.25
1308	A55	16k Prus grn	7.00 1.00
1309	A55	16.50k red brn	6.00 5.25
1310	A55	17k sl grn	6.25 5.25
1311	A55	17.50k purple	6.25 5.25
1312	A55	20k blue	8.25 1.75
1312A	A55	20.50k purple	9.25 1.75
1313	A55	22k brn vio	8.25 6.00
Nos. 1295-1313 (20)			94.95 52.40

Issued: 7.50k, 16.50k, 22k, 1/3. 4.75k, 8k, 11/11. 4.75k, 10k, 17k, 1/2/06. 7.25k, 8.25k, 11/10/06. 13.50k, 17.50k, 1/2/07. 20k, 11/8/07. 5.50k, 6.50k, 7.75k, 8.75k, 1/2/08. Nos. 1296b, 1308, 1312, 3/27/08. Nos. 1303, 1304A, 1/2/09. Type A55 stamps with diagonal engraving lines have engraver's name of Mörck at lower right. Earlier stamps of type A55 have vertical and horizontal engraving

DENMARK

lines. The lettering was also changed slightly in the Mörck engraving.

Danish House Architecture Type of 2002

Designs: 4.25k, Hjarup Manse, Vamdrup, c. 1665. 4.50k, Ejdersted Farm, Southwest Schleswig, 1653. 7.50k, Provstegade, Randers, c. 1650. 9.50k, Smith's Yard, Koge, c. 1550. 16.50k, Carmelite Monastery, Elsinore, c. 1500.

Litho. & Engr.

2005, Jan. 12			Perf. 12¾	
1317	A432	4.25k multi	1.75	1.75
1318	A432	4.50k multi	1.75	.65
	Complete booklet, 10 #1318		17.50	
a.	Booklet pane, 4 #691, 8 #1318		17.00	—
	Complete booklet, #1318a		17.00	
1319	A432	7.50k multi	2.90	2.90
1320	A432	9.50k multi	3.50	3.50
1321	A432	16.50k multi	7.25	7.25
	Nos. 1317-1321 (5)		17.15	16.05

Bonn-Copenhagen Declaration, 50th Anniv. — A447

2005, Mar. 2			Litho.	
1322	A447	6.50k multi	2.50	2.00

See Germany No. 2330.

Hans Christian Andersen (1805-75), Author A448

Paper Cutting by Andersen, Scissors A449

Designs: 6.50k, Pen, inkwell, illustration of duckling, manuscript handwritten by Andersen. 7.50k, Andersen's drawing of Casino dell'Orlogio, Rome, and boots.

2005, Mar. 2			Engr.	
1323	A448	4.50k black	1.60	1.60
a.	Sheet of 8 + central label		20.00	20.00

Litho. & Engr.

1324	A449	5.50k multi	2.00	2.00
	Complete booklet, 10 #1324		20.00	
a.	Sheet of 8 + central label		25.00	25.00
1325	A449	6.50k multi	2.25	2.00
1326	A449	7.50k multi	3.00	2.50
	Nos. 1323-1326 (4)		8.85	8.10

A spiral-bound booklet, enclosed in a slipcase, with four booklet panes containing single stamps of Nos. 1323-1326, and a booklet pane containing a strip of Nos. 1323-1326, sold for 99k. Value, $40.

See Malta Nos. 1196-1199.

August Bournonville (1805-79), Choreographer A450

Bournonville and: 4.50k, Dancer. 5.50k, Dancers.

Litho. & Engr.

2005, May 4			Perf. 13¼x13	
1327	A450	4.50k multi	1.75	1.75
	Complete booklet, 10 #1327		17.50	
a.	Sheet of 8 + central label		19.00	—
1328	A450	5.50k multi	2.00	2.00
a.	Sheet of 8 + central label		17.50	—
b.	Souvenir sheet, #1327-1328		4.00	4.00

Sailors in World War II — A451

Designs: 4.50k, Ship convoy. 7.50k, Unloading of ship's cargo.

2005, May 4			Litho.	Perf. 13
1329	A451	4.50k multi	1.60	1.60
1330	A451	7.50k multi	2.75	2.75

Europa — A452

2005, May 4			Perf. 12¾	
1331	A452	6.50k Hot dog	3.00	1.90
1332	A452	9.50k Fish	4.50	3.75

Contemporary Art Type of 1998

Designs: 5.50k, Telepathy, by Anna Fro Vodder, vert. 6.50k, Home Again, by Kaspar Bonnén, vert. 7.50k, Unrest, by John Korner, vert. 12.50k, Palace in the Morning, by Tal Rosenzweig.

Perf. 13x12½, 12½x13

2005, Aug. 24			Litho.	
1333	A401	5.50k multi	2.40	2.40
1334	A401	6.50k multi	2.75	2.75
1335	A401	7.50k multi	3.00	3.00
1336	A401	12.50k multi	6.00	6.00
	Nos. 1333-1336 (4)		14.15	14.15

INDEX:2005 Intl. Design Exhibition, Copenhagen — A453

2005, Aug. 24		Engr.	Perf. 13¼	
1337	A453	4.50k black	1.75	1.25
	Complete booklet, 10 #1337		17.50	

Wavy Lines Type of 1905-17

2005-08			Engr.	Perf. 12¾
1338	A10	25o indigo	.25	.25
a.	Booklet pane, 2 each #1295, 1338 ('06)		4.00	—
	Complete booklet, #1338a		4.00	
1339	A10	50o brown	.25	.25
1340	A10	100o bright blue	.35	.25
1341	A10	200o dark green	.70	.25
1342	A10	450o green	1.60	.65
1342A	A10	500o brt yel grn	2.25	.65
	Nos. 1338-1342A (6)		5.40	2.30

Wavy Line stamps, cent.

Issued: Nos. 1338-1342, 10/28/05. No. 1338a, 1/2/06. No. 1342A, 3/27/08.

Seals — A454

Designs: 4.50k, Phoca vitulina. 5.50k, Halichoerus grypus.

2005, Nov. 11		Engr.	Perf. 13x13¼	
1343	A454	4.50k multi	1.75	1.25
	Complete booklet, 10 #1343		17.50	
1344	A454	5.50k indigo	2.00	1.50
a.	Souvenir sheet, #1343-1344		4.00	4.00

Flowers — A455

Designs: 4.75k, Calanthus nivalis. 5.50k, Eranthis hyemalis. 7k, Crocus vernus hybrid. 8k, Anemone nemorosa.

2006, Jan. 11		Engr.	Perf. 12¾	
1345	A455	4.75k multi	1.60	.90
	Complete booklet, 10 #1345		16.00	
a.	Sheet of 8 + central label		15.00	—
1346	A455	5.50k multi	1.75	1.75
	Complete booklet, 10 #1346		17.50	
a.	Sheet of 8 + central label		17.00	—
1347	A455	7k multi	2.25	2.25
1348	A455	8k multi	2.50	2.50
	Nos. 1345-1348 (4)		8.10	7.40

Creatures in Norse Mythology — A456

Designs: 4.75k, Elf king and elf girls. 7k, Incubi, werewolves, hel-horse, gnome and troll.

Litho. & Engr.

2006, Mar. 29			Perf. 13¼x13	
1349	A456	4.75k multi	1.60	1.60
1350	A456	7k multi	2.40	2.40
a.	Souvenir sheet, #1349-1350		4.50	7.00

Rosenborg Castle, 400th Anniv. — A457

Designs: 4.75k, Castle exterior. 5.50k, Silver lion, thrones of king and queen. 13k, Royal coat of arms ceiling decoration.

2006, Mar. 29				
1351	A457	4.75k multi	1.60	1.60
	Complete booklet, 10 #1351		16.00	
1352	A457	5.50k multi	2.00	2.00
1353	A457	13k multi	4.50	4.50
	Nos. 1351-1353 (3)		8.10	8.10

A spiral-bound booklet, enclosed in a slipcase, with four booklet panes containing single stamps of Nos. 1351-1353 and a booklet pane containing a strip of Nos. 1351-1353, sold for 99k. Value, $35.

New Carlsberg Glyptotek, Cent. — A458

Designs: 4.75k, Marble relief from Athenian graveyard. 5.50k, Conservatory dome. 8k, Dancer Looking at the Sole of Her Right Foot, sculpture by Edgar Degas.

2006, June 7				
1354	A458	4.75k multi	1.60	1.60
	Complete booklet, 10 #1354		16.00	
1355	A458	5.50k multi	2.00	2.00
1356	A458	8k multi	2.75	2.75
a.	Souvenir sheet, #1354-1356		6.50	6.50
	Nos. 1354-1356 (3)		6.35	6.35

Race Cars — A459

Designs: 4.75k, 1958 Alfa Dana Midget, Swebe Jap. 5.50k, 1965 Austin Mini Cooper S, 1965 Ford Cortina GT, 1965 Alfa Romeo 1600 GTA. 10k, 1963 Jaguar E Type, 1967 Volvo P 1800. 17k, 1965 Lotus Elan, Renault Alpine A 110.

2006, June 7			Perf. 13x13¼	
1357	A459	4.75k multi	1.75	1.75
	Complete booklet, 10 #1357		17.50	
1358	A459	5.50k multi	2.00	2.00
	Complete booklet, 10 #1358		20.00	
1359	A459	10k multi	3.75	3.75
1360	A459	17k multi	6.00	6.00
	Nos. 1357-1360 (4)		13.50	13.50

Europa — A460

Winning designs in children's stamp design contest: 4.75k, Smiling children, by Rikke Veber Rasmussen. 7k, Two smiling children, by Anette Bertram Nielsen.

2006, Aug. 23		Litho.	Perf. 13¼x13	
1361	A460	4.75k multi	1.90	.90
	Booklet, 10 #1361		19.00	
1362	A460	7k blk & dull grn	2.75	1.25

Airplanes — A461

Designs: 4.50k, J. C. H. Ellehammer's 1906 biplane. 4.75k, KZ II, 1946. 5.50k, KZ IV, 1944. 13k, KZ VII, 1947.

Litho. & Engr.

2006, Aug. 23			Perf. 12¾	
1363	A461	4.50k multi	1.75	1.75
1364	A461	4.75k multi	1.75	1.75
a.	Miniature sheet of 8 + central label		14.00	14.00
1365	A461	5.50k multi	2.00	2.00
a.	Miniature sheet of 8 + central label		16.00	16.00
1366	A461	13k multi	4.50	4.50
	Nos. 1363-1366 (4)		10.00	10.00

Paintings by COBRA Group Artists — A462

Designs: 4.75k, Untitled, by Asger Jorn. 5.50k, Landscape of the Night, by Else Alfelt, vert. 7k, New Skin, by Pierre Alechinsky. 8k, The Olive Eater, by Egill Jacobsen, vert.

Perf. 13x13¼, 13¼x13

2006, Nov. 10			Litho.	
1367	A462	4.75k multi	1.75	1.75
	Booklet, 10 #1367		17.50	
1368	A462	5.50k multi	2.00	2.00
1369	A462	7k multi	2.75	2.75
1370	A462	8k multi	3.00	3.00
	Nos. 1367-1370 (4)		9.50	9.50

See Belgium Nos. 2168-2169.

Danish Soldiers in United Nations Peacekeeping Forces, 50th Anniv. — A463

Litho. & Engr.

2007, Jan. 10			Perf. 13	
1371	A463	4.75k multi	1.75	1.75

Intl. Polar Year — A464

Designs: 7.25k, Wooden and walrus tusk carvings of Norse, Late Dorset and Thule cultures of Greenland. 13.50k, Research airplane used for measuring thickness of polar ice.

2007, Jan. 10			Perf. 13¼	
1372	A464	7.25k multi	2.50	2.50
1373	A464	13.50k multi	4.75	4.75
a.	Souvenir sheet, #1372-1373		5.00	5.00

Windmills — A465

Designs: 4.50k, Askov Mill, 1891. 4.75k, Gedser Mil, 1957. 6k, Bogo Mill, 1989. 8.25k, Middelgrunden, 2000.

2007, Jan. 10			Engr.	
1374	A465	4.50k brown	1.75	1.75
1375	A465	4.75k red	1.75	1.75
	Complete booklet, 10 #1375		17.50	
a.	Sheet of 8 + central label		15.00	15.00
1376	A465	6k green	2.00	2.00
	Complete booklet, 10 #1376		20.00	
a.	Sheet of 8 + central label		19.00	19.00
1377	A465	8.25k blue	3.00	3.00
	Nos. 1374-1377 (4)		8.50	8.50

DENMARK

Galathea 3 Scientific Expedition — A466

Satellite, ship and: 4.75k, Marine life. 7.25k, Globe showing route of expedition.

Litho. & Engr.

2007, Mar. 28			Perf. 12¾	
1378	A466	4.75k multi	1.75	1.75
1379	A466	7.25k multi	2.50	2.50
a.		Souvenir sheet, #1378-1379	4.50	4.50

National Museum, Bicent. — A467

Designs: 4.75k, Ceremonial axes. 6k, Funen aquaemanale. 8.25k, Armillary sphere. 10.25k, Wooden mask, Borneo.

2007, Mar. 28			Perf. 13¼	
1380	A467	4.75k Prus bl & blk	1.75	1.75
		Complete booklet, 10 #1380	17.50	
1381	A467	6k brn lake & blk	2.00	2.00
1382	A467	8.25k orange & blk	3.00	3.00
1383	A467	10.25k bl gray, blk & org	3.75	3.75
		Nos. 1380-1383 (4)	10.50	10.50

A spiral-bound booklet, enclosed in a slipcase, with four booklet panes containing single stamps of Nos. 1380-1383 and a booklet pane containing a strip of Nos. 1380-1383, sold for 109k. Value, $40.

Europa — A468

Scouts: 4.75k, On hike. 7.25k, Around campfire.

2007, June 6			Perf. 13x13¼	
1384	A468	4.75k multi	1.75	1.76
		Complete booklet, 10 #1384	17.50	
1385	A468	7.25k multi	2.75	2.75

Scouting, cent.

Modern Art — A469

Designs: 4.75k, The Traveler, by Arne Haugen Sorensen. 8.25k, Trionfale, by Seppo Mattinen.

2007, June 6	Litho.		Perf. 13x12½	
1386	A469	4.75k multi	1.75	1.60
a.		Miniature sheet of 8 + central label	15.00	15.00
1387	A469	8.25k multi	3.00	2.50

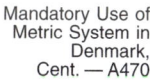

Mandatory Use of Metric System in Denmark, Cent. — A470

Litho. & Engr.

2007, Aug. 22			Perf. 12¾	
1388	A470	4.75k black & red	1.90	.85

Nature of Denmark — A471

Flora and fauna of Rabjerg Dune: 4.75k, Niobe fritillary butterfly (klitperlemorsommerfugl). 6k, Northern dune tiger beetle (sandspringer). 7.25k, Sand lizard (markfirben). 13.50k, Seaside pansy (klitstedmoderblomst).

2007, Aug. 22				
1389	A471	4.75k multi	1.75	.70
		Complete booklet, 10 #1389	17.50	
1390	A471	6k multi	2.25	.90
		Complete booklet, 10 #1390	22.50	
1391	A471	7.25k multi	2.75	1.00
1392	A471	13.50k multi	5.00	1.75
a.		Souvenir sheet, #1389-1392	12.50	12.50
		Nos. 1389-1392 (4)	11.75	4.35

Famous Men — A472

Designs: 4.75k, Poul Henningsen (1894-1967), designer, and Artichoke lamp. 6k, Victor Borge (1909-2000), comedian, and piano keys. 7.25k, Arne Jacobsen (1902-71), architect, and Egg chair. 8.25k, Piet Hein (1905-96), inventor, and superellipse.

2007, Nov. 8	Engr.		Perf. 12¾	
1393	A472	4.75k multi	1.75	.85
		Complete booklet, 10 #1393	17.50	
1394	A472	6k blk & blue	2.00	1.00
1395	A472	7.25k multi	2.75	1.25
1396	A472	8.25k blk & purple	0.00	1.00
		Nos. 1393-1396 (4)	9.50	4.70

See Nos. 1412-1415, 1502-1505.

Danish National Theater — A473

Designs: 5.50k, Old Stage. 6.50k, Playhouse. 7.75k, Copenhagen Opera House.

Litho. & Engr.

2008, Jan. 9			Perf. 13x13¼	
1397	A473	5.50k multi	2.25	1.10
		Complete booklet, 10 #1397	22.50	
a.		Sheet of 8 + central label	19.00	
1398	A473	6.50k multi	2.60	1.25
		Complete booklet, 10 #1398	26.00	
1399	A473	7.75k multi	3.25	1.60
		Nos. 1397-1399 (3)	0.10	0.95

Royal Life Guards, 350th Anniv. — A474

Guards in: 5.50k, Red dress uniforms. 10k, Camouflage uniforms.

Litho. & Engr.

2008, Mar. 27			Perf. 13¼x13	
1400	A474	5.50k multi	2.50	1.25
		Complete booklet, 10 #1400	25.00	
1401	A474	10k multi	4.50	2.10
a.		Souvenir sheet, #1400-1401	7.00	7.00

Nordic Mythology A475

Places associated with mythology: 5.50k, Lindholm Hoje burial grounds. 7.75k, Feggeklit.

2008, Mar. 27		Litho.		
1402	A475	5.50k black	2.40	1.25
1403	A475	7.75k black	3.25	1.60
a.		Souvenir sheet, #1402-1403	6.00	6.00

Europa — A476

Designs: 5.50k, Boy writing letter. 7.75k, Girl reading letter.

2008, June 4	Litho.		Perf. 13	
1404	A476	5.50k multi	2.40	1.25
		Complete booklet, 10 #1404	24.00	
1405	A476	7.75k multi	3.25	1.60

Allotment Gardens — A477

Designs: 5.50k, Man tending Hjelm Allotment Association garden. 6.50k, Men sitting in Vennelyst Allotment Association garden.

Litho. & Engr.

2008, June 4			Perf. 13x13¼	
1406	A477	5.50k multi	2.40	1.25
		Complete booklet, 10 #1406	24.00	
a.		Miniature sheet of 8 + central label	20.00	
1407	A477	6.50k multi	2.75	1.40
a.		Miniature sheet of 8 + central label	23.00	

Louisiana Museum of Art, Humlebaek, 50th Anniv. — A478

Designs: 5.50k, Original Museum building, Figures in Landscape, by Roy Lichtenstein, I Am in You, by Doug Aitken. 7.75k, I Am in You, glass corridor, A Closer Grand Canyon, by David Hockney. 8.75k, Reclining Figure No. 5, by Henry Moore, Walking Man, by Alberto Giacometti, Big Head, by Giacometti, Slender Ribs, by Alexander Calder. 16k, Slender Ribs, people in concert hall, Untitled, by Sam Francis, seat designed by Poul Kjaerholm.

2008, June 4				
1408	A478	5.50k multi	2.40	1.25
1409	A478	7.75k multi	3.25	1.60
a.		Booklet pane, #1408-1409	8.00	
1410	A478	8.75k multi	3.75	1.90
1411	A478	16k multi	6.75	3.50
a.		Booklet pane, #1410-1411	14.50	
b.		Booklet pane, #1408-1411	22.00	
c.		Horiz. strip of 4, #1408-1411	19.00	19.00
		Complete booklet, #1409a, 1411a, 1411b	50.00	
		Nos. 1408-1411 (4)	16.15	8.25

Complete booklet sold for 102.40k.

Famous Men Type of 2007

Designs: 5k, Halfdan Rasmussen (1915-2002), poet, and line from poem. 5.50k, Erik Balling (1924-2005), film and television director, and actors in movie. 6.50k, Bodil Kjer (1917-2003), actress. 10k, Niels-Henning Orsted Pedersen (1946-2005), jazz musician, and bass.

2008, Aug. 27	Engr.		Perf. 12¾	
1412	A472	5k blk & claret	2.40	.90
1413	A472	5.50k multi	2.75	1.10
		Complete booklet, 10 #1413	27.50	
1414	A472	6.50k multi	3.25	1.10
		Complete booklet, 10 #1414	32.50	
1415	A472	10k multi	4.60	1.75
		Nos. 1412-1415 (4)	12.90	4.85

Art Photography A479

Designs: 5.50k, Trappe, by Viggo Rivad. 7.75k, Berlin, by Krass Clement, horiz.

2008, Aug. 27	Litho.		Perf. 13x12¾	
1416	A479	5.50k black	2.50	2.00
		Perf. 12¾x13		
1417	A479	7.75k black	3.25	2.50

Winter Berries and Flowers — A480

Designs: 5.50k, Ilex aquifolium berries. 6.50k, Helleborus niger flower. 7.75k, Taxus baccata berries. 8.75k, Symphoricarpos rivularis berries.

Litho. & Engr.

2008, Nov. 7			Perf. 13	
1418	A480	5.50k multi	1.90	.95
		Complete booklet, 10 #1418	19.00	
a.		Booklet pane of 4	7.75	—
1419	A480	6.50k multi	2.25	1.10
1420	A480	7.75k multi	2.75	1.40
1421	A480	8.75k multi	3.00	1.50
a.		Souvenir sheet, #1418-1421	10.00	5.00
b.		Booklet pane of 4, #1418-1421	10.00	—
		Complete booklet, #1418a, 1421b	18.00	
		Nos. 1418-1421 (1)	0.00	1.05

No. 1421b is No. 1421a sewn into the booklet.

COP15 Climate Change Conference, Copenhagen A481

Designs: 5.50k, Bioenergy. 9k, Low-energy building.

2009, Jan. 7	Engr.		Perf. 13x13¼	
1422	A481	5.50k dark blue	2.00	1.00
1423	A481	9k dark blue	3.25	1.75

Old Town Open-Air Museum, Aarhus, Cent. — A482

Designs: 5.50k, Mintmaster's Mansion, drummer. 6.50k, Mayor's House, woman in period costume. 8k, Museum of Clocks and Watches and Danish Poster Museum, painter. 10.50k, Steps to Kerteminde School, farm hand.

Litho. & Engr.

2009, Jan. 7			Perf. 13x13¼	
1424	A482	5.50k multi	2.00	1.00
		Complete booklet, 10 #1424	20.00	
1425	A482	6.50k multi	2.40	1.25
		Complete booklet, 10 #1425	24.00	
1426	A482	8k multi	3.00	1.50
1427	A482	10.50k multi	3.75	1.90
a.		Souvenir sheet, #1424-1427	11.00	11.00
		Nos. 1424-1427 (4)	11.15	5.65

Europa — A483

Designs: 5.50k, Round Tower, Copenhagen. 8k, Tycho Brahe Planetarium.

2009, Mar. 25	Litho.		Perf. 13¼	
1428	A483	5.50k multi	2.00	.95
		Complete booklet, 10 #1428	20.00	
1429	A483	8k multi	3.25	1.40

Flora and Fauna — A484

Designs: 5k, Anacamptus pyramidalis. 5.50k, Falco peregrinus. 8k, Zygaena purpuralis. 17k, Tooth of Mosasaurus lemonnieri.

2009, Mar. 25   Litho.   Perf. 12¾

1430	A484	5k multi	1.90	.85
1431	A484	5.50k multi	2.40	.95
		Complete booklet, 10 #1431	24.00	
a.		Miniature sheet of 8 + central label	17.00	17.00
1432	A484	8k multi	3.00	1.40
1433	A484	17k multi	6.75	3.00
		Souvenir sheet, #1430-1433	13.50	13.50
		Nos. 1430-1433 (4)	14.05	6.20

Copenhagen Zoo, 150th Anniv. — A485

Designs: 5.50k, Zoo Tower, rhinoceros. 6.50k, Elephants. 8k, Red-eyed tree frog, flamingos. 9k, Tiger python, golden lion tamarin.

2009, June 10   Litho.   Perf. 13¼x13

1434	A485	5.50k multi	2.10	1.10
		Complete booklet, 10 #1434	21.00	
a.		Miniature sheet of 8 + central label	17.00	17.00
1435	A485	6.50k multi	2.50	1.25
a.		Miniature sheet of 8 + central label	20.00	20.00
b.		Booklet pane of 2, #1434-1435	8.00	—
1436	A485	8k multi	3.00	1.50
1437	A485	9k multi	3.50	1.75
a.		Booklet pane of 2, #1436-1437	12.00	—
b.		Booklet pane of 4, #1434-1437	20.00	—
		Complete booklet, #1435b, 1437a, 1437b	40.00	
		Nos. 1434-1437 (4)	11.10	5.60

Complete booklet containing Nos. 1435b, 1437a, 1437b sold for 109k.

Historic Maps — A486

Maps of Denmark by: 5.50k, Royal Danish Academy of Sciences and Letters, 1841. 6.50k, Johannes Mejer, 1650. 12k, Marcus Jordan, 1585. 18k, Abraham Ortelius, 1570.

2009, July 15   Litho.   Perf. 12½

1438	A486	5.50k multi	2.10	1.10

Size: 41x24mm

Perf. 12¾

1439	A486	6.50k multi	2.50	1.25
1440	A486	12k multi	4.75	2.40
1441	A486	18k multi	7.00	3.50
		Nos. 1438-1441 (4)	16.35	8.25

Intl. Conference on the History of Cartography, Copenhagen.

Metropolitanskolen, 800th Anniv. — A487

Designs: 5.50k, Author Hans Scherfig as boy and Metropolitanskolen building, Copenhagen. 6.50k, Two students and current school building, Norrebro.

2009, Sept. 9   Engr.   Perf. 13x13¼

1442	A487	5.50k red & black	2.25	1.10
1443	A487	6.50k black & grn	2.60	1.40

COP15, United Nations Climate Conference, Copenhagen A488

Designs: 5.50k, Fuel cell technology. 8k, Wind turbine.

2009, Sept. 9

1444	A488	5.50k dark blue	2.25	1.10
		Complete booklet, 10 #1444	22.00	
1445	A488	8k dark blue	3.25	1.60

Modern Art — A489

Designs: 5.50k, Houses in Motion, by Jes Fomsgaard. 12k, Garlic, by Karin Birgitte Lund, vert.

2009   Litho.   Perf. 12¾x13

1446	A489	5.50k multi	2.25	1.10
a.		Sheet of 8 + central label	18.00	18.00

Perf. 12½x12¾

1447	A489	12k multi	5.00	2.40

Issued: 5.50k, 9/9; 12k, 10/27.

Children Playing in Snow A490

Designs: 5.50k, Child rolling snow into large ball, snowman. 6.50k, Child in snow, child sledding. 8k, Child throwing snowball at two children. 9k, Two children making snow angels.

2009, Oct. 27   Litho.   Perf. 12½x12¾

1448	A490	Sheet of 4	12.50	12.50
a.		5.50k multi	2.25	1.10
b.		6.50k multi	2.60	1.40
c.		8k multi	3.25	1.60
d.		9k multi	3.75	1.90

Self-Adhesive
Die Cut Perf. 13x13½

1449	A490	5.50k multi	2.40	1.10
a.		Booklet pane of 12	29.00	
1450	A490	6.50k multi	2.75	1.40
a.		Booklet pane of 12	33.00	
1451	A490	8k multi	3.25	1.60
1452	A490	9k multi	3.75	1.90
a.		Sheet of 8, 2 each #1449-1452	25.00	
		Nos. 1449-1452 (4)	12.15	6.00

Nos. 1449a and 1450a each exist with six different booklet covers.

Flora and Fauna — A491

Designs: 8.50k, Bufo calamita. 9.50k, Lycaena phlaeas. 12.50k, Alauda arvensis. 18.50k, Astragalus danicus.

2010, Jan. 2   Litho.   Perf. 12¼

1453		Souvenir sheet of 4	19.00	19.00
a.	A491	8.50k multi	3.25	1.60
b.	A491	9.50k multi	3.50	1.75
c.	A491	12.50k multi	4.75	2.40
d.	A491	18.50k multi	7.00	3.50

Self-Adhesive
Die Cut Perf. 13x13½

1454	A491	8.50k multi	3.25	1.60
1455	A491	9.50k multi	3.50	1.75
1456	A491	12.50k multi	5.00	2.40
1457	A491	18.50k multi	7.00	3.50
		Nos. 1454-1457 (4)	18.75	9.25

Queen Margrethe II — A492

Die Cut Perf. 13
2010, Feb. 10   Litho. & Engr.
Self-Adhesive
Panel Color

1458	A492	5.50k red	2.25	1.00
1459	A492	6.50k Prus blue	2.60	1.40
a.		Booklet pane of 10	26.00	

1460	A492	8.50k yel green	3.25	1.60
1461	A492	9.50k dark blue	3.75	1.75
a.		Miniature sheet of 8, 2 each #1458-1461	25.00	
		Nos. 1458-1461 (4)	11.85	5.60

No. 1458 was issued in coils as well as sheets. Every fifth coil stamp has a control number printed on the backing paper.
No. 1461a sold for 99k. See Nos. 1516-1519, 1574-1575, 1619-1620, 1635, 1665-1666, 1697-1700.
Issued: No. 1459a, 1/2/14.

Queen Margrethe II and Family — A493

Die Cut Perf. 13¼
2010, Mar. 24   Litho. & Engr.
Self-Adhesive

1462	A493	5.50k multi	2.25	2.00
a.		Booklet pane of 12	27.00	

Queen Margrethe II, 70th birthday.

Ribe, 1300th Anniv. — A494

Designs: 5.50k, Ribe Cathedral. 6.50k, Statue of Queen Dagmar.

2010, Mar. 24   Engr.

1463	A494	5.50k black	2.25	1.00
1464	A494	6.50k black	2.40	1.25
a.		Booklet pane of 12	29.00	
b.		Miniature sheet of 6, 3 each #1463-1464	16.00	

Nordic Coastlines — A495

Designs: 5.50k, Ship at Lindo Shipyard. 8.50k, Crane, Port of Aarhus.

Perf. 12¼x12½

2010, Mar. 24   Litho.

1465		Sheet of 2	5.50	6.00
a.	A495	5.50k multi	2.00	1.00
b.	A495	8.50k multi	3.25	1.60

Self-Adhesive
Die Cut Perf. 13¼

1466	A495	5.50k multi	2.00	1.00
1467	A495	8.50k multi	3.25	1.60

Wavy Lines Type of 1905 and Small State Seal Type of 1946

2010   Engr.   Die Cut Perf. 13
Self-Adhesive

1468	A10	50o brown	.25	.25
1469	A10	100o blue	.40	.25
1470	A10	200o dark green	.75	.25
1471	A10	300o orange	1.20	.25
1472	A10	400o purple	1.60	.35
1473	A10	500o green	1.90	.45
1474	A55	10k lemon	3.75	.80
1475	A55	15k blue	5.50	1.25
1476	A55	20k dark blue	7.50	1.60
1477	A55	30k red brown	11.50	2.75
1478	A55	50k red	18.00	4.00
		Nos. 1468-1478 (11)	52.35	12.20

Issued: 50o, 100o, 200o, 5000o, 4/28; 300o, 400o, 30k, 3/24; 10k, 15k, 20k, 50k, 6/1.
Nos. 1474, 1476, 1478 were reissued in slightly different shades Mar. 10, 2014. No. 1476 was reissued Dec. 17, 2015. No. 1478 was reissued Oct. 1, 2016 in a pinker shade.

Album Cover for Gasolin' 3, by Gasolin' — A496

Die Cut Perf. 13½x13¼
2010, Apr. 28   Litho.
Self-Adhesive

1479	A496	5.50k multi	2.25	1.50
a.		Booklet pane of 12	27.00	
b.		Sheet of 4	19.00	15.00

Klampenborg Racetrack, Cent. — A497

Designs: 5.50k, Horses at finish line. 24k, Spectators watching race.

2010, June 1   Self-Adhesive

1480	A497	5.50k multi	2.25	1.10
1481	A497	24k multi	9.25	4.50

Europa — A498

Children's book characters: 5.50k, Sporge-Jorgen. 8.50k, Orla Fro-Snapper, horiz.

Die Cut Perf. 13¼x13½
2010, June 1   Self-Adhesive

1482	A498	5.50k multi	2.10	1.00
a.		Sheet of 8	18.00	

Die Cut Perf. 13½x13¼

1483	A498	8.50k multi	3.25	2.00

Booklet Stamp
Serpentine Die Cut 13½

1484	A498	5.50k multi	8.00	3.50
a.		Booklet pane of 12	96.00	
b.		Serpentine Die Cut 10	8.00	3.50
c.		Booklet pane of 12 #1484b	96.00	

Royal Danish Navy, 500th Anniv. — A499

Designs: 5.50k, Frigate Iver Huitfeldt. 6.50k, Artillery ship Niels Iuel. 8.50k, Ironclad warship Todenskjold. 9.50k, Screw frigate Jylland. 16k, Caravel Maria.

Die Cut Perf. 13¼x13
2010, June 1   Litho. & Engr.
Self-Adhesive (#1485-1489, 1491-1495)

1485	A499	5.50k red & black	2.00	.90
1486	A499	6.50k red & black	2.50	1.10
a.		Booklet pane of 12	25.00	
1487	A499	8.50k red & black	3.25	1.40
1488	A499	9.50k red & black	4.00	1.60
1489	A499	16k red & black	6.25	2.60
		Nos. 1485-1489 (5)	18.00	7.60

Booklet Stamps
Perf. 12¼x12½

1490		Booklet pane of 5	30.00	—
a.		A499 5.50k red & black	3.00	2.60
b.		A499 6.50k red & black	3.75	3.00
c.		A499 8.50k red & black	5.25	4.25
d.		A499 9.50k red & black	5.75	4.75
e.		A499 16k red & black	9.50	7.75

Booklet Panes of 1
Serpentine Die Cut 13¼x13½

1491	A499	5.50k red & black	3.25	2.75
1492	A499	6.50k red & black	4.00	3.50
1493	A499	8.50k red & black	5.50	4.50
1494	A499	9.50k red & black	6.25	5.00
1495	A499	16k red & black	10.00	8.00
		Complete booklet, #1490-1495	60.00	
		Nos. 1491-1495 (5)	29.00	23.75

Complete booklet sold for 139k.

Greetings A500

Die Cut Perf. 13x13¼
2010, June 1   Litho.
Self-Adhesive

1496	A500	5.50k Heart	2.25	.90
1497	A500	5.50k Danish Flag	2.25	.90
1498	A500	5.50k "Tillykke"	2.25	.90

DENMARK

1499	A500	5.50k Gift	2.25	.90
1500	A500	5.50k Flower	2.25	.90
a.		Sheet of 10, 2 each #1496-1500	22.50	
		Nos. 1496-1500 (5)	11.25	4.50

The right third of Nos. 1496-1500 has straight-edged die cutting. See Nos. 1552-1556.

A501

A502

A503

A504

A505

A506

A507

A508

A509

Post Danmark Rundt Bicycle Race — A510

2010, Aug. 4   **Die Cut Perf. 13x13¼**

1501		Sheet of 10	65.00	
a.	A501	5.50k multi	6.50	3.25
b.	A502	5.50k multi	6.50	3.25
c.	A503	5.50k multi	6.50	3.25
d.	A504	5.50k multi	6.50	3.25
e.	A505	5.50k multi	6.50	3.25
f.	A506	5.50k multi	6.50	3.25
g.	A507	5.50k multi	6.50	3.25
h.	A508	5.50k multi	6.50	3.25
i.	A509	5.50k multi	6.50	3.25
j.	A510	5.50k multi	6.50	3.25

The right third of Nos. 1501a-1501j has straight-edged die cutting.

Famous Men Type of 2007

Designs: 5.50k, Dan Turèll (1946-93), writer, and lines from poem. 6.50k, Tove Ditlevsen (1917-76), poet, and her childhood home. 9.50k, Henry Heerup (1907-93), and "Love in the Coffee Pot." 12.50k, Dea Trier Morch (1941-2001), writer and artist, and illustation from her novel, *Winter's Child*.

Die Cut Perf. 13½x12¾
2010, Aug. 25   **Litho. & Engr.**
Self-Adhesive

1502	A472	5.50k multi	2.25	.80
a.		Souvenir sheet of 8	17.50	
b.		Booklet pane of 12	27.50	
1503	A472	6.50k multi	2.50	1.10
1504	A472	9.50k multi	3.50	1.60
1505	A472	12.50k multi	5.00	3.25
		Nos. 1502-1505 (4)	13.25	6.75

Art — A511

Designs: 5.50k, Two Roses, by Inge Ellegaard. 18.50k, Night Flower, by Kirstine Roepstorff, vert.

Die Cut Perf. 13¼x13½
2010, Aug. 25   **Litho.**
Self-Adhesive

1506	A511	5.50k multi	2.25	1.50

Die Cut Perf. 13½x13¼

1507	A511	18.50k multi	7.25	5.00

Small State Seal Type of 1946

Die Cut Perf. 13
2010, Oct. 26   **Engr.**
With Diagonal Engraving Lines

1508	A55	25k green	9.50	4.75

"Winter Tales" — A512

Designs: 5.50k, Woman on park bench, ducks. 6.50k, Woman on park bench hugging snowman. 8.50k, Woman kissing snowman. 12.50k, Snowman coming to life, dog.

2010, Oct. 26   **Litho.**   **Perf. 12¼x13**

1509		Sheet of 4	13.00	6.50
a.	A512	5.50k multi	2.10	1.10
b.	A512	6.50k multi	2.50	1.25
c.	A512	8.50k multi	3.25	1.60
d.	A512	12.50k multi	4.75	2.40

Self-Adhesive
Die Cut Perf. 13¼

1510	A512	5.50k multi	2.10	1.10
1511	A512	6.50k multi	2.50	1.25
1512	A512	8.50k multi	3.25	1.60
1513	A512	12.50k multi	4.75	2.40
a.		Sheet of 8, #1511-1513, 5 #1510	21.00	
		Nos. 1510-1513 (4)	12.60	6.35

Booklet Stamps
Serpentine Die Cut 13½

1514	A512	5.50k multi	5.00	5.00
a.		Booklet pane of 12	60.00	
1515	A512	6.50k multi	5.00	5.00
a.		Booklet pane of 12	60.00	

Queen Margrethe II Type of 2010

Die Cut Perf. 13
2011, Mar. 9   **Litho. & Engr.**
Self-Adhesive
Panel Color

1516	A492	6k Prus blue	2.50	1.10
1517	A492	8k red	3.25	1.50
a.		With "Postnord" printer inscription at LL		
1518	A492	9k yel green	3.75	1.75
1519	A492	11k dark blue	4.50	2.10
		Nos. 1516-1519 (4)	14.00	6.45

Issued: No. 1517a, 12/1/15. Nos. 1516 and 1517 were issued in coils as well as sheets. Every fifth coil stamp has a control number printed on the backing paper.

Art — A513

Designs: 8k, Untitled (for Karl Pichert), by Claus Carstensen. 13k, Det Her Sted (This Place), by Lise Harlev.

Die Cut Perf. 13½x13¼
2011, Mar. 23   **Litho. & Engr.**
Self-Adhesive

1520	A513	8k sil & black	3.25	1.60

Litho.

1521	A513	13k multi	5.00	2.50

Supreme Court, 350th Anniv. — A514

Designs: 6k, Supreme Court decree of King Frederik III, 1661. 8k, Court and judges.

Litho. & Engr.
2011, Mar. 23   **Perf. 13x12½**

1522		Sheet of 2	5.75	6.25
a.		A514 6k multi	2.40	2.40
b.		A514 8k multi	3.25	1.60

Self-Adhesive
Die Cut Perf. 13x13½

1523	A514	6k multi	2.40	1.25
1524	A514	8k multi	3.25	1.00

Camping — A515

Designs: 6k, Man wearing t-shirt and shorts in front of trailer. 8k, Garden gnome in front of trailer.

Die Cut Perf. 13x13¼
2011, Mar. 23   **Litho.**
Self-Adhesive

1525	A515	6k multi	2.50	1.25
1526	A515	8k multi	3.25	1.60

Serpentine Die Cut 13½

1527	A515	6k multi	2.50	1.25
a.		Booklet pane of 12	30.00	
1528	A515	8k multi	3.25	1.60
a.		Booklet pane of 12	39.00	
b.		Pair, #1527-1528	5.75	
		Nos. 1525-1528 (4)	11.50	5.70

Nos. 1527-1528 were printed in sheets of 8 containing four of each stamp. Sheet sold for 56k.

Europa — A516

Designs: 8k, Caterpillar on branch in spring. 11k, Squirrel, tree in autumn.

2011, May 4   **Die Cut Perf. 13x13¼**
Self-Adhesive

1529	A516	8k multi	3.25	1.60
1530	A516	11k multi	4.25	2.10

Booklet Stamp
Serpentine Die Cut 13½

1531	A516	8k multi	3.25	3.00
a.		Booklet pane of 12	39.00	

Intl. Year of Forests.

Manor Houses — A517

Designs: No. 1532, Norre Vosborg, near Holstebro. No. 1533, Voergaard Castle, Vendsyssel. No. 1534, Englesholm Castle, near Vejle. No. 1535, Gammel Estrup, near Randers.

Die Cut Perf. 13¼x13
2011, May 4   **Litho. & Engr.**
Self-Adhesive

1532	A517	6k multi	2.40	1.25
1533	A517	6k multi	2.40	1.25
1534	A517	8k multi	3.25	1.60
1535	A517	8k multi	3.25	1.60
		Nos. 1532-1535 (4)	11.30	5.70

Arabian Expedition of Carsten Niebuhr, 250th Anniv. — A518

Compass rose and: 8k, Niebuhr (1733-1815), explorer. 13k, Horse-drawn grain mill from Egypt.

2011, May 4   **Die Cut Perf. 13x13¼**
Self-Adhesive

1536	A518	8k multi	3.50	1.60
1537	A518	13k multi	5.25	2.50
a.		Souvenir sheet of 2, #1536-1537, + label	8.75	

Booklet Stamp
Serpentine Die Cut 13½

1538	A518	8k multi	3.25	1.60
a.		Booklet pane of 12	39.00	

Paddle Steamer SS Hjejlen, 150th Anniv. — A519

2011, June 8   **Die Cut Perf. 13**
Self-Adhesive

1539	A519	8k multi	3.50	1.60
a.		Miniature sheet of 6	21.00	

Children's Television Characters — A520

Designs: 6k, Bruno the Bear and French fries. 8k, Bamse the Bear and balloons.

Die Cut Perf. 13¼x13
2011, June 8   **Litho.**
Self-Adhesive

1540	A520	6k multi	2.50	1.25
a.		Miniature sheet of 6	15.00	
1541	A520	8k multi	3.50	1.60
a.		Miniature sheet of 6	21.00	

Booklet Stamps
Serpentine Die Cut 13½

1542	A520	6k multi	2.50	2.00
a.		Booklet pane of 10 + 10 etiquettes	25.00	
1543	A520	8k multi	3.50	3.00
a.		Booklet pane of 12	35.00	

Summer Flowers — A521

Designs: 2k, Papaver rhoeas. 6k, Geranium. 8k, Astrantia major. 10k, Papaver nudicaule.

2011, June 8   **Perf. 12x12¾**

1544		Miniature sheet of 4	11.00	11.00
a.	A521	2k multi	.80	.40
b.	A521	6k multi	2.40	1.25
c.	A521	8k multi	3.25	1.60
d.	A521	10k multi	4.00	2.00

Self-Adhesive
Die Cut Perf. 13x13¼

1545	A521	2k multi	.80	.40
1546	A521	6k multi	2.40	1.25
1547	A521	8k multi	3.25	1.60
1548	A521	10k multi	4.00	2.00
		Nos. 1545-1548 (4)	10.45	5.25

Booklet Stamp
Serpentine Die Cut 13½

1549	A521	6k multi	2.50	2.25
a.		Booklet pane of 10 + 10 etiquettes	25.00	

DENMARK

Sketch of Woman's Clothing Designed by Malene Birger — A522

Fashion Accessories Designed by Silas Adler — A523

Die Cut Perf. 13x13¼
2011, Aug. 4 Litho. & Engr.
Self-Adhesive
1550	A522	6k black	2.40	1.25
1551	A523	8k multi	3.25	1.60
a.	Souvenir sheet of 2, #1550-1551		5.75	

Greetings Type of 2010
Die Cut Perf. 13x13¼
2011, Aug. 4 Litho.
Self-Adhesive
1552	A500	8k Heart	3.25	1.60
1553	A500	8k Danish Flag	3.25	1.60
1554	A500	8k "Tillykke"	3.25	1.60
1555	A500	8k Open envelope	3.25	1.60
1556	A500	8k Flower	3.25	1.60
a.	Sheet of 10, 2 each #1552-1556		32.50	
	Nos. 1552-1556 (5)		16.25	8.00

The right third of Nos. 1552-1556 has straight-edged die cutting.

International Cycling Union Road World Championships, Denmark — A524

2011, Aug. 4 **Die Cut Perf. 13x13¼**
Self-Adhesive
| 1557 | A524 | 8k multi | 3.25 | 1.60 |
| a. | Souvenir sheet of 6 | | 19.50 | |

Copenhagen Central Railway Station, Cent. — A525

People and: 6k, Station's front. 8k, Clock. 9k, Arches. 16k, Train at platform.

2011, Sept. 10 Litho. & Engr. **Perf. 13x12¼**
Booklet Stamps (#1558-1561, 1566)
1558	A525	6k multi	6.00	6.00
1559	A525	8k multi	6.00	6.00
a.	Booklet pane of 2, #1558-1559		12.00	—
1560	A525	9k multi	9.00	9.00
1561	A525	16k multi	9.00	9.00
a.	Booklet pane of 4, #1558-1561		30.00	—
b.	Booklet pane of 2, #1560-1561		18.00	—
	Complete booklet, #1559a, 1561a, 1561b		60.00	
	Nos. 1558-1561 (4)		30.00	30.00

Self-Adhesive
Die Cut Perf. 13¼x13
1562	A525	6k multi	2.25	1.25
1563	A525	8k multi	3.00	1.75
1564	A525	9k multi	3.50	2.00
1565	A525	16k multi	6.00	3.00
	Nos. 1562-1565 (4)		14.75	8.00

Serpentine Die Cut 13½
| 1566 | A525 | 8k multi | 3.25 | 3.00 |
| a. | Booklet pane of 12 | | 39.00 | |

The complete booklet sold for 139k.

People in Winter — A526

Designs: 6k, Bathing Viking. 8k, Woman feeding duck. 11k, Man walking dog. 13k, Ice fisherman.

2011, Oct. 25 Litho. **Perf. 12¼**
1567	Sheet of 4		15.00	7.50
a.	A526 6k multi		2.40	1.25
b.	A526 8k multi		3.00	1.75
c.	A526 11k multi		4.25	2.90
d.	A526 13k multi		5.00	3.25

Self-Adhesive
Die Cut Perf. 13x13¼
1568	A526	6k multi	2.40	1.25
1569	A526	8k multi	3.00	1.75
1570	A526	11k multi	4.25	2.90
1571	A526	13k multi	5.00	3.25
	Nos. 1568-1571 (4)		14.65	9.15

Booklet Stamps
Serpentine Die Cut 13½
1572	A526	6k multi	2.50	2.25
a.	Booklet pane of 10 + 10 etiquettes		25.00	
1573	A526	8k multi	3.50	3.25
a.	Booklet pane of 12		42.50	

Queen Margrethe II Type of 2010
Die Cut Perf. 13
2012, Jan. 2 Litho. & Engr.
Self-Adhesive
Panel Color
| 1574 | A492 12k purple | 4.50 | 3.75 |
| 1575 | A492 14k black | 5.25 | 2.90 |

Armillary Spheres — A527

Designs: No. 1576, Equatorial armillary sphere built by Tycho Brahe, 1595. No. 1577, Simplified armillary sphere built by Guo Shoujing, 1276.

Die Cut Perf. 13¾
2012, Jan. 4 Litho. & Engr.
Self-Adhesive
| 1576 | A527 6k multi | 2.50 | 1.50 |
| 1577 | A527 6k multi | 2.50 | 1.50 |

See People's Republic of China Nos. 3980-3981.

Reign of Queen Margrethe II, 40th Anniv. — A528

2012, Jan. 4 **Perf. 13½**
Souvenir Sheet
| 1578 | A528 8k multi | 3.00 | 3.00 |

Self-Adhesive
Die Cut Perf. 13¼x13½
| 1579 | A528 8k multi | 3.00 | 3.00 |

Bridges — A529

Designs: 6k, Queen Alexandrine Bridge. 8k, Faro Bridge.

2012, Jan. 4 Litho. **Perf. 13¼**
Souvenir Sheet
1580	Sheet of 2		8.25	8.25
a.	A529 6k multi		3.00	2.00
b.	A529 8k multi		5.00	3.00

Self-Adhesive
Die Cut Perf. 13¼
| 1581 | A529 6k multi | 2.10 | 1.40 |
| 1582 | A529 8k multi | 3.25 | 2.00 |

Booklet Stamps
Serpentine Die Cut 13½
1583	A529 6k multi	2.10	1.40
a.	Booklet pane of 10 + 10 etiquettes		21.00	
1584	A529 8k multi	3.25	2.00
a.	Booklet pane of 10 + 10 etiquettes		32.50	

Nordia 2012 Stamp Exhibition, Roskilde.

Europa A530

2012, Mar. 21 **Perf. 14**
Souvenir Sheet
| 1585 | A530 12k multi | 4.50 | 4.50 |

Self-Adhesive
Die Cut Perf. 14
| 1586 | A530 12k multi | 4.50 | 2.75 |

No. 1586 was printed in sheets of 30.

Sea Rescue A531

Designs: 6k, Helicopter and rescue boat. 11k, Helicopter over Copenhagen University Hospital helipad.

2012, Mar. 21 **Perf. 13½x13¼**
Souvenir Sheet
1587	A531 Sheet of 2		6.50	6.50
a.	6k multi		2.40	1.60
b.	11k multi		4.00	2.40

Self-Adhesive
Die Cut Perf. 13½x13¼
| 1588 | A531 6k multi | 2.40 | 1.60 |
| 1589 | A531 11k multi | 4.00 | 2.40 |

Scenes From Tales by Hans Christian Andersen — A532

Designs: 2k, The Shepherdess and the Chimney Sweep. 3k, The Nightingale. 6k, The Wild Swans. 8k, What the Old Man Does Is Always Right.

Die Cut Perf. 13½x13¼
2012, June 1 Litho. & Engr.
Self-Adhesive
1590	A532 2k multi	1.10	.70
1591	A532 3k multi	1.00	1.00
1592	A532 6k multi	2.10	1.40
1593	A532 8k multi	2.75	1.75
	Nos. 1590-1593 (4)	6.95	4.85

Booklet Stamps
Serpentine Die Cut 13½x13¼
1594	A532 6k multi	2.25	1.50
a.	Booklet pane of 10 + 10 etiquettes	22.50	
1595	A532 8k multi	3.00	1.75
a.	Booklet pane of 10 + sticker	30.00	

Sandwiches
A533 A534

Designs: Nos. 1596, 1600, 1604, Egg and shrimp sandwich. Nos. 1597, 1601, 1605, Rolled sausage sandwich. 8k, Potato sandwich. 16k, Roast beef sandwich.

2012, June 1 Litho. **Perf. 13x13¼**
Booklet Stamps
1596	A533 6k multi	4.00	4.00
a.	Booklet pane of 1	4.00	
1597	A534 6k multi	4.00	4.00
a.	Booklet pane of 1	4.00	
1598	A534 8k multi	5.25	5.25
a.	Booklet pane of 1	5.25	
1599	A534 16k multi	10.50	10.50
a.	Booklet pane of 1	10.50	—
b.	Booklet pane of 1 #1596-1599	24.00	—
	Complete booklet, #1596a, 1597a, 1598a, 1599a, 1599b	48.00	
	Nos. 1596-1599 (4)	23.75	23.75

Self-Adhesive
Die Cut Perf. 13x13¼
1600	A533 6k multi	2.00	1.00
1601	A534 6k multi	2.00	1.00
1602	A534 8k multi	2.75	1.40
1603	A534 16k multi	5.50	2.75
	Nos. 1600-1603 (4)	12.25	6.15

Serpentine Die Cut 13½
1604	A534 6k multi	2.10	1.10
1605	A534 6k multi	2.10	1.10
a.	Booklet pane of 10, 5 each #1604-1605 + 10 etiquettes	20.00	
1606	A534 8k multi	2.90	1.75
a.	Booklet pane of 10	27.50	
	Nos. 1604-1606 (3)	7.10	3.95

Complete booklet sold for 139k. Nos. 1604-1606 weree printed in a sheet of 8 containing 3 each nos. 1604-1605 and 2 No. 1606.

Portrait of Johanne Luise Heiberg, by Emilius Baerentzen A535

Die Cut Perf. 14x13¾
2012, Sept. 5 Litho. & Engr.
| 1607 | A535 8k multi | 3.00 | 1.75 |

Heiberg (1812-90), theater actress and director.

Flowers — A536

Designs: 8k, Saponaria officinalis. 12k, Centaurea scabiosa. 14k, Leontodon autumnalis.

Die Cut Perf. 13x13½
2012, Sept. 5 Litho.
Self-Adhesive
1608	A536 8k multi	3.00	1.75
1609	A536 12k multi	4.50	2.40
1610	A536 14k multi	5.25	3.75
	Nos. 1608-1610 (3)	12.75	7.90

Booklet Stamp
Serpentine Die Cut 13½
| 1611 | A536 8k multi | 3.00 | 2.50 |
| a. | Booklet pane of 10 | 30.00 | |

Copenhagen Central Post Office, Cent. — A537

2012, Sept. 12 Engr. **Perf. 13x13¼**
| 1612 | A537 8k dark red | 3.00 | 3.00 |

Post Scriptum, by Christian Vind — A538

Die Cut Perf. 14x13¾
2012, Nov. 2 Litho. & Engr.
Self-Adhesive
| 1613 | A538 16k blk & yel org | 5.75 | 4.00 |

DENMARK

Tree in Winter — A539

Tree and: 6k, Bird and musical notes. 8k, Birdhouse, bird. 12k, Moon, bird on branch of bush.

Die Cut Perf. 13x13¼
2012, Nov. 2 Litho. Self-Adhesive
1614	A539	6k blue	2.10	1.10
1615	A539	8k dull blue	2.90	1.75
1616	A539	12k blue	4.25	3.50
	Nos. 1614-1616 (3)		9.25	6.35

Booklet Stamps
Serpentine Die Cut 13½
1617	A539	6k blue	2.10	1.10
a.	Booklet pane of 10 + 10 etiquettes		21.00	
1618	A539	8k dull blue	2.90	1.75
a.	Booklet pane of 10		29.00	

Queen Margrethe II Type of 2010
Self-Adhesive
Die Cut Perf. 13
Litho. & Engr.
2013, Jan. 2 Panel Color
1619	A492	12.50k purple	4.75	2.75
1620	A492	14.50k dark gray	5.25	2.75

Kaj and Andrea — A540
Mr. Beard — A541

Die Cut Perf. 13½x13¼
2013, Jan. 7 Self-Adhesive Litho.
1621	A540	8k multi	3.00	2.50
a.	Sheet of 6		18.00	15.00

Die Cut Perf. 13¼x13½
1622	A541	8k multi	3.00	2.50

Booklet Stamps
Serpentine Die Cut 13½
1623	A540	8k multi	3.00	2.50
1624	A541	8k multi	3.00	2.50
a.	Booklet pane of 10, 5 each #1623-1624		30.00	

Characters on children's television programs.

Fish — A542

Designs: 6k, Clupea harengus. 8k, Gadus morhua. 12.50k, Platichthys flesus. 14.50k, Anguilla anguilla.

Booklet Stamps (#1625-1628, 1633-1634)
2013, Jan. 7 Litho. Perf. 13
1625	A542	6k multi	3.50	3.50
a.	Booklet pane of 1		3.50	—
1626	A542	8k multi	5.00	5.00
a.	Booklet pane of 1		5.00	
1627	A542	12.50k multi	7.50	7.50
a.	Booklet pane of 1		7.50	
1628	A542	14.50k multi	9.00	9.00
a.	Booklet pane of 1		9.00	
b.	Booklet pane of 4, #1625-1628		25.00	—
	Complete booklet #1625a, 1626a, 1627a, 1628a, 1628b		50.00	
	Nos. 1625-1628 (4)		25.00	25.00

Self-Adhesive
Die Cut Perf. 13
1629	A542	6k multi	2.25	1.20
1630	A542	8k multi	3.00	1.75
1631	A542	12.50k multi	4.50	3.75
1632	A542	14.50k multi	5.25	3.75
	Nos. 1629-1632 (4)		15.00	10.45

Serpentine Die Cut 13¼
1633	A542	6k multi	2.25	1.20
a.	Booklet pane of 10 + 10 etiquettes		22.50	
1634	A542	8k multi	3.00	1.75
a.	Booklet pane of 10		30.00	

Complete booklet sold for 139k.

Queen Margrethe II Type of 2010
Die Cut Perf. 13
2013, Mar. 4 Litho. & Engr.
Self-Adhesive Panel Color
1635	A492	16k orange	6.00	5.00
a.	With "Postnord" printer inscription at LL ('16)		—	—

Soren Kierkegaard (1813-55), Philosopher — A543

2013, Mar. 4 Die Cut Perf. 13¼x13
1636	A543	8k multi	3.00	2.50

Electric Postal Bicycle, Europa — A544

2013, Mar. 4 Perf. 13½x13
Souvenir Sheet
1637	A544	12.50k multi	4.75	3.00

Self-Adhesive
Die Cut Perf. 13¼x13
1638	A544	12.50k multi	4.75	2.25

Manor Houses — A545

Designs: Nos. 1639, 1641, Egeskov Castle. Nos. 1640, 1642, Valdemar's Castle.

2013, Mar. 4 Die Cut Perf. 13¼x13
Self-Adhesive
1639	A545	8k multi	3.00	2.50
1640	A545	8k multi	3.00	2.50

Booklet Stamps
Serpentine Die Cut 13½
1641	A545	8k multi	3.00	2.50
1642	A545	8k multi	3.00	2.50
a.	Booklet pane of 10, 5 each #1641-1642		30.00	

The Little Mermaid Statue, Copenhagen, Cent. — A546

Litho. & Engr.
2013, May 27 Perf. 13½x13
Souvenir Sheet
1643	A546	14.50k multi	5.25	5.25

Self-Adhesive
Die Cut Perf. 13¼x13
1644	A546	14.50k multi	5.25	4.50

Danish Rock Music — A547

Designs: Nos. 1645, 1647, Crowd at rock concert. Nos. 1646, 1648, Electric guitar of Kasper Eistrup.

Die Cut Perf. 13¼x13
2013, May 27 Litho.
Self-Adhesive
1645	A547	8k multi	3.00	1.75
1646	A547	8k multi	3.00	1.75

Serpentine Die Cut 13½
1647	A547	8k multi	3.00	1.75
1648	A547	8k multi	3.00	1.75
a.	Booklet pane of 10, 5 each #1647-1648		30.00	
	Nos. 1645-1648 (4)		12.00	7.00

Nos. 1647-1648 were printed in sheets containing 3 of each stamp.

Culture Yard, Elsinore A548

Designs: 8k, Wing of building and reflecting pond. 12.50k, Building entrance and reflecting pond.

2013, Aug. 29 Litho. Perf. 13x13¼
Souvenir Sheet
1649	A548	Sheet of 2	7.50	4.50
a.	8k multi		3.00	1.75
b.	12.50k multi		4.50	2.75

Self-Adhesive
Die Cut Perf. 13x13¼
1650	A548	8k multi	3.00	1.75
1651	A548	12.50k multi	4.50	2.75

Fifth INDEX: Intl. Design award ceremonies, Elsinore.

Best Wishes, by Jytte Hoy — A549

Die Cut Perf. 13¼x13½
2013, Sept. 2 Litho. & Engr.
Self-Adhesive
1652	A549	8k multi	3.00	1.75

Scenes from Stories by Hans Christian Andersen — A550

Scenes from: 6k, The Tinderbox. 8k, The Flying Trunk. 12.50k, The Sweethearts (The Top and the Ball). 14.50k, The Little Match Girl.

Die Cut Perf. 13¼x13
2013, Sept. 2 Litho. & Engr.
Self-Adhesive
1653	A550	6k multi	2.25	1.50
a.	Booklet pane of 10 + 10 etiquettes		22.50	
1654	A550	8k multi	3.00	1.75
a.	Booklet pane of 10		30.00	
1655	A550	12.50k multi	4.50	3.00
1656	A550	14.50k multi	5.25	3.75
	Nos. 1653-1656 (4)		15.00	10.00

Christmas — A551

Designs: 6k, Christmas rose. 8k, Skating girl. 12.50k, Robins.

2013, Oct. 29 Litho. Perf. 13x12¾
Souvenir Sheet
1657		Sheet of 3	9.75	9.75
a.	A551	6k multi	2.25	1.20
b.	A551	8k multi	3.00	1.75
c.	A551	12.50k multi	4.50	3.75

Self-Adhesive
Die Cut Perf. 13x13¼
1658	A551	6k multi	2.25	1.20
1659	A551	8k multi	3.00	1.75
1660	A551	12.50k multi	4.50	3.00
	Nos. 1658-1660 (3)		9.75	5.95

Booklet Stamps
Serpentine Die Cut 13½
1661	A551	6k multi	2.25	1.20
a.	Booklet pane of 10 + 10 etiquettes		22.50	
1662	A551	8k multi	3.00	1.75
a.	Booklet pane of 10		30.00	

Trade Treaty Between Denmark and France, 350th Anniv. — A552

Map and compass rose with ship at: 8k, Right. 12.50k, Left.

Die Cut Perf. 13½x13¼
2013, Nov. 7 Litho. & Engr.
Self-Adhesive
1663	A552	8k rose & blue	3.00	1.75
1664	A552	12.50k blue & rose	4.50	2.75

See France Nos. 4526-4527.

Queen Margrethe II Type of 2010
Die Cut Perf. 13
2014, Jan. 2 Litho. & Engr.
Self-Adhesive Panel Color
1665	A492	9k red	3.75	2.50
a.	Booklet pane of 10		37.50	
1666	A492	18k blue	7.50	4.50
a.	Booklet pane of 10		75.00	

Nordic Cuisine — A553

Aebleflaesk: 6.50k, Raw ingredients (Pig and apples). 14k, Finished dish.

Die Cut Perf. 13½x13
2014, Jan. 2 Litho.
Self-Adhesive
1667	A553	6.50k multi	2.50	1.50
a.	Booklet pane of 10		25.00	
1668	A553	14k multi	5.25	2.60

Flowers — A554

Designs: No. 1669, Fritillaria meleagris. No. 1670, Muscari botryoides.

Die Cut Perf. 13¾
2014, Jan. 2 Litho.
Self-Adhesive
1669	A554	9k multi	3.50	1.75
1670	A554	9k multi	3.50	1.75
a.	Horiz. pair, #1669-1670 on backing paper without printing		7.00	
b.	Booklet pane of 10, 5 each #1669-1670		35.00	

Nos. 1669 and 1670 were printed in sheets of 6 containing 3 of each stamp.

PH Grand Piano — A555

Die Cut Perf. 13½x13
2014, Mar. 15 Litho. & Engr.
Self-Adhesive
1671	A555	14k multi	5.25	3.75

Europa.

156 DENMARK

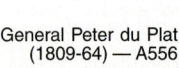
General Peter du Plat (1809-64) — A556

Prussian Soldiers at Battle of Dybbol A557

Litho. & Engr.
2014, Mar. 15   Perf. 13x12¾
Souvenir Sheet
1672	Sheet of 2 + label	10.50	10.50
a.	A556 9k multi	3.50	1.75
b.	A557 18k multi	6.75	3.50

Self-Adhesive
Die Cut Perf. 13½
| 1673 | A556 | 9k multi | 3.50 | 1.75 |
| a. | Booklet pane of 10 | | 35.00 | |

Die Cut Perf. 13x13½
| 1674 | A557 | 18k multi | 6.75 | 3.50 |

Battle of Dybbol, 150th anniv.

Chairs — A558

Designs: 6.50k, Three-legged shell chair, designed by Hans J. Wegner (1914-2007). 16k, Spanish chair, designed by Borge Mogensen (1914-72).

Die Cut Perf. 13½x13
2014, Mar. 15   Litho. & Engr.
Self-Adhesive
1675	A558 6.50k org & gray	2.40	1.50
a.	Booklet pane of 10	24.00	
1676	A558 16k brn & lt brn	6.00	3.00
a.	Booklet pane of 5	30.00	

A booklet containing perf. 13½x13 stamps with water-activated gum having designs identical to Nos. 1675 and 1676 sold for 139k. The booklet contained a pane containing one example of the 6.50k, another containing one example of the 16k, and another containing one example each of the 6.50k and 16k.

Sailboats — A559

Designs: 6.50k, Laser Radial dinghy. 14k, Hanse 430e yacht.

Perf. 12½x12¾
2014, Mar. 17   Litho.
Souvenir Sheet
1677	Sheet of 2	7.75	7.75
a.	A559 6.50k multi	2.40	1.50
b.	A559 14k multi	5.25	2.75

Self-Adhesive
Die Cut Perf. 13x13½
1678	A559 6.50k multi	2.40	1.50
a.	Booklet pane of 10	24.00	
1679	A559 14k multi	5.25	2.60

Princess Benedikte and Scouts — A560

Die Cut Perf. 13x13½
2014, Apr. 29   Litho.
Self-Adhesive
| 1680 | A560 9k multi + label | 3.50 | 3.50 |
| a. | Booklet pane of 5 + 5 labels | 17.50 | |

Princess Benedikte, 70th birthday.

Danish School System, 200th Anniv. — A561

Die Cut Perf. 13½
2014, June 11   Litho.
Self-Adhesive
| 1681 | A561 6.50k multi | 2.40 | 1.50 |
| a. | Booklet pane of 10 | 24.00 | |

Prince Henrik, 80th Birthday — A562

Die Cut Perf. 13½
2014, June 11   Litho.
Self-Adhesive
| 1682 | A562 9k multi | 3.50 | 1.75 |
| a. | Booklet pane of 4 | 14.00 | |

Den Frie Center of Contemporary Art, Cent. — A563

Die Cut Perf. 13½
2014, June 11   Litho. & Engr.
Self-Adhesive
| 1683 | A563 9k multi | 3.50 | 1.75 |
| a. | Booklet pane of 2 | 7.00 | |

Manor Houses — A564

Designs: 6.50k, Knuthenborg. 9k, Ledreborg Palace.

Die Cut Perf. 13x13½
2014, June 11   Litho. & Engr.
Self-Adhesive
1684	A564 6.50k multi	2.40	1.25
a.	Booklet pane of 10	24.00	
1685	A564 9k multi	3.50	1.75
a.	Booklet pane of 10	35.00	

Guard Hussar Regiment, 400th Anniv. — A565

Die Cut Perf. 13½
2014, Aug. 30   Litho. & Engr.
Self-Adhesive
| 1686 | A565 6.50k multi | 2.40 | 1.25 |
| a. | Booklet pane of 10 | 24.00 | |

Blank Space for Greetings, by Olafur Eliasson A566

Serpentine Die Cut 10¼
2014, Aug. 30   Litho. & Engr.
Self-Adhesive
| 1687 | A566 9k blk & olive | 3.25 | 1.60 |
| a. | Booklet pane of 4 | 13.00 | |

The central portion of the stamp is die cut.

Characters from Stories by Hans Christian Andersen — A567

Designs: 6.50k, Klods-Hans (Clumsy Hans) and dead crow. 9k, Tommelise (Thumbelina) and toad.

Perf. 12¾x13¼
2014, Aug. 30   Litho. & Engr.
Souvenir Sheet
1688	Sheet of 2	5.75	3.00
a.	A567 6.50k multi	2.40	1.25
b.	A567 9k multi	3.25	1.60

Self-Adhesive
Die Cut Perf. 13½x13
1689	A567 6.50k multi	2.40	1.25
a.	Booklet pane of 10	24.00	
1690	A567 9k multi	3.25	1.60
a.	Booklet pane of 10	32.50	

Manuscripts A568

Designs: 9k, Valdemar's Law of Zealand, 13th cent. 14k, Njáls Saga, c. 1350.

Litho. & Engr.
2014, Aug. 30   Perf. 13x12¾
Souvenir Sheet
1691	Sheet of 2	8.25	4.25
a.	A568 9k multi	3.25	1.60
b.	A568 14k multi	5.00	2.50

Self-Adhesive
Die Cut Perf. 13½
1692	A568 9k multi	3.25	1.60
a.	Booklet pane of 10	32.50	
1693	A568 14k multi	5.00	2.50
a.	Booklet pane of 5	25.00	

See Iceland Nos. 1350-1352.

Berries — A569

Designs: 6.50k, Snowberries. 9k, Lingonberries. 14k, Firethorn.

Die Cut Perf. 13½x13¼
2014, Oct. 18   Litho.
Self-Adhesive
1694	A569 6.50k multi	2.25	1.10
a.	Booklet pane of 10	22.50	
1695	A569 9k multi	3.00	1.50
a.	Booklet pane of 10	30.00	
1696	A569 14k multi	4.75	2.40
a.	Booklet pane of 5	24.00	
	Nos. 1694-1696 (3)	10.00	5.00

Queen Margrethe II Type of 2010
Die Cut Perf. 13
2014, Nov. 17   Litho. & Engr.
Self-Adhesive
Panel Color
1697	A492 7k Prus blue	2.40	1.25
a.	Booklet pane of 10	24.00	
1698	A492 10k red	3.50	1.75
a.	Booklet pane of 10	35.00	
1699	A492 16.50k orange	5.50	2.75
a.	Booklet pane of 10	55.00	
1700	A492 19k blue	6.50	3.25
a.	Booklet pane of 10	65.00	
	Nos. 1697-1700 (4)	17.90	9.00

Children's Poems by Halfdan Rasmussen (1915-2002) — A570

Poems from *Halfdans ABC*: No. 1701, Bennys Bukser Braendte (Benn's Trouser's Burned). No. 1702, Kanonkongen Knold (Cannon King Knold).

Die Cut Perf. 13¾x13½
2015, Jan. 2   Litho. & Engr.
Self-Adhesive
1701	A570 7k blue & multi	2.25	1.10
1702	A570 7k dl grn & multi	2.25	1.10
a.	Booklet pane of 10, 6 #1701, 4 #1702	22.50	

Lego Blocks — A571

Blocks of various colors and: 10k, Boy. 14.50k, Girl.

Die Cut Perf. 13½x13
2015, Jan. 2   Self-Adhesive   Litho.
1703	A571 10k multi	3.25	1.60
a.	Booklet pane of 10	32.50	
b.	Sheet of 6 + 20 stickers	22.50	
1704	A571 14.50k multi	4.75	2.40
a.	Booklet pane of 10	4.75	2.40

No. 1703b sold for 70k.

Animals in Wadden Sea National Park — A572

Designs: Nos. 1705a, 1706, Texel sheep. Nos. 1705b, 1707, Black-tailed godwit, vert. Nos. 1705c, 1708, Harbor seals.

Litho. & Engr.
2015, Jan. 2   Perf. 13
| 1705 | Souvenir sheet of 3 | 9.75 | 5.00 |
| a.-c. | A572 10k Any single | 3.25 | 1.60 |

Self-Adhesive
Die Cut Perf. 13¼x13½, 13½x13½
1706	A572 10k multi	3.25	1.60
1707	A572 10k multi	3.25	1.60
1708	A572 10k multi	3.25	1.60
a.	Booklet pane of 10, 4 #1706, 6 #1708	32.50	
	Nos. 1706-1708 (3)	9.75	4.80

Herlufsholm, 450th Anniv. — A573

Die Cut Perf. 13½x13
2015, Mar. 14   Litho.
Self-Adhesive
| 1709 | A573 10k multi | 3.00 | 1.50 |
| a. | Booklet pane of 10 | 30.00 | |

Inventions — A574

Inventions: Nos. 1710a, 1711, Dry cell battery, by Wilhelm Hellesen, 1887. Nos. 1710b, 1712, Ready-mix concrete truck, by Kristian Hindhede, 1929, horiz. Nos. 1710c, 1713, Long John delivery bicycle, by Morten Rasmussen Mortensen, 1929, horiz. Nos. 1710d, 1714, Writing ball, by Rasmus Mallin-Hansen, 1867.

DENMARK

2015, Mar. 14 Litho. Perf. 13
Souvenir Sheet
| 1710 | | Sheet of 4 | 12.00 | 6.00 |
| a.-d. | A574 | 10k Any single | 3.00 | 1.50 |

Booklet Stamps
Self-Adhesive
Litho. & Engr.
Die Cut Perf. 13½x13, 13x13½
1711	A574	10k multi	3.00	1.50
1712	A574	10k multi	3.00	1.50
1713	A574	10k multi	3.00	1.50
a.		Booklet pane of 10, 6 #1713, 4 #1712	30.00	
1714	A574	10k multi	3.00	1.50
a.		Booklet pane of 10, 6 #1711, 4 #1714	30.00	
		Nos. 1711-1714 (4)	12.00	6.00

Medal of Merit — A575

Order of the Elephant — A576

Order of Dannebrog — A577

Die Cut Perf. 13½x13
2015, Mar. 14 Litho. & Engr.
Self-Adhesive
| 1715 | A575 | 7k multi | 2.10 | 1.10 |

Booklet Stamps
1716	A576	7k multi	2.10	1.10
1717	A577	7k multi	2.10	1.10
a.		Booklet pane of 10, 6 #1716, 4 #1717	21.00	
		Nos. 1715-1717 (3)	6.30	3.30

A booklet containing perforated examples of Nos. 1715-1717 (three booklet panes containing one of each stamp and one booklet pane containing all three stamps) sold for 199k.

Woman Suffrage, Cent. — A578

Die Cut Perf. 13¼
2015, June 13 Litho.
Self-Adhesive
| 1718 | A578 | 10k multi | 3.00 | 1.50 |

Samosvej 8, 2300 Kobenhaven S, Danmark, by Jesper Christiansen A579

Die Cut Perf. 13¼
2015, June 13 Litho. & Engr.
Self-Adhesive
| 1719 | A579 | 10k multi | 3.00 | 1.50 |

Copenhagen Carpenters' Guild, 500th Anniv. — A580

Die Cut Perf. 13½x13
2015, June 13 Litho. & Engr.
Self-Adhesive
| 1720 | A580 | 10k multi | 3.00 | 1.50 |
| a. | | Booklet pane of 10 | 30.00 | |

Ships A581

Designs: Nos. 1721a, 1723, Georg Stage. Nos. 1721b, 1722, Danmark. Nos. 1721c, 1724, Kobenhavn. Nos. 1721d, 1725, Fulton.

2015, June 13 Litho. Perf. 13x12¾
| 1721 | A581 | Sheet of 4 | 8.50 | 8.50 |
| a.-d. | | 7k Any single | 2.10 | 1.10 |

Self-Adhesive
Die Cut Perf. 13x13½
1722	A581	7k multi	2.10	1.10
1723	A581	7k multi	2.10	1.10
a.		Vert. pair, #1722-1723, on backing paper without printing	4.25	
1724	A581	7k multi	2.10	1.10
1725	A581	7k multi	2.10	1.10
a.		Vert. pair, #1724-1725, on backing paper without printing	4.25	
b.		Booklet pane of 10, 2 each #1723-1725, 4 #1722	21.00	
		Nos. 1722-1725 (4)	8.40	4.40

Miniature Sheet

25th Post Danmark Rundt Bicycle Race A582

No. 1726: a, Moreno Argentin. b, Jakob Fuglsang. c, Cyclists in Randers. d, Matti Breschel. e, Cyclists on Kiddesvej climb, Velje. f, Fabian Cancellara. g, Cyclists on Storebaelts Bridge. h, Cyclist on Frederiksberg Allé, Copenhagen. i, Mark Cavendish. j, Michael Valgren.

Die Cut Perf. 13x13¼ on 3 Sides
2015, June 27 Litho.
Self-Adhesive
1726	A582	Sheet of 10	25.50	
a.-e.		7k Any single	2.10	1.10
f.-j.		10k Any single	3.00	1.50

Christmas — A583

Honey cakes shaped as: Nos. 1727a, 1728, Man. Nos. 1727b, 1729, Woman. Nos. 1727c, 1730, Heart.

2015, Oct. 17 Litho. Perf. 12¾x13¼
Souvenir Sheet
1727		Sheet of 3	7.25	3.75
a. b.	A583	7k Either single	2.10	1.10
c.	A583	10k multi	3.00	1.50

Self-Adhesive
Die Cut Perf. 13½x13
1728	A583	7k multi	2.10	1.10
1729	A583	7k multi	2.10	1.10
a.		Booklet pane of 10, 6 #1728, 4 #1729	21.00	

Size: 22x32mm
Die Cut Perf. 12¼x13 Syncopated
| 1730 | A583 | 10k multi | 3.00 | 1.50 |
| | | Nos. 1728-1730 (3) | 7.20 | 3.70 |

Maribo Cathedral, 600th Anniv. — A584

2016, Jan. 4 Litho. & Engr. Perf. 13½x13
Self-Adhesive
| 1731 | A584 | 19k multi | 5.50 | 2.75 |
| a. | | Booklet pane of 10 | 55.00 | |

Nordic Food Culture A585 A586

2016, Jan. 4 Litho. Perf. 13
Souvenir Sheet
1732		Sheet of 2	4.80	2.50
a.	A585	8k multi	2.40	1.25
b.	A586	8k multi	2.40	1.25

Self-Adhesive
Die Cut Perf. 13 Syncopated
1733	A585	8k multi	2.40	1.25
a.		Booklet pane of 5	12.00	
1734	A586	8k multi	2.40	1.25
a.		Booklet pane of 5	12.00	

Souvenir Sheet

Europa A587

No. 1735: a, Hands holding Earth wrapped in leaves. b, Bicyclist, wind generators, paint roller.

2016, Mar. 31 Litho. Perf. 13
| 1735 | A587 | Sheet of 2 | 15.50 | 15.50 |
| a.-b. | | 25k Either single | 7.75 | 3.75 |

Think Green Issue.

Sports — A588

Designs: No. 1736, Runner in Lillebaelt Half Marathon. No. 1737, Cyclists in Fyen Rundt Bicycle Race. No. 1738, Cyclist in Haervejslobet Mountain Bike Race. No. 1739, Swimmer in Christiansborg Rundt Swimming Race. No. 1740, Bicycle helmet, running shoes, swimming goggles.

Die Cut Perf. 13¼ Syncopated
2016, Mar. 31 Litho.
Booklet Stamps
Self-Adhesive
1736	A588	8k multi	2.50	1.25
1737	A588	8k multi	2.50	1.25
1738	A588	8k multi	2.50	1.25
1739	A588	8k multi	2.50	1.25
1740	A588	8k multi	2.50	1.25
a.		Booklet pane of 10, 2 each #1736-1740	25.00	
		Nos. 1736-1740 (5)	12.50	6.25

Prize-Winning Animals at Agricultural Shows — A589

Designs: No. 1741, Wyandotte cockerel. No. 1742, Danish Red Holstein cow. No. 1743, Oldenburg stallion. No. 1744, Shropshire ram. No. 1745, Satin rabbit.

Die Cut Perf. 13¼ Syncopated
2016, Mar. 31 Litho.
Booklet Stamps
Self-Adhesive
1741	A589	8k multi	2.50	1.25
1742	A589	8k multi	2.50	1.25
1743	A589	8k multi	2.50	1.25
1744	A589	8k multi	2.50	1.25
1745	A589	8k multi	2.50	1.25
a.		Booklet pane of 10, 2 each #1741-1745	25.00	
		Nos. 1741-1745 (5)	12.50	6.25

Famous Men — A590

Designs: No. 1746, Maersk Mc-Kinney Moller (1913-2012), shipping magnate, and M/S Emma Maersk. No. 1747, Jorn Utzon (1918-2008), architect, and Sydney Opera House.

Die Cut Perf. 13¼ Syncopated
2016, Mar. 31 Litho. & Engr.
Booklet Stamps
Self-Adhesive
1746	A590	19k multi	6.00	3.00
1747	A590	19k multi	6.00	3.00
a.		Booklet pane of 10, 6 #1746, 4 #1747	60.00	

Souvenir Sheet

Art by Irine Sondergaard — A591

No. 1748: a, Interior #12. b, Guldnakke #16.

2016, June 23 Litho. Perf. 12½
| 1748 | A591 | Sheet of 2 | 15.00 | 15.00 |
| a.-b. | | 25k Either single | 7.50 | 3.75 |

Children's Songs — A592

Illustrations by Bitte Böcher from children's songbook *De Sma Synger*. Nos. 1749a, 1751, Den Lille Ole Med Paraplyen. Nos. 1749b, 1750, Der Sad to Katte pa et Bord. Nos. 1749c, 1753, Bro, Bro, Brille. Nos. 1749d, 1752, Mors Lille Ole.

2016, June 23 Litho. Perf. 12¾x13
| 1749 | | Sheet of 4 | 9.75 | 9.75 |
| a.-d. | A592 | 8k Any single | 2.40 | 1.25 |

Booklet Stamps
Self-Adhesive
Litho. & Engr.
Die Cut Perf. 13¼ Syncopated
1750	A592	8k blk & brt grn	2.40	1.25
1751	A592	8k blk & brt org	2.40	1.25
1752	A592	8k blk & brt grn	2.40	1.25
1753	A592	8k blk & brt org	2.40	1.25
a.		Booklet pane of 10, 2 each #1751-1753, 4 #1750	24.00	
		Nos. 1750-1753 (4)	9.60	5.00

Danish Porcelain Designs — A593

Designs: No. 1754, Magestellet (Seagull), 1892. No. 1755, Flora Danica, 1790. No. 1756, Bla Blomst Svejfet (Blue Flower Curved), 1775. No. 1757, Sort Mega Riflet (Black Fluted Mega), 2006. No. 1758, Musselmalet Halvblonde (Blue Fluted Half Lace), 1888.

Die Cut Perf. 13¼ Syncopated
2016, June 23 Litho.
Booklet Stamps
Self-Adhesive
1754	A593	8k multi	2.40	1.25
1755	A593	8k multi	2.40	1.25
1756	A593	8k multi	2.40	1.25
1757	A593	8k multi	2.40	1.25
1758	A593	8k multi	2.40	1.25
a.		Booklet pane of 10, 2 each #1754-1758	24.00	
		Nos. 1754-1758 (5)	12.00	6.25

A booklet containing 11 perf. 12¾x13¼ stamps with the designs of Nos. 1754-1758 and four perforated progressive proofs of the Flora Danica design sold for 199k.

DENMARK

Illustrations of Pixies by Peter Moller (1838-1910) — A594

Designs: No. 1759, Pixie carrying baskets of toys and balloon. No. 1760, Pixie dancing with cat. No. 1761, Dog biting pixie's cap. No. 1762, Pixies dancing and playing concertina. No. 1763, Five pixie musicians.

Die Cut Perf. 13¼ Syncopated
2016, Sept. 29   Litho.
Booklet Stamps
Self-Adhesive

1759	A594	8k multi	2.40	1.25
1760	A594	8k multi	2.40	1.25
1761	A594	8k multi	2.40	1.25
1762	A594	8k multi	2.40	1.25
1763	A594	8k multi	2.40	1.25
a.	Booklet pane of 5, #1759-1763		12.00	
	Nos. 1759-1763 (5)		12.00	6.25

Christmas.

Souvenir Sheet

Frederksborg Castle, Hillerod — A595

No. 1764 — Aerial views of: a, Baroque Gardens. b, Castle.

2017, Jan. 2   Litho.   **Perf. 13**
| 1764 | A595 | Sheet of 2 | 14.00 | 7.00 |
| a.-b. | 25k Either single | | 7.00 | 3.50 |

Shellfish — A596

Designs: No. 1765, Taskekrabbe (crab). No. 1766, Jomfruhummer (lobster). No. 1767, Nordsoreje (shrimp). No. 1768, Blamusling (mussel). No. 1769, Limfjordsosters (oyster).

Die Cut Perf. 13¾ Syncopated
2017, Jan. 2   Litho.
Booklet Stamps
Self-Adhesive

1765	A596	8k multi	2.25	1.10
1766	A596	8k multi	2.25	1.10
1767	A596	8k multi	2.25	1.10
1768	A596	8k multi	2.25	1.10
1769	A596	8k multi	2.25	1.10
a.	Booklet pane of 10, 2 each #1765-1769		22.50	
	Nos. 1765-1769 (5)		11.25	5.50

Heart With Gay Pride Flag Stripes — A597

Heart at: No. 1770, Top. No. 1771, Bottom.

Die Cut Perf. 13¼ Syncopated
2017, Mar. 30   Litho.
Booklet Stamps
Self-Adhesive

1770	A597	8k multi	2.40	2.40
1771	A597	8k multi	2.40	2.40
a.	Booklet pane of 10, 6 #1770, 4 #1771		24.00	

Aarhus, 2017 European Capital of Culture — A598

Buildings in Aarhus: No. 1772, ARoS Art Museum. No. 1773, Moesgaard Museum. No. 1774, DOKK1 Culture Center. No. 1775, The Iceberg Apartment Complex. No. 1776, City Hall.

Die Cut Perf. 13¼ Syncopated
2017, Mar. 30   Litho.
Booklet Stamps
Self-Adhesive

1772	A598	25k multi	7.25	7.25
1773	A598	25k multi	7.25	7.25
1774	A598	25k multi	7.25	7.25
1775	A598	25k multi	7.25	7.25
1776	A598	25k multi	7.25	7.25
a.	Booklet pane of 10, 2 each #1772-1776		72.50	
	Nos. 1772-1776 (5)		36.25	36.25

Souvenir Sheet

Queen Margrethe II and Prince Henrik, 50th Wedding Anniversary — A599

2017, May 15   Litho.   **Perf. 13½**
| 1777 | A599 | 50k gold & multi | 15.00 | 15.00 |

See Faroe Islands No. 686, Greenland No. 754.

 A600   A601

 A602   A603

Summer Houses — A604

Die Cut Perf. 13¼ Syncopated
2017, June 15   Litho.
Booklet Stamps
Self-Adhesive

1778	A600	8k multi	2.50	2.50
1779	A601	8k multi	2.50	2.50
1780	A602	8k multi	2.50	2.50
1781	A603	8k multi	2.50	2.50
1782	A604	8k multi	2.50	2.50
a.	Booklet pane of 10, 2 each #1778-1782		25.00	
	Nos. 1778-1782 (5)		12.50	12.50

Automobiles — A605

No. 1783: a, 1960 BMW Isetta 300. b, 1959 Volkswagen 1200 De Luxe. c, 1973 Citroen DS21 Pallas.

2017, June 15   Litho.   **Perf. 13x13¼**
1783	A605	Sheet of 3	23.50	23.50
a.-c.	25k Any single		7.75	7.75
d.	Booklet pane of 1 #1783a		15.00	—
e.	Booklet pane of 1 #1783b		15.00	—
f.	Booklet pane of 1 #1783c		15.00	—
g.	Booklet pane of 1 #1783c + 4 invalid for postage progressive proofs of #1783		15.00	—
	Complete booklet, #1783d, 1783e, 1783f, 1783g		60.00	
h.	As #1783, with Nordia 2017 emblem and text in sheet margin		23.50	23.50

Complete booklet sold for 199k. Issued: No. 1783h, 10/27.

 A606   A607

 A608   A609

Flowers — A610

Die Cut Perf. 13¼ Syncopated
2017, Sept. 28   Litho.
Booklet Stamps
Self-Adhesive

1784	A606	8k multi	2.60	2.60
1785	A607	8k multi	2.60	2.60
1786	A608	8k multi	2.60	2.60
1787	A609	8k multi	2.60	2.60
1788	A610	8k multi	2.60	2.60
a.	Booklet pane of 10, 2 each #1784-1788		26.00	
	Nos. 1784-1788 (5)		13.00	13.00

 A611   A612

 A613   A614

Art by Bjorn Wiinblad (1918-2006) — A615

Die Cut Perf. 13¼ Syncopated
2018, Jan. 2   Litho.
Booklet Stamps
Self-Adhesive

1789	A611	9k multi	3.00	3.00
1790	A612	9k multi	3.00	3.00
1791	A613	9k multi	3.00	3.00
1792	A614	9k multi	3.00	3.00
1793	A615	9k multi	3.00	3.00
a.	Booklet pane of 10, 2 each #1789-1793		30.00	
	Nos. 1789-1793 (5)		15.00	15.00

A booklet, issued on Sept. 6, 2018, containing 11 perf. 14¼ water-activated gum examples of Nos. 1789-1793 and four progressive proofs of No. 1790, sold for 199k.

Rose Varieties — A616

Designs: No. 1794, Jubilee Celebration. No. 1795, Rhapsody in Blue. No. 1796, Sekel. No. 1797, Ingrid Bergman. No. 1798, Crocus Rose.

Die Cut Perf. 13¾ Syncopated
2018, Jan. 2   Litho.
Booklet Stamps
Self-Adhesive

1794	A616	27k multi	8.75	8.75
1795	A616	27k multi	8.75	8.75
1796	A616	27k multi	8.75	8.75
1797	A616	27k multi	8.75	8.75
1798	A616	27k multi	8.75	8.75
a.	Booklet pane of 10, 2 each #1794-1798		87.50	
	Nos. 1794-1798 (5)		43.75	43.75

Souvenir Sheet

A617

No. 1799 — Stamps designed by Yoko Ono: a, Moon and "Dream." b, Sun and "Smile."

2018, Jan. 2   Litho.   **Perf. 13¼x13¾**
| 1799 | A617 | Sheet of 2 | 17.50 | 17.50 |
| a.-b. | 27k Either single | | 8.75 | 8.75 |

Souvenir Sheet

Great Belt Bridge A618

No. 1800: a, Bridge towers. b, Bridge approach.

2018, May 17   Litho.   **Perf. 13¼**
| 1800 | A618 | Sheet of 2 | 17.00 | 17.00 |
| a.-b. | 27k Either single | | 8.50 | 4.25 |

Europa.

Souvenir Sheet

Fish A619

No. 1801: a, Esox lucius (75x36mm). b, Perca fluviatilis (25x36mm).

2018, May 17   Litho.   **Perf. 13½x13¼**
| 1801 | A619 | Sheet of 2 | 17.00 | 17.00 |
| a.-b. | 27k Either single | | 8.50 | 4.25 |

Europa.

Wild Food — A620

Designs: No. 1802, Braende naelde (stinging nettles). No. 1803, Karljohan svamp (Karl Johan mushroom). No. 1804, Japansk pileurt (Japanese knotweed). No. 1805, Skvalder kal (ground elder). No. 1806, Hyben rose (rosehips).

Die Cut Perf. 13¼ Syncopated
2018, Sept. 6   Litho.
Booklet Stamps
Self-Adhesive

1802	A620	9k multi	3.00	3.00
1803	A620	9k multi	3.00	3.00
1804	A620	9k multi	3.00	3.00
1805	A620	9k multi	3.00	3.00
1806	A620	9k multi	3.00	3.00
a.	Booklet pane of 10, 2 each #1802-1806		30.00	

Lines and Hearts — A621

2019, Jan. 2   Litho.   **Die Cut Perf. 13**
Booklet Stamp
Self-Adhesive

| 1807 | A621 | 1k dark blue | .30 | .30 |
| a. | Booklet pane of 10 | | 3.00 | |

DENMARK

Thor's Hammer with Runic Inscriptions
A622

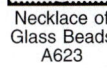
Necklace of Glass Beads
A623

Buckle in Shape of Ship
A624

Valkyrie Figurine
A625

Decorative Clip — A626

Die Cut Perf. 13¼x13½ Syncopated
2019, Jan. 2   Litho.
Booklet Stamps
Self-Adhesive

1808	A622	30k multi	9.25	9.25
1809	A623	30k multi	9.25	9.25
1810	A624	30k multi	9.25	9.25
1811	A625	30k multi	9.25	9.25
1812	A626	30k multi	9.25	9.25

a. Booklet pane of 10, 2 each #1808-1812   92.50

Nos. 1808-1812 (5)   46.25   46.25

Viking era artifacts.

Danish Flag, 800th Anniv. — A627

Flags and: Nos. 1813, 1818, Christianborg Palace Tower. Nos. 1814, 1819, Birthday cake, horiz. Nos. 1815, 1820, Soccer ball and net. Nos. 1816, 1821, Royal Yacht Dannebrog, horiz. Nos. 1817, 1822, Houses.

2019   Litho.   Perf. 13¼
Booklet Stamps

| 1813 | A627 | 10k multi | 5.50 | 5.50 |
| 1814 | A627 | 10k multi | 5.50 | 5.50 |

a. Booklet pane of 1 + 4 perforated progressive proofs   5.50   —

| 1815 | A627 | 10k multi | 5.50 | 5.50 |
| 1816 | A627 | 10k multi | 5.50 | 5.50 |

a. Booklet pane of 2, #1814, 1816   11.00   —

| 1817 | A627 | 10k multi | 5.50 | 5.50 |

a. Booklet pane of 5, #1813-1817   27.50   —
b. Booklet pane of 6, #1813, 1815, 1817   16.50
Complete booklet, #1814a, 1816a, 1817a, 1817b   61.00

Nos. 1813-1817 (5)   27.50   27.50

Self-Adhesive
Die Cut Perf. 13¼ Syncopated

| 1818 | A627 | 10k multi | 3.00 | 3.00 |

a. Coil single on translucent paper   3.00

1819	A627	10k multi	3.00	3.00
1820	A627	10k multi	3.00	3.00
1821	A627	10k multi	3.00	3.00
1822	A627	10k multi	3.00	3.00

a. Booklet pane of 10, 2 each #1818-1822   30.00

Nos. 1818-1822 (5)   15.00   15.00

Issued: Nos. 1813-1817, 5/16; Nos. 1818-1822, 1/2. Complete booklet sold for 199k.

Lighthouses — A628

Designs: No. 1823, Hammeren Lighthouse. No. 1824, Lyngvig Lighthouse. No. 1825, Hirtshals Lighthouse. No. 1826, Taksensand Lighthouse. No. 1827, Omo Lighthouse.

Die Cut Perf. 13¼x13 Syncopated
2019, May 16   Litho.
Booklet Stamps
Self-Adhesive

1823	A628	10k multi	3.00	3.00
1824	A628	10k multi	3.00	3.00
1825	A628	10k multi	3.00	3.00
1826	A628	10k multi	3.00	3.00
1827	A628	10k multi	3.00	3.00

a. Booklet pane of 10, 2 each #1823-1827   30.00

Nos. 1823-1827 (5)   15.00   15.00

Souvenir Sheet

Europa A629

No. 1828: a, Mute swans and chicks (60x40mm). b, Mute swan and chick (30x40mm).

2019, May 16   Litho.   Perf. 13¼x13

| 1828 | A629 | Sheet of 2 | 18.00 | 18.00 |

a.-b. 30k Either single   9.00   9.00

Dogs — A630

Designs: No. 1829, Labrador retriever named Audi. No. 1830, Golden retriever named Chivas. No. 1831, Smooth fox terrier named Mille. No. 1832, Icelandic sheepdogs named Pila, Gaia and Blidha. No. 1833, German shepherd named Theo.

Die Cut Perf. 13x13½ Syncopated
2019, Sept. 19   Litho.
Booklet Stamps
Self-Adhesive

1829	A630	10k multi	3.00	3.00
1830	A630	10k multi	3.00	3.00
1831	A630	10k multi	3.00	3.00
1832	A630	10k multi	3.00	3.00
1833	A630	10k multi	3.00	3.00

a. Booklet pane of 10, 2 each #1829-1833   30.00

Nos. 1829-1833 (5)   15.00   15.00

Miniature Sheet

Trying to Touch the Sun, by Morten Schelde A631

No. 1834 — Hand with country name and denomination at: a, LR. b, LL, country name on two lines. c, LL, country name on one line, palm visible. d, UL, country name on two lines. e, Left. f, LL, country name on one line, palm not visible.

2019, Sept. 19   Litho.   Perf. 13½

| 1834 | A631 | Sheet of 6 | 18.00 | 18.00 |

a.-f. 10k Any single   3.00   3.00

Mammals — A632

Designs: No. 1835, Capreolus capreolus. No. 1836, Erinaceus europaeus. No. 1837, Sciurus vulgaris. No. 1838, Muscardinus avellanarius. No. 1839, Mustela erminea.

Die Cut Perf. 13¼x13½ Syncopated
2020, Jan. 2   Litho.
Booklet Stamps
Self-Adhesive

1835	A632	10k multi	3.00	3.00
1836	A632	10k multi	3.00	3.00
1837	A632	10k multi	3.00	3.00
1838	A632	10k multi	3.00	3.00
1839	A632	10k multi	3.00	3.00

a. Booklet pane of 10, 2 each #1835-1839   30.00

Nos. 1835-1839 (5)   15.00   15.00

UNESCO World Heritage Sites in Denmark — A633

Designs: No. 1840, Par Force Hunting Landscapes in North Zealand. No. 1841, Kronborg Castle. No. 1842, Stevns Klint. No. 1843, Jelling Mounds. No. 1844, Christiansfeld.

Die Cut Perf. 13¼ Syncopated
2020, Jan. 2   Litho.
Booklet Stamps
Self-Adhesive

1840	A633	30k multi	9.00	9.00
1841	A633	30k multi	9.00	9.00
1842	A633	30k multi	9.00	9.00
1843	A633	30k multi	9.00	9.00
1844	A633	30k multi	9.00	9.00

a. Booklet pane of 10, 2 each #1840-1844   90.00

Nos. 1840-1844 (5)   45.00   45.00

See Nos. 1846-1850.

Miniature Sheet

Queen Margrethe II, 80th Birthday — A634

No. 1845: a, King Frederik IX and Princesses Margrethe, Benedikte and Anne-Marie (21x28mm). b, Princess Margrethe and Prince Consort Henrik on wedding day (21x28mm). c, Princess Margrethe and infant son, Frederik (21x28mm). d, Queen Margrethe II wearing tiara (21x28mm). e, Queen Margrethe II (42x56mm).

2020, Jan. 2   Litho.   Perf. 13x13½

| 1845 | A634 | Sheet of 5 | 21.00 | 21.00 |

a.-d. 10k Any single   3.00   3.00
e. 30k multi   9.00   9.00

UNESCO World Heritage Type of 2020

Designs: No. 1846, Par Force Hunting Landscapes in North Zealand. No. 1847, Kronborg Castle. No. 1848, Stevns Klint. No. 1849, Jelling Mounds. No. 1850, Christiansfeld.

2020, May 11   Litho.   Perf. 13¼
Booklet Stamps

| 1846 | A633 | 30k multi | 12.00 | 12.00 |
| 1847 | A633 | 30k multi | 12.00 | 12.00 |

a. Booklet pane of 2, #1846-1847   24.00

| 1848 | A633 | 30k multi | 12.00 | 12.00 |

a. Booklet pane of 1 + 4 progressive proofs   12.00

| 1849 | A633 | 30k multi | 12.00 | 12.00 |
| 1850 | A633 | 30k multi | 12.00 | 12.00 |

a. Booklet pane of 2, #1848-1850   24.00
Complete booklet, #1847a, 1848a, 1850a   60.00

Nos. 1846-1850 (5)   60.00   60.00

Complete booklet sold for 199k.

Souvenir Sheet

Europa A635

No. 1851: a, Post rider. b, Copenhagen and two ships. c, Lutheran Church, Altona Borough of Hamburg, Germany, and ship on Elbe River.

2020, May 11   Litho.   Perf. 13

| 1851 | A635 | Sheet of 3 | 21.00 | 21.00 |

a. 10k multi   3.00   3.00
b.-c. 30k Either single   9.00   9.00

Ancient Postal Routes.

Souvenir Sheet

Reunification of Denmark and Part of Schleswig, Cent. — A636

No. 1852: a, Residents of Aabenraa, 1918. b, King Christian X on horseback, 1920.

2020, May 11   Litho.   Perf. 13

| 1852 | A636 | Sheet of 2 | 18.00 | 18.00 |

a.-b. 30k Either single   9.00   9.00

"What You Write Is Yourself" A637

"Wait to Send" A638

"Spread a Little Joy" A639

"Who Do You Choose?" A640

"Control Yourself, Troll" — A641

Die Cut Perf. 13¾x13 Syncopated
2020, Sept. 16   Litho.
Booklet Stamps
Self-Adhesive

1853	A637	10k multi	3.25	3.25
1854	A638	10k multi	3.25	3.25
1855	A639	10k multi	3.25	3.25
1856	A640	10k multi	3.25	3.25
1857	A641	10k multi	3.25	3.25

a. Booklet pane of 10, 2 each #1853-1857   32.50

Nos. 1853-1857 (5)   16.25   16.25

Campaign for courteous writing.

Desserts — A642

Designs: No. 1858, Citrus cake with vanilla (citruskage med vanilje). No. 1859, Raspberry pie with pistachios (hindbaertaert). No. 1860, Chocolate cake with lime (chokoladekage med lime). No. 1861, Meringue cake with apricot and licorice (marengskager med abrikos & lakrids). No. 1862, Summer layer cake with rhubarb and strawberries (sommerlagkage).

Die Cut Perf. 13½x13 Syncopated
2021, Jan. 4   Litho.
Booklet Stamps
Self-Adhesive

1858	A642	11k multi	3.75	3.75
1859	A642	11k multi	3.75	3.75
1860	A642	11k multi	3.75	3.75
1861	A642	11k multi	3.75	3.75
1862	A642	11k multi	3.75	3.75

a. Booklet pane of 10, 2 each #1858-1862   37.50

Nos. 1858-1862 (5)   18.75   18.75

See Nos. 1873-1877.

DENMARK

Denmark's Golden Age — A643

Designs: No. 1863, Ballet dancer from *La Sylphide,* by August Bournonville (1805-79). No. 1864, Odin steam locomotive. No. 1865, Statue of Adam Oehlenschläger in Sondermarken Park. No. 1866, Acoustic pattern on vibrating plate studied by Hans Christian Oersted (1777-1851). No. 1867, Thorvaldsen Museum, Copenhagen.

Die Cut Perf. 13½x13 Syncopated
2021, Jan. 4   Litho.
Booklet Stamp Self-Adhesive

1863	A643	33k multi	11.00	11.00
1864	A643	33k multi	11.00	11.00
1865	A643	33k multi	11.00	11.00
1866	A643	33k multi	11.00	11.00
1867	A643	33k multi	11.00	11.00
a.	Booklet pane of 10, 2 each #1863-1867		110.00	
Nos. 1863-1867 (5)			55.00	55.00

Endangered Butterflies — A644

Designs: No. 1868, Boloria euphrosyne. No. 1869, Carterocephalus silvicola. No. 1870, Pengaris alcon. No. 1871, Papilio machaon. No. 1872, Lycaena hippothoe.

Die Cut Perf. 13¼x13½ Syncopated
2021, May 20   Litho.
Booklet Stamps Self-Adhesive

1868	A644	11k multi	3.75	3.75
1869	A644	11k multi	3.75	3.75
1870	A644	11k multi	3.75	3.75
1871	A644	11k multi	3.75	3.75
1872	A644	11k multi	3.75	3.75
a.	Booklet pane of 10, 2 each #1868-1872		37.50	
Nos. 1868-1872 (5)			18.75	18.75

Europa (Nos. 1868-1869).

Desserts Type of 2021

Designs: No. 1873, Summer layer cake with rhubarb and strawberries (sommerlagkage). No. 1874, Meringue cakes with apricot and licorice (marengskager med abrikos & lakrids). No. 1875, Raspberry pie with pistachios (hindbaertaert). No. 1876, Chocolate cake with lime (chokoladekage med lime). No. 1877, Citrus cake with vanilla (citruskage med vanilje).

2021, May 20   Litho.   Perf. 13¼
Booklet Stamps

1873	A642	11k multi	6.50	6.50
a.	Booklet pane of 1 + 4 progressive proofs		6.50	—
1874	A642	11k multi	6.50	6.50
1875	A642	11k multi	6.50	6.50
a.	Booklet pane of 2, #1874-1875		13.00	—
1876	A642	11k multi	6.50	6.50
1877	A642	11k multi	6.50	6.50
a.	Booklet pane of 2, #1876-1877		13.00	—
b.	Booklet pane of 5, #1873-1877		32.50	—
	Complete booklet, #1873a, 1875a, 1877a, 1877b		65.00	—
Nos. 1873-1877 (5)			32.50	32.50

Complete booklet sold for 199k.

Miniature Sheet

The Olsen Gang in Jutland, 50th Anniv. of Movie's Premiere A645

No. 1878: a, Egon Olsen carrying shovels (24x30mm). b, Egon, Benny Fransen and Kjell Jensen drinking beer (48x30mm). c, Benny, Egon and Kjell on beach (48x30mm). d, Kjell and Benny with shovels (24x30mm).

2021, May 20   Litho.   Perf. 13¼

| 1878 | A645 | Sheet of 4 | 14.50 | 14.50 |
| a.-d. | 11k Any single | | 3.50 | 3.50 |

Souvenir Sheet

Czeslaw Slania (1921-2005), Engraver of Postage Stamps — A646

No. 1879 — Color of portrait: a, Deep blue green. b, Dark blue.

2021, Aug. 12   Litho. & Engr.   Perf. 13¾x13¼

| 1879 | A646 | Sheet of 2 | 21.00 | 21.00 |
| a.-b. | 33k Either single | | 10.50 | 10.50 |

See Faroe Islands No. 788, Greenland No. 874.

Everyday Heroes — A647

Designs: No. 1880, Mikkel Madsen, boy who raised funds for children affected by COVID-19 with can and bottle deposit money. No. 1881, Nancy Maati, community volunteer organizer for Christmas projects. No. 1882, Leif Framke, rescuer of drowning child. No. 1883, Luni Smil, hospital clown. No. 1884, Villy Ronn, volunteer for local organizations.

Die Cut Perf. 13¼ Syncopated
2021, Sept. 16   Litho.
Booklet Stamps Self-Adhesive

1880	A647	11k multi	3.50	3.50
1881	A647	11k multi	3.50	3.50
1882	A647	11k multi	3.50	3.50
1883	A647	11k multi	3.50	3.50
1884	A647	11k multi	3.50	3.50
a.	Booklet pane of 10, 2 each #1880-1884		35.00	
Nos. 1880-1884 (5)			17.50	17.50

Souvenir Sheet

Reign of Queen Margrethe II, 50th Anniv. — A648

No. 1885: a, Queen Margrethe II (facing right) in 1972. b, Royal coat of arms. c, Queen Margrethe II (facing left) in 2022.

2022, Jan. 3   Litho.   Perf. 14

| 1885 | A648 | Sheet of 3 | 11.50 | 11.50 |
| a.-c. | 12k Any single | | 3.75 | 3.75 |

"Every Bird Sings With Its Beak" A649

"Many Small Streams Make a Big One" A650

"First Come First Served" A651

"When the Cat is Out, the Mice Play on the Table" A652

"Once Bitten, Twice Shy" — A653

Die Cut Perf. 13¾x13 Syncopated
2022, Jan. 3   Litho.
Booklet Stamps Self-Adhesive

1886	A649	12k multi	3.75	3.75
1887	A650	12k multi	3.75	3.75
1888	A651	12k multi	3.75	3.75
1889	A652	12k multi	3.75	3.75
1890	A653	12k multi	3.75	3.75
a.	Booklet pane of 10, 2 each #1886-1890		37.50	
Nos. 1886-1890 (5)			18.75	18.75

Danish proverbs.

Danish Astronomical and Space Achievements — A654

Designs: No. 1891, Supernova of 1572 seen by Tycho Brahe (1546-1601). No. 1892, 1676 observations of eclipses of Jupiter's moon Io and first determination of the speed of light, by Ole Romer (1644-1710). No. 1893, Brorfelde Astronomical Observatory. No. 1894, Andreas Mogensen, first Danish astronaut, 2015. No. 1895, Mars 2020 Mission.

Die Cut Perf. 13¼x13¾ Syncopated
2022, Jan. 3   Litho.
Booklet Stamps Self-Adhesive

1891	A654	36k sil & multi	11.00	11.00
1892	A654	36k sil & multi	11.00	11.00
1893	A654	36k sil & multi	11.00	11.00
1894	A654	36k sil & multi	11.00	11.00
1895	A654	36k sil & multi	11.00	11.00
a.	Booklet pane of 10, 2 each #1891-1895		110.00	
Nos. 1891-1895 (5)			55.00	55.00

Souvenir Sheet

Legend of Bonavedde and the Subterraneans — A655

No. 1896: a, Mermaid with Bonavedde in womb (24x30mm). b, Ellestingeren, King of the Subterraneans on horse (24x30mm). c, Mound of the Subterraneans (48x30mm).

2022, May 19   Litho.   Perf. 13¼x13

1896	A655	Sheet of 3	17.50	17.50
a.-b.	12k Either single		3.50	3.50
c.	36k multi		10.50	10.50

Europa (No. 1896c).

Famous Women — A656

Designs: No. 1897, Nielsine Nielsen (1850-1916), physician. No. 1898, Anne Marie Carl Nielsen (1863-1945), sculptor. No. 1899, Karen Volf (1864-1946), commercial baker. No. 1900, Nina Bang (1866-1928), education minister. No. 1901, Inge Lehmann (1888-1993), seismologist. No. 1902, Bodil Begtrup (1903-87), diplomat. No. 1903, Lis Hartel (1921-2009), Olympic silver medalist in dressage. No. 1904, Inger Christensen (1935-2009), writer. No. 1905, Tine Bryld (1939-2011), writer and radio personality. No. 1906, Natasja Saad (1974-2007), musician.

Die Cut Perf. 13½x13 Syncopated
2022, May 19   Litho.
Booklet Stamps Self-Adhesive

1897	A656	12k multi	3.50	3.50
1898	A656	12k multi	3.50	3.50
1899	A656	12k multi	3.50	3.50
1900	A656	12k multi	3.50	3.50
1901	A656	12k multi	3.50	3.50
1902	A656	12k multi	3.50	3.50
1903	A656	12k multi	3.50	3.50
1904	A656	12k multi	3.50	3.50
1905	A656	12k multi	3.50	3.50
1906	A656	12k multi	3.50	3.50
a.	Booklet pane of 10, #1897-1906		35.00	
Nos. 1897-1906 (10)			35.00	35.00

Miniature Sheet

Danish Theater, 300th Anniv. A657

No. 1907: a, Theater exterior, seats, stage, curtain, pianist, emblem for rock band Gasolin. b, Stage, drawn curtain, actors, and male dancer. c, Male and female dancers, 1722 poster for a performance, theater exterior. d, Actor in *Jeppe paa Bjerget* (Jeppe on the Hill), dancer wearing neck ruff, and theater backdrop.

Perf. 13¼x13¾
2022, Sept. 21   Litho.

| 1907 | A657 | Sheet of 4 | 13.00 | 13.00 |
| a.-d. | 12k Any single | | 3.25 | 3.25 |

Worldwide Fund for Nature (WWF) — A658

Endangered species: No. 1908, Kongeorn (Golden eagles). No. 1909, Snaebel (Houting). No. 1910, Isfugl (Kingfisher). No. 1911, Eremit (Hermit beetle). No. 1912, Marsvin (Porpoise).

Die Cut Perf. 13¼ Syncopated
2022, Sept. 21   Litho.
Booklet Stamps Self-Adhesive

1908	A658	12k multi	3.25	3.25
1909	A658	12k multi	3.25	3.25
1910	A658	12k multi	3.25	3.25
1911	A658	12k multi	3.25	3.25
1912	A658	12k multi	3.25	3.25
a.	Booklet pane of 10, 2 each #1908-1912		32.50	
Nos. 1908-1912 (5)			16.25	16.25

Miniature Sheet

Restored Buildings A659

No. 1913: a, Kornerup Town Hall, Vordingborg. b, Bindesboll Town Hall, Thisted. c, Kochs Courthouse, Store Heddinge. d, Meldahl Town Hall, Courthouse and Jail, Fredericia.

2023, Jan. 2   Litho.   Perf. 13¼

| 1913 | A659 | Sheet of 4 | 14.00 | 14.00 |
| a.-d. | 12k Any single | | 3.50 | 3.50 |

A660   A661

DENMARK

A662   A663

People on Bicycles — A664

Die Cut Perf. 13½x13 Syncopated
2023, Jn. 2   Litho.
Booklet Stamps
Self-Adhesive

1914	A660	12k multi	3.50	3.50
1915	A661	12k multi	3.50	3.50
1916	A662	12k multi	3.50	3.50
1917	A663	12k multi	3.50	3.50
1918	A664	12k multi	3.50	3.50
a.	Booklet pane of 10, 2 each #1914-1918		35.00	
	Nos. 1914-1918 (5)		17.50	17.50

Customized Dress by Annette Orts Hansen A665

Embroidered Insect by Karen Marie Dehn A666

 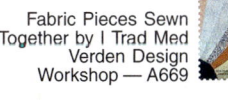

Knitted Sweater by Mette Wendelboe Okkels A667

Crocheted Insect by Jeanette Bogelund Bentzen A668

Fabric Pieces Sewn Together by I Trad Med Verden Design Workshop — A669

Die Cut Perf. 13¼x13½ Syncopated
2023, Jan. 2   Litho.
Booklet Stamps
Self-Adhesive

1919	A665	36k multi	10.50	10.50
1920	A666	36k multi	10.50	10.50
1921	A667	36k multi	10.50	10.50
1922	A668	36k multi	10.50	10.50
1923	A669	36k multi	10.50	10.50
a.	Booklet pane of 10, 2 each #1919-1923		105.00	
	Nos. 1919-1923 (5)		52.50	52.50

Peace Candle A670

Interlocking Hands A671

2023, May 4   Litho.   Perf. 13½
1924		Souvenir sheet of 2	14.00	14.00
a.	A670 12k multi		3.50	3.50
b.	A671 36k multi		10.50	10.50

Self-Adhesive
Die Cut Perf. 13½x13¼ Syncopated
1925	A670	12k multi	3.50	3.50

Europa (No. 1924b).

The Blue-Eyed Pussy, by Egon Mathiesen (1907-76) A672

Carl, by Ida Jessen and Hanne Bartholin A674

When Sally's Dad Was Young, by Thomas Brunstrom and Thorbjorn Christoffersen A676

The Magic Knomes, by Jan Kjaer A678

All the Stories About the Snow, by Benny Andersen A680

Otto is a Rhinoceros, by Ole Lund Kirkegaard (1940-79) A673

The Incredible Story of the Giant Pear, by Jakob Martin Strid A675

Cirkeline Is Created, by Hanne Hastrup A677

Betty Decides Everything, by Alberte Winding and Rasmus Bregnhoi A679

Rasmus Klump Builds a Ship, by Carla and Vilhelm Hansen A681

Die Cut Perf. 13½x13¼ Syncopated
2023, May 4   Litho.
Booklet Stamps
Self-Adhesive

1926	A672	12k multi	3.50	3.50
1927	A673	12k multi	3.50	3.50
1928	A674	12k multi	3.50	3.50
1929	A675	12k multi	3.50	3.50
1930	A676	12k multi	3.50	3.50
1931	A677	12k multi	3.50	3.50
1932	A678	12k multi	3.50	3.50
1933	A679	12k multi	3.50	3.50
1934	A680	12k multi	3.50	3.50
1935	A681	12k multi	3.50	3.50
a.	Booklet pane of 10, #1926-1935		35.00	
	Nos. 1926-1935 (10)		35.00	35.00

Danish children's books.

SEMI-POSTAL STAMPS

Nos. 159, 157 Surcharged in Red

Wmk. Multiple Crosses (114)
1921, June 17   Perf. 14½x14
B1	A20	10o + 5o green	27.50	60.00
B2	A21	20o + 10o slate	30.00	77.50
	Set, never hinged		167.50	

Crown and Staff of Aesculapius — SP1

1929, Aug. 1   Engr.
B3	SP1	10o yellow green	4.50	7.00
a.	Booklet pane of 2		27.50	
B4	SP1	15o brick red	9.00	12.00
a.	Booklet pane of 2		32.50	
B5	SP1	25o deep blue	25.00	40.00
a.	Booklet pane of 2		135.00	
	Nos. B3-B5 (3)		38.50	59.00
	Set, never hinged		100.00	

These stamps were sold at a premium of 5 öre each for benefit of the Danish Cancer Committee.

Dybbol Mill — SP2

1937, Jan. 20   Unwmk.   Perf. 13
B6	SP2	5o + 5o green	.60	1.40
B7	SP2	10o + 5o lt brown	2.25	9.00
B8	SP2	15o + 5o carmine	3.25	9.00
	Nos. B6-B8 (3)		6.10	19.40
	Set, never hinged		13.00	

The surtax was for a fund in memory of H. P. Hanssen, statesman.
Nos. 223a and B6, Nos. 229 and B7, Nos. 238A and B8 are found se-tenant in booklets. For booklet panes, see Nos. 223d, 229b and 238Al.

Queen Alexandrine — SP3

1939-40   Perf. 13
B9	SP3	5o + 3o rose lake & red ('40)	.25	.35
a.	Booklet pane of 4		2.00	2.00
B10	SP3	10o + 5o dk violet & red	.35	.25
B11	SP3	15o + 5o scarlet & red	.30	.50
	Nos. B9-B11 (3)		.90	1.10
	Set, never hinged		1.35	

The surtax was for the Danish Red Cross.
Nos. 230 and B10 have been issued se-tenant in booklets. See No. 230b. In this pane No. 230 measures 23½x31mm from perf. to perf.

Crown Princess Ingrid and Princess Margrethe — SP4

1941-43
B12	SP4	10o + 5o dk violet	.25	.25
a.	Booklet pane of 10		32.50	
B13	SP4	20o + 5o red ('43)	.25	.25
	Set, never hinged		.60	

Surtax for the Children's Charity Fund.

No. 288 Surcharged in Red

1944, May 11
B14	A48	10o + 5o violet	.25	.25
	Never hinged		.30	
a.	Booklet pane of 10		27.50	

The surtax was for the Danish Red Cross.

> **Catalogue values for unused stamps in this section, from this point to the end of the section, are for Never Hinged items.**

Symbols of Freedom SP5

Explosions at Rail Junction SP6

Danish Flag — SP7

1947, May 4   Engr.   Perf. 13
B15	SP5	15o + 5o green	.35	.35
B16	SP6	20o + 5o dark red	.35	.35
B17	SP7	40o + 5o deep blue	.85	.85
	Nos. B15-B17 (3)		1.55	1.55

Issued in memory of the Danish struggle for liberty and the liberation of Denmark. The surtax was for the Liberty Fund.
For surcharges see Nos. B22-B23.

Princess Anne-Marie — SP8

1950, Oct. 19   Unwmk.
| B18 | SP8 | 25o + 5o rose brown | .55 | .50 |

The surtax was for the National Children's Welfare Association.

S. S. Jutlandia — SP9

1951, Sept. 13   Perf. 13
| B19 | SP9 | 25o + 5o red | .65 | .60 |

The surtax was for the Red Cross.

No. 335 Surcharged in Black

1953, Feb. 13
| B20 | A61 | 30o + 10o brown red | 1.50 | 1.50 |

The surtax was for flood relief in the Netherlands.

Stone Memorial — SP10

1953, Mar. 26   Perf. 13
| B21 | SP10 | 30o + 5o dark red | 1.40 | 1.25 |

The surtax was for cultural work of the Danish Border Union.

Nos. B15 and B16 Surcharged in Black

DENMARK

1955, Feb. 17
B22 SP5 20o + 5o on No. B15   1.00   .85
B23 SP6 30o + 5o on No. B16   1.00   .85
The surtax was for the Liberty Fund.

No. 341 Surcharged

1957, Mar. 25
B24 A61 30o + 5o on 95o red org   .65   .65
The surtax went to the Danish Red Cross for aid to Hungary.

No. 335 Surcharged in Black

1959, Feb. 23
B25 A61 30o + 10o brown red   .80   .90
The surtax was for the Greenland Fund.

Globe Encircled by Red Cross Flags — SP11

1959, June 24   *Engr.*   *Perf. 13*
B26 SP11 30o + 5o rose red   .50   .50
B27 SP11 60o + 5o lt ultra & car   .75   .75
Centenary of the Intl. Red Cross idea. The surtax was for the Red Cross. Crosses photogravure on No. B27.

Queen Ingrid — SP12

1960, Oct. 25   *Unwmk.*
B28 SP12 30o + 10o dark red   1.00   1.00
Queen Ingrid's 25th anniv. as a Girl Scout. The surtax was for the Scouts' fund for needy and sick children.

African Mother, Child — SP13

1962, May 24
B29 SP13 30o + 10o dark red   .75   1.00
Issued to aid underdeveloped countries.

Healthy and Crippled Hands — SP14

1963, June 24   *Perf. 13*
B30 SP14 35o + 10o dark red   1.10   1.10
a.   Fluorescent paper   1.10   1.10
The surtax was for the benefit of the Cripples' Foundation.

Old Bridge at Danish-German Border — SP15

1964, May 28   *Engr.*
B31 SP15 35o + 10o henna brn   .85   .90
Surtax for the Danish Border Union.

Princesses Margrethe, Benedikte, Anne-Marie — SP16

1964, Aug. 24
B32 SP16 35o + 10o dull red   .85   .75
B33 SP16 60o + 10o dk bl & red   1.10   .95
The surtax was for the Red Cross.

Happy Child — SP17

1965, Oct. 21   *Engr.*   *Perf. 13*
B34 SP17 50o + 10o brick red   .65   .65
The surtax was for the National Children's Welfare Association.

"Red Cross" in 32 Languages and Red Cross, Red Lion and Sun, and Red Crescent Emblems — SP18

1966, Jan. 20   *Engr.*   *Perf. 13*
B35 SP18 50o + 10o red   .65   .65
Engraved and Photogravure
B36 SP18 80o + 10o dk bl & red   .80   .80
The surtax was for the Red Cross.

"Refugees 66" — SP19

1966, Oct. 24   *Engr.*   *Perf. 13*
B37 SP19 40o + 10o sepia   .80   .80
B38 SP19 50o + 10o rose red   .80   .80
B39 SP19 80o + 10o blue   1.60   1.60
Nos. B37-B39 (3)   3.20   3.20
The surtax was for aid to refugees.

Symbolic Rose — SP20

1967, Oct. 12
B40 SP20 60o + 10o brown red   .50   .55
The surcharge was for the Salvation Army.

Two Greenland Boys in Round Tower — SP21

1968, Sept. 12   *Engr.*   *Perf. 13*
B41 SP21 60o + 10o dark red   .65   .65
The surtax was for child welfare work in Greenland.

Princess Margrethe and Prince Henrik with Prince Frederik — SP22

1969, Dec. 11
B42 SP22 50o + 10o brn & red   .65   .65
B43 SP22 60o + 10o brn red & red   .65   .65
The surtax was for the Danish Red Cross.

Child Seeking Help — SP23

1970, Mar. 13
B44 SP23 60o + 10o brown red   .65   .65
Surtax for "Save the Children Fund."

Child — SP24

1971, Apr. 29   *Engr.*   *Perf. 13*
B45 SP24 60o + 10o copper red   .65   .65
Surtax was for the National Children's Welfare Association.

Marsh Marigold — SP25

1972, Aug. 17
B46 SP25 70o + 10o green & yel   .50   .55
Soc. and Home for the Disabled, cent.

Heimaey Town and Volcano — SP26

1973, Oct. 17   *Engr.*   *Perf. 13*
B47 SP26 70o + 20o vio blue & red   1.00   1.00
The surtax was for the victims of the eruption of Heimaey Volcano, Jan. 23, 1973.

Queen Margrethe, IWY Emblem — SP27

1975, Mar. 20   *Engr.*   *Perf. 13*
B48 SP27 90o + 20o red & cream   .95   .80
International Women's Year 1975. Surtax was for a foundation to benefit women primarily in Greenland and Faroe Islands.

Skuldelev I SP28

Ships: 90o+20o, Thingvalla, emigrant steamer.   100o+20o, Liner Frederick VIII, c. 1930.   130o+20o, Three-master Danmark.

1976, Jan. 22   *Engr.*   *Perf. 13*
B49 SP28   70 + 20o olive brown   .75   .85
B50 SP28   90 + 20o brick red   .75   .85
B51 SP28 100 + 20o olive green   .85   1.10
B52 SP28 130 + 20o violet blue   .90   1.60
Nos. B49-B52 (4)   3.25   4.40
American Declaration of Independence, 200th anniv.

People and Red Cross — SP29

1976, Feb. 26   *Engr.*   *Perf. 13*
B53 SP29 100o + 20o red & black   .65   .65
B54 SP29 130o + 20o bl, red & blk   .80   .80
Centenary of Danish Red Cross.

Invalid in Wheelchair — SP30

1976, May 6   *Engr.*   *Perf. 13*
B55 SP30 100o + 20o ver & blk   .65   .65
The surtax was for the Foundation to Aid the Disabled.

Mother and Child — SP31

1977, Mar. 24   *Engr.*   *Perf. 12½*
B56 SP31 1k + 20o multicolored   .80   .80
Danish Society for the Mentally Handicapped, 25th anniv. Surtax was for the Society.

Anti-Cancer Campaign — SP32

1978, Oct. 12   *Engr.*   *Perf. 13*
B57 SP32 120o + 20o red   .65   .65
Danish Anti-Cancer Campaign, 50th anniversary. Surtax was for campaign.

Child and IYC Emblem — SP33

1979, Jan. 25   *Engr.*   *Perf. 12½*
B58 SP33 1.20k + 20o red & brown   .65   .65
International Year of the Child.

Foundation for the Disabled, 25th Anniversary — SP34

1980, Apr. 10   *Engr.*   *Perf. 13*
B59 SP34 130o + 20o brown red   .65   .70

Children Playing Ball — SP35

1981, Feb. 5   *Engr.*   *Perf. 12½x13*
B60 SP35 1.60k + 20o brown red   .70   .90
Surtax was for child welfare.

Intl. Year of the Disabled — SP36

1981, Sept. 10   *Engr.*   *Perf. 12½x13*
B61 SP36 2k + 20o dark blue   1.00   1.10

Stem and Broken Line — SP37

1982, May 3   *Engr.*   *Perf. 13*
B62 SP37 2k + 40o dull red   1.10   1.20
Surtax was for Danish Multiple Sclerosis Society.

DENMARK

Nurse with Patient — SP38

1983, Jan. 27   Engr.
B63 SP38 2k + 40o multicolored   1.40   1.40

1984 Olympic Games — SP39

1984, Feb. 23   Litho. & Engr.
B64 SP39 2.70k + 40o multi   1.75   1.40

Electrocardiogram Reading, Heart — SP40

1984, Sept. 6   Engr.   Perf. 12½
B65 SP40 2.70k + 40o red   1.75   2.00
Surtax was for Heart Foundation.

SP41

1985, May 2   Litho.   Perf. 13
B66 SP41 2.80k + 50o multi   1.40   2.25
Liberation from German Occupation, 40th Anniv. Surtax for benefit of World War II veterans.

SP42

Design: Tapestry detail, by Caroline Ebbeson (1852-1936), former patient, St. Hans Hospital, Roskilade.

1985, Oct. 3   Litho. & Engr.
B67 SP42 2.80k + 40o multi   1.40   1.90
Natl. Soc. for the Welfare of the Mentally Ill, 25th Anniv. Surtax benefited the mentally ill.

Danish Arthritis Assoc., 50th Anniv. — SP43

1986, Mar. 20   Litho.   Perf. 13
B68 SP43 2.80k + 50o multi   2.25   2.25
Surtax for the Arthritis Assoc.

Poul Reichhart (1913-1985), as Papageno in The Magic Flute — SP44

1986, Feb. 6   Litho.   Perf. 13
B69 SP44 2.80k + 50o multi   2.25   2.25
Surtax for the physically handicapped.

Danish Society for the Blind, 75th Anniv. — SP45

1986, Feb. 20   Litho. & Engr.   Perf. 13
B70 SP45 2.80k + 50o blk, vio brn & dk red   2.25   2.75

Danish Assoc. of Epileptics, 25th Anniv. — SP46

1987, Sept. 24   Engr.   Perf. 13
B71 SP46 2.80k +50o dk red, brt ultra & dk grn   2.40   3.00

Folkekirkens Nodhjaelp Relief Organization — SP47

1988, Mar. 10   Engr.
B72 SP47 3k +50o multicolored   2.25   2.75
Surtax for the relief organization.

Natl. Council for Unwed Mothers, 5th Anniv. — SP48

1988, Sept. 22   Photo.
B73 SP48 3k +50o dk rose brn   2.50   3.25

Salvation Army — SP49

1989, Feb. 16   Litho.
B74 SP49 3.20k +50o multi   2.50   3.00

Insulin Crystal — SP50

1990, Aug. 30   Litho.   Perf. 13
B75 SP50 3.50k +50o multi   3.25   4.50
Danish Diabetes Assoc., 50th anniv.

Children's Telephone — SP51

1991, June 6   Engr.   Perf. 13
B76 SP51 3.50k +50o dark blue   2.40   2.75
Surtax benefits Borns Vilkar, children's welfare organization.

Danish Dyslexia Assoc., 50th Anniv. — SP52

1992, Aug. 27   Litho. & Engr.   Perf. 13
B77 SP52 3.75k +50o multi   2.75   5.00

YMCA Social Work, 75th Anniv. — SP53

1993, Aug. 19   Litho.   Perf. 13
B78 SP53 3.75k +50o multi   2.75   3.25

Prince Henrik, 60th Birthday — SP54

1994, June 9   Litho. & Engr.   Perf. 13
B79 SP54 3.75k +50o multi   2.10   3.00
Surtax for Danish Red Cross.

Natl. Society of Polio and Accident Victims, 50th Anniv. — SP55

1995, June 8   Litho.   Perf. 13
B80 SP55 3.75k +50o red   1.90   2.75

The AIDS Foundation — SP56

1996, Oct. 10   Litho.   Perf. 13
B81 SP56 3.75k +50o red & black   3.50   2.25

Asthma-Allergy Assoc. — SP57

1997, May 15   Litho.   Perf. 13
B82 SP57 3.75k +50o multi   2.50   2.75

Danish Cancer Society — SP58

1998, Sept. 3   Litho.   Perf. 13
B83 SP58 3.75k +50o multi   2.25   2.50

SP59

1999, Aug. 25   Litho.   Perf. 13
B84 SP59 4k +50o blue & red   2.00   2.25
For the Alzheimer's Association.

SP60

2000, Sept. 27   Engr.   Perf. 13
B85 SP60 4k +50o red & blue   1.60   2.00
For the Cerebral Palsy Association.

Amnesty International SP61

2001, Jan. 24   Engr.   Perf. 12¾
B86 SP61 4k +50o blk & red   2.25   2.25

LEV National Association SP62

2002, Mar. 13   Engr.   Perf. 12¾
B87 SP62 4k + 50o multi, greenish   2.25   2.25

Doctors Without Borders — SP63

2003, Mar. 12   Litho.   Perf. 12¾
B88 SP63 4.25k +50o multi   1.60   1.25
Booklet, 10 #B88   16.00

Children's Aid Day — SP64

2004, Jan. 14   Litho.   Perf. 12¾
B89 SP64 4.50k +50o multi   1.75   2.10
Booklet, 10 #B89   17.50

SOS Children's Villages — SP65

2005, Jan. 12   Litho.   Perf. 12¾
B90 SP65 4.50k +50o multi   2.40   2.75
Complete booklet, 10 #B90   24.00

Surtax was originally intended for an SOS Children's Village in Burundi, but surtax went to the relief fund for Dec. 26, 2004 tsunami victims. A sticker noting this change was to be applied to the front covers of the booklets.

Danish Refugee Council, 50th Anniv. — SP66

2006, Jan. 11   Engr.   Perf. 12¾
B91 SP66 4.75k +50o blk & red, tan   2.75   2.75
Complete booklet, 10 #B91   27.50

Crown Prince Frederik, Crown Princess Mary, and Prince Christian — SP67

2007, Jan. 10   Engr.   Perf. 13x13¼
B92 SP67 4.75k +50o multi   2.75   2.40
Complete booklet, 10 #B92   27.50

Surtax for Crown Prince Frederik and Crown Princess Mary's Fund for Charitable and Humanitarian Purposes.

Danish Cancer Society, 80th Anniv. — SP68

2008, Jan. 9   Engr.   Perf. 12¾
B93 SP68 5.50k +50o blk & red   2.50   2.40
Complete booklet, 10 #B93   25.00

SP69

Design: Prince Henrik, Farm Field, Viet Nam, Emblem of Worldwide Fund for Nature (WWF).

DENMARK

2009, Jan. 7   Litho.   Perf. 13x13¼
B94 SP69 5.50k + 50o multi   2.75 3.25
   Complete booklet, 10 #B94   27.50
Surtax for Worldwide Fund for Nature.

Danish Children's Cancer Foundation — SP70

Die Cut Perf. 13¼x13½
2010, Jan. 6   Self-Adhesive   Litho.
B95 SP70 5.50k +50o multi   2.40 2.50
  a. Souvenir sheet of 4   9.75
Booklet Stamp
Serpentine Die Cut 10
B96 SP70 5.50k +50o multi   2.40 2.50
  a. Booklet pane of 12   29.00
Issued: No. B95a, 8/4.

Eight People — SP71

2011   Litho.   Die Cut Perf. 13½x13
Self-Adhesive
B97 SP71 5.50k+50o blk & red   2.50 2.50
B98 SP71 8k+50o blk & red   3.50 3.50
Booklet Stamps
Serpentine Die Cut 13½
B99 SP71 5.50k+50o blk & red   2.50 2.50
  a. Booklet pane of 10   25.00
B100 SP71 8k+50o blk & red   3.50 3.50
  a. Booklet pane of 10   35.00
  b. Sheet of 6 + 7 labels   21.00 21.00
Surtax for Danish Rheumatism Association. Issued: Nos. B97, B99, 1/6; Nos. B98, B100, 3/9. No. B100b, 8/4.

Crown Princess Mary — SP72

2012, June 10   Die Cut Perf. 13x13½
Self-Adhesive
B101 SP72 8k+50o multi   3.00 3.00
Booklet Stamp
Serpentine Die Cut 13½
B102 SP72 8k+50o multi   3.00 3.00
  a. Booklet pane of 10 + sticker 30.00
Surtax for Danish Heart Foundation.

Crown Princess Mary Type of 2012
Serpentine Die Cut 13½
2012, June 10   Self-Adhesive
Stochastic Litho. Printing
B103 SP72 8k+50o multi   3.50 3.50
The black dots that make up the design on No. B102 are arranged in lines, but are randomly placed on No. B103. No. B103 was printed in sheets of 6.

Girl's Head — SP73

Die Cut Perf. 13x13¼
2013-14   Litho.
B104 SP73 8k+1k multi   3.25 3.25

Booklet Stamp
Serpentine Die Cut 13½
B105 SP73 8k+1k multi   3.25 3.25
  a. Booklet pane of 10   32.50
Self-Adhesive
Die Cut Perf. 13½x13
B106 SP73 9k+1k multi   3.75 3.75
  a. Booklet pane of 10   37.50
Surtax for Save the Children charity. Issued: Nos. B104-B105, 5/27; No. B106, 1/2/14.
No. B106 was printed in sheets of 6. Surtax was for Save the Children charity.

Red Cross, 150th Anniv. — SP74

2014-15   Litho.   Die Cut Perf. 13½
Self-Adhesive
B107 SP74 9k+1k gray & red   3.75 3.75
  a. Booklet pane of 10   37.50
B108 SP74 10k+1k gray & red   3.50 3.50
  a. Booklet pane of 10   35.00
Surtax for Red Cross. Issued: No. B107, 6/3; No. B108, 1/2/15.

Worldwide Fund for Nature (WWF) — SP75

Sun, bird and: No. B109, Deer. No. B110, Farmhouse and wind generator.

Die Cut Perf. 13¼ Syncopated
2015, May 7   Self-Adhesive   Litho.
B109 SP75 10k+1k multi   3.25 3.25
B110 SP75 10k+1k multi   3.25 3.25
  a. Booklet pane of 10, 6 #B109, 4 #B110   32.50
Surtax for Worldwide Fund for Nature. See Sweden No. B63.

WWF Type of 2015
Designs: No. B111, Like #B109. No. B112, Like #B110.

Die Cut Perf. 13½ Syncopated
2016, Jan. 4   Self-Adhesive   Litho.
B111 SP75 8k+1k multi   2.60 2.60
B112 SP75 8k+1k multi   2.60 2.60
  a. Booklet pane of 5, 3 #B111, 2 #B112   13.00

AIR POST STAMPS

Airplane and Plowman — AP1

Wmk. Multiple Crosses (114)
1925-29   Typo.   Perf. 12x12½
C1 AP1 10o yellow green   27.50   50.00
C2 AP1 15o violet ('26)   70.00 110.00
C3 AP1 25o scarlet   45.00   72.50
C4 AP1 50o lt gray ('29)   130.00 315.00
C5 AP1 1k choc ('29)   105.00 300.00
   Nos. C1-C5 (5)   377.50 847.50
Set, never hinged   975.00

Towers of Copenhagen — AP2

Unwmk.
1934, June 9   Engr.   Perf. 13
C6   AP2 10o orange   .75   1.10
C7   AP2 15o red   2.60   5.50
C8   AP2 20o Prus blue   2.60   5.50
C9   AP2 50o olive black   2.60   5.50
C10 AP2 1k brown   10.50   19.00
   Nos. C6-C10 (5)   19.05   36.60
Set, never hinged   40.00

LATE FEE STAMPS

LF1

Perf. 14x14½
1923   Typo.   Wmk. 114
I1 LF1 10o green   17.00   5.25
  Never hinged   50.00
  a. Double overprint   3,000.
No. I1 was, at first, not a postage stamp but represented a tax for the services of the post office clerks in filling out postal forms and writing addresses. In 1923 it was put into use as a Late Fee stamp.

Coat of Arms — LF2

1926-31
I2 LF2 10o green   13.50   1.00
I3 LF2 10o brown ('31)   9.00   .70
Set, never hinged   60.00

1934   Unwmk.   Engr.   Perf. 13
I4 LF2 5o green   .35   .30
I5 LF2 10o orange   .35   .30
Set, never hinged   1.30

POSTAGE DUE STAMPS

Regular Issues of 1913-20 Overprinted

Perf. 14x14½
1921, May 1   Wmk. 114
J1   A10 1o deep orange   2.50   7.00
J2   A16 5o green   7.00   7.00
J3   A16 7o orange   4.50   8.50
J4   A16 10o red   30.00   17.00
J5   A16 20o deep blue   22.50   14.00
J6   A16 25o brown & blk   30.00   10.00
J7   A16 50o claret & blk 13.50   8.50
   Nos. J1-J7 (7)   110.00   72.00
Set, never hinged   300.00

Same Overprint in Dark Blue On Military Stamp of 1917
1921, Nov. 23
J8   A16 10o red   15.00   20.00
   Never hinged   37.50
  a. "S" inverted   175.00 240.00
   Never hinged   350.00

Numeral of Value — D1

Typographed (Solid Panel)
1921-30   Perf. 14x14½
J9   D1 1o orange ('22)   2.00   2.50
J10 D1 4o blue ('25)   3.75   3.25
J11 D1 5o brown ('22)   3.25   2.50
J12 D1 5o lt green ('30)   3.75   2.50
J13 D1 7o apple grn ('27) 18.00   24.00
J14 D1 7o dk violet ('30) 50.00   40.00
J15 D1 10o yellow grn ('22) 4.50   2.25
J16 D1 10o lt brown ('30) 4.50   2.25
J17 D1 20o grnsh blue ('21) 3.50   3.25
  a. Double impression   2,700.
J18 D1 20o gray ('30)   4.75   5.00
J19 D1 25o scarlet ('23)   4.50   6.00
J20 D1 25o violet ('26)   3.75   7.75
J21 D1 25o lt blue ('30)   7.25   10.75
J22 D1 1k dk blue ('21)   90.00   20.00

J23 D1 1k brn & dk bl ('25) 10.00 18.00
J24 D1 5k purple ('25)   22.50 18.00
   Nos. J9-J24 (16)   236.00 168.00
Set, never hinged   615.00

Engraved (Lined Panel)
1934-55   Unwmk.   Perf. 13
J25 D1 1o slate   .30   .30
J26 D1 2o carmine   .35   .30
J27 D1 5o yellow green   .45   .30
J28 D1 6o dk olive ('41)   .45   .30
J29 D1 8o magenta ('50)   2.00   4.00
J30 D1 10o orange   .35   .30
J31 D1 12o dp ultra ('55)   .55   .50
J32 D1 15o lt violet ('54) .85   .30
J33 D1 20o gray   .65   .30
J34 D1 25o blue   .75   .30
J35 D1 30o green ('53)   .50   .30
J36 D1 40o claret ('49)   .60   .25
J37 D1 1k brown   .80   .30
   Nos. J25-J37 (13)   8.60   8.75
Set, never hinged   14.50

No. 96 Surcharged in Black

1934   Wmk. 114   Perf. 14x14½
J38 A10 15o on 12o violet   6.00   4.50
   Never hinged   18.00

MILITARY STAMPS

Nos. 97 and 100 Overprinted in Blue

1917   Wmk. 114   Perf. 14x14½
M1 A16 5o green   19.00   40.00
  a. "S" inverted   300.00 375.00
M2 A16 10o red   16.00   27.00
  a. "S" inverted   225.00 375.00
   Set, never hinged   70.00
  #M1a, M2a, never hinged 975.00
The letters "S F" are the initials of "Soldater Frimaerke" (Soldier's Stamp).
For overprint see No. J8.

OFFICIAL STAMPS

Small State Seal — O1

Wmk. Crown (112)
1871   Typo.   Perf. 14x13½
O1 O1 2s blue   275.00 200.00
  a. 2s ultra   275.00 200.00
  b. Imperf   450.00
O2 O1 4s carmine   77.50   40.00
  a. Imperf   450.00
O3 O1 16s green   450.00 350.00
  a. Imperf   450.00
     Perf. 12½
O4 O1 4s carmine   6,500.   650.00
O5 O1 16s green   450.00 600.00
  #O1-O3, O5, never hinged 3,575.
Nos. O4-O5 values are for stamps with defective perfs.
Nos. O1-O3 were reprinted in 1886 upon white wove paper, unwatermarked and imperforate. Value $10 each.

1875   Perf. 14x13½
O6 O1 3o violet   15.00   55.00
O7 O1 4o blue (shades)   18.00   6.25
O8 O1 8o carmine   15.00   2.00
  a. Imperf   —
O9 O1 32o green   32.50   30.00
   Nos. O6-O9 (4)   80.50   93.25
Set, never hinged   245.00
For surcharge see No. 81.

1899-02   Perf. 13
O9A O1 3o red lilac ('02) 4.50 15.00
  c. Imperf   400.00
    As "c," pair   1,100.
O9B O1 4o blue   3.75   4.50
O10 O1 8o carmine   20.00 26.00
   Nos. O9A-O10 (3)   28.25 45.50
Set, never hinged   85.00
For surcharge see No. 137.

DENMARK — DIEGO-SUAREZ

1902-06   Wmk. 113
O11	O1	1o orange	2.25	3.25
O12	O1	3o red lilac ('06)	1.50	1.90
O13	O1	4o blue ('03)	3.00	4.50
O14	O1	5o green	3.00	.85
O15	O1	10o carmine	4.50	3.50
		Nos. O11-O15 (5)	14.25	14.00
		Set, never hinged	36.00	

1914-23   Wmk. 114   Perf. 14x14½
O16	O1	1o orange	1.25	2.75
O17	O1	3o gray ('18)	4.50	17.00
O18	O1	4o blue ('16)	30.00	60.00
O19	O1	5o green ('15)	3.00	2.00
O20	O1	5o choc ('23)	7.50	17.00
O21	O1	10o red ('17)	15.00	8.00
O22	O1	10o green ('21)	5.25	6.00
O23	O1	15o violet ('19)	20.00	37.50
O24	O1	20o indigo ('20)	22.50	20.00
		Nos. O16-O24 (9)	109.00	170.50
		Set, never hinged	250.00	

For surcharges see Nos. 185-191.
No. O20 is valued CTO.
Official stamps were discontinued Apr. 1, 1924.

NEWSPAPER STAMPS

Numeral of Value — N1

1907   Typo.   Wmk. 113   Perf. 13
P1	N1	1o olive	20.00	3.00
P2	N1	5o blue	30.00	15.00
P3	N1	7o carmine	18.00	1.25
P4	N1	10o deep lilac	57.50	5.00
P5	N1	20o green	45.00	1.50
P6	N1	38o orange	62.50	2.50
P7	N1	68o yellow brown	150.00	27.50
P8	N1	1k bl grn & claret	37.50	6.00
P9	N1	5k rose & yel grn	225.00	45.00
P10	N1	10k bister & blue	225.00	45.00
		Nos. P1-P10 (10)	870.50	151.75
		Set, never hinged	3,050.	

For surcharges see Nos. 138-144.

1914-15   Wmk. 114   Perf. 14x14½
P11	N1	1o olive gray	18.00	2.00
P12	N1	5o blue	45.00	12.50
P13	N1	7o rose	45.00	3.00
P14	N1	8o green ('15)	45.00	7.00
P15	N1	10o deep lilac	75.00	3.00
P16	N1	20o green	300.00	3.25
a.		Imperf., pair	1,200.	
P17	N1	29o orange yel ('15)	75.00	8.00
P18	N1	38o orange	2,000.	190.00
P19	N1	41o yellow brn ('15)	95.00	5.75
P20	N1	1k blue grn & mar	125.00	3.25
		Nos. P11-P17, P19-P20 (9)	823.00	47.75
		Set, never hinged	3,200.	

For surcharges see Nos. 145-154.

PARCEL POST STAMPS

These stamps were for use on postal packets sent by the Esbjerg-Fano Ferry Service.

Regular Issues of 1913-30 Overprinted

1919-41   Wmk. 114   Perf. 14x14½
Q1	A10	10o green ('22)	20.00	20.00
Q2	A10	10o bister brn ('30)	15.00	8.50
Q3	A16	10o red	45.00	90.00
a.		"POSTFAERGE"	200.00	500.00
Q4	A16	15o violet	20.00	35.00
a.		"POSTFAERGE"	250.00	525.00
Q5	A16	30o orange ('22)	22.50	47.50
Q6	A16	30o dk blue ('26)	4.50	8.00
Q7	A16	50o cl & blk ('20)	300.00	350.00
Q8	A16	50o lt gray ('22)	30.00	30.00
		50o olive gray ('22)	225.00	450.00
Q9	A16	1k brn & bl ('24)	60.00	30.00
Q9A	A16	5k vio & brn ('41)	3.75	3.25
Q10	A16	10k ver & grn ('30)	80.00	150.00

Engr.
Q11	A17	1k yellow brn	120.00	225.00
a.		"POSTFAERGE"	1,500.	2,600.
		Nos. Q1-Q11 (12)	720.75	997.25
		Set, never hinged	1,750.	

1927-30
Q12	A30	15o red ('27)	27.00	15.00
Q13	A30	30o ocher ('27)	18.00	20.00
Q14	A30	40o yel grn ('30)	27.00	17.00
		Nos. Q12-Q14 (3)	72.00	52.00
		Set, never hinged	180.00	

Overprinted on Regular Issues of 1933-40

1936-42   Unwmk.   Perf. 13
Q15	A32	5o rose lake ('42)	.35	.35
Q16	A32	10o yellow org	35.00	35.00
Q17	A32	10o lt brown ('38)	1.50	2.75
Q18	A32	10o purple ('39)	.35	.35
Q19	A30	15o deep red	1.50	2.00
Q20	A30	30o blue, I	4.50	7.50
Q21	A30	30o blue, II ('40)	15.00	32.50
Q22	A30	30o org, II ('42)	.60	1.25
Q23	A30	40o yel grn, I	4.50	7.00
Q24	A30	40o yel grn, II ('40)	15.00	32.50
Q25	A30	40o blue, II ('42)	.60	1.10
Q26	A33	50o gray	1.20	2.40
Q27	A33	1k lt brown	1.40	1.40
		Nos. Q15-Q27 (13)	81.50	126.75
		Set, never hinged	160.00	

> **Catalogue values for unused stamps in this section, from this point to the end of the section, are for Never Hinged items.**

Overprinted on Nos. 284, 286, 286B

1945
Q28	A47	30o orange	4.00	2.40
Q29	A47	40o blue	1.90	1.90
Q30	A47	50o gray	2.00	2.00
		Nos. Q28-Q30 (3)	7.90	6.30

Ovptd. on #318, 309, 310, 312, 297

1949-53
Q31	A32	10o green ('53)	.65	.50
Q32	A61	30o orange	5.50	2.25
Q33	A61	40o dull blue	4.50	2.25
Q34	A61	50o gray ('50)	24.00	1.25
Q35	A55	1k brown ('50)	2.40	1.50
		Nos. Q31-Q35 (5)	37.05	7.75

Ovptd. on #335, 323, 336, 326, 397

1955-65
Q36	A61	30o brown red	2.25	2.25
Q37	A61	40o gray	2.25	2.25
Q38	A61	50o aqua	2.25	2.25
Q39	A61	70o deep green	2.25	2.25
Q40	A55	1.25k orange ('65)	10.00	12.00
		Nos. Q36-Q40 (5)	19.00	21.00

Overprinted on Nos. 417 and 419

1967   Engr.   Perf. 13
Q41	A86	40o brown	.65	1.25
Q42	A86	80o ultra	.65	1.25

Nos. 224, 438, 441, 297-299 Overprinted

1967-74   Engr.   Perf. 13
Q43	A32	5o rose lake	.60	.50
Q44	A86	50o brown ('74)	.65	.90
Q45	A86	90o ultra ('70)	1.10	1.60
Q46	A55	1k brown	2.50	2.75
Q47	A55	2k red ('72)	2.90	4.25
Q48	A55	5k dull bl ('72)	3.50	4.50
		Nos. Q43-Q48 (6)	11.25	14.50

Nos. Q44-Q45, Q47-Q48 are on fluorescent paper.

Overprinted on No. 541

1975, Feb. 27
Q49	A161	100o deep ultra	1.60	2.40

DIEGO-SUAREZ

dē-ˌā-gō 'swär-əs

LOCATION — A town at the northern end of Madagascar
GOVT. — French colony
POP. — 12,237

From 1885 to 1896 Diego-Suarez, (Antsirane), a French naval base, was a separate colony and issued its own stamps. These were succeeded by stamps of Madagascar.

100 Centimes = 1 Franc

Values for unused stamps are for examples with original gum as defined in the catalogue introduction except for Nos. 6-10 and J1-J2 which are valued without gum.

Stamps of French Colonies Handstamp Surcharged in Violet

1890   Unwmk.   Perf. 14x13½
1	A9	15c on 1c blk, bl	300.00	100.00
2	A9	15c on 5c grn, grnsh	650.00	100.00
3	A9	15c on 10c blk, lav	300.00	92.50
4	A9	15c on 20c red, grn	650.00	80.00
5	A9	15c on 25c blk, rose	130.00	52.50

This surcharge is found inverted, double, etc. See the *Scott Classic Catalogue*. Counterfeits exist.

Ship Flying French Flag A2   France A5

Symbolical of Union of France and Madagascar
A3   A4

1890   Litho.   Imperf.
6	A2	1c black	190.	240.00
7	A3	5c black	1,100.	200.00
8	A4	15c black	210.00	95.00
9	A5	25c black	225.00	110.00

Counterfeits exist of Nos. 6-9.

A6

1891
10	A6	5c black	350.00	100.00

Excellent counterfeits exist of No. 10.

Stamps of French Colonies Surcharged in Red or Black

No. 11   No. 12

1892   Perf. 14x13½
11	A9	5c on 10c blk, lav (R)	210.00	105.00
a.		Inverted surcharge	475.00	400.00
12	A9	5c on 20c red, grn	190.00	72.50
a.		Inverted surcharge	450.00	400.00

Stamps of French Colonies Overprinted in Black or Red

1892
13	A9	1c blk, lilac blue (R)	32.50	20.00
14	A9	2c brown, buff	32.50	20.00
15	A9	4c claret, lav	55.00	45.00
16	A9	5c green, grnsh	120.00	80.00
17	A9	10c black, lavender	40.00	32.50
b.		Double overprint	240.00	180.00
18	A9	15c blue, pale blue	32.50	20.00
19	A9	20c red, grn	40.00	20.00
20	A9	25c black, rose	36.00	20.00
21	A9	30c brown, bis (R)	1,300.	925.00
22	A9	35c black, yellow	1,300.	925.00
23	A9	75c carmine, rose	72.50	52.50
a.		Double overprint		400.00
24	A9	1fr brnz grn, straw (R)	80.00	52.50
a.		Double overprint	240.00	210.00

Inverted Overprint
13a	A9	1c	225.00	190.00
14a	A9	2c	225.00	190.00
15a	A9	4c		325.00
16a	A9	5c	240.00	200.00
17a	A9	10c	240.00	200.00
20a	A9	25c	240.00	200.00
21a	A9	30c		1,700.
22a	A9	35c		1,700.

Navigation and Commerce
A10   A11

1892   Typo.   Perf. 14x13½
Name of Colony in Blue or Carmine
25	A10	1c black, blue	2.00	2.00
26	A10	2c brown, buff	2.75	2.75
27	A10	4c claret, lav	3.25	3.25
28	A10	5c green, grnsh	6.50	6.50
29	A10	10c black, lavender	8.75	7.25
30	A10	15c bl, quadrille paper	16.50	11.00
31	A10	20c red, green	22.50	16.00
32	A10	25c black, rose	17.50	14.50
33	A10	30c brown, bister	22.50	16.00
34	A10	40c red, straw	27.50	21.00
35	A10	50c carmine, rose	45.00	35.00
36	A10	75c violet, org	52.50	45.00
37	A10	1fr brnz grn, straw	75.00	60.00
		Nos. 25-37 (13)	302.25	240.25

Perf. 13½x14 stamps are counterfeits.

1894   Perf. 14x13½
38	A11	1c black, blue	2.00	2.00
39	A11	2c brown, buff	2.75	2.40
40	A11	4c claret, lav	3.25	2.75
41	A11	5c green, grnsh	5.50	4.75
42	A11	10c black, lavender	7.25	7.25
43	A11	15c blue, quadrille paper	12.00	6.50
44	A11	20c red, grn	20.00	13.50
45	A11	25c black, rose	12.00	9.50
46	A11	30c brown, bister	13.50	6.50
47	A11	40c red, straw	13.50	10.50
48	A11	50c carmine, rose	20.00	13.50
49	A11	75c violet, org	10.00	8.75
50	A11	1fr brnz grn, straw	27.50	24.00
		Nos. 38-50 (13)	151.25	107.90

Bisected stamps of type A11 are mentioned in note after Madagascar No. 62.
For surcharges see Madagascar Nos. 56-57, 61-62.
Perf. 13½x14 stamps are counterfeits.

DIEGO-SUAREZ — DJIBOUTI

POSTAGE DUE STAMPS

D1 D2

1891 Unwmk. Litho. Imperf.
| J1 | D1 | 5c violet | 240.00 | 120.00 |
| J2 | D2 | 50c black | 260.00 | 140.00 |

Excellent counterfeits exist of Nos. J1-J2.

Postage Due Stamps of French Colonies Ovptd. Like Nos. 13-24

1892
J3	D1	1c black	130.00	72.50
J4	D1	2c black	130.00	65.00
a.		Inverted overprint	450.00	300.00
J5	D1	3c black	130.00	65.00
J6	D1	4c black	130.00	60.00
J7	D1	5c black	130.00	72.50
J8	D1	10c black	40.00	32.50
a.		Inverted overprint	460.00	450.00
J9	D1	15c black	36.00	32.50
a.		Double overprint	575.00	500.00
J10	D1	20c black	200.00	135.00
a.		Double overprint	600.00	500.00
J11	D1	30c black	120.00	60.00
a.		Inverted overprint	450.00	300.00
J12	D1	60c black	1,200.	775.00
J13	D1	1fr brown	2,800.	1,500.

DJIBOUTI

jə-ˈbü-tē

LOCATION — East Africa
GOVT. — Republic
AREA — 8,958 sq. mi.
POP. — 988,000 (2020 est.)
CAPITAL — Djibouti

Djibouti franc (1977)

The French territory of Afars and Issas became the Republic of Djibouti June 27, 1977. For 1894-1902 issues with "Djibouti" or "DJ," see Somali Coast.

Catalogue values for all unused stamps in this country are for Never Hinged items.

Afars and Issas Issues of 1972-1977 Ovptd. and Srchd. in Black, Dark Green, Blue or Brown

No. 439

No. 440

No. 441

Nos. 442, 447

Nos. 443, 445

Nos. 444, 451

No. 446

Nos. 448, 453

No. 449

No. 450

No. 452

No. 454

No. 455   No. 456

Printing and Perforations as Before
1977
439	A63	1fr on 4fr (#358;B)	2.50	.25
440	A81	2fr on 5fr (#433;B)	2.50	.25
441	A75	5fr on 20fr (#421;B)	.40	.25
442	A70	8fr (#380;B)	.40	.25
443	A71	20fr (#387;DG)	3.75	1.00
444	A81	30fr (#434;B)	4.00	.80
445	A71	40fr (#388;DG)	5.50	1.25
446	A71	45fr (#389;Bl)	5.50	5.50
447	A78	45fr (#428;B)	8.00	5.00
448	A72	50fr (#394;B)	2.50	2.50
449	A71	60fr (#391;Br)	7.50	2.50
450	A79	70fr (#430;B)	8.50	3.50
451	A81	70fr (#435;B)	6.50	3.00
452	A74	100fr (#418;B)	12.00	4.00
453	A71	150fr (#399;B)	12.00	5.00
454	A76	200fr (#422;B)	6.00	4.50
455	A80	200fr (#432;B)	10.00	10.00
456	A74	300fr (#419;B)	10.00	10.00

Nos. 439-456, C106-C108 (21) 140.05 77.80

Map and Flag of Djibouti — A83

Design: 65fr, Map and flag of Djibouti, map of Africa, horiz.

1977, June 27 Litho. Perf. 12½
| 457 | A83 | 45fr multicolored | 1.50 | .85 |
| 458 | A83 | 65fr multicolored | 2.25 | .85 |

Independence, June 27.

A84

1977, July 4
459	A84	10fr Headrest, horiz.	.35	.25
460	A84	20fr Water cask	.70	.25
461	A84	25fr Pitcher	1.00	.45

Nos. 459-461 (3) 2.05 .95

Ostrich — A85

1977, Aug. 11 Litho. Perf. 12½
| 462 | A85 | 90fr shown | 3.00 | .80 |
| 463 | A85 | 100fr Weaver | 4.50 | 1.25 |

Snail — A86

Designs: 15fr, Fiddler crab. 50fr, Klipspringers. 70fr, Green turtle. 80fr, Priacanthus hamrur (fish). 150fr, Dolphinfish.

1977 Litho. Perf. 12½
464	A86	15fr multicolored	.65	.25
465	A86	45fr multicolored	1.25	.60
466	A86	50fr multicolored	1.75	.50
467	A86	70fr multicolored	1.75	.60
468	A86	80fr multicolored	2.25	.85
469	A86	150fr multicolored	4.50	1.75

Nos. 464-469 (6) 12.15 4.55

Issued: 45fr, 70fr, 80fr, 9/14; others, 12/5.

Pres. Hassan Gouled Aptidon and Djibouti Flag — A87

1978, Feb. 12 Litho. Perf. 13
| 470 | A87 | 65fr multicolored | 1.50 | .50 |

Charaxes Hansali — A88

Butterflies: 20fr, Colias electo. 25fr, Acraea chilo. 150fr, Junonia hierta.

1978, Mar. 13 Litho. Perf. 12½x13
471	A88	5fr multicolored	.50	.25
472	A88	20fr multicolored	.85	.25
473	A88	25fr multicolored	1.25	.75
474	A88	150fr multicolored	5.50	2.50

Nos. 471-474 (4) 8.10 3.75

Necklace — A89

Design: 55fr, Necklace, diff.

1978, May 29 Litho. Perf. 12½x13
| 475 | A89 | 45fr pink & multi | 1.25 | .35 |
| 476 | A89 | 55fr blue & multi | 1.25 | .45 |

Bougainvillea — A90

Flowers: 35fr, Hibiscus schizopetalus. 250fr, Caesalpinia pulcherrima.

1978, July 10 Photo. Perf. 12½x13
477	A90	15fr multicolored	.50	.25
478	A90	35fr multicolored	.85	.25
479	A90	250fr multicolored	6.00	.90

Nos. 477-479 (3) 7.35 1.40

Charonia Nodifera A91

Sea Shell: 80fr, Charonia variegata.

1978, Oct. 9 Litho. Perf. 13
| 480 | A91 | 10fr multicolored | 1.10 | .25 |
| 481 | A91 | 80fr multicolored | 4.25 | .95 |

Chaetodon — A92

30fr, Yellow surgeonfish. 40fr, Harlequinfish.

1978, Nov. 20 Litho. Perf. 13x12½
482	A92	8fr multicolored	.55	.25
483	A92	30fr multicolored	1.10	.25
484	A92	40fr multicolored	2.75	.75

Nos. 482-484 (3) 4.40 1.25

Alsthom BB 1201 at Dock — A93

55fr, Steam locomotive 231. 60fr, Steam locomotive 130 and map of route. 75fr, Diesel.

1979, Jan. 29 Litho. Perf. 13
485	A93	40fr multicolored	1.25	.25
486	A93	55fr multicolored	1.40	.30
487	A93	60fr multicolored	1.75	.30
488	A93	75fr multicolored	2.25	.40

Nos. 485-488 (4) 6.65 1.25

Djibouti-Addis Ababa railroad.

Children and IYC Emblem A94

Design: 200fr, Mother, child, IYC emblem.

DJIBOUTI

1979, Feb. 26   Litho.   *Perf. 13*
489 A94   20fr multicolored   .50   .25
490 A94   200fr multicolored   4.00   1.10
International Year of the Child.
Nos. 489-490 exist in souvenir sheets of one. Value, set, $20.

Plane over Ardoukoba Volcano — A95

30fr, Helicopter over Ardoukoba Volcano.

1979, Mar. 19
491 A95   30fr multi, vert.   1.00   .35
492 A95   90fr multi   3.00   .65

Rowland Hill, Postal Clerks, No. C109 — A96

100fr, Somali Coast #22, Djibouti #457, letters, Rowland Hill. 150fr, Letters hoisted onto ship, smoke signals, Rowland Hill.

1979, Apr. 17   Litho.   *Perf. 13x12½*
493 A96   25fr multicolored   .40   .25
494 A96   100fr multicolored   2.00   .45
495 A96   150fr multicolored   3.00   .70
      Nos. 493-495 (3)   5.40   1.40
Sir Rowland Hill (1795-1879), originator of penny postage.
Nos. 493-495 exist in souvenir sheets of one. Value, set, $50.

View of Djibouti, Bird and Local Woman — A97

Design: 80fr, Map and flag of Djibouti, UPU emblem, Boeing 747, train and mail runner.

1979, June 8   Litho.   *Perf. 13x12½*
496 A97   55fr multicolored   4.00   .85
497 A97   80fr multicolored   4.75   1.10
Philexafrique II, Libreville, Gabon, June 8-17. Nos. 496, 497 each printed in sheets of 10 with 5 labels showing exhibition emblem.

Solanacea — A98

Flowers: 2fr, Opuntia, vert. 15fr, Trichodesma. 45fr, Acacia etbaica. 50fr, Thunbergia alata, vert.

Perf. 13x13½, 13½x13
1979, June 18
498 A98   2fr multicolored   .25   .25
499 A98   8fr multicolored   .25   .25
500 A98   15fr multicolored   .50   .25
501 A98   45fr multicolored   1.00   .25
502 A98   50fr multicolored   1.25   .25
      Nos. 498-502 (5)   3.25   1.25

Running — A99

Olympic Emblem and: 70fr, Basketball, vert. 200fr, Soccer.

Perf. 12½x13, 13x12½
1979, Oct. 22   Litho.
503 A99   70fr multicolored   1.50   .25
504 A99   120fr multicolored   2.25   .50
505 A99   200fr multicolored   3.75   .75
      Nos. 503-505 (3)   7.50   1.50
Pre-Olympic Year.

Cypraecassis Rufa — A100

Shells: 40fr, Lambis chiragra arthritica. 300fr, Harpa connaidalis.

1979, Dec. 22   Litho.   *Perf. 13*
506 A100   10fr multicolored   .25   .25
507 A100   40fr multicolored   1.00   .25
508 A100   300fr multicolored   6.50   1.50
      Nos. 506-508 (3)   7.75   2.00

Rotary International, 75th Anniversary — A101

1980, Feb. 19   Litho.   *Perf. 13x12½*
509 A101   90fr multicolored   2.25   .75
   a.   Souvenir sheet of 1 #509   15.00   15.00

Lions Club of Djibouti — A102

1980, Feb. 19
510 A102   100fr multicolored   2.25   .75

Colotis Danae — A103

1980, Mar. 17   *Perf. 13x13½*
511 A103   5fr shown   .90   .50
512 A103   55fr Danaus chrysippus   3.75   1.50

Chess Players, Knight — A104

Chess Federation Creation: 75fr, Chess Game, Florence, 1493.

1980, June 9   Litho.   *Perf. 13*
513 A104   20fr multicolored   1.25   .25
514 A104   75fr multicolored   3.25   .35

Cribraria — A105

1980, Aug. 12   Litho.   *Perf. 13*
515 A105   15fr shown   .75   .25
516 A105   85fr Nautilus pompilius   2.75   .50

Alexander Fleming, Discoverer of Penicillin — A106

Design: 130fr, Jules Verne, French science fiction writer; earth, moon and spacecraft.

1980, Sept. 1
517 A106   20fr multicolored   1.00   .35
518 A106   130fr multicolored   3.00   .60

Capt. Cook and Endeavor — A107

Capt. James Cook Death Bicentenary: 90fr, Ships and Maps of voyages.

1980, Nov. 20   Litho.   *Perf. 13*
519 A107   55fr multicolored   1.40   .65
520 A107   90fr multicolored   2.25   .90
Souvenir sheets of 1 exist, perf. 12½x12. Value, each $10.

Angel Fish — A108

1981, Apr. 13   Litho.   *Perf. 12½*
521 A108   25fr shown   1.75   .25
522 A108   55fr Moorish idol   3.25   .50
523 A108   70fr Scad   3.75   1.50
     Nos. 521-523 (3)   8.75   2.25

13th World Telecommunications Day — A109

1981, May 17   Litho.   *Perf. 13*
524 A109   140fr multicolored   2.75   .70

Type 231 Steam Locomotive, Germany, 1958 and Amtrak, US, 1980 — A110

Locomotives: 55fr, Stephenson and his Rocket, Djibouti Railways 230 engine. 65fr, Type TGV, France. Type 962, Japan.

1981, June 9   Litho.   *Perf. 13*
525 A110   40fr multicolored   1.50   .30
526 A110   55fr multicolored   2.00   .35
527 A110   65fr multicolored   2.50   .40
     Nos. 525-527 (3)   6.00   1.05

Radio Amateurs Club — A111

1981, June 25
528 A111   250fr multicolored   5.00   1.00

Prince Charles and Lady Diana — A112

1981, June 29
529 A112   180fr shown   2.50   .75
530 A112   200fr Couple, diff.   3.00   1.00
Royal Wedding.

Nos. 529-530 exist in souvenir sheets of one. Value, set, $30.

Lord Nelson and Victory — A113

1981, July 6   Litho.   *Perf. 13x12½*
531 A113   100fr multicolored   1.90   .45
532 A113   175fr multicolored   3.25   .90
Lord Horatio Nelson (1758-1805).

Scout Tending Campfire — A114

Design: 105fr, Scout giving sign.

1981, July 16   Litho.   *Perf. 13*
533 A114   60fr shown   3.00   .70
534 A114   105fr multicolored   3.75   .80
28th World Scouting Conference, Dakar, Aug. (60fr); 4th Pan-African Scouting Conference, Abidjan, Aug. (105fr).

Pawn and Queen, Swedish Bone Chess Pieces, 13th Cent. — A115

130fr, Pawn, knight, Chinese, 19th cent., vert.

1981, Oct. 15   Litho.   *Perf. 13*
535 A115   50fr shown   1.50   .35
536 A115   130fr multicolored   3.00   .85
For overprints see Nos. 542-543.

Sheraton Hotel Opening — A116

1981, Nov. 15   Litho.   *Perf. 13x12½*
537 A116   75fr multicolored   1.50   .45
For surcharge see No. 623.

Acacia Mollifora — A117

Designs: 10fr, Clitoria ternatea, vert. 35fr, Punica granatum. 45fr, Malvaceous plant, vert.

1981, Dec. 21   *Perf. 10*
538 A117   10fr multicolored   .40   .25
539 A117   30fr shown   .80   .25
540 A117   35fr multicolored   1.15   .25
541 A117   45fr multicolored   1.40   .30
     Nos. 538-541 (4)   3.75   1.05
See Nos. 558-560.

Nos. 535-536 Overprinted

DJIBOUTI

1981, Dec.	Litho.	Perf. 13
542 A115 50fr multicolored	2.00	.50
543 A115 130fr multicolored	4.00	1.00

World Chess Championship.

TB Bacillus Centenary — A117a

Design: Koch, slide, microscope.

1982, Mar. 24	Litho.	Perf. 13
544 A117a 305fr multicolored	7.00	1.50

A117b

Designs: 125fr, Ivory bishop. 175fr, Queen, pawn, 19th cent.

1982, Apr. 8	Litho.	Perf. 13
545 A117b 125fr multi	3.50	.75
546 A117b 175fr multi	4.25	1.25

1982 World Chess Championship.

A118

1982, May 17		
547 A118 150fr multicolored	3.00	.85

14th World Telecommunications Day. For surcharge see No. 647.

Bus and Jeep — A119

1982, July 27	Litho.	Perf. 13
548 A119 20fr shown	.55	.25
549 A119 25fr Dhow, ferry	.70	.25
550 A119 55fr Train, jet	1.50	.45
Nos. 548-550 (3)	2.75	.95

Nos. 548-550 exist in souvenir sheets of one. Value, set, $25.

Shells from the Red Sea — A120

10fr, Cypraea erythraeensis. 15fr, Conus sumatrensis. 25fr, Cypraea pulchra. 30fr, Conus inscriptus. 70fr, Casmaria ponderosa. 150fr, Cypraea exusta.

1982, Nov. 20	Litho.	Perf. 12½
551 A120 10fr multicolored	.45	.25
552 A120 15fr multicolored	.75	.30
553 A120 25fr multicolored	.90	.35
554 A120 30fr multicolored	1.10	.40
555 A120 70fr multicolored	2.25	.50
556 A120 150fr multicolored	4.50	1.50
a. Strip of 6, #551-556	9.95	3.30
Nos. 551-556 (6)	9.95	3.30

See Nos. 563-567.

Intl. Palestinian Solidarity Day — A121

1982, Nov. 29	Litho.	Perf. 13
557 A121 40fr multicolored	1.00	.25

Local Flowers type of 1981

Various flowers. 5fr, 55fr, vert.

1983, Apr. 14	Litho.	Perf. 13
558 A117 5fr multicolored	.25	.25
559 A117 50fr multicolored	1.25	.40
560 A117 55fr multicolored	1.40	.40
Nos. 558-560 (3)	2.90	1.05

World Communications Year — A123

1983, June 20	Litho.	Perf. 13
561 A123 500fr multicolored	9.00	2.25

Conference of Donors, Nov. 21-23 — A124

1983, Nov. 21	Litho.	Perf. 13x12½
562 A124 75fr multicolored	1.50	.40

Shell Type of 1982

15fr, Marginella obtusa. 30fr, Conus jickelli. 55fr, Cypraea macandrewi. 80fr, Conus cuvieri. 100fr, Turbo petholatus.

1983, Dec. 20	Litho.	Perf. 12½
563 A120 15fr multicolored	.50	.25
564 A120 30fr multicolored	1.00	.25
565 A120 55fr multicolored	1.60	.40
566 A120 80fr multicolored	2.25	.50
567 A120 100fr multicolored	2.50	.65
Nos. 563-567 (5)	7.85	2.05

Local Butterflies — A125

5fr, Colotis chrysonome. 20fr, Colias erate. 30fr, Junonia orithyia. 75fr, Acraea doubledayi. 110fr, Byblia ilithya.

1984, Jan. 24	Litho.	Perf. 13½x13
568 A125 5fr multicolored	.50	.25
569 A125 20fr multicolored	1.00	.25
570 A125 30fr multicolored	1.50	.35
571 A125 75fr multicolored	4.25	1.00
572 A125 110fr multicolored	5.50	1.50
Nos. 568-572 (5)	12.75	3.35

Landscapes and Animals — A126

2fr, Randa Klipspringer. 8fr, Ali Sabieh, gazelles. 10fr, Lake Assal, oryx. 15fr, Tadjoura, gazelle. 40fr, Alaila Dada, jackal, vert. 45fr, Lake Abbe, warthog. 55fr, Obock, seagull. 125fr, Presidential Palace, bird.

1984, Apr. 29	Litho.	Perf. 13
573 A126 2fr multicolored	.25	.25
574 A126 8fr multicolored	.25	.25
575 A126 10fr multicolored	.25	.25
576 A126 15fr multicolored	.25	.25
577 A126 40fr multicolored	.75	.25
578 A126 45fr multicolored	.75	.30
579 A126 55fr multicolored	1.90	.75
580 A126 125fr multicolored	3.75	1.25
Nos. 573-580 (8)	8.15	3.55

For surcharges see Nos. 646, 657-658, 660.

Fire Prevention — A127

1984, Sept. 9	Litho.	Perf. 13
581 A127 25fr Fire truck	1.00	.25
582 A127 95fr Hook & ladder	3.25	.50
583 A127 100fr Fire plane	3.25	1.00
Nos. 581-583 (3)	7.50	1.75

International Olympic Committee Membership — A128

1984, July 22	Litho.	Perf. 13
584 A128 45fr Runners	.90	.35

Motor Carriage, 1886 — A128a

1984, Nov. 11	Litho.	Perf. 12½
585 A128a 35fr shown	.80	.30
586 A128a 65fr Cabriolet, 1896	1.60	.65
587 A128a 90fr Phoenix, 1900	2.25	.95
Nos. 585-587 (3)	4.65	1.90

Gottlieb Daimler (1834-1900), pioneer automobile manufacturer.

Marie and Pierre Curie — A129

1984, Dec. 3	Litho.	Perf. 12½
588 A129 150fr Pierre Curie	3.25	1.10
589 A129 150fr Marie Curie	3.25	1.10

Nos. 588-589 exist in souvenir sheet of two. Value, set, $30.

A130

Audubon Bicentenary — A130a

5fr, Merops albicollis. 15fr, Pterocles exustus. 20fr, Trachyphonus margaritatus somalicus. 25fr, Coracias garrulus. 200fr, Pandion haliaetus, vert.

1985, Jan. 27	Litho.	Perf. 13
590 A130 5fr multi	.75	.35
591 A130 15fr multi	3.25	.85
592 A130 20fr multi	3.75	1.00
593 A130 25fr multi	4.50	1.10
Nos. 590-593 (4)	12.25	3.30

Souvenir Sheet
Self-Adhesive
Perf. 12½

593A A130a 200fr multi	27.50	27.50

No. 593A is airmail and printed on wood.

Intl. Youth Year — A131

1985, Mar. 26	Litho.	Perf. 13
594 A131 10fr multicolored	.30	.25
595 A131 30fr multicolored	.65	.30
596 A131 40fr multicolored	.90	.40
Nos. 594-596 (3)	1.85	.95

German Railways, 150th Anniv. — A132

Designs: 55fr, Engine No. 29, Addis Ababa-Djibouti Railways. 75fr, Adler, museum facsimile of the first German locomotive.

1985, Apr. 22	Litho.	Perf. 13
597 A132 55fr multicolored	2.25	.65
598 A132 75fr multicolored	3.25	.90

Scouting — A133

35fr, Planting saplings. 65fr, Hygiene, family health care.

1985, May 23		
599 A133 35fr multicolored	1.00	.45
600 A133 65fr multicolored	1.75	.75

A134

80fr, Victor Hugo (1802-1885), Novelist. 100fr, Arthur Rimbaud (1854-1891), poet.

1985, June 24		Litho.
601 A134 80fr brt blue & slate	1.60	.80
602 A134 100fr multicolored	2.00	1.00

Sea Shells — A135

Designs: 10fr, Cypraea nebrites. 15fr, Cypraea turdus. 30fr, Conus acuminatus. 40fr, Cypraea camelopardalis. 55fr, Conus terebra.

1985, July 15	Litho.	Perf. 12½
603 A135 10fr multicolored	.40	.25
604 A135 15fr multicolored	.60	.25
605 A135 30fr multicolored	1.50	.30
606 A135 40fr multicolored	1.75	.55
607 A135 55fr multicolored	2.75	.70
Nos. 603-607 (5)	7.00	2.05

DJIBOUTI

1st World Cup Marathon '85, Hiroshima — A136

Designs: 75fr, Winners. 100fr, Approaching finish.

1985, Sept. 2				**Perf. 12½x13**	
608	A136	75fr multicolored		1.25	.75
609	A136	100fr multicolored		2.00	1.00

Halley's Comet — A137

Designs: 85fr, Bayeux Tapestry, Comet and Halley. 90fr, Vega I, Giotto space probes, map of planets, comet trajectory.

1986, Jan. 27		**Litho.**		**Perf. 13**	
610	A137	85fr multicolored		1.50	.50
611	A137	90fr multicolored		1.75	.85

ISERST Solar Energy Installation — A138

Designs: 50fr, Runners on beach. 150fr, Windmill, headquarters, power control station.

1986, Mar. 20					
612	A138	50fr multicolored		.95	.40
613	A138	150fr multicolored		2.75	1.25

Ships from Columbus's Fleet, 1492 — A139

1986, Apr. 14					
614	A139	60fr Santa Maria		1.90	.55
615	A139	90fr Nina, Pinta		3.25	.95

Fish, Red Sea — A140

Designs: 20fr, Elagatis bipinnulatus. 25fr, Valamugil seheli. 55fr, Lutjanus rivulatus.

1986, June 16		**Litho.**		**Perf. 13½x13**	
616	A140	20fr multicolored		.65	.30
617	A140	25fr multicolored		.75	.45
618	A140	55fr multicolored		2.00	.75
		Nos. 616-618 (3)		3.40	1.50

Public Buildings — A141

105fr, People's Palace. 115fr, Ministry of the Interior, Posts & Telecommunications.

1986, July 21		**Litho.**		**Perf. 13**	
619	A141	105fr multicolored		1.75	.90
620	A141	115fr multicolored		2.10	1.00

Sea-Me-We Building, Keyboard — A142

1986, Sept. 8		**Litho.**		**Perf. 13**	
621	A142	100fr multicolored		2.00	.70
		Souvenir Sheet			
		Perf. 12½			
622	A142	250fr multicolored		13.50	13.50

Southeast Asia, Middle East, Western Europe Submarine Cable System inauguration.

No. 537 Surcharged

1986, Nov. 15				**Perf. 13x12½**	
623	A116	55fr on 75fr multi		1.40	.50

Pasteur Institute, Cent. — A143

1987, Feb. 19		**Litho.**		**Perf. 13**	
624	A143	220fr multicolored		5.00	1.60

Natl. Vaccination Campaign.

Edible Mushrooms — A144

35fr, Macrolepiota imbricata. 50fr, Lentinus squarrosulus. 95fr, Terfezia boudieri.

1987, Apr. 16		**Litho.**		**Perf. 13x12½**	
625	A144	35fr multicolored		1.50	.65
626	A144	50fr multicolored		2.25	.85
627	A144	95fr multicolored		3.00	1.50
		Nos. 625-627 (3)		6.75	3.00

Wildlife — A145

1987, May 14				**Perf. 12½x13**	
628	A145	5fr Hare		.50	.25
629	A145	30fr Dromedary		1.25	.30
630	A145	140fr Cheetah		5.00	1.00
		Nos. 628-630 (3)		6.75	1.55

1988 Olympics, Seoul and Calgary — A146

85fr, Pierre de Coubertin (1863-1937), founder of the modern Olympics, & lighting of the flame. 135fr, Ski jumping. 140fr, Running.

1987, July 16				**Perf. 13**	
631	A146	85fr multicolored		1.60	.55
632	A146	135fr multicolored		2.75	.95
633	A146	140fr multicolored		3.00	1.00
		Nos. 631-633 (3)		7.35	2.50

Traditional Art — A147

1988, Jan. 20		**Litho.**		**Perf. 13**	
634	A147	30fr Nomad's comb		.60	.30
635	A147	70fr Wash jug		1.25	.60

UN Universal Immunization by 1990 Campaign — A148

1988, Apr. 10				**Perf. 12½**	
636	A148	125fr multicolored		2.50	1.00

16th Africa Cup Soccer Championships, Morocco — A149

Design: Athletes, view of Rabat.

1988, Mar. 13				**Perf. 13**	
637	A149	55fr multicolored		1.20	.50

1988 Winter Olympics, Calgary — A150

1988, May 7		**Litho.**		**Perf. 13**	
638	A150	45fr Ski jump		1.00	.40

Campaign Against Thirst — A151

1988, Sept. 10		**Litho.**		**Perf. 12½x13**	
639	A151	50fr multicolored		1.25	.45

Intl. Fund for Agricultural Development, 10th Anniv. — A152

1988, Nov. 14				**Perf. 13**	
640	A152	135fr multicolored		2.50	1.00

Michel Lafoux Air Club, 40th Anniv. — A153

Design: 145fr, 1948 Tiger Moth, 1988 Tobago-10.

1988, Dec. 8					
641	A153	145fr multi		2.75	1.00

Marine Life — A154

Designs: 90fr, Lobophyllia costata. 160fr, Lambis truncata.

1989, Jan. 20		**Litho.**		**Perf. 12½**	
642	A154	90fr multicolored		2.25	.30
643	A154	160fr multicolored		4.25	1.40

Colotis protomedia — A155

1989, Feb. 15					
644	A155	70fr multicolored		5.00	2.10

Nos. 573 and 547 Surcharged

1989				**Perf. 13**	
646	A126	70fr on 2fr No. 573		2.25	.50
647	A118	70fr on 150fr No. 547		2.25	.50

Issued: 646, 12/20; 647, 12/29.

Folk Dances — A157

1989, Mar. 20					
648	A157	30fr shown		.50	.25
649	A157	70fr multicolored, diff.		1.40	.50

Francolin of Djibouti — A159

1989, Apr. 10		**Litho.**		**Perf. 12½**	
651	A159	35fr multicolored		2.50	.75

Rare Flora — A160

1989, June 12					
652	A160	25fr Calotropis procera		.60	.25

A161

1989, Aug. 10		**Litho.**		**Perf. 13**	
653	A161	70fr multicolored		1.60	.75

Interparliamentary Union, cent.

Intl. Literacy Year — A162

1989, Oct. 1					
654	A162	145fr multicolored		2.75	1.10

DJIBOUTI

170

Petroglyph A163

1989, Nov. 18   Litho.   *Perf. 13*
655   A163   5fr multicolored   1.00   .40

Girl — A164

1989, Dec. 6
656   A164   55fr multicolored   1.60   .65

Nos. 574, 576-577 Surcharged

1989-1990   Litho.   *Perf. 13*
657   A126   30fr on 8fr multi   .50   .30
658   A126   50fr on 40fr multi   2.00   .55
660   A126   120fr on 15fr multi   2.25   1.00
    Nos. 657-660 (3)   4.75   1.85
Issue dates: 30fr, 12/20/89; 50fr, 7/3/90; 120fr, 3/17/90.

Water Conservation A165

1990, May 5   Litho.   *Perf. 11½*
665   A165   120fr multicolored   2.25   .90

Traditional Jewelry — A166

1990, Mar. 10
666   A166   70fr multicolored   1.75   .45

Commiphora A167

1990, Feb. 20   *Perf. 12*
667   A167   30fr multicolored   1.50   .35

Baskets A168

1990, July 3
668   A168   30fr multicolored   .70   .40

A169

1990, June 12   *Perf. 11½*
669   A169   100fr multicolored   2.00   .80
World Cup Soccer Championships, Italy.

A170

1990, Apr. 16   *Perf. 11½*
670   A170   55fr shown   1.50   .45
20 kilometer race of Djibouti.

Vaccination Campaign — A171

1990, Aug. 22   Litho.   *Perf. 11½*
Granite Paper
671   A171   300fr multicolored   4.75   2.00

Charles de Gaulle — A172

1990, Sept. 16   **Granite Paper**
672   A172   200fr multicolored   4.00   1.25

African Tourism Year — A173

1991, Jan. 23   Litho.   *Perf. 13*
673   A173   115fr multicolored   2.25   .80

Corals — A174

1991, Jan. 28   *Perf. 12½*
674   A174   40fr Acropora   .90   .50
675   A174   45fr Seriatopora hytrise   1.25   .50

Aquatic Birds — A175

10fr, Pelecanus rufescens. 15fr, Egretta gularis. 20fr, Ardea goliath, horiz. 25fr, Platalea leucorodia, horiz.

1991, Feb. 12
676   A175   10fr multicolored   .70   .25
677   A175   15fr multicolored   1.50   .25
678   A175   20fr multicolored   1.75   .30
679   A175   25fr multicolored   1.90   .35
    Nos. 676-679 (4)   5.85   1.15

UNO Development Conference — A176

1990, Oct. 9   Litho.   *Perf. 11½x12*
Granite Paper
680   A176   45fr multicolored   1.10   .45

Fossils — A177

1990, Nov. 1   **Granite Paper**
681   A177   90fr pur, org & blk   5.25   1.75

Papio Hamadryas — A178

1990, Dec. 6   **Granite Paper**
682   A178   50fr multicolored   1.75   .55

Pandion Haliaetus — A179

1991, Mar. 20   Litho.   *Perf. 12x11½*
683   A179   200fr multicolored   5.00   1.60

Traditional Game — A180

1991, Apr. 4
684   A180   250fr multicolored   5.25   3.25
See No. 696.

Djibouti-Ethiopia Railroad — A181

1991, May 25   Litho.   *Perf. 11½*
685   A181   85fr multicolored   4.00   2.25

World Environment Day — A182

1991, June 10
686   A182   110fr multicolored   2.75   .65

Philexafrique A183

1991, Jul. 16   Litho.   *Perf. 11½*
687   A183   120fr Islands   3.25   1.75

Pre-Olympic Year — A184

1991, Sept. 25
688   A184   175fr Handball   4.50   3.00

World Food Day — A185

1991, Oct. 16   Litho.   *Perf. 11½x12*
689   A185   105fr multicolored   2.50   1.10

Underwater Cable Network — A186

1991, Nov. 28   *Perf. 12x11½*
690   A186   130fr multicolored   3.00   1.00

Discovery of America, 500th Anniv. — A187

1991, Dec. 19   Litho.   *Perf. 11½*
691   A187   145fr multicolored   3.25   1.60

Arthur Rimbaud (1854-1891) Poet and Merchant — A188

1991-92   *Perf. 11½*
692   A188   90fr Young man, ship   2.75   .90
693   A188   150fr Old man, camels   3.00   .90
Issued: 90fr, 2/5/92; 150fr, 12/23/91.

Djibouti-Ethiopia Railroad — A189

Design: 250fr, Locomotive, map.

1992   Litho.   *Perf. 12x11½*
694   A189   70fr multicolored   2.75   1.10

DJIBOUTI

Souvenir Sheet
Perf. 13x12½
695 A189 250fr multicolored 5.25 5.25
Issue dates: 70fr, Feb. 2; 250fr, Jan. 30.

Traditional Game Type of 1991
1992, Feb. 10   *Perf. 11½*
696 A180 100fr Boys playing Go 2.10 .85

A190

1992, June 9   Litho.   *Perf. 14*
697 A190 80fr multicolored 2.10 1.25
1992 Summer Olympics, Barcelona.

A191

Traditional food preparation — 30fr, Pounding grain. 45fr, Preparing mofo. 70fr, Winnowing grain. 75fr, Cooking mofo.

1992   Litho.   *Perf. 14x13½*
698 A191 30fr multi 1.25 .50
698A A191 45fr multi 90.00 —
699 A191 70fr multi 1.25 .65
699A A191 75fr multi 90.00 —
Issued: Nos. 698, 699, 4/20; No. 698A, 12/6.

Discovery of America, 500th Anniv. — A192

1992, May 16   Litho.   *Perf. 11½*
700 A192 125fr multicolored 3.25 .95

African Soccer Championships A193

1992, July 22   *Perf. 14*
701 A193 15fr multicolored .75 .25

Intl. Space Year — A194

Designs: 120fr, Rocket, satellite. 135fr, Astronaut, satellite, horiz.

Perf. 14x13½, 13½x14
1992, Sept. 28
702 A194 120fr multi 2.75 .85
703 A194 135fr multi 2.75 .95

Wildlife — A195

1992, Nov. 11   *Perf. 14*
704 A195 5fr Dik-dik 1.25 .25
705 A195 200fr Caretta caretta 5.00 1.60

Taeniura Lymma — A195a

Perf. 11½x11¾
1990, Mar. 24   Litho.
Panel Color
705A A195a 30fr pink — —
705B A195a 70fr yellow — —
705C A195a 100fr green — —
705D A195a 120fr lilac — —

Nomad Girls in Traditional Costumes — A196

1993, Jan. 26   Litho.   *Perf. 13*
706 A196 70fr Girl beside hut 1.75 .45
707 A196 120fr shown 2.75 .75

White-eyed Seagull — A197

1993, Feb. 28   Litho.   *Perf. 12½*
708 A197 300fr multicolored 5.75 1.75

Amin Salman Mosque A198

1993, Feb. 17   Litho.   *Perf. 13¾x14*
709 A198 500fr multicolored 52.50 5.50

Handcrafts A199

1993, Apr. 23   Litho.   *Perf. 13¾x14*
710 A199 100fr Neck rest 100.00 15.00
711 A199 125fr Sword 100.00 15.00

Cercopithecus Aethiops — A200

1993, May 29   Litho.   *Perf. 14¼x13½*
712 A200 150fr multi 80.00 5.00

Organization of African Unity, 30th Anniv. — A201

Perf. 14¼x13½
1993, June 20   Litho.
713 A201 200fr multi 100.00 2.25

Water Carriers — A202

1993, July 6   Litho.   *Perf. 14x13¾*
714 A202 30fr Woman 100.00 —
715 A202 50fr Man 100.00 —

Conquest of Space — A203

1993, Sept. 30   Litho.   *Perf. 14x13¾*
716 A203 90fr multicolored — —

A204

Traditional utensils.

1993, Sept. 30   Litho.   *Perf. 13½*
717 A204 15fr Weyso .45 .25
718 A204 20fr Hangol .90 .25
719 A204 25fr Saqaf 1.00 .25
720 A204 30fr Subrar 1.40 .45
Nos. 717-720 (4) 3.75 1.20

A205

Traditional musical instruments.

1993, Nov. 10   Litho.   *Perf. 14*
721 A205 5fr Flute 1.00 1.00
722 A205 10fr Drum 1.00 1.00

Souvenir Sheet
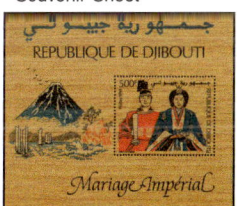
Wedding of Japan's Crown Prince Naruhito and Masako Owada A206

1994, Jan. 10   Litho.   *Perf. 13x12½*
Self-Adhesive
723 A206 500fr multicolored 22.50 22.50
No. 723 printed on wood.

20 Kilometer Race of Djibouti — A207

1994   Litho.   *Perf. 11½*
724 A207 50fr multicolored 2.50 1.00

Promotion of Breastfeeding — A208

1994
725 A208 40fr shown 1.90 .40
726 A208 45fr Mother, infant 2.10 .40

Hassan Gouled Aptidon Stadium — A209

1994
727 A209 70fr multicolored 2.50 1.10

Stenella Longirostris A210

1994, May 1   Litho.   *Perf. 11¾x11½*
728 A210 120fr multicolored — —

World Housing Day — A211

1994, May 9   Litho.   *Perf. 11½x11¾*
729 A211 30fr multi 100.00 —

Eupodotis Senegalensis A212

Perf. 11¾x11½
1994, June 16   Litho.
730 A212 10fr multicolored 180.00 —

1994 World Cup Soccer Tournament A213

1994, Sept. 7
731 A213 200fr multicolored 150.00 —

Dress of a Village Leader — A214

Design: 100fr, Traditional nomad costume.

172 DJIBOUTI

Perf. 11½x11¾
1994, Sept. 18   Litho.
732 A214 100fr multicolored   100.00

Perf. 11¾
733 A214 150fr multicolored   10.00

Canis Aureus — A215

Perf. 11¾x11½
1994, Sept. 28   Litho.
734 A215 400fr multi   135.00

World Walking Day — A216

1994, Oct. 19   Litho.   **Perf. 11¾x11½**
735 A216 75fr multicolored   150.00

A217

1994, Nov. 26   Litho.   **Perf. 11¾**
736 A217 55fr Book stand   75.00

A218

1994, Dec. 6   Litho.   **Perf. 11½x11¾**
737 A218 35fr Traditional dance   60.00   12.00

Souvenir Sheet

Sea-Me-We 2 Submarine Cable — A218a

1994   **Perf. 12½**
737A A218a 350fr multi   175.00

Volleyball, Cent. — A219

1995, Feb. 25   Litho.   **Perf. 11¾**
738 A219 70fr multicolored

United Nations, 50th Anniv. — A220

1995, Feb. 25
739 A220 120fr multicolored

Fight Against Thirst — A221

Perf. 11¾x11½
1995, Mar. 29   Litho.
740 A221 100fr multicolored

Threskiornis Aethiopica — A222

Design: 30fr, Phoenicopterus ruber

1995, Apr. 5   Litho.   **Perf. 11¾**
741 A222 30fr multicolored
742 A222 50fr multicolored

World Telecommunications Day — A223

Perf. 11¾x11½
1995, June 10   Litho.
743 A223 125fr multicolored   70.00   1.25

Crocuta Crocuta — A224

1995, June 12   Litho.   **Perf. 11¾**
744 A224 200fr multi   105.00

People Meeting Under Tree — A225

1995, July 3   Litho.   **Perf. 11¾x11½**
745 A225 150fr multi   65.00

Nomads Around Fire — A226

1995, Aug. 9   **Perf. 11¾**
746 A226 45fr multi   60.00   12.00

FAO, 50th Anniv. — A227

1995, Sept. 27   **Perf. 11½x11¾**
747 A227 250fr multi   70.00   12.00

Traditional Costume — A228

1995, Dec. 6   **Perf. 11¾**
748 A228 90fr multicolored   — 12.00

African Development Bank, 30th Anniv. — A229

1995, Dec. 18   **Perf. 11¾x11½**
749 A229 300fr multi   60.00   12.00

African Soccer Cup — A230

1996, Feb. 28
750 A230 70fr multicolored   180.00

Ostrich — A231

1996, Apr. 23
751 A231 120fr multi   100.00

Leopard — A232

1996, May 6
752 A232 70fr multi   105.00

Amber Necklace — A233

1996, June 13   Litho.
753 A233 30fr multi   100.00

1996 Summer Olympic Games, Atlanta — A234

Perf. 11½x11¾
1996, Sept. 21   Litho.
754 A234 105fr multicolored   125.00   12.00

Commicarpus Grandiflorus — A236

1996, Oct. 6   Litho.   **Perf. 11½x11¾**
756 A236 350fr multi   60.00   12.00

Djibouti Folklore — A237

1996, Nov. 28   Litho.   **Perf. 11¾**
757 A237 95fr multi   60.00

Legend of the Lion and Three Bulls — A238

1996, Nov. 28   Litho.   **Perf. 11¾**
758 A238 95fr multi   80.00   12.00

Children's Day — A239

1996, Dec. 17   **Perf. 11¾x11½**
759 A239 130fr multi   60.00   12.00

A240

Legend of the Tortoise and the Fox: No. 760, Tortoise and fox at starting line. No. 761, Fox leaves tortoise behind. No. 762, Tortoise passes sleeping fox.

1997, Jan. 17   **Perf. 11¾**
760 A240 60fr multi
761 A240 60fr multi
762 A240 60fr multi
   a. Horiz. strip, #760-762   135.00

UNICEF, 50th Anniv. — A241

1997, Feb. 9   Litho.   **Perf. 11¾**
763 A241 80fr Mother, child   50.00   10.00
764 A241 90fr Hands around globe   100.00   12.00

Dancers — A242

1997, May 14   Litho.   **Perf. 11¾**
765 A242 70fr multi   70.00   12.00

Fortune Teller — A243

Designs: 200fr, Fortune teller and woman. 300fr, Fortune teller, camel.

1997, May 29   Litho.   **Perf. 11¾**
766 A243 200fr multi   60.00   12.00
767 A243 300fr multi   60.00   12.00

DJIBOUTI

Woman's Day — A244

1997, May 30   Litho.   Perf. 11¾
768 A244 250fr multi   160.00 12.00

Traditional Objects — A245

Design: 30fr, Writing board, horiz. 400fr, Bowl and spoon.

1997, June 5   Litho.   Perf. 11¾
769 A245 30fr multi   45.00 10.00
770 A245 400fr multi   45.00 10.00

Telecommunications A246

Designs: 30fr, Arta post office. 100fr, Map, building with antenna and satellite dishes. 120fr, Ships, map showing submarine cable route, horiz.

1997, June 27   Litho.   Perf. 11¾
771 A246 30fr multi   —   12.00
772 A246 100fr multi   —   12.00
773 A246 120fr multi   —   12.00

Goats in Tree — A247

1997, July 26   Litho.   Perf. 11¾
774 A247 120fr multi   50.00 15.00

A248

Portrait of Diana: a, 125fr. b, 130fr. c, 150fr.

1998, Mar. 25   Litho.   Perf. 13½
775 A248 Strip of 3, #a.-c.   5.00   5.00

Diana, Princess of Wales (1961-97).
No. 775 was issued in sheets of 6 stamps.

Mother Teresa (1910-97) — A249

1998   Litho.   Perf. 13½
776 A249 130fr multicolored   2.75   1.40

No. 776 was issued in sheets of 4.

Intl. Year of the Ocean — A250

a, Tangara chilensis. b, Agalychnis callidryas. c, Delphinus delphis, megaptera novaeangliae. d, Cercopithecus aethiops (h). e, Laticaudia colubrina (i), sphyrna mokarran. f, Lactoria cornuta, delphinus delphis (g). g, Delphinus delphis (k). h, Aspidontus taeniatus,

lo vulpinus. i, Sepioteuthis lessoniana. j, Prionace glauca (i), chaetodon ornatissimus. k, Eupagurus bernherdus. l, Octopus vulgaris (k).

1998, Apr. 20   Litho.   Perf. 13½
777 A250 75fr Sheet of 12,
           #a.-l.   16.00 16.00

Mahatma Gandhi (1869-1948) — A251

1998, Apr. 20   Litho.   Perf. 11¾
778 A251 250fr multi   80.00 12.00

Traditional Art — A252

1998, Apr. 25 Litho. Perf. 11½x11¾
779 A252 30fr multicolored   120.00 12.00

Women's Rights and International Peace — A253

1998, May 3   Perf. 11¾x11½
780 A253 70fr multicolored   60.00 12.00

1998 World Cup Soccer Championships, France — A255

1998, June 10   Litho.   Perf. 11¾
782 A255 200fr multi   145.00   —

Marine Life — A256

Perf. 11½x11¾, 11¾x11½
1998, July 2   Litho.
783 A256 20fr Octopus   135.00
784 A256 25fr Shark, horiz.   135.00

Cats and Bush — A257

1998, Aug. 30   Perf. 11½x11¾
785 A257 120fr multi   135.00   —

World Telecommunications Day — A258

1996, Sept. 27   Litho.   Perf. 11¾
786 A258 150fr multi   100.00   —

National Bank — A259

1998, Sept. 30   Litho.   Perf. 11¾
787 A259 100fr multi   135.00 12.00

Flags and IGAD Emblem — A260

Perf. 11½x11¾
1998, Sept. 30   Litho.
788 A260 85fr multi   75.00   —

Traditional Game Goos — A261

1998, Oct. 1   Perf. 11¾x11½
789 A261 110fr multi   60.00   —

Fishing Port — A262

1998
790 A262 100fr multi   115.00   —

Maskali Island — A263

1998
791 A263 500fr multi   140.00   —

Fish — A264

1999   Litho.   Perf. 13¼x13½
792 A264 70fr multi   100.00   —

Antelope — A264a

Perf. 13¼x13½
1999, Mar. 16   Litho.
792A A264a 120fr multi   90.00   —

Djibouti Franc, 50th Anniv. — A265

1999
793 A265 100fr multi   60.00   —

World Telecommunications Day — A266

1999
794 A266 125fr multi   55.00   —

Worldwide Fund for Nature (WWF) — A267

Phacochoerus africanus aeliani: a, Adult and young. b, Adult standing. c, Head. d, Adult walking.

2000, Apr. 13   Litho.   Perf. 14
795 A267 100fr Block of 4, #a-d 9.00   9.00

Wild Animals A268

No. 796: a, Flamingo. b, Ostrich. c, Sifaka. d, Yellow-billed stork. e, Scarlet macaw. f, Dwarf puff adder. g, Toucan. h, Whooping crane.

2000, Apr. 13
796 A268 100fr Sheet of 8, #a-
           h   22.50 22.50

Butterflies — A269

No. 797: a, Doxocopa cherubina. b, Heliconius charitonius. c, Cantonephele numili. d, Danaus gilippus. e, Morpho peleides. f, Heliconius doris.
No. 798, 250fr, Agraulis vanillae. No. 799, 250fr, Strymon melinus.

2000, Apr. 13
797 A269 100fr Sheet of 6, #a-
           f   12.00 12.00

Souvenir Sheets
798-799 A269 Set of 2   11.00 11.00

No. 797 contains six 28x42mm stamps.

DJIBOUTI

Water Resources — A270

2000, Apr. 13
800 A270 500fr multi   8.00 8.00

Trains and Landmarks — A271

No. 801: a, 5fr, Class OJ 2-10-2, China. b, 25fr, Eurostar, France-England. c, 15fr, Glacier Express, Switzerland. d, 40fr, Unidentified train. e, 35fr, Class WP 4-6-2, India.
No. 802, 110fr: a, Nord Chapelon Pacific, France. b, Class 23 2-6-2, Germany. c, Class GS-4 4-8-4, US. d, Class A4 4-6-2, Great Britain. e, Pacific 4-6-2, South Africa. f, Class HP, India.
No. 803, 120fr: a, VT601, Germany. b, ICIII Bo-Bo EMU, Netherlands. c, TGV, France. d, ETR 450, Italy. e, AVE, Spain. f, Bullet Train, Japan.
No. 804, 250fr, GM War Bonnet, US. No. 805, 250fr, Class 8 Pacific, Great Britain.

2000, Apr. 28
801 A271 Horiz. strip of 5, #a-e   3.00 3.00
Sheets of 6, #a-f
802-803 A271 Set of 2   15.00 15.00
Souvenir Sheets
804-805 A271 Set of 2   6.00 6.00

Dancers — A272

2000, Apr. 28
806 A272 75fr multi   4.00 1.50

Blacksmith A273

2000, May 14
807 A273 100fr multi   6.00 2.50

Marine Life A274

No. 808, vert.: a, Dendrochirus biocellatus. b, Hippocampus. c, Amphiprion ocellaris, Amphiprion percula. d, Periclimenes imperator. e, Pomacentridae. f, Octopus vulgaris.
No. 809, 50fr: a, Cephalopholis miniata. b, Ptereleotris hanae. c, Sphyraena genie. d, Tripterygion segmentatum. e, Odontaspididae. f, Cirrhitidae. g, Amphiprion. h, Capros aper. i, Balistidae. j, Trygonorhina fasciata. k, Cephalopholis. l, Corythoichthys ocellatus.
No. 810, 60fr: a, Lutjanus kasmira. b, Chaetodon fasciatus. c, Epinephelinae. d, Hypoplectrus gutavarius. e, Loligo opalescens. f, Diodontinae. g, Coelenterata. h, Sargocentron xanthyrthum. i, Thalassoma lunare. j, Hemichromis bimaculatus. k, Dasyatis. l, Fromia monilis.
No. 811, 250fr, Eschrichtius robustus. No. 812, 250fr, Cheloniidae.

2000, May 14
808 A274 55fr Sheet of 6, #a-f   8.00 8.00
Sheets of 12, #a-l
809-810 A274 Set of 2   30.00 30.00
Souvenir Sheets
811-812 A274 Set of 2   8.00 8.00

Camels and Tender — A275

2000, June 26
813 A275 35fr multi   4.75 .90

Ships — A276

Designs: 10fr, Thomas W. Lawson, 1902. 15fr, BT Global Challenge, 2000. 20fr, Reliance and Shamrock III, 1903. 25fr, Archibald Russell, 1905. 50fr, Greek merchantman, 8th cent. B.C.
No. 819, 130fr: a, Norman warship, 1066. b, Hanseatic cog, c. 1300. c, Santa Maria, 1492. d, Mary Rose, 1510. e, Golden Hind, 1577. f, Sovereign of the Seas, 1637.
No. 820:, 135fr: a, HMS Endeavour, 1768. b, USS Constitution, 1797. c, Chasse-Maree, 1800. d, Baltimore clipper, 1812. e, Lightning, 1853. f, Bluenose, 1921.
No. 821, 250fr, HM Yacht Britannia, 1893. No. 822, 250fr, Herzogin Cecilie, 1902.

2000, June 26
814-818 A276 Set of 5   2.00 2.00
Sheets of 6, #a-f
819-820 A276 Set of 2   25.00 25.00
Souvenir Sheets
821-822 A276 Set of 2   8.00 8.00

Millennium A277

2000, July 18
823 A277 125fr multi   2.75 2.75

Birds — A278

2000, Aug. 23
824   Horiz. strip of 5   2.75 2.75
  a. A278 5fr Lanius excubitor   .35 .35
  b. A278 10fr Phoenicopterus minor   .35 .35
  c. A278 15fr Eupodatis senegalensis   .35 .35
  d. A278 40fr Noephron perchopterus   .60 .60
  e. A278 50fr Pterocles lichtensteinii   .75 .75

Space Exploration — A279

No. 825, 100fr, vert.: a, John Glenn and Mercury capsule, 1962. b, Soyuz capsule, Apollo-Soyuz mission, 1975. c, Hubble Telescope, 1990. d, Apollo capsule, Apollo-Soyuz mission, e, Glenn at speaker's stand, 1974. f, Space Shuttle Columbia, 1981.
No. 826, 100fr, vert.: a, Apollo 11 service module, 1969. b, Telstar, 1962. c, Ariane 4, 1988. d, Apollo 11 lunar module. e, Neil Armstrong, 1969. f, Splashdown of Apollo 11, 1969.
No. 827, 200fr, Astronaut on moon saluting. No. 828, 250fr, Astronauts conducting experiments on moon. No. 829, 250fr, Space Shuttle Challenger.

2000, Aug. 23 **Sheets of 6, #a-f**
825-826 A279 Set of 2   20.00 20.00
Souvenir Sheets
827-829 A279 Set of 3   12.00 12.00

2000 Summer Olympics, Sydney — A280

Olympic flame, flag and: 80fr, Runner. 90fr, Tennis player.

2000   **Perf. 14**
830-831 A280 Set of 2   4.00 4.00

Unknown Soldier Monument—A280a

2004, Apr. 18 **Litho.** **Perf. 13x12¾**
832 A280a 175fr multi   50.00 20.00

Independence, 27th Anniv. — A281

2004, June 27 **Litho.** **Perf. 13**
833 A281 45fr multi   — —

Dragon Tree A282

Pregnant Woman at Hospital A283

Camel Caravan A284

Natl. Union of Djibouti Women A285

National Arms — A286

Perf. 12¾x13, 13x12¾
2004, Dec. 18   **Litho.**
834 A282 15fr multi   37.50 20.00
835 A283 25fr multi   37.50 20.00
836 A284 45fr multi   37.50 20.00
837 A285 70fr multi   37.50 20.00
838 A286 100fr multi   25.00 20.00
Nos. 834-838 (5)   175.00 100.00

Friendship Between Djibouti and People's Republic of China, 25th Anniv.

Designs: 5fr, Djibouti Electricity Building. 10fr, Hassan Gouled Stadium. 15fr, Djibouti Central Bank. 30fr, People's Palace. 45fr, Ministry of Foreign Affairs Building.

2004, Dec. 27   **Perf. 12**
839-843 A286a Set of 5   115.00 115.00

Items commemorating the death of Pope John Paul II were declared as "fraudulent" by Djibouti Post.

2006 World Cup Soccer Championships, Germany — A287

2005, June 8 **Litho.** **Perf. 13**
844 A287 100fr multi   95.00 —

Tanker in Port of Doraleh A288

2006, Nov. 6 **Litho.** **Perf. 13**
845 A288 120fr multi   50.00 —
Printed in sheets of 4.

Common Market for Eastern and Southern Africa Summit, Djibouti A289

2006, Nov. 6 **Litho.** **Perf. 13¼x13**
846 A289 150fr multi   50.00 —

Djibouti Chamber of Commerce, Cent. — A290

2007   **Litho.**   **Perf. 12¾**
847 A290 50fr multi   12.00 —
  a. Souvenir sheet of 2   52.50

Independence, 30th Anniv. — A291

2007, June 27 **Litho.** **Perf. 13**
848 A291 75fr multi   25.00 —
  a. Souvenir sheet of 2   50.00

Mahamoud Harbi (1921-60), Politician — A292

2007, Aug. 17 **Litho.** **Perf. 13x12¾**
849 A292 165fr multi   30.00 5.00

DJIBOUTI 175

Indo-Suez Red Sea Bank — A293

2008, Oct. 19   Litho.   Perf. 13x13½
850	A293	220fr multi	25.00	6.00
a.		Souvenir sheet of 2	50.00	—

2010 World Cup Soccer Championships, South Africa — A295

2010, May   Litho.   Perf. 13
852	A295	105fr multi	25.00	
a.		Souvenir sheet of 1	27.50	—

Djibouti postal authorities have declared "illegal" the following items:
Sheets of 8 stamps of various values: Mushrooms
Sheets of 6 stamps of various values: Fire trucks and Scouts (3 different)
Sheets of 6 700f stamps: Butterflies and Orchids, Butterflies and Scouts, Trains
Sheets of 6 300f stamps: Birds
Sheets of 4 800f stamps: Bonsai
Sheets of 4 700f stamps: Dogs (4 different), Cats (4 different), Babe Ruth and Tiger Woods, Dinosaurs
Sheets of 2 stamps of various values: Fire trucks (2 different)

2014 Africa Internet Summit, Djibouti A296

2014   Litho.   Perf. 13
853	A296	170fr multi	15.00	—
a.		Souvenir sheet of 1	50.00	—

A297

A298 / A299

Personalized Stamps — A300

2016, Jan. 25   Litho.   Perf. 13¼x13
854	A297	250fr multi	3.00	3.00
855	A298	250fr multi	3.00	3.00
856	A299	250fr multi	3.00	3.00
857	A300	250fr multi	3.00	3.00
		Nos. 854-857 (4)	12.00	12.00

Nos. 854-857 were each printed in sheets of 16 that could be personalized. A generic image showing Santa Claus with the inscription "Bonne Année 2016!" was made available. Values are for stamps with or without any printed vignette.

Fauna
A301

No. 858, 260fr — Primates: a, Lemur catta. b, Leontopithecus rosalia. c, Macaca fuscata. d, Mandrillus sphinx.
No. 859, 260fr — Bats: a, Plecotus auritus. b, Erophylla sezekorni. c, Sturnira lilium. d, Desmodus rotundus.
No. 860, 260fr — Wild cats: a, Panthera tigris. b, Panthera pardus melas. c, Panthera onca. d, Panthera leo.
No. 861, 260fr — Lions: a, Panthera leo nubica. b, Panthera leo bleyenberghi. c, Panthera leo leo. d, Panthera leo azandica.
No. 862, 260fr — Dugong: a, One dugong surfacing, fish at LR. b, Two dugongs, and calf. c, Dugong swimming, surrounded by fish. d, One dugong on sea floor, two fish at UL.
No. 863, 260fr — Dolphins: a, Delphinus capensis. b, Lagenorhynchus obscurus. c, Stenella frontalis. d, Delphinus delphis.
No. 864, 260fr — Whales: a, Delphinapterus leucas. b, Megaptera novaeangliae. c, Eubalaena australis. d, Physeter macrocephalus.
No. 865, 260fr — Eagles: a, Lophaetus occipitalis. b, Geranoaetus melanoleucus. c, Haliaeetus leucogaster. d, Aquila heliaca.
No. 866, 260fr — Parrots: a, Eclectus roratus. b, Anodorhynchus hyacinthinus. c, Conuropsis carolinensis. d, Trichoglossus moluccanus.
No. 867, 260fr — Owls: a, Megascops asio. b, Pulsatrix perspicillata. c, Bubo sumatranus. d, Ptilopsis leucotis.
No. 868, 260fr — Starlings: a, Sturnus vulgaris. b, Spreo fischeri. c, Sturnia sinensis. d, Mino dumontii.
No. 869, 260fr — Sunbirds: a, Leptocoma minima. b, Nectarinia famosa. c, Leptocoma sperata and Aetopyga siparaja. d, Anthreptes malacensis and Nectarinia tacazze.
No. 870, 260fr — Warblers: a, Lloparus chrysotis. b, Psittiparus gularis. c, Sylvia rueppelli. d, Parophasma galinieri.
No. 871, 260fr — Butterflies: a, Limenitis archippus. b, Apatura iris. c, Teinopalpus imperialis. d, Iphiclides podalirius.
No. 872, 260fr — Turtles: a, Terrapene carolina bauri. b, Chelonoidis nigra. c, Testudo graeca. d, Stigmochelys pardalis.
No. 873, 260fr — Snakes: a, Bitis arietans. b, Diopholidus typus. c, Echio pyramidum. d, Atractaspis fallax.
No. 874, 260fr — Crocodiles: a, Crocodylus siamensis. b, Crocodylus porosus. c, Crocodylus rhombifer. d, Crocodylus acutus.
No. 875, 260fr — Chameleons: a, Chamaeleo calyptratus. b, Chameleon hoehnelii. c, Chamaeleo chamaeleon. d, Furcifer pardalis.
No. 876, 260fr — Scorpions: a, Centruroides margaritatus. b, Parabuthus liosoma. c, Androctonus crassicauda. d, Babycurus jacksoni.
No. 877, 960fr, Cebus capucinus. No. 878, 960fr, Aceredon jubatus. No. 879, 960fr, Puma concolor. No. 880, 960fr, Panthera leo senegalensis. No. 881, 960fr, Two dugong dugon. No. 882, 960fr, Stenella coeruleoalba. No. 883, 960fr, Physeter macrocephalus, diff. No. 884, 960fr, Aquila rapax. No. 885, 960fr, Psittacus erithacus. No. 886, 960fr, Strix nebulosa. No. 887, 960fr, Lamprotornis hildebrandti. No. 888, 960fr, Cinnyris chalybeus. No. 889, 960fr, Myzornis pyrrhoura. No. 890, 960fr, Lasiommata megera. No. 891, 960fr, Aldabrachelys gigantea. No. 892, 960fr, Naja pallida. No. 893, 960fr, Crocodylus acutus, diff. No. 894, 960fr, Kinyongia fischeri. No. 895, 960fr, Hottentotta tamulus.

2016, Jan. 25   Litho.   Perf. 13¼
Sheets of 4, #a-d
858-876	A301	Set of 19	225.00	225.00

Souvenir Sheets
| 877-895 | A301 | Set of 19 | 205.00 | 205.00 |

A302

No. 896, 260fr — Nelson Mandela (1918-2013), President of South Africa, and: a, Three doves. b, Prison cell. c, Amethyst crystal. d, Dove and flag of South Africa.
No. 897, 270fr — Mahatma Gandhi (1869-1948), Indian nationalist leader: a, Sitting at small table. b, With spinning wheel, automobile. c, Seated, pulling thread. d, Seated in chair.
No. 898, 270fr — St. John Paul II (1920-2005): a, With two doves. b, With Nelson Mandela. c, With Mother Teresa. d, Holding crucifix.
No. 899, 270fr — Queen Elizabeth II, longest-reigning British monarch, wearing: a, Crown and blue sash. b, Pink hat. c, Green hat. d, Tiara and orange sash.
No. 900, 270fr — Princess Diana (1961-97), with: a, Princes William and Harry. b, Mother Teresa. c, Child and Red Cross flag. d, Princes Charles and William.
No. 901, 270fr — Lord Robert Baden-Powell (1857-1941), founder of Scouting movement, Scouting emblem: a, Wearing military uniform. b, Wearing Indian headdress. c, Holding animal horn, British flag in background. d, With Scout bugler.
No. 902, 270fr — Nobel laureates: a, Ei-ichi Negishi, 2010 Chemistry laureate. b, Malala Yousafzai, 2014 Peace laureate. c, James D. Watson, 1962 Physiology or Medicine laureate. d, Doris Lessing, 2007 Literature laureate.
No. 903, 270fr — Soccer players and stadiums for 2016 European Soccer Championships, France: a, Stade Pierre Mauroy, Lille. b, Stade Vélodrome, Marseille. c, Stade de Lyon, Lyon. d, Stade de Bordeaux, Bordeaux.
No. 904, 270fr — Sports of the 2016 Summer Olympics, Rio de Janeiro: a, Artistic gymnastics. b, Kayak slalom. c, Women's beach volleyball. d, Rugby.
No. 905, 270fr — Attack on Pearl Harbor, 75th anniv.: a, USS Arizona. b, U.S. P-40B airplane. c, Japanese Mitsubishi A6M Zero airplane. d, USS Missouri.
No. 906, 270fr — Walt Disney (1901-66), animated filmmaker, and: a, Bavarian Castle. b, Awards. c, Film camera. d, Drawing board and sketches.
No. 907, 270fr — Marilyn Monroe (1926-62), actress, wearing: a, Necklace. b, Black bathing suit. c, Blue bathing suit. d, White dress and gloves.
No. 908, 270fr — Elvis Presley (1935-77): a, Playing guitar. b, Holding microphone. c, Wearing striped shirt. d, With Hollywood Walk of Fame star.
No. 909, 270fr — Wolfgang Amadeus Mozart (1756-91), composer, and: a, His father, Johann Georg Leopold Mozart (1719-87). b, His mother, Anna Maria Pertl Mozart (1720-78). c, His wife, Maria Constanze Mozart (1762-1842). d, Young Mozart blind folded playing piano.
No. 910, 270fr — Georg Albert Schumann (1866-1952), composer: a, Violin, score, hands of conductor. b, Wearing black suit. c, At piano. d, Conducting musicians.
No. 911, 270fr — Paintings by Vincent van Gogh (1853-90): a, Self-portrait, 1889. b, Vase with Twelve Sunflowers, 1889. c, Portrait of Doctor Gachet, 1890. d, Starry Night Over the Rhône, 1888.
No. 912, 270fr — Paintings by Claude Monet (1840-1926): a, Flowering Garden in Saint-Adresse, 1866. b, Les Meules à Giverny, 1884. c, The Bridge at Argenteuil, 1874. d, The Bridge Over the Water Lily Pond, 1905.
No. 913, 270fr — Paintings by Pablo Picasso (1881-1973): a, Self-portrait, 1907. b, Boy with a Pipe, 1905. c, The Old Guitarist, 1903. d, Portrait of Daniel-Henry Kahnweiler, 1910.
No. 914, 270fr — Christmas: a, Ded Moroz and Snegurochka. b, Santa Claus and reindeer. c, Saint Nicholas on horse. d, Joulupukki.

No. 915, 270fr — New Year 2016 (Year of the Monkey): a, Monkey on branch. b, Monkey with open mouth. c, Head of monkey. d, Adult and juvenile monkey.
No. 916, 960fr, Mandela, diff. No. 917, 960fr, Gandhi and tiger. No. 918, 960fr, St. John Paul II and 14th Dalai Lama. No. 919, 960fr, Queen Elizabeth II and Prince Philip. No. 920, 960fr, Princess Diana and Queen Elizabeth II. No. 921, 960fr, Baden-Powell, Boy Scout and Scouting emblem. No. 922, 960fr, 14th Dalai Lama receiving 1989 Nobel Peace Prize. No. 923, 960fr, Soccer player, Stade de France, Saint-Denis. No. 924, 960fr, Women's 100-meter sprint, boxers. No. 925, 960fr, Explosion on USS Shaw, Herbert C. Jones, Medal of Honor. No. 926, 960fr, Disney, diff. No. 927, 960fr, Monroe, diff. No. 928, 960fr, Presley playing guitar, diff. No. 929, 960fr, Mozart, Masonic compass and square. No. 930, 960fr, Schumann conducting musicians, diff. No. 931, 960fr, Self-portrait with Bandaged Ear and Pipe, by van Gogh, 1889. No. 932, 960fr, Woman with a Parasol, by Monet, 1875. No. 933, 960fr, Seated Woman, by Picasso, 1937. No. 934, 960fr, Saint Nicholas waving. No. 935, 960fr, Adult and juvenile monkeys, diff.

2016, Mar. 15   Litho.   Perf. 13¼
Sheets of 4, #a-d
896-915	A302	Set of 20	245.00	245.00

Souvenir Sheets
| 916-935 | A302 | Set of 20 | 220.00 | 220.00 |

Inscriptions on Nos. 911b and 932 are incorrect.

A303

No. 936, 280fr — Campaign against malaria: a, Two adults watching sleeping child. b, Mosquito, person tending to patient. c, Mother watching sleeping child. d, Child behind mosquito netting.
No. 937, 280fr — Rugby players: a, Player kicking ball. b, Two players with red shirts attempting tackle. c, Player running with ball and opponent. d, Player with black shirt tackling ball carrier.
No. 938, 280fr — Table tennis players: a, Fan Zhendong. b, Liu Shiwen. c, Kasumi Ishikawa. d, Xu Xin.
No. 939, 280fr — Chess players: a, Magnus Carlsen. b, Sergey Karjakin. c, Viswanathan Anand. d, Judit Polgár.
No. 940, 280fr — Pilgrimage to Mecca: a, Pilgrims circling Ka'aba. b, Stoning of the devil. c, Great Mosque of Mecca, Koran. d, Shaving of heads.
No. 941, 280fr — Lighthouses: a, Les Eclaireurs Lighthouse, Argentina. b, Jeddah Lighthouse, Saudi Arabia. c, Lindau Lighthouse, Germany. d, New London Ledge Lighthouse, U.S.
No. 942, 280fr — Ships: a, Kruzenshtern. b, Flying Dutchman and Phocéa. c, Götheborg. d, Europa.
No. 943, 280fr — Steam locomotives: a, Class C38, Australia. b, Class 19D, South Africa. c, DRB Class 52, Germany. d, Class P36, Russia.
No. 944, 280fr — High-speed trains: a, CRH380A, People's Republic of China. b, Shinkansen Series E6, Eb21-1, Japan. c, Shinkansen Series N700A, Japan. d, Shinkansen Series N700, N2020-1, Japan.
No. 945, 280fr — Race cars: a, Aston Martin DBRS 9. b, Ferrari F150 Italia. c, Ford Fiesta RS WRC. d, Maserati MC12 GT1.
No. 946, 280fr — Fire trucks: a, 1964 Bedford. b, 1962 Chevrolet Apache. c, 1959 Ford Galaxie. d, 1937 Chevrolet.
No. 947, 280fr — First commercial flight of the Concorde, 40th anniv.: a, Concorde in flight, passenger cabin. b, Concorde in flight, nose of Concorde. c, Concorde taking off. d, Under wing view of Concorde.
No. 948, 280fr — Scenes from Apollo space missions: a, Apollo 11. b, Apollo 16. c, Apollo 15. d, Apollo 17.
No. 949, 280fr — Sled dogs: a, Samoyeds. b, Siberian huskies and Alaskan malamutes. c, Alaskan malamutes. d, Man carrying Siberian husky.

DJIBOUTI

No. 950, 280fr — Raptors: a, Melierax poliopterus. b, Torgos tracheliotus. c, Glaucidium passerinum. d, Terathopius ecaudatus.
No. 951, 280fr — Butterflies: a, Boloria aquilonaris. b, Pontia protodice. c, Strymon melinus. d, Aricia agestis.
No. 952, 280fr — Dinosaurs: a, Tyrannosaurus rex. b, Microraptor zhaoianus. c, Dakotaraptor steini. d, Chasmosaurus.
No. 953, 280fr — Orchids: a, Caucaea mimetica. b, Diuris magnifica. c, Thelymitra pulcherrima. d, Thelymitra campanulata.
No. 954, 280fr — Mushrooms: a, Craterellus tubaeformis. b, Tricholoma matsutake. c, Cantharellus cibarius. d, Stropharia rugoso.
No. 955, 280fr — Minerals: a, Sulfur. b, Chalcanthite. c, Colemanite. d, Legrandite.
No. 956, 960fr, Malaria-carrying mosquito, horiz. No. 957, 960fr, Rugby players, horiz. No. 958, 960fr, Ma Long playing table tennis, horiz. No. 959, 960fr, Chess players Anatoly Karpov and Garry Kasparov, horiz. No. 960, 960fr, Pilgrims on Mount Arafat, horiz. No. 961, 960fr, Cape Hatteras Lighthouse, U.S., Onychoprion fuscatus, horiz. No. 962, 960fr, El Galeón, horiz. No. 963, 960fr, Erie Berkshire locomotive, horiz. No. 964, 960fr, Frecciarossa 1000 train, Italy, horiz. No. 965, 960fr, Aston Martin DBR9, horiz. No. 966, 960fr, 1927 Ahrens-Fox fire truck, horiz. No. 967, 960fr, Concorde in flight and cockpit, horiz. No. 968, 960fr, Apollo 16 astronaut John Young on Moon, horiz. No. 969, 960fr, Dogs pulling sled, horiz. No. 970, 960fr, Aquila pomarina, horiz. No. 971, 960fr, Colotis danae, horiz. No. 972, 960fr, Deinocheirus mirificus, horiz. No. 973, 960fr, Cattleya schroederae, horiz. No. 974, 960fr, Boletus edulis, horiz. No. 975, 960fr, Galèna and fluorite, horiz.

2016, May 5   Litho.   Perf. 13¼
Sheets of 4, #a-d
936-955 A303 Set of 20 255.00 255.00

Souvenir Sheets
956-975 A303 Set of 20 220.00 220.00

No. 940a inscription is missing "c" of circumambulation. Nos. 956-975 each contain one 66x42mm stamp.

Investiture of Pres. Ismail Omar Guelleh
A304

2016, May 8   Litho.   Perf. 13¼
976 A304 1000fr bister & multi 11.50 11.50

Litho. With Foil Application
Souvenir Sheet
977 A304 5000fr gold & multi 57.50 57.50

No. 976 was printed in sheets of 4. No. 977 contains one 51x51mm stamp.

A305

Independence, 39th Anniv. — A306

2016, June 27   Litho.   Perf. 13½x13
978 A305 250fr multi 3.00 3.00

Souvenir Sheet
Perf. 13¼
979 A306 500fr multi 5.75 5.75

Souvenir Sheet

Hassan Gouled Aptidon (1916-2006), First President of Djibouti — A307

2016, June 27   Litho.   Perf. 13¼
980 A307 500fr multi 5.75 5.75

Muhammad Ali (1942-2016), Boxer — A308

No. 981 — Ali: a, With sign taped to wall. b, Wearing boxing gloves and headgear. c, In boxing ring. d, With hand touching face. 960fr, Ali running.

2016, July 28   Litho.   Perf. 13¼
981 A308 260fr Sheet of 4, #a-d 12.00 12.00

Souvenir Sheet
982 A308 960fr multi 11.00 11.00

No. 982 contains one 38x54mm stamp.

A309

No. 983, 260fr — Steve Jobs (1955-2011), co-founder and chief executive officer of Apple Inc., and: a, Steve Wozniak, co-founder of Apple. b, Three computers. c, Apple 1 computer. d, Computer and apple.
No. 984, 260fr — Pope Francis: a, With Patriarch Cyril of Moscow. b, With child and dove. c, With statue and rosary beads. d, Washing feet of refugees.
No. 985, 260fr — Paintings by Pierre-Auguste Renoir (1841-1919): a, Young Woman Sewing, 1879. b, Luncheon of the Boating Party, 1880-81. c, Two Girls at the Piano, 1892. d, The Bridge at Chatou, 1875.
No. 986, 260fr — Paintings by Francisco de Goya (1746-1828): a, The Umbrella, 1777. b, Clothed Maja, 1800. c, Saturn Devouring His Son, 1819-23. d, Charles IV of Spain and His Family, 1800.
No. 987, 260fr — Paintings by Berthe Morisot (1841-95): a, The Garden at Bougival, 1884. b, Hide-and-Seek, 1873. c, Lucie Leon at the Piano, 1892. d, Dahlias, 1876.
No. 988, 260fr — Paintings by Paul Cézanne (1839-1906): a, Kitchen Table, 1888-90. b, The Bridge at Maincy, 1879. c, Still Life with Apples and Oranges, 1895. d, Mont Sainte-Victoire with Large Pine, 1887.
No. 989, 260fr — Museum visitors looking at paintings in the Musée d'Orsay: a, Yellow Haystacks, by Paul Gauguin, 1889. b, Luncheon on the Grass, by Edouard Manet, 1862-63. c, The Floor Scrapers, by Gustave Caillebotte, 1875. d, Self-portrait, by Vincent van Gogh, 1889.
No. 990, 260fr — Items from ancient Egypt: a, Bust of Nefertiti. b, Gayer-Anderson Cat. c, Horus and Temple of Amun, Luxor. d, Funerary mask of Tutankhamun and Giza Pyramids.
No. 991, 260fr — Royal Mail, 500th anniv.: a, Postman emptying pillar box, Morris J Type mail van. b, Horse-drawn mail wagon. c, Postal worker rowing to SS Mona's Queen. d, Postmen on bicycles.
No. 992, 260fr — Battle of Moscow, 75th anniv.: a, German soldier and battlefield map. b, T-34 tank. c, Telegrapher and telegraph key. d, German General Erich Hoepner (1886-1944) and Sturmgeschütz III.
No. 993, 260fr — First flight of LZ-129 (Hindenburg), 80th anniv.: a, Pianist and singer on Hindenburg. b, Workers under docked Hindenburg. c, Hindenburg and hangar. d, Hindenburg, tables and chairs.
No. 994, 260fr — Yuri Gagarin (1934-68), 55th anniv. of first spaceflight, and: a, Launch of rocket. b, Vostok 1 in space. c, Gagarin seated in spacesuit. d, Monument to Gagarin, Moscow.
No. 995, 260fr — Intl. Year of Pulses: a, Woman, child and legumes. b, Hands holding seedling. c, Farm machinery, sprout. d, Poicephalus senegalus, legume.
No. 996, 260fr — Gold medalists at 2014 Winter Olympics, Sochi, Russia: a, Alexander Tretyakov, skeleton. b, Matthias Mayer, downhill skiing. c, Darya Domracheva, mass start, pursuit and individual biathlon. d, Michel Mulder, speed skating.
No. 997, 260fr — Host cities for 2018 World Cup soccer championships, Russia: a, Yekaterinburg. b, St. Petersburg. c, Kazan. d, Volgograd.
No. 998, 260fr — Cat breeds: a, Ragdoll, standing. b, Siamese. c, Ragdoll, prone. d, Australian Mist.
No. 999, 260fr — Dolphins: a, Stenella longirostris. b, Tursiops truncatus with open mouth, beak of Stenella longirostris. c, Stenella coeruleoalba. d, Two Tursiops truncatus.
No. 1000, 260fr — Owls: a, Asio stygius. b, Strix leptogrammica. c, Surnia ulula. d, Tyto alba.
No. 1001, 260fr — Turtles: a, Cuora flavomarginata, Terrapene carolina carolina. b, Terrapene carolina carolina, Geochelone elegans. c, Trachemys scripta elegans. d, Terrapene ornata ornata, Stigmochelys pardalis.
No. 1002, 960fr, Jobs, computer and iPhone. No. 1003, 960fr, Pope Francis and dove. No. 1004, 960fr, Portrait of Marie-Thérèse Durand Ruel, by Renoir, 1882. No. 1005, 960fr, Witches' Sabbath, by Goya, 1789. No. 1006, 960fr, On the Balcony of Eugene Manet's room at Bougival, by Morisot, 1881. No. 1007, 960fr, A Modern Olympia, by Cézanne, 1870. No. 1008, 960fr, Visitor looking at Portrait of Doctor Paul Gachet , 1890 at Musée d'Orsay. No. 1009, 960fr, Painting from Tomb of Userhat. No. 1010, 960fr, British postman, pillar box, Titan Airways Boeing 737. No. 1011, 960fr, Soviet General Georgy Zhukov (1896-1974), anti-aircraft fire of Battle of Moscow. No. 1012, 960fr, Mooring of the Hindenburg at Lakehurst, New Jersey. No. 1013, 960fr, Gagarin, Vostok 1, flag of Soviet Union. No. 1014, 960fr, Hands holding legumes. No. 1015, 960fr, Sage Kotsenburg, 2014 Winter Olympics snowboarding gold medalist. No. 1016, 960fr, Moscow, host city for 2018 World Cup. No. 1017, 960fr, Burmese cat. No. 1018, 960fr, Inia geoffrensis. No. 1019, 960fr, Bubo scandiacus. No. 1020, 960fr, Centrochelys sulcata.

2016, July 28   Litho.   Perf. 13¼
Sheets of 4, #a-d
983-1001 A309 Set of 19 225.00 225.00

Souvenir Sheets
1002-1020 A309 Set of 19 205.00 205.00

A310

No. 1021, 260fr — Ursus maritimus: a, Head of bear with open mouth. b, Looking at water. c, Two adults and cub. d, Bear walking.
No. 1022, 260fr — Hippopotamus amphibius: a, One animal with head near ground. b, One animal with open mouth, Latin name on two lines. c, Adult and juvenile. d, One adult with open mouth, Latin name on one line.
No. 1023, 260fr — Pandas: a, Ailuropoda melanoleuca eating. b, Ailurus fulgens, feet on mound. c, Ailurus fulgens, prone. d, Adult and juvenile Ailuropoda melanoleuca.
No. 1024, 260fr — Tigers: a, Head of Panthera tigris altaica. b, Panthera tigris tigris with open mouth. c, Panthera tigris tigris with closed mouth. d, Panthera tigris altaica walking.
No. 1025, 260fr — Dog breeds: a, Brussels griffon. b, Neapolitan mastiff. c, Canary Island hound. d, Kerry Blue terrier.
No. 1026, 260fr — Elephants: a, Loxodonta africana and tree. b, Two Loxodonta africana. c, Loxodonta africana and man. d, Loxodonta cyclotis.
No. 1027, 260fr — Water birds: a, Morus bassanus. b, Tadorna ferruginea. c, Dendrocygna bicolor. d, Cygnus atratus.
No. 1028, 260fr — Kingfishers: a, Corythornis cristatus, Halcyon smyrnensis. b, Alcedo atthis. c, Corythornis cristatus. d, Ceyx erithaca, Halcyon smyrnensis.
No. 1029, 260fr — Pigeons: a, Columba palumbus. b, Gymnophaps albertisii. c, Columba livia. d, Patagioenas leucocephala.
No. 1030, 260fr — Falcons: a, Falco vespertinus. b, Falco fasciinucha. c, Falco amurensis. d, Falco sparverius.
No. 1031, 260fr — Bees: a, Xylocopa micans. b, Euglossa dilemma. c, Anthidium manicatum. d, Augochlorella aurata.
No. 1032, 260fr — Butterflies: a, Cupidopsis cissus. b, Graphium porthaon. c, Myrina silenus. d, Tarucus sybaris.
No. 1033, 260fr — Fish: a, Acanthurus leucosternon, Acanthurus triostegus. b, Pterois volitans. c, Pygoplites diacanthus. d, Manta alfredi.
No. 1034, 260fr — Shells: a, Cypraecassis rufa. b, Charonia tritonis. c, Trochus nodulosus. d, Conus mustelinus.
No. 1035, 260fr — Extinct animals: a, Mammuthus columbi. b, Moropus elatus. c, Elasmotherium sibiricum. d, Smilodon populator.
No. 1036, 260fr — Prehistoric aquatic animals: a, Enchodus. b, Mosasaurus hoffmannii. c, Ammonoidea. d, Helicoprion bessonovi.
No. 1037, 260fr — Mushrooms: a, Rhodotus palmatus. b, Phallus indusiatus. c, Lactarius deliciosus. d, Leccinum scabrum.
No. 1038, 260fr — Minerals: a, Chalcanthite. b, Legrandite. c, Gadolinite. d, Fluorite.
No. 1039, 260fr — Cartoon characters on stamps: a, U.S. Nos. 4399-4402 (Characters from *The Simpsons*). b, U.S. No. 4470, Switzerland Nos. 1536-1537 (Characters from *Garfield*). c, U.S. Zazzle personalized stamps depicting *SpongeBob SquarePants*. d, Switzerland No. 1497, Belgium Nos. 2320-2321 (Characters from *The Smurfs*).
No. 1040, 960fr, Ursus maritimus adult and cub. No. 1041, 960fr, Hippopotamus amphibius adult and juvenile, diff. No. 1042, 960fr, Two Ailuropoda melanoleuca. No. 1043, 960fr, Two Panthera tigris altaica. No. 1044, 960fr, Akita. No. 1045, 960fr, Elephas maximus. No. 1046, 960fr, Gavia immer. No. 1047, 960fr, Alcedo atthis, diff. No. 1048, 960fr, Goura scheepmakeri. No. 1049, 960fr, Falco peregrinus. No. 1050, 960fr, Andrena cineraria. No. 1051, 960fr, Myrina silenus ficedula. No. 1052, 960fr, Plectorhinchus vittatus, Heniochus pleurotaenia. No. 1053, 960fr, Lambis lambis. No. 1054, 960fr, Glyptodon clavipes. No. 1055, 960fr, Djnichthys terrelli. No. 1056, 960fr, Morchella esculenta. No. 1057, 960fr, Cassiterite. No. 1058, 960fr, Netherlands No.1080a, U.S. Zazzle srtamps depicting *Tom and Jerry*.

2016, Sept. 26   Litho.   Perf. 13¼
Sheets of 4, #a-d
1021-1039 A310 Set of 19 225.00 225.00

Souvenir Sheets
1040-1058 A310 Set of 19 210.00 210.00

Worldwide Fund for Nature (WWF) — A311

No. 1059 — Torgos tracheliotos: a, Bird on branch. b, Two birds. c, Two birds and carrion. d, Bird and animal bones.
960fr, Torgos tracheliotos in flight.

2016, Sept. 26   Litho.   Perf. 13¼
1059 A311 260fr Sheet of 4, #a-d 12.00 12.00

Souvenir Sheet
1060 A311 960fr multi 11.00 11.00

No. 1060 lacks the WWF emblem on the stamp and sheet margin. For surcharges, see Nos. 1814-1821.

Miniature Sheet

First Batallion of Somali Snipers, Cent. A312

DJIBOUTI

No. 1061: a, Medal, Battle of Douaumont. b, Tank and Malmaison, 1917. c, Monument. d, Airplane over Pointe de Grave and Cordouan Lighthouse, France, 1945.

2016, Oct. 24   Litho.   Perf. 13¼

1061	A312 500fr Sheet of 4,		
	#a-d	22.50	22.50

A313

No. 1062, 280fr — Rotary International in Djibouti: a, Boy holding stick and water bottle. b, Woman and children at well. c, Woman holding child to receive vaccination. d, Children.

No. 1063, 280fr — Red Cross-Red Crescent in Djibouti: a, Red Crescent, map of Africa, Red Crescent workers carrying litter. b, Red Crescent worker assisting woman. c, Red Crescent worker looking at notebook. d, Red Crescent worker holding water bucket.

No. 1064, 280fr — Canonization of Mother Teresa (1910-97): a, Mother Teresa and building. b, Mother Teresa, dove, Pres. Ronald Reagan and wife, Nancy. c, Mother Teresa holding child. d, Mother Teresa and flag of India.

No. 1065, 280fr — Extraordinary Jubilee of Mercy: a, Pope Francis in Kenya. b, Pope Francis opening holy doors. c, Pope Benedict XVI. d, Dove and Popes Francis, Benedict XVI.

No. 1066, 280fr — British royal family: a, Queen Elizabeth II. b, Duke and Duchess of Cambridge. c, Prince George and Princess Charlotte. d, Duke and Duchess of Cambridge, Prince George and Princess Charlotte.

No. 1067, 280fr — Publication of Albert Einstein's Theory of General Relativity, cent.: a, Einstein, globes, equation, model of atom. b, Einstein and equation. c, Hand holding orb depicting Einstein. d, Einstein and light bulb.

No. 1068, 280fr — Battle of the Somme, cent.: a, Mark I tank. b, British Gen. Ivor Maxse (1862-1958) and soldiers. c, French soldiers at munitions wagon. d, German soldier on horse.

No. 1069, 280fr — Navy ships: a, San Marco, Italy. b, Zubr Class hovercraft, Russia, and tank. c, USS Coronado, United States. d, BSF Azov 151, BF Minsk 127, Russia.

No. 1070, 280fr — Submarines.: a, Type 035, People's Republic of China. b, Typhoon Class Project 941, Russia. c, A26 submarine. d, HMS Triumph, Great Britain.

No. 1071, 280fr — High-speed trains.: a, ETR 500 Frecciarossa, Italy. b, SNCF TGV Duplex, France. c, AVE Class 103, Spain. d, Eurostar e320, Great Britain.

No. 1072, 200fr — Motorcycles. a, BMW K1600GTL. b, Suzuki TU250X. c, MV Agusta F3 800. d, Yamaha Star VMAX.

No. 1073, 280fr — Russian military aircraft: a, Sukhoi Su-35. b, Mil Mi-28 helicopter. c, Kamov KA-50 helicopter. d, Mikoyan MiG-41.

No. 1074, 280fr — Space exploration: a, Mars Rover Spirit, 2004. b, Neil Armstrong (1930-2012) on ladder of Lunar Module, 1969. c, Yuri Gagarin (1934-68), and Vostok 1, 1961. d, Final mission of Space Shuttle Atlantis, 2011.

No. 1075, 280fr — 2016 Ice Hockey World Championships, Russia: a, Players fighting for puck near goaltender. b, U.S. player and Russian goaltender. c, Canadian and Russian players. d, Finnish player and Canadian goaltender.

No. 1076, 280fr — Chess players: a, Magnus Carlsen. b, Anatoly Karpov. c, Bobby Fischer. d, Mariya Muzychuk.

No. 1077, 280fr — Islamic art: a, Battle scene from the Shahnameh. b, Interior of Cathedral-Mosque of Córdoba, Spain. c, Jameh Mosque, Isfahan, Iran. d, Pyxis of al-Mughira.

No. 1078, 280fr — Lighthouses: a, Petit Minou Lighthouse, France. b, Hornby Lighthouse, Australia. c, Store Faerder Lighthouse, Norway. d, Point Betsie Lighthouse, Michigan.

No. 1079, 280fr — Orchids: a, Cattleya labiata. b, Cypripedium kentuckiense. c, Vanda denisoniana. d, Orchis purpurea.

No. 1080, 280fr — New Year 2017 (Year of the Rooster): a, Rooster with leg raised and wings extended. b, Rooster facing right, pagoda in background. c, Rooster facing right, torii in background. d, Rooster in air, flapping wings.

No. 1081, 960fr, Child and containers, Rotary International emblem. No. 1082, 960fr, Red Crescent worker with water bottle tending to injured person. No. 1083, 960fr, Mother Teresa and child, diff. No. 1084, 960fr, Pope Francis kissing creche figure of infant Jesus. No. 1085, 960fr, Queen Elizabeth II, diff. No. 1086, 960fr, Einstein at blackboard. No. 1087, 960fr, German soldier at Battle of the Somme. No. 1088, 960fr, USS Essex and CH-53E helicopters. No. 1089, 960fr, USS Scorpion. No. 1090, 960fr, IC3 3 train, Germany. No. 1091, 960fr, Beta 450 RR motorcycle. No. 1092, 960fr, Mikoyan MiG-35. No. 1093, 960fr, Sputnik 1, 1957. No. 1094, 960fr, Russian ice hockey player sprawled on ice. No. 1095, 960fr, Sergey Karjakin, chess pieces. No. 1096, 960fr, Qutub Minar and Alai Darwaza, India. No. 1097, 960fr, La Vieille Lighthouse, France. No. 1098, 960fr, Vanda coerulea. No. 1099, 960fr, Rooster and Great Wall of China.

2016, Nov. 25   Litho.   Perf. 13¼
Sheets of 4, #a-d

1062-1080	A313	Set of 19	240.00	240.00

Souvenir Sheets

1081-1099	A313	Set of 19	205.00	205.00

Election of Donald Trump as U.S. President — A314

No. 1100: a, Trump and stars. b, Trump and Republican Party emblem. c, Trump with wife, Melania, and son, Barron. d, Trump and running mate, Mike Pence.
960fr, Trump, diff.

2016, Nov. 25   Litho.   Perf. 13¼

1100	A314 280fr Sheet of 4,		
	#a-d	12.50	12.50

Souvenir Sheet

1101	A314 960fr multi	11.00	11.00

No. 1101 contains one 51x90mm stamp.

A315

No. 1102, 280fr — St. John Paul II (1920-2005), with: a, Boy and girl. b, Crowd worshiping. c, Candles. d, Religious sculpture.

No. 1103, 280fr — Michèle Morgan (1920-2016), actress, with: a, Unidentified actor. b, Hand on head. c, Clapboard and film reel. d, Gérard Philips (1022-50), actor.

No. 1104, 280fr — John Glenn, Jr. (1921-2016), astronaut: a, U.S. flag, Mercury capsule, launch of Atlas 8 rocket. b, Glenn and Space Shuttle Discovery. c, Glenn, military airplane and Pres. John F. Kennedy (1917-63). d, Glenn, U.S. flag and rocket launch.

No. 1105, 280fr — Rotary International emblem and: a, Paul P. Harris (1868-1947), founder of Rotary International, holding book. b, Rotary volunteer giving vaccine to child. c, Children reading. d, Harris with reversed Paul Harris Fellow pin.

No. 1106, 280fr — Scouting, 110th anniv.: a, Scouts in canoe, Nettapus auritus. b, Scout with binoculars, Circaetus cinereus. c, Scouts with Scouting flag. d, Scout and Lentinus squarrosulus.

No. 1107, 280fr — Paintings by Ivan Aivazovsky (1817-1900): a, Portrait of Loris-Melikov, 1888. b, Battle of Cesme at Night, 1848. c, Boat Ride by Kumpaki in Constantinople, 1846. d, Odessa, 1840.

No. 1108, 280fr — Paintings by Edgar Degas (1834-1917): a, In a Café, 1875-76. b, Emma Dobigny, 1869. c, A Cotton Office in New Orleans, 1873. d, Ballet Rehearsal on Stage, 1874.

No. 1109, 280fr — Paintings by Frida Kahlo (1907-54): a, Tree of Hope, Keep Firm, 1946. b, Still Life with Parrot, 1951. c, The Wounded Deer, 1946. d, Portrait of Lucha Maria, a Girl from Tehuacan, 1942.

No. 1110, 280fr — Sculptures by Auguste Rodin (1840-1917): a, The Thinker, 1903. b, Lady Sackville-West, 1913. c, Young Woman with Flowered Hat, 1870-75. d, The Clenched Hand, 1885. The Gates of Hell, 1880-90.

No. 1111, 280fr — Primates: a, Pongo pygmaeus. b, Indri indri. c, Loris tardigradus. d, Papio hamadryas.

No. 1112, 280fr — Wild cats: a, Panthera tigris altaica. b, Panthera neofelis nebulosa. c, Puma concolor. d, Panthera pardus kotiya.

No. 1113, 280fr — Dolphins: a, Stenella longirostris. b, Grampus griseus. c, Lagenorhynchus obscurus. d, Tursiops truncatus.

No. 1114, 280fr — Whales: a, Balaena mysticetus. b, Delphinapterus leucas. c, Physeter macrocephalus. d, Balaenoptera musculus.

No. 1115, 280fr — Owls: a, Aegolius harrisii, Aegolius acadicus. b, Athene noctua. c, Bubo virginianus. d, Glaucidium passerinum.

No. 1116, 280fr — Birds of prey: a, Caracara plancus. b, Aegolius acadicus. c, Coragyps atratus. d, Gymnogyps californianus.

No. 1117, 280fr — Water birds: a, Rynchops niger. b, Eudocimus ruber. c, Gavia immer. d, Mycteria leucocephala.

No. 1118, 280fr — Butterflies: a, Perrhybris pamela. b, Junonia lemonias lemonias. c, Ixias pyrene. d, Colotis euippe.

No. 1119, 280fr — Fish: a, Acanthurus leucosternon. b, Ostracion cubicus. c, Antennarius coccineus. d, Scarus coelestinus.

No. 1120, 280fr — Turtles: a, Batagur trivittata. b, Chelus fimbriatus. c, Lepidochelys kempii. d, Lepidochelys olivacea.

No. 1121, 280fr — Snakes: a, Pituophis catenifer. b, Diadophis punctatus. c, Oxyrhopus trigeminus. d, Natrix natrix.

No. 1122, 280fr — Dinosaurs: a, Iguanodon. b, Spinops sternbergorum. c, Cryolophosaurus. d, Spinosaurus.

No. 1123, 280fr — Endangered animals: a, Campephilus principalis. b, Panthera pardus orientalis. c, Helarctos malayanus. d, Lepilemur septentrionalis.

No. 1124, 280fr — Mushrooms: a, Cantharellus cibarius. b, Gyromitra esculenta. c, Ramaria formosa. d, Tylopilus felleus.

No. 1125, 280fr — Orchids: a, Vanda coerulea. b, Cattleya. c, White Phalaenopsis. d, Zygopetalum.

No. 1126, 280fr — Minerals: a, Amazonite. b, Wulfenite. c, Rhodochrosite. d, Aquamarine.

No. 1127, 960fr, St. John Paul II and crosses. No. 1128, 960fr, Morgan with strings of pearls. No. 1129, 960fr, Glenn receiving Presidential Medal of Freedom from Pres. Barack Obama. No. 1130, 960fr, Rotary International emblem and bust of Harris. No. 1131, 960fr, Scout blowing horn, Colotis danae. No. 1132, 960fr, The Roads at Kronstadt, by Aivazovsky, 1840. No. 1133, 960fr, The Dance Class, by Degas, 1874. No. 1134, 960fr, Portrait of My Father, by Kahlo, 1951. No. 1135, 960fr, The Burghers of Calais, by Rodin, 1884-89. No. 1136, 960fr, Leontopithecus rosalia. No. 1137, 960fr, Lynx pardinus. No. 1138, 960fr, Cephalorhynchus heavisidii. No. 1139, 960fr, Megaptera novaeangliae. No. 1140, 900fr, Aslo capensis. No. 1141, 960fr, Buteo lagopus. No. 1142, 960fr, Anas rhynchotis. No. 1143, 960fr, Delias eucharis. No. 1144, 960fr, Sparisoma cretense. No. 1145, 900fr, Geochelone elephantopus. No. 1146, 960fr, Naja sumatrana. No. 1147, 960fr, Parasaurolophus. No. 1148, 960fr, Gyps indicus. No. 1149, 960fr, Clitocybe phyllophila. No. 1150, 960fr, Black Phalaenopsis orchid. No. 1151, 960fr, Pyromorphite.

2017, Jan. 20   Litho.   Perf. 13¼
Sheets of 4, #a-d

1102-1126	A315	Set of 25	310.00	310.00

Souvenir Sheets

1127-1151	A315	Set of 25	265.00	265.00

Varanus Komodoensis — A316

No. 1152 — Komodo dragon: a, With head down, tongue out. b, With head raised, tongue not visible. c, Climbing rock. d, With head raised, tongue out.

950fr, Komodo dragon, tongue touching ground.

2017, Mar. 15   Litho.   Perf. 13¼

1152	A316 240fr Sheet of 4,		
	#a-d	11.00	11.00

Souvenir Sheet

1153	A316 950fr multi	10.50	10.50

Bandung 2017 World Stamp Exhibition. No. 1153 contains one 48x48mm stamp.

A317

No. 1154, 240fr — Wilbur Wright (1867-1912), aviation pioneer: a, Wright, with brother, Orvillo (1871-1948) and Wright Flyer. b, Wind testing of Wright Flyer, 1901. c, Wilbur and Wright Flyer in flight. d, Wilbur at controls of airplane.

No. 1155, 240fr — Concorde: a, British Airways Concorde over Paris. b, British Airways Concorde over Nice, France. c, Air France Concorde over London. d, British Airways Concorde over Mecca, Saudi Arabia.

No. 1156, 240fr — Military aircraft: a, Mikoyan-Gurevich MiG-29. b, A-10 Thunderbolt II. c, Junkers Ju 52. d, Boeing-Bell V-22 Osprey.

No. 1157, 240fr — Disappearance of Amelia Earhart (1897-1937), pilot: a, Earhart and her airplane. b, Earhart, airplane and hangar. c, Earhart and husband, George P. Putnam (1887-1970). d, Electra 10E in flight.

No. 1158, 240fr — Ferdinand von Zeppelin (1838-1917), airship manufacturer: a, Zeppelin, passengers boarding Graf Zeppelin. b, Zeppelin LZ-1. c, Zeppelin LZ-4. d, Zeppelin and schematic drawings of airship.

No. 1159, 240fr — 80th birthday of Valentina Tereshkova, first woman in space: a, In car with Russia Premier Nikita Khrushchev (1894-1971). b, With Yuri Gagarin (1934-68), first man in space. c, With obverse and reverse of 1983 1-ruble Russian coin depicting her. d, With Vostok 6.

No. 1160, 240fr — Steam trains: a, Pennsylvania Railroad 1223. b, London and North Eastern Railway Class A4 Mallard 4468. c, Great Western Railway 4-4-0 City of Truro 3717. d, Doutoohe Reichebahn 10 201.

No. 1161, 240fr — High-speed trains: a, Talgo 350. b, NTV Alstom AGV 575. c, Shinkansen Series 500. d, Renfe Series S-103.

No. 1162, 240fr — Sinking of the Titanic, 105th anniv.: a, Titanic and map of voyage. b, Titanic sinking and overturned lifeboat. c, Titanic and iceberg. d, Titanic and Thomas Andrews (1873-1912), designer of Titanic.

No. 1163, 240fr — Submarines: a, HMAS Collins, Australia. b, SSK Kilo Class Type 636 and icebreaker Ivan Kruzenshtern, Russia. c, HMS Ambush, Great Britain. d, Terrible, France.

No. 1164, 240fr — Donald Campbell (1921-67), land and water speed record holder: a, Wearing helmet. b, In Bluebird K7, waving. c, Sitting. d, With wife, Tonia Bern-Campbell.

No. 1165, 240fr — Special transportation: a, Telescope transporter. b, Victoria, Australia police vehicle. c, Euclid dump truck. d, Snowcat.

No. 1166, 240fr — Fire-fighting vehicles: a, Caterpillar CT660 fire truck, United States. b, Foremost Nodwell 240, Canada. c, Delta 2 wheeled carrier, Canada. d, Hopedale, Massachusets Tanker 1, United States.

No. 1167, 240fr — 1947 Ferrari 125 S, 70th anniv., with background design of: a, Trees. b, Ferrari emblem. c, Steering wheel and dashboard. d, Clouds.

No. 1168, 240fr — Motorcycles: a, 1912 Henderson 4-cylinder. b, 1923 BMW R32. c, 1962-63 BSA Rocket Gold Star A10. d, 1974 Hercules-Wankel 2000.

No. 1169, 240fr — Transportation for Pres. Donald Trump: a, Sikorsky S-76 helicopter. b, 2015 Mercedes-Benz Class S600. c, 1997 Lamborghini Diablo. d, Boeing 757.

No. 1170, 240fr — Sled dogs: a, Five sled dogs and two drivers. b, Two Seppala Siberian sled dogs. c, Husky and Malamutes. d, Sled dogs resting with driver.

No. 1171, 240fr — Jacques Cousteau (1910-97), conservationist and filmmaker: a, Calypso and hot air balloon in Antarctica. b, Cousteau and SP-350 Denise. c, Cousteau holding cup. d, Cousteau and Calypso.

DJIBOUTI

No. 1172, 240fr — Charles Darwin (1809-82), naturalist: a, Portrait of Darwin and his wife, Emma, by George Richmond. b, HMS Beagle and map of its voyage, Conolophus subcristatus. c, Darwin, primate and skulls of Homo neanderthalensis and Homo sapiens. d, Darwin and specimens of Pseudoscarus lepidus, Eleginops maclovinus, and Ceroglossus darwinii.
No. 1173, 240fr — Russian October Revolution, cent.: a, Barricades at St. Isaac Cathedral, St. Petersburg. b, Soldiers at Hermitage and Winter Palace, St. Petersburg. c, Deomonstrators in St. Petersburg. d, Lenin (1870-1924), and Cruiser Aurora.
No. 1174, 240fr — Battle of Stalingrad, 75th anniv.: a, Aug. 23, 1942 air raid. b, Soviet Gen. Georgi Zhukov (1896-1974). c, German Gen. Friedrich Paulus (1890-1957). d, Soviet troops, Feb. 1943.
No. 1175, 240fr — Lighthouses: a, Punta Palascia Lighthouse, Italy. b, Lindesnes Lighthouse, Norway. c, Pointe aux Barques Lighthouse, Michigan. d, North Head Lighthouse, Washington.
No. 1176, 240fr — Windmills and tulips: a, Kinderddijk, Netherlands windmills, red and white tulips. b, Kuremaa, Estonia windmill, yellow tulips. c, Sonderho, Denmark windmill, orange tulips. d, Halanker, Great Britain windmill, red tulips.
No. 1177, 240fr — Endangered animals: a, Anolis gorgonae. b, Anolis proboscis. c, Neurergus kaiseri. d, Tokay gecko.
No. 1178, 950fr, Orville Wright on bicycle, Wright Flyer in flight. No. 1179, 950fr, British Airways Concorde over New York City. No. 1180, 950fr, F-16 Fighting Falcon. No. 1181, 950fr, Earhart holding propeller. No. 1182, 950fr, Zeppelin and his signature. No. 1183, 950fr, Tereshkova and stylized rocket. No. 1184, 950fr, St. Louis-San Francisco train. No. 1185, 950fr, Shinkansen Series E6. No. 1186, 950fr, Titanic and its captain, Edward Smith (1850-1912). No. 1187, 950fr, Victoria Class submarine, Canada. No. 1188, 950fr, Campbell in Bluebird K7. No. 1189, 950fr, Lockheed Martin hybrid dirigibles. No. 1190, 950fr, San José, California fire truck. No. 1191, 950fr, Enzo Ferrari (1898-1988), automobile manufacturer in 1947 Ferrari 125 S. No. 1192, 950fr, 2006 Royal Enfield Bullet motorcycle. No. 1193, 950fr, Gold Trump motorcycle. No. 1194, 950fr, Siberian husky sled dogs. No. 1195, 950fr, Cousteau holding walkie-talkie. No. 1196, 950fr, Darwin, Geospiza fortis, heads of Galapagos finches. No. 1197, 950fr, Lenin and Cruiser Aurora, diff. No. 1198, 950fr, Vasily Zaytsev (1915-91), Soviet sniper at Battle of Stalingrad. No. 1199, 950fr, Petit Minou Lighthouse, France. No. 1200, 950fr, Mostert, South Africa windmill, red and yellow tulips. No. 1201, 950fr, Neurergus kaiseri, diff.

2017, Mar. 15   Litho.   Perf. 13¼
Sheet of 4, #a-d
1154-1177 A317 Set of 24 260.00 260.00
Souvenir Sheets
1178-1201 A317 Set of 24 255.00 255.00

Miniature Sheets

Opening of Djibouti-Ethiopia Electric Rail Line — A318

Nos. 1202 and 1203: a, Tracks and catenary network. b, Electric train. c, Holl Holl Bridge. d, Nagad Station.

2017, Apr. 25   Litho.   Perf. 12¾x13¼
1202 A318 200fr Sheet of 4, #a-d   9.00 9.00
1203 A318 250fr Sheet of 4, #a-d   11.00 11.00

No. 1204, 240fr — Ailuropoda melanoleuca (Giant panda): a, On branch. b, Adult and cub. c, On back. d, Facing left.
No. 1205, 240fr — Dogs: a, Papillons. b, French bulldog. c, English cocker spaniel. d, Basset hounds.
No. 1206, 240fr — Dolphins: a, Lagenorhynchus obscurus. b, Tursiops truncatus. c, Cephalorhynchus commersonii. d, Stenella frontalis.
No. 1207, 240fr — Owls: a, Tyto alba. b, Bubo cinerascens. c, Bubo lacteus. d, Glaucidium perlatum.
No. 1208, 240fr — Bees and orchids: a, Euglossa imperialis, Cattleya aclandiae. b, Exaerete frontalis, Cymbidium madidum. c, Euglossa tridentata, Maxillaria tenufolia. d, Euglossa dilemma, Cattleya lueddemanniana.
No. 1209, 240fr — Butterflies: a, Batesia hypochorica. b, Papilio demoleus. c, Melitaea didyma. d, Phengaris arion.
No. 1210, 240fr — Turtles: a, Graptemys pseudogeographica kohni. b, Rhinoclemmys pulcherrima. c, Trachemys scripta scripta. d, Trachemys scripta elegans.
No. 1211, 240fr — Extinct animals: a, Mammuthus meridionalis. b, Raphus cucullatus. c, Megacerops coloradensis. d, Thalassocnus antiquus.
No. 1212, 240fr — Mahatma Gandhi (1869-1948), Indian nationalist: a, With spinning wheel. b, Walking, holding walking stick. c, With building. d, With decorated cow.
No. 1213, 240fr — Princess Diana (1961-97): a, With Prince Charles and coat of arms. b, Wearing white blouse. c, Wearing white blouse, with sunglasses in hair. d, Holding Prince Harry.
No. 1214, 950fr, Ailuropoda melanoleuca adult and cub, diff. No. 1215, 950fr, Rottweilers. No. 1216, 950fr, Sotalia fluviatilis. No. 1217, 950fr, Otus senegalensis. No. 1218, 950fr, Euglossa imperialis, Laelia anceps. No. 1219, 950fr, Colotis ione. No. 1220, 950fr, Apalone mutica. No. 1221, 950fr, Glyptodon clavipes. No. 1222, 950fr, Gandhi and Taj Mahal. No. 1223, 950fr, Princess Diana, Duke and Duchess of Cambrige, Prince Harry.

2017, July 5   Litho.   Perf. 13¼
Sheets of 4, #a-d
1204-1213 A319 Set of 10 110.00 110.00
Souvenir Sheets
1214-1223 A319 Set of 10 105.00 105.00

International Day of Girls in Information and Communications Technology — A319a

2017, July 13   Litho.   Perf. 13¼
1223A A319a 100fr multi   1.10 1.10
Souvenir Sheet
1223B A319a 200fr multi   2.25 2.25

"Eid Mubarak" — A319b

Designs: 150fr, Lantern at right, Arabic text at left.
300fr, Lantern and star at left, Arabic text at right.

2017, July 20   Litho.   Perf. 13x13¼
1223C A319b 150fr multi   1.75 1.75
Souvenir Sheet
Perf. 13½x13¼
1223D A319b 300fr multi   3.50 3.50

A319c

Independence, 40th Anniv. — A319d

No. 1223E — Flag of Djibouti and: g, "Unité" at LL. h, Arabic inscription at LL. i, "Inkitino" at LL. j, "Midnimo" at LL.

2017, July 20   Litho.   Perf. 13¼
1223E A319c 150fr Sheet of 4, #g-j   6.75 6.75
Souvenir Sheet
Litho. With Foil Application
1223F A319d 500fr sil & multi   5.75 5.75

A320

No. 1224, 240fr — Formula I race cars: a, Blue and yellow cars. b, Orange car. c, Bright red car. d, Red and orange cars.
No. 1225, 240fr — Ice hockey: a, Norwegian player in dark blue jersey, player in white and blue jersey. b, Henrik Lundqvist, goaltender for New York Rangers. c, Referee and Washington Capitals player with stick raised. d, Boston Bruins player in black and yellow jersey, player in red and white jersey.
No. 1226, 240fr — Cricket players: a, Batsman swinging and falling fielder. b, Shikhar Dhawan. c, Josh Hazlewood. d, Batsman holding bat behind back, celebrating player.
No. 1227, 240fr — Tennis players: a, Rafael Nadal. b, Stan Wawrinka. c, Angelique Kerber. d, Serena Williams.
No. 1228, 240fr — Table tennis players: a, Zhang Jike. b, Liu Shiwen. c, Ding Ning. d, Liu Guoliang.
No. 1229, 240fr — Golfers: a, Dustin Johnson. b, So-yeon Ryu. c, Lydia Ko. d, Rory McIlroy.
No. 1230, 240fr — Pierre de Coubertin (1863-1937), President of International Olympic Committee: a, Coubertin, wrestlers in background. b, Statue of Coubertin, Beijing. c, Coubertin facing right. d, Coubertin, ancient Greek soldiers in background.
No. 1231, 240fr — Chess pieces: a, Black knight, queen in silhouette. b, White queen, hand moving black piece. c, White queen and king, black king. d, Carved piece depicting elephant carrying howdah, queen in background.
No. 1232, 240fr — Metropolitan Museum of Art, 145th anniv.: a, Fragment of bust of Roman Emperor Caracalla. b, Jean Engelhard Court. c, Bust of Young Girl Identified as Anne Audéoud of Geneva, by Jean Antoine Houdon. d, Silver Buffalo Figure from Benin, 19th cent.
No. 1233, 240fr — Red Cross-Red Crescent Campaign Against Malaria: a, Man spraying insecticide in village. b, Woman and mosquito netting. c, Medical worker examining child. d, Medical worker taking blood sample from child.

No. 1234, 240fr — Pres. John F. Kennedy (1917-63), and: a, U.S. flag. b, Wife, Jacqueline. c, Daughter, Caroline. d, Wife, daughter, and son, John, Jr.
No. 1235, 240fr — 35th birthday of Prince William of Cambridge: a, In helicopter. b, With wife and children. c, As child, with parents and brother. d, Playing polo with brother, Prince Harry.
No. 1236, 240fr — Tall ships: a, Royal Clipper, Sweden. b, Belem, France. c, Palinuro, Italy. d, Juan Sebastián de Elcano, Spain.
No. 1237, 240fr — Naval vessels: a, Gloire, France, 1859. b, USS Texas, 1912. c, Yamato, Japan, 1940. d, La Fayette, France, 1996.
No. 1238, 240fr — European high-speed trains: a, TGV Thalys PBKA, France. b, TGV Lyria, France and Switzerland. c, ICE 3, Germany. d, TCDD HT80000, Turkey.
No. 1239, 240fr — Fire trucks: a, Citroen 46 CDU. b, Rosenbauer Panther. c, MAZ7310 Airfield Crash Tender. d, Ladder truck with tank treads.
No. 1240, 240fr — Opel automobiles: a, Opel Ascona A. b, Opel Kapitän. c, Opel Mokka. d, Opel Tigra.
No. 1241, 240fr — Supersonic aircraft: a, Aerion SBJ. b, North American XB-70 Valkyrie. c, Tupolev Tu-22M. d, Lockheed SR-71 Blackbird.
No. 1242, 240fr — Sergei Korolev (1907-66), spacecraft designer: a, Luna 3, Sputnik 1. b, Korolev and Luna 8K72. c, Korolev and R-7 Semyorka missile. d, Yuri Gagarin (1934-68), cosmonaut, and Vostok 1.
No. 1243, 240fr — Birds of Djibouti: a, Dendropicos namaquus. b, Phoeniculus somaliensis. c, Caprimulgus stellatus. d, Trachyphonus darnaudii.
No. 1244, 950fr, Nico Rosberg, 2016 Formula 1 racing champion and car. No. 1245, 950fr, Ice hockey player taking shot. No. 1246, 950fr, Cricket batsman and wicket-keeper. No. 1247, 950fr, Tennis player Andy Murray. No. 1248, 950fr, Table tennis player Ma Long. No. 1249, 950fr, Golfer Jason Day. No. 1250, 950fr, Coubertin and hurdlers. No. 1251, 950fr, King and queen chess pieces. No. 1252, 950fr, Statue of William Shakespeare, by John Quincy Adams Ward. No. 1253, 950fr, Woman carrying child, Anopheles maculipennis. No. 1254, 950fr, Pres. Kennedy and U.S. flag, diff. No. 1255, 950fr, Wedding of Prince William of Cambridge and Catherine Middleton. No. 1256, 950fr, Tovarishch, Russia. No. 1257, 950fr, Gloire, France, 1935. No. 1258, 950fr, Renfe Series S-114, Spain. No. 1259, 950fr, Bulldog 4x4 fire truck. No. 1260, 950fr, Opel Astra J. No. 1261, 950fr, Panavia Tornado IDS. No. 1262, 950fr, Korolev and Vostok 1. No. 1263, 950fr, Tricholaema melanocephala.

2017, July 28   Litho.   Perf. 13¼
Sheets of 4, #a-d
1224-1243 A320 Set of 20 215.00 215.00
Souvenir Sheets
1244-1263 A320 Set of 20 215.00 215.00

Birdpex 8 Philatelic Exhibition, Mondorf-les-Bains, Luxembourg (Nos. 1243, 1263).

A321

No. 1264, 240fr — Marilyn Monroe (1926-62), actress: a, Wearing white fur coat. b, With signature. c, With star from Hollywood Walk of Fame. d, Wearing black sweater.
No. 1265, 240fr — Paul McCartney, rock musician, and: a, Emblem of the Beatles. b, Wife, Linda. c, Beatle bandmates, John Lennon, Ringo Starr and George Harrison. d, Musical score and curved piano keyboard.
No. 1266, 240fr — Charlie Chaplin (1889-1977), film actor, and: a, Actor Ben Turpin. b, Signature. c, Woman holding flower. d, Child actor.
No. 1267, 240fr — Marie Curie (1867-1934), chemist and physicist, and: a, Pitchblende, husband, Pierre (1859-1906). b, Nobel medals and Daughter, Irène Joliot-Curie (1897-1956). c, Curie Pavilion of Institut du Radium. d, World War I mobile radiological unit.
No. 1268, 240fr — Nelson Mandela (1918-2013), President of South Africa: a, With F. W. de Klerk, Pres. of South Africa, and Nobel medals and diplomas. b, With fist raised. c,

DJIBOUTI

Holding dove. d, With trophy and South African rugby player.
No. 1269, 240fr — Pres. Franklin D. Roosevelt (1882-1945): a, Signing declaration of war against Germany. b, Wearing top hat. c, With wife, Eleanor (1884-1962). d, Signing Social Security legislation.
No. 1270, 240fr — Battle of Dunkirk: a, British Admiral Bertram Home Ramsay (1883-1945). b, Airplane flying over battle. c, Battle aftermath. d, Troops in water.
No. 1271, 240fr — Pompidou Center, Paris, 40th anniv.: a, La Roue Rouge, by Fernand Léger. b, Quatre Passagers Roses de Face, by Jean Dubuffet. c, Blue in Violet, by Wassily Kandinsky. d, Vieilles Maisons, Saint-Ilpize en Haute Loire.
No. 1272, 240fr — Alexander Pushkin (1799-1837), poet: a, Portrait. b, Dueling pistols. c, Pushkin sitting on railing, signature. d, Sculpture and drawing of Pushkin.
No. 1273, 240fr — Tigers: a, Panthera tigris altaica. b, Panthera tigris tigris cub. c, Two Panthera tigris tigris. d, Panthera tigris tigris with white fur.
No. 1274, 240fr — Shells: a, Lunella smaragdus. b, Nautilus macromphalus. c, Cymbiola innexa. d, Bolinus brandaris.
No. 1275, 240fr — Mushrooms: a, Suillus luteus. b, Macrolepiota rhacodes. c, Boletus edulis. d, Tricholoma portentosum.
No. 1276, 240fr — Windmills and birds: a, Oud-Zuilen, Netherlands windmill and Alopochen aegyptiaca. b, East Hampton, New York windmill and Tyrannus tyrannus. c, Ramsey, United Kingdom windmill and Carduelis carduelis. d, Lautrec, France windmill and Cyanistes caeruleus.
No. 1277, 240fr — Lighthouses: a, Lorain Lighthouse, Ohio. b, Big Sable Point Lighthouse, Michigan. c, Cape Lookout Lighthouse, North Carolina. d, Block Island Southeast Lighthouse, Rhode Island.
No. 1278, 240fr — Japanese high-speed trains: a, Shinkansen Series E3. b, Shinkansen Series E4. c, Shinkansen Series 800. d, Shinkansen Series E5.
No. 1279, 240fr — Louis Renault (1877-1944), automobile manufacturer, and: a, Renault Dauphinoise Juvaquatre fire vehicle. b, Renault FT-17 tank. c, Renault Type B. d, Renault Reinastella, Arc de Triomphe.
No. 1280, 240fr — Louis Blériot (1872-1936), aviation pioneer: a, Blériot XI airplane on ground. b, Blériot and Eiffel Tower. c, Blériot and mountains. d, Blériot XI in flight.
No. 1281, 240fr — Outer Space Treaty, 50th anniv.: a, World Map. b, Moon, planets, balance. c, Earth, satellites in orbit, gavel. d, Satellite and nuclear missile.
No. 1282, 240fr — Christmas: a, Children placing ornaments on Christmas tree. b, Carolers and violinist near Christmas tree. c, Santa Claus and child. d, Child pulling sled carrying Christmas tree.
No. 1283, 240fr — New Year 2018 (Year of the Dog): a, Pekingese dog facing right. b, Pekingese dog facing forward, Chinese characters at top left. c, Pekingese dog facing forward, Chinese characters at top right. d, Pekingese dog facing left.
No. 1284, 950fr, Monroe in automobile. No. 1285, 950fr, McCartney playing guitar. No. 1286, 950fr, Chaplin dancing. No. 1287, 950fr, Marie Curie and model of atom. No. 1288, 950fr, Mandela with fist raised, diff. No. 1289, 950fr, Roosevelt at desk. No. 1290, 950fr, Map of Battle of Dunkirk, troops boarding ship. No. 1291, 950fr, Rythmes, by Robert Delaunav. No. 1292, 950fr, Pushkin holding quill pen. No. 1293, 950fr, Two Panthera tigris altaica. No. 1294, 950fr, Ceratosoma amoenum, Cypraea aurantia. No. 1295, 950fr, Lycoperdon perlatum. No. 1296, 950fr, Kuremaa, Estonia windmill and Ciconia ciconia. No. 1297, 950fr, Greens Ledge Lighthouse, Connecticut. No. 1298, 950fr, Shinkansen Series 500 Type EVA. No. 1299, 950fr, Renault and Renault 4CV. No. 1300, 950fr, Blériot and Eiffel Tower, diff. No. 1301, 950fr, Sputnik 1. No. 1302, 950fr, Santa Claus and reindeer. No. 1303, 950fr, Pekingese dog, diff.

2017, Sept. 29   Litho.   Perf. 13¼
Sheets of 4, #a-d
1264-1283 A321 Set of 20   215.00 215.00
Souvenir Sheets
1284-1303 A321 Set of 20   215.00 215.00

Television Broadcasting in Djibouti, 50th Anniv. — A321a

2017, Nov. 9   Litho.   Perf. 13¼x13
1303A A321a 50fr multi   .60   .60

Miniature Sheet

Landscapes — A321b

No. 1303B: c, Grand Bara. d, Port of Obock (land at top). e, Sable Blanc. f, Ras Bir. g, Port of Obock (no land at top). h, Dikhil Region. i, Village of Assamo ("humilité, jaillir, slalomer" inscription). j, Tewo Daba. k, Village of Assamo ("apurer, adepte, décuivrer" inscription). l, Djibouti City.

2017, Nov. 9   Litho.   Perf. 13¼
1303B A321b 300fr Sheet of 10, #c-l   34.00 34.00

A322   A323

A324   Polar Bear — A325

Design: 950fr, Polar bear, diff.

2017, Dec. 11   Litho.   Perf. 12¾x13¼
1304 A322 240fr multi   2.75 2.75
1305 A323 240fr multi   2.75 2.75
1306 A324 240fr multi   2.75 2.75
1307 A325 240fr multi   2.75 2.75
Nos. 1304-1307 (4)   11.00 11.00
Souvenir Sheet
Perf. 13¼
1308 A325 950fr multi   11.00 11.00

Nos. 1304-1307 were each printed in sheets of 16 + 4 labels. No. 1308 contains one 45x38mm stamp.

A326

No. 1309, 240fr — Ursus maritimus: a, One polar bear, tree at left. b, Polar bear with head at right. c, Adult and two cubs. d, Polar bear with head at left, mouth open.
No. 1310, 240fr — Cat breeds: a, Korat. b, Toyger. c, Selkirk Rex. d, Chantilly.
No. 1311, 240fr — Wild dogs: a, Cuon alpinus. b, One Canis lupus dingo. c, Lycaon pictus. d, Two Canis lupus dingo.
No. 1312, 240fr — Loxodonta africana: a, One elephant facing right. b, One elephant facing left. c, Two elephants with trunks touching. d, Two elephants walking.
No. 1313, 240fr — Dolphins: a, Inia geoffrensis. b, Stenella coeruleoalba. c, Cephalorhynchus commersonii. d, Grampus griseus.
No. 1314, 240fr — Parrots: a, One Ara ararauna in flight. b, Psittacula krameri. c, Two Ara ararauna. d, Eolophus roseicapilla.
No. 1315, 240fr — Pigeon breeds: a, African Owl. b, Bouclier de Saxe (Saxon Shield). c, American Domestic Show Flight. d, Barbe Anglais (English Barb).
No. 1316, 240fr — Bee-eaters: a, Merops apiaster. b, Merops variegatus. c, Merops malimbicus. d, Merops breweri.
No. 1317, 240fr — Owls: a, Bubo scandiacus. b, Bubo lacteus. c, Bubo bubo. d, Strix seloputo.
No. 1318, 240fr — Butterflies: a, Apatura iris. b, Papilio glaucus. c, Battus philenor. d, Callophrys rubi.
No. 1319, 240fr — Turtles: a, Aldabrachelys gigantea. b, Malaclemys terrapin. c, Trachemys scripta elegans. d, Chelonia mydas.
No. 1320, 240fr — Dinosaurs: a, Lambeosaurus lambei. b, Oviraptor philoceratops. c, Archaeopteryx siemensii. d, Stegosaurus ungulatus.
No. 1321, 240fr — Prehistoric marine animals: a, Pteraspis stensioei, Prognathodon solvayi. b, Dearcmhara shawcrossi. c, Parapuzosia seppenradensis. d, Shastasaurus pacificus.
No. 1322, 240fr — Global warming: a, Giraffa camelopardalis tippelskirchi and text. b, Ursus maritimus and text. c, Cervus elaphus and text. d, Turbinaria reniformis and text.
No. 1323, 240fr — Orchids: a, Odontoglossum crispum. b, Cattleya "Blc. Greenwich." c, Vanda coerulea. d, Miltonia regnellii.
No. 1324, 240fr — Minerals: a, Brookite, quartz. b, Uvarovite. c, Andradite. d, Willemite.
No. 1325, 240fr — Fire trucks: a, 2010 Oshkosh Striker 3000. b, 2012 Iveco Trakker. c, 2011 DAF LF. d, 2011 Scania P.
No. 1326, 240fr — Protestant Reformation, 500th anniv.: a, Martin Luther (1483-1546). b, Martin Bucer (1491-1551). c, Ulrich Zwingli (1484-1531). d, John Calvin (1509-64).
No. 1327, 240fr — 2017 Nobel Laureates: a, Michael Rosbach (Physiology or Medicine). b, Joachim Frank (Chemistry). c, Beatrice Fihn, director of International Campaign to Abolish Nuclear Weapons (Peace). d, Kazuo Ishiguro (Literature).
No. 1328, 950fr, Ursus maritiumus, diff. No. 1329, 950fr, Abyssinian cat. No. 1330, 950fr, Cuon alpinus, diff. No. 1331, 950fr, Loxodonta africana, diff. No. 1332, 950fr, Lagenorhynchus acutus. No. 1333, 950fr, Guaruba guarouba. No. 1334, 950fr, Belgian Ringbeater pigeon. No. 1335, 950fr, Merops nubicoides. No. 1336, 950fr, Megascops kennicottii. No. 1337, 950fr, Papilio troilus. No. 1338, 950fr, Graptemys geographica. No. 1339, 950fr, Pterodactylus antiquus. No. 1340, 950fr, Dunkleosteus terrelli. No. 1341, 950fr, Aptenodytes forsteri. No. 1342, 950fr, Beallara marfitch "Howard's Dream." No. 1343, 950fr, Brazilianite. No. 1344, 950fr, 1984 Oshkosh P19 fire truck. No. 1345, 950fr, Luther, diff. No. 1346, 950fr, Richard H. Thaler, 2017 Nobel Laureate in Economics, Nobel medal, Robert Fludd (1574-1637), mathematician.

2017, Dec. 11   Litho.   Perf. 13¼
Sheets of 4, #a-d
1309-1327 A326 Set of 19 200.00 200.00
Souvenir Sheets
1328-1346 A326 Set of 19 200.00 200.00

Souvenir Sheet

Djibouti Chamber of Commerce, 110th Anniv. — A326a

Perf. 13¼x13½
2017, Dec. 21   Litho.
1346A A326a 110fr multi   1.25 1.25

Souvenir Sheet

Emblem of Djibouti International Fair — A326b

Perf. 13¼x13½
2017, Dec. 21   Litho.
1346B A326b 110fr multi   1.25 1.25

A327

No. 1347, 240fr — Bobby Fischer (1943-2008), World Chess Champion: a, Scratching face and holding clock. b, Playing against Mikhail Tal (1936-92). c, Without hands visible. d, With hand on forehead.
No. 1348, 240fr — Garry Kasparov, World Chess Champion: a, With hands covering ears. b, Holding chess piece. c, Scratching head. d, Looking down at chess board, two chess pieces.
No. 1349, 240fr — Golf: a, Player wearing green shirt addressing ball, player in red shirt carrying golf bag and club. b, Golf bag and player in red shirt swinging. c, Golf ball and player finishing swing. d, Player carrying golf bag.
No. 1350, 240fr — Ice hockey players: a, Nikita Gusev. b, Nathan MacKinnon. c, Nikita Kucherov. d, Bogdan Kiselevich.
No. 1351, 240fr — Formula 1 race cars of team: a, Mercedes-AMG Petronas. b, Renault Sport. c, Sauber. d, McLaren.
No. 1352, 240fr — Ferrari automobiles: a, Ferrari Enzo. b, Ferrari F12 Berlinetta. c, Ferrari Pininfarina Sergio Concept, Ferrari F40. d, Ferrari 125 S.
No. 1353, 240fr — Special transportation: a, B-377-SG/SGT Super Guppy airplane. b, GAZ 47 all-terrain vehicle. c, ZIL-4906 Blue Bird all-terrain vehicle. d, Mil V-12 Homer helicopter.
No. 1354, 240fr — Wright Flyer and Orville Wright (1871-1948): a, Wright Flyer. b, Wright and Wright Flyer. c, Wright Flyer, Orville and Wilbur Wright. d, Wright Flyer, Orville and Wilbur Wright, American flag.
No. 1355, 240fr — Concorde: a, British Airways airplane, nose at UL. b, British Airways airplane, nose at LL. c, Air France airplane, nose at UR. d, Air France airplane, nose at UL.
No. 1356, 240fr — Sailing ships: a, Palinuro, Italy. b, ARC Gloria, Colombia. c, Coast Guard Cutter Eagle, United States. d, STS Sedov, Russia.
No. 1357, 240fr — Submarines: a, Victoria Class submarine. b, HMAS Collins. c, K-535 Yury Dolgorukiy. d, USS Virginia.
No. 1358, 240fr — Steam trains: a, Jacobite, flag of Great Britain. b, Class 520 Sir Malcolm Barclay Harvey, flag of Australia. c, North and Western Class J611, flag of Great Britain. d, Class 26 4-8-4 Red Devil, flag of South Africa.
No. 1359, 240fr — High-speed trains: a, 0 series Shinkansen, flag of Japan. b, NTV ETR575, flag of Italy. c, TGV Lyria, flag of Switzerland. d, CRH, flag of People's Republic of China.
No. 1360, 240fr — Launch of Vostok 6, 55th anniv.: a, Earth, arrow and rocket. b, Statue of Valentina Tereshkova, Moscow, and medal. c, Tereshkova and Vostok 6. d, Vostok 6 and red star.
No. 1361, 240fr — End of World War I, cent.: a, 155-mm cannon of Saint Chamond tank. b, Signing of armistice, 1910. c, Marshal Ferdinand Foch (1851-1929). d, Two soldiers.
No. 1362, 240fr — 50th birthday of King Felipe VI of Spain: a, With Prince William. b, With Queen Elizabeth II. c, With Pope Francis. d, With father, King Juan Carlos I.
No. 1363, 240fr — Dogs: a, Bedlington terrier. b, Chihuahua. c, Lancashire heeler. d, Pomeranian.
No. 1364, 240fr — Butterflies: a, Euphaedra themis. b, Bebearia tentyris. c, Cymothoe egesta. d, Junonia sophia.
No. 1365, 240fr — Marine life: a, Eretmochelys imbricata. b, Octopus vulgaris. c, Amphiprion ocellaris. d, Paguristes cadenati.
No. 1366, 950fr, Fischer, diff. No. 1367, 950fr, Kasparov, diff. No. 1368, 950fr, Golfer placing ball on ground. No. 1369, 950fr, Artemi Panarin. No. 1370, 950fr, Red Bull Racing Team Formula I car. No. 1371, 950fr, Ferrari 250. No. 1372, 950fr, Mil Mi-6 Hook helicopter. No. 1373, 950fr, Orville Wright, wearing hat and aviation headgear. No. 1374, 950fr, British Airways Concorde, diff. No. 1375, 950fr, Royal Clipper, Sweden. No. 1376, 950fr, Seawolf Class submarine. No. 1377, 950fr, Japan Railways C11 171 SL Hakodate Onuma Go, flag of Japan. No. 1378, 950fr, N700 Series Shinkansen, flag of Japan. No. 1379, 950fr, Launch of Vostok 6, red star and dove. No. 1380, 950fr, Foch and soldiers, diff. No. 1381, 950fr, King Felipe VI of Spain. No. 1382, 950fr, Swedish vallhund. No. 1383, 950fr, Rhetus periander. No. 1384, 950fr, Synchiropus splendidus.

2018, Feb. 19   Litho.   Perf. 13¼
Sheets of 4, #a-d
1347-1365 A327 Set of 19 205.00 205.00
Souvenir Sheets
1366-1384 A327 Set of 19 205.00 205.00
See Nos. 1387-1388.

2018 Winter Olympics, PyeongChang, South Korea — A328

DJIBOUTI

No. 1385 — Venues of 2014 and 2018 Winter Olympics: a, Fisht Olympic Stadium, Sochi, Russia. b, PyeongChang Olympic Stadium. c, Sochi Olympic Complex. d, Speed skating venue, PyeongChang.
950fr, Yin yang with Russian and South Korean flags.

2018, Feb. 19	Litho.	Perf. 13¼		
1385	A328	240fr	Sheet of 4, #a-d, + central label	11.00 11.00

Souvenir Sheet

| 1386 | A328 | 950fr multi | | 11.00 11.00 |

No. 1386 contains one 72x72mm diamond-shaped stamp.

Type of 2018

No. 1387 — Fire trucks: a, Robur LO 2002A. b, Barkas B 1000 KLF. c, Ural-43206. d, 1960 Ford Thames 800.
950fr, American-La France Type 0-11A.

2018, Mar. 15	Litho.	Perf. 13¼		
1387	A327	240fr	Sheet of 4, #a-d	11.00 11.00

Souvenir Sheet

| 1388 | A327 | 950fr multi | | 11.00 11.00 |

February 6, 2018 SpaceX Flight A329

No. 1389: a, Launch of Falcon Heavy rocket. b, Tesla Roadster in opened rocket hatch. c, Recovery of two launched rockets. d, Tesla Roadster in space.
950fr, View from front seat of Tesla Roadster in space.

2018, Mar. 15	Litho.	Perf. 13¼		
1389	A329	240fr	Sheet of 4, #a-d	11.00 11.00

Souvenir Sheet

| 1390 | A329 | 950fr multi | | 11.00 11.00 |

A330

No. 1391, 240fr — Ursus maritimus: a, Leaping. b, Two adult bears on ice. c, Two cubs in ice den. d, Swimming underwater.
No. 1392, 240fr — Ailuropoda melanoleuca: a, Eating in bamboo forest. b, Walking. c, Rolling on back. d, Eating on hillside.
No. 1393, 240fr — Wild cats: a, Felis chaus. b, Puma concolor. c, Catopuma temminckii. d, Caracal caracal.
No. 1394, 240fr — Whales: a, Kogia breviceps. b, Mesoplodon mirus. c, Eubalaena glacialis. d, Balaenoptera brydei.
No. 1395, 240fr — Owls: a, Tyto alba. b, Bubo bubo sibiricus. c, Glaucidium passerinum. d, Bubo scandiacus.
No. 1396, 240fr — Birds of prey: a, Terathopius ecaudatus. b, Pandion haliaetus. c, Aquila nipalensis. d, Lophaetus occipitalis.
No. 1397, 240fr — Turtles: a, Malaclemys terrapin. b, Emydoidea blandingii. c, Graptemys pseudogeographica. d, Stigmochelys pardalis.
No. 1398, 240fr — Extinct animals a, Diprotodon optatum. b, Coelodonta antiquitatis. c, Megatherium americanum. d, Incilius periglenes (incorrect Latin name).
No. 1399, 240fr — Mushrooms: a, Cantharellus cibarius, Parnassius mnemosyne. b, Entoloma hochstetteri, Vespa mandarinia. c, Laccaria amethystina, Chrysodeixis chalcites. d, Boletus edulis.
No. 1400, 240fr — Bird illustrations of Alexander Wilson (1766-1813), ornithologist: a, Portrait of Wilson and Bonasa umbellus. b, Anas strepera, Somateria mollissima, Mergellus albellus, Oxyura jamaicensis. c, Charadrius wilsonia, Fulica atra, Porphyrio martinicus, Phalaropus fulicarius. d, Tympanuchus cupido.
No. 1401, 240fr — Paintings by Edouard Manet (1832-83): a, The Railway, 1873. b, The Execution of Emperor Maximilian, 1867. c, Music in the Tuileries Gardens, 1862. d, At Father Lathuille, 1879.
No. 1402, 240fr — Paintings by Paul Gauguin (1848-1903): a, Winter at Pont-Aven, and Small Breton Shepherd, 1888. b, The Siesta, c. 1892-94. c, Pastorales Tahitiennes, 1892. d, Sacred Spring, Sweet Dreams (Nave Nave Moe), 1894.
No. 1403, 240fr — Paintings by Vincent van Gogh (1853-90) and various self-portraits: a, A Pair of Shoes, 1887. b, The Old Mill, 1888. c, Prisoners Exercising, 1890. d, Old Man in Sorrow, 1890.
No. 1404, 240fr — Paintings by Pablo Picasso (1881-1973): a, Cat Devouring a Bird, 1939. b, Au Lapin Agile, 1905. c, Mother and Child, 1921. d, Portrait of Dora Maar, 1937.
No. 1405, 240fr — Paintings in the Louvre Museum, Paris: a, Mona Lisa, by Leonardo da Vinci (1452-1519). b, An Old Man and His Grandson, by Domenico Ghirlandaio (1448-94). c, The Veiled Woman, by Raphael (1483-1520). d, Portrait of Daniele Barbaro, by Paolo Veronese (1528-88).
No. 1406, 240fr — Famous people associated with the International Red Cross: a, Agatha Christie (1890-1976), writer. b, Jackie Chan, actor. c, LL Cool J, actor. d, Marie Curie (1867-1934), physicist and chemist.
No. 1407, 240fr — Paul P. Harris (1868-1947), founder of Rotary International: a, Three people near modern bookmobile sponsored by Rotary International. b, Harris, his wife, Jean (1881-1963), Sarcochilus falcatus. c, Harris, Rotary International emblem, Cymbidium sanderae. d, Two children near old bookmobile sponsored by Rotary International.
No. 1408, 240fr — Princess Diana (1961-97): a, Skiing with young sons, Princes William and Harry. b, With small boy. c, With small girl. d, With sons, as adults.
No. 1409, 950fr, Ursus maritimus, diff. No. 1410, 950fr, Ailuropoda melanoleuca, diff., No. 1411, 950fr, Felis margarita. No. 1412, 950fr, Delphinapterus leucas. No. 1413, 950fr, Aegolius funereus. No. 1414, 950fr, Falco hypoleucos. No. 1415, 950fr, Chelonia mydas. No. 1416, 950fr, Incilius periglenes (frog). No. 1417, 950fr, Russula emetica and Rana sylvatica. No. 1418, 950fr, Haliaeetus leucocephala illustration by Wilson. No. 1419, 950fr, A Studio at Batignolles, by Henri Fantin-Latour (1836-1904). No. 1420, 950fr, Self-portrait with Portrait of Emile Bernard (Les Misérables), by Gauguin. No. 1421, 950fr, Self-portraits by van Gogh. No. 1422, 950fr, Acrobat's Family with a Monkey, by Picasso. No. 1423, 950fr, Portrait of a Man, by Antonello da Messina (c. 1430-79). No. 1424, 950fr, Walt Disney (1901-66), movie producer, Ford Model T Red Cross vehicle. No. 1425, 950fr, Harris and Rotary International emblem. No. 1426, 950fr, Princess Diana and Queen Elizabeth II.

2018, Mar. 15	Litho.	Perf. 13¼	
Sheets of 4, #a-d			
1391-1408	A330	Set of 18	195.00 195.00

Souvenir Sheets

| 1409-1426 | A330 | Set of 18 | 195.00 195.00 |

A331

No. 1427, 240fr — Marilyn Monroe (1926-62), actress: a, Brushing hair. b, Sitting on staircase. c, Sitting near plants. d, Near movie camera.
No. 1428, 240fr — Pres. John F. Kennedy (1917-63): a, And Frank Sinatra (1915-98), singer. b, Wearing naval uniform, sitting behind desk. c, And wife, Jacqueline (1929-94). d, With U.S. flag.
No. 1429, 240fr — Nelson Mandela (1918-2013), President of South Africa, and minerals: a, Phosphophyllite. b, Spessartine. c, Anglesite. d, Red beryl.
No. 1430, 240fr — Fifth birthday of Prince George of Cambridge: a, With mother, Catherine, Duchess of Cambridge. b, With sister, Princess Charlotte. c, Sitting alone. d, With father, Prince William.
No. 1431, 240fr — Wedding of Prince Harry and Meghan Markle: a, Couple, flags of Great Britain and United States. b, Couple and foliage. c, Couple kissing in background. d, Couple and castle in background.
No. 1432, 240fr — Ferdinand von Zeppelin (1838-1917), airship builder: a, Zeppelin wearing helmet and Hindenburg (LZ129). b, Zeppelin LZ4. c, Medal depicting Zeppelin and Graf Zeppelin (LZ127). d, Zeppelin wearing red tie.
No. 1433, 240fr — Motorcycle racers in Isle of Man TT races: a, Morgan Govignon, 2016. b, Bruce Anstey, 2007. c, Gary Johnson, 2016. d, James Hillier, 2011.
No. 1434, 240fr — Lamborghini automobiles, 55th anniv.: a, Lamborghini Centenario. b, Lamborghini Gallardo. c, Lamborghini Aventador. d, Lamborghini Diablo.
No. 1435, 240fr — Fire trucks: a, GPM-54. b, CCFM. c, Mercedes-Benz Zetros. d, OES Type III.
No. 1436, 240fr — European high-speed trains: a, Eurostar, France. b, ICE 3, Germany. c, Bombardier Zefiro V300, Italy. d, RENFE Series S-130, Spain.
No. 1437, 240fr — 1958 Munich airplane crash, 60th anniv.: a, Airplane and Manchester United soccer team. b, Refueling of Airspeed Ambassador airplane. c, Rescuers at crash site. d, Nose of crashed airplane.
No. 1438, 240fr — Yuri Gagarin (1934-68), first man in space: a, Gagarin waving. b, Vostok-K rocket, statue of Gagarin, Moscow. c, Gagarin and dove. d, Gagarin in spacesuit.
No. 1439, 240fr — Lighthouses: a, Vlaming Head Lighthouse, Australia. b, Esopus Meadows Lighthouse, New York. c, Cabo de la Huerta Lighthouse, Spain. d, Eckmühl Lighthouse, France.
No. 1440, 240fr — Scouts: a, Two Boy Scouts and campfire. b, Four Girl Scouts and leader. c, Two Boy Scouts saluting. d, Boy Scout and Scoutmaster.
No. 1441, 240fr — Organization of African Unity (African Union), 55th anniv.: a, Pan-African Parliament. b, Roger Nkodo Dang, Parliamentary President. c, African Union building, Addis Ababa, Ethiopia. d, Amara Essy, 2001-02 Secretary-General of OAU.
No. 1442, 240fr — Dolphins: a, Two Tursiops truncatus, one facing right. b, Stenella longirostris. c, Two Tursiops truncatus facing left. d, Orcinus orca.
No. 1443, 240fr — Butterflies: a, Papilio machaon. b, Melanargia galathea. c, Parnassius apollo. d, Morpho helenor.
No. 1444, 240fr — Dinosaurs: a, Velociraptor mongoliensis. b, Triceratops horridus. c, Tyrannosaurus rex. d, Parasaurolophus walkeri.
No. 1445, 240fr — Orchids: a, Laeliocattleya. b, Ophrys apifera. c, Vanda coerulea. d, Anacamptis papilionacea.
No. 1446, 240fr — Minerals: a, Kunzite, California. b, Red beryl, New Mexico. c, Anglesite, Morocco. d, Celestine, Madagascar.
No. 1447, 950fr, Monroe, diff. No. 1448, 950fr, Pres. Kennedy, diff. No. 1449, 950fr, Mandela and Brookite. No. 1450, 950fr, Prince George of Cambridge. No. 1451, 950fr, Prince Harry and Meghan Markle, diff. No. 1452, 950fr, Graf Zeppelin (LZ127) and LZ4. No. 1453, 950fr, Motorcycle racer Ryan Farquhar, 2015. No. 1454, 950fr, Ferruccio Lamborghini (1916-93), industrialist, and Lamborghini Urraco. No. 1455, 950fr, Russian fire truck. No. 1456, 950fr, RABDe 500, Switzerland. No. 1457, 950fr, Harry Gregg, goaltender for Manchester United soccer team who survived plane crash. No. 1458, 950fr, Gagarin in spacesuit. No. 1459, 950fr, St. Nicholas Church Lighthouse, Ukraine. No. 1460, 950fr, Two Boy Scouts following map. No. 1461, 950fr, Gamal Abdel Nasser (1918-70), 1964-65 Chairman of Organization of African Unity. No. 1462, 950fr, One Tursiops truncatus. No. 1463, 950fr, Ypthima baldus. No. 1464, 950fr, Compsognathus longipes. No. 1465, 950fr, Phalaenopsis lueddemanniana. No. 1466, 950fr, Brookite, Pakistan.

2018, June 12	Litho.	Perf. 13¼	
Sheets of 4, #a-d			
1427-1446	A331	Set of 20	215.00 215.00

Souvenir Sheets

| 1447-1466 | A331 | Set of 20 | 215.00 215.00 |

Medals — A332

DesignsL Nos. 1467, 1470a, 200fr, Star of Devotion Military Order. Nos. 1468, 1470b, 300fr, Order of June 27. Nos. 1469, 1470c, 400fr, Order of the Grand Star of Djibouti.

2018, June 27	Litho.	Perf. 13¼x13	
1467-1469	A332	Set of 3	10.00 10.00

Souvenir Sheet
Perf. 13¼

| 1470 | A332 | Sheet of 3, #a-c | 10.00 10.00 |

No. 1470 contains three 30x51mm stamps.

Armed Forces Emblem A333

Police Emblem A334

Republican Guard Emblem A335

Gendarmerie Emblem A336

Coast Guard Emblem — A337

2018, June 27	Litho.	Perf. 13¼x13	
1471	A333	400fr multi	4.50 4.50
1472	A334	400fr multi	4.50 4.50
1473	A335	400fr multi	4.50 4.50
1474	A336	400fr multi	4.50 4.50
1475	A337	400fr multi	4.50 4.50
Nos. 1471-1475 (5)			22.50 22.50

Souvenir Sheets
Stamps With Colored Frames
Perf. 13¼

1476	A333	500fr multi	5.75 5.75
1477	A334	500fr multi	5.75 5.75
1478	A335	500fr multi	5.75 5.75
1479	A336	500fr multi	5.75 5.75
1480	A337	500fr multi	5.75 5.75
Nos. 1476-1480 (5)			28.75 28.75

Nos. 1476-1480 each contain one 39x51mm stamp.

Homage to Army Martyrs — A338

2018, June 27	Litho.	Perf. 13x13¼	
1481	A338	400fr multi	4.50 4.50

Souvenir Sheet
Stamp With Colored Frame
Perf. 13¼

| 1482 | A338 | 500fr multi | 5.75 5.75 |

No. 1482 contains one 51x39mm stamp.

Soldiers of African Union Mission in Somalia — A339

2018, June 27	Litho.	Perf. 13¼x13	
1483	A339	400fr multi	4.50 4.50

Souvenir Sheet
Stamp With Colored Frame
Perf. 13¼

| 1484 | A339 | 500fr multi | 5.75 5.75 |

No. 1484 contains one 39x51mm stamp.

Firefighters — A340

DJIBOUTI

2018, June 27 Litho. Perf. 13¼x13
1485 A340 400fr multi 4.50 4.50

Souvenir Sheet
Stamp With Colored Frame
Perf. 13¼
1486 A340 500fr multi 5.75 5.75
No. 1486 contains one 33x51mm stamp.

Souvenir Sheets

Flags
A341

Flag of: No. 1487, 500fr, United States. No. 1488, 500fr, People's Republic of China. No. 1489, 500fr, France. No. 1490, 500fr, Germany. No. 1491, 500fr, Italy. No. 1492, 500fr, Japan. No. 1493, 500fr, Spain.

2018, June 27 Litho. Perf. 13¼
1487-1493 A341 Set of 7 40.00 40.00

Souvenir Sheet

Imploration, by Rifki Abdoulkader Bamakhrama — A342

2018, June 27 Litho. Perf. 13¼
1494 A342 3000fr multi 34.00 34.00
Aid for orphans.

Flag of Djibouti and Barkat Gourad Hamadou (1930-2001), Prime Minister — A343

2018, June 27 Litho. Perf. 13¼x13
1495 A343 500fr multi 5.75 5.75
  a. Souvenir sheet of 1 5.75 5.75

Isao Takahata (1935-2018), Film Director — A344

No. 1496 — Takahata and: a, Hayao Miyazaki, film director. b, Firefly. c, Japanese raccoon dog. d, Princess Kaguya. 950fr, Takahata and Miyazaki, diff.

2018, July 27 Litho. Perf. 13¼
1496 A344 240fr Sheet of 4, #a-d 11.00 11.00

Souvenir Sheet
1497 A344 950fr multi 11.00 11.00

A345

No. 1498, 240fr — Milos Forman (1932-2018), film director, and: a, Scene from *Amadeus*. b, Clapboard and signature. c, Poster for *One Flew Over the Cuckoo's Nest*. d, Poster for *Loves of a Blonde*.
No. 1499, 240fr — Frank Sinatra (1915-98), singer and actor, and: a, Microphone. b, Luciano Pavarotti (1935-2007), opera singer. c, Kim Novak, actress. d, Academy Award.
No. 1500, 240fr — Film actors who have portrayed James Bond: a, Daniel Craig. b, Timothy Dalton. c, Roger Moore (1927-2017). d, Pierce Brosnan.
No. 1501, 240fr — Composers: a, Ludwig van Beethoven (1770-1827). b, Johann Sebastian Bach (1685-1750). c, Franz Schubert (1797-1828). d, Joseph Haydn (1732-1809).
No. 1502, 240fr — David Livingstone (1813-73), African explorer and missionary, and: a, David Livingstone Memorial Church, Blantyre, Scotland. b, Henry Morton Stanley (1841-1904), journalist and explorer. c, Livingstone Monument, Zambia. d, African people.
No. 1503, 240fr — Mahatma Gandhi (1869-1948), Indian nationalist: a, Gandhi Assassination Memorial, Delhi. b, Gandhi and *Mountain Landscape with Indians*, by John Mix Stanley. c, Gandhi, dove, flag of India. d, Birthplace of Gandhi, Porbandar, India.
No. 1504, 240fr — Queen Elizabeth II, 65th anniv. of coronation: a, With coat of arms. b, With husband, Prince Philip. c, Riding in coach. d, At coronation.
No. 1505, 240fr — Dr. Martin Luther King, Jr. (1929-68), civil rights activist, and: a, Malcolm X (1925-65), civil rights activist. b, Iwo Jima Memorial. c, Pres. John F. Kennedy (1917-63). d, Bald eagle.
No. 1506, 240fr — Ships and airplanes used by Roald Amundsen (1872-1928), polar explorer: a, Gjoa. b, Dornier Wal N25. c, Maud. d, Latham 47.
No. 1507, 240fr — André Citroen (1878-1935), automobile manufacturer: a, Citroen GT. b, Citroen ZX Rallye-Raid. c, Citroen and Citroen Traction Avant. d, Citroen and Citroen Mehari.
No. 1508, 240fr — Motorcycles from Isle of Man Tourist Trophy Races: a, Suzuki GSX-R1000. b, BMW S1000RR. c, Yamaha YZF R1. d, Honda CBR1000RR.
No. 1509, 240fr — Japanese high-speed trains: a, Shinkansen Series E5. b, Shinkansen Series E3. c, SC Maglev L0. d, Shinkansen Series E6.
No. 1510, 240fr — Naval vessels: a, USS Coronado. b, HMS Gloucester. c, HMAS Anzac. d, USS San Antonio.
No. 1511, 240fr — World War II watercraft and tanks: a, Type VII U-boat. b, Tiger II tank. c, Churchill tank. d, USS Missouri.
No. 1512, 240fr — Sled dogs: a, Greenland dogs. b, Siberian huskies. c, Chinooks. d, Samoyeds.
No. 1513, 240fr — Henry Dunant (1828-1910), founder of Red Cross: a, On horse carrying flag, nurse caring for patient. b, With Nobel medal, 1864 Geneva Convention. c, With Red Cross flag, medic treating injured soldier. d, With nurses and Red Crescent flags.
No. 1514, 240fr — Launch of Apollo 8, 50th anniv.: a, Frank Borman, mission commander and rocket launch. b, Apollo 8 crew members, Jim Lovell, William Anders and Borman. c, Lovell and Apollo 8 capsule in ocean. d, Anders and Apollo 8 in space.
No. 1515, 240fr — Rugby players: a, Player wearing No. 6 at left. b, Player with green shirt at left. c, Player with white and red shirt at left. d, Female rugby players.
No. 1516, 240fr — Chess: a, Chess Players, by Ernest Meissonier. b, 12th century chess pieces. c, Chess clock, pieces on chess board. d, Game of Chess, by Benjamin Eugène Fichel.
No. 1517, 950fr, Forman and Jim Carrey, actor. No. 1518, 950fr, Sinatra shooting revolver. No. 1519, 950fr, Sean Connery, actor, and diamonds. No. 1520, 950fr, Wolfgang Amadeus Mozart (1756-91), composer. No. 1521, 950fr, Livingstone and Victoria Falls. No. 1522, 950fr, Gandhi, dove and flag of India, diff. No. 1523, 950fr, Queen Elizabeth II at coronation, diff. No. 1524, 950fr, Dr. King, White House. No. 1525, 950fr, Amundsen and airship Norge. No. 1526, 950fr, Citroen and Citroen DS21. No. 1527, 950fr, Yamaha YZR-M1, Tower of Refuge. No. 1528, 950fr, Shinkansen Series E7. No. 1529, 950fr, USS Oakland. No. 1530, 950fr, Lockheed P-38 Lightning. No. 1531, 950fr, Alaskan malamutes. No. 1532, 950fr, Dunant, Red Cross flag, Red Cross workers carrying corpse. No. 1533, 950fr, Moon and Apollo 8 crew members. No. 1534, 950fr, American football players. No. 1535, 950fr, Magnus Carlsen, chess player, chess board and pieces.

2018, July 27 Litho. Perf. 13¼
Sheets of 4, #a-d
1498-1516 A345 Set of 19 205.00 205.00

Souvenir Sheets
1517-1535 A345 Set of 19 205.00 205.00

Beagle
A346

2018, Aug. 27 Litho. Perf. 13¼
1536 A346 240fr multi 2.75 2.75

Souvenir Sheet
1537 A346 950fr multi 11.00 11.00
No. 1536 was printed in sheets of 4.

A347

No. 1538, 240fr — Panthera leo: a, Male lion roaring. b, Female lion and cubs. c, Male lion standing on rock. d, Female lion roaring.
No. 1539, 240fr — Panthera tigris: a, Tiger with mouth open. b, Tiger and trees. c, Streak of tigers. d, Tiger in snow.
No. 1540, 240fr — Cats: a, American bobtail. b, Canadian Sphynx. c, Mekong bobtail. d, Abyssinian.
No. 1541, 240fr — Elephants: a, Two Elephas maximus. b, Loxodonta africana and zebras. c, Loxodonta africana with trunk raised. d, One Elephas maximus calf.
No. 1542, 240fr — Primates: a, Rhinopithecus roxellana. b, Hylobates lar. c, Nasalis larvatus. d, Colobus guereza.
No. 1543, 240fr — Water birds: a, Anas platyrhynchos. b, Chauna torquata. c, Bucephala albeola. d, Cygnus olor.
No. 1544, 240fr — Owls: a, Tyto alba. b, Bubo bubo. c, Strix nebulosa. d, Strix aluco.
No. 1545, 240fr — Pigeons: a, Phaps chalcoptera. b, Columbina inca. c, Zenaida graysoni. d, Columba guinea.
No. 1546, 240fr — Kingfishers: a, Tanysiptera sylvia. b, Megaceryle maxima. c, Ceryle rudis. d, Syma torotoro.
No. 1547, 240fr — Apis mellifera: a, Bee on flower, facing right. b, Swarm of bees. c, Line of bees. d, Bee on flower facing left.
No. 1548, 240fr — Butterflies: a, Papilio glaucus. b, Vanessa virginiensis. c, Pochliopta aristolochiae. d, Aglais io.
No. 1549, 240fr — Turtles: a, Aldobrachelys gigantea. b, Chelodina longicollis. c, Chelydra serpentina. d, Eretmochelys imbricata.
No. 1550, 240fr — Snakes: a, Lampropeltis getula. b, Lampropeltis zonata. c, Morelia viridis. d, Trimeresurus albolabris.
No. 1551, 240fr — Prehistoric marine creatures: a, Drepanaspis gemuendenensis. b, Eurhinosaurus longirostris. c, Plesiosaurus dolichodeirus. d, Dinichthys terrelli.
No. 1552, 240fr — Orchids: a, Paphiopedilum hennisianum. b, Paphiopedilum callosum. c, Oncidium incurvum. d, Anguloa superba.
No. 1553, 240fr — Mushrooms: a, Mycena polygramma. b, Cantharellus miniatus. c, Lactarius deliciosus. d, Macrolepiota procera.
No. 1554, 240fr — High-speed Japanese trains: a, Train with two blue stripes on side and orange lights. b, Train with hot pink stripe on front in foreground. c, Train with one blue and two brown stripes. d, Train with two blue stripes, no lights.
No. 1555, 950fr, Panthera leo, diff. No. 1556, 950fr, Panthera tigris, diff. No. 1557, 950fr, American curl cat. No. 1558, 950fr, Loxodonta africana, diff. No. 1559, 950fr, Mandrillus sphinx. No. 1560, 950fr, Chen caerulescens. No. 1561, 950fr, Bubo scandiacus. No. 1562, 950fr, Spilopelia chinensis. No. 1563, 950fr, Ceyx erithaca. No. 1564, 950fr, Apis mellifera on flower, diff. No. 1565, 950fr, Troides helena. No. 1566, 950fr, Chelonia mydas. No. 1567, 950fr, Elaphe obsoleta lindheimeri. No. 1568, 950fr, Carcharocles megalodon. No. 1569, 950fr, Miltonia vexillaria. No. 1570, 950fr, Handkea utriformis. No. 1571, 950fr, JR700 Japanese bullet train on bridge.

2018, Aug. 27 Litho. Perf. 13¼
Sheets of 4, #a-d
1538-1554 A347 Set of 17 185.00 185.00

Souvenir Sheets
1555-1571 A347 Set of 17 185.00 185.00

New Year 2019 (Year of the Pig) A348

No. 1572 — Pig: a, Facing right. b, Facing forward. c, Sleeping. d, Facing left. 950fr, Pig wearing santa hat.

2018, Aug. 27 Litho. Perf. 13¼
1572 A348 240fr Sheet of 4, #a-d 11.00 11.00

Souvenir Sheet
1573 A348 950fr multi 11.00 11.00

Miniature Sheets

Chinese Zodiac Animals
A349

Nos. 1574 and 1575: a, Rat. b, Ox (buffle). c, Tiger (tigre). d, Rabbit (lapin). e, Dragon. f, Snake (serpent). g, Horse (cheval). h, Goat (chèvre). i, Monkey (singe). j, Rooster (coq). k, Dog (chien). l, Pig (cochon).

2018, Aug. 27 Litho. Perf. 13¼x13
1574 A349 300fr Sheet of 12, #a-l 40.00 40.00
  m. Souvenir sheet of 1, #1574a 3.25 3.25
  n. Souvenir sheet of 1, #1574b 3.25 3.25
  o. Souvenir sheet of 1, #1574c 3.25 3.25
  p. Souvenir sheet of 1, #1574d 3.25 3.25
  q. Souvenir sheet of 1, #1574e 3.25 3.25
  r. Souvenir sheet of 1, #1574f 3.25 3.25
  s. Souvenir sheet of 1, #1574g 3.25 3.25
  t. Souvenir sheet of 1, #1574h 3.25 3.25
  u. Souvenir sheet of 1, #1574i 3.25 3.25
  v. Souvenir sheet of 1, #1574j 3.25 3.25
  w. Souvenir sheet of 1, #1574k 3.25 3.25
  x. Souvenir sheet of 1, #1574l 3.25 3.25

Printed on Wood Veneer
Self-Adhesive
1575 A349 300fr Sheet of 12, #a-l 40.00 40.00
See Central Africa No. , Guinea No. , Sierra Leone No.

Diplomatic Relations Between Djibouti and Japan, 40th Anniv. — A349a

2018, Dec. 1 Litho. Perf. 13¼x13
1575M A349a 400fr multi 4.50 4.50

182 DJIBOUTI

Labor Inspection Laws — A349b

2018, Dec. 1   Litho.   Perf. 13¼
1575N A349b 5000fr multi   57.50 57.50

Nelson Mandela (1918-2013), President of South Africa — A350

2018, Dec. 13   Litho.   Perf. 13¼
1576 A350 210fr multi   2.40 2.40

Souvenir Sheet
1577 A350 500fr multi   5.75 5.75

A351

No. 1578, 240fr — Michael Jackson (1958-2009), singer: a, With hand over groin at right. b, With heart in background at right. c, As child at right. d, With both arms extended to side at right.
No. 1579, 240fr — 2018 Chess Olympics gold medalists: a, Ju Wenjun, flag of People's Republic of China. b, Ding Liren, flag of People's Republic of China. c, Nguyen Ngoc Truong Son, flag of Viet Nam. d, Mariya Muzychuk, flag of Ukraine.
No. 1580, 240fr — 2018 Nobel laureates: a, Nadia Murad, Peace. b, George P. Smith, Chemistry. c, Gregory P. Winter, Chemistry. d, Denis Mukwege, Peace.
No. 1581, 240fr — Scouts: a, Three Scouts lighting campfire. b, Queen Elizabeth II greeting Scout leaders. c, Girl Scouts raising U.S. flag. d, Scouts and Lord Robert Baden-Powell (1857-1941), founder of Scouting movement.
No. 1582, 240fr — Russian trains: a, Sinara GT1s at Balashikha Station. b, ER-200 at Riga Station, Moscow. c, L-3653 locomotive at Kazan Station. d, Novocherkassk VL85 at Velsk Station.
No. 1583, 240fr — Japanese Shinkansen high-speed trains: a, Series 500. b, Series N700. c, Series E2. d, Series 700.
No. 1584, 240fr — Voyage of USS Nautilus under North Pole, 60th anniv.: a, USS Nautilus under water, emblem. b, USS Nautilus, Commander William R. Anderson (1921-2007), Legion of Merit medal. c, USS Nautilus, Admiral Hyman G. Rickover (1900-86). d, USS Nautilus, map of Arctic, Presidential Unit Citation and National Defense Service Medal.
No. 1585, 240fr — Streamliner motorcycles that broke motorcycle speed records: a, Harley-Davidson, 1970. b, BUB Seven, 2009. c, Yamaha Silver Bird, 1975. d, Ack Attack, 2010.
No. 1586, 240fr — Fire engines: a, FAUN TLF 20 Crashtender. b, Oshkosh MB1. c, Oshkosh P-23 ARFF. d, MAZ-543.
No. 1587, 240fr — Airplanes: a, Antonov An-225 Mriya carrying Buran space shuttle. b, Airbus A300-600ST Beluga. c, Lockheed C-5 Galaxy and F-15s. d, N911NA shuttle carrier with Space Shuttle Endeavour.
No. 1588, 240fr — Space exploration: a, TESS. b, InSight on Mars. c, OSIRIS-REx. d, Falcon Heavy.
No. 1589, 240fr — Minerals: a, Disthene (kyanite). b, Anatase. c, Andradite. d, Cassiterite.
No. 1590, 240fr — Dolphins: a, Lagenorhynchus obscurus. b, Delphinus delphis. c, Stenella frontalis. d, Tursiops truncatus.
No. 1591, 240fr — Fish: a, Acanthurus xanthopterus. b, Zebrasoma xanthurum. c, Carangoides bajad. d, Acanthurus leucopareius.
No. 1592, 240fr — Shells and lighthouses: a, Cypraea mappa and La Vieille Lighthouse, France. b, Cypraecassis rufa and Ile Verte Lighthouse, Canada. c, Cassis cornuta and Cape Meares Lighthouse, Oregon. d, Cymbiola imperialis and Point Loma Lighthouse, California.

No. 1593, 240fr — Dinosaurs: a, Dilophosaurus wetherilli. b, Brontosaurus excelsus. c, Stegosaurus stenops. d, Therizinosaurus cheloniformis.
No. 1594, 240fr — Endangered species: a, Elephas maximus. b, Panthera tigris. c, Aloeides nubilus. d, Equus grevyi.
No. 1595, 240fr — Animals threatened by climate change: a, Pygoscelis antarcticus. b, Ursus maritimus. c, Bombus pascuorum. d, Phascolarctos cinereus.
No. 1596, 240fr — Animals on stamps: a, Panthera tigris on Russia #6181. b, Coracias garrulus on Lithuania #877. c, Lutra lutra on German Democratic Republic #2620. d, Vulpes corsac on Kyrgyzstan #384a.
No. 1597, 950fr, Jackson, diff. No. 1598, 950fr, Jorge Cori, chess gold medalist, flag of Peru. No. 1599, 950fr, Arthur Ashkin 2018 Nobel Physics laureate. No. 1600, 950fr, Two scouts practicing first aid. No. 1601, 950fr, ER-9 train at Yalutorovsk Station, Russia. No. 1602, 950fr, Shinkansen Series 200. No. 1603, 950fr, USS Nautilus under water. No. 1604, 950fr, Gyronaut X-1, 1966. No. 1605, 950fr, Dennis Mk9 fire truck. No. 1606, 950fr, Antonov An-124 and MiG-29. No. 1607, 950fr, Hayabusa 2. No. 1608, 950fr, Red beryl. No. 1609, 950fr, Platanista gangetica. No. 1610, 950fr, Balistapus undulatus. No. 1611, 950fr, Pinctada margaritifera and Point Reyes Lighthouse, California. No. 1612, 950fr, Giganotosaurus carolinii. No. 1613, 950fr, Ailurus fulgens. No. 1614, 950fr, Two Ursus maritimus on Russia #119. No. 1615, 950fr, Castor fiber on Belarus #119.

2018, Dec. 13   Litho.   Perf. 13¼
Sheets of 4, #a-d
1578-1596 A351 Set of 19   205.00 205.00

Souvenir Sheets
1597-1615 A351 Set of 19   205.00 205.00

Mohandas K. Gandhi (1869-1948), Indian Nationalist Leader — A352

2019, Feb. 27   Litho.   Perf. 13¼x13
1616 A352 100fr multi   1.10 1.10

Fauna and Mushrooms — A353

No. 1617, 240fr — Ailuropoda melanoleuca: a, Eating. b, Sitting. c, Climbing on tree. d, Walking.
No. 1618, 240fr — Bats: a, Rhinolophus hipposideros. b, Pteropus lylei. c, Micropteropus pussilus. d, Pteropus poliocephalus.
No. 1619, 240fr — Dogs: a, Airedale terrier. b, Akitai. c, American pit bull terrier. d, Boston terrier.
No. 1620, 240fr — Orcinus orca: a, Head above water, fins at right. b, Pair leaping out of water to right. c, Head above water, fins at left. d, Pair leaping out of water to left.
No. 1621, 240fr — Owls: a, Athene brama. b, Aegolius acadicus. c, Bubo virginianus. d, Bubo scandiacus.
No. 1622, 240fr — Bee-eaters: a, Nyctiornis amictus. b, Merops viridis. c, Merops orientalis. d, Merops nubicoides.
No. 1623, 240fr — Butterflies: a, Papilio glaucus. b, Limenitis arthemis. c, Pachliopta hector. d, Papilio dardanus.
No. 1624, 240fr — Turtles: a, Caretta caretta. b, Emys orbicularis. c, Carettochelys insculpta. d, Pangshura smithii.
No. 1625, 240fr — Spiders: a, Latrodectus mactans. b, Hogna radians. c, Verrucosa arenata. d, Aranea pilipes.
No. 1626, 240fr — Mushrooms: a, Macrolepiota procera. b, Leccinum aurantiacum. c, Boletus edulis. d, Lactarius deterrimus.
No. 1627, 950fr, Ailuropoda melanoleuca, diff. No. 1628, 950fr, Eptesicus fuscus. No. 1629, 950fr, Dalmatian. No. 1630, 950fr, Orcinus orca, diff. No. 1631, 950fr, Athene noctua. No. 1632, 950fr, Merops leschenaulti. No. 1633, 950fr, Battus philenor. No. 1634, 950fr, Geoclemys hamiltonii. No. 1635, 950fr, Araneus diadematus. No. 1636, 950fr, Leccinum versipelle.

2019, Feb. 27   Litho.   Perf. 13¼
Sheets of 4, #a-d
1617-1626 A353 Set of 10   110.00 110.00

Souvenir Sheets
1627-1636 A353 Set of 10   110.00 110.00

Nos. 1627-1636 each contain one 45x60mm stamp.

No. 1637, 240fr — Princess Diana (1961-97): a, With British flags in background. b, Holding infant. c, Touching face of young boy. d, With building and statue in background.
No. 1638, 240fr — Princess Grace of Monaco (1929-82): a, In automobile with Frank Sinatra (1915-98). b, With two children. c, With royal monogram. d, With her coat of arms.
No. 1639, 240fr — Yuri Gagarin (1934-68), first man in space: a, Standing beside automobile. b, Wearing spacesuit, with Vostok 1. c, Wearing military uniform. d, With wife, Valentina and infant daughter.
No. 1640, 240fr — Niki Lauda (1949-2019), race car driver: a, Lauda and McLaren MP4/1. b, Ferrari 312 T2. c, March 721 G. d, Brabham BT48 and Brabham BT46.
No. 1641, 240fr — European high-speed trains: a, Frecciarossa 1000, flag of Italy. b, TGV Réseau, flag of France. c, ICE 4, flag of Germany. d, Eurostar e320, flag of Great Britain.
No. 1642, 240fr — Submarines: a, USS Los Angeles. b, Akula II class SSN Project 971U, Russia. c, USS Skate. d, Alfa class Project 705 Lyra, Russia.
No. 1643, 240fr — Red Cross campaign against malaria: a, Insect exterminator and Anopheles gambiae. b, Medical staffer, Plasmodium malariae and chemical structure of Primaquine. c, Doctor inoculating child. d, Malaria patient and hand holding hypodermic needle.
No. 1644, 240fr — Ice hockey players: a, Sidney Crosby, Canada. b, Alexander Ovechkin, Russia. c, Patrick Kane, U.S. d, Erik Karlsson, Sweden.
No. 1645, 950fr, Princess Diana and Prince Charles on wedding day. No. 1646, 950fr, Princess Grace and Academy Award. No. 1647, 950fr, Gagarin and technician. No. 1648, 950fr, Lauda and Ferrari 312 B3 cars. No. 1649, 950fr, Eurostar e300, flag of Great Britain. No. 1650, 950fr, USS Triton. No. 1651, 950fr, Hands of malaria patient and medical staffer, mosquito and giraffe. No. 1652, 950fr, Evgeni Malkin, Russia.

2019, Feb. 27   Litho.   Perf. 13¼
Sheets of 4, #a-d
1637-1644 A354 Set of 8   87.50 87.50

Souvenir Sheets
1645-1652 A354 Set of 8   87.50 87.50

First Man on the Moon, 50th Anniv. A355

No. 1653: a, Apollo 11 astronaut Neil Armstrong (1930-2012), patch of Gemini 8. b, Apollo 11 astronaut Edwin E. "Buzz" Aldrin, Jr. patch of Gemini 12. c, Apollo 11 astronaut Michael Collins, patch of Gemini 10. c, Aldrin, Armstrong, Collins and patch of Apollo 11.
950fr, Aldrin on moon, Pres. John F. Kennedy (1917-63).

2019, Feb. 27   Litho.   Perf. 13¼
1653 A355 240fr Sheet of 4,
  #a-d   11.00 11.00

Souvenir Sheet
1654 A355 950fr multi   11.00 11.00

No. 1654 contains one 45x51mm stamp.

Paintings by Pablo Picasso (1881-1973) — A356

No. 1655: a, Mother and Child, 1902. b, Le Pigeon aux Petits Pois, 1911. c, Vase of Flowers on a Table, 1969. d, The Card Player, 1913-14.
1000fr, Portrait of Woman with an Ermine Collar (Olga), 1923.

2019, Mar. 14   Litho.   Perf. 13¼x13
1655 A356 250fr Sheet of 4,
  #a-d   11.50 11.50

Souvenir Sheet
1656 A356 1000fr multi   11.50 11.50

A357

No. 1657, 250fr — Napoleon Bonaparte (1769-1821), Emperor of France, with denomination in: a, Gray lilac (66x40mm triangular stamp). b, Rose (30x42mm). c, Dull violet blue (30x42mm). d, Bright green (30x42mm).
No. 1658, 250fr — Composers: a, Ludwig van Beethoven (1770-1827) (66x40mm triangular stamp). b, Franz Schubert (1797-1828) (30x42mm). c, Johann Sebastian Bach (1685-1750) (30x42mm). d, Joseph Haydn (1732-1809) (30x42mm).
No. 1659, 250fr — Tennis players: a, Novak Djokovic (66x40mm triangular stamp). b, Rafael Nadal (30x42mm). c, Petra Kvitova (30x42mm). d, Alexander Zverev (30x42mm).
No. 1660, 250fr — Chess players: a, Bobby Fischer (1943-2008) (66x40mm triangular stamp). b, Ding Liren (30x42mm). c, Judit Polgár (30x42mm). d, Magnus Carlsen (30x42mm).
No. 1661, 250fr — Scouts: a, Scout examining rocks (66x40mm triangular stamp). b, Scout cooking (30x42mm). c, Scout holding laptop computer (30x42mm). d, Scout writing in notebook (30x42mm).
No. 1662, 250fr — Trains of India: a, Jabalpur Express (66x40mm triangular stamp). b, WAG 9 electric locomotive (30x42mm). c, Maharajas' Express car interior (30x42mm). d, DEMU (30x42mm).
No. 1663, 250fr — Fire engines: a, Ford C series (66x40mm triangular stamp). b, ZIL-157 (30x42mm). c, GAZ-51 (30x42mm). d, IFA W 50 (30x42mm).
No. 1664, 250fr — Concorde, 50th anniv., with denomination in: a, Gray violet (66x40mm triangular stamp). b, Rose (30x42mm). c, Dull violet blue (30x42mm). d, Bright green (30x42mm).
No. 1665, 250fr — Prehistoric aquatic animals: a, Nothosaurus mirabilis (66x40mm triangular stamp). b, Carcharocles megalodon (30x42mm). c, Mosasaurus hoffmanni (30x42mm). d, Plesiosaurus dolichodeirus (30x42mm).
No. 1666, 1000fr, Bonaparte, diff. No. 1667, 1000fr, Wolfgang Amadeus Mozart (1756-91), composer. No. 1668, 1000fr, Tennis player Naomi Osaka. No. 1669, 1000fr, Chess player Garry Kasparov. No. 1670, Lord Robert

DJIBOUTI

Baden-Powell (1857-1941), founder of Scouting movement. No. 1671, 1000fr, WCP1 Diesel locomotive. No. 1672, 1000fr, Dennis F2 fire engine. No. 1673, 1000fr, Concorde, diff. No. 1674, 1000fr, Geosaurus giganteus.

2019, Mar. 14   Litho.   Perf. 13¼
Sheets of 4, #a-d
1657-1665   A357   Set of 9   100.00 100.00
Souvenir Sheets
1666-1674   A357   Set of 9   100.00 100.00

Nos. 1666-1674 each contain one 66x40mm triangular stamp.

A358

No. 1675, 250fr — Primates: a, Leontopithecus rosalia (40mm diameter). b, Pan paniscus (40mm diameter). c, Saimiri sciureus (50x30mm). d, Macaca sinica (50x30mm).
No. 1676, 250fr — Cats: a, Korat (40mm diameter). b, Selkirk Rex (40mm diameter). c, Turkish Angora (50x30mm). d, American Shorthair (50x30mm).
No. 1677, 250fr — Sharks: a, Sphyrna lewini (40mm diameter). b, Triaenodon obesus (40mm diameter). c, Prionace glauca (50x30mm). d, Rhincodon typus (50x30mm).
No. 1678, 250fr — Kingfishers: a, Alcedo azurea (40mm diameter). b, Alcedo atthis (40mm diameter). c, Ceyx erithaca (50x30mm). d, Pelargopsis capensis (50x30mm).
No. 1679, 250fr — Bees: a, Bombus sylvarum (40mm diameter). b, Megachile lagopoda (40mm diameter). c, Apis mellifera facing right (50x30mm). d, Apis mellifera facing left (50x30mm).
No. 1680, 250fr — Orchids: a, Paphiopedilum hirsutissimum (40mm diameter). b, Brassovola nodosa (40mm diameter). c, Phalaenopsis hybrid (50x30mm). d, Dendrobium kingianum (50x30mm).
No. 1681, 250fr — Minerals: a, Apophyllite (40mm diameter). b, Amethyst (40mm diameter). c, Grossular (50x30mm). d, Apatite (50x30mm).
No. 1682, 250fr — Lighthouses and various unnamed shells: a, Marblehead Light, Ohio (40mm diameter). b, Tawas Point Light, Michigan (40mm diameter). c, Castle Hill Lighthouse, Rhode Island (50x30mm). d, West Point Light, Washington (50x30mm).
No. 1683, 1000fr, Pongo abelii. No. 1684, 1000fr, Ocicat. No. 1685, 1000fr, Carcharodon carcharias. No. 1686, 1000fr, Dacelo leachii. No. 1687, 1000fr, Bombus ruderarius. No. 1688, 1000fr, Phalaenopsis Sogo Yukidian. No. 1689, 1000fr, Emerald. No. 1690, 1000fr, Fastnet Lighthouse, Ireland, shell and starfish.

2019, Mar. 14   Litho.   Perf. 13¼
Sheets of 4, #a-d
1675-1682   A358   Set of 8   90.00 90.00
Souvenir Sheets
Perf.
1683-1690   A358   Set of 8   90.00 90.00

Nos. 1683-1690 each conatin one 40mm diameter stamp.

Souvenir Sheets

Nobel Laureates — A359

Designs: No. 1691, 1000fr, Dr. Martin Luther King, Jr. (1929-68), 1964 Peace laureate. No. 1692, 1000fr, Pablo Neruda (1904-73), 1971 Literature laureate. No. 1693, 1000fr, Mikhail Gorbachev, 1990 Peace laureate. No. 1694, 1000fr, Tu Youyou, 2015 Physiology or Medicine laureate.

2019, Mar. 14   Litho.   Perf.
1691-1694   A359   Set of 4   45.00 45.00

New Year 2019 (Year of the Pig) A360

No. 1695: a, Pig and bowl. b, Pig facing left. c, Pig sitting. d, Pig in mud.
1000fr, Pig snout.

Litho. With Foil Application
2019, Mar. 14   Perf.
1695   A360   250fr Sheet of 4, #a-d   11.50 11.50
Souvenir Sheet
1696   A360   1000fr multi   11.50 11.50

Naval Vessels of the People's Republic of China — A361

Flag of the Navy of People's Republic of China and: No. 1697, 200fr, Type 001A aircraft carrier. No. 1698, 200fr, Type 075 amphibious assault ship.
No. 1699, 500fr, Like #1697. No. 1700, 500fr, Like #1698.

2019, May 27   Litho.   Perf. 13
1697-1698   A361   Set of 2   4.50 4.50
Souvenir Sheets
1699-1700   A361   Set of 2   11.50 11.50

Eid ul-Fitr Activities — A362

Emblem and: 1000fr, People making art for disabled children. 3000fr, People in march for equality, horiz.

Litho. & Embossed
2019, May 27   Perf. 13
1701-1702   A362   Set of 2   45.00 45.00

A363

No. 1703, 250fr — 50th birthday of Vassily Ivanchuk, chess player: a, Touching chess piece at bottom. b, With chin resting on hands at bottom. c, Writing. d, With hands on forehead at left.
No. 1704, 250fr — Richard F. Gordon, Jr. (1929-2017), astronaut: a, Apollo 12 service and command modules, mission patch. b, Wearing spacesuit without helmet. c, Wearing spacesuit and helmet. d, With astronaut Pete Conrad (1930-99).
No. 1705, 250fr — Ernest H. Shackleton (1874-1922), Antarctic explorer: a, Standing with penguins. b, Marine chronometer. c, Sled dog. d, His ship, Endurance.
No. 1706, 250fr — Birth of Archie Harrison Mountbatten-Windsor, son of the Duke and Duchess of Sussex: a, With parents. b, With mother. c, Duke of Sussex. d, Duke of Sussex as child, with his mother, Princess Diana.
No. 1707, 250fr — Paintings by Pierre-Auguste Renoir (1841-1919): a, Children at the Seashore, Guernsey, 1883. b, The Swing, 1876. c, Riding in the Bois du Boulogne, 1873. d, Woman Sitting by the sea, 1883.
No. 1708, 250fr — Japanese high-speed trains: a, Shinkansen Series E6. b, Shinkansen Series 500, blue black trim. c, Shinkansen Series E7. d, Shinkansen Series 500, blue trim.
No. 1709, 250fr — Fire trucks: a, Isuzu Elf. b, Opel Blitz 1.75t. c, Opel Blitz LF8 TS. d, Ford Transit MK1.
No. 1710, 250fr — Motorcycles: a, Moto Guzzi V85TT. b, 2019 BMW R 1250 GS. c, Suzuki GSX1100S Katana. d, Kawasaki Z125.
No. 1711, 250fr — Dinosaurs: a, Beipiaosaurus inexpectus. b, Caudipteryx dongi. c, Archaeoceratops oshimai. d, Rubeosaurus ovatus.
No. 1712, 1000fr, Ivanchuk and Magnus Carlsen playing chess, horiz. No. 1713, 1000fr, Gordon and Apollo 12 mission patch, horiz. No. 1714, 1000fr, Shackleton and foundering ship, horiz. No. 1715, 1000fr, Feet of Mountbatten-Windsor, horiz. No. 1716, 1000fr, Odalisque, by Renoir, horiz. No. 1717, 1000fr, Shinkansen Series E5, horiz. No. 1718, 1000fr, IFA W50 La fire truck, horiz. No. 1719, 1000fr, Yamaha YZF-R125 motorcycle, horiz. No. 1720, 1000fr, Brachylophosaurus canadensis, horiz.

Perf. 13¼x12¾
2019, June 12   Litho.
Sheets of 4, #a-d
1703-1711   A363   Set of 9   100.00 100.00
Souvenir Sheets
Perf. 12¾x13¼
1712-1720   A363   Set of 9   100.00 100.00

Animals A364

No. 1721, 250fr — Hippopotamus amphibius: a, Adult and calf. b, Bird sitting on adult. c, Adult. d, Adult underwater.
No. 1722, 250fr — Wild cats: a, Panthera tigris tigris. b, Panthera uncia. c, Puma concolor. d, Panthera pardus orientalis.
No. 1723, 250fr — Sled dogs: a, Siberian huskies. b, Sakhalin husky. c, Alaskan malamute. d, Greenland dogs.
No. 1724, 250fr — Dolphins: a, Lagenorhynchus obscurus. b, Delphinus capensis. c, Tursiops truncatus. d, Stenella frontalis.
No. 1725, 250fr — Birds of prey: a, Aquila rapax. b, Pandion haliaetus. c, Milvus migrans. d, Aquila clanga.
No. 1726, 250fr — Hummingbirds: a, Chlorostilbon lucidus. b, Mellisuga helenae. c, Calypte anna. d, Archilochus colubris.
No. 1727, 250fr — Hornbills: a, Rhyticeros cassidix. b, Buceros bicornis. c, Tockus erythrorhynchus. d, Anthracoceros albirostris.
No. 1728, 250fr — Fish and coral: a, Paracanthurus hepatus, Acabaria splendens. b, Pomacanthus xanthometopon, Zoanthus gigantus. c, Pomacanthus imperator, Discosoma nummiforme. d, Balistoides conspicillum, Ricordea florida.
No. 1729, 250fr — Snakes: a, Trimeresurus insularis. b, Natrix natrix. c, Morelia viridis. d, Atheris ceratophora.
No. 1730, 250fr — Extinct animals: a, Ara gossei. b, Numenius borealis. c, Macropus greyi. d, Pyrenean ibex.
No. 1731, 1000fr, Choeropsis liberiensis. No. 1732, 1000fr, Panthera onca. No. 1733, 1000fr, Alaskan malamute, diff. No. 1734, 1000fr, Stenella coeruleoalba. No. 1735, 1000fr, Aquila heliaca. No. 1736, 1000fr, Calypte anna, diff. No. 1737, 1000fr, Tockus leucomelas. No. 1738, 1000fr, Zebrasoma desjardinii, Annella mollis. No. 1739, 1000fr, Drepanoides anomalus and Heliconia rostrata. No. 1740, 1000fr, Ectopistes migratorius.

Perf. 13¼x12¾
2019, June 12   Litho.
Sheets of 4, #a-d
1721-1730   A364   Set of 10   115.00 115.00
Souvenir Sheets
1731-1740   A364   Set of 10   115.00 115.00

Chinese Bridges — A365

Various unnamed Chinese bridges numbered: 100fr, (15-01). 125fr, (15-02). 150fr, (15-03). 175fr, (15-04). 200fr, (15-05). 225fr, (15-06). 250fr, (15-07). 275fr, (15-08). 300fr, (15-09). 325fr, (15-10). 350fr, (15-11). 375fr, (15-12). 400fr, (15-13). 425fr, (15-14). 450fr, (15-15).

2019, June 12   Litho.   Perf. 13x13¼
1741-1755   A365   Set of 15   46.50 46.50

Diplomatic relations between Djibouti and People's Republic of China, 40th anniv. Nos. 1741-1755 were each printed in sheets of 15 + label.

Chinese Buildings — A366

Various unnamed Chinese buildings numbered: 100fr, (15-01). 125fr, (15-02). 150fr, (15-03). 175fr, (15-04). 200fr, (15-05). 225fr, (15-06). 250fr, (15-07). 275fr, (15-08). 300fr, (15-09). 325fr, (15-10). 350fr, (15-11). 375fr, (15-12). 400fr, (15-13). 425fr, (15-14). 450fr, (15-15).

2019, June 12   Litho.   Perf. 13x13¼
1756-1770   A366   Set of 15   46.50 46.50

Diplomatic relations between Djibouti and People's Republic of China, 40th anniv. Nos. 1756-1770 were each printed in sheets of 15 + label.

Stamps With Emblem of Worldwide Fund for Nature (WWF) — A367

No. 1771: a, Dominica #827. b, Domincan Republic #1158c. c, Djibouti #795b. d, Dominica #2520b.
No. 1772, 300fr, Dominica #829. No. 1773, 300fr, Dominican Republic #1158b. No. 1774, 300fr, Djibouti #795a. No. 1775, 300fr, Dominica #2520a.

2019, July 27   Litho.   Perf. 13x13¼
1771   A367   200fr Sheet of 4, #a-d   9.00 9.00
Souvenir Sheets
1772-1775   A367   Set of 4   13.50 13.50

Nos. 1772-1775 each contain one 50x39mm stamp.

A368

No. 1776, 250fr — Mohandas K. Gandhi (1869-1948), Indian nationalist leader: a, With spinning wheel. b, Holding walking stick. c, Facing right, flag of India and Taj Mahal in background. d, Facing left with hands together, flags of India and Taj Mahal in background.
No. 1777, 250fr — 50th birthday of Michael Schumacher, race car driver: a, With race car in background. b, With Eddie Irvine and Jean Todt. c, In race car. d, With arms raised.

DJIBOUTI

No. 1778, 250fr — Golfers: a, Phil Mickelson. b, Tiger Woods. c, Rory McIlroy. d, Brooks Koepka.
No. 1779, 250fr — 2018 Nobel laureates: a, Peace laureates Nadia Murad and Denis Mukwege. b, Physiology or Medicine laureates Tasuku Honjo and James P. Allison. c, Economics laureates Paul Romer and William Nordhaus. d, Chemistry laureates George Smith, Gregory Winter and Frances Arnold.
No. 1780, 250fr — Paintings by Vincent van Gogh (1853-90): a, The Drinkers, 1890. b, The Langlois Bridge at Arles with Women Washing, 1888. c, Boats on the Banks of the Oise at Auvers, 1890. d, Two Peasants Digging (After Millet), 1889.
No. 1781, 250fr — World War II tanks: a, TKS, Poland. b, 7TP, Poland. c, Panzer IV, Germany. d, Panzer I, Germany.
No. 1782, 250fr — Spaceflight of Apollo 11, 50th anniv.: a, Launch. b, Lunar Module landing on Moon. c, Command and Service Modules above Moon. d, Capsule returning to Earth.
No. 1783, 1000fr, Gandhi and crowd holding flags of India. No. 1784, 1000fr, Schumacher and race car, diff. No. 1785, 1000fr, Woods, diff. No. 1786, 1000fr, 2018 Nobel laureates in Physics, Donna Strickland, Arthur Ashkin, and Gérard Mourou. No. 1787, 1000fr, Self-portrait with Straw Hat, by van Gogh. No. 1788, 1000fr, Panzer III tank, Germany. No. 1789, 1000fr, Astronaut Neil Armstrong on Moon, holding U.S. flag, Apollo 11 mission patch.

2019, July 27   Litho.   Perf. 13¼x12¾
Sheets of 4, #a-d
1776-1782   A368   Set of 7   80.00   80.00
Souvenir Sheets
1783-1789   A368   Set of 7   80.00   80.00

A369

No. 1790, 250fr — Panthera tigris tigris: a, Two tigers. b, One tiger facing forward with front legs apart. c, One tiger, standing in water. d, Tiger, reclining, with cub.
No. 1791, 250fr — Elephants: a, Three Loxodonta africana. b, Loxodonta cyclotis looking forward. c, Loxodonta cyclotis walking to right. d, Two Loxodonta africana.
No. 1792, 250fr — Whales: a, Megaptera novaeangliae, head at right. b, Megaptera novaeangliae, head at left. c, Two Megaptera novaeangliae. d, Physeter macrocephalus.
No. 1793, 250fr — Pigeons: a, Streptopelia turtur. b, Streptopelia decaocto. c, Ocyphaps lophotes. d, Goura victoria.
No. 1794, 250fr — Owls: a, Glaucidium californicum. b, Bubo africanus. c, Megascops asio. d, Bubo sumatranus.
No. 1795, 250fr — Parrots: a, Ara ararauna. b, Anodorhynchus hyacinthinus. c, Psittacus erithacus. d, Nymphicus hollandicus.
No. 1796, 250fr — Butterflies: a, Danaus eresimus. b, Gonepteryx cleopatra. c, Graphium sarpedon. d, Caligo eurilochus.
No. 1797, 250fr — Turtles: a, Clemmys guttata. b, Apalone spinifera. c, Trachemys scripta. d, Chelydra serpentina.
No. 1798, 250fr — Endangered animals: a, Canis lupus baileyi. b, Grus americana. c, Lynx pardinus. d, Gorilla beringei.
No. 1799, 250fr — Mushrooms: a, Tricholoma equestre. b, Gyroporus cyanescens. c, Boletus betulicola. d, Boletus aereus.
No. 1800, 250fr — Volcanoes: a, Volcán de Fuego, Guatemala. b, Piton de la Fournaise, Reunion Island. c, Parinacota, Bolivia, and Vicugna pacos. d, Sakurajima, Japan.
No. 1801, 250fr — Ships: a, HMS Diadem. b, Lai Fong. c, HMS Prince Royal. d, HMS Bounty.
No. 1802, 1000fr, Panthera tigris tigris, diff. No. 1803, 1000fr, Loxodonta cyclotis adult and calf. No. 1804, 1000fr, Megaptera novaeangliae, diff. No. 1805, 1000fr, Columba livia domestica. No. 1806, 1000fr, Aegolius funereus. No. 1807, 1000fr, Psittacula krameri. No. 1808, 1000fr, Agalis io. No. 1809, 1000fr, Pseudemys nelsoni. No. 1810, 1000fr, Crocodylus siamensis. No. 1811, 1000fr, Hydnum repandum. No. 1812, 1000fr, Popocatepetl, Mexico. No. 1813, 1000fr, USS Providence.

2019, July 27   Litho.   Perf. 13¼x12¾
Sheets of 4, #a-d
1790-1801   A369   Set of 12   135.00   135.00
Souvenir Sheets
1802-1813   A369   Set of 12   135.00   135.00

Nos. 1059a-1059d Surcharged in Gold or Metallic Red

Methods and Perfs. As Before
2019, Aug. 27
1814   A311   590fr on 260fr #1059a (G)   6.75   6.75
1815   A311   590fr on 260fr #1059a (MR)   6.75   6.75
1816   A311   590fr on 260fr #1059b (G)   6.75   6.75
1817   A311   590fr on 260fr #1059b (MR)   6.75   6.75
1818   A311   590fr on 260fr #1059c (G)   6.75   6.75
1819   A311   590fr on 260fr #1059c (MR)   6.75   6.75
1820   A311   590fr on 260fr #1059d (G)   6.75   6.75
1821   A311   590fr on 260fr #1059d (MR)   6.75   6.75
   Nos. 1814-1821 (8)   54.00   54.00

A370

No. 1822, 250fr — Cats: a, Balinese. b, American Shorthair. c, Russian Blue. d, Japanese bobtail.
No. 1823, 250fr — Horses: a, Paint horse. b, Lusitano. c, Knabstruper. d, Holsteiner.
No. 1824, 250fr, vert. — Bee-eaters: a, Merops albicollis. b, Merops apiaster. c, Merops leschenaulti. d, Merops bulocki.
No. 1825, 250fr, vert. — Sunbirds: a, Hedydipna collaris. b, Aethopyga gouldiae. c, Aethopyga siparaja. d, Aethopyga nipalensis.
No. 1826, 250fr, vert. — Ducks: a, Netta rufina. b, Aythya fuligula. c, Bucephala clangula. d, Tadorna tadorna.
No. 1827, 250fr, vert. — Bees: a, Bombus pascuorum. b, Xylocopa virginica. c, Apis cerana. d, Bombus terrestris.
No. 1828, 250fr, vert. — Orchids: a, Prosthechea brassavolae. b, Phalaenopsis mariae. c, Zygopetalum crinitum. d, Ondinium flexuosum.
No. 1829, 250fr, vert. — Minerals: a, Azurite. b, Pyrite. c, Celestine. d, Demantoid.
No. 1830, 1000fr, Abyssinian cats. No. 1831, 1000fr, Shire horses. No. 1832, 1000fr, Merops nubicus, vert. No. 1833, 1000fr, Arachnothera magna, vert. No. 1834, 1000fr, Marmaronetta angustirostris, vert. No. 1835, 1000fr, Apis mellifera, vert. No. 1836, 1000fr, Catasetum fimbriatum, vert. No. 1837, 1000fr, Heliodor.

Perf. 13x13¼, 13¼x13
2019, Aug. 27   Litho.
Sheets of 4, #a-d
1822-1829   A370   Set of 8   90.00   90.00
Souvenir Sheets
1830-1837   A370   Set of 8   90.00   90.00

No. 1838, 250fr — Marilyn Monroe (1926-62), actress: a, Holding dogs. b, Wearing blue dress at right. c, Wearing red dress at right. d, Seated in chair.
No. 1839, 250fr — Charlie Chaplin (1889-1977), actor, in scene from 1914 film: a, Charlot garde-malade (His New Profession). b, Charlot est content de lui (Kid Auto Races at Venice). c, Charlot et le Mannequin (Mabel's Married Life). d, Charlot artiste peintre (The Face on the Bar Room Floor).
No. 1840, 250fr — Tigran Petrosian (1929-84), chess player, wearing: a, Gray pinstripe suit. b, Brown suit. c, White shirt and tie. d, White and green plaid shirt.
No. 1841, 250fr — Rotary International emblem and: a, Paul P. Harris (1868-1947), founder, world map and doves. b, Child at water spigot. c, Doctor examining child. d, Children carrying blackboard.
No. 1842, 250fr — Duke and Duchess of Sussex: a, Duke and Duchess with son Archie carried by Duke. b, Duke of Sussex holding baby clothes. c, Archie Mountbatten-Windsor. d, Duke and Duchess with son carried by Duchess.
No. 1843, 250fr — Robert Stephenson (1803-59), civil engineer: a, With flag of Great Britain. b, Signature of Stephenson and Rocket locomotive. c, Standing on Planet locomotive. d, With his yacht, Titania.
No. 1844, 250fr — Scout: a, Fishing. b, At campfire. c, Birdwatching. d, Playing guitar.
No. 1845, 250fr — Japanese Shinkansen high-speed trains: a, Series 400. b, Series N700. c, Series 700. d, Series E3-1000.
No. 1846, 250fr — Operation Market Garden, 75th anniv.: a, DeHavilland DH.98 Mosquitos. b, Douglas C-47 Skytrains. c, Airspeed AS.51 Horsa gliders and Short Stirling Mark IV airplanes. d, Spitfire F Mk II and Messerschmitt Bf 109 airplanes.
No. 1847, 250fr — Flying dinosaurs: a, Eudimorphodon ranzii. b, Caviramus schesaplanensis. c, Caulkicephalus trimicrodon. d, Pterosaur.
No. 1848, 1000fr, Monroe, diff. No. 1849, 1000fr, Chaplin in Making a Living. No. 1850, 1000fr, Petrosian, diff. No. 1851, 1000fr, Harris and Rotary International emblem. No. 1852, 1000fr, Archie Mountabtten-Windsor, diff. No. 1853, 1000fr, Britannia Bridge, built by Stephenson. No. 1854, 1000fr, Scout, badge and canoe. No. 1855, 1000fr, Shinkansen Series 500. No. 1856, 1000fr, Hawker Tempest and Junkers Ju88 airplanes. No. 1857, 1000fr, Harpactognathus gentryii.

2019, Aug. 27   Litho.   Perf. 13¼x13
1838-1847   A371   Set of 10   115.00   115.00
Souvenir Sheets
1848-1857   A371   Set of 10   115.00   115.00

No. 1858 — Rat and: a, "2020." b, Fireworks. c, Lantern. d, Fireworks and "2020." 1000fr, Rat with gift.

New Year 2020 (Year of the Rat) A372

Litho. With Foil Application
2019, Aug. 27   Perf. 13¼x13
1858   A372   250fr Sheet of 4, #a-d   11.50   11.50
Souvenir Sheet
1859   A372   1000fr multi   11.50   11.50

Norwegian Navy Ships — A373

No. 1860 — Norwegian state flag and: a, HNoMS Trygvason. b, NoCGV Svalbard. c, KNM Storm. d, Rauma.
1000fr, KNM Fridtjof Nansen.

2019, Dec. 12   Litho.   Perf. 13x13¼
1860   A373   250fr Sheet of 4, #a-d   11.50   11.50
Souvenir Sheet
1861   A373   1000fr multi   11.50   11.50

No. 1862, 250fr — Paul Morphy (1837-84), chess champion, and: a, Queen. b, Bishop. c, Rook. d, Knight.
No. 1863, 250fr — Formula 1 race cars and drivers: a, Ferrari SF90 and Charles Leclerc. b, Ferrari SF90 and Sebastian Vettel. c, Mercedes AMG F1 W10 and Lewis Hamilton. d. Mercedes AMG F1 W10 and Valteri Bottas.
No. 1864, 250fr — Bentley automobiles, cent.: a, Bentley MH7580. b, Bentley EXP 10 Speed 6. c, Bentley Mark VI Drophead Coupe. d. Bentley Benayga.
No. 1865, 250fr — Fire trucks: a, Mercedes-Benz Zetros. b, Pierce. c, Seagrave Marauder II. d. Kenworth T800.
No. 1866, 250fr — Early locomotives: a, Locomotion No. 1, 1825. b, Salamanca, 1812. c, Atlantic, 1832. d. Cherepanov steam locomotive, 1833.
No. 1867, 250fr — African trains: a, South African Class SE1 Series 5. b, South African Gautrain. c, EMD G22C Series. d. South African Class 33-400.
No. 1868, 250fr — Start of World War I, 105th anniv.: a, Mark V tank, Great Britain. b, French soldier. c, A7V tank, Germany. d. British soldier.
No. 1869, 250fr — Dinosaurs: a, Triceratops horridus. b, Gallimimus bullatus. c, Ankylosaurus magniventris. d. Tyrannosaurus rex.
No. 1870, 1000fr, Morphy and king. No. 1871, 1000fr, Red Bull RB15 and Max Verstappen. No. 1872, 1000fr, Bentley Flying Spur. No. 1873, 1000fr, E-One fire truck. No. 1874, 1000fr, Catch Me Who Can (M'attrape qui peut) locomotive, 1808. No. 1875, 1000fr, South African Class 19D4-8-2. No. 1876, 1000fr, Fokker Dr. I airplane, Germany. No. 1877, 1000fr, Parasaurolophus walkeri.

2019, Dec. 12   Litho.   Perf. 13¼
Sheets of 4, #a-d
1862-1869   A374   Set of 8   90.00   90.00
Souvenir Sheets
1870-1877   A374   Set of 8   90.00   90.00

A375

No. 1878, 250fr — Dogs: a, Shetland sheepdog. b, Papillon. c, English bulldog. d, English cocker spaniel.
No. 1879, 250fr — Dolphins: a, Tursiops aduncus. b, Stenella longirostris, Stenella coeruleoalba. c, Tursiops truncatus. d, Lagenorhynchus obliquidens, Cephalorhynchus hectori.
No. 1880, 250fr — Kingfishers: a, Ceyx erithaca. b, Halcyon pileata. c, Ceryle rudis. d, Megaceryle alcyon.
No. 1881, 250fr — Birds of prey: a, Accipiter gentilis. b, Gyps fulvus. c, Haliaeetus leucocephalus. d, Otus scops.
No. 1882, 250fr — Aquatic birds: a, Anas platyrhynchos. b, Ardea alba modesta. c, Alcedo atthis. d, Fratercula arctica.

DJIBOUTI

No. 1883, 250fr — Butterflies: a, Tithorea harmonia. b, Ornithoptera euphorion. c, Papilio rutulus. d, Myscelia cyaniris.
No. 1884, 250fr — Fish: a, Apistogramma cacatuoides. b, Pomacanthus imperator. c, Paracanthurus hepatus. d, Chelmon rostratus.
No. 1885, 250fr — Antarctic animals: a, Leptonychotes weddellii. b, Leucocarbo bransfieldensis. c, Lobodon carcinophaga. d, Pygoscelis antarctica.
No. 1886, 250fr — Mushrooms: a, Leccinum versipelle. b, Hypsizygus tessellatus. c, Leccinum scabrum. d, Morchella esculenta.
No. 1887, 250fr — Lighthouses: a, Bodie Island Lighthouse, North Carolina. b, Split Rock Lighthouse, Minnesota. c, Punta Carena Lighthouse, Italy. d, Tower of Hercules Lighthouse, Spain.
No. 1888, 1000fr, Mastiff. No. 1889, 1000fr, Inia geoffrensis. No. 1890, 1000fr, Dacelo novaeguineae. No. 1891, 1000fr, Sarcoramphus papa. No. 1892, 1000fr, Recurvirostra avosetta. No. 1893, 1000fr, Parnassius tianschanicus. No. 1894, 1000fr, Pterois antennata. No. 1895, 1000fr, Megaptera novaeangliae. No. 1896, 1000fr, Boletus edulis. No. 1897, 1000fr, Point Cabrillo Lighthouse, California.

2019, Dec. 12   Litho.   Perf. 13¼
Sheets of 4, #a-d
1878-1887 A375 Set of 10   115.00   115.00
Souvenir Sheets
1888-1897 A375 Set of 10   115.00   115.00

 A376   A377

A378   A379

A380   A381

A382   A383

A384   A385

A386   A387

 A388   A389

 A390

 Chinese Paintings — A391

2019, Dec. 12   Litho.   Perf. 13¼

1898	A376	250fr multi	3.00	3.00
1899	A377	250fr multi	3.00	3.00
1900	A378	250fr multi	3.00	3.00
1901	A379	250fr multi	3.00	3.00
1902	A380	250fr multi	3.00	3.00
1903	A381	250fr multi	3.00	3.00
1904	A382	250fr multi	3.00	3.00
1905	A383	250fr multi	3.00	3.00
1906	A384	250fr multi	3.00	3.00
1907	A385	250fr multi	3.00	3.00
1908	A386	250fr multi	3.00	3.00
1909	A387	250fr multi	3.00	3.00
1910	A388	250fr multi	3.00	3.00
1911	A389	250fr multi	3.00	3.00
1912	A390	250fr multi	3.00	3.00
1913	A391	250fr multi	3.00	3.00
a.	Sheet of 16, #1898-1913		48.00	48.00

Nos. 1898-1913 (16)   48.00   48.00

Global Compact on Migration — A392

2019   Litho.   Perf. 13¼x12¾
1914 A392 100fr multi   1.25   1.25

Djibouti's Candidacy for 2021-22 United Nations Security Council Seat — A393

2019   Litho.   Perf. 13¼x13
1915 A393 100fr multi + label   1.25   1.25

Kiwis A394

No. 1916: a, Apteryx mantelli. b, Apteryx australis. c, Apteryx owenii. d, Apteryx rowi. 1000fr, Apteryx mantelli, diff.

Litho., Sheet Margin Litho With Foil Application
2020, Feb. 27   Perf. 13¼
1916 A394 250fr Sheet of 4, #a-d   11.50   11.50

Litho. With Foil Application
Souvenir Sheet
1917 A394 1000fr multi   11.50   11.50
New Zealand 2020 International Stamp Exhibition, Auckland. No. 1917 contains one 52x52mm stamp.

Famous Men — A395

Designs: No. 1918, 250fr, St. John Paul II (1920-2005). No. 1919, 250fr, Nelson Mandela (1918-2013), President of South Africa. No. 1920, 250fr, Mohandas K. Gandhi (1869-1948), Indian nationalist leader.

2020, Feb. 27   Perf. 13¼x12¾   Litho.
1918-1920 A395 Set of 3   8.50   8.50
   1920a Souvenir sheet of 6, 2 each #1918-1920   17.00   17.00
Nos. 1918-1920 were each printed in sheets of 8 + central label.

 A396

Butterflies: No. 1921, 250fr, Ornithoptera euphorion. No. 1922, 250fr, Vanessa cardui. No. 1923, 250fr, Idea malabarica. No. 1924, 250fr, Euploea core.
No. 1925, 1000fr, Heliconius ismenius, horiz.
Orchids: No. 1926, 250fr, Vanda coerulea. No. 1927, 250fr, Cattleya harrisoniana. No. 1928, 250fr, Platanthera chlorantha. No. 1929, 250fr, Neottia nidus-avis.
No. 1930, 1000fr, Cattleya Nancy Off "Linwood," horiz.
Mushrooms: No. 1931, 250fr, Cantharellus cibarius. No. 1932, 250fr, Rhodotus palmatus. No. 1933, 250fr, Morchella esculenta. No. 1934, 250fr, Boletus edulis.
No. 1935, 1000fr, Amanita muscaria, horiz.

Perf. 13¼x12¾, 12¾x13¼ (horiz. stamps)
2020, Feb. 27   Litho.
Butterflies
1921-1924 A396 Set of 4   11.50   11.50
   a. Souvenir sheet of 4, #1921-1924   11.50   11.50
Souvenir Sheet
1925 A396 1000fr multi   11.50   11.50
Orchids
1926-1929 A396 Set of 4   11.50   11.50
   a. Souvenir sheet of 4, #1926-1929   11.50   11.50
Souvenir Sheet
1930 A396 1000fr multi   11.50   11.50
Mushrooms
1931-1934 A396 Set of 4   11.50   11.50
   a. Souvenir sheet of 4, #1931-1934   11.50   11.50
Souvenir Sheet
1935 A396 1000fr multi   11.50   11.50

 A397

Alain Prost, Formula 1 race car driver: No. 1936, 250fr, Close-up of Prost, Prost driving race car. No. 1937, 250fr, Prost driving race car, flag of France. No. 1938, 250fr, Prost driving race car. No. 1939, 250fr, Close-up of Prost in race car.
No. 1940, 1000fr, Prost and Ayrton Senna (1960-94) Formula 1 race car driver.

Senna: No. 1941, 250fr, Signature of Senna, Senna driving Lotus 97T. No. 1942, 250fr, Close-up of Senna, crowd watching race. No. 1943, 250fr, Senna driving McLaren MP4/4. No. 1944, 250fr, Senna driving Lotus 99T.
No. 1945, 1000fr, Senna as child, seated in toy Jeep.
Elvis Presley (1935-77), with: No. 1946, 250fr, Guitar in background. No. 1947, 250fr, Guitar and crown. No. 1948, 250fr, Guitar and star. No. 1949, 250fr, Bill Haley (1925-81), rock musician.
No. 1950, 1000fr, Presley holding microphone.
St. John Paul II (1920-2005): No. 1951, 250fr, And St. Peter's Basilica. No. 1952, 250fr, Kissing baby. No. 1953, 250fr, With St. Teresa of Calcutta (1910-97). No. 1954, 250fr, And his coat of arms.
No. 1955, 1000fr, Wearing miter, St. Peter's Basilica in background.
Rotary International, 115th anniv.: No. 1956, 250fr, Child writing at desk. No. 1957, 250fr, Paul P. Harris (1868-1947), founder, microscope and medical supplies. No. 1958, 250fr, Seedling, hands holding Earth. No. 1959, 250fr, Child drinking water from spigot.
No. 1960, 1000fr, Harris and stack of books.
Discovery of Antarctica, 200th anniv.: No. 1961, 250fr, Edward Bransfield (1785-1852), sailor on Antarctic expeditions, and penguins. No. 1962, 250fr, Map of Antarctica, medal commemorating 1819 Bellingshausen expedition. No. 1963, 250fr, Bird, seal and ship. No. 1964, 250fr, Nathaniel Palmer (1799-1877), Antarctic explorer, and sculpture.
No. 1965, 1000fr, Fabian Gottlieb von Bellingshausen (1778-1852), Antarctic explorer.
Battle of Iwo Jima, 75th anniv.: No. 1966, 250fr, LVT(A)-1 tank. No. 1967, 250fr, Lockheed P-38 Lightning and A6M5. No. 1968, 250fr, F4U Corsair and A6M5. No. 1969, 250fr, Soldier and M4A2 Sherman tank.
No. 1970, 1000fr, Jeep and tank.
MiG-17 prototype jet, 70th anniv.: No. 1971, 250fr, Three silver jets flying to right. No. 1972, 250fr, Two green jets flying to left, mechanical drawing. No. 1973, 250fr, Red jet flying to right. No. 1974, 250fr, Silver jet taking off.
No. 1975, 1000fr, Silver jet and Artem Mikoyan (1905-70), aircraft designer.
Treaty of Versailles, cent.: No. 1976, 250fr, Soldier and David Lloyd George (1863-1945), British Prime Minister. No. 1977, 250fr, Woodrow Wilson (1856-1924), U.S. President, and people at peace conference. No. 1978, 250fr, Dirigibles over battlefield and Milenko Vesnic (1863-1921), Serbian representative at Paris Peace Conference. No. 1979, 250fr, Airplane, tank and Vittorio Emanuele Orlando (1860-1952), Italian representative at Paris Peace Conference.
No. 1980, 1000fr, People at peace conference and Georges Clemenceau (1841-1929), French Prime Minister.
Yalta Conference, 75th anniv: No. 1981, 250fr, Winston Churchill (1874-1965), British Prime Minister, Franklin D. Roosevelt (1882-1945), U.S. President, and Joseph Stalin (1878-1953), General Secretary of the Soviet Union. No. 1982, 250fr, Churchill and British flag. No. 1983, 250fr, Roosevelt and U.S. flag. No. 1984, 250fr, Stalin and flag of Soviet Union.
No. 1985, 1000fr, Roosevelt and U.S flag, diff.
90th birthday of Edwin E. "Buzz" Aldrin, Jr., astronaut: No. 1986, 250fr, Gemini 12 mission patch and Titan II rocket on launch pad. No. 1987, 250fr, Apollo 11 mission patch, command and service modules. No. 1988, 250fr, Gemini 12 capsule in space. No. 1989, 250fr, Aldrin in spacesuit.
No. 1990, 1000fr, Gemini 12 mission patch and capsule, and its crew members, Aldrin and James A. Lovell, Jr.
Launch of Osumi, first Japanese satellite: No. 1991, 250fr, Osumi satellite and Japanese flag. No. 1992, 250fr, Osumi in space, antennae at bottom. No. 1993, 250fr, Osumi in space, antennae at top. No. 1994, 250fr, Uchinoura launch pad and rocket.
No. 1995, 1000fr, Drawing of Osumi satellite and Hideo Itokawa (1912-99), rocketry pioneer.
Sir Alexander Fleming (1881-1955), discoverer of penicillin: No. 1996, 250fr, Fleming, molecular diagram of benzylpenicillin, Morchella rufobrunnea. No. 1997, 250fr, Passer domesticus, Amanita phalloides and chemistry apparatus. No. 1998, 250fr, Microscope, Amanita muscaria. No. 1999, 250fr, Fleming, Chrysuronia oenone, Cantharellus cibarius.
No. 2000, 1000fr, Fleming and Penecillium chrysogenum.
COVID-19 pandemic: No. 2001, 250fr, Diamond Princess, quarantined cruise ship on which many passengers contracted COVID-19. No. 2002, 250fr, COVID-19 virus, map of People's Republic of China. No. 2003, 250fr, Li Wenliang (1985-2020), ophthalmologist who noted early COVID-19 cases in Wuhan. No. 2004, 250fr, Foton G9 ambulance, flag of People's Republic of China, Red Cross/Red Crescent emblem.
No. 2005, 1000fr, Li Wenliang and COVID-19 virus.

DJIBOUTI

Dinosaurs: No. 2006, 250fr, Tyrannosaurus rex. No. 2007, 250fr, Spinosaurus aegyptiacus. No. 2008, 250fr, Velociraptor mongoliensis. No. 2009, 250fr, Tarbosaurus bataar. No. 2010, 1000fr, Triceratops horridus.

Perf. 12¾x13¼
2020, Feb. 27   Litho.

Alain Prost
| 1936-1939 | A397 | Set of 4 | 11.50 | 11.50 |
| a. | Souvenir sheet of 4, #1936-1939 | | 11.50 | 11.50 |

Souvenir Sheet
| 1940 | A397 | 1000fr multi | 11.50 | 11.50 |

Ayrton Senna
| 1941-1944 | A397 | Set of 4 | 11.50 | 11.50 |
| a. | Souvenir sheet of 4, #1941-1944 | | 11.50 | 11.50 |

Souvenir Sheet
| 1945 | A397 | 1000fr multi | 11.50 | 11.50 |

Elvis Presley
| 1946-1949 | A397 | Set of 4 | 11.50 | 11.50 |
| a. | Souvenir sheet of 4, #1946-1949 | | 11.50 | 11.50 |

Souvenir Sheet
| 1950 | A397 | 1000fr multi | 11.50 | 11.50 |

St. John Paul II
| 1951-1954 | A397 | Set of 4 | 11.50 | 11.50 |
| a. | Souvenir sheet of 4, #1951-1954 | | 11.50 | 11.50 |

Souvenir Sheet
| 1955 | A397 | 1000fr multi | 11.50 | 11.50 |

Rotary International
| 1956-1959 | A397 | Set of 4 | 11.50 | 11.50 |
| a. | Souvenir sheet of 4, #1956-1959 | | 11.50 | 11.50 |

Souvenir Sheet
| 1960 | A397 | 1000fr multi | 11.50 | 11.50 |

Discovery of Antarctica
| 1961-1964 | A397 | Set of 4 | 11.50 | 11.50 |
| a. | Souvenir sheet of 4, #1961-1964 | | 11.50 | 11.50 |

Souvenir Sheet
| 1965 | A397 | 1000fr multi | 11.50 | 11.50 |

Battle of Iwo Jima
| 1966-1969 | A397 | Set of 4 | 11.50 | 11.50 |
| a. | Souvenir sheet of 4, #1966-1969 | | 11.50 | 11.50 |

Souvenir Sheet
| 1970 | A397 | 1000fr multi | 11.50 | 11.50 |

MiG-17
| 1971-1974 | A397 | Set of 4 | 11.50 | 11.50 |
| a. | Souvenir sheet of 4, #1971-1974 | | 11.50 | 11.50 |

Souvenir Sheet
| 1975 | A397 | 1000fr multi | 11.50 | 11.50 |

Treaty of Versailles
| 1976-1979 | A397 | Set of 4 | 11.50 | 11.50 |
| a. | Souvenir sheet of 4, #1976-1979 | | 11.50 | 11.50 |

Souvenir Sheet
| 1980 | A397 | 1000fr multi | 11.50 | 11.50 |

Yalta Conference
| 1981-1984 | A397 | Set of 4 | 11.50 | 11.50 |
| a. | Souvenir sheet of 4, #1981-1984 | | 11.50 | 11.50 |

Souvenir Sheet
| 1985 | A397 | 1000fr multi | 11.50 | 11.50 |

Edwin E. "Buzz" Aldrin, Jr.
| 1986-1989 | A397 | Set of 4 | 11.50 | 11.50 |
| a. | Souvenir sheet of 4, #1986-1989 | | 11.50 | 11.50 |

Souvenir Sheet
| 1990 | A397 | 1000fr multi | 11.50 | 11.50 |

Osumi Satellite
| 1991-1994 | A397 | Set of 4 | 11.50 | 11.50 |
| a. | Souvenir sheet of 4, #1991-1994 | | 11.50 | 11.50 |

Souvenir Sheet
| 1995 | A397 | 1000fr multi | 11.50 | 11.50 |

Sir Alexander Fleming
| 1996-1999 | A397 | Set of 4 | 11.50 | 11.50 |
| a. | Souvenir sheet of 4, #1996-1999 | | 11.50 | 11.50 |

Souvenir Sheet
| 2000 | A397 | 1000fr multi | 11.50 | 11.50 |

COVID-19 Pandemic
| 2001-2004 | A397 | Set of 4 | 11.50 | 11.50 |
| a. | Souvenir sheet of 4, #2001-2004 | | 11.50 | 11.50 |

Souvenir Sheet
| 2005 | A397 | 1000fr multi | 11.50 | 11.50 |

Dinosaurs
| 2006-2009 | A397 | Set of 4 | 11.50 | 11.50 |
| a. | Souvenir sheet of 4, #2006-2009 | | 11.50 | 11.50 |

Souvenir Sheet
| 2010 | A397 | 1000fr multi | 11.50 | 11.50 |

 A398

Albert Einstein (1879-1955), physicist, and: No. 2011, 250fr, Chalkboard with model of atom and mass-energy equation. No. 2012, 250fr, Sun, Moon, and mathematical calculations. No. 2013, 250fr, Diagram of curvature of space-time and Nobel medal. No. 2014, 250fr, Gravitational lens.
No. 2015, 1000fr, Einstein and diagram of theory of special relativity.
Dr. Albert Schweitzer (1875-1965), 1952 Nobel peace laureate: No. 2016, 250fr, Holding child. No. 2017, 250fr, Playing pipe organ. No. 2018, 250fr, With Nobel medal. No. 2019, 250fr, Examining child.
No. 2020, 1000fr, Schweitzer and Nobel medal, diff.
Eva Gabor (1919-95), actress: No. 2021, 250fr, With Liberace (1919-87), pianist. No. 2022, 250fr, Wearing green hat. No. 2023, 250fr, With Louis Jourdan (1921-2015), in movie, Gigi. No. 2024, 250fr, With suitcases.
No. 2025, 1000fr, Gabor dancing with Jourdan in Gigi.
Johann Sebastian Bach (1685-1750), composer: No. 2026, 250fr, Portrait of Bach. No. 2027, 250fr, Nativity scene and statue of Bach. No. 2028, 250fr, Felix Mendelssohn (1809-47), composer. No. 2029, 250fr, Violin and sheet music.
No. 2030, 1000fr, Portrait of Bach, diff.
Illustrations by Alphonse Mucha (1860-1939): No. 2031, 250fr, The Arts: Dance, 1898. No. 2032, 250fr, Poster for Job Cigarette Paper, 1896. No. 2033, 250fr, The Arts: Poetry, 1898. No. 2034, 250fr, Princess Hyacinth, 1911.
No. 2035, 1000fr, Woman with a Daisy, by Mucha, 1900.
Paintings by Vincent van Gogh (1853-90): No. 2036, 250fr, The Church at Auvers, 1890. No. 2037, 250fr, The Shepherdess (After Millet), 1889. No. 2038, 250fr, Portrait of Doctor Gachet, 1890. No. 2039, 250fr, Wheat Field Behind Saint-Paul Hospital, 1889.
No. 2040, 1000fr, Wheat Fields with Reaper at Sunrise, by van Gogh, 1889.
Penny Black stamp (Great Britain #1), 180th anniv.: No. 2041, 250fr, Gibraltar 50p coin depicting Penny Black. No. 2042, 250fr, Penny Black held by stamp tongs. No. 2043, 250fr, Penny Black under magnifying glass. No. 2044, 250fr, Sir Rowland Hill (1795-1879), postal reformer.
No. 2045, 1000fr, Hill and Penny Black.
Charles de Gaulle (1890-1970), President of France: No. 2046, 250fr, With Britsh Prime Minister Winston Churchill (1874-1965). No. 2047, 250fr, With flag of France. No. 2048, 250fr, With flag of France, saluting. No. 2049, 250fr, Behind microphones, with arms raised.
No. 2050, 1000fr, Behind microphone, holding script for speech.
Battle of France, 80th anniv.: No. 2051, 250fr, German soldiers and Sd Kfz 231 armored car. No. 2052, 250fr, German Panzer IV tank. No. 2053, 250fr, French soldier, T13 tank destroyer. No. 2054, 250fr, French SOMUA S35 tank.
No. 2055, 1000fr, German Panzer IV tank, diff.
Battle of Okinawa, 75th anniv: No. 2056, 250fr, Mitsubishi Ki-67, Japan. No. 2057, 250fr, USS Chilton, United States. No. 2058, 250fr, Yamato-class battleship, Japan. No. 2059, 250fr, Lockheed P-38 Lightning, United States.
No. 2060, 1000fr, Mitsubishi A6M Zero and USS Idaho.
Minerals: No. 2061, 250fr, Fluorine. No. 2062, 250fr, Quartz. No. 2063, 250fr, Magnesite. No. 2064, 250fr, Azurite.
No. 2065, 1000fr, Amazonite.
Volcanoes: No. 2066, 250fr, Mount Etna, Italy. No. 2067, 250fr, Mount Aso, Japan. No. 2068, 250fr, Sakurajima, Japan. No. 2069, 250fr, Arenal Volcano, Costa Rica.
No. 2070, 1000fr, Mount Fuji, Japan.
Jacques-Yves Cousteau (1910-97), marine conservationist: No. 2071, 250fr, With Katsuwonus pelamis. No. 2072, 250fr, SP-350 Denise submarine and Albula vulpes. No. 2073, 250fr, Cousteau's ship, Calypso, and Plectropomus pessuliferus. No. 2074, 250fr, Cousteau and Esox sphyraena.
No. 2075, 1000fr, Cousteau and Manta alfredi.
Spaceflight of Apollo 13, 50th anniv.: No. 2076, 250fr, Service module explosion. No. 2077, 250fr, Crew members James A. Lovell, Jr., Fred W. Haise, Jr., and Jack Swigert, Jr. (1931-82), and mission patch. No. 2078, 250fr, Separation and transposition of Apollo 13 modules and Lovell at rest. No. 2079, 250fr, Recovery of Apollo 13 capsule.
No. 2080, 1000fr, Launch of Apollo 13, mission patch separation and transposition of modules.
Launch of Hubble Space Telescope, 30th anniv.: No. 2081, 250fr, Telescope in space, aperture at UR. No. 2082, 250fr, Space Shuttle Discovery deploying telescope, and commemorative medal. No. 2083, 250fr, Space Shuttle Discovery deploying teleescope, STS-31 mission patch. No. 2084, 250fr, Telescope in space, aperture at LL.
No. 2085, 1000fr, Launch of Space Shuttle Discovery mission STS-31.
Cats: No. 2086, 250fr, Himalayan cat. No. 2087, 250fr, Singapura cat. No. 2088, 250fr, Bombay cat. No. 2089, 250fr, Bengal cat.
No. 2090, 1000fr, Manx cat.
Dolphins: No. 2091, 250fr, Delphinus delphis. No. 2092, 250fr, Stenella attenuata. No. 2093, 250fr, Cephalorhynchus commersonii. No. 2094, 250fr, Stenella frontalis.
No. 2095, 1000fr, Inia geoffrensis.
Bees: No. 2096, 250fr, Osmia cornuta. No. 2097, 250fr, Eucera longicornis. No. 2098, 250fr, Nomada subcornuta. No. 2099, 250fr, Xylocopa violacea.
No. 2100, 1000fr, Bombus magnus.

Perf. 13¼x12¾
2020, Mar. 13   Litho.

Albert Einstein
| 2011-2014 | A398 | Set of 4 | 11.50 | 11.50 |
| a. | Souvenir sheet of 4, #2011-2014 | | 11.50 | 11.50 |

Souvenir Sheet
| 2015 | A398 | 1000fr multi | 11.50 | 11.50 |

Dr. Albert Schweitzer
| 2016-2019 | A398 | Set of 4 | 11.50 | 11.50 |
| a. | Souvenir sheet of 4, #2016-2019 | | 11.50 | 11.50 |

Souvenir Sheet
| 2020 | A398 | 1000fr multi | 11.50 | 11.50 |

Eva Gabor
| 2021-2024 | A398 | Set of 4 | 11.50 | 11.50 |
| a. | Souvenir sheet of 4, #2021-2024 | | 11.50 | 11.50 |

Souvenir Sheet
| 2025 | A398 | 1000fr multi | 11.50 | 11.50 |

Johann Sebastian Bach
| 2026-2029 | A398 | Set of 4 | 11.50 | 11.50 |
| a. | Souvenir sheet of 4, #2026-2029 | | 11.50 | 11.50 |

Souvenir Sheet
| 2030 | A398 | 1000fr multi | 11.50 | 11.50 |

Alphonse Mucha Illustrations
| 2031-2034 | A398 | Set of 4 | 11.50 | 11.50 |
| a. | Souvenir sheet of 4, #2031-2034 | | 11.50 | 11.50 |

Souvenir Sheet
| 2035 | A398 | 1000fr multi | 11.50 | 11.50 |

Vincent van Gogh Paintings
| 2036-2039 | A398 | Set of 4 | 11.50 | 11.50 |
| a. | Souvenir sheet of 4, #2036-2039 | | 11.50 | 11.50 |

Souvenir Sheet
| 2040 | A398 | 1000fr multi | 11.50 | 11.50 |

Penny Black
| 2041-2044 | A398 | Set of 4 | 11.50 | 11.50 |
| a. | Souvenir sheet of 4, #2041-2044 | | 11.50 | 11.50 |

Souvenir Sheet
| 2045 | A398 | 1000fr multi | 11.50 | 11.50 |

Charles de Gaulle
| 2046-2049 | A398 | Set of 4 | 11.50 | 11.50 |
| a. | Souvenir sheet of 4, #2046-2049 | | 11.50 | 11.50 |

Souvenir Sheet
| 2050 | A398 | 1000fr multi | 11.50 | 11.50 |

Battle of France
| 2051-2054 | A398 | Set of 4 | 11.50 | 11.50 |
| a. | Souvenir sheet of 4, #2051-2054 | | 11.50 | 11.50 |

Souvenir Sheet
| 2055 | A398 | 1000fr multi | 11.50 | 11.50 |

Battle of Okinawa
| 2056-2059 | A398 | Set of 4 | 11.50 | 11.50 |
| a. | Souvenir sheet of 4, #2056-2059 | | 11.50 | 11.50 |

Souvenir Sheet
| 2060 | A398 | 1000fr multi | 11.50 | 11.50 |

Minerals
| 2061-2064 | A398 | Set of 4 | 11.50 | 11.50 |
| a. | Souvenir sheet of 4, #2061-2064 | | 11.50 | 11.50 |

Souvenir Sheet
| 2065 | A398 | 1000fr multi | 11.50 | 11.50 |

Volcanoes
| 2066-2069 | A398 | Set of 4 | 11.50 | 11.50 |
| a. | Souvenir sheet of 4, #2066-2069 | | 11.50 | 11.50 |

Souvenir Sheet
| 2070 | A398 | 1000fr multi | 11.50 | 11.50 |

Jacques-Yves Cousteau
| 2071-2074 | A398 | Set of 4 | 11.50 | 11.50 |
| a. | Souvenir sheet of 4, #2071-2074 | | 11.50 | 11.50 |

Souvenir Sheet
| 2075 | A398 | 1000fr multi | 11.50 | 11.50 |

Apollo 13
| 2076-2079 | A398 | Set of 4 | 11.50 | 11.50 |
| a. | Souvenir sheet of 4, #2076-2079 | | 11.50 | 11.50 |

Souvenir Sheet
| 2080 | A398 | 1000fr multi | 11.50 | 11.50 |

Hubble Space Telescope
| 2081-2084 | A398 | Set of 4 | 11.50 | 11.50 |
| a. | Souvenir sheet of 4, #2081-2084 | | 11.50 | 11.50 |

Souvenir Sheet
| 2085 | A398 | 1000fr multi | 11.50 | 11.50 |

Cats
| 2086-2089 | A398 | Set of 4 | 11.50 | 11.50 |
| a. | Souvenir sheet of 4, #2086-2089 | | 11.50 | 11.50 |

Souvenir Sheet
| 2090 | A398 | 1000fr multi | 11.50 | 11.50 |

Dolphins
| 2091-2094 | A398 | Set of 4 | 11.50 | 11.50 |
| a. | Souvenir sheet of 4, #2091-2094 | | 11.50 | 11.50 |

Souvenir Sheet
| 2095 | A398 | 1000fr multi | 11.50 | 11.50 |

Bees
| 2096-2099 | A398 | Set of 4 | 11.50 | 11.50 |
| a. | Souvenir sheet of 4, #2096-2099 | | 11.50 | 11.50 |

Souvenir Sheet
| 2100 | A398 | 1000fr multi | 11.50 | 11.50 |

Nos. 2015, 2020, 2025, 2030, 2035, 2040, 2045, 2050, 2055, 2060, 2065, 2070, 2075, 2080, 2085, 2090, 2095, and 2100 each contain one 40x60mm stamp.

Souvenir Sheets

 Pandas A399

 Horses A400

2020, Mar. 13   Litho.   Perf. 13¼
Self-Adhesive
On Textured Paper Simulating Wood Veneer
| 2101 | A399 | 4000fr multi | 45.00 | 45.00 |
| 2102 | A400 | 4000fr multi | 45.00 | 45.00 |

Mohandas K. Gandhi (1869-1948), Indian Nationalist Leader — A401

2020, Mar. 13   Litho.   Perf. 13¼x13
| 2103 | A401 | 60fr multi | .70 | .70 |

No. 2103 was printed in sheets of 10 + 2 central labels.

Worldwide Fund for Nature Stamps of Various Countries — A402

No. 2104, 200fr: a, Laos #519. b, Liberia #1009. c, Lesotho #512. d, Libya #1326. e, Liechtenstein #907. f, Laos #1174. g, Latvia #381. h, Lithuania #529. i, Libya #1594a.

DJIBOUTI

No. 2105, 200fr: a, Lesotho #1091c. b, Liberia #1321b. c, Lesotho, #1336a. d, Laos #1625b. e, Liberia #2370c. f, Laos, #1719. g, Latvia #703. h, Libya #1718. i, Lithuania #876.

No. 2106, 300fr, Laos #520, vert. No. 2107, 300fr, Laos #1177. No. 2108, 300fr, Laos #1625c. No. 2109, 300fr, Laos #1722. No. 2110, 300fr, Latvia #384. No. 2111, 300fr, Latvia #706, vert. No. 2112, 300fr, Lesotho #515, vert. No. 2113, 300fr, Lesotho #1091a. No. 2114, 300fr, Lesotho #1336c. No. 2115, 300fr, Liberia #1010. No. 2116, 300fr, Liberia #1321d. No. 2117, 300fr, Liberia #2370a. No. 2118, 300fr, Libya #1328. No. 2119, 300fr, Libya #1594d. No. 2120, 300fr, Libya #1717. No. 2121, 300fr, Liechtenstein #908, vert. No. 2122, 300fr, Lithuania #530. No. 2123, 300fr, Lithuania #877.

2020, June 12   Litho.   Perf. 13x13¼
Sheets of 9 #a-i
2104-2105 A402 Set of 2   41.00 41.00

Souvenir Sheets
Perf. 13¼x13, 13x13¼
2106-2123 A402 Set of 18   61.00 61.00

Nos. 2106-2123 each contain one 39x50mm vertical stamp or one 50x39mm horizontal stamp.

A403

No. 2124, 250fr — Scouts: a, Reading and starting fire. b, Carrying backpack and reading compass. c, Standing near campfire. d, Cooking on campfire and saluting.

No. 2125, 250fr — International Year of Plant Health: a, Scientist using microscope. b, Scientist examining Petri dish, parrot in flight. c, Hands holding seedling. d, Scientist using eyedropper.

No. 2126, 250fr — Paintings by Caravaggio (1571-1610): a, Saint Jerome Writing, 1605-06. b, Cardsharps, c. 1595. c, Supper at Emmaus, 1601-02. d, Fortune Teller, 1598-99.

No. 2127, 250fr — Owls: a, Tyto alba. b, Bubo virginianus. c, Strix varia. d, Strix aluco.

No. 2128, 250fr — Shells: a, Gyrineum perca. b, Cymbiola nobilis. c, Nerita lineata. d, Strombus sinuatus.

No. 2129, 1000fr, Scouts near campfire, diff. No. 2130, 1000fr, Hands touching over flowers. No. 2131, 1000fr, Still Life with Flowers and Fruit, c. 1590, by Caravaggio. No. 2132, 1000fr, Bubo scandiacus. No. 2133, 1000fr, Cymatium femorale.

2020, June 12   Litho.   Perf. 13x13¼
Sheets of 4, #a-d
2124-2128 A403 Set of 5   57.00 57.00

Souvenir Sheets
2129-2133 A403 Set of 5   57.00 57.00

Dorje Chang Buddha III, Religious Leader — A404

2020, June 12   Litho.   Perf. 13¼x13
2134 A404 250fr multi   3.00 3.00

A405

A406

St. John Paul II (1920-2005) — A408

2020, June 12   Litho.   Perf. 13
2135 A405 100fr multi   1.25 1.25
  a. Souvenir sheet of 6 + 6 labels   7.50 7.50
2136 A406 100fr multi   1.25 1.25
  a. Souvenir sheet of 5 + 7 labels   6.25 6.25
2137 A407 100fr multi   1.25 1.25
  a. Souvenir sheet of 5 + 7 labels   6.25 6.25
2138 A408 100fr multi   1.25 1.25
  a. Souvenir sheet of 5 + 7 labels   6.25 6.25
  Nos. 2135-2138 (4)   5.00 5.00

A409

Ingrid Bergman (1915-82), Actress — A410

Designs: 1000fr, Bergman, diff. No. 2142: a, Like #2139. b, Like #2140.

2020, June 12   Litho.   Perf. 13¼x13
2139 A409 200fr multi   2.25 2.25
2140 A410 200fr multi   2.25 2.25
  a. Souvenir sheet of 2, #2139-2140   4.50 4.50

Souvenir Sheets
2141 A410 1000fr multi   11.50 11.50
Perf. 13¼
2142   400fr Sheet of 2, #a-b   9.00 9.00

Nos. 2139-2140 were each printed in sheets of 8 + central label. No. 2142 contains two 51x71mm stamps.

A411

Greta Garbo (1905-90), Actress — A412

Designs: 1000fr, Garbo, diff. No. 2146: a, Like #2143. b, Like #2144.

2020, June 12   Litho.   Perf. 13¼x13
2143 A411 200fr multi   2.25 2.25
2144 A412 200fr multi   2.25 2.25
  a. Souvenir sheet of 2, #2143-2144   4.50 4.50

Souvenir Sheets
2145 A412 1000fr multi   11.50 11.50
Perf. 13¼
2146   400fr Sheet of 2, #a-b   9.00 9.00

Nos. 2143-2144 were each printed in sheets of 8 + central label. No. 2146 contains two 51x71mm stamps.

Rock Band Queen, 50th Anniv. — A414

Designs: 1000fr, Band members. No. 2150: a, Like #2147. b, Like #2148.

2020, June 12   Litho.   Perf. 13¼x13
2147 A413 200fr multi   2.25 2.25
2148 A414 200fr multi   2.25 2.25
  a. Souvenir sheet of 2, #2147-2148   4.50 4.50

Souvenir Sheets
2149 A414 1000fr multi   11.50 11.50
Perf. 13¼
2150   400fr Sheet of 2, #a-b   9.00 9.00

Nos. 2147-2148 were each printed in sheets of 8 + central label. No. 2150 contains two 51x71mm stamps.

Magnus Carlsen, Chess Player, 30th Birthday A415

Carlsen and Garry Kasparov A416

Designs: 1000fr, Carlsen, Norwegian flag. No. 2154: a, Like #2151. b, Like #2152.

2020, June 12   Litho.   Perf. 13¼x13
2151 A415 200fr multi   2.25 2.25
2152 A416 200fr multi   2.25 2.25
  a. Souvenir sheet of 2, #2151-2152   4.50 4.50

Souvenir Sheets
2153 A416 1000fr multi   11.50 11.50
Perf. 13¼
2154   400fr Sheet of 2, #a-b   9.00 9.00

Nos. 2151-2152 were each printed in sheets of 8 + central label. No. 2154 contains two 51x71mm stamps.

Salvation Army Worker Writing Letter for World War II Soldier A417

Salvation Army Worker Giving Doughnuts to World War I Soldier A418

Designs: 1000fr, William Booth (1829-1912), founder of Salvation Army. No. 2158: a, Like #2155. b, Like #2156.

2020, June 12   Litho.   Perf. 13¼x13
2155 A417 200fr multi   2.25 2.25
2156 A418 200fr multi   2.25 2.25
  a. Souvenir sheet of 2, #2155-2156   4.50 4.50

Souvenir Sheets
2157 A418 1000fr multi   11.50 11.50
Perf. 13¼
2158   400fr Sheet of 2, #a-b   9.00 9.00

Salvation Army, 155th anniv. Nos. 2155-2156 were each printed in sheets of 8 + central label. No. 2158 contains two 51x71mm stamps.

Messerschmitt Bf 110C Over Parliament Buiilding, London A419

Hurricane Mk I and Hugh Dowding (1882-1970), British Air Chief Marshal A420

Designs: 1000fr, Hurricane Mk i over St. Paul's Cathedral, London. No. 2162: a, Like #2159. b, Like #2160.

2020, June 12   Litho.   Perf. 13¼x13
2159 A419 200fr multi   2.25 2.25
2160 A420 200fr multi   2.25 2.25
  a. Souvenir sheet of 2, #2159-2160   4.50 4.50

Souvenir Sheets
2161 A420 1000fr multi   11.50 11.50
Perf. 13¼
2162   400fr Sheet of 2, #a-b   9.00 9.00

Battle of Britain, 80th anniv. Nos. 2159-2160 were each printed in sheets of 8 + central label. No. 2162 contains two 51x71mm stamps.

Mil Mi-8 Helicopter A421

DAF YA-328 Military Truck A422

Designs: 1000fr, FV-107 Scimitar tank. No. 2166: a, Like #2163. b, Like #2164.

2020, June 12   Litho.   Perf. 13¼x13
2163 A421 200fr multi   2.25 2.25
2164 A422 200fr multi   2.25 2.25
  a. Souvenir sheet of 2, #2163-2164   4.50 4.50

Souvenir Sheets
2165 A422 1000fr multi   11.50 11.50
Perf. 13¼
2166   400fr Sheet of 2, #a-b   9.00 9.00

United Nations, 75th anniv. Nos. 2163-2164 were each printed in sheets of 8 + central label. No. 2166 contains two 51x71mm stamps.

International Loadstar 1700 Fire Truck — A423

Kenworth T300 Fire Truck — A424

Designs: 1000fr, Ford L9000 fire truck. No. 2170: a, Like #2167. b, Like #2168.

2020, June 12   Litho.   Perf. 13¼x13
2167 A423 200fr multi   2.25 2.25
2168 A424 200fr multi   2.25 2.25
  a. Souvenir sheet of 2, #2167-2168   4.50 4.50

Souvenir Sheets
2169 A424 1000fr multi   11.50 11.50
Perf. 13¼
2170   400fr Sheet of 2, #a-b   9.00 9.00

Nos. 2167-2168 were each printed in sheets of 8 + central label. No. 2170 contains two 51x71mm stamps.

DJIBOUTI

Zeppelin LZ 1 — A425

Zeppelin LZ 4 — A426

Designs: 1000fr, LZ 129 Hindenburg and Ferdinand von Zeppelin (1838-1917), airship manufacturer.
No. 2174: a, Like #2171. b, Like #2172.

2020, June 12 Litho. Perf. 13¼x13

2171	A425	200fr multi	2.25	2.25
2172	A426	200fr multi	2.25	2.25
a.		Souvenir sheet of 2, #2171-2172	4.50	4.50

Souvenir Sheets

2173	A426	1000fr multi	11.50	11.50

Perf. 13¼

2174		400fr Sheet of 2, #a-b	9.00	9.00

First Zeppelin flight, 120th anniv. Nos. 2171-2172 were each printed in sheets of 8 + central label. No. 2174 contains two 51x71mm stamps.

Saturn V Rocket and Neil Armstrong (1930-2012), First Man on Moon — A427

Armstrong and Apollo 11 Crewmate, Edwin E. "Buzz" Aldrin, Jr. — A428

Designs: 1000fr, Armstrong and Lunar Module on Moon.
No. 2178: a, Like #2175. b, Like #2176.

2020, June 12 Litho. Perf. 13¼x13

2175	A427	200fr multi	2.25	2.25
2176	A428	200fr multi	2.25	2.25
a.		Souvenir sheet of 2, #2175-2176	4.50	4.50

Souvenir Sheets

2177	A428	1000fr multi	11.50	11.50

Perf. 13¼

2178		400fr Sheet of 2, #a-b	9.00	9.00

Nos. 2175-2176 were each printed in sheets of 8 + central label. No. 2178 contains two 51x71mm stamps.

Lunokhod I on Moon — A429

Lunokhod I and Luna 17 — A430

Designs: 1000fr, Lunokhod I on Moon, diff.
No. 2182: a, Like #2179. b, Like #2180.

2020, June 12 Litho. Perf. 13¼x13

2179	A429	200fr multi	2.25	2.25
2180	A430	200fr multi	2.25	2.25
a.		Souvenir sheet of 2, #2179-2180	4.50	4.50

Souvenir Sheets

2181	A430	1000fr multi	11.50	11.50

Perf. 13¼

2182		400fr Sheet of 2, #a-b	9.00	9.00

Lunokhod I on Moon, 50th anniv. Nos. 2179-2180 were each printed in sheets of 8 + central label. No. 2182 contains two 51x71mm stamps.

A431

Prehistoric Painters of Lascaux Cave Paintings — A432

Designs: 1000fr, Prehistoric painters, diff.
No. 2186: a, Like #2183. b, Like #2184.

2020, June 12 Litho. Perf. 13¼x13

2183	A431	200fr multi	2.25	2.25
2184	A432	200fr multi	2.25	2.25
a.		Souvenir sheet of 2, #2183-2184	4.50	4.50

Souvenir Sheets

2185	A432	1000fr multi	11.50	11.50

Perf. 13¼

2186		400fr Sheet of 2, #a-b	9.00	9.00

Discovery of Lascaux Cave Paintings, 80th anniv. Nos. 2183-2184 were each printed in sheets of 8 + central label. No. 2186 contains two 51x71mm stamps.

Italian Soldier Looking for COVID-19 Curfew Breakers — A433

Stylized Globe and COVID-19 Health Workers — A434

Vaccine Researcher A435

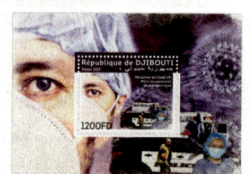

Ambulance and COVID-19 Health Workers — A436

Stadium, Soccer Balls and COVID-19 Virus — A437

Perf. 12¾x13¼

2020, June 12 Litho.

2187		Horiz. strip of 3	10.50	10.50
a.	A433	300fr multi	3.50	3.50
b.	A434	300fr multi	3.50	3.50
c.	A435	300fr multi	3.50	3.50

Souvenir Sheets
Perf. 13x13¼

2188	A436	1200fr multi	13.50	13.50

Perf. 13¼

2189	A437	2000fr multi	22.50	22.50

Stylized Depictions of COVID-19 Viruses — A438

No. 2190 — Various depictions, as shown.
1000fr, Depiction of virus, diff.

2020, June 12 Litho. Perf.

2190	A438	250fr Sheet of 4, #a-d	11.50	11.50

Souvenir Sheet

2191	A438	1000fr multi	11.50	11.50

Miniature Sheet

Queen Victoria on Great Britain #1 Wearing Protective Face Masks — A439

No. 2192: a, White mask. b, Black and red mask. c, Blue mask. d, Blue and white plaid mask. e, Brown patterned mask. f, Gray, white and blue mask.

Perf. 13¼x12¾

2020, June 12 Litho.

2192	A439	160fr Sheet of 6, #a-f	11.00	11.00

Ludwig van Beethoven 91770-1827), Composer — A440

2020, July 27 Litho. Perf. 12¾x13¼

2193	A440	250fr multi + label	3.00	3.00

Presentation of Medal to Chinese Medical Team — A441

Nos. 2194 and 2195: a, Doctors, patient and child. b, Medals.

2020, July 27 Litho. Perf. 13¼

2194	A441	300fr Horiz. pair, #a-b	6.75	6.75

Souvenir Sheet
Self-Adhesive

2195	A441	2000fr Sheet of 2, #a-b	45.00	45.00

No. 2195 was printed on silk.

A442

No. 2196, 250fr — Concorde and: a, British flag, London Eye, Big Ben. b, French flag, Arc de Triomphe. c, French flag, Eiffel Tower. d, British flag, silhouettes of London Eye, Houses of Parliament, Tower Bridge.
No. 2197, 250fr — Steam trains: a, New York Central Hudson. b, E 3/3 No. 456. c, British Rail Class 5. d, Pennsylvania Railroad Class T1.
No. 2198, 250fr — High-speed trains: a, CRH2C. b, EVS1/EVS2 Sapsan. c, SBB ETR 610. d, British Rail Class 370.
No. 2199, 250fr — The Titanic: a, RMS Titanic. b, Edward Smith (1850-1912), captain of the Titanic. c, Thomas Andrews (1873-1912), builder of the Titanic. d, RMS Titanic and newspaper front page announcing the ship's sinking.
No. 2200, 250fr — Submarines: a, Akula-class submarine, flag of Russia. b, Vanguard-class submarine, flag of Great Britain. c, Ohio-class submarine, flag of United States. d, Typhoon-class submarine, flag of Russia.
No. 2201, 250fr — Flying dinosaurs: a, Anhanguera blittersdorffi. b, Peteinosaurus zambelli. c, Quetzalcoatlus northropi. d, Pteranodon longiceps.
No. 2202, 1000fr, Concorde, flag of France, silhouettes of Eiffel Tower, Arc de Triomphe, Brandenburg Gate and buildings. No. 2203, 1000fr, LMS Stanier Class 5 4-6-0 No. 44871. No. 2204, 1000fr, Amtrak Acela Express. No. 2205, 1000fr, RMS Titanic, diff. No. 2206, 1000fr, Triomphant-class submarine, flag of France. No. 2207, 1000fr, Ornithocephalus banthensis.

2020, July 27 Litho. Perf. 12¾x13¼
Sheets of 4, #a-d

2196-2201	A442	Set of 6	67.50	67.50

Souvenir Sheets

2202-2207	A442	Set of 6	67.50	67.50

A443

No. 2208, 250fr — Dogs: a, Poodle (caniche). b, Rhodesian ridgeback (chien de Rhodésie à crête dorsale). c, Soft-coated Irish terrier (terrier irlandaise à poil doux). d, Labrador retriever.
No. 2209, 250fr — Warblers: a, Phylloscopus sibilatrix. b, Setophaga petechia. c, Acrocephalus arundinaceus. d, Iduna caligata.
No. 2210, 250fr — Bee-eaters: a, Merops philippinus. b, Merops orientalis. c, Merops bulocki. d, Merops nubicoides.
No. 2211, 250fr — Birds of prey: a, Aquila rapax. b, Buteo rufofuscus. c, Circus aeruginosus. d, Melierax canorus.
No. 2212, 250fr — Butterflies: a, Pieris rapae. b, Agraulis vanillae. c, Kallima inachus. d, Melanargia galathea.
No. 2213, 250fr — Fish: a, Coryphaena hippurus. b, Oncorhynchus mykiss. c, Esox lucius. d, Silurus glanis.
No. 2214, 250fr — Turtles: a, Podocnemis expansa. b, Malaclemys terrapin. c, Kinosternon leucostomum. d, Clemmys insculpta.
No. 2215, 250fr — Fossils: a, Tooth of Carcharocles megalodon. b, Triceratops horridus and Ammonite. c, Ammonite. d, Trilobite.
No. 2216, 250fr — Orchids: a, Brassavola nodosa. b, Ophrys apifera. c, Anacamptis coriophora. d, Cattleya walkeriana.
No. 2217, 250fr — Mushrooms: a, Pleurotus eryngii. b, Craterellus cornucopioides. c, Russula decolorans. d, Geastrum triplex.
No. 2218, 250fr — Lighthouses: a, Skongenes Lighthouse, Norway. b, Tyrhaug Lighthouse, Norway. c, Portland Head Lighthouse, Maine. d, Utsira Lighthouse, Norway.
No. 2219, 1000fr, Hungarian viszla (braque hongrois à poil court). No. 2220, 1000fr, Sylvia

DJIBOUTI

atricapilla. No. 2221, 1000fr, Merops ornatus. No. 2222, 1000fr, Milvus milvus. No. 2223, 1000fr, Vanessa atalanta. No. 2224, 1000fr, Betta splendens. No. 2225, 1000fr, Deirochelys reticularia. No. 2226, 1000fr, Seymouria fossil. No. 2227, 1000fr, Vanda coerulea. No. 2228, 1000fr, Coprinus comatus. No. 2229, 1000fr, Montauk Lighthouse, New York.

2020, July 27   Litho.   Perf. 13¼x12¾
Sheets of 4, #a-d
2208-2218 A443 Set of 11   125.00 125.00
Souvenir Sheets
2219-2229 A443 Set of 11   125.00 125.00

Miniature Sheet

Zoonotic Viruses A444

No. 2230 — Virus and vector animal: a, Hantavirus (rodent). b, West Nile virus (mosquito). c, Influenza A virus subtype H1N1 (pig). d, Dengue virus (Aedes mosquito). e, Rabies virus (dog). f, Tick-borne meningoencephalitis (tick). g, Ebolavirus (fruit bat). h, Zika virus (Aedes mosquito). i, SARS-CoV-2 (bats).

2020, July 27   Litho.   Perf. 13x13¼
2230 A444 120fr Sheet of 9,
#a-i   12.50 12.50

Miniature Sheet

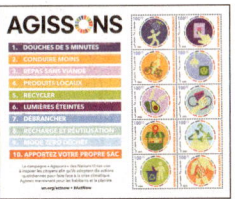

Act Now Climate Action Campaign — A445

No. 2231: a, Man in shower. b, Hand on light switch. c, Bicyclist. d, Electric plug and socket. e, Knife, fork, vegetables. f, Hand, container, and recycling arrow. g, Produce stand. h, Clothing on clothes hanger. i, Man placing bottle in recycling bin. j, Man carrying reusable shopping bag.

2020, July 27   Litho.   Perf. 13x13¼
2231 A445 100fr Sheet of 10,
#a-j   11.50 11.50

Campaign Against COVID-19 — A446

No. 2232 — Red Cross and Red Crescent emblem, COVID-19 virus and: a, Two medical workers. b, Medical worker using microscope. c, Medical worker examining x-ray image. d, Medical worker with arms raised.
1000fr, Medical workers with clipboard and vial of blood.

Perf. 13¼x12¾
2020, Nov. 25   Litho.
2232 A446 250fr Sheet of 4,
#a-d   11.50 11.50
Souvenir Sheet
2233 A446 1000fr multi   11.50 11.50

A447

No. 2234, 250fr — Loxodonta africana: a, Adult and juvenile. b, Adult facing forward. c, Adult walking to right. d, Adult near water puddle.
No. 2235, 250fr — Pandas: a, Ailuropoda melanoleuca standing on tree branch. b, Ailurus fulgens standing on log. c, Ailurus fulgens on log, tail at front. d, Ailuropoda melanoleuca laying on tree branch.
No. 2236, 250fr — Lions: a, Panthera leo bleyenberghi. b, Panthera leo nubica. c, Panthera leo krugeri. d, Panthera leo persica.
No. 2237, 250fr — Whales: a, Balaena mysticetus. b, Eubalaena australis. c, Megaptera novaeangliae. d, Balaenoptera musculus.
No. 2238, 250fr — Water birds: a, Actophilornis africanus. b, Plegadis falcinellus. c, Phalacrocorax carbo. d, Platalea leucorodia.
No. 2239, 250fr — Kingfishers: a, Megaceryle alcyon. b, Chloroceryle americana. c, Alcedo meninting. d, Corythornis cristatus.
No. 2240, 250fr — Endangered animals: a, Panthera pardus orientalis. b, Elephas maximus. c, Pongo abelii. d, Lycaon pictus.
No. 2241, 250fr — Minerals: a, Apatite. b, Amethyst. c, Carnelian (cornaline). d, Calcite.
No. 2242, 250fr — Museums and their works: a, Louvre Museum, Paris, France, Psyche Revived by Cupid's Kiss, sculpture by Antonio Canova (1757-1822). b, Rijksmuseum, Amsterdam, Netherlands, The Night Watch, painting by Rembrandt van Rijn (1606-69). c, State Hermitage Museum, St. Petersburg, Russia, Combat of a Tiger and a Buffalo, painting by Henri Rousseau (1844-1910). d, Uffizi Gallery, Florence, Italy, Leonardo da Vinci, sculpture by Luigi Pampaloni (1791-1847).
No. 2243, 1000fr, Loxodonta cyclotis. No. 2244, 1000fr, Ailuropoda melanoleuca on ground. No. 2245, 1000fr, Panthera leo krugeri, diff. No. 2246, 1000fr, Physeter macrocephalus. No. 2247, 1000fr, Xenus cinereus. No. 2248, 1000fr, Todiramphus chloris. No. 2249, 1000fr, Gorilla gorilla gorilla. No. 2250, 1000fr, Tricolor calcite. No. 2251, 1000fr, Musée d'Orsay, Paris, France, The Floor Scrapers, painting by Gustave Caillebotte (1848-94).

Perf. 12¾x13¼
2020, Nov. 25   Litho.
Sheets of 4, #a-d
2234-2242 A447 Set of 9   100.00 100.00
Souvenir Sheets
2243-2251 A447 Set of 9   100.00 100.00

A448

Grace Kelly (1929-82), actress and Princess of Monaco: No. 2252, 250fr, And her signature. No. 2253, 250fr, Touching railing, and her royal monogram. No. 2254, 250fr, With Bing Crosby (1903-77), in movie, *High Society*. No. 2255, 250fr, Wearing striped blouse, and her royal monogram.
No. 2256, 1000fr, Kelly and her husband Prince Rainier III of Monaco (1923-2005), flag of Monaco.
Marilyn Monroe (1926-62), actress, and movie poster for: No. 2257, 250fr, *How to Marry a Millionaire*. No. 2258, 250fr, *Niagara*. No. 2259, 250fr, *The Asphalt Jungle*. No. 2260, 250fr, *Gentlemen Prefer Blondes*.
No. 2261, 1000fr, *Some Like It Hot*.
Masonic emblem and: No. 2262, 250fr, Shaquille O'Neal, basketball player. No. 2263, 250fr, Sir Winston Churchill (1874-1965), Prime Minister of Great Britain. No. 2264, 250fr, Edwin E. "Buzz" Aldrin, astronaut. No. 2265, 250fr, Leonardo DiCaprio, actor.
No. 2266, 1000fr, Sir Alexander Fleming (1881-1955), discoverer of penicillin.
Red Cross/Red Crescent emblem and: No. 2267, 250fr, Map of Djibouti, mother and child at water spigot. No. 2268, 250fr, Volunteers unloading medical supplies from truck. No. 2269, 250fr, Flag of Djibouti, man spraying chemical, child with protective mask having his temperature taken. No. 2270, 250fr, Volunteer assisting flood victims.
No. 2271, 1000fr, Cardiopulmonary resuscitation lesson with dummy.
Ships: No. 2272, 250fr, Bluenose II, Canada. No. 2273, 250fr, STV Black Jack, Canada. No. 2274, 250fr, Kaljaasi Ansio, Finland. No. 2275, 250fr, Alexander von Humboldt II, Germany.
No. 2276, 1000fr, Europa, Netherlands.
African trains: No. 2277, 250fr, SDJ6 DMU train, flag of Nigeria. No. 2278, 250fr, HXD1C train, flags of Djibouti and Ethiopia. No. 2279, 250fr, Gautrain, flag of South Africa. No. 2280, 250fr, DF8B train, flag of Kenya.
No. 2281, 1000fr, DF11GN train, flag of Kenya.
Fire trucks: No. 2282, 250fr, Mercedes Atego fire truck. No. 2283, 250fr, Pierce Quantum fire truck. No. 2284, 250fr, Crimson GMC Midi fire pumper. No. 2285, 250fr, Deep South International fire truck.
No. 2286, 1000fr, HME 4x4 pumper truck.
Extinct animals: No. 2287, 250fr, Thylacinus cynocephalus. No. 2288, 250fr, Conuropsis carolinensis. No. 2289, 250fr, Bolyeria multocarinata. No. 2290, 250fr, Panthera pardus adersi.
No. 2291, 1000fr, Raphus cucullatus.

Perf. 13¼x12¾
2020, Nov. 25   Litho.
Grace Kelly
2252-2255 A448 Set of 4   11.50 11.50
2253a   Souvenir sheet of 4, 2
           each #2252-2253, + 2
           central labels   11.50 11.50
2255a   Souvenir sheet of 4, 2
           each #2254-2255, + 2
           central labels   11.50 11.50
Souvenir Sheet
2256 A448 1000fr multi   11.50 11.50
Marilyn Monroe
2257-2260 A448 Set of 4   11.50 11.50
2258a   Souvenir sheet of 4, 2
           each #2257-2258, + 2
           central labels   11.50 11.50
2260a   Souvenir sheet of 4, 2
           each #2259-2260, + 2
           central labels   11.50 11.50
Souvenir Sheet
2261 A448 1000fr multi   11.50 11.50
Famous Masons
2262-2265 A448 Set of 4   11.50 11.50
2263a   Souvenir sheet of 4, 2
           each #2262-2263, + 2
           central labels   11.50 11.50
2265a   Souvenir sheet of 4, 2
           each #2264-2265, + 2
           central labels   11.50 11.50
Souvenir Sheet
2266 A448 1000fr multi   11.50 11.50
Red Cross/Red Crescent
2267-2270 A448 Set of 4   11.50 11.50
2268a   Souvenir sheet of 4, 2
           each #2267-2268, + 2
           central labels   11.50 11.50
2270a   Souvenir sheet of 4, 2
           each #2269-2270, + 2
           central labels   11.50 11.50
Souvenir Sheet
2271 A448 1000fr multi   11.50 11.50
Tall Ships
2272-2275 A448 Set of 4   11.50 11.50
2273a   Souvenir sheet of 4, 2
           each #2272-2273, + 2
           central labels   11.50 11.50
2275a   Souvenir sheet of 4, 2
           each #2274-2275, + 2
           central labels   11.50 11.50
Souvenir Sheet
2276 A448 1000fr multi   11.50 11.50
African Trains
2277-2280 A448 Set of 4   11.50 11.50
2278a   Souvenir sheet of 4, 2
           each #2277-2278, + 2
           central labels   11.50 11.50
2280a   Souvenir sheet of 4, 2
           each #2279-2280, + 2
           central labels   11.50 11.50
Souvenir Sheet
2281 A448 1000fr multi   11.50 11.50
Fire Trucks
2282-2285 A448 Set of 4   11.50 11.50
2283a   Souvenir sheet of 4, 2
           each #2282-2283, + 2
           central labels   11.50 11.50
2285a   Souvenir sheet of 4, 2
           each #2284-2285, + 2
           central labels   11.50 11.50
Souvenir Sheet
2286 A448 1000fr multi   11.50 11.50
Extinct Animals
2287-2290 A448 Set of 4   11.50 11.50
2288a   Souvenir sheet of 4, 2
           each #2287-2288, + 2
           central labels   11.50 11.50
2290a   Souvenir sheet of 4, 2
           each #2289-2290, + 2
           central labels   11.50 11.50
Souvenir Sheet
2291 A448 1000fr multi   11.50 11.50

 A449
 A450
 A451
 A452
 A453
 A454
 A455
 A456
 A457
 A458
 A459
 A460
 A461
 A462
 A463
 A464
 A465
 A466

DJIBOUTI

A467

Chinese Opera — A468

2020, Nov. 25 Litho. Perf. 13¼x13

2292		Sheet of 20	48.00	48.00
a.	A449	210fr multi	2.40	2.40
b.	A450	210fr multi	2.40	2.40
c.	A451	210fr multi	2.40	2.40
d.	A452	210fr multi	2.40	2.40
e.	A453	210fr multi	2.40	2.40
f.	A454	210fr multi	2.40	2.40
g.	A455	210fr multi	2.40	2.40
h.	A456	210fr multi	2.40	2.40
i.	A457	210fr multi	2.40	2.40
j.	A458	210fr multi	2.40	2.40
k.	A459	210fr multi	2.40	2.40
l.	A460	210fr multi	2.40	2.40
m.	A461	210fr multi	2.40	2.40
n.	A462	210fr multi	2.40	2.40
o.	A463	210fr multi	2.40	2.40
p.	A464	210fr multi	2.40	2.40
q.	A465	210fr multi	2.40	2.40
r.	A466	210fr multi	2.40	2.40
s.	A467	210fr multi	2.40	2.40
t.	A468	210fr multi	2.40	2.40

A469   A470

A471   A472

A473   A474

A475   A476

A477   A478

A479   A480

A481   A482

A483   A484

A485   A486

A487   A488

A489   A490

A491   A492

A493   A494

A495   A496

A497   A498

A499   A500

A501   A502

A503   A504

A505   A506

A507   A508

A509   A510

A511   A512

A513   A514

Paintings Depicting Mao Zedong (1893-1976), Chairman of the Communist Party of the People's Republic of China — A515

Perf. 12¾x13¼

2020, Nov. 25 Litho.

2293		Sheet of 16	40.00	40.00
a.	A469	225fr multi	2.50	2.50
b.	A470	225fr multi	2.50	2.50
c.	A471	225fr multi	2.50	2.50
d.	A472	225fr multi	2.50	2.50
e.	A473	225fr multi	2.50	2.50
f.	A474	225fr multi	2.50	2.50
g.	A475	225fr multi	2.50	2.50
h.	A476	225fr multi	2.50	2.50
i.	A477	225fr multi	2.50	2.50
j.	A478	225fr multi	2.50	2.50
k.	A479	225fr multi	2.50	2.50
l.	A480	225fr multi	2.50	2.50
m.	A481	225fr multi	2.50	2.50
n.	A482	225fr multi	2.50	2.50
o.	A483	225fr multi	2.50	2.50
p.	A484	225fr multi	2.50	2.50
2294		Sheet of 16	40.00	40.00
a.	A485	225fr multi	2.50	2.50
b.	A486	225fr multi	2.50	2.50
c.	A487	225fr multi	2.50	2.50
d.	A488	225fr multi	2.50	2.50
e.	A489	225fr multi	2.50	2.50
f.	A490	225fr multi	2.50	2.50
g.	A491	225fr multi	2.50	2.50
h.	A492	225fr multi	2.50	2.50
i.	A493	225fr multi	2.50	2.50
j.	A494	225fr multi	2.50	2.50
k.	A495	225fr multi	2.50	2.50
l.	A496	225fr multi	2.50	2.50
m.	A497	225fr multi	2.50	2.50
n.	A498	225fr multi	2.50	2.50
o.	A499	225fr multi	2.50	2.50
p.	A500	225fr multi	2.50	2.50
2295		Sheet of 15	42.00	42.00
a.	A501	240fr multi	2.75	2.75
b.	A502	240fr multi	2.75	2.75
c.	A503	240fr multi	2.75	2.75
d.	A504	240fr multi	2.75	2.75
e.	A505	240fr multi	2.75	2.75
f.	A506	240fr multi	2.75	2.75
g.	A507	240fr multi	2.75	2.75
h.	A508	240fr multi	2.75	2.75
i.	A509	240fr multi	2.75	2.75
j.	A510	240fr multi	2.75	2.75
k.	A511	240fr multi	2.75	2.75
l.	A512	240fr multi	2.75	2.75
m.	A513	240fr multi	2.75	2.75
n.	A514	240fr multi	2.75	2.75
o.	A515	240fr multi	2.75	2.75

Nos. 2293-2295 (3)   122.00 122.00

Communist Party of China, cent.

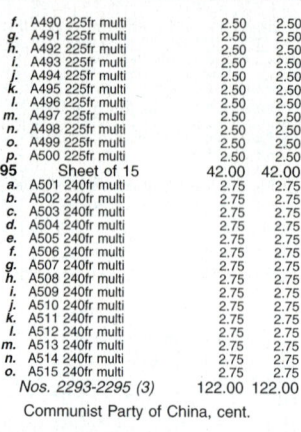

New Year 2021 (Year of the Ox) — A516

Various depictions of an ox: 250fr, 550fr.

2020, Nov. 25 Litho. Perf. 13¼

| 2296-2297 | A516 | Set of 2 | 9.00 | 9.00 |

A517   A518

A519   A520

A521   A522

A523   A524

A525   A526

A527   A528

DJIBOUTI

A529

A530

A531

A532

A533

A534

A535

A536

A537

A538

A539

A539

Chinese Paintings Depicting Oxen — A540

Perf. 12¾x13¼

2020, Nov. 25   Litho.

2298		Sheet of 24	42.00	42.00
a.	A517	150fr multi	1.75	1.75
b.	A518	150fr multi	1.75	1.75
c.	A519	150fr multi	1.75	1.75
d.	A520	150fr multi	1.75	1.75
e.	A521	150fr multi	1.75	1.75
f.	A522	150fr multi	1.75	1.75
g.	A523	150fr multi	1.75	1.75
h.	A524	150fr multi	1.75	1.75
i.	A525	150fr multi	1.75	1.75
j.	A526	150fr multi	1.75	1.75
k.	A527	150fr multi	1.75	1.75
l.	A528	150fr multi	1.75	1.75
m.	A529	150fr multi	1.75	1.75
n.	A530	150fr multi	1.75	1.75
o.	A531	150fr multi	1.75	1.75
p.	A532	150fr multi	1.75	1.75
q.	A533	150fr multi	1.75	1.75
r.	A534	150fr multi	1.75	1.75
s.	A535	150fr multi	1.75	1.75
t.	A536	150fr multi	1.75	1.75
u.	A537	150fr multi	1.75	1.75
v.	A538	150fr multi	1.75	1.75
w.	A539	150fr multi	1.75	1.75
x.	A540	150fr multi	1.75	1.75

New Year 2021 (Year of the Ox).

A541

Mohandas K. Gandhi (1869-1948), Indian Nationalist Leader — A542

Perf. 12¾x13¼

2020, Dec. 30   Litho.

2299	A541	100fr multi	1.10	1.10

Perf. 13¼x13

2300	A542	100fr multi	1.10	1.10

Souvenir Sheet

2301	A542	1000fr multi	11.50	11.50

A543

Giraffes: No. 2302, 250fr, Giraffa camelopardalis facing right, No. 2303, 250fr, Giraffa camelopardalis facing left. No. 2304, 250fr, Two Giraffa camelopardalis. No. 2305, 250fr, Giraffa camelopardalis on ground.
Wild cats: No. 2306, 250fr, Panthera leo. No. 2307, 250fr, Panthera tigris. No. 2308, 250fr, Acinonyx jubatus. No. 2309, 250fr, Lynx lynx.
Owls: No. 2310, 250fr, Tyto alba. No. 2311, 250fr, Strix nebulosa. No. 2312, 250fr, Bubo scandiacus. No. 2313, 250fr, Glaucidium brasilianum.
Butterflies: No. 2314, 250fr, Chetone phyleis. No. 2315, 250fr, Heliconius wallacei. No. 2316, 250fr, Chetone angulosa. No. 2317, 250fr, Ituna phenarete.
Dinosaurs: No. 2318, 250fr, Vulcanodon karibaensis. No. 2319, 250fr, Proceratosaurus bradleyi. No. 2320, 250fr, Melanorosaurus readi. No. 2321, 250fr, Xiaosaurus dashanpensis.
Mushrooms: No. 2322, 250fr, Cantharellus cibarius. No. 2323, 250fr, Armillaria mellea. No. 2324, 250fr, Boletus edulis. No. 2325, 250fr, Amanita muscaria.
Meteorites: No. 2326, 250fr, Diablo Canyon meteorite. No. 2327, 250fr, Campo del Cielo meteorite. No. 2328, 250fr, Chelyabinsk meteorite. No. 2329, 250fr, Sikhote-Aline meteorite.
Lighthouses: No. 2330, 250fr, San Giorgio Maggiore Lighthouse, Italy. No. 2331, 250fr, Saint-Tropez Lighthouse, France. No. 2332, 250fr, Peggys Cove Lighthouse, Nova Scotia, Canada. No. 2333, 250fr, Aniva Lighthouse, Russia.
Scouts: No. 2334, 250fr, Two Scouts, one holding bugle. No. 2335, 250fr, Two Scouts, one holding guitar. No. 2336, 250fr, Two Scouts, one holding pennant on pole. No. 2337, 250fr, Two Scouts, tent and mountain in background.

2020, Dec. 30   Litho.   **Perf. 13¼**

Giraffes

2302-2305	A543	Set of 4	11.50	11.50
2303a		Souvenir sheet of 2, #2302-2303, + central label	5.75	5.75
2305a		Souvenir sheet of 2, #2304-2305, + central label	5.75	5.75

Wild Cats

2306-2309	A543	Set of 4	11.50	11.50
2307a		Souvenir sheet of 2, #2306-2307, + central label	5.75	5.75
2309a		Souvenir sheet of 2, #2308-2309, + central label	5.75	5.75

Owls

2310-2313	A543	Set of 4	11.50	11.50
2311a		Souvenir sheet of 2, #2310-2311, + central label	5.75	5.75
2313a		Souvenir sheet of 2, #2312-2313, + central label	5.75	5.75

Butterflies

2314-2317	A543	Set of 4	11.50	11.50
2315a		Souvenir sheet of 2, #2314-2315, + central label	5.75	5.75
2317a		Souvenir sheet of 2, #2316-2317, + central label	5.75	5.75

Dinosaurs

2318-2321	A543	Set of 4	11.50	11.50
2319a		Souvenir sheet of 2, #2318-2319, + central label	5.75	5.75
2321a		Souvenir sheet of 2, #2320-2321, + central label	5.75	5.75

Mushrooms

2322-2325	A543	Set of 4	11.50	11.50
2323a		Souvenir sheet of 2, #2322-2323, + central label	5.75	5.75
2325a		Souvenir sheet of 2, #2324-2325, + central label	5.75	5.75

Meteorites

2326-2329	A543	Set of 4	11.50	11.50
2327a		Souvenir sheet of 2, #2326-2327, + central label	5.75	5.75
2329a		Souvenir sheet of 2, #2328-2329, + central label	5.75	5.75

Lighthouses

2330-2333	A543	Set of 4	11.50	11.50
2331a		Souvenir sheet of 2, #2330-2331, + central label	5.75	5.75
2333a		Souvenir sheet of 2, #2332-2333, + central label	5.75	5.75

Scouts

2334-2337	A543	Set of 4	11.50	11.50
2335a		Souvenir sheet of 2, #2334-2335, + central label	5.75	5.75
2337a		Souvenir sheet of 2, #2336-2337, + central label	5.75	5.75

Orchids of Venezuela — A544

No. 2338, 330fr: a, Catasetum pileatum. b, Schomburgkia undulata. c, Oncidium cebolleta.
No. 2339, 330fr, horiz.: a, Sobralia violacea. b, Cattleya mossiae. c, Telipogon latifolius.
No. 2340, 1000fr, Bletia purpurea. No. 2341, 1000fr, Catasetum barbatum. No. 2342, 1000fr, Catasetum callosum, horiz.

Perf. 13x13¼, 13¼x13 (#2339)

2020, Dec. 30   Litho.

Sheets of 3, #a-c

2338-2339	A544	Set of 2	22.50	22.50

Souvenir Sheets

Perf. 13¼

2340-2342	A544	Set of 3	34.00	34.00

No. 2340 contains one 51x64mm stamp; No. 2341, one 51x83mm stamp; No. 2342, one 67x51mm stamp.

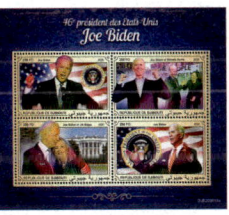
A545

No. 2343, 250fr — Joseph R. Biden, Jr., 46th President of the United States, with: a, Blue, red and white tie, Presidential seal, U.S. flag. b, Vice-President Kamala Harris. c, Wife, Jill, and White House. d, Red and white tie, Presidential seal, U.S. flag.
No. 2344, 250fr — Mohandas K. Gandhi (1869-1948), Indian nationalist leader, with: a, Spinning wheel, flag of India, Nelumbo nucifera. b, Asoka pillar, flag of India. c, Taj Mahal, Dandi March sculpture. d, Taj Mahal, Nelumbo nucifera sculpture of Gandhi.
No. 2345, 250fr — Princess Diana (1961-97), with: a, Nelson Mandela (1918-2013), President of South Africa. b, Castle and gates. c, Houses of Parliament. d, Queen Elizabeth II, flag of Great Britain.
No. 2346, 250fr — Diego Maradona (1960-2020), soccer player: a, In stadium. b, Shaking hands with Brazilian player. c, With flag of Argentina and Italian player. d, Wearing Barcelona team uniform.
No. 2347, 250fr — 2020 Nobel laurates: a, Physics laureates Reinhard Genzel, Andrea M. Ghez, and Roger Penrose. b, Literature laureate Louise Glück. c, Economics laureates Paul Milgrom and Robert B. Wilson. d, Chemistry laureates Emmanuelle Charpentier and Jennifer Doudna.
No. 2348, 250fr — Norwegian trains: a, NSB BM70. b, NSB BM75. c, NSB EL 18. d, NSB BM73.
No. 2349, 250fr — Japanese high-speed trains: a, Shinkansen Series 200. b, Shinkansen Series E4. c, ALFA-X. d, Shinkansen Series E6.
No. 2350, 250fr — Motorcycles: a, Indian Scout. b, Ducati 848. c, Suzuki DR 650. d, Harley-Davidson FXDF Dyna Fat Bob.
No. 2351, 250fr — Special transport: a, Aérospatiale HH-65 Dolphin helicopter. b, MAN KAT.1 16.422 Buffalo truck. c, Lenco BearCat armored vehicle. d, BMW R1200RT motorcycle.
No. 2352, 1000fr, Biden, his signature, and U.S. flag. No. 2353, 1000fr, Gandhi and sculpture of Gandhi. No. 2354, 1000fr, Princess Diana and Prince William. No. 2355, 1000fr, Maradona holding World Cup trophy. No. 2356, 1000fr, 2020 Nobel laurieates in Physiology or Medicine Michael Houghton, Harvey J. Alter, and Charles M. Rice. No. 2357, 1000fr, NSB BM72. No. 2358, 1000fr, Shinkansen Series 500. No. 2359, 1000fr, Honda CBR1000RR motorcycle. No. 2360, 1000fr, Lamborghini Gallardo LP560-4.

2020, Dec. 30   Litho.   **Perf. 13¼**

Sheets of 4, #a-d

2343-2351	A545	Set of 9	100.00	100.00

Souvenir Sheets

2352-2360	A545	Set of 9	100.00	100.00

Chinese Zodiac Animals — A546

Designs: No. 2361, 100fr, Rat. No. 2362, 100fr, Ox. No. 2363, 100fr, Tiger. No. 2364, 100fr, Rabbit. No. 2365, 100fr, Dragon. No. 2366, 100fr, Snake. No. 2367, 100fr, Horse. No. 2368, 100fr, Ram. No. 2369, 100fr, Monkey. No. 2370, 100fr, Rooster. No. 2371, 100fr, Dog. No. 2372, 100fr, Pig.

2020, Dec. 30   Litho.   **Perf. 13¼x13**

2361-2372	A546	Set of 12	13.50	13.50
2372a		Souvenir sheet of 12, #2361-2372	13.50	13.50

Participants in 2020 Education Relief Foundation Forum, Djibouti — A547

2021, Mar. 1   Litho.   **Perf. 13¼x13**

2373	A547	250fr multi	3.00	3.00

Two stamps from some sheets of No. 2373 are inscribed "000FDJ" instead of denomination.

First Djibouti Satellite A548

2021, Mar. 1   Litho.   **Perf. 13¼x13**

2374	A548	100fr multi	1.10	1.10

Souvenir Sheet

2375	A548	250fr multi	3.00	3.00

Two stamps from some sheets of No. 2374 are inscribed "000FDJ" instead of denomination.

DJIBOUTI

Reversals of Policies of U. S. Pres. Donald Trump by Pres. Joseph R. Biden, Jr. — A549

No. 2376: a, Biden and Eiffel Tower (rejoining of Paris Accord on Climate Change). b, Biden, U.S. flag, World Health Organization emblem (rejoining of World Health Organization). c, United States-Mexico border wall (cessation of wall construction). d, Biden signing documents.
1000fr, Biden, syringe and vials of COVID-19 vaccine (accelerated vaccine availability).

2021, Mar. 1   Litho.   Perf. 12¾x13¼

| 2376 | A549 | 250fr Sheet of 4, #a-d | 11.50 | 11.50 |

Souvenir Sheet

| 2377 | A549 | 1000fr multi | 11.50 | 11.50 |

Paintings by Pierre-Auguste Renoir (1841-1919) — A550

No. 2378: a, Woman with a Cat, c. 1875. b, The Lovers, 1875. c, Madame Camille Monet Reading, 1872. d, Algerian Woman, 1881. 1000fr, By the Seashore, 1883.

2021, Mar. 1   Litho.   Perf. 13¼x12¾

| 2378 | A550 | 250fr Sheet of 4, #a-d | 11.50 | 11.50 |

Souvenir Sheet   Perf. 13x13¼

| 2379 | A550 | 1000fr multi | 11.50 | 11.50 |

No. 2379 contains one 40x60mm stamp.

Flora and Fauna — A551

Cats: No. 2380, 250fr, Black and white British Shorthair cats. No. 2381, 250fr, Tortoiseshell Persian cats. No. 2382, 250fr, Abyssinian and Indian cats. No. 2383, Gray and white Persian cats.
No. 2384, 1000fr, Manx and Siamese cats.
Dogs: No. 2385, 250fr, Airedale terrier and Bedlington terrier. No. 2386, 250fr, Three Great Danes (dogue allemand). No. 2387, 250fr, English pointer. No. 2388, 250fr, English foxhound and American foxhound.
No. 2389, 1000fr, Three greyhounds.
Horses: No. 2390, 250fr, Hackney horse. No. 2391, 250fr, Polo ponies. No. 2392, 250fr, Thoroughbred horse and colt (Pur-sang). No. 2393, Standardbred pony (Etalon).
No. 2394, 1000fr, Thoroughbre horse.
Birds of prey: No. 2395, 250fr, Circus pygargus, vert. No. 2396, 250fr, Circaetus gallicus, vert. No. 2397, 250fr, Milvus milvus, vert. No. 2398, 250fr, Buteo lagopus, vert.
No. 2399, 1000fr, Circus hudsonius, vert.
Parrots: No. 2400, 250fr, Lorius domicella, vert. No. 2401, 250fr, Agapornis roseicollis, vert. No. 2402, 250fr, Agapornis roseicollis, vert. No. 2403, 250fr, Cacatua alba, vert.
No. 2404, 1000fr, Eolophus roseicapilla, vert.
Fish: No. 2405, 250fr, Scorpaenodes guamensis. No. 2406, 250fr, Pterois radiata. No. 2407, 250fr, Centropyge bispinosa. No. 2408, 250fr, Acanthurus lineatus.
No. 2409, 1000fr, Heniochus acuminatus, vert.

Shells: No. 2410, 250fr, Bulinus wrighti. No. 2411, 250fr, Turcica monilifera. No. 2412, 250fr, Kelletia kelletii. No. 2413, 250fr, Naquetia barclayi.
No. 2414, 1000fr, Neptunea heros.
Turtles: No. 2415, 250fr, Caretta caretta. No. 2416, 250fr, Hydromedusa maximiliani. No. 2417, 250fr, Testudo graeca. No. 2418, 250fr, Eretmochelys imbricata.
No. 2419, 1000fr, Lissemys punctata.
Orchids: No. 2420, 250fr, Cattleya mossiae, vert. No. 2421, 250fr, Cattleya skinneri alba, vert. No. 2422, 250fr, Cattleya aliciae, vert. No. 2423, 250fr, Cattleya skinneri, vert.
No. 2424, 1000fr, Cattleya trianae, vert.

2021, Mar. 1   Litho.   Perf. 13¼

Cats

| 2380-2383 | A551 | Set of 4 | 11.50 | 11.50 |
| 2383a | | Souvenir sheet of 4, #2380-2383 | 11.50 | 11.50 |

Souvenir Sheet

| 2384 | A551 | 1000fr multi | 11.50 | 11.50 |

Dogs

| 2385-2388 | A551 | Set of 4 | 11.50 | 11.50 |
| 2388a | | Souvenir sheet of 4, #2385-2388 | 11.50 | 11.50 |

Souvenir Sheet

| 2389 | A551 | 1000fr multi | 11.50 | 11.50 |

Horses

| 2390-2393 | A551 | Set of 4 | 11.50 | 11.50 |
| 2393a | | Souvenir sheet of 4, #2390-2393 | 11.50 | 11.50 |

Souvenir Sheet

| 2394 | A551 | 1000fr multi | 11.50 | 11.50 |

Birds of Prey

| 2395-2398 | A551 | Set of 4 | 11.50 | 11.50 |
| 2398a | | Souvenir sheet of 4, #2395-2398 | 11.50 | 11.50 |

Souvenir Sheet

| 2399 | A551 | 1000fr multi | 11.50 | 11.50 |

Parrots

| 2400-2403 | A551 | Set of 4 | 11.50 | 11.50 |
| 2403a | | Souvenir sheet of 4, #2400-2403 | 11.50 | 11.50 |

Souvenir Sheet

| 2404 | A551 | 1000fr multi | 11.50 | 11.50 |

Fish

| 2405-2408 | A551 | Set of 4 | 11.50 | 11.50 |
| 2408a | | Souvenir sheet of 4, #2405-2408 | 11.50 | 11.50 |

Souvenir Sheet

| 2409 | A551 | 1000fr multi | 11.50 | 11.50 |

Shells

| 2410-2413 | A551 | Set of 4 | 11.50 | 11.50 |
| 2413a | | Souvenir sheet of 4, #2410-2413 | 11.50 | 11.50 |

Souvenir Sheet

| 2414 | A551 | 1000fr multi | 11.50 | 11.50 |

Turtles

| 2415-2418 | A551 | Set of 4 | 11.50 | 11.50 |
| 2418a | | Souvenir sheet of 4, #2415-2418 | 11.50 | 11.50 |

Souvenir Sheet

| 2419 | A551 | 1000fr multi | 11.50 | 11.50 |

Orchids

| 2420-2423 | A551 | Set of 4 | 11.50 | 11.50 |
| 2423a | | Souvenir sheet of 4, #2420-2423 | 11.50 | 11.50 |

Souvenir Sheet

| 2424 | A551 | 1000fr multi | 11.50 | 11.50 |

A552

No. 2425, 250fr — Emanuel Lasker (1868-1941), chess player: a, As young man, with glasses, and older man, chess pieces. b, As young man, chess board and knight. c, As young man, chess pieces and knight. d, As older man, chess board and king.
No. 2426, 250fr — Wolfgang Amadeus Mozart (1756-91), composer: a, Portraits in purple and blue, musical notes and clefs. b, Portraits in orange and green, curved keyboard. c, Portrait, G clef, sheet music and bass. d, Portrait as child, at harpsichord.
No. 2427, 250fr — Sir Alexander Fleming (1881-1955), discoverer of penicillin: a, Fleming examining Petri dish, mold sample. b, Sculpture and photograph of Fleming, medicine bottle and Cantharellus cibarius. c, Fleming examining Petri dish, Clitocybe nuda. d, Two photographs of Fleming.
No. 2428, 250fr — Vostok I flight of Yuri Gagarin (1934-68), 60th anniv.: a, Gagarin wearing military uniform and Vostok 3KA. b, Gagarin in spacesuit, red star, and Vostok rocket. c, Gagarin in space suit, cutaway view of Vostok 3KA. d, Gagarin wearing headgear, and Vostok rocket launch.
No. 2429, 250fr — Marilyn Monroe (1926-62), actress: a, Holding glass. b, With star. c, With husband, Joe DiMaggio (1914-99). d, With Pres. John F. Kennedy (1917-63).
No. 2430, 250fr — Queen Elizabeth II, 95th birthday: a, With husband, Prince Philip (1921-2021). b, Two photographs as young woman. c, Holding purse. d, As young woman, wearing military uniform.
No. 2431, 250fr — High-speed trains: a, ETR 610, flag of Italy. b, Sapsan, flag of Russia. c, BM 71, flag of Norway. d, TGV Duplex, flag of France.
No. 2432, 250fr — Concorde passenger service, 45th anniv.: a, Concorde, Arc de Triomphe, flag of France. b, Concorde, Tower Bridge, flag of Great Britain. c, Concorde, Eiffel Tower, flag of France. d, Concorde, St. Paul's Cathedral, flag of Great Britain.
No. 2433, 1000fr, Lasker as young man, chess pieces. No. 2434, 1000fr, Portrait and sculpture of Mozart, keyboard. No. 2435, 1000fr, Fleming and Boletus edulis. No. 2436, 1000fr, Gagarin and monument to Gagarin, Moscow. No. 2437, 1000fr, Two photographs of Monroe. No. 2438, 1000fr, Queen Elizabeth II and Prince Philip, diff. No. 2439, 1000fr, Shinkansen Seried E3-700, flag of Japan. No. 2440, 1000fr, Concorde and Eiffel Tower.

2021, Mar. 1   Litho.   Perf. 13¼
Sheets of 4, #a-d

| 2425-2432 | A552 | Set of 8 | 90.00 | 90.00 |

Souvenir Sheets

| 2433-2440 | A552 | Set of 8 | 90.00 | 90.00 |

Miniature Sheet

Minerals From Bou-Azzer, Morocco — A553

No. 2441: a, Erythrite. b, Gersdorffite. c, Imiterite. d, Talmessite. e, Spherocobaltite. f, Xanthoconite. g, Karibibite. h, Roselite.

2021, Mar. 1   Litho.   Perf. 12¾x13¼

| 2441 | A553 | 270fr Sheet of 8, #a-h | 24.50 | 24.50 |

Miniature Sheet

International Sporting Events Affected by the COVID-19 Pandemic — A554

No. 2442: a, 2020 Summer Olympics, Tokyo (postponed to 2021). b, 44th International Chess Olympiad, Moscow (postponed to 2022). c, 2020 Wimbledon Tennis Championships (canceled). d, 2020 Arctic Winter Games (canceled). e, 2020 African Cup of Nations Soccer Championships (postponed to 2022). f, 2020 Archery World Cup (canceled).

2021, May 20   Litho.   Perf. 13x13¼

| 2442 | A554 | 200fr Sheet of 6, #a-f | 13.50 | 13.50 |

Paintings by Pablo Picasso (1881-1973) — A555

No. 2443: a, Girl Before a Mirror, 1932. b, Head of a Woman, 1960. c, Woman in a Chemise in an Armchair, 1914. d, Harlequin, 1901. 1000fr, The Weeping Woman, 1937.

2021, May 20   Litho.   Perf. 13¼x13

| 2443 | A555 | 250fr Sheet of 4, #a-d | 11.50 | 11.50 |

Souvenir Sheet   Perf. 13¼

| 2444 | A555 | 1000fr Sheet of 4, #a-d | 11.50 | 11.50 |

No. 2444 contains one 39x50mm stamp.

A556

No. 2445, 250fr — Wild cats: a, Panthera leo. b, Felis lynx. c, Panthera tigris. d, Panthera onca.
No. 2446, 250fr — Dolphins: a, Tursiops truncatus, white denomination. b, Tursiops truncatus, black denomination. c, Stenella frontalis. d, Stenella coeruleoalba.
No. 2447, 250fr — Bee-eaters: a, Nyctyornis amictus. b, Merops nubicoides. c, Merops ornatus. d, Merops leschenaulti.
No. 2448, 250fr — Pigeons: a, Columba livia. b, Columba livia domestica. c, Patagioenas fasciata. d, Columba palumbus.
No. 2449, 250fr — Butterflies: a, Graphium tyndereus. b, Papilio glaucus. c, Papilio polyxenes. d, Papilio bianor.
No. 2450, 250fr — Flying dinosaurs: a, Rhamphorhynchus muensteri. b, Dsungaripterus weii. c, Ornithodesmus latidens. d, Pterodactylus simus.
No. 2451, 250fr — Mushrooms: a, Russula emetica. b, Amanita vaginata, Trichodes alvearius. c, Amanita muscaria, Rosalia batesi. d, Armillaria mellea.
No. 2452, 250fr — Volcanoes: a, Rishiri-to, Japan. b, Mount Usu, Japan. c, Mount Asama, Japan. d, Mount Kaimon, Japan.
No. 2453, 250fr — Lighthouses and birds: a, Fastnet Lighthouse, Ireland, Larus smithsonianus. b, Pontusval Lighthouse, France, Larus pacificus. c, Dyrhólaey Lighthouse, Iceland, Creagrus furcatus. d, Skudenes Lighthouse, Norway, Larus delawarensis.
No. 2454, 1000fr, Felis lynx, diff. No. 2455, 1000fr, Tursiops truncatus, diff. No. 2456, 1000fr, Merops persicus. No. 2457, 1000fr, Columba arquatrix. No. 2458, 1000fr, Euploea mulciber. No. 2459, 1000fr, Pterodactylus antiquus. No. 2460, 1000fr, Leccinum aurantiacum, Chrysomela populi. No. 2461, 1000fr, Mount Daisen, Japan. No. 2462, 1000fr, La Madonetta Lighthouse, France, Larus smithsonianus.

2021, May 20   Litho.   Perf. 12¾x13¼
Sheets of 4, #a-d

| 2445-2453 | A556 | Set of 9 | 100.00 | 100.00 |

Souvenir Sheets

| 2454-2462 | A556 | Set of 9 | 100.00 | 100.00 |

DJIBOUTI

A557

No. 2463, 250fr — Antonio Vivaldi (1678-1741) composer: a, With musical score and violin. b, With his signature, musical score and violin. c, With his signature and small cup. d, Holding violin, musical score.
No. 2464, 250fr — Napoleon Bonaparte (1769-1821), Emperor of France: a, With flag of France, wearing hat. b, Napoleon in Egypt, painting by Edouard Detaille (1848-1912). c, With hand in vest. d, With eagle.
No. 2465, 250fr — Wedding of Prince Charles and Lady Diana Spencer, 40th anniv.: a, Couple, Prince Charles in military uniform, castle. b, Couple on wedding day. c, Couple, flag of Great Britain, Diana. d, Prince Charles, Obverse of 1981 Australian 50-cent coin commemorating the wedding.
No. 2466, 250fr — William Speirs Bruce (1867-1921), Antarctic explorer: a, Playing bagpipes, with penguin. b, Penguins and map of Antarctica. c, With ship. d, With sled dog.
No. 2467, 250fr — Steam trains: a, DR 18 201, buildings in Dresden, Germany. b, DRG Class 05, buildings in Berlin, Germany. c, Great Western Railway Class 0440 City of Truro, Conwy Castle, Wales. d, Nilgiri Mountain Railway Class X, buildings in Udaipur, India.
No. 2468, 250fr — Bugatti automobiles: a, Bugatti Type 35 and Ettore Bugatti (1881-1947), automobile manufacturer. b, Bugatti 16C Galibier c, Bugatti Type 57. d, Bugatti and Bugatti Type 57 Stelvio.
No. 2469, 250fr — Fire engines: a, KamAZ-53213. b, Bedford RL. c, Merceds-Benz Atego 1325F. d, Merceedes-Benz 614D.
No. 2470, 250fr — First flight of LZ 129 Hindenburg airship, 85th anniv.: a, Airship and its pilot, Max Pruss (1891-1960). b, Airship in flight, and nameplate. c, Globe, airship over New York City. d, Airship and Paul von Hindenburg (1847-1934), President of Germany.
No. 2471, 250fr — Operation Barbarossa (German invasion of the Soviet Union), 80th anniv.: a, T-26 tank and Soviet soldiers. b, PzKpfW IV tank and German soldier. c, Junkers Ju87 divebomber, tank and soldiers. d, MiG-3 fighter plane and Soviet soldiers.
No. 2472, 250fr — Landing of Perseverance rover on Mars: a, Perseverance on Mars. b, Descent stage lowering Perseverance to Mars. c, Atlas V 541 rocket and Launchpad 41, Cape Canaveral, Florida. d, Perseverance and emblem.
No. 2473, 1000fr, Vivaldi and musical score. No. 2474, 1000fr, Portrait and medal depicting Napoleon Bonaparte. No. 2475, 1000fr, Prince Charles and Princess Diana, diff. No. 2476, 1000fr, Bruce, ship and bird in flight. No. 2477, 1000fr, London and North Eastern Railway Class A4 No. 4468 Mallard, and Big Ben, London. No. 2478, 1000fr, Bugatti and Bugatti Type 57 Ventoux. No. 2479, 1000fr, Scania P360 fire truck. No. 2480, 1000fr, LZ 129 Hindenburg over New York City. No. 2481, 1000fr, KV-1 tanks, barbed wire, and battle map. No. 2482, 1000fr, Perseverence rover on Mars, diff.

2021, May 20 Litho. Perf. 13¼x12¾
Sheets of 4, #a-d
2463-2472 A557 Set of 10 115.00 115.00
Souvenir Sheets
2473-2482 A557 Set of 10 115.00 115.00

Paintings by Paul Cézanne (1839-1906) — A558

No. 2483: a, Self-portrait in a White Cap, 1882. b, Still Life with Fruit and a Pot of Ginger, c. 1895. c, Bibemus Quarry, c. 1898. d, Boy with a Red Vest, c. 1890.
1000fr, Madame Cézanne in a Red Armchair, 1878.

2021, Aug. 9 Litho. Perf. 13¼x13
2483 A558 250fr Sheet of 4, #a-d 11.50 11.50
Souvenir Sheet
Perf. 13¼
2484 A558 1000fr multi 11.50 11.50
No. 2484 contains one 40x60mm stamp.

A559

No. 2485, 330fr — Mikhail Lomonosov (1711-65), scientist: a, Lomonosov, Lomonosovite, Lomonosov State University of Moscow. b, Lomonosov Shows Catherine the Great Her Own Mosaic Works in Her Office, painting by Alexey D. Kivshenko (1851-95). c, Lomonosov and telescope.
No. 2486, 330fr — Anatoly Karpov, chess player, and: a, Salvador Dalí (1904-89), painter. b, Boris Spassky, chess player. c, Garry Kasparov, chess player and Russia #5291.
No. 2487, 330fr — First flight of Virgin Galactic commercial spacecraft: a, Virgin Galactic spacecraft facing right. b, Richard Branson, founder of Virgin Galactic, Space Ship Two and White Knight Two. c, Virgin Galactic spacecraft facing left.
No. 2488, 330fr — Flag of People's Republic of China and high-speed Chinese trains: a, Shanghai Transrapid. b, CRH380A. c, CRH6.
No. 2489, 330fr — Fire trucks: a, 1911 Christie. b, 1941 Ford. c, 1925 Ahrens Fox NS4.
No. 2490, 1000fr, Lomonosov. No. 2491, 1000fr, Karpov playing chess. No. 2492, 1000fr, Virgin Galactic Space Ship Two and White Knight Two. No. 2493, 1000fr, DJJ2 China Star train. No. 2494, 1000fr, 1926 American LaFrance fire truck.

2021, Aug. 9 Litho. Perf.
Sheets of 3, #a-c
2485-2489 A559 Set of 5 56.00 56.00
Souvenir Sheets
2490-2494 A559 Set of 5 57.50 57.50

A560

No. 2495, 330fr — Cats: a, Aphrodite's giant cat. b, Somali cat. c, Bengal cat.
No. 2496, 330fr — Dogs: a, German shorthaired pointer, flag of Germany. b, Estonian hound, Lithuanian hound, flags of Estonia and Lithuania. c, English cocker spaniel, flag of United Kingdom.
No. 2497, 330fr — Birds of prey: a, Aquila adelberti. b, Buteo rufinus. c, Necrosyrtes monachus.
No. 2498, 330fr — Bees: a, Coelioxys argenteus. b, Andrena nubecula. c, Andrena gravida.
No. 2499, 330fr — Greta oto: a, On yellow flower at left. b, On lilac flower. c, On yellow flower at right.
No. 2500, 330fr — Fish: a, Pterophyllum scalare. b, Paracanthurus hepatus. c, Amphiprion ocellaris.
No. 2501, 330fr — Shells: a, Doxander vittatus. b, Pleuroploca trapezium paeteli. c, Sinistrofulgur perversum.
No. 2502, 330fr — Turtles: a, Pseudemys rubriventris. b, Aldabrachelys gigantea. c, Trachemys scripta elegans.
No. 2503, 330fr — Extinct animals: a, Viverra leakeyi. b, Iniopteryx. c, Arctodus simus.
No. 2504, 330fr — Orchids: a, Laelia x Cattleya hybrid. b, Paphiopedilum "Rosy Dawn." c, Cattleya bicolor brasiliensis.
No. 2505, 330fr — Mushrooms: a, Cortinarius archeri. b, Amanita phalloides. c, Galerina marginata.
No. 2506, 330fr — Lighthouses: a, Anorisaki Lighthouse, Japan, and Lsarus heermanni. b, Landsort Lighthouse, Sweden. c, Erie Harbor North Pier Lighthouse, Pennsylvalnia, and Creagrus furcatus.
No. 2507, 1000fr, Scottish Fold cat. No. 2508, 1000fr, Irish setter, flag of Ireland. No. 2509, 1000fr, Neophron percnopterus. No. 2510, 1000fr, Osmia cornuta. No. 2511, 1000fr, Greta oto on white and yellow fllower. No. 2512, 1000fr, Scarus frenatus. No. 2513, 1000fr, Liguus virgineus. No. 2514, 1000fr, Chelydra serpentina. No. 2515, 1000fr, Pachycrocuta brevirostris. No. 2516, 1000fr, Epicattleya Kyoguchi. No. 2517, 1000fr, Cortinarius caperatus. No. 2518, 1000fr, Kyogamisaki Lighthouse, Japan.

2021, Aug. 9 Litho. Perf.
Sheets of 3, #a-c
2495-2506 A560 Set of 12 135.00 135.00
Souvenir Sheets
2507-2518 A560 Set of 12 135.00 135.00

COVID-19 Delta Variant — A561

No. 2519 — Map of India and: a, Vial of vaccine, man wearing protective face mask, health care worker vaccinating patient. b, Health care worker with large vaccine vial and hypodermic needle, COVID-19 virus. c, Vial of vaccine, health care workers administering vaccine.

2021, Aug. 9 Litho. Perf. 12¾x13¼
2519 A561 330fr Sheet of 3, #a-c 11.50 11.50

Souvenir Sheets

27th Universal Postal Union Congress, Abidjan, Ivory Coast — A562

Denominations: 500fr, 1000fr.

2021, Aug. 9 Litho. Perf. 12¾x13¼
2520-2521 A562 Set of 2 17.00 17.00

Souvenir Sheet

Chinese Communist Party, Cent. — A563

No. 2522: a, "1921." b, "2021."

2021, Aug. 9 Litho. Perf.
2522 A563 500fr Sheet of 2, #a-b 11.50 11.50

Paintings by Henri de Toulouse-Lautrec (1864-1901) — A564

No. 2523: a, In the Salon of the Rue des Moulins, 1894. b, Monsieur Boileau, 1893. c, Woman with Gloves, 1891. d, At the Moulin-Rouge, 1890.
1000fr, Marcelle Lender Dancing the Bolero in Chilpéric, 1895-96.

2021, Aug. 30 Litho. Perf. 13¼x13
2523 A564 250fr Sheet of 4, #a-d 11.50 11.50
Souvenir Sheet
Perf. 13¼
2524 A564 1000fr multi 11.50 11.50
No. 2524 contains one 40x60mm stamp.

Miniature Sheet

Mohandas K. Gandhi (1869-1948), Indian Nationalist Leader — A565

No. 2525 — Portrait of Gandhi in: a, 250fr, Green (30x40mm). b, 250fr, Purple (30x40mm). c, 250fr, Red (30x40mm). d, 250fr, Violet (30x40mm). e, 1000fr, Maroon (60x80mm).

2021, Aug. 30 Litho. Perf. 13x13¼
Self-Adhesive
On Wood Veneer
2525 A565 Sheet of 5, #a-e 22.50 22.50

Souvenir Sheet

Chinese Vaccine Against COVID-19 in Africa — A566

No. 2526: a, 250fr, Flag of People's Republic of China at left, map of Africa, COVID-19 virus and hypodermic noodles (50x39mm). b, 250fr, Flag of People's Republic of China at rigth, map of Africa, COVID-19 virus and hypodermic needles (50x39). c, 500fr, Map of Africa and emblem of Sinopharm (40mm diameter).

Perf. 13x13¼ (#2526a, 2526b), Perf. (#2526c)
2021, Aug. 30 Litho.
2526 A566 Sheet of 3, #a-c 11.50 11.50

194 DJIBOUTI

Souvenir Sheet

Fabergé Egg
A567

Perf. 13¼, 9½ on Diagonal Perfs.
2021, Aug. 30   Litho.
2527 A567 1000fr multi   11.50 11.50

A568

No. 2528, 330fr — Scouts with: a, Tent in background. b, Campfire. c, Folding chair and backpack in background.
No. 2529, 330fr — Large cats: a, Panthera tigris. b, Panthera leo leo. c, Panthera tigris with its kill.
No. 2530, 330fr — Whales: a, Globicephala sp. b, Physeter macrocephalus. c, Balaena mysticetus.
No. 2531, 330fr — Owls: a, Glaucidium passerinumi. b, Strix nebulosa. c, Athene noctua.
No. 2532, 330fr — Kingfishers: a, Halcyon coromanda. b, Halcyon albiventris. c, Todiramphus sanctus.
No. 2533, 330fr — Butterflies: a, Morpho adonis. b, Meandrusa sciron. c, Dasyophthalma creusa.
No. 2534, 330fr — Dinosaurs: a, Euplocephalus tutus. b, Tyrannosaurus rex. c, Alioramus remotus.
No. 2535, 330fr — Fruits and vegetables: a, Citrus sinensis. b, Raphanus raphanistrum subsp. sativus. c, Prunus domestica.
No. 2536, 330fr — Fossils: a, Cyclurus minor. b, Sphyraenodus priscus. c, Vomer longispinus.
No. 2537, 330fr — Prehistoric humans: a, Australopithecus afarensis. b, Cro-Magnon woman and child. c, Homo neanderthalensis.
No. 2538, 330fr — Minerals: a, Tanzanite. b, Malachite. c, Aragonite.
No. 2539, 1000fr, Scouts, chopped log and recreational vehicle. No. 2540, 1000fr, Panthera leo. No. 2541, 1000fr, Delphinapterus leucas. No. 2542, 1000fr, Otus scops. No. 2543, 1000fr, Ceryle rudis. No. 2544, 1000fr, Parnassius phoebus. No. 2545, 1000fr, Alectrosaurus olseni. No. 2546, 1000fr, Allium cepa. No. 2547, 1000fr, Fossil of Anguilla pachyura. No. 2548, 1000fr, Homo neanderthalensis, diff. No. 2549, 1000fr, Halite.

Perf. 12¾x13¼
2021, Aug. 30   Litho.
Sheets of 3, #a-c
2528-2538 A568 Set of 11 122.50 122.50
Souvenir Sheets
2539-2549 A568 Set of 11 125.00 125.00

A569

No. 2550, 330fr — Michael Collins (1930-2021), Apollo 11 Command Module pilot, and : a, Apollo 11 Command Module. b, Astronaut and Lunar Module on Moon. c, Earth in background.
No. 2551, 330fr — Sergei Korolev (1907-66), rocket engineer: a, Sputnik 1. b, Korolev and medal. c, Vostok 1.
No. 2552, 330fr — Circumnavigation of the Earth by crew of Ferdiand Magellan (1480-1521), 500th anniv.: a, 2021 Nicaraguan gold coin depicting Magellan and his ship. b, Magellan, compass and ship. c, Monument to Magellan in Punta Arenas, Chile, and Spheniscus magellanicus.
No. 2553, 330fr — The Titanic: a, Titanic at sea. b, Titanic and iceberg. c, Titanic, iceberg and flag of United Kingdom.
No. 2554, 330fr — African trains and animals: a, SNCFT Hyundai Rotem EMU, Macaca sylvanus. b, Madaraka Express, Xerus inauris. c, Blue Train, Oreotrgus.
No. 2555, 330fr — Mikhail Botvinnik 1911-95), chess player, and chess players: a, Mikhail Tal (1936-92). b, José Raúl Capablanca (1888-1942). c, Tigran Petrossian (1929-84).
No. 2556, 1000fr, Collins and Saturn V rocket. No. 2557, 1000fr, Korolev and Yuri Gagarin (1934-68), first man in space. No. 2558, 1000fr, Magellan and ships. No. 2559, 1000fr, Titanic at sea, flag of United Kingdom. No. 2560, 1000fr, South African class train No. E1114, Lucaon pictus. No. 2561, 1000fr, Botvinnik.

Perf. 12¾x13¼
2021, Aug. 30   Litho.
Sheets of 3, #a-c
2550-2555 A569 Set of 6 67.00 67.00
2556-2561 A569 Set of 6 67.50 67.50

Paintings and Drawings by Vincent van Gogh (1853-90) — A570

No. 2562: a, The Church at Auvers, 1890. b, Young Man with a Pipe, 1884. c, Head of a Woman, 1885. d, Willows at Sunset, 1888. 1000fr, Self-portrait, 1888.

2021, Nov. 1   Litho.   *Perf. 13¼x12¾*
2562 A570 250fr Sheet of 4,
#a-d   11.50 11.50
Souvenir Sheet
Perf. 13¼
2563 A570 1000fr multi   11.50 11.50

No. 2563 contains one 40x80mm stamp.

Miniature Sheet

COVID-19 Variants — A571

No. 2564: a, Alpha, flag of Great Britain. b, Beta, flag of South Africa. c, Gamma, flag of Brazil. d, Delta, flag of India.

2021, Nov. 1   Litho.   *Perf. 13x13¼*
2564 A571 250fr Sheet of 4,
#a-d   11.50 11.50

Doves, Flag of the Palestinian Authority, and Dome of the Rock, Jerusalem A572

2021, Nov. 1   Litho.   *Perf. 13x13¼*
2565 A572 250fr multi   3.00 3.00

2566 A572 400fr multi   4.75 4.75
Souvenir Sheets
Perf. 13¼x13
2567 A572 1000fr multi   11.50 11.50
Litho. With Foil Application
2568 A572 1000fr gold & multi 11.50 11.50

Nos. 2567 and 2568 each contain one 80x40mm stamp.

A573

No. 2569, 250fr — Birds of Djibouti: a, Melierax poliopterus. b, Phoenicopterus roseus. c, Sula dactylatra. d, Centropus superciliosus. e, Circaetus gallicus. f, Himantopus himantopus.
No. 2570, 250fr — Butterflies: a, Melanitis leda. b, Acraea cabira. c, Acraea horta. d, Papilio dardanus. e, Graphium antheus. f, Papilio demodocus.
No. 2571, 250fr — Sharks: a, Rhincodon typus, country name in red. b, Notorhynchus cepedianus. c, Isurus oxyrinchus. d, Carcharodon carcharias. e, Ginglymostoma cirratum. f, Galeocerdo cuvier.
No. 2572, 250fr — Fauna of Djibouti: a, Orycteropus afer. b, Papio hamadryas. c, Orcinus orca with tail underwater. d, Buteo buteo vulpinus. e, Rhinolophus hipposideros. f, Gazella dorcas.
No. 2573, 250fr — Marine biodiversity: a, Orcinus orca with tail above water. b, Octopus vulgaris. c, Taseniura lymma. d, Chelonia mydas. e, Chrysaora melanaster. f, Rhincodon typus, country name in blue.
No. 2574, 250fr — Prehistoric aquatic animals: a, Otodus megalodon. b, Archelon ischyros. c, Dunkleosteus terrelli. d, Ichthyosaurus communis. e, Utatsusaurus hataii. f, Helicoprion bessonowi.
No. 2575, 250fr — Cacti: a, Mammillaria elongata "Cristata." b, Opuntia basilaris. c, Mammillaria bocasana. d, Astrophytum coahuilense. e, Echinocactus grusonii. f, Mammillaria haageana.
No. 2576, 250fr — Minerals: a, Tetrahedrite. b, Rhodonite. c, Fuchsite. d, Okenite. e, Prehnite. f, Strontianite.
No. 2577, 250fr — Art by Albrecht Dürer: a, Portrait of Barbara Dürer, 1490. b, Lamentation for Christ, 1500. c, Virgin and Child with a Pear, 1512. d, Young Hare, 1502. e, Portrait of Dürer's Father at 70, 1497. f, Great Piece of Turf, 1503.
No. 2578, 1000fr, Terathopius ecaudatus. No. 2579, 1000fr, Danaus chrysippus. No. 2580, 1000fr, Shyrna mokarran. No. 2581, 1000fr, Panthera pardus pardus. No. 2582, 1000fr, Dugong dugon. No. 2583, 1000fr, Mosasaurus hoffmannii. No. 2584, 1000fr, Jasminocereus thouarsii. No. 2585, 1000fr, Apophyllite. No. 2586, 1000fr, St. Jerome, by Dürer, 1521.

2021, Nov. 1   Litho.   *Perf. 13¼x13*
Sheets of 6, #a-f
2569-2577 A573 Set of 9 150.00 150.00
Souvenir Sheets
Perf. 13¼x12¾
2578-2586 A573 Set of 9 100.00 100.00

Nos. 2578-2586 each contain one 40x50mm stamp.

A574

No. 2587, 330fr — Nona Gaprindashvili, chess player: a, Playing chess on blue table. b, Scene from movie *Glory to the Queen*. c, With male chess player in background.
No. 2588, 330fr — Elvis Presley (1935-77): a, Dancing with Ann-Margret. b, Dancing and wearing horizontally striped shirt. c, Wearing vertically striped shirt.

No. 2589, 330fr — Marilyn Monroe (1926-62), actress: a, With her husband, Joe DiMaggio (1914-99). b, Holding fur stole. c, Wearing black strapless dress.
No. 2590, 330fr — Princess Diana (1961-97), with: a, Flowers. b, Big Ben and flag of Great Britain. c, Queen Elizabeth II.
No. 2591, 330fr — Red Cross: a, Worker distributing sacks of food. b, People waiting near Red Cross building. c, Worker monitoring flood waters.
No. 2592, 330fr — Steam trains: a, Fairy Queen, flag of India. b, London and North Eastern Railway A3 60103 Flying Scotsman, flag of Great Britain. c, Union Pacific 4014 Big Boy, flag of United States.
No. 2593, 330fr — Indian trains: a, WAP-4, Buceros bicornis. b, WDM-3D, Panthera tigris tigris. c, WDG-4, Panthera uncia.
No. 2594, 330fr — Space flight of Shenzhou-12: a, Mission emblem and lauch of Shenzhou-12. b, Shenzhou-12 docking in space. c, Crew members, Tang Hongbo, Nie Haisheng and Liu Boming, capsule returning to Earth.
No. 2595, 330fr — Space flight of Inspiration4: a, Lauch of Inspiration4. b, Crew members Christopher Sembroski and Sian Proctor. c, Crew members Jared Isaacman and Hayley Arceneaux.
No. 2596, 1000fr, Gaprindashvili and Garry Kasparov playing chess. No. 2597, 1000fr, Presley playing guitar. No. 2598, 1000fr, Monroe and poster for her movie, *Niagara*. No. 2599, 1000fr, Princess Diana and Nelson Mandela (1918-2013), president of South Africa. No. 2600, 1000fr, Red Cross water distribution project site. No. 2601, 1000fr, Japanese National Railways Class C55 locomotive, flag of Japan. No. 2602, 1000fr, WAG-9H locomotive, buildings of Mumbai, India. No. 2603, 1000fr, Shenzhou-12 above Earth. No. 2604, 1000fr, Inspiration4 and flag of United States.

2021, Nov. 1   Litho.   *Perf. 13¼x13*
Sheets of 3, #a-c, + 3 labels
2587-2595 A574 Set of 9 100.00 100.00
Souvenir Sheets
Perf. 13¼x12¾
2596-2604 A574 Set of 9 100.00 100.00

Nos. 2596-2604 each contain one 40x50mm stamp.

A575   New Year 2022 (Year of the Tiger) — A576

2021, Nov. 1   Litho.   *Perf. 13¼*
2605 A575 250fr multi   3.00 3.00
2606 A575 550fr multi   6.25 6.25
  a. Souvenir sheet of 2, #2605-2606   9.25 9.25
Souvenir Sheets
2607 A575 1000fr multi   11.50 11.50
2608 A576 1000fr multi   11.50 11.50

No. 2606a was printed with two different sheet margins, one with a blue green background and the other with a maroon background. Value is for either sheet.

Miniature Sheet

COVID-19 Revaccination — A577

No. 2609: a, Male health care worker vaccinating woman wearing yellow blouse. b, Female health care worker vaccinating man wearing red shirt. c, Female health care worker vaccinating man wearing green shirt. d, Male health care worker vaccinating woman wearing red blouse. e, Vials of vaccine.

DJIBOUTI

2021, Dec. 20   Litho.   Perf. 13¼x13
2609 A577 200fr Sheet of 5, #a-e, + 4 labels   11.50 11.50

Miniature Sheet

Rotary International COVID-19 Pandemic Relief Efforts — A578

No. 2610: a, Truck, vaccine vials, COVID-19 virus (delivery of vaccines). b, Vaccine vials and arrows (equal distribution of vaccines). c, Worker carrying box, coin, protective glove and mask (purchase of medical supplies). d, Teacher, hypodermic needle, COVID 19 virus and pill bottle vaccination education). e, COVID-19 virus, antiseptic spray and hands under faucet (promotion of hygiene). f, People, loudspeaker and Earth (diffusion of precise information). g, Man wearing protective mask (promotion of mask wearing). h, Hands, money, box of groceries (promotion of donations).

Perf. 12¾x13¼
2021, Dec. 20   Litho.
2610 A578 200fr Sheet of 8, #a-h, + central label   18.00 18.00

A579

No. 2611, 250fr — Concorde: a, Over street view of European city. b, Over skyscrapers. c, Over Eiffel Tower. d, Over Arc de Triomphe, Paris.
No. 2612, 250fr — Flying Hospitals: a, McDonnell Douglas DC-10, attendant laying out medical tools. b, Lockheed L-1011-100 Tristar, medical workers, patient on gurney. c, McDonnell Douglas DC-10 and schematic diagram of Flying Hospital. d, Lockheed L-1011-100 Tristar, gurney, chair and medical equipment.
No. 2613, 250fr — Fire trucks: a, International B180. b, International KB-7. c, Commer. d, Mack B85FSW.
No. 2614, 250fr — Japanese high-speed trains: a, Hikari, Kyoto skyline. b, Shinkansen Series N700S, Himeji Castle. c, Shinkansen Series 0, Osaka skyline. d, Shinkansen Series E3, aerial view of Asahikawa.
No. 2615, 250fr — German trains: a, MVG Class, Siegestor, Munich. b, Munich-Nuremberg Express Class 101, Marienplatz, Munich. c, ICE3, Berlin Konzerthaus. d, Bombardier Talent 2, Cologne skyline.
No. 2616, 250fr — Space flight of William Shatner: a, Shatner and launch of Blue Origin rocket. b, New Shepard-18 over Earth. c, New Shepard-18 and diagram of its flight. d, Shatner with members of flight crew, Audrey Powers, Chris Boshuizen, and Glen de Vries.
No. 2617, 250fr — Space flight of Shenzhou-13: a, Launch of Long March 2F rocket. b, Crew members Zhai Zhigang, Wang Yaping, and Ye Guangfu. c, Chinese Space Station over Earth. d, Docking of Shenzhou-13 and Chinese Space Station.
No. 2618, 250fr — Creation of first film in space on Soyuz MS-19 flight: a, Soyuz MS-19 at International Space Station, and crew members. b, Soyuz MS-19, map of Russia. c, Launch of Soyuz-19, Yulia Peresild, crew member and actress. d, Peresild and mission emblem.
No. 2619, 250fr — Russian lighthouses: a, Anapa Lighthouse, Phoebastria immutabilis. b, Tolbukhin Lighthouse. c, Tokarevsky Lighthouse. d, Basargin Lighthouse, Rissa brevirostris.
No. 2620, 250fr — Scouts: a, At campfire near tent. b, With medical bag. c, With knapsack, bow and arrow. d, With musical instruments, firewood and tent.

No. 2621, 250fr — Hornbills: a, Rhinoplax vigil. b, Buceros rhinoceros. c, Anthracoceros albirostris. d, Anorrhinus galeritus.
No. 2622, 250fr — Butterflies: a, Hebomoia leucippe. b, Idea idea. c, Consul fabius, Cyrestis cocles. d, Papilio ulysses.
No. 2623, 250fr — Dinosaurs: a, Bactrosaurus johnsoni. b, Massospondylus carinatus. c, Alectrosaurus olseni. d, Haplocanthosaurus priscus.
No. 2624, 250fr — African mammals: a, Panthera pardus. b, Equus zebra. c, Giraffa camelopardalis. d, Panthera leo leo.
No. 2625, 250fr — Orchids: a, Paphiopedilum bellatulum. b, Odontoglossum hallii. c, Anguloa clowesii. d, Vanda coerulea alba.
No. 2626, 250fr — Mushrooms: a, Ramaria flava. b, Lactarius deliciosus. c, Cortinarius violaceus. d, Lactarius piperatus.
No. 2627, 250fr — 2021 Nobel laureates: a, Peace laureate Dmitri Muratov, Spassky Tower, Moscow, and Anna Politkovskaya (1958-2006), murdered Russian journalist. b, Peace laureate Maria Ressa, dove and flag of Philippines. c, Physiology or Medicine laureates Ardem Patapoutian and David Julius. d, Chemistry laureates David MacMillan and Benjamin List, amethyst crystal.
No. 2628, 250fr — Paintings by Jan Brueghel the Younger (1601-78): a, A Basket of Flowers, c. 1620. b, A Village Street, 1630. c, Farmyard, 1650. d, Paradise, c. 1620.
No. 2629, 1000fr, Concorde flying over the Beatles on rooftop. No. 2630, 1000fr, McDonnell Douglas DC-10 Flying Hospital, gurneys, chair and medical equipment. No. 2631, 1000fr, International Loadstar 1700 fire truck and fire plane. No. 2632, 1000fr, Shinkansen Series 6 train and Tokyo skyline. No. 2633, 1000fr, DB Class 103 Blauer Enzian train, Neuschwanstein Castle. No. 2634, 1000fr, Shatner and New Shepard-18 rocket. No. 2835, 1000fr, Shenzhou-13 and its crew, flag of People's Republic of China. No. 2636, 1000fr, Peresild and Soyuz MS-19 mission emblem. diff. No. 2637, 1000fr, Gelendzhik Lighthouse, Russia, Haliaeetus pelagicus. No. 2638, 1000fr, Scouts with ax and lantern. No. 2639, 1000fr, Rhyticeros undulatus. No. 2640, 1000fr, Cepora judith, Appias libythea. No. 2641, 1000fr, Tyrannosaurus rex. No. 2642, 1000fr, Loxodonta africana. No. 2643, 1000fr, Cattleya candida. No. 2644, 1000fr, Helvella crispa, Clitocybe laccata. No. 2645, 1000fr, Giorgio Parisi, 2021 Nobel laureate in Physics, Space X Dragon. No. 2646, 1000fr, Allegory of the Tulipomania. c. 1640, by Brueghel the Younger.

Perf. 13¼x12¾
2021, Dec. 20   Litho.
Sheets of 4, #a-d, + 2 labels
2611-2628 A579 Set of 18 205.00 205.00

Souvenir Sheets
2629-2646 A579 Set of 18 205.00 205.00

AIR POST STAMPS

Afars and Issas Nos. C104-C105, C103 Overprinted in Brown or Black

Nos. C106, C107

No. C108

1977   Engr.   Perf. 13
C106 AP37 55fr multi (Br)   2.00 1.75
C107 AP37 75fr multi   9.00 4.00
             Litho.   Perf. 12
C108 AP36 500fr multi   15.00 13.50
      Nos. C106-C108 (3)   26.00 19.25

Map of Djibouti, Dove, UN Emblem AP38

1977, Oct. 19   Photo.   Perf. 13
C109 AP38 300fr multi   6.50 4.25
Djibouti's admission to the United Nations.

Marcel Brochet MB 101, 1955 AP39

Djibouti Aero Club: 85fr, Tiger Moth, 1960. 200fr, Rallye-Commodore, 1973.

1978, Feb. 27   Litho.   Perf. 13
C110 AP39 60fr multi   1.10 .40
C111 AP39 85fr multi   1.60 .65
C112 AP39 200fr multi   4.00 1.10
      Nos. C110-C112 (3) 6.70 2.15

Old Man, by Rubens — AP40

500fr, Hippopotamus Hunt, by Rubens.

1978, Apr. 24   Photo.   Perf. 13
C113 AP40 50fr multi   1.50 .50
C114 AP40 500fr multi, horiz. 11.00 5.00
Peter Paul Rubens (1577-1640).

Player Holding Soccer Cup — AP41

Design: 300fr, Soccer player, map of South America with Argentina, Cup and emblem.

1978, June 20   Litho.   Perf. 13
C115 AP41 100fr multi   1.75 .50
C116 AP41 300fr multi   5.50 1.25
11th World Cup Soccer Championship, Argentina, June 1-25.
For overprints see Nos. C117-C118.

Nos. C115-C116 Overprinted

a   b

1978, Aug. 20   Litho.   Perf. 13
C117 AP41 (a) 100fr multi   1.60 .75
C118 AP41 (b) 300fr multi   5.50 2.00
Argentina's victory in 1978 Soccer Championship.

Tahitian Women, by Gauguin AP42

Young Hare, by Dürer — AP43

Perf. 13x12½, 12½x13
1978, Sept. 25   Litho.
C119 AP42 100fr multi   2.75 .40
C120 AP43 250fr multi   5.50 2.50
Paul Gauguin (1848-1903) and Albrecht Dürer (1471-1528), painters.

Common Design Types pictured following the introduction.

Philexafrique II-Essen Issue
Common Design Types

Designs: No. C121, Lynx and Djibouti No. 456. No. C122, Jay and Brunswick No. 3.

1978, Dec. 13   Litho.   Perf. 13x12½
C121 CD138 90fr multi   3.00 1.50
C122 CD139 90fr multi   3.00 1.50
  a. Pair, Nos. C121-C122 + label 6.50 6.50

UPU Emblem, Map of Djibouti, Dove — AP44

1978, Dec. 18   Engr.   Perf. 13
C123 AP44 200fr multi   3.25 1.10
Centenary of Congress of Paris.

Junkers JU-52 and Dewoitine D-338 AP45

Powered Flight, 75th Anniversary: 250fr, Potez P63-11, 1941 and Supermarine Spitfire HF-VII, 1942. 500fr, Concorde, 1969 and Sikorsky S-40 "American Clipper," 1931.

1979, May 21   Litho.   Perf. 13x12½
C124 AP45 140fr multi   3.00 .60
C125 AP45 250fr multi   4.50 1.00
C126 AP45 500fr multi   9.00 1.75
      Nos. C124-C126 (3)   16.50 3.35

The Laundress, by Honore Daumier — AP46

1979, July 10   Litho.   Perf. 12½x13
C127 AP46 500fr multi   12.00 3.00

Olympic Emblem, Skis, Sleds AP47

1980, Jan. 21   Litho.   Perf. 13
C128 AP47 150fr multi   3.00 .60
13th Winter Olympic Games, Lake Placid, N.Y., Feb. 12-24.
For surcharges see Nos. C133-C134.

Cathedral of the Archangel, Basketball, Moscow '80 Emblem — AP48

DJIBOUTI

120fr, Lomonossov Univ., Moscow, soccer.
250fr, Cathedral of the Annunciation, running.

1980, Apr. 10   Litho.   Perf. 13
C129 AP48 60fr multi   1.05 .25
C130 AP48 120fr multi   2.10 .40
C131 AP48 250fr multi   4.25 1.00
    Nos. C129-C131 (3)   7.40 1.65

22nd Summer Olympic Games, Moscow, July 18-Aug. 3.

Air Djibouti, 1st Anniversary AP49

1980, Mar. 29   Litho.   Perf. 13x12½
C132 AP49 400fr multi   9.00 2.50

No. C128 Surcharged in Black and Blue or Purple

1980, Apr. 5   Litho.   Perf. 13
C133 AP47 80fr on 150fr   1.75 .50
C134 AP47 200fr on 150fr (P) 4.00 1.50

Apollo 11 Moon Landing, 10th Anniversary AP50

Space Conquests: 300fr, Apollo-Soyuz space project, 5th anniversary.

1980, May 8
C135 AP50 200fr multi   4.00 .75
C136 AP50 300fr multi   6.50 1.25

Nos. C135-C136 exist in souvenir sheets of one. Value, set, $22.50.

Satellite Earth Station Inauguration AP51

1980, July 3   Litho.   Perf. 13
C137 AP51 500fr multi   9.50 1.75

Graf Zeppelin AP52

1980, Oct. 2   Litho.   Perf. 13
C138 AP52 100fr shown   2.25 .40
C139 AP52 150fr Ferdinand von
             Zeppelin, blimp   3.25 .60

Zeppelin flight, 80th anniversary.

Voyager Passing Saturn AP53

1980, Dec. 21   Litho.   Perf. 13
C140 AP53 250fr multi   5.50 1.00

AP54

World Cup Soccer Preliminary Games: 200fr, Players, diff.

1981, Jan. 14
C141 AP54 80fr multi   1.75 .30
C142 AP54 200fr multi   4.25 .65

AP55

1981, Feb. 10   Litho.   Perf. 13
C143 AP55 100fr multi   3.50 .50

European-African Economic Convention.

5th Anniversary of Viking I Take-off to Mars AP56

20th Anniversary of Various Space Flights: 75fr, Vostok I, Yuri Gagarin, vert. 150fr, Freedom 7, Alan B. Shepard, vert.

1981, Mar. 9   Litho.   Perf. 13
C144 AP56 75fr multi   1.75 .35
C145 AP56 120fr multi   2.25 .45
C146 AP56 150fr multi   3.00 .65
    Nos. C144-C146 (3)   7.00 1.45

Football Players, by Picasso (1881-1973) AP57

Design: 400fr Man Wearing a Turban, by Rembrandt (1606-1669), vert.

Perf. 13x12½, 12½x13
1981, Aug. 3   Litho.
C147 AP57 300fr multi   7.00 1.40
C148 AP57 400fr multi   7.50 1.75

Columbia Space Shuttle AP58

90fr, Shuttle launching.

1981, Sept. 24   Litho.   Perf. 13
C149 AP58 90fr multicolored   1.75 .40
C150 AP58 120fr shown   2.50 .60

Nos. C149-C150 exist in souvenir sheets of one. Value, set, $22.50.

Nos. C149-C150 Overprinted in Brown

No. C151

No. C152

1981, Nov. 12   Litho.   Perf. 13
C151 AP58 90fr multi   1.75 .50
C152 AP58 120fr multi   2.50 .75

1982 World Cup Soccer AP59

Designs: Various soccer players.

1982, Jan. 20
C153 AP59 110fr multi   2.10 .60
C154 AP59 220fr multi   4.75 1.25

For overprints see Nos. C166-C167.

Space Anniversaries — AP60

Designs: 40fr, Luna 9 moon landing, 15th, vert. 60fr, John Glenn's flight, 20th, vert. 180fr, Viking I Mars landing, 5th.

1982, Feb. 15
C155 AP60 40fr multi   .70 .25
C156 AP60 60fr multi   1.10 .30
C157 AP60 180fr multi   3.00 1.00
    Nos. C155-C157 (3)   4.80 1.55

21st Birthday of Princess Diana of Wales — AP61

1982, Apr. 29   Litho.   Perf. 12½x13
C158 AP61 120fr Portrait   2.25 .75
C159 AP61 180fr Portrait, diff. 3.50 1.00

For overprints see Nos. C168-C169.

No. 489, Boy Examining Collection AP62

1982, May 10   Perf. 13x12½
C160 AP62 80fr shown   2.50 .75
C161 AP62 140fr No. 495   3.75 1.00
    a. Pair, Nos. C160-C161 + label 6.50 6.50

PHILEXFRANCE '82 Stamp Exhibition, Paris, June 11-21.

1350th Anniv. of Mohammed's Death at Medina — AP63

1982, June 8   Litho.   Perf. 13
C162 AP63 500fr Medina
             Mosque   9.00 2.00

Scouting Year AP64

1982, June 28
C163 AP64 95fr Baden-Powell   1.75 .50
C164 AP64 200fr Camp, scouts 4.00 1.25

AP65

Design: 2nd UN conference on peaceful uses of outer space, Vienna, Aug. 9-21.

1982, Aug. 19
C165 AP65 350fr multi   6.75 3.00

Nos. C153-C154 Overprinted

1982, July 21   Litho.   Perf. 13
C166 AP59 110fr multi   2.00 .60
C167 AP59 220fr multi   4.00 1.10

Italy's victory in 1982 World Cup.

Nos. C158-C159 Overprinted in Blue or Red

No. C168

No. C169

1982, Aug. 9   Perf. 12½x13
C168 AP61 120fr multi   2.50 .75
C169 AP61 180fr multi (R)   3.50 1.00

Birth of Prince William of Wales, June 21.

DJIBOUTI

Franklin D. Roosevelt
(1882-1945) — AP66

1982, Oct. 7   **Litho.**   **Perf. 13**
C170	AP66	115fr shown	2.00	.50
C171	AP66	250fr George Washington	5.25	1.00

Manned Flight Bicentenary — AP67

35fr, Montgolfiere, 1783. 45fr, Giffard, Paris Exposition, 1878. 120fr, Double Eagle II, 1978.

1983, Jan. 20   **Litho.**
C172	AP67	35fr multi	.80	.25
C173	AP67	45fr multi	1.35	.30
C174	AP67	120fr multi	3.50	.80
		Nos. C172-C174 (3)	5.65	1.35

Pre-olympic Year — AP68

1983, Feb. 15
C175	AP68	75fr Volleyball	1.50	.55
C176	AP68	125fr Wind surfing	2.75	.85

Nos. C175-C176 exist in souvenir sheets of one. Value, set, $25.

50th Anniv. of Air France AP69

1983, Mar. 20   **Litho.**   **Perf. 13**
C177	AP69	25fr Bloch 220	.50	.25
C178	AP69	100fr DC-4	1.75	.70
C179	AP69	175fr Boeing 747	3.50	1.10
		Nos. C177-C179 (3)	5.75	2.05

AP70

180fr, Martin Luther King, Jr. (1929-68), civil rights leader. 250fr, Alfred Nobel (1833-96).

1983, May 18   **Perf. 13**
C180	AP70	180fr multi	3.50	1.25
C181	AP70	250fr multi	4.50	2.00

AP71

Service Clubs: 90fr, Rotary Club Intl., Sailing Show, Toronto, June 5-9. 150fr, Lions Club Intl., Honolulu Meeting, June 22-24, Djibouti lighthouse.

1983, July 18   **Litho.**   **Perf. 13**
C182	AP71	90fr multi	3.00	1.50
C183	AP71	150fr multi	3.00	1.00
a.		Pair, Nos. C182-C183 + label	5.50	5.50

Vintage Motor Cars AP72

Designs: 60fr, Renault, 1904. 80fr, Mercedes, 1910, vert. 110fr, Lorraine-Dietrich, 1912.

1983, Sep. 20   **Litho.**   **Perf. 13x12½**
C184	AP72	60fr multi	1.90	.50
C185	AP72	80fr multi	2.50	.65
C186	AP72	110fr multi	3.00	.85
		Nos. C184-C186 (3)	7.40	2.00

Souvenir Sheet

Air France, 50th Anniv. AP73

1983, Oct. 7   **Litho.**   **Perf. 12½**
Self-Adhesive
C187	AP73	250fr multicolored	25.00	25.00

Printed on wood.

Vostok VI — AP74

1983, Oct. 20   **Litho.**   **Perf. 12**
C188	AP74	120fr shown	2.25	.80
C189	AP74	200fr Explorer I	3.75	1.10

1984 Winter Olympics AP75

1984, Feb. 14   **Litho.**   **Perf. 13**
C190	AP75	70fr Speed skating	1.50	.55
C191	AP75	130fr Figure skating	2.50	1.10

For overprints see Nos. C196-C197.

Souvenir Sheet

Ship — AP76

1984, Feb. 14   **Litho.**   **Perf. 12½**
C192	AP76	250fr multi	11.00	11.00

Sea-Me-We (South-east Asia-Middle East-Western Europe) submarine cable construction agreement.
No. C192 exists in a souvenir sheet of one. Value, $12.50.

Motorized Hang Gliders AP77

Various hang gliders.

1984, Mar. 12   **Perf. 13x12½**
C193	AP77	65fr multi	1.25	.50
C194	AP77	85fr multi	1.60	.60
C195	AP77	100fr multi	2.10	.75
		Nos. C193-C195 (3)	4.95	1.85

Nos. C190-C191 Overprinted with Winners' Names and Country

1984, Mar. 28   **Perf. 13**
C196	AP75	70fr multi	1.50	.50
C197	AP75	130fr multi	2.75	1.00

Portrait of Marguerite Matisse, 1910, by Henri Matisse — AP78

Design: 200fr, Portrait of Mario Varvogli, by Amedeo Modigliani.

1984, Apr. 15   **Litho.**   **Perf. 12½x13**
C198	AP78	150fr multi	3.75	1.00
C199	AP78	200fr multi	4.75	1.40

1984 Summer Olympics AP79

1984, May 24   **Perf. 13**
C200	AP79	50fr Running	1.00	.40
C201	AP79	60fr High jump	1.25	.40
C202	AP79	80fr Swimming	1.50	.60
		Nos. C200-C202 (3)	3.75	1.40

Nos. C200-C202 exist in a souvenir sheet of 3. Value, $32.50.

Battle Scene AP80

1984, June 16   **Litho.**   **Perf. 13x12½**
C203	AP80	300fr multi	6.00	2.75

125th anniv. of Battle of Solferino and 120th anniv. of Red Cross.

Bleriot's Flight over English Channel, 75th Anniv. AP81

Designs: 40fr, 14-Bis plans. 75fr, Britten-Norman Islander. 90fr, Air Djibouti jet.

1984, July 8
C204	AP81	40fr multi	.90	.40
C205	AP81	75fr multi	1.40	.75
C206	AP81	90fr multi	1.50	1.00
		Nos. C204-C206 (3)	3.80	2.15

375th Anniv., Galileo's Telescope — AP82

120fr, Telescopes, spacecraft. 180fr, Galileo, telescopes.

1984, Oct. 7   **Litho.**   **Perf. 13**
C207	AP82	120fr multicolored	2.50	.80
C208	AP82	180fr multicolored	3.50	1.10

1984 Soccer Events AP83

Designs: No. C209, Euro Cup. No. C210, Los Angeles Olympics.

1984, Oct. 20   **Litho.**   **Perf. 13**
C209	AP83	80fr multi	2.50	.60
C210	AP83	80fr multi	2.50	.60
a.		Pair, Nos. C209-C210 + label	4.50	4.00

Service Clubs — AP84

50fr, Lions, World Leprosy Day. 60fr, Rotary, chess board, pieces.

1985, Feb. 23   **Litho.**   **Perf. 13**
C211	AP84	50fr multicolored	1.40	.60
C212	AP84	60fr multicolored	1.60	.55

Nos. C211-C212 exist in souvenir sheets of 1.

Telecommunications Technology — AP85

No. C213, Technician, researchist, operator. No. C214, Offshore oil rig, transmission tower, government building.

1985, July 2   **Perf. 13x12½**
C213	AP85	80fr multi	2.50	.55
C214	AP85	80fr multi	2.50	.55
a.		Pair, Nos. C213-C214 + label	6.25	1.25

PHILEXAFRICA '85, Lome.

DJIBOUTI

Telecommunications Development — AP86

50fr, Intl. transmission center. 90fr, Ariane rocket, vert. 120fr, ARABSAT satellite.

1985, Oct. 2   *Perf. 13*
C215 AP86 50fr multi .90 .35
C216 AP86 90fr multi 1.60 .65
C217 AP86 120fr multi 2.00 .90
    Nos. C215-C217 (3) 4.50 1.90

Youths Windsurfing, Playing Tennis AP87

No. C219, Tadjoura Highway construction.

1985, Nov. 13   *Perf. 13x12½*
C218 AP87 100fr multi 2.50 1.00
C219 AP87 100fr multi 2.50 1.00
  a. Pair, Nos. C218-C219 + label 6.00 5.00

PHILEXAFRICA '85, Lome, Togo, 11/16-24.

1986 World Cup Soccer Championships, Mexico — AP88

Design: 100fr, Players, stadium.

1986, Feb. 24   *Litho.*   *Perf. 13*
C220 AP88 75fr shown 1.50 .50
C221 AP88 100fr multi 2.00 .70

For overprints see Nos. C223-C224.

Statue of Liberty, Cent. AP89

1986, May 21
C222 AP89 250fr multi 4.50 1.75

Nos. C220-C221 Ovptd. with Winners

1986, Sept. 15   *Litho.*   *Perf. 13*
C223 AP88 75fr "FRANCE - BELGIQUE / 4-2" 1.25 .65
C224 AP88 100fr "3-2 ARGENTINE-RFA" 1.75 .80

1986 World Chess Championships, May 1-19 — AP89a

Malayan animal chess pieces: 80fr, Knight, bishops. 120fr, Rook, king, pawn.

1986, Oct. 13   *Litho.*   *Perf. 13*
C225 AP89a 80fr multi 2.00 .60
C226 AP89a 120fr multi 3.25 .90

Yuri Gagarin, Vostok Spacecraft AP90

Design: 200fr, Space rendezvous, 1966.

1986, Nov. 27   *Litho.*   *Perf. 13*
C227 AP90 150fr shown 3.00 1.10
C228 AP90 200fr multi 4.25 1.25

First man in space, 25th anniv.; Gemini 8-Agena link-up, 20th anniv.

Historic Flights AP91

Designs: 55fr, Amiot 370. 80fr, Spirit of St. Louis. 120fr, Voyager.

1987, Jan. 22   *Litho.*   *Perf. 13*
C229 AP91 55fr multi 1.25 .40
C230 AP91 80fr multi 1.75 .55
C231 AP91 120fr multi 2.50 .90
    Nos. C229-C231 (3) 5.50 1.85

First flight from Istria to Djibouti, 1942; Lindbergh's Transatlantic flight, 1927; nonstop world circumnavigation without refueling. For surcharge see No. C240.

Souvenir Sheet

Fight Against Leprosy AP91a

Design: Raoul Follereau (b. 1903), care giver to lepers, Gerhard Hansen (1841-1912), discoverer of bacillus of leprosy.

1987, Mar. 23   *Litho.*   *Perf. 13x12½*
Self-Adhesive
C231A AP91a 500fr multi 20.00 15.00

No. C231A printed on wood.

Pres. Aptidon, Natl. Crest and Flag — AP92

1987, June 27   *Litho.*   *Perf. 12½x13*
C232 AP92 250fr multi 4.50 1.50

Natl. independence, 10th anniv.

Telstar, 25th Anniv. AP93

Design: 250fr, Samuel Morse, telegraph key.

1987, Oct. 1   *Perf. 13*
C233 AP93 190fr shown 3.50 1.25
  a. Souvenir sheet, 1 #C233 14.00
C234 AP93 250fr multi 4.50 1.50
  a. Souvenir sheet, 1 #C234 14.00

Invention of the telegraph, 150th anniv. (250fr).
Nos. C233a and C234a also exist imperf. Value, set of 2, $40.

City of Djibouti, Cent. AP94

100fr, Djibouti Creek & quay, 1887. 150fr, Aerial view of city, 1987. 250fr, Somali Coast #6, 20, postmarks of 1898 & 1903.

1987, Nov. 15   *Litho.*   *Perf. 13x12½*
C235 AP94 100fr blk & buff 2.00 1.10
C236 AP94 150fr multi 3.00 1.60
  a. Pair, Nos. C235-C236 + label 6.00 2.75

Souvenir Sheet
C237 AP94 250fr multi 6.00 5.50

No. C237 has decorative margin like design of 100fr.

Intl. Red Cross and Red Crescent Organizations, 125th Anniv. — AP95

1988, Feb. 17   *Litho.*   *Perf. 13*
C238 AP95 300fr multi 6.00 3.25

1988 Summer Olympics, Seoul AP96

1988, June 15   *Litho.*   *Perf. 13*
C239 AP96 105fr multi 3.00 1.00

For overprint see No. C242.
No. C239 exists in a souvenir sheet of one. Value, $25.

No. C229 Surcharged in Black

1988, June 28
C240 AP91 70fr on 55fr multi 3.00 1.50

Air race in memory of the Paris-Djibouti-St. Denis flight of French aviator Roland Garros (1888-1913).

World Post Day AP97

1988, Oct. 9   *Litho.*   *Perf. 13*
C241 AP97 1000fr multi 18.00 10.00

No. C239 Overprinted

1988, Dec. 15   *Litho.*   *Perf. 13*
C242 AP96 105fr multi 2.25 1.50

World Telecommunications Day — AP98

1989, May 17   *Litho.*   *Perf. 12½*
C243 AP98 150fr multi 2.75 1.50

PHILEXFRANCE '89, Declaration of Human Rights and Citizenship Bicent. — AP99

1989, July 14   *Litho.*   *Perf. 12½x13*
C244 AP99 120fr multi 2.75 1.25

Salt, Lake Assal AP100

1989, Sept. 15   *Litho.*   *Perf. 13*
C245 AP100 300fr multicolored 6.75 3.50

POSTAGE DUE STAMP

Urn for Milking Camel — D1

1988, Jan. 20   *Litho.*   *Perf. 13*
J1 D1 60fr multicolored 1.20 .65

DOMINICA

,dä-mə-'nē-kə

LOCATION — The largest island of the Windward group in the West Indies. Southeast of Puerto Rico.
GOVT. — Republic in British Commonwealth
AREA — 290 sq. mi.
POP. — 72,000 (2020 est.)
CAPITAL — Roseau

Formerly a Presidency of the Leeward Islands, Dominica became a separate colony under the governor of the Windward Islands on January 1, 1940. Dominica joined the West Indies federation April 22, 1958. In 1968, Dominica became an associate state of Britain; in 1978, an independent nation.

12 Pence = 1 Shilling
20 Shillings = 1 Pound
100 Cents = 1 Dollar (1949)

Catalogue values for unused stamps in this country are for Never Hinged items, beginning with Scott 112.

Watermark

Wmk. 334 — Rectangles

Queen Victoria — A1

1874, May 4   Typo.   Wmk. 1   Perf. 12½

1	A1	1p violet	170.00	55.00
a.	Vertical half used as ½p on cover			9,000.
2	A1	6p green	625.00	115.00
3	A1	1sh deep lilac rose	375.00	80.00
	Nos. 1-3 (3)		1,170.	250.00

During 1875-87 some issues were manuscript dated with village names. These are considered postally used. Stamps with entire village names sell for much more, starting at $100.

1877-79   Perf. 14

4	A1	½p bister ('79)	20.00	62.50
5	A1	1p violet	24.00	3.75
a.	Diagonal or vertical half used as ½p on cover			2,600.
6	A1	2½p red brown ('79)	275.00	45.00
7	A1	4p blue ('79)	130.00	3.75
8	A1	6p green	170.00	22.50
9	A1	1sh dp lilac rose	140.00	57.50
	Nos. 4-9 (6)		759.00	195.00

For surcharges see Nos. 10-15.

No. 5 Bisected and Surcharged in Black or Red

a   b   c

1882

10	A1(a)	½p on half of 1p	240.00	57.50
a.	Inverted surcharge		1,150.	900.00
b.	Surcharge tete beche pair		2,600.	2,000.
11	A1(b)	½p on half of 1p	72.50	42.50
a.	Surch. reading downward		72.50	42.50
b.	Double surcharge		900.00	
12	A1(c)	½p on half of 1p (R)	40.00	20.00
a.	Inverted surcharge		1,150.	550.00
b.	Double surcharge		1,850.	750.00
	Nos. 10-12 (3)		352.50	120.00

The existence of genuine examples of No. 10b has been questioned.

Nos. 8 and 9 Surcharged in Black

1886

13	A1	½p on 6p green	13.00	15.00
14	A1	1p on 6p green	45,000.	12,500.
15	A1	1p on 1sh	24.00	22.00
a.	Double surcharge		11,500.	4,250.

All examples of No. 14 may have small pin marks which may have been part of the surcharging process.

1883-89   Wmk. 2

16	A1	½p bister ('83)	7.50	11.50
17	A1	½p green ('86)	6.00	5.75
18	A1	1p violet ('86)	60.00	16.00
a.	Half used as ½p on cover			2,350.
19	A1	1p dp carmine ('89)	5.75	15.00
a.	1p rose ('87)		19.00	28.00
b.	Vert. half used as ½p on cover			2,100.
20	A1	2½p red brn ('84)	160.00	5.00
21	A1	2½p ultra ('88)	4.25	9.00
22	A1	4p gray ('86)	9.00	7.75
23	A1	6p orange ('88)	23.00	92.50
24	A1	1sh dp lil rose ('88)	200.00	500.00
	Nos. 16-24 (9)		475.50	662.50

Roseau, Capital of Dominica — A6

King Edward VII — A7

1903   Wmk. 1   Perf. 14
Ordinary Paper

25	A6	½p gray green	5.25	4.75
26	A6	1p car & black	17.50	.80
27	A6	2p brn & gray grn	6.00	8.00
28	A6	2½p ultra & blk	13.00	5.25
29	A6	3p black & vio	11.50	4.50
30	A6	6p org brn & blk	15.00	22.50
31	A6	1sh gray grn & red vio	42.50	52.50
32	A6	2sh red vio & blk	40.00	35.00
33	A6	2sh6p ocher & gray grn	23.00	92.50
34	A7	5sh brown & blk	125.00	175.00
	Nos. 25-34 (10)		298.75	400.00

Nos. 25 to 29 and 31 are on both ordinary and chalky paper. For detailed listings, see the *Scott Classic Specialized Catalogue of Stamps & Covers.*

1907-20   Chalky Paper   Wmk. 3

35	A6	½p gray green	15.00	11.00
36	A6	1p car & black	2.50	.55
37	A6	2p brn & gray grn	16.00	24.00
38	A6	2½p ultra & black	5.50	27.50
39	A6	3p black & vio	5.00	20.00
40	A6	3p vio, yel, chalky paper ('08)	3.75	3.25
41	A6	6p org brn & blk ('08)	65.00	100.00
42	A6	6p vio & dl vio, chalky paper ('09)	12.50	19.00
43	A6	1sh gray grn & red vio	4.75	67.50
44	A6	1sh blk, green, chalky paper ('10)	3.75	5.00
45	A6	2sh red vio & blk ('08)	30.00	40.00
46	A6	2sh ultra & vio, bl ('19)	32.50	110.00
47	A6	2sh6p ocher & gray grn ('08)	27.50	75.00
48	A6	2sh6p red & blk, bl ('20)	32.50	125.00
49	A7	5sh brn & blk ('08)	75.00	75.00
	Nos. 35-49 (15)		331.25	704.80

Nos. 40, 42 and 44 are on both ordinary and chalky paper. For detailed listings, see the *Scott Classic Specialized Catalogue of Stamps & Covers.*

1908-09   Ordinary Paper

50	A6	½p green	9.50	6.25
51	A6	1p scarlet	2.00	.75
a.	1p carmine		4.50	.45
52	A6	2p gray ('09)	5.00	17.50
53	A6	2½p ultramarine	9.50	9.75
a.	2½p bright blue ('18)		5.75	10.50
	Nos. 50-53 (4)		26.00	34.25

King George V — A8

1914   Chalky Paper   Perf. 14

54	A8	5sh grn & scar, yel	70.00	100.00

Type of 1903 Surcharged

1920

55	A6	1½p on 2½p orange	8.25	4.75

1921   Ordinary Paper   Wmk. 4

56	A6	½p green	3.50	25.00
57	A6	1p rose red	3.00	4.00
58	A6	1½p orange	4.75	21.00
59	A6	2p gray	4.25	4.00
60	A6	2½p ultra	3.25	17.50
61	A6	6p vio & dl vio	5.00	50.00
62	A6	2sh ultra & vio, bl	50.00	145.00
63	A6	2sh6p red & blk, bl	45.00	165.00
	Nos. 56-63 (8)		118.75	431.50

No. 61 is on chalky paper.

Seal of Colony and George V — A9

1923-33   Chalky Paper   Wmk. 4

65	A9	½p green & blk	2.50	.85
66	A9	1p violet & blk	7.50	2.25
67	A9	1p scar & black	18.00	1.40
68	A9	1½p car & black	6.75	.90
69	A9	1½p dp brn & blk	15.50	.95
70	A9	2p gray & black	4.50	.65
71	A9	2½p org & black	4.50	10.00
72	A9	2½p ultra & black	7.75	2.25
73	A9	3p ultra & black	4.50	19.00
74	A9	3p red & blk, yel	4.75	1.40
75	A9	4p brown & blk	5.25	7.25
76	A9	6p red vio & blk	5.50	9.00
77	A9	1sh blk, emerald	3.50	4.25
78	A9	2sh ultra & blk, bl	26.00	40.00
79	A9	2sh6p red & blk, bl	27.50	40.00
80	A9	3sh vio & blk, yel	4.50	15.00
81	A9	4sh red & blk, emer	23.00	40.00
82	A9	5sh grn & blk, yel	42.50	62.50
	Nos. 65-82 (18)		214.00	257.65

Issue years: Nos. 80, 82, 1927; Nos. 72, 74, 1928; Nos. 67, 69, 1933; others, 1923. Many values of this set are known with a forged G.P.O. cancellation dated "MY 19 27".

1923   Wmk. 3

83	A9	3sh vio & blk, yel	5.75	72.50
84	A9	5sh grn & blk, yel	10.00	65.00
85	A9	£1 vio & blk, red	240.00	375.00
	Nos. 83-85 (3)		255.75	512.50

Common Design Types pictured following the introduction.

Silver Jubilee Issue
Common Design Type
Perf. 13½x14

1935, May 6   Wmk. 4   Engr.

90	CD301	1p car & blue	1.60	.35
91	CD301	1½p gray blk & ultra	5.75	3.25
92	CD301	2½p blue & brn	5.75	4.75
93	CD301	1sh brt vio & ind	5.75	11.50
	Nos. 90-93 (4)		18.85	19.85
	Set, never hinged		27.50	

Coronation Issue
Common Design Type
1937, May 12   Perf. 11x11½

94	CD302	1p dark carmine	.25	.25
95	CD302	1½p brown	.25	.25
96	CD302	2½p deep ultra	.35	1.90
	Nos. 94-96 (3)		.85	2.40
	Set, never hinged		1.50	

Fresh-Water Lake — A10

Layou River — A11

Picking Limes — A12

Boiling Lake — A13

1938-47   Wmk. 4   Perf. 12½

97	A10	½p grn & red brn	.25	.25
98	A11	1p car & gray	.25	.25
99	A12	1½p rose vio & grn	.25	.75
100	A13	2p brn blk & dp rose	.35	2.25
101	A12	2½p ultra & rose vio	.25	2.25
a.	2½p bl & rose vio		2.75	1.90
102	A11	3p red brn & ol	.25	.60
103	A12	3½p red vio & brt ultra	1.00	2.10
104	A10	6p grn & yel grn	.50	1.60
105	A10	7p org brn & grn	1.00	1.60
106	A13	1sh olive & blk	2.50	1.60
107	A11	2sh red vio & blk	4.50	12.50
108	A10	2sh6p scar ver & blk	10.00	5.75
109	A11	5sh dk brn & bl	8.00	12.00
110	A13	10sh dl org & blk	10.00	22.50
	Nos. 97-110 (14)		39.10	66.00
	Set, never hinged		80.00	

Issued: No. 101, 8/42; 3½p, 7p, 2sh, 10sh, 10/15/47; others, 8/15/38.

King George VI — A14

1940, Apr. 15   Photo.   Perf. 14½x14

111	A14	¼p brown violet	1.00	.25
a.	Ordinary paper ('42)		.25	1.50

No. 111 is on chalky paper.

Catalogue values for unused stamps in this section, from this point to the end of the section, are for Never Hinged items.

Peace Issue
Common Design Type
1946, Oct. 14   Engr.   Perf. 13½x14

112	CD303	1p crimson	.25	.25
113	CD303	3½p deep blue	.25	.25

Silver Wedding Issue
Common Design Types
1948, Dec. 1   Photo.   Perf. 14x14½

114	CD304	1p scarlet	.25	.25

Engraved; Name Typographed
Perf. 11½x11

115	CD305	10sh orange brn	25.00	32.50

UPU Issue
Common Design Types
Engr.: Name Typo. on 6c and 12c
1949, Oct. 10   Perf. 13½, 11x11½

116	CD306	5c blue	.25	.25
117	CD307	6c chocolate	1.25	3.00
118	CD308	12c rose violet	.50	2.10
119	CD309	24c olive	.30	.30
	Nos. 116-119 (4)		2.30	5.65

University Issue
Common Design Types
1951, Feb. 16   Engr.   Perf. 14x14½

120	CD310	3c purple & green	.60	1.25
121	CD311	12c dp car & dk bl grn	.80	.50

DOMINICA

George VI
A15

Drying Cocoa
A16

Picking Oranges — A17

Designs: 2c and 60c, Carib Baskets. 3c and 48c, Lime Plantation. 4c, Picking Oranges. 5c, Bananas. 6c, Botanical Gardens. 8c, Drying Vanilla Beans. 12c and $1.20, Fresh Water Lake. 14c, Layou River. 24c, Boiling Lake.

Perf. 14½x14

1951, July 1		Photo.		Wmk. 4
122	A15	½c brown	.25	.25

Perf. 13x13½
Engr.

123	A16	1c red org & blk	.25	.30
124	A16	2c dp grn & red brn	.25	.25
125	A16	3c red vio & bl grn	.25	3.50
126	A16	4c dk brn & brn org	.75	3.75
127	A16	5c rose red & blk	.85	.30
128	A16	6c org brn & ol grn	1.00	.30
129	A16	8c dp bl & dp grn	3.00	1.75
130	A16	12c emer & gray	.75	1.25
131	A16	14c pur & blue	1.25	3.50
132	A16	24c rose car & red vio	1.00	.40
133	A16	48c red org & bl grn	5.00	13.50
134	A16	60c gray & car	4.00	9.25
135	A16	$1.20 gray & emer	8.25	7.25

Perf. 13½x13

136	A17	$2.40 gray & org	30.00	52.50
		Nos. 122-136 (15)	56.85	98.05

Nos. 125, 127, 129 and 131 Overprinted in Black or Carmine

1951, Oct. 15   Perf. 13x13½

137	A16	3c red vio & bl green	.25	.60
138	A16	5c rose red & black	.25	1.75
139	A16	8c dp blue & dp grn (C)	.30	.30
140	A16	14c purple & blue (C)	1.75	.30
		Nos. 137-140 (4)	2.55	2.90

Adoption of a new constitution for the Windward Islands, 1951.

Coronation Issue
Common Design Type

1953, June 2   Engr.   Perf. 13½x13

141	CD312	2c dk green & black	.40	.40

Types of 1951 with Portrait of Queen Elizabeth II

1954, Oct. 1   Photo.   Perf. 14½x14

142	A15	½c brown	.25	1.25

Perf. 13x13½
Engr.

143	A16	1c red org & blk	.25	.30
144	A16	2c dp grn & red brn	1.10	2.00
145	A16	3c red vio & bl grn	1.50	.40
146	A16	4c dk brn & brn org	.25	.30
147	A16	5c rose red & blk	2.75	1.00
148	A16	6c org brn & ol grn	.55	.30
149	A16	8c dp bl & dp grn	1.50	.30
150	A16	12c emer & gray	.60	.25
151	A16	14c pur & bl	.45	.25
152	A16	24c rose car & red vio	.55	.30
153	A16	48c red org & bl grn	2.75	11.00
154	A16	60c gray & car	3.50	1.50
155	A16	$1.20 gray & emer	22.50	7.00

Perf. 13½x13

156	A17	$2.40 gray & org	22.50	14.00
		Nos. 142-156 (15)	61.00	40.15

Mat Making — A18

5c, Canoe making. 10c, Bananas.

1957, Oct. 15   Wmk. 4   Perf. 13x13½

157	A18	3c car rose & black	4.00	2.50
158	A18	5c brown & blue	12.00	1.10
159	A18	10c redsh brn & brt grn	6.00	3.25
160	A18	48c violet & brown	3.25	2.75
		Nos. 157-160 (4)	25.25	9.60

West Indies Federation
Common Design Type
Perf. 11½x11

1958, Apr. 22   Wmk. 314

161	CD313	3c green	.50	.35
162	CD313	6c blue	.60	1.10
163	CD313	12c car rose	.85	.40
		Nos. 161-163 (3)	1.95	1.85

Sailing Canoe
A19

Traditional Costume
A20

Type I

Type II

Two types of 14c:
I — Mountain light violet. Girl's eyes look straight out.
II — Mountain blue. Eyes look sideways.
Designs: 1c, Seashore, Rosalie. 2c, 5c, Queen Elizabeth II by Annigoni. 4c, Sulphur Springs. 6c, Road making. 8c, Dugout canoe. 10c, Frog (mountain chicken). 12c, Boats and Scotts Head. 15c, Bananas. 24c, Imperial parrot. 48c, View of Goodwill. 60c, Cacao tree. $1.20, Coat of Arms. $2.40, Trafalgar Falls. $4.80, Coconut palm.

Perf. 14½x14, 14x14½

1963, May 16   Photo.   Wmk. 314

164	A19	1c bl, brn & grn	.25	.90
165	A20	2c ultramarine	.30	.25
166	A19	3c lt ultra & blk	1.50	1.10
167	A19	4c sl, grn & brn	.25	.25
168	A20	5c magenta	.30	.25
169	A19	6c lt grn, vio & buff	.25	.50
170	A19	8c tan, blk & lt grn	.30	.25
171	A19	10c pink & brn	.25	.25
172	A19	12c bl, blk, grn & brn	.90	.25
173	A20	14c multi (II)	2.50	2.50
a.		Type I	.90	.30
174	A19	15c grn, yel & brn	1.25	.25
175	A20	24c multicolored	8.50	.25
176	A19	48c bl, blk & grn	.90	.90
177	A19	60c blk, grn, org & brn	1.00	.75
178	A19	$1.20 multicolored	6.25	1.60
179	A20	$2.40 grn, bl, brn & blk	4.75	4.00
180	A20	$4.80 bl, brn & grn	20.00	30.00
		Nos. 164-180 (17)	49.45	44.25

For overprints see Nos. 211-232.

1966-67   Wmk. 314 Sideways

167a	A19	4c ('67)	1.25	.90
169a	A19	6c	.25	.80
170a	A19	8c	.45	.90
171a	A19	10c ('67)	.70	.95
174a	A19	15c	.85	1.50
		Nos. 167a-174a (5)	3.50	5.05

Freedom from Hunger Issue
Common Design Type

1963, June 4   Perf. 14x14½

181	CD314	15c lilac	.30	.30

Red Cross Centenary Issue
Common Design Type
Wmk. 314

1963, Sept. 2   Litho.   Perf. 13

182	CD315	5c black & red	.25	.25
183	CD315	15c ultra & red	.45	.80

Shakespeare Issue
Common Design Type

1964, Apr. 23   Photo.   Perf. 14x14½

184	CD316	15c lilac rose	.35	.35

ITU Issue
Common Design Type

1965, May 17   Photo.   Perf. 11x11½

185	CD317	2c emerald & blue	.25	.25
186	CD317	48c grnsh blue & slate	.30	.30

Intl. Cooperation Year Issue
Common Design Type

1965, Oct. 25   Perf. 14½

187	CD318	1c blue grn & claret	.25	.25
188	CD318	15c lt violet & grn	.30	.30

Churchill Memorial Issue
Common Design Type

1966, Jan. 24   Photo.   Perf. 14
Design in Black, Gold and Carmine Rose

189	CD319	1c bright blue	.25	.25
a.		Gold omitted	2,000.	
190	CD319	5c green	.25	.25
191	CD319	15c brown	.30	.30
192	CD319	24c violet	.35	.35
		Nos. 189-192 (4)	1.15	1.15

Royal Visit Issue
Common Design Type

1966, Feb. 4   Litho.   Perf. 11x12

193	CD320	5c violet blue	.75	.25
194	CD320	15c dk car rose	2.25	.35

World Cup Soccer Issue
Common Design Type

1966, July 1   Litho.   Perf. 14

195	CD321	5c multicolored	.35	.25
196	CD321	24c multicolored	.85	.50

WHO Headquarters Issue
Common Design Type

1966, Sept. 20   Litho.   Perf. 14

197	CD322	5c multicolored	.25	.25
198	CD322	24c multicolored	.50	.50

UNESCO Anniversary Issue
Common Design Type

1966, Dec. 1   Litho.   Perf. 14

199	CD323	5c "Education"	.35	.25
200	CD323	15c "Science"	.45	.25
201	CD323	24c "Culture"	.80	.25
		Nos. 199-201 (3)	1.60	.75

Carib, Negro and Caucasian Children — A21

10c, Columbus' ship Santa Maria & banderol. 15c, Hands with banderol. 24c, Belaire dancers.

Perf. 14½x14

1967, Nov. 3   Photo.   Wmk. 314

202	A21	5c multicolored	.25	.25
203	A21	10c multicolored	.25	.25
204	A21	15c multicolored	.25	.25
205	A21	24c multicolored	.25	.25
		Nos. 202-205 (4)	1.00	1.00

Issued for National Day, Nov. 3.

John F. Kennedy and Human Rights Flame — A22

Human Rights Flame and: 10c, Cecil E. A. Rawle (1891-1938), Dominican crusader for human rights. 12c, Pope John XXIII. 48c, Florence Nightingale. 60c, Dr. Albert Schweitzer.

Wmk. 314 Sideways

1968, Apr. 20   Litho.   Perf. 14

206	A22	1c multicolored	.25	.25
207	A22	10c multicolored	.25	.25
208	A22	12c multicolored	.25	.25
209	A22	48c multicolored	.25	.25
210	A22	60c multicolored	.25	.25
		Nos. 206-210 (5)	1.25	1.25

International Human Rights Year.

Stamps and Types of 1963-67 Overprinted in Silver or Black: "ASSOCIATED / STATEHOOD"
Perf. 14½x14, 14x14½

1968, July 8   Photo.   Wmk. 314

211	A19	1c multi	.25	.25
212	A20	2c ultra	.25	.25
213	A19	3c lt ultra & blk	.25	.25
214	A19	4c multi	.25	.25
215	A20	5c magenta	.25	.25
216	A19	6c multi (B)	.25	.25
217	A19	8c multi (B)	.25	.25
218	A19	10c pink & brn	.55	.25
219	A19	12c multi	.25	.50
a.		Watermark upright	.25	.25
220	A20	14c multi (II)	.25	.25
221	A19	15c multi	.25	.25
222	A20	24c multi	4.00	.25
223	A19	48c multi	.55	2.25
a.		Watermark upright	.50	1.00
224	A19	60c multi (B)	.90	.75
225	A19	$1.20 multi (B)	1.00	3.00
226	A20	$2.40 multi	1.00	2.25
227	A20	$4.80 multi	1.25	8.00
		Nos. 211-227 (17)	11.75	19.50

In this set, overprint was applied to 2c, 3c, 12c, 14c, 24c, 48c, 60c, $1.20, $2.40 and $4.80 with watermark upright. A reprinting of the 1c, 4c, 6c, 8c, 10c, 12c, No. 219, 15c and 48c, No. 223 on paper with watermark sideways was made. Same value.

Nos. 164-166, 173 and 178 Overprinted: "NATIONAL DAY / 3 NOVEMBER 1968"
Perf. 14½x14, 14x14½

1968, Nov. 3   Photo.   Wmk. 314

228	A19	1c blue, brn & grn	.25	.25
229	A20	2c ultra	.25	.25
230	A19	3c lt ultra & blk	.25	.25
231	A20	14c multi (I)	.25	.25
232	A19	$1.20 multicolored	.55	.55
		Nos. 228-232 (5)	1.55	1.55

A23

No. 233: a, 3 soccer players; b, Soccer player, goalie. No. 234: a, Swimmers at start; b, Divers. No. 235: a, Javelin thrower, hurdlers; b, Hurdlers. No. 236: a, Basketball; b, 3 basketball players.

Perf. 11½

1968, Nov. 23   Unwmk.   Litho.

233	A23	1c Pair, #a-b	.25	.25
234	A23	5c Pair, #a-b	.25	.25
235	A23	48c Pair, #a-b	.50	.50
236	A23	60c Pair, #a-b	1.40	1.40
		Nos. 233-236 (4)	2.40	2.40

19th Olympic Games, Mexico City, 10/12-27.

The Small Cowper Madonna, by Raphael — A24

Perf. 12½x12

1968, Dec. 23   Photo.   Unwmk.

241	A24	5c multicolored	.30	.30

Christmas. No. 241 printed in sheets of 20. Sheets of 6 (3x2) exist containing two each of 12c, 24c, and $1.20 stamps, each picturing a different madonna painting. Value $6.

Venus and Adonis, by Rubens — A25

DOMINICA

Paintings: 15c, The Death of Socrates, by Louis Jacques David. 24c, Christ at Emmaus, by Velazquez. 50c, Pilate Washing his Hands, by Rembrandt.

1969, Jan. 30 Litho. Perf. 14½x15 Wmk. 314
242	A25	5c lilac & multi	.25	.25
243	A25	15c emerald & multi	.25	.25
244	A25	24c lt blue & multi	.25	.25
245	A25	50c crimson & multi	.45	.45
		Nos. 242-245 (4)	1.20	1.20

20th anniv. (in 1968) of the WHO.

Citrus Fruit Picker — A26

No. 247, Woman and child. No. 248, Hotel. No. 249, Red-necked parrots. No. 250, Calypso band. No. 251, Women dancers. No. 252, Tropical fish and coelenterates. No. 253, Diver and turtle.

1969, Mar. 10 Perf. 14½
246	A26	10c multicolored	.25	.25
247	A26	10c multicolored	.25	.25
a.	Pair, #246-247		.25	.25
248	A26	12c multicolored	.25	.25
249	A26	12c multicolored	.25	.25
a.	Pair, #248-249		.25	.25
250	A26	24c multicolored	.25	.25
251	A26	24c multicolored	.25	.25
a.	Pair, #250-251		.50	.50
252	A26	48c multicolored	.65	.65
253	A26	48c multicolored	.65	.65
a.	Pair, #252-253		1.30	1.30
		Nos. 246-253 (8)	2.80	2.80

Tourist publicity.

Spinning, by Millet, Flags and ILO Emblem — A27

50th anniv. of the ILO (Etchings by Jean F. Millet, Flags and ILO Emblem): 30c, Threshing. 30c, Flax pulling.

1969, July Unwmk. Perf. 13½
254	A27	15c multicolored	.25	.25
255	A27	30c multicolored	.30	.30
256	A27	38c multicolored	.30	.30
		Nos. 254-256 (3)	.85	.85

"Strength in Unity," Bananas and Cacao — A28

"Strength in Unity" Emblem and: 8c, Map of Dominica and Hawker Siddeley 748. 12c, Map of Caribbean. 24c, Ships in harbor.

1969, July Litho.
257	A28	5c orange & multi	.30	.30
258	A28	8c gray & multi	.30	.30
259	A28	12c lilac & multi	.30	.30
260	A28	24c lt blue & multi	.30	.30
		Nos. 257-260 (4)	1.20	1.20

Caribbean Free Trade Area (CARIFTA).

Gandhi at Spinning Wheel and Big Ben, London — A29

38c, Gandhi, Nehru and Fatehpur Sikri Mausoleum. $1.20, Gandhi & Taj Mahal.

1969, Oct. Litho. Perf. 14½
261	A29	6c multicolored	.55	.25
262	A29	38c multicolored	.75	.25
263	A29	$1.20 multicolored	.85	.85
		Nos. 261-263 (3)	2.15	1.35

Mohandas K. Gandhi (1869-1948), leader in India's fight for independence. "Gandhi" is misspelled "Ghandi" on Nos. 261-263.

St. Joseph — A30

Stained Glass Windows, from 17th Century French Churches: 8c, St. John. 12c, St. Peter. 60c, St. Paul.

1969, Nov. 10 Litho. Perf. 14
264	A30	6c black & multi	.25	.25
265	A30	8c black & multi	.25	.25
266	A30	12c black & multi	.25	.25
267	A30	60c black & multi	.40	.40
		Nos. 264-267 (4)	1.15	1.15

National Day, Nov. 3. Issued in sheets of 16 (4x4) with control numbers and 4 tabs with a patriotic poem by W. O. M. Pond.

Queen Elizabeth II A31

Purplethroated Carib (Hummingbird) A32

2c, Poinsettia. 3c, Red-necked pigeon. 4c, Imperial parrot. 5c, Swallowtail butterfly. 6c, Brown Julia butterfly. 8c, Banana shipment. 10c, Portsmouth Harbor. 12c, Copra processing plant. 15c, Women with straw work. 25c, Timber plant. 30c, Mining pumice. 38c, Cricket, Grammar School. 50c, Roman Catholic Cathedral. 60c, Government headquarters. $1.20, Melville Hall Airport. $2.40, Coat of Arms. $4.80, Queen Elizabeth II.

Perf. 13½
1969, Nov. 26 Unwmk. Photo.
Chalky Paper
268	A31	½c silver & multi	.25	1.50
269	A32	1c yellow & multi	.75	2.00
270	A32	2c yellow & multi	.25	.25
271	A32	3c yellow & multi	2.50	2.50
272	A32	4c yellow & multi	2.50	2.50
273	A32	5c yellow & multi	2.50	2.50
274	A32	6c brown & multi	2.00	3.50
275	A32	8c brown & multi	.25	.25
276	A32	10c yellow & multi	.25	.25
277	A32	12c citron & multi	.25	.25
278	A32	15c blue & multi	.25	.25
279	A32	25c pink & multi	.40	.25
280	A32	30c olive & multi	1.50	.25
281	A32	38c multicolored	8.50	1.75
282	A32	50c brown & multi	.65	.65

Wmk. Rectangles (334)
Perf. 14
Size: 38x26mm, 26x38mm
283	A31	60c yel & multi	1.00	1.50
284	A32	$1.20 yel & multi	2.00	2.00
285	A32	$2.40 gold & multi	1.50	4.00
286	A31	$4.80 gold & multi	3.00	7.50
		Nos. 268-286 (19)	30.30	33.65

1972 On glazed Paper
268a	A31	½c silver & multi	.30	2.00
269a	A32	1c yellow & multi	1.40	1.50
270a	A32	2c yellow & multi	.50	.50
271a	A32	3c yellow & multi	3.00	1.50
272a	A32	4c yellow & multi	3.00	1.50
273a	A32	5c yellow & multi	2.75	1.25
274a	A32	6c brown & multi	2.75	2.75
275a	A32	8c brown & multi	.45	.60
276a	A32	10c yellow & multi	.35	.25
277a	A32	12c citron & multi	.35	.25
278a	A32	15c blue & multi	.35	.30
279a	A32	25c pink & multi	.30	.25
280a	A32	30c olive & multi	1.50	.65
281a	A32	38c multicolored	8.00	14.00
282a	A32	50c brown & multi	.85	1.25
		Nos. 268a-282a (15)	25.85	28.55

Madonna and Child, by Filippino Lippi — A33

Paintings: 10c, Holy Family with Lamb, by Raphael. 15c, Virgin and Child, by Perugino. $1.20, Madonna of the Rose Hedge, by Botticelli.

Perf. 14½
1969, Dec. Unwmk. Litho.
287	A33	6c lt blue & multi	.25	.25
288	A33	10c multicolored	.25	.25
289	A33	15c lilac & multi	.25	.25
290	A33	$1.20 lt grn & multi	.25	.25
a.	Souvenir sheet of 2		1.25	1.25
		Nos. 287-290 (4)	1.00	1.00

Christmas. No. 290a contains 2 imperf. stamps with simulated perforations similar to Nos. 289-290.

Neil A. Armstrong, First Man on the Moon — A34

Designs: 5c, American flag and astronauts on moon. 8c, Astronauts collecting moon rocks. 30c, Landing module, moon and earth. 50c, Memorial tablet left on moon. 60c, Astronauts Armstrong, Aldrin and Collins.

1970, Feb. 2 Litho. Perf. 12½
291	A34	½c lilac & multi	.25	.25
292	A34	5c lt blue & multi	.25	.25
293	A34	8c orange & multi	.25	.25
294	A34	30c blue & multi	.25	.25
295	A34	50c red brn & multi	.40	.30
296	A34	60c rose & multi	.50	.45
a.	Souvenir sheet of 4		2.60	2.60
		Nos. 291-296 (6)	1.90	1.75

See note after US No. C76. No. 296a contains 4 stamps similar to Nos. 293-296, but imperf. with simulated perforations.

Giant Green Turtle — A35

Designs: 24c, Flying fish. 38c, Anthurium lily. 60c, Imperial and red-necked parrots.

1970, Sept. 6 Litho. Perf. 13½x13
297	A35	6c lt green & multi	.50	.50
298	A35	24c multicolored	.65	.65
299	A35	38c green & multi	.75	.75
300	A35	60c yellow & multi	3.50	3.50
a.	Souvenir sheet of 4, #297-300		8.50	8.50
		Nos. 297-300 (4)	5.40	5.40

Women in 18th Century Dress — A36

Natl. Day: 8c, Carib mace & wife leader, 18th cent. $1, Map & flag of Dominica.

1970, Nov. 3 Litho. Perf. 14
301	A36	5c yellow & multi	.25	.25
302	A36	8c green & multi	.25	.25
303	A36	$1 lt blue & multi	.40	.40
a.	Souv. sheet of 3, #301-303 + 3 labels		1.25	1.50
		Nos. 301-303 (3)	.90	.90

Marley's Ghost — A37

Designs (from A Christmas Carol, by Dickens): 15c, Fezziwig's Ball. 24c, Scrooge and his Nephew's Christmas Party. $1.20, The Ghost of Christmas Present.

1970, Nov. 23 Litho. Perf. 14x14½
304	A37	2c blue & multi	.25	.25
305	A37	15c multicolored	.25	.25
306	A37	24c red & multi	.25	.25
307	A37	$1.20 org & multi	.75	.75
a.	Souvenir sheet of 4, #304-307		2.75	2.75
		Nos. 304-307 (4)	1.50	1.50

Christmas; Charles Dickens (1812-1870).

Hands and Red Cross — A38

Designs: 8c, The Doctor, by Sir Luke Fildes. 15c, Dominica flag and Red Cross. 50c, The Sick Child, by Edvard Munch.

1970, Dec. 28 Perf. 14½x14
308	A38	8c multicolored	.25	.25
309	A38	10c multicolored	.25	.25
310	A38	15c multicolored	.25	.25
311	A38	50c multicolored	.50	.50
a.	Souvenir sheet of 4, #308-311		2.00	2.00
		Nos. 308-311 (4)	1.25	1.25

Centenary of the British Red Cross Society.

Marigot Primary School — A39

Education Year Emblem and: 8c, Goodwill Junior High School. 14c, University of the West Indies. $1, Trinity College, Cambridge, England.

1971, Mar. 1 Litho. Perf. 13½
312	A39	5c multicolored	.25	.25
313	A39	8c multicolored	.25	.25
314	A39	14c multicolored	.25	.25
315	A39	$1 multicolored	.45	.45
a.	Souvenir sheet of 2, #314-315		1.50	1.50
		Nos. 312-315 (4)	1.20	1.20

International Education Year.

Waterfall and Bird-of-Paradise Flower — A40

Tourist Publicity: 10c, Boat building. 30c, Sailboat along North Coast. 50c, Speed boat and steamer.

1971, Mar. 22 Perf. 13½x14
316	A40	5c multicolored	.25	.25
317	A40	10c multicolored	.25	.25
318	A40	30c multicolored	.25	.25
319	A40	50c multicolored	.35	.35
a.	Souvenir sheet of 4, #316-319		1.10	1.10
		Nos. 316-319 (4)	1.10	1.10

UNICEF Emblem, Letter "D" — A41

1971, June 14 Litho. Perf. 14
320	A41	5c multicolored	.25	.25
321	A41	10c multicolored	.25	.25
322	A41	38c multicolored	.25	.25
323	A41	$1.20 multicolored	.25	.25
a.	Souvenir sheet of 2, #321, 323		.85	.85
		Nos. 320-323 (4)	1.00	1.00

25th anniv. of UNICEF.

Boy Scout, Jamboree Emblem, Torii, Camp and Mt. Fuji — A42

24c, British Scout, flag. 30c, Japanese Scout, flag. $1, Dominican Scout, flag.

1971, Oct. 18 Unwmk. Perf. 11
324	A42	20c bister & multi	.25	.25
325	A42	24c green & multi	.30	.30
326	A42	30c red lilac & multi	.40	.40

DOMINICA

327	A42	$1 blue & multi	.80	.80
a.		Souvenir sheet of 2, #326-327	1.75	1.75
		Nos. 324-327 (4)	1.75	1.75

13th Boy Scout World Jamboree, Asagiri Plain, Japan, Aug. 2-10.

Boats at Portsmouth — A43

15c, Carnival street scene. 20c, $1.20, Anthea Mondesire, Carifta Queen. 50c, Rock of Atkinson.

Perf. 13½x14, 14x13½

1971, Nov. 15 Litho.

328	A43	8c multi	.25	.25
329	A43	15c multi	.25	.25
330	A43	20c multi, vert.	.25	.25
331	A43	50c multi, vert.	.25	.25
		Nos. 328-331 (4)	1.00	1.00

Souvenir Sheet
Perf. 15

| 332 | A43 | $1.20 multi, vert. | .85 | .85 |

National Day.

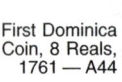

First Dominica Coin, 8 Reals, 1761 — A44

Early Dominica Coins: 30c, Eleven and 3-bit pieces, 1798. 35c, Two-real coin, 1770, vert. 50c, Three "mocos" and piece of 8, 1798.

1972, Feb. 7 Litho. **Perf. 14**

333	A44	10c violet, silver & blk	.25	.25
334	A44	30c green, silver & blk	.25	.25
335	A44	35c ultra, silver & blk	.25	.25
336	A44	40c red, silver & blk	.25	.25
a.		Souvenir sheet of 2, #335-336	1.00	1.00
		Nos. 333-336 (4)	1.00	1.00

Margin of No. 336a inscribed "Christmas 1971."

Common Opossum, Environment Emblem — A45

Environment Emblem and: 35c, Agouti. 60c, Oncidium papillo (orchid). $1.20, Hibiscus.

1972, June 5

337	A45	½c yel grn & multi	.25	.25
338	A45	35c org brn & multi	.30	.30
339	A45	60c lt blue & multi	2.25	2.25
340	A45	$1.20 yellow & multi	1.75	1.75
a.		Souvenir sheet of 4, #337-340	6.75	6.75
		Nos. 337-340 (4)	4.55	4.55

UN Conf. on Human Environment, Stockholm, June 5-16.

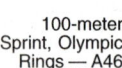

100-meter Sprint, Olympic Rings — A46

Olympic Rings and: 35m, 400-meter hurdles. 58c, Hammer throw, vert. 72c, Broad jump, vert.

1972, Oct. 9 Litho. **Perf. 14**

341	A46	30c dp org & multi	.25	.25
342	A46	35c blue & multi	.25	.25
343	A46	58c lilac rose & multi	.30	.30
344	A46	72c yel green & multi	.40	.40
a.		Souv. sheet of #343-344, perf. 15	1.25	1.25
		Nos. 341-344 (4)	1.20	1.20

20th Olympic Games, Munich, Aug. 26-Sept. 11.

General Post Office — A47

1972, Nov. 1 **Perf. 13½**

345	A47	10c shown	.25	.25
346	A47	20c Morne Diablotin Mountain	.25	.25
347	A47	30c Rodney's Rock	.25	.25
a.		Souv. sheet, #346-347, perf. 15	.60	.60
		Nos. 345-347 (3)	.75	.75

National Day.

Adoration of the Shepherds, by Caravaggio — A48

Paintings: 14c, Madonna and Child, by Rubens. 30c, Madonna and Child, with St. Anne by Orazio Gentileschi. $1, Adoration of the Kings, by Jan Mostaert. (On 8c, painting is mistakenly attributed to Boccaccino, according to Fine Arts Philatelist.)

1972, Dec. 4.

348	A48	8c gold & multi	.25	.25
349	A48	14c gold & multi	.25	.25
350	A48	30c gold & multi	.25	.25
351	A48	$1 gold & multi	.35	.35
a.		Souvenir sheet of 2	1.10	1.10
		Nos. 348-351 (4)	1.10	1.10

Christmas. No. 351a contains one each of Nos. 350-351 with simulated perforations.

Silver Wedding Issue, 1972
Common Design Type

Design: Queen Elizabeth II, Prince Philip, bananas, sisseron parrot.

Perf. 14x14½

1972, Nov. 13 Photo. Wmk. 314

352	CD324	5c olive & multi	.25	.25
353	CD324	$1 multicolored	.40	.40

See note after Antigua No. 296.

Launching of Tiros Weather Satellite — A49

1c, Nimbus satellite. 2c, Radiosonde balloon & equipment. 30c, Radarscope. 35c, General circulation of atmosphere. 50c, Picture of hurricane transmitted by satellite. $1, Computer weather map. 30c, 35c, 50c, $1, horiz.

Perf. 14½

1973, July 16 Unwmk. Litho.

354	A49	½c black & multi	.25	.25
355	A49	1c black & multi	.25	.25
356	A49	2c black & multi	.25	.25
357	A49	30c black & multi	.25	.25
358	A49	35c black & multi	.25	.25
359	A49	50c black & multi	.30	.30
360	A49	$1 black & multi	.55	.55
a.		Souvenir sheet of 2, #359-360	1.40	1.40
		Nos. 354-360 (7)	2.10	2.10

Intl. meteorological cooperation, cent.

Going to the Hospital — A50

WHO Emblem and: 1c, Maternity and infant care. 2c, Inoculation against smallpox. 30c, Emergency service. 35c, Waiting patients. 50c, Examination. $1, Traveling physician.

1973, Aug. 20 Unwmk. **Perf. 14½**

361	A50	½c lt blue & multi	.25	.25
362	A50	1c gray grn & multi	.25	.25
363	A50	2c yellow & multi	.25	.25
364	A50	30c lt vio & multi	.25	.25
365	A50	35c yel grn & multi	.30	.30
366	A50	50c multicolored	.30	.30
367	A50	$1 bister & multi	.45	.45
a.		Souvenir sheet of 2, #366-367, perf. 14x14½	1.25	1.25
		Nos. 361-367 (7)	2.05	2.05

WHO, 25th anniv. No. 367a exists perf. 14½.

Flora and Fauna — A51

1973, Oct.

368	A51	½c Cyrique Crab	.25	.25
369	A51	22c Blue land crab	.35	.35
370	A51	25c Breadfruit	.45	.45
371	A51	$1.20 Sunflower	1.00	1.00
a.		Souvenir sheet of 4, #368-371	2.75	2.75
		Nos. 368-371 (4)	2.05	2.05

Princess Anne and Mark Phillips — A52

1973, Nov. 14 **Perf. 13½**

372	A52	25c salmon & multi	.25	.25
373	A52	$2 blue & multi	.60	.60
a.		Souv. sheet of 2 (75c, $1.20)	.60	.60

Wedding of Princess Anne and Capt. Mark Phillips.

Nos. 372-373 were issued in sheets of 5 + label. No. 373a contains 2 stamps of type A52: 75c in colors of the 25c, and $1.20 in colors of the $2.

Nativity, by Brueghel — A53

Paintings of the Nativity by: 1c, Botticelli. 2c, Dürer. 12c, Botticelli. 22c, Rubens. 35c, Dürer. $1, Giorgione (inscribed "Giorgeone").

1973 Unwmk. **Perf. 14½x15**

374	A53	½c gray & multi	.25	.25
375	A53	1c gray & multi	.25	.25
376	A53	2c gray & multi	.25	.25
377	A53	12c gray & multi	.25	.25
378	A53	22c gray & multi	.25	.25
379	A53	35c gray & multi	.25	.25
380	A53	$1 gray & multi	.60	.60
a.		Souvenir sheet of 2	1.30	1.30
		Nos. 374-380 (7)	2.10	2.10

Christmas. No. 380a contains one each of Nos. 379-380 in changed colors.

National Day — A54

Designs: 5c, Carib basket weaving. 10c, Staircase of the Snake. 50c, Miss Caribbean Queen, Kathleen Telemacque, vert. 60c, Miss Carifta Queen, Esther Fadelle, vert. $1, La Jeune Etoille Dancers.

1973, Dec. 17 **Perf. 13½x14, 14x13½**

381	A54	5c buff & multi	.25	.25
382	A54	10c multicolored	.25	.25
383	A54	50c multicolored	.25	.25
384	A54	60c multicolored	.25	.25
385	A54	$1 multicolored	.25	.25
a.		Souv. sheet of 3, #381-382, 385	.75	.75
		Nos. 381-385 (5)	1.25	1.25

U.W.I. Center, Dominica — A55

30c, Graduation. $1, University coat of arms.

1974, Jan. 21 Litho. **Perf. 13½x14**

386	A55	12c dp orange & multi	.25	.25
387	A55	30c violet & multi	.25	.25
388	A55	$1 multicolored	.35	.35
a.		Souvenir sheet of 3, #386-388	.50	.50
		Nos. 386-388 (3)	.85	.85

University of the West Indies, 25th anniv.

Dominica No. 1 and Map of Island — A56

Designs: 1c, 50c, No. 8 and post horn. 2c, $1.20, No. 9 and coat of arms. 10c, Like ½c.

1974, May 4 Litho. **Perf. 14½**

389	A56	½c brt pur & multi	.25	.25
390	A56	1c salmon & multi	.25	.25
391	A56	2c ultra & multi	.25	.25
392	A56	10c violet & multi	.25	.25
393	A56	50c yel grn & multi	.40	.40
394	A56	$1.20 rose & multi	.65	.65
a.		Souv. sheet, #392-394, perf. 15	1.60	1.60
		Nos. 389-394 (6)	2.05	2.05

Centenary of Dominican postage stamps.

Soccer Player and Cup, Brazilian Flag — A57

Soccer cup, various players and flags: 1c, Germany, Fed. Rep. 2c, Italy. 30c, Scotland. 40c, Sweden. 50c, Netherlands. $1, Yugoslavia.

1974, July Litho. **Perf. 14½**

395	A57	½c shown	.25	.25
396	A57	1c multicolored	.25	.25
397	A57	2c multicolored	.25	.25
398	A57	30c multicolored	.25	.25
399	A57	40c multicolored	.30	.30
400	A57	50c multicolored	.75	.75
401	A57	$1 multicolored	1.10	1.10
a.		Souvenir sheet of 2, #400-401, perf. 13½	1.25	1.25
		Nos. 395-401 (7)	3.15	3.15

World Cup Soccer Championship, Munich, June 13-July 7.

Indian Hole — A58

40c, Teachers' Training College. $1, Petite Savane Co-operative Bay Oil Distillery.

1974, Nov. 1 Litho. **Perf. 13½x14**

402	A58	10c multicolored	.25	.25
403	A58	40c multicolored	.25	.25
404	A58	$1 multicolored	.50	.50
a.		Souvenir sheet of 3, #402-404	.80	.80
		Nos. 402-404 (3)	1.00	1.00

Churchill at Race Track — A59

Sir Winston Churchill (1874-1965): 1c, with Gen. Eisenhower. 2c, with Franklin D. Roosevelt. 20c, as First Lord of the Admiralty. 45c, painting outdoors. $2, giving "V" sign.

1974, Nov. 25 Litho. **Perf. 14½**

405	A59	½c multicolored	.25	.25
406	A59	1c multicolored	.25	.25
407	A59	2c multicolored	.25	.25
408	A59	20c multicolored	.25	.25
409	A59	45c multicolored	.25	.25
410	A59	$2 multicolored	.50	.50
a.		Souvenir sheet of 2, #409-410, perf. 13½	1.25	1.25
		Nos. 405-410 (6)	1.75	1.75

Virgin and Child, by Oronzo Tiso — A60

Paintings (Virgin and Child): 1c, by Lorenzo Costa. 2c, by unknown Master. 10c, by G. F. Romanelli. 25c, Holy Family, by G. S. da Sermoneta. 45c, Adoration of the Shepherds,

DOMINICA

by Guido Reni. $1, Adoration of the Kings, by Cristoforo Caselli.

1974, Dec. 16   Litho.   Perf. 14

411	A60	½c multicolored	.25	.25
412	A60	1c multicolored	.25	.25
413	A60	2c multicolored	.25	.25
414	A60	10c multicolored	.25	.25
415	A60	25c multicolored	.25	.25
416	A60	45c multicolored	.35	.25
417	A60	$1 multicolored	.65	.50
a.		Souvenir sheet of 2, #416-417	1.10	1.10
		Nos. 411-417 (7)	2.25	2.00

Christmas.

Seamail, "Orinoco," 1851, and "Geesthaven," 1966 — A61

Cent. of UPU: $2, $2.40, Airmail, De Havilland 4, 1918, and Boeing 747, 1974.

1974, Dec. 4   Litho.   Perf. 13½

418	A61	10c multicolored	.25	.25
419	A61	$2 multicolored	1.25	1.25

Souvenir Sheet

419A		Sheet of 2	1.50	1.50
b.	A61 $1.20 multicolored		.45	.45
c.	A61 $2.40 multicolored		.90	.90

Nos. 418-419 were each printed in sheets of 50 and 5 + label.

Oldwife — A62

1c, Ocyurus chrysurus. 2c, Blue marlin. 3c, Swordfish. 20c, Great barracuda. $2, Grouper.

1975, June 2   Litho.   Perf. 14½

421	A62	½c shown	.25	.25
422	A62	1c multicolored	.25	.25
423	A62	2c multicolored	.25	.25
424	A62	3c multicolored	.25	.25
425	A62	20c multicolored	.90	.90
426	A62	$2 multicolored	2.75	2.75
a.		Souvenir sheet, perf. 13½	4.00	4.00
		Nos. 421-426 (6)	4.65	4.65

Myscelia Antholia — A63

Butterflies: 1c, Lycorea ceres. 2c, Siderone nemesis. 6c, Battus polydamas. 30c, Anartia lytrea. 40c, Morpho peleides. $2, Dryas Julia.

1975, July 28   Litho.   Perf. 14½

427	A63	½c shown	.25	.25
428	A63	1c multicolored	.25	.25
429	A63	2c multicolored	.25	.25
430	A63	6c multicolored	.75	.75
431	A63	30c multicolored	1.50	1.00
432	A63	40c multicolored	1.50	1.00
433	A63	$2 multicolored	2.25	6.75
a.		Souvenir sheet, perf. 13½	4.00	4.00
		Nos. 427-433 (7)	6.75	10.25

Royal Mail Ship Yare — A64

Ships Tied in with Dominican History: 1c, Royal mail ship Thames. 2c, Canadian National S.S. Lady Nelson. 20c, C.N. S.S. Lady Rodney. 45c, Harrison Line M.V. Statesman. 50c, Geest Line M.V. Geestcape. $2, Geest Line M.V. Geeststar.

1975, Sept. 1   Perf. 14

434	A64	½c black & multi	.40	.35
435	A64	1c black & multi	.40	.35
436	A64	2c black & multi	.45	.40
437	A64	20c black & multi	1.25	.60
438	A64	45c black & multi	1.50	.80
439	A64	50c black & multi	1.50	1.00
440	A64	$2 black & multi	2.50	4.50
a.		Souvenir sheet of 2, #439-440	4.00	4.00
		Nos. 434-440 (7)	8.00	8.00

IWY Emblem, Farm Women — A65

$2, IWY emblem, dressmaker & saleswoman.

1975, Oct. 30   Litho.   Perf. 14

441	A65	10c pink & multi	.25	.25
442	A65	$2 yellow & multi	.65	.65

International Women's Year.

Public Library — A66

5c, Miss Caribbean Queen 1975. 30c, Citrus factory. $1, National Day Cup.

1975, Nov. 6

443	A66	5c multi, vert.	.25	.25
444	A66	10c multi	.25	.25
445	A66	30c multi	.25	.25
446	A66	$1 multi, vert	.40	.40
a.		Souvenir sheet of 3	.90	.90
		Nos. 443-446 (4)	1.15	1.15

National Day. No. 446a contains 3 stamps similar to Nos. 444-446 with simulated perforations.

Virgin and Child, by Mantegna — A67

Christmas: Paintings of the Virgin and Child.

1975, Nov. 24

447	A67	½c shown	.25	.25
448	A67	1c Fra Filippo Lippi	.25	.25
449	A67	2c Bellini	.25	.25
450	A67	10c Botticelli	.25	.25
451	A67	25c Bellini	.25	.25
452	A67	45c Correggio	.25	.25
453	A67	$1 Durer	.50	.50
a.		Souvenir sheet of 2, #452-453	1.25	1.25
		Nos. 447-453 (7)	2.00	2.00

Hibiscus — A68   Queen Elizabeth II — A69

Designs: 1c, African tulip. 2c, Castor oil tree. 3c, White cedar flower. 4c, Eggplant. 5c, Garfish. 6c, Okra. 8c, Zenaida doves. 10c, Screw pine. 20c, Mangoes. 25c, Crayfish. 30c, Manicou. 40c, Bay leaf groves. 50c, Tomatoes. $1, Lime factory. $2, Rum distillery. $5, Bay oil distillery.

1975, Dec. 8   Litho.   Perf. 14½

454	A68	½c ultra & multi	.25	.80
455	A68	1c lilac & multi	.25	.80
456	A68	2c orange & multi	.25	.80
457	A68	3c multicolored	.25	.80
458	A68	4c pink & multi	.25	.80
459	A68	5c multicolored	.25	.80
460	A68	6c gray & multi	.25	1.00
461	A68	8c multicolored	3.25	1.10
462	A68	10c violet & multi	.25	.25
a.		Perf. 13½	30.00	—
463	A68	20c yellow & multi	.35	.25
464	A68	25c lemon & multi	.40	.25
465	A68	30c salmon & multi	.85	.80
466	A68	40c multicolored	.85	.80
467	A68	50c red & multi	.50	.50
468	A68	$1 citron & multi	.75	.65
469	A68	$2 multicolored	1.30	3.25
470	A68	$5 multicolored	1.60	5.00

471	A69	$10 blue & multi	2.25	14.50
		Nos. 454-471 (18)	14.10	33.15

Nos. 454-465 measure 38½mm x 25mm; nos. 466-470 measure 44½mm x 28mm. For overprints see Nos. 584-601, 640-643. All except 3c and 25c exist imperf.

American Infantry — A70

Designs: 1c, English three-decker, 1782. 2c, George Washington. 45c, English sailors. 75c, English ensign with regimental flag. $2, Admiral Hood. All designs have old maps in background.

1976, Apr. 12   Litho.   Perf. 14½

472	A70	½c green & multi	.25	.25
473	A70	1c purple & multi	.25	.25
474	A70	2c orange & multi	.25	.25
475	A70	45c brown & multi	.45	.25
476	A70	75c ultra & multi	.75	.75
477	A70	$2 red & multi	.90	1.50
a.		Souvenir sheet of 2	2.75	2.75
		Nos. 472-477 (6)	2.85	3.25

American Bicentennial. No. 477a contains 2 stamps similar to Nos. 476-477, perf. 13.

Rowing — A71

1c, Shot put. 2c, Swimming. 40c, Relay race. 45c, Gymnastics. 60c, Sailing. $2, Archery.

1976, May 24   Litho.   Perf. 14½

478	A71	½c ocher & multi	.25	.25
479	A71	1c ocher & multi	.25	.25
480	A71	2c ocher & multi	.25	.25
481	A71	40c ocher & multi	.25	.25
482	A71	45c ocher & multi	.25	.25
483	A71	60c ocher & multi	.25	.25
484	A71	$2 ocher & multi	.65	.65
a.		Souv. sheet of #483-484, perf 13	1.75	1.75
		Nos. 478-484 (7)	2.15	2.15

21st Olympic Games, Montreal, Canada, July 17-Aug. 1.

Ringed Kingfisher — A72

Birds: 1c, Mourning dove. 2c, Green heron. 15c, Broad-winged hawk. 30c, Blue-headed hummingbird. 45c, Banana-quit. $2, Imperial parrot. 15c, 30c, 45c, $2, vert.

1976, June 28

485	A72	½c multicolored	.25	.25
486	A72	1c multicolored	.25	.25
487	A72	2c multicolored	.25	.25
488	A72	15c multicolored	.90	.90
489	A72	30c multicolored	1.25	1.25
490	A72	45c multicolored	1.50	1.50
491	A72	$2 multicolored	3.00	3.00
a.		Souv. sheet of 3, #489-491, perf. 13	7.00	7.00
		Nos. 485-491 (7)	7.40	7.40

Map of West Indies, Bats, Wicket and Ball — A72a   Prudential Cup — A72b

1976, July 26   Litho.   Perf. 14

492	A72a	15c lt blue & multi	.45	.45
493	A72b	25c lilac rose & black	.85	.85

World Cricket Cup, won by West Indies Team, 1975.

Viking Spacecraft — A73

1c, Titan launch center, horiz. 2c, Titan 3-D & Centaur D-IT. 3c, Orbiter & landing capsule. 45c, Capsule with closed parachute. 75c, Capsule with open parachute. $1, Landing capsule descending on Mars, horiz. $2, Viking on Mars, horiz.

1976, Sept. 20   Litho.   Perf. 15

494	A73	½c multicolored	.25	.25
495	A73	1c multicolored	.25	.25
496	A73	2c multicolored	.25	.25
497	A73	3c multicolored	.25	.25
498	A73	45c multicolored	.25	.25
499	A73	75c multicolored	.30	.30
500	A73	$1 multicolored	.35	.35
501	A73	$2 multicolored	.00	.00
a.		Souvenir sheet of 2, #500, 501, perf. 13	1.75	1.75
		Nos. 494-501 (8)	2.50	2.50

Viking mission to Mars.

Virgin and Child, by Giorgione — A74

Virgin and Child by: 1c, Bellini. 2c, Mantegna. 6c, Mantegna. 25c, Memling. 45c, 50c, Correggio. $1, $3, Raphael.

1976, Nov. 1   Litho.   Perf. 14

502	A74	½c multicolored	.25	.25
503	A74	1c multicolored	.25	.25
504	A74	2c multicolored	.25	.25
505	A74	6c multicolored	.25	.25
506	A74	25c multicolored	.25	.25
507	A74	45c multicolored	.25	.25
508	A74	$3 multicolored	.60	.60
		Nos. 502-508 (7)	2.10	2.10

Souvenir Sheet

509		Sheet of 2	1.10	1.10
a.	A74 50c multicolored		.35	.35
b.	A74 $1 multicolored		.75	.75

Christmas.

Island Craft Co-operative — A75

National Day: 50c, Banana harvest, Castle Bruce Co-operative. $1, Banana shipping plant, Bourne Farmers' Co-operative.

1976, Nov. 22   Litho.   Perf. 13½x14

510	A75	10c multicolored	.25	.25
511	A75	50c multicolored	.25	.25
512	A75	$1 multicolored	.30	.30
a.		Souvenir sheet of 3, #510-512	.75	.75
		Nos. 510-512 (3)	.80	.80

Common Sundial — A76

Sea Shells: 1c, Flame helmet. 2c, Mouse cone. 20c, Caribbean vase. 40c, West Indian fighting conch. 50c, Short coral shell. $2, Long-spined star shell. $3, Apple murex.

1976, Dec. 20   Litho.   Perf. 14

513	A76	½c black & multi	.25	.25
514	A76	1c black & multi	.25	.25
515	A76	2c black & multi	.25	.25

DOMINICA

516	A76	20c black & multi	.30	.25
517	A76	40c black & multi	.55	.45
518	A76	50c black & multi	.60	.60
519	A76	$3 black & multi	2.25	2.25
		Nos. 513-519 (7)	4.45	4.20

Souvenir Sheet

520	A76	$2 black & multi	2.00	2.00

Queen Enthroned — A77

Designs: 1c, Imperial crown. 45c, Elizabeth II and Princess Anne. $2, Coronation ring. $2.50, Ampulla and spoon. $5, Royal visit to Dominica.

1977, Feb. 7   *Perf. 14*

521	A77	½c multicolored	.25	.25
522	A77	1c multicolored	.25	.25
523	A77	45c multicolored	.25	.25
524	A77	$2 multicolored	.35	.35
525	A77	$2.50 multicolored	.50	.50
		Nos. 521-525 (5)	1.60	1.60

Souvenir Sheet

526	A77	$5 multicolored	1.40	1.40

25th anniv. of the reign of Elizabeth II.
Nos. 521-525 were printed in sheets of 40 (4x10), perf. 14, and sheets of 5 plus label, perf. 12, in changed colors.
For overprints see Nos. 549-554.

Joseph Haydn — A78

Designs: 1c, Fidelio, act I, scene IV. 2c, Dancer Maria Casentini. 15c, Beethoven working on Pastoral Symphony. 30c, "Wellington's Victory." 40c, Soprano Henriette Sontag. $2, Young Beethoven.

1977, Apr. 25   *Litho.*   *Perf. 14*

527	A78	½c multicolored	.25	.25
528	A78	1c multicolored	.25	.25
529	A78	2c multicolored	.25	.25
530	A78	15c multicolored	.50	.50
531	A78	30c multicolored	.50	.50
532	A78	40c multicolored	.50	.50
533	A78	$2 multicolored	1.60	1.60
a.		Souvenir sheet of 3, #531-533	2.60	2.60
		Nos. 527-533 (7)	3.85	3.85

Ludwig van Beethoven (1770-1827), composer.

Boy Scouts on Hike — A79

Saluting Boy Scout and: 1c, First aid. 2c, Scouts setting up camp. 45c, Rock climbing. 50c, Kayaking. 75c, Map reading. $2, Campfire. $3, Sailing.

1977, Aug. 8   *Litho.*   *Perf. 14*

534	A79	½c multicolored	.25	.25
535	A79	1c multicolored	.25	.25
536	A79	2c multicolored	.25	.25
537	A79	45c multicolored	.35	.35
538	A79	50c multicolored	.50	.50
539	A79	$3 multicolored	2.00	2.00
		Nos. 534-539 (6)	3.60	3.60

Souvenir Sheet

540		Sheet of 2	1.90	1.90
a.		A79 75c multicolored	.55	.55
b.		A79 $2 multicolored	1.35	1.35

6th Caribbean Jamboree, Kingston, Jamaica, Aug. 5-14.

Nativity — A80

Christmas: 1c, Annunciation to the Shepherds. 2c, 45c, Presentation at the Temple (different). 6c, $2, $3, Flight into Egypt (different). 15c, Adoration of the Kings. 50c, Virgin and Child with Angels. ½c to 45c are illustrations from De Lisle Psalter, 14th century. 50c, $2, $3 are from other Psalters.

1977, Nov. 14   *Litho.*   *Perf. 14*

541	A80	½c multicolored	.25	.25
542	A80	1c multicolored	.25	.25
543	A80	2c multicolored	.25	.25
544	A80	6c multicolored	.25	.25
545	A80	15c multicolored	.25	.25
546	A80	45c multicolored	.35	.35
547	A80	$3 multicolored	.85	.85
		Nos. 541-547 (7)	2.45	2.45

Souvenir Sheet

548		Sheet of 2	1.35	1.35
a.		A80 50c multicolored	.25	.25
b.		A80 $2 multicolored	1.10	1.10

Nos. 521-526 Overprinted

1977, Nov. 24   *Litho.*   *Perf. 12, 14*

549	A77	½c multicolored	.25	.25
550	A77	1c multicolored	.25	.25
551	A77	45c multicolored	.25	.25
552	A77	$2 multicolored	.40	.40
553	A77	$2.50 multicolored	.45	.45
		Nos. 549-553 (5)	1.60	1.60

Souvenir Sheet
Perf. 14

554	A77	$5 multicolored	1.10	1.10

Caribbean visit of Queen Elizabeth II. Nos. 549-550 are perf. 12, others perf. 12 and 14.
Two types of No. 554: I. Overprinted only on stamp. II. Overprinted "W.I. 1977" on stamp and "Royal Visit W.I. 1977" on margin.

Masqueraders — A81

Designs: 1c, Sensay costume. 2c, Street musicians. 45c, Douiette band. 50c, Pappy Show wedding. $2, $2.50, Masquerade band.

1978, Jan. 9   *Perf. 14*

555	A81	½c multicolored	.25	.25
556	A81	1c multicolored	.25	.25
557	A81	2c multicolored	.25	.25
558	A81	45c multicolored	.25	.25
559	A81	50c multicolored	.30	.30
560	A81	$2 multicolored	.50	.50
		Nos. 555-560 (6)	1.80	1.80

Souvenir Sheet

561	A81	$2.50 multicolored	1.50	1.50

History of Carnival.

Lindbergh and Spirit of St. Louis — A82

Designs: 10c, Spirit of St. Louis take-off, Long Island, May 20, 1927. 15c, Lindbergh and map of route New York to Paris. 20c, Lindbergh and plane in Paris. 40c, 1st Zeppelin, trial over Lake Constance. 50c, Spirit of St. Louis. 60c, Count Zeppelin and Zeppelin LZ-2, 1906. $2, Graf Zeppelin, 1928. $3, LZ-127, 1928.

1978, Mar. 13   *Litho.*   *Perf. 14½*

562	A82	6c multicolored	.25	.25
563	A82	10c multicolored	.25	.25
564	A82	15c multicolored	.30	.30
565	A82	20c multicolored	.40	.40
566	A82	40c multicolored	.60	.60
567	A82	60c multicolored	.85	.85
568	A82	$3 multicolored	2.25	2.25
		Nos. 562-568 (7)	4.90	4.90

Souvenir Sheet

569		Sheet of 2	2.00	2.00
a.		A82 50c multicolored	.40	.40
b.		A82 $2 multicolored	1.60	1.60

Charles A. Lindbergh's solo transatlantic flight from New York to Paris, 50th anniv., and flights of Graf Zeppelin.

Royal Family on Balcony — A83

Designs: 45c, Coronation. $2.50, Elizabeth II and Prince Philip. $5, Elizabeth II.

1978, June 2   *Litho.*   *Perf. 14*

570	A83	45c multicolored	.25	.25
571	A83	$2 multicolored	.45	.45
572	A83	$2.50 multicolored	.55	.55
		Nos. 570-572 (3)	1.25	1.25

Souvenir Sheet

573	A83	$5 multicolored	1.00	1.00

Coronation of Queen Elizabeth II, 25th anniv. Nos. 570-572 were issued in sheets of 50, and in sheets of 3 stamps and label, in changed colors, perf. 12.

Wright Plane Coming out of Hangar — A84

Designs: 40c, 1908 plane. 60c, Flyer I gliding. $2, Flyer I taking off. $3, Wilbur and Orville Wright and Flyer I.

1978, July 10   *Litho.*   *Perf. 14½*

574	A84	30c multicolored	.25	.25
575	A84	45c multicolored	.25	.25
576	A84	60c multicolored	.30	.30
577	A84	$2 multicolored	1.25	1.25
		Nos. 574-577 (4)	2.05	2.05

Souvenir Sheet

578	A84	$3 multicolored	1.75	1.75

75th anniv. of first powered flight.
A set of 30 stamps embossed on gold foil exists. Value, $400.

Two Apostles, by Rubens — A85

Rubens Paintings: 45c, Descent from the Cross. 50c, St. Ildefonso Receiving Chasuble. $2, Holy Family. $3, Assumption of the Virgin.

1978, Oct. 16   *Litho.*   *Perf. 14*

579	A85	20c multicolored	.25	.25
580	A85	45c multicolored	.25	.25
581	A85	50c multicolored	.25	.25
582	A85	$3 multicolored	.90	.90
		Nos. 579-582 (4)	1.65	1.65

Souvenir Sheet

583	A85	$2 multicolored	1.00	1.00

Christmas.

Nos. 454-471 Overprinted

1978 Nov. 1   *Litho.*   *Perf. 14½*

584	A68	½c ultra & multi	.25	.25
585	A68	1c lilac & multi	.25	.25
586	A68	2c orange & multi	.30	.25
587	A68	3c multicolored	.30	.25
588	A68	4c pink & multi	.30	.25
589	A68	5c multicolored	.30	.25
590	A68	6c gray & multi	.35	.25
591	A68	8c multicolored	3.00	.25
592	A68	10c violet & multi	1.00	.25
a.		Perf. 13½ ('79)	.50	.25
593	A68	20c yellow & multi	.60	.25
594	A68	25c lemon & multi	.65	.25
595	A68	30c salmon & multi	.70	.25
596	A68	40c multicolored	.70	.55
597	A68	50c red & multi	.75	.75
598	A68	$1 citron & multi	.80	1.40
599	A68	$2 multicolored	1.50	2.75
600	A68	$5 multicolored	2.00	5.50

Perf. 14

601	A69	$10 blue & multi	3.00	12.50
		Nos. 584-601 (18)	16.75	26.50

Map of Dominica with Parishes — A86

25c, Sabinea carinalis, natl. flower, & map. 45c, New flag & map. 50c, Coat of arms & map. $2, Prime Minister Patrick John.

1978, Nov. 1   *Perf. 14*

602	A86	10c multicolored	.75	.40
603	A86	25c multicolored	.55	.25
604	A86	45c multicolored	1.50	.35
605	A86	50c multicolored	.65	.35
606	A86	$2 multicolored	1.50	2.75
		Nos. 602-606 (5)	4.95	4.10

Souvenir Sheet

607	A86	$2.50 multicolored	2.60	2.60

Dominican independence.

Rowland Hill — A87

45c, Great Britain #2. 50c, Dominica #1. $2, Maltese Cross handstamps. $5, Penny Black.

1979, Mar. 19

608	A87	25c multicolored	.25	.25
609	A87	45c multicolored	.25	.25
610	A87	50c multicolored	.25	.25
611	A87	$2 multicolored	.35	.35
		Nos. 608-611 (4)	1.10	1.10

Souvenir Sheet

612	A87	$5 multicolored	1.40	1.40

Sir Rowland Hill (1795-1879), originator of penny postage.
Nos. 608-611 printed in sheets of 5 plus label, perf. 12x12½, in changed colors.
For overprints see Nos. 663A-663D.

Boys and Dugout Canoe — A88

IYC Emblem and: 40c, Children carrying bananas. 50c, Boys playing cricket. $3, Child feeding rabbits. $5, Boy showing catch of fish.

1979, Apr. 23   *Litho.*   *Perf. 14*

613	A88	20c multicolored	.30	.30
614	A88	40c multicolored	.45	.45
615	A88	50c multicolored	.50	.50
616	A88	$3 multicolored	2.00	2.00
		Nos. 613-616 (4)	3.25	3.25

Souvenir Sheet

617	A88	$5 multicolored	2.00	2.00

Grouper — A89

30c, Striped dolphin. 50c, White-tailed tropic birds. 60c, Brown pelicans. $1, Pilot whale. $2, Brown booby. $3, Elkhorn coral.

1979, May 21   *Litho.*   *Perf. 14*

618	A89	10c multicolored	.50	.25
619	A89	30c multicolored	1.00	.50
620	A89	50c multicolored	1.75	.75
621	A89	60c multicolored	2.00	2.00
622	A89	$1 multicolored	2.50	2.50
623	A89	$2 multicolored	4.25	4.25
		Nos. 618-623 (6)	12.00	10.25

Souvenir Sheet

624	A89	$3 multicolored	2.75	2.75

Wildlife protection.

DOMINICA 205

Capt. Cook, Bark
Endeavour
A90

Capt. Cook and: 50c, Resolution, map of 2nd voyage. 60c, Discovery, map of 3rd voyage. $2, Cook's map of New Zealand, 1770. $5, Portrait.

1979, July 16   Litho.   *Perf. 14*
625	A90	10c multicolored	.60 .40
626	A90	50c multicolored	1.00 1.00
627	A90	60c multicolored	1.25 1.25
628	A90	$2 multicolored	1.50 2.50
	Nos. 625-628 (4)		4.35 5.15

Souvenir Sheet
629	A90	$5 multicolored	2.00 2.00

200th death anniv. of Capt. James Cook (1728-1779).

Girl Guides
Cooking — A91

Girl Guides: 20c, Setting up emergency rain tent. 50c, Raising flag of independent Dominica. $2.50, Playing accordion and singing. $3, Leader and Guides of different ages.

1979, July 30
630	A91	10c multicolored	.25 .25
631	A91	20c multicolored	.25 .25
632	A91	50c multicolored	.60 .60
633	A91	$2.50 multicolored	1.25 1.25
	Nos. 630-633 (4)		2.05 2.05

Souvenir Sheet
634	A91	$3 multicolored	1.50 1.50

50th anniv. of Dominican Girl Guides.

Colvillea — A92

Flowering Trees: 40c, Lignum vitae. 60c, Dwarf poinciana. $2, Fern tree. $3, Perfume tree.

1979, Sept. 3   Litho.   *Perf. 14*
635	A92	20c multicolored	.25 .25
636	A92	40c multicolored	.25 .25
637	A92	60c multicolored	.35 .35
638	A92	$2 multicolored	.90 .90
	Nos. 635-638 (4)		1.75 1.75

Souvenir Sheet
639	A92	$3 multicolored	1.75 1.75

Nos. 459, 466, 470-471 Overprinted

No. 640   No. 643

Perf. 14½, 13½, 13½x14, 14
1979, Oct. 29   Litho.
640	A68	5c multicolored	.25 .25
641	A68	40c multicolored	.30 .30
642	A68	$5 multicolored	2.00 2.00
643	A69	$10 multicolored	3.50 3.50
	Nos. 640-643 (4)		6.05 6.05

Hurricane devastation, Aug. 29. Vertical overprint on No. 643, others horizontal.

Music
Scenes — A92a

½c, Mickey Mouse. 1c, Goofy playing guitar. 2c, Mickey Mouse and Goofy. 3c, Donald Duck. 4c, Minnie Mouse. 5c, Goofy playing accordion. 10c, Horace Horsecollar and Dale. $2, Huey, Dewey, Louie. $2.50, Donald and Huey.
$3, Mickey Mouse playing piano.

1979, Nov. 2   Litho.   *Perf. 11*
644	A92a	½c multicolored	.25 .25
645	A92a	1c multicolored	.25 .25
646	A92a	2c multicolored	.25 .25
647	A92a	3c multicolored	.25 .25
648	A92a	4c multicolored	.25 .25
649	A92a	5c multicolored	.25 .25
650	A92a	10c multicolored	.25 .25
651	A92a	$2 multicolored	1.50 1.50
652	A92a	$2.50 multicolored	1.50 1.50
	Nos. 644-652 (9)		4.75 4.75

Souvenir Sheet
Perf. 13
653	A92a	$3 multicolored	3.25 3.25

Cathedral of the
Assumption
A93

Cathedrals: 40c, St. Patrick's, New York. 45c, St. Paul's, London, vert. 60c, St. Peter's, Rome. $2, Cologne Cathedral. $3, Notre Dame, Paris, vert.

1979, Nov. 26   Litho.   *Perf. 14*
654	A93	6c multicolored	.25 .25
655	A93	45c multicolored	.25 .25
656	A93	60c multicolored	.25 .25
657	A93	$3 multicolored	.90 .90
	Nos. 654-657 (4)		1.65 1.65

Souvenir Sheet
658		Sheet of 2	.80 .80
a.		A93 40c multicolored	.25 .25
b.		A93 $2 multicolored	.55 .55

Christmas.

Nurse and
Patients, Rotary
Emblem — A94

20c, Electrocardiogram machine. 40c, Mental hospital. $2.50, Paul Harris, founder. $3, Map of Africa and Europe.

1980, Mar. 31   Litho.   *Perf. 14*
659	A94	10c shown	.25 .25
660	A94	20c multicolored	.25 .25
661	A94	40c multicolored	.25 .25
662	A94	$2.50 multicolored	.75 .75
	Nos. 659-662 (4)		1.50 1.50

Souvenir Sheet
663	A94	$3 multicolored	1.25 1.25

Rotary International, 75th anniv. Nos. 659-662 each contain quadrant of Rotary emblem.

Nos. 608-611
Overprinted in Black

1980, May 6   Litho.   *Perf. 12*
663A	A87	25c multicolored	.35 .35
663B	A87	45c multicolored	.55 .55
663C	A87	50c multicolored	.60 .60
663D	A87	$2 multicolored	1.50 1.50
	Nos. 663A-663D (4)		3.00 3.00

London 80 Intl. Stamp Exhib., May 6-14.

Shot Put,
Moscow '80
Emblem — A95

1980, May 27   Litho.   *Perf. 14*
664	A95	30c shown	.25 .25
665	A95	40c Basketball	.60 .30
666	A95	60c Swimming	.40 .40
667	A95	$2 Gymnast	.70 .70
	Nos. 664-667 (4)		1.95 1.65

Souvenir Sheet
668	A95	$3 Running	1.25 1.25

22nd Summer Olympic Games, Moscow, July 19-Aug. 3.

Embarkation
for Cythera,
by Watteau
A96

Paintings: 20c, Supper at Emmaus, by Caravaggio. 25c, Charles I Hunting, by van Dyck, vert. 30c, The Maids of Honor, by Velazquez, vert. 45c, Rape of the Sabine Women, by Poussin. $1, Embarkation for Cythera, by Watteau. $3, Holy Family, by Rembrandt. $5, Girl before a Mirror, by Picasso, vert.

Perf. 14x13½, 13½x14
1980, July 22   Litho.
669	A96	20c multicolored	.25 .25
670	A96	25c multicolored	.25 .25
671	A96	30c multicolored	.25 .25
672	A96	45c multicolored	.25 .25
673	A96	$1 multicolored	.40 .40
674	A96	$5 multicolored	1.50 1.50
	Nos. 669-674 (6)		2.90 2.90

Souvenir Sheet
675	A96	$3 multicolored	1.10 1.10

Queen Mother
Elizabeth, 80th
Birthday — A97

1980, Aug. 4   *Perf. 12, 14*
676	A97	40c multicolored	.25 .25
677	A97	$2.50 multicolored	.50 .50

Souvenir Sheet
678	A97	$3 multicolored	.75 .75

Tinkerbell
A98

Designs: Scenes from Disney's Peter Pan.

1980, Oct. 1   Litho.   *Perf. 11*
679	A98	½c multicolored	.25 .25
680	A98	1c multicolored	.25 .25
681	A98	2c multicolored	.25 .25
682	A98	3c multicolored	.25 .25
683	A98	4c multicolored	.25 .25
684	A98	5c multicolored	.25 .25
685	A98	10c multicolored	.25 .25
686	A98	$2 multicolored	2.25 1.60
687	A98	$2.50 multicolored	2.25 1.75
	Nos. 679-687 (9)		6.25 5.10

Souvenir Sheet
688	A98	$4 multicolored	5.00 5.00

Christmas.

Douglas
Bay — A99

30c, Valley of Desolation. 40c, Emerald Pool, vert. $3, Indian River, vert.
$4, Trafalgar Falls.

1981, Feb. 12   Litho.   *Perf. 14*
689	A99	20c shown	.25 .25
690	A99	30c multicolored	.25 .25
691	A99	40c multicolored	.25 .25
692	A99	$3 multicolored	.70 .70
	Nos. 689-692 (4)		1.45 1.45

Souvenir Sheet
693	A99	$4 multicolored	1.40 1.40

Pluto and
Fifi — A100

$4, Pluto in Blue Note (1947 cartoon).

1981, Apr. 30   Litho.   *Perf. 13½x14*
694	A100	$2 multicolored	1.75 1.75

Souvenir Sheet
695	A100	$4 multicolored	2.75 2.75

50th anniversary of Walt Disney's Pluto.

Forest
Thrush — A101

30c, Stolid flycatcher. 40c, Blue-hooded euphonia. $5, Lesser antillean peewee.
$3, Sisserou parrot.

1981, Apr. 30   *Perf. 14*
696	A101	20c shown	.60 .25
697	A101	30c multicolored	.70 .35
698	A101	40c multicolored	.80 .45
699	A101	$5 multicolored	4.75 4.75
	Nos. 696-699 (4)		6.85 5.80

Souvenir Sheet
700	A101	$3 multicolored	3.75 3.75

Royal Wedding Issue
Common Design Type

45c, Couple. 60c, Windsor Castle. $4, Charles.
$5, Helicopter.

1981, June 16   Litho.   *Perf. 14*
701	CD331a	45c multi	.25 .25
702	CD331a	60c multi	.25 .25
703	CD331a	$4 multi	.60 .60
	Nos. 701-703 (3)		1.10 1.10

Souvenir Sheet
704	CD331	$5 multi	1.25 1.25

Booklet
705	CD331	multi	6.00
a.		Pane of 6 (3x25c, Lady Diana, 3x$2, Charles)	2.25 4.50
b.		Pane of 1, $5, Couple	3.00 3.50

No. 705 contains imperf., self-adhesive stamps.

Nos. 701-703 also printed in sheets of 5 plus label, perf. 12, in changed colors. Value, set of three sheets $10.

Elves
Repairing
Santa's
Sleigh
A102

Christmas: Scenes from Walt Disney's Santa's Workshop.

1981, Nov. 2   Litho.   *Perf. 14*
706	A102	½c multicolored	.25 .25
707	A102	1c multicolored	.25 .25
708	A102	2c multicolored	.25 .25
709	A102	3c multicolored	.25 .25
710	A102	4c multicolored	.25 .25
711	A102	5c multicolored	.25 .25
712	A102	10c multicolored	.25 .25
713	A102	45c multicolored	2.00 .40
714	A102	$5 multicolored	4.00 5.50
	Nos. 706-714 (9)		7.75 7.65

Souvenir Sheet
715	A102	$4 multicolored	5.75 5.75

DOMINICA

Ixora — A103

2c, Flamboyant. 4c, Poinsettia. 5c, Sabinea carinalis. 8c, Annatto roucou. 10c, Passion fruit. 15c, Breadfruit. 20c, Allamanda buttercup. 25c, Cashew. 35c, Soursop. 40c, Bougainvillea. 45c, Anthurium. 60c, Cacao. 90c, Pawpaw tree. $1, Coconut palm. $2, Coffee tree. $5, Lobster claw. $10, Banana fig.

1981, Dec. 1		Litho.	Perf. 14	
716	A103	1c shown	.25	.90
717	A103	2c multicolored	.25	.90
718	A103	4c multicolored	.25	.90
719	A103	5c multicolored	.25	.60
720	A103	8c multicolored	.25	.90
721	A103	10c multicolored	.30	.90
722	A103	15c multicolored	.50	.50
723	A103	20c multicolored	.35	.25
724	A103	25c multicolored	.40	.25
725	A103	35c multicolored	.45	.40
726	A103	40c multicolored	.45	.65
727	A103	45c multicolored	.50	.70
728	A103	60c multicolored	1.00	.95
729	A103	90c multicolored	.75	1.40
730	A103	$1 multicolored	2.00	1.50
731	A103	$2 multicolored	1.50	3.00
732	A103	$5 multicolored	2.00	7.00
c.		Perf. 12½x12 ('85)	3.25	5.00
733	A103	$10 multicolored	3.50	13.00
		Nos. 716-733 (18)	14.95	34.05

For overprints see Nos. 852-853.

1984	Inscribed "1984"		Perf. 12	
721a	A103	10c	1.75	.40
730a	A103	$1	2.50	3.00
732a	A103	$5	3.25	5.00
733a	A103	$10	5.25	10.00
		Nos. 721a-733a (4)	12.75	18.40

1985	Inscribed "1985"		Perf. 14	
721b	A103	10c	1.00	.65
722b	A103	15c Breadfruit	4.00	2.00
728b	A103	60c Cacao	5.00	3.50
732b	A103	$5 Lobster claw	3.25	5.00
		Nos. 721b-732b (4)	13.25	11.15

Intl. Year of the Disabled — A104

45c, Ramp curb. 60c, Bus steps. 75c, Hand-operated car. $4, Bus lift. $5, Elevator buttons.

1981, Dec. 22		Litho.	Perf. 14	
734	A104	45c multicolored	.45	.30
735	A104	60c multicolored	.55	.40
736	A104	75c multicolored	.65	.50
737	A104	$4 multicolored	2.00	2.40
		Nos. 734-737 (4)	3.65	3.60
		Souvenir Sheet		
738	A104		5.00	5.00

Bathers, by Picasso — A105

45c, Olga in Armchair. 75c, Woman in Spanish Costume. $4, Dog and Cock. $5, Sleeping Peasants.

1981, Dec. 30			Perf. 14½	
739	A105	45c multicolored	.30	.30
740	A105	60c shown	.40	.40
741	A105	75c multicolored	.50	.50
742	A105	$4 multicolored	2.25	2.25
		Nos. 739-742 (4)	3.45	3.45
		Souvenir Sheet		
743	A105	$5 multicolored	4.00	4.00

1982 World Cup Soccer A106

Various Disney characters playing soccer.

1982, Jan. 29			Perf. 14	
744	A106	½c multicolored	.25	.25
745	A106	1c multicolored	.25	.25
746	A106	2c multicolored	.25	.25
747	A106	3c multicolored	.25	.25
748	A106	4c multicolored	.25	.25
749	A106	5c multicolored	.25	.25
750	A106	10c multicolored	.25	.25
751	A106	60c multicolored	1.25	1.25
752	A106	$5 multicolored	6.25	6.25
		Nos. 744-752 (9)	9.25	9.25
		Souvenir Sheet		
753	A106	$4 multicolored	5.75	5.75

Golden Days, by Norman Rockwell — A107

25c, The Morning News. 45c, The Marbles Champ. $1, Speeding Along.

1982, Mar. 10		Litho.	Perf. 14x13½	
754	A107	10c shown	.25	.25
755	A107	25c multicolored	.25	.25
756	A107	45c multicolored	.30	.30
757	A107	$1 multicolored	.55	.55
		Nos. 754-757 (4)	1.35	1.35

Intl. Decade for Women (1975-85) A108

Famous Women: 10c, Elma Napier (1890-1973), first woman elected to Legislative Council in British West Indies, 1940. 45c, Margaret Mead (1901-1978), anthropologist. $1, Mabel Caudiron (1909-1968), musician and folk historian. $3, Florence Nightingale, founder of modern nursing. $4, Eleanor Roosevelt.

1982, Apr. 15		Litho.	Perf. 14	
758	A108	10c multicolored	.25	.25
759	A108	45c multicolored	.35	.35
760	A108	$1 multicolored	.60	.60
761	A108	$4 multicolored	2.50	2.50
		Nos. 758-761 (4)	3.70	3.70
		Souvenir Sheet		
762	A108	$3 multicolored	3.00	3.00

A109

Washington or Roosevelt and: 45c, George Washington and Independence Hall, Philadelphia. 60c, The Capitol Building. 90c, The Surrender of Cornwallis, by John Trumbull. $2, Dam construction during New Deal (mural by William Gropper). $5, Washington, Roosevelt.

1982, May 1			Perf. 14½	
763	A109	45c multicolored	.35	.35
764	A109	60c multicolored	.40	.40
765	A109	90c multicolored	.55	.55
766	A109	$2 multicolored	1.00	1.00
		Nos. 763-766 (4)	2.30	2.30
		Souvenir Sheet		
767	A109	$5 multicolored	3.00	3.00

George Washington's 250th birth anniv. and Franklin D. Roosevelt's birth cent.

Godman's Leaf Butterfly — A110

45c, Zebra. 60c, Mimic. $3, Red rim. $5, Southern dagger tail.

1982, June 1		Litho.	Perf. 14	
768	A110	15c shown	1.75	1.75
769	A110	45c multicolored	2.75	2.75
770	A110	60c multicolored	3.00	3.00
771	A110	$3 multicolored	6.25	6.25
		Nos. 768-771 (4)	13.75	13.75
		Souvenir Sheet		
772	A110	$5 multicolored	7.00	7.00

Princess Diana Issue
Common Design Type

45c, Buckingham Palace. $2, Engagement portrait. $4, Diana in wedding dress. $5, Diana sitting in chair in white dress.

1982, July 1		Litho.	Perf. 14½x14	
773	CD332	45c multicolored	.30	.30
774	CD332	$2 multicolored	1.00	1.00
775	CD332	$4 multicolored	2.25	2.25
		Nos. 773-775 (3)	3.55	3.55
		Souvenir Sheet		
776	CD332	$5 multicolored	3.50	3.50

Also issued in sheet of 5 plus label. For overprints see Nos. 782-785.

Scouting Year — A111

45c, Cooking. 60c, Meteorological study. 75c, Sisserou parrot, cub scouts. $3, Canoeing, Indian River. $5, Flagbearer.

1982, July 1		Litho.	Perf. 14	
777	A111	45c multicolored	1.25	1.25
778	A111	60c multicolored	1.75	1.75
779	A111	75c multicolored	2.25	2.25
780	A111	$3 multicolored	5.25	5.25
		Nos. 777-780 (4)	10.50	10.50
		Souvenir Sheet		
781	A111	$5 multicolored	3.50	3.50

Nos. 773-776 Overprinted

1982, Sept. 1		Litho.	Perf. 14½x14	
782	CD332	45c multicolored	.30	.30
783	CD332	$2 multicolored	1.00	1.00
784	CD332	$4 multicolored	2.25	2.25
		Nos. 782-784 (3)	3.55	3.55
		Souvenir Sheet		
785	CD332	$5 multicolored	3.50	3.50

Birth of Prince William of Wales, June 21. Also issued in sheet of 5 plus label.

Christmas — A112

Holy Family Paintings by Raphael.

1982, Oct. 18		Litho.	Perf. 14	
786	A112	25c multicolored	.25	.25
787	A112	30c multicolored	.25	.25
788	A112	90c multicolored	.40	.40
789	A112	$4 multicolored	1.75	1.75
		Nos. 786-789 (4)	2.65	2.65
		Souvenir Sheet		
790	A112	$5 multicolored	3.50	3.50

Goosebeak Whale Eating Squid — A113

60c, Humpback whale. 75c, Great right whale. $3, Melonhead whale. $5, Pygmy sperm whale.

1983, Feb. 15		Litho.	Perf. 14	
791	A113	45c shown	1.75	1.75
792	A113	60c multicolored	2.00	2.00
793	A113	75c multicolored	2.25	2.25
794	A113	$3 multicolored	7.50	7.50
		Nos. 791-794 (4)	13.50	13.50
		Souvenir Sheet		
795	A113	$5 multicolored	6.25	6.25

Commonwealth Day — A113a

25c, Banana industry. 30c, Road construction. 90c, Community nursing. $3, Basket weavers.

1983, Mar. 14				
796	A113a	25c multicolored	.25	.25
797	A113a	30c multicolored	.25	.25
798	A113a	90c multicolored	.40	.40
799	A113a	$3 multicolored	1.25	1.25
		Nos. 796-799 (4)	2.15	2.15

World Communications Year — A114

45c, Hurricane pattern, map. 60c, Air-to-ship communication. 90c, Columbia shuttle, dish antenna. $2, Walkie-talkie. $5, Satellite.

1983, Apr. 18		Litho.	Perf. 14	
800	A114	45c multicolored	.30	.30
801	A114	60c multicolored	.35	.35
802	A114	90c multicolored	.50	.50
803	A114	$2 multicolored	1.00	1.00
		Nos. 800-803 (4)	2.15	2.15
		Souvenir Sheet		
804	A114	$5 multicolored	2.50	2.50

Manned Flight Bicentenary A115

45c, Mayo Composite. 60c, Macchi M-39. 90c, Fairey Swordfish. $4, Zeppelin LZ-3. $5, Double Eagle II, vert.

1983, July 19		Litho.	Perf. 15	
805	A115	45c multicolored	.50	.50
806	A115	60c multicolored	.60	.60
807	A115	90c multicolored	.85	.85
808	A115	$4 multicolored	3.00	3.00
		Nos. 805-808 (4)	4.95	4.95
		Souvenir Sheet		
809	A115	$5 multicolored	3.00	3.00

Duesenberg SJ, 1935 — A116

45c, Studebaker Avanti, 1962. 60c, Cord 812, 1936. 75c, MG-TC, 1945. 90c, Camaro 350-SS, 1967. $3, Porsche 356, 1948. $5, Ferrari 312-T, 1975.

1983, Sept. 1		Litho.	Perf. 14	
810	A116	10c shown	.35	.35
811	A116	45c multicolored	.45	.45
812	A116	60c multicolored	.50	.50
813	A116	75c multicolored	.55	.55
814	A116	90c multicolored	.60	.60
815	A116	$3 multicolored	1.75	1.75
		Nos. 810-815 (6)	4.20	4.20
		Souvenir Sheet		
816	A116	$5 multicolored	3.00	3.00

DOMINICA 207

Christmas
A117

Raphael Paintings.

1983, Oct. 4	Litho.	Perf. 13½
817 A117 45c multicolored	.30	.30
818 A117 60c multicolored	.35	.35
819 A117 90c multicolored	.50	.50
820 A117 $4 multicolored	2.00	2.00
Nos. 817-820 (4)	3.15	3.15
Souvenir Sheet		
821 A117 $5 multicolored	3.00	3.00

23rd Olympic Games, Los Angeles, July 28-Aug. 12 — A118

30c, Gymnastics. 45c, Javelin. 60c, Diving. $4, Fencing.
$5, Equestrian.

1984, Mar.	Litho.	Perf. 14
822 A118 30c multicolored	.25	.25
823 A118 45c multicolored	.35	.35
824 A118 60c multicolored	.45	.45
825 A118 $4 multicolored	2.50	2.50
Nos. 822-825 (4)	3.55	3.55
Souvenir Sheet		
826 A118 $5 multicolored	3.75	3.75

Local Birds — A119

5c, Plumbeous warbler. 45c, Imperial parrot. 60c, Blue-headed hummingbird. 90c, Red-necked parrot.
$5, Roseate flamingoes.

1984, May		Litho.
827 A119 5c multicolored	3.00	3.00
828 A119 45c multicolored	7.00	7.00
829 A119 60c multicolored	8.50	8.50
830 A119 90c multicolored	11.00	11.00
Nos. 827-830 (4)	29.50	29.50
Souvenir Sheet		
831 A119 $5 multicolored	9.00	9.00

Easter — A120

Various Disney characters and Easter bunnies.

1984, Apr. 15	Litho.	Perf. 14
832 A120 ½c multicolored	.25	.25
833 A120 1c multicolored	.25	.25
834 A120 2c multicolored	.25	.25
835 A120 3c multicolored	.25	.25
836 A120 4c multicolored	.25	.25
837 A120 5c multicolored	.25	.25
838 A120 10c multicolored	.25	.25
839 A120 $2 multicolored	3.00	3.00
840 A120 $4 multicolored	6.25	6.25
Nos. 832-840 (9)	11.00	11.00
Souvenir Sheet		
Perf. 14		
841 A120 $5 multicolored	5.75	5.75

Ships — A121

45c, Atlantic Star. 60c, Atlantic fishing pirogue. $4, Norway.
$5, Santa Maria.

1984, June 14	Litho.	Perf. 14
842 A121 45c multicolored	1.75	1.75
843 A121 60c multicolored	2.00	2.00
844 A121 90c multicolored	2.50	2.50
845 A121 $4 multicolored	6.75	6.75
Nos. 842-845 (4)	13.00	13.00
Souvenir Sheet		
846 A121 $5 multicolored	5.00	5.00

Local Plants — A122

45c, Guzmania lingulata. 60c, Pitcairnia angustifolia. 75c, Tillandsia fasciculata. $3, Aechmea smithiorum.
$5, Tillandsia utriculata.

1984, Aug. 13		
847 A122 45c multicolored	.40	.40
848 A122 60c multicolored	.50	.50
849 A122 75c multicolored	.60	.60
850 A122 $3 multicolored	2.40	2.40
Nos. 847-850 (4)	3.90	3.90
Souvenir Sheet		
851 A122 $5 multicolored	3.75	3.75

Ausipex Intl. Stamp Exhibition.

Nos. 721, 732 Overprinted

1984	Litho.	Perf. 14
852 A103 10c multicolored	.25	.25
853 A103 $5 multicolored	4.00	4.00

Correggio & Degas — A122a

Correggio: 25c, Virgin and Child with Young St. John. 60c, Christ Bids Farewell to the Virgin Mary. 90c, Do Not Touch Me. $4, The Mystical Marriage of St. Catherine. No. 862, Adoration of the Magi.
Degas, horiz.: 30c, Before the Start. 45c, On the Racecourse. $1, Jockeys at the Flagpole. $3, Racehorses at Longchamp. No. 863, Self-portrait.

1984, Nov.	Litho.	Perf. 15
854 A122a 25c multicolored	.35	.35
855 A122a 30c multicolored	.40	.40
856 A122a 45c multicolored	.45	.45
857 A122a 60c multicolored	.50	.50
858 A122a 90c multicolored	.65	.65
859 A122a $1 multicolored	.75	.75
860 A122a $3 multicolored	1.75	1.75
861 A122a $4 multicolored	1.90	1.90
Nos. 854-861 (8)	6.75	6.75
Souvenir Sheets		
862 A122a $5 multicolored	3.00	3.00
863 A122a $5 multicolored	3.00	3.00

A123

1984, Dec.		Perf. 14
864 A123 30c Avro 748	1.25	1.25
865 A123 60c Twin Otter	2.25	2.25
866 A123 $1 Islander	2.50	2.50
867 A123 $3 Casa	4.75	4.75
Nos. 864-867 (4)	10.75	10.75
Souvenir Sheet		
868 A123 $5 Boeing 747	5.50	5.50

Intl. Civil Aviation Org., 40th anniv.

A124

Scenes from various Donald Duck movies.

1984, Nov.		Litho.
869 A124 45c multicolored	1.25	1.25
870 A124 60c multicolored	1.50	1.50
871 A124 90c multicolored	2.00	2.00
872 A124 $2 multicolored, perf. 12x12½	3.50	3.50
873 A124 $4 multicolored	5.75	5.75
Nos. 869-873 (5)	14.00	14.00
Souvenir Sheet		
Perf. 13½x14		
874 A124 $5 multicolored	5.50	5.50

Christmas and 50th anniv. of Donald Duck.

Cats — A125

10c, Tabby. 15c, Calico shorthair. 20c, Siamese. 25c, Manx. 45c, Abyssinian. 60c, Tortoise shell longhair. $1, Rex. $2, Persian. $3, Himalayan. No. 884, $5, Burmese.
No. 885, $5, Gray Burmese, Persian, American shorthair.

1984, Nov. 12	Litho.	Perf. 15
875 A125 10c multicolored	.25	.25
876 A125 15c multicolored	.25	.25
877 A125 20c multicolored	.25	.25
878 A125 25c multicolored	.25	.25
879 A125 45c multicolored	.40	.40
880 A125 60c multicolored	.50	.50
881 A125 $1 multicolored	.75	.75
882 A125 $2 multicolored	1.00	1.00
883 A125 $3 multicolored	2.00	2.00
884 A125 $5 multicolored	3.50	3.50
Nos. 875-884 (10)	9.15	9.15
Souvenir Sheet		
885 A125 $5 multicolored	5.50	5.50

Girl Guides, 75th Anniv. — A126

35c, Lady Baden-Powell. 45c, Inspecting Dominican troop. 60c, With Dominican troop leaders. $3, Lord and Lady Baden-Powell, vert.
$5, Flag ceremony.

1985, Feb. 18		Perf. 14
886 A126 35c multicolored	.60	.60
887 A126 45c multicolored	.70	.70
888 A126 60c multicolored	.90	.90
889 A126 $3 multicolored	3.50	3.50
Nos. 886-889 (4)	5.70	5.70
Souvenir Sheet		
890 A126 $5 multicolored	5.50	5.50

John James Audubon
A127

45c, King rails. $1, Black & white warbler, vert. $2, Broad-winged hawks, vert. $3, Ring-necked ducks.
$5, Reddish egrets, vert.

1985, Apr. 4		
891 A127 45c multicolored	1.25	1.25
892 A127 $1 multicolored	2.00	2.00
893 A127 $2 multicolored	3.25	3.25
894 A127 $3 multicolored	4.25	4.25
Nos. 891-894 (4)	10.75	10.75
Souvenir Sheet		
895 A127 $5 multicolored	5.50	5.50

Nos. 891-894 exist vertically se-tenant with labels showing additional bird species. See Nos. 965-969.

Duke of Edinburgh Awards, 1984 — A128

45c, Woman at computer terminal. 60c, Medical staff, patient. 90c, Runners. $4, Family jogging.
$5, Duke of Edinburgh.

1985, Apr. 30		
896 A128 45c multicolored	.50	.50
897 A128 60c multicolored	1.60	1.60
898 A128 90c multicolored	2.00	2.00
899 A128 $4 multicolored	3.25	3.25
Nos. 896-899 (4)	7.35	7.35
Souvenir Sheet		
900 A128 $5 multicolored	4.00	4.00

Intl. Youth Year — A129

45c, Cricket match. 60c, Environmental study, parrot. $1, Stamp collecting. $3, Boating, leisure.
$5, Youths join hands.

1985, July 8	Litho.	Perf. 14
901 A129 45c multicolored	3.00	2.00
902 A129 60c multicolored	3.75	2.50
903 A129 $1 multicolored	4.00	3.50
904 A129 $3 multicolored	5.25	7.50
Nos. 901-904 (4)	16.00	15.50
Souvenir Sheet		
905 A129 $5 multicolored	4.00	4.00

Queen Mother, 85th Birthday — A130

60c, Visiting Sadlers Wells. $1, Fishing. $3, At Clarence House, 1984.
$5, Attending Windsor Castle Garter Ceremony.

1985, July 15		
906 A130 60c multicolored	1.00	.75
907 A130 $1 multicolored	1.50	.75
908 A130 $3 multicolored	2.00	2.00
Nos. 906-908 (3)	4.50	3.50
Souvenir Sheet		
909 A130 $5 multicolored	3.75	3.75

Johann Sebastian Bach — A131

Portrait, signature, music from Explication and: 45c, Cornett. 60c, Coiled trumpet. $1, Piccolo. $3, Violoncello piccolo.

DOMINICA

1985, Sept. 2
910	A131	45c multicolored	1.00	1.00
911	A131	60c multicolored	1.50	1.50
912	A131	$1 multicolored	2.00	2.00
913	A131	$3 multicolored	4.25	4.25
		Nos. 910-913 (4)	8.75	8.75

Souvenir Sheet
914	A131	$5 Portrait	4.00	4.00

State Visit of Elizabeth II, Oct. 25 — A132

60c, Flags of UK, Dominica. $1, Elizabeth II, vert. $4, HMS Britannia. $5, Map.

1985, Oct. 25   *Perf. 14½*
915	A132	60c multicolored	.75	.75
916	A132	$1 multicolored	.75	.75
917	A132	$4 multicolored	3.50	3.50
		Nos. 915-917 (3)	5.00	5.00

Souvenir Sheet
918	A132	$5 multicolored	3.75	3.75

Mark Twain — A133

Disney characters in Tom Sawyer.

1985, Nov. 11   *Litho.*   *Perf. 14*
919	A133	20c multicolored	.75	.35
920	A133	60c multicolored	1.50	.35
921	A133	$1 multicolored	2.00	2.00
922	A133	$1.50 multicolored	2.50	2.50
923	A133	$2 multicolored	3.00	3.00
		Nos. 919-923 (5)	9.75	8.20

Souvenir Sheet
924	A133	$5 multicolored	6.50	6.50

Christmas.

The Brothers Grimm — A134

Disney characters in Little Red Cap (Little Red Riding Hood).

1985, Nov. 11
925	A134	10c multicolored	.40	.40
926	A134	45c multicolored	1.00	.50
927	A134	90c multicolored	2.00	2.00
928	A134	$1 multicolored	2.25	2.25
929	A134	$3 multicolored	4.25	4.25
		Nos. 925-929 (5)	9.90	9.40

Souvenir Sheet
930	A134	$5 multicolored	7.75	7.75

Christmas.

UN, 40th Anniv. — A135

Stamps of UN, famous men and events: 45c, No. 442 and Lord Baden-Powell. $2, No. 157 and Maimonides (1135-1204) Judaic scholar. $3, No. 278 and Sir Rowland Hill. $5, Apollo-Soyuz Mission, 10th anniv.

1985, Nov. 22   *Perf. 14½*
931	A135	45c multicolored	.90	.90
932	A135	$2 multicolored	2.00	2.00
933	A135	$3 multicolored	2.00	2.00
		Nos. 931-933 (3)	4.90	4.90

Souvenir Sheet
934	A135	$5 multicolored	3.75	3.75

1986 World Cup Soccer Championships, Mexico — A136

Various soccer plays.

1986, Mar. 26   *Perf. 14*
935	A136	45c multicolored	1.25	1.25
936	A136	60c multicolored	1.75	1.75
937	A136	$1 multicolored	2.25	2.25
938	A136	$3 multicolored	5.50	5.50
		Nos. 935-938 (4)	10.75	10.75

Souvenir Sheet
939	A136	$5 multicolored	8.50	8.50

For overprints see Nos. 974-978.

Statue of Liberty, Cent. — A137

Statue and: 15c, New York police pursuing river pirates, c. 1890. 25c, Police patrol boat. 45c, Hoboken Ferry Terminal, c. 1890. $4, Holland Tunnel. $5, Statue, vert.

1986, Mar. 26
940	A137	15c multicolored	1.50	.75
941	A137	25c multicolored	1.50	1.00
942	A137	45c multicolored	2.50	1.00
943	A137	$4 multicolored	5.00	5.00
		Nos. 940-943 (4)	10.50	7.75

Souvenir Sheet
944	A137	$5 multicolored	5.50	5.50

Halley's Comet — A138

5c, Jantal Mantar Observatory, Delhi, India, Nasir al Din al Tusi (1201-1274), astronomer. 10c, US Bell X-1 rocket plane breaking sound barrier. 45c, Astronomicum Caesareum, 1540, manuscript diagram of comet's trajectory, 1531. $4, Mark Twain, comet appeared at birth and death. $5, Comet.

1986, Apr. 17
945	A138	5c multicolored	.60	.60
946	A138	10c multicolored	.60	.60
947	A138	45c multicolored	1.25	1.25
948	A138	$4 multicolored	3.25	3.25
		Nos. 945-948 (4)	5.70	5.70

Souvenir Sheet
949	A138	$5 multicolored	3.75	3.75

For overprints see Nos. 984-988.

Queen Elizabeth II, 60th Birthday
Common Design Type

2c, Wedding, 1947. $1, With Pope John Paul II, 1982. $4, Royal visit, 1971. $5, Age 10.

1986, Apr. 21   *Litho.*   *Perf. 14*
950	CD339	2c multicolored	.25	.25
951	CD339	$1 multicolored	.75	.75
952	CD339	$4 multicolored	2.50	2.50
		Nos. 950-952 (3)	3.50	3.50

Souvenir Sheet
953	CD339	$5 multicolored	3.75	3.75

AMERIPEX '86 — A139

Walt Disney characters involved in stamp collecting: 25c, Mickey Mouse and Pluto. 45c, Donald Duck. 60c, Chip-n-Dale. $4, Donald, nephews. $5, Uncle Scrooge.

1986, May 22   *Perf. 11*
954	A139	25c multicolored	.75	.75
955	A139	45c multicolored	.95	.95
956	A139	60c multicolored	1.25	1.25
957	A139	$4 multicolored	4.00	4.00
		Nos. 954-957 (4)	6.95	6.95

Souvenir Sheet
Perf. 14
958	A139	$5 multicolored	6.00	6.00

British Monarchs — A140

1986, June 9   *Perf. 14*
959	A140	10c William I	.40	.40
960	A140	40c Richard II	.75	.75
961	A140	50c Henry VIII	.90	.90
962	A140	$1 Charles II	1.00	1.00
963	A140	$2 Queen Anne	1.50	1.50
964	A140	$4 Queen Victoria	3.00	3.00
		Nos. 959-964 (6)	7.55	7.55

Audubon Type of 1985

25c, Black-throated diver. 60c, Great blue heron. 90c, Yellow-crowned night heron. $4, Shoveler duck. $5, Goose.

Perf. 12½x12, 12x12½
1986, June 18
965	A127	25c multicolored	1.25	.50
966	A127	60c multicolored	1.75	1.75
967	A127	90c multicolored	2.25	2.25
968	A127	$4 multicolored	4.50	4.50
		Nos. 965-968 (4)	9.75	9.00

Souvenir Sheet
Perf. 14
969	A127	$5 multicolored	10.00	10.00

Nos. 966-967 vert.

Royal Wedding Issue, 1986
Common Design Type

1986, July 23   *Perf. 14*
970	CD340	45c Couple	.40	.40
971	CD340	60c Prince Andrew	.60	.60
972	CD340	$4 Prince, aircraft	2.50	2.50
		Nos. 970-972 (3)	3.50	3.50

Souvenir Sheet
973	CD340	$5 Couple, diff.	3.75	3.75
		Nos. 970-973 (4)	7.25	7.25

Nos. 935-939 Overprinted in Gold

1986, Sept. 15   *Litho.*   *Perf. 14*
974	A136	45c multicolored	1.25	.50
975	A136	60c multicolored	1.50	1.50
976	A136	$1 multicolored	2.00	2.00
977	A136	$3 multicolored	4.75	4.75
		Nos. 974-977 (4)	9.50	8.75

Souvenir Sheet
978	A136	$5 multicolored	8.75	8.75

Paintings by Albrecht Durer — A141

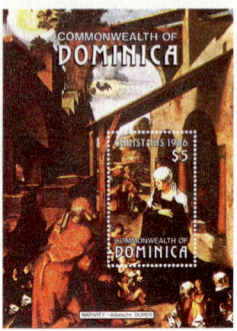

A142

45c, Virgin in Prayer. 60c, Madonna and Child. $1, Madonna and Child, diff. $3, Madonna and Child with St. Anne. $5, Nativity.

1986, Dec. 2   *Litho.*   *Perf. 14*
979	A141	45c multicolored	.85	.35
980	A141	60c multicolored	1.40	1.40
981	A141	$1 multicolored	2.00	2.00
982	A141	$3 multicolored	5.50	5.50
		Nos. 979-982 (4)	9.75	9.25

Souvenir Sheet
983	A142	$5 multicolored	8.75	8.75

Nos. 945-949 Printed with Halley's Comet Logo in Black or Silver

1986, Dec. 16
984	A138	5c multicolored	.25	.25
985	A138	10c multicolored	.25	.25
986	A138	45c multicolored	.50	.50
987	A138	$4 multicolored	3.75	3.75
		Nos. 984-987 (4)	4.75	4.75

Souvenir Sheet
988	A138	$5 multi (S)	4.50	4.50

Birds — A143

1c, Broad-winged hawk. 2c, Ruddy quail dove. 5c, Red-necked pigeon. 10c, Green heron. 15c, Common gallinule. 20c, Ringed kingfisher. 25c, Brown pelican. 35c, White-tailed tropicbird. 45c, Red-legged thrush. 60c, Purple throated carib. 90c, Magnificent frigatebird. $1, Trembler. $2, Black-capped petrel. $5, Barn owl. $10, Imperial parrot.

1987, Jan. 20   *Litho.*   *Perf. 15*
989	A143	1c multicolored	.25	.75
990	A143	2c multicolored	.25	.75
991	A143	5c multicolored	.30	.75
992	A143	10c multicolored	.30	.25
993	A143	15c multicolored	.40	.30
994	A143	20c multicolored	.40	.30
995	A143	25c multicolored	.40	.30
996	A143	35c multicolored	.40	.30
997	A143	45c multicolored	.50	.45
998	A143	60c multicolored	.60	.55
999	A143	90c multicolored	.70	.70
1000	A143	$1 multicolored	.80	.80
1001	A143	$2 multicolored	1.50	1.50
1002	A143	$5 multicolored	3.75	3.75
1003	A143	$10 multicolored	6.25	6.25
		Nos. 989-1003 (15)	16.80	17.60

Inscribed "1989" and "Questa"

1989, Aug. 31   *Litho.*   *Perf. 14*
990a	A143	2c	.35	.90
991a	A143	5c	.35	.80
992a	A143	10c	.40	.25
993a	A143	15c	.55	.30
994a	A143	20c	.65	.35
995a	A143	25c	.65	.35
996a	A143	35c	.85	.35
997a	A143	45c	1.00	.30
998a	A143	60c	1.50	.30
1000a	A143	$1	1.75	1.00
1001a	A143	$2	3.00	3.00
1002a	A143	$5	6.00	6.00
1003a	A143	$10	8.00	8.00
		Nos. 990a-1003a (13)	25.05	22.05

Inscribed "1989" and "Questa"

DOMINICA

1990 Litho. Perf. 12

990b	A143	2c	.40	.95
991b	A143	5c	.40	.85
992b	A143	10c	.45	.35
993b	A143	15c	.45	.35
994b	A143	20c	.70	.40
995b	A143	25c	.70	.40
996b	A143	35c	.85	.35
997b	A143	45c	1.00	.35
998b	A143	60c	1.50	1.60
1000b	A143	$1	1.75	1.00
1001b	A143	$2	3.00	3.00
1002b	A143	$5	6.25	6.25
1003b	A143	$10	8.25	8.25
Nos. 990b-1003b (13)			25.70	24.10

Inscribed "1989" and "Questa"

1991 Litho. Perf. 13x11½

990c	A143	2c	.50	1.10
991c	A143	5c	.50	.95
992c	A143	10c	.55	.40
993c	A143	15c	.55	.35
994c	A143	20c	.75	.35
995c	A143	25c	.75	.40
996c	A143	35c	.85	.40
997c	A143	45c	1.40	1.25
998c	A143	60c	2.00	1.40
1000c	A143	$1	2.00	1.50
1001c	A143	$2	3.50	3.50
1002c	A143	$5	7.00	7.00
1003c	A143	$10	10.00	10.00
Nos. 990c-1003c (13)			30.35	28.60

Paintings by Marc Chagall (1887-1985) A144

Designs: 25c, Artist and His Model. 35c, Midsummer Night's Dream. 45c, Joseph the Shepherd. 60c, the Cellist. 90c, Woman with Pigs. $1, the Blue Circus. $3, For Vava. $4, the Rider. No. 1012, Purim. No. 1013, Firebird design for the curtain of the Stravinsky Ballet production.

1987, Mar. 2 Perf. 14

1004	A144	25c multicolored	.50	.25
1005	A144	35c multicolored	.65	.30
1006	A144	45c multicolored	.85	.35
1007	A144	60c multicolored	1.00	.50
1008	A144	90c multicolored	1.10	.70
1009	A144	$1 multicolored	1.25	1.25
1010	A144	$3 multicolored	2.50	2.50
1011	A144	$4 multicolored	3.50	3.50

Size: 110x95mm Imperf

1012	A144	$5 multicolored	4.00	4.00
1013	A144	$5 multicolored	4.00	4.00
Nos. 1004-1013 (10)			19.35	17.35

A145

America's Cup — A146

45c, Reliance, 1903. 60c, Freedom, 1980. $1, Mischief, 1881. $3, Australia, 1977. $5, Courageous, Australia, 1977.

1987, Feb. 5 Perf. 15

1014	A145	45c multicolored	.60	.45
1015	A145	60c multicolored	.70	.50
1016	A145	$1 multicolored	.90	1.00
1017	A145	$3 multicolored	2.75	2.00
Nos. 1014-1017 (4)			4.95	3.95

Souvenir Sheet

| 1018 | A146 | $5 multicolored | 3.75 | 3.75 |

Conch Shells — A147

Designs: 35c, Morch Poulsen's triton. 45c, Swainson globe purple sea snail. 60c, Banded tulip. No. 1022, Lamarck deltoid rock shell. No. 1023, Junoia volute.

1987, Apr. 13 Litho.

1019	A147	35c multicolored	.35	.35
1020	A147	45c multicolored	.45	.45
1021	A147	60c multicolored	.55	.55
1022	A147	$5 multicolored	3.50	3.50
Nos. 1019-1022 (4)			4.85	4.85

Souvenir Sheet

| 1023 | A147 | $5 multicolored | 4.50 | 4.50 |

CAPEX '87 — A148

Mushrooms: 45c, Cantharellus cinnabarinus. 60c, Boletellus cubenis. $2, Eccilia cystiophorus. $3, Xeroconus guadelupae. $5, Gymnopilus chrysopellus.

1987, June 15 Litho. Perf. 14

1024	A148	45c multicolored	1.50	.75
1025	A148	60c multicolored	2.00	2.00
1026	A148	$2 multicolored	3.75	3.75
1027	A148	$3 multicolored	4.50	4.50
Nos. 1024-1027 (4)			11.75	11.00

Souvenir Sheet

| 1028 | A148 | $5 multicolored | 10.00 | 10.00 |

A149

Discovery of America, 500th Anniv. (in 1992) — A150

Explorations of Christopher Columbus: 10c, Discovery of Dominica. 15c, Ships greeted by Carib Indians. 45c, Claiming New World for Spain. 60c, Wrecking of the Santa Maria. 90c, Fleet setting sail. $1, Sighting land. $3, Trading with the Indians. No. 1036, First settlement. No. 1037, Arrival of Second Fleet at Dominica, Nov. 3, 1493. No. 1038, Map of exploration of the Leeward Islands.

1987, July 27 Perf. 15

1029	A149	10c multicolored	.40	.40
1030	A149	15c multicolored	.50	.50
1031	A149	45c multicolored	.75	.75
1032	A149	60c multicolored	.95	.95
1033	A149	90c multicolored	1.20	1.20
1034	A149	$1 multicolored	1.25	1.25
1035	A149	$3 multicolored	2.50	2.50
1036	A149	$5 multicolored	3.25	3.25
Nos. 1029-1036 (8)			10.80	10.80

Souvenir Sheets

1037	A150	$5 multicolored	4.75	4.75
1038	A150	$5 multicolored	4.75	4.75

For overprints see Nos. 1083-1084.

Transportation A151

10c, Warrior, 1st iron-clad warship. 15c, Maglev-MLU 001, fastest passenger train. 25c, Clipper Flying Cloud, fastest NYC-San Francisco voyage, 1852. 35c, 1st elevated railway, NYC. 45c, Tom Thumb, 1st US passenger train locomotive. 60c, Joshua Slocum, 1st solo circumnavigation of the world in a sloop. 90c, Se-Land Commerce, fastest Pacific crossing. $1, 1st cable car, San Francisco. $3, Orient Express. $4, The North River Steamboat of Clermont, invented by Robert Fulton, 1st successful commercial steamboat.

1987 Litho. Perf. 14

1039	A151	10c multicolored	.50	.50
1040	A151	15c multicolored	.75	.75
1041	A151	25c multi.	.80	.80
1042	A151	35c multi, vert.	1.00	1.00
1043	A151	45c multi, vert.	1.10	1.10
1044	A151	60c multi, vert.	1.25	1.25
1045	A151	90c multi, vert.	1.40	1.40
1046	A151	$1 multicolored	1.50	1.50
1047	A151	$3 multicolored	3.75	3.75
1048	A151	$4 multicolored	4.00	4.00
Nos. 1039-1048 (10)			16.05	16.05

Issued: 10c, 15c, 45c, 60c, $4, 9/28; others 8/1.

For overprints see Nos. 1081-1082.

Christmas — A152

Paintings (details): 20c, Virgin and Child with St. Anne, by Durer. 25c, The Virgin and Child, by Murillo. $2, Madonna and Child, by Vincenzo Foppa (c. 1427-1516). $4, Madonna and Child, by Paolo Veronese (1528-1588). $5, Angel of the Annunciation, anonymous.

1987, Nov. 16

1049	A152	20c multicolored	.30	.30
1050	A152	25c multicolored	.30	.30
1051	A152	$2 multicolored	2.00	2.00
1052	A152	$4 multicolored	4.25	4.25
Nos. 1049-1052 (4)			6.85	6.85

Souvenir Sheet

| 1053 | A152 | $5 multicolored | 3.75 | 3.75 |

Mickey Mouse, 60th Anniv. — A153

Disney theme parks and trains: 20c, People Mover, Disney World. 25c, Horse-drawn Trolley, Disneyland. 45c, Roger E. Broggie, Disney World. 60c, Big Thunder Mountain, Disneyland. 90c, Walter E. Disney, Disneyland. $1, Monorail, Disney World. $3, Casey Jr. from Dumbo. $4, Lilly Belle, Disney World. No. 1062, Rainbow Caverns Mine Train, Disneyland, horiz. No. 1063, Toy train from movie Out of Scale, horiz.

1987, Dec. 7 Litho. Perf. 14

1054	A153	20c multicolored	.55	.55
1055	A153	25c multicolored	.55	.55
1056	A153	45c multicolored	.90	.90
1057	A153	60c multicolored	1.00	1.00
1058	A153	90c multicolored	1.60	1.60
1059	A153	$1 multicolored	1.75	1.75
1060	A153	$3 multicolored	4.00	4.00
1061	A153	$4 multicolored	5.25	5.25
Nos. 1054-1061 (8)			15.60	15.60

Souvenir Sheets

1062	A153	$5 multicolored	4.00	4.00
1063	A153	$5 multicolored	4.00	4.00

40th Wedding Anniv. of Queen Elizabeth II and Prince Philip — A154

45c, Couple, wedding party, 1947. 60c, Elizabeth, Charles, c. 1952. $1, Royal Family, c. 1952. $3, Queen with tiara, c. 1960. $5, Elizabeth, 1947.

1988, Feb. 15 Litho. Perf. 14

1064	A154	45c multicolored	.75	.75
1065	A154	60c multicolored	.80	.80
1066	A154	$1 multicolored	1.00	1.00
1067	A154	$3 multicolored	2.40	2.40
Nos. 1064-1067 (4)			4.95	4.95

Souvenir Sheet

| 1068 | A154 | $5 multicolored | 3.50 | 3.50 |

1988 Summer Olympics, Seoul — A155

1988, Mar. 15

1069	A155	45c Kayaking	.85	.85
1070	A155	60c Tae kwon-do	1.25	1.25
1071	A155	$1 Diving	1.40	1.40
1072	A155	$3 Parallel bars	2.50	2.50
Nos. 1069-1072 (4)			6.00	6.00

Souvenir Sheet

| 1073 | A155 | $5 Soccer | 3.25 | 3.25 |

For overprints see Nos. 1151-1155.

Reunion '88 Tourism Campaign A156

10c, Carib Indian, vert. 25c, Mountainous interior. 35c, Indian River, vert. 60c, Belaire dancer, vert. 90c, The Boiling Lake, vert. $3, Coral reef. $5, Belaire dancer, diff., vert.

1988, Apr. 13 Litho. Perf. 15

1074	A156	10c multicolored	.25	.25
1075	A156	25c multicolored	.25	.25
1076	A156	35c multicolored	.25	.25
1077	A156	60c multicolored	.25	.25
1078	A156	90c multicolored	.30	.30
1079	A156	$3 multicolored	.90	.90
Nos. 1074-1079 (6)			2.20	2.20

Souvenir Sheet

| 1080 | A156 | $5 multicolored | 3.00 | 3.00 |

Independence, 10th anniv.

Nos. 1046-1047, 1037-1038 Ovptd. for Philatelic Exhibitions in Black

a

b

c

d

1988, June 1 Litho. Perf. 14

1081	A151(a)	$1 multi	1.00	1.00
1082	A151(b)	$3 multi	3.75	3.75

DOMINICA

Souvenir Sheets
Perf. 15
| 1083 | A150(c) | $5 multi | 4.00 | 4.00 |
| 1084 | A150(d) | $5 multi | 4.00 | 4.00 |

Miniature Sheet

Rain Forest Flora and Fauna — A157

Designs: a, White-tailed tropicbirds. b, Blue-throated euphonia. c, Smooth-billed ani. d, Scaly-breasted thrasher. e, Purple-throated carib. f, Southern daggertail and Clench's hairstreak. g, Trembler. h, Imperial parrot. i, Mangrove cuckoo. j, Hercules beetle. k, Orion. l, Red-necked parrot. m, Tillandsia. n, Polystacha luteola and bananaquit. o, False chameleon. p, Iguana. q, Hypolimnas. r, Green-throated carib. s, Heliconia. t, Agouti.

1988, July 25   *Perf. 14½*
| 1085 | A157 | Sheet of 20 | 14.00 | 14.00 |
| a.-t. | | 45c any single | .60 | .60 |

Intl. Fund for Agricultural Development (IFAD), 10th Anniv. — A158

1988, Sept. 5   *Litho.*   *Perf. 14*
1086	A158	45c Hen house	.65	.65
1087	A158	60c Pig farm	.90	.90
1088	A158	90c Cattle	1.25	1.25
1089	A158	$3 Black-belly sheep	3.50	3.50
	Nos. 1086-1089 (4)		6.30	6.30

Souvenir Sheet
| 1090 | A158 | $5 Mixed crops, vert. | 3.75 | 3.75 |

Entertainers — A159

10c, Gary Cooper. 35c, Josephine Baker. 45c, Maurice Chevalier. 60c, James Cagney. $1, Clark Gable. $2, Louis Armstrong. $3, Liberace. $4, Spencer Tracy.
No. 1099, Elvis Presley. No. 1100, Humphrey Bogart.

1988, Sept. 8
1091	A159	10c multicolored	.40	.25
1092	A159	35c multicolored	.50	.25
1093	A159	45c multicolored	.55	.30
1094	A159	60c multicolored	.75	.30
1095	A159	$1 multicolored	1.00	.30
1096	A159	$2 multicolored	1.75	1.75
1097	A159	$3 multicolored	2.00	2.00
1098	A159	$4 multicolored	2.50	2.50
	Nos. 1091-1098 (8)		9.45	7.65

Souvenir Sheets
| 1099 | A159 | $5 multicolored | 4.25 | 4.25 |
| 1100 | A159 | $5 multicolored | 4.25 | 4.25 |

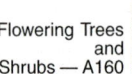

Flowering Trees and Shrubs — A160

1988, Sept. 29   *Litho.*   *Perf. 14*
1101	A160	15c Sapodilla	.25	.25
1102	A160	20c Tangerine	.25	.25
1103	A160	25c Avocado pear	.25	.25
1104	A160	45c Amherstia	.30	.30
1105	A160	90c Lipstick tree	.55	.55
1106	A160	$1 Cannonball tree	.60	.60
1107	A160	$3 Saman	1.50	1.50
1108	A160	$4 Pineapple	2.00	2.00
	Nos. 1101-1108 (8)		5.70	5.70

Souvenir Sheets
| 1109 | A160 | $5 Lignum vitae | 3.75 | 3.75 |
| 1110 | A160 | $5 Sea grape | 3.75 | 3.75 |

Paintings by Titian — A161

Designs: 25c, Jacopo Strada, c. 1567. 35c, Titian's Daughter Lavinia, c. 1565. 45c, Andrea Navagero, c. 1515. 60c, Judith with Head of Holoferenes, c. 1570. $1, Emilia di Spilimbergo, c. 1560. $2, Martyrdom of St. Lawrence, c. 1548. $3, Salome With the Head of St. John the Baptist, 1560. $4, St. John the Baptist, c. 1540. No. 1119, Self-portrait, c. 1555. No. 1120, Sisyphus, 1549.

1988, Oct. 10   *Litho.*   *Perf. 13½x14*
1111	A161	25c multicolored	.25	.25
1112	A161	35c multicolored	.25	.25
1113	A161	45c multicolored	.35	.35
1114	A161	60c multicolored	.45	.45
1115	A161	$1 multicolored	.90	.90
1116	A161	$2 multicolored	1.25	1.25
1117	A161	$3 multicolored	2.00	2.00
1118	A161	$4 multicolored	2.50	2.50
	Nos. 1111-1118 (8)		7.95	7.95

Souvenir Sheets
| 1119 | A161 | $5 multicolored | 3.50 | 3.50 |
| 1120 | A161 | $5 multicolored | 3.50 | 3.50 |

Independence, 10th Anniv. — A162

20c, Imperial parrot. 45c, No. 1, landscape. $2, No. 602, waterfall. $3, Carib wood. $5, Natl. band performing.

1988, Oct. 31   *Litho.*   *Perf. 14*
1121	A162	20c multicolored	1.75	.50
1122	A162	45c multicolored	1.00	.40
1123	A162	$2 multicolored	1.75	1.75
1124	A162	$3 multicolored	2.00	3.00
	Nos. 1121-1124 (4)		6.50	5.65

Souvenir Sheet
| 1125 | A162 | $5 multicolored | 3.75 | 3.75 |

Nos. 1122-1123 horiz.

John F. Kennedy — A163

20c, With Jackie. 25c, Sailing Vicuna. $2, Walking in Hyannis Port. $4, Berlin Wall speech. $5, Portrait.

1988, Nov. 22
1126	A163	20c multicolored	.25	.25
1127	A163	25c multicolored	.25	.25
1128	A163	$2 multicolored	.95	.95
1129	A163	$4 multicolored	2.25	2.25
	Nos. 1126-1129 (4)		3.70	3.70

Souvenir Sheet
| 1130 | A163 | $5 multicolored | 3.50 | 3.50 |

Nos. 1126-1128 horiz.

Miniature Sheet

Christmas, Mickey Mouse 60th Anniv. — A164

No. 1131: a, Huey, Dewey, Louie. b, Daisy Duck. c, Winnie-the-Pooh. d, Goofy. e, Donald Duck. f, Mickey Mouse. g, Minnie Mouse. h, Chip-n-Dale.
No. 1132, Mickey, Morty and Ferdy. No. 1133, Characters visiting shopping mall Santa.

1988, Dec. 1   *Perf. 13½x14*
| 1131 | A164 | Sheet of 8 | 6.75 | 6.75 |
| a.-h. | | 60c any single | .80 | .80 |

Souvenir Sheets
| 1132 | A164 | $6 multi | 5.00 | 5.00 |
| 1133 | A164 | $6 multi, horiz. | 5.00 | 5.00 |

UN Declaration of Human Rights, 40th Anniv. — A165

Designs: $3, Flag of Sweden and Raoul Wallenberg, who helped save 100,000 Jews in Budapest from deportation to Nazi concentration camps. $5, Human Rights Flame.

1988, Dec. 12   *Perf. 14*
| 1134 | A165 | $3 multicolored | 3.00 | 3.00 |

Souvenir Sheet
| 1135 | A165 | $5 multi, vert. | 4.00 | 4.00 |

Coastal Game Fish — A166

10c, Greater amberjack. 15c, Blue marlin. 35c, Cobia. 45c, Dolphin. 60c, Cero. 90c, Mahogany snapper. $3, Yellowfin tuna. $4, Rainbow parrotfish.
No. 1144, Manta ray. No. 1145, Tarpon.

1988, Dec. 22   *Litho.*   *Perf. 14*
1136	A166	10c multicolored	.25	.25
1137	A166	15c multicolored	.25	.25
1138	A166	35c multicolored	.40	.40
1139	A166	45c multicolored	.50	.50
1140	A166	60c multicolored	.75	.75
1141	A166	90c multicolored	1.00	1.00
1142	A166	$3 multicolored	2.50	2.50
1143	A166	$4 multicolored	3.50	3.50
	Nos. 1136-1143 (8)		9.15	9.15

Souvenir Sheets
| 1144 | A166 | $5 multicolored | 5.00 | 5.00 |
| 1145 | A166 | $5 multicolored | 5.00 | 5.00 |

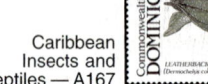

Caribbean Insects and Reptiles — A167

10c, Leatherback turtle. 25c, Monarch butterfly. 60c, Green anole. $3, Praying mantis. $5, Hercules beetle.

1988, Dec. 29
1146	A167	10c multicolored	.60	.60
1147	A167	25c multicolored	1.75	1.75
1148	A167	60c multicolored	2.00	2.00
1149	A167	$3 multicolored	5.50	5.50
	Nos. 1146-1149 (4)		9.85	9.85

Souvenir Sheet
| 1150 | A167 | $5 multicolored | 5.00 | 5.00 |

Nos. 1069-1073 Overprinted

a

b

c   d

e

1989, Mar. 20   *Litho.*   *Perf. 14*
1151	A155(a)	45c multi	.30	.30
1152	A155(b)	60c multi	.40	.40
1153	A155(c)	$1 multi	.75	.75
1154	A155(d)	$3 multi	1.90	1.90
	Nos. 1151-1154 (4)		3.35	3.35

Souvenir Sheet
| 1155 | A155(e) | $5 multi | 3.75 | 3.75 |

Pre-Columbian Societies and Their Customs — A168

UPAE and discovery of America anniv. emblems and: 20c, Carib Indians canoeing. 35c, Bow hunting. $1, Canoe making. $3, Shield wrestling. $6, Dancing.

1989, May 8   *Litho.*   *Perf. 14*
1156	A168	20c multicolored	.25	.25
1157	A168	35c multicolored	.35	.35
1158	A168	$1 multicolored	1.00	1.00
1159	A168	$3 multicolored	2.75	2.75
	Nos. 1156-1159 (4)		4.35	4.35

Souvenir Sheet
| 1160 | A168 | $6 multicolored | 4.25 | 4.25 |

Discovery of America 500th anniv. (in 1992).

Paintings by Yokoyama Taikan (1868-1958) — A169

Designs: 10c, Lao-tzu. 20c, Red Maple Leaves (panels 1-2). 45c, King Wen Learns a Lesson from His Cook. 60c, Red Maple Leaves (panels 3-4). $1, Wild Flowers. $2, Red Maple Leaves (panels 5-6). $3, Red Maple Leaves (panels 7-8). $4, The Indian Ceremony of Floating Lamps on the River. No. 1169, Innocence. No. 1170, Red Maple Leaves (4 panels).

1989, Aug. 8   *Litho.*   *Perf. 13½x14*
1161	A169	10c multicolored	.25	.25
1162	A169	20c multicolored	.25	.25
1163	A169	45c multicolored	.30	.30
1164	A169	60c multicolored	.40	.40
1165	A169	$1 multicolored	.65	.65
1166	A169	$2 multicolored	1.25	1.25
1167	A169	$3 multicolored	1.75	1.75
1168	A169	$4 multicolored	2.25	2.25
	Nos. 1161-1168 (8)		7.10	7.10

Souvenir Sheets
| 1169 | A169 | $5 multicolored | 3.75 | 3.75 |
| 1170 | A169 | $5 multicolored | 3.75 | 3.75 |

Hirohito (1901-89) and enthronement of Akihito as emperor of Japan.

PHILEXFRANCE '89, July 7-17, Paris — A170

Designs: 10c, Map of Dominica with French place names, 1766. 35c, French coin, 1688. $1, French ship, 1720. $4, Introduction of coffee to Dominica by the French, 1772. $5, Text.

DOMINICA

1989, July 17   Litho.   *Perf. 14*
1171	A170	10c multi, vert.	1.00	1.00
1172	A170	35c shown	1.00	1.00
1173	A170	$1 multicolored	1.50	1.50
1174	A170	$4 multicolored	3.00	3.00
		Nos. 1171-1174 (4)	6.50	6.50

Souvenir Sheet
| 1175 | A170 | $5 multicolored | 5.25 | 5.25 |

The sheet margin of No. 1175 shows imperforate reproductions of Nos. 1171-1174 that were not valid for postage.

Butterflies — A171

Designs: 10c, Homerus swallowtail. 15c, *Morpho peleides*. 25c, Julia. 35c, Gundlach's swallowtail. 60c, Monarch. $1, Gulf fritillary. $3, Red-splashed sulphur. $5, *Papilio andraemon*. No. 1184, *Heliconius doris, Adelpha cytherea, Calliona argenissa, Eurema proterpia*. No. 1185, *Adelpha iphicla, Dismorphia spio, Lucinia sida*.

1989, Sept. 11   Litho.   *Perf. 14*
1176	A171	10c multicolored	.40	.40
1177	A171	15c multicolored	.40	.40
1178	A171	25c multicolored	.70	.70
1179	A171	35c multicolored	.80	.80
1180	A171	60c multicolored	1.10	1.10
1181	A171	$1 multicolored	1.50	1.50
1182	A171	$3 multicolored	3.50	3.50
1183	A171	$5 multicolored	6.00	6.00
		Nos. 1176-1183 (8)	14.40	14.40

Souvenir Sheets
| 1184 | A171 | $6 multicolored | 6.50 | 6.50 |
| 1185 | A171 | $6 multicolored | 6.50 | 6.50 |

Misspellings: No. 1181, "Frittillary"; No. 1182, "Sulper."

Orchids — A172

10c, *Oncidium pusillum*. 35c, *Epidendrum cochleata*. 45c, *Epidendrum ciliare*. 60c, *Cyrtopodium andersonii*. $1, *Habenaria pauciflora*. $2, *Maxillaria alba*. $3, *Selenipedium palmifolium*. $4, *Brassavola cucullata*. No. 1194, *Oncidium lanceanum*. No. 1195, *Comparettia falcata*.

1989, Sept. 28
1186	A172	10c multicolored	.40	.40
1187	A172	35c multicolored	.75	.75
1188	A172	45c multicolored	.85	.85
1189	A172	60c multicolored	1.10	1.10
1190	A172	$1 multicolored	1.50	1.50
1191	A172	$2 multicolored	2.50	2.50
1192	A172	$3 multicolored	3.00	3.00
1193	A172	$4 multicolored	4.75	4.75
		Nos. 1186-1193 (8)	14.85	14.85

Souvenir Sheets
| 1194 | A172 | $5 multicolored | 6.50 | 6.50 |
| 1195 | A172 | $5 multicolored | 6.50 | 6.50 |

1st Moon Landing, 20th Anniv. — A173

10c, Columbia in lunar orbit. 60c, Aldrin descending ladder. $2, Aldrin, Sea of Tranquility. $3, Flag raising. $6, Liftoff.

1989, Oct. 31   Litho.   *Perf. 14*
1196	A173	10c multicolored	.35	.35
1197	A173	60c multicolored	.80	.80
1198	A173	$2 multicolored	2.25	2.25
1199	A173	$3 multicolored	3.25	3.25
		Nos. 1196-1199 (4)	6.65	6.65

Souvenir Sheet
| 1200 | A173 | $6 multicolored | 7.00 | 7.00 |

Souvenir Sheets

A174

1990 World Cup Soccer Championships, Italy — A175

Past championship match scenes, flags and soccer ball: a, Brazil vs. Italy, Mexico, 1970. b, England vs. West Germany, England, 1966. c, West Germany vs. Netherlands, West Germany, 1974. d, Italy vs. West Germany, Spain, 1982.

1989, Nov. 7   *Perf. 14*
| 1201 | A174 | Sheet of 4 | 8.75 | 8.75 |
| a.-d. | | $1 any single | 2.00 | 2.00 |

   Perf. 14
| 1202 | A175 | $6 shown | 6.00 | 6.00 |

Souvenir Sheet

The Capitol, Washington, DC — A176

1989, Nov. 17   Litho.   *Perf. 14*
| 1203 | A176 | $4 multicolored | 3.75 | 3.75 |

World Stamp Expo '89.

Miniature Sheets

American Presidency, 200th Anniv. — A177

US presidents, historic events and monuments.
No. 1204: a, Washington, 1st inauguration. b, John Adams, presidential mansion, 1800. c, Jefferson, Graff House in Philadelphia, excerpt from the 1st draft of the Declaration of Independence. d, Madison, USS *Constitution* at the defeat of HMS *Guerriere*, 1812. e, Monroe, freed slaves settle Liberia, 1822. f, John Quincy Adams, opening of the Erie Canal, 1825.
No. 1205: a, Fillmore, Commodore Perry laying groundwork for US trade agreement with Japan. b, Pierce, Jefferson Davis and San Xavier del Bac mission, Tucson, AZ, Gadsden Purchase, 1853. c, Buchanan, Pony Express stamp, Buffalo Bill Cody as express rider. d, Lincoln, UPU emblem, Intl. Postal Congress, Paris, 1863. e, Andrew Johnson, polar bear, purchase of Alaska from Russia, 1867. f, Grant, 1st transcontinental railway link, Promontory Point, Utah, 1869.
No. 1206: a, Theodore Roosevelt, construction of the Panama Canal, 1904. b, Taft, Adm. Peary becomes 1st man to reach the North Pole, 1909. c, Wilson, US #C3, cancel commemorating the 1st scheduled airmail service, 1918. d, Harding, airship USS *Shenandoah* at Lakehurst, NJ. e, Coolidge, Lindbergh's solo transatlantic flight, 1927. f, Mt. Rushmore, by Gutzon Borglum, 1927.
No. 1207: a, Lyndon B. Johnson, space exploration. b, Nixon visiting PRChina, 1971. c, Ford, tall ship in NY Harbor for Operation Sail, 1976, US bicentennial celebrations. d, Carter, Sadat of Egypt and Begin of Israel during the Camp David Accords, 1979. e, Reagan, European Space Agency emblem, flags and *Columbia* space shuttle. f, Bush, Grumman Avenger bomber he piloted during WWII.

1989, Nov. 17   *Perf. 14*
1204	A177	Sheet of 6	6.50	6.50
a.-f.		60c any single	1.00	1.00
1205	A177	Sheet of 6	6.50	6.50
a.-f.		60c any single	1.00	1.00
1206	A177	Sheet of 6	6.50	6.50
a.-f.		60c any single	1.00	1.00
1207	A177	Sheet of 6	6.50	6.50
a.-f.		60c any single	1.00	1.00

Mickey Mouse as a Hollywood Star — A178

Walt Disney characters: 20c, Reading script. 35c, Television interview. 45c, Named a star in tabloid headline. 60c, Signing autographs. $1, In dressing room, holding fans at bay. $2, Riding in limousine. $3, With Minnie in the limelight. $4, Accepting award. No. 1216, Giving interview during celebrity tennis tournament. No. 1217, Footprint impression in cement outside theater.

1989, Nov. 30   Litho.   *Perf. 14x13½*
1208	A178	20c multicolored	.50	.50
1209	A178	35c multicolored	.70	.70
1210	A178	45c multicolored	.80	.80
1211	A178	60c multicolored	.90	.90
1212	A178	$1 multicolored	1.25	1.25
1213	A178	$2 multicolored	2.25	2.25
1214	A178	$3 multicolored	3.00	3.00
1215	A178	$4 multicolored	4.00	4.00
		Nos. 1208-1215 (8)	13.40	13.40

Souvenir Sheets
| 1216 | A178 | $5 multicolored | 5.50 | 5.50 |
| 1217 | A178 | $5 multicolored | 5.50 | 5.50 |

Christmas — A179

Religious paintings by Botticelli: 20c, *Madonna in Glory with Seraphim*. 25c, *The Annunciation*. 35c, *Madonna of the Pomegranate*. 45c, *Madonna of the Rose Garden*. 60c, *Madonna of the Book*. $1, *Madonna and Child Under a Baldachin with Three Angels*. $4, *Madonna and Child with Angels*. No. 1225, *Bardi Madonna*. No. 1226, *The Mystic Nativity*. No. 1227, *The Adoration of the Magi*.

1989, Dec. 4   *Perf. 14*
1218	A179	20c multicolored	.45	.45
1219	A179	25c multicolored	.45	.45
1220	A179	35c multicolored	.60	.60
1221	A179	45c multicolored	.75	.75
1222	A179	60c multicolored	.90	.90
1223	A179	$1 multicolored	1.10	1.10
1224	A179	$4 multicolored	3.00	3.00
1225	A179	$5 multicolored	4.75	4.75
		Nos. 1218-1225 (8)	12.00	12.00

Souvenir Sheets
| 1226 | A179 | $5 multicolored | 5.00 | 5.00 |
| 1227 | A179 | $5 multicolored | 5.00 | 5.00 |

Nehru — A180

$5, Parliament House, New Delhi, horiz.

1989, Dec. 27   Litho.   *Perf. 14*
| 1228 | A180 | 60c shown | 2.00 | 2.00 |

Souvenir Sheet
| 1229 | A180 | $5 multicolored | 6.00 | 6.00 |

Jawaharlal Nehru (1889-1964), 1st prime minister of independent India.

Girl Guides — A181

Guide movement in Dominica, 60th anniv.: 60c, Lady Baden-Powell and Agatha Robinson, former Guide leader on Dominica. $5, Doris Stockmann, chairman of the world committee of the World Assoc. of Girl Guides and Girl Scouts, and Judith Pestaina, chief commissioner of the Dominica Girl Guides Assoc., horiz.

1989, Dec. 29
| 1230 | A181 | 60c multicolored | 1.25 | 1.25 |

Souvenir Sheet
| 1231 | A181 | $5 multi, horiz. | 5.25 | 5.25 |

Miniature Sheet

Marine Life — A182

Designs: a, Cocoa damselfish. b, Stinging jellyfish. c, Dolphin. d, Queen angelfish. e, French angelfish. f, Blue striped grunt. g, Pork fish. h, Hammerhead shark. i, Spadefish. j, Great barracuda. k, Stingray. l, Black grunt. m, Two-spotted butterflyfish. n, Dog snapper. o, Southern puffer. p, Four-eyed butterflyfish. q, Lane snapper. r, Green moray.

1990   Litho.   *Perf. 14*
| 1232 | A182 | Sheet of 18 | 11.00 | 11.00 |
| a.-r. | | 45c any single | .55 | .55 |

Penny Black, 150th Anniv. — A183

Stamp World London '90: 50c, Post Office accelerator, 1830. 60c, $4, No. 1239, London skyline, St. Paul's Cathedral. 90c, Railway post car, 1838. $3, Center cycle, 1883. No. 1240, Mail truck, 1899.

1990, May 3   Litho.   *Perf. 13½*
1233	A183	45c green & black	.60	.60
1234	A183	50c blk & slate blue	.80	.80
1235	A183	60c dk blue & blk	.85	.85
1236	A183	90c black & green	1.50	1.50
1237	A183	$3 blk & dk bl vio	2.75	2.75
1238	A183	$4 dk bl vio & blk	3.75	3.75
		Nos. 1233-1238 (6)	10.25	10.25

Souvenir Sheet
| 1239 | A183 | $5 beige & black | 4.50 | 4.50 |
| 1240 | A183 | $5 gray & red brn | 4.50 | 4.50 |

A184

Birds: 10c, Blue-headed hummingbird. 20c, Black-capped petrel. 45c, Red-necked parrot. 60c, Black swift. $1, Troupial. $2, Brown noddy. $4, Lesser Antillean pewee. $5, Little blue heron. No. 1249, House wren. No. 1250, Imperial parrot.

1990, July 16   Litho.   *Perf. 14*
1241	A184	10c multicolored	.40	.40
1242	A184	20c multicolored	.55	.55
1243	A184	45c multicolored	.75	.75

DOMICA

1244	A184	60c multicolored	.95	.95
1245	A184	$1 multicolored	1.60	1.60
1246	A184	$2 multicolored	2.25	2.25
1247	A184	$4 multicolored	3.75	3.75
1248	A184	$5 multicolored	4.25	4.25
	Nos. 1241-1248 (8)		14.50	14.50

Souvenir Sheets

1249	A184	$6 multicolored	5.00	5.00
1250	A184	$6 multicolored	5.00	5.00

A185

Shells: 10c, Reticulated cowrie-helmet. 20c, West Indian chank. 35c, West Indian fighting conch. 60c, True tulip. $1, Sunrise tellin. $2, Crown cone. $3, Common dove shell. $4, Atlantic fig shell. No. 1259, Giant tun. No. 1260, King helmet.

1990, July 19

1251	A185	10c multicolored	.40	.40
1252	A185	20c multicolored	.55	.55
1253	A185	35c multicolored	.70	.70
1254	A185	60c multicolored	1.00	1.00
1255	A185	$1 multicolored	1.40	1.40
1256	A185	$2 multicolored	2.25	2.25
1257	A185	$3 multicolored	3.00	3.00
1258	A185	$4 multicolored	3.75	3.75
	Nos. 1251-1258 (8)		13.05	13.05

Souvenir Sheets

1259	A185	$5 multicolored	5.00	5.00
1260	A185	$5 multicolored	5.00	5.00

A186

Queen Mother, 90th Birthday: various photos.

1990, Sept. 10

1261	A186	20c multicolored	.25	.25
1262	A186	45c multicolored	.40	.40
1263	A186	60c multicolored	.60	.60
1264	A186	$3 multicolored	2.50	2.50
	Nos. 1261-1264 (4)		3.75	3.75

Souvenir Sheet

1265	A186	$5 multicolored	3.50	3.50

A187

45c, Men's singles, tennis. 60c, Men's foil fencing. $2, 100m freestyle swimming. $3, Star class yachting. $5, Coxless pairs, rowing.

1990, Nov. 5   Litho.   Perf. 14

1266	A187	45c multicolored	1.25	1.25
1267	A187	60c multicolored	1.40	1.40
1268	A187	$2 multicolored	2.25	2.25
1269	A187	$3 multicolored	3.25	3.25
	Nos. 1266-1269 (4)		8.15	8.15

Souvenir Sheet

1270	A187	$5 multicolored	6.75	6.75

1992 Summer Olympics, Barcelona.

Christmas — A188

Walt Disney characters on carousel animals: 10c, Mickey, frog. 15c, Huey, Dewey &

Louie, white elephant. 25c, Donald, polar bear. 45c, Goofy, goat. $1, Donald, giraffe. $2, Daisy, stork. $4, Goofy, lion. $5, Daisy, horse. No. 1279, Mickey, swan chariot, horiz. No. 1280, Mickey, Minnie & Goofy, griffin chariot.

1990, Dec. 13   Perf. 13½x14

1271	A188	10c multicolored	.40	.40
1272	A188	15c multicolored	.50	.50
1273	A188	25c multicolored	.60	.60
1274	A188	45c multicolored	.90	.90
1275	A188	$1 multicolored	1.25	1.25
1276	A188	$2 multicolored	2.00	2.00
1277	A188	$4 multicolored	4.00	4.00
1278	A188	$5 multicolored	5.00	5.00
	Nos. 1271-1278 (8)		14.65	14.65

Souvenir Sheets
Perf. 14x13½

1279	A188	$6 multicolored	7.00	7.00
1280	A188	$6 multicolored	7.00	7.00

World Cup Soccer Championships, Italy — A189

Players and coaches from participating countries.

1990, Dec. 28   Litho.   Perf. 14

1281	A189	15c England	.45	.45
1282	A189	45c Brazil	.75	.75
1283	A189	60c West Germany	1.00	1.00
1284	A189	$4 Austria	4.25	4.25
	Nos. 1281-1284 (4)		6.45	6.45

Souvenir Sheets

1285	A189	$6 Ireland, vert.	5.00	5.00
1286	A189	$6 USSR, vert.	5.00	5.00

Cog Trains of Switzerland A190

Designs: 10c, Glion-Roches de Naye, 1890. 35c, Electric cog rail car ascending Mt. Pilatus. 45c, Cog railway to Schynige Platte, view of Eiger, Monch and Jungfrau Mountains. 60c, Furka-Oberalp train on Bugnli Viaduct, vert. $1, 1910 Jungfraubahn Cog Railway, Jungfrau Mountain, 1910. $2, Testing Swiss rail cars built for Pike's Peak on Arth-Rigibahn, 1963. $4, Brienz-Rothorn Bahn, 1991. $5, Private 1870 Rigi-Scheideck Hotel post stamp, 1890 Arth-Rigi Railway Engine. No. 1295, Sherlock Holmes watching Brunigline train descending from Brunig Pass. No. 1296, Switzerland #738 and first passenger train to ascend Mt. Rigi, 1871.

1991, Mar. 26   Litho.   Perf. 14

1287	A190	10c multicolored	.60	.60
1288	A190	35c multicolored	1.00	1.00
1289	A190	45c multicolored	1.10	1.10
1290	A190	60c multicolored	1.25	1.25
1291	A190	$1 multicolored	1.40	1.40
1292	A190	$2 multicolored	2.00	2.00
1293	A190	$4 multicolored	3.00	3.00
1294	A190	$5 multicolored	3.50	3.50
	Nos. 1287-1294 (8)		13.85	13.85

Souvenir Sheets
Perf. 13½

1295	A190	$6 multicolored	6.00	6.00
1296	A190	$6 multicolored	6.00	6.00

Nos. 1295-1296 each contain one 50x37mm stamp.

Voyages of Discovery A191

Explorer's ships: 10c, Gil Eannes, 1433-1434. 25c, Alfonso Gonclaves Baldaya, 1436. 45c, Bartolomeu Dias, 1487. 60c, Vasco da Gama, 1497-1499. $1, Vallarte the Dane. $2, Aloisio Cadamosto, 1456-1458. $4, Diogo Gomes, 1457. $5, Diogo Cao, 1482-1485.

No. 1305, Blue and yellow macaw. No. 1306, Red and yellow macaw.

1991, Apr. 8   Litho.   Perf. 14

1297	A191	10c multicolored	.45	.45
1298	A191	25c multicolored	.55	.55
1299	A191	45c multicolored	.65	.65
1300	A191	60c multicolored	.75	.75
1301	A191	$1 multicolored	1.10	1.10
1302	A191	$2 multicolored	1.60	1.60
1303	A191	$4 multicolored	2.75	2.75
1304	A191	$5 multicolored	3.25	3.25
	Nos. 1297-1304 (8)		11.10	11.10

Souvenir Sheets

1305	A191	$6 multicolored	4.75	4.75
1306	A191	$6 multicolored	4.75	4.75

Discovery of America, 500th anniv. (in 1992).

Japanese Costumes A192

Walt Disney characters wearing Japanese costumes: 10c, Donald as soldier. 15c, Mickey as Kabuki actor. 25c, Mickey, Minnie in traditional wedding clothes. 45c, Daisy as Geisha girl, vert. $1, Mickey in sokutai dress of high government official, vert. $2, Goofy as mino farmer, vert. $4, Pete as shogun, vert. $5, Donald as warlord. No. 1315, Mickey, as Noh player, vert. No. 1316, Goofy as Kabubei-Jishi street performer, vert.

1991, May 22   Litho.   Perf. 14

1307	A192	10c multicolored	.65	.65
1308	A192	15c multicolored	.75	.75
1309	A192	25c multicolored	.90	.90
1310	A192	45c multicolored	1.10	1.10
1311	A192	$1 multicolored	2.00	2.00
1312	A192	$2 multicolored	2.75	2.75
1313	A192	$4 multicolored	3.50	3.50
1314	A192	$5 multicolored	4.25	4.25
	Nos. 1307-1314 (8)		15.90	15.90

Souvenir Sheets

1315	A192	$6 multicolored	7.50	7.50
1316	A192	$6 multicolored	7.50	7.50

Phila Nippon '91.

Mushrooms — A193

10c, Horn of plenty. 15c, Shaggy mane. 45c, Yellow morel. 60c, Chanterelle. $1, Blewit. $2, Slippery jack. $4, Emetic russula. $5, Honey mushroom.

No. 1326, Beefsteak polypore. No. 1327, Voluminous-latex milky.

1991, June 3   Litho.   Perf. 14

1318	A193	10c multicolored	.25	.25
1319	A193	15c multicolored	.45	.45
1320	A193	45c multicolored	.55	.55
1321	A193	60c multicolored	.65	.65
1322	A193	$1 multicolored	1.00	1.00
1323	A193	$2 multicolored	1.75	1.75
1324	A193	$4 multicolored	3.00	3.00
1325	A193	$5 multicolored	4.00	4.00
	Nos. 1318-1325 (8)		11.65	11.65

Souvenir Sheets

1326	A193	$6 multicolored	5.00	5.00
1327	A193	$6 multicolored	5.00	5.00

Royal Family Birthday, Anniversary
Common Design Type

1991, June 17   Litho.   Perf. 14

1328	CD347	10c multicolored	.45	.45
1329	CD347	15c multicolored	.90	.90
1330	CD347	40c multicolored	1.00	1.00
1331	CD347	60c multicolored	1.10	1.10
1332	CD347	$1 multicolored	2.00	2.00
1333	CD347	$2 multicolored	2.75	2.75
1334	CD347	$4 multicolored	4.00	4.00
1335	CD347	$5 multicolored	4.50	4.50
	Nos. 1328-1335 (8)		16.70	16.70

Souvenir Sheets

1336	CD347	$5 Elizabeth, Philip	5.00	5.00
1337	CD347	$5 Charles, Diana, sons	8.50	8.50

10c, 60c, $2, $4, No. 1336, Queen Elizabeth II, 65th birthday. Others, Charles and Diana, 10th wedding anniversary.

Vincent Van Gogh (1853-1890), Painter A194

Paintings: 10c, Thatched Cottages. 25c, The House of Pere Eloi. 45c, The Midday Siesta. 60c, Portrait of a Young Peasant, vert. $1, Still Life: Vase with Irises Against a Yellow Background, vert. $2, Still Life Vase with Irises. $4, Blossoming Almond Tree. $5, Irises. No. 1346, A Meadow in the Mountains: Le Mas De Saint-Paul. No. 1347, Doctor Gachet's Garden in Auvers, vert.

1991, July 8   Litho.   Perf. 13½

1338	A194	10c multicolored	.65	.65
1339	A194	25c multicolored	.90	.90
1340	A194	45c multicolored	1.10	1.10
1341	A194	60c multicolored	1.40	1.40
1342	A194	$1 multicolored	2.00	2.00
1343	A194	$2 multicolored	2.50	2.50
1344	A194	$4 multicolored	3.75	3.75
1345	A194	$5 multicolored	4.00	4.00
	Nos. 1338-1345 (8)		16.30	16.30

Size: 101x75mm
Imperf

1346	A194	$6 multicolored	6.50	6.50
1347	A194	$6 multicolored	6.50	6.50

Intl. Literacy Year — A195

Scenes from Walt Disney's "The Little Mermaid": 10c, Ariel with Flounder and Sebastian. 25c, King Triton. 45c, Sebastian drums in "Kiss De Girl" concert. 60c, Flotsam and Jetsam taunt Ariel. $1, Scuttle, Flounder and Ariel. $2, Ariel and Flounder discover a book. $4, Prince Eric, dog Max, manservant Grimsby, and crew. $5, Ursula the sea witch. No. 1356, Ariel transformed into human being. No. 1357, Ariel and Prince Eric dancing in town, vert.

1991, Aug. 6   Perf. 14

1348	A195	10c multicolored	.35	.35
1349	A195	25c multicolored	.45	.45
1350	A195	45c multicolored	.65	.65
1351	A195	60c multicolored	.90	.90
1352	A195	$1 multicolored	1.50	1.50
1353	A195	$2 multicolored	2.75	2.75
1354	A195	$4 multicolored	4.50	4.50
1355	A195	$5 multicolored	5.50	5.50
	Nos. 1348-1355 (8)		16.60	16.60

Souvenir Sheets

1356	A195	$6 multicolored	6.50	6.50
1357	A195	$6 multicolored	6.50	6.50

World Landmarks A196

Designs: 10c, Empire State Building, US, vert. 25c, Kremlin, USSR. 45c, Buckingham Palace, United Kingdom. 60c, Eiffel Tower, France, vert. $1, Taj Mahal, India. $2, Sydney Opera House, Australia. $4, Colosseum, Italy. $5, Pyramids, Egypt. No. 1366, Galileo demonstrating laws of physics from Tower of Pisa, Italy. No. 1367, Great Wall of China and Emperor Shi Huang Ti.

1991, Aug. 12   Litho.   Perf. 14

1358	A196	10c multicolored	.45	.45
1359	A196	25c multicolored	.55	.55
1360	A196	45c multicolored	.90	.90
1361	A196	60c multicolored	1.10	1.10
1362	A196	$1 multicolored	2.00	2.00
1363	A196	$2 multicolored	3.00	3.00
1364	A196	$4 multicolored	4.75	4.75
1365	A196	$5 multicolored	5.50	5.50
	Nos. 1358-1365 (8)		18.25	18.25

Souvenir Sheets

1366	A196	$6 multicolored	8.00	8.00
1367	A196	$6 multicolored	8.00	8.00

DOMICA

Japanese Attack on Pearl Harbor, 50th Anniv. — A197

Designs: 10c, 6:00am, First wave of Japanese planes leave carrier Akagi. 15c, 6:40am, Destroyer Ward and PBY attack midget submarine. 45c, 7:00am, Second wave of Japanese planes leave carriers. 60c, 7:48am, Japanese Zeros attack on Kaneohe Air Station. $1, 8:30am, Destroyers Breeze, Medusa and Curtiss sink midget submarine. $2, 8:45am, Damaged battleship Nevada sorties. $4, 8:10am, Battleship Arizona explodes, killing 1,177 men. $5, 9:45am, Japanese attack ends. No. 1376, 8:00am, Japanese fighters and bombers attack Hickam Air Base. No. 1377, 7:55am, Pearl Harbor attack begins.

1991, Sept. 2
1368	A197	10c multicolored	.60	.60
1369	A197	15c multicolored	.70	.70
1370	A197	45c multicolored	1.10	1.10
1371	A197	60c multicolored	1.25	1.25
1372	A197	$1 multicolored	1.50	1.50
1373	A197	$2 multicolored	2.00	2.00
1374	A197	$4 multicolored	2.75	2.75
1375	A197	$5 multicolored	3.00	3.00
	Nos. 1368-1375 (8)		12.90	12.90

Souvenir Sheets
1376	A197	$6 multicolored	5.25	5.25
1377	A197	$6 multicolored	5.25	5.25

Butterflies — A198

1c, Little yellow. 2c, Gulf fritillary. 5c, Monarch. 10c, Red rim. 15c, Flambeau. 20c, Large orange sulphur. 25c, Caribbean buckeye. 35c, Polydamas swallowtail. 45c, Cassius blue. 55c, Great southern white. 60c, Godman's leaf. 65c, Hanno blue. 90c, Mimic. $1, Long-tailed skipper. $1.20, Orion. $2, Cloudless sulphur. $5, Painted lady. $10, Southern daggertail. $20, White peacock.

Perf. 13½x13, 13½x14 (2c, 10c, 15c, 25c, 45c, 90c, $1, $20)

1991-93
1378	A198	1c multi	.35	.90
1379	A198	2c multi	.35	.90
1380	A198	5c multi	.65	.90
1381	A198	10c multi	.65	.25
1382	A198	15c multi	.75	.25
1383	A198	20c multi	.75	.25
1384	A198	25c multi	.75	.25
1385	A198	35c multi	.85	.35
1386	A198	45c multi	.85	.35
1386A	A198	55c multi	1.25	.60
1387	A198	60c multi	1.00	.40
1387A	A198	65c multi	1.25	.60
1388	A198	90c multi	1.40	.60
1389	A198	$1 multi	1.40	.75
1389A	A198	$1.20 multi	1.50	1.50
1390	A198	$2 multi	2.25	2.25
1391	A198	$5 multi	3.75	5.50
1391A	A198	$10 multi	9.00	11.00
1391B	A198	$20 multi	14.00	16.00
	Nos. 1378-1391B (19)		42.75	43.60

Issued: 55c, 65c, $1.20, 1/11/93; others, 10/14/91.

Charles de Gaulle, Birth Cent. — A199

1991, Nov. 1
1392	A199	45c shown	2.25	2.25

Souvenir Sheet
1393	A199	$5 blk & bl, horiz.	6.00	6.00

Creole Week — A200

45c, Man in 18th cent. costume. 60c, Accordion player. $1, Dancers. $5, Stick fight c. 1785.

1991, Nov. 1 — Perf. 14
1394	A200	45c multicolored	.60	.60
1395	A200	60c multicolored	.90	.90
1396	A200	$1 multicolored	1.50	1.50
	Nos. 1394-1396 (3)		3.00	3.00

Souvenir Sheet
1397	A200	$5 multicolored	6.50	6.50

Credit Union, 40th Anniv. — A201

60c, Emblem, founder, horiz.

1991, Nov. 1
1398	A201	10c black	.55	.55
1399	A201	60c blk, red, org, yel	1.50	1.50

Year of the Environment and Shelter — A202

15c, Keep the beaches clean. 60c, No. 1402, Amazona imperialis. No. 1403, Lagoon outlet.

1991, Nov. 18
1400	A202	15c multicolored	.50	.50
1401	A202	60c multicolored	2.75	2.75

Souvenir Sheets
1402	A202	$5 multicolored	7.75	7.75
1403	A202	$5 multicolored	7.75	7.75

Paintings by Jan van Eyck: 10c, The Virgin Enthroned with Child (detail). 20c, The Madonna at the Fountain. 35c, The Virgin in a Church. 45c, The Madonna with Canon van der Paele. 60c, The Madonna with Canon van der Paele (detail). $1, The Madonna in an Interior. $3, The Annunciation. $5, The Annunciation, diff. No. 1412, The Madonna with Chancellor Rolin. No. 1413, Virgin and Child with Saints and Donor.

Christmas — A203

1991, Dec. 2 — Perf. 12
1404	A203	10c multicolored	.55	.55
1405	A203	20c multicolored	.75	.75
1406	A203	35c multicolored	.90	.90
1407	A203	45c multicolored	1.00	1.00
1408	A203	60c multicolored	1.50	1.50
1409	A203	$1 multicolored	1.75	1.75
1410	A203	$3 multicolored	2.75	2.75
1411	A203	$5 multicolored	4.00	4.00
	Nos. 1404-1411 (8)		13.20	13.20

Souvenir Sheets
Perf. 14x14½
1412	A203	$6 multicolored	6.50	6.50
1413	A203	$6 multicolored	6.50	6.50

Queen Elizabeth II's Accession to the Throne, 40th Anniv.
Common Design Type

1992, Feb. 6 — Litho. — Perf. 14
1414	CD348	10c multicolored	.25	.25
1415	CD348	15c multicolored	.25	.25
1416	CD348	$1 multicolored	.75	.75
1417	CD348	$5 multicolored	3.75	3.75
	Nos. 1414-1417 (4)		5.00	5.00

Souvenir Sheets
1418	CD348	$6 River scene	3.75	3.75
1419	CD348	$6 Seaside village	3.75	3.75

Botanical Gardens, Cent. — A204

Designs: 10c, Cricket match. 15c, Scenic entrance. 45c, Traveller's tree. 60c, Bamboo house. $1, Old pavilion. $2, Ficus benjamina. $4, Cricket ground. $5, Thirty-five steps. No. 1428, Fountain. No. 1429, Cricket masters.

1992, Mar. 30 — Litho. — Perf. 14
1420	A204	10c multicolored	.40	.40
1421	A204	15c multicolored	.40	.40
1422	A204	45c multicolored	.40	.40
1423	A204	60c multicolored	.60	.60
1424	A204	$1 multicolored	1.00	1.00
1425	A204	$2 multicolored	1.75	1.75
1426	A204	$4 multicolored	4.25	4.25
1427	A204	$5 multicolored	4.50	4.50
	Nos. 1420-1427 (8)		13.30	13.30

Souvenir Sheets
1428	A204	$6 multicolored	5.00	5.00
1429	A204	$6 multicolored	5.00	5.00

Spanish Art — A205

Paintings or details from paintings by Velazquez: 10c, Pope Innocent X. 15c, 45c The Forge of Vulcan (different details). 60c, Queen Mariana of Austria. $1, Pablo de Valladolid. $2, Sebastian de Morra. $3, Felipe IV (detail). $4, Felipe IV. No. 1438, Surrender of Breda. No. 1439, The Drunkards.

1992, May 4 — Perf. 13
1430	A205	10c multicolored	.25	.25
1431	A205	15c multicolored	.25	.25
1432	A205	45c multicolored	.45	.45
1433	A205	60c multicolored	.55	.55
1434	A205	$1 multicolored	.80	.80
1435	A205	$2 multicolored	1.50	1.50
1436	A205	$3 multicolored	2.25	2.25
1437	A205	$4 multicolored	2.75	2.75

Size: 120x95mm
Imperf
1438	A205	$6 multicolored	4.75	4.75
1439	A205	$6 multicolored	4.75	4.75
	Nos. 1430-1439 (10)		18.30	18.30

Granada '92.

Easter — A206

Paintings: 10c, The Supper at Emmaus, studio of Gerrit Van Honthorst. 15c, Christ before Caiaphas, by Van Honthorst. 45c, The Taking of Christ, by Valentin de Boulogne. 60c, Pilate Washing his Hands, by Mattia Preti, vert. $1, The Last Supper (detail), by Master of the Heredos of The Chapel of the Church of S. Francisco D'Evora. $2, The Three Marys at the Tomb (detail), by Adolphe William Bouguereau, vert. $3, Denial of St. Peter, by Hendrik Terbrugghen. $5, Doubting Thomas, by Bernardo Strozzi, vert. No. 1448, The Crucifixion (detail), by Mathias Grunewald, vert. No. 1449, The Resurrection (detail), by Caravaggio, vert.

1992 — Perf. 14
1440	A206	10c multicolored	.25	.25
1441	A206	15c multicolored	.25	.25
1442	A206	45c multicolored	.50	.50
1443	A206	60c multicolored	.75	.75
1444	A206	$1 multicolored	.90	.90
1445	A206	$2 multicolored	1.50	1.50
1446	A206	$3 multicolored	2.25	2.25
1447	A206	$5 multicolored	3.75	3.75
	Nos. 1440-1447 (8)		10.15	10.15

Souvenir Sheets
1448	A206	$6 multicolored	5.00	5.00
1449	A206	$6 multicolored	5.00	5.00

Columbus and New World Flora and Fauna — A207

10c, Hercules beetle. 25c, Crapaud frog. 75c, Parrot. $2, Anole. $4, Royal gramma. $5, Hibiscus.

No. 1456, Giant katydid. No. 1457, Columbus' fleet.

1992, May 18
1450	A207	10c multicolored	.50	.50
1451	A207	25c multi	1.00	1.00
1452	A207	75c multi	1.75	1.75
1453	A207	$2 multi	2.00	2.00
1454	A207	$4 multi	2.75	2.75
1455	A207	$5 multi	3.50	3.50
	Nos. 1450-1455 (6)		11.50	11.50

Souvenir Sheets
1456	A207	$6 multi	5.00	5.00
1457	A207	$6 multi	5.00	5.00

Nos. 1456-1457 are horiz.

Hummingbirds — A208

10c, Purple throated carib. 15c, Rufous breasted hermit. 45c, Puerto Rican emerald. 60c, Antillean mango. $1, Green throated carib. $2, Blue headed. $4, Eastern streamertail. $5, Antillean crested. No. 1466, Green mango. No. 1467, Vervain hummingbird.

1992, May 28
1458	A208	10c multicolored	.50	.50
1459	A208	15c multicolored	.50	.50
1460	A208	45c multicolored	.75	.75
1461	A208	60c multicolored	.90	.90
1462	A208	$1 multicolored	1.25	1.25
1463	A208	$2 multicolored	2.25	2.25
1464	A208	$4 multicolored	3.75	3.75
1465	A208	$5 multicolored	4.50	4.50
	Nos. 1458-1465 (8)		14.40	14.40

Souvenir Sheets
1466	A208	$6 multicolored	6.75	6.75
1467	A208	$6 multicolored	6.75	6.75

Genoa '92.

Dinosaurs A209

10c, Camptosaurus. 15c, Edmontosaurus. 25c, Corythosaurus. 60c, Stegosaurus. $1, Torosaurus. $3, Euoplocephalus. $4, Tyrannosaurus. $5, Parasaurolophus.

1992, June 23 — Litho. — Perf. 14
1468	A209	10c multi	.60	.60
1469	A209	15c multi	.60	.60
1470	A209	25c multi	.75	.75
1471	A209	60c multi	.85	.85
1472	A209	$1 multi	1.00	1.00
1473	A209	$3 multi	1.90	1.90
1474	A209	$4 multi	3.00	3.00
1475	A209	$5 multi	3.50	3.50
	Nos. 1468-1475 (8)		12.10	12.10

Souvenir Sheets
1476	A209	$6 like #1472	4.75	4.75
1477	A209	$6 like #1470	4.75	4.75

DOMINICA

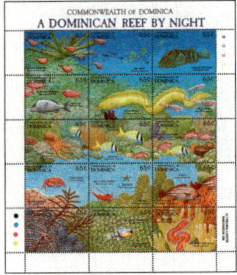

Marine Life — A210

No. 1478: a, Copper sweeper (b). b, Sea wasp (c). c, Nassau grouper. d, Glasseye snapper, margate. e, Green moray (f). f, Reef squid. g, Octopus. h, Porkfish (g, i). i, Reef squirrelfish (h). j, Coral crab, flower coral. k, Red coral shrimp, sea star, pillar coral (l, n). l, Cubbyu, brain coral (o). m, Basket starfish, thick finger coral. n, Belted cardinal fish, boulder coral (k, m). o, Fire worm, crenelated fire coral.

No. 1479: a, Trumpetfish, blue chromis. b, Queen triggerfish. c, Hawksbill turtle. d, Sergeant major, rock beauty. e, Sharksucker. f, Lemon shark. g, Spotted trunkfish, bluehead. h, Blue tang, yellowtail damselfish. i, Queen angelfish, banded butterflyfish. j, Spotted seahorse, flower coral. k, Stoplight parrotfish, pillar coral. l, Smallmouth grunt, brain coral. m, Flamingo tongue, thick finger coral. n, Arrow crab, boulder coral. o, Sharknose goby, crenelated fire coral.

No. 1480, Harlequin bass. No. 1481, Flamefish.

1992, July 20		Litho.		Perf. 14	
1478	A210	65c	Sheet of 15, #a.-o.	7.75	7.75
1479	A210	65c	Sheet of 15, #a.-o.	7.75	7.75
		Souvenir Sheets			
1480	A210	$6	multicolored	6.50	6.50
1481	A210	$6	multicolored	6.50	6.50

A211

10c, Archery. 15c, Two-man canoeing. 25c, 110-meter hurdles. 60c, Men's high jump. $1, Greco-Roman wrestling. $2, Men's rings. $4, Men's parallel bars. $5, Equestrian.

No. 1490, Field hockey. No. 1491, Women's platform diving.

1992, Aug. 10		Litho.	Perf. 14	
1482	A211	10c multi	.30	.30
1483	A211	15c multi	.35	.35
1484	A211	25c multi	.40	.40
1485	A211	60c multi	.65	.65
1486	A211	$1 multi	.90	.90
1487	A211	$2 multi	1.50	1.50
1488	A211	$4 multi	2.75	2.75
1489	A211	$5 multi	3.25	3.25
		Nos. 1482-1489 (8)	10.10	10.10
		Souvenir Sheets		
1490	A211	$6 multi	5.50	5.50
1491	A211	$6 multi	5.50	5.50

1992 Summer Olympics, Barcelona.

A212

1992		Litho.	Perf. 14½	
1492	A212	$1 Coming ashore	1.00	1.00
1493	A212	$2 Natives, ships	1.75	2.00

Discovery of America, 500th anniv. Organization of East Caribbean States.

Walt Disney's Goofy, 60th Anniv. A213

Scenes from Disney cartoon films: 10c, Two Weeks Vacation, 1952. 15c, Aquamania, 1961. 25c, Goofy Gymnastics, 1949. 45c, How to Ride a Horse, 1941. $1, Foul Hunting, 1947. $2, For Whom the Bulls Toil, 1953. $4, Tennis Racquet, 1949. $5, Double Dribble, 1946. No. 1502, Aquamania, 1961, vert. No. 1503, The Goofy Sports Story, 1956, vert.

1992, Nov. 11		Litho.	Perf. 14x13½	
1494	A213	10c multicolored	.45	.45
1495	A213	15c multicolored	.55	.55
1496	A213	25c multicolored	.80	.80
1497	A213	45c multicolored	.90	.90
1498	A213	$1 multicolored	1.50	1.50
1499	A213	$2 multicolored	2.75	2.75
1500	A213	$4 multicolored	4.75	4.75
1501	A213	$5 multicolored	5.25	5.25
		Nos. 1494-1501 (8)	16.95	16.95
		Souvenir Sheets		
		Perf. 13½x14		
1502	A213	$6 multicolored	7.75	7.75
1503	A213	$6 multicolored	7.75	7.75

Model Trains — A214

15c, Brass Reno 4-4-0, HO scale, c. 1963. 25c, Union Pacific Golden Classic, G gauge, 1992. 55c, LMS 3rd class brake coach, OO scale, 1970s. 65c, Brass Wabash 2-6-0, HO scale, c. 1958. 75c, Pennsylvania RR T-1 duplex, O gauge, 1991. $1, Streamline engine 2-6-0, O gauge, post World War II. $3, Japanese Natl. Railways class C62, HO scale, c. 1960. No. 1512, 1st "toy" train in Japan, 1854. No. 1513, Stephenson's Rocket, 1:26 scale, c. 1972, vert.

1992, Nov. 11			Perf. 14	
1504	A214	15c multicolored	.45	.45
1505	A214	25c multicolored	.50	.55
1506	A214	55c multicolored	.75	.75
1507	A214	65c multicolored	.90	.90
1508	A214	75c multicolored	1.00	1.00
1509	A214	$1 multicolored	1.25	1.25
1510	A214	$3 multicolored	2.75	2.75
1511	A214	$5 multicolored	4.50	4.50
		Nos. 1504-1511 (8)	12.10	12.15
		Souvenir Sheets		
		Perf. 13		
1512	A214	$6 multicolored	5.50	5.50
1513	A214	$6 multicolored	5.50	5.50

No. 1512 contains one 52x40mm stamp, No. 1513 one 39x51mm stamp.

Hummel Figurines — A215

Angel: 20c, Playing violin. 25c, Playing horn. 55c, Playing mandolin. 65c, Seated, playing trumpet. 90c, On cloud with lantern. $1, Holding candle. $1.20, Flying. $6, On cloud with candle.

1992, Nov. 2			Perf. 14	
1514	A215	20c multicolored	.35	.35
1515	A215	25c multicolored	.35	.35
1516	A215	55c multicolored	.55	.55
1517	A215	65c multicolored	.70	.70
a.		Sheet of 4, #1514-1517	2.25	2.25
1518	A215	90c multicolored	1.00	1.00
1519	A215	$1 multicolored	1.25	1.25
1520	A215	$1.20 multicolored	1.50	1.50
1521	A215	$6 multicolored	3.25	3.25
a.		Sheet of 4, #1518-1521	8.00	8.00
		Nos. 1514-1521 (8)	8.95	8.95

Anniversaries and Events A216 A217

Designs: 25c, Graf Zeppelin, 1929. No. 1523, Elderly man, plant. No. 1524, Elderly man on bicycle. No. 1525, Elderly man helping boy bait hook. No. 1526, Konrad Adenauer. No. 1527, Space shuttle. No. 1528, Wolfgang Amadeus Mozart. No. 1529, Snowy egret. No. 1530, Sir Thomas Lipton, Shamrock V, 1930. $2, Men pulling fishing net toward beach. $3, Helen Keller. No. 1533, Earth Resources Satellite. No. 1534, Map of Germany, 1949. No. 1535, Eland. $5, Count Ferdinand von Zeppelin. No. 1537, Cologne Cathedral, Germany. No. 1538, Scene from the Magic Flute. No. 1539, Mir Space Station. No. 1540, Engine of Graf Zeppelin. No. 1541, Rhinoceros hornbill.

1992		Litho.	Perf. 14	
1522	A216	25c multicolored	.60	.60
1523	A216	45c multicolored	.80	.80
1524	A216	45c multicolored	.80	.80
1525	A216	45c multicolored	.80	.80
1526	A216	90c multicolored	.90	.90
1527	A216	90c multicolored	.90	.90
1528	A217	$1.20 multicolored	2.00	2.00
1529	A216	$1.20 multicolored	1.50	1.50
1530	A216	$1.20 multicolored	1.75	1.75
1531	A216	$2 multicolored	1.75	1.75
1532	A216	$3 multicolored	3.00	3.00
1533	A216	$4 multicolored	3.00	3.00
1534	A216	$4 multicolored	4.25	4.25
1535	A216	$4 multicolored	4.25	4.25
1536	A216	$5 multicolored	5.00	5.00
		Nos. 1522-1536 (15)	31.30	31.30
		Souvenir Sheets		
1537	A216	$6 multicolored	6.25	6.25
1538	A217	$6 multicolored	6.75	6.75
1539	A216	$6 multicolored	6.25	6.25
1540	A216	$6 multicolored	6.25	6.25
1541	A216	$6 multicolored	5.75	5.75

Konrad Adenauer, 25th anniv. of death (Nos. 1526, 1534, 1537). Intl. Space Year (Nos. 1527, 1533, 1539). Mozart, 200th anniv. of death (in 1991) (Nos. 1528, 1538). Count Zeppelin, 75th anniv. of death (Nos. 1522, 1536, 1540). Intl. Day of the Elderly (Nos. 1523-1525). UN Earth Summit, Rio (Nos. 1529, 1535, 1541). America's Cup yacht race (No. 1530). WHO Intl. Conference on Nutrition, Rome (No. 1531). Lions Intl., 75th anniv. (No. 1532).

Issued: Nos. 1528, 1539, Oct.; Nos. 1523-1527, 1533-1534, 1537-1538, Nov.; Nos. 1522, 1529, 1535-1536, 1540-1541, Dec.

Miniature Sheet

Louvre Museum, Bicent. A218

Details or entire paintings by Titian: a-b, Madonna and Child with St. Catherine and a Rabbit (diff. details). c, A Woman at Her Toilet. d-e, The Supper at Emmaus (diff. details). f, The Pastoral Concert. g-h, An Allegory, Perhaps of Marriage (diff. details).

Painting by Hieronymus Bosch: $6, The Ship of Fools.

1993, Mar. 24		Litho.	Perf. 12	
1542	A218	$1 Sheet of 8, #a.-h. + label	9.50	9.50
		Souvenir Sheet		
		Perf. 14½		
1543	A218	$6 multicolored	5.75	5.75

No. 1543 contains one 55x88mm stamp.

Elvis Presley, 15th Anniv. of Death (in 1992) — A219

a, Portrait. b, With guitar. c, Holding microphone.

1993, Feb.			Perf. 14	
1544	A219	$1 Strip of 3, #a.-c.	3.75	3.75

Miniature Sheet

Birds of Dominica A220

a, Plumbeous warbler. b, Black swift. c, Blue-hooded euphonia. d, Rufous-throated solitaire. e, Ringed kingfisher. f, Blue-headed hummingbird. g, Bananaquit. h, Trembler. i, Forest thrush. j, Purple-throated carib. k, Ruddy quail dove. l, Least bittern.

No. 1546, Imperial parrot. No. 1547, Red-necked parrot (Amazona arausiaca).

1993, Apr. 30				
1545	A220	90c Sheet of 12, #a.-l.	18.00	18.00
		Souvenir Sheets		
1546	A220	$6 multicolored	6.50	6.50
1547	A220	$6 multicolored	6.50	6.50

Turtles — A221

25c, Leatherback laying eggs. 55c, Hawksbill. 65c, Atlantic Ridley. 90c, Green turtle laying eggs. $1, Green turtle at sea. $2, Hawksbill, diff. $4, Loggerhead. $5, Leatherback at sea. No. 1556, Green turtle hatchling. No. 1557, Head of hawksbill.

1993, May 26		Litho.	Perf. 14	
1548	A221	25c multicolored	.45	.45
1549	A221	55c multicolored	.55	.55
1550	A221	65c multicolored	.75	.75
1551	A221	90c multicolored	.95	.95
1552	A221	$1 multicolored	1.10	1.10
1553	A221	$2 multicolored	1.75	1.75
1554	A221	$4 multicolored	3.25	3.25
1555	A221	$5 multicolored	4.25	4.25
		Nos. 1548-1555 (8)	13.05	13.05
		Souvenir Sheets		
1556	A221	$6 multicolored	5.75	5.75
1557	A221	$6 multicolored	5.75	5.75

For overprints see Nos. 2103-2107.

Automobiles A222

Designs: 90c, 1928 Model A Ford. $1.20, Mercedes-Benz winning Swiss Grand Prix, 1936. $4, Mercedes-Benz winning German Grand Prix, 1935. $5, 1915 Model T Ford.

No. 1562: a, 1993 Mercedes-Benz coupe/roadster. b, 1893 Benz Viktoria.

No. 1563, Ford GT-40.

1993, May		Litho.	Perf. 14	
1558	A222	90c multicolored	.80	.80
1559	A222	$1.20 multicolored	1.10	1.10
1560	A222	$4 multicolored	2.75	2.75
1561	A222	$5 multicolored	3.75	3.75
		Nos. 1558-1561 (4)	8.40	8.40

DOMINICA

Souvenir Sheets
1562	A222	$3 Sheet of 2, #a.-b.	5.00	5.00
1563	A222	$6 multicolored	5.00	5.00

No. 1563 contains one 57x42mm stamp. First Ford gasoline engine, cent. (Nos. 1558, 1561, 1563). Benz's first four-wheeled vehicle, cent. (Nos. 1559-1560, 1562).

Dominica Grammar School, Cent. — A223

Designs: 25c, School crest. 30c, V. A. A. Archer, first West Indian headmaster. 65c, Hubert A. Charles, first Dominican headmaster. 90c, Present school building.

1993, May
1564	A223	25c multicolored	.25	.25
1565	A223	30c multicolored	.30	.30
1566	A223	65c multicolored	.60	.60
1567	A223	90c multicolored	.85	.85
		Nos. 1564-1567 (4)	2.00	2.00

Aviation Anniversaries A224

Designs: 25c, New York ticker tape parade, 1920. 55c, BAC Lightning F2. 65c, Graf Zeppelin over Sphinx, pyramids, 1929. $1, Boeing 314 flying boat. $2, Astronaut stepping onto moon. $4, Viktoria Louise over Kiel harbor, 1912. $5, Supermarine Spitfire, vert. No. 1575, Royal Air Force Crest, vert. No. 1576, Hugo Eckener in airship cockpit, vert. No. 1577, Jean-Pierre Blanchard's hot air balloon, 1793, vert.

1993, May 28   Litho.   Perf. 14
1568	A224	25c multicolored	.90	.90
1569	A224	55c multicolored	1.10	1.10
1570	A224	65c multicolored	1.50	1.50
1571	A224	$1 multicolored	1.75	1.75
1572	A224	$2 multicolored	3.00	3.00
1573	A224	$4 multicolored	4.00	4.00
1574	A224	$5 multicolored	4.25	4.25
		Nos. 1568-1574 (7)	16.50	16.50

Souvenir Sheets
1575	A224	$6 multicolored	6.25	6.25
1576	A224	$6 multicolored	6.25	6.25
1577	A224	$6 multicolored	5.75	5.75

Zeppelin Capt. Hugo Eckener, 125th anniv. of birth (Nos. 1568, 1570, 1573, 1576). Royal Air Force, 75th anniv. (Nos. 1569, 1574-1575). Nos. 1575-1576 each contain one 42x57mm stamp.

Miniature Sheet

Coronation of Queen Elizabeth II, 40th Anniv. — A225

Designs: No. 1578a, 20c, Official coronation photograph. b, 25c, Ceremony. c, 65c, Gold State Coach. d, $5, Queen Elizabeth II, Queen Mother.

$6, Portrait, by Norman Hutchinson, 1969.

1993, June 2   Litho.   Perf. 13½x14
1578	A225	Sheet, 2 each #a.-d.	13.00	13.00

Souvenir Sheet
Perf. 14
1579	A225	$6 multicolored	6.75	6.75

No. 1579 contains one 28x42mm stamp. For overprints see Nos. 1688-1689.

A226

Cameo photos of couple and: 90c, Crown Prince holding flowers. $5, Princess wearing full-length coat.

$6, Princess riding in limousine.

1993, June 14   Litho.   Perf. 14
1580	A226	90c multicolored	.75	.75
1581	A226	$5 multicolored	5.00	5.00

Souvenir Sheet
1582	A226	$6 multicolored	6.00	6.00

Wedding of Japan's Crown Prince Naruhito and Masako Owada.

Inauguration of Pres. William J. Clinton — A227

$5, Bill, Hillary Clinton. $6, Bill Clinton, vert.

1993, July 30   Litho.   Perf. 14
1583	A227	$5 multicolored	4.25	4.25

Souvenir Sheet
1584	A227	$6 multicolored	6.00	6.00

Willy Brandt (1913-92), German Chancellor A228

Brandt and: 65c, Pres. Eisenhower, 1959. $5, N.K. Winoton, 1064. $6, Portrait.

1993, July 30
1585	A228	65c black & brown	.90	.90
1586	A228	$5 black & brown	4.75	4.75

Souvenir Sheet
1587	A228	$6 black & brown	6.00	6.00

Picasso (1881-1973) — A229

Paintings: 25c, Bather with Beach Ball, 1929. 90c, Portrait of Leo Stein, 1906. $5, Portrait of Wilhelm Unde, 1910. $6, Man with a Pipe, 1915.

1993, July 30
1588	A229	25c multicolored	.40	.40
1589	A229	90c multicolored	.85	.85
1590	A229	$5 multicolored	4.75	4.75
		Nos. 1588-1590 (3)	6.00	6.00

Souvenir Sheet
1591	A229	$6 multicolored	6.00	6.00

Polska '93 — A230

Paintings: 90c, Self-portrait, by Marian Czorybuła, 1921. $3, Portrait of Bruni Jasieński, by Tytus Czyzewski, 1921. $6, Miser, by Tadeusz Makowski, 1973.

1993, July 30
1592	A230	90c multicolored	1.50	1.50
1593	A230	$3 multicolored	3.50	3.50

Souvenir Sheet
1594	A230	$6 multicolored	6.00	6.00

A231

90c, Monika Holzner, speedskating, 1984. $4, US hockey players, Ray Leblanc, Tim Sweeney, 1992. $6, Men's ski jump.

1993, July 30
1595	A231	90c multicolored	1.50	1.50
1596	A231	$4 multicolored	4.00	4.00

Souvenir Sheet
1597	A231	$6 multicolored	5.75	5.75

1994 Winter Olympics, Lillehammer, Norway.

Copernicus (1473-1543) — A232

Designs: $1.20, Astronomer using quadrant. $3, Observatory. $5, Copernicus.

1993, July 30
1598	A232	$1.20 multicolored	1.50	1.50
1599	A232	$3 multicolored	3.75	3.75

Souvenir Sheet
1600	A232	$5 multicolored	6.00	6.00

Opening of New General Post Office — A233

New General Post Office and: 25c, Prince Philip. 90c, Queen Elizabeth II.

1993, July 30
1601	A233	25c multicolored	.25	.25
1602	A233	90c multicolored	1.00	1.00

1994 World Cup Soccer Championships, US — A234

25c, Maradona, Buchwald. 55c, Gullit. 65c, Chavarria, Bliss. No. 1606, 90c, Maradona. No. 1607, 90c, Alvares. $1, Altobelli, Yonghwang. $2, Referee, Stopyra. $5, Renquin, Yaremtchuk. No. 1611, Brehme. No. 1612, Fabbri.

1993, Sept. 8   Litho.   Perf. 14
1603	A234	25c multicolored	.65	.65
1604	A234	55c multicolored	.75	.75
1605	A234	65c multicolored	.85	.85
1606	A234	90c multicolored	1.00	1.00
1607	A234	90c multicolored	1.00	1.00
1608	A234	$1 multicolored	1.25	1.25
1609	A234	$2 multicolored	2.00	2.00
1610	A234	$5 multicolored	0.00	0.00
		Nos. 1603-1610 (8)	10.50	10.50

Souvenir Sheets
1611	A234	$6 multicolored	4.50	4.50
1612	A234	$6 multicolored	4.50	4.50

Taipei '93 — A235

25c, Tiger Balm Gardens. 65c, Building, Kenting Park. 90c, Tzu-en Tower. $5, Villa, Lan Tao Island.
No. 1617 — Chinese kites: a, Chang E Rising up to the Moon. b, Red Phoenix and Rising Sun. c, Heavenly Judge. d, Monkey King. e, Goddess of the Luo River. f, Heavenly Maiden Scatters Flowers.
$6, Jade Girl, Liao Dynasty.

1993, Oct. 4   Litho.   Perf. 13½x14
1613	A235	25c multi	.30	.30
1614	A235	65c multi	.55	.55
1615	A235	90c multi	1.00	1.00
1616	A235	$5 multi	4.25	4.25
		Nos. 1613-1616 (4)	6.10	6.10

Miniature Sheet
1617	A235	$1.65 Sheet of 6, #a.-f.	10.00	10.00

Souvenir Sheet
1618	A235	$6 multi	5.25	5.25

With Bangkok '93 Emblem
25c, Tugu Monument, Java. 55c, Candi Cangkuang, West Java. 90c, Pura Taman Ayun, Mengwi. $5, Stone mosaics, Ceto.
No. 1623 — Puppets: a, Thai, Rama and Sita. b, Burmese, Tha Khi Lek. c, Burmese, diff. d, Thai, Demons, Wat Phra Kaew. e, Thai, Hun Lek performing Khun Chang, Khun Phaen. f, Thai, Hun Lek performing Ramakien.
$6, Stone carving, Thailand.

1993
1619	A235	25c multi	.30	.30
1620	A235	55c multi	.55	.55
1621	A235	90c multi	1.00	1.00
1622	A235	$5 multi	4.00	4.00
		Nos. 1619-1622 (4)	5.85	5.85

Miniature Sheet
1623	A235	$1.65 Sheet of 6, #a.-f.	10.00	10.00

Souvenir Sheet
1624	A235	$6 multi	5.25	5.25

With Indopex '93 Emblem
Designs: 25c, Ornate Chedi, Wat Phra Boromathat Chaiya. 55c, Preserved temple ruins, Sukhothai Historical Park. 90c, Prasat Hin Phimai, Thailand. $5, Main sanctuary, Prasat Phanom Rung, Thailand.
Indonesian puppets: No. 1629: a, Arjuna & Prabu Gilling Wesi. b, Loro Blonyo. c, Yogyanese puppets, Menak cycle. d, Wayang gedog, Ng Setro. e, Wayang golek, Kencana Wungu. f, Wayang gedog, Raden Damar Wulan.
$6, Sculpture of Majapahit noble, Pura Sada, Kapel.

1993, Oct. 4   Litho.   Perf. 13½x14
1625	A235	25c multicolored	.40	.40
1626	A235	55c multicolored	.60	.60
1627	A235	90c multicolored	1.25	1.25
1628	A235	$5 multicolored	4.00	4.00
		Nos. 1625-1628 (4)	6.25	6.25

Miniature Sheet
1629	A235	$1.65 Sheet of 6, #a.-f.	10.00	10.00

Souvenir Sheet
1630	A235	$6 multicolored	5.25	5.25

Miniature Sheet

Willie the Operatic Whale — A236

Nos. 1631-1633, Characters and scenes from Disney's animated film Willie the Operatic Whale.

1993, Nov. 1   Litho.   Perf. 14x13½
1631	A236	$1 Sheet of 9, #a.-i.	14.00	14.00

Souvenir Sheets
1632	A236	$6 multicolored	5.00	5.00

Perf. 13½x14
1633	A236	$6 multi, vert.	5.00	5.00

Christmas A237

25c, 55c, 65c, 90c (No. 1637), Details or entire woodcut, The Adoration of the Magi, by Durer.
90c (No. 1638), $1, $3, $5, Details or entire painting, The Foligni Madonna, by Raphael.

216 DOMINICA

Souvenir Sheets: No. 1642, $6, The Adoration of the Magi, by Durer. No. 1643, $6, The Foligni Madonna, by Raphael.

1993, Nov. 8   Litho.   Perf. 13
1634-1643	A237	Set of 10	20.00	20.00

A238

Hong Kong '94 — A239

Stamps, scene from Peak Tram: No. 1644, Hong Kong #527, city buildings, trees. No. 1645, Trees, tram, #1292.
Chinese jade: No. 1646a, Horse. b, Cup with handle. c, Vase with birthday peaches. d, Vase. e, Fu dog and puppy. f, Drinking vessel.

1994, Feb. 18   Litho.   Perf. 14
1644	A238	65c multicolored	.50	.50
1645	A238	65c multicolored	.50	.50
a.		Pair, #1644-1645	1.10	1.10

Miniature Sheet
1646	A239	65c Sheet of 6, #a.-f.	5.75	5.75

Nos. 1644-1645 issued in sheets of 5 pairs. No. 1645a is a continuous design.
New Year 1994 (Year of the Dog) (No. 1646e).

Insects, Butterflies, & Birds — A240

Various Hercules beetles: 20c, 25c, 65c, Male. 90c, Female.
$1, Imperial parrot. $2, Southern dagger tail. $3, The mimic. $5, Purple-throated carib.
Each $6: No. 1655, Snout butterfly. No. 1656, Blue-headed hummingbird.

1994, Mar. 15   Litho.   Perf. 14
1647-1654	A240	Set of 8	11.00	11.00
1650a		Min. sheet, 3 each #1647-1650	10.00	10.00

Souvenir Sheets
1655-1656	A240	Set of 2	12.00	12.00

World Wildlife Fund (Nos. 1647-1650).

Mushrooms — A241

Designs: 20c, Russula matoubenis. 25c, Leptonia caeruleocapita. 65c, Inocybe littoralis. 90c, Russula hygrophytica. $1, Pyrrhoglossum lilaceipes. $2, Hygrocybe konradii. $3, Inopilus magnificus. $5, Boletellus cubensis.
No. 1665, Gerronema citrinum. No. 1666, Lentinus strigosus.

1994, Apr. 18
1657	A241	20c multicolored	.45	.45
1658	A241	25c multicolored	.50	.50
1659	A241	65c multicolored	.65	.65
1660	A241	90c multicolored	.80	.80
1661	A241	$1 multicolored	.95	.95
1662	A241	$2 multicolored	1.50	1.50
1663	A241	$3 multicolored	2.00	2.00
1664	A241	$5 multicolored	3.00	3.00
		Nos. 1657-1664 (8)	9.85	9.85

Souvenir Sheets
1665	A241	$6 multicolored	4.75	4.75
1666	A241	$6 multicolored	4.75	4.75

Orchids — A242

Designs: 20c, Laeliocattleya. 25c, Sophrolaeliocattleya. 65c, Odontocidium. 90c, Laeliocattleya, diff. $1, Cattleya. $2, Odontocidium, diff. $3, Epiphronitis. $4, Oncidium.
Each $6: No. 1675, Schombocattleya. No. 1676, Cattleya, diff.

1994, May 3
1667-1674	A242	Set of 8	10.00	10.00

Souvenir Sheets
1675-1676	A242	Set of 2	10.00	10.00

New Year 1994 (Year of the Dog) — A243

Designs: 20c, Dachshund. 25c, Beagle. 55c, Greyhound. 90c, Jack Russell terrier. $1, Pekingese. $2, White fox terrier. $4, English toy spaniel. $5, Irish setter.
No. 1686, Welsh corgi. No. 1687, Labrador retriever.

1994, May 17
1678	A243	20c multicolored	.30	.30
1679	A243	25c multicolored	.35	.35
1680	A243	55c multicolored	.50	.50
1681	A243	90c multicolored	.80	.80
1682	A243	$1 multicolored	1.00	1.00
1683	A243	$2 multicolored	1.50	1.50
1684	A243	$4 multicolored	2.50	2.50
1685	A243	$5 multicolored	3.00	3.00
		Nos. 1678-1685 (8)	9.95	9.95

Souvenir Sheets
1686	A243	$6 multicolored	5.00	5.00
1687	A243	$6 multicolored	5.00	5.00

Nos. 1578-1579 Ovptd. in Black or Silver

1994, June 27   Litho.   Perf. 13½x14
1688	A225	Sheet, 2 ea #a-d	15.00	15.00

Souvenir Sheet
1689	A225	$6 multicolored (S)	7.25	7.25

Overprint on No. 1689 appears in sheet margin.

Miniature Sheet

1994 World Cup Soccer Championships, US — A244

No. 1690: a, Dos Armstrong, US. b, Dennis Bergkamp, Netherlands. c, Roberto Baggio, Italy. d, Rai, Brazil. e, Cafu, Brazil. f, Marco Van Basten, Netherlands.
Each $6: No. 1691, Roberto Mancini, Italy. No. 1692, Stanford Stadium, Palo Alto.

1994, July 5   Perf. 14
1690	A244	$1 Sheet of 6, #a.-f.	6.00	6.00

Souvenir Sheets
1691-1692	A244	Set of 2	10.00	10.00

Butterflies A245

20c, Florida white. 25c, Red rim. 55c, Barred sulphur. 65c, Mimic. $1, Large orange sulphur. $2, Southern dagger tail. $3, Dominican snout butterfly. $5, Caribbean buckeye.
No. 1700, Clench's hairstreak. No. 1701, Painted lady.

1994, May 3   Litho.   Perf. 14
1693	A245	20c multi	.40	.40
1694	A245	25c multi	.40	.40
1695	A245	55c multi	.75	.75
1696	A245	65c multi	.80	.80
1697	A245	$1 multi	1.00	1.00
1698	A245	$2 multi	1.50	1.50
1698A	A245	$3 multi	2.00	2.00
1699	A245	$5 multi	3.50	3.50
		Nos. 1693-1699 (8)	10.35	10.35

Souvenir Sheets
1700	A245	$6 multi	5.50	5.50
1701	A245	$6 multi	5.50	5.50

 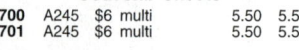

10th Caribbean Scout Jamboree A246

Designs: 20c, Backpacking. 25c, Cooking over campfire. 55c, Making camp. 65c, Camping. $1, Scout drum unit. $2, Planting trees. $4, Sailing. $5, Scout salute.
Each $6: No. 1710, Early Scout troop. No. 1711, Pres. C.A. Sorhaindo, vert.

1994, July 18   Litho.   Perf. 14
1702-1709	A246	Set of 8	11.50	11.50

Souvenir Sheets
1710-1711	A246	Set of 2	11.50	11.50

For overprints see Nos. 1762-1766.

D-Day, 50th Anniv. — A247

Designs: 65c, US Waco glider brings reinforcements. $2, British Horsa gliders land more troops. $3, Glider troops take Pegasus Bridge.
$6, Hadrian glider.

1994, July 26
1712-1714	A247	Set of 3	5.00	5.00

Souvenir Sheet
1715	A247	$6 multicolored	4.75	4.75

A248

Intl. Olympic Committee, Cent. — A249

Designs: 55c, Ulrike Meyfarth, Germany, high jump, 1984. $1.45, Dieter Baumann, Germany, 5000-meter run, 1992.
$6, Ji Hoon Chae, South Korea, 500-meter short track speed skating, 1994.

1994, July 26
1716	A248	55c multicolored	.90	.90

1717	A248	$1.45 multicolored	2.00	2.00

Souvenir Sheet
1718	A249	$6 multicolored	5.75	5.75

English Touring Cricket, Cent. — A250

Designs: 55c, D.I. Goweer Leics, England, vert. 90c, E.C.L. Ambrose, Leeward Islands. $1, G.A. Gooch, England, vert.
$3, First English team, 1895.

1994, July 26
1719-1721	A250	Set of 3	4.00	4.00

Souvenir Sheet
1722	A250	$3 multicolored	5.75	5.75

Miniature Sheet of 6

First Manned Moon Landing, 25th Anniv. A251

No. 1723: a, Apollo 14 crew. b, Apollo 14 patch. c, Apollo 14 lunar module Antares at Fra Mauro Crater. d, Apollo 15 crew. e, Apollo 15 patch. f, Apollo 15 mission, Mount Hadley from rover.
$6, 25th anniv. emblem, lunar surface.

1994, July 26
1723	A251	$1 #a.-f.	7.75	7.75

Souvenir Sheet
1724	A251	$6 multicolored	6.50	6.50

A252

PHILAKOREA '94 — A253

Designs: 65c, P'alsang-jon Hall, Korea. 90c, Popchu-sa Temple. $2, Uhwajong Pavillion, Korea.
Screen, Late Choson Dynasty showing flowers and: No. 1728a, c, e, Birds. b, g, Butterfly. d, Roosters. f, Duck. h, Pheasant. i, Cranes. j, Deer.
$4, Stylized "spirit post" guardian.

1994, July 26   Perf. 14, 13 (#1728)
1725-1727	A252	Set of 3	3.50	3.50

Miniature Sheet of 10
1728	A253	55c #a.-j.	6.00	6.00

Souvenir Sheet
1729	A252	$4 multicolored	3.00	3.00

Mickey Mouse, 65th Birthday — A254

Disney characters: 20c, Dippy dawg. 25c, Clarabelle Cow. 55c, Horace Horsecollar. 65c, Mortimer Mouse. $1, Joe Piper. $3, Mr. Casey. $4, Chief O'Hara. $5, Mickey and the Blot.
Each $6: No. 1738, Minnie, Tanglefoot. No. 1739, Pluto, Minnie, horiz.

DOMICA

Perf. 13½x14, 14x13½ (#1739)
1994, Oct. 3
1730-1737 A254 Set of 8   14.00 14.00
Souvenir Sheets
1738-1739 A254 Set of 2   13.00 13.00

A255

Local Entertainers: 20c, Sonia Llyod, folk singer. 25c, Ophelia Marie, singer. 55c, Edney Francis, accordionist. 65c, Norman Letang, saxophonist. 90c, Edie Andre, steel drummer.

1994, Dec. 1   Litho.   Perf. 14
1740-1744 A255 Set of 5   3.25 3.25

Miniature Sheet

A256

Marilyn Monroe (1926-62), Actress: Nos. 1745a-1745i, Various portraits. No. 1746, $6, Hands above head. No. 1747, $6, Holding hat.

1994, Dec. 1
1745 A256 90c #a.-i.   11.50 11.50
Souvenir Sheets
1746-1747 A256 Set of 2   10.00 10.00

Christmas — A257

Details or entire Spanish paintings: 20c, Madonna and child, by Luis de Morales. 25c, Madonna and Child with Yarn Winder, by Morales. 55c, Our Lady of the Rosary, by Zurbaran. 65c, Dream of the Patrician, by Bartolome Murillo. 90c, Madonna of Charity, by El Greco. $1, The Annunciation, by Zurbaran. $2, Mystical Marriage of St. Catherine, by Jusepe de Ribera. $3, The Holy Family with St. Bruno and Other Saints, by Ribera.
Each $6: No. 1756, Vision of the Virgin to St. Bernard, by Murillo. No. 1757, Adoration of the Shepherds, by Murillo.

1994, Dec. 2   Perf. 13½x14
1748-1755 A257 Set of 8   7.00 7.00
Souvenir Sheets
1756-1757 A257 Set of 2   10.00 10.00

Order of the Caribbean Community A258

First award recipients: 25c, Sir Shridath Ramphal, statesman, Guyana. 65c, William Gilbert Demas, economist, Trinidad & Tobago. 90c, Derek Walcott, writer, St. Lucia.

1994, Dec. 16   Perf. 14
1758-1760 A258 Set of 3   2.00 2.00

Jeffrey Edmund, 1994 World Cup Soccer Player — A259

1994, Dec. 28
1761 A259 25c multicolored   .35 .35

Nos. 1705, 1708-1711 Ovptd.

1995, Mar. 21   Litho.   Perf. 14
1762-1764 A246 Set of 3   7.00 7.00
Souvenir Sheets
1765-1766 A246 Set of 2   10.00 10.00
Location of overprint varies.

New Year 1995 (Year of the Boar) — A260

Stylized boar: a, 25c, Facing right. b, 65c, Facing forward. c, $1, Facing left.
$2, Two facing each other, horiz.

1995, Apr. 15   Litho.   Perf. 14½
1767 A260 Strip of 3, #a.-c.   1.60 1.60
    d. Souv. sheet of 3, #1767a-
        1767c   1.60 1.60
Souvenir Sheet
1768 A260 $2 multicolored   1.50 1.50
No. 1767 was issued in sheets of 4 strips.

Birds — A261

Designs: 25c, Wood duck. 55c, Mallard. 65c, Blue-winged teal. $5, Blood eared parakeet.
No. 1773, vert.: a, Cattle egret. b, Snow goose (a, c). c, Peregrine falcon. d, Barn owl. e, Black-crowned night heron. f, Common grackle. g, Brown pelican. h, Great egret. i, Ruby-throated hummingbird. j, Laughing gull. k, Greater flamingo. l, Common moorhen.
No. 1774, Trumpeter swan, vert. No. 1775, White-eyed vireo.

1995, Apr. 15   Litho.   Perf. 14
1769-1772 A261 Set of 4   5.00 5.00
Miniature Sheet of 12
1773 A261 65c #a.-l.   16.00 16.00
Souvenir Sheets
1774 A261 $5 multicolored   5.00 5.00
1775 A261 $6 multicolored   6.00 6.00

Miniature Sheets

End of World War II, 50th Anniv. — A262

No. 1776: a, Mitsubishi A6M2 Zero. b, Aichi D3A1 Type 99 "Val." c, Nakajima 97-B5N "Kate." d, Zuikaku. e, Akagi. f, Ryuho.
No. 1777: a, German Panther tank, Ardennes. b, Allied fighter bomber. c, Patton's army crosses the Rhine. d, Rocket-powered ME 163. e, V-2 rocket on launcher. f, German U-boat surrenders in North Atlantic. g, Round the clock bombardment of Berlin. h, Soviet soldiers reach center of Berlin.

Each $6: No. 1778, Statue atop Dresden's town hall after Allied bombing. No. 1779, Japanese attack plane.

1995   Litho.   Perf. 14
1776 A262 $2 #a.-f. + label   9.00 9.00
1777 A262 $2 #a.-h. + label   13.00 13.00
Souvenir Sheets
1778-1779 A262 Set of 2   14.00 14.00
Issued: Nos. 1777-1778, 5/18; others, 7/21.

1996 Summer Olympics, Atlanta — A263

Designs: 15c, Mark Breland, boxing. 20c, Lou Banach, Joseph Atiyeh, freestyle wrestling. 25c, Judo. 55c, Fencing. 65c, Matt Biondi, swimming. $1, Gushiken on rings, vert. $2, Cycling, vert. $5, Volleyball.
Each $6: No. 1788, Joe Fargis on Touch of Class, equestrian. No. 1789, Soccer, vert.

1995, July 21
1780-1787 A263 Set of 8   9.50 9.50
Souvenir Sheets
1788-1789 A263 Set of 2   10.60 10.60

UN, 50th Anniv. — A264

No. 1790: a, 65c, Signatures on UN charter, attendee. b, $1, Attendee. $2, Attendees. $6, Winston Churchill.

1995, Aug. 16   Litho.   Perf. 14
1790 A264 Strip of 3, #a.-c.   2.75 2.75
Souvenir Sheet
1791 A264 $6 multicolored   5.00 5.00
No. 1790 is a continuous design.

Souvenir Sheets

FAO, 50th Anniv. — A265

Street market scene: a, 90c, Woman in red dress. b, $1, Woman seated. c, $2, Vendors, women.
$6, Woman in field, woman holding water cans, vert.

1995, Aug. 16
1792 A265 Sheet of 3, #a.-c.   2.50 2.50
1793 A265 $6 multicolored   4.50 4.50
No. 1792 is a continuous design.

Queen Mother, 95th Birthday — A266

No. 1794: a, Drawing. b, Wearing crown, green dress. c, Formal portrait. d, Blue dress. $6, Portrait as younger woman.

1995, Aug. 16   Perf. 13½x14
1794 A266 $1.65 Strip or block of
              4, #a.-d.   5.50 5.50
Souvenir Sheet
1795 A266 $6 multicolored   5.50 5.50
No. 1794 was issued in sheets of 8 stamps. Sheet margins of Nos. 1794-1795 exist with black frame and text "In Memoriam — 1900-2002" overprinted in sheet margins.

Rotary, 90th Anniv. — A267

1995   Perf. 14
1796 A267 $1 Paul Harris, emblem   1.00 1.00
Souvenir Sheet
1797 A267 $6 Rotary emblems   4.75 4.75

Dinosaurs A268

20c, Monoclonius. 25c, Euoplocephalus. 55c, Coelophysis. 65c, Compsognathus.
No. 1802: a, Dimorphodon. b, Ramphorynchus. c, Giant alligator. d, Pentaceratops.
No. 1803, vert: a, Ceratosaurus. b, Comptosaurus (a). c, Stegosaur. d, Camarasaurus. e, Baronyx. f, Dilophosaurus. g, Dromaeosaurids (f). h, Deinonychus. i, Dinicthys. j, Carcharodon (k) k, Nautiloid, l, Trilobite.
$5, Sauropelta. $6, Triceratops, vert.

1995, Sept. 8
1798-1801 A268 Set of 4   1.75 1.75
1802 A268 90c Strip of 4, #a.-
              d.   3.00 3.00
Miniature Sheet of 12
1803 A268 $1 #a.-l.   10.00 10.00
Souvenir Sheets
1804 A268 $5 multicolored   5.00 5.00
1805 A268 $6 multicolored   5.00 5.00
Singapore '95 (Nos. 1798-1801, 1803-1805).

Miniature Sheets of 6

Nobel Prize Fund Established, Cent. — A269

Recipients, each $2: No. 1806a, Oscar A. Sanchez, peace, 1987. b, Ernst B. Chain, medicine, 1945. c, Aage Bohr, physics, 1975. d, Jaroslav Seifert, literature, 1984. e, Joseph E. Murray, medicine, 1990. f, Jaroslav Heyrovsky, chemistry, 1959.
No. 1807, each $2: a, Adolf von Baeyer, chemistry, 1905. b, Edward Buchner, chemistry, 1907. c, Carl Bosch, chemistry, 1931. d, Otto Hahn, chemistry, 1944. e, Otto Paul Herman Diels, chemistry, 1950. f, Kurt Alder, chemistry, 1950.
No. 1808, Emil A. von Behring, medicine, 1901.

1995, Oct. 24   Litho.   Perf. 14
1806-1807 A269 Set of 2   19.00 19.00
Souvenir Sheet
1808 A269 $2 multicolored   1.75 1.75

Christmas — A270

Details or entire paintings: 20c, Madonna and Child, by Pontormo. 25c, The Immaculate Conception, by Murillo. 55c, The Adoration of the Magi, by Filippino Lippi. 65c, Rest on the Flight into Egypt, by Van Dyck. 90c, Sacred Family, by Van Dyck. $5, The Annunciation, by Van Eyck.
No. 1815, The Virgin and the Infant, by Van Eyck. No. 1816, The Holy Family, by Ribera.

1995, Nov. 30   Litho.   Perf. 13½x14
1809-1814 A270 Set of 6   6.00 6.00
Souvenir Sheets
1815 A270 $5 multicolored   3.75 3.75
1816 A270 $6 multicolored   4.75 4.75

DOMINICA

Miniature Sheets

Sierra Club, Cent. — A271

Designs: No. 1817, each $1: a, Florida panther with mouth open. b, Florida panther looking right. c, Manatee. d, Two manatees. e, Three sockeye salmon. f, Group of sockeye salmon. g, Two southern sea otters. h, Southern sea otter. i, Southern sea otter showing both front paws.
No. 1818, vert, each $1: a, Florida panther. b, Manatee. c, Sockeye salmon. d, Key deer facing left. e, Key deer. f, Key deer with antlers, up close. g, Wallaby with young in pouch. h, Wallaby. i, Wallaby with young.

1995, Dec. 10   Perf. 14
1817-1818   A271   Set of 2   13.00   13.00

Chinese Paintings, A City of Cathay — A272

No. 1819, brown lettering, each 90c: a, Boats docked, people on shore. b, River, bridge. c, Two boats on river. d, River, pavilion along shore. e, Open sea, people in courtyard.
No. 1820, black lettering, each 90c: a, City scene. b, City scene, wall. c, Outside wall, river. d, Large boat on river. e, People crossing over bridge.
No. 1821, $2: a, Boat on river, city above. b, People walking across bridge.
No. 1822, $2: a, Lifting ramp to another boat, vert. b, Holding lines in water, tree, vert.

1995, Dec. 27   Litho.   Perf. 14½
Strips of 5
1819-1820   A272   Set of 2   7.50   7.50
Souvenir Sheets of 2
1821-1822   A272   Set of 2   6.00   6.00

Nos. 1819-1822 are each continuous designs.

Classic Western Art — A273

Paintings by Raphael: No. 1823, Agony in the Garden. No. 1824, Pope Leo X with Two Cardinals. No. 1825, Bindo Altoviti.
$6, Triumphant entry of Constantine into Rome, by Rubens.

1995, Dec. 27   Perf. 14
1823-1825   A273 $2 Set of 3   5.25   5.25
Souvenir Sheet
1826   A273 $6 multicolored   5.25   5.25

New Year 1996 (Year of the Rat) — A274

Stylized rats, Chinese inscriptions: No. 1827a, 25c, purple & brown. b, 65c, orange & green. c. $1, red lilac & blue.
$2, Two rats, horiz.

1996, Jan. 16   Perf. 14½
1827   A274   Strip of 3, #a.-c.   1.90   1.90
Miniature Sheet
1828   A274   Sheet of 1 #1827   1.60   1.60
Souvenir Sheet
1829   A274 $2 multicolored   1.75   1.75

No. 1827 was issued in sheets of 12 stamps.

Miniature Sheet

Disney Lunar New Year — A275

Disney characters representing year of the: No. 1830a, Rat. b, Ox. c, Tiger. d, Hare. e, Dragon. f, Snake. g, Horse. h, Sheep. i, Monkey. j, Rooster. k, Dog. l, Pig.
$3, Rat character. $6, Pig, rat, ox characters on lunar calendar wheel.

1996, Jan. 16   Perf. 14x13½
1830   A275   55c Sheet of 12, #a.-l.   11.00   11.00
Souvenir Sheets
1831   A275 $3 multicolored   4.00   4.00
1832   A275 $6 multicolored   8.00   8.00

Methods of Transportation A276

Designs: 65c, Donkey cart, 1965. 90c, 1910 Car. $2, 1950 Taxi. $3, 1955 Bus.

1996, Jan. 29   Litho.   Perf. 14
1833-1836   A276   Set of 4   8.00   8.00

Miniature Sheets

Locomotives — A277

No. 1837, each $2: a, "Dragon," Hawaii. b, "Regina," Italy. c, Calazo to Padua, Italy. d, "Mogul," Philippines. e, Nuremberg, Germany. f, "Stanislas," French Natl. Railway. g, "Black Five," Scotland. h, SNCF diesel electric, France. i, "Sir Nigel Gresley," England.
No. 1838, each $2: a, Hohi Line 9600 class, Japan. b, Peloponnese Express, Greece. c, Porter 2-4-0S, Hawaii. d, Norway-Swedish Jodemans Railway. e, 220 Diesel, Federal German Railway. f, 2-8-4T Indian Railways. g, East African Railways. h, Electrical trains, USSR. i, 0-8-0, Austria.
$5, "Duchess of Hamilton," England. $6, Diesel engine, China.

1996, Jan. 29
1837-1838   A277   Set of 2   28.00   28.00
Souvenir Sheets
1839   A277 $5 multicolored   4.75   4.75
1840   A277 $6 multicolored   5.25   5.25

No. 1837h has a face value of $1.

Giant Panda — A278

Designs: a, With right leg up on rock. b, Front legs up on rock. c, Seated. d, Holding head down.

1996, May 15   Litho.   Perf. 13½x14
1841   A278   55c Block of 4, #a.-d.   4.50   4.50

Souvenir Sheet
Perf. 14x13½
1842   A278 $3 Panda, horiz.   3.75   3.75

CHINA '96, 9th Asian Intl. Philatelic Exhibition. No. 1841 was issued in sheets of 8 stamps.
See No. 1911.

Queen Elizabeth II, 70th Birthday A279

No. 1843: a, Portrait. b, Wearing regalia of Order of the Garter. c, Wearing bright blue dress, pearls.
$6, In uniform.

1996, May 16   Litho.   Perf. 13½x14
1843   A279 $2 Strip of 3, #a.-c.   4.25   4.25
Souvenir Sheet
1844   A279 $6 multicolored   4.25   4.25

No. 1843 was issued in sheets of 9 stamps.

Legendary Film Detectives — A280

Designs: a, Humphrey Bogart as Sam Spade. b, Sean Connery as James Bond. c, Warren Beatty as Dick Tracy. d, Basil Rathbone as Sherlock Holmes. e, William Powell as the Thin Man. f, Sidney Toler as Charlie Chan, g, Peter Sellers as Inspector Clouseau. h, Robert Mitchum as Philip Marlowe. i, Peter Ustinov as Inspector Poirot.
$6, Margaret Rutherford as Miss Marple.

1996, July
1845   A280 $1 Sheet of 9, #a.-i.   13.00   13.00
Souvenir Sheet
1846   A280 $6 multicolored   6.00   6.00

1996 Summer Olympics, Atlanta — A281

Designs: 20c, Olympic Stadium, Moscow, 1980. 25c, Hermine Joseph, vert. 55c, Women's field hockey, Zimbabwe, 1980. 90c, Jerome Romain, vert. $1, Polo, discontinued sport, vert. $2, Greg Louganis, diving.

1996   Perf. 14
1847-1852   A281   Set of 6   4.25   4.25
See Nos. 1897-1900.

Local Entertainers A282

Designs: 25c, Irene Peltier, national dress of Dominica. 55c, Rupert Bartley, street band player. 65c, Rosemary Cools-Lartigue, pianist. 90c, Celestine "Orion" Theophile, belle queen, Grand Bay. $1, Cecil Bellot, former government band master.

1996, July 31   Litho.   Perf. 14
1853-1857   A282   Set of 5   2.75   2.75

Jerusalem, 3000th Anniv. — A283

Designs: a, 90c, Shrine of the Book, Israel Museum. b, $1, Church of All Nations. c, $2, The Great Synagogue.
$5, Hebrew University, Mount Scopus.

1996, July 31
1858   A283   Sheet of 3, #a.-c.   3.00   3.00
Souvenir Sheet
1859   A283 $5 multicolored   4.50   4.50

Radio, Cent. — A284

Entertainers: 90c, Artie Shaw. $1, Benny Goodman. $2, Duke Ellington. $4, Harry James.
$6, Tommy Dorsey, Jimmy Dorsey, horiz.

1996, July 31
1860-1863   A284   Set of 4   6.25   6.25
Souvenir Sheet
1864   A284 $6 multicolored   5.00   5.00

UNICEF, 50th Anniv. — A285

20c, Girl looking at globe. 55c, Boy with stethoscope, syringe. $5, Doctor examining child.
No. 1868, Girl, vert.

1996, July 31
1865-1867   A285   Set of 3   4.25   4.25
Souvenir Sheet
1868   A285 $5 multicolored   4.50   4.50

World Post Day — A286

Scenes of 18th cent. life in Dominica: 10c, Captain of ship taking letters by hand. 25c, Anthony Trollope vists Dominica to organize postal service. 55c, Steam vessel "Yare" carries mail around island. 65c, Post offices and agencies. 90c, Country postman carrying mail around mountain tracks. $1, West Indies Federation stamp, first airmail sent on German "goose" seaplane. $2, #602, General Post Office, old and new.
$5, Captain of ship.

1996, Oct. 1   Litho.   Perf. 14
1869-1875   A286   Set of 7   6.25   6.25
Souvenir Sheet
1876   A286 $5 multicolored   5.50   5.50

Fish — A287

Designs: 1c, Scrawled filefish. 2c, Lion fish. 5c, Porcupine fish. 10c, Powder blue surgeonfish. 15c, Red hind. 20c, Golden butterfly fish. 25c, Long-nosed butterfly fish. 35c, Pennant butterfly fish. 45c, Spotted drum. 55c, Blue-girdled angelfish. 60c, Scorpion fish. 65c, Harlequin sweetlips. 90c, Flame angelfish. $1, Queen trigger. $1.20, Stoplight parrot. $1.45,

DOMINICA

Black durgon. $2, Glasseye snapper. $5, Balloon fish. $10, Creole wrasse. $20, Seabass.

1996, Oct. 1   Litho.   Perf. 14

1877	A287	1c multicolored	.30	.50
1878	A287	2c multicolored	.30	.50
1879	A287	5c multicolored	.35	.50
1880	A287	10c multicolored	.45	.45
1881	A287	15c multicolored	.50	.50
1882	A287	20c multicolored	.55	.55
1883	A287	25c multicolored	.55	.55
1884	A287	35c multicolored	.70	.70
1885	A287	45c multicolored	.90	.90
1886	A287	55c multicolored	1.00	1.00
1887	A287	60c multicolored	1.00	1.00
1888	A287	65c multicolored	1.00	1.00
1889	A287	90c multicolored	1.25	1.00
1890	A287	$1 multicolored	1.50	1.00
1891	A287	$1.20 multicolored	1.60	1.00
1892	A287	$1.45 multicolored	1.75	1.25
1893	A287	$2 multicolored	2.00	2.00
1894	A287	$5 multicolored	5.00	5.00
1895	A287	$10 multicolored	10.00	10.00
1896	A287	$20 multicolored	19.00	19.00
		Nos. 1877-1896 (20)	49.70	48.40

See Nos. 2024-2039B for size 20x18mm stamps.

1996 Summer Olympic Games Type

Past Olympic medalists, vert, each 90c: No. 1897a, Ulrike Meyfarth, high jump. b, Pat McCormick, diving. c, Takeichi Nishi, equestrian. d, Peter Farkas, Greco-Roman wrestling. e, Carl Lewis, track & field. f, Agnes Keleti, gymnastics. g, Yasuhiro Yamashita, judo. h, John Kelly, single sculls. i, Naim Suleymanoglu, weight lifting.

No. 1898, vert, each 90c: a, Sammy Lee, diving. b, Bruce Jenner, decathlon. c, Olga Korbut, gymnastics. d, Steffi Graf, tennis. e, Florence Griffith-Joyner, track and field. f, Mark Spitz, swimming. g, Li Ning, gymnastics. h, Erika Salumae, cycling. i, Abebe Bikila, marathon.

#1899, $5, Joan Benoit, 1st women's marathon, vert.

#1900, $5, Milt Campbell, discus.

1996, June 7   Litho.   Perf. 14
Sheets of 9

1897-1898	A281	Set of 2	15.00	15.00

Souvenir Sheets

1899-1900	A281	Set of 2	8.25	8.25

A288

Christmas (Details or entire paintings): 25c, Enthroned Madonna and Child, by Stefano Veneziano. 55c, Noli Me Tangere, by Beato Angelico. 65c, Madonna and Child, by Angelico. 90c, Madonna of Corneta Tarquinia, by Filippo Lippi. $2, Annunciation, by Angelico. $5, Madonna with Child, by Angelico, diff.

Each $6: No. 1907, Coronation of the Virgin, by Beato Angelico. No. 1908, Holy Family with St. Barbara, by Veronese, horiz.

1996, Nov. 25

1901-1906	A288	Set of 6	8.50	8.50

Souvenir Sheets

1907-1908	A288	Set of 2	10.00	10.00

A289

Paintings of "Herdboy and Buffalo," by Li Keran (1907-89): No. 1909: a, f, Herdboy Plays the Flute. b, g, Playing Cricket in the Autumn. c, h, Listen to the Summer Cicada. d, i, Grazing in the Spring.
$2, Return in Wind and Rain.

1997   Litho.   Perf. 14

1909	A289	90c Strip of 4, #a.-d.	3.25	3.25

Souvenir Sheets

1909E	A289	55c Sheet of 4, #f.-i.	2.00	2.00

Perf. 15x14½

1910	A289	$2 multicolored	2.00	2.00

New Year 1997 (Year of the Ox).
No. 1909 was printed in sheets of 8 stamps.
No. 1910 contains one 34x52mm stamp.

Souvenir Sheet

Huangshan Mountain, China — A290

1996, May 15   Litho.   Perf. 12

1911	A290	$2 multicolored	2.25	2.25

China '96. No. 1911 was not available until March 1997.

A291

Lee Lai-Shan, 1996 Olympic Gold Medalist in Wind Surfing — A291a

1997   Litho.   Perf. 15x14

1912	A291	$2 multicolored	1.75	1.75

Souvenir Sheet
Perf. 14

1913	A291	$5 multicolored	4.25	4.25

No. 1912 was issued in sheets of 3.
No. 1913 contains one 38x51mm stamp.

Litho. & Embossed
Perf. 9
Without Gum

1913A	A291a	$35 gold & multi, like #1013		

Butterflies
A292

No. 1014: a, Melitaea motis. b, Coeliades forestan. c, Papilio dardanus. d, Mylothris chloris. e, Poecilmitis thyshe. f, Myrina silenus. g, Bematistes aganice. h, Euphaedra neophron. i, Precis hierta.

No. 1915, vert: a, Striped policeman. b, Mountain sandman. c, Brown-veined white. d, Bowker's widow. e, Foxy charaxes. f, Pirate. g, African clouded yellow. h, Garden inspector.

Each $6: No. 1916, Acraea natalica. No. 1917, Eurytela dryope.

1997, Apr. 1   Litho.   Perf. 14

1914	A292	55c Sheet of 9, #a.-i.	4.75	4.75
1915	A292	90c Sheet of 8, #a.-h.	6.75	6.75

Souvenir Sheets

1916-1917	A292	Set of 2	12.00	12.00

UNESCO, 50th Anniv. — A293

55c, View from temple, China. 65c, Palace of Diocletian, Croatia. 90c, St. Mary's Cathedral, Hildesheim, Germany. $1, Monastery of Rossanou, Mount Athos, Greece. $2, Scandola Nature Reserve, France. $4, Church of San Antao, Portugal.

No. 1924: a, Ruins of Copan, Honduras. b, Cuzco Cathedral, Peru. c, Olinda, Brazil. d, Canaima Natl. Park, Venezuela. e, Galapagos Islands Natl. Park, Ecuador. f, Ruins of Church, Jesuit missions of Santisima, Paraguay. g, Fortress, San Lorenzo, Panama. h, Natl. Park, Fortress, Haiti.

Each $6: No. 1925, Chengde Lakes, China. No. 1926, Kyoto, Japan.

1997, Apr. 7   Perf. 13½x14

1918-1923	A293	Set of 6	8.75	8.75
1924	A293	$1 Sheet of 8, #a.-h. + label	7.75	7.75

Souvenir Sheets

1925-1926	A293	Set of 2	10.50	10.50

Disney Scenes "Sealed with a Kiss" — A294

Cartoon film, year released: 25c, Mickey's Horse, Tanglefoot, 1933. 35c, Shanghaied, 1935. 55c, Pluto's Judgment Day, 1935. 65c, Race for Riches, 1935. 90c, Elmer Elephant, 1936. $1, Brave Little Tailor, 1938. $2, Donald's Crime, 1945. $4, In Dutch, 1946.

Each $6: No. 1935, Nifty Nineties, 1941. No. 1936, Mickey's Surprise Party, 1939.

1997, Apr. 15   Perf. 13½x14

1927-1934	A294	Set of 8	11.00	11.00

Souvenir Sheets

1935-1936	A294	Set of 2	10.00	10.00

Cats — A295

25c, Cream Burmese. $1, Snowshoe. $2, Sorrell Abyssinian. $5, Torbie Persian.

No. 1041: a, British bicolor chorthair (d, e). b, Maine coon kitten, Somali kitten (c). c, Maine coon kitten, diff. d, Lynx point Siamese (e). e, Blue Burmese kitten, white Persian (odd-eyed) (f). f, Persian kitten.

No. 1942, Silver tabby.

1997, Apr. 24   Perf. 14

1937-1940	A295	Set of 4	7.00	7.00
1941	A295	$2 Sheet of 6, #a.-f.	10.50	10.50

Souvenir Sheet

1942	A295	$6 multicolored	5.50	5.50

Dogs — A296

Designs: 20c, Afghan hound. 55c, Cocker spaniel. 65c, Smooth fox terrier. 90c, West Highland white terrier.

No. 1947a, St. Bernard. b, Boy with grand basset. c, Rough collie. d, Golden retriever. e, Golden retriever, Tibetan spaniel, smooth fox terrier. f, Smooth fox terrier, diff.

$6, Shetland sheepdog.

1997, Apr. 24

1943-1946	A296	Set of 4	2.00	2.00
1947	A296	90c Sheet of 6, #a.-f.	5.25	5.25

Souvenir Sheet

1948	A296	$6 multicolored	5.50	5.50

A297

No. 1949: a, Queen Elizabeth II. b, Royal Arms. c, Prince, Queen walking among crowd. d, Queen, Prince in military attire. e, Buckingham Palace. f, Prince Philip.

$6, Portrait of Queen and Prince on balcony.

1997, May 29   Litho.   Perf. 14

1949	A297	$1 Sheet of 6, #a.-f.	5.50	5.50

Souvenir Sheet

1950	A297	$6 multicolored	5.00	5.00

Queen Elizabeth II and Prince Philip, 50th wedding anniv.

Paintings by Hiroshige (1797-1858) — A298

No. 1951: a, Ichigaya Hachiman Shrine. b, Blossoms on the Tama River Embankment. c, Kumano Junisha Shrine, Tsunohazu ("Junso"). d, Benkei Moat from Soto-Sakurada to Kojimachi. e, Kinokuni Hill & View of Akasak Tameike. f, Naito Shinjuku, Yotsuya.

Each $6: No. 1952, Kasumigaseki. No. 1952A, Sanno Festival Procession at Kojimachi I-chome.

1997, May 29

1951	A298	$1.55 Sheet of 6, #a.-f.	10.50	10.50

Souvenir Sheets

1952-1952A	A298	Set of 2	12.50	12.50

Orchids — A299

Designs, vert: 20c, Oncidium altissimum. 25c, Oncidium papilio. 55c, Epidendrum fragrans. 65c, Oncidium lanceanum. 90c, Campylocentrum micranthum. $4, Pogonia rosea.

No. 1959: a, Brassavola cucculata. b, Epidendrum ibaguense. c, Ionopsis utricularioides. d, Rodriguezia lanceolata. e, Oncidium cebolleta. f, Epidendrum ciliare.

Each $5: No. 1960, Stanhopea grandiflora. No. 1961, Oncidium ampliatum.

1997, May 10   Litho.   Perf. 14

1953-1958	A299	Set of 6	8.00	8.00
1959	A299	$1 Sheet of 6, #a.-f.	7.00	7.00

Souvenir Sheets

1960-1961	A299	Set of 2	11.00	11.00

Paul P. Harris (1868-1947), Founder of Rotary, Intl. — A300

Portrait of Harris and: $2, Rotary Village Corps, irrigation project, Honduras. $6, Emblems, world community service.

1997, May 29

1962	A300	$2 multicolored	1.60	1.60

Souvenir Sheet

1963	A300	$6 multicolored	6.00	6.00

Heinrich von Stephan (1831-97) — A301

Portraits of Von Stephan and: No. 1964 a, Kaiser Wilhelm II. b, UPU emblem. c, Postal messenger, ancient Japan.

220 DOMINICA

$6, Von Stephan, Russian dog team carrying post, 1859.

1997, May 29
| 1964 | A301 | $2 Sheet of 3, #a.-c. | 4.25 | 4.25 |

Souvenir Sheet
| 1965 | A301 | $6 multicolored | 4.50 | 4.50 |

PACIFIC 97.

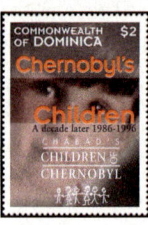

Chernobyl Disaster, 10th Anniv. — A302

Designs: No. 1966, Chabad's Children of Chernobyl. No. 1967, UNESCO.

1997, May 29   *Perf. 13½x14*
| 1966 | A302 | $2 multicolored | 2.25 | 2.25 |
| 1967 | A302 | $2 multicolored | 2.25 | 2.25 |

Grimm's Fairy Tales — A303

Mother Goose Rhymes A304

The Goose Girl: No. 1968: a, Girl with horse. b, Geese, pond, castle. c, Girl. No. 1969, Girl, horiz.
No. 1970: Mary, Mary, Quite Contrary.

1997, May 29   *Perf. 13½x14*
| 1968 | A303 | $2 Sheet of 3, #a.-c. | 6.00 | 6.00 |

Souvenir Sheets
Perf. 14x13½
| 1969 | A303 | $6 multicolored | 6.00 | 6.00 |

Perf. 14
| 1970 | A304 | $6 multicolored | 5.00 | 5.00 |

Return of Hong Kong to China — A305

Designs: $1, View of Hong Kong at night. $1.45, View of Hong Kong in daytime. $2, View of Hong Kong at night, diff.
Hong Kong skyline at dusk: No. 1974: a, 65c, b, 90c. c, $1. d, $3.

1997, July 1   *Perf. 14*
| 1971-1973 | A305 | Set of 3 | 3.75 | 3.75 |
| 1974 | A305 | Sheet of 4, #a.-d. | 5.00 | 5.00 |

Nos. 1971-1973 were issued in sheets of 4.

1998 Winter Olympics, Nagano — A306

Medal winners: 20c, Yukio Kasaya, 1972 ski jump. 25c, Jens Weissflog, 1994 ski jump. No. 1977, 55c, Anton Maier, 1968 men's speed skating. No. 1978, 55c, Ljubov Egorova, 1994 women's cross-country skiing. 65c, 1994 Ice hockey, Sweden. 90c, Bernhard Glass, 1980 men's luge. $4, Frank-Peter Roetsch, 1988 men's biathlon.
No. 1982: a, like #1975. b, like #1976. c, like #1977. d, Christa Rothenburger, 1988 women's speed skating.
Each $5: No. 1983, Jacob Tullin Thams, 1924 ski jumping. No. 1984, Charles Jewtraw, 1924 men's speed skating.

1997, July 15
| 1975-1981 | A306 | Set of 7 | 8.75 | 8.75 |
| 1982 | A306 | $1 Strip or block of 4, #a.-d. | 5.00 | 5.00 |

Souvenir Sheets
| 1983-1984 | A306 | Set of 2 | 9.00 | 9.00 |

No. 1982 issued in sheets of 8 stamps.

1998 World Cup Soccer Championships, France — A307

Players, vert: 20c, Klinsmann, Germany. 55c, Bergkamp, Holland. 65c, Ravanelli, Italy. 90c, Kinkladze, Georgia. $2, Shearer, England. $4, Dani, Portugal.
Stadiums: No. 1991, each 65c: a, Wembley, England. b, Bernabeu, Spain. c, Maracana, Brazil. d, Torino, Italy. e, Centenary, Uruguay. f, Olympic, Germany. g, Rose Bowl, US. h, Azteca, Mexico.
Team Captains: No. 1992, each 65c: a, Meazza, Italy, 1934. b, Matthaus, Germany, 1990. c, Walter, W. Germany, 1954. d, Maradona, Argentina, 1986. e, Beckenbauer, Germany, 1974. f, Moore, England, 1966. g, Dunga, Brazil, 1994. h, Zoff, Italy, 1982.
$5, Mario Kempes, Argentina, vert. $6, Ally McCoist, Scotland, vert.

1997, July 21   *Litho.*   *Perf. 14*
| 1985-1990 | A307 | Set of 6 | 8.00 | 8.00 |

Sheets of 8 + Label
| 1991-1992 | A307 | Set of 2 | 9.00 | 9.00 |

Souvenir Sheets
| 1993 | A307 | $5 multicolored | 4.50 | 4.50 |
| 1994 | A307 | $6 multicolored | 5.50 | 5.50 |

Dominica Credit Union — A308

25c, Joffre Robinson, former Credit Union president. 55c, Sister Alicia, founder credit union movement in Dominica. 65c, Lorrel Bruce, 1st Cooperative Credit Union president. 90c, Roseau Credit Union Building.
$5, Bruce, Robinson, Sister Alicia.

1997, Aug. 15   *Litho.*   *Perf. 14x13½*
| 1995-1998 | A308 | Set of 4 | 2.25 | 2.25 |

Souvenir Sheet
Perf. 14
| 1999 | A308 | $5 multicolored | 4.50 | 4.50 |

No. 1999 contains one 28x60mm stamp.

A309

Medical Pioneers: 20c, Louis Pasteur, father of bacteriology. 25c, Christiaan Barnard, performed first heart transplant. 55c, Sir Alexander Fleming, developer of penicillin. 65c, Camillo Golgi, neurologist. 90c, Jonas Salk, developer of polio vaccine. $1, Har Ghobind Khorana, geneticist. $2, Elizabeth Blackwell, first woman physician. $3, Sir Frank Macfarlane Burnet, immunologist.
$5, Fleming, diff. $6, Pasteur, diff.

1997, Sept. 1   *Litho.*   *Perf. 14*
| 2000-2007 | A309 | Set of 8 | 10.00 | 10.00 |

Souvenir Sheets
| 2008 | A309 | $5 multicolored | 5.25 | 5.25 |
| 2009 | A309 | $6 multicolored | 6.25 | 6.25 |

A310

Diana, Princess of Wales (1961-97): Various portraits.

1997, Oct. 20   *Litho.*   *Perf. 14*
| 2010 | A310 | $2 Sheet of 4, #a.-d. | 6.50 | 6.50 |

Souvenir Sheet
| 2011 | A310 | $5 multicolored | 4.75 | 4.75 |

Christmas — A311

Entire paintings or details: 20c, Echo and Narcissus, by Poussin. 55c, Angel Departing from the Family of Tobias, by Rembrandt. 65c, Seated Nymphs with Flute, by Francois Boucher. 90c, Angel, by Rembrandt. $2, Dispute of the Holy Sacrament, by Raphael. $4, Garden of Love, by Rubens.
Each $6: No. 2018, Annunciation, by Botticelli. No. 2019, Christ on the Mount of Olives, by El Greco.

1997, Nov. 10   *Litho.*   *Perf. 14*
| 2012-2017 | A311 | Set of 6 | 7.00 | 7.00 |

Souvenir Sheets
| 2018-2019 | A311 | Set of 2 | 11.00 | 11.00 |

The $4 is incorrectly inscribed Holy Trinity, by Raphael. No. 2018 is incorrectly inscribed Study of a Muse, by Raphael.

A312

Paintings of tigers, by Ling-Nan School: No. 2020: a, 55c, Gao Qifeng. b, 65c, Zhao Shao'ang. c, 90c, Gao Jianfu. d, $1.20, Gao Jianfu, diff.
$3, Tiger running down mountain, by Gao Jianfu.

1998, Jan. 5   *Litho.*   *Perf. 14½*
| 2020 | A312 | Sheet of 4, #a.-d. | 3.00 | 3.00 |

Souvenir Sheet
Perf. 14x14½
| 2021 | A312 | $3 multicolored | 2.25 | 2.25 |

New Year 1998 (Year of the Tiger). No. 2021 contains one 44x36mm stamp.

Fish Type of 1996

5c, Porcupine fish. 10c, Powder-blue surgeonfish. 15c, Red hind. 20c, Golden butterflyfish. 25c, Long-nosed butterflyfish. 35c, Pennant butterflyfish. 45c, Spotted drum. 55c, Blue-girdled angelfish. 60c, Scorpion fish. 65c, Harlequin sweetlips. 90c, Flame angelfish. $1, Queen trigger. $1.20, Stoplight parrot. $1.45, Black durgon. $2, Glasseye snapper. $5, Balloon fish. $10, Creole wrasse. $20, Seabass.

1998   *Perf. 13x13½*
Size: 20x18mm
2024	A287	5c multi	.30	.50
2025	A287	10c multi	.30	.50
2026	A287	15c multi	.40	.50
2027	A287	20c multi	.40	.40
2028	A287	25c multi	.45	.45
2029	A287	35c multi	.50	.50
2030	A287	45c multi	.70	.70
2031	A287	55c multi	.80	.80
2032	A287	60c multi	.90	.90
2033	A287	65c multi	.90	.90
2034	A287	90c multi	1.00	.90
2035	A287	$1 multi	1.25	1.25
2036	A287	$1.20 multi	1.50	1.40
2037	A287	$1.45 multi	1.75	1.75
2038	A287	$2 multi	2.25	2.25
2039	A287	$5 multi	5.00	5.00
2039A	A287	$10 multi	9.50	9.50
2039B	A287	$20 multi	20.00	20.00
Nos. 2024-2039B (18)			47.90	48.20

A313

Famous 20th cent. athletes — No. 2040: a, Jesse Owens. b, Owens jumping in 1936 Summer Olympic Games, Berlin. c, Isaac Berger lifting weights. d, Berger. e, Boris Becker. f, Becker playing tennis. g, Arthur Ashe playing tennis, holding Wimbledon trophy. h, Ashe.
No. 2041, Franz Beckenbauer, soccer player, horiz.

1998, Feb. 9   *Litho.*   *Perf. 14*
Sheet of 8
| 2040 | A313 | $1 #a.-h. | 7.50 | 7.50 |

Souvenir Sheet
| 2041 | A313 | $6 multi | 6.25 | 6.25 |

Nos. 2040b-2040c, 2040f-2040g are each 53x38mm.

A314

Japanese Cinema Stars — No. 2042: a, Akira Kurosawa. b, Kurosawa's 1950 film, "Rashomon." c, Toshiro Mifune in 1954 film, "Seven Samurai." d, Mifune. e, Yasujiro Ozu. f, Ozu's 1949 film, "Late Spring." g, Sessue Hayakawa in 1957 film, "Bridge on the River Kwai." h, Hayakawa.
No. 2043, Akira Kurosawa, director.

1998, Feb. 9   *Litho.*   *Perf. 14*
Sheet of 8
| 2042 | A314 | $1 #a.-h. | 7.50 | 7.50 |

Souvenir Sheet
| 2043 | A314 | $6 multi | 6.25 | 6.25 |

Nos. 2042b-2042c, 2042f-2042g are each 53x38mm.

A315

DOMINICA

Mushrooms: 10c, Omphalotus illudens. 15c, Inocybe fastigiata. 20c, Marasmius plicatulus. 50c, Mycena lilacifolia. 55c, Armillaria straminea. 90c, Tricholomopsis rutilans.
No. 2050, each $1: a, Lepiota naucina. b, Cortinarius violaceus. c, Boletus aereus. d, Tricholoma aurantium. e, Lepiota procera. f, Clitocybe geotropa. g, Lepiota acutes-quamosa. h, Tricholoma saponaceum. i, Lycoperdon gemmatum.
No. 2051, each $1: a, Boletus ornatipes. b, Russula xerampelina. c, Cortinarius collinitus. d, Agaricus meleagris. e, Coprinus comatus. f, Amanita caesarea. g, Amanita brunnescens. h, Amanita muscaria. i, Morchella esculenta.
$6, Cortinarius violaceus.

1998, Mar. 2	Litho.	Perf. 14
2044-2049 A315 Set of 6	3.00	3.00
Sheets of 9		
2050-2051 A315 Set of 2	17.50	17.50
Souvenir Sheet		
2052 A315 $6 multicolored	5.25	5.25

Sailing Ships — A316

Designs: 65c, Greek bireme. 90c, Egyptian felucca. $1, Viking longboat. $2, Chinese junk.
No. 2057: a, Two-masted topsail schooner. b, The Golden Hinde. c, Roman merchant ship. d, Gazela Primeiro. e, Moshulu. f, Bluenose.
Each $5: No. 2058, Pinta. No. 2059, Chesapeake Bay skipjack.

1998, Mar. 16	Litho.	Perf. 14
2053-2056 A316 Set of 4	4.50	4.50
2057 A316 55c Block of 6, #a.-f.	3.25	3.25
Souvenir Sheets		
2058-2059 A316 Set of 2	10.00	10.00

No. 2053 incorrectly inscribed "Egyptian felucca."
No. 2057 was issued in sheets of 12 stamps.

Mickey & Minnie Mouse's 70th Anniv. A317

25c, Steamboat Willie, 1928. 55c, The Brave Little Tailor, 1938. 65c, Nifty Nineties, 1941. 90c, Mickey Mouse Club, 1955. $1, Mickey, Minnie at the opening of Walt Disney World, 1971. $1.45, Mousercise Mickey & Minnie, 1980.
Each $5: No. 2061, Walt Disney, Mickey, Minnie. No. 2062, Surprise Party for Mickey & Minnie.

1998, June 16	Litho.	Perf. 14x13½
2060A A317 25c black	.30	.30
2060B A317 55c multi	.60	.60
2060C A317 65c multi	.75	.75
2060D A317 90c multi	1.00	1.00
2060E A317 $1 multi	1.10	1.10
2060F A317 $1.45 multi	1.60	1.60
Nos. 2060A-2060F (6)	5.35	5.35
Souvenir Sheet of 7		
2060G #2060A-2060F, 2060h	11.50	11.50
h. $5 Runaway brain, perf 13½ at left	3.50	3.50

Size: 130x104mm
Imperf
2061-2062 A317 Set of 2   10.00   10.00

Souvenir Sheet

Disney's The Lion King A318

1998, June 16	Litho.	Perf. 13½x14
2063 A318 $5 multicolored	7.00	7.00

Sea Birds — A319

25c, Erect crested penguin. 65c, Humboldt penguin. 90c, Red knot. $1, Audubon's shearwater.
No. 2068: a, Crested tern. b, Franklin's gull. c, Australian pelican. d, Fairy prion. e, Andean gull. f, Imperial shag. g, Red phalarope. h, Hooded grebe. i, Least auklet. j, Little grebe. k, Cape petrel. l, Horned grebe.
Each $5: No. 2069, Sula nebouxii. No. 2070, Fulmarus glacialis.

1998, Aug. 4		Perf. 14
2064-2067 A319 Set of 4	2.50	2.50
2068 A319 90c Sheet of 12, #a.-l.	10.00	10.00
Souvenir Sheets		
2069-2070 A319 Set of 2	10.50	10.50

Airplanes A320

20c, Jetstar II. 25c, AN 225. 55c, Dash-8. 65c, Beech-99. 90c, American Eagle. $2, HFB 320 Itansa Jet.
No. 2077, each $1: a, SR 71 "Blackbird." b, Stealth bomber. c, Northrop YF23. d, F-14 A "Tomcat." e, F-15 "Eagle S." f, MiG 29 "Fulcrum." g, Europa X5. h, Camlon.
No. 2078, each $1: a, E400. b, CL-215 C-GKDN Amphibian. c, Piper jet. d, Beech Hawker. e, Lockheed YF22. f, Piper Seneca V. g, CL-215 Amphibian. h, Vantase.
Each $6: No. 2079, F-1 Fighter. No. 2080, Sea Hopper.

1998, Aug. 17		
2071-2076 A320 Set of 6	4.50	4.50
Sheets of 8		
2077-2078 A320 Set of 2	17.00	17.00
Souvenir Sheets		
2079-2080 A320 Set of 2	11.00	11.00

Intl. Year of the Ocean — A321

Marine life: 25c, Fridman fish. 55c, Hydrocoral. 65c, Feather star. 90c, Royal angelfish.
No. 2085, each $1: a, Monk seal. b, Galapagos penguin. c, Manta ray. d, Hawksbill turtle. e, Moorish idol. f, Nautilus. g, Giant clam. h, Tubeworms. i, Nudibranch.
No. 2086, each $1: a, Spotted dolphin. b, Atlantic sailfish. c, Sailfin flying fish. d, Fairy basslet. e, Atlantic spadefish. f, Leatherback turtle. g, Blue tang. h, Coral banded shrimp. i, Rock beauty.
No. 2087, Humpback whale. No. 2088, Leafy sea dragon.

1998, Sept. 7	Litho.	Perf. 14
2081-2084 A321 Set of 4	2.50	2.50
Sheets of 9		
2085-2086 A321 Set of 2	19.00	19.00
Souvenir Sheets		
2087 A321 $5 multicolored	4.75	4.75
2088 A321 $6 multicolored	5.50	5.50

Organization of American States, 50th Anniv. — A322

1998, Sept. 1	Litho.	Perf. 14
2089 A322 $1 multicolored	1.25	1.25

Ferrari Sports Cars — A323

55c, 365 GT 2+2. 90c, Boano/Ellena 250 GT. $1, 375 MM coupe. $5, 212.

1998, Sept. 1		
2090-2092 A323 Set of 3	3.75	3.75
Souvenir Sheet		
2093 A323 $5 multicolored	5.50	5.50

No. 2093 contains one 91x35mm stamp.

Gandhi — A324

1998, Sept. 1		
2094 A324 90c shown	1.50	1.50
Souvenir Sheet		
2095 A324 $6 Seated	5.25	5.25

No. 2094 was issued in sheets of 4.

Pablo Picasso — A325

Paintings: 90c, The Painter and His Model, 1926. $1, The Crucifixion, 1930. $2, Nude with Raised Arms, 1908, vert.
$6, Cafe at Royan, 1940.

1998, Sept. 1		Perf. 14½
2096-2098 A325 Set of 3	4.50	4.50
Souvenir Sheet		
2099 A325 $6 multicolored	5.75	5.75

Royal Air Force, 80th Anniv. — A326

No. 2100: a, Nimrod MR2P. b, C-130 Hercules Mk3. c, Panavia Tornado GR1. d, C-130 Hercules landing.
$5, Biplane, hawk. $6, Hawker Hart, jet.

1998, Sept. 1		Perf. 14
2100 A326 $2 Sheet of 4, #a.-d.	7.00	7.00
Souvenir Sheets		
2101 A326 $5 multicolored	4.75	4.75
2102 A326 $6 multicolored	5.25	5.25

No. 2100d incorrectly inscribed Panavia Tornado GR1.

Nos. 1548-1549, 1551-1552, 1554 Ovptd.

1998, Sept. 14		
2103-2107 A221 Set of 5	6.00	6.00

A327

1998 World Scouting Jamboree, Chile: 65c, Scout sign. $1, Scout handshake. $2, World Scout flag.
$5, Lord Baden-Powell.

1998		
2108-2110 A327 Set of 3	3.25	3.25
Souvenir Sheet		
2111 A327 $5 multicolored	5.25	5.25

A328

Birds: 25c, Northern cardinal. 55c, Eastern bluebird. 65c, Carolina wren. 90c, Blue jay. $1, Evening grosbeak. $2, Bohemian waxwing.
$5, Northern parula. $6, Painted bunting.

1998, Dec. 1	Litho.	Perf. 14
2112-2117 A328 Set of 6	5.50	5.50
Souvenir Sheets		
2118 A328 $5 multicolored	5.25	5.25
2119 A328 $6 multicolored	6.25	6.25

Christmas.

New Year 1999 (Year of the Rabbit) — A329

1999, Jan. 4	Litho.	Perf. 14
2120 A329 $1.50 multicolored	2.00	2.00

No. 2120 was issued in sheets of 4.

Orchids — A330

55c, Broughtonia sanguinea. 65c, Cattleyonia Keith Roth "Roma". 90c, Comparettia falcata. $2, Cochleanthes discolor.
No. 2125, each $1: a, Dracula erythrochaete. b, Lycaste aromatica. c, Masdevallia marguerile. d, Encyclia marfae. e, Laelia gouldiana. f, Huntleya meleagris. g, Galeandria baueri. h, Lycale deppei.
No. 2126, each $1: a, Anguloa clowesii. b, Lemboglossum cervantesii. c, Oncidium cebolleta. d, Millonia. e, Pescatorea lehmannII. f, Sophronitis coccinea. g, Pescatorea cerina. h, Encyclia vitellina.
Each $5: No. 2127, Lepanthes ovalis. No. 2128, Encyclia cochleata.

1999, Apr. 26	Litho.	Perf. 14
2121-2124 A330 Set of 4	4.50	4.50
Sheets of 8		
2125-2126 A330 Set of 2	17.50	17.50
Souvenir Sheets		
2127-2128 A330 Set of 2	10.00	10.00

Trains — A331

No. 2129, each $1: a, Class 103.1 Co-Co, Germany. b, Class .24, "Trans Pennine," UK. c, GG1 2-Co-Co-2, US. d, LRC Bo-Bo, Canada. e, Class EW, New Zealand. f, Class SS1 "Shao-Shani," China. g, Gulf, Mobile Ohio, US. h, Class 9100 2-Do-2, France.
No. 2130, each $1: a, County Donegal Petrol Rail Car No. 10, Ireland. b, RDC Single Rail Car, US. c, WDM Class Co-Co, India. d, Bi-Polar No. E-2, US. e, Class X Co-Co, Australia. f, Beijing Bo-Bo, China. g, Class E428 2-

DOMINICA

Bo-Bo-2, Italy. h, Class 581 Twelve-Car Train, Japan.
$5, X-2000 Tilting Express Train, Sweden, vert. $6, Class 87 Bo-Bo, Great Britain, vert.

1999, May 10	Litho.	Perf. 14

Sheets of 8

2129-2130	A331	Set of 2	13.00	13.00

Souvenir Sheets

| 2131 | A331 | $5 multicolored | 4.00 | 4.00 |
| 2132 | A331 | $6 multicolored | 5.00 | 5.00 |

Australia '99, World Stamp Expo.

Prehistoric Animals — A332

25c, Tyrannosaurus, vert. 65c, Hypacrosaurus. 90c, Sauropelta. $2, Zalambdalestes.
No. 2137, each $1: a, Barosaurus. b, Rhamphorhynchus. c, Apatosaurus. d, Archaeopteryx. e, Diplodocus. f, Ceratosaurus. g, Stegosaurus. h, Elaphrosaurus. i, Vulcanodon.
No. 2138, each $1: a, Psittacosaurus. b, Pteranodon. c, Ichthyornis. d, Spinosaurus. e, Parasaurolophus. f, Ornithomimus. g, Anatosaurus. h, Triceratops. i, Baronyx.
$5, Yangchuanosaurus. $6, Brachiosaurus.

1999, June 1	Litho.	Perf. 14

| 2133-2136 | A332 | Set of 4 | 3.50 | 3.50 |

Sheets of 9

| 2137-2138 | A332 | Set of 2 | 18.00 | 18.00 |

Souvenir Sheets

| 2139 | A332 | $5 multicolored | 4.50 | 4.50 |
| 2140 | A332 | $6 multicolored | 5.50 | 5.50 |

Wedding of Prince Edward and Sophie Rhys-Jones — A333

No. 2141: a, Sophie. b, Sophie, Edward. c, Edward.
$6, like No. 2141b.

1999, June 19	Litho.	Perf. 13½
2141	A333	$3 Sheet of 3, #a.-c.	7.25	7.25

Souvenir Sheet

| 2142 | A333 | $6 multicolored | 5.00 | 5.00 |

IBRA '99, World Philatelic Exhibition, Nuremberg — A334

Exhibition emblem, sailing ship Eendraght and: 65c, Cameroun #58, #56. 90c, Cameroun #11, #9.
Emblem, early German train and: $1, Cameroun #19. $2, Cameroun #6.
$6, Cover with Cameroun #19.

1999, June 22		Perf. 14
2143-2146	A334	Set of 4	4.00	4.00

Souvenir Sheet

| 2147 | A334 | $6 multicolored | 6.25 | 6.25 |

Souvenir Sheets

PhilexFrance '99 — A335

Trains: $5, L'Aigle, 1855. $6, Mainline diesel locomotive, 1963.

1999, June 22		Perf. 13¾
2148	A335	$5 multicolored	4.50	4.50
2149	A335	$6 multicolored	5.50	5.50

Apollo 11 Moon Landing, 30th Anniv. — A336

No. 2150: a, Command Module separation. b, Service Module separation. c, 3rd Stage Booster separation. d, Landing, Command Modules go to the moon. e, Apollo Ground Tracker. f, Goldstone Radio Telescope.
$6, Apollo 11 after splashdown.

1999, June 22		Perf. 14
2150	A336	$1.45 Sheet of 6, #a.-f.	9.00	9.00

Souvenir Sheet

| 2151 | A336 | $6 multicolored | 6.00 | 6.00 |

Paintings by Hokusai (1760-1849) — A337

Details or entire paintings — No. 2152:, each $2 a, Pilgrims at Kirifuri Waterfall. b, Kakura-Sato (rats looking at book, pulling on rope). c, Travelers on the Bridge by Ono Waterfall. d, Fast Cargo Boat Battling the Waves. e, Kakura-Sato (rats working with bales). f, Buufinfinh and Weeping cherry.
No. 2153, each $2: a, Cuckoo and Azalea. b, Soldiers (spear in left hand). c, Lover in the snow. d, Ghost of Koheiji. e, Soldiers (spear in right hand). f, Chinese Poet in Snow.
$5, Empress Jitó. $6, One Hundred Poems by One Hundred Poets.

		Perf. 13½x13¾
1999, June 22		Litho.

Sheets of 6

| 2152-2153 | A337 | Set of 2 | 19.00 | 19.00 |

Souvenir Sheets

| 2154 | A337 | $5 multicolored | 4.50 | 4.50 |
| 2155 | A337 | $6 multicolored | 5.50 | 5.50 |

Johann Wolfgang von Goethe (1749-1832), Poet — A338

No. 2156: a, Faust perceives an astrological sign. b, Portrait of Goethe and Friedrich von Schiller (1759-1805). c, Faust tempted by Mephistopheles.
$6, Profile portrait of Goethe.

1999, June 22		Perf. 14
2156	A338	$2 Sheet of 3, #a.-c.	5.00	5.00

Souvenir Sheet

| 2157 | A338 | $6 multicolored | 5.00 | 5.00 |

Rights of the Child — A339

No. 2158: a, Woman, child. b, Child in blue sweater. c, Two children.
$6, Dove, horiz.

1999, June 22	Litho.	Perf. 14
2158	A339	$3 Sheet of 3, #a.-c.	7.50	7.50

Souvenir Sheet

| 2159 | A339 | $6 multicolored | 5.00 | 5.00 |

Queen Mother (b. 1900) — A340

Gold Frames

No. 2160: a, In 1939. b, In Australia, 1958. c, At Badminton, 1982. d, Hatless, in 1982.
$6, In 1953.

1999, Aug. 4		Perf. 14
2160	A340	$2 Sheet of 4, #a.-d. + label	7.50	7.50

Souvenir Sheet
Perf. 13¾

| 2161 | A340 | $6 multicolored | 5.00 | 5.00 |

No. 2161 contains one 38x51mm stamp.
Compare with Nos. 2345-2346. Backdrop of photo is more pink on No. 2161 than on No. 2346. No. 2161 has embossed arms in margin, while No. 2346 does not.

Litho. & Embossed
Die Cut Perf. 8¾
Without Gum

| 2161A | A340a | $20 gold & multi | 20.00 | 20.00 |

See Nos. 2345-2346.

Flora & Fauna — A341

Designs: 25c, Heliconia lobster claw. 65c, Broad winged hawk. $1, Anthurium. $1.55, Blue-headed hummingbird. $2, Bananaquit. $4 Agouti.
No. 2168: a, White-throated sparrow. b, Blue-winged teal. c, Raccoon. d, Alfalf butterfly. e, Bridge. f, Whitetail deer. g, Gray squirrel. h, Banded purple butterfly. i, Snowdrop. j, Bullfrog. k, Mushrooms. l, Large-blotched ensatina.
$5, Eastern chipmunk. $6, Black-footed ferret.

1999

| 2162-2167 | A341 | Set of 6 | 9.00 | 9.00 |

Sheet of 12

| 2168 | A341 | 90c #a.-l. | 10.00 | 10.00 |

Souvenir Sheets

| 2169 | A341 | $5 multicolored | 5.00 | 5.00 |
| 2170 | A341 | $6 multicolored | 6.00 | 6.00 |

Dominica Festival Commission: 25c, Domfesta. 55c, $5, Dominica's 21st anniv. as a republic. 65c, Carnival development committee. 90c, World Creole Music Festival.

1999		Perf. 12½
2171-2174	A342	Set of 4	2.00	2.00

Souvenir Sheet
Perf. 13¼

| 2175 | A342 | $5 multicolored | 4.50 | 4.50 |

No. 2175 contains one 38x51mm stamp.

A343

Intl. Year of the Elderly: 25c, Family. 65c, Four people. 90c, Four people, one in chair.

1999, Aug. 4		Perf. 14
2176	A343	Sheet of 3, #a.-c.	1.50	1.50

A345

Christmas: 25c, Yellow-crowned parrot. 55c, Red bishop. 65c, Troupial. 90c, Puerto Rican woodpecker. $2, Mangrove cuckoo. $3, American robin.
$6, Mary with Child Beside the Wall, by Albrecht Dürer.

1999, Dec. 7	Litho.	Perf. 14
2178-2183	A345	Set of 6	6.75	6.75

Souvenir Sheet

| 2184 | A345 | $6 multi | 5.25 | 5.25 |

Inscription on No. 2181 is misspelled.

A346

Millennium (Highlights of the early 13th Cent.) — No. 2185: a, Leonardo Fibonacci publishes "Liber Abaci", 1202. b, St. Francis of Assisi. c, Mongols conquer China. d, Children's Crusade begins, 1212. e, Magna Carta signed, 1215. f, Founding of Salamanca University, 1218. g, Snorri Sturluson writes "Prose Edda". h, Chinese painter Ma Yuan dies, 1225. i, Genghis Khan dies, 1227. j, Zen Buddhism in Japan. k, Sixth Crusade. l, Lubeck-Hamburg League. m, Inquisitions begin, 1231. n, Cordoba conquered by Castilians, 1236. o, Democracy in San Marino. p, Maimonides (60x40mm). q, Notre Dame Cathedral, Paris.
Highlights of the 1940s — No. 2186: a, Japan bombs Pearl Harbor. b, Churchill becomes Prime Minister of Great Britain. c, Regular television broadcasting begins in the US. d, Anne Frank hid in Amsterdam. e, D-Day Invasion. f, Yalta Conference. g, Establishment of the UN. h, Germany surrenders, concentration camps exposed. i, Russians hoist flag over gutted Reichstag building. j, Eniac computer. k, Independence for India. l, Bell Laboratories produce 1st transistor. m, Gandhi assassinated. n, Israel achieves statehood. o, Blockade of West Berlin, Berlin Airlift. p, Atomic bomb tested in New Mexico (60x40mm). q, Establishment of People's Republic of China.

Perf. 12¾x12½

1999, Dec. 31	Sheets of 17	Litho.
2185	A346	55c #a.-q. + label	8.50	8.50
2186	A346	55c #a.-q. + label	8.50	8.50

See Nos. 2249-2252.

New Year 2000 (Year of the Dragon) — A347

DOMINICA

2000, Feb. 5		Perf. 13¾
2187 A347 $1.50 shown		1.25 1.25

Souvenir Sheet

| 2188 A347 | $4 Dragon, horiz. | 3.75 3.75 |

No. 2187 printed in sheets of 4.

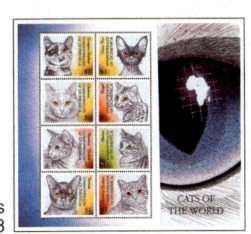

Cats — A348

No. 2189, each $1: a, European Shorthair. b, Devon Rex. c, Chartreux. d, Bengal. e, American Wirehair. f, Siberian. g, Burmese. h, American Shorthair.
No. 2190, each $1: a, Asian Longhair. b, Burmilla. c, Snowshoe. d, Pekeface Persian. e, Himalayan Persian. f, Japanese Bobtail. g, Seychelles Longhair. h, Exotic Shorthair.
Each $6: No. 2191, Awake cat. No. 2192, Sleeping cat.

2000, Feb. 21		Perf. 14¼
Sheets of 8, #a.-h.		
2189-2190 A348 Set of 2		16.00 16.00

Souvenir Sheets

| 2191-2192 A348 Set of 2 | | 12.00 12.00 |

Puppies — A349

No. 2193: a, Jack Russell Terrier. b, Shar Peis. c, Basset Hound. d, Boxers. e, Wirehaired Terrier. f, Golden Retrievers.
No. 2194, Beagle.

2000, Feb. 21		Perf. 14½x14¼
2193 A349 $1 Sheet of 6, #a.-f.		6.00 6.00

Souvenir Sheet

| 2194 A349 $6 multi | | 6.00 6.00 |

Flowers — A350

Various flowers making up a photomosaic of Princess Diana.

2000, Apr. 3		Perf. 13¾
2195 A350 $1 Sheet of 8, #a.-h.		7.50 7.50

See No. 2225.

Butterflies A351

No. 2196, each $1.50: a, Giant swallowtail. b, Tiger pierid. c, Orange theope. d, White peacock. e, Blue tharops. f, Mosaic.
No. 2197, each $1.50: a, Banded king shoemaker. b, Figure-of-eight. c, Grecian shoemaker. d, Blue night. e, Monarch. f, Common morpho.
No. 2198, each $1.50: a, Orange-barred sulphur. b, Clorinde. c, Small flambeau. d, Small lace-wing. e, Polydamas swallowtail. f, Atala.
Each $6: No. 2199, Polydamas swallowtail, vert. No. 2200, Sloane's urania, vert. No. 2201, Blue-green reflector, vert.

2000, Apr. 10		Perf. 14
Sheets of 6, #a.-f.		
2196-2198 A351 Set of 3		24.00 24.00

Souvenir Sheets

| 2199-2201 A351 Set of 3 | | 17.50 17.50 |

Flowers — A352

Designs: 65c, Passion flower. 90c, Spray orchid. $1, Peach angel's trumpet. $4, Allamanda.
No. 2206, each $1.65: a, Bird of paradise. b, Lobster claw heliconia. c, Candle bush. d, Flor de San Miguel. e, Hibiscus. f, Oleander.
No. 2207, each $1.65: a, Anthurium. b, Fire ginger. c, Shrimp plant. d, Sky vine thunbergia. e, Ceriman. f, Morning glory.
Each $6: No. 2208, Bird of paradise, diff. c, Hibiscus, diff.
No. 2109, Hibiscus, diff.

2000, Apr. 25	Litho.	Perf. 14
2202-2205 A352 Set of 4		6.00 6.00
Sheets of 6, #a-f		
	Perf. 13¾	
2206-2207 A352 Set of 2		17.00 17.00
Souvenir Sheets		
	Perf. 13½x13¾	
2208-2209 A352 Set of 2		12.00 12.00

Size of stamps: Nos. 2106-2107, 32x48mm; Nos. 2108-2109, 38x51mm.

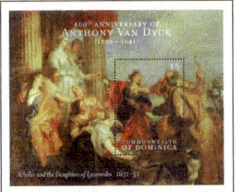

Paintings of Anthony Van Dyck A353

No. 2210, each $1.65: a, Lady Jane Goodwin. b, Philip Herbert, 4th Earl of Pembroke. c, Philip, Lord Wharton. d, Sir Thomas Hammer. e, Olivia Porter, Wife of Enymion Porter. f, Sir Thomas Chaloner.
No. 2211, horiz, each $1.65: a, Ladies in Waiting. b, Thomas Wentworth, Earl of Strafford, with Sir Philip Mainwaring. c, Dorothy Rivers Savage, Viscountess Andover and Her Sister Lady Elizabeth Thimbleby. d, Mountjoy Blount, Earl of Newport, and Lord George Goring with a Page. e, Thomas Killigrew and an Unidentified Man. f, Elizabeth Villiers, Lady Dalkeith, and Cecilia Killigrew.
No. 2212, horiz, each $1.65: a, The Ages of Man. b, Portrait of a Girl as Erminia Accompanied by Cupid. c, Cupid and Psyche. d, Vertumnus and Pomona. e, The Continence of Scipio. f, Diana and Endymion Surprised by a Satyr.
No. 2213, $5, Achilles and the Daughters of Lycomedes. No. 2214, $5, Amaryllis and Mirtillo. No. 2215, $6, Thomas Howard, 2nd Earl of Arundel, with Alathea, Countess of Arundel.

2000, May 29		Perf. 13¾
Sheets of 6, #a-f		
2210-2212 A353 Set of 3		27.00 27.00
Souvenir Sheets		
2213-2214 A353 Set of 2		9.00 9.00
2215 A353 $6 multi		5.50 5.50

First Zeppelin Flight, Cent. A354

No. 2216: a, Count Ferdinand von Zeppelin (1838-1917). b, First takeoff of LZ-1. c, LZ-10 over field. d, LZ-6 and Deutschland in hangar. e, Arrival of Z-4 at Luneville. f, Victoria Luise. No. 2217, LZ-1, diff.

2000, June 21	Litho.	Perf. 14
2216 A354 $1.65 Sheet of 6, #a-f		9.00 9.00

Souvenir Sheet

| 2217 A354 $6 multi | | 5.50 5.50 |

Berlin Film Festival, 50th Anniv. A355

No. 2218: a, Director Satyajit Ray. b, Mahangar. c, Fanfan La Tulipe. d, Le Salaire de la Peur. e, Les Cousins. f, Hon Dansade en Sommar.
No. 2219, Buffalo Bill and the Indians.

2000, June 21		
2218 A355 $1.65 Sheet of 6, #a-f		9.00 9.00

Souvenir Sheet

| 2219 A355 $6 multi | | 5.50 5.50 |

100th Test Match at Lord's Ground — A356

2000, June 21		
2220 A356 $4 Norbert Phillip		3.50 3.50

Souvenir Sheet

| 2221 A356 $6 Lord's Ground | | 5.50 5.50 |

2000 Summer Olympics, Sydney — A357

a, Jesse Owens. b, Pole vault. c, Lenin Stadium Moscow, Soviet Union flag. d, Ancient Greek discus thrower.

2000, June 21		
2222 A357 $2 Sheet of 4, #a-d		8.00 8.00

Public Railways, 175th Anniv. — A358

No. 2223: a, Locomotion No. 1, George Stephenson. b, Brother Jonathon.

2000, June 21		
2223 A358 $3 Sheet of 2, #a-b		6.25 6.25

The Stamp Show 2000, London.

Johann Sebastian Bach — A359

2000, June 21		
2224 A359 $6 multi		5.50 5.50

Flower Type of 2000

Various pictures of religious sites making up a photomosaic of Pope John Paul II.

2000, June 21	Litho.	Perf. 13¾
2225 A350 $1 Sheet of 8, #a-h		8.00 8.00

Apollo-Soyuz Mission, 25th Anniv. — A360

No. 2226, vert.: a, Saturn IB launch vehicle. b, Apollo 18. c, Donald K. Slayton. $6, Apollo and Soyuz docking.

2000, June 21		Perf. 14
2226 A360 $3 Sheet of 3, #a-c		9.50 9.50

Souvenir Sheet

| 2227 A360 $6 multi | | 6.00 6.00 |

Souvenir Sheet

Albert Einstein (1879-1955) — A361

2000, June 21		Perf. 14¼
2228 A361 $6 multi		5.50 5.50

Prince William, 18th Birthday A362

No. 2229: a, In ski gear. b, In jacket and red sweater. c, In suit and tie. d, In plaid shirt. $6, With Prince Harry.

2000, June 22		Perf. 14
2229 A362 $1.65 Sheet of 4, #a-d		6.25 6.25

Souvenir Sheet

		Perf. 13¾
2230 A362 $6 multi		5.50 5.50

No. 2229 contains four 28x42mm stamps.

223

DOMINICA

Bob Hope A363

No. 2231: a, Microphone at right. b, Entertaining troops. c, Wearing bowler. d, Standing in cake. e, Microphone at left. f, With moon.

2000, Aug. 7   **Perf. 14**
2231 A363 $1.65 Sheet of 6, #a-f   10.00 10.00

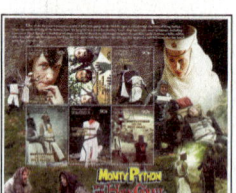

Monty Python and the Holy Grail, 25th Anniv. A364

No. 2232: a, Close-up of Eric Idle. b, Terry Jones, Graham Chapman and John Cleese as three-headed giant, horiz. c, Knights facing castle wall. d, Chapman as King Arthur, with helmeted knight. e, Beheaded knight. f, Armless and legless Black Knight and King Arthur.

2000, Aug. 7   **Perf. 13¾**
2232 A364 90c Sheet of 6, #a-f   5.25 5.25

Popes A365

No. 2233: a, Clement X, 1670-76. b, Innocent X, 1644-55. c, Nicholas V, 1447-55. d, Martin V, 1417-31. e, Julius III, 1550-55. f, Innocent XII, 1691-1700.
$6, Clement XIV, 1769-74.

2000, Sept. 5
2233 A365 $1.65 Sheet of 6, #a-f   10.00 10.00
Souvenir Sheet
2234 A365 $6 multi   5.50 5.50

Monarchs — A366

No. 2235: a, Edward IV of England, 1461-83. b, Peter the Great of Russia, 1682-1725. c, Henry VI of England, 1422-61. d, Henry III of England, 1216-72. e, Richard III of England, 1483-85. f, Edward I of England, 1272-1307.
$6, Henry VIII of England, 1509-47.

2000, Sept. 5
2235 A366 $1.65 Sheet of 6, #a-f   10.00 10.00
Souvenir Sheet
2236 A366 $6 multi   5.50 5.50

World Stamp Expo 2000, Anaheim A367

Spacecraft — No. 2237, $1.65: a, Explorer 14. b, Luna 16. c, Copernicus. d, Explorer 16. e, Luna 10. f, Arybhattan.
No. 2238, $1.65: a, ESSA 8. b, Echo 1. c, Topex Poseidon. d, Diademe. e, Early Bird. f, Molniya.
No. 2239, $6, Hipparcos. No. 2240, $6, Eole.

2000, June 21   **Litho.**   **Perf. 14¼x14**
Sheets of 6, #a-f
2237-2238 A367   Set of 2   20.00 20.00
Souvenir Sheets
2239-2240 A367   Set of 2   11.00 11.00

David Copperfield, Magician — A368

2000, Aug. 8   **Perf. 14**
2241 A368 $2 multi   1.75 1.75
Printed in sheets of 4.

Souvenir Sheet

Female Recording Groups of the 1960s — A369

No. 2242 — The Crystals, yellow spotlight covering: a, UR, LL and LR corners. b, UL and LL corners. c, UR and LR corners. d, UL, LL and LR corners.

2000, Aug. 8
2242 A369 90c Sheet of 4, #a-d   3.50 3.50

Christmas — A370

Angel: 25c, No. 2247a, Looking right, purple and yellow green background. 65c, No. 2247b, At left, looking left, purple background. 90c, No. 2247c, At right, purple and orange background. $5, No. 2247d, At center, blue and purple background.

2000, Dec. 4
2243-2246 A370   Set of 4   6.25 6.25
Sheet of 4
2247 A370 $1.90 #a-d   7.00 7.00
Souvenir Sheet
2248 A370 $6 Angel   5.50 5.50

Millennium Type of 1999

Chinese Art — No. 2249, 55c: a, Eight Prize Steeds, by Giuseppe Castiglione. b, Oleanders, by Wu Hsi Tsai. c, Mynah and Autumn Flowers, by Chang Hsiung. d, Hen and Chicks Beneath Chrysanthemums, by Chu Ch'ao. e, Long Living Pine and Crane, by Xugu. f, Flowers and Fruits, by Chu Lien. g, Lotus and Willow, by Pu Hua. h, Kuan-Yin, by Ch'ien Hui-An. i, Human Figures, by Jen hsun. j, Han-Shan and Shih-Te, by Ren Yi. k, Landscape and Human Figure, by Jen Yu. l, Poetic Thoughts While Walking With a Staff, by Wangchen. m, Peony, by Chen Heng Ko. n, Plum and Orchids, by Wu Chang-Shih. o, Monkey, by Kao Chi-Feng. p, Grapes and Locust, by Ch'i Pai-Shih and Galloping Horse, by Xu Beihong (60x40mm). q, The Beauty, by Lin Fengmian.
History of Change — No. 2250, 55c: a, Star charts. b, Precision tools. c, Science of the stars. d, Investigation into healing a human being. e, Sharing of medical information. f, Church. g, Water alarm clock. h, Weighted clock. i, Spring-loaded miniature clock. j, New technology of glass blowing. k, First screws. l, Wood lathe. m, New systems for assembly blocks for ships. n, Interchangeable parts for rifles. o, Study of movement. p, Efficiency and the Industrial Revolution (60x40mm). q, Concept of efficiency.
Highlights of the 1960s — No. 2251, 55c: a, First birth control pill developed. b, Yuri Gagarin becomes first man in space. c, The first hit for the Beatles in Britain. d, Assassination of John F. Kennedy. e, Dr. Martin Luther King's "I Have a Dream" speech. f, Betty Friedan writes "The Feminine Mystique." g, Kenya gains independence. h, U.S. Surgeon General warns about smoking-related health hazards. i, U.S. Congress passes Civil Rights Act. j, U.S. increases military presence in South Viet Nam. k, Ernesto "Che" Guevara. l, First heart transplant. m, Israel wins Six-day War. n, Ho Chi Minh dies. o, First man on the Moon. p, Communists build wall to divide East and West Berlin (60x40mm). q, Woodstock rock concert.
Highlights of the late 14th Century — No. 2252: a, Minnesingers. b, Acampitzin, King of the Aztecs. c, Black Death eases. d, Giotto's campanile built. e, First French franc. f, Ming Dynasty in China. g, Tamerlane begins conquest of Asia. h, Triumph of Death painted by Francesco Traini. i, Robin Hood. j, Geoffrey Chaucer writes "The Canterbury Tales." k, Succession dispute in Japan. l, Jewish exodus from France. m, Temple of the Golden Pavilion built. n, Strasbourg Cathedral built. o, Alhambra Palace (60x40mm). p, Ife bronzes in Nigeria.

2000, Dec. 31   **Perf. 12¾x12½**
Sheets of 17, #a-q
2249-2251 A346   Set of 3   26.00 26.00
2252 A347 65c Sheet of 17,
   #a-h, j-p, 2 #i   10.00 10.00

Hummingbirds — A371

No. 2253, $1.25: a, Green-throated carib. b, Bee, on branch. c, Bee, in flight. d, Bahama woodstar. e, Antillean mango. f, Blue-headed.
No. 2254, $1.65: a, Eastern streamertail. b, Purple-throated carib. c, Vervain. d, Bahama woodstar. e, Puerto Rican emerald. f, Antillean crested.
No. 2255, $5, Feeders. No. 2256, $6, Hispaniolan.

2000, Dec. 18   **Litho.**   **Perf. 14**
Sheets of 6, #a-f
2253-2254 A371   Set of 2   16.00 16.00
Souvenir Sheets
2255-2256 A371   Set of 2   10.00 10.00
Misspellings abound on Nos. 2253-2254.

New Year 2001 (Year of the Snake) — A372

2001, Jan. 2   **Perf. 12x12¼**
2257 A372 $1.20 multi   1.00 1.00
Printed in sheets of 4.

Fauna — A373

Designs: 15c, Puerto Rican crested toad. 20c, Axolotl. $1.90, Panamanian golden frog. $2.20, Manatee. No. 2262, $1.45: a, St. Vincent parrot. b, Indigo macaw. c, Cock of the rock. d, Cuban solenodon. e, Cuban hutia. f, Chinchilla.
No. 2263, $1.45: a, South American flamingo. b, Golden conure. c, Ocelot. d, Giant armadillo. e, Margay. f, Maned wolf.
No. 2264, $6, Anteater. No. 2265, $6, Hawksbill turtle.

2000, Dec. 18   **Litho.**   **Perf. 14**
2258-2261 A373   4.75 4.75
Sheets of 6, #a-f
2262-2263 A373   Set of 2   17.00 17.00
Souvenir Sheets
2264-2265 A373   Set of 2   12.00 12.00

Pokémon A374

No. 2266, horiz.: a, Butterfree. b, Bulbasaur. c, Caterpie. d, Charmander. e, Squirtle. f, Pidgeotto.

2001, Feb.   **Perf. 13¾**
2266 A374 $1.65 Sheet of 6, #a-f   7.00 7.00
Souvenir Sheet
2267 A374 $6 Nidoking   4.25 4.25

A375

Marine Life — A376

Designs: No. 2268, 15c, Banded sea snake. 25c, Soldier fish. 55c, Banner fish. No. 2271, 90c, Crown of thorns starfish.
No. 2272, 15c, Fish. 65c, Ray. No. 2274, 90c, Octopus. $3, Fish, diff.
No. 2276, $1.65: a, White-tip reef shark, lionfish, sergeant major. b, Blue-striped snappers. c, Great hammerhead shark, stovepipe sponge, pink vase sponge. d, Hawaiian monk seal, blue tube coral. e, Seahorse, common clownfish, red feather star coral. f, Bat starfish, brown octopus.
No. 2277, $1.65: a, Red sponge, shoal of Anthias. b, Orange-striped triggerfish. c, Coral grouper, soft tree coral. d, Peacock fan worms, gorgonian sea fan. e, Sweetlips, sea fan. f, Giant clam, golden cup coral.
No. 2278: a, Shark. b, Starfish. c, Seahorse. d, Fish. e, Crab. f, Eel.
No. 2279, $5, Royal angelfish. No. 2280, $5, Pink anemone fish. No. 2281, Turtle.

2001, Feb. 27   **Perf. 14**
2268-2271 A375   Set of 4   2.00 2.00
2272-2275 A376   Set of 4   5.00 5.00
Sheets of 6, #a-f
2276-2277 A375   Set of 2   19.00 19.00
2278 A376 $2 Sheet of 6, #a-f   11.00 11.00
Souvenir Sheets
2279-2280 A375   Set of 2   10.00 10.00
2281 A376 $5 multi   5.00 5.00

DOMINICA

Phila Nippon '01, Japan — A377

Art: 25c, Gathering of Chinese Women, by Tsuji Kako. 55c, Village by Bamboo Grove, by Takeuchi Seiho. 65c, Mountain Village in Spring, by Suzuki Hyakunen. 90c, Gentleman Amusing Himself, by Domoto Insho. $1, Calmness of Spring Light, by Seiho. $2, Su's Embankment on a Spring Morning, by Tomioka Tessai.
No. 2288, $1.65: a, Thatched Cottages in the Willows, by Kako. b, Joy in the Garden, by Kako. c, Azalea and butterfly, by Kikuchi Hobun. d, Pine Grove, by Kako. e, Woodcutters Talking in Autumn Valley, by Kubota Beisen.
No. 2289, $1.65: a, Waterfowl in Snow, by Kako. b, Heron and Willow, by Kako. c, Crow and Cherry Blossoms, by Hobun. d, Chrysanthemum Immortal, by Yamamoto Shunkyo. e, Cranes of Immortality, by Kako.
No. 2290, $6, Kamo Riverbank in the Misty Rain, by Kako. No. 2291, $6, Diamond Gate, by Kako. No. 2292, $6, Woman, by Suzuki Harunobu.

2001, May 15	Litho.		Perf. 14	
2282-2287	A377	Set of 6	5.25	5.25
		Sheets of 5, #a-e		
2288-2289	A377	Set of 2	15.00	15.00
		Souvenir Sheets		
		Perf. 13¾		
2290-2292	A377	Set of 3	12.00	12.00

Nos. 2290-2292 each contain one 38x51mm stamp.

Queen Victoria (1819-1901) — A378

No. 2293: a, Prince Albert in uniform. b, Victoria with silver crown. c, Victoria with gold crown. d, Albert in suit.
$6, Victoria as old woman.

2001, May 15			Perf. 14	
2293	A378	$2 Sheet of 4, #a-d	7.25	7.25
		Souvenir Sheet		
		Perf. 13¾		
2294	A378	$6 multi	5.50	5.50

No. 2294 contains one 38x51mm stamp.

Queen Elizabeth II, 75th Birthday A379

No. 2295: a, With crown. b, With white dress. c, Formal portrait by Pietro Annigoni. d, With orange coat. e, With child. f, With green dress.
$6, In uniform.

2001, May 15			Perf. 14	
2295	A379	$1.20 Sheet of 6, #a-f	6.25	6.25
		Souvenir Sheet		
2296	A379	$6 multi	5.50	5.50

Toulouse-Lautrec Paintings — A380

No. 2297: a, Two Women Waltzing. b, The Medical Inspection. c, The Two Girlfriends. d, Woman Pulling Up Her Stocking.

2001, May 15	Litho.		Perf. 13¾	
2297	A380	$2 Sheet of 4, #a-d	7.25	7.25
		Souvenir Sheet		
2298	A380	$6 Self-portrait	5.50	5.50

Giuseppe Verdi (1813-1901), Opera Composer — A381

No. 2299: a, Verdi. b, Lady Macbeth. c, Orchestra. d, Score.

2001, May 15			Perf. 14	
2299	A381	$2 Sheet of 4, #a-d	7.25	7.25
		Souvenir Sheet		
2300	A381	$6 Verdi, score	5.50	5.50

Mushrooms — A382

Designs: 15c, Cantharellus cibarius. 25c, Hygrocybe pratensis. 55c, Leccinum aurantiacum. $3, Mycena haematopus.

No. 2305, 90c, horiz.: a, Caesar's amanita. b, Agaricus augustus. c, Clitocybe nuda. d, Hygrocybe plavescens. e, Stropharia kaufmanii. f, Hygrophorus speciosus.
No. 2306, $2: a, Marasmiellus candidus. b, Calostoma cinnabarina. c, Cantharellus infundibuliformis. d, Hygrocybe punicea. e, Basket stinkhorn. f, Agrocybe praecox.
No. 2307, $5, Fly agaric, horiz. No. 2308, $5, Gymnopilus spectabilis, horiz.

2001, June 18				
2301-2304	A382	Set of 4	4.50	4.50
		Sheets of 6, #a-f		
2305-2306	A382	Set of 2	18.00	18.00
		Souvenir Sheets		
2307-2308	A382	Set of 2	10.00	10.00

Mao Zedong (1893-1976) — A383

No. 2309 — Picture from: a, 1945. b, 1926. c, 1949.
$3, 1930.

2001, May 15	Litho.		Perf. 14	
2309	A383	$2 Sheet of 3, #a-c	5.25	5.25
		Souvenir Sheet		
2310	A383	$3 multi	2.75	2.75

Monet Paintings A384

No. 2311, horiz.: a, The Basin of Argenteuil. b, The Bridge at Argenteuil. c, The Railway Bridge, Argenteuil. d, The Seine Bridge at Argenteuil.
$6, Woman with a Parasol — Madame Monet and Her Son.

2001, May 15			Perf. 13¾	
2311	A384	$2 Sheet of 4, #a-d	7.25	7.25
		Souvenir Sheet		
2312	A384	$6 multi	5.25	5.25

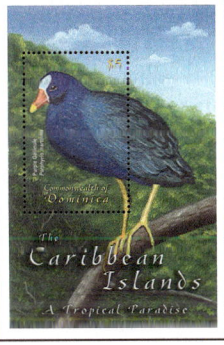

Fauna A385

No. 2313: a, St. Vincent parrot. b, Painted bunting. c, Jamaican giant anole. d, White-fronted capuchin. e, Strand racerunner. f, Agouti.
No. 2314: a, Cook's tree boa. b, Tamandua. c, Common iguana. d, Solenodon.
No. 2315, $5, Purple gallinule. No. 2316, $5, Rufous-tailed jacamar. No. 2317, $5, Ruby-throated hummingbird, horiz. No. 2318, $5, Bottlenose dolphins, horiz.

2001, Sept. 3			Perf. 14	
2313	A385	$1.45 Sheet of 6, #a-f	8.75	8.75
2314	A385	$2 Sheet of 4, #a-d	8.25	8.25
		Souvenir Sheets		
2315-2318	A385	Set of 4	19.00	19.00

Birds — A386

Designs: 5c, Yellow warbler. 10c, Palmchat. 15c, Snowy cotinga. 20c, Blue-gray gnatcatcher. 25c, Belted kingfisher. 55c, Red-legged thrush. 65c, Bananaquit. 90c, Yellow-bellied sapsucker. $1, White-tailed tropicbird. $1.45, Ruby-throated hummingbird. $1.90, Painted bunting. $2, Great frigatebird. $5, Brown trembler. $10, Red-footed booby. $20, Sooty tern.

2001, Sept. 3		Litho.	Perf. 14¾x14	
2319	A386	5c multi	.30	.80
2320	A386	10c multi	.30	.80
2321	A386	15c multi	.35	.35
2322	A386	20c multi	.35	.35
2323	A386	25c multi	.35	.35
2324	A386	55c multi	.65	.65
2325	A386	65c multi	.75	.75
2326	A386	90c multi	1.00	.80
2327	A386	$1 multi	1.25	1.25
2328	A386	$1.45 multi	1.60	1.60
2329	A386	$1.90 multi	2.00	2.00
2330	A386	$2 multi	2.50	2.50
2331	A386	$5 multi	5.00	5.00
2332	A386	$10 multi	8.50	8.50
2333	A386	$20 multi	17.50	17.50
Nos. 2319-2333 (15)			42.40	43.20

No. 2323 exists dated "2005."
See No. 2513.

Photomosaic of Queen Elizabeth II — A387

2001, Nov. 15			Perf. 14	
2334	A387	$1 multi	1.00	1.00

Issued in sheets of 8.

Christmas — A388

Paintings by Giovanni Bellini: 25c, Madonna and Child. 65c, Madonna and Child, diff. 90c, Baptism of Christ. $1.20, Madonna and Child, diff. $4, Madonna and Child, diff.
$6, Madonna and Child with Sts. Catherine and Mary Magdalene.

2001, Dec. 3				
2335-2339	A388	Set of 5	6.75	6.75
		Souvenir Sheet		
2340	A388	$6 multi	5.50	5.50

2002 World Cup Soccer Championships, Japan and Korea — A389

No. 2341, $2: a, US team, 1950. b, Poster, 1954. c, Poster, 1958. d, Zozimo, 1962. e, Gordon Banks, 1966. f, Pelé, 1970.
No. 2342, $2: a, Daniel Passarella, 1978. b, Paolo Rossi, 1982. c, Diego Maradona, 1986. d, Poster, 1990. e, Seo Jungulon, 1994. f, Jürgen Klinsmann, 1998.
No. 2343, $5, Face on World Cup, 1930. No. 2344, $5, Face and globe on Jules Rimet Trophy, 2002.

2001, Dec. 13			Perf. 13¾x14¼	
		Sheets of 6, #a-f		
2341-2342	A389	Set of 2	21.00	21.00
		Souvenir Sheets		
		Perf. 14¼		
2343-2344	A389	Set of 2	10.00	10.00

DOMINICA

Queen Mother Type of 1999 Redrawn
No. 2345: a, In 1939. b, In Australia, 1958. c, At Badminton, 1982. d, Hatless, in 1982. $6, In 1953.

2001, Dec.   *Perf. 14*
Yellow Orange Frames
2345 A340 $2 Sheet of 4, #a-d, + label   7.00 7.00

Souvenir Sheet
Perf. 13¾
2346 A340 $6 multi   5.25 5.25

Queen Mother's 101st birthday. No. 2346 contains one 38x51mm stamp with a bluer backdrop than that found on No. 2161. Sheet margins of Nos. 2345-2346 lack embossing and gold arms and frames found on Nos. 2160-2161.

Souvenir Sheets

Betty Boop A390

Betty Boop: No. 2347, $5, In chair, pink rose background. No. 2348, $5, Wearing blue blouse, in jungle. No. 2349, $5, With heart and stars, cat with film reel. No. 2350, $5, Wearing nurse's cap.

2001, Oct. 1   *Litho.*   *Perf. 13¾*
2347-2350 A390   Set of 4   18.00 18.00

The Three Stooges A391

No. 2351: a, Man, Larry, Moe with sledgehammer, Joe Besser. b, Larry, woman, Joe Besser, Moe. c, Joe Besser, Larry and Moe on hands and knees. d, Larry grabbing throat of woman holding Joe Besser and Moe. e, Joe Besser drinking from baby bottle, pony, Moe and Larry. f, Military policeman, Joe Besser, Larry, woman. g, Larry. h, Joe Besser. i, Moe.
No. 2352, $5, Moe and Larry, "On the air" sign. No. 2353, $5, Larry and pony.

2001, Oct. 1   *Litho.*   *Perf. 13¾*
2351 A391 $1 Sheet of 9, #a-i   8.00 8.00
Souvenir Sheets
2352-2353 A391   Set of 2   9.00 9.00

Souvenir Sheet

New Year 2002 (Year of the Horse) A392

No. 2354: a, Man with pole, horse. b, Horses grazing. c, Man currying horse. d, Horses with heads up.

2001, Dec. 17   *Perf. 14*
2354 A392 $1.65 Sheet of 4, #a-d   6.00 6.00

Reign of Queen Elizabeth II, 50th Anniv. A393

No. 2355: a, Wearing blue coat. b, With Prince Philip. c, Wearing tiara. d, Wearing flowered hat.
$6, With Prince Philip, diff.

2002, Feb. 6   *Perf. 14¼*
2355 A393 $2 Sheet of 4, #a-d   7.00 7.00
Souvenir Sheet
2356 A393 $6 multi   5.00 5.00

United We Stand — A394

2002, Feb.   *Perf. 13½x13¼*
2357 A394 $2 multi   1.50 1.50
Printed in sheets of 4.

Shirley Temple in "Just Around the Corner" A395

No. 2358, horiz.: a, Temple, woman with dogs. b, Temple, man and woman. c, Temple and man. d, Boy eating turkey leg, Temple carving turkey. e, Temple with old man. f, Temple with group of boys.
No. 2359: a, Boy, Temple with purse. b, Man and Temple using fingers as guns. c, Temple and man. d, Temple cutting boy's hair.
$6, Temple with black man on toadstool.

2002, Apr. 8   *Perf. 12¼*
2358 A395 $1.90 Sheet of 6, #a-f   10.00 10.00
2359 A395 $2 Sheet of 4, #a-d   7.25 7.25
Souvenir Sheet
2360 A395 $6 multi   5.25 5.25

Japanese Art — A396

No. 2361, $1.20: a, The Courtesan Tsukioka of the Teahouse Hyogo-Ya, by Eisui Ichirakutei. b, Woman and Servant in the Snow, by Choki Eishosai. c, The Courtesan Shiratsuyu of the Teahouse Wakana-Ya, by Eisho Chokosai. d, Ohisa of the Takashima-Ya, by Toyokuni Utagawa. e, Woman and a Cat, by Kunimasa Utagawa. f, One of "Genre Scenes of Beauties," by Eisen Keisai.
No. 2362, $1.65: a, Women Inside and Outside of a Mosquito Net, by Harushige Suzuki. b, Komachi at Shimizu, by Harushige Suzuki. c, Women Viewing Plum Blossoms, by Harunobu Suzuki. d, Women Cooling Themselves at Shijogawara in Kyoto, by Toyohiro Utagawa. e, Woman Reading a Letter, by Utamaro Kitagawa. f, Women Dressed for the Kashima Dance at the Niwaka Festival, by Utamaro Kitagawa.
No. 2363, $1.90: a, Actor Kiyotaro Iwai, by Kunimasa Utagawa. b, Actors Hiriji Otani III and Ryuzo Arashi, by Sharaku Toshusai. c, Actor Komazo Ichikawa II, by Shunko Katsukawa. d, Actors Yaozo Ichikawa and Hangoro Sakata III, by Sharaku Toshusai. e, Actor Torazo Tanimura, by Sharaku Toshusai. f, Actor Kiyotaro Iwai as Oishi, by Toyokuni Utagawa.
No. 2464, $5, Actor Riko Nakamura, by Shunsho Katsukawa. No. 2365, $5, Actors Hanshiro Iwai IV and Sojuro Sawamura III, by Kiyonaga Torii, horiz. No. 2366, $6, Ofuji, Daughter of the Motoyanagi-Ya, by Harunobu Suzuki.

2002, June 17   *Perf. 14¼*
Sheets of 6, #a-f
2361-2363 A396   Set of 3   24.00 24.00
Souvenir Sheets
2364-2366 A396   Set of 3   12.00 12.00

Souvenir Sheet

Intl. Year of Mountains — A397

No. 2367: a, Mt. Everest. b, Mt. Kilimanjaro. c, Mt. McKinley.

2002, July 15   *Perf. 14*
2367 A397 $2 Sheet of 3, #a-c   5.00 5.00

2002 Winter Olympics, Salt Lake City — A398

Designs: No. 2368, $2, Skiing. No. 2369, $2, Bobsled.

2002, July 15   *Perf. 13½*
2368-2369 A398   Set of 2   3.50 3.50
    a. Souvenir sheet, #2368-2369   3.50 3.50

First Solo Trans-Atlantic Flight, 75th Anniv. — A399

No. 2370: a, Charles Lindbergh and Spirit of St. Louis. b, Charles and Anne Morrow Lindbergh.
$6, Charles Lindbergh and Spirit of St. Louis, diff.

2002, July 15   *Perf. 14*
2370 A399 $3 Sheet of 2, #a-b   5.00 5.00
Souvenir Sheet
2371 A399 $6 multi   5.00 5.00

Popeye in New York A400

No. 2372, $1: a, Olive Oyl. b, Brutus. c, Sweet Pea. d, Wimpy. e, Jeep. f, Popeye.
No. 2373, $1.90: a, Popeye and Olive Oyl, giraffe at Bronx Zoo. b, Popeye and Olive Oyl, Statue of Liberty. c, Popeye, Olive Oyl, Empire State Building. d, Popeye skating at Rockefeller Center. e, Popeye at Yankee Stadium. f, Popeye helping firefighters.
No. 2374, $6, Popeye, Atlas Statue, Rockefeller Center. No. 2375, $6, Popeye, Olive Oyl and Radio City Music Hall Rockettes, horiz.

2002, July 22
Sheets of 6, #a-f
2372-2373 A400   Set of 2   15.00 15.00
Souvenir Sheets
2374-2375 A400   Set of 2   10.50 10.50

20th World Scout Jamboree, Thailand — A401

No. 2376: a, Lord Robert Baden-Powell (facing forward). b, Lady Olave Baden-Powell. c, Maceo Johnson.
$6, Lord Baden-Powell (profile).

2002, July 15   *Litho.*   *Perf. 14¼x14*
2376 A401 $3 Sheet of 3, #a-c   8.00 8.00
Souvenir Sheet
2377 A401 $6 multi   5.25 5.25

Birds, Insects, Moths and Whales A402

No. 2378, $1.50, vert. — Birds: a, Brown trembler. b, Snowy ctinga. c, Bananaquit. d, Painted bunting. e, Belted kingfisher. f, Ruby-throated hummingbird.
No. 2379, $1.50, vert. — Insects: a, Field cricket. b, Migratory grasshopper. c, Honey bee. d, Hercules beetle. e, Black ant. f, Cicada.
No. 2380, $1.50, vert. — Moths: a, Carolina sphinx. b, White-lined sphinx. c, Orizaba silkmoth. d, Hieroglyphic moth. e, Hickory tussock moth. f, Diva moth.
No. 2381, $1.50, vert. — Whales: a, Sei. b, Killer. c, Blue. d, White. e, Pygmy. f, Sperm.
No. 2382, $6, Yellow-bellied sapsucker. No. 2383, $6, Bumble bee. No. 2384, $6, Ornate moth. No. 2385, $6, Gray whale.

2002, July 29   *Perf. 14*
Sheets of 6, #a-f
2378-2381 A402   Set of 4   28.00 28.00
Souvenir Sheets
2382-2385 A402   Set of 4   22.00 22.00

DOMINICA

A403

A404

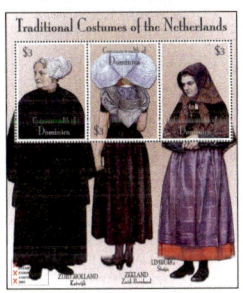

Amphilex 2002 Intl. Stamp Exhibition, Amsterdam — A405

No. 2386 — Dutch Nobel Prize winners: a, Willem Einthoven, Medicine, 1924. b, Nobel Economics medal. c, Peter J. W. Debye, Chemistry, 1936. d, Frits Zernike, Physics, 1953. e, Jan Tinbergen, Economics, 1969. f, Simon van der Meer, Physics, 1984.
No. 2387 — Dutch lighthouses: a, Marken. b, Harlingen. c, Den Oever. d, De Ven. e, Urk. f, Oosterleek.
No. 2388 — Traditional women's costumes: a, South Holland woman with small white head covering (facing forward). b, Zeeland woman with large white head covering (facing backwards). c, Limburg woman with black scarf.

2002, Aug. 30		Perf. 13½x13¼	
2386	A403	$1.50 Sheet of 6, #a-f	8.00 8.00
2387	A404	$1.50 Sheet of 6, #a-f	0.00 0.00
		Perf. 13½	
2388	A405	$3 Sheet of 3, #a-c	8.00 8.00

Intl. Year of Ecotourism — A406

Island scenes and cartoon characters: 45c, Detective H2O. 50c, Factman. 55c, B.B. 60c, Stanley the Starfish. 90c, Toxi. $1.20, Adopt. $6, Litterbit.

2002, Oct. 16		Perf. 14¼	
2389-2394	A406	Set of 6	3.25 3.25
		Souvenir Sheet	
2395	A406	$6 multi	5.00 5.00

Elvis Presley (1935-77) — A407

2002, Oct. 28		Perf. 13¾	
2396	A407	$1.50 multi	1.10 1.10

Printed in sheets of 6 stamps with slightly differing frames.

Amerigo Vespucci (1454-1512), Explorer — A408

No. 2397: a, Compass rose. b, Vespucci with map. c, Map scroll.
$5, Two men.

2002, Nov. 28		Perf. 13¾	
2397	A408	$3 Sheet of 3, #a-c	8.00 8.00
		Souvenir Sheet Perf. 14	
2398	A408	$5 multi	4.50 4.50

No. 2397 contains three 50x38mm stamps.

Pres. John F. Kennedy (1917-63) — A409

No. 2399, $1.90: a, Wearing military uniform. b, With red denomination at UL. c, With blue denomination at UR. d, Wearing tan suit.
No. 2400, $1.90 (denominations at UL in blue): a, Wearing red tie. b, Wearing blue tie (profile). c, Wearing black tie. d, With hand on chin.

2002, Dec. 16		Perf. 14	
		Sheets of 4, #a-d	
2399-2400	A409	Set of 2	13.50 13.50

Pres. Ronald Reagan A410

No. 2401, $1.00: a, Wearing cowboy hat. b, Wearing blue green sweater. c, Wearing red sweater. d, Wearing blue sweater.
No. 2402, $1.90, horiz.: a, Wearing blue shirt, and with wife, Nancy. b, Nancy and US flag. c, Ronald. d, Wearing pink shirt, and with wife.

2002, Dec. 16	Litho.	Perf. 14	
	Sheets of 4, #a-d		
2401-2402	A410	Set of 2	13.50 13.50

Princess Diana (1961-97) — A411

No. 2403 — Various depictions of Princess Diana with background colors of: a, Tan. b, Pink. c, Light blue. d, Light green.

2002, Dec. 16			
2403	A411	$1.90 Sheet of 4, #a-d	7.00 7.00
		Souvenir Sheet	
2404	A411	$5 multi	4.50 4.50

Elizabeth "Ma Pampo" Israel, 128th Birthday — A412

2003, Jan. 27		Perf. 13½x13¼	
2405	A412	90c multi	.70 .70

New Year 2003 (Year of the Ram) — A413

2003, Feb. 10		Perf. 13¾	
2406	A413	$1.65 multi	1.25 1.25

Printed in sheets of 4.

Souvenir Sheets

Science Fiction A414

Designs: No. 2407, $6, Mayan calendar. No. 2408, $6, Atlas. No. 2409, $6, Confucius. No. 2410, $6, Nazca Lines. No. 2411, $6, Pres. Franklin D. Roosevelt and Pres. John F. Kennedy. No. 2412, $6, Zoroaster.

2003, Feb. 10		Perf. 13¼	
2407-2412	A414	Set of 6	27.50 27.50

A415

Coronation of Queen Elizabeth II, 50th Anniv. — A416

No. 2413: a, Wearing white dress, no crown. b, Wearing black robe. c, Wearing crown.
$6, Wearing crown, diff. $20, Wearing red robe.

2003	Litho.	Perf. 14	
2413	A415	$3 Sheet of 3, #a-c	6.25 6.25
		Souvenir Sheet	
2414	A415	$6 multi	4.25 4.25
		Miniature Sheet Litho. & Embossed Perf. 13¼x13	
2415	A416	$20 gold & multi	14.00 14.00

Issued: Nos. 2413-2414, 5/13; No. 2415, 2/24.

Prince William, 21st Birthday A417

No. 2416: a, Wearing dark blue shirt. b, Wearing blue suit, holding flowers. c, In polo uniform.
$6, Wearing black suit.

2003, June 21	Litho.	Perf. 14	
2416	A417	$3 Sheet of 3, #a-c	6.50 6.50
		Souvenir Sheet	
2417	A417	$6 multi	4.50 4.50

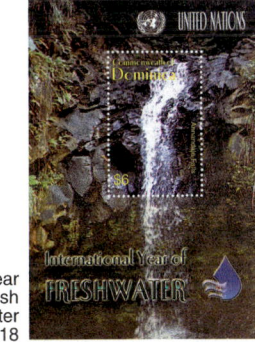

Intl. Year of Fresh Water A418

No. 2418: a, Trafalgar Falls. b, YS Falls. c, Dunn's River.
$6, Annandale Falls.

2003, June 21		Perf. 13½	
2418	A418	$3 Sheet of 3, #a-c	6.75 6.75
		Souvenir Sheet	
2419	A418	$6 multi	4.50 4.50

Teddy Bears, Cent. A419

No. 2420 — Bear with: a, Purple shirt. b, Pink shirt and party favor. c, Green shirt and party favor. d, Black hat. e, Purple hat. f, Pink shirt and birthday cake.

DOMINICA

No. 2421 — Bear with: a, Reindeer sweater, text at top. b, Santa Claus costume, text at top. c, Santa Claus costume, text at bottom. d, Reindeer sweater, text at bottom.

2003, June 21   **Perf. 13½**
2420 A419 $1.65 Sheet of 6, #a-f   7.50 7.50
2421 A419 $2 Sheet of 4, #a-d   6.00 6.00

No. 2421 contains four 37x51mm stamps.

General Motors Automobiles — A420

No. 2422, $2 — Cadillacs: a, 1903 Model A Runabout. b, 1912 Model 30. c, 1918 Type 57 Victoria Coupe. d, 1927 Lasalle Convertible Coupe.
No. 2423, $2 — Corvettes: a, 1953. b, 1956. c, 1957. d, 1962.
No. 2424, $5, 1933 Cadillac 355-C V8 sedan. No. 2425, $5, 1959 Corvette.

2003, June 21   **Perf. 13¼**
Sheets of 4, #a-d
2422-2423 A420 Set of 2   12.00 12.00
Souvenir Sheets
2424-2425 A420 Set of 2   7.50 7.50

Tour de France Bicycle Race, Cent. A421

No. 2426 — Champions: a, Firmin Lambot, 1919. b, Phillippe Thys, 1920. c, Léon Scieur, 1921. d, Lambot, 1922.
$5, François Faber.

2003, June 21   **Perf. 13¼**
2426 A421 $2 Sheet of 4, #a-d   6.00 6.00
Souvenir Sheet
2427 A421 $5 multi   3.75 3.75

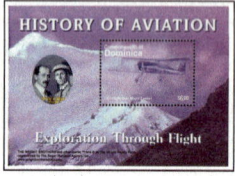

History of Aviation A422

No. 2428: a, Sputnik, first orbiting satellite, 1957. b, Yuri Gagarin, first man in space, 1961. c, Neil Armstrong, first man on the Moon, 1969. d, Skylab 1, 1973.
$6, Flight over Mt. Everest, 1933.

2003, June 21   **Perf. 14**
2428 A422 $2 Sheet of 4, #a-d   6.50 6.50
Souvenir Sheet
2429 A422 $6 multi   5.00 5.00

Lewis & Clark Expedition A423

Designs: 20c, Dealing with the Chinook Indians. 50c, Compass used in expedition. 55c, Rocky Mountains. 65c, Medals presented to the Indians, vert. 90c, First encounter with grizzly bear. $1, Befriending Shoshone Indians. $2, Lewis after the expedition, vert. $4, Lewis & Clark, vert.
No. 2438, $5, Meriwether Lewis, vert. No. 2439, $5, William Clark, vert.

2003, June 21
2430-2437 A423 Set of 8   7.50 7.50
Souvenir Sheets
2438-2439 A423 Set of 2   7.00 7.00

2002 World Cup Soccer Championships, Japan and Korea — A424

No. 2440, $1.45: a, Danny Mills. b, Paul Scholes. c, Darius Vassell. d, Michael Owen. e, Emile Heskey. f, Rio Ferdinand.
No. 2441, $1.45: a, Bobby Moore. b, Roger Hunt. c, Gordon Banks. d, Bobby Charlton. e, Alan Ball. f, Geoff Hurst.
No. 2442, $3: a, Ashley Cole. b, David Seaman.
No. 2443, $3: a, Sven-Goran Eriksson. b, Nikki Butt.
No. 2444, $3: a, Robbie Fowler. b, Sol Campbell.
No. 2445, $3: a, Charlton, Ball and Hunt. b, Nobby Stiles.
No. 2446: a, Franz Beckenbauer. b, Oliver Kahn.

2003, June 21   **Perf. 13¼**
Sheets of 6, #a-f
2440-2441 A424 Set of 2   11.00 11.00
Souvenir Sheets of 2, #a-b
2442-2446 A424 Set of 5   20.00 20.00

CARICOM, 30th Anniv. — A425

2003, July 25   **Perf. 13½**
2447 A425 $1 multi   .75 .75

Christmas — A426

Painting details: 50c, Madonna and Child with the Young St. John, by Correggio. 90c, Madonna in Glory with the Christ Child and Sts. Frances and Alvise with the Donor, by Titian. $1.45, Madonna and Child with Angels Playing Musical Instruments, by Correggio. $3, Madonna of the Cherries, by Titian.
$6, Holy Family with John the Baptist, by Andrea del Sarto.

2003, Nov. 17   **Litho.**   **Perf. 14¼**
2448-2451 A426 Set of 4   4.50 4.50
Souvenir Sheet
2452 A426 $6 multi   4.50 4.50

New Year 2004 (Year of the Monkey) A427

No. 2453: a, Orange monkey, hindquarters of brown monkey. b, Monkey with brown face. c, Brown monkey drinking water. d, Monkey with blue face.

2004, Jan. 5   **Litho.**   **Perf. 14**
2453 A427 $1.50 Sheet of 4, #a.-d.   4.50 4.50

Paintings of Pablo Picasso A428

No. 2454, vert.: a, Portrait of Manuel Pallarés. b, Woman with Vase of Flowers. c, Woman with a Fan (Fernande). d, Portrait of Clovis Sagot.
$5, Brick Factory at Torosa (The Factory).

2004, Mar. 8   **Perf. 14¼**
2454 A428 $1 Sheet of 4, #a.-d.   3.00 3.00
Imperf
2455 A428 $5 multi   3.75 3.75

No. 2454 contains four 38x50mm stamps.

Paintings of Paul Gauguin A429

No. 2456: a, Village Tahitien avec la Femme en Marche. b, La Barriere. c, Bonjour, Monsieur Gauguin. d, Vegetation Tropicale.
$5, Petites Bretonnes Devant la Mer.

2004, Mar. 8   **Perf. 14¼**
2456 A429 $2 Sheet of 4, #a.-d.   6.00 6.00
Imperf
2457 A429 $5 multi   3.75 3.75

No. 2456 contains four 38x50mm stamps.

Paintings of Presidents by Norman Rockwell A430

No. 2458: a, Dwight D. Eisenhower. b, John F. Kennedy. c, Lyndon B. Johnson. d, Richard M. Nixon.
$5, Abraham Lincoln.

2004, Mar. 8   **Perf. 14¼**
2458 A430 $2 Sheet of 4, #a.-d.   6.00 6.00
Imperf
2459 A430 $5 multi   3.75 3.75

No. 2458 contains four 38x50mm stamps.

Paintings of James McNeill Whistler A431

Designs: 50c, Symphony in White No. 3. $1, The Artist's Studio, vert. $1.65, The Thames in Ice, vert. No. 2463, $2, Arrangement in Black: Portrait of F. R. Leyland, vert.
No. 2464, $2, vert.: a, Arrangement in Brown & Black: Portrait of Miss Rosa Corder. b, Harmony in Red: Lamplight. c, Symphony in Flesh Color & Pink: Portrait of Mrs. Frances Leyland. d, Arrangement in Yellow & Gray: Effie Deans.

$5, Harmony in Gray and Green: Miss Cicely Alexander, vert.

2004, Mar. 8   **Perf. 14¼**
2460-2463 A431 Set of 4   4.00 4.00
2464 A431 $2 Sheet of 4, #a-d   6.00 6.00
Imperf
Size: 71x103mm
2465 A431 $5 multi   3.75 3.75

No. 2464 contains four 35x70mm stamps.

Fish — A432

Designs: 20c, Banded butterflyfish. 25c, Queen angelfish. 55c, Porkfish. No. 2469, $5, Redband parrotfish.
No. 2470: a, Beaugregory. b, Porkfish, diff. c, Bicolor cherubfish. d, Rock beauty. e, Blackfin snapper. f, Blue tang.
No. 2471, $5, Indigo hamlet.

2004, Mar. 8   **Perf. 14¼x14¾**
2466-2469 A432 Set of 4   4.50 4.50
Perf. 14
2470 A432 $2 Sheet of 6, #a-f   9.00 9.00
Souvenir Sheet
2471 A432 $5 multi   3.75 3.75

Nos. 2470-2471 each contain 42x28mm stamps.

Shells A433

Designs: 20c, Siratus perelegans. 90c, Polystira albida. $1.45, Cypraea cervus. $2, Strombus gallus.
No. 2476: a, Strombus pugilis. b, Cittarium pica. c, Distorsio clathrata. d, Melongena morio. e, Prunum labiata. f, Chione paphia.
$5, Strombus alatus, vert.

2004, Mar. 8   **Perf. 14¼x14¾**
2472-2475 A433 Set of 4   3.50 3.50
Perf. 14
2476 A433 $1.90 Sheet of 6, #a-f 8.50 8.50
Souvenir Sheet
2477 A433 $5 multi   3.75 3.75

No. 2476 contain six 42x28mm stamps; No. 2477 contains one 28x42mm stamp.

Orchids A434

Designs: 25c, Epidendrum pseudepidendrum. 55c, Aspasia epidendroides. $1.50, Cochleanthes discolor. $4, Brassavola nodosa.
No. 2482: a, Laelia anceps. b, Caularthron bicornutum. c, Cattleya velutina. d, Cattleya warneri. e, Oncidium splendidum. f, Psychlis atropurpurea.
$5, Maxillaria cuculata, vert.

2004, Mar. 8   **Perf. 14¼x14¾**
2478-2481 A434 Set of 4   4.75 4.75
Perf. 14
2482 A434 $1.90 Sheet of 6, #a-f 8.50 8.50
Souvenir Sheet
2483 A434 $5 multi   3.75 3.75

No. 2482 contains six 42x28mm stamps; No. 2483 contains one 28x42mm stamp.

Butterflies A435

DOMICICA

Designs: 50c, Small flambeau. 90c, Tiger pierid. $1, White peacock. No. 2469, $2, Cramer's mesene.
No. 2488, $2: a, Figure-of-eight. b, Orange theope. c, Clorinde. d, Grecian shoemaker. e, Orange-barred sulphur. f, Common morpho. $5, Giant swallowtail, vert.

2004, Mar. 8		Perf. 14¼x13¾
2484-2487 A435	Set of 4	3.00 3.00
	Perf. 14	
2488 A435	$2 Sheet of 6, #a-f	8.00 8.00
	Souvenir Sheets	
2489 A435	$5 multi	3.75 3.75

No. 2488 contains six 42x28mm stamps; No. 2489 contains one 28x42mm stamp.

Olympic Gold Medalists — A436

Designs: 20c, Elizabeth Robinson, Amsterdam, 1928. 25c, Károly Takács, London, 1948. 55c, Bob Beamon, Mexico City, 1968. 65c, Mildred Didrikson, Los Angeles, 1932. $1, Ville Ritola, Paris, 1924. $1.65, Alfred Hajós (Guttman), Athens, 1896. $2, Paavo Nurmi, Antwerp, 1920. $4, Nedo Nadi, Antwerp, 1920.

2004, Apr. 12		Perf. 13¼
2490-2497 A436	Set of 8	7.75 7.75

Election of Pope John Paul II, 25th Anniv. (in 2003) A437

No. 2498: a, Praying for peace in Falkland Islands, 1982. b, In Croatia, 1998. c, Seated, 1998. d, With Franciscan monks, 1999. e, Remembering the Holocaust, 2001.

2004, June 21	Litho.	Perf. 14
2498 A437	$2 Sheet of 5, #a-e	7.50 7.50

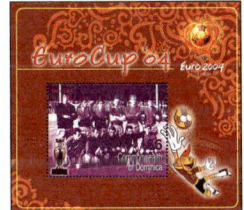

European Soccer Championships, Portugal — A438

No. 2499, vert.: a, Jose Luis Villalonga. b, Lev Yashin. c, Marcelino Martinez. d, Santiago Bernabeu Stadium. $6, 1964 Spain team.

2004, June 21		Perf. 14
2499 A438	$2 Sheet of 4, #a-d	6.00 6.00
	Souvenir Sheet	
	Perf. 14¼	
2500 A438	$6 multi	4.50 4.50

No. 2499 contains four 28x42mm stamps.

Trains A439

No. 2501, $1: a, Engine #22, V7 T4-4-0. V7T4-6-0. b, Don J12. c, Baldwin 2-D-D. d, Southern Engine #20. e, 143-890 2DB class electric locomotive. f, Engine #1.
No. 2502, $1: a, Canadian Pacific freight train. b, Queensland Rail IM U railroad. c, Green and white Shinkansen locomotive. d, Amtrak locomotive. e, Shinkansen locomotive in station. f, YPDMU rail cars.
No. 2503, $1: a, Santa Fe Railroad locomotive. b, Via Rail train, Canada. c, Two Conrail road switchers. d, Strasburg Railroad #90. e, Deltic diesel-electric engine. f, Brighton Belle.
No. 2504, $6, Golsdorf two cylinder compound locomotive 4-4-0. No. 2505, $6, Southern Pacific 4449 4-8-4. No. 2506, $6, White, yellow and blue Shinkansen.

2004, July 12		Perf. 13¼x13½
	Sheets of 6, #a-f	
2501-2503 A439	Set of 3	13.50 13.50
	Souvenir Sheets	
2504-2506 A439	Set of 3	13.50 13.50

D-Day, 60th Anniv. — A440

Designs: $1, Eddie Hannath. $4, Pres. Franklin D. Roosevelt.
No. 2509: a, Rangers make their way towards the cliffs of Pointe du Hoc. b, Rangers begin scaling the cliffs of Pointe du Hoc. c, British troops advance on Sword Beach. d, An AVRE Petard heads inland off Sword Beach. $6, British troops landing on Sword Beach.

2004, July 22		Perf. 14
	Stamp + Label (#2507-2508)	
2507-2508 A440	Set of 2	3.75 3.75
2509 A440	$2 Sheet of 4, #a-d	6.00 6.00
	Souvenir Sheet	
2510 A440	$6 multi	4.50 4.50

George Herman "Babe" Ruth (1895-1948), Baseball Player — A441

No. 2511: a, Swinging bat. b, Swinging bat, looking up. c, Holding three bats. d, Hand on knee.

2004, Aug. 18		Perf. 13½x13¼
2511 A441	$2 Sheet of 4, #a-d	6.00 6.00

Marilyn Monroe (1926-62), Actress — A442

No. 2512: a, Wearing earrings and necklace. b, Wearing earrings. c, Wearing no earrings or necklace. d, Wearing necklace.

2004, Aug. 18		
2512 A442	$2 Sheet of 4, #a-d	6.00 6.00

Bird Type of 2001

2004, Sept. 3		Perf. 14¾x14
2513 A386	50c Baltimore oriole	.45 .45

Exists dated "2005."

Queen Juliana of the Netherlands (1909-2004) A443

2004, Sept. 21		Perf. 13¼
2514 A443	$2 multi	1.50 1.50

Printed in sheets of 6.

Intl. Year of Peace A444

No. 2515: a, Mother Teresa, UN emblem. b, Mother Teresa feeding poor. c, Dove.

2004, Sept. 21		Perf. 14
2515 A444	$2 Sheet of 3, #a-c	4.50 4.50

Souvenir Sheet

Deng Xiaoping (1904-97) and Mao Zedong (1893-1976), Chinese Leaders — A445

2004, Sept. 21		Perf. 14
2516 A445	$6 multi	4.50 4.50

National Soccer Team A446

2004, Nov. 8	Litho.	Perf. 12
2517 A446	90c multi	.70 .70

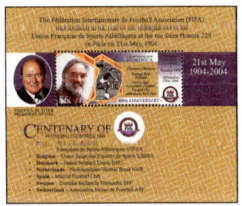

FIFA (Fédération Internationale de Football Association), Cent. — A447

No. 2518: a, Ferenc Puskas. b, Rivaldo. c, Carsten Jancker. d, Johan Cruyff. $6, George Best.

2004, Nov. 8		Perf. 12¾x12½
2518 A447	$2 Sheet of 4, #a-d	6.00 6.00
	Souvenir Sheet	
2519 A447	$6 multi	4.50 4.50

Worldwide Fund for Nature (WWF) — A448

No. 2520: a, Green-throated Carib (denomination in blue). b, Purple-throated Carib (denomination in white). c, Green-throated Carib (denomination in white). d, Purple-throated Carib (denomination in red).

2005, Jan. 10		Perf. 14
2520 A448	$2 Block of 4, #a-d	5.50 5.50
e.	Miniature sheet, 2 each #2520a-2520d	11.00 11.00

Prehistoric Animals — A449

No. 2521, $2: a, Tyrannosaurus rex. b, Velociraptor. c, Stegosaurus. d, Psittacosaurus.
No. 2522, $2: a, Mammuthus columbi. b, Spinosaurus. c, Ankylosaurus. d, Mammuthus primigenius.
No. 2523, $2: a, Pterodactylus. b, Pteranodon. c, Sordes. d, Caudipteryx zoui. $3, Compsognathus. $5, Archaeopteryx. $6, Mammuthus primigenius, diff.

2005, Jan. 10		Perf. 12¾
	Sheets of 4, #a-d	
2521-2523 A449	Set of 3	18.00 18.00
	Souvenir Sheets	
2524-2526 A449	Set of 3	10.50 10.50

Birds — A450

Designs: 25c, Brown booby. 90c, Brown pelican. $1, Red-billed tropicbird. $4, Northern gannet.
No. 2531: a, Great egret. b, Black-necked grebe. c, Turkey vulture. d, Snail kite. $6, Red knot.

2005, Jan. 10		Perf. 14
2527-2530 A450	Set of 4	4.50 4.50
2531 A450	$2 Sheet of 4, #a-d	5.75 5.75
	Souvenir Sheet	
2532 A450	$6 multi	4.00 4.00

Mushrooms — A451

No. 2533: a, Cortinarius mucosus. b, Cortinarius splendens. c, Cortinarius rufoolivaceus. d, Inocybe erubescens. $6, Split fibercap.

2005, Jan. 10		
2533 A451	$2 Sheet of 4, #a-d	6.00 6.00
	Souvenir Sheet	
2534 A451	$6 multi	4.50 4.50

DOMINICA

Miniature Sheet

Flowers A452

No. 2535: a, Sweetshrub. b, Pink turtle-heads. c, Flowering quince. d, Water lily. $6, Glory of the snow, vert.

2005, Jan. 10   Litho.   *Perf. 14*
2535   A452 $2 Sheet of 4, #a-d   6.00 6.00

Souvenir Sheet
2535E   A452 $6 multi   4.50 4.50

New Year 2005 (Year of the Rooster) — A453

2005, Jan. 24   *Perf. 12¾x12½*
2536   A453 $1 shown   .75 .75

Souvenir Sheet
Perf. 12
2537   A453 $4 Roosters   3.00 3.00
No. 2537 contains one 56x36mm stamp.

A454

Elvis Presley (1935-77) — A455

Elvis Presley (1935-77) — A455a

No. 2538: a, Green background under country name and near shirt collar. b, Guitar. c, Large red violet areas at side of head. d, Dark green background under country name, blue background near shirt collar. e, Purple background near shirt collar. f, Small red violet areas at side of head.
No. 2539: a, Country name in white, blue background at UR. b, Country name in white, pink background at UR. c, Country name in white, orange background at UR. d, Country name in blue, green background at UR. e, Presley and guitar. f, Country name in blue, yellow background at UR. g, Country name in blue, blue background at UR.
No. 2539H illustration reduced.

2005, Apr. 5   *Perf. 13½*
2538   A454 $1 Sheet of 9, #a-c, 2 each #d-f   6.75 6.75
2539   A455 $1 Sheet of 9, #a, c, e-g, 2 each #b, d   6.75 6.75

Litho. & Embossed
Variable Serpentine Die Cut Without Gum
2539H   A455a $20 gold & multi   14.00 14.00
No. 2539H was not available in the marketplace until 2006.

Miniature Sheet

Rotary International, Cent. — A456

No. 2540: a, Globe and Rotary emblem. b, Rotary emblem. c, Women and children.

2005, Sept. 7   *Perf. 12½x12¾*
2540   A456 $3 Sheet of 3, #a-c   6.75 6.75

Battle of Trafalgar, Bicent. A457

Designs: 55c, Admiral Horatio Nelson explaining plan of attack before battle. 65c, Orient explodes during the Battle of the Nile, vert. $1, Nelson and his men board San Nicolas during the Battle of Cape St. Vincent, vert. $2, Ships Agamemnon and Ca Ira in battle. $6, HMS Victory.

2005, Sept. 7   *Perf. 13¼*
2541-2544   A457 Set of 4   3.25 3.25

Souvenir Sheet
Perf. 12
2545   A457 $6 multi   4.50 4.50

Hans Christian Andersen (1805-75), Author — A458

No. 2546: a, The Swineherd. b, The Nightingale. c, The Fir Tree. $6, The Ugly Duckling.

2005, Sept. 7   *Perf. 12¾*
2546   A458 $2 Sheet of 3, #a-c   4.50 4.50

Souvenir Sheet
Perf. 12
2547   A458 $6 multi   4.50 4.50
No. 2546 contains three 42x28mm stamps.

Friedrich von Schiller (1759-1805), Writer — A459

No. 2548, vert. — Schiller and German Democratic Republic stamps: a, #241. b, #242. c, #243. $6, Statue of Schiller.

2005, Sept. 7   *Perf. 12¾*
2548   A459 $3 Sheet of 3, #a-c   6.75 6.75

Souvenir Sheet
2549   A459 $6 multi   4.50 4.50

Jules Verne (1828-1905), Writer — A460

No. 2550: a, Men, dog and rooster in space. b, Astronauts. c, Men looking at undersea creature. d, Submarine. $6, Portrait of Verne.

2005, Sept. 7   *Perf. 12¾*
2550   A460 $2 Sheet of 4, #a-d   6.00 6.00

Souvenir Sheet
2551   A460 $6 multi   4.50 4.50

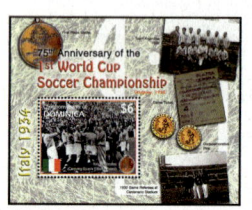

World Cup Soccer Championships, 75th Anniv. — A461

No. 2552: a, 1934 Italy team. b, Scene from 1934 Italy victory over Czechoslovakia. c, Flaminio Stadium. d, Angelos Schiavo. $6, Italian team celebrating.

2005, Sept. 7   *Perf. 12*
2552   A461 $2 Sheet of 4, #a-d   6.00 6.00

Souvenir Sheet
2553   A461 $6 multi   4.50 4.50

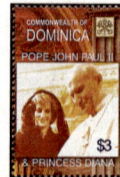

Christmas — A462

Painting details: 25c, Madonna and Child with Two Angels, by Sandro Botticelli. 50c, Madonna and Child with Angels, by Botticelli. 65c, Madonna and Child, by Pietro Lorenzetti. 90c, Madonna del Roseto, by Botticelli. $1.20, Adoration of the Magi, by Lorenzetti. $3, Madonna in Glory with the Seraphim, by Botticelli.
$5, Madonna of Frari, by Titian, horiz.

2005, Nov. 15   *Perf. 12¾*
2554-2559   A462 Set of 6   5.00 5.00

Souvenir Sheet
2560   A462 $5 multi   3.75 3.75

Pope John Paul II (1920-2005) and Princess Diana (1961-97) — A463

2005   *Perf. 13½x13¼*
2561   A463 $3 multi   2.25 2.25

Pope Benedict XVI — A464

2005   Litho.   *Perf. 13½x13¼*
2562   A464 $2 multi   1.50 1.50
Printed in sheets of 4.

Souvenir Sheet

New Year 2006 (Year of the Dog) A465

No. 2563 — Dog figurines with background colors of: a, Pale green and green. b, Orange and pink. c, Rose pink and yellow.

2006, Jan. 3   *Perf. 13¼x13½*
2563   A465 $1 Sheet of 3, #a-c   2.25 2.25

Miniature Sheets

National Basketball Association Players and Team Emblems — A466

No. 2564, 90c: a, Orlando Magic emblem. b, Hedo Turkoglu.
No. 2565, 90c: a, Denver Nuggets emblem. b, Kenyon Martin.
No. 2566, 90c: a, Miami Heat emblem. b, Antoine Walker.
No. 2567, 90c: a, Golden State Warriors emblem. b, Jason Richardson.
No. 2568, 90c: a, Phoenix Suns emblem. b, Amaré Stoudemire.
No. 2569, 90c: a, Los Angeles Clippers emblem. b, Elton Brand.

2006, Feb. 14   *Perf. 14*
Sheets of 12, 2 each #a, 10 each #b
2564-2569   A466 Set of 6   47.50 47.50

Léopold Sédar Senghor (1906-2001), First President of Senegal — A467

2006, Mar. 20   *Perf. 13¼*
2570   A467 $2 multi   1.50 1.50

DOMINICA

2006 Winter Olympics, Turin — A468

Designs: 75c, Yugoslavia #1670. 90c, 1984 Sarajevo Winter Olympics poster, vert. $2, Japan #2607g, vert. $3, 1998 Nagano Winter Olympics poster, vert.

2006, Mar. 29
2571-2574 A468 Set of 4   5.00 5.00
Each stamp printed in sheets of 4.

Queen Elizabeth II, 80th Birthday — A469

No. 2575: a, As infant, with mother. b, As young child. c, As baby, wearing bonnet. d, As young girl, wearing jacket. $5, Wearing tiara and sash.

2006, Mar. 29
2575 A469 $2 Sheet of 4, #a-d   6.00 6.00
Souvenir Sheet
2576 A469 $5 multi   3.75 3.75

Marilyn Monroe (1926-62), Actress — A470

2006, Apr. 7
2577 A470 $3 multi   2.25 2.25
Printed in sheets of 4.

Space Achievements — A471

No. 2578 — Viking I. a, Trenches dug by Viking I. b, Sunset at Viking I landing site. c, Chryse Planitia looking northwest over Viking I. d, First panoramic image of Chryse Planitia, country name and denomination in white. e, As "d," country name in black, denomination in white. f, As "d," country name and denomination in black.
No. 2579, $3, vert. — Luna 9: a, Flight apparatus. b, Modified SS-6 Sapwood rocket. c, Luna 9 Soft Lander. d, Tyuratam.
No. 2580, $3, vert. — Giotto Comet Probe: a, Launch of Giotto. b, Giotto during solar simulation test. c, Halley's Comet develops seven tails. d, Giotto and Comet Grigg-Skjellerup approach trajectories.
No. 2581, $6, Intl. Space Station. No. 2582, $6, Mars Reconnaissance Orbiter. No. 2583, $6, Venus Express Orbiter.

2006, June 6   Litho.   Perf. 14
2578 A471 $2 Sheet of 4, #a-f   9.00 9.00
Sheets of 4, #a-d
2579-2580 A471 Set of 2   18.00 18.00
Souvenir Sheets
2581-2583 A471 Set of 3   13.50 13.50

Wolfgang Amadeus Mozart (1756-91), Composer — A472

No. 2584: a, Oval portrait. b, Playing harpsichord. c, Wearing red coat. d, Head of Mozart.

2006, Sept. 1   Perf. 13¼
2584 A472 $3 Sheet of 4, #a-d   9.00 9.00

Miniature Sheet

Purchase of Graceland by Elvis Presley, 50th Anniv. — A473

No. 2585: a, View of path leading to front door. b, Graceland, columns at right. c, Graceland, columns at left. d, Room with Presley's costumes.

2006, Sept. 1   Perf. 13¼
2585 A473 $3 Sheet of 4, #a-d   9.00 9.00

Miniature Sheets

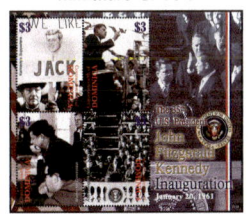

Pres. John F. Kennedy (1917-63) — A474

No. 2586, $3: a, Supporters holding campaign sign. b, Kennedy campaigning. c, Kennedy waiting for concession. d, Kennedy addressing the nation.
No. 2587, $3: a, Kennedy on crutches from war injuries. b, Kennedy on stretcher. c, Dust jacket of *Profiles in Courage*. d, Kennedy as senator.

2006, Oct. 1   Perf. 13¼
Sheets of 4, #a-d
2586-2587 A474 Set of 2   18.00 18.00

Shells — A475

Designs: 5c, Turbinella angulata. 10c, Vasum muricatum. 15c, Fusinus closter. 20c, Crasispira gibbosa. 25c, Terebra strigata. 50c, Prunum carneum. 65c, Purpura patula. 90c, Oliva circinata. $1, M. nodulosa. $2, Oniscia regius. $3.50, Conus hieroglyphus. $5, Anodontia alba, vert. $10, C. cassidiformis. $20, Strigilla carnaria, vert.

2006, Oct. 1   Perf. 14x15, 15x14
2588 A475 5c multi   .30 .50
2589 A475 10c multi   .30 .50
2590 A475 15c multi   .40 .80
2591 A475 20c multi   .40 .30
2592 A475 25c multi   .40 .30
2593 A475 50c multi   .55 .35
2594 A475 65c multi   .75 .50
2595 A475 90c multi   1.00 .75
2596 A475 $1 multi   1.25 1.25
2597 A475 $2 multi   2.00 2.00
2598 A475 $3.50 multi 3.25 3.25
2599 A475 $5 multi   4.00 4.00
2600 A475 $10 multi   7.00 7.00
2601 A475 $20 multi   14.00 14.00
Nos. 2588-2601 (14)   35.60 35.50

Souvenir Sheet

Ludwig Durr (1878-1956), Engineer — A476

2006, Nov. 15   Litho.   Perf. 12¾
2602 A476 $5 multi   3.75 3.75

Betty Boop A477

No. 2603, vert.: a, Betty Boop with black background and leg raised. b, Lips. c, Betty Boop with black background. d, Dog on leash, star. e, Betty Boop, white background. f, Dog, two stars.
No. 2604 — Betty Boop with: a, Light blue panel at top. b, Light yellow panel at top.

2006, Nov. 15
2603 A477 $2 Sheet of 6, #a-f   9.00 9.00
Souvenir Sheet
2604 A477 $3.50 Sheet of 2, #a-b   5.25 5.25

Christmas — A478

Christmas stocking showing: No. 2605, 25c, No. 2609a, $2, Christmas tree. No. 2606, 50c, No. 2609b, $2, Bell. No. 2607, 90c, No. 2609c, $2, Candy canes. No. 2608, $1, No. 2609d, $2, Stars.

2006, Dec. 1   Perf. 14¼
2605-2608 A478 Set of 4   2.00 2.00
Souvenir Sheet
2609 A478 $2 Sheet of 4, #a-d   5.00 3.00

Souvenir Sheet

Christopher Columbus (1451-1506), Explorer — A479

2007, Jan. 10   Perf. 12
2610 A479 $5 brn & black   3.75 3.75

Scouting, Cent. A480

2007, Jan. 10
2611 A480 $3.50 blue & multi   2.60 2.60
Souvenir Sheet
2612 A480 $5 org & multi   3.75 3.75
No. 2611 was printed in sheets of 3.

Concorde Prototype 001 F-WTSS — A481

No. 2613: a, $1, Airplane in hangar. b, $2, Airplane out of hangar.

2007, Jan. 23   Perf. 13¼
2613 A481 Pair, #a-b   2.25 2.25
Printed in sheets containing 3 of each stamp.

Rembrandt (1606-69), Painter — A482

No. 2614, vert. — Details from Christ Driving the Money Changers from the Temple: a, Christ. b, Man with moustache looking up. c, Man with striped headdress. d, Man protecting face with hands. $5, Jesus and His Disciples.

2007, Jan. 23   Perf. 13¼
2614 A482 $2 Sheet of 4, #a-d   6.00 6.00
Imperf
2615 A482 $5 shown   3.75 3.75
No. 2614 contains four 38x50mm stamps.

Cricket World Cup — A483

Designs: 90c, Cricket bats, ball and wicket, map and flag of Dominica. $1, Umpire Billy Doctrove. $5, Cricket bats, ball and wicket.

2007, Apr. 11   Perf. 14
2616-2617 A483 Set of 2   2.50 2.50
Souvenir Sheet
2618 A483 $5 multi   4.00 4.00

Birds — A484

Designs: 10c, Great frigatebird. 25c, Peruvian booby. 90c, Black stork, vert. No. 2622, $1, Linklu, vert. No. 2623: a, Antillean crested hummingbird. b, Rufous-breasted hermit. c, Cuban hummingbird. d, Blue-headed hummingbird. No. 2624, $6, Red capped manakin, vert.

2007, Apr. 11   Perf. 12¾
2619-2622 A484 Set of 4   5.25 5.25
2623 A484 $2 Sheet of 4, #a-d   7.50 7.50
Souvenir Sheet
2624 A484 $5 multi   5.25 5.25

Flowers — A485

232 DOMINICA

Designs: 10c, Red jasmine. 25c, Bougainvillea. 90c, Portia tree. No. 2628, $5, Rose bay.
No. 2629 — Orchids: a, $1, Tolumnia urophylla. b, $1, Brassavola cucullata. c, $2, Isochilus linearis. d, Spathoglottis plicata.
No. 2630, horiz.: a, Red ginger. b, Baobab. c, Purple wreath. d, Thunbergia.
No. 2631, $5, Flamboyant. No. 2632, $5, Oncidium altissimum.

2007, Apr. 11		Litho.		Perf. 12¾
2625-2628	A485	Set of 4	4.75	4.75
2629	A485	Sheet of 4, #a-d	4.50	4.50
2630	A485	$2 Sheet of 4, #a-d	6.00	6.00
Souvenir Sheets				
2631-2632	A485	Set of 2	7.50	7.50

Princess Diana (1961-97) — A486

No. 2633: a, Holding flowers, wearing purple hat. b, Without hat. c, Not holding flowers, wearing purple hat. d, Close-up of #2633a, lines on face. e, Close-up of #2633b, lines on face. f, Close-up of #2633c, lines on face.
$5, Wearing purple sweater.

2007, June 11			Perf. 13½
2633	A486	$1 Sheet of 6, #a-f	4.50 4.50
Souvenir Sheet			
2634	A486	$5 multi	3.75 3.75

No. 2633 contains six 28x42mm stamps.

Texas Rangers A487

No. 2635, horiz.: a, Two Rangers on horses. b, Seven Rangers in front of building with pillars. c, Ten rangers showing rifles. d, Rangers on horses. e, Rangers around still. f, Three Rangers at Justice of the Peace office. g, Rangers and tents. h, Rangers and locomotive. i, Five Rangers on horses near house.
$5, Statue of Charles Goodnight.

2007, June 15			Perf. 13½
2635	A487	$1 Sheet of 9, #a-i	6.75 6.75
Souvenir Sheet			
2636	A487	$5 multi	3.75 3.75

American Topical Association National Topical Stamp Show, Irving, TX.

Miniature Sheet

New Year 2007 (Year of the Pig) A488

No. 2637 — Text in: a, Red. b, Green. c, Blue green. d, Purple.

2007, July 2			
2637	A488	$2 Sheet of 4, #a-d	6.00 6.00

A489

A490

A491

Christmas A492

2007, Nov. 19		Litho.	Perf. 14¾x14
2638	A489	25c multi	.25 .25
2639	A490	50c multi	.40 .40
2640	A491	90c multi	.70 .70
2641	A492	$1 multi	.75 .75
	Nos. 2638-2641 (4)		2.10 2.10

New Year 2008 (Year of the Rat) — A493

2008, Feb. 28			Perf. 12
2642	A493	$1 multi	.75 .75

Printed in sheets of 4.

University of the West Indies, 60th Anniv. — A494

University crest, Dr. Bernard A. Sorhaindo and denomination in: 50c, Red brown. 65c, Green. 90c, Brown.
No. 2646, $5, Crest, Sorhaindo, denomination in black. No. 2647, $5, Crest, Sorhaindo, denomination in blue. No. 2648, $5, Crest, diploma, 60th anniversary emblem.

2008, Apr. 8			Perf. 13¼
2643-2645	A494	Set of 3	1.60 1.60
Souvenir Sheets			
2646-2648	A494	Set of 3	11.50 11.50

Miniature Sheet

2008 Summer Olympics, Beijing — A495

No. 2649: a, Archery. b, Men's gymnastics. c, Badminton. d, Boxing.

2008, Apr. 8			Perf. 13¼x13
2649	A495	$1.40 Sheet of 4, #a-d	4.25 4.25

Miniature Sheet

Visit of Pope Benedict XVI to New York A496

No. 2650 — Pope and part of St. Patrick's Cathedral in background: a, Small circular window under spire. b, Large central circular window. c, Archway below spire. d, Archway above main door.

2008, June 16		Litho.	Perf. 13½
2650	A496	$1.40 Sheet of 4, #a-d	4.25 4.25

Miniature Sheet

Wedding of Queen Elizabeth II and Prince Philip, 60th Anniv. A497

No. 2651: a, Couple, denomination in white. b, Queen, denomination in red violet. c, Couple, denomination in black. d, Queen, denomination in white. e, Couple, denomination in red violet. f, Queen, denomination in black.

2008, June 16			
2651	A497	$1 Sheet of 6, #a-f	4.50 4.50

Miniature Sheet

Elvis Presley (1935-77) — A498

No. 2652 — Presley and: a, Black and red background, Prussian blue denomination. b, Gray and black background, purple denomination. c, Blue and black background, Prussian blue denomination. d, Purple and black background, purple denomination. e, Gray and black background, Prussian blue denomination. f, Brown and black background, purple denomination.

2008, June 16			
2652	A498	$1.50 Sheet of 6 #a-f	6.75 6.75

A499

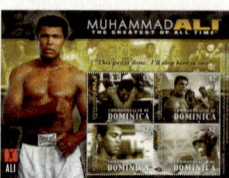

Muhammad Ali, Boxer — A500

No. 2653 — Ali: a, Sweating, denomination in white. b, Smiling, denomination in black. c, Wearing headgear. d, With arms raised.
No. 2654 — Ali: a, Seated in corner of boxing ring. b, Speaking to the press. c, Punching bag. d, Wearing headgear and mouth guard.

2008, July 7			
2653	A499	$2 Sheet of 4, #a-d	6.25 6.25
2654	A500	$2 Sheet of 4, #a-d	6.25 6.25

Convent High School, 150th Anniv. — A501

Panel color: 50c, Red violet. 65c, Yellow orange. 90c, Blue. $1, Red.
$5, Denomination in LR corner.

2008, Oct. 1			Perf. 12½
2655-2658	A501	Set of 4	2.40 2.40
Souvenir Sheet			
2659	A501	$5 multi	4.00 4.00

Dogs — A502

Designs: 25c, Dandie Dinmont terrier. 50c, Alaskan malamute. 90c, Welsh Springer spaniel. $1, Pug. $2, Norfolk terrier. $5, Vizsla.
No. 2666: a, Akita. b, Australian cattle dog. c, Border collie. d, Staffordshire bull terrier cross.

		Perf. 14¼x14¾	
2008, Dec. 11			Litho.
2660-2665	A502	Set of 6	8.50 8.50
2666	A502	$2.50 Sheet of 4, #a-d	9.00 9.00

Miniature Sheet

Marilyn Monroe (1926-62), Actress — A503

No. 2667 — Monroe wearing: a, Purple sweater, hand on arm. b, Orange sweater, looking in mirror. c, Purple sweater, holding post. d, Orange sweater, holding wine glass.

2008, Dec. 11			Perf. 14
2667	A503	$2 Sheet of 4, #a-d	6.00 6.00

Christmas A504

Designs: 25c, Santa Claus. 50c, Palm tree with Christmas ornaments. 90c, Christmas stocking. $1, Poinsettias.

2008, Dec. 15			Perf. 12
2668-2671	A504	Set of 4	2.00 2.00

DOMINICA

New Year 2009 (Year of the Ox) — A505

2009, Jan. 5			Perf. 14¾x14¼
2672	A505	$2 multi	1.50 1.50

Printed in sheets of 4.

Inauguration of Barack Obama as US President — A506

Pres. Obama: 65c, With raised hand. 90c, Hand not showing.
No. 2675: a, $2.25, Like 65c. b, $2.25, Looking over shoulder. c, $2.25, Like 90c. d, $2.25, Like 90c. e, $2.50, Looking over shoulder. f, $2.50, Like 65c.

2009, Jan. 20			Perf. 11½
2673-2674	A506	Set of 2	1.25 1.25
2675	A506	Sheet of 6, #a-f	11.00 11.00

A507

Denominations: 50c, 65c, 90c, $1.

2009, Mar. 23			Perf. 14¾x14¼
2676-2679	A507	Set of 4	2.40 2.40

Souvenir Sheet

| 2680 | A507 | $5 multi | 3.75 3.75 |

Diplomatic relations between Dominica and People's Republic of China, 5th anniv.

Peony — A508

2009, Apr. 10			Perf. 13¼
2681	A508	75c shown	.55 .55

Souvenir Sheet

| 2682 | A508 | $5 Peonies | 3.75 3.75 |

No. 2682 contains one 44x44mm stamp.

Miniature Sheet

Elvis Presley (1935-77) — A509

No. 2683 — Various photos of Presley with background colors of: a, Yellow orange. b, Gray and blue. c, Blue. d, Gray.

2009, May 23			Perf. 13¼
2683	A509	$2.50 Sheet of 4, #a-d	7.75 7.75

Miniature Sheet

Joseph Haydn (1732-1809), Composer — A510

No. 2684: a, Haydn. b, Haydn's birthplace, Rohrau, Austria. c, Wolfgang Amadeus Mozart. d, St. Stephen's Cathedral, Vienna. e, Nikolaus Esterházy, sponsor of Haydn. f, Esterházy Palace, Fertod, Hungary.

2009, June 10			Perf. 11½
2684	A510	$2.25 Sheet of 6, #a-f	10.00 10.00

Mushrooms — A511

Designs: 50c, Leucopaxillus gracillimus. 65c, Calvatia cyathiformis. 90c, Hygrocybe viridiphylla. $1, Boletellus coccineus.
No. 2689, $2: a, Hygrocybe acutoconica. b, Lepiota sulphureocyanescens. c, Lactarius rubrilacteus. d, Lactarius ferrugineus. e, Asterophera lycoperdoides. f, Amanita polypyramis.

2009, Sept. 8	Litho.		Perf. 14x14¾
2685-2688	A511	Set of 4	2.25 2.25
2689	A511	$2 Sheet of 6, #a-f	9.00 9.00

A512

Corals and Marine Life A513

Designs: 50c, Lobed star coral and shark. 65c, Orange cup coral and fish. 90c, Grooved brain coral and turtle. $1, Elkhorn coral and fish.
No. 2694, $2: a, Rough star coral and fish. b, Branched finger coral and fish. c, Wire coral and ray. d, Great star coral and fish. e, Pillar coral and fish. f, Rose lace coral and fish.

2009, Sept. 8			Perf. 14¾x14
2690-2693	A512	Set of 4	2.25 2.25
2694	A513	$2 Sheet of 6, #a-f	9.00 9.00

Butterflies A514

Designs: 90c, Banded orange heliconian. $1, Gulf fritillary. $2, Julia longwing. $5, Zebra longwing.
No. 2699: a, Cuban cattleheart. b, White peacock. c, Bahamian swallowtail. d, Tropical buckeye.
No. 2700, $6, Purple emperor. No. 2701, $6, Atala black.

2009, Sept. 8			Perf. 14¾x14
2695-2698	A514	Set of 4	6.75 6.75
2699	A514	$2.50 Sheet of 4, #a-d	7.50 7.50

Souvenir Sheets
Perf. 14¼

| 2700-2701 | A514 | Set of 2 | 9.00 9.00 |

Nos. 2700-2701 each contain one 50x38mm stamp.

Dolphins and Whales — A515

Designs: 50c, Irawaddy dolphin. 65c, Pantropical spotted dolphin. 90c, Atlantic humpback dolphin. $1, Indian humpback dolphin.
No. 2706: a, Melon-headed whale. b, Striped dolphin. c, Atlantic spotted dolphin. d, Clymene dolphin. e, Pantropical spotted dolphin (Stenella attenuata graffmani). f, Pantropical spotted dolphin (Stenella attenuata).

2009, Sept. 8	Litho.		Perf. 14¾x14
2702-2705	A515	Set of 4	2.25 2.25
2706	A515	$2 Sheet of 6, #a-f	9.00 9.00

See No. 2732.

Shells — A516

Designs: 50c, Oliva reticularis. 65c, Vasum muricatum. 90c, Olivella nivea. $1, Olivella mutica.
No. 2711: a, Hyalina avena. b, Persicula fluctuata. c, Agatrix agassizi. d, Trigonostoma rugosum. e, Olivella floralia. f, Marginella eburneola.

2009, Sept. 8			
2707-2710	A516	Set of 4	2.25 2.25
2711	A516	$2 Sheet of 6, #a-f	9.00 9.00

Miniature Sheet

Expo 2010, Shanghai — A517

No. 2712: a, Bund. b, Shanghai Museum. c, Yangpu Bridge. d, Shanghai Theater.

2009, Oct. 16			Perf. 13x12¾
2712	A517	$1.50 Sheet of 4, #a-d	4.50 4.50

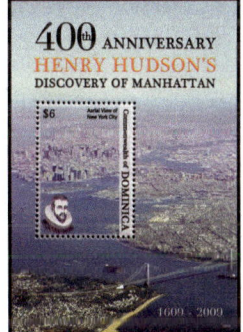

Discovery of Manhattan Island by Henry Hudson, 400th Anniv. — A518

No. 2713, horiz.: a, Panoramic view of New York City, 1913. b, Hudson, the Dreamer, by Jean L.G. Ferris. c, Henry Hudson. d, Hudson's ship, Half Moon. e, Map of Hudson River, c. 1600. f, Henry Hudson Memorial Column, Bronx, NY.
$6, Hudson, aerial view of New York City.

2009, Oct. 16			Perf. 13x12¾
2713	A518	$2.25 Sheet of 6, #a-f	10.00 10.00

Souvenir Sheet
Perf. 12¾x13

| 2714 | A518 | $6 multi | 4.50 4.50 |

Miniature Sheet

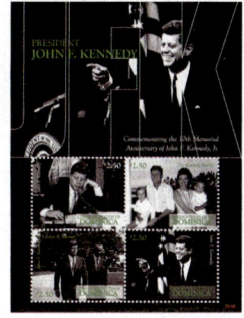

Pres. John F. Kennedy (1917-63) — A519

No. 2715 — Pres. Kennedy: a, On telephone. b, With family. c, With Vice-president Lyndon B. Johnson. d, Pointing.

2009, Oct. 30			Perf. 11½x12
2715	A519	$2.50 Sheet of 4, #a-d	7.50 7.50

Miniature Sheet

First Man on the Moon, 40th Anniv A520

No. 2716: a, Apollo 11 crew. b, Moon landing on television. c, Apollo 11 capsule with parachutes. d, Earth, Apollo 11 modules and patch. e, Command Module in Moon orbit. f, Project Orion.

2009, Nov. 2			Perf. 11½
2716	A520	$2 Sheet of 6, #a-f	9.00 9.00

Chinese Aviation, Cent. A521

No. 2717: a, H-5. b, H-6. c, H-6H. d, H-6L. $6, H 6U.

2009, Nov. 12			Perf. 14
2717	A521	$2 Sheet of 4, #a-d	6.50 6.50

Souvenir Sheet
Perf. 14¼

| 2718 | A521 | $6 multi | 4.75 4.75 |

Aeropex 2009 Intl. Philatelic Exhibition, Beijing. No. 2717 contains four 42x28mm stamps.

Christmas — A522

Designs: 50c, Bell-shaped Christmas tree ornament. 65c, Candles and poinsettia. 90c, Gingerbread man. $1.10, Decorated palm tree. $2.25, Christmas tree ornaments. $2.75, Women dancers.

2009, Nov. 16			Perf. 11½
2719-2724	A522	Set of 6	6.25 6.25

233

234 DOMINICA

Personalized Stamp — A523

2009, Dec. 18   Perf. 14x14¾
2725 A523 $3 gray   2.25 2.25

The vignette on the stamp shown is a generic image. Stamps without a vignette were also made available. Printed in sheets of 12.

Pope John Paul II (1920-2005) — A524

2010, Jan. 4   Perf. 12x11½
2726 A524 $2.75 multi   2.10 2.10

Printed in sheets of 4.

Miniature Sheet

Chinese Zodiac Animals — A524a

No. 2726A — Various stamps of People's Republic of China depicting Zodiac animals: b, Monkey. c, Rooster. d, Dog. e, Pig. f, Rat. g, Ox. h, Tiger. i, Rabbit. j, Dragon. k, Snake. l, Horse. m, Ram.

2010, Jan. 4   Litho.   Perf. 12¾
2726A A524a 60c Sheet of 12, #b-m   6.00 6.00

Souvenir Sheet

New Year 2010 (Year of the Tiger) A525

2010, Jan. 4   Perf. 12¾
2727 A525 $5 multi   4.00 4.00

Miniature Sheet

Elvis Presley (1935-77) — A526

Various drawings of Presley.

2010, Jan. 8   Perf. 11½
2728 A526 $2.50 Sheet of 4, #a-d   7.75 7.75

Miniature Sheet

NASCAR Drivers and Their Cars A527

No. 2729: a, Denny Hamlin. b, Kyle Busch. c, Joey Logano. d, Hamlin's car (#11). e, Busch's car (#18). f, Logano's car (#20).

2010, Jan. 19   Litho.
2729 A527 $3.25 Sheet of 6, #a-f   15.00 15.00

Miniature Sheets

Dogs A528

No. 2730, $2.50 — Dalmatian and: a, Books. b, Stone wall. c, Swimming pool. d, Stack of logs.
No. 2731, $2.50 — Boxer and: a, Brick wall. b, Bush. c, Window. d, Fence.

2010, Jan. 19   Perf. 11½x11¾
2730-2731 A528 Set of 2   15.50 15.50

No. 2706 With "Haiti Earthquake Relief Fund" and Map of Haiti Added to Stamps and Sheet Margin

Miniature Sheet

Designs as before.

2010, Feb. 4   Perf. 14¾x14
2732 A515 $2 Sheet of 6, #a-f   9.25 9.25

Position of added text varies on each stamp.

Ferraris and Their Parts — A529

No. 2733, $1.25: a, Engine of 1982 208 GTB Turbo. b, 1982 208 GTB Turbo.
No. 2734, $1.25: a, Engine of 1983 126 C3. b, 1983 126 C3.
No. 2735, $1.25: a, Side panel and rear wheel of 1984 Testarossa. b, 1984 Testarossa.
No. 2736, $1.25: a, Suspension of 1987 408 4RM. b, 1987 408 4RM.

2010, Feb. 17   Perf. 12
Vert. Pairs, #a-b
2733-2736 A529 Set of 4   8.00 8.00

Nos. 2733-2736 each were printed in sheets containing four pairs.

Miniature Sheet

Mother Teresa (1910-97), Humanitarian — A530

No. 2737 — Mother Teresa: a, Denomination in black. b, Holding rosary. c, Wearing white habit. d, Kissing hand of Pope John Paul II.

2010, Feb. 24   Perf. 11¼x11½
2737 A530 $2.50 Sheet of 4, #a-d   8.00 8.00

Boy Scouts of America, Cent. A531

No. 2738, $2.50: a, Outdoor skills. b, Campfire inspirations.
No. 2739, $2.50: a, Emergency one-man carry. b, Swimming fun with safety.

2010, Feb. 24   Perf. 13¼
Pairs, #a-b
2738-2739 A531 Set of 2   8.00 8.00

Nos. 2738-2739 each were printed in sheets containing two pairs.

Miniature Sheet

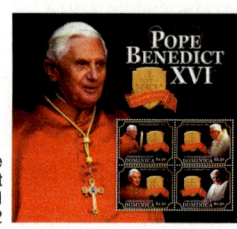

Pope Benedict XVI A532

No. 2740 — Pope Benedict XVI: a, Wearing red, holding candle. b, Wearing white, hands clasped. c, Wearing red, not holding candle. d, Wearing white, hands not clasped.

2010, Mar. 23   Perf. 11½x12
2740 A532 $2.50 Sheet of 4, #a-d   7.50 7.50

Caravaggio Paintings — A533

No. 2741, vert.: a, Mary Magdalene. b, Sick Bacchus. c, Bacchus. d, The Inspiration of Saint Matthew.
$6, Saint Gerolamo.

2010, Mar. 23   Perf. 12x11½
2741 A533 $2.50 Sheet of 4, #a-d   7.50 7.50

Souvenir Sheet
Perf. 11½

2742 A533 $6 multi   4.50 4.50

Miniature Sheet

Girl Guides, Cent. A534

No. 2743: a, Rainbows. b, Brownies. c, Guides. d, Senior Section. $6, Girl Guide, vert.

2010, Apr. 19   Perf. 11½x12
2743 A534 $2.75 Sheet of 4, #a-d   8.25 8.25

Souvenir Sheet
Perf. 11¼x11½

2743E A534 $6 multi   4.50 4.50

Souvenir Sheets

A535

A536

A537

Elvis Presley (1935-77) — A538

2010, May 12   Perf. 13½
2744 A535 $6 multi   4.50 4.50
2745 A536 $6 multi   4.50 4.50
2746 A537 $6 multi   4.50 4.50
2747 A538 $6 multi   4.50 4.50
Nos. 2744-2747 (4)   18.00 18.00

DOMINICA   235

Miniature Sheets

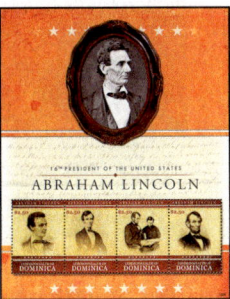

Pres. Abraham Lincoln (1809-65) — A539

No. 2748, $2.50 — Photographs of Lincoln: a, Without beard. b, Without beard, arms crossed. c, Reading to son, Tad. d, With beard.
No. 2749, $2.50: a, Statue of Lincoln, Bascom Hill, University of Wisconsin. b, Aerial view of Lincoln Memorial. c, Statue of Lincoln in Lincoln Memorial. d, Sculpture of Lincoln, Mount Rushmore.

2010, June 22 Litho. Perf. 11½
Sheets of 4, #a-d
2748-2749 A539 Set of 2   15.00 15.00

Whales A540

No. 2750: a, Sowerby's beaked whale. b, Blainville's beaked whale. c, Short-finned pilot whale. d, True's beaked whale. e, False killer whale. f, Dwarf sperm whale.
$6, Sperm whale.

2010, June 22 Litho. Perf. 13x13½
2750 A540 $2 Sheet of 6, #a-f   9.00 9.00
Souvenir Sheet
2751 A540 $6 multi   4.50 4.50

Miniature Sheets

A541

Princess Diana (1901-97) — A542

No. 2752 — Princess Diana wearing: a, Plaid jacket. b, Wedding gown. c, Black jacket. d, Red and white dress.
No. 2753 — Princess Diana with: a, Prince Charles. b, Princes Charles, William and Harry. c, Crowd, holding flowers. d, Small child

2010, May 12 Litho. Perf. 13x13¼
2752 A541 $2.75 Sheet of 4, #a-d 8.25 8.25
2753 A542 $2.75 Sheet of 4, #a-d 8.25 8.25

Christmas — A543

Painting details: 90c, Geburt Christi (Birth of Christ), by Hans Baldung. $1.45, Thomas Altar, by Meister Francke. $2, Nativity, by Baldung.

2010, Dec. 1 Perf. 13x13½
2754-2756 A543 Set of 3   3.25 3.25
Nos. 2754-2756 each were printed in sheets of 6.

Henri Dunant (1828-1910), Founder of Red Cross — A544

No. 2757 — Red Cross, nurses aiding wounded and portrait of Dunant in: a, Green. b, Brown. c, Purple. d, Blue.
$5, Red Cross, nurses, Dunant in purplish gray.

2010, Dec. 15 Perf. 12½x12
2757 A544 $3.50 Sheet of 4, #a-d   10.50 10.50
Souvenir Sheet
2758 A544 $5 multi   3.75 3.75

Tenth Cricket World Cup, India, Sri Lanka and Bangladesh A545

Designs: 90c, Chris Gayle. $2, Windsor Park Sports Stadium, Roseau, horiz. $5, Cricket World Cup.

2011, June 1 Litho. Perf. 12½
2759-2760 A545 Set of 2   2.25 2.25
Souvenir Sheet
Perf. 12
2761 A545 $5 multi   3.75 3.75
No. 2761 contains one 30x40mm stamp.

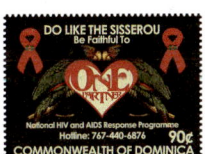

National HIV and AIDS Response Program — A545a

2011, June 1 Litho. Perf. 13½
2761A A545a 90c multi

Lizards — A546

Designs: 5c, Golden skink. 10c, Dominican ground lizard. 15c, Crested anole. 20c, Dominican tree lizard. 25c, Pygmy skink. 50c, House gecko. 65c, Fantastic gecko. 90c, Iguana. $1, Vincent's least gecko. $2, Turnip-tailed gecko. $5, House gecko, diff. $10, Fantastic gecko, diff. $20, Vincent's least gecko, diff.

2011, Oct. 1 Perf. 14
2762 A546   5c multi   .25 .25
2763 A546 10c multi   .25 .25
2764 A546 15c multi   .25 .25
2765 A546 20c multi   .25 .25
2766 A546 25c multi   .25 .25
2767 A546 50c multi   .40 .40
2768 A546 65c multi   .50 .50
2769 A546 90c multi   .70 .70
2770 A546 $1 multi   .75 .75
2771 A546 $2 multi   1.50 1.50
2772 A546 $5 multi   3.75 3.75
2773 A546 $10 multi   7.50 7.50
2774 A546 $20 multi   15.00 15.00
Nos. 2762-2774 (13)   31.35 31.35

Christmas — A547

Paintings: 90c, The Annunciation, by Andrea del Sarto. $1.45, Madonna with Child, by Jacopo Bellini. $2, The Virgin, by Carlo Dolci.

2011, Nov. 1
2775-2777 A547 Set of 3   3.25 3.25

Christmas — A548

Paintings: 50c, Virgin in Adoration Before the Christ Child, by Peter Paul Rubens. 90c, Altarpiece of the Rose Garlands, by Albrecht Dürer. $3.50, Crowning of St. Catherine, by Rubens. $6, Adoration of the Magi, by Dürer.

2012, Nov. 19 Perf. 13¾
2778-2781 A548 Set of 4   7.50 7.50

New Year 2011 (Year of the Rabbit) — A549

2013, Aug. 29 Litho. Perf. 12
2782 A549 $4 multi   3.00 3.00
No. 2782 was printed in sheets of 2.

Cats A550

No. 2783: a, Cat with brown-tipped tail, eyes not visible. b, Cat with black tail and four white paws. c, Head of cat and two front paws. d, Cat with black tail, paw touching "A" in "Cats." e, Cat with white tail, with one black paw visible. f, Cat with one black and three white paws.
$5, Cat, diff.

2013, Sept. 2 Litho. Perf. 14
2783 A550 $1 Sheet of 6, #a-f   4.50 4.50
Souvenir Sheet
Perf. 12
2784 A550 $5 multi   3.75 3.75

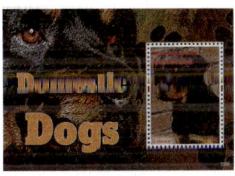

Dogs A551

No. 2785, $1.45: a, Airedale terrier. b, Bernese mountain dog. c, Pekingese. d, Samoyed.
No. 2786, $1.45, horiz.: a, Labrador retriever. b, Border collie. c, Cocker spaniel. d, Dalmatian.
No. 2787, $5, Rottweiler. No. 2788, $5, Great Dane.

2013, Sept. 2 Litho. Perf. 12
Sheets of 4, #a-d
2785-2786 A551 Set of 2   8.75 8.75
Souvenir Sheets
2787-2788 A551 Set of 2   7.50 7.50

Bees and Wasps A552

No. 2789: a, Carpenter bee. b, Golden digger wasp. c, Bumblebee. d, Yellowjacket.
$5, Golden paper wasp.

2013, Sept. 2 Litho. Perf. 13¾
2789 A552 $2 Sheet of 4, #a-d   6.00 6.00
Souvenir Sheet
2790 A552 $5 multi   3.75 3.75

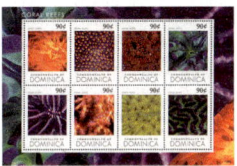

Corals A553

No. 2791 — Various unnamed corals with colors of: a, Pink (with anemone-like tips). b, Purple and pink (small bead-like appearance). c, Dark red. d, Blue (tubes). e, Purple and pink (with lines). f, Pink (with branches). g, Yellow green. h, Blue (with black curved lines).
$5, Nephthyigorgia sp.

2013, Sept. 2 Litho. Perf. 14
2791 A553 90c Sheet of 8, #a-h   6.50 6.50
Souvenir Sheet
Perf. 12¾x12½
2792 A553 $5 multi   3.75 3.75
No. 2792 contains one 38x51mm stamp.

Election of Pope Francis A554

No. 2793 — Pope Francis: a, With top of head visible (40x60mm). b, Waving, without eyeglasses, horiz. (40x30mm). c, With top of head not visible, horiz. (40x30mm). d, Waving, wearing eyeglasses, horiz. (40x30mm).
$5, Pope Francis, horiz.

2013, Sept. 2 Litho. Perf. 14
2793 A554 $3.50 Sheet of 4, #a-d   10.50 10.50
Souvenir Sheet
Perf. 12¾x12½
2794 A554 $5 multi   3.75 3.75
No. 2794 contains one 51x38mm stamp.

236 DOMICA

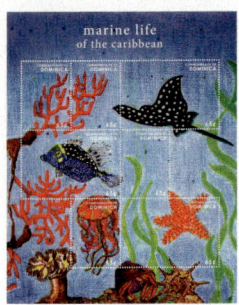

Painting of Marine Life A555

Painting of Parrot A556

No. 2795: a, Coral, denomination on coral (30x40mm). b, Coral, denomination on blue background (30x40mm). c, Ray (60x40mm). d, Fish and coral (60x40mm). e, Sea grass (30x40mm). f, Jellyfish (30x40mm). g, Sea grass and starfish (60x40mm).

2013, Sept. 2	Litho.		Perf. 14	
2795 A555	65c Sheet of 7, #a-g		3.50	3.50
Souvenir Sheet				
Perf. 12				
2796 A556	$5 multi		3.75	3.75

Butterflies — A557

No. 2797, $2: a, Malachite. b, Silver-banded hairstreak.
No. 2798, $2: a, Gold rim swallowtail. b, Mangrove buckeye.

2013, Sept. 2	Litho.	Perf. 13¾		
Pairs, #a-b				
2797-2798 A557	Set of 2		6.00	6.00

Nos. 2797 and 2798 each were printed in sheets containing two pairs.

Birth of Prince George of Cambridge — A558

No. 2799: a, Duke and Duchess of Cambridge, Prince George. b, Duke of Cambridge holding Prince George. c, Duchess of Cambridge holding Prince George. d, Close-up of Prince George.
$6, Duke and Duchess of Cambridge, Prince George, diff.

2013	Litho.		Perf. 14	
2799 A558	$2 Sheet of 4, #a-d		6.00	6.00
Souvenir Sheet				
2800 A558	$6 multi		4.50	4.50

A559

Nelson Mandela (1918-2013), President of South Africa — A560

No. 2801 — Mandela: a, Holding loudspeaker. b, Wearing green and black shirt and jacket. c, With arms raised, color photograph. d, With arms raised, black-and-white photograph. e, Wearing black and gray shirt. f, Wearing black shirt.
$5, Mandela wearing gray shirt. $20, Mandela wearing shirt with leaf design.

2014, Jan. 6	Litho.	Perf. 13¾		
2801 A559	$2.50 Sheet of 6, #a-f		11.00	11.00
Souvenir Sheets				
2802 A559	$5 multi		3.75	3.75
Litho., Margin Embossed With Foil Application				
Imperf				
2803 A560	$20 multi		15.00	15.00

New Year 2014 (Year of the Horse) A561

No. 2804 — Various Chinese characters for "horse" and: a, Horse in red at left, red chop at right, orange background. b, Horse in yellow at left, yellow chop at left, red orange background. c, Horse in red at left, red chop at left, yellow orange background. d, Horse in yellow at right, red chop at left, brown background. e, Horse in red at right, red chop at left, yellow orange background. f, Horse in yellow at right, red chop at left, dull orange background.
No. 2805 — Chinese characters for "horse" and: a, Horse in red at right. b, Horse in yellow brown at right.

2014, Jan. 8	Litho.		Perf. 14	
2804 A561	$2.50 Sheet of 6, #a-f		11.00	11.00
Souvenir Sheet				
2805 A561	$5 Sheet of 2, #a-b		7.50	7.50

Sea Turtles A562

No. 2806: a, Leatherback turtle. b, Green sea turtle. c, Hawksbill turtle.
$5, Green sea turtle, diff.

2014, May 1	Litho.	Perf. 11½x12		
2806 A562	$3.50 Sheet of 3, #a-c		7.75	7.75
Souvenir Sheet				
2807 A562	$5 multi		3.75	3.75

Morne Trois Pitons National Park UNESCO World Heritage Site, 70th Anniv. — A563

No. 2808: a, Fumarole, mountain in background. b, Fumarole, rocks in foreground. c, Lesser Antillean iguana. d, Smoke-enshrouded landscape. e, Smoke above waterfall. g, Waterfall.
$10, Waterfall, diff.

2015, Dec. 1	Litho.		Perf. 12	
2808 A563	$3.50 Sheet of 6, #a-f		15.50	15.50
Souvenir Sheet				
2809 A563	$10 multi		7.50	7.50

First Man on the Moon, 50th Anniv. (in 2019) A564

No. 2810: a, Michael Collins (1930-2021), Apollo 11 Command Module pilot. b, Neil Armstrong (1930-2012), Apollo 11 commander, and first man on the Moon. c, Edwin E. Aldrin, Jr., Apollo 11 Lunar Module pilot.
$5, Aldrin on Moon, vert.

2020, Nov. 3	Litho.		Perf. 14	
2810 A564	$2.50 Sheet of 3, #a-c		5.75	5.75
Souvenir Sheet				
Perf. 12				
2811 A564	$5 multi		3.75	3.75

No. 2811 contains one 30x80mm stamp.

Miniature Sheet

Tribute to Workers in COVID-19 Pandemic — A565

No. 2812: a, Police officer wearing cap and protective mask and face shield. b, Health care worker wearing hair net, protective eyeglasses and face mask. c, Medical emblem. d, Vial of coronavirus vaccine.

2020, Nov. 3	Litho.		Perf. 14	
2812 A565	$5 Sheet of 4, #a-d		15.00	15.00

Dorje Chang Buddha III, Religious Leader — A566

2020, Nov. 18	Litho.	Perf. 13¼		
2813 A566	$5 multi		3.75	3.75

No. 2813 was printed in sheets of 5.

A567

Wildlife of Dominica A568

Nos. 2814, 2821a, 5c, Black land crab. Nos. 2815, 2821b, 25c, Dominica cloud boa. Nos. 2816, 2821c, 90c, Mountain chicken. Nos. 2817, 2821d, $1, Lesser Antillean iguana. Nos. 2818, 2821e, $5, Red-necked Amazon. Nos. 2819, 2821f, $20, Imperial Amazon. $250, Flag of Dominica.

Perf. 12½x13¼

2020, Nov. 18		Litho.		
2814 A567	5c multi		.25	.25
2815 A567	25c multi		.25	.25
2816 A567	90c multi		.65	.65
2817 A567	$1 multi		.75	.75
2818 A567	$5 multi		3.75	3.75
2819 A567	$20 multi		15.00	15.00
2820 A567	$250 multi		185.00	185.00
Nos. 2814-2819 (6)			20.65	20.65

Miniature Sheet
Perf. 14

| 2821 A568 | Sheet of 6, #a-f | | 21.00 | 21.00 |

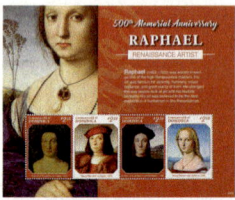

Paintings by Raphael (1483-1520) — A569

No. 2822: a, Portait of Elisabetta Gonzaga, 1505. b, Young Man with an Apple, 1505. c, Portrait of Guidobaldo da Montefeltro, 1506. d, Young Woman with Unicorn, 1506.
$5, Portrait of Maddalena Doni, 1506.

2020, Nov. 18	Litho.		Perf. 14	
2822 A569	$2.50 Sheet of 4, #a-d		7.50	7.50
Souvenir Sheet				
Perf. 12½				
2823 A569	$5 multi		3.75	3.75

No. 2823 contains one 38x51mm stamp.

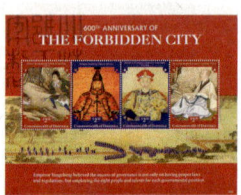

Forbidden City, Beijing, People's Republic of China, 600th Anniv. — A570

No. 2824: a, Yongzheng Emperor (1678-1735) holding off tiger with trident. b, Yongzheng Emperor in armor. c, Yongzheng Emperor in court dress. d, Yongzheng Emperor wearing robe.
$5, Yongzheng Emperor Offering Sacrifice at the Xiannong Altar, horiz.

2020, Nov. 18	Litho.	Perf. 12½		
2824 A570	$2.50 Sheet of 4, #a-d		7.50	7.50
Souvenir Sheet				
Perf. 12				
2825 A570	$5 multi		3.75	3.75

No. 2825 contains one 50x30mm stamp.

Visit to United Kingdom of Pres. Donald Trump A571

DOMINICA — DOMINICAN REPUBLIC

No. 2826: a, First Lady Melania Trump. b, Pres. Trump, with wife Melania in background. c, Donald Trump. d, John Hall, Dean of Westminster. $5, Pres. Trump and wife, Melania, diff.

2020, Nov. 18	Litho.	Perf. 14
2826 A571 $2.50 Sheet of 4, #a-d		7.50 7.50

Souvenir Sheet
Perf. 13¾
| 2827 A571 $5 multi | 3.75 3.75 |

No. 2827 contains one 35x35mm stamp.

New Year 2020 (Year of the Rat) — A572

2020, Nov. 18	Litho.	Perf. 12½
2828 A572 $5 multi		3.75 3.75

No. 2828 was printed in sheets of 2.

WAR TAX STAMPS

No. 50 Surcharged in Red

1916	Wmk. 3	Perf. 14
MR1 A6 ½p on ½p green		3.50 .85

No. 50 Overprinted in Black

1918
MR2 A6 ½p green 7.50 6.25

Nos. 50, 40 in Black or Red

1918
MR3 A6 ½p green   .25 .30
MR4 A6 3p violet, yel (R) 5.50 4.50

Type of 1908-09 Surcharged in Red

1919
MR5 A6 1½p on 2½p orange .25 .60

DOMINICAN REPUBLIC
də-ˈmi-ni-kən ri-ˈpə-blik

LOCATION — Comprises about two-thirds of the island of Hispaniola in the West Indies
GOVT. — Republic
AREA — 18,700 sq. mi.
POP. — 10,850,000 (2020 est.)

CAPITAL — Santo Domingo

8 Reales = 1 Peso
100 Centavos = 1 Peso (1880)
100 Centimos = 1 Franco (1883)
100 Centavos = 1 Peso (1885)

> Catalogue values for unused stamps in this country are for Never Hinged items, beginning with Scott 437 in the regular postage section, Scott B1 in the semipostal section, Scott C75 in the airpost section, Scott CB1 in the airpost semi-postal section, Scott E7 in the special delivery section, Scott G13 in the insured letter section, Scott J14 in the postage due section, Scott O26 in the officials section, and Scott RA20 in the postal tax section.

Watermarks

Wmk. 115
Diamonds

Wmk. 116
Crosses and Circles

Coat of Arms
A1   A2

1865	Unwmk.	Typo.	Imperf.

Wove Paper
| 1 | A1 | ½r black, rose | 700. 650. |
| 2 | A1 | 1r black, dp green | 1,100. 1,000. |

Twelve varieties of each.

Laid Paper
| 3 | A2 | ½r black, pale green | 550. 475. |
| 4 | A2 | 1r black, straw | 1,800. 1,200. |

Twelve varieties of the ½r, ten of the 1r.

A3   A4

1866	Laid Paper	Unwmk.
5	A3 ½r black, straw	200.00 160.00
6	A3 1r black, pale green	2,500. 2,000.
7	A4 1r black, pale green	175.00 125.00

Nos. 5-8 have 21 varieties (sheets of 21).

Wmk. 115
| 8 | A3 1r blk, pale grn | 13,000. 13,000. |
| a. | "CORREOS" and "Un Real" doubled | 21,000. |

The unique example of No. 8a is centered in the grade of fine, has a shallow thin spot and pinhole.

1866-67	Wove Paper	Unwmk.
9	A3 ½r blk, rose ('67)	60.00 60.00
10	A3 1r blk, pale green	85.00 75.00
a.	Inscription dbl., top & bottom	400.00 400.00
11	A3 1r black, blue ('67)	60.00 37.50
a.	1r black, light blue ('67)	50.00 30.00
b.	No space btwn. "Un" and "real"	600.00 500.00
c.	Without inscription at top & bottom	1,500. 1,000.
d.	Inscription invtd., top & bottom	—

Nos. 9-11 (3) 205.00 172.50

1867-71		Pelure Paper
13	A3 ½r black, rose	150.00 75.00
15	A3 ½r black, lav ('68)	250.00 210.00
a.	Without inscription at top and bottom	525.00
b.	Dbl. inscriptions, one invtd.	425.00

16	A3 ½r black, grnsh gray ('68)	260.00 225.00
17	A3 ½r black, yel ('68)	12,000.
18	A3 ½r blk, ol ('69)	3,000. 5,500.
22	A3 1r black, blue	4,000.
23	A3 1r black, lav	225.00 200.00
24	A4 1r blk, rose ('68)	225.00 225.00
25	A4 1r blk, mag ('69)	2,250. 1,300.
26	A4 1r blk, sal ('71)	300.00 225.00

Value for No. 17 is for an example with very fine centering and small faults. Value for No. 22 is for a faulty example with very fine centering and appearance.

1870-73		Ordinary Paper
27	A3 ½r blk, mag	2,500. 4,750.
28	A3 ½r blue, rose (blk inscription) ('71)	50.00 42.50
a.	Blue inscription	500.00 500.00
b.	Without inscription at top and bottom	
29	A3 ½r blk, yel ('73)	30.00 21.00
a.	Without inscription at top and bottom	700.00 700.00
30	A4 1r blk, vio ('73)	30.00 21.00
a.	Without inscription at top and bottom	700.00 700.00
31	A4 1r black, dk grn	60.00 50.00

Nos. 9-31 have 21 varieties (sheets of 21). Nos. 29 and 30 are known pin-perforated, unofficially.

Bisects are known of several of the early 1r stamps.

A5

1879		Perf. 12½x13
32	A5 ½r violet	3.00 2.10
a.	Imperf., pair	9.00 9.00
b.	Horiz. pair, imperf. vert.	17.00
33	A5 ½r violet, bluish	2.50 1.80
a.	Imperf., pair	9.00 7.50
34	A5 1r carmine	4.50 2.10
a.	Imperf., pair	11.50 9.00
b.	Perf. 13	11.50 7.50
c.	Perf. 13x12½	11.50 7.50
35	A5 1r carmine, sal	2.50 1.50
a.	Imperf., pair	10.00 10.00

Nos. 32-35 (4) 12.50 7.50

In 1891 15 stamps of 1879-83 were surcharged "U P U," new values and crossed diagonal lines.

A6

1880	Typo.	Rouletted in Color
36	A6 1c green	1.40 .90
a.	Laid paper	50.00 50.00
37	A6 2c red	1.00 .75
a.	Pelure paper	40.00 40.00
b.	Laid paper	40.00 40.00
38	A6 5c blue	1.50 .70
39	A6 10c rose	3.25 .90
40	A6 20c brown	2.00 .75
41	A6 25c lilac	2.25 1.25
42	A6 50c orange	3.00 1.75
43	A6 75c ultra	5.75 3.00
a.	Laid paper	40.00 40.00
44	A6 1p bister	7.50 4.50
a.	Laid paper	50.00 50.00
b.	Double impression	42.50 42.50

Nos. 36-44 (9) 27.65 14.50

1881		Network Covering Stamp
45	A6 1c green	.90 .50
46	A6 2c red	.90 .50
47	A6 5c blue	1.25 .50
48	A6 10c rose	1.50 .65
49	A6 20c org brown	1.50 .90
50	A6 25c lilac	1.75 1.00
51	A6 50c orange	2.00 1.40
52	A6 75c ultra	6.00 4.50
53	A6 1p bister	8.00 7.00

Nos. 45-53 (9) 23.80 16.95

Preceding Issues (Type A6) Srch. with Value in New Currency

a

b

(c) 50 céntimos

(d) 1 franco

(e) 1 Franco.

(f) 1 franco

(g) 1 franco, 25 céntimos

(h) 5 francos

(i) 5 francos

1883		Without Network
54	(a) 5c on 1c green	1.50 1.60
b.	Inverted surcharge	21.00 21.00
c.	Surcharged "25 céntimos"	50.00 50.00
d.	Surcharged "10 céntimos"	27.50 27.50
55	(b) 5c on 1c green	25.00 9.00
b.	Double surcharge	100.00
c.	Inverted surcharge	65.00 65.00
56	(c) 5c on 1c green	17.00 9.50
b.	Surcharged "10 céntimos"	35.00 35.00
c.	Surcharged "25 céntimos"	37.50 37.50
57	(a) 10c on 2c red	5.00 3.00
a.	Inverted surcharge	27.50 27.50
d.	Surcharged "5 céntimos"	52.50 52.50
e.	Surcharged "25 céntimos"	75.00 75.00
58	(c) 10c on 2c red	4.50 3.50
a.	"Céntimso"	
b.	Inverted surcharge	37.50 37.50
c.	Surcharged "25 céntimos"	60.00 60.00
d.	"10" omitted	60.00
59	(a) 25c on 5c blue	7.00 4.50
a.	Surcharged "5 céntimos"	52.50
b.	Surcharged "10 céntimos"	52.50 52.50
c.	Surcharged "50 céntimos"	75.00 75.00
d.	Inverted surcharge	50.00 50.00
60	(c) 25c on 5c blue	7.50 3.50
a.	Inverted surcharge	45.00 37.50
b.	Surcharged "10 céntimos"	45.00 37.50
e.	"25" omitted	75.00
f.	Surcharged on back	75.00
61	(a) 50c on 10c rose	27.50 12.50
a.	Inverted surcharge	70.00 60.00
62	(c) 50c on 10c rose	35.00 17.50
a.	Inverted surcharge	52.50 52.50
63	(d) 1fr on 20c brn	15.00 10.00
64	(e) 1fr on 20c brn	17.50 10.00
a.	Comma after "Franco,"	27.50 27.50
65	(f) 1fr on 20c brn	25.00 20.00
a.	Inverted surcharge	75.00
66	(g) 1fr25c on 25c violet	21.00 15.00
a.	Inverted surcharge	65.00 65.00
67	(g) 2fr50c on 50c org	16.00 12.00
a.	Inverted surcharge	35.00 27.50
68	(g) 3fr75c on 75c ultra	30.00 25.00
b.	Inverted surcharge	60.00 60.00
c.	Laid paper	75.00 75.00
70	(i) 5fr on 1p gold	550.00 500.00
a.	"s" of "francos" inverted	700.00 700.00

With Network
71	(a) 5c on 1c green	3.00 2.50
b.	Inverted surcharge	22.50 22.50
c.	Double surcharge	22.50 22.50
d.	Surcharged "25 céntimos"	42.50 42.50
e.	"5" omitted	75.00 75.00
72	(b) 5c on 1c green	21.00 9.00
b.	Inverted surcharge	60.00 60.00
73	(c) 5c on 1c green	27.50 11.50
b.	Surcharged "10 céntimo"	50.00 42.50
c.	Surcharged "25 céntimos"	60.00
74	(a) 10c on 2c red	3.75 2.25
a.	Surcharged "5 céntimos"	52.50 45.00
b.	Surcharged "25 céntimos"	67.50 67.50
c.	"10" omitted	57.50
75	(b) 10c on 2c red	6.00 6.00
a.	Inverted surcharge	30.00 20.00
76	(a) 25c on 5c blue	7.50 3.50
a.	Surcharged "10 céntimos"	75.00
b.	Surcharged "5 céntimos"	60.00
c.	Surcharged "50 céntimos"	67.50
77	(c) 25c on 5c blue	60.00 30.00
a.	Inverted surcharge	
b.	Surcharged on back	
78	(a) 50c on 10c rose	25.00 7.50
a.	Inverted surcharge	50.00 30.00
b.	Surcharged "25 céntimos"	60.00
79	(c) 50c on 10c rose	30.00 9.50
a.	Inverted surcharge	60.00
80	(d) 1fr on 20c brn	12.00 10.00
81	(e) 1fr on 20c brn	14.50 12.50
a.	Comma after "Franco"	35.00 35.00
b.	Inverted surcharge	75.00
82	(f) 1fr on 20c brown	25.00 20.00
83	(g) 1fr25c on 25c violet	45.00 30.00
a.	Inverted surcharge	75.00
84	(g) 2fr50c on 50c org	19.00 12.50
a.	Inverted surcharge	35.00 27.50

DOMINICAN REPUBLIC

85	(g)	3fr75c on 75c ultra	45.00	42.50
86	(h)	5fr on 1p gold	140.00	140.00
a.		Inverted surcharge		
87	(i)	5fr on 1p gold	190.00	190.00

Many minor varieties exist in Nos. 54-87: accent on "i" of "centimos"; "5" with straight top; "1" with straight serif.

A7

A7a

1885-91   Engr.   Perf. 12

88	A7	1c green	1.00	.50
89	A7	2c vermilion	1.00	.50
90	A7	5c blue	1.40	.50
91	A7a	10c orange	2.25	.65
92	A7a	20c dark brown	2.25	.80
93	A7a	50c violet ('91)	7.50	7.50
94	A7	1p carmine ('91)	35.00	25.00
95	A7	2p red brown ('91)	31.00	31.00
		Nos. 88-95 (8)	81.40	66.45

Nos. 93, 94, 95 were issued without gum. Imperf. varieties are proofs.
For surcharges see Nos. 166-168.

In 1891 certain denominations of the 1879-83 issues were overprinted with a large "X" separating the stamp into four triangles. The top triangle has the letter "U," and the left and right triangles have the letter "P". The bottom triangle is surcharged with a new value. Although this issue was authorized by the president, the entire supply was given to a single French dealer. A few covers exist, most addressed to the dealer's wife in New York. Numerous forgeries exist.

Coat of Arms — A8

1895   Perf. 12½x14

96	A8	1c green	1.25	.50
97	A8	2c orange red	1.25	.50
98	A8	5c blue	1.40	.50
99	A8	10c orange	3.25	1.60
		Nos. 96-99 (4)	7.15	3.10

Exist imperforate but were not issued.

1897   Perf. 14

96a	A8	1c green	1.50	.50
97a	A8	2c orange red	8.75	.75
98a	A8	5c blue	1.50	.75
99a	A8	10c orange	3.25	1.50
		Nos. 96a-99a (4)	15.00	3.50

Voyage of Diego Méndez from Jamaica — A9

Enriquillo's Revolt — A10

Sarcophagus of Columbus A11

Toscanelli Replying to Columbus A13

Bartolomé de las Casas Defending Indians A14

Columbus at Salamanca A15

"Española" Guarding Remains of Columbus A12

Columbus' Mausoleum A16

1899, Feb. 27   Litho.   Perf. 11½

100	A9	1c brown violet	9.75	5.25
102	A10	2c rose red	2.25	.70
103	A11	5c blue	2.60	.70
104	A12	10c orange	6.75	1.60
a.		Tête bêche pair	42.50	42.50
105	A13	20c brown	13.00	8.25
106	A14	50c yellow green	15.00	9.75
		Tête bêche pair	60.00	60.00
107	A15	1p black, gray bl	35.00	22.00
108	A16	2p bister brown	60.60	47.50

1900, Jan.

109	A11	¼c black	1.00	1.60
110	A15	½c black	1.00	1.60
110A	A9	1c gray green	1.00	.65
		Nos. 100-110A (11)	147.95	99.60

Nos. 100-110A were issued to raise funds for a Columbus mausoleum.

Imperf., Pairs

100a	A9	1c brown violet	16.50	16.50
102a	A10	2c rose red	5.00	
103a	A11	5c blue	5.75	
104b	A12	10c orange	8.75	
105a	A13	20c brown	15.00	
106b	A14	50c yellow green	17.50	
c.		As "b", tête bêche pair	125.00	
107a	A15	1p black, gray blue	42.50	
108a	A16	2p bister brown	70.00	
109a	A11	¼c black	3.75	4.25
110b	A15	½c black	3.75	4.25
110c	A9	1c gray green	3.50	

Map of Hispaniola — A17

1900, Oct. 21   Unwmk.   Perf. 14

111	A17	¼c dark blue	.75	.40
112	A17	½c rose	.75	.40
113	A17	1c olive green	.75	.40
114	A17	2c deep green	.75	.40
115	A17	5c red brown	.75	.40
a.		Vertical pair, imperf. between	17.50	

Perf. 12

116	A17	10c orange	.75	.40
117	A17	20c lilac	3.00	2.50
a.		20c rose (error)	25.00	
118	A17	50c black	2.75	2.50
119	A17	1p brown	3.00	2.50
		Nos. 111-119 (9)	13.25	9.90

Several varieties in design are known in this issue. They were deliberately made. Counterfeits of Nos. 111-119 abound.

A18

1901-06   Typo.   Perf. 14

120	A18	½c carmine & vio	.70	.40
121	A18	½c blk & org ('05)	1.80	.95
122	A18	½c grn & blk ('06)	.85	.40
123	A18	1c ol grn & vio	.70	.40
124	A18	1c blk & ultra ('05)	1.80	.85
125	A18	1c car & blk ('06)	1.00	.45
126	A18	2c dp grn & vio	.80	.40
127	A18	2c blk & vio ('05)	2.25	.70
128	A18	2c org brn & blk ('06)	1.40	.40
129	A18	5c org brn & vio	.80	.40
130	A18	5c blk & cl ('05)	2.50	1.25
131	A18	5c blue & blk ('06)	1.25	.40
132	A18	10c orange & vio	1.40	.45
133	A18	10c blk & grn ('05)	4.25	2.25
134	A18	10c red vio & blk ('06)	1.40	.40
135	A18	20c brn vio & vio	2.50	.95
136	A18	20c blk & ol ('05)	13.50	8.75
137	A18	20c ol grn & blk ('06)	7.25	3.25
138	A18	50c gray blk & vio	8.00	5.50
139	A18	50c blk & red brn ('05)	47.50	34.00
140	A18	50c brn & blk ('06)	8.75	7.75
141	A18	1p org brn & lil ('05)	18.00	10.00
142	A18	1p blk & gray ('05)	200.00	225.00
143	A18	1p vio & blk ('06)	21.00	13.50
		Nos. 120-143 (24)	349.40	318.80

Issued: 11/15/01; 5/11/05; 8/17/06.

See Nos. 172-176. For surcharges see Nos.151-156.

Francisco Sánchez A19

Juan Pablo Duarte A20

Ramón Mella A21

Ft. Santo Domingo A22

1902, Feb. 25   Engr.   Perf. 12

144	A19	1c dk grn & blk	.35	.35
145	A20	2c scarlet & blk	.35	.35
146	A20	5c blue & blk	.35	.35
147	A19	10c orange & blk	.35	.35
148	A21	12c purple & blk	.35	.35
149	A21	20c rose & blk	.60	.60
150	A22	50c brown & blk	.90	.90
		Nos. 144-150 (7)	3.25	3.25

Center Inverted

144a	A19	1c	25.00	25.00
145a	A20	2c	25.00	25.00
146a	A20	5c	25.00	25.00
148a	A21	12c	25.00	25.00
149a	A21	20c	25.00	25.00
150a	A22	50c	25.00	25.00
		Nos. 144a-150a (6)	150.00	150.00

400th anniversary of Santo Domingo. Imperforate varieties of Nos. 144 to 150 were never sold to the public.

Nos. 138, 141 Surcharged in Black

1904, Aug.

151	A18	2c on 50c	9.25	7.25
152	A18	2c on 1p	13.50	9.25
b.		"2" omitted	50.00	50.00
153	A18	5c on 50c	4.25	2.25
154	A18	5c on 1p	5.25	4.00
155	A18	10c on 50c	8.25	6.75
156	A18	10c on 1p	8.75	6.75
		Nos. 151-156 (6)	49.25	36.25

Inverted Surcharge

151a	A18	2c on 50c	15.00	15.00
152a	A18	2c on 1p	15.00	15.00
c.		As "a", "2" omitted	85.00	85.00
153a	A18	5c on 50c	5.50	5.50
154a	A18	5c on 1p	7.00	6.50
155a	A18	10c on 50c	14.00	14.00
156a	A18	10c on 1p	10.00	10.00
		Nos. 151a-156a (6)	66.50	66.00

Official Stamps of 1902 Overprinted

1904, Aug. 16   Red Overprint

157	O1	5c dk blue & blk	5.75	3.00
a.		Inverted overprint	7.25	5.75

Black Overprint

158	O1	2c scarlet & blk	17.00	5.25
a.		Inverted overprint	20.00	6.50
159	O1	5c dk blue & blk	3,500.	3,500.
160	O1	10c yellow grn & blk	10.50	10.50
a.		Inverted overprint	15.00	15.00

Official Stamps of 1902 Surcharged

1904-05   Surcharged "CENTAVOS"

161	O1	1c on 20c yellow & blk	4.75	3.00
a.		Inverted surcharge	7.25	7.25

Nos. J1-J2 Surcharged or Overprinted in Black

1904-05   Surcharged "CENTAVOS"

162	D1	1c on 2c olive gray	250.00	200.00
a.		"entavos"		
b.		"Dominican"	350.00	300.00

c.		"Centavo"	350.00	300.00

Carmine Surcharge or Overprint

163	D1	1c on 2c olive gray	3.50	1.10
a.		Inverted surcharge	4.75	4.75
b.		"Domihicana"	15.00	15.00
c.		As "b," inverted	40.00	40.00
d.		"Dominican"	10.50	10.50
e.		"Centavos" omitted	30.00	30.00
g.		"entavos"	30.00	
163F	D1	1c on 4c olive gray	35.00	7.00
164	D1	2c olive gray	.95	.60
a.		"Domihicana"	11.00	11.00
b.		Inverted overprint	2.00	2.00
c.		As "a," inverted	25.00	25.00
d.		"Dominican"	25.00	25.00
e.		"Centavo" omitted	12.50	10.00
f.		"entavos"	12.50	12.50
g.		As "f," inverted	40.00	40.00
h.		As "d," inverted	40.00	40.00

Surcharged "CENTAVO"

165	D1	1c on 4c olive gray	.95	.70
a.		"Domihicana"	10.00	10.00
c.		Inverted surcharge	1.75	1.75
d.		"1" omitted	3.50	3.50
e.		As "a," inverted	32.50	32.50
f.		As "d," inverted	40.00	40.00
g.		Double surcharge	30.00	30.00

No. 92 Surcharged in Red

1905, Apr. 4

166	A7a	2c on 20c dk brown	8.75	7.25
a.		Inverted surcharge	15.00	15.00
167	A7a	5c on 20c dk brown	4.75	2.50
a.		Inverted surcharge	16.00	16.00
b.		Double surcharge	25.00	25.00
168	A7a	10c on 20c dk brown	8.75	7.25
		Nos. 166-168 (3)	22.25	17.00

Nos. 166-168 exist with inverted "A" for "V" in "CENTAVOS" in surcharge.

No. J2 Surcharged in Red

1906, Jan. 16   Perf. 14

169	D1	1c on 4c olive gray	.95	.50
a.		Inverted surcharge	10.50	10.50
b.		Double surcharge	25.00	

Nos. J4, J3 Surcharged in Black

1906, May 1

170	D1	1c on 10c olive gray	1.10	.40
a.		Inverted surcharge	10.50	10.50
b.		Double surcharge	14.00	14.00
c.		"OMINICANA"	20.00	20.00
d.		As "c," inverted	150.00	
171	D1	2c on 5c olive gray	1.10	.40
a.		Inverted surcharge	10.50	10.50
b.		Double surcharge	35.00	

The varieties small "C" or small "A" in "REPUBLICA" are found on Nos.169, 170, 171.

Arms Type of 1901-06

1907-10   Wmk. 116

172	A18	½c grn & blk ('08)	.85	.25
173	A18	1c carmine & blk	.85	.25
174	A18	2c orange brn & blk	.85	.25
175	A18	5c blue & blk	.85	.25
176	A18	10c red vio & blk ('10)	8.00	1.00
		Nos. 172-176 (5)	11.40	2.00

No. O6 Overprinted in Red

1911, July 11   Perf. 13½x14, 13½x13

177	O2	2c scarlet & brn blk	1.60	.60
a.		"HABILITAOO"	8.75	6.00
b.		Inverted overprint	21.00	
c.		Double overprint	21.00	

A23

DOMINICAN REPUBLIC

1911-13		Center in Black	Perf. 14	
178	A23	½c orange ('13)	.25	.25
179	A23	1c green	.25	.25
180	A23	2c carmine	.25	.25
181	A23	5c gray blue ('13)	.80	.25
182	A23	10c red violet	1.60	.45
183	A23	20c olive green	11.50	11.50
184	A23	50c yellow brn ('12)	3.75	3.75
185	A23	1p violet ('12)	5.75	4.25
		Nos. 178-185 (8)	24.15	20.95

See Nos. 230-232.

Juan Pablo Duarte — A24

1914, Apr. 13			Perf. 13x14	
		Background Red, White and Blue		
186	A24	½c orange & blk	.60	.30
187	A24	1c green & blk	.60	.30
188	A24	2c rose & blk	.60	.30
189	A24	5c slate & blk	.60	.40
190	A24	10c magenta & blk	1.40	.70
191	A24	20c olive grn & blk	2.50	1.90
192	A24	50c brown & blk	3.50	2.75
193	A24	1p dull lilac & blk	5.50	4.00
		Nos. 186-193 (8)	15.30	10.65

Cent. of the birth of Juan Pablo Duarte (1813-1876), patriot and revolutionary.

Official Stamps of 1909-12 Surcharged in Violet or Overprinted in Red

a   b

1915, Feb.			Perf. 13½x13, 13½x14	
194	O2 (a)	½c on 20c org & blk	.50	.35
a.		Inverted surcharge	6.00	6.00
b.		Double surcharge	8.75	8.75
c.		"Habilitado" omitted	5.25	5.25
195	O2 (b)	1c blue grn & blk	.80	.35
a.		Inverted overprint	6.00	6.00
b.		Double overprint	6.00	
c.		Overprinted "1915" only	12.50	
196	O2 (b)	2c scarlet & blk	1.25	.35
a.		Inverted overprint	5.25	5.25
b.		Double overprint	8.00	8.00
c.		Overprinted "1915" only	8.75	
d.		"1915" double		
197	O2 (b)	5c dk blue & blk	1.00	.35
a.		Inverted overprint	7.00	7.00
b.		Double overprint	8.75	8.75
c.		Double ovpt., one invtd.	27.50	
d.		Overprinted "1915" only	8.50	
198	O2 (b)	10c yel grn & blk	2.75	2.50
a.		Inverted overprint	15.00	
199	O2 (b)	20c orange & blk	9.25	7.25
a.		"Habilitado" omitted		
		Nos. 194-199 (6)	15.55	11.15

Nos. 194, 196-198 are known with both perforations. Nos. 195, 199 are only perf. 13½x13.

The variety capital "I" for "1" in "Habilitado" occurs once in each sheet in all denominations.

Type of 1911-13 Redrawn

A25

SMALL LETTERS

LARGE LETTERS

TWO CENTAVOS:
Type I — "DOS" in small letters.
Type II — "DOS" in larger letters with white dot at each end of the word.

Overprinted "1915" in Red

1915		Unwmk.	Litho.	Perf. 11½	
200	A25	½c violet & blk		.85	.25
a.		Imperf., pair		5.75	
201	A25	1c yel brn & blk		.85	.25
a.		Imperf., pair		6.50	
b.		Vert. pair, imperf. horiz.		10.50	
c.		Horiz. pair, imperf. vert.		10.50	
202	A25	2c ol grn & blk (I)		3.75	.25
a.		Imperf., pair		10.00	
203	A25	2c ol grn & blk (II)		6.00	.25
a.		Center omitted		87.50	
b.		Frame omitted		87.50	
c.		Imperf., pair		15.00	
d.		Horiz. pair, imperf. vert.		12.50	
204	A25	5c magenta & blk		3.75	.25
a.		Pair, one without overprint		65.00	
b.		Imperf., pair		6.50	
205	A25	10c gray blue & blk		3.75	.50
a.		Imperf., pair		10.00	
b.		Horiz. pair, imperf. vert.		35.00	
206	A25	20c rose red & blk		8.25	1.40
a.		Imperf., pair		25.00	
207	A25	50c green & blk		10.50	4.00
a.		Imperf., pair		12.50	
208	A25	1p orange & blk		21.00	7.00
a.		Imperf., pair		52.50	
		Nos. 200-208 (9)		58.70	14.15

Type of 1915 Overprinted "1916" in Red

1916				
209	A25	½c violet & blk	2.75	.40
a.		Imperf., pair	21.00	
210	A25	1c green & blk	3.75	.40
a.		Imperf., pair	21.00	

Type of 1915 Overprinted "1917" in Red

1917-19				
213	A25	½c red lilac & blk	3.50	.30
a.		Horiz. pair, imperf. btwn.	47.50	47.50
214	A25	1c yellow grn & blk	1.60	.25
a.		Vert. pair, imperf. btwn.	50.00	
215	A25	2c olive grn & blk	2.25	.25
a.		Imperf., pair	35.00	
216	A25	5c magenta & blk	23.00	.85
		Nos. 213-216 (4)	30.35	1.65

Type of 1915 Overprinted "1919" in Red

1919				
219	A25	2c olive grn & blk	17.00	.40

Type of 1915 Overprinted "1920" in Red

1920-27				
220	A25	½c lilac rose & blk	.60	.40
a.		Horiz. pair, imperf. btwn.	25.00	25.00
b.		Inverted overprint		
c.		Double overprint		
d.		Double overprint, one invtd.		
221	A25	1c yellow grn & blk	.75	.40
a.		Overprint omitted	70.00	
b.		Horiz. pair, imperf. btwn.	40.00	
222	A25	2c olive grn & blk	.75	.40
a.		Vertical pair, imperf. between	27.50	
223	A25	5c dp rose & blk	9.00	.90
224	A25	10c blue & black	6.75	.10
225	A25	20c rose red & blk	7.75	.60
226	A25	50c green & blk ('27)	65.00	22.50
		Nos. 220-226 (7)	89.60	25.30

Type of 1915 Overprinted "1921" in Red

1921				
227	A25	1c yellow grn & blk	5.25	.40
a.		Horiz. pair, imperf. btwn.	45.00	45.00
b.		Imperf., pair	45.00	45.00
228	A25	2c olive grn & blk	5.75	.40
a.		Vert. pair, imperf. btwn.	45.00	

Redrawn Design of 1915 without Overprint

1922				
230	A25	1c green	3.75	.40
231	A25	2c carmine (II)	3.75	.40
232	A25	5c blue	5.75	.40
		Nos. 230-232 (3)	13.25	1.20

Nos. 230-232 exist imperf.

Type I

Type II

TEN CENTAVOS:
Type I — Numerals 2mm high. "DIEZ" in thick letters with large white dot at each end.
Type II — Numerals 3mm high. "DIEZ" in thin letters with white dot with colored center at each end.

1924-27		Second Redrawing		
233	A26	1c green	1.60	.25
a.		Vert. pair, imperf. btwn.	35.00	35.00
234	A26	2c red	.85	.25
235	A26	5c blue	2.25	.25
236	A26	10c pale bl & blk (I) ('26)	12.00	3.00
236A	A26	10c pale bl & blk (II)	22.50	1.10
236B	A26	50c gray grn & blk ('26)	60.00	33.00
237	A26	1p org & blk ('27)	19.00	12.50
		Nos. 233-237 (7)	118.20	50.35

In the second redrawing the shield has a flat top and the design differs in many details from the stamps of 1911-13 and 1915-22.

A27

1927				
238	A27	½c lilac rose & blk	.40	.40

Exhibition Pavilion — A28

1927		Unwmk.	Perf. 12	
239	A28	2c carmine	1.10	.50
240	A28	5c ultra	2.10	.50

Natl. and West Indian Exhib. at Santiago de los Caballeros.

Ruins of Columbus' Fortress — A29

1928				
241	A29	½c lilac rose	.95	.35
242	A29	1c deep green	.70	.25
a.		Horiz. pair, imperf. btwn.	25.00	
243	A29	2c red	.95	.25
244	A29	5c dark blue	2.75	.35
245	A29	10c light blue	2.75	.30
246	A29	20c rose	4.75	.40
247	A29	50c yellow green	13.50	8.25
248	A29	1p orange yellow	35.00	27.00
		Nos. 241-248 (8)	61.35	37.15

Reprints exist of 1c, 2c and 10c.
Issued: 1c, 2c, 10c, Oct. 1; others, Dec.

Horacio Vasquez — A30

1929, May-June				
249	A30	½c dull rose	.60	.30
250	A30	1c gray green	.60	.30
251	A30	2c red	.70	.30
252	A30	5c dark ultra	1.40	.35
253	A30	10c pale blue	2.10	.50
		Nos. 249-253 (5)	5.40	1.75

Signing of the "Frontier" treaty with Haiti.
Issue dates: 2c, May; others, June.

Imperf., Pairs

249a	A30	½c	12.50
250a	A30	1c	12.50
251a	A30	2c	12.50
252a	A30	5c	14.50

Convent of San Ignacio de Loyola — A31

1930, May 1			Perf. 11½	
254	A31	½c red brown	.70	.45
a.		Imperf., pair	55.00	55.00
255	A31	1c deep green	.65	.25
256	A31	2c vermilion	.65	.25
a.		Imperf., pair	60.00	
257	A31	5c deep blue	2.10	.35
258	A31	10c light blue	4.25	1.25
		Nos. 254-258 (5)	8.35	2.55

Cathedral of Santo Domingo, First Church in America — A32

1931			Perf. 12	
260	A32	1c deep green	.85	.25
a.		Imperf., pair	50.00	
261	A32	2c scarlet	.60	.25
a.		Imperf., pair	50.00	
262	A32	3c violet	.85	.25
263	A32	7c dark blue	2.50	.25
264	A32	8c bister	3.00	.85
265	A32	10c light blue	5.75	1.25
a.		Imperf., pair	35.00	
		Nos. 260-265 (6)	13.55	3.10

Issued: 3c-7c, Aug. 1; others, July 11.
For overprint see No. RAC8.

A33

Overprinted or Surcharged in Black

1932, Dec. 20			Perf. 12	
		Cross in Red		
265B	A33	1c yellow green	.55	.50
265C	A33	3c on 2c violet	.80	.60
265D	A33	5c blue	4.50	4.75
265E	A33	7c on 10c pale bl	6.00	6.25
		Nos. 265B-265E (4)	11.85	12.10

Proceeds of sale given to Red Cross. Valid Dec. 20 to Jan. 5, 1933.
Inverted and pairs, one without surcharge or overprint, exist on Nos. 265B-265D, as well as missing letters.

Fernando Arturo de Merino (1833-1906) as President A35

Cathedral of Santo Domingo A36

Designs: ½c, 5c, 8c, Tomb of Merino. 1c, 3c, 10c, as Archbishop.

DOMINICAN REPUBLIC

1933, Feb. 27		Engr.	Perf. 14	
266	A35	½c lt violet	.45	.35
267	A35	1c yellow green	.60	.25
268	A35	2c lt red	1.00	.75
269	A35	3c deep violet	.70	.30
270	A35	5c dark blue	.80	.35
271	A35	7c ultra	1.40	.50
272	A35	8c dark green	1.75	1.00
273	A35	10c orange yel	1.50	.60
274	A35	20c carmine rose	3.00	1.75
275	A36	50c lemon	11.25	7.75
276	A36	1p dark brown	26.00	19.00
		Nos. 266-276 (11)	48.45	32.60

For surcharges see Nos. G1-G7.

Tower of Homage, Ozama Fortress — A37

1932		Litho.	Perf. 12	
278	A37	1c green	1.75	.40
279	A37	3c violet	1.10	.40

Issue dates: 1c, July 2; 3c, June 22.

"CORREOS" added at left

1933, May 28				
283	A37	1c dark green	.50	.35

President Rafael L. Trujillo
A38 A39

1933, Aug. 16		Engr.	Perf. 14	
286	A38	1c yellow grn & blk	1.75	.35
287	A39	3c dp violet & blk	2.50	.35
288	A38	7c ultra & blk	5.75	.75
		Nos. 286-288 (3)	10.00	1.45

42nd birthday of President Rafael Leonidas Trujillo Molina.

San Rafael Bridge — A40

1934		Litho.	Perf. 12	
289	A40	½c redsh lil	.70	.40
290	A40	1c dp bl grn	1.00	.40
291	A40	3c violet	1.75	.40
		Nos. 289-291 (3)	3.45	1.20

Opening of San Rafael Bridge.
Issue dates: ½c, 3c, Mar. 3; 1c, Feb. 17.

Trujillo Bridge — A41

1934

292	A41	½c red brown	.70	.40
293	A41	1c dp grn	1.00	.40
294	A41	3c violet	1.40	.40
		Nos. 292-294 (3)	3.10	1.20

Opening of the General Trujillo Bridge near Ciudad Trujillo.
Issue dates: 1c, Aug. 24. Others, Sept. 7.

Ramfis Bridge — A42

1935, Apr. 6				
295	A42	1c bl grn	.70	.25
296	A42	3c org brown	.70	.25
297	A42	5c dp redsh pur	2.10	1.00
298	A42	10c rose	4.25	1.40
		Nos. 295-298 (4)	7.75	2.90

Opening of the Ramfis Bridge over the Higuamo River.

President Trujillo A43

A44

A45

1935			Perf. 11	
299	A43	3c yellow & brown	.40	.40
300	A44	5c org red, bl, red & bis	.40	.40
301	A45	7c ultra, bl, red & brn	.60	.40
302	A44	10c red vio, bl, red & bis	1.00	.40
		Nos. 299-302 (4)	2.40	1.60

Ratification of a treaty setting the frontier between Dominican Republic and Haiti.
Issued: 3c, 10/29; 5c, 10c, 11/25; 7c, 11/8.

National Palace — A46

1935, Apr. 1			Perf. 11½	
303	A46	25c yellow orange	3.75	.40

Obligatory for all mail addressed to the president and cabinet ministers.

Post Office, Santiago — A47

1936

304	A47	½c bright violet	.40	.40
305	A47	1c green	.40	.40

Issue dates: ½c, Jan. 14; 1c, Jan. 4.

George Washington Ave., Ciudad Trujillo A48

1936, Feb. 22

306	A48	½c brn & vio brn	.40	.45
a.		Imperf., pair	52.50	
307	A48	2c carmine & brn	.40	.30
308	A48	3c yel org & red brn	.70	.25
309	A48	7c ultra, blue & brn	1.60	1.25
a.		Imperf., pair	52.50	
		Nos. 306-309 (4)	3.10	2.25

Dedication of George Washington Avenue, Ciudad Trujillo.

José Nuñez de Cáceres A49

Felix M. del Monte A55

Proposed National Library — A56

1c, Gen. Gregorio Luperon. 2c, Emiliano Tejera. 3c, Pres. Trujillo. 5c, Jose Reyes. 7c, Gen. Antonio Duverge. 25c, Francisco J. Peynado. 30c, Salome Urena. 50c, Gen. Jose M. Cabral. 1p, Manuel de Jesus Galvan. 2p, Gaston F. Deligne.

1936	Unwmk.	Engr.	Perf. 13½, 14	
310	A49	½c dull violet	.50	.25
311	A49	1c dark green	.35	.25
312	A49	2c carmine	.35	.25
313	A49	3c violet	.50	.25
314	A49	5c deep ultra	.80	.30
315	A49	7c slate blue	1.50	.60
316	A55	10c orange	1.50	.30
317	A56	20c olive green	6.00	3.00
318	A55	25c gray violet	7.00	8.75
319	A55	30c scarlet	8.50	11.50
320	A55	50c black brown	10.00	6.25
321	A55	1p black	30.00	35.00
322	A55	2p yellow brown	85.00	90.00
		Nos. 310-322 (13)	152.00	156.70

The funds derived from the sale of these stamps were returned to the National Treasury Fund for the erection of a building for the National Library and Archives.
Issued: 3c, 7c, Mar. 18; others, May 22.

President Trujillo and Obelisk — A62

1937, Jan. 11		Litho.	Perf. 11½	
323	A62	1c green	.30	.25
324	A62	3c violet	.40	.25
325	A62	7c blue & turq blue	1.10	1.10
		Nos. 323-325 (3)	1.80	1.60

1st anniv. of naming Ciudad Trujillo.

Discus Thrower and Flag — A63

Flag in Red and Blue

1937, Aug. 14				
326	A63	1c dark green	6.00	.75
327	A63	3c violet	9.00	.75
328	A63	7c dark blue	15.00	3.50
		Nos. 326-328 (3)	30.00	5.00

1st Natl. Olympic Games, Aug. 16, 1937.

Symbolical of Peace, Labor and Progress — A64

1937, Sept. 18			Perf. 12	
329	A64	3c purple	.50	.40

"8th Year of the Benefactor."

Monument to Father Francisco Xavier Billini (1837-90) — A65

1937, Dec. 29				
330	A65	½c deep orange	.40	.40
331	A65	5c purple	.60	.40

Globe and Torch of Liberty — A66

1938, Feb. 22			Perf. 11½	
332	A66	1c green	.50	.40
333	A66	3c purple	.70	.40
334	A66	10c orange	1.40	.40
		Nos. 332-334 (3)	2.60	1.20

150th anniv. of the Constitution of the US.

Pledge of Trinitarians, City Gate and National Flag — A67

1938, July 16			Perf. 12	
335	A67	1c green, red & dk bl	.50	.40
336	A67	3c purple, red & bl	.60	.40
337	A67	10c orange, red & bl	1.25	.40
		Nos. 335-337 (3)	2.35	1.20

Trinitarians and patriots, Francisco Del Rosario Sanchez, Matías Ramón Mella and Juan Pablo Duarte, who helped free their country from foreign domination.

Seal of the University of Santo Domingo — A68

1938, Oct. 28				
338	A68	½c orange	.40	.40
339	A68	1c dp green & lt green	.40	.40
340	A68	3c purple & pale vio	.50	.40
341	A68	7c dp blue & lt blue	1.00	.50
		Nos. 338-341 (4)	2.30	1.70

Founding of the University of Santo Domingo, on Oct. 28, 1538.

A69

Design: Trylon and perisphere, flag and proposed Columbus lighthouse.

Flag in Blue and Red

1939, Apr. 30		Litho.	Perf. 12	
342	A69	½c red org & org	.35	.25
343	A69	1c green & lt green	.40	.25
344	A69	3c purple & pale vio	.40	.25
345	A69	10c orange & yellow	1.40	.65
		Nos. 342-345,C33 (5)	4.55	2.25

New York World's Fair.

A70

1939, Sept.			Typo.	
346	A70	½c black & pale gray	.40	.25
347	A70	1c black & yel grn	.50	.25
348	A70	3c black & yel brn	.50	.25
349	A70	7c black & dp ultra	1.10	.90
350	A70	10c black & brt red vio	2.10	.40
		Nos. 346-350 (5)	4.60	2.05

José Trujillo Valdez (1863-1935), father of President Trujillo Molina.

A71

Map of the Americas and flags of 21 American republics.

Flags in National Colors

1940, Apr. 14		Litho.	Perf. 11½	
351	A71	1c deep green	.35	.25
352	A71	2c carmine	.45	.25
353	A71	3c red violet	.60	.25
354	A71	10c orange	1.25	
355	A71	1p chestnut	18.00	13.50
		Nos. 351-355 (5)	20.65	14.50

Pan American Union, 50th anniv.

DOMINICAN REPUBLIC

Sir Rowland Hill — A72

1940, May 6   **Perf. 12**
356 A72 3c dp mag & rose lil   3.25 .40
357 A72 7c dk blue & lt blue   6.75 1.75

Centenary of first postage stamp.

Julia Molina Trujillo — A73

1940, May 26
358 A73 1c grn, lt grn & dk grn   .40 .35
359 A73 2c brt red, buff & dp rose   .40 .35
360 A73 3c org, dl org & brn org   .55 .35
361 A73 7c bl, pale bl & dk bl   1.10 .35
    Nos. 358-361 (4)   2.45 1.40

Issued in commemoration of Mother's Day.

Map of Caribbean — A74

1940, June 6   **Perf. 11½**
362 A74 3c brt car & pale rose   .50 .25
363 A74 7c dk blue & lt blue   1.00 .25
364 A74 1p yel & pale grn   10.00 9.00
    Nos. 362-364 (3)   11.50 9.50

2nd Inter-American Caribbean Conf. held at Ciudad Trujillo, May 31 to June 6.

Marion Military Hospital — A75

1940, Dec. 24
365 A75 ½c chestnut & fawn   .40 .40

Fortress, Ciudad Trujillo — A76

Statue of Columbus, Ciudad Trujillo — A77

1941
366 A76 1c dk green & lt green   .35 .25
367 A77 2c brt red & rose   .25 .25
368 A77 10c orange brn & buff   .70 .25
    Nos. 366-368 (3)   1.30 .75

Issue dates: 1c, Mar. 27; others, Apr. 7.

Sánchez, Duarte, Mella and Trujillo — A78

1941, May 16
369 A78 3c brt red lil & red vio   .30 .25
370 A78 4c brt red, crim & pale rose   .40 .25
371 A78 13c dk blue & lt blue   .85 .35
372 A78 15c orange brn & buff   2.75 2.10
373 A78 17c lt bl, bl & pale bl   2.75 2.10
374 A78 1p org, yel brn & pale org   11.50 10.50

375 A78 2p lt gray & pale gray   25.00 10.50
    Nos. 369-375 (7)   43.55 26.05

Trujillo-Hull Treaty signed Sept. 24, 1940 and effective Apr. 1, 1941.

Bastion of February 27 — A79

1941, Oct. 20
376 A79 5c brt blue & lt blue   .50 .35

School, Torch of Knowledge, Pres. Trujillo — A80

1941
377 A80 ½c chestnut & fawn   .35 .35
378 A80 1c dk green & lt green   .35 .35

Education campaign.
Issue dates: ½c, Dec. 12, 1c, Dec. 2.

Reserve Bank of Dominican Republic — A81

1942   **Unwmk.**
379 A81 5c lt brown & buff   .50 .25
380 A81 17c dp blue & lt blue   1.00 .45

Founding of the Reserve Bank, 10/24/41.

Representation of Transportation — A82

1942, Aug. 15
381 A82 3c dk brn, grn yel & lt bl   4.25 .50
382 A82 15c vio, grn, yel & lt bl   11.00 5.50

Day of Posts and Telegraph, 8th anniv.

Virgin of Altagracia — A83

1942, Aug. 15
383 A83 ½c gray & pale gray   1.00 .25
384 A83 1c dp grn & lt grn   2.10 .25
385 A83 3c brt red lil & lil   13.50 .25
386 A83 5c dk vio brn & vio brn   2.75 .25
387 A83 10c rose pink & pink   4.75 .25
388 A83 15c dp blue & lt blue   10.50 .30
    Nos. 383-388 (6)   34.60 1.55

20th anniv. of the coronation of Our Lady of Altagracia.

Bananas A84   Cows A85

1942-43
389 A84 3c dk brn & grn ('43)   .60 .25
390 A84 4c vermilion & blk ('43)   .60 .40
391 A85 5c dp blue & cop brn   .60 .25
392 A85 15c dk pur & blue grn   1.00 .50
    Nos. 389-392 (4)   2.80 1.40

Issue date: 5c, 15c, Aug. 18.

Emblems of Dominican and Trujillista Parties — A86

1943, Jan. 15
393 A86 3c orange   .50 .25
394 A86 4c dark red   .60 .25
395 A86 13c brt red lilac   1.40 .25
396 A86 1p lt blue   6.75 1.60
    Nos. 393-396 (4)   9.25 2.35

Re-election of President Rafael Trujillo Molina, May 16, 1942.

Model Market, Ciudad Trujillo — A87

1944
397 A87 2c dk brown & buff   .35 .35

Bastion of Feb. 27 and National Flag — A88

1944, Feb. 27   **Unwmk.**
Flag in Dark Blue and Carmine
398 A88 ½c ocher   .25 .25
399 A88 1c yellow green   .25 .25
400 A88 2c scarlet   .25 .25
401 A88 3c brt red vio   .25 .25
402 A88 5c yellow orange   .25 .25
403 A88 7c brt blue   .25 .25
404 A88 10c orange brown   .40 .30
405 A88 20c olive green   .65 .60
406 A88 50c lt blue   1.90 1.75
    Nos. 398-406,C46-C48 (12)   7.25 6.15

Souvenir Sheet
Imperf
407 A88 Sheet of 12   110.00 110.00
   a.-l. Single stamp   3.00 3.00

Centenary of Independence.
No. 407 contains 1 each of Nos. 398-406 and C46-C48 with simulated perforations. Size: 141x205mm.

Battlefield and Nurse with Child — A90

1944, Aug. 1
408 A90 1c gray grn, buff & red   .35 .35
   a. Vertical pair, imperf. btwn.   15.00
   b. Horiz. pair, imperf. vert.   15.00
409 A90 2c dk brn, buff & red   .40 .35
410 A90 3c brt bl, buff & red   .40 .35
411 A90 10c rose car, buff & red   .80 .35
    Nos. 408-411 (4)   1.95 1.40

80th anniv. of the Intl. Red Cross.

Municipal Building, San Cristóbal — A91

Unwmk.
1945, Jan. 10   **Litho.**   **Perf. 12**
412 A91 ½c blue & lt blue   .35 .35
413 A91 1c dk green & green   .35 .35
414 A91 2c red org & org   .35 .35
415 A91 3c dk brown & brown   .35 .35
416 A91 10c ultra & gray blue   1.25 .35
    Nos. 412-416 (5)   2.65 1.75

Centenary of the constitution.

Emblem of Communications A92

1945, Sept. 1
Center in Dark Blue and Carmine
417 A92 3c orange   .25 .25
418 A92 20c yellow green   .85 .25
419 A92 50c light blue   1.75 .70
    Nos. 417-419,C53-C56 (7)   5.00 2.20

Palace of Justice, Ciudad Trujillo — A93

1946   **Perf. 11½**
420 A93 3c dk red brown & buff   .35 .35

Map of Hispaniola A94

1946, Aug. 4   **Perf. 12**
421 A94 10c multicolored   .75 .35
    Nos. 421,C62-C63 (3)   2.85 1.05

450th anniv. of the founding of Santo Domingo.

Waterfall of Jimenoa — A95

1946-47   **Center Multicolored**
422 A95 1c yellow grn ('47)   .25 .25
423 A95 2c carmine ('47)   .25 .25
424 A95 3c deep blue   .25 .25
425 A95 13c red violet ('47)   .45 .35
426 A95 20c chocolate ('47)   .80 .35
427 A95 50c orange ('47)   1.75 1.25
    Nos. 422-427,C64-C67 (10)   11.45 5.50

Nos. 422-423, 425-427 issued Mar. 18.
For surcharge see No. 540.

Executive Palace — A96

1948, Feb. 27
428 A96 1c yellow green   .25 .25
429 A96 3c deep blue   .25 .25
    Nos. 428-429,C68-C69 (4)   8.35 3.60

Church of San Francisco Ruins — A97

1949, Apr. 13   **Perf. 11½**
430 A97 1c dk grn & pale grn   .25 .25
431 A97 3c dp bl & pale bl   .25 .25
    Nos. 430-431,C70-C73 (6)   4.30 1.90

Gen. Pedro Santana — A98

1949, Aug. 10
432 A98 3c deep blue & blue   .35 .35

Battle of Las Carreras, cent. See No. C74.

DOMINICAN REPUBLIC

Pigeon and Globe — A99

Center and Inscriptions in Brown

1950, Mar. 23

433	A99	1c green & pale green	.35	.35
434	A99	2c yel grn & yel	.35	.35
435	A99	5c blue & pale blue	.35	.35
436	A99	7c dk vio bl & pale bl	.40	.35
		Nos. 433-436 (4)	1.45	1.40

75th anniv. of the UPU.

Catalogue values for unused stamps in this section, from this point to the end of the section, are for Never Hinged items.

Hotel Jimani — A100

Hotels: 1c, 2c, Hamaca. 5c, Montana. 15c, San Cristobal. 20c, Maguana.

1950-52

437	A100	½c org brn & buff	.30	.25
438	A100	1c dp grn & grn ('51)	.30	.25
439	A100	2c red org & sal ('52)	.30	.25
440	A100	5c blue & lt blue	.60	.25
441	A100	15c dp orange & yel	.90	.25
442	A100	20c lilac & rose lilac	1.60	.25
443	A100	1p brn & yel	6.75	1.90
		Nos. 437-443,C75-C76 (9)	15.10	6.15

Issue dates: 1c, Dec. 1, 1951; 2c, Jan. 11, 1952; others, Sept. 8, 1950.
The ½c, 15c and 20c exist imperf.

Ruins of Church and Hospital of San Nicolas de Bari A101

School of Medicine A102

1950, Oct. 2

444	A101	2c dk green & rose brn	.75	.35
445	A102	5c vio blue & org brn	.90	.35
		Nos. 444-445,C77 (3)	2.95	1.05

13th Pan-American Health Conference. Nos. 444-445 and C77 exist imperf.

Queen Isabella I — A103

1951, Oct. 12

| 446 | A103 | 5c dk blue & red brn | 1.10 | .35 |

500th anniversary of the birth of Queen Isabella I of Spain. Exists imperf.

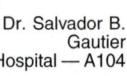

Dr. Salvador B. Gautier Hospital — A104

1952, Aug.

447	A104	1c dark green	.40	.25
448	A104	2c red	.40	.25
449	A104	5c violet blue	.65	.25
		Nos. 447-449,C78-C79 (5)	6.85	4.20

Columbus Lighthouse and Flags of 21 Republics — A105

1953, Jan. 6 Engr. Perf. 13

450	A105	2c dark green	.55	.30
451	A105	5c deep blue	.75	.30
452	A105	10c deep carmine	1.30	.30
		Nos. 450-452,C80-C86 (10)	12.55	5.05

Treasury Building, Ciudad Trujillo — A106

Sugar Industry, "Central Rio Haina" — A107

1953 Litho. Perf. 11½

453	A106	½c brown	.60	.35
454	A106	2c dark blue	.60	.35
455	A107	5c blue & vio brn	.60	.35
456	A106	15c orange	1.90	.35
		Nos. 453-456 (4)	3.70	1.40

For surcharge see No. 539.

José Marti — A108

1954 Perf. 12½

| 457 | A108 | 10c dp blue & dk brown | 1.10 | .35 |

Centenary of the birth of Jose Marti (1853-1895), Cuban patriot.

Monument to the Peace of Trujillo — A109

1954, May 25

458	A109	2c green	.60	.35
459	A109	7c blue	.60	.35
460	A109	20c orange	2.10	.25
		Nos. 458-460 (3)	3.30	.95

See No. 493.

Rotary Emblem — A110

1955, Feb. 23 Perf. 12

| 461 | A110 | 7c deep blue | 1.25 | .35 |

50th anniv., Rotary Intl. See No. C90.

Gen. Rafael L. Trujillo — A111

4c, Trujillo in civilian clothes. 7c, Trujillo statue. 10c, Symbols of culture & prosperity.

1955, May 16 Engr. Perf. 13½x13

462	A111	2c red	.60	.25
463	A111	4c lt olive green	.60	.25
464	A111	7c dp blue	.80	.25
465	A111	10c brown	1.50	.25
		Nos. 462-465,C91-C93 (7)	8.75	2.05

25th anniversary of the Trujillo era.

General Rafael L. Trujillo — A112

1955, Dec. 20 Unwmk. Perf. 13

466	A112	7c deep claret	.85	.35
467	A112	10c dark blue	1.10	.35
		Nos. 466-467,C94 (3)	2.80	1.05

Angelita Trujillo — A113

1955, Dec. 20 Litho. Perf. 12½

| 468 | A113 | 10c blue & ultra | 1.00 | .35 |

Nos. 466-468 were issued to publicize the International Fair of Peace and Brotherhood in Ciudad Trujillo, Dec. 1955.

Airport — A114

1956, Apr. 6 Perf. 12½

469	A114	1c brown	.35	.35
470	A114	2c red orange	.35	.35
		Nos. 469-470,C95 (3)	2.45	1.05

3rd Caribbean conf. of the ICAO.

Cedar — A115

1956, Dec. 8 Perf. 11½x12

471	A115	5c car rose & grn	2.00	.35
472	A115	6c red vio & grn	2.25	.35
		Nos. 471-472,C96 (3)	6.75	1.05

Reforestation program.

Fair Emblem — A116

1957, Jan. 10 Perf. 12½

| 473 | A116 | 7c blue, lt brn & ver | .65 | .35 |

2nd International Livestock Show, Ciudad Trujillo, Jan. 10-20, 1957. Exists imperf.

Fanny Blankers-Koen, Netherlands — A117

Olympic Winners and Flags: 2c, Jesse Owens, US. 3c, Kee Chung Sohn, Japan. 5c, Lord Burghley, England. 7c, Bob Mathias, US.

Flags in National Colors
Engraved & Lithographed

1957, Jan. 24 Perf. 11½, Imperf.

474	A117	1c brn, lt bl, vio & mar	.50	.35
475	A117	2c dk brn, lt bl & vio	.50	.35
476	A117	3c red lilac & red	.50	.35
477	A117	5c red org & vio	.70	.30
478	A117	7c green & violet	.85	.35
		Nos. 474-478,C97-C99 (8)	4.70	2.75

16th Olympic Games, Melbourne, Nov. 22-Dec. 8, 1956.
Miniature sheets of 5 exist, perf. and imperf., containing Nos. 474-478. Value, 2 sheets, perf. and imperf., $16.
For surcharges see Nos. B1-B5, B26-B30, CB1-CB3, CB16-CB18.

Lars Hall, Sweden, Pentathlon A118

Olympic Winners and Flags: 2c, Betty Cuthbert, Australia, 100 & 200 meter dash. 3c, Egil Danielsen, Norway, javelin. 5c, Alain Mimoun, France, marathon. 7c, Norman Read, New Zealand, 50 km. walk.

Perf. 13½, Imperf.
1957, July 18 Photo. Unwmk.
Flags in National Colors

479	A118	1c brn & brt bl	.80	.35
480	A118	2c org ver & dk bl	.80	.35
481	A118	3c dark blue	.80	.35
482	A118	5c ol & dk bl	.80	.35
483	A118	7c rose brn & dk bl	.80	.35
		Nos. 479-483,C100-C102 (8)	5.50	2.80

1956 Olympic winners.
Miniature sheets of 8 exist, perf. and imperf., containing Nos. 479-483 and C100-C102. The center label in these sheets is printed in two forms: Olympic gold medal or Olympic flag. Sheets measure 140x140mm. Value, 4 sheets, perf. and imperf., medal and flag, $24.
A third set of similar miniature sheets (perf. and imperf.) with center label showing an incorrect version of the Dominican Republic flag (colors transposed) was printed. These sheets are said to have been briefly sold on the first day, then withdrawn as the misprint was discovered. Value, 2 sheets, perf. & imperf., $150.
For surcharges see Nos. B6-B10, CB4-CB6.

Gerald Ouellette, Canada, Small Bore Rifle, Prone — A119

Ron Delaney, Ireland, 1,500 Meter Run A120

Olympic Winners and Flags: 3c, Tenley Albright, US, figure skating. 5c, Joaquin Capilla, Mexico, platform diving. 7c, Ercole Baldini, Italy, individual road race (cycling).

Engraved and Lithographed
1957, Nov. 12 Perf. 13½, Imperf.
Flags in National Colors

484	A119	1c red brown	.50	.35
485	A120	2c gray brown	.50	.35
486	A119	3c violet	.50	.35
487	A120	5c red orange	.50	.35
488	A119	7c Prus green	.50	.35
		Nos. 484-488,C103-C105 (8)	4.35	2.80

1956 Olympic winners.
Miniature sheets of 5 exist, perf. and imperf., containing Nos. 484-488. Value, 2 sheets, perf. and imperf., $5.50.
For surcharges see Nos. B11-B20, CB7-CB12.

DOMINICAN REPUBLIC

Mahogany Flower — A121

1957-58   **Litho.**   **Perf. 12½**
489 A121   2c bl grn & red brn   .45   .35

Perf. 12
490 A121   4c brt mauve & ver ('58)   .45   .35
491 A121   7c blue & gray grn   .60   .35
492 A121   25c brown & org ('58)   1.75   .35
Nos. 489-492 (4)   3.25   1.40

Sizes: No. 489, 25x29¼mm; Nos. 490-492, 24x28¾mm. In 1959, the 2c was reissued in size 24¼x28½mm with slightly different tones of green and maroon.
Issued: 2c, 10/24; 7c, 11/6; 4c, 25c, 4/7/58.
For surcharges see Nos. 537-538.

Type of 1954, Redrawn
Perf. 12x11½
1957, June 12   **Unwmk.**
493 A109   7c bright blue   1.00   .35

On No. 493 the cent symbol is smaller, the shading of the sky and steps stronger and the letters in "Correos" shorter and bolder.

Cervantes, Globe, Book — A122

1958, Apr. 23   **Litho.**   **Perf. 12½**
494 A122   4c yellow green   .65   .35
495 A122   7c red lilac   .65   .35
496 A122   10c lt olive brown   1.10   .35
Nos. 494-496 (3)   2.40   1.05

4th Book Fair, Apr. 23-28. Exist imperf.

Gen. Rafael L. Trujillo — A123

1958, Aug. 16   **Perf. 12**
497 A123   2c red lilac & yel   .60   .35
498 A123   4c green & yel   .60   .35
499 A123   7c brown & yel   .60   .35
  a. Souv. sheet of 3, #497-499, imperf.   2.00   1.00
Nos. 497-499 (3)   1.80   1.05

25th anniv. of Gen. Trujillo's designation as "Benefactor of his country."

S. S. Rhadames A124

1958, Oct. 27   **Perf. 12½**
500 A124   7c bright blue   1.75   .35

Day of the Dominican Merchant Marine. Exists imperf.

Shozo Sasahara, Japan, Featherweight Wrestling — A125

Olympic Winners and Flags: 1c, Gillian Sheen, England, fencing, vert. 2c, Milton Campbell, US, decathlon, vert. 5c, Madeleine Berthod, Switzerland, downhill skiing. 7c, Murray Rose, Australia, 400 & 1,500 meter freestyle.

Perf. 13½, Imperf.
1958, Oct. 30   **Photo.**
Flags in National Colors
501 A125   1c rose, ind & ultra   .65   .35
502 A125   2c brown & blue   .65   .35
503 A125   3c gray, vio, blk & buff   .65   .35
504 A125   5c rose, dk bl, brn & red   .65   .35
505 A125   7c lt brn, dk bl & red   .65   .35
Nos. 501-505,C106-C108 (8)   5.10   2.80

1956 Olympic winners.
Miniature sheets of 5 exist, perf. and imperf. containing Nos. 501-505. Value, 2 sheets, perf. and imperf., $5.
For surcharges see Nos. B21-B25, CB13-CB15.

Globe and Symbolic Fire — A126

1958, Nov. 3   **Litho.**   **Perf. 11½**
506 A126   7c blue & dp carmine   .75   .35

UNESCO Headquarters in Paris opening, Nov. 3.

Dominican Republic Pavilion, Brussels Fair — A127

1958, Dec. 9   **Unwmk.**   **Perf. 12½**
507 A127   7c blue green   .45   .30
Nos. 507,C109-C110 (3)   2.15   1.05

Universal & Intl. Exposition at Brussels.

Gen. Trujillo Placing Wreath on Altar of the Nation — A128

1959, July 10   **Perf. 12**
508 A128   9c brn, grn, red & gold   .70   .30
  a. Souv. sheet of 1, imperf.   1.50   1.00

29th anniversary of the Trujillo regime.

Lt. Leonidas Rhadames Trujillo, Team Captain A129

Jamaican Polo Team A130

Design: 10c, Lt. Trujillo on polo pony.

1959, May 15
509 A129   2c violet   .40   .35
510 A130   7c yellow brown   .80   .35
511 A130   10c green   .95   .35
Nos. 509-511,C111 (4)   2.75   1.40

Jamaica-Dominican Republic polo match at Ciudad Trujillo.

Symbolical of Census — A131

1959, Aug. 15   **Litho.**   **Perf. 12½**
Flag in Ultramarine and Red
512 A131   1c blue & black   .45   .35
513 A131   9c green & black   .75   .35
514 A131   13c orange & black   .95   .35
Nos. 512-514 (3)   2.15   1.05

Issued to publicize the 1960 census.

Trujillo Stadium A132

1959, Aug. 27
515 A132   9c green & gray   .85   .35

Issued to publicize the 3rd Pan American Games, Chicago, Aug. 27-Sept. 7.

Charles V — A133

1959, Oct. 12   **Unwmk.**   **Perf. 12**
516 A133   5c bright pink   .60   .35
517 A133   9c violet blue   .90   .35

400th anniv. of the death of Charles V (1500-1558), Holy Roman Emperor.

Rhadames Bridge — A134

1c and No. 520, Different view of bridge.

1959-60   **Litho.**   **Perf. 12**
518 A134   1c green & gray ('60)   .60   .35
519 A134   2c ultra & gray   .60   .35
520 A134   2c red & gray ('60)   .60   .35
521 A134   5c brn & dull red brn   .60   .35
Nos. 518-521 (4)   2.40   1.40

Issued: No. 519, 10/22; 5c, 11/30; 1c, No. 520, 2/6.
For surcharge see No. 536.

Sosua Refugee Settlement and WRY Emblem — A135

1960, Apr. 7   **Perf. 12½**
Center in Gray
522 A135   5c red brn & yel grn   .35   .35
523 A135   9c carmine & lt blue   .35   .35
524 A135   13c orange & green   .75   .35
Nos. 522-524,C113-C114 (5)   3.80   1.75

World Refugee Year, 7/1/59-6/30/60.
For surcharges see Nos. B31-B33.

Sholam Takhti, Iran, Lightweight Wrestling A136

Olympic Winners: 2c, Masaru Furukawa, Japan, 200 meter breast stroke. 3c, Mildred McDaniel, US, high jump. 5c, Terence Spinks, England, featherweight boxing. 7c, Carlo Pavesi, Italy, fencing.

Perf. 13½, Imperf.
1960, Sept. 14   **Photo.**
Flags in National Colors
525 A136   1c red, yel grn & blk   .60   .35
526 A136   2c org, grnsh bl & brn   .60   .35
527 A136   3c henna brn & bl   .60   .35
528 A136   5c brown & ultra   .60   .35
529 A136   7c grn, bl & rose brn   .60   .35
Nos. 525-529,C115-C117 (8)   4.80   2.80

17th Olympic Games, Rome, 8/25-9/11.
Miniature sheets of 5 exist, perf. and imperf., containing Nos. 525-529. Value, 2 sheets, perf. & imperf., $5.
For surcharges see Nos. B34-B38, CB21-CB23.

Post Office, Ciudad Trujillo — A137

1960, Aug. 26   **Litho.**   **Perf. 11½x12**
530 A137   2c ultra & gray   .60   .35
Exists imperf.

Cattle — A138

1960, Aug. 30
531 A138   9c carmine & gray   .60   .35

Issued to publicize the Agricultural and Industrial Fair, San Juan de la Maguana.

Nos. 518, 490-491, 453, 427 Surcharged in Red, Black or Blue

1960-61   **Perf. 12**
536 A134   2c on 1c grn & gray (R)   .35   .35
537 A121   9c on 4c lilac & rose   .70   .35
  a. Inverted surcharge   21.00
538 A121   9c on 7c ultra & gray grn (R)   .70   .35
539 A106   36c on ½c brown   2.25   1.75
  a. Inverted surcharge   18.00
540 A95   1p on 50c multi (Bl)   5.00   3.25
Nos. 536-540 (5)   9.00   6.05

Issue dates: No. 536, Dec. 30, 1960; No. 537, Dec. 20, 1960; others, Feb. 4, 1961.

Trujillo Memorial — A139

1961   **Unwmk.**   **Perf. 11½**
548 A139   1c brown   .35   .35
549 A139   2c green   .35   .35
550 A139   4c rose lilac   .60   .35
551 A139   5c light blue   .70   .35
552 A139   9c red orange   .60   .35
Nos. 548-552 (5)   2.60   1.75

Gen. Rafael L. Trujillo (1891-1961).
Issued: 2c, 8/7; 4c, 10/24; others 8/30.

Coffee, Cacao — A140

1961, Dec. 30   **Litho.**   **Perf. 12½**
553 A140   1c blue green   .55   .35
554 A140   2c orange brown   .55   .35
555 A140   4c violet   .55   .35
556 A140   5c blue   .55   .35
557 A140   9c gray   .70   .35
Nos. 553-557,C118-C119 (7)   4.70   2.95

Nos. 553-557 exist imperf.

Dagger Pointing at Mosquito — A141

1962, Apr. 29   **Photo.**   **Perf. 12**
558 A141   10c brt pink & red lilac   .40   .25
559 A141   20c pale brn & brn   .80   .30
560 A141   25c pale grn & yel grn   1.20   .40
Nos. 558-560,B39-B40,C120-C121 (9)   7.20   3.75

WHO drive to eradicate malaria.

DOMINICAN REPUBLIC

Broken Fetters and Laurel — A142

"Justice," Map of Dominican Republic — A143

Design: 20c, Flag, torch and inscription.

1962, May 30   Litho.   Perf. 12½
561	A142	1c grn, yel, ultra & red	.30	.25
562	A143	9c bister ultra & red	.50	.25
563	A142	20c lt blue, ultra & red	1.00	.25
a.		Souvenir sheet of 3, #561-563	2.25	2.25
564	A143	1p lilac, ultra & red	2.50	2.50
		Nos. 561-564,C122-C123 (6)	6.35	4.55

1st anniv. of end of Trujillo era. Nos. 561-564 exist imperf.

Farm, Factory and Flag — A144

1962, May 22
565	A144	1c ultra, red & green	.60	.35
566	A144	2c ultra & red	.60	.35
567	A144	3c ultra, red & brown	.60	.35
568	A144	5c ultra, red & blue	.60	.35
569	A144	15c ultra, red & orange	.60	.35
		Nos. 565-569 (5)	3.00	1.75

Map and Laurel — A145

1962, June 14   Litho.
570	A145	1c black	.70	.35

Honoring the martyrs of June 1959 revolution.

Western Hemisphere and Carrier Pigeon — A146

1962, Oct. 23   Unwmk.   Perf. 12½
571	A146	2c rose red	.45	.35
572	A146	9c orange	.45	.35
573	A146	14c blue green	.90	.35
		Nos. 571-573,C124-C125 (5)	3.35	1.90

50th anniv. of the founding of the Postal Union of the Americas and Spain, UPAE.

Archbishop Adolfo Alejandro Nouel — A147

1962, Dec. 18
574	A147	2c bl grn & dull bl	.35	.35
575	A147	9c orange & red brn	.40	.35
576	A147	13c maroon & vio brn	.55	.35
		Nos. 574-576,C126-C127 (5)	2.70	1.90

Cent. of the birth of Archbishop Adolfo Alejandro Nouel, President of Dominican Republic in 1911.

Globe, Banner and Emblems — A148

1963, Apr. 15   Unwmk.   Perf. 11½
Banner in Dark Blue & Red
577	A148	2c green	.50	.35
578	A148	5c brt rose lilac	.50	.35
579	A148	9c orange	1.00	.35
		Nos. 577-579,B41-B43 (6)	3.80	2.10

FAO "Freedom from Hunger" campaign.

Juan Pablo Duarte — A149

1963, July 7   Litho.   Perf. 12x11½
580	A149	2c shown	.50	.35
581	A149	7c Francisco Sanchez	.60	.35
582	A149	9c Ramon Mella	.75	.35
		Nos. 580-582 (3)	1.85	1.05

120th anniv. of separation from Haiti. See No. C128.

Ulises F. Espaillat, Benigno F. de Rojas and Pedro F. Bono — A150

Designs: 4c, Generals Santiago Rodriguez, Jose Cabrera and Benito Moncion. 5c, Capotillo monument. 9c, Generals Gaspar Polanco, Gregorio Luperon and Jose A. Salcedo.

1963, Aug. 16   Unwmk.   Perf. 11½
583	A150	2c green	.50	.35
584	A150	4c red orange	.50	.35
585	A150	5c brown	1.20	.35
586	A150	9c bright blue	.55	.35
a.		Souvenir sheet of 4	1.50	1.25
		Nos. 583-586 (4)	2.75	1.40

Cent. of the Restoration. No. 586a contains 4 imperf. stamps similar to Nos. 583-586.

Patient and Nurse — A151

1963, Oct. 25   Unwmk.   Perf. 12½
587	A151	3c gray & carmine	.55	.35
588	A151	6c emerald & red	.55	.35
		Nos. 587-588,C129 (3)	1.85	1.05

Centenary of International Red Cross. Nos. 587-588 exist imperf. Value, set of pairs $18. See No. C129.

Scales, Globe, UNESCO Emblem — A152

1963, Dec. 10   Litho.
589	A152	6c pink & deep pink	.45	.35
590	A152	50c lt green & green	1.30	.35
		Nos. 589-590,C130-C131 (4)	2.65	1.40

Universal Declaration of Human Rights, 15th anniv. Nos. 589-590 exist imperf.

Ramses II Battling the Hittites (from Abu Simbel) A153

Design: 6c, Two heads of Ramses II.

1964, Mar. 8   Unwmk.   Perf. 12½
591	A153	3c pale pink & ver	.45	.35
592	A153	6c pale blue & ultra	.45	.35
593	A153	9c pale rose & red brn	.45	.35
		Nos. 591-593,C132-C133 (5)	2.25	1.75

UNESCO world campaign to save historic monuments in Nubia. For surcharges see Nos. B44-B46.

Maximo Gomez — A154

1964, Apr. 30   Litho.
594	A154	2c lt blue & blue	.60	.35
595	A154	6c dull pink & dull claret	.60	.35

Bicent. of the founding of the town of Bani.

Palm Chat — A155

Design: 6c, Hispaniolan parrot.

Size: 27x37½mm

1964, June 8   Unwmk.   Perf. 12½
596	A155	3c ultra, brn & yel	2.60	.35
597	A155	6c gray & multi	3.50	.35
		Nos. 596-597,C134 (3)	12.10	1.05

See Nos. 602-604.

Rocket Leaving Earth — A156

Designs: 1c, Launching of rocket, vert. 3c, Space capsule orbiting earth. 6c, As 2c.

1964, July 28   Litho.
598	A156	1c sky blue	.50	.35
599	A156	2c emerald	.50	.35
600	A156	3c blue	.50	.35
601	A156	6c sky blue	.65	.35
		Nos. 598-601,C135-C136 (6)	3.30	2.05

Conquest of space.

Bird Type of 1964

Designs: 1c, Narrow-billed tody. 2c, Hispaniolan emerald hummingbird. 6c, Hispaniolan trogon.

1964, Nov. 7   Perf. 11½
Size: 26x37mm
Birds in Natural Colors
602	A155	1c bright pink	2.75	.35
603	A155	2c dark brown	2.75	.35
604	A155	6c blue	4.50	.35
		Nos. 602-604 (3)	10.00	1.05

Universal Postal Union and United Nations Emblems A157

1964, Dec. 5   Litho.   Perf. 12½
605	A157	1c red	.50	.35
606	A157	4c green	.50	.35
607	A157	5c orange	.50	.35
		Nos. 605-607,C138 (4)	2.00	1.40

15th UPU Cong., Vienna, May-June 1964.

International Cooperation Year Emblem — A158

1965, Feb. 16   Unwmk.   Perf. 12½
608	A158	2c lt blue & ultra	.60	.35
609	A158	3c emerald & dk grn	.60	.35
610	A158	6c salmon pink & red	.60	.35
		Nos. 608-610,C139 (4)	2.55	1.40

UN Intl. Cooperation Year.

Virgin of Altagracia — A159

Design: 2c, Hands holding lily.

1965, Mar. 18   Unwmk.   Perf. 12½
611	A159	2c grn, emer & dp rose	.55	.35
612	A159	6c multicolored	.75	.35
		Nos. 611-612,C140 (3)	2.10	1.05

4th Mariological Cong. and 11th Intl. Marian Cong. No. 612 exists imperf.

Flags of 21 American Nations — A160

1965, Apr. 14   Litho.   Perf. 11½
613	A160	2c brown, yel & multi	.50	.35
614	A160	6c red lilac & multi	.80	.35

Organization of American States.

Stamp of 1865 (No. 1) — A161

1965, Dec. 28   Litho.   Perf. 12½
615	A161	1c pink, buff & blk	.60	.35
616	A161	2c blue, buff & blk	.60	.35
617	A161	6c emerald, buff & blk	.60	.35
a.		Souvenir sheet of 2	1.75	1.50
		Nos. 615-617,C142-C143 (5)	3.20	1.75

Cent. of 1st Dominican postage stamps. No. 617a shows replicas of Nos. 1-2. Sold for 50c.

WHO Headquarters, Geneva — A162

1966, May 21   Litho.   Perf. 12½
618	A162	6c blue	.45	.35
619	A162	10c red lilac	.75	.35

New WHO Headquarters, Geneva.

Man Holding Map of Republic — A163

1966, May 23
620	A163	2c black & brt green	.45	.35
621	A163	6c black & dp orange	.75	.35

General elections, June 1, 1966.

Ascia Monuste — A164

1966   Litho.   Perf. 12½
Various Butterflies in Natural Colors
Size: 31x21mm
622	A164	1c blue & vio bl	1.90	.25
623	A164	2c lt grn & brt grn	1.90	.25
624	A164	3c lt gray & gray	2.50	.25
625	A164	6c pink & magenta	2.90	1.00
626	A164	8c buff & brown	5.00	1.40
		Nos. 622-626,C146-C148 (8)	52.45	7.90

Issued: 1c, 9/7; 3c, 9/11; others, 11/8.

DOMINICAN REPUBLIC

For surcharges see Nos. B47-B51, CB28-CB30.

Natl. Altar — A165

1967, Jan. 18   Litho.   *Perf. 11½*
627 A165 1c bright blue .50 .35
628 A165 2c carmine rose .50 .35
629 A165 3c emerald .50 .35
630 A165 4c gray .50 .35
631 A165 5c orange yellow .50 .35
632 A165 6c orange .50 .35
   Nos. 627-632,C149-C151 (9)   4.95 3.15

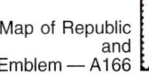

Map of Republic and Emblem — A166

1967, Mar. 30   Litho.   *Perf. 12½*
633 A166 2c yellow, blue & blk .45 .30
634 A166 6c orange, blue & blk .45 .30
635 A166 10c emerald, blue & blk   1.25 .45
   Nos. 633-635 (3)   2.15 1.05

Development Year, 1967.

Rook and Knight — A167

1967, June 23   Litho.   *Perf. 12½*
636 A167 25c multicolored   3.25 .50

5th Central American Chess Championships, Santo Domingo. See Nos. C152-C152a.

Alliance for Progress — A168

1967, Sept. 16   Litho.   *Perf. 12½*
637 A168 1c bright green .50 .35
   Nos. 637,C153-C154 (3)   2.15 1.05

6th anniv. of the Alliance for Progress.

Institute Emblem — A169

1967, Oct. 7
638 A169 3c bright green .50 .35
639 A169 6c salmon pink .50 .35
   Nos. 638-639,C155 (3)   2.20 1.05

25th anniversary of the Inter-American Agriculture Institute.

Globe and Satellite A170

1968, June 15   Typo.   *Perf. 12*
640 A170 6c black & multi .55 .35
   Nos. 640,C156-C157 (3)   1.90 1.05

World Meteorological Day, Mar. 23.

Boxers — A171

1968, June 29
641 A171 6c rose red & dp claret .50 .35
   Nos. 641,C158-C159 (3)   2.45 1.05

Fight between Carlos Ortiz, Puerto Rico, and Teo Cruz, Dominican Republic, for the World Lightweight Boxing Championship.

Lions Emblem — A172

1968, Aug. 9   Litho.   *Perf. 11½*
642 A172 6c brown & multi .60 .35

Lions Intl., 50th anniv. (in 1967). See No. C160.

Wrestling and Olympic Emblem — A173

1968, Nov. 12   Litho.   *Perf. 11½*
643 A173 1c shown .40 .25
644 A173 6c Running .45 .25
645 A173 25c Boxing   1.75 .40
   Nos. 643-645,C161-C162 (5)   4.80 1.90

19th Olympic Games, Mexico City, 10/12-27.

Map of Americas and House — A174

1969, Jan. 25   Litho.   *Perf. 12½*
646 A174 6c brt bl, lt bl & grn .55 .35

7th Inter-American Conference for Savings and Loans, Santo Domingo, Jan. 25-31. See No. C163.

Stool in Human Form — A175

Taino Art: 2c, Wood carved mother figure, vert. 3c, Face carved on 3-cornered stone. 4c, Stone hatchet, vert. 5c, Clay pot.

1969, Jan. 31   Litho.   *Perf. 12½*
647 A175 1c yellow, org & blk .80 .35
648 A175 2c lt grn, grn & blk .80 .35
649 A175 3c citron, ol & brt grn .80 .35
650 A175 4c lt lil, lil & brt grn .80 .35
651 A175 5c yellow, org & brn .80 .35
   Nos. 647-651,C164-C166 (8)   7.00 2.80

Taino art flourished in the West Indies at the time of Columbus.

Community Day Emblem — A176

1969, Mar. 25   Litho.   *Perf. 12½*
652 A176 6c dull green & gold .60 .35

Community Development Day, Mar. 22.

COTAL Emblem A177

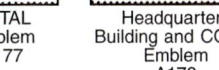

Headquarters Building and COTAL Emblem A178

Design: 2c, Boy and COTAL emblem.

1969, May 25   Litho.   *Perf. 12½*
653 A177 1c lt & dk blue & red .65 .35
654 A177 2c emerald & dk grn .65 .35
655 A178 6c vermilion & pink .65 .35
   Nos. 653-655,C167 (4)   2.60 1.40

12th Congress of the Confederation of Latin American Tourist Organizations (COTAL), Santo Domingo, May 25-29.

ILO Emblem — A179

1969, June 27   Litho.   *Perf. 12½*
656 A179 6c lt grnsh bl, grnsh bl & blk .65 .35

50th anniv. of the ILO. See No. C168.

Sliding into Base — A180

Designs: 1c, Catching a fly ball. 2c, View of Cibao Stadium, horiz.

Size: 21x31mm (1c, 3c); 43x30mm (2c)

1969, Aug. 15   Litho.   *Perf. 12½*
657 A180 1c green & gray .40 .30
658 A180 2c green & lt green .40 .30
659 A180 3c purple & red brown .40 .30
   Nos. 657-659,C169-C171 (6)   8.10 5.00

17th World Amateur Baseball Championships, Santo Domingo.

Las Damas Dam — A181

Tavera Dam — A182

Designs: 2c, Las Damas hydroelectric station, vert. 6c, Arroyo Hondo substation.

1969   Litho.   *Perf. 12*
660 A181 2c green & multi .50 .30
661 A181 3c dk blue & multi .50 .30
662 A181 6c brt rose lilac .50 .30
663 A182 6c multicolored .70 .30
   Nos. 660-663,C172-C173 (6)   3.45 1.80

National electrification plan. Issued: Nos. 660-662, Sept. 15; No. 663, Oct. 15.

Juan Pablo Duarte — A183

1970, Jan. 26   Litho.   *Perf. 12*
664 A183 1c emerald & dk grn .55 .35
665 A183 2c sal pink & dp car .55 .35
666 A183 3c brt pink & plum .55 .35
667 A183 6c blue & violet blue .55 .35
   Nos. 664-667,C174 (5)   3.40 1.75

Issued for Duarte Day in memory of Juan Pablo Duarte (1813-1876), liberator.

Map of Republic, People, Census Emblem — A184

Design: 6c, Census emblem and inscription.

1970, Feb. 6   *Perf. 11*
668 A184 5c emerald & blk .50 .35
669 A184 6c ultra & blue .50 .35
   Nos. 668-669,C175 (3)   2.20 1.05

Census of 1970.

Abelardo Rodriguez Urdaneta A185

"One of Many" A186

1970, Feb. 20   Litho.   *Perf. 12½*
670 A185 3c ultramarine .55 .35
671 A186 6c green & yel grn .55 .35
   Nos. 670-671,C176 (3)   2.00 1.05

Issued to honor Abelardo Rodriguez Urdaneta, sculptor.

Masonic Symbols — A187

1970, Mar. 2
672 A187 6c green   2.75 .35

8th Inter-American Masonic Conference, Santo Domingo, Mar. 1-7. See No. C177.

Communications Satellite — A188

1970, May 25   Litho.   *Perf. 12½*
673 A188 20c olive & gray   1.10 .35

World Telecommunications Day. See No. C178.

UPU Headquarters, Bern — A189

1970, June 5   *Perf. 11*
674 A189 6c gray & brown .65 .35

Inauguration of the new UPU headquarters in Bern. See No. C179.

246 DOMINICAN REPUBLIC

Education Year Emblem — A190

1970, June 26   Litho.   Perf. 12½
675 A190 4c rose lilac   .60 .35

Issued for International Education Year, 1970. See No. C180.

Pedro Alejandrino Pina — A191

1970, Aug. 24   Litho.   Perf. 12½
676 A191 6c lt red brn & blk   .60 .35

Pedro Alejandrino Pina (1820-70), author.

Children Reading — A192

1970, Oct. 12   Litho.   Perf. 12½
677 A192 5c dull green   .75 .35
Nos. 677,C181-C182 (3)   2.00 1.05

1st World Exhibition of Books and Culture Festival, Santo Domingo, Oct. 11-Dec. 11.

Virgin of Altagracia — A193

1971, Jan. 20   Litho.   Perf. 12½
678 A193 3c multicolored   .60 .35

Inauguration of the Basilica of Our Lady of Altagracia. See No. C184.

Rodriguez Objio — A194

1971, June 18   Litho.   Perf. 11
679 A194 6c light blue   .70 .35

Manuel Rodriguez Objio (1838-1871), poet.

Boxing and Canoeing — A195

1971, Sept. 10
680 A195 2c shown   .55 .35
681 A195 5c Basketball   .55 .35
Nos. 680-681,C186 (3)   1.80 1.05

2nd National Games.

Goat and Fruit — A196

Designs: 2c, Cow and goose. 3c, Cacao and horse. 6c, Bananas, coffee and pig.

1971, Sept. 29   Perf. 12½
682 A196 1c brown & multi   .70 .35
683 A196 2c plum & multi   .70 .35
684 A196 3c green & multi   .70 .35
685 A196 6c blue & multi   .70 .35
Nos. 682-685,C187 (5)   6.30 1.75

6th Natl. agriculture and livestock census.

José Nuñez de Cáceres — A197

1971, Dec. 1   Perf. 11
686 A197 6c lt bl, lil & dk bl   .65 .35

Sesquicentennial of first national independence. See No. C188.

Shepherds and Star — A198

1971, Dec. 10   Perf. 12½
687 A198 6c blue, brown & yel   .55 .35

Christmas 1971. See No. C189.

UNICEF Emblem, Child on Beach — A199

1971, Dec. 14   Litho.   Perf. 11
688 A199 6c gray blue & multi   .50 .35

UNICEF, 25th anniv. See No. C190.

Book Year Emblem — A200

1972, Jan. 25   Perf. 12½
689 A200 1c green, ultra & red   .45 .35
690 A200 2c brown, ultra & red   .45 .35
Nos. 689-690,C191 (3)   2.10 1.05

Intl. Book Year 1972.

Taino Mask — A201

4c, Ladle and amulet. 6c, Human figure.

1972, May 10   Litho.   Perf. 11
691 A201 2c pink & multi   .60 .35
692 A201 4c black, bl & ocher   .60 .35
693 A201 6c gray & multi   .60 .35
Nos. 691-693,C194-C196 (6)   4.95 2.25

Taino art. See note after No. 651.

Globe — A202

1972, May 17   Perf. 12½
694 A202 6c blue & multi   .45 .35

4th World Telecommunications Day. See No. C197.

"1972," Stamps and Map of Dominican Republic — A203

1972, June 3
695 A203 2c green & multi   .40 .25

First National Philatelic Exhibition, Santo Domingo, June 3-17. See No. C198.

Basketball — A204

1972, Aug. 25   Litho.   Perf. 12½
696 A204 2c blue & multi   .40 .30

20th Olympic Games, Munich, Aug. 26-Sept. 11. See No. C199.

Club Emblem — A205

1972, Sept. 29   Litho.   Perf. 10½
697 A205 1c lt green & multi   .45 .35

50th anniversary of the Club Activo 20-30 International. See No. C200.

Emilio A. Morel — A206

1972, Oct. 20   Perf. 12½
698 A206 6c brt pink & multi   .50 .35

Emilio A. Morel (1884-1958), poet and journalist. See No. C201.

Central Bank Building A207

1972, Oct. 23
699 A207 1c shown   .40 .25
700 A207 5c 1-peso note   .40 .25
Nos. 699-700,C202 (3)   2.55 1.05

25th anniv. of Central Bank.

Holy Family A208   Poinsettia A209

1972, Nov. 21
701 A208 2c rose lil, pur & gold   .40 .30
702 A209 6c red & multi   .40 .30
Nos. 701-702,C203 (3)   2.05 .90

Christmas 1972.

Mail Box and Student — A210

1972, Dec. 15
703 A210 2c rose red   .50 .35
704 A210 6c blue   .50 .35
705 A210 10c emerald   .85 .35
Nos. 703-705 (3)   1.85 1.05

Publicity for correspondence schools.

Tavera Dam — A211

1973, Feb. 26   Litho.   Perf. 12½
706 A211 10c multicolored   .65 .35

Inauguration of the Tavera Dam.

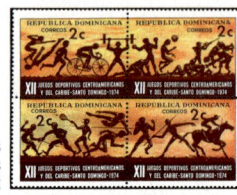

Various Sports A212

Designs: a, UL. b, UR. c, LL. d, LR.

1973, Mar. 30   Perf. 13½x13
707 A212 Block of 4   5.00 5.00
a.-d.   2c, any single   .75 .50
708 A212 Block of 4   27.50 27.50
a.-d.   25c, any single   4.00 2.00
Nos. 707-708,C204-C205 (4)   54.75 54.75

12th Central American and Caribbean Games, Santo Domingo, Summer 1974.

Christ Carrying the Cross — A213

6c, Belfry of Church of Our Lady of Carmen.

1973, Apr. 18   Litho.   Perf. 10½
709 A213 2c multicolored   .45 .35
710 A213 6c multicolored, vert.   .45 .35
Nos. 709-710,C206 (3)   2.10 1.05

Holy Week, 1973.

WMO Emblem, Weather Satellite, "Weather" — A214

1973, Aug. 10   Litho.   Perf. 13½x13
711 A214 6c magenta & multi   .55 .35

Centenary of international meteorological cooperation. See No. C208.

Mask, Cibao — A215

1973, Oct. 12   Litho.   Perf. 10½
712 A215 1c Maguey drum, horiz   .55 .35
713 A215 2c Carved amber, horiz   .55 .35
714 A215 4c shown   .55 .35
715 A215 6c Pottery   .55 .35
Nos. 712-715,C210-C211 (6)   4.80 2.10

Opening of Museum of Mankind in Santo Domingo.

DOMINICAN REPUBLIC

Nativity — A216

Christmas: 6c, Stained glass window, vert.

Perf. 13½x13, 13x13½

1973, Nov. 26
716 A216 2c black, bl & yel .55 .35
717 A216 6c rose & multi .55 .35
Nos. 716-717,C212 (3) 1.95 1.05

No. 717 exists imperf.

Dominican Scout Emblem — A217

Design: 5c, Scouts and flag.

1973, Dec. 7   Litho.   Perf. 12
Size: 35x35mm
718 A217 1c ultra & multi .35 .25
Size: 26x36mm
719 A217 5c black & multi .35 .25
Nos. 718-719,C213 (3) 1.95 1.25

Dominican Republic Boy Scouts, 50th anniv.

Sports Palace, Basketball Players — A218

Design: 6c, Bicyclist and race track.

1974, Feb. 25   Litho.   Perf. 13½
720 A218 2c red brown & multi .45 .35
721 A218 6c yellow & multi .45 .35
Nos. 720-721,C214-C215 (4) 3.00 1.40

12th Central American and Caribbean Games, Santo Domingo, 1974.

Bell Tower, Cathedral of Santo Domingo A219

Mater Dolorosa A220

1974, June 27   Litho.   Perf. 13½
722 A219 2c multicolored .35 .25
723 A220 6c multicolored .50 .25
Nos. 722-723,C216 (3) 1.50 .75

Holy Week 1974.

Francisco del Rosario Sanchez Bridge — A221

1974, July 12   Perf. 12
724 A221 6c multicolored .65 .35

See No. C217.

Map, Emblem and Patient A222

Design: 5c, Map of Dominican Republic, diabetics' emblem and pancreas.

1974, Aug. 22   Litho.   Perf. 13
725 A222 4c blue & multi .40 .25
726 A222 5c yellow grn & multi .40 .25
Nos. 725-726,C218-C219 (4) 3.85 1.50

Fight against diabetes.

Train and UPU Emblem — A223

Design: 6c, Mail coach and UPU emblem.

1974, Oct. 9   Litho.   Perf. 13½
727 A223 2c blue & multi .70 .60
728 A223 6c brown & multi .55 .25
Nos. 727-728,C220-C221 (4) 6.50 1.95

Cent. of UPU.

Golfers — A224

Design: 2c, Championship emblem and badge of Dominican Golf Association, horiz.

1974, Oct. 24   Perf. 13x13½, 13½x13
729 A224 2c yellow & blk 2.40 .50
730 A224 6c blue & multi 3.00 .50
Nos. 729-730,C222-C223 (4) 8.50 2.50

World Amateur Golf Championships.

Christmas Decorations A225

Virgin and Child A226

1974, Dec. 3   Litho.   Perf. 12
731 A225 2c multicolored .45 .35
732 A226 6c multicolored .60 .35
Nos. 731-732,C224 (3) 1.95 1.05

Christmas 1974.

Tomatoes, FAO Emblem A227

1974, Dec. 5
733 A227 2c shown 1.25 .35
734 A227 3c Avocados 1.25 .35
735 A227 5c Coconuts 1.25 .35
Nos. 733-735,C225 (4) 5.75 1.40

World Food Program, 10th anniv.

Dr. Fernando A. Defillo (1874-1949), Physician — A228

1975, Feb. 14   Litho.   Perf. 13½x13
736 A228 1c dull brown .65 .35
737 A228 6c dull green .65 .35

Tower, Our Lady of the Rosary Convent — A229

Design: 2c, Jesus saying "I am the Resurrection and the Life."

1975, Mar. 26   Litho.   Perf. 13½
738 A229 2c brown & multi .45 .35
739 A229 6c multicolored .45 .35
Nos. 738-739,C226 (3) 2.00 1.05

Holy Week 1975.

Hands (Steel Beams) with Symbols of Agriculture, Industry — A230

1975, May 19   Litho.   Perf. 10½x10
740 A230 6c dull blue & multi .50 .35

16th Assembly of the Governors of the International Development Bank, Santo Domingo, May 1975. See No. C228.

Satellite Tracking Station — A231

1975, June 21   Litho.   Perf. 13½
741 A231 5c multicolored .45 .35

Opening of first earth satellite tracking station in Dominican Republic. See No. C229.

Apollo — A232

1975, July 24   Size: 35x25mm
742 A232 1c shown .35 .25
743 A232 4c Soyuz .35 .25
Nos. 742-743,C230 (3) 7.20 4.50

Apollo Soyuz space test project (Russo-American cooperation), launching July 15; link-up, July 17.

Father Rafael C. Castellanos — A233

1975, Aug. 6   Litho.   Perf. 12
744 A233 6c brown & buff .70 .35

Castellanos (1875-1934), 1st Apostolic Administrator in Dominican Republic.

Women and Men Around IWY Emblem A234

1975, Aug. 6   Perf. 13
745 A234 3c orange & multi .70 .35

International Women's Year 1975.

Guacanagarix — A235

Indian Chiefs: 2c, Guarionex. 3c, Caonabo. 4c, Bohechio. 5c, Cayacoa. 6c, Anacona (woman). 9c, Hatuey.

1975, Sept. 27   Litho.   Perf. 12
746 A235 1c yellow & multi .85 .50
747 A235 2c salmon & multi .85 .50
748 A235 3c violet bl & multi .85 .50
749 A235 4c green & multi .85 .50
750 A235 5c blue & multi .85 .50
751 A235 6c violet & multi .85 .50
752 A235 9c rose & multi 1.40 .50
Nos. 746-752,C231-C233 (10) 10.00 5.20

Basketball — A236

Design: 6c, Baseball and Games' emblem.

1975, Oct. 24   Litho.   Perf. 12
753 A236 2c pink & multi .75 .35
754 A236 6c orange & multi .75 .35
Nos. 753-754,C234-C235 (4) 4.50 1.40

7th Pan-American Games, Mexico City, Oct. 13-26.

Carolers A237

6c, Dominican nativity with farmers & shepherds.

1975, Dec. 12   Litho.   Perf. 13x13½
755 A237 2c yellow & multi .60 .35
756 A237 6c blue & multi .60 .35
Nos. 755-756,C236 (3) 2.10 1.05

Christmas 1975.

Abudefdul Marginatus A238

1976, Jan. 23   Litho.   Perf. 13
757 A238 10c shown 1.25 .85
758 A238 10c Doncella 1.25 .85
759 A238 10c Carajuelo 1.25 .85
760 A238 10c Reina de los Angeles 1.25 .85
761 A238 10c Pargo Colorado 1.25 .85
a. Strip of 5, #757-761 11.00 11.00

Ascension, by J. Priego — A239

2c, Mary Magdalene, by Enrique Godoy.

1976, Apr. 14   Litho.   Perf. 13½
762 A239 2c blue & multi .60 .35
763 A239 6c yellow & multi .60 .35
Nos. 762-763,C238 (3) 2.30 1.05

Holy Week 1976.

"Separacion Dominicana" and Adm. Cambiaso — A240

1976, Apr. 15   Perf. 13½x13
764 A240 20c multicolored 1.50 .45

Naval Battle off Tortuga, Apr. 15, 1844.

DOMINICAN REPUBLIC

Maps of US and Dominican Republic — A241

Design: 9c, Maps within cogwheels.

1976, May 29   Litho.   Perf. 13½
765 A241 6c violet bl & multi   .50 .35
766 A241 9c violet bl & multi   .50 .35
   Nos. 765-766,C239-C240 (4)   4.20 2.30
American Bicentennial.

Flags of Dominican Republic and Spain — A242

1976, May 31
767 A242 6c multicolored   .80 .25
Visit of King Juan Carlos I and Queen Sofia of Spain. See No. C241.

Various Telephones — A243

1976, July 15   Perf. 12x12½
768 A243 6c multicolored   .60 .35
Cent. of 1st telephone call by Alexander Graham Bell, Mar. 10, 1876. See No. C242.

Vision of Duarte, by Luis Desangles — A244

Juan Pablo Duarte, by Rhadames Mejia — A245

1976, July 20   Litho.   Perf. 13x13½
769 A244 2c multicolored   .40 .25
   Perf. 13½
770 A245 6c multicolored   .40 .25
   Nos. 769-770,C243-C244 (4)   4.25 1.85
Juan Pablo Duarte, liberation hero, death centenary.

Fire Hydrant — A246

Design: 6c, Firemen's emblem.

1976, Sept. 13   Litho.   Perf. 12
771 A246 4c multicolored   .65 .50
772 A246 6c multicolored   .65 .50
   Nos. 771-772,C245 (3)   5.80 2.50
Honoring firemen. Nos. 771-772 inscribed "Corrreos."

Radio and Atom Symbols — A247

1976, Oct. 8   Litho.   Perf. 13½
773 A247 6c red & black   .60 .35
Dominican Radio Club, 50th anniv. See No. C246.

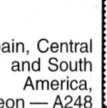

Spain, Central and South America, Galleon — A248

1976, Oct. 22   Litho.   Perf. 13½
774 A248 6c multicolored   .55 .25
Spanish heritage. See No. C247.

Boxing and Montreal Emblem — A249

Design: 3c, Weight lifting.

1976, Oct. 22   Perf. 12
775 A249 2c blue & multi   .55 .25
776 A249 3c multicolored   .55 .25
   Nos. 775-776,C248-C249 (4)   3.90 1.50
21st Olympic Games, Montreal, Canada, July 17-Aug. 1.

Virgin and Child A250

Three Kings A251

1976, Dec. 8   Litho.   Perf. 13½
777 A250 2c multicolored   .60 .35
778 A251 6c multicolored   .60 .35
   Nos. 777-778,C250 (3)   2.30 1.00
Christmas 1976.

Cable Car and Beach Scenes A252

1977, Jan. 7
779 A252 6c multicolored   .60 .50
   Nos. 779,C251-C253 (4)   3.35 2.40
Tourist publicity.

Championship Emblem — A253

1977, Mar. 4   Litho.   Perf. 13½
780 A253 3c rose & multi   .55 .50
781 A253 5c yellow & multi   .55 .50
   Nos. 780-781,C254-C255 (4)   3.90 3.00
10th Central American and Caribbean Children's and Young People's Swimming Championships, Santo Domingo.

Christ Carrying Cross — A254

Design: 6c, Head with crown of thorns.

1977, Apr. 18   Litho.   Perf. 13½x13
782 A254 2c multicolored   .60 .50
783 A254 6c black & rose   .60 .50
   Nos. 782-783,C256 (3)   2.30 1.50
Holy Week 1977.

Doves, Lions Emblem — A255

1977, May 6   Perf. 13½x13
784 A255 2c lt blue & multi   .60 .45
785 A255 6c salmon & multi   .60 .45
   Nos. 784-785,C257 (3)   2.10 1.35
12th annual Dominican Republic Lions Convention.

Battle Scene — A256

1977, June 15   Litho.   Perf. 13x13½
786 A256 20c multicolored   1.40 .35
Dominican Navy.

Water Lily — A257

National Botanical Garden: 4c, "Flor de Mayo" (orchid). 6c, Sebesten.

1977, Aug. 19   Litho.   Perf. 12
787 A257 2c multicolored   .60 .35
788 A257 4c multicolored   .60 .35
789 A257 6c multicolored   .75 .35
   Nos. 787-789,C259-C260 (5)   6.20 2.65

Chart and Computers A258

1977, Nov. 30   Litho.   Perf. 13
790 A258 6c multicolored   .55 .35
7th Interamerican Statistics Conf. See No. C261.

Solenodon Paradoxus A259

Design: 20c, Iguana and Congress emblem.

1977, Dec. 29   Litho.   Perf. 13
791 A259 6c multicolored   2.75 1.00
792 A259 20c multicolored   4.50 1.20
   Nos. 791-792,C262-C263 (4)   15.75 8.95
8th Pan-American Veterinary and Zoo-technical Congress.

Main Gate, Casa del Cordon, 1503 — A260

1978, Jan. 19   Perf. 13x13½
   Size: 26x36mm
793 A260 6c multicolored   .55 .35
Spanish heritage. See No. C264.

Crown of Thorns, Tools at the Cross — A261

6c, Head of Jesus with crown of thorns.

   Size: 22x33mm

1978, Mar. 21   Litho.   Perf. 12
794 A261 2c multicolored   .50 .30
795 A261 6c slate   .50 .30
   Nos. 794-795,C265-C266 (4)   3.10 1.25
Holy Week 1978.

Cardinal Octavio A. Beras Rojas — A262

1978, May 5   Litho.   Perf. 13
796 A262 6c multicolored   .60 .35
First Cardinal from Dominican Republic, consecrated May 24, 1976. See No. C268.

Pres. Manuel de Troncoso — A263

1978, June 12   Litho.   Perf. 13½
797 A263 2c black, rose & brn   .75 .50
798 A263 6c black, gray & brn   .75 .50
Manuel de Jesus Troncoso de la Concha (1878-1955), pres. of Dominican Republic, 1940-42.

Father Juan N. Zegri y Moreno — A264

1978, July 11   Litho.   Perf. 13x13½
799 A264 6c multicolored   .55 .35
Congregation of the Merciful Sisters of Charity, centenary. See No. C273.

Boxing and Games' Emblem — A265

1978, July 21   Perf. 12
800 A265 2c shown   .80 .50
801 A265 6c Weight lifting   1.20 .50
   Nos. 800-801,C274-C275 (4)   6.00 3.75
13th Central American & Caribbean Games, Medellin, Colombia.

DOMINICAN REPUBLIC

Sun over Landscape — A266

Design: 6c, Sun over beach and boat.

1978, Sept. 12   Litho.   *Perf. 12*
802 A266 2c multicolored   .55   .40
803 A266 6c multicolored   .55   .40
    Nos. 802-803,C280-C281 (4)   3.50 2.35
Tourist publicity.

Ships of Columbus, Map of Dominican Republic — A267

1978, Oct. 12   Litho.   *Perf. 13½*
804 A267 2c multicolored   .55   .40
Spanish heritage. See No. C282.

Dove, Lamp, Poinsettia — A268

Design: 6c, Dominican family and star, vert.

1978, Dec. 5   Litho.   *Perf. 12*
805 A268 2c multicolored   .55   .40
806 A268 6c multicolored   .70   .40
    Nos. 805-806,C284 (3)   2.00 1.15
Christmas 1978.

Starving Child, IYC Emblem — A269

1979, Feb. 26   Litho.   *Perf. 12*
807 A269 2c orange & black   .50   .40
    Nos. 807,C287-C289 (4)   4.05 3.15
Intl. Year of the Child.

Crucifixion — A270

Design: 3c, Jesus carrying cross, horiz.

1979, Apr. 9   Litho.   *Perf. 13½*
808 A270 2c multicolored   .55   .40
809 A270 3c multicolored   .80   .40
    Nos. 808-809,C290 (3)   6.60 3.80
Holy Week.

Stigmaphyllon Periplocifolium A271

1979, May 17   Litho.   *Perf. 12*
810 A271 50c multicolored   3.00   .75
    Nos. 810,C293-C295 (4)   11.00 5.00
Dr. Rafael M. Moscoso National Botanical Garden.

Heart, Diseased Blood Vessel — A272

Design: 1p, Cardiology Institute and heart.

1979, June 2   Litho.   *Perf. 13½*
811 A272 3c multicolored   .50   .40
812 A272 1p multicolored   3.25 2.75
    Nos. 811-812,C296 (3)   4.65 3.90
Dominican Cardiology Institute.

Baseball, Games' Emblem — A273

3c, Bicycling and Games' emblem, vert.

1979, June 20
813 A273 2c multicolored   .55   .40
814 A273 3c multicolored   .55   .40
    Nos. 813-814,C297 (3)   3.20 2.55
8th Pan American Games, Puerto Rico, June 30-July 15.

Soccer — A274

Design: 25c, Swimming, horiz.

1979, Aug. 9   Litho.   *Perf. 12*
815 A274 2c multicolored   .60   .40
816 A274 25c multicolored   .75   .40
    Nos. 815-816,C298 (3)   2.35 1.40
Third National Games.

Thomas A. Edison — A275

1979, Aug. 27   *Perf. 13½*
817 A275 25c multicolored   1.25 1.00
Cent. of invention of electric light. See No. C300.

Hand Holding Electric Plug — A276

Design: 6c, Filling automobile gas tank.

1979, Aug. 30
818 A276 2c multicolored   .60   .40
819 A276 6c multicolored   .80   .50
Energy conservation.

Parrot — A277

Birds: 6c, Temnotrogon roseigaster.

1979, Sept. 12   Litho.   *Perf. 12*
820 A277 2c multicolored   2.25   .60
821 A277 6c multicolored   2.25   .60
    Nos. 820-821,C301-C303 (5)   22.00 5.20

A278

Lions Emblem, Map of Dominican Republic.

1979, Nov. 13   Litho.   *Perf. 12*
822 A278 20c multicolored   1.40   .60
Lions International Club of Dominican Republic, 15th anniversary. See No. C304.

Christmas — A279

1979, Dec. 18   Litho.   *Perf. 12*
823 A279 2c Holy Family   .60   .40
See No. C305.

Holy Week — A280

Design: Jesus Carrying Cross.

1980, Mar. 27   Litho.   *Perf. 12*
824 A280 3c multicolored   .60   .40
    Nos. 824,C306-C307 (3)   2.20 1.55

A281

1980, May 15   Litho.   *Perf. 13½*
825 A281 1c shown   .85   .60
826 A281 2c Coffee   .85   .60
827 A281 3c Plantain   .85   .60
828 A281 4c Sugar cane   .85   .60
829 A281 5c Corn   .85   .60
    Nos. 825-829 (5)   4.25 3.00
Cacao Harvest (Agriculture Year)

Cotuf Gold Mine, Pueblo Viejo, Flag of Dominican Republic — A282

1980, July 8   Litho.   *Perf. 13½*
830 A282 6c multicolored   .55   .40
    Nos. 830,C310-C311 (3)   3.15 2.00
Nationalization of gold mining

Blind Man's Buff — A283

1980, July 21   *Perf. 12*
831 A283 3c shown   .60   .40
832 A283 4c Marbles   .60   .40
833 A283 5c Drawing in sand   .75   .50
834 A283 6c Hopscotch   .75   .50
    Nos. 831-834 (4)   2.70 1.80

Iguana — A284

1980, Aug. 30   Litho.   *Perf. 12*
835 A284 20c multicolored   3.00 1.00
    Nos. 835,C314-C317 (5)   17.25 5.05

Dance, by Jaime Colson A285

50c, Woman, by Gilberto Hernandez Ortega, vert.

Perf. 13x13½, 13½x13

1980, Sept. 23   Litho.
836 A285 3c shown   .50   .40
837 A285 50c multicolored   2.00 1.50
    Nos. 836-837,C318-C319 (4)   4.50 3.40

Three Kings — A286

1980, Dec. 5   Litho.   *Perf. 13½*
838 A286 3c shown   .60   .40
839 A286 6c Carolers   .60   .40
    Nos. 838-839,C327 (3)   2.20 1.45
Christmas 1980.

Salcedo Province Cent. — A287

1981, Jan. 14   Litho.   *Perf. 13½*
840 A287 6c multicolored   .60   .40
See No. C328.

Juan Pablo Duarte, Liberation Hero. 105th Anniv. of Death — A288

1981, Feb. 6   Litho.   *Perf. 12*
841 A288 2c sepia & deep bister   .85   .60

Gymnast — A289

1981, Mar. 31   Litho.   *Perf. 13½*
842 A289 1c shown   .65   .50
843 A289 2c Running   .65   .50
844 A289 3c Pole vault   .65   .50
845 A289 6c Boxing   1.25 1.00
    Nos. 842-845,C331 (5)   6.20 5.00
5th National Games.

DOMINICAN REPUBLIC

Mother Mazzarello — A290

1981, Apr. 14   *Perf. 12*
846   A290   6c multicolored   .70   .45

Mother Maria Mazzarello (1837-1881), founder of Daughters of Mary.

 A291

1981, May 18   Litho.   *Perf. 13½*
847   A291   6c gray vio & lt gray   .55   .40

Pedro Henriquez Urena, Historian (1884-1946).

Forest Conservation — A292

1981, June 30   Litho.   *Perf. 12*
848   A292   2c shown   .70   .45
849   A292   6c River, forest   .70   .45

Family in House, Census Emblem — A293

1981, Aug. 14   Litho.   *Perf. 12*
850   A293   3c shown   .70   .45
851   A293   6c Farmer   .70   .45

1981 natl. population and housing census.

Christmas — A294

1981, Dec. 23   Litho.   *Perf. 13½*
852   A294   2c Bells   .65   .45
853   A294   3c Poinsettia   .65   .45
    Nos. 852-853, C353 (3)   2.55   1.80

 A295

1982, Jan. 29   Litho.   *Perf. 13½*
854   A295   2c Juan Pablo Duarte   1.00   .80

National Elections — A296

Designs: Voters casting votes. 3c, 6c vert.

1982, Mar. 30   Litho.   *Perf. 13½*
855   A296   2c multicolored   .65   .40
856   A296   3c multicolored   .65   .40
857   A296   6c multicolored   .80   .50
    Nos. 855-857 (3)   2.10   1.30

 A297

Energy Conservation: Various forms of energy.

1982, May 10   Litho.   *Perf. 12*
858   A297   1c multicolored   .60   .40
859   A297   2c multicolored   .60   .40
860   A297   3c multicolored   .60   .40
861   A297   4c multicolored   .75   .50
862   A297   5c multicolored   .75   .50
863   A297   6c multicolored   .75   .50
    Nos. 858-863 (6)   4.05   2.70

 A298

1982, Aug. 2   *Perf. 12x12½*
864   A298   6c multicolored   .65   .40

Emilio Prud'Homme (1856-1932), composer.

Pres. Antonio Guzman Fernandez (1911-1982) — A299

1982, Aug. 4   *Perf. 13x13½*
865   A299   6c multicolored   .55   .40

14th Central American and Caribbean Games — A300

1982, Aug. 13   *Perf. 12, Imperf.*
866   A300   3c Baseball   2.00   1.00

See Nos. C368-C370.

San Pedro de Macoris Province Centenary A301

Designs: 1c, Wagon. 2c, Stained-glass window. 5c, Views.

1982, Aug. 26   *Perf. 13*
867   A301   1c multicolored   .60   .40
868   A301   2c multicolored   .60   .40
869   A301   5c multicolored   .75   .50
    Nos. 867-869, C375 (4)   3.05   2.05

Size of 2c, 25x35mm.

St. Teresa of Jesus of Avila (1515-1582) — A302

1982, Nov. 17   Litho.   *Perf. 13½*
870   A302   6c multicolored   .85   .60

Christmas 1982 — A303

Various Christmas balls.

1982, Dec. 8
871   A303   6c multicolored   1.40   1.10

See No. C380.

Environmental Protection — A304

1982, Dec. 15   *Perf. 12*
872   A304   2c Bird   .55   .40
873   A304   3c Water   .55   .40
874   A304   6c Forest   .55   .40
875   A304   20c Fish   1.75   1.25
    Nos. 872-875 (4)   3.40   2.45

Natl. Literacy Campaign A305

Designs: 2c, Vowels on blackboard. 3c, Writing, reading. 6c, Children, pencil.

1983, Mar. 9   Litho.   *Perf. 13½*
876   A305   2c multicolored   .65   .40
877   A305   3c multicolored   .65   .40
878   A305   6c multicolored   .80   .50
    Nos. 876-878 (3)   2.10   1.30

 A306

5c, similar arms, incorporating stylized centenary monument.

1983, Apr. 4   *Perf. 12*
879   A306   1c multicolored   .60   .40
880   A306   5c multicolored   .80   .50

Mao City centenary.

 A307

Dominican Historians: 2c, Antonio del Monte y Tejada (1780-1861). 3c, Manuel Ubaldo Gomez (1857-1941). 5c, Emiliano Tejera (1841-1923). 6c, Bernardo Pichardo (1877-1924). 7c, Americo Lugo (1870-1952). 10c, José Gabriel Garcia (1834-1910). 7c, 10c airmail.

1983, Apr. 25   Litho.   *Perf. 12*
881   A307   2c multicolored   .60   .40
882   A307   3c multicolored   .60   .40
883   A307   5c multicolored   .60   .40
884   A307   6c multicolored   .60   .40
885   A307   7c multicolored   .75   .40
886   A307   10c multicolored   1.10   .75
    Nos. 881-886 (6)   4.25   2.75

National Anthem, 100th Anniv. — A308

Emilio Prud'Homme, & Jose Reyes, composer.

1983, Sept. 13   Litho.   *Perf. 13½*
887   A308   6c copper red & blk   .70   .45

Free Masons, 125th Anniv. — A309

1983, Oct. 24   Litho.   *Perf. 12*
888   A309   4c Emblem   1.75   1.50

Church of Our Lady of Regla, 300th Anniv. — A310

1983, Nov. 5   *Perf. 13½*
889   A310   3c Church   .60   .40
890   A310   6c Statue   .80   .50

450th Anniv. of Monte Cristi Province — A311

Designs: 1c, Tower. 2c, Arms. 5c, Cuban independence site, horiz. 7c, Workers, horiz.

1983, Nov. 25   *Perf. 12*
891   A311   1c dark grn & blk   .65   .45
892   A311   2c multicolored   .65   .45
893   A311   5c gray   .65   .45
894   A311   7c gray & blue   .65   .45
    Nos. 891-894 (4)   2.60   1.80

6th Natl. Games — A312

6c, Bicycling, boxing, baseball. 10c, Runner, weight lifting, swimming.

1983, Dec. 9
895   A312   6c multicolored   .60   .40
896   A312   10c multicolored   .90   .65

10c airmail.

Restoration of the Republic, 120th Anniv. — A313

Design: 1c, Capotillo Heroes Monument.

1983, Dec. 30   Litho.   *Perf. 13½*
897   A313   1c multicolored   .70   .45

DOMINICAN REPUBLIC

140th Anniv. of Independence — A314

Designs: 6c, Matia Ramon Mella (Patriot), flag. 25c, Mella's Blunderbuss rifle, Gate of Deliverance (independence declaration site).

1984, Feb. 24   Litho.   *Perf. 13½*
898 A314 6c multicolored .55 .40
899 A314 25c multicolored 1.40 1.00

Heriberto Pieter (1884-1972), Physician, First Negro Graduate — A315

1984, Mar. 16
900 A315 3c multicolored .70 .45

Battle of Barranquita, 67th Anniv. — A316

1983, Dec. 30   *Perf. 12*
901 A316 5c multicolored .70 .45

Battle of Santiago, 140th Anniv. — A317

1984, Mar. 29   *Perf. 13½*
902 A317 7c multicolored .70 .45

Coast Guard Ship DC-1, 1934 — A318

1984, Apr. 13   Litho.
903 A318 10c multicolored .90 .65

Navy Day and 140th anniv. of Battle of Tortuguero.

Salome Urena — A319   Poem "Mi Pedro" — A319a

Designs: 22c, Pedro Henriquez Urena.

1984, June 29   Litho.   *Perf. 12*
904 A319 7c pink & brown .65 .45
905 A319a 10c cream & chestnut .95 .65
906 A319 22c cream & brown .85 .60
    Nos. 904-906 (3) 2.45 1.70

Birth centenary of Pedro Henriquez Urena.

Monument to Heroes of June 1959 — A320

1984, June 20   *Perf. 13½*
907 A320 6c silver & blue .85 .60

Costal towns of Constanza, Maimon and Estero Hondo - sites of attempted overthrow of Rafael Trujillo, 25th anniv.

1984 Summer Olympics — A321

1984, Aug. 1
908 A321 1p Hurdles 3.50 2.50
909 A321 1p Weightlifting 3.50 2.50
910 A321 1p Boxing 3.50 2.50
911 A321 1p Baseball 3.50 2.50
  a. Block of 4, #908-911 27.50 18.00
    Nos. 908-911 (4) 14.00 10.00

Protection of Fauna — A322

1984, Oct. 3   Litho.   *Perf. 12*
912 A322 10c Owl 4.50 2.00
913 A322 15c Flamingo 5.75 2.50
914 A322 25c Wild Pig 8.00 3.50
915 A322 35c Solenodon 5.25 .70
    Nos. 912-915 (4) 23.50 8.70

500th Anniv. of Discovery of America — A323

10c, Landing on Hispaniola. 35c, Destruction of Ft. Navidad. 65c, First Mass in America. 1p, Battle of Santo Cerro.

1984, Oct. 10   Litho.   *Perf. 13½x13*
916 A323 10c multicolored .55 .45
917 A323 35c multicolored .95 .80
918 A323 65c multicolored 1.75 1.50
919 A323 1p multicolored 3.00 2.50
    Nos. 916-919 (4) 6.25 5.25

Visit of Pope John Paul II — A324

1984, Oct. 11   Litho.   *Perf. 13x13½*
920   Block of 4 11.00 10.00
  a. A324 75c shown 2.00 2.00
  b. A324 75c Pope, map of Caribbean 2.00 2.00
  c. A324 75c Pope, globe 2.00 2.00
  d. A324 75c Bishop's crozier 2.00 2.00

150th Anniv. of Birth of Maximo Gomez (1986) — A325

10c, Gomez on horseback. 20c, Maximo Gomez.

1984, Dec. 6   Litho.   *Perf. 13½*
921 A325 10c multicolored .65 .45
922 A325 20c multicolored .85 .55

Christmas 1984 — A326

Perf. 13½x13, 13x13½
1984, Dec. 14   Litho.
923 A326 5c multicolored .60 .40
924 A326 10c multicolored, vert. .80 .50

Sacrifice of the Goat, by Eligio Pichardo — A327

Paintings and sculpture: 10c, The Pumpkin Sellers, by Gaspar Mario Cruz; 25c, The Market, by Celeste Woss y Gil; 50c, Horses in the Rain, by Dario Suro.

1984, Dec. 19   Litho.   *Perf. 13½*
925 A327 5c multi .65 .50
926 A327 10c multi, vert. .65 .50
927 A327 25c multi 1.10 .85
928 A327 50c multi 1.90 1.50
    Nos. 925-928 (4) 4.30 3.35

Day of Our Lady of Altagracia A328

5c, Old church at Higuey, 1572. 10c, Our Lady of Altagracia 1514, vert. 25c, Basilica of the Protector, Higuey 1971, vert.

1985, Jan. 21
929 A328 5c multicolored .60 .40
930 A328 10c multicolored .70 .50
931 A328 25c multicolored 1.10 .75
    Nos. 929-931 (3) 2.40 1.65

Independence, 141st Anniv. — A329

Painting: The Fathers of Our Country (Duarte, Sanchez and Mella).

1985, Mar. 8   *Perf. 12½*
932 A329 5c multicolored .60 .40
933 A329 10c multicolored .65 .45
934 A329 25c multicolored 1.00 .70
    Nos. 932-934 (3) 2.25 1.55

Battle of Azua, 141st Anniv. — A330

10c, Gen. Antonio Duverge, Statue.

1985, Apr. 8   Litho.   *Perf. 13½*
935 A330 10c multicolored .80 .50

Santo Domingo Lighthouse, 1853 — A331

1985, Apr. 15   Litho.
936 A331 25c multicolored 1.25 .85

Battle of Tortuguero, 141st anniv.

A332

1985, Apr. 15   Litho.   *Perf. 12*
937 A332 35c multicolored 1.40 1.00

American Airforces Cooperation System, 25th anniv.

Espaillat Province Cent. — A333

10c, Don Carlos M. Rojas, 1st governor.

1985, May 24   Litho.   *Perf. 13½*
938 A333 10c multicolored .80 .55

A334

1985, July 5   Litho.   *Perf. 12*
939 A334 5c Table tennis .60 .40
940 A334 10c Walking race .80 .50

MOCA '85, 7th Natl. Games.

Intl. Youth Year — A335

1985, July 29   *Perf. 13½*
941 A335 5c Youth .40 .35
942 A335 25c The Haitises 1.20 1.10
943 A335 35c Mt. Duarte summit 1.40 1.25
944 A335 2p Mt. Duarte 8.00 7.25
    Nos. 941-944 (4) 11.00 9.95

Interamerican Development Bank, 25th Anniv. — A336

10c, Haina Harbor. 25c, Map of development sites. 1p, Tavera-Bao-Lopez Hydroelectric Complex.

1985, Aug. 23
945 A336 10c multicolored .45 .40
946 A336 25c multicolored 1.00 .85
947 A336 1p multicolored 3.25 2.75
    Nos. 945-947 (3) 4.70 4.00

Intl. Decade for Women — A337

Design: Evangelina Rodriguez (1879-1947), first Dominican woman doctor.

1985, Sept. 26
948 A337 10c multicolored .80 .55

252　　　　　　　　　　　　　　　　　　　DOMINICAN REPUBLIC

15th Central American and Caribbean Games, Santiago — A338

1985, Oct. 9　　　　　　　　　　**Perf. 12**
949　A338　5c multicolored　　　　.65　.50
950　A338　25c multicolored　　　1.75　1.40

4th Adm. Christopher Columbus Regatta, Casa de Espana — A339

Designs: 50c, Founding of Santo Domingo, 1496. 65c, Chapel of Our Lady of the Rosary, 1496, Santo Domingo. 1p, Columbus, American Indian and old Spanish coat of arms.

1985, Oct. 10　　　　　　　　　**Perf. 13½**
951　A339　35c multicolored　　　1.50　1.40
952　A339　50c multicolored　　　2.00　1.80
953　A339　65c multicolored　　　2.75　2.50
954　A339　1p multicolored　　　　5.00　4.50
　　Nos. 951-954 (4)　　　　　　11.25　10.20

Discovery of America, 500th anniv. (in 1992).

Cacique Enriquillo — A340

Designs: 5c, Enriquillo in the Bahuroco Mountains, mural detail.

1985, Oct. 31
955　A340　5c multicolored　　　　.75　.50
956　A340　10c multicolored　　　1.00　.75

Enriquillo (d. 1536), leader of revolution against Spain. Size of No. 955: 47x33mm.

Archbishop Fernando Arturo de Merino — A341

1985, Dec. 3　　　　　　　　　　**Perf. 12**
957　A341　25c multicolored　　　1.00　.75

Cent. of holy orders granted to Merino (1833-1906), pres. of the republic 1880-82.

Mirabal Sisters, Political Martyrs 1960 — A342

1985, Dec. 18　　　　　　　　　**Perf. 13½**
958　A342　10c multicolored　　　　.75　.50

Christmas A343

1985, Dec. 18
959　A343　10c multicolored　　　　.55　.40
960　A343　25c multicolored　　　1.25　.90

Day of Independence, Feb. 27 — A344

Design: Mausoleum of founding fathers Duarte, Sanchez and Mella.

1986, Feb. 26　　**Litho.**　　**Perf. 13½**
961　A344　5c multicolored　　　　.60　.40
962　A344　10c multicolored　　　　.80　.50

Holy Week — A345

Colonial churches.

1986, Apr. 10
963　A345　5c San Miguel　　　　　.85　.60
964　A345　5c San Andres　　　　　.85　.60
965　A345　10c Santa Barbara　　　.90　.65
966　A345　10c San Lazaro　　　　.90　.65
967　A345　10c San Carlos　　　　.90　.65
　　Nos. 963-967 (5)　　　　　　4.40　3.15

Navy Day — A346

Design: Juan Bautista Cambiaso, Juan Bautista Maggiolo and Juan Alejandro Acosta, 1844 independence battle heroes.

1986, Apr. 15
968　A346　10c multicolored　　　　.85　.60

Natl. Elections — A347

1986, Apr. 29
969　A347　5c Voters, map　　　　.65　.45
970　A347　10c Ballot box　　　　.85　.55

Natl. Postal Institute Inauguration — A348

1986, June 10
971　A348　10c gold, blue & red　.50　.40
972　A348　25c silver, blue & red　1.25　1.00
973　A348　50c black, blue & red　2.10　1.75
　　Nos. 971-973 (3)　　　　　　3.85　3.15

Central America and Caribbean Games, Santiago — A349

1986, July 17　**Litho.**　**Perf. 13½**
974　A349　10c Weight lifting　　.50　.40
975　A349　25c Gymnastics　　　1.00　.85
976　A349　35c Diving　　　　　1.60　1.25
977　A349　50c Equestrian　　　1.90　1.50
　　Nos. 974-977 (4)　　　　　　5.00　4.00

Historians A350

Designs: 5c, Ercilia Pepin (b. 1886), vert. 10c, Ramon Emilio Jimenez (b. 1886) and Victor Garrido (1886-1972).

1986, Aug. 1　**Litho.**　**Perf. 13½**
978　A350　5c silver & dull brn　　.60　.40
979　A350　10c silver & dull brn　.85　.55

A351　　　　　　　　　　A352

Discovery of America, 500th Anniv. (in 1992) — A353

Designs: 25c, Yachts racing, 5th Adm. Christopher Columbus Regatta, Casa de Espana. 50c, Columbus founding La Isabela City. 65c, Exploration of the hidalgos. 1p, Columbus returning to the Court of Ferdinand and Isabella. 1.50p, Emblems.

1986, Oct. 10　**Litho.**　**Perf. 13½**
980　A351　25c multicolored　　　.80　.75
981　A352　50c multicolored　　　1.60　1.50
982　A352　65c multicolored　　　2.25　2.00
983　A352　1p multicolored　　　3.75　3.50

Textured Paper
Size: 86x58mm
Imperf
984　A353　1.50p multicolored　　6.50　6.25
　　Nos. 980-984 (5)　　　　　14.90　14.00

1986 World Cup Soccer Championships, Mexico — A354

Various soccer plays.

1986, Oct. 21　　　　　　　　**Perf. 13½**
985　A354　50c multicolored　　　1.75　1.60
986　A354　75c multicolored　　　3.50　3.25

Medicinal Plants — A355

5c, Zea mays. 10c, Bixa orellana. 25c, Momordica charantia. 50c, Annona muricata.

1986, Dec. 5
987　A355　5c multicolored　　　　.50　.40
988　A355　10c multicolored　　　.60　.45
989　A355　25c multicolored　　1.00　.75
990　A355　50c multicolored　　2.10　1.60
　　Nos. 987-990 (4)　　　　　　4.20　3.20

Second Caribbean Pharmacopeia Seminar.

Christmas A356

1986, Dec. 19
991　A356　5c Urban scene　　　　.60　.50
992　A356　25c Rural scene　　　1.90　1.50

A357

1986, Dec. 31　**Litho.**　**Perf. 13½**
993　A357　10c shown　　　　　　.55　.40
994　A357　25c Portrait, c. 1900　1.50　1.00

Maximo Gomez (1836-1905), revolutionary, statesman.

A358

1987, Mar. 30　**Litho.**　**Perf. 13½**
995　A358　50c brt blue, blk & red　1.60　1.40

16th Pan American Ophthalmological Conf., Apr. 5-10.

A359

Stained-glass window, San Juan Bosco church, Santo Domingo: Ascension of Christ to Heaven.

1987, May 28
996　A359　35c multicolored　　　1.75　1.50

Edible Plants — A360

5c, Sorghum bicolor. 25c, Martanta arundinacea. 65c, Calathaea allouia. 1p, Voandzeia subterranea.

1987, Aug. 21
997　A360　5c multicolored　　　　.25　.25
998　A360　25c multicolored　　　1.00　.90
999　A360　65c multicolored　　　2.00　1.75
1000　A360　1p multicolored　　　3.50　3.00
　　Nos. 997-1000 (4)　　　　　　6.75　5.90

Activo 20-30 Intl., 25th Anniv. — A361

1987, Aug. 26
1001　A361　35c multicolored　　　2.00　1.75

Adm. Christopher Columbus Regatta — A362

A363

Columbus Memorial, Santo Domingo — A364

DOMINICAN REPUBLIC

1p, Building Ft. Santiago. 1.50p, Columbus imprisoned by Bombadilla.

1987, Oct. 14
1002	A362	50c shown	1.60	1.50
1003	A363	75c shown	2.50	2.25
1004	A363	1p multicolored	3.25	3.00
1005	A363	1.50p multicolored	5.00	4.50

Size: 82x70mm
Imperf
| 1006 | A364 | 2.50p shown | 12.75 | 12.25 |
| | | Nos. 1002-1006 (5) | 25.10 | 23.50 |

Discovery of America, 500th anniv. in 1992.

A365

1987, Sept. 28
| 1007 | A365 | 40c multicolored | 1.40 | 1.20 |

Junior Olympics, La Vega, 50th anniv.

A366

Historians and authors: 10c, Jose Antonio Hungria. 25c, Joaquin Sergio Inchaustegui.

1987, Nov. 10 Litho. Perf. 13½
| 1008 | A366 | 10c buff & brown | .50 | .35 |
| 1009 | A366 | 25c pale grn & grn | 1.25 | .90 |

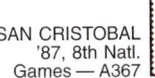
SAN CRISTOBAL '87, 8th Natl. Games — A367

1987, Nov. 19
1010	A367	5c Baseball	1.10	.90
1011	A367	10c Boxing	1.20	1.00
1012	A367	50c Judo	3.50	3.00
		Nos. 1010-1012 (3)	5.80	4.90

Christmas 1987 — A368

1987, Dec. 9 Litho. Perf. 13½
| 1013 | A368 | 10c Roasting pig | .70 | .55 |
| 1014 | A368 | 50c Arriving at airport | 2.10 | 1.75 |

Fr. Xavier Billini (b. 1837) — A369

10c, Statue. 25c, Portrait. 75c, Ana Hernandez de Billini, his mother.

1987, Dec. 18 Litho. Perf. 13½
1015	A369	10c blue gray & dark blue	.45	.35
1016	A369	25c cream & dark grn	.90	.75
1017	A369	75c pink & blkish pur	2.75	2.25
		Nos. 1015-1017 (3)	4.10	3.35

Frank Feliz, Sr., and Aircraft — A370

1987, Dec. 22
| 1018 | A370 | 25c shown | 1.00 | .80 |

Size: 86x106mm
Imperf
| 1019 | A370 | 2p No. C30, map | 15.50 | 12.50 |

Pan-American goodwill flight to South American countries by the planes Colon, Pinta, Nina and Santa Maria, 50th anniv.

Flora — A371

No. 1020, Bromelia pinguin. No. 1021, Tillandsia fasciculata. No. 1022, Tillandsia hotteana, vert. No. 1023, Tillandsia compacta, vert.

1988, Feb. 3 Litho. Perf. 13½
1020	A371	50c multi	2.40	2.10
1021	A371	50c multi	2.40	2.10
1022	A371	50c multi	2.40	2.10
1023	A371	50c multi	2.40	2.10
		Nos. 1020-1023 (4)	9.60	8.40

St. John Bosco (1815-1888) — A372

1988, Feb. 23 Litho. Perf. 13½
| 1024 | A372 | 10c shown | .50 | .40 |
| 1025 | A372 | 70c Stained-glass window | 3.00 | 2.25 |

Dominican Rehabilitation Assoc., 25th Anniv. — A373

1988, Mar. 1
| 1026 | A373 | 20c multicolored | 1.00 | .75 |

A374

1988, Apr. 6 Litho. Perf. 13½
| 1027 | A374 | 20c dk red brn & lt fawn | 1.00 | .75 |

Dr. Manuel Emilio Perdomo (b.1886).

A375

1988, Apr. 29 Litho. Perf. 13½
| 1028 | A375 | 20c multicolored | 1.00 | .75 |

Dominican College of Engineers, Architects and Surveyors (CODIA), 25th Anniv.

Independence Day, Mexico — A376

Flags and: No. 1029, Fr. Miguel Hidalgo y Costilla (1753-1811), Mexican revolutionary. No. 1030, Juan Pablo Duarte (1813-1876), father of Dominican independence.

1988, Sept. 12 Litho. Perf. 13½
| 1029 | A376 | 50c multicolored | 1.60 | 1.40 |
| 1030 | A376 | 50c multicolored | 1.60 | 1.40 |

1988 Summer Olympics, Seoul — A377

50c, Running, vert. 70c, Table tennis, vert. 1p, Judo, vert. 1.50p, Mural by Tete Marella.

1988, Sept. 21 Litho. Perf. 13½
1031	A377	50c multicolored	1.25	1.10
1032	A377	70c multicolored	1.75	1.60
1033	A377	1p multicolored	2.75	2.50
1034	A377	1.50p multicolored	4.00	3.75
		Nos. 1031-1034 (4)	9.75	8.95

A378

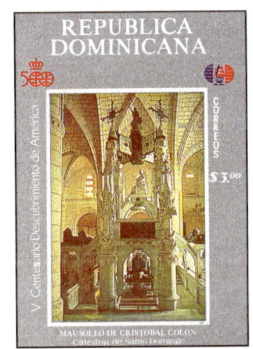
Discovery of America, 500th Anniv. (in 1992) — A379

Designs: 50c, 7th Adm. Christopher Columbus Regatta, Casa de Espana, 1988. 70c, La Concepcion Fortress, La Vega Real, 1494. 1.50p, Ft. Bonao. 2p, Nicolas de Ovando (c. 1451-1511), governor of Spanish possessions in America from 1502 to 1509. 3p, Mausoleum of Christopher Columbus, Santo Domingo Cathedral.

1988, Oct. 14 Perf. 13½
1035	A378	50c multicolored	1.20	1.10
1036	A378	70c multicolored	1.90	1.75
1037	A378	1.50p multicolored	3.75	3.50
1038	A378	2p multicolored	5.50	5.00

Size: 78x109mm
Imperf
| 1039 | A379 | 3p multicolored | 6.50 | 6.25 |
| | | Nos. 1035-1039 (5) | 18.85 | 17.60 |

Discovery of America, 500th anniv. (in 1992). No. 1038 inscribed "1501-1509."

Duverge Parish, Cent. — A380

1988, July 13 Litho. Perf. 13½
| 1040 | A380 | 50c multicolored | 1.50 | 1.25 |

A381

Trinitarians, 150th Anniv. — A382

Designs: 10c, Freedom fighters. 1p, Trinitarian Plaza. 5p, Independence Plaza.

1988, Nov. 11
1041	A381	10c red, blue, gray	.50	.45
1042	A382	1p multicolored	2.10	2.00
1043	A382	5p mutlicolored	13.50	13.00
		Nos. 1041-1043 (3)	16.10	15.45

See footnote after No. 337.

Pharmacology and Biochemistry — A383

1988, Nov. 28 Litho. Perf. 13½
| 1044 | A383 | 1p multicolored | 2.25 | 2.00 |

13th Pan American and 16th Central American Congresses.

The Holy Family, 1504, by Miguel Angel — A384

Design: 20c, Stained-glass window.

1988, Dec. 12
| 1045 | A384 | 10c shown | .65 | .45 |
| 1046 | A384 | 20c multicolored | 1.00 | .70 |

Christmas.

Municipal Technical Advisory Organization (LIGA), 50th Anniv. — A385

1988, Dec. 23
| 1047 | A385 | 20c multicolored | 1.00 | .75 |

Ana Teresa Paradas (1890-1960), 1st Female Lawyer of the Republic, 1913 — A386

1988, Dec. 26
| 1048 | A386 | 20c deep claret | 1.00 | .75 |

French Revolution Bicent. — A387

1989, Mar. 10 Litho. Perf. 13½
| 1049 | A387 | 3p red & violet blue | 3.50 | 3.25 |

Battle of Tortuga, Apr. 15, 1844 — A388

1989, Apr. 14 Litho. Perf. 13½
| 1050 | A388 | 40c multicolored | 1.40 | 1.10 |

Natl. Anti-drug Campaign A389

1989, May 15
1051	A389	10c multicolored	.35	.30
1052	A389	20c multicolored	.40	.35
1053	A389	50c multicolored	.70	.65

1054	A389	70c multicolored	1.00	.90
1055	A389	1p multicolored	1.50	1.40
1056	A389	1.50p multicolored	2.00	1.90
1057	A389	2p multicolored	2.75	2.60
1058	A389	5p multicolored	7.00	6.50
1059	A389	10p multicolored	13.50	12.50
		Nos. 1051-1059 (9)	29.20	27.10

Mother's Day — A390

1989, May 30   Litho.   Perf. 13½
| 1060 | A390 | 20c multicolored | .95 | .70 |

Eugenio Maria de Hostos (b. 1839) — A391

1989, Aug. 22   Litho.   Perf. 13½
| 1061 | A391 | 20c multicolored | .95 | .70 |

Gen. Gregorio Luperon (b. 1839) — A392

1989, Aug. 28
| 1062 | A392 | 20c multicolored | .95 | .70 |

Little League Baseball, 50th Anniv. — A393

1989, Sept. 29
| 1063 | A393 | 1p multicolored | 2.00 | 1.75 |

Diabetes '89, 7th Latin American Congress — A394

1989, Oct. 9   Litho.   Perf. 13½
| 1064 | A394 | 1p multicolored | 2.00 | 1.75 |

America Issue — A395

UPAE emblem, pre-Columbian artifacts and customs: 20c, Cohoba silver statue and ritual dance. 1p, Taina mortar, pestle and family preparing cazabe.

1989, Oct. 12
| 1065 | A395 | 20c multicolored | .80 | .75 |
| 1066 | A395 | 1p multicolored | 4.00 | 3.75 |

8th Adm. Christopher Columbus Regatta, Casa de Espana A396

European Colonization of the Americas A397

Designs: 70c, Fr. Pedro de Cordoba converting the Indians to Catholicism. 1p, Christopher Columbus trading with the Indians. 3p, Sermon of Pedro de Cordoba.

1989, Oct. 13
1067	A396	50c shown	.75	.65
1068	A397	70c shown	1.00	.85
1069	A397	1p multicolored	2.00	1.75
1070	A397	3p multicolored	3.75	3.25
		Nos. 1067-1070 (4)	7.50	6.50

Discovery of America, 500th anniv. (in 1992).

Natl. Afforestation — A398

Designs: 20c, Tree. 50c, Forest. 1p, Sapling, mature trees.

1989, Oct. 30   Litho.   Perf. 13½
1071	A398	10c shown	.35	.30
1072	A398	20c multicolored	.45	.35
1073	A398	50c multicolored	1.40	1.10
1074	A398	1p multicolored	2.75	2.25
		Nos. 1071-1074 (4)	4.95	4.00

9th Natl. Games, La Vega — A399

1990, Mar. 20   Litho.   Perf. 13½
1075	A399	10c Cycling	.40	.30
1076	A399	20c Running	.60	.45
1077	A399	50c Basketball	1.90	1.40
		Nos. 1075-1077 (3)	2.90	2.15

Holy Week (Easter) — A400

Design: 50c, Jesus carrying cross.

1990, Apr. 5
| 1078 | A400 | 20c shown | .65 | .50 |
| 1079 | A400 | 50c multicolored | 1.60 | 1.25 |

Labor Day, Cent. — A401

1990, Apr. 30   Litho.   Perf. 13½
| 1080 | A401 | 1p multicolored | 1.60 | .65 |

Urban Renewal — A402

Designs: 20c, Highway underpass. 50c, Library. 1p, City street.

1990, May 10
1081	A402	10c shown	.40	.30
1082	A402	20c multi	.50	.40
1083	A402	50c multi	1.10	.85
1084	A402	1p multi	2.50	2.00
		Nos. 1081-1084 (4)	4.50	3.55

No. 1084 inscribed $100 instead of $1.00.

Penny Black, 150th Anniv. — A403

Design: 3p, Sir Rowland Hill, Penny Black.

1990, May 29
| 1085 | A403 | 1p multicolored | 2.50 | 2.25 |

Size: 62x80mm
Imperf
| 1086 | A403 | 3p multi | 6.50 | 6.25 |

A404

1990, Oct. 5   Litho.   Perf. 13½
| 1087 | A404 | 2p Flags | 4.25 | 4.00 |

Organization of American States, Cent.

Children's Drawings — A405

No. 1088, House of Tostado. No. 1089, Ruins of St. Nicolas of Bari.

1990, Aug. 7
| 1088 | A405 | 50c multicolored | 1.50 | 1.25 |
| 1089 | A405 | 50c multicolored | 1.50 | 1.25 |

Discovery of America, 500th Anniv. (in 1992) — A406

Designs: 1p, Fight at the Gulf of Arrows. 2p, Columbus talking with Guacanagari Indians. 5p, Columbus and Caonabo Indian prisoner.

1990, Oct. 12
1090	A406	1p multicolored	2.40	2.25
1091	A406	2p multicolored	4.75	4.50
1092	A406	5p multicolored	11.50	11.00
		Nos. 1090-1092 (3)	18.65	17.75

9th Adm. Christopher Columbus Regatta — A407

1990, Oct. 12
| 1093 | A407 | 50c multicolored | 1.75 | 1.50 |

America Issue — A408

UPAE emblem and: 50c, Men in canoe. 3p, Man on hammock.

1990, Nov. 7   Litho.   Perf. 13½
| 1094 | A408 | 50c multicolored | 2.00 | 1.90 |
| 1095 | A408 | 3p multicolored | 8.50 | 8.00 |

A409

Discovery of Hispaniola: 50c, 1st official mass in Americas. 1p, Arms of 1st religious order in Americas. 3p, Map of island, horiz. 4p, Christopher Columbus, 1st viceroy and governor in Americas.

1991, July 17   Litho.   Perf. 13½
1096	A409	50c multicolored	.95	.90
1097	A409	1p multicolored	1.90	1.75
1098	A409	3p multicolored	5.00	4.75
1099	A409	4p multicolored	8.75	8.25
		Nos. 1096-1099 (4)	16.60	15.65

A410

1991
1100	A410	30c Boxing	.45	.40
1101	A410	50c Cycling	1.50	1.25
1102	A410	1p Bowling	3.00	2.50
		Nos. 1100-1102 (3)	4.95	4.15

11th Pan American Games, Havana.

Dr. Tomas Eudoro Perez Rancier, Birth Cent. — A411

1991, July 3
| 1103 | A411 | 2p yellow & black | 7.75 | 7.50 |

10th Columbus Regatta, Casa de Espana A412

Discovery of America, 500th Anniv. (in 1992) A413

Designs: 50c, Encounter of three cultures. 3p, Columbus and Dr. Alvarez Chanca caring for sick. 4p, Rebellion of Enriquillo.

1991, Oct. 15   Litho.   Perf. 13½
1104	A412	30c multicolored	.70	.65
1105	A413	50c multicolored	.95	.90
1106	A413	3p multicolored	6.00	5.50
1107	A413	4p multicolored	8.00	7.50
		Nos. 1104-1107 (4)	15.65	14.55

See No. 1116.

A414

1991, Nov. 18
| 1108 | A414 | 3p black & red | 5.00 | 4.75 |

Cornea Bank.

DOMINICAN REPUBLIC

America Issue — A415

Designs: 1p, Santa Maria. 3p, Christopher Columbus.

1991		Litho.	Perf. 13½
1109	A415	1p multi	3.25 3.00
1110	A415	3p multi	7.25 7.00

33rd Meeting of Inter-American Development Bank Governors, Santo Domingo — A416

1992		Litho.	Perf. 13½
1111	A416	1p multicolored	2.00 1.75

A417

1992		Litho.	Perf. 13½
1112	A417	3p multicolored	5.50 5.25

Espanola '92 Philatelic Exposition.

A418

Valentin Salinero, Order of the Apostles founder.

1992		Litho.	Perf. 13½
1113	A418	1p blue & brown	2.00 1.75

Order of the Apostles, cent.

Ruins of Monastery of San Francisco — A419

Designs: 3p, Ruins of San Nicolas hospital, first in the Americas

1992, July 28			
1114	A419	50c multicolored	1.00 .75
1115	A419	3p multicolored	5.75 5.50

Type of 1991 and

A420

Designs: 50c, Racing yacht. 1p, Native women, Columbus. 2p, Natives offering Columbus tobacco. 3p, Native woman, Columbus, corn.

1992, Oct. 6		Litho.	Perf. 13½
1116	A412	50c multicolored	.75 .70
1117	A420	1p multicolored	1.75 1.60
1118	A420	2p multicolored	4.75 4.50
1119	A420	3p multicolored	7.00 6.50
		Nos. 1116-1119 (4)	14.25 13.30

11th Columbus Regatta (No. 1116), Discovery of America, 500th anniv. (Nos. 1117-1119).

23rd Convention of the Alliance of Panamerican Round Tables, Santo Domingo — A421

1992, Oct. 14			
1120	A421	1p multicolored	2.00 1.75

Visit by Pope John Paul II — A422

Cathedrals: 50c, Vega. 3p, Santo Domingo.

1992, Oct. 1			Photo.
1121	A422	50c multicolored	1.50 1.40
1122	A422	3p multicolored	5.00 4.75

Columbus Lighthouse A423

Design: 3p, Lighthouse at night.

1992, Oct. 12			Litho.
1123	A423	30c multicolored	1.10 1.00
1124	A423	1p multicolored	2.40 2.00

Size: 70x133mm
Imperf
| 1125 | A423 | 3p multicolored | 10.25 10.00 |

America Issue — A424

Designs: 50c, First royal residence in America, Santo Domingo. 3p, First viceregal residence in America, Royal Palace, Colon.

1992, Nov. 13		Litho.	Perf. 13½
1126	A424	50c multicolored	.80 .75
1127	A424	3p multicolored	4.50 4.00

A425

1992, Dec. 2		Litho.	Perf. 13½
1128	A425	30c Torch bearer	.50 .45
1129	A425	1p Emblems	1.00 1.50
1130	A425	4p Judo	7.25 7.00
		Nos. 1128-1130 (3)	9.35 8.95

1992 Natl. Sports Games, San Juan. Secretary of Sports, Education, Exercise and Recreation (No. 1129).

Natl. Census — A426

1992-93		Litho.	Perf. 13½
1131	A426	50c black, buff & blue	.75 .70
1132	A426	1p blk, brn & blue	1.50 1.40
1133	A426	3p blk, gray & bl	5.00 4.75
1134	A426	4p blk, yel grn & bl	6.50 6.00
		Nos. 1131-1134 (4)	13.75 12.85

Issued: 50c, 1p, 5/12/92; 3p, 4p, 9/9/93.

A427

1993, May 30
1135	A427	30c multicolored	.60 .50
1136	A427	50c multicolored	1.10 .90
1137	A427	1p multicolored	2.25 1.90
		Nos. 1135-1137 (3)	3.95 3.30

Ema Balaguer, humanitarian.

A428

1993, Oct. 7		Litho.	Perf. 13½
1138	A428	30c shown	1.25 1.00
1139	A428	1p Emblem, flags	3.00 2.75

Rotary Club of Santo Domingo, 50th anniv.

17th Central American & Caribbean Games, Ponce — A429

1993, Dec. 21		Litho.	Perf. 13½
1140	A429	50c Tennis	.65 .40
1141	A429	4p Swimming	7.50 5.00

Natl. Education Plan — A430

1993, Dec. 8
| 1142 | A430 | 1.50p multicolored | 2.60 1.25 |

Spanish America — A431

Designs: 50c, First university lecture. 3p, First city coat of arms.

1993, Dec. 28
| 1143 | A431 | 50c multi | .75 .40 |
| 1144 | A431 | 3p multi | 6.50 3.00 |

America Issue — A432

Designs: 1p, Aratinga chloroptera. 3p, Cyclura cornuta.

1993, Dec. 30
| 1145 | A432 | 1p multi | 1.50 .75 |
| 1146 | A432 | 3p multi | 5.50 3.00 |

Opening of New Natl. Post Office — A433

1993, Nov. 12
Color of Inscription
1147	A433	1p olive	1.00 .55
1148	A433	3p red	3.00 1.60
1149	A433	4p blue	4.00 1.90
1150	A433	5p green	5.00 2.25
1151	A433	10p black	10.00 4.50

Size: 105x96mm
Imperf
| 1152 | A433 | 5p black | 13.00 12.50 |
| | | Nos. 1147-1152 (6) | 36.00 23.30 |

First Mass in America, 500th Anniv. — A434

1994, Feb. 3		Litho.	Perf. 13½
1153	A434	2p multicolored	3.25 1.75

5th Natl. Philatelic Exhibition — A435

1994, Feb. 25
| 1154 | A435 | 3p multicolored | 4.75 2.50 |

Natl. Independence, 150th Anniv. — A436

No. 1155: a, Men with document, left side of table. b, Document on right side of table, men. c, Flag. d, Couple at window. e, Child holding material, mother making flag.

No. 1156: a, Men looking upward, shooting muskets. b, Men with guns, swords looking backwards. c, Natl. coat of arms. d, Men with guns, swords, one pointing upward. e, Men with weapons, one with flag.

10p, Three men, angel carrying musket, flag.

1994, Feb. 26			Strips of 5
1155	A436	2p #a.-e.	9.50 6.50
1156	A436	3p #a.-e.	13.50 7.50

Size: 161x104mm
Imperf
| 1157 | A436 | 10p multicolored | 13.50 13.50 |
| | | Nos. 1155-1157 (3) | 36.50 27.50 |

Nos. 1155a-1155b, 1155d-1155e, 1156a-1156b, 1156d-1156e have a continuous design.

Solenodon Paradoxus — A437

Designs: a, Crawling on rock. b, Walking in leaves. c, Looking up. d, With food in mouth.

1994, Mar. 15		Litho.	Perf. 13½
1158	A437	1p Block of 4, #a.-d.	10.00 7.50

World Wildlife Fund.

Battle of March 19, 150th Anniv. — A438

No. 1160, Soldiers advancing uphill toward fort.

1994
| 1159 | A438 | 2p multicolored | 3.25 2.00 |
| 1160 | A438 | 2p multicolored | 3.25 2.00 |

Issued: No. 1159, Mar. 18; No. 1160, Mar. 29.

DOMINICAN REPUBLIC

Virgin of Amparo — A439

1994, Apr. 15 Litho. Perf. 13½
1161 A439 3p multicolored 4.75 3.00

Battle of Puerto Tortuguero, 150th anniv.

Natl. Elections, May 16 — A440

1994, Apr. 4
1162 A440 2p multicolored 3.25 2.00

1994 World Cup Soccer Championships, US — A441

1994, June 24 Litho. Perf. 13½
1163 A441 4p multicolored 5.00 3.00
1164 A441 6p multicolored 7.50 5.00

Ema Balaguer City of Children — A442

1994, July 20 Litho. Perf. 13½
1165 A442 1p magenta & brown 3.00 2.00

Stamp Day — A443

1994, Oct. 18 Litho. Perf. 13½
1166 A443 5p Type A3 8.00 5.00

America Issue — A444

1994, Oct. 28
1167 A444 2p Pony Express 3.00 2.00
1168 A444 6p Sailing ship 10.50 6.50

Province of LaVega, 500th Anniv. — A445

3p, Ruins of San Francisco Monastery.

1994, Nov. 24 Litho. Perf. 13½
1169 A445 3p multicolored 7.50 4.00

First Church the New World, 500th Anniv. A446

a, "La Isabela," cradle of evangelization. b, "Temple of the Americas," first mission.

1994, Dec. 5 Perf. 11½
1170 A446 3p Pair, #a.-b. 10.50 5.00

Constitution, 150th Anniv. — A447

1994, Nov. 6 Perf. 13½
1171 A447 3p multicolored 5.25 3.00

Christmas — A448

2p, Holy family's flight into Egypt. 3p, Modern family of three standing at river's edge.

1994, Nov. 18
1172 A448 2p multicolored 3.50 2.00
1173 A448 3p multicolored 5.25 3.00

Intl. Year of the Family.

Firsts in America — A449

1994, Dec. 21 Litho. Perf. 13½
1174 A449 2p Circulating coins 3.50 2.00
1175 A449 5p Sermon for Justice 8.25 4.50

Snakes — A450

No. 1176, Hypsirhynchus ferox. No. 1177, Antillophis parvifrons. No. 1178, Uromacer catesbyi. No. 1179, Epicrates striatus.

1994, Dec. 26
1176 2p multicolored 3.00 1.50
1177 2p multicolored 3.00 1.50
  a. A450 Pair, #1176-1177 6.50 6.00
1178 2p multicolored 3.00 1.50
1179 2p multicolored 3.00 1.50
  a. A450 Pair, #1178-1179 6.50 6.00

Nos. 1177a, 1179a are continuous designs.

Pan American Games, Mar Del Plata, Argentina — A451

1995, Apr. 20 Perf. 13½
1180 A451 4p Tae kwon do 4.75 2.50
1181 A451 13p Tennis 15.00 7.50

FAO, 50th Anniv. A452

1995, Apr. 21 Litho. Perf. 11½
1182 A452 4p multicolored 4.75 2.50

A453

Designs: 2p, Jose Marti, Maximo Gomez. 3p, Marti. 4p, Marti seated at desk, Gomez.

1995, May 19 Litho. Perf. 13½
1183 A453 2p multicolored 2.00 1.00
1184 A453 3p multicolored 2.75 1.50
1185 A453 4p multicolored 4.00 2.50
  Nos. 1183-1185 (3) 8.75 5.00

Jose Marti (1853-95), Montecristi Manifesto, cent.

Basketball, Cent. — A454

1995, May 22
1186 A454 3p multicolored 3.25 1.50

Medicinal Plants — A455

Designs: No. 1187, Pimenta ozua. No. 1188, Melocactus communis. No. 1189, Smilax. No. 1190, Zamia.

1995, May 26
1187 A455 2p multicolored 2.25 1.50
1188 A455 2p multicolored 2.25 1.50
1189 A455 3p multicolored 3.25 2.00
1190 A455 3p multicolored 3.25 2.00
  Nos. 1187-1190 (4) 11.00 7.00

Tourism — A456

4p, San Souci Port. 5p, Barahona Airport. 6p, G. Luperon Airport. 13p, Airport of the Americas.

1995, June 21
1191 A456 4p multicolored 3.25 1.50
1192 A456 5p multicolored 4.00 2.00
1193 A456 6p multicolored 5.00 2.50
1194 A456 13p multicolored 10.00 5.00
  Nos. 1191-1194 (4) 22.25 11.00

Santiago de Los Caballeros, 500th Anniv. — A457

1995, July 29 Litho. Perf. 13½
1195 A457 3p Jacagua ruins 5.00 4.75

Whales — A458

Designs: No. 1196, Physeter macrocephalus. No. 1197, Balaenoptera borealis. No. 1198, Ziphius cavirostris. No. 1199, Megaptera novaeangliae.

1995, Aug. 14
1196 A458 3p multicolored 3.25 1.50
1197 A458 3p multicolored 3.25 1.50
1198 A458 3p multicolored 3.25 1.50
1199 A458 3p multicolored 3.25 1.50
  Nos. 1196-1199 (4) 13.00 6.00

Stamp Day — A459

1995, Oct. 18 Litho. Perf. 13½
1200 A459 4p No. 37 3.50 2.00

Popular Singers — A460

1995, Oct. 8
1201 A460 2p Rafael Colon 2.00 1.00
1202 A460 3p Casandra Damiron 2.50 1.25

Cathedral of Santiago, Cent. — A461

1995, Dec. 28 Litho. Perf. 13½
1203 A461 3p multicolored 2.75 1.50

4th World Conference of Women, Beijing — A462

1995, Nov. 23
1204 A462 2p multicolored 5.50 2.50

Volleyball, Cent. — A463

Norceca '95 — A464

DOMINICAN REPUBLIC

1995, Oct. 19 — Imperf.
1205 A463 5p multicolored — 5.00 2.50
Perf. 13½
1206 A464 6p multicolored — 5.25 4.50

Singers — A465

1995, Dec. 27 — Perf. 13½
1207 A465 2p Antonio Mesa — 2.00 1.00
1208 A465 2p Julieta Otero — 2.00 1.00
1209 A465 2p Susano Polanco — 2.00 1.00
Nos. 1207-1209 (3) — 6.00 3.00

Columbus Lighthouse — A466

1995, Dec. 5
1210 A466 10p dk bl, bl & gray — 11.00 6.00
See Nos. 1241, 1265, 1299, 1337, 1371, 1375, 1382.

A467 UN, 50th Anniv. — A468

1995, Oct. 24
1211 A467 2p multicolored — 2.00 1.00
Perf. 11½
1212 A468 6p multicolored — 5.25 2.75

Environmental Protection A469

America issue: 2p, Flamingos, sea gull. 6p, Manglar.

1995, Dec. 19 — Perf. 13½
1213 A469 2p multicolored — 2.00 1.00
1214 A469 6p multicolored — 5.25 3.75

Dominican Republic Air Force, 50th Anniv. — A470

Aircraft: a, O2U-35D Corsair. b, PT-17 Stearman. c, AT-6 Texan. d, PBY-5A Catalina. e, TF-10 Beaufighter. f, FB-6 Mosquito. g, P-38 Lightning. h, P-51D Mustang. i, B-17G Flying Fortress. j, P-47D Thunderbolt. k, FB-5 Vampire. l, C-46 Commander. m, B-26 Invader. n, C-47 Skytrain. o, T-28B Trojan. p, T-33A Silverstar. q, Cessna T-41D. r, T-34 Mentor. s, Cessna O-2A. t, A-37B Dragonfly.

1995, Dec. 30
1215 A470 2p Sheet of 20, #a-t — 35.00 30.00
See No. 1228.

UNICEF, 50th Anniv. — A471

1996, Feb. 23
1216 A471 2p shown — 1.75 1.00
1217 A471 4p Mirror image of #1216 — 3.25 2.00

Intl. Sailing Competition A472

1996, Mar. 8
1218 A472 5p multicolored — 3.50 2.00

Eduardo Brito, Singer, 50th Death Anniv. — A473

1996, Jan. 15
1219 A473 1p shown — .75 .40
1220 A473 2p With maracas — 1.60 .90
1221 A473 3p Portrait — 2.10 1.25
Nos. 1219-1221 (3) — 4.45 2.55
No. 1220 is 54x35mm.

Natl. Journalist Day — A474

Design: Arturo J. Pellerano Alfau, Dr. Freddy Gaton Arce, Rafael Herrera Cabral.

1996, Apr. 17 — Litho. Perf. 13½
1222 A474 5p multicolored — 4.00 2.00

ESPAMER '96, Seville — A475

1996, June 7 — Litho. Perf. 13½
1223 A475 15p multicolored — 9.75 5.00

1996 Summer Olympic Games, Atlanta — A476

1996, July 5
1224 A476 5p Judo — 4.00 2.00
1225 A476 15p Torch — 10.00 5.00

Modern Olympic Games, Cent. — A477

1996, July 5
1226 A477 6p Greece No. 118 — 3.75 1.90
1227 A477 15p No. 328 — 9.50 4.50

Dominican Republic Air Force, 50th Anniv. Type of 1995

Helicopters: a, Sikorsky S-55. b, Alouette II. c, Alouette III. d, OH-6A Cayuse. e, Bell 205 A-1. f, Dauphin II SA.365C.

1996, July 31 — Litho. Perf. 13½
1228 A470 3p Sheet of 6, #a.-f. — 9.50 9.50

World Day Against Illegal Drugs — A478

1996, Sept. 23 — Litho. Perf. 13½
1229 A478 15p multicolored — 10.00 5.00

Mail Delivery — A479

No. 1230, World delivery, putting mail in letter box, mailman receiving mail on motorcycle. No. 1231, Woman giving mail to man on horseback, vert. No. 1232, Child holding letter beside mailbox.

1996, July 17 — Litho. Perf. 13½
1230 A479 3p multicolored — 2.75 1.50
1231 A479 0p multicolored — 2.75 1.50
1232 A479 3p multicolored — 2.75 1.50
Nos. 1230-1232 (3) — 8.25 4.50

America Issue — A480

1996, Oct. 15 — Litho. Perf. 13½
1233 A480 2p Men's costume — 1.50 .75
1234 A480 6p Women's costume — 4.00 2.00

Stamp Day — A481

1996, Oct. 18
1235 A481 5p No. 142 — 3.50 1.75

26th Intl. Sunfish Championships A482

6p, Sun, natl. flag, sailboat, vert. 10p, Man sailing boat.

1996, Oct. 16
1236 A482 6p multicolored — 4.00 2.00
1237 A482 10p multicolored — 6.50 3.25

A483

1996, Nov. 25 — Litho. Perf. 13½
1238 A483 5p green & multi — 3.50 1.75
1239 A483 10p pink & multi — 6.50 3.25
Intl. Day to End Violence Against Women.

Birds — A484

a, Buteo ridgwayi. b, Aratinga chloroptera. c, Amazona ventralis. d, Hyetornis rufigularis. e, Saurothera longirostris. f, Siphonorhis brewsteri. g, Chlorostilbon swainsonii. h, Todus angustirostris. i, Todus subulatus. j, Temnotrogon roseigaster. k, Nesoctites micromegas. l, Melanerpes striatus. m, Turdus swalesi. n, Carduelis dominicensis. o, Dulus dominicus. p, Microligea palustris. q, Vireo nanus. r, Xenoligea montanta. s, Turdus swalesi dodae. t, Calyptophilus frugivorus tertius. u, Corvus leucognaphalus. v, Calyptophilus frugivorus neibae.

1996, Nov. 11
1240 A484 2p Sheet of 22, #a-v — 50.00 45.00

Lighthouse Type of 1995
1996, Dec. 27 — Litho. Perf. 13½
1241 A466 10p grn, sil & gray — 7.25 3.75

Turtles — A485

a, Dermochelys coriacea. b, Caretta caretta. c, Chelonia mydas. d, Eretmochelys imbricata.

1996, Dec. 30
1242 A485 5p Block of 4, #a.-d. — 13.00 11.00

Natl. Youth Day — A486

1997, Jan. 31
1243 A486 3p multicolored — 2.25 1.25

National Anthem — A487

Designs: 2p, Lyrics, by Emilio Prudhome. 3p, Music, by Jose Reyes.

1997, Feb. 26
1244 A487 2p multicolored — 1.75 1.00
1245 A487 3p multicolored — 2.25 1.25

Salomé Urena (1850-97), Poet — A488

1997, Mar. 6 — Perf. 13½
1246 A488 3p multicolored — 2.10 1.00

DOMINICAN REPUBLIC

Comet Hale-Bopp — A489

1997, Apr. 1
1247 A489 5p multicolored 4.50 2.25
Size: 72x47mm Imperf
1248 A489 10p multicolored 11.50 11.50

A490

11th Natl. Sports Games, Mao '97 — A491

2p, Mascot running with torch. 3p, Mascot in batting stance, vert. 5p, Runner breaking finish line.

1997, Apr. 3
1249 A490 2p multicolored 2.00 1.00
1250 A491 3p multicolored 3.00 1.50
1251 A491 5p multicolored 4.50 2.25
Nos. 1249-1251 (3) 9.50 4.75

A492

Design: 10p, 5p, Heinrich von Stephan (1831-97), founder of UPU.

1997, Apr. 8 Litho. Perf. 13½
1252 A492 10p multicolored 6.50 4.00

Souvenir Sheet Imperf
1253 A492 5p like #1252 3.50 2.75
No. 1253 has simulated perforations.

A493

1997, Apr. 29 Perf. 13½
1254 A493 10p multicolored 9.75 5.00

25th Intl. Congress of CLAHT (Caracas and Latin American Group of Hemostasis and Thrombosis).

Gregorio Luperón (1839-1897), Politician — A494

1997, May 21
1255 A494 3p multicolored 2.25 1.25

House of Spain, 80th Anniv. — A495

1997, July 4
1256 A495 5p multicolored 3.50 1.75

First Peso Coin, Cent. — A496

1997, Aug. 6 Litho. Perf. 13½
1257 A496 2p multicolored 1.75 1.00

A497

Coronation of the Image of Our Lady of Alta Gracia, 75th Anniv. — A498

1997, Aug. 12
1258 A497 3p multicolored 2.00 1.00
1259 A498 5p multicolored 3.25 1.60

America Issue — A499

Life of a postman: 2p, Dog grabbing pants leg of postman on motorcycle. 6p, Dog tearing pants leg of postman with letter.

1997, Oct. 9 Litho. Perf. 13½
1260 A499 2p multicolored 1.50 .75
Size: 35½x35½mm
1261 A499 6p multicolored 3.50 1.75

Mother Teresa (1910-97) — A500

1997, Oct. 17
1262 A500 5p multicolored 3.25 1.60

Stamp Day — A501

1997, Oct. 18
1263 A501 5p Nos. 108, 322 3.00 1.60

Central Bank of the Dominican Republic, 50th Anniv. — A502

1997, Oct. 30 Perf. 11½
1264 A502 10p multicolored 5.75 3.25

Lighthouse Type of 1995
1997, Dec. 15 Perf. 13½
1265 A466 10p bright rose & gray 7.75 3.75

Bats — A503

a, Erophylius bombifrons. b, Brachyphylla nana. c, Molossus molossus. d, Lasiurus borealis.

1997, Nov. 11
1266 A503 5p Block of 4, #a.-d. 12.00 11.00

Dominican Air Force, 50th Anniv. — A504

Insignias: a, Air Force, red, white, and blue target. b, Northern Air Command, "shark plane." c, Air Command, eagle's wings over target. d, Rescue Force, eagle. e, Maintenance Command. f, Combat Force, dragon, target.

1997, Dec. 19
1267 A504 3p Sheet of 6, #a.-f. 12.50 11.00

Construction of the National Palace, 50th Anniv. — A505

1997, Dec. 30 Litho. Perf. 13½
1268 A505 10p multicolored 6.50 3.50

First Regional Symposium on Pre-Columbian Culture and Caribbean Contemporary Art — A506

1998, Jan. 28
1269 A506 6p multicolored 4.00 2.00

A507

1998, Apr. 2 Litho. Perf. 13½
1270 A507 10p multicolored 6.50 3.25

American Chamber of Commerce of the Dominican Republic, 75th anniv.

A508

Book Fair: 3p, Natl. Book Fair, 25th anniv. 5p, Intl. Book Fair, Santo Domingo '98.

1998, Apr. 26
1271 A508 3p black, blue & red 2.10 1.00
Size: 35x33mm
1272 A508 5p black, blue & red 3.50 1.75

Organization of American States, 50th Anniv. — A509

1998, Apr. 30
1273 A509 5p blue & multi 3.50 1.75
1274 A509 5p pink & multi 3.50 1.75

Establishment of the State of Israel, 50th Anniv. — A510

1998, Apr. 30
1275 A510 10p multicolored 9.25 4.50

Dominican Air Force, 50th Anniv. — A511

a, Gen. Frank Felix Miranda, portrait at left. b, Early aircraft. c, Col. Ernesto Tejeda, portrait at right. d, As "c," portrait at left. e, As "a," portrait at right.

1998, June 26 Sheet of 6
1276 A511 3p Sheet of 6, #a, c-e, 2 #b 12.50 11.00

City of Santo Domingo, 500th Anniv. — A512

2p, Sun clock. 3p, St. Lazaro Church & Hospital. 4p, First Cathedral in America. 5p, Royal Palace. 6p, Tower of Honor. 10p, St. Nicolas of Bari Church & Hospital.

1998, Aug. 6 Litho. Perf. 13½
1277 A512 2p multi, vert. 1.30 .65
1278 A512 3p multi 2.10 .90
1279 A512 4p multi 2.75 1.25
1280 A512 5p multi 3.50 1.60
1281 A512 6p multi 4.00 1.90
1282 A512 10p multi, vert. 4.75 3.25
Nos. 1277-1282 (6) 18.40 9.55

National Theater, 25th Anniv. — A513

1998, Aug. 14 Perf. 13x13½
1283 A513 10p multicolored 6.50 3.00

Latin Union, 44th Anniv. — A514

1998, Aug. 26 Perf. 13½
1284 A514 10p multicolored 6.50 6.25

DOMINICAN REPUBLIC

ICCO (Intl. Cocoa Organization of America & Europe), 25th Anniv. — A515

1998, Sept. 3
1285   A515   10p multicolored   8.00   4.50

Nino Ferrua (1909-79), Stamp Designer — A516

1998, Oct. 18   Litho.   Perf. 13½x13
1286   A516   5p multicolored   3.50   1.75
Stamp Day.

Pontificate of John Paul II, 20th Anniv. — A517

1998, Oct. 22   Perf. 13½
1287   A517   5p shown   3.50   1.75
1288   A517   10p Portrait, diff.   7.00   3.50

Medicinal Plants — A518

a, Pimenta racemosa. b, Pimenta haitiensis. c, Cymbopogon citratus. d, Citrus aurantium.

1998, Nov. 2
1289   A518   3p Block of 4, #a.-d.   8.00   7.00

Famous Women — A519

America Issue: 2p, Juana Saltitopa standing with cannon. 6p, Anacaona, Indian maiden, group of Indians.

1998, Nov. 5
1290   A519   2p multicolored   2.00   1.00
1291   A519   6p multicolored   5.00   2.50

Intl. Year of the Ocean — A520

1998, Nov. 20
1292   A520   5p multicolored   4.25   2.25

A521

1998, Nov. 23
1293   A521   5p multicolored   3.00   1.50
Expofila '98, Santo Domingo. Santo Domingo, 500th anniv.

National Military Heroes — A522

Designs: a, Fernando Valerio. b, Benito Moncion. c, Jose Maria Cabral. d, Antonio Duverge. e, Gregorio Luperon. f, Jose A. Salcedo. g, Fco. A. Salcedo. h, Gaspar Polanco. i, Santiago Rodriguez. j, Juan Bta. Cambiaso. k, Jose J. Puello. l, Jose Ma. Imbert. m, Juan A. Acosta. n, Marcos Adon. o, Matias R. Mella. p, Francisco R. Sanchez. q, Juan Pablo Duarte. r, Olegario Tenares. s, Pedro Santana. t, Juan Sanchez Ramirez.

1998, Nov. 29
1294   A522   3p Sheet of 20, #a.-t.   32.50   27.50

1st Natl. Paper Money, 150th Anniv. A523

1998, Nov. 30   Perf. 11½
1295   A523   10p multicolored   5.00   3.00

Christmas A524

1998, Dec. 7   Perf. 13½
1296   A524   2p Roasting hog   1.00   .50
1297   A524   5p Magi   3.50   1.75

Universal Declaration of Human Rights, 50th Anniv. — A525

1998, Dec. 10
1298   A525   10p multicolored   5.00   2.50

Columbus Lighthouse Type of 1995
1998, Dec. 11
1299   A466   10p orange & black   6.25   3.25

Shells — A526

Designs: a, Lyria vegai. b, Strombus gigas. c, Cittarium pica. d, Nerita peloronta.

1998, Dec. 16
1300   A526   5p Block of 4, #a.-d.   12.00   11.00

Gaspar Hernandez (1798-1858), Priest — A527

1998, Dec. 18
1301   A527   3p multicolored   1.60   .80

Dominican Society of Endocrinology and Nutrition, 25th Anniv. — A528

1999, Feb. 24   Litho.   Perf. 13¼
1302   A528   10p multicolored   4.25   2.25

Office of Comptroller General A529

1999, May 4   Litho.   Perf. 13¼
1303   A529   2p multicolored   1.25   .60

Export Industries — A530

Perf. 13½x13¼, 13¼x13½
1999, Apr. 30   Litho.
1304   A530   6p Tobacco   2.50   1.25
1305   A530   10p Textiles, vert.   4.00   2.00

Pan American Games, Winnipeg   A530a

1999, July 29   Litho.   Perf. 13¼x13¼
1306   A530a   5p Baseball   3.00   1.50
1307   A530a   6p Weight lifting   3.50   1.75

Native Plants — A531

Designs: a, Pseudophoenix ekmanii. b, Murtigia calabura. c, Pouteria dominguensis. d, Rubus dominguensis focke.

1999, July 13
1308   A531   5p Block of 4, #a.-d.   10.50   9.50

Presidents of the Dominican Republic — A532

Designs: a, Tomas Bobadilla y Briones. b, Pedro Santana. c, Manuel Jimenez. d, Buenaventura Baez. e, Manuel de Regla Mota. f, José Desiderio Valverde. g, José A. Salcedo. h, Gaspar Polanco.

1999, Aug. 31   Perf. 13½x13¼
1309   A532   3p Sheet of 8, #a.-h. + label   12.00   10.00

A533

Sovereign Military Order of Malta — A534

Perf. 13¼x13½
1999, Sept. 20   Litho.
1310   A533   2p multicolored   1.10   .60
Perf. 13½
1311   A534   10p multicolored   4.75   3.00

Paintings by José Vela Zanetti (1913-99) — A535

Various paintings.

Perf. 13½x13¼, 13¼x 13½
1999, Sept. 8
1312   A535   2p multi, vert.   .80   .65
1313   A535   3p multi, vert.   1.40   .90
1314   A535   5p multi   2.10   1.25
1315   A535   6p multi, vert.   2.75   1.75
1316   A535   10p multi, vert.   4.25   2.50
Nos. 1312-1316 (5)   11.30   7.05

Insects A536

Designs: a, Strataegus quadrifoveatus. b, Anetia jaegeri. c, Polyancistroydes tettigonidae. d, Aploppus phasmidae.

1999, Sept. 10   Perf. 13½x13¼
1317   A536   5p Block of 4, #a.-d.   9.00   8.00

SOS Children's Villages, 50th Anniv. — A537

1999, Sept. 29   Perf. 13¼x13½
1318   A537   10p multicolored   4.25   2.25

Intl. Year of the Elderly — A538

1999, Oct. 1
1319   A538   2p Man   1.00   .50
1320   A538   5p Woman   2.25   1.25

World Education Day — A539

1999, Oct. 5
1321   A539   5p multicolored   2.25   1.25

DOMINICAN REPUBLIC

A540

Designs: 2p, Skull and crossbones, land mines, shattered gun. 6p, Mushroom cloud.

1999, Oct. 18
| 1322 | A540 | 2p multicolored | 1.00 | .50 |
| 1323 | A540 | 6p multicolored | 2.90 | 1.50 |

America Issue, a new millennium without arms.

Stamp Day — A541

1999, Oct. 22
| 1324 | A541 | 5p Luis F. Thomen | 2.25 | 1.25 |

Account of Gen. Juan Pablo Duarte — A542

1999, July 16 — Perf. 13½
| 1325 | A542 | 3p multicolored | 1.50 | .75 |

A543

Contemporary Writers — A544

Perf. 13¼x13½, 13½x13¼
1999, June 23
| 1326 | A543 | 2p multicolored | 1.00 | .50 |
| 1327 | A544 | 10p multicolored | 5.00 | 2.50 |

Dermatological Society, 50th Anniv. — A545

1999, Sept. 15 Litho. Perf. 13¼
| 1328 | A545 | 3p multi | 2.00 | 1.00 |

Millennium A546

3p, Earth, trees. 5p, Scientific achievements.

Perf. 13¼x13½
1999, Nov. 10 Litho.
| 1329 | A546 | 3p multi | 1.50 | .75 |
| 1330 | A546 | 5p multi | 2.50 | 1.25 |

2nd Summit of African, Caribbean and Pacific Heads of State — A547

Emblem and: 5p, Map of Caribbean area, whale. 6p, Map of Pacific area, Easter Island statues. 10p, Map of Africa, lion.

1999, Nov. 23
1331	A547	5p multi	2.25	1.25
1332	A547	6p multi	2.75	1.40
1333	A547	10p multi	4.25	2.25
		Nos. 1331-1333 (3)	9.25	4.90

UPU, 125th Anniv. — A548

6p, Globe, envelope, computer, electronic circuits. 10p, Envelope, electronic circuits.

1999, Nov. 29
| 1334 | A548 | 6p multi | 2.50 | 1.25 |

Size: 50x75mm
Imperf
| 1335 | A548 | 10p multi | 4.75 | 2.50 |

Union of Latin American Universities, 50th Anniv. — A549

1999, Dec. 3 Perf. 13½x13¼
| 1336 | A549 | 6p multi | 2.50 | 1.25 |

Lighthouse Type of 1995
1999, Dec. 14 Perf. 13¼x13½
| 1337 | A466 | 10p brown & silver | 4.75 | 2.50 |

Classical Musicians — A550

No. 1338, José de Jésus Ravelo (1876-1951), clarinet. No. 1339, Juan Francisco Garcia (1892-1974), cornet. No. 1340, Manuel Simo (1916-88), saxophone.

1999, Dec. 17
1338	A550	5p multi	2.25	1.50
1339	A550	5p multi	2.25	1.50
1340	A550	5p multi	2.25	1.50
		Nos. 1338-1340 (3)	6.75	4.50

Municipal Notes, Cent. — A551

Notes and background colors — No. 1341: a, Santo Domingo, San Pedro de Macorís, deep purple. b, Puerto Plata, Moca, purple. No. 1342, vert.: a, Santiago, Cotui, blue green. b, San Francisco de Macorís, La Vega, golden brown. c, San Cristobal, Samana, peacock blue. No. 1343: a, As No. 1342a, green background. b, As No. 1342b, brown background. c, As No. 1342c, Prussian blue background.

1999, Dec. 30 Perf. 13¼
| 1341 | A551 | 2p Pair, #a.-b. | 2.25 | 1.25 |
| 1342 | A551 | 2p Strip of 3, #a.-c. | 2.75 | 1.50 |

Souvenir Sheet
Imperf
| 1343 | A551 | 2p Sheet of 5, Nos. 1341a-1341b, 1343a-1343c | 5.75 | 3.00 |

Chamber of Spanish Commerce and Industry, 75th Anniv. — A552

1999, Dec. 30 Perf. 13¼x13½
| 1344 | A552 | 10p multi | 4.75 | 2.50 |

Fight Against Drugs — A553

2000, Feb. 17 Litho. Perf. 13½
| 1345 | A553 | 5p multi | 2.50 | 1.25 |

Hogar Crea Dominicana Inc., 25th anniv.

Duarte Institute A554

2000, Feb. 25 Perf. 13¼
| 1346 | A554 | 2p multi | 1.25 | .65 |

Prevention of Child Abuse — A555

2000, Mar. 31
| 1347 | A555 | 2p multi | 1.25 | .65 |

National Police — A556

2000, Apr. 6 Perf. 13½
| 1348 | A556 | 2p shown | 1.50 | .75 |

Size: 37x28mm
Perf. 13½x13¼
| 1349 | A556 | 5p Crest | 3.50 | 1.75 |

Dominican Institute of Industrial Technology, 25th Anniv. — A557

2000, Apr. 11 Perf. 13½
| 1350 | A557 | 2p multi | 1.25 | .65 |

Independencia Province, 50th Anniv. — A558

2000, Apr. 15
| 1351 | A558 | 3p multi | 1.50 | .75 |

A559

12th Natl. Games, La Romana — A560

2000, Apr. 27 Perf. 13½x13¼
| 1352 | A559 | 2p Baseball | 1.25 | .65 |
| 1353 | A559 | 3p Boxing | 2.25 | 1.25 |

Perf. 13½
| 1354 | A560 | 5p Emblem | 3.50 | 1.75 |
| | | Nos. 1352-1354 (3) | 7.00 | 3.65 |

Paintings — A561

Designs: 5p, The Violinist, by Darío Suro. 10p, Self-portrait, by Théodore Chassériau.

2000, May 5 Perf. 13¼
| 1355 | A561 | 5p multi | 4.00 | 2.00 |
| 1356 | A561 | 10p multi | 6.50 | 3.50 |

Presidential Elections — A562

2000, May 12
| 1357 | A562 | 2p multi | 1.60 | .80 |

Classical Musicians A563

No. 1358, Julio Alberto Hernandez Camejo (1900-99), pianist. No. 1359, Ramon Diaz (1901-76), bassoonist. No. 1360, Enrique de Marchena Dujarric (1908-88), pianist.

2000, May 31 Perf. 13½
1358	A563	5p multi	3.50	1.75
1359	A563	5p multi	3.50	1.75
1360	A563	5p multi	3.50	1.75
		Nos. 1358-1360 (3)	10.50	5.25

Expo 2000, Hanover — A564

2000, June 1
| 1361 | A564 | 5p shown | 2.50 | 1.25 |
| 1362 | A564 | 10p Emblem, diff. | 4.75 | 2.50 |

DOMINICAN REPUBLIC

Art by Jaime Colson — A565

Designs: 2p, Woman on horseback. 3p, Abstract. 5p, Musicians and dancers, horiz. 6p, Nudes. 10p, Colson.

2000	Litho.		Perf. 13¼	
1363-1367	A565	Set of 5	21.00	12.00

Holy Year 2000 — A566

Churches: 2p, Santo Cristo de los Milagros de Bayaguana Sanctuary. 5p, Santa Maria la Menor Cathedral, first in the Americas, vert. 10p, Nuestra Señora de la Altagracia Basilica, vert.

2000	Perf. 13½x13¼, 13¼x13½			
1368-1370	A566	Set of 3	11.00	5.50

Lighthouse Type of 1995

2000		Perf. 13¼x13½	
1371	A466 10p buff, brn & sil	8.25	7.25

Dominican Republic — Republic of China Diplomatic Relations — A566a

Flags of Dominican Republic and Republic of China and: 5p, Illustration of dragon. 10p, Carved dragon.

Serpentine Die Cut 11¼

2000, Dec. 15		Litho.	
	Self-Adhesive		
1371A-1371B	A566a	Set of 2	14.50 7.50

America Issue — Campaign Against AIDS — A566b

Designs: 2p, Child. 6p, AIDS patient (38x38mm).

2000, Dec. 21		Self-Adhesive	
1371C-1371D	A566b	Set of 2	4.50 2.50

UN High Commissioner for Refugees, 50th Anniv. — A566c

2000, Dec. 29		Self-Adhesive	
1371E	A566c 10p multi	4.75	2.50

Environmental Protection — A567

Designs: 2p, Lizard on leaf, vert. $3, House. $5, River rapids, vert.

Serpentine Die Cut 11¼

2000		Litho.	
	Self-Adhesive		
1372-1374	A567	Set of 3	7.75 4.00

Lighthouse Type of 1995

2001	Litho.	Perf. 13¼x13½	
1375	A466 15p lt bl, dk bl & sil	10.50	9.00

Concepcion Bona, Seamstress of First Dominican Republic Flag, Cent. of Death — A568

2001		Perf. 13½x13¼	
1376	A568 10p multi	5.75	3.00

Stamp Day — A569

2001			
1377	A569 5p multi	3.50	1.75

Year of Dialogue Among Civilizations — A570

2001		Perf. 13¼x13½	
1378	A570 12p multi	7.75	4.00

America Issue — UNESCO World Heritage — A571

Designs: 4p, San Felipe Fort. 15p, Ruins of San Nicolas de Bari Hospital (27x37mm).

2001	Perf. 13½, 13¼x13½ (15p)		
1379-1380	A571 Set of 2	12.00	6.00

Lighthouse Type of 1995

2002, Oct. 17	Litho.	Perf. 13½x13¾	
1382	A466 15p yel & multi	5.75	3.00

Mushrooms — A572

No. 1383: a, Pycnoporus sanguineus. b, Morchella elata. c, Mycena epipterygia. d, Coriolopsis polyzona.

Perf. 13¼x13½

2001, Sept. 13		Litho.	
1383	A572 6p Block of 4, #a-d	14.00	10.00

National Botanical Gardens, 25th Anniv. A573

No. 1384: a, Isidorea pungens. b, Pereskia quisqueyana. c, Goetzea ekmanii. d, Cubanola domingensis.

Perf. 13¼x13½

2001, Sept. 20		Litho.	
1384	A573 4p Block of 4, #a-d	11.00	11.00

Presidents of the Dominican Republic — A574

No. 1385: a, Gen. José María Cabral. b, Gen. Gregório Luperón. c, Gen. Ignacio María González. d, Ulises Espaillat. e, Pedro A. Pimentel. f, Federico de Jesús García. g, Frenando Arturo de Mariño. h, Gen. Ulises Heureaux.

2001, Sept. 27	Litho.	Perf. 13¼	
1385	A574 6p Sheet of 8, #a-h, + label	33.50	30.00

Blessed Josemaría Escrivá de Balaguer (1902-75), Founder of Opus Dei — A575

2002, Aug. 29		Perf. 13½x13¼	
1386	A575 10p multi	7.50	5.00

Loyola Polytechnic Institute, 50th Anniv. — A576

2002, Oct. 24		Perf. 13¼x13½	
1387	A576 6p multi	2.75	2.00

12th Iberoamerican Heads of State Summit A577

Designs: 12p, Flags below map. 15p, Flags above map.

Perf. 13¾x13½

2002, Nov. 14		Litho.	
1388-1389	A577 Set of 2	14.00	10.00

Compare with Type A637a.

America Issue — Youth Education and Literacy — A578

Designs: 4p, Teacher helping child write. 15p, Child writing on blackboard.

2002, Dec. 20		Perf. 13¼x13½	
1390-1391	A578 Set of 2	9.50	5.00

Coccothrinax Spissa — A579

Perf. 13¼x13½

2002, Dec. 20		Litho.	
1392	A579 10p multi	4.50	2.50

2003 Pan American Games, Santo Domingo — A580

Color of "2003" in design: 4p, Light green blue. 6p, Blue. 12p, Red.

2003, Feb. 25			
1393-1395	A580 Set of 3	7.25	4.00

Medicinal Plants — A581

No. 1396: a, Hymenaea courbaril. b, Spondias mombin. c, Genipa americana. d, Guazuma ulmifonia.

2003, June 17			
1396	A581 5p Block of 4, #a-d	7.00	4.00

Dr. José Francisco Peña Gomez (1937-98), Politician — A582

Litho. & Engr.

2003, Dec. 17		Perf. 11½	
1397	A582 10p multi	4.50	2.50

José Marti (1853-95), Cuban Patriot — A583

2003, Nov. 5	Litho.	Perf. 13x13¼	
1398	A583 15p multi	5.00	3.00

262 DOMINICAN REPUBLIC

Pan American Health Organization, Cent. (in 2002) — A583a

2006, July. 12   Perf. 13½x13¼   Litho.
1398A A583a 20p multi   5.75 3.00

America Issue — Flora and Fauna A584

Designs: 5p, Aristelliger lar. 15p, Cornpernicia berteroana, vert.

Perf. 13½x13¼, 13¼x13½
2004, Jan. 19
1399-1400 A584 Set of 2   9.50 5.00
Nos. 1399-1400 are dated "2003."

Election of Pope John Paul II, 25th Anniv. — A585

Pope John Paul II: 10p, With hand touching face. 15p, Blessing crowd, horiz. 25p, Vignettes of 10p and 15p stamps.

Perf. 13¼x13½, 13½x13¼
2005, Nov. 26
1401-1402 A585   Set of 2   14.00 7.00
Size: 57x85mm
Imperf
1403 A585 25p multi   14.50 7.50

National Council for Children — A586

2004, Mar. 10   Perf. 13½x13¼
1404 A586 7p multi   3.50 2.50

Exfilna National Philatelic Exhibition A587

2004, Dec. 8   Litho.   Perf. 13½x13¼
1405 A587 7p multi   3.75 2.00

America Issue — Fight Against Poverty — A588

Design: 10p, Shack. 20p, Poor woman.

2004, Dec. 23
1406-1407 A588   Set of 2   13.50 7.00

Dominican Republic - Canada Diplomatic Relations, 50th Anniv. — A589

2004, Dec. 31
1408 A589 20p multi   9.25 5.00

Interexpo '05 Intl. Philatelic Exhibition A590

Designs: 7p, Dove and stamp. 20p, Map highlighting Dominican Republic, vert. 10p, Similar to 7p.

Perf. 13½x13¼, 13¼x13½
2005   Litho.
1409-1410 A590 Set of 2   12.50 6.50
Souvenir Sheet
1410A A590 10p multi   32.50 20.00
Dominican Republic Philatelic Society, 50th anniv.
Issued: 20p, 10/16; 7p, 10/17; 10p, 2005.

America Issue — Environmental Protection — A591

Prevention of: 10p, Water pollution. 20p, Air pollution.

2005   Perf. 13¼x13½
1411-1412 A591 Set of 2   12.50 6.50

Monte Plata Maternity Clinic — A592

Perf. 13½x13¼
2005, Nov. 14   Litho.
1413 A592 15p multi   7.25 4.00

Proclamation of Sister City Status of Santo Domingo and La Guardia, Spain — A593

2005, Nov. 11
1414 A593 10p multi   4.50 2.50

Stamp Day — A594

2005   Litho.   Perf. 13½x13¼
1415 A594 10p multi   4.50 2.50

Palace of Fine Arts, 50th Anniv. A595

2006, Oct. 10   Litho.   Perf. 13¾x13¼
1416 A595 7p multi   3.50 2.00

Dominican History Academy, 75th Anniv. A596

2006, Oct. 30   Perf. 13¼
1417 A596 10p multi   4.50 2.50

16th Intl. Boxing Congress, Santo Domingo — A597

2006, Nov. 2   Perf. 13¼x13½
1418 A597 20p multi   7.25 4.00

Pope John Paul II (1920-2005) — A598

Pope and: 10p, Crucifix. 20p, Dove, horiz.

2006, Nov. 4   Perf. 13½
1419-1420 A598   Set of 2   13.00 7.00

Blessing of Natl. Sacred Heart of Jesus Sanctuary, 50th Anniv. — A599

2006, Nov. 24   Perf. 13½x13¼
1421 A599 10p multi   5.25 2.75

Ninth Latin American Botanical Congress — A600

2007, Feb/ 26   Perf. 13¼x13½
1422 A600 20p multi   8.50 4.50

America Issue, Energy Conservation A601

Designs: 10p, Light bulb in hands. 20p, Transmission lines and tower.

2007, June 11   Perf. 13x13½
1423-1424 A601   Set of 2   9.50 5.00

Pres. Joaquin Balaguer (1906-2002) — A602

Balaguer: 7p, Wearing bow tie. 10p, Holding book.

2006, Sept. 1   Perf. 13¼x13½
1425-1426 A602   Set of 2   8.25 4.50

Office of the First Lady — A603

Emblem and: 10p, Tree. 25p, Computer and keyboard.

2007, Mar. 1   Perf. 13½x13¼
1427-1428 A603   Set of 2   13.00 7.00

Selection of Nicolás de Jesus Cardinal López Rodríguez as Archbishop of Santo Domingo, 25th Anniv. — A604

López Rodríguez: 10p, Standing next to chair. 15p, With Pope John Paul II. 25p, Holding crucifix.

2007, May 25   Perf. 13¼x13½
1429-1431 A604 Set of 3   17.50 10.00

2007 Pan American Games, Rio de Janeiro — A605

Designs: 15p, High jump. 20p, Weight lifting.

2007, July 6   Litho.
1432-1433 A605 Set of 2   13.00 7.00

Podilymbus Podiceps — A606

2007, Sept. 7   Litho.   Perf. 13½x13¼
1434 A606 20p multi   8.50 4.50
Dated 2006.

Stamp Day — A607

2007, Oct. 4   Perf. 13¼x13½
1435 A607 15p multi   5.75 3.00

America Issue, Education For All — A608

Top panel in: 10p, Red. 20p, Blue.

2007, Dec. 26
1436-1437 A608 Set of 2   13.00 7.00

Treaty of Friendship With the Netherlands, 150th Anniv. — A609

2007, Nov. 9   Perf. 13½x13¼
1438 A609 25p multi   8.50 4.50

Palace of Columbus A610

2008, Apr. 18
1439 A610 10p multi   4.50 2.50

DOMINICAN REPUBLIC

Barahona Province, Cent. — A611

2007, Nov. 23   Perf. 13¼x13
1440   A611   10p multi   3.00   1.75

Salvaléon de Higuey, 500th Anniv. — A612

2008, Jan. 17   Perf. 13½
1441   A612   15p multi   4.50   2.50

Friendship and Cooperation Between Dominican Republic and Republic of China — A613

Designs: 10p, Prunus mume, Swietenia mahagonii. 15p, Uroctssa caeruela, Dulus dominicus. 35p, Buildings from China and Dominican Republic.

2008, Feb. 6
1442-1444   A613   Set of 3   16.00   9.00

Children's Book Illustrations by Dr. Sophie Jakowska — A614

Initials of Dr. Jakowska and: No. 1445, 7p, Trichechus manatus manatus. No. 1446, 7p, Eretmochelys imbricata, horiz. No. 1447, 10p, Photograph of Jakowska. No. 1448, 10p, Amazona ventralis. 15p, Crocodylus acutus, horiz.

2007, Dec. 7   Perf. 13¼x13, 13x13¼
1445-1449   A614   Set of 5   15.00   8.00

Scouting, Cent. — A615

Designs: 10p, Dominican Republic Scouting emblem. 15p, Scouts, knotted rope.

2008, Jun. 5   Litho.   Perf. 13½
1450-1451   A615   Set of 2   7.50   4.00

Dominican Diaspora — A616

2008, Apr. 5   Perf. 13¼x13
1452   A616   15p multi   4.50   2.50

Freemasonry in Dominican Republic, 150th Anniv. — A617

2008, Oct. 25   Perf. 13¼x13½
1453   A617   25p multi   7.25   4.00

Stamp Day — A618

2008, Oct. 2   Perf. 13¼
1454   A618   20p brown   6.50   3.50

2008 Summer Olympics, Beijing — A619

No. 1455: a, Taekwondo. b, Boxing. c, Table tennis. d, Judo.

2008, Aug. 15   Perf. 13x13¼
1455   A619   10p Block of 4, #a-d   12.00   7.00

Women Involved in Fight for Independence — A620

No. 1456: a, Juana de la Merced Trinidad (d. 1860). b, Joaquina Filomena Gomez de la Cova (1800-93). c, Maria Baltasara de los Reyes (1789-1867). d, Rosa Protomartir Duarte y Diaz (1820-88). e. Manuela Diaz y Jimenez (1786-1858). f, Petronila Abreu y Delgado (1815-1904). g, Micaela de Rivera de Santana (1785-1854). h, Froilana Febles de Santana (1814-88). i, Rosa Montas de Duvergé (1813-95). j, Josefa Antonia Perez de la Paz (1788-1855). k, Ana Valverde (1798-1864). l, Maria de la Concepción Bona y Hernandez (1824-1901). m, Maria de Jesus Pina y Benitez (1825-58). n, Maria Trinidad Sanchez y Ramona (1794-1845).

2008, Mar. 10   Perf. 13¼x13½
1456   A620   Sheet of 14 + 31 labels   35.00   35.00
   a.-n.   10p Any single   1.75   .90

Arms of Santiago, 500th Anniv. — A621

2008, Dec. 7   Litho.   Perf. 13x13¼
1457   A621   10p multi   1.75   1.00

Discovery of Quisqueya (Hispaniola) by Christopher Columbus, 1492 — A622

2008, Dec. 17
1458   A622   10p multi   1.75   1.00

General Timoteo Ogando Encarnación (1818-1908) — A623

2008   Perf. 13¼x13
1459   A623   10p multi   1.75   1.00

Campaign Against Commercial Sexual Exploitation — A624

2008, Nov. 14
1460   A624   10p multi   1.75   1.00

Intl. Swimming Federation, Cent. — A625

2009, Feb. 23   Perf. 13½
1461   A625   15p multi   1.75   1.00

America Issue, National Festivals A626

No. 1462: a, 15p, Shot of Independence. b, 25p, Sword of the Restoration.

2008   Perf. 13¼x13
1462   A626   Horiz. pair, #a-b   7.50   4.00

Duarte y Díez Family Tree A627

No. 1463: a, Juan J. Duarte (1768-1843) and wife, Manuela Díez (1786-1858). b, Juan J. Duarte's sons, Juan Pablo (1813-76), Dominican independence leader, and Vicente (1802-65). c, Juan J. Duarte's son, Manuel (1826-90), and daughter, Rosa (1820-88). d, Juan J. Duarte's daughters, Francisca (1831-99), and Filomena (1818-65).

2009, Feb. 26   Perf. 13½x13¼
1463   A627   10p Block of 4, #a-d   8.00   4.50

Chinatown, Santo Domingo — A628

Designs: 15p, Confucius Plaza. 20p, Gateway.

2009, Apr. 17
1464-1465   A628   Set of 2   9.00   5.00

De La Salle Schools in Dominican Republic, 75th Anniv. A629

St. Jean Baptiste de la Salle (1651-1719) A630

2009, May 14   Perf. 13½x13¼
1466   A629   7p multi   2.00   1.00
   Perf. 13¼x13½
1467   A630   10p multi   3.50   2.00

Invasion of Constanza, Maimón and Estero Hondo by Dominican Exiles, 50th Anniv. — A631

2009, June 17   Perf. 13½
1468   A631   10p multi   3.50   2.00

Pres. Juan Bosch (1909-2001) — A632

2009, Jun. 19   Perf. 13¼x13
1469   A632   20p multi   5.50   3.00

Crabs A633

No. 1470: a, Epilobocera haytensis. b, Gecarcinus ruricola. c, Coenobita clypeatus. d, Callinectes sapidus.

   Perf. 13½x13¼
2009, Sept. 17   Litho.
1470   A633   10p Block of 4, #a-d   6.00   3.50

Winning Designs in Children's Christmas Stamp Design Contest — A634

No. 1471: a, Dancers and musicians in front of house. b, Parade. c, Family and livestock. d, Villagers, manger and Christmas tree.

2009, Oct. 5   Litho.   Perf. 13x13¼
1471   A634   10p Block of 4, #a-d   7.00   4.00

Plazas A635

DOMINICAN REPUBLIC

Designs: 15p, Galicia Plaza, Santo Domingo. 25p, Santo Domingo Plaza, La Guardia, Spain.

2009, Oct. 15 — Perf. 13¼
1472-1473 A635 Set of 2   6.00 3.50

15th American Genealogical Reunion — A636

2009, Nov. 3 — Perf. 13x13¼
1474 A636 75p multi   13.00 7.00

Natl. School of Judicature A637

2009, Nov. 4 — Perf. 13½
1475 A637 7p multi   1.10 .60

12th Iberoamerican Heads of State Summit — A637a

Designs: 12p, Ribbon of flags below map. 15p, Flags above and to sides of map.

2009   Litho.   Perf. 13¾x13½
1475A-1475B A637a Set of 2   8.00 4.50

Dated 2002. Compare with type A577.

America Issue, Toys and Games — A638

Designs: 10p, Fu-fu. 15p, Hopscotch, horiz. 20p, Pañuelo, horiz.

2009, Dec. 15 — Perf. 13x13, 13x13¼
1476-1477 A638 Set of 2   7.50 4.00

Imperf.
Size: 76x50mm
1478 A638 20p multi   5.75 3.00

Miniature Sheet

Dominican Republic Presidents — A639

No. 1479: a, Benigno Filomeno De Rojas. b, Jacinto B. De Castro. c, Maetos Cabral. d, Gen. Cesáreo Guillermo. e, Francisco G. Billini. f, Alejandro Woss y Gil. g, Carlos Felipe Morales Languasco. h, Ramón Cáceres.

2009 — Perf. 13¼
1479 A639 7p Sheet of 8, #a-h, + central label   10.00 6.00

See Nos. 1531, 1585.

National Coat of Arms — A640

2010, Feb. 10 — Perf. 13¼x13½
1480 A640 50p multi   7.25 4.00

14th Ibero-American Notaries Meeting — A641

2010, June 3   Litho.   Perf. 13¼x13
1481 A641 26p multi   3.75 2.00

Preservation of Polar Regions — A642

2010, July 7 — Perf. 13½x13¼
1482 A642 20p multi   2.75 1.50

Solenodon Paradoxus A643

2010, July 28
1483 A643 25p multi   3.75 2.00

Biodiversity protection.

National Philatelic and Numismatic Museum, 25th Anniv. — A644

2010, Aug. 10 — Perf. 13¼x13
1484 A644 33p ocher & black   4.75 2.50

Juan Pablo Duarte (1813-76), Independence Leader, and Birthplace, Santo Domingo — A645

2010, Aug. 30 — Perf. 11½x13¼
1485 A645 25p multi   3.75 2.00

Delivery of the Flag A646

National Pantheon A647

2010, Oct. 12   Litho.   Perf. 13½
1486 A646 26p multi   3.75 2.00

Perf. 13¼x13
1487 A647 33p multi   5.00 2.75

America Issue.

Stamp Day — A648

2010, Oct. 18 — Perf. 13x13¼
1488 A648 15p multi   2.25 1.25

Miniature Sheet

Tourism A649

No. 1489 — Tourist attractions: a, Los Tres Ojos. b, Juan Dolio Beach. c, Altos de Chavón. d, Bayahibe Beach. e, Bávaro Beach. f, Cayo Levantado. g, Las Terrenas Beach. h, Cabarete Beach. i, River rafters, Jarabacoa. j, Lake Enriquillo.

2010, Nov. 4
1489 A649 10p Sheet of 10, #a-j, + 2 labels   16.00 13.50

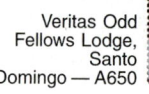

Veritas Odd Fellows Lodge, Santo Domingo — A650

2010, Nov. 26 — Perf. 13½x13¼
1490 A650 60p multi   8.50 4.50

World AIDS Day — A651

Designs: 15p, Hands with AIDS ribbons on thumbs. 46p, Flower with AIDS ribbon petals.

2010, Dec. 1 — Perf. 13¼x13
1491-1492 A651 Set of 2   8.75 4.50

Dominican Order in the Americas, 500th Anniv. — A652

Designs: 15p, Monastery. 26p, Dominican monk and native boy, vert.

2010, Dec. 7 — Perf. 13x13¼, 13¼x13
1493-1494 A652 Set of 2   6.00 3.50

National Archives, 75th Anniv. — A653

2010, Dec. 14 — Perf. 13½x13¼
1495 A653 20p multi   3.00 1.75

Santo Domingo, 2010 American Capital of Culture — A654

2010, Dec. 16 — Imperf.
1496 A654 26p multi   3.75 2.00

Santo Domingo Gates A655

No. 1497: a, Puerta de la Misericordia, "Republica" at bottom. b, Puerta del Conde, "Republica" at left. c, Puerta del Conde, "Republica" at top. d, Puerta de la Misericordia, "Republica" at left.
20p, Puerta de la Misericordia, Puerta del Conde, arms of Dominican Republic.

2011, Feb. 21 — Perf. 13x13¼
1497 A655 10p Block of 4, #a-d   6.50 3.50

Size: 90x70mm
Imperf
1498 A655 20p multi   3.00 3.00

Sur Futuro Foundation — A656

Designs: 15p, Tree and rainbow. 20p, Lake.

2011, Mar. 3 — Perf. 13¼x13½
1499-1500 A656 Set of 2   5.25 2.75

Caves A657

No. 1501: a, Pomier Caves, San Cristobal. b, Fun Fun Cave, Hato Mayor del Rey. c, Guácara de Hernando Alonzo, La Mata, Sánchez Ramírez. d, Golondrinas Cave, Río San Juan.

2011, Mar. 15 — Perf. 13½x13¼
1501 A657 10p Block of 4, #a-d   6.25 3.50

Dated 2010.

Postal Union of the Americas, Spain and Portugal (UPAEP), Cent. — A658

Designs: 20p, "100" with map of Americas and Iberian peninsula in zeroes. 26p, Map of Americas and Iberian peninsula, doves with letters.

2011, Mar. 18 — Litho.
1502-1503 A658 Set of 2   6.75 3.50

DOMINICAN REPUBLIC

Flowers
A659

No. 1504: a, Pereskia quisqueyana. b, Cereus hexagonus. c, Catalpa longissima. d, Tolumnia variegata.

2011, Mar. 31		Perf. 13¼x13	
1504	A659 10p Block of 4, #a-d	6.25	3.50

Dated 2010.

Colonel Rafael T. Fernandez Dominguez (1934-65) — A660

2011, May 19	Litho.	Perf. 13¼x13	
1505	A660 15p multi	2.25	1.25

Liberty Day, 50th Anniv. A661

2011, June 2		Imperf.	
1506	A661 33p multi	4.75	2.50

Assassination of Pres. Rafael Trujillo, 50th anniv.

Aviation — A662

No. 1507: a, 20p, Airplane of Zoilo H. Garcia. b, 25p, Garcia (1849-1922), first Dominican pilot.

2011, June 16		Perf. 13x13¼	
1507	A662 Vert. pair, #a-b	6.75	3.50

Places Associated With Independence Leader Juan Pablo Duarte — A663

Designs: 15p, Santa Barbara Church, Santo Domingo. 20p, Baptismal font.

2011, Aug. 30			
1508-1509	A663 Set of 2	5.25	2.75

Worldwide Fund for Nature (WWF) — A664

No. 1510 — Hypsiboas heilprini: a, Blue denomination at LR. b, Red denomination at LL. c, Red denomination at LR. d, Blue denomination at LL.

2011, Sept. 7			
1510	A664 10p Block of 4, #a-d	6.50	3.50

Father of the Fatherland, by Martin de San Juan — A665

2011, Nov. 9	Litho.	Imperf.	
1511	A665 20p multi	3.25	3.25

Execution of Francisco del Rosario Sánchez, 150th anniv.

Pastoral and Social Work in Dominican Republic of Bishop Francisco José Arnáiz, 50th Anniv. — A666

2011, Dec. 21			
1512	A666 33p multi	5.00	2.75

Juan Pablo Duarte and Camara de Cuentas (Governmental Accounting Office) Document — A667

2011			
1513	A667 20p multi	3.25	1.75

Sermon Denouncing Mistreatment of Indians of Friar Antonio de Montesinos, 500th Anniv. (in 2011) — A668

2012, Jan. 5		Perf. 11½	
1514	A668 60p multi	9.00	5.00

Dated 2011.

National Police, 75th Anniv. (in 2011) — A669

2012, Jan. 12		Perf. 13x13¼	
1515	A669 20p multi	3.25	1.75

Dated 2011.

Order of the Pilgrims of the Way of St. James — A670

2012, Feb. 8		Perf. 13¼x13½	
1516	A670 33p multi	5.00	2.75

Miniature Sheets

A671

A672

A673

A674

Carnival Masks and Painted Faces
A675

No. 1517: a, Azua (white face with headband). b, Bani. c, Barahona (red and black face). d, Barahona (green, yellow and red face). e, Cotuí (black and red face). f, La Romana (red, white and blue face with hat). g, La Romana (red and blue face with flower). h, Montecristi (yellow face with black and yellow hat). i, San Luis. j, Santo Domingo (red and yellow face with blue spots).
No. 1518: a, Cotuí (pink and red woman's face mask with blue eye lashes), horiz. b, Navarrette. c, Puerto Plata (white and brown mask). d, La Vega (mask with large pointed teeth), horiz. e, Rio San Juan (fish-head mask with large teeth), horiz. f, Samaná. g, San Juan de la Maguana. h, San Pedro de Macoris. i, Santo Domingo (green mask with horns). j, Villa Rivas.
No. 1519: a, Bonao (blue, green and red dragon's head mask). b, Cotuí (hat in flag colors with slits for eyes and mouth). c, La Vega (green and red dragon's head mask). d, Montecristi (red, gold, white, black and green mask). e, La Joya, Guerra, horiz. f, La Romana (yellow and blue bull's head mask with open mouth), horiz. g, Rio San Juan (blue, yellow, green and red demon-head mask with projections). h, Salcedo. i, Santiago (red, white and blue mask with spiked horns). j, Santo Domingo (mask with yellow beard).
No. 1520: a, Barahona (red, white and blue bull's head mask with horns), horiz. b, Bonao (mask with beard, moustache and gold hat). c, Constanza. d, Cabral, horiz. e, Elias Piña. f, La Vega (black, green and red cat's head mask). g, Valverde-Mao, horiz. h, Santiago (white, red and orange mask with spiked horns). i, Santo Domingo (red and yellow mask with horns). j, Puerto Plata (green, white and black pottery head mask), horiz.
No. 1521: a, Azua (red face with green hair). b, Barahona (blue, red, white and black face). c, Cotuí (black and white striped face with green hat). d, Cotuí (black face with flag hat). e, Cotuí (yellow, green, red and black face), horiz. f, Puerto Plata (brown and red mask, black, red and white face), horiz. g, Santo Domingo (yellow and black striped face). h, Santo Domingo (red, blue, white, green and black face). i, Rio San Juan (black face). j, Santiago (red, white and blue face).

Perf. 13¼x13 (vert. stamps), 13x13¼ (horiz. stamps)

2012, Feb. 27			
1517	A671 20p Sheet of 10, #a-j, + 2 central labels	30.00	30.00
1518	A672 20p Sheet of 10, #a-j, + 2 central labels	30.00	30.00
1519	A673 20p Sheet of 10, #a-j, + 2 central labels	30.00	30.00
1520	A674 20p Sheet of 10, #a-j, + 2 central labels	30.00	30.00
1521	A675 20p Sheet of 10, #a-j, + 2 central labels	30.00	30.00
Nos. 1517-1521 (5)		150.00	150.00

A676

2012, Mar. 1		Perf. 13½x13¼	
1522	A676 20p multi	3.25	1.75

Dated 2011.
Diplomatic Relations Between Dominican Republic and Ecuador, 125th Anniv.

Pontifical Catholic University, Santo Domingo, 50th Anniv. — A677

2012, Apr. 17		Perf. 13¼x13	
1523	A677 25p multi	7.75	4.00

Mailboxes — A678

DOMINICAN REPUBLIC

Designs: 20p, Mailbox with legs. 25p, Mailbox without legs.

2012, May 8   *Perf. 13¼x13½*
1524-1525 A678 Set of 2   7.25 4.00
America Issue. Dated 2011.

Maria Montez (1912-51), Actress — A679

2012, June 2   *Perf. 13¼x13*
1526 A679 100p multi   15.00 8.00

Juan Pablo Duarte (1813-76), Patriot — A680

No. 1527: a, 15p, Photograph of Duarte in Hamburg. b, 25p, Oath of the Trinitaria.

2012, July 24   *Perf. 13½x13¼*
1527 A680 Pair, #a-b   6.50 3.50

Expo Cibao, 25th Anniv. — A681

2012, Sept. 5   *Perf. 13¼x13*
1528 A681 20p multi   3.00 2.00
a. Tete-beche pair   6.50 6.50

Miniature Sheet

Birds A682

No. 1529: a, Caprimulgus eckmani. b, Contopus hispaniolensis. c, Phaenicophilus palmarum. d, Icterus dominicensis. e, Loxia megaplaga. f, Calyptophilus frugivorus. g, Geotrygon leucometopia. h, Spindalis dominicensis. i, Corvus palmarum. j, Tyto glaucops.

2012, Sept. 19
1529 A682 20p Sheet of 10, #a-j, + 2 central labels   32.50 32.50

No. 1529d in the sheet of 10 was inscribed "CIGUA AMARILLA" in the first part of the print run. The error was discovered and corrected to "CIGUA CANARIA" on the remainder of the printing. Same values.

Orchids A683

No. 1530: a, Sudamerylcaste peguerol. b, Tolumnia calochila. c, Quisqueya ekmanii. d, Tolumnia henekenii.

2012, Oct. 18
1530 A683 15p Block of 4, #a-d   10.50 6.50

Presidents Type of 2009
Miniature Sheet

No. 1531: a, Pedro Guillermo. b, Wenceslao Figuereo. c, Horacio Vásquez. d, Juan Isidro Jiménez. e, Eladio Victoria. f, Adolfo Alejandro Nouel. g, José Bordas Valdéz. h, Ramón Báez Machado.

2012   *Perf. 13¼*
1531 A639 15p Sheet of 8, #a-h, + central label   20.00 20.00

America Issue A684

No. 1532 — Legend of: a, El Caracaracol. b, La Ciguapa.

2012, Dec. 18   *Perf. 13¼x13*
1532 A684 20p Horiz. pair, #a-b   15.00 15.00

Miniature Sheet

Tourism A685

No. 1533: a, Beach, Saona Island. b, Beach, Bahia de las Aguilas. c, San Rafael Beach. d, Gri-Gri Lagoon. e, Dominican Republic flag. f, Playa Dorada. g, El Morro Beach. h, Puerto Plata. i, Monument to the Heroes of the Restoration, Santiago. j, Historic center of Santiago. k, Jordobadas Whale Sanctuary. l, Beach, Punta Cana.

2013, May 23   *Perf. 13½x13¼*
1533 A685 10p Sheet of 12, #a-l   21.00 19.00

Arachnids — A686

No. 1534: a, Phrynus longipes. b, Mastigoproctus proscorpio. c, Phormictopus canceroides. d, Rhopalurus princeps.

2013, May 28
1534 A686 20p Block of 4, #a-d   13.00 10.00

Pedro Mir (1913-2000), Poet — A687

2013, June 24   *Perf. 13¼x13*
1535 A687 50p multi   3.50 2.40

La Trinitaria Secret Society, 175th Anniv. A688

2013, July 15   *Imperf.*
1536 A688 60p multi   4.00 4.00

María Ugarte (1914-2011), Investigative Reporter — A689

2013, July 31   *Litho.*   *Perf. 13¼x13*
1537 A689 33p multi   2.50 1.75

A690

General Gregoio Luperón (1839-97) — A691

Perf. 13½x13¼
2013, Aug. 12   *Litho.*
1538 A690 15p multi   1.40 .90

Imperf
1539 A691 33p multi   2.40 2.40

Dominican War of the Restoration, 150th anniv.

Dominican Rehabilitation Association, Inc., 50th Anniv. — A692

2013, Oct. 23   *Litho.*   *Perf. 13½x13*
1540 A692 15p red & blue   1.40 1.00

Dominican Postal Institute (Inposdom), 50th Anniv. — A693

Designs: 15p, Emblem for InposPak service. 20p, Inposdom emblem, vert. 25p, Exhibit frames at stamp exhibition. 80p, Inposdom Headquarters.

2013, Nov. 28   *Litho.*   *Perf. 13¼*
1541 A693 15p multi   .90 .90
Size: 30x40mm
Perf. 13¼x13½
1542 A693 20p multi   1.25 1.25
Size: 40x30mm
Perf. 13½x13¼
1543 A693 25p multi   1.50 1.50
Nos. 1541-1543 (3)   3.65 3.65
Size: 80x50mm
Imperf
1544 A693 80p multi   5.50 5.50

A694

Juan Pablo Duarte (1813-76), Leader of Independence Movement — A695

No. 1545: a, Atarazana School where Duarte taught fencing. b, House of Josefa Pérez de la Paz, birthplace of La Trinitaria Secret Society. c, Duarte directing "La Dramatica." d, 1844 return of Duarte from exile. e, Duarte and Dominican Republic Constitution and flag.

2013, Dec. 9   *Litho.*   *Perf. 13*
1545   Horiz. strip of 5   6.25 5.00
a.-e. A694 15p Any single   1.00 1.00
Imperf
1546 A695 25p multi   2.10 1.90

Campaign Against Discrimination A696

Designs: 15p, Five children. 20p, Map of Dominican Republic, hands.

2014, Jan. 30   *Litho.*   *Perf. 13x13¼*
1547-1548 A696 Set of 2   3.25 2.25
America issue. Dated 2013.

A697

Designs: 20p, Building. 25p, Buildings and university crest.

2014, Feb. 14   *Litho.*   *Perf. 13x13¼*
1549 A697 20p multi   1.60 1.40
Size: 89x60mm
Imperf
1550 A697 25p multi   2.00 1.75
Dated 2013.
Founding of St. Thomas Aquinas University, Santo Domingo, 475th Anniv. (in 2013). Reopening of university as Autonomous University of Santo Domingo, cent.

Julia de Burgos (1914-53), Poet — A698

2014, Mar. 28   *Litho.*   *Perf. 13¼x13*
1551 A698 100p multi   7.00 5.00

Souvenir Sheets

Centro León Museum — A699

DOMINICAN REPUBLIC

National Botanical Gardens — A700

Bellapart Museum — A701

Numismatic and Philatelic Museum — A702

National Museum of Natural History — A703

Museum of Modern Art — A704

No. 1552: a, Entrance to Jimenes Cultural Center. b, Caribeño Patio of Eduardo León Jimenes Cultural Center.
No. 1553: a, Bridge in Japanese Garden. b, Path in Japanese Garden.
No. 1554: a, Permanent Gallery. b, Merongue, painting by Jaime Colson.
No. 1555: a, Exhibit of money with metal ingot. b, Display case in Numismatics Gallery.
No. 1556: a, Museum entrance. b, Skeleton of humpback whale.
No. 1557: a, Sculptures. b, Sculptures and paintings in Permanent Gallery.

2014, May 21   Litho.   Perf. 13½
1552 A699 50p Sheet of 2, #a-b, + 2 labels   7.25 6.50
1553 A700 50p Sheet of 2, #a-b, + 2 labels   7.25 6.50
1554 A701 50p Sheet of 2, #a-b, + 2 labels   7.25 6.50
1555 A702 50p Sheet of 2, #a-b, + 2 labels   7.25 6.50
1556 A703 50p Sheet of 2, #a-b, + 2 labels   7.25 6.50
1557 A704 50p Sheet of 2, #a-b, + 2 labels   7.25 6.50
Nos. 1552-1557 (6)   43.50 39.00
World Museum Day.

Duarte Institute, 50th Anniv. — A705

2014, June 24   Litho.   Perf. 13½
1558 A705 50p multi   3.75 3.00

Flowers — A706

No. 1559: a, Salcedoa mirabaliarum. b, Ekmanianthe longiflora, vert. c, Coccothrinax jienezii, vert. d, Rhytidophyllum daisyanum.

2014, Aug. 27   Litho.   Perf. 13x13¼
1559 A706 20p Block of 4, #a-d   6.75 5.75
Dated 2013.

National Literacy Plan — A707

2014, Sept. 8   Litho.   Perf. 13½
1560 A707 15p multi   1.30 1.10
Dated 2013.

Miniature Sheets

Heroes and Flags of Nations of North and South America — A708

No. 1561, 50p: a, José de San Martín, flag of Argentina. b, Joaquim José Da Silva Xavier (Tiradentes), flag of Brazil. c, Francisco de Paula Santander, flag of Colombia. d, Pedro Alvarado y Bonilla, flag of Costa Rica. e, José Martí, flag of Cuba. f, Juan Pablo Duarte (standing), flag of Dominican Republic. g, Quote by Duarte, flag of Dominican Republic. h, Bernardo O'Higgins Riquelme, flag of Chile. i, José Matías Delgado de León, flag of El Salvador. j, George Washington, flag of United States. k, Jean Jacques Dessalines, flag of Haiti. l, Francisco Morazán Quezada, flag of Honduras.
No. 1562, 50p: a, Simón Bolívar, flag of Bolivia. b, Georges-Etienne Cartier, flag of Canada. c, Máximo Gómez y Báez, flag of Cuba. d, Manuela Sáenz y Aizpuru, flag of Ecuador. e, Pedro Molina Mazariegos, flag of Guatemala. f, Miguel Hidalgo y Costilla, flag of Mexico. g, Head of Duarte, flag of Dominican Republic. h, Augusto César Sandino, flag of Nicaragua. i, Gaspar Rodríguez de Francia, flag of Paraguay. j, José Gabriel Condorcanqui (Túpac Amaru II), flag of Peru. k, José Gervado Artigas Arnal, flag of Uruguay. l, Bolívar, flag of Venezuela.

2014, Sept. 30   Litho.   Perf. 13¼x13
Sheets of 12, #a-l
1561-1562 A708 Set of 2   81.00 75.00
America issue.

World Food Day — A709

No. 1563: a, Boy holding apple. b, Boy eating broccoli, vert. c, Fruit picker on ladder. d, Girl eating cob of corn, vert.

2014, Oct. 15   Litho.   Perf. 13½
1563 A709 25p Block of 4, #a-d   8.00 7.00

Miniature Sheet

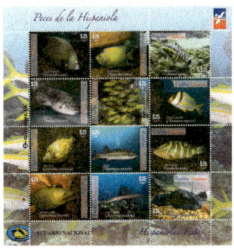
Wildlife A710

No. 1564, 25p — Fish: a, Pomacanthus paru. b, Holacanthus ciliaris. c, Serranus tigrinus. d, Nandopsis haitensis. e, Haemulon flavolineatum. f, Anisotremus virginicus. g, Cantherhines macrocerus. h, Agonostomus monticola. i, Epinephelus striatus. j, Gymnothorax funebris. k, Aulostomus maculatus. l, Dasyatis americana.
No. 1565, 25p — Butterflies: a, Anaea troglodyta. b, Anartia lytrea. c, Burca stillmani. d, Burca hispaniolae. e, Myscelia aracynthia. f, Archimestra teleboas. g, Atlante cryptadia. h, Greta diaphanus quisqueya. i, Heraclides machaonides. j, Choranthus haitensis. k, Memphis verticordia. l, Pyrisitia pyro.

Perf. 13½x13¼
2014, Nov. 20   Litho.
Sheets of 12, #a-l
1564-1565 A710 Set of 2   45.00 40.00

Miniature Sheet

Merengue Musicians and Instruments — A711

No. 1566: a, Nico Lora playing accordion. b, Accordion, horiz. c, Tatico Henriquez playing accordion, horiz. d, Güira. e, Tambora. f, Trio Reynosa performing, horiz. g, Marimba. g, Guandulito playing accordion, horiz.

Perf. 13¼x13½, 13½x13¼
2014, Nov. 26   Litho.
1566 A711 15p Sheet of 8, #a-h, + central label   9.75 7.75

Scouting in the Dominican Republic, Cent — A712

2014, Dec. 3   Litho.   Perf. 13½x13¼
1567 A712 20p multi   1.60 1.25

ISA University, 50th Anniv. (in 2014) — A713

2015, Mar. 5   Litho.   Perf. 13½
1568 A713 200p multi   12.50 12.00

Bani, 250th Anniv. (in 2014) — A714

2015, Mar. 6   Litho.   Perf. 13¼
1569 A714 100p multi   6.50 5.00
Dated 2014.

Gustavo A. Moré González (1925-2002), President of Dominican Philatelic Society — A715

2015, Apr. 9   Litho.   Perf. 13½
1570 A715 75p multi   5.00 4.00
Stamp Day. Dated 2014.

Programs Run Through Office of the First Lady — A716

No. 1571: a, Newborn Screening Program. b, Comprehensive Care Center for Disability.

2015, Apr. 28   Litho.   Perf. 13¼x13
1571 A716 250p Horiz. pair, #a-b   31.00 31.00

Miniature Sheets

National Parks A717

No. 1572, 20p: a, Pyramids, Valle Nuevo National Park. b, Rio Grande Waterfall, Francisco Alberto Caamaño Deñó National Park. c, Coral reef and fish, Monte Cristi Underwater National Park. d, Hatillo Dam Reservoir with small islands at left, Aniana Vargas National Park. e, Hoyo de Pelempito, Sierra de Bahoruco National Park. f, Aerial view of El Morro Beach, El Morro National Park. g, Coastal hills, Los Haitises National Park. h, Sierra de Neiba, Sierra de Neiba National Park. i, Salado de Neiba, La Gran Sabana National Park. j, Haemulon spp., La Caleta Underwater National Park. k, Quita Coraza, Anacona National Park. l, La Isabela ruins, La Hispaniola National Park.
No. 1573, 20p: a, Baiguate Waterfall, Baiguate National Park. b, Punta Aguila Cliffs, Jaragua National Park. c, Waterfall, Saltos de la Jalda National Park, vert. d, Cliffs, Sierra Martín García National Park. e, Cyclura ricordii, Lago Enriquillo e Isla Cabritos National Park. f, Offshore rocks, Los Haitises National Park. g, Rock art, Aniana Vargas National Park, vert. h, Whales, Cabo Cabrón National Park. i, Plagiodontia aedium, Sierra de Bahoruco National Park. j, Mountains, Nalga de Maco National Park. k, Sea level view of cliffs and El Morro Beach, El Morro National Park. l, Palm trees, Sierra Martín García National Park.
No. 1574, 20p: a, Tetero Valley, José del Carmen Ramírez National Park. b, Isla Saona, Este National Park. c, Frogata magnifioono, Este National Park. d, Mountains, Armando Bermúdez National Park. e, Sun over water, Lago Enriquillo e Isla Cabritos National Park. f, Cabo Cabrón, Cabo Cabrón National Park. g, Callubocera weihenbeel, Valle Nuevo National Park. h, Punta Espada, Punta Espada National Park. i, Río Amina, Manolo Tavárez Justo National Park. j, La Humeadora, La Humeadora National Park. k, Rivers, Humedales del Ozama National Park. l, Río Mana, Máximo Gómez National Park, vert.
No. 1575, 20p: a, Balsa Estuary, Mangiares de Estero Balsa National Park. b, Río Mao, Piky Lora National Park. c, Lakes, Humedales del Ozama National Park. d, Shoreline, Mangiares del Bajo Yuna National Park. e, Foggy landscape, Valle Nuevo National Park. f, Bahia de las Aguilas, Jaragua National Park. g, Siproeta stelenes, Máximo Gómez National Park, vert. h, Hatillo Dam Reservoir with rocks at LR, Aniana Vargas National Park. i, Phaenicophilus palmarum, Luis Quin National Park. j, Loma La Tachuela, Luis Quin National Park. k, Shoreline, Este National Park. l, Mountains, Manolo Tavárez Justo National Park.

2015, May 22   Litho.   Perf. 13½
Sheets of 12, #a-l
1572-1575 A717 Set of 4   70.00 60.00

DOMINICAN REPUBLIC

Dominican Chapter of Lions International, 50th Anniv. — A718

2015, May 24 Litho. *Perf. 13¼*
1576 A718 50p multi 3.25 2.75

Matías Ramón Mella Castillo (1816-64), Vice-President — A719

2015, June 10 Litho. *Imperf.*
1577 A719 300p multi 16.00 16.00
Dated 2014.

Cooperation Between Brazilian and Dominican Republic Universities, 50th Anniv. — A720

2015, June 22 Litho. *Perf. 13½*
1578 A720 50p multi 3.00 2.50

Santiago Chamber of Commerce, Cent. — A721

2015, July 9 Litho. *Perf. 13¼*
1579 A721 50p multi 3.00 2.50

Oscar de la Renta (1932-2014), Fashion Designer — A722

2015, Oct. 13 Litho. *Perf. 13¼x13*
1580 A722 250p multi 14.50 12.50

St. Teresa of Avila (1515-82) — A723

2015, Oct. 16 Litho. *Perf. 13¼x13½*
1581 A723 45p multi 2.75 2.50

Rights for Disabled People A724

2015, Nov. 16 Litho. *Perf. 13¼*
1582 A724 100p multi 5.75 5.00

Campaign to End Violence Against Women — A725

Perf. 13¼x13½
2015, Nov. 25 Litho.
1583 A725 35p multi 2.10 1.75
See Ecuador No. 2173, Guatemala No. 717, El Salvador No. 1747, and Venezuela No. 1731.

Religious Objects — A726

No. 1584: a, Pax, 17th cent. (portapaz). b, Processional cross, 18th cent. (cruz procesional). c, Monstrance, 19th cent. (custodia). d, Eucharistic ark, 16th cent. (arca eucaristica). e, Chalice, 16th cent. (cáliz).

2015, Dec. 1 Litho. *Perf. 13¼x13½*
1584 Strip of 5 13.50 12.50
a.-e. A726 45p Any single 2.00 2.00

Presidents Type of 2009
Miniature Sheet

No. 1585: a, Francisco Henríquez y Carvajal. b, Juan Bautista Vicini Burgos. c, Rafael Estrella Ureña. d, Inscriptions "1930-1938" (rule of Rafael Trujillo). e, Inscription "1952-1960" (rule of Hector Trujillo). f, Jacinto Bienvenido Peynado. g, Manuel de Jesús Troncoso de la Concha. h, Joaquín Balaguer Ricardo.

2015, Dec. 18 Litho. *Perf. 13¼*
1585 A639 20p Sheet of 8, #a-h, + central label 11.00 9.00
Dated 2014.

Campaign Against Human Trafficking — A727

No. 1586: a, People in suitcase. b, Chained hands holding Earth.

2015, Dec. 18 Litho. *Perf. 13x13½*
1586 A727 50p Pair, #a-b 6.00 5.25
America Issue.

Dominican Republic Postage Stamps, 150th Anniv. — A728

Designs: 30p, Dominican Republic #1. 35p, Dominican Republic #2. 45p, Dominican Republic #3. 50p, Dominican Republic #4. 150p, Dominican Republic #1-4, cover bearing #1, printing press.

2015, Dec. 18 Litho. *Perf. 13x13½*
1587-1590 A728 Set of 4 9.25 8.00
Size: 140x100mm
Imperf
1591 A728 150p multi 8.50 8.00

Luis María "Billo" Frómeta (1915-88), Orchestra Conductor A729

2016, Mar. 30 Litho. *Perf. 13½*
1592 A729 150p multi 8.75 7.00

Pedro Henriquez Ureña National University, 50th Anniv. — A730

2016, Apr. 20 Litho. *Perf. 13½*
1593 A730 50p multi 3.00 2.50

Marine Mammals — A731

No. 1594: a, Tursiops truncatus. b, Trichechus manatus manatus. c, Megaptera novaeangliae. d, Globicephala.

Perf. 13½x13¼
2016, June 15 Litho.
1594 A731 50p Block of 4, #a-d 12.50 12.50

Anoles A732

No. 1595: a, Anolis divius. b, Anolis prasinorius. c, Anolis viridius. d, Anolis eladioi.

Perf. 13½x13¼
2016, June 15 Litho.
1595 A732 50p Block of 4, #a-d 12.50 12.50

Miniature Sheet

Dominican Scientists — A733

No. 1596: a, Dr. Pedro Troncoso Sánchez (1904-89), ambassador and historian. b, Dr. Henri Alain Liogier (1916-2009), botanist. c, Dr. Pablo Rafael Iñiguez Pérez (1925-2007), gastroenterologist. d, Dr. José Luís Alemán Dupuy (1928-2007), economist. e, Dr. Juan Manuel Taveras Rodríguez (1919-2002), neuroradiologist. f, Dr. José Altagracia Silié Gatón (1919-2014), judge. g, Dr. Hugo R. Mendoza Tapia (1930-2009), pediatrician. h, Dr. Francisco R. Guarocuya Batista del Villar (1934-2013), cardiologist.

2016, Aug. 10 Litho. *Perf. 13½*
1596 A733 20p Sheet of 8, #a-h 13.00 13.00

Matías Ramón Mella Castillo (1816-64), National Hero — A734

2016, Sept. 29 Litho. *Imperf.*
1597 A734 150p multi 9.75 9.75

A735

Designs: 35p, Florence Terry Griswold (1875-1941), Founder of Pan America Round Tables, and Hotel Menger, San Antonio, Texas.

2016, Oct. 12 Litho. *Perf. 13x13¼*
1598 A735 35p multi 3.00 2.50
First Pan American Round Table, cent.

2016 Summer Olympics, Rio de Janeiro — A736

No. 1599: a, Track and field. b, Boxing. c, Weight lifting. d, Taekwondo.

2016, Oct. 18 Litho. *Perf. 13½x13¼*
1599 A736 15p Block of 4, #a-d 5.75 4.75
America Issue.

Miniature Sheet

National Botanical Garden A737

No. 1600: a, Peltophorum berteroanum. b, Phyllostylon rhamnoides. c, Guarea guidonia. d, Haematoxylon campechianum. e, Magnolia pallescens. f, Capparis cynophollophora. g, Guaiacum officinale. h, Coccoloba pubescens. i, Calophyllum calaba. j, Krugiodendron ferreum. k, Ekmanianthe longiflora. l, Juniperus gracilior.

2016, Oct. 27 Litho. *Perf. 13x13¼*
1600 A737 10p Sheet of 12, #a-l 12.50 9.50

No. 1600h "pubescens" is spelled wrong on stamp.

Dr. Román Bautista Brache (1905-65), Physician and Politician — A738

2016, Nov. 4 Litho. *Perf. 13¼x13½*
1601 A738 20p multi 1.50 1.25

Mountains — A739

No. 1602: a, Matterhorn, Switzerland. b, Loma Isabel de Torres, Dominican Republic.

Perf. 13½x13¼
2016, Nov. 17 Litho.
1602 A739 60p Pair, #a-b 8.50 8.00
80th anniv. of relations between Dominican Republic and Switzerland.
See Switzerland Nos. 1617.

DOMINICAN REPUBLIC

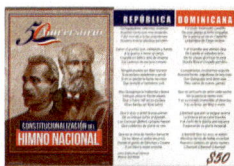

Specification of Dominican Republic National Anthem in National Constitution, 50th Anniv. — A740

2016, Nov. 28 Litho. Imperf.
1603 A740 50p multi 3.75 3.50

Miguel de Cervantes (1547-1616), Writer — A741

2017, Jan. 31 Litho. Perf. 13¼x13½
1604 A741 100p multi + label 6.25 5.00

BanReservas (Reserve Bank), 75th Anniv. — A742

2017, Mar. 2 Litho. Perf. 13¼x13½
1605 A742 75p multi 4.50 4.00

Popes A743

No. 1606: a, Pope Emeritus Benedict XVI, denomination at LL. b, Pope Francis, denomination at LR. c, Pope Francis, denomination at LL. d, Pope Emeritus Benedict XVI, denomination at LR.

2017, Mar. 14 Litho. Perf. 13½
1606 A743 60p Block of 4, #a-d 15.00 12.50

Francisco del Rosario Sánchez (1817-61), Leader in Dominican War of Independence — A744

2017, Mar. 29 Litho. Imperf.
1607 A744 150p multi 9.00 7.50

Bridges A745

No. 1608: a, Mauricio Báez Bridge. b, Matías Ramón Mella Bridge. c, Rio Chavón Bridge. d, Hermanos Patiño Bridge.

2017, Apr. 24 Litho. Perf. 13½x13¼
1608 A745 50p Block of 4, #a-d 11.00 10.00

Painters and Their Paintings A746

No. 1609: a, Silvano Lora (1931-2003). b, Domingo Líz (1931-2013), horiz. c, Gordas en Bicicletas, by Líz, horiz. d, Serie Concieno Ecologico, by Lora.

Perf. 13¼x13½, 13½x13¼ (horiz. stamps)
2017, Apr. 24 Litho.
1609 A746 25p Block of 4, #a-d 6.00 5.00

YMCA in Dominican Republic, 50th Anniv. — A747

2017, Apr. 28 Litho. Perf. 13¼x13½
1610 A747 50p multi 3.25 2.75

Miniature Sheet

Buildings Designed by José Antonio Caro Alvarez (1910-78) — A748

No. 1611: a, University of Santo Domingo Faculty of Medical Science Building, 1944. b, Menendez Building, 1941. c, Faculty of Engineering and Architecture Building, 1959. d, Rodriguez Building, 1949. e, Central Bank Building, 1956. f, National Library, 1971.

2017, May 9 Litho. Perf. 13½x13¼
1611 A748 15p Sheet of 6, #a-f, + 6 labels 6.75 5.25

Fe y Alegría Organization in Dominican Republic, 25th Anniv. — A749

2017, May 17 Litho. Perf. 13¼x13½
1612 A749 25p multi 1.75 1.50

Lions Clubs International, Cent. (in 2016) — A750

2017, May 21 Litho. Perf. 13½x13¼
1613 A750 100p multi 6.00 5.00

Casa de España Organization, Cent. — A751

2017, June 14 Litho. Perf. 13½
1614 A751 12p multi 1.00 .75

Miniature Sheet

Fruit A752

No. 1615: a, Annona squamosa. b, Chrysophyllum cainito. c, Malpighia punicifolia. d, Eugenia domingensis e, Chrisobalanus icaco. f, Genipa americana. g, Spondias mombin. h, Mammea americana. i, Annona reticulata. j, Byrsonima spicata. k, Ziziphus rhodoxylon. l, Coccoloba uvifera.

Perf. 13½x13¼
2017, Sept. 12 Litho.
1615 A752 20p Sheet of 12, #a-l 16.00 13.00

Miniature Sheets

Historic Maps of Hispaniola — A753

No. 1616, 10p — Map by: a, Christopher Columbus, 1493. b, Bologna, 1516. c, Benedetto Bordone, 1528. d, Giovanni B. Ramusio, 1534. e, Giacomo Gastaldi, 1548. f, Giacomo Ruscelli, 1561. g, Paolo Forlani, 1564. h, Ramusio, 1565. i, Bertelli Lafreri, 1566. j, Tomasso Porcacchi, 1572. k, Girolamo Ruscelli, 1580. l, Cornelius Wytfliet, 1597.
No. 1617, 10p — Map by: a, Laugenes, 1598. b, Metellus, 1598. c, Petrus Bertius, 1616. d, Arent Roggeveen, 1675. e, P. Coronelli, 1696. f, Guillaume de l'Isle, 1722-23. g, Emanuel Bowen, 1747. h, M. Bollin, 1754. i, M. Bonne, 1788. j, William Foden, 1795. k, I. Sonis, 1796. l, Tardieu, 1802.

2017, Sept. 26 Litho. Perf. 13x13¼
Sheets of 12, #a-l
1616-1617 A753 Set of 2 19.00 13.00

Martin Luther (1483-1546), Religious Reformer — A754

2017, Oct. 9 Litho. Perf. 13½x13¼
1618 A754 100p multi 5.75 5.00
Protestant Reformation, 500th anniv.

Women's Citizenship and Suffrage, 75th Anniv. — A755

2017, Nov. 7 Litho. Perf. 13½x13¼
1619 A755 75p multi 4.25 4.00

Manuel Corripio García (1908-2004), Businessman, and His House — A756

2017, Nov. 29 Litho. Perf. 13½
1620 A756 20p multi 1.40 1.10
A vertical column of perforations runs through the center of No. 1620.

Miniature Sheet

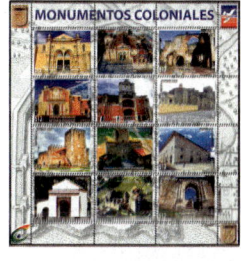

Santo Domingo Colonial Era Buildings A757

No. 1621: a, Santa Maria de la Encarnacion Basilica Cathedral. b, Ruins of San Nicolás di Bari Hospital. c, Imperial Convent. d, Church of the Convent of Our Lady of Mercy. e, Ozama Fortress. f, Museum of the Royal Houses. g, Rosario Chapel. h, Ruins of Monastery of San Francisco.

2017, Dec. 11 Litho. Perf. 13½
1621 A757 12p Sheet of 8, #a-h, + 4 central labels 7.25 6.00

Jarabacoa — A758

2017, Dec. 20 Litho. Perf. 13¼
1622 A758 25p multi 1.60 1.40
International Year of Sustainable Tourism for Development.

Miniature Sheet

Tourist Attractions — A759

No. 1623: a, Lago Enriquillo, Bahoruco Province. b, Salinas Sand Dunes, Baní. c, Playa Macao, La Altagracia Province. d, Waterfall, Constanza. e, Cathedral of the Immaculate Conception, La Vega. f, Clock tower designed by Gustave Eiffel, Montecristi, vert. g, Bahia de las Aguilas, Pedernales Province. h, Lighthouse, Puerto Plata Province. i, Playa Rincón, Samaná Province. j, Cueva de las Maravillas, San Pedro de Macoris Province. k, St. James the Apostle Cathedral, Santiago de los Caballeros. l, Colonial City, Santo Domingo.

2017, Dec. 20 Litho. Perf. 13½
1623 A759 15p Sheet of 12, #a-l 12.50 9.50
America Issue.

DOMINICAN REPUBLIC

Introduction of Basketball in the Dominican Republic, Cent. (in 2017) — A760

2018, Jan. 23   Litho.   Perf. 13x13¼
1624 A760 25p multi   1.75 1.50
Dated 2017.

Vincentian Charism, 400th Anniv. (in 2017) — A761

2018, Jan. 25   Litho.   Perf. 13x13¼
1625 A761 100p multi   6.00 5.00
Dated 2017.

Souvenir Sheet

Friendship Between Dominican Republic and Peru — A762

No. 1626: a, Ramón Castilla y Marquesado (1797-1867), 20th President of Peru, and flag of Peru. b, Gregorio Luperón (1839-97), 20th President of Dominican Republic, flag of Dominican Republic.

2018, Feb. 7   Litho.   Perf. 13½
1626 A762 50p Sheet of 2, #a-b   6.00 5.00
Dated 2017. See Peru No. 1957.

Miniature Sheet

Buildings Designed by Guillermo González Sánchez (1900-70) — A763

No. 1627: a, Ramfis Park, 1936. b, Feria de la Paz (Peace Fair), 1955. c, Copello Building, 1938. d, Hotel Jaragua. e, Centro Social Obrero (Social Worker Center), 1945. f, Hotel Hamaca, 1949.

Perf. 13½x13¼
2018, Feb. 15   Litho.
1627 A763 15p Sheet of 6, #a-f,
         + 6 labels   6.75 5.00
Dated 2017.

Rotary International in Dominican Republic, 75th Anniv. — A764

2018, May 15   Litho.   Perf. 13½
1628 A764 75p multi   4.50 3.50

Miniature Sheet

Buildings Designed by Humberto Ruiz Castillo (1897-1966) — A765

No. 1629: a, St. John Cosco Church, 1938. b, Santo Domingo College, 1939. c, San Rafael Chapel, 1942. d, Anatomy Faculty Building, University of Santo Domingo, 1945. e, Gonzalez Ramos Building, 1946. f, Alma Mater, University of Santo Domingo, 1955.

2018, May 29   Litho.   Perf. 13½x13¼
1629 A765 15p Sheet of 6, #a-f,
         + 6 labels   6.75 5.25

Inter-American Institute for Cooperation on Agriculture, 50th Anniv. — A766

Perf. 13½x13¼
2018, June 27   Litho.
1630 A766 50p multi   3.25 2.50

Miniature Sheet

23rd Central American and Caribbean Games, Barranquilla, Colombia — A767

No. 1631: a, Basketball. b, Baseball. c, Artistic gymnastics. d, Volleyball.

2018, July 4   Litho.   Perf. 13½x13¼
1631 A767 25p Sheet of 4, #a-d   6.00 5.00

Miniature Sheets

Artists and Their Works — A768

No. 1632, 50p: a, Celeste Woss y Gil (1891-1985). b, Nude, by Woss y Gil. c, Mother Selling Dolls, by Cándido Bidó (1936-2011). d, Bidó.
No. 1633, 50p: a, Rooster, by Guillo Perez (1923-2014). b, Perez. c, Marianela Jiménez (1925-2008). d, Carnaval, by Jiménez.
No. 1634, 50p: a, Soucy de Pellerano (1928-2014). b, Maqui-barca del Progresso, sculpture by de Pellerano. c, Untitled work by Fernando Ureña Rib (1951-2014). d, Ureña Rib.

2018, July 18   Litho.   Perf. 13¼x13½
Sheets of 4, #a-d
1632-1634 A768 Set of 3   32.50 30.00

National Symphony Orchestra — A769

2018, Aug. 22   Litho.   Imperf.
1635 A769 100p multi   5.25 4.50

Miniature Sheets

Aviators and Flags of Their Countries — A770

No. 1636, 20p: a, Ramón Franco (1896-1938), Spain. b, Frank Andrés Féliz Miranda (1901-54), Dominican Republic. c, Charles Lindbergh (1902-74), United States. d, Juan Guillermo Villasana López (1891-1959), Mexico. e, Silvio Pettirossi (1887-1916), Paraguay. f, Jorge Antonio Chávez Dartnell (1887-1910), Peru. g, Cesáreo L. Berisso (1887-1971), Uruguay. h, Artur de Sacadura Cabral (1881-1924) and Carlos Viegas Gago Cutinho (1869-1959), Portugal, horiz.
No. 1637, 20p: a, Jorge Alejandro Newbery (1875-1914), Argentina, horiz. b, Rafael Pabón Cuevas (1903-34), Bolivia. c, Alberto Santos-Dumont (1873-1932), Brazil. d, Arturo Meriño Benítez (1888-1970), Chile. e, Camilo Daza Alvarez Mutiscua (1898-1975), Colombia. f, Domingo Rosillo del Toro (1878-1957), Cuba. g, Zoilo Hermógenes García (1881-1916), Dominican Republic. h, Cosme Rennella Barbatto (1890-1937), Ecuador.

Perf. 13¼x13½, 13½x13¼ (#1636h, 1637a)
2018, Oct. 3   Litho.
Sheets of 8, #a-h
1636-1637 A770 Set of 2   20.00 16.00

Spanish International Cooperation Agency in the Dominican Republic — A771

2018, Oct. 17   Litho.   Perf. 13½
1638 A771 60p multi   3.25 2.50

17th Congress of Aeronautical and Space History, Santo Domingo — A772

2018, Nov. 19   Litho.   Perf. 13½
1639 A772 25p multi   1.50 1.25

Dr. Salvador B. Gautier (1868-1938), First President of Dominican Republic Red Cross — A773

Perf. 13¼x13½
2018, Nov. 27   Litho.
1640 A773 100p multi   5.25 4.50

Miniature Sheet

Winning Art In Zero Hunger Generation Children's Stamp Design Contest — A774

No. 1641: a, Child licking bowl, by Anabelys Estévez. b, Child and plate of food, by Angela María Ramírez Ciriaco. c, Children watering seedling and dreaming of giving apples to other children, by Victor Manuel Pérez. d, Children on globe, by Anderson Alvarez Carpio.

2018, Dec. 12   Litho.   Perf. 13x13¼
1641 A774 25p Sheet of 4, #a-d   6.00 5.00

Miniature Sheet

Bromeliads — A775

No. 1642: a, Bromelia pinguin. b, Captosis floribunda. c, Guzmania monestachya. d, Tillandsia baliophylla. e, Tillandsia compressa. f, Tillandsia fasciculata. g, Tillandsia hotteana. h, Tillandsia paucifolia. i, Tillandsia pruinosa. j, Vriesea capituligera. k, Vriesea incurva. l, Vriesea sintenisii.

2019, Feb. 26   Litho.   Perf. 13x13¼
1642 A775 15p Sheet of 12,
          #a-l   13.00 10.00

Expo-Independencia 2019 Numismatic and Philatelic Exhibition, Santo Domingo — A776

2019, Apr. 21   Litho.   Imperf.
1643 A776 25p multi   1.75 1.25

Cooperation Between the Dominican Republic and the European Union — A777

2019, May 8   Litho.   Perf. 13¼
1644 A777 60p multi   3.25 3.00

A778

A779

DOMINICAN REPUBLIC

A780

A781

Santo Domingo Rotary Club, 50th Anniv. — A782

2019, May 24   Litho.   Perf. 13½x13¼
1645	Horiz. strip of 5	7.00	5.50
a.	A778 20p multi	1.10	.90
b.	A779 20p multi	1.10	.90
c.	A780 20p multi	1.10	.90
d.	A781 20p multi	1.10	.90
e.	A782 20p multi	1.10	.90

Miniature Sheets

North and South American Icons of the Virgin Mary — A783

No. 1646, 50p — Icon from: a, Argentina. b, Bolivia. c, Brazil. d, Canada. e, Colombia. f, Costa Rica. g, Dominican Republic (Nuestra Señora de las Mercedes). h, Chile. i, Cuba. j, Ecuador. k, El Salvador. l, United States.

No. 1647, 50p — Icon from: a, Guatemala. b, Haiti. c, Honduras. d, Mexico. e, Nicaragua. f, Dominican Republic (Nuestra Señora de la Altagracia). g, Panama. h, Paraguay. i, Peru. j, Puerto Rico. k, Uruguay. l, Venezuela.

Perf. 13¼x13½
2019, June 13   Litho.
Sheets of 12, #a-l
| 1646-1647 | A783 | Set of 2 | 75.00 | 67.50 |

A784

Dominican Numismatic Society, 50th Anniv. — A785

Designs: 60p, Dominican Numismatic Society 50th anniversary emblem.

No. 1649 — Obverse and reverse of: a, King Ferdinand II era real coin (denomination at UR). b, Two reales silver coin minted in Santo Domingo (denomination at LR). c, 1844 quarter real coin (denomination at UL). d, 1937 half peso coin (denomination at LL).

2019, June 21   Litho.   Perf. 13½
| 1648 | A784 60p multi | | 3.50 | 2.75 |

Perf. 13x13¼
| 1649 | A785 20p Sheet of 4, #a-d | 5.50 | 4.00 |

Dr. Zoraida Heredia Suncar (1917-2011), Educator — A786

2019, July 17   Litho.   Perf. 13¼x13
| 1650 | A786 60p multi | | 3.75 | 3.00 |

Establishment of Diplomatic Relations Between the Dominican Republic and People's Republic of China — A787

2019, Aug. 2   Litho.   Imperf.
| 1651 | A787 75p multi | | 4.50 | 3.50 |

Miniature Sheet

Mushrooms — A788

No. 1652: a, Chlorophyllum molybdites, vert. b, Amanita cruzii. c, Clathrus roseovolvatus, vert. d, Coockeina sulcipes. e, Entoloma aff. altissimum. f, Leucocoprinus fragilissimus. g, Leucopaxillus gracillimus. h, Marasmius tageticolor. i, Phallus indusiatus. j, Geastrum violaceum, vert. k, Phillipsia domingensis. l, Laternea pusilla, vert.

Perf. 13½x13¼, 13¼x13½ (vert. stamps)
2019, Aug. 21   Litho.
| 1652 | A788 20p Sheet of 12, #a-l | 15.00 | 12.00 |

Mohandas K. Gandhi (1869-1948), Indian Nationalist Leader — A789

Perf. 13¼x13½
2019, Aug. 27   Litho.
| 1653 | A789 100p multi | 5.25 | 4.50 |

Alexander von Humboldt (1769-1859), Naturalist, and Andira Inermis — A790

Perf. 13¼x13½
2019, Sept. 18   Litho.
| 1654 | A790 250p multi | 13.00 | 12.00 |

A vertical column of perforations runs through the center of the stamp, with the denomination on the left side, and the country name on the right side.

Miniature Sheets

Corals A791

No. 1655, 20p: a, Plexaurella nutans. b, Madracis auretenra. c, Black fish over blue and red Montastraea cavernosa. d, Antipathes gracilis. e, Acropora palmata. f, Yellow Montastraea cavernosa. g, Orbicella annularis. h, Two fish over Colpophyllia natans. i, Iciligorgia schrammi. j, Fish and close-up view of Colpophyllia natans. k, Stylaster roseus. l, Mycetophyllia aliciae.

No. 1656, 20p: a, Acroporia cervicornis. b, Neospongodes portoricensis. c, Mycetophyllia ferox. d, Dendrogyra cylindrus. e, Pseudopterogorgia sp. f, Tubastraea coccinea. g, Antipathes caribbeana. h, Orbicella faveolata. i, Millepora complenata. j, Agaricia tenuifolia. k, Gorgonia ventalina. l, Helioseris cucullata.

2019, Oct. 9   Litho.   Perf. 13½x13¼
Sheets of 12, #a-l
| 1655-1656 | A791 | Set of 2 | 30.00 | 24.00 |

Color Television Broadcasting in Dominican Republic, 50th Anniv. — A792

2019, Nov. 7   Litho.   Perf. 13½x13¼
| 1657 | A792 50p multi | 3.00 | 2.50 |

Miniature Sheet

America Issue A793

No. 1658 — Native cuisine: a, Chicharrón de cerdo (pork rinds). b, Buñuelos de yuca con almíbar (yucca fritters with syrup). c, Chicharrón de pollo (fried chicken). d, Mangú (pureed plantains). e, Habichuelas con dulce (sweet beans). f, Sancocho siete carnes (stew with seven meats). g, Pastel en hoja (Dominican tamales). h, Majarete (corn pudding). i, Chambre (meat and vegetable soup). j, Sopión o sancocho de habichuelas (bean soup). k, Plátano maduro al caldero (plantains in sweet syrup). l, Chivo liniero (goat stew).

Perf. 13½x13¼
2019, Nov. 14   Litho.
| 1658 | A793 15p Sheet of 12, #a-l | 12.50 | 9.00 |

Miniature Sheet

Paintings by Ramón Oviedo (1924-2015) — A794

No. 1659: a, Mi Mundo. b, 24 de Abril. c, Maternidad. d, Perrotoroburro.

Perf. 13½x13¼
2019, Nov. 29   Litho.
| 1659 | A794 25p Sheet of 4, #a-d | 6.25 | 4.50 |

First Catholic Mass in the Americas, 525th Anniv. — A795

No. 1660: a, Temple of the Americas, 1994. b, Church at La Isabela, 1494.

Perf. 13½x13¼
2019, Dec. 10   Litho.
| 1660 | A795 60p Pair, #a-b | 6.75 | 5.50 |

Miniature Sheet

Founding of La Isabela (First Spanish Settlement in North America), 525th Anniv. (in 2018) — A796

No. 1661 — Various La Isabela archaeological sites with denomination at: a, LR. b, LL. c, UR. d, UL.

Perf. 13½x13¼
2019, Dec. 10   Litho.
| 1661 | A796 60p Sheet of 4, #a-d | 13.50 | 12.50 |

Order of the Blessed Virgin Mary of Mercy, 800th Anniv. — A797

Perf. 13¼x13½
2019, Dec. 11   Litho.
| 1662 | A797 60p multi | 3.50 | 2.75 |

Miniature Sheet

Puerto Plata Province Tourism A798

No. 1663: a, Parque Central Bandstand and statues, Puerto Plata. b, 27 Waterfalls of the Damajagua River. c, Punta Rucia. d, Cofresí. e, Victorian house, Puerto Plata. f, Playa Dorada. g, Sosua. h, Cabarete. i, Fuerte San Felipe. j, Cruise Terminal, Maimón. k, Aerial cable car, Puerto Plata. l, Christ the Redeemer statue, Loma Isabel de Torres.

2020, Jan. 14   Litho.   Perf. 13½x13¼
| 1663 | A798 25p Sheet of 12, #a-l | 17.00 | 14.00 |

Dated 2016.

A799

DOMINICAN REPUBLIC

Dominican Republic Declaration of Independence, 175th Anniv. — A800

Designs: 15p, Oath of the Trinitarians, Masonic square and compass. 20p, Puerta de la Misericordia and General Matías Ramón Mella Castillo (1816-64). 25p, Puerta del Conde. 30p, Flag of the Dominican Republic, national heroes Francisco del Rosario Sánchez (1817-61), Juan Pablo Duarte (1813-76), and Mella.
150p, Dominican Republic coats of arms from 1844, 1848, 1865, 1889, 1898, 1905, 1913 and 2010.

2020, Feb. 5   Litho.   Perf. 13¼x13½
1664-1667 A799 Set of 4   5.25 4.00
                Imperf
1668 A800 150p multi   7.25 7.25
Dated 2019.

First Census, Cent. — A801

2020, July 16   Litho.   Perf. 13¼x13½
1669 A801 100p multi   5.00 4.00

Domesticated Animals — A802

Designs: No. 1670, 20p, Cat. No. 1671, 20p, Dog. No. 1672, 20p, Horse. No. 1673, 20p, Hen and rooster.

2020, July 31   Litho.   Perf. 13½
1670-1673 A802 Set of 4   4.75 3.50
America issue.

Miniature Sheet

16th Century Colonial Houses of Santo Domingo A803

No. 1674: a, Rodrigo de Bastidas House. b, Patio of Rodrigo de Bastidas House. c, Quinta Dominica Art Gallery. d, Patio of Quinta Dominica. e, La Bricola Restaurant (house of Alonso de Peña). f, Patio of La Bricola. g, Juan de Villoria House. h, Patio of Juan de Villoria House.

2020, Aug. 4   Litho.   Perf. 13½x13¼
1674 A803 20p Sheet of 8, #a-h,
            + 4 central labels   9.50 7.50

María Victoria de la Cruz (1859-1967), Founder of Doña Chucha Girls' School Home — A804

Perf. 13½x13¼
2020, Sept. 30   Litho.
1675 A804 15p multi   1.00   .75
Dated 2017.

Dominican School of Notaries, 50th Anniv. (in 2017) — A805

Perf. 13½x13¼
2020, Sept. 30   Litho.
1676 A805 20p multi   1.30 1.00

Musicians and Composers — A806

No. 1677: a, Salvador Sturla (1891-1975), musician. b, Luis Alberti (1906-76), musician. c, Juan Lockward (1915-2006), singer. d, Manuel Troncoso (1927-2012), composer.

Perf. 13¼x13½
2020, Sept. 30   Litho.
1677 A806 20p Block of 4, #a-d   5.00 4.00
Dated 2017.

Juan Antonio Alix Rodríguez (1833-1918), Writer — A807

2020, Sept. 30   Litho.   Imperf.
1678 A807 100p multi   5.25 4.00
Dated 2018.

Souvenir Sheet

Juan Hipolito Yrigoyen (1852-1933), President of Argentina — A808

2020, Oct. 28   Litho.   Perf. 13¼x13
1679 A808 100p multi + 2 labels 5.25 4.00
Order of Yrigoyen for Argentine ship 9 de Julio to fly Dominican Republic flag in protest of American occupation of the Dominican Republic, cent.

Dr. Angel Amado Pared Gómez (1917-2016), Organizer of Merchants in National District — A809

2020, Nov. 3   Litho.   Perf. 13¼x13
1680 A809 42p multi   2.40 2.00
A column of perforations was placed in the middle of the stamp.

Rosa Duarte Díez (1820-88), Independence Activist and Sister of Pres. Juan Pablo Duarte — A810

2020, Dec. 16   Litho.   Perf. 13½
1681 A810 60p multi   2.40 2.25

Manuel Bello Cabral (1927-91), Philatelic Publisher, and Dominican Republic No. C198 — A811

2021, Jan. 20   Litho.   Perf. 13½
1682 A811 60p multi   3.00 2.50
Stamp Day. Dated 2020.

María Trinidad Sánhez (1794-1845), National Heroine — A812

2021, Mar. 9   Litho.   Imperf.
1683 A812 200p multi   9.50 8.00
Dated 2020.

Ludwig van Beethoven (1770-1827), Composer A813

2021, Mar. 19   Litho.   Perf. 13½
1684 A813 250p multi   11.50 10.00
Dated 2020.

Diplomatic Relations Between Dominican Republic and Morocco, 60th Anniv. — A814

No. 1685: a, 60p, Kasbah of the Oudaias, Rabat, Morocco. b, 72p, Alcázar de Colón, Santo Domingo.

2021, Mar. 25   Litho.   Perf. 13x13¼
1685 A814 Horiz. pair, #a-b   6.50 5.50
Dated 2020. See Morocco No. 1298.

Hotel Tortuga Bay and 50th Anniversary Emblem of Grupo Puntacana A815

2021, June 11   Litho.   Perf. 13½
1686 A815 42p multi   2.25 1.50
Dated 2020.

Juan Pablo Duarte (1813-77), Giuseppe Garibaldi (1807-82) and Flags of Dominican Republic and Italy — A816

2021, July 7   Litho.   Imperf.
1687 A816 60p multi   3.25 3.00
Diplomatic relations between Dominican Republic and Italy. Dated 2019.

Gregorio Urbano Gilbert Suero (1898-1970), Guerilla Fighter Against United States Occupations of Dominican Republic — A817

2021, July 12   Litho.   Perf. 13½
1688 A817 100p multi   5.25 4.50

Dominican Academy of History, 90th Anniv. — A818

2021, Aug. 4   Litho.   Perf. 13x13¼
1689 A818 60p multi   3.25 2.50

Pedro Henriquez Ureña National Library, 50th Anniv. — A819

2021, Sept. 16   Litho.   Perf. 13½
1690 A819 50p multi   2.75 2.50

Architects — A820

Designs: No. 1691, 60p, Mario Rafael Lluberes Abreu (1906-67) and Herrera Báez Residence. No. 1692, 60p, Edgardo Vega Malagón (1924-99) and Banco Nacional de la Vivienda

2021, Nov. 4   Litho.   Perf. 13¼x13
1691-1692 A820 Set of 2   6.50 6.00
America issue. A column of perforations runs through the center of Nos. 1691 and 1692.

Miniature Sheet

Architecture of Marcial (1905-76) and Leo Pou Ricart (1908-65) — A821

No. 1693: a, Dr. Martos Anti-tuberculosis Hospital, 1942. b, Education Secretariat building, 1944. c, Salomé Ureña Institute, 1944. d, Dr. Morgan Hospital, 1946. e, Odontology Faculty Building of the University of Santo Domingo, 1949. f, Men's Normal School, 1950.

2021, Nov. 4   Litho.   Perf. 13½x13¼
1693 A821 15p Sheet of 6, #a-f, + 6 labels   6.00 4.50

Larimar, National Mineral of the Dominican Republic — A822

2021, Nov. 22   Litho.   Perf. 13¼x13
1694 A822 20p multi   1.25 1.00

José Núñez de Cáceres (1772-1846), Leader of Independence Movement — A823

2021, Dec. 1   Litho.   Perf. 13¼
1695 A823 200p multi   10.00 8.00

Independence of Central America, 200th Anniv. — A824

2021, Dec. 17   Litho.   Imperf.
1696 A824 200p multi   10.00 8.00

Independence of Mexico, 200th Anniv. — A825

Perf. 13½x13¼
2021, Dec. 21   Litho.
1697 A825 200p multi   10.00 8.00

Dr. Antonio Zaglul (1920-96), Psychiatrist — A826

2021, Dec. 23   Litho.   Perf. 13¼
1698 A826 100p multi   5.25 4.00

Type A6 Redrawn With Denominations in Pesos and "2020" Year Date — A827

Color of denomination numerals: 15p, Yellow green. 25p, Red. 45p, Bright mauve. 60p, Bister.

2022, Feb. 7   Litho.   Rouletted 5
1699-1702 A827 Set of 4   5.50 5.50
Dated 2020.

Dominican Republic Coats of Arms — A828

Coat of arms from: No. 1703, 15p, 1844 (with cannons). No. 1704, 15p, 1844 (without cannons). No. 1705, 15p, 1848 (foliage around arms). No. 1706, 15p, 1848 (blue banner above arms). No. 1707, 15p, 1849. No. 1708, 15p, 1853. No. 1709, 15p, 1857. No. 1710, 15p, 1860. No. 1711, 15p, 1864. No. 1712, 15p, 1866. No. 1713, 15p, 1867. No. 1714, 15p, 1870. No. 1715, 15p, 1874. No. 1716, 15p, 1886. No. 1717, 15p, 1889. No. 1718, 15p, 1898. No. 1719, 15p, 1905. No. 1720, 15p, 1909. No. 1721, 15p, 1913. No. 1722, 15p, 1914. No. 1723, 15p, 1943. No. 1724, 15p, 1983. No. 1725, 15p, 2010.

2022, Feb. 7   Litho.   Perf. 13½
1703-1725 A828 Set of 23   13.00 13.00
Dated 2021.

Fire Fighting A829

No. 1726: a, Firefighters on aerial ladder at building fire. b, Rescue vehicle. c, Fire station, San Pedro de Macorís. d, Firefighter spraying water.

2022, Mar. 11   Litho.   Perf. 13x13¼
1726 A829 15p Block of 4, #a-d   2.25 2.25

Miguel Canela Lázaro (1894-1977), Physician, and Ankle Showing Rouvière-Canela Ligament — A830

2022, May 3   Litho.   Perf. 13½
1727 A830 20p multi   .75 .75
Dated 2020.

Ana Emilia Abigail Mejía Soliere (1895-1941), Educator and Feminist — A831

2022, May 3   Litho.   Perf. 13½
1728 A831 100p multi   3.75 3.75
Dated 2020.

Constitutional Court — A832

2022, June 23   Litho.   Perf. 13½
1729 A832 75p multi   2.75 2.75
Dated 2021.

Central Bank of the Dominican Republic, 75th Anniv. — A833

2022, July 19   Litho.   Perf. 13¼x13
1730 A833 75p multi   2.75 2.75

Santo Domingo Technological Institute, 50th Anniv. — A834

2022, Aug. 10   Litho.   Perf. 13½
1731 A834 50p multi   1.90 1.90

Coronation of the Virgin of Altagracia Icon, Cent. — A835

2022, Sept. 6   Litho.   Perf. 13½
1732 A835 100p multi   3.75 3.75

A836

Miguel de Cervantes (1547-1616), Writer — A837

No. 1733: a, Cervantes, denomination at UL. b, Drawing of Don Quixote and his horse, Rocinante, denomination at UR. c, Drawing of Don Quixote and his horse, denomination at UL. d, Cervantes, denomination at UR.

Perf. 13¼x13½
2022, Sept. 29   Litho.
1733 A836 100p Block of 4, #a-d   15.00 15.00
Imperf
1734 A837 75p multi   3.00 3.00

Enriquillo (c.1500-c. 1536), Taíno Cacique Who Led Rebellions Against Spaniards A838

2022, Oct. 5   Litho.   Perf. 13½
1735 A838 60p multi   2.25 2.25

Altagracia Casandra Damirón Santana (1919-83), Singer — A839

2022, Oct. 13   Litho.   Perf. 13½
1736 A839 100p multi   3.75 3.75
Dated 2019.

Market, Painting by Fernando Arturo Báez González (1895-1960) — A840

2022, Oct. 18   Litho.   Perf. 13¼x13½
1737 A840 42p multi   1.60 1.60

A column of perforations runs through the center of No. 1737.

Werner Gunther Hennig (1920-2016), Philatelist — A841

2022, Oct. 18   Litho.   Perf. 13½
1738 A841 60p multi   2.25 2.25
Stamp Day.

A842

Paintings A843

No. 1739: a, Peasant House, by Yoryi Morel (1906-79). b, Old Man, by Hilario Rodriguez (1936-87). c, Untitled 1969 painting by Clara Ledesma (1924-99). d, Bride, by Jorge Severino (1935-2020).
No. 1740: a, Crazy Cow, by Alberto Ulloa (1950-2011). b, Sowers, by Dionisio Blanco. c, Ingenuity, by Guillo Pérez (1923-2014). d, Untitled 1967 painting by Ledesma, horiz.

2022, Oct. 18   Litho.   Perf. 13¼x13
1739 A842 42p Block of 4, #a-d   6.25 6.25
Perf. 13x13¼
1740 A843 42p Block of 4, #a-d   6.25 6.25
America issue.

DOMINICAN REPUBLIC

Constituents' Monument, San Cristóbal — A844

2022, Nov. 3   Litho.   *Perf. 13½*
1741 A844 200p multi   7.50 7.50

Granting of municipal status to San Cristóbal, 200th anniv.

Tenth Census — A845

2022, Nov. 4   Litho.   *Perf. 13x13¼*
1742 A845 60p multi   2.25 2.25

First Revolt of African Slaves in the Americas, 500th Anniv. (in 2021) — A846

Perf. 13½x13¼   Litho.
2022, Nov. 15
1743 A846 100p multi   3.75 3.75

Soccer and Baseball Players — A847

Perf. 13½x13¼
2022, Dec. 13   Litho.
1744 A847 100p multi   3.75 3.75

Friendship and cooperation between Dominican Republic and Brazil.

Tourist Attractions — A848

2022   Litho.   *Perf. 13x13¼*
1745 A848 25p Block of 4, #a-d   3.75 3.75

America issue. Dated 2021.

No. 1745: a, Statue and buildings, Santo Domingo. b, Boats on shore of Cayo Arena. c, La Caleta Underwater National Park. d, Columbus Lighthouse, Santo Domingo Este.

Rafael Fradique Lizardo Barinas (1930-97), Folklorist — A851

2023, Apr. 18   Litho.   *Perf. 13x13¼*
1748 A851 20p multi   .75 .75

Dated 2022.

United Nations, 75th Anniv. (in 2020) — A852

2023, Apr. 18   Litho.   *Perf. 13½*
1749 A852 75p multi   2.75 2.75

Dated 2020.

United Nations Food and Agriculture Organization, 75th Anniv. (in 2021) — A853

2023, Apr. 18   Litho.   *Perf. 13½*
1750 A853 75p multi   2.75 2.75

Dated 2021.

Women Writers — A854

No. 1751: a, Joséfa Antonia Perdomo y Heredia (1834-96), poet. b, Amelia Francisca Marchena Sánchez (1850-1941), novelist. c, Virginia Elena Ortea Mella (1866-1903), journalist and novelist. d, Flérida Lamarche Henríquez de Nolasco (1891-1976), folklorist and historian.

2023, Apr. 18   Litho.   *Perf. 13x13¼*
1751 A854 20p Block of 4, #a-d   3.00 3.00

Dated 2022.

Fourth International Convention of Historians and Numismatists, Santo Domingo — A856

2023, June 28   Litho.   *Perf. 13½*
1753 A856 100p multi   3.75 3.75

Sinking of the USS Memphis in Santo Domingo Harbor, 107th Anniv. — A857

2023, July 6   Litho.   *Perf. 13½*
1754 A857 60p multi   2.25 2.25

SEMI-POSTAL STAMPS

Catalogue values for unused stamps in this section are for Never Hinged items.

Nos. 474-478 Surcharged in Red

Engraved and Lithographed
1957, Feb. 8   Unwmk.   *Perf. 11½*
Flags in National Colors

B1	A117	1c + 2c brn, lt bl, vio & mar	.60	.40
B2	A117	2c + 2c dk brn, lt bl & vio	.60	.40
B3	A117	3c + 2c red lilac & red	.60	.40
B4	A117	5c + 2c red orange & vio	.60	.40
B5	A117	7c + 2c green & violet	.75	.50
		Nos. B1-B5,CB1-CB3 (8)	5.85	3.90

The surtax was to aid Hungarian refugees. A similar 25c surcharge was applied to the miniature sheets described in the footnote following No. 478. Value, 2 sheets, perf. and imperf., $45

Nos. 479-483 Surcharged in Red Orange

1957, Sept. 9   Photo.   *Perf. 13½*
Flags in National Colors

B6	A118	1c + 2c brown & brt bl	.40	.30
B7	A118	2c + 2c org ver & dk bl	.50	.35
B8	A118	3c + 2c dark blue	.55	.40
B9	A118	5c + 2c olive & dk bl	.75	.55
B10	A118	7c + 2c rose brn & dk bl	.85	.60
		Nos. B6-B10,CB4-CB6 (8)	6.65	4.15

Cent. of the birth of Lord Baden Powell and the 50th anniv. of the Scout Movement. The surtax was for the Dominican Republic Boy Scouts.

A similar 5c surcharge was applied to the miniature sheets described in the footnote following No. 483. Value 4 sheets, perf. and imperf., medal and flag, $66.50

Types of Olympic Regular Issue, 1957, Surcharged in Carmine

a

b

1958, May 26   Engr. & Litho.
Flags in National Colors
Pink Paper

B11	A119(a)	1c + 2c red brown	.45	.30
B12	A119(b)	1c + 2c red brown	.45	.30
B13	A120(a)	2c + 2c gray brown	.60	.40
B14	A120(b)	2c + 2c gray brown	.60	.40
B15	A119(a)	3c + 2c violet	.60	.40
B16	A119(b)	3c + 2c violet	.60	.40
B17	A120(a)	5c + 2c red orange	.85	.55
B18	A120(b)	5c + 2c red orange	.85	.55
B19	A119(a)	7c + 2c Prus green	.95	.65
B20	A119(b)	7c + 2c Prus green	.95	.65
		Nos. B11-B20,CB7-CB12 (16)	10.10	7.80

Surtax for the UN Relief and Works Agency for Palestine Refugees.

A similar 5c surcharge, plus marginal United Nations emblem and "UNRWA," was applied to the miniature sheets described in the footnote following No. 488. Value, 4 sheets, perf. and imperf., $20.

Nos. 501-505 Surcharged

Perf. 13½
1959, Apr. 13   Photo.   Unwmk.
Flags in National Colors

B21	A125	1c + 2c rose, indigo & ultra	.60	.45
B22	A125	1c + 2c brown & blue	.60	.45
B23	A125	3c + 2c gray, vio, blk & buff	.70	.55
B24	A125	5c + 2c rose, dk bl, brn & red	.90	.70
B25	A125	7c + 2c lt brn, dk bl & red	1.00	.80
		Nos. B21-B25,CB13-CB15 (8)	8.30	6.45

International Geophysical Year, 1957-58.

A similar 5c surcharge was applied to the miniature sheets described in the footnote following No. 505. Value, 2 sheets, perf. and imperf., $40.

Type of 1957 Surcharged in Red

Engraved and Lithographed
1959, Sept. 10   Unwmk.   *Imperf.*
Flags in National Colors

B26	A117	1c + 2c brn, lt bl, vio & mar	.55	.40
B27	A117	2c + 2c dk brn, lt bl & vio	.55	.40
B28	A117	3c + 2c red lilac & red	.65	.45
B29	A117	5c + 2c red org & vio	.65	.45
B30	A117	7c + 2c green & violet	.80	.55
		Nos. B26-B30,CB16-CB18 (8)	6.80	4.85

3rd Pan American Games, Chicago, Aug. 27-Sept. 7, 1959.

Nos. 522-524 Surcharged in Red

1960, Apr. 7   Litho.   *Perf. 12½*
Center in Gray

B31	A135	5c + 5c red brn & yel grn	.50	.35
B32	A135	9c + 5c car & lt bl	.50	.35
B33	A135	13c + 5c org & grn	1.20	.80
		Nos. B31-B33,CB19-CB20 (5)	3.55	2.40

World Refugee Year, July 1, 1959-June 30, 1960. The surtax was for aid to refugees. Souvenir sheets exist perf. and imperf., containing one each of Nos. B31-B33 and CB19-CB20. Value, 2 sheets, perf. and imperf., $13.50

Nos. 525-529 Surcharged

1962, Jan. 8   Photo.   *Perf. 13½*
Flags in National Colors

B34	A136	1c + 2c red, yel grn & blk	.55	.35
B35	A136	2c + 2c org, grnsh bl & brn	.55	.35
B36	A136	3c + 2c henna brn & bl	.55	.35
B37	A136	5c + 2c brown & ultra	.55	.35
B38	A136	7c + 2c grn, bl & rose brn	.55	.35
		Nos. B34-B38,CB21-CB23 (8)	4.90	3.10

15th anniv. (in 1961) of UNESCO.

A similar 5c surcharge was applied to the miniature sheets described in the footnote following No. 529. Value, 2 sheets, perf. and imperf., $20.

Anti-Malaria Type of 1962
1962, Apr. 29   Litho.   *Perf. 12*

B39	A141	10c + 2c brt pink & red lil	.50	.40
B40	A141	20c + 2c pale brn & brn	.75	.55

DOMINICAN REPUBLIC

Freedom from Hunger Type of 1963
1963, Apr. 15   Unwmk.   Perf. 11½
Banner in Dark Blue & Red

B41	A148 2c + 1c green	.60	.35
B42	A148 5c + 2c brt rose lil	.60	.35
B43	A148 9c + 2c orange	.60	.35
	Nos. B41-B43 (3)	1.80	1.05

A souvenir sheet contains three imperf. stamps similar to Nos. B41-B43. Value, $2.25.

Nos. 591-593 Surcharged

1964, Mar. 8   Perf. 12½

B44	A153 3c + 2c pale pink & ver	.65	.35
B45	A153 6c + 2c pale bl & ultra	.65	.35
B46	A153 9c + 2c pale rose & red brn	.65	.35
	Nos. B44-B46,CB26-CB27 (5)	3.30	1.80

UNESCO world campaign to save historic monuments in Nubia.

Nos. 622-626 Surcharged

1966, Dec. 9   Litho.   Perf. 12½
Size: 31x21mm

B47	A164 1c + 2c multi	8.75	1.25
B48	A164 2c + 2c multi	8.75	1.25
B49	A164 3c + 2c multi	8.75	1.25
B50	A164 6c + 4c multi	8.75	1.25
B51	A164 8c + 4c multi	8.75	1.25
	Nos. B47-B51,CB28-CB30 (8)	58.00	14.00

Surtax for victims of Hurricane Inez.

AIR POST STAMPS

 Map of Hispaniola AP1

Perf. 11½
1928, May 31   Litho.   Unwmk.

C1	AP1 10c deep ultra	5.25	2.50

1930

C2	AP1 10c ocher	3.50	3.00
a.	Vert. pair, imperf. btwn.	600.00	
C3	AP1 15c scarlet	6.75	4.00
C4	AP1 20c green	3.25	.85
C5	AP1 30c redsh vio	6.75	4.50
	Nos. C2-C5 (4)	20.25	12.35

Nos. C2-C5 have only "CENTAVOS" in lower panel. Issued: 10c, 20c, 1/24; 15c, 30c, 2/14.

1930

C6	AP1 10c light blue	1.75	.60
C7	AP1 15c blue green	3.25	1.00
C8	AP1 20c org brown	3.50	.85
a.	Horiz. pair, imperf. vert.	450.00	450.00
C9	AP1 30c brown	6.25	1.75
	Nos. C6-C9 (4)	14.75	4.20

Issue dates: 10c, 15c, 20c, Sept.; 30c, Oct.

  Batwing Sundial Erected in 1753 — AP2

1931-33   Perf. 12

C10	AP2 10c carmine	3.50	.50
C11	AP2 10c light blue	1.75	.50
C12	AP2 10c dp bl grn	6.25	2.75
C13	AP2 15c rose lilac	2.75	.50
C14	AP2 20c dark blue	6.25	2.25
a.	Numerals reading up at left and down at right	5.75	2.75
b.	Imperf., pair	250.00	

C15	AP2 30c turq grn	2.50	.25
C16	AP2 50c red brown	6.25	.50
C17	AP2 1p deep orange	10.00	2.75
	Nos. C10-C17 (8)	39.25	10.00

Issued: No. C11, 7/2/32; No. C12, 5/28/33; others 8/16.

 Airplane and Ozama Fortress — AP3

1933, Nov. 20

C18	AP3 10c dark blue	3.50	.60

 Airplane and Trujillo Bridge — AP4

1934, Sept. 20

C19	AP4 10c dark blue	3.00	.50

 Symbolic of Flight — AP5

1935, Apr. 29

C20	AP5 10c lt blue & dk blue	1.60	.50

 AP6

1936, Feb. 11   Perf. 11½

C21	AP6 10c dk bl & turq grn	2.50	.50

 Allegory of Flight — AP7

1936, Oct. 17

C22	AP7 10c dk bl, grnsh bl & turq bl	2.25	.40

 Macoris Airport AP8

1937, Oct. 22

C23	AP8 10c green	1.00	.35

 Fleet of Columbus AP9

 Air Fleet — AP10

 Proposed Columbus Lighthouse AP11

1937, Nov. 9   Perf. 12

C24	AP9 10c rose red	1.75	1.40
C25	AP10 15c purple	1.40	.95
C26	AP11 20c dk bl & lt bl	1.40	1.25
C27	AP10 25c red violet	2.00	1.25
C28	AP11 30c yellow green	1.75	1.25
C29	AP10 50c brown	3.50	1.75

C30	AP11 75c dk olive grn	10.50	10.50
C31	AP9 1p orange	6.25	2.50
	Nos. C24-C31 (8)	28.55	20.85

Goodwill flight to all American countries by the planes "Colon", "Pinta", "Nina" and "Santa Maria."

No. C30 was reproduced imperf. on No. 1019.

 Pan American Clipper — AP12

1938, July 30

C32	AP12 10c green	1.25	.40

 Trylon and Perisphere, Plane and Proposed Columbus Lighthouse AP13

1939, Apr. 30

C33	AP13 10c green & lt green	2.00	.85

New York World's Fair.

 Airplane AP14

1939, Oct. 18

C34	AP14 10c green & dp green	1.60	.40
a.	Pair, imperf. btwn.	450.00	

 Proposed Columbus Lighthouse, Plane and Caravels AP15

 Christopher Columbus and Proposed Lighthouse AP16

 Proposed Lighthouse AP17

 Christopher Columbus AP18

 Caravel AP19

1940, Oct. 12

C35	AP15 10c sapphire & lt bl	1.10	.60
C36	AP16 15c org brn & brn	1.60	1.00
C37	AP17 20c rose red & red	1.60	1.00
C38	AP18 25c brt red lil & red vio	1.60	.50
C39	AP19 50c green & lt green	3.00	1.75
	Nos. C35-C39 (5)	8.90	4.85

Discovery of America by Columbus and proposed Columbus memorial lighthouse in Dominican Republic.

 Posts and Telegraph Building, San Cristobal — AP20

1941, Feb. 21

C40	AP20 10c brt red lil & pale lil rose	.50	.35

 Globe, Wing and Letter — AP21

1942, Feb. 13

C41	AP21 10c dark violet brn	.60	.30
C42	AP21 75c deep orange	3.25	2.00

 Plane — AP22

1943, Sept. 1

C43	AP22 10c brt red lilac	.40	.25
C44	AP22 20c dp blue & blue	.40	.25
C45	AP22 25c yellow olive	5.75	3.25
	Nos. C43-C45 (3)	6.55	3.75

 Plane, Flag, Coat of Arms and Torch of Liberty — AP23

1944, Feb. 27   Perf. 11½
Flag in Gray, Dark Blue, Carmine

C46	AP23 10c multicolored	.35	.25
C47	AP23 20c multicolored	.45	.25
C48	AP23 1p multicolored	2.00	1.50
	Nos. C46-C48 (3)	2.80	2.00

Centenary of Independence. See No. 407 for souvenir sheet listing.

 Communications Building, Ciudad Trujillo — AP24

1944, Nov. 12   Litho.   Perf. 12

C49	AP24 9c yel grn & blue	.25	.25
C50	AP24 13c dull brn & rose car	.25	.25
C51	AP24 25c org & dull red	.35	.25
b.	Vert. pair, imperf. btwn.	45.00	
C52	AP24 30c black & ultra	.75	.65
	Nos. C49-C52 (4)	1.60	1.40

Twenty booklets of 100 (25 panes of 4) of the 25c were issued. All booklets are still intact.

Communications Type
1945, Sept. 1
Center in Dark Blue and Carmine

C53	A92 7c deep yellow green	.35	.25
C54	A92 12c red orange	.40	.25
C55	A92 13c deep blue	.50	.25
C56	A92 25c orange brown	.90	.25
	Nos. C53-C56 (4)	2.15	1.00

AP26   Flags and National Anthem — AP27

Unwmk.
1946, Feb. 27   Litho.   Perf. 12
Center in Dark Blue, Deep Carmine and Black

C57	AP26 10c carmine	.95	.40
C58	AP26 15c blue	2.10	.85
C59	AP26 25c chocolate	2.50	.85
C60	AP26 35c orange	3.00	.95

275

DOMINICAN REPUBLIC

C61	AP27	1p grn, yel grn & cit	25.00	10.00
		Nos. C57-C61 (5)	33.55	13.05

Nos. C57-C61 exist imperf.

Map Type of Regular Issue
1946, Aug. 4

C62	A94	10c multicolored	.75	.35
C63	A94	13c multicolored	1.35	.35

Waterfall Type of Regular Issue
1947, Mar. 18   **Litho.**
Center Multicolored

C64	A95	18c light blue	1.00	.50
C65	A95	23c carmine	1.60	.60
C66	A95	50c red violet	2.10	.60
C67	A95	75c chocolate	3.00	1.10
		Nos. C64-C67 (4)	7.70	2.80

Palace Type of Regular Issue
1948, Feb. 27

C68	A96	37c orange brown	2.10	1.00
C69	A96	1p orange yellow	5.75	2.10

Ruins Type of Regular Issue
1949   **Unwmk.**   **Perf. 11½**

C70	A97	7c ol grn & pale ol grn	.40	.25
C71	A97	10c orange brn & buff	.40	.25
C72	A97	15c brt rose & pale pink	1.25	.40
C73	A97	20c green & pale green	1.75	.60
		Nos. C70-C73 (4)	3.80	1.40

Issue dates: 10c, Apr. 4; others, Apr. 13.

Las Carreras Monument — AP32

1949, Aug. 10

C74	AP32	10c red & pink	.75	.35

Cent. of the Battle of Las Carreras.

> **Catalogue values for unused stamps in this section, from this point to the end of the section, are for Never Hinged items.**

Hotel Type of Regular Issue
Hotels: 12c, Montana. 37c, San Cristobal.
1950, Sept. 8

C75	A100	12c dk blue & blue	.60	.25
C76	A100	37c carmine & pink	3.75	2.50

Map, Plane and Caduceus — AP34

1950, Oct. 2

C77	AP34	12c orange brn & yel	1.30	.35

13th Pan-American Health Conf. Exists imperf.

Hospital Type of Regular Issue
1952, Aug.

C78	A104	23c deep blue	1.40	1.20
C79	A104	29c carmine	4.00	2.25

Columbus Lighthouse and Plane — AP36

1953, Jan. 6   **Engr.**   **Perf. 13**

C80	AP36	12c ocher	.55	.30
C81	AP36	14c dark blue	.55	.30
C82	AP36	20c black brown	1.30	.60
C83	AP36	23c deep plum	.75	.40
C84	AP36	25c dark blue	1.75	.70
C85	AP36	29c deep green	1.30	.60

C86	AP36	1p red brown	3.75	1.25
a.		Miniature sheet of 10	77.50	75.00
		Nos. C80-C86 (7)	9.95	4.15

No. C86a is lithographed and contains Nos. 450-452 and C80-C86, in slightly different shades. Sheet measures 190x130mm and is imperf. with simulated perforations.
A miniature sheet similar to No. C86a, but measuring 200x163mm and in folder, exists. Value $130.

Ano Mariano Initials in Monogram — AP37

1954, Aug. 5   **Litho.**   **Perf. 11½**

C87	AP37	8c claret	.40	.25
C88	AP37	11c blue	.50	.25
C89	AP37	33c brown orange	1.60	.60
		Nos. C87-C89 (3)	2.50	1.10

Marian Year. Nos. C87-C89 exist imperf.

Rotary Type of Regular Issue
1955, Feb. 23   **Perf. 12**

C90	A110	11c rose red	.75	.35

Flags — AP39

Portraits of General Hector B. Trujillo: 25c, In civilian clothes. 33c, In uniform.

1955, May 16   **Engr.**   **Perf. 13½x13**

C91	AP39	11c blue, yel & car	1.00	.25
C92	AP39	25c rose violet	1.75	.30
C93	AP39	33c brown orange	2.50	.50
		Nos. C91-C93 (3)	5.25	1.05

The center of No. C91 is litho. 25th anniv. of the inauguration of the Trujillo era.

Fair Type of Regular Issue
1955, Dec. 20   **Unwmk.**   **Perf. 13**

C94	A112	11c vermilion	.85	.35

ICAO Type of Regular Issue
1956, Apr. 6   **Litho.**   **Perf. 12½**

C95	A114	11c ultra	1.75	.35

Tree Type of Regular Issue
Design: 13c, Mahogany tree.

1956, Dec. 8   **Litho.**   **Perf. 11½x12**

C96	A115	13c orange & green	2.50	.35

Type of Regular Issue, 1957
Olympic Winners and Flags: 11c, Paavo Nurmi, Finland. 16c, Ugo Frigerio, Italy. 17c, Mildred Didrikson ("Didrickson" on stamp), US.

Engraved and Lithographed
Perf. 11½, Imperf.
1957, Jan. 24   **Unwmk.**
Flags in National Colors

C97	A117	11c ultra & red org	.45	.35
C98	A117	16c carmine & It grn	.50	.35
C99	A117	17c black, vio & red	.70	.35
		Nos. C97-C99 (3)	1.65	1.05

16th Olympic Games, Melbourne, Nov. 22-Dec. 8, 1956.
Souvenir sheets of 3 exist, perf. and imperf., containing Nos. C97-C99. Value, 2 sheets, perf. & imperf., $15.
For surcharges see Nos. CB1-CB3, CB16-CB18.

Type of Regular Issue
Olympic Winners and Flags: 11c, Robert Morrow, US, 100 & 200 meter dash. 16c, Chris Brasher, England, steeplechase. 17c, A. Ferreira Da Silva, Brazil, hop, step and jump.

Perf. 13½, Imperf.
1957, July 18   **Photo.**
Flags in National Colors

C100	A118	11c yellow grn & dk bl	.40	.35
C101	A118	16c lilac & dk blue	.50	.35
C102	A118	17c brown & blue grn	.60	.35
		Nos. C100-C102 (3)	1.50	1.05

1956 Olympic winners.

See note on miniature sheets following No. 483.
For surcharges see Nos. CB4-CB6.

Types of Regular Issue
Olympic Winners and Flags: 11c, Hans Winkler, Germany, individual jumping. 16c, Alfred Oerter, US, discus throw. 17c, Shirley Strickland, Australia, 800 meter hurdles.

Engraved and Lithographed
Perf. 13½, Imperf.
1957, Nov. 12   **Unwmk.**
Flags in National Colors

C103	A119	11c ultra	.45	.35
C104	A120	16c rose carmine	.70	.35
C105	A119	17c claret	.70	.35
		Nos. C103-C105 (3)	1.85	1.05

1956 Olympic winners.
Miniature sheets of 3 exist, perf. and imperf., containing Nos. C103-C105. Value, 2 sheets, perf. and imperf., $5.50.
For surcharges see Nos. CB7-CB12.

Type of Regular Issue
Olympic Winners and Flags: 11c, Charles Jenkins, 400 & 800 meter run, and Thomas Courtney, 1,600 meter relay, US. 16c, Field hockey team, India. 17c, Yachting team, Sweden.

Perf. 13½, Imperf.
1958, Oct. 30   **Unwmk.**   **Photo.**
Flags in National Colors

C106	A125	11c blue, olive & brn	.55	.35
C107	A125	16c lt grn, org & dk bl	.65	.35
C108	A125	17c ver, blue & yel	.65	.35
		Nos. C106-C108 (3)	1.85	1.05

1956 Olympic winners.
Miniature sheets of 3 exist, perf. and imperf., containing Nos. C106-C108. Value, 2 sheets, perf. and imperf., $5.
For surcharges see Nos. CB13-CB15.

Fair Type of Regular Issue
1958, Dec. 9   **Litho.**   **Perf. 12½**

C109	A127	9c gray	.45	.35
C110	A127	25c lt violet	1.25	.40
a.		Souv. sheet of 3, #C109-C110, 507, imperf.	2.25	2.25

Polo Type of Regular Issue
1959, May 15   **Perf. 12**

C111	A130	11c Dominican polo team	.60	.35

"San Cristobal" Plane — AP42

Perf. 11½
1960, Feb. 25   **Unwmk.**   **Litho.**

C112	AP42	13c org, bl, grn & gray	.75	.35

Dominican Civil Aviation.

Children and WRY Emblem AP43

1960, Apr. 7   **Perf. 12½**

C113	AP43	10c plum, gray & grn	.95	.35
C114	AP43	13c gray & green	1.40	.35

World Refugee Year, 7/1/59-6/30/60.
For surcharges see Nos. CB19-CB20.

Olympic Type of Regular Issue
Olympic Winners: 11c, Pat McCormick, US, diving. 16c, Mithat Bayrack, Turkey, welterweight wrestling. 17c, Ursula Happe, Germany, 200 meter breast stroke.

Perf. 13½, Imperf.
1960, Sept. 14   **Photo.**
Flags in National Colors

C115	A136	11c blue, gray & brn	.60	.35
C116	A136	16c red, brown & ol	.60	.35
C117	A136	17c black, blue & ocher	.60	.35
		Nos. C115-C117 (3)	1.80	1.05

17th Olympic Games, Rome, 8/25-9/11.

Miniature sheets of 3 exist, perf. and imperf., containing Nos. C115-C117. Value, 2 sheets, perf. and imperf. $3.75.
For surcharges see Nos. CB21-CB23.

Coffee-Cacao Type of Regular Issue
1961, Dec. 30   **Litho.**   **Perf. 12½**

C118	A140	13c orange ver	.55	.35
C119	A140	33c brt yellow	1.25	.85

Nos. C118-C119 exist imperf.

Anti-Malaria Type of Regular Issue
1962, Apr. 29   **Unwmk.**   **Perf. 12**

C120	A141	13c pink & red	.65	.25
C121	A141	33c org & dp org	1.30	.50

See Nos. CB24-CB25.

Type of Regular Issue
Designs: 13c, Broken fetters and laurel. 50c, Flag, torch and inscription.

1962, May 30   **Perf. 12½**

C122	A142	13c brn, yel, ol, ultra & red	.45	.30
C123	A142	50c rose lilac, ultra & red	1.60	1.00

No. C122 exists imperf.

UPAE Type of Regular Issue
1962, Oct. 23   **Perf. 12½**

C124	A146	13c bright blue	.65	.35
C125	A146	22c dull red brown	.90	.35

Nos. C124-C125 exist imperf.

Nouel Type of Regular Issue
Design: Frame altered with rosary and cross surrounding portrait.

1962, Dec. 18

C126	A147	13c blue & pale blue	.55	.35
C127	A147	25c vio & pale vio	.85	.50
a.		Souv. sheet, #C126-C127, imperf	2.00	1.25

Nos. C126-C127 exist imperf.

Sanchez, Duarte, Mella — AP44

1963, July 7   **Litho.**   **Perf. 11½x12**

C128	AP44	15c orange	.75	.35

120th anniv. of separation from Haiti.

World Map — AP45

1963, Oct. 25   **Unwmk.**   **Perf. 12½**

C129	AP45	10c gray & carmine	.75	.35

Cent. of Intl. Red Cross. Exists imperf.

Human Rights Type
1963, Dec. 10   **Litho.**

C130	A152	7c fawn & red brn	.45	.35
C131	A152	10c lt blue & blue	.45	.35

Nos. C130-C131 exist imperf.

Ramses II Battling the Hittites (from Abu Simbel) — AP46

1964, Mar. 8   **Perf. 12½**

C132	AP46	10c brt violet	.45	.35
C133	AP46	13c yellow	.45	.35

UNESCO world campaign to save historic monuments in Nubia.
Nos. C132-C133 exist imperf.
For surcharges see Nos. CB26-CB27.

DOMINICAN REPUBLIC

Striated
Woodpecker
AP47

1964, June 8   Litho.
C134   AP47   10c multicolored   6.00   .35

Type of Space Issue
Designs: 7c, Rocket leaving earth. 10c, Space capsule orbiting earth.

1964, July 28   Unwmk.   Perf. 12½
C135   A156   7c brt green   .50   .35
C136   A156   10c violet blue   .65   .30
     a.   Souvenir sheet   4.75   4.25

No. C136a contains 7c and 10c stamps similar to Nos. C135-C136 with simulated perforations.

Pres. John F.
Kennedy — AP48

1964, Nov. 22   Perf. 11½
C137   AP48   10c buff & dk brown   .85   .35

President John F. Kennedy (1917-63). Sheets of 10 (5x2) and sheets of 50.

UPU Type of Regular Issue
1964, Dec. 5   Litho.   Perf. 12½
C138   A157   7c blue   .50   .35

ICY Type of Regular Issue
1965, Feb. 16   Unwmk.   Perf. 12½
C139   A158   10c lilac & violet   .75   .35

Basilica of Our
Lady of
Altagracia
AP49

1965, Mar. 18   Unwmk.   Perf. 12½
C140   AP49   10c multicolored   .80   .35

Fourth Mariological Congress and the Eleventh International Marian Congress.

Abraham
Lincoln — AP50

1965, Apr. 15   Litho.   Perf. 12½
C141   AP50   17c bright blue   .90   .40

Cent. of the death of Abraham Lincoln.

Stamp Centenary Type of 1965
Design: Stamp of 1865, (No. 2).

1965, Dec. 28   Litho.   Perf. 12½
C142   A161   7c violet, lt grn & blk   .70   .35
C143   A161   10c yellow, lt grn & blk   .70   .35

ITU Emblem, Old
and New
Communication
Equipment — AP51

1966, Apr. 6   Litho.   Perf. 12½
C144   AP51   28c rose pink & scar   1.00   .85
C145   AP51   45c lt grn & dp grn   1.90   1.50

Cent. (in 1965) of the ITU.

Butterfly Type of Regular Issue
1966, Nov. 8   Litho.   Perf. 12½
Various Butterflies in Natural Colors
Size: 35x24mm
C146   A164   10c lt violet & violet   9.75   .75
C147   A164   50c org & dp org   12.50   1.50
C148   A164   75c pink & rose red   16.00   2.50
     Nos. C146-C148 (3)   38.25   4.75

For surcharges see Nos. CB28-CB30.

Altar Type of Regular Issue
1967, Jan. 18   Litho.   Perf. 11½
C149   A165   7c lt olive green   .60   .35
C150   A165   10c lilac   .60   .35
C151   A165   20c yellow brown   .75   .35
     Nos. C149-C151 (3)   1.95   1.05

Chess Type of Regular Issue
Design: 10c, Pawn and Bishop.

1967, June 23   Litho.   Perf. 12½
C152   A167   10c ol, lt ol & blk   1.40   .30
     a.   Souvenir sheet   10.50   5.00

No. C152a contains 2 imperf. stamps similar to Nos. 636 and C152.

Alliance for Progress Type
1967, Sept. 16   Litho.   Perf. 12½
C153   A168   8c gray   .75   .35
C154   A168   10c blue   .90   .35

Cornucopia and
Emblem — AP52

1967, Oct. 7
C155   AP52   12c multicolored   1.20   .75

25th anniversary of the Inter-American Agriculture Institute.

Satellite Type of Regular Issue
1968, June 15   Typo.   Perf. 12
C156   A170   10c dp blue & multi   .55   .35
C157   A170   15c purple & multi   .80   .35

Boxing Type of Regular Issue
Designs: Two views of boxing match.

1968, June 29
C158   A171   7c orange yel & grn   .85   .35
C159   A171   10c gray & blue   1.10   .35

See note after No. 641.

Lions Type of Regular Issue
1968, Aug. 9   Litho.   Perf. 11½
C160   A172   10c ultra & multi   .60   .35

Olympic Type of Regular Issue
Designs (Olympic Emblem and): 10c, Weight lifting. 33c, Pistol shooting.

1968, Nov. 12   Litho.   Perf. 11½
C161   A173   10c buff & multi   .45   .25
C162   A173   33c pink & multi   1.75   .75

Latin American
Flags — AP53

1969, Jan. 25   Litho.   Perf. 12½
C163   AP53   10c pink & multi   .75   .35

7th Inter-American Savings and Loan Conference, Santo Domingo, Jan. 25-31.

Taino Art Type of Regular Issue
7c, Various vomiting spoons with human heads, vert. 10c, Female torso forming drinking vessel. 20c, Vase with human head, vert.

1969, Jan. 31   Litho.   Perf. 12½
C164   A175   7c lt bl, bl & lem   .80   .35
C165   A175   10c pink, ver & brn   1.00   .35
C166   A175   20c yellow, org & brn   1.20   .35
     Nos. C164-C166 (3)   3.00   1.05

COTAL Type of Regular Issue
10c, Airport of the Americas and COTAL emblem.

1969, May 25   Litho.   Perf. 12½
C167   A178   10c brown & pale fawn   .65   .35

ILO Type of Regular Issue
1969, June 27   Litho.   Perf. 12½
C168   A179   10c rose, red & black   .65   .35

Baseball Type of Regular Issue
Designs: 7c, Bleachers, Tetelo Vargas Stadium, horiz. 10c, Batter, catcher and umpire. 1p, Quisqueya Stadium, horiz.

1969, Aug. 15   Litho.   Perf. 12½
Size: 43x30mm (7c, 1p); 21x31mm (10c)
C169   A180   7c magenta & org   .65   .30
C170   A180   10c mar & rose red   .75   .30
C171   A180   1p violet blue & brn   5.50   3.50
     Nos. C169-C171 (3)   6.90   4.10

Electrification Types of Regular Issue
Design: No. C172, Rio Haina steam plant. No. C173, Valdesa Dam.

1969   Litho.   Perf. 12
C172   A181   10c orange ver   .60   .30
C173   A182   10c multicolored   .65   .30

Issued: No. C172, Sept. 15; No. C173, Oct. 15.

Duarte Type of Regular Issue
1970, Jan. 26   Litho.   Perf. 12
C174   A183   10c brown & dk brown   1.20   .35

Census Type of Regular Issue
Design: 10c, Buildings and census emblem.

1970, Feb. 6   Perf. 11
C175   A184   10c lt blue & multi   1.20   .35

Sculpture Type of Regular Issue
Design: 10c, The Prisoner, by Abelardo Rodriguez Urdaneta, vert.

1970, Feb. 20   Litho.   Perf. 12½
C176   A186   10c bluish gray   .90   .35

Masonic Type of Regular Issue
1970, Mar. 2
C177   A187   10c brown   2.75   .35

Satellite Type of Regular Issue
1970, May 25   Litho.   Perf. 12½
C178   A188   7c blue & gray   .60   .35

UPU Type of Regular Issue
1970, June 5   Perf. 11
C179   A189   10c yellow & brown   .65   .35

Education Year Type of Regular Issue
1970, June 26   Litho.   Perf. 12½
C180   A190   15c bright pink   .90   .35

Dancers — AP54

Design: 10c, UN emblem and wheel.

1970, Oct. 12   Litho.   Perf. 12½
C181   AP54   7c blue & multi   .50   .35
C182   AP54   10c pink & multi   .75   .35

1st World Exhib. of Books and Culture Festival, Santo Domingo, Oct. 11-Dec. 11.

Album, Globe and
Emblem — AP55

1970, Oct. 26   Litho.   Perf. 11
C183   AP55   10c multicolored   .90   .35

EXFILCA 70, 2nd Interamerican Philatelic Exhibition, Caracas, Venezuela, 11/27-12/6.

Basilica of Our Lady of
Altagracia — AP56

1971, Jan. 20   Litho.   Perf. 12½
C184   AP56   17c multicolored   1.30   .45

Inauguration of the Basilica of Our Lady of Altagracia.

Map of Dominican
Republic, CARE
Package — AP57

1971, May 28   Litho.   Perf. 12½
C185   AP57   10c blue & green   .70   .35

25th anniversary of CARE, a US-Canadian Cooperative for American Relief Everywhere.

Sports Type of Regular Issue
1971, Sept. 10   Perf. 11
C186   A195   7c Volleyball   .70   .35

Animal Type of Regular Issue
Design: 25c, Cock and grain.

1971, Sept. 29   Perf. 12½
C187   A196   25c black & multi   3.50   .35

Independence Type
10c, Dominican-Colombian flag of 1821.

1971, Dec. 1   Perf. 11
C188   A197   10c vio bl, yel & red   1.10   .35

Christmas Type of Regular Issue
1971, Dec. 10   Perf. 12½
C189   A198   10c Bell, 1493   .55   .35

UNICEF Type of Regular Issue
Design: UNICEF emblem & child on beach.

1971, Dec. 14   Perf. 11
C190   A199   15c multicolored   .90   .35

Book Year Type of Regular Issue
1972, Jan. 25   Litho.   Perf. 12½
C191   A200   12c lilac, dk bl & red   1.20   .35

Magnifying Glass over
Peru on Map of
Americas — AP58

1972, Mar. 7   Litho.   Perf. 12
C192   AP58   10c blue & multi   .85   .35

EXFILIMA '71, 3rd Inter-American Philatelic Exposition, Lima, Peru, Nov. 6-14, 1971.

DOMINICAN REPUBLIC

"Your Heart is your Health" — AP59

1972, Apr. 27   Litho.   Perf. 11
C193 AP59 7c red & multi   .75   .35
World Health Day.

Taino Art Type of 1972
Taino Art: 8c, Ritual vessel showing human figures. 10c, Trumpet (shell). 25c, Carved vomiting spoons. All horiz.

1972, May 10   Litho.   Perf. 11
C194 A201 8c multicolored   .60   .35
C195 A201 10c lt blue & multi   .80   .35
C196 A201 25c multicolored   1.75   .50
Nos. C194-C196 (3)   3.15 1.20

Telecommunications Type of Regular Issue
1972, May 17   Perf. 12½
C197 A202 21c yellow & multi   1.20   .45

Exhibition Type of Regular Issue
1972, June 3
C198 A203 33c orange & multi   1.25   .55

Olympic Type of Regular Issue
1972, Aug. 25   Litho.   Perf. 12½
C199 A204 33c Running   1.50   .75

Club Type of Regular Issue
1972, Sept. 29   Litho.   Perf. 10½
C200 A205 20c blue & multi   1.10   .35

Morel Type of Regular Issue
1972, Oct. 20   Litho.   Perf. 12½
C201 A206 10c multicolored   .80   .35

Bank Type of Regular Issue
25c, 1947 silver coin, entrance to the Mint.

1972, Oct. 23
C202 A207 25c ocher & multi   1.75   .55

"La Navidad" Fortress, 1492 — AP60

1972, Nov. 21   Litho.   Perf. 12½
C203 AP60 10c multicolored   1.25   .30
Christmas 1972.

Sports Type of Regular Issue
Various sports; a, UL. b, UR. c, LL. d, LR.

1973, Mar. 30   Litho.   Perf. 13½x13
C204 A212 Block of 4   8.75 8.75
  a.-d.   8c, any single   1.00   .75
C205 A212 Block of 4   13.50 13.50
  a.-d.   10c, any single   2.00 1.50

Easter Type 1973
10c, Belfry of Church of Our Lady of Help.

1973, Apr. 18   Litho.   Perf. 10½
C206 A213 10c multi, vert.   1.20   .35

North and South America on Globe — AP61

1973, May 29   Litho.   Perf. 12
C207 AP61 7c multicolored   .70   .35
Pan-American Health Organization, 70th anniversary (in 1972).

WMO Type of Regular Issue
1973, Aug. 10   Litho.   Perf. 13½x13
C208 A214 7c green & multi   .80   .35

INTERPOL Emblem Police Scientist — AP62

1973, Sept. 28   Litho.   Perf. 10½
C209 AP62 10c vio bl, bl & emer .85   .35
50th anniversary of International Criminal Police Organization.

Handicraft Type of Regular Issue
1973, Oct. 12
C210 A215 7c Sailing ship, mosaic   1.10   .35
C211 A215 10c Maracas rattles, horiz. 1.50   .35

Christmas Type of Regular Issue
Design: 10c, Angels adoring Christ Child.

1973, Nov. 26   Litho.   Perf. 13½x13
C212 A216 10c multicolored   .85   .35

Scout Type of Regular Issue
21c, Scouts cooking, Lord Baden-Powell.

1973, Dec. 7   Litho.   Perf. 12
C213 A217 21c red & multi   1.25   .75

Sport Type of Regular Issue
10c, Olympic swimming pool and diver. 25c, Olympic Stadium, soccer and discus.

1974, Feb. 25   Litho.   Perf. 13½
C214 A218 10c blue & multi   .60   .35
C215 A218 25c multicolored   1.50   .35

The Last Supper — AP63

1974, June 27   Litho.   Perf. 13½
C216 AP63 10c multicolored   .65   .25
Holy Week 1974.

Bridge Type
Design: 10c, Higuamo Bridge.

1974, July 12   Perf. 12
C217 A221 10c multicolored   .95   .35

Diabetes Type
Map of Dominican Republic, Diabetics' Emblem and: 7c, Kidney. 33c, Eye & heart.

1974, Aug. 22   Litho.   Perf. 13
C218 A222 7c yellow & multi   .65   .25
C219 A222 33c lt blue & multi 2.40   .75

UPU Type
1974, Oct. 9   Litho.   Perf. 13½
C220 A223 7c Ships   2.00   .35
C221 A223 33c Jet   3.25   .75
  a.   Souvenir sheet of 4   8.50 8.50
No. C221a contains Nos. 727-728, C220-C221 forming continuous design.

Golfers and Championship Emblem AP64

20c, Golfer and Golf Association emblem.

1974, Oct. 24   Litho.   Perf. 13x13½
C222 AP64 10c green & multi   1.20   .50
C223 AP64 20c green & multi   1.90 1.00
World Amateur Golf Championships.

Hand Holding Dove — AP65

1974, Dec. 3   Litho.   Perf. 12
C224 AP65 10c multicolored   .90   .35
Christmas 1974.

FAO Type
10c, Bee, beehive and barrel of honey.

1974, Dec. 5
C225 A227 10c multicolored   2.00   .35

Chrismon, Lamb, Candle and Palm — AP66

1975, Mar. 26   Litho.   Perf. 13½
C226 AP66 10c gold & multi   1.10   .35
Holy Week 1975.

Spain No. 1, España 75 Emblem — AP67

1975, Apr. 10
C227 AP67 12c red, yel & blk   .65   .30
Espana 75, International Philatelic Exhibition, Madrid, Apr. 4-13.

Development Bank Type
1975, May 19   Litho.   Perf. 10½x10
C228 A230 10c rose car & multi .95   .35

Three Satellites and Globe — AP68

1975, June 21   Litho.   Perf. 13½
C229 AP68 15c multicolored   .95   .35
Opening of first earth satellite tracking station in Dominican Republic.

Apollo Type
Design: 2p, Apollo-Soyuz link-up over earth.

1975, July 24   Perf. 13
Size: 42x28mm
C230 A232 2p multicolored   6.50 4.00

Indian Chief Type
7c, Mayobanex. 8c, Cotubanama & Juan de Esquivel. 10c, Enriquillo & Mencia.

1975, Sept. 27   Litho.   Perf. 12
C231 A235 7c lt green & multi   .85   .50
C232 A235 8c orange & multi   1.25   .60
C233 A235 10c gray & multi   1.40   .60
Nos. C231-C233 (3)   3.50 1.70

Volleyball — AP69

10c, Weight lifting and Games' emblem.

1975, Oct. 24   Litho.   Perf. 12
C234 AP69 7c blue & multi   1.10   .35
C235 AP69 10c multicolored   1.90   .35
7th Pan-American Games, Mexico City, Oct. 13-26.

Christmas Type
Design: 10c, Dove and peace message.

1975, Dec. 12   Litho.   Perf. 13x13½
C236 A237 10c yellow & multi   .90   .35

Valdesia Dam — AP70

1976, Jan. 26   Litho.   Perf. 13
C237 AP70 10c multicolored   .75   .35

Holy Week Type 1976
Design: 10c, Crucifixion, by Eliezer Castillo.

1976, Apr. 14   Litho.   Perf. 13½
C238 A239 10c multicolored   1.10   .35

Bicentennial Type and

George Washington, Independence Hall — AP71

Design: 10c, Hands holding maps of US and Dominican Republic.

1976, May 29   Litho.   Perf. 13½
C239 A241 10c vio bl, grn & blk .80   .35
C240 AP71 75c black & orange   2.40 1.25
American Bicentennial; No. C240 also for Interphil 76 International Philatelic Exhibition, Philadelphia, Pa., May 29-June 6.

King Juan Carlos I and Queen Sofia — AP72

1976, May 31
C241 AP72 21c multicolored   1.60   .85
Visit of King Juan Carlos I and Queen Sofia of Spain.

Telephone Type
Design: 10c, Alexander Graham Bell and telephones, 1876 and 1976.

1976, July 15
C242 A243 10c multicolored   .95   .35

Duarte Types
10c, Scroll with Duarte letter and Dominican flag. 33c, Duarte return from Exile, by E. Godoy.

1976, July 20   Litho.   Perf. 13½
C243 A245 10c blue & multi   .85   .25
                             Perf. 13x13½
C244 A244 33c brown & multi   2.60 1.10

Fire Engine — AP73

1976, Sept. 13   Litho.   Perf. 12
C245 AP73 10c multicolored   4.50 1.50
Honoring firemen.

Radio Club Type
1976, Oct. 8   Litho.   Perf. 13½
C246 A247 10c blue & black   .90   .35

DOMINICAN REPUBLIC

Various People — AP74

1976, Oct. 22   Litho.   Perf. 13½
C247 AP74 21c multicolored   1.25   .55
Spanish heritage.

Olympic Games Type
1976, Oct. 22   Perf. 12
C248 A249 10c Running   .80   .25
C249 A249 25c Basketball   2.00   .75

Christmas Type
Design: 10c, Angel with bells.
1976, Dec. 8   Litho.   Perf. 13½
C250 A251 10c multicolored   1.10   .30

Tourist Activities — AP75

Tourist publicity: 12c, Angling and hotel. 25c, Horseback riding and waterfall, vert.
1977, Jan. 7   Size: 36x36mm
C251 AP75 10c multicolored   .65   .50
Size: 34x25½mm, 25½x34mm
C252 AP75 12c multicolored   .70   .50
C253 AP75 25c multicolored   1.40   .90
    Nos. C251-C253 (3)   2.75 1.90

Championship Type
1977, Mar. 4   Litho.   Perf. 13½
C254 A253 10c yel grn & multi   .80   .50
C255 A253 25c lt brown & multi   2.00 1.50

Holy Week Type 1977
Design: 10c, Belfry and open book.
1977, Apr. 18   Litho.   Perf. 13½x13
C256 A254 10c multicolored   1.10   .50

Lions Type
1977, May 6   Perf. 13½x13
C257 A255 7c lt green & multi   .90   .45

Caravel under Sail — AP76

1977, July 16   Litho.   Perf. 13
C258 AP76 10c multicolored   .95   .35
Miss Universe Contest, held in Dominican Republic.

Melon Cactus — AP77

Design: 33c, Coccothrinax (tree).
1977, Aug. 19   Litho.   Perf. 12
C259 AP77   7c multicolored   1.25   .35
C260 AP77 33c multicolored   3.00 1.25
National Botanical Garden.

Chart and Factories — AP78

1977, Nov. 30   Litho.   Perf. 13x13½
C261 AP78 28c multicolored   1.40 1.00
7th Interamerican Statistics Conference.

Animal Type
Congress Emblem and: 10c, "Dorado," red Roman stud bull. 25c, Flamingo, vert.
1977, Dec. 29   Litho.   Perf. 13
C262 A259 10c multicolored   3.25 4.50
C263 A259 25c multicolored   5.25 2.25

Spanish Heritage Type
21c, Window, Casa del Tostado, 16th cent.
1978, Jan. 19   Perf. 13x13½
    Size: 28x41mm
C264 A260 21c multicolored   1.20   .90

Holy Week Type, 1978
7c, Facade, Santo Domingo Cathedral. 10c, Facade of Dominican Convent.
1978, Mar. 21   Litho.   Perf. 12
    Size: 27x36mm
C265 A261   7c multicolored   .70   .30
C266 A261 10c multicolored   1.40   .35

Schooner Duarte — AP79

1978, Apr. 15   Litho.   Perf. 13½
C267 AP79 7c multicolored   .95   .35
Dominican naval forces training ship.

Cardinal Type
1978, May 5   Litho.   Perf. 13
C268 A262 10c multicolored   .90   .65

Antenna — AP80

1978, May 17   Litho.   Perf. 13½
C269 AP80 25c silver & multi   1.25   .55
10th World Telecommunications Day.

No. C1 and Map — AP81

1978, June 6
C270 AP81 10c multicolored   .85   .35
1st Dominican Rep. airmail stamp, 50th anniv.

Globe, Soccer Ball, Emblem — AP82

33c, Soccer field, Argentina '78 emblem, globe.
1978, June 29
C271 AP82 12c multicolored   .80   .50
C272 AP82 33c multicolored   1.75 1.50
11th World Cup Soccer Championship, Argentina, June 1-25.

Crown, Cross and Rosary Emblem — AP83

1978, July 11   Perf. 13x13½
C273 AP83 21c multicolored   1.20   .90
Congregation of the Merciful Sisters of Charity, centenary.

Sports Type
1978, July 21   Litho.   Perf. 13½
C274 A265   7c Baseball, vert.   1.60 1.25
C275 A265 10c Basketball, vert. 2.40 1.50

Wright Brothers and Glider, 1902 — AP84

Designs: 7c, Diagrams of Flyer I and jet, vert. 13c, Diagram of air flow over wing. 45c, Flyer I over world map.
1978, Aug. 8   Perf. 12
C276 AP84   7c multicolored   .30   .30
C277 AP84 10c multicolored   .75   .50
C278 AP84 13c multicolored   1.00   .60
C279 AP84 45c multicolored   2.75 2.00
    Nos. C276-C279 (4)   4.80 3.40
75th anniversary of first powered flight.

Tourist Type
Designs: 7c, Sun and musical instruments. 10c, Sun and plane over Santo Domingo.
1978, Sept. 12   Litho.   Perf. 12
C280 A266   7c multicolored   1.00   .65
C281 A266 10c multicolored   1.40   .90

People and Globe — AP85

1978, Oct. 12   Litho.   Perf. 13½
C282 AP85 21c multicolored   1.25   .60
Spanish heritage.

Dominican Republic and UN Flags — AP86

1978, Oct. 23   Perf. 12
C283 AP86 33c multicolored   1.75   .75
33rd anniversary of the United Nations.

Statue of the Virgin — AP87

1978, Dec. 5   Litho.   Perf. 12
C284 AP87 10c multicolored   .75   .35
Christmas 1978.

Pope John Paul II — AP88

1979, Jan. 25   Litho.   Perf. 13½
C285 AP88 10c multicolored   4.00 3.75
Visit of Pope John Paul II to the Dominican Republic, Jan. 25-26.

Map of Beata Island — AP89

1979, Jan. 25   Perf. 12
C286 AP89 10c multicolored   2.25 1.50
1st expedition of radio amateurs to Beata Is.

Year of the Child Type, 1979
Designs (ICY Emblem and): 7c, Children reading book. 10c, Symbolic head and protective hands. 33c, Hands and jars.
1979, Feb. 26
C287 A269   7c multicolored   .50   .40
C288 A269 10c multicolored   .80   .60
C289 A269 33c multicolored   2.25 1.75
    Nos. C287-C289 (3)   3.55 2.75

Pope John Paul II Giving Benediction — AP90

1979, Apr. 9   Litho.   Perf. 13½
C290 AP90 10c multicolored   5.25 3.00
Holy Week.

Adm. Juan Bautista Cambiaso — AP91

1979, Apr. 14   Perf. 12
C291 AP91 10c multicolored   .85   .60
135th anniv. of the Battle of Tortuguero.

Map of Dominican Rep., Album, Magnifier — AP92

1979, Apr. 18
C292 AP92 33c multicolored   1.40 1.10
EXFILNA 3rd National Philatelic Exhibition, Apr. 18-22.

Flower Type
Designs: 7c, Passionflower. 10c, Isidorea pungens. 13c, Calotropis procera.
1979, May 17   Litho.   Perf. 12
C293 A271   7c multicolored   1.60 1.00
C294 A271 10c multicolored   2.40 1.25
C295 A271 13c multicolored   4.00 2.00
    Nos. C293-C295 (3)   8.00 4.25

Cardiology Type, 1979
10c, Figure of man showing blood circulation.
1979, June 2   Litho.   Perf. 13½
C296 A272 10c multi, vert.   .90   .75

DOMINICAN REPUBLIC

Sports Type
7c, Runner and Games' emblem, vert.

1979, June 20
C297 A273 7c multicolored — 2.10 1.75

Soccer Type
1979, Aug. 9   Litho.   *Perf. 12*
C298 A273 10c Tennis, vert. — 1.00 .60

Rowland Hill, Dominican Republic No. 1 — AP93

1979, Aug. 21   *Perf. 13½*
C299 AP93 2p multicolored — 5.00 4.75

Sir Rowland Hill (1795-1879), originator of penny postage.

Electric Light Type
Design: 10c, "100" and light bulb, horiz.

1979, Aug. 27   *Perf. 13½*
C300 A275 10c multicolored — 1.00 .50

Bird Type
Birds: 7c, Phaenicophilus palmarum. 10c, Calyptophilus frugivorus tertius. 45c, Icterus dominicensis.

1979, Sept. 12   Litho.   *Perf. 12*
C301 A277 7c multicolored — 3.00 .75
C302 A277 10c multicolored — 4.00 .75
C303 A277 45c multicolored — 10.50 2.50
Nos. C301-C303 (3) — 17.50 4.00

Lions Type
10c, Melvin Jones, organization founder.

1979, Nov. 13   Litho.   *Perf. 12*
C304 A278 10c multicolored — .85 .50

Christmas Type
Christmas: 10c, Three Kings riding camels.

1979, Dec. 18   Litho.   *Perf. 12*
C305 A279 10c multicolored — .75 .50

Holy Week Type
1980, Mar. 27   Litho.   *Perf. 12*
C306 A280 7c Crucifixion — .60 .40
C307 A280 10c Resurrection — 1.00 .75

Navy Day — AP94

1980, Apr. 15   Litho.   *Perf. 13½*
C308 AP94 21c multicolored — 1.00 .55

Dominican Philatelic Society, 25th Anniversary AP95

1980, Apr. 18
C309 AP95 10c multicolored — .80 .55

Gold Type
1980, July 8   Litho.   *Perf. 13½*
C310 A282 10c Drag line mining — 1.00 .60
C311 A282 33c Mine — 1.60 1.00

Tourism Secretariat Emblem — AP96

1980, Aug. 26   Litho.   *Perf. 13½*
C312 AP96 10c shown — .55 .35
C313 AP96 33c Conf. emblem — 2.00 1.50

World Tourism Conf., Manila, Sept. 27.

Iguana Type
Designs: 7c, American crocodile. 10c, Cuban rat. 25c, Manatee. 45c, Turtle.

1980, Aug. 30   *Perf. 12*
C314 A284 7c multi — 2.25 .75
C315 A284 10c multi — 2.50 .80
C316 A284 25c multi — 4.00 1.00
C317 A284 45c multi — 5.50 1.50
Nos. C314-C317 (4) — 14.25 4.05

Painting Type
Designs: 10c, Abstract, by Paul Guidicelli, vert. 17c, Farmer, by Yoryi Morel, vert.

1980, Sept. 23   Litho.   *Perf. 13½x13*
C318 A285 10c multi — .80 .60
C319 A285 17c multi — 1.20 .90

Visit of Radio Amateurs to Catalina Island — AP97

1980, Oct. 3
C320 AP97 7c multicolored — .85 .60

Rotary International, 75th Anniversary AP98

Design: 10c, Globe, emblem, vert.

1980, Oct. 23   Litho.   *Perf. 12*
C321 AP98 10c multi — .75 .65
C322 AP98 33c shown — 1.60 1.20

Carrier Pigeons, UPU Emblem — AP99

1980, Oct. 31   *Perf. 13½*
C323 AP99 33c shown — .95 .80
C324 AP99 45c Pigeons, diff. — 1.25 1.10
C325 AP99 50c Pigeon, stamp — 1.75 1.25
Nos. C323-C325 (3) — 3.95 3.15

Souvenir Sheet
Imperf
C326 AP99 1.10p UPU emblem — 2.00 2.00

UPU cent. No. C326 contains one 48½x31mm stamp.

Christmas Type
1980, Dec. 5   Litho.   *Perf. 13½*
C327 A286 10c Holy Family — 1.00 .65
Christmas 1980.

Salcedo Type
Design: Map and arms of Salcedo.

1981, Jan. 14   Litho.   *Perf. 13½*
C328 A287 10c multicolored — .75 .50

AP100

Industrial Symbols, Seminar Emblem.

1981, Feb. 18   Litho.   *Perf. 13½*
C329 AP100 10c shown — .70 .50
C330 AP100 33c Seminar emblem — 1.25 .95

CODIA Chemical Engineering Seminar.

National Games Type
1981, Mar. 31   Litho.   *Perf. 13½*
C331 A289 10c Baseball — 3.00 2.50

AP101

Design: Admiral Juan Alejandro Acosta.

1981, Apr. 15
C332 AP101 10c multicolored — .65 .40

Battle of Tortuguero anniversary.

13th World Telecommunications Day — AP102

1981, May 16   Litho.   *Perf. 12*
C333 AP102 10c multicolored — .90 .65

Heinrich von Stephan — AP103

1981, July 15   Litho.   *Perf. 13½*
C334 AP103 33c tan & lt red brn — 1.40 1.10

Birth sesquicentennial of UPU founder.

Worker in Wheelchair — AP104

1981, July 24
C335 AP104 7c Stylized people — .65 .50
C336 AP104 33c shown — 1.60 1.25

Intl. Year of the Disabled.

EXPURIDOM '81 Intl. Stamp Show, Santo Domingo, July 31-Aug. 2 — AP105

1981, July 31
C337 AP105 7c multicolored — 1.00 .75

Bullet Holes in Target, Competition Emblem — AP106

1981, Aug. 12
C338 AP106 10c shown — .50 .40
C339 AP106 15c Riflemen — .75 .45
C340 AP106 25c Pistol shooting — 1.75 1.00
Nos. C338-C340 (3) — 3.00 1.85

2nd World Sharpshooting Championship.

Exports — AP107

1981, Oct. 16   Litho.   *Perf. 12*
C341 AP107 7c Jewelry — .75 .55
C342 AP107 10c Handicrafts — .85 .65
C343 AP107 11c Fruit — 1.00 .80
C344 AP107 17c Vegetables — 1.30 1.00
Nos. C341-C344 (4) — 3.90 3.00

World Food Day — AP108

1981, Oct. 16   Litho.   *Perf. 13½*
C345 AP108 10c Fruits — .90 .50
C346 AP108 50c Vegetables — 2.10 2.00

5th Natl. Games — AP109

1981, Dec. 5   Litho.   *Perf. 13½*
C347 AP109 10c Javelin, vert. — .55 .45
C348 AP109 50c Cycling — 2.50 2.10

Orchids — AP110

7c, Encyclia cochleata. 10c, Broughtonia domingensis. 25c, Encyclia truncata. 75c, Elleanthus capitatus.

1981, Dec. 14
C349 AP110 7c multicolored — 1.25 .85
C350 AP110 10c multicolored — 1.50 1.00
C351 AP110 25c multicolored — 2.40 1.60
C352 AP110 75c multicolored — 6.00 4.00
Nos. C349-C352 (4) — 11.15 7.45

Christmas Type
1981, Dec. 23
C353 A294 10c Dove, sun — 1.25 .90

Battle of Tortuguero Anniv. — AP111

Design: Naval Academy, cadets.

1982, Apr. 15   Litho.   *Perf. 13½*
C354 AP111 10c multi — .85 .60

1982 World Cup Soccer — AP112

Designs: Various soccer players.

1982, Apr. 19
C355 AP112 10c multicolored — .75 .60
C356 AP112 21c multicolored — .90 .75
C357 AP112 33c multicolored — 1.90 1.40
Nos. C355-C357 (3) — 3.55 2.75

DOMINICAN REPUBLIC

American Air Forces Cooperation System — AP113

1982, Apr. 12   **Perf. 12**
C358 AP113 10c multicolored   .95   .70

Scouting Year — AP114

10c, Baden-Powell, vert. 15c, Globe. 25c, Baden-Powell, scout, vert.

1982, Apr. 30   **Litho.**   **Perf. 13½**
C359 AP114 10c multi   .60   .45
C360 AP114 15c multi   .90   .65
C361 AP114 25c multi   1.30   .90
    Nos. C359-C361 (3)   2.80   2.00

Dancers — AP115

7c, Emblem. 10c, Cathedral, Casa del Tostado, Santo Domingo.

1982, June 1   **Litho.**   **Perf. 13½**
C362 AP115 7c multi   .40   .30
C363 AP115 10c multi   .45   .35
C364 AP115 33c multi   2.25   1.75
    Nos. C362-C364 (3)   3.10   2.40

Tourist Org. of the Americas, 25th Congress (COTAL '82), Santo Domingo.

Espamer '82 Emblem — AP116

Espamer '82 Intl. Stamp Exhibition, San Juan, Oct. 12-17: Symbolic stamps.

1982, July 5
C365 AP116 7c multi   .40   .30
C366 AP116 13c multi, horiz.   .65   .50
C367 AP116 50c multi   2.00   2.10
    Nos. C365-C367 (3)   3.65   2.90

Sports Type

1982, Aug. 13   **Perf. 12, Imperf.**
C368 A300 10c Basketball   2.00   1.00
C369 A300 13c Boxing   3.00   1.50
C370 A300 25c Gymnast   4.00   2.00
    Nos. C368-C370 (3)   9.00   4.50

Harbor, by Alejandro Bonilla AP117

Paintings: 10c, Portrait of a Woman, by Leopoldo Navarro. 45c, Amelia Francasci, by Luis Desangles. 2p, Portrait, by Abelardo Rodriguez Urdaneta. 10c, 45c, 2p vert.

1982, Aug. 20   **Perf. 13**
C371 AP117 7c multicolored   .30   .30
C372 AP117 10c multicolored   .55   .45
C373 AP117 45c multicolored   2.25   2.10
C374 AP117 2p multicolored   9.75   9.00
    Nos. C371-C374 (4)   12.85   11.85

Nos. C371-C374 exist imperf. Value, $25.

San Pedro de Macoris Type

1982, Aug. 26
    Size: 42x29mm
C375 A301 7c Lake   1.10   .75

35th Anniv. of Central Bank — AP118

1982, Oct. 22   **Litho.**   **Perf. 13½x13**
C376 AP118 10c multicolored   .85   .60

490th Anniv. of Discovery of America — AP119

Designs: 7c, Map. 10c, Santa Maria, vert. 21c, Columbus, vert.

1982, Oct. 7   **Litho.**   **Perf. 13½**
C377 AP119 7c multi   1.50   1.25
C378 AP119 10c multi   1.00   1.00
C379 AP119 21c multi   2.40   2.10
    Nos. C377-C379 (3)   5.80   4.95

Christmas Type

1982, Dec. 8
C380 A303 10c multicolored   .80   .55

French Alliance Centenary — AP120

1983, Mar. 31   **Litho.**   **Perf. 13½**
C381 AP120 33c multicolored   1.10   .85

Battle of Tortuguero Anniv. — AP121

Design: 15c, Frigate Mella-451.

1983, Apr. 15   **Litho.**   **Perf. 13½**
C382 AP121 15c multi   1.20   .95

World Communications Year — AP122

1983, May 6   **Litho.**   **Perf. 13½**
C383 AP122 10c dk blue & blue   .85   .60

AP123

1983, July 5   **Litho.**   **Perf. 13½**
C384 AP123 9c multicolored   .85   .60

Simon Bolivar (1783-1830).

AP124

7c, Gymnast, basketball. 10c, Highjump, boxing. 15c, Baseball, weight lifting, bicycling.

1983, Aug. 22   **Litho.**   **Perf. 12**
C385 AP124 7c multi   1.00   .85
C386 AP124 10c multi   1.30   .95
C387 AP124 15c multi   1.50   1.20
    Nos. C385-C387 (3)   3.80   3.00

9th Pan American Games, Caracas, Aug. 13-28.

491st Anniv. of Discovery of America — AP125

10c, Columbus' ships, map. 21c, Santa Maria (trophy). 33c, Yacht Sotavento, vert. 50c, Ship models.

1983, Oct. 11   **Litho.**   **Perf. 13½**
C388 AP125 10c multi   1.40   1.25
C389 AP125 21c multi   2.10   1.90
C390 AP125 33c multi   2.50   2.10
    Nos. C388-C390 (3)   6.00   5.25

Size: 103x103mm

Imperf
C391 AP125 50c multi   16.00   16.00

10th Anniv. of Latin American Civil Aviation Commission AP126

1983, Dec. 7
C392 AP126 10c dark blue   .85   .60

Funeral Procession, by Juan Bautista Gomez AP127

Designs: 15c, Meeting of Maximo Gomez and Jose Marti in Guayubin, by Enrique Garcia Godoy. 21c, St. Francis, by Angel Perdomo, vert. 33c, Portrait of a Girl, by Adriana Billini, vert.

1983, Dec. 26   **Perf. 13½**
C393 AP127 10c multicolored   .60   .40
C394 AP127 15c multicolored   .60   .40
C395 AP127 21c multicolored   .75   .60
C396 AP127 33c multicolored   1.10   .75
    Nos. C393-C396 (4)   3.05   2.05

Christmas 1983 — AP128

1983, Dec. 13   **Litho.**   **Perf. 13½**
C397 AP128 10c Bells, ornaments   .85   .60

AIR POST SEMI-POSTAL STAMPS

> Catalogue values for unused stamps in this section are for Never Hinged items.

Nos. C97-C99 Surcharged in Red like Nos. B1-B5
Engraved and Lithographed

1957, Feb. 8   **Unwmk.**   **Perf. 11½**
Flags in National Colors
CB1 A117 11c + 2c ultra & red org   .60   .40
CB2 A117 16c + 2c car & lt grn   1.00   .70
CB3 A117 17c + 2c blk, vio & red   1.10   .70
    Nos. CB1-CB3 (3)   2.70   1.80

The surtax was to aid Hungarian refugees. A similar 25c surcharge was applied to the souvenir sheets described in the footnote following No. C99. Value, 2 sheets, perf. and imperf., $17.50.

Nos. C100-C102 Surcharged in Red Orange like Nos. B6-B10

1957, Sept. 9   **Photo.**   **Perf. 13½**
Flags in National Colors
CB4 A118 11c + 2c yel grn & dk bl   1.00   .50
CB5 A118 16c + 2c lilac & dk bl   1.20   .70
CB6 A118 17c + 2c brn & bl grn   1.40   .75
    Nos. CB4-CB6 (3)   3.60   1.95

See note after No. B10.
A similar 5c surcharge was applied to the miniature sheets described in the footnote following No. 483. Value, 4 sheets, perf. & imperf., medal and flag, $40.

Types of Olympic Air Post Stamps, 1957, Surcharged in Carmine like Nos. B11-B20

1958, May 26   **Engr. & Litho.**
Flags in National Colors
Pink Paper
CB7 A119(a) 11c + 2c ultra   .40   .40
CB8 A119(b) 11c + 2c ultra   .40   .40
CB9 A120(a) 16c + 2c rose car   .55   .55
CB10 A120(b) 16c + 2c rose car   .55   .55
CB11 A119(a) 17c + 2c claret   .65   .65
CB12 A119(b) 17c + 2c claret   .65   .65
    Nos. CB7-CB12 (6)   3.20   3.20

A similar 5c surcharge, plus marginal UN emblem and "UNRWA," was applied to the miniature sheets described in the footnote following No. C105. Value, 2 sheets, perf. and imperf., $20.

Nos. C106-C108 Surcharged like Nos. B21-B25

1959, Apr. 13   **Photo.**   **Perf. 13½**
Flags in National Colors
CB13 A125 11c + 2c blue, ol & brn   1.00   .80
CB14 A125 16c + 2c lt grn, org & dk bl   1.40   1.10
CB15 A125 17c + 2c ver bl & yel   2.10   1.60
    Nos. CB13-CB15 (3)   4.50   3.50

A similar 5c surcharge was applied to the miniature sheets described in the footnote following No. C108. Value, 2 sheets, perf. and imperf., $25.

Type of Regular Issue 1957 Surcharged in Red like Nos. B28-B30
Engraved and Lithographed

1959, Sept. 10   **Imperf.**
Flags in National Colors
CB16 A117 11c + 2c ultra & red org   1.10   .80
CB17 A117 16c + 2c carmine & lt grn   1.25   .90
CB18 A117 17c + 2c black, vio & red   1.25   .90
    Nos. CB16-CB18 (3)   3.60   2.60

Nos. C113-C114 Surcharged in Red like Nos. B31-B33

1960, Apr. 7   **Litho.**   **Perf. 12½**
CB19 AP43 10c + 5c plum, gray & grn   .50   .35
CB20 AP43 13c + 5c gray & green   .85   .55

World Refugee Year.
For souvenir sheets see note after No. B33.

DOMINICAN REPUBLIC

Nos. C115-C117 Surcharged

Perf. 13½

1962, Jan. 8   Unwmk.   Photo.
Flags in National Colors

CB21	A136	11c + 2c blue, gray & brn	.55 .35
CB22	A136	16c + 2c red, brn & ol	.80 .50
CB23	A136	17c + 2c blk, bl & ocher	.80 .50
		Nos. CB21-CB23 (3)	2.15 1.35

See note after No. B38.
A similar 5c surcharge was applied to the miniature sheets described in the footnote following No. C117. Value, 2 sheets, perf. and imperf., $9.

Anti-Malaria Type of 1962

1962, Apr. 29   Litho.   Perf. 12

CB24	A141	13c + 2c pink & red	.50 .35
CB25	A141	33c + 2c org & dp org	1.10 .75

Souvenir sheets exist, perf. and imperf. containing one each of Nos. B39-B40, CB24-CB25 and a 25c+2c pale grn and yel grn. Value, 2 sheets, perf. and imperf., $7.50.

Nos. C132-C133 Surcharged like Nos. B44-B46

1964, Mar. 8

CB26	AP46	10c + 2c brt violet	.65 .35
CB27	AP46	13c + 2c yellow	.70 .40

Nos. C146-C148 Surcharged like Nos. B47-B51

1966, Dec. 9   Litho.   Perf. 12½
Size: 35x24mm

CB28	A164	10c + 5c multi	3.25 1.00
CB29	A164	50c + 10c multi	4.75 3.00
CB30	A164	75c + 10c multi	6.25 3.75
		Nos. CB28-CB30 (3)	14.25 7.75

AIR POST OFFICIAL STAMPS

Nos. O13-O14 Overprinted in Blue

1930, Dec. 3   Unwmk.   Typo.   Perf. 12

CO1	O3	10c light blue	20.00 17.50
a.		Pair, one without ovpt.	1,100.
CO2	O3	20c orange	20.00 17.50

SPECIAL DELIVERY STAMPS

Biplane — SD1

Perf. 11½

1920, Apr.   Unwmk.   Litho.

E1	SD1	10c deep ultra	6.75 1.40
a.		Imperf., pair	

Special Delivery Messenger SD2

1925

E2	SD2	10c dark blue	21.00 5.75

SD3

1927

E3	SD3	10c red brown	8.00 1.40
a.		"E EXPRESO" at top	55.00 55.00

Type of 1927

1941   Redrawn

E4	SD3	10c yellow green	3.00 3.25
E5	SD3	10c dark blue green	2.75 .60

The redrawn design differs slightly from SD3. Issue dates: No. E4, Mar. 27; No. E5, Aug. 7.

Emblem of Communications — SD4

1945, Sept. 1   Perf. 12

E6	SD4	10c rose car, car & dk bl	1.50 .35

> Catalogue values for unused stamps in this section, from this point to the end of the section, are for Never Hinged items.

SD5

1950   Litho.   Unwmk.

E7	SD5	10c multicolored	.95 .35

Exists imperf.

Modern Communications System — SD6

1956, Aug. 18   Perf. 11½

E8	SD6	25c green	1.50 .35

Carrier Pigeon — SD7

1967   Litho.   Perf. 11½

E9	SD7	25c light blue	1.00 .35

Carrier Pigeon, Globe — SD8

1978, Aug. 2   Litho.   Perf. 13½

E10	SD8	25c multicolored	1.30 .60

Messenger, Plane — SD9

1979, Nov. 30   Perf. 13½

E11	SD9	25c multicolored	1.00 .45

Motorcycling SD10

1989, May   Litho.   Perf. 13½

E12	SD10	1p multicolored	2.75 1.10

Postman — SD11

1999   Litho.   Perf. 13½x13¼

E13	SD11	8p multicolored	3.50 2.75

INSURED LETTER STAMPS

Merino Issue of 1933 Surcharged in Red or Black

1935, Feb. 1   Unwmk.   Perf. 14

G1	A35	8c on 7c ultra	.60 .25
a.		Inverted surcharge	18.00 18.00
G2	A35	15c on 10c org yel	.65 .25
a.		Inverted surcharge	18.00 18.00
G3	A35	30c on 8c dk green	2.25 .90
G4	A35	45c on 20c car rose (Bk)	3.25 1.10
G5	A36	70c on 50c lemon	7.75 1.75
		Nos. G1-G5 (5)	14.50 4.25

Merino Issue of 1933 Surcharged in Red

1940

G6	A35	8c on ½c lt vio	2.75 2.75
G7	A35	8c on 7c ultra	3.25 3.25

Coat of Arms — IL1

1940-45   Litho.   Perf. 11½
Arms in Black

G8	IL1	8c brown red	.85 .40
a.		8c dk red, no shading on inner frame	1.10 .40
G9	IL1	15c dp orange ('45)	1.75 .40
G10	IL1	30c dk green ('41)	2.00 .40
a.		30c yellow green	2.00 .40
G11	IL1	45c ultra ('44)	2.25 .40
G12	IL1	70c olive brn ('44)	2.10 .40
		Nos. G8-G12 (5)	8.95 2.00

See Nos. G13-G16, G24-G27.

> Catalogue values for unused stamps in this section, from this point to the end of the section, are for Never Hinged items.

Redrawn Type of 1940-45

1952-53   Arms in Black

G13	IL1	8c car lake ('53)	4.00 .50
G14	IL1	15c red orange ('53)	2.50 .75
G15	IL1	70c dp brown car	9.50 1.75
		Nos. G13-G15 (3)	16.00 3.00

Larger and bolder numerals on 8c and 15c. Smaller and bolder "70." There are many other minor differences in the design.

Type of 1940-45

1954   Arms in Black, 15x16mm

G16	IL1	10c carmine	1.10 .35

Coat of Arms — IL2

1955-69   Unwmk.   Litho.   Perf. 11½
Arms in Black, 13½x11½mm

G17	IL2	10c carmine rose	.65 .35
G18	IL2	15c red orange ('56)	5.25 2.25
G19	IL2	20c red orange ('58)	3.75 .35
a.		20c orange ('69)	3.25 .35
b.		20c orange, retouched ('69)	3.75 1.25
G20	IL2	30c dark green ('55)	2.25 1.25
G21	IL2	40c dark green ('58)	2.40 .90
a.		40c lt yellow grn ('62)	2.40 .40
G22	IL2	45c ultra ('56)	4.00 3.75
G23	IL2	70c dp brn car ('56)	7.00 2.25
		Nos. G17-G23 (7)	25.30 11.10

On No. G19b the horizontal shading lines of shield are omitted.
See Nos. G28-G37.

Type of 1940-45
Second Redrawing

1963   Perf. 12½
Arms in Black, 17x16mm

G24	IL1	10c red orange	1.60 .30
G25	IL1	20c orange	2.25 1.25

Third Redrawing

1966   Litho.   Perf. 12½
Arms in Black, 14x14mm

G26	IL1	10c violet	.50 .25
G27	IL1	40c orange	1.90 1.00

Type of 1955-62

1968   Litho.   Perf. 11½
Arms in Black, 13½x11½mm

G28	IL2	20c red	3.00 1.00
G29	IL2	60c yellow	2.50 2.10

1973-76   Litho.   Perf. 12½
Arms in Black, 11x11mm

G30	IL2	10c car rose ('76)	.50 .35
G31	IL2	20c yellow	2.00 .90
G32	IL2	20c orange ('76)	2.00 .50
G33	IL2	40c yel grn	1.90 1.00
a.		40c green ('76)	3.25 3.00
G34	IL2	70c blue	2.10 1.90
		Nos. G30-G34 (5)	8.50 4.65

1973   Perf. 11½
Arms in Black, 13½x11½mm

G35	IL2	10c dark violet	1.10 .35

1978, Aug. 9   Perf. 10½
Arms in Black, 11x11mm

G36	IL2	10c rose magenta	.55 .25
G37	IL2	40c bright green	2.10 1.50

IL3

1982-83   Litho.   Perf. 10½
Arms in Black

G38	IL3	10c deep magenta	.30 .25
G39	IL3	20c deep orange	.45 .30
G40	IL3	40c bluish green	1.00 .50
		Nos. G38-G40 (3)	1.75 1.05

IL4

1986   Litho.   Perf. 10½
Arms in Black

G41	IL4	20c brt rose lilac	.35 .25
G42	IL4	60c orange	1.25 .85
G43	IL4	1p light blue	2.10 1.40
G44	IL4	1.25p pink	2.90 1.75
G45	IL4	1.50p vermilion	8.50 2.50
G46	IL4	3p light green	6.50 4.25
G47	IL4	3.50p olive bister	7.25 4.50
G48	IL4	4p yellow	9.00 5.50
G49	IL4	4.50p lt blue grn	10.00 6.25
G50	IL4	5p brown olive	10.75 7.00
G51	IL4	6p gray	13.00 8.50
G52	IL4	6.50p lt ultra	15.00 9.50
		Nos. G41-G52 (12)	86.60 52.25

Issue dates: Nos. G42-G43, G45, July 16. Nos. G46-G52, Sept. 2. Nos. G41, G44, Nov. 6.

DOMINICAN REPUBLIC

Coat of Arms — IL5

1989-90   Litho.   Perf. 13½
Arms in Black
G53	IL5	20c brt lilac rose	.40	.30
G54	IL5	60c orange ('90)	1.20	.45
G55	IL5	1p sky blue	1.90	.75
G56	IL5	1.25p lt salmon pink	2.25	.90
G57	IL5	1.50p dark red	2.75	1.40
		Nos. G53-G57 (5)	8.50	3.80

"RD$" in lower left square on Nos. G55-G57.

IL6

1994, Oct.   Litho.   Perf. 13½
Arms in Black
G58	IL6	50c lilac rose	.50	.35
G59	IL6	1p sky blue	.70	.35
G60	IL6	1.50p red	.90	.35
G61	IL6	2p pink	1.10	.50
G62	IL6	3p violet blue	1.90	.60
G63	IL6	5p yellow	2.60	.75
G64	IL6	6p apple green	3.25	1.25
G65	IL6	8p green	4.00	1.50
G66	IL6	10p silver gray	5.75	2.00
		Nos. G58-G66 (9)	20.70	7.80

POSTAGE DUE STAMPS

D1

1901   Unwmk.   Typo.   Perf. 14
J1	D1	2c olive gray	.90	.25
J2	D1	4c olive gray	1.10	.25
J3	D1	5c olive gray	1.90	.30
J4	D1	10c olive gray	3.25	.95
		Nos. J1-J4 (4)	7.15	1.75

For surcharges and overprint see Nos. 162-165, 169-171.

1909   Wmk. 116
J5	D1	2c olive gray	1.50	.50
J6	D1	4c olive gray	1.50	.50
J7	D1	6c olive gray	2.00	.75
J8	D1	10c olive gray	4.00	2.50
		Nos. J5-J8 (4)	9.00	4.25

1913
J9	D1	2c olive green	.60	.30
J10	D1	4c olive green	.70	.40
J11	D1	6c olive green	1.10	.50
J12	D1	10c olive green	1.25	.60
		Nos. J9-J12 (4)	3.65	1.80

1922   Unwmk.   Litho.   Perf. 11½
J13	D1	1c olive green	.70	.70

Catalogue values for unused stamps in this section, from this point to the end of the section, are for Never Hinged items.

D2

1942
J14	D2	1c dk red & pale pink	.50	.30
J15	D2	2c dk bl & pale bl	.50	.30
J16	D2	4c dk grn & pale grn	.50	.30
J17	D2	6c green & buff	.60	.30
J18	D2	8c yel org & pale yel	.60	.40
J19	D2	10c mag & pale pink	.90	.60
		Nos. J14-J19 (6)	3.60	2.20

1955   Size: 20½x25mm
J20	D2	2c dark blue	1.40	1.00

D3

1959   Litho.   Perf. 11½
Size: 21x25½mm
J21	D3	1c dark car rose	1.50	1.50
J22	D3	2c dark blue	1.50	1.25
J23	D3	4c green	3.50	3.00
		Nos. J21-J23 (3)	6.50	5.75

OFFICIAL STAMPS

Bastion of February 27 — O1

1902, Feb. 25   Unwmk.   Litho.   Perf. 12
O1	O1	2c scarlet & blk	.65	.40
O2	O1	5c dk blue & blk	.85	.40
O3	O1	10c yel grn & blk	1.00	.60
O4	O1	20c yellow & blk	1.25	.60
a.		Imperf., pair	11.00	
		Nos. O1-O4 (4)	3.75	2.00

For overprints and surcharge see Nos. 157-161.

Bastion of Feb. 27 — O2

Perf. 13½x13, 13½x14
1909-12   Wmk. 116   Typo.
O5	O2	1c blue grn & blk	.40	.25
O6	O2	2c scarlet & blk	.50	.30
O7	O2	5c dk blue & blk	1.00	.40
O8	O2	10c yel grn & blk ('12)	1.60	.95
O9	O2	20c orange & blk ('12)	2.75	2.25
		Nos. O5-O9 (5)	6.25	4.15

The 2c, 5c are found in both perforations; 1c, 20c perf. 13½x13; 10c perf. 13½x14.
For overprints and surcharge see Nos. 177, 194-199.

Columbus Lighthouse — O3

1928   Unwmk.   Perf. 12
O10	O3	1c green	.30	.30
O11	O3	2c red	.30	.30
O12	O3	5c ultramarine	.35	.35
O13	O3	10c light blue	.40	.40
O14	O3	20c orange	.60	.60
		Nos. O10-O14 (5)	1.95	1.95

For overprints see Nos. CO1-CO2.

Proposed Columbus Lighthouse — O4

1937   Litho.   Perf. 11½
O15	O4	3c dark purple	1.60	.50
O16	O4	7c indigo & blue	1.90	.60
O17	O4	10c orange yellow	2.25	.85
		Nos. O15-O17 (3)	5.75	1.95

Proposed Columbus Lighthouse — O5

1939-41
O18	O5	1c dp grn & lt grn	1.00	.40
O19	O5	2c crim & pale pink	1.00	.40
O20	O5	3c purple & lt vio	1.00	.40
O21	O5	5c dk bl & lt bl ('40)	1.40	.60
O21A	O5	5c lt blue ('41)	2.75	1.25
O22	O5	7c brt bl & lt bl ('41)	2.40	.40
O23	O5	10c yel org & pale org ('41)	2.40	.60
O24	O5	20c org brn & buff ('41)	8.00	1.00
O25	O5	50c dp mag & pink ('41)	9.75	3.00
		Nos. O18-O25 (9)	29.70	8.05

Catalogue values for unused stamps in this section, from this point to the end of the section, are for Never Hinged items.

Type of 1939

1950   Redrawn
O26	O5	50c dp car & rose	13.00	2.00

The numerals "50" measure 3mm, and are close to left and right frames; numerals measure 4mm on No. O25. There are other minor differences.

Denominations in "Centavos Oro"

1950
O27	O5	5c light blue	1.20	.40
O28	O5	10c yel & pale yel	1.50	.60
O29	O5	20c dl org brn & buff	3.00	2.25
		Nos. O27-O29 (3)	5.70	3.25

Letters of top inscription are 1½mm high.

Second Redrawing
Type of 1939-41 Denominations in "Centavos Oro"

1956   Unwmk.   Perf. 11½
O30	O5	7c blue & lt blue	1.20	1.00
O31	O5	20c yellow brn & buff	3.00	2.50
O32	O5	50c red lil & brt pink	7.25	6.00
		Nos. O30-O32 (3)	11.45	9.50

The letters of top inscription are 2mm high, the trees at base of monument have been redrawn, etc. On No. O32 the numerals are similar to No. O26.

POSTAL TAX STAMPS

Santo Domingo after Hurricane — PT1

Hurricane's Effect on Capital — PT2

1930, Dec.   Unwmk.   Litho.   Perf. 12
RA1	PT1	1c green & rose	.40	.40
RA2	PT1	2c red rose	.40	.40
RA3	PT2	5c ultra & rose	.40	.40
RA4	PT2	10c yellow & rose	.40	.40

Imperf
RA5	PT1	1c green & rose	.40	.40
RA6	PT1	2c red rose	.50	.40
RA7	PT2	5c ultra & rose	.60	.50
RA8	PT2	10c yellow & rose	.90	.75
		Nos. RA1-RA8 (8)	4.00	3.65

For surcharges see Nos. RAC1-RAC7.

Tête bêche Pairs
RA1a	PT1	1c green & rose	1.75	1.75
RA2a	PT1	2c red rose	1.75	1.50
RA3a	PT1	5c ultra & rose	1.75	2.10
RA4a	PT1	10c yellow & rose	2.10	2.10
RA5a	PT1	1c green & rose	1.75	1.75
RA6a	PT1	2c red rose	1.75	1.75
RA7a	PT1	5c ultra & rose	2.10	2.10
RA8a	PT1	10c yellow & rose	2.10	2.10
		Nos. RA1a-RA8a (8)	15.05	15.15

Dr. Martos Sanatorium — PT3

1944, Apr. 1   Litho.   Perf. 11½
RA9	PT3	1c dp bl, sl bl & red	.40	.35

Nurse and Child — PT4

1947, Apr. 1   Unwmk.
RA10	PT4	1c dp bl, pale bl & car	.50	.35

Sanatorium of the Holy Help — PT5

1949, Apr. 1
RA11	PT5	1c dp bl, pale bl & car	.35	.35

Youth Holding Banner — PT6

1950, Apr. 1   Perf. 11½
RA12	PT6	1c dp bl, pale bl & car	.35	.35

"Suffer Little Children to Come Unto Me" — PT7

1950, Dec. 1   Perf. 12
Size: 22½x32mm
RA13	PT7	1c lt bl & pale bl	1.25	.35
b.		Perf. 12½ ('52)	4.50	.35

Vertical line centering side borders merges into dots toward the bottom. See Nos. RA13A, RA17, RA19, RA26, RA32, RA35.
The tax was for child welfare.

1951, Dec. 1   Redrawn
RA13A	PT7	1c lt blue & pale blue	6.25	.35

In the redrawn stamp, the standing child, a blonde in No. RA13, is changed to a brunette; more foliage has been added above child's head and to branches showing in upper right corner. Vertical dashes in side borders.

Tuberculosis Sanatorium, Santiago — PT8

1952, Apr. 1   Litho.   Perf. 11½
RA14	PT8	1c lt blue & car	.35	.35

Sword, Serpent and Crab — PT9

1953, Feb. 1   Unwmk.   Perf. 12.
RA15	PT9	1c carmine	.50	.35

The tax was for the Dominican League Against Cancer. See Nos. RA18, RA21, RA43, RA46, RA51, RA56, RA61, RA67, RA72, RA76, RA82, RA88, RA93, RA96.

283

DOMINICAN REPUBLIC

Tuberculosis Dispensary for Children — PT10

1953, Apr. 1   Litho.   Perf. 12½
RA16 PT10 1c dp bl, pale bl & red   .40   .35
See No. RA22.

Jesus Type of 1950
Second Redrawing
1953, Dec. 1   Perf. 11½
Size: 22x31mm
RA17 PT7 1c blue   .35   .35
Solid shading in sky reduced to a few scattered dots. Girl's left arm indicated. Rough white dots in side borders.

Cancer Type of 1952
1954, Oct. 1   Redrawn   Perf. 12½
RA18 PT9 1c rose carmine   .35   .35
a. 1c red orange ('58)   .40   .40
b. 1c carmine ('70)   1.25   .35
Upper right serif of numeral "1" eliminated; diagonal line added through "C" and period removed; sword extended, placing top on a line with top of "1." Dots of background screen arranged diagonally. Many other differences.
The tax was for the Dominican League Against Cancer. No. RA18a exists imperf.
On No. RA18b background screen eliminates white outline of crab.

Jesus Type of 1950
1954, Dec. 1   Third Redrawing
Size: 23x32¾mm
RA19 PT7 1c bright blue   .40   .35
a. 1c pale blue ('59)   .40   .30
Center completely screened. Tiny white horizontal rectangles in side borders.

Catalogue values for unused stamps in this section, from this point to the end of the section, are for Never Hinged items.

Lorraine Cross as Bell Clapper — PT11

1955, Apr. 1   Litho.   Perf. 11½x12
RA20 PT11 1c black, yel & red   .75   .35

Cancer Type of 1952
Second Redrawing
1956, Oct. 1   Perf. 12½
RA21 PT9 1c carmine   .90   .35
a. 1c red orange ('64)   1.50   .50
Similar to No. RA18, but dots of background screen arranged in vertical and horizontal rows. Outlines of central device, lettering and frame clearly delineated. "C" of cent-sign smaller. Upper claw in solid color.

TB Dispensary Type of 1953
Redrawn
1954, Apr. 1
RA22 PT10 1c blue & red   1.10   .35
a. Red (cross) omitted   55.00
No. RA22 has third color omitted; clouds added; bolder letters and numerals.

Angelita Trujillo — PT12

1955, Dec. 1   Unwmk.   Perf. 12½
RA23 PT12 1c violet   1.20   .35
The tax was for child welfare.

Lorraine Cross — PT13

1956, Apr. 1   Litho.   Perf. 11½
RA24 PT13 1c blk, grn, lem & red   .75   .35
The tax was for the Anti-Tuberculosis League. Inscribed: B.C.G. (Bacillus Calmette-Guerin).

PT14

1957, Apr. 1
RA25 PT14 1c red, blk, yel, grn & bl   .75   .35

Jesus Type of 1950
Fourth Redrawing
1956, Dec. 1   Unwmk.   Perf. 12
Size: 21¾x31¼mm
RA26 PT7 1c blue   .75   .35
Thin white lines around numeral boxes. Girl's bouquet touches Jesus' sleeve. Tiny white squares or rectangles in side borders. Foliage at either side of "Era de Trujillo" panel.

PT15

1958, Apr. 1   Litho.   Perf. 12½
RA27 PT15 1c brown car & red   .70   .35

1959, Apr. 1   Inscribed "1959"
RA28 PT15 1c brown car & red   .70   .35

PT16

1960, Apr. 1   Litho.   Perf. 12
RA29 PT16 1c bl, pale yel & red   .80   .35

PT17

1961, Apr. 1   Unwmk.   Perf. 11½
RA30 PT17 1c blue & red   .65   .35
Nos. RA29-RA30: tax was for the Anti-Tuberculosis League. See No. RA33.

PT18

1961, Aug. 1   Litho.   Perf. 12
RA31 PT18 1c carmine rose   .65   .35
The tax was for aid to the needy.
Nos. RA31-RA33 exist imperf.

Jesus Type of 1950
Fifth Redrawing
1961, Dec. 1   Unwmk.   Perf. 12½
RA32 PT7 1c blue   .65   .35
No. RA32 is similar to No. RA19, but "Era de Trujillo" has been replaced by a solid color panel.

Type of 1961 Dated "1962"
1962, Apr. 2   Perf. 12½
RA33 PT17 1c blue & red   1.20   .35
Tax for the Anti-Tuberculosis League.

Man's Chest — PT19

1963, Apr. 1   Perf. 12x11½
RA34 PT19 1c ultra & red   .75   .35

Jesus Type of 1950
Sixth Redrawing
1963, Dec. 1   Perf. 11½
Size: 21¾x32mm
RA35 PT7 1c blue   .65   .35
a. 1c deep blue ('64)   .65   .35
No. RA35 is similar to No. RA26, but "Era de Trujillo" panel has been omitted.

Hibiscus — PT20

1966, Apr. 1   Litho.   Perf. 11½
RA36 PT20 1c emerald & car   .65   .35
Tax for the Anti-Tuberculosis League.

Domingoa Nodosa — PT21

1967, Apr. 1   Litho.   Perf. 12½
RA37 PT21 1c lilac & red   1.25   .35
Tax for the Anti-Tuberculosis League.

Civil Defense Emblem — PT22

1967, July 1   Litho.   Rouletted 13
RA38 PT22 1c multicolored   .65   .35
Tax for the Civil Defense Organization.

Boy, School and Yule Bells — PT23

1967, Dec. 1   Litho.   Perf. 12½
RA39 PT23 1c rose red & pink   .75   .35

1968   Perf. 11
RA40 PT23 1c vermilion   .70   .35
No. RA40 has screened background; No. RA39, smooth background.
The tax was for child welfare.
See Nos. RA49A, RA52, RA57, RA62, RA68, RA73, RA77, RA81.

Hand Holding Invalid — PT24

1968, Mar. 19   Litho.   Perf. 12½
RA41 PT24 1c green & yellow   .65   .35
a. 1c olive green & deep yellow, perf. 11½x12 ('69)   .40   .25
The tax was for the rehabilitation of the handicapped. See Nos. RA47, RA50, RA54.

Dogbane — PT25

1968, Apr. 25   Litho.   Perf. 12½
RA42 PT25 1c emerald, yel & red   .65   .35
The tax was for the Anti-Tuberculosis League. See Nos. RA45, RA49.

Redrawn Cancer Type of 1955
1968, Oct. 1   Litho.   Perf. 12
RA43 PT9 1c emerald   .65   .35
The tax was for the Dominican League against Cancer.

Schoolyard, Torch — PT26

1969, Feb. 1   Litho.   Perf. 12½
RA44 PT26 1c light blue   .65   .35
Issued for Education Year 1969.

Flower Type of 1968
Design: No. RA45, Violets.

1969, Apr. 25   Litho.   Perf. 12½
RA45 PT25 1c emerald, lil & red   .95   .35
Tax for the Anti-Tuberculosis League.

Redrawn Cancer Type of 1955
1969, Oct. 1   Litho.   Perf. 11
RA46 PT9 1c brt rose lilac   .65   .35
Tax for Dominican League against Cancer.

Invalid Type of 1968
1970, Mar. 2   Perf. 12½
RA47 PT24 1c blue   .65   .35
The tax was for the rehabilitation of the handicapped.

Book, Sun and Education Year Emblem — PT27

1970, Feb. 6   Perf. 11
RA48 PT27 1c bright pink   .65   .35
International Education Year.

Flower Type of 1968
Design: 1c, Elleanthus capitatus; cross in upper left corner, denomination in lower right.

1970, Apr. 30   Perf. 11
RA49 PT25 1c emerald, red & yel   1.30   .35
Tax for Anti-Tuberculosis League.

Boy Type of 1967
1970, Dec. 1   Perf. 12½
RA49A PT23 1c orange   .70   .35

DOMINICAN REPUBLIC

Communications Emblem — PT28

1971, Jan. 2 Litho. *Perf. 11*
Size: 17½x20½mm
RA49B PT28 1c vio bl & red (white frame) .80 .35
Tax was for Postal and Telegraph Communications School.
See Nos. RA53, RA58, RA63, RA69, RA78, RA91.

Invalid Type of 1968
1971, Mar. 1 Litho. *Perf. 11*
RA50 PT24 1c brt rose lilac .65 .35
Tax for rehabilitation of the handicapped.

Cancer Type of 1952
Third Redrawing
1971, Oct. 1 *Perf. 11½*
RA51 PT9 1c dp yellow green .65 .35
Background of No. RA51 appears white and design stands out. No. RA43 has greenish background and design appears faint. Numeral "1" on No. RA51 is 3½mm high, on No. RA43 it is 3mm.

Boy Type of 1967
1971, Dec. 1 Litho. *Perf. 11*
RA52 PT23 1c green .70 .35

Communications Type of 1971
1972, Jan. 3 Litho. *Perf. 12½*
Size: 19x22mm
RA53 PT28 1c dk bl & red (bl frame) .65 .35
Tax was for the Postal and Telegraph Communications School.

Invalid Type of 1968
1972, Mar. 1 Litho. *Perf. 11½*
RA54 PT24 1c brown 1.00 .35

Orchid — PT29

1972, Apr. 2 *Perf. 11*
RA55 PT29 1c lt grn, red & yel 1.80 .50
Tax was for the Anti-Tuberculosis League.

Redrawn Cancer Type of 1954-58
1972, Oct. 2 *Perf. 12½*
RA56 PT9 1c orange .70 .35
Tax for Dominican League against Cancer.

Boy Type of 1967
1972, Dec. 1 *Perf. 12*
RA57 PT23 1c violet .65 .35
Tax was for child welfare.

Communications Type of 1971
1973, Jan. 2 Litho. *Perf. 10½*
Size: 19x22mm
RA58 PT28 1c dk bl & red (red frame) .65 .35
Tax was for Postal and Telegraph Communications School.

Invalid — PT30

1973, Mar. 1 Litho. *Perf. 12½*
Size: 21x25mm
RA59 PT30 1c .65 .35
Tax was for the Dominican Rehabilitation Association. See Nos. RA66, RA70, RA74, RA79, RA86.

Hibiscus — PT31

1973, Apr. 17 Litho. *Perf. 10½*
RA60 PT31 1c multicolored 1.50 .35
Tax was for Anti-Tuberculosis League. Exists imperf.

Cancer Type of 1952 Redrawn and "1973" Added
1973, Oct. 1 *Perf. 13½*
RA61 PT9 1c olive green .60 .35
Tax was for Dominican League Against Cancer.

Boy Type of 1967
1973, Dec. 1 Litho. *Perf. 13x13½*
RA62 PT23 1c blue .95 .35

Communications Type of 1971
1973, Nov. 3 *Perf. 10½*
Size: 19x22mm
RA63 PT28 1c bl & red (lt grn frame) .65 .35
Tax was for Postal and Telegraph Communications School. Exists imperf.

Invalid Type of 1973
1974, Mar. 1 Litho. *Perf. 10½*
Size: 22x27½mm
RA66 PT30 1c light ultra .65 .35
See note after No. RA59.

Cancer Type of 1952 Redrawn and "1974" Added
1974, Oct. 1 *Perf. 12*
RA67 PT9 1c orange .80 .35
Tax for Dominican League Against Cancer.

Boy Type of 1967
1974, Dec. 2 Litho. *Perf. 11½*
RA68 PT23 1c dk brown & buff .60 .35

Communications Type of 1971
1974, Nov. 13 *Perf. 10½*
RA69 PT28 1c blue & red (yel frame) .60 .35

Invalid Type of 1973 Dated "1975"
1975, Mar. 1 *Perf. 13½x13*
Size: 21x32mm
RA70 PT30 1c olive brown .80 .35
See note after No. RA59.

Catteeyopsis Rosea — PT32

1975, Apr. 1 *Perf. 12*
RA71 PT32 1c blue & multi 1.60 1.00
Tax was for Anti-Tuberculosis League

Cancer Type of 1952 Redrawn and "1975" Added
1975, Oct. 1 Litho. *Perf. 12*
RA72 PT9 1c violet blue .80 .35
Tax was for Dominican League Against Cancer. Exists imperf.

Boy Type of 1967
1975, Dec. 1 Litho. *Perf. 12*
RA73 PT23 1c red orange .60 .35
Tax was for child welfare.

Invalid Type of 1973 Dated "1976"
1976, Mar. 1 Litho. *Perf. 12*
Size: 21x31mm
RA74 PT30 1c ultra .80 .35
See note after No. RA59.

Oncidium Colochilum — PT33

1976, Apr. 6 *Perf. 13x13½*
RA75 PT33 1c green & multi 1.25 .35
Tax was for Anti-Tuberculosis League.
See Nos. RA80, RA84.

Cancer Type of 1952 Redrawn and "1976" Added
1976, Oct. 1 Litho. *Perf. 13½*
RA76 PT9 1c green .80 .35
Tax was for Dominican League Against Cancer.

Boy Type of 1967
1976, Dec. 1 Litho. *Perf. 13½*
RA77 PT23 1c purple .80 .35
Tax was for child welfare.

Communications Type of 1971
1977, Jan. 7 Litho. *Perf. 10½*
Size: 19x22mm
RA78 PT28 1c blue & red (lil frame) .65 —
 a. Perf. 12½x10½
Tax was for Postal and Telegraph Communications School.

Invalid Type of 1973 Dated "1977"
1977, Mar. 11 *Perf. 12*
Size: 21x31mm
RA79 PT30 1c ultra .85 .35
See note after No. RA59.

Orchid Type of 1976 Dated "1977"
Orchid: Oncidium variegatum.
1977, Apr. 22 Litho. *Perf. 13½*
RA80 PT33 1c multicolored 1.50 .35
Tax was for Anti-Tuberculosis League.

Boy Type of 1967
1977, Dec. 27 Litho. *Perf. 12*
RA81 PT23 1c emerald .65 .35
Tax was for child welfare.

Cancer Type of 1952 Redrawn and "1977" Added
1978, Oct. 2 Litho. *Perf. 13½*
RA82 PT9 1c lilac rose .80 .35
Tax for Dominican League Against Cancer.

Mother, Child, Holly — PT34

1978, Dec. 1 Litho. *Perf. 13½*
RA83 PT34 1c green .65 .35
Tax was for child welfare.
See Nos. RA89, RA92, RA97.

Orchid Type of 1973 Dated "1978"
Flower: Yellow alder.
1979, Apr. Litho. *Perf. 13½*
RA84 PT33 1c lt blue & multi 1.30 .35
Tax was for Anti-Tuberculosis League.

University Seal — PT35

1979, Feb. 10 Litho. *Perf. 13½*
RA85 PT35 2c ultra & gray .65 .35
450th anniv. of University of Santo Domingo.

Invalid Type of 1973 Dated "1978"
1979, Mar. 1 Litho. *Perf. 12*
RA86 PT30 1c emerald 1.25 .35
See note after No. RA59.

Invalid — PT36

1980, Mar. 28 Litho. *Perf. 13½*
RA87 PT36 1c olive & citron 1.25 .35

Cancer Type of 1952 Redrawn and "1980" Added
1980, Oct. 1
RA88 PT9 1c violet & dk pur .65 .35

Mother and Child Type of 1978
1980, Dec. 1 Litho. *Perf. 13½*
RA89 PT34 1c bright blue .65 .35

Turnera Ulmifolia (Marilope) — PT37

1981, Apr. 27 Litho. *Perf. 12*
RA90 PT37 1c multicolored .75 .50
Tax was for Anti-Tuberculosis League.
See Nos. RA98-RA99.

Communications Type of 1971
1981, Feb. Litho. *Perf. 10½*
RA91 PT28 1c blue & red (lt bl frame) 1.00 .35

Mother and Child Type of 1978
1982, Dec. 1 Litho. *Perf. 12x12½*
RA92 PT34 1c lt bluish green .65 .35
Inscribed 1981.

Cancer Type of 1952 Redrawn and "1981" Added
1982 Litho. *Perf. 13½*
RA93 PT9 1c blue & dp blue 1.25 .35

PT38

1983, Apr. 29 Litho. *Perf. 12*
RA94 PT38 1c multicolored .65 .35
Tax was for Red Cross.

Disabled — PT39

1984 Litho. *Perf. 13½*
RA95 PT39 1c sky blue .80 .35

Cancer Type of 1952 Redrawn and "1983" Added
1983, Oct. 1 Litho. *Perf. 13½*
RA96 PT9 1c lt bluish grn & dk grn 1.30 .35

Mother and Child Type of 1978
1983, Dec. 1 Litho. *Perf. 12*
RA97 PT34 1c light green 1.30 .35
Inscribed 1983.

DOMINICAN REPUBLIC — DUBAI

Flower Type of 1981 Dated "1983" or "1984"
1983-85   Litho.   Perf. 12x12½
| RA98 | PT37 | 1c 1983 | 2.25 | .35 |
| RA99 | PT37 | 1c 1984 | 2.25 | .35 |

Issued: #RA98, 4/19/83; #RA99, 4/1/85.

POSTAL TAX AIR POST STAMPS

Postal Tax Stamps Surcharged in Red or Gold

1930, Dec. 3   Unwmk.   Perf. 12
RAC1	PT2	5c + 5c blk & rose (R)	55.00	60.00
a.	Tête bêche pair		125.00	
b.	"Habilitado Para" missing		52.50	
RAC2	PT2	10c + 10c blk & rose (R)	55.00	60.00
a.	Tête bêche pair		125.00	
b.	"Habilitado Para" missing		52.50	
c.	Gold surcharge		95.00	95.00
d.	As "c," tête bêche pair		450.00	
e.	As "c" and "b"		250.00	

Nos. RAC1-RAC2 were on sale one day.

RAC4	PT2	5c + 5c ultra & rose (R)	13.50	13.50
a.	Tête bêche pair		45.00	
b.	Inverted surcharge		42.50	
c.	Tête bêche pair, inverted surcharge		600.00	
d.	Pair, one without surcharge		190.00	
e.	"Habilitado Para" missing		50.00	
RAC5	PT2	10c + 10c yel & rose (G)	10.00	10.00
a.	Tête bêche pair		42.50	
b.	"Habilitado Para" missing		36.00	

Imperf
RAC6	PT2	5c + 5c ultra & rose (R)	13.50	13.50
a.	Tête bêche pair		52.50	
b.	"Habilitado Para" missing		18.00	
RAC7	PT2	10c + 10c yel & rose (G)	13.50	13.50
a.	Tête bêche pair		52.50	
b.	"Habilitado Para" missing		18.00	
Nos. RAC1-RAC7 (6)			160.50	170.50

It was obligatory to use Nos. RA1-RA8 and RAC1-RAC7 on all postal matter, in amounts equal to the ordinary postage.

This surtax was for the aid of sufferers from the hurricane of Sept. 3, 1930.

No. 261 Overprinted in Green

1933, Oct. 11
RAC8	A32	2c scarlet	.50	.40
a.	Double overprint		9.00	
b.	Pair, one without overprint		375.00	
c.	Inverted overprint			25.00

By official decree this stamp, in addition to the regular postage, had to be used on every letter, etc., sent by the internal air post service.

DUBAI

dü-'bī

LOCATION — Oman Peninsula, Arabia, on Persian Gulf
GOVT. — Sheikdom under British protection
AREA — 1,500 sq. mi.
POP. — 60,000
CAPITAL — Dubai

Dubai is one of six Persian Gulf sheikdoms to join the United Arab Emirates which proclaimed its independence Dec. 2, 1971. See United Arab Emirates.

100 Naye Paise = 1 Rupee
100 Dirhams = 1 Riyal (1966)

Imperforate
Many issues were accompanied by smaller quantities of imperforate stamps.

Catalogue values for all unused stamps in this country are for Never Hinged items.

Hermit Crab — A1   Sheik Rashid bin Said al Maktum — A2

2np, 20np, Cuttlefish. 3np, 25np, Snail. 4np, 30np, Crab. 5np, 35np, Sea urchin. 10np, 50np, Sea shell. 1r, Fortress wall. 2r, View of Dubai. 3r, Fortress wall. 5r, View of Dubai.

Perf. 12x11½
1963, June 15   Litho.   Unwmk.
1	A1	1np dl bl & car bne	.30	.25
2	A1	2np lt bl & bis brn	.35	.25
3	A1	3np green & sepia	.35	.25
4	A1	4np pink & orange	.35	.25
5	A1	5np violet & blk	.35	.25
6	A1	10np brn org & blk	.35	.25
7	A1	15np gray ol & dp car	.70	.25
8	A1	20np rose red & org brn	.75	.40
9	A1	25np ap grn & red brn	.90	.40
10	A1	30np gray & red	1.50	.40
11	A1	35np dl lil & dl vio	1.50	.40
12	A1	50np org & sepia	2.25	.75
13	A1	1r brt bl & red org	6.00	1.50
14	A1	2r dull yel & brn	9.50	3.50
15	A1	3r rose car & blk	16.00	5.50
16	A1	5r grn & dl red brn	27.50	9.50

Perf. 12
| 17 | A2 | 10r rose lake, grnsh bl & blk | 60.00 | 19.00 |
| Nos. 1-17 (17) | | | 128.65 | 43.10 |

Nos. 13-17 exist perf 10½. Values are much higher.

Dhows — A3

Designs: 2np, First-aid tent. 3np, Camel caravan. 4np, Butterfly.

1963, Sept. 1   Unwmk.   Perf. 12
18	A3	1np ultra, yel & red	.80	.35
19	A3	2np brn, yel & red	.80	.35
20	A3	3np red brn, org & red	.80	.35
21	A3	4np brn, brt grn & red	.80	.35
Nos. 18-21, C9-C12 (8)			11.00	4.10

Intl. Red Cross, cent. Exist perf. 10½. Values, each $1.75.

Four imperf. souvenir sheets exist in the denominations and designs of Nos. C9-C12, with "Air-Mail" omitted and colors changed. Size: 119x99mm. Value $50.

For overprints see Nos. C52-C54.

A4

Anopheles Mosquito: 2np, Mosquito and entwined snakes. 3np, Mosquitoes over swamp.

1963, Dec. 20   Unwmk.   Perf. 12
22	A4	1np emer & red brn	.35	.25
23	A4	1np red & dark brn	.35	.25
24	A4	1np blue & carmine	.35	.25
25	A4	2np brn & orange	.35	.25
26	A4	2np carmine & blue	.35	.25
27	A4	3np org brn & blue	.35	.25
Nos. 22-27, C13-C15 (9)			4.55	2.35

WHO drive to eradicate malaria.

A5

Designs: 1np, Scouts forming pyramid. 2np, Bugler. 3np, Cub Scouts. 4np, Scouts and bugler. 5np, Scouts presenting flag.

1964   Unwmk.
28	A5	1np dk brn & ocher	.25	.25
29	A5	2np car rose & sep	.25	.25
30	A5	3np blue & red org	.25	.25
31	A5	4np carmine & blue	.25	.25
32	A5	5np ind & bluish grn	.35	.25
Nos. 28-32, C20-C24 (10)			6.35	3.20

11th Boy Scout Jamboree, Marathon, Greece, Aug., 1963.

For overprints see Nos. C47-C51.

Unisphere, New York Skyline and Dubai Harbor — A6

2np, 4np, 10np, Views of NYC and Dubai.

1964, Apr. 22   Litho.   Perf. 12
33	A6	1np dk bl & rose red	.25	.25
34	A6	2np dl red, lil rose & bl	.25	.25
35	A6	3np brown & green	.25	.25
36	A6	4np emer, brt grn & red	.25	.25
37	A6	5np ol, sl grn & lil	.25	.25
38	A6	10np brn org, red org & blk	.70	.50
Nos. 33-38, C36-C38 (9)			6.15	4.05

New York World's Fair, 1964-65.

Gymnast A8

Designs: 2np, 5np, 20np, 40np, Various exercises on bar. 3np, 30np, Various exercises on vaulting horse. 4np, 10np, 1r, Various exercises on rings.

1964   Photo.   Perf. 14
43	A8	1np org brn & yel grn	.25	.25
44	A8	2np dk brn & grnsh bl	.25	.25
45	A8	3np ultra & org brn	.25	.25
46	A8	4np dk pur & yel	.25	.25
47	A8	5np ocher & dk bl	.25	.25
48	A8	10np brt bl & ocher	.30	.25
49	A8	20np ol & lil rose	.40	.25
50	A8	30np dk bl & yel	.75	.25
51	A8	40np Prus grn & dl org	1.25	.50
52	A8	1r rose vio & grnsh bl	2.50	1.25
Nos. 43-52 (10)			6.45	3.75

18th Olympic Games, Tokyo, Oct. 10-25, 1964. An imperf. miniature sheet contains a 67x67mm stamp similar to No. 52. Value $11.

Palace A9   Sheik Rashid bin Said A10

Designs: 20np, 25np, View of new Dubai. 35np, 40np, Bridge and dhow. 60np, 1r, Bridge. 1.25r, Minaret. 1.50r, 3r, Old Dubai.

1966, May 30   Photo.   Perf. 14x14½
Size: 23x18mm
53	A9	5np brown & indigo	.25	.25
54	A9	10np black & orange	.30	.25
55	A9	15np ultra & brown	.40	.25

Perf. 13
Size: 27½x20½mm
56	A9	20np blue & red brn	.50	.30
57	A9	25np org ver & ultra	.55	.40
58	A9	35np violet & emer	.75	.50
59	A9	40np grnsh bl & bl	1.10	.50

Perf. 14½
Size: 31½x24mm
60	A9	60np yel grn & org ver	1.75	1.00
61	A9	1r ultra & blue	2.75	1.50
62	A9	1.25r brn org & blk	3.00	2.00
63	A9	1.50r rose lil & yel grn	5.50	2.10
64	A9	3r dk ol bis & vio	10.00	4.00

Engr.
Perf. 14
65	A10	5r rose carmine	18.00	7.50
66	A10	10r dark blue	37.50	16.00
Nos. 53-66 (14)			82.35	36.55

Nos. 53-62, 64-66 Overprinted with New Currency Names and Bars

1967
67	A9	5d on 5np	.30	.25
68	A9	10d on 10np	.35	.25
69	A9	15d on 15np	.50	.25
70	A9	20d on 20np	1.00	.25
71	A9	25d on 25np	1.25	.25
72	A9	35d on 35np	1.50	.25
73	A9	40d on 40np	1.75	.30
74	A9	60d on 60np	3.00	.40
75	A9	1r on 1r	4.00	.95
76	A9	1.25r on 1.25r	7.25	1.30
77	A9	3r on 3r	15.00	3.75
78	A10	5r on 5r	27.50	7.50
79	A10	10r on 10r	40.00	14.00
Nos. 67-79 (13)			103.40	29.70

Sheik and Falcon — A11   Dhow — A12

Litho. & Engr.
1967, Aug. 21   Perf. 13½
80	A11	5d dp car & org	1.10	.30
81	A11	10d sepia & green	1.25	.25
82	A11	20d dp cl & bl gray	1.40	.30
83	A11	35d slate & car	1.75	.30
84	A11	60d vio bl & emer	3.25	.30
85	A11	1r green & lilac	4.50	.50
86	A12	1.25r lt bl & claret	5.50	.65
87	A12	3r dull vio & claret	11.00	1.75
88	A12	5r brt grn & vio	22.50	3.75
89	A12	10r lil rose & grn	30.00	6.75
Nos. 80-89 (10)			82.25	15.05

S. S. Bamora, 1914 — A13

35d, De Havilland 66 plane, 1930. 60d, S. S. Sirdhana, 1947. 1r, Armstrong Whitworth 15 "Atlanta," 1938. 1.25r, S. S. Chandpara, 1949. 3r, BOAC Sunderland amphibian plane, 1943. No. 96, Freighter Bombala, 1961, and BOAC Super VC10, 1967.

DUBAI

1969, Feb. 12   Litho.   Perf. 14x13½
90	A13	25d lt grn, bl & blk	.25	.25
91	A13	35d multicolored	.25	.25
92	A13	60d multicolored	.70	.25
93	A13	1r lil, blk & dl yel	1.15	.25
94	A13	1.25r gray, blk & dp org	1.60	.25
95	A13	3r pink, blk & bl grn	2.50	.35
	Nos. 90-95 (6)		6.45	1.60

Miniature Sheet
Imperf
| 96 | A13 | 1.25r pink, blk & bl grn | 16.00 | 16.00 |

60 years of postal service.

Mother and Children, by Rubens — A14

Arab Mother's Day: 60d, Madonna and Child, by Murillo. 1r, Mother and Child, by Francesco Mazzuoli. 3r, Madonna and Child, by Correggio.

1969, Mar. 21   Litho.   Perf. 13½
97	A14	60d silver & multi	.75	.25
98	A14	1r silver & multi	1.50	.25
99	A14	1.25r silver & multi	1.75	.25
100	A14	3r silver & multi	3.50	.45
	Nos. 97-100 (4)		7.60	1.20

Porkfish A15

1969, May 26   Litho.   Perf. 11
101	A15	60d shown	2.00	.35
102	A15	60d Spotted grouper	2.00	.35
103	A15	60d Moonfish	2.00	.35
104	A15	60d Sweetlips	2.00	.35
105	A15	60d Blue angel	2.00	.35
106	A15	60d Texas skate	2.00	.35
107	A15	60d Striped butterf-lyfish	2.00	.35
108	A15	60d Imperial angelfish	2.00	.35
a.	Block of 8, #101-108		35.00	
	Nos. 101-108 (8)		16.00	2.80

Nos. 101-108 printed in se-tenant blocks of 8, each sheet containing two such blocks.

Explorers and Map of Arabia — A16

1969, July 21   Litho.   Perf. 13½x13
109	A16	35d brown & green	1.50	.35
110	A16	60d vio & sepia	2.00	.45
111	A16	1r green & dl bl	5.50	.55
112	A16	1.25r gray & rose car	7.00	.65
	Nos. 109-112 (4)		16.00	2.00

European explorers of Arabia: Sir Richard Francis Burton (1821-1890), Charles Montagu Doughty (1843-1926), Johann Ludwig Burckhardt (1784-1817) and Wilfred Patrick Thesiger (1910-).

Construction of World's First Underwater Oil Storage Tank — A17

Designs: 20d, Launching of oil storage tank. 35d, Oil storage tank in place on ocean ground. 60d, Sheik Rashid bin Said, offshore drilling platform and monument commemorating first oil export. 1r, Offshore production platform and helicopter port.

1969, Oct. 13   Litho.   Perf. 11
113	A17	5d blue & multi	.30	.25
114	A17	20d blue & multi	1.00	.25
115	A17	35d blue & multi	1.90	.25
116	A17	60d blue & multi	2.75	.25
117	A17	1r blue & multi	4.00	.25
	Nos. 113-117 (5)		9.95	1.25

Astronauts Collecting Moon Rocks — A18

Designs: 1r, Astronaut at foot of ladder. 1.25r, Astronauts planting American flag.

1969, Dec. 15   Litho.   Perf. 14½
118		Strip of 3	3.75	1.00
a.	A18	60d multicolored	.40	.25
b.	A18	1r multicolored	.80	.25
c.	A18	1.25r multicolored (airmail)	1.50	.25

The 1.25r is inscribed "AIRMAIL."
Sizes: 60d and 1r, 28½x41mm; 1.25r, 60½x41mm.
See note after US No. C76.

Ocean Weather Ship Launching Radio Sonde, and Hastings Plane — A19

WMO Emblem and: 1r, Kew-type radio sonde, weather balloon and radar antenna. 1.25r, Tiros satellite and weather sounding rocket. 3r, Ariel satellite and rocket launching.

1970, Mar. 23   Litho.   Perf. 11
121	A19	60d dl grn, brn & blk	.40	.25
122	A19	1r brown & multi	.75	.25
123	A19	1.25r dk blue & multi	.90	.25
124	A19	3r multicolored	2.00	.30
	Nos. 121-124 (4)		4.05	1.05

10th World Meteorological Day.

UPU Headquarters and Monument, Bern — A20

60d, UPU monument, Bern, telecommunications satellite and London PO tower.

1970, May 20   Litho.   Perf. 13½x14
| 125 | A20 | 5d lt green & multi | .75 | .25 |
| 126 | A20 | 60d dp blue & multi | 1.00 | .25 |

UPU Headquarters opening, May 20.

Charles Dickens, London Skyline — A21

60d, Dickens' portrait, vert. 1.25r, Dickens & "Old Curiosity Shop." 3r, Bound volumes.

1970, July 23   Litho.   Perf. 13½
127	A21	60d olive & multi	.85	.25
128	A21	1r multicolored	1.00	.25
129	A21	1.25r buff & multi	1.20	.25
130	A21	3r multicolored	4.00	.50
	Nos. 127-130 (4)		7.05	1.25

Dickens (1812-70), English novelist.

The Graham Children, by William Hogarth A22

Paintings: 60d, Caroline Murat and her Children, by François Pascal Gerard, vert. 1r,

Napoleon with the Children on the Terrace in St. Cloud, by Louis Ducis.

1970, Oct. 1   Litho.   Perf. 13½
131	A22	35d multicolored	.75	.25
132	A22	60d multicolored	1.25	.25
133	A22	1r multicolored	2.00	.25
	Nos. 131-133 (3)		4.00	.75

Issued for Children's Day.

 Sheik Rashid bin Said A23

 Television Station A25

National Bank of Dubai — A24

Designs: 10d, Boat building. 20d, Al Maktum Bascule Bridge. 35d, Great Mosque, Dubai, vert. 1r, Dubai International Airport, horiz. 1.25r, Port Rashid harbor project, horiz. 3r, Rashid Hospital, horiz. 5r, Dubai Trade School, horiz.

Perf. 14x14½, 14½x14
1970-71   Litho.
134	A23	5d multi ('71)	.30	.25
135	A24	10d multi ('71)	.30	.25
136	A24	20d multi ('71)	.40	.25
137	A24	35d multi ('71)	.55	.25
138	A24	60d multicolored	.80	.25

Perf. 14
139	A25	1r multicolored	1.20	.25
140	A25	1.25r multicolored	1.20	.25
141	A25	3r multicolored	3.75	.25
142	A25	5r multicolored	6.00	.40
143	A25	10r multi ('71)	14.00	.85
	Nos. 134-143 (10)		28.50	3.25

Dubai Airport — A26

Designs: 1.25r, Airport entrance.

1971, May 15   Litho.   Perf. 13½x14
| 144 | A26 | 1r multicolored | 3.25 | .25 |
| 145 | A26 | 1.25r multicolored | 4.00 | .25 |

Opening of Dubai International Airport.

Map With Tracking Stations, Satellites — A27

1971, June 21   Litho.   Perf. 14½
| 146 | A27 | 60d multicolored | .60 | .30 |

Outer Space Telecommunications Cong., Paris, Mar. 29-Apr. 2. See Nos. C55-C56.

Fan, Scout Emblem, Map of Japan — A28

Designs: 1r, Boy Scouts in kayaks. 1.25r, Mountaineering. 3r, Campfire, horiz.

Albrecht Dürer, Self-portrait — A29

1971, Aug. 30   Litho.
147	A28	60d multicolored	.45	.25
148	A28	1r multicolored	.90	.25
149	A28	1.25r multicolored	1.15	.25
150	A28	3r multicolored	2.50	.30
	Nos. 147-150 (4)		5.00	1.05

13th Boy Scout World Jamboree, Asagiri Plain, Japan, Aug. 2-10.

1971, Oct. 18   Perf. 14x13½
| 151 | A29 | 60d gold & multi | .80 | .25 |

See Nos. C57-C59.

Boy in Meadow — A30

5r, Boys playing and UNICEF emblem.

1971, Dec. 11   Perf. 13½
| 152 | A30 | 60d multi | .45 | .25 |
| 153 | A30 | 5r multi, horiz. | 3.50 | .50 |

25th anniv. of UNICEF. See No. C60.

Ludwig van Beethoven — A31

Portrait: 10d, Leonardo da Vinci.

1972, Feb. 7
| 154 | A31 | 10d lt tan & multi | .30 | .25 |
| 155 | A31 | 35d lt tan & multi | .45 | .25 |

See Nos. C61-C62.

Olympic Emblems, Gymnast on Rings — A32

1972, July 31   Litho.   Perf. 13½
156	A32	35d shown	.55	.25
157	A32	40d Fencing	.65	.25
158	A32	65d Hockey	.80	.25
	Nos. 156-158,C65-C67 (6)		7.50	1.50

20th Olympic Games, Munich, 8/26-9/11.
Stamps of Dubai were replaced in 1972 by those of United Arab Emirates.

AIR POST STAMPS

Type of Regular Issue and

Peregrine Falcon — AP1

DUBAI — EAST AFRICA & UGANDA PROTECTORATES

Design: A1, Falcon over bridge.

Perf. 12x11½, 11½x12

		1963, June 15 Litho.	Unwmk.	
C1	A1	20np dk red brn & lt blue	2.50	.35
C2	AP1	25np ol & blk brn	2.75	.45
C3	A1	30np red org & blk	3.25	.55
C4	AP1	40np grayish brn & dk violet	3.50	.65
C5	A1	50np emer & rose cl	4.25	.75
C6	AP1	60np brn org & blk	5.25	.85
C7	A1	75np vio & dp grn	6.50	1.00
C8	AP1	1r org & red brn	9.00	1.25
		Nos. C1-C8 (8)	37.00	5.85

Red Cross Type

Designs: 20np, Dhows. 30np, First-aid tent. 40np, Camel caravan. 50np, Butterfly.

		1963, Sept. 1 Unwmk.	Perf. 12	
C9	A3	20np brown, yel & red	1.40	.50
C10	A3	30np dk bl, buff & red	1.40	.50
C11	A3	40np black, yel & red	1.75	.60
C12	A3	50np vio, lt bl & red	3.25	1.10
		Nos. C9-C12 (4)	7.80	2.70

Malaria Type

Designs: 30np, Anopheles mosquito. 40np, Mosquito and coiled arrows. 70np, Mosquitoes over swamp.

		1963, Dec. 20 Unwmk.	Perf. 12	
C13	A4	30np purple & emer	.65	.25
C14	A4	40np red & dull grn	.75	.25
C15	A4	70np slate & citron	1.05	.35
		Nos. C13-C15 (3)	2.45	.85

Three imperf. souv. sheets exist containing 4 stamps each in changed colors similar to Nos. C13-C15. Value $30.

Wheat — AP2

40np, Wheat and palm tree. 70np, Hands holding wheat. 1r, Woman carrying basket.

		1963, Dec. 30	Litho.	
C16	AP2	30np vio bl & ocher	.50	.30
C17	AP2	40np red & olive	.75	.45
C18	AP2	70np green & orange	1.15	.65
C19	AP2	1r org brn & Prus bl	1.75	1.00
		Nos. C16-C19 (4)	4.15	2.40

Boy Scout Type

Designs: 20np, Human pyramid. 30np, Bugler. 40np, Cub Scouts. 70np, Scouts and bugler. 1r, Scouts presenting flag.

		1964, Jan. 20		
C20	A5	20np green & dk brn	.30	.25
C21	A5	30np lilac & ocher	.60	.25
C22	A5	40np vio bl & yel grn	.80	.30
C23	A5	70np dk grn & gray	1.40	.45
C24	A5	1r vio bl & red org	1.90	.70
		Nos. C20-C24 (5)	5.00	1.95

Five imperf. souv. sheets exist containing 4 stamps each in changed colors similar to Nos. C20-C24. Value $60.

For overprints see Nos. C47-C51.

John F. Kennedy and US Seal — AP3

		1964, Jan. 15	Litho.	
C25	AP3	75np grn & blk, *lt grn*	.90	.55
C26	AP3	1r ocher & blk, *tan*	1.25	.60
C27	AP3	1.25r mag & blk, *gray*	1.60	.85
		Nos. C25-C27 (3)	3.75	2.00

Pres. John F. Kennedy (1917-1963).
Nos. C25-C27 exist imperf. Value, set $9.50.
A souvenir sheet contains one imperf. 1.25r in buff and black with simulated perforations. Value $5.

For overprints see Nos. C52-C54.

Spacecraft — AP4

Designs: 1np, 5np, Ascending rocket, vert. 2np, 1r, Mercury capsule, vert. 4np, 2r, Twin spacecraft.

		1964, Jan. 25 Unwmk.	Perf. 12	
C28	AP4	1np emerald & org	.25	.25
C29	AP4	2np multicolored	.30	.25
C30	AP4	3np multicolored	.35	.25
C31	AP4	4np multicolored	.40	.25
C32	AP4	5np blue & orange	.45	.25
C33	AP4	1r vio bl, dp car & buff	1.25	.70
C34	AP4	1.50r vio bl, dp car & buff	2.00	1.25
C35	AP4	2r blue, yel & red	2.75	1.50
		Nos. C28-C35 (8)	7.75	4.70

Issued to honor the astronauts.
Nos. C28-C35 exist imperf. Value, set $10.
An imperf. souvenir sheet contains one stamp similar to No. C35. Value $7.

New York World's Fair Type

Statue of Liberty and ships in Dubai harbor.

		1964, Apr. 22	Litho.	
C36	A6	75np gray bl, ultra & blk	.80	.40
C37	A6	2r gray grn, dk brn & bis	1.40	.80
C38	A6	3r dl grn, gray ol & dp org	2.00	1.10
		Nos. C36-C38 (3)	4.20	2.30

An imperf. souvenir sheet contains 2 stamps in Statue of Liberty design: 2r dark brown and rose carmine, and 3r ultramarine and gold. Value $10.

Scales and Flame — AP5

		1964, Apr. 30 Litho.	Perf. 12	
C39	AP5	35np bl, brn & scar	.60	.30
C40	AP5	50np lt bl, dk grn & scar	.75	.35
C41	AP5	1r grnsh bl, blk & scar	1.40	.60
C42	AP5	3r lt ultra, ultra, & scar	4.00	2.00
		Nos. C39-C42 (4)	6.75	3.25

15th anniv. of the Universal Declaration of Human Rights. An imperf. souvenir sheet contains one 3r light green, ultramarine and scarlet stamp. Value $7.50.

Nos. C20-C24 Overprinted in Red and Black (Shield in Red)

		1964, June 20		
C47	A5	20np green & dk brn	1.15	.40
C48	A5	30np lilac & ocher	1.35	.50
C49	A5	40np vio bl & yel grn	2.00	.75
C50	A5	70np dk grn & gray	3.25	1.50
C51	A5	1r vio bl & red org	4.50	2.00
		Nos. C47-C51 (5)	12.25	5.15

9th Winter Olympic Games, Innsbruck, Austria, Jan. 29-Feb. 9, 1964.
A similar but unauthorized overprint, with shield in black, exists on Nos. 28-32, C20-C24, and the five souvenir sheets mentioned below No. C24. The Dubai G.P.O. calls this black-shield overprint "bogus."

Nos. C25-C27 Overprinted in Brown or Green

		1964, Sept. 15		
C52	AP3	75np (Br)	2.00	2.00
C53	AP3	1r (G)	2.40	2.40
C54	AP3	1.25r (G)	3.00	3.00
		Nos. C52-C54 (3)	7.40	7.40

Pres. John F. Kennedy 48th birth anniv. The same overprint in black was applied to the souv. sheet noted after No. C27.

Communications Type

Designs: 1r, Intelsat 4, tracking station on globe and rocket. 5r, Eiffel Tower, Syncom 3 and Goonhilly radar station.

		1971, June 21 Litho.	Perf. 14½	
C55	A27	1r lt brown & multi	.60	.25
C56	A27	5r multicolored	3.00	.45

Portrait Type

1r, Newton. 1.25r, Avicenna. 3r, Voltaire.

		1971, Oct. 18 Litho.	Perf. 14x13½	
C57	A29	1r gold & multi	1.10	.25
C58	A29	1.25r gold & multi	1.40	.25
C59	A29	3r gold & multi	4.00	.25
		Nos. C57-C59 (3)	6.50	1.00

UNICEF Type

1r, Mother, children, UNICEF emblem.

		1971, Dec. 11	Perf. 13½	
C60	A30	1r gold & multi	1.00	.25

Portrait Type

75d, Khalil Gibran. 5r, Charles de Gaulle.

		1972, Feb. 7 Litho.	Perf. 13½	
C61	A31	75d lt tan & multi	.75	.25
C62	A31	5r lt tan & multi	5.25	.35

Infant Health Care — AP6

Design: 75d, Nurse supervising children at meal, and WHO emblem, vert.

		1972, Apr. 7 Litho.	Perf. 14x13½	
C63	AP6	75d multicolored	1.60	.25
C64	AP6	1.25r multicolored	2.40	.25

World Health Day.

Olympic Type

		1972, July 31 Litho.	Perf. 13½	
C65	A32	75d Water polo	1.50	.25
C66	A32	1r Steeplechase	1.75	.25
C67	A32	1.25r Running	2.25	.25
		Nos. C65-C67 (3)	5.50	.60

POSTAGE DUE STAMPS

Type of Regular Issue

Designs: 1np, 4np, 15np, Clam. 2np, 5np, 25np, Mussel. 3np, 10np, 35np, Oyster.

Perf. 12x11½

		1963, June 15 Litho.	Unwmk.	
J1	A1	1np gray grn & ver	1.00	.35
J2	A1	2np lemon & brt bl	1.50	.45
J3	A1	3np dl rose & green	1.75	.75
J4	A1	4np light grn & mag	2.50	1.00
J5	A1	5np vermilion & blk	3.00	1.25
J6	A1	10np citron & violet	3.50	1.50
J7	A1	15np brt ultra & ver	4.50	1.90
J8	A1	25np buff & olive grn	6.00	2.00
J9	A1	35np turq bl & dp org	6.50	2.75
		Nos. J1-J9 (9)	30.25	11.95

Sheik Rashid bin Said — D1

		1972, May 22 Litho.	Perf. 14x14½	
J10	D1	5d blk & gray grn	2.00	.75
J11	D1	10d vio bl, blk & bis	2.50	.85
J12	D1	20d sl grn, blk & brick red	4.25	1.50
J13	D1	30d grnsh gray, blk & lil	7.00	2.25
J14	D1	50d lilac, brn & bis	11.00	4.50
		Nos. J10-J14 (5)	26.75	9.85

EAST AFRICA & UGANDA PROTECTORATES

ˈēst ˈa-fri-kə and ü-ˈgan-də prə-ˈtek-tə-ˌrəts

LOCATION — Central East Africa, bordering on the Indian Ocean
GOVT. — British Protectorate
AREA — 350,000 sq. mi. (approx.)
POP. — 6,503,507 (approx.)
CAPITAL — Mombasa

This territory, formerly administered by the British East Africa Colony, was divided between Kenya Colony and the Uganda Protectorate. See Kenya, Uganda and Tanzania.

16 Annas = 1 Rupee
100 Cents = 1 Rupee (1907)

Altered high value stamps of East Africa and Uganda are plentiful. Expertization by competent authorities is recommended.

A1   A2

King Edward VII

		1903 Typo. Wmk. 2	Perf. 14	
1	A1	½a gray green	7.00	23.00
2	A1	1a car & black	3.00	2.00
3	A1	2a vio & dull vio	10.50	3.00
4	A1	2½a ultramarine	14.50	60.00
5	A1	3a gray grn & brn	30.00	75.00
6	A1	4a blk & gray grn	13.50	27.50
7	A1	5a org brn & blk	22.50	60.00
8	A1	8a pale blue & blk	28.00	50.00

Wmk. 1

9	A2	1r gray green	27.50	65.00
10	A2	2r vio & dull vio	95.00	100.00
11	A2	3r blk & gray grn	175.00	325.00
12	A2	4r lt green & blk	175.00	350.00
13	A2	5r car & black	175.00	350.00
14	A2	10r ultra & black	475.00	675.00
15	A2	20r ol gray & blk	850.00	1,950.
16	A2	50r org brn & blk	2,600.	4,750.
		Nos. 1-14 (14)	1,252.	2,166.

Nos. 9 and 14 are on both ordinary and chalky paper. Values are for examples on ordinary paper. Values are for the least expensive varieties. See Scott Classic Specialized Catalogue of Stamps & Covers for detailed listings.

		1904-07 Wmk. 3	Chalky Paper	
17	A1	½a gray green	16.00	3.75
18a	A1	1a car & black	11.00	1.00
19	A1	2a vio & dull vio	3.50	3.25
20	A1	2½a blue	10.00	37.50
a.		2½a blue & ultramarine	9.50	35.00
21	A1	3a gray grn & brn	4.75	45.00
22	A1	4a blk & gray grn	9.25	22.50
23	A1	5a org brn & blk	8.00	32.50
24a	A1	8a pale blue & blk	8.75	10.50
25	A2	1r gray green	35.00	75.00
26	A2	2r vio & dl vio	50.00	77.50
27	A2	3r blk & gray grn	100.00	160.00
28	A2	4r lt green & blk	140.00	200.00
29	A2	5r car & black	175.00	700.00
29A	A2	10r ultra & black	400.00	450.00
30	A2	20r ol gray & blk	875.00	1,600.
30A	A2	50r org brn & blk	2,750.	4,500.
		Nos. 17-29 (10)	541.50	1,320.

Nos. 17-19, 21-24 are on both ordinary and chalky paper. No. 20 is on ordinary paper. Values are for the least expensive varieties. See Scott Classic Specialized Catalogue of Stamps & Covers for detailed listings.

		1907-08		
31	A1	1c brown ('08)	3.00	.25
32	A1	3c gray green	22.50	.80
33	A1	6c carmine	3.25	.25
34	A1	10c citron & violet	13.00	10.00
35	A1	12c red vio & dl vio	12.00	3.50
36	A1	15c multicolored	34.00	11.00
37	A1	25c blk & blue green	22.50	8.50
38	A1	50c org brn & green	20.00	17.50
39	A1	75c pale bl & gray blk ('08)	5.50	40.00
		Nos. 31-39 (9)	135.75	91.80

Nos. 31-33, 36 are on ordinary paper. There are two dies of the 6c differing very slightly in many details.

EAST AFRICA & UGANDA PROTECTORATES — EASTERN RUMELIA — EASTERN SILESIA

A3

King George V — A4

1912-18		Ordinary Paper	Wmk. 3	
40	A3	1c black	.40	2.10
41	A3	3c green	2.50	.75
a.		Booklet pane of 6		
42	A3	6c carmine	1.50	.70
a.		Booklet pane of 6		
43	A3	10c yel orange	2.50	.65
44	A3	12c gray	3.25	.65
45	A3	15c ultramarine	3.25	1.00
		Chalky Paper		
46	A3	25c scar & blk, yel	.65	1.60
47	A3	50c violet & black	1.90	1.60
48	A3	75c black, green	1.90	21.00
a.		75c black, emerald	13.50	65.00
b.		75c blk, bl grn, olive back	12.00	9.25
c.		75c blk, emer, olive back	50.00	175.00
49	A4	1r black, green	3.00	5.25
a.		1r black, emerald	6.00	60.00
50	A4	2r blk & red, bl	26.00	45.00
51	A4	3r gray grn & vio	32.50	130.00
52	A4	4r grn & red, yel	65.00	130.00
53	A4	5r dl vio & ultra	65.00	160.00
54	A4	10r grn & red, grn	260.00	375.00
55	A4	20r vio & blk, red	500.00	475.00
56	A4	20r bl & violet, blue ('18)	575.00	875.00
57	A4	50r gray grn & rose red	925.00	975.00
58	A4	100r blk & vio, red	9,750.	4,000.
59	A4	500r red & grn, grn	40,000.	
		Nos. 40-54 (15)	469.35	875.30

1914
Chalky Surface-colored Paper
| 60 | A3 | 25c scarlet & blk, yel | .65 | 5.50 |
| 61 | A3 | 75c black, green | 1.25 | 19.50 |

Stamps of types A3 and A4 with watermark 4 are listed under Kenya, Uganda and Tanzania.

The 1r through 50r with revenue cancellations sell for minimal prices. The 100r and 500r were available for postage but were nearly always used fiscally.

For surcharge see No. 62.

No. 42 Surcharged

1919
62	A3	4c on 6c carmine	1.50	.25
a.		Double surcharge	160.00	250.00
b.		Without squares over old value	50.00	85.00
c.		Pair, one without surcharge	2,000.	2,250.
d.		Inverted surcharge	350.00	475.00

For later issues see Kenya, Uganda and Tanzania.
For stamps of East Africa and Uganda overprinted "G. E. A." see German East Africa.

EASTERN RUMELIA

ē-stərn rü-'mēl-yə

(South Bulgaria)

LOCATION — In southern Bulgaria
GOVT. — An autonomous unit of the Turkish Empire.
CAPITAL — Philippopolis (Plovdiv)

In 1885 the province of Eastern Rumelia revolted against Turkish rule and united with Bulgaria, adopting the new name of South Bulgaria. This union was assured by the Treaty of Bucharest in 1886, following the war between Serbia and Bulgaria.

40 Paras = 1 Piaster

Counterfeits of all overprints are plentiful.

Stamps of Turkey, 1876-84, Overprinted in Blue

No. 1

A2

A3

1880		Unwmk.	Perf. 13½	
1	A5	½pi on 20pa yel grn	67.50	57.50
a.		Horiz. pair, one without overprint		400.00
3	A2	10pa blk & rose	55.00	
4	A2	20pa vio & grn	87.50	67.50
6	A2	2pi blk & buff	115.00	100.00
7	A2	5pi red & bl	450.00	500.00
8	A3	10pa blk & red lil	57.50	

Nos. 3 & 8 were not placed in use.
Inverted and double overprints of all values exist.

Same, with Extra Overprint "R. O."
| 9 | A3 | 10pa blk & red lil | 97.50 | 95.00 |

Crescent and Turkish Inscriptions of Value — A4

1881		Typo.	Perf. 13½	
10	A4	5pa blk & olive	17.00	1.35
11	A4	10pa blk & green	65.00	1.35
12	A4	20pa blk & rose	1.75	1.25
13	A4	1pi blk & blue	5.75	4.50
14	A4	5pi rose & blue	57.50	82.50

Tête bêche pairs, imperforates and all perf. 11½ examples of Nos. 10-14 were not placed in use, and were found only in the remainder stock. This is true also of a 10pa cliché in the 20pa plate, and of a cliché of Turkey No. 63 in the 1pi plate. See the *Scott Classic Catalogue*.

1884			Perf. 11½	
15	A4	5pa lil & pale lil	.75	.45
16	A4	10pa grn & pale grn	.25	.45
17	A4	20pa car & pale rose	.55	
18	A4	1pi bl & pale bl	1.15	
19	A4	5pi brn & pale brn	400.00	

Nos. 17-19 were not placed in use, and were found only in the remainder stock.
Nos. 15-19 imperf. are from remainders.
See the *Scott Classic Catalogue* for perf 13½ listings.
For overprints see Turkey Nos. 542-545.

South Bulgaria
Counterfeits of all overprints are plentiful.
Nos. 10-14 Overprinted in Two Types

a   b

Type a — Four toes on each foot.
Type b — Three toes on each foot.

Blue Overprint
1885		Unwmk.	Perf. 13½	
20	A4 (a)	5pa blk & olive	325.00	375.00
21	A4 (a)	10pa blk & grn	875.00	825.00
22	A4 (a)	20pa blk & rose	325.00	
23	A4 (a)	1pi blk & blue	37.50	72.50
24	A4 (b)	5pi rose & blue	1,100.	

See the *Scott Classic Catalogue* for Nos. 22-23, type A, No. 24, type a, and No. 22, perf 11½, types a and b.

Black Overprint
24B		A4	20pa blk & green	275.00	
25	A4 (a)	1pi blk & bl	55.00	115.00
26	A4 (b)	5pi rose & bl	675.00	

See the *Scott Classic Catalogue* for No. 25 type b.

Same Overprint on Nos. 15-17
Blue Overprint
Perf. 11½
27	A4 (b)	5pa lil & pale lil, type "b"	22.50	57.50
28	A4 (b)	10pa grn & pale grn	40.00	75.00
29	A4 (b)	20pa car & pale rose	275.00	375.00

Black Overprint
Perf. 13½
| 30 | A4 (b) | 5pa lil & pale lil | 40.00 | 67.50 |

Perf. 11½
| 31 | A4 (a) | 10pa grn & pale grn | 42.50 | 85.00 |
| 32 | A4 (b) | 20pa car & pale rose | 55.00 | 65.00 |

See the *Scott Classic Catalogue* for detailed listings of Nos. 27-32.

Nos. 10-17 Handstamped in Black in Two Types

a   b

Type a — First letter at top circular.
Type b — First letter at top oval.

1885			Perf. 13½	
33	A4 (b)	5pa blk & olive	300.00	250.00
34	A4 (b)	10pa blk & grn	225.00	250.00
35	A4 (b)	20pa blk & rose	72.50	85.00
36	A4 (a)	1pi blk & bl	87.50	115.00
37	A4 (a)	5pi rose & blue, type "a"	2,500.	—

Perf. 13½
| 38 | A4 (a) | 5pa lil & pale lil | 26.00 | 44.00 |

Perf. 11½
| 39 | A4 (a) | 10pa grn & pale grn | 29.00 | 35.00 |
| 40 | A4 (a) | 20pa car & pale rose | 29.00 | 50.00 |

See the *Scott Classic Catalogue* for Nos. 38-40, type a, and No. 38, perf 11½, types a and b.
Nos. 20-40 exist with inverted and double handstamps. Overprints in unlisted colors are proofs.
The stamps of South Bulgaria were superseded in 1886 by those of Bulgaria.

EASTERN SILESIA

ē-stərn sī-'lē-zh ē-ə

LOCATION — In central Europe
GOVT. — Austrian crownland
AREA — 1,987 sq. mi.
POP. — 680,422 (estimated 1920)
CAPITAL — Troppau

After World War I, this territory was occupied by Czechoslovakia and eventually was divided between Poland and Czechoslovakia, the dividing line running through Teschen.

100 Heller = 1 Krone
100 Fennigi = 1 Marka

Plebiscite Issues

Stamps of Czechoslovakia 1918-20, Overprinted in Black, Blue, Violet or Red

1920		Unwmk.	Imperf.	
1	A2	1h dark brown	.25	.30
2	A1	3h red violet	.25	.25
3	A2	5h blue green	23.50	22.50
4	A2	15h red	11.50	11.00
5	A1	20h blue green	.25	.25
6	A2	25h dull violet	.75	.75
7	A1	30h bister (R)	.25	.25
8	A1	40h red orange	.30	.30
9	A2	50h dull violet	.60	.45
10	A2	50h dark blue	2.60	1.50
11	A2	60h orange (Bl)	.75	.75
12	A2	75h slate (R)	.50	.50
13	A2	80h olive grn (R)	.75	

14	A1	100h brown	1.10	1.10
15	A2	120h gray blk (R)	1.60	2.25
16	A1	200h ultra (R)	1.60	2.00
17	A2	300h green (R)	6.25	7.50
18	A1	400h purple (R)	2.60	3.00
20	A2	500h red brn (Bl)	5.25	6.00
a.		Black overprint	6.25	9.00
21	A2	1000h violet (Bl)	13.00	13.50
a.		Black overprint	62.50	75.00
		Nos. 1-21 (20)	74.40	75.15

Perf. 11½, 13¾
22	A2	1h dark brown	.25	.25
23	A2	5h blue green	.30	.25
24	A2	10h yellow green	.30	.25
a.		Imperf.	260.00	210.00
25	A2	15h red	.50	.25
26	A2	20h rose	.50	.35
a.		Imperf.	300.00	250.00
27	A2	25h dull violet	.50	.35
28	A2	30h red violet (Bl)	.35	.35
29	A2	60h orange (Bl)	.50	.50
30	A1	200h ultra (R)	3.00	3.00
		Nos. 22-30 (9)	6.20	5.55

The letters "S. O." are the initials of "Silésie Orientale."
Forged cancellations are found on Nos. 1-30.

Overprinted in Carmine or Violet

| 31 | A4 | 500h sl, grysh (C) | 40.00 | |
| 32 | A4 | 1000h blk brn, brnsh | 40.00 | |

Excellent counterfeits of this overprint exist.

Stamps of Poland, 1919, Overprinted

1920			Perf. 11½	
41	A10	5f green	.25	.25
42	A10	10f red brown	.25	.25
43	A10	15f light red	.25	.25
44	A11	25f olive green	.25	.25
45	A11	50f blue green	.25	.25

Overprinted

46	A12	1k deep green	.25	.25
47	A12	1.50k brown	.25	.25
48	A12	2k dark blue	.25	.25
49	A13	2.50k dull violet	.30	.25
50	A14	5k slate blue	.50	.50
		Nos. 41-50 (10)	2.80	2.50

SPECIAL DELIVERY STAMPS

Czechoslovakia Special Delivery Stamps Ovptd. in Blue

1920		Unwmk.	Imperf.	
E1	SD1	2h red violet, yel	.25	.25
a.		Black overprint	4.75	.80
E2	SD1	5h yellow green, yel	.25	.25
a.		Black overprint	8.00	5.00

Nos. E1-E2a exist on white paper.

POSTAGE DUE STAMPS

Czechoslovakia Postage Due Stamps Overprinted In Blue or Red

1920		Unwmk.	Imperf.	
J1	D1	5h deep bis (Bl)	.25	.25
a.		Black overprint	72.50	62.50

EASTERN SILESIA — ECUADOR

J2	D1	10h deep bister	.25	.25
J3	D1	15h deep bister	.25	.25
J4	D1	20h deep bister	.25	.25
J5	D1	25h deep bister	.25	.25
J6	D1	30h deep bister	.25	.25
J7	D1	40h deep bister	.50	.25
J8	D1	50h deep bister	2.60	3.00
J9	D1	100h blk brn (R)	2.60	3.00
J10	D1	500h gray grn (R)	5.75	4.50
J11	D1	1000h purple (R)	8.50	11.50
		Nos. J1-J11 (11)	21.45	23.75

Forged cancellations exist.

NEWSPAPER STAMPS

Czechoslovakia Newspaper Stamps Overprinted in Black like Nos. 1-30

1920		Unwmk.		Imperf.
P1	N1	2h gray green	.30	.30
P2	N1	6h red	.25	.25
P3	N1	10h dull violet	.40	.25
P4	N1	20h blue	.65	.25
P5	N1	30h gray brown	.65	.25
		Nos. P1-P5 (5)	2.25	1.30

ECUADOR

'e-kwə-,dor

LOCATION — Northwest coast of South America, bordering on the Pacific Ocean
GOVT. — Republic
AREA — 99,112 sq. mi.
POP. — 17,640,000 (2020 est.)
CAPITAL — Quito

The Republic of Ecuador was so constituted on May 11, 1830, after the Civil War that separated the original members of the Republic of Colombia, founded by Simon Bolivar by uniting the Presidency of Quito with the Viceroyalty of New Grenada and the Captaincy of Venezuela. The Presidency of Quito became the Republic of Ecuador.

8 Reales = 1 Peso
100 Centavos = 1 Sucre (1881)
100 Cents = 1 Dollar (2000)

Catalogue values for unused stamps in this country are for Never Hinged items, beginning with Scott 453 in the regular postage section, Scott C147 in the airpost section, Scott CO19 in the airpost officials section, Scott O201 in the officials section, Scott RA60 in the postal tax section, and all entries in the Galapagos section.

Watermarks

Wmk. 117 — Liberty Cap

Wmk. 127 — Quatrefoils

Wmk. 233 — "Harrison & Sons, London" in Script Letters

Wmk. 340 — Alternating Interlaced Wavy Lines

Wmk. 367 — Liberty Cap, Emblem, Inscription

Wmk. 377 — Interlocking Circles

Wmk. 395 — Emblem, Inscription

Coat of Arms
A1   A2

1865-72   Unwmk.   Typo.   Imperf.
Quadrille Paper

1	A1	1r yellow ('72)	60.00	55.00

Wove Paper

2	A1	½r ultra	40.00	20.00
a.		½r gray blue ('67)	40.00	15.00
b.		Batonne paper ('70)	50.00	25.00
c.		Blue paper ('72)	250.00	100.00
3	A1	1r buff	25.00	18.00
a.		1r orange buff	30.00	20.00
4	A1	1r yellow	25.00	15.00
a.		1r olive yellow ('66)	32.50	22.50
b.		Laid paper	175.00	110.00
c.		Half used as ½r on cover		900.00
d.		Batonne paper	40.00	30.00
5	A1	1r green	300.00	55.00
a.		Half used as ½r on cover		900.00
6	A2	4r red ('66)	500.00	200.00
a.		4r red brown ('66)	700.00	200.00
b.		Arms in circle	500.00	250.00
c.		Printed on both sides	550.00	—
d.		Half used as 2r on cover		1,600.
		Nos. 1-6 (6)	950.00	363.00

Letter paper embossed with arms of Ecuador was used in printing a number of sheets of Nos. 2, 4-6.
On the 4r the oval holding the coat of arms is usually 13½-14mm wide, but on about one-fifth of the stamps in the sheet it is 15-15½mm wide, almost a circle.
The 2r, 8r and 12r, type A1, are bogus.
Proofs of the ½r, type A1, are known in black and green.
An essay of type A2 shows the condor's head facing right.

1871-72   Blue-surface Paper

| 7 | A1 | ½r ultra | 50.00 | 25.00 |
| 8 | A1 | 1r yellow | 300.00 | 100.00 |

Unofficial reprints of types A1-A2 differ in color, have a different sheet makeup and lack gum. Type A1 reprints usually have a double frameline at left. All stamps on blue paper with horiz. blue lines are reprints.

A3

A4

1872   White Paper   Litho.   Perf. 11

9	A3	½r blue	30.00	5.00
10	A4	1r orange	40.00	7.00
11	A3	1p rose	5.00	25.00
		Nos. 9-11 (3)	75.00	37.00

The 1r surcharged 4c is fraudulent.

A5   A6

A7   A8

A9   A10

1881, Nov. 1   Engr.   Perf. 12

12	A5	1c yellow brn	.40	.25
13	A6	2c lake	.40	.25
14	A7	5c blue	10.00	.50
15	A8	10c orange	.40	.25
16	A9	20c gray violet	.40	.25
17	A10	50c blue green	2.00	3.00
		Nos. 12-17 (6)	13.60	4.50

The 1c surcharged 3c, and 20c surcharged 5c are fraudulent.
For overprints see Nos. O1-O6.

No. 17 Surcharged in Black

1883, Apr.

| 18 | A10 | 10c on 50c blue grn | 50.00 | 30.00 |
| a. | | Double surcharge | | |

Dangerous forgeries exist.

A12   A13

A14   A15

1887

19	A12	1c blue green	.50	.40
20	A13	2c vermilion	1.00	.40
21	A14	5c blue	3.00	.50
22	A15	80c olive green	6.00	15.00
		Nos. 19-22 (4)	10.50	16.30

For overprints see Nos. O7-O10.

President Juan Flores — A16

1892

23	A16	1c orange	.30	1.00
24	A16	2c dk brown	.30	1.00
25	A16	5c vermilion	.30	1.00
26	A16	10c green	.30	1.00
27	A16	20c red brown	.30	1.00
28	A16	50c maroon	.30	2.00
29	A16	1s blue	.30	4.00
30	A16	5s purple	1.00	8.00
		Nos. 23-30 (8)	3.10	19.00

The issues of 1892, 1894, 1895 and 1896 were printed by the Hamilton Bank Note Co., New York, to the order of N. F. Seebeck, who held a contract for stamps with the government of Ecuador.
No. 30 in green is said to be an essay or color trial.

For surcharges and overprints see Nos. 31-37, O11-O17.

Nos. 29 and 30 Surcharged in Black

1893

Surcharge Measures 25½x2½mm

31	A16	5c on 1s blue	6.00	6.00
32	A16	5c on 5s redsh pur	10.00	9.00
a.		Double surcharge		

Surcharge Measures 24x2¼mm

33	A16	5c on 1s blue	3.00	3.00
a.		Double surcharge, one inverted		
34	A16	5c on 5s purple	12.00	10.00
a.		Double surcharge, one invtd.		

Nos. 28-30 Surcharged in Black

35	A16	5c on 50c maroon	2.00	2.00
a.		Inverted surcharge	5.00	
36	A16	5c on 1s blue	2.50	2.00
37	A16	5c on 5s purple	10.00	10.00
		Nos. 31-37 (7)	45.50	42.00

Pres. Juan Flores — A19

| 38 | A19 | 5c on 5s lake | 4.00 | 4.00 |

It is stated that No. 38 was used exclusively as a postage stamp and not for telegrams.

Pres. Vicente Rocafuerte — A20

Dated "1894"

1894		Various Frames		Perf. 12
39	A20	1c blue	.40	.40
40	A20	2c yellow brn	.40	.40
41	A20	5c green	.40	.40
b.		Perf. 14	6.00	2.00
42	A20	10c vermilion	.70	.60
43	A20	20c black	1.10	.70
44	A20	50c orange	6.00	2.00
45	A20	1s carmine	9.50	4.00
46	A20	5s dark blue	12.00	6.00
		Nos. 39-46 (8)	30.50	14.50

1895   Same, Dated "1895"

47	A20	1c blue	.90	.70
48	A20	2c yellow brn	.90	.70
49	A20	5c green	.70	.50
50	A20	10c vermilion	.70	.40
51	A20	20c black	1.00	1.00
52	A20	50c orange	3.50	2.25
53	A20	1s carmine	21.00	8.00
54	A20	5s dark blue	8.50	4.00
		Nos. 47-54 (8)	37.20	17.55

Reprints of the 2c, 10c, 50c, 1s and 5s of the 1894-95 issues are generally on thick paper. Original issues are on thin to medium thick paper. To distinguish reprints from originals, a comparison of paper thickness, paper color, gum, printing clarity and direction of paper weave is necessary. Value 30 cents each.

For overprints see Nos. 77-112, O20-O33, O50-O91.

A21

A22

A23

A24

ECUADOR

A25

A26

A27

A28

1896			Wmk. 117	
55	A21	1c dk green	.70	.60
56	A22	2c red	.70	.40
57	A23	5c blue	.70	.40
58	A24	10c bister brn	.60	.90
59	A25	20c orange	1.40	2.00
60	A26	50c dark blue	5.00	3.00
61	A27	1s yellow brn	4.00	4.00
62	A28	5s violet	14.00	5.50
		Nos. 55-62 (8)	27.10	16.80

Unwmk.

62A	A21	1c dk green	1.00	.40
62B	A22	2c red	1.10	.40
62C	A23	5c blue	1.10	.70
62D	A24	10c bister brn	.70	1.40
62E	A25	20c orange	6.00	5.50
62F	A26	50c dark blue	2.00	2.75
62G	A27	1s yellow brn	6.00	8.00
62H	A28	5s violet	15.00	6.00
		Nos. 62A-62H (8)	32.90	25.15

Reprints of Nos. 55-62H are on very thick paper, with paper weave direction vertical. Value 30 cents each.

For surcharges and overprints see Nos. 74, 76, 113-114, O34-O49.

Vicente Roca, Diego Noboa and José Olmedo
A28a

General Juan Francisco Elizalde
A28b

Perf. 11½

1896, Oct. 9		Unwmk.		Litho.
63	A28a	1c rose	.55	.55
64	A28b	2c blue	.55	.55
65	A28a	5c green	.75	.75
66	A28b	10c ocher	.76	.76
67	A28a	20c red	1.10	3.25
68	A28b	50c violet	1.75	4.75
69	A28a	1s orange	3.25	8.00
		Nos. 63-69 (7)	8.70	18.60

Success of the Liberal Party in 1845 & 1895.
For overprints see Nos. 115-125.

A29

Black Surcharge

1896, Nov. Perf. 12

70	A29	1c on 1c vmt "1893-1894"	1.00	.60
a.		Inverted surcharge	2.50	2.00
b.		Double surcharge	8.00	7.00
71	A29	2c on 2c bl, "1893-1894"	2.00	1.75
a.		Inverted surcharge	4.00	3.50
72	A29	5c on 10c org. "1887-1888"	2.00	.60
a.		Inverted surcharge	4.00	1.75
b.		Double surcharge	7.00	4.00
c.		Surcharged "2cts"	5.00	5.00
d.		"1893-1894"	6.00	5.00
73	A29	10c on 4c brn, "1887-1888"	2.00	1.10
a.		Inverted surcharge	4.00	1.75
b.		Double surcharge	6.00	3.50
c.		Double surcharge, one inverted		
d.		Surcharged "1 cto"	2.00	2.75
e.		"1891-1892"	17.00	13.50
		Nos. 70-73 (4)	7.00	4.05

Similar surcharges of type A29 include:
Dated "1887-1888" — 1c on 1c blue green, 1c on 2c red, 1c on 4c brown, 1c on 10c yellow; 2c on 2c red, 2c on 10c yellow; 10c on 1c green.

Dated "1891-1892" — 1c on 1c blue green, 1c on 4c brown.
Dated "1893-1894" — 2c on 10c yellow; 10c on 1c vermilion, 10c on 10s black.
For overprints see Nos. O18-O19.

Nos. 59-60 Surcharged in Black or Red

1896, Oct. Wmk. 117

74	A25	5c on 20c orange	40.00	40.00
76	A26	10c on 50c dk bl (R)	50.00	50.00
a.		Double surcharge		

The surcharge is diag., horiz. or vert.

Nos. 39-54 Overprinted

On Issue of 1894

1897			Unwmk.	
77	A20	1c blue	2.25	2.25
78	A20	2c yellow brn	1.90	1.00
79	A20	5c green	.90	.90
80	A20	10c vermilion	2.75	2.25
81	A20	20c black	3.00	2.75
82	A20	50c orange	6.50	3.25
83	A20	1s carmine	19.00	6.50
84	A20	5s dark blue	110.00	90.00
		Nos. 77-84 (8)	146.30	109.20

On Issue of 1895

85	A20	1c blue	6.00	5.50
86	A20	2c yellow brn	2.25	2.25
87	A20	5c green	1.90	1.60
88	A20	10c vermilion	7.00	6.00
89	A20	20c black	1.90	1.75
90	A20	50c orange	32.50	13.00
91	A20	1s carmine	14.50	7.50
92	A20	5s dark blue	14.50	14.50
		Nos. 85-92 (8)	80.55	52.10

Nos. 39-54 Overprinted

On Issue of 1894

93	A20	1c blue	1.40	.90
94	A20	2c yellow brn	1.20	.75
95	A20	5c green	.60	.50
96	A20	10c vermilion	3.50	1.75
97	A20	20c black	3.75	2.50
98	A20	50c orange	7.00	2.75
99	A20	1s carmine	13.00	8.50
100	A20	5s dark blue	115.00	85.00
		Nos. 93-100 (8)	145.45	102.65

On Issue of 1895

101	A20	1c blue	3.25	1.60
102	A20	2c yellow brn	1.60	1.60
103	A20	5c green	1.75	1.00
104	A20	10c vermilion	5.50	4.50
105	A20	20c black	5.00	1.20
106	A20	50c orange	1.75	1.75
107	A20	1s carmine	8.00	7.00
108	A20	5s dark blue	9.50	9.50
		Nos. 101-108 (8)	36.35	28.15

Overprints on Nos. 77-108 are to be found reading upward from left to right and downward from left to right, as well as inverted.

Overprinted

1897 On Issue of 1894

109	A20	10c vermilion	—	—

On Issue of 1895

110	A20	2c yellow brn	—	—
111	A20	1s carmine	—	—
112	A20	5s dark blue	—	—

Nos. 56, 59 Overprinted like Nos. 93-108

1897, June Wmk. 117

113	A22	2c red	100.00	100.00
114	A25	20c orange	—	100.00

Many forged overprints on Nos. 77-114 exist, made on original stamps and reprints.

Stamps or Types of 1896 Overprinted in Black

1897 Unwmk. Perf. 11½

115	A28a	1c rose	3.75	3.75
116	A28b	2c blue	3.00	3.00
117	A28b	10c ocher	3.00	3.00
118	A28a	1s yellow	15.00	15.00
		Nos. 115-118 (4)	24.75	24.75

No. 63 Overprinted in Black

1897

119	A28a	1c rose	.60	.50

Nos. 63-66 Overprinted in Black

1897

122	A28a	1c rose	4.50	4.00
123	A28b	2c blue	4.50	4.00
124	A28a	5c green	4.50	4.00
125	A28b	10c yellow	4.50	4.00
a.		Double overprint	10.50	9.50
		Nos. 122-125 (4)	18.00	16.00

The 20c, 50c and 1s with this overprint in black and all values of the issue overprinted in blue are reprints.

Overprint Inverted

122a	A28a	1c	6.00	5.50
123a	A28b	2c	6.00	5.50
124a	A28a	5c	6.00	5.50
125b	A28b	10c	6.00	5.50

Coat of Arms — A33

1897, June 23 Engr. Perf. 14-16

127	A33	1c dk yellow grn	.35	.25
128	A33	2c orange red	.35	.25
129	A33	5c lake	.35	.25
130	A33	10c dk brown	.35	.25
131	A33	20c yellow	.45	.40
132	A33	50c dull blue	.45	.65
133	A33	1s gray	.90	1.25
134	A33	5s dark lilac	4.00	5.00
		Nos. 127-134 (8)	7.20	8.30

No. 135

No. 136

1899, May

135	A33	1c on 2c orange red	3.00	1.50
136	A33	5c on 10c brown	2.50	1.00
a.		Double surcharge		

Luis Vargas Torres
A36

Abdón Calderón
A37

Juan Montalvo
A38

José Mejía
A39

Santa Cruz y Espejo
A40

Pedro Carbo
A41

José Joaquin Olmedo
A42

Pedro Moncayo
A43

1899 Perf. 12½-16

137	A36	1c gray blue & blk	.40	.25
a.		Horiz. pair, imperf. vert.		
138	A37	2c brown lil & blk	.40	.25
139	A38	5c lake & blk	.70	.25
140	A39	10c reddsh lil & blk	.70	.25
141	A40	20c green & blk	.70	.25
142	A41	50c lil rose & blk	1.75	.55
143	A42	1s ocher & blk	8.00	2.75
144	A43	5s lilac & blk	14.50	7.50
		Nos. 137-144 (8)	27.15	12.05

1901

145	A36	1c scarlet & blk	.45	.25
146	A37	2c green & blk	.45	.25
147	A38	5c gray lil & blk	.45	.25
148	A39	10c dp blue & blk	.50	.25
149	A40	20c gray & blk	.50	.25
150	A41	50c lt blue & blk	1.75	.95
151	A42	1s brown & blk	6.00	2.75
152	A43	5s gray blk & blk	9.00	5.75
		Nos. 145-152 (8)	19.10	10.70

In July, 1902, following the theft of a quantity of stamps during a fire at Guayaquil, the Government authorized the governors of the provinces to handstamp their stocks. Many varieties of these handstamps exist.
Other control marks were used in 1907.
For overprints see Nos. O103-O106, O167.

A44

Surcharged on Revenue Stamp Dated 1901-1902

1903-06 Perf. 14, 15

153	A44	1c on 5c gray lil ('06)	.75	.40
154	A44	1c on 20c gray	10.00	4.50
155	A44	1c on 25c yellow	1.50	.40
a.		Double surcharge		
156	A44	1c on 1s bl ('06)	77.50	50.00
157	A44	3c on 5c gray lil ('06)	10.00	4.00
158	A44	3c on 20c gray ('06)	25.00	15.00
159	A44	3c on 25c yel ('06)	24.00	15.00
159A	A44	3c on 1s blue ('06)	3.75	2.25
		Nos. 153-159A (8)	152.50	91.55

Counterfeits are plentiful.
See Nos. 191-197.

Capt. Abdón Calderón
A45 A46

1904, July 31 Perf. 12

160	A45	1c red & blk	.45	.30
161	A45	2c blue & blk	.50	.35
162	A46	5c yellow & blk	1.90	1.00

292 ECUADOR

163	A45	10c red & blk	6.00	2.00
164	A45	20c blue & blk	10.00	8.00
165	A46	50c yellow & blk	85.00	120.00
		Nos. 160-165 (6)	103.85	131.65

Centenary of the birth of Calderón.

Presidents

Vicente Roca A47

Diego Noboa A48

Francisco Robles A49

José M. Urvina A50

García Moreno A51

Jerónimo Carrión A52

Javier Espinoza A53

Antonio Borrero A54

1907, July — Perf. 14, 15

166	A47	1c red & blk	1.00	.25
167	A48	2c pale blue & blk	2.00	.25
168	A49	3c orange & blk	3.00	.25
169	A50	5c lilac rose & blk	3.75	.25
170	A51	10c dp blue & blk	7.50	.25
171	A52	20c yellow grn & blk	10.00	.35
172	A53	50c violet & blk	22.50	.70
173	A54	1s green & blk	30.00	2.00
		Nos. 166-173 (8)	79.75	4.30

The stamps of the 1907 issue frequently have control marks similar to those found on the 1899 and 1901 issues. These marks were applied to distinguish the stamps issued in the various provinces and to serve as a check on local officials.

Locomotive — A55

García Moreno A56

Gen. Eloy Alfaro A57

Abelardo Moncayo A58

Archer Harman A59

James Sivewright A60

Mt. Chimborazo — A61

1908, June 25

174	A55	1c red brown	1.10	2.10
175	A56	2c blue & blk	1.30	2.25
176	A57	5c claret & blk	2.75	5.25
177	A58	10c ocher & blk	1.75	2.75
178	A59	20c green & blk	1.75	3.75
179	A60	50c gray & blk	1.75	3.75
180	A61	1s black	3.50	8.00
		Nos. 174-180 (7)	13.90	27.85

Opening of the Guayaquil-Quito Railway.

José Mejía Vallejo A62

Principal Exposition Building A70

Designs: 2c, Francisco J. E. Santa Cruz y Espejo. 3c, Francisco Ascásubi. 5c, Juan Salinas. 10c, Juan Pio de Montúfar, el Marques de Selva Alegre. 20c, Carlos de Montúfar. 50c, Juan de Dios Morales. 1s, Manuel R. de Quiroga.

1909, Aug. 10 — Perf. 12

181	A62	1c green	.35	.65
182	A62	2c blue	.35	.65
183	A62	3c orange	.35	.75
184	A62	5c claret	.35	.75
185	A62	10c yellow brn	.45	.75
186	A62	20c gray	.45	1.10
187	A62	50c vermilion	.45	1.10
188	A62	1s olive grn	.45	1.40
189	A70	5s violet	1.25	2.75
		Nos. 181-189 (9)	4.45	9.90

National Exposition of 1909.

No. 187 Surcharged

1909

| 190 | A62 | 5c on 50c vermilion | .90 | .75 |

Revenue Stamps Surcharged as in 1903

1910 — Perf. 14, 15

Stamps Dated 1905-1906

191	A44	1c on 5c green	2.25	1.75
192	A44	5c on 20c blue	9.50	2.00
193	A44	5c on 25c violet	18.00	3.50

Stamps Dated 1907-1908

194	A44	1c on 5c green	.40	.40
195	A44	5c on 20c blue	14.00	9.50
196	A44	5c on 25c violet	1.20	.40

Stamp Dated 1909-1910

| 197 | A44 | 5c on 20c blue | 80.00 | 60.00 |
| | | Nos. 191-197 (7) | 125.35 | 77.55 |

Presidents

Roca A71

Noboa A72

Robles A73

Urvina A74

Moreno A75

Borrero A76

1911-28 — Perf. 12

198	A71	1c scarlet & blk	.80	.25
199	A71	1c orange ('16)	.80	.25
200	A71	1c lt blue ('25)	.40	.25
201	A72	2c blue & blk	1.10	.25
202	A72	2c green ('16)	1.10	.25
203	A72	2c dk violet ('25)	1.10	.25
204	A73	3c orange & blk ('13)	2.25	.30
205	A73	3c black ('15)	1.50	.25
206	A74	5c scarlet & blk	1.90	.25
207	A74	5c violet ('15)	1.90	.25
208	A74	5c rose ('25)	.70	.25
209	A74	5c dk brown ('28)	.70	.25
210	A75	10c dp blue & blk	2.25	.25
211	A75	10c dp blue ('15)	2.25	.25
212	A75	10c yellow grn ('25)	.70	.25
213	A75	10c black ('28)	1.60	.25
214	A76	1s green & blk	12.00	1.50
215	A76	1s orange & blk ('27)	8.00	.25
		Nos. 198-215 (18)	41.05	5.80

For overprints see Nos. 260-262, 264-265, O107-O122, O124-O134, O156-O157, O160-O162, O164-O166, O168-O173, O175-O178, O183-O184, O189, RA1.

A77

1912 — Perf. 14, 15

216	A77	1c on 1s green	1.00	1.00
217	A77	2c on 2s carmine	2.50	1.50
218	A77	2c on 5s dull blue	1.50	1.50
219	A77	2c on 10s yellow	5.00	5.00
a.		Inverted surcharge	16.00	12.00
		Nos. 216-219 (4)	10.00	9.00

No. 216 exists with narrow "V" and small "U" in "UN" and Nos. 217, 218 and 219 with "D" with serifs or small "O" in "DOS."

Enrique Váldez A78

Jerónimo Carrión A79

Javier Espinoza — A80

1915-17 — Perf. 12

220	A78	4c red & blk	1.00	.25
221	A79	20c green & blk ('17)	6.50	.25
222	A80	50c dp violet & blk	12.50	.45
		Nos. 220-222 (3)	20.00	.95

For overprints see Nos. O123, O135, O163, O174.

Olmedo A86

Monument to "Fathers of the Country" A95

Laurel Wreath and Star — A104

Designs: 2c, Rafael Ximena. 3c, Roca. 4c, Luis F. Vivero. 5c, Luis Febres Cordero. 6c, Francisco Lavayen. 7c, Jorge Antonio de Elizalde. 8c, Baltazar Garcia. 9c, Jose de Antepara. 15c, Luis Urdaneta. 20c, Jose M. Villamil. 30c, Miguel Letamendi. 40c, Gregorio Escobedo. 50c, Gen. Antonio Jose de Sucre. 60c, Juan Illingworth. 70c, Roca. 80c, Rocafuerte. 1s, Simon Bolivar.

1920

223	A86	1c yellow grn	.35	.25
224	A86	2c carmine	.35	.25
225	A86	3c yellow brn	.35	.25
226	A86	4c myrtle green	.55	.25
227	A86	5c pale blue	.55	.25
228	A86	6c red orange	.90	.25
229	A86	7c brown	2.25	.75
230	A86	8c apple green	1.25	.35
231	A86	9c lake	4.25	1.50
232	A95	10c lt blue	1.50	.25
233	A86	15c dk gray	2.25	.35
234	A86	20c dk violet	2.25	.25
235	A86	30c brt violet	4.25	1.40
236	A86	40c dk brown	7.50	2.10
237	A86	50c dk green	5.25	.55
238	A86	60c dk blue	9.50	2.10
239	A86	70c bluish gray	16.00	4.75
240	A86	80c orange yel	16.50	4.75
241	A104	90c green	17.00	4.75
242	A86	1s pale blue	24.00	8.50
		Nos. 223-242 (20)	116.80	33.90

Cent. of the independence of Guayaquil.
For overprints and surcharges see Nos. 263, 274-292, O136-O155, O179-O182, O185-O188.

No. RA12 Overprinted in Black

1925

| 259 | PT6 | 20c bister brown | 4.00 | 1.50 |

Stamps of 1915-25 Overprinted in Black or Red Upright (1c, 3c, 5c) or Inverted (2c, 4c, 10c)

1926

260	A71	1c lt blue	12.50	10.50
261	A72	2c dk violet	12.50	10.50
262	A73	3c black (R)	12.50	10.50
263	A86	4c myrtle green	12.50	10.50
264	A74	5c rose	17.50	10.50
265	A75	10c yellow grn	17.50	10.50
		Nos. 260-265 (6)	85.00	63.00

Quito-Esmeraldas railway opening.
Upright overprints on 2c, 4c, 10c and inverted overprints on 1c, 3c, 5c sell for more.

Nos. RA10-RA12 Overprinted in Black

1927

266	PT6	1c olive green	.50	.30
a.		"POSTAI"	1.40	.85
b.		Double overprint	2.00	.85
c.		Inverted overprint	2.00	.85
267	PT6	2c deep green	.50	.30
a.		"POSTAI"	1.40	.85
b.		Double overprint	2.00	.85
268	PT6	20c bister brown	1.00	.30
a.		"POSTAI"	8.50	5.00
		Nos. 266-268 (3)	2.00	.90

Quito Post Office — A109

1927, June

269	A109	5c orange	.50	.30
270	A109	10c dark green	.70	.30
271	A109	20c violet	.80	.30
		Nos. 269-271 (3)	2.00	.90

Opening of new Quito P.O.
For overprint see No. O190.

No. RA12 Overprinted in Dark Blue

ECUADOR

1928
273 PT6 20c bister brown .50 .30
  a. Double overprint, one inverted 2.00 .70
See No. 339 for 10c with same overprint.

Nos. 235, 239-240 Ovptd. in Red Brown and Srchd. in Bluish Black

1928, July 8
274 A86 10c on 30c violet 16.00 16.00
275 A86 50c on 70c bluish gray 20.00 20.00
276 A86 1s on 80c org yel 22.50 22.50
  Nos. 274-276 (3) 58.50 58.50
Quito-Cayambe railway opening.

Stamps of 1920 Surcharged

1928, Oct. 9
277 A86 1c on 1c yel grn 15.00 15.00
278 A86 1c on 2c car .30 .30
279 A86 2c on 3c yel brn 2.25 2.25
  a. Dbl. surch., one reading up 30.00 30.00
280 A86 2c on 4c myr grn 1.60 1.60
281 A86 2c on 5c lt blue .60 .45
  a. Dbl. surch., one reading up 30.00 30.00
282 A86 2c on 7c brown 75.00 75.00
283 A86 5c on 6c red org .40 .30
  a. "5 ctvos." omitted 40.00 40.00
284 A86 10c on 7c brown 1.25 1.25
285 A86 20c on 8c apple grn .35 .35
  a. Double surcharge
286 A95 40c on 10c blue 4.25 4.25
287 A86 40c on 15c dk gray 1.25 1.25
288 A86 50c on 20c dk vio 13.25 13.25
289 A86 1s on 40c dk brown 4.50 4.50
290 A86 5s on 50c dk green 5.25 5.25
291 A86 10s on 60c dk blue 19.50 19.50

With Additional Surcharge in Red

292 A86 10c on 2c on 7c brn .65 .65
  a. Red surcharge double 30.00 30.00
  Nos. 277-292 (16) 145.20 144.90

National Assembly of 1928.
Counterfeit overprints exist of Nos. 277-291.

A111

Surcharged in Various Colors

1928, Oct. 31   *Perf. 14*
293 A111 5c on 20c gray lil (Bk) 3.00 1.75
294 A111 10c on 20c gray lil (R) 3.00 1.75
295 A111 20c on 1s grn (O) 3.00 1.75
296 A111 50c on 1s grn (Bl) 3.75 1.40
297 A111 1s on 1s grn (V) 4.75 1.75
298 A111 5s on 2s red (G) 15.00 9.00
299 A111 10s on 2s red (Br) 18.00 12.00
  a. Black surcharge 15.00 10.00
  Nos. 293-299 (7) 50.50 29.40

Quito-Otavalo railway opening.
See Nos. 586-587.

No. RA11 Overprinted in Red

1929   *Perf. 12*
302 PT6 2c deep green .50 .30
There are two types of overprint on No. 302 differing slightly.

A112

1929   **Red Overprint**
303 A112 1c dark blue .50 .30
  a. Overprint reading down .75 .50
See Nos. 586-587.

Plowing A113   Cultivating Cacao A114

Cacao Pod A115   Growing Tobacco A116

Exportation of Fruits — A117   Landscape — A118

Loading Sugar Cane — A119   Scene in Quito — A120

Scene in Quito A121   Olmedo A122

Monument to Simón Bolívar — A125

Designs: 2s, Sucre. 5s, Bolivar.

1930, Aug. 1   *Perf. 12½*
304 A113 1c yellow & car .30 .25
305 A114 2c yellow & grn .30 .25
306 A115 5c dp grn & vio brn .35 .25
307 A116 6c yellow & red .45 .25
308 A117 10c orange & ol grn .45 .25
309 A118 16c red & yel grn .55 .25
310 A119 20c ultra & yel .90 .25
311 A120 40c orange & sepia 1.10 .35
312 A121 50c orange & sepia 1.10 .40
313 A122 1s dp green & blk 4.25 .45
314 A122 3s dk blue & blk 6.50 2.00
315 A122 5s dk violet & blk 11.50 3.00
316 A122 10s car rose & blk 40.00 6.50
  Nos. 304-316 (13) 67.75 14.45

Centenary of founding of republic.
For surcharges and overprints see Nos. 319-320, 331-338, RA25, RA33, RA43.

A126   A127

1933   **Red Overprint**   *Perf. 15*
317 A126 10c olive brown 1.15 .30

Blue Overprint
318 A127 10c olive brown .70 .30
  a. Inverted overprint 5.00 5.00

For overprint see No. 339.

Nos. 307, 309 Surcharged in Black

1933   *Perf. 12½*
319 A116 5c on 6c yellow & red 1.00 .30
320 A118 10c on 16c red & yel grn 2.00 .30
  a. Inverted overprint 4.00 4.00

Landscape A128   Mt. Chimborazo A129

1934-45   *Perf. 12*
321 A128 5c violet 4.00 .55
322 A128 5c blue 4.00 .55
323 A128 5c dark brown 4.00 .55
323A A128 5c slate blk ('45) 4.00 .55
324 A128 10c rose 4.00 .55
325 A128 10c dark green 4.00 .55
326 A128 10c brown 4.00 .55
327 A128 10c orange 4.00 .55
328 A128 10c olive green 4.00 .55
329 A128 10c gray blk ('36) 4.00 .55
329A A128 10c red lilac ('44) 4.00 .55

Perf. 14
330 A129 1s carmine rose 6.00 .55
  Nos. 321-330 (12) 50.00 6.60

Stamps of 1930 Srchd. or Ovptd. in various colors

1935   *Perf. 12½*
331 A116 5c on 6c (Bl) .90 .35
332 A116 10c on 6c (G) 1.25 .35
333 A119 20c on 20c (R) 1.75 .35
334 A120 40c on 40c (G) 2.50 .35
335 A121 50c on 50c (G) 3.00 .45
336 A122 1s on 5s (Gold) 7.00 1.25
337 A122 2s on 5s (Gold) 9.50 1.75
338 A125 5s on 10s (Bl) 12.00 5.00
  Nos. 331-338,C35-C38 (12) 87.90 29.85

Unveiling of a monument to Bolivar at Quito, July 24, 1935.

A129a

1935, Oct. 13   *Photo.*   *Perf. 11½x11*
338A A129a 5c ultra & black .85 .30
338B A129a 10c org & blue .85 .30
338C A129a 40c dk car & red .85 .30
338D A129a 1S blue grn & red 1.00 .70
338E A129a 2S violet & red 1.90 1.20
  Nos. 338A-338E,C38A-C38E (10) 14.85 7.70

Columbus Day. Nos. 338A-338E and C38A-C38E were prepared by the Sociedad Colombista Panamericana and were sold by the Ecuadorian post office through Oct. 30.

Telegraph Stamp Overprinted Diagonally in Red like No. 273

1935   *Perf. 14½*
339 A126 10c olive brown .75 .30

Map of Galápagos Islands A130   Galapagos Land Iguana A131

Galápagos Tortoise A132   Charles R. Darwin A133

Columbus A134   Island Scene A135

1936   *Perf. 14*
340 A130 2c black 1.50 .35
341 A131 5c olive grn 1.75 .35
342 A132 10c brown 3.50 .45
343 A133 20c dk violet 5.00 .65
344 A134 1s dk carmine 7.50 1.20
345 A135 2s dark blue 11.50 2.00
  Nos. 340-345 (6) 30.75 5.00

Cent. of the visit of Charles Darwin to the Galápagos Islands, Sept. 17, 1835.
For overprints see Nos. O191-O195.

Tobacco Stamp Overprinted in Black

1936   *Rouletted 7*
346 PT7 1c rose red .50 .30
  a. Horiz. pair, imperf. vert.
  b. Double surcharge

No. 346 is similar to type PT7 but does not include "CASA CORREOS."

Louis Godin, Charles M. de la Condamine and Pierre Bouguer — A136

Portraits: 5c, 20c, Antonio Ulloa, La Condamine and Jorge Juan.

1936   *Engr.*   *Perf. 12½*
347 A136 2c deep blue .50 .30
348 A136 5c dark green .50 .30
349 A136 10c deep orange .50 .30
350 A136 20c violet .80 .30
351 A136 50c dark red 1.25 1.00
  Nos. 347-351,C39-C42 (9) 6.60 2.60

Bicentenary of Geodesical Mission to Quito.

ECUADOR

Independence Monument — A137

1936   *Perf. 13½x14*
352 A137 2c green 2.50 1.25
353 A137 5c dark violet 2.50 1.25
354 A137 10c carmine rose 2.50 1.25
355 A137 20c black 2.50 1.25
356 A137 50c blue 3.50 2.10
357 A137 1s dark red 4.00 3.25
   Nos. 352-357,C43-C48 (12) 50.50 43.35
1st Intl. Philatelic Exhibition at Quito.

Coat of Arms — A138

Overprint in Black or Red
1937   *Perf. 12½*
359 A138 5c olive green 2.00 .30
360 A138 10c dark blue (R) 2.00 .30
For overprint see No. 562.

Andean Landscape A139

Atahualpa, the Last Inca A140

Hat Weavers A141

Coast Landscape A142

Gold Washing — A143

1937, Aug. 19   *Perf. 11½*
361 A139 2c green .50 .25
362 A140 5c deep rose .50 .25
363 A141 10c blue .50 .25
364 A142 20c deep rose 1.50 .30
365 A143 1s olive green 2.00 .35
   Nos. 361-365 (5) 5.00 1.40
For overprints see Nos. O196-O200.

"Liberty" Carrying Flag of Ecuador A144

Engraved and Lithographed
1938, Feb. 22   *Perf. 12*
Center Multicolored
366 A144 2c blue .25 .25
367 A144 5c violet .35 .25
368 A144 10c black .55 .25
369 A144 20c brown .65 .25
370 A144 50c black 1.10 .25
371 A144 1s olive blk 1.75 .30
372 A144 2s dk brn 3.55 .55
   Nos. 366-372,C57-C63 (14) 22.40 4.50
US Constitution, 150th anniversary.
For overprints and surcharges see Nos. 413-415, 444-446, RA46, RA52.

A145

A146

A147

A148

Designs: 10c, Winged figure holding globe. 50c, Cactus, winged wheel. 1s, "Communications." 2s, "Construction."

Perf. 13, 13x13½
1938, Oct. 30   *Engr.*
373 A145 10c bright ultra .40 .30
374 A146 50c deep red violet .40 .30
375 A147 1s copper red .70 .30
376 A148 2s dark green 1.10 .30
   Nos. 373-376 (4) 2.60 1.20
Progress of Ecuador Exhibition.
For overprints see Nos. C105-C113.

Parade of Athletes — A149

Runner A150

Basketball A151

Wrestlers A152

Diver A153

1939, Mar.   *Perf. 12*
377 A149 5c carmine rose 3.00 .55
378 A150 10c deep blue 3.50 .65
379 A151 50c gray olive 5.75 .85
380 A152 1s dull violet 7.75 .85
381 A153 2s dull olive green 12.50 .95
   Nos. 377-381,C65-C69 (10) 78.35 6.30
First Bolivarian Games (1938), Bogota.

Dolores Mission — A154

1939, June 16   *Perf. 12½x13*
382 A154 2c blue green .50 .25
383 A154 5c rose red .50 .25
384 A154 10c ultra .50 .25
385 A154 50c yellow brown 1.20 .25
386 A154 1s black 1.90 .25
387 A154 2s purple 1.25 .40
   Nos. 382-387,C73-C79 (13) 11.25 3.75
Golden Gate International Exposition.
For surcharges see Nos. 429, 436.

Trylon and Perisphere — A155

1939, June 30
388 A155 2c lt olive green .80 .35
389 A155 5c red orange .80 .35
390 A155 10c ultra .80 .35
391 A155 50c slate gray 1.10 .35
392 A155 1s rose carmine 1.90 .35
393 A155 2s black brown 2.25 .40
   Nos. 388-393,C80-C86 (13) 16.55 4.25
New York World's Fair.
For surcharge see No. 437.

Flags of the 21 American Republics — A156

1940   *Perf. 12*
394 A156 5c dp rose & blk 1.00 .25
395 A156 10c dk blue & blk .40 .25
396 A156 50c Prus green & blk .60 .25
397 A156 1s dp violet & blk 1.00 .30
   Nos. 394-397,C87-C90 (8) 8.30 2.90
Pan American Union, 50th anniversary.

Francisco J. E. Santa Cruz y Espejo — A157

1941, Dec. 15
398 A157 30c blue 1.25 .25
399 A157 1s red orange 2.50 .35
   Nos. 398-399,C91-C92 (4) 21.50 1.30
Exposition of Journalism held under the auspices of the Natl. Newspaper Men's Union.

Francisco de Orellana A158

Gonzalo Pizarro A159

View of Guayaquil A160

View of Quito A161

1942, Jan. 30
400 A158 10c sepia .90 .35
401 A159 40c deep rose 2.50 .35
402 A160 1s violet 3.50 .35
403 A161 2s dark blue 4.50 .45
   Nos. 400-403,C93-C96 (8) 23.45 3.35
400th anniv. of the discovery and exploration of the Amazon River by Orellana.

Remigio Crespo Toral — A162

1942   *Perf. 13½*
404 A162 10c green .60 .25
405 A162 50c brown 1.00 .25
   Nos. 404-405,C97 (3) 2.85 1.00

Alfredo Baquerizo Moreno — A163

1942
406 A163 10c green .25 .25

Mt. Chimborazo — A164

1942-47   *Perf. 12*
407 A164 30c red brown 1.50 .30
407A A164 30c lt blue ('43) 1.50 .30
407B A164 30c red orange ('44) 1.50 .30
407C A164 30c green ('47) 1.50 .30
   Nos. 407-407C (4) 6.00 1.20

View of Guayaquil — A165

1942-44
408 A165 20c red 1.50 .25
408A A165 20c deep blue ('44) 1.50 .25

Gen. Eloy Alfaro A166

Devil's Nose A167

President Alfaro (1842-1912): 30c, Military College. 1s, Montecristi, Alfaro's birthplace.

1942
409 A166 10c dk rose & blk .60 .25
410 A167 20c ol blk & red brn .60 .25
411 A167 30c ol gray & grn .75 .25
412 A167 1s slate & salmon 1.80 .25
   Nos. 409-412,C98-C101 (8) 20.15 4.40

Nos. 370-372 Overprinted in Red Brown

1943, Apr. 15   *Perf. 11½*
413 A144 50c multicolored .65 .65
414 A144 1s multicolored 1.25 1.25
415 A144 2s multicolored 2.75 2.75
   Nos. 413-415,C102-C104 (6) 14.65 10.25
Visit of US Vice-Pres. Henry A. Wallace.

"30 Centavos" — A170

1943 Black Surcharge   *Perf. 12½*
416 A170 30c on 50c red brn 1.00 .25
  a. Without bars 1.00 .25

Map Showing US and Ecuador A171

1943, Oct. 9   *Perf. 12*
417 A171 10c dull violet .75 .50
418 A171 20c red brown .75 .50
419 A171 30c orange .75 .50
420 A171 50c olive green .90 .60
421 A171 1s deep violet 1.00 .65
422 A171 10s olive bister 8.25 5.25
   Nos. 417-422,C114-C118 (11) 32.70 15.10
Good will tour of Pres. Arroyo del Rio in 1942.

1944, Feb. 7
423 A171 10c yellow green .65 .45
424 A171 20c rose pink .65 .45
425 A171 30c dark gray brown .65 .45
426 A171 50c deep red lilac .65 .45
427 A171 1s olive gray 1.00 .65
428 A171 10s red orange 10.50 6.00
   Nos. 423-428,C119-C123 (11) 24.90 13.40
For surcharges see Nos. B1-B6.

ECUADOR

No. 385 Surcharged in Black

1944		Unwmk.	Perf. 12½x13
429	A154	30c on 50c yel brn	2.00 .25

Archbishop Federico González Suárez, Birth Cent. — A172

1944			Perf. 12
430	A172	10c deep blue	.40 .25
431	A172	20c green	.40 .25
432	A172	30c dk violet brn	.50 .25
433	A172	1s dull violet	.90 .25
	Nos. 430-433,C124-C127 (8)		15.50 4.30

Air Post Stamps Nos. C76 and C83 Surcharged in Black

1944			Perf. 12½x13
434	AP15	30c on 50c rose vio	.40 .25
435	AP16	30c on 50c sl grn	.40 .25

Nos. 382 and 388 Surcharged in Black

1944-45			
436	A154	5c on 2c bl grn	.50 .25
a.	Double surcharge		4.00
437	A155	5c on 2c lt ol grn ('45)	.50 .25

Government Palace, Quito — A173

1944		Engr.	Perf. 11
438	A173	10c dark green	.50 .25
439	A173	30c blue	.50 .25

See Nos. C128-C130, C221. For surcharges see Nos. 452, RAC1-RAC2.

Symbol of the Red Cross — A174

1945, Apr. 25			Perf. 12
		Cross in Rose	
440	A174	30c bister brown	1.90 .35
441	A174	1s red brown	2.75 .45
442	A174	6s turq green	4.75 .45
443	A174	10s scarlet	13.00 3.00
	Nos. 440-443,C131-C134 (8)		58.40 14.75

International Red Cross, 80th anniversary.

Nos. 370 to 372 Overprinted in Dark Blue and Gold

1945, Oct. 2			Perf. 11½
		Center Multicolored	
444	A144	50c black	.80 .70
a.	Double overprint		22.50

445	A144	1s olive black	1.40 1.40
446	A144	2s dark brown	2.75 2.50
a.	Double overprint		22.50
Nos. 444-446,C139-C141 (6)		10.45 8.25

Visit of Pres. Juan Antonio Rios of Chile.

General Antonio José de Sucre, 150th Birth Anniv. — A175

1945, Nov. 14		Engr.	Perf. 12
447	A175	10c olive	.55 .25
448	A175	20c red brown	.55 .25
449	A175	40c olive gray	.55 .25
450	A175	1s dark green	1.10 .25
451	A175	2s sepia	2.25 .75
Nos. 447-451,C142-C146 (10)			13.20 6.10

No. 438 Surcharged in Blue

1945			Perf. 11
452	A173	20c on 10c dark green	.50 .25
a.	Fancy bar omitted		

Catalogue values for unused stamps in this section, from this point to the end of the section, are for Never Hinged items.

Map of Pan-American Highway and Arms of Loja — A176

1946, Apr. 22		Engr.	Perf. 12
453	A176	20c red brown	.75 .40
454	A176	30c bright green	.75 .45
455	A176	1s bright ultra	.75 .45
456	A176	5s deep red lilac	2.50 1.50
457	A176	10s scarlet	4.75 2.00
Nos. 453-457,C147-C151 (10)			20.25 7.95

Torch of Democracy A177   Popular Suffrage A178

Flag of Ecuador A179   Pres. José M. Velasco Ibarra A180

1946, Aug. 9		Unwmk.	Perf. 12½
458	A177	5c dark blue	.35 .25
459	A178	10c Prus green	.35 .25
460	A179	20c carmine	.45 .25
461	A180	30c chocolate	.65 .25
Nos. 458-461,C152-C155 (8)			5.10 2.35

Revolution of May 28, 1944, 2nd anniv.

"30 Ctvs." — A181

1946			Black Surcharge
462	A181	30c on 50c red brown	.65 .25

For overprint see No. 484.

Nos. CO13-CO14 With Additional Ovpt. in Black

1946			Perf. 11½
463	AP7	10c chestnut	.60 .25
464	AP7	20c olive black	.60 .25

Instructor and Student — A182

1946, Sept. 16			Perf. 12½
465	A182	10c deep blue	.40 .50
466	A182	20c chocolate	.40 .50
467	A182	30c dark green	.40 .50
468	A182	50c bluish blk	.55 .65
469	A182	1s dark red	1.10 1.00
470	A182	10s dark violet	6.50 1.90
Nos. 465-470,C156-C160 (11)			22.30 11.05

Campaign for adult education.

Mariana de Jesus Paredes y Flores A183   Urn A184

1946, Nov. 28			
471	A183	10c black brown	.35 .25
472	A183	20c green	.35 .25
473	A183	30c purple	.35 .25
474	A184	1s rose brown	.45 .30
Nos. 471-474,C161-C164 (8)			5.55 3.10

300th anniv. of the death of the Blessed Mariana de Jesus Paredes y Flores.

Pres. Vicente Rocafuerte A185   Jesuits' Church Quito A186

45c, 50c, 80c, F.J.E. de Santa Cruz y Espejo.

1947, Nov. 27			Perf. 12
475	A185	5c redsh brown	.30 .25
476	A185	10c sepia	.30 .25
477	A185	15c gray black	.30 .25
478	A186	20c redsh brown	.35 .25
479	A186	30c red violet	.60 .25
480	A186	40c brt ultra	.75 .25
481	A185	45c dk slate grn	1.00 .30
482	A185	50c olive black	1.05 .30
483	A185	80c orange red	1.50 .35
Nos. 475-483,C165-C171 (16)			11.00 4.55

For overprints and surcharges see Nos. 489, 496, 525-527, C215.

Type of 1946, Overprinted "POSTAL" in Black but Without Additional Surcharge

1948			Engr.
484	A181	10c orange	.50 .25

Andrés Bello — A188

1948, Apr. 21			Perf. 13
485	A188	20c lt blue	.40 .25
486	A188	30c rose carmine	.40 .25
487	A188	40c blue green	.40 .25
488	A188	1s black brown	.80 .25
Nos. 485-488,C172-C174 (7)			4.65 1.90

83rd anniversary of the death of Andrés Bello (1781-1865), educator.

No. 480 Overprinted in Black

1948, May 24			Perf. 12
489	A186	40c bright ultra	.60 .35

See No. C175.

Flagship of Columbus — A189

1948			Perf. 14
490	A189	10c dark blue green	.50 .25
491	A189	20c brown	.50 .25
492	A189	30c dark purple	1.20 .25
493	A189	50c deep claret	1.60 .25
494	A189	1s ultra	2.40 .40
495	A189	5s carmine	6.50 .80
Nos. 490-495,C176-C180 (11)			30.50 8.15

Issued to publicize the proposed Columbus Memorial Lighthouse near Ciudad Trujillo, Dominican Republic.

No. 483 Overprinted in Blue, "MANANA" Reading Down

1948			Perf. 12
496	A185	80c orange red	.25 .25

Issued to publicize the National Fair of Today and Tomorrow, 1948. See No. C181.

Telegrafo I in Flight — A190

1948		Engr.	Perf. 12½
497	A190	30c red orange	.70 .25
498	A190	40c rose lilac	.70 .25
499	A190	60c violet blue	.70 .25
500	A190	1s brown red	.70 .25
501	A190	3s brown	2.25 .35
502	A190	5s gray black	2.50 .35
Nos. 497-502,C182-C187 (12)			10.00 6.70

25th anniversary (in 1945) of the first postal flight in Ecuador.

Book and Pen — A191

1948, Oct. 12		Unwmk.	Perf. 14
503	A191	10c deep claret	.60 .30
504	A191	20c brown	.60 .30
505	A191	30c dark green	1.25 .30
506	A191	50c red	2.00 .30
507	A191	1s purple	3.00 .35
508	A191	10s dull blue	8.00 1.25
Nos. 503-508,C188-C192 (11)			34.15 9.65

Campaign for adult education.

ECUADOR

A192

Franklin D. Roosevelt and Two of "Four Freedoms" — A193

1948, Oct. 24   **Perf. 12½**
509	A192	10c rose brn & gray	.50	.30
510	A192	20c brn ol & bl	.60	.40
511	A193	30c ol bis & car rose	.60	.40
512	A193	40c red vio & sep	.75	.40
513	A193	1s org brn & car	.80	.50

Nos. 509-513,C193-C197 (10) 8.95 3.70

Maldonado and Map A194   Riobamba Aqueduct A195

Maldonado on Bank of Riobamba A196   Pedro V. Maldonado A197

1948, Nov. 17   **Engr.**   **Unwmk.**
514	A194	5c gray blk & ver	.50	.25
515	A195	10c car & gray blk	.60	.25
516	A196	30c bis brn & ultra	.70	.25
517	A195	40c sage grn & vio	.90	.25
518	A194	50c grn & car	1.20	.30
519	A197	1s brn & slate bl	1.50	.35

Nos. 514-519,C198-C201 (10) 10.00 2.85

Bicentenary of the death of Pedro Vicente Maldonado, geographer.
For overprints and surcharges see Nos. 537-540.

A198

Miguel de Cervantes Saavedra — A199

1949, May 2   **Perf. 12½x12**
520	A198	30c dk car rose & dp ultra	.75	.25
521	A199	60c bis & brn vio	1.25	.30
522	A198	1s grn & rose car	1.75	.25
523	A199	2s gray blk & red brn	3.25	.30
524	A198	5s choc & aqua	6.50	1.25

Nos. 520-524,C202-C206 (10) 26.70 5.95

400th anniv. of the birth of Miguel de Cervantes Saavedra, novelist, playwright and poet.

No. 480 Surcharged in Carmine

1949, June 15   **Perf. 12**
525	A186	10c on 40c brt ultra	.55	.25
526	A186	20c on 40c brt ultra	.75	.25
a.		Double surcharge		
527	A186	30c on 40c brt ultra	.75	.25

Nos. 525-527,C207-C209 (6) 4.35 1.65

2nd Natl. Eucharistic Cong., Quito, 6/49.
No. 526 exists se-tenant with No. 527.

Monument on Equator — A200

1949, June   **Engr.**   **Perf. 12½x12**
| 528 | A200 | 10c deep plum | .50 | .25 |

For overprint see No. 536.

No. 542 Surcharged in Black and Carmine

1949   **Perf. 12½x12**
529	A203	10c on 50c green	.60	.25
530	A203	20c on 50c green	.60	.25
531	A203	30c on 50c green	.70	.25

Nos. 529-531,C210-C213 (7) 7.15 2.25

Universal Postal Union, 75th anniversary.

Consular Service Stamps Surcharged in Black

Arms of Ecuador — R1

1949   **Perf. 12**
| 532 | R1 | 20c on 25c red brown | .85 | .25 |
| 533 | R1 | 30c on 50c gray | .85 | .25 |

For other overprints and surcharges on type R1 see Nos. 544-549, 566-570, C214 C245, C249-C252, RA60-RA62, RA72.

Nos. RA49A and RA55 Overprinted in Black — a

1950   **Unwmk.**   **Perf. 12**
| 534 | PT18 | 5c green | .45 | .25 |
| 535 | PT21 | 5c blue | .45 | .25 |

Overprint 15mm on No. 534.

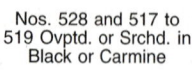

Nos. 528 and 517 to 519 Ovptd. or Srchd. in Black or Carmine

1950, Feb. 10   **Perf. 12½x12**
| 536 | A200 | 10c dp plum | .50 | .50 |

    Perf. 12½
537	A195	20c on 40c sage grn & vio	1.00	1.00
538	A195	30c on 40c sage grn & vio	1.25	1.25
539	A194	50c grn & car	2.00	2.00
540	A197	1s brn & slate bl (C)	2.50	2.50

No. C220 Overprinted in Carmine

Overprint 15mm long   **Perf. 11**
| 541 | A173 | 10s violet | 6.00 | 3.00 |

Nos. 536-541,C216-C220 (11) 34.90 22.25
Nos. 536-541 publicize adult education.

San Pablo Lake — A203

  Perf. 12x12½
1950, May   **Engr.**   **Unwmk.**
| 542 | A203 | 50c green | .60 | .25 |

For surcharges see Nos. 529-531.

Consular Service Stamp Surcharged Vertically in Black

1950   **Perf. 12**
| 544 | R1 | 30c on 50c gray | .60 | .25 |

Consular Service Stamps Overprinted or Surcharged in Black

 b   c

 d   e

 f   g

1951   **Unwmk.**   **Perf. 12**
545	R1 (b)	5c on 10c car rose	.60	.25
546	R1 (c)	10c car rose	.60	.25
547	R1 (d)	10c car rose	.60	.25
548	R1 (e)	20c on 25c red brn	.60	.25
549	R1 (e)	30c on 50c gray	.60	.25
550	R2 (f)	40c on 25c blue	.60	.25
551	R2 (g)	50c on 25c blue	.60	.25

Nos. 545-551 (7) 4.20 1.75

See Nos. 552-554, C233-C234, C246-C248, RA67.

Consular Service Stamps Surcharged in Black

1951
| 552 | R2 | 20c on 25c blue | .50 | .25 |
| 553 | R2 | 30c on 25c blue | .50 | .25 |

Adult education. See Nos. C225-C226.

Consular Service Stamp Surcharged in Black

1951
| 554 | R2 | $0.30 on 50c car rose | .60 | .25 |

Reliquary of St. Mariana and Vatican — A204

  Perf. 12½x12
1952, Feb.   **Engr.**   **Unwmk.**
555	A204	10c emer & red brn	1.00	.70
556	A204	20c dp bl & pur	1.00	.70
557	A204	30c car & bl grn	1.00	.70

Nos. 555-557,C227-C230 (7) 7.05 3.30

Issued to publicize the canonization of Mariana de Jesus Paredes y Flores.

Presidents Galo Plaza and Harry Truman — A205

2s, Pres. Plaza addressing US Congress.

1952, Mar. 26   **Perf. 12**
| 558 | A205 | 1s rose car & gray blk | .75 | .60 |
| 559 | A205 | 2s dl bl & sepia | 1.90 | .90 |

Nos. 558-559,C231-C232 (4) 5.95 3.70

1951 visit of Pres. Galo Plaza y Lasso to the US.

R3

Fiscal Stamps Srchd. or Ovptd. Horiz. in Carmine or Black

Type of 1937 Overprinted Diagonally

1952   **Unwmk.**   **Engr.**   **Perf. 12**
560	R3	20c on 30c dp bl (C)	.80	.25
561	R3	30c deep blue	.80	.25
562	A138	50c purple	.80	.25

Nos. 560-562 (3) 2.40 .75

For overprints and surcharge see Nos. RA68-RA69, RA71.

Pres. José M. Urvina, Slave and "Liberty" — A206

Hyphen-hole Perf. 7x6½
1952   **Litho.**
563	A206	20c red & green	.70	.45
564	A206	30c red & vio bl	.90	.45
565	A206	50c blue & car	1.50	.45

Nos. 563-565,C236-C239 (7) 18.10 3.15

Centenary of abolition of slavery in Ecuador. Counterfeits exist.

Consular Service Stamps Surcharged in Black — h

1952-53   **Unwmk.**   **Perf. 12**
566	R1	10c on 20s blue ('53)	.85	.25
567	R1	20c on 10s gray ('53)	.85	.25
568	R1	20c on 20s blue	.85	.25
569	R1	30c on 10s gray ('53)	.85	.25
570	R1	30c on 20s blue	.85	.25

Nos. 566-570 (5) 4.25 1.25

Similar surcharges of 60c and 90c on the 20s blue are said to be bogus.

ECUADOR

Teacher and Students
A207

New Citizens Voting
A208

Designs: 10c, Instructor with student. 30c, Teaching the alphabet.

1953, Apr. 13			Engr.	
571	A207	5c lt bl	.35	.25
572	A207	10c dk car rose	.55	.25
573	A208	20c brt brn org	.60	.25
574	A208	30c dp red lil	.90	.25
	Nos. 571-574,C240-C241 (6)		5.80	1.60

1952 adult education campaign.

A209

1953   **Black Surcharge**
575   A209   40c on 50c purple   1.00 .25

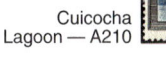
Cuicocha Lagoon — A210

Designs: 10c, Equatorial Line monument. 20c, Quininde countryside. 30c, Tomebamba river. 40c, La Chilintosa rock. 50c, Iliniza Mountains.

Frames in Black

1953		Engr.	Perf. 13x12½	
576	A210	5c brt bl	.60	.50
577	A210	10c brt grn	.60	.50
578	A210	20c purple	.60	.50
579	A210	30c brown	.60	.50
580	A210	40c orange	.60	.50
581	A210	50c dp car	1.10	.50
	Nos. 576-581 (6)		4.10	3.00

A211

Carlos Maria Cardinal de la Torre and arches.

1954, Jan.		Photo.	Perf. 8½	
582	A211	30c blk & ver	.70	.65
583	A211	50c blk & rose lil	.70	.65
	Nos. 582-583,C253-C255 (5)		4.75	2.35

1st anniv. of the elevation of Archbishop de la Torre to Cardinal.

A212

1954, Apr. 22				
584	A212	30c blk & gray	1.50	1.40
585	A212	50c blk & yel	1.50	1.40
	Nos. 584-585,C256-C260 (7)		8.10	4.80

Queen Isabella I (1451-1504) of Spain, 500th birth anniv.

Type of 1929 Overprint Larger, No Letterspacing

1954-55		Unwmk.	Perf. 12	
586	A112	5c ol grn ('55)	.80	.25
587	A112	10c orange	.80	.25

The normal overprint on Nos. 586-587 reads up. It also exists reading down.

Indian Messenger — A213

1954, Aug. 2		Litho.	Perf. 11	
588	A213	30c dk brn	1.00	.25

Day of the Postal Employee. See No. C263.

Products of Ecuador — A214

1954, Sept. 24			Photo.	
589	A214	10c orange	.45	.25
590	A214	20c vermilion	.45	.25
591	A214	30c rose pink	.45	.25
592	A214	40c dk gray grn	.70	.25
593	A214	50c yel brn	.90	.25
	Nos. 589-593 (5)		2.95	1.25

José Abel Castillo — A215

		Perf. 11½x11		
1955, Oct. 19		Engr.	Unwmk.	
594	A215	30c olive bister	.65	.25
595	A215	50c dk gray	.65	.25
	Nos. 594-595,C282-C286 (7)		11.80	2.10

30th anniv. of the 1st flight of the "Telegrafo I" and to honor Castillo, aviation pioneer.

Babahoyo River Los Rios — A216

Designs: 5c, Palms, Esmeraldas. 10c, Fishermen, Manabi. 30c, Guayaquil, Guayas. 50c, Pital River, El Oro. 70c, Cactus, Galapagos Isls. 80c, Orchids, Napo-Pastaza. 1s, Aguacate Mission, Zamora-Chinchipe. 2s, Jibaro Indian, Morona-Santiago.

1955-56			Photo.	Perf. 13
596	A216	5c yel grn ('56)	1.50	.30
597	A216	10c blue ('56)	1.50	.30
598	A216	20c brown	1.50	.30
599	A216	30c dk gray	1.50	.30
600	A216	50c bl grn	1.50	.30
601	A216	70c ol ('56)	1.50	.30
602	A216	80c dp vio ('56)	3.75	.30
603	A216	1s dry ('56)	2.00	.30
604	A216	2s rose red ('56)	3.75	.30
	Nos. 596-604 (9)		18.50	2.70

See Nos. 620-630, 670, C288-C297, C310-C311.

Brother Juan Adam Schwarz, S. J. — A217

1956, Aug. 27			Engr.	Perf. 13½
605	A217	5c yel grn	.55	.25
606	A217	10c org red	.55	.25
607	A217	20c lt vio	.55	.25
608	A217	30c dk grn	.55	.25
609	A217	40c blue	.55	.25
610	A217	50c dp ultra	.55	.25
611	A217	70c orange	.55	.25
	Nos. 605-611,C302-C305 (11)		6.85	3.35

Bicentennial of printing in Ecuador and honoring Brother Juan Adam Schwarz, S.J.

Andres Hurtado de Mendoza
A218

Gil Ramirez Davalos
A219

Designs: 20c, Brother Vincent Solano.

1957, Apr. 7		Unwmk.	Perf. 12	
612	A218	5c dk bl, pink	.80	.25
613	A219	10c grn, grnsh	.80	.25
614	A218	20c choc, buff	.80	.25
a.	Souvenir sheet of 4, imperf.		3.50	3.50
	Nos. 612-614,C312-C314 (6)		3.75	1.65

4th cent. of the founding of Cuenca.
No. 614a contains 2 5c gray & 2 20c brown red stamps in designs similar to #612, 614. It was printed on white ungummed paper.

A220

Design: 40c, 50c, 2s, Francisco Marcos, Gen. Pedro Alcantara Herran and Santos Michelena.

1957, Sept. 5		Engr.	Perf. 14½x14	
615	A220	40c yellow	.40	.25
616	A220	50c ultra	.40	.25
617	A220	2s dk red	1.00	.25
	Nos. 615-617 (3)		1.80	.75

7th Postal Congress of the Americas and Spain (in 1955).

Souvenir Sheets

Various Railroad Scenes A221

1957		Litho.	Perf. 10½x11	
618	A221	20c Sheet of 5	9.25	4.25
619	A221	30c Sheet of 5	9.25	4.25

Issued to commemorate the opening of the Quito-Ibarra-San Lorenzo railroad.
Nos. 618-619 contain 2 orange yellow, 1 ultramarine and 2 carmine stamps, each in a different design.

Scenic Type of 1955-56.

Designs as before, except: 40c, as 70c. 90c, as 80c. No. 629, San Pablo, Imbabura.

1957-58			Photo.	Perf. 13
620	A216	5c light blue	1.75	.25
621	A216	10c brown	1.75	.25
622	A216	20c crimson rose	1.75	.25
623	A216	20c yel green	1.75	.25
624	A216	30c rose red	2.50	.25
625	A216	40c chalky blue	1.75	.25
626	A216	50c lt vio	2.50	.25
627	A216	90c brt ultra	1.75	.25
628	A216	1s dark brown	1.75	.25
629	A216	1s gray blk ('58)	1.75	.25
630	A216	2s brown	2.75	.25
	Nos. 620-630 (11)		21.75	2.75

Blue and Yellow Macaw — A222

Birds: 20c, Red-breasted toucan. 30c, Condor. 40c, Black-tailed and sword-tailed hummingbirds.

	Perf. 13½x13			
1958, Jan. 7		Litho.	Unwmk.	
	Birds in Natural Colors			
634	A222	10c red brn	1.40	.25
635	A222	20c dk gray	1.40	.25
636	A222	30c brt yel grn	3.50	.25
637	A222	40c red org	3.50	.25
	Nos. 634-637 (4)		9.80	1.00

Carlos Sanz de Santamaria
A223

Richard M. Nixon and Flags
A224

No. 640, Dr. Ramon Villeda Morales, flags. 2.20s, José Carlos de Macedo Soares, horizontal flags.

1958			Perf. 12	
	Flags in Red, Blue, Yellow & Green			
638	A223	1.80s dl vio	.65	.25
639	A224	2s dk grn	.65	.25
640	A224	2s dk brn	.65	.25
641	A223	2.20s blk brn	.65	.25
	Nos. 638-641 (4)		2.60	1.00

Visits: Colombia's Foreign Minister Dr. Carlos Sanz de Santamaria; US Vice Pres. Nixon, May 9-10; Pres. Ramon Villeda Morales of Honduras; Brazil's Foreign Minister José Carlos de Macedo Soares. See Nos. 775-775C, C419-C421, C460. For overprints and surcharges see Nos. 775-775C, C419-C421, C460.

Locomotive of 1908 — A225

Garcia Moreno, Jose Caamano, L. Plaza and Eloy Alfaro
A226

Design: 50c, Diesel locomotive.

	Perf. 13½x14, 14			
1958, Aug. 9		Photo.	Unwmk.	
642	A225	30c brn blk	.30	.25
643	A225	50c dk car	.40	.25
644	A226	5s dk brn	1.80	.70
	Nos. 642-644 (3)		2.50	1.20

Guayaquil-Quito railroad, 50th anniv.

Cardinal — A227

Birds: 30c, Andean cock-of-the-rock. 50c, Glossy cowbird. 60c, Red-fronted Amazon.

1958			Perf. 13½x13	
	Birds in Natural Colors			
645	A227	20c blush grn, blk & red	1.40	.25
646	A227	30c buff, blk & brt bl	1.65	.25
647	A227	50c org, blk & grn	1.90	.55
648	A227	60c pale rose, blk & bluish grn	3.75	.55
	Nos. 645-648 (4)		8.70	1.60

UNESCO Building and Eiffel Tower, Paris — A228

1958, Nov. 3			Engr.	Perf. 12½
649	A228	80c brown	.65	.35

UNESCO Headquarters in Paris opening, Nov. 3.

ECUADOR

Globe and Satellites — A229

1958, Dec. 20   Photo.   Perf. 14x13½
650   A229   1.80s dark blue   1.25   .45

International Geophysical Year, 1957-58. For overprints see Nos. 718, C422.

Virgin of Quito — A230

1959, Sept. 8   Unwmk.   Perf. 13
651   A230   5c ol grn   .30   .25
652   A230   10c yel brn   .30   .25
653   A230   20c purple   .30   .25
654   A230   30c ultra   .30   .25
655   A230   80c dk car rose   .30   .25
     Nos. 651-655 (5)   1.50   1.25

See No. C290. For surcharges and overprint see Nos. 695-699.

Uprooted Oak Emblem — A231

1960, Apr. 7   Litho.   Perf. 14x13
656   A231   80c rose car & grn   .60   .25

World Refugee Year, 71/59-630/60. For overprints see Nos. 709, 719, O205.

Great Anteater and Arms — A232

Animals: 40c, Tapir and map. 80c, Spectacled bear and arms. 1s, Puma and map.

1960, May 14   Photo.   Perf. 13
657   A232   20c org, grn & blk   .60   .25
658   A232   40c yel grn, bl grn & brn   .90   .25
659   A232   80c bl, blk & red brn   1.50   .25
660   A232   1s Prus bl, plum & ocher   2.75   .60
     Nos. 657-660 (4)   5.75   1.35

Founding of the city of Baeza, 4th cent. See Nos. 676-679.

Hotel Quito — A233

No. 662, Dormitory, Catholic University. No. 663, Dormitory, Central University. No. 664, Airport, Quito. No. 665, Overpass on Highway to Quito. No. 666, Security Bank. No. 667, Ministry of Foreign Affairs. No. 668, Government Palace. No. 669, Legislative Palace.

Perf. 11x11½
1960, Aug. 8   Engr.   Unwmk.
661   A233   1s dk pur & redsh brn   .55   .25
662   A233   1s dk bl & brn   .55   .25
663   A233   1s blk & red   .55   .25
664   A233   1s dk bl & ultra   .55   .25
665   A233   1s dk pur & dk car rose   .55   .25
666   A233   1s blk & ol bis   .55   .25
667   A233   1s dk pur & turq   .55   .25
668   A233   1s dk bl & grn   .55   .25
669   A233   1s blk & vio   .55   .25
     Nos. 661-669 (9)   4.95   2.25

11th Inter-American Conference, Quito. For surcharges see Nos. 700-708.

Type of Regular Issue, 1955-56
Souvenir Sheet
Design: Orchids, Napo-Pastaza.

1960   Photo.   Perf. 13
     Yellow Paper
670   Sheet of 2   5.00   5.00
  a.   A216 80c deep violet   .85   .45
  b.   A216 90c deep green   .85   .45

25th anniv. of Asociacion Filatelica Ecuatoriana. Marginal inscription in silver. Exists with silver inscription omitted.

"Freedom of Expression" A234   Manabi Bridge A235

10c, "Freedom to vote." 20c, "Freedom to work." 30c, Coins, "Monetary stability."

1960, Aug. 29   Litho.   Perf. 13
671   A234   5c dk bl   .80   .25
672   A234   10c lt vio   .80   .25
673   A234   20c orange   .80   .25
674   A234   30c bluish grn   .80   .25
675   A235   40c brn & bluish grn   .80   .25
     Nos. 671-675 (5)   4.00   1.25

Achievements of President Camilo Ponce Enriquez. See Nos. C370-C374.

Animal Type of 1960
Animals: 10c, Collared peccary. 20c, Kinkajou. 80c, Jaguar. 1s, Mountain coati.

Unwmk.
1961, July 13   Photo.   Perf. 13
676   A232   10c grn, rose red & blk   .60   .25
677   A232   20c vio, grnsh bl & brn   1.10   .25
678   A232   80c red org, dl yel & blk   1.70   .55
679   A232   1s org brn & pale bl grn   2.20   .65
     Nos. 676-679 (4)   5.60   1.70

Founding of the city of Tena, 400th anniv.

Graphium Pausianus — A236

Butterflies: 30c, Papilio torquatus leptalea. 50c, Graphium molops molops. 80c, Battus lycidas.

1961, July 13   Litho.   Perf. 13½
680   A236   20c pink & multi   .70   .25
681   A236   30c lt ultra & multi   1.20   .25
682   A236   50c org & multi   1.40   .25
683   A236   80c bl grn & multi   2.40   .25
     Nos. 680-683 (4)   5.70   1.00

See Nos. 711-713.

Galapagos Islands Nos. L1-L3 Overprinted in Black or Red

1961, Oct. 31   Photo.   Perf. 12
684   A1   20c dk brn   1.00   .25
685   A2   50c violet   1.00   .25
686   A1   1s dk ol grn (R)   2.40   1.50
     Nos. 684-686, C389-C391 (6)   11.30   3.30

Establishment of maritime biological stations on Galapagos Islands by UNESCO. Overprint arranged differently on 20c, 1s. See Nos. C389-C391.

Daniel Enrique Proano School — A237

Designs: 60c, Loja-Zamora highway, vert. 80c, Aguirre Abad College, Guayaquil. 1s, Army quarters, Quito.

Perf. 11x11½, 11½x11
1962, Jan. 10   Engr.   Unwmk.
687   A237   50c dl bl & blk   .50   .25
688   A237   60c ol grn & blk   .50   .25
689   A237   80c org red & blk   .50   .25
690   A237   1s rose lake & blk   .50   .25
     Nos. 687-690 (4)   2.00   1.00

Pres. Arosemena, Flags of Ecuador, US — A238

Designs (Arosemena and): 10c, Flags of Ecuador. 20c, Flags of Ecuador and Panama.

1963, July 1   Litho.   Perf. 14
691   A238   10c buff & multi   .30   .25
692   A238   20c multi   .30   .25
693   A238   60c multi   .30   .25
     Nos. 691-693, C409-C411 (6)   3.65   1.70

Issued to commemorate Pres. Carlos J. Arosemena's friendship trip, July 1962. Imperfs exist. Value $9.

Protection for The Family — A239

1963, July 9   Unwmk.   Perf. 14
694   A239   10c ultra, red, gray & blk   .25   .25

Social Insurance, 25th anniv. See No. C413.

No. 655 Ovptd. or Srchd. in Black or Blue

1963   Photo.   Perf. 13
695   A230   10c on 80c dk car rose   .35   .25
696   A230   20c on 80c dk car rose   .35   .25
697   A230   50c on 80c dk car rose   .35   .25
698   A230   60c on 80c dk car rose (Bl)   .35   .25
699   A230   80c dk car rose   .40   .25
     Nos. 695-699 (5)   1.80   1.25

Nos. 661-669 Surcharged

1964, Apr. 20   Engr.   Perf. 11x11½
700   A233   10c on 1s dk pur & redsh brn   .65   .25
701   A233   10c on 1s dk pur & turq   .65   .25
702   A233   20c on 1s dk bl & brn   .65   .25
703   A233   20c on 1s dk bl & grn   .65   .25
704   A233   30c on 1s dk pur & dk car rose   .65   .25
705   A233   40c on 1s blk & ol bis   .65   .25
706   A233   60c on 1s blk & red   .65   .25
707   A233   80c on 1s dk bl & ultra   .65   .25
708   A233   80c on 1s blk & vio   .65   .25
     Nos. 700-708 (9)   5.85   2.25

No. 656 Overprinted in Black or Light Ultramarine

1964   Litho.   Perf. 14x13
709   A231   80c rose car & grn   5.00   1.25

Butterfly Type of 1961
Butterflies: Same as on Nos. 680, 682-683.

1964, June   Litho.   Perf. 13½
711   A236   20c brt grn & multi   .80   .25
712   A236   50c sal pink & multi   1.60   .25
713   A236   80c lt red brn & multi   3.25   .25
     Nos. 711-713 (3)   5.65   .75

Alliance for Progress Emblem, Agriculture and Industry — A240

Designs: 50c, Emblem, gear wheels, mountain and seashore. 80c, Emblem, banana worker, fish, factory and ship.

1964, Aug. 26   Unwmk.   Perf. 12
715   A240   40c bis brn & vio   .35   .25
716   A240   50c red org & blk   .35   .25
717   A240   80c bl & dk brn   .55   .25
     Nos. 715-717 (3)   1.25   .75

Issued to publicize the Alliance for Progress which aims to stimulate economic growth and raise living standards in Latin America.

No. 650 Overprinted in Red

1964   Photo.   Perf. 14x13½
718   A229   1.80s dark blue   2.75   2.25

No. 656 Overprinted

1964, July   Litho.   Perf. 14x13
719   A231   80c block of 4   4.00   4.00

Organization of American States.

World Map and Banana Tree — A241

1964, Oct. 26   Perf. 12½x12
720   A241   50c dk brn, gray & gray ol   .30   .25
721   A241   80c blk, org & gray ol   .30   .25

Issued to publicize the Banana Conference, Oct.-Nov. 1964. See Nos. C427-C428a.

King Philip II of Spain and Map of Upper Amazon River — A242

Designs (Map and): 20c, Juan de Salinas de Loyola. 30c, Hernando de Santillan.

1964, Dec. 6   Litho.   Perf. 13½
722   A242   10c rose, blk & buff   .40   .25
723   A242   20c bl grn, blk & buff   .40   .25
724   A242   30c bl, blk & buff   .40   .25
     Nos. 722-724 (3)   1.20   .75

4th centenary of the establishment of the Royal High Court in Quito.

Pole Vaulting — A243

ECUADOR

1964, Dec. 16   *Perf. 14x13½*
725	A243	80c vio bl, yel grn & brn	.35 .25

18th Olympic Games, Tokyo, Oct. 10-25. See Nos. C432-C434.

Peter Fleming and Two-toed Sloth — A244

Designs: 20c, James Elliot and armadillo. 30c, T. Edward McCully, Jr., and squirrel. 40c, Roger Youderian and deer. 60c, Nathaniel (Nate) Saint and plane over Napo River.

1965   *Unwmk.*   *Perf. 13½*
726	A244	20c emerald & multi	1.00 .25
727	A244	30c yellow & multi	1.00 .25
728	A244	40c lilac & multi	1.00 .25
729	A244	60c multi	1.00 .25
730	A244	80c multi	1.00 .25
		Nos. 726-730 (5)	5.00 1.25

Issued in memory of five American Protestant missionaries, killed by the Auca Indians, 1/8/56.
Issue dates: 80c, May 11; others, July 8.

Juan B. Vázquez and Benigno Malo College A245

1965, June 6   *Litho.*   *Perf. 14*
731	A245	20c blk, yel & vio bl	.35 .25
732	A245	60c blk, red, yel & vio bl	.35 .25
733	A245	80c blk, emer, yel & vio bl	.35 .25
		Nos. 731-733 (3)	1.05 .75

Centenary (in 1964) of the founding of Benigno Malo National College.

National Anthem, Juan Leon Mera and Antonio Neumane — A246

1965, Aug. 10   *Litho.*   *Perf. 13½*
734	A246	50c pink & blk	.30 .25
735	A246	80c lt grn & blk	.40 .25
736	A246	5s blu & blk	.95 .35
737	A246	10s lt ultra & blk	1.75 .90
		Nos. 734-737 (4)	3.40 1.75

Cent. of the national anthem. The name of the poet Juan Leon Mera is misspelled on the stamps.
For surcharges see Nos. 766C, 766H.

Torch and Athletes (Shot Put, Discus, Javelin and Hammer Throw) A247

50c, 1s, Runners. 60c, 1.50s, Soccer.

1965, Nov. 30   *Perf. 12x12½*
738	A247	40c org, gold, & blk	.30 .25
739	A247	50c org ver, gold & blk	.30 .25
740	A247	60c bl, gold & blk	.30 .25
741	A247	80c brt yel grn, gold & blk	.50 .25
742	A247	1s lt vio, gold & blk	.50 .25
743	A247	1.50s brt pink, gold & blk	.85 .50
		Nos. 738-743,C435-C440 (12)	7.70 3.95

Issued to publicize the 5th Bolivarian Games, held at Guayaquil and Quito.
For surcharges see Nos. 766B, 766D, C449.

Stamps of 1865 — A248

1965, Dec. 30   *Litho.*   *Perf. 13½*
Stamps of 1865 in Yellow, Ultramarine & Green
744	A248	80c rose red	.40 .25
745	A248	1.30s rose lilac	.45 .25
746	A248	2s chocolate	.60 .25
747	A248	4s black	.90 .25
a.		Souv. sheet, #744-747, imperf.	4.00 4.00
		Nos. 744-747 (4)	2.35 1.00

Cent. of Ecuadorian postage stamps.

The postal validity of some of the following sets has been questioned.

ITU Centenary — A248a

No. 748, Telstar. No. 748A, Syncom. No. 748B, Relay. No. 748C, Luna 3. No. 748D, Echo II. No. 748E, E. Branly, Marconi, Bell, E. Belin.

1966, Jan. 27   *Litho.*   *Perf. 12x12½*
748	A248a	10c multi	.30 .25
748A	A248a	10c multi	.30 .25
748B	A248a	80c multi	.30 .25
748C	A248a	1.50s multi	.50 .35
748D	A248a	3s multi	2.25 1.25
f.		Souv. sheet of 3, #748, 748B, 748D, perf. 14x12½	17.50
748E	A248a	4s multi	2.25 1.50
g.		Souv. sheet of 3, #748A, 748C, 748E, perf. 14x12½	17.50
		Nos. 748-748E (6)	5.90 3.85

1.50s, 3s, 4s are airmail.
Nos. 748Df, 748Eg are printed on surface colored paper. Exist imperf. Value, each $20.

Space Exploration A248b

10c, Edward White's space walk, June 8, 1965. 1s, Gemini 5, Aug. 21, 1965. 1.30s, Solar system. 2s, Charles Conrad, L. Gordon Cooper, Gemini 5, Aug. 21-29, 1965. 2.50s, Gemini 6. 3.50s, Alexei L. Leonov's space walk, Mar. 18, 1965.

1966, Jan. 27   *Perf. 12x12½*
749	A248b	10c multi	.30 .25
749A	A248b	1s multi	.40 .25
749B	A248b	1.30s multi	.40 .25
749C	A248b	2s multi	1.40 .65
749D	A248b	2.50s multi	1.40 .65
749E	A248b	3.50s multi	3.25 2.50
f.		Souv. sheet of 3, #749, 749B, 749E, perf. 14x12½	15.00 10.00
		Nos. 749-749E (6)	7.15 4.55

1.30s, 2s, 2.50s, 3.50s are airmail.
No. 749Ef is printed on surface colored paper. Exists imperf. Value $15.

Dante's Dream by Rossetti A248c

Designs: 80c, Dante and Beatrix by Holliday. 2s, Galileo Galilei, 400th birth cent., vert. 3s, Dante, 700th birth cent., vert.

1966, June   *Perf. 13½x14, 14x13½*
750	A248c	10c multicolored	.30 .25
750A	A248c	80c multicolored	.30 .25
750B	A248c	2s multi	3.00 1.50
750C	A248c	3s multicolored	3.00 1.60
d.		Souv. sheet of 3, #750, 750A, 750C, perf. 12x12½	18.00 18.00
		Nos. 750-750C (4)	6.60 3.60

Nos. 750A-750B are airmail. No. 750Cd exists imperf. Value $18.

Pavonine Quetzal — A249

Birds: 50c, Blue-crowned motmot. 60c, Paradise tanager. 80c, Wire-tailed manakin.

1966, June 17   *Litho.*   *Perf. 13½*
Birds in Natural Colors
751	A249	40c dl rose & blk	1.60 .25
751A	A249	50c sal & blk	1.60 .25
751B	A249	60c lt ocher & blk	1.60 .25
751C	A249	80c lt bl & blk	1.60 .25
		Nos. 751-751C,C441-C448 (12)	34.25 6.25

For surcharges see Nos. 766E-766F, C450, C455-C457.

Pope Paul VI — A249a

Pope Paul VI and: 1.30s, Nativity. 3.50s, Virgin of Merced.

1966, June 24   *Perf. 12½x12*
752	A249a	10c multicolored	.30 .25
752A	A249a	1.30s multicolored	.90 .35
752B	A249a	3.50s multicolored	2.50 .75
c.		Souv. sheet of 3, #752, perf. 14x13½, 752A-752B, perf. 12½x12	15.00 15.00
		Nos. 752-752B (3)	3.70 1.35

Nos. 752A-752B are airmail.
No. 752Bc is printed on surface colored paper. Exists imperf. Value $18.

Sir Winston Churchill, (1874-1965) A249b

Famous Men: 10c, Dag Hammarskjold, vert. 1.50s, Albert Schweitzer, vert. 2.50s, John F. Kennedy, vert. 4s, Churchill, Kennedy.

Perf. 14x13½, 13½x14
1966, June 24
753	A249b	10c vio bl, brn & blk	.30 .25
753A	A249b	1s ver, bl & blk	.40 .25
753B	A249b	1.50s brn, lil rose & blk	.90 .30
753C	A249b	2.50s ver, bl & blk	2.25 1.00
753D	A249b	4s bl, blk & brn	2.50 1.50
e.		Souv. sheet of 3, #753, 753B, 753D	30.00 27.50
		Nos. 753-753D (5)	6.35 3.30

Nos. 753C-753D are airmail.
No. 753De is printed on surface colored paper. 10c stamp is perf. 14x13½, 1.50s is perf. 14x13½x14x12, 4s is perf. 12x12½x13x12½. Exists imperf. Value $30.

History of Summer Olympics A249c

No. 754, Long jump. No. 754A, Wrestling. No. 754B, Discus, javelin. No. 754C, Chariot racing. No. 754D, High jump. No. 754E, Discus.

1966, June 27   *Perf. 12x12½*
754	A249c	10c multi	.30 .25
754A	A249c	10c multi	.30 .25
754B	A249c	80c multi	.35 .25
754C	A249c	1.30s multi	1.40 .45
754D	A249c	3s multi	2.25 .90
f.		Souv. sheet of 3, #754, 754B, 754D	12.00 5.00
754E	A249c	3.50s multi	3.50 1.10
g.		Souv. sheet of 3, #754A, 754C, 754E	12.50 5.00
		Nos. 754-754E (6)	8.10 3.20

Nos. 754C-754D are airmail.
Nos. 754Df, 754Eg are printed on surface colored paper.
Nos. 754Df and 754Eg exist imperf. Value $13.50.

1968 Winter Olympics, Grenoble A249d

Designs: 10c, Speedskating. 1s, Ice hockey. 1.50s, Ski jumping. 2s, Cross country skiing. 2.50s, Downhill skiing. 4s, Figure skating.

1966, June 27   *Perf. 14*
755	A249d	10c multi	.25 .25
755A	A249d	1s multi	.40 .25
755B	A249d	1.50s multi	.60 .30
755C	A249d	2s multi	1.20 .45
755D	A249d	2.50s multi	1.60 1.25
755E	A249d	4s multi	2.00 1.50
f.		Souv. sheet of 3, #755, 755B, 755E, perf. 14x13½	8.50 6.00
		Nos. 755-755E (6)	6.05 4.00

Nos. 755B-755E are airmail.
No. 755Ef is printed on surface colored paper. Exists imperf. Value same as perf.

French-American Cooperation in Space — A249e

Designs: 1.50s, French satellite D-1, Mt. Gros observatory, vert. 4s, John F. Kennedy, satellites.

1966   *Perf. 13½x14, 14x13½*
756	A249e	10c multicolored	.30 .25
756A	A249e	1.50s multicolored	1.75 1.10
756B	A249e	4s multicolored	4.25 2.25
c.		Sheet of 3, #756-756B	15.00 12.00
		Nos. 756-756B (3)	6.30 3.60

Nos. 756A-756B are airmail.
No. 756Bc exists imperf. Value same as perf.

Italian Space Program A249n

Designs: 10c, San Marco satellite. 1.30s, San Marco satellite, diff. 3.50s, Leonardo da Vinci, Moon, and Johannes Kepler.

1966   *Litho.*   *Unwmk.*   *Perf. 14*
757	A249n	10c multi	.25 .15
757A	A249n	1.30s multi		
757B	A249n	3.50s multi	2.00 1.10
c.		Souvenir sheet of 3, #757, 757A, 757B	13.00 8.00
		Nos. 757- (3)	3.00 1.80

Nos. 757A and 757B are airmail. No. 757Bc is printed on paper with a gray pattern, and exists imperforate on paper printed with a green pattern. Value same as perf.

Moon Exploration A249f

Designs: 10c, Surveyor. 80c, Luna 10. 1s, Luna 9. 2s, Astronaut flight trainer. 2.50s, Ranger 7. 3s, Lunar Orbiter 1.

ECUADOR

1966   *Perf. 14*
758	A249f	10c multi	.25	.25
758A	A249f	80c multi	.25	.25
758B	A249f	1s multi	.25	.25
758C	A249f	2s multi	.80	.45
758D	A249f	2.50s multi	1.00	.75
758E	A249f	3s multi	1.20	.90
f.	Sheet of 3, #758, 758A, 758E		12.00	6.00
	Nos. 758-758E (6)		3.75	2.85

Nos. 758C-758E are airmail. Stamps in No. 758Ef have colored pattern in border.

No. 758Ef exists imperf. Value same as perf.

1968 Summer Olympics, Mexico City — A249g

Paintings by Mexican artists: 10c, Wanderer by Diego Rivera. 1s, Workers by Jose Orozco. 1.30s, Pres. Juarez by Orozco. 2s, Mother and Child by David Siqueiros. 2.50s, Two Women by Rivera. 3.50s, New Democracy by Siqueiros.

1967, Mar. 13   *Perf. 14*
759	A249g	10c multicolored	.25	.25
759A	A249g	1s multicolored	.55	.25
759B	A249g	1.30s multicolored	.80	.35
759C	A249g	2s multicolored	1.00	.60
759D	A249g	2.50s multicolored	1.20	1.00
759E	A249g	3.50s multicolored	2.25	2.00
f.	Sheet of 3, #759, 759B, 759E		15.00	
	Nos. 759-759E (6)		6.05	4.45

Nos. 759B-759E are airmail.

No. 759f is printed on surface colored paper that differs slightly from Nos. 759-759E. Exists imperf. Value same as perf.

1968 Summer Olympics, Mexico City A249h

No. 760, Soccer. No. 760A, Hurdles. No. 760B, Track. No. 760C, Fencing. No. 760D, High jump. No. 760E, Swimming.

1967, Mar. 13
760	A249h	10c multi	.25	.25
760A	A249h	10c multi	.25	.25
760B	A249h	80c multi	.25	.25
760C	A249h	1.50s multi	.75	.30
760D	A249h	3s multi	1.50	1.00
f.	Souv. sheet of 3, #760A, 760B, 760D		15.00	7.50
760E	A249h	4s multi	3.25	1.50
g.	Souv. sheet of 3, #760, 760C, 760E		12.00	7.00
	Nos. 760-760E (6)		6.25	3.55

Nos. 760C-760E are airmail.

Nos. 760f-760g are printed on surface colored paper. Exist imperf. Value same as perf.

4th Natl. Eucharistic Congress A249i

Paintings: 10c, Madonna and Child by unknown artist. 60c, Holy Family by Rodriguez. 80c, Madonna and Child by Samaniego. 1s, Good Shepherd by Samaniego. 1.50s, Assumption of the Virgin by Vargas. 2s, Man in Prayer by Santiago.

10s, Chalice, eucharist, church, wheat.

1967, May 10
761	A249i	10c multicolored	.30	.25
761A	A249i	60c multicolored	.60	.30
761B	A249i	80c multicolored	.90	.30
761C	A249i	1s multicolored	.90	.50
761D	A249i	1.50s multicolored	1.60	.75
761E	A249i	2s multicolored	2.75	.75
	Nos. 761-761E (6)		7.05	2.85

Souvenir Sheet
761F	A249i	10s multi	7.50	6.50

Nos. 761D-761E are airmail. Frames and inscriptions vary greatly.

No. 761F exists imperf. with an orange margin color. Value, same.

Madonna and Child Enthroned by Guido Reni — A249j

Paintings of the Madonna and Child by: 40c, van Hemesen. 50c, Memling. 1.30s, Durer. 2.50s, Raphael. 3s, Murillo.

1967, May 25   *Perf. 14x13½*
762	A249j	10c multicolored	.25	.25
762A	A249j	40c multicolored	.25	.25
762B	A249j	50c multicolored	.25	.25
762C	A249j	1.30s multicolored	.70	.30
762D	A249j	2.50s multicolored	1.75	.95
762E	A249j	3s multicolored	2.75	1.20
	Nos. 762-762E (6)		5.95	3.20

Nos. 762C-762E are airmail.

Portrait of a Young Woman by Rogier van der Weyden — A249k

Designs: 1s, Helene Fourment by Rubens. 1.50s, Venetian Woman by Durer. 2s, Lady Sheffield by Gainsborough. 2.50s, Suzon by Manet. 4s, Lady with a Unicorn by Raphael.

1967, Sept. 9   *Perf. 14x13½*
763	A249k	10c multicolored	.30	.25
763A	A249k	1s multicolored	.60	.30
763B	A249k	1.50s multicolored	1.40	.50
763C	A249k	2s multicolored	1.90	.65
763D	A249k	2.50s multicolored	2.75	.80
763E	A249k	4s multicolored	3.25	1.25
f.	Sheet of 3, #763, 763B, 763E, perf. 14		12.00	8.00
	Nos. 763-763E (6)		10.20	3.75

Nos. 763B-763E are airmail.

Stamps in No. 763f have colored pattern in border. Exists imperf. Value same as perf.

John F. Kennedy, 50th Birth Anniv. — A249l

JFK and: No. 764A, Dag Hammarskjold. 80c, Pope Paul VI. 1.30s, Konrad Adenauer. 3s, Charles de Gaulle. 3.50s, Winston Churchill.

Perf. 14x13½, 13½x14

1967, Sept. 11
764	A249l	10c lil, brn & bl	.25	.25
764A	A249l	10c yel, brn & sky bl	.25	.25
764B	A249l	80c yel, brn & sal	.25	.25
764C	A249l	1.30s brn & pink	2.00	.75
764D	A249l	3s yel, brn & yel grn	2.90	1.25
764E	A249l	3.50s yel, brn & bl	4.00	1.75
	Nos. 764-764E (6)		9.65	4.50

Souvenir Sheets
764F		Sheet of 3	19.00	8.00
h.	like #764, 35x27mm			
i.	like #764A, 35x27mm			
j.	like #764D, 35x27mm			
764G		Sheet of 3	19.00	8.00
k.	like #764A, 35x27mm			
l.	like #764C, 35x27mm			
m.	like #764E, 35x27mm			

Nos. 764C-764E are airmail. Nos. 764A-764E horiz. Stamps in Nos. 764F-764G have colored pattern in border.

Nos. 764F and 764G exist imperf. Values same as perf.

Christmas A249m

Designs: No. 765A, Children's procession. 40c, Candlelight procession. 50c, Children singing. 60c, Processional. 2.50s, Christmas celebration.

1967, Dec. 29   *Perf. 13x14*
765	A249m	10c multi	.40	.25
765A	A249m	10c multi	.40	.25
765B	A249m	40c multi	.40	.25
765C	A249m	50c multi	.40	.25
765D	A249m	60c multi	.40	.25
765E	A249m	2.50s multi	11.00	9.75
	Nos. 765-765E (6)		13.00	11.00

No. 765E is airmail. See Nos. 768-768F.

Various Surcharges on Issues of 1956-66

1967-68
766	AP72	30c on 1.10s (C337)	.35	.25
766A	AP66	40c on 1.70s (C292)	.35	.25
766B	A247	40c on 3.50s (C438)	.35	.25
766C	A246	50c on 5s (736) ('68)	.35	.25
766D	A247	80c on 1.50s (743)	.40	.25
766E	A249	80c on 2.50s (C445)	.40	.25
766F	A249	1s on 4s (C447)	.50	.25
766G	AP66	1.30s on 1.90s (C293)	.65	.55
766H	A246	2s on 10s (737) ('68)	.80	.25
	Nos. 766-766H,C449-C450 (11)		5.65	3.20

The surcharge on Nos. 766B-766C, 766E and 766G-766H includes "Resello." The obliteration of old denomination and arrangement of surcharges differ on each stamp.

Bust of Peñaherrera, Central University, Quito — A250

50c, Law books. 80c, Open book, laurel, horiz.

Perf. 12x12½, 12½x12

1967, Dec. 29   *Litho.*
767	A250	50c brt grn & blk	.25	.25
767A	A250	60c rose & blk	.25	.25
767B	A250	80c rose lil & blk	.25	.25
	Nos. 767-767B,C451-C452 (5)		1.65	1.25

Cent. (in 1964) of the birth of Dr. Victor Manuel Peñaherrera (1864-1932), author of the civil and criminal codes of Ecuador.

Christmas Type of 1967

Native Christian Art: 10c, Mourning of the Death of Christ, by Manuel Chili. 80c, Ascension of the Holy Virgin, vert. 1s, The Holy Virgin. 1.30s, Coronation of the Holy Virgin, by Bernardo Rodriguez, vert. 1.50s, Madonna and Child with the Heavenly Host, vert. 2s, Madonna and Child, by Manuel Samaniego, vert. 3s, Immaculate Conception, by Bernardo de Legranda, vert. 3.50s, Passion of Christ, by Chili, vert. 4s, The Holy Virgin of Quito, by de Legranda, vert.

1968, Jan. 19   *Perf. 13½x14, 14x13½*
768	A249m	10c multi	.25	.25
768A	A249m	80c multi	.25	.25
768B	A249m	1s multi	.25	.25
768C	A249m	1.30s multi	.25	.25
768D	A249m	1.50s multi	.50	.30
768E	A249m	2s multi	.80	.75
	Nos. 768-768E (6)		2.30	2.05

Souvenir Sheet
    Perf. 14
768F		Sheet of 3	19.00	8.00
g.	A249m 3s multicolored			
h.	A249m 3.50s multicolored			
i.	A249m 4s multicolored			

Nos. 768C-768F are airmail. No. 768F exists imperf. Value same.

Tourism Year — A250a

20c, Woman from Otavalo. 30c, Colorado Indian. 40c, Petroglyph of a cat. 50c, Petroglyph of a mythological predator. 60c, Woman in a bazaar. 80c, 1s, 1.30s, Petroglyphs, diff. 1.50s, Colonial street, Quito. 2s, Amulet.

1968, Apr. 1   *Perf. 13½x14*
769	A250a	20c multicolored	.30	.25
769A	A250a	30c multicolored	.30	.25
769B	A250a	40c multicolored	.30	.25
769C	A250a	50c multicolored	.30	.25
769D	A250a	60c multicolored	.30	.25
769E	A250a	80c multicolored	.30	.25
769F	A250a	1s multicolored	.35	.25
769G	A250a	1.30s multicolored	.30	.25
769H	A250a	1.50s multicolored	.35	.25
769I	A250a	2s multicolored	.40	.25
	Nos. 769-769I (10)		3.20	2.50

Eleventh Congress of the Confederation of Latin American Tourist Organizations (COTAL). Nos. 769G-769I are airmail.

Otto Arosemena Gomez — A251

Design: 1s, Page from the Constitution.

1968, May 9   *Litho.*   *Perf. 13½x14*
770	A251	80c lil & multi	.35	.25
770A	A251	1s multi	.35	.25
	Nos. 770-770A,C453-C454 (4)		2.15	1.30

First anniversary of the administration of Pres. Otto Arosemena Gomez.

Lions Emblem — A252

1968, May 24   *Litho.*   *Perf. 13½x14*
771	A252	80c multi	.35	.25
771A	A252	1.30s multi	.35	.25
771B	A252	2s pink & multi	.40	.25
c.	Souvenir sheet of 1		4.75	4.75
	Nos. 771-771B (3)		1.10	.75

50th anniv. (in 1967) of Lions Intl. No. 771c contains one 5s 39x49mm stamp. Exists imperf. Value same as perf.

Pope Paul VI, Visit to Latin America A252a

ECUADOR

39th Intl. Eucharistic Congress, Bogota, Colombia — A252b

60c, Pope Paul VI, vert. 1s, Madonna by Botticelli. 1.30s, Pope Paul VI with flags of South American nations. 2s, Madonna and Child by Durer.

1969		Perf. 13½x14, 14x13½		
772	A252a	40c multicolored	.35	.25
772A	A252a	60c multicolored	.45	.25
772B	A252b	1s multicolored	1.25	.30
772C	A252a	1.30s multicolored	.90	.40
e.		Souv. sheet of 3, #772, 772A, 772C, imperf.	4.00	2.50
772D	A252b	2s multicolored	1.90	.75
f.		Souv. sheet of 2, #772B, 772D, imperf.	4.75	2.50
		Nos. 772-772D (5)	4.85	1.95

Nos. 772C-772D are airmail. Nos. 772-772f overprinted in silver with the national coat of arms.

Madonna with the Angel by Rogier van der Weyden — A252c

Paintings by various artists showing the life of the Virgin Mary: 40c, Annunciation of the Lord, by van der Weyden. 60c, Presentation of the Lord, by van der Weyden. 1s, Holy Family, by Raphael. 1.30s, Adoration of the Shepherds, by Bonifazio Veronese. 2s, Adoration of the Magi, by van der Weyden

1969		Perf. 14x13½, 13½x14		
773	A252c	40c shown	.25	.25
773A	A252c	60c multi	.25	.25
773B	A252c	1s multi	.35	.25
773C	A252c	1.30s multi	1.25	.65
e.		Souv. sheet of 2, #773B-773C, imperf.	6.25	2.50
773D	A252c	2s multi	2.00	.80
f.		Souv. sheet of 3, #773-773A, 773D, imperf.	6.25	2.50
		Nos. 773-773D (5)	4.10	2.20

Nos. 773-773Df overprinted in silver with the national coat of arms. Sizing of No. 773Df stamps, side stamps are 25mm x 50mm; center stamp is 54.5mm x 50mm. Nos. 773C-773D are airmail.

Nos. C331 and C326 Surcharged in Violet and Dark Blue

a

b

1969, Jan. 10		Perf. 11½, 14x13½		
774	AP79	(a) 40c on 1.30s (V)	.60	.25
774A	AP76	(b) 50c on 1.30s (DBl)	.60	.25

Types of 1958

No. 775 & 775B Srchd. and Ovptd. in Plum and Black

No. 775A Srchd. and Ovptd. in Plum and Black

No. 775C Overprinted in Red & Black

Design: Ignacio Luis Arcaya, Foreign Minister of Venezuela.

1969, Mar.		Litho.	Perf. 12	
		Flags in Red, Blue and Yellow		
775	A223	50c on 2s sepia	.35	.25
775A	A223	80c on 2s sepia	.35	.25
775B	A223	1s on 2s sepia	.35	.25
775C	A223	2s sepia	.35	.25
		Nos. 775-775C,C455-C457 (7)	6.35	1.75

Nos. 775-775C were not issued without overprint. The obliteration of old denomination on No. 775A is a small square around a star. Overprint is plum, except for the black small coat of arms on right flag.

Map of Ecuador and Oriental Region — A253

Surcharge typographed in Dark Blue, Red Brown, Black or Lilac

1969		Litho.	Perf. 14	
776	A253	20c on 30c (DBl)	.40	.25
776A	A253	40c on 30c (RBr)	.40	.25
777	A253	50c on 30c (DBl)	.40	.25
778	A253	60c on 30c (DBl)	.40	.25
778A	A253	60c on 30c (Bk)	.45	.40
778B	A253	80c on 30c (DBl)	—	20.00
779	A253	80c on 30c (Bk)	.40	.25
780	A253	1s on 30c (L)	.40	.25
780A	A253	1s on 30c (Bk)	1.35	.80
781	A253	1.30s on 30c (Bk)	.60	.25
782	A253	1.50s on 30c (Bk)	.60	.25
783	A253	2s on 30c (DBl)	.75	.25
784	A253	3s on 30c (DBl)	.85	.25
784A	A253	4s on 30c (DBl)	2.40	2.00
785	A253	4s on 30c (Bk)	.90	.25
786	A253	5s on 30c (Bk)	1.20	.35
		Nos. 776-786 (16)	11.50	26.30

Not issued without surcharge.

M. L. King, John and Robert Kennedy — A254

1969-70		Typo.	Perf. 12½	
787	A254	4s blk, bl, grn & buff	.65	.25
		Perf. 13½		
788	A254	4s blk, lt bl & grn ('70)	.65	.25

In memory of John F. Kennedy, Robert F. Kennedy and Martin Luther King, Jr.

Thecla Coronata — A255

Butterflies: 20c, Papilio zabreus. 30c, Heliconius chestertoni. 40c, Papilio pausanias. 50c, Pereute leucodrosime. 60c, Metamorpha dido. 80c, Morpho cypris. 1s, Catagramma astarte.

1970		Litho.	Perf. 12½	
789	A255	10c buff & multi	3.25	.45
790	A255	20c lt grn & multi	3.25	.45
791	A255	30c pink & multi	3.25	.45
792	A255	40c lt bl & multi	3.25	.25
793	A255	50c gold & multi	3.25	.25
794	A255	60c salmon & multi	3.25	.25
795	A255	80c silver & multi	3.25	.25
796	A255	1s lt grn & multi	3.25	.25

Same, White Background

		Perf. 13½		
797	A255	10c multi	3.25	.45
798	A255	20c multi	3.25	.45
799	A255	30c multi	3.25	.45
800	A255	40c multi	3.25	.25
801	A255	50c multi	3.25	.25
802	A255	60c multi	3.25	.25
803	A255	80c multi	3.25	.25
804	A255	1s multi	3.25	.25
		Nos. 789-804,C461-C464 (20)	66.50	6.60

Surcharged Revenue Stamps — A256

1970, June 16		Litho.	Perf. 14	
		Red Surcharge		
805	A256	1s on 1s light blue	.30	.25
806	A256	1.30s on 1s light blue	.30	.25
807	A256	1.50s on 1s light blue	.35	.30
808	A256	2s on 1s light blue	.40	.25
809	A256	5s on 1s light blue	.90	.25
810	A256	10s on 1s light blue	1.60	.55
		Nos. 805-810 (6)	3.75	1.90

Surcharged Revenue Stamps — A257

1970		Typo.	Perf. 12	
		Black Surcharge		
811	A257	60c on 1s violet	.35	.25
812	A257	80c on 1s violet	.35	.25
813	A257	1s on 1s violet	.35	.25
814	A257	1.10s on 1s violet	.35	.25
815	A257	1.30s on 1s violet	.35	.25
816	A257	1.50s on 1s violet	.40	.25
817	A257	2s on 1s violet	.40	.25
818	A257	2.20s on 1s violet	.45	.25
819	A257	3s on 1s violet	.55	.25
		Nos. 811-819 (9)	3.55	2.25

1970				
820	A257	1.10s on 2s green	.35	.25
821	A257	1.30s on 2s green	.35	.25
822	A257	1.50s on 2s green	.40	.25
823	A257	2s on 2s green	.40	.25
824	A257	3.40s on 2s green	.60	.25
825	A257	5s on 2s green	.90	.25
826	A257	10s on 2s green	1.40	.25
827	A257	20s on 2s green	2.40	.70
828	A257	50s on 2s green	6.00	2.25
		Nos. 820-828 (9)	12.80	4.70

1970				
829	A257	3s on 5s blue	.60	.25
830	A257	5s on 5s blue	.70	.35
831	A257	10s on 40s orange	1.35	.65
		Nos. 829-831 (3)	2.65	1.25

In the surcharge applied to Nos. 811-831, the word "POSTAL" is not locked into horizontal and vertical position relative to the "1970". On some stamps the "P" is directly below the numeral "1", on others the "O" is below the "1". The top of "POSTAL" can vary from 1mm-8mm from the bottom of the date.

Arms of Zamora Chinchipe — A258

Design: 1s, Arms and flag of Esmeraldas.

1971		Litho.	Perf. 10½	
832	A258	50c pale yel & multi	.30	.25
833	A258	1s sal & multi	.30	.25
		Nos. 832-833,C465-C469 (7)	4.95	2.30

Flags of Ecuador and Chile — A259

1971, Sept.			Perf. 12½	
840	A259	1.30s blk & multi	.30	.25
		Nos. 840,C481-C482 (3)	1.40	.85

Visit of Pres. Salvador Allende of Chile, Aug. 24.

Ismael Pérez Pazmiño — A260

1971, Sept. 16			Perf. 12x11½	
841	A260	1s grn & multi	.35	.25
		Nos. 841,C485-C486 (3)	1.50	.85

"El Universo," newspaper founded by Ismael Pérez Pazmiño, 50th anniv.

CARE Package — A261

1971-72			Perf. 12½	
842	A261	30c lilac ('72)	.35	.25
843	A261	40c emerald ('72)	.35	.25
844	A261	50c blue	.35	.25
845	A261	60c carmine	.35	.25
846	A261	80c lt brn ('72)	.35	.25
		Nos. 842-846 (5)	1.75	1.25

25th anniversary of CARE, a US-Canadian Cooperative for American Relief Everywhere.

Flags of Ecuador and Argentina — A262

1972			Perf. 11½	
847	A262	1s blk & multi	.30	.25
		Nos. 847,C491-C492 (3)	1.65	.90

Visit of Lt. Gen. Alejandro Agustin Lanusse, president of Argentina, Jan. 25.

Jesus Giving Keys to St. Peter, by Miguel de Santiago — A263

Ecuadorian Paintings: 1.10s, Virgin of Mercy, Quito School. 2s, Virgin Mary, by Manuel Samaniego.

1972, Apr. 24		Litho.	Perf. 14x13½	
848	A263	50c black & multi	.30	.25
849	A263	1.10s black & multi	.40	.30
850	A263	2s black & multi	.60	.50
a.		Souvenir sheet of 3	2.50	2.50
		Nos. 848-850,C494-C495 (5)	3.60	2.10

No. 850a contains 3 imperf. stamps similar to Nos. 848-850.

1972, May 4

Ecuadorian Statues: 50c, Our Lady of Sorrow, by Caspicara. 1.10s, Nativity, Quito School, horiz. 2s, Virgin of Quito, anonymous.

851	A263	50c blk & multi	.35	.25
852	A263	1.10s blk & multi	.45	.35
853	A263	2s blk & multi	.60	.50
a.		Souv. sheet of 3	2.90	2.40
		Nos. 851-853,C496-C497 (5)	3.45	2.15

Letters of "Ecuador" 3mm high on Nos. 851-853, 7mm high on Nos. 848-850. No. 853a contains 3 imperf. stamps similar to Nos. 851-853.

ECUADOR

A264

Designs: 30c, Gen. Juan Ignacio Pareja. 40c, Juan José Flores. 50c, Leon de Febres Cordero. 60c, Ignacio Torres. 70c, Francisco de Paula Santander. 1s, José M. Cordova.

1972, May 24   **Perf. 12½**

854	A264	30c blue & multi	.35	.25
855	A264	40c blue & multi	.35	.25
856	A264	50c blue & multi	.35	.25
857	A264	60c blue & multi	.35	.25
858	A264	70c blue & multi	.35	.25
859	A264	1s blue & multi	.35	.35
	Nos. 854-859,C498-C503 (12)		11.55	4.65

Sesquicentennial of the Battle of Pichincha and the liberation of Quito.

A265

Designs: 2s, Woman Wearing Poncho. 3s, Striped poncho. 5s, Embroidered poncho. 10s, Metal vase.

1972, July   **Photo.**   **Perf. 13**

860	A265	2s multicolored	.35	.25
861	A265	3s multicolored	.60	.25
862	A265	5s multicolored	.75	.40
863	A265	10s dp blue & multi	1.75	.90
a.	Souvenir sheet of 4		4.00	4.00
	Nos. 860-863,C504-C507 (8)		8.95	3.90

Handicraft of Ecuador. No. 863a contains 4 imperf. stamps similar to Nos. 860-863.

Sucre Statue, Santo Domingo — A266

1.80s, San Agustin Convent. 2.30s, Plaza de la Independencia. 2.50s, Bolivar statue, La Alameda. 4.75s, Chapel door.

1972, Dec. 6   **Litho.**   **Perf. 11½**

864	A266	1.20s yel & multi	.40	.25
865	A266	1.80s yel & multi	.40	.25
866	A266	2.30s yel & multi	.45	.25
867	A266	2.50s yel & multi	.60	.25
868	A266	4.75s yel & multi	.90	.30
	Nos. 864-868,C518-C524 (12)		12.30	4.40

Sesquicentennial of the Battle of Pichincha.

Radar Station — A267

1973, Apr. 5   **Wmk. 367**

869	A267	1s multicolored	.40	.25

Inauguration of earth telecommunications station, Oct. 19, 1972.

Blue-footed Boobies — A268

Designs: 40c, Blue-faced booby. 50c, Oyster-catcher. 60c, California sea lions. 70c, Galapagos giant tortoise. 1s, California sea lion.

Wmk. 367, Unwmkd. (#872)
1973   **Litho.**   **Perf. 11½x12**

870	A268	30c shown	.55	.30
871	A268	40c multicolored	.55	.30
872	A268	50c multicolored	.55	.30
873	A268	60c multicolored	1.10	.30
874	A268	70c multicolored	1.25	.30
875	A268	1s multicolored	1.75	.30
	Nos. 870-875,C527-C528 (8)		11.553.00	

Elevation of Galapagos Islands to a province of Ecuador.
Issue dates: 50c, Oct. 3; others Aug. 16.

Black-chinned Mountain Tanager — A269

Birds of Ecuador: 2s, Moriche oriole. 3s, Toucan barbet, vert. 5s, Masked crimson tanager, vert. 10s, Blue-necked tanager, vert.

Perf. 11x11½, 11½x11
1973, Dec. 6   **Litho.**   **Unwmk.**

876	A269	1s brick red & multi	.65	.25
877	A269	2s lt blue & multi	1.10	.25
878	A269	3s lt green & multi	1.10	.25
879	A269	5s pale lilac & multi	2.40	.65
880	A269	10s pale yel grn & multi	4.75	1.40
	Nos. 876-880 (5)		10.00	2.80

Two souvenir sheets exist: one contains 2 imperf. stamps similar to Nos. 876-877 with yellow margin and black inscription; the other 3 stamps similar to Nos. 878-880; gray margin and black inscription including "Aereo." Both sheets dated "1972." Size: 143x84mm. Value, each $9.50.

Marco T. Varea, Botanist — A270

Portraits: 60c, Pio Jaramillo Alvarado, writer. 70c, Prof. Luciano Andrade M. No. 883, Marco T. Varea, botanist. No. 884, Dr. Juan Modesto Carbo Noboa, medical researcher. No. 885, Alfredo J. Valenzuela. No. 886, Capt. Edmundo Chiriboga G. 1.20s, Francisco Campos R., scientist. 1.80s, Luis Vernaza Lazarte, philanthropist.

1974   **Unwmk.**   **Perf. 12x11½**

881	A270	60c crimson rose	.40	.25
882	A270	70c lilac	.40	.25
883	A270	1s ultra	.30	.25
884	A270	1s orange	.30	.25
885	A270	1s emerald	.30	.25
886	A270	1s brown	.30	.25
887	A270	1.20s apple green	.40	.25
889	A270	1.80s lt blue	.50	.25
	Nos. 881-889 (8)		2.90	2.00

Arcade — A271

Designs: 30c, Monastery, entrance. 40c, Church. 50c, View of Church through gate, vert. 60c, Chapel, vert. 70c, Church and cemetery, vert.

Perf. 11½x12, 12x11½
1975, Feb. 4   **Litho.**

896	A271	20c yellow & multi	.35	.25
897	A271	30c yellow & multi	.35	.25
898	A271	40c yellow & multi	.35	.25
899	A271	50c yellow & multi	.35	.25
900	A271	60c yellow & multi	.35	.25
901	A271	70c yellow & multi	.35	.25
	Nos. 896-901 (6)		2.10	1.50

Colonial Monastery, Tilipulo, Cotopaxi Province.

Angel Polibio Chaves, Founder of Bolivar Province — A272

Portrait: No. 903, Emilio Estrada Ycaza (1916-1961), archeologist.

1975   **Litho.**   **Perf. 12x11½**

902	A272	80c violet bl & lt bl	.35	.25
903	A272	80c vermilion & pink	.35	.25

Issue dates: No. 902, 2/21; No. 903, 3/25.

R. Rodriguez Palacios and A. Duran Quintero — A273

1975, Apr. 1   **Litho.**   **Perf. 12x11½**

910	A273	1s multicolored	.30	.25
	Nos. 910,C547-C548 (3)		1.40	.85

Meeting of the Ministers for Public Works of Ecuador and Colombia, July 27, 1973.

"Woman of Action" — A274

Design: No. 912, "Woman of Peace."

1975, June

911	A274	1s yellow & multi	.40	.25
912	A274	1s blue & multi	.50	.25

International Women's Year 1975.

Planes, Soldier and Ship — A275

1975, July 9   **Perf. 11½x12**

913	A275	2s multicolored	.45	.25

3 years of Natl. Revolutionary Government.

Hurdling — A276

Designs: Modern sports drawn Inca style.

1975, Sept. 11   **Litho.**   **Perf. 11½**

914	A276	20c shown	.55	.40
915	A276	20c Chess	.55	.40
916	A276	30c Basketball	.55	.40
917	A276	30c Boxing	.55	.40
918	A276	40c Bicycling	.55	.40
919	A276	40c Steeplechase	.55	.40
920	A276	50c Soccer	.55	.40
921	A276	50c Fencing	.55	.40
922	A276	60c Golf	.55	.40
923	A276	60c Vaulting	.55	.40
924	A276	70c Judo (standing)	.55	.40
925	A276	70c Wrestling	.55	.40
926	A276	80c Swimming	.55	.40
927	A276	80c Weight lifting	.55	.40
928	A276	1s Table Tennis	.55	.40
929	A276	1s Paddle ball	.55	.40
	Nos. 914-929,C554-C558 (21)		14.05	8.65

3rd Ecuadorian Games.

Genciana — A277

Ecuadorian plants — 20c, Phragmipedium caudatum, vert. 40c, Bromeliaceae cactacceae, vert. 50c, Cochlioda vulcanica. 60c, Odontoglossum hallii. 80c, Pitahaya flowering cactus. 1s, Odontoglossum cirrhosum.

Perf. 12x11½, 11½x12
1975, Nov. 18   **Litho.**

930	A277	20c multicolored	.25	.25
931	A277	30c shown	.25	.25
932	A277	40c multicolored	.35	.35
933	A277	50c multicolored	.35	.35
934	A277	60c multicolored	.45	.40
935	A277	80c multicolored	.45	.40
936	A277	1s multicolored	.75	.50
	Nos. 930-936,C559-C563 (12)		10.80	7.70

Venus, Chorrera Culture A278

Female Mask, Tolita Culture A279

Designs: 30c, Venus, Valdivia Culture. 40c, Seated man, Chorrera Culture. 50c, Man with poncho, Panzaleo Culture (late). 60c, Mythical head, Cashaloma Culture. 80c, Musician, Tolita Culture. No. 943, Chief Priest, Mantefia Culture. No. 945, Ornament, Tolita Culture. No. 946, Angry mask, Tolita Culture.

1976, Feb. 12   **Litho.**   **Perf. 11½**

937	A278	20c multicolored	.45	.30
938	A278	30c multicolored	.45	.30
939	A278	40c multicolored	.45	.30
940	A278	50c multicolored	.45	.30
941	A278	60c multicolored	.45	.30
942	A278	80c multicolored	.45	.30
943	A278	1s multicolored	.45	.30
944	A279	1s multicolored	.45	.30
945	A279	1s multicolored	.45	.30
946	A279	1s multicolored	.45	.30
	Nos. 937-946,C568-C572 (15)		11.156.80	

Archaeological artifacts.

Strawberries — A280

1976, Mar. 30

947	A280	1s blue & multi	.45	.30
	Nos. 947,C573-C574 (3)		2.60	1.40

25th Flower and Fruit Festival, Ambato.

Carlos Amable Ortiz (1859-1937) — A281

No. 949, Sixto Maria Duran (1875-1947). No. 950, Segundo Cueva Celi (1901-1969). No. 951, Cristobal Ojeda Davila (1910-1952). No. 952, Luis Alberto Valencia (1918-1970).

1976, Mar. 15   **Litho.**   **Perf. 11½**

948	A281	1s ver & multi	.40	.25
949	A281	1s orange & multi	.40	.25
950	A281	1s lt green & multi	.40	.25
951	A281	1s blue & multi	.40	.25
952	A281	1s lt brn & multi	.40	.25
	Nos. 948-952 (5)		2.00	1.25

Ecuadorian composers and musicians.

Institute Emblem — A282

1977, Aug. 15   **Litho.**   **Perf. 11½x12**

953	A282	2s multicolored	.40	.25

11th General Assembly of Pan-American Institute of Geography and History, Quito, Aug. 15-30. See Nos. C597-C597a.

ECUADOR

Hands Holding Rotary Emblem — A283

1977, Aug. 31   Litho.   Perf. 12
| 954 | A283 | 1s multicolored | .30 | .25 |
| 955 | A283 | 2s multicolored | .50 | .25 |

Souvenir Sheets
Imperf
| 956 | A283 | 5s multicolored | 1.25 | 1.25 |
| 957 | A283 | 10s multicolored | 1.50 | 1.50 |

Rotary Club of Guayaquil, 50th anniv.

José Peralta — A284

Design: 2.40s, Peralta statue.

1977   Litho.   Perf. 11½
958	A284	1.80s multi	.35	.25
959	A284	2.40s multi	.35	.25
Nos. 958-959, C009 (3)			1.45	.80

José Peralta (1855-1937), writer.

Blue-faced Booby — A285

Galapagos Birds: 1.80s, Red-footed booby. 2.40s, Blue-footed boobies. 3.40s, Gull. 4.40s, Galapagos hawk. 5.40s, Map of Galapagos Islands and boobies, vert.

Perf. 11½x12, 12x11½
1977, Nov. 29   Litho.
960	A285	1.20s multi	.50	.25
961	A285	1.80s multi	.70	.25
962	A285	2.40s multi	1.15	.25
963	A285	3.40s multi	1.60	.25
964	A285	4.40s multi	2.40	.30
965	A285	5.40s multi	3.25	.30
Nos. 960-965 (6)			9.60	1.60

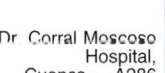

Dr. Corral Moscoso Hospital, Cuenca — A286

1978, Apr. 12   Litho.   Perf. 11½x12
| 966 | A286 | 3s multicolored | .30 | .25 |
| Nos. 966, C613-C614 (3) | | | 2.65 | .85 |

Inauguration (in 1977) of Dr. Vicente Corral Moscoso Regional Hospital, Cuenca.

Surveyor Plane over Ecuador — A287

1978, Apr. 12   Litho.   Perf. 11½
| 967 | A287 | 6s multicolored | .75 | .35 |
| Nos. 967, C619-C620 (3) | | | 4.75 | 2.95 |

Military Geographical Institute, 50th anniv.

Latin-American Lions Emblem — A288

1978, May 24
968	A288	3s multi	.60	.25
969	A288	4.20s multi	.90	.25
Nos. 968-969, C621-C623 (5)			6.40	2.80

7th meeting of Latin American Lions, Jan. 25-29.

70th Anniversary Emblem — A289

1978, Sept.   Litho.   Perf. 11½
| 970 | A289 | 4.20s gray & multi | .70 | .30 |

70th anniversary of Filanbanco (Philanthropic Bank). See No. C626.

Goalmouth and Net A290

Designs: 1.80s, "Gauchito" and Games emblem, vert. 4.40s, "Gauchito," vert.

1978, Nov. 1   Litho.   Perf. 12
971	A290	1.20s multi	.30	.25
972	A290	1.80s multi	.30	.25
973	A290	4.40s multi	.70	.25
Nos. 971-973, C627-C629 (6)			4.35	2.05

11th World Cup Soccer Championship, Argentina, June 1-25.

Symbols for Male and Female — A291

1979, Feb. 15   Litho.   Perf. 12x11½
| 974 | A291 | 3.40s multi | .75 | .30 |

Inter-American Women's Commission, 50th anniversary.

Emblem — A292

1979, June 21   Litho.   Perf. 11½x12
| 975 | A292 | 4.40s multi | .45 | .30 |
| 976 | A292 | 5.40s multi | .55 | .30 |

Ecuadorian Mortgage Bank, 16th anniv.

Street Scene, Quito — A293

Perf. 12x11½
1979, Aug. 3   Litho.   Unwmk.
| 977 | A293 | 3.40s multi | .35 | .25 |
| Nos. 977, C651-C653 (4) | | | 8.60 | 3.70 |

Natl. heritage. Quito & Galapagos Islands.

Jose Joaquin de Olmedo (1780-1847), Physician — A294

1980, Apr. 29   Litho.   Perf. 12x11½
978	A294	3s multi	.35	.25
979	A294	5s multi	.55	.40
Nos. 978-979, C662 (3)			2.50	1.30

First Pres. of Free State of Guayaquil, 1820.

Chief Enriquillo, Dominican Republic — A295

Indo-American Tribal Chiefs: 3.40s, Guaycapyuro, Venezuela. No. 982, Abayuba, Uruguay. No. 983, Atlacatl, Salvador.

Wmk. 367, Unwmkd. (#981-983)
1980, May 12
980	A295	3s multi	.70	.35
981	A295	3.40s multi	.90	.40
982	A295	5s multi	1.75	.55
983	A295	5s multi	1.75	.55
Nos. 980-983, C663-C678 (20)			46.35	18.60

King Juan Carlos and Queen Sofia, Visit to Ecuador — A296

Perf. 11½x12
1980, May 18   Unwmk.
| 984 | A296 | 3.40s multi | .55 | .30 |

See No. C679.

Cofan Indian, Napo Province — A297

3.40s, Zuleta man, Imbabura. 5s, Chota woman, Imbabura.

1980, June 10   Litho.   Perf. 12x11½
985	A297	3s shown	.55	.25
986	A297	3.40s multicolored	.55	.25
987	A297	5s multicolored	.85	.30
Nos. 985-987, C681-C684 (7)			11.55	4.55

Basilica, Our Lady of Mercy Church, Quito — A298

1980, July 7   Litho.   Perf. 11½
988	A298	3.40s shown	.45	.25
989	A298	3.40s Balcony	.45	.25
989A	A298	3.40s Dome and cupolas	.45	.25

Sizes: 91x116mm, 116x91mm
Imperf
990	A298	5s multi	1.75	1.60
990A	A298	5s multi, horiz.	1.75	1.60
990B	A298	5s multi	1.75	1.60
Nos. 988-990B, C685-C691 (13)			15.60	10.05

Virgin of Mercy, patron saint of Ecuadorian armed forces. No. 990 contains designs of Nos. C688, C685, 989. No. 990A contains designs of Nos. C688, C691, C690. No. 990B contains designs of Nos. C689, C687, 989A, 988.

Olympic Torch and Rings — A299

Perf. 12x11½
1980, July 19   Wmk. 395
991	A299	5s multi	.70	.25
992	A299	7.60s multi	.80	.30
Nos. 991-992, C695-C696 (4)			4.80	2.30

Souvenir Sheet
Imperf
| 993 | A299 | 30s multi | 7.00 | 6.75 |

22nd Summer Olympic Games, Moscow, July 19-Aug. 3.
No. 993 contains vignettes in designs of Nos. 991 and C695.

Coronation of Virgin of Cisne, 50th Anniv. — A300

1980   Litho.   Perf. 11½
| 994 | A300 | 1.20s shown | .30 | .25 |
| 995 | A300 | 3.40s Different statue | .60 | .30 |

J.J. Olmedo, Father de Velasco, Flags of Ecuador and Riobamba, Constitution A301

1980, Sept. 20   Litho.   Perf. 11½
996	A301	3.40s multi	.30	.25
997	A301	5s multi	.80	.40
Nos. 996-997, C700-C701 (4)			3.35	1.45

Souvenir Sheet
Imperf
| 998 | A301 | 30s multi | 6.00 | 3.00 |

Constitutional Assembly of Riobamba sesquicentennial. No. 998 contains vignettes in designs of #996-997.

Young Indian Girl — A302

1980, Oct. 9   Perf. 12x11½   Wmk. 395
Litho.
999	A302	1.20s multi	.25	.25
1000	A302	3.40s multi	.55	.25
Nos. 999-1000, C703-C704 (4)			3.10	1.60

Democratic government, 1st anniversary.

OPEC Emblem — A303

1980, Nov. 8   Perf. 11½x12
| 1001 | A303 | 3.40s multi | .50 | .25 |

20th anniversary of OPEC. See No. C706.

Decorative Hedges, Capitol Gardens, Carchi — A304

1980, Nov. 21   Perf. 13
| 1002 | A304 | 3s multi | .50 | .25 |
| Nos. 1002, C707-C708 (3) | | | 5.00 | 1.75 |

Carchi province centennial.

Cattleya Maxima — A305

Orchids: 3s, Comparattia speciosa. 3.40s, Cattleya iricolor.

1980, Nov. 22   Perf. 11½x12
1003	A305	1.20s shown	.75	.25
1004	A305	3s multicolored	1.00	.30
1005	A305	3.40s multicolored	1.10	.35
Nos. 1003-1005, C709-C712 (7)			26.35	5.60

ECUADOR

Souvenir Sheet
Imperf

| 1006 | A305 | 20s multi | 14.00 | 10.00 |

No. 1006 contains vignettes in designs of Nos. 1003-1005.

Pope John Paul II and Children — A306

1980, Dec. 27   *Perf. 12*

| 1007 | A306 | 3.40s multi | .60 | .30 |
| | Nos. 1007,C715-C716 (3) | | 5.50 | 1.60 |

Christmas and visit of Pope John Paul II.

Carlos and Jorge Mantilla Ortega, Editors of El Comercio — A307

El Comercio Newspaper, 75th Anniv.: 3.40s, Editors Cesar & Carlos Mantilla Jacome.

1981, Jan. 6

| 1008 | A307 | 2s multi | .40 | .25 |
| 1009 | A307 | 3.40s multi | .65 | .25 |

Soldier on Map of Ecuador — A308

1981, Mar. 10   *Litho.*   *Perf. 13*

1010	A308	3.40s shown	.40	.30
1011	A308	3.40s Pres. Roldos	.40	.30
a.		Pair, #1010-1011	1.90	1.25

National defense.

Theodore E. Gildred and Ecuador I — A309

1981, Mar. 31   *Litho.*   *Perf. 13*

| 1012 | A309 | 2s lt bl & blk | .60 | .30 |

Ecuador-US flight, 50th anniv.

A310

1981, Apr. 10

| 1013 | A310 | 2s multi | .70 | .30 |

Octavio Cordero Palacios (1870-1930), humanist.

Radio Station HCJB, 50th Anniv. — A311

1981   *Litho.*   *Perf. 13*

| 1014 | A311 | 2s multi | 1.20 | .30 |
| | Nos. 1014,C721-C722 (3) | | 5.05 | 1.85 |

Virgin of Dolorosa — A312

1981, Apr. 30   *Litho.*   *Perf. 12*

| 1015 | A312 | 2s shown | .60 | .30 |
| 1016 | A312 | 2s San Gabriel College Church | .60 | .30 |

Miracle of the painting of the Virgin of Dolorosa at San Gabriel College, 75th anniv.

Dr. Rafael Mendoza Aviles Bridge Inauguration — A313

1981, July 25   *Perf. 13*

| 1017 | A313 | 2s multi | .70 | .30 |

Pablo Picasso (1881-1973), Painter — A313a

1981, Oct. 26   *Litho.*   *Imperf.*

| 1017A | A313a | 20s multi | 3.00 | 2.75 |
| | Nos. 1017A,C728-C731 (5) | | 10,357.50 |

No. 1017A contains design of No. C728, additional portrait.

World Food Day — A314

1981, Dec. 31   *Litho.*   *Perf. 13½x13*

| 1018 | A314 | 5s multi | .75 | .30 |

See No. C732.

Transnave Shipping Co. 10th Anniv. — A315

1982, Jan. 21   *Litho.*   *Perf. 13*

| 1019 | A315 | 3.50s Freighter Isla Salango | .90 | .30 |

Intl. Year of the Disabled — A316

1982, Feb. 25

| 1020 | A316 | 3.40s Man in wheelchair | .60 | .30 |
| | Nos. 1020,C733-C734 (3) | | 3.10 | 1.30 |

Arch — A317

1982, May   *Litho.*   *Perf. 13*

| 1021 | A317 | 2s shown | .60 | .30 |
| 1022 | A317 | 3s Houses | .80 | .30 |

Miniature Sheet
Perf. 12½ on 2 Sides

| 1023 | | Sheet of 4, 18th cent. map of Quito | 6.00 | 4.50 |
| a.-d. | | A317 6s multi | .90 | .50 |

QUITEX '82, 4th Natl. Stamp Exhib., Quito, Apr. 16-22. No. 1023 contains 4 48x35mm stamps.

Juan Montalvo Birth Sesqui. — A318

1982   *Perf. 13*

1024	A318	2s Portrait	.50	.30
1025	A318	3s Mausoleum	.50	.30
	Nos. 1024-1025,C735 (3)		2.75	1.35

American Air Forces Cooperation System — A319

1982

| 1026 | A319 | 5s Emblem | .80 | .35 |

4th World Swimming Champ., Guayaquil — A320

1982, July 30

1027	A320	1.80s Stadium	.40	.30
1028	A320	3.40s Water polo	.50	.35
	Nos. 1027-1028,C736-C737 (4)		3.90	1.90

A321

1982, Dec.   *Litho.*   *Perf. 13*

| 1029 | A321 | 5.40s shown | .55 | .30 |
| 1030 | A321 | 6s Statue | .80 | .30 |

Juan L. Mera (1832-?), Writer, by Victor Mideros.

A322

1983, Mar. 28   *Litho.*   *Perf. 13*

| 1031 | A322 | 2s multi | .75 | .30 |

St. Teresa of Jesus of Avila (1515-82).

Sea Lions A323   Flamingoes A324

1983, June 17   *Litho.*   *Perf. 13*

| 1032 | A323 | 3s multi | 1.60 | .30 |
| 1033 | A324 | 5s multi | 2.50 | .30 |

Ecuadorian rule over Galapagos Islds., sesqui. (3s); Charles Darwin (1809-1882).

Pres. Rocafuerte A325   Simon Bolivar A326

Perf. 13x13½

1983, Aug. 26   *Litho.*   *Wmk. 395*

1034	A325	5s Statue	.35	.30
1035	A325	20s Portrait	1.20	.35
1036	A326	20s Portrait	1.20	.35
	Nos. 1034-1036 (3)		2.75	1.00

Vicente Rocafuerte Bejarano, president, 1833-39 (Nos. 1034-1035).

A327

1983, Sept. 3

| 1037 | A327 | 5s River | .90 | .30 |
| 1038 | A327 | 10s Dam | 1.40 | .85 |

Size: 110x89mm
Imperf

| 1039 | A327 | 20s Dam, river | 3.75 | 2.75 |
| | Nos. 1037-1039 (3) | | 6.05 | 3.90 |

Paute hydroelectric plant opening. No. 1039 is airmail.

World Communication Year — A328

Wmk. 395

1983, Oct. 11   *Litho.*   *Perf. 13*

| 1040 | A328 | 2s multi | .75 | .30 |

World Communication Year.

A329

1983, Sept.   *Litho.*   *Perf. 13*

| 1041 | A329 | 3s multi | .75 | .30 |

Cent. of Bolivar and El Oro Provinces (1984).

A330

1984, Mar.   *Litho.*   *Perf. 13*

| 1042 | A330 | 15s Engraving | 1.20 | .55 |

Atahualpa (1497-1529), last Incan ruler.

A331

ECUADOR

Christmas
1983 — A331a

Creche figures: No. 1043, Jesus & the teachers. No. 1044, Three kings. No. 1045, Holy Family. No. 1046, Priest.

Perf. 13½x13, 13x13½
1984, July 7			Litho.		
1043	A331	5s multicolored		.60	.30
1044	A331	5s multicolored		.60	.30
1045	A331	5s multicolored		.60	.30
1046	A331a	6s multicolored		.60	.30
	Nos. 1043-1046 (4)			2.40	1.20

Foreign Policy of Pres. Hurtado — A332

State visits: 8s, Brazil. 9s, PRC. 24s, UN. 28s, USA. 29s, Venezuela. 37s, Latin American Economic Conf., Quito.

1984, July 10			Perf. 13½x13		
1047	A332	8s multicolored		.55	.30
1048	A332	9s multicolored		.70	.30
1049	A332	24s multicolored		1.75	.75
1050	A332	28s multicolored		2.25	.80
1051	A332	29s multicolored		2.25	.80
1052	A332	37s multicolored		2.60	1.25
	Nos. 1047-1052 (6)			10.10	4.20

Miguel Diaz Cueva (1884-1942), Lawyer — A333

1984, Aug. 8		Litho.	Perf. 13½x13		
1053	A333	10s multicolored		1.10	.35

1984 Winter Olympics — A334

Designs: 2s, Emblem. 4s, Ice skating, right leg in air. 6s, Ice skating, left leg in air. 10s, Skiing. 20s, Figure skating.

Perf. 13x13½, 12x11½ (6s)
1984, Aug. 15					
1054	A334	2s multi		.70	.30
1055	A334	4s multi		.70	.30
1056	A334	6s multi		.70	.30
1057	A334	10s multi		1.20	.30
	Nos. 1054-1057 (4)			3.30	1.20

Size: 90x100mm
Imperf
| 1057A | A334 | 20s multi | | 40.00 | 17.50 |

No. 1057A is airmail.

Manned Flight Bicentenary — A335

3s, Montgolfier. 6s, Charlier's balloon, Paris, 1789. 20s, Graf Zeppelin, Montgolfier.

1984, Aug. 15		Perf. 13x13½		
1058	A335	3s multicolored	.50	.30
1059	A335	6s multicolored	1.00	.30

Souvenir Sheet
| 1060 | A335 | 20s multicolored | 2.75 | 1.50 |

No. 1060 is airmail and contains one imperf. stamp (50x37mm).

SAN MATEO '83, Esmeraldas A336

8s, La Marimba folk dance. 15s, La Marimba, 8 dancers in white.

1984		Litho.	Perf. 13	
1061	A336	8s multi	2.50	.30

Size: 89x110mm
| 1061A | A336 | 15s multi | 2.75 | 1.75 |

No. 1061A is airmail.

Jose Maria de Jesus Yerovi (b. 1824), 4th Archbishop of Quito — A337

1984				
1062	A337	5s multi	.75	.30

Canonization of Brother Miguel — A338

Designs: 9s, Academy of Languages. 24s, Vatican City, vert. 28s, Home of Brother Miguel.

1984		Litho.	Perf. 13	
1063	A338	9s multi	.65	.30
1064	A338	24s multi	1.60	.60

Imperf
Size: 110x90mm
| 1065 | A338 | 28s multi | 4.25 | 2.00 |
| | Nos. 1063-1065 (3) | | 6.50 | 2.90 |

No. 1065, airmail, has black control number.

State Visit of Pope John Paul II — A339

Designs: 1.60s, Papal arms. 5s, Blessing crowd. 9s, World map, itinerary. 28s, Pope waving. 29s, Portrait. 30s, Pope holding crosier.

1985, Jan. 23		Litho.	Perf. 13x13½	
1066	A339	1.60s multi	2.00	.40
1067	A339	5s multi	2.00	.40
1068	A339	9s multi	2.00	.40
1069	A339	28s multi	5.30	.40
1070	A339	29s multi	6.00	.40

Size: 90x109mm
Imperf
| 1071 | A339 | 30s multi | 10.50 | 10.50 |
| | Nos. 1066-1071 (6) | | 27.80 | 12.50 |

Beatification of Mercedes de Jesus Molina — A340

Paintings, sculpture: 1.60s, Portrait. 5s, Czestochowa Madonna. 9s, Alborada Madonna. 20s, Mercedes de Jesus, children.

1985, Jan. 23				
1072	A340	1.60s multi	.65	.30
1073	A340	5s multi	.65	.30
1074	A340	9s multi	.70	.30

Size: 90x110mm
Imperf
| 1075 | A340 | 20s multi | 8.50 | 7.50 |
| | Nos. 1072-1075 (4) | | 10.50 | 8.40 |

Visit of Pope John Paul II, birth bimillennium of the Virgin Mary.

Samuel Valarezo Delgado, Naturalist, Politician — A341

1985, Feb.				
1076	A341	2s Bird	.45	.30
1077	A341	3s Swordfish, tuna	.45	.30
1078	A341	6s Portrait	.80	.30
	Nos. 1076-1078 (3)		1.70	.90

ESPAÑA '84, Madrid — A342

Designs: 6s, Emblem. 10s, Spanish royal family. 15s, Retiro Park, exhibition site.

1985, Apr. 25		Perf. 13½x13	
1079	A342	6s multi	.60	.30
1080	A342	10s multi	.95	.30

Size: 110x90mm
Imperf
| 1081 | A342 | 15s multi | 2.00 | 1.50 |

Dr. Pio Jaramillo Alvarado (1884-1968), Historian — A343

1985, May 17				
1082	A343	6s multi	.60	.30

Ingenio Valdez Sugar Refinery A344

Designs: 50s, Sugar cane, emblem. 100s, Rafael Valdez Cervantes, founder.

1985, June		Litho.	Perf. 13	
1082A	A344	50s multi	1.60	.50
1082B	A344	100s multi	3.25	1.00

Size: 110x90mm
Imperf
| 1083 | A344 | 30s multi | 2.50 | 2.00 |
| | Nos. 1082A-1083 (3) | | 7.35 | 3.50 |

Chamber of Commerce, 10th Anniv. — A345

50s, Natl. and American Statues of Liberty.

1985, Aug. 15		Perf. 13½x13	
1084	A345	24s multicolored	1.25	.30
1085	A345	28s multicolored	1.50	.45

Size: 110x90mm
Imperf
| 1086 | A345 | 50s multicolored | 3.00 | 2.50 |
| | Nos. 1084-1086 (3) | | 5.75 | 3.25 |

Natl. Philatelic Assoc., AFE, 50th Anniv. — A346

1985, Aug. 25			Perf. 12	
1087	A346	25s AFE emblem	1.00	.50
1088	A346	30s No. 357, horiz.	1.50	.60

Guayaquil Fire Dept., 150th Anniv. — A347

6s, Steam fire pump, 1882. 10s, Fire Wagon, 1899. 20s, Anniv. emblem, natl. flag.

1985, Oct. 10		Perf. 13½x13	
1089	A347	6s multi	.60	.25
1090	A347	10s multi	1.00	.25
1091	A347	20s multi	2.10	.75
	Nos. 1089-1091 (3)		3.70	1.25

Natl. Infant Survival Campaign — A348

1985, Oct.		Perf. 13x13½	
1092	A348	10s Boy, girl, tree	.75	.30

1st Natl. Phil. Cong., Quito, Nov. 25-28 — A349

20th cent. illustrations, natl. cultural collection: 5s, Supreme Court, Quito, by J. M. Roura. 10s, Riobamba Cathedral, by O. Munaz. 15s, House of 100 Windows, by J. M. Roura, horiz. 20s, Rural cottage near Cuenca, by J. M. Roura.

No. 1097: a, Stampless cover, 1779, Riobamba. b, Hand press, 1864, Quito. c, Postrider, 1880, Cuenca. d, Monoplane, 1st airmail flight, 1919, Guayaquil.

1985, Nov.		Perf. 13x13½, 13½x13	
1093	A349	5s multi	.35	.30
1094	A349	10s multi	.85	.30
1095	A349	15s multi	.95	.50
1096	A349	20s multi	1.50	.65
	Nos. 1093-1096 (4)		3.65	1.75

Souvenir Sheet
| 1097 | | Sheet of 4 | 1.50 | 1.50 |
| a.-d. | A349 5s, any single | | .25 | .25 |

AFE, 50th anniv. No. 1097 contains 53x42mm stamps, perf. 13x12½ on 2 sides.

10th Bolivarian Games, Cuenca — A350

Designs: 10s, Boxing. 25s, Women's gymnastics. 30s, Discus.

1985, Nov.		Perf. 13½x13	
1098	A350	10s multi	.70	.30
1099	A350	25s multi	1.20	.35
1100	A350	30s multi	1.40	.60
	Nos. 1098-1100 (3)		3.30	1.25

BAF Calderon, Navy Cent. — A351

Military anniv.: No. 1102, Fighter plane, Air Force 65th anniv. No. 1103, Army & paratroops emblems, Special Forces 30th anniv.

1985, Dec.		Perf. 13x13½	
1101	A351	10s multi	.80	.30
1102	A351	10s multi	.80	.30
1103	A351	10s multi	.80	.30
	Nos. 1101-1103 (3)		2.40	.90

UN, 40th Anniv. — A352

ECUADOR

1985, Oct.   Litho.   Perf. 13
| 1104 | A352 | 10s UN flag | .80 | .30 |
| 1105 | A352 | 20s Natl. flag | .80 | .30 |

Size: 110x90mm
Imperf
| 1106 | A352 | 50s UN Building | 2.00 | 1.50 |
| | | Nos. 1104-1106 (3) | 3.60 | 2.10 |

No. 1106 is airmail.

Christmas — A353

Designs: 5s, Little girl riding donkey. 10s, Baked goods. 15s, Little boy riding donkey.

1985, Nov.
1107	A353	5s multicolored	.40	.30
1108	A353	10s multicolored	.80	.35
1109	A353	15s multicolored	1.10	.55

Size: 90x110mm
Imperf
| 1110 | A353 | 30s like 5s | 2.10 | 1.60 |
| | | Nos. 1107-1110 (4) | 4.40 | 2.80 |

Indigenous Flowers — A354

Designs: 24s, Embotrium grandiforum. 28s, Topobea sp. 29s, Befaria resinosa mutis.

1986, Feb.
1111	A354	24s multi	1.50	.30
1112	A354	28s multi	2.25	.30
1113	A354	29s multi	3.00	.40

Size: 110x90mm
Imperf
| 1114 | A354 | 15s multi | 9.00 | 4.00 |
| | | Nos. 1111-1114 (4) | 15.75 | 5.00 |

No. 1114 contains designs of Nos. 1111, 1113, 1112; black control number.

Discovery of the Galapagos Islds., 450th Anniv. — A355

Map of the Islands A356

Designs: 10s, Land iguana. 20s, Sea lion. 30s, Frigate birds. 40s, Penguins. 50s, Giant tortoise. 100s, Charles Darwin. 200s, Bishop Tomas de Berlenga, discoverer.

1986, Feb. 12
1115	A355	10s multi	.65	.35
1116	A355	20s multi	1.25	.75
1117	A355	30s multi	2.00	1.25
1118	A355	40s multi	2.50	1.75
1119	A355	50s multi	3.00	2.00
1120	A355	100s multi	6.25	4.00
1121	A355	200s multi	12.50	8.00

Perf. 12½ on 2 Sides
1122	A356	Sheet of 4	13.50	13.00
a.-d.		50s, any single	1.75	1.75
		Nos. 1115-1122 (8)	41.65	31.10

No. 1122 contains 53x42mm stamps.

Inter-American Development Bank, 25th Anniv. — A357

5s, Antonio Ortiz Mena, pres. 1971-88. 10s, Felipe Herrera, pres. 1960-71. 50s, Emblem.

1986, Mar. 6
1123	A357	5s multicolored	.60	.25
1124	A357	5s multicolored	.85	.25
1125	A357	50s multicolored	1.60	.80
		Nos. 1123-1125 (3)	3.05	1.30

Guayaquil Tennis Club, 75th Anniv. — A358

Designs: No. 1126, Emblem. No. 1127, Francisco Segura Cano, vert. No. 1128, Andres Gomez Santos, vert.

1986, Mar. 7
1126	A358	10s multicolored	.85	.40
1127	A358	10s multicolored	.85	.40
1128	A358	10s multicolored	.85	.40
		Nos. 1126-1128 (3)	2.55	1.20

1986 World Cup Soccer Championships, Mexico — A359

1986, May 5
| 1129 | A359 | 5s Shot | .55 | .40 |
| 1130 | A359 | 10s Block | 1.10 | .40 |

An imperf. stamp exists picturing flags, player and emblem. Value $9.75.

Meeting of Presidents Cordero and Betancourt of Colombia, Feb. 1985 — A360

1986   Litho.   Perf. 13½x13
| 1131 | A360 | 20s Presidents | .85 | .40 |
| 1132 | A360 | 20s Embracing | .85 | .40 |

Exports — A361

35s, No. 1137c, Shrimp. 40s, No. 1137b, Tuna. 45s, No. 1137a, Sardines. No. 1137d, MICIP emblem.

1986, Apr. 12
1133	A361	35s ultra & ver	1.50	.40
1134	A361	40s red & yel grn	1.50	.40
1135	A361	45s car & dk yel	1.65	.70

Perf. 12½ on 2 Sides
1137		Sheet of 4	3.75	2.75
a.-d.		A361 10s, any single	.60	.50
		Nos. 1133-1137 (4)	8.40	4.25

No. 1137 contains 4 53x42mm stamps.

A362

La Condamine's First Geodesic Mission, 250th Anniv. — A363

Designs: 10s, La Condamine. 15s, Maldonado. 20s, Middle of the World, Quito. No. 1141a, Triangulation map for determining equatorial meridian, 1736. No. 1141b, Partial map of the Maranon & Amazon Rivers, by Samuel Fritz, 1743-1744. No. 1141c, Base of measurement, Yaruqui plains. No. 1141d, Caraburo & Dyambaru Pyramids near Quito. No. 1141 has a continuous design.

1986, July 10   Litho.   Perf. 13½x13
1138	A362	10s multicolored	.65	.40
1139	A362	15s multicolored	.80	.45
1140	A362	20s multicolored	.95	.45
		Nos. 1138-1140 (3)	2.40	1.25

Souvenir Sheet
Perf. 12½ on 2 Sides
| 1141 | A363 | Sheet of 4 | 6.00 | 5.00 |
| a.-d. | | 10s any single | .75 | .50 |

Chambers of Commerce — A364

1986   Litho.   Perf. 13½x13
1142	A364	10s Pichincha	.70	.45
1143	A364	10s Cuenca	.70	.45
1144	A364	10s Guayaquil	.70	.45
		Nos. 1142-1144 (3)	2.10	1.35

Civil Service and Communications Ministry, 57th Anniv. — A365

Organization emblems: 5s, State railway. 10s, Post office. 15s, Communications. 20s, Ministry of Public Works.

1986, Dec.   Litho.   Perf. 13x13½
1145	A365	5s multicolored	.45	.40
1146	A365	10s multicolored	.50	.40
1147	A365	15s multicolored	.95	.40
1148	A365	20s multicolored	1.10	.75
		Nos. 1145-1148 (4)	3.00	1.95

A366

1987, Feb. 16   Litho.   Perf. 13x13½
| 1149 | A366 | 5s multi | .90 | .40 |

Chamber of Agriculture of the 1st Zone, 50th anniv.

Col. Luis Vargas Torres (d. 1887) — A367

Combat unit, c. 1885 — A367a

A367b

No. 1152a, Torres & his mother, Delfina. No. 1152b, Letter to Delfina written by Torres during imprisonment, 1882. No. 1152c, Arms of Ecuador & combat unit.

Litho. & Typo.
1988, Jan. 6   Perf. 13
| 1150 | A367 | 50s yel grn, blk & gold | 1.50 | 1.00 |
| 1151 | A367a | 100s ver, gold & ultra | 3.00 | 1.75 |

Size: 95x140mm
Perf. 12 on One or Two Sides
1152	A367b	Block of 3	8.75	8.00
a.-c.		100s any single	1.75	1.60
		Nos. 1150-1152 (3)	13.25	10.75

Sizes: Nos. 1152a, 1152c, 95x28mm, No. 1152b, 95x83mm.

Founding of Guayaquil, 450th Anniv. — A368

15s, Street in Las Penas. 30s, Rafael Mendoza Aviles Bridge. 40s, Francisco de Orellana (c. 1490-1546), Spanish explorer, founder, & reenactment of landing, 1538.

1988, Feb. 19   Litho.   Perf. 13
1153	A368	15s multi, vert.	.50	.40
1154	A368	30s multi	.90	.40
1155	A368	40s multi	1.00	.40
		Nos. 1153-1155 (3)	2.40	1.20

Social Security Foundation (IESS), 60th Anniv. — A369

1988, Mar. 11
| 1156 | A369 | 50s shown | 1.00 | .65 |
| 1157 | A369 | 100s multi, diff. | 2.25 | 1.25 |

Dr. Pedro Moncayo y Esparza (1807-1888), Author, Politician — A370

Designs: 10s, Yaguarcocha Lake. 20s, Residence. 100s, Full-length portrait.

1988, Apr. 28   Litho.   Perf. 14x13½
1158	A370	10s multicolored	.65	.40
1159	A370	15s shown	.65	.40
1160	A370	20s multicolored	.65	.40

Size: 89x110mm
Imperf
| 1161 | A370 | 100s multi | 1.90 | 1.60 |
| | | Nos. 1158-1161 (4) | 3.85 | 2.80 |

A371

Avianca Airlines, 60th Anniv. — A372

10s, Junkers F-13. 20s, Dornier Wal seaplane. 30s, Ford 5AT trimotor. 40s, Boeing 247-D. 50s, Boeing 720-059B. 100s, Douglas DC-3. 200s, Boeing 727-200. 300s, Sikorsky S-38.

1988, May 12   Litho.   Perf. 14x13½
1162	A371	10s shown	.40	.40
1163	A371	20s multi	.40	.40
1164	A371	30s multi	.50	.40
1165	A371	40s multi	.60	.40
1166	A371	50s multi	.75	.55
1167	A371	100s multi	1.60	1.00
1168	A371	200s multi	3.00	2.50
1169	A371	300s multi	5.25	3.50

Perf. 13½x14
| 1170 | A372 | 500s shown | 8.00 | 4.50 |
| | | Nos. 1162-1170 (9) | 20.50 | 13.65 |

ECUADOR

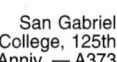

San Gabriel College, 125th Anniv. — A373

15s, Contemporary facility. 35s, College entrance, 19th cent.

1988, July 25   Litho.   Perf. 14x13½
| 1171 | A373 | 15s multicolored | .50 | .40 |
| 1172 | A373 | 35s multicolored | 1.20 | .45 |

A374

Military Geographical Institute, 60th Anniv. — A375

25s, Planetarium. 50s, Zeiss projector. 60s, Anniv. emblem. 500s, Creation, mural by E. Kingman.

1988, July 25   Perf. 12½ on 2 Sides
Size of No. 1173: 110x90mm
| 1173 | A374 | Block of 4 | 3.25 | 2.25 |
| a.-d. | | 5s any single | .40 | .40 |

Perf. 13½
1174	A375	25s multi	.55	.45
1175	A375	50s multi	1.00	.45
1176	A375	60s multi	1.25	.60
1177	A375	500s multi	7.75	5.00
	Nos. 1173-1177 (5)		13.80	8.75

In 1996 Nos. 1174, 1183, 1265 were surcharged 800s, 2600s 400s respectively. Only a few sets were sold to the public. The balance were sold by postal employees at greatly inflated prices.

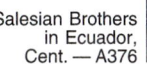

Salesian Brothers in Ecuador, Cent. — A376

Designs: 10s, St. John Bosco (1815-88), vert. 50s, 1st Salesian Cong. in Ecuador. 100s, Bosco, Salesian Brothers monument and Andes Mountains.

1988, July 29   Litho.   Perf. 13½
| 1178 | A376 | 10s multi | .40 | .40 |
| 1179 | A376 | 50s multi | 1.40 | .40 |

Size: 89x110mm
Imperf
| 1180 | A376 | 100s multi | 3.00 | 1.75 |
| | Nos. 1178-1180 (3) | | 4.80 | 2.55 |

Francisco Coello, Founder — A377

Social Services Council, Guayaquil, Cent. — A378

Designs: 20s, Eduardo Arosemena, 1st Director. 45s, Emblem.
No. 1184 — Flag: a, Emblem (upper left portion). b, Emblem (upper right portion). c, Emblem (lower left portion) and "100 ANOS." d, Emblem (lower right portion) and "DE TRADICION DE FE, AMPARO Y ESPERANZA."

1988, Nov. 24   Litho.   Perf. 13½x14
1181	A377	15s shown	.40	.40
1182	A377	20s multicolored	.50	.40
1183	A377	45s multicolored	1.10	.40

Size: 110x90mm
Perf. 12½ on 2 Sides
1184	A378	Block of 4	2.00	1.75
a.-d.		10s any single	.40	.40
	Nos. 1181-1184 (4)		4.00	2.95

For surcharge see note following No. 1177.

A379

Azuay Bank, 75th Anniv. — A380

Perf. 14x13½, 13½x14
1989, Mar. 1   Litho.
| 1185 | A379 | 20s shown | .60 | .45 |
| 1186 | A379 | 40s multi, vert. | .80 | .45 |

Size: 90x110mm
Imperf
| 1187 | A380 | 500s shown | 11.50 | 3.00 |
| | Nos. 1185-1187 (3) | | 12.90 | 3.90 |

1988 Summer Olympics, Seoul — A381

Character trademark demonstrating sports.

1989, Mar. 20   Perf. 13½x14
1188	A381	10s Running	.40	.40
1189	A381	20s Boxing	.40	.40
1190	A381	30s Cycling	.60	.40
1191	A381	40s Shooting	.60	.40
1192	A381	100s Diving	1.50	.80
1193	A381	200s Weight lifting	2.75	2.00
1194	A381	300s Tae kwon do	4.25	3.00

Size: 90x110mm
Imperf
| 1195 | A381 | 200s Emblems | 3.75 | 3.50 |
| | Nos. 1188-1195 (8) | | 14.25 | 10.90 |

RUMINAHUI '88 — A382

Designs: 50s, Bird, by Joaquin Tinta, vert. 70s, Matriz Church, Sangolqui. 300s, Monument to Ruminahui in Sangolqui, Pichincha.

Perf. 14x13½, 13½x14
1989, May 2   Litho.   Wmk. 395
| 1196 | A382 | 50s multi | 1.10 | .40 |
| 1197 | A382 | 70s multi | 1.50 | .60 |

Size: 90x111mm
Imperf
| 1198 | A382 | 300s multi | 7.50 | 2.50 |
| | Nos. 1196-1198 (3) | | 10.10 | 3.50 |

Cantonization, 50th anniv.

Benjamin Carrion Mora, Educator — A383

50s, Portrait, vert. 70s, Loja landscape. 1000s, University. 200s, Portrait, diff.

Perf. 13½x14, 14x13½
1989, May 10   Litho.
1199	A383	50s multi	.50	.40
1200	A383	70s multi	.70	.40
1201	A383	1000s multi	11.00	6.00

Size: 110x90mm
Imperf
| 1202 | A383 | 200s multi | 2.25 | 2.00 |
| | Nos. 1199-1202 (4) | | 14.45 | 8.80 |

2nd Intl. Art Biennial — A384

Prize-winning art: 40s, The Gilded Frame, by Myrna Baez. 70s, Paraguay III, by Carlos Colorabino, vert. 100s, Ordinanoo ootablishing the art exhibition. 180s, Modulation 892, by Julio Le Parc, vert.

Perf. 14x13½, 13½x14, Imperf. (100s)
1989, June 2   Litho.
Size of No. 1205: 110x90mm
1203	A384	40s multi	.85	.40
1204	A384	70s multi	1.60	.40
1205	A384	100s multi	2.50	1.00
1206	A384	200s multi	2.50	1.25
	Nos. 1203-1206 (4)		7.45	3.05

Guayaquil Chamber of Commerce, Cent. — A385

50s, Founder Ignacio Molestina, vert. 200s, Flags. 300s, Headquarters. 500s, Flags, diff.

Perf. 13½x14, 14x13½, Imperf. (No. 1208)
1989, June 20   Litho.
Size of No. 1208: 110x91mm
1207	A385	50s multi	.95	.40
1208	A385	200s multi	4.00	2.25
1209	A385	300s multi	2.75	2.50
1210	A385	500s multi	2.00	1.75
	Nos. 1207-1210 (4)		9.70	6.90

French Revolution, Bicent. — A386

20s, French natl. colors, anniv. emblem. 50s, Cathedral fresco. 100s, Rooster. 200s, Symbols of the revolution. 600s, Story board showing events of the revolution.

1989, July 11   Perf. 13½x14, 14x13½
1211	A386	20s multi, vert.	.40	.40
1212	A386	50s multi	.80	.40
1213	A386	100s multi, vert.	1.30	.65

Size: 90x110mm
Imperf
1214	A386	200s multi, vert.	2.00	2.00
1215	A386	600s multi, vert.	7.50	7.50
	Nos. 1211-1215 (5)		12.00	10.95

A387

Ministry of Public Works and Communications A388

No. 1216a, MOP emblem, 2-lane roadway. No. 1216b, State railway emblem, train. No. 1216c, Postal service emblem, airmail cover. No. 1216d, Telecommunications (IETEL) emblem, wall telephone. No. 1217, MOP, IETEL, postal service & state railway emblems. 100s, IETEL emblem. 200s, MOP emblem.

1989, July 7   Perf. 12½ on 2 Sides
| 1216 | A387 | Block of 4 | 3.00 | 3.00 |
| a.-d. | | 50s any single | .60 | .60 |

Perf. 13½x14
1217	A388	50s shown	.55	.40
1218	A388	100s multi	1.10	.75
1219	A388	200s multi	2.40	1.30
	Nos. 1216-1219 (4)		7.05	5.45

MOP, 60th anniv.; national communications, 105th anniv. (No. 1216d, 100s).

A389

Designs: 10s, Medical volunteer, vert. 200s, Two volunteers.

1989, Sept. 14   Litho.   Perf. 13½
1220	A389	10s multi	.35	.35
1221	A389	30s shown	.35	.35
1222	A389	200s multi	2.50	1.00
	Nos. 1220-1222 (3)		3.20	1.70

Natl. Red Cross, Intl. Red Cross and Red Crescent Societies, 125th Annivs.

Juan Montalvo (1832-1889), Writer — A390

Designs: 50s, Mausoleum, Ambato. 100s, Portrait (detail). No. 1225, Monument, Ambato. No. 1226, Portrait.

1989, Nov. 11   Litho.   Perf. 14x13½
1223	A390	50s multi	.55	.25
1224	A390	100s multi	1.40	.65
1225	A390	200s multi	2.60	1.40

Size: 90x110mm
Imperf
| 1226 | A390 | 200s multi | 2.00 | 1.75 |
| | Nos. 1223-1226 (4) | | 6.55 | 4.05 |

America Issue — A391

UPAE emblem and pre-Columbian pottery: 200s, La Tolita incensory, vert. 300s, Warrior (plate).

1990, Mar. 6   Litho.   Perf. 13½
| 1227 | A391 | 200s multi | 2.25 | 1.25 |
| 1228 | A391 | 300s multi | 3.50 | 2.00 |

Dated 1989.

Dr. Luis Carlos Jaramillo Leon, Founder — A392

No. 1233a, Dr. Leon. Nos. 1230, 1233b, Federico Malo Andrade, honorary president. 130s, No. 1233c, Roberto Crespo Toral, 1st president. 200s, Alfonso Jaramillo Leon, founder.

1990, Jan. 17   Litho.   Perf. 13½
1229	A392	100s shown	1.10	.60
1230	A392	100s multicolored	1.10	.60
1231	A392	130s multicolored	1.50	.75
1232	A392	200s multicolored	2.10	1.25

ECUADOR

Size: 91x38mm
Perf. 12½ Horiz. on 1 or 2 sides
1233		Block of 3	3.25	3.00
a.-c.	A392	100s any single	.50	.50
		Nos. 1229-1233 (5)	9.05	6.20

Chamber of Commerce, 70th anniversary.

World Cup Soccer, Italy — A393

Designs: No. 1235, Soccer player. No. 1236, Map of Italy, trophy. No. 1237, Player, flags. No. 1238, World Cup Trophy.

1990, July 12   Litho.   Perf. 13½
1234	A393	100s shown	.70	.35
1235	A393	200s multi	1.50	.60
1236	A393	300s multi	2.25	.90

Imperf
Size: 110x90mm
| 1237 | A393 | 200s multi | 1.90 | 1.75 |

Size: 60x90mm
| 1238 | A393 | 300s multi | 2.90 | 2.50 |
| | | Nos. 1234-1238 (5) | 9.25 | 6.10 |

Nos. 1235-1236, 1238 vert.

A394

Design: 200s, Church tower, book.

1990, June 12   Perf. 13½
| 1239 | A394 | 100s multi | .85 | .25 |
| 1240 | A394 | 200s multi | 1.50 | .60 |

College of St. Mariana, cent.

A395

Tourism: No. 100s, No. 1244c, Iguana. 200s, No. 1244b, La Compania Church, Quito. 300s, No. 1244a, Old man from Vilcabamba. No. 1244d, Locomotive.

1990, Sept. 7   Litho.   Perf. 13½
1241	A395	100s multi	.95	.25
1242	A395	200s multi, vert.	2.00	.55
1243	A395	300s multi	2.90	.75

Size: 111x90mm
Perf. 12½ on 2 sides
1244		Block of 4	8.50	4.00
a.-d.	A395	100s any single	.40	.30
		Nos. 1241-1244 (4)	14.35	5.55

A396

National Census: 100s, No. 1248a, People and house. 200s, No. 1248b, Map. 300s, No. 1248c, Census breakdown, pencil.

1990, Sept. 1   Perf. 13½
1245	A396	100s multicolored	.75	.25
1246	A396	200s multi, horiz.	1.50	.55
1247	A396	300s multicolored	2.10	.75

Size: 109x88mm
Perf. 12½ on 2 sides
1248		Block of 3	2.60	1.90
a.-c.	A396	100s any single	.40	.30
		Nos. 1245-1248 (4)	6.95	3.45

A397

1990, Nov. 2   Litho.   Perf. 14
| 1249 | A397 | 200s Flags | 2.40 | .55 |
| 1250 | A397 | 300s shown | 3.25 | .75 |

Organization of Petroleum Exporting Countries (OPEC), 30th anniv.

A398

Designs: No. 1251, Emblem. No. 1252, Four wooden parrots. No. 1253, Wooden parrots, diff.

1990, Oct. 31   Perf. 13½x14
| 1251 | A398 | 200s multi | 1.40 | .55 |
| 1252 | A398 | 300s multi | 2.25 | .75 |

Size: 92x110mm
Imperf
| 1253 | A398 | 200s multi | 2.40 | 2.10 |
| | | Nos. 1251-1253 (3) | 6.05 | 3.40 |

Artisans' Organization, 25th anniv.

Flowers — A399

Wmk. 395
1990, Nov. 12   Litho.   Perf. 13½
1254	A399	100s Sobralia	1.50	.30
1255	A399	100s Blakea, vert.	1.50	.30
1256	A399	100s Cattleya, vert.	1.50	.30
1257	A399	100s Loasa, vert.	1.50	.30
		Nos. 1254-1257 (4)	6.00	1.20

Discovery of America, 500th Anniv. (in 1992) — A400

Designs: 100s, Ancient dwelling. 200s, Mangrove swamp.

1990, Dec. 31   Litho.   Perf. 13½
| 1258 | A400 | 100s multi | .80 | .25 |
| 1259 | A400 | 200s multi | 2.00 | .35 |

Natl. Union of Journalists, 50th Anniv. — A401

Designs: 300s, Eugenio Espejo, writer. 400s, Union emblem.

1991, Feb. 28
1260	A401	200s shown	1.25	.70
1261	A401	300s multicolored	2.00	.80
1262	A401	400s multicolored	2.25	1.10
		Nos. 1260-1262 (3)	5.50	2.60

Radio Quito, 50th Anniv. — A402

Designs: 200s, Man with microphone, vert. 500s, Family listening to radio.

1991, Apr. 10
| 1263 | A402 | 200s multicolored | 1.00 | .35 |
| 1264 | A402 | 500s multicolored | 2.10 | .95 |

Dr. Pablo A. Suarez, Birth Cent. — A403

1991, Sept. 16   Wmk. 395
| 1265 | A403 | 70s multicolored | 1.00 | .30 |

Dated 1990.
For surcharge see note following No. 1177. Value $20.

America Issue — A404

UPAEP emblem and: 200s, Columbus' ships. 500s, Columbus, landing in America.

1991, Oct. 18   Litho.   Perf. 13½x13
| 1266 | A404 | 200s multicolored | 1.50 | .65 |
| 1267 | A404 | 500s multicolored | 2.50 | 1.25 |

Cultural Artifacts — A405

Designs: 100s, Cat censer. 200s, Statue of old man's head. 300s, Zoomorphic statue.

Wmk. 395
1991, Nov. 14   Litho.   Perf. 13½
1268	A405	100s multi	.65	.25
1269	A405	200s multi	1.25	.35
1270	A405	300s multi	2.25	.60
		Nos. 1268-1270 (3)	4.15	1.20

Dated 1990. See No. 1291.

A406

Design: 500s, Woman in profile.

1991   Perf. 13
| 1271 | A406 | 300s shown | 1.25 | .55 |
| 1272 | A406 | 500s multicolored | 2.25 | 1.00 |

Day of Non-violence Toward Women.

Jacinto Jijon y Caamano, Archaeologist, Birth Cent. — A407

1991, Dec. 11   Perf. 13½
| 1273 | A407 | 200s Portrait, vert. | 1.00 | .40 |
| 1274 | A407 | 300s shown | 1.50 | .60 |

Pres. Rodrigo Borja, Ecuador and Pres. Jaime Paz Zamora, Bolivia A408

1991, Dec. 10   Perf. 14x13½
| 1275 | A408 | 500s multicolored | 2.25 | 1.00 |

Pres. Rodrigo Borja's Visit to the UN A409

Designs: 1000s, Flags, world map.

Wmk. 395
1992, Jan. 24   Litho.   Perf. 14
| 1276 | A409 | 100s multicolored | .40 | .25 |
| 1277 | A409 | 1000s multicolored | 3.50 | 1.60 |

Battle of Jambeli, 50th Anniv. A410

No. 1278, Gunboat Calderon and Capt. Raphael Moran Valverde. No. 1279, Dispatch boat Atahualpa and Ens. Victor Naranjo Fiallo. No. 1280, Valverde, Fiallo and ships.

1992, Apr. 7
| 1278 | A410 | 300s multicolored | .95 | .40 |
| 1279 | A410 | 500s multicolored | 2.90 | .90 |

Size: 110x90mm
Imperf
| 1280 | A410 | 500s multicolored | 3.00 | 2.40 |
| | | Nos. 1278-1280 (3) | 6.85 | 3.70 |

Galapagos Islands Wildlife — A411

Designs: No. 1281, Giant tortoise. No. 1282, Galapagos penguin, vert. No. 1283, Zalophus californianus, vert. No. 1284, Swallow-tailed gull. No. 1285, Fregata minor. No. 1286, Land iguana.

1992, Apr. 9   Litho.   Perf. 13½
1281	A411	100s multicolored	2.00	1.00
1282	A411	100s multicolored	2.00	1.00
1283	A411	100s multicolored	2.00	1.00
1284	A411	100s multicolored	2.00	1.00
1285	A411	100s multicolored	2.00	1.00
1286	A411	100s multicolored	2.00	1.00
		Nos. 1281-1286 (6)	12.00	6.00

Vicente Rocafuerte National College, 150th Anniv. (in 1991) — A412

Designs: 400s, Vicente Rocafuerte.

Perf. 14x13½
1992, Apr. 29   Litho.   Wmk. 395
| 1287 | A412 | 200s shown | 1.00 | .35 |
| 1288 | A412 | 400s multicolored | 1.75 | .65 |

Eloy Alfaro (1842-1912), President — A413

Designs: 300s, Portrait, vert.

Perf. 13½x14, 14x13½
1992, Aug. 26   Litho.   Wmk. 395
| 1289 | A413 | 300s multicolored | 1.10 | .70 |
| 1290 | A413 | 700s multicolored | 1.90 | 1.00 |

Cultural Artifacts Type of 1991
Designs: 400s, Ceremonial mask.

1992, Sept. 6   Litho.   Perf. 13½
| 1291 | A405 | 400s multi | 1.90 | .75 |

Dated 1990.

Discovery of America, 500th Anniv. — A414

Designs: 200s, Sailing ship. 400s, Columbus, map, vert.

ECUADOR

Wmk. 395
1992, Oct. 15	**Litho.**	**Perf. 13½**	
1292	A414	200s multi	.90 .55
1293	A414	400s multi	1.75 .95

Andres F. Cordova (b. 1892) — A415

1992, Nov. 17	**Litho.**	**Perf. 13½**	
1294	A415	300s multicolored	1.40 .60

Beatification of Narcisa of Jesus — A416

1992, Nov. 30		**Perf. 13½**	
1295	A416	100s multicolored	1.00 .30

A417

Christmas: 300s, Infant Jesus of Saqueo, 18th cent. 600s, Stable scene, Infant Jesus asleep on hay.

1992, Dec. 14		**Perf. 13½**	
1296	A417	300s multicolored	1.50 .60
1297	A417	600s multicolored	3.25 1.25

A418

1992, Dec. 29			
1298	A418	200s multicolored	1.30 .45

Father Juan de Velasco, Death Bicent.

Frogs — A419

No. 1299, Agalychnis spurelli. No. 1300, Atelopus homolochos. No. 1301, Gastrotheca plumbea. No. 1302, Hyla picturata. No. 1303, Dendrobates sp. No. 1304, Sphaenorhyncus lacteus.

	Perf. 13½x14		
1993, Jan. 28	**Litho.**	**Wmk. 395**	
1299	A419	300s multi	1.00 .35
1300	A419	300s multi	1.00 .35
1301	A419	600s multi	2.40 .90
1302	A419	600s multi	2.40 .90
1303	A419	900s multi	3.00 1.10
1304	A419	900s multi	3.00 1.10
Nos. 1299-1304 (6)			12.80 5.30

A420

1993, Feb. 16	**Litho.**	**Perf. 13x13½**	
1305	A420	300s blue	1.00 .30

J. Roberto Paez, (1893-1983), co-founder of social security.

Francisco Robles (1811-93) — A421

1993, Mar. 16		**Perf. 13½x14**	
1306	A421	500s No. 168	1.75 .55

National Police — A422

	Perf. 13½x14		
1993, Mar. 25	**Litho.**	**Wmk. 395**	
1307	A422	300s multicolored	1.25 .60

Pres. Jose Maria Velasco Ibarra (1893-1979) — A423

	Perf. 14x13½		
1993, Mar. 31	**Litho.**	**Wmk. 395**	
1308	A423	500s multicolored	1.75 .55

Insects — A424

150s, Fulgora laternaria. 200s, Semiotus ligneus. 300s, Taeniotes pulverulenta. 400s, Danaus plexippus. 600s, Erotylus onagga. 700s, Xylocopa darwini.

	Wmk. 395		
1993, May 27	**Litho.**	**Perf. 13½**	
1309	A424	150s multi	.85 .30
1310	A424	200s multi	1.10 .30
1311	A424	300s multi	1.75 .45
1312	A424	400s multi	2.25 .60
1313	A424	600s multi	3.25 .95
1314	A424	700s multi	3.75 1.10
Nos. 1309-1314 (6)			12.95 3.70

A425

	Wmk. 395		
1993, May 31	**Litho.**	**Perf. 13½**	
1315	A425	1000s multicolored	3.25 1.50

Pedro Fermin Cevallos Villacreces (1812-93), historian and founder of Academy of Language.

First Latin-American Children's Peace Assembly, Quito — A426

1993, June 7			
1316	A426	300s multicolored	1.20 .50

Juan Benigno Vela Hervas (1843-97), Jurist — A427

	Perf. 13x13½		
1993, July 8	**Litho.**	**Wmk. 395**	
1317	A427	2000s multicolored	5.25 3.00

Guillermo Bustamante, Birth Cent. — A428

1993, Sept. 23		**Perf. 13½**	
1318	A428	1500s multicolored	4.25 1.75

University of Ecuador School of Medicine, 300th Anniv. — A429

	Perf. 14x13½		
1993, Sept. 7	**Litho.**	**Wmk. 395**	
1319	A429	300s multicolored	1.25 .45

Maldonado-La Condamine Amazon Expedition, 250th Anniv. — A430

Designs: 150s, Cinchona cordifolia. 200s, Pedro V. Maldonado, 1500s, Charles La Condamine (1701-74), explorer.

1993, Aug. 20			
1320	A430	150s multicolored	.40 .30
1321	A430	200s multicolored	.55 .30
1322	A430	1500s multicolored	4.90 2.10
Nos. 1320-1322 (3)			5.85 2.70

A431

	Wmk. 395		
1993, Nov. 27	**Litho.**	**Perf. 13**	
1323	A431	500s multicolored	1.40 .55

Dr. Carlos A. Arroyo del Rio, birth cent.

Endangered Species — A432

400s, Dinomys branickii, horiz. 800s, Ara aovora.

1993, Oct. 15	**Perf. 13½x13, 13x13½**		
1324	A432	400s multicolored	2.25 .60
1325	A432	800s multicolored	3.25 1.25

America issue.

Christmas — A433

600s, Holy Family, 18th cent. Tagua miniatures. 900s, Mother and child, vert.

	Wmk. 395		
1993, Dec. 1	**Litho.**	**Perf. 13**	
1326	A433	600s multicolored	1.60 .90
1327	A433	900s multicolored	2.50 1.40

Intl. Year of the Family — A434

	Wmk. 395		
1994, Jan. 18	**Litho.**	**Perf. 13**	
1328	A434	300s grn, blk & org	.85 .35

A435

1994, Jan. 25			
1329	A435	500s multicolored	2.00 .90

Dr. Julio Tobar Donoso, birth cent.

Orchids — A436

No. 1330, Dracula hirtzii. No. 1331, Sobralia dichotoma. No. 1332, Encyclia pulcherrima. No. 1333, Lepanthes delhierroi. No. 1334, Macdovallia rosca. No. 1335, Telipogon andicola.

	Wmk. 395		
1994, Feb. 7	**Litho.**	**Perf. 13½**	
1330	A436	150s multicolored	.60 .30
1331	A436	150s multicolored	.60 .30
1332	A436	300s multicolored	1.20 .40
1333	A436	300s multicolored	1.20 .40
1334	A436	600s multicolored	2.40 .90
1335	A436	600s multicolored	2.40 .90
Nos. 1330-1335 (6)			8.40 3.20

First Convention on the Conservation of Andean Orchids.

Federico Gonzalez Suarez (1844-1917) — A437

1994, Apr. 12		**Perf. 13**	
1336	A437	200s multicolored	1.00 .40

Scouting in Ecuador — A438

1994, Jan. 11			
1337	A438	400s multicolored	1.50 .60

Dr. Miguel Egas Cabezas (1823-04) A439

	Wmk. 395		
1994, Mar. 10	**Litho.**	**Perf. 13**	
1338	A439	100s multicolored	1.00 .40

Father Aurelio Espinosa, Birth Cent. — A440

1994, July 12			
1339	A440	200s multicolored	.95 .50

ECUADOR

A441

Nos. 1341, 1343d, Mascot. 900s, Player.
No. 1343: a, Emblem. b, "COPA MUNDIAL FUTBOL '94," emblem. c, "COPA MUNDIAL, USA 94."

Wmk. 395
1994, June 10   Litho.   Perf. 13
1340	A441	300s shown	1.40	.60
1341	A441	600s Mascot	2.60	1.25
1342	A441	900s Soccer player	4.00	1.75

Perf. 12 on 2 Sides
| 1343 | A441 | 600s Block of 4, #a.-d. | 10.75 | 7.50 |
| | | Nos. 1340-1343 (4) | 18.75 | 11.10 |

1994 World Cup Soccer Championships, US. No. 1343 contains two 50x25mm stamps, two 50x51mm stamps.

Ecuador in Antarctica — A442

1994, July 19   Perf. 13
| 1344 | A442 | 600s Outpost | 2.50 | 1.10 |
| 1345 | A442 | 900s Ship, B/1 Orion | 3.75 | 1.75 |

ILO, 75th Anniv. — A443

1994   Litho.   Wmk. 395   Perf. 13
| 1346 | A443 | 100s multicolored | .75 | .40 |

Ecuadorian Culture Center, 50th Anniv. — A444

700s, Benjamin Carrion, vert. 900s, Cultural center.

1994
| 1347 | A444 | 700s multi | 2.60 | 1.40 |
| 1348 | A444 | 900s multi | 3.75 | 1.60 |

Natl. Lottery, Cent. — A445

1994
| 1349 | A445 | 1000s multicolored | 4.00 | 1.75 |

Junior World Cycling Championships, Quito — A446

Design: No. 1351, Stylized cyclist, vert.

Wmk. 395
1994, June 22   Litho.   Perf. 13
| 1350 | A446 | 300s shown | 1.00 | .40 |
| 1351 | A446 | 400s multi | 1.25 | .50 |

Postal Transportation — A447

America Issue: No. 1352, Van, airplane, ship, horiz. No. 1353, Airplane, mail bag.

1994
| 1352 | A447 | 600s multicolored | 1.10 | .40 |
| 1353 | A447 | 600s multicolored | 1.50 | .50 |

Christmas — A448

No. 1354, Simulated stamp showing globe circled by envelope, horiz. No. 1355, Nativity.

1994
| 1354 | A448 | 600s multicolored | 1.50 | .75 |
| 1355 | A448 | 900s multicolored | 2.25 | .85 |

Juan Leon Mera, Death Cent.
A449   A450

Wmk. 395
1994, Dec. 21   Litho.   Perf. 13
| 1356 | A449 | 600s Mera's home | 1.25 | .65 |
| 1357 | A450 | 900s multicolored | 2.50 | 1.40 |

Gen. Antonio Jose de Sucre (1795-1830) — A451

Designs: 2000s, Portrait at right. 3000s, In military uniform.

Perf. 14x13½
1995, Mar. 14   Litho.   Wmk. 395
| 1358 | A451 | 1500s shown | 3.75 | 1.75 |
| 1359 | A451 | 2000s multi | 5.50 | 2.50 |

Size: 80x105
Imperf
| 1360 | A451 | 3000s multi | 5.75 | 5.50 |
| | | Nos. 1358-1360 (3) | 15.00 | 9.75 |

Beatification of Josemaria Escriva, 3rd Anniv. — A452

1995, May 17   Perf. 13x13½
| 1361 | A452 | 900s multicolored | 2.25 | .90 |

Gen. Eloy Alfaro (1842-1912), Alfarista Revolution, Cent. — A453

1995, June 5   Perf. 13½x13
| 1362 | A453 | 800s multicolored | 1.60 | .80 |

A454

Conflict Between Ecuador & Peru — A455

Designs: 200s, Soldier writing to children. 400s, Hand holding flag of Ecuador. 800s, Soldier in wilderness.

1995, July   Perf. 13½, 13 (#1364)
1363	A454	200s multicolored	.60	.25
1364	A455	400s multicolored	1.25	.45
1365	A455	800s multicolored	2.15	.90
		Nos. 1363-1365 (3)	4.00	1.60

CARE, 50th Anniv. — A456

1995, July 14   Perf. 13½
| 1366 | A456 | 400s Girl, vert. | .75 | .30 |
| 1367 | A456 | 800s shown | 2.10 | 1.00 |

CAF (Andes Development Corporation), 25th Anniv. — A457

1995, Aug. 22   Perf. 13
| 1368 | A457 | 1000s multicolored | 3.25 | 1.25 |

Virgin of Cisne — A458

1995, Sept. 2   Litho.   Perf. 13
| 1369 | A458 | 500s multi | 1.00 | .50 |

A459

1995, Sept. 28
| 1370 | A459 | 400s multicolored | 1.10 | .45 |

Natl. Institute of Children and Families (INNFA), 35th anniv.

UN, 50th Anniv. — A460

Wmk. 395
1995, Oct. 6   Litho.   Perf. 13
| 1371 | A460 | 1000s bl, blk & bis | 2.25 | 1.00 |

Intl. Decade for Natural Disaster Reduction — A461

Civil defense emblem and: No. 1372, House surrounded by flood waters. No. 1373, Family leaving site of erupting volcano. No. 1374, People under table during earthquake. No. 1375, Couple planting seedlings on hillside. No. 1376, Man reading instruction booklet for natural disaster preparation.

1995, Oct. 11
1372	A461	1000s multicolored	2.25	1.00
1373	A461	1000s multicolored	2.25	1.00
1374	A461	1000s multicolored	2.25	1.00
1375	A461	1000s multicolored	2.25	1.00
1376	A461	1000s multicolored	2.25	1.00
		Nos. 1372-1376 (5)	11.25	5.00

FAO, 50th Anniv. — A462

1995, Oct. 16
| 1377 | A462 | 1300s multicolored | 3.00 | 1.50 |

Women's Culture Club, 50th Anniv. — A463

1995, Oct. 20
| 1378 | A463 | 1500s multicolored | 3.00 | 1.50 |

29th Assembly of Inter-America Philatelic Federation, Quito — A464

1995, Nov. 11
| 1379 | A464 | 1000s blue & red | 2.00 | 1.00 |

A465

Christmas: 2000s, Santa, sleigh, reindeer on top of world. 2600s, Man on decorated horse, children.

Wmk. 395
1995, Dec.   Litho.   Perf. 13
| 1380 | A465 | 2000s multicolored | 5.00 | 2.40 |
| 1381 | A465 | 2600s multicolored | 6.50 | 2.40 |

A466

Indigenous Birds: No. 1382, Aglaiocercus kingi.
No. 1383: a, Coeligena torquata. b, Phaethornis superciliosus. c, Oreatus underwoodii. d, Oreotrochilus chimborazo. e, Aglaiocercus coelestis.

1995, Dec.
| 1382 | A466 | 1000s multicolored | 2.50 | .85 |
| 1383 | A466 | 1000s Strip of 5, #a.-e. | 12.50 | 6.25 |

Ecuadoran Air Force, 75th Anniv. — A467

1995, Dec.
| 1384 | A467 | 1000s multicolored | 2.25 | 1.00 |

Year of Folk Music — A468

2000s, Julio Jaramillo (1935-78), musician, composer. 3000s, Jaramillo, wall.

1996, Jan. 16   Litho.   Perf. 13
| 1385 | A468 | 2000s multicolored | 4.00 | 2.00 |

Imperf
| 1386 | A468 | 3000s multicolored | 5.25 | 4.25 |

ECUADOR

Advancement of Ecuador, 4 Year Program — A469

Designs show symbols for: 1500s, Mail delivery. 2000s, Customs crossing. 2600s, Telecommunications. 3000p, Ports.

1996, July 23   Wmk. 395   Litho.   Perf. 13
1387	A469	1000s multicolored	1.90	.80
1388	A469	1500s multicolored	2.90	1.25
1389	A469	2000s multicolored	3.50	1.75
1390	A469	2600s multicolored	4.75	1.90
a.		Pair, #1388, #1390	8.50	8.50
b.		Pair, #1389, #1390	9.00	9.00
1391	A469	3000s multicolored	5.75	3.00
a.		Pair, #1387, #1391	8.50	8.50
b.		Pair, #1389, #1391	10.00	10.00
		Nos. 1387-1391 (5)	18.80	8.70
		Nos. 1390a-1391b (4)	36.00	36.00

Nos. 1387-1391 were issued in strips of 2 each.

Esmeraldas '96, 8th National Games — A470

Mascot depicting two sports on each stamp: No. 1392, Tennis, boxing. No. 1393, Basketball, soccer. 600s, Racketball, swimming. 800s, Weight lifting, karate. 1000s, Volleyball, gymnastics. 1200s, Athletics, judo. No. 1398, Chess, wrestling.
No. 1399, Mascot holding flag, emblem, surrounded by flags.

1996, July 30
1392	A470	400s multicolored	.65	.25
1393	A470	400s multicolored	.65	.25
1394	A470	600s multicolored	1.10	.45
a.		Pair, #1392, #1394	1.75	1.75
1395	A470	800s multicolored	1.50	.60
a.		Pair, #1394-1395	2.60	2.60
1396	A470	1000s multicolored	1.90	.75
a.		Pair, #1393, #1396	2.90	2.90
b.		Pair, #1395-1396	3.50	3.50
1397	A470	1200s multicolored	2.10	.95
1398	A470	2000s multicolored	3.75	1.40
		Nos. 1392-1398 (7)	11.65	4.65
		Nos. 1394a-1396b (4)	10.75	10.75

Size: 120x100mm
1399	A470	2000s multicolored	4.25	3.50

Nos. 1392-1396 were printed in strips of 2 each.

Civil Aviation, 50th Anniv. — A471

1996, Aug. 8
1400	A471	2000s multicolored	3.25	1.25

1996 Summer Olympic Games, Atlanta — A472

Atlanta Games emblem and: 1000s, Mascot carrying torch. No. 1402, Emblem of Olympic Committee of Ecuador. 3000s, Jefferson Perez, vert.
No. 1404, Perez, gold medalist, 20-kilometer walk, walking.

1996
1401	A472	1000s multicolored	2.00	.75
1402	A472	2000s multicolored	4.50	2.25
a.		Pair, #1401-1402	7.00	6.00
1403	A472	3000s multicolored	5.50	2.50
		Nos. 1401-1403 (3)	12.00	5.50

Size: 100x120mm
Imperf
1404	A472	2000s multicolored	4.75	3.50

Fight Against Drug Abuse — A473

1996   Litho.   Wmk. 395   Perf. 13
1408	A473	2000s multicolored	4.25	2.00

Dr. Eduardo Salazar Gomez, Birth Cent. — A474

1996
1409	A474	1000s multicolored	2.75	1.25

Catholic University, Quito, 50th Anniv. — A475

Designs: 400s, Outside view of building, horiz. 800s, Entrance.

1996
1410	A475	400s multicolored	1.00	.45
1411	A475	800s multicolored	2.10	.85

Junior Chamber International — A476

2000s, Children's faces, horiz.

1996
1412	A476	2000s multi	4.50	2.75
1413	A476	2600s shown	6.00	3.50

Catholic University, Quito, 50th Anniv. — A477

1996, Nov.
1414	A477	2000s multicolored	4.25	2.00

The Universe Daily Newspaper, 75th Anniv. — A478

1996, Dec.
1415	A478	2000s multicolored	4.25	2.00

Private Technical University, Loja — A479

1996, Dec. 9
1416	A479	4700s multicolored	11.25	5.50

UNICEF, 50th Anniv. — A480

1996, Dec. 11
1417	A480	2000s multicolored	4.75	2.25

Christmas — A481

Children's paintings: 600s, Merry Chrismas All Over the World. 800s, World of Peace and Love. 2000s, Christmas.

1996, Dec. 19
1418	A481	600s multicolored	1.50	1.00
1419	A481	800s multicolored	2.00	1.25

Size: 51x31mm
Perf. 13½
1420	A481	2000s multicolored	5.75	2.50
		Nos. 1418-1420 (3)	9.25	4.75

Preserving the Ecological System — A482

America '95: 1000s, Voltur grypus. 1500s, Harpia harpyja, vert.

1996, Dec. 30   Perf. 13
1421	A482	1000s multicolored	2.75	1.50
1422	A482	1500s multicolored	4.00	2.00

Typical Children's Costumes — A483

America '96: No. 1423, "Bordando" girl, Zuleta. No. 1424, Girl from Otavalo.

1996, Dec. 30
1423	A483	2600s multicolored	5.25	1.75
1424	A483	2600s multicolored	5.25	4.25
a.		Pair, #1423-1424	14.00	12.50

Mejia Natl. Institute, Cent. — A484

Design: Jose Mejia Lequerica, building.

1997, Jan. 10
1425	A484	1000s multicolored	2.50	1.25

Army Polytechnical School, 75th Anniv. — A485

Wmk. 395
1997, June 16   Typo.   Perf. 13
1426	A485	400s multicolored	1.50	.75

Natl. Experimental College, Ambato, 50th Anniv. — A486

1997, June 20
1427	A486	600s multicolored	1.75	1.00

Vicente Rocafuerte (1783-1847), First Constitutional President of Ecuador — A487

1997, July 1
1428	A487	400s multicolored	1.50	.75

49th Intl. Congress of the Americanists — A488

1997, July 3
1429	A488	2000s multicolored	5.25	3.25

Butterflies — A489

Designs: 400s, Actinote equatoria. 600s, Dismorphia amphione. 800s, Marpesia corinna. 2000s, Marpesia berania. 2600s, Morpho helenor.

1997, July 21
1430	A489	400s multicolored	1.30	.80
1431	A489	600s multicolored	1.60	1.00
1432	A489	800s multicolored	2.10	1.25
1433	A489	2000s multicolored	5.25	3.25
1434	A489	2600s multicolored	7.50	4.75
		Nos. 1430-1434 (5)	17.75	11.05

Air Club of Ecuador, 66th Anniv. — A490

1997, July 23
1435	A490	2600s multicolored	6.25	3.00

Orchids — A491

400s, Epidendrum secundum. 600s, Epidendrum. 800s, Oncidium cultratrum. 2000s, Oncidium sp mariposa. 2600s, Pleurothalis corrulensis.

1997, Aug. 14   Litho.   Perf. 13
1436	A491	400s multicolored	1.30	.80
1437	A491	600s multicolored	1.60	1.00
1438	A491	800s multicolored	2.10	1.25
1439	A491	2000s multicolored	5.25	3.25
1440	A491	2600s multicolored	7.50	4.75
		Nos. 1436-1440 (5)	17.75	11.05

Rocks and Minerals — A492

Designs: 400s, Quartz. 600s, Chalcopyrite. 800s, Gold. 2000s, Petrified wood. 2600s, Pyrite.

1997, Oct. 6   Litho.   Perf. 13
1441	A492	400s multi	1.30	.80
1442	A492	600s multi	1.60	1.00
1443	A492	800s multi	2.10	1.25
1444	A492	2000s multi	5.25	3.25
1445	A492	2600s multi	7.50	4.75
		Nos. 1441-1445 (5)	17.75	11.05

A493

Christmas (Children's designs): 400s, Santa as postman delivering letters over world. 2600s, Star on Christmas tree reaching for letters, airplane under tree. 3000s, Child dreaming of angels carrying letters.

1997, Dec. 22   Litho.   Perf. 13
1446	A493	400s multicolored	1.30	.80
1447	A493	2600s multicolored	7.00	4.75
1448	A493	3000s multicolored	9.00	5.50
		Nos. 1446-1448 (3)	17.30	11.05

ECUADOR

America Issue — A494

Designs: 800s, Life of a Postman. 2000s, On bicycle.

1997, Dec. 29
| 1449 | A494 | 800s multi | 2.00 | 1.00 |
| 1450 | A494 | 2000s multi | 5.50 | 2.50 |

Intl. Women's Day — A495

Matilde Hidalgo de Procel (1889-1974), physician, social reformer.

1998, Mar. 6   Litho.   Perf. 13
| 1451 | A495 | 2000s multicolored | 5.00 | 3.25 |

Dr. Misael Acosta Solis, Botanist — A496

Wmk. 395
1998, Apr. 22   Litho.   Perf. 13
| 1452 | A496 | 2000s multicolored | 8.50 | 5.50 |

Organization of American States (OAS), 50th Anniv. — A497

1998, Apr. 30
| 1453 | A497 | 2600s multicolored | 5.25 | 3.25 |

1998 World Cup Soccer Championships, France — A498

Designs: 2600s, Trophy, mascot, vert. 3000s, Two players, trophy.

1998, May
1454	A498	2000s multicolored	4.25	2.25
1455	A498	2600s multicolored	5.25	2.75
1456	A498	3000s multicolored	6.25	3.25
		Nos. 1454-1456 (3)	15.75	8.25

Flowers — A499

600s, Gypsophila paniculata. 800s, Banana flowers. 2000s, Roses. 2600s, Asters.

1998, June
1457	A499	600s multicolored	1.50	.60
1458	A499	800s multicolored	1.90	.90
1459	A499	2000s multicolored	4.25	2.25
1460	A499	2600s multicolored	5.50	2.75
		Nos. 1457-1460 (4)	13.15	6.50

Galapagos Flora — A500

Designs: 600s, Jasminocereus thouarsii. 1000s, Cordia lutea lamarck. 2600s, Momordica charantia.

1998, July
1461	A500	600s multicolored	1.25	.60
1462	A500	1000s multicolored	2.00	1.00
1463	A500	2600s multicolored	5.50	2.75
		Nos. 1461-1463 (3)	8.75	4.35

Tourism — A501

Designs: 600s, St. Augustine Church, Quito. 800s, Monument to the Heroes of the Independence, Guayaquil. 2000s, Equator Monument, Quito. 2600s, Mojanda Lake.

1998, July
1464	A501	600s multi, vert.	1.25	.60
1465	A501	800s multi, vert.	1.60	.90
1466	A501	2000s multi	3.75	2.25
1467	A501	2600s multi	5.00	2.75
		Nos. 1464-1467 (4)	11.60	6.50

Emiliano Ortega Espinosa (1898-1974), Educator — A502

Perf. 13¼x13, 13x13¼
1998   Litho.   Wmk. 395
| 1468 | A502 | 400s shown | .90 | .50 |
| 1469 | A502 | 4700s Portrait, vert. | 11.50 | 8.25 |

Carlos Cueva Tamariz (1898-1991), Educator — A503

Perf. 13x13¼
1998, Nov.   Litho.   Wmk. 395
| 1470 | A503 | 2600s multicolored | 5.25 | 3.50 |

Radio Club of Guayaquil, 75th Anniv. — A504

Wmk. 395
1998, Nov. 20   Litho.   Perf. 13
| 1471 | A504 | 600s multicolored | 1.50 | .90 |

6th South American Games — A505

Designs: 400s, Mascot. 1000s, Games poster, tennis rackets, hurdles, sailing, hammer throw, bowling, boxing. 2600s, Mascot, parallel bars, wrestling, judo, fencing, running, swimming, shooting, cycling.

1998
1472	A505	400s multicolored	1.25	.50
1473	A505	1000s multicolored	2.00	1.00
1474	A505	2600s multicolored	5.50	2.75
		Nos. 1472-1474 (3)	8.75	4.25

Paintings by Eduardo Kingman (1913-85) — A506

Designs: 600s, Ecuadoran Woman, vert. 800s, World Without Answers.

1998, Dec. 10
| 1475 | A506 | 600s multicolored | 1.40 | .65 |
| 1476 | A506 | 800s multicolored | 2.25 | 1.00 |

Manuela Sáenz (1797-1856), Mistress of Simon Bolívar — A507

1999, Jan. 19
| 1477 | A507 | 1000s multicolored | 2.25 | .95 |

America issue. Exists imperf. Value, $30.

Christmas — A508

Children's drawings: 1000s, Santa posting letters on tree. 2600s, People holding up giant letter, vert. 3000s, Santas parachuting with letters, nativity scene, tree, vert.

1998, Dec. 22
1478	A508	1000s multicolored	1.75	.95
1479	A508	2600s multicolored	5.00	2.50
1480	A508	3000s multicolored	5.25	2.75
		Nos. 1478-1480 (3)	12.00	6.20

Los Tayos Caves — A509

Design: 1000s, Man in cave, vert.

1999, Feb. 25   Litho.   Perf. 13
| 1481 | A509 | 1000s multi | 1.75 | .90 |
| 1482 | A509 | 2600s shown | 5.25 | 2.50 |

Napal, the Age of Wrath, by Oswaldo Guayasamin (1919-99) — A510

Wmk. 395
1999, May 12   Litho.   Perf. 13
| 1483 | A510 | 2000s multicolored | 4.50 | 2.10 |

Iberoamerica art exhibition.

Universal Day of Human Rights — A511

1999, May 28
| 1484 | A511 | 4000s multicolored | 7.75 | 4.50 |

Eloy Alfaro Superior Military College, Cent. — A512

5200s, Cannon, monument, flags, buildings. 9400s, Honor Guard, modern building.

1999, June 4
| 1485 | A512 | 5200s multicolored | 11.00 | 7.00 |
| 1486 | A512 | 9400s multicolored | 20.00 | 11.50 |

Puyo, 100th Anniv. — A513

Designs: a, Bromeliad. b, Ara chloroptera.

1999, June 2
| 1487 | A513 | 4000s Pair, #a.-b. | 15.00 | 10.00 |

Dr. Rafael Barahona Andrade (1827-98) — A514

Perf. 13¼x13
1999, June 17   Litho.   Wmk. 395
| 1488 | A514 | 5200s multi | 11.50 | 4.50 |

Generals — A515

Designs: 2000s, Manuel Antonio de Luzarraga y Echezurria (1776-1859). 4000s, Tomas Carlos Wright (1799-1868).

1999, Aug. 11   Perf. 13x13¼
| 1489-1490 | A515 | Set of 2 | 13.75 | 6.00 |

Galapagos Islands Flora and Fauna — A516

No. 1491, vert.: a, Phoenicopterus ruber. b, Buteo galapagoensis. c, Amblyrhynchus cristatus. d, Conolophus subcristatus. e, Opuntia galapageia. f, Pyrocephalus rubinus. g, Sula nebouxii. h, Sula dactylatra. i, Scalesia villosa. j, G. elephantopus abingdoni.
No. 1492: a, Brachycereus nesioticus. b, Dendroica petechia. c, Nannopterum harrisi. d, Tursiops truncatus. e, Pentaceraster cumingi. f, G. elephantopus porteri. g, Microlophus albemarlensis. h, Arctocephalus galapagoensis. i, Spheniscus mendiculus. j, Geospiza scandens.

Perf. 13x13¼, 13¼x13
1999, Sept. 3   Litho.   Wmk. 395
1491		Strip of 10	125.00	75.00
a.-j.	A516	7000s Any single	7.50	1.75
1492		Strip of 10	240.00	125.00
a.-j.	A516	15,000s Any single	16.00	5.00

Intl. Year of Older Persons — A517

Designs: No. 1493, 1000s, Hands of child and old person. No. 1494, 1000s, Emblem.

Perf. 13¼x13
1999, Sept. 22   Wmk. 395
| 1493-1494 | A517 | Set of 2 | 5.75 | 1.75 |

SOS Children's Villages, 50th Anniv. — A518

a, 2000s, Two children. b, 2000s, One child.

1999, Sept. 30
| 1495 | A518 | Pair, #a-b | 8.00 | 2.50 |

America Issue, A World Without Arms — A519

No. 1496: a, World map. b, Tree, bird, Earth.

Perf. 13¼x13
1999, Dec. 11   Litho.   Wmk. 395
| 1496 | A519 | 4000s Pair, #a-b | 15.00 | 10.00 |

ECUADOR

UPU, 125th
Anniv. — A520

Designs: 1000s, Ecuadorian Postal Service mascot, vert. 4000s, Dove with letter, vert. 8000s, UPU emblem.

1999, Dec. 11   Litho.   Wmk. 395   Perf. 13¼x12¾

1497	A520	1000s multi	1.10	.45
1498	A520	4000s multi	4.50	1.75
1499	A520	8000s multi	9.00	4.00
	Nos. 1497-1499 (3)		14.60	6.20

Ecuador as Secretary General of Permanent South Pacific Commission — A521

Design: León Dormido.

1999, Dec. 21   Litho.   Wmk. 395   Perf. 13x13¼

| 1500 | A521 | 7000s multi | 9.75 | 5.50 |

Machala Tourism — A522

Designs: No. 1501, Banana flower and city. No. 1502, vert.: a, Monument to banana plantation workers. b, City Hall.

1999, Dec. 28   Perf. 13¼x13, 13x13¼

| 1501 | A522 | 3000s multi | 4.25 | 1.60 |
| 1502 | A522 | 3000s Pair, #a-b | 8.50 | 3.25 |

EMELEC Soccer Team A523

No. 1503: a, Jorge Bolanos. b, Carlos Raffo. No. 1504, EMELEC team photo, 1957. No. 1505, Player, vert.

Perf. 13x13¼, 13¼x13
2000, Jan. 7   Litho.

1503	A523	1000s Pair, #a-b	4.25	2.25
1504	A523	2000s multi	4.25	1.50
1505	A523	2000s multi	4.25	1.50

Guayas Philanthropic Society, 150th Anniv. — A524

Designs: 1000s, Building. 2000s, Founder Juan Maria Martinez Coello. 4000s, Emblem.

Perf. 13¼x13
2000, Jan. 19   Litho.   Wmk. 395

| 1506-1508 | A524 | Set of 3 | 4.75 | 1.90 |

Dual Nationality Day — A525

2000, Jan. 24   Perf. 13¼x13

| 1509 | A525 | 7000s multi | 3.25 | 1.50 |

Cuenca, World Heritage Site — A526

No. 1510: a, Buildings. b, Puente Roto and Tomebamba River. c, Church bell gable, Concepcion Monastery. d, Cathedral and city skyline. e, San José Church.

2000, Mar. 24   Perf. 13¼x13

| 1510 | | Strip of 5 | 8.25 | 6.00 |
| a.-e. | A526 | 4000s Any single | .85 | .50 |

Nicolas Lapentti, Tennis Player — A527

2000, Mar. 26   Perf. 13¼x13¼

| 1511 | A527 | 8000s multi | 3.25 | 1.50 |

Birds — A528

No. 1512: a, Diglossa cyanea. b, Oreotrochilus chimborazo. c, Trogon personatus. d, Colibri coruscans. e, Atlapetes rufinucha.

2000, Apr. 7

| 1512 | | Horiz. strip of 5 | 15.25 | 11.50 |
| a.-e. | A528 | 8000s Any single | 3.00 | 1.50 |

Relocation of Riobamba, Bicent. — A529

Designs: No. 1513, Mt. Chimborazo. No. 1514: a, Riobamba Cathedral. b, Statue of Pedro Vicente Maldonado.

2000, Apr. 13   Perf. 13¼x13, 13x13¼

| 1513 | A529 | 8000s multi | 3.25 | 1.00 |
| 1514 | A529 | 8000s Pair, #a-b | 5.75 | 3.50 |

Gen. Eloy Alfaro, Founder of Natl. Music Conservatory — A530

2000, Apr. 19   Perf. 13¼x13¼

| 1515 | A530 | 10,000s multi | 4.25 | 1.60 |

Natl. Music Conservatory, cent.

Climbing of Mt. Everest by Ivan Vallejo Ricaurte — A531

2000, May 23   Perf. 13¼x13

| 1516 | A531 | 8000s multi | 5.50 | 2.00 |

100 Cents=1 Dollar

Dolores Sucre Fiscal College, 50th Anniv. — A532

Perf. 13x13¼
2000   Litho.   Wmk. 395

| 1517 | A532 | 32c multi | 3.00 | 1.25 |

Training Ship Guayas — A533

2000, July 5   Perf. 13x13¼

| 1518 | A533 | 68c multi | 2.25 | .80 |

Imperf
Size: 90x110mm

| 1519 | A533 | $1 multi | 7.25 | 3.25 |

Battle of Jambeli, 59th Anniv., Navy Day — A534

2000   Perf. 13¼x13

| 1520 | A534 | 16c multi | 1.80 | .25 |

Guayaquil Civic Renovation — A535

2000, July   Perf. 13x13¼

| 1521 | A535 | 84c multi | 7.75 | 3.75 |

Megaptera Novaeangliae A536

2000, Aug. 3   Perf. 13¼x13

| 1522 | A536 | 84c multi | 8.75 | 4.25 |

Imperf
Size: 90x110mm

| 1523 | A536 | $1 Two whales | 12.00 | 5.75 |

American and Caribbean Dog Show, Quito — A537

2000, Aug.   Perf. 13¼x13

| 1524 | A537 | 68c multi | 5.75 | 2.25 |

Guayaquil Tennis Club, 90th Anniv. — A538

2000, Aug.   Wmk. 395

| 1525 | A538 | 84c multi | 7.25 | 2.50 |

Alberto Spencer, Soccer Player — A539

2000   Perf. 13¼x13

| 1526 | A539 | 68c multi | 5.75 | 2.50 |

Imperf
Size: 69x99mm

| 1527 | A539 | $1 Spencer, crowd | 9.25 | 4.50 |

2000 Summer Olympics, Sydney — A540

Ecuadoran team emblem, Games emblem and: 32c Mascots. 68c, Runner Jefferson Perez Marchista. 84c, Weight lifter Boris Burov, Olympic flag, horiz.

2000, Sept.   Perf. 13¼x13, 13¼x13

| 1528-1530 | A540 | Set of 3 | 16.00 | 6.00 |

Salinas Yacht Club, 60th Anniv. — A541

Designs: No. 1531a, Lighthouse, vert. Nos. 1531b, 1533, Sailboat, vert. 68c, Sailboats, fisherman, waterskier, scuba diver.

2000, Oct.   Perf. 13x13¼

| 1531 | A541 | 32c Horiz. pair, #a-b | 5.50 | 2.75 |

Perf. 13¼x13

| 1532 | A541 | 68c multi | 6.50 | 2.75 |

Imperf
Size: 69x100mm

| 1533 | A541 | $1 multi | 9.25 | 4.50 |

Inter-American Development Bank, 40th Anniv. — A542

Designs: No. 1534a, 68c, No. 1536a, 25c, Salsipuedes Bridge, Felipe Herrera. No. 1534b, 68c, No. 1536b, 25c, Daule-Peripa Dam, Antonio Ortiz Mena. No. 1535a, 84c, No. 1536c, 25c, Enrique Iglesias, Ucubamba Water Treatment Plant. No. 1535b, 84c, No. 1536d, 25c, Bank emblem, History Museum, Quito.

2000, Oct. 27   Perf. 13¼x13
Horiz. Pairs, #a-b

| 1534-1535 | A542 | Set of 2 | 26.00 | 10.00 |

Rouletted 14 on 2 sides

| 1536 | A542 | 25c Sheet of 4, #a-d | 9.75 | 3.75 |

Size of Nos. 1536a-1536b, 75x48mm; Nos. 1536c-1536d, 75x42mm.

National Union of Journalists A543

2000, Nov. 1   Perf. 13¼x13

| 1537 | A543 | 16c multi | 1.60 | .25 |

Civil Registry, Cent. A544

No. 1538: a, People, flag, computer. b, Fingerprint, family.

2000, Oct. 27   Perf. 13¼x13

| 1538 | A544 | 68c Horiz. pair, #a-b | 11.75 | 4.50 |

Mama Negra Festival, Latacunga — A545

ECUADOR

No. 1539: a, Mama Negra with doll. b, Man in Moor King costume.

2000, Nov.   *Perf. 13x13¼*
1539 A545 32c Horiz. pair, #a-b   6.00 2.75
Imperf
Size: 100x68mm
1540 A545 $1 Mama Negra, doll, diff.   8.25 3.00

Ministry of Labor, 75th Anniv. — A546

2000, Nov. 15   *Perf. 13x13¼*
1541 A546 68c multi   5.50 2.25

Intl. Fruits and Flowers Festival, Ambato, 50th Anniv. — A547

No. 1542, horiz.: Design inside "0" of 50 — a, Tungurahua Volcano. b, Aerial view of Ambato.
No. 1544, horiz.: Design inside "0" of 50 — a, Flower. b, Fruit.

2000, Nov.   *Perf. 13¾*
1542 A547 32c Vert. pair, #a-b   5.50 2.10
1543 A547 84c shown   7.50 2.75
1544 A547 84c Vert. pair, #a-b   15.50 6.00
   Nos. 1542-1544 (3)   28.50 10.85
Imperf
Size: 68x100mm
1545 A547 $1 Ambato   8.25 3.00

Christmas — A548

Children's art by — No. 1546, 68c: a, Giannina Rhor Isaias. b, Josue Remache Romero.
No. 1547, 84c: a, Maria Cedeño Bazurtto. b, Juan Alban Salazar.
$1, Walther Carvache.

2000, Dec. 15   *Perf. 13¼x13*
   Horiz. Pairs, #a-b
1546-1547 A548 Set of 2   26.00 11.00
Imperf
Size: 100x69mm
1548 A548 $1 multi   8.25 3.00

Expoflores Flower Producer and Exporter Association — A549

2000   *Perf. 13x13¼*
1549 A549 68c multi   5.75 2.50

Man's Chapel, Guayasamin A550

2000   *Perf. 13¼x13*
1550 A550 16c multi   1.80 .25

Spanish Chamber of Commerce in Ecuador, 80th Anniv. — A551

2000, Dec.   *Perf. 13x13¼*
1551 A551 16c multi   1.80 .25

Intl. Volunteers Year — A552

2000   *Wmk. 395*
1552 A552 16c multi   1.80 .25

Restoration of Bolivar Theater, Quito — A553

Designs: 16c, Piano, banquet room. 32c, Stage, orchestra, horiz.

2000, Dec.   *Perf. 13x13¼, 13¼x13*
1553-1554 A553 Set of 2   6.00 1.75

Spondylus Princeps — A554

2000, Dec. 16   *Perf. 13¾*
1555 A554 84c multi   7.25 3.00
Imperf
Size: 69x99mm
1556 A554 $1 multi   8.25 3.50

America Issue, Fight Against AIDS A555

No. 1557: a, Strands. b, Earth.

2000   *Perf. 13x13¼*
1557 A555 84c Horiz. pair, #a-b   16.00 7.50

Guayas Province Red Cross, 90th Anniv. — A556

2000   *Perf. 13¼x13*
1558 A556 16c multi   1.80 .60

Guayas Sports Federation, 78th Anniv. — A557

2000, Dec.   *Perf. 13x13¼*
1559 A557 16c multi   1.80 .60

Landscapes A557a

Designs: No. 1559A, 16c, Andean region. No. 1559B, 16c, Pacific coast. 32c, Tourism emblem. 68c, Amazonia. 84c, Galápagos Islands.

Perf. 13¼x12¾
2001, Jan. 24   *Litho.*   *Wmk. 395*
1559A A557a 16c multi   1.80 .60
1559B A557a 16c multi   1.80 .60
1559C A557a 32c multi   3.75 1.10
1559D A557a 68c multi   7.00 2.40
1559E A557a 84c multi   7.00 2.40
   Nos. 1559A-1559E (5)   21.35 7.10

Guayas Soccer Team, 50th Anniv. — A558

2001, Mar. 8   *Perf. 13¼x13*
1560 A558 68c multi   5.75 2.50

Census — A558a   Census — A558b

Perf. 12¾x13¼
2001, Mar. 12   *Litho.*   *Wmk. 395*
1560A A558a 68c multi   5.00 4.50
1560B A558b 68c multi   5.00 4.50
   c.   Horiz. pair, #1560A-1560B   11.50 11.50

Dr. Raúl Clemente Huerta — A559

2001, Apr. 4   *Perf. 13¼x13*
1561 A559 68c multi   6.75 2.75

Dr. Antonio J. Quevedo, Birth Cent. — A560

2001, Apr. 5   *Litho.*
1562 A560 84c multi   8.00 3.25

Military Geographic Institute — A560a

No. 1562A: b, Soldier, building. c, Computer, printing press.

Perf. 13¼x12¾
2001, Apr. 11   *Litho.*   *Wmk. 395*
1562A A560a 68c Vert. pair, #b-c   13.00 6.00

Automobile Club of Ecuador, 50th Anniv. — A561

2001, May 15   *Wmk. 395*
1563 A561 84c multi   8.00 3.25

San Francisco de Peleusí Church, Azogues — A561a

Perf. 12¾x13¼
2001, May   *Litho.*   *Wmk. 395*
1563A A561a 84c multi   8.00 3.25

Women's Training Institute — A562

2001, Apr. 10   *Perf. 13x13¼*
1564 A562 84c multi   8.00 3.25

Intl. Women's Day — A563

No. 1565: a, Woman, child, corn. b, Woman, emblem.

2001, Apr. 2   *Perf. 13¼x13*
1565 A563 84c Vert. pair, #a-b   16.00 6.25

Secular Education at Manuela Cañizares University, Cent. — A564

2001, Mar. 29   *Wmk. 395*
1566 A564 84c multi   8.00 3.25

Ecuador Merchant Marines, Cent. — A565

2001, Jan. 2001   *Perf. 13x13¼*
1567 A565 16c multi   1.80 .60

Ambato Technical University, 32nd Anniv. — A566

No. 1568: a, Building. b, Painting.

2001   *Perf. 13¼x13*
1568 A566 32c Vert. pair, #a-b   8.25 2.75

Galapagos Islands Scenes A567

No. 1569: a, Española Island (shown). b, San Cristobal Island. c, Bartolome Island. d,

ECUADOR

Española Island, diff. e, Bartolome and Santiago Islands.
$1, Bird on rock, Española Island.

2001, Feb. 17   **Perf. 13¾**
1569   Horiz. strip of 5   10.25 3.00
a.-e.   A567 16c Any single   1.00 .40

Imperf
Size: 100x70mm
1570 A567 $1 multi   9.75 4.00

Alexander von Humboldt (1769-1859), Naturalist — A568

Perf. 13x13¼
2001, June 14   **Litho.**   **Wmk. 395**
1571 A568 84c multi   7.25 3.00

Ecuadorian Atomic Energy Commission — A568a

2001, Aug. 3   **Litho.**   **Perf. 12¾x13¼**
1571A A568a 70c multi   6.50 2.75

Lebanese Union, 80th Anniv. — A569

No. 1572: a, Building and emblem. b, Emblem.

2001, Aug. 30   **Perf. 13¼x13**
1572 A569 16c Horiz. pair, #a-b   4.00 1.50

Manta Port Authority A570

No. 1573: a, Emblem. b, Ships in port.

2001, Sept. 28
1573 A570 68c Horiz. pair, #a-b   11.75 5.00

Esmereldas Province Tourism — A571

No. 1574: a, Beach. b, Musicians and dancers on beach.

2001
1574 A571 86c Horiz. pair, #a-b   14.50 6.25

Latin American Writers A572

No. 1575: a, Claudia Lars (1899-1974), Salvadoran poet. b, Federico Proaño (1848-94), Ecuadoran journalist.

2001, Aug. 28   **Perf. 13¼x13¼**
1575 A572 86c Horiz. pair, #a-b   17.50 6.75

Andean Condor Preservation — A573

No. 1576: a, Condor and chick. b, Condor heads, FRAPZOO emblem.
$1, Condor in flight, FRAPZOO emblem.

2001, July 23   **Perf. 13x13¼**
1576 A573 86c Horiz. pair, #a-b   15.00 6.25

Imperf
Size: 68x99mm
1577 A573 $1 multi   9.00 3.75

Ecuador — Peru Peace Accords — A574

No. 1578: a, Map of Ecuador and Peru. b, Soldier. c, Flags of military obeservers. d, Amazon River. e, Men in field.

2001, May 22   **Perf. 13¼x13**
1578   Horiz. strip of 5   32.50 16.00
a.-e.   A574 68c Any single   5.00 2.50

Archidona Canton — A575

No. 1579: a, Phragmipedium orchid. b, Saimiri sciureus. c, B. macrophylla. d, Church. e, Kichwa Indian family.

2001, Apr. 28   **Perf. 13¼x13¼**
1579   Vert. strip of 5   40.00 20.00
a.-e.   A575 84c Any single   8.00 4.00

Ecotourism in Baños — A576

No. 1580: a, Orchid. b, Basilica, Baños. c, Tungurahua Volcano. d, Pailon del Diablo Waterfall. e, Statue of Virgin of Rosario de Agua Santa.
$1, Pailon del Diablo Waterfall, orchid.

2001   **Perf. 13¼x13**
1580   Horiz. strip of 5   35.00 17.50
a.-e.   A576 86c Any single   6.50 3.25

Imperf
Size: 68x99mm
1581 A576 $1 multi   9.00 3.75

Guayas Educational Journalists Association, 30th Anniv. — A577

Perf. 13¼x13¼
2001, Oct. 15   **Litho.**   **Wmk. 395**
1582 A577 16c multi   1.80 .60

Foundation for Development of Cattle Ranching, 15th Anniv. — A578

2001, Aug. 15   **Perf. 13x13¼**
1583 A578 16c multi   1.80 .60

City Gates, Loja — A579

2001   **Perf. 13¼x13**
1584 A579 32c multi   3.20 1.25

Quito Municipal District Directorate of Security — A580

2001, Nov. 26
1585 A580 68c multi   5.75 2.50

Salvador Bustamante Celi (1876-1935), Musician — A581

2001
1586 A581 68c multi   6.50 2.75

Marcel Laniado de Wind (1927-98), First Pres. of Natl. Modernization Council — A582

2001, Aug. 6   **Perf. 13¼x13¼**
1587 A582 70c multi   6.50 2.75

Bernardino Cardinal Echeverria (1912-2000) — A583

2001, Nov. 14
1588 A583 84c multi   8.00 3.25

José Joaquin Olmedo (1780-1847), Statesman and Poet — A584

2001, Nov. 8
1589 A584 84c multi   8.00 3.25

El Angel Ecological Reserve — A585

No. 1590: a, Paja de Paramo. b, Fraileján.

2001   **Perf. 13¼x13**
1590 A585 16c Horiz. pair, #a-b   3.50 1.40

Yahuarcocha Race Track — A586

No. 1591: a, Race track and lake. b, Lake.

2001, Nov. 30
1591 A586 68c Horiz. pair, #a-b   11.75 5.00

World Food Day A587

No. 1592: a, Wheat ears. b, Food baskets.

2001, Nov. 5
1592 A587 84c Horiz. pair, #a-b   16.00 6.25

Art of Voroshilov Bazante — A588

No. 1593: a, Spatial composition. b, Abstract, artists name at LR. c, Urban landscape. d, Abstract, diff. "Abstracto" at UL, denomination at LL. e, Abstract, denomination at LR.

2001, Nov.
1593   Horiz. strip of 5   40.00 20.00
a.-e.   A588 84c Any single   7.00 3.50

Wilson Popenoe Private Foundation — A589

2001, Nov. 19   **Litho.**   **Perf. 13¼x13**
1594 A589 16c multi   1.80 .60

FAO Food Program — A590

2001, Aug. 15
1595 A590 84c multi   8.00 3.25

Rotary District 4400, 75th Anniv. — A591

2001, Nov. 30   **Perf. 13¼x13¼**
1596 A591 84c multi   8.00 3.25

Pres. Camilo Ponce Enriquez (1912-76) — A592

2001
1597 A592 84c multi   8.00 3.25

Pedro Vicente Maldonado (1702-48), Geographer — A593

2001, Dec. 12
1598 A593 84c multi   8.00 3.25

Otonga Foundation A595

No. 1599: a, Frog on branch. b, Mustela frenata.

2001, Oct. 31
1599 A595 16c Horiz. pair, #a-b   3.50 1.40

Tourism in Zaruma A596

No. 1600: a, Virgen del Carmen. b, Orchid.

2001, Dec. 12   **Perf. 13¼x13**
1600 A596 68c Horiz. pair, #a-b   11.50 5.00

Radio HCJB, 70th Anniv. A597

ECUADOR

No. 1601: a, Microphone. b, Announcer.

2001, Dec. 21
1601 A597 68c Horiz. pair, #a-b 11.50 5.00

Tennis — A598

No. 1602: a, Davis Cup. b, K. Lapentti, G. Lapentti, L.A. Morejón, A. Intriago and R. Viver. c, Francisco Guzman and Miguel Olvera. d, Pancho Segura. e, Andres Gomez.

2001, Nov. 1
1602   Horiz. strip of 5   30.00 15.00
a.-e. A598 68c Any single   5.00   2.50

Church Paintings of Wilfrido Martínez A599

No. 1603: a, San Francisco (artist's name is vert.). b, Guapulo. c, San Francisco (artist's name is horiz.). d, La Compania. e, El Rosario.

2002, Apr. 9   *Perf. 13¾*
1603   Horiz. strip of 5   35.00 17.50
a.-e. A599 90c Any single   7.00   3.50

First Judicial Summit of the Americas, Quito — A600

                          Perf. 13¼x13
2002, Jan. 8 Litho.   Wmk. 395
1604 A600 68c multi   5.75   2.50

Union Club, Guayaquil — A601

2002, Apr. 25   *Perf. 13x13¼*
1605 A601 90c multi   8.00   2.75

South American Soccer Confederation — A602

Designs: 25c, Confederation Pres. Nicolás Leoz. 40c, Confederation emblem, soccer players. 70c, Emblem of Emelec team.

2002, Jan. 29
1606-1608 A602 Set of 3   12.00   5.00

World Conservation Union — A603

Designs: 70c, Fish, man's head. 85c, Leopard, man, horiz.
$1, Bird, animals, women and children, horiz.

2002, Feb. 21 *Perf. 13x13¼, 13¼x13*
1609-1610 A603 Set of 2   13.00   5.75
Imperf
Size: 100x70mm
1611 A603 $1 multi   9.00   3.75

UN High Commissioner for Refugees — A604

Designs: 70c, Emblem. 85c, Child.
$1, Refugees carrying belongings, horiz.

2002, Feb. 28   *Perf. 13x13¼*
1612-1613 A604 Set of 2   13.00   5.75
Imperf
Size: 100x70mm
1614 A604 $1 multi   9.00   3.75

Ecuadorian Educational Credit and Scholarship Institute — A605

No. 1615: a, Student using microscope. b, Emblem.

2002, Apr. 30   *Perf. 13x13¼*
1615 A605 25c Horiz. pair, #a-b 4.00 1.50

Cuenca Soccer Team A606

No. 1616: a, Team photo. b, Emblem, player dribbling.

2002, Apr. 19   *Perf. 13x13¼*
1616 A606 25c Horiz. pair, #a-b 4.00 1.50

Imbabura Province History A607

No. 1617: a, Building. b, Statue.

2002, Mar. 27   *Perf. 13x13¼*
1617 A607 40c Horiz. pair, #a-b 7.50 3.00

Crucita A608

No. 1618: a, Parachutist with sun on horizon. b, Prachutist above beach.

2002, Mar. 28   *Perf. 13¼x13*
1618 A608 40c Horiz. pair, #a-b 7.50 3.00

Mountains — A609

No. 1619: a, Mt. Altar (trees in foreground). b, Mt. Chimborazo. c, Mt. Carihuayrazo. d, Mt. Altar (lake in foreground). e, Mt. Cubillin.

2002, Apr. 19
1619   Horiz. strip of 5   35.00 17.50
a.-e. A609 90c Any single   6.00   3.00

Endangered Frogs — A610

No. 1620: a, Atelopus bomolochos. b, Atelopus longirostris. c, Atelopus pachydermus. d, Atelopus arthuri. e, Atelopus sp.
$1, Atelopus ignescens.

2002, Mar. 25   *Perf. 13¼x13*
1620   Horiz. strip of 5   35.00 17.50
a.-e. A610 $1.05 Any single 6.00   3.00
Imperf
Size: 100x70mm
1621 A610 $1 multi   10.50   9.00

National Anti-narcotics Police — A611

No. 1622: a, Policeman and dog. b, Emblem.

              Perf. 13x13¼
2002, Apr. 23 Litho.   Wmk. 395
1622 A611 40c Horiz. pair, #a-b 7.50 3.00

2002 World Cup Soccer Championships, Japan and Korea — A612

Designs: 90c, Ecuadorian Soccer Federation emblem, vert. $1.05, $2, Emblem, team photo, players in action.

2002, Apr. 28 *Perf. 13x13¼, 13¼x13*
1623-1624 A612 Set of 2   10.50   5.00
Imperf
Size: 100x70mm
1625 A612 $2 multi   10.50   5.00

Dr. Servio Aguirre Villamagua, Forest Conservationist — A613

No. 1626: a, Aguirre. b, Plant.

2002, May 22   *Perf. 13¼x13*
1626 A613 40c Horiz. pair, #a-b 4.75 2.00

Food and Agriculture Organization in Ecuador, 50th Anniv. — A614

2002, May 30
1627 A614 $1.05 multi   5.75   2.50

Galapagos Islands Fauna — A615

No. 1628: a, Grapsus grapsus. b, Conolophus subcristatus.
No. 1629, vert.: a, Sula sula websteri. b, Phoenicopterus ruber.
No. 1630, Amblyrhynchus cristatus.
No. 1631, vert.: a, Pair of Zalophus californianus wollebacki. b, One Zalophus californianus wollebacki.
No. 1632, Sula nebouxii excisa, vert.
No. 1633, vert.: a, Sula dactylatra granti. b, Emblem of Iberoamerican Summit on Tourism and Environment.
$2, Bird, tourists, tourist ship.

2002, May 31 *Perf. 13¼x13, 13x13¼*
1628 A615   25c Horiz. pair,
                 #a-b   3.75   1.50
1629 A615   40c Horiz. pair,
                 #a-b   5.00   2.00
1630 A615   90c multi   7.75   3.00
1631 A615   90c Horiz. pair,
                 #a-b   11.50   4.50
1632 A615 $1.05 multi   6.25   2.50
1633 A615 $1.05 Horiz. pair,
                 #a-b   13.00   5.00
Nos. 1628-1633 (6)   47.25 18.50

Imperf
Size: 100x68mm
1634 A615 $2 multi   20.00 10.00

Ministry of Foreign Relations — A616

2002, June 5   *Perf. 13x13¼*
1635 A616 90c multi   4.75   2.25

Army Polytechnic School, 80th Anniv. — A617

2002, June 13   *Perf. 13¼x13*
1636 A617 25c multi   2.00   .90

Military Engineers, Cent. — A618

Designs: No. 1637, 40c, Castle of Engineering. No. 1638, 40c, Castle of Engineering, Military engineers in action, vert.
$2, Castle of Engineering, engineers in action, emblems of military groups.

              Perf. 13¼x13, 13x13¼
2002, June 19
1637-1638 A618 Set of 2   5.00   2.00
Imperf
Size: 100x68mm
1639 A618 $2 multi   10.50   4.50

Dr. Alfredo Pérez Guerrero (1901-66), Academic — A619

2002, July 4   *Perf. 13x13¼*
1640 A619 25c multi   2.00   .90

20th Anniv. of Ecuador's Second Place Finish In World Taekwondo Championships A620

2002, July 18   *Perf. 13¼x13*
1641 A620 40c multi   2.50   1.00

Orellana Province A621

No. 1642: a, Three native men. b, Man in tree.

2002, July 30   Wmk. 395
1642 A621 25c Horiz. pair, #a-b 4.00 1.50

CARE in Ecuador, 40th Anniv. A622

No. 1643: a, Two children. b, Boy.

2002, July 30   *Perf. 13x13¼*
1643 A622 90c Horiz. pair, #a-b 10.50 4.50

ECUADOR

Macará Region — A623

2002, Aug. 10   **Perf. 13¼x13**
1644 A623 40c multi   2.50   1.00

Intl. Organization for Migration, 50th Anniv. — A624

2002, Aug. 18   **Perf. 13x13¼**
1645 A624 $1.05 multi   5.75   2.50

Quito Philharmonic Society, 50th Anniv. — A625

2002, Aug. 29
1646 A625 25c multi   2.00   .90

Comptroller General, 75th Anniv. — A625a

Perf. 13x13¼
2002, Sept. 26   **Litho.**   **Wmk. 395**
1646A A625a 40c multi   2.50   1.00

Second World Meeting of Mountain People — A626

No. 1647 — Emblem of World Meeting and: a, Mountain. b, Group of people. c, Houses in valley. d, Town. e, Other emblems.

2002, Sept. 18
1647   Horiz. strip of 5   31.00 15.00
  a.-e. A626 90c Any single   6.00   3.00

Pujili Dancer — A627

Perf. 13x13¼
2002, Oct. 14   **Litho.**   **Wmk. 395**
1648 A627 $1.05 multi   5.75   2.50

Paintings of Milton Estrella Gavidia — A628

No. 1649 — Various paintings with background colors of: a, Blue violet. b, Brown violet. c, Olive green. d, Blue. e, Gray lilac.

Wmk. 395
2002, May 17   **Litho.**   **Perf. 13¾**
1649   Horiz. strip of 5   31.00 15.00
  a.-e. A628 90c Any single   6.00   3.00

Paintings of Leonardo Hidalgo — A629

No. 1650: a, La Dolorosa. b, El Hombre Cargando su Fruto. c, Frida Kahlo. d, El Hombre Fuerte del Mar. e, Jesus.

Wmk. 395
2002, Oct. 3   **Litho.**   **Perf. 13¾**
1650   Horiz. strip of 5   26.00 13.00
  a.-e. A629 90c Any single   4.50   2.25

Pan-American Health Organization, Cent. — A630

2002, Dec. 2   **Perf. 13¼x12¾**
1651 A630 $1.05 multi   5.75   2.50

Lo Nuestro Art Exhibition — A631

No. 1652: a, Wall with six works of art. b, Walls with 16 works of art.

2002, Dec. 15
1652 A631 25c Horiz. pair, #a-b   3.25 1.25

Catholic University, 40th Anniv. — A632

2002, Dec. 18
1653 A632 40c multi   2.50   1.00

America Issue — UNESCO World Heritage Sites A633

No. 1654: a, Cupola of San Blas Church, Cuenca. b, Society of Jesus Church, Quito.

2002, Dec. 18   **Perf. 12¾x13¼**
1654 A633 25c Horiz. pair, #a-b   4.50 1.50
   Dated 2001.

America Issue — Youth, Education and Literacy — A634

No. 1655: a, Students and blackboard. b, Toddler and books.

2002, Dec. 18   **Perf. 13¼x12¾**
1655 A634 25c Horiz. pair, #a-b   4.00 1.50

Second Meeting of South American Presidents, Guayaquil — A635

No. 1656: a, Meeting emblem. b, Emblem, presidents and flags.

2003, Jan. 13
1656 A635 $1.05 Horiz. pair, #a-b   10.50 4.00

Papal Benediction for Ecuadorian Emigrants — A636

2003, Jan. 24   **Perf. 12¾x13¼**
1657 A636 $1.05 multi   5.25   2.25
   Size: 68x100mm
   Imperf
1658 A636 $2 multi   10.50 4.50

World Vision — A637

2003, Feb. 6   **Perf. 12¾x13¼**
1659 A637 40c multi   2.25   .95

Intl. Women's Day — A638

2003, Mar. 8   **Wmk. 395**
1660 A638 $1.05 multi   5.25   2.50

Agustin Cueva Vallejo (1820-73), Physician — A639

2003, Mar. 13   **Litho.**
1661 A639 40c multi   2.25   .95

Blasco Moscoso Cuesta, Founder of Pichincha Sports Writers Association — A640

2003, Mar. 14
1662 A640 25c multi   1.75   .75

Cuenca Artisan Products — A641

No. 1663: a, Azuay University domes. b, Tinware. c, Jewelry. d, Fireworks. e, Saddles.
No. 1664: a, Engraving. b, Metallurgy. c, Baskets. d, Embroidery. e, Ceramics.
$2, Assorted products.

2003, Mar. 27   **Perf. 13¼x12¾**
1663   Horiz. strip of 5   7.00 3.50
  a.-e. A641 25c Any single   1.00   .50
1664   Horiz. strip of 5   27.00 13.50
  a.-e. A641 $1.05 Any single   5.00   2.50
   Size: 100x68mm
   Imperf
1665 A641 $2 multi   10.50 4.50

Flora and Fauna — A642

No. 1666: a, Curculionidae. b, Lycidae. c, Acridoidea. d, Arachnidae. e, Liliacea.

2003, Apr. 4   **Perf. 13¼x12¾**
1666   Horiz. strip of 5   26.00 13.00
  a.-e. A642 $1.05 Any single   4.50   2.25

Military Geographic Institute, 75th Anniv. — A643

Designs: No. 1667, 40c, No. 1669, $2, Painting by Eduardo Kingman. No. 1668, 40c, Institute emblem, vert.

Perf. 13¼x12¾, 12¾x13¼
2003, Apr. 11
1667-1668 A643 Set of 2   4.50 1.75
   Size: 100x68mm
   Imperf
1669 A643 $2 multi   10.50 4.50

Galápagos Marine Reserve — A644

Designs: 40c, Stylized butterfly.
No. 1671, $1.05, horiz.: a, Sphyrna lewini. b, Chelonia mydas agassisi.
No. 1672, $1.05, horiz.: a, Xanthichthys mento. b, Zanclus cornutus.
$2, Tubastrea coccinea, horiz.

Perf. 12¾x13¼, 13¼x12¾
2003, May 9
1670 A644 40c multi   2.00   .90
   Horiz. Pairs, #a-b
1671-1672 A644 Set of 2   21.00 10.50
   Size: 100x68mm
   Imperf
1673 A644 $2 multi   10.50 5.25

Intl. Tourism Trade Fair of Ecuador — A645

No. 1674: a, Monkey in tree. b, Birds. c, Embroidery. d, Mountain. e, Hat seller on beach.

2003, May 14   **Perf. 13¼x12¾**
1674   Vert. strip of 5   7.50 3.75
  a.-e. A645 25c Any single   1.25   .65

Artifacts of Pre-Columbian Cultures — A646

No. 1675, 25c: a, Gold bell with monkey. b, Amphora.
No. 1676, 25c: a, Sculpture of a man. b, Three-footed pot.

Perf. 13x13¼
2003, May 16   **Litho.**   **Wmk. 395**
   Horiz. pairs, #a-b
1675-1676 A646 Set of 2   6.00 2.25

Central Bank of Ecuador — A647

No. 1677, vert.: a, Tolita Culture mask. b, Guayaquil Historic Park.
$1.05, Pumapungo Museum.

Perf. 13x13¼, 13¼x13
2003, June 5   **Litho.**
1677 A647 25c Horiz. pair, #a-b   2.00   .75
1678 A647 $1.05 multi   3.50   1.40

ECUADOR

Philately and Guayaquil — A648

No. 1679, horiz.: a, British consular cover to Veracruz with British stamp and cancel. b, Stampless cover.
No. 1680, horiz.: a, SCADTA first flight cover. b, French consular cover to Lima with French stamps and cancels.
$1.05, Philatelic magazines.
$2, Guayaquil Philatelic Club emblem, Ecuadoran stamps, horiz.

2003, July 22   Perf. 13¾
1679 A648   40c Vert. pair, #a-b   4.25 1.60
1680 A648   40c Vert. pair, #a-b   4.25 1.60
1681 A648 $1.05 multi   5.25 2.00
   Nos. 1679-1681 (3)   13.75 5.20
Size: 100x69mm
Imperf
1682 A648 $2 multi   9.25 4.50

Guayaquil Urban Renewal — A649

No. 1683: a, Punta Cerro Santa Ana. b, Plaza Colón. c, Malecón Gardens. d, Crystal Palace. e, Plaza de San Francisco.

2003, July 26   Perf. 13¼x13
1683   Horiz. strip of 5   22.00 11.00
a.-e. A649 90c Any single   4.00 2.00

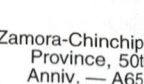

World Bird Festival — A650

Designs: No. 1684, $1.05, Geranoaetus melanoleucus. No. 1685, $1.05, Harpia harpyja, vert.

2003, Sept. 2   Perf. 13¼x13, 13x13¼
1684-1685 A650 Set of 2   10.50 4.50

Zamora-Chinchipe Province, 50th Anniv. — A651

No. 1686: a, Shown. b, Eira barbara. c, Boa constrictor. d, Tapirus terrestris. e, Psophia crepitans.

2003, Nov. 7   Perf. 13¼x13
1686   Vert. strip of 5   7.50 3.75
a.-e. A651 25c Any single   1.10 .55

America Issue — Flora and Fauna A652

No. 1687: a, Semnornis ramphastinus. b, Bomarea glaucescens.

2003, Nov. 1   Perf. 13x13¼
   Litho.   Wmk. 395
1687 A652 $1.05 Horiz. pair, #a-b   9.25 4.50

Selection of Quito as World Heritage Site, 25th Anniv. — A653

Churches: 40c, El Sagrario. No. 1689a, La Compañía de Jesus. No. 1689b, Santa Barbara. $1.05, San Francisco, vert.

2003, Nov. 1   Perf. 13¼x13, 13x13¼
1688 A653   40c multi   1.40 .60
1689 A653   90c Horiz. pair, #a-b   7.00 3.00
1690 A653 $1.05 multi   4.25 1.90
   Nos. 1688-1690 (3)   12.65 5.50

Christmas — A654

Children's art by: No. 1691a, Stephanie Pacheco. b, Sebastián Tejada. 40c, María Claudia Iturralde, vert. 90c, Luis Antonio Ortega. $1.05, Angel Andrés Castro, vert.

2003, Nov. 1
1691 A654   25c Horiz. pair, #a-b   2.25 .95
1692 A654   40c multi   1.80 .75
1693 A654   90c multi   4.25 1.75
1694 A654 $1.05 multi   4.50 1.90
   Nos. 1691-1694 (4)   12.80 5.35

Treasures of Guayaquil Municipal Museum — A655

No. 1695: a, Santiago de Guayaquil Act of Independence. b, Punaes ceremonial stone. c, Proclamation of Mariano Donoso. d, Tzantzas. e, Manteño-Huancavilca totem.

2003, Dec. 1   Perf. 13¼x13
1695   Horiz. strip of 5   10.50 5.25
a.-e. A655 40c Any single   1.75 .85

Selection of Galapagos Islands as World Heritage Site, 25th Anniv. — A656

No. 1696: a, Zalophus californianus wollebacki. b, Fregata minor palmerstoni. c, Sula nebouxxi excisa. d, Isla Bartolomé. e, Two Sula nebouxxi excisa shaped as "25."

2003, Nov. 26   Perf. 13x13¼
1696   Horiz. strip of 5   10.50 5.00
a.-e. A656 40c Any single   1.75 .85

Army Aviation Instruction, 50th Anniv. — A657

No. 1697, 40c: a, Mountain, airplanes, emblem. b, Airplane in flight, men on ground.
No. 1698, 40c, horiz.: a, Helicopter and soldiers. b, Airplanes, mountain, people.

2004, Jan. 21   Perf. 13¼x13, 13¼x13
   Horiz. pairs, #a-b
1697-1698 A657 Set of 2   6.75 3.00

Military Geographical Institute's Role in National Development A658

2004, Apr. 14   Perf. 13¼x13
1699 A658 $1.05 multi   4.50 1.90

Commander Rafael Morán Valverde, Military Hero — A659

2004, Apr. 5   Perf. 13x13¼
1700 A659 $1.05 multi   4.50 1.90

Intl. Philately Day A660

No. 1701: a, Ecuador #2, Greece #1. b, Cover with six stamps.
$2, Various stamps, tongs, magnifying glass, stamp catalogues.

2004, May 6   Perf. 13¼x13
1701 A660 75c Horiz. pair, #a-b   7.50 3.00
Imperf
Size: 100x68mm
1702 A660 $2 multi   7.50 3.75

Ecuadorian Volleyball Federation — A661

Perf. 13x13¼
2004, May 27   Litho.   Wmk. 395
1703 A661 75c multi   3.75 1.50

2004 Miss Universe Pageant — A662

2004, May 29   Perf. 13¾
1704 A662 75c multi   3.75 1.50

Sculpture by Mario Tapia — A663

No. 1705: a, Adolescencia. b, Beato Chaminade. c, Delfin de Galapagos. d, Pelicano. e, Homenaje a Carlo Vidano.
$2, Similar to No. 1705b.

2004, June 1   Perf. 13¼x13
1705   Horiz. strip of 5   20.00 8.00
a.-e. A663 90c Any single   2.50 1.25
Imperf
Size: 100x69mm
1706 A663 $2 multi   10.50 4.50

Pedro Vicente Maldonado (1704-48), Cartographer — A664

2004, June 25   Perf. 13x13¼
1707 A664 90c multi   3.75 1.50

Dr. Agustín Cueva Tamariz (1903-79) — A665

2004, June 30   Litho.
1708 A665 90c multi   3.75 1.50

34th General Assembly of the Organization of American States — A666

2004, July 4   Wmk. 395
1709 A666 75c multi   3.75 1.50

Dr. Angel Felicísmo Rojas (b. 1909), Writer — A667

2004, July 11
1710 A667 50c multi   2.50 1.00

Ecuadoran and Spanish Postal Money Orders — A668

2004, Aug. 3   Perf. 13¼x13
1711 A668 $1.05 multi   4.50 1.90

2004 Summer Olympics, Athens — A669

No. 1712 — 2004 Summer Olympics emblem, Ecuadoran Olympic Committee emblem and, a, 2004 Olympics mascots. b, Alexandra Escobar Guerrero.

2004, Aug. 3   Perf. 13x13¼
1712 A669 $1.05 Horiz. pair, #a-b   9.25 3.75

Ecuador Orchid Association, 30th Anniv. — A670

Designs: 25c, Cattleya maxima. $1.05, Epidendrum bracteolatum.

2004, Sept. 30
1713-1714 A670 Set of 2   5.75 2.50

Guayaquil Symphony Orchestra — A671

Perf. 13x13¼
2004, Nov. 19   Litho.   Wmk. 395
1715 A671 90c multi   3.75 1.50

ECUADOR

Christmas — A672

Children's art: 40c, Christmas stocking with envelopes. $1.05, Santa Claus giving letter to Christmas tree, horiz.

2004, Dec. 12   *Perf. 13x13¼, 13¼x13*
1716-1717   A672   Set of 2   6.00   2.50

America Issue - Environmental Protection — A673

Designs: 40d, Buddha and trees. $1.05, Mother Earth.

2004, Dec. 23   *Perf. 13x13¼*
1718-1719   A673   Set of 2   6.00   2.50

Galapagos Islands Fauna — A674

Designs: 40c, Chelonoidis abingdonii. 90c, Amblyrhynchus cristatus, vert. $2.15, Sula granti. $3, Fregata magnificens. $2, Creagrus furcatus, vert.

2005, Feb. 18   *Perf. 13¼x13, 13x13¼*
1720-1723   A674   Set of 4   28.00   12.00

Imperf.
Size: 68x98mm
1724   A674 $2 multi   9.25   3.75

El Mercurio Newspaper, 80th Anniv. — A675

Designs: $1.25, Masthead. $2, Dr. Nicanor Merchan Bermeo, newspaper co-founder. $2.25, Miguel Merchan Ochoa.

2005, Mar. 4   *Perf. 13¼x13, 13x13¼*
1725-1727   A675   Set of 3   23.00   11.00

Tourism — A676

2005, Mar. 22   *Perf. 13¼x13*
1728   A676 $3.75 multi   14.00   7.00

Ecuadorian Chess Federation, 25th Anniv. — A677

2005, Apr. 1   *Perf. 13¼x13*
1729   A677 $1.25 multi   5.25   2.50

Ecuadorian Olympic Academy, 25th Anniv. — A678

Perf. 13x13¼
2005, June 20   *Litho.*   *Wmk. 395*
1730   A678 $1.25 shown   5.25   2.50

Imperf.
Size: 69x100mm
1731   A678 $2 Emblems   9.25   4.50

Rotary International, Cent. — A679

Rotary emblem and: 40c, Man on Mt. Chimborazo. 90c, People on Mt. Cotopaxi. $2, Man on Mt. Shisha Pangma, Nepal.

2005, June 29   *Perf. 13¼x13*
1732-1734   A679   Set of 3   13.00   6.25

Guayaquil Conference, 183rd Anniv. — A680

No. 1735 — Guayaquil Philatelic Club emblem and: a, José de San Martín, Argentina #1. b, Simón Bolívar, Venezuela #1. $2, Bolívar, San Martín, monument.

2005, July 22   *Perf. 13¼x13*
1735   A680   90c Horiz. pair, #a-b   8.00   3.75

Imperf
Size: 98x68mm
1736   A680 $2 multi   9.25   4.50

Intl. Year of Books and Reading — A681

Perf. 13x13¼
2005, July 22   *Litho.*   *Wmk. 395*
1737   A681   25c multi   1.50   .60

Dr. Juan Isaac Lovato Vargas (1904-2001), Judge — A682

Perf. 13¼x13
2005, July 28   *Litho.*   *Wmk. 395*
1738   A682 $1.25 multi   6.25   3.00

Mountain and Eastern Cattleman's Association — A683

No. 1739 — Emblem and: a, Mountains. b, Head of cow.

2005, Aug. 4   *Perf. 13x13¼*
1739   A683   40c Horiz. pair, #a-b   3.50   3.00

University Sports League of Quito, 75th Anniv. — A684

No. 1740: a, University Sports League Stadium. b, 1969 University Sports League soccer team. c, Emblem. d, Children playing at school. e, Statue of emblem, League Country Club. $2, Soccer shirt, vert.

2005, Aug. 4   *Perf. 13¼x13*
1740   Horiz. strip of 5   9.25   4.00
a.-e.   A684 40c Any single   1.50   .75

Imperf.
Size: 68x98mm
1741   A684 $2 multi   9.25   4.50

15th Bolivarian Games, Armenia and Pereira — A685

2005, Aug. 8   *Perf. 13¼x13*
1742   A685   25c multi   1.50   .60

A686

Design: 1938 South American Swimming Champions, Trophy and Swimming Federation Emblem.

2005, Aug. 8   *Litho.*
1743   A686   25c multi   1.50   .60

First Ecuadoran victory in international sports competition.

Virgin of Cisne — A687

2005, Sept. 6   *Perf. 13¾*
1744   A687 $1.25 multi   6.25   3.00

History of the Ecuadoran Army — A688

No. 1745: a, Troops in Esmeraldas, 1916. b, Military school cadets, 1928. c, Cayambe Battalion. d, Arms and Grandsons of Gen. Eloy Alfaro. e, Imbabura Battalion. $2, Battle for emancipation of Guayaquil.

2005, Sept. 15   *Perf. 13¼x13*
1745   Horiz. strip of 5   9.25   4.00
a.-e.   A688 40c Any single   1.50   .75

Imperf.
Size: 98x67mm
1746   A688 $2 multi   9.25   4.50

Carchi Province Arms — A689

No. 1747: a, Tulcán Canton. b, Bolívar Canton.
No. 1748: a, Carchi Province. b, Huaca Canton. c, Mira Canton. d, Espejo Canton. e, Montúfar Canton.

2005, Sept. 26   *Perf. 13x13¼*
1747   Horiz. pair   3.50   1.50
a.-b.   A689 40c Either single   1.50   .75
1748   Horiz. strip of 5   8.75   3.75
a.-e.   A689 40c Any single   1.50   .75

Tourism A690

No. 1749: a, Cerro Santa Ana, Guayaquil. b, Esmereldas. c, Misahualli. d, Tsunki Shuar, Pastaza.
No. 1750: a, Cisne Church, Loja. b, Ingapirca Ruins. c, Seal, Galapagos Islands. d, Sea turtle, Galapagos Islands.

Perf. 13¼x13   *Wmk. 395*
2005, Sept. 26   *Litho.*
1749   A690   30c Block of 4, #a-d   6.00   2.50
1750   A690   40c Block of 4, #a-d   7.50   3.25

St. Mariana de Jesús Paredes y Flores — A691

2005, Oct. 19
1751   A691   25c multi   1.50   .60

Popes Reigning in 2005 A692

No. 1752: a, $1.25, Pope John Paul II (1920-2005). b, $2, Pope Benedict XVI.

2005, Oct. 19
1752   A692   Horiz. pair, #a-b   18.00   6.25

Cenepa War With Peru, 10th Anniv. A693

No. 1753: a, Mirage F1-JA airplanes. b, Cessna A-37B airplanes. c, Kfir-C2 airplanes. d, Lt. Col. Carlos Uscategui and airplane.

2005, Oct. 26
1753   A693 $1.25 Block of 4, #a-d   23.00   11.00

First Guayaquil to Cuenca Airmail Flight, 85th Anniv. — A694

No. 1754: a, 25c, Tail of Telegrafo I airplane, flight manager José Abel Castillo. b, $1, Front of Telegrafo I airplane, pilot Elia Liut.

2005, Nov. 12
1754   A694   Horiz. pair, #a-b   6.00   2.75

Ecuadorian Armed Forces in United Nations Peacekeeping Forces — A695

No. 1755: a, Female soldier. b, Two soldiers wearing helmets. c, Soldiers with flags. d, United Nations and Ecuadorian flags, beret of Peacekeeping forces.

2005, Nov. 25   *Perf. 13x13¼*
1755   A695   75c Block of 4, #a-d   13.00   6.00

ECUADOR

Christmas A696

No. 1756 — Children's drawings by: a, Pamela Alejandra Castillo Rocha. b, Kira Cedeño. c, Silvia Moran Burgos. d, Carol Garcia.

2005, Nov. 25
1756 A696 $1.25 Block of 4,
 #a-d   23.00 11.00

19th Cent. Watercolors of Ecuadorians A697

No. 1757: a, Water bearer. b, Indian governor's wife. c, Dancer. d, Cuenca Indian. e, Municipal council piper. f, Indian carrying skyrockets. g, Woman (Mina gigante). h, Majordomo. i, Society woman (Chola pinganilla). j, Street sweeper.

2005, Nov. 30   *Perf. 13¾*
1757   Block of 10   15.00 6.25
 a.-j. A697 25c Any single 1.20 .60

Publication of Don Quixote, 400th Anniv. — A698

No. 1758 — Drawings of Don Quixote and: a, Windmills. b, Tree.

2005, Dec. 7   *Perf. 13x13¼*
1758 A698 $2 Horiz. pair, #a-b 17.50 8.50

Colonial Religious Art A699

Colonial Religious Art A700

No. 1759: a, St. Joseph and Baby Jesus. b, Resurrected Christ. c, Virgin of Quito. d, St. Augustine.
No. 1760: $2, The Divine Shepherd.

2005, Dec. 9
1759 A699 40c Block of 4, #a-d 7.00 3.00

Souvenir Sheet
Imperf
1760 A700 $2 multi   9.25 4.50

El Comercio Newspaper, Cent. (in 2006) — A701

"100" and: No. 1761, Statue at LL, newspaper masthead. No. 1762a, Statue at LR. No. 1762b, Statue in "0." No. 1763, Statue in seal. No. 1764, Statue at LL, newspaper masthead, simulated perforations.

              Perf. 13¼x13
2006, Jan. 2   *Litho.*   *Wmk. 395*
1761 A701 40c multi   2.00   .85
1762 A701 40c Horiz. pair, #a-b 3.75 1.60
         Size: 55x35mm
              Perf. 13¾
1763 A701 50c multi   2.25 1.00
   Nos. 1761-1763 (3)   8.00 3.45
         Size: 100x69mm
              Imperf
1764 A701 $2 multi   8.25 4.00
         Dated 2006.

Quito Tourism — A702

2006, Jan. 11   *Perf. 13¼x13*
1765 A702 25c multi   1.50   .60
         Dated 2005.

35th Latin American and Caribbean Lions' Club Forum, Quito — A703

Color of oceans: 90c, White. $2, Orange.

2006, Jan. 19   *Perf. 13x13¼*
1766 A703 90c multi   4.25 2.00
         Size: 68x99mm
              Imperf
1767 A703 $2 multi   8.25 4.00

Biodiversity of Puyo — A704

Designs: $1, Cromacris sp. $1.20, Desmodus rotundus.

2006, Mar. 22   *Perf. 13¼x13*
1768-1769 A704 Set of 2   10.50 5.00

America Issue, Fight Against Poverty — A705

Various Pre-Columbian Guayasamin figurines: 40c, 80c, $1, $1.20.

2006, Feb. 12
1770-1773 A705 Set of 4   15.00 7.25

Benito Juarez (1806-72), President of Mexico — A706

2006, Mar. 21   *Perf. 13x13¼*
1774 A706 $1.20 multi   5.25 2.50

Manteña Raft — A707

2006, Mar. 23   *Perf. 13¼x13*
1775 A707 $1 multi   4.75 2.25

Straw Hat Makers — A708

Designs: No. 1776, 40c, Hat maker. No. 1777, 40c, Hat maker wearing hat, vert.

2006, Apr. 8   *Perf. 13¼x13, 13x13¼*
1776-1777 A708 Set of 2   4.25 1.90

Federation of University Students — A709

2006, Apr. 21   *Perf. 13x13¼*
1778 A709 30c multi   1.50   .60

Miracle of Colegio San Gabriel, Cent. — A710

2006, Apr. 21   *Wmk. 395*
1779 A710 80c multi   4.00 1.90

Ibarra, 400th Anniv. — A711

2006, Apr. 28   *Perf. 13¼x13*
1780 A711 20c shown   1.20   .25
         Size: 68x100mm
              Imperf
1781 A711 $2.50 Painting, diff. 11.25 5.50

Baltazara Calderon — A712

2005, May 16   *Perf. 13x13¼*
1782 A712 $1 multi   4.75 2.25

18th Cent. Military Uniforms — A713

No. 1783: a, Compañia Fija de Quito. b, Dragones de Quito. c, Infanteria de Quito. d, Dragones de Guayaquil (gray horse). e, Dragones de Guayaquil (brown horse).

2006, May 18   *Perf. 13¾*
1783   Horiz. strip of 5   5.50 2.10
 a.-e. A713 20c Any single   .90   .45

Mushrooms and Fauna of Podocarpus Park — A714

Designs: 20c, Basidiomicetes. 25c, Tremarctus ornatus. 90c, Harpya harpyja, vert.

           Perf. 13¼x13, 13x13¼
2006, May 22   *Litho.*   *Wmk. 395*
1784-1786 A714 Set of 3   9.75 3.00

Wolfgang Amadeus Mozart (1756-91), Composer — A715

2006, May 31   *Perf. 13¼x13*
1787 A715 20c multi   1.00   .25

UNICEF, 60th Anniv. — A716

Designs: 75c, Child, butterfly, and sun. $1, Children and books.

              Perf. 13¼x13
2006, June 1   *Litho.*   *Wmk. 395*
1788-1789 A716 Set of 2   12.50 4.00

Eloy Alfaro Military School — A717

2006, June 5
1790 A717 80c multi   4.00 1.90

Banco Pichincha, Cent. — A718

Designs: No. 1791, 1906 1-sucre banknote. No. 1792 — First bank building: a, Denomination at left. b, Denomination at right.

2006, June 8
1791 A718 40c shown   2.00   .90
1792 A718 40c Horiz. pair, #a-b 4.25 1.90

2006 World Cup Soccer Championships, Germany — A719

FIFA emblem and: 40c, World Cup. 80c, 2006 World Cup emblem. $1, Mascot. $1.20, World Cup and flags of competing countries.

              Perf. 13¼x13
2006, June 9   *Litho.*   *Wmk. 395*
1793-1796 A719 Set of 4   15.00 7.25

ECUADOR

World Cup Type of 2006
Perf. 13¼x13
2006, June 9 Litho. Wmk. 395
Stamps Without FIFA Emblem
With Inscription "COPA MONDIAL de la FIFA"

1796A	A719	40c Like #1793	23.00	23.00
1797	A719	80c Like #1794	7.50	7.50
1797A	A719	$1 Like #1795	9.75	9.75
1797B	A719	$1.20 Like #1795	11.50	11.50
		Nos. 1796A-1797B (4)	51.75	51.75

2006 Litho. Wmk. 395 Imperf.
Size: 60x40mm

Designs: No. 1797C, Like #1796. No. 1797D, Similar to #1796, but with scores of Ecuador team's first round victories.

1797C	A719	$2 multi	32.50	4.00
1797D	A719	$2 multi	32.50	4.00

A720

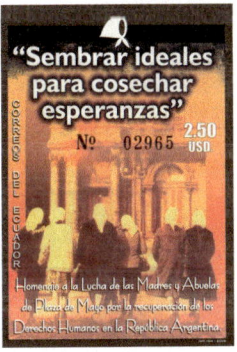
Plaza de Mayo Mothers of Argentina — A721

Perf. 13¼x13
2006, June 19 Litho. Wmk. 395
1798 A720 80c multi   4.00 1.90

Imperf
1799 A721 $2.50 multi   14.50 5.50

Machala Canton, 182nd Anniv. — A722

2006, June 20 Perf. 13¼x13
1800 A722 30c multi   1.50 .60

Machala Canton, 182nd Anniv. A723

Flags of 2006 World Cup Soccer Championship participants, FIFA emblem and: No. 1801, Flag of Ecuador. No. 1802, Soccer shoes and ball.

2006 Litho. Wmk. 395 Imperf.
1801 A723 $2 multi   10.50 4.00
1802 A723 $2 multi   10.50 4.00

2006 World Cup Soccer Championships, Germany.

Garibaldi Italian Assistance Society — A724

2006, July 7 Perf. 13x13¼
1803 A724 90c multi   4.25 2.00

Municipal Railroads — A725

Designs: No. 1804, $1, Steam locomotive. No. 1805, $1, Steam locomotive, vert.

Perf. 13¼x13, 13x13¼
2006, July 20 Litho. Wmk. 395
1804-1805 A725 Set of 2   8.50 8.00

Souvenir Sheet

Municipal Railroads — A726

Wmk. 395
2006, July 20 Litho. Imperf.
1806 A726 $2 multi   10.50 4.00

Simón Bolívar Experimental College A727

Bolívar A728

2006, July 25 Litho. Perf. 13x13¼
1807 A727 20c multi   1.00 .25

Imperf
1808 A728 $10 multi   52.00 20.00

Spondylus Shell Carvings in National Institute of Cultural Heritage — A729

Designs: 25c, Necklace. No. 1810, vert.: a, Figurine of trader. b, Figurine of fishermen in boat.

2006, July 26 Perf. 13¼x13, 13x13¼
1809 A729 25c multi   1.50 .75
1810 A729 $1 Horiz. pair, #a-b   8.75 8.00

Indian Postal Runner and Ecuador Post Emblem — A730

Background colors: 25c, White. 30c, Dark blue. 40c, Black. 60c, Beige. 80c, Olive green

2006, Aug. 5 Perf. 13x13¼
1811-1815 A730 Set of 5   13.00 5.00

Ecuadorian Olympic Committee — A731

2006, Aug. 15 Litho.
1816 A731 30c multi   1.80 .60

Writers — A732

Designs: $1, Jorge Icaza (1906-78). $1.20, Pablo Palacio (1906-47).

2006, Sept. 18 Wmk. 395
1817-1818 A732 Set of 2   11.50 5.00

Ecuadorian Food — A733

No. 1819: a, Bandera Manabi. b, Viche de Manabi.

2006, Sept. 23 Perf. 13¼x13
1819 A733 $1 Horiz. pair, #a-b   10.25 4.25

Orchid — A734

No. 1820: a, Caucaea olivaceum. b, Cyrtochilum macranthum. c, Miltoniopsis vexillaria. d, Odontoglossum harryanum. e, Cyrtochilum pastasae. f, Cyrtochilum loxense. g, Cyrtochilum eduardii. h, Odontoglossum epidendroides. i, Cyrtochilum retusum. j, Cyrtochilum geniculatum.
$2, Cyrtochilum macranthum, diff.

2006, Sept. 29 Perf. 13x13¼
1820 Block of 10   18.00 6.50
 a.-j. A734 30c Any single   1.50 .75

Imperf
Size: 66x95mm
1821 A734 $2 multi   10.00 4.25

America Issue, Energy Conservation A735

Background color: $1, Brown. $1.20, Blue.

2006, Oct. 4 Perf. 13¼x13
1822-1823 A735 Set of 2   11.75 5.00

Natural Fiber Art, by Citi Nouman — A736

Designs: No. 1824, En la Ventana. No. 1825: a, Forma en Movimiento. b, Caminantes. No. 1826, horiz.: a, Caminando. b, Cabezas Huecas.

2006, Oct. 4 Perf. 13x13¼, 13¼x13
1824 A736 30c multi   1.50 .60
1825 A736 30c Vert. pair, #a-b   3.75 1.40
1826 A736 30c Horiz. pair, #a-b   3.75 1.40
  Nos. 1824-1826 (3)   9.00 3.40

Tourism in Otavalo — A737

Designs: 25c, El Lechero tree. 30c, El Jordan Church. 75c, Young girl, vert. $1, Costume for El Coraza Festival, vert.

2006, Oct. 18 Perf. 13¼x13, 13x13¼
1827-1830 A737 Set of 4   13.00 5.25

Eruption of Tungurahua Volcano — A738

No. 1831: a, Ash cloud above volcano. b, Lava flowing down volcano.

2006, Oct. 20 Perf. 13x13¼
1831 A738 $1 Horiz. pair, #a-b   10.25 4.25

Urban Renewal of Guayaquil — A739

No. 1832: a, Municipal Palace, denomination at left. b, Municipal Palace, denomination at right. c, Vulcan forge. d, José Joaquín de Olmedo Airport. e, Bus station.

2006, Oct. 24 Perf. 13¼x13
1832 Horiz. strip of 5   26.00 11.00
 a.-e. A739 $1 Any single   4.75 2.40

Radio Station HCJB, 75th Anniv. — A740

2006, Oct. 26 Wmk. 395
1833 A740 $1 multi   5.50 2.25

Millennium Development Objectives of the United Nations — A741

2006, Oct. 27 Perf. 13¾
1834 A741 $2 multi   10.00 4.25

Pres. Galo Plaza Lasso (1906-87) — A742

Designs: 40c, Photograph. 80c, Tree.

2006, Oct. 27 Perf. 13x13¼
1835-1836 A742 Set of 2   6.50 2.50

German Shepherd Breeding Association A743

2006, Oct. 28 Litho. Perf. 13¼x13
1837 A743 $1 multi   5.50 2.25

Military Parachuting, 50th Anniv. — A744

Designs: 20c, Soldiers. 40c, Soldiers and airplane. 60c, Soldier and troop emblem. 80c, Paratrooper in air.

Perf. 13¼x13, 13x13¼
2006, Oct. 31 Litho. Wmk. 395
1838-1841 A744 Set of 4   10.50 4.00

322 ECUADOR

Galapagos Islands Fauna — A745

No. 1842, horiz.: a, Sea turtle. b, Sea gull. c, Marine iguana. d, Blue-footed boobies. e, Sea lion.
80c, Flamingo. $1, Crab. $1.20, Fish.

2006, Nov. 1
1842	A745	30c Horiz. strip of 5, #a-e	8.50	3.25
1843	A745	80c multi	4.25	1.60
1844	A745	$1 multi	5.25	2.00
1845	A745	$1.20 multi	6.50	2.50
		Nos. 1842-1845 (4)	24.50	9.35

Christmas — A746

2006, Nov. 28 **Perf. 13x13¼**
| 1846 | A746 | 80c multi | | 4.00 | 1.60 |

Monsignor Juan I. Larrea Holguín (1927-2006) — A747

No. 1847: a, In bishop's robes. b, In judicial robes.

2006, Dec. 8 **Perf. 13¾**
| 1847 | A747 | 40c Horiz. pair, #a-b | 4.75 | 1.90 |

Freemasonry — A748

Designs: 25c, Masonic altar, beehive. 40c, Compass and square.

2006, Dec. 11 **Perf. 13x13¼**
| 1848-1849 | A748 | Set of 2 | 4.00 | 1.50 |

Quito Zoo Animals A749

No. 1850: a, Parrot. b, Frog.
No. 1851: a, Harpy eagle. b, Jaguar.
$2, Parrot on branch.

2006, Dec. 11 **Perf. 13x13¼**
| 1850 | A749 | 60c Horiz. pair, #a-b | 8.00 | 2.40 |
| 1851 | A749 | 80c Horiz. pair, #a-b | 10.75 | 3.25 |

Imperf
Size: 40x65mm
| 1852 | A749 | $2 multi | 10.00 | 4.25 |

Erotic and Fertility Figurines — A750

Designs: 10c, Nursing mother. 20c, Copulating couple. $1.20, Pregnant woman. $2, Man with erect penis.

2006, Dec. 12 **Perf. 13x13¼**
| 1853-1856 | A750 | Set of 4 | 19.00 | 7.50 |

Admiral Juan Illingworth Naval Museum — A751

Emblem of Ecuador Navy and Illingworth: 20c, On rope ladder, 1880. 25c, As Marine Guard, 1854.

2006, Dec. 15 **Litho.**
| 1857-1858 | A751 | Set of 2 | 2.75 | 1.00 |

Colors of Ecuador Flag — A752

2006, Dec. 15 **Wmk. 395**
| 1859 | A752 | $10 multi | 50.00 | 19.00 |

Postmen and Bicycles — A753

Color of photograph: 20c, Gray brown. 40c, Gray blue. 80c, Red.

2006, Dec. 17 **Perf. 13¼x13**
| 1860-1862 | A753 | Set of 3 | 7.75 | 3.00 |

Pets — A754

Designs: 25c, Puppy. 40c, Dog, vert. 50c, Cat with brown and blue eyes, vert. 80c, Dog running. $1, Cat with blue eyes, vert.

2006, Dec. 17 **Perf. 13¼x13, 13x13¼**
| 1863-1867 | A754 | Set of 5 | 15.00 | 6.00 |

Cuenca Biennale — A755

Art by: 5c, Alexander Apóstol. 15c, Ricardo González Elias, vert.

2006, Dec. 20
| 1868-1869 | A755 | Set of 2 | 1.80 | .25 |

Independence Monument, 50th Anniv. — A756

No. 1870: a, Head of statue. b, Entire statue.

2006, Dec. 21 **Perf. 13¾**
| 1870 | A756 | 20c Horiz. pair, #a-b | 2.60 | .90 |

Quito Fair — A757

Designs: No. 1871, Matador Manolo Caena. No. 1872 — Matadors: a, Sebastián Castella. b, El Juli.
No. 1873, horiz. — Quito Bull Ring: a, At right. b, At left.
$3, Sculpture of Jesus, horiz.

Perf. 13x13¼, 13¼x13
2006, Dec. 27 **Litho.**
1871	A757	50c multi	3.00	1.25
1872	A757	50c Horiz. pair, #a-b	5.50	2.10
1873	A757	50c Horiz. pair, #a-b	5.50	2.10
			14.00	5.45

Litho. With Foil Application
Imperf
Size: 65x40mm
| 1874 | A757 | $3 multi | 16.00 | 6.50 |

Pirates — A758

No. 1875, vert.: a, Jolly Roger flag, ship, sea lions. b, Sea lions, ships. c, Ships, Jolly roger flag. d, Armed pirate on ship. e, Ship, Jolly Roger flag.
No. 1876: a, Map of Galapagos Islands, Jolly Roger flag, Sir Francis Drake. b, Ship, map, skull.
$1, Ship, map, skull, William Dampier.

Perf. 13x13¼, 13¼x13
2006, Dec. 27 **Litho.**
1875	A758	30c Horiz. strip of 5, #a-e	9.00	3.50
1876	A758	40c Horiz. pair, #a-b	4.50	1.90
1877	A758	$1 multi	6.75	2.50
		Nos. 1875-1877 (3)	20.25	7.90

SEK International University, Quito — A759

Perf. 13¼x13
2006, Dec. 29 **Wmk. 395**
| 1878 | A759 | 10c multi | 1.00 | .40 |

Scouting, Cent. — A760

Scout emblem and: 25c, Circles. $2, Scout and circles.

Perf. 13x13¼
2007, Mar. 29 **Litho.** **Wmk. 395**
| 1879-1880 | A760 | Set of 2 | 10.00 | 4.00 |

Hispanic-American Poetry Festival — A761

2007, Apr. 19
| 1881 | A761 | 10c multi | 1.00 | .30 |

Cuenca, 450th Anniv. — A762

Designs: 40c, Casa de los Arcos (Arch House). 75c, Vergel Plaza. 80c, Tomebamba River Gorge, horiz. $3, Cathedral of the Immaculate Conception.

2007, Apr. 27 **Perf. 13x13¼, 13¼x13**
| 1882-1885 | A762 | Set of 4 | 18.50 | 8.75 |

Prehistoric Animals — A763

Designs: No. 1886, 80c, Megatherium. No. 1887, 80c, Smilodon, horiz.

2007, May 10
| 1886-1887 | A763 | Set of 2 | 7.25 | 3.75 |

Beetles — A764

Designs: No. 1888, Golopha eaucus. No. 1889: a, Chrysophora chrysochlora. b, Dynastes hercules.

2007, May 10 **Perf. 13¼x13**
| 1888 | A764 | 40c multi | 2.00 | .75 |
| 1889 | A764 | 40c Horiz. pair, #a-b | 4.00 | 1.50 |

Guayaquil Rotary Club, 80th Anniv. — A765

2007, June 1 **Wmk. 395**
| 1890 | A765 | 25c multi | 1.40 | .45 |

America Issue, Education For All — A766

Designs: 40c, Children on school bus. 80c, Girl doing geometry work. $1, Children flying kites, vert. $1.20, Student in wheelchair, vert. $2, Girl and handprints, vert.

2007, June 6 **Perf. 13¼x13, 13x13¼**
| 1891-1894 | A766 | Set of 4 | 15.00 | 6.00 |

Imperf
Size: 40x65mm
| 1895 | A766 | $2 multi | 8.75 | 3.75 |

Naval Institute of Oceanography, 75th Anniv. — A767

Antarctic research: 10c, Penguin, ship. $3, Scientists and scientific equipment, horiz.

2007, July 18 **Perf. 13x13¼**
| 1896 | A767 | 10c multi | .55 | .40 |

Perf. 12
Size: 52x32mm
| 1897 | A767 | $3 multi | 13.00 | 5.50 |

Central Bank of Ecuador, 80th Anniv. A768

2007, Aug. 28 **Perf. 12**
| 1898 | A768 | $2 multi | 8.75 | 3.75 |

ECUADOR

Guayaquil Firefighters — A769

Various firefighters at fires: 5c, 10c, 15c, 25c, $1. 25c and $1 are horiz.

2007, Oct. 10   Perf. 13x13¼, 13¼x13
1899-1903 A769 Set of 5   7.50   2.75

Breast Cancer Prevention A770

2007, Oct. 15   Perf. 13¼x13
1904 A770 $3 multi   13.00   5.50

Guayaquil Tourism — A771

Designs: 5c, Las Peñas. 10c, Lighthouse, Santa Ana Hill. 15c, El Velero Bridge. 25c, Mercado Sur, horiz. $1, June 5 Bridge, horiz.

2007, Oct. 23   Perf. 13x13¼, 13¼x13
1905-1909 A771 Set of 5   7.50   2.25

Cuenca Chamber of Industries, 70th Anniv. — A772

2007, Oct. 25   Perf. 13¼x13
1910 A772 $1.20 multi   5.00   2.10

Operation Smile — A773

2007, Nov. 16   Litho.
1911 A773 $1 multi   4.50   1.90

Vistazo Magazine, 50th Anniv. — A774

2007, Nov. 29   Perf. 12
1912 A774 20c multi   1.10   .40

Galapagos Islands Fauna — A775

Designs: 40c, Sea turtle. 80c, Penguin. $1, Dolphin. $1.20, Tropicbird.

2007, Nov. 30   Perf. 13¼x13
1913-1916 A775 Set of 4   15.00   6.00
Compare with type A780.

Comptroller General, 80th Anniv. — A776

2007, Dec. 3   Perf. 12
1917 A776 20c multi   1.10   .40

2007 Pan American Games, Rio de Janeiro — A777

No. 1918 — Athletes and text noting gold medalists: a, Alexandra Escobar. b, Seledina Nieve. c, Jefferson Perez. d, Xavier Moreno. e, Under-18 soccer team.

2007, Dec. 18   Perf. 13x13¼
1918   Horiz. strip of 5   9.50   3.00
a.-e. A777 40c Any single   1.50   .75

Christmas — A778

No. 1919: a, The Annunciation. b, The Three Magi. c, Nativity. d, Flight into Egypt.

2007, Dec. 20   Perf. 13¼x13
1919 A778 20c Block of 4, #a-d   4.50   1.40

Guayas Province Transit Commission, 60th Anniv. — A779

   Perf. 13x13¼
2008, Jan. 29   Litho.   Wmk. 395
1920 A779 $1 multi   4.00   1.90

Galapagos Islands — A780

Map of islands and: 40c, Pelecanus occidentalis. 80c, Aetobatus narinari. $1, Carcharhinus galapagensis. $1.20, San Cristóbal Windmill Project.

2008, Mar. 18   Perf. 13¼x13
1921-1924 A780 Set of 4   13.00   6.00
Compare with Type A775.

Free Maternity and Infant Care A781

2008, Mar. 28   Perf. 12
1925 A781 $1 multi   4.00   1.90

Guayaquil Port Authority, 50th Anniv. — A782

2008, Apr. 8
1926 A782 20c multi   1.00   .25

Tungurahua Chamber of Industry, 80th Anniv. — A783

   Wmk. 395
2000, Apr. 24   Litho.   Perf. 12
1927 A783 $3 multi   11.00   5.50

Father Carlos Crespi (1891-1982) — A784

2008, Apr. 30
1928 A784 $2 multi   7.50   3.00

Santiago de Guayaquil Medallion — A785

2008, June 3
1929 A785 30c multi   1.40   .55
Intl. Philately Day.

Jorge Pérez Concha, Historian and Diplomat, Birth Cent. — A786

2008, June 4
1930 A786 $3 multi   11.00   5.50

Los Pinos College, Quito, 40th Anniv. — A787

2008, June 6
1931 A787 20c multi   1.00   .25

Guayaquil-Quito Railway, Cent. — A788

Ecuador No. 174 and: 56c, Steam locomotive. $5, Steam locomotives, Gabriel García Moreno and Gen. Eloy Alfaro.

2008, June 23   Perf. 12
1932 A788 56c multi   2.25   1.00
   Imperf
   Size: 100x70mm
1933 A788 $5 multi   18.50   9.00

Polytechnic School of the Coast, 50th Anniv. — A789

   Wmk. 395
2008, July 28   Litho.   Perf. 12
1934 A789 32c multi   1.40   .55

Latin American Youth Year A790

2008, Aug. 20
1935 A790 30c multi   1.40   .55

Ecuadorian Cacao — A791

No. 1936: a, Cacao pod, UL corner of #306. b, Cacao flower, UR corner of #306. c, Cacao processing, LL corner of #306. d, Cacao pods and beans, chocolate candy, LR corner of #306.

2008, Oct. 1   Perf. 13¼x13
1936 A791 56c Block of 4, #a-d   9.00   4.00

Meridiano Newspaper, 25th Anniv. — A792

2008, Oct. 22   Perf. 13x13¼
1937 A792 60c multi   2.25   1.00

Intl. Swimming Federation, Cent. — A793

No. 1938: a, World Map. b, Ecuadorian swimmer.
30c, Swimmer from underwater.

2008, Oct. 31   Perf. 13¼x13
1938 A793 24c Horiz. pair, #a-b   1.40   .60
1939 A793 30c multi   1.00   .30

324 ECUADOR

Office of the Procurator General, 80th Anniv. — A794

2008, Nov. 11   Perf. 13x13¼
1940   A794   25c multi   .90   .25

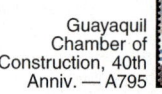

Guayaquil Chamber of Construction, 40th Anniv. — A795

2008, Nov. 27   Perf. 13¼x13
1941   A795 $1 multi   2.75   1.10

New Constitution — A796

Flag and: 32c, Sun behind clouds. $5, People, vert.

2008, Nov. 29   Perf. 12
1942   A796   32c multi   1.00   .30
Size: 66x95mm
Imperf
1943   A796 $5 multi   12.75   6.00

Santiago de Guayaquil Municipal Museum, Cent. — A797

No. 1944: a, Old musuem building. b, New musuem building with murals. $2, Entrance to old musuem building.

2008, Dec. 16   Perf. 13¼x13
1944   A797   60c Horiz. pair, #a-b   3.50   1.50
1945   A797 $2 multi   5.75   2.50

Friendship Between Ecuador and Japan, 90th Anniv. — A798

No. 1945: a, Cotopaxi Volcano, Ecuador. b, Mt. Fuji, Japan.

2008, Dec. 17
1946   A798   30c Horiz. pair, #a-b   2.00   .75

America Issue, National Festivals A799

No. 1947 — Festival of Sts. Peter and Paul: a, Dancers. b, Guitarist.
No. 1948, vert. — Diablada Pillareña: a, Figure with red mask. b, Figure with black mask.

2008, Dec. 23   Perf. 13¼x13
1947   A799   20c Horiz. pair, #a-b   1.25   .50
             Perf. 13x13¼
1948   A799 $1 Horiz. pair, #a-b   5.75   2.50

Christmas — A800

Various creche figurines of Holy Family and animals with background color of: 30c, Blue. No. 1949: a, Green. b, Yellow brown.

2008, Dec. 23   Perf. 13¼x13
1949   A800   30c multi   1.00   .40
1950   A800   80c Horiz. pair, #a-b   4.50   2.00

A801

A802

A803

A804

Jacchigua National Folk Ballet — A805

             Perf. 13¼x13
2009, Feb. 18   Litho.   Wmk. 395
1951   Horiz. strip of 5   13.50   6.00
   a.   A801 $1 multi   2.25   1.00
   b.   A802 $1 multi   2.25   1.00
   c.   A803 $1 multi   2.25   1.00
   d.   A804 $1 multi   2.25   1.00
   e.   A805 $1 multi   2.25   1.00

Preservation of Polar Regions and Glaciers — A806

Designs: 20c, Feet of polar bear. 80c, Earth in water.

2009, Mar. 31
1952-1953   A806   Set of 2   3.00   1.25

A807

Tourism — A808

Designs: No. 1954, Babahoyo River, Los Ríos Province. No. 1955, Ingapirca Ruins, Cañar Province. No. 1956, Rafters on Quijos River, Napo Province. No. 1957, Marimba group, Esmeraldas Province. $1.25, Tulcán cemetery, Carchi Province. $2, Train and Mt. Chimborazo, Chimborazo Province. $3, Alcea rosea flowers, Morona-Santiago Province. $5, Acrocinus longimanus, Sucumbíos Province.
No. 1962: a, Like #1954. b, Like #1957. c, Like #1958. d, Like #1955. e, Like #1959. f, Like #1956. g, Like #1960. h, Like #1961.
No. 1963: a, Equator Monument, Pichincha Province. b, Colorado Indians, Santo Domingo de los Tsáchilas Province. c, Los Frailes Beach, Manabí Province. d, Banana plantation, El Oro Province. e, Arctocephalus galapagoensis, Galápagos Province. f, Cuicocha Lake, Imbabura Province. g, Harpia harpyja, Pastaza Province. h, Shuar community, Orellana Province.
No. 1964: a, Bolívar and San Martín Monument, Guayas Province. b, The Lovers of Sumpa, Santa Elena Province. c, Pillaro devil, Tungurahua Province. d, Mt. Cotopaxi, Cotopaxi Province. e, Guaranga Indian Monument, Bolívar Province. f, Virgin of Cisne, Loja Province. g, Tomebamba River, Azuay Province. h, Leopardus pardalis, Zamora Province.

          Perf. 13¼x13
2009   Litho.   Wmk. 395
1954   A807   25c multi   .65   .25
1955   A807   50c multi   1.40   .60
1956   A807   75c multi   1.90   .90
1957   A807 $1 multi   2.75   1.25
1958   A807 $1.25 multi   3.25   1.50
1959   A807 $2 multi   5.00   2.40
1960   A807 $3 multi   7.75   3.50
1961   A807 $5 multi   13.00   6.00
    Nos. 1954-1961 (8)   35.70   16.40

Booklet Stamps
Self-Adhesive
Die Cut
Unwmk.

1962   Booklet pane of 8 + 2 labels   14.50
  a.-b.   A808 25c Either single   .70   .40
  c.-d.   A808 50c Either single   1.40   .70
  e.-f.   A808 75c Either single   2.00   1.00
  g.-h.   A808 $1 Either single   3.00   1.50
1963   Booklet pane of 8 + 2 labels   14.50
  a.-b.   A808 25c Either single   .70   .40
  c.-d.   A808 50c Either single   1.40   .70
  e.-f.   A808 75c Either single   2.00   1.00
  g.-h.   A808 $1 Either single   3.00   1.50
1964   Booklet pane of 8 + 2 labels   14.50
  a.-b.   A808 25c Either single   .70   .40
  c.-d.   A808 50c Either single   1.40   .70
  e.-f.   A808 75c Either single   2.00   1.00
  g.-h.   A808 $1 Either single   3.00   1.50
    Nos. 1962-1964 (3)   43.50

Issued: Nos. 1954-1961, 4/29; Nos. 1962-1964, July.
See Nos. 1985-2000, 2021-2022.

Intl. Philately Day — A809

       Perf. 13¼x13
2009, May 6   Wmk. 395
1965   A809   75c multi   2.10   .90

Icons of Santa Clara Monastery — A810

No. 1966: a, Angel. b, Jesus Christ. c, Pensive child. d, Protective Virgin. e, Virgin of Quito.

2009, June 9   Perf. 13x13¼
1966   Horiz. strip of 5   13.50   6.00
  a.-e.   A810 $1 Any single   2.00   1.00

National Finance Corporation, 45th Anniv. — A811

2009, June 22   Perf. 13¼x13
1967   A811 $1.25 multi   3.25   1.50

Ambato Electric Company, 50th Anniv. — A812

2009, June
1968   A812 $1 multi   2.75   1.25

Paute-Molino Dam, 25th Anniv. — A813

2009, July 22
1969   A813 $2 multi   5.25   2.50

El Telégrafo Newspaper, 125th Anniv. — A814

2009, July 30   Perf. 12
1970   A814 $1.75 multi   4.50   2.10

Call for Independence, Bicent. — A815

Nos. 1971 and 1972 — Doves, butterflies, bell and: a, Open mouth. b, Monument.

2009, Aug. 14   Perf. 13¼x13
1971   A815 $3 Horiz. pair, #a-b   15.00   7.25

Souvenir Sheet
With Horizontal Blue Stripe Added to Middle of Stamps
1972   A815 $3 Sheet of 2, #a-b   15.00   7.25

Call for Independence, Bicent. — A816

Serpentine Die Cut 12½x12¼
2009, Aug. 14   Litho.   Unwmk.
Self-Adhesive
Printed on Cork
1973   A816 $3.50 multi   8.75   4.25

Chinese Benevolent Society, Cent. — A817

No. 1974: a, Galápagos tortoise. b, Giant panda.

         Perf. 13¼x13
2009, Aug. 18   Wmk. 395
1974   A817   25c Horiz. pair, #a-b   1.90   .60

Famous People — A818

No. 1975: a, Carlos Silva Pareja (1909-68), musician. b, Tránsito Amaguaña (1909-2009), Indian rights advocate. c, Demetrio Aguilera Malta (1909-81), writer, diplomat. d, Carlos Zevallos Menéndez (1909-81), archaeologist. e, Humberto Salvador Guerra (1909-82), writer.

2009, Aug. 28   Litho.
1975   Horiz. strip of 5   4.25   1.50
  a.-e.   A818 25c Any single   .75   .40

Ecuadorian Olympic Committee, 50th Anniv. — A819

Designs: No. 1976, 25c, Shooting, cycling, equestrian, wrestling, archery and basketball. No. 1977, 25c, Diving, running, weight lifting, tennis, boxing and soccer, vert.

2009, Oct. 17   Perf. 13¼x13, 13x13¼
1976-1977   A819   Set of 2   1.75   .60

ECUADOR

Exportation of Cooperative Open Banking Information System — A820

No. 1984: a, Paddle and ball. b, Go-cart.

Perf. 13¼x13
2009, Nov. 5		Litho.		Wmk. 395	
1978	A820	50c multi		1.50	1.00

Loja National University, 150th Anniv. A821

Wmk. 395   Litho.   Perf. 12
2009, Nov. 27					
1979	A821	$2 multi		5.25	2.50

Independence, Bicent. — A822

No. 1980: a, Juan Pío Montúfar (1758-1010), Chairman of Supreme Council of Government. b, José Mejía Lequerica (1777-1813), representative to Cortes of Cadiz. c, Eugenio Espejo (1747-95), journalist, medical pioneer. d, Manuela Cañizares (1769-1814), patriot. e, Bicentenary emblem.

2009, Nov. 28
1980		Horiz. strip of 5		11.50	4.50
a.-e.	A822	75c Any single		1.75	.85

A823

Charles Darwin (1809-82), Naturalist — A824

No. 1982 — Darwin and: a, Phoenicopterus ruber. b, Ardea herodias. c, Calandria galapagosa. d, Conolopus marthae. e, Sula granti. f, Rhincodon typus. g, Zalophus wollebaeki. h, Phalacrocorax harrisi. i, Geochelone nigra abingdoni. Nos. 1982a-1982h are 35x35mm, No. 1982i ic 38mm diameter.

Perf. 13¾x14
2009, Nov. 30				Unwmk.	
		Granite Paper			
1981	A823	$5 multi		12.50	6.00

Perf. 13¼ ($1), 13¾ ($2)
1982	A824	Sheet of 9		27.00	12.00
a.-h.		$1 Any single		2.25	1.10
i.		$2 multi		4.25	2.10

Christmas — A825

Perf. 13¼x13
2009, Dec. 10				Wmk. 395	
1983	A825	$1 multi		2.75	1.25

America Issue, Toys and Games A826

No. 1984: a, Paddle and ball. b, Go-cart.

2009, Dec. 18
1984	A826	$1 Horiz. pair, #a-b		5.75	2.50

Tourism Type of 2009

Designs: No. 1985, The Lovers of Sumpa, Santa Elena Province. No. 1986, Colorado Indians, Santo Domingo de los Tsáchilas Province. No. 1987, Shuar community, Orellana Province. No. 1988, Guaranga Indian Monument, Bolívar Province. No. 1989, Banana plantation, El Oro Province. No. 1990, Virgin of Cisne, Loja Province. No. 1991, Pillaro devil, Tungurahua Province. No. 1992, Equator Monument, Pichincha Province. No. 1993, Cuicocha Lake, Imbabura Province. $1.75, Bolívar and San Martín Monument, Guayas Province. No. 1995, Tomebamba River, Azuay Province. No. 1996, Leopardus pardalis, Zamora Province. No. 1997, Los Frailes Beach, Manabí Province. No. 1998, Harpia harpyja, Pastaza Province. No. 1999, Arctocephalus galapagoensis, Galápagos Province. $5, Mt. Cotopaxi, Cotopaxi Province.

Wmk. 395, 377 (#1986-1987, 1989, 1992, 1993, 1997-1999)

2010-11   Litho.   Perf. 13¼x13
1985	A807	25c multi	.65	.25
1986	A807	25c multi	.65	.25
1987	A807	25c multi	.65	.25
1988	A807	50c multi	1.30	.50
1989	A807	50c multi	1.30	.50
1990	A807	$1 multi	2.60	1.00
1991	A807	$1.25 multi	3.25	1.25
1992	A807	$1.25 multi	3.25	1.25
1993	A807	$1.25 multi	3.25	1.25
1994	A807	$1.75 multi	4.50	1.75
1995	A807	$2 multi	5.25	2.00
1996	A807	$2 multi	5.25	2.00
1997	A807	$2 multi	5.75	2.00
1998	A807	$3 multi	8.00	3.00
1999	A807	$3 multi	8.00	3.00
2000	A807	$5 multi	13.00	5.00
		Nos. 1985-2000 (16)	66.65	25.25

Issued: Nos. 1985, 1988, 1991, 1995, 1/20; Nos. 1990, 1994, 1996, 2000, 4/12; Nos. 1986, 1992, 1997, 1998, 9/30; Nos. 1987, 1989, 1993, 1999, 1/24/11.

Miniature Sheet

First Unmanned Ecuadorian Airship — A827

No. 2001: a, $1, Pilot with remote-control device (40x18mm) b, $1, Airship over coastline (40x18mm). c, $1, Airship and mountain (40x18mm). d, $3, Airship (115x42mm).

Wmk. 395
2010, Feb. 7   Litho.   Perf. 14
2001	A827	Sheet of 4, #a-d		16.00	6.00

Ecuadorian Red Cross, Cent. — A828

No. 2002: a, Old ambulance, blood drop inscribed "Ayuda." b, New ambulance, blood drop inscribed "Cuida." c, Modern Red Cross hard hat, blood drop inscribed "Salva." d, Old Red Cross hard hat, blood drop inscribed "Vida."

Perf. 13¼x13
2010, Mar. 18				Wmk. 395	
2002	A828	50c Block of 4, #a-d		6.00	2.00

Birds A829

No. 2003: a, Tachycineta albiventer. b, Momotus momota. c, Semnornis ramphastinus. d, Aulacorhynchus haematopygus.
No. 2004, horiz.: a, Ramphocelus carbo. b, Tangara vitriolina.

2010, Apr. 16   Wmk. 395   Perf. 14
2003	A829	25c Block of 4, #a-d	3.50	1.00	

Souvenir Sheet
Perf. 13¼x13
2004	A829	$1.50 Sheet of 2, #a-b		8.00	3.00

No. 2004 contains two 38x27mm stamps. Birdpex 2010, Antwerp, Belgium (No. 2004).

Tall Ships in Velas Sudamérica 2010 — A830

No. 2005, vert. (27x38mm) — Various knots, ships and flags: a, Cisne Branco, Brazil. b, Libertad, Argentina. c, Sagres, Portugal. d, Capitán Miranda, Uruguay. e, Europa, Netherlands. f, Esmerelda, Chile. g, Gloria, Colombia. h, Simón Bolívar, Venezuela. i, Cuauhtémoc, Mexico. j, Juan Sebastián Elcano, Spain.

$1, Training Ship Guayas, Ecuador.

Perf. 13x13¼
2010, May 7				Wmk. 377	
2005		Block of 10		21.50	7.50
a.-j.	A830	75c Any single		2.00	1.00

Perf. 12
2006	A830	$1 shown		2.75	1.00

Miniature Sheet

Manuela Sáenz (c. 1797-1856), Mistress of Simón Bolívar — A831

Litho. with Foil Application
2010, May 24   Imperf.
2007	A831	$3 multi		7.75	4.00

See Venezuela No. 1707.

2010 World Cup Soccer Championships, South Africa — A832

No. 2008 — Emblem of 2010 World Cup, soccer player, ball and: a, Lion. b, Elephant. c, Zebra.
$5, Mascot of 2010 World Cup, giraffe.

2010, June 9   Litho.   Perf. 13¼x13
2008		Horiz. strip of 3		8.25	4.00
a.-c.	A832	$1 Any single		2.50	1.25

Souvenir Sheet
Imperf
2009	A832	$5 multi		13.00	6.50

No. 2009 contains one 45x36mm stamp with simulated perforations. Animals on No. 2009 have blurred appearance, but have a three-dimensional appearance when seen through 3-D glasses.

Creation of Tungurahua Province, 150th Anniv. — A833

No. 2010: a, Atelopus ignescens. b, Mt. Tungurahua, flag at Parque de la Familia. c, Casa del Portal Museum.

Perf. 13¼x13
2010, July 1				Wmk. 377	
2010		Horiz. strip of 3		2.60	.75
a.-c.	A833	25c Any single		.75	.35

Las Floristas, by Camilo Egas A834

2010, July 21   Perf. 12
2011	A834	$1.25 multi		3.50	1.25

Campaign against illegal trafficking in historical objects.

Souvenir Sheet

Massacre of Patriots, Bicent. — A835

No. 2012: a, Soldier with sword threatening woman, man and child. b, Soldier threatening to shoot man.

2010, Aug. 2   Perf. 13x13¼
2012	A835	$2 Sheet of 2, #a-b, + central label		10.50	5.00

Souvenir Sheet

Philatelic Firsts of Ecuador A836

No. 2013: a, First postmark of Ecuador, 1770, emblem of Philatelic Association of Ecuador. b, First Ecuadorian stamps (#2, 3, 5, 6), emblem of Intl. Federation of Philately. c, Cover from first SCADTA flight, 1928, emblem of 2010 Philatelic Association of Ecuador Expo.

2010, Aug. 25   Perf. 10¼x10
2013	A836	$1 Sheet of 3, #a-c		8.25	4.00

Philatelic Association of Ecuador, 75th anniv., and its admission to Intl. Federation of Philately.

Organization of Petroleum Exporting Countries, 50th Anniv. — A837

2010, Sept. 14   Wmk. 377   Perf. 12
2014	A837	50c multi		1.50	.50

ECUADOR

Citigroup in Ecuador, 50th Anniv. — A838

2010, Oct. 7   Perf. 13¼x13
2015   A838 $1 multi   2.75   1.00

General Directorate of Civil Registration, Identification and Certification — A839

2010, Oct. 29   Litho.   Perf. 12
2016   A839   50c multi   1.60   .50

America Issue, National Symbols — A840

No. 2017 — National: a, Flag. b, Coat of arms. c, Anthem.

2010, Nov. 24   Perf. 13¼x13
2017   Horiz. strip of 3   8.25   4.00
   a.-c.   A840 $1 Any single   2.25   1.10

Christmas — A841

2010, Dec. 3   Perf. 13x13¼
2018   A841 $2 multi   5.25   2.00

San José-La Salle College, Guayaquil, Cent. — A842

2010, Dec. 16   Litho.   Wmk. 377
2019   A842   25c multi   1.10   .40

Children's Christmas Parade, Cuenca — A843

2010, Dec. 21   Perf. 13¼x13
2020   A843   50c multi   1.25   .50

Tourism Type of 2009

No. 2021 — Galapagos Islands fauna: a, Fregata magnificens. b, Sula dactylatra. c, Spheniscifome. d, Sula nebouxi. e, Conolophus subcristatus. f, Geochelone nigra. g, Chelonia mydas agassisi. h, Oxycirrhites typus.

No. 2022 — Galapagos Islands sites and fauna: a, Bartolomé Island, denomination at L. b, Bartolomé Island, denomination at R. c, Zoluphus wallebaeki, denomination at L. d, Zoluphus wallebaeki, denomination at R. e, Darwin's Arch, denomination at L. f, Darwin's Arch, denomination at R. g, Amblyrhynchus cristatus, denomination at L. h, Amblyrhynchus cristatus, denomination at R.

2011, Mar. 18   Unwmk.   Die Cut
Self-Adhesive
2021   Booklet pane of 8 + 2 labels   14.50
   a.-b.   A808 25c Either single   .60   .30
   c.-d.   A808 50c Either single   1.20   .60
   e.-f.   A808 75c Either single   1.80   .90
   g.-h.   A808 $1 Either single   2.40   1.20
   i.   Booklet pane of 8, #a-h, with lilac pane margins   12.00

2022   Booklet pane of 8 + 2 labels   14.50
   a.-b.   A808 25c Either single   .60   .30
   c.-d.   A808 50c Either single   1.20   .60
   e.-f.   A808 75c Either single   1.80   .90
   g.-h.   A808 $1 Either single   2.40   1.20
   i.   Booklet pane of 8, #a-h, with lilac pane margins   12.00

Issued: Nos. 2021i, 2022i, 1/13/12. Nos. 2021 and 2022 have gray pane margins.

Souvenir Sheet

Postal Union of the Americas, Spain and Portugal (UPAEP), Cent. — A844

2011, Mar. 18   Wmk. 377   Perf. 12
2023   A844 $3 multi   8.25   3.00

Souvenir Sheet

Yuri Gagarin, First Man in Space, 50th Anniv. A845

2011, May 6   Perf. 13x13¼
2024   A845 $5 multi   13.50   6.50

Intl. Year of Forests A846

No. 2025, 50c: a, Chinchona officinalis. b, Ceiba tichistandra.
No. 2026, 75c, horiz.: a, Jacaranda sp. b, Prosopis sp.

2011, May 19   Perf. 13x13¼, 13¼x13
Horiz. pairs, #a-b
2025-2026   A846   Set of 2   7.50   3.75

Pichincha Chamber of Industries and Production, 75th Anniv. A847

Wmk. 377
2011, June 16   Litho.   Perf. 12
2027   A847 $2 multi   5.25   4.00

Christopher Columbus College, Guayaquil, Cent. — A848

2011, July 7   Perf. 13¼x13
2028   A848 $1 multi   2.75   2.00

National Telecommunications Day — A849

No. 2029: a, First Bell telephone, 1876. b, Western Electric magneto wall telephone, 1894. c, Ericsson wall pay telephone, 1970. d, Apple iPhone, 2011.

2011, July 8
2029   A849   50c Block of 4, #a-d   6.00   5.00

Miniature Sheet

Seven Wonders of Quito A850

No. 2030: a, Basilica of the National Vow. b, Virgin of the Panecillo. c, Chimbacalle Railway Station. d, San Francisco Convent. e, Independence Plaza. f, Church of the Society of Jesus. g, Sanctuary of the Virgin of El Quinche.

2011, Sept. 8
2030   A850   75c Sheet of 7, #a-g, + label   15.00   15.00

Quito, 2011 American Capital of Culture.

Yasuni- ITT Initiative — A851

No. 2031 — Reptiles: a, Chelonoidis denticulata. b, Anolis trachyderma. c, Thecadactylus solimoensis. d, Epicrates cenchria. e, Dendropsophus bifurcus. f, Osteocephalus taurinus. g, Ranitomeya ventrimaculata. h, Melanosuchus niger.
No. 2032: a, Clavija procera. b, Duguetia hadrantha. c, Hymenaea oblongifolia. d, Connarus ruber. e, Fungi. f, Theobroma speciosum. g, Brownea gradiceps. h, Apeiba membranacea.

Unwmk.
2011, Sept. 20   Litho.   Die Cut
Self-Adhesive
2031   Booklet pane of 8 + 2 labels   14.50
   a.-b.   A851 25c Either single   .65   .30
   c.-d.   A851 50c Either single   1.30   .65
   e.-f.   A851 75c Either single   2.00   1.00
   g.-h.   A851 $1 Either single   2.60   1.30
2032   Booklet pane of 8 + 2 labels   14.50
   a.-b.   A851 25c Either single   .65   .30
   c.-d.   A851 50c Either single   1.30   .65
   e.-f.   A851 75c Either single   2.00   1.00
   g.-h.   A851 $1 Either single   2.60   1.30

See Nos. 2061-2062.

Intl. Year For People of African Descent A852

No. 2033 — Musical instruments: a, Marimba. b, Guasá. c, Maracas. d, Cununos.

Perf. 13¼x13
2011, Sept. 26   Litho.   Wmk. 395
2033   A852 $1 Block of 4, #a-d   11.00   10.00

Flowers — A853

Designs: 25c, Passiflora manicata. $2, Passiflora pinnatistipula. $3, Herrania balaensis. $5, Passiflora arborea.

Perf. 13x13¼
2011, Sept. 26   Litho.   Wmk. 377
2034-2037   A853   Set of 4   26.00   20.50

Trains A854   Railroad Stations A855

No. 2038 — Locomotives: a, 1992 GEC Alsthon. b, 1900 Baldwin. c, 1900 Baldwin, diff. d, 1935 Baldwin. e, 1992 GEC Alsthon on hillside. f, Front of 1992 GEC Alsthon. g, 1953 Baldwin. h, Baldwin XXXX.
No. 2039 — Stations at: a, Machachi. b, Latacunga. c, Sibambe. d, Durán. e, El Tambo. f, Riobamba. g, Chimbacalle. h, Boliche.

2011, Oct. 3   Unwmk.   Die Cut
Self-Adhesive
2038   Booklet pane of 8 + 2 labels   14.50
   a.-b.   A854 25c Either single   .65   .40
   c.-d.   A854 50c Either single   1.30   .65
   e.-f.   A854 75c Either single   2.00   1.00
   g.-h.   A854 $1 Either single   2.60   1.30
2039   Booklet pane of 8 + 2 labels   14.50
   a.-b.   A855 25c Either single   .65   .40
   c.-d.   A855 50c Either single   1.30   .65
   e.-f.   A855 75c Either single   2.00   1.00
   g.-h.   A855 $1 Either single   2.60   1.30

Exports A856

No. 2040: a, Wicker basket. b, Chocolate. c, Wooden automobile. d, Hats. e, Textiles. f, Leather goods. g, Filigree. h, Tagua carvings.

Perf. 13¼x13
2011, Oct. 11   Wmk. 395
2040   A856   50c Block of 8, #a-h, + central label   12.00   9.00

Intl. Day for Disaster Reduction — A857

No. 2041: a, Volcano eruption. b, Landslide. c, Flood, d, Earthquake.

2011, Oct. 12   Perf. 13¼
2041   A857 $1.25 Block of 4, #a-d   13.50   10.00

Mail Boxes and Postal Transportation — A858

Designs: No. 2042, $1.75, 1928 mailbox, bicycle. No. 2043, $1.75, 2011 mailbox, motorcycle.
$5, Mailbox, Post Office Bay, Galápagos Islands, vert.

Perf. 13½x13¾
2011, Nov. 28   Wmk. 377
2042-2043   A858   Set of 2   9.25   7.00

Souvenir Sheet
Perf. 13x13¼
2044   A858 $5 multi   13.00   10.00

America issue. No. 2044 contains one 28x38mm stamp.

ECUADOR

Christmas A859

No. 2045: a, Holy Family. b, Angel.

2011, Nov. 29		Perf. 13½x13¾
2045 A859	$1 Horiz. pair, #a-b	5.50 4.50

2011 Pan-American Games, Guadalajara, Mexico — A860

Emblem, sports equipment and athletes: a, Karate. b, Weight lifting. c, Kayaking. d, Boxing. e, Rollerblading.

2011, Nov. 30			
2046	Horiz. strip of 5	4.25	3.00
a.-e.	A860 25c Any single	.75	.60

Guayaquil Chamber of Industries, 75th Anniv. A861

2011, Dec. 14		Wmk. 377
2047 A861	$2 multi	5.25 4.25

Ecuador Cancer Society, 60th Anniv. — A862

2011, Dec. 19		Perf. 13¼x13
2048 A862	75c multi	2.10 1.00

Pres. Luis Cordero (1833-1912) A864

2012, Mar. 1		Perf. 13¾x13½
2051 A864	$1 multi	2.75 2.25

Flowers — A865

Designs: $1, Barnadesia spinosa. $2, Bixa orellana. $3, Espeletia pycnophylla. $5, Brugmansia sanguinea.

		Perf. 13½x13¾
2012, Mar. 28		Unwmk.
2052-2055 A865	Set of 4	29.00 25.00

Souvenir Sheets

Sinking of the Titanic, Cent. A866

Designs: No. 2056, $4, Titanic, sepia-toned image. No. 2056, $4, Titanic and Olympic at dock.

		Perf. 13¾x13½
2012, Apr. 20		Wmk. 377
2056-2057 A866	Set of 2	20.00 17.50

Bananas A867

		Perf. 13½x13¾
2012, May 17		Litho. Wmk. 377
2058 A867	$2 multi	5.25 4.50

Banco de Machala, 50th anniv.

Catholic University of Santiago, Guayaquil, 50th Anniv. — A868

2012, May 31		Perf. 13¾
2059 A868	$1 multi	2.75 2.25

Miniature Sheet

Guayaquil Tourist Attractions — A869

No. 2060: a, Hemiciclo la Rotonda (monument honoring meeting of Simón Bolívar and José de San Martín). b, Malecón del ío Guayas (Guayas River Walk). c, Metropolitan Cathedral. d, Torre del Reloj (Clock Tower). e, Malecón del Salado (Salado Walk). f, Edificio del Municipio (City Hall). g, Las Peñas Cerro Santa Ana (Santa Ana Hill).

2012, June 8		Wmk. 377
2060 A869	75c Sheet of 7, #a-g, + label	17.50 12.50

Yasuni-ITT Type of 2011

No. 2061 — Flora and fauna: a, Dasypodidae. b, Saimiri sciureus. c, Tettigoniidae. d, Automeris postalbida. e, Brownea sp. f, Aristolochia sp. g, Hypsiboas sp. h, Hypsiboas geographicus.
No. 2062 — Birds: a, Morphnus guianensis. b, Sarcorhamphus papa. c, Ara ararauna. d, Harpia harpyja. e, Trochilidae sp. f, Ramphastos tucanus. g, Pteroglossus pluricinctus. h, Pionus menstruus.

2012, Juno 11		Unwmk.
	Self-Adhesive	Die Cut
2061	Booklet pane of 8 + 2 labels	14.50
a.-b.	A851 25c Either single	.65 .40
c.-d.	A851 50c Either single	1.30 .65
e.-f.	A851 75c Either single	2.00 2.00
g.-h.	A851 $1 Either single	2.60 2.60
2062	Booklet pane of 8 + 2 labels	14.50
a.-b.	A851 25c Either single	.65 .40
c.-d.	A851 50c Either single	1.30 .05
e.-f.	A851 75c Either single	2.00 2.00
g.-h.	A851 $1 Either single	2.60 2.60

Galapagos Islands Landscapes and Fauna — A870

No. 2063: a, Rocks in surf. b, Head of Amblyrhynchus cristatus. c, Numenius phaeopus. d, South Plaza Island. e, Pinnacle Rock, Bartolomé Island. f, Sula nebouxi. g, Chelonoidis sp. h, Kicker Rock (Leon Dormido), San Cristóbal Island.
No. 2064: a, Zalophus wollebaeki. b, Geospiza magnirostris. c, Sula granti. d, Fregata magnificens. e, Microlophus bivittatus. f, Spheniscus mendiculus. g, Anas bahamensis. h, Sphyrna lewini.

2012, July 11		Unwmk. Die Cut
	Self-Adhesive	
Water Droplets on Blue Depicted in Frames Around Stamps		
2063	Booklet pane of 8	14.50
a.-b.	A870 25c Either single	.65 .40
c.-d.	A870 50c Either single	1.30 .65
e.-f.	A870 75c Either single	2.00 1.00
g.-h.	A870 $1 Either single	2.60 1.30
i.	Booklet pane of 8, #a-h, with pane margins depicting rocks	12.50
2064	Booklet pane of 8	14.50
a.-b.	A870 25c Either single	.65 .40
c.-d.	A870 50c Either single	1.30 .65
e.-f.	A870 75c Either single	2.00 1.00
g.-h.	A870 $1 Either single	2.60 1.30
i.	Booklet pane of 8, #a-h, with pane margins depicting rocks	12.50

Issued: Nos. 2063i, 2064i, 10/8. See Nos. 2094-2095.

Guayas Sports Federation, 90th Anniv. — A871

No. 2065: a, Shooting (tiro). b, Wrestling (lucha). c, Kayaking (canotaje). d, Boxing (boxeo). e, Weight lifting (pesas).

		Perf. 13¾x13½
2012, July 25		Wmk. 377
2065	Horiz. strip of 5	7.50 4.00
a.-e.	A871 50c Any single	1.50 .75

A872

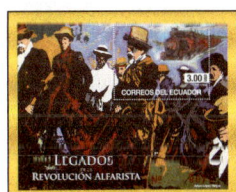

Legacy of the Revolution of 1895 — A873

No. 2066: a, Ecuador #129, Matilde Huerta, first Ecuadoran female postal official, 1895. b, Bolívar College, Tulcán, first lay college, 1896. c, Civil Registration Law, 1900. d, School of Fine Arts, Quito, 1904. e, Opening of Guayaquil-Quito Railroad, 1908. f, Founding of Guayaquil Worker's Society, Creation of Independence Plaza, Quito, 1909. h, Map of South America, José Marti, Eloy Alfaro, and Augusto Cesar Sandino, 1911.
$3, Alfaro, locomotive.

2012, July 31		Perf. 13¾x13½
2066 A872	25c Sheet of 8, #a-h	7.00 3.50

Souvenir Sheet
Imperf

2067 A873	$3 multi	8.00 4.00

Enrique Gil Gilbert (1912-73), Writer — A874

2012, Aug. 8		Perf. 13¾x13½
2068 A874	$1 multi	2.75 1.40

Souvenir Sheet

Steamship Ecuador — A875

No. 2069 — Emblem of 2012 Ecuador Philatelic Society Stamp Exposition and: a, Ship's stern and flag. b, Ship's bow.

Litho. (Foil Application in Margin)

2012, Aug. 16		Perf. 13½x13¾
2069 A875	$3 Sheet of 2, #a-b, gold inscription in sheet margin	15.00 6.00
c.	As #2069, silver inscription in sheet margin	15.00 6.00
d.	As #2069, red metallic inscription in sheet margin	15.00 6.00

Miniature Sheet

Moths — A876

No. 2070: a, Getta baetifica. b, Sematura diana. c, Xylophanes pyrrhus. d, Leucanella contempta.

		Perf. 13¾x13½
2012, Aug. 28		Litho.
2070 A876	50c Sheet of 4, #a-d	6.00 2.50

Quito Chamber of Construction, 50th Anniv. — A877

Construction materials: No. 2071, $1, Timber (madera). No. 2072, $1, Bamboo (guadua). No. 2073, $1, Wattle (baharaque). No. 2074, $1, Compacted mud (tapial).

2012, Sept. 4		Perf. 13½x13¾
2071-2074 A877	Set of 4	11.50 4.50

America Issue — A878

Myths and legends: No. 2075, $2, Legend of Ayer. No. 2076, $2, Legend of the Rooster of the Cathedral, vert.

		Perf. 13¾x13½, 13½x13¾
2012, Sept. 17		
2075-2076 A878	Set of 2	5.50 4.50

Nelson Estupiñán Bass (1912-2002), Writer — A879

2012, Sept. 20		Perf. 13¾x13½
2077 A879	$2 multi	5.25 2.25

327

328 ECUADOR

Alexander von Humboldt (1769-1859), Naturalist — A880

Denominations: 50c, $2.

2012, Sept. 26			Wmk. 377
2078-2079	A880	Set of 2	6.75 3.00

Friendship between Ecuador and Germany, 125th anniv.

A881 Trains — A882

No. 2080: a, Baldwin No. 3 Ingenio Valdez. b, Baldwin No. 2 Inés María. c, Baldwin No. 12 C.F.F.E. d, Baldwin No. 37 G&Q. e, Baldwin No. 7 G&Q. f, Baldwin No. 3 Quito-Esmeraldas train. g, Baldwin No. 2 Yaguachi train. h, Baldwin No. 1 Curaray train.

No. 2081: a, Baldwin No. 53. b, Gec Alsthom No. 2408. c, Gec Alsthom No. 2405. d, Baldwin No. 17. e, Baldwin No. 58. f, Gec Alsthom No. 2407 and station. g, Gec Alsthom No. 2404. h, Gec Alsthom No. 2407.

No. 2082: a, Baldwin No. 58, diff. b, Gec Alsthom No. 2404, diff. c, Gec Alsthom No. 2406. d, Baldwin No. 53, diff. e, Gec Alsthom No. 2402. f, Baldwin No. 58 on bridge. g, Baldwin No. 17, diff. h, Gec Alsthom No. 2405, diff.

2012, Oct. 8	Unwmk.	Die Cut
	Self-Adhesive	
2080	Booklet pane of 8	14.50
a.-b.	A881 25c Either single	.65 .40
c.-d.	A881 50c Either single	1.30 .65
e.-f.	A881 75c Either single	2.00 1.00
g.-h.	A881 $1 Either single	2.60 1.30
2081	Booklet pane of 8	14.50
a.-b.	A882 25c Either single	.65 .40
c.-d.	A882 50c Either single	1.30 .65
e.-f.	A882 75c Either single	2.00 1.00
g.-h.	A882 $1 Either single	2.60 1.30
2082	Booklet pane of 8	14.50
a.-b.	A882 25c Either single	.65 .40
c.-d.	A882 50c Either single	1.30 .65
e.-f.	A882 75c Either single	2.00 1.00
g.-h.	A882 $1 Either single	2.60 1.30

Jesuit Institutions — A883

Schools: No. 2083, $1, Unidad Educativa Borja, 75th anniv. No. 2084, $1, Unidad Educativa San Felipe Neri, 175th anniv. No. 2085, $1.25, Colegio San Gabriel, 150th anniv. $5, Jesuit church and emblem.

	Perf. 13¾x13½	
2012, Oct. 29		Wmk. 377
2083-2085	A883 Set of 3	9.75 3.50
	Size: 100x70mm	
	Imperf	
2086	A883 $5 multi	13.00 13.00

Permanent return of Jesuits to Ecuador, 150th anniv.

Renovation of Guayas Government Palace — A884

2012, Nov. 6		Perf. 13½x13¾
2087	A884 $5 multi	13.00 10.00

Ecuadorian Army's Communications Group, 50th Anniv. — A885

No. 2088: a, Indian messenger. b, Men and wagon transporting radiotelegraphic station, 1924. c, Bicycle messengers, 1932. d, Communication transmission school building, 1942.

2012, Nov. 14		
2088	Horiz. strip of 4	3.50 2.50
a.-d.	A885 25c Any single	.65 .40

Guayaquil Beneficence Council, 125th Anniv. — A886

2012, Nov. 27		Perf. 13¾x13½
2089	A886 $3 multi	7.50 6.00

Miniature Sheet

Guayas Tourism A887

No. 2090: a, Crucifix. b, Rock climbers. c, Fishermen in boats. d, Rice farmer. e, Cacao farmer. f, Sugar processing.

2012, Nov. 29		
2090	A887 75c Sheet of 6, #a-f, + 2 labels	12.50 10.00

Christmas — A888

Icons: No. 2091, $1, Bethlehem Portal, Concepción Monastery, Quito. No. 2092, $1, Mystery, Carmen Alto Monastery, Quito.

2012, Dec. 3		Wmk. 377
2091-2092	A888 Set of 2	5.50 4.50

Military Leaders A889

No. 2093: a, Gen. Eloy Alfaro (1842-1912). b, Col. Carlos Concha Torres (1864-1919). c, Col. Luis Vargas Torres (1855-87).

2012, Dec. 14		Rouletted 13½
2093	Horiz. strip of 3	10.00 7.50
a.-c.	A889 $1.25 Any single	2.50 2.50

Galapagos Islands Type of 2012

No. 2094: a, Rock with carving of face, Isla Floreana. b, Phoebastria irrorata. c, Carcharhinus galapagensis. d, Chelonia mydas. e, Pterophyllum scalare. f, Sleeping Lion Rock, San Cristóbal. g, Flower. h, Isla Plaza Sur.

No. 2095: a, Fregata magnificens. b, Post barrel, Post Office Bay, Isla Floreana. c, Camarhynchus pallidus. d, Pyrocephalus rubinus. e, Buteo galapagoensis. f, Isla Bartolomé. g, Red reef fish. h, Vicente Roca Point.

2013, Jan. 16	Unwmk.	Die Cut
	Self-Adhesive	
2094	Booklet pane of 8	15.00
a.-b.	A870 25c Either single	.65 .40
c.-d.	A870 50c Either single	1.40 1.40
e.-f.	A870 75c Either single	2.00 2.00
g.-h.	A870 $1 Either single	2.60 2.60
2095	Booklet pane of 8	15.00
a.-b.	A870 25c Either single	.65 .40
c.-d.	A870 50c Either single	1.40 1.40
e.-f.	A870 75c Either single	2.00 2.00
g.-h.	A870 $1 Either single	2.60 2.60

Nos 2094 and 2095 were each printed with two different background designs, one depicting a wood grain, and the other depicting a tortoise shell pattern. Values are the same.

Miniature Sheet

TAME Airlines, 50th Anniv. A890

No. 2096: a, DC-3. b, DC-6B. c, Avro 748. d, Electra II. e, Boeing 727-200. f, Embraer E-190. g, Airbus A320. h, ATR 42-500.

2013, Feb. 8	Wmk. 377	Perf. 13½
2096	A890 25c Sheet of 8, #a-h, + central label	7.50 5.00

Hat Making A891

No. 2097: a, Unfinished hats (orange panel). b, Hat maker (blue panel). c, Hat maker, diff. (red panel).

2013, Mar. 18		Perf. 13¼
2097	Horiz. strip of 3	4.50 3.50
a.-c.	A891 50c Any single	1.25 1.00

Scout Group No. 14, Guayaquil, 50th Anniv. — A892

Litho. With Foil Application
Perf. 13½x13¾

2013, June 21		Wmk. 377
2098	A892 $1 multi	4.00 3.00

Launch of Pegasus NEE-01 (First Ecuadorian Satellite) — A893

Perf. 13¾x13½

2013, June 28		Litho.
2099	A893 $2 multi	5.25 4.50

Diplomatic Relations Between Dominican Republic and Ecuador, 75th Anniv. A894

2013, July 2		Perf. 13½x13¾
2100	A894 $1 multi	2.75 2.25

Popes Francis and Benedict XVI A895

Litho. With Foil Application

2013, July 3		Wmk. 377
2101	A895 $5 multi	12.00 12.00

June 24, 2012 Death of Pinta Island Tortoise, Lonesome George — A896

Lonesome George and: $3, Surf spray. $25, Trees.

Litho. With Grit Affixed
Perf. 13½x13¼

2013, July 4		Unwmk.
2102	A896 $3 multi	7.75 6.50

Litho.
Wmk. 377
Size: 91x71mm
Imperf

2103	A896 $25 multi	63.00 60.00

Dr. Ricardo Descalzi (1912-90), Writer and Physician — A897

Perf. 13½x13¾

2013, Aug. 1	Litho.	Wmk. 377
2104	A897 $3 multi	7.75 6.50

Volcanos — A898

No. 2105: a, Mt. Chimborazo. b, Mt. Cotopaxi. c, Mt. Tungurahua.

Perf. 13¾x13½

2013, Aug. 21	Litho.	Wmk. 377
2105	Horiz. strip of 3	2.75 2.25
a.-c.	A898 25c Any single	.80 .60

Flower With Black and White Faces, Dr. Martin Luther King, Jr. — A899

Perf. 13¾x13½

2013, Oct. 22	Litho.	Wmk. 377
2106	A899 $1 multi	3.00 2.50

America issue (campaign against discrimination).

Royal Audience of Quito, 450th Anniv. — A900

Designs: 25c, Hernando de Santillán y Figueroa (1519-75), First President of the Royal Audience of Quito. $5, Map of the Royal Audience of Quito.

ECUADOR

Perf. 13¾x13½
2013, Nov. 13   Litho.   Wmk. 377
2107   A900   25c multi   .95   .70
Size: 74x94mm
Imperf
2108   A900 $5 multi   13.00   13.00

Ecuadorian Presence in the Antarctic, 25th Anniv. — A901

No. 2109: a, Pygoscelis papua. b, Leptonychotes weddellii. c, Catharacta lonnbergi.

Wmk. 377
2013, Nov. 21   Litho.   Perf. 13½
2109   Horiz. strip of 3   4.50   3.50
   a.-c.   A901 50c Any single   1.50   1.10

Miniature Sheet

Christmas — A902

No. 2110: a, Annunciation (Primer día). b, Visitation of St. Elizabeth (Segundo día). c, St. Joseph's dream (Tercer día). d, Journey to Bethlehem (Cuarto día). e, Arrival at the inn (Quinto día). f, Star of Bethlehem (Sexto día). g, Shepherds (Séptimo día). h, Angels (Octavo día). i, Holy Family (Noveno día).

Perf. 13½x13¼
2013, Nov. 29   Litho.   Wmk. 377
2110   A902   25c Sheet of 9, #a-i   8.00   5.50

Intl. Year of Quinoa — A903

No. 2111: a, Chenopodium quinoa. b, Amaranthus caudatus. c, Lupinus mutabilis.

Perf. 13¾x13½
2013, Dec. 16   Litho.   Wmk. 377
2111   Horiz. strip of 3   16.00   14.00
   a.-c.   A903 $2 Any single   5.00   4.25

Imbabura Textile Mill A904

No. 2112: a, Workers near weaving machines. b, Workers near machines with thread spools.

Rouletted 12¼
2014, Jan. 27   Litho.   Wmk. 377
2112   A904 $1 Horiz. pair, #a-b   5.75   5.00

Resolution of Ecuador-Peru Border Dispute, 15th Anniv. — A905

Rouletted 12¼
2014, Jan. 30   Litho.   Wmk. 377
2113   A905 $5 multi   13.00   12.00

Presidents of Ecuador — A906

No. 2114: a, Juan José Flores A. (1800-64). b, Vicente Rocafuerte B. (1783-1847). c, Vicente Roca R. (1792-1858). d, Diego Noboa A. (1789-1870). e, José M. Urbina V. (1808-91). f, Francisco Robles G. (1811-93). g, Gabriel García M. (1821-75). h, Jerónimo Carrión P. (1804-73). i, Javier Espinosa E. (1815-70). j, Antonio Borrero C. (1827-1911). k, Ignacio de Vientemilla V. (1828-1908). l, José M. Camaño (1837-1900). m, Antonio Flores J. (1833-1915). n, Luis Cordero C. (1833-1912). o, Eloy Alfaro D. (1842-1912). p, Leonidas Plaza G. (1865-1932). q, Lizardo García S. (1844-1937). r, Emilio Estrada C. (1855-1911). s, Alfredo Baquerizo M. (1859-1951). t, José L. Tamayo T. (1858-1947). u, Gonzalo S. córdova R. (1863-1928). v, Isidro Ayora C. (1879-1978). w, Juan D. Martínez M. (1875-1955). x, José M. Velasco I. (1893-1979). y, Aurelio Mosquera N. (1883-1939). z, Carlos A. Arroyo (1893-1969). aa, Mariano Suárez V. (1897-1980). ab, Carlos J. Arosemena T. (1888-1952). ac, Galo Plaza L. (1906-87). ad, Camilo Ponce E. (1912-76). ae, Carlos J. Arosemena M. (1919-2004). af, Otto Arosemena G. (1925-84). ag, Jaime Roldós A. (1940-81). ah, León Febres Cordero R. (1931-2008).

Perf. 13¾x13½
2014, Apr. 1   Litho.   Wmk. 377
2114   Sheet of 34 + label   30.00   21.00
   a.-ah.   A906 25c Any single   .85   .60

Hugo R. Chávez (1954-2013), President of Venezuela — A907

Perf. 13¾x13½
2014, Apr. 14   Litho.   Wmk. 377
2115   A907   50c multi   1.50   1.25

Parade of Tall Ships, Manabí A908

No. 2116 — Ship and national flag: a, Cisne Branco, Brazil. b, Cuauhtémoc, Mexico. c, Gloria, Colombia. d, Libertad, Argentina. e, Esmerelda, Chile. f, Guayas, Ecuador. g, Simón Bolívar, Venezuela.

Perf. 13½x13¾
2014, May 3   Litho.   Wmk. 377
2116   Sheet of 7 + label   15.00   13.00
   a.-g.   A908 75c Any single   2.00   1.75

Intl. Philately Day A909

Magnifying glass over: $2, Ecuadorian stamps. $3, Text from *El Nacional*.

2014, May 22   Litho.   Perf. 13½x13¾
2117   A909 $2 multi   5.50   5.00
Size: 90x70mm
Wmk. 395
Imperf
2118   A909 $3 multi   8.00   7.50

Regional Platform for Disaster Risk Reduction in the Americas, Guayaquil A910

Perf. 13½x13¾
2014, May 27   Litho.   Wmk. 377
2119   A910 $1 multi   2.75   2.50

2014 World Cup Soccer Championships, Brazil — A911

Designs: 50c, Stadium and stylized Ecuador soccer player. $3, Stylized Ecuador soccer player in stadium, Christ the Redeemer Statue, Rio de Janeiro, horiz. $5, Soccer player and field, horiz.

Perf. 13½x13¾, 13¾x13½
2014, June 18   Litho.   Wmk. 377
2120-2121   A911   Set of 2   9.50   8.50
Size: 55x35mm
Imperf
2122   A911 $5 multi   13.00   12.50

Pancho Segura, Ecuadorian-born Tennis Player — A912

Designs: 25c, Segura on tennis court as young man. $5, Segura, tennis ball and racquet, Ecuadoran flag.

Perf. 13½x13¾
2014, July 25   Litho.   Wmk. 377
2123-2124   A912   Set of 2   14.00   13.00

Intl. Year of Family Farming — A913

Designs: 75c, Woman near tree. $1, Woman spinning yarn from wool. $2, Man pulling down cacao pod from tree.

Perf. 13¾x13½
2014, Aug. 11   Litho.   Wmk. 377
2125-2127   A913   Set of 3   10.00   9.00

2014 Latin American Integration Expo, Montevideo, Uruguay — A914

Perf. 13½x13¾
2014, Aug. 28   Litho.   Wmk. 377
2128   A914 $3 multi   8.00   7.00

Mural by Oswaldo Guayasamín — A915

No. 2129: a, Denomination at left. b, Denomination at right.

Perf. 13¾x13½
2014, Aug. 29   Litho.   Wmk. 377
2129   A915   25c Horiz. pair, #a-b   1.75   1.25
Latin American Parliament, 50th anniv.

Luis Vernaza Hospital, 450th Anniv. A916

No. 2130: a, Hospital building. b, Doctor examining patient.

Perf. 13½x13¾
2014, Sept. 10   Litho.   Wmk. 377
2130   A916   50c Horiz. pair, #a-b   3.25   2.50

Miniature Sheet

Scorpions — A917

No. 2131: a, Centruroides margaritatus. b, Touthrauotoo atramontariuo. o, Tityuo asthenes. d, Tityus crassicauda. e, Tityus ythieri.

Perf. 13¾x13½
2014, Sept. 30   Litho.   Wmk. 377
2131   A917 $5 Sheet of 5, #a-e, + label   65.00   60.00

Yachay University Buildings — A918

No. 2132: a, Capitular Building. b, Library.

Perf. 13¾x13½
2014, Oct. 21   Litho.   Wmk. 377
2132   A918 $2 Horiz. pair, #a-b   11.50   9.50

Oryx Leucoryx, Vultur Gryphus, Flags of Ecuador and Qatar — A919

Litho. With Foil Application
Perf. 13½x13¾
2014, Oct. 22   Wmk. 377
2133   A919 $10 multi   25.00   20.00
See Qatar No. 1101.

Manuela Espejo (c. 1757-c. 1829), Writer — A920

Litho. With Foil Application
Perf. 10¼x10¼
2014, Oct. 28   Wmk. 377
2134   A920 $5 metallic blue & blue   13.00   10.00
America issue.

Electricity Generation Projects — A921

Designs: 75c, Baba Dam. $1.25, Wind generators, Villonaco. $2, Mazar Dam.

Perf. 13½x13¾
2014, Oct. 31   Litho.   Wmk. 377
2135-2137   A921   Set of 3   11.00   10.00

ECUADOR

Fall of the Berlin Wall, 25th Anniv. — A922

Perf. 13¾x13½
2014, Nov. 10   Litho.   Wmk. 377
2138 A922 75c multi   2.25 2.00

Christmas — A923

Designs: 50c, Ivory creche figurines, 18th cent. $1, Wood carving of Infant Jesus, by Caspicara, vert.

Perf. 13¾x13½, 13½x13¾
2014, Nov. 25   Litho.   Wmk. 377
2139-2140 A923 Set of 2   4.25 3.50

Miniature Sheet

Cuenca Tourist Attractions — A924

No. 2141: a, Rio Tomebamba. b, Mayor's office (Alcaldía). c, Benigno Malo College. d, Interamerican Artisans Center. e, New Cathedral. f, Azuay Provincial Court. g, Plaza de las Flores.

Perf. 13¾x13½
2014, Dec. 2   Litho.   Wmk. 377
2141 A924 75c Sheet of 7, #a-g, + label   15.00 13.50

Miniature Sheet

First Ecuadorian Postage Stamps, 150th Anniv. — A925

No. 2142: a, Emilia Rivadeneira (1839-1916), engraver. b, Printing press, Ecuador #3. c, Printing press, Ecuador #2. d, Printing press, Ecuador #5. e, Manuel Rivadeneira (1814-94), printer.

Litho. With Foil Application
Perf. 13¾x13½
2015, Mar. 19   Wmk. 377
2142 A925 $5 Sheet of 5, #a-e, + 4 labels   65.00 50.00

Insects — A926

No. 2143: a, Antianthe expansa. b, Heteronotus abbreviatus. c, Cyphonia clavata. d, Guayaquila gracilicornis. e, Stegaspis frondtia. f, Thuris depressus. g, Tritropidia galeata. h, Membracis mexicana.

Unwmk.
2015, Apr. 21   Litho.   **Die Cut**
Self-Adhesive
2143   Booklet pane of 8   14.50 14.50
 a.-b. A926 25c Either single   .75   .75
 c.-d. A926 50c Either single   1.40 1.40
 e.-f. A926 75c Either single   2.10 2.10
 g.-h. A926 $1 Either single   3.00 3.00

Pres. Sixto Durán Ballén and Dove — A927

Perf. 13½x13¾
2015, May 15   Litho.   Wmk. 377
2144 A927 $1.25 multi   3.25 3.00

Insects — A928

No. 2145: a, Alchisme grossa. b, Membracis foliata. c, Cladonota apicalis. d, Cyphonia trifida. e, Adippe histrio.

Perf. 13½x13¾
2015, May 28   Litho.   Wmk. 377
2145   Horiz. strip of 5   39.00 35.00
 a.-e. A928 $3 Any single   7.00   6.50

Cattle — A929

Breeds: 75c, Aberdeen Angus. $1.25, Brahman. $3, Holstein Friesian.

Perf. 13½x13¾
2015, June 2   Litho.   Wmk. 377
2146-2148 A929 Set of 3   15.00 10.00

Eradication of hoof-and-mouth disease in Ecuador.

Renovation of San Francisco Monastery, Quito — A930

Designs: 25c, Friar Jodoco Ricke baptizing indigenous people. 50c, Icon of Jesus, San Francisco Church. $1, San Francisco Church and Plaza. $1.75, Franciscan monk making beer. $2, Religious procession.

Perf. 13½x13¾
2015, June 11   Litho.   Wmk. 377
2149-2153 A930 Set of 5   15.00 13.50

Birds — A931

Designs: 25c, Grallaria ridgelyi. 50c, Amazona lilacina. $1, Atlapetes pallidiceps. $2, Pyrrhura albipectus. $3, Chaetocercus berlepschi.

Perf. 13½x13¾
2015, June 16   Litho.   Wmk. 377
2154-2158 A931 Set of 5   18.00 15.00

Visit of Pope Francis to Ecuador — A932

Perf. 13¾x13½
2015, June 30   Litho.   Wmk. 377
2159 A932 $3 multi   8.75 6.00

Litho. With Foil Application
Size: 100x70mm
Imperf
2160 A932 $5 Pope Francis, diff.   14.00 10.00

Official Registrar, 120th Anniv. — A933

Perf. 13¾x13½
2015, Sept. 1   Litho.   Wmk. 377
2161 A933 $1.50 multi   4.00 3.50

Famous People — A934

No. 2162: a, Antonio Bastidas y Carranza (1615-81), poet. b, Raúl Clemente Huerta (1915-91), politician. c, Morayma Ofyr Carvajal (1915-51), writer. d, José Modesto Espinosa (1833-1915), writer. e, José Cuero y Caicedo (1735-1815), bishop of Quito.

Perf. 13¾x13½
2015, Sept. 22   Litho.   Wmk. 377
2162   Horiz. strip of 5   17.00 15.00
 a.-e. A934 $1.25 Any single   3.00   3.00

Miniature Sheet

ExpoAFE, 150th Anniv. — A935

No. 2163: a, Argentina #594, flag of Argentina. b, Unissued Bolivia stamp of 1863, flag of Bolivia. c, Brazil #3252c, flag of Brazil. d, Canada #322, flag of Canada. e, Chile #348A, flag of Chile. f, Colombia #C56, flag of Colombia. g, Costa Rica #1, flag of Costa Rica. h, Cuba #432, flag of Cuba. i, Ecuador #306, flag of Ecuador. j, El Salvador #509, flag of El Salvador. k, Cover of El Coleccionista Ecuatoriano, emblem of Ecuadorian Philatelic Association. l, Block of six of Ecuador #2, ExpoAFE 80th anniv. emblem. m, Cover to Lima, emblem of ExpoAFE thematic stamp exhibition. n, Cover depicting airplane, emblem of FIAF thematic stamp exhibition. o, Postal card, FIAF emblem. p, Spain #345, flag of Spain. q, United States #C3a, flag of United States. r, Guatemala #21, flag of Guatemala. s, Mexico #246, flag of Mexico. t, Panama #214, flag of Panama. u, Paraguay #407, flag of Paraguay. v, Peru #C338, flag of Peru. w, St. Pierre & Miquelon #136, flag of St. Pierre & Miquelon. x, Uruguay #1167, flag of Uruguay. y, Venezuela #C9, flag of Venezuela.

Perf. 13½x13¾
2015, Sept. 29   Litho.   Wmk. 377
2163 A935 Sheet of 25   40.00 37.50
 a.-y.   75c Any single   1.50   1.50

Birds — A936

No. 2164: a, Tangara florida. b, Acropternis orthonyx. c, Pipreola jucunda. d, Pionopsitta pyrilia. e, Semnornis ramphastinus. f, Trogon chionurus. g, Pipra filicauda. h, Dacnis egregia.
No. 2165: a, Thryothorus nigricapillus. b, Neomorphus radiolosus. c, Phoenicircus nigricollis. d, Tangara gyrola. e, Aegolius harrisii. f, Grallaricula lineifrons. g, Melanopareia elegans. h, Piculus rivolii.

Unwmk.
2015, Oct. 20   Litho.   **Die Cut**
Self-Adhesive
2164   Booklet pane of 8   14.50
 a.-b. A936 25c Either single   .65   .65
 c.-d. A936 50c Either single   1.30 1.30
 e.-f. A936 75c Either single   2.00 2.00
 g.-h. A936 $1 Either single   2.60 2.60
2165   Booklet pane of 8   14.50
 a.-b. A936 25c Either single   .65   .65
 c.-d. A936 50c Either single   1.30 1.30
 e.-f. A936 75c Either single   2.00 2.00
 g.-h. A936 $1 Either single   2.60 2.60

Don Quixote in Art A937

No. 2166, $1 — Depictions of Don Quixote by: a, Carlos Monsalve. b, Ernesto Saá Sevilla.
No. 2167, $1.50 — Depictions of Don Quixote by: a, Oswaldo Viteri. b, Vilma Vargas.
No. 2168, $1.75, horiz. — Depictions of Don Quixote by: a, Joaquín Pinto. b, Karlomán Villota.

Perf. 13½x13¾, 13¾x13½
2015, Oct. 30   Litho.   Wmk. 377
Horiz. Pairs, #a-b
2166-2168 A937 Set of 3   23.00 20.00

A938

A939

Tourism — A940

No. 2169: a, Chelonia mydas. b, Vicugna vicugna. c, Paleosuchus trigonatus. d, Megaptera novaeangliae. e, Marine iguana. $5, Tortoise, caiman, whale, condor.
No. 2171: a, Corallus batesii. b, San Rafael Waterfall. c, Dasyatis brevis. d, Gardner Bay Beach, Española Island, Galapagos Islands. e, Ceratophrys stolzmanni. f, Ship on Guayas River. g, Coeligena torquata. h, El Vado, Cuenca.
No. 2172: a, Hippocampus ingens. b, Amblyrhynchus cristatus. c, Prionurus laticlavius. d, Fregata magnificens. e, Spheniscus mendiculus. f, Boats near Isabela Island, Galapagos Islands. g, Roca Pináculo, Bartolomé Island, Galapagos Islands. h, Boats near Plaza Islands, Galapagos Islands.

Perf. 13¾x13½
2015, Nov. 11   Litho.   Wmk. 377
2169   Horiz. strip of 5   14.00 12.50
 a.-e. A938 $1 Any single   2.75   2.75

Imperf
2170 A939 $5 multi   13.00 12.00

Self-Adhesive
Unwmk.
Die Cut
2171   Booklet pane of 8   14.50
 a.-b. A940 25c Either single   .65   .65
 c.-d. A940 50c Either single   1.30 1.30
 e.-f. A940 75c Either single   2.10 2.10
 g.-h. A940 $1 Either single   2.60 2.60
2172   Booklet pane of 8   14.50
 a.-b. A940 25c Either single   .65   .65
 c.-d. A940 50c Either single   1.30 1.30
 e.-f. A940 75c Either single   2.10 2.10
 g.-h. A940 $1 Either single   2.60 2.60

ECUADOR 331

Campaign to End Violence Against Women — A941

Perf. 13¾x13½
2015, Nov. 25   Litho.   Wmk. 377
2173 A941 $5 multi   13.00 12.00
See Dominican Republic No. 1583, Guatemala No. 717, El Salvador No. 1747, Venezuela No. 1731.

Campaign Against Human Trafficking — A942

Perf. 13½x13¾
2015, Nov. 22   Litho.   Wmk. 377
2174 A942 $1.50 multi   4.00 3.50
America Issue.

Christmas — A943

Perf. 13½x13¾
2015, Dec. 3   Litho.   Wmk. 377
2175 A943 $2 multi   5.25 4.50

Yachay, City of Knowledge — A944

Perf. 13¾x13½
2016, Mar. 31   Litho.   Wmk. 377
2176 A944 $2 multi   5.75 4.00

Amphibians — A945

Amphibians — A945

No. 2177: a, Epipedobates anthonyi. b, Hyloscirtus princecharlesi. c, Oophaga sylvatica. d, Ceratophrys stolzmanni. e, Gastrotheca riobambae. f, Hyalinobatrachium aureoguttatum. g, Hypsiboas picturatus. h, Atelopus balios.

Unwmk.
2016, Mar. 31   Litho.   Die Cut
Self-Adhesive
2177   Booklet pane of 8   14.50
  a.-b. A945 25c Either single   .60   .60
  c.-d. A945 50c Either single   1.10 1.10
  e.-f. A945 75c Either single   1.75 1.75
  g.-h. A945 $1 Either single   2.25 2.25

Quito Central Lions Club, 70th Anniv. — A946

Perf. 13½x13¾
2016, Apr. 27   Litho.   Wmk. 377
2178 A946 $5 multi   14.00 10.00

Ecuador Postal Service, 185th Anniv. A947

No. 2179: a, Chasqui (relay messenger). b, Postman on bicycle. c, Postal worker on motorcycle. d, Old Quito Post Office, 185th anniv. emblem.

Perf. 13½x13¾
2016, May 25   Litho.   Wmk. 377
2179 A947 10c Block of 4, #a-d   2.60 1.30

2016 Summer Olympics, Rio de Janeiro — A948

No. 2180: a, Swimming. b, Running. c, Weight lifting. d, Boxing.

Perf. 13¾x13½
2016, Aug. 16   Litho.   Wmk. 377
2180 A948 $1.25 Sheet of 4, #a-d   13.50 12.00

Colegio Intisana, Quito, 50th Anniv. — A949

Perf. 13½x13¾
2016, Oct. 24   Litho.   Wmk. 377
2181 A949 $2 multi   6.00 4.00

Jamaica Letter, by Simón Bolívar, 200th Anniv. (in 2015) A950

No. 2182: a, Portrait of Bolívar, by Antonio Salguero. b, Jamaica Letter, ribbon in colors of Ecuadorian flag.

Perf. 13½x13¾
2016, Oct. 28   Litho.   Wmk. 377
2182 A950 $10 Horiz. pair, #a-b 55.00 40.00

Coca Codo Sinclair Hydroelectric Project — A951

Designs: $1.25, Dam. $1.50, Compensating reservoir. $1.75, Generators.

Perf. 13¾x13½
2016, Oct. 25   Litho.   Wmk. 377
2183-2185 A951 Set of 3   13.00 9.00

Flowers — A952

No. 2186: a, Cyrtocaucaea. b, Masdevallia. c, Hippeastrum sp. d, Gentianella hirculus. e, Bomarea caldasii.

Perf. 13¾x13½
2016, Nov. 12   Litho.   Wmk. 395
2186   Horiz. strip of 5   14.00 12.00
  a.-e. A952 $1 Any single   2.25   2.00

Third French-Ecuadorian Geodesic Mission — A953

No. 2187: a, Drawing of people near globe. b, Mt. Chimborazo.

Perf. 13¾x13½
2016, Nov. 14   Litho.   Wmk. 377
2187 A953 10c Horiz. pair, #a-b   1.25   .65

Society for Protection of Children — A954

Perf. 13½x13¾
2016, Nov. 22   Litho.   Wmk. 377
2188 A954 $5 multi   14.00 10.00

Santa Elena Petroleum Ancón Oil Well — A955

Perf. 13¾x13½
2016, Nov. 30   Litho.   Wmk. 377
2189 A955 30c multi   1.00   .75

Christmas — A956

No. 2190: a, Shepherd and sheep, volcano. b, Star of Bethlehem, Andean village. c, Annunciation, Galapagos turtle. d, Three Magi in Ecuadorian Indian costumes. e, Afro American Holy Family.

Perf. 13¾x13½
2016, Dec. 12   Litho.   Wmk. 377
2190   Horiz. strip of 5   29.00 21.00
  a.-e. A956 $2 Any single   4.25   4.00

Union of South American Nations Summit, Quito — A957

Perf. 13¾x13½
2016, Dec. 22   Litho.   Wmk. 377
2191 A957 $3 multi   8.75 6.00

Ecuadorian Institute for Promotion of Exportation and Investment — A958

No. 2192: a, Dam, emblem for 2016 Ecuador Investment Summit. b, Spiral and "love life." c, Hats. d, Cacao pods. e, Onions, bananas, herbs, shrimp.

Perf. 13½x13¾
2016, Dec. 29   Litho.   Wmk. 377
2192   Horiz. strip of 5   16.00 10.00
  a.-e. A958 $1 Any single   2.00   2.00

A959

Schools A960

No. 2193: a, Hands, emblem of Ecuador University of Arts. b, Book, quill pen, emblem of National University of Ecuador.
No. 2194: a, Buckminsterfullerene molecule, emblem for Yachay Tech. b, Frog, emblem for Amazon Regional University.

ECUADOR

Perf. 13½x13¾
2016, Dec. 30   Litho.   **Wmk. 377**
| 2193 | A959 | $3 Horiz. pair, #a-b | 17.50 | 12.00 |
| 2194 | A960 | $3 Horiz. pair, #a-b | 17.50 | 12.00 |

Carnival, Guaranda — A961

No. 2195: a, Aerial view of Guaranda. b, Guitarist.

Perf. 13¾x13½
2017, Feb. 24   Litho.
| 2195 | A961 | $1 Horiz. pair, #a-b | 6.25 | 4.50 |

Ants — A962

No. 2196: a, Atta cephalotes (Hormiga arriera). b, Eciton hamatum (Hormiga legionaria). c, Daceton armigerum (Hormiga cazadora). d, Acanthoponera minor (Conga enana). e, Ectatomma tuberculatum (Hormiga rugosa). f, Gigantiops destructor (Hormiga ojona). g, Neoponera villosa (Hormiga peluda). h, Cephalotes atratus (Cabezona negra).

No. 2197: a, Cephalotes spinosus (Hormiga paracaidista). b, Odontomachus hastatus (Hormiga mandibula). c, Pheidole xanthogaster (Hormiga zanahoria). d, Myrmelachista ruszkii (Hormiga limón). e, Leptogenys pucuna (Hormiga de Lattke). f, Eciton rapax (Hormiga rapaz). g, Paraponera clavata (Conga). h, Camponotus sericeiventris (Hormiga aterciopelada).

Unwmk.
2017, Mar. 31   Litho.   *Die Cut*
Self-Adhesive
2196		Booklet pane of 8	18.00	
a.-b.	A962	25c Either single	.55	.55
c.-d.	A962	50c Either single	1.10	1.10
e.-f.	A962	75c Either single	1.60	1.60
g.-h.	A962	$1 Either single	2.25	2.25
2197		Booklet pane of 8	18.00	
a.-b.	A962	25c Either single	.55	.55
c.-d.	A962	50c Either single	1.10	1.10
e.-f.	A962	75c Either single	1.60	1.60
g.-h.	A962	$1 Either single	2.25	2.25

Miniature Sheet

World Philately Day A963

No. 2198: a, Emblem of Olympic and Sports Philatelic Association of Ecuador. b, 1883 cover with Ecuador #18. c, 1895 cover with Guaranda provisional surcharge stamps. d, 1896 cover with bisected Seebeck stamp and other Ecuador stamps.

Litho., Litho With Foil Application (#2198a)
Perf. 13¾x13½
2017, May 18   **Wmk. 377**
| 2198 | A963 | $2.50 Sheet of 4, #a-d | 32.50 | 20.00 |

German School, Quito, Cent. — A964

Perf. 13¼x13
2017, Oct. 3   Litho.   **Wmk. 377**
| 2199 | A964 | $5 multi | 16.00 | 10.00 |

Darwin and Wolf Islands Marine Sanctuary — A965

No. 2200: a, Darwin Island and Darwin Arch. b, Sphyrna lewini. c, Rhincodon typus. d, Aetobatus narinari. e, Darwin Arch. f, Chelonia mydas. g, Delphinus delphis. h, Sula nebouxii.

Unwmk.
2017, Oct. 24   Litho.   *Die Cut*
Self-Adhesive
2200		Booklet pane of 8	19.00	
a.-b.	A965	25c Either single	.55	.55
c.-d.	A965	50c Either single	1.10	1.10
e.-f.	A965	75c Either single	1.60	1.60
g.-h.	A965	$1 Either single	2.25	2.25

Amazon Regional Economic Development Institute (ECORAE) — A966

No. 2201: a, Communication between Amazon cultures. b, Bridge, Morona-Santiago Province.

Perf. 13¼x13
2017, Nov. 2   Litho.   **Wmk. 377**
| 2201 | A966 | $2.50 Horiz. pair, #a-b | 16.00 | 10.00 |

A967

Tourism — A968

No. 2202: a, Train, Guamote Canton. b, Chimborazo Volcano. c, San Rafael Waterfall. d, San Lorenzo Beach. e, Negra Beach.
No. 2203: a, Caucaea nubigena. b, Handroanthus chrysanthus. c, Sula granti. d, Podocnemis expansa. e, Oreotrochilus. f, Cuyabeno River. g, Los Frailes Beach. h, San Francisco Church, Quito.

Perf. 13¼x13
2017   Litho.   **Wmk. 377**
| 2202 | | Horiz. strip of 5 | 47.50 | 40.00 |
| a.-e. | A967 | $3 Any single | 7.50 | 7.50 |

Self-Adhesive
Unwmk.
Die Cut
2203		Booklet pane of 8	16.00	
a.-b.	A968	25c Either single	.65	.65
c.-d.	A968	50c Either single	1.25	1.25
e.-f.	A968	75c Either single	1.90	1.90
g.-h.	A968	$1 Either single	2.50	2.50

America issue. Issued: No. 2202, 12/27; No. 2203, 11/27.

Christmas — A969

Perf. 13x13¼
2017, Dec. 18   Litho.   **Wmk. 377**
| 2204 | A969 | $2 multi | 5.75 | 4.50 |

Eugenio Espejo National Prize — A970

Perf. 13x13¼
2017, Dec. 21   Litho.   **Wmk. 377**
| 2205 | A970 | $10 multi | 31.00 | 20.00 |

15th Interamerican Scout Jamboree, Ecuador — A971

Perf. 13x13¼
2017, Dec. 29   Litho.   **Wmk. 377**
| 2206 | A971 | $5 multi | 15.00 | 12.00 |

Souvenir Sheet

Locomotives — A972

No. 2207: a, Model of Sapucai locomotive. b, Baldwin steam locomotive.

Perf. 13¼x13
2018, Apr. 27   Litho.   **Wmk. 377**
| 2207 | A972 | $2.50 Sheet of 2, #a-b, + 2 labels | 15.00 | 15.00 |

Joint Issue between Ecuador & Paraguay. See Paraguay No. 3083.

Spiders — A973

No. 2208: a, Micrathena pilaton. b, Patrera fulvastra.
No. 2209: a, Argiope argentata. b, Chrysometa tenuipes.
No. 2210: a, Micrathena raimondi. b, Micrathena pichincha.
$5, Linothele quori.

Perf. 13x13¼
2018, May 9   Litho.   **Wmk. 377**
2208		Horiz. pair	1.25	.80
a.-b.	A973	20c Either single	.40	.40
2209		Horiz. pair	3.25	2.00
a.-b.	A973	50c Either single	1.00	1.00
2210		Horiz. pair	12.50	8.00
a.-b.	A973	$2 Either single	4.00	4.00
2211	A973	$5 multi	15.50	10.00
		Nos. 2208-2211 (4)	32.50	20.80

A974

Domesticated Animals — A975

No. 2212: a, Lama glama. b, Cavia porcellus. c, Bos primigenius taurus. d, Ovis orientalis aries. e, Equus ferus caballus.
No. 2213: a, Anser anser. b, Gallus gallus. c, Canis lupus familiaris. d, Felis silvestris catus. e, Capra aegagrus hircus. f, Oryctolagus cuniculus. g, Equus ferus caballus. h, Lama glama.

Perf. 13¼x13
2018, May 18   Litho.   **Wmk. 377**
| 2212 | | Horiz. strip of 5 | 30.00 | 20.00 |
| a.-e. | A974 | $2 Any single | 4.00 | 4.00 |

Self-Adhesive
Unwmk.
Die Cut
2213		Booklet pane of 8	16.00	
a.-b.	A975	25c Either single	.65	.65
c.-d.	A975	50c Either single	1.25	1.25
e.-f.	A975	75c Either single	1.90	1.90
g.-h.	A975	$1 Either single	2.50	2.50

University of Azuay, 50th Anniv. — A976

Designs: $3, Emblem. $5, Emblem and trees, horiz.

Perf. 13x13¼
2018, June 14   Litho.   **Wmk. 377**
| 2214 | A976 | $3 multi | 9.00 | 6.00 |

Imperf
Size: 96x71mm
| 2215 | A976 | $5 multi | 15.00 | 10.00 |

Nelson Mandela (1918-2013), President of South Africa, and Flag of South Africa — A977

Perf. 13¼x13
2018, July 18   Litho.   **Wmk. 377**
| 2216 | A977 | $10 multi | 30.00 | 20.00 |

Miniature Sheet

Diplomatic Relations Between Ecuador and Japan, Cent. — A978

No. 2217: a, Kinkaku-ji Temple, Kyoto, Japan. b, Torii, Itsukushima Shrine, Miyajima, Japan. c, Church of the Society of Jesus, Quito. d, Darwin's Arch, Galapagos Islands.

Wmk. 377
2018, Aug. 13   *Perf. 13*
| 2217 | A978 | $2.50 Sheet of 4, #a-d | 30.00 | 20.00 |

Volcanoes — A979

No. 2218: a, Corazón Volcano. b, Imbabura Volcano. c, Cotacachi Volcano.

Wmk. 377
2018, Aug. 20   Litho.   *Perf. 13*
| 2218 | | Horiz. strip of 3 | 17.50 | 12.00 |
| a.-c. | A979 | $2 Any single | 4.25 | 4.00 |

Souvenir Sheet

12th Latin American Botanical Congress, Quito — A980

Perf. 13¾x13½
2018, Aug. 29   Litho.   **Wmk. 377**
| 2219 | A980 | $4 multi | 11.50 | 9.00 |

A981

ECUADOR

Green Tourism — A982

No. 2220: a, Amblyrhynchus cristatus. b, Mount Carihuairazo. c, Machalilla National Park. d, Paleosuchus trigonatus.
No. 2221: a, Zalophus wollebaeki. b, Isabela Island. c, Chalcostigma herrani. d, Espelitia plants, Páramo el Angel Ecological Reserve. e, Oophaga sylvatica. f, Cayapas Mataje Reserve. g, Cebuella pygmaea. h, Lake, Orellana Province.

Perf. 13¾x13½
2018, Sept. 13 Litho. Wmk. 377
2220 A981 $2 Block of 4, #a-d 26.00 16.00
Self-Adhesive
Die Cut
Unwmk.
2221 Booklet pane of 8 16.00
a.-b. A982 25c Either single .50 .50
c.-d. A982 50c Either single 1.00 1.00
e.-f. A982 75c Either single 1.50 1.50
g.-h. A982 $1 Either single 2.00 2.00

A983 A984

Image of the Motherland Mural, by Oswaldo Guayasamín
A985

Perf. 13¾x13½
2018, Sept. 18 Litho. Wmk. 377
2222 Horiz. strip of 3 9.50 6.00
a. A983 $1 multi 2.00 2.00
b. A984 $1 multi 2.00 2.00
c. A985 $1 multi 2.00 2.00

Christmas — A986

No. 2223: a, Buildings. b, Magi on camels. c, Holy Family. d, Angel with horn. e, Shepherd and sheep.

Perf. 13¾x13½
2018, Nov. 30 Litho. Wmk. 377
2223 Horiz. strip of 5 3.00 1.75
a.-e. A986 10c Any single .40 .30

Miniature Sheet

Scientific Contributions of San Francisco University, Quito — A987

No. 2224: a, 25c, Rhincodon typus. b, 50c, Geospiza magnirostri. c, 75c, Oreotrochilus cyanolaemus. d, $1, Tiputinia foetida. e, $1.25, Cebuella pygmaea. f, $1.50, Vaccinium floribundum. g, $2, Microlophus bivittatus. h, $2.50, Chimerella mariaelenae. i, $5, University crest.

Perf. 13½x13¾
2018, Dec. 11 Litho. Wmk. 377
2224 A987 Sheet of 9, #a-i 45.00 35.00

A988

Cotacachi-Cayapas Ecological Reserve, 50th Anniv. — A989

No. 2225: a, Podiceps occipitalis. b, Odocoileus virginiannus. c, Cuicocha Lake. d, Elaenia albiceps. e, Epidendrum jamiesonis.
No. 2226: a, Eira barbara. b, Tremarctos ornatus. c, Geranoaetus melanoleucus. d, Anisogomathus igniventris. e, Eriocnemis nigrivestis. f, Cerro Pilavo. g, Bomarea glaucenscens. h, Vaccinium floribundum.

Perf. 13¾x13½
2018, Dec. 27 Litho. Wmk. 377
2225 Horiz. strip of 5 42.50 35.00
a.-e. A988 $3 Any single 7.50 6.00

Self-Adhesive
Unwmk.
Die Cut
2226 Booklet pane of 8 16.00
a.-b. A989 25c Either single .65 .65
c.-d. A989 50c Either single 1.25 1.25
e.-f. A989 75c Either single 1.90 1.90
g.-h. A989 $1 Either single 2.50 2.50

National Development Plan — A990

Perf. 13¾x13½
2018 Litho. Wmk. 377
2227 A990 $5 multi 16.50 10.00

2019 Global Forum on Miigration and Development, Quito — A991

Perf. 13¾x13½
2019, Apr. 8 Litho. Wmk. 377
2228 A991 $1 multi 3.00 2.25

Birds — A992

No. 2229: a, Turdus fuscater. b, Zonotrichia capensis. c, Sicalis flaveola. d, Thraupis bonariensis. e, Mimus gilvus. f, Pyrocephalus rubinus. g, Diglossa sittoides. h, Notiochleidon cyanoleuca.
No. 2230: a, Sporophila luctuosa. b, Dendroica fusca. c, Thraupis episcopus. d, Zenaida auriculata. e, Camptostoma obsoletum. f, Patagona gigas. g, Phoeticus chrysogaster. h, Euphonia cyanocephala.

Unwmk.
2019, May 2 Litho. Die Cut
Self-Adhesive
2229 Booklet pane of 8 16.00
a.-b. A992 25c Either single .80 .80
c.-d. A992 50c Either single 1.60 1.60
e.-f. A992 75c Either single 2.40 2.40
g.-h. A992 $1 Either single 3.25 3.25
2230 Booklet pane of 8 16.00
a.-b. A992 25c Either single .80 .80
c.-d. A992 50c Either single 1.60 1.60
e.-f. A992 75c Either single 2.40 2.40
g.-h. A992 $1 Either single 3.25 3.25

Frogs — A993

No. 2231: a, Hyalinobatrachium pellucidum. b, Nymphargus anomalus. c, Nymphargus cochranae. d, Nymphargus grandisonae facing forward. e, Nymphargus griffithsi facing left. f, Sachatamia albomaculata. g, Sachatamia ilex. h, Overhead view of Teratohyla pulverata.
No. 2232: a, Centrolene ballux. b, Centrolene buckleyi. c, Centrolene condor. d, Centrolene heloderma. e, Chimerella mariaelenae. f, Espadarana callistomma. g, Espadarana prosoblepon. h, Overhead view of Hyalinobatrachium aureoguttatum.
No. 2233: a, Cochranella balionota. b, Cochranella litoralis. c, Cochranella mache. d,

Nymphargus grandisonae facing right. e, Underside view of Hyalinobatrachium aureoguttatum. f, Underside view of Teratohyla pulverata. g, Underside view of Nymphargus griffithsi. h, Two Terarohyla spinosa.

Unwmk.
2019, May 29 Litho. Die Cut
Self-Adhesive
2231 Booklet pane of 8 16.50
a.-b. A993 25c Either single .50 .50
c.-d. A993 50c Either single 1.00 1.00
e.-f. A993 75c Either single 1.50 1.50
g.-h. A993 $1 Either single 2.00 2.00
2232 Booklet pane of 8 16.50
a.-b. A993 25c Either single .50 .50
c.-d. A993 50c Either single 1.00 1.00
e.-f. A993 75c Either single 1.50 1.50
g.-h. A993 $1 Either single 2.00 2.00
2233 Booklet pane of 8 16.50
a.-b. A993 25c Either single .50 .50
c.-d. A993 50c Either single 1.00 1.00
e.-f. A993 75c Either single 1.50 1.50
g.-h. A993 $1 Either single 2.00 2.00
Nos. 2231-2233 (3) 49.50

Paintings by Oswaldo Guayasamín (1919-99) — A994

No. 2234: a, Manos del Mendigo (Hands of a Beggar). b, Manos de la Ternura (Hands of Tenderness). c, Autoretrato (Self-portrait). d, Manos de la Oración (Hands in Prayer). e, Manos de la Esperanza (Hands of Hope).

Perf. 13½x13¾
2019, June 28 Litho. Wmk. 377
2234 Horiz. strip of 5 29.50 20.00
a.-e. A994 $2 Any single 4.00 4.00

National Symphony Orchestra, 70th Anniv. — A995

Perf. 13¾x13½
2019, Sept. 12 Litho. Wmk. 377
2235 A995 25c multi .95 .65

A996

No. 2236: a, Telipogon humboldtiana. b, Dichaea bonplandiana. c, Flowers and Alexander von Humboldt (1769-1859), naturalist and explorer. d, Caucaea kunthiana. e, Telipogon montufariana.

Wmk. 377
2019, Sept. 26 Litho. Perf. 13¾
2236 Horiz. strip of 5 15.00 12.00
a.-e. A996 $1 Any single 2.40 2.00

A997

A998

ECUADOR

A999

A1000

Items in Mindalae Ethnohistoric and Crafts Museum of Ecuador, Quito — A1001

No. 2237 — Inscription: a, Pirotecnia Festiva. b, Máscara Andina. c, Fiesta Andina. d, Aya Huma de Imbabura. e, Máscara de Tigua. f, Máscara Lobo Andino. g, Rondador Andino. h, Danzante de Corpus Christi.

No. 2238 — Inscription: a, Shigra Andina. b, Shakap Shuar. c, Canasto Zápara. d, Cesta Huaorani. e, Peinilla Achuar. f, Collar Amazónico. g, Canasto Epera. h, Tambor Andino.

No. 2239 — Inscription: a, Shigras de Simiatug. b, Bordado de Zuleta. c, Fajas Andinas. d, Ikat de Gualaceo. e, Tapiz de Salasaca. f, Chal de Imbabura. g, Máscara afro del Chota. h, Coquero del Carchi.

No. 2240 — Inscription: a, Rostro Manteño. b, Murciélago Jama Coaque. c, Zarigüeya Manteña. d, Hombre Pájaro Ancestral. e, Jaguar Jama Coaque. f, Emplumado Jama Coaque. g, Mujer Chorrera. h, Mindalae Tolita.

No. 2241 — Inscription: a, Banco Chamánico Shiwiar. b, Boa Quichua. c, Tinaja Quichua. d, Supai Quichua. e, Ollas Huaorani. f, Mukawa Quichua. g, Arte Plumario. h, Tawasapa Shuar.

Unwmk.
2019, Oct. 22   Litho.   Die Cut
Self-Adhesive

2237	A997	Booklet pane of 8	16.00
a.-b.		25c Either single	.80 .80
c.-d.		50c Either single	1.60 1.60
e.-f.		75c Either single	2.40 2.40
g.-h.		$1 Either single	3.25 3.25
2238	A998	Booklet pane of 8	16.00
a.-b.		25c Either single	.80 .80
c.-d.		50c Either single	1.60 1.60
e.-f.		75c Either single	2.40 2.40
g.-h.		$1 Either single	3.25 3.25
2239	A999	Booklet pane of 8	16.00
a.-b.		25c Either single	.80 .80
c.-d.		50c Either single	1.60 1.60
e.-f.		75c Either single	2.40 2.40
g.-h.		$1 Either single	3.25 3.25
2240	A1000	Booklet pane of 8	16.00
a.-b.		25c Either single	.80 .80
c.-d.		50c Either single	1.60 1.60
e.-f.		75c Either single	2.40 2.40
g.-h.		$1 Either single	3.25 3.25
2241	A1001	Booklet pane of 8	16.00
a.-b.		25c Either single	.80 .80
c.-d.		50c Either single	1.60 1.60
e.-f.		75c Either single	2.40 2.40
g.-h.		$1 Either single	3.25 3.25
		Nos. 2237-2241 (5)	80.00

Miniature Sheet

Tiputini Biodiversity Station, 25th Anniv. — A1002

No. 2242: a, 25c, Amorphochilus schnablii. b, 50c, Anoura peruana. c, 75c, Desmodus rotundus. d, $1, Diclidurus albus. e, $1.25, Eumops maurus. f, $1.50, Noctilio albiventris. g, $1.75, Sphaeronycteris toxophyllum. h, $3, Trachops cirrhosus. i, $5, Emblem of Tiputini Biodiversity Station.

Perf. 13½x13¾
2019, Oct. 29   Litho.   Wmk. 377
2242 A1002 Sheet of 9, #a-i   45.00 45.00

Elias Cedeño Jerves (1902-71), Poet — A1003

Perf. 13¾x13½
2019, Nov. 20   Litho.   Wmk. 377
2243 A1003 $5 multi   15.00 10.00

A1004

A1005

Tourism A1006

No. 2244: a, Driftwood on beach. b, Bicyclist near Cotopaxi. c, Cuyabeno River. d, Land iguana, Galapagos Islands. e, Canyon explorers near Puyo.

No. 2245: a, Puerto Baquerizo Moreno, Isla San Cristóbal. b, Isla Bartolomé, Galapagos Islands. c, Iguana, Galapagos Islands. d, Sea lions, Galapagos Islands. e, Albatrosses, Galapagos Islands. f, Two Swallow-tailed gulls, Galapagos Islands. g, Diver and school of fish in Galapagos Islands waters. h, Shark in Galapagos Islands waters.

No. 2246: a, Train on bridge. b, Cuenca. c, Guayaquil. d, Whale breaching water. e, Head of reptile, Yasuní National Park. f, Butterflies, Zamora. g, Rafters on Pastaza River. h, Montubio Rodeo, Pimocha.

Perf. 13¾x13½
2019, Nov. 22   Litho.   Wmk. 377
2244		Horiz. strip of 5	50.00 30.00
a.-e.		A1004 $3 Any single	6.00 6.00

Booklet Stamps
Self-Adhesive
Die Cut
Unwmk.

2245	A1005	Booklet pane of 8	17.00	
a.-b.		25c Either single	.55	.55
c.-d.		50c Either single	1.10	1.10
e.-f.		75c Either single	1.75	1.75
g.-h.		$1 Either single	2.25	2.25
2246	A1006	Booklet pane of 8	17.00	
a.-b.		25c Either single	.55	.55
c.-d.		50c Either single	1.10	1.10
e.-f.		75c Either single	1.75	1.75
g.-h.		$1 Either single	2.25	2.25

Traditional Dishes — A1007

No. 2247 — Inscriptions: a, Trilogía de helados, jucho, canelazo y colada morada. b, Sudado de mariscos con piña y curry ecuatoriano. c, Cascarita de cerdo con tubérculos del páramo. d, Sopa de los siete mares. e, Seco de chivo. f, Brocheta de chontacuro. g, Caldo de patas. h, Pangora fría de anconcito. i, Maito de paiche y palmito. j, Dulces típicos.

Perf. 13¾x13½
2019, Nov. 26   Litho.   Wmk. 377
2247		Block of 10	27.50 15.00
a.-j.		A1007 75c Any single	1.60 1.50

America issue.

ECUADOR

Christmas — A1008

No. 2248: a, Village in circle. b, Angel and people. c, Christmas tree. d, Three candles. e, Angel.

Perf. 13½x13¾
2019, Dec. 3   Litho.   Wmk. 377
2248	Horiz. strip of 5	32.50	20.00
a.-e.	A1008 $2 Any single	4.00	4.00

Baños de Agua Santa Tourism A1009

No. 2249: a, Treehouse. b, Cara de Perro hiker. c, Bridge over Pailón del Diablo Waterfall. d, Las Antenas Mountains. e, Basílica, Baños de Agua Santa. f, Bridge jumper. g, Thermal baths. h, Hikers near Cascada del Silencio.

Unwmk.
2019, Dec. 26   Litho.   Die Cut
Self-Adhesive
2249	A1009 Booklet pane of 8	19.00	
a.-b.	25c Either single	.55	.55
c.-d.	50c Either single	1.10	1.10
e.-f.	75c Either single	1.60	1.60
g.-h.	$1 Either single	2.25	2.25

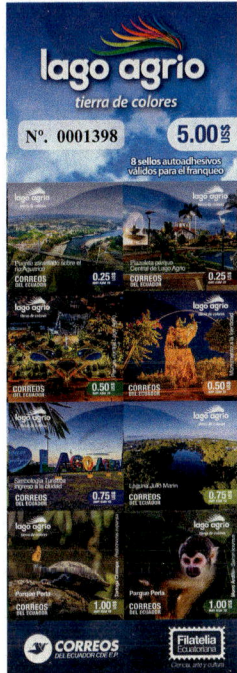

Lake Agrio A1010

No. 2250: a, Aguarico River cable-stayed bridge. b, Central plaza in Lago Agrio. c, Central plaza in Lago Agrio at night. d, Monument, Plaza de Toros, Lago Agrio. e, Lago Agrio town sign. f, Julio Marín Lagoon. g, Turtle and butterfly in Perla Park. h, Saimin sciureus.

2020   Litho.   Unwmk.   Die Cut
Self-Adhesive
2250	A1010 Booklet pane of 8	19.00	
a.-b.	25c Either single	.55	.55
c.-d.	50c Either single	1.10	1.10
e.-f.	75c Either single	1.60	1.60
g.-h.	$1 Either single	2.25	2.25

SEMI-POSTAL STAMPS

Nos. 423-428 Surcharged in Carmine or Blue

1944, May 9   Unwmk.   Perf. 12
B1	A171 10c + 10c yel grn (C)	.60	.30
B2	A171 20c + 20c rose pink	.60	.30
B3	A171 30c + 20c dk gray brn	.60	.30
B4	A171 50c + 20c dp red lil	1.20	.60
B5	A171 1s + 50c ol gray (C)	2.00	1.00
B6	A171 10s + 2s red orange	7.00	3.50
	Nos. B1-B6 (6)	12.00	6.00

The surtax aided Mendez Hospital.

AIR POST STAMPS

In 1928-30, the internal airmail service of Ecuador was handled by the Sociedad Colombo-Alemana de Transportes Aereos ("SCADTA") under government sanction. During this period SCADTA issued stamps which were the only legal franking for airmail service except that handled under contract with Pan American-Grace Airways. SCADTA issues are Nos. C1-C6, C16-C25, CF1-CF2.

Colombia Air Post Stamps of 1923 Surcharged in Carmine

"Provisional" at 45 degree Angle
Perf. 14x14½
1928, Aug. 28   Wmk. 116
C1	AP6 50c on 10c green	110.00	70.00
C2	AP6 75c on 15c car	210.00	160.00
C3	AP6 1s on 20c gray	70.00	42.50
C4	AP6 1½s on 30c blue	45.00	35.00
C5	AP6 3s on 60c brown	85.00	52.50
	Nos. C1-C5 (5)	520.00	360.00

"Provisional" at 41 degree Angle
1929, Mar. 20
C1a	AP6 50c on 10c green	125.00	110.00
C2a	AP6 75c on 15c carmine	225.00	175.00
C3a	AP6 1s on 20c gray	225.00	175.00
	Nos. C1a-C3a (3)	575.00	460.00

C6	AP6 50c on 10c green	700.00	1,700.

A 75c on 15c carmine with "Cts." between the surcharged numerals exists. There is no evidence that it was regularly issued or used.
For overprints see Nos. CF1-CF1a.

Plane over River Guayas — AP1

Unwmk.
1929, May 5   Engr.   Perf. 12
C8	AP1 2c black	.40	.25
C9	AP1 5c carmine rose	.40	.25
C10	AP1 10c deep brown	.40	.25
C11	AP1 20c dark violet	.90	.25
C12	AP1 50c deep green	1.60	.45
C13	AP1 1s dark blue	6.00	2.75
C14	AP1 5s orange yellow	25.00	11.00
C15	AP1 10s orange red	135.00	57.50
	Nos. C8-C15 (8)	169.70	72.70

Establishment of commercial air service in Ecuador. The stamps were available for all forms of postal service and were largely used for franking ordinary letters.
Nos. C13-C15 show numerals in color on white background. Counterfeits of No. C15 exist.
See Nos. C26-C31. For overprints and surcharge see Nos. C32-C38, C287, CO1-CO12.

Jesuit Church La Compania AP2

Mount Chimborazo AP3

Wmk. 127
1929, Apr. 1   Litho.   Perf. 14
C16	AP2 50c red brown	4.50	2.25
C17	AP2 75c green	4.50	2.25
C18	AP2 1s rose	7.00	2.25
C19	AP2 1½s gray blue	7.00	2.25
C20	AP2 2s violet	11.50	4.50
C21	AP2 3s brown	11.50	4.50
C22	AP3 5s lt blue	50.00	15.00
C23	AP3 10s lt red	100.00	32.50
C24	AP3 15s violet	160.00	65.00
C25	AP3 25s olive green	225.00	75.00
	Nos. C16-C25 (10)	581.00	205.50

For overprint see No. CF2.

Plane Type of 1929
1930-44   Unwmk.   Engr.   Perf. 12
C26	AP1 1s carmine lake	6.50	.55
C27	AP1 1s green ('44)	1.00	.25
C28	AP1 5s olive green	10.00	3.75
C29	AP1 5s purple ('44)	2.00	.25
C30	AP1 10s black	30.00	5.50
C31	AP1 10s brt ultra ('44)	4.50	.30
	Nos. C26-C31 (6)	54.00	10.60

Nos. C26-C31 show numerals in color on white background.
For surcharge see No. C287.

Nos. C26, C28, C30 Ovptd. in Various Colors

1930, June 4
C32	AP1 1s car lake (Bk)	22.50	22.50
a.	Double ovpt. (R Br + Bk)	75.00	
C33	AP1 5s olive grn (Bl)	22.50	22.50
C34	AP1 10s black (R Br)	22.50	22.50
	Nos. C32-C34 (3)	67.50	67.50

Flight of Capt. Benjamin Mendez from Bogota to Quito, bearing a crown of flowers for the tomb of Grand Marshal Sucre.

Air Post Official Stamps of 1929-30 Ovptd. in Various Colors or Srchd. Similarly in Upper & Lower Case

1935, July 24
C35	AP1 50c deep green (Bl)	12.50	5.00
C36	AP1 50c olive brn (R)	12.50	5.00
C37	AP1 1s on 5s ol grn (Bk)	12.50	5.00
a.	Double surcharge	95.00	
C38	AP1 2s on 10s black (R)	12.50	5.00
	Nos. C35-C38 (4)	50.00	20.00

Unveiling of a monument to Bolívar at Quito, July 24th, 1935.

AP5

1935, Oct. 13   Photo.   Perf. 11½x11
C38A	AP5 5c ultra & red	.85	.30
C38B	AP5 10c brown & black	.85	.50
C38C	AP5 50c green & red	.85	.50
C38D	AP5 1S carmine & blue	2.60	1.20
C38E	AP5 5S gray grn & red	4.25	2.40
	Nos. C38A-C38E (5)	9.40	4.90

Columbus Day. Nos. 338A-338E and C38A-C38E were prepared by the Sociedad Colombista Panamericana and were sold by the Ecuadorian post office through Oct. 30. Nos. C38B-C38E exist imperf.

Geodesical Mission Issue
Type of Regular Issue and Nos. 349-351 Overprinted in Blue or Black

1936, July 3   Perf. 12½
C39	A136 10c deep orange (Bl)	.60	.25
C40	A136 20c violet (Bk)	.60	.25
C41	A136 50c dark red (Bl)	.60	.25
C42	A136 70c black	1.25	.35
	Nos. C39-C42 (4)	3.05	1.10

For surcharge see No. RA42.

Philatelic Exhibition Issue
Type of Regular Issue Overprinted "AEREA"

1936, Oct. 20   Perf. 13½x14
C43	A137 2c rose	5.50	5.50
C44	A137 5c brown orange	5.50	5.50
C45	A137 10c brown	5.50	5.50
C46	A137 20c ultra	5.50	5.50
C47	A137 50c red violet	5.50	5.50
C48	A137 1s green	5.50	5.50

Condor and Plane — AP6

Perf. 13½
C49	AP6 70c orange brown	2.25	.50
C50	AP6 1s dull violet	2.25	.50
	Nos. C43-C50 (8)	37.50	34.00

Nos. C43-C50 were issued for the 1st Intl. Phil. Exhib. at Quito.

ECUADOR

Condor over "El Altar" — AP7

1937-46		Perf. 11½, 12	
C51	AP7	10c chestnut	5.00	.25
C52	AP7	20c olive black	6.50	.25
C53	AP7	40c rose car ('46)	6.50	.25
C54	AP7	70c black brown	9.00	.25
C55	AP7	1s gray black	14.00	.25
C56	AP7	2s dark violet	24.00	.65
		Nos. C51-C56 (6)	65.00	1.90

Issue dates: 40c, Oct. 7; others, Aug. 19.
For overprints see Nos. 463-464, CO13-CO17.

Portrait of Washington, American Eagle and Flags — AP8

Engraved and Lithographed

1938, Feb. 9		Perf. 12	
		Center Multicolored	
C57	AP8	2c brown	.40	.25
C58	AP8	5c black	.40	.25
C59	AP8	10c brown	.40	.25
C60	AP8	20c dark blue	.80	.25
C61	AP8	50c violet	1.75	.25
C62	AP8	1s black	3.25	.25
C63	AP8	2s violet	7.50	.90
		Nos. C57-C63 (7)	14.50	2.40

150th anniv. of the US Constitution.
In 1947, Nos. C61-C63 were overprinted in dark blue: "Primero la Patria!" and plane. These revolutionary propaganda stamps were later renounced by decree. Value $20.
For overprints see Nos. C102-C104, C139-C141.

No. RA35 Surcharged in Red

1938, Nov. 16		Perf. 13½	
C64	PT12	65c on 3c ultra	.40	.30

A national airmail concession was given to the Sociedade Ecuatoriano de Transportes Aereos (SEDTA) in July, 1938. No. RA35 was surcharged for SEDTA postal requirements. SEDTA operated through 1940.

Army Horseman AP9

Woman Runner AP10

Tennis AP11

Boxing AP12

Olympic Fire — AP13

1939, Mar.	Engr.	Perf. 12	
C65	AP9	5c lt green	1.60	.30
C66	AP10	10c salmon	2.25	.30
C67	AP11	50c redsh brown	11.50	.30
C68	AP12	1s black brown	13.50	.45
C69	AP13	2s rose carmine	17.00	1.10
		Nos. C65-C69 (5)	45.85	2.45

First Bolivarian Games (1938).

Plane over Chimborazo — AP14

1939, May 1		Perf. 13x12½	
C70	AP14	1s yellow brown	.40	.30
C71	AP14	2s rose violet	.70	.30
C72	AP14	5s black	1.90	.30
		Nos. C70-C72 (3)	3.00	.90

Golden Gate Bridge and Mountain Peak — AP15

1939		Perf. 12½x13	
C73	AP15	2c black	.40	.30
C74	AP15	5c rose red	.40	.30
C75	AP15	10c indigo	.40	.30
C76	AP15	50c rose violet	.40	.30
C77	AP15	1s chocolate	.80	.30
C78	AP15	2s yellow brown	1.00	.30
C79	AP15	5s emerald	2.00	.30
		Nos. C73-C79 (7)	5.40	2.10

Golden Gate International Exposition.
For surcharge & overprint see Nos. 434, CO18.

Empire State Building and Mountain Peak — AP16

1939			
C80	AP16	2c brown orange	.65	.30
C81	AP16	5c dark carmine	.65	.30
C82	AP16	10c indigo	.65	.30
C83	AP16	50c slate green	.65	.30
C84	AP16	1s deep orange	1.30	.30
C85	AP16	2s dk red violet	1.50	.30
C86	AP16	5s dark gray	3.50	.30
		Nos. C80-C86 (7)	8.90	2.10

New York World's Fair.
For surcharge see No. 435.

Map of the Americas and Airplane — AP17

1940, July 9			
C87	AP17	10c red org & blue	.45	.30
C88	AP17	70c sepia & blue	.45	.30
C89	AP17	1s copper brn & blue	.90	.30
C90	AP17	10s black & blue	3.50	.95
		Nos. C87-C90 (4)	5.30	1.85

Pan American Union, 50th anniversary.

Journalism Type

1941, Dec. 15			
C91	A157	3s rose carmine	5.75	.25
C92	A157	10s yellow orange	12.00	.45

See note after No. 399.

Old Map of South America Showing Amazon River AP19

Panoramic View of Amazon River AP20

1942, Jan. 30			
C93	AP19	40c black & buff	1.90	.25
C94	AP19	70c olive	2.90	.25
C95	AP20	2s dark green	3.25	.25
C96	AP19	5s rose	4.00	1.10
		Nos. C93-C96 (4)	12.05	1.85

See note after No. 403.

Remigio Crespo Toral Type

1942, Sept. 1		Perf. 13½	
C97	A162	10c dull violet	1.25	.50

Alfaro Types

70c, Gen. Eloy Alfaro. 1s, Devils's Nose. 3s, Military College. 5s, Montecristi, Alfaro's birthplace.

1943, Feb. 16		Perf. 12	
C98	A166	70c dk rose & blk	1.90	.25
C99	A167	1s ol blk & red brn	3.25	.70
C100	A167	3s ol gray & grn	4.50	1.10
C101	A167	5s slate & salmon	6.75	1.30
		Nos. C98-C101 (4)	16.40	3.40

Nos. C61-C63 Overprinted in Red Brown

1943, Apr. 15		Perf. 11½	
		Center Multicolored	
C102	AP8	50c violet	2.75	1.50
C103	AP8	1s black	3.25	1.60
C104	AP8	2s violet	4.00	2.50
		Nos. C102-C104 (3)	10.00	5.60

Visit of US Vice-Pres. Henry A. Wallace.

Nos. 374-376 Overprinted "AEREO LOOR A BOLIVIA JUNIO 11-1943" (like Nos. C111-C113)

1943, June 11		Perf. 13	
C105	A146	50c dp red violet	.40	.40
C106	A147	1s copper red	.60	.40
C107	A148	2s dark green	.70	.40
		Nos. C105-C107 (3)	1.70	1.20

Visit of Pres. Eurique Penaranda of Bolivia.
Vertical overprints on Nos. C105-C106.

Nos. 374-376 Overprinted "AEREO LOOR A PARAGUAY JULIO 5-1943" (like Nos. C111-C113)

1943, July 5			
C108	A146	50c dp red violet	.45	.25
a.	Double overprint		75.00	
C109	A147	1s copper red	1.10	.50
C110	A148	2s dark green	1.50	.70
		Nos. C108-C110 (3)	3.05	1.45

Visit of Pres. Higinio Moringo of Paraguay.
Vertical overprints on Nos. C108-C109.

Nos. 374-376 Overprinted in Black

1943, July 23			
C111	A146	50c dp red violet	.45	.40
C112	A147	1s copper red	.65	.40
C113	A148	2s dark green	.75	.40
		Nos. C111-C113 (3)	1.85	1.20

Issued to commemorate the visit of President Isaias Medina Angarita of Venezuela. Vertical overprint on Nos. C111-C112.
See Nos. C105-C110.

President Arroyo del Rio Addressing US Congress AP26

1943, Oct. 9		Perf. 12	
C114	AP26	50c dark brown	1.00	.50
C115	AP26	70c brt rose	1.30	.50
C116	AP26	3s dark blue	1.50	.65
C117	AP26	5s dark green	3.50	1.20
C118	AP26	10s olive black	13.00	4.25
		Nos. C114-C118 (5)	20.30	7.10

Good will tour of Pres. Arroyo del Rio in 1942.
For surcharges see Nos. CB1-CB5.

1944, Feb. 7			
C119	AP26	50c dp red lilac	.90	.65
C120	AP26	70c red brown	1.75	.65
C121	AP26	3s turq green	1.75	.65

C122	AP26	5s brt ultra	2.90	1.40
C123	AP26	10s scarlet	3.50	1.60
		Nos. C119-C123 (5)	10.80	4.95
		Nos. C114-C123 (10)	31.10	12.05

Church of San Francisco, Quito — AP27

1944, Feb. 13			
C124	AP27	70c turq green	1.90	.45
C125	AP27	1s olive	1.90	.45
C126	AP27	3s red orange	4.25	1.10
C127	AP27	5s carmine rose	5.25	1.30
		Nos. C124-C127 (4)	13.30	3.30

Palace Type

1944	Engr.	Perf. 11	
C128	A173	3s orange	1.00	.40
C129	A173	5s dark brown	1.75	.40
C130	A173	10s dark red	4.00	.25
		Nos. C128-C130 (3)	6.75	1.05

See No. C221. For overprints and surcharges see Nos. 541, C136-C138, C210-C213, C218-C220, C223-C224, C277-C279.

Red Cross Type

1945, Apr. 25	Unwmk.	Perf. 12	
		Cross in Rose	
C131	A174	2s deep blue	4.00	1.10
C132	A174	3s green	4.50	1.25
C133	A174	5s dark violet	6.50	1.75
C134	A174	10s carmine rose	21.00	5.75
		Nos. C131-C134 (4)	36.00	9.85

No. RA55 Surcharged in Black

1945, June 8			
C135	PT21	40c on 5c blue	1.00	.25
a.	Double surcharge		10.00	

Counterfeits exist.

Nos. C128-C130 Overprinted in Green

1945, Sept. 6		Perf. 11	
C136	A173	3s orange	1.00	.50
a.	Inverted overprint		50.00	
b.	Double overprint		50.00	
C137	A173	5s dark brown	1.25	.65
C138	A173	10s dark red	3.25	1.25
		Nos. C136-C138 (3)	5.50	2.40

Nos. C61-C63 Overprinted in Dark Blue and Gold like Nos. 444-446

1945, Oct. 2		Perf. 12	
		Center Multicolored	
C139	AP8	50c violet	1.40	.25
C140	AP8	1s black	1.60	1.50
C141	AP8	2s violet	2.50	1.90
		Nos. C139-C141 (3)	5.50	3.65

Visit of Pres. Juan Antonio Rios of Chile.

Monument to Liberty — AP30

1945, Nov. 14		Engr.	
C142	AP30	30c blue	.45	.25
C143	AP30	40c rose carmine	.45	.25
C144	AP30	1s dull violet	1.30	.55
C145	AP30	3s gray black	2.50	1.40
C146	AP30	5s purple brown	3.50	1.90
		Nos. C142-C146 (5)	8.20	4.35

Gen. Antonio Jose de Sucre, 150th birth anniv.

Catalogue values for unused stamps in this section, from this point to the end of the section, are for Never Hinged items.

ECUADOR

Highway Type
1946, Apr. 22   **Unwmk.**
C147	A176	1s carmine rose	.95	.40
C148	A176	2s violet	1.20	.55
C149	A176	3s turq green	2.10	.60
C150	A176	5s red orange	2.50	.80
C151	A176	10s dark blue	4.00	.80
		Nos. C147-C151 (5)	10.75	3.15

Revolution Types
1946, Aug. 9   **Perf. 12½**
C152	A177	40c deep claret	.40	.30
C153	A178	1s sepia	.40	.30
C154	A179	2s indigo	.60	.30
C155	A180	3s olive green	1.90	.45
		Nos. C152-C155 (4)	3.30	1.35

National Union of Journalists, Initials and Quill Pen — AP36

1946, Sept. 16
C156	AP36	50c dull purple	.85	.65
C157	AP36	70c dark green	1.00	.80
C158	AP36	3s red	1.60	1.00
C159	AP36	5s indigo	2.25	1.30
C160	AP36	10s chocolate	7.25	2.25
		Nos. C156-C160 (5)	12.95	6.00

Campaign for adult education.

The Blessed Mariana Teaching Children AP37

"Lily of Quito" AP38

1946, Nov. 28   **Unwmk.**
C161	AP37	40c chocolate	.40	.25
C162	AP37	60c deep blue	.55	.35
C163	AP38	3s orange yellow	1.10	.60
C164	AP38	5s green	2.00	.85
		Nos. C161-C164 (4)	4.05	2.05

300th anniv. of the death of the Blessed Mariana de Jesus Paredes y Flores.

Rocafuerte Type
60c-1.10s, Jual de Velasco. 1.30s-2s, Riobamba Irrigation Canal.

1947, Nov. 27   **Perf. 12**
C165	A185	60c dark green	.35	.30
C166	A185	70c purple	.35	.30
C167	A185	1s black brown	.35	.30
C168	A185	1.10s car rose	.35	.30
C169	A185	1.30s deep blue	.45	.30
C170	A185	1.90s olive bister	1.40	.30
C171	A185	2s olive green	1.60	.30
		Nos. C165-C171 (7)	4.85	2.10

For overprints & surcharges see Nos. C175, C181, C207-C209, C215, C216-C217, C222, C235.

Bello Type
1948, Apr. 21   **Perf. 13**
C172	A188	60c magenta	.65	.30
C173	A188	1.30s dk blue grn	1.10	.30
C174	A188	1.90s dk rose car	.90	.30
		Nos. C172-C174 (3)	2.65	.90

No. C166 Overprinted in Black

1948, May 24   **Perf. 12**
C175	A185	70c purple	.90	.35

Columbus — AP42

1948, May 26   **Perf. 14**
C176	AP42	50c olive green	.35	.30
C177	AP42	70c rose carmine	.70	.45
C178	AP42	3s ultra	2.25	1.20
C179	AP42	5s brown	3.50	1.75
C180	AP42	10s deep violet	11.00	2.25
		Nos. C176-C180 (5)	17.80	5.95

See note after No. 495.

No. C169 Overprinted in Carmine like No. 496 (MANANA reads up)
1948, Aug. 26   **Unwmk.**   **Perf. 12**
C181	A185	1.30s deep blue	.70	.30

National Fair of Today and Tomorrow, 1948.

Elia Liut and Telegrafo I — AP43

1948, Sept. 10   **Perf. 12½**
C182	AP43	60c rose red	.95	.30
C183	AP43	1s green	.95	.30
C184	AP43	1.30s deep claret	.95	.30
C185	AP43	1.90s deep violet	.95	.30
C186	AP43	2s dark brown	1.40	.30
C187	AP43	5s blue	2.75	.50
		Nos. C182-C187 (6)	7.95	2.00

25th anniv. (in 1945) of the 1st postal flight in Ecuador.

Teacher and Pupils — AP44

1948, Oct. 12   **Perf. 14**
C188	AP44	50c violet	1.60	.60
C189	AP44	70c deep blue	1.60	.60
C190	AP44	3s dark green	2.75	1.25
C191	AP44	5s red	4.50	1.90
C192	AP44	10s brown	8.25	2.50
		Nos. C188-C192 (5)	18.70	6.85

Campaign for adult education.

AP45

Franklin D. Roosevelt and Two of "Four Freedoms" — AP46

1948, Oct. 24   **Perf. 12½**
C193	AP45	60c omor & org brn	.65	.25
C194	AP45	1s car rose & slate	.80	.30
C195	AP46	1.50s grn & red brn	1.00	.55
C196	AP46	2s red & black	1.10	.30
C197	AP46	5s ultra & blk	2.25	.30
		Nos. C193-C197 (5)	5.70	1.70

Maldonado Types
1948, Nov. 17
C198	A196	60c dp org & rose car	1.00	.30
C199	A197	90c red & gray blk	1.00	.30
C200	A196	1.30s pur & dp org	1.30	.30
C201	A197	2s dp bl & dull grn	1.30	.30
		Nos. C198-C201 (4)	4.60	1.20

See note after No. 519.

Juan Montalvo and Cervantes AP47

Don Quixote AP48

1949, May 2   **Engr.**   **Perf. 12½x12**
C202	AP47	1.30s ol brn & ultra	3.25	2.50
C203	AP48	1.90s grn & rose car	1.10	.30
C204	AP47	3s vio & org brn	1.60	.30
C205	AP48	5s red & gray blk	3.00	.25
C206	AP47	10s red lil & aqua	4.25	.25
		Nos. C202-C206 (5)	13.20	3.60

400th anniv. of the birth of Miguel de Cervantes Saavedra, novelist, playwright and poet, and the 60th anniv. of the death of Juan Montalvo (1832-89), Ecuadorean writer.

For surcharges see Nos. C225-C226.

No. C168 Surcharged in Blue

1949, June 15   **Perf. 12**
C207	A185	50c on 1.10s car rose	.65	.30
C208	A185	60c on 1.10s car rose	.65	.30
C209	A185	90c on 1.10s car rose	1.00	.30
		Nos. C207-C209 (3)	2.30	.90

2nd Eucharistic Cong., Quito, June 1949.

No. C128 Surcharged in Black

1949, Oct. 11   **Perf. 11**
C210	A173	60c on 3s orange	.90	.40
a.		Double surcharge	30.00	
C211	A173	90c on 3s orange	1.00	.30
C212	A173	1s on 3s orange	1.25	.40
C213	A173	2s on 3s orange	2.10	.40
		Nos. C210-C213 (4)	5.25	1.50

"SUCRE(S)" in capitals on Nos. C212-C213. 75th anniv. of the UPU.

Consular Service Stamps Type of 1949 Surcharged in Black

1950   **Unwmk.**   **Perf. 12**
C214	R1	60c on 50c gray	1.00	.40
a.		Double surcharge	15.00	

No. C170 Surcharged with New Value in Black
C215	A185	90c on 1.90s ol bis	1.00	.40

See Nos. 475-483, 532-533.

Nos. C168, C128-C129 and Type of 1944 Srchd. or Ovptd. in Black or Carmine

1950, Feb. 10   **Perf. 12**
C216	A185	50c on 1.10s	1.90	1.75
C217	A185	70c on 1.10s	2.50	1.75

Perf. 11
C218	A173	3s orange	3.50	3.00
C219	A173	5s dark brown (C)	5.50	2.50
C220	A173	10s violet (C)	8.25	3.00
		Nos. C216-C220 (5)	21.65	12.00

Issued to publicize adult education.
For overprint see No. 541.

Govt. Palace Type of 1944

1950, May 15   **Engr.**   **Perf. 11**
C221	A173	10s violet	2.25	.40

For surcharges see Nos. C277-C279.

No. C169 Surcharged with New Value in Black

1950   **Perf. 12**
C222	A185	90c on 1.30s dp blue	.65	.40

See No. C235.

Nos. C128-C129 Overprinted in Black

1951, July 28   **Unwmk.**   **Perf. 11**
C223	A173	3s orange	1.90	.90
C224	A173	5s dark brown	3.75	1.25

20,000th crossing of the equator by Pan American-Grace Airways planes.

Nos. C202-C203 Surcharged in Black

1951   **Unwmk.**   **Perf. 12½x12**
C225	AP47	60c on 1.30s	.65	.30
C226	AP48	1s on 1.90s	.65	.30
a.		Inverted surcharge	20.00	

Issued to publicize adult education.

St. Mariana de Jesus — AP50

1952, Feb. 15   **Engr.**
C227	AP50	60c plum & aqua	.70	.30
C228	AP50	90c dk grn & lt ultra	1.00	.30
C229	AP50	1s car & dk grn	1.10	.30
C230	AP50	2s indigo & rose lil	1.25	.30
		Nos. C227-C230 (4)	4.05	1.20

Canonization of Mariana de Jesus Paredes y Flores.

Plaza Visit to US Issue
3s, as No. 558. 5s, as No. 559.

1952, Mar. 26   **Perf. 12**
C231	A205	3s lilac & bl grn	.80	.45
C232	A205	5s red brn & ol gray	2.50	1.75
a.		Souv. sheet of 2, #C231-C232	5.00	9.00

Consular Service Stamps Surcharged in Black

1952   **Unwmk.**   **Perf. 12**
C233	R2	60c on 1s green	.65	.40
C234	R2	1s on 1s green	.65	.40

Type R2 illustrated above No. 545.

No. C169 Surcharged with New Value in Carmine
C235	A185	90c on 1.30s dp bl	.65	.40
		Nos. C233-C235 (3)	1.95	1.20

See No. C222.

Pres. José M. Urvina and Allegory of Freedom — AP52

Hyphen-hole Perf. 7x6½
1952, Nov. 18   **Litho.**
C236	AP52	60c rose red & blue	3.75	.45
C237	AP52	90c lilac & red	3.75	.60
C238	AP52	1s orange & green	3.75	.30
C239	AP52	2s red brn & blue	3.75	.45
		Nos. C236-C239 (4)	15.00	1.80

Centenary of abolition of slavery in Ecuador. Counterfeits exist.

338 ECUADOR

Torch of Knowledge — AP53

Design: 2s, Aged couple studying alphabet.

Unwmk.
1953, Apr. 13   **Engr.**   **Perf. 12**
C240 AP53 1s dark blue   1.50 .30
C241 AP53 2s red orange   1.90 .30

1952 adult education campaign.

Globe Showing Part of Western Hemisphere — AP54

1953, June 5   **Perf. 12½x12**
C242 AP54 60c orange yellow   .45 .40
C243 AP54 90c dark blue   .60 .40
C244 AP54 3s carmine   1.00 .40
   Nos. C242-C244 (3)   2.05 1.20

Issued to publicize the crossing of the equator by the Pan-American highway.

Consular Service Stamps Surcharged in Black

   a   b

1953-54   **Perf. 12**
C245 R1 (a) 60c on 2s brown   .65 .40
C246 R2 (a) 60c on 5s sep ('54)   .65 .40
C247 R2 (a) 70c on 5s sep ('54)   .65 .40
C248 R2 (a) 90c on 50c car rose ('54)   .65 .40
C249 R1 (b) 1s on 2s brown   .65 .40
C250 R1 (a) 1s on 2s brn ('54)   .65 .40
C251 R1 (a) 2s on 2s brn ('54)   .75 .40
C252 R1 (a) 3s on 5s vio ('54)   1.00 .40
   Nos. C245-C252 (8)   5.65 3.20

Surcharge is horizontal on Nos. C245-C248.

Carlos Maria Cardinal de la Torre — AP55

1954, Jan. 13   **Photo.**   **Perf. 8½**
Center in Black
C253 AP55 60c rose lilac   .65 .30
C254 AP55 90c green   1.10 .30
C255 AP55 3s orange   1.60 .45
   Nos. C253-C255 (3)   3.35 1.05

1st anniv. of the elevation of Archbishop de la Torre to Cardinal.

Queen Isabella I — AP56

1954, Apr. 22
C256 AP56 60c dk grn & grn   .65 .40
C257 AP56 90c lil rose   .65 .40
C258 AP56 1s blk & pale lil   .65 .40
C259 AP56 2s blk brn & pale bl   .90 .40
C260 AP56 5s blk brn & sepia   2.25 .40
   Nos. C256-C260 (5)   5.10 2.00

See note with No. 585.

Post Office, Guayaquil AP57

1954, May 19   **Engr.**   **Perf. 12½x12**
Black Surcharge
C261 AP57 80c on 20c red   .65 .40
C262 AP57 1s on 20c red   .65 .40

25th anniversary of Pan American-Grace Airways' operation in Ecuador.

Plane, Gateway and Wheel — AP58

Unwmk.
1954, Aug. 2   **Litho.**   **Perf. 11**
C263 AP58 80c blue   .65 .40

Day of the Postal Employee.

San Pablo Lagoon — AP59

1954, Sept. 24   **Photo.**
C264 AP59 60c orange   .55 .40
C265 AP59 70c rose pink   .55 .40
C266 AP59 90c dp grn   .55 .40
C267 AP59 1s dk gray grn   .55 .40
C268 AP59 2s blue   .65 .40
C269 AP59 3s yel brn   1.25 .40
   Nos. C264-C269 (6)   4.10 2.40

Glorification of Abdon Calderon Garaicoa AP60   Capt. Calderon AP61

1954, Oct. 1
C270 AP60 80c rose pink   .70 .40
C271 AP61 90c blue   .70 .40

150th anniversary of the birth of Capt. Abdon Calderon Garaicoa.

El Cebollar College AP62   Brother Miguel Instructing Boys AP63

Designs: 90c, Francisco Febres Cordero (Brother Miguel). 2.50s, Tomb of Brother Miguel. 3s, Monument to Brother Miguel.

1954, Dec. 3   **Unwmk.**   **Perf. 11**
C272 AP62 70c dk grn   .45 .40
C273 AP63 80c dk brn   .45 .40
C274 AP63 90c dk gray bl   .45 .40
C275 AP63 2.50s indigo   .85 .40
C276 AP62 3s lil rose   1.00 .40
   Nos. C272-C276 (5)   3.20 2.00

Centenary of the birth of Francisco Febres Cordero (Brother Miguel).

No. C221 Surcharged in Various Colors

1955, May 25
C277 A173 1s on 10s vio (Bk)   .45 .40
C278 A173 1.70s on 10s vio (C)   .60 .40
C279 A173 4.20s on 10s vio (Br)   .65 .40
   Nos. C277-C279 (3)   2.05 1.20

Denomination in larger type on No. C279. National Exhibition of Daily Periodicals.

"La Rotonda," Guayaquil, and Rotary Emblem — AP64

Design: 90c, Eugenio Espejo hospital, Quito, and Rotary emblem.

1955, July 9   **Engr.**   **Perf. 12½**
C280 AP64 80c dark brown   .50 .40
C281 AP64 90c dark green   .80 .45

50th anniv. of the founding of Rotary Intl.

José Abel Castillo — AP65

2s, 5s, José Abel Castillo, Map of Ecuador.

1955, Oct. 19   **Perf. 11x11½**
C282 AP65 60c chocolate   1.30 .25
C283 AP65 90c light olive green   1.50 .25
C284 AP65 1s lilac   1.60 .25
C285 AP65 2s vermilion   2.10 .30
C286 AP65 5s ultra   4.00 .55
   Nos. C282-C286 (5)   10.50 1.60

See note after No. 595.

No. C29 Surcharged in Black

1955, Oct. 24   **Perf. 12**
C287 AP1 1s on 5s purple   1.00 .40

A similar surcharge on No. C29, set in two lines with letters 5mm high and no X's or black-out line of squares, was privately applied.

San Pablo, Imbabura — AP66

50s, Rumichaca Caves. 1.30s, Virgin of Quito. 1.50s, Cotopaxi Volcano. 1.70s, Tungurahua Volcano, Tungurahua. 1.90s, Guanacos. 2.40s, Mat market. 2.50s, Ruins at Ingapirca. 4.20s, El Carmen, Cuenca, Azuay. 4.80s, Santo Domingo Church.

1956, Jan. 2   **Photo.**   **Perf. 13**
C288 AP66 50c slate blue   3.75 .40
C289 AP66 1s ultra   3.75 .40
C290 AP66 1.30s crimson   6.00 .40
C291 AP66 1.50s dp grn   3.75 .40
C292 AP66 1.70s yel brn   2.50 .40
C293 AP66 1.90s olive   5.00 .40
C294 AP66 2.40s red org   5.25 .40
C295 AP66 2.50s violet   5.25 .40
C296 AP66 4.20s black   6.50 .40
C297 AP66 4.80s yel org   1.00 .40
   Nos. C288-C297 (10)   42.75 4.00

See Nos. C310-C311. For surcharges see Nos. 766A, 766G.

Honorato Vazquez — AP67

1956, May 28   **Engr.**
Various Portraits
C298 AP67 1s yellow green   .75 .40
C299 AP67 1.50s red   .75 .40
C300 AP67 1.70s bright blue   .75 .40
C301 AP67 1.90s slate blue   .75 .40
   Nos. C298-C301 (4)   3.00 1.60

Birth centenary (in 1955) of Honorato Vazquez, statesman.

Title Page of First Book — AP68

1956, Aug. 27   **Unwmk.**   **Perf. 13½**
C302 AP68 1s black   .75 .40
C303 AP68 1.70s slate bl   .75 .40
C304 AP68 2s blk brn   .75 .40
C305 AP68 3s redsh brn   .75 .40
   Nos. C302-C305 (4)   3.00 1.60

Bicentenary of printing in Ecuador.

Hands Reaching for UN Emblem — AP69

1956, Oct. 24   **Perf. 14**
C307 AP69 1.70s red org   1.30 .40

10th anniv. of the UN (in 1955). See No. C319. For overprint see No. C426.

Coat of Arms and Basketball Player — AP70

Designs: 1.70s, Map of South America with flags and girl basketball players.

1956, Dec. 28   **Photo.**   **Perf. 14½x14**
C308 AP70 1s red lilac   1.20 .40
C309 AP70 1.70s deep green   1.50 .40

6th South American Women's Basketball Championship, Aug. 1956.

Scenic Type of 1956
1957, Jan. 2   **Perf. 13**
C310 AP66 50c bl grn   2.00 .40
C311 AP66 1s orange   2.00 .40

Type of Regular Issue, 1957

Designs: 50c, Map of Cuenca, 16th century. 80c, Cathedral of Cuenca. 1s, Modern City Hall.

Unwmk.
1957, Apr. 7   **Photo.**   **Perf. 12**
C312 A219 50c brn, cr   .45 .30
   a. Souvenir sheet of 4   1.30 1.30
C313 A219 80c red, bluish   .45 .30
C314 A219 1s pur, yel   .45 .30
   a. Souvenir sheet of 3   2.60 2.60
   Nos. C312-C314 (3)   1.35 .90

No. C312a contains 4 imperf. 50c stamps similar to No. 613, but inscribed "AEREO" and printed in green. The sheet is printed on white ungummed paper.

No. C314a contains 3 imperf. stamps in designs similar to Nos. C312-C314, but with colors changed to orange (50c), brown (80c), violet (1s). The sheet is printed on white ungummed paper.

Gabriela Mistral — AP71

Unwmk.
1957, Sept. 18   **Litho.**   **Perf. 14**
C315 AP71 2s lt bl, blk & red   .80 .40

Issued to honor Gabriela Mistral (1889-1957), Chilean poet and educator. See Nos. C406-C407.

Arms of Espejo, Carchi — AP72

Arms of Cantons: 2s, Montufar. 4.20s, Tulcan.

1957, Nov. 16   **Perf. 14½x13½**
Coat of Arms Multicolored
C316 AP72 1s carmine   .75 .40
C317 AP72 2s black   .75 .40
C318 AP72 4.20s ultra   1.40 .40
   Nos. C316-C318 (3)   2.90 1.20

Province of Carchi.
See Nos. C334-C337, C355-C364, C392-C395. For surcharge see No. 766.

ECUADOR

Redrawn UN Type of 1956
1957, Dec. 10 Engr. *Perf. 14*
C319 AP69 2s greenish blue 1.00 .40

Honoring the UN. Dates, as on No. C307, are omitted; inscribed: "Homenaje a las Naciones Unidas."

Mater Dolorosa, San Gabriel College — AP73

No. C321, 1s, Door of San Gabriel College, Quito.

1958, Apr. 27 Engr. *Perf. 14*
C320	AP73	30c rose cl, dp rose	.65	.40
C321	AP73	30c rose cl, dp rose	.65	.40
a.		Pair, #C320-C321	1.30	.80
C322	AP73	1s dk bl, lt bl	.65	.40
C323	AP73	1.70s dk bl, lt bl	.65	.40
a.		Pair, #C322-C323	1.30	.80

Miracle of San Gabriel College, Quito, 50th anniv.

Rafael Maria Arizaga (1858-1933), Writer — AP74

1958, July 21 Litho.
C324 AP74 1s multi 1.00 .40
See Nos. C343, C350, C412.

Daule River Bridge — AP75

1958, July 25 Engr. *Perf. 13½x14*
C325 AP75 1.30s green .95 .40

Issued to commemorate the opening of the River Daule bridge in Guayas province. See Nos. C367-C369.

Basketball Player — AP76

1958, Sept. 1 Photo. *Perf. 14x13½*
C326 AP76 1.30s dk grn & lt brn .95 .45

South American basketball championships. For surcharge see No. 774A.

Symbolical of the Eucharist — AP77

Design: 60c, Cathedral of Guayaquil.

1958, Sept. 25 Litho. Unwmk.
C327	AP77	10c vio & buff	.80	.40
C328	AP77	60c org & vio brn	.80	.40
C329	AP77	1s brn & lt bl	.80	.40
		Nos. C327-C329 (3)	2.40	1.20

Souvenir Sheet

Symbolical of the Eucharist — AP78

Perf. 13½x14
C330 AP78 Sheet of 4 3.75 2.75
 a.-d. 40c dark blue, any single .60 .40
3rd National Eucharistic Congress.

Stamps of 1865 and 1920 — AP79

Designs: 2s, Stamps of 1920 and 1948. 4.20s, Municipal museum and library.

1958, Oct. 8 Photo. *Perf. 11½*
Granite Paper
C331	AP79	1.30s grn & brn red	.55	.40
C332	AP79	2s bl & vio	1.00	.40
C333	AP79	4.20s dk brn	1.30	.40
		Nos. C331-C333 (3)	2.85	1.20

National Philatelic Exposition (EXFIGUA), Guayaquil, Oct. 4-14.
For surcharge see No. 774.

Coat of Arms Type of 1957
Province of Imbabura

Arms of Cantons: 50c, Cotacachi. 60c, Antonio Ante. 80c, Otavalo. 1.10s, Ibarra.

1958, Nov. 9 Litho. *Perf. 14½x13½*
Coats of Arms Multicolored
C334	AP72	50c blk & red	.80	.40
C335	AP72	60c blk, bl & red	.80	.40
C336	AP72	80c blk & yel	.80	.40
C337	AP72	1.10s blk & red	.80	.40
		Nos. C334-C337 (4)	3.20	1.60

Charles V — AP80

Engr. & Photo.
1958, Dec. 12 *Perf. 14x13½*
C338 AP80 2s brn red & dk brn .75 .30
C339 AP80 4.20s dk gray & red brn .95 .45

400th anniv. of the death of Charles V, Holy Roman Emperor.

Paul Rivet — AP81

1958, Dec. 29 Photo. *Perf. 11½*
Granite Paper
C340 AP81 1s brown 1.00 .40

Issued in honor of Paul Rivet (1876-1958), French anthropologist.

1959, May 6
Portrait: 2s, Alexander von Humboldt.
C341 AP81 2s slate .95 .40
Cent. of the death of Alexander von Humboldt, German naturalist and geographer.

Front Page of "El Telegrafo" AP82

1959, Feb. Litho. *Perf. 13½*
C342 AP82 1.30s bl grn & blk .95 .40
75th anniv. of Ecuador's oldest newspaper.

Portrait Type of 1958
José Luis Tamayo (1858-1947), lawyer.

1959, June 26 Unwmk. *Perf. 14*
Portrait Multicolored
C343 AP74 1.30s lt grn, bl & sal .95 .40

El Sagrario & House of Manuela Canizares AP83

Condor AP84

Designs: 80c, Hall at San Agustin. 1s, First words of the constitutional act. 2s, Entrance to Cuartel Real. 4.20s, Allegory of Liberty.

Unwmk.
1959, Aug. 28 Photo. *Perf. 14*
C344	AP83	20c ultra & lt brn	.45	.25
C345	AP83	80c brt bl & dp org	.45	.25
C346	AP83	1s dk red & dk ol	.45	.25
C347	AP84	1.30s brt bl & org	.45	.25
C348	AP84	2s ultra & org brn	.45	.25
C349	AP84	4.20s scar & brt bl	1.10	.50
		Nos. C344-C349 (6)	3.35	1.75

Sesquicentennial of the revolution.

Portrait Type of 1958
1s, Alfredo Baquerizo Moreno (1859-1951), statesman.

1959, Sept. 26 Litho. *Perf. 14*
C350 AP74 1s gray, red & salmon .75 .40

Pope Pius XII — AP85

1959, Oct. 9 Unwmk. *Perf. 14½*
C351 AP85 1.30s multi .95 .40
Issued in memory of Pope Pius XII.

Flags of Argentina, Bolivia, Brazil, Guatemala, Haiti, Mexico and Peru — AP86

Flags of: 80c, Chile, Costa Rica, Cuba, Dominican Republic, Panama, Paraguay, United States. 1.00s, Colombia, Ecuador, Honduras, Nicaragua, Salvador, Uruguay, Venezuela.

1959, Oct. 12 *Perf. 13½*
C352	AP86	50c multi	.50	.40
C353	AP86	80c yel, red & bl	.60	.40
C354	AP86	1.30s multi	.80	.40
		Nos. C352-C354 (3)	1.90	1.20

Organization of American States.
For overprints see Nos. C423-C425, CO19-CO21.

Arms of the Cantons Type of 1957
Province of Pichincha

10c, Rumiñahui. 40c, Pedro Moncayo. 1s, Mejia. 1.30s, Cayambe. 4.20s, Quito.

Perf. 14½x13½
1959-60 Unwmk. Litho.
Coat of Arms Multicolored
C355	AP72	10c blk & dk red ('60)	.75	.40
C356	AP72	40c blk & yel	.75	.40
C357	AP72	1s blk & brn ('60)	.75	.40
C358	AP72	1.30s blk & grn ('60)	.75	.40
C359	AP72	4.20s blk & org	.75	.40
		Nos. C355-C359 (5)	3.75	2.00

Province of Cotopaxi
40c, Pangua. 60c, Pujili. 70c, Saquisili. 1s, Salcedo. 1.30s, Latacunga.

1960 **Coat of Arms Multicolored**
C360	AP72	40c blk & car	.65	.40
C361	AP72	60c blk & bl	.65	.40
C362	AP72	70c blk & turq	.65	.40
C363	AP72	1s blk & red org	.65	.40
C364	AP72	1.30s blk & org	.65	.40
		Nos. C360-C364 (5)	3.25	2.00

Flags of American Nations AP87

1960, Feb. 23 *Perf. 13x12½*
C365 AP87 1.30s multi .65 .40
C366 AP87 2s multi .65 .40
11th Inter-American Conference, Feb. 1960.

Bridge Type of 1958.
Bridges: No. C367, Juntas. No. C368, Saracay. 2s, Railroad bridge, Ambato.

1960 Litho. *Perf. 13½*
C367 AP75 1.30s chocolate .55 .40

Photo. *Perf. 12½*
C368 AP75 1.30s emerald .55 .40
C369 AP75 2s brown .85 .40
Nos. C367-C369 (3) 1.95 1.20
Building of three new bridges.

Bahia-Chone Road — AP88

Pres. Camilo Ponce Enriquez — AP89

Designs: 4.20s, Public Works Building, Cuenca. 5s, El Coca airport. 10s, New Harbor, Guayaquil.

1960, Aug. Litho. *Perf. 14*
C370	AP88	1.30s blk & dl yel	.35	.25
C371	AP88	4.20s rose car & lt grn	.55	.45
C372	AP88	5s dk brn & yel	.80	.55
C373	AP88	10s dk bl & bl	1.80	.55

Perf. 11x11½
C374 AP89 2s org brn & blk 2.75 .30
Nos. C370-C374 (5) 6.25 2.10

Nos. C370-C374 publicize the achievements of Pres. Camilo Ponce Enriquez (1956-1960).
Issued: Nos. C370-C373, 8/24; No. C374, 8/31.

Red Cross Building, Quito and Henri Dunant — AP90

1960, Oct. 5 Unwmk. *Perf. 13x14*
C375 AP90 2s rose vio & car .95 .40
Centenary (in 1959) of Red Cross idea.
For overprint see No. C408.

ECUADOR

El Belen Church,
Quito — AP91

1961, Jan. 14   *Perf. 12½*
C376   AP91   3s multi   1.00   .40
Ecuador's participation in the 1960 Barcelona Philatelic Congress.

Map of Ecuador
and Amazon
River System
AP92

1961, Feb. 27   *Litho.*   *Perf. 10½*
C377   AP92   80c salmon, claret & grn   .50   .40
C378   AP92   1.30s gray, slate & grn   .80   .40
C379   AP92   2s beige, red & grn   1.10   .40
   Nos. C377-C379 (3)   2.40   1.20
Amazon Week, and the 132nd anniversary of the Battle of Tarqui against Peru.

Juan Montalvo, Juan
Leon Mera, Juan
Benigno
Vela — AP93

1961, Apr. 13   *Unwmk.*   *Perf. 13*
C380   AP93   1.30s salmon & blk   1.00   .40
Centenary of Tungurahua province.

Hugo Ortiz G. — AP94

Design: No. C382, Ortiz monument.

1961, May 25   *Perf. 14x14½*
C381   AP94   1.30s grnsh bl, blk & yel   .70   .40
C382   AP94   1.30s grnsh bl, pur, ol & brn   .70   .40
Lt. Hugo Ortiz G., killed in battle 8/2/41.

Condor and
Airplane Stamp
of
1936 — AP95

1.30s, Map of South America and stamp of 1865. 2s, Bolivar monument stamp of 1930.

   Perf. 10½
1961, May 25   *Litho.*   *Unwmk.*
   Size: 41x28mm
C383   AP95   80c org & vio   .55   .40
   Size: 41x34mm
C384   AP95   1.30s bl, yel, ol & car   .85   .40
   Size: 40½x37mm
C385   AP95   2s car rose & blk   1.40   .40
   Nos. C383-C385 (3)   2.80   1.20
Third National Philatelic Exhibition, Quito, May 25-June 3, 1961.

Arms of Los Rios and
Egret — AP96

1961, May 27   *Perf. 14½x13½*
   Coat of Arms Multicolored
C386   AP96   2s bl & blk   1.00   .40
Centenary (in 1960) of Los Rios province.

Gabriel Garcia
Moreno — AP97

1961, Sept. 24   *Unwmk.*   *Perf. 12*
C387   AP97   1s bl, brn & buff   1.00   .40
Centenary of the restoration of national integrity.

Remigio Crespo
Toral — AP98

1961, Nov. 3   *Unwmk.*   *Perf. 14*
C388   AP98   50c multi   .90   .40
Centenary of the birth of Remigio Crespo Toral, poet laureate of Ecuador.

**Galapagos Islands Nos. LC1-LC3
Overprinted in Black or Red (Similar
to #684-686)
"ESTACION DE BIOLOGIA MARITIMA
DE GALAPAGOS" and " UNESCO
1961"**

1961, Oct. 31   *Photo.*   *Perf. 12*
C389   A1   1s dp bl   1.90   .30
   a. "de Galapagos" on top line   6.50   6.00
C390   A1   1.80s rose vio   2.00   .40
   a. UNESCO emblem omitted   6.50   6.00
C391   A1   4.20s blk (R)   3.00   .60
   Nos. C389-C391 (3)   6.90   1.30
Establishment of maritime biological stations on Galapagos Islands by UNESCO.

Arms of the Cantons Type of 1957
Province of Tungurahua

50c, Pillaro. 1s, Pelileo. 1.30s, Baños. 2s, Ambato.

   Perf. 14½x13½
1962, Mar. 30   *Litho.*   *Unwmk.*
   Coats of Arms Multicolored
C392   AP72   50c black   .40   .40
C393   AP72   1s black   .55   .40
C394   AP72   1.30s black   .70   .40
C395   AP72   2s black   1.10   .40
   Nos. C392-C395 (4)   2.75   1.60

AP99

Designs: 1.30s, 2s, Pres. Arosemena and Prince Philip, Arms of Ecuador and Great Britain and Equator Monument.

   Perf. 14x13½
1962, Feb. 17   *Wmk. 340*
C396   AP99   1.30s bl, sepia, red & yel   .55   .40
C397   AP99   2s multi   .90   .40
Visit of Prince Philip, Duke of Edinburgh, to Ecuador, Feb. 17-20, 1962.

Mountain
Farming — AP100

   Perf. 12½
1963, Mar. 21   *Unwmk.*   *Litho.*
C398   AP100   30c emer, yel & blk   .40   .40
C399   AP100   3s dl red, grn & org   .95   .40
C400   AP100   4.20s bl, blk & yel   1.50   .40
   Nos. C398-C400 (3)   2.85   1.20
FAO "Freedom from Hunger" campaign.
Exist imperf. Value $32.50.

Mosquito and
Malaria
Eradication
Emblem — AP101

1963, Apr. 17   *Unwmk.*   *Perf. 12½*
C401   AP101   50c multi   .55   .40
C402   AP101   80c multi   .55   .40
C403   AP101   2s multi   .85   .40
   Nos. C401-C403 (3)   1.95   1.20
WHO drive to eradicate malaria.

Stagecoach and
Jet Plane — AP102

1963, May 7   *Litho.*
C404   AP102   2s org & car rose   .70   .40
C405   AP102   4.20s claret & ultra   1.20   .40
1st Intl. Postal Conference, Paris, 1863.

**Type of 1957 Inscribed "Islas
Galapagos," Surcharged with New
Value and Overprinted "Ecuador" in
Black or Red**

1963, June 19   *Unwmk.*   *Perf. 14*
C406   AP71   5s on 2s gray, dk bl & red   1.20   .80
C407   AP71   10s on 2s gray, dk bl & red (R)   2.40   1.60
The basic 2s exists without surcharge and overprint. No. C407 exists with "ECUADOR" omitted, and with both "ECUADOR" and "10 SUCRES" double.

**No. C375 Overprinted: "1863-
1963/Centenario/de la Fundación/ de
la Cruz Roja/Internacional"**

1963, June 21   *Photo.*   *Perf. 13x14*
C408   AP90   2s rose vio & car   1.00   .40
Intl. Red Cross, centenary.

Type of Regular Issue, 1963
Arosemena and: 70c, Flags of Ecuador. 2s, Flags of Ecuador, Panama. 4s, Flags of Ecuador, US.

1963, July 1   *Litho.*   *Perf. 14*
C409   A238   70c pale bl & multi   .40   .30
C410   A238   2s pink & multi   .75   .30
C411   A238   4s lt bl & multi   1.60   .35
   Nos. C409-C411 (3)   2.75   .95
Imperfs exist. Value $15.

Portrait Type of 1958
Portrait: 2s, Dr. Mariano Cueva (1812-82).

   Unwmk.
1963, July 4   *Litho.*   *Perf. 14*
C412   AP74   2s lt grn & multi   .70   .25

Social Insurance
Symbol — AP103

1963, July 9   *Litho.*
C413   AP103   10s brn & multi   1.50   .90
25th anniversary of Social Insurance.
Exists imperf. Value $9.

Mother and
Child — AP104

1963, July 28   *Perf. 12½*
C414   AP104   1.30s org, dk bl & blk   .80   .40
C415   AP104   5s gray, red & brn   1.10   .75
7th Pan-American and South American Pediatrics Congresses, Quito.

Simon Bolivar
Airport,
Guayaquil — AP105

1963, July 25   *Perf. 14*
C416   AP105   60c gray   .65   .40
C417   AP105   70c dk grn   .75   .40
C418   AP105   5s brn vio   1.10   .40
   Nos. C416-C418 (3)   2.50   1.20
Opening of Simon Bolivar Airport, Guayaquil, July 15, 1962.
Exist imperf. Value $5.25.

**Nos. 638, 640-641 Overprinted
"AEREO"**

1964   *Perf. 12*
   Flags in National Colors
C419   A223   1.80s dl vio   .85   .40
C420   A224   2s dk brn   .85   .40
C421   A223   2.20s blk brn   .85   .40
   Nos. C419-C421 (3)   2.55   1.20
On 1.80s and 2.20s, "AEREO" is vertical, reading down.

**No. 650 Overprinted in Gold: "FARO
DE COLON / AEREO"**

1964   *Photo.*   *Perf. 14x13½*
C422   A229   1.80s dk bl   4.25   2.00

Nos. C352-C354 Overprinted

1964   *Litho.*   *Perf. 13½*
C423   AP86   50c bl & multi   1.00   .45
C424   AP86   80c yel & multi   1.00   .45
C425   AP86   1.30s pale grn & multi   1.00   .45
   Nos. C423-C425 (3)   3.00   1.35

**No. C307 Overprinted:
"DECLARACION / DERECHOS
HUMANOS / 1964 / XV-ANIV"**

   Unwmk.
1964, Sept. 29   *Engr.*   *Perf. 14*
C426   AP69   1.70s red org   .95   .40
15th anniversary (in 1963) of the Universal Declaration of Human Rights.

Banana Type

1964, Oct. 26   *Litho.*   *Perf. 12½x12*
C427   A241   4.20s blk, bis & gray ol   .75   .30
C428   A241   10s blk, scar & gray ol   1.25   .50
   a. Souv. sheet of 4   4.25   3.50
No. C428a contains imperf. stamps similar to Nos. 720-721 and C427-C428.

John F.
Kennedy,
Flag-draped
Coffin and
John
Jr. — AP106

1964, Nov. 22   *Litho.*   *Perf. 14*
C429   AP106   4.20s multi   1.40   .95
C430   AP106   5s multi   1.75   1.25
C431   AP106   10s multi   3.25   1.60
   a. Souv. sheet of 3   11.00   10.00
   Nos. C429-C431 (3)   6.40   3.80
President John F. Kennedy (1917-63).
No. C431a contains stamps similar to Nos. C429-C431, imperf.

ECUADOR

Olympic Type
1.30s, Gymnast, vert. 1.80s, Hurdler. 2s, Basketball.

Perf. 13½x14, 14x13½
1964, Dec. 16   Unwmk.
C432	A243	1.30s vio bl, ver & brn	.70 .35
C433	A243	1.80s vio bl & multi	.70 .35
C434	A243	2s red & multi	.70 .35
a.		Souv. sheet of 4	4.75 4.25
		Nos. C432-C434 (3)	2.10 1.05

No. C434a contains stamps similar to Nos. 725 and C432-C434, imperf.

Sports Type
Torch and Athletes: 2s, 3s, Diver, gymnast, wrestlers and weight lifter. 2.50s, 4s, Bicyclists. 3.50s, 5s, Jumpers.

1965, Nov. 20   Litho.   *Perf. 12x12½*
C435	A247	2s bl, gold & blk	.65 .30
C436	A247	2.50s org, gold & blk	.65 .30
C437	A247	3s brt pink, gold & blk	.65 .30
C438	A247	3.50s lt vio, gold & bl	.95 .65
C439	A247	4s brt yel grn, gold & blk	.95 .35
C440	A247	5s red org, gold & blk	1.10 .35
a.		Souv. sheet of 12	15.00 12.00
		Nos. C435-C440 (6)	4.95 2.20

No. C440a contains 12 imperf. stamps similar to Nos. 738-743 and C435-C440.
For surcharges see Nos. 766B, C449.

Bird Type
Birds: 1s, Yellow grosbeak. 1.00s, Black-headed parrot. 1.50s, Scarlet tanager. 2s, Sapphire quail-dove. 2.50s, Violet-tailed sylph. 3s, Lemon-throated barbet. 4s, Yellow-tailed oriole. 10s, Collared puffbird.

1966, June 17   Litho.   *Perf. 13½*
Birds in Natural Colors
C441	A249	1s lt red brn & blk	1.20 .25
C442	A249	1.30s pink & blk	1.20 .25
C443	A249	1.50s pale grn & blk	1.20 .25
C444	A249	2s sal & blk	3.00 .45
C445	A249	2.50s lt yel grn & blk	3.00 .45
C446	A249	3s sal & blk	4.25 .65
C447	A249	4s gray & blk	5.50 .85
C448	A249	10s beige & blk	8.50 2.10
		Nos. C441-C448 (8)	27.85 5.25

For surcharges see Nos. 766E-766F, C450, C455-C457.

Nos. C436 and C443 Surcharged

1967
C449	A247	80c on 2.50s multi	.75 .35
C450	A249	80c on 1.50s multi	.75 .30

Old denomination on No. C449 is obliterated with heavy bar; the surcharge on No. C450 includes "Resello" and an ornament over old denomination.

Peñaherrera Monument, Quito — AP107

Design: 2s, Peñaherrera statue.

1967, Dec. 29   Litho.   *Perf. 12x12½*
C451	AP107	1.30s blk & org	.45 .25
C452	AP107	2s blk & lt ultra	.45 .25

See note after No. 767B.

Arosemena Type
1.30s, Inauguration. 2s, Pres. Arosemena speaking in Punta del Este.

1968, May 9   Litho.   *Perf. 13½x14*
C453	A251	1.30s multi	.65 .35
C454	A251	2s multi	.80 .45

No. C448 Srchd. in Plum, Dark Blue or Green

1969, Jan. 9   Litho.   *Perf. 13½*
Bird in Natural Colors
C455	A249	80c on 10s beige (P)	1.65 .25
C456	A249	1s on 10s beige (DBl)	1.65 .25
C457	A249	2s on 10s beige (G)	1.65 .25
		Nos. C455-C457 (3)	4.95 .75

"Operation Friendship" — AP108

1969-70   Typo.   *Perf. 13½*
C458	AP108	2s yel, blk, red & lt bl	.65 .40
a.		Perf. 12½	.65 .40
C459	AP108	2s bl, blk, car & yel ('70)	.65 .40

Friendship campaign. Medallion background on Nos. C458 and C458a is blue; on No. C459, yellow.
No. C459 exists imperf. Value, $12.50.

No. 639 Surcharged in Gold "S/. 5 AEREO" and Bar

1969, Nov. 25   Litho.   *Perf. 12*
C460	A224	5s on 2s multi	2.25 .75

Butterfly Type
Butterflies: 1.30s, Morpho peleides. 1.50s, Anartia amathea.

1970   Litho.   *Perf. 12½*
C461	A255	1.30s multi	3.50 .40
C462	A255	1.50s pink & multi	3.50 .40

Same, White Background

1970   *Perf. 13½*
C463	A255	1.30s multi	3.75 .30
C464	A255	1.50s multi	3.75 .30

Arms Type
Provincial Arms and Flags: 1.30s, El Oro. 2s, Loja. 3s, Manabi. 5s, Pichincha. 10s, Guayas.

1971   Litho.   *Perf. 10½*
C465	A258	1.30s pink & multi	.40 .30
C466	A258	2s multi	.50 .30
C467	A258	3s multi	.75 .35
C468	A258	5s multi	.95 .35
C469	A258	10s multi	1.75 .50
		Nos. C465-C469 (5)	4.35 1.00

Presentation of the Virgin — AP109

Art of Quito: 1.50s, Blessed Anne at Prayer. 2s, St. Theresa de Jesus. 2.50s, Altar of Carmen, horiz. 3s, Descent from the Cross. 4s, Christ of St. Mariana de Jesus. 5s, Shrine of St. Anthony. 10s, Cross of San Diego.

1971   *Perf. 11½*
Inscriptions in Black
C473	AP109	1.30s multi	.45 .40
C474	AP109	1.50s multi	.45 .40
C475	AP109	2s multi	.45 .40
C476	AP109	2.50s multi	.75 .40
C477	AP109	3s multi	.95 .40
C478	AP109	4s multi	1.20 .40
C479	AP109	5s multi	1.20 .40
C480	AP109	10s multi	2.25 .40
		Nos. C473-C480 (8)	7.70 3.20

Pres. Allende and Chilean Flag — AP110

2.10s, Pres. José M. Velasco Ibarra of Ecuador, Pres. Salvador Allende of Chile, national flags.

1971, Aug. 24   *Perf. 12½*
C481	AP110	2s multi	.55 .30
C482	AP110	2.10s multi	.55 .30

Visit of Pres. Salvador Allende of Chile, Aug. 24.

Globe and Emblem — AP111

1971
C483	AP111	5s black	1.30 .45
C484	AP111	5.50s dl pur & blk	1.30 .45

Opening of Postal Museum, Aug. 24, 1971.
Exist imperf. Value $7.50.

Pazmiño Type

1971, Sept. 16   *Perf. 12x11½*
C485	A260	1.50s grn & multi	.50 .30
C486	A260	2.50s grn & multi	.65 .30

AP112

Designs: 5s, Map of Americas. 10s, Converging roads and map. 20s, Map of Americas and Equator. 50s, Mountain road and monument on Equator.

1971   *Perf. 11½*
C487	AP112	5s org & multi	.90 .30
C488	AP112	10s org & blk	1.40 .55
C489	AP112	20s blk, bl & brt rose	2.25 1.00
C490	AP112	50s bl, blk & gray	3.50 1.50
		Nos. C487-C490 (4)	8.05 3.35

11th Pan-American Road Congress. Issued: 5s, 10s, 50s, 11/15; 20s, 11/22.
No. C488 exists imperf. Value $8.

AP113

Design: 3s, Arms of Ecuador and Argentina. 5s, Presidents José M. Velasco Ibarra and Alejandro Agustin Lanusse.

1972
C491	AP113	3s blk & multi	.40 .30
C492	AP113	5s blk & multi	.95 .35

Visit of Lt. Gen. Alejandro Agustin Lanusse, president of Argentina. Jan. 25.

Flame, Scales, Map of Americas — AP114

1972, Apr. 24   Litho.   *Perf. 12½*
C493	AP114	1.30s bl & red	.75 .40

17th Conference of the Interamerican Federation of Lawyers, Quito, Apr. 24.

Religious Paintings Type of Regular Issue
Ecuadorian Paintings: 3s, Virgin of the Flowers, by Miguel de Santiago. 10s, Virgin of the Rosary, by Quito School.

1972, Apr. 24   *Perf. 14x13½*
C494	A263	3s blk & multi	.55 .40
C495	A263	10s blk & multi	1.75 .65
a.		Souv. sheet of 2, #C494-C495	2.25 2.25

1972, May 4
Ecuadorian Statues: 3s, St. Dominic, Quito School. 10s, St. Rosa of Lima, by Bernardo de Legarda.
C496	A263	3s blk & multi	.55 .40
C497	A263	10s blk & multi	1.50 .65
a.		Souv. sheet of 2, #C496-C497	3.25 3.00

Letters of "Ecuador" 3mm high on Nos. C496-C497, 7mm high on Nos. C494-C495.

Portrait Type
Designs (Generals, from Paintings): 1.30s, José Maria Saenz. 3s, Tomás Wright. 4s, Antonio Farfan. 5s, Antonio José de Sucre. 10s, Simon Bolivar. 20s, Arms of Ecuador.

1972, May 24
C498	A264	1.30s bl & multi	.60 .30
C499	A264	3s bl & multi	.60 .30
C500	A264	4s bl & multi	.80 .30
C501	A264	5s bl & multi	1.10 .35
C502	A264	10s bl & multi	2.10 .65
C503	A264	20s bl & multi	4.25 1.25
		Nos. C498-C503 (6)	9.45 3.15

Artisan Type
Handicraft of Ecuador: 2s, Woman wearing flowered poncho. 3s, Striped poncho. 5s, Poncho with roses. 10s, Gold sunburst sculpture.

1972, July   Photo.   *Perf. 13*
C504	A265	2s multi	.55 .30
C505	A265	3s multi	.95 .30
C506	A265	5s multi	1.50 .50
C507	A265	10s org red & multi	2.50 1.00
a.		Souv. sheet of 4, #C504-C507	5.75 5.75
		Nos. C504-C507 (4)	5.50 2.10

Epidendrum Orchid AP115

1972   Photo.   *Perf. 12½*
C508	AP115	4s shown	1.60 1.30
C509	AP115	6s Canna	2.50 2.10
C510	AP115	10s Jimson weed	3.50 3.00
a.		Souv. sheet of 3, #C508-C510	13.00 8.00
		Nos. C508-C510 (3)	7.60 6.40

Exists imperf.

Oil Drilling Towers — AP116

1972, Oct. 17   Litho.   *Perf. 11½*
C511	AP116	1.30s bl & multi	.75 .40

Ecuadorian oil industry.

Coat of Arms — AP117

Arms Multicolored

1972, Nov. 18   Litho.   *Perf. 11½*
C512	AP117	2s black	.40 .40
C513	AP117	3s black	.40 .40
C514	AP117	4s black	.40 .40
C515	AP117	4.50s black	.40 .40
C516	AP117	6.30s black	1.30 .40
C517	AP117	6.90s black	1.30 .40
		Nos. C512-C517 (6)	4.20 2.40

Pichincha Type
Designs: 2.40s, Corridor, San Agustin. 4.50s, La Merced Convent. 5.50s, Column base. 6.30s, Chapter Hall, San Agustin. 6.90s, Interior, San Agustin. 7.40s, Crucifixion, Cantuña Chapel. 7.90s, Decorated ceiling, San Agustin.

ECUADOR

1972, Dec. 6			Wmk. 367	
C518	A266	2.40s yel & multi	.65	.30
C519	A266	4.50s yel & multi	.95	.35
C520	A266	5.50s yel & multi	.95	.35
C521	A266	6.30s yel & multi	1.40	.40
C522	A266	6.90s yel & multi	1.40	.40
C523	A266	7.40s yel & multi	2.10	.65
C524	A266	7.90s yel & multi	2.10	.65
	Nos. C518-C524 (7)		9.55	3.10

UN Emblem — AP118

1973, Mar. 23			Unwmk.	
C525	AP118	1.30s lt bl & blk	.95	.40

25th anniversary of the Economic Committee for Latin America (CEPAL).

OAS Emblem — AP119

1973, Apr. 14			Wmk. 367	
C526	AP119	1.50s multi	.90	.40
a.	Unwatermarked		.65	.25

Day of the Americas and "Philately for Peace."

Bird Type

Designs: 1.30s, Blue-footed booby. 3s, Brown pelican.

1973		Unwmk.	Perf. 11½x11	
C527	A268	1.30s multi	2.90	.60
C528	A268	3s multi	2.90	.60

Presidents Lara and Caldera — AP120

1973, June 15			Wmk. 367	
C529	AP120	3s multi	.95	.30

Visit of Venezuela Pres. Rafael Caldera, Feb. 5-7.

Silver Coin, 1934 — AP121

Ecuadorian Coins: 10s, Silver coin, obverse. 50s, Gold coin, 1928.

1973, Dec. 14	Unwmk.	Photo.	Perf. 14	
C530	AP121	5s multi	.65	.40
C531	AP121	10s multi	1.10	.60
C532	AP121	50s multi	5.00	2.50
a.	Souvenir sheet of 3		9.50	7.50
	Nos. C530-C532 (3)		6.75	3.50

No. C532a contains one each of Nos. C530-C532; Dated "1972." Exists imperf. Value, same.

A gold marginal overprint was applied in 1974 to No. C532a (perf. and imperf.): "X Campeonato Mundial de Football / Munich - 1974." Value, each $75.

A carmine overprint was applied in 1974 to No. C532a (perf. and imperf.): "Seminario de Telecommunicaciones Rurales, / Septiembre-1974 / Quito-Ecuador" and ITU emblem. Value, each $12.50.

Globe, OPEC Emblem, Oil Derrick — AP122

1974, June 15		Litho.	Perf. 11½	
C533	AP122	2s multi	.70	.40

Meeting of Organization of Oil Exporting Countries, Quito, June 15-24.

Ecuadorian Flag, UPU Emblem — AP123

1974, July 15		Litho.	Perf. 11½	
C534	AP123	1.30s multi	.90	.40

Centenary of Universal Postal Union. Two 25s souvenir sheets exist. These were sold on a restricted basis. Value, each $75.

Teodoro Wolf AP124

Capt. Edmundo Chiriboga AP125

1974		Litho.	Perf. 12x11½	
C535	AP124	1.30s blk & ultra	.55	.40
C536	AP125	1.50s gray	.70	.40

Teodoro Wolf, geographer; Edmundo Chiriboga, national hero. Issued: No. C535, 11/29; No. C536, 12/4.

Congress Emblem — AP126

1974, Dec. 8		Litho.	Perf. 11½x12	
C537	AP126	5s bl & multi	.95	.40

8th Inter-American Postmasters' Cong., Quito.

Map of Americas and Coat of Arms — AP127

1975, Feb. 1			Perf. 12x11½	
C538	AP127	3s bl & multi	.95	.40

EXFIGUA Stamp Exhibition and 5th General Assembly of Federation Inter-Americana de Filatelia, Guayaquil, Nov. 1973.

Prominent Ecuadorians — AP128

1975			Perf. 12x11½	
C539	AP128	5s lilac rose	.85	.40
C540	AP128	5s gray	.85	.40
C541	AP128	5s violet	.85	.40
C542	AP128	5s blk & rose red	.85	.40
	Nos. C539-C542 (4)		3.40	1.60

Pres. Guillermo Rodriguez Lara AP129

1975		Unwmk.	Perf. 12	
C546	AP129	5s vermilion & blk	1.10	.40

State visit of Pres. Guillermo Rodriguez Lara to Algeria, Romania and Venezuela.

Meeting Type of 1975

1.50s, Rafael Rodriguez Palacios & Argelino Duran Quintero meeting at border in Rumichaca. 2s, Signing border agreement.

1975, Apr. 1		Litho.	Perf. 12x11½	
C547	A273	1.50s multi	.55	.30
C548	A273	2s multi	.55	.30

Sacred Heart (Painting) AP130

Quito Cathedral AP131

Design: 2s, Monstrance.

1975, Apr. 28		Litho.	Perf. 12x11½	
C549	AP130	1.30s yel & multi	.55	.40
C550	AP130	2s bl & multi	.60	.40
C551	AP131	3s multi	.80	.40
	Nos. C549-C551 (3)		1.95	1.20

3rd Bolivarian Eucharistic Congress, Quito, June 9-16, 1974.

J. Delgado Panchana with Trophy AP132

J. Delgado Panchana Swimming AP133

	Perf. 12x11½, 11½x12			
1975, June 12			Unwmk.	
C552	AP132	1.30s bl & multi	.55	.40
C553	AP133	3s blk & multi	.65	.40

Jorge Delgado Panchana, South American swimming champion, 1971 and 1974.

Sports Type of 1975

1975, Sept. 11		Litho.	Perf. 11½	
C554	A276	1.30s Tennis	.65	.45
C555	A276	2s Target shooting	.85	.45
C556	A276	2.80s Volleyball	1.00	.45
C557	A276	3s Raft with sails	1.00	.45
C558	A276	5s Mask	1.75	.45
	Nos. C554-C558 (5)		5.25	2.25

Flower Type of 1975

Designs: 1.30s, Pitcairnia pungens. 2s, Scarlet sage. 3s, Amaryllis. 4s, Opuntia quitense. 5s, Bomarea.

1975, Nov. 18		Litho.	Perf. 11½x12	
C559	A277	1.30s multi	.65	.65
C560	A277	2s multi	1.00	.65
C561	A277	3s multi	1.40	.90
C562	A277	4s multi	2.00	1.40
C563	A277	5s multi	2.90	1.60
	Nos. C559-C563 (5)		7.95	5.20

No. C539, Manuel J. Calle, Journalist. No. C540, Leopoldo Benites V., president of UN General Assembly, 1973-74; No. C541, Adolfo H. Simmonds G. (1892-1969), journalist; No. C542, Juan de Dios Martinez Mera, President of Ecuador, birth centenary.

Tail Assemblies and Emblem AP134

Planes over Map of Ecuador AP135

1975, Dec. 17		Litho.	Perf. 11½	
C564	AP134	1.30s bl & multi	.65	.40
C565	AP135	3s multi	.85	.40

TAME, Military Transport Airline, 13th anniv.

Benalcázar Statue — AP136

1976, Feb. 6		Litho.	Perf. 11½	
C566	AP136	2s multi	.75	.40
C567	AP136	3s multi	.75	.40

Sebastián de Benalcázar (1495-1550), Spanish conquistador, founder of Quito.

Archaeology Type of 1975

1.30s, Seated man, Carchi Culture. 2s, Funerary urn, Tuncahuan Culture. 3s, Priest, Bahia de Caraquez Culture. 4s, Snail's shell, Cuasmal Culture. 5s, Bowl supported by figurines, Guangala Culture.

1976, Feb. 12		Litho.	Perf. 11½	
C568	A278	1.30s multi	.65	.60
C569	A278	2s multi	.80	.60
C570	A278	3s multi	1.20	.60
C571	A278	4s multi	1.75	1.00
C572	A278	5s multi	2.25	1.00
	Nos. C568-C572 (5)		6.65	3.80

Fruit Type of 1976

1976, Mar. 30				
C573	A280	2s Apples	.65	.40
C574	A280	5s Rose	1.50	.70

Lufthansa Jet — AP137

1976, June 25		Litho.	Perf. 12	
C575	AP137	10s bl & multi	1.75	.50

Lufthansa, 50th anniversary.

An imperf. 20s miniature sheet exists, similar to No. C575 enlarged, with overprinted black bar covering line below "Lufthansa." Size: 90x115mm. Value, $32.50.

Projected PO, Quito — AP138

1976, Aug. 10		Litho.	Perf. 12	
C576	AP138	5s blk & multi	.85	.40

Design for new General Post Office, Quito.

Fruit Peddler — AP139

ECUADOR

No. C578, Longshoreman. No. C579, Cerros del Carmen & Santa Ana, hills of Guayaquil, horiz. No. C580, Sebastián de Belalcázar. No. C581, Francisco de Orellana. No. C582, Chief Guayas & his wife Quila.

1976, July 25

C577	AP139	1.30s red & multi	.65	.40
C578	AP139	1.30s red & multi	.65	.40
C579	AP139	1.30s red & multi	.65	.40
C580	AP139	2s red & multi	.65	.40
C581	AP139	2s red & multi	.65	.40
C582	AP139	2s red & multi	.65	.40
Nos. C577-C582 (6)			3.90	2.40

Founding of Guayaquil, 441st anniversary.

Emblem and Laurel — AP140

1976, Aug. 9

C583 AP140 1.30s yel & multi   .90 .40

Bolivarian Soc. of Ecuador, 50th anniv.

Western Hemisphere and Equator Monument — AP141

1976, Sept. 6

C584 AP141 2s multi   .85 .40

Souvenir Sheet
Imperf

C585 AP141 5s multi   4.25 4.00

3rd Conf. of Pan-American Transport Ministers, Quito, Sept. 6-11. No. C585 contains design similar to No. C584 with black denomination and red control number in margin.

Congress Emblem — AP142

1976, Sept. 27 Litho. Perf. 11½

| C586 | AP142 | 1.30s bl & multi | .60 | .40 |
| C587 | AP142 | 3s bl & multi | .80 | .40 |

Souvenir Sheet
Imperf

C588 AP142 10s bl & multi   2.40 1.20

10th Inter-American Congress of the Construction Industry, Quito, Sept. 27-30

George Washington — AP143

American Bicentennial: 5s, Naval battle, Sept. 23, 1779, in which the Bonhomme Richard, commanded by John Paul Jones, defeated and captured the Serapis, British man-of-war, off Yorkshire coast, horiz.

1976, Oct. 18 Litho. Perf. 12

| C589 | AP143 | 3s blk & multi | .90 | .40 |
| C590 | AP143 | 5s red brn & yel | 1.60 | .60 |

Dr. Hideyo Noguchi — AP144

1976 Litho. Perf. 11½

C591 AP144 3s yel & multi   .65 .40

Dr. Hideyo Noguchi (1876-1928), bacteriologist (at Rockefeller Institute). A 10s imperf. miniature sheet in same design exists without "Aereo." Size: 95x114mm. Value $6.50.

Luis Cordero — AP145

1976, Dec. Litho. Perf. 11½

C592 AP145 2s multi   .95 .40

Luis Cordero (1833-1912), president of Ecuador.

Mariuxi Febres Cordero — AP146

1976, Dec. Perf. 11½

C593 AP146 3s multi   .95 .40

Mariuxi Febres Cordero, South American swimming champion.

Flags and Monument — AP147

1976, Nov. 9 Perf. 12

C594 AP147 3s multi   .75 .40

Miniature Sheet
Imperf

C595 AP147 5s multi   2.75 1.50

2nd Meeting of the Agriculture Ministers of the Andean Countries, Quito, Nov. 8-10.

Sister Catalina — AP148

1977, June 17 Litho. Perf. 12x11½

C596 AP148 1.30s blk & pale salmon   .95 .40

Sister Catalina de Jesus Herrera (1717-1795), writer.

Congress Hall, Quito — AP149

1977, Aug. 15 Litho. Perf. 12x11½

C597 AP149 5s multi   .85 .40
  a. 10s souvenir sheet   2.25 2.25

11th General Assembly of Pan-American Institute of Geography and History, Quito, Aug. 15-30. No. C597a contains the designs of types A282 and AP149 without denominations and with simulated perforations.

Pres. Alfonso López Michelsen, Flag of Colombia — AP150

Designs: 5s, Pres. López Michelsen of Colombia, Pres. Alfredo Poveda Burbano of Ecuador and aide. 7s, as 5s, vert. 9s, 10s, Presidents with aides.

1977, Sept. 13 Perf. 12

C598	AP150	2.60s multi	.75	.40
C599	AP150	5s multi	1.10	.40
C600	AP150	7s multi	1.30	.50
C601	AP150	9s multi	1.75	.70

Imperf

C602 AP150 10s multi   4.00 2.00
  Nos. C598-C602 (5)   8.90 4.00

Meeting of the Presidents of Ecuador and Colombia and Declaration of Putumayo, Feb. 25, 1977. Nos. C598-C602 are overprinted in multiple fluorescent, colorless rows: INSTITUTO GEOGRAFICO MILITAR GOBIERNO DEL ECUADOR.

Ceramic Figure, Tolita Culture — AP151

9s, Divine Shepherdess, sculpture by Bernardo de Legarda. 11s, The Fruit Seller, sculpture by Legarda. 20s, Sun God, pre-Columbian gold mask.

1977, Aug. 24 Perf. 12

C603	AP151	7s gold & multi	1.50	.30
C604	AP151	9s gold & multi	2.00	.35
C605	AP151	11s gold & multi	2.50	.70
Nos. C603-C605 (3)			6.00	1.35

Souvenir Sheet
Gold Embossed
Imperf

C606 AP151 20s vio, bl, blk & gold   8.50 3.50

Central Bank of Ecuador, 50th anniversary. Nos. C603-C605 overprinted like Nos. C598-C602.

Lungs — AP152

1977, Oct. 5 Litho. Perf. 12x11½

C607 AP152 2.60s multi   .90 .40

3rd Cong. of the Bolivarian Pneumonic Soc. and cent. of the founding of the medical faculty of the University of Guayaquil.

Brother Miguel, St. Peter's, Rome — AP153

1977

C608 AP153 2.60s multi   .75 .40

Beatification of Brother Miguel.

Peralta Type

2.60s, Titles of works by Peralta & his bookmark.

1977 Perf. 11½

C609 A284 2.60s multi   .75 .30

Broadcast Tower — AP154

1977, Dec. 2 Litho. Perf. 12x11½

C610 AP154 5s multi   .75 .45

9th World Telecommunications Day.

Remigio Romero y Cordero (1895-1967), Poet — AP155

1978, Mar. 2 Litho. Perf. 12½x11½

| C611 | AP155 | 3s multi | .70 | .40 |
| C612 | AP155 | 10.60s multi | .95 | .40 |

Imperf

C612A AP155 10s multi   1.90 1.50
  Nos. C611-C612A (3)   3.55 2.30

No. C612A contains a vignette similar to Nos. C611-C612.

Dr. Vicente Corral Moscoso — AP156

5s, Hospital emblem with Caduceus.

1978, Apr. 12 Litho. Imperf.

C613 AP156 5s multi   .75 .30

Perf. 12x11½

C614 AP156 7.60s multi   1.60 .30

Inauguration (in 1977) of Dr. Vicente Corral Moscoso Regional Hospital, Cuenca.

Faces — AP157

Designs: 9s, Emblems and flags of Ecuador. 10s, 11s, Hands reaching for light.

1978, Mar. 17

C615	AP157	7s multicolored	.95	.40
C616	AP157	9s multicolored	1.30	.40
C617	AP157	11s multicolored	1.75	.40

Imperf

C618 AP157 10s multicolored   2.00 1.50
  Nos. C615-C618 (4)   6.00 2.70

Ecuadorian Social Security Institute, 50th anniv.

Geographical Institute Type

7.60s, Plane over map of Ecuador with mountains.

1978, Apr. 12 Litho. Perf. 11½

C619 A287 7.60s multi   1.50 .60

Imperf

C620 A287 10s multi   2.50 2.00

No. C620 contains 2 vignettes with simulated perforations in designs of Nos. 967 and C619.

Lions Type

1978 Perf. 11½

| C621 | A288 | 5s multi | .90 | .30 |
| C622 | A288 | 6.20s multi | 1.00 | .50 |

Imperf

C623 A288 10s multi   3.00 1.50
  Nos. C621-C623 (3)   4.90 2.30

No. C623 contains a vignette similar to Nos. C621-C622.

ECUADOR

San Martin — AP158

1978, Apr. 13   Litho.   *Perf. 12*
C624 AP158   10.60s multi   1.90   .75
Imperf
C625 AP158   10s multi   3.25   2.25

Gen. José de San Martin (1778-1850), soldier and statesman. No. C625 contains a vignette similar to No. C624.

Bank Type
Design: 5s, Bank emblem.

1978, Sept.   Litho.   *Perf. 11½*
C626 A289   5s gray & multi   .70   .35

Soccer Type
Designs: 2.60s, "Gauchito" and Games' emblem. 5s, "Gauchito." 7s, Soccer ball. 9s, Games' emblem, vert. 10s, Games' emblem.

1978, Nov. 1   *Perf. 12*
C627 A290   2.60s multi   .45   .25
C628 A290   7s multi   1.10   .40
C629 A290   9s multi   1.50   .65
Imperf
C630 A290   5s blk & bl   9.00   9.00
C631 A290   10s blk & bl   9.00   9.00
Nos. C627-C631 (5)   21.05   19.30

Bernardo O'Higgins — AP159

1978, Nov. 11   Litho.   *Perf. 12x11½*
C632 AP159   10.60s multi   1.25   .40
Imperf
C633 AP159   10s multi   1.75   .60

Gen. Bernardo O'Higgins (1778-1842), Chilean soldier and statesman. No. C633 contains a vignette similar to No. C632.

Old Men of Vilcabamba — AP160

1978, Nov. 11   *Perf. 12x11½*
C634 AP160   5s multi   1.00   .40

Vilcabamba, valley of longevity.

Humphrey — AP161

1978, Nov. 27   Litho.   *Perf. 12x11½*
C635 AP161   5s multi   1.00   .40

Hubert H. Humphrey (1911-1978), Vice President of the US.

Virgin and Child — AP162

Children's Drawings: 4.60s, Holy Family. 6.20s, Candle and children.

1978
C636 AP162   2.20s multi   .55   .40
C637 AP162   4.60s multi   .85   .40
C638 AP162   6.20s multi   1.30   .40
Nos. C636-C638 (3)   2.70   1.20

Christmas 1978.

Village, by Anibal Villacis — AP163

Ecuadorian Painters: No. C640, Mountain Village, by Gilberto Almeida. No. C641, Bay, by Roura Oxandaberro. No. C642, Abstract, by Luis Molinari. No. C643, Statue, by Oswaldo Viteri. No. C644, Tools, by Enrique Tabara.

1978, Dec. 9   *Perf. 12*
C639 AP163   5s multi   .85   .40
C640 AP163   5s multi   .85   .40
C641 AP163   5s multi   .85   .40
C642 AP163   5s multi   .85   .40
C643 AP163   5s multi   .85   .40
C644 AP163   5s multi   .85   .40
Nos. C639-C644 (6)   5.10   2.40

House and Monument AP164

Design: 3.40s, Monument, vert.

1979, Feb. 27   Litho.   *Perf. 12*
C645 AP164   2.40s multi   .70   .40
C646 AP164   3.40s multi   .70   .40
Imperf
C647 AP164   10s multi   1.60   1.00
Nos. C645-C647 (3)   3.00   1.80

Sesquicentennial of Battle of Portete and Tarqui. No. C647 contains vignettes similar to Nos. C645-C646.

Fish and Ship — AP165

7s, Map of Ecuador & Galapagos showing territorial waters. 9s, Map of South America with west-coast territorial waters.

Perf. 12x11½, 11½x12
1979, July 23   Litho.   Wmk. 367
C648 AP165   5s multi   .90   .35
C649 AP165   7s multi, horiz.   1.25   .35
C650 AP165   9s multi   1.75   .50
Nos. C648-C650 (3)   3.90   1.20

Declaration of 200-mile territorial limit, 25th anniversary.

National Heritage Type
Designs: 10.60s, Bells in Quito clock tower, horiz. 13.60s, Aerial view of Galapagos coast.

1979, Aug. 3   *Perf. 12x11½*
C651 A293   10.60s multi   1.40   .60
C652 A293   13.60s multi   1.60   .75
Size: 115x91mm
Imperf Unwmk.
C653 A293   10s multi   5.25   2.10
Nos. C651-C653 (3)   8.25   3.45

National heritage: Quito and Galapagos Islands. No. C653 contains vignettes similar to Nos. 977, C651-C652.

Flags of Ecuador and U.S. — AP166

1979, Aug.   Wmk. 367   *Perf. 11½x12*
C654 AP166   7.60s multi   .80   .50
C655 AP166   10.60s multi   1.20   .75
Size: 115x91mm
Imperf Unwmk.
C656 AP166   10s multi   1.50   .75
Nos. C654-C656 (3)   3.50   2.00

5th anniv. of Ecuador-US Chamber of Commerce. No. C656 contains vignettes similar to Nos. C654-C655.

Smiling Girl, IYC Emblem — AP167

Perf. 12x11½
1979, Sept. 7   Litho.   Wmk. 367
C657 AP167   10s multi   1.40   .40

International Year of the Child.

Citizens and Flag of Ecuador — AP168

Design: 10.60s, Pres. Jaime Roldos Aguilera, flag of Ecuador, vert.

Perf. 11½
1979, Sept. 27   Litho.   Unwmk.
C658 AP168   7.60s multi   1.25   .45
Wmk. 367
C659 AP168   10.60s multi   1.50   .40

Restoration of democracy to Ecuador.

Ecuador Coat of Arms, Olympic Rings and Eagle — AP169

Perf. 12x11½
1979, Nov. 23   Unwmk.
C660 AP169   28s multi   2.50   1.25

5th National Games, Cuenca.

CIESPAL Building, Quito — AP170

Perf. 11½x12½
1979, Dec. 26   Wmk. 367
C661 AP170   10.60s multi   1.30   .40

Opening of Ecuadorian Institute of Engineers building.

Olmedo Type
Perf. 12x11½
1980, Apr. 29   Litho.   Unwmk.
C662 A294   10s multi   1.60   .65

Tribal Chief Type
Indo-American Tribal Chiefs: No. C663, Cuauhtemoc, Mexico. No. C664, Lempira, Honduras. No. C665, Nicaragua. No. C666, Lambaré, Paraguay. No. C667, Urraca, Panama. No. C668, Anacaona, Haiti. #C669, Caupolican, Chile. No. C670, Tacun-Uman, Guatemala. No. C671, Calarca, Colombia. No. C672, Garabito, Costa Rica. No. C673, Hatuey, Cuba. No. C674, Camarao, Brazil. No. C675, Tehuelche, Argentina. No. C676, Tupaj Katri, Bolivia. 17.80s, Sequoyah, US. 22.80s, Ruminahui, Ecuador.

Wmk. 367 (#C663, C667), Unwmkd.
1980, May 12
C663 A295   7.60s multi   1.75   .75
C664 A295   7.60s multi   1.75   .75
C665 A295   7.60s multi   1.75   .75
C666 A295   10s multi   2.10   .85
C667 A295   10s multi   2.10   .85
C668 A295   10.60s multi   2.10   .85
C669 A295   10.60s multi   2.10   .85
C670 A295   10.60s multi   2.10   .85
C671 A295   12.80s multi   3.00   1.10
C672 A295   12.80s multi   3.00   1.10
C673 A295   12.80s multi   3.00   1.10
C674 A295   13.60s multi   3.00   1.10
C675 A295   13.60s multi   3.00   1.10
C676 A295   13.60s multi   3.00   1.10
C677 A295   17.80s multi   3.50   1.25
C678 A295   22.80s multi   4.00   2.40
Nos. C663-C678 (16)   41.25   16.75

Royal Visit Type
Perf. 11½x12
1980, May 18   Unwmk.
C679 A296   10.60s multi   1.00   .65

Pichincha Provincial Development Council Building — AP171

1980, June 1   *Perf. 12x11½*
C680 AP171   10.60s multi   1.60   .60

Progress in Pichincha Province.

Indian Type
Designs: 7.60s, Salasaca boy, Tungurahua. 10s, Amula woman, Chimborazo. 10.60s, Canar woman, Canar. 13.60s, Colorado Indian, Pichincha.

1980, June 10   Litho.   *Perf. 12x11½*
C681 A297   7.60s multi   1.75   .75
C682 A297   10s multi   2.10   .85
C683 A297   10.60s multi   2.50   .90
C684 A297   13.60s multi   3.25   1.25
Nos. C681-C684 (4)   9.60   3.75

Virgin of Mercy Type
Designs: No. C685, Cupola, cloisters. No. C686, Gold screen. No. C687, Quito from basilica tower. No. C688, Retable. No. C689, Pulpit. No. C690, Cupola. No. C691, Statue of Virgin.

1980, July 7   Litho.   *Perf. 11½*
C685 A298   7.60s multi   1.00   .50
C686 A298   7.60s multi   1.00   .50
C687 A298   7.60s multi   1.00   .50
C688 A298   10.60s multi   1.25   .60
C689 A298   10.60s multi   1.25   .60
C690 A298   13.60s multi   1.75   .90
C691 A298   13.60s multi   1.75   .90
Nos. C685-C691 (7)   9.00   4.50

Nos. C685-C691 are vert.

UPU Monument — AP172

Design: 17.80s, Mail box, 1880.

1980, July 7   *Perf. 12*
C692 AP172   10.60s multi   1.60   .75
C693 AP172   17.80s multi   2.90   1.25
Souvenir Sheet
C694 AP172   25s multi   3.75   3.00

UPU membership cent. No. C694 contains designs of C692 and C693, horiz., perf. 11½.

Olympic Type.
Design: 10.60s, 13.60s, Moscow '80 emblem, Olympic rings.

Perf. 12x11½
1980, July 19   Wmk. 395
C695 A299   10.60s multi   1.40   .75

ECUADOR

C696	A299 13.60s multi	1.90	1.00

Souvenir Sheet

C697	A299 30s multi	7.50	7.00

No. C697 contains vignettes in designs of Nos. 991 and C695.

Marshal Sucre, by Marco Sales — AP173

1980

C698	AP173 10.60s multi	1.30	.60

Marshal Antonio Jose de Sucre, death sesquicentennial.

Rotary International, 75th Anniversary — AP174

1980, Aug. 4 — *Perf. 11½*

C699	AP174 10s multi	1.75	.50

Riobamba Type

Design: 7.60s, 10.60s, Monstrance, Riobamba Cathedral, vert.

1980, Sept. 20 — *Litho.* *Perf. 11½*

C700	A301 7.60s multi	.95	.35
C701	A301 10.60s multi	1.30	.45

Souvenir Sheet
Imperf

C702	A301 30s multi	2.25	2.25

No. C702 contains vignettes in designs of Nos. 996 and C701.

Democracy Type

7.60s, 10.60s, Pres. Aguilera and voter.

Perf. 12x11½

1980, Oct. 9 — *Litho.* *Wmk. 395*

C703	A302 7.60s multi	.70	.50
C704	A302 10.60s multi	1.60	.60

Souvenir Sheet
Imperf

C705	A302 15s multi	2.00	1.50

No. C705 contains vignettes in designs of Nos. 999 and C703.

OPEC Type

20th Anniversary of OPEC: 7.60s, Men holding OPEC emblem, vert.

1980, Nov. 8 — *Perf. 11½x12*

C706	A303 7.60s multi	1.10	.65

Carchi Province Type

10.60s, Governor's Palace, vert. 17.80s, Victory Museum, Central Square, vert.

1980, Nov. 21 — *Perf. 13*

C707	A304 10.60c multi	1.75	.65
C708	A304 17.80s multi	2.75	.90

Orchid Type

Designs: No. C709, Anguloa uniflora. No. C710, Scuticaria salesiana. C711, Helcia sanguinolenta, vert. No. C712, Anguloa virginalis.

Perf. 12x11½, 11½x12

1980, Nov. 22

C709	A305 7.60s multi	2.75	.65
C710	A305 10.60s multi	4.00	.40
C711	A305 50s multi	7.25	1.25
C712	A305 100s multi	9.50	2.40
	Nos. C709-C712 (4)	23.50	4.70

Souvenir Sheets
Imperf

C713	A305 20s multi	9.00	6.00
C714	A305 20s multi	9.00	6.00

Nos. C713-C714 contain vignettes in designs of Nos. C709, C711 and C710, C712 respectively.

Christmas Type

7.60s, Pope blessing crowd. 10.60s, Portrait.

1980, Dec. 27 — *Perf. 12*

C715	A306 7.60s multi, vert.	2.00	.60
C716	A306 10.60s multi, vert.	2.90	.70

Isidro Cueva — AP175

1980, Nov. 20 — *Perf. 13*

C717	AP175 18.20s multi	2.75	1.25

Dr. Isidro Ayora Cueva, former president, birth centenary.

Simon Bolivar, by Marco Salas — AP176

1980, Dec. 17 — *Perf. 11½*

C718	AP176 13.60s multi	2.25	1.00

Simon Bolivar death sesquicentennial.

Turtle, Galapagos Islands — AP177

100s, Oldest Ecuadorian mail box, 1793.

1981, Feb. 12 — *Litho.* *Perf. 13*

C719	AP177 50s multi	6.50	4.00
C720	AP177 100s multi, vert.	8.50	5.00

HCJB Type

1981 — *Litho.* *Perf. 13*

C721	A311 7.60s Emblem, horiz.	1.60	.65
C722	A311 10.60s Emblem, diff.	2.25	.90

Soccer Players — AP178

1981, July 8

C723	AP178 7.60s Emblem	1.30	.45
C724	AP178 10.60s shown	1.60	.45
C725	AP178 13.60s World Cup	2.00	.75
	Nos. C723-C725 (3)	4.90	1.65

Souvenir Sheets

C726	AP178 20s multi	4.50	3.50
C727	AP178 20s multi	4.50	3.50

1982 World Cup Soccer Championship. Nos. C726-C727 contain vignettes in designs of Nos. C723 and C725 respectively.

Picasso Type

7.60s, Still-life. 10.60s, First Communion, vert. 13.60s, Las Meninas, vert.

1981, Oct. 26 — *Litho.* *Perf. 13*

C728	A313a 7.60s multi	1.10	.45
C729	A313a 10.60s multi	1.50	.60
C730	A313a 13.60s multi	1.75	.70

Size: 110x90mm
Imperf

C731	A313a 20s multi	3.00	3.00
	Nos. C728-C731 (4)	7.35	4.75

No. C731 contains designs of Nos. C730, C729.

World Food Day Type

1981, Dec. 31 — *Litho.* *Perf. 13x13½*

C732	A314 10.60s Farming, vert.	1.75	.70

IYD Type

Designs: No. C733, Emblem. No. C734, Man with crutch.

1982, Feb. 25 — *Litho.* *Perf. 13*

C733	A316 7.60s multi	1.10	.35
C734	A316 10.60s multi	1.40	.65

Montalvo Type

1982 — *Litho.* *Perf. 13*

C735	A318 5s Home, horiz.	1.75	.75

Swimming Type

1982, July 30

C736	A320 10.20s Emblem, vert.	1.25	.50
C737	A320 14.20s Diving, vert.	1.75	.75

Pres. Jaime Roldos, (1940-81), Mrs. Martha Roldos, Independence Monument, Quito — AP179

1983, May 25 — *Litho.* *Perf. 12*

C738	AP179 13.60s multi	1.10	.50

Souvenir Sheet
Imperf

C739	AP179 20s multi	2.00	1.75

AIR POST SEMI-POSTAL STAMPS

Nos. C119-C123 Surcharged in Blue or Red

1944, May 9 — *Unwmk.* *Perf. 12*

CB1	AP26 50c + 50c	7.00	3.50
CB2	AP26 70c + 30c	7.00	3.50
CB3	AP26 3s + 50c (R)	7.00	3.50
CB4	AP26 5s + 1s (R)	7.00	3.50
CB5	AP26 10s + 2s	7.00	3.50
	Nos. CB1-CB5 (5)	35.00	17.50

The surtax aided Mendez Hospital

AIR POST REGISTRATION STAMPS

Issued by Sociedad Colombo-Alemana de Transportes Aereos (SCADTA)

Nos. C3 and C3a Overprinted in Carmine

1928-29 — *Wmk. 116* *Perf. 14x14½*

CF1	AP6 1s on 20c (#C3)	110.00	100.00
a.	1s on 20c (#C3a) (29)	140.00	110.00

No. C18 Overprinted in Black

1929, Apr. 1 — *Wmk. 127* *Perf. 14*

CF2	AP2 1s rose	85.00	55.00

AIR POST OFFICIAL STAMPS

Nos. C8-C15 Overprinted in Red or Black

1929, May — *Unwmk.* *Perf. 12*

CO1	AP1 2c black (R)	1.00	.50
CO2	AP1 5c carmine rose	1.00	.50
CO3	AP1 10c deep brown	1.00	.50
CO4	AP1 20c dark violet	1.00	.50
CO5	AP1 50c deep green	4.00	2.00
CO6	AP1 1s dark blue	4.00	2.00
a.	Inverted overprint	240.00	
CO7	AP1 5s orange yellow	18.00	7.75
CO8	AP1 10s orange red	210.00	75.00
	Nos. CO1-CO8 (8)	240.00	88.75

Establishment of commercial air service in Ecuador.
Counterfeits of No. CO8 exist.
See Nos. CO9-CO12. For overprints and surcharges see No. C35.

1930, Jan. 9

CO9	AP1 50c olive brown	3.50	1.75
CO10	AP1 1s carmine lake	4.50	2.25
CO11	AP1 5s olive green	11.00	5.50
CO12	AP1 10s black	21.00	10.50
	Nos. CO9-CO12 (4)	40.00	20.00

For surcharges and overprint see Nos. C32-C34, C36-C38.

Air Post Stamps of 1937 Overprinted in Black

1937, Aug. 19

CO13	AP7 10c chestnut	.50	.30
CO14	AP7 50c olive black	.50	.30
CO15	AP7 70c black brown	.60	.30
CO16	AP7 1s gray black	.70	.30
CO17	AP7 2s dark violet	.70	.30
	Nos. CO13-CO17 (5)	3.00	1.50

For overprints see Nos. 463-464.

No. C79 Overprinted in Black

1940, Aug. 1 — *Perf. 12½x13*

CO18	AP15 5s emerald	2.00	.60

Catalogue values for unused stamps in this section, from this point to the end of the section, are for Never Hinged items.

Nos. C352-C354 Overprinted

1964 — *Perf. 13½*

CO19	AP86 50c multi	2.25	.85
CO20	AP86 80c multi	2.25	.85
CO21	AP86 1.30s multi	2.25	.85
	Nos. CO19-CO21 (3)	6.75	2.55

SPECIAL DELIVERY STAMPS

SD1

SD1a

ECUADOR

	1928	Unwmk.		Perf. 12	
E1	SD1	2c on 2c blue		8.00	9.00
a.		"DOS CVTOS." inverted		35.00	37.50
E2	SD1a	5c on 2c blue		7.00	9.00
E3	SD1a	10c on 2c blue		7.00	6.00
a.		"10 CENTAVOS" inverted		21.00	25.00
E4	SD1a	20c on 2c blue		10.00	9.00
E5	SD1a	50c on 2c blue		12.00	9.00
		Nos. E1-E5 (5)		44.00	42.00

No. E1 surcharge reads "CTVOS". Nos. E2-E5 surcharge reads "CENTAVOS".

No. RA49A Surcharged in Red

1945				
E6	PT18	20c on 5c green	4.50	2.00

LATE FEE STAMP

No. RA49A Surcharged in Black

1945		Unwmk.	Perf. 12	
I1	PT18	10c on 5c green	1.50	1.00

POSTAGE DUE STAMPS

Numeral — D1

1896		Engr.	Wmk. 117	Perf. 12	
J1	D1	1c blue green		6.00	6.50
J2	D1	2c blue green		6.00	6.50
J3	D1	5c blue green		6.00	6.50
J4	D1	10c blue green		6.00	6.50
J5	D1	20c blue green		6.00	8.50
J6	D1	50c blue green		6.00	13.00
J7	D1	100c blue green		6.00	17.00
		Nos. J1-J7 (7)		42.00	64.50

Reprints are on very thick paper with distinct watermark and vertical paper-weave direction. Value 30c each.

		Unwmk.		
J8	D1	1c blue green	5.00	6.00
J9	D1	2c blue green	5.00	6.00
J10	D1	5c blue green	5.00	6.00
J11	D1	10c blue green	5.00	6.00
J12	D1	20c blue green	5.00	7.50
J13	D1	50c blue green	5.00	10.50
J14	D1	100c blue green	5.00	15.00
		Nos. J8-J14 (7)	35.00	57.00

Coat of Arms — D2

1929				
J15	D2	5c deep blue	.40	.40
J16	D2	10c orange yellow	.40	.40
J17	D2	20c red	.60	.60
		Nos. J15-J17 (3)	1.40	1.40

Numeral — D3

		Perf. 13½		
1958, Nov.		Unwmk.	Litho.	
J18	D3	10c bright lilac	.60	.40
J19	D3	50c emerald	.60	.40
J20	D3	1s maroon	.75	.40
J21	D3	2s red	.90	.40
		Nos. J18-J21 (4)	2.85	1.60

OFFICIAL STAMPS

Regular Issues of 1881 and 1887 Handstamped in Black

1886		Unwmk.	Perf. 12	
O1	A5	1c yellow brown	2.50	2.50
O2	A6	2c lake	3.00	3.00
O3	A7	5c blue	6.75	8.75
O4	A8	10c orange	5.25	3.25
O5	A9	20c gray violet	5.25	5.25
O6	A10	50c blue green	15.00	11.50
		Nos. O1-O6 (6)	37.75	34.25

1887				
O7	A12	1c green	3.25	2.50
O8	A13	2c vermilion	3.25	3.25
O9	A14	5c blue	5.25	2.50
O10	A15	80c olive green	17.50	10.00
		Nos. O7-O10 (4)	29.25	18.25

Nos. O1-O10 are known with red handstamp but these are believed to be speculative.
The overprint on the 1886-87 issues is handstamped and is found in various positions.

Flores — O1

1892		Carmine Overprint		
O11	O1	1c ultramarine	.30	.40
O12	O1	2c ultramarine	.30	.40
O13	O1	5c ultramarine	.30	.40
O14	O1	10c ultramarine	.30	.60
O15	O1	20c ultramarine	.30	.90
O16	O1	50c ultramarine	.30	.90
O17	O1	1s ultramarine	.35	1.00
		Nos. O11-O17 (7)	2.15	4.60

Arms — O1a

1894				
O18	O1a	1c slate green (R)	15.00	
O19	O1a	2c lake (Bk)	20.00	

Nos. O18 and O19 were not placed in use.

Rocafuerte — O2

Dated "1894"

1894		Carmine Overprint		
O20	O2	1c gray black	.60	1.00
O21	O2	2c gray black	.60	.60
O22	O2	5c gray black	.60	.60
O23	O2	10c gray black	.75	1.00
O24	O2	20c gray black	1.00	1.00
O25	O2	50c gray black	3.75	3.75
O26	O2	1s gray black	6.00	6.00
		Nos. O20-O26 (7)	13.30	13.95

Dated "1895"

1895		Carmine Overprint		
O27	O2	1c gray black	5.25	5.25
O28	O2	2c gray black	7.50	7.50
O29	O2	5c gray black	1.50	1.50
O30	O2	10c gray black	7.50	7.50
O31	O2	20c gray black	11.00	10.50
O32	O2	50c gray black	75.00	75.00
O33	O2	1s gray black	3.75	3.75
		Nos. O27-O33 (7)	111.50	111.00

Reprints of 1894-95 issues are on very thick paper with paper weave found both horizontal and vertical for all denominations. Values: Nos. O20-O26, 35c each; O27-O33, 20c each. Generally they are blacker than originals.
For overprints see Nos. O50-O91.

Types of 1896 Overprinted in Carmine

1896			Wmk. 117	
O34	A21	1c olive bister	1.00	1.00
O35	A22	2c olive bister	1.00	1.00
O36	A23	5c olive bister	1.00	1.00
O37	A24	10c olive bister	1.00	1.00
O38	A25	20c olive bister	1.00	1.00
O39	A26	50c olive bister	1.00	1.00
O40	A27	1s olive bister	3.00	3.00
O41	A28	5s olive bister	6.00	6.00
		Nos. O34-O41 (8)	15.00	15.00

Reprints of Nos. O34-O41 are on thick paper with vertical paper weave direction.

		Unwmk.		
O42	A21	1c olive bister	3.00	3.00
O43	A22	2c olive bister	3.00	3.00
O44	A23	5c olive bister	3.00	3.00
O45	A24	10c olive bister	3.00	3.00
O46	A25	20c olive bister	3.00	3.00
O47	A26	50c olive bister	3.00	3.00
O48	A27	1s olive bister	7.50	7.50
O49	A28	5s olive bister	10.50	10.50
		Nos. O42-O49 (8)	36.00	36.00

Reprints of Nos. O42-O49 all have overprint in black. Value 30 cents each.

Nos. O20-O26 Overprinted

1897-98				
O50	O2	1c gray black	20.00	20.00
O51	O2	2c gray black	35.00	35.00
O52	O2	5c gray black	200.00	200.00
O53	O2	10c gray black	30.00	30.00
O54	O2	20c gray black	20.00	20.00
O55	O2	50c gray black	35.00	35.00
O56	O2	1s gray black	55.00	55.00
		Nos. O50-O56 (7)	395.00	395.00

Nos. O20-O26 Overprinted

O57	O2	1c gray black	4.00	4.00
O58	O2	2c gray black	9.00	9.00
O59	O2	5c gray black	90.00	90.00
O60	O2	10c gray black	100.00	100.00
O61	O2	20c gray black	25.00	25.00
O62	O2	50c gray black	15.00	15.00
O63	O2	1s gray black	165.00	165.00
		Nos. O57-O63 (7)	408.00	408.00

Nos. O20-O26 Overprinted

O64	O2	1c gray black	40.00	40.00
O65	O2	2c gray black	40.00	40.00
O66	O2	5c gray black	40.00	40.00
O67	O2	10c gray black	40.00	40.00
O68	O2	20c gray black	40.00	40.00
O69	O2	50c gray black	40.00	40.00
O70	O2	1s gray black	40.00	40.00
		Nos. O64-O70 (7)	280.00	280.00

Nos. O27-O33 Overprinted in Black like Nos. O50-O56

O71	O2	1c gray black	20.00	20.00
O72	O2	2c gray black	20.00	20.00
O73	O2	5c gray black	20.00	20.00
O74	O2	10c gray black	20.00	20.00
O75	O2	20c gray black	30.00	30.00
O76	O2	50c gray black	275.00	275.00
O77	O2	1s gray black	100.00	100.00
		Nos. O71-O77 (7)	485.00	485.00

Nos. O27-O33 Overprinted

O78	O2	1c gray black	35.00	35.00
O79	O2	2c gray black	30.00	30.00
O80	O2	5c gray black	30.00	30.00
O81	O2	10c gray black	32.50	32.50
O82	O2	20c gray black	42.50	42.50

O83	O2	50c gray black	30.00	30.00
O84	O2	1s gray black	30.00	30.00
		Nos. O78-O84 (7)	230.00	230.00

Nos. O27-O33 Overprinted like #O64-O70

O85	O2	1c gray black	90.00	90.00
O86	O2	2c gray black	20.00	20.00
O87	O2	5c gray black	80.00	80.00
O88	O2	10c gray black	80.00	80.00
O89	O2	20c gray black	140.00	140.00
O90	O2	50c gray black	85.00	85.00
O91	O2	1s gray black	165.00	165.00
		Nos. O85-O91 (7)	660.00	660.00

Many forged overprints of Nos. O50-O91 exist, made on the original stamps and reprints.

O3

1898-99			Perf. 15, 16	
		Black Surcharge		
O92	O3	5c on 50c lilac	10.00	10.00
a.		Inverted surcharge	25.00	25.00
O93	O3	10c on 20s org	15.00	15.00
a.		Double surcharge	40.00	30.00
O94	O3	10c on 50c lilac	140.00	140.00
O95	O3	20c on 50c lilac	30.00	30.00
O96	O3	20c on 50s green	30.00	30.00
		Nos. O92-O96 (5)	225.00	225.00
		Green Surcharge		
O97	O3	5c on 50c lilac	10.00	10.00
a.		Double surcharge	5.00	
b.		Double surcharge, blk and grn	12.00	
c.		Same as "b," blk surch. invtd.	5.00	
1899		Red Surcharge		
O98	O3	5c on 50c lilac	10.00	10.00
a.		Double surcharge	20.00	
b.		Dbl. surch., blk and red	25.00	
O99	O3	20c on 50s green	15.00	15.00
a.		Inverted surcharge	40.00	
b.		Dbl. surch., red and blk	60.00	

Similar Surcharge in Black Value in Words in Two Lines

O100	O3	1c on 5c blue	650.00	
		Red Surcharge		
O101	O3	2c on 5c blue	1,150.	
O102	O3	4c on 20c blue	800.00	

Types of Regular Issue of 1899 Ovptd. in Black

1899			Perf. 14, 15	
O103	A37	2c orange & blk	.70	1.60
O104	A39	10c orange & blk	.70	1.60
O105	A40	20c orange & blk	.50	2.50
O106	A41	50c orange & blk	.50	3.25
		Nos. O103-O106 (4)	2.40	8.95

For overprint see No. O167.

The above overprint was applied to remainders of the postage stamps of 1904 with the idea of increasing their salability. They were never regularly in use as official stamps.

Regular Issue of 1911-13 Overprinted in Black

1913			Perf. 12	
O107	A71	1c scarlet & blk	3.50	3.50
O108	A72	2c blue & blk	3.50	3.50
O109	A73	3c orange & blk	2.25	2.25

ECUADOR

O110	A74	5c scarlet & blk	4.50	4.50
O111	A75	10c blue & blk	4.50	4.50
		Nos. O107-O111 (5)	18.25	18.25

Regular Issue of 1911-13 Overprinted

1916-17   **Overprint 22x3½mm**

O112	A72	2c blue & blk	25.00	18.00
O113	A74	5c scarlet & blk	25.00	18.00
O114	A75	10c blue & blk	15.00	12.00
		Nos. O112-O114 (3)	65.00	48.00

Overprint 25x4mm

O115	A71	1c scarlet & blk	1.10	1.10
O116	A72	2c blue & blk	1.60	1.60
a.		Inverted overprint	5.00	5.00
O117	A73	3c orange & blk	1.00	1.00
O118	A74	5c scarlet & blk	1.60	1.60
O119	A75	10c blue & blk	1.60	1.60
		Nos. O115-O119 (5)	6.90	6.90

Same Overprint On Regular Issue of 1915-17

O120	A71	1c orange	1.40	1.40
O121	A72	2c green	1.40	1.40
O122	A73	3c black	2.25	2.25
O123	A78	4c red & blk	2.25	2.25
a.		Inverted overprint	15.00	
O124	A74	5c violet	1.40	1.40
O125	A75	10c blue	2.75	2.75
O126	A79	20c green & blk	15.00	15.00
		Nos. O120-O126 (7)	26.45	26.45

Regular Issues of 1911-17 Overprinted in Black or Red

O127	A71	1c orange	1.10	.90
O128	A72	2c green	.95	.70
O129	A73	3c black (Bk)	1.10	.90
O130	A73	3c black (R)	1.10	.70
a.		Inverted overprint	15.00	
O131	A78	4c red & blk	1.10	.90
O132	A74	5c violet	2.10	.90
O133	A75	10c blue & blk	5.75	1.75
O134	A75	10c blue	1.10	.90
O135	A79	20c green & blk	5.50	1.75
		Nos. O127-O135 (9)	19.80	9.40

Regular Issue of 1920 Overprinted

1920

O136	A86	1c green	1.25	1.25
a.		Inverted overprint	17.00	—
O137	A86	2c carmine	1.00	1.00
a.		Inverted overprint	5.00	
O138	A86	3c yellow brn	1.25	1.25
O139	A86	4c dark green	2.00	2.00
a.		Inverted overprint	17.00	
O140	A86	5c blue	2.00	2.00
O141	A86	6c orange	1.25	1.25
O142	A86	7c brown	2.00	2.00
O143	A86	8c yellow green	2.50	2.50
O144	A86	9c red	3.25	3.25
O145	A95	10c blue	2.00	2.00
O146	A86	15c gray	11.00	11.00
O147	A86	20c deep violet	14.50	14.50
O148	A86	30c violet	17.00	17.00
O149	A86	40c dark brown	21.00	21.00
O150	A86	50c dark green	14.50	14.50
O151	A86	60c dark blue	17.00	17.00
O152	A86	70c bluish gray	17.00	17.00
O153	A86	80c yellow	21.00	21.00
O154	A104	90c green	21.00	21.00
O155	A86	1s deep blue	45.00	45.00
		Nos. O136-O155 (20)	217.50	217.50

Cent. of the independence of Guayaquil.

Stamps of 1911 Overprinted

1922

O156	A71	1c scarlet & blk	9.00	9.00
O157	A72	2c blue & blk	4.50	4.50

Revenue Stamps of 1919-1920 Overprinted like Nos. O156 and O157

1924

O158	PT3	1c dark blue	2.00	2.00
O159	PT3	2c green	12.50	12.50

Regular Issues of 1911-17 Overprinted

1924

O160	A71	1c orange	7.00	7.00
a.		Inverted overprint	15.00	

Overprinted in Black or Red

O161	A72	2c green	.60	.60
O162	A73	3c black (R)	.80	.80
O163	A78	4c red & blk	1.25	1.25
O164	A74	5c violet	1.25	1.25
O165	A75	10c deep blue	1.25	1.25
O166	A76	1s green & blk	7.00	7.00
		Nos. O160-O166 (7)	19.15	19.15

No. O106 with Additional Overprint

1924   **Perf. 14, 15**

O167	A41	50c orange & blk	2.25	2.25

Nos. O160-O167 exist with inverted overprint.

No. 199 Overprinted

1924   **Perf. 12**

O168	A71	1c orange	5.50	5.50

Regular Issues of 1911-25 Overprinted

1925

O169	A71	1c scarlet & blk	10.00	4.25
a.		Inverted overprint	15.00	
O170	A71	1c orange	.60	.60
a.		Inverted overprint	4.00	
O171	A72	2c green	.60	.60
a.		Inverted overprint	4.00	
O172	A73	3c black (Bk)	.60	.60
O173	A73	3c black (R)	1.10	1.10
O174	A78	4c red & blk	.60	.60
O175	A74	5c violet	.80	.80
O176	A74	5c rose	.80	.80
O177	A75	10c deep blue	.60	.60
		Nos. O169-O177 (9)	15.70	9.95

Regular Issues of 1916-25 Ovptd. Vertically Up or Down

1927, Oct.

O178	A71	1c orange	2.00	2.00
O179	A86	2c carmine	2.00	2.00
O180	A86	3c yellow brown	2.00	2.00
O181	A86	4c myrtle green	2.00	2.00
O182	A86	5c pale blue	2.00	2.00
O183	A75	10c yellow green	2.00	2.00
		Nos. O178-O183 (6)	12.00	12.00

Regular Issues of 1920-27 Overprinted

1928

O184	A71	1c lt blue	1.25	1.25
O185	A86	2c carmine	1.25	1.25
O186	A86	3c yellow brown	1.25	1.25
a.		Inverted overprint	5.00	
O187	A86	4c myrtle green	1.25	1.25
O188	A86	5c lt blue	1.25	1.25
O189	A75	10c yellow green	1.25	1.25
O190	A109	20c violet	11.00	2.50
a.		Overprint reading up	3.50	2.25
		Nos. O184-O190 (7)	18.50	10.00

The overprint is placed vertically reading down on No. O190.

Regular Issues of 1936 Overprinted in Black

1936   **Perf. 14**

O191	A131	5c olive green	2.25	1.50
O192	A132	10c brown	2.25	1.50
O193	A133	20c dark violet	2.75	.70
O194	A134	1s dark carmine	3.25	1.10
O195	A135	2s dark blue	3.75	1.75
		Nos. O191-O195 (5)	14.25	6.55

The overprint is placed vertically reading up on No. O192.

Regular Postage Stamps of 1937 Overprinted in Black

1937   **Perf. 11½**

O196	A139	2c green	.40	.40
O197	A140	5c deep rose	.40	.40
O198	A141	10c blue	.40	.40
O199	A142	20c deep rose	.40	.40
O200	A143	1s olive green	.40	.40
		Nos. O196-O200 (5)	2.00	2.00

Catalogue values for unused stamps in this section, from this point to the end of the section, are for Never Hinged items.

Tobacco Stamp, Overprinted in Black

1946   **Unwmk.**   **Rouletted**

O201	PT7	1c rose red	2.00	1.75

Communications Building, Quito — O4

1947   **Unwmk.**   **Litho.**   **Perf. 11**

O202	O4	30c brown	.85	.40
O203	O4	30c greenish blue	.85	.40
a.		Imperf., pair		
O204	O4	30c purple	.85	.40
		Nos. O202-O204 (3)	2.55	1.20

Nos. O202 to O204 overprinted "Primero la Patria!" and plane in dark blue were issued in August, 1947, by a revolutionary group. They were later repudiated by decree.

No. 719 with Additional Diagonal Overprint

1964   **Perf. 14x13**

O205	A231	80c block of 4	7.00	6.00

The "OEA" overprint covers four stamps, the "oficial" overprint is applied to every stamp.

A set of 20 imperforate items in the above Roosevelt design, some overprinted with the initials of various government ministries, was released in 1949. Later that year a set of 8 miniature sheets, bearing the same design plus a marginal inscription, "Presidencia (or Vicepresidencia) de la Republica," and a frame-line were released. In the editors' opinion, information justifying the listing of these issues has not been received.

POSTAL TAX STAMPS

Roca — PT1

1920   **Unwmk.**   **Perf. 12**

RA1	PT1	1c orange	2.00	.30
a.		Double overprint	10.00	

PT2   PT3

RA2	PT2	1c red & blue	1.10	.30
a.		"de" inverted	10.50	5.25
b.		Double overprint	10.00	.60
c.		Inverted overprint	10.00	.60
RA3	PT3	1c deep blue	1.25	.20
a.		Inverted overprint	6.00	1.00
b.		Double overprint	6.00	1.00

For overprints see Nos. O158-O159.

PT4   PT5

Red or Black Surcharge or Overprint
Stamp Dated 1911-1912

RA4	PT4	20c deep blue	—	30.00

Stamp Dated 1913-1914

RA5	PT4	20c deep blue (R)	2.25	.35

ECUADOR

Stamp Dated 1917-1918

RA6	PT4	20c olive green (R)	6.50	.55
a.		Dated 1919-20	25.00	25.00
RA7	PT5	1c on 2c green	.90	.30

Stamp Dated 1911-1912

RA8	PT5	1c on 5c green	.90	.30

Stamp Dated 1913-1914

RA9	PT5	1c on 5c green	8.00	.75
a.		Double surcharge	12.00	4.00

On Nos. RA7, RA8 and RA9 the surcharge is found reading upward or downward.
For surcharges see Nos. RA15-RA16.

Post Office — PT6

1920-24 Engr.

RA10	PT6	1c olive green	.40	.25
RA11	PT6	2c deep green	.40	.25
RA12	PT6	20c bister brn ('24)	1.75	.25
RA13	PT6	2s violet	11.50	3.25
RA14	PT6	5s blue	20.00	5.75
		Nos. RA10-RA14 (5)	34.05	9.75

For overprints and surcharge see Nos. 259, 266-268, 273, 302, RA17, RA28.

Revenue Stamps of 1917-18 Srchd. Vertically in Red reading up or down

1921-22

RA15	PT5	20c on 1c dk blue	55.00	6.50
RA16	PT5	20c on 2c green	55.00	6.50

No. RA12 Surcharged in Green

1924

RA17	PT6	2c on 20c bis brn	.60	.25
a.		Inverted surcharge	14.00	5.00
b.		Double surcharge	4.00	2.00

PT7

1924 Rouletted 7

RA18	PT7	1c rose red	.90	.30
a.		Inverted overprint	3.50	

Similar Design, Eagle at left
Perf. 12

RA19	PT7	2c blue	.90	.30
a.		Inverted overprint	3.50	1.75

For overprints and surcharges see Nos. 346, O201, RA32, RA34, RA37, RA44-RA45, RA47.

PT8

Inscribed "Timbre Fiscal"

1924

RA20	PT8	1c yellow	4.50	.85
RA21	PT8	2c dark blue	1.40	.35

Inscribed "Region Oriental"

RA22	PT8	1c yellow	.70	.30
RA23	PT8	2c dark blue	1.40	.35
		Nos. RA20-RA23 (4)	8.00	1.85

Overprint on No. RA22 reads down or up.

Revenue Stamp Overprinted in Blue

1934

RA24		2c green	.50	.30
a.		Blue overprint inverted	3.50	1.75
b.		Blue ovpt. dbl., one invtd	4.00	1.25

Postage Stamp of 1930 Overprinted in Red
Perf. 12½

RA25	A119	20c ultra & yel	.50	.25

Telegraph Stamp Overprinted in Red, like No. RA24, and Surcharged diagonally in Black

1934 Perf. 14

RA26		2c on 10c olive brn	.70	.30
a.		Double surcharge		5.50

Overprint Blue, Surcharge Red

RA27		2c on 10c olive brn	.70	.30

PT9

1934-36 Perf. 12

RA28	PT9	2c green	.60	.30
a.		Both overprints in red ('36)	.60	.30

Postal Tax stamp of 1920-24, overprinted in red "POSTAL" has been again overprinted "CASA de Correos y Teleg. de Guayaquil" in black.

PT10

Perf. 14½x14

1934 Photo. Wmk. 233

RA29	PT10	2c yellow green	.50	.30

For the rebuilding of the GPO at Guayaquil. For surcharge see No. RA31.

Symbols of Post and Telegraph Service — PT11

1935

RA30	PT11	20c claret	.50	.30

For the rebuilding of the GPO at Guayaquil.

No. RA29 Surcharged in Red and Overprinted in Black

1935

RA31	PT10	3c on 2c yel grn	.40	.30
a.		Double surcharge		
b.		Inverted surcharge (R)	4.50	

Social and Rural Workers' Insurance Fund.

Tobacco Stamp Surcharged in Black

1936 Unwmk. Rouletted 7

RA32	PT7	3c on 1c rose red	.60	.30
a.		Lines of words reversed	4.00	.75
b.		Horiz. pair, imperf. vert.		

Issued for the Social and Rural Workers' Insurance Fund.

No. 310 Overprinted in Black

1936 Perf. 12½

RA33	A119	20c ultra & yel	.60	.30
a.		Double overprint		

Tobacco Stamp Surcharged in Black

1936 Rouletted 7

RA34	PT7	3c on 1c rose red	.60	.30

Social and Rural Workers' Insurance Fund.

Worker — PT12

1936 Engr. Perf. 13½

RA35	PT12	3c ultra	.40	.30

Social and Rural Workers' Insurance Fund. For surcharges see Nos. C64, RA36, RA53-RA54.

Surcharged in Black

1936

RA36	PT13	5c on 3c ultra	.60	.30

This combines the 2c for the rebuilding of the post office with the 3c for the Social and Rural Workers' Insurance Fund.

National Defense Issue
Tobacco Stamp Surcharged in Black

1936 Rouletted 7

RA37	PT7	10c on 1c rose	.90	.30
a.		Double surcharge		

Symbolical of Defense — PT14

1937-42 Perf. 12½

RA38	PT14	10c deep blue	.90	.30

A 1s violet and 2s green exist in type PT14. For surcharge see No. RA40.

Overprinted or Surcharged in Black

PT15

1937 Engr. & Typo. Perf. 13½

RA39	PT15	5c lt brn & red	2.00	.30
d.		Inverted overprint	20.00	

1942 Perf. 12, 11½

RA39A	PT15	20c on 5c rose pink & red	75.00	20.00
RA39B	PT15	20c on 1s yel brn & red	75.00	20.00
		Surcharge omitted		
RA39C	PT15	20c on 2s grn & red	75.00	20.00
		Nos. RA39A-RA39C (3)	225.00	60.00

A 50c dark blue and red exists.

No. RA38 Surcharged in Red

1937 Engr. Perf. 12½

RA40	PT14	5c on 10c dp blue	1.10	.30

Map of Ecuador — PT16

1938 Perf. 14x13½

RA41	PT16	5c carmine rose	.70	.30

Social and Rural Workers' Insurance Fund.

No. C42 Surcharged in Red

1938 Perf. 12½

RA42	A136	20c on 70c black	1.10	.30

No. 307 Surcharged in Red

1938

RA43	A116	5c on 6c yel & red	.40	.30

This stamp was obligatory on all mail from Nov. 23rd to 30th, 1938. The tax was for the Intl. Union for the Control of Cancer.

Tobacco Stamp Surcharged in Black

1939 Rouletted

RA44	PT7	5c on 1c rose	.70	.30
a.		Double surcharge		
b.		Triple surcharge		

Tobacco Stamp Surcharged in Blue

1940

RA45	PT7	5c on 1c rose red	1.00	.30
a.		Double surcharge	3.50	3.50

No. 370 Surcharged in Carmine

1940 Perf. 11½

RA46	A144	20c on 50c blk & multi	.50	.30
a.		Double surcharge, one inverted		

Tobacco Stamp Surcharged in Black

1940 Rouletted

RA47	PT7	20c on 1c rose red	6.00	.50

ECUADOR

Farmer Plowing — PT17

1940   **Perf. 13x13½**
RA48   PT17   5c carmine rose   .70   .30

Communication Symbols — PT18

1940-43   **Perf. 12**
RA49   PT18   5c copper brown   .70   .40
RA49A   PT18   5c green ('43)   .70   .40

For overprint and surcharges see #534, E6, I1.

Pursuit Planes — PT19

1941   **Perf. 11½x13**
RA50   PT19   20c ultra   1.10   .40

The tax was used for national defense.

Warrior Shielding Women — PT20

1942-46   **Engr.**   **Perf. 12**
RA51   PT20   20c dark blue   1.10   .40
RA51A   PT20   40c blk brn ('46)   1.10   .40

The tax was used for national defense.
A 20c carmine, 20c brown and 30c gray exist lithographed in type PT20.

No. 370 Surcharged in Carmine

1942   **Perf. 11½**
RA52   A144   20c on 50c multi   1.10   .40
   a.   Double surcharge   10.00

No. RA35 Surcharged in Red

1943   **Perf. 13½**
RA53   PT12   5c on 3c ultra   .60   .40

No. RA53 with Additional Surcharge in Black

1943
RA54   PT12   5c on 5c on 3c ultra   1.10   .40

Peons — PT21

1943   **Perf. 12**
RA55   PT21   5c blue   .90   .40

The tax was for farm workers.
For overprint & surcharge see #535, C135.

Revenue Stamp (as No. RA64) Overprinted or Surcharged in Black

1943   **Perf. 12½**
RA56   20c red orange   75.00   5.00

Revenue Stamp (as No. RA64) Overprinted or Surcharged in Black

1943   **Perf. 12**
RA57   20c on 10c orange   2.25   .40
   a.   Double surcharge

Coat of Arms — PT22

1943   **Perf. 12½**
RA58   PT22   20c orange red   .70   .40

The tax was for national defense.

No. RA58 Surcharged in Black

1944
RA59   PT22   30c on 20c org red   .70   .40
   a.   Double surcharge   20.00

> Catalogue values for unused stamps in this section, from this point to the end of the section, are for Never Hinged items.

Consular Service Stamps Surcharged in Black

1951   **Unwmk.**   **Perf. 12**
RA60   R1   20c on 1s red   .85   .40
RA61   R1   20c on 2s brown   .85   .40
RA62   R1   20c on 5s violet   .85   .40
Nos. RA60-RA62 (3)   2.55   1.20

Teacher and Pupils in Schoolyard — PT23

1952   **Engr.**   **Perf. 13**
RA63   PT23   20c blue green   .85   .40

Revenue Stamp Overprinted — PT24

1952   **Perf. 12**
RA64   PT24   40(c) olive green   1.50   .40

For overprints & surcharges see #RA56-RA57.

Woman Holding Flag — PT25

1953   **Perf. 12½**
RA65   PT25   40c ultra   1.50   .40

Telegraph Stamp Surcharged in Black — PT26

1954   **Unwmk.**   **Perf. 13**
RA66   PT26   20c on 30c red brn   1.25   .40

Revenue Stamps Surcharged or Overprinted Horizontally in Black

PT26a   PT26b

PT26c

1954   **Unwmk.**   **Perf. 12**
RA67   PT26a   10c on 25c blue   1.50   .40
RA68   PT26b   10c on 50c org red   1.50   .40
RA69   PT26c   10c carmine   1.50   .40
Nos. RA67-RA69 (3)   4.50   1.20

Telegraph Stamp Surcharged — PT27

1954   **Perf. 13**
RA70   PT27   10c on 30c red brn   2.50   .40

Revenue Stamp Overprinted in Black

1954   **Perf. 12**
RA71   R3   20c olive black   3.00   .40

Consular Service Stamp Surcharged in Black

1954
RA72   R1   20c on 10s gray   3.00   .40

Young Student at Desk — PT28

Imprint: "Heraclio Fournier.-Vitoria"

1954   **Photo.**   **Perf. 11**
RA73   PT28   20c rose pink   1.30   .40

See No. RA76.

Globe, Ship, Plane — PT29

1954   **Engr.**   **Perf. 12**
RA74   PT29   10c dp magenta   2.50   .40

Soldier Kissing Flag — PT30

1955   **Photo.**   **Perf. 11**
RA75   PT30   40c blue   2.50   .40

See No. RA77.

Types of 1954-55 Redrawn. Imprint: "Thomas de la Rue & Co. Ltd."

1957   **Unwmk.**   **Perf. 13**
RA76   PT28   20c rose pink   1.30   .40
    Perf. 14x14½
RA77   PT30   40c blue   2.50   .40

No. RA77 is inscribed "Republica del Ecuador."

The above stamp is believed to have been used only for fiscal purposes.

AIR POST POSTAL TAX STAMPS

No. 438 Surcharged in Black or Carmine

1945   **Unwmk.**   **Perf. 11**
RAC1   A173   20c on 10c dk grn   .75   .40
   a.   Pair, one without surcharge   90.00
RAC2   A173   20c on 10c dk grn (C)   .75   .40

Obligatory on letters and parcel post carried on planes in the domestic service.

Liberty, Mercury and Planes — PTAP1

1946   **Engr.**   **Perf. 12**
RAC3   PTAP1   20c orange brown   .75   .40

GALAPAGOS ISLANDS

Issued for use in the Galapagos Islands (Columbus Archipelago), a province of Ecuador, but were commonly used throughout the country.

> Catalogue values for unused stamps in this section are for Never Hinged items.

Sea Lions — A1   Map — A2

Design: 1s, Marine iguana.

ECUADOR — EGYPT

Unwmk.
1957, July 15 Photo. Perf. 12
L1	A1	20c dark brown	1.50	.30
L2	A2	50c violet	1.00	.30
L3	A1	1s dull olive green	4.75	.80
		Nos. L1-L3 (3)	7.25	1.40
		Nos. L1-L3,LC1-LC3 (6)	18.50	3.65

125th anniv. of Ecuador's possession of the Galapagos Islands, and publicizing the islands.
See Nos. LC1-LC3. For overprints see Nos. 684-686, C389-C391.

GALAPAGOS AIR POST STAMPS

Type of Regular Issue

1s, Santa Cruz Island. 1.80s, Map of Galapagos archipelago. 4.20s, Galapagos giant tortoise.

Unwmk.
1957, July 19 Photo. Perf. 12
LC1	A1	1s deep blue	1.25	.30
LC2	A1	1.80s rose violet	2.50	.70
LC3	A1	4.20s black	7.50	1.25
		Nos. LC1-LC3 (3)	11.25	2.25

For overprints see Nos. C389-C391.

Redrawn Type of Ecuador, 1956

1959, Jan. 3 Engr. Perf. 14
| LC4 | AP69 | 2s lt olive green | 1.50 | .70 |

Issued to honor the United Nations.
See note after No. C407.

EGYPT

ē-jəpt

LOCATION — Northern Africa, bordering on the Mediterranean and the Red Sea
GOVT. — Republic
AREA — 386,900 sq. mi.
POP. — 102,330,000 (2020 est.)
CAPITAL — Cairo

Modern Egypt was a part of Turkey until 1914 when a British protectorate was declared over the country and the Khedive was deposed in favor of Hussein Kamil under the title of sultan. In 1922 the protectorate ended and the reigning sultan was declared king of the new monarchy. Egypt became a republic on June 18, 1953. Egypt merged with Syria in 1958 to form the United Arab Republic. Syria left this union in 1961. In 1971 Egypt took the name of Arab Republic of Egypt.

40 Paras = 1 Piaster
1000 Milliemes = 100 Piasters = 1 Pound (1888)
1000 Milliemes = 1 Pound (1953)
1000 Milliemes = 100 Piasters = 1 Pound (1982)

> Catalogue values for unused stamps in this country are for Never Hinged items, beginning with Scott 241 in the regular postage section, Scott B1 in the semi-postal section, Scott C38 in the airpost section, Scott CB1 in the airpost semi-postal section, Scott E5 in the special delivery section, Scott J40 in the postage due section, Scott M16 in the military stamps section, Scott O60 in the officials section, Scott N1 in the occupation section, Scott NC1 in the occupation airpost section, Scott NE1 in the occupation special delivery section, and Scott NJ1 in the occupation postage due section.

Watermarks

Wmk. 118 — Pyramid and Star

Wmk. 119 — Crescent and Star

Wmk. 120 — Triple Crescent and Star

Wmk. 195 — Multiple Crown and Arabic F

"F" in watermark stands for Fuad.

Wmk. 315 — Multiple Eagle

Wmk. 318 — Multiple Eagle and "Misr"

Wmk. 342 — Coat of Arms, Multiple

Wmk. 328 — U A R

Values for unused stamps are for examples with original gum as defined in the catalogue introduction. Very fine examples of Nos. 1-15 will have perforations that are clear of the framelines but with the design noticeably off center. Well centered stamps are extremely scarce and will command substantial premiums.

A1

A2

Turkish Numerals

١٢٣٤٥
1 2 3 4 5

٦٧٨٩٠
6 7 8 9 0

Turkish Suzerainty

A3

A5

A4   A6

A7

Surcharged in Black

Wmk. 118
1866, Jan. 1 Litho. Perf. 12½

1	A1	5pa greenish gray	62.50	37.50
a.		Imperf., pair	250.00	
b.		Pair, imperf. between	400.00	
c.		Perf. 12½x13	82.50	62.50
d.		Perf. 13	325.00	370.00
2	A2	10pa brown	75.00	37.50
a.		Imperf., pair	210.00	
b.		Pair, imperf. between	550.00	
c.		Perf. 13	300.00	340.00
d.		Perf. 12½x15	325.00	350.00
e.		Perf. 13½	100.00	65.00
3	A3	20pa blue	105.00	40.00
a.		Imperf., pair	300.00	
b.		Pair, imperf. between	500.00	
c.		Perf. 12½x13	140.00	95.00
d.		Perf. 13	575.00	375.00
4	A4	2pi yellow	125.00	52.50
a.		Imperf.	150.00	125.00
b.		Pair, imperf. vert. or horiz., pair	525.00	450.00
c.		Perf. 12½x15	210.00	
d.		Diagonal half used as 1pi on cover		3,000.
e.		Perf. 12½x13, 13x12½	200.00	75.00
f.		Pair, imperf. between	650.00	550.00
5	A5	5pi rose	325.00	250.00
a.		Imperf.	425.00	375.00
b.		Pair, imperf. vert. or horiz., pair	1,300.	
c.		Inscription of 10pi, imperf.	1,100.	950.00
e.		Perf. 12½x13, 13x12½	350.00	275.00
f.		As "d," perf. 12½x15	1,050.	1,000.
g.		Perf. 13	850.00	
6	A6	10pi slate bl	375.00	325.00
a.		Imperf.	550.00	450.00
b.		Pair, imperf. between	2,750.	
c.		Perf. 12½x13, 13x12½	575.00	575.00
d.		Perf. 13	2,000.	

Unwmk.
Typo.
7	A7	1pi rose lilac	80.00	6.00
a.		Imperf.	125.00	
b.		Horiz. pair, imperf. vert.	525.00	
c.		Perf. 12½x13, 13x12½	110.00	25.00
d.		Perf. 13	475.00	325.00
e.		Perf. 12½x15	350.00	
		Nos. 1-7 (7)	1,148.	748.50

Single imperforates of types A1-A10 are sometimes simulated by trimming wide-margined examples of perforated stamps.
No. 4d must be dated between July 16 and July 31, 1867.
Proofs of Nos. 1-7 are on smooth white paper, unwatermarked and imperforate. Proofs of No. 7 are on thinner paper than No. 7a.

Sphinx and Pyramid — A8

Perf. 15x12½
1867 Litho. Wmk. 119
8	A8	5pa orange	42.50	11.00
a.		Imperf.	250.00	
b.		Horiz. pair, imperf between	200.00	
c.		Vert. pair, imperf between		
9	A8	10pa lilac ('69)	70.00	11.00
a.		10pa violet	95.00	14.00
b.		Half used as 5pa on newspaper piece		900.00
11	A8	20pa yel grn ('69)	135.00	14.00
a.		20pa blue green	135.00	17.00
13	A8	1pi rose red	27.50	1.10
a.		Imperf., pair	150.00	
b.		Pair, imperf. between	325.00	
d.		Rouletted	70.00	
e.		1pi lake red	175.00	32.50
14	A8	2pi blue	150.00	18.00
a.		Imperf.	325.00	
b.		Horiz. pair, imperf. vert.	525.00	
c.		Perf. 12½	275.00	
15	A8	5pi brown	375.00	200.00
		Nos. 8-15 (6)	800.00	255.10

There are 4 types of each value, so placed that any block of 4 contains all types.

A9

Clear Impressions
Thick Opaque Paper
Typographed by the Government at Boulac
Perf. 12½x13½ Clean-cut
1872 Wmk. 119
19	A9	5pa brown	10.00	5.50
20	A9	10pa lilac	9.00	3.75
21	A9	20pa blue	67.50	4.75
22	A9	1pi rose red	72.50	2.25
h.		Half used as 20pa on cover		750.00
23	A9	2pi dull yellow	100.00	15.00
j.		Half used as 1p on cover		1,200.
24	A9	2½pi dull violet	95.00	25.00
25	A9	5pi green	325.00	42.50
i.		Tête bêche pair	8,000.	
		Nos. 19-25 (7)	679.00	98.75

Perf. 13½ Clean-cut
19a	A9	5pa brown	27.50	10.00
20a	A9	10pa dull lilac	7.00	3.50
21a	A9	20pa blue	95.00	22.00
22a	A9	1pi rose red	95.00	4.00
23a	A9	2pi dull yellow	20.00	4.50
24a	A9	2½pi dull violet	800.00	225.00
25a	A9	5pi green	325.00	62.50

Litho.
21m	A9	20pa blue, perf. 12½x13½	160.00	80.00
21n	A9	20pa blue, perf. 13½	250.00	65.00
21p	A9	20pa blue, imperf.	—	
21q	A9	20pa blue, pair, imperf. between		2,000.
22m	A9	1pi rose red, perf. 12½x13½	550.00	20.00
22n	A9	1pi rose red, perf. 13½	875.00	50.00

A10

Blurred Impressions
Thinner Paper
Perf. 12½ Rough
1874-75 Typo. Wmk. 119
26	A10	5pa brown ('75)	22.50	3.75
e.		Imperf.	200.00	200.00
f.		Vert. pair, imperf. horiz.	1,000.	
g.		Tête bêche pair	45.00	45.00
20b	A9	10pa gray lilac	16.00	3.75
g.		Tête bêche pair	225.00	225.00
21b	A9	20pa gray blue	105.00	4.00
k.		Half used as 10pa on cover		
22b	A9	1pi vermilion	12.00	1.75
f.		Imperf.	—	150.00
g.		Tête bêche pair	150.00	125.00
23b	A9	2pi yellow	90.00	5.75
i.		Tête bêche pair	600.00	600.00
24b	A9	2½pi deep violet	9.25	6.25
e.		Imperf.		
f.		Tête bêche pair	600.00	600.00
25b	A9	5pi yellow green	65.00	22.50
e.		Imperf.	400.00	

No. 26f normally occurs tête-bêche.

Perf. 13½x12½ Rough
26c	A10	5pa brown	24.00	4.50
i.		Tête bêche pair	62.50	62.50
20c	A9	10pa gray lilac	37.50	3.50
i.		Tête bêche pair	225.00	225.00
h.		Pair, imperf. between	350.00	
21c	A9	20pa gray blue	11.00	3.75
22c	A9	1pi vermilion	90.00	3.25
i.		Tête bêche pair	500.00	500.00
23c	A9	2pi yellow	10.00	6.25
i.		Tête bêche pair	500.00	500.00
k.		Half used as 1pi on cover		4,000.

Perf. 12½x13½ Rough
23d	A9	2pi yellow ('75)	80.00	17.00
h.		Tête bêche pair	1,250.	
24d	A9	2½pi dp violet ('75)	80.00	20.00
i.		Tête bêche pair	1,150.	800.00
25d	A9	5pi yel grn ('75)	375.00	300.00

Nos. 24b, 24d Surcharged in Black

1879, Jan. 1 Perf. 12½ Rough
27	A9	5pa on 2½pi dull vio	10.00	12.00
a.		Imperf.	450.00	450.00
b.		Tête bêche pair	7,500.	
c.		Inverted surcharge	125.00	75.00
d.		Perf. 12½x13½ rough	12.00	12.00
e.		As "d," tête bêche pair	7,500.	
f.		As "d," inverted surcharge	150.00	150.00
28	A9	10pa on 2½pi dull vio	12.50	12.50
a.		Imperf.	400.00	400.00
b.		Tête bêche pair	2,500.	
c.		Inverted surcharge	125.00	82.50
d.		Perf. 12½x13½ rough	17.00	17.00
e.		As "d," tête bêche pair	3,000.	
f.		As "d," inverted surcharge	150.00	125.00

A11

A12

EGYPT

A13

A14

Ras-el-Tin Palace A26

Giza Pyramids A27

	Perf. 14		
72	A30 20m olive green	12.50	.40
73	A31 50m maroon	10.00	1.25
74	A32 100m black	95.00	7.50
	Nos. 61-74 (14)	237.50	40.60

For overprints see Nos. O28-O29.

Perf. 14
Size: 22x28mm

99	A36 20m dk green	6.25	.25
100	A36 50m myrtle grn	10.00	.25
101	A36 100m red violet	25.00	.55
102	A36 200m violet ('24)	45.00	2.00
a.	Imperf., pair	325.00	
103	A37 £1 ultra & dk vio ('24)	175.00	27.50
a.	Imperf., pair	1,750.	
	Nos. 92-103 (12)	270.30	32.95

A15, A16

1879-1902 Typo. Perf. 14x13½
Ordinary Paper

29	A11 5pa brown	4.25	1.25
30	A12 10pa violet	57.50	7.50
31	A12 10pa lilac rose ('81)	70.00	10.00
32	A12 10pa gray ('82)	8.00	1.75
33	A12 10pa green ('84)	2.50	2.00
34	A13 20pa ultra	67.50	2.25
35	A13 20pa rose ('84)	22.00	1.25
36	A14 1pi rose	42.50	.30
37	A14 1pi ultra ('84)	5.75	.30
38	A15 2pi orange yel	42.50	1.50
39	A15 2pi orange brn	27.50	.75
40	A16 5pi green	77.50	11.50
41	A16 5pi gray ('84)	25.00	.50
	Nos. 29-41 (13)	452.50	38.10

Nos. 29-31, 35-41 imperf are proofs.
Nos. 37, 39, 41, exist on both ordinary and chalky paper. See *Scott Classic Specialized Catalogue of Stamps & Covers* for detailed listings.

For overprints see Nos. 42, O6-O7.

A17

1884, Feb. 1

42	A17 20pa on 5pi green	14.00	2.25
a.	Inverted surcharge	70.00	62.50
b.	Double surcharge	—	

A18

Sphinx A28

Pylon of Karnak and Temple of Khonsu A30

For overprints see Nos. O28-O29.

Independent Kingdom

Stamps of 1921-22 Overprinted

Thoth Carving Name of King Fuad — A38

1925, Apr. Litho. Perf. 11

105	A00 5m brown	11.00	8.00
106	A38 10m rose	22.50	12.50
107	A38 15m ultra	22.50	14.00
	Nos. 105-107 (3)	56.00	32.50

International Geographical Congress, Cairo.
Nos. 106-107 exist with both white and yellowish gum.

Oxen Plowing — A39

1926 Wmk. 195 Perf. 13½x13½

108	A39 5m lt brown	3.00	2.00
109	A39 10m brt rose	2.75	2.00
110	A39 15m dp blue	3.00	2.00
111	A39 50m Prus green	14.00	5.00
112	A39 100m brown vio	22.50	8.00
113	A39 200m brt violet	32.50	17.50
	Nos. 108-113 (6)	77.75	36.50

12th Agricultural and Industrial Exhibition at Gezira.
For surcharges see Nos. 115-117.

1922, Oct. 10

78	A24 1m olive brown	1.50	1.10
a.	Inverted overprint	475.00	450.00
b.	Double overprint	225.00	
79	A25 2m red	1.10	.65
a.	Double overprint	225.00	
80	A26 3m orange	2.25	1.10
81	A27 4m green	1.50	1.00
b.	Inverted overprint	225.00	
82	A28 5m pink	2.75	.25
83	A29 10m lake	2.75	.25
84	A34 15m indigo	5.75	1.10
85	A35 15m indigo	4.50	1.10

Perf. 14

86	A30 20m olive green	6.00	1.10
a.	Inverted overprint	200.00	
b.	Double overprint	300.00	
87	A31 50m maroon	9.00	1.10
a.	Inverted overprint	400.00	500.00
88	A32 100m black	22.50	1.25
a.	Inverted overprint	500.00	160.00
b.	Double overprint	400.00	250.00
	Nos. 78-88 (11)	59.60	10.15

Same Overprint on Nos. 58-59
Wmk. Crescent and Star (119)

90	A32 100m black	90.00	50.00
91	A33 200m plum	30.00	1.60

Proclamation of the Egyptian monarchy. The overprint signifies "The Egyptian Kingdom, March 15, 1922." It exists in four types, one lithographed and three typographed on Nos. 78-87, but lithographed only on Nos. 88-91.

A36

King Fuad — A37

1923-24 Wmk. 120 Photo. Perf. 13½
Size 18x22½mm

92	A36 1m orange	.35	.25
93	A36 2m black	1.10	.25
94	A36 3m brown	1.00	.65
a.	Imperf., pair	225.00	
95	A36 4m yellow grn	.90	.50
96	A36 5m orange brn	.45	.25
a.	Imperf., pair	50.00	
97	A36 10m rose	2.00	.25
98	A36 15m ultra	3.25	.25

A19

A20, A21

Rock Temple of Abu Simbel A32

Citadel at Cairo A31

Colossi of Thebes A29

Aswan Dam A33

Perf. 13½x14
1914, Jan. 8 Wmk. 119
Chalk-surfaced Paper

50	A24 1m olive brown	1.25	.80
51	A25 2m dp green	3.75	.25
52	A26 3m orange	3.50	.50
53	A27 4m red	4.50	.75
54	A28 5m lake	4.25	.25
a.	Booklet pane of 6	250.00	
55	A29 10m dk blue	7.50	.40

Perf. 14

56	A30 20m olive grn	8.00	.70
57	A31 50m red violet	24.00	1.10
58	A32 100m black	25.00	1.40
59	A33 200m plum	42.50	4.00
	Nos. 50-59 (10)	124.25	10.15

All values of this issue exist imperforate on both watermarked and unwatermarked paper but are not known to have been issued in that condition.
See Nos. 61-69, 72-74. For overprints and surcharge see Nos. 60, 78-91, O11-O13, O16-O27, O30.

British Protectorate

No. 52 Surcharged

1915, Oct. 15

60	A26 2m on 3m orange	1.25	2.25
a.	Inverted surcharge	250.00	250.00

Scenic Types of 1914 and

Statue of Ramses II A34, A35

1921-22 Wmk. 120 Perf. 13½x14
Chalk-surfaced Paper

61	A24 1m olive brown	1.50	3.00
62	A25 2m dp green	9.00	4.75
63	A25 2m red ('22)	6.00	2.50
64	A26 3m orange	9.00	6.00
65	A27 4m green ('22)	8.00	6.50
66	A28 5m lake	7.00	1.75
67	A28 5m pink	14.00	.25
68	A29 10m dp blue	12.00	.70
69	A29 10m lake ('22)	3.50	.70
70	A34 15m indigo ('22)	10.00	.30
71	A35 15m indigo ('22)	40.00	5.00

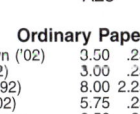
A22, A23

1888-1906 Ordinary Paper

43	A18 1m pale brown ('02)	3.50	.25
44	A19 2m green ('02)	3.00	.25
45	A20 3m maroon ('92)	8.00	2.25
46	A20 3m yel org ('02)	5.75	.25
48	A22 5m carmine rose	6.50	.25
49	A23 10p purple ('89)	35.00	1.00
	Nos. 43-49 (6)	61.75	4.25

Chalky Paper

43a	A18 1m pale brown ('02)	4.00	.25
44a	A19 2m green ('02)	1.25	.25
46a	A20 3m yel org ('02)	3.00	.25
47	A21 4m brown red ('06)	4.75	.25
a.	Half used as 2m on cover		
48b	A22 5m rose ('02)	3.00	.25
49b	A23 10p mauve ('02)	22.50	.55

Nos. 43-44, 47-48 imperf are proofs.
For overprints see Nos. O2-O5, O8-O10, O14-O15.

Boats on Nile A24

Cleopatra A25

EGYPT

King Fuad — A40

Perf. 14x14½

1926, Apr. 2		Photo.	Wmk. 120
114	A40	50p brn vio & red vio	140.00 22.50

58th birthday of King Fuad.
For overprint and surcharge see Nos. 124, 166.

Nos. 111-113 Surcharged

Perf. 13x13½

1926, Aug. 24			Wmk. 195
115	A39	5m on 50m Prus green	2.50 2.50
116	A39	10m on 100m brn vio	2.50 2.50
117	A39	15m on 200m brt vio	2.50 2.50
a.		Double surcharge	300.00
		Nos. 115-117 (3)	7.50 7.50

Ship of Hatshepsut A41

1926, Dec. 9		Litho.	Perf. 13x13½
118	A41	5m brown & blk	3.00 1.40
119	A41	10m dp red & blk	3.50 1.50
120	A41	15m dp blue & blk	4.00 1.50
		Nos. 118-120 (3)	10.50 4.40

International Navigation Congress, Cairo.
For overprints see Nos. 121-123.

Nos. 118-120, 114 Overprinted — a | No. 114 Overprinted — b

1926, Dec. 21			
121	A41 (a)	5m	300.00 250.00
122	A41 (a)	10m	300.00 250.00
123	A41 (a)	15m	300.00 250.00

Perf. 14x14½
Wmk. 120

| 124 | A40 (b) | 50p | 1,600. 875.00 |

Inauguration of Port Fuad opposite Port Said.
Nos. 121-123 have a block over "Le Caire" at lower left.
Forgeries of Nos. 121-124 exist.

Branch of Cotton — A42

Perf. 13x13½

1927, Jan. 25			Wmk. 195
125	A42	5m dk brown & sl grn	1.75 .80
126	A42	10m dp red & slate grn	2.75 1.50
127	A42	20m dp blue & slate grn	3.50 1.50
		Nos. 125-127 (3)	8.00 3.80

International Cotton Congress, Cairo.

King Fuad
A43 A44

A45 A46

Type I   Type II

Early printings of the seven values indicated were printed from plates with screens of vertical dots in the vignettes (type I). All values were printed later from plates with screens of diagonal dots (type II).

Perf. 13x13½

1927-37		Wmk. 195	Photo.
		Type II	
128	A43	1m orange	.35 .25
a.		Type I	3.25 .60
129	A43	2m black	.35 .25
a.		Type I	11.00 6.00
130	A43	3m olive brn	.35 .55
a.		Type I	2.50 1.00
131	A43	3m dp green ('30)	.65 .25
132	A43	4m yellow grn	1.25 1.10
a.		Type I	65.00 12.50
133	A43	4m brown ('30)	1.10 .55
134	A43	4m dp green ('34)	.85 .40
135	A43	5m dk red brn ('29)	.95 .40
a.		Type I	3.50 1.00
136	A43	10m dk red ('29)	1.40 .25
a.		10m orange red, type I	2.50 .45
137	A43	10m purple ('34)	3.75 .25
138	A43	13m car rose ('32)	1.50 .40
139	A43	15m ultra	2.50 .25
a.		Type I	12.00 .65
140	A43	15m dk violet ('34)	5.25 .25
141	A43	20m ultra ('34)	9.25 .30

Perf. 13½x14

142	A44	20m olive grn	3.25 .40
143	A44	20m ultra ('32)	7.50 .25
144	A44	40m olive brn ('32)	4.25 .25
145	A44	50m Prus green	3.50 .25
a.		50m greenish blue	6.00 .35
146	A44	100m brown vio	10.00 .35
a.		100m claret	14.00 .50
147	A44	200m deep violet	9.00 1.25

Printings of Nos. 142, 145 and 146, made in 1929 and later, were from new plates with stronger impressions and darker colors.

Perf. 13x13½

148	A45	500m choc & Prus bl, entirely photo ('32)	100.00 25.00
a.		Frame litho, vignette photo	125.00 11.50
149	A46	£1 dk grn & org brn, entirely photo ('37)	125.00 8.25
a.		Frame litho, vignette photo	140.00 7.00
		Nos. 128-149 (22)	292.00 41.45

Statue of Amenhotep, Son of Hapu — A47

1927, Dec. 29		Photo.	Perf. 13½x13
150	A47	5m orange brown	1.50 1.00
151	A47	10m copper red	2.00 1.00
152	A47	15m deep blue	3.25 1.00
		Nos. 150-152 (3)	6.75 3.00

Statistical Congress, Cairo.

Imhotep A48 | Mohammed Ali Pasha A49

1928, Dec. 15			
153	A48	5m orange brown	1.10 .65
154	A49	10m copper red	1.25 .65

Intl. Congress of Medicine at Cairo and the cent. of the Faculty of Medicine at Cairo.

Prince Farouk — A50

1929, Feb. 11			Litho.
155	A50	5m choc & gray	2.00 1.40
156	A50	10m dull red & gray	3.00 1.50
157	A50	15m ultra & gray	3.00 1.50
158	A50	20m Prus blue & gray	3.50 1.50
		Nos. 155-158 (4)	11.50 5.90

Ninth birthday of Prince Farouk.
Nos. 155-158 with black or brown centers are trial color proofs. They were sent to the UPU, but were never placed on sale to the public, although some are known used.

Tomb Fresco at El-Bersheh A51

1931, Feb. 15			Perf. 13x13½
163	A51	5m brown	1.50 1.00
164	A51	10m copper red	2.50 1.75
165	A51	15m dark blue	3.50 2.00
		Nos. 163-165 (3)	7.50 4.75

14th Agricultural & Industrial Exhib., Cairo.

Nos. 114 and 103 Surcharged in Black

1932		Wmk. 120	Perf. 14x14½
166	A40	50m on 50p	20.00 3.00

Perf. 14

| 167 | A37 | 100m on £1 | 250.00 190.00 |

Locomotive of 1852 — A52

1933, Jan. 19		Litho.	Wmk. 195
		Perf. 13x13½	
168	A52	5m shown	14.00 8.00
169	A52	13m 1859	21.00 12.00
170	A52	15m 1862	21.00 12.00
171	A52	20m 1932	21.00 12.00
		Nos. 168-171 (4)	77.00 44.00

International Railroad Congress, Heliopolis.

Commercial Passenger Airplane — A56

Dornier Do-X — A57

Graf Zeppelin — A58

1933, Dec. 20			Photo.
172	A56	5m brown	7.50 4.00
173	A56	10m brt violet	17.50 12.00
174	A57	13m brown car	20.00 15.00
175	A57	15m violet	20.00 13.00
176	A58	20m blue	25.00 20.00
		Nos. 172-176 (5)	90.00 64.00

International Aviation Congress, Cairo.

A59

Khedive Ismail Pasha — A60

1934, Feb. 1			Perf. 13½
177	A59	1m dp orange	.60 1.10
178	A59	2m black	.60 1.10
179	A59	3m brown	.75 1.25
180	A59	4m blue green	1.25 .40
181	A59	5m red brown	1.40 .25
182	A59	10m violet	2.50 .35
183	A59	13m copper red	4.00 2.25
184	A59	15m dull violet	4.50 1.75
185	A59	20m ultra	3.00 .40
186	A59	50m Prus blue	9.50 .65
187	A59	100m olive grn	9.50 1.25
188	A59	200m dp violet	75.00 7.25

Perf. 13½x13

189	A60	50p brown	225.00 95.00
190	A60	£1 Prus blue	400.00 150.00
		Nos. 177-190 (14)	737.60 263.00

10th Congress of UPU, Cairo.

King Fuad — A61

1936-37			Perf. 13½
191	A61	1m dull orange	.55 .90
192	A61	2m black	1.75 .25
193	A61	4m dk green	2.00 .25
194	A61	5m chestnut	1.40 .55
195	A61	10m purple ('37)	2.50 .35
196	A61	15m brown violet	2.75 .50
197	A61	20m sapphire	3.25 .35
		Nos. 191-197 (7)	14.20 3.15

Entrance to Agricultural Building A62 | Agricultural Building A63

Design: 15m, 20m, Industrial Building.

1936, Feb. 15			Perf. 13½x13
198	A62	5m brown	1.75 1.25

Perf. 13x13½

199	A63	10m violet	2.00 1.50
200	A63	13m copper red	3.25 2.50
201	A63	15m dark violet	1.75 1.25
202	A63	20m blue	3.75 2.25
		Nos. 198-202 (5)	12.50 8.75

15th Agricultural & Industrial Exhib., Cairo.

EGYPT

Signing of Treaty A65

1936, Dec. 22   Perf. 11x11½
203	A65	5m brown	.80	.80
204	A65	15m dk violet	1.00	1.00
205	A65	20m sapphire	1.75	1.75
		Nos. 203-205 (3)	3.55	3.55

Signing of Anglo-Egyptian Treaty, Aug. 26, 1936.

King Farouk — A66

1937-44   Wmk. 195   Perf. 13x13½
206	A66	1m brown org	.30	.25
207	A66	2m vermilion	.30	.25
208	A66	3m brown	.30	.25
209	A66	4m green	.30	.25
210	A66	5m red brown	.50	.25
211	A66	6m lt yel grn ('40)	.60	.25
212	A66	10m purple	.30	.25
213	A66	13m rose car	.60	.35
214	A66	15m dk vio brn	.50	.25
215	A66	20m blue	.75	.35
216	A66	20m lil gray ('44)	.75	.25
		Nos. 206-216 (11)	5.20	2.95

For overprints see Nos. 301, 303, 345, 348, 360E, N3, N6, N8, N22, N25, N27.

Medal for Montreux Conf. — A67

1937, Oct. 15   Perf. 13½x13
217	A67	5m red brown	.75	.55
218	A67	15m dk violet	1.25	1.10
219	A67	20m sapphire	1.50	1.25
		Nos. 217-219 (3)	3.50	2.90

Intl. Treaty signed at Montreux, Switzerland, under which foreign privileges in Egypt were to end in 1949.

Eye of Ré — A68

1937, Dec. 8   Perf. 13x13½
220	A68	5m brown	1.25	1.00
221	A68	15m dk violet	1.50	.90
222	A68	20m sapphire	1.75	1.00
		Nos. 220-222 (3)	4.50	2.70

15th Ophthalmological Congress, Cairo, December, 1937.

King Farouk, Queen Farida A69

1938, Jan. 20   Perf. 11
223	A69	5m red brown	6.50	5.00

Royal wedding of King Farouk and Farida Zulficar.

Inscribed: "11 Fevrier 1938"
1938, Feb. 11
224	A69	£1 green & sepia	200.00	150.00

King Farouk's 18th birthday.
No. 224 is valued CTO; postally used examples: Value, $300.

Cotton Picker — A70

1938, Jan. 26   Perf. 13½x13
225	A70	5m red brown	.75	.75
226	A70	15m dk violet	2.25	1.50
227	A70	20m sapphire	2.00	1.75
		Nos. 225-227 (3)	5.00	4.00

18th International Cotton Congress at Cairo.

Pyramids of Giza and Colossus of Thebes — A71

1938, Feb. 1   Perf. 13x13½
228	A71	5m red brown	1.40	1.00
229	A71	15m dk violet	2.00	1.25
230	A71	20m sapphire	2.25	1.25
		Nos. 228-230 (3)	5.65	3.50

Intl. Telecommunication Conf., Cairo.

Branch of Hydnocarpus A72

1938, Mar. 21   Perf. 13x13½
231	A72	5m red brown	1.50	1.25
232	A72	15m dk violet	2.25	1.25
233	A72	20m sapphire	2.50	1.25
		Nos. 231-233 (3)	6.25	3.75

International Leprosy Congress, Cairo.

King Farouk and Pyramids — A73

King Farouk
A74   A75

Backgrounds: 40m, Hussan Mosque. 50m, Cairo Citadel. 100m, Aswan Dam. 200m, Cairo University.

1939-46   Photo.   Perf. 14x13½
234	A73	30m gray	.75	.25
a.		30m slate gray	.75	.25
234B	A73	30m ol grn ('46)	.80	.25
235	A73	40m dk brown	.85	.25
236	A73	50m Prus green	1.00	.25
237	A73	100m brown vio	1.40	.50
238	A73	200m dk violet	5.00	.50

   Perf. 13½x13
239	A74	50p green & sep	11.00	4.00
240	A75	£1 dp bl & dk brn	26.00	7.00
		Nos. 234-240 (9)	46.80	10.00

For £1 with A77 portrait, see No. 269D. See Nos. 267-269D. For overprints see Nos. 310-314, 316, 355-358, 360, 363-364, N13-N19, N32-N38.

Catalogue values for unused stamps in this section, from this point to the end of the section, are for Never Hinged items.

King Fuad — A76

1944, Apr. 28   Perf. 13½x13
241	A76	10m dk violet	.50	.25

8th anniv. of the death of King Fuad.

King Farouk — A77

1944-50   Wmk. 195   Perf. 13x13½
242	A77	1m yellow brn ('45)	.45	.25
243	A77	2m red org ('45)	.45	.25
244	A77	3m sepia ('46)	1.00	1.00
245	A77	4m dp green ('45)	.45	.25
246	A77	5m red brown ('46)	.45	.25
247	A77	10m dp violet	.45	.25
247A	A77	13m rose red ('50)	12.00	4.25
248	A77	15m dk violet ('45)	1.25	.25
249	A77	17m olive grn	1.25	.25
250	A77	20m dk gray ('45)	1.40	.25
251	A77	22m dp blue ('45)	1.40	.25
		Nos. 242-251 (11)	20.55	7.50

For overprints see Nos. 299-300, 302, 304-309, 343-344, 346-347, 349-354, 360B, 361-362, N1-N2, N4-N5, N7, N9-N12, N20-N21, N23-N24, N26, N28-N31.

King Farouk — A78

1945, Feb. 10   Perf. 13½x13
252	A78	10m deep violet	.40	.25

25th birthday of King Farouk.

Khedive Ismail Pasha — A79

1945, Mar. 2   Photo.
253	A79	10m dark olive	.35	.25

50th anniv. of death of Khedive Ismail Pasha.

Flags of Arab Nations — A80

1945, July 29
254	A80	10m violet	.35	.25
255	A80	22m dp yellow grn	.45	.25

League of Arab Nations Conference, Cairo, Mar. 22, 1945.

Flags of Egypt and Saudi Arabia — A81

   Perf. 13x13½   Wmk. 195
1946, Jan. 10
256	A81	10m dp yellow grn	.35	.25

Visit of King Ibn Saud, Jan. 1946.

Citadel, Cairo — A82

1946, Aug. 9
257	A82	10m yel brn & dp yel grn	.40	.25

Withdrawal of British troops from Cairo Citadel, Aug. 9, 1946.

King Farouk and Inchas Palace, Cairo — A83

2m, Prince Abdullah, Yemen. 3m, Pres. Bechara el-Khoury, Lebanon. 4m, King Abdul Aziz ibn Saud, Saudi Arabia. 5m, King Faisal II, Iraq. 10m, Amir Abdullah ibn Hussein, Jordan. 15m, Pres. Shukri el Kouatly, Syria.

1946, Nov. 9
258	A83	1m dp yellow grn	.60	.25
259	A83	2m sepia	.60	.25
260	A83	3m deep blue	.60	.25
261	A83	4m brown orange	.60	.25
262	A83	5m brown red	.60	.25
263	A83	10m dark gray	.75	.25
264	A83	15m deep violet	.75	.25
		Nos. 258-264 (7)	4.50	1.75

Arab League Cong. at Cairo, May 28, 1946.

Parliament Building, Cairo — A84

1947, Apr. 7   Photo.
265	A84	10m green	.35	.25

36th conf. of the Interparliamentary Union, Apr. 1947.

Raising Egyptian Flag over Kasr-el-Nil Barracks — A85

1947, May 6   Perf. 13½x13
266	A85	10m dp plum & yel grn	.40	.25

Withdrawal of British troops from the Nile Delta.

Farouk Types 1939 Redrawn and

King Farouk — A85a

1947-51   Wmk. 195   Perf. 14x13½
267	A73	30m olive green	.75	.25
268	A73	40m dk brown	.60	.25
269	A73	50m Prus grn ('48)	.90	.25
269A	A73	100m dk brn vio ('49)	6.00	.90
269B	A73	200m dk vio ('49)	14.00	1.40

   Perf. 13½x13
269C	A85a	50p green & sep ('51)	27.50	9.50
269D	A75	£1 dp bl & dk brn ('50)	37.50	3.75
		Nos. 267-269D (7)	87.25	16.30

The king faces slightly to the left and clouds have been added in the sky on Nos. 267-269B. Backgrounds as in 1939-46 issue. Portrait on £1 as on type A77.

For overprints see Nos. 315, 359.

354 EGYPT

Field and Branch of Cotton — A86

Perf. 13½x13
1948, Apr. 1 Wmk. 195
270 A86 10m olive green .65 .25
Intl. Cotton Cong. held at Cairo in Apr. 1948.

Map and Infantry Column — A87

1948, June 15 Perf. 11½x11
271 A87 10m green 1.40 .25
Arrival of Egyptian troops at Gaza, 5/15/48.

Ibrahim Pasha (1789-1848) A88

1948, Nov. 10 Perf. 13x13½
272 A88 10m brn red & dp grn .40 .25

Statue, "The Nile" A89

Protection of Industry and Agriculture A90

Perf. 13x13½
1949, Mar. 1 Photo. Wmk. 195
273 A89 1m dk green .40 .25
274 A89 10m purple 1.00 .25
275 A89 17m crimson 1.00 .25
276 A89 22m deep blue 1.00 .45

Perf. 11½x11
277 A90 30m dk brown 1.50 .60
Nos. 273-277 (5) 4.90 1.80

Souvenir Sheets
Photo. & Litho.
Imperf
278 Sheet of 4 3.75 3.75
  a. A89 1m red brown .75 .75
  b. A89 10m dark brown .75 .75
  c. A89 17m brown orange .75 .75
  d. A89 22m dark Prussian green .75 .75
279 Sheet of 2 3.75 3.75
  a. A90 10m violet gray 1.60 1.60
  b. A90 30m red orange 1.60 1.60

16th Agricultural & Industrial Expo., Cairo.

Mohammed Ali and Map — A93

Perf. 11½x11
1949, Aug. 2 Photo. Wmk. 195
280 A93 10m orange brn & grn .60 .25
Centenary of death of Mohammed Ali.

Globe — A94

1949, Oct. 9 Perf. 13½x13
281 A94 10m rose brown 1.00 .60
282 A94 22m violet 2.00 .90
283 A94 30m dull blue 2.75 1.20
Nos. 281-283 (3) 5.75 2.70
75th anniv. of the UPU.

Scales of Justice — A95

1949, Oct. 14 Perf. 13x13½
284 A95 10m deep olive green .40 .25
End of the Mixed Judiciary System, 10/14/49.

Desert Scene — A96

1950, Dec. 27
285 A96 10m violet & red brn .90 .75
Opening of the Fuad I Institute of the Desert.

Fuad I University — A97

1950, Dec. 27
286 A97 22m dp green & claret .90 .75
Founding of Fuad I University, 25th anniv.

Globe and Khedive Ismail Pasha — A98

1950, Dec. 27
287 A98 30m claret & dp grn .90 .75
75th anniv. of Royal Geographic Society of Egypt.

Picking Cotton — A99

1951, Feb. 24
290 A99 10m olive green .40 .35
International Cotton Congress, 1951.

King Farouk and Queen Narriman A100

1951, May 6 Photo. Perf. 11x11½
291 A100 10m green & red brn 3.00 2.25
  a. Souvenir sheet 17.50 19.00
Marriage of King Farouk and Narriman Sadek, May 6, 1951.

Stadium Entrance A101

Arms of Alexandria and Olympic Emblem A102

King Farouk — A103

1951, Oct. 5 Perf. 13x13½, 13½x13
292 A101 10m brown 1.10 1.10
293 A102 22m dp green 1.40 1.40
294 A103 30m blue & dp grn 1.40 1.40
  a. Souvenir sheet of 3, #292-294 14.00 16.00
Nos. 292-294 (3) 3.90 3.90

Issued to publicize the first Mediterranean Games, Alexandria, Oct. 5-20, 1951.

Winged Figure and Map — A105

Designs: 22m, King Farouk and Map. 30m, King Farouk and Flag.

Dated "16 Oct. 1951"
1952, Feb. 11 Perf. 13½x13
296 A105 10m dp green .75 .40
297 A105 22m plum & dp grn 1.00 .75
298 A105 30m green & brown 1.25 .95
  a. Souvenir sheet of 3, #296-298 14.00 14.00
Nos. 296-298 (3) 3.00 2.10

Abrogation of the Anglo-Egyptian treaty.

Stamps of 1937-51 Overprinted in Various Colors

Perf. 13x13½
1952, Jan. 17 Wmk. 195
299 A77 1m yellow brown .85 .25
300 A77 2m red org (Bl) .25 .25
301 A66 3m brown (Bl) .35 .50
302 A77 4m dp green (RV) .35 .25
303 A66 6m lt yel grn (RV) 1.25 1.25
304 A77 10m dp vio (C) .45 .25
305 A77 13m rose red (Bl) 1.75 1.60
306 A77 15m dk violet (C) 2.75 1.75
307 A77 17m olive grn (C) 2.00 .35
308 A77 20m dk gray (RV) 1.60 .35
309 A77 22m dp blue (C) 3.00 3.00

No. 244, the 3m sepia, exists with this overprint but was not regularly issued or used.

Same Overprint, 24½mm Wide, on Nos. 267 to 269B

310 A73 30m olive grn (DkBl) 3.75 .25
  a. Black overprint 2.25 1.00
311 A73 40m dk brown (G) .90 .25
312 A73 50m Prus grn (C) 1.75 .25
313 A73 100m dk brn vio (C) 3.00 .50
314 A73 200m dk violet (C) 15.00 2.25

Same Overprint, 19mm Wide, on Nos. 269C-269D

315 A85a 50p grn & sep (C) 25.00 8.00
316 A75 £1 dp bl & dk brn (Bl) 45.00 9.00
Nos. 299-316 (18) 109.10 30.30

The overprint translates: King of Egypt and the Sudan, Oct. 16, 1951.
Overprints in colors other than as listed are color trials.

Egyptian Flag — A106

Perf. 13½x13
1952, May 6 Photo. Wmk. 195
317 A106 10m org yel, dp bl & dp grn 1.00 .25
  a. Souvenir sheet of 1 7.50 5.25

Issued to commemorate the birth of Crown Prince Ahmed Fuad, Jan. 16, 1952.

"Dawn of New Era" A107

Symbolical of Egypt Freed A108

Designs: 10m, "Egypt" with raised sword. 22m, Citizens marching with flag.

Dated: "23 Juillet 1952"
Perf. 13x13½, 13½x13
1952, Nov. 23
318 A107 4m dp green & org .35 .25
319 A107 10m dp grn & cop brn .35 .75
320 A108 17m brn org & dp grn .75 .90
321 A108 22m choc & dp grn 1.25 .60
Nos. 318-321 (4) 2.70 2.50

Change of government, July 23, 1952.

Republic

Farmer A109

Soldier A110

Mosque of Sultan Hassan A111

Queen Nefertiti A112

1953-56 Perf. 13½x13
322 A109 1m red brown .50 .25
323 A109 2m dk lilac .35 .25
324 A109 3m brt blue .50 .45
325 A109 4m dk green .35 .25
326 A110 10m dk brown ("Defence") .40 .40
327 A110 10m dk brown ("Defense") .80 .25
328 A110 15m gray .55 .25
329 A110 17m dk grnsh blue .75 .25
330 A110 20m purple .35 .25

EGYPT

Perf. 13¼x13¾

331	A111	30m dull green	.35	.25
332	A111	32m brt blue	.90	.25
333	A111	35m violet ('55)	1.10	.25
334	A111	37m gldn brn ('56)	1.75	.60
335	A111	40m red brown	.90	.25
336	A111	50m violet brn	1.75	.25
337	A112	100m henna brn	2.75	.30
338	A112	200m dk grnsh blue	4.50	.75
339	A112	500m purple	12.00	1.75
340	A112	£1 dk grn, blk & red	22.50	3.25
		Nos. 322-340 (19)	53.05	10.50

Nos. 327-330 are inscribed "Defense."
See No. 490. For overprints and surcharges see Nos. 460, 500, N44-N56, N72.

Stamps of 1939-51 Overprinted in Black

1953   Perf. 13x13½, 13½x13

343	A77	1m yellow brn	.35	.25
344	A77	2m red orange	.35	.25
345	A66	3m brown	.75	.75
346	A77	3m sepia	.35	.25
347	A77	4m dp green	.35	.25
348	A66	6m lt yel grn	.35	.25
349	A77	10m dp violet	.35	.25
350	A77	13m rose red	1.00	1.00
351	A77	15m dk violet	.75	.25
352	A77	17m olive grn	.75	.25
353	A77	20m dk gray	.90	.25
354	A77	22m deep blue	1.25	.25
355	A73	30m ol grn (#267)	.75	.35
356	A73	50m Prus grn (#269)	1.20	.35
357	A73	100m dk brn vio (#269A)	2.00	.75
358	A73	200m dk vio (#269B)	7.50	1.60
359	A85a	50p grn & sepia	19.00	7.00
360	A75	£1 dp bl & dk brn (#269D)	24.00	4.75
		Nos. 343-360 (18)	61.95	19.05

No. 206 with this overprint is a forgery.

Same Overprint on Nos. 300, 303-305, 311 and 314

360B	A77	2m red orange	.40	.25
360E	A66	6m lt yel grn	35.00	
361	A77	10m dp violet	4.00	4.00
362	A77	13m rose red	1.25	.75
363	A73	40m dk brown	6.00	.75
364	A73	200m dk violet	4.00	.90
		Nos. 360B,361-364 (5)	15.65	6.65

Practically all values of Nos. 343-364 exist with double overprint. Other values of the 1952 overprinted issue are known only with counterfeit bars.

Symbols of Electronic Progress — A113

1953, Nov. 23   Photo.   Perf. 13x13½

| 365 | A113 | 10m brt blue | .75 | .50 |

Electronics Exposition, Cairo, Nov. 23.

Crowd Acclaiming the Republic — A114

Design: 30m, Crowd, flag and eagle.

Perf. 13½x13

1954, June 18   Wmk. 195

| 366 | A114 | 10m brown | .55 | .25 |
| 367 | A114 | 30m deep blue | .90 | .60 |

Proclamation of the republic, 1st anniv.

Farmer — A115

1954-55   Perf. 13x13½

368	A115	1m red brown	.35	.25
369	A115	2m dark lilac	.35	.25
370	A115	3m brt blue	.35	.25
371	A115	4m dk green ('55)	1.25	.95
372	A115	5m dp car ('55)	.35	.25
		Nos. 368-372 (5)	2.65	1.95

For overprints see Nos. N39-N43.

Egyptian Flag, Map — A116

Design: 35m, Bugler, soldier and map.

1954, Nov. 4   Perf. 13½x13

| 373 | A116 | 10m rose vio & grn | .50 | .30 |
| 374 | A116 | 35m ver, blk & bl grn | .80 | .70 |

Agreement of Oct. 19, 1954, with Great Britain for the evacuation of the Suez Canal zone by British troops.

Arab Postal Union Issue

Globe — A117

1955, Jan. 1

375	A117	5m yellow brn	.60	.30
376	A117	10m green	.60	.50
377	A117	37m violet	1.25	.95
		Nos. 375-377 (3)	2.45	1.75

Founding of the Arab Postal Union, 7/1/54. For overprints see Nos. 381-383.

Paul P. Harris and Rotary Emblem — A118

35m, Globe, wings and Rotary emblem.

Perf. 13½x13

1955, Feb. 23   Wmk. 195

| 378 | A118 | 10m claret | 1.10 | .35 |
| 379 | A118 | 35m blue | 1.50 | .75 |

50th anniv. of the founding of Rotary Intl.

Nos. 375-377 Overprinted

1955, Nov. 1

381	A117	5m yellow brown	1.00	.80
382	A117	10m green	1.25	1.00
383	A117	37m violet	1.75	1.25
		Nos. 381-383 (3)	4.00	3.05

Arab Postal Union Congress held at Cairo, Mar. 15, 1955.

Map of Africa and Asia, Olive Branch and Rings A119

Globe, Torch, Dove and Olive Branch A120

1956, July 29   Perf. 13x13½, 13½x13

| 384 | A119 | 10m chestnut & green | .40 | .25 |
| 385 | A120 | 35m org yel & dull pur | 1.00 | .70 |

Afro-Asian Festival, Cairo, July, 1956.

Map of Suez Canal and Ship — A121

Perf. 11½x11

1956, Sept. 26   Wmk. 195

| 386 | A121 | 10m blue & buff | .60 | .60 |

Nationalization of the Suez Canal, July 26, 1956. See No. 393.

Queen Nefertiti — A122

1956, Oct. 15   Perf. 13½x13

| 387 | A122 | 10m dark green | 1.40 | 1.25 |

Intl. Museum Week (UNESCO), Oct. 8-14.

Egyptians Defending Port Said — A123

1956, Dec. 20   Litho.   Perf. 11x11½

| 388 | A123 | 10m brown violet | 1.00 | .75 |

Honoring the defenders of Port Said.

No. 388 Overprinted in Carmine Rose

1957, Jan. 14

| 389 | A123 | 10m brown violet | 1.00 | .60 |

Evacuation of Port Said by British and French troops, Dec. 22, 1956.

Old and New Trains — A124

1957, Jan. 30   Photo.   Perf. 13x13½

| 390 | A124 | 10m red violet & gray | 1.10 | 1.00 |

100th anniv. of the Egyptian Railway System (in 1956).

Mother and Children — A125

1957, Mar. 21

| 391 | A125 | 10m crimson | .90 | .35 |

Mother's Day, 1957.

Battle Scene — A126

Perf. 13x13½

1957, Mar. 28   Wmk. 195

| 392 | A126 | 10m bright blue | .40 | .35 |

Victory over the British at Rosetta, 150th anniv.

Type of 1956; New Inscriptions in English

1957, Apr. 15   Perf. 11½x11

| 393 | A121 | 100m blue & yel grn | 1.60 | 1.25 |

Reopening of the Suez Canal.
No. 393 is inscribed: "Nationalisation of Suez Canal Co. Guarantees Freedom of Navigation" and "Reopening 1957."

Map of Gaza Strip — A127

Perf. 13½x13

1957, May 4   Photo.   Wmk. 195

| 394 | A127 | 10m Prus blue | 1.50 | .70 |

"Gaza Part of Arab Nation."
For overprint see No. N57.

Al Azhar University A128

1957, Apr. 27   Perf. 13x13½

New Arabic Date in Red

395	A128	10m brt violet	.50	.40
396	A128	15m violet brown	.80	.60
397	A128	20m dark gray	1.30	.90
		Nos. 395-397 (3)	2.60	1.90

Millenary of Al Azhar University, Cairo.

Shepheard's Hotel, Cairo — A129

Perf. 13½x13

1957, July 20   Wmk. 195

| 398 | A129 | 10m brt violet | .70 | .45 |

Reopening of Shepheard's Hotel, Cairo.

Gate, Palace and Eagle — A130

Perf. 11½x11

1957, July 22   Wmk. 315

| 399 | A130 | 10m yellow & brown | .70 | .40 |

First meeting of New National Assembly.

Amasis I in Battle of Avaris, 1580 B.C. — A131

EGYPT

Designs: No. 401, Sultan Saladin, Hitteen, 1187 A. D. No. 402, Louis IX of France in chains, Mansourah, 1250, vert. No. 403, Map of Middle East, Ein Galout, 1260. No. 404, Port Said, 1956.

Inscribed: "Egypt Tomb of Aggressors 1957"

1957, July 26   Perf. 13x13½, 13½x13
400	A131	10m carmine rose	1.50	1.50
401	A131	10m dk olive grn	1.50	1.50
402	A131	10m brown violet	1.50	1.50
403	A131	10m grnsh blue	1.50	1.50
404	A131	10m yellow brown	1.50	1.50
		Nos. 400-404 (5)	7.50	7.50

No. 400 exists with Wmk. 195.

Ahmed Arabi Speaking to the Khedive — A132

Perf. 13x13½
1957, Sept. 16   Wmk. 315
| 405 | A132 | 10m deep violet | .80 | .25 |

75th anniversary of Arabi Revolution.

Hafez Ibrahim — A133

Portrait: No. 407, Ahmed Shawky.

1957, Oct. 14   Perf. 13½x13
406	A133	10m dull red brn	.30	.25
407	A133	10m olive green	.30	.25
a.		Pair, #406-407	1.00	1.00

25th anniv. of the deaths of Hafez Ibrahim and Ahmed Shawky, poets.

MiG and Ilyushin Planes — A134

Design: No. 409, Viscount plane.

1957, Dec. 19   Perf. 13x13½
408	A134	10m ultra	.70	.50
409	A134	10m green	.70	.50
a.		Pair, #408-409	1.60	1.60

25th anniv. of the Egyptian Air Force and of Misrair, the Egyptian airline.

Pyramids, Dove and Globe — A135

1957, Dec. 26   Photo.   Wmk. 315
410	A135	5m brown orange	.60	.40
411	A135	10m green	.60	.30
412	A135	15m brt violet	.60	.40
		Nos. 410-412 (3)	1.70	1.10

Afro-Asian Peoples Conf., Cairo, 12/26-1/2.

Farmer's Wife A136   Ramses II A137

1957-58   Wmk. 315   Perf. 13½
| 413 | A136 | 1m blue green ('58) | .30 | .25 |
| 414 | A137 | 10m violet | .30 | .25 |

"Industry" — A138

1958   Wmk. 318
415	A136	1m lt blue green	.30	.25
416	A138	5m brown	.35	.25
417	A137	10m violet	.60	.25
		Nos. 413-417 (5)	1.85	1.25

See Nos. 438-444, 474-488, 535. For overprints see Nos. N58-N63, N66-N68, N75, N77-N78.

Cyclists — A139

Perf. 13½x13
1958, Jan. 12   Wmk. 315
| 418 | A139 | 10m lt red brown | .65 | .45 |

5th Intl. Bicycle Race, Egypt, Jan. 12-26.

Mustafa Kamel — A140

1958, Feb. 10   Photo.   Wmk. 318
| 419 | A140 | 10m blue gray | .80 | .25 |

50th anniversary of the death of Mustafa Kamel, orator and politician.

United Arab Republic

Linked Maps of Egypt and Syria — A141

Perf. 11½x11
1958, Mar. 22   Wmk. 318
| 436 | A141 | 10m yellow & green | .75 | .25 |

Birth of United Arab Republic. See No. C90. See also Syria-UAR Nos. 1 and C1.

Cotton — A142

1958, Apr. 5   Perf. 13½x13
| 437 | A142 | 10m Prussian blue | .35 | .25 |

Intl. Fair for Egyptian Cotton, Apr., 1958.

Types of 1957-58 Inscribed "U.A.R. EGYPT" and

Princess Nofret — A143

Designs: 1m, Farmer's wife. 2m, Ibn-Tulun's Mosque. 4m, 14th century glass lamp (design lacks "1963" of A217). 5m, "Industry" (factories and cogwheel). 10m, Ramses II. 35m, "Commerce" (eagle, ship and cargo).

1958   Perf. 13½x14
438	A136	1m crimson	.30	.30
439	A138	2m blue	.25	.25
440	A143	3m dk red brown	.25	.25
441	A217	4m green	.30	.25
442	A138	5m brown	.30	.25
443	A137	10m violet	.85	.30
444	A138	35m lt ultra	3.75	.45
		Nos. 438-444 (7)	6.00	2.05

See Nos. 474-488, 532-533, N62-N68, N75-N78.

Qasim Amin — A144

1958, Apr. 23   Perf. 13½x13
| 445 | A144 | 10m deep blue | .60 | .25 |

50th anniversary of the death of Qasim Amin, author of "Emancipation of Women."

Doves, Broken Chain and Globe — A145

1958, June 18
| 446 | A145 | 10m violet | .60 | .25 |

5th anniv. of the republic and to publicize the struggle of peoples and individuals for freedom.
For overprint see No. N69.

Cement Industry — A146

UAR Flag A147

Industries: No. 448, Textile. No. 449, Iron & steel. No. 450, Petroleum (Oil). No. 451, Electricity and fertilizers.

Perf. 13½x13
1958, July 23   Photo.   Wmk. 318
447	A146	10m red brown	.40	.25
448	A146	10m blue green	.40	.25
449	A146	10m bright red	.40	.25
450	A146	10m olive green	.40	.25
451	A146	10m dark blue	.40	.25
a.		Strip of 5, #447-451	2.75	2.75

Souvenir Sheet
Imperf
| 452 | A147 | 50m grn, dp car & blk | 16.00 | 14.00 |

Revolution of July 23, 1952, 6th anniv.

Sayed Darwich — A148

1958, Sept. 15   Perf. 13½x13
| 453 | A148 | 10m violet brown | .50 | .25 |

35th anniv. of the death of Sayed Darwich, Arab composer.

Hand Holding Torch, Broken Chain and Flag — A149

1958, Oct. 14   Photo.   Wmk. 318
| 454 | A149 | 10m carmine rose | .40 | .25 |

Establishment of the Republic of Iraq.
See Syria-UAR No. 13.

Maps and Cogwheels A150

1958, Dec. 8   Perf. 13½x13
| 455 | A150 | 10m blue | .50 | .25 |

Issued to publicize the Economic Conference of Afro-Asian Countries, Cairo, Dec. 8.

Ovptd. in Red in English and Arabic in 3 Lines "Industrial and Agricultural Production Fair"
1958, Dec. 9
| 456 | A150 | 10m lt red brown | .50 | .25 |

Issued to publicize the Industrial and Agricultural Production Fair, Cairo, Dec. 9.

Dr. Mahmoud Azmy and UN Emblem — A151

1958, Dec. 10
| 457 | A151 | 10m dull violet | .45 | .25 |
| 458 | A151 | 35m green | 1.00 | .75 |

10th anniv. of the signing of the Universal Declaration of Human Rights.
For overprints see Nos. N70-N71.

University Building, Sphinx, "Education" and God Thoth — A152

1958, Dec. 21   Photo.   Wmk. 318
| 459 | A152 | 10m grnsh black | .40 | .25 |

50th anniversary of Cairo University.

No. 337 Surcharged

1959, Jan. 20   Wmk. 195   Perf. 13½
| 460 | A112 | 55m on 100m henna brn | 3.00 | .75 |

For overprint see No. N72.

Emblem — A153

1959, Feb. 2   Perf. 13x13½
| 461 | A153 | 10m lt olive green | .35 | .25 |

Afro-Asian Youth Conf., Cairo, Feb. 2.

See Syria UAR issues for stamps of designs A141, A149, A154, A156, A157, A162, A170, A172, A173, A179 with denominations in piasters (p).

EGYPT

Arms of UAR — A154

1959, Feb. 22 Photo. Perf. 13½x13 Wmk. 318
462 A154 10m green, blk & red .35 .25
First anniversary, United Arab Republic.
See Syria UAR No. 17.

Nile Hilton Hotel — A155

1959, Feb. 22 Perf. 13x13½
463 A155 10m dark gray .35 .25
Opening of the Nile Hilton Hotel, Cairo.

Globe, Radio and Telegraph A156

1959, Mar. 1
464 A156 10m violet .40 .25
Arab Union of Telecommunications.
See Syria-UAR Nos. C20-C21.

United Arab States Issue

Flags of UAR and Yemen — A157

1959, Mar. 8
465 A157 10m sl grn, car & blk .35 .25
First anniversary of United Arab States.
See Syria-UAR No. 16.

Oil Derrick and Pipe Line — A158

1959, Apr. 16 Litho. Perf. 13½x13 Wmk. 318
466 A158 10m lt bl & dk bl .65 .25
First Arab Petroleum Congress, Cairo.

Railroad — A159

Designs: No. 468, Bus on highway. No. 469, River barge. No. 470, Ocean liner. No. 471, Telecommunications on map. No. 472, Stamp printing building, Heliopolis. No. 472A, Ship, train, plane and motorcycle mail carrier.

1959, July 23 Photo. Perf. 13½x13
Frame in Gray
467 A159 10m maroon 1.10 .50
468 A159 10m green 1.10 .50
469 A159 10m violet 1.10 .50
470 A159 10m dark blue 1.10 .50
471 A159 10m dull purple 1.10 .50
472 A159 10m scarlet 1.10 .50
 Nos. 467-472 (6) 6.60 3.00

Souvenir Sheet
Imperf
472A A159 50m green & red 12.00 12.00
No. 472A for the 7th anniv. of the Egyptian revolution of 1952 and was sold only with 5 sets of Nos. 467-472.

Globe, Swallows and Map — A160

1959, Aug. 8 Perf. 13½x13
473 A160 10m lake brn .40 .25
Convention of the Assoc. of Arab Emigrants in the US.

Types of 1953-58 without "Egypt" and

St. Simon's Gate, Bosra, Syria — A161

Designs: 1m, Farmer's wife. 2m, Ibn-Tulun's Mosque. 3m, Princess Nofret. 4m, 14th century glass lamp (design lacks "1963" of A217). 5m, "Industry" (factories and cogwheel). 10m, Ramses II. 15m, Omayyad Mosque, Damascus. 20m, Lotus vase, Tutankhamun treasure. 35m, Eagle, ship and cargo. 40m, Scribe statue. 45m, Saladin's citadel, Aleppo. 55m, Eagle, cotton and wheat. 60m, Dam and factory. 100m, Eagle, hand, cotton and grain. 200m, Palmyra ruins, Syria. 500m, Queen Nefertiti, inscribed "UAR" (no ovpt.).

Perf. 13½x14, 14x13½
1959-60		Wmk. 328	Photo.	
474	A136	1m vermilion	.25	.25
475	A138	2m dp blue ('60)	.25	.25
476	A143	3m maroon	.25	.25
477	A217	4m green ('60)	.25	.25
478	A138	5m black ('60)	.25	.25
479	A137	10m dk ol grn	.30	.25
480	A138	15m deep claret	.30	.25
481	A138	20m crimson ('60)	.90	.25
482	A161	30m brown vio	.65	.25
483	A138	35m lt vio bl ('60)	.75	.25
484	A143	40m sepia	1.10	.25
485	A161	45m lil gray ('60)	2.25	.35
486	A138	55m brt blue grn	2.00	.25
487	A138	60m dp purple ('60)	2.75	.25
488	A138	100m org & sl grn ('60)	2.25	.30
489	A161	200m lt blue & mar	4.50	.30
490	A112	500m dk gray & red ('60)	14.00	1.60
		Nos. 474-490 (17)	33.00	6.00

See Nos. 532-535.

Shield and Cogwheel — A162

1959, Oct. 20 Photo. Perf. 13½x13 Wmk. 328
491 A162 10m brt car rose .35 .25
Issued for Army Day, 1959.
See Syria-UAR No. 32.

Cairo Museum — A163

1959, Nov. 18 Perf. 13x13½
492 A163 10m olive gray .40 .25
Centenary of Cairo museum.

Abu Simbel Temple of Ramses II — A164

1959, Dec. 22 Perf. 11x11½
493 A164 10m lt red brn, pnksh .70 .30
Issued as propaganda to save historic monuments in Nubia threatened by the construction of Aswan High Dam.

Postrider, 12th Century — A165

1960, Jan. 2 Perf. 13x13½
494 A165 10m dark blue .35 .25
Issued for Post Day, Jan. 2.

Hydroelectric Power Station, Aswan Dam — A166

1960, Jan. 9
495 A166 10m violet blk .35 .25
Inauguration of the Aswan Dam hydroelectric power station, Jan. 9.

A167

10m, Arabic and English Description of Aswan High Dam. 35m, Architect's Drawing of Aswan High Dam.

1960, Jan. 9 Perf. 11x11½
496 10m claret .75 .60
497 35m claret 1.10 .75
a. A167 Pair, #496-497 2.00 2.00
Start of work on the Aswan High Dam.

Symbols of Agriculture and Industry — A169

1960, Jan. 16 Perf. 13½x13
498 A169 10m gray grn & sl grn .35 .25
Industrial and Agricultural Fair, Cairo.

Arms and Flag — A170

1960, Feb. 22 Photo. Wmk. 328
499 A170 10m green, blk & red .35 .25
2nd anniversary of the proclamation of the United Arab Republic.
See Syria-UAR No. 38.

No. 340 Overprinted in Red

1960 Wmk. 195 Perf. 13½
500 A112 £1 dk grn, blk & red 19.00 4.25

"Art" — A171

1960, Mar. 1 Perf. 13½x13 Wmk. 328
501 A171 10m brown .35 .25
Issued to publicize the 3rd Biennial Exhibition of Fine Arts in Alexandria.

Arab League Center, Cairo — A172

1960, Mar. 22 Photo. Perf. 13½x13
502 A172 10m dull grn & blk .35 .25
Opening of Arab League Center and Arab Postal Museum, Cairo.
See Syria-UAR No. 40.

Refugees Pointing to Map of Palestine — A173

1960, Apr. 7
503 A173 10m orange ver .55 .30
504 A173 35m Prus blue .80 .65
World Refugee Year, 7/1/59-6/30/60.
See Nos. N73-N74. See also Syria-UAR Nos. 43-44.

Weight Lifter — A174

Stadium, Cairo — A175

Sports: No. 506, Basketball. No. 507, Soccer. No. 508, Fencing. No. 509, Rowing. 30m, Steeplechase, horiz. 35m, Swimming, horiz.

Perf. 13½x13
1960, July 23		Photo.	Wmk. 328	
505	A174	5m gray	.60	.30
506	A174	5m brown	.60	.30
507	A174	5m dp claret	.60	.30
508	A174	10m brt carmine	.60	.30
509	A174	10m gray green	.60	.30
a.		Vert. or horiz. strip, #505-509	3.75	
510	A174	30m purple	.85	.50
511	A174	35m dark blue	1.10	.60
		Nos. 505-511 (7)	4.95	2.60

Souvenir Sheet
Imperf
512 A175 100m car & brown 3.25 3.25
Nos. 505-511 for the 17th Olympic Games, Rome, Aug. 25-Sept. 11.

EGYPT

Dove and UN Emblem — A176

35m, Lights surrounding UN emblem, horiz.

Perf. 13½x13
1960, Oct. 24 **Wmk. 328**
513 A176 10m purple   .25 .25
514 A176 35m brt rose .50 .30

15th anniversary of United Nations.

Abu Simbel Temple of Queen Nefertari A177

Perf. 11x11½
1960, Nov. 14 **Photo.** **Wmk. 328**
515 A177 10m ocher, *buff* .80 .50

Issued as propaganda to save historic monuments in Nubia and in connection with the UNESCO meeting, Paris, Nov. 14.

Model Post Office — A178

1961, Jan. 2 **Perf. 13x13½**
516 A178 10m brt car rose .40 .25

Issued for Post Day, Jan. 2.

Eagle, Fasces and Victory Wreath — A179

1961, Feb. 22 **Perf. 13½x13**
517 A179 10m dull violet .35 .25

3rd anniversary of United Arab Republic. See Syria-UAR No. 50.

Wheat and Globe Surrounded by Flags — A180

1961, Mar. 21 **Wmk. 328**
518 A180 10m vermilion .35 .25

Intl. Agricultural Exhib., Cairo, 3/21-4/20.

Patrice Lumumba and Map — A181

1961, Mar. 30 **Perf. 13½x13**
519 A181 10m black .35 .25

Africa Day, Apr. 15 and 3rd Conf. of Independent African States, Cairo, Mar. 25-31.

Reading Braille and WHO Emblem — A182

1961, Apr. 6 **Photo.**
520 A182 10m red brown .35 .25

WHO Day. See Nos. B21, N80.

Tower of Cairo — A183

1961, Apr. 11 **Perf. 13½x13**
521 A183 10m grnsh blue .35 .25

Opening of the 600-foot Tower of Cairo, on island of Gizireh. See No. C95.

Arab Woman and Son, Palestine Map — A184

1961, May 15 **Wmk. 328**
522 A184 10m brt green .45 .30

Issued for Palestine Day. See No. N79.

Symbols of Industry and Electricity A185

Chart and Workers — A186

1961, July 23 **Photo.** **Perf. 13½x13**
523 A185 10m dp carmine .65 .30
524 A185 10m brt blue .65 .30
525 A185 10m dk vio brown .65 .30
526 A185 35m dk green .85 .40
527 A185 35m brt purple .85 .40
Nos. 523-527 (5) 3.65 1.70

Souvenir Sheet
Imperf
528 A186 100m red brown 4.00 3.75

9th anniv. of the revolution.

Map of Suez Canal and Ships — A187

Perf. 11½x11
1961, July 26 **Unwmk.**
529 A187 10m olive .50 .30

Suez Canal Co. nationalization, 5th anniv.

Various Enterprises of Misr Bank — A188

Perf. 13x13½
1961, Aug. 22 **Wmk. 328**
530 A188 10m red brn, *pnksh* .35 .25

The 41st anniversary of Misr Bank.

Flag, Ship's Wheel and Battleship — A189

1961, Aug. 29 **Photo.** **Perf. 13½x13**
531 A189 10m deep blue .45 .25

Issued for Navy Day.

Type A136 Redrawn, Type A138, Type A217 and

Eagle of Saladin over Cairo — A190

Designs: 1m, Farmer's wife. 4m, 14th cent. glass lamp. 35m, "Commerce."

1961, Aug. 31 **Unwmk.** **Perf. 11½**
532 A136 1m blue .25 .25
533 A217 4m olive .25 .25
534 A190 10m purple .40 .25
535 A138 35m slate blue .70 .25
Nos. 532-535 (4) 1.60 1.00

Smaller of two Arabic inscriptions in new positions: 1m, at right above Egyptian numeral; 4m, upward to spot beside waist of lamp; 35m, upper left corner below "UAR." On 4m, "UAR" is 2mm deep instead of 1mm. "Egypt" omitted as in 1959-60.

UN Emblem, Book, Cogwheel, Corn — A191

Design: 35m, Globe and cogwheel, horiz.

Perf. 13½x13
1961, Oct. 24 **Photo.** **Wmk. 328**
536 A191 10m black & ocher .30 .25
537 A191 35m blue grn & brn .65 .35

UN Technical Assistance Program and 16th anniv. of the UN. See Nos. N81-N82.

Trajan's Kiosk, Philae A192

1961, Nov. 4 **Unwmk.** **Perf. 11½**
Size: 60x27mm
538 A192 10m dp vio blue .85 .40

15th anniv. of UNESCO, and to publicize UNESCO's help in safeguarding the monuments of Nubia.

Palette, Brushes, Map of Mediterranean — A193

1961, Dec. 14 **Wmk. 328** **Perf. 13½**
539 A193 10m dk red brown .35 .25

Issued to publicize the 4th Biennial Exhibition of Fine Arts in Alexandria.

Atom and Educational Symbols — A194

1961, Dec. 18
540 A194 10m dull purple .35 .25

Issued to publicize Education Day. See No. N83.

Arms of UAR — A195

1961, Dec. 23 **Unwmk.** **Perf. 11½**
541 A195 10m brt pink, brt grn & blk .35 .25

Victory Day. See No. N84.

Sphinx at Giza — A196

1961, Dec. 27 **Perf. 11x11½**
542 A196 10m black .55 .35

Issued to publicize the "Sound and Light" Project, the installation of floodlights and sound equipment at the site of the Pyramids and Sphinx.

Post Office Printing Plant, Nasser City — A197

1962, Jan. 2 **Photo.** **Perf. 11½x11**
543 A197 10m dk brown .40 .25

Issued for Post Day, Jan. 2.

Map of Africa, King Mohammed V of Morocco and Flags — A198

1962, Jan. 4 **Perf. 11x11½**
544 A198 10m indigo .35 .25

African Charter, Casablanca, 1st anniv.

Girl Scout Saluting and Emblem — A199

EGYPT

Perf. 13x13½
1962, Feb. 22 — **Wmk. 328**
545 A199 10m bright blue .95 .30
Egyptian Girl Scouts' 25th anniversary.

Arab Refugees, Flag and Map — A200

1962, Mar. 7 — **Perf. 13½x13**
546 A200 10m dark slate green .40 .25
5th anniv. of the liberation of the Gaza Strip. See No. N85.

Mother and Child — A201

1962, Mar. 21 — **Photo.**
547 A201 10m dk violet brn .40 .25
Issued for Arab Mother's Day, Mar. 21.

Map of Africa and Post Horn — A202

1962, Apr. 23 — **Wmk. 328**
548 A202 10m crimson & ocher .40 .30
549 A202 50m dp blue & ocher .80 .55
Establishment of African Postal Union.

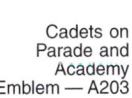
Cadets on Parade and Academy Emblem — A203

1962, June 18 — **Perf. 13x13½**
550 A203 10m green .35 .25
Egyptian Military Academy, 150th anniv.

Malaria Eradication Emblem — A204

1962, June 20 — **Perf. 13½x13**
551 A204 10m dk brown & red .25 .25
552 A204 35m dk green & blue .70 .50
WHO drive to eradicate malaria. See Nos. N87-N88.

Theodor Bilharz — A205

1962, June 24 — **Perf. 11x11½**
553 A205 10m brown orange .55 .25
Dr. Theodor Bilharz (1825-1862), German physician who first described bilharziasis, an endemic disease in Egypt.

Patrice Lumumba and Map of Africa — A206

1962, July 1 — **Photo.** — **Wmk. 342**
554 A206 10m rose & red .35 .25
Issued in memory of Patrice Lumumba (1925-61), Premier of Congo.

Hand on Charter — A207

1962, July 10 — **Perf. 11x11½**
555 A207 10m brt blue & dk brn .35 .25
Proclamation of the National Charter. Stamps with 20m denominations depicting the hand on charter and having different background colors are revenue stamps.

"Birth of the Revolution" A208

Symbolic Designs: No. 557, Proclamation (Scroll and book). No. 558, Agricultural Reform (Farm and crescent). No. 559, Bandung Conference (Dove, globe and olive branch). No. 560, Birth of UAR (Eagle and flag). No. 561, Industrialization (cogwheel, factory, ship and bus). No. 562, Aswan High Dam. No. 563, Social Revolution (Modern buildings and emblem). 100m, Arms of UAR, emblems of Afro-Asian and African countries and UN.

1962, July 23 — **Perf. 11½**
556 A208 10m brn, dk red brn & pink .40 .30
557 A208 10m dk blue & sepia .40 .30
558 A208 10m sepia & brt bl .40 .30
559 A208 10m olive & dk ultra .40 .30
560 A208 10m blk & red .40 .30
561 A208 10m brn org & indigo .40 .30
562 A208 10m brn org & vio blk .40 .30
563 A208 10m orange & blk .40 .30
Nos. 556-563 (8) 3.20 2.40

Souvenir Sheets
Perf. 11½
564 A208 100m grn, pink, red & blk 2.75 2.50
10th anniv. of the revolution. No. 564 exists imperf. Same value.

Mahmoud Moukhtar, Museum and Sculpture A209

1962, July 24 — **Perf. 11½x11**
565 A209 10m lt vio bl & olive .40 .25
Opening of the Moukhtar Museum, Island of Gezireh. The sculpture is "La Vestale de Secrets" by Moukhtar.

Flag of Algeria and Map of Africa Showing Algeria — A210

1962, Aug. 15 — **Perf. 11x11½**
566 A210 10m multicolored .35 .25
Algeria's independence, July 1, 1962.

Rocket, Arms of UAR and Atom Symbol — A211

1962, Sept. 1 — **Photo.** — **Wmk. 342**
567 A211 10m brt grn, red & blk .45 .25
Launching of UAR rockets.

Rifle and Target A212

Map of Africa, Table Tennis Paddle, Net and Ball A213

1962, Sept. 18 — **Perf. 11½**
568 A212 5m green, blk & red .55 .45
569 A213 5m green, blk & red .55 .45
 a. Pair, #568-569 1.25 1.25
570 A212 10m bister, bl & dk grn .65 .55
571 A213 10m bictor, bl & dk grn .65 .55
 a. Pair, #570-571 1.50 1.50
572 A212 35m dp ultra, red & blk 1.50 1.50
573 A213 35m dp ultra, red & blk 1.50 1.50
 a. Pair, #572-573 3.25 3.25
Nos. 568-573 (6) 5.40 5.00

38th World Shooting Championships and the 1st African Table Tennis Tournament. Types A212 and A213 are printed se-tenant at the base.

Dag Hammarskjold and UN Emblem — A214

Perf. 11½x11
1962, Oct. 24 — **Photo.** — **Wmk. 342**
574 A214 5m deep lilac .65 .25
575 A214 10m olive .75 .25
576 A214 35m deep ultra 1.10 .50
Nos. 574-576 (3) 2.50 1.00

Dag Hammarskjold, Secretary General of the UN, 1953-61, and 17th anniv. of the UN. See Nos. N89-N91.

Queen Nefertari Crowned by Isis and Hathor — A215

1962, Oct. 31 — **Perf. 11½**
577 A215 10m blue & ocher 1.25 .40
Issued to publicize the UNESCO campaign to safeguard the monuments of Nubia.

Jet Trainer, Hawker Hart Biplane and College Emblem — A216

1962, Nov. 2 — **Perf. 11½x11**
578 A216 10m bl, dk bl & crim .40 .25
25th anniversary of Air Force College.

14th Century Glass Lamp and "1963" — A217

1963, Feb. 20 — **Perf. 11x11½**
579 A217 4m dk brn, grn & car .35 .25
Issued for use on greeting cards. See Nos. 441, 477, 533, N76, N92. For overprint see No. N65.

Yemen Flag and Hand with Torch — A218

1963, Mar. 14 — **Photo.** — **Wmk. 342**
580 A218 10m olive & brt car .45 .25
Establishment of Yemen Arab Republic.

Tennis Player, Pyramids and Globe — A219

Perf. 11½x11
1963, Mar. 20 — **Unwmk.**
581 A219 10m gray, blk & brn .75 .30
Intl. Lawn Tennis Championships, Cairo.

Cow, UN and FAO Emblems A220

Designs: 10m, Corn, wheat and emblems, vert. 35m, Wheat, corn and emblems.

Perf. 11½x11, 11x11½
1963, Mar. 21 — **Wmk. 342**
582 A220 5m violet & dp org .45 .30
583 A220 10m ultra & yel .55 .30
584 A220 35m blue, yel & blk .75 .75
Nos. 582-584 (3) 1.75 1.35
FAO "Freedom from Hunger" campaign. See Nos. N93-N95.

Centenary Emblem — A221

Design: 35m, Globe and emblem.

1963, May 8 — **Unwmk.** — **Perf. 11x11½**
585 A221 10m lt blue, red & mar .30 .25
586 A221 35m lt blue & red .85 .85
Centenary of the Red Cross. See Nos. N96-N97.

Arab Socialist Union Emblem — A222

50m, Tools, torch & symbol of National Charter.

Wmk. 342
1963, July 23 — **Photo.** — **Perf. 11½**
587 A222 10m slate & rose pink .35 .25

EGYPT

Souvenir Sheets
Perf. 11½

588 A222 50m vio bl & org yel 2.25 2.25

11th anniv. of the revolution and to publicize the Arab Socialist Union.

No. 588 exists imperf. Same value.

Television Station, Cairo, and Screen — A223

1963, Aug. 1 *Perf. 11½x11*
589 A223 10m dk blue & yel .35 .25

2nd Intl. Television Festival, Alexandria, 9/1-10.

Queen Nefertari — A224

Designs: 10m, Great Hypostyle Hall, Abu Simbel. 35m, Ramses in moonlight.

Size: 25x42mm (5m, 35m); 28x61mm (10m)

Wmk. 342
1963, Oct. 1 *Photo.* *Perf. 11*
590 A224 5m brt vio blue & yel .65 .40
591 A224 10m gray, blk & red org .75 .45
592 A224 35m org yel & blk 1.60 .85
  Nos. 590-592 (3) 3.00 1.70

UNESCO world campaign to save historic monuments in Nubia.
See Nos. N98-N100.

Swimmer and Map of Suez Canal — A225

1963, Oct. 15
593 A225 10m blue & sal rose .35 .25

Intl. Suez Canal Swimming Championship.

Ministry of Agriculture A226

Perf. 11½x11
1963, Nov. 20 **Wmk. 342**
594 A226 10m multicolored .35 .25

50th anniv. of the Ministry of Agriculture.

Modern Building and Map of Africa and Asia — A227

1963, Dec. 7
595 A227 10m multicolored .35 .25

Afro-Asian Housing Congress, Dec. 7-12.

Scales, Globe, UN Emblem — A228

1963, Dec. 10
596 A228 5m dk green & yel .30 .25
597 A228 10m blue, gray & blk .35 .25
598 A228 35m rose red, pink & red .85 .45
  Nos. 596-598 (3) 1.50 .95

15th anniv. of the Universal Declaration of Human Rights.
See Nos. N101-N103.

Sculpture, Arms of Alexandria and Palette with Flags — A229

1963, Dec. 12 *Perf. 11x11½*
599 A229 10m pale bl, dk bl & brn .35 .25

Issued to publicize the 5th Biennial Exhibition of Fine Arts in Alexandria.

Lion and Nile Hilton Hotel A230

Vase, 13th Century A231

Pharaoh Userkaf (5th Dynasty) — A232

Designs: 1m, Long Necked Mamluke glass bottle, 14th century. 2m, Ivory headrest. 3m, Pharaonic calcite boat. 4m, Minaret and gate. 5m, Nile and Aswan High Dam. 10m, Eagle of Saladin over pyramids. 15m, Window, Ibn Tulun's mosque. No. 608, Mitwalli Gate, Cairo. 35m, Nefertari. 40m, Tower Hotel. 55m, Sultan Hassan's Mosque. 60m, Courtyard, Al Azhar University. 200m, Head of Ramses II. 500m, Funerary mask of Tutankhamun.

1964-67 *Unwmk.* *Photo.* *Perf. 11*
Size: Nos. 608, 612, 19x24mm; others, 24x29mm

600	A231	1m citron & ultra	.25	.25
601	A230	2m magenta & bis	.25	.25
602	A230	3m sal, org & bl	.25	.25
603	A235	4m och, blk & ultra	.35	.25
604	A230	5m brn & brt blue	.25	.25
a.		5m brown & dark blue	.50	.25
605	A231	10m green, dk brn & lt brn	.30	.25
606	A230	15m ultra & yel	.30	.25
607	A230	20m brn org & blk	.90	.25
608	A231	20m lt olive grn ('67)	1.60	.25
609	A231	30m yellow & brown	.75	.25
610	A231	35m sal, och & ultra	.90	.25
611	A231	40m ultra & yellow	1.75	.40
612	A231	55m brt red lil ('67)	2.00	.25
613	A231	60m grnsh bl & yel brn	1.25	.55

Wmk. 342
614	A232	100m dk vio brn & sl	3.50	.85
615	A232	200m bluish blk & yel brn	8.00	1.00
616	A232	500m ultra & dp org	17.50	3.25
		Nos. 600-616 (17)	40.10	9.05

Nos. 603 & N107 lack the vertically arranged dates which appear at lower right on No. 619.
See Nos. N104-N116.

HSN Commission Emblem — A233

Perf. 11x11½
1964, Jan. 10 **Wmk. 342**
617 A233 10m dull bl, dk bl & yel .35 .25

1st conf. of the Commission of Health, Sanitation and Nutrition.

Arab League Emblem A234

1964, Jan. 13 *Perf. 11*
618 A234 10m brt green & blk .35 .25

1st meeting of the Heads of State of the Arab League, Cairo, January.
See No. N117.

Minaret at Night — A235

1964 *Unwmk.* *Perf. 11*
619 A235 4m emerald, blk & red .35 .25

Issued for use on greeting cards.
See Nos. 603, N107, N118.

Old and New Dwellings and Map of Nubia — A236

Perf. 11½x11
1964, Feb. 27 *Photo.* **Wmk. 342**
620 A236 10m dull vio & yel .35 .25

Resettlement of Nubian population.

Map of Africa and Asia and Train — A237

1964, Mar. 21
621 A237 10m dull bl, dk bl & yel .90 .50

Asian Railway Conference, Cairo, Mar. 21.

Ikhnaton and Nefertiti with Children — A238

1964, Mar. 21 *Perf. 11x11½*
622 A238 10m dk brown & ultra .90 .30

Issued for Arab Mother's Day, Mar. 21.

APU Emblem — A239

1964, Apr. 1 *Photo.* **Wmk. 342**
623 A239 10m org brn & bl, *sal* .35 .25

Permanent Office of the APU, 10th anniv.
See No. N119.

WHO Emblem — A240

1964, Apr. 7
624 A240 10m dk blue & red .35 .25

World Health Day (Anti-Tuberculosis).
See No. N120.

Statue of Liberty, World's Fair Pavilion and Pyramids A241

1964, Apr. 22 *Perf. 11½x11*
625 A241 10m brt green & ol, *grysh* .35 .25

New York World's Fair, 1964-65.

Nile and Aswan High Dam — A242

1964, May 15 *Unwmk.* *Perf. 11½*
626 A242 10m black & blue .35 .25

The diversion of the Nile.

"Land Reclamation" A243

A423a

Design: No. 628, "Electricity," Aswan High Dam hydroelectric station. No. 628A, Aswan High Dam before and after diversion of the Nile.

1964, July 23 *Perf. 11½*
627 A243 10m yellow & emer .35 .25
628 A243 10m green & blk .35 .25

Souvenir Sheet
Imperf
628A A243a 50m blue & black 2.00 2.00

Land reclamation and hydroelectric power due to the Aswan High Dam.

Map of Africa and 34 Flags A244

1964, July 17 *Photo.*
629 A244 10m brn, brt bl & blk .40 .25

Assembly of Heads of State and Government of the Organization for African Unity at Cairo in July.

EGYPT

Jamboree Emblem — A245

Design: No. 631, Emblem of Air Scouts.

1964, Aug. 28   Unwmk.   Perf. 11½
630 A245 10m red, grn & blk   .60   .40
631 A245 10m green & red   .60   .40
   a.   Pair, #630-631   2.50   2.50

The 6th Pan Arab Jamboree, Alexandria.

Flag of Algeria — A246

1964, Sept. 5   Perf. 11½x11
Flags in Original Colors
632 A246 10m Algeria   .75   .40
633 A246 10m Iraq   .75   .40
634 A246 10m Jordan   .75   .40
635 A246 10m Kuwait   .75   .40
636 A246 10m Lebanon   .75   .40
637 A246 10m Libya   .75   .40
638 A246 10m Morocco   .75   .40
639 A246 10m Saudi Arabia   .75   .40
640 A246 10m Sudan   .75   .40
641 A246 10m Syria   .75   .40
642 A246 10m Tunisia   .75   .40
643 A246 10m UAR   .75   .40
644 A246 10m Yemen   .75   .40
   Nos. 632-644 (13)   9.75   5.20

2nd meeting of the Heads of State of the Arab League, Alexandria, Sept. 1964.

World Map, Dove, Olive Branches and Pyramids A247

1964, Oct. 5   Perf. 11½
645 A247 10m slate blue & yel   .35   .25

Conference of Heads of State of Non-Aligned Countries, Cairo, Oct. 1964.

Pharaonic Athletes — A248

Designs from ancient decorations: 10m, Four athletes, vert. 35m, Wrestlers, vert. 50m, Pharaoh in chariot hunting.

Perf. 11½x11, 11x11½
1964, Oct. 10   Photo.   Unwmk.
   Sizes: 39x22mm, 22x39mm
646 A248 5m lt green & org   .40   .25
647 A248 10m slate bl & lt brn   .45   .25
648 A248 35m dull vio & lt brn   1.10   .75
   Size: 58x24mm
649 A248 50m ultra & brn org   1.75   1.00
   Nos. 646-649 (4)   3.70   2.25

18th Olympic Games, Tokyo, Oct. 10-25.

Emblem, Map of Africa and Asia — A249

1964, Oct. 10   Perf. 11x11½
650 A249 10m violet & yellow   .35   .25

First Afro-Asian Medical Congress.

Map of Africa, Communication Symbols — A250

1964, Oct. 24
651 A250 10m green & dp sepia   .35   .25

Pan-African and Malagasy Posts and Telecommunications Cong., Cairo, Oct. 24-Nov. 6.

Horus and Facade of Nefertari Temple, Abu Simbel — A251   Ramses II — A252

Designs: 35m, A god holding rope of life, Abu Simbel. 50m, Isis of Kalabsha, horiz.

1964, Oct. 24   Perf. 11½, 11x11½
652 A251 5m grnsh bl & yel brn   .70   .35
653 A252 10m sepia & brt yel   1.10   .40
654 A251 35m brown org & indigo   2.50   1.25
   Nos. 652-654 (3)   4.30   2.00

Souvenir Sheet
Imperf
655 A252 50m olive & vio blk   15.00   15.00

"Save the Monuments of Nubia" campaign. No. 655 contains one horiz. stamp.

Emblems of Cooperation, Rural Handicraft and Women's Work — A253

Perf. 11½x11
1964, Dec. 8   Photo.   Unwmk.
656 A253 10m yellow & dk blue   .35   .25

25th anniv. of the Ministry of Social Affairs.

UN, UNESCO Emblems, Pyramids — A254

1964, Dec. 24   Perf. 11x11½
657 A254 10m ultra & yellow   .35   .25

Issued for UNESCO Day.

Minaret, Mardani Mosque — A255

1965, Jan. 20   Photo.   Perf. 11
658 A255 4m blue & dk brown   .35   .25

Issued for use on greeting cards. See No. N121.

Police Emblem over City — A256

Perf. 11x11½
1965, Jan. 25   Wmk. 342
659 A256 10m dp sepia & yellow   .85   .40

Issued for Police Day.

Oil Derrick and Emblem — A257

1965, Mar. 16   Photo.
660 A257 10m dk brown & yellow   .45   .25

5th Arab Petroleum Congress and the 2nd Arab Petroleum Exhibition.

Flags and Emblem of the Arab League — A258

Design: 20m, Arab League emblem, horiz.

1965, Mar. 22   Wmk. 342
661 A258 10m green, red & blk   .80   .40
662 A258 20m ultra & brown   1.00   .55

20th anniversary of the Arab League. See Nos. N122-N123.

Red Crescent and WHO Emblem — A259

1965, Apr. 7   Photo.
663 A259 10m blue & crimson   .55   .35

World Health Day (Smallpox: Constant Alert). See No. N124.

Dagger in Map of Palestine — A260

1965, Apr. 9   Perf. 11x11½
664 A260 10m black & red   1.50   .35

Deir Yassin massacre, Apr. 9, 1948. See No. N125.

ITU Emblem, Old and New Communication Equipment — A261

1965, May 17   Perf. 11x11½
665 A261 5m violet blk & yel   .40   .30
666 A261 10m red & yellow   .65   .30
667 A261 35m dk blue, ultra & yel   1.75   .80
   Nos. 665-667 (3)   2.80   1.40

Cent. of the ITU. See Nos. N126-N128.

Library Aflame and Lamp — A262

1965, June 7   Photo.   Wmk. 342
668 A262 10m black, grn & red   .60   .25

Burning of the Library of Algiers, 6/7/62.

Sheik Mohammed Abdo (1850-1905), Mufti of Egypt — A263

1965, July 11   Perf. 11x11½
669 A263 10m Prus blue & bis brn   .35   .25

Pouring Ladle (Heavy Industry) — A264

President Gamal Abdel Nasser and Emblems of Arab League, African Unity Organization, Afro-Asian Countries and UN — A265

No. 670, Search for off-shore oil. No. 672, Housing, construction in Nasser City (diamond shaped).

1965, July 23   Perf. 11½
670 A264 10m indigo & lt blue   .85   .50
671 A264 10m brown & yellow   .85   .50
672 A264 10m yel brn & blk   .85   .50
673 A265 100m lt green & blk   5.75   3.25
   Nos. 670-673 (4)   8.30   4.75

13th anniversary of the revolution. The 100m was printed in sheets of six, consisting of two singles and two vertical pairs. Margins and gutters contain multiple UAR coat of arms in light green. Size: 240x330mm.

4th Pan Arab Games Emblem — A266

Map and Emblems of Previous Games A267

No. 675, Swimmers Zeitun & Abd el Gelil. Arms of Alexandria. 35m, Race horse "Saadoon."

Perf. 11½x11; 11½ (#676)
1965, Sept. 2   Photo.   Wmk. 342
674 A266 5m blue & red   .40   .40
675 A266 10m dp blue & dk brn   .65   .30
676 A267 10m org brn & dp bl   .80   .45
677 A266 35m green & brown   1.40   1.00
   Nos. 674-677 (4)   3.25   2.15

4th Pan Arab Games, Cairo, Sept. 2-11. No. 675 for the long-distance swimming competition at Alexandria, a part of the Games.

362 EGYPT

Map of Arab Countries, Emblem of Arab League and Broken Chain — A268

1965, Sept. 13 Photo. Perf. 11½
678 A268 10m brown & yellow .40 .25
3rd Arab Summit Conf., Casablanca, 9/13.

Land Forces Emblem and Sun — A269

Perf. 11x11½
1965, Oct. 20 Wmk. 342
679 A269 10m bister brn & blk .65 .30
Issued for Land Forces Day.

Map of Africa, Torch and Olive Branches A270

1965, Oct. 21 Perf. 11½
680 A270 10m dull pur & car rose .40 .25
Assembly of Heads of State of the Organization for African Unity.

Ramses II, Abu Simbel, and ICY Emblem A271

Pillars, Philae, and UN Emblem A272

Designs: 35m, Two Ramses II statues, Abu Simbel and UNESCO emblem. 50m, Cartouche of Ramses II and ICY emblem, horiz.

Wmk. 342
1965, Oct. 24 Photo. Perf. 11½
681 A271 5m yellow & slate grn 1.00 .50
682 A272 10m blue & black 2.00 .50
683 A271 35m dk violet & yel 3.75 2.00
Nos. 681-683 (3) 6.75 3.00

Souvenir Sheet
Imperf
684 A272 50m brt ultra & dk brn 5.00 4.00
Intl. cooperation in saving the Nubian monuments. No. 684 also for the 20th anniv. of the UN. No. 684 contains one 42x25mm stamp.

Al-Maqrizi, Buildings and Books — A273

Perf. 11½x11
1965, Nov. 20 Photo. Wmk. 342
685 A273 10m olive & dk slate grn .40 .25
Ahmed Al-Maqrizi (1365-1442), historian.

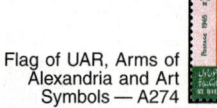

Flag of UAR, Arms of Alexandria and Art Symbols — A274

1965, Dec. 16 Perf. 11x11½
686 A274 10m multicolored .40 .25
6th Biennial Exhibition of Fine Arts in Alexandria, Dec. 16, 1965-Mar. 31, 1966.

Parchment Letter, Carrier Pigeon and Postrider — A275

1966, Jan. 2 Wmk. 342 Perf. 11½
687 A275 10m multicolored .80 .25
Nos. 687,CB1-CB2 (3) 8.30 6.50
Post Day, Jan. 2.

Lamp and Arch — A276

1966, Jan. 10 Unwmk. Perf. 11
688 A276 4m violet & dp org .40 .25
Issued for use on greeting cards.

Exhibition Poster — A277

Perf. 11x11½
1966, Jan. 27 Wmk. 342
689 A277 10m lt blue & blk .40 .25
Industrial Exhibition, Jan. 29-Feb.

Arab League Emblem — A278

1966, Mar. 22 Photo. Wmk. 342
690 A278 10m brt yellow & pur .40 .25
Arab Publicity Week, Mar. 22-28.

Printed Page and Torch — A279

1966, Mar. 25 Perf. 11½x11
691 A279 10m dp orange & sl blue .40 .25
Centenary of the national press.

Traffic Signal at Night — A280

1966, May 4 Photo. Wmk. 342
692 A280 10m green & red .85 .25
Issued for Traffic Day.

Hands Holding Torch, Flags of UAR & Iraq — A281

1966, May 26 Perf. 11x11½
693 A281 10m dp claret, rose red & brt grn .40 .25
Friendship between UAR and Iraq.

Workers and UN Emblem — A282

Perf. 11½x11
1966, June 1 Photo. Wmk. 342
694 A282 5m blue grn & blk .35 .25
695 A282 10m brt rose lil & grn .40 .25
696 A282 35m orange & black 1.25 .85
Nos. 694-696 (3) 2.00 1.35
50th session of the ILO.

Mobilization Dept. Emblem, People and City — A283

1966, June 30 Perf. 11x11½
697 A283 10m dull pur & brn .35 .25
Population sample, May 31-June 16.

"Salah el Din," Crane and Cogwheel A284

Present-day Basket Dance and Pharaonic Dance — A285

No. 699, Transfer of first stones of Abu Simbel. No. 700, Development of Sinai (map of Red Sea area and Sinai Peninsula). No. 701, El Maadi Hospital and nurse with patient.

Wmk. 342
1966, July 23 Photo. Perf. 11½
698 A284 10m orange & multi .65 .30
699 A284 10m brt green & multi .65 .30
700 A284 10m yellow & multi .65 .30
701 A284 10m lt blue & multi .65 .30
Nos. 698-701 (4) 2.60 1.20

Souvenir Sheet
Imperf
702 A285 100m multicolored 5.00 3.75
14th anniv. of the revolution.

Suez Canal Headquarters, Ships and Map of Canal — A286

1966, July 26 Perf. 11½
703 A286 10m blue & crimson 1.10 .50
Suez Canal nationalization, 10th anniv.

Cotton, Farmers with Plow and Tractor — A287

Perf. 11½x11
1966, Sept. 9 Photo. Wmk. 342
704 A287 5m shown .35 .25
705 A287 10m Rice .35 .25
706 A287 35m Onions 1.10 .90
Nos. 704-706 (3) 1.80 1.40
Issued for Farmer's Day.

WHO Headquarters, Geneva — A288

Designs: 10m, UN refugee emblem. 35m, UNICEF emblem.

Perf. 11½x11
1966, Oct. 24 Wmk. 342
707 A288 5m olive & brt pur .40 .25
708 A288 10m orange & brt pur .40 .25
709 A288 35m lt blue & brt pur .90 .80
Nos. 707-709 (3) 1.70 1.30
21st anniversary of the United Nations. See Nos. N129-N131.

World Map and Festival Emblem — A289

1966, Nov. 8 Photo.
710 A289 10m brt purple & yellow .55 .25
5th Intl. Television Festival, Nov. 1-10.

Arms of UAR, Rocket and Pylon — A290

1966, Dec. 23 Wmk. 342 Perf. 11½
711 A290 10m brt grn & car rose .55 .25
Issued for Victory Day. See No. N132.

Jackal — A291

35m, Alabaster head from Tutankhamun treasure.

1967, Jan. 2 Photo.
712 A291 10m slate, yel & brn 1.50 .35
713 A291 35m bl, dk vio & ocher 2.75 .70
Issued for Post Day, Jan. 2.

EGYPT

Carnations — A292

1967, Jan. 10 Unwmk. Perf. 11
714 A292 4m citron & purple .50 .25
Issued for use on greeting cards.

Workers Planting Tree — A293

Perf. 11x11½
1967, Mar. 15 Wmk. 342
715 A293 10m brt green & blk vio .40 .25
Issued to publicize the Tree Festival.

Gamal el-Dine el-Afaghani and Arab League Emblem — A294

1967, Mar. 22 Photo. Wmk. 342
716 A294 10m dp green & dk brn .40 .25
Arab Publicity Week, Mar. 22-28.
See No. N133.

Census Emblem, Man, Woman and Factory — A295

1967, Apr. 23 Perf. 11½x11
717 A295 10m black & dp org .40 .25
First industrial census.

Brickmaking Fresco, Tomb of Rekhmire, Thebes, 1504-1450 B.C. — A296

1967, May 1 Photo. Wmk. 342
718 A296 10m olive & orange .55 .30
Issued for Labor Day, 1967.
See No. N134.

Ramses II and Queen Nefertari A297

Design: 35m, Shooting geese frieze from tomb of Atet at Meidum, c. 2724 B.C.

Perf. 11½x11
1967, June 7 Photo. Wmk. 342
719 A297 10m multicolored 1.00 .50
720 A297 35m dk green & org 4.25 1.40
Nos. 719-720,C113-C115 (5) 13.60 6.15
Issued for International Tourist Year, 1967.

President Nasser, Crowd and Map of Palestine — A298

1967, June 22 Perf. 11½
721 A298 10m dp org, yel & ol 2.75 1.50
Issued to publicize Arab solidarity for "the defense of Palestine."

Souvenir Sheet

National Products A299

1967, July 23 Wmk. 342 Imperf.
722 A299 100m multicolored 4.00 3.50
15th anniv. of the revolution.

Salama Higazi — A300

Perf. 11x11½
1967, Oct. 14 Photo. Wmk. 342
723 A300 20m brown & dk blue .80 .40
50th anniversary of the death of Salama Higazi, pioneer of Egyptian lyric stage.

Stag on Ceramic Disk — A301

Design: 55m, Apse showing Christ in Glory, Madonna and Saints, Coptic Museum, and UNESCO Emblem.

1967, Oct. 24 Perf. 11½
724 A301 20m dull rose & dk bl .95 .40
725 A301 55m dk slate grn & yel 1.75 .85
Nos. 724-725,C117 (3) 4.20 2.15
22nd anniv. of the UN.

Savings Bank and Postal Authority Emblems A302

1967, Oct. 31 Perf. 11½x11
726 A302 20m sal pink & dk blue .60 .30
International Savings Day.

Rose — A303

Unwmk.
1967, Dec. 15 Photo. Perf. 11
727 A303 5m green & rose lilac .50 .25
Issued for use on greeting cards.

Pharaonic Dress — A304

Designs: Various pharaonic dresses from temple decorations.

Perf. 11x11½
1968, Jan. 2 Wmk. 342
728 A304 20m brown, grn & buff 1.40 .35
729 A304 55m lt grn, yel & sepia 2.25 .85
730 A304 80m dk brn, bl & brt rose 3.75 1.25
Nos. 728-730 (3) 7.40 2.45
Issued for Post Day, Jan. 2.
See Nos. 752-755.

Aswan High Dam and Power Lines — A305

1968, Jan. 9
731 A305 20m yel, bl & dk brn .35 .25
1st electricity generated by the Aswan Hydroelectric Station.

Alabaster Vessel, Tutankhamun Treasure A306

Capital of Coptic Limestone Pillar A307

Perf. 11x11½, 11½
1968, Jan. 20 Photo. Wmk. 342
732 A306 20m dk ultra, yel & brn .75 .30
733 A307 80m lt grn, dk pur & ol grn 1.60 1.00
2nd International Festival of Museums.

Girl, Moon and Paint Brushes — A308

1968, Feb. 15 Perf. 11x11½
734 A308 20m brt blue & black .40 .30
7th Biennial Exhibition of Fine Arts, Alexandria, Feb. 15.

Cattle and Veterinarian A309

Perf. 11½x11
1968, May 4 Photo. Wmk. 342
735 A309 20m brown, yel & grn .75 .25
8th Arab Veterinary Congress, Cairo.

Human Rights Flame — A310

Perf. 11x11½
1968, July 1 Photo. Wmk. 342
736 A310 20m citron, crim & grn .50 .25
737 A310 60m sky blue, crim & grn 1.00 .90
International Human Rights Year, 1968.

Open Book with Symbols of Science, Victory Election Result — A311

Workers, Cogwheel with Coat of Arms and Open Book — A312

1968, July 23 Perf. 11½
738 A311 20m rose red & sl grn .50 .25

Souvenir Sheet
Imperf
739 A312 100m lt grn, org & pur 3.25 3.00
16th anniversary of the revolution.

Imhotep and WHO Emblem — A313

No. 741, Avicenna and WHO emblem.

Perf. 11½x11
1968, Sept. 1 Photo. Wmk. 342
740 A313 20m blue, yel & brn 1.10 .55
741 A313 20m yellow, bl & brn 1.10 .55
a. Pair, #740-741 3.00 3.00
20th anniv. of the WHO. Nos. 740-741 printed in checkerboard sheets of 50 (5x10).

Table Tennis — A314

Perf. 11x11½
1968, Sept. 20 Photo. Wmk. 342
742 A314 20m lt green & dk brn .90 .35
First Mediterranean Table Tennis Tournament, Alexandria, Sept. 20-27.

Factories and Fair Emblem — A315

1968, Oct. 20 Wmk. 342 Perf. 11½
743 A315 20m bl gray, red & sl bl .45 .25
Cairo International Industrial Fair.

Temples of Philae A316

EGYPT

Refugees, Map of Palestine, Refugee Year Emblem — A317

55m, Temple at Philae & UNESCO emblem.

1968, Oct. 24   **Photo.**
744 A316 20m multicolored   1.25 .30
745 A317 30m multicolored   1.75 .85
746 A317 55m lt blue, yel & blk   3.00 1.10
    Nos. 744-746 (3)   6.00 2.25

Issued for United Nations Day, Oct. 24.

Egyptian Boy Scout Emblem — A318

1968, Nov. 1
747 A318 10m dull org & vio bl   .80 .30

50th anniversary of Egyptian Boy Scouts.

Pharaonic Sports — A319

Design: 30m, Pharaonic sports, diff.

1968, Nov. 1
748 A319 20m pale ol, pale sal & blk   .80 .25
749 A319 30m pale blue, buff & pur   1.25 .75

19th Olympic Games, Mexico City, 10/12-27.

Aly Moubarak — A320

1968, Nov. 9   **Perf. 11½**
750 A320 20m green, brn & bister   .55 .25

Aly Moubarak (1823-93), founder of the modern educational system in Egypt.

Lotus — A321

1968, Dec. 11   **Photo.**   **Wmk. 342**
751 A321 5m brt blue, grn & yel   .55 .25

Issued for use on greeting cards.

Ramses IV — A322

Pharaonic Dress: No. 753, Ramses III. No. 754, Girl carrying basket on her head. 55m, Queen of the New Empire in transparent dress.

1969, Jan. 2   **Photo.**   **Perf. 11½**
752 A322 5m blue & multi   .75 .30
753 A322 20m blue & multi   1.25 .50
754 A322 30m blue & multi   1.50 .60
755 A322 55m blue & multi   3.75 1.75
    Nos. 752-755 (4)   7.25 3.15

Issued for Post Day, Jan. 2.

Hefni Nassef — A323

Portrait: No. 757, Mohammed Farid.

Perf. 11x11½
1969, Mar. 2   **Photo.**   **Wmk. 342**
756 A323 20m purple & brown   .55 .30
757 A323 20m emerald & brown   .55 .30
   a. Pair, #756-757   1.25 1.25

50th anniv. of the death of Hefni Nassef (1860-1919) writer and government worker, and Mohammed Farid (1867-1919), lawyer and Speaker of the Nationalist Party.

Teacher and Children — A324

1969, Mar. 2   **Perf. 11x11½**
758 A324 20m multicolored   .55 .25

Arab Teacher's Day.

ILO Emblem and Factory Chimneys — A325

1969, Apr. 11   **Photo.**   **Wmk. 342**
759 A325 20m brown, ultra & car   .55 .25

50th anniv. of the ILO.

A326

Design: Flag of Algeria, Africa Day and Tourist Year Emblems.

Perf. 11½x11
1969, May 25   **Litho.**   **Wmk. 342**
760 A326 10m Algeria   .95 .55
761 A326 10m Botswana   .95 .55
762 A326 10m Burundi   .95 .55
763 A326 10m Cameroun   .95 .55
764 A326 10m Cent. Afr. Rep.   .95 .55
765 A326 10m Chad   .95 .55
766 A326 10m Congo (Brazzaville)   .95 .55
767 A326 10m Congo (Kinshassa)   .95 .55
768 A326 10m Dahomey   .95 .55
769 A326 10m Equatorial Guinea   .95 .55
770 A326 10m Ethiopia   .95 .55
771 A326 10m Gabon   .95 .55
772 A326 10m Gambia   .95 .55
773 A326 10m Ghana   .95 .55
774 A326 10m Guinea   .95 .55
775 A326 10m Ivory Coast   .95 .55
776 A326 10m Kenya   .95 .55
777 A326 10m Lesotho   .95 .55
778 A326 10m Liberia   .95 .55
779 A326 10m Libya   .95 .55
780 A326 10m Malagasy   .95 .55
781 A326 10m Malawi   .95 .55
782 A326 10m Mali   .95 .55
783 A326 10m Mauritania   .95 .55
784 A326 10m Mauritius   .95 .55
785 A326 10m Morocco   .95 .55
786 A326 10m Niger   .95 .55
787 A326 10m Nigeria   .95 .55
788 A326 10m Rwanda   .95 .55
789 A326 10m Senegal   .95 .55
790 A326 10m Sierra Leone   .95 .55
791 A326 10m Somalia   .95 .55
792 A326 10m Sudan   .95 .55
793 A326 10m Swaziland   .95 .55
794 A326 10m Tanzania   .95 .55
795 A326 10m Togo   .95 .55
796 A326 10m Tunisia   .95 .55
797 A326 10m Uganda   .95 .55
798 A326 10m UAR   .95 .55
799 A326 10m Upper Volta   .95 .55
800 A326 10m Zambia   .95 .55
    Nos. 760-800 (41)   38.95 22.55

El Fetouh Gate, Cairo — A327

Sculptures from the Egyptian Museum, Cairo — A328

Millenary of Cairo A329

No. 802, Al Azhar University. No. 803, The Citadel. No. 805, Sculptures, Coptic Museum. No. 806, Glass plate and vase, Fatimid dynasty, Islamic Museum. No. 807: a, Islamic coin. b, Fatimist era jewelry. c, Copper vase. d, Coins and plaque.

Perf. 11½x11
1969, July 23   **Photo.**   **Wmk. 342**
801 A327 10m dk brown & multi   .55 .25
802 A327 10m green & multi   .55 .25
803 A327 10m blue & multi   .55 .25
Perf. 11½
804 A328 20m yellow grn & multi   .95 .40
805 A328 20m dp ultra & multi   .95 .40
806 A328 20m brown & multi   .95 .40
    Nos. 801-806 (6)   4.50 1.95
807 A329 Souvenir Sheet
    Sheet of 4   15.00 14.00
   a. 20m dark blue & multi   2.50 2.00
   b. 20m lilac & multi   2.50 2.00
   c. 20m yellow & multi   2.50 2.00
   d. 20m dark green & multi   2.50 2.00

Millenium of the founding of Cairo.

African Development Bank Emblem — A330

Perf. 11x11½
1969, Sept. 10   **Photo.**   **Wmk. 342**
808 A330 20m emerald, yel & vio   .40 .25

African Development Bank, 5th anniv.

Pharaonic Boat and UN Emblem — A331

Temple of Philae Inundated and UNESCO Emblem — A332

Design: 5m, King and Queen from Abu Simbel Temple and UNESCO Emblem (size: 21x38mm).

Perf. 11x11½, 11½x11
1969, Oct. 24   **Photo.**   **Wmk. 342**
809 A332 5m brown & multi   .45 .30
810 A331 20m yellow & ultra   1.40 .55
Perf. 11½
811 A332 55m yellow & multi   1.60 .75
    Nos. 809-811 (3)   3.45 1.60

Issued for United Nations Day.

Ships of 1869 and 1967 and Maps of Africa and Suez Canal A333

1969, Nov. 15   **Perf. 11½x11**
812 A333 20m lt blue & multi   1.50 .55

Centenary of the Suez Canal.

Cairo Opera House and Performance of Aida — A334

1969, Nov. 15
813 A334 20m multicolored   1.00 .45

Centenary of the Cairo Opera House.

Crowd with Egyptian and Revolutionary Flags — A335

1969, Nov. 15   **Perf. 11½x11**
814 A335 20m brt grn, dull lil & red   1.00 .45

Revolution of 1919.

Ancient Arithmetic and Computer Cards — A336

Perf. 11½x11
1969, Dec. 17   **Photo.**   **Wmk. 342**
815 A336 20m multicolored   .55 .30

Intl. Congress for Scientific Accounting, Cairo, Dec. 17-19.

Poinsettia — A337

1969, Dec. 24   **Unwmk.**   **Perf. 11**
816 A337 5m yellow, grn & car   .30 .25

Issued for use on greeting cards.

Sakkara Step Pyramid A338

El Fetouh Gate, Cairo A339

Fountain, Sultan Hassan Mosque, Cairo A340

King Khafre (Ruled c. 2850 B.C.) A341

EGYPT

Designs: 5m, Al Azhar Mosque. 10m, Luxor Temple. 50m, Qaitbay Fort, Alexandria.

Wmk. 342 (20m, £1), Unwmkd.
Photo.; Engr. (20m, 55m)

1969-70			Perf. 11	
817	A338	1m multi ('70)	.30	.40
818	A338	5m multi ('70)	.50	.25
819	A338	10m multi ('70)	.50	.25
820	A339	20m dark brown	2.25	.35
821	A340	50m multi ('70)	2.25	.50
822	A340	55m slate green	3.50	.30

Perf. 11½
Photo. & Engr.

823	A341	£1 org & sl grn ('70)	40.00	9.50
		Nos. 817-823 (7)	49.30	11.55

See Nos. 889-891, 893-897, 899, 901-902, 904.

Veiled Women, by Mahmoud Said — A342

Perf. 11x11½
1970, Jan. 2   Photo.   Wmk. 342

824	A342	100m blue & multi	3.50	3.00

Post Day. Sheet of 8 with 2 panes of 4.

Parliament, Scales, Globe and Laurel — A343

1970, Feb. 2   Perf. 11½x11

825	A343	20m blue, vio bl & ocher	.75	.25

Intl. Conf. of Parliamentarians on the Middle East Crisis, Cairo, Feb. 2-5.

Map of Arab League Countries, Flag and Emblem — A344

Perf. 11½x11
1970, Mar. 22   Photo.   Wmk. 342

826	A344	30m brn org, grn & dk pur	.65	.40

Arab League, 25th anniv. See No. B42.

Mena House and Sheraton Hotel — A345

1970, Mar. 23

827	A345	20m olive, org & bl	.55	.25

Centenary of Mena House and the inauguration of the Cairo Sheraton Hotel.

Manufacture of Medicine — A346

1970, Apr. 20

828	A346	20m brown, yel & bl	1.25	.35

Production of medicines in Egypt, 30th anniv.

Mermaid — A347

1970, Apr. 20   Perf. 11x11½

829	A347	20m orange, blk & ultra	.65	.25

8th Biennial Exhibition of Fine Arts, Alexandria, March 12.

Misr Bank and Talaat Harb — A348

1970, May 7   Photo.   Wmk. 342

830	A348	20m multicolored	.65	.25

50th anniversary of Misr Bank.

ITU Emblem — A349

1970, May 17   Perf. 11x11½

831	A349	20m dk brn, yel & dull bl	.65	.25

World Telecommunications Day.

UPU Headquarters, Bern — A350

1970, May 20   Perf. 11½x11

832	A350	20m multicolored	.80	.35

Inauguration of the UPU Headquarters in Bern. See No. C128.

Basketball Player and Map of Africa A351

UPU, UN and U.P.A.F. Emblems A352

Perf. 11x11½, 11½x11
1970, May 25   Photo.   Wmk. 342

833	A351	20m lt blue, yel & brn	1.25	.40
834	A351	20m yellow & multi	.80	.35
835	A352	20m ocher, grn & blk	.70	.25
		Nos. 833-835 (3)	2.75	1.00

Africa Day. No. 833 also for the 5th African basketball championship for men; No. 834 the annual African Soccer championship; No. 835 publicizes the African Postal Union seminar.

Fist and Freed Bird — A353

Al Aqsa Mosque on Fire — A354

1970, July 23   Photo.   Perf. 11

836	A353	20m lt green, org & blk	.95	.25

Souvenir Sheet
Imperf

837	A353	100m lt blue, dp org & blk	3.25	2.40

18th anniv. of the revolution.

1970, Aug. 21   Wmk. 342   Perf. 11

838	A354	20m multicolored	1.25	.40
839	A354	60m brt blue & multi	2.75	1.60

1st anniv. of the burning of Al Aqsa Mosque, Jerusalem.

Standardization Emblems A355

1970, Oct. 14   Wmk. 342   Perf. 11

840	A355	20m yellow, ultra & grn	.75	.25

World Standards Day and 25th anniv. of the Intl. Standardization Organization, ISO.

UN Emblem, Scales and Dove — A356

Temple at Philae — A357

Child, Education Year and UN Emblems — A358

Designs: 10m, UN emblem. No. 845, 2nd Temple at Philae (denomination at left)

Perf. 11 (5m), 11½ (others)
1970, Oct. 24   Photo.   Wmk. 342

841	A356	5m lt bl, rose lil & sl	.25	.25
842	A357	10m yel, brn & lt bl	.25	.25
843	A358	20m slate & multi	.65	.30
844	A357	55m brn, bl & ocher	1.10	.75
845	A357	55m brn, bl & ocher	1.10	.75
a.		Strip of 3, #842, 844-845	4.00	4.00
		Nos. 841-845,B43 (6)	4.25	3.10

25th anniv. of the UN. No. 843 also for Intl. Education Year; Nos. 842, 844-845, the work of UNESCO in saving the Temples of Philae. No. 845a printed in sheets of 35 (15 No. 842, 10 each Nos. 844-845), Nos. 844-845 show continuous picture of the Temples at Philae.

Gamal Abdel Nasser — A359

1970, Nov. 6   Wmk. 342   Perf. 11

846	A359	5m sky blue & blk	.25	.25
847	A359	20m gray green & blk	.55	.25
		Nos. 846-847,C129-C130 (4)	4.55	2.15

Gamal Abdel Nasser (1918-70), Pres. of Egypt.

Medical Association Building — A360

No. 849, Old & new National Library. No. 850, Egyptian Credo (Nasser quotation). No. 851, Engineering Society, old & new buildings. No. 852, Government Printing Offices, old & new buildings.

1970, Dec. 20   Photo.   Perf. 11

848	A360	20m yel, grn & brn	.80	.40
849	A360	20m green & multi	.80	.40
850	A360	20m lt blue & brn	.80	.40
851	A360	20m blue, yel & brn	.80	.40
852	A360	20m blue, yel & brn	.80	.40
a.		Strip of 5, #848-852	4.50	4.25

50th anniv. of Egyptian Medical Assoc. (No. 848); cent. of Natl. Library (No. 849); Egyptian Engineering Assoc. (No. 851); sesqui. of Government Printing Offices (No. 852).

Map and Flags of UAR, Libya, Sudan — A361

1970, Dec. 27   Perf. 11½

853	A361	20m lt grn, car & blk	.75	.25

Signing of the Charter of Tripoli affirming the unity of UAR, Libya & the Sudan, 12/27/70.

Qalawun Minaret — A362

Designs (Minarets): 10m, As Saleh. 20m, Isna. 55m, Al Hakim.

1971, Jan. 2   Wmk. 342   Perf. 11

854	A362	5m green & multi	.60	.25
855	A362	10m green & multi	1.25	.40
856	A362	20m green & multi	2.50	.80
857	A362	55m green & multi	4.00	2.25
a.		Strip of 4, #854-857 + label	10.00	9.00

Post Day, 1971.
See Nos. 905-908, 932-935.

Gamal Abdel Nasser — A363

Design: Nos. 860a-860b, Portrait facing right.

Photogravure and Engraved
1971   Wmk. 342   Perf. 11½

858	A363	200m brn vio & dk bl	5.00	1.25
859	A363	500m blue & black	12.00	3.25

Souvenir Sheet
Imperf

860		Sheet of 2	13.00	13.00
a.	A363	100m lt green & black	4.00	2.75
b.	A363	200m blue & black	6.00	4.50

No. 860 commemorates inauguration of the Aswan High Dam, which is shown in margin. Issued: No. 860, 1/15; Nos. 858-859, 2/1. See No. 903.

EGYPT

Cotton and Globe — A364

1971, Mar. 6   Photo.   Perf. 11½x11
861   A364   20m lt grn, blue & brn   .65   .25
Egyptian cotton.

Arab Countries, and Arab Postal Union Emblem — A365

1971, Mar. 6   Wmk. 342
862   A365   20m lt bl, org & sl grn   .65   .25
9th Arab Postal Cong., Cairo, 3/6-25. See No. C131.

Cairo Fair Emblem — A366

1971, Mar. 6   Perf. 11x11½
863   A366   20m plum, blk & org   .65   .25
Cairo International Fair, March 2-23.

Nesy Ra, Apers Papyrus and WHO Emblem — A367

Perf. 11½x11
1971, Apr. 30   Photo.   Wmk. 342
864   A367   20m yellow bis & pur   1.25   .30
World Health Organization Day.

Gamal Abdel Nasser — A368

1971, May 1   Perf. 11
865   A368   20m purple & bl gray   .90   .30
866   A368   55m blue & purple   2.75   .95

Map of Africa, Telecommunications Symbols — A369

1971, May 17   Perf. 11½x11
867   A369   20m blue & multi   .65   .25
Pan-African telecommunications system.

Wheelwright A370

Hand Holding Wheat and Laurel A371

Candle Lighting Africa A372

Perf. 11x11½
1971, July 23   Photo.   Wmk. 342
868   A370   20m yellow & multi   .60   .25
869   A371   20m tan, grn & ocher   .60   .25

Souvenir Sheet
Imperf
870   A372   100m blue & multi   6.00   4.75
19th anniv. of the July Revolution. No. 870 contains one stamp with simulated perforations in gold.

Arab Postal Union Emblem — A373

1971, Aug. 3   Perf. 11½
871   A373   20m black, yel & grn   .65   .25
25th anniv. of the Conf. of Sofar, Lebanon, establishing the APU. See No. C135.

Arab Republic of Egypt

Three Links — A374

Perf. 11½x11
1971, Sept. 28   Photo.   Wmk. 342
872   A374   20m gray, org brn & blk   .65   .30
Confederation of Arab Republics (Egypt, Syria and Libya). See No. C136.

Gamal Abdel Nasser — A375

1971, Sept. 28   Perf. 11x11½
873   A375   5m slate grn & vio brn   .45   .25
874   A375   20m violet brn & ultra   .65   .25
875   A375   30m ultra & brown   1.25   .75
876   A375   55m brown & emerald   2.10   1.10
Nos. 873-876 (4)   4.45   2.35
Death of Pres. Gamal Abdel Nasser, 1st anniv.

Blood Donation — A376

1971, Oct. 24
877   A376   20m green & carmine   1.10   .25
"Blood Saves Lives."

Princess Nursing Child, UNICEF Emblem A377

Submerged Pillar, Philae, UNESCO Emblem A379

Equality Year Emblem — A378

Perf. 11x11½, 11½x11
1971, Oct. 24   Photo.   Wmk. 342
878   A377   5m buff, blk & org brn   .55   .30
879   A378   20m red brn, grn, yel & blk   .90   .30
880   A379   55m black, lt bl, yel & brn   2.25   .30
Nos. 878-880,C137 (4)   5.45   1.35
UN Day. No. 878 honors UN Intl. Children's Fund; No. 879 for Intl. Year Against Racial Discrimination; No. 880 honors UNESCO.

Postal Traffic Center, Alexandria A380

1971, Oct. 31   Perf. 11x11½
881   A380   20m blue & bister   1.00   .30
Opening of Postal Traffic Center in Alexandria.

Sunflower — A381

1971, Nov. 13   Perf. 11
882   A381   5m lt blue & multi   .45   .25
For use on greeting cards.

Abdalla El Nadim — A382

1971, Nov. 14   Perf. 11x11½
883   A382   20m green & brown   .65   .25
Abdalla El Nadim (1845-1896), journalist, publisher, connected with Orabi Revolution.

Section of Earth's Crust, Map of Africa on Globe — A383

1971, Nov. 27   Perf. 11½x11
884   A383   20m ultra, yel & brn   1.25   .25
75th anniv. of Egyptian Geological Survey and Intl. Conference, Nov. 27-Dec. 1.

Postal Union Emblem, Letter and Dove — A384

55m, African Postal Union emblem and letter.

1971, Dec. 2
885   A384   5m multicolored   .45   .25
886   A384   20m olive, blk & org   .90   .25
887   A384   55m red, blk & blue   2.00   1.10
Nos. 885-887,C138 (4)   4.75   2.00
10th anniversary of African Postal Union.

Money and Safe Deposit Box — A385

1971, Dec. 23   Perf. 11½
888   A385   20m rose, brn & grn   .85   .30
70th anniversary of Postal Savings Bank.

Types of 1969-70, 1971 Inscribed "A. R. Egypt" and

Ramses II — A385a

Designs as before and: No. 894, King Citi I. No. 897, View of Alexandria. No. 898, Queen Nefertari. No. 900, Sphinx and Middle Pyramid. 100m, Cairo Mosque. 200m, Head of Pharaoh Userkaf.

Wmk. 342 (892A, 901-904)
1972-76   Photo.   Unwmk.   Perf. 11
889   A338   1m multi   .25   .25
890   A338   1m dk brn ('73)   .30   .25
891   A338   5m multi   .40   .25
892   A385a   5m olive ('73)   .45   .25
892A   A385a   5m bister ('76)   .45   .25
893   A338   10m multi   .70   .25
894   A338   10m lt brn ('73)   .70   .25
895   A339   20m olive   1.10   .25
896   A339   20m purple ('73)   1.10   .25
897   A338   50m multi   2.25   .30
898   A385a   50m dull bl ('73)   2.25   .30
899   A340   55m red lilac   4.00   .90
900   A340   55m green ('74)   2.00   .50
901   A339   100m lt blue, dp org & blk   3.00   .70

Perf. 11½
Photo. & Engr.
902   A341   200m yel grn & brn   6.75   1.50
903   A363   500m bl & choc   17.50   4.00
904   A341   £1 org & sl grn   32.50   9.00
Nos. 889-904 (17)   75.70   19.45

Minaret Type of 1971

5m, West Minaret, Nasser Mosque. 20m, East Minaret, Nasser Mosque. 30m, Minaret, Al Gawli Mosque. 55m, Minaret, Ibn Tulun Mosque.

Wmk. 342
1972, Jan. 2   Photo.   Perf. 11
905   A362   5m dk green & multi   .45   .25
906   A362   20m dk green & multi   1.25   .25
907   A362   30m dk green & multi   2.75   .50
908   A362   55m dk green & multi   3.75   1.50
a.   Strip of 4, #905-908 + label   11.00   3.50
Post Day, 1972.

Police Emblem and Activities A386

1972, Jan. 25   Perf. 11½
909   A386   20m dull blue, brn & yel   2.25   .35
Police Day 1972.

UNESCO, UN and Book Year Emblems — A387

EGYPT

1972, Jan. 25   **Perf. 11x11½**
910 A387 20m lt yel grn, vio bl & yel   1.10   .25
International Book Year 1972.

Alexandria Biennale — A388

1972, Feb. 15   **Wmk. 342**   **Perf. 11½**
911 A388 20m black, brt rose & yel   .85   .30
9th Biennial Exhibition of Fine Arts, Alexandria, Mar., 1972.

Fair Emblem — A389

1972, Mar. 5   **Perf. 11x11½**
912 A389 20m blue, org & yel grn   1.10   .30
International Cairo Fair.

Abdel Moniem Riad — A390

1972, Mar. 21   **Photo.**   **Wmk. 342**
913 A390 20m blue & brown   1.25   .30
In memory of Brig. Gen. Abdel Moniem Riad (1919-1969), military hero.

Bird Feeding Young — A391

1972, Mar. 21   **Perf. 11½**
914 A391 20m yellow & multi   1.00   .25
Mother's Day.

Tutankhamun A392

Design: 55m, Back of chair with king's name and symbols of eternity.

1972, May 22   **Unwmk.**
915 A392 20m gray, blk & ocher   2.25   .65
916 A392 55m purple & yellow   6.25   1.75
Nos. 915-916,C142-C143 (4)   28.50   13.40
Discovery of the tomb of Tutankhamun by Howard Carter & Lord Carnarvon, 50th anniv. See No. C144.

Queen Nefertiti — A393

1972, May 22   **Wmk. 342**   **Photo.**   **Perf. 11½**
917 A393 20m red, blk & gold   1.25   .30
Soc. of the Friends of Art, 50th anniv.

Map of Africa — A394

1972, May 25   **Perf. 11x11½**
918 A394 20m purple, bl & brn   .75   .30
Africa Day.

Atom Symbol, "Faith and Science" — A395

Design: No. 920, Egyptian coat of arms.

1972, July 23   **Perf. 11½**
919 A395 20m blue, claret & blk   1.10   .30
920 A395 20m ol grn, gold & blk   1.10   .30
20th anniversary of the revolution.

Boxing, Olympic and Motion Emblems A396

Designs (Olympic and Motion Emblems and): 10m, Wrestling. 20m, Basketball.

1972, Aug. 17   **Perf. 11½x11**
921 A396 5m blue & multi   .35   .25
922 A396 10m yellow & multi   .50   .25
923 A396 20m ver & multi   .60   .30
Nos. 921-923,C149-C152 (7)   6.65   3.70
20th Olympic Games, Munich, 8/26-9/11.

Flag of Confederation of Arab Republics — A397

1972, Sept. 1   **Wmk. 342**   **Perf. 11½**
924 A397 20m carmine, bis & blk   .85   .30
Confederation of Arab Republics, 1st anniv.

Red Crescent, TB and UN Emblems A398   Heart and WHO Emblem A399

Refugees, UNRWA Emblem, Map of Palestine A400

Design: 55m, Inundated Temple of Philae, UNESCO emblem.

Perf. 11x11½ (#925), 11½ (#926, 928), 11 (#927)
1972, Oct. 24   **Photo.**
925 A398 10m brn org, red & bl   .55   .30
926 A399 20m green, yel & blk   1.00   .40
927 A400 30m lt bl, pur & lt brn   3.00   .75
928 A399 55m brn, gold & bluish gray   3.25   1.00
Nos. 925-928 (4)   7.80   2.45
UN Day. No. 925 is for the 14th Regional Tuberculosis Conf., Cairo, 1972; No. 926 World Health Month; No. 927 publicizes aid to refugees and No. 928 the UN campaign to save the Temples at Philae.

Morning Glory — A401

1972, Oct. 24   **Perf. 11**
929 A401 10m yel, lilac & grn   .65   .25
For use on greeting cards.

"Seeing Eye" — A402

1972, Nov. 30   **Perf. 11½**
930 A402 20m multicolored   1.00   .25
Social Work Day.

Sculling Race, View of Luxor A403

1972, Dec. 17   **Wmk. 342**   **Perf. 11**
931 A403 20m blue & brown   1.40   .40
3rd Nile Intl. Rowing Festival, Dec. 1972.

Minaret Type of 1971
10m, Al Maridani, 1338. 20m, Bashtak, 1337. 30m, Qusun, 1330. 55m, Al Gashankir, 1306.

1973, Jan. 2
Frame in Bright Yellow Green
932 A362 10m multicolored   .80   .25
933 A362 20m multicolored   1.25   .30
934 A362 30m multicolored   2.75   .75
935 A362 55m multicolored   3.75   2.00
 a. Strip of 4, #932-935 + Label   11.00   10.00
Post Day, 1973.

Cairo Fair Emblem — A404

Perf. 11½x11
1973, Mar. 21   **Photo.**   **Wmk. 342**
936 A404 20m gray & multi   .55   .25
International Cairo Fair.

Family — A405

1973, Mar. 21   **Perf. 11x11½**
937 A405 20m multicolored   .65   .25
Family planning.

Sania Girls' School and Hoda Sharawi — A406

Perf. 11½x11
1973, July 15   **Photo.**   **Wmk. 342**
938 A406 20m ultra & green   .65   .25
Centenary of education for girls and 50th anniversary of the Egyptian Women's Union, founded by Hoda Sharawi.

Rifaa el Tahtawi — A407

1973, July 15   **Perf. 11x11½**
939 A407 20m brt green, ol & brn   .70   .30
Centenary of the death of Rifaa el Tahtawi, champion of democracy and principal of language school.

Omar Makram A408   Abdel Rahman al Gabarti, Historian A409

"Reconstruction and Battle" — A410

No. 941, Mohamed Korayem, martyr.

1973, July 23
940 A408 20m yel grn, bl & brn   .65   .30
941 A408 20m lt grn, bl & brn   .65   .30
942 A409 20m ocher & brown   .65   .30
Nos. 940-942 (3)   1.95   .90

Souvenir Sheet
Imperf
943 A410 110m gold, bl & blk   3.25   3.00
Revolution establishing the republic, 21st anniv.

Grain, Cow, FAO Emblem — A411

Perf. 11½x11
1973, Oct. 24   **Wmk. 342**
944 A411 10m brn, dk bl & yel grn   .65   .25
10th anniv. of the World Food Org.

EGYPT

Inundated Temples at Philae — A412

1973, Oct. 24   *Perf. 11½*
945 A412 55m blue, pur & org   4.00   1.40
UNESCO campaign to save the temples at Philae.

Bank Building — A413

1973, Oct. 24
946 A413 20m brn org, grn & blk   .75   .30
75th anniv. of the National Bank of Egypt.

Rose — A414

1973, Oct. 24   *Perf. 11*
947 A414 10m blue & multi   .55   .25
For use on greeting cards.

Human Rights Flame — A415

Perf. 11x11½
1973, Dec. 8   *Photo.*   *Wmk. 342*
948 A415 20m yel grn, dk bl & car   .75   .25
25th anniversary of the Universal Declaration of Human Rights.

Taha Hussein — A416

1973, Dec. 10
949 A416 20m dk blue, brn & emer   .75   .25
Dr. Taha Hussein (1893-1973), "Father of Education" in Egypt, writer, philosopher.

Pres. Sadat, Flag and Battle of Oct. 6 A417

1973, Dec. 23   *Perf. 11x11½*
950 A417 20m yellow, blk & red   1.25   .60
October War against Israel (crossing of Suez Canal by Egyptian forces, Oct. 6, 1973). See No. 959.

WPY Emblem and Chart — A418

1974, Mar. 21   *Wmk. 342*   *Perf. 11*
951 A418 55m org, grn & dk bl   1.10   .50
World Population Year.

Cairo Fair Emblem — A419

1974, Mar. 21   *Photo.*
952 A419 20m blue & multi   .65   .25
Cairo International Fair.

Nurse and Medal of Angels of Ramadan 10 — A420

1974, May 15   *Perf. 11½*
953 A420 55m multicolored   2.00   .65
Nurses' and World Hospital Day.

Workers, Relief Carving from Queen Tee's Tomb, Sakhara A421

1974, May 15   *Perf. 11*
954 A421 20m yellow, blue & brn   .85   .30
Workers' Day.

Pres. Sadat, Troops Crossing Suez Canal — A422

"Reconstruction," Map of Suez Canal and New Building — A423

Sheet of Aluminum — A424

Design: 110m, Pres. Sadat's "October Working Paper," symbols of science and development.

1974, July 23   *Photo.*   *Perf. 11x11½*
955 A422 20m multicolored   .75   .40
956 A423 20m blue, gold & blk   .75   .40
     Perf. 11½
957 A424 20m plum & silver   .75   .40
    Nos. 955-957 (3)   2.25   1.20

Souvenir Sheet
Imperf
958 A424 110m green & multi   3.75   3.75
22nd anniv. of the revolution establishing the republic and for the end of the October War. No. 958 contains one 52x59mm stamp.

Pres. Sadat and Flag — A425

Perf. 11x11½
1974, Oct. 6   *Wmk. 342*
959 A425 20m yellow, blk & red   1.50   .75
1st anniv. of Battle. See No. 950.

Palette and Brushes — A426

1974, Oct. 6   *Perf. 11½*
960 A426 30m purple, yel & blk   1.00   .40
6th Exhibition of Plastic Art.

Teachers and Pupils — A427

1974, Oct. 6   *Perf. 11x11½*
961 A427 20m multicolored   .75   .25
Teachers' Day.

Souvenir Sheet

UPU Monument, Bern — A428

1974, Oct. 6   *Imperf.*
962 A428 110m gold & multi   5.50   5.00
Cent. of the UPU.

Emblems, Cogwheel and Calipers A429

Refugee Camp under Attack and UN Refugee Organization Emblem — A430

Child and UNICEF Emblem A431

Temple of Philae A432

1974, Oct. 24   *Perf. 11½, 11x11½*
963 A429 10m black, bl & yel   .55   .25
964 A430 20m dp org, bl & blk   .85   .25
965 A431 30m green, bl & brn   1.25   .40
966 A432 55m black, bl & yel   3.00   .85
   Nos. 963-966 (4)   5.65   1.75
UN Day. World Standards Day (10m); Palestinian refugee repatriation (20m); Family Planning (30m); Campaign to save Temple of Philae (55m).

Calla Lily — A433

1974, Nov. 7   *Perf. 11*
967 A433 10m ultra & multi   .55   .25
For use on greeting cards.

10m-coins, Smokestacks and Grain — A434

1974, Nov. 7   *Perf. 11½x11*
968 A434 20m yel grn, dk bl & sil   .60   .25
International Savings Day.

Organization Emblem and Medical Services — A435

1974, Nov. 7   *Perf. 11½*
969 A435 30m vio, red & gold   .90   .30
Health Insurance Organization, 10th anniv.

Mustafa Lutfy El Manfalouty A436

Abbas Mahmoud El Akkad A437

Perf. 11x11½
1974, Dec. 8   *Photo.*   *Wmk. 342*
970 A436 20m blue blk & brn   .55   .30
971 A437 20m brown & bl blk   .55   .30
  a. Pair, #970-971   1.30   1.30
Arab writers; El Manfalouty (1876-1924) and El Akkad (1889-1964).

Goddess Maat Facing God Thoth A438

Fish-shaped Vase — A439

EGYPT

Pharaonic Golden Vase — A440

Sign of Life, Mirror — A441

Wmk. 342
1975, Jan. 2   Photo.   Perf. 11½
972	A438	20m silver & multi	1.00	.30
973	A439	30m multicolored	1.25	.30
974	A440	55m multicolored	1.75	1.00
975	A441	110m blue & multi	3.00	1.75
		Nos. 972-975 (4)	7.00	3.35

Post Day 1975. Egyptian art works from 12th-5th centuries B.C.

Om Kolthoum — A442

Perf. 11¼
1975, Mar. 3   Photo.   Unwmk.
| 976 | A442 | 20m brown | .85 | .25 |

In memory of Om Kolthoum, singer.

Crescent, Globe, Al Aqsa and Kaaba — A443

1975, Mar. 25
| 977 | A443 | 20m multicolored | .85 | .25 |

Mohammed's Birthday.

Cairo Fair Emblem — A444

Perf. 11x11½
1975, Mar. 25   Wmk. 342
| 978 | A444 | 20m multicolored | .65 | .25 |

International Cairo Fair.

Kasr El Ainy Hospital WHO Emblem — A445

Perf. 11½x11
1975, May 7   Photo.   Wmk. 342
| 979 | A445 | 20m dk brown & blue | .85 | .25 |

World Health Organization Day.

Children Reading Book A446

Children and Line Graph A447

1975, May 7   Perf. 11x11½
| 980 | A446 | 20m multicolored | 1.00 | .40 |
| 981 | A447 | 20m multicolored | 1.00 | .40 |

Science Day.

A448

Design: Suez Canal, globe, ships, Pres. Sadat.

1975, June 5   Perf. 11½
| 982 | A448 | 20m blue, brn & blk | .85 | .25 |
| | | Nos. 982, C166-C167 (3) | 5.35 | 2.90 |

Reopening of the Suez Canal, June 5.

Belmabgoknis Flowers — A449

1975, July 30   Photo.   Wmk. 342
| 983 | A449 | 10m green & blue | .65 | .25 |

For use on greeting cards.

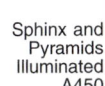

Sphinx and Pyramids Illuminated A450

Rural Electrification A451

Map of Egypt with Tourist Sites A452

1975, July 23
| 984 | A450 | 20m black, org & grn | .75 | .25 |
| 985 | A451 | 20m dk blue & brown | .75 | .25 |

Perf. 11
| 986 | A452 | 110m multicolored | 5.75 | 5.00 |
| | | Nos. 984-986 (3) | 7.25 | 5.50 |

23rd anniversary of the revolution establishing the republic. No. 986 printed in sheets of 6 (2x3). Size: 71x80mm.

Volleyball — A453

No. 988, Running. No. 989, Torch and flag bearers. No. 990, Basketball. No. 991, Soccer.

1975, Aug. 2   Photo.   Perf. 11x11½
987	A453	20m shown	.90	.45
988	A453	20m multicolored	.90	.45
989	A453	20m multicolored	.90	.45
990	A453	20m multicolored	.90	.45
991	A453	20m multicolored	.90	.45
a.		Strip of 5, #987-991	5.75	5.75

6th Arab School Tournament.

Egyptian Flag and Tanks — A454

1975   Photo.   Unwmk.   Perf. 11½
| 992 | A454 | 20m multicolored | 1.40 | .40 |

Two-line Arabic Inscription in Bottom Panel, "M" over "20"
| 992A | A454 | 20m multicolored | 1.40 | .40 |

No. 992 for 2nd anniv. of October War against Israel, "The Spark;" No. 992A, the Intl. Symposium on October War against Israel 1073, Cairo University, Oct. 27-31.

Issue dates: No. 992, Oct. 6; No. 992A, Oct. 24.

Arrows Pointing to Fluke, and Emblems A455

Submerged Wall and Sculpture, UNESCO Emblem A456

Perf. 11x11½
1975, Oct. 24   Wmk. 342
| 993 | A455 | 20m multicolored | .95 | .40 |
| 994 | A456 | 55m multicolored | 2.50 | 1.25 |

UN Day. 20m for Intl. Conf. on Schistosomiasis (Bilharziasis); 55m for UNESCO help in saving temples at Philae. See Nos. C169-C170.

Pharaonic Gate, University Emblem — A457

1975, Nov. 15   Photo.   Wmk. 342
| 995 | A457 | 20m multicolored | .55 | .25 |

Ain Shams University, 25th anniversary.

Al Biruni — A458

Arab Philosophers: No. 997, Al Farabi and lute. No. 998, Al Kanady, book and compass.

1975, Dec. 23   Photo.   Perf. 11x11½
996	A458	20m blue, brn & grn	1.50	.50
997	A458	20m blue, brn & grn	1.50	.50
998	A458	20m blue, brn & grn	1.50	.50
		Nos. 996-998 (3)	4.50	1.50

Ibex (Prow) — A459

Post Day (from Tutankhamun's Tomb): 30m, Lioness. 55m, Cow's head (Goddess Hawthor). 110m, Hippopotamus' head (God Horus).

1976, Jan. 2   Unwmk.   Perf. 11½
| 999 | A459 | 20m multicolored | 4.75 | 2.00 |

Wmk. 342
1000	A459	30m brown, gold & ultra	7.50	2.50
1001	A459	55m multicolored	12.50	6.50
1002	A459	110m multicolored	18.00	13.50
		Nos. 999-1002 (4)	42.75	24.50

Lake, Aswan Dam, Industry and Agriculture A460

Perf. 11½x11
1976, Jan. 27   Photo.   Wmk. 342
| 1003 | A460 | 20m multicolored | .90 | .25 |

Filling of lake formed by Aswan High Dam.

Fair Emblem — A461

1976, Mar. 15   Perf. 11x11½
| 1004 | A461 | 20m orange & purple | .50 | .25 |

9th International Cairo Fair, Mar. 8-27.

Commemorative Medal — A462

1976, Mar. 15   Wmk. 342
| 1005 | A462 | 20m olive, yel & blk | .60 | .25 |

11th Biennial Exhibition of Fine Arts, Alexandria.

Hands Shielding Invalid — A463

1976, Apr. 7   Photo.   Perf. 11½
| 1006 | A463 | 20m dk grn, lt grn & yel | .65 | .30 |

Founding of Faithfulness and Hope Society.

Eye and WHO Emblem — A464

1976, Apr. 7
| 1007 | A464 | 20m dk brn, yel & grn | .85 | .25 |

World Health Day: "Foresight prevents blindness."

EGYPT

Pres. Sadat, Legal Department Emblem — A465

Perf. 11½x11
1976, May 15   Photo.   Wmk. 342
1008 A465 20m olive & multi   .65 .30
Centenary of State Legal Department.

Scales of Justice — A466

1976, May 15   Perf. 11x11½
1009 A466 20m carmine, blk & grn   .60 .30
5th anniversary of Rectification Movement.

Al-Ahram Front Page, First Issue — A467

Perf. 11½x11
1976, June 25   Photo.   Wmk. 342
1010 A467 20m bister & multi   .65 .30
Centenary of Al-Ahram newspaper.

World Map, Pres. Sadat and Emblems A468

1976, July 23   Perf. 11x11½
1011 A468 20m bl, blk & yel   .85 .35
Size: 240x216mm
Imperf
1012 A468 110m bl, brn & yel   7.00 6.75
24th anniv. of the revolution. No. 1012 design is similar to No. 1011.

Scarborough Lily — A469

1976, Sept. 10   Photo.   Perf. 11
1013 A469 10m multicolored   .55 .25
For use on greeting cards.

Reconstruction of Sinai by Irrigation A470

Abu Redice Oil Wells and Refinery A471

Unknown Soldier, Memorial Pyramid for October War A472

1976, Oct. 6   Perf. 11x11½
1014 A470 20m multicolored   .85 .40
1015 A471 20m multicolored   .85 .40
Size: 65x77mm
1016 A472 110m grn, bl & blk   7.50 7.00
October War against Israel, 3rd anniv.

Papyrus with Children's Animal Story — A473

Al Aqsa Mosque, Palestinian Refugees A474

55m, Isis, from Philae Temple, UNESCO emblem, vert. 110m, UNESCO emblem & "30."

Perf. 11½, 11½x11
1976, Oct. 24   Photo.   Wmk. 342
1017 A473 20m dk bl, bis & brn   .65 .30
1018 A474 30m brn, grn & blk   .80 .35
1019 A473 55m dk blue & bister   1.50 .50
1020 A474 110m lt grn, vio bl & red   2.50 1.40
Nos. 1017-1020 (4)   5.45 2.55
30th anniversary of UNESCO.

Census Chart — A475

1976, Nov. 22   Photo.   Perf. 11½x11
1021 A475 20m multicolored   .65 .25
10th General Population and Housing Census.

A476

Nile and commemorative medal.

1976, Nov. 22   Perf. 11x11½
1022 A476 20m green & brown   .65 .25
Geographical Soc. of Egypt, cent. (in 1975).

A477

Post Day: 20m, Akhnaton. 30m, Akhnaton's daughter. 55m, Nefertiti, Akhnaton's wife. 110m, Akhnaton, front view.

1977, Jan. 2   Photo.   Perf. 11x11½
1023 A477 20m multicolored   .65 .30
1024 A477 30m multicolored   .65 .35
1025 A477 55m multicolored   1.10 .55
1026 A477 110m multicolored   3.50 1.50
Nos. 1023-1026 (4)   5.90 2.70

Policeman, Emblem and Emergency Car — A478

Perf. 11½x11
1977, Feb. 25   Photo.   Wmk. 342
1027 A478 20m multicolored   1.10 .30
Police Day.

Map of Africa, Arab League Emblem — A479

1977, Mar 7   Perf. 11x11½
1028 A479 55m multicolored   .90 .50
First Afro-Arab Summit Conference, Cairo.

Fair Emblem, Pharaonic Ship — A480

1977, Mar. 7   Perf. 11x11½
1029 A480 20m green, blk & red   .65 .30
10th International Cairo Fair.

King Faisal — A481

1977, Mar. 22   Photo.   Perf. 11x11½
1030 A481 20m indigo & brown   .65 .25
King Faisal Ben Abdel-Aziz Al Saud of Saudi Arabia (1906-1975).

Healthy and Crippled Children — A482

1977, Apr. 12   Wmk. 342
1031 A482 20m multicolored   .95 .30
National campaign to fight poliomyelitis.

APU Emblem, Members' Flags — A483

1977, Apr. 12   Perf. 11½
1032 A483 20m blue & multi   .45 .25
1033 A483 30m gray & multi   .65 .25
25th anniv. of Arab Postal Union (APU).

Children's Village — A484

Perf. 11½x11
1977, May 7   Photo.   Wmk. 342
1034 A484 20m multicolored   .55 .35
1035 A484 55m multicolored   1.25 .70
Inauguration of Children's Village, Cairo.

Loom, Spindle and Factory — A485

1977, May 7
1036 A485 20m multicolored   .55 .25
Egyptian Spinning and Weaving Company, El Mehalla el Kobra, 50th anniv.

Satellite, Globe, ITU Emblem — A486

1977, May 17   Perf. 11x11½
1037 A486 110m dk blue & multi   2.00 .50
World Telecommunications Day.

Flag and "25" — A487

Egyptian Flag and Eagle A488

Perf. 11½x11
1977, July 23   Photo.   Wmk. 342
1038 A487 20m silver, car & blk   .65 .25
Perf. 11x11½
1039 A488 110m multicolored   3.00 3.00
25th anniversary of July 23rd Revolution. No. 1039 printed in sheets of six. Size: 75x83mm.

Saad Zaghloul — A489

Perf. 11x11½
1977, Aug. 23   Photo.   Wmk. 342
1040 A489 20m dk green & dk brn   .40 .25
Saad Zaghloul, leader of 1919 Revolution, 50th death anniversary.

Archbishop Capucci, Map of Palestine — A490

1977, Sept. 1
1041 A490 45m emerald & blue   1.10 .50
Palestinian Archbishop Hilarion Capucci, jailed by Israel in 1974.

EGYPT

Bird-of-Paradise Flower — A491

1977, Sept. 3
1042 A491 10m multicolored .45 .25
For use on greeting cards.

Proclamation Greening the Land — A492

1977, Sept. 25 Photo. **Perf. 11x11½** Wmk. 342
1043 A492 20m multicolored .50 .25
Agrarian Reform Law, 25th anniversary.

Soldier, Tanks, Medal of Oct. 6 — A493

Anwar Sadat A494

1977, Oct. 6 **Perf. 11½x11**
1044 A493 20m multicolored .55 .25

Unwmk. **Perf. 11**
1045 A494 140m dk brn, gold & red 8.50 8.50
October War against Israel, 4th anniv. No. 1045 printed in sheets of 16.

Refugees Looking at Al Aqsa Mosque — A495

Goddess Taueret and Spirit of Flight (Horus) A496 — Mural Relief, Temple of Philae A497

Wmk. 342
1977, Oct. 24 Photo. **Perf. 11**
1046 A495 45m grn, red & blk .80 .35
1047 A496 55m dp blue & yel 1.50 .45
1048 A497 140m ol bis & dk brn 2.50 1.25
Nos. 1046-1048 (3) 4.80 2.05
United Nations Day.

Electric Trains, First Egyptian Locomotive A498

1977, Oct. 22
1049 A498 20m multicolored 1.75 .40
125th anniversary of Egyptian railroads.

Film and Eye — A499

1977, Nov. 16 **Perf. 11½x11**
1050 A499 20m gray, blk & gold .75 .25
50th anniversary of Egyptian cinema.

Natural Gas Well and Refinery — A500

1977, Nov. 17 Photo.
1051 A500 20m multicolored 1.25 .30
National Oil Festival, celebrating the acquisition of Sinai oil wells.

Pres. Sadat and Dome of the Rock — A501

Perf. 11½x11
1977, Dec. 31 Photo. Wmk. 342
1052 A501 20m green, brn & blk .60 .25
1053 A501 140m green, blk & brn 2.00 .80
Pres. Sadat's peace mission to Israel.

Ramses II — A502

Post Day: 45m, Queen Nefertari, bas-relief.

1978, Jan. 2 **Perf. 11½**
1054 A502 20m green, blk & gold .85 .40
1055 A502 45m orange, blk & ol 1.75 .90
Post Day 1978.

Water Wheels, Fayum A503 — Flying Duck, from Floor in Ikhnaton's Palace A504

5m, Birdhouse, 10m, Statue of Horus, 20m, 30m, Al Rifa'i Mosque, Cairo. 50m, Monastery of Baramus, Wadi el Natrun. 55m, Ruins of Edfu Temple. 70m, 80m, Bridge of Oct. 6. 85m, Medum pyramid. 100m, Facade, El Morsi Mosque, Alexandria. 200m, Column, Alexandria, Sphinx. 500m, Arabian stallion.

Wmk. 342, Unwmkd. (30m, 70m, 80m)
1978-85 **Perf. 11½**
1056 A503 1m slate blue .25 .25
  a. Unwmkd. ('79) .25 .25
  b. 1m gray ('83) .25 .25
  c. 1m gray, unwmkd. ('83) .25 .25
1057 A503 5m lt brn .25 .25
  a. 5m dull brn, unwmkd. ('79) .25 .25
1058 A503 10m brt green .25 .25
1059 A503 20m dk brown .25 .25
  a. 20m ('79) .25 .25
1059A A503 30m sepia .60 .50
  c. Wmk. 342 ('82) — —
1060 A503 50m lt blue .25 .25
  a. Unwmkd. ('79) .25 .25
  b. Unwmkd., brt blue ('87) .25 .25

1061 A503 55m olive .25 .25
1062 A503 70m olive ('79) .40 .25
1062A A503 80m olive ('82) .50 .30
1063 A503 85m dp purple .70 .30
  a. Unwmkd. ('85) .70 .35
1064 A503 100m yel brn .95 .30
  a. Unwmkd. ('85) 1.25 .40
1065 A503 200m lt bl & ind 2.25 .80
  a. Unwmkd. ('85) 2.25 .85
1066 A504 500m multicolored 7.00 2.00
  a. Unwmkd. ('85) 7.00 2.00
1067 A504 £1 multicolored 11.00 4.00
  a. Unwmkd. ('85) 11.00 4.00
Nos. 1056-1067 (14) 24.90 9.95

Issued: 500m, £1, 2/27/78; 70m, 8/22/79; others, 7/23/78.

Fair Emblem and Wheat — A505

1978, Mar. 15 **Perf. 11½**
1072 A505 20m multicolored .45 .25
11th Cairo International Fair, Mar. 11-25.

Emblem, Kasr El Ainy School — A506

1978, Mar. 18 **Perf 11½x11**
1073 A506 20m lt blue, blk & gold .55 .25
Kasr El Ainy School of Medicine, 150th anniv.

A507

No. 1074, Soldiers and Emblem. No. 1075, Youssef El Sebai.

1978, Mar. 30 **Perf. 11x11½**
1074   20m multicolored .50 .30
1075   20m bister brown .50 .30
  a. A507 Pair, #1074-1076 1.25 1.25
Youssef El Sebai, newspaper editor, assassinated on Cyprus and in memory of the commandos killed in raid on Cyprus.

Biennale Medal, Statue for Entrance to Port Said — A509

1978, Apr. 1 **Perf. 11½**
1076 A509 20m blue, grn & blk .55 .25
12th Biennial Exhibition of Fine Arts, Alexandria.

Child with Smallpox, UN Emblem — A510

1978, Apr. 7 Photo. **Perf. 11½**
1077 A510 20m multicolored .55 .35
Eradication of smallpox.

Heart & Arrow, UN Emblem — A511

1978, Apr. 7 Wmk. 342
1078 A511 20m multicolored .55 .35
Fight against hypertension.

Anwar Sadat — A512

1978, May 15 Photo. **Perf. 11½x11**
1079 A512 20m grn, brn & gold .65 .30
7th anniversary of Rectification Movement.

Social Security Emblem A513

1978, May 16 **Perf. 11**
1080 A513 20m lt green & dk brn .35 .25
General Organization of Insurance and Pensions (Social Security), 25th anniversary.

New Cities on Map of Egypt A514 — Map of Egypt and Sudan, Wheat A515

Wmk. 342
1978, July 23 Photo. **Perf. 11½**
1081 A514 20m multicolored .85 .30
1082 A515 45m multicolored 1.75 .50
26th anniversary of July 23rd revolution.

Symbols of Egyptian Ministries — A516

1978, Aug. 28 Photo. **Perf. 11½x11**
1083 A516 20m multicolored .65 .30
Centenary of Egyptian Ministerial System.

Pres. Sadat and "Spirit of Egypt" Showing Way — A517

1978, Oct. 6 Photo. **Perf. 11x11½**
1084 A517 20m multicolored .85 .30
October War against Israel, 5th anniv.

EGYPT

Fight Against Racial Discrimination Emblem — A518

Kobet al Sakra Mosque, Refugee Camp — A519

Dove and Human Rights Emblem — A520

UN Day: 55m, Sanctuary of Isis at Philae and UNESCO emblem, horiz.

Perf. 11, 11½ (45m)
1978, Oct. 24   Photo.   Wmk. 342
1085 A518 20m multicolored .45 .25
1086 A519 45m multicolored .90 .50
1087 A518 55m multicolored 1.00 .60
1088 A520 140m multicolored 2.25 1.00
Nos. 1085-1088 (4) 4.60 2.35

Pilgrims, Mt. Arafat and Holy Kaaba — A521

1978, Nov. 7   Photo.   Perf. 11
1089 A521 45m multicolored 1.00 .40
Pilgrimage to Mecca.

Tahtib Horse Dance — A522

1978, Nov. 7
1090 A522 10m multicolored .50 .25
1091 A522 20m multicolored .50 .25
For use on greeting cards.

UN Emblem, Globe and Grain — A523

1978, Nov. 11   Photo.   Perf. 11½
1092 A523 20m green, dk bl & yel .45 .25
Technical Cooperation Among Developing Countries Conf., Buenos Aires, Sept. 1978.

Pipes, Map and Emblem of Sumed Pipeline — A524

1978, Nov. 11
1093 A524 20m brown, bl & yel .65 .25
Inauguration of Sumed pipeline from Suez to Alexandria, 1st anniversary.

Mastheads — A525

1978, Dec. 24   Perf. 11x11½
1094 A525 20m brown & black .65 .25
El Wakea el Masriya newspaper, 150th anniv.

Abu el Walid — A526

1978, Dec. 24
1095 A526 45m brt grn & indigo .85 .30
800th death anniv. of Abu el Walid ibn Rashid.

Helwan Observatory and Sky — A527

1978, Dec. 30   Wmk. 342
1096 A527 20m multicolored .95 .35
Helwan Observatory, 75th anniversary.

Second Daughter of Ramses II A528

Ramses Statues, Abu Simbel, and Cartouches A529

1979, Jan. 2   Photo.   Perf. 11
1097 A528 20m brown & yellow .65 .30
Perf. 11½x11
1098 A529 140m multicolored 2.25 .80
Post Day 1979.

Book, Reader and Globe — A530

Perf. 11½x11
1979, Feb. 1   Photo.   Wmk. 342
1099 A530 20m yel grn & brn .45 .25
Cairo 11th International Book Fair.

Wheat, Globe, Fair Emblem A531

Perf. 11x11½
1979, Mar. 17   Photo.   Unwmk.
1100 A531 20m blue, org & blk .50 .25
12th Cairo International Fair, Mar.-Apr.

Skull, Poppy, Agency Emblem A532

1979, Mar. 20   Perf. 11
1101 A532 70m multicolored 1.90 .65
Anti-Narcotics General Administration, 50th anniv.

Isis Holding Horus — A533

1979, Mar. 21
1102 A533 140m multicolored 3.25 1.00
Mother's Day.

World Map and Book A534

Perf. 11x11½
1979, Mar. 22   Wmk. 342
1103 A534 45m yellow, bl & brn .55 .25
Cultural achievements of the Arabs.

Pres. Sadat's Signature, Peace Doves — A535

Wmk. 342
1979, Mar. 31   Photo.   Perf. 11½
1104 A535 70m brt green & red 1.25 .45
1105 A535 140m yel grn & red 2.25 1.00
Signing of Peace Treaty between Egypt and Israel, Mar. 26.

1979, May 26   Photo.   Perf. 11½
1106 A535 20m yellow & dk brn .55 .30
Return of Al Arish to Egypt.

Honeycomb with Food Symbols — A536

1979, May 15
1107 A536 20m multicolored .35 .25
8th anniversary of movement to establish food security.

Coins, 1959, 1979 — A537

Perf. 11½x11
1979, June 1   Wmk. 342   Photo.
1108 A537 20m yellow & gray .45 .25
25th anniversary of the Egyptian Mint.

Egypt No. 1104 under Magnifying Glass A538

1979, June 1   Perf. 11
1109 A538 20m green, blk & brn .55 .25
Philatelic Society of Egypt, 50th anniversary.

Book, Atom Symbol, Rising Sun — A539

"23 July," "Revolution" and "Peace" A540

Perf. 11½x11
1979, July 23   Wmk. 342
1110 A539 20m multicolored .50 .25
Miniature Sheet
Imperf
1111 A540 140m multicolored 3.75 3.75
27th anniversary of July 23rd revolution.

Musicians — A541

1979, Aug. 22   Perf. 11½
1112 A541 10m multicolored .25 .25
For use on greeting cards.

Dove over Map of Suez Canal — A542

Wmk. 342
1979, Oct. 6   Photo.   Perf. 11½
1113 A542 20m blue & brown .65 .30
October War against Israel, 6th anniv.

Prehistoric Mammal Skeleton, Map of Africa — A543

Perf. 11½x11
1979, Oct. 9   Photo.   Wmk. 342
1114 A543 20m multicolored 2.00 .35
Egyptian Geological Museum, 75th anniv.

EGYPT

T Square on Drawing Board
A544

1979, Oct. 11   **Perf. 11**
1115 A544 20m multicolored   .65   .25
Engineers Day.

Human Rights Emblem Over Globe
A545

Boy Balancing IYC Emblem
A546

Perf. 11½
1979, Oct. 24   **Photo.**   **Unwmk.**
1116 A545 45m multicolored   .65   .30
1117 A546 140m multicolored   1.50   1.25
UN Day and Intl. Year of the Child.

International Savings Day — A547

1979, Oct. 31
1118 A547 70m multicolored   1.00   .45

A548

Design: Shooting championship emblem.
1979, Nov. 16
1119 A548 20m multicolored   .65   .25
20th International Military Shooting Championship, Cairo.

International Palestinian Solidarity Day — A549

1979, Nov. 29   **Perf. 11x11½**
1120 A549 45m multicolored   .85   .30

Dove Holding Olive Branch, Rotary Emblem, Globe — A550

1979, Dec. 3   **Photo.**   **Perf. 11½**
1121 A550 140m multicolored   1.60   1.00
Rotary Intl., 75th anniv.; Cairo Rotary Club, 50th anniv.

Arms Factories, 25th Anniversary
A551

Perf. 11½x11
1979, Dec. 23   **Photo.**   **Wmk. 342**
1122 A551 20m lt olive grn & brn   .55   .25

Aly El Garem (1881–1949) — A552

Poets: No. 1124, Mahmoud Samy El Baroudy (1839–1904).

1979, Dec. 25   **Perf. 11x11½**
1123 A552 20m dk brn & yel brn   .50   .30
1124 A552 20m brn & dk brn   .50   .30
   a. Pair, #1123-1124   1.25   1.25

Pharaonic Capital — A553

Post Day: Various Pharaonic capitals.

1980, Jan. 2   **Unwmk.**   **Perf. 11½**
1125 A553 20m multicolored   .45   .30
1126 A553 45m multicolored   .65   .65
1127 A553 70m multicolored   1.00   .75
1128 A553 140m multicolored   2.75   1.50
   a. Strip of 4, #1125-1128   6.50   .650

Golden Goddess of Writing, Fair Emblem — A554

1980, Feb. 2   **Photo.**   **Perf. 11½**
1129 A554 20m multicolored   1.10   .25
12th Cairo Intl. Book Fair, Jan. 24-Feb. 4.

Exhibition Catalogue and Medal — A555

1980, Feb. 2
1130 A555 20m multicolored   .60   .30
13th Biennial Exhibition of Fine Arts, Alexandria.

13th Cairo International Fair — A556

1980, Mar. 8   **Photo.**   **Perf. 11x11½**
1131 A556 20m multicolored   .60   .25

Kiosk of Trajan
A557

a, Kiosk of Trajan. b, Temple of Korasy, entry at right. c, Temple of Ksalabsha, carvings on frame. d, Temple of Philae, 5 columns..

1980, Mar. 10   **Perf. 11½**
1132 Strip of 4 + label   5.50   5.50
   a.-d. A557 70m, any single   1.10   .85
UNESCO campaign to save Nubian monuments, 20th anniversary. Shown on stamps are Temples of Philae, Kalabsha, Korasy.

Physicians' Day — A558

1980, Mar. 18   **Perf. 11x11½**
1133 A558 20m multicolored   .60   .25

Rectification Movement, 9th Anniversary
A559

Perf. 11½x11
1980, May 15   **Photo.**   **Wmk. 342**
1134 A559 20m multicolored   .60   .25

Re-opening of Suez Canal, 5th Anniversary — A560

1980, June 5   **Perf. 11½**
1135 A560 140m multicolored   1.50   1.00

Prevention of Cruelty to Animals Week — A561

1980, June 5
1136 A561 20m lt yel grn & gray   .85   .25

Industry Day — A562

Perf. 11½x11
1980, July 12   **Photo.**   **Wmk. 342**
1137 A562 20m multicolored   .55   .25

Leaf with Text — A563

Family Protection Emblem
A564

1980, July 23   **Perf. 11½**
1138 A563 20m multicolored   .60   .25
Souvenir Sheet
Imperf
1139 A564 140m multicolored   3.75   3.75
July 23rd Revolution, 28th anniv.; Social Security Year.

Erksous Seller and Nakrazan Player — A565

Perf. 11½
1980, Aug. 8   **Unwmk.**   **Photo.**
1140 A565 10m multicolored   .50   .25
For use on greeting cards.

October War Against Israel, 7th Anniv.
A566

1980, Oct. 6   **Litho.**
1141 A566 20m multicolored   .75   .25

Islamic and Coptic Columns — A567

International Telecommunications Union Emblem — A568

Wmk. 342
1980, Oct. 24   **Photo.**   **Perf. 11½**
1142 A567 70m multicolored   .80   .60
1143 A568 140m multicolored   1.60   1.25
UN Day. Campaign to save Egyptian monuments (70m), Intl. Telecommunications Day (140m).

Hegira (Pilgrimage Year) — A569

1980, Nov. 9   **Litho.**   **Perf. 11x11½**
1144 A569 45m multicolored   .70   .30

374 EGYPT

Opening of Suez Canal Third Branch — A570

Perf. 11½x11
1980, Dec. 16   Photo.   Wmk. 342
1145 A570 70m multicolored   1.10   .60

Mustafa Sadek El-Rafai (1880-1927), Writer — A571

No. 1147, Ali Mustafa Mousharafa (1898-1950), mathematician (with glasses). No. 1148, Ali Ibrahim (1880-1947), surgeon.

1980, Dec. 23   Perf. 11x11½
1146 A571 20m green & brown   .50   .30
1147 A571 20m green & brown   .50   .30
1148 A571 20m green & brown   .50   .30
  a.   Strip of 3, #1146-1148   2.00 2.00
      See Nos. 1178-1179.

Ladybug Scarab Emblem — A572

Perf. 11½
1981, Jan. 2   Photo.   Unwmk.
1149 A572 70m shown   1.25   .50
1150 A572 70m Scarab, reverse 1.25   .50
      Post Day.

von Stephan, UPU — A573

Perf. 11x11½
1981, Jan. 7   Wmk. 342
1151 A573 140m grnsh bl & dk brn   1.75   .70

Heinrich von Stephan (1831-97), founder of UPU.

13th Cairo International Book Fair — A574

1981, Feb. 1   Perf. 11½x11
1152 A574 20m multicolored   .60   .25

14th Cairo International Fair, Mar. 14-28 — A575

Perf. 11x11½
1981, Mar. 14   Photo.   Wmk. 342
1153 A575 20m multicolored   .60   .25

Rural Electrification Authority, 10th Anniversary A576

1981, Mar. 18
1154 A576 20m multicolored   .60   .25

Veterans' Day — A577

1981, Mar. 26
1155 A577 20m multicolored   .60   .25

Intl. Dentistry Conf., Cairo — A578

Perf. 11x11½
1981, Apr. 14   Photo.   Wmk. 342
1156 A578 20m red & olive   .60   .25

Trade Union Emblem — A579

Perf. 11x11½
1981, May 1   Photo.   Wmk. 342
1157 A579 20m brt blue & dk brn   .60   .25

International Confederation of Arab Trade Unions, 25th anniv.

Nurses' Day — A580

1981, May 12
1158 A580 20m multicolored   .60   .25

Irrigation Equipment (Electrification Movement) A581

1981, May 15   Perf. 11½
1159 A581 20m multicolored   .60   .25

Air Force Day — A582

Perf. 11x11½
1981, June 30   Photo.   Wmk. 342
1160 A582 20m multicolored   .60   .25

A583

Designs: No. 1161, Flag Surrounding Map of Suez Canal. No. 1162, Emblems.

Wmk. 342
1981, July 23   Photo.   Perf. 11½
1161 A583 20m multicolored   .60   .25
1162 A583 20m multicolored   .60   .25

July 23rd Revolution, 29th anniv.; Social Defense Year.

Lotus — A584

Wmk. 342
1981, July 29   Photo.   Perf. 11
1163 A584 10m multicolored   .60   .25
For use on greeting cards.

Kemal Ataturk — A585

1981, Aug. 10   Perf. 11x11½
1164 A585 140m dp bluish grn, brn   2.25 1.25

Orabi Revolution Centenary — A586

20m, Orabi Pasha, Leader of Egyptian Force.

Perf. 11x11½
1981, Sept. 9   Photo.   Wmk. 342
1165 A586 20m dp bluish grn, brn   .60   .25

A587

1981, Sept. 14
1166 A587 45m ochre, blk, brn   .85   .25
World Muscular Athletics Championships, Cairo.

A588

Perf. 11x11½
1981, Sept. 26   Photo.   Wmk. 342
1167 A588 45m multicolored   .60   .25
Ministry of Industry and Mineral Resources, 25th anniv.

20th Intl. Occupational Health Congress, Cairo — A589

1981, Sept. 28   Perf. 11½x11
1168 A589 20m multicolored   .60   .25

October War Against Israel, 8th Anniv. — A590

1981, Oct. 6
1169 A590 20m multicolored   .65   .25

World Food Day — A591

13th World Telecommunications Day — A592

Intl. Year of the Disabled A593   Fight Against Apartheid A594

Perf. 11½x11, 11x11½
1981, Oct. 24   Photo.   Wmk. 342
1170 A591 10m multicolored   .45   .25
1171 A592 20m multicolored   .60   .25
1172 A593 45m multicolored   .80   .55
1173 A594 230m multicolored 3.75 1.10
      Nos. 1170-1173 (4)   5.60 2.15
United Nations Day.

Pres. Anwar Sadat (1917-81) A595

Perf. 11x11½
1981, Nov. 14   Unwmk.
1174 A595 30m multicolored   1.25   .75
1175 A595 230m multicolored 5.50 3.00

Establishment of Shura Council — A596

Perf. 11½x11
1981, Dec. 12   Photo.   Wmk. 342
1176 A596 45m purple & yellow   .60   .30

Agricultural Credit and Development Bank, 50th Anniv. — A597

1981, Dec. 15   Perf. 11x11½
1177 A597 20m multicolored   .50   .25

EGYPT 375

Famous Men Type of 1980
30m, Ali el-Ghayati (1885-1956), journalist.
60m, Omar Ebn sl-Fared (1181-1234), Sufi poet.

Perf. 11x11½
1981, Dec. 21   Photo.   Wmk. 342
1178   A571   30m green & brown   .40   .30
1179   A571   60m green & brown   .65   .45
   a.   Pair, #1178-1179   1.50   1.50

20th Anniv. of African Postal Union — A598

1981, Dec. 21   Perf. 11½x11
1180   A598   60m multicolored   .95   .35

14th Cairo Intl. Book Fair — A599

1982, Jan. 28
1181   A599   3p brown & yellow   .65   .25

Arab Trade Union of Egypt, 25th Anniv. — A600

1982, Jan. 30
1182   A600   3p multicolored   .45   .25

Khartoum Branch of Cairo University, 25th Anniv. — A601

Perf. 11½x11
1982, Mar. 4   Wmk. 342
1183   A601   6p blue & green   .75   .35

15th Cairo Intl. Fair — A602

1982, Mar. 13   Perf. 11x11½
1184   A602   3p multicolored   .60   .25

50th Anniv. of Al-Ghardaka Marine Biological Station — A603

Fish of the Red Sea: 10m, Lined butterfly fish. 30m, Blue-banded sea perch. 60m, Batfish. 230m, Blue-spotted boxfish.

1982, Apr. 24   Litho.   Perf. 11½x11
1185   10m multicolored   .90   .60
1186   30m multicolored   1.10   .70
1187   60m multicolored   1.50   .90
1188   230m multicolored   3.50   2.00
   a.   A603 Block of 4, #1185-1188   7.50   7.50

Liberation of the Sinai — A604

1982, Apr. 25   Photo.   Perf. 11x11½
1189   A604   3p multicolored   .65   .25

50th Anniv. of Egypt Air — A605

1982, May 7   Photo.   Perf. 11½x11
1190   A605   23p multicolored   3.25   2.25

Minaret — A606

Al Azhar Mosque A607

a, shown. b, Two terraces. c, Three terraces. d, Two turrets at top.

Perf. 11x11½
1982, June 28   Photo.   Wmk. 342
1191   Strip of 4 + label   5.00   5.00
   a.-d.   A606 6p any single, multi   .75   .55

Souvenir Sheet
Unwmk.   **Imperf.**
1192   A607   23p multicolored   6.25   6.25
Al Azhar Mosque millennium.
No. 1192 airmail.

Dove — A608

Flower in Natl. Colors A609

Perf. 11x11½
1982, July 23   Photo.   Wmk. 342
1193   A608   3p multicolored   .50   .25

Souvenir Sheet
Imperf
1194   A609   23p multicolored   4.00   4.00
30th anniv. of July 23rd Revolution.

World Tourism Day — A610

Design: Sphinx, pyramid of Cheops, St. Catherine's Tower.

Perf. 11½x11
1982, Sept. 27   Photo.   Wmk. 342
1195   A610   23p multicolored   3.50   2.25

October War Against Israel, 9th Anniv. — A611

1982, Oct. 6
1196   A611   3p Memorial, map   .65   .25

Biennale of Alexandria Art Exhibition — A612

1982, Oct. 17   Perf. 11x11½
1197   A612   3p multicolored   .60   .25

10th Anniv. of UN Conference on Human Environment A613

2nd UN Conference on Peaceful Uses of Outer Space, Vienna, Aug. 9-21 — A614

Scouting Year — A615

TB Bacillus Centenary A616

Perf. 11½x11, 11½ (A615)
1982, Oct. 24
1198   A613   3p multicolored   .50   .35
1199   A614   6p multicolored   .80   .55
1200   A615   6p multicolored   1.10   .55
1201   A616   8p multicolored   1.25   .75
   Nos. 1198-1201 (4)   3.65   2.20
United Nations Day.

50th Anniv. of Air Force — A617

1982, Nov. 2   Perf. 11x11½
1202   A617   3p Jet, plane   .70   .25

Ahmed Chawki (1868-1932) and Hafez Ibrahim (1871-1932), Poets — A618

Perf. 11½x11
1982, Nov. 25   Photo.   Wmk. 342
1203   A618   6p multicolored   .65   .50

Natl. Research Center, 25th Anniv. — A619

1982, Dec. 12   Photo.   Perf. 11x11½
1204   A619   3p red & blue   .70   .30

50th Anniv. of Arab Language Society — A620

1982, Dec. 25   Perf. 11½x11
1205   A620   6p multicolored   .80   .50

Year of the Aged — A621

1982, Dec. 25   Perf. 11x11½
1206   A621   23p multicolored   3.25   2.00

Post Day — A622

1983, Jan. 2   Perf. 11½
1207   A622   3p multicolored   .60   .25

15th Cairo Intl. Book Fair — A623

Perf. 11x11½
1983, Jan. 25   Photo.   Wmk. 342
1208   A623   3p blue & red   .65   .25

Police Day — A624

1983, Jan. 25   Perf. 11½x11
1209   A624   3p multicolored   .65   .25

16th Cairo Intl. Fair — A625

Perf. 11x11½
1983, Mar. 2   Photo.   Wmk. 342
1210   A625   3p multicolored   .65   .30

EGYPT

5th UN African Map
Conf., Cairo — A626

1983, Mar. 2
1211 A626 3p lt green & blue   .70 .30

A627

Design: African ministers of transport, communications and planning, 3rd conference.

1983, Mar. 8   *Perf. 11½x11*
1212 A627 23p green & blue   1.75 1.00

Victory in African Soccer
Cup — A628

1983, Mar. 20   *Perf. 11x11½*
1213 A628 3p Heading   .55 .30
1214 A628 3p Kick   .55 .30
 a. Pair, #1213-1214   1.25 1.25

World Health Day and
Natl. Blood Donation
Campaign — A629

Perf. 11x11½
1983, Apr. 2 Photo. Wmk. 342
1215 A629 3p olive & red   .70 .25

Org. of African
Trade Union
Unity — A630

Perf. 11½x11
1983, Apr. 21 Photo. Wmk. 342
1216 A630 3p multicolored   .65 .30

1st Anniv. of Sinai
Liberation — A631

1983, Apr. 25   *Perf. 11x11½*
1217 A631 3p multicolored   .70 .30

75th Anniv. of
Entomology
Society — A632

3p, Emblem (Holy Scarab).

1983, May 23
1218 A632 3p blue & black   .70 .30

Chrysanthemums
A633

1983, June 11 Photo. Perf. 11½x11
1219 A633 20m green & org red   .40 .25
For use on greeting cards.

5th African
Handball
Championship,
Cairo — A634

Perf. 11½x11
1983, July 22 Photo. Wmk. 342
1220 A634 6p brown & dk grn   .65 .30

31st Anniv. of
Revolution — A635

1983, July 23   *Perf. 11½*
1221 A635 3p multicolored   .45 .25

Simon Bolivar (1783-
1830) — A636

1983, Aug.   *Perf. 11x11½*
1222 A636 23p brown & dull grn   1.75 1.00

Centenary of
Arrival of Natl.
Hero Orabi in
Ceylon — A637

3p, Map, Orabi, El-Zahra School.

Perf. 11½x11
1983, Aug. 25 Photo. Wmk. 342
1223 A637 3p multicolored   .55 .25

Islamic Vase,
Museum
Building — A638

1983, Sept. 14 Photo. Perf. 11½x11
1224 A638 3p yel brn & dk brn   .85 .30
Reopening of Islamic Museum.

October War Against
Israel, 10th
Anniv. — A639

1983, Oct. 6   *Perf. 11½*
1225 A639 3p multicolored   .70 .25

2nd Pharaonic
Race — A640

1983, Oct. 17   *Perf. 11½*
1226 A640 23p multicolored   2.25 1.25

United Nations
Day — A641

1983, Oct. 24 Photo. Perf. 11
1227 A641 3p IMO, ships, horiz.   .60 .25
1228 A641 6p ITU, UPU   .75 .50
1229 A641 6p FAO, UN, grain   .75 .50
1230 A641 23p UN, ocean   2.50 1.75
 Nos. 1227-1230 (4)   4.60 3.00

4th World Karate
Championship,
Cairo — A642

1983, Nov. Photo. Perf. 13
1231 A642 3p multicolored   .70 .30

Intl. Palestinian
Cooperation
Day — A643

1983, Nov. 29 Photo. Perf. 13x13½
1232 A643 6p Dome of the Rock   1.00 .30

75th Anniv. of
Faculty of Fine
Arts,
Cairo — A644

1983, Nov. 30   *Perf. 13*
1233 A644 3p multicolored   .55 .25

75th Anniv. of Cairo
University — A645

1983, Nov. 30   *Perf. 11x11½*
1234 A645 3p multicolored   .55 .25
 a. Perf. 13¼x12¾

Intl. Egyptian
Society of
Mother and Child
Care — A646

1983, Nov. 30   *Perf. 11½x11*
1235 A646 3p multicolored   .55 .25

Org. of African Unity,
20th Anniv. — A647

Perf. 11x11½
1983, Dec. 20 Photo. Wmk. 342
1236 A647 3p multicolored   .55 .25

World Heritage Convention, 10th
Anniv. — A648

1983, Dec. 24
1237 A648 Strip of 3   2.25 2.25
 a. 3p Wood carving, Islamic   .70 .45
 b. 3p Coptic tapestry   .70 .45
 c. 3p Ramses II Thebes   .70 .45

Post Day — A649

Restored Forts: 6p, Quatbay. 23p, Mosque,
Salah El-Din.

1984, Jan. 2   *Perf. 13*
1238 A649 6p multicolored   .80 .45
1239 A649 23p multicolored   2.50 1.25

Misr Insurance
Co., 50
Anniv. — A650

1984, Jan. 14   *Perf. 11½x11*
1240 A650 3p multicolored   .55 .30

16th Cairo Intl. Book
Fair — A651

Perf. 13½x13
1984, Jan. 26 Photo. Wmk. 342
1241 A651 3p multicolored   .55 .25

17th Cairo Intl.
Fair — A652

Perf. 11½x11
1984, Mar. 10 Photo. Wmk. 342
1242 A652 3p multicolored   .55 .30

25th Anniv. of Asyut
University — A653

1984, Mar. 10   *Perf. 11x11½*
1243 A653 3p multicolored   .55 .25

75th Anniv. of
Cooperative
Unions — A654

1984, Mar. 17
1244 A654 3p multicolored   .55 .25

EGYPT

377

World Theater Day A655

Mahmoud Mokhtar (1891-1934), Sculptor A656

Perf. 11x11½, 11½x11
1984, Mar. 27   Photo.   Unwmk.
1245 A655 3p Masks   .55 .25
1246 A656 3p Pride of the Nile .55 .25

World Health Day and Fight Against Polio — A657

Perf. 11½x11
1984, Apr. 7   Photo.   Wmk. 342
1247 A657 3p Polio vaccine   1.00 .30

2nd Anniv. of Sinai Liberation — A658

1984, Apr. 25
1248 A658 3p Doves, map   .55 .25

Africa Day — A659

Perf. 12½x13½
1984, May 25   Photo.   Wmk. 342
1249 A659 3p Map, UN emblem   .55 .25

Satellite, Waves — A660

1984, May 31   Perf. 11x11½
1250 A660 3p multicolored   .55 .25
Radio broadcasting in Egypt, 50th anniv.

Carnations — A661

1984, June 1
1251 A661 2p red & green   .45 .25
For use on greeting cards.

Intl. Cairo Arab Arts Biennale — A662

1984, June 1   Perf. 13½x12½
1252 A662 3p multicolored   .55 .25

July Revolution, 32nd Anniv. — A663

3p, Atomic energy, agriculture.

Wmk. 342
1984, July 23   Photo.   Perf. 11
1253 A663 3p multicolored   .55 .25

A664

1984 Summer Olympics: a, Boxing. b, Basketball. c, Volleyball. d, Soccer.

1984, July 28
1254 Strip of 4 + label   5.75 5.75
a.-d. A664 3p any single   .45 .25

Size: 130x80mm
Imperf
1255 A664 30p like No. 1254   4.25 4.25

A665

Wmk. 342
1984, Aug. 13   Photo.   Perf. 11
1256 A665 3p bl & multi   .55 .25
1257 A665 23p grn & multi   2.50 1.40
2nd Genl. Conference of Egyptians Abroad, Aug. 11-15, Cairo.

Youth Hostels, 30th Anniv. — A666

Perf. 11x11½
1984, Sept. 22   Photo.   Wmk. 342
1258 A666 3p Youths, emblem   .55 .25

Egypt Tour Co., 50th Anniv. — A667

1984, Sept. 27
1259 A667 3p Emblem, sphinx   .60 .25

October War Against Israel, 11th Anniv. — A668

1984, Oct. 6
1260 A668 3p Map, eagle   .55 .25

Egypt-Sudan Unity — A669

1984, Oct. 12
1261 A669 3p Map of Nile, arms   .55 .25

UN Day — A670

Perf. 13½x12½
1984, Oct. 24   Photo.   Wmk. 342
1262 A670 3p UNICEF Emblem, child   .55 .25
UN campaign for infant survival.

Tanks, Emblem — A671

1984, Nov. 10
1263 A671 3p multicolored   .60 .25
Military Equipment Exhibition, Cairo, Nov. 10-14.

Tolon Mosque, Egypt — A672

1984, Dec. 23   Photo.   Perf. 11½x11
1264 A672 3p multicolored   .65 .25
Ahmed Ebn Tolon (A.D. 835-884), Gov. of Egypt, founder of Kataea City.

A673

1984, Dec. 23   Perf. 11x11½
1265 A673 3p multicolored   .55 .25
Kamel el-Kilany (1897-1959), author.

Globe and Congress Emblem — A674

Perf. 11x11½
1984, Dec. 26   Photo.   Wmk. 342
1266 A674 3p lt blue, ver & blk   .65 .25
29th Intl. Congress on the History of Medicine, Dec. 27, 1984-Jan. 1, 1985, Cairo.

Academy of the Arts, 25th Anniv. — A675

1984, Dec. 31   Perf. 13
1267 A675 3p Emblem in spotlights   .60 .25

A676

Design: Pharaoh Receiving Message, Natl. Postal Museum, Cairo.

1985, Jan. 2   Perf. 11½x11
1268 A676 3p brown, lt bl & ver   .65 .25
Postal Museum, 50th anniv.

Intl. Union of Architects, 15th Conference, Jan. 14-Feb. 15 — A677

1985, Jan. 20
1269 A677 3p multicolored   .60 .25

Seated Pharaonic Scribe — A678

1985, Jan. 22   Perf. 11x11½
1270 A678 3p brt org & dk blue grn   .70 .30
17th Intl. Book Fair, Jan. 22-Feb. 3, Cairo.

Wheat, Cogwheels, Fair Emblem — A679

1985, Mar. 9   Perf. 13½x13
1271 A679 3p multicolored   .60 .25
18th Intl. Fair, Mar. 9-22, Cairo.

Return of Sinai to Egypt, 3rd Anniv. — A680

1985, Apr. 25   Wmk. 342   Litho.
1272 A680 5p multicolored   1.00 .30

Ancient Artifacts — A681

A681a

A681b

378 EGYPT

A681c

A681e

A681g

A681i

A681k

A681m

A681d

A681f

A681h

A681j

A681l

A681n

A681o

Designs: 1p, God Mout, limestone sculpture, 360-340 B.C. 2p, No. 1281, Five wading birds, bas-relief. 3p, No. 1276, Seated statue, Ramses II, Temple of Luxor. No. 1276A, Vase. 8p, 15p, Slave bearing votive fruit offering, mural. 10p, Double-handled flask. 11p, Sculpted head of woman. No. 1282, Pitcher. 30p, 50p, Decanter. 35p, Temple of Karnak carved capitals. £1, Mosque.

1985-90 Photo. Unwmk. Perf. 11½
1273	A681	1p brown olive	.40	.25
1274	A681a	2p brt grnsh bl	.40	.25
1275	A681b	3p yel brn	.40	.25
1276	A681c	5p dk violet	.50	.25
1276A	A681d	5p bister	.40	.25
1277	A681e	8p pale ol grn, sep & brn	.75	.25
1278	A681f	10p dk vio & bl	.60	.25
1279	A681g	11p blksh pur	.90	.30
1280	A681h	15p pale yel, sep & brn	1.40	.30
1281	A681i	20p yel grn	.60	.30
1282	A681j	20p dk grn & yel	.60	.30
1283	A681k	30p ol bis & buff	.70	.30
1284	A681l	35p sep & pale yel	1.00	.60
1285	A681m	50p vio & buff	1.25	.50
1285A	A681n	£1 brn & buff	3.00	1.25
1286	A681o	£2 sepia & yel	6.00	2.00
		Nos. 1273-1286 (16)	18.90	7.60

No. 1276A is 18x23mm. No. 1278 exists dated "1990."
See Nos. 1467, 1470, 1472.
Issued: 1p, 2p, 3p, No. 1276, 8p, 11p, 15p, 5/1/85; 35p, 7/7/85; No. 1281, 4/1/86; 10p, 10/1/89; £2, 12/1/89; No. 1282, 2/1/90; 30p, 50p, 2/5/90; £1, 2/8/90; No. 1276A, 12/15/90.

Helwan University School of Music, 50th Anniv. — A682

1985, May 15
1287 A682 5p multicolored   .75 .30

El-Moulid Bride, Folk Doll — A683

1985
1288 A683 2p orange & multi   .50 .25
1289 A683 5p red & multi   .60 .30
Festivals 1985. Issued: 2p, 6/11; 5p, 8/10. For use on greeting cards.

A684

Winning teams: a, b, Cairo Sports Stadium. c, El-Zamalek Club, white uniform, 1983. d, Natl. Club, red uniform, 1984. e, El-Mokawiloon Club (Arab Contractor Club), orange uniform, 1984.

1985, June 17   Perf. 13½x13
1290 Strip of 5   5.50 5.50
  a.-e. A684 5p any single   .80 .50
1985 Africa Cup Soccer Championships. Cairo Sports Stadium, 25th anniv. Nos. 1290a-1290b have continuous design.

A685

1985, July 23   Perf. 11½x11
1291 A685 5p blue, brn & yel   .80 .30
Egyptian Television, 25th anniv. Egyptian Revolution, 33rd anniv.

Suez Canal Reopening, 10th Anniv. A686

Perf. 13x13½
1985, July 23   Litho.   Wmk. 342
1292 A686 5p multicolored   .80 .30
Egyptian Revolution, 33rd anniv.

Ahmed Hamdi Memorial Underwater Tunnel — A687

1985, July 23   Perf. 13½x13
1293 A687 5p blue, vio & org   .60 .25
Egyptian Revolution, 33rd anniv.

Souvenir Sheet
Aswan High Dam, 25th Anniv. A688

Wmk. 342
1985, July 23   Photo.   Imperf.
1294 A688 30p multicolored   4.00 4.00

Heart, Map, Olive Laurel, Conference Emblem — A689

1985, Aug. 10   Litho.   Perf. 13½x13
1295 A689 15p multicolored   1.25 .85
Egyptian Emigrants, 3rd general conference, Aug. 10-14, Cairo.

Natl. Tourism Ministry, 50th Anniv. A690

1985, Sept. 10   Perf. 13x13½
1296 A690 5p multicolored   .55 .30

October War Against Israel, 12th Anniv. A691

1985, Oct. 6
1297 A691 5p multicolored   .60 .30

Air Scouts Assoc., 30th Anniv. A692

1985, Oct. 15   Photo.   Perf. 11½
1298 A692 5p Emblem   .80 .30

UN Day, Meteorology Day — A693

5p, UN emblem, weather map.
1985, Oct. 24
1299 A693 5p multicolored   .55 .25

UN, 40th Anniv. — A694

1985, Oct. 24
1300 A694 15p multicolored   1.25 .85

Intl. Youth Year — A695

1985, Oct. 24
1301 A695 5p multicolored   .55 .25

A696

1985, Oct. 24
1302 A696 15p blue & int blue   1.25 .85
Intl. Communications Development Program.

2nd Intl. Dentistry Conference — A697

Emblem, hieroglyphics of Hassi Raa, 1st known dentist.
1985, Oct. 29   Perf. 11x11½
1303 A697 5p beige & pale bl vio   .75 .30

Emblem, Squash Player — A698

1985, Nov. 18   Photo.   Perf. 11½
1304 A698 5p multicolored   .65 .25
1985 World Squash Championships, Nov. 18-Dec. 4.

A699

1985, Nov. 2   Litho.   Perf. 13½x13
1305 A699 5p multicolored   .55 .30
4th Intl. Conference on the Biography and Sunna of Mohammed.

A700

1985, Dec. 1   Photo.   Perf. 11x11½
1306 A700 5p multicolored   .55 .30
1st Conference on the Development of Vocational Training.

EGYPT

Natl. Olympic Committee, 75th Anniv. — A701

1985, Dec. 28   *Photo.*   *Perf. 13x13½*
1307   A701   5p multicolored   .60   .30

18th Intl. Book Fair, Cairo — A702

1986, Jan. 21   *Perf. 11x11½*
1308   A702   5p Pharaonic scribe   .55   .25

CODATU III — A703

1986, Jan. 26   *Perf. 11½*
1309   A703   5p lt ol grn, ver & grnsh bl   .55   .25

3rd Intl. Conference on Urban Transportation in Developing Countries, Cairo.

Central Bank, 25th Anniv. A704

1986, Jan. 30   *Perf. 13x13½*
1310   A704   5p multicolored   .55   .25

Cairo Postal Traffic Center Inauguration A705

1986, Jan. 30   *Perf. 11½x11*
1311   A705   5p blue & dk brown   .55   .25

Pharaonic Mural, Btah Hotteb's Tomb at Saqqara — A706

1986, Feb. 27   *Photo.*   *Perf. 11½x11*
1312   A706   5p yel, gldn brn & brn   .70   .36

Faculty of Commerce, Cairo Univ., 75th anniv.

Cairo Intl. Fair, Mar. 8-21 — A707

1986, Mar. 8   *Litho.*   *Perf. 13½x13*
1313   A707   5p multicolored   .55   .25

Queen Nefertiti, Sinai — A708

Perf. 13x13½   **Wmk. 342**
1986, Apr. 25   *Litho.*
1314   A708   5p multicolored   .70   .30

Return of the Sinai to Egypt, 4th anniv.

Ministry of Health, 50th Anniv. — A709

1986, Apr. 10   *Perf. 13½x13*
1315   A709   5p multicolored   .55   .30

1986 Census A710

1986, May 26   *Photo.*   *Perf. 11½*
1316   A710   15p brn, grnsh bl & yel bis   1.00   .50

Egypt, Winner of African Soccer Cup — A711

No. 1317, English inscription below cup. No. 1318, Arabic inscription below cup.

1986, May 31   *Perf. 13½x13*
1317   A711   5p multicolored   .65   .45
1318   A711   5p multicolored   .65   .45
   a.   Pair, #1317-1318   1.50   1.50

Festivals, Roses — A712

1986, June 2   *Perf. 11½*
1319   A712   5p multicolored   .55   .25

For use on greeting cards.

World Environment Day — A713

15p, Emblem, smokestacks.

1986, June 5   *Perf. 13½x13*
1320   A713   15p multicolored   1.25   .50

July 23rd Revolution, 34th Anniv. — A714

1986, July 23   *Litho.*   *Perf. 13*
1321   A714   5p gray grn, scar & yel bis   .60   .25

6th African Roads Conference, Cairo, Sept. 22-26 — A715

Perf. 13½x13
1986, Sept. 21   *Litho.*   **Wmk. 342**
1322   A715   15p multicolored   1.25   .55

October War Against Israel, 13th Anniv. — A716

1986, Oct. 6   *Litho.*   *Perf. 13*
1323   A716   5p multicolored   1.00   .30

Engineers' Syndicate, 40th Anniv. — A717

1986, Oct. 11   *Photo.*   *Perf. 11½*
1324   A717   5p lt blue, brn & pale grn   .55   .25

Workers' Cultural Education Assoc., 25th Anniv. — A718

1986, Oct. 11   *Perf. 11x11½*
1325   A718   5p orange & rose vio   .55   .25

Intl. Peace Year — A719

1986, Oct. 24
1326   A719   5p blue, grn & pale sal   .55   .25

First Oil Well in Egypt, Cent. — A720

1986, Nov. 7   *Photo.*   *Perf. 11½*
1327   A720   5p dull grn, blk & pale yel   .65   .25

UN Child Survival Campaign A721

1986, Nov. 20   *Litho.*   *Perf. 13*
1328   A721   5p multicolored   .60   .25

Ahmed Amin, Philosopher — A722

1986, Dec. 20   *Perf. 11½*
1329   A722   5p pale grn, pale yel & brn   .55   .25

National Theater, 50th Anniv. — A723

1986, Dec. 20   *Perf. 13½x13*
1330   A723   5p multicolored   .55   .25

Post Day — A724

Step Pyramid, Saqqara, King Zoser.

Perf. 13x13½
1987, Jan. 2   *Litho.*   **Wmk. 342**
1331   A724   5p multicolored   .65   .30

19th Intl. Book Fair, Cairo — A725

1987, Jan. 25   *Litho.*   *Perf. 13*
1332   A725   5p multicolored   .60   .30

5th World Conference on Islamic Education A726

Wmk. 342
1987, Mar. 8   *Litho.*   *Perf. 13*
1333   A726   5p multicolored   .55   .25

20th Intl. Fair, Cairo — A727

5p, Good workers medal.

1987, Mar. 21　Photo.　Perf. 11½
1334　A727　5p multicolored　　.55　.25

Veteran's Day — A728

1987, Mar. 26
1335　A728　5p multicolored　　.55　.30

Intl. Gardens Inauguration, Nasser City — A729

1987, Mar. 30　Litho.　Perf. 13
1336　A729　15p multicolored　　1.10　.60

World Health Day — A730

No. 1337, Mother feeding child. No. 1338, Oral rehydration therapy.

1987, Apr. 7　Photo.　Perf. 11½
1337　A730　5p multicolored　　.55　.30
　　　　　Litho.
　　　　　　Perf. 13
1338　A730　5p multicolored　　.55　.30

A731

Natl. Team Victory at 1986 Intl. Soccer Championships — A732

Trophies: No. 1339a, Al Ahly Cup. No. 1339b, National Cup. No. 1339c, Al Zamalek Cup. No. 1340, Natl. flag, Cairo Stadium and trophies pictured on No. 1339.

1987, Apr. 19　Litho.　Perf. 13½x13
1339　A731　Strip of 3　　1.75　1.75
a.-c.　　5p any single　　.55　.30
　　　　Size: 115x85mm
　　　　　Imperf
1340　A732　30p multicolored　　4.00　4.00

Salah El Din Citadel, Pharoah's Is., Sinai.

1987, Apr. 25
1341　A733　5p sky blue & lt brown　.65　.30
Return of the Sinai to Egypt, 5th anniv.

Festivals — A734

1987, May 21　Photo.　Perf. 11½
1342　A734　5p Dahlia　　.55　.25

Cultural Heritage Exhibition A735

1987, June 17　Litho.　Perf. 13x13½
1343　A735　15p multicolored　　1.00　1.00

Tourism Year A736

a, Column and Sphinx, Alexandria. b, St. Catherine's Monastery, Mt. Sinai. c, Colossi of Thebes. d, Temple of Theban Triad, Luxor.

1987, June 18
1344　A736　Block of 4　　5.25　5.25
a.-d.　　15p any single　　1.10　.90
See No. C187.

Loyalty Day — A737

1987, June 26　Perf. 13
1345　A737　5p multicolored　　.55　.25
General Intelligence Service, 32nd anniv.

Industry-Agriculture Exhibition — A738

1987, July 23　Photo.　Perf. 11½
1346　A738　5p grn, dull org & blk　.55　.25

Intl. Year of Shelter for the Homeless — A739

1987, Sept. 2　Litho.　Perf. 13
1347　A739　5p multicolored　　.55　.25
World Architects' Day.

Aida, Performed at Al Ahram Pyramid, Giza — A740

Radamis and troops returning from Ethiopia.

1987, Sept. 21
1348　A740　15p multicolored　　1.50　.65

Size: 70x70mm
Imperf
1349　A740　30p multicolored　　10.00　10.00

Greater Cairo Subway Inauguration A741

1987, Sept. 27　Perf. 13x13½
1350　A741　5p multicolored　　1.20　.30

Industry Day — A742

1987, Oct. 1　Perf. 13
1351　A742　5p multicolored　　.55　.25

Battle of Hettin, 800th Anniv. — A743

1987, Oct. 6　Photo.　Perf. 11x11½
1352　A743　5p multicolored　　.70　.30

UPU Emblem — A744

Perf. 11½
1987, Oct. 24　Unwmk.　Photo.
1353　A744　5p multicolored　　.55　.25
UN Executive Council, 40th anniv.; UPU Consultative Council, 30th anniv.

16th Art Biennial of Alexandria — A745

1987, Nov. 7　Litho.　Perf. 13½x13
1354　A745　5p multicolored　　.55　.25

Second Intl. Defense Equipment Exhibition, Cairo, Nov. 9-13 — A746

Perf. 13x13½
1987, Nov. 9　Litho.　Unwmk.
1355　A746　5p multicolored　　.60　.25

2nd Pan-Arab Congress on Anaesthesia and Intensive Care — A747

Unwmk.
1987, Dec. 1　Litho.　Perf. 13
1356　A747　5p multicolored　　.65　.30

Intl. Orthopedic and Traumatology Conference — A748

1987, Dec. 1　Perf. 13½x13
1357　A748　5p gray, red brn & bl　.55　.25

Selim Hassan (1887-1961), Egyptologist, and Hieroglyphs A749

Abdel Hamid Badawi (1887-1965), Jurist, and Scales of Justice A750

Perf. 13½x13
1987, Dec. 30　Litho.　Unwmk.
1358　A749　5p multicolored　　.55　.25
1359　A750　5p multicolored　　.55　.25

Stamp Day 1988 A751

Pyramids of the Pharaohs and: a, Cheops. b, Chefren. c, Mycerinus. No. 1360 has a continuous design.

1988, Jan. 2
1360　A751　Strip of 3　　5.50　5.50
a.-c.　　15p, any single　　1.40　.90

Afro-Asian Peoples Solidarity Organization, 30th Anniv. A752

1988, Jan. 10　Perf. 13x13½
1361　A752　15p multicolored　　1.00　.55

20th Intl. Book Fair, Cairo — A753

1988, Jan. 26　Perf. 13½x13
1362　A753　5p multicolored　　.55　.25

Martrans (Natl. Shipping Line), 25th Anniv. — A754

Unwmk.
1988, Mar. 3　Litho.　Perf. 13
1363　A754　5p multicolored　　.85　.25

EGYPT

Cairo Intl.
Fair — A755

1988, Mar. 12   Photo.   Perf. 11½x11
1364 A755 5p multicolored   .55 .25

World Health Day 1988:
Diabetes — A756

Perf. 11x11½
1988, Apr. 7   Photo.   Unwmk.
1365 A756 5p multicolored   .55 .25

Prince, Fig Tree — A757

1988, Apr. 17   Perf. 11½
1366 A757 5p grn, brn org & brn   .55 .25
1988 Festival. For use on greeting cards.

African Postal
Union, 25th
Anniv.
A758

1988, Apr. 23   Litho.   Perf. 13x13½
1367 A758 15p brt blue   1.00 1.00

Oppose Racial Discrimination — A759

1988, May 25   Photo.   Perf. 11½
1368 A759 5p multicolored   .50 .25

Taw Fek-Hakem
(1902-1987),
Playwright,
Novelist — A760

1988, Aug. 5   Photo.   Perf. 11½
1369 A760 5p brt grn bl & org brn   .60 .25
See Nos. 1383-1384, 1479-1480, 1486,
1500-1502, 1543-1546.

Faculty of Art
Education, 50th
Anniv. — A761

Perf. 11½
1988, Sept. 10   Photo.   Unwmk.
1370 A761 5p multicolored   .50 .25

A762

1988 Summer Olympics,
Seoul — A763

1988, Sept. 17   Litho.   Perf. 13
1371 A762 15p multicolored   1.25 1.25
Size: 96x91mm
Imperf.
1372 A763 30p multicolored   6.25 6.25
No. 1371 is airmail.

October War
Against
Israel, 15th
Anniv.
A764

Perf. 13x13½
1988, Oct. 6   Litho.   Unwmk.
1373 A764 5p multicolored   .55 .35

A765

Opening
of the
Opera House
A766

1988, Oct. 10   Perf. 11½
1374 A765 5p multicolored   .55 .30
Size: 112x75mm
Imperf
1375 A766 50p multicolored   3.50 3.50

Intl. Red Cross
and Red Crescent
Organizations,
125th
Anniv. — A767

Perf. 11½
1988, Oct. 24   Photo.   Unwmk.
1376 A767 5p green, blk & red   .50 .25

WHO, 40th
Anniv. — A768

1988, Oct. 24   Perf. 11x11½
1377 A768 20p multicolored   1.25 1.10

Naguib
Mahfouz,
1988 Nobel
Prize Winner
for Literature
A769

1988, Nov. 7   Litho.   Perf. 13x13½
1378 A769 5p multicolored   .50 .25
See No. C190.

Arab
Scouting
Organization,
75th Anniv.
A770

1988, Nov. 10
1379 A770 25p multicolored   1.25 1.25

Return of
Taba to
Egypt
A771

1988, Nov. 15
1380 A771 5p multicolored   .50 .25

Intl. Conference
on Orthopedic
Surgery, Cairo,
Nov. 15-
18 — A772

1988, Nov. 15   Photo.   Perf. 11½x11
1381 A772 5p pale yel, brt yel grn & brn   .60 .25

A773

1988, Dec. 3   Perf. 11½
1382 A773 5p multicolored   .50 .25
Ministry of Agriculture, 75th anniv.

A774

Perf. 13½x13
1988, Dec. 29   Litho.   Unwmk.
1383 A774 5p green & red brn   .45 .25
1384 A774 5p green & red brn   .45 .25
 a. Pair, #1383-1384   1.00 1.00

Famous Men: No. 1383, Mohamed Hussein
Hekal (1888-1956), author, politician. No.
1384, Ahmed Lotfi El Sayed (1872-1963), educator, politician.

Stamp Day — A775

Statues: 5p, Statue of K. Abr, a priest, 5th
cent. No. 1386, Queen Nefert, 4th Dynasty.
No. 1387, King Ra Hoteb, 4th Dynasty.

1989, Jan. 2
1385 A775 5p multicolored   .50 .30
1386 A775 25p multicolored   1.60 1.00
1387 A775 25p multicolored   1.60 1.00
 a. Pair, #1386-1387   3.50 3.50
    Nos. 1385-1387 (3)   3.70 2.30

A776

1989, Jan. 10
1388 A776 5p dull green   .55 .25
Jawaharlal Nehru (1889-1964), 1st Prime
Minister of independent India.

Nile Hilton
Hotel, 30th
Anniv.
A777

1989, Feb. 22   Litho.   Perf. 13x13½
1389 A777 5p multicolored   .45 .25

Return of Taba to
Egypt — A778

Unwmk.
1989, Mar. 15   Litho.   Perf. 13
1390 A778 5p multicolored   .45 .25

2nd Stage of
Cairo
Subway — A779

1989, Apr. 12   Litho.   Perf. 13
1391 A779 5p multicolored   1.00 .30

Lantern — A780

1989, May 4   Photo.   Perf. 11½
1392 A780 5p multicolored   .45 .25
1989 Festival. For use on greeting cards.

1st Arab Olympic
Day — A781

1989, May 24
1393 A781 5p tan, blk & dull grn   .50 .25

Interparliamentary Union,
Cent. — A782

Pyramids and the Parliament Building,
Cairo.

382 EGYPT

1989, June 29 Litho. Perf. 13x13½
1394 A782 25p shown 1.60 1.25
Size: 87x76mm
Imperf
1395 A782 25p multi, diff. 2.75 2.75

French Revolution, Bicent. A783

1989, July 14 Photo. Perf. 11½
1396 A783 25p multicolored 1.50 1.25
No. 1396 is an airmail issue.

African Development Bank, 25th Anniv. — A784

Perf. 11½
1989, Oct. 1 Photo. Unwmk.
1397 A784 10p multicolored .45 .25

A785

October War Against Israel, 16th Anniv. — A786

1989, Oct. 6 Perf. 13
1398 Strip of 3 1.50 1.50
  a. A785 10p shown .50 .25
  b. A786 10p shown .50 .25
  c. A785 10p Battle scene .50 .25
See No. 1424.

Aga Khan Award for Architecture — A788

Perf. 11½
1989, Oct. 15 Photo. Unwmk.
1400 A788 35p multicolored 1.25 .60

Natl. Health Insurance Plan, 25th Anniv. — A789

1989, Oct. 24
1401 A789 10p blk, gray & ver .50 .25

World Post Day — A790

1989, Oct. 24 Perf. 11x11½
1402 A790 35p blue, blk & brt yel 1.00 .50

Statues of Memnon, Thebes A791

Perf. 11½
1989, Nov. 12 Photo. Unwmk.
1403 A791 10p lt vio, blk & brt yel grn .50 .25
Intl. Cong. & Convention Assoc. (ICCA) annual convention, Nov. 11-18, Cairo.

Cairo University School of Agriculture, Cent. — A792

1989, Nov. 15
1404 A792 10p pale grn, blk & brt yel .45 .25

Cairo Intl. Conference Center — A793

1989, Nov. 20 Perf. 11½x11
1405 A793 5p multicolored .45 .25

Road Safety Soc., 20th Anniv. A794

1989, Nov. 20 Perf. 11½
1406 A794 10p multicolored .45 .25

Alexandria University, 50th Anniv. — A795

1989, Nov. 30 Perf. 11x11½
1407 A795 10p pale blue & tan .45 .25

Portrait of Pasha, Monument in Opera Square, Cairo — A796

Perf. 11½x11
1989, Dec. 31 Photo. Unwmk.
1408 A796 10p multicolored .45 .25
Ibrahim Pasha (d. 1838), army commander from 1825 to 1828.

Famous Men
A797 A798

1989, Dec. 31 Perf. 11x11½
1409 A797 10p grn & dk ol grn .45 .25
1410 A798 10p golden brown .45 .25
Abd El-Rahman El-Rafei (b. 1889), historian (No. 1409); Abdel Kader El Mazni (b. 1889), man of letters (No. 1410).
See Nos. 1431-1432.

Statue of Priest Ranofr A799 Relief Sculpture of Betah Hoteb A800

1990, Jan. 2 Perf. 13½x13
1411 A799 30p multicolored 1.00 .40
1412 A800 30p multicolored 1.00 .40
  a. Pair, #1411-1412 2.75 2.75
Stamp Day.

Arab Cooperation Council, 1st Anniv. A801

Perf. 13x13½
1990, Feb. 16 Photo. Unwmk.
1413 A801 10p multicolored .45 .25
1414 A801 35p multicolored 1.25 .60

Emblem, Conference Center — A802

Perf. 13½x13
1990, Mar. 10 Litho. Unwmk.
1415 A802 10p brt yel grn, red & blk .50 .25
Size: 80x59mm
Imperf
1416 A802 30p multicolored 1.50 1.50
African Parliamentary Union 13th general conference, Mar. 10-15.

Road Safety Emblems — A803

1990, Mar. 19 Photo. Perf. 11x11½
1417 A803 10p multicolored .60 .25
Intl. Conference on Road Safety & Accidents in Developing Countries, Mar. 19-22.

Egyptian Wild Daisies — A804

1990, Apr. 24 Perf. 11½
1418 A804 10p multicolored .45 .25
1990 Festival. For use on greeting cards.

Sinai Liberation, 8th Anniv. — A805

1990, Apr. 25
1419 A805 10p blue, blk & yel grn .50 .25

World Cup Soccer Championships, Italy — A806

1990, May 26 Litho. Perf. 13½x13
1420 A806 10p multicolored .40 .25
Souvenir Sheet
Imperf
1421 A806 50p Flags, trophy 2.25 2.25

World Basketball Championships, Argentina — A807

1990, Aug. 8 Perf. 13x13½
1422 A807 10p multicolored .50 .25

Natl. Population Council, 5th Anniv. — A808

1990, Sept. 15 Perf. 13½x13
1423 A808 10p brown & yel grn .50 .25

October War Against Israel Type
1990, Oct. 6 Litho. Perf. 13x13½
1424 Strip of 3 1.75 1.75
  a. A785 10p Bunker, tank .40 .25
  b. A786 10p like #1398b .40 .25
  c. A785 10p Troops with flag, flame thrower .40 .25

Egyptian Postal Service, 125th Anniv. A809

1990, Oct. 9
1425 A809 10p lt blue, blk & red .50 .25

Dar El Eloum Faculty, Cent. — A810

1990, Oct. 13 Litho. Perf. 13
1426 A810 10p multicolored .45 .25

UN Development Program, 40th Anniv. A811

ITU, 125th Anniv. — A812

EGYPT

1990, Oct. 24   *Perf. 11½*
1427 A811 30p yel, bl grn & yel grn   .90 .30

Perf. 13
1428 A812 30p multicolored   .90 .30
UN Day.

Ras Mohammed Natl. Park — A813

Designs: a, Crown butterfly fish. b, Lionfish. c, Twobar anemone fish. d, Grouper.

1990, Dec. 22   *Litho.*   *Perf. 13*
1429 A813 Block of 4   3.50 3.50
   a.-b.   10p any single   .50 .30
   c.-d.   20p any single   .80 .40

Day of the Disabled — A814

1990, Dec. 15   *Photo.*   *Perf. 11*
1430 A814 10p multicolored   .50 .25

Mohamed Fahmy Abdel Meguid Bey, Medical Reformer A815

Nabaweya Moussa (1890-1951), Educator A816

Perf. 11x11½
1990, Dec. 30   *Unwmk.*
1431 A815 10p Prus bl, brn & org   .40 .25
1432 A816 10p grn, org brn & blk   .40 .25

Stamp Day   A817

1991, Jan. 1   *Litho.*   *Perf. 13½x13*
1433 A817 5p No. 1   .30 .25
1434 A817 10p No. 2   .45 .25
1435 A817 20p No. 3   .60 .40
   a.   Strip of 3, #1433-1435   1.75 1.75
See Nos. 1443-1446, 1459-1460.

Veterinary Surgeon Syndicate, 50th Anniv. A818

1991, Feb. 28   *Photo.*   *Perf. 11½*
1436 A818 10p multicolored   .45 .25

Syndicate of Journalists, 50th Anniv. A819

1991, Apr.   *Photo.*   *Perf. 11½*
1437 A819 10p multicolored   .40 .25

Narcissus — A820

1991, Apr. 13
1438 A820 10p multicolored   .40 .25
1991 Festival. For use on greeting cards.

Giza Zoo, Cent. — A821

1991, June 15   *Litho.*   *Imperf.*
Size: 80x63mm
1439 A821 50p multicolored   4.00 4.00

Mahmoud Mokhtar (1891-1934), Sculptor A822

Mohamed Nagi (1888-1956), Painter — A823

Perf. 13x13½, 13½x13
1991, June 11   *Litho.*
1440 A822 10p multicolored   .40 .25
1441 A823 10p multicolored   .40 .25

Faculty of Engineering A824

1991, June 30   *Perf. 13x13½*
1442 A824 10p multicolored   .40 .25

Stamp Day Type
Designs: No. 1443, No. 5. No. 1444, No. 4. No. 1445, No. 7. No. 1446, Sphinx, pyramid, No. 6.

1991, July 23   *Perf. 13*
1443 A817 10p orange & blk   .40 .25
1444 A817 10p yellow & blk   .40 .25
1445 A817 10p lilac & blk   .40 .25
   a.   Strip of 3, #1443-1445   1.40 1.40

Size: 80x60mm
Imperf
1446 A817 50p multicolored   2.25 1.75
Nos. 1443-1446 (4)   3.45 2.50

Mohamed Abdel el Wahab, Musician — A825

1991, Aug. 28   *Perf. 13*
1447 A825 10p multicolored   .55 .25

5th Africa Games, Cairo A826

No. 1448, Karate, judo. No. 1449, Table tennis, field hockey, tennis. No. 1450, Running, gymnastics, swimming. No. 1451, Soccer, basketball, shooting. No. 1452, Boxing, wrestling, weightlifting. No. 1453, Handball, cycling, volleyball. No. 1454, Games mascot, vert. No. 1455, Mascot, emblem, torch.

Perf. 13x13½
1991, Sept.   *Litho.*   *Unwmk.*
1448 A826 10p multicolored   .40 .25
1449 A826 10p multicolored   .40 .25
   a.   Pair, #1448-1449   .90 .90
1450 A826 10p multicolored   .40 .25
1451 A826 10p multicolored   .40 .25
   a.   Pair, #1450-1451   .90 .90
1452 A826 10p multicolored   .40 .25
1453 A826 10p multicolored   .40 .25
   a.   Pair, #1452-1453   .90 .90

Perf. 13½x13
1454 A826 10p multicolored   .45 .25

Size: 80x60mm
Imperf
1455 A826 50p multicolored   1.75 1.75
Nos. 1448-1455 (8)   4.60 3.50

Intl. Statistics Institute, 48th Session — A827

1991, Sept. 9
1456 A827 10p multicolored   .40 .25

Opening of Dar Al Eftaa Religious Center — A828

1991, Oct. 1   *Litho.*   *Perf. 13*
1457 A828 10p multicolored   .40 .25

October War Against Israel, 18th Anniv. A829

1991, Oct. 6   *Perf. 13x13½*
1458 A829 10p multicolored   .55 .25

Stamp Day Type
Designs: 10p, No. 6. £1, Stamp exhibition emblem, hieroglyphics, pyramids, sphinx.

1991, Oct. 7   *Perf. 13*
1459 A817 10p blue & black   .50 .25

Size: 90x60mm
Imperf
1460 A817 £1 multicolored   5.50 5.50
Natl. Philatelic Exhibition, Cairo, 10/7-12 (No. 1460). No. 1460 sold only with £1 admission ticket at exhibition.

Ancient Artifacts Type of 1985
Perf. 11½x11
1990-92   *Unwmk.*   *Photo.*
Size: 18x23mm
1467 A681 10p like #1278   .60 .25
1470 A681 30p like #1283   1.00 1.00
1472 A681 50p like #1285   1.75 1.75
Nos. 1467-1472 (3)   3.35 3.00

Issued: 10p, 1/20/90; 30p, 9/1/91; 50p, 7/11/92.

United Nations Day — A830

No. 1477, Brick hands housing people. No. 1478, Woman learning to write, fingerprint, vert.

Perf. 13x13½, 13½x13
1991, Oct. 24   *Litho.*
1476 A830 10p shown   .40 .25
1477 A830 10p multicolored   .40 .25
1478 A830 10p multicolored   .40 .25
Nos. 1476-1478 (3)   1.20 .75

Famous Men Type of 1988
Inscribed "1991"

Designs: No. 1479, Dr. Zaki Mubarak (1891-1952), writer and poet. No. 1480, Abd El Kader Hamza (1879-1941), journalist.

1991, Dec. 23   *Photo.*   *Perf. 13½x13*
1479 A760 10p olive brown   .40 .25
1480 A760 10p gray   .40 .25

A831

Post Day — A832

1992, Jan. 2   *Litho.*   *Perf. 13*
1481 A831 10p shown   .40 .25
1482 A831 45p Bird mosaic   1.00 1.00

Perf. 14
1483 A832 70p multicolored   1.75 1.75
Nos. 1481-1483 (3)   3.15 3.00
Nos. 1482-1483 are airmail.

Police Day — A833

1992, Jan. 25   *Perf. 14*
1484 A833 10p multicolored   .40 .25

25th Cairo Intl. Fair — A834

1992, Feb. 15   *Litho.*   *Perf. 14*
1485 A834 10p multicolored   .40 .25

Famous Men Type of 1988
Inscribed "1992"
10p, Sayed Darwish (1892-1923), musician.

1992, Mar. 17   *Photo.*   *Perf. 14x13½*
1486 A760 10p dull org & olive   .40 .25

Festivals — A835

1992, Mar. 18   *Perf. 11½*
1487 A835 10p Egyptian hoopoe   .40 .25
For use on greeting cards.

EGYPT

World Health Day — A836

1992, Apr. 20   Litho.   *Perf. 13*
1488 A836 10p multicolored   .50   .25

Aswan Dam, 90th Anniv. — A837

1992, July   Litho.   *Perf. 13*
1489 A837 10p No. 487   .50   .25

20th Arab Scout Jamboree A838

1992, July 10   *Perf. 13x13½*
1490 A838 10p multicolored   .50   .25

A839
70p, Summer Games' emblem.

1992, July 20   *Perf. 13½x13*
1491 A839 10p multicolored   .45   .25
    Size: 80x60mm
    Imperf
1492 A839 70p multicolored   5.00   2.50
1992 Summer Olympics, Barcelona.

El Helal Magazine, Cent. — A840

1992, Sept. 14   Litho.   *Perf. 13½x13*
1493 A840 10p multicolored   .45   .25

Alexandria World Festival A841

1992, Sept. 27   *Perf. 13x13½*
1494 A841 70p multicolored   1.60   1.60

Congress of Federation of World and American Travel Companies, Cairo A842

1992, Sept. 20
1495 A842 70p multicolored   1.50   1.50

World Post Day — A843

1992, Oct. 9   Litho.   *Perf. 13*
1496 A843 10p dk bl, lt bl & blk   .45   .25

Children's Day — A844

1992, Oct. 24   Litho.   *Perf. 13½x13*
1497 A844 10p multicolored   .55   .25

Intl. Conference on Food, Agriculture and World Health — A845

1992, Oct. 24   *Perf. 13*
1498 A845 70p multicolored   1.50   1.50

A846

1992, Nov. 21   *Perf. 13½x13*
1499 A846 10p multicolored   .50   .25
20th Arab Scout Conference, Cairo.

Famous Men Type of 1988
Inscribed "1992"

No. 1500, Talaat Harb, economist. No. 1501, Mohamed Taymour, writer. No. 1502, Dr. Ahmed Zaki Abu Shadi (with glasses), physician & poet.

1992, Dec. 23   Photo.   *Perf. 13½x13*
1500 A760 10p blue & brown   .40   .25
1501 A760 10p citron & blue gray   .40   .25
1502 A760 10p citron & blue gray   .40   .25
   a. Pair, #1501-1502   .90   .90
     Nos. 1500-1502 (3)   1.20   .75

A847

Pharaohs: 10p, Sesostris I. 45p, Amenemhet III. 70p, Hur I.

1993, Jan. 2   Litho.   *Perf. 13½x13*
1503 A847 10p brown & yellow   .45   .25
1504 A847 45p brown & yellow   .75   .65
1505 A847 70p brown & yellow   1.20   1.00
   a. Strip of 3, #1503-1505   3.00   3.00
Post Day.

25th Intl. Book Fair, Cairo — A848

1993, Jan. 26   Litho.   *Perf. 13½x13*
1506 A848 15p multicolored   .40   .25

A849   A849a

A849b   A849c

A849d   A849e

A849f   A849g

A849h

Artifacts: A849, Bust. A849a, Sphinx. A849b, Bust of princess. A849c, Ramses II. A849d, Queen Ti. A849e, Horemheb. A849f, As A849b. A849g, Amenhotep III. £1, Head of a woman. £2, Woman wearing headdress. £5, Pharaonic capital.

Photo., Litho. (#1511)
1993-99   Unwmk.   *Perf. 11½x11,*
1507 A849   5p multi   .55   .25
1508 A849a 15p brn & bis   .55   .25
1509 A849a 15p brn & bis   .30   .25
1510 A849b 25p brn & org
         brn   .35   .25
1511 A849c 55p blk & bl   .90   .50
     Size: 21x25mm
     Perf. 11¼
1512 A849   5p dp cl &
         brick red   .50   .25
1513 A849d 5p brown   .30   .25
   a. Wmk. 342   .30   .25
1514 A849a 15p brn & bis   .50   .25
1515 A849e 20p blk & gray   .30   .25
   a. Wmk. 342   .30   .25
1516 A849f 25p brn & org
         brn   .70   .30
1517 A849f 25p black brown   .30   .25
1518 A849c 55p blk & lt bl   .60   .60
1519 A849g 75p blk & brn   .90   .80
     Perf. 11½
1520 A849h £1 slate & blk   2.25   2.25
1521 A849h £2 brn & grn   5.00   5.00
1521A A849h £5 brn & gold   10.00   10.00
    Nos. 1507-1521A (16)   24.00   21.70

Warning: Avoid using watermark fluid on Nos. 1513-1513a and 1515-1515a. Images will be adversely affected.
Body of Sphinx on Nos. 1509, 1514 stops above value, and extends through value on No. 1508.
Issued: Nos. 1507-1508, 2/1; No. 1509, 3/10; £1, £2, 4/1; No. 1511, 7/1/93; £5, 8/1/93; Nos. 1512, 1514, 1518, 10/30/94; No. 1516, 6/25/94; 20p, 2/1/97; 75p, 3/25/97; No. 1517, 1998; Nos. 1513a, 1515a, 1999.
See Nos. C204-C206.

Architects' Association, 75th Anniv. A850

1993, Feb. 28   Litho.   *Perf. 13x13½*
1522 A850 15p multicolored   .45   .25

New Building for Ministry of Foreign Affairs — A851

1993, Mar. 15   *Perf. 13*
1523 A851 15p multicolored   .45   .25
1524 A851 80p multicolored   1.50   1.50
Diplomacy Day (No. 1523). No. 1524 is airmail.

Feasts — A852

1993, Mar. 20   Litho.   *Perf. 13x13½*
1525 A852 15p Opuntia   .45   .25
For use on greeting cards.

Newspaper, Le Progres Egyptien, Cent. A853

1993, Apr. 15   Litho.   *Perf. 13x13½*
1526 A853 15p multicolored   .40   .25

A854

1993, May 15   Litho.   *Perf. 13x13½*
1527 A854 15p multicolored   .50   .25
World Telecommunications Day.

A855

1993, June 15   Litho.   *Perf. 13½x13*
1528 A855 15p multicolored   .45   .25
UN Conference on Human Rights, Vienna.

Organization of African Unity — A856

1993, June 26   *Perf. 13*
1529 A856 15p yel grn & multi   .45   .25
1530 A856 80p red violet & multi   1.10   1.10
No. 1530 is airmail.

EGYPT

World PTT Conference, Cairo — A857

1993, Sept. 4   Litho.   Perf. 13
1531   A857   15p multicolored   .45   .25

Salah El-Din El Ayubi (1137-1193), Dome of the Rock — A858

1993, Sept. 4
1532   A858   55p multicolored   1.10   1.10

A859

1993, Oct. 6
1533   A859   15p multicolored   .50   .25

October War Against Israel, 20th Anniv.

A860

1993, Oct. 12   Perf. 13½x13
1534   A860   15p cream & multi   .45   .25
1535   A860   55p silver & multi   1.10   .55
1536   A860   80p gold & multi   1.50   .85

Imperf
Size: 90x70mm
1537   A860   80p multicolored   2.00   2.00
Nos. 1534-1537 (4)   5.05   3.65

Pres. Mohamed Hosni Mubarak, Third Term.

Reduction of Natural Disasters — A861

1993, Oct. 24   Litho.   Perf. 13
1538   A861   80p multicolored   1.10   1.10

Electricity in Egypt, Cent. — A862

1993, Oct. 24   Perf. 13½x13
1539   A862   15p multicolored   .45   .25

Intl. Conference on Big Dams, Cairo A863

1993, Nov. 19   Litho.   Perf. 13
1540   A863   15p multicolored   .45   .25

35th Military Intl. Soccer Championship — A864

1993, Dec. 1   Litho.   Perf. 13x13½
1541   A864   15p orange & multi   .40   .25
1542   A864   15p Trophy, emblem   .40   .25

9th Men's Junior World Handball Championship (No. 1542).

Famous Men Type of 1988
Inscribed "1993"

No. 1543, Abdel Aziz Al-Bishry. No. 1544, Mohammad Farid Abu Hadid. No. 1545, Mahmud Beyram el-Tunsi. No. 1546, Ali Moubarak.

1993, Dec. 25   Perf. 13½x13
1543   A760   15p blue   .40   .25
1544   A760   15p blue black   .40   .25
1545   A760   15p light violet   .40   .25
1546   A760   15p green   .40   .25
Nos. 1543-1546 (4)   1.60   1.00

Post Day — A865

15p, Amenhotep III. 55p, Queen Hatshepsut. 80p, Thutmose III.

1994, Jan. 2
1547   A865   15p multicolored   .45   .25
1548   A865   55p multicolored   1.10   .30
1549   A865   80p multicolored   1.75   .40
Nos. 1547-1549 (3)   3.30   .95

Congress of Egyptian Sedimentary Geology Society A866

1994, Jan. 4   Litho.   Perf. 13x13½
1550   A866   15p multicolored   .45   .25

Birds — A867

1994, Mar. 3   Litho.   Perf. 13
1551   A867   Block of 4, #a.-d.   2.75   2.75
   a.   15p Egyptian swallow   .45   .30
   b.   15p Fire crest   .45   .30
   c.   15p Rose-ringed parrot   .45   .30
   d.   15p Goldfinch   .45   .30

Festivals 1994.

Arab Scouting, 40th Anniv. — A868

1994, Mar. 25   Perf. 13½x13
1552   A868   15p multicolored   .45   .25

27th Cairo Intl. Fair — A869

1994, Apr. 9   Litho.   Perf. 13½x13
1553   A869   15p multicolored   .45   .25

A870

1994, Apr. 15   Litho.   Perf. 13
1554   A870   15p green & brown   .45   .25

1994 African Telecommunications Exhibition, Cairo.

A871

1994, Apr. 30   Litho.   Perf. 13
1555   A871   15p grn, blk & blue   .45   .25

Natl. Afforestation Campaign.

5th Arab Energy Conference, Cairo. — A872

1994, July 5   Litho.   Perf. 13
1556   A872   15p multicolored   .45   .25

Signing of Washington Accord for Palestinian Self-Rule in Gaza and Jericho A873

1994, May 4   Litho.   Perf. 13
1557   A873   15p multicolored   .60   .25

18th Biennial Art Exhibition, Alexandria A874

1994, May 21
1558   A874   15p yel, blk & gray   .45   .25

Organization of African Unity — A875

1994, May 25
1559   A875   15p multicolored   .45   .25

Natl. Reading Festival A876

1994, June 15
1560   A876   15p multicolored   .45   .25

ILO, 75th Anniv. — A877

1994, June 28   Litho.   Perf. 13½x13
1561   A877   15p multicolored   .45   .25

Intl. Conference on Population and Development, Cairo A878

15p, Conference, UN emblems. 80p, Drawings, hieroglyphics, conference emblem.

1994, Sept. 5   Litho.   Perf. 13
1562   A878   15p multi   .45   .25
1563   A878   80p multi, vert.   1.10   .75

No. 1563 is airmail.

World Junior Squash Championships — A879

1994, Sept. 14   Litho.   Perf. 13
1564   A879   15p multicolored   .45   .25

World Post Day — A880

1994, Oct. 9   Litho.   Perf. 13
1565   A880   15p multicolored   .50   .25

EGYPT

Intl. Red Cross & Red Crescent Societies, 75th Anniv. — A881

1994, Oct. 24
1566 A881 80p multicolored 1.50 .90

Akhbar El-Yom Newspaper, 50th Anniv. A882

1994, Nov. 11
1567 A882 15p multicolored .45 .25

African Field Hockey Club Championships — A883

1994, Nov. 14 *Litho.* *Perf. 13*
1568 A883 15p multicolored .45 .25

A884

Opera Aida, by Verdi A885

1994, Nov. 26
1569 A884 15p multicolored .45 .25
Imperf
Size: 58x69mm
1570 A885 80p multicolored 2.25 2.25
No. 1570 is airmail.

Intl. Olympic Committee, Cent. — A886

1994, Dec. 10 *Perf. 13*
1571 A886 15p multicolored .45 .25

Egyptian Youth Hostels Assoc., 40th Anniv. — A887

1994, Dec. 24
1572 A887 15p multicolored .45 .25

Intl. Speed Ball Federation, 10th Anniv. — A888

1994, Dec. 25
1573 A888 15p multicolored .45 .25

African Development Bank, 30th Anniv. — A889

1994, Dec. 26
1574 A889 15p multicolored .45 .25

Opening of Suez Canal, 125th Anniv. A890

Design: 80p, Map, inaugural ceremony.
1994, Dec. 27
1575 A890 15p multicolored .65 .25
1576 A890 80p multicolored 1.25 .75
No. 1576 is airmail.

Famous Men — A891

No. 1577, Hassan Fathy, engineer. No. 1578, Mahmoud Taimour, writer.
1994, Dec. 29
1577 A891 15p multicolored .40 .25
1578 A891 15p multicolored .40 .25

Post Day — A892

15p, Statue of Akhenaton. 55p, Golden mask of King Tutankhamun. 80p, Statue of Nefertiti.
1995, Jan. 2 *Litho.* *Perf. 13½x13*
1579 A892 15p multicolored .50 .25
1580 A892 55p multicolored 1.10 .40
1581 A892 80p multicolored 1.50 .50
Nos. 1579-1581 (3) 3.10 1.15

World Tourism Organization, 20th Anniv. A893

1995, Jan. 2 *Perf. 13x13½*
1582 A893 15p multicolored .45 .25

Festivals A894

1995, Feb. 25 *Litho.* *Perf. 13x13½*
1583 A894 15p multicolored .45 .25
For use on greeting cards.

Egyptian Women's Day — A895

1995, Mar. 16 *Litho.* *Perf. 13x13½*
1584 A895 15p multicolored .45 .25

Arab League, 50th Anniv. — A896

1995, Mar. 22 *Perf. 13½x13*
1585 A896 15p blue & multi .45 .25
1586 A896 55p green & multi .75 .75

Sheraton Hotel, Cairo, 25th Anniv. A897

1995, Mar. 28 *Perf. 13x13½*
1587 A897 15p multicolored .45 .25

Misr Bank, 75th Anniv. — A898

1995, May 7 *Litho.* *Perf. 13x13½*
1588 A898 15p multicolored .50 .25

World Telecommunications Day — A899

1995, May 31 *Perf. 13x13½*
1589 A899 80p multicolored 1.00 .50

Wilhelm Roentgen (1845-1923), Discovery of the X-Ray, Cent. — A900

1995, May *Litho.* *Perf. 13½x13*
1590 A900 15p multicolored .50 .25

Membership in World Heritage Committee, 20th Anniv. (in 1994) — A901

Artifacts from the Shaft of Luxor: No. 1591, Goddess Hathor. No. 1592, God Atoum. 80p, God Amon and Horemheb.
1995, July 23 *Litho.* *Perf. 13½x13*
1591   15p multicolored .45 .25
1592   15p multicolored .45 .25
  a. A901 Pair, #1591-1592 1.10 1.10
1593 A901 80p multicolored 1.10 1.10
  Nos. 1591-1593 (3) 2.00 1.60
No. 1592a is a continuous design. No. 1593 is airmail.

21st Intl. Conference on Pediatrics, Cairo — A902

1995, Sept. 10 *Litho.* *Perf. 13*
1594 A902 15p multicolored .50 .25

Intl. Ozone Day — A903

1995, Sept. 16 *Litho.* *Perf. 13x12½*
1595 A903 15p green & multi .45 .25
1596 A903 55p brown & multi .90 .45
1597 A903 80p blue & multi 1.40 .55
  Nos. 1595-1597 (3) 2.75 1.25
See Nos. 1622-1623, 1824.

World Tourism Day — A904

1995, Sept. 25 *Perf. 12½x13*
1598 A904 15p multicolored 1.00 .25

Government Printing House, 175th Anniv. — A905

1995, Sept. 27
1599 A905 15p multicolored .45 .25

EGYPT

Sun Verticality on Abu Simbel Temple — A906

1995, Oct. 22   Litho.   Perf. 12½x13
1600 A906 15p multicolored   .95   .30

Opening of New Esna Dam — A907

1995, Nov. 25   Perf. 12½
1601 A907 15p multicolored   .75   .30

Egyptian Engineers Assoc., 75th Anniv. — A908

1995, Dec. 20   Perf. 13
1602 A908 15p multicolored   .45   .25

A909

Famous entertainers.

1995, Dec. 9   Litho.   Perf. 13x12½
1603 A909 15p Abdel Halim Hafez   .40   .25
1604 A909 15p Youssef Wahbi   .40   .25
1605 A909 15p Naquib el-Rihani   .40   .25
   Nos. 1603-1605 (3)   1.20   .75

A910

1995, Dec. 23   Litho.   Perf. 13x12½
1606 A910 15p multicolored   .45   .25
Motion Pictures, cent.

Post Day — A911

Ancient paintings: 55p, Man facing right. 80p, Man facing left. 100p, Playing flute, dancers.

1996, Jan. 2   Litho.   Perf. 13½x13
1607   55p multicolored   1.10   .60
1608   80p multicolored   1.50   .90
   a. A911 Pair, Nos. 1607-1608   2.75 2.75
Imperf
Size: 88x72mm
1609 A911 100p multicolored   3.00 3.00
   Nos. 1607-1608 are airmail.

Feasts — A912

1996, Feb. 15   Perf. 12½
1610 A912 15p Blue convolvulus   .45   .25
1611 A912 15p Red poppies   .45   .25
   a. Pair, No. 1610-1611   .95   .95
For use on greeting cards.

A913

1996, Mar. 13   Litho.   Perf. 13x12½
1612 A913 15p pink & multi   .40   .25
1613 A913 80p brown & multi   .90   .60
Summit of Peace Makers, Sharm al-Sheikh. No. 1613 is airmail.

A914

1996, Mar. 16
1614 A914 15p multicolored   .45   .25
29th Intl. Fair, Cairo.

Egyptian Geological Survey, Cent. — A915

1996, Mar. 18   Perf. 12½x13
1615 A915 15p multicolored   .45   .25

A916

1996, Apr. 11   Litho.   Perf. 13x12½
1616 A916 15p blue & multi   .45   .25
1617 A916 80p pink & multi   .95   .50
Signing of African Nuclear Weapon-Free Zone Treaty.

A917

1996, Apr. 20   Litho.   Perf. 13x12½
1618 A917 15p multicolored   .45   .25
Egyptian Society of Accountants and Auditors, 50th anniv.

General Census — A918

1996, May 4
1619 A918 15p multicolored   .45   .25

A919

1996 Summer Olympics, Atlanta: 15p, Atlanta 1996 emblem. £1, Emblem surrounded by sports pictograms.

1996, July 15   Litho.   Perf. 13x12½
1620 A919 15p lilac & multi   .50   .25
Size: 63x103mm
Imperf
1621 A919 £1 black & multi   2.75 2.75
   No. 1621 is airmail.

Intl. Ozone Day Type of 1995
1996, Sept. 16   Litho.   Perf. 13x12½
1622 A903 15p pink & multi   .40   .25
1623 A903 80p gray & multi   1.10   .55
   No. 1623 is airmail.
   See Nos. 1595-1597, 1824.

A920

1996, Sept. 19
1624 A920 80p multicolored   .75   .45
2nd Alexandria World Festival.

A921

1996, Sept. 21
1625 A921 15p grn, blk & bl   .45   .25
Scientific Research and Technology Academy, 25th anniv.

A922

1996, Oct. 7   Perf. 12½x13
1626 A922 15p multicolored   .50   .25
Opening of 2nd Line of Greater Cairo Subway System.

Rowing Festival — A923

1996, Sept. 27
1627 A923 15p multicolored   .75   .25
Intl. Tourism Day. See Nos. C215-C216.

Courts of the State Council, 50th Anniv. — A924

1996, Nov. 2   Litho.   Perf. 12½x13
1628 A924 15p blue & claret   .45   .25

A925

1996, Nov. 4   Perf. 13x12½
1629 A925 15p yel, blk & blue   .40   .25
25th World Conference of Intl. Federation of Training and Development Organizations.

A926

Cairo Economic Summit (MENA): £1, Graph, earth, gear, olive branch, wheat.

1996, Nov. 12   Litho.   Perf. 13x12½
1630 A926 15p shown   .45   .25
Size: 65x45mm
Imperf
1631 A926 £1 multicolored   1.75 1.75
   No. 1631 is airmail.

A927

1996, Nov. 13   Perf. 13x12½
1632 A927 15p multicolored   .45   .25
1996 World Food Summit, Rome.

A928

National Day of El-Gharbia Governorate: Al Sayd Ahmed El-Badawy mosque, Tanta.

1996, Nov. 16
1633 A928 15p multicolored   .45   .25

A929

Famous artists: No. 1634, Ali El-Kassar. No. 1635, George Abyad. No. 1636, Mohamed Kareem. No. 1637, Fatma Roshdi.

1996, Dec. 28   Litho.   Perf. 13x12½
1634 A929 20p black   .45   .25
1635 A929 20p red brown   .45   .25
1636 A929 20p brown   .45   .25
1637 A929 20p black   .45   .25
   Nos. 1634-1637 (4)   1.80 1.00
   See Nos. 1666-1669.

EGYPT

A930

1997, Jan. 2
1638 A930 20p multicolored .45 .25
Size: 61x80mm
Imperf
1639 A930 £1 multicolored 2.00 2.00
Post Day; Discovery of Tutankhamun's tomb, 75th anniv.
No. 1639 is airmail.

Police Day — A931

1997, Jan. 25 *Litho.* **Perf. 13x13½**
1640 A931 20p multicolored .45 .25

Feasts — A932

1997, Feb. 1 **Perf. 13**
1641 A932 20p Pink asters .40 .25
1642 A932 20p White asters .40 .25
 a. Pair, #1641-1642 .95 .95
For use on greeting cards.

World Civil Defense Day — A933

1997, Mar. 10 *Litho.* **Perf. 13x13½**
1643 A933 20p multicolored .45 .25

30th Cairo Intl. Fair — A934

1997, Mar. 19 **Perf. 13½x13**
1644 A934 20p multicolored .45 .25

Mahmoud Said, Photographer, Artist, Birth Cent. — A935

The City, By Mahmoud Said — A936

1997, Apr. 12 *Litho.* **Perf. 12½**
1645 A935 20p multicolored .45 .25
Size: 80x60mm
Imperf
1646 A936 £1 multicolored 1.25 1.25
No. 1646 is airmail.

Institute of African Research and Studies, 50th Anniv. — A937

1997, May 27 *Litho.* **Perf. 13**
1647 A937 75p multicolored .65 .65

New Headquarters of State Information Service — A938

1997, Aug. 16 *Litho.* **Perf. 12½**
1648 A938 20p multicolored .45 .25

A939

1997, Sept. 4 **Perf. 13x12½**
1649 A939 20p multicolored .45 .25
1650 AP81 75p multicolored .70 .65
Size: 75x55mm
Imperf
1651 A939 £1 multicolored 1.75 1.75
Nos. 1650-1651 are airmail. Under 17 FIFA World Soccer Championships, Egypt.
£1, Mascot, soccer ball, playing field, emblems.

A940

1997, Sept. 16 **Perf. 13**
1652 A940 20p lt bl grn & multi .60 .30
1653 A940 £1 pink & multi 1.60 1.25
Montreal Protocol on Substances that Deplete the Ozone Layer, 10th anniv. No. 1653 is airmail.

Completion of Second Stage of Metro Line No. 2 — A941

1997, Sept. 27 **Perf. 12½x13**
1654 A941 20p multicolored .45 .25

Premiere in Egypt of Opera Aida, by Verdi, 125th Anniv. — A942

1997, Oct. 12 **Perf. 13**
1655 A942 20p multicolored .60 .25
Size: 80x75mm
Imperf
1656 A942 £1 like #1655 4.00 4.00
No. 1656 is airmail.

Queen Nefertari — A943

1997, Oct. 25 *Litho.* **Perf. 13**
1657 A943 £1 multicolored 1.25 1.25
 a. Perf. 14¼x14 —

A944

1997, Nov. 17 *Litho.* **Perf. 13**
1658 A944 20p multicolored .50 .25
Intl. Congress of Orthopedics, Cairo.

A945

Designs: 20p, Goddess Selket. £1, Scarab, baboon pendant.

1997, Nov. 22 **Perf. 13x12½**
1659 A945 20p black & gold .50 .25
Size: 73x62mm
Imperf
1660 A945 £1 multicolored 1.50 1.50
No. 1660 is airmail. Discovery of King Tutanhkamen's tomb, 75th anniv.

Inauguration of Nubia Monument Museum A946

1997, Nov. 23 **Perf. 13**
1661 A946 20p multicolored .95 .25

Arab Land Bank, 50th Anniv. — A947

1997, Dec. 10 **Perf. 12½**
1662 A947 20p multicolored .60 .25

5th Pan Arab Congress on Anesthesia and Intensive Care — A948

1997, Dec. 9 *Litho.* **Perf. 13**
1663 A948 20p multicolored .45 .25

El Salaam Canal A949

1997, Dec. 28
1664 A949 20p multicolored .60 .25
Liberation of Sinai, 15th anniv.

Famous Artists Type of 1996 and

A950

1997, Dec. 23 *Litho.* **Perf. 13x12½**
1665 A950 20p blue .40 .25
1666 A929 20p Zaky Tolaimat .40 .25
1667 A929 20p Ismael Yassen .40 .25
1668 A929 20p Zaky Roustom .40 .25
1669 A929 20p Soliman Naguib .40 .25
 a. Strip of 5, #1665-1669 2.00 2.00

A951

Post Day: 20p, King Tutankhamun's guard. 75p, King Ramses III. £1, Cover of King Tutankhamun's coffin.

1998, Jan. 2 **Perf. 13**
1670 A951 20p multicolored .45 .25
1671 A951 75p multicolored 1.10 .65
Size: 26x43mm
1672 A951 £1 multicolored 1.75 .85
Nos. 1671-1672 are airmail.

Feasts A952

1998, Jan. 20
1673 20p multicolored .40 .25
1674 20p multicolored .40 .25
 a. A952 Pair, #1673-1674 .80 .80
For use on greeting cards.

Intl. Cairo Fair — A954

1998, Mar. 11 *Litho.* **Perf. 13**
1675 A954 20p multicolored .50 .25

Natl. Bank of Egypt, Cent. — A955

1998, Mar. 12
1676 A955 20p multicolored .50 .25

Tutankhamun A956

Thutmose IV A957

EGYPT

1998   Litho.   Perf. 13½x12½
1677	A956	£2 pink & multi	1.75	1.75
1677A	A956	£2 Like #1677, with white background	—	—
b.		Perf. 14x14¼		
1678	A957	£5 purple & black	5.00	3.75
		Nos. 1677-1678 (3)	6.75	5.50

Issued: £2, 4/23; £5, 3/23.

A958

1998, Apr. 14   Perf. 13
| 1679 | A958 | 20p green & multi | .45 | .25 |
| 1680 | A958 | 75p blue & multi | 1.10 | .75 |

Size: 70x52mm
Imperf
| 1681 | A958 | £1 Natl. flags, map, trophy | 1.50 | 1.00 |

Egypt, winner of 21st African Cup of Nations soccer competition.
Nos. 1680-1681 are airmail.

Egyptian Satellite "Nile Sat" — A959

1998, May 30   Litho.   Perf. 13
| 1682 | A959 | 20p multicolored | .50 | .25 |

World Environment Day — A960

1998, June 5
| 1683 | A960 | 20p shown | .60 | .25 |

Size: 43x62mm
Imperf
| 1684 | A960 | £1 Fauna, emblems | 3.75 | 3.75 |

No. 1684 is airmail.

A961

1998, June 14
| 1685 | A961 | 20p blue & black | .40 | .25 |
| 1686 | A961 | £1 yel, grn & blk | 1.10 | .80 |

Dr. Ahmed Zewail, winner of Franklin Institute award.
No. 1686 is airmail.

A962

Imam Sheikh Mohamed Metwalli Al-Shaarawi.

1998, July 15
| 1687 | A962 | 20p buff & multi | .40 | .25 |
| 1688 | A962 | £1 green & multi | 1.10 | .80 |

No. 1688 is airmail.

Day of the Nile Flood — A963

1998, Sept. 12   Litho.   Perf. 13
| 1689 | A963 | 20p multicolored | .50 | .25 |

A964

1998, Sept. 30   Litho.   Perf. 13
| 1690 | A964 | 20p multicolored | .50 | .25 |

Chemistry Administration, cent.

October War Against Israel, 25th Anniv. — A965

1998, Oct. 6   Litho.   Perf. 13
| 1691 | A965 | 20p multicolored | .60 | .25 |

Size: 50x70mm
Imperf
| 1692 | A965 | £2 like No. 1691 | 3.25 | 3.25 |

No. 1692 is airmail.

Egyptian Survey Authority, Cent. A966

1998, Oct. 15   Perf. 13
| 1693 | A966 | 20p multicolored | .50 | .25 |

Cairo University, 90th Anniv. A967

1998, Dec. 7   Litho.   Perf. 13
| 1694 | A967 | 20p multicolored | .50 | .25 |

A968

1998, Dec. 17   Litho.   Perf. 13
| 1695 | A968 | 20p multicolored | .45 | .25 |

Egyptian trade unions, cent.

A970

Post Day (19th Dynasty): 20p, Queen Nefertari, Goddess Isis. 125p, God Osiris, Goddess Isis.

1999, Jan. 2   Litho.   Perf. 13
| 1696 | A970 | 20p multicolored | .50 | .25 |

Size: 41x61mm
Imperf
| 1697 | A970 | 125p multicolored | 2.00 | 2.00 |

No. 1697 is airmail.

Feasts A971

1999, Jan. 5   Perf. 13
1698		20p multicolored	1.00	.30
1699		20p multicolored	.40	.25
a.	A971	Pair, #1698-1699	1.75	1.75

For use on greeting cards.

Intl. Women's Day — A973

1999, Mar. 7   Litho.   Perf. 13
| 1700 | A973 | 20p multicolored | .50 | .25 |

Cairo Intl. Fair — A974

1999, Mar. 9
| 1701 | A974 | 20p multicolored | .50 | .25 |

Opening of Metro Line Beneath Nile River — A975

1999, Apr.   Litho.   Perf. 13
| 1702 | A975 | 20p multicolored | .60 | .25 |

A976

UPU, 125th Anniv. — A977

1999, Apr. 21
1703	A976	20p shown	.45	.25
1704	A976	£1 multi	1.25	.85
1705	A977	125p shown	1.50	1.20

Size: 50x70mm
Imperf
| 1706 | A977 | 125p multi | 2.10 | 2.10 |
| | | Nos. 1703-1706 (4) | 5.30 | 4.40 |

Nos. 1704-1706 are airmail.

A978

1999, May 8   Perf. 13
| 1707 | A978 | 20p green & multi | .45 | .25 |
| 1708 | A978 | 125p buff, red & multi | 1.25 | 1.00 |

Geneva Conventions, 50th anniv. No. 1708 is airmail.

A980

1999, May 20   Litho.   Perf. 13x12¾
| 1710 | A980 | 20p green & multi | .45 | .25 |
| 1711 | A980 | £1 buff & multi | .95 | .85 |

African Development Bank, 35th Meeting, Cairo. No. 1711 is airmail.

16th Men's Handball World Championship — A981

20p, Stylized player with ball, pyramids. 1£, Mascot with ball, Sphinx, pyramids, globe. 125p, Mascot with ball, goalie, pyramids.

1999, June 1   Perf. 13
1712	A901	20p multicolored	.45	.25
1713	A981	£1 multicolored	.90	.85
1714	A981	125p multicolored	1.10	1.00
		Nos. 1712-1714 (3)	2.45	2.10

Nos. 1713-1714 are airmail.

Goddess Selket — A982

1999, June 23   Litho.   Perf. 13
| 1715 | A982 | 25p multicolored | .40 | .25 |

See Nos. 1750, 1754.

SOS Children's Village, 50th Anniv. A983

1999, June 23   Perf. 12¾x13¼
| 1716 | A983 | 20p grn, blk & blue | .45 | .25 |
| 1717 | A983 | 125p pale yel, blk & bl | 1.25 | 1.10 |

No. 1717 is airmail.

390 EGYPT

A984

No. 1718, Sameera Moussa (1917-52), Physicist. No. 1719, Aisha Abdul Rahman (1913-98), writer. No. 1720, Ahmed Eldemerdash Touny (1907-97), member of Intl. Olympic Committee.

1999   **Litho.**   *Perf. 13x12¾*

1718	A984	20p multicolored	.45	.25
1719	A984	20p multicolored	.45	.25
1720	A984	20p multicolored	.45	.25
		Nos. 1718-1720 (3)	1.35	.75

Issued: Nos. 1718-1719, 7/23; No. 1720, 8/13.
See Nos. 1730-1733.

A985

1999, Oct. 5   **Litho.**   *Perf. 13x12¾*

1721	A985	20p org & multi	.45	.25
1722	A985	£1 silver & multi	.90	.85
1723	A985	125p gold & multi	1.10	1.00

Imperf

1724	A985	125p multicolored	2.00	2.00
		Nos. 1721-1724 (4)	4.45	4.10

Pres. Hosni Mubarak, 4th term.
Nos. 1722-1724 are airmail.

A986

1999, Nov. 15   **Litho.**   *Perf. 13¼x13*
Background Color

1725	A986	20p green	.45	.25
1726	A986	£1 red vio	.90	.85
1727	A986	125p purple	1.10	1.00
		Nos. 1725-1727 (3)	2.45	2.10

Intl. Year of the Elderly. Nos. 1726-1727 are airmail.

A987

1999, Nov. 20

| 1728 | A987 | 20p multi | .50 | .25 |

Children's Day.

Famous People Type of 1999

No. 1730, Farid El Attrash (1913-76), singer, movie star. No. 1731, Laila Mourad (1918-95), singer, movie star. No. 1732, Anwar Wagdi (1911-55), actor, director. No. 1733, Asia Dagher (1901-86), actor, producer.

1999, Dec. 30   **Litho.**   *Perf. 13x12¾*

1730	A984	20p lt bl & blk	.40	.25
1731	A984	20p lt bl & blk	.40	.25
1732	A984	20p lt bl & blk	.40	.25
1733	A984	20p lt bl & blk	.40	.25
		Nos. 1730-1733 (4)	1.60	1.00

Millennium — A989

2000, Jan. 1

1734	A989	20p multi	.45	.25
1735	A989	125p multi	1.25	1.10

Size: 70x50mm
Imperf

1736	A989	£2 multi, horiz.	4.00	4.00
		Nos. 1734-1736 (3)	5.70	5.35

20p, "1999" & "2000." 125p, Countdown of years. £2, Holy Family, Virgin Tree.
Nos. 1735-1736 are airmail.

A990   Post Day — A991

2000, Jan. 2   *Perf. 13¼x12¾*

1737	A990	20p multi	.50	.25
1738	A991	125p multi	.50	.25
a.		Pair, #1737-1738	1.25	1.25

Size: 70x50mm
Imperf

1739	A991	125p Chariot, horiz.	2.00	2.00
		Nos. 1737-1739 (3)	3.00	2.50

Ain Shams University, 50th Anniv. A992

2000, Jan. 3   *Perf. 13¼x13*

| 1740 | A992 | 20p multi | .50 | .25 |

Festivals
A993   A994

2000, Jan. 5   *Perf. 13¼x13¼*

1741	A993	20p multi	.40	.25
1742	A994	20p multi	.40	.25
a.		Pair, #1741-1742	.90	.90

For use on greeting cards.

A995

2000, Jan. 20   *Perf. 13¼x13*

| 1743 | A995 | 20p multi | .50 | .25 |

Islamic Development Bank, 25th anniv.

A996

2000, Feb. 28   *Perf. 13¼x12¾*

| 1744 | A996 | 125p multi | 1.25 | 1.25 |

Common Market for Eastern and Southern Africa Economic Conference.

Death of Om Kolthoum, 25th Anniv. — A997

2000, Mar. 11   *Perf. 13¼x13*

| 1745 | A997 | 20p grnsh yel & blk | .50 | .25 |

8th Intl. Congress of Egyptologists — A998

2000, Mar. 28   *Perf. 13¼x13¼*

| 1746 | A998 | 20p multi | .50 | .25 |

Europe-Africa Summit, Cairo — A999

2000, Apr. 3   *Perf. 13¼x13*

| 1747 | A999 | 125p multi | 1.25 | 1.25 |

Group of 15 Developing Nations, 10th Summit, Cairo A1000

Perf. 12¾x13¼

2000, June 19   **Litho.**

| 1748 | A1000 | 125p multi | 1.25 | 1.25 |

Goddess Selket Type of 1999 and

Scene from 20th Dynasty A1003

Nofret, Wife of Rahotep A1004

King Seostris A1005

Princess Merit Aton A1006

20th Dynasty A1007

Pyramid at Snefru A1008

Wife of Sheikh-el-Balad A1009

King Psusennes I A1010

King Tutankhamun A1011

Obelisk of Ramses II A1011a

Temple of Karnak — A1012

Without Dots

With Dots

Perf. 12¾x13¼, 11¼ (#1750A, 1752-1755, 1757), 11x11½ (#1758-1760), 13¼x12¾ (#1756, 1761, 1763)

Photo., Litho. (#1750, 1750A, 1751, 1754, 1754A, 1761, 1763)

2000-2002

1750	A982	10p multi, type I	.40	.25
1750A	A982	10p multi, Type II	3.00	3.00
1751	A1003	10p multi	.40	.25
1752	A1004	20p multi	.40	.25
a.		With dot pattern in headdress and on chest and face ('07)	—	—
1753	A1005	25p multi	.40	.25
1754	A982	30p multi, Type I	.60	.45
1754A	A982	30p multi, Type II	—	—
1755	A1006	30p multi	.50	.35
1756	A1007	50p multi	.65	.45
1757	A1008	£1 multi	.60	.25
1758	A1009	110p multi	1.25	.95
1759	A1010	125p multi	1.40	1.00
1760	A1011	150p multi	1.75	1.25
1761	A1011a	225p multi	2.75	2.00

EGYPT

1763	A1012	£5 multi	5.75	5.50
a.		Perf. 14x14¼		
	Nos. 1750-1763 (15)		19.85	16.20

Issued: 20p, 6/25; No. 1750, 3/25/01; Nos. 1750A, 1754A, 2007; No. 1754, 6/11/01. Nos. 1751, 1755, 225p, 5/25/02; 110p, 6/4/02; 125p, 6/20/02; 150p, 6/15/02; £5, 6/1/02. 25p, 50p, £1, 6/30/02.

Type I (Nos. 1750, 1754), has "Goddess" in smaller type than "Silakht." Type II (No. 1750A, 1754A), has "Goddess" and "Silakht" in type the same height.

See No. 2174 for smaller stamp of type A1010.

Intl. Day Against Drug Abuse A1013

2000, June 26   Perf. 12¾x13¼   Litho.
1764   A1013   20p multi   .50   .25
See No. 1796.

Natl. Insurance Company, Cent. — A1014

125p, Emblem, building, horiz.

2000, Aug. 20   Perf. 13¼x12¾   Litho.
1765   A1014   20p shown   .50   .25

Imperf
Size: 96x75mm
1766   A1014   125p multi   2.25   2.25

2000 Summer Olympics, Sydney — A1015

Background colors: 20p, Light blue. 125p, Pink.

2000, Sept. 9   Perf. 13¼x12¾
1767-1768   A1015   Set of 2   1.75   1.50
No. 1768 is airmail.

Productive Cooperative Union, 25th Anniv. A1016

2000, Sept. 15   Perf. 12¾x13¼
1769   A1016   20p multi   .50   .25

Opening of Fourth Stage of Second Cairo Subway Line A1017

2000, Oct. 7
1770   A1017   20p multi   .60   .25

World Post Day A1018

2000, Oct. 9
1771   A1018   125p multi   1.40   1.40

Solidarity with Palestinians — A1019

Palestinian Authority flag and: 20p, Dome of the Rock, Jerusalem, vert. No. 1773, 125p, shown. No. 1774, 125p, Dome of the Rock, father and boy, vert.

Perf. 13¼x12¾, 12¾x13¼
2000, Nov. 29
1772-1774   A1019   Set of 3   3.25   3.25
No. 1774 is airmail.

Opening of El-Ferdan Railway Bridge A1020

2000, Dec. 2
1775   A1020   20p multi   .70   .25

Disabled Person's Day — A1021

2000, Dec. 9   Perf. 13¼x12¾
1776   A1021   20p multi   .50   .25

Opening of Al-Azhar Professorial Building A1022

2000, Dec. 10   Perf. 12¾x13¼
1777   A1022   20p multi   .50   .25

Famous Egyptians — A1023

No. 1778: a, Karem Mahmoud, artist (yellow background). b, Mahmoud El-Miligi, artist (green background). c, Mohamed Fawzi, musician (pink background). d, Hussein Riyad, artist (lilac background). e, Abdel Wares Asser, artist (light blue background).

2000, Dec. 24   Perf. 13¼x12¾
1778   Horiz. strip of 5   2.00   2.00
a.-e.   A1023 20p Any single   .40   .25

Feasts A1024

a, Red and yellow flowers. b, Purple flowers.

Perf. 12¾x13¼
2000, Dec. 23   Litho.
1779   A1024   20p Pair, #a-b   .90   .90
For use on greeting cards.

Jerusalem, City of Peace — A1025

2001, Jan. 1   *Imperf.*
1780   A1025   £2 multi   2.00   2.00

Post Day A1026

Ancient Egyptian art: 20p, 8 standing figures. No. 1782, 125p, 3 large standing figures.

2001, Jan. 2   Perf. 12¾x13¼
1781-1782   A1026   Set of 2   1.75   1.75

Imperf
Size: 80x60mm
1783   A1026   125p Chariot   2.00   2.00
No. 1782 is airmail.

Arab Labor Organization, 36th Anniv. — A1027

Perf. 13¼x12¾
2001, Feb. 10   Litho.
1784   A1027   20p multi   .50   .25

Postal Savings Bank, Cent. — A1028

2001, Mar. 1
1785   A1028   20p multi   .50   .25

Natl. Council for Women, 1st Anniv. A1029

Background colors: 30p, Pink. 125p, Blue.

2001, Mar. 16   Perf. 12¾x13¼
1786-1787   A1029   Set of 2   2.00   1.40
No. 1787 is airmail.

Cairo Intl. Fair — A1030

2001, Mar. 21   Perf. 13¼x12¾
1788   A1030   30p multi   .50   .25

Helwan University, 25th Anniv. A1031

2001, May 4   Perf. 12¾x13¼
1789   A1031   30p multi   .50   .25

Inauguration of Alexandria Library A1032

2001, May 20
1790   A1032   125p multi   1.40   1.25

African Conference on the Future of Children — A1033

Background color: 30p, Blue. 125p, Red.

2001, May 28   Perf. 13¼x12¾
1791-1792   A1033   Set of 2   1.75   1.40
No. 1792 is airmail.

World Environment Day — A1034

2001, June 5   Litho.   Perf. 13¼x12¾
1793   A1034   125p multi   1.40   1.25

World Military Soccer Championships A1035

Designs: 30p, Emblem. 125p, Emblem and map.

Perf. 13¼x12¾
2001, June 21   Litho.
1794-1795   A1035   Set of 2   1.75   1.50

Intl. Day Against Drug Abuse Type of 2000

2001, June 26   Perf. 12¾x13¼
1796   A1013   30p multi   .50   .25

EGYPT

Egypt's Victory in World Military Soccer Championships — A1036

2001, July 6   **Litho.**   *Imperf.*
1797 A1036 125p multi   1.75 1.75

Egyptian Railways, 150th Anniv. A1037

2001, July 12   *Perf. 12¾x13¼*
1798 A1037 30p multi   .75 .25

Poets A1038

No. 1799: a, Aziz Abaza Pasha (1898-73), blue background. b, Ahmed Rami (1892-1981), pink background.

2001, July 28   *Perf. 13¼x12¾*
1799 A1038 30p Horiz. pair, #a-b   .80 .80

Intl. Volunteers Year — A1039

2001, Aug. 18
1800 A1039 125p multi   1.40 1.10

Ismailia Folklore Festival — A1040

2001, Aug. 20
1801 A1040 30p multi   .60 .25

Satellite Telecommunications Ground Stations, 25th Anniv. — A1041

2001, Sept. 8   *Perf. 12¾x13¼*
1802 A1041 30p multi   .60 .25

Year of Dialogue Among Civilizations — A1042

Designs: No. 1803, 125p, Emblem. No. 1804, 125p, UN emblem, globe, symbols of various civilizations, horiz.

Perf. 13¼x12¾, 12¾x13¼
2001, Oct. 9
1803-1804 A1042 Set of 2   3.00 2.50

Opening of Suez Canal Bridge A1043

No. 1805: a, 30p, Bridge, ship. b, 125p, Bridge, road.
No. 1806, Bridge, ship and flags of Egypt and Japan.

2001, Oct. 10   *Perf. 12¾x13¼*
1805 A1043 Horiz. pair, #a-b   1.75 1.75

Imperf
Size: 81x60mm
1806 A1043 125p multi   2.00 2.00

Ancient Gold Masks A1044

Designs: No. 1807, 30p, Mask of San Xing Dui, China, green background. No. 1808, 30p, Funerary mask of King Tutankhamun, brown background.

2001, Oct. 12   *Perf. 12¾x13¼*
1807-1808 A1044 Set of 2   .80 .60
See People's Republic of China 3141-3142.

Opening of Azhar Tunnels, Cairo — A1045

2001, Oct. 28   *Perf. 13¼x12¾*
1809 A1045 30p multi   .60 .25

El-Menoufia University, 25th Anniv. — A1046

2001, Nov. 25
1810 A1046 30p multi   .60 .25

Feasts A1047

No.1811: a, Black and white bird on branch. b, Sea gulls. c, Parrot. d, Blue bird on branch.

2001, Dec. 5
1811 A1047 30p Block of 4, #a-d   2.50 2.00
For use on greeting cards.

Musicians — A1048

No. 1812: a, Zakaria Ahmed (1896-1961) with scarf around neck (4). b, Riyadh El-Sonbati (1908-81) with glasses with rectangular lenses (3). c, Mahmoud El-Sherif (1912-90) (2). d, Mohamed El-Kasabgi (1898-1966) with glasses with round lenses (1). Stamp numbers, shown in parentheses, are found at the bottom center in Arabian script.

2001, Dec.
1812 A1048 30p Horiz. strip of 4   2.00 1.40

Painting From Tomb of Anhur Khawi A1049

Painting from Tomb of Irinefer A1050

2002, Jan. 2   **Litho.**   *Perf. 12¾x13¼*
1813 A1049 30p multi   .45 .25

Imperf
Size: 79x60mm
1814 A1050 125p multi   2.25 2.25
Post Day.

Intl. Nephrology Congress — A1051

2002, Jan. 16   **Litho.**   *Perf. 13¼x12¾*
1815 A1051 30p multi   .45 .25

Police Day, 50th Anniv. A1052

2002, Jan. 25   *Perf. 12¾x13¼*
1816 A1052 30p multi   .45 .25

Imperf
Size: 79x50mm
1817 A1052 30p multi   1.60 1.50

Return of Sinai to Egypt, 20th Anniv. — A1053

2002, Apr. 25   *Perf. 13¼x12¾*
1818 A1053 30p multi   .60 .25

Cairo Bank, 50th Anniv. — A1054

2002, May 15
1819 A1054 30p multi   .50 .25

Weight Lifters A1055

No. 1820: a, Ibrahim Shams, 1948 (weights over head). b, Khidre el Touney, 1936 (weights at knees).

2002, June 1
1820 A1055 30p Horiz. pair, #a-b   .80 .80

Al Akhbar Newspaper, 50th Anniv. A1056

2002, June 15   *Perf. 12¾x13¼*
1821 A1056 30p multi   .45 .25

Nos. 318-321 and Egyptian Arms A1057

2002, July 23   **Litho.**   *Imperf.*
1822 A1057 125p multi   1.40 1.40
July 23rd Revolution, 50th anniv.

Aswan Dam, Cent. A1058

No. 1823: a, Dam. b, Dam and buildings.

2002, Aug. 15   *Perf. 12¾x13¼*
1823 A1058 30p Horiz. pair, #a-b   .90 .90

Intl. Ozone Day — A1059

2002, Sept. 16   *Perf. 13¼x12¾*
1824 A1059 125p multi   1.40 1.25
See Nos. 1595-1597, 1622-1623.

18th Intl. Conference on Road Safety, Cairo — A1060

2002, Sept. 22
1825 A1060 30p multi   .50 .25

EGYPT 393

17th Congress of Ear-
Nose-Throat (ENT)
Associations — A1061

2002, Sept. 28
1826 A1061 30p multi   .50 .25
17th Congress of Intl. Federation of Otorhi-
nolaryngological Societies, Cairo.

World Post
Day — A1062

2002, Oct. 9
1827 A1062 125p multi   1.10 1.10

Opening of
Alexandria
Library
A1063

Ancient Alexandria Library — A1064

Designs: 30p, Library exterior. 125p, Pillar,
sun on horizon, vert.

Perf. 12¾x13¼, 13¼x12¾
2002, Oct. 16
1828-1829 A1063 Set of 2   1.75 1.50
Size: 60x80mm
Imperf
1830 A1064 125p multi   1.60 1.60

Hassan Faek,
Actor
A1065

Aziza Amir,
Actress
A1066

Farid Shawki,
Actor
A1067

Mary Mounib,
Actress
A1068

2002, Nov. 23   **Perf. 13¼x12¾**
1831   Horiz. strip of 4   1.75 1.60
  a. A1065 30p tan & black   .40 .25
  b. A1066 30p tan & black   .40 .25
  c. A1067 30p tan & black   .40 .25
  d. A1068 30p tan & black   .40 .25

A1069

A1070

A1071

Birds — A1072

2002, Dec. 3   **Perf. 13¼x12¾**
1832   Block of 4   1.75 1.60
  a. A1069 30p multi   .40 .25
  b. A1070 30p multi   .40 .25
  c. A1071 30p multi   .40 .25
  d. A1072 30p multi   .40 .25

Egyptian
Museum,
Cent.
A1073

125p, Entrance, statue of Cheops.

2002, Dec. 11   **Perf. 12¾x13¼**
1833 A1073 30p shown   .50 .25
Size: 80x60mm
Imperf
1834 A1073 125p multi   1.40 1.40

Opening of Aswan Suspension
Bridge — A1074

No. 1835: a, Bridge and support cables. b,
Bridge towers.

2002, Dec. 17   **Perf. 12¾x13¼**
1835 A1074 30p Horiz. pair, #a-b .90 .90

Suez Canal University,
25th Anniv. — A1075

2002, Dec. 29   **Perf. 13¼x12¾**
1836 A1075 30p multi   .45 .25

Toshka Land
Reclamation
Project
A1076

2002, Dec. 31   **Perf. 12¾x13¼**
1837 A1076 30p multi   .45 .25

A1077

A1078

Post
Day — A1079

2003, Jan. 2
1838 A1077 30p multi   .45 .25
1839 A1078 30p multi   .45 .25
1840 A1079 125p multi   1.10 1.00
  Nos. 1838-1840 (3)   2.00 1.50

Cairo Intl.
Communications and
Information Technology
Fair — A1080

2003, Jan. 12 Litho. Perf. 13¼x12¾
1841 A1080 30p multi   .50 .25

Intl. Nile
Children's
Song Festival
A1081

Background color: 30p, Brown. 125p,
Green.

2003, Jan. 28   **Perf. 12¾x13¼**
1842-1843 A1081 Set of 2   1.50 1.25

Intl. Table Tennis
Championships — A1082

Background color: 30p, Blue. 125p, Orange.

2003, Feb. 3
1844-1845 A1082 Set of 2   1.50 1.25

Tenth Intl. Building and
Construction
Conference — A1083

Background color: 30p, Orange. 125p, Blue.

2003, Apr. 1   **Perf. 13¼x12¾**
1846-1847 A1083 Set of 2   1.50 1.10

Arab
Lawyer's
Union, 60th
Anniv.
A1084

Background color: 30p, Blue. 125p, Lilac.

2003, Apr. 25   **Perf. 12¾x13¼**
1848-1849 A1084 Set of 2   1.40 1.10

Inauguration
of First Phase
of Smart
Village Project
A1085

Denomination color: 30p, White. 125p, Yellow. £1, White.

2003, July 1   **Perf. 12¾x13¼**
1850-1851 A1085 Set of 2   1.50 1.50
Size: 79x59mm
Imperf
1852 A1085 £1 multi   1.50 1.50

Writers
A1086

No. 1853: a, Ihsan Abdul Qudous (1919-90)
(wearing checked tie). b, Youssef Idris (1927-
91) (wearing solid tie).

2003, July 28   **Perf. 13¼x12¾**
1853 A1086 30p Horiz. pair, #a-b .90 .90

African Men's
Basketball
Championships
A1087

Background color: 30p, Black. 125p, Blue.

2003, Aug. 12
1854-1855 A1087 Set of 2   1.50 1.10

Natl. Institute of Astronomical and
Geophysical Research, Cent.
A1088

2003, Sept. 7   **Perf. 12¾x13¼**
1856 A1088 30p multi   .60 .30

World
Tourism
Day — A1089

Denomination color: 30p, White. 125p, Red.

Perf. 12¾x13¼
2003, Sept. 27   **Litho.**
1857-1858 A1089 Set of 2   1.50 1.10

Egypt's Bid for Hosting
2010 World Cup
Soccer Championships
A1090

Designs: 30p, Emblem, vert. 125p, Emblem,
funerary mask of King Tutankhamun.

Perf. 13¼x12¾, 12¾x13¼
2003, Sept. 27
1859-1860 A1090 Set of 2   1.50 1.10

EGYPT

October War Against Israel, 30th Anniv. — A1091

2003, Oct. 6   Perf. 13¼x12¾
1861   A1091   30p multi   1.00   .30

World Post Day — A1092

2003, Oct. 9
1862   A1092   125p multi   1.00   .80

National Bar Association, 91st Anniv. — A1093

2003, Oct. 30
1863   A1093   30p multi   .60   .25

Festivals A1094

No. 1864: a, Pink orchids. b, White rose. c, Red rose. d, Sunflower.

2003, Nov. 23   Perf. 14
1864   A1094   30p Block of 4, #a-d   1.50   1.50
For use on greeting cars.

Film Directors A1095

No. 1865: a, Salah Abou Seif (balding man with open collar). b, Kamal Selim (round eyeglasses) c, Henri Barakat (square eyeglasses). d, Hassan El Emam.

2003, Dec. 1   Perf. 13¼x12¾
1865   A1095   30p Horiz. strip of 4, #a-d   1.50   1.50

El Gomhoreya Newspaper, 50th Anniv. — A1096

2003, Dec. 7
1866   A1096   30p multi   .50   .25

Cairo Bourse, Cent. A1097

2003, Dec. 7   Perf. 12¾x13¼
1867   A1097   30p multi   .45   .25

Mrs. Suzanne Mubarak, Emblems of Fifth E-9 Ministerial Review Meeting and UNESCO A1098

Background color: 30p, Blue. 125p, Orange. £2, Blue.

2003, Dec. 18   Perf. 12¾x13¼   Litho.
1868-1869   A1098   Set of 2   1.50   1.10
Imperf
Size: 79x60mm
1870   A1098   £2 multi   2.00   2.00

Delta International Bank, 25th Anniv. — A1099

Background color: 30p, Green. 125p, Blue. £2, Green and blue, horiz.

2004, Jan. 1   Perf. 12¾x13¼
1871-1872   A1099   Set of 2   1.40   1.00
Imperf
Size: 80x60mm
1873   A1099   £2 multi   2.00   2.00

Post Day — A1100

Denominations: 30p, 125p.

2004, Jan. 2   Perf. 12¾x13¼
1874-1875   A1100   Set of 2   1.50   1.25

Eighth Intl. Telecommunications Conference — A1101

2004, Jan. 17
1876   A1101   30p multi   .80   .30

Treasures of Egypt — A1102

No. 1877: a, Sinai. b, Pyramids at dusk. c, Egyptian Bedouin. d, Red Sea corals. e, Suez Canal, Ferdinand-Marie de Lesseps, Khedive Ismail. f, Ramadan lanterns. g, Nile felucca. h, White Western Desert. i, Maydum Pyramid.
No. 1878: a, St. Catherine Monastery, Sinai. b, Icon of Sts. Paul and Anthony. c, Mosque of Muhammad Ali. d, Lamp, Old Cairo. e, Emblem of Sultan Qaytbay. f, Minaret, Cairo. g, Mosque of al-Azhar. h, Coptic priest and icon, Cairo. i, Ben Ezra Synagogue.
No. 1879: a, Ankh. b, Rosetta Stone. c, Sarcophagus of Ahmes Meritamun. d, Stela of Amenmhat. e, Sphinx. f, Udjat. g, Canopic jars of Tutankhamun. h, Cartouche of Tutankhamun. i, Egyptian scribe.
No. 1880: a, Sphinx, diff. b, Queen Nefertiti. c, Tutankhamun.

2004, Jan. 22   Litho.   Perf. 13x13¼
1877   Booklet pane of 9   2.25   —
   a.-i.   A1102 30p Any single   .40   .25
1878   Booklet pane of 9   8.25   —
   a.-i.   A1102 125p Any single   .90   .80

Litho. & Embossed, Litho. & Embossed With Foil Application (£10)

1879   Booklet pane of 9   13.50   —
   a.-i.   A1102 £2 Any single   1.50   1.25

Perf. 13¼

1880   Booklet pane of 3   15.00   —
   a.-b.   A1102 £5 Either single, 38x51mm   3.75   3.75
   c.   A1102 £10 gold & multi, 38x51mm   7.00   7.00
   Complete booklet, #1877-1880   39.00

Complete booklet sold for £80.

Morkos Hanna A1103

Mahmoud Abu el Nasr A1105

Ibrahim el Helbawi A1107

Mohammad Naguib el Gharabli A1109

Mohammad Hafez Ramadan A1111

Ahmed Lotfi A1104

Abd el Aziz Fahmy A1106

Makram Ebeid A1108

Mohammad Bassiouni A1110

Mohammad Abu Shadi A1112

Mahmoud Fahmi Goundia A1113

Abd el Hamid Abd el Hakk A1115

Kamel Sedki Beck A1117

Abd el Rahman el Rafei A1119

Mohammad Sabri Abu Alam A1121

Sameh Ashour A1123

Kamel Youssof Saleh A1114

Mohammad Ali Allouba A1116

Bar Association Emblem A1118

Abd el Fattah el Shalkany A1120

Omar Omar A1122

Ahmed el Khawaga A1124

EGYPT

Abd el Aziz el Shorgabi
A1125

Mostafa el Baradei
A1126

2004, Feb.	Litho.	Perf. 13¼x12¾
1881	Block of 25	8.75 8.75
a.	A1103 30p bright blue & black	.35 .25
b.	A1104 30p bright blue & black	.35 .25
c.	A1105 30p bright blue & black	.35 .25
d.	A1106 30p bright blue & black	.35 .25
e.	A1107 30p bright blue & black	.35 .25
f.	A1108 30p pink & black	.35 .25
g.	A1109 30p pink & black	.35 .25
h.	A1110 30p pink & black	.35 .25
i.	A1111 30p pink & black	.35 .25
j.	A1112 30p pink & black	.35 .25
k.	A1113 30p orange & black	.35 .25
l.	A1114 30p orange & black	.35 .25
m.	A1115 30p orange & black	.35 .25
n.	A1116 30p orange & black	.35 .25
o.	A1117 30p orange & black	.35 .25
p.	A1118 30p green & multi	.35 .25
q.	A1119 30p green & black	.35 .25
r.	A1120 30p green & black	.35 .25
s.	A1121 30p green & black	.35 .25
t.	A1122 30p green & black	.35 .25
u.	A1118 30p dark blue & multi	.35 .25
v.	A1123 30p dark blue & black	.35 .25
w.	A1124 30p dark blue & black	.35 .25
x.	A1125 30p dark blue & black	.35 .25
y.	A1126 30p dark blue & black	.35 .25

National Bar Association, 92nd anniv.

IBM Corporation in Egypt, 50th Anniv. — A1127

2004, Feb. 24
1882 A1127 30p multi .60 .25

Cairo Rotary Club, 75th Anniv. — A1128

2004, Mar. 11
1883 A1128 30p multi .60 .25

Egyptian Victory in Regional Computer Programming and Information Technology Competition — A1129

2004, Mar. 15
1884 A1129 30p multi .60 .25

National Women's Day — A1130

Background colors: 30p, Blue. 125p, Red orange.

2004, Mar. 16 Litho.
1885-1886 A1130 Set of 2 1.50 1.00

Anti-Narcotics General Administration, 75th Anniv. — A1131

2004, Mar. 20 Perf. 12¾x13¼
1887 A1131 30p multi .75 .30
Imperf
Size: 80x60mm
1888 A1131 125p multi 1.50 1.50

Orphan's Day — A1132

2004, Apr. 2 Perf. 13¼x12¾
1889 A1132 30p multi .60 .25
Compare with Types A1169 and A1199.

Telecom Africa Fair and Conference, Cairo A1133

2004, May 4 Perf. 12¾x13¼
1890 A1133 30p multi .60 .25

Egyptian Philatelic Society, 75th Anniv. — A1134

Designs: 30p, Emblem. 125p, Emblem, stamp, magnifying glass, tongs.

2004, May 20 Perf. 13¼x12¾
1891 A1134 30p multi .60 .25
Imperf
Size: 80x60mm
1892 A1134 125p multi 1.50 1.50

State Information Service, 50th Anniv. A1135

2004, May 30 Perf. 12¾x13¼
1893 A1135 30p multi .75 .25

Tenth Radio and Television Festival, Cairo — A1136

Designs: 30p, Festival emblem, green background. £1, Festival emblem, brown background. 125p, Sphinx, festival emblem, film, horiz.
£2, Like 125p, horiz.

Perf. 13¼x12¾, 12¾x13¼
2004, June 1
1894-1896 A1136 Set of 3 2.00 2.00
Imperf
Size: 80x60mm
1897 A1136 £2 multi 2.00 2.00

Pres. Hosni Mubarak, "Education for All" Arab Regional Conference Emblem A1137

Stylized Children, Emblems — A1138

Perf. 12¾x13¼, 13¼x12¾
2004, June 1
1898 A1137 30p yel & multi .35 .25
1899 A1137 125p red org & multi .60 .25
1900 A1138 125p multi .60 .60
Nos. 1898-1900 (3) 1.55 1.45
Imperf
Size: 80x60mm
1901 A1137 £2 blue & multi 1.75 1.75

Construction and Housing Bank, 25th Anniv. — A1139

2004, June 24 Perf. 13¼x12¾
1902 A1139 30p multi .60 .25

2004 Summer Olympics, Athens — A1140

Background color: 30p, Gray. 150p, Orange yellow.

Perf. 13¼x12¾
2004, Aug. 13 Litho.
1903-1904 A1140 Set of 2 1.50 1.40

Scouting in Egypt, 90th Anniv. A1141

2004, Aug. 15 Perf. 12¾x13¼
1905 A1141 30p multi .80 .30

14th Intl. Folklore Festival, Ismailia — A1142

2004, Aug. 24 Perf. 13¼x12¾
1906 A1142 30p multi .70 .25

Administrative Attorneys, 50th Anniv. — A1143

2004, Sept. 16 Perf. 13¼x12¾
1907 A1143 30p multi .60 .25
Imperf
Size: 60x80mm
1908 A1143 £1 multi 1.50 1.50

Egyptian National Archives, 50th Anniv. A1144

2004, Sept. 20 Perf. 12¾x13¼
1909 A1144 30p multi .75 .25

Light and Hope Society, 50th Anniv. A1145

2004, Sept. 26
1910 A1145 30p multi .70 .25

General Arab Journalists Union, 10th Conference — A1146

2004, Oct. 2 Perf. 13¼x12¾
1911 A1146 125p multi 1.00 .80

Telecom Egypt, 150th Anniv. A1146a

2004, Oct. 3 Litho. Perf. 12¾x13¼
1911A A1146a 30p multi 18.50 18.50

No. 1911A was withdrawn from sale after a few days as anniversary emblem was incorrect.

Military Production Day, 50th Anniv. A1147

2004, Oct. 6 Perf. 12¾x13¼
1912 A1147 30p multi .60 .30

World Post Day — A1148

2004, Oct. 9
1913 A1148 150p multi 1.10 1.00

EGYPT

Egyptian Youth Hostels Association, 50th Anniv. — A1149

2004, Oct. 20
1914 A1149 30p multi .80 .25

Rose
A1150

Songbird
A1151

Perf. 12¾x13¼   Litho.
1915 A1150 30p multi .50 .25
Perf. 13¼x12¾
1916 A1151 30p multi .50 .25

24th Arab Scouting Congress
A1152

2004, Nov. 27 *Perf. 12¾x13¼*
1917 A1152 30p multi .65 .25

Arab Scouting Organization, 50th Anniv.
A1153

2004, Dec. 4
1918 A1153 30p multi .65 .25

Islamic Art Museum Foundation, Cent. — A1154

2004, Dec. 15 *Perf. 13¼x12¾*
1919 A1154 30p multi .65 .25

FIFA (Fédération Internationale de Football Association), Cent.
A1155

2004, Dec. 15 *Perf. 12¾x13¼*
1920 A1155 150p multi 1.25 1.00

Fekri Abaza (1896-1979), Journalist
A1156

Abd El Rahman El Sharqawi (1920-87), Journalist
A1157

2004, Dec. 28 *Perf. 13¼x12¾*
1921 A1156 30p multi .40 .25
1922 A1157 30p multi .40 .25

Telecom Egypt, 150th Anniv.
A1158

Color of central panel: 30p, White. 125p, Gray.

2004, Dec. 30 *Perf. 12¾x13¼*
1923-1924 A1158 Set of 2 1.50 1.10

First Sale of Natural Gas to Jordan
A1159

2005, Jan. 1
1925 A1159 30p multi .90 .30

Post Day — A1160

2005, Jan. 2 *Perf. 13¼x12¾*
1926 A1160 30p multi .80 .30

Opening of Om El Massrean — El Moneib Subway Line, Cairo
A1161

2005, Jan. 16 *Perf. 12¾x13¼*
1927 A1161 30p multi .65 .30
Imperf
Size: 80x59mm
1928 A1161 150p multi 1.40 1.40

Police Day — A1162

Pres. Hosni Mubarak and flag stripes aligned: 30p, Vertically. £1, Horizontally.

2005, Jan. 25 *Perf. 13¼x12¾*
1929 A1162 30p multi .60 .25
Imperf
Size: 80x59mm
1930 A1162 £1 multi 1.25 1.25

El Mohandes Insurance Company, 25th Anniv. — A1163

2005, Jan. 26 *Perf. 13¼x12¾*
1931 A1163 30p multi .65 .30

9th Intl. Telecommunications and Information Conference, Cairo — A1164

2005, Feb. 1
1932 A1164 30p multi .65 .25

7th University Youth Week — A1165

2005, Feb. 5
1933 A1165 30p multi .65 .25

Rotary International, Cent. — A1166

2005, Feb. 23 *Litho.*
1934 A1166 30p multi .75 .30

38th Intl. Fair, Cairo — A1167

2005, Mar. 15
1935 A1167 30p multi .50 .25

Arab League, 60th Anniv. — A1168

2005, Mar. 22
1936 A1168 30p multi .55 .25

Orphan's Day — A1169

2005, Apr. 2
1937 A1169 30p multi .70 .30

Compare with Types A1132 and A1199. See also Nos. 2035, 2053.

Heliopolis Foundation, Cent.
A1170

2005, May 5 *Perf. 12¾x13¼*
1938 A1170 30p multi .65 .25

National Center of Social and Criminological Research, 50th Anniv. — A1171

2005, May 22 *Litho.* *Perf. 13¼x12¾*
1939 A1171 30p multi .70 .30

Egyptian-European Association Agreement, 1st Anniv. — A1172

2005, June 1
1940 A1172 150p multi .90 .50

World Environment Day — A1173

2005, June 5 *Perf. 12¾x13¼*
1941 A1173 30p multi .80 .30

World Summit on the Information Society, Tunis — A1174

2005, July 31 *Litho.* *Perf. 13¼x12¾*
1942 A1174 150p multi 1.40 1.40

Ministry of Youth, 50th Anniv. — A1175

Background colors: 30p, Green. 125p, Olive green.

2005, Aug. 13
1943-1944 A1175 Set of 2 1.25 1.10

Presidential Elections — A1176

2005, Sept. 7
1945 A1176 30p multi .65 .30

13th World Psychiatry Congress, Cairo — A1177

Designs: 30p, Emblem. 150p, Emblem and funerary mask of King Tutankhamun, horiz.

2005, Sept. 10
1946 A1177 30p multi .65 .30
Imperf
Size: 80x60mm
1947 A1177 150p multi 1.90 1.90

World Literacy Day — A1178

2005, Sept. 24 Perf. 12¾x13¼
1948 A1178 30p multi .70 .30

Re-election of Pres. Hosni Mubarak — A1179

2005, Sept. 27 Perf. 13¼x12¾
1949 A1179 30p multi .60 .25

Mohamed El-Baradei, Director General of Intl. Atomic Energy Agency — A1180

Background colors: 30p, Blue green. 150p, Rose lilac.

2005, Oct. 8
1950-1951 A1180 Set of 2 1.75 1.50

Awarding of 2005 Nobel Peace Prize to El-Baradei and IAEA.

World Post Day — A1181

Denominations: 30p, 150p.

2005, Oct. 9
1952-1953 A1181 Set of 2 1.40 1.25

Intl. Year of Sports and Physical Education — A1182

2005, Oct. 24
1954 A1182 150p multi 1.25 1.00

United Nations, 60th Anniv. A1183

2005, Oct. 24 Perf. 12¾x13¼
1955 A1183 150p multi 1.25 1.00

Festivals — A1184

2005, Nov. 1 Perf. 13¼x12¾
1956 A1184 30p multi .70 .30

Alexandria Biennale, 50th Anniv. — A1185

2005, Dec. 1
1957 A1185 30p multi .65 .30

K-8 Training Airplane A1186

Denominations: 30p, 150p.

2005, Dec. 26 Perf. 12¾x13¼ Litho.
1958-1959 A1186 Set of 2 2.00 1.50

Sayed Mekawi, Musician A1187

Mohamed El Mogi (1923-95), Musician A1188

Kamal El Taweel, Composer A1189

Ali Ismael (1921-75), Composer A1190

Mohamed Roshdi, Folk Singer — A1191

2005, Dec. 31 Perf. 13¼x12¾
1960 Horiz. strip of 5 1.75 1.75
  a. A1187 30p green & multi .30 .25
  b. A1188 30p blue & multi .30 .25
  c. A1189 30p lilac & black .30 .25
  d. A1190 30p org & black .30 .25
  e. A1191 30p brt org & black .30 .25

Post Day — A1192

2006, Jan. 2
1961 A1192 30p multi .75 .30

25th Africa Cup of Nations Soccer Tournament — A1193

2006, Jan. 20
1962 A1193 30p multi .60 .25

Arab University Youth Week A1194

2006, Feb. 4 Perf. 12¾x13¼
1963 A1194 30p multi .55 .25

Intl. Telecommunications, Information and Networking Exhibition, Cairo — A1195

2006, Feb. 5 Perf. 13¼x12¾
1964 A1195 30p multi .55 .25

Pres. Hosni Mubarak Holding African Cup of Nations A1196

2006, Feb. 10 Perf. 12¾x13¼
1965 A1196 30p multi .75 .35
Size: 80x60mm
Imperf
1966 A1196 150p multi 1.75 1.60

Information and Decision Support Center, 20th Anniv. — A1197

2006, Mar. 27 Perf. 13¼x12¾
1967 A1197 30p multi .55 .25

Total Solar Eclipse of March 29, 2006 A1198

2006, Mar. 29 Perf. 12¾x13¼
1968 A1198 30p multi .55 .35
Size: 82x60mm
Imperf
1969 A1198 150p multi 2.25 1.90

Orphan's Day — A1199

2006, Apr. 2 Perf. 13¼x12¾
1970 A1199 30p multi .70 .30

Compare with types A1132 and A1169. See also Nos. 2035, 2053.

Gamal Hemdan (1928-93), Geographical Historian — A1200

2006, Apr. 16
1971 A1200 30p lilac & black .55 .30

Abd El Rahman ibn Khaldun (1332-1406), Historian — A1201

2006, May 27
1972 A1201 30p multi .70 .30

World Environment Day — A1202

Designs: 30p, Stone pillar in White Desert. 150p, Trees in desert.

2006, June 5 Perf. 12¾x13¼
1973-1974 A1202 Set of 2 1.50 1.25

EGYPT

Diplomatic Relations Between Egypt and People's Republic of China, 50th Anniv. — A1203

No. 1975, £1.50: a, Abu Simbel Temple, Egypt. b, South Gate Pavilion, China.

2006, July 13	Litho.	Perf. 12		
1975	A1203	Horiz. pair, #a-b, + central label	1.75	1.75
c.		Souvenir sheet, #1975	25.00	25.00

Military Academy Headquarters, Heliopolis, 50th Anniv. — A1204

2006, July 19		Perf. 12¾x13¼		
1976	A1204	30p multi	.70	.30

Nationalization of the Suez Canal, 50th Anniv. — A1205

2006, July 26		Perf. 13¼x12¾		
1977	A1205	30p multi	.55	.25

World Post Day — A1206

Denominations: 30p, 150p.

2006, Oct. 9				
1978-1979	A1206	Set of 2	1.50	1.25

China - Africa Summit — A1206a

No. 1979A: b, Chinese mask. c, African mask.

2006, Nov. 5	Litho.	Perf. 12		
1979A	A1206a	Horiz. pair with central label	2.25	2.25
b.-c.		£1.50 Either single	.80	.60

National Housing Census — A1207

2006, Nov. 21	Litho.	Perf. 13¼x13		
1980	A1207	30p multi	.55	.25

Al-Ahram Newspaper — A1208

No. 1981: a, Newspaper headquarters. b, Newspaper emblem. 150p, Headquarters and emblem.

2006, Nov. 26		Perf. 13x13¼		
1981	A1208	30p Horiz. pair, #a-b, + central label	1.00	1.00

Imperf
Size: 80x60mm

1982	A1208	150p multi	1.00	1.00

Egyptian Initiative to Support Lebanon A1209

2006, Dec. 27		Perf. 13x13¼		
1983	A1209	150p multi	1.00	1.00

Feasts A1210

2006, Dec. 30				
1984	A1210	30p multi	.45	.25

Post Day — A1211

2007, Jan. 2				
1985	A1211	30p multi	.45	.25

Ali El Kassar (1888-1957), Artist — A1212

2007, Jan. 15		Perf. 13¼x13		
1986	A1212	30p multi	.45	.25

Automobile and Touring Club of Egypt A1213

2007, Jan. 14	Litho.	Perf. 12¾x13¼		
1987	A1213	30p multi	.55	.30

Imperf
Size: 80x60mm

1988	A1213	150p multi	1.50	1.50

Police Day — A1214

2007, Jan. 25		Perf. 12¾x13¼		
1989	A1214	30p multi	.55	.30

Imperf
Size: 80x60mm

1990	A1214	150p multi	1.00	1.00

Rededication of National Library A1215

2007, Feb. 25		Perf. 12¾x13¼		
1991	A1215	30p multi	.55	.30

Arabic Language Academy, 75th Anniv. — A1216

2007, Mar. 17		Perf. 13¼x12¾		
1992	A1216	30p multi	.55	.30

World Health Day — A1217

2007, Apr. 7	Litho.	Perf. 12¾x13¼		
1993	A1217	30p multi	.55	.30

Egyptian Trade Union Federation, 50th Anniv. — A1218

2007, May 1		Perf. 13¼x12¾		
1994	A1218	30p multi	.45	.25

Egypt Air, 75th Anniv. — A1219

Anniversary emblem and: 30p, Biplane. 150p, Biplane and jet.

2007, May 7		Perf. 12¾x13¼		
1995-1996	A1219	Set of 2	1.00	.75

Return of Sinai to Egypt, 25th Anniv. A1220

No. 1997: a, Monastery of St. Catherine. b, Salah el Din Castle. c, Sharm el-Sheikh. d, Oasis of Nabq.

2007, Apr. 25	Litho.	Perf. 12¾x13¼		
1997	A1220	30p Block of 4, #a-d	1.90	1.25

Mevlana Jalal ad-Din Rumi (1207-73), Islamic Philosopher — A1221

2007, May 8		Perf. 13¼x12¾		
1998	A1221	150p multi	.55	.30

World Environment Day — A1222

Designs: 30p, Sinai baton blue butterfly. 150p, Melting ice, horiz.

Perf. 13¼x12¾, 12¾x13¼

2007, June 5				
1999-2000	A1222	Set of 2	1.50	.75

Scouting, Cent. A1223

2007, June 6		Perf. 12¾x13¼		
2001	A1223	150p multi	1.25	.80

EuroMed Postal Conference, Marseille, France A1224

2007, July 9				
2002	A1224	150p multi	1.10	.75

Diplomatic Relations Between Egypt and Nepal, 50th Anniv. A1225

2007, July 16				
2003	A1225	150p multi	1.10	.75

Egyptian Air Force, 75th Anniv. A1226

2007, Oct. 14	Litho.	Perf. 13x13¼		
2004	A1226	30p multi	.55	.25

A1227

11th Arab Games A1228

2007, Oct. 26	Litho.	Perf. 13¼x12¾		
2005	A1227	150p multi	1.25	.90

Imperf
Size: 95x75mm

2006	A1228	150p multi	1.25	1.00

Assiut University, 50th Anniv. — A1229

2007, Nov. 27		Perf. 13¼x12¾		
2007	A1229	30p brn & blk	.45	.25

EGYPT

Hafez Ibrahim (1872-1932), Poet — A1230

Ahmed Shawky (1868-1932), Poet — A1231

2007, Dec. 16
2008 A1230 30p multi .45 .25
2009 A1231 30p multi .45 .25

A 150p stamp issued in December 2007 depicting riders on horses on a beach with a se-tenant label was created exclusively for the Utopia Resort in Marsa Alam. The resort sold the stamps to its guests.

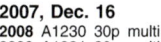

Egyptian Handball Federation, 50th Anniv. — A1232

2007, Dec. 30
2010 A1232 30p multi .50 .25

Musicians A1233

2008, Jan. 1 Perf. 12¾x13¼
2011 A1233 30p multi .45 .25

Post Day A1234

2008, Feb. 7 Litho. Imperf.
2012 A1234 150p multi 1.00 1.00

Africa Cup of Nations Soccer Championships, Ghana — A1235

2008, Feb. 10 Perf. 13¼x13
2013 A1235 30p multi .45 .25

Wadi El-Hitan UNESCO World Heritage Site — A1236

No. 2014: a, Whale bones on ground. b, Reconstructed whale skeleton.

2008, Feb. 10 Perf. 13x13¼
2014 Horiz. pair with central label 1.00 1.00
a.-b. A1236 30p Either single .45 .25

Cairo University, Cent. — A1237

2008, Apr. 14 Perf. 13¼x13
2015 A1237 30p multi .45 .25

Land Mine Clearance in Northwest Egypt A1238

No. 2016 — Map and: a, Amputee surrounded by land mines. b, Hand, "no land mines" symbol, vert.

Perf. 13x13¼, 13¼x13 (#2016b)
2008, Apr. 22
2016 A1238 150p Pair, #a-b 1.10 1.10

Telecom Africa Conference — A1239

2008, May 12 Perf. 13¼x13
2017 A1239 30p multi .45 .25

World Environment Day — A1240

Background colors: 30p, Blue. 150p, Lilac.

2008, June 5
2018-2019 A1240 Set of 2 1.00 .70

Faculty of Fine Arts, Cent. A1241

No. 2020 — Background color: a, 30p, Blue. b, 150p, Green.

2008, June 21 Litho. Perf. 13¼x13
2020 A1241 Horiz. pair, #a-b 1.25 1.25

Pan African Postal Union Plenipotentiary Conference, Cairo — A1242

2008, June 28 Perf. 13x13¼
2021 A1242 150p multi 1.25 .60

Cairo University, Cent. — A1237 (cont.)

2008, July 11
2022 A1243 150p multi 1.25 .85

Egypt Air Joining Star Alliance A1243

Alexandria, 2008 Islamic Cultural Capital A1244

2008, July 26
2023 A1244 150p multi .85 .60

Arab Post Day A1245

No. 2024 — Emblem and: a, World map, pigeon. b, Camel caravan.

2008, Aug. 3
2024 Horiz. pair 2.00 2.00
a.-b. A1245 150p Either single .75 .60

24th Universal Postal Union Congress, Geneva, Switzerland A1246

2008, Aug. 4 Litho. Perf. 12¾x13¼
2025 A1246 150p multi 1.00 .75

Men's Sports Education Faculty, 50th Anniv. — A1247

2008, Oct. 15 Litho. Perf. 13¼x13
2026 A1247 30p multi .50 .30

Postech 2008 Intl. Postal Technology Conference, Sharm El-Sheikh A1248

Map and: 30p, Queen Nefertari holding Postech 2008 emblem. 150p, Statue of King Tutankhamun, hand holding Postech emblem.

Perf. 12¾x13¼
2008, Nov. 17 Litho.
2027-2028 A1248 Set of 2 1.40 .90

Egyptian Cooperative Movement, Cent. — A1249

2008, Dec. 22 Perf. 13¼x12¾
2029 A1249 30p multi .45 .25

Natl. Telecommunications Institute, 25th Anniv. — A1250

2008, Dec. 31 Perf. 12¾x13¼
2030 A1250 30p multi .55 .30

Natl. Sports Council — A1251

2009, Mar. 3 Perf. 13¼x12¾
2031 A1251 150p multi .95 .75

Constitutional Judiciary, 40th Anniv. — A1252

Designs: 30p, Emblem, text below. 150p, Emblem, text at right, horiz.

2009, Mar. 7 Perf. 13¼x12¾
2032 A1252 30p multi .65 .40

Size:80x60mm
Imperf
2033 A1252 150p multi 1.00 1.00

Intl. Francophone Day — A1253

2009, Mar. 20 Perf. 12¾x13¼
2034 A1253 150p multi .95 .55

Orphan's Day — A1254

2009, Apr. 3 Perf. 13¼x12¾
2035 A1254 150p multi 1.00 .60

Compare with Types A1132, A1169 and A1199. See also No. 2053.

Intl. Labor Organization, 90th Anniv. A1255

2009, Apr. 21 Perf. 12¾x13¼
2036 A1255 150p multi .90 .60

399

EGYPT

Suzanne Mubarak Women's International Peace Movement — A1256

2009, May 14   Perf. 13¼x12¾
2037 A1256 150p multi   .75 .55

Yehia Hakki (1905-92), Writer A1257

2009, May 11   Litho.   Perf. 12¾x13¼
2038 A1257 150p multi   .95 .55

Nobel Laureates From Africa A1258

No. 2039: a, Ahmed Zewail, Chemistry, 1999. b, Bishop Desmond Tutu, Peace, 1984. c, Wangari Maathai, Peace 2004. d, Anwar al-Sadat, Peace, 1978. e, Naguib Mahfouz, Literature, 1988. f, Allan M. Cormack, Physiology or Medicine, 1979. g, Nelson Mandela, Peace, 1993. h, Wole Soyinka, Literature, 1986. i, Sydney Brenner, Physiology or Medicine, 2002. j, F.W. de Klerk, Peace, 1993. k, Nadine Gordimer, Literature, 1991. l, Max Theiler, Physiology or Medicine, 1951. m, Mohamed El Baradei, Peace, 2005. n, Albert Luthuli, Peace, 1960. o, Kofi Annan, Peace, 2001. p, J.M. Coetzee, Literature, 2003.

2009, June 9
2039   Sheet of 16, #a-p, + 9 labels   22.50 22.50
a.-p. A1258 150p Any single   .95 .75

Fourth Extraordinary Session of the Pan-African Postal Union Plenipotentiary Conference, Cairo.

Fifteenth Non-Aligned Movement Summit, Sharm el-Sheikh — A1259

2009, July 15   Perf. 13¼x12¾
2040 A1259 150p multi   .55 .55

Opening of Mubarak Public Library, Damanhour A1260

2009, May 7   Litho.   Perf. 13x13¼
2041 A1260 150p multi   .95 .70

Jerusalem, Capital of Arab Culture — A1261

2009, Aug. 3   Perf. 13¼x13
2042 A1261 150p multi   .95 .75

FIFA Under-20 World Cup Soccer Championships, Egypt — A1262

No. 2042 — Tournament emblem, trophy and flag of participating team: a, Paraguay. b, Brazil. c, Uruguay. d, Germany. e, Nigeria. f, South Korea. g, Venezuela. h, Ghana. i, United Arab Emirates. j, South Africa. k, Egypt. l, Spain. m, Italy. n, Hungary. o, Czech Republic. p, Costa Rica.

2009, Oct. 5   Perf. 13x13¼
2043   Sheet of 16, #a-p, + 9 labels   19.50 19.50
a.-p. A1262 150p Any single   .95 .75

Fourth Ministerial Conference of Forum on China-African Cooperation, Sharm El Sheikh A1263

2009, Nov. 8
2044 A1263 150p multi   .95 .75

Fourth Meeting of Internet Governance Forum, Sharm El Sheikh A1264

2009, Nov. 15
2045 A1264 150p multi   .95 .75

Luxor Governate — A1264a

2009, Dec. 9   Litho.   Perf. 12¾x13¼
2045A A1264a 250p multi   1.25 1.25

Egyptian Society of Political Economy, Statistics and Legislation, Cent. A1265

2009, Dec. 19
2046 A1265 150p multi   .95 .95

Pharmaceutical Industry Drug Holding Company, 75th Anniv. — A1266

Background colors: 30p, Pink, yellow and pale green. 150p, Green.

2009, Dec. 19   Perf. 13¼x13
2047-2048 A1266   Set of 2   .95 .95

Egyptian Stock Exchange, 125th Anniv. A1267

Stock Exchange Building with anniversary emblem at left in: 30p, Gold and white. 150p, Gold (75x30mm).

2009, Dec. 21   Perf. 13x13¼
2049-2050 A1267   Set of 2   .95 .95

Pan-African Postal Union, 30th Anniv. A1268

2010, Jan. 18
2051 A1268 150p multi   .85 .85

National Council for Women, 10th Anniv. A1269

2010, Mar. 16
2052 A1269 30p multi   .65 .65

Orphan's Day — A1270

2010, Jan. 4   Litho.   Perf. 13¼x12¾
2053 A1270 30p multi   .55 .55

Compare with Types A1132, A1169 and A1199. See also No. 2035.

Edfu Temple A1271

2010, Jan. 5   Perf. 12¾x13¼
2054 A1271 250p multi   1.50 1.50

Aswan High Dam, 50th Anniv. A1272

No. 2055 — Part of dam: a, 30p. b, £1.

2010, Jan. 15
2055 A1272   Horiz. pair, #a-b   1.50 1.50

Arab League Center, 50th Anniv. A1273

2010, Mar. 22
2056 A1273 200p multi   1.25 1.25

Egyptian Soccer Team, 2010 Winner of African Cup of Nations A1274

No. 2057 — Pyramid, African Cup of Nations, tournament emblems and: a, 30p, Crocodile mascot. b, 200p, Eagle mascot. c, 250p, Antelope mascot.
No. 2058, 250p, Soccer players, African Cup of nations, years of Egyptian championships, horiz.

2010, Jan. 31   Litho.   Perf. 13¼x12¾
2057 A1274   Horiz. strip of 3, #a-c   4.50 4.50
Size: 80x60mm
Imperf.
2058 A1274 250p multi   1.50 1.50

Egyptian Gazette, 130th Anniv. — A1275

2010, Apr. 20   Perf. 13¼x12¾
2059 A1275 30p multi   .55 .55

Egypt Pavilion, Expo 2010, Shanghai A1276

2010, May 1   Litho.   Perf. 12¾x13¼
2060 A1276 £2.50 multi   1.75 1.75

Opening of Road to Red Sea — A1277

2010, May 27   Perf. 13¼x12¾
2061 A1277 £1 multi   .95 .95

World Environment Day A1278

2010, June 5   Perf. 12¾x13¼
2062 A1278 £2.50 multi   1.50 1.50

Tawfiq al-Hakim (1898-1987), Writer — A1279

2010, June 6   Litho.   Perf. 13¼x12¾
2063 A1279 150p multi   .95 .95

Second Egyptian Post Innovation Meeting.

Reading for All, 20th Anniv. — A1280

2010, June 21
2064 A1280 £1 multi   .95 .95

EGYPT

Egyptian Television, 50th Anniv. — A1281

2010, July 21
2065 A1281 £1.50 multi   1.25 1.25

Alexandria, 2010 Capital of Arab Tourism — A1282

2010, July 22 Perf. 12¾x13¼
2066 A1282 150p multi   1.25 1.25

2010 Asia-Pacific Broadcasting Union Robotics Competition, Cairo A1283

2010, Sept. 19
2067 A1283 £2.50 multi   1.50 1.50

2010 Euromed Postal Conference, Alexandria A1284

2010, Sept. 28
2068 A1284 £2.50 multi   1.75 1.75

Alabaster Canopic Jar — A1285

2010, Oct. 8 Perf. 13¼x12¾
2069 A1285 £2.50 multi   1.75 1.75
See Slovakia No. 601.

Second Arab University Games, Cairo — A1286

2010, Oct. 17 Perf. 13¼x12¾
2070 A1286 30p multi   .55 .55

World Statistics Day — A1287

2010, Oct. 20
2071 A1287 30p multi   .55 .55

Reopening of Museum of Islamic Art, Cairo — A1288

No. 2072: a, 30p, Goblet. £2, Bas-relief. £2.50, Plate with antelope design.

2010, Oct. 25
2072 A1288 Horiz. strip of 3, #a-c   2.50 2.50

Egyptian Olympic Committee, Cent. — A1289

2010, Dec. 11
2073 A1289 30p multi   .60 .60

Information and Decision Support Center, 25th Anniv. A1290

2010, Dec. 20 Perf. 12¾x13¼
2074 A1290 30p multi   .55 .55

Cairo Stadium, 50th Anniv. A1291

2010, Dec. 30 Imperf.
2075 A1291 £2.50 multi   1.50 1.50

Post Day A1292

No. 2076 — Egyptian stamps: a, #3. b, #57. c, #107. d, #183. e, #271. f, #321. g, #386. h, #389. i, #873. j, #C1.

2011, Jan. 2 Perf. 13
2076   Block of 10   5.50 5.50
a.-h. A1292 30p Any single   .40 .30
i. A1292 £2 multi   1.00 .75
j. A1292 £2.50 multi   1.25 1.00

Cairo Tower, 50th Anniv. A1293

No. 2077 — Tower: a, 30p, In daylight. b, £2.50, At night.

2011, Apr. 11 Perf. 13¼x12¾
2077 A1293 Horiz. pair, #a-b   2.25 2.25

World Environment Day — A1294

2011, June 5
2078 A1294 £2.50 multi   1.50 1.50

War Academy, 200th Anniv. A1295

2011, July 20 Perf. 12¾x13¼
2079 A1295 30p multi   .80 .80

Rivers A1296

No. 2080: a, 30p, Pyramids, Nile River. b, 30p, Downtown Singapore, Singapore River. c, £2, Ancient Egyptian boat, Nile River. d, £2, Modern boat, Singapore River. e, £2.50, Cairo skyline, yellow flowers, Nile River. f, £2.50, Singapore buildings, pink flowers, Singapore River.

2011, Oct. 17
2080 A1296 Block of 6, #a-f   3.25 3.25
See Singapore Nos. 1513-1515.

Post Day A1297

No. 2081: a, Dove, flowers, Egypt Post emblem. b, Post office, air mail envelopes. c, Eye of Horus, flowers, Egypt Post emblem.

2012, Jan. 2 Perf. 13¼x12¾
2081 A1297 £2.50 Horiz. strip of 3, #a-c   2.50 2.50

Temple — A1297a

2011 Litho. Perf. 11¼
2081D A1297a £2.50 multi   — —

January 25 Revolution, 1st Anniv. — A1298

2012, Jan. 25 Imperf.
2082 A1298 £2.50 multi   .85 .85

Pope Shenouda III of Alexandria (1923-2012) — A1299

2012, Mar. 17 Imperf.
2083 A1299 £5 multi   1.75 1.75

Diplomatic Relations Between Egypt and Azerbaijan, 20th Anniv. — A1300

No. 2084: a, Arches and Maiden Tower, Baku, Azerbaijan. b, Sphinx and Pyramids, Egypt.

2012, May 28 Perf. 12¾x13¼
2084 A1300 £2.50 Horiz. pair, #a-b   1.75 1.75

Environment Day — A1301

2012, June 5 Perf. 13¼x12¾
2085 A1301 £2 multi   .70 .70

A1302

Overthrow of King Farouk by Gamal Abdel Nasser, 60th Anniv. — A1303

2012, July 23 Perf. 12¾x13¼
2086 A1302 £2 multi   .65 .65
 Imperf
2087 A1303 £4 multi   1.40 1.40

2012 Summer Olympics, London — A1304

No. 2088 — Mascot and: a, Cycling. b, Running. c, Emblem of 2012 Summer Olympics. d, Basketball. e, Soccer.

2012, July 27 Perf. 13¼x12¾
2088   Horiz. strip of 5   4.25 4.25
a.-e. A1304 £2.50 Any single   .85 .85

EGYPT

Arab Postal Day — A1305

2012, Aug. 3   *Perf. 12¾x13¼*
2089 A1305 £3 multi   1.00 1.00

Festivals A1306

No. 2090: a, Rider on blue gray horse, heads of white and black horses. b, Two riders, black horse, head of brown horse. c, Rider on brown horse.

2012, Aug. 18   *Perf. 13¼x12¾*
2090 A1306 £1 Horiz. strip of 3, #a-c   1.00 1.00

Lawyers Trade Union, Cent. A1307

2012, Sept. 12   *Perf. 12¾x13¼*
2091 A1307 £1 multi   .35 .35

Tourism and Sustainable Energy — A1308

2012, Sept. 27   *Perf. 13¼x12¾*
2092 A1308 £1 multi   .35 .35

Helwan University Art Education Faculty, 75th Anniv. — A1309

2012, Nov. 12   Litho.
2093 A1309 £2 multi   .65 .65

Post Day A1310

No. 2094: a, Ancient Egyptian art with Isis seated at right, envelopes. b, Lotus flowers, funerary mask of King Tutankhamun. c, Anceit Egyptian art with Isis seated at left.

2013, Jan. 2   *Perf. 13¼x13*
2094 A1310 £3 Horiz. strip of 3, #a-c   3.00 3.00

January 25th Revolution, 2nd Anniv. A1311

2013, Jan. 25   *Perf. 13x13¼*
2095 A1311 £1 multi   .30 .30

Victory of Egyptian Team at African Cup of Nations Youth Soccer Championships A1312

2013, Apr. 24   *Perf. 13¼x13*
2096 A1312 £3 multi   .90 .90

Return of Sinai to Egypt, 31st Anniv. A1313

No. 2097 — Various tourist attractions and Sinai Peninsula map showing: a, Northwestern section. b, Northeastern section. c, Southwestern section. d, Southeastern section.

2013, Apr. 25   *Perf. 13x13¼*
2097 A1313 £2 Block of 4, #a-d   2.40 2.40

World Environment Day — A1314

2013, June 5   *Perf. 13¼x13*
2098 A1314 £3 multi   .85 .85

July 23rd Revolution, 61st Anniv. A1315

2013, July 23   Litho.   *Perf. 12¾x13¼*
2099 A1315 £3 multi   .85 .85

Day of the Nile Inundation — A1316

2013, Aug. 25   Litho.   Imperf.
2100 A1316 £4 multi   1.25 1.25

Intl. Islamic Council for Da'wa and Relief — A1317

   Perf. 13¼x12¾
2013, Sept. 21   Litho.
2101 A1317 £2 multi   .60 .60

World Tourism Day — A1318

Perf. 13¼x12¾
2013, Sept. 27   Litho.
2102 A1318 £3 multi   .90 .90

A1319

October War Against Israel, 40th Anniv. A1320

2013, Oct. 6   Litho.   *Perf. 12¾x13¼*
2103 A1319 £1 multi   .30 .30
2104 A1320 £4 multi   1.25 1.25

Thutmosis III — A1321   Thutmosis III — A1321a

Sculptures of Egyptian Pharaohs — A1322

Designs: £1, Senusret I. £3, Ramesses II. £4, Akhenaten.

2013-20   Litho.   *Perf. 11¼*
2105 A1321 50p org & multi   .25 .25
2106 A1321 50p grn & multi   .25 .25
   Perf. 11x11½
2107 A1322 £1 multi   .30 .30
2108 A1322 £3 lil & multi   .90 .90
2108A A1322 £3 blue & multi   — —
2109 A1322 £4 brn & multi   1.25 1.25
2109A A1322 £4 rose brn & multi   — —

Star Punched Out in Upper Left Corner
   Perf. 13½x14
2109B A1321a 50p multi ('20)   — —
Nos. 2105-2109A (7)   2.95 2.95
Issued: Nos. 2105-2109A, 10/7. See Nos. 2174-2175.

World Post Day — A1323

2013, Oct. 9   Litho.   *Perf. 12¾x13¼*
2110 A1323 £4 multi   1.25 1.25

Tourists on Horseback, Utopia Resort, Marsa Alam — A1324

Old Town, Hurghada — A1325

Madinat Makadi Resort, Hurghada — A1326

Perf. 12¾x13¼
2013, Dec. 17   Litho.
2111 A1324 £4 multi   1.25 1.25
2112 A1325 £4 multi   1.25 1.25
2113 A1326 £4 multi   1.25 1.25
Nos. 2111-2113 (3)   3.75 3.75

Nile Meter, by M. Sabry A1327

2014, Jan. 2   Litho.   Imperf.
2114 A1327 £4 multi   1.25 1.25
Post Day.

January 25th Revolution, 3rd Anniv. A1328

2014, Jan. 25   Litho.   *Perf. 12¾x13¼*
2115 A1328 £2 multi   .60 .60

Intl. Women's Day — A1329

2014, Mar. 8   Litho.   *Perf. 12¾x13¼*
2116 A1329 £2 multi   .60 .60

World Heritage Day A1330

No. 2117: a, Two women. b, Men and camel. c, Men playing board game. d, Man, pottery in windows.

2014, Apr. 18   Litho.   *Perf. 12¾x13¼*
2117 A1330 £1 Block of 4 #a-d   1.25 1.25

Diversion of the Nile River, 50th Anniv. A1331

2014, May 15   Litho.   Imperf.
2118 A1331 £4 multi   1.10 1.10

African Regional Postal Training Center A1332

2014, June 1   Litho.   *Perf. 12¾x13¼*
2119 A1332 £2 multi   .55 .55

Day of the African Child A1333

Perf. 12¾x13¼
2014, June 17   Litho.
2120 A1333 £3 multi   .85 .85

EGYPT

Euromed Postal Emblem and
Mediterranean Sea — A1334

2014, July 9 Litho. Perf. 13x13¼
2121 A1334 £4 multi   1.10 1.10

July 23rd Revolution,
62nd Anniv. — A1335

2014, July 23 Litho. Perf. 13¼x13
2122 A1335 £2 multi   .55 .55

Start of Construction on Second Suez
Canal — A1336

No. 2123: a, Suez Canal emblem, ship, map of northern portion of canal. b, Map of central portion of canal, ships near locks of Panama Canal. c, Map of southern portion of canal, Administration building, ship.

2014, Aug. 5 Litho. Perf. 13¼x13
2123 A1336 £2 Horiz. strip of
3, #a-c   55.00 37.50

No. 2123 was withdrawn shortly after the error in stamp design (the Suez Canal has no locks) was made known to Egypt Post.

General Arab
Insurance Federation,
50th Anniv. — A1337

50th anniversary emblem: No. 2124, Above map of Arab countries. No. 2125, To left of map of Arab countries.

2014, Sept. 1 Litho. Perf. 13¼x13
2124 A1337 £4 multi   1.10 1.10

Imperf
Size: 90x70mm
2125 A1337 £4 multi   1.10 1.10

Start of Construction on New Suez
Canal — A1338

No. 2126: a, Map of canal, Administration Building, ship in canal. b, Map of canal, ship approaching canal. c, Suez Canal emblem, ship in canal.

2014, Sept. 16 Litho. Perf. 13¼x13
2126 A1338 £2 Horiz. strip of 3,
#a-c   1.75 1.75

No. 2126 replaces the hastily withdrawn No. 2123. First day covers of No. 2126 show the Aug. 5 first day cancel of No. 2123, though the stamps were printed after the discovery of the design error on No. 2123.

Shali Siwa
Oasis
A1339

Perf. 12¾x13¼
2014, Sept. 27
2127 A1339 £4 multi   1.10 1.10

October War
Against
Israel, 41st
Anniv.
A1340

2014, Oct. 6 Litho. Perf. 12¾x13¼
2128 A1340 £2 multi   .55 .55

World Post
Day — A1341

2014, Oct. 9 Litho. Perf. 13¼x12¾
2129 A1341 £4 multi   1.10 1.10

Scouting in
Egypt, Cent.
A1342

2014, Oct. 15 Litho. Perf. 12¾x13¼
2130 A1342 £1.25 multi   .35 .35

Arabic Calligraphy — A1343

2014, Dec. 6 Litho. Imperf.
2131 A1343 £5 multi   1.40 1.40

Central Agency for
Public Mobilization and
Statistics,
Cent. — A1344

2014, Dec. 8 Litho. Perf. 13¼x12¾
2132 A1344 £3 multi   .85 .85

Birds
A1345

No. 2133, £1.25: a, Palm dove. b, Hoopoe. c, Roller. d, Bee-eater. e, Sooty falcon. f, Golden oriole.

Perf. 13¼x12¾
2014, Dec. 10 Litho.
2133 A1345 Block of 6, #a-f, + 3
central labels   2.10 2.10

Re-opening of
National
Theater
A1346

Perf. 12¾x13¼
2014, Dec. 20 Litho.
2134 A1346 £1.50 multi   .45 .45

A1347

Amenhotep, Son of Hapu — A1347a

2015-20 Litho. Perf. 11¼
2135 A1347 £3 multi   .85 .85
 a.   Perf. 13x13¼ ('15)

Perf. 13½x14
**Star Punched Out in Upper Left
Corner**
2135B A1347a £3 multi ('20) — —

A1348

Egyptian
Post, 150th
Anniv.
A1349

2015, Jan. 2 Litho. Perf. 12¾x13¼
2136 A1348 £1.50 multi   .45 .45

Imperf
2137 A1349 £4 multi   1.10 1.10

January 25
Revolution,
4th Anniv.
A1350

2015, Jan. 25 Litho. Perf. 12¾x13¼
2138 A1350 £2 multi   .55 .55

Faten Hamama (1931-
2015),
Actress — A1351

2015, Mar. 8 Litho. Perf. 13¼x12¾
2139 A1351 £3 black   .80 .80

Egypt
Economic
Development
Conference
A1352

Perf. 12¾x13¼
2015, Mar. 13 Litho.
2140 A1352 £2 multi   .55 .55

26th Arab Summit,
Sharm el-
Sheikh — A1353

Perf. 13¼x12¾
2015, Mar. 23 Litho.
2141 A1353 £3 multi   .80 .80

International Telecommunication
Union, 150th Anniv — A1354

2015, May 17 Litho. Perf. 12¾x13¼
2142 A1354 £4 multi   1.10 1.10

Dar al-Ifta al-
Misriyyah
Educational
Institute,
120th Anniv.
A1355

2015, June 1 Litho. Perf. 12¾x13¼
2143 A1355 £2 multi   .55 .55

July 23rd
Revolution,
63rd Anniv.
A1356

2015, July 23 Litho. Perf. 12¾x13¼
2144 A1356 £2 multi   .55 .55

Campaign to
Save the Nile
River
A1357

2015, July 25 Litho. Perf. 12¾x13¼
2145 A1357 £2 multi   .55 .55

A1358

New
Suez
Canal
A1359

2015, Aug. 6 Litho. Perf. 12¾x13¼
2146   Horiz. strip of 3   2.40 2.40
 a. A1358 £3 lilac & multi   .80 .80
 b. A1358 £3 beige & multi   .80 .80
 c. A1358 £3 lt blue green & multi   .80 .80
Imperf
2147 A1359 £4 multi   1.10 1.10

EGYPT

Poets A1360

No. 2148: a, Fouad Hadad (1927-85). b, Salah Jaheen (1930-86). c, Abd el Rahman El Abnody (1938-2015).

Perf. 13¼x12¾
2015, Aug. 10   Litho.
2148 A1360 £2 Horiz. strip of 3,
       #a-c   1.60 .80

Food and Agricultural Organization, 70th Anniv. A1361

2015, Oct. 1   Litho.   **Perf. 12¾x13¼**
2149 A1361 £3 multi   .80 .40

October War With Israel, 42nd Anniv. A1362

2015, Oct. 6   Litho.   **Perf. 12¾x13¼**
2150 A1362 £2 multi   .50 .25

A1363

Federation of Afro-Asian Insurers and Reinsurers, 50th Anniv. — A1364

2015, Oct. 12   Litho.   **Perf. 13¼x12¾**
2151 A1363 £4 multi   1.00 .50
   Imperf
2152 A1364 £4 multi   1.00 .50

World Statistics Day — A1365

2015, Oct. 20   Litho.   **Perf. 12¾x13¼**
2153 A1365 £3 multi   .75 .35

Yacht "Mahrousa," 150th Anniv. — A1366

Perf. 12¾x13¼
2015, Dec. 15   Litho.
2154 A1366 £2 multi   .55 .55

Al-Ahram Newspaper, 140th Anniv. — A1367

Perf. 13¼x12¾
2015, Dec. 20   Litho.
2155 A1367 £2 multi   .55 .55

Helwan University Faculty of Applied Arts, 175th Anniv. A1368

Perf. 12¾x13¼
2015, Dec. 31   Litho.
2156 A1368 £2 multi   .55 .55

A1369

First Egyptian Postage Stamps, 150th Anniv. A1370

No. 2157: a, Egypt #4-7, dove, boat. b, Egyptian man on donkey. c, Egypt #1-3, Egyptian man on camel. £4, Emblem of Philatelic Society of Egypt, dove, boat, train, mail carrier on bicycle, mail box.

2016, Jan. 1   Litho.   **Perf. 13¼x12¾**
2157 A1369 £2 Horiz. strip of 3,
       #a-c   1.60 1.60
   Imperf
2158 A1370 £4 multi   1.10 1.10

Syndicate of Journalists, 75th Anniv. — A1371

Perf. 13¼x12¾
2016, Mar. 31   Litho.
2159 A1371 £3 multi   .70 .70

Famous Men A1372

No. 2160: a, United Nations emblem and Boutros Boutros-Ghali (1922-2016), United Nations Secretary-General. b, Muhammad Husayn Haykal (1888-1956), Minister of Education.

2016, May 31   Litho.   **Perf. 13¼x12¾**
2160 A1372 £2 Horiz. pair, #a-b .90 .90

World Day to Combat Drugs A1373

2016, June 26   Litho.
2161 A1373 £2 multi   .45 .45

Egypt Nos. 356, 374, 386, 388 and 393 A1374

2016, July 23   Litho.   *Imperf.*
2162 A1374 £4 multi   .90 .90

July 23 Revolution, 64th anniv.

Arab Postal Day A1375

No. 2163 — Area behind denomination in: a, White. b, Green.

2016, Aug. 3   Litho.   **Perf. 12¾x13¼**
2163 A1375 £3 Horiz. pair, #a-b 1.40 1.40

Gezera Youth Center — A1376

Perf. 13¼x12¾
2016, Aug. 15   Litho.
2164 A1376 £2 multi   .45 .45

Relocation of Abu Simbel Temples, 50th Anniv. — A1377

No. 2165: a, Moving of statues. b, Man wearing glasses. c, Face of Ramesses II statue.

Perf. 13¼x12¾
2016, Aug. 18   Litho.
2165 A1377 £2 Horiz. strip of 3,
       #a-c   1.40 1.40

World Tourism Day A1378

No. 2166: a, Hanging Church, Cairo. b, Al-Moez Street, Cairo. c, Philae Temple, Aswan. d, Qaitbay Castle, Alexandria.

Perf. 12¾x13¼
2016, Sept. 27   Litho.
2166 A1378 £2 Block of 4, #a-d 1.90 1.90

October War Against Israel, 43rd Anniv. A1379

2016, Oct. 6   Litho.   **Perf. 12¾x13¼**
2167 A1379 £2 multi   .45 .45

Egyptian Parliament, 150th Anniv. — A1380

2016, Oct. 22   Litho.   **Perf. 12¾x13¼**
2168 A1380 £2 multi + label   .45 .45

Ahmed Zewail (1946-2016), 1999 Nobel Laureate in Chemistry A1381

2016, Oct. 25   Litho.   **Perf. 12¾x13¼**
2169 A1381 £2 multi   .45 .45

Actors A1382

No. 2170: a, Mahmoud Abd El-Aziz (1946-2016). b, Nour El-Sherif (1946-2015). c, Ahmed Zaki (1949-2005).

Perf. 13¼x12¾ Syncopated
2016, Nov. 27   Litho.
2170 A1382 £2 Horiz. strip of 3,
       #a-c   .70 .70

Miniature Sheet

Giza Zoo, 125th Anniv. A1383

No. 1383: a, Barbary sheep. b, Giraffe. c, Elephant. d, Crocodile. e, Hippopotamus. f, Pelicans. g, Lion. h, Tiger.

2016, Dec. 2   Litho.   **Perf. 12¾x13¼**
2171 A1383 £2 Sheet of 8, #a-h 1.90 1.90

World Day of the Arabic Language — A1384

No. 2172: a, £1, Arabic calligraphy. b, £2, Arabic calligraphy, diff., circle arc at left. c, £2, Arabic calligraphy, diff., circle arc at right.

2016, Dec. 18   Litho.   **Perf. 11½**
2172 A1384 Horiz. strip of 3,
       #a-c   .55 .55

National Circus, 50th Anniv. A1385

2016, Dec. 25   Litho.   *Imperf.*
2173 A1385 £4 multi   .45 .45

Sculptures of Egyptian Pharaohs Type of 2013

Designs: 125p, Pseusennes I (image used on #1759). £4, Akhenaten.

2017   Litho.   **Perf. 11¼**
2174 A1321 125p multi   —   —
2175 A1321 £4 multi   —   —

EGYPT

Dendera Temple — A1385a

Perf. 12¾x13¼
2017, Nov. 19 Litho.
2176 A1385a £5 multi .60 .60

Central Agency for Public Mobilization and Statistics — A1386

Perf. 13¼x12¾ Syncopated
2017, Apr. 10 Litho.
2177 A1386 £2 multi .25 .25

Modern Egypt Heritage, 150th Anniv. A1387

Perf. 12¾x13¼ Syncopated
2017, July 5 Litho.
2178 A1387 £2 multi .25 .25

July 23 Revolution, 65th Anniv. A1388

Perf. 12¾x13¼ Syncopated
2017, July 23 Litho.
2179 A1388 £4 multi .45 .45

General Sports Union for Businesses, 50th Anniv. — A1389

Perf. 13¼x12¾ Syncopated
2017, Sept. 14 Litho.
2180 A1389 £2 multi .25 .25

Forum on Heavenly Religions, Sharm el Sheikh — A1390

Perf. 13¼x12¾ Syncopated
2017, Sept. 28 Litho.
2181 A1390 £4 multi .45 .45

October War Against Israel, 44th Anniv. A1391

Perf. 12¾x13¼ Syncopated
2017, Oct. 6 Litho.
2182 A1391 £2 multi .25 .25

No. 2182 has simulated perfs to look like a label is attached.

A1392

Discovery of Abu Simbel Temples, 200th Anniv. — A1393

Perf. 12¾x13¼ Syncopated
2017, Oct. 21 Litho.
2183 A1392 £4 multi .45 .45

Size: 90x70mm
Imperf
2184 A1393 £5 multi .60 .60

Egyptian Women's Year A1394

Perf. 12¾x13¼ Syncopated
2017, Dec. 10 Litho.
2185 A1394 £2 multi .25 .25

The National Post Organization of Egypt has declared as "illegal" miniature sheets of 3 depicting Renaissance painters and miniature sheets of 4 depicting Coins, Napoleonic Wars, High Speed Trains, and the 2018 Winter Olympics.

Post Day — A1395

Perf. 13¼x12¾ Syncopated
2018, Jan. 2 Litho.
2186 A1395 £2.50 multi .30 .30

2018 World Cup Soccer Championships, Russia — A1396

Designs: £2.50, World Cup trophy, silhouette of soccer player running ball. £5, World Cup trophy, soccer ball, player kicking ball, horiz.

Perf. 13¼x12¾ Syncopated
2018, June 14 Litho.
2187 A1396 £2.50 multi .30 .30

Size: 90x70mm
Imperf
2188 A1395 £5 multi .55 .55

Luxor Temple — A1397

2018, Sept. 12 Litho. **Perf. 11¼**
2189 A1397 £2.50 multi .30 .30

October War Against Israel, 45th Anniv. A1398

Perf. 12¾x13¼ Syncopated
2018, Oct. 6 Litho.
2190 A1398 £4 multi .45 .45

Ministry of Culture, 60th Anniv. A1399

2018, Oct. 14 Litho. **Perf. 12¾x13¼**
2191 A1399 £2.50 multi .30 .30

Post Day — A1400

Perf. 12¾x13¼ Syncopated
2019, Jan. 2 Litho.
2192 A1400 £3 multi .35 .35

Cairo International Book Fair, 50th Anniv. A1401

2019, Jan. 23 Litho. **Perf. 12¾x13¼**
2193 A1401 £2.50 multi .30 .30

Egyptian Chairmanship of African Union A1402

Perf. 12¾x13¼ Syncopated
2019, Feb. 10 Litho.
2194 A1402 £4 multi .45 .45

National Institute of Oceanography and Fisheries, Cent. — A1403

Perf. 12¾x13¼ Syncopated
2019, Feb. 12 Litho.
2195 A1403 £3 multi .35 .35

International Women's Day — A1405

Perf. 13¼x12¾ Syncopated
2019, Mar. 8 Litho.
2198 A1405 £4 multi .50 .50

Saad Zaghloul (1859-1927), Leader of 1919 Egyptian Revolution and Prime Minister A1406

Perf. 12¾x13¼ Syncopated
2019, Mar. 9 Litho.
2199 A1406 £4 multi .50 .50

Return of Sinai to Egypt, 37th Anniv. — A1407

Perf. 13¼x12¾ Syncopated
2019, Apr. 25 Litho.
2200 A1407 £4 multi .50 .50

Labor Day — A1408

Perf. 13¼x12¾ Syncopated
2019, May 1 Litho.
2201 A1408 £5 multi .60 .60

World Telecommunications Day — A1410

Perf. 13¼x12¾ Syncopated
2019, May 17 Litho.
2203 A1410 £5 multi .60 .60

World Environment Day — A1411

Perf. 13¼x12¾ Syncopated
2019, June 5 Litho.
2204 A1411 £4 multi .50 .50

A1412

Africa Cup of Nations Soccer Tournament, Egypt — A1413

No. 2205 — Silhouettes of Egyptian buildings and: a, Flags of African countries on map of Africa, emblem of African Cup of Nations. b, Arabic text in red, "2019" in violet. c, Mascot and African Cup of Nations.

EGYPT

Perf. 13¼x12¾ Syncopated
2019, June 21   Litho.
2205 A1412 £4 Horiz. strip of 3, #a-c   1.50 1.50

Imperf
2206 A1413 £5 multi   .60 .60

Traditional Costumes — A1414

No. 2207 — Euromed Postal emblem and: a, Man and woman dancing, ship's wheel and anchor. b, Women in robes. c, Women in ancient Egyptian costumes.

Perf. 13¼x12¾ Syncopated
2019, July 8   Litho.
2207 A1414 £4 Horiz. strip of 3, #a-c   1.50 1.50

July 23rd Revolution, 67th Anniv. — A1415

Perf. 13¼x12¾ Syncopated
2019, July 23   Litho.
2208 A1415 £4 multi   .50 .50

Egyptian Team's Victory at World Under-19 Handball Championships — A1416

Perf. 12¾x13¼ Syncopated
2019, Aug. 16   Litho.
2209 A1416 £5 multi   .60 .60

Egyptian Philatelic Society, 90th Anniv. — A1417

Perf. 13¼x12¾ Syncopated
2019, Sept. 9   Litho.
2210 A1417 £5 multi   .65 .65

Egypt as Host of African Space Agency — A1418

Perf. 13¼x12¾ Syncopated
2019, Sept. 19   Litho.
2211 A1418 £5 multi   .65 .65

Cairo University School of Law, 150th Anniv. — A1419

Perf. 13¼x12¾ Syncopated
2019, Sept. 23   Litho.
2212 A1419 £5 multi   .65 .65

Opening of the Suez Canal, 150th Anniv. — A1420

Perf. 13¼x12¾ Syncopated
2019, Oct. 3   Litho.
2213 A1420 £5 multi   .65 .65

October War Against Israel, 46th Anniv. — A1421

Perf. 13¼x12¾ Syncopated
2019, Oct. 6   Litho.
2214 A1421 £5 multi   .65 .65

World Post Day — A1422

Perf. 12¾x13¼ Syncopated
2019, Oct. 9   Litho.
2215 A1422 £5 multi   .65 .65

A1423

Design: Dome of the Rock, Jerusalem, doves, and flag of Palestinian Authority.

Perf. 12¾x13¼ Syncopated
2019, Oct.   Litho.
2216 A1423 £5 multi   .65 .65

Supreme Constitutional Court, 50th Anniv. — A1424

Perf. 13¼x12¾ Syncopated
2019, Oct.   Litho.
2217 A1424 £5 multi   .65 .65

Mohandas K. Gandhi (1869-1948), Indian Nationalist Leader
A1425

Perf. 12¾x13¼ Syncopated
2019, Nov. 6   Litho.
2218 A1425 £5 multi   .65 .65

International Civil Aviation Organization, 75th Anniv. — A1426

Perf. 13¼x12¾ Syncopated
2019, Dec. 7   Litho.
2219 A1426 £5 blue   .65 .65

Ministry of Social Solidarity, 80th Anniv. — A1427

2019   Litho.   Perf. 11½
2220 A1427 £5 multi   .65 .65

Post Day
A1428

Perf. 13¼x12¾ Syncopated
2020, Jan. 2   Litho.
2221 A1428 £5 multi   .65 .65

Pan-African Postal Union, 40th Anniv. — A1429

Perf. 13¼x12¾ Syncopated
2020, Jan. 18   Litho.
2222 A1429 £5 multi   .65 .65

International Organization of La Francophonie, 50th Anniv. — A1430

Perf. 13¼x12¾ Syncopated
2020, Mar. 20   Litho.
2223 A1430 £5 multi   .65 .65

Arab League, 75th Anniv. — A1431

Perf. 13¼x12¾ Syncopated
2020, Mar. 22   Litho.
2224 A1431 £5 multi   .65 .65

Economic Census — A1432

Perf. 13¼x12¾ Syncopated
2020, Mar. 31   Litho.
2225 A1432 £4 multi   .50 .50

Government Printing Offices, 200th Anniv. — A1432a

Perf. 12¾x13¼ Syncopated
2020, July 16   Litho.
2225A A1432a £5 multi   — —

October War Against Israel, 47th Anniv. — A1433

2020, Oct. 6   Litho.   Perf. 11½
2226 A1433 £4 multi   .50 .50

Misr Bank, Cent. — A1434

Perf. 13x13¼ Syncopated
2020   Litho.
2227 A1434 £5 multi   .65 .65

World Statistics Day — A1435

Perf. 13¼x13 Syncopated
2020   Litho.
2228 A1435 £4 multi   .50 .50

Country name is spelled incorrectly.

Tribute to Medical Professionals Combatting COVID-19 — A1436

Perf. 13¼x13 Syncopated
2020, Nov. 1   Litho.
2229 A1436 £5 multi   .65 .65

EGYPT

United Nations, 75th Anniv. — A1437

2020, Oct. 24   *Litho.*   *Perf. 11½*
2230   A1437   £5 multi   .65   .65

Egyptian Engineers Society, Cent. A1438

Perf. 13x13¼ Syncopated
2020, Dec. 3   *Litho.*
2231   A1438   £4 multi   .50   .50

Post Day — A1439

Perf. 13½x14 Syncopated
2021, Jan. 2   *Litho.*
2232   A1439   £5 multi   .65   .65

2021 Men's World Handball Championships, Egypt — A1440

Perf. 14x13½ Syncopated
2021, Jan. 13   *Litho.*
2233   A1440   £5 multi   .65   .65

Police Day — A1441

Perf. 13½x14 Syncopated
2021, Jan. 25   *Litho.*
2234   A1441   £5 multi   .65   .65

Diplomatic Relations Between Egypt and the Philippines, 75th Anniv. A1442

Perf. 13x13¼ Syncopated
2021, Mar. 3   *Litho.*
2235   A1442   £5 multi   .65   .65

Martyr's Day A1443

No. 2236: a, General Abd El Moniem Riad (1919-69). b, Monument.

Perf. 13¼x13 Syncopated
2021, Mar. 9   *Litho.*
2236   A1443   £4 Horiz. pair, #a-b   1.10   1.10

A1444

A1445

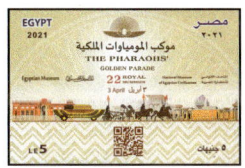
Golden Parade of the Pharaohs — A1446

No. 2237 — Walls with hieroglyphs and: a, QR code, left side of emblem. c, Central part of emblem. d, Right side of emblem.
No. 2238: a, Hatshepsut. b, Thutmose II. c, Thutmose I. d, Merytamon. e, Amenhotep I. f, Ahmose-Nefertari. g, Seqenenre. h, Amenhotep III. i, Thutmose IV. j, Amenhotep II. k, Thutmose III. l, Merenptah. m, Ramesses II. n, Sety I. o, Tiye. p, Ramesses IX. q, Ramesses VI. r, Ramesses V. s, Ramesses IV. t, Ramesses III. u, Siptah. v, Sety II.
No. 2239, Museums and procession, emblem and QR code.

Perf. 13¼x12¾ Syncopated
2021, Apr. 3   *Litho.*
2237   A1444   £5 Horiz. strip of 3, #a-c   1.90   1.90
2238   A1445   £5 Sheet of 22, #a-v, + 6 central labels   14.00   14.00

Size: 120x79mm
Imperf.
2239   A1446   £5 multi   .65   .65

Move of 22 pharaoh mummies from Egyptian Museum to National Museum of Egyptian Civilization.

Museums — A1447

No. 2240 — QR code and: a, Mohamed Mahmoud Khalil Museum, Giza, and Mohamed Mahmoud Khalil Pasha (1877-1941), Prime minister of Egypt. b, National Museum of Egyptian Civilization, Cairo. c, Baron Empain Palace, Heliopolis. d, Royal Carriages Museum, Cairo.

Perf. 13½x13¾ Syncopated
2021, Apr. 18   *Litho.*
2240   A1447   £5 Block of 4, #a-d   —   —

World Heritage Day.

Sinai Liberation Day, 39th Anniv. A1448

Perf. 12¾x13¼ Syncopated
2021, Apr. 25   *Litho.*
2241   A1448   £5 multi   —   —

Labor Day — A1449

Perf. 13¼x12¾ Syncopated
2021, May 1   *Litho.*
2242   A1449   £5 multi   —   —

World Telecommunication and Information Society Day — A1450

Perf. 13½x13¾ Syncopated
2021, May 17   *Litho.*
2243   A1450   £5 multi   —   —

Misr Life Insurance Company, 120th Anniv. — A1451

Perf. 13¼x13 Syncopated
2021, May 20   *Litho.*
2244   A1451   £5 multi   —   —

World Environment Day — A1452

2021, June 5   *Litho.*   *Imperf.*
2245   A1452   £5 multi   —   —

Good Life to All Egyptians Presidential Initiative — A1453

Perf. 13¼x13 Syncopated
2021, June 30   *Litho.*
2246   A1453   £5 multi   —   —

Good Life to All Egyptians Campaign — A1454

2021, June 30   *Litho.*   *Imperf.*
2247   A1454   £5 multi   —   —

July 23rd Revolution, 69th Anniv. — A1455

Perf. 13¼x13 Syncopated
2021, July 23   *Litho.*
2248   A1455   £5 multi   —   —

2020 Summer Olympics, Tokyo — A1456

Perf. 14x13½ Syncopated
2021, July 23   *Litho.*
2249   A1456   £5 multi   —   —

The 2020 Summer Olympics were postponed until 2021 because of the COVID-19 pandemic.

World Day Against Human Trafficking A1457

Perf. 14x13½ Syncopated
2021, July 30   *Litho.*
2250   A1457   £5 multi   —   —

Establishment of Egypt University of Informatics A1458

Perf. 14x13½ Syncopated
2021, Aug. 5   *Litho.*
2251   A1458   £5 multi   —   —

Egyptian Medalists at 2020 Summer Olympics — A1459

2021, Aug. 8   *Litho.*   *Imperf.*
2252   A1459   £5 multi   —   —

The 2020 Summer Olympics were postponed until 2021 because of the COVID-19 pandemic.

International Youth Day — A1460

408 EGYPT

Perf. 14x13½ Syncopated
2021, Aug. 13   Litho.
2253 A1460 £5 multi

Egyptian Medalists at the 2020 Summer Paralympics, Tokyo — A1461

2021, Sept. 2   Litho.   Imperf.
2254 A1461 £5 multi

The 2020 Summer Paralympics were postponed until 2021 because of the COVID-19 pandemic.

World Tourism Day — A1462

Perf. 14x13½ Syncopated
2021, Sept. 27   Litho.
2255 A1462 £10 multi

Egyptian Judiciary Day — A1463

Perf. 12¾x13¼ Syncopated
2021, Oct. 1   Litho.
2256 A1463 £5 multi

Field Marshal Mohamed Hussein Tantawi (1935-2021) — A1464

2021, Oct. 6   Litho.   Perf. 14
2257 A1464 £5 multi

October War Against Israel, 48th Anniv. A1465

Perf. 13¼x14 Syncopated
2021, Oct. 6   Litho.
2258 A1465 £5 multi

Sports Culture A1466

Perf. 12¾x13¼ Syncopated
2021, Oct.   Litho.
2259 A1466 £5 multi

Restoration of the Avenue of the Sphinxes — A1467

No. 2260: a, Sphinx statues facing right. b, "Luxor" and QR code. c, Sphinx statues facing left.

Perf. 13½x13 Syncopated
2021, Nov. 25   Litho.
2260 A1467 £5 Horiz. strip of 3, #a-c

First Public Film Presentation, 125th Anniv. (in 2020) A1468

2021, Nov. 26   Litho.   Perf. 13½x14
2261 A1468 £5 multi

Post Day — A1469

2022, Jan. 2   Litho.   Perf. 11½
2262 A1469 £10 multi

Miniature Sheet

World Youth Forum, Sharm el-Sheikh A1470

No. 2263: a. Flowers, youths, ankhs, QR code (100x100mm). b, Ankh, olive branch in ellipse (58x38mm). c, Olive branch, sun over pyramid (58x38mm). d, Youths and sun over pyramid in diamond (58x58mm). e, Greek key border in circle, sun over pyramid (58x58mm).

2022, Jan. 10   Litho.   Perf. 14
2263 A1470 £5 Sheet of 5, #a-e

Independence, Cent. — A1472

Perf. 14x13½ Syncopated
2022, Mar. 15   Litho.
2265 A1472 £10 multi

Diplomatic Relations Between Egypt and Armenia, 30th Anniv. A1473

Perf. 13½x14 Syncopated
2022, Mar. 22   Litho.
2266 A1473 £10 multi

Cairo, 2022 Capital of Islamic Culture A1474

2022, Apr. 10   Litho.   Perf. 14x13½
2267 A1474 £10 multi

Egypt Air, 90th Anniv. A1475

QR code and: No. 2268, Tail of Egypt Air plane. No. 2269, Egypt Air plane in flight.

Perf. 13x13¼ Syncopated
2022, May   Litho.
2268 A1475 £10 multi

Size: 81x60mm

Imperf
2269 A1475 £10 multi

Ain Shams University Faculty of Medicine, 75th Anniv. — A1476

Perf. 14x13½ Syncopated
2022   Litho.
2270 A1476 £10 multi

Egyptian-Tunisian Cultural Year — A1477

2022, June 30   Litho.   Perf. 13½x14
2271 A1477 £10 multi

See Tunisia No. 1785.

Underwater Archaeology — A1478

No. 2272 — Fish and: a, Coral and ancient Egyptian statue. b, Diver, coral and QR code. c, Jellyfish, amphora, head of statue.

Perf. 13¼x12¾ Syncopated
2022, July 11   Litho.
2272 A1478 £10 Horiz. strip of 3, #a-c

July 23rd Revolution, 70th Anniv. A1479

Perf. 13½x14 Syncopated
2022, July 23   Litho.
2273 A1479 £10 multi

Diplomatic Relations Between Egypt and India, 75th Anniv. A1480

2022, Aug.   Litho.   Perf. 13½x14
2274 A1480 £10 multi

National Beheira Governorate Day — A1481

2022, Sept. 19   Litho.   Perf. 14x13½
2275 A1481 £10 multi

Council of State, 75th Anniv. A1482

2022   Litho.   Perf. 13½x14
2276 A1482 £10 multi

Fine Arts Lovers Association, Cent. — A1483

Perf. 14x13½ Syncopated
2022   Litho.
2277 A1483 £10 multi

Restoration of Historic Aswan Post Office A1484

2022, July   Litho.   Perf. 13½x13¾
2278 A1484 £10 multi

EGYPT

A1485

A1486

A1487

A1488

Opening of Postal Museum of Egypt — A1489

2022, July   Litho.   Perf. 13¾
2279   Block of 5   —   —
  a. A1485 £10 multi   —   —
  b. A1486 £10 multi   —   —
  c. A1487 £10 multi   —   —
  d. A1488 £10 multi   —   —
  e. A1489 £10 multi   —   —

A strip of selvage separates Nos. 2279b-2279c from 2279d-2279e.

October War Against Israel, 49th Anniv. A1503

Perf. 13½x14 Syncopated
2022, Oct. 6   Litho.
2285   A1503   £10 multi

World Post Day — A1504

2022, Oct. 9   Litho.   Perf. 13½x14
2286   A1504   £10 multi

27th United Nations Climate Change Conference, Sharm El Sheikh — A1509

2022, Nov. 6   Litho.   Perf. 14x13½
2291   A1509   £10 multi

Federation of Egyptian Industries, Cent. — A1510

Perf. 13¾x13½ Syncopated
2022   Litho.
2292   A1510   £10 multi

Inauguration of Sultan Hussein Kamel Palace Digital Egypt Innovation Center — A1511

2022   Litho.   Imperf.
2293   A1511   £10 multi

A1512

Restoration of Cairo Main Post Office, Ataba A1513

2023, Jan. 2   Litho.   Perf. 13x13¼
2294   Horiz. pair, #a-b, + central label
  a. A1512 £10 multi   —   —
  b. A1513 £10 multi   —   —

Post Day.

Souvenir Sheet

"50" and Flags of Egypt and United Arab Emirates A1514

Litho. With Foil Application
2023, Jan. 19   Perf. 13½x14
2295   A1514   £10 multi

Diplomatic relations between Egypt and United Arab Emirates, 50th anniv.

Egyptian Media Production City Company, 25th Anniv. A1515

2023, Jan. 23   Litho.   Perf. 13½x14
2296   A1515   £10 multi

Sports Federation for Intellectual Disabilities — A1517

2023, Mar. 21   Litho.   Perf. 13¼x13
2298   A1517   £10 multi

National Telecom Regulatory Authority, 25th Anniv. A1518

Perf. 13½x14 Syncopated
2023, Apr. 4   Litho.
2299   A1518   £10 multi

Miniature Sheet

Completion of Egypt's Islamic Cultural Center, Cairo — A1519

No. 2300: a, Building exterior, QR code (90x80mm). b, Hallway (60x40mm). c, Doorways (60x40mm). d, Chandelier and ceiling (60x40mm). e, Corner of room (60x40mm).

2023, Mar. 23   Litho.   Perf. 14
2300   A1519   £10 Sheet of 5, #a-e   3.25   3.25

1923 Constitution, Cent. — A1520

Perf. 14¼x13½ Syncopated
2023, Apr. 19   Litho.
2301   A1520   £10 multi   .65   .65

Pres. Gamal Abdel Nasser (1918-70) and Pres. Mohamed Naguib (1901-84), 1953 Revolution Leaders A1521

Perf. 13½x14 Syncopated
2023, June 18   Litho.
2302   A1521   £10 multi   .65   .65

Republic of Egypt, 70th anniv.

Mediterranean Festivals — A1522

No. 2303: a, Man on horse, Euromed Postal emblem. b, Three dancers and QR code. c, Two dancers.

Perf. 13½x13 Syncopated
2023, July 10   Litho.
2303   A1522   £10 Horiz. strip of 3, #a-c   2.00   2.00

World Day Against Trafficking in Persons A1523

Perf. 13½x14 Syncopated
2023, July 30   Litho.
2304   A1523   £10 multi   .65   .65

A1524

Pan African Postal Union Headquarters, Arusha, Tanzania — A1525

2023, Sept. 2   Litho.   Perf. 14x13¾
2305   A1524   £10 multi   .65   .65

Souvenir Sheet
Perf. 13½x14
2306   A1525   £10 multi   .65   .65

Sayed Darwish (1892-1923), Singer and Composer A1526

2023, Sept. 28   Litho.   Perf. 14
2307   A1526   £10 multi   .65   .65

409

EGYPT

Miniature Sheet

October War With Israel, 50th Anniv. A1527

No. 2308: a, Soldiers, tank, airplanes, "50" in Arabic script. b, Tank, Pres. Anwar Sadat (1918-81) saluting. c, Unknown Soldier Memorial. d, Airplane, people, "50" in Arabic script.

Litho., Sheet Margin Litho With Foil Application

2023, Oct. 6			Perf. 14x13¾
2308	A1527	£10 Sheet of 4, #a-d	2.60 2.60

World Post Day A1528

2023, Oct. 9	Litho.	Perf. 13¾x14¼
2309	A1528	£10 multi	.65 .65

Re-opening of the Greco-Roman Museum, Alexandria — A1529

No. 2310: a, Bust of Emperor Augustus (30x40mm). b, Museum exterior (90x40mm). c, Statue of Emperor Marcus Aurelius (30x40mm). d, Mosaic of Alexandria (30x40mm). e, Statue of Apis dedicated to Serapis (30x40mm). f, Statue of Isis (30x40mm). g, Canopic jars (30x40mm).

2023, Oct. 11	Litho.	Perf. 14
2310	A1529	£10 Sheet of 7, #a-g + label	4.50 4.50

Miniature Sheet

Migratory Birds A1530

No. 2311: a, Goldfinch. b, Golden oriole. c, Bluethroat. d, Kingfisher.

Perf. 14x13½ Syncopated

2023, Oct. 24			Litho.
2311	A1530	£10 Sheet of 4, #a-d	2.60 2.60

Taha Hussein (1889-1973), Writer — A1531

2023, Oct. 28	Litho.	Perf. 14
2312	A1531	£10 multi	.65 .65

SEMI-POSTAL STAMPS

Catalogue values for unused stamps in this section are for Never Hinged items.

Princess Ferial — SP1

Perf. 13½x14

1940, May 17	Photo.	Wmk. 195
B1	SP1 5m + 5m copper brown	4.50 1.25

No. B1 Overprinted in Green

1943, Nov. 17

B2	SP1 5m + 5m	14.00 9.00
a.	Arabic date "1493"	300.00 300.00

The surtax on Nos. B1 and B2 was for the children's fund.

First Postage Stamp of Egypt — SP2

King Fuad — SP3

No. B4, Khedive Ismail Pasha. No. B6, King Farouk.

Perf. 13¼x13½

1946, Feb. 28		Wmk. 195
B3	SP2 1m + 1m gray	.40 .25
B4	SP3 10m + 10m violet	.50 .25
B5	SP3 17m + 17m brown	.50 .40
B6	SP3 22m + 22m yel grn	.75 .60
a.	Souv. sheet, #B3-B6, perf. 8½	85.00 85.00
b.	As "a," imperf.	85.00 85.00
	Nos. B3-B6 (4)	2.15 1.50

80th anniv. of Egypt's 1st postage stamp. Nos. B6a, B6b measure 129x171mm.

Goddess Hathor, King Menkau-Re (Mycerinus) and Jackalheaded Goddess SP7

Ramesseum, Thebes SP8

Queen Nefertiti SP9

Funerary Mask of King Tutankhamun SP10

Perf. 13½x13¼, 13¼x13½

1947, Mar. 9		Wmk. 195
B9	SP7 5m + 5m slate	1.75 .80
B10	SP8 15m + 15m dp blue, perf. 13¼x13½	2.00 1.00
B11	SP9 30m + 30m henna brn	2.50 1.75
B12	SP10 50m + 50m brown	3.50 2.25
	Nos. B9-B12 (4)	9.75 5.80

Intl. Exposition of Contemporary Art, Cairo.

Boy Scout Emblem — SP11

Scout Emblems: 20m+10m, Sea Scouts. 35m+15m, Air Explorers.

1956, July 25	Photo.	Perf. 13½x13
B13	SP11 10m + 10m green	1.00 .55
B14	SP11 20m + 10m ultra	1.50 .85
B15	SP11 35m + 15m blue	2.00 1.25
	Nos. B13-B15 (3)	4.50 2.65

2nd Arab Scout Jamboree, Alexandria-Aboukir, 1956. Souvenir sheets, perf. and imperf., contain one each of Nos. B13-B15. Size: 118x158mm. Values: $1,750 unused each, $1,100 used each.

Ambulance SP12

1957, May 13		Perf. 13x13½
B16	SP12 10m + 5m rose red	.80 .55

50th anniv. of the Public Aid Society.

United Arab Republic

Eye and Map of Africa, Europe and Asia — SP13

Perf. 13½x13

1958, Mar. 1	Photo.	Wmk. 318
B17	SP13 10m + 5m orange	1.25 1.00

1st Afro-Asian Cong. of Ophthalmology, Cairo.

The surtax was for centers to aid the blind.

Postal Emblem — SP14

1959, Jan. 2

| B18 | SP14 10m + 5m bl grn, red & blk | .40 .30 |

Post Day. The surtax went to the social fund for postal employees.
See Syria UAR issues No. B1 for similar stamp with denominations in piasters (p).

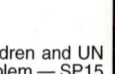

Children and UN Emblem — SP15

1959, Oct. 24		Wmk. 328
B19	SP15 10m + 5m brown lake	.60 .30
B20	SP15 35m + 10m dk blue	.90 .40

Issued for International Children's Day and to honor UNICEF.

Braille Type of Regular Issue, 1961

1961, Apr. 6		Perf. 13½x13
B21	A182 35m + 15m yel & brn	.80 .50

Arab League Building, Cairo, and Emblem — SP16

1962, Mar. 22	Photo.	Wmk. 328
B22	SP16 10m + 5m gray	.60 .40

Arab Publicity Week, Mar. 22-28.
See No. N86.

Postal Emblem SP17

Stamp of 1866 SP18

1963, Jan. 2	Wmk. 342	Perf. 11½
B23	SP17 20m +10m brt grn, red & blk	1.25 1.25
B24	SP18 40m +20m blk & brn org	1.75 1.75
B25	SP18 40m + 20m brn org & blk	1.75 1.75
a.	Pair, #B24-B25	4.00 4.00
	Nos. B23-B25 (3)	4.75 4.75

Post Day, Jan. 2 and 1966 exhibition of the FIP.

Arms of UAR and Pyramids — SP19

1964, Jan. 2	Wmk. 342	Perf. 11
B26	SP19 10m + 5m org yel & grn	1.75 1.00
B27	SP19 80m + 40m grnsh bl & blk	3.00 1.75
B28	SP19 115m + 55m org brn & blk	4.00 2.25
	Nos. B26-B28 (3)	8.75 5.00

Issued for Post Day. Jan. 2.

Type of 1963 and

SP20

EGYPT

Postal Emblem — SP20a

No. B30, Emblem of Postal Secondary School. 80m+40m, Postal emblem, gear-wheel, laurel wreath.

		Perf. 11½		
1965, Jan. 2		**Unwmk.**		**Photo.**
B29	SP20	10m + 5m lt grn & car	1.00	.50
B30	SP20	10m + 5m ultra, car & blk	1.00	.50
a.		Pair, #B29-B30	2.50	2.00
B31	SP20a	80m + 40m rose, brt grn & blk	2.75	2.00
		Nos. B29-B31 (3)	4.75	3.00

Issued for Post Day, Jan. 2. No. B31 also publicizes the Stamp Centenary Exhibition.

Souvenir Sheet

Stamps of Egypt, 1866 — SP21

1966, Jan. 2		**Wmk. 342**		**Imperf.**
B32	SP21	140m + 60m blk, sl bl & rose	4.50	4.50

Post Day, 1966, and cent. of the 1st Egyptian postage stamps.

Pharaonic "Mediator" — SP22

Design: 115m+40m, Pharaonic guard.

1967, Jan. 2		**Wmk. 342**		**Perf. 11½**
B33	SP22	80m + 20m multi	3.75	2.75
B34	SP22	115m + 40m multi	6.00	3.00

Issued for Post Day, Jan. 2.

Grand Canal, Doges' Palace, Venice, and Santa Maria del Fiore, Florence — SP23

115m+30m, Piazzetta and Campanile, Venice, and Palazzo Vecchio, Florence.

		Perf. 11½x11		
1967, Dec. 9		**Photo.**		**Wmk. 342**
B35	SP23	80m + 20m grn, yel & brn	1.75	1.25
B36	SP23	115m + 30m ol, yel & sl bl	2.75	2.00

The surtax was to help save the cultural monuments of Venice and Florence, damaged in the 1966 floods.

Boy and Girl — SP24

Design: No. B38, Five children and arch.

		Wmk. 342		**Perf. 11**
1968, Dec. 11		**Photo.**		
B37	SP24	20m + 10m car, bl & lt brn	.80	.60
B38	SP24	20m + 10m vio bl, sep & lt grn	.80	.60

Children's Day & 22nd anniv. of UNICEF.

Emblem and Flags of Arab League — SP25

1969, Mar. 22				**Perf. 11x11½**
B39	SP25	20m + 10m multi	.80	.60

Arab Publicity Week, Mar. 22-28.

Refugee Family — SP26

1969, Oct. 24		**Photo.**		**Perf. 11½**
B40	SP26	30m + 10m multi	.80	.60

Issued for United Nations Day.

Men of Three Races, Human Rights Emblem — SP27

1970, Mar. 21				**Perf. 11½x11**
B41	SP27	20m + 10m multi	1.00	.75

Issued to publicize the International Day for the Elimination of Racial Discrimination.

Arab League Type

1970, Mar. 22				**Wmk. 342**
B42	A344	20m + 10m bl, grn & brn	.90	.60

Map of Palestine and Refugees — SP28

		Perf. 11½x11		
1970, Oct. 24		**Photo.**		**Wmk. 342**
B43	SP28	20m + 10m multi	.90	.60

25th anniv. of the UN and to draw attention to the plight of the Palestinian refugees.

Arab Republic of Egypt

Blind Girl, WHO and Society Emblems — SP29

1973, Oct. 24		**Photo.**		**Perf. 11x11½**
B44	SP29	20m + 10m blue & gold	.85	.75

25th anniv. of WHO and for the Light and Hope Soc., which educates and helps blind girls.

Map of Africa, OAU Emblem — SP30

		Perf. 11x11½		
1973, Dec. 8		**Photo.**		**Wmk. 342**
B45	SP30	55m + 20m multi	2.25	1.50

Organization for African Unity, 10th anniv.

Social Work Day Emblem — SP31

1973, Dec. 8				
B46	SP31	20m + 10m multi	.75	.65

Social Work Day.

Jihan al Sadat Consoling Wounded Man — SP32

1974, Mar. 21		**Wmk. 342**		**Perf. 11**
B47	SP32	20m + 10m multi	1.25	.90

Faithfulness and Hope Society.

Afghan Solidarity — SP33

		Wmk. 342		
1981, July 15		**Photo.**		**Perf. 11½**
B48	SP33	20m + 10m multi	1.00	.75

		Size: 30x25mm		
1981		**Photo.**		**Perf. 11½**
B49	SP33	20m + 10m multi	4.25	3.75

Map of Sudan, Dunes, Dead Tree — SP34

1986, Mar. 25		**Photo.**		**Perf. 13x13½**
B50	SP34	15p + 5p multi	1.75	1.25

Fight against drought and desertification of the Sudan. Surtax for drought relief.

Organization of African Unity, 25th Anniv. — SP35

1988, May 25		**Litho.**		**Perf. 13**
B51	SP35	15p +10p multi	1.25	1.00

AIR POST STAMPS

Mail Plane in Flight — AP1

		Perf. 13x13½		
1926, Mar. 10		**Wmk. 195**		**Photo.**
C1	AP1	27m deep violet	32.50	32.50

1929, July 17				
C2	AP1	27m orange brown	10.00	2.50

Zeppelin Issue
No. C2 Surcharged in Blue or Violet

1931, Apr. 6				
C3	AP1	50m on 27m (Bl)	90.00	77.50
a.		"1951" instead of "1931"	125.00	115.00
C4	AP1	100m on 27m (V)	90.00	82.50

Airplane over Giza Pyramids — AP2

			Perf. 13x13½	
1933-38		**Litho.**		
C5	AP2	1m orange & blk	.30	.50
C6	AP2	2m gray & blk	.80	1.50
C7	AP2	2m org red & blk ('38)	2.75	2.00
C8	AP2	3m ol brn & blk	.60	.35
C9	AP2	4m green & blk	.90	.30
C10	AP2	5m dp brown & blk	.75	.25
C11	AP2	6m dk green & blk	1.50	1.25
C12	AP2	7m dk blue & blk	1.25	1.00
C13	AP2	8m violet & blk	.80	.25
C14	AP2	9m dp red & blk	2.00	1.50
C15	AP2	10m violet & brn	.75	.70
C16	AP2	20m dk green & brn	.60	.25
C17	AP2	30m dull blue & brn	.75	.25
C18	AP2	40m dp red & brn	15.00	.60
C19	AP2	50m orange & brn	13.00	.25
C20	AP2	60m gray & brn	6.00	1.10
C21	AP2	70m dk blue & bl grn	3.50	1.00
C22	AP2	80m ol brn & bl grn	3.50	1.00
C23	AP2	90m org & bl grn	4.00	1.00
C24	AP2	100m vio & bl grn	9.00	.80
C25	AP2	200m dp red & bl grn	15.00	1.75
		Nos. C5-C25 (21)	82.75	18.20

See Nos. C34-C37. For overprint see No. C38.

Type of 1933

1941-43				**Photo.**
C34	AP2	5m copper brn ('43)	.30	.30
C35	AP2	10m violet	.55	.30
C36	AP2	25m dk vio brn ('43)	.55	.30
C37	AP2	30m green	.70	.30
		Nos. C34-C37 (4)	2.10	1.20

Catalogue values for unused stamps in this section, from this point to the end of the section, are for Never Hinged items.

No. C37 Overprinted in Black

1946, Oct. 1				
C38	AP2	30m green	.85	.40
a.		Double overprint	425.00	—
b.		Inverted overprint	425.00	—

Middle East Intl. Air Navigation Congress, Cairo, Oct. 1946.

King Farouk, Delta Dam and DC-3 Plane — AP3

EGYPT

Perf. 13x13½

1947, Feb. 19 Photo. Wmk. 195
C39	AP3	2m red orange	.30	.85
C40	AP3	3m dk brown	.30	1.00
C41	AP3	5m red brown	.30	.30
C42	AP3	7m dp yellow org	.60	.30
C43	AP3	8m green	.60	.90
C44	AP3	10m violet	.60	.30
C45	AP3	20m brt blue	.90	.30
C46	AP3	30m brown violet	1.20	.30
C47	AP3	40m carmine rose	2.00	.75
C48	AP3	50m Prus green	2.50	.85
C49	AP3	100m olive green	5.00	2.50
C50	AP3	200m dark gray	11.00	5.00
		Nos. C39-C50 (12)	25.30	13.35

For overprints see Nos. C51-C64, C67-C89, NC1-NC30.

Nos. C49 and C50 Surcharged in Black

1948, Aug. 23
C51	AP3	13m on 100m	.60	.55
C52	AP3	22m on 200m	.85	.85
a.		Date omitted		

Inaugural flights of "Services Aeriens Internationaux d'Egypte" from Cairo to Athens and Rome, Aug. 23, 1948.

Nos. C39 to C50 Overprinted in Various Colors

Overprint 27mm Wide

1952, Jan. Wmk. 195 Perf. 13x13½
C53	AP3	2m red orange (Bl)	.45	.30
C54	AP3	3m dark brown (R)	1.60	1.25
C55	AP3	5m red brown	.55	.55
C56	AP3	7m dp yel org (Bl)	.85	.50
C57	AP3	8m green (R)	2.50	1.60
C58	AP3	10m violet (G)	1.75	1.60
C59	AP3	20m brt blue (R)	4.25	2.50
C60	AP3	30m brown vio (G)	1.90	1.60
C61	AP3	40m carmine rose	4.00	2.50
C62	AP3	50m Prus green (R)	4.25	2.75
C63	AP3	100m olive green	7.50	3.75
C64	AP3	200m dark gray (R)	15.00	7.50
		Nos. C53-C64 (12)	44.60	26.40

See notes after No. 316.

Delta Dam and Douglas DC-3 — AP4

1953 Photo.
C65	AP4	5m red brown	.60	.60
C66	AP4	15m olive green	1.50	1.25

For overprints see Nos. NC31-NC32.

Nos. C39-C49 Overprinted in Black

1953
C67	AP3	2m red orange	3.00	3.00
C68	AP3	3m dk brown	1.25	1.25
C69	AP3	5m red brown	1.60	1.60
C70	AP3	7m dp yellow org	.60	.60
C71	AP3	8m green	2.00	2.00
C72	AP3	10m violet	32.50	37.50
C73	AP3	20m brt blue	2.10	.60
C74	AP3	30m brown violet	3.00	1.60
C75	AP3	40m carmine rose	3.00	1.90
C76	AP3	50m Prus green	5.00	2.00
C77	AP3	100m olive green	9.25	4.75
C77A	AP3	200m gray	55.00	

No. C77A is in question. It is not known postally used.

Nos. C53-C64 Overprinted in Black with Three Bars to Obliterate Portrait

1953
C78	AP3	2m red orange	.90	.50
C79	AP3	3m dark brown	1.90	1.60
C80	AP3	5m red brown	.50	.35
C82	AP3	8m green	1.10	2.50
C83	AP3	10m violet	.90	2.00
C85	AP3	30m brown violet	2.00	2.00
C87	AP3	50m Prus green	4.25	1.60
C88	AP3	100m olive green	6.25	3.75
C89	AP3	200m dark gray	12.50	12.50
		Nos. C78-C89 (9)	30.30	26.80

Practically all values of Nos. C67-C89 exist with double overprint. The 7m, 20m and 40m with this overprint have been considered forgeries. Values: 7m, $8 mint and used; 20m, $5 mint and used; 40m, $20 mint, $25 used.

United Arab Republic
Type of Regular Issue
Perf. 11½x11

1958, Mar. 22 Photo. Wmk. 318
C90	A141	15m ultra & red brn	.65	.30

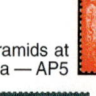

Pyramids at Giza — AP5

Al Azhar University — AP6

Designs: 15m, Colossi of Memnon, Thebes. 90m, St. Catherine Monastery, Mt. Sinai.

1959-60 Wmk. 328 Perf. 13x13½
C91	AP5	5m bright red	.35	.25
C92	AP5	15m dk dull violet	.40	.35
C93	AP6	60m dk green	.95	.60
C94	AP5	90m brown car ('60)	2.00	1.25
		Nos. C91-C94 (4)	3.70	2.45

Nos. C91-C93 exist imperf. See Nos. C101, C105, NC33.

Tower of Cairo Type, Redrawn

1961, May 1 Perf. 13½x13
C95	A183	50m bright blue	1.10	.55

Top inscription has been replaced by two airplanes.

Weather Vane, Anemometer and UN World Meteorological Organization Emblem — AP7

Perf. 11½x11

1962, Mar. 23 Photo. Unwmk.
C96	AP7	60m yellow & dp blue	2.00	1.00

2nd World Meteorological Day, Mar. 23.

Patrice Lumumba and Map of Africa — AP8

Perf. 13½x13

1962, July 1 Wmk. 328
C97	AP8	35m multicolored	.65	.40

Patrice Lumumba (1925-61), Premier of Congo.

Maritime Station, Alexandria AP9

Designs: 30m, International Airport, Cairo. 40m, Railroad Station, Luxor.

1963, Mar. 18 Perf. 13x13½
C98	AP9	20m dark brown	.70	.30
C99	AP9	30m carmine rose	.95	.40
C100	AP9	40m black	1.50	1.00
		Nos. C98-C100 (3)	3.15	1.70

Type of 1959-60 and

Temple of Queen Nefertari, Abu Simbel AP10

Arch and Tower of Cairo AP11

Designs: 80m, Al Azhar University seen through arch. 140m, Ramses II, Abu Simbel.

Perf. 11½x11, 11x11½

1963-65 Photo. Wmk. 342
C101	AP6	80m vio blk & brt bl	3.75	1.60
C102	AP10	115m brown & yel	4.00	1.50
C103	AP10	140m pale vio, blk & org red	4.00	2.00

Unwmk.
C104	AP11	50m yel brn & brt bl	2.25	1.00
C105	AP6	80m vio bl & lt bl	3.75	1.60
		Nos. C101-C105 (5)	17.75	7.70

Issued: 50m, 11/2/64; No. C105, 2/13/65; others, 10/24/63.
See Nos. NC34-NC36.

Weather Vane, Anemometer and WMO Emblem — AP12

Perf. 11½x11

1965, Mar. 23 Wmk. 342
C106	AP12	80m dk blue & rose lil	2.75	1.50

Fifth World Meteorological Day.
See No. NC37.

Game Board from Tomb of Tutankhamun AP13

1965, July 1 Photo. Unwmk.
C107	AP13	10m yellow & dk blue	2.00	.45

See No. NC38.

Temples at Abu Simbel AP14

1966, Apr. 28 Wmk. 342 Perf. 11½
C108	AP14	20m multicolored	1.10	.55
C109	AP14	80m multicolored	2.50	1.75

Issued to commemorate the transfer of the temples of Abu Simbel to a hilltop, 1963-66.

Scout Camp and Jamboree Emblem — AP15

1966, Aug. 10 Perf. 11½x11
C110	AP15	20m olive & rose	1.60	.50

7th Pan-Arab Boy Scout Jamboree, Good Daim, Libya, Aug. 12.

St. Catherine Monastery, Mt. Sinai — AP16

1966, Nov. 30 Photo. Wmk. 342
C111	AP16	80m multicolored	2.25	1.75

St. Catherine Monastery, Sinai, 1400th anniv.

Cairo Airport — AP17

1967, Apr. 26 Perf. 11½x11
C112	AP17	20m sky bl, sl grn & lt brn	1.00	.40

Hotel El Alamein and Map of Nile Delta — AP18

Intl. Tourist Year: 80m, The Virgin's Tree, Virgin Mary and Child. 115m, Fishing in the Red Sea.

1967, June 7 Wmk. 342 Perf. 11½
C113	AP18	20m dull pur, sl grn & dl org	1.10	.50
C114	AP18	80m blue & multi	2.50	1.50
C115	AP18	115m brown, org & bl	4.75	2.25
		Nos. C113-C115 (3)	8.35	4.25

Oil Derricks, Map of Egypt — AP19

1967, July 23 Photo.
C116	AP19	50m org & bluish blk	1.25	.85

15th anniversary of the revolution.

Type of Regular Issue, 1967

Design: 80m, Back of Tutankhamun's throne and UNESCO emblem.

1967, Oct. 24 Wmk. 342 Perf. 11½
C117	A301	80m blue & yellow	1.50	.90

Koran AP20

1968, Mar. 25 Wmk. 342 Perf. 11½
C118	AP20	30m lilac, bl & yel	1.25	1.00
C119	AP20	80m lilac, bl & yel	2.25	1.25
a.		Pair, #C118-C119 + label	4.50	3.50

1400th anniv. of the Koran. Nos. C118-C119 are printed in miniature sheets of 4 containing 2 each of Nos. C118-C119.

St. Mark and St. Mark's Cathedral — AP21

1968, June 25 Wmk. 342 Perf. 11½
C120	AP21	80m brt grn, dk brn & dp car	1.75	1.00

Martyrdom of St. Mark, 1900th anniv. and the consecration of St. Mark's Cathedral, Cairo.

EGYPT

AP22

Design: No. C121, Map of United Arab Airlines and Boeing 707. No. C122, Ilyushin 18 and routes of United Arab Airlines.

1968-69   Photo.   Perf. 11½x11
C121 AP22 55m blue, ocher & car   1.75 .90
C122 AP22 55m bl, yel & vio blk ('69)   1.25 .90

1st flights of a Boeing 707 and an Ilyushin 18 for United Arab Airlines.

Mahatma Gandhi, Arms of India and UAR — AP23

1969, Sept. 10   Perf. 11x11½
C123 AP23 80m lt blue, ocher & brn   4.00 1.75

Mohandas K. Gandhi (1869-1948), leader in India's fight for independence.

Imam El Boukhary — AP24

1969, Dec. 27   Photo.   Wmk. 342
C124 AP24 30m lt ol & dk brn   .70 .25

1100th anniv. of the death of the Imam El Boukhary (824-870), philosopher and writer.

Azzahir Beybars Mosque — AP25

1969, Dec. 27   Engr.   Perf. 11½x11
C125 AP25 30m red lilac   .70 .25

700th anniv. of the founding of the Azzahir Beybars Mosque, Cairo.

Lenin (1870-1924) — AP26

Perf. 11x11½
1970, Apr. 22   Photo.   Wmk. 342
C126 AP26 80m lt grn & brn   2.00 1.25

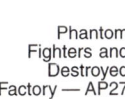
Phantom Fighters and Destroyed Factory — AP27

1970, May 1   Perf. 11½x11
C127 AP27 80m yel, grn & dk vio brn   2.00 1.00

Issued to commemorate the destruction of the Abu-Zaabal factory by Israeli planes.

UPU Type of Regular Issue
1970, May 20   Photo.   Wmk. 342
C128 A350 80m multicolored   1.40 .85

Nasser and Burial Mosque AP28

1970, Nov. 6   Wmk. 342   Perf. 11
C129 AP28 30m olive & blk   1.00 .40
C130 AP28 80m brown & blk   2.75 1.25

Gamal Abdel Nasser (1918-70), Pres. of Egypt.

Postal Congress Type
1971, Mar. 6   Photo.   Wmk. 342
C131 A365 30m lt ol, org & sl grn   .90 .45

Nasser, El Rifaei and Sultan Hussein Mosques AP29

Designs: 85m, Nasser and Ramses Square, Cairo. 110m, Nasser, Sphinx and pyramids.

Perf. 11½x11
1971, July 1   Photo.   Wmk. 342
C132 AP29 30m multicolored   2.50 .80
C133 AP29 85m multicolored   4.50 1.25
C134 AP29 110m multicolored   5.75 2.50
Nos. C132-C134 (3)   12.75 4.55

APU Type of Regular Issue
1971, Aug. 3   Wmk. 342   Perf. 11½
C135 A373 30m brown, yel & bl   1.40 .50

Arab Republic of Egypt Confederation Type
Perf. 11½x11
1971, Sept. 28   Photo.   Wmk. 342
C136 A374 30m gray, sl grn & dk pur   1.25 .50

Al Aqsa Mosque and Woman — AP30

Wmk. 342
1971, Oct. 24   Photo.   Perf. 11½
C137 AP30 30m bl, yel, brn & grn   1.75 .45

25th anniv. of the UN (in 1970) and return of Palestinian refugees.

Postal Union Type
30m, African Postal Union emblem & letter.

1971, Dec. 2   Perf. 11½x11
C138 A384 30m green, blk & bl   1.40 .40

Aida, Triumphal March — AP31

1971, Dec. 23   Wmk. 342   Perf. 11½
C139 AP31 110m dk brn, yel & sl grn   5.75 3.00

Centenary of the first performance of the opera Aida, by Giuseppe Verdi.

Globe, Glider, Rocket Club Emblem — AP32

1972, Feb. 11   Perf. 11x11½
C140 AP32 30m blue, ocher & yel   1.50 .50

International Aerospace Education Conference, Cairo, Jan. 11-13.

St. Catherine's Monastery on Fire — AP33

Perf. 11½x11
1972, Feb. 15   Unwmk.
C141 AP33 110m dp car, org & blk   4.75 4.00

The burning of St. Catherine's Monastery in Sinai Desert, Nov. 30, 1971.

Tutankhamun in Garden — AP34

Tutankhamun, from 2nd Sarcophagus — AP35

Design: No. C143, Ankhesenamun.

1972, May 22   Photo.   Perf. 11½
C142 110m brn org, bl & grn   10.00 5.50
C143 110m brn org, bl & grn   10.00 5.50
  a. AP34 Pair, #C142-C143   26.00 22.50

Souvenir Sheet
Imperf
C144 AP35 200m gold & multi   32.50 32.50

50th anniv. of the discovery of the tomb of Tutankhamun.

Souvenir Sheet

Flag of Confederation of Arab Republics — AP36

1972, July 23   Photo.   Imperf.
C145 AP36 110m gold, dp car & blk   4.50 4.25

20th anniversary of the revolution.

Temples at Abu Simbel — AP37

Designs: 30m, Al Azhar Mosque and St. George's Church. 110m, Pyramids at Giza.

1972   Wmk. 342   Perf. 11½x11
C146 AP37 30m blue, brn & buff   2.50 .40
C147 AP37 85m bl, brn & ocher   3.50 1.75
C148 AP37 110m multicolored   5.25 1.75
Nos. C146-C148 (3)   11.25 3.90

Issued: Nos. C146, C148, 11/22; No. C147, 8/1.

Olympic Type of Regular Issue
Olympic and Motion Emblems and: No. C149, Handball. No. C150, Weight lifting. 50m, Swimming. 55m, Gymnastics. All vertical.

1972, Aug. 17   Perf. 11x11½
C149 A396 30m multicolored   .80 .40
C150 A396 30m yellow & multi   .80 .40
C151 A396 50m blue & multi   1.60 1.00
C152 A396 55m multicolored   2.00 1.10
Nos. C149-C152 (4)   5.20 2.90

Champollion, Rosetta Stone, Hieroglyphics AP38

1972, Oct. 16
C153 AP38 110m gold, grn & blk   7.50 2.50

Sesquicentennial of the deciphering of Egyptian hieroglyphics by Jean-François Champollion.

World Map, Telephone, Radar, ITU Emblem AP39

1973, Mar. 21   Photo.   Perf. 11
C154 AP39 30m lt bl, dk bl & blk   .90 .25

5th World Telecommunications Day.

Karnak Temple, Luxor — AP40

1973, Mar. 21
C155 AP40 110m dp ultra, blk & rose   4.75 2.50

Sound and light at Karnak.

Hand Dripping Blood and Falling Plane — AP41

1973, May 1   Perf. 11x11½
C156 AP41 110m multicolored   6.25 3.00

Israeli attack on Libyan civilian plane, Feb. 1973.

WMO Emblem, Weather Vane — AP42

1973, Oct. 24   Perf. 11x11½
C157 AP42 110m blue, gold & pur   3.00 1.75

Cent. of intl. meteorological cooperation.

EGYPT

Refugees, Map of Palestine — AP43

1973, Oct. 24   *Perf. 11½*
C158   AP43   30m dk brn, yel & bl   1.60   .50
Plight of Palestinian refugees.

INTERPOL Emblem — AP44

Perf. 11x11½
1973, Dec. 8   Photo.   Wmk. 342
C159   AP44   110m black & multi   3.75   2.00
Intl. Criminal Police Organization, 50th anniv.

Postal and UPU Emblems — AP45

Post Day (UPU Emblems and): 30m, APU emblem. 55m, African Postal Union emblem. 110m, UPU emblem.

Size: 26x46½mm
1974, Jan. 2   Unwmk.   *Perf. 11*
C160   AP45   20m gray, red & blk   .45   .25
C161   AP45   30m sal, blk & pur   .65   .25
C162   AP45   55m emerald, blk & brt mag   1.25   .85

Size: 37x37½mm
Perf. 11½
C163   AP45   110m lt bl, blk & gold   1.75   1.50
Nos. C160-C163 (4)   4.10   2.85

Solar Bark of Khufu (Cheops) AP46

Wmk. 342
1974, Mar. 21   Photo.   *Perf. 11½*
C164   AP46   110m blue, gold & brn   3.75   2.25
Solar Bark Museum.

Hotel Meridien — AP47

1974, Oct. 6   *Perf. 11½x11*
C165   AP47   110m multicolored   2.25   1.25
Opening of Hotel Meridien, Cairo.

Suez Canal Type of 1975
1975, June 5   *Perf. 11½*
C166   A448   30m bl, yel grn & ind   1.75   .60
C167   A448   110m indigo & blue   2.75   2.00

Irrigation Commission Emblem — AP48

1975, July 20
C168   AP48   110m orange & dk grn   2.25   1.25
9th Intl. Congress on Irrigation and Drainage, Moscow, and 25th anniv. of the Intl. Commission on Irrigation and Drainage.

Refugees and UNWRA Emblem AP49   Woman and IWY Emblem AP50

Perf. 11x11½
1975, Oct. 24   Photo.   Wmk. 342
C169   AP49   30m multicolored   1.40   .50

Unwmk.
C170   AP50   110m olive, org & blk   3.50   2.00
UN Day. 30m publicizes UN help for refugees; 110m is for Intl. Women's Year 1975.

Step Pyramid, Sakhara, and Entrance Gate — AP51

Designs: 45m, 60m, Plane over Giza Pyramids. 140m, Plane over boats on Nile.

Perf. 11½x11
1978-82   Photo.   Wmk. 342
C171   AP51   45m yel & brown   .60   .25
   b.   Unwatermarked
C171A   AP51   60m olive   2.00   1.00
   c.   Unwatermarked
C172   AP51   115m blue & brn   1.10   .55
C173   AP51   140m blue & pur   2.00   1.00
C173A   AP51   185m bl, sep & gray brn   5.00   2.25
Nos. C171-C173A (5)   10.70   5.05
Issued: 60m, 1/15/82; 185m, 1982; others, 1/1/78.

Flyer and UN ICAO Emblem — AP52

Perf. 11x11½
1978, Dec. 30   Photo.   Wmk. 342
C174   AP52   140m blue, blk & brn   2.50   1.25
75th anniversary of 1st powered flight.

Seeing Eye Medallion AP53

Perf. 11½x11
1981, Oct. 1   Photo.   Wmk. 342
C175   AP53   230m multicolored   2.50   1.25

Hilton Ramses Hotel Opening — AP54

Perf. 11x11½
1982, Mar. 15   Photo.   Wmk. 342
C176   AP54   18½p multi   2.00   1.00

Temple of Horus, Edfu — AP55

Designs: 15p, like 6p. 18½p, 25p, Statue of Akhnaton, Thebes, hieroglyphics, vert. 23p, 30p, Giza pyramids.

Perf. 11½x11, 11x11½
1985   Photo.   Wmk. 342
C177   AP55   6p lt blue & dk bl grn   1.00   .40
C178   AP55   15p grnsh bl & brn   1.75   .50
   a.   Unwatermarked
C179   AP55   18½p grn, sep & dp yel   2.00   1.25
C180   AP55   23p grnsh bl, sep & yel bis   2.50   1.50
C181   AP55   25p lt bl, sep & yel bis   2.10   .95
   a.   Unwmkd. ('87)   2.75   1.10
C182   AP55   30p grnsh bl, sep & org yel   2.10   .85
   a.   Unwmkd. ('87)   2.75   1.10
Nos. C177-C182 (6)   11.45   5.45
Issued: 6p, 18½p, 23p, 3/1; 15p, 25p, 30p, 5/1.
See No. C236.

Post Day AP56

Narmer Board, oldest known hieroglyphic inscriptions: No. C183a, Tablet obverse. No. C183b, Reverse.

1986, Jan. 2   Photo.   *Perf. 13½x13*
C183   AP56   Pair   2.50   2.50
   a.-b.   15p any single   1.10   1.00

Map, Jet, AFRAA Emblem — AP57

1986, Apr. 7   Photo.   *Perf. 11½*
C184   AP57   15p blue, yel & blk   1.25   .50
African Airlines Assoc., 18th General Assembly, Cairo, Apr. 7-10.

World Food Day — AP58

UNESCO, 40th Anniv. AP59

Perf. 13½x13, 13x13½
1986, Oct. 24   Litho.
C185   AP58   15p multicolored   1.00   1.00
C186   AP59   15p multicolored   1.00   1.00
UN Day.

Tourism Year AP60

Design: Column and Sphinx in Alexandria, St. Catherine's Monastery in Mt. Sinai, Colossi of Thebes and Temple of Theban Triad in Luxor.

Unwmk.
1987, Sept. 30   Litho.   *Imperf.*
Size: 140x90mm
C187   AP60   30p multicolored   4.25   4.25
See No. 1344.

Palestinian Uprising AP61

1988, Sept. 28   Litho.   *Perf. 12x13½*
C188   AP61   25p multicolored   1.60   1.40

UN Day — AP62

1988, Oct. 20   Litho.   *Perf. 13x13½*
C189   AP62   25p multicolored   1.60   1.40

Nobel Prize Type of 1988
1988, Nov. 7
C190   A769   25p multicolored   1.60   1.40

Arab Cooperation Council — AP63

1989, May 10   Litho.   *Perf. 13½x13*
C191   AP63   25p Flags   1.25   .55

Size: 89x80mm
Imperf
C192   AP63   50p Flags, seal   3.50   3.50

Architecture and Art — AP64

1989-91   Photo.   *Perf. 11x11½*
C193   AP64   20p Balcony   .75   .45
C194   AP64   25p Brazier   1.10   .60
C195   AP64   35p shown   1.25   .75
C196   AP64   45p Tapestry   1.60   .75
C197   AP64   45p like #C195   1.40   .40
C198   AP64   50p Stag (dish)   2.00   1.00
C199   AP64   55p 4 animals (plate)   1.90   .90
C200   AP64   60p like #C198   2.25   1.25
C201   AP64   65p like #C198   2.50   1.50
C202   AP64   70p like #C193   2.50   1.50
C203   AP64   85p like #C199   3.00   1.75
Nos. C193-C203 (11)   20.25   10.85
Issued: 35p, 60p, 10/1/89; 55p, 1/1/90; No. C197, C202, 1/25/91; 65p, 85p, 7/20/91; others, 4/1/89.

AP65

EGYPT

Funerary Mask of King Tutankhamun AP66 — King Tutankhamun AP66a

No. C205, 21mm between "EGYPT" and Arabic text at top.
No. C205A, 17mm between "Egypt" and Arabic text at top ('00).

1993-2000   Litho.   **Perf. 11½**
C204   AP65   55p black & sepia   2.00   .95
C205   AP66   80p black & drab   3.25   1.25
C205A   AP66   80p black & sepia   —   —

Photo.
Perf. 11x11¼
C206   AP66a   £1 black & brown   1.50   1.25
  b.   Wmk. 342   2.00   1.25
  Nos. C204-C206 (4)   6.75   3.45

Issued: 55p, 80p, 3/1/93; £1, 1997; No. C206b, 1999.
See No. C231.

ICAO, 50th Anniv. — AP67

1994, Sept. 16   Litho.   **Perf. 13**
C207   AP67   80p multicolored   1.00   .45

Intl. Year of the Family AP68

1994, Oct. 24   Litho.   **Perf. 13**
C208   AP68   80p multicolored   1.50   1.00

Arab League for Education, Culture, & Science Organization AP69

1995, July 25   Litho.   **Perf. 13x13½**
C209   AP69   55p multicolored   .80   .50

UN Organizations, 50th Anniv. — AP70

Perf. 12½x13, 13x12½
1995, Oct. 24   Litho.
C210   AP70   80p UN   2.00   1.00
C211   AP70   80p FAO   2.00   1.00
C212   AP70   80p UNESCO, vert.   2.00   1.00
  Nos. C210-C212 (3)   6.00   3.00

Arab Summit, Cairo — AP71

1996, June 21   Litho.   **Perf. 13x12½**
C213   AP71   55p multicolored   .70   .30

16th Intl. Conference on Irrigation and Drainage, Cairo — AP72

1996, Sept. 15   Litho.   **Perf. 12½x13**
C214   AP72   80p multicolored   1.10   1.10

Intl. Tourism Day — AP73

1996, Sept. 27   **Perf. 13**
C215   AP73   80p multicolored   1.50   .60

Arabian Horse Day — AP74

1996, Sept. 27   **Perf. 13x12½**
C216   AP74   55p grn, blk & gray   1.00   .35

World Post Day — AP75

1996, Oct. 9   Litho.   **Perf. 13x12½**
C217   AP75   80p multicolored   1.25   .60

AP76

1996, Oct. 24
C218   AP76   55p multicolored   .70   .40
Cairo, Arab cultural capital of 1996.

UNICEF, 50th Anniv. — AP77

1996, Oct. 24
C219   AP77   80p multicolored   1.10   .55

World Meteorological Day — AP78

1997, Mar. 23   Litho.   **Perf. 13x12½**
C220   AP78   £1 multicolored   1.75   1.00

Thutmose III — AP79

1997, Mar. 25   Photo.   **Perf. 11x11½**
C221   AP79   75p blk, bl & gray   1.10   1.10

Heinrich von Stephan (1831-97) AP80

1997, Apr. 15   Litho.   **Perf. 13**
C222   AP80   £1 multicolored   1.60   1.25

AP81

1997, Sept. 11
C223   AP81   £1 multicolored   1.00   .90
98th Intl. Parliamentary Conference, Cairo.

AP82

1997, Sept. 10   Litho.   **Perf. 13**
C224   AP82   75p multicolored   1.00   .90
1997 Egyptian Team, top medal winners of 8th Pan Arab Games, Beirut, Lebanon.

AP83

1997, Sept. 27   **Perf. 13x12½**
C225   AP83   £1 multicolored   1.90   1.00
Sarabas (180-211), mumified Egyptian.

World Book and Copyright Day — AP84

1997, Oct. 24   Litho.   **Perf. 12½x13**
C226   AP84   £1 multicolored   1.75   1.00

African Ministries of Transport and Communications, 11th Conference — AP85

1997, Nov. 22   Litho.   **Perf. 13x12½**
C227   AP85   75p multicolored   .80   .70

Arab Scout Movement, 85th Anniv. — AP86

1997, Nov. 24   **Perf. 12½x13**
C228   AP86   75p multicolored   1.00   .90

8th G-15 Summit Meeting — AP87

1998, May 11   Litho.   **Perf. 13**
C229   AP87   £1 multicolored   1.10   .90

Lighthouse of Alexandria — AP88

1998, May 20   Litho.   **Perf. 13**
C230   AP88   £1 multicolored   1.75   1.00

King Tut Type of 1997
1998, July 25   Litho.   **Perf. 11x11¼**
C231   AP66a   125p Tutankhamun   1.75   1.25
  a.   Wmk. 342 ('99)   5.50   4.00

Arab Post Day — AP90

1998, Aug. 3   **Perf. 13**
C232   AP90   £1 multicolored   1.10   .90

World Post Day — AP91

1998, Oct. 9   Litho.   **Perf. 13**
C233   AP91   125p multicolored   1.40   1.25

67th Interpol Meeting, Cairo — AP92

1998, Oct. 22
C234   AP92   125p multicolored   1.40   1.25

EGYPT

AP93

1998, Oct. 24
C235 AP93 125p multicolored 1.40 1.25
Universal Declaration of Human Rights, 50th anniv.

Statue of Akhnaton Type of 1985
1998 Litho. *Perf. 13*
C236 AP55 25p lt bl, brn & tan 1.75 1.00

AP94

1999, Oct. 12 Litho. *Perf. 13x12¾*
C237 AP94 125p multicolored 2.25 1.75
Performance of opera "Aida" at the Pyramids.

AP95

1999, Oct. 16
C238 AP95 125p multicolored 2.50 1.75
Discovery of the Rosetta Stone, bicent.

World Tourism Day — AP96

Perf. 13¼x12¾
2000, Sept. 27 Litho.
C239 AP96 125p multi 1.50 1.25

Awarding of Nobel Prize for Chemistry to Dr. Ahmed Zewail — AP97

1999, Dec. 10 Imperf.
C240 AP97 125p multi 2.00 2.00

UN High Commissioner for Refugees, 50th Anniv. — AP98

2000, Dec. 13
C241 AP98 125p multi 1.50 1.25

AIR POST SEMI-POSTAL STAMPS

Catalogue values for unused stamps in this section are for Never Hinged items.

United Arab Republic

Pharaonic Mail Carriers and Papyrus Plants — SPAP1

Design: 115m+55m, Jet plane, world map and stamp of Egypt, 1926 (No. C1).

Wmk. 342
1966, Jan. 2 Photo. *Perf. 11½*
CB1 SPAP1 80m + 40m multi 3.25 2.75
CB2 SPAP1 115m + 55m multi 4.25 3.50
 a. Pair, #CB1-CB2 10.00 8.00
Post Day, Jan. 2.

SPECIAL DELIVERY STAMPS

Motorcycle Postman — SD1

Perf. 13x13½
1926, Nov. 28 Photo. Wmk. 195
E1 SD1 20m dark green 35.00 9.50

1929, Sept.
E2 SD1 20m brown red & black 6.75 1.75

Inscribed "Postes Expres"
1943-44 Litho.
E3 SD1 26m brn red & gray blk 6.75 6.75
E4 SD1 40m dl brn & pale gray ('44) 6.00 4.00
For overprints see Nos. E5, NE1.

Catalogue values for unused stamps in this section, from this point to the end of the section, are for Never Hinged items.

No. E4 Overprinted in Black

1952, Jan. Overprint 27mm Wide
E5 SD1 40m dl brn & pale gray 3.50 2.00
See notes after No. 316.

POSTAGE DUE STAMPS

D1

Wmk. Crescent and Star (119)
1884, Jan. 1 Litho. *Perf. 10½*
J1 D1 10pa red 57.50 9.50
 a. Horiz. pair, imperf. vert. 175.00
J2 D1 20pa red 175.00 50.00
J3 D1 1pi red 145.00 52.50
J4 D1 2pi red 240.00 12.50
J5 D1 5pi red 20.00 65.00
 Nos. J1-J5 (5) 637.50 189.50

1886, Aug. 1 Unwmk.
J6 D1 10pa red 75.00 17.50
 a. Horiz. pair, imperf. vert. 150.
J7 D1 20pa red 260.00 50.00
J8 D1 1pi red 37.50 10.00
 a. Pair, imperf. between 225.00 150.00
J9 D1 2pi red 37.50 5.00
 a. Pair, imperf. between 200.00
 Nos. J6-J9 (4) 410.00 82.50

D2

1888, Jan. 1 *Perf. 11½*
J10 D2 2m green 22.50 27.50
 a. Horiz. pair, imperf. between 250.00 225.00
J11 D2 5m rose red 45.00 27.50
J12 D2 1pi blue 145.00 40.00
 a. Pair, imperf. between 325.00
J13 D2 2pi yellow 155.00 20.00
J14 D2 5pi gray 240.00 210.00
 a. Period after "PIASTRES" 325.00 250.00
 Nos. J10-J14 (5) 607.50 325.00

Excellent counterfeits of #J1-J14 are plentiful.
There are 4 types of each of Nos. J1-J14, so placed that any block of 4 contains all types.

D3

Perf. 14x13½
1889 Wmk. 119 Typo.
J15 D3 2m green 10.00 .70
 a. Half used as 1m on cover 400.00
J16 D3 4m maroon 3.75 .70
J17 D3 1pi ultra 7.75 .70
J18 D3 2pi orange 7.50 1.00
 a. Half used as 1p on cover
 Nos. J15-J18 (4) 29.00 3.10

Nos. J15-J18 exist on both ordinary and chalky paper. Imperf. examples of Nos. J15-J17 are proofs.

Black Surcharge

Type I — D4

1898
J19 D4 3m on 2pi orange 2.10 6.25
 a. Inverted surcharge 67.50 90.00
 b. Pair, one without surcharge —
 f. Double surcharge 250.00 —

There are two types of this surcharge. In type I, the spacing between the last two Arabic characters at the right is 2mm. In type II, this spacing is 3mm, and there is an added sign on top of the second character from the right. See *Scott Classic Specialized Catalogue of Stamps & Covers* for detailed listing.

D5 D6

1921 Wmk. 120 *Perf. 14x13½*
J20 D5 2m green 3.75 6.75
J21 D5 4m vermilion 7.50 19.00
J22 D6 10m deep blue 12.50 25.00
 Nos. J20-J22 (3) 23.75 50.75

1921-22
J23 D5 2m vermilion 1.00 2.25
J24 D5 4m green 6.00 2.00
J25 D6 10m lake ('22) 6.50 1.50
 Nos. J23-J25 (3) 13.50 5.75

Nos. J18, J23-J25 Overprinted

1922, Oct. 10 Wmk. 119
J26 D3 2pi orange 7.50 10.50
 a. Overprint right side up 32.50 32.50

Wmk. 120
J27 D5 2m vermilion 1.00 3.25
J28 D5 4m green 1.60 3.25
J29 D6 10m lake 2.75 2.00
 Nos. J26-J29 (4) 12.85 19.00
Overprint on Nos. J26-J29 is inverted.

Arabic Numeral — D7

Perf. 13x13½
1927-56 Litho. Wmk. 195
 Size: 18x22½mm
J30 D7 2m slate .85 .50
J31 D7 2m orange ('38) 1.00 1.10
J32 D7 4m gray green .85 .55
J33 D7 4m ol brn ('32) 8.00 5.25
J34 D7 5m brown 4.25 1.10
J35 D7 6m grn gray ('41) 2.75 2.10
J36 D7 8m brn vio 1.60 .65
J37 D7 10m brick red ('29) 1.25 .35
 a. 10m deep red 1.90 1.00
J38 D7 12m rose lake ('41) 1.90 3.75
J38A D7 20m dk red ('56) 2.50 2.50

Perf. 13½x14
Size: 22x28mm
J39 D7 30m purple 5.25 3.75
 Nos. J30-J39 (11) 30.20 21.60

See Nos. J47-J59. For overprints see Nos. J40-J46, NJ1-NJ7.

Catalogue values for unused stamps in this section, from this point to the end of the section, are for Never Hinged items.

Postage Due Stamps and Type of 1927 Overprinted in Various Colors

1952, Jan. 16 *Perf. 13x13½*
J40 D7 2m orange (Bl) 1.60 1.60
J41 D7 4m green 1.60 1.60
J42 D7 6m gray grn (RV) 1.90 1.90
J43 D7 8m brn vio (Bl) 2.50 2.50
J44 D7 10m dl rose (Bl) 4.25 3.50
 a. 10m brown red (Bk) 4.00 3.75
J45 D7 12m rose lake (Bl) 2.10 2.10

Perf. 14
J46 D7 30m purple (C) 3.50 3.50
 Nos. J40-J46 (7) 17.45 16.70
See notes after No. 316.

United Arab Republic

1960 Wmk. 318 *Perf. 13x13½*
 Size: 18x22½mm
J47 D7 2m orange 1.00 1.00
J48 D7 4m light green 1.50 1.50
J49 D7 6m green 2.50 2.50
J50 D7 8m brown vio 5.00 5.00
J51 D7 12m rose brown 12.00 10.00
J52 D7 20m dull rose brn 2.00 .50

Perf. 14
Size: 22x28mm
J53 D7 30m violet 12.00 6.00
 Nos. J47-J53 (7) 36.00 26.50

1962 Wmk. 328 *Perf. 13x13½*
 Size: 18x22½mm
J54 D7 2m salmon 1.00 1.00
J55 D7 4m light green 1.50 1.50
J56 D7 10m red brown 2.50 2.50
J57 D7 12m rose brown 5.00 5.00
J58 D7 20m dull rose brn 11.00 11.00

EGYPT

Perf. 14
Size: 22x28mm

J59	D7	30m light violet	16.00	16.00
		Nos. J54-J59 (6)	37.00	37.00

D8

1965   Unwmk.   Photo.   Perf. 11

J60	D8	2m org & vio blk	1.25	1.00
J61	D8	8m lt bl & dk bl	1.50	1.50
J62	D8	10m yel & emer	2.25	1.50
J63	D8	20m lt bl & vio blk	2.75	2.25
J64	D8	40m grn & emer	4.75	2.00
		Nos. J60-J64 (5)	12.50	8.25

MILITARY STAMPS

The "British Forces" and "Army post" stamps were special issues provided at a reduced rate for the purchase and use by the British military forces in Egypt and their families for ordinary letters sent to Great Britain and Ireland by a concessionary arrangement made with the Egyptian government. From Nov. 1, 1932 to Feb. 29, 1936, in order to take advantage of the concessionary rate, it was mandatory to use #M1-M11 by affixing them to the backs of envelopes. An "Egypt Postage Prepaid" handstamp was applied to the face of the envelopes. Envelopes bearing these stamps were to be posted only at British military post boxes. Envelopes bearing the 1936-39 "Army Post" stamps (#M12-M15, issued by the Egyptian Postal Administration) also were sold at the concessionary rate and also were to be posted only at British military post boxes. The "Army Post" stamps were withdrawn in 1941, but the concession continued without the use of special stamps. The concession was finally canceled in 1951.

Imperf examples of Nos. M1-M4, M6, M9 (without overprint) and M10 are proofs.

M1

Unwmk.
1932, Nov. 1   Typo.   Perf. 11

M1	M1	1pi red & blue	70.00	4.50

For similar design see No. M3.

M2

1932, Nov. 26   Typo.   Perf. 11½

M2	M2	3m blk, sage grn	57.50	80.00

See Nos. M4, M6, M10

M3

1933, Aug.   Typo.   Perf. 11

M3	M3	1pi red & blue	47.50	1.10

Camel Type of 1932
1933, Nov. 13   Typo.   Perf. 11½

M4	M2	3m brown lake	40.00	57.50

M4

1934, June 1   Photo.   Perf. 14½x14

M5	M4	1pi bright carmine	40.00	1.25

See Nos. M7-M8. For overprint and surcharge see Nos. M9, M11.

Camel Type of 1932
1934, Nov. 17   Typo.   Perf. 11½

M6	M2	3m deep blue	30.00	30.00

Type of 1934
1934, Dec. 5   Photo.   Perf. 14½x14

M7	M4	1pi green	6.00	6.00

Type of 1934
1935, Apr. 24   Perf. 13½x14

M8	M4	1pi bright carmine	2.90	3.75

Type of 1934 Overprinted in Red

1935, May 6   Perf. 14

M9	M4	1pi ultramarine	350.00	275.00

Camel Type of 1932
1935, Nov. 23   Typo.   Perf. 11½

M10	M2	3m vermilion	30.00	45.00

No. M8 Surcharged

1935, Dec. 16   Photo.   Perf. 13½x14

M11	M4	3m on 1pi brt car	40.00	100.00

Fuad Type of 1927

Inscribed "Army Post" — M5

1936, Mar. 1   Wmk. 195

M12	M5	3m green	2.50	2.50
M13	M5	10m carmine	7.00	.25

King Farouk — M6

1939, Dec. 16   Perf. 13x13½

M14	M6	3m green	6.00	12.00
M15	M6	10m carmine rose	8.00	.25

Catalogue values for unused stamps in this section, from this point to the end of the section, are for Never Hinged items.

United Arab Republic

Arms of UAR and Military Emblems — M7

Perf. 11x11½
1971, Apr. 15   Photo.   Wmk. 342

M16	M7	10m purple	.75	.50

OFFICIAL STAMPS

O1

Wmk. Crescent and Star (119)
1893, Jan. 1   Typo.   Perf. 14x13½

O1	O1	orange brown	3.75	.25

No. O1 exists on ordinary and chalky paper. Imperf. examples of No. O1 are proofs.

Regular Issues of 1884-93 Overprinted

1907

O2	A18	1m brown	2.40	.35
O3	A19	2m green	4.25	.25
O4	A20	3m orange	4.75	1.25
O5	A22	5m car rose	7.75	.25
O6	A14	1pi ultra	4.75	.25
O7	A16	5pi gray	17.00	6.00
		Nos. O2-O7 (6)	40.90	8.35

Nos. O2-O3, O5-O7 imperf. are proofs.

No. 48 Overprinted

1913

O8	A22	5m carmine rose	9.50	.70
a.		Inverted overprint	90.00	
b.		No period after "S"	65.00	19.00

Regular Issues Overprinted

1914-15   On Issues of 1888-1906

O9	A19	2m green	5.00	10.00
a.		Inverted overprint	42.50	42.50
b.		Double overprint	450.00	
c.		No period after "S"	16.00	16.00
O10	A21	4m brown red	7.50	5.50
a.		Inverted overprint	225.00	160.00

On Issue of 1914

O11	A24	1m olive brown	2.50	5.00
a.		No period after "S"	14.00	30.00
O12	A26	3m orange	3.75	6.00
a.		No period after "S"	16.00	30.00
O13	A28	5m lake	4.75	2.75
a.		No period after "S"	17.50	26.00
b.		Two periods after "S"	17.50	26.00
		Nos. O9-O13 (5)	23.50	29.25

Regular Issues Overprinted

1915, Oct.   On Issues of 1888-1906

O14	A19	2m green	5.50	5.00
a.		Inverted overprint	24.00	24.00
b.		Double overprint	30.00	
O15	A21	4m brown red	11.00	11.00

On Issue of 1914

O16	A28	5m lake	15.00	1.75
a.		Pair, one without overprint	1,000.	
		Nos. O14-O16 (3)	31.50	17.75

Nos. 50, 63, 52, 67 Overprinted

1922   Wmk. 120

O17	A24	1m olive brown	4.25	16.00
O18	A25	2m red	10.00	24.00
O19	A26	3m orange	77.50	150.00
O20	A28	5m pink	21.00	6.00
		Nos. O17-O20 (4)	112.75	196.00

Regular Issues of 1921-22 Overprinted

1922

O21	A24	1m olive brn	1.50	3.25
O22	A25	2m red	2.00	4.50
O23	A26	3m orange	3.25	5.00
O24	A27	4m green	7.00	9.00
a.		Two periods after "H" none after "S"	175.00	175.00
O25	A28	5m pink	4.00	1.00
a.		Two periods after "H" none after "S"	75.00	75.00
O26	A29	10m deep blue	7.00	8.00
O27	A29	10m lake ('23)	10.00	4.00
a.		Two periods after "H" none after "S"	100.00	100.00

O28	A34	15m indigo	8.00	7.00
O29	A35	15m indigo	160.00	160.00
a.		Two periods after "H" none after "S"	250.00	250.00
O30	A31	50m maroon	20.00	18.00

Regular Issue of 1923 Overprinted in Black or Red

1924   Perf. 13½x14

O31	A36	1m orange	2.10	2.25
O32	A36	2m gray (R)	2.75	3.50
O33	A36	3m brown	6.75	6.75
O34	A36	4m yellow green	8.50	8.50
O35	A36	5m orange brown	2.00	1.05
O36	A36	10m rose	5.50	4.00
O37	A36	15m ultra	9.25	6.75

Perf. 14

O38	A36	50m myrtle green	25.00	13.50
		Nos. O31-O38 (8)	61.85	46.30

O2

Perf. 13x13½
1926-35   Litho.   Wmk. 195
Size: 18½x22mm

O39	O2	1m lt orange	1.05	.55
O40	O2	2m black	.70	.40
O41	O2	3m olive brn	2.00	1.35
O42	O2	4m lt green	1.75	1.60
O43	O2	5m brown	2.10	.55
O44	O2	10m dull red	5.25	.55
O45	O2	10m brt vio ('34)	3.00	.60
O46	O2	15m dp blue	5.25	1.25
O47	O2	15m brown vio ('34)	5.25	1.10
O48	O2	20m dp blue ('35)	5.50	1.60

Perf. 13½
Size: 22½x27½mm

O49	O2	20m olive green	7.50	2.75
O50	O2	50m myrtle green	10.00	2.00
		Nos. O39-O50 (12)	49.35	14.30

O3

1938, Dec.   Size: 22½x19mm

O51	O3	1m orange	.35	.35
O52	O3	2m red	.35	.35
O53	O3	3m olive brown	1.60	1.60
O54	O3	4m yel green	1.00	1.00
O55	O3	5m brown	.50	.50
O56	O3	10m brt violet	.60	.60
O57	O3	15m rose violet	1.60	1.60
O58	O3	20m blue	1.60	1.60

Perf. 14x13½
Size: 26½x22mm

O59	O3	50m myrtle green	3.75	3.00
		Nos. O51-O59 (9)	11.35	10.60

Catalogue values for unused stamps in this section, from this point to the end of the section, are for Never Hinged items.

Nos. O51 to O59 Overprinted in Various Colors

Overprint 19mm Wide
1952, Jan.   Perf. 13x13½

O60	O3	1m orange (Br)	2.10	2.10
O61	O3	2m red (Br)	2.10	2.10
O62	O3	3m olive brn (Bl)	2.50	2.50
O63	O3	4m yel green (Bl)	2.50	2.50
O64	O3	5m brown (Bl)	2.50	2.50
O65	O3	10m brt violet (Bl)	2.50	2.50
O66	O3	15m rose violet (Bl)	3.00	3.00
O67	O3	20m blue	3.75	3.75

EGYPT

Overprint 24½mm Wide
Perf. 14x13½

O68	O3 50m myrtle grn (RV)	8.00	8.00
	Nos. O60-O68 (9)	28.95	28.95

See notes after No. 316.

United Arab Republic

 O4

Perf. 13x13½

1959		Litho.	Wmk. 318
O69	O4 10m brown violet	.65	.25
O70	O4 35m chalky blue	1.75	.30

1962-63			Wmk. 328
O71	O4 1m orange ('63)	.30	.30
O72	O4 4m yel grn ('63)	.60	.60
O73	O4 5m brown	.60	.25
O74	O4 10m dk brown	.75	.30
O75	O4 35m dark blue	2.25	.60
O76	O4 50m green	3.50	.60
O77	O4 100m violet ('63)	7.00	1.75
O78	O4 200m rose red ('63)	15.00	8.00
O79	O4 500m gray ('63)	22.50	15.00
	Nos. O71-O79 (9)	52.50	27.30

Arms of UAR — O5

Perf. 11½x11

1966-68		Unwmk.	Photo.
O80	O5 1m ultra	.25	.25
O81	O5 4m brown	.25	.25
O82	O5 5m olive	.30	.25
O83	O5 10m brown blk	1.00	.85
O84	O5 20m magenta	.60	.30
O85	O5 35m dk purple	1.00	.35
O86	O5 50m dk orange	1.10	.45
O87	O5 55m dk purple	1.10	.45

		Wmk. 342	
O88	O5 100m brt grn & brick red	2.25	1.00
O89	O5 200m blue & brick red	4.50	2.00
O90	O5 500m olive & brick red	10.00	6.25
	Nos. O80-O90 (11)	22.35	11.90

1969			Wmk. 342
O91	O5 10m magenta	1.10	.65

Arab Republic of Egypt

Arms of Egypt — O6

Wmk. 342

1972, June 30		Photo.	Perf. 11
O92	O6 1m black & vio blue	.30	.25
a.	1m black & light blue ('75)	.25	.25
O93	O6 10m black & car	.65	.30
a.	10m black & rose red ('76)	.25	.25
O94	O6 20m black & olive	.90	.40
O95	O6 50m black & orange	.60	.55
O96	O6 55m black & purple	3.00	1.00

1973			
O97	O6 20m lilac & sepia	.90	.40
a.	20m purple & light brown ('76)	2.50	.75
O98	O6 70m black & grn ('79)	.85	.45

1982		Photo. Unwmk.	Perf. 11
O99	O6 30m purple & brown	.60	.30
O100	O6 60m black & orange	.70	.30
O101	O6 80m black & green	.95	.35
	Nos. O92-O101 (10)	9.45	4.30

Issued: 30m, 2/12; 60m, 2/24; 80m, 2/18.

Arms of Egypt — O7

1985-89		Photo.	Perf. 11
		Size: 21x25mm	
O102	O7 1p vermilion	.25	.25
O103	O7 2p brown	.25	.25
O104	O7 3p sepia	.25	.25
O105	O7 5p orange yel	.35	.30
O106	O7 8p green	.70	.35
O107	O7 10p brown olive	.25	.25
O108	O7 15p dull violet	1.50	.70
O109	O7 20p blue	.85	.80
O110	O7 25p red	1.50	1.00
O111	O7 30p dull violet	.90	.70
O112	O7 50p green	2.25	2.25
O113	O7 60p myrtle green	2.00	1.40
	Nos. O102-O113 (12)	11.05	8.50

Issued: 1p, 3p, 5p, 8p, 15p, 5/1/85; 20p, 50p, 4/88; 10p, 30p, 60p, 12/1/89; 2p, 25p, 1989.

1991-99	Wmk. 342	Perf. 11½x11
	Size: 18x22mm	
O114	O7 5p orange yellow	.25	.25
O115	O7 10p brown violet	.25	.25
O116	O7 15p brown	.25	.25
O117	O7 20p blue	.35	.25
O118	O7 20p violet	.25	.25
O119	O7 25p purple	.45	.25
O120	O7 30p dk violet	.50	.25
O121	O7 50p green	.80	.60
O122	O7 55p red	.70	.55
O123	O7 75p brown	.75	.55
O124	O7 £1 green blue	1.25	.75
O125	O7 £2 green	2.50	1.50
	Nos. O114-O125 (12)	8.30	5.70

Issued: 10p, 30p, 7/1/91; 50p, 12/1/91; 55p, 4/1/93; £1, £2, 3/22/94; No. O123, 75p, 2/1/97; No. O118, 4/11/99.

Arms Type of 1985-89
Perf. 11½x11

2001-02?	Photo.	Unwmk.
	Size: 18x22mm	
O126	O7 5p orange yellow	—	—
O127	O7 10p brown	2.75	.50
O128	O7 20p dark blue	—	—
O129	O7 25p purple	—	—
O130	O7 30p violet	3.75	.60
O131	O7 75p olive brown	—	—
O132	O7 £1 greenish blue	—	—

Issued: Nos. O126-O129, O131-O132, 3/25/01; No. O130, 2002?.

Arms Type of 1985-89
Perf. 11½x11

2018, Aug. 16	Photo.	Unwmk.
	Size: 18x22mm	
O133	O7 50p brown	.25	.25
O134	O7 £2.50 Prus blue	.30	.30
O135	O7 £3 blksh pur	.35	.35
O136	O7 £4 dark brown	.45	.45
O137	O7 £5 green	.55	.55
	Nos. O133-O137 (5)	1.90	1.90

OCCUPATION STAMPS

Catalogue values for unused stamps in this section are for Never Hinged items.

For Use in Palestine

Stamps of 1939-46 Overprinted in Red, Green or Black — a

Perf. 13x13½, 13½x13

1948, May 15		Wmk. 195
N1	A77 1m yellow brn (G)	.40	.40
N2	A77 2m red org (G)	.40	.40
N3	A66 3m brown (G)	.40	.40
N4	A77 4m dp green	.40	.40
N5	A77 5m red brown (Bk)	.40	.40
N6	A66 6m lt yel grn (Bk)	.40	.40
N7	A77 10m dp violet	.40	.40
N8	A66 13m rose car (G)	2.00	2.50
N9	A77 15m dk violet	.50	.50
N10	A77 17m olive green	.50	.50
N11	A77 20m dk gray	.50	.50
N12	A77 22m deep blue	.55	.55
N13	A74 50pi green & sep	30.00	30.00
N14	A75 £1 dp bl & dk brn	50.00	50.00

The two lines of the overprint are more widely separated on Nos. N13 and N14.

Nos. 267-269, 237 and 238 Ovptd. in Red — b

Perf. 14x13½

N15	A73 30m olive green	1.35	1.35
N16	A73 40m dark brown	1.75	1.75
N17	A73 50m Prus green	3.25	3.25
N18	A73 100m brown violet	5.00	5.00
N19	A73 200m dark violet	15.00	15.00
	Nos. N1-N19 (19)	113.20	113.70

Overprint arranged to fit size of stamps.

Nos. N1-N19 Overprinted in Black with Three Bars to Obliterate Portrait
Perf. 13x13½, 13½x13, 14x13½

1953		Wmk. 195
N20	A77 1m yellow brown	.75	.75
N21	A77 2m red orange	.75	.75
N22	A66 3m brown	.75	.75
N23	A77 4m deep green	.75	.75
N24	A77 5m red brown	.75	.75
N25	A66 6m lt yel grn	.85	.85
N26	A77 10m deep violet	.90	.90
N27	A66 13m rose carmine	.95	.95
N28	A77 15m dark violet	1.00	1.00
N29	A77 17m olive green	1.00	1.00
N30	A77 20m dark gray	1.15	1.5
N31	A77 22m deep blue	1.50	1.50
N32	A73 30m olive green	1.50	1.50
N33	A73 40m dark brown	2.75	2.75
N34	A73 50m Prus green	8.00	8.00
N35	A73 100m brown violet	17.00	17.00
N36	A73 200m dark violet	40.00	40.00
N37	A74 50pi green & sepia	80.00	75.00
N38	A75 £1 dp bl & dk brn	170.00	170.00
	Nos. N20-N38 (19)	330.35	325.70

Regular Issue of 1953-55 Overprinted Type "a" in Blue or Red

1954-56		Perf. 13x13½
N39	A115 1m red brown	.50	.50
N40	A115 2m dark lilac	.50	.50
N41	A115 3m brt blue (R)	.50	.50
N42	A115 4m dark green (R)	.50	.50
N43	A115 5m deep carmine	.50	.50
N44	A110 10m dark brown	.50	.50
N45	A110 15m gray (R)	.50	.50
N46	A110 17m dk grnsh bl (R)	.50	.50
N47	A110 20m purple (R) ('54)	.65	.65

Nos. 331-333 and 335-340 Overprinted in Blue or Red — c

Perf. 13½

N48	A111 30m dull green (R)	.90	.90
N49	A111 32m brt blue (R)	1.00	1.00
N50	A111 35m violet (R)	1.30	1.30
N51	A111 40m red brown	2.00	2.00
N52	A111 50m violet brown	2.50	2.50
N53	A112 100m henna brown	6.00	6.00
N54	A112 200m dk grnsh bl (R)	20.00	20.00
N55	A112 500m purple (R)	70.00	70.00
N56	A112 £1 dk grn, blk & red (R) ('56)	115.00	115.00
	Nos. N39-N56 (18)	223.35	223.35

Type of 1957 Overprinted in Red — d

1957	Wmk. 195	Perf. 13x13½
N57	A127 10m blue green	5.00	5.00

Nos. 414-417 Overprinted Type "d" in Red

1957-58	Wmk. 315	Perf. 13
N58	A137 10m violet	3.25	3.25

	Wmk. 318	
N59	A136 1m lt bl grn ('58)	.65	.65
N60	A138 5m brown ('58)	.65	.65
N61	A137 10m violet ('58)	.95	.95
	Nos. N58-N61 (4)	5.50	5.50

United Arab Republic

Nos. 438-444 Overprinted in Red or Green

Perf. 13½x14

1958	Wmk. 318	Photo.
N62	A136 1m crimson	.40	.40
N63	A138 2m blue	.40	.40
N64	A143 3m dk red brn (G)	.40	.40
N65	A217 4m green	.40	.40
N66	A138 5m brown	.40	.40
N67	A137 10m violet	.50	.40
N68	A138 35m lt ultra	3.50	3.25
	Nos. N62-N68 (7)	6.00	5.65

Freedom Struggle Type of 1958 Overprint in Red

1958		Perf. 13½x13
N69	A145 10m dark brown	2.25	2.25

Declaration of Human Rights Type of 1958 Overprinted in Green

1958		Perf. 13½x13
N70	A151 10m rose violet	3.50	3.50
N71	A151 35m red brown	8.50	8.50

No. 460 Overprinted in Green

1959	Wmk. 195	Perf. 13½
N72	A112 55m on 100m henna brn	4.25	4.25

World Refugee Year Type "PALESTINE" Added in English and Arabic to Stamps of Egypt

 OS1

1960	Wmk. 328	Perf. 13x13½
N73	OS1 10m orange brown	.80	.80
N74	OS1 35m dk blue gray	1.75	1.50

Type of Regular Issue 1957-63

1960		Perf. 13½x14
N75	A136 1m brown orange	.40	.40
N76	A217 4m olive gray	.40	.40
N77	A138 5m dk dull pur	.40	.40
N78	A137 10m olive grn	.40	.40
	Nos. N75-N78 (4)	1.60	1.60

Palestine Day Type

1961, May 15		Perf. 13½x13
N79	A184 10m purple	1.00	1.00

WHO Day Type

1961	Wmk. 328	Perf. 13½x13
N80	A182 10m blue	1.30	.75

U.N.T.A.P. Type

1961, Oct. 24		
N81	A191 10m dk blue & org	.55	.55
N82	A191 35m vermilion & blk	.80	.80

Education Day Type

1961, Dec. 18	Photo.	Perf. 13½
N83	A194 10m red brown	.55	.55

Victory Day Type

1961, Dec. 23	Unwmk.	Perf. 11½
N84	A195 10m brn org & brn	.45	.45

Gaza Strip Type
Perf. 13½x13

1962, Mar. 7		Wmk. 328
N85	A200 10m red brown	.45	.45

EGYPT

Arab Publicity Week Type
1962, Mar. 22   *Perf. 13½x13*
N86 SP16 10m dark purple .35 .35

Anti-Malaria Type
1962, June 20   *Photo.*
N87 A204 10m brn & dk car rose .50 .50
N88 A204 35m black & yellow .60 .60

Hammarskjold Type
Perf. 11½x11
1962, Oct. 24   *Wmk. 342*
Portrait in Slate Blue
N89 A214 5m bright rose .40 .40
N90 A214 10m brown .50 .50
N91 A214 35m blue .80 .80
   Nos. N89-N91 (3) 1.70 1.70

Lamp Type of Regular Issue
Perf. 11x11½
1963, Feb. 20   *Unwmk.*
N92 A217 4m dk brn, org & ultra .35 .35

"Freedom from Hunger" Type
Perf. 11½x11, 11x11½
1963, Mar. 21   *Wmk. 342*
N93 A220 5m blue grn & brn org .35 .35
N94 A220 10m olive & yellow .45 .45
N95 A220 35m lt pur, yel & blksh pur .65 .65
   Nos. N93-N95 (3) 1.45 1.45

Red Cross Centenary Type
Designs: 10m, Centenary emblem, bottom panel added. 35m, Globe and emblem, top and bottom panels added.

1963, May 8   *Unwmk.*   *Perf. 11x11½*
N96 A221 10m blue & brt red .35 .35
N97 A221 35m brt red & blue .60 .60

"Save Abu Simbel" Type, 1963
1963, Oct. 15   *Wmk. 342*   *Perf. 11*
N98 A224 5m black & yellow .40 .40
N99 A224 10m gray, blk & yellow .50 .50
N100 A224 35m org yel, vio & pur 1.25 .95
   Nos. N98-N100 (3) 2.15 1.85

Human Rights Type
1963, Dec. 10   *Photo.*   *Perf. 11½x11*
N101 A228 5m dk brown & yellow .35 .35
N102 A228 10m dp claret, gray & blk .40 .40
N103 A228 35m lt grn, pale grn & blk .95 .95
   Nos. N101-N103 (3) 1.70 1.70

Types of Regular Issue
1964   *Unwmk.*   *Perf. 11*
N104 A231 1m citron & lt vio .40 .40
N105 A230 2m orange & slate .40 .40
N106 A230 3m blue & ocher .40 .40
N107 A230 4m ol gray, ol, brn & rose .40 .40
N108 A230 5m rose & brt blue .40 .40
   a. 5m rose & dark blue 1.25 1.25
N109 A231 10m ol, rose & brn .40 .40
N110 A230 15m lilac & yellow .50 .50
N111 A230 20m brown blk & ol .80 .80
N112 A231 30m dp org & ind 1.60 1.60
N113 A231 35m buff, ocher & emer 1.40 1.40
N114 A231 40m ultra & emer 1.75 1.75
N115 A231 60m grnsh bl & brn org 2.50 2.50
Wmk. 342
N116 A232 100m bluish blk & yel brn 3.50 3.50
   Nos. N104-N116 (13) 14.45 14.45

Arab League Council Type
1964, Jan. 13   *Photo.*
N117 A234 10m olive & black .35 .35

Minaret Type
1964   *Unwmk.*   *Perf. 11*
N118 A235 4m ol, red brn & green .35 .35

Arab Postal Union Type
1964, Apr. 1   *Wmk. 342*   *Perf. 11*
N119 A239 10m emer & ultra, lt grn .35 .35

WHO Type
1964, Apr. 7
N120 A240 10m violet blk & red .35 .35

Minaret Type
1965, Jan. 20   *Unwmk.*   *Perf. 11*
N121 A255 4m green & dk brn .35 .35

Arab League Type
1965, Mar. 22   *Wmk. 342*   *Perf. 11*
N122 A258 10m green, red & blk .35 .35
N123 A258 20m green & brown .35 .35

World Health Day Type
1965, Apr. 7   *Wmk. 342*   *Perf. 11*
N124 A259 10m brt green & crim .35 .35

Massacre Type
1965, Apr. 9   *Photo.*
N125 A260 10m slate blue & red .60 .60

ITU Type
1965, May 17   *Wmk. 342*   *Perf. 11*
N126 A261 5m sl grn, sl bl & yel .40 .40
N127 A261 10m car, rose red & gray .50 .50
N128 A261 35m vio bl, ultra & yel 1.40 .95
   Nos. N126-N128 (3) 2.30 1.85

United Nations Type
5m, WHO Headquarters Building, Geneva. 10m, UN Refugee emblem. 35m, UNICEF emblem.

1966, Oct. 24   *Wmk. 342*   *Perf. 11*
N129 A288 5m rose & brt pur .35 .35
N130 A288 10m yel brn & brt pur .40 .40
N131 A288 35m brt green & brt pur .80 .80
   Nos. N129-N131 (3) 1.55 1.55

Victory Day Type
Wmk. 342
1966, Dec. 23   *Photo.*   *Perf. 11½*
N132 A290 10m olive & car rose .40 .40

Arab Publicity Week Type
Perf. 11x11½
1967, Mar. 22   *Photo.*   *Wmk. 342*
N133 A294 10m vio blue & brn .35 .35

Labor Day Type
Perf. 11½x11
1967, May 1   *Photo.*   *Wmk. 342*
N134 A296 10m olive & sepia .35 .35

OCCUPATION AIR POST STAMPS

Catalogue values for unused stamps in this section are for Never Hinged items.

Nos. C39-C50 Overprinted Type "b" in Black, Carmine or Red

Perf. 13x13½
1948, May 15   *Wmk. 195*
NC1 AP3 2m red org (Bk) .75 .75
NC2 AP3 3m dk brn (C) .75 .75
NC3 AP3 5m red brn (Bk) .75 .75
NC4 AP3 7m dp yel org (Bk) 1.00 1.00
NC5 AP3 8m green (C) 1.05 1.05
NC6 AP3 10m violet 1.20 1.20
NC7 AP3 20m brt bl 1.90 1.90
NC8 AP3 30m brn vio (Bk) 4.50 4.50
NC9 AP3 40m car rose (Bk) 3.00 3.00
NC10 AP3 50m Prus grn 4.00 4.00
NC11 AP3 100m olive grn 6.75 6.75
NC12 AP3 200m dark gray 34.00 34.00
   Nos. NC1-NC12 (12) 59.70 59.70

Nos. NC1-NC12 Overprinted in Black with Three Bars to Obliterate Portrait

1953
NC13 AP3 2m red org 1.90 1.90
NC14 AP3 3m dk brn 1.20 1.20
NC15 AP3 5m red brn 20.00 20.00
NC16 AP3 7m dp yel org 1.25 1.25
NC17 AP3 8m green 3.75 3.75
NC18 AP3 10m violet 3.75 3.75
NC19 AP3 20m brt bl 3.75 3.75
NC20 AP3 30m brn vio 3.75 3.75
NC21 AP3 40m car rose 6.75 6.75
NC22 AP3 50m Prus grn 28.00 28.00
NC23 AP3 100m olive grn 115.00 115.00
NC24 AP3 200m dk gray 15.00 15.00
   Nos. NC13-NC24 (12) 204.10 204.10

Nos. NC1-NC3, NC6, NC10, NC11 with Additional Overprint in Various Colors

1953
NC25 AP3 2m red org (Bk + Bl) 1.00 1.00
NC26 AP3 3m dk brn (Bk + RV) 19.00 19.00
NC27 AP3 5m red brn (Bk) 2.75 2.75
NC28 AP3 10m vio (R + G) 28.00 28.00
NC29 AP3 50m Prus grn (R + RV) 8.75 8.75
NC30 AP3 100m ol grn (R + Bk) 62.50 62.50
   Nos. NC25-NC30 (6) 122.00 122.00

Nos. C65-C66 Overprinted Type "b" in Black or Red
1955   *Wmk. 195*   *Perf. 13x13½*
NC31 AP4 5m red brn 7.00 5.75
NC32 AP4 15m ol grn (R) 10.00 8.25

United Arab Republic

OAP1

Designs: 80m, Al Azhar University. 115m, Temple of Queen Nefertari, Abu Simbel. 140m, Ramses II, Abu Simbel.

Perf. 11½x11
1963, Oct. 24   *Photo.*   *Wmk. 342*
NC33 OAP1 80m blk & brt bl 2.50 2.50
NC34 OAP1 115m blk & yel 3.50 3.50
NC35 OAP1 140m bl, ultra & org red 4.00 4.00
   Nos. NC33-NC35 (3) 10.00 10.00

Cairo Tower Type, 1964
1964, Nov. 2   *Unwmk.*   *Perf. 11x11½*
NC36 AP11 50m dl vio & lt bl 1.25 1.25

World Meteorological Day Type
1965, Mar. 23   *Wmk. 342*   *Perf. 11*
NC37 AP12 80m dk bl & org 3.00 3.00

Tutankhamun Type of 1965
1965, July 1   *Photo.*   *Perf. 11*
NC38 AP13 10m brn org & brt grn 1.75 1.75

OCCUPATION SPECIAL DELIVERY STAMP

Catalogue values for unused stamps in this section are for Never Hinged items.

No. E4 Overprinted Type "b" in Carmine
1948   *Wmk. 195*   *Perf. 13x13½*
NE1 SD1 40m dl brn & pale gray 12.50 12.50

OCCUPATION POSTAGE DUE STAMPS

Catalogue values for unused stamps in this section are for Never Hinged items.

Postage Due Stamps of Egypt, 1927-41, Overprinted Type "a" in Black or Rose
1948   *Wmk. 195*   *Perf. 13x13½*
NJ1 D7 2m orange 2.25 2.40
NJ2 D7 4m green (R) 1.60 2.00
NJ3 D7 6m gray green 1.60 2.00
NJ4 D7 8m brown violet 1.60 2.00
NJ5 D7 10m brick red 1.60 2.00
NJ6 D7 12m rose lake 1.60 2.00

Overprinted Type "b" in Red
Perf. 14
Size: 22x28mm
NJ7 D7 30m purple 5.00 9.00
   Nos. NJ1-NJ7 (7) 15.25 21.40

ELOBEY, ANNOBON & CORISCO

ˌel-ə-ˈbā, ˌan-ə-ˈbän and kə-ˈris-ˌkō

LOCATION — A group of islands near the Guinea Coast of western Africa.
GOVT. — Spanish colonial possessions administered as part of the Continental Guinea District. A second district under the same governor-general included Fernando Po.
AREA — 13¾ sq. mi.
POP. — 2,950 (estimated 1910)
CAPITAL — Santa Isabel

100 Centimos = 1 Peseta

King Alfonso XIII — A1

1903		Unwmk. Typo. Perf. 14		
		Control Numbers on Back		
1	A1	¼c carmine	.75	.55
2	A1	½c dk violet	.75	.55
3	A1	1c black	.75	.55
4	A1	2c red	.75	.55
5	A1	3c dk green	.75	.55
6	A1	4c dk blue grn	.75	.55
7	A1	5c violet	.75	.55
8	A1	10c rose lake	1.50	1.60
9	A1	15c orange buff	4.50	1.75
10	A1	25c dark blue	7.75	6.00
11	A1	50c red brown	9.00	10.50
12	A1	75c black brn	9.00	14.50
13	A1	1p orange red	15.00	20.00
14	A1	2p chocolate	40.00	60.00
15	A1	3p dp olive grn	60.00	75.00
16	A1	4p claret	140.00	100.00
17	A1	5p blue green	165.00	110.00
18	A1	10p dull blue	300.00	165.00
		Nos. 1-18 (18)	757.00	568.20
		Set, never hinged	1,500.	

Dated "1905"

1905		Control Numbers on Back		
19	A1	1c carmine	1.25	.70
20	A1	2c dp violet	5.00	.70
21	A1	3c black	1.25	.70
22	A1	4c dull red	1.25	.70
23	A1	5c dp green	1.25	.70
24	A1	10c blue grn	4.50	.90
25	A1	15c violet	5.00	4.75
26	A1	25c rose lake	5.00	4.75
27	A1	50c orange buff	9.00	7.25
28	A1	75c dark blue	9.00	7.25
29	A1	1p red brown	18.50	16.00
30	A1	2p black brn	20.00	22.50
31	A1	3p orange red	20.00	23.00
32	A1	4p dk brown	150.00	72.50
33	A1	5p bronze grn	160.00	80.00
34	A1	10p claret	350.00	225.00
		Nos. 19-34 (16)	761.00	467.40
		Set, never hinged	1,500.	

Nos. 19-22 Surcharged in Black or Red

1906

35	A1 10c on 1c rose (Bk)	11.50	6.50
a.	Inverted surcharge	11.50	6.50
b.	Value omitted	30.00	16.00
c.	Frame omitted	16.00	7.50
d.	Double surcharge	11.50	6.50
e.	Surcharged "15 cents"	30.00	16.00
f.	Surcharged "25 cents"	52.50	22.50
g.	Surcharged "50 cents"	37.50	22.50
h.	"1906" omitted	17.50	7.50
36	A1 15c on 2c dp vio (R)	11.50	6.50
a.	Frame omitted	12.50	6.50
b.	Surcharged "25 cents"	16.00	9.00
c.	Inverted surcharge	11.50	6.50
d.	Double surcharge	11.50	6.50
37	A1 25c on 3c blk (R)	11.50	6.50
a.	Inverted surcharge	11.50	6.50
b.	Double surcharge	11.50	6.50
c.	Surcharged "15 cents"	16.00	6.50
d.	Surcharged "25 cents"	25.00	11.00
38	A1 50c on 4c red (Bk)	11.50	6.50
a.	Inverted surcharge	11.50	6.50
b.	Value omitted	35.00	17.50
c.	Frame omitted	17.50	8.00
d.	Double surcharge	11.50	6.50
f.	"1906" omitted	17.50	8.00
g.	Surcharged "10 cents"	32.50	16.00
h.	Surcharged "25 cents"	32.50	16.00
	Nos. 35-38 (4)	46.00	26.00

Eight other surcharges were prepared but not issued: 10c on 50c, 75c, 1p, 2p and 3p; 15c on 50c and 5p; 50c on 5c.

Exist with surcharges in different colors; #35 in blue, red or violet; #36 in black or violet, #37

in black or violet, #38 in blue, violet or red. Value, set of 10, $135.

King Alfonso XIII — A2

1907		Control Numbers on Back		
39	A2	1c dk violet	.50	.45
40	A2	2c black	.50	.45
41	A2	3c red orange	.50	.45
42	A2	4c dk green	.50	.45
43	A2	5c blue green	.50	.45
44	A2	10c violet	5.50	5.50
45	A2	15c carmine	1.60	1.75
46	A2	25c orange	1.60	1.75
47	A2	50c blue	1.60	1.75
48	A2	75c brown	6.00	2.75
49	A2	1p black brn	9.00	4.75
50	A2	2p orange red	12.00	8.00
51	A2	3p dk brown	12.00	9.00
52	A2	4p bronze grn	18.00	8.50
53	A2	5p claret	22.00	10.00
54	A2	10p rose	45.00	27.50
		Nos. 39-54 (16)	136.80	83.50
		Set, never hinged	350.00	

Stamps of 1907 Surcharged

1908-09		Black Surcharge		
55	A2	5c on 3c red org ('09)	2.25	1.25
56	A2	5c on 4c dk grn ('09)	2.25	1.25
57	A2	5c on 10c violet	4.50	5.00
58	A2	5c on 10c violet	30.00	15.00
		Nos. 55-58 (4)	39.00	22.50
		Set, never hinged	70.00	

1910		Red Surcharge		
59	A2	5c on 1c dark violet	1.75	.90
60	A2	5c on 2c black	1.75	.90

Nos. 55-60 exist with surcharge inverted (value set, $125 unused or used); with double surcharge, one black, one red (value set, $300 unused or used); with "PARA" omitted (value set, $150.00 unused or used).

The same 5c surcharge was also applied to Nos. 45-54, but these were not issued (value set, $250).

In 1909, stamps of Spanish Guinea replaced those of Elobey, Annobon and Corisco.

Revenue stamps surcharged as above were unauthorized although some were postally used.

For postally valid examples similar to the item shown above see Rio de Oro Nos. 44-45 and Spanish Guinea Nos. 98-101C.

For revenue stamps with the arms at the left surcharged for postal use see Spanish Guinea Nos. 8A-8J.

EPIRUS

i-ˈpī-rəs

LOCATION — A region of southeastern Europe, now divided between Greece and Albania.

During the First Balkan War (1912-13), this territory was occupied by the Greek army, and the local Greek majority wished to be united with Greece. Italy and Austria-Hungary favored its inclusion in the newly created Albania, however, which both powers expected to dominate. Greek forces were withdrawn subsequently in early 1914. The local population resisted inclusion in Albania and established the Autonomous Republic of Northern Epirus on Feb. 28, 1914. Resistance to Albanian control continued until October, when

Greece reoccupied the country. Northern Epirus was administered as an integral part of Greece, and it was expected that Greece's annexation of the territory would become official following World War I. Instead, in 1916, Italian pressure and its own military reverses in Anatolia caused Greece to withdraw from Epirus and to formally cede the territory to Albania.

100 Lepta = 1 Drachma

Chimarra Issue

Double-headed Eagle, Skull and Crossbones — A1

Handstamped

1914, Feb. 10		Unwmk. Imperf.		
		Control Mark in Blue		
		Without Gum		
1	A1	1 l black & blue	475.00	250.00
a.		Tête-bêche pair	3,000.	
2	A1	5 l blue & red	475.00	250.00
3	A1	10 l red & blk	475.00	250.00
4	A1	25 l blue & red	475.00	250.00
		Nos. 1-4 (4)	1,900.	1,000.

All values exist without control mark. This mark is a solid blue oval, about 12x8mm, containing the colorless Greek letters "SP," the first two letters of Spiromilios, the Chimarra commander.

All four exist with denomination inverted and the 1 l, 5 l and 10 l with denomination double. The values above are for the first printing on somewhat transparent shiny, white, thin, wove paper, which is sometimes known as "rice paper."

A second printing was made from original handstamps, on similar thin wove paper, but not translucent, known as "Spetsiotis Reprints." Value, unused or canceled to order, each $55. Later printings were made from original handstamps on other papers, generally thicker and whiter, sometimes surfaced. Value, unused or canceled to order, each $45.

Values above are for genuine stamps expertized by knowledgeable authorities. Most of the stamps offered as Nos. 1-4 in the marketplace are forgeries. Most resemble the stamps from the second reprinting, but the designs differ in details of the lettering, monogram and skull. Such forgeries have only nominal commercial value.

Some experts question the official character of this issue.

Argyrokastro Issues

Stamps of Turkey surcharged "AUTONOMOUS EPIRUS" and new denominations in several formats in Greek currency.

On Turkish stamps of 1908

No. 4A   No. 4B

1914, Mar. 2

4A	A19	1d on 2½pi (#137)	11.00	12.50
4B	A19	2d on 2½pi (#137)	11.00	12.50

No. 4C   No. 4D

4C	A19	5d on 25pi (#140)	80.00	92.50
4D	A19	5d on 50pi (#141)	127.50	140.00

On Turkish stamps of 1909-10

| 4E | A21 | 5 l on 5pa (#151) | 80.00 | — |

No. 4F   No. 4G

4F	A21	5 l on 10pa (#152)	3.50	4.00
4G	A21	10 l (oval "O") on 20pa (#153)	2.50	2.75
a.		Double surcharge	80.00	

No. 4H   No. 4I

4H	A21	10 l (round "O") on 20pa (#153)	2.50	2.75
a.		Double surcharge	80.00	
4I	A21	20 l on 1pi (#154)	2.50	2.75
a.		Double surcharge	80.00	

No. 4J   No. 4K

4J	A21	25 l on 1pi (#154)	2.50	2.75
a.		Double surcharge	80.00	
4K	A21	40 l on 2pi (#155)	3.50	3.75

No. 4L   No. 4M

4L	A21	80 l on 2pi (#155)	3.50	3.75
4M	A21	1d on 5pi (#157)	13.00	14.00

No. 4N   No. 4O

4N	A21	2d on 5pi (#157)	13.00	14.00
4O	A21	5d on 10pi (#158)	80.00	92.50
a.		Double surcharge		
4P	A21	5d on 10pa (#152)	135.00	170.00
4Q	A21	5d on 20pa (#153)	135.00	170.00
4R	A21	5d on 1pi (#154)	135.00	170.00
4RR	A21	5d on 2½pi (#156)	135.00	170.00
4S	A21	5d on 50pi (#160)	135.00	170.00

On Turkish stamps of 1909-11 (with "Béhié")

4T	A21	5 l on 5pa (#161)	80.00	
4U	A21	10 l (oval "O") on 20pa (#162)	80.00	
4V	A21	10 l (round "O") on 20pa (#162)	80.00	
4W	A21	20 l on 1pi (#163)	80.00	
4X	A21	25 l on 1pi (#163)	80.00	
4Y	A21	40 l on 2pi (#164)	80.00	
4Z	A21	80 l on 2pi (#164)	80.00	
4AA	A21	5d on 10pa (#161)	135.00	
4BB	A21	5d on 20pa (#162)	135.00	
4CC	A21	5d on 1pi (#163)	135.00	
4CA	A21	5d on 2pi (#164)	135.00	

On Turkish Printed Matter stamps of 1910-11

No. 4DD   No. 4EE

4DD	A21	30 l on 2pa on 5pa (#P67)	87.50	
4EE	A21	50 l on 2pa on 5pa (#P67)	87.50	

EPIRUS

No. 4FF

4FF	A21	30 l on 2pa (#P68)	2.50	2.75
4GG	A21	50 l on 2pa (#P68)	2.50	2.75

Provisional Government Issues

Infantryman with Rifle
A2   A3

Serrate Roulette 13½

1914, Mar. Litho.
5	A2	1 l orange	.50	1.00
a.		Imperf., pair	60.00	
6	A2	5 l green	.50	1.00
a.		Imperf., pair	60.00	
7	A3	10 l carmine	.50	1.00
8	A3	25 l deep blue	.50	1.00
9	A2	50 l brown	1.50	1.50
10	A2	1d violet	2.25	2.50
11	A2	2d blue	14.00	14.00
12	A2	5d gray green	18.00	19.00
		Nos. 5-12 (8)	37.75	41.00

Issue dates: 10 l, 25 l, Mar. 5; balance of set, Mar. 26.

Flag of Epirus — A5

1914, Aug. 28
15	A5	1 l brown & blue	.35	.40
16	A5	5 l green & blue	.35	.40
17	A5	10 l rose red & blue	.40	.65
18	A5	25 l dk blue & blue	1.00	1.10
19	A5	50 l violet & blue	1.00	1.10
20	A5	1d carmine & blue	5.75	6.50
21	A5	2d orange & blue	1.50	2.25
b.		Double impression, one inverted	1,000.	
22	A5	5d dk green & blue	9.50	11.00
a.		Double impression		1,000.
		Nos. 15-22 (8)	19.85	23.40

Nos. 16 and 21 exist with the blue color inverted.

Koritsa Issue

A7

1914, Sept. 25
26	A7	25 l dk blue & blue	6.00	5.25
27	A7	50 l violet & blue	12.00	13.50

Nos. 26 and 27 were issued at Koritsa (Korce) to commemorate that city's occupation by Epirot forces.

Chimarra Issues

King Constantine I — A8

1914, Oct.
28	A8	1 l yellow green	135.00	77.50
29	A8	2 l red	120.00	42.50
30	A8	5 l dark blue	120.00	77.50
31	A8	10 l orange brown	80.00	90.00
32	A8	20 l carmine	87.50	62.50
33	A8	25 l gray blue	115.00	77.50
33A	A8	50 l yellow green	170.00	90.00
33B	A8	1d carmine	170.00	90.00
33C	A8	2d pale yellow green	255.00	125.00
33D	A8	5d orange brown	425.00	290.00
		Nos. 28-33D (10)	1,678.	962.50

Nos. 28-33D were printed by Papachrysanthou, Athens. The papermaker's watermark "PARCHIMINE JOHANNOT" appears on some stamps in the set.

1911-23 Issues of Greece Overprinted

1914, Aug. 24 *Perf. Perf. 11 ½*
34	A24	1 l green	55.00	62.50
35	A25	2 l carmine	45.00	52.50
36	A24	3 l vermilion	45.00	52.50
37	A26	5 l green	45.00	52.50
38	A24	10 l carmine	60.00	65.00
39	A25	20 l slate	80.00	87.50
40	A25	25 l blue	175.00	185.00
41	A26	50 l violet brn	220.00	225.00
		Nos. 34-41 (8)	725.00	782.50

The 2 l and 3 l are engraved stamps of the 1911-21 issue; the others are lithographed stamps of the 1912-23 issue.
Overprint reads: "Greek Chimarra 1914."
Stamps of this issue are with or without a black monogram (S.S., for S. Spiromilios) in manuscript. Counterfeits are plentiful.

Moschopolis Issue

Arms
A9

Ancient Epirot Coins/Medals
A10

1914, Sept. Engr. *Perf. 14 ½*
42	A9	1 l yellow brown	.75	3.50
43	A9	2 l black	.75	3.50
44	A9	3 l yellow	.75	3.50
45	A9	5 l green	.75	3.50
46	A9	10 l red	.75	3.50
47	A9	25 l deep blue	.75	3.50
48	A9	30 l violet	.75	3.50
49	A9	40 l olive gray	.75	3.50
50	A9	50 l violet black	.75	3.50
51	A10	1d yellow brown & olive	5.00	11.50
52	A10	2d carmine & gray	6.00	11.50
53	A10	3d gray green & red brown	5.00	11.50
54	A10	5d olive & yellow brown	5.00	11.50
55	A10	10d orange & blue	5.00	14.50
56	A10	25d violet & black	5.00	20.00
		Nos. 42-56 (15)	37.75	112.00

Nos. 42-56 were privately printed in early 1914. In June 1914, the Epirots occupied Moschopolis (Voskopoj), and these stamps were authorized for use by the local military commander in Sept. After the occupation of Moschopolis by Greek forces in Nov., remaining stocks of this issue were sent to Athens, where they were destroyed in 1931.

All values exist imperf., and all but the 5 l and 10 l stamps exist in different colors. For details, see the *Scott Classic Specialized Catalogue of Stamps and Covers*.

The 1d exists with center omitted. Value $100. The 1d, 2d, 10d and 25d exist with center inverted. Values, each $305.

Stamps of the following designs were locals, privately produced. Issued primarily for propaganda and for philatelic purposes, their postal use is in dispute. The 1917 and 1920 designs are fantasy items, created long after Epirus was annexed by Albania.

From 1914: 1st design, 3 varieties.
2nd design, 6 varieties. 3rd design, 7 varieties.
From 1917: 4th design, 8 varieties, + 1 surcharged; perforated and imperforate.
From 1920: 5th design, 4 varieties.

OCCUPATION STAMPS

Issued under Greek Occupation

Greek Occupation Stamps of 1913 Overprinted Horizontally

Serrate Roulette 13½

1914-15 Black Overprint Unwmk.
N1	O1	1 l brown	.90	.90
b.		Inverted overprint	25.00	25.00
c.		Double overprint	25.00	25.00
d.		Double overprint, one inverted	25.00	25.00
N2	O2	2 l red	.90	.90
b.		2 l rose	1.35	1.35
c.		As #N2, inverted overprint	25.00	25.00
d.		As "b", inverted overprint	32.50	32.50
e.		As #N2, double overprint	26.00	32.50
f.		As "b", double overprint	32.50	32.50
g.		As #N2, double overprint, one inverted	25.00	25.00
N4	O2	3 l orange	.90	.90
b.		Inverted overprint	20.00	17.50
c.		Double overprint	20.00	17.50
d.		Double overprint, one inverted	20.00	20.00
N5	O1	5 l green	2.50	2.50
b.		Inverted overprint	37.50	37.50
N6	O1	10 l rose red	3.00	3.00
a.		Inverted overprint	52.50	52.50
b.		Double overprint	52.50	52.50
N7	O1	20 l violet	7.00	7.00
a.		Inverted overprint	52.50	52.50
b.		Double overprint	87.50	87.50
N8	O2	25 l pale blue	3.00	3.25
N9	O1	30 l gray green	14.50	15.00
N10	O2	40 l indigo	19.50	21.00
N11	O1	50 l dark blue	22.00	24.00
N12	O2	1d violet brown	140.00	150.00
a.		Inverted overprint	325.00	225.00
b.		Double overprint	400.00	300.00
		Nos. N1-N12 (11)	214.20	228.45

Red Overprint
N1a	O1	1 l brown		5.75
N2a	O2	2 l red		5.75
N4a	O2	3 l orange		5.75
N5a	O1	5 l green		5.75

Nos. N1a-N5a were not issued. Exist canceled.

Regular Issues of Greece, 1911-23, Ovptd. Reading Up

On Issue of 1911-21

1916 Engr.
N17	A24	3 l vermilion	11.50	11.50
a.		Overprint reading down	15.00	
N18	A26	30 l carmine rose	52.50	40.00
a.		Overprint reading down	225.00	
N18B	A25	40 l dark blue	—	—
N19	A27	1d ultra	85.00	85.00
N20	A27	2d vermilion	95.00	95.00
N21	A27	3d carmine rose	130.00	130.00
N22	A27	5d ultra		
a.		Double overprint	1,300.	
b.		Overprint reading down	725.00	
		Nos. N17-N22 (6)	374.00	361.50

On Issue of 1912-23

1916 Litho.
N23	A24	1 l green	2.75	2.75
b.		Overprint reading down	10.00	
N24	A25	2 l carmine	2.75	2.75
a.		Double overprint	13.00	
b.		Overprint reading down	10.00	
N25	A24	3 l vermilion	2.75	2.75
a.		Double overprint	13.00	
b.		Overprint reading down	15.00	
N26	A26	5 l green	2.75	2.75
a.		Double overprint	15.00	
b.		Overprint reading down	15.00	
N27	A24	10 l carmine	2.75	2.75
a.		Double overprint	15.00	
b.		Overprint reading down	15.00	
N28	A25	20 l slate	2.75	2.75
a.		Double overprint	17.50	
N29	A25	25 l blue	3.75	3.75
a.		Double overprint	30.00	
N30	A26	30 l rose	22.00	22.00
a.		Double overprint	250.00	
N31	A25	40 l indigo	16.50	16.50
a.		Overprint reading down	475.00	
N32	A26	50 l violet brown	26.50	26.50
		Nos. N23-N32 (10)	85.25	85.25

In each sheet, there are two varieties in the overprint. For listings, see the *Scott Classic Catalogue*.
Counterfeits exist of Nos. N1-N32.
Postage stamps issued in 1940-41, during Greek occupation, are listed under Greece.

EQUATORIAL GUINEA

ē-kwə-'tō-ē-əl 'gi-nē

LOCATION — Gulf of Guinea, West Africa
GOVT. — Republic
AREA — 10,832 sq. mi.
POP. — 1,400,000 (2020 est.)
CAPITAL — Malabo

The Spanish provinces Fernando Po and Rio Muni united and became independent as the Republic of Equatorial Guinea, Oct. 12, 1968.

100 Centimos = 1 Peseta
100 centimos = 1 ekuele, bipkwele is plural (1973)
100 centimes = 1 CFA franc (1985)

Catalogue values for all unused stamps in this country are for Never Hinged items.

Clasped Hands and Laurel — A1

Unwmk.

1968, Oct. 12		Photo.		Perf. 13
1	A1	1p dp bl, gold & sep	.35	.35
2	A1	1.50p dk grn, gold & brn	.35	.35
3	A1	6p cop red, gold & brn	.35	.35
		Nos. 1-3 (3)	1.05	1.05

Attainment of independence, Oct. 12, 1968.

Pres. Francisco Macias Nguema — A2

1970, Jan. 27			Perf. 13x12½	
4	A2	50c dl org, brn & crim	.25	.25
5	A2	1p pink, grn & lil	.25	.25
6	A2	1.50p pale ol, brn & bl grn	.25	.25
7	A2	2p buff, grn & ol	.25	.25
8	A2	2.50p pale ol, dk grn & dk bl	.30	.25
9	A2	10p bis, Prus bl & vio brn	1.00	.25
10	A2	25p gray, blk & brn	2.10	.25
		Nos. 4-10 (7)	4.40	1.75

Pres. Macias Nguema and Cock — A3

1971, Apr.		Photo.		Perf. 13
11	A3	3p lt bl & multi	.25	.25
12	A3	5p buff & multi	.30	.25
13	A3	10p pale lilac & multi	.75	.25
14	A3	25p pale grn & multi	1.50	.35
		Nos. 11-14 (4)	2.80	1.10

2nd anniv. of independence, Oct. 12, 1970.

Torch, Bow and Arrows A4

1972		Photo.		Perf. 11½
15	A4	50p ocher & multi	1.50	.55

"3rd Triumphal Year."

Upon achieving independence from Spain in 1968, Francisco Macias Nguema was elected the first president of Equatorial Guinea. By May 1971, Nguema controlled a government that essentially performed no functions except internal security. From 1972 to 1979, the country's main post office was padlocked and completely inoperative. Nonetheless, European agents continued to produce postage stamps for Equatorial Guinea that were promoted by so-called press releases from Madrid, Spain.

With the exception of Nos. 16-25, the editors question whether any of the stamps described below could have reached Equatorial Guinea or been placed on sale in that country. As such, they do not meet the criteria for listing in the Scott catalogue. See the Catalogue Listing Policy section in the catalogue introduction for additional details.

Apollo 15, set of seven, 1p, 3p, 5p, 8p, 10p, airmail 15p, 25p, plus two airmail semi-postal gold foil perf. 200p+25p, imperf. 250p+50p, and two souv. sheets, perf. 25p+200p, imperf. 50p+250p, issued Jan. 28. Nos. 7201-7211.

1972 Winter Olympics, Sapporo, set of seven, 1p, 2p, 3p, 5p, 8p, airmail 15p, 50p, plus two airmail semi-postal gold foil perf., imperf., 200p+25p, 250p+50p, and two souv. sheets, perf. 200p+25p, imperf. 250p+50p, issued Feb. 3, 1972. Nos. 7212-7222.

Christmas, paintings, set of seven, 1p, 3p, 5p, 8p, 10p, airmail 15p, 25p, plus two airmail semi-postal gold foil perf. 200p+25p, imperf. 250p+50p, and two souv. sheets, perf. 25p+200p, imperf. 50p+250p (Virgin and Child by da Vinci, Murillo, Raphael, Mabuse, van der Weyden, Durer), issued Feb. 20. Nos. 7223-7233.

Easter, set of seven, 1p, 3p, 5p, 8p, 10p, airmail 15p, 25p, plus two airmail semi-postal gold foil perf., imperf., 200p+25p, 250p+50p (designs by Velazquez and El Greco), two souv. sheets, perf. (25p, 200p), and imperf. 250p+50p, issued Apr. 28. Nos. 7234-7244.

1972 Summer Olympics, Munich, set of seven, 1p, 2p, 3p, 5p, 8p, airmail 15p, 50p, plus two airmail semi-postal souv. sheets, perf. 200p+25p, imperf. 250p+50p, and presentation folder with two gold foil, perf. 200p+25p, imperf. 250p+50p, issued May 5, 1972. Nos. 7245-7255.

Gold Medal Winners, Sapporo, set of seven, 1p, 2p, 3p, 5p, 8p, airmail 15p, 50p, plus 12 airmail semi-postal gold foil perf. 200p+25p (6), imperf. 250p+50p (6), imperf. souv. sheet 250p+50p, and perf. souv. sheet of two (25p, 200p), issued May 25. Nos. 7256-7276.

Black Gold Medal Winners, Munich, set of seven, 1p, 2p, 3p, 5p, 8p, airmail 15p, 50p, plus 18 gold foil airmail semi-postal perf. 200p+25p (9), imperf. 250p+50p (9), and two souv. sheets, perf. 200p+25p, imperf. 250p+50p, issued June 26. Nos. 7277-72103.

Olympic Games, Regatta in Kiel and Oberschleissheim, set of seven, 1p, 2p, 3p, 5p, 8p, airmail 15p, 50p, plus four airmail semi-postal gold foil, perf. 200p+25p (2), imperf. 250p+50p (2), and two souv. sheets, perf. 200p+25p, imperf. 250p+50p, issued July 25. Nos. 72104-72116.

1972 Summer Olympics, Munich, set of seven, 1p, 2p, 3p, 5p, 8p, airmail 15p, 50p, plus two airmail semi-postal souv. sheets, perf. 200p+25p, imperf. 250p+50p, issued Aug. 10, 1972; and 20 gold foil, perf. 200p+25p (10), imperf. 250+50p (10), issued Aug. 17. Nos. 72117-72145.

Olympic Equestrian Events, set of seven, 1p, 2p, 3p, 5p, 8p, airmail 15p, 50p, plus two airmail semi-postal souv. sheets, perf. 200p+25p, imperf. 250p+50p, two gold foil, perf. 200p+25p, imperf. 250p+50p, four gold foil souv. sheets of two, 200p+25p (2 perf., 2 imperf.), and 16 souv. sheets, perf. 200p+25p (8), imperf. 250p+50p (8), issued Aug. 24. Nos. 72146-72176.

Japanese Railroad Cent. (locomotives), set of seven, 1p, 3p, 5p, 8p, 10p, airmail 15p, 25p, plus 2 airmail postal souv. sheets, perf. 200p+25p, imperf. 250p+50p, 11 gold foil souv. sheets of 1, perf. 200p+25p (9), imperf. 200p+25p (2), and 2 souv. sheets of 2, perf., imperf., 200p+25p, issued Sept. 21. Nos. 72177-72198.

Gold Medal Winners, Munich, set of seven, 1p, 2p, 3p, 5p, 8p, airmail 15p, 50p, plus two airmail semi-postal souv. sheets, perf. 200p+25p, imperf. 250p+50p, and four gold foil souv. sheets, perf. 200p+25p (2), imperf. 250p+50p (2), issued Oct. 30. Nos. 72199-72211.

Christmas and 500th Birth Anniv. of Lucas Cranach, Madonnas and Christmas seals, set of seven, 1p, 3p, 5p, 8p, 10p, airmail 15p, 25p (Giotto, Schongauer, Fouquet, de Morales, Fini, David, Sassetta), plus two airmail semi-postal souv. sheets, perf. 200p+25p, imperf. 250p+50p, 12 gold foil souv. sheets, perf. 200p+25p (6), imperf. 250p+50p (6), two souv. sheets of two, perf., imperf., 200p+25p, and ovptd. 200p+25p stamp, issued Nov. 22. Nos. 72212-72234.

American and Russian Astronaut Memorial, set of seven, 1p, 3p, 5p, 8p, 10p, airmail 15p, 25p, plus two airmail semi-postal souv. sheets, perf. 200p+25p, imperf. 250p+50p, and four gold foil ovptd. "Apollo 16 and 17" perf. 200p+25p (2), imperf. 250p+50p (2), issued Dec. 14. Nos. 72235-72247.

United Natl. Workers' Party Emblem — A5

1973		Litho.		Perf. 13½x13
16	A5	1p multi	.25	.25
17	A5	1.50p multi	.25	.25
18	A5	2p multi	.25	.25
19	A5	4p multi	.30	.25
20	A5	5p multi	.40	.25
		Nos. 16-20 (5)	1.45	1.25

Natl. Independence, 4th Anniv. — A6

Pres. Macias Nguema and: 1.50p, Agriculture. 2p, 4p, Education. 3p, 5p, Natl. defense.

1973				Perf. 13½
21	A6	1.50p multi	.25	.25
22	A6	2p multi	.25	.25
23	A6	3p multi	.35	.25
24	A6	4p multi	.40	.25
25	A6	5p multi	.60	.35
		Nos. 21-25 (5)	1.85	1.35

1973

Transatlantic Yacht Race, set of seven, 1p, 2p, 3p, 5p, 8p, airmail 15p, 50p, and two airmail semi-postal souv. sheets, perf. 200p+25p, imperf. 250p+50p, issued Jan. 22. Nos. 7301-7309.

Renoir paintings, set of seven, 1p, 2p, 3p, 5p, 8p, airmail 15p, 50p, plus two airmail semi-postal gold foil, perf. 200p+25p, imperf. 250p+50p, and two souv. sheets, perf. 200p+25p, imperf. 250p+50p, issued Feb. 22. Nos. 7310-7320.

Conquest of Venus (spacecraft), set of seven, 1p, 3p, 5p, 8p, 10p, airmail 5p, 25p, and two airmail semi-postal souv. sheets, perf. 200p+25p, imperf. 250p+50p, issued Mar. 22. Nos. 7321-7329.

Apollo 11-17 Flights, gold foil airmail semi-postal souv. sheets, perf. 200p+25p (7), 250p+50p (7), and four souv. sheets of two, perf. 200p+25p (2), imperf. 250p+50p (2), issued Mar. 22. Nos. 7330-7347.

Easter, paintings, set of seven, 1p, 3p, 5p, 8p, 10p, airmail 15p, 25p (Verrocchio, Perugino, Tintoretto, Witz, Pontormo), plus two airmail semi-postal souv. sheets, perf. 200p+25p, imperf. 250p+50p, and four gold foil issue of 1972 souv. sheets ovptd., perf. 200p+25p (2), imperf. 250p+50p (2), issued Apr. 25. Nos. 7348-7360.

Copernicus, 500th birth anniv. (US and USSR space explorations), four gold foil airmail semi-postal souv. sheets, perf. 200p+25p (2), imperf. 250p+50p (2), issued May 15. Nos. 7361-7364.

Tour de France bicycle race, set of seven, 1p, 2p, 3p, 5p, 8p, airmail 15p, 50p, and two airmail semi-postal souv. sheets, perf. 200p+25p, imperf. 250p+50p, issued May 22. Nos. 7365-7373.

Paintings, set of seven, 1p, 2p, 3p, 5p, 8p, airmail 15p, 50p, and two airmail semi-postal souv. sheets, 200p+25p, imperf. 250p+50p, issued June 29. Nos. 7374-7382.

1974 World Cup Soccer Championships, Munich, set of nine, 5c, 10c, 15c, 20c, 25c, 55c, 60c, airmail 5p, 70p, and two airmail souv. sheets, perf. 130p, imperf. 200p, issued Aug. 30. Nos. 7383-7393.

Rubens paintings, set of seven, 1p, 2p, 3p, 5p, 8p, airmail 15p, 50p, and two airmail semi-postal souv. sheets, perf. (25p, 200p), imperf. (50p, 250p), issued Sept. 23. Nos. 7394-73102.

1974 World Cup Soccer Championships, Munich, four gold foil airmail souv. sheets, perf. 130e (2), imperf. 200e (2), and two souv. sheets of two, perf. 130e, imperf. 200e, issued Oct. 24. Nos. 73103-73108.

Christmas, paintings, set of seven, 1p, 3p, 5p, 8p, 10p, airmail 15p, 25p, and two airmail semi-postal souv. sheets, perf. 200p+25p, imperf. 250p+50p (Nativity, by van der Weyden, Bosco, de Carvajal, Mabuse, Lucas Jordan, P. Goecke, Maino, Fabriano, Lochner), issued Oct. 30. Nos. 73109-73117.

Apollo Program and J.F. Kennedy, two gold foil airmail semi-postals, perf. 200p+25p, imperf. 250p+50p, and two souv. sheets, perf. 200p+25p, imperf. 250p+50p, issued Nov. 10. Nos. 73118-73121.

World Cup Soccer (famous players), set of nine, 30c, 35c, 40c, 45c, 50c, 65c, 70c, airmail 8p, 60p, and two airmail souv. sheets, perf. 130p, imperf. 200p, issued Nov. 20. Nos. 73122-73132.

EQUATORIAL GUINEA

Princess Anne's Wedding, six gold foil airmail souv. sheets, perf., imperf., two sheets of one, each 250e, one sheet of two 250e, issued Dec. 17. Nos. 73133-73141.

Pablo Picasso Memorial (Blue Period paintings), set of seven, 30c, 35c, 40c, 45c, 50c, airmail 8e, 60e, and two airmail souv. sheets, perf. 130e, imperf. 200e, issued Dec. 20. Nos. 73142-73150.

1974

Copernicus, 500th birth anniv., set of seven, 5c, 10c, 15c, 20c, 4e, airmail 10e, 70e, two airmail souv. sheets, perf. 130e, imperf. 200e, issued Feb. 8, 1974; eight gold foil airmail souv. sheets, perf. 130e (3), 250e, imperf. 200e (3), 300e, and four souv. sheets of two, perf. 250e (2), imperf. 250e (2), issued Apr. 10. Nos. 7401-7421.

World Cup Soccer Championships (final games), set of nine, 75c, 80c, 85c, 90c, 95c, 1e, 1.25e, airmail 10c, 50e, and two airmail souv. sheets, perf. 130e, imperf. 200e, issued Feb. 28. Nos. 7422-7432.

Easter, paintings, set of seven, 1p, 3p, 5p, 8p, 10p, airmail 15p, 25p (Fra Angelico, Castagno, Allori, Multscher, della Francesca, Pleydenwurff, Correggio), and two airmail semi-postal souv. sheets, perf. 200p+25p, imperf. 250p+50p, issued Mar. 27. Nos. 7433-7441.

Holy Year 1975 (famous churches), set of seven, 5c, 10c, 15c, 20c, 3.50e, airmail 10e, 70e, and two airmail souv. sheets, perf. 130e, imperf. 200e, issued Apr. 11. Nos. 7442-7450.

World Cup Soccer (contemporary players), set of nine, 1.50, 1.75, 2, 2.25, 2.50, 3, 3.50e, airmail 10, 60e, and 2 airmail souv. sheets of 2, perf. (2x65e), imperf. (2x100e), issued Apr. 30. Nos. 7451-7461.

UPU Cent. (transportation from messenger to rocket), set of seven, 60c, 70c, 80c, 1e, 1.50e, airmail 30e, 50e, and two airmail souv. sheets, perf. 225e, imperf. (150e, 150e), issued May 30; three airmail deluxe souv. sheets, 130e, and 2x130e, issued June 8. Nos. 7462-7472A.

Picasso Memorial (Pink Period paintings), set of seven, 55c, 60c, 65c, 70c, 75c, airmail 10e, 50e, and two airmail souv. sheets, perf. 130e, imperf. 200e, issued June 28. Nos. 7473-7481.

World Cup Soccer Championships, gold foil airmail souv. sheets, four sheets of one, 130e (2), 250e (2), two sheets of two (2x130e; 2x250e), issued July 8. Nos. 7482-7487.

Aleksander Solzhenitsyn, two gold foil airmail souv. sheets, perf. 250e, imperf. 300e, issued July 25. Nos. 7488-7489.

Opening of American West, set of seven, 30c, 35c, 40c, 45c, 50c, airmail 8p, 60p, and two souv. sheets, perf. 130p, imperf. 200p, issued July 30. Nos. 7490-7498.

Flowers, set of 14, 5c, 10c, 15c, 20c, 25c, 1p, 3p, 5p, 8p, 10p, airmail 5p, 15p, 25p, 70p, and 4 airmail souv. sheets, perf. 130p, 25p+200p, imperf. 200p, 50p+250p, issued Aug. 20. Nos. 7499-74116.

Christmas, set of seven, 60c, 70c, 80c, 1e, 1.50e, airmail 30e, 50e, and two souv. sheets, perf. 225e, imperf. 300e, issued Sept. 16. Nos. 74117-74125.

Barcelona Soccer Team, 75th anniv., set of seven, 1e, 3e, 5e, 8e, 10e, airmail 15e, 60e, miniature sheet of seven plus label, two airmail souv. sheets, perf. 200e, imperf. 300e, and two gold foil airmail souv. sheets, imperf., 200e each, issued Sept. 25. Nos. 74126-74137.

UPU Cent. and ESPANA 75, set of seven, 1.25e, 1.50e, 1.75e, 2e, 2.25e, airmail 35e, 60e, and 2 airmail souv. sheets, perf. 225e, imperf. 300e, issued Oct. 9; 6 gold foil sheets, perf. 250e, 250e, 2x250e, imperf. 300e, 300e, 2x300e, issued Oct. 14. Nos. 74138-74152.

Nature Protection

Australian Animals, set of seven, 80c, 85c, 90c, 95c, 1e, airmail 15e, 40e, and two airmail souv. sheets, perf. 130e, imperf. 200e, issued Oct. 25. Nos. 74153-74161.

African Animals, set of seven, 55c, 60c, 65c, 70c, 75c, airmail 10e, 70e, and two airmail souv. sheets, perf. 130e, imperf. 200e, issued Nov. 6. Nos. 74162-74170.

Australian and South American Birds, set of 14, 1.25p, 1.50p, 1.75p, 2p, 2.25p, 2.50p, 2.75p, 3p, 3.50p, 4p, airmail 20p, 25p, 30p, 35p, and four souv. sheets, perf. 130p (2), imperf. 200p (2), issued Nov. 26. Nos. 74171-74188.

Endangered Species, set of 15, 10c, 15c, 20c, 25c, 30c, 35c, 40c, 45c, 50c, 55c, 60c, 1e, 2e, airmail 10e, 70e, se-tenant in sheet of 15, issued Dec. 17. Nos. 74189-74203.

Monkeys, various species, set of 16, 5c, 10c, 15c, 20c, 25c, 30c, 35c, 40c, 45c, 50c, 55c, 60c, 1e, 2e, airmail 10e, 70e, se-tenant in sheet of 16, issued Dec. 27. Nos. 74204-74219.

Cats, various species, set of 16, 5c, 10c, 15c, 20c, 25c, 30c, 35c, 40c, 45c, 50c, 55c, 60c, 1e, 2e, airmail 10e, 70e, se-tenant in sheet of 16, issued Dec. 27. Nos. 74220-74235.

Fish, various species, set of 16, 5c, 10c, 15c, 20c, 25c, 30c, 35c, 40c, 45c, 50c, 55c, 60c, 1e, 2e, airmail 10e, 70e, se-tenant in sheet of 16, issued Dec. 27. Nos. 74236-74251.

Butterflies, various species, set of 16, 5c, 10c, 15c, 20c, 25c, 30c, 35c, 40c, 45c, 50c, 55c, 60c, 1e, 2e, airmail 10e, 70e, se-tenant in sheet of 16, issued Dec. 27. Nos. 74252-74267.

1975

Picasso Memorial (paintings from last period), set of seven, 5c, 10c, 15c, 20c, 25c, airmail 5e, 70e, and two souv. sheets, perf. 130e, imperf. 200e, issued Jan. 27. Nos. 7501-7509.

ARPHILA 75 Phil. Exhib., Paris, 8 gold foil airmail souv. sheets: perf. 3 sheets of 1 250e, 1 sheet of 2 250e, imperf. 3 sheets of 1 300e, 1 sheet of 2 300e, issued Jan. 27. Nos. 7510-7517.

Easter and Holy Year 1975, set of seven, 60c, 70c, 80c, 1e, 1.50e, airmail 30e, 50e, and two airmail souv. sheets, perf. 225e, imperf. 300e, issued Feb. 15. Nos. 7518-7526.

1976 Winter Olympics, Innsbruck, set of 11, 5c, 10c, 15c, 20c, 25c, 30c, 35c, 40c, 45c, 25e, 70e, two airmail souv. sheets, perf. 130e, imperf. 200e, and two gold foil airmail souv. sheets, 1 sheet of 1 250e, 1 sheet of 2 250e, issued Mar. 10. Nos. 7527-7541.

Don Quixote, set of seven, 30c, 35c, 40c, 45c, 50c, airmail 25e, 60e, and two airmail souv. sheets, perf. 130e, imperf. 200e, issued Apr. 4. Nos. 7542-7550.

American Bicent. (1st issue), set of nine, 5c, 20c, 40c, 75c, 2e, 5e, 8e, airmail 25e, 30e, and two airmail souv. sheets, perf. 130c, imperf. 200e, issued Apr. 30. Nos. 7551-7561.

American Bicent. (2nd issue), set of nine, 10c, 30c, 50c, 1e, 3e, 6e, 10e, airmail 12e, 40e, and two airmail souv. sheets, perf. 130e, imperf. 200e, issued Apr. 30. Nos. 7562-7572.

American Bicent. (Presidents), set of 18, 5c, 10c, 20c, 30c, 40c, 50c, 75c, 1e, 2e, 3e, 5e, 6e, 8e, 10e, airmail 12e, 25e, 30e, 40e, four airmail souv. sheets, perf. 225e (2), imperf. 300e (2), and six embossed gold foil airmail souv. sheets, perf. 200e, 200e, 2x200e, imperf. 300e, 300e, 2x300e, issued July 4. Nos. 7573-75100.

Bull Fight, set of seven, 80c, 85c, 90c, 95c, 8e, airmail 35e, 40e, and two airmail souv. sheets, perf. 130e, imperf. 200e, issued May 26. Nos. 75101-75109.

Apollo-Soyuz Space Project, set of 11, 1e, 2e, 3e, 5e, 5.50e, 7e, 7.50e, 9e, 15e, airmail 20e, 30e, and two airmail souv. sheets, perf. 225e, imperf. 300e, issued June 20, 1975; airmail souv. sheet, perf. 250e, issued July 17. Nos. 75110-75123.

Famous Painters, Nudes, set of 16, 5c, 10c, 15c, 20c, 25c, 30c, 35c, 40c, 45c, 50c, 55c, 60c, 1e, 2e, airmail 10e, 70e (Egyptian Greek, Roman, Indian art, Goes, Durer, Liss, Beniort, Renoir, Gauguin, Stenlen, Picasso, Modigliani, Matisse, Padua), se-tenant in sheet of 16, and 20 airmail embossed gold foil souv. sheetlets, perf. 200p+25p (10), imperf. 250p+50p (10), issued Aug. 10. Nos. 75124-75159.

Conquerors of the Sea, set of 14, 30c, 35c, 40c, 45c, 50c, 55c, 60c, 65c, 70c, 75c, airmail 8p, 10p, 50p, 60p, and four airmail souv. sheets, perf. 130p (2), imperf. 200p (2), issued Sept. 5. Nos. 75160-75177.

Christmas and Holy Year, 1975, set of seven, 60c, 70c, 80c, 1e, 1.50e, airmail 30e, 50e (Jordan, Barocci, Vereycke, Rubens, Mengs, Del Castillo, Cavedone), two airmail souv. sheets, perf. 225e, imperf. 300e, plus four embossed gold foil souv. sheets, perf. 200e (2), imperf. 300e (2), and two gold foil miniature sheets of two, perf. 200e+200e, imperf. 300e+300e, issued Oct. 25. Nos. 75178-75192.

President Macias, IWY, set of eight, 1.50e, 3e, 3.50e, 5e, 7e, 10e, airmail 100e, 300e, and two imperf. airmail souv. sheets (world events), 100e (US 2c Yorktown), 300e, issued Dec. 25. Nos. 75193-75202.

1976

Cavalry Uniforms, set of seven, 5c, 10c, 15c, 20c, 25c, airmail 5p, 70p, and two airmail souv. sheets, perf. 130p, imperf. 200p, issued Feb. 2. Nos. 7601-7609.

1976 Winter Olympics, Innsbruck, set of 11, 50c, 55c, 60c, 65c, 70c, 75c, 80c, 85c, 90c, airmail 35e, 60e, and two airmail souv. sheets, perf. 130e, imperf. 200e, issued Feb. 10. Nos. 7610-7622.

1976 Summer Olympics, Montreal, Ancient to Modern Games, set of seven, 50c, 60c, 70c, 80c, 90c, airmail 35e, 60e, and two airmail souv. sheets, perf. 225e, imperf. 300e, issued Feb. Nos. 7623-7631.

1976 Summer Olympics, Montreal, set of seven, 50c, 60c, 70c, 80c, 90c, airmail 30e, 60e, plus two airmail souv. sheets, perf. 225e, imperf. 300e, four embossed gold foil airmail souv. sheets, per. 250e (2), imperf. 300e (2), and two imperf. miniature sheets of two, perf. 2x250e, imperf. 2x300e, issued Mar. 5. Nos. 7632-7646.

El Greco, paintings, set of seven, 1e, 3e, 5e, 8e, 10e, airmail 15e, 25e, and two airmail semi-postal souv. sheets, perf. 200e+25e, imperf. 250e+50e, issued Apr. 5. Nos. 7647-7655.

1976 Summer Olympics, modern games, set of 11, 50c, 55c, 60c, 65c, 70c, 75c, 80c, 85c, 90c, airmail 35e, 60e, plus two airmail souv. sheets, perf. 225e, imperf. 300e, four embossed gold foil airmail souv. sheets, perf. 250e (2), imperf. 300e (2), and two miniature sheets of two, perf. 2x250e, imperf. 2x300e, issued May 7. Nos. 7656-7674.

UN 30th Anniv., airmail souv. sheet, 250e, issued June. No. 7675.

Contemporary Automobiles, set of seven, 1p, 3p, 5p, 8p, 10p, airmail 15p, 25p, and two airmail semi-postal souv. sheets, perf. 200p+25p, imperf. 250p+50p, issued June 10. Nos. 7675-7684.

Nature Protection

European Animals, set of seven, 5c, 10c, 15c, 20c, 25c, airmail 5p, 70p, and two airmail souv. sheets, perf. 130p, imperf. 200p, issued July 1. Nos. 7685-7693.

Asian Animals, set of seven, 30c, 35c, 40c, 45c, 8p, airmail 50c, 60p, and two airmail souv. sheets, perf. 130p, imperf. 200p, issued Sept. 20. Nos. 7694-74102.

Asian Birds, set of seven, 55c, 60c, 65c, 70c, 75c, airmail 10p, 50p, and two airmail souv. sheets, perf. 130p, imperf. 200p, issued Sept. 20. Nos. 76103-76111.

European Birds, set of seven, 5c, 10c, 15c, 20c, 25c, airmail 5p, 70p, and two airmail souv. sheets, perf. 130p, imperf. 200p, issued Sept. 20. Nos. 76112-76120.

North American Birds, set of seven, 80c, 85c, 90c, 95c, 1p, airmail 15p, 40p, and two airmail souv. sheets, perf. 130p, imperf. 200p, issued Sept. 20. Nos. 76121-76129.

Motorcycle Aces, set of 16, two each 1e, 2e, 3e, 4e, 5e, 10e, 30e, 40e, in se-tenant blocks of eight diff. values, issued July 22. Nos. 76130-76145.

1976 Summer Olympics, Montreal, set of five, 10e, 25e se-tenant strip of 3, airmail 200e, and imperf. airmail souv. sheet, 300e, issued Aug. 7. Nos. 76146-76151.

South American Flowers, set of seven, 30c, 35c, 40c, 45c, 50c, airmail 8p, 60p, and two airmail souv. sheets, perf. 130p, imperf. 200p, issued Aug. 16. Nos. 76152-76160.

Oceania, set of seven, 80c, 85c, 90c, 95c, 1p, airmail 15p, 40p, and two airmail souv. sheets, perf. 130p, imperf. 200p, issued 1976. Nos. 76161-76169.

1977

Butterflies, set of seven, 80c, 85c, 90c, 95c, 8e, airmail 35e, 40e, and two airmail souv. sheets, perf. 130e, imperf. 200e, issued Jan. Nos. 7701-7709.

Madrid Real, 75th Anniv., set of nine, 2e, 4e, 5e, 8e, 10e, 15e, airmail 20e, 35e, 150e, issued Jan. Nos. 7710-7718.

Ancient Carriages, set of 16, 5c, 10c, 15c, 20c, 25c, 30c, 35c, 40c, 45c, 50c, 55c, 60c, 1e, 2e, airmail 10e, 70e, issued Feb. Nos. 7719-7734.

Chinese Art, set of seven, 60c, 70c, 80c, 1e, 1.50e, airmail 30e, 50e, and two airmail souv. sheets, perf. 130e, imperf. 200e, issued Feb. Nos. 7735-7743.

African Masks, set of seven, 5c, 10c, 15c, 20c, 25c, airmail 5p, 70p, and two airmail souv. sheets, perf. 130e, imperf. 200e, issued Mar. Nos. 7744-7752.

North American Animals, set of seven, 1.25e, 1.50e, 1.75e, 2e, 2.25e, airmail 20e, 50e, and two airmail souv. sheets, perf. 130e, imperf. 200e, issued 1977. Nos. 7753-7761.

World Cup Soccer Championships, Argentina '78 (famous players), set of eight, 2e, 4e, 5e, 8e, 10e, 15e, airmail 20e, 35e, and two airmail souv. sheets, perf. 150e, imperf. 250e, issued July 25. Nos. 7762-7771.

World Cup Soccer (famous teams), se-tenant set of eight, 2e, 4e, 5e, 8e, 10e, 15e, airmail 20e, 35e, and two gold foil embossed souv. sheets, 500e (AMPHILEX '77, Cutty Sark, Concorde), airmail 500e (World Cup), issued Aug. 25. Nos. 7772-7781.

Napoleon, Life and Battle Scenes, se-tenant sheet of 16, 5c, 10c, 15c, 20c, 25c, 30c, 35c, 40c, 45c, 50c, 55c, 60c, 1e, 2e, airmail 10e, 70e, Aug. 20. Nos. 7782-7797.

Napoleon, Military Uniforms, se-tenant sheet of 16, 5c, 10c, 15c, 20c, 25c, 30c, 35c, 40c, 45c, 50c, 55c, 60c, 1e, 2e, airmail 10e, 70e, issued Aug. 20. Nos. 7798-77113.

424 EQUATORIAL GUINEA

South American Animals, set of seven, 2.50e, 2.75e, 3e, 3.50e, 4e, airmail 25e, 35e, and two airmail souv. sheets, perf. 130e, imperf. 200e, issued Aug. Nos. 77114-77122.

USSR Space Program, 20th Anniv., set of eight, 2e, 4e, 5e, 8e, 10e, 15e, airmail 20e, 35e, and two airmail souv. sheets, imperf. 150e, perf. 250e, issued Dec. 15. Nos. 77123-77132.

1978

Ancient Sailing Ships, set of 12, 5c, 10c, 15c, 20c, 25c, airmail 5e, 10e, also 5e, 10e, 20e, 25e, 70e, plus four airmail souv. sheets, perf. 150e, 225e, imperf. 250e, 300e, and two embossed gold foil airmail souv. sheets, perf., imperf., 500e, issued Jan. 6. Nos. 7801-7818.

1980 Winter Olympics, Lake Placid, set of five, 5e, 10e, 20e, 25e, airmail 70e, two airmail souv. sheets, perf. 150e, imperf. 250e, and two embossed gold foil airmail souv. sheets, perf., imperf., 500e, issued Jan. 17. Nos. 7819-7827.

1980 Summer Olympics, Moscow, set of eight, 2e, 3e, 5e, 8e, 10e, 15e, airmail 30e, 50e, two airmail souv. sheets, perf. 150e, imperf. 250e, and two embossed gold foil airmail souv. sheets, perf., imperf., 500e, issued Jan. 17. Nos. 7828-7839.

1980 Summer Olympic Water Games, Tallinn, set of five, 5e, 10e, 20e, 25e, airmail 70e, two airmail souv. sheets, perf. 150e, imperf. 250e, and two embossed gold foil airmail souv. sheets, perf., imperf., 500e, issued Jan. 17. Nos. 7840-7848.

Eliz. II Coronation, 25th Anniv., set of eight, 2e, 5e, 8e, 10e, 12e, 15e, airmail 30e, 50e, and two airmail souv. sheets, perf. 150e, imperf. 250e, issued Apr. 25. Nos. 7849-7858.

English Knights of 1200-1350 A.D., set of seven, 5e, 10e, 15e, 20e, 25e, airmail 15e, 70e, and two airmail souv. sheets, perf. 130e, imperf. 200e, issued Apr. 25. Nos. 7859-7867.

Old Locomotives, set of seven, 1e, 2e, 3e, 5e, 10e, airmail 25e, 70e, and two airmail souv. sheets, perf. 150e, imperf. 250e, issued Aug. Nos. 7868-7876.

Prehistoric Animals, set of seven, 30e, 35e, 40e, 45e, 50e, airmail 25e, 60e, and airmail souv. sheets, 130e, 200e, issued Aug. Nos. 7877-7884, 7884A.

Francisco Goya, "Maja Vestida," airmail souv. sheet, 150e, issued Aug. No. 7885.

Peter Paul Rubens — UNICEF, airmail souv. sheet, 250e, issued Aug. No. 7886.

Europa — CEPT — Europhila '78, airmail souv. sheet, 250e, issued Aug. No. 7887.

30th Intl. Stamp Fair, Riccione, airmail souv. sheet, 150e, issued Aug. No. 7888.

Eliz. II Coronation, 25th anniv., airmail souv. sheet of three, 150e, issued CEPT, airmail souv. sheet, 250e, issued Aug. No. 7890.

World Cup Soccer Championships, Argentina '78 and Spain '82, airmail souv. sheet, 150e, issued Aug. Nos. 7891.

Christmas, Titian painting, "The Virgin," airmail souv. sheet, 150e, issued Aug. Nos. 7892.

Natl. Independence, 5th Anniv. (in 1973) — A7

1979   Perf. 13x13½
26 A7 1e Ekuele coin   1.10 .25

Natl. Independence, 5th Anniv. (in 1973) — A8

1e, Port Bata. 1.50e, State Palace. 2b, Central Bank, Bata. 2.50b, Nguema Biyogo Bridge. 3b, Port, palace, bank, bridge.

1979
27	A8	1e multicolored	.25	.25
28	A8	1.50e multicolored	.25	.25
29	A8	2b multicolored	.30	.30
30	A8	2.50b multicolored	.35	.35
31	A8	3b multicolored	.60	.60
		Nos. 27-31 (5)	1.75	1.75

Pres. Nguema — A9

1979   Perf. 13½x13
32 A9 1.50e multi   .50 .35

United Natl. Workers's Party (PUNT), 3rd Congress.

Independence Martyrs — A10

1e, Enrique Nvo. 1.50e, Salvador Ndongo Ekang. 2b, Acacio Mane.

1979
33	A10	1e multicolored	.30	.30
34	A10	1.50e multicolored	.35	.35
35	A10	2b multicolored	.45	.45
		Nos. 33-35 (3)	1.10	1.10

Agricultural Experiment Year — A11

1979   Perf. 13x13½
| 36 | A11 | 1e multi | .65 | .25 |
| 37 | A11 | 1.50e multi, diff. | .95 | .35 |

Independence Martyrs A12   Natl. Coat of Arms A13

5b, Obiang Esono Nguema. 15b, Fernando Nvara Engonga. 25b, Ela Edjodjomo Mangue. 35b, Obiang Nguema Mbasogo, president. 50b, Hipolito Micha Eworo.

1981, Mar.   Photo.   Perf. 13½x12½
38	A12	5b multicolored	.40	.25
39	A12	15b multicolored	.40	.25
40	A12	25b multicolored	.40	.25
41	A12	35b multicolored	.55	.25
42	A12	50b multicolored	.80	.30
43	A13	100b multicolored	1.60	.45
		Nos. 38-43 (6)	4.15	1.75

Dated 1980.

Christmas 1980 — A14

1981, Mar. 30   Perf. 13½
| 44 | A14 | 8b Cathedral, infant | .30 | .25 |
| 45 | A14 | 25b Bells, youth | .35 | .25 |

Dated 1980.

Souvenir Sheet

Pres. Obiang Nguema Mbasogo A15

1981, Aug. 30   Litho.   Imperf.
46 A15 400b multi   5.00 2.25

State Visit of King Juan Carlos of Spain A16

50b, Government reception. 100b, Arrival at airport. 150b, King, Pres. Mbasogo, vert.

Perf. 13x13½, 13½x13
1981, Nov. 30
47	A16	50b multicolored	.90	.25
48	A16	100b multicolored	1.75	.50
49	A16	150b multicolored	2.75	.75
		Nos. 47-49 (3)	5.40	1.50

State Visit of Pope John Paul II A17

100b, Papal and natl. arms. 200b, Pres. Mbasogo greeting Pope. 300b, Pope, vert.

1982, Feb. 18
50	A17	100b multicolored	1.50	.80
51	A17	200b multicolored	3.25	1.60
52	A17	300b multicolored	4.75	2.40
		Nos. 50-52 (3)	9.50	4.80

Christmas 1981 — A18

1982, Feb. 25   Photo.
| 53 | A18 | 100b Carolers, vert. | 1.25 | .40 |
| 54 | A18 | 150b Magi, African youth | 1.90 | .70 |

Dated 1981.

1982 World Cup Soccer Championships, Spain — A19

40b, Emblem. 60b, Naranjito character trademark. 100b, World Cup trophy. 200b, Players, palm tree, emblem.

1982, June 13   Perf. 13½
55	A19	40b multicolored	.45	.25
56	A19	60b multicolored	.70	.35
57	A19	100b multicolored	1.25	.60
58	A19	200b multicolored	2.50	1.10
		Nos. 55-58 (4)	4.90	2.30

Fauna — A20

1983, Feb. 4   Litho.
59	A20	40b Gorilla	.75	.25
60	A20	60b Hippopotamus	1.25	.40
61	A20	80b Atherurus africanus	1.75	.50
62	A20	120b Felis pardus	2.75	.75
		Nos. 59-62 (4)	6.50	1.90

Dated 1982.

Christmas 1982 — A21

1983, Feb. 25   Photo.
| 63 | A21 | 100b Stars | .95 | .35 |
| 64 | A21 | 200b King offering frankincense | 2.25 | .75 |

Dated 1982.

World Communications Year — A22

Designs: 150b, Postal runner. 200b, Microwave station, drummer.

1983, July 18   Litho.
| 65 | A22 | 150b multicolored | 1.00 | .45 |
| 66 | A22 | 200b multicolored | 2.25 | .80 |

Banana Trees — A23

1983, Oct. 8
| 67 | A23 | 300b shown | 3.25 | 1.00 |
| 68 | A23 | 400b Forest, vert. | 4.50 | 1.40 |

Christmas 1983 — A24

Designs: 80b, Folk dancer, musical instruments. 100b, Holy Family.

1984
| 69 | A24 | 80b multicolored | 1.00 | .35 |
| 70 | A24 | 100b multicolored | 1.25 | .50 |

Dated 1983.

Constitution of State Powers — A25

Scales of justice, fundamental lawbook and various maps.

1984, Feb. 15
| 71 | A25 | 50b Annobon and Bioko | .60 | .30 |
| 72 | A25 | 100b Mainland regions | 1.40 | .65 |

Inscription at the UR on No. 71 reads "Region Insular". No. 71 also exists with inscription reading "Regiones Insulares".

Turtle Hunting, Rio Muni — A26

1984, May 1
| 73 | A26 | 125b Hunting Whales, horiz. | 1.75 | .75 |
| 74 | A26 | 150b shown | 2.00 | .85 |

EQUATORIAL GUINEA

World Food Day — A27

1984, Sept.
| 75 | A27 | 60b Papaya | 1.25 | .50 |
| 76 | A27 | 80b Malanga | 1.50 | .65 |

Abstract Wood-Carved Figurines and Art — A28

Designs: 25b, *Black Gazelle* and *Anxiety.* 30b, *Black Gazelle,* diff., and *Woman.* 60b, *Man and woman,* vert. 75b, *Poster,* vert. 100b, *Mother and Child,* vert. 150b, *Man and Woman,* diff., and *Bust of a Woman.*

1984, Nov. 15
77	A28	25b multi	.25	.25
78	A28	30b multi	.35	.25
79	A28	60b multi	.75	.35
80	A28	75b multi	1.00	.40
81	A28	100b multi	1.50	.50
82	A28	150b multi	2.00	.90
		Nos. 77-82 (6)	5.85	2.65

Christmas — A29

60b, Mother and child, vert. 100b, Musical instruments.

1984, Dec. 24
| 83 | A29 | 60b multicolored | .75 | .25 |
| 84 | A29 | 100b multicolored | 1.25 | .55 |

Immaculate Conception Missions, Cent. — A30

50fr, Emblem, vert. 60fr, Map, nun and youths, vert. 80fr, First Guinean nuns. 125fr, Missionaries landing at Bata Beach, 1885.

1985, Apr. *Perf. 14*
85	A30	50fr multi	.45	.25
86	A30	60fr multi	.60	.25
87	A30	80fr multi	.90	.30
88	A30	125fr multi	1.40	.60
		Nos. 85-88 (4)	3.35	1.40

José Mavule Ndjong, First Postmaster — A31

1985, July *Perf. 13½*
| 89 | A31 | 50fr Postal emblem, vert. | 1.00 | .25 |
| 90 | A31 | 80fr shown | 1.75 | .55 |

Equatorial Guinea Postal Service.

Christmas — A32

Designs: 40fr, Nativity. 70fr, Folk band, dancers, mother and child.

1985, Dec.
| 91 | A32 | 40fr multicolored | .65 | .25 |
| 92 | A32 | 70fr multicolored | 1.10 | .35 |

Nature Conservation — A33

15fr, Crab, snail. 35fr, Butterflies, bees, birds. 45fr, Flowering plants. 65fr, Spraying and harvesting cacao.

1985
93	A33	15fr multicolored	.30	.25
94	A33	35fr multicolored	.85	.30
95	A33	45fr multicolored	.85	.30
96	A33	65fr multicolored	1.25	.45
		Nos. 93-96 (4)	3.25	1.30

Folklore — A34

10fr, Ndowe dance, Mekuyo, horiz. 50fr, Fang dance, Mokom. 65fr, Cacha Bubi, Bisila. 80fr, Fang dance, Ndong-Mba.

1986, Apr. 15
97	A34	10fr multicolored	.25	.25
98	A34	50fr multicolored	.60	.25
99	A34	65fr multicolored	.90	.30
100	A34	80fr multicolored	1.00	.40
		Nos. 97-100 (4)	2.75	1.20

A35

1986 World Cup Soccer Championships, Mexico: Various soccer plays.

1986, June 25
101	A35	50fr multi, horiz.	.30	.25
102	A35	100fr multi, horiz.	.80	.30
103	A35	150fr multi	1.25	.45
104	A35	200fr multi	1.60	.60
		Nos. 101-104 (4)	3.95	1.60

Christmas — A36

Designs: 100fr, Musical instruments, horiz. 150fr, Holy Family, lamb.

1986, Dec. 12
| 105 | A36 | 100fr multicolored | 1.10 | .35 |
| 106 | A36 | 150fr multicolored | 1.60 | .60 |

Conf. of the Union of Central African States — A37

Designs: 80fr, Flags, map. 100fr, Emblem, map, horiz.

1986, Dec. 29
| 107 | A37 | 80fr multicolored | .90 | .35 |
| 108 | A37 | 100fr multicolored | 1.25 | .40 |

Campaign Against Hunger — A38

1987, June 5
109	A38	60fr Chicken	.65	.25
110	A38	80fr Fish	.95	.35
111	A38	100fr Wheat	1.25	.45
		Nos. 109-111 (3)	2.85	1.05

Intl. Peace Year — A39

1987, July 15 *Litho. Perf. 13½*
| 112 | A39 | 100fr shown | .85 | .40 |
| 113 | A39 | 200fr Hands holding dove | 1.90 | .80 |

Stamp Day 1987 — A40

1987, Oct. 5 *Litho. Perf. 13½*
| 114 | A40 | 150fr shown | 1.25 | .50 |
| 115 | A40 | 300fr Posting envelope | 2.25 | .90 |

Christmas 1987 — A41

Mother and child (wood carvings).

1987, Dec. 22 *Litho. Perf. 13½*
| 116 | A41 | 80fr multi | 1.00 | .35 |
| 117 | A41 | 100fr multi, diff. | 1.40 | .45 |

Climbing Palm Tree — A42

75fr, Woman carrying fish. 150fr, Chopping down trees.

1988, May 4 *Litho. Perf. 13½*
118	A42	50fr shown	.45	.25
119	A42	75fr multicolored	.65	.35
120	A42	150fr multicolored	1.40	.65
		Nos. 118-120 (3)	2.50	1.25

Democratic Party — A43

40fr, Crest. 75fr, Torch, motto, horiz. 100fr, Torch, flag, weaving, horiz.

1988, Nov. 16
121	A43	40fr multicolored	.40	.25
122	A43	75fr multicolored	.65	.30
123	A43	100fr multicolored	.95	.40
		Nos. 121-123 (3)	2.00	.95

Cultural Revolution Day — A44

Geometric shapes.

1988, June 4
124	A44	35fr shown	.40	.25
125	A44	50fr Squares, sphere	.60	.25
126	A44	100fr Bird	1.00	.40
		Nos. 124-126 (3)	2.00	.90

Christmas — A45

1988, Dec. 22
| 127 | A45 | 50fr shown | .55 | .25 |
| 128 | A45 | 100fr Mother and child | 1.20 | .40 |

Natl. Independence, 20th Anniv. — A46

Designs: 10fr, Lumber on truck. 35fr, Folk dancers. 45fr, Officials on dais.

1989, Apr. 14 *Litho. Perf. 14*
129	A46	10fr multicolored	.35	.25
130	A46	35fr multicolored	.40	.35
131	A46	45fr multicolored	.55	.40
		Nos. 129-131 (3)	1.30	1.00

Youths Bathing, Ilachi Falls — A47

25fr, Waterfall in the jungle. 60fr, Boy drinking from fruit, boys swimming at Luba Beach.

1989, July 7 *Perf. 13½*
132	A47	15fr shown	.45	.25
133	A47	25fr multicolored	.50	.25
134	A47	60fr multicolored	.75	.40
		Nos. 132-134 (3)	1.70	.90

1st Congress of the Democratic Party of Equatorial Guinea — A48

1989, Oct. 23 *Litho. Perf. 13½*
135	A48	25fr shown	.35	.25
136	A48	35fr Torch, vert.	.60	.25
137	A48	40fr Proc. Nguoma, vert.	.70	.25
		Nos. 135-137 (3)	1.65	.75

Christmas — A49

1989, Dec. 18 *Litho. Perf. 13½*
| 138 | A49 | 150fr shown | 1.60 | .50 |
| 139 | A49 | 300fr Nativity, horiz. | 2.00 | .75 |

Boy Scouts — A50

Designs: 100fr, Lord Baden-Powell. 250fr, Salute. 350fr, Bugler.

1990, Mar. 23 *Litho. Perf. 13*
140	A50	100fr multi	1.50	.50
141	A50	250fr multi	3.50	1.10
142	A50	350fr multi	4.75	1.50
		Nos. 140-142 (3)	9.75	3.10

World Cup Soccer Championships, Italy — A51

EQUATORIAL GUINEA

Designs: 100fr, Soccer player, map. 250fr, Goalkeeper. 350fr, Trophy.

1990, June 8   Litho.   Perf. 13
143	A51	100fr multicolored	.60	.35
144	A51	250fr multicolored	1.50	.65
145	A51	350fr multicolored	2.00	1.00
	Nos. 143-145 (3)		4.10	2.00

Musical Instruments of the Ndowe People — A52

Instruments of the: 250fr, Fang. 350fr, Bubi.

1990, June 19
146	A52	100fr multicolored	.50	.30
147	A52	250fr multicolored	1.50	.75
148	A52	350fr multicolored	2.00	1.00
	Nos. 146-148 (3)		4.00	2.05

Discovery of America, 500th Anniv. (in 1992) — A53

Designs: 170fr, Arrival in New World. 300fr, Columbus' fleet.

1990, Oct. 10
149	A53	170fr multicolored	2.00	.60
150	A53	300fr multicolored	2.50	1.00

Christmas — A54

1990, Dec. 23   Litho.   Perf. 13½
151	A54	170fr shown	1.00	.45
152	A54	300fr Bubi tribesman	2.00	.90

1992 Summer Olympics, Barcelona — A55

1991, Apr. 22   Litho.   Perf. 13½x14
153	A55	150fr Tennis	1.25	.75
154	A55	250fr Cycling	2.25	1.25

Souvenir Sheet

155	A55	500fr Equestrian	20.00	20.00

La Maja Desnuda by Goya — A56

Designs: 250fr, Eve by Durer, vert. 350fr, The Three Graces by Rubens, vert.

1991, May 6   Litho.   Perf. 14
156	A56	100fr shown	1.50	.50
157	A56	250fr multicolored	2.75	1.00
158	A56	350fr multicolored	3.75	1.25
	Nos. 156-158 (3)		8.00	2.75

Madrillus Sphinx — A57

1991, July 1   Litho.   Perf. 13½x14
159	A57	25fr shown	2.50	1.25
160	A57	25fr Face	2.50	1.25
161	A57	25fr Seated	2.50	1.25
162	A57	25fr Walking, horiz.	2.50	1.25
	Nos. 159-162 (4)		10.00	5.00

World Wildlife Fund.

Discovery of America, 500th Anniv. — A58

Captains, ships: 150fr, Vicente Yanez Pinzon, Nina. 260fr, Martin Alonso Pinzon, Pinta. 350fr, Christopher Columbus, Santa Maria.

1991   Litho.   Perf. 13½x14
163	A58	150fr multicolored	1.50	.60
164	A58	250fr multicolored	2.75	1.00
165	A58	350fr multicolored	3.75	1.50
	Nos. 163-165 (3)		8.00	3.10

Locomotives A59

150fr, Electric, Japan, 1932. 250fr, Steam, US, 1873. 500fr, Steam, Germany, 1841.

1991, Sept. 10
166	A59	150fr multicolored	1.00	.50
167	A59	250fr multicolored	2.50	.75

Souvenir Sheet

168	A59	500fr multicolored	22.50	22.50

1992 Summer Olympics, Barcelona — A60

1992, Feb. 12   Litho.   Perf. 13½x14
169	A60	200fr Basketball	1.75	.75
170	A60	300fr Swimming	2.50	1.10

Souvenir Sheet

171	A60	400fr Baseball	22.50	22.50

Souvenir Sheet

Discovery of America, 500th Anniv. — A61

Columbus: a, 300fr, Departing from Palos, Spain. b, 500fr, Landing in New World.

1992, Apr. 8
172	A61	Sheet of 2, #a.-b.	22.50	22.50

Motion Pictures, Cent. — A61a

Scenes from movies: 100fr, Humphrey Bogart, Ingrid Bergman, Dooley Wilson in "Casablanca," 1942. 250fr, "Viridiana," 1961. 350fr, Laurel and Hardy in "Sons of the Desert," 1933.

1992, Sept.   Litho.   Perf. 14
172C	A61a	100fr multicolored	1.00	.65
172D	A61a	250fr multicolored	1.50	1.00
172E	A61a	350fr multicolored	2.50	1.50
	Nos. 172C-172E (3)		5.00	3.15

Mushrooms — A62

75fr, Termitomyces globulus. 125fr, Termitomyces le testui. 150fr, Termitomyces robustus.

1992, Nov.   Litho.   Perf. 14x13½
173	A62	75fr multicolored	1.00	.25
174	A62	125fr multicolored	1.50	.50
175	A62	150fr multicolored	2.00	.65
	Nos. 173-175 (3)		4.50	1.40

A62a

Wildlife Protection: 150fr, Halcyon malimbicus. 250fr, Corythaeola cristata. 500fr, Mariposa nymphalidae, horiz.

1992   Litho.   Perf. 14x13½
175A	A62a	150fr multicolored	2.50	1.00
175B	A62a	250fr multicolored	4.25	1.50

Souvenir Sheet Perf. 13½x14

175C	A62a	500fr multicolored	25.00	25.00

Virgin and Child with Virtuous Saints, by Claudio Coello (c. 1635-1693) A63

Paintings, by Jacob Jordaens (1593-1678): 300fr, Apollo Conquering Marsias. 400fr, Meleager and Atalanta.

1993, Mar.   Litho.   Perf. 13½x14
176	A63	200fr multicolored	2.25	.75
177	A63	300fr multicolored	3.00	1.10

Souvenir Sheet

178	A63	400fr multicolored	20.00	20.00

1992 Olympic Gold Medalists — A64

Designs: 100fr, Quincy Watts, 400-meter dash, US. 250fr, Martin Lopez Zubero, swimming, Spain. 350fr, Petra Kronberger, women's slalom, Austria. 400fr, Flying Dutchman class yachting, Spain.

1993   Litho.   Perf. 13½x14
179	A64	100fr multicolored	.90	.35
180	A64	250fr multicolored	2.25	.75
181	A64	350fr multicolored	3.25	1.00
182	A64	400fr multicolored	4.00	1.25
	Nos. 179-182 (4)		10.40	3.35

Scene from Romeo and Juliet, by Tchaikovsky A65

Design: 200fr, Scene from Faust, by Charles-Francois Gounod (1818-93).

1993, June   Litho.   Perf. 13½x14
183	A65	100fr multicolored	1.40	.40
184	A65	200fr multicolored	2.40	.65

First Ford Gasoline Engine, Cent. — A66

1993   Perf. 13½x14, 14x13½
185	A66	200fr First Ford vehicle	2.00	.75
186	A66	300fr Ford Model T	2.75	1.00
187	A66	400fr Henry Ford, vert.	4.00	1.25
	Nos. 185-187 (3)		8.75	3.00

25th Anniv. of Independence A67

Designs: 150fr, Pres. Obiang Nguema Mbasogo, vert. 250fr, Cargo ship, map, communications. 300fr, Hydroelectric plant, Riaba. 350fr, Bridge.

Perf. 14x13½, 13½x14

1993, Oct. 12   Litho.
188	A67	150fr multicolored	1.10	.50
189	A67	250fr multicolored	1.90	.75
190	A67	300fr multicolored	2.50	.85
191	A67	350fr multicolored	3.00	.95
	Nos. 188-191 (4)		8.50	3.05

1994 World Cup Soccer Championships, US — A68

Designs: 200fr, German team, 1990 champions. 300fr, Rose Bowl Stadium, Pasadena, Calif. 500fr, Player kicking ball, vert.

1994   Litho.   Perf. 13½x14, 14x13½
192	A68	200fr multicolored	1.35	.50
193	A68	300fr multicolored	1.90	.70
194	A68	500fr multicolored	3.50	1.20
	Nos. 192-194 (3)		6.75	2.40

First Manned Moon Landing, 25th Anniv. — A69

Designs: 500fr, Lunar module, Eagle. 700fr, "Buzz" Aldrin, Michael Collins, Neil Armstrong. 900fr, Footprint on moon, astronaut.

1994   Perf. 13½x14
195	A69	500fr multicolored	2.75	1.10
196	A69	700fr multicolored	4.25	1.50
197	A69	900fr multicolored	6.50	2.00
	Nos. 195-197 (3)		13.50	4.60

Dinosaurs — A70

Designs: 300fr, Chasmosaurus. 500fr, Tyrannosaurus rex. 700fr, Triceratops. 800fr, Styracosaurus, deinonychus.

1994
198	A70	300fr multicolored	2.00	.65
199	A70	500fr multicolored	3.25	1.10
200	A70	700fr multicolored	6.00	1.60
	Nos. 198-200 (3)		11.25	3.35

Souvenir Sheet

201	A70	800fr multicolored	21.00	21.00

Famous Men — A71

Designs: 300fr, Jean Renoir (1894-1979), French film director. 500fr, Ferdinand de Lesseps (1805-94), French diplomat, promoter of Suez Canal. 600fr, Antoine de Saint Exupery (1900-44), French aviator, writer. 700fr, Walter Gropius (1883-1969), architect.

1994   Litho.   Perf. 13½x14
202	A71	300fr multicolored	2.25	.75
203	A71	500fr multicolored	3.75	1.40
204	A71	600fr multicolored	4.50	1.50
205	A71	700fr multicolored	5.50	2.00
	Nos. 202-205 (4)		16.00	5.65

Establishment of The Bauhaus, 75th anniv. (No. 205).

Minerals — A72

1994   Litho.   Perf. 13½x14
206	A72	300fr Auricalcite	2.50	.90
207	A72	400fr Pyromorphite	3.50	1.25
208	A72	600fr Fluorite	5.00	1.75
209	A72	700fr Halite	6.00	2.00
	Nos. 206-209 (4)		17.00	5.90

EQUATORIAL GUINEA

Domestic Animals — A73

Designs: a, Cat. b, Dog. c, Pig.

1995	Litho.		Perf. 13½x14	
210	Strip of 3, #a.-c.		8.50	8.50
a.-c.	A73 500fr Any single		1.60	1.40

Butterflies & Orchids — A74

a, Hypolimnas salmacis. b, Myrina silenus. c, Palla ussheri. d, Pseudacraea boisduvali.

1995				
211	Strip of 4, #a.-d.		14.00	14.00
a.-d.	A74 400fr Any single		2.75	1.50

Anniversaries A75

Designs: a, 350fr, End of World War II, 50th Anniv. b, 450fr, UN, 50th anniv. c, 600fr, Sir Rowland Hill, birth bicent.

1995	Litho.		Perf. 13½x14	
212	Strip of 3, #a.-c.		11.00	11.00
a.	A75 350fr multi		2.50	1.25
b.	A75 450fr multi		3.25	1.50
c.	A75 600fr multi		4.00	2.25

Trains — A76

Designs: No. 213a, English steam engine. b, German diesel engine. c, Japanese Shinkansen train.
800fr, Swiss electric locomotive.

1995				
213	Strip of 3, #a.-c.		13.00	13.00
a.-c.	A76 500fr Any single		2.75	2.25

Souvenir Sheet

214	A76 800fr multicolored	11.00	11.00

Formula 1 Driving Champions A77

Designs: a, Juan Manuel Fangio. b, Ayrton Senna. c, Jim Clark. d, Jochen Rindt.

1995	Litho.		Perf. 14	
215	Strip of 4, #a.-d.		12.00	12.00
a.-d.	A77 400fr Any single		2.25	1.50

Motion Pictures, Cent. — A78

Designs: a, Marilyn Monroe. b, Elvis Presley. c, James Dean. d, Vittorio de Sica.

1996	Litho.		Perf. 14	
216	Strip of 4, #a.-d.		9.00	9.00
a.-d.	A78 350fr Any single		1.50	1.50

Famous People — A79

Designs: a, Alfred Nobel (1833-96), inventor, philanthropist. b, Anton Bruckner (1824-96), composer. c, Abraham and Three Angels, by Giovanni B. Tiepolo (1696-1770).

800fr, Family of Charles IV, by Francisco de Goya, (1746-1828).

1996				
217	Strip of 3, #a.-c.		13.50	13.50
a.-c.	A79 500fr Any single		2.75	2.00

Souvenir Sheet

218	A79 800fr multicolored	8.00	7.75

Chess — A80

Designs: a, World Chess Festival for youth and children, Minorca, Spain. b, Women's World Chess Championship, Jaén, Spain. c, Men's World Chess Championship, Karpov versus Kamsky, Elista, Kalmyk. d, Chess Olympiad, Yerevan, Armenia.

1996	Litho.		Perf. 14	
219	Strip of 4, #a.-d.		14.00	14.00
a.-d.	A80 400fr Any single		3.00	1.50

1996 Summer Olympic Games, Atlanta — A81

Designs: a, Olympic Stadium, Athens, 1896. b, Cycling. c, Tennis. d, Equestrian show jumping.

1996	Litho.		Perf. 14	
220	Strip of 4, #a.-d.		10.00	10.00
a.-d.	A81 400fr Any single		1.75	1.50

Ships — A82

Designs: a, Paddle steamer with sails, 19th cent. b, Bark "Galatea," 1896. c, Modern ferry.

1996				
221	Strip of 3, #a.-c.		12.00	12.00
a.-c.	A82 500fr Any single		2.75	2.00

Franz Schubert (1797-1828), Composer — A83

Miguel de Cervantes (1547-1616), Novelist — A84

Designs: a, shown. b, Chinese Lunar New Year, 1997, (Year of the Ox). c, Johannes Brahms (1833-97), composer.

1997, Apr. 23	Litho.		Perf. 14	
222	Strip of 3, #a.-c.		10.00	10.00
a.-c.	A83 500fr Any single		2.50	2.00

Souvenir Sheet

223	A84 800fr multicolored	11.00	11.00

Mushrooms A85

a, Sparassis laminosa. b, Amanita pantherina. c, Morchella esculenta. d, Aleuria aurantia.

1997				
224	Strip of 4, #a.-d.		13.50	13.50
a.-d.	A85 400fr Any single		2.25	1.75

1998 World Cup Soccer Championships, France — A86

Designs: a, Players with ball on field. b, Stadium. c, Kicking ball.

1997	Litho.		Perf. 14	
225	Strip of 3, #a.-c.		7.00	7.00
a.-c.	A86 300fr Any single		1.50	1.10

Fauna — A88

a, Snake. b, Snail. c, Turtle. d, Monitor lizard.

1998	Litho.		Perf. 14	
230	Strip of 4, #a.-d.		14.00	14.00
a.-d.	A88 400fr Any single		2.25	1.50

A89

Military Uniforms: a, Alsace Regiment, French Infantry, 18th cent. b, English Marine, 18th cent. c, Georgian Hussars Regiment, Russian Calvary, 18th cent. d, Prussian Artillery, 19th cent.

1998				
231	Strip of 4, #a.-d.		10.00	10.00
a.-d.	A89 400fr Any single		1.75	1.50

A90

Easter (Museum paintings): a, Crucifixion of Christ, by Velázquez. b, Adoration of the Magi, by Rubens. c, Holy Family, by Michelangelo.

1999	Litho.		Perf. 14	
232	Strip of 3, #a.-c.		10.00	10.00
a.-c.	A90 500fr Any single		2.25	2.00

Orchids — A91

Designs: a, Angraecum eburneum. b, Paphiopedilum insigne. c, Ansellia africana. d, Cattleya leopoldii.

1999				
233	Strip of 4, #a.-d.		16.00	16.00
a.-d.	A91 400fr Any single		3.00	1.50

Birth and Death Anniversaries — A92

No. 234: a, 750fr, Portrait of Frederic Chopin (1810-49), by Eugene Delacroix. b, 100fr, Christ Crowned With Thorns, by Anthony Van Dyck (1599-1641). c, 250fr, Portrait of Johann Wolfgang von Goethe (1749-1832), by Joseph Carl Stieler. d, 500fr, Jacques-Etienne Montgolfier (1745-1799) and balloon.

1999	Litho.		Perf. 14x13¾	
234	Horiz. strip of 4, #a-d		11.00	11.00
a.	A92 750fr multi		4.00	3.00
b.	A92 100fr multi		.45	.35
c.	A92 250fr multi		1.25	1.10
d.	A92 500fr multi		2.75	2.00

Parrots — A93

No. 235: a, Aratinga guarouba. b, Ara ambigua. c, Anodorhynchus hyacinthinus. 800fr, Alisterus amboinensis.

1999				
235	Vert. strip of 3, #a-c		13.00	13.00
a.-c.	A93 500fr any single		3.00	2.25

Souvenir Sheet

236	A93 800fr multi	11.00	11.00

Economic and Monetary Community of Central Africa Week (CEMAC) — A93a

Designs: 100fr, Map of Africa, flags of member nations.

1999	Litho.		Perf. 14½	
236A	A93a 100fr multi			—

An additional stamp was issued in this set. The editors would like to examine any example.

Locomotives A94

No. 237: a, Swiss. b, German. c, Japanese.

2000	Litho.		Perf. 13¾x14	
237	Horiz. strip of 3		12.00	12.00
a.-c.	A94 500fr Any single		3.00	2.50

Souvenir Sheet

238	A94 800fr AVE Train	7.25	7.25

Butterflies — A95

a, Fabriciana niobe. b, Palaeochrysophanus hippothoe. c, Inachis io. d, Apatura iris.

2000				
239	Horiz. strip of 4		16.00	16.00
a.-d.	A95 400fr Any single		3.00	1.75

UPU, 125th Anniv. (in 1999) — A96

2000	Litho.		Perf. 13¾	
240	A96 400fr multi		3.00	2.60

Mushrooms A97

EQUATORIAL GUINEA

No. 241: a, Gyroporus cyanescens. b, Terfezia arenaria. c, Battarrea stevenii. d, Amanita muscaria.

2001	Litho.		Perf. 13¾	
241	Horiz. strip of 4		12.00	12.00
a.-d.	A97 400fr Any single		2.25	1.75

Fire Trucks — A98

No. 242: a, Truck, 1915. b, Tanker, 1943. c, Ladder truck, 1966. d, Merryweather pumper, 1888.

2001				
242	Horiz. strip of 4		13.00	13.00
a.-d.	A98 400fr Any single		2.50	2.00

Soldiers — A99

No. 243: a, Infantry officer, 1700. b, Harquebusier, 1534. c, Musketeer, 17th cent. d, Fusilier, 1815.

2001	Litho.		Perf. 14x13¾	
243	Horiz. strip of 4		12.00	12.00
a.-d.	A99 400fr Any single		2.50	1.75

Prehistoric Animals — A100

No. 244: a, Carnotaurus sastrei. b, Iberomesornis romerali. c, Troodon. 800fr, Diplodocus carnegiei.

2001			Perf. 13¾x14	
244	Horiz. strip of 3		12.00	12.00
a.-c.	A100 500fr Any single		3.00	2.50

Souvenir Sheet
245	A100 800fr multi	10.00	10.00

Millennium A101

Designs: No. 246, 200fr, Intl. Conference Center. No. 247, 200fr, Offshore petroleum exploration. No. 248, 200fr, Women's Plaza, Malabo. 400fr, Statue at Intl. Conference Center, vert.

2001	Litho.		Perf. 13¾x14	
246-248	A101 Set of 3		10.50	10.50

Souvenir Sheet
Perf. 14x13¾
249	A101 400fr multi	7.75	7.75

Flora — A102

No. 250: a, Alstonia congensis. b, Harongana madagascariensis. c, Caloncoba glauca. d, Cassia occidentalis.

2002			Perf. 14x13¾	
250	Horiz. strip of 4		12.00	12.00
a.-d.	A102 400fr Any single		2.60	2.10

Automobiles A103

No. 251: a, 1924 Rochet Schneider 20,000. b, 1930 Bugatti T49. c, 1931 Ford Model A. d, 1925 Alfa Romeo RLSS.

2002			Perf. 13¾x14	
251	Vert. strip of 4		12.00	12.00
a.-d.	A103 400fr Any single		2.60	2.10

Butterflies A104

No. 252: a, Papilio menestheus canui. b, Papilio policenes. c, Papilio tyndaerus. d, Papilio zalmoxis.

2002				
252	Strip of 4		12.00	12.00
a.-d.	A104 400fr Any single		2.60	2.10

Famous Men — A105

No. 253: a, Victor Hugo (1802-85), writer. b, Santiago Ramón y Cajal (1852-1934), histologist. c, Emile Zola (1840-1902), writer.

2002				
253	Horiz. strip of 3		7.25	7.25
a.-c.	A105 400fr Any single		1.90	1.75

2002 World Cup Soccer Championships, Japan and Korea — A106

No. 254: a, Player with yellow shirt with knee on ground. b, Stadium. c, Player with yellow shirt on ground.

2002				
254	Horiz. strip of 3		11.00	11.00
a.-c.	A106 500fr Any single		3.00	2.75

Souvenir Sheet

2002 Chess Olympiad, Bled, Slovenia — A107

2002				
255	A107 800fr multi		7.50	7.50

Anniversaries and Events — A108

No. 256: a, Painting by Henri de Toulouse-Lautrec (1864-1901). b, Year of Dialogue Among Civilizations. c, Giuseppe Verdi (1813-1901), composer.

2004 ?	Litho.		Perf. 14x13¾	
256	Vert. strip of 3		8.00	8.00
a.-c.	A108 400fr Any single		2.50	2.50

Dated 2001. Stamps did not appear in philatelic market until 2004.

Anniversaries and Events — A109

No. 257: a, Tour de France bicycle race, cent. b, Painting by Vincent van Gogh (1853-90). c, Wright Brothers and Wright Flyer.

2004 ?			Perf. 13¾x14	
257	Horiz. strip of 3		10.00	10.00
a.	A109 400fr multi		2.75	2.75
b.	A109 500fr multi		3.25	3.25
c.	A109 600fr multi		4.00	4.00

Dated 2003. Stamps did not appear in philatelic market until 2004.

Minerals — A110

2004 ?				
258	Vert. strip of 4		12.00	12.00
a.	A110 400fr Realgar		2.25	2.25
b.	A110 450fr Gypsum		2.75	2.75
c.	A110 550fr Red quartz		3.25	3.25
d.	A110 600fr Chrysoberyl		3.50	3.50

Dated 2003. Stamps did not appear in philatelic market until 2004.

Lighthouses — A111

Designs: a, Marina Lighthouse, Luba, Equatorial Guinea. b, La Plata Lighthouse, Spain. c, Prodecao Lighthouse, Luba. d, Torre de Hércules, Spain.

2004 ?			Perf. 14x13¾	
259	Horiz. strip of 4		12.50	12.50
a.	A111 400fr multi		2.50	2.50
b.	A111 450fr multi		2.75	2.75
c.	A111 550fr multi		3.00	3.00
d.	A111 600fr multi		3.75	3.75

Dated 2003. Stamps did not appear in philatelic market until 2004.

Space Shuttle Columbia Accident — A112

No. 260: a, Rocket lift-off. b, Rocket on launch pad. c, Flight crew patch. 1000fr, View of earth from outer space.

2004 ?				
260	Vert. strip of 3		10.50	10.50
a.	A112 500fr multi		3.00	3.00
b.	A112 600fr multi		3.25	3.25
c.	A112 700fr multi		3.75	3.75

Souvenir Sheet
261	A112 1000fr multi	8.00	8.00

Dated 2003. Stamps did not appear in philatelic market until 2004.

Motorcycles A113

No. 262: a, 1944-47 Soriano Tigre. b, 1970 Derbi 50 Grand Prix. c, 1938 DKW 250 with sidecar. 1000fr, Harley-Davidson VRSCA V-Rod.

2004 ?			Perf. 13¾x14	
262	Horiz. strip of 3		8.50	8.50
a.	A113 450fr multi		2.00	2.00
b.	A113 500fr multi		2.50	2.50
c.	A113 550fr multi		3.00	3.00

Souvenir Sheet
263	A113 1000fr multi	7.50	7.50

Dated 2003. Stamps did not appear in philatelic market until 2004.

Souvenir Sheet

Wedding of Spanish Prince Felipe and Letizia Ortiz Rocasolano — A114

2004	Litho.		Perf. 13¾x14	
264	A114 1400fr multi		11.00	11.00

2004 Summer Olympics, Athens — A115

2004				
265	Horiz. strip of 4		10.00	10.00
a.	A115 400fr Basketball		1.90	1.90
b.	A115 450fr Track		2.25	2.25
c.	A115 550fr Tennis		2.75	2.75
d.	A115 600fr Cycling		3.00	3.00

2004 Anniversaries — A116

No. 266: a, FIFA (Fédération Internationale de Football Association), cent. b, Pablo Neruda (1904-73), poet. c, Anton Dvorak (1841-1904), composer.

2005 ?	Litho.		Perf. 14x13¾	
266	Vert. strip of 3		10.00	10.00
a.	A116 450fr multi		2.75	2.75
b.	A116 500fr multi		3.00	3.00
c.	A116 550fr multi		3.50	3.50

Dated 2004. Stamps did not appear in philatelic marketplace until 2005.

Airplanes A117

No. 267: a, Concorde. b, Airbus A340-600. c, Boeing 747-400. d, Eurofighter C-16 Typhoon.

2005 ?			Perf. 13¾x14	
267	Vert. strip of 4		11.00	11.00
a.	A117 400fr multi		2.00	2.00
b.	A117 450fr multi		2.50	2.50
c.	A117 500fr multi		2.75	2.75
d.	A117 600fr multi		3.25	3.25

Dated 2004. Stamps did not appear in philatelic marketplace until 2005.

Churches — A118

No. 268: a, Cathedral, Pisa, Italy. b, Notre-Dame-la-Grande Church, Poitiers, France. c, Speyer Cathedral, Germany. d, Cathedral, Santiago de Compostela, Spain.

2005			Perf. 14x13¾	
268	Horiz. strip of 4		12.00	12.00
a.	A118 400fr multi		2.00	2.00
b.	A118 450fr multi		2.50	2.50
c.	A118 550fr multi		3.00	3.00
d.	A118 600fr multi		3.25	3.25

EQUATORIAL GUINEA

Paintings by Salvador Dali (1904-89) — A119

Various unnamed paintings.

2005			Perf. 14x13¾	
269	Vert. strip of 3		10.00	10.00
a.	A119 500fr multi		2.50	2.50
b.	A119 600fr multi		3.00	3.00
c.	A119 700fr multi		3.50	3.50
	Souvenir Sheet			
270	A119 1000fr multi		9.00	9.00

Art and Architecture — A120

No. 271: a, Statue of African Woman, Malabo. b, Building, Bioko Sur. c, Eyi Muan Ndong, troubador.

2005	Litho.		Perf. 13¾x14	
271	Horiz. strip of 3		8.00	8.00
a.	A120 450fr multi		2.25	2.25
b.	A120 550fr multi		2.60	2.60
c.	A120 600fr multi		3.00	3.00

Trains — A121

No. 272: a, Tren Basculante. b, Tren Talgo Pendular. c, Tren Electrotrén. d, Tren T. A. F.

2005				
272	Strip of 4		11.00	11.00
a.	A121 400fr multi		2.10	2.10
b.	A121 450fr multi		2.25	2.25
c.	A121 550fr multi		3.00	3.00
d.	A121 600fr multi		3.25	3.25

Publication of Don Quixote, 400th Anniv. — A122

No. 273: a, Emblem. b, Don Quixote and Sancho Panza riding. c, Quixote catching falling Panza. d, Quixote on horse, windmill.

2005			Perf. 14x13¾	
273	Horiz. strip of 4		11.00	11.00
a.	A122 400fr multi		2.10	2.10
b.	A122 450fr multi		2.25	2.25
c.	A122 550fr multi		3.00	3.00
d.	A122 600fr multi		3.25	3.25

Famous People — A123

No. 274: a, Christopher Columbus (1451-1506), explorer. b, Federico García Lorca (1898-1936), poet. c, Wolfgang Amadeus Mozart (1756-91), composer.

2006			Perf. 13¾x14	
274	Horiz. strip of 3		11.00	11.00
a.	A123 450fr multi		3.00	3.00
b.	A123 550fr multi		3.50	3.50
c.	A123 600fr multi		3.75	3.75

Pope Benedict XVI — A124

No. 275: a, Coat of Arms. b, St. Peter's Basilica. 1000fr, Pope Benedict XVI.

2006				
275	Vert. pair		6.00	6.00
a.	A124 450fr multi		2.50	2.50
b.	A124 550fr multi		3.50	3.50
	Souvenir Sheet			
276	A124 1000fr multi		7.00	7.00

Tourism — A125

No. 277: a, Road from Boloko to Luba. b, Malabo Intl. Airport Terminal. c, Sculpture, Avenida de Juan Pablo II. d, National Parliament.

2006	Litho.		Perf. 13¾x14	
277	Strip of 4		12.00	12.00
a.	A125 400fr multi		2.40	2.40
b.	A125 450fr multi		2.60	2.60
c.	A125 550fr multi		3.25	3.25
d.	A125 600fr multi		3.50	3.50

Spain, 2006 World Basketball Champions — A126

No. 278: a, Emblem of Spanish Basketball Federation. b, Basketball and hoop. c, Players.

2006			Perf. 14x13¾	
278	Vert. strip of 3		10.00	10.00
a.	A126 450fr multi		2.50	2.50
b.	A126 550fr multi		3.25	3.25
c.	A126 600fr multi		3.50	3.50

Christmas — A127

No. 279 — Baby and: a, People and drummer. b, People. c, People and airplane.

2006			Perf. 13¾x14	
279	Horiz. strip of 3		9.00	9.00
a.	A127 450fr multi		2.25	2.25
b.	A127 550fr multi		3.00	3.00
c.	A127 600fr multi		3.25	3.25

European Economic Community, 50th Anniv. — A128

No. 280: a, Orchard, Spain. b, Mountain, France. c, Farm fields, Italy. d, Village, Germany.

2007	Litho.		Perf. 13¾x14	
280	Horiz. strip of 4		13.00	13.00
a.	A128 400fr multi		2.25	2.25
b.	A128 500fr multi		2.75	2.75
c.	A128 550fr multi		3.00	3.00
d.	A128 600fr multi		3.25	3.25

Locomotives in Madrid Train Museum — A129

No. 281: a, Steam locomotive 242F-2009. b, Diesel locomotive 1615. c, Electric locomotive 6101. d, Talgo II train. 1000fr, Steam locomotive, diff.

2007				
281	Strip of 4		13.00	13.00
a.	A129 450fr multi		2.25	2.25
b.	A129 500fr multi		2.75	2.75
c.	A129 600fr multi		3.50	3.50
d.	A129 650fr multi		3.75	3.75
	Souvenir Sheet			
282	A129 1000fr multi		5.75	5.75

Native Toys — A130

2007	Litho.		Perf. 13¾x14	
283	Horiz. strip of 4		10.00	10.00
a.	A130 400fr Airplane		2.00	2.00
b.	A130 450fr Car		2.40	2.40
c.	A130 500fr Scooter		2.60	2.60
d.	A130 550fr Songo game		3.00	3.00

Flora — A131

No. 284: a, Artocarpus communis. b, Hibiscus sabdariffa. c, Spathodea campanulata. d, Theobroma cacao.

2007	Litho.		Perf. 13¾x14	
284	Horiz. strip of 4		12.00	12.00
a.	A131 400fr multi		2.25	2.25
b.	A131 450fr multi		2.60	2.60
c.	A131 550fr multi		3.25	3.25
d.	A131 600fr multi		3.50	3.50

African Children — A132

No. 285: a, Child and basket. b, Five children and toy cars. c, Six children and net.

2008	Litho.		Perf. 13¾	
285	Horiz. strip of 3		8.50	8.50
a.	A132 400fr multi		2.50	2.50
b.	A132 450fr multi		2.75	2.75
c.	A132 500fr multi		3.00	3.00

2008 African Cup of Nations Soccer Championships, Ghana — A133

No. 286 — Emblem and: a, Soccer ball and player's foot. b, Soccer ball being caught. c, Goalie. d, Goalie, diff.

2008				
286	Horiz. strip of 4		12.00	12.00
a.	A133 400fr multi		2.50	2.50
b.	A133 450fr multi		2.75	2.75
c.	A133 500fr multi		3.00	3.00
d.	A133 600fr multi		3.50	3.50

Flora and Fauna — A134

No. 287: a, Sitatunga. b, Passiflora quadrangularis. c, Pachylobus edulis.

2008				
287	Horiz. strip of 3		8.00	8.00
a.	A134 450fr multi		2.25	2.25
b.	A134 500fr multi		2.60	2.60
c.	A134 600fr multi		3.00	3.00

Intl. Year of Planet Earth — A135

No. 288: a, Seedlings. b, Parched earth. c, Waterfall.

2008				
288	Horiz. strip of 3		7.50	7.50
a.	A135 400fr multi		2.25	2.25
b.	A135 450fr multi		2.40	2.40
c.	A135 550fr multi		2.75	2.75

Declaration of the Rights of Children, 50th Anniv. — A136

No. 289: a, Child drinking glass of milk. b, Children playing with ball. c, Children reading. d, Child coloring.

2009, Mar. 27	Litho.		Perf. 14x13¾	
289	Horiz. strip of 4		11.00	11.00
a.	A136 400fr multi		2.00	2.00
b.	A136 500fr multi		2.75	2.75
c.	A136 550fr multi		3.00	3.00
d.	A136 600fr multi		3.25	3.25

Women's Soccer — A137

No. 290: a, Cheering crowd. b, Soccer ball hitting net. c, Players battling for ball. d, Corner of field.

2009, May 14	Litho.		Perf. 13¾	
290	Vert. strip of 4		13.00	13.00
a.	A137 450fr multi		2.50	2.50
b.	A137 550fr multi		3.00	3.00
c.	A137 600fr multi		3.25	3.25
d.	A137 650fr multi		3.50	3.50

Medicinal Plants — A138

No. 291: a, Asystasia gangetica. b, Bryophyllum pinnatum. c, Solanum torvum. 1000fr, Cassia alata.

2009, Aug. 14				
291	Vert. strip of 3		10.00	10.00
a.	A138 400fr multi		2.75	2.75
b.	A138 450fr multi		3.25	3.25
c.	A138 550fr multi		3.75	3.75
	Souvenir Sheet			
292	A138 1000fr multi		7.25	7.25

Christmas — A139

No. 293 — Paintings: a, Birth of Christ, by Federico Barocci. b, Adoration of the Kings, by J. B. Maíno. c, Adoration of the Shepherds, by Maíno. d, Nativity, by Master of Sopetrán.

2009, Sept. 25				
293	Horiz. strip of 4		11.00	11.00
a.	A139 400fr multi		2.00	2.00
b.	A139 450fr multi		2.75	2.75
c.	A139 500fr multi		3.00	3.00
d.	A139 550fr multi		3.25	3.25

Paintings by Joaquin Sorolla y Bastida — A140

No. 294: a, Paseo a Orillas del Mar. b, El Balandrito. c, La Hora del Baño. d, Self-portrait.

2010, Mar. 15		Perf. 13¾x13¼	Litho.	
294	Horiz. strip of 4		14.00	14.00
a.	A140 475fr multi		2.75	2.75
b.	A140 575fr multi		3.50	3.50
c.	A140 625fr multi		3.75	3.75
d.	A140 675fr multi		4.00	4.00

EQUATORIAL GUINEA

Architecture — A141

No. 295: a, La Paz Medical Center, Bata. b, Gepetrol Building, Malabo. c, Gecotel Building, Bata. d, Central African Economic and Monetary Community Parliament Building, Malabo.

2010, June 15
295	Horiz. strip of 4	14.00	14.00
a.	A141 475fr multi	2.75	2.75
b.	A141 575fr multi	3.50	3.50
c.	A141 625fr multi	3.75	3.75
d.	A141 675fr multi	4.00	4.00

2010 World Cup Soccer Championships, South Africa — A142

No. 296: a, Emblem of 2010 tournament. b, Mascot. c, World Cup. d, Colors of Spain, World Cup champions.

2010   Litho.   Perf. 13¼x13¾
296	Horiz. strip of 4	14.00	14.00
a.	A142 475fr multi	2.75	2.75
b.	A142 575fr multi	3.50	3.50
c.	A142 625fr multi	3.75	3.75
d.	A142 675fr multi	4.00	4.00

Miniature Sheet

Christmas — A143

No. 297: a, 375fr, Adoration of the Shepherds, by Anton Rafael Mengs. b, 425fr, Adoration of the Magi, by Diego Velázquez. c, 475fr, Nativity, by Hans Memling. d, 525fr, Adoration of the Shepherds, by El Greco.

2010
| 297 | A143 | Sheet of 4, #a-d | 12.00 | 12.00 |

Intl. Women's Day, Cent. — A144

No. 298 — Stylized woman as: a, Doctor. b, Police officer. c, Chemist. d, Chef.

2011   Perf. 13¾x14
298	Horiz. strip of 4	16.00	16.00
a.	A144 525fr black	3.25	3.25
b.	A144 625fr green	3.75	3.75
c.	A144 675fr red violet	4.25	4.25
d.	A144 725fr blue	4.50	4.50

Intl. Year of Chemistry — A145

No. 299 — Emblem and: a, Chemical glassware. b, Molecular model and textbook. c, Children in school. d, Water.

2011   Perf. 14x13¾
299	Horiz. strip of 4	16.00	16.00
a.	A145 525fr multi	3.25	3.25
b.	A145 625fr multi	3.75	3.75
c.	A145 675fr multi	4.25	4.25
d.	A145 725fr multi	4.50	4.50

Gustavo Adolfo Bécquer (1836-70), Poet — A146

No. 300: a, Drawing of Woman. b, Windows of Veruela Monastery. c, Portrait of Bécquer by his brother, Valeriano.

2011
300	Horiz. strip of 3	11.00	11.00
a.	A146 525fr multi	3.00	3.00
b.	A146 625fr multi	3.75	3.75
c.	A146 675fr multi	4.00	4.00

Christmas — A147

No. 301 — Christmas-themed paintings by: a, Nicolás Francés. b, Fra Angelico. c, Luca di Tommè. d, Jaume Serra.

2011   Perf. 13¾x14
301	Horiz. strip of 4	13.00	13.00
a.	A147 525fr multi	2.60	2.60
b.	A147 625fr multi	3.00	3.00
c.	A147 675fr multi	3.25	3.25
d.	A147 725fr multi	3.50	3.50

Paintings by Juan Gris (1887-1927) — A148

Various paintings.

2012   Perf. 14x13¾
302	Horiz. strip of 4	12.00	12.00
a.	A148 525fr multi	2.40	2.40
b.	A148 625fr multi	2.75	2.75
c.	A148 675fr multi	3.00	3.00
d.	A148 725fr multi	3.25	3.25

Spices — A149

No. 303: a, Xylopia aethiopica. b, Piper guineense. c, Capsicum frutescens. d, Zingiber officinale.

2012
303	Horiz. strip of 4	12.00	12.00
a.	A149 525fr multi	2.40	2.40
b.	A149 625fr multi	2.75	2.75
c.	A149 675fr multi	3.00	3.00
d.	A149 725fr multi	3.25	3.25

Sports — A150

No. 304: a, Gymnastics. b, Table tennis. c, Running. d, Kayaking.

2012   Perf. 14x13¾
304	Horiz. strip of 4	12.00	12.00
a.	A150 525fr multi	2.40	2.40
b.	A150 625fr multi	2.75	2.75
c.	A150 675fr multi	3.00	3.00
d.	A150 725fr multi	3.25	3.25

Christmas — A151

No. 305 — Religious painting by: a, Pietro de Lignis. b, Francisco and Rodrigo de Osona. c, Pietro da Cortona. d, Hans Memling.

2012   Perf. 14x13¾
305	Horiz. strip of 4	12.00	12.00
a.	A151 525fr multi	2.40	2.40
b.	A151 625fr multi	2.75	2.75
c.	A151 675fr multi	3.00	3.00
d.	A151 725fr multi	3.25	3.25

Tourist Areas — A152

No. 306: a, Sipopo. b, Luba. c, Mbini. d, Bata.

2013   Perf. 13¾x13¼
306	Horiz. strip of 4	12.00	12.00
a.	A152 550fr multi	2.50	2.50
b.	A152 600fr multi	2.75	2.75
c.	A152 650fr multi	3.00	3.00
d.	A152 700fr multi	3.25	3.25

Intl. Red Cross, 150th Anniv. — A153

No. 307: a, Students in classroom. b, Man carrying large pot on head. c, Red Cross worker. d, Flags on building.

2013   Perf. 13¾x14
307	Horiz. strip of 4	12.00	12.00
a.	A153 550fr multi	2.50	2.50
b.	A153 600fr multi	2.75	2.75
c.	A153 650fr multi	3.00	3.00
d.	A153 700fr multi	3.25	3.25

Pope John XXIII (1881-1963) — A154

No. 307: a, Pope John XXIII. b, Pope John XXIII, diff. c, Pope John XXIII, diff. d, Arms of Pope John XXIII.

2013   Perf. 13¼x13¾
308	Horiz. strip of 4	12.00	12.00
a.	A154 550fr multi	2.60	2.60
b.	A154 600fr multi	2.75	2.75
c.	A154 650fr multi	3.00	3.00
d.	A154 700fr multi	3.50	3.50

Christmas — A155

No. 308: a, Nativity. b, Adoration of the Magi. c, Nativity, diff. d, Nativity, diff.

2013   Perf. 13¼x13¾
309	Horiz. strip of 4	12.00	12.00
a.	A155 550fr multi	2.60	2.60
b.	A155 600fr multi	2.75	2.75
c.	A155 650fr multi	3.00	3.00
d.	A155 700fr multi	3.50	3.50

Bolondo-Mbini Bridge — A156

Various views of bridge.

2014   Litho.   Perf. 13¼x13¾
310	Horiz. strip of 4	11.50	11.50
a.	A156 600fr multi	2.50	2.50
b.	A156 650fr multi	2.75	2.75
c.	A156 700fr multi	3.00	3.00
d.	A156 750fr multi	3.25	3.25

Intl. Year of Family Farms — A157

No. 311: a, Hands leveling earth. b, Woman tending cows. c, Woman tending goats. d, Farmer inspecting crops.

2014   Litho.   Perf. 13¾x13¼
311	Horiz. strip of 4	11.50	11.50
a.	A157 600fr multi	2.50	2.50
b.	A157 650fr multi	2.75	2.75
c.	A157 700fr multi	3.00	3.00
d.	A157 750fr multi	3.25	3.25

Religious Paintings by El Greco (1541-1614) — A158

No. 312: a, St. Andrew and St. Francis. b, Christ Carrying the Cross. c, St. Peter. d, The Disrobing of Christ.

2014   Litho.   Perf. 13¼x13¾
312	Horiz. strip of 4	11.50	11.50
a.	A158 600fr multi	2.50	2.50
b.	A158 650fr multi	2.75	2.75
c.	A158 700fr multi	3.00	3.00
d.	A158 750fr multi	3.25	3.25

Christmas — A159

No. 313: a, Adoration of the Shepherds, by Bartolomé Esteban Murillo. b, Adoration of the Magi, by Peter Paul Rubens. c, Adoration of the Magi, by Luis de Morales. d, Adoration of the Shepherds, by de Morales.

2014   Litho.   Perf. 13¼x13¾
313	Horiz. strip of 4	11.50	11.50
a.	A159 600fr multi	2.50	2.50
b.	A159 650fr multi	2.75	2.75
c.	A159 700fr multi	3.00	3.00
d.	A159 750fr multi	3.25	3.25

Sipopo Congress Center, Malabo — A160

No. 314: a, Seats and video screen in meeting hall (29x41mm). b, Seats in auditorium (29x41mm). c, Building exterior (29x41mm). d, Building entrance (58x41mm).

2015   Litho.   Perf. 13¼x13¾
314	Horiz. strip of 4	14.50	14.50
a.	A160 650fr multi	2.25	2.25
b.	A160 700fr multi	2.40	2.40
c.	A160 750fr multi	2.60	2.60
d.	A160 2100fr multi	7.25	7.25

Paintings of Women by Federico de Madrazo y Kuntz (1815-94) — A161

No. 315 — Various women wearing: a, Blue dress. b, White dress. c, Lilac dress. d, Black dress.

2015   Litho.   Perf. 13¾
315	Horiz. strip of 4	9.25	9.25
a.	A161 600fr multi	2.00	2.00
b.	A161 650fr multi	2.25	2.25
c.	A161 700fr multi	2.40	2.40
d.	A161 750fr multi	2.60	2.60

EQUATORIAL GUINEA — ERITREA

International Year
of Light — A162

No. 316: a, Fiber optic cord connector. b, Ends of optical fibers. c, Ends of optical fibers, diff. d, Close-up of ends of bound optical fibers.

2015	Litho.	Perf. 13¾x13¼		
316	Horiz. strip of 4		8.75	8.75
a.	A162 600fr multi		2.00	2.00
b.	A162 650fr multi		2.10	2.10
c.	A162 700fr multi		2.25	2.25
d.	A162 750fr multi		2.40	2.40

Christmas — A163

No. 317 — Various Nativity paintings by unknown artists from: a, Prado, Madrid. b, Museum of Fine Arts, Bilbao. c, Prado, diff. d, Museum of Fine Arts, diff.

2015	Litho.	Perf. 13¼x13¾		
317	Horiz. strip of 4		8.75	8.75
a.	A163 600fr multi		2.00	2.00
b.	A163 650fr multi		2.10	2.10
c.	A163 700fr multi		2.25	2.25
d.	A163 750fr multi		2.40	2.40

Paintings by
Hieronymus Bosch
(c.1450-1516) — A164

No. 318 — Details of paintings: a, Garden of Earthly Delights (left panel). b, Garden of Earthly Delights (center panel). c, The Hay Wagon (center panel). d, St. John the Baptist in the Wilderness.

2016	Litho.	Perf. 13¾		
318	Horiz. strip of 4		8.75	8.75
a.	A164 600fr multi		2.00	2.00
b.	A164 650fr multi		2.25	2.25
c.	A164 700fr multi		2.40	2.40
d.	A164 750fr multi		2.60	2.60

Miguel de
Cervantes (1547-
1616),
Writer — A165

No. 319 — Various paintings from Prado Museum, Madrid.

2016	Litho.	Perf. 13¾		
319	Horiz. strip of 4		8.75	8.75
a.	A165 600fr multi		2.00	2.00
b.	A165 650fr multi		2.25	2.25
c.	A165 700fr multi		2.40	2.40
d.	A165 750fr multi		2.60	2.60

Flora and
Fauna — A166

No. 320: a, Hibisco (hibiscus). b, Geranio de la jungla (jungle geranium). c, Pangolín arborícola (tree pangolin). d, Barbasco guineano (Vogel's tephrosia).

2016	Litho.	Perf. 13¾x14		
320	Horiz. strip of 4		8.75	8.75
a.	A166 600fr multi		1.90	1.90
b.	A166 650fr multi		2.10	2.10
c.	A166 700fr multi		2.25	2.25
d.	A166 750fr multi		2.40	2.40

Christmas — A167

Various paintings depicting the Nativity from the Prado Museum, Madrid.

2016	Litho.	Perf. 14x13¾		
321	Horiz. strip of 4		8.75	8.75
a.	A167 600fr multi		1.90	1.90
b.	A167 650fr multi		2.10	2.10
c.	A167 700fr multi		2.25	2.25
d.	A167 750fr multi		2.40	2.40

International Year
for Sustainable
Tourism for
Development
A168

No. 322: a, Bicyclist walking bicycle. b, Boat near dock. c, Cyclist on trail. d, Canoers.

2017	Litho.	Perf. 13¾		
322	Horiz. strip of 4		9.50	9.50
a.	A168 600fr multi		2.10	2.10
b.	A168 650fr multi		2.25	2.25
c.	A168 700fr multi		2.40	2.40
d.	A168 750fr multi		2.60	2.60

Paintings by Bartolomé
Esteban Murillo (1617-
82) — A169

No. 323: a, Leander and St. Bonaventure. b, Saints Justa and Rufina. c, Christ the Good Shepherd. d, Immaculate Conception.

2017	Litho.	Perf. 13¾		
323	Horiz. strip of 4		9.50	9.50
a.	A169 600fr multi		2.10	2.10
b.	A169 650fr multi		2.25	2.25
c.	A169 700fr multi		2.40	2.40
d.	A169 750fr multi		2.60	2.60

Malabo National
Park — A170

No. 324: a, Bridge. b, Sculptures. c, Island. d, Park entrance.

2017	Litho.	Perf. 13¾		
324	Horiz. strip of 4		10.00	10.00
a.	A170 600fr multi		2.25	2.25
b.	A170 650fr multi		2.40	2.40
c.	A170 700fr multi		2.60	2.60
d.	A170 750fr multi		2.75	2.75

Christmas — A171

Various unattributed Nativity paintings from the Prado Museum.

2017	Litho.	Perf. 13¾		
325	Horiz. strip of 4		10.00	10.00
a.	A171 600fr multi		2.25	2.25
b.	A171 650fr multi		2.40	2.40
c.	A171 700fr multi		2.60	2.60
d.	A171 750fr multi		2.75	2.75

Paintings by
Tintoretto (1518-
94)
A172

No. 326: a, Christ Washing the Feet of His Disciples. b, The Queen of Sheba and Solomon. c, Susanna and the Elders. d, Esther Before Ahasuerus.

2018	Litho.	Perf. 13¾		
326	Horiz. strip of 4		9.75	9.75
a.	A172 600fr multi		2.10	2.10
b.	A172 650fr multi		2.40	2.40
c.	A172 700fr multi		2.50	2.50
d.	A172 750fr multi		2.75	2.75

A173

Independence, 50th Anniv. — A174

No. 326: a, Mongomo Basilica. b, Coat of arms of Equatorial Guinea. c, Presidential Palace. d, President Teodoro Obiang Nguema Mbasogo.
1000fr, Pres. Obiang, diff.

2018	Litho.	Perf. 13¾		
327	Horiz. strip of 4		9.75	9.75
a.	A173 600fr multi		2.10	2.10
b.	A173 650fr multi		2.40	2.40
c.	A173 700fr multi		2.50	2.50
d.	A173 750fr multi		2.75	2.75

Souvenir Sheet
Perf. 13¾x13½

328	A174 1000fr multi		3.50	3.50

Items Made by
Artisans — A175

No. 329: a, Decorated gourds. b, Comb. c, Basket. d, Carved wooden shelf.

2018	Litho.	Perf. 13¾		
329	Horiz. strip of 4		9.50	9.50
a.	A175 600fr multi		2.10	2.10
b.	A175 650fr multi		2.25	2.25
c.	A175 700fr multi		2.40	2.40
d.	A175 750fr multi		2.60	2.60

Christmas — A176

Various unnamed works of religious art from the Prado, Madrid.

2018	Litho.	Perf. 13¾		
330	Horiz. strip of 4		9.50	9.50
a.	A176 600fr multi		2.10	2.10
b.	A176 650fr multi		2.25	2.25
c.	A176 700fr multi		2.40	2.40
d.	A176 750fr multi		2.60	2.60

SPECIAL DELIVERY STAMPS

Archer with
Crossbow
SD1

1971, Oct. 12	Photo.	Perf. 12½x13		
E1	SD1 4p blue & multi		.75	.25
E2	SD1 8p rose & multi		1.25	.35

3rd anniversary of independence.

ERITREA

ˌer-ə-ˈtrē-ə

LOCATION — In northeast Africa, bordering on the Red Sea, Sudan, Ethiopia and Djibouti.
GOVT. — Independent state
AREA — 45,300 (?) sq. mi.
POP. — 3,550,000 (2020 est.)
CAPITAL — Asmara

Formerly an Italian colony, Eritrea was incorporated as a State of Italian East Africa in 1936.
Under British occupation (1941-52) until it became part of Ethiopia as its northernmost region. Eritrea became independent May 24, 1993.

100 Centesimi = 1 Lira
100 cents = 1 birr (1991)
100 cents = 1 nakfa (1997)

Catalogue values for unused stamps in this country are for Never Hinged items, beginning with Scott 200 in the regular postage section.

All used values to about 1916 are for postally used stamps. From 1916-1934, used values in italics are for postally used stamps. CTO's, for stamps valued postally used, sell for about the same as unused, hinged stamps.

Watermark

Wmk. 140 — Crown

Stamps of Italy Overprinted

a   b

1892		Wmk. 140	Perf. 14		
Overprinted Type "a" in Black					
1	A6	1c bronze grn		6.00	12.00
a.		Inverted overprint		725.00	750.00
b.		Double overprint		2,150.	
		Never hinged		3,200.	
c.		vert. pair, one without overprint		4,800.	
		Never hinged		7,250.	
2	A7	2c org brn		3.75	6.00
a.		Inverted overprint		725.00	750.00
b.		Double overprint		9,150.	
		Never hinged		3,200.	
3	A33	5c green		75.00	16.00
a.		Inverted overprint		9,500.	4,275.
		Never hinged		13,500.	
Overprinted Type "b" in Black					
4	A17	10c claret		100.00	15.00
5	A17	20c orange		185.00	12.00
6	A17	25c blue		675.00	50.00
7	A25	40c brown		7.50	27.50
8	A26	45c slate grn		7.50	30.00
9	A27	60c violet		7.50	60.00
10	A28	1 l brn & yel		37.50	75.00
11	A38	5 l bl & rose		300.00	500.00
		Nos. 1-11 (11)		1,405.	803.50
		Set, never hinged		3,600.	

ERITREA

1895-99
Overprinted type "a" in Black
12	A39	1c brown ('99)	12.50	9.00
13	A40	2c org brn ('99)	3.00	1.85
14	A41	5c green	3.00	1.90
a.		Inverted overprint	500.00	4,500.

Overprinted type "b" in Black
15	A34	10c claret ('98)	3.00	1.90
16	A35	20c orange	3.00	2.50
17	A36	25c blue	3.00	3.75
18	A37	45c olive grn	24.00	22.00
		Nos. 12-18 (7)	51.50	42.90

1903-28
Overprinted type "a" in Black
19	A42	1c brown	1.25	1.10
a.		Inverted overprint	125.00	100.00
20	A43	2c orange brn	1.25	.55
21	A44	5c blue green	35.00	.50
22	A45	10c claret	40.00	.55
23	A45	20c orange	6.00	1.10
24	A45	25c blue	340.00	13.75
a.		Double overprint	1,400.	
25	A45	40c brown	375.00	22.00
26	A45	45c olive grn	6.00	7.50
27	A45	50c violet	135.00	25.00
28	A46	75c dk red & rose ('28)	85.00	6.00
29	A46	1 l brown & grn	5.00	.75
30	A46	1.25 l bl & ultra ('28)	37.50	3.00
31	A46	2 l dk grn & org ('25)	85.00	100.00
32	A46	2.50 l dk grn & org ('28)	250.00	75.00
33	A46	5 l blue & rose	24.00	35.00
		Nos. 19-33 (15)	1,426.	291.80

Surcharged in Black

1905
34	A45	15c on 20c orange	100.00	18.50
		Never hinged	250.00	

1908-28
Overprinted type "a" in Black
35	A48	5c green	.90	.85
36	A48	10c claret ('09)	.90	.85
37	A48	15c slate ('20)	17.00	11.00
38	A48	20c green ('25)	24.50	11.00
39	A49	20c lilac brn ('28)	8.50	3.00
40	A49	25c blue ('09)	5.00	2.00
41	A49	30c gray ('25)	24.00	15.00
42	A49	40c brown ('16)	75.00	30.00
43	A49	50c violet ('16)	30.00	1.60
44	A49	60c brown car ('18)	21.00	21.50
a.		Printed on both sides		2,000.
45	A49	60c brown org ('28)	135.00	240.00
46	A51	10 l gray grn & red ('16)	340.00	625.00
		Nos. 35-46 (12)	681.80	961.80

See No. 53.

A1

Government Building at Massaua — A2

1910-29 Unwmk. Engr. Perf. 13½
47	A1	15c slate	500.00	24.00
a.		Perf. 11 ('29)	50.00	55.00
		Never hinged	125.00	
48	A2	25c dark blue	12.50	13.50
a.		Perf. 12	925.00	925.00

For surcharges see Nos. 51-52.

A3 | Farmer Plowing — A4

1914-28
49	A3	5c green	2.50	2.00
a.		Perf. 11 ('28)	250.00	75.00
		Never hinged	625.00	
50	A4	10c carmine	12.00	13.50
a.		Perf. 11 ('28)	21.00	42.50
		Never hinged	52.50	
b.		Perf. 13½x14	55.00	55.00

No. 47 Surcharged in Red or Black

1916
51	A1	5c on 15c slate (R)	8.50	13.00
52	A1	20c on 15c slate	3.75	3.75
a.		"CEN" for "CENT"	27.50	30.00
b.		"CENT" omitted	160.00	160.00
c.		"ENT"	44.00	44.00

Italy No. 113 Overprinted in Black — f

1921 Wmk. 140 Perf. 14
53	A50	20c brown orange	3.75	11.00
		Never hinged	9.00	

Victory Issue
Italian Victory Stamps of 1921 Overprinted type "f" 13mm long
1922
54	A64	5c olive green	1.90	6.00
55	A64	10c red	1.90	5.50
56	A64	15c slate green	1.90	8.50
57	A64	25c ultra	1.90	8.50
		Nos. 54-57 (4)	7.60	28.50

Somalia Nos. 10-16 Overprinted In Black g

1922 Wmk. 140
58	A1	2c on 1b brn	5.00	14.75
a.		Pair, one missing "ERITREA"	2,450.	
59	A1	5c on 2b bl grn	5.00	10.25
60	A2	10c on 1a claret	5.00	2.25
61	A2	15c on 2a brn org	5.00	2.25
62	A2	25c on 2½a blue	5.00	2.25
63	A2	50c on 5a yellow	20.00	10.25
a.		"ERITREA" double		950.00
64	A2	1 l on 10a lilac	20.00	18.50
a.		"ERITREA" double	1,850.	950.00
b.		Pair, one missing "ERITREA"	3,750.	
		Nos. 58-64 (7)	65.00	60.50

See Nos. 81-87.

Propagation of the Faith Issue
Italy Nos. 143-146 Overprinted

1923
65	A68	20c ol grn & brn org	11.00	45.00
66	A68	30c claret & brn org	11.00	45.00
67	A68	50c vio & brn org	7.00	52.50
68	A68	1 l bl & brn org	7.00	82.50
		Nos. 65-68 (4)	36.00	225.00

Fascisti Issue
Italy Nos. 159-164 Overprinted in Red or Black — j

1923 Unwmk. Perf. 14
69	A69	10c dk green (R)	12.00	17.00
70	A69	30c dk violet (R)	12.00	17.00
71	A69	50c brown carmine	12.00	23.50
		Wmk. 140		
72	A70	1 l blue	12.00	42.50
73	A70	2 l brown	12.00	52.50
74	A71	5 l black & blue (R)	12.00	80.00
		Nos. 69-74 (6)	72.00	232.50

Manzoni Issue
Italy Nos. 165-170 Overprinted in Red

1924 Perf. 14
75	A72	10c brown red & blk	12.00	62.50
76	A72	15c blue grn & blk	12.00	62.50
77	A72	30c black & slate	12.00	62.50
78	A72	50c org brn & blk	12.00	62.50
79	A72	1 l blue & blk	75.00	375.00
80	A72	5 l violet & blk	375.00	2,750.
		Nos. 75-80 (6)	498.00	3,375.

On Nos. 79 and 80 the overprint is placed vertically at the left side.

Somalia Nos. 10-16 Overprinted type "g" in Blue or Red
Bars over Original Values in Black
1924
81	A1	2c on 1b brn	17.00	22.50
a.		Pair, one without "ERITREA"	2,750.	
82	A1	5c on 2b bl grn (R)	17.00	14.00
83	A2	10c on 1a rose red	8.50	12.00
84	A2	15c on 2a brn org	8.50	13.50
a.		Pair, one without "ERITREA"	2,750.	
b.		"ERITREA" inverted	1,950.	2,000.
85	A2	25c on 2½a bl (R)	8.50	8.50
a.		Double surcharge	1,475.	
86	A2	50c on 5a yellow	8.50	16.00
87	A2	1 l on 10a lil (R)	8.50	22.50
		Nos. 81-87 (7)	76.50	109.00

Stamps of Italy, 1901-08 Overprinted type "j" in Black
1924
88	A42	1c brown	8.50	8.75
a.		Inverted overprint	250.00	
b.		Vertical pair, one without ovpt.	1,850.	
89	A43	2c orange brown	6.25	7.50
b.		Vertical pair, one without ovpt.	1,850.	
90	A48	5c green	8.50	8.75
		Nos. 88-90 (3)	23.25	25.00

Victor Emmanuel Issue
Italy Nos. 175-177 Overprinted — k

1925-26 Unwmk. Perf. 11
91	A78	60c brown car	2.25	9.25
a.		Perf. 13½	12.50	37.50
92	A78	1 l dark blue	2.25	14.50
a.		Perf. 13½	24,000.	9,300.
		Never hinged	36,000.	
		Perf. 13½		
93	A78	1.25 l dk blue ('26)	4.00	32.50
a.		Perf. 11	8.00	40.00
		Nos. 91-93 (3)	8.50	56.25

Saint Francis of Assisi Issue
Italian Stamps of 1926 Overprinted

1926 Wmk. 140 Perf. 14
94	A79	20c gray green	2.40	14.00
95	A80	40c dark violet	2.40	14.00
96	A81	60c red violet	2.40	25.00

Overprinted in Red

Unwmk. Perf. 11
97	A82	1.25 l dark blue	2.40	36.00
		Perf. 14		
98	A83	5 l + 2.50 l ol grn	8.00	72.50
		Nos. 94-98 (5)	17.60	161.50

Italian Stamps of 1926 Overprinted type "f" in Black
1926 Wmk. 140 Perf. 14
99	A46	75c dk red & rose	70.00	20.00
a.		Double overprint	450.00	
100	A46	1.25 l blue & ultra	40.00	20.00
101	A46	2.50 l dk green & org	175.00	72.50
		Nos. 99-101 (3)	285.00	112.50

Volta Issue
Type of Italy, 1927, Overprinted — o

1927
102	A84	20c purple	6.50	35.00
103	A84	50c deep orange	9.50	23.50
a.		Double overprint	160.00	
104	A84	1.25 l brt blue	14.00	57.50
		Nos. 102-104 (3)	30.00	116.00

Italian Stamps of 1925-28 Overprinted type "a" in Black
1928-29
105	A86	7½c lt brown ('29)	24.00	72.50
106	A86	50c brt violet	87.50	65.00

Italian Stamps of 1927-28 Overprinted type "f"
1928-29
107	A86	50c brt violet	72.50	60.00
		Never hinged	175.00	
		Unwmk. Perf. 11		
107A	A85	1.75 l deep brown	95.00	47.50
		Never hinged	240.00	

Italy No. 192 Overprinted type "o"
1928 Wmk. 140 Perf. 14
108	A85	50c brown & slate	24.00	12.00
		Never hinged	60.00	

Monte Cassino Issue
Types of 1929 Issue of Italy Overprinted in Red or Blue

1929 Perf. 14
109	A96	20c dk green (R)	6.50	18.50
110	A96	25c red orange (Bl)	6.50	18.50
111	A98	50c + 10c crim (Bl)	6.50	23.50
112	A98	75c + 15c ol brn (R)	6.50	23.50
113	A96	1.25 l + 25c dl vio (R)	14.50	42.50
114	A98	5 l + 1 l saph (R)	14.50	47.50

Overprinted in Red

Unwmk.
115	A100	10 l + 2 l gray brn	14.50	70.00
		Nos. 109-115 (7)	69.50	244.00

ERITREA

Royal Wedding Issue
Type of Italian Stamps of 1930 Overprinted

			Wmk. 140	
1930				
116	A101	20c yellow green	2.60	7.50
117	A101	50c + 10c dp org	1.90	9.25
118	A101	1.25 l + 25c rose red	1.90	19.00
		Nos. 116-118 (3)	6.40	35.75

Lancer A5   Scene in Massaua A6

2c, 35c, Lancer. 5c, 10c, Postman. 15c, Lineman. 25c, Askari (infantryman). 2 l, Railroad viaduct. 5 l, Asmara Deghe Selam. 10 l, Camels.

1930		**Wmk. 140**	**Litho.**	**Perf. 14**
119	A5	2c brt bl & blk	4.75	20.00
120	A5	5c dk vio & blk	8.00	2.40
121	A5	10c yel brn & blk	8.00	1.25
122	A5	15c dk grn & blk	8.00	1.60
123	A5	25c gray grn & blk	8.00	1.25
124	A5	35c red brn & blk	12.50	35.00
125	A6	1 l dk brn & blk	8.00	1.25
126	A6	2 l choc & blk	12.50	35.00
127	A6	5 l ol grn & blk	24.00	52.50
128	A6	10 l dl bl & blk	32.50	100.00
		Nos. 119-128 (10)	126.25	250.25

Ferrucci Issue
Types of Italian Stamps of 1930 Overprinted type "f" in Red or Blue

1930				
129	A102	20c violet (R)	5.25	5.25
130	A103	25c dk green (R)	5.25	5.25
131	A103	50c black (R)	5.25	12.00
132	A103	1.25 l dp blue (R)	5.25	18.00
133	A104	5 l + 2 l dp car (Bl)	17.00	37.50
		Nos. 129-133 (5)	38.00	78.00

Virgil Issue
Types of Italian Stamps of 1930 Overprinted in Red or Blue

1930			**Photo.**	
134	A106	15c violet black	1.00	9.50
135	A106	20c org brn	1.00	3.75
136	A106	25c dark green	1.00	3.75
137	A106	30c lt brown	1.00	3.75
138	A106	50c dull violet	1.00	3.75
139	A106	75c rose red	1.00	7.50
140	A106	1.25 l gray blue	1.00	9.00
			Unwmk.	**Engr.**
141	A106	5 l + 1.50 l dk vio	6.75	47.50
142	A106	10 l + 2.50 l ol brn	6.75	72.50
		Nos. 134-142 (9)	20.50	161.50

Saint Anthony of Padua Issue
Types of Italian Stamps of 1931 Overprinted type "f" in Blue, Red or Black

1931			**Photo.**	**Wmk. 140**
143	A116	20c brown (Bl)	2.00	18.00
144	A116	25c green (R)	2.00	7.00
145	A118	30c gray brn (R)	2.00	7.00
146	A118	50c dl violet (Bl)	2.00	7.00
147	A120	1.25 l slate bl (R)	3.00	40.00
			Unwmk.	**Engr.**
148	A121	75c black (R)	3.00	19.00
149	A122	5 l + 2.50 l dk brn (Bk)	6.75	80.00
		Nos. 143-149 (7)	20.75	178.00

Victor Emmanuel III — A13

1931		**Photo.**	**Wmk. 140**	
150	A13	7½c olive brown	1.40	5.25
151	A13	20c slate bl & car	1.40	.25
152	A13	30c ol grn & brn vio	1.40	.25
153	A13	40c bl & yel grn	2.40	.50
154	A13	50c bis brn & ol	1.40	.25
155	A13	75c carmine rose	4.75	.35
156	A13	1.25 l vio & indigo	5.75	5.25
157	A13	2.50 l dull green	5.75	12.00
		Nos. 150-157 (8)	24.25	24.00

Camel A14   Temple Ruins A18

Designs: 2c, 10c, Camel. 5c, 15c, Shark fishery. 25c, Baobab tree. 35c, Pastoral scene. 2 l, African elephant. 5 l, Eritrean man. 10 l, Eritrean woman.

1934		**Photo.**	**Wmk. 140**	
158	A14	2c deep blue	2.40	4.75
159	A14	5c black	4.00	.40
160	A14	10c brown	4.00	.35
161	A14	15c orange brn	4.75	1.60
162	A14	25c gray green	4.00	.35
163	A14	35c purple	12.50	9.50
164	A18	1 l dk blue gray	.80	.35
165	A18	2 l olive black	35.00	3.25
166	A18	5 l carmine rose	19.00	6.50
167	A18	10 l red orange	27.50	22.50
		Nos. 158-167 (10)	113.95	49.55

Abruzzi Issue
Types of 1934 Issue Overprinted in Black or Red

1934				
168	A14	10c dull blue (R)	22.50	29.00
169	A14	15c blue	16.00	29.00
170	A14	35c green (R)	9.50	29.00
171	A18	1 l copper red	9.50	29.00
172	A14	2 l rose red	27.50	29.00
173	A18	5 l purple (R)	19.00	57.50
174	A18	10 l olive grn (R)	19.00	70.00
		Nos. 168-174 (7)	123.00	272.50

Grant's Gazelle — A22

1934			**Photo.**	
175	A22	5c ol grn & brn	5.50	22.50
176	A22	10c yel brn & blk	5.50	22.50
177	A22	20c scar & indigo	5.50	20.00
178	A22	50c dk vio & brn	5.50	20.00
179	A22	60c org brn & ind	5.50	27.50
180	A22	1.25 l dk brn & grn	5.50	47.50
		Nos. 175-180 (6)	33.00	160.00

Second Colonial Arts Exhibition, Naples. See Nos. C1-C6.

Catalogue values for unused stamps in this section, from this point to the end of the section, are for Never Hinged items.

Between 1981 and 1986 unofficial labels appeared showing such non-Eritrean subjects as the British royal weddings, Queen Mother, Queen's birthday, and the Duke & Duchess of York. These labels are not listed.

In 1978, two sets of stamps were issued for use within liberated areas of Eritrea and to publicize the liberation effort. A May 26 set of 5c, 10c, 80c and 1b commemorated the 8th anniv. of the Eritrean People's Liberation Front (EPLF). An August 1 set of 80c, 1b, 1.50b featured the Future of Eritrea theme. A September 1, 1991 set of 5c, 15c and 20c was issued with a Freedom Fighter design in orange and black almost identical to design A24. Although the 80c from the 1st 1978 issue was available at the Asmara post office in late 1992 and early 1993, there is no evidence that any of these stamps were available at the time of independence. Thus these stamps are more properly considered locals and provisionals.

A23

Designs: Freedom fighter with EPLF flags.

1991, Jan. 16		**Typo.**	**Perf. 11 rough**	
192	A23	5c lt bl, blk & org	30.00	40.00
193	A23	15c pale green, blk & org	30.00	40.00
194	A23	20c pale yel, blk & org	30.00	40.00
195	A23	3b silver, blk & org	25.00	25.00
196	A23	5b gold, blk & org	25.00	25.00

See footnotes following No. 199.

A24

1993, Feb. 1		**Litho.**	**Perf. 10**	
197	A24	5c lt bl, blk & org	25.00	25.00
198	A24	15c pale grn, blk & org	25.00	25.00
199	A24	20c pale yel, blk & org	25.00	25.00

Nos. 192-199 commemorate 30 years of the war for national liberation.

Nos. 192-199 were issued for local use, and became valid for international mail on Sept. 13, 1993.

Referendum for Independence — A25

Designs: 15c, Placing ballot in box. 60c, Group of arrows pointing right, one pointing left. 75c, Signs indicating "yes" & "no." 1b, Candle burning. 2b, Peace dove, horn over country map.

Perf. 14x15

1993, Apr. 22		**Litho.**	**Wmk. 373**	
200	A25	15c multicolored	1.50	1.50
201	A25	60c multicolored	2.75	2.75
202	A25	75c multicolored	4.00	4.00
203	A25	1b multicolored	7.50	7.50
204	A25	2b multicolored	10.00	10.00
		Nos. 200-204 (5)	25.75	25.75

Natl. Flag — A26

1993		**Litho.**	**Perf. 11 rough**	
		Blue Border		
205	A26	5c multicolored	2.50	.50
206	A26	20c multicolored		
207	A26	35c multicolored	4.25	2.00
208	A26	50c multicolored	11.00	2.50
209	A26	70c multicolored	3.50	3.50
210	A26	80c multicolored	3.50	4.00

The border of the 40c, No. 215, is similar to that of this issue but it was issued with next set. And the type face of the "0.40" matches that set.

1994		**Litho.**	**Perf. 11 rough**	
		Color of Border		
211	A26	5c brown	2.00	1.50
212	A26	15c red	2.00	1.50
213	A26	20c gold	15.00	—
214	A26	35c lt blue	2.00	1.50
215	A26	40c blue	15.00	15.00
216	A26	60c yellow	3.00	2.00
217	A26	70c purple	3.00	2.25
218	A26	3b light green	7.50	6.00
219	A26	5b silver	9.00	6.00

Flag & Map — A27

1994, Sept. 2		**Litho.**	**Perf. 13½x14**	
		Color of Border		
220	A27	5c deep yellow	.45	.40
221	A27	10c yellow green	.50	.45
222	A27	20c salmon	.70	.65
223	A27	25c red	1.25	1.25
224	A27	40c lilac rose	1.40	1.25
225	A27	60c blue green	1.50	1.25
226	A27	70c dark green	1.60	1.50
227	A27	1b yellow	1.60	1.50
228	A27	2b orange	1.75	1.50
229	A27	3b blue violet	1.90	1.75
230	A27	5b red lilac	2.25	2.00
231	A27	10b pale violet	3.75	3.50
		Nos. 220-231 (12)	18.65	17.00

See Nos. 277A-277D.

World Tourism Organization, 20th Anniv. — A29

Perf. 14x13½, 13½x14

1995, Jan. 2			**Litho.**	
232	A29	10c Fishing from boat	1.50	1.50
233	A29	35c Monument, vert.	1.50	1.50
234	A29	85c Winding road	3.00	3.00
235	A29	2b Stone dwelling, vert.	5.00	5.00
		Nos. 232-235 (4)	11.00	11.00

Fish — A30

Designs: 30c, Horned butterflyfish. 55c, Gonochaetodon larvatus. 70c, Shrimp lobster. 1b, Bluestripe snapper.

1995, Apr. 1			**Perf. 14x13½**	
236	A30	30c multicolored	.60	.60
237	A30	55c multicolored	.85	.85
238	A30	70c multicolored	1.25	1.25
239	A30	1b multicolored	1.50	1.50
		Nos. 236-239 (4)	4.20	4.20

Independence Day — A31

Designs: 25c, Breaking chains, mountain, buildings, animals. 40c, Raising natl. flag, vert. 70c, Three men, holding natl. flag, sword, vert. 3b, Natl. flag, fireworks, vert.

Perf. 14x13½, 13½x14

1995, May 23				**Litho.**
240	A31	25c multicolored	.40	.40
241	A31	40c multicolored	.45	.45
242	A31	70c multicolored	.70	.70
243	A31	3b multicolored	1.40	1.40
		Nos. 240-243 (4)	2.95	2.95

ERITREA

Future Development Plan — A32

1995, Aug. 28 Litho. Perf. 13
244	A32	60c	Building bridge	.60	.60
245	A32	80c	Trees	.75	.75
246	A32	90c	Rural village	.90	.90
247	A32	1b	Camels	1.00	1.00
			Nos. 244-247 (4)	3.25	3.25

A33

1995, Oct. 23 Perf. 13½x14
248	A33	40c	shown	.30	.30
249	A33	60c	Tree, emblem	.40	.40
250	A33	70c	Dove, "50," emblem	.50	.50
251	A33	2b	like No. 248	2.25	2.25
			Nos. 248-251 (4)	3.45	3.45

UN, 50th anniv.

A34

COMESA, Committee for Economic Growth and Development in Southern Africa: 40c, Map of African member countries. 50c, Tree with country names on branches. 60c, Emblem, 3b, Emblem surrounded by country flags, horiz.

1995, Oct. 2 Perf. 13½x14, 14x13½
252	A34	40c	multicolored	.30	.30
253	A34	50c	multicolored	.50	.50
254	A34	60c	multicolored	.60	.60
255	A34	3b	multicolored	2.25	2.25
			Nos. 252-255 (4)	3.65	3.65

FAO, 50th Anniv. — A35

5c, Food bowl with world map on it, spoon. 25c, Men with tractor. 80c, Mother bird feeding chicks. 3b, Vegetables in horn of plenty.

1995, Dec. 18 Litho. Perf. 13x14
256	A35	5c	multicolored	.40	.40
257	A35	25c	multicolored	.40	.40
258	A35	80c	multicolored	.80	.80
259	A35	3b	multicolored	2.50	2.50
			Nos. 256-259 (4)	4.10	4.10

Endangered Fauna — A36

No. 260: a, Green monkey. b, Aardwolf. c, Dugong. d, Maned rat.
Beisa oryx: No. 261: a, With young. b, One facing left. c, Two with heads together. d, One facing right.
White-eyed gull: No. 262: a, Preening. b, In flight. c, Two standing. d, One facing right.

1996, July 15 Litho. Perf. 14
| 260-262 | A36 | 3b | Set of 3 strips | 26.00 | 26.00 |

Nos. 260-262 were each issued in sheets of 12 stamps, containing three strips of four stamps, Nos. a.-d. #261 for World Wildlife Fund.

Martyrs Day — A37

1996, June 17 Litho. Perf. 13½x14
263	A37	40c	People, flag	.40	.40
264	A37	60c	At grave	.40	.40
265	A37	70c	Mother, child	.80	.80
266	A37	80c	Planting crops	1.00	1.00
			Nos. 263-266 (4)	2.60	2.60

1996 Summer Olympic Games, Atlanta — A38

No. 267, Cycling. No. 268, Basketball, vert. No. 269, Volleyball, vert. No. 270, Soccer.
No. 271, vert: a, Volleyball. b, Laurel wreath. c, Basketball. d, Torch. e, Cycling, yellow shirt. f, Torch, diff. g, Cycling, green shirt. h, Gold medal. i, Soccer.
Each 10b: No. 272, Soccer, vert. No. 273, Cycling, vert.

1996, Nov. 20 Litho. Perf. 14
| 267-270 | A38 | 3b | Set of 4 | 7.50 | 7.50 |
| 271 | A38 | 2b | Sheet of 9, #a.-i. | 11.00 | 11.00 |

Souvenir Sheets
| 272-273 | A38 | | Set of 2 | 11.00 | 11.00 |

UNICEF, 50th Anniv. — A39

UNICEF emblem and: 40c, Mother with child. 55c, Nurse helping child. 60c, Weighing baby. 95c, Boy with one leg walking with crutch.

1996, Dec. 9 Litho. Perf. 14x13½
274	A39	40c	multicolored	.45	.45
275	A39	55c	multicolored	.45	.45
276	A39	60c	multicolored	1.00	1.00
277	A39	95c	multicolored	1.00	1.00
			Nos. 274-277 (4)	2.90	2.90

Flag and Map Type of 1994 Redrawn With Islands Added on Map at Lower Right

1996, Dec. 25 Litho. Perf. 13½x14
Color of Border
277A	A27	20c	salmon	—	—
277B	A27	40c	lilac rose	—	—
277C	A27	60c	blue green	—	—
277D	A27	3b	blue violet	—	—

Revival of Eritrea Railway — A40

Designs: 40c, Repairing track. 55c, Steam train arriving at station. 60c, Train shuttle transporting people. 95c, Train tunnel.

1997, Jan. 10
278	A40	40c	multicolored	.50	.50
279	A40	55c	multicolored	.50	.50
280	A40	60c	multicolored	.50	.50
281	A40	95c	multicolored	1.50	1.50
			Nos. 278-281 (4)	3.00	3.00

National Service — A41

40c, Service members, speaker's platform, flags, vert. 55c, People looking over mountainside, vert. 60c, People digging ditches. 95c, Man standing on mountain top, overlooking valley, lake.

1996, Dec. 28 Perf. 13½x14, 14x13½
282	A41	40c	multicolored	.75	.75
283	A41	55c	multicolored	.75	.75
284	A41	60c	multicolored	1.25	1.25
285	A41	95c	multicolored	2.00	2.00
			Nos. 282-285 (4)	4.75	4.75

Butterflies and Moths — A42

1b, Pieris napi. 2b, Heliconius melpomerie. 4b, Ornithoptera goliath. 8b, Heliconius astraea.
No. 290, vert, each 3b: a, Psaphis eusehemoides. b, Papilio brookiana. c, Parnassius charitonius. d, Morpho cypris. e, Dariaus plexippus. f, Precis octavia. g, Teinopalpus imperialis. h, Samia gloreri. i, Automeris nyctimene.
No. 291, each 3b: a, Papilio polymnestar. b, Ornithoptera paradiseo. c, Graphium marcellus. d, Panaxia quadripuncataria. e, Cardui japonica. f, Papilio childrence. g, Philosamea cynthis. h, Actias luna. i, Heticopis acit.
Each 10b: No. 292, Papilio glaucus. No. 293, Parnassius phoebus.

1997, June 16 Litho. Perf. 14
| 286-289 | A42 | | Set of 4 | 12.00 | 12.00 |

Sheets of 9
| 290-291 | A42 | 3b | Set of 2 Sheets, #a.-i. | 30.00 | 30.00 |

Souvenir Sheets
| 292-293 | A42 | 10b | Set of 2 Sheets | 15.00 | 15.00 |

Environmental Protection — A43

1997, Aug. 15 Litho. Perf. 14x13½
294	A43	60c	Irrigation	.90	.90
295	A43	90c	Reforestation	.90	.90
296	A43	95c	Preventing erosion	2.00	2.00
			Nos. 294-296 (3)	3.80	3.80

Marine Life — A44

No. 297, each 3n: a, Sergeant major, white tipped reef shark. b, Hawksbill turtle, devil ray (e). c, Surgeonfish (d), Red sea houndfish, humpback whale (a, g). e, Devil ray (b, f, h). f, Devil ray (e, c), two-banded clownfish. g, Long-nosed butterflyfish. h, Red sea houndfish (g), yellow sweetlips (i). i, White moray eel.
No. 298, each 3n: a, Masked butterflyfish. b, Suckerfish (a), whale shark (a). c, Sunrise dottyback, bluefin trevally. d, Moon wrasse (a), purple moon angel (a), two-banded anemonefish. e, Lionfish (b, f). f, White tipped shark, sand diver fish. g, Golden jacks (d), lunar tailed grouper. h, Batfish (e, i). i, Black triggerfish.
Each 10n: No. 299, Powder-blue surgeonfish. No. 300, Twin-spot wrasse.

1997, Dec. 29 Litho. Perf. 14
Sheets of 9, #a.-i.
| 297-298 | A44 | | Set of 2 | 20.00 | 20.00 |

Souvenir Sheets
| 299-300 | A44 | | Set of 2 Sheets | 12.50 | 12.50 |

A45

Natl. Constitution: 10c, Speaker, crowd seated beneath tree. 40c, Dove, scales of justice. 85c, Hands holding constitution.

1997, Oct. 24 Litho. Perf. 13½x14
| 301-303 | A45 | | Set of 3 | 3.50 | 3.50 |

A46

Birds — No. 304, each 3n: a, African darter (b, d, e). b, White-headed vulture (e). c, Egyptian vulture (f). d, Yellow-billed hornbill (g). e, Helmeted guineafowl (d, f). f, Secretary bird (d, e, i). g, Martial eagle (h). h, Bateleur eagle (i). i, Red-billed queleas.
No. 305, each 3n: a, Black-headed weaver. b, Abyssinian roller (c, f). c, Abyssinian ground hornbill (b, e, f). d, Lichtenstein's sandgrouse. e, Erckel's francolin (d, g, h). f, Arabian bustard (e, i). g, Chestnut-backed finch-lark. h, Desert lark. i, Bifasciated lark.
Each 10n: #306, Peregrine falcon. #307, Hoopoe.

1998, Mar. 16 Litho. Perf. 14
Sheets of 9, #a.-i.
| 304-305 | A46 | | Set of 2 | 25.00 | 25.00 |

Souvenir Sheets
| 306-307 | A46 | | Set of 2 Sheets | 12.00 | 12.00 |

Dwellings — A47

1998, July 1 Litho. Perf. 13½x14
308	A47	50c	Highlanders	1.50	1.50
309	A47	60c	Lowlanders	1.50	1.50
310	A47	85c	Danakils (Afars)	1.50	1.50
			Nos. 308-310 (3)	4.50	4.50

Traditional Hair Styles — A48

1998, Nov. 23 Litho. Perf. 13½x14
311	A48	10c	Cunama	.30	.30
312	A48	50c	Tignnys	.60	.60
313	A48	85c	Bllen	1.00	1.00
314	A48	95c	Tigre	1.25	1.25
			Nos. 311-314 (4)	3.15	3.15

Dated 1997.

A49

Traditional Musical Instruments: 15c, Chirawata. 60c, Imbilta, malaket, shambeko. 75c, Kobero. 85c, K'rar.

1998, Dec. 28 Litho. Perf. 13½x14
315	A49	15c	multicolored	.35	.35
316	A49	60c	multicolored	.60	.60
317	A49	75c	multicolored	.80	.80
318	A49	85c	multicolored	1.00	1.00
			Nos. 315-318 (4)	2.75	2.75

A50

1999, May 25 Litho. Perf. 13¼x14
319	A50	60c	green & multi	.60	.60
320	A50	1n	red & multi	1.00	1.00
321	A50	3n	blue & multi	4.00	4.00
			Nos. 319-321 (3)	5.60	5.60

Independence, 8th Anniv.

ERITREA

1997 Introduction of Nakfa Currency — A51

Bank notes: 10c, 1 Nakfa. 60c, 5 Nakfa. 80c, 10 Nakfa. 1n, 20 Nakfa. 2n, 50 Nakfa. 3n, 100 Nakfa.

1999, Nov. 8 Litho. **Perf. 13¼**
322	A51	10c multicolored	.45	.45
323	A51	60c multicolored	.60	.60
324	A51	80c multicolored	.75	.75
325	A51	1n multicolored	1.00	1.00
326	A51	2n multicolored	2.00	2.00
327	A51	3n multicolored	3.50	3.50
		Nos. 322-327 (6)	8.30	8.30

Natl. Union of Eritrean Women, 20th Anniv. — A52

Designs: 5c, Woman and child, vert. 10c, Three women. 25c, Women and flag. 1n, Woman with binoculars.

Perf. 13¼x14, 14x13¼
1999, Nov. 26
328	A52	5c multicolored	.35	.35
329	A52	10c multicolored	.35	.35
330	A52	25c multicolored	.50	.50
331	A52	1n multicolored	.75	.75
		Nos. 328-331 (4)	1.95	1.95

A53

Marine Life — A54

No. 332, each 3n: a, Coachwhip ray. b, Sulfur damselfish. c, "Gray moray." d, Sabre squirrelfish. e, Rusty parrotfish. f, "Striped eel catfish."
No. 333, each 3n: a, Spangled emperor. b, Devil scorpionfish. c, Crown squirrelfish. d, Vanikoro sweeper. e, Sergeant major. f, Giant manta.
No. 334, each 3n: a, Chilomycterus spilostylus. b, Dascyllus marginatus. c, Balistapus undulatus. d, Pomacanthus semicirculatus. e, Rhinecanthus assasi. f, Millepora.
No. 335, each 3n: a, Epinephalus fasciata. b, Pygoplites diacanthus. c, Cephalopholis miniata. d, Centropyge eibli. e, Ostracion cubicus. f, Heniochus acuminatus.
Each 10n: No. 336, Centropyge flavissimus. No. 337, Larabicus quadrilineatus. No. 338, Anthias squamipinnis. 15n. Pomacanthus maculosus.

2000, Apr. 17 Litho. **Perf. 14**
Sheets of 6, #a.-f.
332-333	A53	Set of 2	13.50	13.50
334-335	A54	Set of 2	13.50	13.50

Souvenir Sheets
336-338	A54	Set of 3	15.00	15.00
339	A54	15n multi	6.00	6.00

Illustrations on Nos. 332c and 332f were switched.

A55

Flag and: 5c, Man with sword. 10c, Ship Denden Assab. 25c, Independence Day festivities. 60c, Soldiers and barracks. 1n, Finger, heart and map. 2n, People under tree. 3n, Ballot box. 5n, Eritrean seal, military plane, tank, ship. 7n, Seal. 10n, Ten-nakfa note.

Perf. 13¾x13¼
2000, Mar. 17 Litho.
Denominations in Sans-Serif Type
340-349	A55	Set of 10	16.00	16.00

See Nos. 363A-363F.

Worldwide Fund for Nature (WWF) — A56

Proteles cristatus: a, Laying down. b, Pair in den. c, Walking. d, Close-up.

2001, Oct. 1 Litho. **Perf. 14**
350	A56	3n Block or strip of 4, #a-d	4.50	4.50

Wild Animals A57

No. 351, 3n: a, Salt's dik-dik. b, Klipspringer. c, Greater kudu. d, Soemmering's gazelle. e, Dorcas gazelle. f, Somali wild ass.
No. 352, 3n: a, Aardvark. b, Black-backed jackal. c, Striped hyena. d, Spotted hyena. e, East African leopard. f, African elephant.

2001, Oct. 29 **Sheets of 6, #a-f**
351-352	A57	Set of 2	10.00	10.00

Struggle for Independence, 10th Anniv. — A58

Designs: 20c, Women, flag, jewelry. 60c, Doves, stylized flag, vert. 1n, Bees, honeycomb, flag, vert. 3n, Men with sticks, vert.

Perf. 13x13¼, 13¼x13
2001, May 23 Litho.
353-356	A58	Set of 4	3.00	3.00

Liberation of Nakfa, 25th Anniv. — A59

Designs: 50c, Denden. 1n, Town of Nakfa, 1977 (77x27mm). 3n, First Organizational Congress of the Eritrean People's Liberation Front (77x27mm).

2002, Mar. 23 Litho. **Perf. 14x13¼**
357-359	A59	Set of 3	2.00	2.00

Martyr's Day — A60

Designs: 1n, People and map. 2n, Hand, map of Badma area, and flag. 3n, Map and ship. 5n, Dove, map and dead man (49x29mm, triangular).

Perf. 14x13¼, 13½ (5n)
2002, June 20
360-363	A60	Set of 4	4.50	4.50

Type of 2000 Redrawn

Flag and: 30c, People under tree. 45c, Man with sword. 50c, Independence Day festivities. 60c, Soldiers and barracks. 75c, Ship Denden Assab. 3n, Ballot box.

2002, Oct. 21 Litho. **Perf. 13¼x14¼**
Denominations in Serifed Type
363A	A55	30c multi	—	—
363B	A55	45c multi	—	—
363C	A55	50c multi	—	—
363D	A55	60c multi	—	—
363E	A55	75c multi	—	—
363F	A55	3n multi	—	—

Denominations on Nos. 340-349 are in sans-serif type.

Dr. Fred C. Hollows (1929-93), Ophthalmologist — A61

Designs: 50c, Portrait. 1n, Hollows wearing ophthalmological equipment. 2n, Hollows with man.

2003, Feb. 10 **Perf. 13¼x14**
364-366	A61	Set of 3	2.00	2.00

Eritrea — People's Republic of China Diplomatic Relations, 10th Anniv. — A62

2003, May 24 **Perf. 12**
367	A62	4.50n multi	2.50	2.50

Eritrean postal authorities have declared "illegal" the following items:
Sheetlet of nine 5n stamps depicting Trains;
Sheetlets of nine 3n stamps depicting Marilyn Monroe (two different), Dogs, The Beatles "Yellow Submarine," September 11 firefighters, Brigitte Bardot, Grace Kelly, Sophia Loren, Golf etiquette, Sexy actresses, Sexy models, Boris Vallejo nudes, Dorian Cleavenger, Michael Möbius, Olivia, Ricky Carralero, Concorde;
Sheetlets of six stamps with various denominations depicting Lighthouses (with Rotary emblem) (two different), Hopper paintings (two different), Vettriano paintings (two different), Marilyn Monroe (two different), Elvgren pin-ups (two different), Teddy bears (two different);
Sheetlets of six 3n stamps depicting Van Gogh paintings, Paintings of nudes;
Sheetlets of five 3n stamps depicting Corot paintings, Pisarro paintings, Renoir paintings, Elvis Presley, Marilyn Monroe;
Sheetlets of four stamps with various denominations depicting Pandas (with Scouting emblem), Crocodiles (with Scouting emblem), Buffalos (with Rotary emblem), Elephants (with Rotary emblem), Monkeys (with Scouting emblem), Lizards (with Scouting emblem), Snakes (with Scouting Emblem), Turtles (with Rotary emblem), Wild cats (with Scouting emblem), Birds of prey (with Rotary emblem), Fowl (with Rotary emblem), Parrots (with Scouting emblem), Penguins (with Rotary emblem), Fish (with Rotary emblem), Marine life (with Scouting emblem), Mushrooms (with Rotary emblem), Butterflies (with Scouting emblem), Bees (with Scouting emblem), Spiders (with Scouting emblem);
Sheetlets of four 3n stamps depicting Dinosaurs (with Scouting emblem), Dinosaurs (with Rotary emblem) Elephants (with Scouting emblem), Elephants (with Rotary emblem), Horses (with Scouting emblem), Horses (with Rotary emblem), Birds (with Scouting emblem), Birds (with Rotary emblem), Penguins (with Scouting emblem), Penguins (with Rotary emblem), Orchids (with Scouting emblem), Orchids (with Rotary emblem), Butterflies (with Scouting emblem), Butterflies (with Rotary emblem), Cars (with Scouting emblem), Cars (with Rotary emblem), Motorcycles (with Scouting emblem), Motorcycles (with Rotary emblem), Trains (with Scouting emblem), Trains (with Rotary emblem);
Sheetlets of three 5n stamps depicting Dinosaurs (with Rotary emblem) (two different), Pandas;
Strips of three 5n stamps depicting Steam trains (four different);
Souvenir sheet with one 8n stamp depicting Steam Trains (with Rotary emblem) (two different), Dinosaurs (with Rotary emblem), Pandas (with Scouting emblem), Elephants (with Scouting emblem), Tigers (with Scouting emblem), Birds of prey (with Scouting emblem);
Souvenir sheets with one 5n stamp depicting Marilyn Monroe (six different), Lighthouses (with Rotary emblem) (four different), Teddy bears (four different), Hopper paintings (two different), Vettriano paintings (two different).

Eritrean Railway A63

436 ERITREA

Independence Celebrations A63a

Massawa A63b

2003		Litho.	Perf. 14x13¼
Denomination	Color		
368	A63	5c Prussian blue	.25 .25
369	A63	10c greenish blk	.25 .25
370	A63	15c lilac	.25 .25
371	A63	35c violet	.25 .25
372	A63	50c orange	.25 .25
373	A63	90c olive green	.25 .25
374	A63	1n red	.25 .25
375	A63	2n blue violet	.55 .55
376	A63	10n red	2.75 2.75
376A	A63a	50n white	12.00 12.00
376B	A63b	75n white	18.00 18.00
376C	A63	100n white	24.00 24.00
		Nos. 368-376C (12)	59.05 59.05

Issued: 50n, 75n, 100n, 8/29.

Liberation of Massawa, 14th Anniv. — A64

Designs: 40c, Tanks as fountains. 50c, Boat with soldiers.
No. 379: a, 3n, Crashed airplane, people, soldiers in shallow water. b, 3n, Tank, soldier, flag, boat. c, 4n, People, buildings at shore.

2004
377-378 A64 Set of 2   1.00 1.00

Miniature Sheet
379 A64 Sheet of 3, #a-c   4.00 4.00

Man and Camels — A65

Man and Cattle — A66

Highland Woman, Child and Camel — A67

2004, July 12		Litho.	Perf. 12
Frame	Color		
380	A65	20c violet blue	.25 .25
381	A65	25c red violet	.25 .25
382	A65	40c brown	.25 .25
383	A66	50c red	.25 .25
384	A66	55c green	.25 .25
385	A66	60c light blue	.25 .25
386	A67	80c olive green	.50 .50
387	A67	1n orange	.50 .50
388	A67	4.50n blue	1.25 1.25
		Nos. 380-388 (9)	3.75 3.75

A68

A69

Monuments and Statues — A70

Perf. 13¼x14, 14x13¼
2006, Jan. 5 Litho.
389 A68 1.50n multi .25 .25
390 A69 6n multi .80 .80
391 A70 25n multi 3.50 3.50
Nos. 389-391 (3) 4.55 4.55

China - Africa Cooperation Forum, Beijing — A71

2006, Nov. 3		Litho.	Perf. 12
392	A71	7n multi	.95 .95

African Soccer Confederation, 50th Anniv. — A72

Anniversary emblem and: 3n, Eritrean soccer players and flags. 5n, Soccer field. 10n, Soccer players in action.

2007, May 29	Litho.	Perf. 13x13¼
393-395 A72 Set of 3	2.40 2.40

Soldiers Carrying Flag — A73

2008, Dec. 31		Litho.	Perf. 14x13¼
Denomination	Color		
396	A73	15c dark blue	.25 .25
397	A73	35c green	.25 .25
398	A73	50c orange	.25 .25
399	A73	70c red	.25 .25
400	A73	75c blue	.25 .25
401	A73	90c brown	.25 .25
402	A73	1.50n red violet	.25 .25
403	A73	2n indigo	.25 .25
404	A73	3n org yellow	.40 .40
405	A73	5n gray	.65 .65
406	A73	10n yel green	1.25 1.25
		Nos. 396-406 (11)	4.30 4.30

Eritrean National Festival — A74

Ethnic groups in costume: 5c, Afars. 10c, Bilens. 30c, Hedarebs. 95c, Kunamas. 1n, Naras. 1.50n, Rashaidas. 4n, Sahos. 7n, Tigres. 8n, Tigrinyas.

2010, Nov. 15			
407-415	A74	Set of 9	4.25 4.25

Independence, 20th Anniv. — A75

Designs: 70c, Eritrean flag, stylized people defining border. 95c, Map of Eritrea, hand holding torch, vert. 8n, Map of Africa, flag of Eritrea, vert.

2011, Mar. 24	Perf. 14x13¼, 13¼x14
416-418 A75 Set of 3	2.00 2.00

Eritrean Martyr's Day, 20th Anniv. — A76

Designs: 80c, Eritreans and woman holding shining square. 9n, Woamn and child lighting candles.

2011, June 17	Perf. 13¾x13¼
419-420 A76 Set of 2	2.10 2.10

Eritrean Armed Struggle, 50th Anniv. — A77

Designs: 1.50n, Arm holding rifle, "50," flame, stylized people. 7n, Flame, arms holding rifles.

2011, Sept. 3	Perf. 13¼x14
421-422 A77 Set of 2	1.75 1.75

Miniature Sheet

Diplomatic Relations Between Eritrea and People's Republic of China, 20th Anniv. — A78

No. 423: a, 1n, Mosque, Nakfa, Eritrea. b, 1n, Harbor, Massawa, Eritrea. c, 1.50n, Pagoda and bridge, Yan'an, People's Republic of China. d, 1.50n, Harbor, Qingdao, People's Republic of China. e, 7n, Buildings, Asmara, Eritrea. f, 7n, Camels. g, 10n, Buildings, Datong, People's Republic of China. h, 10n, Antelopes.

2013, May 27	Litho.	Perf. 12
423 A78 Block of 8, #a-h	8.50 8.50
i. Souvenir sheet of 8, #423a-423h	8.50 8.50

Gelaalo — A79

2013, June 27		Litho.	Perf. 13x13¼
Frame	Color		
424	A79	55c orange yellow	.50 .50
425	A79	60c green	.55 .55
426	A79	70c purple	.60 .60
427	A79	80c blue	.70 .70
428	A79	90c red	.80 .80
429	A79	95c olive yellow	.85 .85
430	A79	1.50n yellow brown	1.40 1.40
431	A79	50n light blue	42.50 42.50
		Nos. 424-431 (8)	47.90 47.90

Operation Fenkil, 25th Anniv. — A80

Designs: 3n, Soldiers watching man in water. 7n, Tank in Massawa. 10n, Soldiers watching people in boats.

2015, Feb. 10	Perf. 13¼x13¾	Litho.
432-434 A80 Set of 3	4.25 4.25

A81

Liberation of Eritrea, 25th Anniv. — A82

2016		Litho.	Perf. 14x14¼
435	A81	7n multi	1.40 1.40
436	A82	8n multi	1.60 1.60

Souvenir Sheet

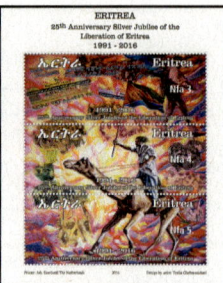

Liberation of Eritrea, 25th Anniv. — A83

No. 437: a, 3n, Eritrean flag. b, 4n, Flagbearer and camel's head. c, 5n, Body of camel.

2016		Litho.	Perf. 14x13½
437	A83	Sheet of 3, #a-c	2.75 2.75

SEMI-POSTAL STAMPS

Many issues of Italy and Italian Colonies include one or more semipostal denominations. To avoid splitting sets, these issues are generally listed as regular postage, airmail, etc., unless all values carry a surtax.

Italy Nos. B1-B3 Overprinted type "ɛ"

1915-16	Wmk. 140		Perf. 14
B1	SP1 10c + 5c rose	4.00	16.00
a.	"EPITREA"	32.50	45.00
b.	Inverted overprint	800.00	800.00
B2	SP2 15c + 5c slate	32.50	27.50
B3	SP2 20c + 5c orange	4.75	35.00
a.	"EPITREA"	80.00	110.00
b.	Inverted overprint	800.00	800.00
c.	Pair, one without ovpt.		4,500.
	Nos. B1-B3 (3)	41.25	78.50

No. B2 Surcharged

1916			
B4	SP2 20c on 15c+5c slate	32.50	35.00
	Never hinged	80.00	
a.	"EPITREA"	80.00	110.00
b.	Pair, one without overprint	2,000.	

Counterfeits exist of the minor varieties of Nos. B1, B3-B4.

Holy Year Issue
Italy Nos. B20-B25 Overprinted in Black or Red

1925			Perf. 12
B5	SP4 20c + 10c dk grn & brn	4.00	24.00
B6	SP4 30c + 15c dk brn & brn	4.00	27.50
a.	Double overprint		
B7	SP4 50c + 25c vio & brn	4.00	24.00
B8	SP4 60c + 30c dp rose & brn	4.00	32.50
a.	Inverted overprint		

ERITREA

B9	SP8	1 l + 50c dp bl & vio (R)	4.00	40.00
B10	SP8	5 l + 2.50 l org brn & vio (R)	4.00	60.00
	Nos. B5-B10 (6)		24.00	208.00

Colonial Institute Issue

"Peace" Substituting Spade for Sword — SP1

1926   **Typo.**   **Perf. 14**

B11	SP1	5c + 5c brown	1.20	9.50
B12	SP1	10c + 5c olive grn	1.20	9.50
B13	SP1	20c + 5c blue grn	1.20	9.50
B14	SP1	40c + 5c brown red	1.20	9.50
B15	SP1	60c + 5c orange	1.20	9.50
B16	SP1	1 l + 5c blue	1.20	20.00
	Nos. B11-B16 (6)		7.20	67.50

The surtax of 5c on each stamp was for the Italian Colonial Institute.

Italian Semi-Postal Stamps of 1926 Overprinted

1927   **Unwmk.**   **Perf. 11½**

B17	SP10	40c + 20c dk brn & blk	4.00	45.00
B18	SP10	60c + 30c brn red & ol brn	4.00	45.00
B19	SP10	1.25 l + 60c dp bl & blk	4.00	65.00
B20	SP10	5 l + 2.50 l dk grn & blk	6.50	100.00
	Nos. B17-B20 (4)		18.50	255.00

The surtax on these stamps was for the charitable work of the Voluntary Militia for Italian National Defense.

Fascism and Victory — SP2

1928   **Wmk. 140**   **Typo.**   **Perf. 14**

B21	SP2	20c + 5c blue grn	3.25	14.00
B22	SP2	30c + 5c red	3.25	14.00
B23	SP2	50c + 10c purple	0.25	6.00
B24	SP2	1.25 l + 20c dk blue	4.00	32.50
	Nos. B21-B24 (4)		13.75	84.50

The surtax was for the Society Africana d'Italia, whose 46th anniv. was commemorated by the issue.

Types of Italian Semi-Postal Stamps of 1928 Overprinted type "f"

1929   **Unwmk.**   **Perf. 11**

B25	SP10	30c + 10c red & blk	4.75	27.50
B26	SP10	50c + 20c vio & blk	4.75	30.00
B27	SP10	1.25 l + 50c brn & bl	7.25	52.50
B28	SP10	5 l + 2 l olive grn & blk	7.25	100.00
	Nos. B25-B28 (4)		24.00	210.00

Surtax for the charitable work of the Voluntary Militia for Italian Natl. Defense.

Types of Italian Semi-Postal Stamps of 1930 Overprinted type "f" in Black or Red

1930   **Perf. 14**

B29	SP10	30c + 10c dk grn & bl grn (Bk)	35.00	65.00
B30	SP10	50c + 10c dk grn & vio	35.00	100.00
B31	SP10	1.25 l + 30c ol brn & red brn	35.00	100.00
B32	SP10	5 l + 1.50 l ind & grn	120.00	275.00
	Nos. B29-B32 (4)		225.00	540.00

Surtax for the charitable work of the Voluntary Militia for Italian Natl. Defense.

Agriculture — SP3

1930   **Photo.**   **Wmk. 140**

B33	SP3	50c + 20c ol brn	4.00	25.00
B34	SP3	1.25 l + 20c dp bl	4.00	25.00
B35	SP3	1.75 l + 20c green	4.00	27.50
B36	SP3	2.55 l + 50c purple	9.50	45.00
B37	SP3	5 l + 1 l dp car	9.50	67.50
	Nos. B33-B37 (5)		31.00	190.00

Italian Colonial Agricultural Institute, 25th anniv. The surtax aided that institution.

AIR POST STAMPS

Desert Scene — AP1

Design: 80c, 1 l, 2 l, Plane and globe.

Wmk. Crowns (140)

1934, Oct. 17   **Photo.**   **Perf. 14**

C1	AP1	25c sl bl & org red	5.50	22.50
C2	AP1	50c grn & indigo	5.50	20.00
C3	AP1	75c brn & org red	5.50	20.00
C4	AP1	80c org brn & ol grn	5.50	22.50
C5	AP1	1 l scar & ol grn	5.50	27.50
C6	AP1	2 l dk bl & brn	5.50	47.50
	Nos. C1-C6 (6)		33.00	160.00

Second Colonial Arts Exhibition, Naples.

Plowing — AP3

Plane and Cacti — AP6

Designs: 25c, 1.50 l, Plowing. 50c, 2 l, Plane over mountain pass. 60c, 6 l, Plane and trees. 75c, 10 l, Plane and cacti. 1 l, 3 l, Bridge.

1936   **Photo.**

C7	AP3	25c deep green	4.75	4.75
C8	AP3	50c dark brown	3.25	.35
C9	AP3	60c brn org	6.50	16.00
C10	AP6	75c org brn	4.75	1.60
C11	AP3	1 l deep blue	1.60	.35
C12	AP3	1.50 l purple	6.50	.85
C13	AP3	2 l gray blue	6.50	3.25
C14	AP3	3 l copper red	25.00	27.50
C15	AP3	5 l green	19.00	8.00
C16	AP6	10 l rose red	45.00	27.50
	Nos. C7-C16 (10)		122.85	90.15
	Set, never hinged		300.00	

AIR POST SEMI-POSTAL STAMPS

King Victor Emmanuel III — SPAP1

1934   **Wmk. 140**   **Photo.**   **Perf. 14**

CB1	SPAP1	25c + 10c ol grn	9.50	27.50
CB2	SPAP1	50c + 10c brn	9.50	27.50
CB3	SPAP1	75c + 15c car	9.50	27.50
CB4	SPAP1	80c + 15c brnsh blk	9.50	27.50
CB5	SPAP1	1 l + 20c redsh brn	9.50	27.50
CB6	SPAP1	2 l + 20c bl	9.50	27.50
CB7	SPAP1	3 l + 25c vio	27.50	125.00
CB8	SPAP1	5 l + 25c org	27.50	125.00
CB9	SPAP1	10 l + 30c lil	27.50	125.00
CB10	SPAP1	25 l + 2 l grn	27.50	125.00
	Nos. CB1-CB10 (10)		167.00	665.00

65th birthday of King Victor Emmanuel III and the nonstop flight from Rome to Mogadiscio. Used values are for stamps canceled to order.

AIR POST SEMI-POSTAL OFFICIAL STAMP

Type of Air Post Semi-Postal Stamps, 1934, Overprinted in Black

1934   **Wmk. 140**   **Perf. 14**

CBO1	SPAP1	25 l + 2 l cop red		2,800.
	Never hinged			5,500.

SPECIAL DELIVERY STAMPS

Special Delivery Stamps of Italy, Overprinted type "a"

1907   **Wmk. 140**   **Perf. 14**

E1	SD1	25c rose red	24.00	20.00
	Never hinged		60.00	
a.	Double overprint			

1909

E2	SD2	30c blue & rose	145.00	240.00
	Never hinged		375.00	

1920

E3	SD1	50c dull red	4.00	24.00
	Never hinged		10.00	

"Italia" — SD1

1924   **Engr.**   **Unwmk.**

E4	SD1	60c dk red & brn	6.50	24.00
a.	Perf. 13½		14.00	40.00
E5	SD1	2 l dk blue & red	17.50	27.50
	Set, never hinged		59.00	

For surcharges see Nos. E6-E8.

Nos. E4 and E5 Surcharged in Dark Blue or Red

v

w

1926

E6	SD1	70c on 60c (Bl)	6.50	16.00
E7	SD1	2.50 l on 2 l (R)	17.50	27.50
	Set, never hinged		60.00	

Type of 1924 Surcharged in Blue or Black

1927-35   **Perf. 11**

E8	SD1	1.25 l on 60c dk red & brn (Bl)	16.00	4.00
	Never hinged		40.00	
a.	Perf. 14 (Bl) ('35)		110.00	24.00
	Never hinged		275.00	
b.	Perf. 11 (Bk) ('35)		9,500.	1,250.
	Never hinged		14,500.	
c.	Perf. 14 (Bk) ('35)		400.00	65.00
	Never hinged		1,000.	

AUTHORIZED DELIVERY STAMP

Authorized Delivery Stamp of Italy, No. EY2, Overprinted Type "f" in Black

1939-41   **Wmk. 140**   **Perf. 14**

EY1	AD2	10c dk brown ('41)	.80	
	Never hinged		2.00	
a.	10c reddish brown		27.50	47.50
	Never hinged		72.50	

On No. EY1a, which was used in Italian East Africa, the overprint hits the figures "10." On No. EY1, which was sold in Rome, the overprint falls above the 10's.

POSTAGE DUE STAMPS

Postage Due Stamps of Italy Overprinted type "a" at Top

1903   **Wmk. 140**   **Perf. 14**

J1	D3	5c buff & mag	24.00	47.50
a.	Double overprint		550.00	
J2	D3	10c buff & mag	16.00	47.50
J3	D3	20c buff & mag	16.00	32.50
J4	D3	30c buff & mag	24.00	35.00
J5	D3	40c buff & mag	80.00	72.50
J6	D3	50c buff & mag	87.50	72.50
J7	D3	60c buff & mag	24.00	72.50
J8	D3	1 l blue & mag	16.00	40.00
J9	D3	2 l blue & mag	200.00	180.00
J10	D3	5 l blue & mag	325.00	340.00
J11	D3	10 l blue & mag	3,600.	875.00
	Never hinged		7,200.	

Same with Overprint at Bottom

1920-22

J1b	D3	5c buff & magenta	4.75	16.00
c.	Numeral and ovpt. inverted		550.00	550.00
J2a	D3	10c buff & magenta	8.00	16.00
J3a	D3	20c buff & magenta	950.00	475.00
J4a	D3	30c buff & magenta	65.00	65.00
J5a	D3	40c buff & magenta	47.50	52.50
J6a	D3	50c buff & magenta	24.00	47.50
J7a	D3	60c buff & magenta	24.00	47.50
J8a	D3	1 l blue & magenta	40.00	47.50
J9a	D3	2 l blue & magenta	1,900.	1,450.
J10a	D3	5 l blue & magenta	475.00	350.00
J11a	D3	10 l blue & magenta l	47.50	100.00

1903   **Wmk. 140**

J12	D4	50 l yellow	875.00	300.00
J13	D4	100 l blue	475.00	180.00

1927

J14	D3	60c buff & brown	160.00	240.00
	Never hinged		325.00	

Postage Due Stamps of Italy, 1934, Overprinted type "j" in Black

1934

J15	D6	5c brown	.80	16.00
J16	D6	10c blue	.80	3.25
J17	D6	20c rose red	4.00	4.75
a.	Inverted overprint			
J18	D6	25c green	4.00	6.50
J19	D6	30c red orange	4.00	10.00
J20	D6	40c black brown	4.00	16.00
J21	D6	50c violet	4.00	2.40
J22	D6	60c black	8.00	24.00
J23	D7	1 l red orange	4.00	3.25
a.	Inverted overprint		550.00	
J24	D7	2 l green	16.00	47.50
J25	D7	5 l violet	28.00	55.00
J26	D7	10 l blue	32.50	65.00
J27	D7	20 l carmine rose	40.00	72.50
a.	Inverted overprint		550.00	
	Nos. J15-J27 (13)		150.10	332.15

PARCEL POST STAMPS

These stamps were used by affixing them to the way bill so that one half remained on it following the parcel, the other half staying on the receipt given the sender. Most used halves are right halves. Complete stamps were obtainable canceled, probably to order. Both unused and used values are for complete stamps.

ERITREA — ESTONIA

Parcel Post Stamps of Italy, 1914-17, Overprinted type "j" in Black on Each Half

1916 Wmk. 140 Perf. 13½

Q1	PP2	5c brown	145.00	225.00
Q2	PP2	10c deep blue	2,600.	4,250.
		Never hinged	5,250.	
Q3	PP2	25c red	290.00	350.00
Q4	PP2	50c orange	72.50	225.00
Q5	PP2	1 l violet	145.00	225.00
Q6	PP2	2 l green	110.00	225.00
Q7	PP2	3 l bister	875.00	625.00
Q8	PP2	4 l slate	875.00	625.00

Halves Used, Each

Q1	4.25
Q2	85.00
Q3	5.50
Q4	3.00
Q5	3.00
Q6	8.50
Q7	19.00
Q8	19.00

Overprinted type "f" on Each Half

1917-24

Q9	PP2	5c brown	3.25	8.00
Q10	PP2	10c deep blue	3.25	8.00
Q11	PP2	20c black	3.25	8.00
Q12	PP2	25c red	3.25	8.00
Q13	PP2	50c orange	6.50	12.00
Q14	PP2	1 l violet	6.50	12.00
Q15	PP2	2 l green	6.50	12.00
Q16	PP2	3 l bister	6.50	12.00
Q17	PP2	4 l slate	6.50	20.00
Q18	PP2	10 l rose lil ('24)	87.50	190.00
Q19	PP2	12 l red brn ('24)	240.00	375.00
Q20	PP2	15 l olive grn ('24)	240.00	375.00
Q21	PP2	20 l brn vio ('24)	325.00	525.00
	Nos. Q9-Q21 (13)	938.00	1,565.

Halves Used, Each

Q9	1.20
Q10	1.20
Q11	1.20
Q12	1.20
Q13	1.20
Q14	1.60
Q15	1.20
Q16	4.25
Q17	4.25
Q18	8.50
Q19	12.50
Q20	12.50
Q21	17.00

Parcel Post Stamps of Italy, 1927-39, Overprinted type "f" on Each Half

1927-37

Q21A	PP3	10c dp blue ('37)	8,750.	1,250.
		Never hinged	13,500.	
Q22	PP3	25c red ('37)	550.00	72.50
Q23	PP3	30c ultra ('29)	4.00	24.00
Q24	PP3	50c org ('36)	725.00	47.50
Q25	PP3	60c red ('29)	4.00	24.00
Q26	PP3	1 l brn vio ('36)	325.00	47.50
a.		1 l lilac	400.00	47.50
Q27	PP3	2 l grn ('36)	325.00	47.50
Q28	PP3	3 l bister	9.50	40.00
Q29	PP3	4 l gray	9.50	40.00
Q30	PP3	10 l rose lil ('36)	525.00	800.00
Q31	PP3	20 l lilac brn ('36)	525.00	800.00
	Nos. Q22-Q31 (10)	3,002.	
	Nos. Q21A-Q31 (11)		3,193.

Halves Used, Each

Q21A	27.50
Q22	1.20
Q23	.65
Q24	1.70
Q25	.85
Q26	1.25
Q26a	1.25
Q27	1.25
Q28	1.25
Q29	1.25
Q30	37.50
Q31	37.50

ESTONIA

e-ˈstō-nē-ə

LOCATION — Northern Europe, bordering on the Baltic Sea and the Gulf of Finland
GOVT. — Independent republic
AREA — 17,462 sq. mi.
POP. — 1,330,000 (2020 est.)
CAPITAL — Tallinn

Formerly a part of the Russia empire, Estonia declared its independence in 1918. In 1940 it was incorporated in the Union of Soviet Socialist Republics.

Estonia declared the restoration of its independence from the USSR on Aug. 20, 1991. Estonian independence was recognized by the Soviet Union on Sept. 6, 1991.

100 Kopecks = 1 Ruble (1918, 1991)
100 Penni = 1 Mark (1919)
100 Sents = 1 Kroon (1928, 1992)
100 Cents = 1 Euro (2011)

Catalogue values for unused stamps in this country are for Never Hinged items, beginning with Scott 200 in the regular postage section, Scott B60 in the semi-postal section, and Scott F1 in the registration section.

Watermark

Wmk. 207 — Arms of Finland in the Sheet

Watermark covers a large part of sheet.

A1 A2

1918-19 Unwmk. Litho. Imperf.

1	A1	5k pale red	.95	.80
2	A1	15k bright blue	.95	.80
3	A2	35p brown ('19)	.80	.80
a.		Printed on both sides	200.00	
b.		35p olive	80.00	80.00
4	A2	70p olive grn ('19)	1.60	2.00
	Nos. 1-4 (4)	4.30	4.40

Nos. 1-4 exist privately perforated.

Russian Stamps of 1909-17 Handstamped in Violet or Black

1919, May 7 Perf. 14, 14½x15, 13½

8	A14	1k orange	8,000.	8,000.
9	A14	2k green	45.00	45.00
10	A14	3k red	52.50	52.50
11	A14	5k claret	45.00	45.00
12	A15	10k dk bl (Bk)	85.00	85.00
13	A15	10k dk bl	500.00	500.00
14	A14	10k on 7k lt bl	2,400.	2,400.
15	A11	15k red brn & bl	67.50	67.50
16	A11	25k grn & vio	80.00	80.00
17	A11	35k red brn & grn	7,000.	7,000.
18	A8	50k vio & grn	190.00	190.00
19	A9	1r pale brn, brn & org	325.00	325.00
20	A13	10r scar, yel & gray	12,000.	12,000.

Imperf

21	A14	1k orange	62.50	62.50
22	A14	2k green	2,000.	2,000.
23	A14	3k red	85.00	85.00
24	A9	1r pale brn, brn & red org	475.00	475.00
25	A12	3½r mar & grn	2,000.	2,000.
26	A13	5r dk bl, grn & pale bl	2,750.	2,750.

Provisionally issued at Tallinn. This overprint has been extensively counterfeited. Values are for genuine examples competently expertized. No. 20 is always creased.

Gulls — A3

1919, May 13 Imperf.

27	A3	5p yellow	2.50	5.50

A4 A5 A6

A7 Viking Ship — A8

1919-20 Perf. 11½

28	A4	10p green	.45	.80

Imperf

29	A4	5p orange	.25	.25
30	A4	10p green	.25	.25
31	A5	15p rose	.25	.30
32	A6	35p blue	.25	.30
33	A7	70p dl vio ('20)	.25	.30
34	A8	1m bl & blk brn	4.25	1.60
a.		Gray granite paper ('20)	1.60	.80
35	A8	5m org yel & blk	6.25	4.75
a.		Gray granite paper ('20)	3.25	1.25
36	A8	15m yel grn & vio ('20)	4.00	2.40
37	A8	25m ultra & blk brn ('20)	6.50	5.50
	Nos. 28-37 (10)	22.70	16.45
	Set, never hinged	32.50	

The 5m exists with inverted center. Not a postal item.
See Nos. 76-77. For surcharges see Nos. 55, 57.

Skyline of Tallinn — A9

1920-24 Pelure Paper Imperf.

39	A9	25p green	.30	.40
40	A9	25p yellow ('24)	.30	.30
41	A9	35p rose	.40	.40
42	A9	50p green ('21)	.60	.25
43	A9	1m vermilion	1.25	.80
44	A9	2m blue	.80	.40
45	A9	2m ultramarine	1.00	1.25
46	A9	2.50m blue	1.25	.80
	Nos. 39-46 (8)	5.90	4.60
	Set, never hinged	16.50	

Nos. 39-46 with sewing machine perforation are unofficial.
For surcharge see No. 56.

Stamps of 1919-20 Surcharged

1920 Imperf.

55	A5	1m on 15p rose	.50	.50
56	A9	1m on 35p rose	.70	.80
57	A7	2m on 70p dl vio	.85	.80
	Nos. 55-57 (3)	2.05	2.10
	Set, never hinged	4.25	

Weaver Blacksmith
A10 A11

1922-23 Typo. Imperf.

58	A10	½m orange ('23)	2.75	8.00
59	A10	1m brown ('23)	4.75	11.00
60	A10	2m yellow green	4.75	8.00
61	A10	2½m claret	5.50	8.00
62	A11	5m rose	8.00	8.00
63	A11	9m red ('23)	12.00	24.00
64	A11	10m deep blue	5.50	16.00
	Nos. 58-64 (7)	43.25	83.00
	Set, never hinged	110.00	

1922-25 Perf. 14

65	A10	½m orange ('23)	1.25	.80
66	A10	1m brown ('23)	2.40	.40
67	A10	2m yellow green	2.40	.40
68	A10	2½m claret	4.75	.40
69	A10	3m blue green ('24)	2.00	.40
70	A11	5m rose	2.75	.40
71	A11	9m red ('23)	4.75	1.60
72	A11	10m deep blue	6.00	.40
73	A11	12m red ('25)	6.00	1.75
74	A11	15m plum ('25)	8.00	1.40
75	A11	20m ultra ('25)	22.00	.80
	Nos. 65-75 (11)	62.30	9.55
	Set, never hinged	130.00	

See No. 89. For surcharges see Nos. 84-88.

Viking Ship Type of 1920

1922, June 8 Perf. 14x13½

76	A8	15m yel grn & vio	20.00	.80
77	A8	25m ultra & blk brn	20.00	3.25
	Set, never hinged	80.00	

Map of Estonia — A13

1923-24 Paper with Lilac Network

78	A13	100m ol grn & bl	24.00	3.50

Paper with Buff Network

79	A13	300m brn & bl ('24)	80.00	17.50
	Set, never hinged	210.00	

For surcharges see Nos. 106-107.

National Theater, Tallinn — A14

Paper with Blue Network

1924, Dec. 9 Perf. 14x13½

81	A14	30m violet & blk	10.00	4.00

Paper with Rose Network

82	A14	70m car rose & blk	15.00	8.00
	Set, never hinged	50.00	

For surcharge see No. 105.

Vanemuine Theater, Tartu — A15

Paper with Lilac Network

1927, Oct. 25

83	A15	40m dp bl & ol brn	10.00	3.50
	Never hinged	20.00	

Stamps of 1922-25 Surcharged in New Currency in Red or Black

1928 Perf. 14

84	A10	2s yellow green	1.25	1.25
85	A11	5s rose red (B)	1.25	1.25
86	A11	10s deep blue	2.40	1.25
a.		Imperf., pair	2,000.	16,000.
87	A11	15s plum (B)	3.75	1.25
88	A11	20s ultra	3.75	1.25
	Nos. 84-88 (5)	12.40	6.25
	Set, never hinged	30.00	

10th anniversary of independence.

3rd Philatelic Exhibition Issue
Blacksmith Type of 1922-23

1928, July 6

89	A11	10m gray	3.00	6.00
	Never hinged	6.00	

Sold only at Tallinn Philatelic Exhibition. Exists imperf. Value $1,000.

Arms — A16

Paper with Network in Parenthesis

ESTONIA

1928-40   *Perf. 14, 14½x14*

90	A16	1s dk gray (bl)	.50	.25
a.		Thick gray-toned laid paper ('40)	10.00	27.50
		5 feet on lowest lion	45.00	32.50
91	A16	2s yel grn (org)	.50	.25
92	A16	4s grn (brn) ('29)	1.10	.25
93	A16	5s red (grn)	.70	.25
94	A16	8s vio (buff) ('29)	2.75	.25
95	A16	10s lt bl (lilac)	1.75	.25
96	A16	12s crimson (grn)	1.75	.25
97	A16	15s car (blue)	2.75	.25
98	A16	15s car (gray) ('35)	12.00	1.50
99	A16	20s slate bl (red)	3.75	.25
100	A16	25s red vio (org) ('29)	9.00	.25
101	A16	25s bl (brn) ('35)	10.00	1.50
102	A16	40s red org (bl) ('29)	5.75	.80
103	A16	60s gray (brn) ('29)	10.00	.80
104	A16	80s brn (bl) ('29)	12.00	1.60
		Nos. 90-104 (15)	74.30	8.70
		Set, never hinged	160.00	

Types of 1924 Issues Surcharged

1930, Sept. 1   *Perf. 14x13½*

Paper with Green Network

105	A14	1k on 70m car & blk	16.00	5.50

Paper with Rose Network

| 106 | A13 | 2k on 300m brn & bl | 32.50 | 16.00 |

Paper with Blue Network

107	A13	3k on 300m brn & bl	60.00	27.50
		Nos. 105-107 (3)	108.50	49.00
		Set, never hinged	215.00	

University Observatory A17   University of Tartu A18

Paper with Network as in Parenthesis

1932, June 1   *Perf. 14*

108	A17	5s red (yellow)	6.00	.80
109	A18	10s light bl (lilac)	4.00	.80
110	A17	12s car (blue)	10.00	4.00
111	A18	20s dk bl (green)	6.00	1.60
		Nos. 108-111 (4)	26.00	7.20
		Set, never hinged	57.50	

University of Tartu tercentenary.

Narva Falls — A19

1933, Apr. 1   *Photo.*   *Perf. 14x13½*

| 112 | A19 | 1k gray black | 6.50 | 3.00 |
| | | Never hinged | 14.00 | |

See No. 149.

Ancient Bard Playing Harp — A20

Paper with Network as in Parenthesis

1933, May 29   *Typo.*   *Perf. 14*

113	A20	2s green (orange)	1.60	.30
114	A20	5s red (green)	2.75	.30
115	A20	10s blue (lilac)	3.50	.30
		Nos. 113-115 (3)	7.85	.90
		Set, never hinged	17.00	

Tenth National Song Festival.
Nos. 113-115 exist imperf. Value $125.

Woman Harvester — A21

1935, Mar. 1   *Engr.*   *Perf. 13½*

| 116 | A21 | 3k black brown | .80 | 6.50 |
| | | Never hinged | 1.75 | |

Pres. Konstantin Päts — A22

1936-40   *Typo.*   *Perf. 14*

117	A22	1s chocolate	.80	.40
118	A22	2s yellow green	.80	.40
119	A22	3s dp org ('40)	8.00	8.00
120	A22	4s rose vio	1.60	.80
121	A22	5s lt blue grn	2.00	.40
122	A22	6s rose lake	1.60	.40
123	A22	6s dp green ('40)	40.00	55.00
124	A22	10s greenish blue	2.00	.40
125	A22	15s crim rose ('37)	2.40	.40
126	A22	15s dp bl ('40)	4.00	3.25
127	A22	18s dp car ('39)	17.50	6.25
128	A22	20s brt vio	4.00	.40
129	A22	25s dk bl ('38)	12.00	1.60
130	A22	25s bister ('38)	18.00	1.60
131	A22	30s ultra ('39)	24.00	6.25
132	A22	50s org brn	8.75	1.60
133	A22	60s brt pink	20.00	5.50
		Nos. 117-133 (17)	167.45	92.65
		Set, never hinged	340.00	

St. Brigitta Convent Entrance A23   Ruins of Convent, Pirita River A24

Front View of Convent A25   Seal of Convent A26

Paper with Network as in Parenthesis

1936, June 10   *Perf. 13½*

134	A23	5s green (buff)	.60	1.60
135	A24	10s blue (lil)	.60	1.60
136	A25	15s red (org)	1.75	4.75
137	A26	25s ultra (brn)	3.00	8.00
		Nos. 134-137 (4)	5.95	15.95
		Set, never hinged	12.00	

St. Brigitta Convent, 500th anniversary.

Harbor at Tallinn — A27

1938, Apr. 11   *Engr.*   *Perf. 14*

| 138 | A27 | 2k blue | .80 | 8.00 |
| | | Never hinged | 1.75 | |

Friedrich R. Faehlmann A28   Friedrich R. Kreutzwald A29

1938, June 15   *Typo.*   *Perf. 13½*

139	A28	5s dark green	.40	.80
140	A29	10s deep brown	.40	.80
141	A29	15s dark carmine	.80	5.50
142	A28	25s ultra	1.25	7.25
a.		Sheet of 4, #139-142	10.00	80.00
		Nos. 139-142 (4)	2.85	14.35
		Set, never hinged	8.00	

Society of Estonian Scholars centenary.

Hospital at Pärnu — A30   Beach Hotel — A31

1939, June 20   *Typo.*   *Perf. 14x13½*

144	A30	5s dark green	1.00	1.00
145	A31	10s deep red violet	.80	1.60
146	A30	18s dark carmine	1.25	5.50
147	A31	30s deep blue	1.60	7.25
a.		Sheet of 4, #144-147	16.00	87.50
		Nos. 144-147 (4)	5.25	15.95
		Set, never hinged	11.00	

Cent. of health resort and baths at Pärnu.

Narva Falls Type of 1933

1940, Apr. 15   *Engr.*

| 149 | A19 | 1k slate green | 1.40 | 12.00 |
| | | Never hinged | 2.75 | |

The sky consists of heavy horizontal lines and the background consists of horizontal and vertical lines.

Carrier Pigeon and Plane — A32

1940, July 30   *Typo.*

150	A32	3s red orange	.25	.25
151	A32	10s purple	.25	.25
152	A32	15s rose brown	.25	.25
153	A32	30s dark blue	1.60	1.25
		Nos. 150-153 (4)	2.35	2.00
		Set, never hinged	4.75	

Centenary of the first postage stamp.
The 15s exists imperf. Value $6.25.

Catalogue values for unused stamps in this section, from this point to the end of the section, are for Never Hinged items.

Natl. Arms — A40

1991, Oct. 1   *Litho.*   *Perf. 13x12½*

200	A40	5k salmon & red	.30	.30
201	A40	10k lt grn & dk bl grn	.30	.30
202	A40	15k lt bl & dk bl	.30	.30
203	A40	30k vio & gray	.35	.35
204	A40	50k org & brn	.40	.40
205	A40	70k pink & purple	.50	.50
206	A40	90k pur & rose lilac	.60	.60

Size: 20½x27mm
Engr.
Perf. 12½ Horiz.

207	A40	1r dark brown	.75	.75
208	A40	2r lt bl & dk bl	1.50	1.50
		Nos. 200-208 (9)		

See Nos. 211-213, 215, 216, 230, 299-301, 314-314A, 317, 333-334, 339-340. For surcharge, see No. 217.

A41

Perf. 13½x14, 14x13½

1991, Nov. 1   *Litho.*

| 209 | A41 | 1.50r Flag, vert. | 1.10 | 1.10 |
| 210 | A41 | 2.50r shown | 1.90 | 1.90 |

National Arms — A42

1992, Mar. 16   *Litho.*   *Perf. 13x12½*

211	A42	E (1r) lemon	.25	.25
212	A42	I (20r) blue green	.85	.85
213	A42	A (40r) blue	1.90	1.90
		Nos. 211-213 (3)	3.00	3.00

No. 211 was valid for postage within Estonia. No. 212 was valid for postage within Europe. No. 213 was valid for overseas mail. See Nos. 214, 219, 220, 224-229.

Arms Types of 1991-1992 and No. 202 Surcharged

Natl. Arms — A42a

Perf. 14, 13x12½ (#214, 217, 219-220)

1992-96

214	A42	E (10s) orange	.25	.25
215	A40	10s blue & gray	.25	.25
216	A40	50s gray & brt bl	.25	.25
a.		Perf. 13x13¼		—
217	A40	60s on 15k #202	.25	.25
218	A40	60s lilac & olive	.25	.25
219	A42	I (1k) emerald	.75	.75
220	A42	A (2k) violet blue	1.50	1.50
221	A42a	5k bis & red vio	1.25	1.25
a.		5k yel orange & red violet	2.75	2.75
222	A42a	10k turq blue & dp bl	2.50	2.50
223	A42a	20k pale lilac & slate grn	4.25	4.25
		Nos. 214-223 (10)	11.50	11.50

Coil Stamps
Engr.
Size: 20½x27mm
Perf. 12½ Horiz.

224	A42	X (10s) brown	.30	.30
225	A42	X (10s) olive	.30	.30
226	A42	X (10s) black	.30	.30
227	A42	Z (30s) red lilac	.30	.30
228	A42	Z (30s) red	.30	.30
229	A42	Z (30s) dark blue	.30	.30

Litho.

| 230 | A40 | 60s lilac brown | .30 | .30 |
| | | Nos. 224-230 (7) | 2.10 | 2.10 |

Issued: Nos. 214, 219-220, 6/22; No. 224, 8/29; No. 225, 9/25; No. 226, 10/31; No. 227, 11/16; No. 228, 12/1; No. 229, 12/22; No. 230, 1/9/93; No. 217, 0/0/00; 10s, 30s, 0/00 1000, 10k, 5/25/93; 5k, 7/7/93; No. 218, 8/6/93; 20k, 9/8/93; No. 221a, 9/19/96; No. 216a, 3/5/96. See note after No. 213. Nos. 224-229 were valid for postage within Estonia. See No. F1.

A44

ESTONIA

Birds of the Baltic shores.

1992, Oct. 3 **Litho. & Engr.** **Perf. 13**
Booklet Stamps
231	A44	1k Pandion haliaetus	.65	.65
232	A44	1k Limosa limosa	.65	.65
233	A44	1k Mergus merganser	.65	.65
234	A44	1k Tadorna todorna	.65	.65
a.		Booklet pane of 4, #231-234	2.60	2.60

See Latvia Nos. 332-335a, Lithuania Nos. 427-430a and Sweden Nos. 1975-1978a.

 A45

1992, Dec. 15 **Litho.** **Perf. 14**
| 235 | A45 | 30s gray & multi | .30 | .30 |
| 236 | A45 | 2k light brown & multi | .70 | .70 |

Christmas.
Exist on ordinary and fluorescent paper. Values are for former. Value for set on fluorescent paper, $30.

 Friendship — A46

1993, Feb. 8 **Litho.** **Perf. 14**
| 237 | A46 | 1k multicolored | .30 | .30 |
| a. | | Booklet pane of 6 | 1.80 | |

See Finland No. 906.

 First Republic, 75th Anniv. — A47

1993, Feb. 16 **Perf. 13x13½**
238	A47	60s black & multi	.25	.25
239	A47	1k violet & multi	.25	.25
240	A47	2k blue & multi	.50	.50
		Nos. 238-240 (3)	1.00	1.00

 First Baltic Sea Games — A48

60s, Wrestling. 1k +25s, Viking ship, map. 2k, Shot put with rock.

1993, June 9 **Litho.** **Perf. 13½x14**
241	A48	60s multi	.25	.25
242	A48	1k +25s multi	.30	.30
243	A48	2k multi	.45	.45
		Nos. 241-243 (3)	1.00	1.00

 Tallinn Castle — A49

Designs: 1k, Toolse Castle. No. 245, Paide Castle, vert. No. 246, Purtse Castle. No. 247, Haapsalu Castle and Cathedral. 2.70k, Narva Fortress. 2.90k, Haapsalu Cathedral. 3k, Monks' Tower, Kiiu. 3.20k, Rakvere Castle. 4k, Kuressaare Castle. 4.80k, Viljandi Castle.

1993-97 **Litho.** **Perf. 14**
244	A49	1k gray & black	.45	.45
245	A49	2k tan & brown	.45	.45
246	A49	2.50k lt vio & dk vio	.55	.55
247	A49	2.50k gray	.55	.55
248	A49	2.70k lt blue & dk blue	.55	.55
249	A49	2.90k lt grn & dk grn	.60	.60
250	A49	3k rose & brown	.60	.60
251	A49	3.20k lt grn & dk grn	.85	.85
252	A49	4k lt gray vio & gray vio	.90	.90
253	A49	4.80k dull org & brn	.95	.95
		Nos. 244-253 (10)	6.45	6.45

Issued: 1k, 2/22/94; 2k, 10/12/93; 2.70k, 12/10/93; 2.90k, 12/23/93; 3k, 3/31/94; 3.20, 12/28/94; 4k, 9/20/94; No. 246, 1/25/96; 247, 7/25/96; 4.80k, 1/21/97.

 First Estonian Postage Stamp, 75th Anniv. — A50

No. 260a

1993, Nov. 13 **Litho.** **Perf. 14**
| 259 | A50 | 1k multicolored | .40 | .40 |

Souvenir Sheet
Imperf
| 260 | A50 | 4k multicolored | 3.00 | 3.00 |
| a. | | Ovptd. in sheet margin | 11.50 | 11.50 |

No. 260 sold for 5k.

 Christmas — A51

80s, Haapsalu Cathedral. 2k, Tallinn Church.

1993, Nov. **Litho.** **Perf. 14**
| 261 | A51 | 80s red | .25 | .25 |
| 262 | A51 | 2k blue, vert. | .40 | .40 |

See Nos. 279-280.

 Lydia Koidula — A52

1993, Dec. 14 **Litho.** **Perf. 14**
| 263 | A52 | 1k multicolored | .35 | .35 |

 1994 Winter Olympics, Lillehammer — A53

1994, Jan. 26
| 264 | A53 | 1k +25s Ski jumping | .40 | .40 |
| 265 | A53 | 2k Speed skating | .50 | .50 |

 Festival Badges — A54

1k+25s, Tartu, 1869. 2k, Tallinn, 1923. 3k, Tallinn, 1969.

15k, Anniversary badge.

1994, May 31 **Litho.** **Perf. 13½x14**
266	A54	1k +25s olive & multi	.25	.25
267	A54	2k blue & brown	.45	.45
268	A54	3k brown, buff & bister	.60	.60
		Nos. 266-268 (3)	1.30	1.30

Souvenir Sheet
| 269 | A54 | 15k multicolored | 3.00 | 3.00 |

All Estonian Song Festival, 125th anniv.

 Flying Squirrel — A55

1994, June 27 **Litho.** **Perf. 13½x14**
270	A55	1k shown	.40	.40
271	A55	2k On leafy branch	.50	.50
272	A55	3k In fir tree	.85	.85
273	A55	4k With young	1.10	1.10
		Nos. 270-273 (4)	2.85	2.85

World Wildlife Fund.

 A56

Europa (Estonian Inventions): 1k, Rotating horizontal millstones, by Aleksander Mikiver. 2.70k, First mini-camera, by Walter Zapp.

1994, July 19
| 274 | A56 | 1k multicolored | .25 | .25 |
| 275 | A56 | 2.70k multicolored | .50 | .50 |

 Folk Costumes — A57

1994, Aug. 23 **Litho.** **Perf. 14**
| 276 | A57 | 1k Jamaja | .25 | .25 |
| 277 | A57 | 1k Mustjala | .25 | .25 |

See Nos. 286-287, 303-304, 325-326, 347-348, 369-370, 476-477, 497-498, 524-525.

 Estonian Art Museum, 75th Anniv. — A58

1994, Sept. 27 **Litho.** **Perf. 13½**
| 278 | A58 | 1.70k multicolored | .35 | .35 |

Christmas Type of 1993
Designs: 1.20k, Ruhnu Church, vert. 2.50k, Urvaste Church.

1994, Nov. 15 **Litho.** **Perf. 14**
| 279 | A51 | 1.20k brown | .30 | .30 |
| 280 | A51 | 2.50k green | .55 | .55 |

For surcharge see No. B63.

 Intl. Year of the Family — A59

1994, Oct. 18
| 281 | A59 | 1.70k multicolored | .40 | .40 |

 A60

Gustavus II Adolphus (1594-1632), King of Sweden.

1994, Dec. 9
| 282 | A60 | 2.50k lilac | 1.00 | 1.00 |

 Matsalu Nature Reserve — A61

1995, Jan. 26 **Litho.** **Perf. 14**
| 283 | A61 | 1.70k Branta leucopsis | .35 | .35 |
| 284 | A61 | 3.20k Anser anser | .60 | .60 |

 FAO, 50th Anniv. — A62

Farm Laborer's Family at Table, by Efraim Allsalu.

1995, Feb. 28 **Litho.** **Perf. 14**
| 285 | A62 | 2.70k multicolored | .55 | .55 |

Folk Costumes Type of 1994
1995, Mar. 30 **Litho.** **Perf. 14**
| 286 | A57 | 1.70k Muhu couple | .40 | .40 |
| 287 | A57 | 1.70k Three Muhu girls | .40 | .40 |

 A63

Via Baltica Highway Project: Nos. 288, 289a, Beach Hotel, Parnu. No. 289b, Castle, Bauska, Latvia. No. 289c, Kaunas, Lithuania.

1995, Apr. 20 **Litho.** **Perf. 14**
| 288 | A63 | 1.70k multicolored | .45 | .45 |

Souvenir Sheet
| 289 | A63 | 3.20k Sheet of 3, #a.-c. | 2.00 | 2.00 |

See Latvia Nos. 394-395, Lithuania Nos. 508-509.

 A64

1995, Apr. 20 **Litho.** **Perf. 14**
| 290 | A64 | 2.70k multicolored | .75 | .75 |

Europa. Liberation of Nazi Concentration Camps, 50th anniv.

 UN, 50th Anniv. — A65

1995, June 1 **Litho.** **Perf. 14**
| 291 | A65 | 4k multicolored | .75 | .75 |

 Pakri Lighthouse — A66

1995, July 5 **Litho.** **Perf. 14**
| 292 | A66 | 1.70k multicolored | .45 | .45 |

See Nos. 309, 318, 338, 356, 388-389, 408, 434, 452, 501-502.

ESTONIA

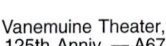

Vanemuine Theater, 125th Anniv. — A67

1995, Aug. 14   Litho.   *Perf. 14*
293   A67   1.70k multicolored   .45   .45

Louis Pasteur (1822-95) — A68

1995, Sept. 20   Litho.   *Perf. 14*
294   A68   2.70k multicolored   .60   .60

Miniature Sheet

Finno-Ugric Peoples — A69

Ethnographic object, languages: a, 2.50k, Drawing on shaman's drum, Saami. b, 3.50k, Duck-shaped brooch, Mordva, Mari. c, 4.50k, Duck-feet necklace pendant, Udmurdi, Komi. d, 2.50k, Khanty band ornament, Ungari, Mansi, Handi. e, 3.50k, Bronze amulet, Neenetsi, Eenetsi, Nganassaani, Solkupi, Kamassi. f, 4.50k, Karelian writing on birchbark, Eesti, Vadia, Soome, Liivi, Isuri, Karjala, Vespa.

1995, Oct. 17   Litho.   *Perf. 14*
295   A69   Sheet of 6, #a.-f.   4.00   4.00

Aleksander Kunileid (1845-75), Composer — A70

1995, Nov. 1   Engr.   *Perf. 12½ Horiz.*
296   A70   2k dark blue black   .45   .45

Christmas — A71

Churches: 2k, St. Martin's, Türi. 3.50k, Charles' Church of the Toompea Congregation, Tallinn.

1995, Nov. 15   Litho.   *Perf. 14*
297   A71   2k yellow orange   .55   .55
298   A71   3.50k dull carmine   .95   .95
See Nos. 315-316, 331.

Natl. Arms Type of 1991

1995, Oct. 26   Litho.   *Perf. 14*
299   A40   20s blue green & black   .25   .25
300   A40   30s gray & magenta   .25   .25
301   A40   00s lilac & blue black   .25   .25
    a.   Perf. 13   .25   .25
    Nos. 299-301 (3)   .75   .75
No. 301a issued in 1996.

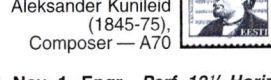

Submarine Lembit — A72

1996, Feb. 29   Litho.   *Perf. 14*
302   A72   2.50k multicolored   .65   .65
See No. 308, 328.

Folk Costume Type of 1994

1996, Mar. 26   Litho.   *Perf. 14*
303   A57   2.50k Emmaste   .65   .65
304   A57   2.50k Reigi   .65   .65

A73

1996, Apr. 25   Litho.   *Perf. 14*
305   A73   Sheet of 3, #a.-c.   2.00   2.00

Designs: a, 2.50k, First gold medal, 1896. b, 3.50k, Alfred Neuland, weight lifter, first to win gold medal for Estonia, 1920. c, 4k, Cyclist.

Modern Olympic Games, Cent. & 1996 Summer Olympics, Atlanta.

A74

Europa: Marie Under (1883-1980), poet.

1996, May 10
306   A74   2.50k multicolored   1.00   1.00

Radio, Cent. — A75

1996, June 27   Litho.   *Perf. 14*
307   A75   3.50k Guglielmo Marconi   .90   .90

Ship Type of 1996

Design: Icebreaker, Suur Tõll.

1996, Aug. 30   Litho.   *Perf. 14*
308   A72   2.50k multicolored   .65   .65

Lighthouse Type of 1995

1996, Sept. 25   Litho.   *Perf. 14*
309   A66   2.50k Vaindloo   .70   .70

Estonian Narrow Gauge Railway, Cent. — A76

Designs: 3.20k, Class Gk steam locomotive. 3.50k, DeM 1 diesel motor wagon. 4.50k, Class Sk steam locomotive.

1996, Oct. 17   Litho.   *Perf. 14*
310   A76   3.20k multicolored   .70   .70
311   A76   3.50k multicolored   .75   .75
312   A76   4.50k multicolored   .85   .85
    Nos. 310-312 (3)   2.30   2.30
See No. 307.

Christmas — A77

1996, Nov. 27   Litho.   *Perf. 14*
313   A77   2.50k multicolored   .60   .60

Natl. Arms Type of 1991

1996-97   *Perf. 14*
314   A40   3.30k lilac and claret   1.25   1.25
    Perf. 13x13¼
314A   A40   3.30k blue & lt claret   1.25   1.25
Issued: No. 314, 12/2; No. 314A, 12/10/97.

Church Type of 1995

Christmas: 3.30k, Harju-Madise Church. 4.50k, Holy Spirit Church, Tallinn.

1996, Dec. 12
315   A71   3.30k blue   .70   .70
316   A71   4.50k pink   .85   .85

Natl. Arms Type of 1991

1996, Oct. 24   Litho.   *Perf. 13½*
317   A40   2.50k grn & dark grn   1.25   1.25

Lighthouse Type of 1995

1997, Feb. 11   Litho.   *Perf. 14*
318   A66   3.30k Ruhnu   .75   .75

Tallinn Zoo A78

a, Haliaeetus pelagicus. b, Mustela lutreola. c, Aegypius monachus. d, Panthera pardus orientalis. e, Diceros bicornis. f, Capra cylindricornis.

1997, Mar. 26   Litho.   *Perf. 14*
319   A78   3.30k Sheet of 6, #a.-f.   3.50   3.50

Heinrich von Stephan (1831-97), Founder of UPU — A79

1997, Apr. 8   Litho.   *Perf. 14*
320   A79   7k black & bister   1.25   1.25

Goldspinners Fairy Tale — A80

1997, May 5   Litho.   *Perf. 14*
321   A80   4.80k multicolored   1.00   1.00
Europa.

A81

No. 323: a, like #322. b, Linijkugis, 17th cent. c, Kurenas, 16th cent.

1997, May 10
322   A81   3.30k multicolored   .70   .70
    Perf. 14x14½
323   A81   4.50k Sheet of 3, #a.-c.   5.25   5.25
Maasilinn ship, 16th cent.
See Latvia Nos. 443-444, Lithuania Nos. 571-572.

Folk Costume Type of 1994

1997, June 10   Litho.   *Perf. 14*
325   A57   3.30k Ruhnu   .55   .55
326   A57   3.30k Vormsi   .55   .55

One Kroon Coin — A82

1997, June 12   Litho.   *Perf. 14*
327   A82   50k bl grn, blk & gray   9.00   9.00
See Nos. 345, 363, 391.

Ship Type of 1996

Design: Four-masted barkentine, Tormilind.

1997, July 2
328   A72   5.50k multicolored   .90   .90

Stone Bridge, Tartu — A83

1997, Sept. 16   Litho.   *Perf. 14*
329   A83   3.30k multicolored   .65   .65

Wastne Testament, Estonian Bible Translation, 1686 — A84

1997, Oct. 14   Litho.   *Perf. 14*
330   A84   3.50k multicolored   .65   .65

Church Type of 1995

Christmas: St. Anne's, Halliste.

1997, Nov. 27   Litho.   *Perf. 14*
331   A71   3.30k brown   .65   .65

Christmas — A85

1997, Dec. 3
332   A85   2.90k Elves   .60   .60

Natl. Arms Type of 1991

1998, Jan. 19   Litho.   *Perf. 13x13½*
333   A40   3.10k lt violet & rose   .60   .60
334   A40   3.60k lt blue & ultra   .70   .70
    a.   3.60k gray & vio bl   .80   .80
Issued: No. 334a, 8/4/98.

1998 Winter Olympic Games, Nagano — A86

1998, Jan. 28   Litho.   *Perf. 14*
335   A86   3.60k multicolored   .70   .70

Republic of Estonia, 80th Anniv. A87

1998, Feb. 6   Litho.   *Imperf.*
336   A87   7k Proclamation, arms   1.40   1.40

Eduard Wiiralt (1898-1954), Print Artist — A88

Various sections of print, "Hell," showing faces: a, 3.60k, shown. b, 3.60k, Explosion coming from center figure. c, 5.50k, Cat on top of one figure's head. d, 5.50k, Faces within faces.

1998, Feb. 18   *Perf. 14*
337   A88   Sheet of 4, #a.-d.   4.00   4.00

Lighthouse Type of 1995

1998, Mar. 12   Litho.   *Perf. 14*
338   A66   3.60k Kunda   .70   .70

Natl. Arms Type of 1991

1998, Mar. 16   *Perf. 13*
339   A40   10s grn bl & dim blk   .25   .25
340   A40   4.50k pale orange & brick red   .80   .80
Issued: 10s, 3/25/97; 4.50k, 3/16/98.

442 ESTONIA

 A88a

1998, Apr. 16 Litho. *Perf. 14*
341 A88a 7k multicolored 1.30 1.30
1998 World Cup Soccer Championship, France.

St. John's Day — A89

1998, May 5 Litho. *Perf. 14*
342 A89 5.20k multi 1.25 1.25
Europa.

Use of Lübeck Charter in Tallinn, 750th Anniv. — A90

1998, June 1
343 A90 4.80k multicolored .95 .95

Beautiful Homes Year — A91

1998, June 16 Litho. *Perf. 14*
344 A91 3.60k multicolored .85 .85

One Kroon Coin Type of 1997
1998, June 18
345 A82 25k green, gray & black 4.75 4.75

 A92

1998, Aug. 4 Litho. *Perf. 14*
346 A92 5.50k multicolored 1.00 1.00
470 Class World Yachting Championships.

Folk Costume Type of 1994
1998, Aug. 21 Litho. *Perf. 14*
347 A57 3.60k Kihnu couple .65 .65
348 A57 3.60k Kihnu family .65 .65

A93

1998, Sept. 3
349 A93 3.60k yel, blue & blk .70 .70
Juhan Jaik (1899-1948), author.

Tallinn Zoo — A94
Design: Panthera tigris altaica.

1998, Sept. 17
350 A94 3.60k multicolored .70 .70
See No. 357.

Estonian Post, 80th Anniv. — A95

1998, Oct. 22 Litho. *Perf. 14*
351 A95 3.60k multicolored .75 .75

Military Aid from Finland, 90th Anniv. — A96

1998, Nov. 5 Litho. *Perf. 14*
352 A96 4.50k Freedom Cross .85 .85

Christmas — A97

1998, Nov. 26 Litho. *Perf. 14*
353 A97 3.10k Santa, child, vert. .60 .60
354 A97 5k shown .90 .90

Friedrich Robert Faehlmann, Founder of Learned Estonian Society, Birth Bicent. — A98

1998, Dec. 2
355 A98 3.60k multicolored .70 .70

Lighthouse Type of 1995
1999, Jan. 20 Litho. *Perf. 14*
356 A66 3.60k Vilsandi .70 .70

Tallinn Zoo Type of 1998
1999, Feb. 18 Litho. *Perf. 14*
357 A94 3.60k Uncia uncia .70 .70

Council of Europe, 50th Anniv. — A99

1999, Mar. 24 Litho. *Perf. 14*
358 A99 5.50k multicolored 1.00 1.00

Estonian Pres. Lennart Meri, 70th Birthday — A100

1999, Mar. 29
359 A100 3.60k multicolored .70 .70

Tolkuse Bog — A101

1999, Apr. 27 Litho. *Perf. 14*
360 A101 5.50k multicolored 1.25 1.25
Europa.

Bank of Estonia, 80th Anniv. — A102

1999, May 3 Litho. *Perf. 14*
361 A102 5k multicolored 1.00 1.00

Olustvere Manor — A103

1999, June 1
362 A103 3.60k multicolored .70 .70
See Nos. 395, 414, 433, 456, 490, 520, 551, 562, 603, 627, 648.

One Kroon Coin Type of 1997
1999, June 18 Litho. *Perf. 14*
363 A82 100k bl, bister & blk 17.00 17.00

Estonian Natl. Anthem — A104

1999, June 30 Litho. *Perf. 14*
364 A104 3.60k multicolored .70 .70
No. 364 is printed se-tenant with label.

Tower on Suur Munamägi, Highest Point in Baltic Countries — A105

1999, July 17
365 A105 5.20k multicolored 1.00 1.00

 A106

Families holding hands and: 3.60k, Estonian flag.
No. 367: a, like #366. b, Latvian flag. c, Lithuanian flag.

1999, Aug. 23 Litho. *Perf. 14*
366 A106 3.60k multicolored .70 .70

Souvenir Sheet
367 A106 5.50k Sheet of 3, #a.-c. 3.00 3.00
Baltic Chain, 10th Anniv.
See Latvia Nos. 493-494, Lithuania Nos. 639-640.

 A107

1999, Sept. 23 Litho. *Perf. 14x13¾*
368 A107 7k multicolored 1.40 1.40
UPU, 125th Anniv.

Folk Costumes Type of 1994
1999, Oct. 12 Litho. *Perf. 13¾x14*
369 A57 3.60k Setu couple .65 .65
370 A57 5k Setu man, boy .90 .90

Three Lions — A108

Perf. 13x13¼, 13¾x14 (#371, 373, 374, 378-382)
1999-2002 Litho.
371 A108 10s brn & dk brn .30 .30
372 A108 30s lt bl & dk bl .30 .30
  a. Perf. 13¾x14 .30 .30
  b. As No. 372, with two "1999" year dates — —
373 A108 30s blue & slate blue, dated 2003 .30 .30
374 A108 50s ol & dk grn .30 .30
375 A108 1k brn & fawn .30 .30
376 A108 2k gray .50 .50
377 A108 3.60k sky bl & dk bl .75 .75
  a. bright blue green ('00) .75 .75
378 A108 4.40k grn & bl grn 1.00 .80
  a. Inscribed "2001" 1.00 .80
  b. Inscribed "2002" 1.00 .80
379 A108 4.40k bl grn & brt bl grn, wide 2001 date 1.00 .30
380 A108 4.40k Prus bl & lt bl, narrow 2001 date 1.00 .30
381 A108 4.40k grn & lt grn, dated 2002 1.00 .30
382 A108 4.40k grn & apple grn, dated 2002 1.00 .30
382A A108 4.40k ol grn & apple grn, dated 2003 1.00 .35
382B A108 5k grn & lt grn, dated "2001" 1.30 1.30
  a. Inscribed "2002" 1.20 1.20
  b. Inscribed "2004" .75 .75
382C A108 6k bis & yel 1.50 1.50
382D A108 6.50k pale org & org 1.50 1.50
382E A108 8k lake & pink 1.75 1.75
Nos. 371-382E (17) 14.80 11.15

Issued: 30s, 2k, 11/4; No. 377, 10/22; No. 377a, 3/31/00; No. 378, 8/21/00; 6k, 10/12/00; 6.50k, 10/5/00; 8k, 10/19/00; No. 372a: 4/17/01; 1k, 5k, 8/28/01; 10s, 2/2/02. 50s, 1/7/03; No. 373, 3/11/03; No. 379, 4/17/01; No. 380, 9/24/01; No. 381, 2/2/02; No. 382, 11/14/02; No. 382A, 3/11/03.
The background color of No. 379 is bolder than that on No. 380. The additional year date on No. 372b is at left below the paw of the lower lion and is found on one cliché (No. 83) of the sheet.
See Nos. 467, 472-474.

Christmas — A109

1999, Nov. 25 Litho. *Perf. 14x13¾*
383 A109 3.10k multicolored .60 .60

 A110

1999, Nov. 25 *Perf. 13¾x14*
384 A110 7k multicolored 1.25 1.25
1st public Christmas tree in Tallinn, 1441.

Christmas Lottery — A110a

1999, Dec. 1 Litho. *Perf. 14x13¾*
384A A110a 3.10k + 1.90k multi 1.75 1.75

 A111

1999, Dec. 14 Litho. *Perf. 13¾x14*
385 A111 5.50k Millennium 1.10 1.10

2000 Census — A112

2000, Jan. 5
386 A112 3.60k multicolored .70 .70

ESTONIA 443

Tartu Peace Treaty, 80th Anniv. — A113

2000, Feb. 2 Litho. Perf. 14x13¾
387 A113 3.60k multi .70 .70

Lighthouse Type of 1995
2000, Feb. 25
388 A66 3.60k Ristna .65 .65
389 A66 3.60k Kopu .65 .65
  a. Pair, #388-389 1.30 1.30

Congress, 10th Anniv. — A114

2000, Mar. 9 Perf. 13¾x14
390 A114 3.60k multi .65 .65

One Kroon Coin Type of 1997
2000, Mar. 14 Perf. 14x13¾
391 A82 10k red, sil & blk 1.75 1.75

Cornflower (Natl. Flower) — A115

2000, Apr. 7
392 A115 4.80k multi .85 .85

Natl. Book Year — A116

2000, Apr. 22 Perf. 13¾x14
393 A116 3.60k multi .65 .65

First book printed in Estonian language, 475th anniv.

Europa, 2000
Common Design Type
2000, May 9
394 CD17 4.80k multi 1.25 1.25

Manor Type of 1999
2000, May 23 Litho. Perf. 14x13¾
395 A103 3.60k Palmse Hall .70 .70

Tallinn Zoo — A117

2000, June 13 Litho. Perf. 14x13¾
396 A117 3.00k Naemorhedus caudatus .70 .70

Railway Type of 1996
4.50k, Viljandi-Tallinn Railway, cent.
2000, June 30
397 A76 4.50k multi .80 .80

9th Intl. Finno-Ugric Congress — A118

2000, Aug. 1
398 A118 5k multi 1.00 1.00

2000 Summer Olympics, Sydney — A119

2000, Sept. 5 Litho. Perf. 13¾x14
399 A119 8k multi 1.50 1.50

Folk Costume Type of 1994
Designs: 4.40k, Hargla. 8k, Polva.
2000, Sept. 12
400-401 A57 Set of 2 2.25 2.25

August Mälk (1900-87), Writer — A120

2000, Sept. 20 Perf. 14x13¾
402 A120 4.40k multi .80 .80

Lake Peipus Fish — A121

No. 403: a, Osmerus eperlanus spirinchus. b, Stizostedion lucioperka.

2000, Oct. 25
403   Horiz. pair + central label 2.50 2.50
 a.-b. A121 6.50k Any single 1.10 1.10
See Russia No. 6607.

Souvenir Sheet

Estonian Bookplates, Cent. — A122

Various bookplates. Denominiations in: a, LR. b, UR.

2000, Nov. 11 Perf. 13¾x14
404 A122 6k Sheet of 2, #a-b 2.25 2.25

Christmas — A123

3.60k, Horn and bow. 6k, Ornament.

2000, Nov. 29 Perf. 14x13¾
405-406 A123 Set of 2 1.60 1.60

Erki Nool, Olympic Decathlon Champion — A124

2001, Jan. 10 Litho. Perf. 14x13¾
407 A124 4.40k multi .75 .75

Lighthouse Type of 1995
2001, Jan. 24
408 A66 4.40k Mohni .80 .80

Valentine's Day — A125

2001, Feb. 6 Litho. Perf. 13¾x14
409 A125 4.40k multi .80 .80

Stenbock House, Seat of Government — A126

2001, Feb. 20 Perf. 14x13¾
410 A126 6.50k multi 1.10 1.10

Souvenir Sheet

Paintings of Johann Köler (1826-99) — A127

No. 411: a, Girl on the Spring, 1858-62. b, Eve of the Pomegranate, 1879-80.

2001, Feb. 27
411 A127 4.40k Sheet of 2, #a-b 1.50 1.50

European Year of Languages — A128

2001, Mar. 6
412 A128 4.40k multi .85 .85

Vanellus Vanellus — A129

2001, Apr. 4 Perf. 12¾x13
413 A129 4.40k multi .85 .85

See No. 435.

Manor Type of 1999
2001, Apr. 17 Perf. 14x13¾
414 A103 4.40k Laupa Hall .80 .80

Europa — A130

2001, May 9 Perf. 13¾x14
415 A130 6.50k multi 1.30 1.30

Kalev Sports Association, Cent. — A131

2001, May 24
416 A131 6.50k multi 1.25 1.25

Pärnu, 750th Anniv. — A132

2001, June 5 Litho. Perf. 14x13¾
417 A132 4.40k multi .85 .85

Illustrations from Pokuland, by Edgar Valter — A133

Characters and — No. 418: a, Lake. b, Owl. c, Crane. d, Bird in nest.
No. 419: a, Fence. b, Flowers. c, Dog. d, Moon.

2001, June 19
418   Booklet pane of 4 2.75
 a.-d. A133 3.60k Any single .75 .75
419   Booklet pane of 4 3.75
 a.-d. A133 4.40k Any single .90 .90
  Booklet, #418-419 7.25

Entire booklet sold for 35k, 3k of which went to the Pokuland Project of the Estonian Nature Fund.

Restoration of Independence, 10th Anniv. — A134

2001, Aug. 7 Perf. 13¾x14
420 A134 4.40k multi .85 .85

Establishment of St. Mary's Land, 800th Anniv. — A135

2001, Aug. 15 Perf. 14x13¾
421 A135 6.50k multi 1.25 1.25

Resumption of Issuing Stamps, 10th Anniv. — A136

2001, Sept. 4 Perf. 13¾x14
422 A136 4.40k #200 .85 .85

Baltic Coast Landscapes — A137

Designs: 4.40k, No. 424a, Lahemaa. No. 424b, Vidzeme. No. 424c, Palanga.

2001, Sept. 15 Perf. 14x13¾
423 A137 4.40k multi .90 .90

Souvenir Sheet
Perf. 13¼x13½
424   Sheet of 3 3.50 3.50
 a.-c. A137 6k Any single 1.10 1.10

No. 424 contains three 35x29mm stamps. See Lithuania Nos.
See Latvia Nos. 534-535, Lithuania Nos. 698-699.

Tallinn Zoo — A138

2001, Oct. 4 Perf. 14x13¾
425 A138 4.40k Alligator sinensis .90 .90

ESTONIA

Estonia 26/9 Racing Car — A139

2001, Oct. 23
426 A139 6k multi   1.15 1.15

Folk Costume Type of 1994
Designs: 4.40k, Paistu woman. 7.50k, Tarvastu man.

2001, Nov. 7   Litho.   *Perf. 13¾x14*
427-428 A57 Set of 2   2.25 2.25

A140

Christmas — A141

Perf. 13¾x14, 14x13¾
2001, Nov. 22
429 A140 3.60k multi   .70 .70
430 A141 6.50k multi   1.40 1.40

Radio Broadcasting in Estonia, 75th Anniv. — A142

2001, Dec. 4   *Perf. 14x13¾*
431 A142 4.40k multi   .90 .90

2002 Winter Olympics, Salt Lake City — A143

2002, Jan. 10   Litho.   *Perf. 14x13¾*
432 A143 8k multi   1.40 1.40

Manor Type of 1999
2002, Jan. 22
433 A103 4.40k Sangaste Hall   .80 .80

Lighthouse Type of 1995
2002, Feb. 20
434 A66 4.40k Laidunina   .80 .80

Bird Type of 2001
Design: Passer domesticus and Passer montanus.

2002, Mar. 7   *Perf. 12¾x13*
435 A129 4.40k multi   .80 .80

Spring Flowers — A144

2002, Mar. 20   *Perf. 14x13¾*
436 A144 4.40k multi   .80 .80

Estonian Puppet Theater, 50th Anniv. A145

2002, Mar. 27   *Perf. 13¾x14*
437 A145 4.40k multi + label   .80 .80

PTO-4 Training Airplane — A146

2002, Apr. 10   *Perf. 14x13¾*
438 A146 6k multi   1.10 1.10

Andrus Veerpalu, Gold Medalist at 2002 Winter Olympics — A147

2002, Apr. 12
439 A147 4.40k multi   .80 .80

Tartu University Anniversaries — A148

No. 440: a, Main building, 1806-09, founding act of 1632. b, University Library, 1982, text from Biblia Latina.

2002, Apr. 24
440 A148 4.40k Horiz. pair, #a-b, + central label   2.25 2.25

Europa — A149

2002, May 9   *Perf. 12¾x13*
441 A149 6.50k multi   1.60 1.60

Re-adoption of Constitution, 10th Anniv. — A150

2002, May 23   *Perf. 13¾x14*
442 A150 4.40k multi   .80 .80

Adoption of Lübeck Charter by Town of Rakvere, 700th Anniv. — A151

2002, June 5
443 A151 4.40k multi   .80 .80

Souvenir Sheet

Re-introduction of the Kroon, 10th Anniv. — A152

No. 444 — Portraits from bank notes: a, Lydia Koidula, poet. b, Carl Rober Jakobson, journalist.

2002, June 10   *Perf. 14x13¾*
444 A152 4.40k Sheet of 2, #a-b   2.00 2.00

Souvenir Sheet

Adamson-Eric (1902-68), Painter — A153

Denomination at: a, LL. b, LR. c, UL. d, UR.

2002, Aug. 8   Litho.   *Perf. 14x13¾*
445 A153 4.40k Sheet of 4, #a-d   3.00 3.00

Sus Scrofa — A154

2002, Aug. 21   *Perf. 12¾x13*
446 A154 4.40k multi   .80 .80

Limestone, Estonia's National Stone — A155

2002, Sept. 18
447 A155 4.40k multi   .80 .80

Folk Costume Type of 1994
Designs: 4.40k, Kolga-Jaani women. 5.50k, Suure-Jaani boy and girl.

2002, Oct. 1   *Perf. 13¾x14*
448-449 A57 Set of 2   1.60 1.60

A156

Christmas — A157

Perf. 14x13¾, 13¾x14
2002, Nov. 20   Litho.
450 A156 3.60k Reindeer   .60 .60
451 A157 6.50k Christmas tree   1.15 1.15

Lighthouse Type of 1995
2003, Jan. 15   *Perf. 14x13¾*
452 A66 4.40k Keri   .80 .80

Anton Hansen Tammsaare (1878-1940), Novelist — A158

2003, Jan. 30   Litho.   *Perf. 14x13¾*
453 A158 4.40k multi   .80 .80

Pica Pica — A159

2003, Feb. 13   *Perf. 12¾x13*
454 A159 4.40k multi   .80 .80

See Nos. 485, 509, 540, 566, 595, 625.

Spring Flowers A160

No. 455: a, Tulips. b, Helleborus purpurascens. c, Narcissus poeticus. d, Crocus vernus.

2003, Mar. 20   *Perf. 13¾x14*
455 A160 4.40k Sheet of 4, #a-d   7.00 7.00
   e. Booklet pane, like #455, without date in margin   3.25 —
   Complete booklet, #455e   3.25

See No. 484.

Manor Type of 1999
2003, Apr. 9   *Perf. 14x13¾*
456 A103 4.40k Alatskivi Hall   .80 .80

Pres. Arnold Rüütel, 75th Birthday — A161

2003, Apr. 24
457 A161 4.40k multi + label   .90 .90

Europa — A162

2003, May 8   *Perf. 13¾x14*
458 A162 6.50k multi   1.60 1.60

Tartu University Botanical Gardens, Bicent. — A163

2003, June 11   Litho.   *Perf. 14x13¾*
459 A163 4.40k multi   .90 .90

14th Junior World Orienteering Championships A164

2003, June 27
460 A164 7.50k multi   1.25 1.25

Circumnavigation of Adam Johann von Krusenstern (1770-1846) — A165

2003, Aug. 6   *Perf. 12½*
461 A165 8k multi   1.40 1.40

ESTONIA 445

Phoca Hispida — A166

2003, Aug. 27   *Perf. 12¾x13*
462   A166   4.40k multi   .80   .80

Adm. Fabian Gottlieb von Bellingshausen (1778-1852) A167

2003, Sept. 10
463   A167   8k multi   1.75   1.75

Ancient Trade Routes A168

Map and: No. 464, 6.50k, Silver coin of Prince Volodymyr Sviatoslavovych, Slavic warship with sail. No. 465, 6.50k, Arrival of Scandinavian Seamen, coin of Danish King Svend Estridsen.

2003, Sept. 10   *Perf. 11½*
464-465   A168   Set of 2   2.10   2.10

See Ukraine No. 524.

Three Lions Type of 1999-2002
2003-04   *Litho.*   *Perf. 13¾x14*
467   A108   20s blk & gray   .30   .30
472   A108   4.40k ol grn & apple grn   .80   .80
473   A108   5k dk grn & apple grn, dated 2004   .90   .90
474   A108   5.50k dk grn & yel grn   1.00   1.00

Issued: 20s, 4.40k, 8/22; 5k, 1/20/04; 5.50k, 3/25/04.

Folk Costume Type of 1994
Designs: 4.40k, Aksi woman and girl. 6.50k, Otepää man, woman and girl.

2003, Oct. 9   *Litho.*   *Perf. 13¾x14*
476-477   A57   Set of 2   1.90   1.90

A169

Christmas — A170

2003, Nov. 26   *Perf. 14x13¾*
478   A169   3.60k multi   .70   .70
479   A170   6k multi   .90   .90

Souvenir Sheet

Friedrich Reinhold Kreutzwald (1803-82), Writer — A171

No. 480: a, 4.40k, Illustration by Kristjan Raud of "Voyage to the End of the World," from "Kalevipoeg," by Kreutzwald. b, 6.50k, Portrait of Kreutzwald.

2003, Dec. 4   *Perf. 13x12¾*
480   A171   Sheet of 2, #a-b   2.10   2.10

Lighthouse Type of 1995
2004, Jan. 7   *Litho.*   *Perf. 14x13¾*
481   A66   4.40k Sorgu   .85   .85

Canis Lupus — A172

2004, Feb. 3   *Perf. 12¾x13*
482   A172   4.40k multi   .85   .85

Voyage Around Cape Horn of the Hioma, 150th Anniv. — A173

2004, Feb. 18   *Perf. 13¾x14*
483   A173   8k multi   1.50   1.50

Spring Flowers Type of 2003
No. 484: a, Viola riviniana. b, Anemone nemorosa. c, Hepatica nobilis. d, Trollius europaeus.

2004, Mar. 17
484   A160   4.40k Sheet of 4, #a-d   3.25   3.25
   e.   Booklet pane, like #484 without date in margin   3.25
     Complete booklet, #484e   3.25

Bird Type of 2003
2004, Apr. 6   *Perf. 12¾x13*
485   A159   4.40k Ciconia ciconia   .80   .80

Admission to European Union — A174

2004, May 1   *Perf. 13¼x13*
486   A174   6.50k multi   1.25   1.25

Europa A175

2004, May 4   *Perf. 13*
487   A175   6.50k multi   1.25   1.25

Tallinn Town Hall, 600th Anniv. — A176

2004, May 13   *Litho.*   *Perf. 12¾x13*
488   A176   4.40k multi   .80   .80

Consecration of Estonian Flag, 120th Anniv. — A177

2004, June 4   *Perf. 13¾x14*
489   A177   4.40k multi   .80   .80

Manor Type of 1999
2004, June 15   *Perf. 14x13¾*
490   A103   4.40k Vasalemma Hall   .80   .80

Admission to NATO — A178

2004, June 28   *Perf. 13¾x14*
491   A178   6k multi   1.10   1.10

2004 Summer Olympics, Athens — A179

2004, July 15   *Litho.*   *Perf. 13¾x14*
492   A179   8k multi   1.40   1.40

Dragon Class Yachting European Championships A180

2004, Aug. 17   *Perf. 14x13¾*
493   A180   6k multi   1.10   1.10

Taraxacum Officinale — A181

Serpentine Die Cut 12½
2004, Sept. 14   *Self-Adhesive*
494   A181   30s multi   .40   .40

See Nos. 547, 560, 572.

County Arms — A182

2004, Sept. 28   *Self-Adhesive*
495   A182   4.40k Harjumaa   .80   .80
496   A182   4.40k Hiiumaa   .80   .80

See Nos. 506-507, 518-519, 532-533, 536, 552, 561, 573, 588, 594, 608.

Folk Costumes Type of 1994
Designs: 4.40k, Viru-Jaagupi boy and girl. 7.50k, Jõhvi woman and girl.

2004, Oct. 5   *Litho.*   *Perf. 13¾x14*
497-498   A57   Set of 2   2.10   2.10

A183

Christmas — A184

2004, Nov. 23   *Perf. 13¾x14*
499   A183   4.40k multi   .90   .90
     Perf. 14x13¾
500   A184   6.50k multi   1.00   1.00

Lighthouse Type of 1995
Norrby Lighthouse with: 4.40k, White top, vert. 6.50k, Red top, vert.

2005, Jan. 11   *Litho.*   *Perf. 14*
501-502   A66   Set of 2   1.75   1.75

Castor Fiber — A185

2005, Jan. 25   *Perf. 12¾x13*
503   A185   4.40k multi   .70   .70

Rotary International, Cent. — A186

2005, Feb. 11   *Perf. 13¾x14*
504   A186   8k multi   1.25   1.25

Flag Over Pikk Hermann Tower, Tallinn — A187

Serpentine Die Cut 12½
2005, Feb. 22   *Self-Adhesive*
505   A187   5k multi   .90   .90

See Nos. 530, 559, 574.

County Arms Type of 2004
2005   *Self-Adhesive*   *Litho.*
506   A182   4.40k Ida-Virumaa   .80   .80
507   A182   4.40k Järvamaa   .80   .80

Issued: No. 506, 3/8; No. 507, 3/15.

Souvenir Sheet

Spring A188

No. 508: a, Two swans, denomination at UL. b, One swan, denomination at UL. c, One swan, denomination at LL. d, Two swans, denomination at LR.

2005, Mar. 22   *Litho.*   *Perf. 14x13¾*
508   A188   4.40k Sheet of 4, #a-d   2.75   2.75

Bird Type of 2003
2005, Apr. 5   *Perf. 12¾x13*
509   A159   4.40k Accipiter gentilis   .80   .80

Mother's Day — A189

2005, Apr. 20   *Perf. 14x13¾*
510   A189   4.40k multi   .80   .80

Europa — A190

Designs: 6k, Vegetable wrap. 6.50k, Tomato, carrots, egg yolk, parsley, fish, onion, beet.

2005, May 3
511-512   A190   Set of 2   2.25   2.25

Eduard Tubin (1905-82), Composer — A191

2005, May 18
513   A191   6k multi   1.00   1.00

Intl. Children's Day — A192

No. 514: a, Birds. b, Butterflies.

2005, June 1   *Perf. 13¼x13¾*
514   A192   4.40k Horiz. pair, #a-b, + central label   1.50   1.50

ESTONIA

Orchids — A193

Designs: 4.40k, Epipactis palustris. 8k, Epipogium aphyllum.

2005, June 16   Litho.   Perf. 13¾x14
515-516 A193 Set of 2   2.50 2.50

Restoration of St. John's Cathedral, Tartu — A194

2005, June 29
517 A194 4.40k multi   .80 .80
Tartu, 975th anniv.

County Arms Type of 2004
Serpentine Die Cut 12½
2005   Self-Adhesive   Litho.
518 A182 4.40k Jõgevamaa   .75 .75
519 A182 4.40k Läänemaa   .75 .75
Issued: No. 518, 7/5; No. 519, 7/8.

Manor Type of 1999
2005, July 12   Perf. 14x13¾
520 A103 4.40k Kiltsi Hall   .75 .75

St. Catherine's Church, Karja — A195

2005, Sept. 20
521 A195 4.40k multi   .75 .75

Souvenir Sheet

Sculptures by Amandus Adamson (1855-1929) — A196

No. 522: a, Igavesti Voidutsev Armastus, 1889. b, Lüüriline Muusika, 1891. c, Memento Mori, 1907. d, Koit ja Hämarik, 1895.

2005, Oct. 12   Perf. 13½
522 A196 650s Sheet of 4, #a-d 4.00 4.00

Dogs A197

No. 523: a, Kazakh hound (Kasaahi hurt). b, Estonian hound (Eesti hagijas).

2005, Oct. 19   Perf. 14x13¾
523 A197 6.50k Horiz. pair, #a-b 2.10 2.10
See Kazakhstan No. 495.

Folk Costumes Type of 1994
Designs: 4.40k, Ambla man, woman and girl. 8k, Türi women.

2005, Oct. 28   Perf. 13¾x14
524-525 A57 Set of 2   2.25 2.25

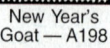
New Year's Goat — A198

Adoration of the Magi — A199

2005, Nov. 22
526 A198 4.40k multi   .80 .80
527 A199 8k sil & red lil   1.45 1.45
Christmas and New Year's Day.

Due to the postponed conversion to the euro, originally scheduled for Jan. 1, 2007, Estonian stamps issued between 2006 and 2010 show denominations in kroons and the at-that-time-uncirculating euros.

Europa Stamps, 50th Anniv. — A200

CEPT emblem and: 6k, Superimposed letters. 6.50k, Map of Europe.

2006, Jan. 4   Litho.   Perf. 14x13¾
528 A200 6k multi   .95 .95

Souvenir Sheet
529 A200 6.50k multi   1.00 1.00

Flag Over Pikk Hermann Tower Type of 2005 With Euro Denominations Added
2006, Jan. 11   Die Cut Perf. 12½
Self-Adhesive
530 A187 11k multi   1.75 1.75

2006 Winter Olympics, Turin, Italy — A201

2006, Jan. 18   Perf. 14x13¾
531 A201 8k multi   1.25 1.25

County Arms Type of 2004 With Euro Denominations Added
2006   Die Cut Perf. 12½
Self-Adhesive
532 A182 4.40k Lääne-Virumaa   .70 .70
533 A182 4.40k Polvamaa   .70 .70
Issued: No. 532, 1/25; No. 533, 2/8.

Alces Alces — A202

2006, Feb. 1   Perf. 12¾x13
534 A202 4.40k multi   .75 .75

Opening of KUMU Art Museum — A203

2006, Feb. 17   Litho.   Perf. 13¾x14
535 A203 4.40k multi   .75 .75

County Arms Type of 2004 With Euro Denominations Added
2006, Mar. 8   Die Cut Perf. 12½
Self-Adhesive
536 A182 4.40k Pärnumaa   .85 .85

Souvenir Sheet

National Opera, Cent. A204

No. 537: a, Characters from Vikerlased, first opera staged in 1928. b, Ballerina.

2006, Mar. 27   Perf. 13¾x14
537 A204 6.50k Sheet of 2, #a-b,
           + central label   2.25 2.25

A205

Gold Medalists at 2006 Winter Olympics — A206

No. 539: a, Andrus Veerpalu. b, Kristina Smigun.

2006, Mar. 30   Perf. 14x13¾
538 A205 4.40k multi   .75 .75

Souvenir Sheet
539 A206 8k Sheet of 2, #a-b   2.50 2.50

Bird Type of 2003 With Euro Denominations Added
2006, Apr. 5   Perf. 12¾x13
540 A159 4.40k multi   .75 .75

Lighthouses — A207

Designs: 4.40k, Tallinn Bay lower lighthouse. 6.50k, Tallinn Bay upper lighthouse.

2006, Apr. 12   Perf. 13¾x14
541-542 A207 Set of 2   1.75 1.75
See Nos. 564, 587, 624.

Estonian Shooting Sport Federation, 75th Anniv. — A208

2006, Apr. 26
543 A208 4.40k car & sil   .75 .75

Europa — A209

2006, May 3
544 A209 6.50k multi   1.25 1.25

Confectionery Industry in Estonia, Bicent. — A210

2006, May 18   Perf. 14x13¾
545 A210 4.40k multi   .75 .75

Posthorns A211

2006, May 22   Die Cut Perf. 10
Self-Adhesive
546 A211 4.40k gray brn + label .75 .75
Labels could be personalized.
See No. 563.

Flower Type of 2004 with Euro Denominations Added
2006, May 24   Die Cut Perf. 12½
Self-Adhesive
547 A181 30s Hepatica nobilis   .35 .35

Souvenir Sheet

Tori Stud Farm, 150th Anniv. A212

No. 548: a, Three horses, denomination at UL. b, Pony and three horses, denomination at UR.

2006, June 7   Perf. 14x13¾
548 A212 4.40k Sheet of 2, #a-b 1.40 1.40

Victory Day — A213

2006, June 23
549 A213 4.40k multi   .75 .75

20th Intl. Organ Music Festival, Tallinn — A214

2006, July 28   Litho.   Perf. 14x13¾
550 A214 4.40k multi   .75 .75

Manor Type of 1999 With Added Euro Denomination
2006, Aug. 16
551 A103 4.40k Taagepera Hall   .75 .75

County Arms Type of 2004 With Added Euro Denomination
2006, Sept. 6   Die Cut Perf. 12½
Self-Adhesive
552 A182 4.40k Raplamaa   .75 .75

St. Lawrence's Church, Noo — A215

2006, Sept. 20   Perf. 13¾x14
553 A215 4.40k multi   .75 .75

Betti Alver (1906-89), Writer — A216

2006, Oct. 11   Perf. 13
554 A216 4.40k multi   .75 .75

Antarctic Wildlife A217

ESTONIA

No. 555 — Estonian and Chilean flags and: a, Aptenodytes forsteri. b, Balaenoptera acutorostrata.

2006, Oct. 25   Perf. 13½
555 A217 8k Pair, #a-b   2.50 2.50
See Chile No. 1468.

A218

Christmas — A219

2006, Nov. 22   Litho.   Perf. 13¾x14
556 A218 4.40k multi   .70 .70
557 A219 6k multi   .95 .95

Lotte From Gadgetville — A220

2007, Jan. 4   Perf. 14x13¾
558 A220 4.40k multi   .85 .85

Flag Over Pikk Hermann Tower Type of 2005 With Euro Denomination Added
2007, Jan. 11   Die Cut Perf. 12½ Self-Adhesive
559 A187 5k tan & multi   .85 .85

Flower Type of 2004 With Euro Denomination Added
2007, Jan. 17   Die Cut Perf. 12½ Self-Adhesive
560 A181 30s Leucanthemum vulgare   .30 .30

County Arms Type of 2004 With Euro Denomination Added
2007, Jan. 25   Die Cut Perf. 12½ Self-Adhesive
561 A182 4.40k Saaremaa   .85 .85

Manor Type of 1999 With Euro Denomination Added
2007, Feb. 14   Perf. 14x13¾
562 A103 5.50k Sagadi Hall   .95 .95

Posthorns Type of 2006
2007, Feb. 22   Die Cut Perf. 10 Self-Adhesive
563 A211 5.50k bl grn + label   1.00 1.00
Labels could be personalized.

Lighthouse Type of 2006
2007, Mar. 8   Perf. 14x13¾
564 A207 6k Juminda, horiz.   1.00 1.00

Meles Meles — A221

2007, Mar. 22   Perf. 12¾x13
565 A221 4.40k multi   .90 .90

Bird Type of 2003 With Euro Denomination Added
2007, Apr. 5   Perf. 12¾x13
566 A159 4.40k Cygnus bewickii   .90 .90

Miniature Sheet

Summer Flowers A222

No. 567: a, Paeonia officinalis. b, Lilium lancifolium. c, Rosa ecae Golden Chersonese. d, Iris latifolia.

2007, Apr. 19   Perf. 13¾x14
567 A222 4.40k Sheet of 4, #a-d   3.25 3.25

Europa A223

2007, May 3   Perf. 12½
568 A223 20.50k multi   3.50 3.50
Scouting, cent.

Intl. Children's Day — A224

2007, June 1   Litho.   Perf. 13½
569 A224 10k multi   1.75 1.75

Souvenir Sheet

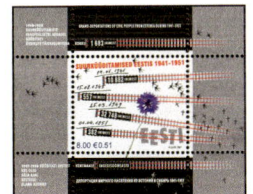

1941-51 Deportation of Estonians — A225

2007, June 14   Perf. 13
570 A225 8k multi   1.40 1.40

Pirita Convent, 600th Anniv. A226

2007, June 15   Litho.   Perf. 12½
571 A226 5.50k multi   1.00 1.00

Flower Type of 2004 With Euro Denominations Added
2007, July 2   Die Cut Perf. 12½ Self-Adhesive
572 A181 1.10k Centaurea phrygia   .30 .30

County Arms Type of 2004 With Euro Denominations Added
2007, July 2   Self-Adhesive
573 A182 5.50k Tartumaa   1.00 1.00

Flag Over Pikk Hermann Tower Type of 2005 With Euro Denominations Added
2007, Aug. 1   Self-Adhesive
574 A187 10k multi   1.75 1.75

Hellenurme Mill — A227

2007, Aug. 9   Perf. 14x13¾
575 A227 5.50k multi   1.00 1.00

Hirvepark Demonstration, 20th Anniv. — A228

2007, Aug. 23   Perf. 14x14¼
576 A228 5.50k multi   1.00 1.00

Souvenir Sheet

Matthias Johann Eisen (1857-1934), Folklorist A229

2007, Sept. 14   Imperf.
577 A229 10k multi   1.75 1.75
No. 577 has simulated perforations.

Ragnar Nurkse (1907-59), Economist A230

2007, Oct. 5   Perf. 13
578 A230 10k multi   1.75 1.75

St. John's Church, Kanepi — A231

2007, Oct. 11   Perf. 13¾x14
579 A231 5.50k multi   1.00 1.00

Arms of Viljandi — A232

2007, Oct. 25   Litho.   Perf. 13¾x14
580 A232 5.50k multi   1.00 1.00

A233

Christmas — A234

Die Cut Perf. 11¼ Syncopated
2007, Nov. 22   Self-Adhesive
581 A233 5.50k multi   .90 .90
582 A234 8k multi   1.40 1.40

Post Horn — A235

2008   Litho.   Die Cut Perf. 12½ Self-Adhesive
583 A235 5.50k brt orange   1.00 1.00
584 A235 6.50k brt yel green   1.15 1.15
585 A235 9k blue   1.60 1.60
Nos. 583-585 (3)   3.75 3.75
Issued: 5.50k, 1/10; 6.50k, 3/6; 9k, 4/1.
See Nos. 600, 638, 649, 658-662, 675-677, 682-684, 696-697, 708, 719-721.

Gustav Ernesaks (1908-93), Composer — A236

2008, Jan. 17   Litho.   Perf. 13
586 A236 5.50k multi   1.00 1.00

Lighthouse Type of 2006
2008, Jan. 24   Perf. 14x13¾
587 A207 5.50k Mehikoorma, horiz.   1.00 1.00

County Arms Type of 2004 With Euro Denominations Added
2008, Feb. 7   Die Cut Perf. 12½ Self-Adhesive
588 A182 5.50k Valgamaa   1.00 1.00

Plecotus Auritus — A237

2008, Feb. 14   Perf. 12¾x13
589 A237 5.50k multi   1.00 1.00

Oak Tree — A238

2008, Feb. 23   Perf. 13
590 A238 5.50k multi   1.00 1.00
Republic of Estonia, 90th anniv.

A239

Design: Kristjan Palusalu (1908-87), olympic wrestling gold medalist.

2008, Mar. 10   Perf. 12½
591 A239 10k multi   1.75 1.75

State Awards of the Baltic Countries — A240

Designs: Nos. 592, 593a, Order of the National Coat of Arms, Estonia. No. 593b, Order of Three Stars, Latvia. No. 593c, Order of Vytautas the Great, Lithuania.

2008, Mar. 15   Litho.   Perf. 13¾
592 A240 5.50k multi   1.00 1.00

Souvenir Sheet
593 A240 10k Sheet of 3, #a-c, + label   5.25 5.25
See Latvia Nos. 701-702, Lithuania Nos. 862-863.

ESTONIA

County Arms Type of 2004 With Euro Denominations Added
2008, Mar. 27 *Die Cut Perf. 12½*
Self-Adhesive
594 A182 5.50k Viljandimaa 1.00 1.00

Bird Type of 2003 With Euro Denomination Added
2008, Apr. 3 *Perf. 12¾x13*
595 A159 5.50k Tetrao tetrix 1.10 1.10

Europa — A241

2008, Apr. 30 *Perf. 14x14¼*
596 A241 9k multi 1.60 1.60

Otto Strandman (1875-1941), Statesman — A242

2008, May 9 Litho. *Perf. 13¾x14*
597 A242 5.50k brown 1.00 1.00

Wavy Lines A243

2008, May 22 *Serpentine Die Cut 10*
Self-Adhesive
598 A243 9k multi + label 1.75 1.75
The label shown is generic. Labels could be personalized for a fee.

Peasant War at Mahtra, 150th Anniv. — A244

2008, May 31 *Perf. 14x13¾*
599 A244 5.50k multi 1.00 1.00

Posthorn Type of 2008
Die Cut Perf. 12½
2008, May 31 Litho.
Self-Adhesive
600 A235 50s gray .35 .35

2008 Summer Olympics, Beijing — A245

2008, Aug. 8 Litho. *Perf. 13¾x14*
601 A245 9k multi 1.60 1.60

Polma Windmill — A246

2008, Aug. 28 *Perf. 14x13¾*
602 A246 5.50k multi 1.00 1.00

Manor Type of 1999 With Euro Denomination Added
2008, Sept. 18 Litho. *Perf. 14x13¾*
603 A103 5.50k Kalvi Hall 1.00 1.00

Gerd Kanter, Olympic Discus Champion — A247

2008, Sept. 25 *Perf. 13½*
604 A247 5.50k multi 1.00 1.00

Church of the Holy Cross, Audru — A248

2008, Oct. 16 Litho. *Perf. 13¾x14*
605 A248 5.50k multi 1.00 1.00

County Arms Type of 2004 With Euro Denominations Added
2008, Oct. 30 *Die Cut Perf. 12½*
Self-Adhesive
606 A182 5.50k Vorumaa 1.00 1.00

Estonia Post, 90th Anniv. — A249

2008, Nov. 13 *Perf. 13¾x14*
607 A249 5.50k multi 1.00 1.00

Christmas — A250

Designs: 5.50k, Gift on skis. 9k, Snowman on gift.

Die Cut Perf. 11¼ Syncopated
2008, Nov. 20 Litho.
Booklet Stamps Self-Adhesive
608 A250 5.50k multi .90 .90
a. Booklet pane of 10 8.25
609 A250 9k multi 1.60 1.60
a. Booklet pane of 10 13.50

Souvenir Sheet

International Polar Year — A251

No. 610 — Antarctic glacier with snowflake emblem in: a, White. b, Blue.

2009, Jan. 15 Litho. *Perf. 13x12¾*
610 A251 15k Sheet of 2, #a-b 5.50 5.50

Battle of Paju, 90th Anniv. — A252

2009, Jan. 29 *Perf. 12¾x13*
611 A252 5.50k multi 1.00 1.00

Gen. Johan Laidoner (1884-1953) A253

2009, Feb. 12 Litho. *Perf. 13*
612 A253 5.50k multi 1.00 1.00

Ants Piip (1884-1942), Prime Minister — A254

2009, Feb. 26 *Perf. 14*
613 A254 5.50k maroon 1.00 1.00

Pres. Lennart Meri (1929-2006) — A255

2009, Mar. 26 Litho. *Perf. 14*
614 A255 5.50k blue 1.00 1.00

Estonian National Museum, Cent. — A256

2009, Apr. 14 *Perf. 13*
615 A256 5.50k multi 1.00 1.00

Estonian Parliament, 90th Anniv. — A257

2009, Apr. 23 *Perf. 14*
616 A257 5.50k multi 1.00 1.00

Europa A258

No. 617: a, Galaxies and hexagonal cells. b, Galaxy and hexagonal cells at left.

2009, May 5 Litho. *Perf. 13¾x14*
617 A258 9k Horiz. pair, #a-b 3.25 3.25
Intl. Year of Astronomy.

Räpina Paper Mill, 275th Anniv. — A259

2009, May 14
618 A259 5.50k multi 1.00 1.00

Estonian Flag, 125th Anniv. — A260

Die Cut Perf. 11¼ Syncopated
2009, June 5
Booklet Stamp Self-Adhesive
619 A260 9k multi 1.50 1.50
a. Booklet pane of 10 15.00

25th Song Festival — A261

2009, June 18 *Perf. 14x13¾*
620 A261 5.50k multi 1.00 1.00

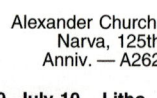

Alexander Church, Narva, 125th Anniv. — A262

2009, July 10 Litho. *Perf. 13¾x13*
621 A262 5.50k multi 1.50 1.50

Ursus Arctos — A263

2009, Sept. 10 *Perf. 12¾x13*
622 A263 5.50k multi 1.00 1.00

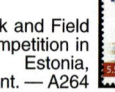

First Track and Field Competition in Estonia, Cent. — A264

2009, Sept. 22 *Perf. 14x13¾*
623 A264 5.50k multi 1.10 1.10

Lighthouse Type of 2006
2009, Sept. 24 *Perf. 14x13¾*
624 A207 5.50k Hara Tuletorn, horiz. 1.10 1.10

Bird Type of 2003 With Euro Denomination Added
2009, Oct. 8 Litho. *Perf. 12¾x13*
625 A159 5.50k Strix aluco 1.10 1.10

Windmill, Angla — A265

2009, Oct. 22 *Perf. 13¾x14*
626 A265 5.50k multi 1.10 1.10

Manor Type of 1999 With Euro Denomination Added
2009, Nov. 5 *Perf. 14x13¾*
627 A103 5.50k Saku Hall 1.10 1.10

A266

Christmas — A267

Die Cut Perf. 11¼ Syncopated
2009, Nov. 19
Booklet Stamps Self-Adhesive
628 A266 5.50k multi .95 .95
a. Booklet pane of 10 9.50
629 A267 9k multi 1.60 1.60
a. Booklet pane of 10 16.00

Fabric Design — A268

Die Cut Perf. 11¼ Syncopated
2010, Jan. 7 Litho.
Booklet Stamp Self-Adhesive
630 A268 50k orange & multi 8.50 8.50
a. Booklet pane of 10 85.00
See Nos. 646, 650.

ESTONIA

Jüri Jaakson (1870-1942), Politician — A269

2010, Jan. 15   Perf. 14
631   A269   5.50k multi   .95   .95

2010 European Figure Skating Championships, Tallinn — A270

2010, Jan. 19   Perf. 12¾x13
632   A270   9k multi   1.50   1.50
   a. Tete-beche pair   3.00   3.00

Tartu Peace Treaty, 90th Anniv. — A271

2010, Feb. 2   Perf. 13
633   A271   5.50k multi   1.00   1.00

Post Horn Type of 2008
2010, Feb. 4   Die Cut Perf. 12½
Self-Adhesive
634   A235   9k deep blue   1.50   1.50
Dated 2010. Compare with No. 585.

2010 Winter Olympics, Vancouver — A272

2010, Feb. 4   Perf. 14
635   A272   9k multi   1.60   1.60

Platanthera Bifolia — A273

2010, Feb. 19
636   A273   5.50k multi   1.00   1.00

Estonia Pavilion, Expo 2010, Shanghai — A274

2010, Mar. 11
637   A274   9k multi   1.50   1.50

Posthorn Type of 2008
Die Cut Perf. 12½
2010, Mar. 23   Litho.
Self-Adhesive
638   A235   5.50k bright pink   1.00   1.00

St. Catherine's Church, Pärnu — A275

2010, Mar. 23   Perf. 13¾x14
639   A275   6.50k multi   1.10   1.10

Juhan Kukk (1885-1942), State Elder — A276

2010, Apr. 13
640   A276   5.50k olive brown   1.00   1.00

Lighthouses Type of 2006
Designs: 6.50k, Suurupi front lighthouse. 8k, Suurupi rear lighthouse.
2010, Apr. 22
641-642   A207   Set of 2   2.50   2.50

Europa — A277

Children's book illustrations: No. 643, 9k, Family of mice, by Jüri Mildeberg. No. 644, 9k, Skaters in snow, by Viive Noor.

2010, May 6   Perf. 14x13¾
643-644   A277   Set of 2   2.50   2.50

Bird Type of 2003 With Euro Denominations Added
2010, May 13   Perf. 12¾x13
645   A159   5.50k Lanius collurio   1.00   1.00

Fabric Design Type of 2010
Die Cut Perf. 11¼ Syncopated
2010, June 1
Booklet Stamp Self-Adhesive
646   A268   26k brt yel grn & multi   4.50   4.50
   a. Booklet pane of 10   45.00

Intl. Children's Day — A278

2010, June 1   Litho.
Booklet Stamp Self-Adhesive
647   A278   5.50k multi   1.00   1.00
   a. Booklet pane of 10   10.00

Manor Type of 1999 With Euro Denominations Added
2010, Aug. 5   Litho.   Perf. 14x13¾
648   A103   5.50k Suuremõisa Hall   .95   .95

Posthorn Type of 2008
2010, Aug. 18   Die Cut Perf. 12
Self-Adhesive
649   A235   9k bright yellow   1.50   1.50

Fabric Design Type of 2010
Die Cut Perf. 11¼ Syncopated
2010, Aug. 18
Booklet Stamp Self-Adhesive
650   A268   26k lilac & multi   4.50   4.50
   a. Booklet pane of 10   45.00

Tallinn, 2011 European Capital of Culture — A279

2010, Sept. 9   Litho.
Self-Adhesive
651   A279   5.50k multi   1.00   1.00

Eliomys Quercinus — A280

2010, Sept. 23   Perf. 12¾x13
652   A280   5.50k multi   .75   .75

A281   A282

A283   Worldwide Fund for Nature (WWF) — A284

Various views of Triturus cristatus.

2010, Oct. 14   Perf. 14x13¾
653   Horiz. strip of 4   6.50   6.50
   a. A281 9k multi   1.60   1.60
   b. A282 9k multi   1.60   1.60
   c. A283 9k multi   1.60   1.60
   d. A284 9k multi   1.60   1.60
   e. Sheet of 8 stamps with two tete-beche strips   13.00   13.00

Lennuk, by Nikolai Triik — A285

2010, Nov. 17   Litho.   Perf. 14
654   A285   9k multi   1.60   1.60
No. 654 was printed in sheets of 8.

A286

Christmas — A287

Die Cut Perf. 11¼ Syncopated
2010, Nov. 25
Booklet Stamps Self-Adhesive
655   A286   5.50k multi   .95   .95
   a. Booklet pane of 10   9.50
656   A287   9k multi   1.60   1.60
   a. Booklet pane of 10   16.00

Stamps in No. 655a are tete-beche in relation to adjacent stamps. Vertical pairs of stamps in No. 656a are tete-beche.

100 Cents = 1 Euro

Introduction of Euro Currency — A288

Die Cut Perf. 11¼ Syncopated
2011, Jan. 1
Booklet Stamp Self-Adhesive
657   A288   €1 multi   2.75   2.75
   a. Booklet pane of 10   27.50

Post Horn Type of 2008 with Euro Denominations Only
2011, Jan. 3   Die Cut Perf. 12½
Self-Adhesive
658   A235   1c orange   .25   .25
659   A235   5c salmon pink   .25   .25
660   A235   10c lilac   .25   .25
661   A235   50c blue   1.40   1.40
662   A235   65c green   1.75   1.75
   Nos. 658-662 (5)   3.90   3.90

New Year 2011 (Year of the Rabbit) — A289

2011, Feb. 3   Litho.   Perf. 12¾x13
663   A289   58c multi   1.60   1.60

Friedebert Tuglas (1886-1971), Writer — A290

2011, Mar. 2   Perf. 13¾x14
664   A290   58c multi   1.60   1.60

Villem Reiman (1861-1917), Historian — A291

2011, Mar. 9
665   A291   35c multi   1.00   1.00

Peony — A292

2011, Mar. 24   Perf. 13x12¾
666   A292   58c multi   1.75   1.75

Printed in sheets of 4 having each stamp rotated 90 degrees in relation to each other.

Folk Costumes — A293

Designs: 35c, Man and woman from Rapla. 58c, Two women from Joelähtme.

2011, Apr. 14   Perf. 13¾x14
667-668   A293   Set of 2   2.50   2.50

Hirundo Rustica — A294

2011, Apr. 21   Perf. 12¾x13
669   A294   35c multi   1.00   1.00

Europa — A295

Designs: No. 670, 58c, Elk in forest. No. 671, 58c, Cut logs.

2011, Apr. 28   Perf. 13
670-671   A295   Set of 2   3.00   3.00
Intl. Year of Forests.

ESTONIA

Souvenir Sheet

Struve Geodetic Arc — A296

No. 672 — Map of arc and: a, Friedrch Georg Wilhelm Struve (1793-1864), astronomer. b, Tartu Observatory.

2011, May 6		Perf. 14x13¾
672 A296 58c Sheet of 2, #a-b		3.25 3.25

Lepus Europaeus — A297

2011, May 19	Perf. 12¾x13
673 A297 35c multi	1.00 1.00

Vergi Lighthouse — A298

2011, June 2	Perf. 14x13¾
674 A298 35c multi	1.00 1.00

Posthorn Type of 2008 With Euro Denominations Only

2011		Die Cut Perf. 12½
	Self-Adhesive	
675 A235 35c brt yel grn		1.00 1.00
676 A235 58c lt purple		1.75 1.75
677 A235 58c green		1.60 1.60

Issued: 35c, No. 676, 6/2. No. 677, 8/25.

21st European Junior Track and Field Championships, Tallinn — A299

2011, July 20 Litho.	Perf. 14x13¾
678 A299 35c multi	1.00 1.00

Restoration of Independence, 20th Anniv. — A300

2011, Aug. 20	Perf. 13¾x14¼
679 A300 35c multi	1.00 1.00

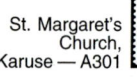

St. Margaret's Church, Karuse — A301

2011, Aug. 25	Perf. 14x13¾
680 A301 35c multi	1.00 1.00

Friedrich Karl Akel (1871-1941), State Elder — A302

2011, Sept. 5	Perf. 13¾x14
681 A302 35c brown	1.00 1.00

Posthorn Type of 2008 With Euro Denominations Only

2011		Die Cut Perf. 12½
	Self-Adhesive	
682 A235 10c sage green		.30 .30
683 A235 35c cerise		.95 .95
684 A235 45c rose		1.25 1.25
Nos. 682-684 (3)		2.50 2.50

Issued: 10c, 45c, 11/1; 35c, 9/15.

Heinrich Mark (1911-2004), Prime Minister — A303

2011, Sept. 30	Perf. 13¾x14
685 A303 35c blue	.95 .95

Michael Andreas Barclay de Tolly (1761-1818), Military Leader — A304

2011, Oct. 20	Perf. 14x13¾
686 A304 €1 multi	2.75 2.75

10-Cent and 2-Euro Coins — A305

Die Cut Perf. 11¼ Syncopated
2011, Nov. 1
Booklet Stamp
Self-Adhesive

687 A305 €2.10 multi	5.50 5.50
a. Booklet pane of 10	55.00

Market, Painting by Henn-Olavi Roode (1924-74) — A306

2011, Nov. 17	Perf. 14
688 A306 €1 multi	2.75 2.75

Christmas — A307

Die Cut Perf. 11¼ Syncopated
2011, Nov. 24
Booklet Stamps
Self-Adhesive

689 A307 45c Angel	1.25 1.25
a. Booklet pane of 10	12.50
690 A307 €1 Ornament	2.75 2.75
a. Booklet pane of 10	27.50

Vertical pairs of stamps in Nos. 689a and 690a are tete-beche.

Oskar Luts (1887-1953), Writer — A308

2012, Jan. 7 Litho.	Perf. 13
691 A308 45c multi	1.25 1.25

Population and Housing Census — A309

Die Cut Perf. 11¼x11½ Syncopated
2012, Jan. 12 **Self-Adhesive**
| 692 A309 45c multi | 1.25 1.25 |

New Year 2012 (Year of the Dragon) — A310

2012, Jan. 23	Perf. 12¾x13
693 A310 €1.10 multi	3.00 3.00

Capreolus Capreolus — A311

2012, Feb. 16	Perf. 12¾x13
694 A311 45c multi	1.25 1.25

Heino Eller (1887-1970), Composer — A312

2012, Mar. 7	Perf. 14x13¾
695 A312 45c multi	1.25 1.25

Posthorn Type of 2008 With Euro Denominations Only
2012, Mar. 29 **Die Cut Perf. 12½**
Self-Adhesive
Dated "2012"

696 A235 10c dull blue green	.25 .25
697 A235 50c pale yel grn	1.40 1.40

Compare Nos. 696 and 750.

Personalized Stamp — A313

Die Cut Perf. 8¾ Syncopated
2012, Mar. 29 **Self-Adhesive**
| 698 A313 45c multi | 1.25 1.25 |

The generic vignette shown, depicting a map of Saaremaa, could be personalized for an additional fee.
See Nos. 773, 901, 966.

Folk Costumes — A314

Designs: 45c, Woman and girl from Hageri. €1, Woman from Nissi.

2012, Apr. 14 Litho.	Perf. 13¾x14
699-700 A314 Set of 2	4.00 4.00

Charadrius Dubius — A315

2012, Apr. 19	Perf. 12¾x13
701 A315 45c multi	1.25 1.25

Johannes Pääsuke (1892-1918), Creator of First Estonian Film in 1912 — A316

2012, Apr. 30	
702 A316 45c multi	1.25 1.25

Europa — A317

Inscriptions: No. 703, €1, "wild est." No. 704, €1, "smart est."

2012, May 3	Perf. 14x13¾
703-704 A317 Set of 2	5.25 5.25

Church of St. Simeon and the Prophet Anne, Tallinn — A318

2012, May 17	Perf. 13¾x14
705 A318 45c multi	1.25 1.25

2012 Summer Olympics, London — A319

2012, June 1	Perf. 14x13¾
706 A319 €1.10 multi	2.75 2.75

Martin Klein (1884-1947), First Estonian Olympic Medalist — A320

2012, July 13	Perf. 14x14¼
707 A320 €1 multi	2.50 2.50

Posthorn Type of 2008 With Euro Denominations Only
2012, Aug. 10	Die Cut Perf. 12½
	Self-Adhesive
708 A235 45c citron	1.25 1.25

One-Euro Coin — A321

Die Cut Perf. 11¼ Syncopated
2012, Aug. 10 **Self-Adhesive**
| 709 A321 €1 multi | 2.60 2.60 |

ESTONIA 451

Amanita Virosa — A322

2012, Aug. 30   *Perf. 13¾x14*
710 A322 45c red & black   1.25 1.25

Käsmu Lighthouse — A323

2012, Sept. 13   *Perf. 14x13¾*
711 A323 45c multi   1.25 1.25

Jaan Teemant (1872-1941), State Elder — A324

2012, Sept. 24   *Perf. 13¾x14*
712 A324 45c brown   1.25 1.25

Railway Bridges — A325

Train and: Nos. 713, 714a, Narva Bridge, Estonia. No. 714b, Carnikava Bridge, Latvia. No. 714c, Lyduvenai Bridge, Lithuania.

2012, Oct. 25   *Perf. 13¼*
713 A325 45c multi   1.25 1.25
Souvenir Sheet
714 A325 €1 Sheet of 3, #a-c   8.00 8.00
See Latvia Nos. 815-816, Lithuania Nos. 985-986.

Scouting in Estonia, Cent. — A326

2012, Nov. 7   *Perf. 14x13¾*
715 A326 45c multi   1.25 1.25

Still Life with Mandolin, by Lepo Mikko — A327

2012, Nov. 16   *Perf. 14*
716 A327 €1.10 multi   3.00 3.00

Santa Claus on Skis A328

Poinsettia A329

Die Cut Perf. 11¼ Syncopated
2012, Nov. 22   *Self-Adhesive*
717 A328 45c multi   1.25 1.25
718 A329 €1 multi   2.60 2.60
Christmas.

Posthorn Type of 2008 With Euro Denominations Only
Self-Adhesive
2013, Jan. 10   *Die Cut Perf. 12½*
719 A235 5c light blue   .30 .30
720 A235 50c green   1.40 1.40
721 A235 65c red violet   1.75 1.75
Nos. 719-721 (3)   3.45 3.45

Kiipsaare Lighthouse — A330

2013, Jan. 31   *Perf. 14x13¾*
722 A330 45c multi   1.25 1.25

New Year 2013 (Year of the Snake) — A331

2013, Feb. 8   *Perf. 12¾x13*
723 A331 €1.10 multi   3.00 3.00

Estonian Flag — A332

Die Cut Perf. 11¼ Syncopated
2013, Feb. 22   *Self-Adhesive*
724 A332 €1 multi   2.60 2.60
   a. Dated "2014"   2.75 2.75
See Nos. 754, 929, 1002. Compare with illustration A449.
Issued No. 724a, 5/22/14.

Perdix Perdix — A333

2013, Mar. 7   *Perf. 12¾x13*
725 A333 45c multi   1.25 1.25

Arms of Cindi A333a

Die Cut Perf. 12½
2013, Mar. 28   *Litho.*
Self-Adhesive
725A A333a 45c multi   1.75 1.75

Folk Costumes — A334

Man and woman from: 45c, Kihelkonna. €1, Karja.

2013, Apr. 12   *Perf. 13¾x14*
726-727 A334 Set of 2   4.00 4.00

Icebreaker "Tarmo" — A335

2013, Apr. 25   *Perf. 14x13¾*
728 A335 €1 multi   2.75 2.75

Europa A336

No. 729 — Postal vehicles: a, Horse-drawn stagecoach, 1840s. b, Modern van.

2013, May 2   *Litho.*
729 A336 €1 Horiz. pair, #a-b   5.25 5.25

Souvenir Sheet

Estcube-1 Satellite — A337

2013, May 2
730 A337 €1.10 multi   3.00 3.00

Kuressaare, 450th Anniv. — A338

2013, May 8   *Perf. 14x14¼*
731 A338 45c multi   1.40 1.40

Kaarel Eenpalu (1888-1942), State Elder and Prime Minister — A339

2013, May 28   *Perf. 13¾x14*
732 A339 45c dk brn violet   1.25 1.25

Mustela Nivalis — A340

2013, June 6   *Perf. 12¾x13*
733 A340 45c multi   1.25 1.25

St. Catherine's Church, Voru — A341

2013, July 24   *Perf. 13¾x14*
734 A341 45c multi   1.25 1.25

Souvenir Sheet

Cultural Heritage Year A342

2013, Aug. 3   *Perf.*
735 A342 €1.10 multi   3.00 3.00

Finn Class Sailing World Championships, Tallinn — A343

2013, Aug. 23   *Perf. 14¼x13¾*
736 A343 €1.10 multi   3.00 3.00

Estonia Theater and Concert House, Tallinn, Cent. A344

2013, Sept. 6   *Perf. 13*
737 A344 €1.10 multi   3.00 3.00

Amanita Phalloides — A345

2013, Sept. 12   *Perf. 13¾x14*
738 A345 45c multi   1.25 1.25

Raimond Valgre (1913-49), Composer A346

2013, Oct. 7   *Litho.*   *Perf. 13*
739 A346 45c multi   1.25 1.25

Arms of Moisaküla — A347

Die Cut Perf. 12½
2013, Oct. 31   *Litho.*
Self-Adhesive
740 A347 45c sil & black   1.50 1.50

Regular Postal Services in Estonia, 375th Anniv. — A348

Perf. 14¼x13¾
2013, Nov. 13   *Litho.*
741 A348 45c multi   1.50 1.50

Aadu (Ado) Birk (1883-1942), Prime Minister — A349

2013, Nov. 14   *Litho.*   *Perf. 13¾x14*
742 A349 45c dull brown   1.25 1.25

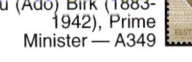
After Dinner, by Elmar Kits (1913-72) — A350

2013, Nov. 15   *Litho.*   *Perf. 14*
743 A350 €1.10 multi   2.50 2.50

A351

Christmas — A352

ESTONIA

Serpentine Die Cut 11¼ Syncopated
2013, Nov. 22   Litho.
Self-Adhesive

| 744 | A351 | 45c multi | 1.25 | 1.25 |
| 745 | A352 | €1 multi | 2.75 | 2.75 |

Estonian Olympic Committee, 90th Anniv. — A353

2013, Dec. 9   Litho.   Perf. 13¾x14
746 A353 45c multi   1.50 1.50

Jaan Tõnisson (1888-c. 1941), Prime Minister — A354

2013, Dec. 20   Litho.   Perf. 13¾x14
747 A354 45c brown   1.25 1.25

2014 Winter Olympics, Sochi, Russia — A355

2014, Jan. 16   Litho.   Perf. 14x13¾
748 A355 €1.10 multi   3.00 3.00

New Year 2014 (Year of the Horse) — A356

2014, Jan. 31   Litho.   Perf. 12¾x13
749 A356 €1.10 multi   3.00 3.00

Post Horn Type of 2008 With Euro Denomination Only
Die Cut Perf. 12½
2014, Feb. 19   Litho.
Self-Adhesive Dated "2014"

| 750 | A235 | 10c brt bl grn | .35 | .35 |
| a. | | Dated "2015" | .35 | .35 |

Issued: No. 750a, 10/16/15. Compare with No. 696.

Estonian History Museum. 150th Anniv. — A357

2014, Feb. 19   Litho.   Perf. 12¾x13
751 A357 45c multi   1.25 1.25

Pres. Konstantin Päts (1874-1956) — A358

2014, Feb. 21   Litho.   Perf. 13¾x14
752 A358 45c blue   1.25 1.25

Arms of Voru — A359

Die Cut Perf. 12½
2014, Mar. 5   Litho.
Self-Adhesive
753 A359 45c multi   1.25 1.25

Estonian Flag Type of 2013
Die Cut Perf. 11¼ Syncopated
2014, Mar. 5   Litho.
Self-Adhesive

| 754 | A332 | €2 multi | 5.50 | 5.50 |
| a. | | Dated "2018" | 4.75 | 4.75 |

Issued: No. 754a, 6/27/18.

Alcedo Atthis — A360

2014, Mar. 20   Litho.   Perf. 12¾x13
755 A360 45c multi   1.25 1.25

Folk Costumes — A361

Designs: 45c, Man and woman from Mihkli. €1, Women from Vigala.

2014, Apr. 12   Litho.   Perf. 13¾x14
756-757 A361 Set of 2   4.00 4.00

Juhan Liiv (1864-1913), Poet — A362

2014, Apr. 30   Litho.   Perf. 13
758 A362 45c multi   1.25 1.25

Inachis Io — A363

Serpentine Die Cut 12½
2014, May 2   Litho.
Booklet Stamp Self-Adhesive

| 759 | A363 | 45c multi | 1.40 | 1.40 |
| a. | | Booklet pane of 4 | 5.60 | |

Europa — A364

Musical instruments: No. 760, €1, Väikekannel (zither). No. 761, €1, Lootspill (accordion).

2014, May 8   Litho.   Perf. 14x13¾
760-761 A364 Set of 2   5.00 5.00

Erinaceus Europaeus A365

2014, May 30   Litho.   Perf. 12¾x13
762 A365 45c multi   1.25 1.25

Estonian Herdbook, Cent. — A366

2014, July 19   Litho.   Perf. 14x13½
Textured and Flocked Granite Paper
763 A366 €1 multi   2.75 2.75

Baltic Chain Demonstration, 25th Anniv. — A367

Designs: 55c, Man and child. No. 765: a, Five adults and one child. b, Three women. c, Like #764

2014, Aug. 23   Litho.   Perf. 13¼
764 A367 55c multi   1.50 1.50

Souvenir Sheet
765 A367 €1 Sheet of 3, #a-c   8.00 8.00

See Latvia Nos. 883-884; Lithuania No. 1031.

Souvenir Sheet

Tallinn Zoo, 75th Anniv. A368

No. 766: a, Gypaetus barbatus. b, Panthera pardus orientalis.

Perf. 14¼x13¾
2014, Aug. 25   Litho.
766 A368 55c Sheet of 2, #a-b   3.00 3.00

Estonian Academy of Arts, Cent. — A369

2014, Sept. 1   Litho.   Perf. 14x13¾
767 A369 55c multi   1.50 1.50

Inocybe Erubescens — A370

2014, Sept. 11   Litho.   Perf. 13¾x14
768 A370 55c red & black   1.40 1.40

Arms of Saue — A371

Die Cut Perf. 12½
2014, Sept. 11   Litho.
Self-Adhesive
769 A371 55c multi   1.40 1.40

1-Euro and 20-Cent Coins — A372

Die Cut Perf. 11¼ Syncopated
2014, Oct. 2   Litho.
Self-Adhesive
770 A372 €1.20 multi   3.00 3.00

Lighthouses — A373

Designs: 55c, Northern Soru Lighthouse. €1.30, Southern Soru Lighthouse.

2014, Oct. 17   Litho.   Perf. 13¾x14
771-772 A373 Set of 2   5.00 5.00

Personalized Stamp Type of 2012
Die Cut Perf. 8¾ Syncopated
2014, Nov. 17   Litho.
Self-Adhesive
773 A313 55c multi   1.40 1.40

The generic vignette, depicting a map of Hiiumaa, could be personalized for an additional fee.

Courtyard, by Herbert Lukk (1892-1919) — A374

2014, Nov. 17   Litho.   Perf. 14
774 A374 €1.30 multi   3.50 3.50

Christmas — A375

Christmas tree, ornaments and: 55c, Ribbon. €1.20, Pine cone.

Die Cut Perf. 11¼ Syncopated
2014, Nov. 20   Litho.
Self-Adhesive
775-776 A375 Set of 2   4.50 4.50

Jüri Uluots (1890-1945), Prime Minister — A376

2015, Jan. 13   Litho.   Perf. 13¾x14
777 A376 55c blue   1.25 1.25

Johannes Kotkas (1915-88), Wrestler A377

2015, Feb. 3   Litho.   Perf. 12½
778 A377 55c multi   1.25 1.25

New Year 2015 (Year of the Ram) — A378

2015, Feb. 19   Litho.   Perf. 12¾x13
779 A378 €1.30 multi   3.00 3.00

Eduard Vilde (1865-1933), Writer — A379

2015, Mar. 4   Litho.   Perf. 13
780 A379 55c multi   1.25 1.25

ESTONIA 453

Arms of Elva — A380

Die Cut Perf. 12½
2015, Mar. 12 Litho.
Self-Adhesive
781 A380 55c multi 1.25 1.25

Souvenir Sheet

Seal and Map of Baltic Sea — A381

2015, Mar. 12 Litho. Perf.
782 A381 €2.55 multi 6.25 6.25

Folk Costumes — A382

Designs: 55c, Man, woman and girl from Lihula. €1.20, Women from Kirbla.

2015, Apr. 14 Litho. Perf. 13¾x14
783-784 A382 Set of 2 4.00 4.00

Europa — A383

Designs: No. 785, €1.20, Toy horses. No. 786, €1.20, Stuffed animals.

2015, May 6 Litho. Perf. 14
785-786 A383 Set of 2 5.50 5.50

Pernis Apivorus — A384

2015, May 21 Litho. Perf. 12¾x13
787 A384 55c multi 1.25 1.25

Characters From Animated Film *Lotte From Gadgetville* — A385

No. 788: a, Bruno the Kitten. b, Albert the Bunny. c, Bruno, Albert and Lotte. d, Lotte the Puppy.

Serpentine Die Cut 5x6
2015, May 30 Litho.
Self-Adhesive
788 A385 Booklet pane of 4 + 6 stickers 5.50
a.-d. 55c Any single 1.35 1.35

Giraffe With Head Above Cloud — A386

Serpentine Die Cut 5x6
2015, June 4 Litho.
Booklet Stamp
Self-Adhesive
789 A386 €1.20 multi 2.75 2.75
a. Booklet pane of 4 11.00

Aleksander Warma (1890-1970), Prime Minister — A387

2015, June 22 Litho. Perf. 13¾x14
790 A387 55c Prus grn 1.25 1.25

European Under 23 Track and Field Championships, Tallinn — A388

2015, July 1 Litho. Perf. 14x13¾
791 A388 55c multi 1.25 1.25

Estonian Business Innovations — A389

No. 792: a, Fortumo. b, GrabCAD. c, Skype. d, TransferWise.

Die Cut Perf. 12½
2015, July 6 Litho.
Self-Adhesive
792 A389 Booklet pane of 4 12.00
a.-d. €1.30 Any single 3.00 3.00

Lutra Lutra — A390

2015, Aug. 25 Litho. Perf. 12¾x13
793 A390 55c multi 1.35 1.35

Arms of Paide — A391

Die Cut Perf. 12½
2015, Sept. 10 Litho.
Self-Adhesive
794 A391 55c multi 1.25 1.25

Cortinarius Rubellus — A392

2015, Sept. 10 Litho. Perf. 13¾x14
795 A392 55c multi 1.35 1.35

Tahkuna Lighthouse — A393

2015, Oct. 16 Litho. Perf. 14x13¾
796 A393 55c multi 1.25 1.25

Penny Black, 175th Anniv. — A394

2015, Nov. 13 Litho. Perf. 13½
797 A394 55c multi 1.25 1.25

A Girl and the Moon, by Karl Pärsimägi (1902-42) — A395

2015, Nov. 17 Litho. Perf. 14
798 A395 55c multi 1.25 1.25

A396

Christmas — A397

Die Cut Perf. 11¼ Syncopated
2015, Nov. 10 Litho.
Self-Adhesive
799 A396 55c multi 1.25 1.25
800 A397 €1.20 multi 2.60 2.60

Arthur Joachim von Oettingen (1836-1920), Meteorologist, and Tartu University Meteorological Observatory A398

2015, Dec. 2 Litho. Perf. 14¼x13¾
801 A398 65c multi 1.60 1.60
Tartu University Meteorological Observatory, 150th anniv.

Paul Keres (1916-75), Chess Player A399

2016, Jan. 7 Litho. Perf. 12½
802 A399 65c multi 1.50 1.50

Souvenir Sheet

Tolkuse Bog A400

2016, Feb. 2 Litho. Perf. 13
803 A400 €3.05 multi 7.25 7.25

New Year 2016 (Year of the Monkey) — A401

2016, Feb. 8 Litho. Perf. 12¾x13
804 A401 €1.50 multi 3.25 3.25

Arms of Keila — A402

Die Cut Perf. 12½
2016, Feb. 10 Litho.
Self-Adhesive
805 A402 65c multi 1.40 1.40

Posthorn — A403

Die Cut Perf. 12½
2016, Feb. 10 Litho.
Self-Adhesive
806 A403 €1.40 multi 3.00 3.00
a. Dated "2017" 3.00 3.00
Issued: No. 806a, 1/18/17.
See Nos. 816-818, 832-833, 926-928.

Parus Major — A404

2016, Feb. 17 Litho. Perf. 12¾x13
807 A404 65c multi 1.40 1.40

Architecture — A405

No. 808: a, Tartu University Narva College, Narva (magenta background). b, Snail Tower, Tartu (green background). c, Estonian Embassy, Beijing (yellow brown background). d, Rotermann Quarter, Tallinn (turquoise green background).

2016, Mar. 17 Litho. Perf. 14
808 A405 65c Block of 4, #a-d 6.00 6.00
e. Booklet pane of 4, #808a-808d 6.00 —
Complete booklet, #808e 6.00

ESTONIA

August Rei (1886-1963), Chairman of Estonian National Council — A406

2016, Mar. 22   Litho.   Perf. 13¾x14
809 A406 65c brown   1.50 1.50

Otepää, 900th Anniv. — A407

2016, Apr. 1   Litho.   Perf. 13¼x12¾
810 A407 65c multi   1.50 1.50

Folk Costumes — A408

Designs: 65c, Man and woman from Audru. €1.50, Girl and woman from Tostamaa.

2016, Apr. 14   Litho.   Perf. 13¾x14
811-812 A408 Set of 2   5.00 5.00

Self-Portrait of Ants Laikmaa (1866-1942), Painter — A409

2016, May 5   Litho.   Perf. 12¾x13
813 A409 65c multi   1.50 1.50

A410   Europa — A411

2016, May 9   Litho.   Perf. 14
814 A410 €1.40 multi   3.25 3.25
815 A411 €1.40 multi   3.25 3.25
Think Green Issue.

Posthorn Type of 2016
Die Cut Perf. 12½
2016, May 19   Self-Adhesive   Litho.
Background Colors
816 A403 5c yel & pale yel   .25   .25
817 A403 20c mag & pale mag   .45   .45
818 A403 40c brt grn & pale grn   .90   .90
     Nos. 816-818 (3)   1.60 1.60

2016 Summer Olympics, Rio de Janeiro — A412

2016, June 9   Litho.   Perf. 13¾x14¼
819 A412 €1.50 multi   3.50 3.50

Souvenir Sheet
Oil Shale Mining in Estonia, Cent. A413

Perf. 13¼x13½
2016, June 15   Litho.
820 A413 €2.95 multi   6.75 6.75

2016 Veterans' World Orienteering Championships, Tallinn and Harju County — A414

2016, Aug. 5   Litho.   Perf. 12¾x13
821 A414 €1.50 multi   3.50 3.50

Tonis Kint (1896-1991), Deputy Prime Minister of Exile Government — A415

2016, Aug. 17   Litho.   Perf. 13¾x14
822 A415 65c blue green   1.50 1.50

Sicista Betulina — A416

2016, Aug. 25   Litho.   Perf. 12¾x13
823 A416 65c multi   1.50 1.50

Amanita Muscaria — A417

2016, Sept. 8   Litho.   Perf. 13¾x14
824 A417 65c multi   1.50 1.50

National Museum A418

2016, Oct. 1   Litho.   Perf. 13
825 A418 €1.50 multi   3.50 3.50

Virtsu Lighthouse — A419

2016, Oct. 27   Litho.   Perf. 14x13¾
826 A419 65c multi   1.50 1.50

Baltic Assembly, 25th Anniv. — A420

2016, Nov. 8   Litho.   Perf. 13½
Stamp With White Frame
827 A420 65c multi   1.50 1.50

Souvenir Sheet
Stamp With Multicolored Frame
828 A420 €1.40 multi   3.25 3.25
  See Latvia Nos. 948-949, Lithuania Nos. 1088-1089.

Fish Above Karlova, by Valve Janov (1921-2003) A421

2016, Nov. 17   Litho.   Perf. 14
829 A421 65c multi   1.50 1.50

Cookies — A422

Stylized Christmas Tree — A423

Die Cut Perf. 13½x14
2016, Nov. 18   Self-Adhesive   Litho.
830 A422 65c multi   1.50 1.50
831 A423 €1.40 multi   3.25 3.25
  Christmas. No. 830 is impregnated with a gingerbread scent.

Posthorn Type of 2016
Die Cut Perf. 12½
2017, Jan. 18   Self-Adhesive   Litho.
Background Colors
832 A403 10c org & pale org   .30   .30
833 A403 65c bl grn & pale bl   1.50 1.50
  a. Dated "2019"   1.50 1.50
  Issued: No. 833a, 11/19/19.

New Year 2017 (Year of the Rooster) — A424

2017, Jan. 28   Litho.   Perf. 12¾x13
834 A424 €1.50 multi   3.50 3.50

Streptopelia Turtur — A425

2017, Feb. 9   Litho.   Perf. 12¾x13
835 A425 65c multi   1.50 1.50

Baltic Herring A426

2017, Feb. 23   Litho.   Perf. 13
836 A426 65c multi   1.50 1.50

Ships Built in Estonia A427

No. 837: a, Patrol 4500 WP patrol vessel. b, AC600PVDB fish feeding barge. c, Saare 46 yacht. d, Koidula ferry.

2017, Mar. 30   Litho.   Perf. 14
837 A427 65c Block of 4, #a-d   6.00 6.00
  e. Booklet pane of 4, #837a-837d   6.00
      Complete booklet, #837e   6.00
  No. 837 was printed in sheets containing two blocks that are tete-beche in relation to each other.

Souvenir Sheet

Figure Skating in Estonia, Cent. A428

2017, Apr. 15   Litho.   Perf. 13¼
838 A428 €3.05 multi + 2 labels   7.00 7.00

Lions Clubs International, Cent. — A429

2017, Apr. 29   Litho.   Perf. 13
839 A429 65c multi   1.50 1.50

Europa — A430

Designs: No. 840, €1.40, Keila-Joa Castle, lion. No. 841, €1.40, Maarjamäe Castle, eagle.

2017, May 8   Litho.   Perf. 12¾x13
840-841 A430 Set of 2   6.50 6.50

Estonian Presidency of the European Union Council in 2017 — A431

2017, May 13   Litho.   Perf. 14¼x14
842 A431 €1.40 multi   3.25 3.25

Statue of Martin Luther — A432

2017, May 27   Litho.   Perf. 13¾x14
843 A432 65c multi   1.50 1.50
  Protestant Reformation, 500th anniv.

Republic of Estonia, Cent. (in 2018) — A433

Die Cut Perf. 11¼ Syncopated
2017, June 1   Self-Adhesive   Litho.
844 A433 €1.50 multi   3.50 3.50

Gustav Boesberg (1867-1922), Weight Lifter — A434

2017, June 19   Litho.   Perf. 12½
845 A434 65c multi   1.50 1.50

ESTONIA

Constitution of Republic of Estonia, 25th Anniv. — A435

2017, June 28 Litho. *Perf. 14x13¾*
846 A435 65c multi 1.50 1.50

World Orienteering Championships, Estonia — A436

2017, July 1 Litho. *Perf. 13¾x14*
847 A436 €1.50 multi 3.50 3.50

Landscape with a Red Cloud, by Konrad Mägi (1878-1925) — A437

2017, Aug. 25 Litho. *Perf. 12¾x13*
848 A437 €1.50 multi 3.75 3.75

Orjaku Lighthouses — A438

Designs: 65c, Lighthouse 26mm tall. €1.40, Lighthouse 29mm tall.

2017, Sept. 8 Litho. *Perf. 13¾x14*
849-850 A438 Set of 2 5.00 5.00

Lynx — A439

2017, Sept. 11 Litho. *Perf. 12¾x13*
851 A439 65c multi 1.60 1.60

Paxillus Involutus — A440

2017, Sept. 21 Litho. *Perf. 13¾x14*
852 A440 65c multi 1.60 1.60

Pres. Kersti Kaljulaid — A441

2017, Oct. 10 Litho. *Perf. 13¾x14*
853 A441 65c multi 1.50 1.50

Juniper Forest, Painting by Ulo Sooster (1924-70) — A442

2017, Nov. 17 Litho. *Perf. 14*
854 A442 65c multi 1.60 1.60

Trees — A443

Designs: No. 855, Picea abies. No. 856, Sorbus aucuparia.

2017, Nov. 24 Litho. *Perf. 14*
855 A443 €1.40 multi 3.50 3.50
  a. Tete-beche pair 7.00 7.00
856 A443 €1.40 multi 3.50 3.50
  a. Tete-beche pair 7.00 7.00

See Romania Nos. 6031-6032.

Miniature Sheet

Christmas — A444

No. 857: a, Bells and cinnamon sticks (43x34mm). b, Two Christmas ornaments on tree (27x31mm). c, Christmas tree with ornaments (33x47mm). d, Snowman and gifts (28x32mm).

2017, Nov. 24 Litho. *Die Cut*
Self-Adhesive
857 A444 Sheet of 4 + 4 stickers, 2 etiquettes 7.00
  a.-d. 75c Any single 1.75 1.75

No. 857 is impregnated with a cinnamon scent.

2018 Winter Olympics, PyeongChang, South Korea — A445

2018, Jan. 12 Litho. *Perf. 13x12¾*
858 A445 €1.50 multi 3.75 3.75

Estonian Defense League, Cent. — A446

2018, Jan. 26 Litho. *Perf. 14x14¼*
859 A446 65c multi 1.60 1.60

New Year 2018 (Year of the Dog) — A447

2018, Feb. 16 Litho. *Perf. 12¾x13*
860 A447 €1.50 multi 3.75 3.75

Republic of Estonia, Cent. — A448

Die Cut Perf. 12¾x12½
Etched on Silver Foil
2018, Feb. 22 **Self-Adhesive**
861 A448 €10 silver 25.00 25.00

No. 861 was sold as a single stamp in a protective plastic box.

Flag of Estonia and Centenary Emblem — A449

Die Cut Perf. 11¼ Syncopated
2018, Mar. 15 Litho.
Self-Adhesive
862 A449 €1.40 multi 3.50 3.50
  a. Dated "2020" 3.25 3.25

Issued: No. 862a, 1/6/20. Compare with Illustration A332.

Tetrao Urogallus — A450

2018, Mar. 29 Litho. *Perf. 12¾x13*
863 A450 65c multi 1.60 1.60

Research Vessel Mare — A451

2018, Apr. 5 Litho. *Perf. 14x13¾*
864 A451 65c multi 1.60 1.60

Estonian Maritime Museum, 50th anniv.

Estonian Ballet, Cent. — A452

2018, Apr. 29 Litho. *Perf. 12¾x13*
865 A452 65c gold & blk 1.60 1.60

Europa — A453

Bridges in Tartu: No. 866, €1.40, Stone bridge. No. 867, €1.40, Arch bridge.

2018, May 3 Litho. *Perf. 14*
866-867 A453 Set of 2 6.50 6.50

Pres. Arnold Rüütel — A454

2018, May 5 Litho. *Perf. 13¾x14*
868 A454 65c cobalt & blue 1.50 1.50

Arms of Tallinn — A455

Die Cut Perf. 12½
2018, May 30 Litho.
Self-Adhesive
869 A455 65c multi 1.60 1.60

Manilaiu Lighthouse — A456

2018, June 7 Litho. *Perf. 14x13¾*
870 A456 65c multi 1.50 1.50

Estonia No. 1 — A457

2018, July 13 Litho. *Perf. 13¾x14*
871 A457 65c multi 1.60 1.60

First Estonian postage stamps, cent.

Kadriorg Palace, Tallinn, 300th Anniv. — A458

2018, July 22 Litho. *Perf. 13¾x14*
872 A458 65c multi 1.60 1.60

Gyromitra Esculenta — A459

2018, Aug. 23 Litho. *Perf. 13¾x14*
873 A459 65c multi 1.50 1.50

Litwinsky House, Tel Aviv — A460

2018, Aug. 28 Litho. *Perf. 14x13¾*
874 A460 €1.50 multi 3.50 3.50

See Israel No. 2192.

Souvenir Sheet

Winning Art in Children's Stamp Design Contest — A461

No. 875: a, Map of Estonia, by Tartu kindergarten students. b, Barn swallow, by Emeli Matjusenko. c, Windmill, by Ann-Elisbeth Sang.

Serpentine Die Cut 5x6
2018, Sept. 1 Litho.
Self-Adhesive
875 A461 Sheet of 3 8.25
  a. 65c multi 1.50 1.50
  b. €1.40 multi 3.25 3.25
  c. €1.50 multi 3.50 3.50

Tallinn University of Technology, Cent. — A462

2018, Sept. 17 Litho. *Perf. 14x13¾*
876 A462 €1.50 multi 3.50 3.50

ESTONIA

Souvenir Sheet

Automobiles From 1933 Tallinn-Monte Carlo Rally — A463

No. 877: a, Hotchkiss AM 80S. b, GAZ-M20 Pobeda.

2018, Sept. 18   Litho.   Perf. 14x13¾
877 A463 €1.50 Sheet of 2, #a-b   7.00 7.00

Canis Aureus — A464

2018, Oct. 18   Litho.   Perf. 12¾x13
878 A464 65c multi   1.50 1.50

Estonian Postal Service, Cent. — A465

Perf. 13¾x14¼
2018, Nov. 12   Litho.
879 A465 65c multi   1.50 1.50

Estonian Paintings A466

No. 880: a, Truu Valvur, by Johann Köler (1826-99). b, Merikapsad, by Konrad Mägi (1878-1925). c, Pühapäev, by Felix Randel (1901-77). d, Comédie-Française, by Karin Luts (1904-93).

2018, Nov. 17   Litho.   Perf. 12¾x13
880 A466 €1.50 Block or
            horiz. strip
            of 4, #a-d   14.00 14.00

Estonian Spelling Dictionary, Cent. — A467

2018, Nov. 20   Litho.   Perf. 14x13¾
881 A467 65c multi   1.50 1.50

Christmas — A468

Die Cut Perf. 13½x14
2018, Nov. 23   Litho.
Self-Adhesive
882 A468 €1.50 multi   3.50 3.50

No. 882 is impregnated with a pine scent.

Toomas Hendrik Ilves, 4th President of Estonia — A469

2018, Dec. 20   Litho.   Perf. 13¾x14
883 A469 65c blue   1.50 1.50

Estonian Red Cross, Cent. — A470

2019, Jan. 24   Litho.   Perf. 14x13¾
884 A470 65c multi   1.50 1.50

Arms of Narva-Joesuu — A471

Die Cut Perf. 12½
2019, Jan. 31   Litho.
Self-Adhesive
885 A471 65c sil & multi   1.50 1.50

New Year 2019 (Year of the Pig) — A472

2019, Feb. 5   Litho.   Perf. 12¾x13
886 A472 €1.50 gold & multi   3.50 3.50

Tallinn Cathedral School, 700th Anniversary — A473

No. 887: a, St. Mary's Cathedral. b, St. Mary's Cathedral school house and crest.

2019, Feb. 11   Litho.   Perf. 13¼
887 A473 €1.50 Sheet of 2,
            #a-b   7.00 7.00

Vello Agori (1894-1944), Cartoonist A474

Perf. 14¼x13¾
2019, Feb. 20   Litho.
888 A474 65c multi   1.50 1.50

Tallinn University, Cent. — A475

Perf. 14¼x13¾
2019, Feb. 22   Litho.
889 A475 65c multi   1.50 1.50

Osmussaare Lighthouse — A476

2019, Mar. 14   Litho.   Perf. 13¾x14
890 A476 65c multi   1.50 1.50

Hepatica Nobilis — A477

Serpentine Die Cut 6x7
2019, Mar. 28   Litho.
Self-Adhesive
891 A477 65c multi   1.50 1.50

Parliament of Estonia, Cent. — A478

2019, Apr. 24   Litho.   Perf. 13¾x14
892 A478 65c multi   1.50 1.50

Europa — A479

Map of Estonia and Hirundo rustica: No. 893, €1.40, Head. No. 894, €1.40, In flight.

2019, Apr. 25   Litho.   Perf. 14x13¾
893-894 A479 Set of 2   6.50 6.50

Estonian Bank, Cent. — A480

2019, May 3   Litho.   Perf. 14
895 A480 65c multi   1.50 1.50

Johann Voldemar Jannsen (1819-90), Journalist A481

2019, May 16   Litho.   Perf. 13
896 A481 65c multi   1.50 1.50

Metrosert (Central Office of Metrology), Cent. — A482

2019, May 20   Litho.   Perf. 14
897 A482 65c multi   1.50 1.50

Estonian Patent Office, Cent. — A483

2019, May 23   Litho.   Perf. 13¾
898 A483 65c multi   1.50 1.50

Battle of Lyndanisse, by Märt Bormeister (1916-91) — A484

2019, May 30   Litho.   Perf. 12¾x13
899 A484 €1.50 multi   3.50 3.50

First mention of Tallinn, 800th anniv.

Battle of Cesis, Cent. — A485

2019, June 21   Litho.   Perf. 14
900 A485 65c multi   1.50 1.50

Personalized Stamp Type of 2012
Die Cut Perf. 8¾ Syncopated
2019, July 5   Litho.
Self-Adhesive
901 A313 65c multi   1.50 1.50

The generic vignette depicting a map of Muhu could be personalized for an additional fee.

Souvenir Sheet

Estonian Song Festival, 150th Anniv. A486

2019, July 5   Litho.   Perf. 13½
On Cotton-faced Paper
902 A486 €10 multi   22.50 22.50

Galerina Marginata — A487

2019, Aug. 29   Litho.   Perf. 13¾x14
903 A487 65c multi   1.50 1.50

Souvenir Sheet

Fire Fighting in Estonia, Cent. A488

No. 904: a, Fire truck and female fire fighters, 1939. b, Fireman and helicopter fighting forest fire.

2019, Sept. 6   Litho.   Perf. 14
904 A488 Sheet of 2   6.50 6.50
a.-b. €1.50 Either single   3.25 3.25

Talpa Europaea — A489

2019, Sept. 11   Litho.   Perf. 12¾x13
905 A489 65c multi   1.40 1.40

ESTONIA 457

St. Peter's Church, Tartu, 150th Anniv. — A490
2019, Oct. 4 Litho. *Perf. 13¾x14*
906 A490 65c multi 1.50 1.50

Caprimulgus Europaeus A491
2019, Oct. 17 Litho. *Perf. 12¾x13*
907 A491 65c multi 1.50 1.50

Christmas — A492
Die Cut Perf. 13½x14
2019, Oct. 17 Litho.
Self-Adhesive
Flocked Paper
908 A492 65c multi 1.50 1.50

The Procession of the Bride, by Pieter Brueghel the Younger (1564-1638) A493
2019, Nov. 17 Litho. *Perf. 14x13¾*
909 A493 65c multi 1.50 1.50

National University, Tartu, Cent. — A494
2019, Nov. 19 Litho. *Perf. 13*
910 A494 65c multi 1.50 1.50

Ugala Theater, Viljandi, Cent. — A495
2020, Jan. 6 Litho. *Perf. 13¾x14*
911 A495 65c multi 1.50 1.50

Estonian Supreme Court, Cent. — A496
2020, Jan. 14 Litho. *Perf. 13*
912 A496 65c multi 1.50 1.50

New Year 2020 (Year of the Rat) — A497
2020, Jan. 25 Litho. *Perf. 12¾x13*
913 A497 €1.50 sil & multi 3.50 3.50

Souvenir Sheet

Discovery of Antarctica, 200th Anniv. — A498
2020, Jan. 28 Litho. *Perf. 14x14¼*
914 A498 €1.50 Sheet of 2, #a-b 6.75 6.75
No. 914: a, Fabian von Bellingshausen (1778-1852), explorer. b, Mikhail P. Lazarev (1788-1851), explorer.
Joint issue between Estonia and Russia. See Russia No. 8114.

Jaan Poska (1866-1920) Signing Tartu Peace Treaty, Cent. — A499
2020, Jan. 29 Litho. *Perf. 13*
915 A499 65c multi 1.50 1.50

Jaan Kross (1920-2007), Writer — A500
2020, Feb. 19 Litho. *Perf. 12¾x13*
916 A500 65c multi 1.50 1.50

St. Nicholas' Church, Paldiski — A501
2020, Feb. 27 Litho. *Perf. 14x13¾*
917 A501 65c multi 1.50 1.50

National Archives, Cent. — A502
2020, Mar. 3 Litho. *Perf. 12¾x13*
918 A502 65c sil & multi 1.50 1.50

Souvenir Sheet

Georg Ots (1920-75), Singer — A503
2020, Mar. 21 Litho. *Perf. 13*
919 A503 €5.50 multi 12.00 12.00

Estonian Internal Security Service, Cent. — A504
2020, Apr. 6 Litho. *Perf. 13*
920 A504 65c multi 1.50 1.50

Estonian Students' Society, 150th Anniv. — A505
2020, Apr. 7 Litho. *Perf. 14x13½*
921 A505 65c multi 1.50 1.50

Estonian Girl Guides, Cent. — A506
2020, Apr. 23 Litho. *Perf. 12½*
922 A506 €1.50 multi 3.25 3.25

Podiceps Cristatus — A507
2020, Apr. 30 Litho. *Perf. 12¾x13*
923 A507 65c multi 1.50 1.50

Tartu-Voru Post Road — A508

Estonian Road Museum, Varbuse — A509
2020, May 14 Litho. *Perf. 14x13¾*
924 A508 €1.90 multi 4.25 4.25
925 A509 €1.90 multi 4.25 4.25
Ancient Postal Routes.
Europa.

Posthorn Type of 2016
Die Cut Perf. 12½
2020, May 26 Litho.
Self-Adhesive
Background Colors
926 A403 5c ol yel & pale grn .25 .25
927 A403 25c purple & lilac .55 .55
928 A403 90c brt org & pale org 2.00 2.00
Nos. 926-928 (2) 2.80 2.80

Estonian Flag Type of 2013
Die Cut Perf. 11¼ Syncopated
2020, May 26 Litho.
Self-Adhesive
929 A332 €1.90 multi 4.25 4.25

Euphydryas Aurinia — A510
Serpentine Die Cut 5x6
2020, June 11 Litho.
Booklet Stamp
Self-Adhesive
930 A510 90c multi 2.00 2.00
a. Booklet pane of 4 8.00

Amanita Pantherina — A511
2020, Aug. 28 Litho. *Perf. 13¾x14*
931 A511 90c multi 2.25 2.25

Alfred Neuland (1895-1966), First Estonian Olympic Gold Medalist — A512
Etched on Silver Foil
2020, Aug. 28 *Die Cut Perf. 13x12½*
Self-Adhesive
932 A512 €13 silver 31.00 31.00
No. 932 was sold individually inside a plastic case.

Souvenir Sheet

Toyota Yaris 2020 Rally Estonia Race Car A513
2020, Sept. 4 Litho. *Perf. 12¾x13¼*
933 A513 €5.90 multi 14.00 14.00

Souvenir Sheet

Estonian Railroads, 150th Anniv. — A514
Litho. With Foil Application
2020, Sept. 10 *Perf. 13¼*
934 A514 €5.90 sil & multi 14.00 14.00

Rattus Rattus — A515
2020, Sept. 11 Litho. *Perf. 12¾x13*
935 A515 90c multi 2.10 2.10

Christmas A516
Designs: 90c, Bells. €1.90, Christmas tree.
Die Cut Perf. 12¼x12¾
2020, Oct. 15 Litho.
Self-Adhesive
936-937 A516 Set of 2 6.50 6.50

458 ESTONIA

Kihnu Lighthouse — A517

2020, Oct. 26   Litho.   *Perf. 14x13¾*
938   A517   90c multi   2.10   2.10

River Seine, by Ado Vabbe (1892-1961) — A518

2020, Nov. 17   Litho.   *Perf. 14*
939   A518   90c multi   2.25   2.25

Voldemar Panso (1920-77), Actor and Director — A519

2020, Nov. 30   Litho.   *Perf. 14x13¾*
940   A519   90c multi   2.25   2.25

Letipea Lighthouse — A520

2021, Jan. 21   Litho.   *Perf. 14x13¾*
941   A520   90c multi   2.25   2.25

Roses — A521

Serpentine Die Cut
2021, Feb. 4   Litho.
Self-Adhesive
942   A521   90c multi   2.25   2.25

Valentine's Day.

New Year 2021 (Year of the Ox) — A522

2021, Feb. 12   Litho.   *Perf. 12¾x13*
943   A522   €1.90 multi   4.75   4.75

Estonian Medical Association, Cent. — A523

2021, Feb. 27   Litho.   *Perf. 12½*
944   A523   90c multi   2.25   2.25

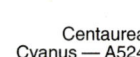
Centaurea Cyanus — A524

Die Cut Perf. 12½
2021, Mar. 1   Litho.
Self-Adhesive
945   A524   90c multi   2.25   2.25

See No. 1001.

Statistics Estonia, Cent. — A525

2021, Mar. 1   Litho.   *Perf. 14x13¾*
946   A525   90c multi   2.25   2.25

Souvenir Sheet

King's Pine, Järvselja Nature Reserve A526

Serpentine Die Cut 6½ Syncopated
2021, Apr. 13   Litho.
On Wood Veneer
Self-Adhesive
947   A526   €7.50 multi   18.00   18.00

Souvenir Sheet

Estonian Ornithological Society, Cent. — A527

No. 948: a, Sturnus vulgaris. b, Society emblem, bird, binoculars and notebook.

2021, Apr. 29   Litho.   *Perf. 12¾x13*
948   A527   €1.90 Sheet of 2, #a-b   9.25   9.25

Upupa Epops — A528

Cypripedium Calceolus A529

2021, May 6   Litho.   *Perf. 13*
949   A528   €1.90 multi   4.75   4.75
950   A529   €1.90 multi   4.75   4.75

Endangered species. Europa.

Papaver Rhoeas — A530

2021, May 20   Litho.   *Perf. 13¼*
951   A530   €4 multi   9.75   9.75

A poppy seed is under a gummed circle of plastic in the center of the stamp.

2020 Summer Olympics, Tokyo — A531

2021, May 26   Litho.   *Perf. 13¾x14¼*
952   A531   €1.90 multi   4.75   4.75

The 2020 Summer Olympics were postponed until 2021 because of the COVID-19 pandemic.

Eighth World Congress of Finno-Ugric Peoples, Tartu — A532

Perf. 14¼x13¾
2021, June 16   Litho.
953   A532   90c multi   2.25   2.25

European Under-23 and Under-20 Track and Field Championships, Tallinn — A533

2021, July 12   Litho.   *Perf. 12½*
954   A533   €1.90 multi   4.50   4.50

People on Village Swing — A534

Perf. 13¾x14¼
2021, Aug. 12   Litho.
955   A534   90c multi   2.25   2.25

Estonian Soccer Federation, Cent. — A535

Silk-Screened
2021, Aug. 30   Die Cut
Self-Adhesive
Printed on Foam-backed Plastic
956   A535   €5.90 blue & black   14.00   14.00

Mustela Erminea — A536

2021, Sept. 10   Litho.   *Perf. 12¾x13*
957   A536   90c multi   2.10   2.10

First Film Screening in Estonia, 125th Anniv. — A537

2021, Sept. 16   Litho.   *Perf. 13*
958   A537   90c multi   2.10   2.10

St. Michael's Church, Keila — A538

2021, Sept. 17   Litho.   *Perf. 13¾x14*
959   A538   90c multi   2.10   2.10

Estonian Civil Aviation, Cent. — A539

Perf. 14¼x13¾
2021, Sept. 20   Litho.
960   A539   €1.90 multi   4.50   4.50

Christmas — A540

Designs: 90c, Eurasian bullfinch. €1.90, Squirrel.

Die Cut Perf. 11¼ Syncopated
2021, Oct. 15   Litho.
Self-Adhesive
961-962   A540   Set of 2   6.50   6.50

Estonian Federation of the Blind, Cent. — A541

Litho. & Embossed
2021, Oct. 19   *Perf. 14x13¾*
963   A541   90c black & blue   2.10   2.10

Canis Lupus — A542

2021, Oct. 19   Litho.   *Perf. 12¾x13*
964   A542   90c multi   2.10   2.10

Ministry of Foreign Affairs, Tallinn, and Itamaraty Palace, Brasilia — A543

2021, Nov. 10   Litho.   *Perf. 13*
965   A543   €1.90 multi   4.50   4.50

Diplomatic relations between Estonia and Brazil, cent. See Brazil No. 3476.

Personalized Stamp Type of 2012
Die Cut Perf. 8¾ Syncopated
2021, Nov. 17   Litho.
Self-Adhesive
966   A313   90c multi   2.10   2.10

The generic vignette shown, depicting a map of Vormsi, could be personalized for an additional fee. A similar 90c stamp, having a generic vignette depicting a map of Naissaar, was issued on Feb. 16, 2023.

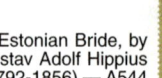
Estonian Bride, by Gustav Adolf Hippius (1792-1856) — A544

2021, Nov. 17   Litho.   *Perf. 14*
967   A544   90c multi   2.10   2.10

ESTONIA

Souvenir Sheet

Estonian Women's Epee Team, Gold Medalists at 2020 Summer Olympics — A545

2021, Dec. 29   Litho.   Perf. 12¾x13
968 A545 €5.90 multi   13.50 13.50

The 2020 Summer Olympics were postponed until 2021 because of the COVID-19 pandemic.

St. Mary's Church, Tartu — A546

2022, Jan. 6   Litho.   Perf. 13¾x14
969 A546 90c multi   2.10 2.10

2022 Winter Olympics, Beijing — A547

2022, Jan. 6   Litho.   Perf. 13
970 A547 €1.90 multi   4.25 4.25

New Year 2022 (Year of the Tiger) — A548

2022, Feb. 1   Litho.   Perf. 12¾x13
971 A548 €1.90 multi   4.25 4.25

Rear Admiral Johan Pitka (1872-1944) A549

2022, Feb. 19   Litho.   Perf. 13
972 A549 90c multi   2.00 2.00

Society of Estonian Writers, 150th Anniv. — A550

2022, Mar. 9   Litho.   Perf. 13
973 A550 90c multi   2.00 2.00

Dove and Flag of Ukraine — A551

Die Cut Perf. 11¼ Syncopated
2022, Mar. 24   Litho.
   Self-Adhesive
974 A551 €1.90 multi   4.25 4.25

Estonian solidarity with Ukraine after its invasion by Russia.

Scolopax Rusticola — A552

2022, Mar. 31   Litho.   Perf. 12¾x13
975 A552 90c multi   2.00 2.00

Town Hall Pharmacy, Tallinn, 600th Anniv. — A553

2022, Apr. 8   Litho.   Perf. 13¾x14¼
976 A553 €1.90 multi   4.00 4.00

Souvenir Sheet

Estonian Tennis Association, Cent. — A554

No. 977: a, Kaia Kanepi (blue background). b, Anett Kontaveit (green background).

2022, Apr. 11   Litho.   Perf. 13¾
977 A554 €1.90 Sheet of 2, #a-b   8.00 8.00

Betula Pendula Var. Carelica — A555

2022, Apr. 20   Litho.   Perf. 13¾x14¼
978 A555 90c multi   1.90 1.90

Tapestry of Siuru Bird, by Oskar Kallis — A556

Doing a Handstand, Painting by Kallis — A557

2022, May 5   Litho.   Perf. 14
979 A556 €1.90 multi   4.25 4.25
980 A557 €1.90 multi   4.25 4.25

Europa. Scenes from *Kalevipoeg*, Estonian national epic poem, by Friedrich Reinhold Kreutzwald (1803-82).

Miniature Sheet

Flowers A558

No. 981: a, Galanthus. b, Anthemis arvensis. c, Aster. d, Symphoricarpos.

Die Cut Perf. 11¼ Syncopated
2022, May 19   Litho.
   Self-Adhesive
981 A558 Sheet of 4   8.00
a.-d.   90c Any single   2.00 2.00

Cat Mailing Postcard — A559

2022, June 1   Litho.   Perf. 12¾x13
982 A559 90c multi   2.00 2.00

Motorized Sailboat Läänemaa — A560

2022, June 9   Litho.   Perf. 14x13¾
983 A560 90c multi   1.90 1.90

Diplomatic Relations Between Estonia and the United States, Cent. — A561

Perf. 14¼x13¾
2022, June 17   Litho.
984 A561 €1.90 multi   4.00 4.00

Tallinn Town Hall, 700th Anniv. — A562

Die Cut Perf. 11¼ Syncopated
2022, July 7   Litho.
   Self-Adhesive
985 A562 90c multi   1.90 1.90

Piano Built by Estonia Klaverivabrik A563

2022, Aug. 25   Litho.   Perf. 12¾x13
986 A563 90c multi   1.90 1.90

Pteromys Volans — A564

2022, Sept. 9   Litho.   Perf. 12¾x13
987 A564 90c multi   1.75 1.75

Riigikogu (Parliament) Building, Tallinn, Cent. — A565

2022, Sept. 12   Litho.   Perf. 14x14¼
988 A565 90c multi   1.75 1.75

Postcrossing — A566

Die Cut Perf. 11¼ Syncopated
2022, Oct. 1   Litho.
   Self-Adhesive
989 A566 €1.90 multi   3.75 3.75

Christmas — A567

Angel: 90c, Playing flute. €1.90, Holding candle.

Die Cut Perf. 8½x9 Syncopated
2022, Oct. 20   Litho.
   Self-Adhesive
990-991 A567 Set of 2   5.75 5.75

Souvenir Sheet

Livonian Diet, 600th Anniv. — A568

Litho. With Foil Application
2022, Oct. 25   Perf. 13¾x14
992 A568 €5.90 multi   12.00 12.00

Narva-Joesuu Lighthouse — A569

2022, Oct. 27   Litho.   Perf. 14x13¾
993 A569 90c multi   1.75 1.75

Souvenir Sheet

Road Safety A570

2022, Nov. 1   Litho.   Impert.
   Self-Adhesive
   On Reflective Plastic Film
994 A570 €4 multi   8.00 8.00

No. 994 has simulated perforations.

A Walk, Painting by Adamson-Eric (1902-68) — A571

2022, Nov. 17   Litho.   Perf. 14
995 A571 90c multi   1.90 1.90

460 ESTONIA

St. Elizabeth's Church, Pärnu — A572

2023, Jan. 6 Litho. *Perf. 13¾x14*
996 A572 90c multi 2.00 2.00

Konstantin Konik (1873-1936), Surgeon and Politician A573

2023, Feb. 21 Litho. *Perf. 13*
997 A573 90c multi 2.00 2.00

Artur Alliksaar (1923-66), Poet — A574

Perf. 14¼x13¾
2023, Mar. 14 Litho.
998 A574 90c multi 2.00 2.00

Picea Abies — A575

2023, Apr. 12 Litho. *Perf. 13¾x14¼*
999 A575 90c multi 2.00 2.00

Clangula Hyemalis — A576

2023, Apr. 20 Litho. *Perf. 12¾x13*
1000 A576 90c multi 2.00 2.00

Centaurea Cyanus Type of 2021
Die Cut Perf. 12½
2023, Apr. 27 Litho.
Self-Adhesive
1001 A524 €1.30 multi 3.00 3.00

Estonian Flag Type of 2013
Die Cut Perf. 11¼ Syncopated
2023, Apr. 27 Litho.
Self-Adhesive
1002 A332 €2.60 multi 5.75 5.75

Looming Magazine, Cent. — A577

2023, Apr. 27 Litho. *Perf. 14¼x13¾*
1003 A577 €1.30 multi 3.00 3.00

Wrecked Hanseatic Merchant Ship — A578

2023, May 2 Litho. *Perf. 14x13¾*
1004 A578 €1.30 multi 2.75 2.75

Danse Macabre (Tallinn Version), Painting by Bernt Notke (c. 1440-c. 1509) — A579

2023, May 18 Litho. *Perf. 13x13¼*
1005 A579 €6 multi 13.00 13.00
No. 1005 is shown sideways.

Europa — A580

2023, May 25 Litho. *Perf. 14¼x13¾*
1006 A580 €2.60 multi 5.75 5.75

Rudolf Tobias (1873-1918), Organist and Composer — A581

2023, May 29 Litho. *Perf. 14x13¾*
1007 A581 €1.30 multi 2.75 2.75

Sipsik, Character From Children's Book by Eno Raud (1928-96) — A582

Die Cut Perf. 8½x8¾ Syncopated
2023, June 1 Litho.
Self-Adhesive
1008 A582 €1.30 multi 2.75 2.75

Admission to North Atlantic Treaty Organization of Finland — A583

Die Cut Perf. 11¼ Syncopated
2023, June 2 Litho.
Self-Adhesive
1009 A583 €2.60 multi 5.75 5.75

SEMI-POSTAL STAMPS

Assisting Wounded Soldier SP1

Offering Aid to Wounded Hero SP2

1920, June Unwmk. Litho. *Imperf.*
B1 SP1 35p + 10p red & ol grn .50 2.00
B2 SP2 70p + 15p dp bl & brn .50 2.00

Surcharged

1920
B3 SP1 1m on No. B1 .35 .30
B4 SP2 2m on No. B2 .35 .30

Nurse and Wounded Soldier — SP3

1921, Aug. 1 *Imperf.*
B5 SP3 2½ (3½)m org, brn & car 2.00 8.00
B6 SP3 5 (7)m ultra, brn & car 2.00 8.00

1922, Apr. 26 *Perf. 13½x14*
B7 SP3 2½ (3½)m org, brn & car 2.00 8.00
 a. Vert. pair, imperf. horiz. 30.00 95.00
B8 SP3 5 (7)m ultra, brn & car 2.00 8.00
 a. Vert. pair, imperf. horiz. 30.00 95.00

Nos. B5-B8 Overprinted

1923, Oct. 8 *Imperf.*
B9 SP3 2½ (3½)m 60.00 160.00
B10 SP3 5 (7)m 60.00 160.00

Perf. 13½x14
B11 SP3 2½ (3½)m 60.00 160.00
 a. Vert. pair, imperf. horiz. 300.00 1,000.
B12 SP3 5 (7)m 60.00 160.00
 a. Vert. pair, imperf. horiz. 300.00 1,000.
Nos. B9-B12 (4) 240.00 640.00
Set, never hinged 480.00
Excellent forgeries are plentiful.

Nos. B7 and B8 Surcharged

1926, June 15
B13 SP3 5 (6)m on #B7 3.75 9.50
 a. Vert. pair, imperf. horiz. 32.50 120.00
B14 SP3 10 (12)m on #B8 4.50 9.50
 a. Vert. pair, imperf. horiz. 32.50 120.00

Nos. B5-B14 had the franking value of the lower figure. They were sold for the higher figure, the excess going to the Red Cross Society.

Kuressaare Castle SP4

Tartu Cathedral SP5

Tallinn Castle SP6 — Narva Fortress SP7

View of Tallinn — SP8

Laid Paper
Perf. 14½x14
1927, Nov. 19 Typo. *Wmk. 207*
B15 SP4 5m + 5m bl grn & ol, *grysh* .60 9.50
B16 SP5 10m + 10m dp bl & brn, *cream* .60 9.50
B17 SP6 12m + 12m rose red & ol grn, *bluish* .60 9.50
Perf. 14x13½
B18 SP7 20m + 20m bl & choc, *gray* .60 9.50
B19 SP8 40m + 40m org brn & slate, *buff* .60 9.50
Nos. B15-B19 (5) 3.00 47.50
Set, never hinged 10.00

The money derived from the surtax was donated to the Committee for the commemoration of War for Liberation.

Red Cross Issue

Symbolical of Succor to Injured SP9

Symbolical of "Light of Hope" SP10

1931, Aug. 1 Unwmk. *Perf. 13½*
B20 SP9 2s + 3s grn & car 10.00 9.50
B21 SP10 5s + 3s red & car 10.00 9.50
B22 SP10 10s + 3s lt bl & car 10.00 9.50
B23 SP9 20s + 3s dk bl & car 12.00 20.00
Nos. B20-B23 (4) 42.00 48.50
Set, never hinged 85.00

Nurse and Child SP11

Taagepera Sanatorium SP12

Lorraine Cross and Flower — SP13

Paper with Network as in Parenthesis
1933, Oct. 1 *Perf. 14, 14½*
B24 SP11 5s + 3s ver (grn) 8.00 8.00
B25 SP12 10s + 3s lt bl & red (vio) 8.00 8.00
B26 SP13 12s + 3s rose & red (grn) 10.00 12.00
B27 SP12 20s + 3s dk bl & red (org) 12.00 16.00
Nos. B24-B27 (4) 38.00 44.00
Set, never hinged 75.00

The surtax was for a fund to combat tuberculosis.

Coats of Arms

Narva SP14

Pärnu SP15

Tartu SP16

Tallinn SP17

Paper with Network as in Parenthesis
1936, Feb. 1 *Perf. 13½*
B28 SP14 10s + 10s grn & ultra (gray) 2.50 8.00
B29 SP15 15s + 15s car & bl (gray) 4.00 12.00
B30 SP16 25s + 25s gray bl & red (brn) 4.50 16.00

ESTONIA

```
B31  SP17 50s + 50s blk & dl
           org (ol)         18.00  52.50
     Nos. B28-B31 (4)       29.00  88.50
     Set, never hinged      57.50
```

Paide SP18

Rakvere SP19

Valga SP20

Viljandi SP21

Paper with Network as in Parenthesis

1937, Jan. 2 Perf. 13½x14
```
B32  SP18 10s + 10s grn (gray)  2.50   9.50
B33  SP19 15s + 15s red brn
              (gray)             3.50   9.50
B34  SP20 25s + 25s dk bl (lil)  4.00  14.50
B35  SP21 50s + 50s dk vlo
              (gray)            10.00  24.00
     Nos. B32-B35 (4)           20.00  57.50
     Set, never hinged          40.00
```

Baltiski SP22

Võru SP23

Haapsalu SP24

Kuressaare SP25

Designs are the armorial bearings of various cities

1938, Jan. 21
Paper with Gray Network
```
B36  SP22 10s + 10s dk brn     2.00   8.00
B37  SP23 15s + 15s car & grn  2.00  12.00
B38  SP24 25s + 25s dk bl &
              car                    4.00  20.00
B39  SP25 50s + 50s blk & org
              yel                12.00  40.00
  a. Sheet of 4, #B36-B39     30.00  95.00
     Nos. B36-B39 (4)          20.00  80.00
     Set, never hinged         40.00
```
Annual charity ball, Tallinn, Jan. 2, 1938.

Viljandimaa SP27

Pärnumaa SP28

Tartumaa SP29

Harjumaa SP30

Designs are the armorial bearings of various cities

1939, Jan. 10 Perf. 13½
Paper with Gray Network
```
B41  SP27 10s + 10s dk bl
              grn                2.00   8.00
B42  SP28 15s + 15s carmine     2.00   8.00
B43  SP29 25s + 25s dk blue     6.00  20.00
B44  SP30 50s + 50s brn lake   16.00  47.50
  a. Sheet of 4, #B41-B44     45.00 175.00
     Nos. B41-B44 (4)          26.00  83.50
     Set, never hinged         52.50
```

Võrumaa SP32

Järvamaa SP33

Läänemaa SP34

Saaremaa SP35

Designs are the armorial bearings of various cities

1940, Jan. 2 Typo. Perf. 13½
Paper with Gray Network
```
B46  SP32 10s + 10s dp grn &
              ultra              2.00  12.00
B47  SP33 15s + 15s dk car &
              ultra              2.00  16.00
B48  SP34 25s + 25s dk bl &
              scar               3.00  24.00
B49  SP35 50s + 50s ocher &
              ultra              8.00  32.50
     Nos. B46-B49 (4)           15.00  84.50
     Set, never hinged          30.00
```

Catalogue values for unused stamps in this section, from this point to the end of the section, are for Never Hinged items.

1992 Summer Olympics, Barcelona — SP40

1992, June 22 Litho. Perf. 14
```
B60  SP40 1r +50k red             .40   .40
B61  SP40 3r +1.50r green        1.75  1.75
B62  SP40 5r +2.50r blue & blk    .80   .80
     Nos. B60-B62 (3)            2.95  2.95
```
While face values are shown in kopecks and rubles, the stamps were sold in the new currency at the rate of 1 ruble = 10 sents.

No. 280 Surcharged

1994, Nov. 18 Litho. Perf. 14
```
B63  A51 2.50k +20k green        6.00  6.00
```
Surtax for benefit of survivors of sinking of ferry "Estonia."

Hallaeetus Albicilla — SP41

1995, Aug. 29 Litho. Perf. 14
```
B64  SP41 2k +26k black & blue    .40   .40
```
Surtax for Keep the Estonian Sea Clean Assoc.

UNICEF, 60th Anniv. — SP42

2006, June 1 Litho. Perf. 13½
```
B65  SP42 4.40k +1k multi        1.00  1.00
```

Stylized Map of Estonia — SP43

Perf. 14¼x13¾
2022, Sept. 16 Litho.
```
B66  SP43 90c +€1 multi          3.75  3.75
```
Estonian Cancer Society, 30th anniv. Surtax for Estonian Cancer Society.

AIR POST STAMPS

Airplane — AP1

Unwmk.
1920, Mar. 13 Typo. Imperf.
```
C1   AP1 5m yel, blk & lt grn    2.50  6.50
     Never hinged                7.00
```

No. C1 Overprinted "1923" in Red
1923, Oct. 1
```
C2   AP1 5m multicolored         8.00  32.50
     Never hinged               16.00
```

No. C1 Surcharged in Red

1923, Oct. 1
```
C3   AP1 15m on 5m multi        16.00  17.50
     Never hinged               32.50
```

Pairs of No. C1 Surcharged in Black or Red

1923, Oct.
```
C4   AP1 10m on 5m+5m           10.00   35.00
C5   AP1 20m on 5m+5m           20.00   55.00
C6   AP1 45m on 5m+5m           60.00  200.00
```
Rough Perf. 11½
```
C7   AP1 10m on 5m+5m
              (B)              650.00 1,600.
C8   AP1 20m on 5m+5m          275.00   725.00
     Nos. C4-C8 (5)           1,015.  2,615.
     Set, never hinged        1,850.
```
The pairs comprising Nos. C7 and C8 are imperforate between. Forged surcharges and perforations abound. Authentication is required.

Monoplane in Flight — AP2

Designs: Various views of planes in flight.

1924, Feb. 12 Imperf.
```
C9   AP2  5m yellow & blk       1.60   8.00
C10  AP2 10m blue & blk         1.60   8.00
C11  AP2 15m red & blk          1.60   8.00
C12  AP2 20m green & blk        1.60   8.00
C13  AP2 45m violet & blk       1.60  16.00
     Nos. C9-C13 (5)            8.00  48.00
     Set, never hinged         16.00
```
The paper is covered with a faint network in pale shades of the frame colors. There are four varieties of the frames and five of the pictures.

1925, July 15 Perf. 13½
```
C14  AP2  5m yellow & blk       1.25   8.00
C15  AP2 10m blue & blk         1.25   8.00
C16  AP2 15m red & blk          1.25   8.00
C17  AP2 20m green & blk        1.25   8.00
C18  AP2 45m violet & blk       1.25  16.00
     Nos. C14-C18 (5)           6.25  48.00
     Set, never hinged         12.00
```
Counterfeits of Nos. C1-C18 are plentiful.

REGISTRATION STAMP

Catalogue values for unused stamps in this section are for Never Hinged items.

Arms Type of 1992
1992, Mar. 16 Litho. Perf. 13x12½
```
F1   A42  R (10r) pink & red     .60   .60
```

OCCUPATION STAMPS

Issued under German Occupation
For Use in Tartu (Dorpat)

Russian Stamps of 1909-12 Surcharged

1918 **Unwmk.** Perf. 14x14½
```
N1   A15 20pf on 10k dk bl     40.00 160.00
N2   A8  40pf on 20k bl &
              car              40.00 160.00
     Set, never hinged        250.00
```
Forged overprints exist.

Estonian Arms and Swastika — OS1

Perf. 11½
1941, Aug. Typo. Unwmk.
```
N3   OS1 15k brown              8.00  16.00
N4   OS1 20k green              5.50  14.50
N5   OS1 30k dark blue          5.50  14.50
     Nos. N3-N5 (3)            19.00  45.00
     Set, never hinged         45.00
```
Exist imperf. Value, set $200.
Nos. N3-N5 were issued on both ordinary paper with colorless gum and thick chalky paper with yellow gum. Value, set on chalky paper $22.50.

OCCUPATION SEMI-POSTAL STAMPS

Castle Tower, Tallinn — OSP1

Designs: 20k+20k, Stone Bridge, Tartu, horiz. 30k+30k, Narva Castle, horiz. 50k+50k, Tallinn view, horiz. 60k+60k, Tartu University. 100k+100k, Narva Castle, close view.

Paper with Gray Network
Perf. 11½
1941, Sept. 29 Photo. Unwmk.
```
NB1  OSP1 15k + 15k dk brn       .60   4.75
NB2  OSP1 20k + 20k red lil      .60   4.75
NB3  OSP1 30k + 30k dk bl        .60   4.75
NB4  OSP1 50k + 50k bluish
              grn                .70   9.50
NB5  OSP1 60k + 60k gar         1.00   9.50
NB6  OSP1 100k + 100k gray      1.50   9.50
     Nos. NB1-NB6 (6)           5.00  41.25
     Set, never hinged         10.00
```
Nos. NB1-NB6 exist imperf. Value, set unused $70, used $200.
A miniature sheet containing one each of Nos. NB1-NB6, imperf., exists in various colors. Value, mint $40, used $60. It was not postally valid. Reproductions are common.

ETHIOPIA

ē-thē-'ō-pē-ə

(Abyssinia)

LOCATION — Northeastern Africa
GOVT. — Republic (1988)
AREA — 426,260 sq. mi.
POP. — 114,960,000 (2020 est.)
CAPITAL — Addis Ababa

During the Italian occupation (1936-1941) Nos. N1-N7 were used, also stamps of Italian East Africa, Eritrea and Somalia.
During the British administration (1941-42) stamps of Great Britain and Kenya were used when available.

16 Guerche = 1 Menelik Dollar or 1 Maria Theresa Dollar
100 Centimes = 1 Franc (1905)
40 Paras = 1 Piaster (1908)
16 Mehalek = 1 Thaler or Talari (1928)
100 Centimes = 1 Thaler (1936)
100 Cents = 1 Ethiopian Dollar (1946)
100 Cents = 1 Birr (1978)

Catalogue values for unused stamps in this country are for Never Hinged items, beginning with Scott 247 in the regular postage section, Scott B6 in the semi-postal section, Scott C18 in the airpost section, Scott E1 in the special delivery section, and Scott J57 in the postage due section.

Watermarks

Wmk. 140 — Crown

Wmk. 282 — Ethiopian Star and Amharic Characters, Multiple

Excellent forgeries of Nos. 1-86 exist.

Very Fine examples of Nos. 1-86 and J1-J42 will have perforations touching the design on one or more sides due to the narrow spacing of the stamps on the plates and imperfect perforating methods. Stamps with margins clear on all sides are scarce and command high premiums.

On March 9, 1894 Menelik II awarded Alfred Ilg a concession to develop a railway, including postal service. Ilg's stamps, Nos. 1-79, were valid locally and to Djibouti. Mail to other countries had to bear stamps of Obock, Somali Coast, etc.
Ethiopia joined the UPU Nov. 1, 1908.

Menelik II
A1

Lion of Judah
A2

Amharic numeral "8"

Perf. 14x13½

1895, Jan.   Unwmk.   Typo.
1	A1	¼g green	4.00	6.00
2	A1	½g red	3.50	5.00
3	A1	1g blue	3.50	5.00
4	A1	2g dark brown	3.00	6.00
5	A2	4g lilac brown	3.00	6.00
6	A2	8g violet	3.00	6.00
7	A2	16g black	4.00	6.00
		Nos. 1-7 (7)	24.00	40.00

For 4g, 8g and 16g stamps of type A1, see Nos. J3a, J4a and J7a.
Earliest reported use is Jan. 29, 1895.
Forged cancellations are plentiful.
For overprints see Nos. 8-86, J8-J28, J36-J42. For surcharges see Nos. 94-100, J29-J35.

Nos. 1-7 Handstamped in Violet or Blue

Overprint 9¼x2½mm, Serifs on "E"

1901, July 18
8	A1	¼g green	27.50	27.50
9	A1	½g red	27.50	27.50
10	A1	1g blue	27.50	27.50
11	A1	2g dark brown	27.50	27.50
12	A2	4g lilac brown	32.50	32.50
13	A2	8g violet	47.50	47.50
14	A2	16g black	60.00	60.00
		Nos. 8-14 (7)	250.00	250.00

Violet overprints were issued July 18, 1901, for postal use, while the blue overprints were issued in Jan. 5 1902 for philatelic purposes. The blue overprints were not used in the mails. Values for unused stamps are for examples with blue overprints. The blue overprints became valid for postage in 1908 only. Unused stamps with violet overprints are worth much more.
Overprints 8¼mm wide are unofficial reproductions.

Nos. 1-7 Handstamped in Violet, Blue or Black

Overprint 11x3mm, Low Colons

1902, Apr. 1
15	A1	¼g green	14.00	14.00
16	A1	½g red	14.00	14.00
17	A1	1g blue	14.00	14.00
18	A1	2g dark brown	14.00	14.00
19	A2	4g lilac brown	24.00	24.00
20	A2	8g violet	30.00	30.00
21	A2	16g black	55.00	55.00
		Nos. 15-21 (7)	165.00	165.00

The handstamp reads "Bosta" (Post).
Overprints 10¾mm and 11mm wide with raised colons are unofficial reproductions.

Nos. 1-7 Handstamped in Black

1903, Jan. 9   **Overprint 16x3¾mm**
22	A1	¼g green	14.00	14.00
23	A1	½g red	20.00	20.00
24	A1	1g blue	22.50	22.50
25	A1	2g dark brown	22.50	22.50
26	A2	4g lilac brown	35.00	35.00
27	A2	8g violet	50.00	50.00
28	A2	16g black	70.00	70.00
		Nos. 22-28 (7)	234.00	234.00

The handstamp reads "Malekt." (Also "Melekt," message).
Original stamps have blurred colons. Unofficial reproductions have clean colons.
Nos. 22-28 have black overprints only. All other colors are fakes.

Nos. 1-7 Handstamped in Violet or Blue

Overprint 18¼mm Wide

1904, Dec.
36	A1	¼g green	30.00	30.00
37	A1	½g red	30.00	
38	A1	1g blue	40.00	
39	A1	2g dark brown	40.00	
40	A2	4g lilac brown	55.00	
41	A2	8g violet	100.00	
42	A2	16g black	140.00	
		Nos. 36-42 (7)	435.00	

The handstamp reads "Malekathe" (message). This set was never issued.

Preceding Issues Surcharged with New Values in French Currency in Blue, Violet, Rose or Black

a

b

On Nos. 1-7

1905, Jan. 1   **Overprint 3mm High**
43	A1 (a)	5c on ¼g	10.00	10.00
44	A1 (a)	10c on ½g	10.00	10.00
45	A1 (a)	20c on 1g	10.00	10.00
46	A1 (a)	40c on 2g	11.00	11.00
47	A2 (a)	80c on 4g	21.00	21.00
48	A2 (b)	1.60fr on 8g	22.50	22.50
49	A2 (b)	3.20fr on 16g	40.00	40.00
		Nos. 43-49 (7)	124.50	124.50

Nos. 48-49 exist with period or comma.

1905, Feb.
On No. 8, "Ethiopie" in Blue
| 50 | A1 (a) | 5c on ¼g | 150.00 | 150.00 |

On No. 15, "Bosta" in Black
| 51 | A1 (a) | 5c on ¼g | 100.00 | 100.00 |

On No. 22, "Malekt" in Black
| 52 | A1 (a) | 5c on ¼g | 75.00 | 75.00 |

Unofficial reproductions exist of Nos. 50, 51, 52. The 5c on No. 36, 10c, 20c, 40c, 80c, and 1.60fr surcharges exist as unofficial reproductions only.

c

d

1905   **On No. 2**
| 54 | A1 (c) | 5c on half of ½g | 10.00 | 10.00 |

On No. 21, "Bosta" in Black
| 55 | A2 (d) | 5c on 16g blk | 200.00 | 100.00 |

On No. 55, "Bosta" is in black.

On No. 28, "Malekt" in Black
| 56 | A2 (d) | 5c on 16g blk | 250.00 | 250.00 |
| | | Nos. 54-56 (3) | 460.00 | 360.00 |

No. 54 issued in March. Nos. 55-56 issued Mar. 30.
The overprints and surcharges on Nos. 8 to 56 inclusive were handstamped, the work being very roughly done.
As is usual with handstamped overprints and surcharges there are many inverted and double, but most of them are fakes or unofficial reproductions.

Surcharged with New Values in Various Colors and in Violet

Overprint 14¾x3½mm

1906, Jan. 1
57	A1	5c on ¼g green	12.50	12.50
58	A1	10c on ½g red	15.00	15.00
59	A1	20c on 1g blue	15.00	15.00
60	A1	40c on 2g dk brn	15.00	15.00
61	A2	80c on 4g lilac brn	22.50	22.50

62	A2	1.60fr on 8g violet	35.00	35.00
63	A2	3.20fr on 16g black	90.00	90.00
		Nos. 57-63 (7)	205.00	205.00

Two types of the 4-character overprint ("Menelik"): 14x¾x3½mm and 16x4mm.

Surcharged in Violet Brown

1906, July 1   **Overprint 16x4¼mm**
64	A1	5c on ¼g grn	12.50	12.50
a.	Surcharged "20"		110.00	110.00
65	A1	10c on ½g red	12.50	12.50
66	A1	20c on 1g blue	22.50	22.50
67	A1	40c on 2g dk brn	22.50	22.50
68	A2	80c on 4g lil brn	35.00	35.00
69	A2	1.60fr on 8g vio	35.00	35.00
70	A2	3.20fr on 16g blk	75.00	75.00
		Nos. 64-70 (7)	215.00	215.00

The control overprint reads "Menelik."

Surcharged in Violet

e

f

1907, June 21
71	A1 (e)	¼ on ¼g grn	8.75	8.75
72	A1 (e)	½ on ½g red	8.75	8.75
73	A1 (f)	1 on 1g blue	11.00	11.00
74	A1 (f)	2 on 2g dk brn	12.00	12.00
a.	Surcharged "40"		65.00	
75	A2 (f)	4 on 4g lil brn	13.00	13.00
a.	Surcharged "80"		57.50	
76	A2 (f)	8 on 8g vio	25.00	25.00
77	A2 (f)	16 on 16g blk	30.00	30.00
		Nos. 71-77 (7)	108.50	108.50

Nos. 71-72 are also found with stars farther away from figures.
The control overprint reads "Dagmawi" ("Second"), meaning Emperor Menelik II.
On stamps with "1" in surcharge, genuine examples have straight serifs, forgeries have curved serifs.

Nos. 2, 23 Surcharged in Bluish Green

1908, Aug. 14
| 78 | A1 | 1pi on ½g red (#2) | 15.00 | 15.00 |
| 79 | A1 | 1pi on ½g red (#23) | 1,150. | |

Official reproductions exist. Value, set $25.
Forgeries exist.
The surcharges on Nos. 57-78 are handstamped and are found double, inverted, etc.

Surcharged in Black

1908, Nov. 1
80	A1	¼p on ¼g grn	2.25	2.25
81	A1	½p on ½g red	2.25	2.25
82	A1	1p on 1g blue	2.75	2.75
83	A1	2p on 2g dk brn	5.00	5.00
84	A2	4p on 4g lil brn	7.50	7.50
85	A2	8p on 8g vio	14.00	14.00
86	A2	16p on 16g blk	18.00	18.00
		Nos. 80-86 (7)	51.75	51.75

Surcharges on Nos. 80-85 are found double, inverted, etc. Forgeries exist.
These are the 1st stamps valid for international mail.

King Solomon's Throne
A3

Menelik in Native Costume
A4

ETHIOPIA 463

Menelik in Royal
Dress — A5

1909, Jan. 29   *Perf. 11½*
87	A3	¼g blue green	.70	.60
88	A3	½g rose	.75	.75
89	A3	1g green & org	4.50	1.50
90	A4	2g blue	3.00	1.75
91	A4	4g green & car	5.00	4.00
92	A5	8g ver & dp grn	9.00	7.00
93	A5	16g ver & car	15.00	10.00
		Nos. 87-93 (7)	37.95	25.60

For overprints see Nos. 101-115, J43-J49, J55-J56. For surcharges see Nos. 116-119.

Nos. 1-7 Handstamped and Surcharged in ms.

1911, Oct. 1   *Perf. 14x13½*
94	A1	¼g on ¼g grn	85.00
95	A1	½g on ½g rod	85.00
96	A1	1g on 1g blue	85.00
97	A1	2g on 2g dk brn	85.00
98	A2	4g on 4g lil brn	85.00
99	A2	8g on 8g violet	85.00
100	A2	16g on 16g black	85.00
		Nos. 94-100 (7)	595.00

Nos. 94-100 were produced as a philatelic speculation by the postmaster at Diro Dawa. The overprint is abbreviated from "Affranchissement Exceptionnel Faute Timbres" (Special Franking Lacking Stamps). The overprints and surcharges were applied to stamps on cover and then canceled. These covers were then sold to dealers in Europe. No. 98 is known postally used on a small number of commercial covers.

Nos. 94-100 without surcharge are forgeries.

Stamps of 1909 Handstamped in Violet or Black

Nos. 101-102

Nos. 104-107

1917, Mar. 30   *Perf. 11½*
101	A3	¼g blue grn (V)	7.50	9.00
a.		Inverted overprint	15.00	18.00
102	A3	½g rose (V)	7.50	9.00
a.		Inverted overprint	15.00	18.00
104	A4	2g blue (Dk)	10.00	9.50
a.		Inverted overprint	20.00	11.00
105	A4	4g grn & car (Bk)	15.00	15.00
a.		Inverted overprint	30.00	15.00
106	A5	8g ver & dp grn (Bk)	25.00	22.50
a.		Inverted overprint	50.00	45.00
107	A5	16g ver & car (Bk)	40.00	45.00
a.		Inverted overprint	80.00	90.00
		Nos. 101-107 (6)	105.00	110.00

Coronation of Empress Zauditu and appointment of Prince Tafari as Regent and Heir to the throne.
Exist with overprint double.

Stamps of 1909 Overprinted in Blue, Black or Red

Nos. 108-111

Nos. 112-115

1917, Apr. 5-Oct. 1
108	A3	¼g blue grn (Bl)	1.25	1.25
109	A3	½g rose (Bl)	1.25	1.25
110	A3	1g grn & org (Bl)	2.25	2.25
111	A4	2g blue (R)	82.50	87.25
112	A4	2g blue (Bk)	1.25	1.25
113	A4	4g grn & car (Bl)	1.25	1.25
a.		Black overprint	11.00	11.00
114	A5	8g ver & dp grn (Bl)	1.25	1.25
115	A5	16g ver & car (Bl)	2.25	2.25
		Nos. 108-115 (8)	93.25	98.00

Coronation of Empress Zauditu.
Nos. 108-115 all exist with double overprint, inverted overprint, double overprint, one inverted, and various combinations.

Nos. 114-115 with Additional Surcharge

k   l

m   n

1917, May 28
116	A5 (k)	¼g on 8g	3.00	3.00
117	A5 (l)	½g on 8g	3.00	3.00
118	A5 (m)	1g on 16g	8.00	8.00
119	A5 (n)	2g on 16g	10.00	9.00
		Nos. 116-119 (4)	24.00	23.00

Nos. 116-119 all exist with the numerals double and inverted and No. 116 with the Amharic surcharge missing.

Sommering's Gazelle A6

Prince Tafari A9

Cathedral of St. George A12   Empress Waizeri Zauditu A18

¼g, Giraffes. ½g, Leopard. 2g, Prince Tafari, diff. 4g, Prince Tafari, diff. 8g, White rhinoceros. 12g, Somali ostriches. 1t, African elephant. 2t, Water buffalo. 3t, Lions. 5t, 10t, Empress Zauditu.

1919, June 16   *Typo.*   *Perf. 11½*
120	A6	⅛g violet & brn	.25	.25
121	A6	¼g bl grn & drab	.25	.25
122	A6	½g scar & ol grn	.25	.25
123	A9	1g rose lil & gray grn	.25	.25
124	A9	2g dp ultra & fawn	.25	.25
125	A9	4g turq bl & org	.25	2.50
126	A12	8g bl blue & org	.25	.25
127	A12	8g ol grn & blk brn	.35	.25
128	A12	12g red vio & gray	.50	.30
129	A12	1t rose & gray blk	.90	.40
130	A12	2t black & brown	2.50	
131	A12	3t grn & dp org	2.50	1.90
132	A18	4t brn & lil rose	3.00	2.50
133	A18	5t carmine & gray	4.00	4.00
134	A18	10t gray grn & bis	8.00	5.25
		Nos. 120-134 (15)	23.50	
		Nos. 120-129, 131-134 (14)		18.25

No. 130 was not issued.
For overprints see Nos. J50-J54. For surcharges see Nos. 135-154.
Reprints have brownish gum that is cracked diagonally. Originals have smooth, white gum. Reprints exist imperf. and some values with inverted centers. Value for set, unused or canceled, $5.

No. 132 Surcharged in Blue

1919, July
| 135 | A18 | 4g on 4t brn & lil rose | 3.00 | 3.00 |

Nos. 135-154
The Amharic surcharge indicates the new value and, therefore, varies on Nos. 135-154. There are numerous defective letters and figures, several types of the "2" of "½," the errors "guerhce," "gnerche," etc.
Many varieties of surcharge, such as double, inverted, lines transposed or omitted, and inverted "2" in "½," exist.
There are many irregularly produced settings in imitation of Nos. 136-154 which differ slightly from the originals. These may be essays or proofs.

Stamps of 1919 Surcharged

1921
136	A6	½g on ⅛g vio & brn	1.00	1.00
137	A6	1g on ¼g grn & db	2.50	1.00
138	A9	2g on 1g lil brn & gray grn	1.00	1.50
139	A18	2g on 4t brn & lil rose	35.00	30.00
140	A6	2½g on ½g scar & ol grn	1.00	1.50
141	A9	4g on 2g ultra & fawn	1.00	1.25
		Nos. 136-141 (6)	41.50	36.25

Forgeries of No. 139 exist.

Stamps and Type of 1919 Surcharged

1925-26
142	A12	½g on 1t rose & gray blk ('26)	1.25	1.25
a.		Without colon ('26)	12.50	12.50
143	A18	½g on 5t car & gray ('26)	1.50	1.50
144	A12	1g on 6g bl & org	1.25	1.25
145	A12	1g on 12g lil & gray	450.00	400.00
146	A12	1g on 3t grn & org ('26)	22.50	16.00
147	A18	1g on 10t gray grn & bis ('26)	1.50	1.50
		Nos. 142-147 (6)	478.00	421.50

On No. 142 the surcharge is at the left side of the stamp, reading upward. On No. 142a it is at the right, reading downward. The two surcharges are from different, though similar, settings. On No. 146 the surcharge is at the right, reading upward. See note following No. 164.

Type of 1919 Srchd.

1925, Oct.
| 147A | A12 | 1g on 12g lil & gray | 400.00 |

Forgeries exist.

Nos. 126-128 Srchd.

1926
148	A12	½g on 8g	3.00	1.25
149	A12	1g on 6g	80.00	50.00
150	A12	1g on 12g	350.00	
		Nos. 148-150 (3)	433.00	51.25

The Amharic line has 7 (½g) or 6 characters (1g).

Nos. 126-128, 131 Srchd.

1925-27
151	A12	½g on 8g ('27)	1.50	1.50
152	A12	1g on 6g ('27)	60.00	40.00
153	A12	1g on 12g ('27)	5.00	1.50
154	A12	1g on 3t	375.00	
		Nos. 151-154 (4)	441.50	43.00

The Amharic line has 7 (½g) or 4 characters (1g). No. 152 has the lines closer together than do the others.
Forgeries of No. 154 exist.

Ras Tafari A22

Empress Zauditu A23

1928, Sept. 5   *Typo.*   *Perf. 13½x14*
155	A22	⅛m org & lt bl	.65	1.40
156	A23	¼m ind & red org	.40	1.40
157	A22	½m gray grn & blk	.65	1.40
158	A23	1m dk car & blk	.40	1.40
159	A22	2m dk bl & blk	.40	1.40
160	A23	4m yel & olive	.40	1.40
161	A22	8m vio & olive	1.00	1.40
162	A22	1t org brn & vio	1.10	1.40
163	A22	2t grn & bister	1.75	3.25
164	A23	3t choc & grn	2.75	3.75
		Nos. 155-164 (10)	9.50	18.20

For overprints and surcharges see Nos. 165-209, 217-230, C1-C10.

Preceding Issue Overprinted in Black, Violet or Red

1928, Sept. 1
165	A22	⅛m (Bk)	1.75	3.25
166	A23	¼m (V)	1.75	3.25
167	A22	½m (V)	1.75	3.25
168	A23	1m (R)	1.75	3.25
169	A22	2m (R)	1.75	3.25
170	A23	4m (Bk)	1.75	3.25
171	A22	8m (R)	1.75	3.25
172	A23	1t (Bk)	1.75	3.25
173	A22	2t (R)	2.75	3.25
174	A23	3t (R)	4.00	3.25
		Nos. 165-174 (10)	20.75	32.50

Opening of General Post Office, Addis Ababa.
Exist with overprint inverted, double, double, one inverted, etc.

Nos. 155, 157, 159, 161, 163 Handstamped in Violet, Red or Black

1928, Oct. 7
175	A22	⅛m (V)	2.10	8.00
176	A22	½m (R)	2.10	8.00
177	A22	2m (R)	2.10	10.00

ETHIOPIA

178	A22	8m (Bk)	2.10	10.00
179	A22	2t (V)	2.10	10.00
		Nos. 175-179 (5)	10.50	46.00

Crowning of Prince Tafari as king (Negus) on Oct. 7, 1928.

Nos. 175-177 exist with overprint vertical, inverted, double, etc.

Forgeries exist.

Nos. 155-164 Overprinted in Red or Green

1930, Apr. 3

180	A22	⅛m org & lt bl (R)	.25	.25
181	A23	¼m ind & red org (R)	.50	.50
182	A22	½m gray grn & blk (R)	.25	.25
183	A23	1m dk car & blk (G)	.55	.55
184	A22	2m dk bl & blk (R)	.55	.55
185	A23	4m yel & ol (R)	.85	.85
186	A22	8m vio & ol (R)	1.60	1.60
187	A23	1t org brn & vio (R)	4.50	4.50
188	A22	2t grn & bis (R)	5.50	5.50
189	A23	3t choc & grn (R)	8.00	8.00
		Nos. 180-189 (10)	22.55	22.55

Proclamation of King Tafari as King of Kings of Abyssinia under the name "Haile Selassie."

A similar overprint, set in four vertical lines, was printed on all denominations of the 1928 issue. It was not considered satisfactory and was rejected. The trial impressions were not placed on sale to the public, but some stamps reached private hands and have been passed through the post.

Nos. 155-164 Overprinted in Red or Olive Brown

1930, Apr. 3

190	A22	⅛m orange & lt bl	.50	.50
191	A23	¼m ind & red org (OB)	.55	.55
192	A22	½m gray grn & blk	1.40	1.40
193	A23	1m dk car & blk (OB)	.55	.55
194	A22	2m dk blue & blk	.55	.55
195	A23	4m yellow & ol	1.00	1.00
196	A22	8m violet & ol	1.60	1.60
197	A23	1t org brn & vio	4.50	4.50
198	A22	2t green & bister	5.50	5.50
199	A23	3t chocolate & grn	8.00	8.00
		Nos. 190-199 (10)	24.15	24.15

Proclamation of King Tafari as Emperor Haile Selassie.

All stamps of this series exist with "H" of "HAILE" omitted and with many other varieties.

Nos. 155-164 Handstamped in Violet or Red

1930, Nov. 2

200	A22	⅛m (V)	1.10	1.10
201	A23	¼m (V)	1.10	1.10
202	A22	½m (R)	1.10	1.10
203	A23	1m (R)	1.10	1.10
204	A22	2m (R)	1.10	1.10
205	A23	4m (V)	1.10	1.10
206	A22	8m (V or R)	1.90	1.90
207	A23	1t (V)	3.00	3.00
208	A22	2t (V or R)	4.50	4.50
209	A23	3t (V or R)	6.50	6.50
		Nos. 200-209 (10)	22.50	22.50

Coronation of Emperor Haile Selassie, Nov. 2, 1930.

Haile Selassie Coronation Monument, Symbols of Empire — A24

1930, Nov. Engr. Perf. 12½

210	A24	1g orange	1.00	1.00
211	A24	2g ultra	1.00	1.00
212	A24	4g violet	1.00	1.00
213	A24	8g dull green	1.00	1.00
214	A24	1t brown	1.25	1.25
215	A24	3t green	2.00	2.00
216	A24	5t red brown	2.00	2.00
		Nos. 210-216 (7)	9.25	9.25

Coronation of Emperor Haile Selassie. Issued: 4g, 11/2; others, 11/23.

Reprints of Nos. 210 to 216 exist. Colors are more yellow and the ink is thicker and slightly glossy. Ink on the originals is dull and granular. Value 50c each.

Nos. 158-160, 164 Surcharged in Green, Red or Blue

Type I

Type II

1931 Perf. 13½x14

217	A23	⅛m on 1m	.55	1.00
218	A22	⅛m on 2m (R)	.55	1.00
219	A23	⅛m on 4m	.55	1.00
220	A23	¼m on 1m (Bl)	.55	1.00
221	A22	¼m on 2m (R)	1.60	2.10
222	A23	¼m on 4m	1.60	2.10
225	A23	½m on 1m (Bl)	1.60	2.10
226	A22	½m on 2m (R)	1.60	2.10
227	A23	½m on 4m, type II	1.60	2.10
	a.	½m on 4m, type I	15.00	15.00
228	A23	½m on 3t (R)	13.00	16.00
230	A22	1m on 2m (R)	2.25	2.75
		Nos. 217-230 (11)	25.45	33.25

The ½m on ⅛m orange & light blue and ½m on ¼m indigo & red orange were clandestinely printed and never sold at the post office.

No. 230 with double surcharge in red and blue is a color trial.

Many varieties exist.

Issued: 1m, Apr.; others, 3/20.

Ras Makonnen
A25

Empress Menen
A27

View of Hawash River and Railroad Bridge — A26

Designs: 2g, 8g, Haile Selassie (profile). 4g, 1t, Statue of Menelik II. 3t, Empress Menen (full face). 5t, Haile Selassie (full face).

Perf. 12½, 12x12½, 12½x12

1931, June 27 Engr.

232	A25	⅛g red	.50	.80
233	A26	¼g olive green	.50	.80
234	A25	½g dark violet	.50	.80
235	A27	1g red orange	.50	.80
236	A25	2g ultra	.80	.80
237	A25	4g violet	.80	1.60
238	A27	8g blue green	2.50	3.00
239	A25	1t chocolate	24.00	10.00
240	A27	3t yellow green	7.00	7.00
241	A27	5t red brown	13.00	13.00
		Nos. 232-241 (10)	49.80	38.60

For overprints see Nos. B1-B5. For surcharges see Nos. 242-246.

Reprints of Nos. 232-236, 238-240 are on thinner and whiter paper than the originals. On originals the ink is dull and granular. On reprints, heavy, caked and shiny. Value 50c each.

Nos. 232-236 Surcharged in Blue or Carmine

1936, Jan. 29 Perf. 12x12½, 12½x12

242	A25	1c on ⅛g red	2.50	2.50
243	A26	2c on ¼g ol grn (C)	2.50	2.50
244	A25	3c on ½g dk vio	2.50	2.50
245	A27	5c on 1g red org	5.00	5.00
246	A27	10c on 2g ultra (C)	6.00	5.00
		Nos. 242-246 (5)	18.50	17.50

Catalogue values for unused stamps in this section, from this point to the end of the section, are for Never Hinged items.

Haile Selassie I — A32

1942, Mar. 23 Litho. Perf. 14x13½

247	A32	4c lt bl grn, ind & blk	.80	.40
248	A32	10c rose, indigo & blk	2.50	.75
249	A32	20c dp ultra, ind & blk	5.00	1.25
		Nos. 247-249 (3)	8.30	2.40

Haile Selassie I — A33

1942-43 Unwmk.

250	A33	4c lt bl grn & indigo	.90	.25
251	A33	8c yel org & indigo	1.00	.25
252	A33	10c rose & indigo	1.25	.25
253	A33	12c dull vio & indigo	1.25	.30
254	A33	20c dp ultra & indigo	2.00	.50
255	A33	25c dull grn & indigo	2.50	.70
256	A33	30c dull brn & indigo	4.75	1.25
257	A33	60c lilac & indigo	7.25	1.50
		Nos. 250-257 (8)	20.90	5.00

Issued: 25c, 50c, 60c, 4/1/43; others, 6/22/42.

For surcharges see Nos. 258-262, 284, C18-C20.

Nos. 250-254 Surcharged in Black or Brown

1943, Nov. 3

258	A33	5c on 4c	65.00	—
259	A33	10c on 8c	65.00	—
260	A33	15c on 10c	65.00	—
261	A33	20c on 12c (Br)	65.00	—
262	A33	30c on 20c (Br)	65.00	—
		Nos. 258-262 (5)	325.00	

Restoration of the Obelisk in Myazzia Place, Addis Ababa, and the 13th anniv. of the coronation of Emperor Haile Selassie.

Nos. 258-262 were almost entirely sold to collectors. Used examples are mostly CTO. Only 10 postally used examples are known.

No. 258 exists with inverted "5" in surcharge. Value $150. On No. 262, "3" is surcharged on "2" of "20" to make "30."

Approximately 40 sets exist with a somewhat different handstamped surcharge. Value, set $2,000. Forgeries exist.

Palace of Menelik II — A34

Menelik II
A35

Statue
A36

50c, Mausoleum. 65c, Menelik II (with scepter).

1944, Dec. 31 Litho. Perf. 10½

263	A34	5c green	1.25	.65
264	A35	10c red lilac	2.25	1.10
265	A36	20c deep blue	4.00	2.25
266	A34	50c dull purple	5.25	2.25
267	A35	65c bister brown	9.25	3.50
		Nos. 263-267 (5)	22.00	9.75

Cent. of the birth of Menelik II, 8/18/44. Printed on gum-impregnated paper.

Unissued Semi-Postal Stamps Overprinted in Carmine

Nurse & Baby — A39

Various Designs Inscribed "Croix Rouge"

1945, Aug. 7 Photo. Perf. 11½

268	A39	5c brt green	.90	1.50
269	A39	10c brt red	1.10	1.50
270	A39	25c brt blue	1.10	1.50
271	A39	50c dk yellow brn	5.00	7.00
272	A39	1t brt violet	7.50	9.00
		Nos. 268-272 (5)	15.60	20.50

Nos. 268-272 without overprint were ordered printed in Switzerland before Ethiopia fell to the invading Italians, so were not delivered to Addis Ababa. After the country's liberation, the set was overprinted "V" and issued for ordinary postage. These stamps exist without overprint, but were not issued. Value, set $17.50.

Some values exist inverted or double. Forged overprints exist.

For surcharges see Nos. B11-B15, B36-B40.

Lion of Judah
A44

Menelik II
A45

Mail Transport, Old and New — A46

Designs: 50c, Old Post Office, Addis Ababa. 70c, Menelik II and Haile Selassie.

1947, Apr. 18 Engr. Perf. 13

273	A44	10c yellow org	3.50	2.00
274	A45	20c deep blue	5.75	2.25
275	A46	30c orange brn	9.50	3.75
276	A46	50c dk slate grn	22.50	7.50
277	A46	70c red violet	37.50	14.00
		Nos. 273-277 (5)	78.75	29.50

50th anniv. of Ethiopia's postal system.

ETHIOPIA

Haile Selassie and Franklin D. Roosevelt — A49

Design: 65c, Roosevelt and US Flags.

Engraved and Photogravure

1947, May 23		Unwmk.		Perf. 12½
278	A49	12c car lake & bl grn	1.60	2.25
279	A49	25c dk blue & rose	3.00	3.50
280	A49	65c blk, red & dp bl	6.00	7.50
		Nos. 278-280,C21-C22 (5)	45.60	51.25

King Sahle Selassie Reclining A50

King Sahle Selassie A52

Design: 30c, View of Ankober.

1947, May 1		Engr.		Perf. 13
281	A50	20c deep blue	2.00	2.40
282	A50	30c dark purple	4.00	4.00
283	A52	$1 deep green	10.00	8.00
		Nos. 281-283 (3)	16.00	14.40

150th anniversary of Selassie dynasty.

No. 255 Surcharged in Orange

1947, July 14			Perf. 14x13½
284	A33	12c on 25c	95.00 95.00

Amba Alaguie — A53

Designs: 2c, Trinity Church. 4c, Debra Sina. 5c, Mecan, near Achanguie. 8c, Lake Tana. 12c, 15c, Parliament Building, Addis Ababa. 20c, Aiba, near Mai Cheo. 30c, Bahr Bridge over Blue Nile. 60c, 70c, Canoe on Lake Tana. $1, Omo Falls. $3, Mt Alamata. $5, Ras Dashan Mountains.

		Perf. 13x13½		
1947-53		Engr.		Wmk. 282
285	A53	1c rose violet	.25	.25
286	A53	2c blue violet	.25	.25
a.		Unwatermarked ('51)	37.50	15.00
287	A53	4c green	.35	.25
288	A53	5c dark green	.35	.25
289	A53	8c deep orange	.65	.25
290	A53	12c red	.80	.25
290A	A53	15c dk ol brn ('53)	.75	.25
291	A53	20c blue	1.10	.40
292	A53	30c orange brown	1.90	.55
292A	A53	60c red ('51)	2.25	.95
293	A53	70c rose lilac	3.25	.70
294	A53	$1 dk carmine rose	5.25	.70
295	A53	$3 bright blue	14.00	2.75
296	A53	$5 olive	22.50	5.50
		Nos. 285-296 (14)	53.65	13.30

Issue dates: 15c, May 25, 1953; 60c, Feb. 10, 1951; others, Aug. 23, 1947.
Shades exist.
For overprints see Nos. 355-356. For surcharges see Nos. B6-B10, B16-B20.

Empress Waizero Menen and Emperor Haile Selassie — A54

1949, May 5		Wmk. 282		Perf. 13
297	A54	20c blue	1.75	.85
298	A54	30c yellow org	1.75	1.10
299	A54	50c purple	4.50	1.75
300	A54	80c green	4.50	2.75
301	A54	$1 red	9.00	4.50
		Nos. 297-301 (5)	21.50	10.95

Central ornaments differ on each denomination.
8th anniv. of Ethiopia's liberation from Italian occupation.

Dejach Balcha Hospital A55

Abuna Petros A56

Designs: 20c, Haile Selassie raising flag. 30c, Lion of Judah statue. 50c, Empress Waizero Menen, Haile Selassie and building.

	Perf. 13x13½, 13½x13			
1950, Nov. 2		Engr.		Wmk. 282
302	A55	5c purple	1.10	.65
303	A56	10c deep plum	3.50	1.60
304	A56	20c deep carmine	4.50	1.60
305	A56	30c green	9.50	3.25
306	A55	50c deep blue	13.50	6.50
		Nos. 302-306 (5)	32.10	13.60

20th anniv. of the coronation of Emperor Haile Selassie and Empress Menen

Abbaye Bridge — A57

1951, Jan. 1		Unwmk.		Perf. 14
308	A57	5c dk green & dk brn	4.25	1.60
309	A57	10c dp orange & blk brn	6.50	2.75
310	A57	15c dp blue & org	11.00	4.50
311	A57	30c olive & lil rose	16.00	6.50
312	A57	60c brown & dp bl	22.50	8.50
313	A57	80c vio & green	32.50	12.50
		Nos. 308-313 (6)	92.75	36.35

Opening of the Abbaye Bridge over the Blue Nile.

Tomb of Ras Makonnen — A58

1951, Mar. 2			Center in Black
314	A58	5c dark green	3.25 1.10
315	A58	10c deep ultra	3.25 1.60
316	A58	15c blue	5.50 2.75
317	A58	30c dp claret	11.00 3.25
318	A58	80c rose carmine	17.00 5.50
319	A58	$1 orange brown	22.50 8.50
		Nos. 314-319 (6)	62.50 22.70

55th anniversary of the Battle of Adwa.

Emperor Haile Selassie — A59

1952, July 23			Perf. 13½
320	A59	5c dark green	.55 .55
321	A59	10c red orange	.85 .55
322	A59	15c black	1.10 .55
323	A59	25c ultra	1.75 .85
324	A59	30c violet	2.75 1.10
325	A59	50c rose red	3.50 1.10
326	A59	65c chocolate	9.00 2.75
		Nos. 320-326 (7)	19.50 7.45

60th birthday of Haile Selassie.

Open Road to Sea — A60

Designs: 25c, 50c, Road and broken chain. 65c, Map. 80c, Allegory: Reunion. $1, Haile Selassie raising flag. $2, Ethiopian flag and seascape. $3, Haile Selassie addressing League of Nations.

		Wmk. 282		
1952, Sept. 11		Engr.		Perf. 13
327	A60	15c brown carmine	.85	.60
328	A60	25c red brown	1.10	1.00
329	A60	30c yellow brown	2.00	1.10
330	A60	50c purple	3.00	1.25
331	A60	65c gray	5.75	1.60
332	A60	80c blue green	6.50	2.25
333	A60	$1 rose carmine	13.00	3.00
334	A60	$2 deep blue	22.50	5.00
335	A60	$3 magenta	47.50	7.50
		Nos. 327-335 (9)	102.20	23.30

Issued to celebrate Ethiopia's federation with Eritrea, effected Sept. 11, 1952.

Haile Selassie and New Ethiopian Port — A61

15c, 30c, Haile Selassie on deck of ship.

1953, Oct. 4				
337	A61	10c red & dk brn	4.75	2.75
338	A61	15c blue & dk grn	5.00	2.75
339	A61	25c orange & dk brn	9.00	5.00
340	A61	30c red brn & dk grn	16.00	8.00
341	A61	50c purple & dk brn	25.00	9.00
		Nos. 337-341 (5)	59.75	27.50

Federation of Ethiopia and Eritrea, 1st anniv.

Princess Tsahai at a Sickbed — A62

		Perf. 13x13½		
1955, July 8		Engr.		Wmk. 282
		Cross Typo. in Red		
342	A62	15c choc & ultra	2.50	1.25
343	A62	20c green & orange	3.75	1.50
344	A62	30c ultra & green	6.25	1.90
		Nos. 342-344 (3)	12.50	4.65

Ethiopian Red Cross, 20th anniv.
For surcharges see Nos. B33-B35.

Promulgating the Constitution A63

Bishops' Consecration by Archbishop A64

25c, Kagnew Battalion. 35c, Reunion with the Motherland. 50c, "Progress." 65c, Empress Waizero Menen & Emperor Haile Selassie.

		Perf. 12½		
1955, Nov. 3		Unwmk.		Engr.
345	A63	5c green & choc	1.25	.55
346	A64	20c carmine & slate grn	2.50	.90
347	A64	25c magenta & gray	3.50	1.40
348	A63	35c brown & red org	4.75	1.75
349	A64	50c dk brn & ultra	7.00	2.50
350	A64	65c violet & car	9.75	4.00
		Nos. 345-350 (6)	28.75	11.10

Silver jubilee of the coronation of Emperor Haile Selassie and Empress Waizero Menen.

Emperor Haile Selassie and Fair Emblem — A65

1955, Nov. 5			Wmk. 282
351	A65	5c green & ol grn	1.00	.35
352	A65	10c car & dp ultra	1.50	.40
353	A65	15c vio blk & grn	2.00	.60
354	A65	50c mag & red brn	3.00	2.00
		Nos. 351-354 (4)	7.50	3.35

Silver Jubilee Fair, Addis Ababa.

Nos. 291 and 292A Overprinted

1960, Apr. 7			Perf. 13x13½
355	A53	20c blue	1.75 1.25
356	A53	60c red	3.00 2.40

WRY, July 1, 1959-June 30, 1960.
The 60c without serifs is a trial printing.

Map of Africa, "Liberty" and Haile Selassie — A66

		Perf. 13½		
1960, June 14		Engr.		Unwmk.
357	A66	20c orange & green	.85	.85
358	A66	80c orange & violet	2.75	.85
359	A66	$1 orange & maroon	2.75	1.10
		Nos. 357-359 (3)	6.35	2.80

2nd Conf. of Independent African States at Addis Ababa. Issued in sheets of 10.

Emperor Haile Selassie — A67

1960, Nov. 2		Wmk. 282		Perf. 14
360	A67	10c brown & blue	.85	.85
361	A67	25c violet & emerald	1.10	1.10
362	A67	50c dk bl & org yel	2.75	2.75
363	A67	60c slate grn & sal pink	4.25	4.25
364	A67	$1 indigo & rose vio	5.00	5.00
		Nos. 360-364 (5)	13.95	13.95

30th anniv. of the coronation of Emperor Haile Selassie.

Africa Hall, UN Economic Commission for Africa — A68

1961, Apr. 15		Wmk. 282		Perf. 14
365	A68	80c ultra	2.75	1.40

Africa Freedom Day, Apr. 15. Sheets of 10.

Map of Ethiopia, Olive Branch — A69

ETHIOPIA

1961, May 5   **Perf. 13x13½**
366	A69	20c green	.40	.40
367	A69	30c blue	.60	.45
368	A69	$1 brown	3.25	1.40
		Nos. 366-368 (3)	4.25	2.25

20th anniv. of Ethiopia's liberation from Italian occupation.

African Wild Ass — A70

1961, June 16   **Wmk. 282**   **Perf. 14**
369	A70	5c shown	1.10	.25
370	A70	15c Eland	1.10	.25
371	A70	25c Elephant	1.25	.40
372	A70	35c Giraffe	3.00	.50
373	A70	50c Beisa	3.00	.50
374	A70	$1 Lion	6.00	1.50
		Nos. 369-374 (6)	15.45	3.40

Issued in sheets of 10. Used values are for CTO's.

Emperor Haile Selassie and Empress Waizero Menen — A71

1961, July 27   **Unwmk.**   **Perf. 11**
375	A71	10c green	.85	.45
376	A71	50c violet blue	1.50	.80
377	A71	$1 carmine rose	3.25	1.60
		Nos. 375-377 (3)	5.60	2.85

Golden wedding anniv. of the Emperor and Empress.

Warlike Horsemanship (Guks) — A72

15c, Hockey. 20c, Bicycling. 30c, Soccer. 50c, 1960 Olympic marathon winner, Abebe Bikila.

Photogravure and Engraved
1962, Jan. 14   **Perf. 12x11½**
378	A72	10c yel grn & car	.50	.35
379	A72	15c pink & dk brn	.85	.60
380	A72	20c red & black	1.00	.70
381	A72	30c ultra & dl pur	1.10	.85
382	A72	50c yellow & green	1.75	1.00
		Nos. 378-382 (5)	5.20	3.50

Third Africa Football (soccer) Cup, Addis Ababa, Jan. 14-22.

Malaria Eradication Emblem, World Map and Mosquito — A73

Wmk. 282
1962, Apr. 7   **Engr.**   **Perf. 13½**
383	A73	15c black	.30	.25
384	A73	30c purple	.55	.25
385	A73	60c red brown	1.20	.65
		Nos. 383-385 (3)	2.05	1.15

WHO drive to eradicate malaria.

Abyssinian Ground Hornbill — A74

Birds: 15c, Abyssinian roller. 30c, Bateleur, vert. 50c, Double-toothed barbet, vert. $1, Didric cuckoo.

Perf. 11½
1962, May 5   **Unwmk.**   **Photo.**
Granite Paper
386	A74	5c multicolored	.85	.25
387	A74	15c emer, brn & ultra	1.10	.50
388	A74	30c lt brn, blk & red	2.25	.85
389	A74	50c multicolored	4.50	1.10
390	A74	$1 multicolored	9.00	2.50
		Nos. 386-390 (5)	17.70	5.20

See Nos. C77-C81, C97-C101, C107-C111.

Assab Hospital — A75

15c, School at Assab. 20c, Church at Massawa. 50c, Mosque at Massawa. 60c, Assab port.

Wmk. 282
1962, Sept. 11   **Engr.**   **Perf. 13½**
391	A75	3c purple	.25	.25
392	A75	15c dark blue	.25	.25
393	A75	20c green	.30	.25
394	A75	50c brown	.55	.30
395	A75	60c carmine rose	.85	.50
		Nos. 391-395 (5)	2.20	1.55

Federation of Ethiopia and Eritrea, 10th anniv.

King Bazen, Madonna and Stars over Bethlehem — A76

15c, Ezana, obelisks & temple. 20c, Kaleb & sailing fleet. 50c, Lalibela, rock-church and frescoes, vert. 60c, King Yekuno Amlak & Abuna Tekle Haimanot preaching in Ankober. 75c, King Zara Yacob & Maskal celebration. $1, King Lebna Dengel & battle against Mohammed Gragn.

Perf. 14½
1962, Nov. 2   **Unwmk.**   **Photo.**
396	A76	10c multicolored	.30	.25
397	A76	15c multicolored	.50	.25
398	A76	20c multicolored	.50	.25
399	A76	50c multicolored	.85	.25
400	A76	60c multicolored	1.10	.50
401	A76	75c multicolored	1.75	.85
402	A76	$1 multicolored	2.25	1.25
		Nos. 396-402 (7)	7.25	3.60

32nd anniv. of the coronation of Emperor Haile Selassie and to commemorate ancient kings and saints.

Map of Ethiopian Telephone Network — A77

Designs: 50c, Radio mast and waves. 60c, Telegraph pole and rising sun.

Perf. 13½x14
1963, Jan. 1   **Engr.**   **Wmk. 282**
403	A77	10c dark red	.50	.25
404	A77	50c ultra	1.10	.50
405	A77	60c red brown	1.75	.60
		Nos. 403-405 (3)	3.35	1.35

10th anniv. of the Imperial Board of Telecommunications.

Wheat Emblem — A78

1963, Mar. 21   **Unwmk.**   **Perf. 13½**
406	A78	5c deep rose	.25	.25
407	A78	10c rose carmine	.25	.25
408	A78	15c violet blue	.25	.25
409	A78	30c emerald	1.25	.25
		Nos. 406-409 (4)	2.00	1.00

FAO "Freedom from Hunger" campaign.

Abuna Salama — A79

Spiritual Leaders: 15c, Abuna Aregawi. 30c, Abuna Tekle Haimanot. 40c. Yared. 60c, Zara Yacob.

1964, Jan. 3   **Unwmk.**   **Perf. 13½**
410	A79	10c blue	.55	.25
411	A79	15c dark green	.85	.25
412	A79	30c brown red	1.10	.50
413	A79	40c dark blue	1.60	.75
414	A79	60c brown	2.75	1.60
		Nos. 410-414 (5)	6.85	3.35

Queen of Sheba — A80

Ethiopian Empresses: 15c, Helen. 50c, Seble Wongel. 60c, Mentiwab. 80c, Taitu, consort of Menelik II.

Granite Paper
1964, Mar. 2   **Photo.**   **Perf. 11½**
415	A80	10c multicolored	.85	.30
416	A80	15c multicolored	.85	.30
417	A80	50c multicolored	1.60	.85
418	A80	60c multicolored	2.75	1.10
419	A80	80c multicolored	4.50	1.60
		Nos. 415-419 (5)	10.55	4.15

Priest Teaching Alphabet to Children — A81

10c, Classroom. 15c, Woman learning to read. 40c, Students in chemistry laboratory. 60c, Graduation procession.

1964, June 1   **Unwmk.**   **Perf. 11½**
Granite Paper
420	A81	5c brown	.25	.25
421	A81	10c emerald	.25	.25
422	A81	15c rose vio, vert.	.25	.25
423	A81	40c vio blue, vert.	1.00	.30
424	A81	60c dark pur, vert.	1.50	.55
		Nos. 420-424 (5)	3.25	1.60

Issued to publicize education.

Eleanor Roosevelt (1884-1962) — A82

1964, Oct. 11   **Photo.**
Granite Paper
Portrait in Slate Blue
425	A82	10c yellow bister	.25	.25
426	A82	60c orange brown	1.10	.75
427	A82	80c green & gold	1.75	1.00
		Nos. 425-427 (3)	3.10	2.00

King Serse Dengel and View of Gondar, 1563 — A83

Ethiopian Leaders: 10c, King Fasiladas and Gondar in 1632. 20c, King Yassu the Great and Gondar in 1682. 25c, Emperor Theodore II and map of Ethiopia. 60c, Emperor John IV and Battle of Gura, 1876. 80c, Emperor Menelik II and Battle of Adwa, 1896.

1964, Dec. 12   **Photo.**   **Perf. 14½x14**
428	A83	5c multicolored	.30	.25
429	A83	10c multicolored	.30	.25
430	A83	20c multicolored	.55	.25
431	A83	25c multicolored	.85	.25
432	A83	60c multicolored	1.60	1.10
433	A83	80c multicolored	1.60	1.10
		Nos. 428-433 (6)	5.20	3.20

Ethiopian Rose — A84

Flowers: 10c, Kosso tree. 25c, St-John's-wort. 35c, Parrot's-beak. 60c, Maskal daisy.

1965, Mar. 30   **Perf. 12x13½**
434	A84	5c multicolored	.30	.25
435	A84	25c multicolored	.30	.25
436	A84	35c multicolored	.85	.55
437	A84	35c multicolored	1.20	1.00
438	A84	60c green, yel & org	2.25	1.60
		Nos. 434-438 (5)	4.90	3.85

ITU Emblem, Old and New Communication Symbols — A85

Perf. 13½x14½
1965, May 17   **Litho.**   **Unwmk.**
439	A85	5c blue, indigo & yel	.25	.25
440	A85	10c blue, indigo & org	.55	.25
441	A85	60c blue, indigo & lil rose	2.00	.95
		Nos. 439-441 (3)	2.80	1.45

Cent. of the ITU.

Laboratory — A86

Designs: 5c, Textile spinning mill. 10c, Sugar factory. 20c, Mountain road. 25c, Autobus. 30c, Diesel locomotive and bridge. 35c, Railroad station, Addis Ababa.

1965, July 19   **Photo.**   **Perf. 11½**
Granite Paper
Portrait in Black
442	A86	3c sepia	.30	.25
443	A86	5c dull pur & buff	.30	.25
444	A86	10c black & gray	.30	.25
445	A86	20c green & pale yel	.30	.25
446	A86	25c dk brown & yel	.55	.30
447	A86	30c maroon & gray	.85	.30
448	A86	35c dk blue & gray	.85	.50
		Nos. 442-448 (7)	3.45	2.10

For overprints see Nos. 609-612.

ICY Emblem — A87

1965, Oct. 24   **Unwmk.**   **Perf. 11½**
Granite Paper
449	A87	10c blue & red brn	.50	.25
450	A87	50c dp blue & red brn	1.40	.75
451	A87	80c vio blue & red brn	2.25	1.10
		Nos. 449-451 (3)	4.15	2.10

International Cooperation Year, 1965.

National Bank Emblem — A88

Designs: 10c, Commercial Bank emblem. 60c, Natl. and Commercial Bank buildings.

1965, Nov. 2   **Photo.**   **Perf. 13**
452	A88	10c dp car, blk & indigo	.45	.25
453	A88	30c ultra, blk & indigo	1.00	.40
454	A88	60c black, yel & indigo	1.50	.65
		Nos. 452-454 (3)	2.95	1.30

Natl. and Commercial Banks of Ethiopia.

ETHIOPIA

"Light and Peace" Press Building — A89

1966, Apr. 5   Engr.   Perf. 13
455	A89	5c pink & black	.25	.25
456	A89	15c lt yel grn & blk	.60	.35
457	A89	30c orange yel & blk	1.10	.55
		Nos. 455-457 (3)	1.95	1.05

Opening of the "Light and Peace" Printing Press building.

Kabaro Drum — A90

Musical Instruments: 10c, Bagana harp. 35c, Messenko guitar. 50c, Krar lyre. 60c, Wachent flutes.

1966, Sept. 9   Photo.   Perf. 13½
458	A90	5c brt green & blk	.30	.25
459	A90	10c dull blue & blk	.30	.25
460	A90	35c orange & blk	1.10	.85
461	A90	50c yellow & blk	1.75	1.10
462	A90	60c rose car & blk	2.75	1.60
		Nos. 458-462 (5)	6.20	4.05

Emperor Haile Selassie A91

1966, Nov. 1   Unwmk.   Perf. 12
463	A91	10c black, gold & grn	.30	.25
464	A91	15c black, gold & dp car	.55	.25
465	A91	40c black & gold	1.10	.85
		Nos. 463-465 (3)	1.95	1.35

50 years of leadership of Emperor Haile Selassie.

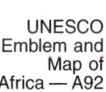

UNESCO Emblem and Map of Africa — A92

Wmk. 282
1966, Nov. 30   Litho.   Perf. 13½
466	A92	15c blue car & blk	.50	.25
467	A92	60c olive, brn & dk bl	1.10	.85

20th anniv. of UNESCO.

WHO Headquarters, Geneva — A93

1966, Nov. 30
468	A93	5c olive, ultra & brn	.80	.25
469	A93	40c brown, pur & emer	1.25	.85

Opening of WHO Headquarters, Geneva.

Expo '67 Ethiopian Pavilion and Columns of Axum (Replica) — A94

Perf. 12x13½
1967, May 2   Photo.   Unwmk.
470	A94	30c brt blue & multi	.75	.30
471	A94	45c multicolored	1.00	.40
472	A94	80c gray & multi	1.25	.60
		Nos. 470-472 (3)	3.00	1.30

EXPO '67, Intl. Exhibition, Montreal, Apr. 28-Oct. 27, 1967.

Diesel Train and Map — A95

1967, June 7   Photo.   Perf. 12
473	A95	15c multicolored	1.10	.55
474	A95	30c multicolored	2.75	1.50
475	A95	50c multicolored	4.25	2.25
		Nos. 473-475 (3)	8.10	4.30

Djibouti-Addis Ababa railroad, 50th anniv.

Papilionidae Aethiops — A96

Various Butterflies.

Perf. 13½x13
1967, June 30   Photo.   Unwmk.
476	A96	5c buff & multi	.60	.25
477	A96	10c lilac & multi	2.00	.40
478	A96	20c multicolored	2.75	.75
479	A96	35c blue & multi	4.75	1.50
480	A96	40c multicolored	7.75	2.00
		Nos. 476-480 (5)	17.85	4.90

Emperor Haile Selassie and Lion of Judah — A97

1967, July 21   Perf. 11½
Granite Paper
481	A97	10c dk brn, emer & gold	.45	.25
482	A97	15c dk brn, yel & gold	.80	.25
483	A97	$1 dk brn, red & gold	3.50	1.50
		Nos. 481-483 (3)	4.75	2.00

Souvenir Sheet
484	A97	$1 dk brn, pur & gold	16.00	22.50

75th birthday of Emperor Haile Selassie.

Microscope and Ethiopian Flag — A98

1967, Nov. 6   Litho.   Perf. 13
Flag in Grn, Yel, Red & Blk
485	A98	5c blue	.25	.25
486	A98	30c ocher	.55	.30
487	A98	$1 violet	1.75	1.10
		Nos. 485-487 (3)	2.55	1.65

2nd Intl. Conf. on the Global Impact of Applied Microbiology, Addis Ababa, 11/6-12.

Wall Painting from Debre Berhan Selassie Church, Gondar, 17th Century — A99

ITY Emblem and: 25c, Votive throne from Atsbe Dera, 4th Cent. B.C., vert. 35c, Prehistoric cave painting, Harar Province. 50c, Prehistoric stone tools, Melke Kontoure, vert.

1967, Nov. 20   Photo.   Perf. 14½
488	A99	15c multicolored	3.00	1.40
489	A99	25c yel grn, buff & blk	3.25	1.40
490	A99	35c green, brn & blk	3.00	1.75
491	A99	50c yellow & blk	5.50	2.75
		Nos. 488-491 (4)	14.75	7.30

International Tourist Year, 1967.

A100

Crosses of Lalibela: 5c, Processional Bronze Cross, Biet-Maryam Church. 10c, Processional copper cross. 15c, Copper cross, Biet-Maryam church. 20c, Lalibela-style cross. 50c, Chiseled copper cross, Madhani Alem church.

1967, Dec. 7   Photo.   Perf. 14½
Crosses in Silver
492	A100	5c yellow & blk	.30	.25
493	A100	10c red orange & blk	.30	.25
494	A100	15c violet & blk	.40	.25
495	A100	20c brt rose & blk	.65	.25
496	A100	50c orange yel & blk	2.00	.60
		Nos. 492-496 (5)	3.65	1.60

A101

Designs: 10c, Emperor Theodore (1818?-1868). 20c, Emperor Theodore and lions, horiz. 50o, Imperial crown.

Perf. 14x13½
1968, Apr. 18   Litho.   Unwmk.
497	A101	10c lt vio, ocher & brn	.50	.25
498	A101	20c lilac, brn & dk vio	.85	.50
499	A101	50c dk grn, org & rose cl	1.75	1.10
		Nos. 497-499 (3)	3.10	1.85

Human Rights Flame — A102

1968, May 31   Unwmk.   Perf. 14½
500	A102	15c pink, red & blk	.55	.55
501	A102	$1 lt bl, brt bl & blk	2.40	2.40

International Human Rights Year, 1968.

Shah Mohammed Reza Pahlavi, Emperor and Flags — A103

1968, June 3   Litho.   Perf. 13½
502	A103	5c multicolored	.25	.25
503	A103	15c multicolored	.30	.30
504	A103	30c multicolored	1.25	1.25
		Nos. 502-504 (3)	1.80	1.80

Visit of Shah Mohammed Riza Pahlavi of Iran.

Emperor Haile Selassie Appealing to League of Nations, 1935 — A104

35c, African Unity Building and map of Africa. $1, World map, symbolizing intl. relations.

1968, July 22   Photo.   Perf. 14x13½
505	A104	15c bl, red, blk & gold	.40	.25
506	A104	35c blk, emer, red & gold	.75	.75
507	A104	$1 dk bl, lil, blk & gold	2.50	2.75
		Nos. 505-507 (3)	3.65	3.75

Ethiopia's struggle for peace. Issued with tabs on bottom row. Value, set $10.

WHO Emblem — A105

Perf. 14x13½
1968, Aug. 30   Litho.   Unwmk.
508	A105	15c brt green & blk	.50	.35
509	A105	60c red lilac & blk	1.75	1.90

20th anniv. of the WHO.

Abebe Bikila, Marathon Runner — A106

1968, Oct. 12   Perf. 11½
510	A106	10c shown	.25	.25
511	A106	15c Soccer	.40	.40
512	A106	20c Boxing	.50	.50
513	A106	40c Basketball	1.25	1.25
514	A106	50c Bicycling	1.90	1.90
		Nos. 510-514 (5)	4.30	4.30

19th Olympic Games, Mexico City, 10/12-27.

Arrussi Woman — A107

Regional Costumes: 15c, Man from Gemu Gefa. 20c, Gojam man. 30c, Kefa man. 35c, Harar woman. 50c, Ilubabor grass coat. 60c, Woman from Eritrea.

Perf. 13½x13
1968, Dec. 10   Photo.   Unwmk.
515	A107	5c silver & multi	.65	.25
516	A107	15c silver & multi	.65	.25
517	A107	20c silver & multi	.65	.25
518	A107	30c silver & multi	.85	.55
519	A107	35c silver & multi	.85	.65
520	A107	50c silver & multi	1.75	1.10
521	A107	60c silver & multi	2.25	1.60
		Nos. 515-521 (7)	7.65	4.65

See Nos. 575-581.

Message Stick and Amharic Postal Emblem — A108

1969, Mar. 10   Litho.   Perf. 14
522	A108	10c emerald, blk & brn	.75	.70
523	A108	15c yellow, blk & brn	.75	.70
524	A108	35c multicolored	1.40	1.25
		Nos. 522-524 (3)	2.90	2.65

Ethiopian postal service, 75th anniv.

ILO Emblem — A109

1969, Apr. 11   Litho.   Perf. 14½
525	A109	15c orange & blk	.50	.50
526	A109	60c emerald & blk	2.00	2.00

50th anniv. of the ILO.

Dove, Red Cross, Crescent, Lion and Sun Emblems A110

ETHIOPIA

1969, May 8   **Wmk. 282**   *Perf. 13*
527	A110	5c lt ultra, blk & red	.25	.25
528	A110	15c lt ultra, grn & red	.65	.65
529	A110	30c lt ultra, vio bl & red	1.40	1.40
		Nos. 527-529 (3)	2.30	2.30

League of Red Cross Societies, 50th anniv.

Endybis Silver Coin, 3rd Century — A111

Ancient Ethiopian Coins: 10c, Gold of Ezana, 4th cent. 15c, Gold of Kaleb, 6th cent. 30c, Bronze of Armah, 7th cent. 40c, Bronze of Wazena, 7th cent. 50c, Silver of Gersem, 8th cent.

1969, June 19   **Photo.**   *Perf. 14½*
530	A111	5c ultra, blk & sil	.30	.25
531	A111	10c brt red, blk & gold	.50	.45
532	A111	15c brown, blk & gold	.80	.70
533	A111	30c dp car, blk & brnz	1.10	1.25
534	A111	40c dk green, blk & brnz	1.60	1.10
535	A111	50c dp violet, blk & sil	1.75	1.75
		Nos. 530-535 (6)	6.05	5.50

Zebras and Tourist Year Emblem — A112

Designs: 10c, Camping. 15c, Fishing. 20c, Water skiing. 25c, Mountaineering, vert.

Perf. 13x13½, 13½x13
1969, Aug. 29   **Litho.**   **Unwmk.**
536	A112	5c multicolored	.30	.30
537	A112	10c multicolored	.55	.30
538	A112	15c multicolored	.85	.55
539	A112	20c multicolored	.85	.85
540	A112	25c multicolored	1.75	1.10
		Nos. 536-540 (5)	4.30	3.10

International Year of African Tourism.

Stylized Bird and UN Emblem — A113

UN 25th anniv.: 30c, Stylized flowers, UN and peace emblems, vert. 60c, Stylized bird, UN emblem and plane.

1969, Oct. 24   **Unwmk.**   *Perf. 11½*
541	A113	10c lt blue & multi	.25	.25
542	A113	30c lt blue & multi	.80	.80
543	A113	60c lt blue & multi	2.00	2.00
		Nos. 541-543 (3)	3.05	3.05

Ancient Cross and Holy Family — A114

Designs: Various ancient crosses.

Perf. 14½x13½
1969, Dec. 10   **Photo.**
544	A114	5c black, yel & dk bl	.25	.25
545	A114	10c black & yellow	.25	.55
546	A114	25c black, yel & grn	1.10	1.10
547	A114	60c black & ocher	2.75	2.25
		Nos. 544-547 (4)	4.35	4.15

Ancient Figurines A115

Ancient Ethiopian Pottery: 20c, Vases, Yeha period, 4th-3rd centuries B.C. 25c, Vases and jugs, Axum, 4th-6th centuries A.D. 35c, Bird-shaped jug and jugs, Matara, 4th-6th centuries A.D. 60c, Decorated pottery, Adulis, 6th-7th centuries A.D.

1970, Feb. 6   **Photo.**   *Perf. 14½*
548	A115	10c black & multi	.65	.55
549	A115	20c black & multi	.65	.55
550	A115	25c black & multi	.65	.55
551	A115	35c black & multi	1.40	1.25
552	A115	60c black & multi	2.50	2.25
		Nos. 548-552 (5)	5.85	5.15

Medhane Alem Church A116

Rock Churches of Lalibela, 12th-13th Centuries: 10c, Bieta Emmanuel. 15c, The four Rock Churches of Lalibela. 20c, Bieta Mariam. 50c, Bieta Giorgis.

1970, Apr. 15   **Unwmk.**   *Perf. 13*
553	A116	5c brown & multi	.30	.25
554	A116	10c brown & multi	.40	.25
555	A116	15c brown & multi	.50	.40
556	A116	20c brown & multi	.75	.65
557	A116	50c brown & multi	1.80	1.50
		Nos. 553-557 (5)	3.65	3.05

Sailfish Tang — A117

Tropical Fish: 10c, Undulate triggerfish. 15c, Orange butterflyfish. 25c, Butterflyfish. 50c, Imperial Angelfish.

1970, June 19   **Photo.**   *Perf. 12½*
558	A117	5c multicolored	.25	.25
559	A117	10c multicolored	.25	.25
560	A117	15c multicolored	.60	.60
561	A117	25c multicolored	1.50	1.50
562	A117	50c multicolored	3.00	3.00
		Nos. 558-562 (5)	5.60	5.60

Education Year Emblem — A118

1970, Aug. 14   **Unwmk.**   *Perf. 13½*
563	A118	10c multicolored	.25	.25
564	A118	20c gold, ultra & emer	.45	.45
565	A118	50c gold, emer & org	1.40	1.40
		Nos. 563-565 (3)	2.10	2.10

Issued for International Education Year.

Map of Africa A119

30c, Flag of Organization of African Unity. 40c, OAU Headquarters, Addis Ababa.

1970, Sept. 21   **Photo.**   *Perf. 13½*
566	A119	20c multicolored	.30	.30
567	A119	30c multicolored	.60	.60
568	A119	40c green & multi	.85	.85
		Nos. 566-568 (3)	1.75	1.75

Africa Unity Day and Organization of African Unity.

Emperor Haile Selassie — A120

1970, Oct. 30   **Unwmk.**   *Perf. 14½*
569	A120	15c Prus bl & multi	.30	.30
570	A120	50c multicolored	1.00	1.00
571	A120	60c multicolored	1.75	1.75
		Nos. 569-571 (3)	3.05	3.05

Coronation, 40th anniv.

Buildings A121

1970, Dec. 30   **Litho.**   *Perf. 13½*
572	A121	10c ver & multi	.30	.30
573	A121	50c brown & multi	1.10	1.10
574	A121	80c multicolored	1.75	1.75
		Nos. 572-574 (3)	3.15	3.15

Opening of new Posts, Telecommunications and General Post Office buildings.

Costume Type of 1968

Regional Costumes: 5c, Warrior from Begemdir and Semien. 10c, Woman from Bale. 15c, Warrior from Welega. 20c, Woman from Shoa. 25c, Man from Sidamo. 40c, Woman from Tigre. 50c, Man from Welo.

1971, Feb. 17   **Photo.**   *Perf. 11½*
Granite Paper
575	A107	5c gold & multi	.30	.30
576	A107	10c gold & multi	.30	.30
577	A107	15c gold & multi	.55	.50
578	A107	20c gold & multi	.60	.60
579	A107	25c gold & multi	.85	.85
580	A107	40c gold & multi	1.10	1.10
581	A107	50c gold & multi	2.25	2.25
		Nos. 575-581 (7)	5.95	5.90

Plane's Tail with Emblem — A122

Designs: 10c, Ethiopian scenes. 20c, Nose of Boeing 707. 60c, Pilots in cockpit, and engine. 80c, Globe with routes shown.

1971, Apr. 8   *Perf. 14½x14*
582	A122	5c multicolored	.30	.30
583	A122	10c multicolored	.30	.30
584	A122	20c multicolored	.60	.60
585	A122	60c multicolored	1.25	1.25
586	A122	80c multicolored	2.00	2.00
		Nos. 582-586 (5)	4.45	4.45

Ethiopian Airlines, 25th anniversary. Issued with tabs on bottom row. Value, set $11.

Fountain of Life, 15th Century Gospel Book — A123

Ethiopian Paintings: 10c, King David, 15th cent. manuscript. 25c, St. George, 17th cent. painting on canvas. 50c, King Lalibela, 18th cent. painting on wood. 60c, Yared singing before King Kaleb. Mural in Axum Cathedral.

1971, June 15   **Photo.**   *Perf. 11½*
Granite Paper
587	A123	5c tan & multi	.25	.25
588	A123	10c pale sal & multi	.25	.25
589	A123	25c lemon & multi	.60	.60
590	A123	50c yellow & multi	1.60	1.60
591	A123	60c gray & multi	2.50	2.50
		Nos. 587-591 (5)	5.20	5.20

Black and White Heads, Globes — A124

Designs: 60c, Black and white hand holding globe. 80c, Four races, globes.

1971, Aug. 31   **Unwmk.**
592	A124	10c org, red brn & blk	.30	.30
593	A124	60c green, bl & blk	1.75	1.75
594	A124	80c bl, org, yel & blk	2.75	2.75
		Nos. 592-594 (3)	4.80	4.80

Intl. Year Against Racial Discrimination.

Emperor Menelik II and Reading of Treaty of Ucciali — A125

Contemporary Paintings: 30c, Menelik II on horseback gathering the tribes. 50c, Ethiopians and Italians in Battle of Adwa. 60c, Menelik II and Taitu at head of their armies.

1971, Oct. 20   **Litho.**   *Perf. 13½*
595	A125	10c multicolored	.35	.35
596	A125	30c multicolored	.95	.95
597	A125	50c multicolored	1.40	1.40
598	A125	60c multicolored	2.40	2.40
		Nos. 595-598 (4)	5.10	5.10

75th anniversary of victory of Adwa over the Italians, March 1, 1896.

Two telephones, 1897, Menelik II and Ras Makonnen A126

Designs: 10c, Haile Selassie Broadcasting and Map of Ethiopia. 30c, Ethiopians around television set. 40c, Telephone microwave circuits. 60c, Map of Africa on globe and telephone dial.

1971, Nov. 2
599	A126	5c brown & multi	.30	.30
600	A126	10c yellow & multi	.30	.30
601	A126	30c vio bl & multi	.30	.30
602	A126	40c black & multi	.85	.85
603	A126	60c vio bl & multi	2.25	2.25
		Nos. 599-603 (5)	4.00	4.00

Telecommunications in Ethiopia, 75th anniv.

UNICEF Emblem, Mother and Child — A127

UNICEF Emblem and: 10c, Children drinking milk. 15c, Man holding sick child. 30c, Kindergarten class. 50c, Father and son.

1971, Dec. 15   **Unwmk.**
604	A127	5c yellow & multi	.30	.30
605	A127	10c pale brn & multi	.30	.30
606	A127	15c rose & multi	.30	.30
607	A127	30c violet & multi	.85	.85
608	A127	50c green & multi	1.60	1.60
		Nos. 604-608 (5)	3.35	3.35

25th anniv. of UNICEF.

Nos. 445-448 Overprinted

1972, Jan. 28   **Photo.**   *Perf. 11*
Portrait in Black
609	A86	20c grn & pale yel	.55	.55
610	A86	25c dk brn & yel	.85	.85
611	A86	30c maroon & gray	3.50	3.50
612	A86	35c dk blue & gray	3.50	3.50
		Nos. 609-612 (4)	8.40	8.40

1st meeting of UN Security Council in Africa.

River Boat on Lake Haik A128

ETHIOPIA

1972, Feb. 7   Litho.   Perf. 11½
Granite Paper
613 A128 10c shown   .30   .30
614 A128 20c Boats on Lake Abaya   .55   .55
615 A128 30c on Lake Tana   .85   .85
616 A128 60c on Baro River   1.75 1.75
  Nos. 613-616 (4)   3.45 3.45

Proclamation of Cyrus the Great — A129

1972, Mar. 28   Photo.   Perf. 14x14½
617 A129 10c red & multi   .50   .50
618 A129 60c emerald & multi 2.00 2.00
619 A129 80c gray & multi 3.00 3.00
  Nos. 617-619 (3) 5.50 5.50

2500th anniversary of the founding of the Persian empire by Cyrus the Great.

Houses, Sidamo Province — A130

Ethiopian Architecture: 10c, Tigre Province. 20c, Eritrea Province. 40c, Addis Ababa. 80c, Shoa Province.

1972, Apr. 11   Litho.   Perf. 13½
620 A130 5c black & multi   .30   .30
621 A130 10c black, gray & brn   .30   .30
622 A130 20c black & multi   .65   .65
623 A130 40c black, bl grn & brn 1.10 1.10
624 A130 80c black, brn & red brn 2.75 2.75
  Nos. 620-624 (5) 5.10 5.10

Hands Holding Map of Ethiopia — A131

10c, Hands shielding Ethiopians. 25c, Map of Africa, hands reaching for African Unity emblem. 50c, Brown & white hands clasped, UN emblem. 60c, Hands protecting dove. Each denomination shows different portrait of the Emperor.

Perf. 14½x14
1972, July 21   Litho.   Unwmk.
625 A131 5c scarlet & multi   .35   .35
626 A131 10c ultra & multi   .35   .35
627 A131 25c vio bl & multi   .60   .60
628 A131 50c lt blue & multi 1.25 1.25
629 A131 60c brown & multi 1.50 1.50
  Nos. 625-629 (5) 4.05 4.05

80th birthday of Emperor Haile Selassie.

Running, Flags of Mexico, Japan, Italy — A132

1972, Aug. 25   Perf. 13½x13
630 A132 10c shown   .35   .35
631 A132 30c Soccer   .80   .80
632 A132 50c Bicycling 1.75 1.75
633 A132 60c Boxing 2.25 2.25
  Nos. 630-633 (4) 5.15 5.15

20th Olympic Games, Munich, Germany, Aug. 26-Sept. 11.

Open Bible, Cross and Orbit — A133

Designs: 50c, First and 1972 headquarters of the British and Foreign Bible Society, vert. 80c, First Amharic Bible.

1972, Sept. 25   Photo.   Perf. 13½
634 A133 20c deep red & multi   .60   .60
635 A133 50c deep red & multi 1.10 1.10
636 A133 80c deep red & multi 2.75 2.75
  Nos. 634-636 (3) 4.45 4.45

United Bible Societies World Assembly, Addis Ababa, Sept. 1972.

Security Council Meeting — A134

Designs: 60c, Building where Security Council met. 80c, Map of Africa with flags of participating members.

1972, Nov. 1   Litho.   Perf. 13½
637 A134 10c lt bl & vio bl   .25   .25
638 A134 50c multicolored 1.10 1.10
639 A134 80c multicolored 1.75 1.75
  Nos. 637-639 (3) 3.10 3.10

First United Nations Security Council meeting, Addis Ababa, Jan. 28-Feb. 4, 1972.

Fish in Polluted Sea — A135

Designs: 30c, Fisherman, beacon, family. 80c, Polluted seashore.

1973, Feb. 23   Photo.   Perf. 13½
640 A135 20c gold & multi   .75   .50
641 A135 30c gold & multi 1.00   .85
642 A135 80c gold & multi 2.25 2.00
  Nos. 640-642 (3) 4.00 3.35

World message from the sea, Ethiopian anti-pollution campaign.

INTERPOL and Ethiopian Police Emblems A136

50c, INTERPOL emblem & General Secretariat, Paris. 60c, INTERPOL emblem.

1973, Mar. 20   Photo.   Perf. 13½
643 A136 40c dull orange & blk 1.25 1.25
644 A136 50c blue, blk & yel 1.75 1.75
645 A136 60c dk carmine & blk 2.00 2.00
  Nos. 643-645 (3) 5.00 5.00

50th anniversary of International Criminal Police Organization (INTERPOL).

Virgin of Emperor Zara Yaqob — A137

Ethiopian Art: 15c, Crucifixion, Zara Yaqob period. 30c, Virgin and Child, from Entoto Mariam Church. 40c, Christ, contemporary mosaic. 80c, The Evangelists, contemporary bas-relief.

1973, May 15   Photo.   Perf. 11½
Granite Paper
646 A137 5c brown & multi   .30   .30
647 A137 15c dp blue & multi   .55   .55
648 A137 30c gray grn & multi   .95   .95
649 A137 40c multicolored 1.10 1.10
650 A137 80c slate & multi 2.75 2.75
  Nos. 646-650 (5) 5.55 5.55

Free African States in 1963 and 1973 — A138

Designs (Map of Africa and): 10c, Flags of OAU members. 20c, Symbols of progress. 40c, Dove and people. 80c, Emblems of various UN agencies.

1973, May 25   Perf. 14½x14
651 A138 5c red & multi   .25   .25
652 A138 10c ol gray & multi   .30   .30
653 A138 20c green & multi   .50   .50
654 A138 40c sepia & multi 1.10 1.10
655 A138 80c lt blue & multi 2.75 2.75
  Nos. 651-655 (5) 4.90 4.90

OAU, 10th anniv.

Scouts Saluting Ethiopian and Scout Flags — A139

Designs: 15c, Road and road sign. 30c, Girl Scout reading to old man. 40c, Scout and disabled people. 60c, Ethiopian Boy Scout.

1973, July 10   Photo.   Perf. 11½
Granite Paper
656 A139 5c blue & multi   .30   .30
657 A139 15c lt green & multi   .55   .55
658 A139 30c yellow & multi   .85   .85
659 A139 40c crimson & multi 1.10 1.10
660 A139 60c violet & multi 2.75 2.75
  Nos. 656-660 (5) 5.55 5.55

24th Boy Scout World Conference, Nairobi, Kenya, July 16-21.

WMO Emblem — A140

50c, WMO emblem, anemometer. 60c, Weather satellite over earth, WMO emblem.

1973, Sept. 4   Photo.   Perf. 13½
661 A140 40c black, bl & dl bl 1.10 1.10
662 A140 50c dull blue & blk 1.25 1.25
663 A140 60c dull blue & multi 1.90 1.90
  Nos. 661-663 (3) 4.25 4.25

Cent. of intl. meteorological cooperation. Printed with tabs at top of sheet inscribed in Amharic and tabs at bottom with "ETHIOPIA."

Ras Makonnen, Duke of Harar — A141

5c, Old wall of Harar. 20c, Operating room. 40c, Boy Scouts learning 1st aid & hospital. 80c, Prince Makonnen & hospital.

1973, Nov. 1   Unwmk.   Perf. 14½
664 A141 5c gray & multi   .30   .30
665 A141 10c red brn & multi   .30   .30
666 A141 20c green & multi   .60   .60
667 A141 40c brown red & multi 1.10 1.10
668 A141 80c ultra & multi 2.75 2.75
  Nos. 664-668 (5) 5.05 5.05

Opening of Ras Makonnen Memorial Hospital.

Human Rights Flame — A142

Perf. 11½
1973, Nov. 16   Unwmk.
Granite Paper
669 A142 40c yel, gold & dk grn   .70   .70
670 A142 50c lt grn, gold & dk grn 1.00 1.00
671 A142 60c org, gold & dk grn 1.25 1.25
  Nos. 669-671 (3) 2.95 2.95

25th anniversary of the Universal Declaration of Human Rights.

Emperor Haile Selassie — A143

1973, Nov. 5   Photo.   Perf. 11½
672 A143 5c yellow & multi   .35   .30
673 A143 10c brt blue & multi   .35   .30
674 A143 15c green & multi   .45   .40
675 A143 20c dull yel & multi   .55   .40
676 A143 25c multicolored   .65   .40
677 A143 30c multicolored   .80   .40
678 A143 35c multicolored   .85   .40
679 A143 40c ultra & multi   .95   .40
680 A143 45c multicolored 1.10   .50
681 A143 50c orange & multi 1.25   .50
682 A143 55c magenta & multi 1.60   .85
683 A143 60c multicolored 1.75 1.10
684 A143 70c red org & multi 2.10 1.25
685 A143 90c brt vio & multi 2.75 1.40
686 A143 $1 multicolored 3.25 1.90
687 A143 $2 orange & multi 6.25 3.25
688 A143 $3 multicolored 10.50 5.00
689 A143 $5 multicolored 17.00 8.25
  Nos. 672-689 (18) 52.50 27.00

Wicker Furniture — A144

Designs: Various wicker baskets, wall hangings, dinnerware.

1974, Jan. 31   Photo.   Perf. 11½
Granite Paper
690 A144 5c violet bl & multi   .25   .25
691 A144 10c violet bl & multi   .30   .30
692 A144 30c violet bl & multi   .60   .60
693 A144 50c violet bl & multi   .95   .95
694 A144 60c violet bl & multi 1.20 1.20
  Nos. 690-694 (5) 3.30 3.30

Cow, Calf, Syringe — A145

Designs: 15c, Inoculation of cattle. 20c, Bullock and syringe. 50c, Laboratory technician, cow's head, syringe. 60c, Map of Ethiopia, cattle, syringe.

1974, Feb. 20   Litho.   Perf. 13½x13
695 A145 5c sepia & multi   .25   .25
696 A145 15c ultra & multi   .40   .40
697 A145 20c ultra & multi   .50   .50
698 A145 50c orange & multi 1.40 1.40
699 A145 60c gold & multi 1.75 1.75
  Nos. 695-699 (5) 4.30 4.30

Campaign against cattle plague.

Umbrella Makers — A146

Designs: 30c, Weaving. 50c, Child care. 60c, Foundation headquarters.

1974, Apr. 17   Photo.   Perf. 14½
700 A146 10c lt lilac & multi   .30   .30
701 A146 30c multicolored   .50   .50
702 A146 50c multicolored 1.00 1.00
703 A146 60c blue & multi 1.25 1.25
  Nos. 700-703 (4) 3.05 3.05

20th anniv. of Haile Selassie Foundation.

470 ETHIOPIA

Ceremonial Robe — A147

Designs: Ceremonial robes.

1974, June 26	Litho.	Perf. 13
704	A147	15c multicolored	.40	.40
705	A147	25c ocher & multi	.60	.60
706	A147	35c green & multi	1.10	1.10
707	A147	40c lt brown & multi	1.25	1.25
708	A147	60c gray & multi	2.50	2.50
		Nos. 704-708 (5)	5.85	5.85

World Population Statistics A148

Designs: 50c, "Larger families-lower living standard." 60c, Rising population graph.

1974, Aug. 19	Photo.	Perf. 14½
709	A148	40c yellow & multi	.85	.85
710	A148	50c violet & multi	.85	.85
711	A148	60c green & multi	.85	.85
		Nos. 709-711 (3)	2.55	2.55

World Population Year 1974.

UPU Emblem, Letter Carrier's Staff — A149

UPU Emblem and: 50c, Letters and flags. 60c, Globe. 70c, Headquarters, Bern.

1974, Oct. 9	Photo.	Perf. 11½
	Granite Paper			
712	A149	15c yellow & multi	.30	.30
713	A149	50c multicolored	.85	.85
714	A149	60c ultra & multi	1.25	1.10
715	A149	70c multicolored	1.25	1.25
		Nos. 712-715 (4)	3.65	3.50

Centenary of Universal Postal Union.

Celebration Around "Damara" Pillar — A150

5c, Site of Gishen Mariam Monastery. 20c, Cross and festivities. 80c, Torch (Chibos) Parade.

1974, Dec. 17	Photo.	Perf. 14x14½
716	A150	5c yellow & multi	.30	.30
717	A150	10c yellow & multi	.30	.30
718	A150	20c yellow & multi	.30	.30
719	A150	80c yellow & multi	1.75	1.75
		Nos. 716-719 (4)	2.65	2.65

Meskel Festival, Sept. 26-27, commemorating the finding in the 4th century of the True Cross, of which a fragment is kept at Gishen Mariam Monastery in Welo Province.

Precis Clelia — A151

Butterflies: 25c, Charaxes achaemenes. 45c, Papilio dardanus. 50c, Charaxes druceanus. 60c, Papilio demodocus.

1975, Feb. 18	Photo.	Perf. 12x12½
720	A151	10c silver & multi	.60	.40
721	A151	25c gold & multi	.90	.75
722	A151	45c purple & multi	1.75	1.75
723	A151	50c green & multi	2.75	2.75
724	A151	60c brt blue & multi	3.50	3.00
		Nos. 720-724 (5)	9.50	8.65

Adoration of the Kings — A152

10c, Baptism of Jesus. 15c, Jesus teaching in the Temple. 30c, Jesus giving sight to the blind. 40c, Crucifixion. 80c, Resurrection.

Granite Paper

1975, Apr. 23	Photo.	Perf. 11½
725	A152	5c brown & multi	.30	.30
726	A152	10c black & multi	.30	.30
727	A152	15c dk brown & multi	.30	.30
728	A152	30c dk brown & multi	.60	.60
729	A152	40c black & multi	1.10	1.10
730	A152	80c slate & multi	2.25	2.25
		Nos. 725-730 (6)	4.85	4.85

Murals from Ethiopian churches.

Wild Animals — A153

1975, May 27	Photo.	Perf. 11½
	Granite Paper			
731	A153	5c Warthog	.60	.60
732	A153	10c Aardvark	.60	.60
733	A153	20c Semien wolf	.85	.85
734	A153	40c Gelada baboon	1.75	1.75
735	A153	80c Civet	4.25	4.25
		Nos. 731-735 (5)	8.05	8.05

"Peace," Dove, Globe, IWY Emblem — A154

50c, Symbols of development. 90c, Equality between men and women.

1975, June 30	Litho.	Perf. 14x14½
736	A154	40c blue & black	.60	.60
737	A154	50c salmon & multi	.85	.85
738	A154	90c multicolored	1.75	1.75
		Nos. 736-738 (3)	3.20	3.20

International Women's Year 1975.

Postal Museum — A155

Various interior views of Postal Museum.

1975, Aug. 19	Photo.	Perf. 13x12½
739	A155	10c ocher & multi	.35	.30
740	A155	30c pink & multi	.65	.50
741	A155	60c multicolored	1.50	1.10
742	A155	70c lt green & multi	1.75	1.25
		Nos. 739-742 (4)	4.25	3.15

Ethiopian Natl. Postal Museum, opening.

Map of Ethiopia and Sun — A156

1975, Sept. 11	Photo.	Perf. 11½
	Granite Paper			
743	A156	5c lilac & multi	.25	.25
744	A156	10c ultra & multi	.25	.25
745	A156	25c brown & multi	.35	.35
746	A156	50c yellow & multi	.90	.90
747	A156	90c brt green & multi	1.75	1.75
		Nos. 743-747 (5)	3.50	3.50

1st anniv. of Ethiopian revolution.

UN Emblem — A157

1975, Oct. 24	Photo.	Perf. 11½
748	A157	40c lilac & multi	.85	.85
749	A157	50c multicolored	.85	.85
750	A157	90c blue & multi	1.75	1.75
		Nos. 748-750 (3)	3.45	3.45

United Nations, 30th anniversary.

Regional Hair Styles — A158

1975, Dec. 15	Photo.	Perf. 11½
751	A158	5c Ilubabor	.30	.30
752	A158	15c Arusi	.40	.40
753	A158	20c Eritrea	.60	.60
754	A158	30c Bale	.85	.85
755	A158	35c Kefa	1.00	1.00
756	A158	50c Begemir	1.40	1.40
757	A158	75c Shoa	1.75	1.75
		Nos. 751-757 (7)	6.30	6.30

See Nos. 832-838.

Delphinium Wellbyi — A159

Flowers: 10c, Plectocephalus varians. 20c, Brachystelma asmarensis, horiz. 40c, Ceropegia inflata. 80c, Erythrina brucei.

1976, Jan. 15	Photo.	Perf. 11½
758	A159	5c multicolored	.35	.35
759	A159	10c multicolored	.40	.40
760	A159	20c multicolored	.60	.60
761	A159	40c multicolored	1.50	1.50
762	A159	80c multicolored	2.50	2.50
		Nos. 758-762 (5)	5.35	5.35

Goalkeeper, Map of Africa, Games' Emblem — A160

Designs: Various scenes from soccer, map of Africa and ball.

1976, Feb. 27	Photo.	Perf. 14½
763	A160	5c orange & multi	.30	.30
764	A160	10c yellow & multi	.30	.30
765	A160	25c lilac & multi	.60	.60
766	A160	50c green & multi	1.10	1.10
767	A160	90c brt grn & multi	2.25	2.25
		Nos. 763-767 (5)	4.55	4.55

10th African Cup of Nations, Addis Ababa and Dire Dawa, Feb. 29-Mar. 14.

Telephones, 1876 and 1976 — A161

Designs: 60c, Alexander Graham Bell. 90c, Transmission tower.

1976, Mar. 10	Litho.	Perf. 12x13½
768	A161	30c lt ocher & multi	.55	.55
769	A161	60c emerald & multi	1.10	1.10
770	A161	90c ver, blk & buff	1.75	1.75
		Nos. 768-770 (3)	3.40	3.40

Centenary of first telephone call by Alexander Graham Bell, Mar. 10, 1876.

Ethiopian Jewelry — A162

Designs: Women wearing various kinds of Ethiopian jewelry.

Granite Paper

1976, May 14	Photo.	Perf. 11½
771	A162	5c blue & multi	.30	.30
772	A162	10c plum & multi	.30	.30
773	A162	20c gray & multi	.60	.60
774	A162	40c green & multi	.90	.90
775	A162	80c orange & multi	1.75	1.75
		Nos. 771-775 (5)	3.85	3.85

Boxing — A163

Designs (Montreal Olympic Emblem and): 80c, Runner and maple leaf. 90c, Bicycling.

1976, July 15	Litho.	Perf. 12½x12
776	A163	10c multicolored	.30	.30
777	A163	80c brt red, blk & grn	1.75	1.75
778	A163	90c brt red & multi	1.75	1.75
		Nos. 776-778 (3)	3.80	3.80

21st Olympic Games, Montreal, Canada, July 17-Aug. 1.

Hands Holding Map of Ethiopia — A164

1976, Aug. 5	Photo.	Perf. 14½
779	A164	5c rose & multi	.25	.25
780	A164	10c olive & multi	.30	.25
781	A164	25c orange & multi	.40	.30
782	A164	50c multicolored	.95	.70
783	A164	90c dk blue & multi	1.75	1.40
		Nos. 779-783 (5)	3.65	2.90

Development through cooperation.

Revolution Emblem: Eye and Map — A165

1976, Sept. 9	Photo.	Perf. 13½
784	A165	5c multicolored	.30	.30
785	A165	10c multicolored	.30	.30
786	A165	25c multicolored	.30	.30
787	A165	50c yellow & multi	.90	.90
788	A165	90c green & multi	1.25	1.25
		Nos. 784-788 (5)	3.05	3.05

2nd anniversary of the revolution.

Sunburst Around Crest — A166

1976, Sept. 13	Photo.	Perf. 11½
789	A166	5c green, gold & blk	.25	.25
790	A166	10c org, gold & blk	.25	.25
791	A166	15c grnsh bl, gold & blk	.55	.25
792	A166	20c lilac, gold & blk	.55	.25
793	A166	25c brt grn, gold & blk	.55	.25
794	A166	30c car, gold & blk	.55	.55
795	A166	35c yel, gold & blk	.85	.55
796	A166	40c ol, gold & blk	.85	.55
797	A166	45c brt grn, gold & blk	.85	.55
798	A166	50c car rose, gold & blk	1.10	.85
799	A166	55c ultra, gold & blk	1.10	.85
800	A166	60c fawn, gold & blk	1.10	.85
801	A166	70c rose, gold & blk	1.75	.90

ETHIOPIA

802	A166	90c blue, gold & blk	1.75	.90
803	A166	$1 dull grn, gold & blk	2.25	.90
804	A166	$2 gray, gold & blk	4.50	1.75
805	A166	$3 brn vio, gold & blk	7.00	2.75
806	A166	$5 slate bl, gold & blk	11.00	4.50
		Nos. 789-806 (18)	36.80	17.70

Denomination Expressed as "BIRR"

1983, June 16

806A	A166	1b dull grn, gold & blk	7.50	2.25
806B	A166	2b gray, gold & blk	20.00	4.50
806C	A166	3b brn vio, gold & blk	25.00	6.25

Plane Over Man with Donkey — A167

10c, Globe showing routes. 25c, Crew and passengers forming star. 50c, Propeller and jet engine. 90c, Airplanes surrounding map of Ethiopia.

1976, Oct. 28   Litho.   Perf. 12x12½

807	A167	5c dull bl & multi	.30	.30
808	A167	10c lilac & multi	.30	.30
809	A167	25c multicolored	.40	.40
810	A167	50c orange & multi	1.25	1.25
811	A167	90c olive & multi	2.00	2.00
		Nos. 807-811 (5)	4.25	4.25

Ethiopian Airlines, 30th anniversary.

Tortoises — A168

Reptiles: 20c, Chameleon. 30c, Python. 40c, Monitor lizard. 80c, Nile crocodiles.

1976, Dec. 15   Photo.   Perf. 14½

812	A168	10c multicolored	.40	.40
813	A168	20c multicolored	.60	.60
814	A168	30c multicolored	.90	.90
815	A168	45c multicolored	1.25	1.25
816	A168	80c multicolored	2.75	2.75
		Nos. 812-816 (5)	5.90	5.90

Hand Holding Makeshift Hammer — A169

Designs: 5c, Hands holding bowl and plane dropping food. 45c, Infant with empty bowl, and bank note. 60c, Map of affected area, footprints and tire tracks. 80c, Film strip, camera and Ethiopian sitting between eggshells.

1977, Jan. 20   Litho.   Perf. 12½

817	A169	5c multicolored	.40	.40
818	A169	10c multicolored	.40	.40
819	A169	45c multicolored	.85	.85
820	A169	60c multicolored	.85	.85
821	A169	80c multicolored	1.60	1.60
		Nos. 817-821 (5)	4.10	4.10

Ethiopian Relief and Rehabilitation Commission for drought and disaster areas.

Elephant and Ruins, Axum, 7th Century — A170

Designs: 10c, Ibex and temple, 5th century, B.C., Yeha. 25c, Megalithic dolmen and pottery, Sourre Kabanawa. 50c, Awash Valley, stone axe, Acheulean period. 80c, Omo Valley, hominid jawbone.

1977, Mar. 15   Photo.   Perf. 13½

822	A170	5c gold & multi	.35	.35
823	A170	10c gold & multi	.35	.35
824	A170	25c gold & multi	.55	.55
825	A170	50c gold & multi	1.00	1.00
826	A170	80c gold & multi	1.40	1.40
		Nos. 822-826 (5)	3.65	3.65

Archaeological sites and finds in Ethiopia.

Map of Africa with Trans-East Highway — A171

1977, Mar. 30   Perf. 14

827	A171	10c gold & multi	.30	.30
828	A171	20c gold & multi	.30	.30
829	A171	40c gold & multi	.85	.85
830	A171	50c gold & multi	.85	.85
831	A171	60c gold & multi	1.10	1.10
		Nos. 827-831 (5)	3.40	3.40

Addis Ababa to Nairobi Highway and projected highways to Cairo, Egypt, and Gaborone, Botswana.

Hairstyle Type of 1975

1977, Apr. 28   Photo.   Perf. 11½

832	A158	5c Welega	.30	.30
833	A158	10c Gojam	.30	.30
834	A158	15c Tigre	.30	.30
835	A158	20c Harar	.60	.60
836	A158	25c Gemu Gefa	.60	.60
837	A158	40c Sidamo	1.10	1.10
838	A158	50c Welo	1.10	1.10
		Nos. 832-838 (7)	4.30	4.30

Addis Ababa — A172

Towns of Ethiopia: 10c, Asmara. 25c, Harar. 50c, Jima. 90c, Dese.

1977, June 20   Photo.   Perf. 14½

839	A172	5c silver & multi	.30	.30
840	A172	10c silver & multi	.30	.30
841	A172	25c silver & multi	.30	.30
842	A172	50c silver & multi	.85	.85
843	A172	90c silver & multi	1.25	1.25
		Nos. 839-843 (5)	3.00	3.00

Terebratula Abyssinica — A173

Fossil Shells: 10c, Terebratula subalata. 25c, Cuculloea lefeburiaua. 50c, Ostrea plicatissima. 90c, Trigonia cousobrina.

1977, Aug. 15   Photo.   Perf. 14x13½

844	A173	5c multicolored	.75	.30
845	A173	10c multicolored	1.25	.30
846	A173	50c multicolored	1.50	.60
847	A173	50c multicolored	2.50	1.10
848	A173	90c multicolored	4.00	1.75
		Nos. 844-848 (5)	10.00	4.05

Fractured Imperial Crown — A174

Designs: 10c, Symbol of the Revolution (spade, axe, torch). 25c, Warriors, hammer and sickle, map of Ethiopia. 60c, Soldier, farmer and map. 80c, Map and emblem of revolutionary government.

1977, Sept. 9   Litho.   Perf. 15

849	A174	5c multicolored	.30	.30
850	A174	10c multicolored	.30	.30
851	A174	25c multicolored	.55	.55
852	A174	60c multicolored	.85	.85
853	A174	80c multicolored	1.10	1.10
		Nos. 849-853 (5)	3.10	3.10

Third anniversary of the revolution.

Cicindela Petitii — A175

Insects: 10c, Heliocopris dillonii. 25c, Poekilocerus vignaudii. 50c, Pepsis heros. 90c, Pepsis dedjaz.

1977, Sept. 30   Photo.   Perf. 14x13½

854	A175	5c multicolored	.40	.30
855	A175	10c multicolored	.50	.30
856	A175	25c multicolored	1.00	.90
857	A175	50c multicolored	2.50	1.75
858	A175	90c multicolored	3.75	2.90
		Nos. 854-858 (5)	8.15	5.85

Lenin, Globe, Map of Ethiopia and Emblem — A176

1977, Nov. 15   Litho.   Perf. 12

859	A176	5c orange & multi	.40	.30
860	A176	10c multicolored	.40	.30
861	A176	25c salmon & multi	.40	.30
862	A176	50c lt blue & multi	1.00	.85
863	A176	90c yellow & multi	1.25	1.10
		Nos. 859-863 (5)	3.45	2.85

60th anniv. of Russian October Revolution.

Chondrostoma Dilloni — A177

Salt-water Fish: 10c, Ostracion cubicus. 25c, Serranus summana. 50c, Serranus luti. 90c, Tetraodon maculatus.

1978, Jan. 20   Litho.   Perf. 15½

864	A177	5c multicolored	.65	.65
865	A177	10c multicolored	.75	.75
866	A177	25c multicolored	1.25	1.25
867	A177	50c multicolored	2.25	2.25
868	A177	90c multicolored	4.00	4.00
		Nos. 864-868 (5)	8.90	8.90

Domestic Animals — A178

1978, Mar. 27   Litho.   Perf. 13½x14

869	A178	5c Cattle	.25	.25
870	A178	10c Mules	.25	.25
871	A178	25c Goats	.60	.55
872	A178	50c Dromedaries	1.25	1.25
873	A178	90c Horses	1.75	1.75
		Nos. 869-873 (5)	4.10	4.05

Weapons and Shield, Map of Ethiopia — A179

"Call of the Motherland." (Map of Ethiopia and): 10c, Civilian fighters. 25c, Map of Africa. 60c, Soldiers. 80c, Red Cross nurse and wounded man.

1978, May 13   Litho.   Perf. 15½

874	A179	5c multicolored	.25	.25
875	A179	10c multicolored	.30	.30
876	A179	25c multicolored	.30	.30
877	A179	60c multicolored	.90	.90
878	A179	80c multicolored	1.25	1.25
		Nos. 874-878 (5)	3.00	3.00

Bronze Ibex, 5th Century B.C. — A180

Ancient Bronzes: 10c, Lion, Yeha, 5th cent. B.C., horiz. 25c, Lamp with ibex attacked by dog, Matara, 1st cent. B.C. 50c, Goat, Axum, 3rd cent. A.D., horiz. 90c, Ax, chisel and sickle, Yeha, 5th-4th centuries B.C.

1978, June 21   Litho.   Perf. 15½

879	A180	5c multicolored	.25	.25
880	A180	10c multicolored	.30	.30
881	A180	25c multicolored	.60	.60
882	A180	50c multicolored	.90	.90
883	A180	90c multicolored	1.75	1.75
		Nos. 879-883 (5)	3.80	3.80

See Nos. 1024-1027.

Globe and Argentina '78 Emblem — A181

20c, Soccer player kicking ball. 30c, Two players embracing, net and ball. 55c, World map and ball. 70c, Soccer field, vert.

Perf. 14x13½, 13½x14

1978, July 19   Litho.

884	A181	5c multicolored	.30	.30
885	A181	20c multicolored	.60	.50
886	A181	30c multicolored	.60	.60
887	A181	55c multicolored	1.10	1.10
888	A181	70c multicolored	1.75	1.75
		Nos. 884-888 (5)	4.35	4.25

11th World Cup Soccer Championship, Argentina, June 1-25.

Map of Africa, Oppressed African — A182

Namibia Day: 10c, Policeman pointing gun. 25c, Sniper with gun. 60c, African caught in net. 80c, Head of free man.

1978, Aug. 25   Perf. 12½x13½

889	A182	5c multicolored	.25	.25
890	A182	10c multicolored	.30	.30
891	A182	25c multicolored	.60	.60
892	A182	60c multicolored	1.10	1.10
893	A182	80c multicolored	1.25	1.25
		Nos. 889-893 (5)	3.50	3.50

Soldiers, Guerrilla and Jets — A183

Design: 1b, People looking toward sun, crushing snake, flags.

1978, Sept. 8   Photo.   Perf. 14

894	A183	80c multicolored	1.10	1.10
895	A183	1b multicolored	1.75	1.75

4th anniversary of revolution.

Hand and Globe with Tools — A184

Designs: 15c, Symbols of energy, communications, education, medicine, agriculture and industry. 25c, Cogwheels and world map. 60c, Globe and hands passing wrench. 70c, Flying geese and turtle over globe.

1978, Nov. 14   Litho.   Perf. 13x13½

896	A184	10c multicolored	.25	.25
897	A184	15c multicolored	.30	.30
898	A184	25c multicolored	.60	.60
899	A184	60c multicolored	1.10	1.00
900	A184	70c multicolored	1.25	1.10
		Nos. 896-900 (5)	3.50	3.15

Technical Cooperation Among Developing Countries Conference, Buenos Aires, Argentina, Sept. 1978.

Human Rights Emblem — A185

ETHIOPIA

1978, Dec. 7   **Photo.**   **Perf. 12½x13½**
901	A185	5c multicolored	.25 .25
902	A185	15c multicolored	.30 .30
903	A185	25c multicolored	.30 .30
904	A185	35c multicolored	.60 .60
905	A185	1b multicolored	1.75 1.75
		Nos. 901-905 (5)	3.20 3.20

Declaration of Human Rights, 30th anniv.

Broken Chain, Anti-Apartheid Emblem — A186

1978, Dec. 28   **Litho.**   **Perf. 12½x12**
906	A186	5c multicolored	.25 .25
907	A186	20c multicolored	.30 .30
908	A186	60c multicolored	.60 .60
909	A186	55c multicolored	.85 .85
910	A186	70c multicolored	1.25 1.25
		Nos. 906-910 (5)	3.25 3.25

Anti-Apartheid Year.

Stele from Osole — A187

Ancient Carved Stones, Soddo Region: 10c, Anthropomorphous stele, Gorashino. 25c, Leaning stone, Wado. 60c, Round stones, Ambeut. 80c, Bas-relief, Tiya.

1979, Jan. 25   **Perf. 14**
911	A187	5c multicolored	.25 .25
912	A187	10c multicolored	.30 .30
913	A187	25c multicolored	.30 .30
914	A187	60c multicolored	1.25 1.25
915	A187	80c multicolored	1.25 1.25
		Nos. 911-915 (5)	3.35 3.35

Cotton Plantation — A188

Shemma Industry: 10c, Women spinning cotton yarn. 20c, Man reeling cotton. 65c, Weaver. 80c, Shemma (Natl. dress).

1979, Mar. 15   **Litho.**   **Perf. 15½**
916	A188	5c multicolored	.25 .25
917	A188	10c multicolored	.30 .30
918	A188	20c multicolored	.60 .60
919	A188	65c multicolored	1.25 1.25
920	A188	80c multicolored	1.75 1.75
		Nos. 916-920 (5)	4.15 4.15

Ethiopian Trees — A189

1979, Apr. 26   **Photo.**   **Perf. 13½x14**
921	A189	5c Grar	.25 .25
922	A189	10c Weira	.30 .30
923	A189	25c Tidh	.60 .40
924	A189	50c Shola	.85 .85
925	A189	90c Zigba	1.75 1.50
		Nos. 921-925 (5)	3.75 3.30

Agricultural Development A190

Revolutionary Development Campaign: 15c, Industry. 25c, Transportation and communication. 60c, Education and health. 70c, Commerce.

1979, July 3   **Litho.**   **Perf. 12x12½**
926	A190	10c multicolored	.25 .25
927	A190	15c multicolored	.30 .30
928	A190	25c multicolored	.30 .30
929	A190	60c multicolored	.85 .85
930	A190	70c multicolored	1.25 1.25
		Nos. 926-930 (5)	2.95 2.95

IYC Emblem — A191

Intl. Year of the Child: 15c, Adults leading children. 25c, Adult helping child. 60c, IYC emblem surrounded by children. 70c, Adult and children embracing.

1979, Aug. 16   **Litho.**   **Perf. 12x12½**
931	A191	10c multicolored	.30 .30
932	A191	15c multicolored	.30 .30
933	A191	25c multicolored	.60 .60
934	A191	60c multicolored	1.10 1.10
935	A191	70c multicolored	1.75 1.75
		Nos. 931-935 (5)	4.05 4.05

Guerrilla Fighters A192

15c, Soldiers. 25c, Map of Africa within cogwheel, star. 60c, Students with book, torch. 70c, Family, hammer & sickle emblem.

1979, Sept. 11   **Photo.**   **Perf. 14**
936	A192	10c multicolored	.30 .30
937	A192	15c multicolored	.30 .30
938	A192	25c multicolored	.60 .60
939	A192	60c multicolored	1.10 1.10
940	A192	70c multicolored	1.75 1.75
		Nos. 936-940 (5)	4.05 4.05

Fifth anniversary of revolution.

Telephone Receiver — A193

Telecom Emblem and: 5c, Symbolic waves. 35c, Satellite beaming to earth. 45c, Dish antenna. 65c, Television cameraman.

1979, Sept. 20   **Photo.**   **Perf. 11½**
941	A193	5c multicolored	.30 .30
942	A193	30c multicolored	.60 .60
943	A193	35c multicolored	.60 .60
944	A193	45c multicolored	.85 .85
945	A193	65c multicolored	1.25 1.25
		Nos. 941-945 (5)	3.60 3.60

3rd World Telecommunications Exhibition, Geneva, Sept. 20-26.

Incense Container — A194

1979, Nov. 15   **Litho.**   **Perf. 15**
946	A194	5c shown	.30 .30
947	A194	10c Vase	.60 .60
948	A194	25c Earthenware cover	.85 .85
949	A194	60c Milk container	1.25 1.25
950	A194	80c Storage container	1.75 1.75
		Nos. 946-950 (5)	4.75 4.75

Wooden Grain Bowl — A195

1980, Jan. 3   **Litho.**   **Perf. 13½x13**
951	A195	5c shown	.30 .30
952	A195	20c Chair, stool	.85 .85
953	A195	35c Mortar, pestle	.85 .85
954	A195	45c Buckets	1.25 1.25
955	A195	65c Storage jars	1.75 1.75
		Nos. 951-955 (5)	5.00 5.00

Lappet-faced Vulture — A196

Birds of Prey: 15c, Long-crested hawk eagle. 25c, Secretary bird. 60c, Abyssinian long-eared owl. 70c, Lanner falcon.

1980, Feb. 12   **Perf. 13½x14**
956	A196	10c multicolored	.60 .60
957	A196	15c multicolored	.85 .85
958	A196	25c multicolored	1.25 1.25
959	A196	60c multicolored	2.90 2.90
960	A196	70c multicolored	4.50 4.50
		Nos. 956-960 (5)	10.10 10.10

Fight Against Cigarette Smoking — A197

1980, Apr. 7   **Photo.**   **Perf. 13x13½**
961	A197	20c shown	.60 .60
962	A197	60c Cigarette	1.25 1.25
963	A197	1b Respiratory system	1.75 1.75
		Nos. 961-963 (3)	3.60 3.60

"110" and Lenin House Museum — A198

Lenin, 110th "Birthday" (Paintings): 15c, In hiding. 20c, As a young man. 40c, Returning to Russia. 1b, Speaking on the Goelro Plan.

1980, Apr. 22   **Litho.**   **Perf. 12x12½**
964	A198	5c multicolored	.30 .30
965	A198	15c multicolored	.30 .30
966	A198	20c multicolored	.30 .30
967	A198	40c multicolored	.85 .85
968	A198	1b multicolored	1.75 1.75
		Nos. 964-968 (5)	3.50 3.50

Grévy's Zebras — A199

Designs: 15c, Gazelles. 25c, Wild hunting dogs. 60c, Swayne's hartebeests. 70c, Cheetahs.

1980, June 10   **Litho.**   **Perf. 12½x12**
969	A199	10c shown	.30 .30
970	A199	15c multi	.60 .60
971	A199	25c multi	.85 .85
972	A199	60c multi	2.25 2.25
973	A199	70c multi	3.00 3.00
		Nos. 969-973 (5)	7.00 7.00

Runner, Moscow '80 Emblem — A200

1980, July 19   **Photo.**   **Perf. 11½x12**
974	A200	30c shown	.85 .85
975	A200	70c Cycling	1.25 1.25
976	A200	80c Boxing	1.75 1.75
		Nos. 974-976 (3)	3.85 3.85

22nd Summer Olympic Games, Moscow, July 19-Aug. 3.

Removing Blindfold — A201

40c, Revolutionary. 50c, Woman breaking chain. 70c, Russian & Ethiopian flags.

1980, Sept. 10   **Photo.**   **Perf. 14x13½**
977	A201	30c shown	.60 .50
978	A201	40c multicolored	.60 .60
979	A201	50c multicolored	.85 .85
980	A201	70c multicolored	1.25 1.25
		Nos. 977-980 (4)	3.30 3.20

6th anniversary of revolution.

Bamboo Folk Craft — A202

Designs: 5c, Bamboo food basket. 15c, Hand basket. 25c, Stool. 35c, Fruit basket. 1b, Lamp shade.

1980, Oct. 23   **Litho.**   **Perf. 14**
981	A202	5c multi	.30 .30
982	A202	15c multi	.30 .30
983	A202	25c multi	.60 .60
984	A202	35c multi	.85 .85
985	A202	1b multi	1.75 1.75
		Nos. 981-985 (5)	3.80 3.80

Mekotkocha (Used in Weeding) — A203

Traditional Harvesting Tools: 15c, Layda (grain separator). 40c, Mensh (fork). 45c, Mededekia (soil turner). 70c, Mofer & Kenber (plow and yoke).

1980, Dec. 18   **Litho.**   **Perf. 12½x12**
986	A203	10c multicolored	.30 .25
987	A203	15c multicolored	.30 .30
988	A203	40c multicolored	.60 .60
989	A203	45c multicolored	.85 .85
990	A203	70c multicolored	1.25 1.25
		Nos. 986-990 (5)	3.30 3.25

Baro River Bridge Opening — A204

1981, Feb. 28   **Photo.**   **Perf. 13½x13**
991	A204	15c Canoes and ferry	.30 .30
992	A204	65c Bridge construction	1.25 1.25
993	A204	1b shown	2.25 2.25
		Nos. 991-993 (3)	3.80 3.80

Semien National Park — A205

World Heritage Year: 5c, Wawel Castle, Poland. 15c, Quito Cathedral, Ecuador. 20c, Old Slave Quarters, Goree Island, Senegal. 30c, Mesa Verde Indian Village, US. 1b, L'Anse aux Meadows excavation, Canada.

Perf. 11x11½, 11½x11
1981, Mar. 10   **Photo.**
994	A205	5c multicolored	.30 .30
995	A205	15c multicolored	.30 .30
996	A205	20c multicolored	.55 .55
997	A205	30c multicolored	.60 .60
998	A205	80c multicolored	1.75 1.75
999	A205	1b multicolored	2.25 2.25
		Nos. 994-999 (6)	5.75 5.75

1981, June 16   **Photo.**

10c, Biet Medhanialem Church, Ethiopia. 15c, Nahanni Natl. Park, Canada. 20c, Yellowstone River Lower Falls, U.S. 30c, Aachen Cathedral, Germany. 80c, Kicker Rock, San Cristobal Island, Ecuador. 1b, The Lizak corridor, Holy Cross Chapel, Cracow, Poland.

1000	A205	10c multi	.30 .30
1001	A205	15c multi	.30 .30
1002	A205	20c multi	.60 .60
1003	A205	30c multi	.85 .80
1004	A205	80c multi	1.75 1.75
1005	A205	1b multi, vert.	2.25 2.25
		Nos. 1000-1005 (6)	6.05 6.00

ETHIOPIA

Ancient Drinking Vessel — A206

Designs: 25c, Spice container. 35c, Jug. 40c, Cooking pot holder. 60c, Animal figurine.

1981, May 5 Litho. Perf. 12½x12
1006	A206	20c shown	.30	.30
1007	A206	25c multicolored	.30	.30
1008	A206	35c multicolored	.60	.60
1009	A206	45c multicolored	.85	.85
1010	A206	60c multicolored	1.25	1.25
	Nos. 1006-1010 (5)		3.30	3.30

Intl. Year of the Disabled — A207

1981, July 16 Photo. Perf. 11½x12
1011	A207	5c Prostheses	.25	.25
1012	A207	15c Boys writing	.30	.30
1013	A207	20c Activities	.60	.50
1014	A207	40c Knitting	.85	.85
1015	A207	1b Weaving	1.75	1.75
	Nos. 1011-1015 (5)		3.75	3.65

7th Anniv. of Revolution A208

1981, Sept. 10 Perf. 14
1016	A208	20c Children's Center	.30	.30
1017	A208	60c Heroes' Center	.85	.85
1018	A208	1b Serto Ader (state newspaper)	1.75	1.75
	Nos. 1016-1018 (3)		2.90	2.90

World Food Day — A209

Designs: 5c, Wheat airlift. 15c, Plowing. 20c, Malnutrition. 40c, Agriculture education. 1b, Cattle, corn.

1981, Oct. 15 Litho. Perf. 13½x12½
1019	A209	5c multi	.25	.25
1020	A209	15c multi	.25	.25
1021	A209	20c multi	.30	.30
1022	A209	40c multi	.85	.85
1023	A209	1b multi	1.75	1.75
	Nos. 1019-1023 (5)		3.40	3.40

Ancient Bronze Type of 1978

Designs: 15c, Bird shaped pitcher. 45c, Tsenatsil (musical instrument). 50c, Pitcher with large handle on top. 70c, Pot.

1981, Dec. 15 Litho. Perf. 14x13½
1024	A180	15c multi	.30	.30
1025	A180	45c multi	.85	.85
1026	A180	50c multi	.85	.85
1027	A180	70c multi	1.25	1.25
	Nos. 1024-1027 (4)		3.25	3.25

Horn Artifacts — A210

Designs: 10c, Tobacco containers. 15c, Horn cup. 40c, Tej container. 45c, Horn goblet. 70c, Horn spoons.

1982, Feb. 18 Photo. Perf. 12x12½
1028	A210	10c multi	.25	.25
1029	A210	15c multi	.30	.30
1030	A210	40c multi	.85	.85
1031	A210	45c multi	.85	.85
1032	A210	70c multi	1.25	1.25
	Nos. 1028-1032 (5)		3.50	3.50

Coffee Cultivation A211

1982, May 6 Photo. Perf. 13½
1033	A211	5c Plants	.25	.25
1034	A211	15c Bushes	.30	.30
1035	A211	25c Mature bushes	.50	.45
1036	A211	35c Picking beans	.85	.85
1037	A211	1b Drinking coffee	2.00	1.75
	Nos. 1033-1037 (5)		3.90	3.55

1982 World Cup — A212

Various soccer plays.

Perf. 13½x12½
1982, June 10 Litho.
1038	A212	5c multicolored	.25	.25
1039	A212	15c multicolored	.30	.30
1040	A212	20c multicolored	.50	.50
1041	A212	40c multicolored	.85	.85
1042	A212	1b multicolored	1.75	1.75
	Nos. 1038-1042 (5)		3.65	3.65

TB Bacillus Centenary — A213

1982, July 12 Litho. Perf. 13½x12½
1043	A213	15c Cow	.30	.30
1044	A213	20c Magnifying glass	.30	.30
1045	A213	30c Koch, microscope	.60	.60
1046	A213	35c Koch	.65	.65
1047	A213	80c Man coughing	1.75	1.75
	Nos. 1043-1047 (5)		3.60	3.60

8th Anniv. of Revolution — A214

Designs: Symbols of justice.

1982, Sept. 10 Perf. 12½x13½
1048	A214	80c multicolored	1.25	1.25
1049	A214	1b multicolored	1.75	1.75

World Standards Day — A215

1982, Oct. 14 Litho. Perf. 13½x12½
1050	A215	5c Hand, foot, square	.30	.30
1051	A215	15c Scales	.30	.30
1052	A215	20c Rulers	.35	.35
1053	A215	40c Weights	.60	.60
1054	A215	1b Emblem	1.75	1.75
	Nos. 1050-1054 (5)		3.30	3.30

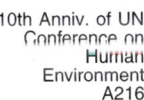

10th Anniv. of UN Conference on Human Environment A216

5c, Wildlife conservation. 15c, Environmental health and settlement. 20c, Forest protection. 40c, Natl. literacy campaign. 1b, Soil and water conservation.

1982, Dec. 13 Litho. Perf. 12
1055	A216	5c multicolored	.25	.25
1056	A216	15c multicolored	.30	.30
1057	A216	20c multicolored	.40	.40
1058	A216	45c multicolored	.85	.85
1059	A216	1b multicolored	1.90	1.90
	Nos. 1055-1059 (5)		3.70	3.70

Cave of Sof Omar — A217

Various views.

1983, Feb. 10 Photo. Perf. 13½
1060	A217	5c multicolored	.25	.25
1061	A217	10c multicolored	.30	.30
1062	A217	15c multicolored	.30	.30
1063	A217	70c multicolored	1.25	1.25
1064	A217	80c multicolored	1.25	1.25
	Nos. 1060-1064 (5)		3.35	3.35

A218

1983, Apr. 29 Photo. Perf. 14
1065	A218	80c multicolored	1.25	1.25
1066	A218	1b multicolored	1.75	1.75

25th Anniv. of Economic Commission for Africa.

A219

Perf. 12½x11½
1983, June 3 Photo.
1067	A219	85c Emblem	1.25	1.25
1068	A219	1b Lighthouse, ship	2.25	2.25

25th Anniv. of Intl. Maritime Org.

WCY — A220

Designs: 25c, UPU emblem. 55c, Dish antenna, emblems. 1b, Bridge, tunnel.

1983, July 22 Litho.
1069	A220	25c multi	.55	.55
1070	A220	55c multi	.85	.85
1071	A220	1b multi	2.75	2.75
	Nos. 1069-1071 (3)		4.15	4.15

9th Anniv. of Revolution — A221

1983, Sept. 10 Litho. Perf. 14½
1072	A221	25c Dove	.30	.30
1073	A221	55c Star	.85	.85
1074	A221	1b Emblems	1.25	1.25
	Nos. 1072-1074 (3)		2.40	2.40

Musical Instruments — A222

1983, Oct. 17 Litho. Perf. 12½x13½
1075	A222	5c Hura	.25	.25
1076	A222	15c Dinke	.30	.30
1077	A222	20c Meleket	.60	.60
1078	A222	40c Embilta	1.25	1.25
1079	A222	1b Tom	1.75	1.75
	Nos. 1075-1079 (5)		4.15	4.15

Charaxes Galawadiwosi A223

15c, Epiphora elianae. 55c, Batuana rougeoti. 1b, Achaea saboeareginae.

1983, Dec. 13 Photo. Perf. 14
1080	A223	10c shown	.85	.85
1081	A223	15c multicolored	1.25	1.25
1082	A223	55c multicolored	2.75	2.75
1083	A223	1b multicolored	3.50	3.50
	Nos. 1080-1083 (4)		8.35	8.35

Intl. Anti-Apartheid Year (1983) — A224

Perf. 13½x12½
1984, Feb. 10 Litho.
1084	A224	5c multicolored	.25	.25
1085	A224	15c multicolored	.30	.30
1086	A224	20c multicolored	.60	.60
1087	A224	40c multicolored	.85	.85
1088	A224	1b multicolored	2.25	2.25
	Nos. 1084-1088 (5)		4.25	4.25

Local Flowers — A225

5c, Protea gaguedi. 25c, Sedum epidendrum. 50c, Echinops amplexicaulis. 1b, Canarina eminii.

1984, Apr. 13 Litho. Perf. 13½
1089	A225	5c multi	.30	.30
1090	A225	25c multi	.85	.85
1091	A225	50c multi	1.75	1.75
1092	A225	1b multi	3.00	3.00
	Nos. 1089-1092 (4)		5.90	5.90

Traditional Houses — A226

1984, June 13 Photo.
1093	A226	15c Konso	.30	.30
1094	A226	65c Dorzo	1.25	1.25
1095	A226	1b Harer	1.75	1.75
	Nos. 1093-1095 (3)		3.30	3.30

10th Anniv. of the Revolution — A227

1984, Sept. 10 Photo. Perf. 11½
1096	A227	5c Sept. 12, 1974	.40	.40
1097	A227	10c Mar. 4, 1975	.40	.40
1098	A227	15c Apr. 20, 1976	.40	.40
1099	A227	20c Feb. 11, 1977	.50	.50
1100	A227	25c Mar. 1978	.65	.65
1101	A227	40c July 8, 1980	1.20	1.20
1102	A227	45c Dec. 17, 1980	1.60	1.50
1103	A227	50c Sept. 15, 1980	1.75	1.75
1104	A227	70c Sept. 18, 1981	2.40	2.40
1105	A227	1b June 6, 1983	2.75	2.75
	Nos. 1096-1105 (10)		12.05	11.95

Traditional Sports — A228

1984, Dec. 7 Photo. Perf. 14
1106	A228	5c Gugs	.25	.25
1107	A228	25c Tigil	.40	.40
1108	A228	50c Genna	.95	.95
1109	A228	1b Gebeta	1.75	1.75
	Nos. 1106-1109 (4)		3.35	3.35

ETHIOPIA

Birds — A229

Designs: 5c, Francolinus harwoodi. 15c, Rallus rougetti. 80c, Merops pusillus. 85c, Malimbus rubriceps.

1985, Jan. 4		Photo.	Perf. 14½	
1110	A229	5c multi	.30	.30
1111	A229	15c multi	.85	.85
1112	A229	80c multi	3.00	3.00
1113	A229	85c multi	3.00	3.00
	Nos. 1110-1113 (4)		7.15	7.15

Indigenous Fauna — A230

20c, Hippopotamus amphibius. 25c, Litocranius walleri. 40c, Sylvicapra grimmia. 1b, Rhynchotragus guentheri.

1985, Feb. 4		Litho.	Perf. 12½x12	
1114	A230	20c multicolored	.85	.85
1115	A230	25c multicolored	1.00	1.00
1116	A230	40c multicolored	2.00	2.00
1117	A230	1b multicolored	3.50	3.50
	Nos. 1114-1117 (4)		7.35	7.35

Freshwater Fish — A231

10c, Barbus degeni. 20c, Labeo cylindricus. 55c, Protopterus annectens. 1b, Alestes dentex.

1985, Apr. 3			Perf. 13½	
1118	A231	10c multicolored	.50	.25
1119	A231	20c multicolored	.90	.50
1120	A231	55c multicolored	2.10	1.20
1121	A231	1b multicolored	3.25	2.50
	Nos. 1118-1121 (4)		6.75	4.45

Medicinal Plants — A232

10c, Securidaca longepedunculata. 20c, Plumbago zeylanicum. 55c, Brucea antidysenteric. 1b, Dorstenia barminiana.

1985, May 23			Perf. 11½x12½	
1122	A232	10c multicolored	.30	.30
1123	A232	20c multicolored	.30	.30
1124	A232	55c multicolored	.85	.85
1125	A232	1b multicolored	2.25	2.25
	Nos. 1122-1125 (4)		3.70	3.70

Ethiopian Red Cross Soc., 50th Anniv. — A233

1985, Aug. 6		Litho.	Perf. 13½x13	
1126	A233	35c multicolored	.60	.60
1127	A233	55c multicolored	.85	.85
1128	A233	1b multicolored	2.25	2.25
	Nos. 1126-1128 (3)		3.70	3.70

Ethiopian Revolution, 11th Anniv. — A234

10c, Kombolcha Mills, Welo Region. 80c, Muger Cement Factory, Mokoda, Shoa. 1b, Relocating famine and drought victims.

1985, Sept. 10		Litho.	Perf. 13½	
1129	A234	10c multicolored	.30	.30
1130	A234	80c multicolored	1.75	1.75
1131	A234	1b multicolored	2.25	2.25
	Nos. 1129-1131 (3)		4.30	4.30

UN 40th Anniv. — A235

1985, Nov. 22		Litho.	Perf. 13½x14	
1132	A235	25c multicolored	.90	.75
1133	A235	55c multicolored	1.75	1.50
1134	A235	1b multicolored	3.25	2.50
	Nos. 1132-1134 (3)		5.90	4.75

Anti-Polio Campaign — A236

Designs: 5c, Boy, prosthesis. 10c, Boy on crutches. 20c, Nurse, boy. 55c, Man, sewing machine. 1b, Nurse, mother, child.

1986, Jan. 10		Litho.	Perf. 11½x12½	
1135	A236	5c multi	.75	.25
1136	A236	10c multi	.30	.30
1137	A236	20c multi	.60	.50
1138	A236	55c multi	1.10	1.10
1139	A236	1b multi	2.75	2.75
	Nos. 1135-1139 (5)		5.50	4.90

Indigenous Trees — A237

10c, Millettia ferruginea. 30c, Syzygium guineense. 50c, Cordia africana. 1b, Hagenia abyssinica.

1986, Feb. 10			Perf. 13½x14½	
1140	A237	10c multicolored	.35	.35
1141	A237	30c multicolored	.60	.60
1142	A237	50c multicolored	.90	.90
1143	A237	1b multicolored	2.25	2.25
	Nos. 1140-1143 (4)		4.10	4.10

Spices — A238

10c, Zingiber officinale rosc. 15c, Ocimum bacilicum. 55c, Sinapsis alba. 1b, Cuminum cyminum.

1986, Mar. 10			Perf. 13½	
1144	A238	10c multicolored	.60	.60
1145	A238	15c multicolored	.60	.60
1146	A238	55c multicolored	1.25	1.25
1147	A238	1b multicolored	2.75	2.75
	Nos. 1144-1147 (4)		5.20	5.20

Current Coins, Obverse and Reverse — A239

1986, May 9		Litho.	Perf. 13½x14	
1148	A239	5c 1-cent	.30	.30
1149	A239	10c 25-cent	.30	.30
1150	A239	35c 5-cent	.85	.85
1151	A239	50c 50-cent	1.25	1.25
1152	A239	1b 10-cent	2.25	2.25
	Nos. 1148-1152 (5)		4.95	4.95

Discovery of 3.5 Million Year-old Hominid Skeleton, "Lucy" — A240

1986, July 4			Perf. 13½	
1153	A240	2b multicolored	6.50	6.50

Ethiopian Revolution, 12th Anniv. — A241

Designs: 20c, Military service. 30c, Tiglachin monument. 55c, Delachin Exhibition emblem. 85c, Food processing plant, Merti.

1986, Sept. 10		Litho.	Perf. 14	
1154	A241	20c multicolored	.40	.40
1155	A241	30c multicolored	.65	.65
1156	A241	55c multicolored	1.10	1.10
1157	A241	85c multicolored	1.40	1.40
	Nos. 1154-1157 (4)		3.55	3.55

Ethiopian Airlines, 40th Anniv. — A242

1986, Oct. 14				
1158	A242	10c DC-7	.30	.30
1159	A242	20c DC-3	.60	.60
1160	A242	30c Personnel, jet tail	.85	.85
1161	A242	40c Engine	.85	.85
1162	A242	1b DC-7, map	2.25	2.25
	Nos. 1158-1162 (5)		4.85	4.85

Intl. Peace Year — A243

1986, Nov. 13			Perf. 13½	
1163	A243	10c multicolored	.30	.30
1164	A243	80c multicolored	2.00	2.00
1165	A243	1b multicolored	2.25	2.25
	Nos. 1163-1165 (3)		4.55	4.55

UN Child Survival Campaign A244

10c, Breast feeding. 35c, Immunization. 50c, Hygiene. 1b, Growth monitoring.

1986, Dec. 11			Perf. 12½	
1166	A244	10c multi	.30	.30
1167	A244	35c multi	.85	.85
1168	A244	50c multi	1.25	1.10
1169	A244	1b multi	2.25	2.00
	Nos. 1166-1169 (4)		4.65	4.25

Umbrellas — A245

1987, Feb. 10			Perf. 13½	
1170	A245	35c Axum	.85	.85
1171	A245	55c Negele-Borena	1.25	1.25
1172	A245	1b Jimma	1.75	1.75
	Nos. 1170-1172 (3)		3.85	3.85

Artwork by Afewerk Tekle (b. 1932) — A246

Designs: 50c, Defender of His Country — Afar, stained glass window. 2b, Defender of His Country — Adwa, painting.

1987, Mar. 19		Litho.	Perf. 13½	
1173	A246	50c multicolored	1.50	1.00
1174	A246	2b multicolored	5.50	4.50

Stained Glass Windows by Afewerk Tekle A247

1987, June 16		Photo.	Perf. 11½x12	
		Granite Paper		
1175	A247	50c multicolored	4.00	2.00
		Size: 26x38mm		
1176	A247	80c multicolored	5.00	2.75
1177	A247	1b multicolored	7.50	.40
	Nos. 1175-1177 (3)		16.50	5.15

Struggle of the African People.
Sold out in Addis Ababa on date of issue.

Simien Fox — A248

1987, June 29		Litho.	Perf. 13½	
1178	A248	5c multicolored	.25	.25
1179	A248	10c multicolored	.25	.25
1180	A248	15c multicolored	.35	.25
1181	A248	20c multicolored	.45	.30
1182	A248	25c multicolored	.60	.30
1183	A248	45c multicolored	1.00	.85
1184	A248	55c multicolored	1.25	.85
	Nos. 1178-1184 (7)		4.15	3.05

For overprints see Nos. 1234-1237. For similar design see A294a.

Ethiopian Revolution, 13th Anniv. — A249

Designs: 5c, Constitution, freedom of press. 10c, Popular elections. 80c, Referendum. 1b, Bahir Dar Airport, map.

1987, Sept. 10			Perf. 12½	
1185	A249	5c multi	.65	.65
1186	A249	10c multi	.65	.40
1187	A249	80c multi	1.75	1.75
1188	A249	1b multi	2.25	2.25
	Nos. 1185-1188 (4)		5.30	5.05

Addis Ababa, Cent. — A251

"100" and views: 5c, Emperor Menelik II, Empress Taitu and city. 10c, Traditional buildings. 80c, Central Addis Ababa. 1b, Aerial view of city.

1987, Sept. 7			Perf. 13½	
1193	A251	5c multicolored	.30	.30
1194	A251	10c multicolored	.30	.30
1195	A251	80c multicolored	1.75	1.75
1196	A251	1b multicolored	2.25	2.25
	Nos. 1193-1196 (4)		4.60	4.60

Wooden Spoons — A252

ETHIOPIA

1987, Nov. 30
| 1197 | A252 | 85c Hurso, Harerge | 1.25 | 1.25 |
| 1198 | A252 | 1b Borena, Sidamo | 1.75 | 1.75 |

Intl. Year of Shelter for the Homeless — A253

10c, Village revitalization program. 35c, Resettlement program. 50c, Urban improvement. 1b, Cooperative and government housing.

1987, Dec. 12   Litho.   Perf. 13
1199	A253	10c multicolored	.30	.30
1200	A253	35c multicolored	.60	.60
1201	A253	50c multicolored	.85	.85
1202	A253	1b multicolored	1.25	1.25
		Nos. 1199-1202 (4)	3.00	3.00

October Revolution, Russia, 70th Anniv. (in 1987) — A254

Painting: 1b, Lenin receiving Workers' Council delegates in the Smolny Institute.

1988, Feb. 17   Perf. 12½x12
| 1203 | A254 | 1b multicolored | 2.25 | 2.00 |

Traditional Hunting Methods and Prey — A255

Designs: 85c, Bow and arrow. 1b, Double-pronged spear.

1988, Mar. 30   Litho.   Perf. 13½
| 1204 | A255 | 85c multi | 1.75 | 1.75 |
| 1205 | A255 | 1b multi | 3.00 | 3.00 |

A256

1988, May 6
| 1206 | A256 | 85c multicolored | 1.25 | 1.25 |
| 1207 | A256 | 1b multicolored | 1.75 | 1.75 |

Intl. Red Cross and Red Crescent Organizations, 125th anniv.

A257

1988, June 7   Photo.   Perf. 11½x12
| 1208 | A257 | 2b multicolored | 3.00 | 2.75 |

Organizaton of African Unity, 25th anniv.

Ethiopian Revolution, 14th Anniv. — A258

Design: Various details of *The Victory of Ethiopia*, six-panel mural by Afewerk Tekle (b. 1932) in the museum of the Heroes Center, Debre Zeit — 10c, Jet over farm, vert. 20c, Farm workers on road, vert. 35c, Allegory of unity, vert. 55c, Jet over industry. 80c, Steel works. 1b, Weaving.

1988, June 28   Litho.   Perf. 13½x13
1209	A258	10c multi	.30	.30
1210	A258	20c multi	.30	.30
1211	A258	35c multi	.60	.60
1212	A258	55c multi	.85	.85
1213	A258	80c multi	1.25	1.25
1214	A258	1b multi	1.25	1.25
		Nos. 1209-1214 (6)	4.55	4.55

Nos. 1209-1211 vert.

Women, Bracelets and Maps — A259

1988, July 27   Litho.   Perf. 13x13½
1215	A259	15c Sidamo	.30	.30
1216	A259	85c Arsi	1.25	1.25
1217	A259	1b Harerge	1.75	1.75
		Nos. 1215-1217 (3)	3.30	3.30

Immunize Every Child — A260

1988, June 14   Litho.   Perf. 13x13½
1218	A260	10c Measles	.30	.30
1219	A260	35c Tetanus	.60	.60
1220	A260	50c Whooping cough	.85	.85
1221	A260	1b Diphtheria	1.75	1.75
		Nos. 1218-1221 (4)	3.50	3.50

Intl. Fund for Agricultural Development (IFAD), 10th Anniv. — A261

1988, Aug. 16   Perf. 13½
1222	A261	15c Monetary aid	.30	.30
1223	A261	85c Farming activities	1.25	1.25
1224	A261	1b Harvest	1.75	1.75
		Nos. 1222-1224 (3)	3.30	3.30

People's Democratic Republic of Ethiopia, 1st Anniv. — A262

5c, 1st Session of the natl. Shengo (congress). 10c, Mengistu Haile-Mariam, 1st president of the republic. 80c, Natl. crest, flag & crowd. 1b, State assembly building.

1988, Sept. 9   Perf. 14
1225	A262	5c multicolored	.30	.30
1226	A262	10c multicolored	.30	.30
1227	A262	80c multicolored	1.25	1.25
1228	A262	1b multicolored	1.75	1.75
		Nos. 1225-1228 (4)	3.60	3.60

Bank Notes — A263

1988, Nov. 10   Photo.   Perf. 13
1229	A263	5c 1-Birr	.30	.30
1230	A263	10c 5-Birr	.30	.30
1231	A263	20c 10-Birr	.50	.50
1232	A263	75c 50-Birr	1.40	1.40
1233	A263	85c 100-Birr	1.75	1.75
		Nos. 1229-1233 (5)	4.25	4.25

Nos. 1181-1184 Ovptd. in Two Languages

1988, Dec. 1   Litho.   Perf. 13½
1234	A248	20c multicolored	4.75	4.50
1235	A248	25c multicolored	6.25	5.50
1236	A248	45c multicolored	12.50	10.50
1237	A248	55c multicolored	13.00	11.00
		Nos. 1234-1237 (4)	36.50	31.50

Intl. Day for the Fight Against AIDS.

WHO, 40th Anniv. — A264

1988, Dec. 30   Litho.   Perf. 14
1238	A264	50c multicolored	.85	.85
1239	A264	65c multicolored	1.10	1.10
1240	A264	85c multicolored	1.25	1.25
		Nos. 1238-1240 (3)	3.20	3.20

Traditional Musical Instruments A265

1989, Feb. 9   Perf. 13x13½
1241	A265	30c Gere	.55	.55
1242	A265	40c Fanfa	.55	.55
1243	A265	50c Chancha	.85	.85
1244	A265	85c Negareet	1.25	1.25
		Nos. 1241-1244 (4)	3.20	3.20

Ethiopian Shipping Lines, 25th Anniv. — A266

1989, Mar. 27   Litho.   Perf. 14
1245	A266	15c Abyot	.30	.30
1246	A266	30c Wolwol	.60	.60
1247	A266	55c Queen of Sheba	1.25	1.25
1248	A266	1b Abbay Wonz	1.75	1.75
		Nos. 1245-1248 (4)	3.90	3.90

Birds — A267

10c, Yellow-fronted parrot. 35c, White-winged cliff chat. 50c, Yellow-throated seed eater. 1b, Black-headed forest oriole.

1989, May 18   Litho.   Perf. 13½x13
1249	A267	10c multicolored	.30	.30
1250	A267	35c multicolored	.85	.85
1251	A267	50c multicolored	1.25	1.25
1252	A267	1b multicolored	2.25	2.25
		Nos. 1249-1252 (4)	4.65	4.65

Production of Early Manuscripts A268

Designs: 5c, Preparing vellum. 10c, Ink horns, pens. 20c, Scribe. 75c, Book binding. 85c, Illuminated manuscript.

1989, June 16   Litho.   Perf. 13½
1253	A268	5c multi	.30	.30
1254	A268	10c multi	.30	.30
1255	A268	20c multi	.35	.35
1256	A268	75c multi	1.25	1.25
1257	A268	85c multi	1.50	1.50
		Nos. 1253-1257 (5)	3.70	3.70

Indigenous Wildlife — A269

1989, July 18
1258	A269	30c Greater kudu	.85	.85
1259	A269	40c Lesser kudu	.95	.95
1260	A269	50c Roan antelope	1.25	1.25
1261	A269	85c Nile lechwe	1.75	1.75
		Nos. 1258-1261 (4)	4.80	4.80

People's Democratic Republic of Ethiopia, 2nd Anniv. — A270

Designs: 15c, Melka Wakana Hydroelectric Power Station. 75c, Adea Berga Dairy Farm. 1b, Pawe Hospital.

1989, Sept. 8
1262	A270	15c multicolored	.30	.25
1263	A270	75c multicolored	1.25	1.25
1264	A270	1b multicolored	2.00	2.00
		Nos. 1262-1264 (3)	3.55	3.50

African Development Bank, 25th Anniv. — A271

1989, Nov. 10   Litho.   Perf. 13½x13
1265	A271	20c multicolored	.30	.30
1266	A271	80c multicolored	1.25	1.25
1267	A271	1b multicolored	1.75	2.00
		Nos. 1265-1267 (3)	3.30	3.55

Pan-African Postal Union, 10th Anniv. — A272

1990, Jan. 18   Litho.   Perf. 13½
1268	A272	50c multicolored	.75	.75
1269	A272	70c multicolored	1.25	1.25
1270	A272	80c multicolored	1.50	1.75
		Nos. 1268-1270 (3)	3.50	3.75

UNESCO World Literacy Year — A273

15c, Illiterate man holding newspaper upside down. 85c, Adults learning alphabet in school. 1b, Literate man holding newspaper upright.

1990, Mar. 13
1271	A273	15c multicolored	.40	.40
1272	A273	85c multicolored	1.40	1.40
1273	A273	1b multicolored	1.75	1.75
		Nos. 1271-1273 (3)	3.55	3.55

Abebe Bikila, Marathon Runner — A274

5c, Race. 10c, Flag bearer, Olympic team. 20c, Race, Rome Olympics. 75c, Race, Tokyo Olympics. 85c, Bikila, trophies, vert.

1990, Apr. 17
1274	A274	5c multicolored	.30	.30
1275	A274	10c multicolored	.30	.30
1276	A274	20c multicolored	.60	.60
1277	A274	75c multicolored	1.25	1.25
1278	A274	85c multicolored	1.75	1.75
		Nos. 1274-1278 (5)	4.20	4.20

Flag — A275

1990, Apr. 30   Litho.   Perf. 13½x13
1279	A275	5c multicolored	.30	.30
1280	A275	10c multicolored	.30	.30
1281	A275	15c multicolored	.30	.30
1282	A275	20c multicolored	.40	.30
1283	A275	25c multicolored	.50	.30
1284	A275	30c multicolored	.60	.30
1285	A275	35c multicolored	.70	.30

ETHIOPIA

1286	A275	40c multicolored	.80	.30
1287	A275	45c multicolored	.85	.60
1288	A275	50c multicolored	1.00	.60
1289	A275	55c multicolored	1.00	.60
1290	A275	60c multicolored	1.25	.60
1291	A275	70c multicolored	1.25	.85
1292	A275	80c multicolored	1.25	.85
1293	A275	85c multicolored	1.25	.85
1294	A275	90c multicolored	1.25	.85
1295	A275	1b multicolored	1.75	1.25
1296	A275	2b multicolored	3.50	2.25
1297	A275	3b multicolored	5.50	4.50
		Nos. 1279-1297 (19)	23.75	16.20

Dated 1989.

Sowing of Teff — A276

Designs: 10c, Harvesting. 20c, Threshing. 75c, Storage, preparation. 85c, Consumption.

1990, May 18 Litho. *Perf. 13½*

1298	A276	5c shown	.30	.30
1299	A276	10c multi	.30	.30
1300	A276	20c multi	.30	.30
1301	A276	75c multi	1.25	1.25
1302	A276	85c multi	1.75	1.75
		Nos. 1298-1302 (5)	3.90	3.90

Walia Ibex — A277

1990, June 18 *Perf. 14x13½*

1303	A277	5c multi	.75	.35
1304	A277	15c multi	1.40	.75
1305	A277	20c multi	2.25	1.10
1306	A277	1b multi, horiz.	8.00	4.25
		Nos. 1303-1306 (4)	12.40	6.45

World AIDS Day — A278

Designs: 15c, Stages of disease. 85c, Education. 1b, Causes, preventatives.

1991, Jan. 31 Litho. *Perf. 14*

1307	A278	15c multi	.30	.30
1308	A278	85c multi	1.50	1.50
1309	A278	1b multi	2.25	2.25
		Nos. 1307-1309 (3)	4.05	4.05

Intl. Decade for Natural Disaster Reduction A279

Map of disaster-prone African areas and: 5c, Volcano. 10c, Earthquake. 15c, Drought. 30c, Flood. 50c, Red Cross health education. 1b, Red Cross assisting fire victims.

1991, Apr. 9 Litho. *Perf. 14*

1310	A279	5c multicolored	.30	.30
1311	A279	10c multicolored	.30	.30
1312	A279	15c multicolored	.30	.30
1313	A279	30c multicolored	.60	.60
1314	A279	50c multicolored	1.10	1.10
1315	A279	1b multicolored	2.25	2.25
		Nos. 1310-1315 (6)	4.85	4.85

The Cannon of Tewodros — A280

Designs: 15c, Villagers receiving cannon. 85c, Warriors leaving with cannon. 1b, Hauling cannon up mountainside.

1991, June 18 Litho. *Perf. 13½*

1316	A280	15c multicolored	.40	.40
1317	A280	85c multicolored	1.50	1.50
1318	A280	1b multicolored	2.25	1.75
		Nos. 1316-1318 (3)	4.15	3.65

Fish — A281

5c, Lacepede. 15c, Black-finned butterflyfish. 80c, Regal angelfish. 1b, Bleeker.

1991, Sept. 6 Litho. *Perf. 13½*

1319	A281	5c multi	.50	.50
1320	A281	15c multi	.50	.50
1321	A281	80c multi	2.25	2.25
1322	A281	1b multi	2.75	2.75
		Nos. 1319-1322 (4)	6.00	6.00

A282

Traditional Ceremonial Robes: Various robes.

1992, Jan. 1 Litho. *Perf. 13½x14*

1323	A282	5c yellow & multi	.30	.30
1324	A282	15c orange & multi	.30	.30
1325	A282	80c yel green & multi	1.75	1.75
1326	A282	1b blue & multi	2.00	2.00
		Nos. 1323-1326 (4)	4.35	4.35

A283

Flowers: 5c, Cissus quadrangularis. 15c, Delphinium dasycaulon. 80c, Epilobium hirsutum. 1b, Kniphofia foliosa.

1992, Mar. 5 Litho. *Perf. 13½x14*

1327	A283	5c multicolored	.30	.30
1328	A283	15c multicolored	.40	.40
1329	A283	80c multicolored	2.00	1.75
1330	A283	1b multicolored	2.50	2.00
		Nos. 1327-1330 (4)	5.20	4.45

Traditional Homes — A284

1992, May 14 Litho. *Perf. 12½x12*

1331	A284	15c Afar	.30	.30
1332	A284	35c Anuak	.60	.60
1333	A284	50c Gimira	.90	.90
1334	A284	1b Oromo	2.25	1.75
		Nos. 1331-1334 (4)	4.05	3.55

A285

Pottery.

1992, July 7 Litho. *Perf. 13x13½*

1335	A285	15c Cover	.30	.30
1336	A285	85c Jug	1.25	1.25
1337	A285	1b Tall jar	2.00	2.00
		Nos. 1335-1337 (3)	3.55	3.55

A286

1992, Sept. 29 *Perf. 14x13½*

1338	A286	20c multicolored	.30	.30
1339	A286	80c multicolored	1.25	1.25
1340	A286	1b multicolored	2.00	1.75
		Nos. 1338-1340 (3)	3.55	3.30

Pan-African Rinderpest campaign.

Musical Instruments — A287

1993, Feb. 16 Litho. *Perf. 14x13½*

1341	A287	15c Catchel	.30	.30
1342	A287	35c Huludwa	.55	.55
1343	A287	50c Dita	.85	.85
1344	A287	1b Atamo	1.75	1.75
		Nos. 1341-1344 (4)	3.45	3.45

Birds — A288

Designs: 15c, Banded barbet. 35c, Ruppell's chat. 50c, Abyssinian catbird. 1b, White-billed starling.

1993, Apr. 22 Litho. *Perf. 14x13½*

1345	A288	15c multi	.30	.30
1346	A288	35c multi	.75	.75
1347	A288	50c multi	1.00	1.00
1348	A288	1b multi	2.00	2.00
		Nos. 1345-1348 (4)	4.05	4.05

Animals — A289

Designs: 15c, Honey badger. 35c, Spotted necked otter. 50c, Rock hyrax. 1b, White-tailed mongoose.

1993, May 14 *Perf. 13½x14*

1349	A289	15c multi	.30	.30
1350	A289	35c multi	.60	.60
1351	A289	50c multi	1.00	1.00
1352	A289	1b multi	2.00	2.00
		Nos. 1349-1352 (4)	3.90	3.90

Herbs — A290

Designs: 5c, Caraway seed. 15c, Garlic. 80c, Turmeric. 1b, Capsicum peppers.

1993, June 10 Litho. *Perf. 14x13½*

1353	A290	5c multi	.60	.60
1354	A290	15c multi	.75	.75
1355	A290	80c multi	1.40	1.40
1356	A290	1b multi	1.50	1.50
		Nos. 1353-1356 (4)	4.25	4.25

Butterflies — A291

20c, Papilio echeriodes. 30c, Papilio rex. 50c, Graphium policenes. 1b, Graphium leonidas.

1993, July 9 Litho. *Perf. 14x13½*

1357	A291	20c multicolored	1.00	.85
1358	A291	30c multicolored	.85	.85
1359	A291	50c multicolored	1.40	1.40
1360	A291	1b multicolored	2.50	2.50
		Nos. 1357-1360 (4)	5.75	5.60

Insects — A292

Designs: 15c, C. Variabilis. 35c, Lycus trabeatus. 50c, Malachius bifasciatus. 1b, Homoeogryllus xanthographus.

1993, Aug. 10

1361	A292	15c multi	.60	.60
1362	A292	35c multi	.60	.60
1363	A292	50c multi	.85	.85
1364	A292	1b multi	1.75	1.75
		Nos. 1361-1364 (4)	3.80	3.80

Trees — A293

15c, Euphorbia amplyphylla. 35c, Erythrina brucei. 50c, Dracaena steudneri. 1b, Allophylus abyssinicus.

1993, Oct. 12 Litho. *Perf. 13½x14*

1365	A293	15c multicolored	.30	.30
1366	A293	35c multicolored	.30	.30
1367	A293	50c multicolored	.30	.30
1368	A293	1b multicolored	1.00	1.00
		Nos. 1365-1368 (4)	1.90	1.90

Lakes — A294

1993, Dec. 14

1369	A294	15c Wonchi	.35	.30
1370	A294	35c Zuquala	.50	.30
1371	A294	50c Ashengi	.70	.50
1372	A294	1b Tana	1.25	1.00
		Nos. 1369-1372 (4)	2.80	2.10

Simien Fox A294a

Rough Perf. 13½

1994, Jan. 18 Litho.

Color of Border

1372A	A294a	5c violet	—	—
1372B	A294a	10c brown	—	—
1372C	A294a	15c lemon	—	—
1372D	A294a	20c salmon	—	—
1372E	A294a	40c pale rose	—	—
1372F	A294a	55c dull green	—	—
1372G	A294a	60c dark blue	—	—
1372H	A294a	80c bright blue	—	—
1372I	A294a	85c gray green	—	—
1372J	A294a	1b bright green	—	3.65
		Nos. 1372A-1372J (10)		3.65

Nos. 1372A-1372J have rough perforations and a poor quality printing impression. Dated "1991."

See Nos. 1393A-1393T.

A295

Transitional government: 15c, First anniversary of EPRDF's control of Addis Ababa. 35c, Transition Conference. 50c, National, regional elections. 1b, Coat of arms of Transitional Government.

1994, Mar. 31 Litho. *Perf. 14*

1373	A295	15c multicolored	.30	.30
1374	A295	35c multicolored	.30	.30
1375	A295	50c multicolored	.40	.40
1376	A295	1b multicolored	.75	.75
		Nos. 1373-1376 (4)	1.75	1.75

ETHIOPIA 477

A296

1994, May 17   **Perf. 13½**
1377	A296	15c blue & multi	.30	.30
1378	A296	85c green & multi	.50	.50
1379	A296	1b violet & multi	.75	.75
		Nos. 1377-1379 (3)	1.55	1.55

Intl. Year of the Family.

Ethiopian Postal Service, Cent. — A297

Designs: 60c, Early, modern postal workers, Scott Type A1. 75c, Early letter carriers. 80c, Older building, methods of transportation. 85c, People, mail buses. 1b, Modern methods of transportation, modern high-rise building.

1994, July 4   **Litho.**   **Perf. 13½**
1380	A297	60c multicolored	.75	.55
1381	A297	75c multicolored	.90	.60
1382	A297	80c multicolored	1.15	.70
1383	A297	85c multicolored	1.20	.75
1384	A297	1b multicolored	1.45	1.05
a.		Souvenir sheet, #1380-1384 + label	10.00	8.00
		Nos. 1380-1384 (5)	5.45	3.65

Enset Plant — A298

1994, Aug. 3
1385	A298	10c shown	.25	.25
1386	A298	15c Young plants, hut	.35	.30
1387	A298	25c Root, women processing leaves	.40	.35
1388	A298	50c Mature plants	.75	.40
1389	A298	1b Uses as food	1.50	.65
		Nos. 1385-1389 (5)	3.25	1.95

Hair Ornaments — A299

1994, Sept. 2
1390	A299	5c Gamo gofa	.40	.30
1391	A299	15c Sidamo	.50	.35
1392	A299	80c Gamo gofa, diff.	.80	.60
1393	A299	1b Wello	1.10	.85
		Nos. 1390-1393 (4)	2.80	2.10

Simien Fox Type of 1994
Size: 39x25mm
Color of Border

1994, Oct. 18   **Litho.**   **Perf. 14**
1393A	A294a	5c dull lilac	—	.35
1393B	A294a	10c brown	—	.45
1393C	A294a	15c lemon	—	.55
1393D	A294a	20c salmon	—	.65
1393E	A294a	25c lemon	—	.75
1393F	A294a	30c yel brn	—	1.00
1393G	A294a	35c orange	—	1.25
1393H	A294a	40c pale rose	—	1.50
1393I	A294a	45c pale red org	—	1.75
1393J	A294a	50c rose lilac	—	2.00
1393K	A294a	55c pale grn	—	2.25
1393L	A294a	60c dark blue	—	2.50
1393M	A294a	65c pale lilac	—	2.75
1393N	A294a	70c brt grn	—	3.00
1393O	A294a	75c pale bl grn	—	3.25
1393P	A294a	80c bright blue	—	3.50
1393Q	A294a	85c dk grnsh blue	—	3.75
1393R	A294a	90c pale brn	—	4.00

1393S	A294a	1b grnsh blue	—	5.00
1393T	A294a	2b yel brn	—	9.00
		Nos. 1393A-1393T (20)		49.25

Nos. 1393A-1393T have sharp impressions, Questa imprint, clean perforations. Dated "1993."
For overprints see Nos. 1393U-1393X, 1396A-1396D.

Nos. 1393L, 1393P-1393Q, 1393S Ovptd. in Blue

1994, Oct. 20   **Litho.**   **Perf. 14**
1393U	A294a	60c on #1393L	—	—
1393V	A294a	80c on #1393P	—	—
1393W	A294a	85c on #1393Q	—	—
1393X	A294a	1b on #1393S	—	—

UNFPA, 50th anniv.

ICAO, 50th Anniv. — A300

1994, Dec. 7   **Litho.**   **Perf. 13½**
1394	A300	20c mag, lt bl & yel	.40	.40
1395	A300	80c yel & lt bl	.60	.60
1396	A300	1b dk bl, lt bl & yel	.90	.90
		Nos. 1394-1396 (3)	1.90	1.90

Nos. 1393M-1393O, 1393R Ovptd.

1994, Dec. 20   **Litho.**   **Perf. 14**
1396A	A294a	65c on #1393M	—	—
1396B	A294a	70c on #1393N	—	—
1396C	A294a	75c on #1393O	—	—
1396D	A294a	90c on #1393R	—	—

African Development Bank, 30th anniv.

Baskets for Serving Food — A301

1995, June 7   **Litho.**   **Perf. 13½**
1397	A301	30c Erbo	.30	.25
1398	A301	70c Sedieka	.50	.50
1399	A301	1b Tirar	.85	.85
		Nos. 1397-1399 (3)	1.65	1.60

Traditional Hair Styles — A302

1995, July 5   **Litho.**   **Perf. 13½**
1400	A302	25c Kuncho	.40	.40
1401	A302	75c Gamme	.60	.60
1402	A302	1b Sadulla	1.00	1.00
		Nos. 1400-1402 (3)	2.00	2.00

FAO, 50th Anniv. — A303

1995, Aug. 29   **Litho.**   **Perf. 13½**
1403	A303	20c green & multi	.75	.65
1404	A303	80c blue & multi	1.25	1.00
1405	A303	1b brown & multi	1.50	1.25
		Nos. 1403-1405 (3)	3.50	2.90

Cultivating Tools — A304

1995, Sept. 7
1406	A304	15c Dangora	.60	.60
1407	A304	35c Gheso	.60	.60
1408	A304	50c Akafa	.60	.60
1409	A304	1b Ankasse	1.10	1.10
		Nos. 1406-1409 (4)	2.90	2.90

UN, 50th Anniv. — A305

1995, Oct. 18   **Litho.**   **Perf. 13½**
Color of UN Emblem
1410	A305	20c black	.40	.30
1411	A305	80c bister	.85	.65
1412	A305	1b blue	1.00	.85
		Nos. 1410-1412 (3)	2.25	1.80

Intergovernmental Authority on Drought and Development (IGADD), 10th Anniv. — A306

Flags of member nations and: 15c, Seedling being planted in arid region. 35c, People carrying supplies through desert. 50c, Person picking fruit. 1b, Map of member nations.

1995, Dec. 27   **Litho.**   **Perf. 13½**
1413	A306	15c multicolored	.45	.35
1414	A306	35c multicolored	.55	.45
1415	A306	50c multicolored	.70	.60
1416	A306	1b multicolored	1.10	1.00
		Nos. 1413-1416 (4)	2.80	2.40

Victory at Battle of Adwa, Cent. A307

Designs: 40c, Battle sites. 50c, Map of Africa focused at Ethiopia. 60c, Troops, ship. 70c, Warriors, soldiers in two battle scenes. 80c, Italians surrendering, Ethiopian troops, cannons. 1b, Emperor Menelik II, constitution, Empress Taitu.

1996, Mar. 2   **Litho.**   **Perf. 13½x14½**
1417	A307	40c multicolored	.35	.35
1418	A307	50c multicolored	.40	.35
1419	A307	60c multicolored	.60	.45
1420	A307	70c multicolored	.75	.55
1421	A307	80c multicolored	1.00	.80
1422	A307	1b multicolored	1.40	1.10
a.		Souvenir sheet, #1417-1422	5.50	5.50
		Nos. 1417-1422 (6)	4.50	3.60

UN Volunteers, 25th Anniv. — A308

Designs: 20c, People, temporary housing huts. 30c, Planting seedlings. 50c, Instructing students. 1b, Caring for infant.

1996, June 6   **Litho.**   **Perf. 13½**
1423	A308	20c multicolored	.25	.25
1424	A308	30c multicolored	.35	.25
1425	A308	50c multicolored	.50	.40
1426	A308	1b multicolored	1.40	1.25
		Nos. 1423-1426 (4)	2.50	2.15

1996 Summer Olympic Games, Atlanta — A310

1996, Aug. 1   **Litho.**   **Perf. 12½x12**
Overprint in Black
1427	A310	15c Boxing	.30	.30
1428	A310	20c Swimming	.30	.30
1429	A310	40c Cycling	.30	.30
1430	A310	85c Athletics	.60	.60
1431	A310	1b Soccer	.90	.90
		Nos. 1427-1431 (5)	2.40	2.40

Nos. 1427-1431 were originally prepared for the 1984 Summer Olympic Games in Los Angeles, but were not released due to the Soviet-led boycott. Nos. 1427-1431 exist without overprint. Value, set $100.

A311

UNICEF, 50th Anniv.: 10c, Emblems. 15c, Mother, child receiving vaccination. 25c, Woman carrying water, boy drinking from faucet. 50c, Children studying. 1b, Mother breastfeeding infant.

1996, Sept. 10   **Litho.**   **Perf. 13½**
1432	A311	10c multicolored	.35	.35
1433	A311	15c multicolored	.40	.35
1434	A311	25c multicolored	.50	.40
1435	A311	50c multicolored	.85	.65
1436	A311	1b multicolored	1.40	1.05
		Nos. 1432-1436 (5)	3.50	2.80

A312

Creation of Federal Democratic Republic of Ethiopia: 10c, People discussing new Constitution, approved Dec. 8, 1994. 20c, Ballot boxes, hand placing ballot in box. 30c, Marking ballot, placing into box, tower building, items from country's environment. 40c, Building, ballot, assembly hall. 1b, Natl. flag, transition of power.

1996, Dec. 26   **Litho.**   **Perf. 13½**
1437	A312	10c multicolored	.30	.30
1438	A312	20c multicolored	.40	.30
1439	A312	30c multicolored	.50	.30
1440	A312	40c multicolored	.60	.30
1441	A312	1b multicolored	.75	.60
		Nos. 1437-1441 (5)	2.55	1.80

Traditional Baskets A313

1997, Feb. 20   **Litho.**   **Perf. 13½**
1442	A313	5c Jimma	.40	.40
1443	A313	15c Wello	.40	.40
1444	A313	80c Welega	1.00	1.00
1445	A313	1b Shewa	1.25	1.25
		Nos. 1442-1445 (4)	3.05	3.05

Traditional Baskets — A314

ETHIOPIA

1997, May 22	Litho.	Perf. 13½
1446 A314 35c Arssi	.40	.40
1447 A314 65c Gojam	.60	.50
1448 A314 1b Harer	1.25	1.00
Nos. 1446-1448 (3)	2.25	1.90

See Nos. 1464-1466.

UN Decade Against Drug Abuse & Illicit Trafficking — A315

1997, Sept. 9	Litho.	Perf. 14
1449 A315 20c green & multi	.60	.60
1450 A315 80c brown & multi	.60	.60
1451 A315 1b blue & multi	1.00	.85
Nos. 1449-1451 (3)	2.20	2.05

Historic Buildings, Addis Ababa — A316

45c, Bitwoded Haile Giorgis' house. 55c, Alfred Ilg's house, vert. 3b, Menelik's Elfign.

Perf. 14½x14, 14x14½

1997, Dec. 23		Litho.
1452 A316 45c multicolored	.30	.30
1453 A316 55c multicolored	.45	.45
1454 A316 3b multicolored	1.50	1.50
Nos. 1452-1454 (3)	2.25	2.25

Addis Ababa's Oldest Historical Buildings — A317

Designs: 60c, Ras Biru W/Gabriel's house. 75c, Sheh Hojele Alhassen's house. 80c, Fitawrari H/Giorgis Dinegde's house. 85c, Etege Taitu Hotel. 1b, Dejazmach Wube Atnafseged's house.

1997, Dec. 30	Litho.	Perf. 14½x14
1455 A317 60c multicolored	.55	.45
1456 A317 75c multicolored	.60	.55
1457 A317 80c multicolored	.70	.60
1458 A317 85c multicolored	.75	.70
1459 A317 1b multicolored	1.15	.90
Nos. 1455-1459 (5)	3.75	3.20

Pan African Postal Union, 18th Anniv. — A318

Union's emblem and wildlife: 45c, Deculla bushback. 55c, Soemmering's gazelle. 1b, Defassa waterbuck. 2b, Black buffalo.

1998, Mar. 25	Litho.	Perf. 14½x14
1460 A318 45c multicolored	.50	.35
1461 A318 55c multicolored	.55	.45
1462 A318 1b multicolored	1.00	.65
1463 A318 2b multicolored	2.00	1.25
Nos. 1460-1463 (4)	4.05	2.70

Traditional Basket Type of 1997

1998, May 21	Litho.	Perf. 13½
1464 A314 45c Gonder	.45	.35
1465 A314 55c Harere	.55	.35
1466 A314 3b Tigray	2.00	1.25
Nos. 1464-1466 (3)	3.00	1.95

Golden-Backed Woodpecker — A319

1998, Jan. 12	Photo.	Perf. 11½
Granite Paper		
Panel Color		
1467 A319 5c green blue	.45	.30
1468 A319 10c yellow	.45	.30
1469 A319 15c blue	.45	.30
1470 A319 20c light brown	15.00	.30
1471 A319 25c violet	.45	.30
1472 A319 30c light blue	.45	.30
1473 A319 35c salmon rose	.45	.30
1474 A319 40c lilac	.45	.30
1475 A319 45c green	.45	.30
1476 A319 50c salmon	.45	.35
1477 A319 55c blue	.45	.35
1478 A319 60c brick red	.45	.40
1479 A319 65c light gray	.45	.45
1480 A319 70c bright yellow	.45	.50
1481 A319 75c pale violet	.70	.65
1482 A319 80c apple green	.75	.70
1483 A319 85c gray	.80	.75
1484 A319 90c orange	.90	.80
1485 A319 1b yellow green	1.25	.95
1486 A319 2b pale rose	1.50	1.25
1487 A319 3b lilac rose	2.50	2.00
1488 A319 5b bister	3.50	3.00
1489 A319 10b orange yellow	7.00	6.00
Nos. 1467-1489 (23)	39.75	20.85

Agreement for Return of Axum Obelisk from Italy — A320

45c, Map of Italy, pieces of obelisk. 55c, Obelisk in Rome. 3b, Map of E. Africa, obelisk, ruins of Axum.

1998, Sept. 3	Litho.	Perf. 13½
1490 A320 45c multicolored	.50	.50
1491 A320 55c multicolored	.60	.40
1492 A320 3b multicolored	2.50	1.50
Nos. 1490-1492 (3)	3.60	2.20

Ethiopia-Djibouti Railway, Cent. — A321

Designs: 45c, Men carrying rails during construction. 55c, Early steam train, CFE 404. 1b, Terminal building. 2b, Modern train, BB 1212.

1998, Nov. 24	Litho.	Perf. 11½
Granite Paper		
1493 A321 45c multicolored	.55	.35
1494 A321 55c multicolored	.70	.45
1495 A321 1b multicolored	1.20	.75
1496 A321 2b multicolored	2.50	1.25
Nos. 1493-1496 (4)	4.95	2.80

Universal Declaration of Human Rights, 50th Anniv. — A322

1998, Dec. 23	Litho.	Perf. 13x13½
1497 A322 45c red & multi	.45	.25
1498 A322 55c yellow & multi	.45	.30
1499 A322 1b green & multi	.75	.50
1500 A322 2b blue & multi	1.10	.75
Nos. 1497-1500 (4)	2.75	1.80

Mother Teresa (1910-97) — A323

Various portraits.

1999, Mar. 9	Litho.	Perf. 13½x13
1501 A323 45c brown & multi	.60	.60
1502 A323 55c green & multi	.60	.60
1503 A323 1b yel org & multi	1.00	.75
1504 A323 2b blue & multi	2.00	1.75
Nos. 1501-1504 (4)	4.20	3.70

Intl. Year of the Ocean A324

1999, May 6	Litho.	Perf. 13½x13¼
1505 A324 45c black & multi	.60	.30
1506 A324 55c red & multi	.75	.30
1507 A324 1b blue & multi	1.00	.60
1508 A324 2b green & multi	2.25	1.25
Nos. 1505-1508 (4)	4.60	2.45

World Environment Day — A325

1999, June 17	Litho.	Perf. 13½
1509 A325 45c pink & multi	.55	.30
1510 A325 55c vio & multi	.70	.40
1511 A325 1b yel org & multi	1.10	.70
1512 A325 2b grn & multi	1.90	1.00
Nos. 1509-1512 (4)	4.25	2.40

National Parks — A326

45c, Abijata, Shalla Lakes. 70c, Nechisar. 85c, Bale Mountains. 2b, Awash.

Perf. 13¾x13¼, 13¼x13¾

1999, Sept. 8		Litho.
1513 A326 45c multi, vert.	.50	.50
1514 A326 70c multi, vert.	.80	.70
1515 A326 85c multi, vert.	1.25	.90
1516 A326 2b multi	3.00	1.50
Nos. 1513-1516 (4)	5.55	3.60

See Nos. 1521-1524.

UPU, 125th Anniv. — A327

1999, Oct. 28		Perf. 13¼x13
1517 A327 20c multicolored	.50	.50
1518 A327 80c multicolored	.70	.35
1519 A327 1b multicolored	.75	.60
1520 A327 2b multicolored	1.50	.85
Nos. 1517-1520 (4)	3.45	2.30

National Parks Type of 1999

Designs: 50c, Omo, vert. 70c, Mago, vert. 80c, Yangudi-Rassa, vert. 2b, Gambella.

1999, Nov. 30	Litho.	Perf. 13¼
1521-1524 A326 Set of 4	5.00	3.00

Intl. Year of Older Persons — A328

45c, Woman attending to sick man. 70c, Older people gardening. 85c, Four men, bench. 2b, Older man, two young people.

1999, Dec. 30		Perf. 13¾x13¼
1525-1528 A328 Set of 4	4.50	3.50

Alexander Pushkin, Writer, Birth Bicent. (in 1999) — A329

Various portraits: 45c, 70c, 85c, 2b.

2000, Mar. 9	Litho.	Perf. 13¾x13¼
1529-1532 A329 Set of 4	3.25	2.25

Worldwide Fund for Nature (WWF) A330

Grevy's zebra: a, Grazing. b, Running. c, Resting. d, Head.

2001, Jan. 30	Litho.	Perf. 13¼x13¾
1533 Strip of 4	4.25	3.50
a. A330 45c multi	.40	.30
b. A330 55c multi	.50	.40
c. A330 1b multi	.80	.70
d. A330 3b multi	2.50	2.25

Operation Sunset — A331

Designs: 45c, President Meles Zenawi, Parliament. 55c, Soldiers, flag ceremony. 1b, People, house. 2b, Agriculture, construction.

2000, June 27		Perf. 13¾
1534-1537 A331 Set of 4	4.50	2.50

Flags — A332

Designs: 25c, Harar Region. 30c, Oromia Region. 50c, Amhara Region. 60c, Tigre Region. 70c, Benishangi Region. 80c, Somalia Region. 90c, Peoples of the South Region. 95c, Gambella Region. 1b, Afar Region. 2b, Ethiopia.

2000, Oct. 26		Perf. 13¼x13¾
1538-1547 A332 Set of 10	7.00	4.50

Afro Ayigeba, Cross of St. Lalibela — A333

2000, Apr. 27		Perf. 13¾x13¼
1548 A333 4b multi	2.50	2.25

Menelik's Bushbuck — A334

ETHIOPIA

2000, June 19   Litho.   Perf. 13¾x13¼
Frame Color

1548A	A334	5c dk Prus blue	2.00	.25
1549	A334	10c lilac	2.00	.25
1549A	A334	15c blue	2.00	.25
1549B	A334	20c yellow bister	2.00	.25
1549C	A334	25c purple	2.00	.25
1549D	A334	30c lt Prus blue	2.00	.25
1549E	A334	35c brt red	2.00	.25
1549F	A334	40c lilac	2.00	.25
1549G	A334	45c emerald	2.00	.25
1549H	A334	50c red	2.25	.25
1549I	A334	55c blue	2.50	.25
1549J	A334	60c yellow orange	2.50	.25
1549K	A334	65c deep blue	2.50	.25
1549L	A334	70c dull blue	2.50	.25
1549M	A334	75c orange yellow	3.00	.35
1549N	A334	80c carmine	3.00	.35
1549O	A334	85c light blue	3.00	.40
1550	A334	90c ocher	3.00	.40
1551	A334	1b green	4.00	.50
1552	A334	2b red violet	9.00	.75
1553	A334	3b purple	16.00	.90
1554	A334	5b dark carmine	27.50	1.75
1555	A334	10b light carmine	37.50	4.00

Nos. 1548A-1555 (23)   136.25   12.90

Haile Gebreselassie, Runner — A335

Gebreselassie: No. 1557, 50c, Running. No. 1557A, 60c, Running, diff. No. 1557B, 90c, Running, diff. No. 1558, 2b, With arms raised.

2000, Nov. 9   Litho.   Perf. 13½
1557-1558   A335   Set of 4   3.50   2.00

World Meteorological Organization, 50th Anniv. — A336

Color of inscriptions: 40c, Gray. 75c, Green. 85c, Brown. 2b, Blue.

2000, Oct. 10   Litho.   Perf. 13½
1559-1562   A336   Set of 4   3.00   2.00

Addis Ababa University, 50th Anniv. — A337

2000, Nov. 30   Perf. 13½x14¼
1563   A337   4b multi   3.25   2.75

UN High Commissioner for Refugees, 50th Anniv. — A338

Frame color: 40c, Brown. 75c, Green. 85c, Blue. 2b, Gold.

2000, Dec. 14   Perf. 13½x14
1564-1567   A338   Set of 4   4.00   2.50

Freshwater Fish — A340

Designs: 45c, Catfish. 55c, Tilapia. 3b, Nile perch.

2001, July 26   Litho.   Perf. 14¼
1572-1574   A340   Set of 3   3.50   1.75

Traditional Means of Transportation A341

Designs: 40c, Man on horseback, horse-drawn cart. 60c, Camel caravan. 1b, Man on horseback, horse carrying load. 2b, Man on donkey, donkeys carrying goods.

2001, Aug. 30   Perf. 13¼x13½
1575-1578   A341   Set of 4   4.25   2.25

Year of Dialogue Among Civilizations — A342

Color of country name: 25c, Light blue. 75c, White. 1b, Light yellow. 2b, Pink.

2001, Oct. 9   Perf. 14
1579-1582   A342   Set of 4   3.50   2.25

Birds — A343

Designs: 50c, White-tailed swallow. 60c, Spot-breasted plover. 90c, Abyssinian long-claw. 2b, Prince Ruspoli's turaco.

2001, Nov. 29   Perf. 14¼
1583-1586   A343   Set of 4   5.00   3.00

Traditional Beehives — A344

Various beehives: 40c, 70c, 90c, 2b.

2002, Jan. 24   Litho.   Perf. 14
1587-1590   A344   Set of 4   4.50   3.50

Traditional Grain Storage — A345

Designs: 30c, Gota. 70c, Bekollo Gotera. 1b, Gotera. 2b, Gotera, diff.

2002, Mar. 28   Perf. 13½x14
1591-1594   A345   Set of 4   4.50   3.50

Lions Club Intl. — A346

Lions Club Intl. emblem and: 45c, Quality emblem. 55c, Woman at pump. 1b, Eye doctor treating patient. 2b, Man in wheelchair.

2002, Apr. 26   Litho.   Perf. 13x13¼
1595-1598   A346   Set of 4   4.50   4.00

Trees — A347

Designs: 50c, Acacia abyssinica. 60c, Boswellia papyrifera, vert. 90c, Aningeria adolfi-friederici, vert. 2b, Prunus africana, vert.

Perf. 13½x13¼, 13¼x13½
2002, June 27
1599-1602   A347   Set of 4   4.50   4.00

Traditional Beehives — A348

Various beehives with panel colors of: 45c, Pink. 55c, Yellow. 1b, Light blue. 2b, Light green.

2002, Sept. 19   Litho.   Perf. 13¼x13
1603-1606   A348   Set of 4   4.50   3.50

Granite — A349

Designs: 45c, Sidamo. 55c, Harrar. 1b, Tigray. 2b, Wollega.

2002, Oct. 24   Perf. 13x13¼
1607-1610   A349   Set of 4   4.50   4.00

Konso Waka — A350

Various wooden sculptures with background colors of: 40c, Green. 60c, Blue. 1b, Yellow. 2b, Red.

2002, Nov. 28   Perf. 14
1611-1614   A350   Set of 4   4.00   2.00

Menelik's Bushbuck — A351

2002, Dec. 12   Perf. 13½x13¾
Frame Color

1615	A351	5c brt grn blue	.30	.25
1616	A351	10c lilac	.30	.25
1617	A351	15c bright blue	.30	.25
1618	A351	20c brn orange	.30	.25
1619	A351	25c purple	.30	.25
1620	A351	30c bright blue	.30	.25
1621	A351	35c carmine	.30	.25
1622	A351	40c purple	.30	.25
1623	A351	45c emerald	.30	.25
1624	A351	50c red	.30	.25
1625	A351	55c blue	.30	.25
1626	A351	60c bright yel	.40	.25
1627	A351	65c red	.40	.25
1628	A351	70c light blue	.40	.25
1629	A351	75c bright yel	.45	.35
1630	A351	80c carmine	.45	.35
1631	A351	85c bright blue	.60	.40
1632	A351	90c orange brn	.60	.40
1633	A351	95c green	.60	.40
1634	A351	1b red violet	.70	.50
1635	A351	2b purple	1.00	.75
1636	A351	3b blue	1.25	.90
1637	A351	5b dull red	2.25	1.50
1638	A351	10b light green	6.50	3.00
1639	A351	20b rose pink	11.00	6.00

Nos. 1615-1639 (25)   29.90   18.05

Oil Crops — A352

Designs: 40c, Abyssinian mustard. 60c, Linseed. 3b, Niger seed.

2002, Dec. 31   Litho.   Perf. 13¼x13
1640-1642   A352   Set of 3   3.00   2.00

Pan-African Postal Union, 23rd Anniv. — A353

Background color: 20c, Green. 80c, Blue green. 1b, Orange brown. 2b, Purple.

2003, Feb. 18   Perf. 13x13¼
1643-1646   A353   Set of 4   3.00   2.00

Opals — A354

Designs: 45c, Milk opal. 60c, Brown precious opal. 95c, Fire opal. 2b, Yellow precious opal.

2003, May 8   Perf. 14
1647-1650   A354   Set of 4   4.00   2.00

Emperor Tewodros's Amulet — A355

Various views with frame color of: 40c, Green. 60c, Yellow orange. 3b, Red.

2003, Sept. 4   Litho.   Perf. 13x13¼
1651-1653   A355   Set of 3   4.50   2.50

Flowers — A356

Designs: 45c, Kniphofia isoetfolia. 55c, Kniphofia insignis. 1b, Crinum bambusetum. 2b, Crinum abyssinicum, horiz.

2003, Nov. 27   Litho.   Perf. 13x13¼
1654-1657   A356   Set of 4   3.00   2.00

Konso Terracing System — A357

Designs: 40c, Village, crops. 60c, Man and woman, ears of grains. 1b, Terraces, tool. 2b, Farmers working on terraces, crops.

2003, Dec. 30   Perf. 13¼x13¾
1658-1661   A357   Set of 4   3.00   2.00

Amaranths — A358

Designs: 20c, Seeds. 80c, White amaranth. 1b, Red amaranth. 2b, Amaranth bread.

2004, Mar. 11   Litho.   Perf. 13¼x14
1662-1665   A358   Set of 4   3.00   2.00

ETHIOPIA

Marble — A359

Designs: 25c, Sabian multicolored marble. 75c, Eshet blue marble. 1b, Sabian rose green marble. 2b, Sabian purple marble.

2004, July 27			Perf. 14	
1666-1669	A359	Set of 4	2.25	2.25

FIFA (Fédération Internationale de Football Association), Cent. — A360

Soccer field, "100" and: 5c, FIFA emblem. 95c, Old soccer ball. 1b, Cleats. 2b, Modern soccer ball.

2004, Sept. 7		Litho.	Perf. 14	
1670-1673	A360	Set of 4	2.25	2.25

2004 Summer Olympics, Athens — A361

Designs: 20c, Track. 35c, Hammer throw. 45c, Boxing. 3b, Cycling.

2004, Dec. 7				
1674-1677	A361	Set of 4	2.25	2.25

Gesho — A362

Designs: 40c, Chopped plant. 60c, Plants, horiz. 1b, Cut logs. 2b, Branch with berries.

2004, Dec. 28				
1678-1681	A362	Set of 4	2.25	2.25

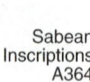
Black Rhinoceros A363

2005, June 20		Litho.	Perf. 14
Background Color			
1682	A363	5c bright blue	.25 .25
1683	A363	10c lilac	.25 .25
1684	A363	15c dark blue	.25 .25
1685	A363	20c bister	1.00 1.00
1686	A363	25c dark purple	1.00 1.00
1687	A363	30c blue	1.00 1.00
1688	A363	35c red	1.00 1.00
1689	A363	40c purple	1.00 1.00
1690	A363	45c green	1.00 1.00
1691	A363	4b bright red	4.25 4.25
Nos. 1682-1691 (10)			11.00 11.00

Sabean Inscriptions A364

Various inscriptions with background colors of: 15c, Green. 40c, Red, vert. 45c, Orange, vert. 3b, Blue, vert.

Perf. 13¾x14, 14x13¾
2005, Aug. 20			Litho.	
1692-1695	A364	Set of 4	2.00	2.00

Surma Hairstyles — A365

Various hairstyles with background colors of: 15c, Red. 40c, Green. 45c, Blue. 3b, Lilac.

2005, Dec. 20			Perf. 14x13¾	
1696-1699	A365	Set of 4	2.00	2.00

Flowers — A366

Designs: 45c, Chlorophytum neghellense. 55c, Aloe bertemariae, vert. 3b, Aloe schelpei, vert.

Perf. 13¾x14, 14x13¾
2006, June 6			Litho.	
1700-1702	A366	Set of 3	2.00	2.00

Ethiopian Airlines, 60th Anniv. — A367

Designs: 15c, Douglas C-47A Dakota III. 40c, Douglas DC-6B Super Cloudmaster. 45c, Boeing 720-060B. 1b, Boeing 767-300ER. 2b, Boeing 787 Dreamliner.

2006, Sept. 28			Perf. 13x13¼	
1703-1707	A367	Set of 5	2.00	2.00

Intl. Year of Deserts and Desertification A368

Emblem and: 15c, United Nations emblem. 40c, Map of Ethiopia showing desertification vulnerability. 45c, Map of Africa showing climate types. 3b, Map of world showing climate types.

2006, Oct. 31			Perf. 14x13½	
1708-1711	A368	Set of 4	2.00	2.00

Ethiopian Millennium — A369

Panel color: 40c, Pink. 60c, Buff. 3b, Green.

2007, Nov. 15		Litho.	Perf. 13¾	
1712-1714	A369	Set of 3	2.00	2.00

Minerals — A370

Designs: 40c, Gypsum. 60c, Quartz. 1b, Ambo sandstone. 2b, Feldspar.

2007, Dec. 25			Perf. 14	
1715-1718	A370	Set of 4	2.00	2.00

Onslaught Martyrs Memorial — A371

Designs: 40c, Martyrs Memorial Center. 60c, Emblem of Association for the Erection of the Martyrs Memorial Monument, vert. 3b, Woman, jail cell, gun, vert.

2008, Aug. 26		Litho.	Perf. 14	
1719-1721	A371	Set of 3	3.00	3.00

Catha Edulis — A372

Designs: 45c, Red leaves. 55c, Harvesting of plant. 3b, Plant.

2008, Sept. 8			Perf. 13¾	
1722-1724	A372	Set of 3	3.00	3.00

Diplomatic Relations Between Ethiopia and India, 60th Anniv. — A373

"60" and: 30c, Ethiopian and Indian flowers. 70c, Rock church, Lalibela, and Taj Mahal, India. 3b, Symbols of India and Ethiopia.

2008, Dec. 30		Litho.	Perf. 14x13¼	
1725-1727	A373	Set of 3	3.00	3.00

Pan-African Tsetse and Trypanosomiasis Eradication Campaign — A374

Designs: 15c, Campaign emblem. 40c, Tsetse fly. 45c, Tsetse fly and blood drop, horiz. 3b, Tsetse fly, cow, silhouette of human, map of Africa, horiz.

Perf. 13½x14, 14x13½
2009, July 21			Litho.	
1728-1731	A374	Set of 4	3.00	3.00

Addis Ababa Monuments A375

Designs: 45c, Arat Kilo, Miazia 27 Square Monument. 55c, Sidist Kilo, Yekatit 12 Square Monument. 3b, Abune Petros Monument, vert.

2009, Sept. 17		Litho.	Perf. 13¾	
1732-1734	A375	Set of 3	3.00	3.00

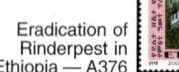
Eradication of Rinderpest in Ethiopia — A376

Designs: 15c, First laboratory in Addis Ababa where rinderpest vaccine was produced. 40c, Certificate from World Organization for Animal Health. 45c, Dead cattle. 3b, Dr. Alemework Beyene, monument to Dr. Engueda Johannes, veterinarians.

2009, Dec. 31			Perf. 14	
1735-1738	A376	Set of 4	3.00	3.00

Pan-African Postal Union, 30th Anniv. — A377

Background color: 45c, Green. 55c, Yellow. 3b, Rose.

2010, Apr. 6		Litho.	Perf. 13¼x14	
1739-1741	A377	Set of 3	3.00	3.00

Writers — A378

Designs: No. 1742, 1b, Tsegaye Gebremedhin (1936-2006). No. 1743, 1b, Dr. Sindehu Gebru (1915-2009). No. 1744, 1b, Dr. Haddis Alemayehu (1910-2003). No. 1745, 1b, Dr. Kebede Michael (1915-98).

2010, Aug. 6			Perf. 14	
1742-1745	A378	Set of 4	3.25	3.25

Ethiopian Red Cross, 75th Anniv. — A379

75th anniversary emblem and: 45c, Ambulance, Red Cross workers and truck. 55c, Bags of blood, boy receiving transfusion. 1b, Amharic letters, vert. 2b, Red Cross building.

2010, Oct. 12		Litho.	Perf. 14	
1746-1749	A379	Set of 4	3.00	3.00

Mosques — A380

Designs: 20c, Goze Mosque. 80c, Al-Nejashi Mosque. 3b, Sheh Hussein Mosque, Dire.

2011, May 24		Litho.	Perf. 14	
1750-1752	A380	Set of 3	3.00	3.00

Monasteries and Churches A381

Designs: 35c, Zoz Amba St. George's Monastery, Gonder. 65c, Meskele Kiristonse Church, Wollo, vert. 3b, Debre Damo Abuna Aregawi Monastery, Tigrai, vert.

2011, June 9				
1753-1755	A381	Set of 3	3.00	3.00

Bridges — A382

Designs: 20c, Tezeke Bridge No. 3. 80c, Hidassie Bridge. 1b, Beshela River Bridge. 2b, Blue Nile Bridge.

2011, Sept. 2		Litho.	Perf. 14x13¼	
1756-1759	A382	Set of 4	3.00	3.00

ETHIOPIA

Martyr's Monuments — A383

Designs: 40c, Amhara Region Martyr's Monument, Bahir Dar. 60c, Oromo Martyr's Monument, Adama. 3b, Tigrai Region Martyr's Monument, Mekelle, horiz.

2011, Sept. 9	Perf. 13¼x13, 13x13¼	
1760-1762 A383	Set of 3	3.00 3.00

Coffee Ceremony — A384

Designs: 20c, Coffee pots. 80c, Preparation of coffee. 1b, Bean roasting. 2b, Pouring of coffee into cups.

2011, Dec. 20	Perf. 13¼x14	
1763-1766 A384	Set of 4	3.00 3.00

Medicinal Plants — A385

Designs: 20c, Lippia adoensis. 35c, Artemisia absinthium. 45c, Thymus schimperi. 3b, Ocimum lamiifolium.

2012, Apr. 10	Perf. 14x13¼	
1767-1770 A385	Set of 4	3.00 3.00

Addis Ababa Monuments A386

Designs: 40c, Lion of Judah Monument. 60c, Ras Mekonen Monument. 1b, Lion of Judah Monument, vert. 2b, Menelik II Monument, vert.

2012, July 5	Perf. 14x13¼, 13¼x14	
1771-1774 A386	Set of 4	3.00 3.00

Writers — A387

Designs: 20c, Temesgen Gebre. 80c, Hiruy Woldeslassie. 1b, Yoftahe Nigussie. 2b, Afework Gebreyesus.

2012, Sept. 7	Perf. 13¼x14	
1775-1778 A387	Set of 4	3.00 3.00

Addis Ababa, 125th Anniv. (in 2011) — A388

Various views of Addis Ababa: 15c, 35c, 2b, 4b.

	Perf. 13¾x13½	
2013, Aug. 20		Litho.
1779-1782 A388	Set of 4	4.00 4.00
	Dated 2012.	

African Union, 50th Anniv. — A389

African Union emblem, "50," and: 10c, Year of Pan-Africanism emblem, building. 40c, Building, diff. 2b, Assembly hall. 4b, Map of Africa, doves, airplane, road, farm field.

2013, Dec. 3	Litho.	Perf. 13¼x14
1783-1786 A389	Set of 4	4.00 4.00

Ethio Telecom — A390

Designs: 10c, Man holding wireless telephone console. 40c, Woman holding mobile telephone, woman using wall-mounted telephone, old dial telephone, vert. 2b, Man and woman using computer. 4b, Satellite, satellite dish, map, vert.

	Perf. 14x13¼, 13¼x14	
2014, May 13		Litho.
1787-1790 A390	Set of 4	4.00 4.00

Traditional Costumes of Southern Ethiopian People — A391

Map and costumes of the: 15c, Karo. 35c, Erbore. 2b, Hamer. 4b, Daasanach.

2014, May 27	Litho.	Perf. 14x13¼
1791-1794 A391	Set of 4	4.00 4.00

Ethiopian Orthodox Tewahedo Churches and Monasteries A392

Designs: 50c, Orra Kidanemihiret Zege (monastery), Tana Island. 1b, Kibran Gebriel (monastery), Tana Island. 2b, Debrebirihan Silassie (church), Gonder, vert. 3b, Tsion Mariam Church, Axum.

	Perf. 14x13¼, 13¼x14	
2014, June 12		Litho.
1795-1798 A392	Set of 4	4.50 4.50

Rift Valley Sites — A393

Designs: 25c, Sulfur deposits, Dallol. 30c, Brine ponds, Dallol. 35c, Salt deposits, Dallol. 45c, Erta Ale Volcano erupting. 65c, Ash plume over Erta Ale Volcano. 4b, Erta Ale caldera.

2014, Aug. 28	Litho.	Perf. 14
1799-1804 A393	Set of 6	4.00 4.00

University of Gondar, 60th Anniv. A394

Designs: 5c, Millennium Steps, Referral Hospital, Health team training group on horses in 1964, new campus. 45c, President's office. 2b, Main gate. 4b, 60th anniv. emblem, vert.

2014, Dec. 2	Litho.	Perf. 13½
1805-1808 A394	Set of 4	3.50 3.50

Ethiopian Airlines — A395

Designs: 15c, Boeing 777-F6N cargo plane. 35c, Boeing 777-200R passenger plane. 2b, Ethiopian Airlines Star Alliance jet. 4b, Boeing 787 Dreamliner.

2014, Dec. 25	Litho.	Perf. 13x13¼
1809-1812 A395	Set of 4	3.50 3.50
1812a	Booklet pane of 16, 4 each #1809-1812, perf. 13x13¼ on 3 sides	15.00 —
	Complete booklet, #1812a	15.00

Ethiopian Visual Artists Association A396

Painters and their works: 10c, Yegezu Bisrat (1926-79). 40c, Emealaf Hiruy (1907-71). 2b, Belachew Yimer (1869-1957). 4b, Agegnehu Engida (1905-50).

2015, Nov. 10	Litho.	Perf. 13¼
1813-1816 A396		3.50 3.50

Ethiopian postal officials have declared as "illegal" sheets of 9 dated "2016" depicting Ferrari automobiles, Michael Schumacher, National Hockey League stars, Soccer stars, Cristiano Ronaldo, Crocodile, Fish, Tigers, Roses, and Nudes, sheets of 9 dated "2009" depicting Pandas, sheets of 6 dated "2009" depicting Chimpanzees, sheets of 5 dated "2015" depicting Netherlands 2018 World Cup soccer players, and sheets of 4 dated "2009" depicting Pandas and Chimpanzees.

Ethiopian National Archives and Libraries Agency, 70th Anniv. — A397

Designs: 10c, Sea of Computs. 15c, Ethiopian Cultural Medicine Book. 25c, Letter from Ethiopian King Theodros to Queen Victoria of Great Britain, 19th cent. 1b, Four Gospels Bible, 14th cent. 2b, Book of Enoch, 15th cent., horiz. 3b, National Archives, horiz.

	Perf. 13¼x13½, 13½x13¼	
2016, Jan. 28		Litho.
1817-1822 A397	Set of 6	3.50 3.50

Palaces — A398

Designs: 10c, Emperor Menelik Palace, Fit Ber Gate. 40c, Emperor Menelik Palace, Entoto. 2b, Guenete Leul Palace and gate, Addis Ababa. 4b, National Palace, Addis Ababa.

	Perf. 13¼x13½	
2016, Feb. 18		Litho.
1823-1826 A398	Set of 4	3.50 3.50

Haramaya University, 60th Anniv. — A399

Designs: 5c, Parking lot and Administration building. 45c, Agricultural research plot, dairy production. 2b, Main gate. 4b, 60th anniv. emblem, vert.

Perf. 13½x13¼, 13¼x13½		
2016, Apr. 21		Litho.
1827-1830 A399	Set of 4	3.50 3.50

Waterfalls — A400

Designs: 10c, Habera River Falls, Bale. 40c, Sor Waterfalls, Ilu Abba Bora. 2b, Blue Nile Falls, Gojam. 4b, Ajora Falls, Wolaitta.

	Perf. 13½x13¼	
2016, June 14		Litho.
1831-1834 A400	Set of 4	3.50 3.50

Ministry of Urban Development and Housing — A401

Designs: 50c, Building under construction. 1b, Housing complexes and bricks. 2b, Main office. 3b, Emblem.

	Perf. 13½x13¼	
2016, Sept. 28		Litho.
1835-1838 A401	Set of 4	3.50 3.50

Snakes — A402

Designs: 50c, Ethiopian house snake. 1b, Abyssinian house snake. 2b, Ethiopian blind snake. 3b, Ethiopian mountain adder.

2016, Oct. 27	Litho.	Perf. 13½x13¼
1839-1842 A402	Set of 4	3.50 3.50

Defeat of Italy In East African Campaign, 75th Anniv. — A403

Designs: No. 1843, 1b, People on gallows, statue at left, monuments, four Ethiopians in foreground, green frame. No. 1844, 1b, Four Ethiopians, monument at center, green frame. No. 1845, 1b, Ethiopians planting flag in ground, monument, train, dam, tractor, red frame. No. 1846, 1b, Eight Ethiopians, monument at center, gray green frame. No. 1847, 1b, Six Ethiopians, monument at center, blue frame. 1.50b, Two Ethiopians, monument at center, blue frame.

2016, Nov. 6	Litho.	Perf. 13½x13¾
1843-1848 A403	Set of 6	4.00 4.00

Fish — A404

Map and: 5c, Labeobarbus marcophtalmus. 45c, Labeobarbus gorguari. 1b, Labeobarbus acutirostris. 5b, Labeobarbus osseensis.

	Perf. 13½x13¼	
2017, Mar. 21		Litho.
1849-1852 A404	Set of 4	3.50 3.50
	Dated 2016.	

Gates of Harar — A405

Designs: 15c, Buda Gate. 35c, Fellana Gate. 1b, Senga Gate. 2b, Showa Gate. 3b, Erer Gate.

ETHIOPIA

Perf. 13¾x13½
2017, Aug. 24   Litho.
1853-1857   A405   Set of 5   3.50   3.50

Commercial Bank of Ethiopia, 75th Anniv. — A406

75th anniversary emblem and: 40c, Tefera Degefe, first general manager of bank. 50c, State Bank of Ethiopia Building, horiz. 60c, Former headquarters, 1964, horiz. 2b, Bank building, automatic teller machine, mobile banking application on cell phone, computer and credit card reader. 3b, Bank emblem, train, ship, dam, wheat and factory.

Perf. 13¾x13¼, 13¼x13¾
2018, Apr. 26   Litho.
1858-1862   A406   Set of 5   3.50   3.50

Churches — A407

Designs: 5c, Narga Selassie Church, Bahar Dar. 45c, Adadi Maryam Church, Oromia. 2b, Medhane Alem Kesho Church, Tigray. 4b, Maryam Korkor Church, Tigray.

2018, June 5   Litho.   Perf. 13½x13¼
1863-1866   A407   Set of 4   3.50   3.50

Ethiopia-Djibouti Electrified Railway — A408

Designs: 50c, Train. 1b, Station. 2b, Trains on multiple tracks. 3b, Construction of railway.

Perf. 13¼x13½
2018, Aug. 31   Litho.
1867-1870   A408   Set of 4   3.50   3.50
1870a   Souvenir sheet of 4, #1867-1870   3.50   3.50

Diplomatic Relations Between Ethiopia and Russia, 120th Anniv. — A409

Designs: 50c, Balcha Safo (1863-1936), Ethiopian military commander, Nikolay S. Leontiev (1862-1910), Russian military officer, and Balcha Hospital. 1b, Musical instruments of Ethiopia and Russia. 2b, Castle of Fasilides, Ethiopia, and Castle of Nizhny Novgorod, Russia, horiz. 3b, Ethiopian jebena (coffee pot), and tagine and Russian Khokhloma bowls, horiz.

Perf. 14¼x14, 14x14¼
2018, Dec. 28   Litho.
1871-1874   A409   Set of 4   .45   .45

Birds — A410

Designs: 40c, White-bellied go-away bird. 50c, Long-tailed nightjar. 60c, Dusky turtle dove. 2b, Black-billed barbet. 3b, Red-fronted tinker bird.

2019, Jan. 24   Litho.   Perf. 13½
1875-1879   A410   Set of 5   .50   .50

Animals — A411

Designs: 50c, Aardwolves. 1b, Striped hyenas. 5b, Spotted hyenas.

2019, Feb. 14   Litho.   Perf. 14
1880-1882   A411   Set of 3   .45   .45

SEMI-POSTAL STAMPS

Types of 1931, Overprinted in Red at Upper Left

Perf. 12x12½, 12½x12
1936, Feb. 24   Unwmk.
B1	A27	1g light green	.60	1.00
B2	A27	2g rose	.60	1.00
B3	A25	4g blue	.60	1.00
B4	A27	8g brown	.85	1.50
B5	A25	1t purple	.85	1.50
		Nos. B1-B5 (5)	3.50	6.00

Nos. B1-B5 were sold at twice face value, the surtax going to the Red Cross.

Catalogue values for unused stamps in this section, from this point to the end of the section, are for Never Hinged items.

Nos. 289, 290, 292-294 Surcharged in Blue

Perf. 13x13½
1949, June 13   Wmk. 282
B6	A53	8c + 8c deep org	2.50	2.50
B7	A53	12c + 5c red	2.50	2.50
B8	A53	30c + 15c org brn	4.00	4.00
B9	A53	70c + 70c rose lilac	25.00	25.00
B10	A53	$1 + 80c dk car rose	32.50	32.50
		Nos. B6-B10 (5)	66.50	66.50

No. B10 exists with "80+" error. See Nos. B16-B20.

Type A39 Surcharged in Red or Carmine

Perf. 11½
1950, May 8   Unwmk.   Photo.
Various Designs
Inscribed "Croix Rouge"
B11	A39	5c + 10c brt grn	.85	1.60
B12	A39	10c + 10c brt red	1.10	1.60
B13	A39	25c + 10c brt bl	2.25	3.25
B14	A39	50c + 10c dk yel brn	5.00	5.50
B15	A39	1t + 10c brt vio	11.00	13.50
		Nos. B11-B15 (5)	21.70	25.45

The surtax was for the Red Cross.
The surcharge includes two dots which invalidate the original surtax. The original surcharge with uneven cross was red, a 1951 printing with even cross was carmine. Forgeries exist.

Nos. B6-B10 Overprinted in Black

Perf. 13x13½
1951, Nov. 17   Wmk. 282
B16	A53	8c + 8c dp org	.70	.70
B17	A53	12c + 5c red	.70	.70
B18	A53	30c + 15c org brn	1.25	1.25
B19	A53	70c + 70c rose lilac	12.00	12.00
B20	A53	$1 + 80c dk car rose	20.00	20.00
		Nos. B16-B20 (5)	34.65	34.65

No. B20 exists with "80 +" error.

Tree, Staff and Snake — SP1

Wmk. 282
1951, Nov. 25   Engr.   Perf. 13
Lower Panel in Red
B21	SP1	5c + 2c dp bl grn	.50	.25
B22	SP1	10c + 3c orange	.55	.30
B23	SP1	15c + 3c dp bl	.85	.50
B24	SP1	30c + 5c red	1.60	1.10
B25	SP1	50c + 7c red brn	4.50	2.75
B26	SP1	$1 + 10c purple	9.00	4.50
		Nos. B21-B26 (6)	17.00	9.40

The surtax was for anti-tuberculosis work.

1958, Dec. 1
Lower Panel in Red
B27	SP1	20c + 3c dl pur	.75	.75
B28	SP1	25c + 4c emerald	1.10	1.10
B29	SP1	35c + 5c rose vio	1.50	1.50
B30	SP1	60c + 7c vio bl	2.75	2.75
B31	SP1	65c + 7c violet	5.00	5.00
B32	SP1	80c + 9c car rose	9.00	9.00
		Nos. B27-B32 (6)	20.10	20.10
		Nos. B21-B32 (12)	37.10	29.50

The surtax was for anti-tuberculosis work.
Nos. B21-B32 were the only stamps on sale from Dec. 1-25, 1958.

Type of Regular Issue, 1955, Overprinted and Surcharged

Engr.; Cross Typo. in Red
1959, May 30   Wmk. 282
B33	A62	15c + 2c olive bister & rose red	.70	.70
B34	A62	20c + 3c vio & emer	.85	.85
B35	A62	30c + 5c rose car & grnsh bl	1.25	1.25
		Nos. B33-B35 (3)	2.80	2.80

Cent. of the Intl. Red Cross idea. Surtax for the Red Cross.
The overprint includes the cross, "RED CROSS CENTENARY" and date in two languages. The surcharge includes the date in Amharic and the new surtax. The surcharge was applied locally.

Design A39 Surcharged

Perf. 11½
1960, May 7   Photo.   Unwmk.
B36	A39	5c + 1c brt green	.85	.85
B37	A39	10c + 2c brt red	1.25	1.25
B38	A39	25c + 3c brt blue	1.60	1.60
B39	A39	50c + 4c dk yel brn	2.75	2.75
B40	A39	1t + 5c brt vio	6.50	6.50
		Nos. B36-B40 (5)	12.95	12.95

25th anniversary of Ethiopian Red Cross. Forgeries exist.

Crippled Boy on Crutches — SP2

Wmk. 282
1963, July 23   Engr.   Perf. 13½
B41	SP2	10c + 2c ultra	.30	.30
B42	SP2	15c + 3c red	.55	.55
B43	SP2	50c + 5c brt green	1.10	1.10
B44	SP2	60c + 5c red lilac	2.25	2.25
		Nos. B41-B44 (4)	4.20	4.20

The surtax was to aid the disabled.

AIR POST STAMPS

Regular Issue of 1928 Handstamped in Violet, Red, Black or Green

Perf. 13½x14
1929, Aug. 17   Unwmk.
C1	A22	⅛m orange & lt bl	1.50	2.00
C2	A23	¼m ind & red org	1.50	2.00
C3	A22	½m gray grn & blk	1.50	2.75
C4	A23	1m dk car & blk	1.50	2.75
C5	A22	2m dk blue & blk	1.50	2.75
C6	A23	4m yellow & olive	1.50	2.75
C7	A22	8m violet & olive	1.50	2.75
C8	A23	1t org brn & vio	2.75	4.25
C9	A22	2t green & bister	4.25	5.25
C10	A23	3t choc & grn	4.25	5.25
		Nos. C1-C10 (10)	21.75	32.50

The overprint signifies "17 August 1929-Airplane of the Ethiopian Government." The stamps commemorate the arrival at Addis Ababa of the 1st airplane of the Ethiopian Government.
There are 3 types of the overprint: (I) 19½mm high; "colon" at right of bottom word. (II) 20mm high; same "colon." (III) 19½mm high; no "colon." Many errors exist.

Symbols of Empire, Airplane and Map — AP1

1931, June 17   Engr.   Perf. 12½
C11	AP1	1g orange red	.25	.50
C12	AP1	2g ultra	.25	.50
C13	AP1	4g violet	.25	.80
C14	AP1	8g blue green	.80	1.40
C15	AP1	1t olive brown	1.60	2.10
C16	AP1	2t carmine	2.75	8.00
C17	AP1	3t yellow green	4.00	9.00
		Nos. C11-C17 (7)	9.90	22.30

Nos. C11 to C17 exist imperforate.
Reprints of C11 to C17 exist. Paper is thinner and gum whiter than the originals and the ink is heavy and shiny. Originals have ink that is dull and granular. Reprints usually sell at about one-third of above values.

Catalogue values for unused stamps in this section, from this point to the end of the section, are for Never Hinged items.

ETHIOPIA

Nos. 250, 255 and 257 Surcharged in Black

a   b

Perf. 14x13½

1947, Mar. 20   **Unwmk.**

C18	A33 (a) 12c on 4c	77.50	77.50
C19	A33 (b) 50c on 25c	72.50	72.50
a.	"26-12-46"	275.00	
C20	A33 (b) $2 on 60c	125.00	125.00
a.	"26-12-46"	340.00	
	Nos. C18-C20 (3)	275.00	275.00
	Set, hinged	175.00	

Resumption of airmail service, 12/29/46.

Franklin D. Roosevelt — AP2

Design: $2, Haile Selassie.

Engraved and Photogravure
1947, May 23   **Perf. 12½**

C21	AP2 $1 dk purple & sepia	12.50	14.00
C22	AP2 $2 carmine & dp blue	22.50	24.00

Farmer Plowing — AP3

Designs: 10c, 25c, Zoquala, extinct volcano. 30c, 35c, Tesissat Falls, Abai River. 65c, 70c, Amba Alaguie. $1, Sacala, source of Nile. $3, Gorgora and Dembia, Lake Tana. $5, Magdala, former capital. $10, Ras Dashan, mountain peak.

Perf. 13x13½

1947-55   **Wmk. 282**   **Engr.**

C23	AP3 8c purple brown	.30	.30
C24	AP3 10c bright green	.30	.30
C25	AP3 25c dull pur ('52)	.45	.30
C26	AP3 30c orange yellow	.85	.30
C27	AP3 35c blue ('55)	.95	.45
C28	AP3 65c purple ('55)	1.10	.80
C29	AP3 70c red	1.25	.55
C30	AP3 $1 deep blue	1.60	.80
C31	AP3 $3 rose lilac	6.50	4.25
C32	AP3 $5 red brown	13.00	5.50
C33	AP3 $10 rose violet	27.50	13.50
	Nos. C23-C33 (11)	53.80	27.05

For overprints see Nos. C64-C70.

UPU Monument, Bern — AP4

1950, Apr. 3   **Unwmk.**   **Perf. 12½**

C34	AP4 5c green & red	1.00	1.00
C35	AP4 15c dk sl grn & car	1.50	1.10
C36	AP4 25c org yel & grn	2.75	1.10
C37	AP4 50c carmine & ultra	4.50	3.25
	Nos. C34-C37 (4)	9.75	5.95

75th anniv. of the UPU.
No. C34 exists in the colors of Nos. C35-C37. These are considered to be trial color proofs.

Convair Plane over Mountains AP5

Engraved and Lithographed
1955, Dec. 30   **Unwmk.**   **Perf. 12½**
Center Multicolored

C38	AP5 10c gray green	1.25	.30
C39	AP5 15c carmine	1.60	.80
C40	AP5 20c violet	2.50	1.25
	Nos. C38-C40 (3)	5.35	2.35

10th anniversary of Ethiopian Airlines.

Promulgating the Constitution — AP6

Perf. 14x13½

1956, July 16   **Engr.**   **Wmk. 282**

C41	AP6 10c redsh brn & ultra	.60	.70
C42	AP6 15c dk car rose & ol grn	.95	1.00
C43	AP6 20c blue & org red	1.25	1.00
C44	AP6 25c purple & green	1.40	1.60
C45	AP6 30c dk grn & red brn	2.40	2.50
	Nos. C41-C45 (5)	6.60	6.80

25th anniversary of the constitution.

Aksum — AP7

Ancient Capitals: 10c, Lalibela. 15c, Gondar. 20c, Mekele. 25c, Ankober.

1957, Feb. 7   **Perf. 14**
Centers in Green

C46	AP7 5c red brown	.75	.40
C47	AP7 10c rose carmine	.75	.40
C48	AP7 15c red orange	.90	.50
C49	AP7 20c ultramarine	1.40	.70
C50	AP7 25c claret	2.10	1.00
	Nos. C46-C50 (5)	5.90	3.00

Amharic "A" — AP8

Designs: Various Amharic characters and views of Addis Ababa. The characters, arranged by values, spell Addis Ababa.

1957, Feb. 14   **Engr.**
Amharic Letters in Scarlet

C51	AP8 5c ultra, *sal pink*	.35	.35
C52	AP8 10c ol grn, *pink*	.35	.35
C53	AP8 15c dl pur, *yel*	.55	.35
C54	AP8 20c grn, *buff*	.90	.40
C55	AP8 25c plum, *pale bl*	2.50	.55
C56	AP8 30c red, *pale grn*	1.75	.60
	Nos. C51-C56 (6)	6.40	2.60

70th anniversary of Addis Ababa.

Map, Rock Church at Lalibela and Obelisk — AP9

1958, Apr. 15   **Wmk. 282**   **Perf. 13½**

C57	AP9 10c green	.50	.50
C58	AP9 20c rose red	1.10	1.10
C59	AP9 30c bright blue	1.75	1.10
	Nos. C57-C59 (3)	3.35	2.70

Conf. of Independent African States, Accra, Apr. 15-22.

Map of Africa and UN Emblem — AP10

1958, Dec. 29   **Perf. 13**

C60	AP10 5c emerald	.25	.25
C61	AP10 20c carmine rose	.55	.25
C62	AP10 25c ultramarine	.75	.55
C63	AP10 50c pale purple	1.50	.75
	Nos. C60-C63 (4)	3.05	1.80

1st session of the UN Economic Conf. for Africa, opened in Addis Ababa Dec. 29.

Nos. C23-C29 Overprinted

Perf. 13x13½
1959, Aug. 16   **Engr.**   **Wmk. 282**

C64	AP3 8c purple brown	.50	.30
C65	AP3 10c brt green	.70	.35
C66	AP3 25c dull purple	1.05	.40
C67	AP3 30c orange yellow	1.15	.60
C68	AP3 35c blue	1.40	.65
C69	AP3 65c purple	2.25	1.00
C70	AP3 70c red	2.75	1.25
	Nos. C64-C70 (7)	9.80	4.55

30th anniv. of Ethiopian airmail service.

Ethiopian Soldier and Map of Congo — AP11

Perf. 11½
1962, July 23   **Unwmk.**   **Photo.**
Granite Paper

C71	AP11 15c org, bl, brn & grn	.30	.25
C72	AP11 50c pur, bl, brn & grn	.90	.50
C73	AP11 60c red, bl, brn & grn	1.60	.65
	Nos. C71-C73 (3)	2.80	1.40

2nd anniv. of the Ethiopian contingent of the UN forces in the Congo and in honor of the 70th birthday of Emperor Haile Selassie.

Globo with Map of Africa — AP12

1963, May 22   **Granite Paper**

C74	AP12 10c magenta & blk	.60	.30
C75	AP12 40c emerald & blk	1.10	.55
C76	AP12 60c blue & blk	1.75	.85
	Nos. C74-C76 (3)	3.45	1.70

Conf. of African heads of state for African Unity, Addis Ababa.

Bird Type of Regular Issue

Birds: 10c, Black-headed forest oriole. 15c, Broad-tailed paradise whydah, vert. 20c, Lammergeier, vert. 50c, White-checked touraco. 80c, Purple indigo bird.

1963, Sept. 12   **Perf. 11½**
Granite Paper

C77	A74 10c multicolored	.75	.25
C78	A74 15c multicolored	.90	.25
C79	A74 20c blue, blk & ocher	1.75	.60
C80	A74 50c lemon & multi	2.60	1.10
C81	A74 80c ultra, blk & brn	5.00	1.90
	Nos. C77-C81 (5)	11.00	4.10

Swimming AP13

Sport: 10c, Basketball, vert. 15c, Javelin. 80c, Soccer game in stadium.

Perf. 14x13½
1964, Sept. 15   **Litho.**   **Unwmk.**

C82	AP13 5c multicolored	.30	.25
C83	AP13 10c multicolored	.40	.25
C84	AP13 15c multicolored	.85	.55
C85	AP13 80c multicolored	2.25	1.10
	Nos. C82-C85 (4)	3.80	2.15

18th Olympic Games, Tokyo, Oct. 10-25.

Queen Elizabeth II and Emperor Haile Selassie AP14

1965, Feb. 1   **Photo.**   **Perf. 11½**
Granite Paper

C86	AP14 5c multicolored	.30	.30
C87	AP14 35c multicolored	.85	.55
C88	AP14 60c multicolored	1.10	.85
	Nos. C86-C88 (3)	2.25	1.70

Visit of Queen Elizabeth II, Feb. 1-8.

Koka Dam and Power Plant — AP15

Designs: 15c, Sugar cane field. 50c, Blue Nile Bridge. 60c, Gondar castles. 80c, Coffee tree. $1, Cattle at water hole. $3, Camels at well. $5, Ethiopian Air Lines jet plane.

1965, July 19   **Unwmk.**   **Perf. 11½**
Granite Paper
Portrait in Black

C89	AP15 15c vio brn & buff	.30	.30
C90	AP15 40c vio bl & lt bl	.50	.40
C91	AP15 50c grn & lt bl	.80	.45
C92	AP15 60c claret & yel	1.30	.70
C93	AP15 80c grn, yel & red	1.75	.80
C94	AP15 $1 brn & lt bl	1.90	.95
C95	AP15 $3 claret & pink	6.50	2.40
C96	AP15 $5 ultra & lt bl	14.00	4.50
	Nos. C89-C96 (8)	27.05	10.50

Bird Type of Regular Issue

Birds: 10c, White-collared kingfisher. 15c, Blue-breasted bee-eater. 25c, African paradise flycatcher. 40c, Village weaver. 60c, White-collared pigeon.

1966, Feb. 15   **Photo.**   **Perf. 11½**
Granite Paper

C97	A74 10c dull yel & multi	.85	.25
C98	A74 15c lt blue & multi	.85	.25
C99	A74 25c gray & multi	1.75	.55
C100	A74 40c pink & multi	3.50	.85
C101	A74 60c multicolored	4.50	1.10
	Nos. C97-C101 (5)	11.45	3.00

Black Rhinoceros AP16

Animals: 10c, Leopard. 20c, Black-and-white colobus (monkey). 30c, Mountain nyala. 80c, Nubian Ibex.

1966, June 20   **Litho.**   **Perf. 13**

C102	AP16 5c dp grn, blk & gray	.55	.30
C103	AP16 10c grn, blk & ocher	.55	.55
C104	AP16 20c cit, blk & grn	1.10	.55
C105	AP16 30c yel grn, blk & ocher	1.75	.85
C106	AP16 60c yel grn, blk & dk brn	4.50	1.00
	Nos. C102-C106 (5)	8.45	3.85

Bird Type of Regular Issue

Birds: 10c, Blue-winged goose, vert. 15c, Yellow-billed duck. 20c, Wattled ibis. 25c, Striped swallow. 40c, Black-winged lovebird, vert.

1967, Sept. 29   **Photo.**   **Perf. 11½**
Granite Paper

C107	A74 10c lt ultra & multi	.55	.25
C108	A74 15c green & multi	.85	.25
C109	A74 20c yellow & multi	1.10	.55
C110	A74 25c salmon & multi	2.25	.55
C111	A74 40c pink & multi	4.50	1.10
	Nos. C107-C111 (5)	9.25	2.70

ETHIOPIA — FALKLAND ISLANDS

SPECIAL DELIVERY STAMPS

Catalogue values for unused stamps in this section are for Never Hinged items.

Motorcycle Messenger SD1

Addis Ababa Post Office — SD2

			Unwmk.	Engr.	Perf. 13
1947, Apr. 24					
E1	SD1	30c orange brown		5.00	1.25
E2	SD2	50c blue		9.00	3.50

1954-62			Wmk. 282		
E3	SD1	30c org brown ('62)		4.50	1.25
E4	SD2	50c blue		5.50	1.45

POSTAGE DUE STAMPS

Very Fine examples of Nos. J1-J42 will have perforations touching the design on one or more sides.

Nos. 1-4 and unissued values Overprinted

Perf. 14x13½

1896, June 10   Unwmk.

Black Overprint
J1	A1	¼g green	1.45
J2	A1	½g red	1.45
J3	A1	4g lilac brown	1.00
a.	Without overprint		1.00
J4	A1	8g violet	1.00
a.	Without overprint		1.00

Red Overprint
J5	A1	1g blue	1.45
J6	A1	2g dark brown	1.45
J7	A1	16g black	1.00
a.	Without overprint		1.00
	Nos. J1-J7 (7)		8.80

Nos. J1-J7 were not issued. Forgeries exist.

Nos. 1-7 Handstamped in Various Colors

a

1905, Apr.
J8	A1 (a)	¼g green	55.00	55.00
J9	A1 (a)	½g red	55.00	55.00
J10	A1 (a)	1g blue	55.00	55.00
J11	A1 (a)	2g dk brown	55.00	55.00
J12	A2 (a)	4g lilac brown	55.00	55.00
J13	A2 (a)	8g violet	55.00	55.00
J14	A2 (a)	16g black	55.00	55.00
	Nos. J8-J14 (7)		385.00	385.00

b

1905, Aug.
J15	A1 (b)	¼g green	55.00	55.00
J16	A1 (b)	½g red	55.00	55.00
J17	A1 (b)	1g blue	55.00	55.00
J18	A1 (b)	2g dark brown	55.00	55.00
J19	A2 (b)	4g lilac brown	55.00	55.00
J20	A2 (b)	8g violet	55.00	55.00
J21	A2 (b)	16g black	55.00	55.00
	Nos. J15-J21 (7)		385.00	385.00

Excellent forgeries of Nos. J8-J42 exist.

Nos. 1-7 Handstamped in Blue or Violet

1905, Sept.
J22	A1	¼g green	14.50	14.50
J23	A1	½g red	14.50	14.50
J24	A1	1g blue	14.50	14.50
J25	A1	2g dark brown	14.50	14.50
J26	A2	4g lilac brown	14.50	14.50
J27	A2	8g violet	21.00	21.00
J28	A2	16g black	25.00	25.00
	Nos. J22-J28 (7)		118.50	118.50

Nos. J22-J27 exist with inverted overprint, also No. J22 with double overprint. Forgeries exist.

With Additional Surcharge of Value Handstamped as on Nos. 71-77

1907, July 1
J29	A1 (e)	¼ on ¼g grn	14.00	14.00
J30	A1 (e)	½ on ½g red	14.00	14.00
J31	A1 (f)	1 on 1g blue	14.00	14.00
J32	A1 (f)	2 on 2g dk brown	14.00	14.00
J33	A2 (f)	4 on 4g lilac brn	14.00	14.00
J34	A2 (f)	8 on 8g violet	14.00	14.00
J35	A2 (f)	16 on 16g blk	22.50	22.50
	Nos. J29-J35 (7)		106.50	106.50

Nos. J30-J35 exist with inverted surcharge. Nos. J30, J33-J35 exist with double surcharge.

Nos. 1-7 Handstamped in Black

1908, Dec. 1
J36	A1	¼g green	1.40	1.25
J37	A1	½g red	1.40	1.25
J38	A1	1g blue	1.40	1.25
J39	A1	2g dark brown	1.75	1.50
J40	A2	4g lilac brown	2.50	2.50
J41	A2	8g violet	5.50	6.25
J42	A2	16g black	17.50	20.00
	Nos. J36-J42 (7)		31.45	34.00

Nos. J36 to J42 exist with inverted overprint and Nos. J36, J37, J38 and J40 with double overprint. Forgeries of Nos. J36-J56 exist.

Same Handstamp on Nos. 87-93

1912, Dec. 1   Perf. 11½
| J43 | A3 | ¼g blue green | 1.75 | 1.25 |
| J44 | A3 | ½g rose | 1.75 | 1.50 |

1913, July 1
J45	A3	1g green & org	6.00	4.25
J46	A4	2g blue	7.00	6.00
J47	A4	4g green & car	11.00	7.00
J48	A5	8g ver & dp grn	14.00	11.00
J49	A5	16g ver & car	35.00	27.50
	Nos. J43-J49 (7)		76.50	58.50

Nos. J43-J49, all exist with inverted, double and double, one inverted overprint.

Same Handstamp on Nos. 120-124 in Blue Black

1925-27   Perf. 11½
J50	A6	⅛g violet & brn	18.00	18.00
J51	A6	¼g bl grn & db	18.00	18.00
J52	A6	½g scar & ol grn	20.00	20.00
J53	A9	1g rose lil & gray grn	20.00	20.00
J54	A9	2g dp ultra & fawn	20.00	20.00
	Nos. J50-J54 (5)		96.00	96.00

Same Handstamp on Nos. 110, 112

1917 (?)
| J55 | A3 (i) | 1g green & org | 30.00 | 30.00 |
| J56 | A4 (j) | 2g blue | 30.00 | 30.00 |

The status of Nos. J55-J56 is questioned.

Catalogue values for unused stamps in this section, from this point to the end of the section, are for Never Hinged items.

D2

Perf. 11½

1951, Apr. 2   Unwmk.   Litho.
J57	D2	1c emerald	.35	.25
J58	D2	5c rose red	.75	.25
J59	D2	10c violet	1.40	.55
J60	D2	20c ocher	2.00	1.25
J61	D2	50c bright ultra	3.75	2.75
J62	D2	$1 rose lilac	7.75	3.75
	Nos. J57-J62 (6)		16.00	8.80

Nos. J57-J62 were reissued in 1968 on slightly yellowish paper.

OCCUPATION STAMPS

Issued under Italian Occupation

100 Centesimi = 1 Lira

OS1

Emperor Victor Emmanuel III — OS2

1936   Wmk. 140   Perf. 14
N1	OS1	10c org brn	16.00	9.50
N2	OS1	20c purple	14.50	4.00
N3	OS2	25c dark green	9.50	.80
N4	OS2	30c dark brown	9.50	1.60
N5	OS2	50c rose car	4.00	.40
N6	OS1	75c deep orange	36.00	8.00
N7	OS1	1.25 l deep blue	36.00	12.00
	Nos. N1-N7 (7)		125.50	36.30
	Set, never hinged		300.00	

Issued: Nos. N3-N5, May 22; others Dec. 5. For later issues see Italian East Africa.

FALKLAND ISLANDS

ˈfȯl-klənd ˈī-lənds

LOCATION — A group of islands about 300 miles east of the Straits of Magellan at the southern limit of South America
GOVT. — British Crown Colony
AREA — 4,700 sq. mi.
POP. — 3,032 (2016)
CAPITAL — Stanley

Dependencies of the Falklands are South Georgia and South Sandwich. In March 1962, three other dependencies — South Shetland Islands, South Orkneys and Graham Land — became the new separate colony of British Antarctic Territory. In 1985 South Georgia and the South Sandwich Islands became a separate colony.

12 Pence = 1 Shilling
20 Shillings = 1 Pound
100 Pence = 1 Pound (1971)

Catalogue values for unused stamps in this country are for Never Hinged items, beginning with Scott 97 in the regular postage section, Scott B1 in the semi-postal section, Scott J1 in the postage due section, Scott 1L1 in Falkland Island Dependencies regular issues, Scott 1LB1 in Falkland Island Dependencies semi-postals, and Scott 2L1, 3L1, 4L1, 5L1 in the Issues for Separate Islands.

Values for unused stamps are for examples with original gum as defined in the catalogue introduction. Nos. 1-4, 7-8, and some printings of Nos. 5-6, exist with straight edges on one or two sides, being the imperforate margins of the sheets. This occurs in 24 out of 60 stamps. Catalogue values are for stamps with perforations on all sides.

Queen Victoria — A1

1878-79   Unwmk.   Engr.   Perf. 14
1	A1	1p claret	850.00	500.00
2	A1	4p dark gray ('79)	1,400.	200.00
3	A1	6p green	125.00	85.00
4	A1	1sh bister brown	85.00	80.00

1883-95   Wmk. 2
5	A1	1p brt claret ('94)	130.00	95.00
a.		1p claret	425.00	190.00
b.		Horiz. pair, imperf. vert.	90.000.	
c.		1p red brown ('91)	375.00	95.00
d.		Diag. half of #5c used as ½p on cover		4,600.
6	A1	4p ol gray ('95)	16.00	27.50
a.		4p gray black	875.00	100.00
b.		4p olive gray black ('89)	200.00	65.00
c.		4p brownish black ('94)	1,300.	400.00

No. 6c has watermark reversed.
For surcharge see No. 19E.

1886   Wmk. 2 Sideways
7	A1	1p claret	95.00	65.00
a.		1p brownish claret	125.00	80.00
b.		Diagonal half of #7a used as ½p on cover		4,250.
8	A1	4p olive gray	525.00	60.00
a.		4p pale gray black	850.00	90.00

For surcharge see No. 19.

1891-1902   Wmk. 2
9	A1	½p green ('92)	19.00	18.00
a.		½p blue green	30.00	29.00
10	A1	½p yel green ('99)	3.75	3.50
11	A1	1p orange brown	130.00	85.00
a.		Diagonal half used as ½p on cover		4,250.
11B	A1	1p pale red ('99)	9.00	3.50
12	A1	1p org red ('02)	17.50	4.75
a.		1p Venetian red ('95)	32.50	20.00
13	A1	2p magenta ('96)	7.00	14.00
14	A1	2½p deep blue ('94)	275.00	160.00
15	A1	2½p ultra ('94)	50.00	14.00
a.		2½p pale ultra ('98)	70.00	20.00
b.		2½p dull blue	350.00	95.00
c.		2½p deep ultra ('01)	50.00	42.50
d.		2½p pale chalky ultra	275.00	60.00
16	A1	6p yellow ('96)	55.00	52.50
a.		6p orange ('92)	325.00	225.00
17	A1	9p ver ('95)	60.00	60.00
a.		9p salmon ('96)	65.00	65.00
18	A1	1sh gray brn ('95)	80.00	65.00
a.		1sh bis brn ('96)	75.00	65.00
	Nos. 9-18 (11)		706.25	480.25

Nos. 7 and 5a Surcharged in Black

1891   Wmk. 2 Sideways
| 19 | A1 | ½p on half of 1p, #7 | 725.00 | 360.00 |
| d. | | Unsevered pair | 4,000. | 1,600. |

Wmk. 2
| 19E | A1 | ½p on half of 1p, #5a | 825.00 | 325.00 |
| f. | | Unsevered pair | | 1,800. |

Genuine used bisects should be canceled with a segmented circular cork cancel. Any other cancel must be linked by date to known mail ship departures. This surcharge exists on "souvenir" bisects, including examples of No. 11, and can be found inverted, double and sideways.

A3

A4

1898   Wmk. 1
| 20 | A3 | 2sh6p dark blue | 290.00 | 290.00 |
| 21 | A4 | 5sh brown red | 260.00 | 260.00 |

A5

A6

FALKLAND ISLANDS

King Edward VII
1904-07   **Wmk. 3**   **Perf. 14**

22	A5	½p yellow green	9.00	1.75
23	A5	1p red, wmk. sideways ('07)	1.50	4.50
a.		Wmk. upright ('04)	17.00	1.75
24	A5	2p dull vio ('04)	25.00	24.00
25	A5	2½p ultramarine	35.00	10.00
a.		2½p deep blue	300.00	200.00
26	A5	6p orange ('05)	50.00	57.50
27	A5	1sh bis brn ('05)	50.00	40.00
28	A6	3sh gray green	180.00	160.00
29	A6	5sh dull red ('05)	240.00	160.00
		Nos. 22-29 (8)	590.50	457.75

 A7   A8

King George V
1912-14   **Perf. 13¾x14, 14 (#36-40)**

30	A7	½p yel grn	3.00	3.75
31	A7	1p red	5.50	2.75
32	A7	2p brn vio	30.00	24.00
33	A7	2½p deep ultra	27.50	25.00
34	A7	6p orange	17.50	22.50
35	A7	1sh bis brn	40.00	37.50
36	A8	3sh dark green	100.00	100.00
37	A8	5sh brown red	120.00	120.00
38	A8	5sh plum ('14)	300.00	300.00
39	A8	10sh red, green	200.00	275.00
40	A8	£1 black, red	550.00	600.00
		Nos. 30-40 (11)	1,394.	1,511.

For overprints see Nos. MR1-MR3.

1921-29   **Wmk. 4**   **Perf. 14**

41	A7	½p yellow green	3.50	4.50
42	A7	1p red ('24)	6.00	2.10
43	A7	2p brown vio ('23)	26.00	8.50
44	A7	2½p dark blue	24.00	20.00
a.		2½p Prussian blue ('29)	375.00	550.00
45	A7	2½p vio, yel ('23)	6.00	42.50
46	A7	6p orange ('25)	11.00	45.00
47	A7	1sh bister brown	24.00	57.50
48	A8	3sh dk green ('23)	100.00	190.00
		Nos. 41-48 (8)	200.50	370.10

Some specialists call into question No. 44a. The editors would like to see authenticated evidence of its existence.

No. 43 Surcharged

1928

52	A7	2½p on 2p brn vio	1,300.	1,400.
a.		Double surcharge	60,000.	

Beware of forged surcharges.

King George V — A9

1929-31   **Perf. 14**

54	A9	½p green	1.40	4.25
55	A9	1p scarlet	4.50	.90
56	A9	2p gray	6.00	3.75
57	A9	2½p blue	6.00	2.50
58	A9	4p deep orange	23.00	15.00
59	A9	6p brown violet	24.00	19.00
60	A9	1sh black, green	32.50	37.50
a.		1sh black, emerald	27.50	37.50
61	A9	2sh6p red, blue	70.00	70.00
62	A9	5sh green, yel	105.00	120.00
63	A9	10sh red, green	225.00	250.00

Wmk. 3

64	A9	£1 black, red	350.00	425.00
		Nos. 54-64 (11)	847.40	972.90

Issue dates: 4p, 1931, others, Sept. 2.

Romney Marsh Ram — A10

 Iceberg — A11

 Whaling Ship — A12

 Port Louis — A13

 Map of the Islands — A14

 South Georgia — A15

 Blue Whale — A16

 Government House A17

 Battle Memorial A18

 King Penguin A19

Coat of Arms A20

1933, Jan. 2   **Wmk. 4**   **Perf. 12**

65	A10	½p grn & blk	4.00	13.00
66	A11	1p dl red & blk	3.75	2.75
67	A12	1½p lt bl & blk	£1.00	£7.50
68	A13	2p ol brn & blk	17.50	32.50
69	A14	3p dl vio & blk	20.00	65.00
70	A15	4p org & blk	26.00	28.00
71	A16	6p gray & blk	75.00	95.00
72	A17	1sh ol grn & blk	75.00	100.00
73	A18	2sh6p dp vio & blk	250.00	400.00
74	A19	5sh yel & blk	950.00	1,500.
a.		5sh yel org & blk	3,250.	3,750.
75	A20	10sh lt brn & blk	850.00	1,500.
76	A21	£1 rose & blk	2,500.	3,500.
		Nos. 65-76 (12)	4,800.	7,224.

Cent. of the permanent occupation of the islands as a British colony.

Common Design Types
pictured following the introduction.

Silver Jubilee Issue
Common Design Type

1935, May 7   **Perf. 11x12**

77	CD301	1p car & blue	3.50	.50
78	CD301	2½p ultra & brn	12.50	2.25
79	CD301	4p indigo & grn	24.00	8.00
80	CD301	1sh brn vio & ind	15.00	4.00
		Nos. 77-80 (4)	55.00	14.75
		Set, never hinged	75.00	
		Set (4), Ovptd. "SPECIMEN"	500.00	

Coronation Issue
Common Design Type

1937, May 12   **Perf. 11x11½**

81	CD302	½p deep green	.25	.25
82	CD302	1p dark carmine	.75	.55
83	CD302	2½p deep ultra	1.90	1.50
		Nos. 81-83 (3)	2.90	2.30
		Set, never hinged	4.00	
		Set (3), Ovptd. "SPECIMEN"	450.00	

Whale Jawbones (Centennial Monument) A22

Nos. 85, 86A, Black-necked swan. Nos. 85B, 86, Battle memorial. 2½p, 3p, Flock of sheep. 4p, Upland goose. 6p, R.R.S. "Discovery II." 9p, R.R.S. "William Scoresby." 1sh, Mt. Sugar Top. 1sh3p, Turkey vultures. 2sh6p, Gentoo penguins. 5sh, Sea lions. 10sh, Deception Island. £1, Arms of Colony.

1938-46   **Perf. 12**

84	A22	½p green & blk	.25	.75
85	A22	1p red & black	2.50	1.00
a.		1p rose carmine & black	22.50	1.00
85B	A22	1p dk vio & blk ('41)	2.00	2.00
86	A22	2p dk vio & blk	1.30	1.00
86A	A22	2p rose car & black ('41)	1.40	4.50
87	A22	2½p ultra & blk	1.00	.50
87A	A22	3p blue & blk ('41)	5.50	8.50
c.		3p dp blue & blk	12.50	4.50
88	A22	4p rose vio & black	2.75	2.00
89	A22	6p sepia & blk	7.50	4.25
90	A22	9p ol bl & blk	15.00	10.00
91	A22	1sh lt dl blue	30.00	19.00
92	A22	1sh3p car & blk	2.00	1.60
93	A22	2sh6p gray black	40.00	22.50
94	A22	5sh org brn & ultra	75.00	95.00
a.		5sh yel brown & indigo	650.00	150.00
95	A22	10sh org & blk	100.00	65.00
96	A22	£1 dk vio & blk	75.00	75.00
		Nos. 84-96 (16)	361.20	308.60
		Set, never hinged	600.00	
		Set (16), perf. "SPECIMEN"	2,500.	

Issued: Nos. 85B, 86A, 3p, 7/14/41; 1sh3p, 12/10/46; No. 94a, 1942; others, 1/3/38.

See Nos. 101-102. For overprints see Nos. 2L1-2L8, 3L1-3L8, 4L1-4L8.

Catalogue values for unused stamps in this section, from this point to the end of the section, are for Never Hinged items.

Peace Issue
Common Design Type

Perf. 13½x14

1946, Oct. 7   **Engr.**   **Wmk. 4**

97	CD303	1p purple	.35	.80
98	CD303	3p deep blue	.55	.55

Silver Wedding Issue
Common Design Types

1948, Nov. 1   **Photo.**   **Perf. 14x14½**

99	CD304	2½p bright ultra	2.10	1.10

Engr.; Name Typo.   **Perf. 11½x11**

100	CD305	£1 purple	110.00	75.00

Types of 1938-46

2½p, Upland goose. 6p, R.R.S. "Discovery II."

Perf. 12

1949, June 15   **Engr.**   **Wmk. 4**

101	A22	2½p dp blue & black	7.50	8.50
102	A22	6p gray black	6.75	5.50

UPU Issue
Common Design Types

Engr.; Name Typo. on 3p, 1sh3p

1949, Oct. 10   **Perf. 13½, 11x11½**

103	CD306	1p violet	1.75	1.10
104	CD307	3p indigo	5.00	5.00
105	CD308	1sh3p green	3.50	2.50
106	CD309	2sh blue	3.75	8.50
		Nos. 103-106 (4)	14.00	17.10

Sheep A35   Arms of the Colony A36

Designs: 1p, R.M.S. Fitzroy. 2p Upland goose. 2½p, Map. 4p, Auster plane. 6p, M.S.S. John Biscoe. 9p, "Two Sisters" peaks. 1sh, Gentoo penguins. 1sh 3p, Kelp goose and gander. 2sh 6p, Sheep shearing. 5sh, Battle memorial. 10sh, Sea lion and clapmatch. £1, Hulk of "Great Britain."

Perf. 13½x13, 13x13½

1952, Jan. 2   **Engr.**   **Wmk. 4**

107	A35	½p green	1.25	1.00
108	A35	1p red	2.40	.55
109	A35	2p violet	4.50	3.00
110	A35	2½p ultra & blk	2.00	.70
111	A36	3p deep ultra	2.25	1.10
112	A35	4p claret	12.50	1.75
113	A35	6p yellow brn	12.00	1.10
114	A35	9p orange yel	9.00	2.25
115	A36	1sh black	24.00	1.10
116	A36	1sh3p red orange	18.00	7.00
117	A36	2sh6p olive	22.50	12.50
118	A36	5sh red violet	20.00	11.00
119	A35	10sh gray	30.00	20.00
120	A35	£1 black	40.00	27.00
		Nos. 107-120 (14)	200.40	90.05

FALKLAND ISLANDS

Coronation Issue
Common Design Type
1953, June 4   **Perf. 13½x13**
121   CD312   1p car & black   .90   1.50

Types of 1952 with Portrait of Queen Elizabeth II
1955-57   **Perf. 13½x13, 13x13½**
122	A35	½p green ('57)	1.00	1.50
123	A35	1p red ('57)	1.25	1.25
124	A35	2p violet ('56)	3.25	4.75
125	A35	6p light brown	9.00	.70
126	A35	9p ocher ('57)	10.50	17.00
127	A36	1sh black	12.00	2.50
		Nos. 122-127 (6)	37.00	27.70

Marsh Starling — A37

Birds: ½p, Falkland Islands Thrush. 1p, Dominican gull. 2p, Gentoo penguins. 3p, Upland geese. 4p, Steamer ducks. 5½p, Rock-hopper penguin. 6p, Black-browed albatross. 9p, Silver grebe. 1sh, Pied oystercatchers. 1sh3p, Yellow-billed teal. 2sh, Kelp geese, 5sh, King shag. 10sh, Guadelupe caracara. £1, Black-necked swan.

Perf. 13½x13
1960, Feb. 10   **Engr.**   **Wmk. 314**
Center in Black
128	A37	½p green	5.00	2.25
a.		Wmk. sideways ('66)	.45	.40
129	A37	1p rose red	3.00	2.00
130	A37	2p blue	4.50	1.25
131	A37	2½p bister brn	2.50	1.00
132	A37	3p olive	1.25	.50
133	A37	4p rose car	1.50	1.25
134	A37	5½p violet	3.25	2.50
135	A37	6p sepia	3.50	.30
136	A37	9p orange	2.50	1.25
137	A37	1sh dull purple	1.25	.40
138	A37	1sh3p ultra	12.50	14.00
139	A37	2sh brown car	30.00	2.50
140	A37	5sh grnsh blue	27.50	11.00
141	A37	10sh rose lilac	42.60	22.00
142	A37	£1 yellow org	45.00	27.00
		Nos. 128-142 (15)	185.85	89.20

Morse Key — A38

1962, Oct. 5   **Photo.**   **Perf. 11½x11**
143	A38	6p dp org & dk red	.85	.50
144	A38	1sh brt ol grn & dp green	.95	.50
145	A38	2sh brt ultra & violet	1.25	1.75
		Nos. 143-145 (3)	3.05	2.75

Falkland Islands radio station, 50th anniv.

Freedom from Hunger Issue
Common Design Type
1963, June 4   **Perf. 14x14½**
146   CD314   1sh ultramarine   10.50   2.50

Red Cross Centenary Issue
Common Design Type
     Wmk. 314
1963, Sept.2   **Litho.**   **Perf. 13**
147	CD315	1p black & red	2.00	.75
148	CD315	1sh ultra & red	16.00	4.75

Shakespeare Issue
Common Design Type
1964, Apr. 23   **Photo.**   **Perf. 14x14½**
149   CD316   6p black   1.60   .50

H.M.S. Glasgow — A39

6p, H.M.S. Kent. 1sh, H.M.S. Invincible. 2sh, Falkland Islands Battle Memorial, vert.

1964, Dec. 8   **Engr.**   **Perf. 13**
150	A39	2½p ver & black	9.00	3.75
151	A39	6p blue & black	.55	.30
a.		"Glasgow" vignette	30,000.	
152	A39	1sh carmine & blk	.55	1.00

Perf. 13x14
153   A39   2sh dk blue & blk   .55   .75
     Nos. 150-153 (4)   10.65   5.80

Battle of the Falkland Islands between the British and German navies, 50th anniv.

ITU Issue
Common Design Type
     Perf. 11x11½
1965, May 26   **Litho.**   **Wmk. 314**
154	CD317	1p blue & dl dk bl	.50	.40
155	CD317	2sh lilac & dl yel	6.25	2.75

Intl. Cooperation Year Issue
Common Design Type
1965, Oct. 25   **Perf. 14½**
156	CD318	1p blue grn & claret	1.25	.40
157	CD318	1sh lt violet & grn	4.75	1.25

Churchill Memorial Issue
Common Design Type
1966, Jan. 24   **Photo.**   **Perf. 14**
Design in Black, Gold and Carmine Rose
158	CD319	½p bright blue	.75	2.25
159	CD319	1p green	2.00	.30
160	CD319	1sh brown	5.50	3.00
161	CD319	2sh violet	4.50	4.00
		Nos. 158-161 (4)	12.75	9.55

Human Rights Flame and Globe — A40

Perf. 14x14½
1968, July 4   **Photo.**   **Wmk. 314**
162	A40	2p brt rose & multi	.40	.25
163	A40	6p brt green & multi	.45	.25
164	A40	1sh orange & multi	.55	.30
165	A40	2sh ultra & multi	.65	.35
		Nos. 162-165 (4)	2.05	1.15

International Human Rights Year.

Dusty Miller — A41

Falkland Islands flora: 1½p, Pig vine, horiz. 2p, Pale maiden. 3p, Dog orchid. 3½p, Sea cabbage, horiz. 4½p, Vanilla daisy. 5½p, Arrowleaf marigold, horiz. 6p, Diddle-dee, horiz. 1sh, Scurvy grass, horiz. 1sh6p, Prickly burr. 2sh, Fachine. 3sh, Lavender. 5sh, Felton's flower, horiz. £1, Yellow orchid.

1968, Oct. 9   **Photo.**   **Perf. 14**
166	A41	½p multicolored	.25	1.75
167	A41	1½p multicolored	.45	.25
168	A41	2p multicolored	.60	.25
169	A41	3p multicolored	6.00	1.00
170	A41	3½p multicolored	.35	1.00
171	A41	4½p multicolored	1.60	2.00
172	A41	5½p multicolored	1.60	2.00
173	A41	6p multicolored	.85	.30
174	A41	1sh multicolored	1.00	1.50
175	A41	1sh6p multicolored	5.00	15.00
176	A41	2sh multicolored	5.50	6.25
177	A41	3sh multicolored	7.75	8.00
178	A41	5sh multicolored	27.00	13.00
179	A41	£1 multicolored	11.50	3.25
		Nos. 166-179 (14)	69.45	55.55

See Nos. 210-222. For surcharges see Nos. 197-209.

Beaver DHC 2 Seaplane — A42

Designs: 6p, Norseman seaplane. 1sh, Auster plane. 2sh, Falkland Islands arms.

1969, Apr. 8   **Litho.**   **Perf. 14**
180	A42	2p multicolored	.45	.30
181	A42	6p multicolored	.65	.35
182	A42	1sh multicolored	.65	.40
183	A42	2sh multicolored	1.20	2.00
		Nos. 180-183 (4)	2.95	3.05

21st anniv. of Government Air Service.

Bishop Stirling — A43

2p, Holy Trinity Church, 1869. 6p, Christ Church Cathedral, 1969. 2sh, Bishop's miter.

1969, Oct. 30   **Perf. 14**
184	A43	2p emerald & black	.40	.60
185	A43	6p red orange & black	.50	.60
186	A43	1sh lilac & black	.50	.60
187	A43	2sh yellow & multi	.60	.75
		Nos. 184-187 (4)	2.00	2.55

Consecration of Waite Hocking Stirling (1829-1923), as first Bishop of the Bishopric of the Falkland Islands, cent.

Gun Emplacement A44

2p, Volunteer on horseback, vert. 1sh, Volunteer in dress uniform, vert. 2sh, Defense Force badge.

     Perf. 13½x13, 13x13½
1970, Apr. 30   **Litho.**   **Wmk. 314**
188	A44	2p ultra & multi	1.15	.70
189	A44	6p multicolored	1.40	.80
190	A44	1sh buff & multi	2.25	.80
191	A44	2sh yellow & multi	3.25	1.00
		Nos. 188-191 (4)	8.05	3.30

Falkland Islands Defense Force, 50th anniv.

The Great Britain, 1843 — A45

The Great Britain in: 4p, 1845. 9p, 1876. 1sh, 1886. 2sh, 1970.

1970, Oct. 30   **Litho.**   **Perf. 14½**
192	A45	2p lemon & multi	1.00	.50
193	A45	4p lilac & multi	1.25	.90
194	A45	9p bister & multi	1.50	.90
195	A45	1sh org brn & multi	1.50	.90
196	A45	2sh multicolored	2.00	1.10
		Nos. 192-196 (5)	7.25	4.30

Nos. 166-178 Surcharged

1971, Feb. 15   **Photo.**   **Perf. 14**
197	A41	½p on ½p multi	.40	.40
198	A41	1p on 1½p multi	.25	.25
a.		5p on 1½p (error)	750.00	
199	A41	1½p on 2p multi	.35	.35
200	A41	2p on 3p multi	.55	.55
201	A41	2½p on 3½p multi	.30	.30
202	A41	3p on 4½p multi	.35	.35
203	A41	4p on 5½p multi	.40	.40
204	A41	5p on 6p multi	.70	.70
205	A41	6p on 1sh multi	6.00	7.00
206	A41	7½p on 1sh6p multi	8.00	8.00
207	A41	10p on 2sh multi	8.00	3.50
208	A41	15p on 3sh multi	3.50	2.75
209	A41	25p on 5sh multi	4.50	3.75
		Nos. 197-209 (13)	33.30	28.30

Flower Type of 1968
"p" instead of "d"

Designs as before. 1p, 2½p, 4p, 5p, 6p, 25p, horizontal.

Wmk. 314, Sideways on Vert. Stamps
1972, June 1   **Perf. 14**
210	A41	½p Dusty miller	.75	4.75
a.		Wmk. upright ('74)	15.00	32.50
b.		Wmk. 373 ('75)	3.25	3.50
211	A41	1p Pig vine	.40	.40
212	A41	1½p Pale maiden	.55	4.50
213	A41	2p Dog orchid	6.00	1.50
a.		Wmk. upright ('74)	30.00	3.25
214	A41	2½p Sea cabbage	.70	4.50
215	A41	3p Vanilla daisy	.75	1.40
216	A41	4p Arrowleaf marigold	1.00	1.10
217	A41	5p Diddle-dee	1.10	.75

218	A41	6p Scurvy grass	18.00	9.50
a.		Wmk. sideways ('74)	2.10	2.50
219	A41	7½p Prickly burr	2.00	3.75
220	A41	10p Fachine	10.00	4.00
221	A41	15p Lavender	4.00	4.50
222	A41	25p Felton's flower	8.00	6.00
		Nos. 210-222 (13)	53.25	46.65

Silver Wedding Issue, 1972
Common Design Type

Design: Queen Elizabeth II, Prince Philip, Romney Marsh sheep and giant sea lions.

1972, Nov 20   **Photo.**   **Perf. 14x14½**
223	CD324	1p sl grn & multi	.30	.30
224	CD324	10p ultra & multi	.70	.85

Princess Anne's Wedding Issue
Common Design Type
1973, Nov. 14   **Litho.**   **Perf. 14**
225	CD325	5p lilac & multi	.25	.25
226	CD325	15p citron & multi	.45	.35

Fur Seals — A46

Tourist Publicity: 4p, Trout fishing. 5p, Rockhopper penguins. 15p, Military starling.

1974, Mar. 6   **Litho.**   **Wmk. 314**
227	A46	2p lt ultra & multi	2.25	2.00
228	A46	4p brt blue & multi	3.25	1.50
229	A46	5p yellow & multi	10.50	2.50
230	A46	15p lt ultra & multi	12.00	5.00
		Nos. 227-230 (4)	28.00	11.00

Early 19th Cent. Mail Coach, UPU Emblem — A47

UPU Cent.: 5p, Packet, 1841. 8p, First British mail planes, 1911. 16p, Catapult mail, 1920's.

1974, July 31   **Perf. 14**
231	A47	2p multicolored	.25	.25
232	A47	5p multicolored	.30	.45
233	A47	8p multicolored	.35	.55
234	A47	16p multicolored	.55	.75
		Nos. 231-234 (4)	1.45	2.00

Churchill, Parliament and Big Ben — A48

Design: 20p, Churchill and warships.

1974, Nov. 30   **Perf. 13x13½**
235	A48	16p multicolored	1.00	1.00
236	A48	20p multicolored	1.50	1.50
a.		Souvenir sheet of 2, #235-236	8.00	8.00

Sir Winston Churchill (1874-1965).

HMS Exeter — A49

Battleships: 6p, HMNZS Achilles. 8p, Admiral Graf Spee. 16p, HMS Ajax.

1974, Dec. 13   **Perf. 14**
237	A49	2p multicolored	2.50	1.75
238	A49	6p multicolored	4.25	3.50
239	A49	8p multicolored	5.25	4.50
240	A49	16p multicolored	10.00	14.00
		Nos. 237-240 (4)	22.00	23.75

35th anniv. of the Battle of the River Plate between British ships and the German battleship Graf Spee.

FALKLAND ISLANDS

Seal and Flag Badge — A50

7½p, Coat of arms, 1925. 10p, Arms, 1948. 16p, Arms (Falkland Islands Dependencies), 1952.

1975, Oct. 28   Litho.   Wmk. 373
241	A50	2p multicolored	1.00	.50
242	A50	7½p multicolored	1.60	1.50
243	A50	10p multicolored	1.75	1.75
244	A50	16p multicolored	2.50	3.25
		Nos. 241-244 (4)	6.85	7.00

Falkland Islands heraldic arms, 50th anniv.

½p-Coin and Trout — A51

New Coinage: 5½p, 1p coin and gentoo penguins. 8p, 2p-coin and upland geese. 10p, 5p-coin and black-browed albatross. 16p, 10p-coin and sea lions.

1975, Dec. 31   Litho.   Wmk. 373
245	A51	2p copper & multi	.75	.50
246	A51	5½p copper & multi	1.75	1.50
247	A51	8p copper & multi	2.00	1.75
248	A51	10p silver & multi	2.50	2.00
249	A51	16p silver & multi	3.00	3.00
		Nos. 245-249 (5)	10.00	8.75

Gathering Sheep — A52

Sheep Farming: 7½p, Shearing. 10p, Dipping sheep. 20p, Motor Vessel Monsunen collecting wool.

1976, Apr. 28   Litho.   Perf. 13½
250	A52	2p multicolored	.90	.75
251	A52	7½p multicolored	1.25	1.25
252	A52	10p multicolored	1.60	1.60
253	A52	20p multicolored	2.50	3.50
		Nos. 250-253 (4)	6.25	7.10

Prince Philip, 1957 Visit — A53

11p, Queen, ampulla and spoon. 33p, Queen awaiting anointment, and Knights of the Garter.

1977, Feb. 7   Perf. 13½x14
254	A53	6p multicolored	.35	.35
a.		Booklet pane of 4, wmk. 314	6.00	
b.		Single stamp from #254a	1.50	4.00
255	A53	11p multicolored	.60	.60
a.		Booklet pane of 4	2.40	
256	A53	33p multicolored	1.50	1.50
a.		Booklet pane of 4	6.00	
		Nos. 254-256 (3)	2.45	2.45

25th anniv. of the reign of Elizabeth II.

Map of West and East Falkland with Communications Centers — A54

Telecommunications: 11p, Ship to shore communications at Fox Bay. 40p, Globe with Telex tape and telephone.

1977, Oct. 24   Litho.   Perf. 14½x14
257	A54	3p yel brown & multi	.90	.25
258	A54	11p lt ultra & multi	1.60	.60
259	A54	40p rose & multi	2.50	2.00
		Nos. 257-259 (3)	5.00	2.85

A.E.S., 1957-1974 A55

Designs: Mail ships.

1978, Jan. 25   Wmk. 373   Perf. 14   No Date Inscription
260	A55	1p shown	.25	.25
261	A55	2p Darwin, 1957-75	.35	.25
262	A55	3p Merak-N 1951-53	.25	1.50
263	A55	4p Fitzroy, 1936-57	.25	1.50
264	A55	5p Lafonia 1936-41	.25	.30
265	A55	6p Fleurus, 1924-33	.30	.40
266	A55	7p S.S. Falkland, 1914-34	.40	2.75
267	A55	8p Oravia, 1900-12	.45	1.25
268	A55	9p Memphis, 1890-97	.45	1.00
269	A55	10p Black Hawk, 1873-80	.60	.50
270	A55	20p Foam, 1963-72	1.00	1.50
271	A55	25p Fairy, 1857-61	1.00	3.25
272	A55	50p Amelia, 1852-54	1.50	3.50
273	A55	£1 Nautilus, 1846-48	2.50	5.50
274	A55	£3 Hebe, 1842-46	9.00	13.00
		Nos. 260-274 (15)	18.55	36.45

The 1p, 3p, 5p, 6p and 10p were also issued in booklet panes of 4.
For overprints see Nos. 352-353.

1982, Dec. 1   Inscribed "1982"
260a	A55	1p shown	.40	2.00
261a	A55	2p Darwin, 1957-75	.50	2.00
262a	A55	3p Merak-N 1951-53	.60	2.00
263a	A55	4p Fitzroy, 1936-57	.60	2.00
264a	A55	5p Lafonia 1936-41	.70	2.00
265a	A55	6p Fleurus, 1924-33	.70	2.00
266a	A55	7p S.S. Falkland, 1914-34	.75	2.00
267a	A55	8p Oravia, 1900-12	.75	2.00
268a	A55	9p Memphis, 1890-97	.80	2.00
269a	A55	10p Black Hawk, 1873-80	.85	2.00
270a	A55	20p Foam, 1963-72	1.50	3.25
271a	A55	25p Fairy, 1857-61	1.50	3.25
272a	A55	50p Amelia, 1852-54	1.75	4.00
273a	A55	£1 Nautilus, 1846-48	3.25	5.00
274a	A55	£3 Hebe, 1842-46	5.00	10.00
		Nos. 260a-274a (15)	19.65	45.50

Elizabeth II Coronation Anniversary Issue
Souvenir Sheet
Common Design Type

1978, June 2   Unwmk.   Perf. 15
275		Sheet of 6	4.00	5.50
a.		CD326 25p Red Dragon of Wales	.60	.85
b.		CD327 25p Elizabeth II	.60	.85
c.		CD328 25p Hornless ram	.60	.85

No. 275 contains 2 se-tenant strips of Nos. 275a-275c, separated by horizontal gutter with commemorative and descriptive inscriptions.

Short Sunderland Mark III — A56

Design: 33p, Plane in flight and route Southampton to Stanley.

1978, Apr. 28   Wmk. 373   Perf. 14
276	A56	11p multicolored	2.75	2.25
277	A56	33p multicolored	4.00	3.25

First direct flight Southampton, England to Stanley, Falkland Islands, 26th anniv.

First Fox Bay PO and No. 1 — A57

Designs: 11p, Second Stanley Post Office and #2. 15p, New Island Post Office and #3. 22p, 1st Stanley Post Office and #4.

1978, Aug. 8   Litho.   Perf. 13½x13
278	A57	3p multicolored	.25	.25
279	A57	11p multicolored	.30	.40
280	A57	15p multicolored	.40	.60
281	A57	22p multicolored	.70	.85
		Nos. 278-281 (4)	1.65	2.00

Falkland Islands postage stamps, cent.

Macrocystis Pyrifera — A58

Kelp: 7p, Durvillea. 11p, Lessoniae, horiz. 15p, Callophyllis, horiz. 25p, Iridea.

1979, Feb. 19   Litho.   Perf. 14
282	A58	3p multicolored	.40	.40
283	A58	7p multicolored	.45	.45
284	A58	11p multicolored	.55	.55
285	A58	15p multicolored	.80	.80
286	A58	25p multicolored	.95	1.10
		Nos. 282-286 (5)	3.15	3.30

Britten-Norman Islander over Map — A59

Opening of Stanley Airport: 11p, Fokker F27 over map. 15p, Fokker F28 over Stanley. 25p, Cessna 172 Skyhawk, Islander and Fokkers F27, F28 over runway.

1979, May 1   Litho.   Perf. 13½
287	A59	3p multicolored	.45	.25
288	A59	11p multicolored	.85	.65
289	A59	15p multicolored	1.00	.65
290	A59	25p multicolored	1.50	1.00
		Nos. 287-290 (4)	3.80	2.55

Rowland Hill and No. 121 — A60

Sir Rowland Hill (1795-1879), originator of penny postage, and: 11p, Falkland Islands No. 1, vert. 25p, Penny Black. 33p, Falkland Islands No. 37, vert.

1979, Aug. 27   Perf. 14
291	A60	3p multicolored	.25	.25
292	A60	11p multicolored	.40	.40
293	A60	25p multicolored	.75	.75
		Nos. 291-293 (3)	1.40	1.40

Souvenir Sheet
| 294 | A60 | 33p multicolored | 1.50 | 1.50 |

Mail Delivery by Air, UPU Emblem — A61

UPU Membership Cent. (Modes of Mail Delivery). 11p, Horseback. 25p, Schooner Gwendolin.

1979, Nov. 26
295	A61	3p multicolored	.25	.25
296	A61	11p multicolored	.45	.55
297	A61	25p multicolored	.65	1.10
		Nos. 295-297 (3)	1.35	1.90

Commerson's Dolphin — A62

Designs: 3p, Peale's porpoise, vert. 7p, Hour-glass dolphin. 11p, Spectacled porpoise, vert. 15p, Dusky dolphin. 25p, Killer whale.

1980, Feb. 25   Wmk. 373   Perf. 14
298	A62	3p multicolored	.40	.40
299	A62	6p shown	.60	.60
300	A62	7p multicolored	.60	.60
301	A62	11p multicolored	.70	.70
302	A62	15p multicolored	.80	.80
303	A62	25p multicolored	.90	1.50
		Nos. 298-303 (6)	4.00	4.60

Miniature Sheet

A63

Designs: a, Falkland Islands Cancel, 1878. b, New Islds., 1915. c, Falklands Islds., 1901. d, Port Stanley, 1935. e, Port Stanley airmail, 1952. f, Fox Bay, 1934.

1980, May 6   Litho.   Perf. 14
304	A63	Sheet of 6	1.60	1.60
a.-f.		11p any single	.25	.25

London 1980 Intl. Stamp Exhib., May 6-14.

Queen Mother Elizabeth Birthday
Common Design Type

1980, Aug. 4   Litho.   Perf. 14
| 305 | CD330 | 11p multicolored | .40 | .40 |

FALKLAND ISLANDS

Striated Caracara — A64

Designs: 11p, Red-backed buzzard. 15p, Crested caracara. 25p, Cassin's falcon.

1980, Aug. 11	Wmk. 373	Perf. 13½		
306	A64	3p shown	.60	.30
307	A64	11p multicolored	.75	.55
308	A64	15p multicolored	.85	.65
309	A64	25p multicolored	1.00	1.00
	Nos. 306-309 (4)		3.20	2.50

Port Egmont, Early Settlement A65

1980, Dec. 22	Litho.	Perf. 14		
310	A65	3p Stanley	.25	.25
311	A65	11p shown	.35	.35
312	A65	25p Port Louis	.75	.75
313	A65	33p Mission House, Keppel Island	.95	.95
	Nos. 310-313 (4)		2.30	2.30

Polwarth Sheep — A66

1981, Jan. 19	Litho.	Perf. 14		
314	A66	3p shown	.25	.25
315	A66	11p Frisian cow and calf	.35	.30
316	A66	25p Horse	.70	1.00
317	A66	33p Welsh collies	.80	1.25
	Nos. 314-317 (4)		2.10	2.80

Map of Falkland Islands, Bowles and Carver, 1779 — A67

10p, Hawkin's Mainland, 1773. 13p, New Isles, 1747. 15p, French & British Islands. 25p, Falklands, 1771. 26p, Falklands, 1764.

1981, May 22	Litho.	Perf. 14		
318	A67	3p shown	.25	.25
319	A67	10p multicolored	.30	.35
320	A67	13p multicolored	.35	.35
321	A67	15p multicolored	.45	.35
322	A67	25p multicolored	.60	.50
323	A67	26p multicolored	.65	.50
	Nos. 318-323 (6)		2.60	2.30

Royal Wedding Issue
Common Design Type

1981, July 22	Litho.	Perf. 13½x13		
324	CD331	10p Bouquet	.25	.25
325	CD331	13p Charles	.40	.45
326	CD331	52p Couple	1.00	1.00
	Nos. 324-326 (3)		1.65	1.70

Duke of Edinburgh's Awards, 25th Anniv. — A68

1981, Sept. 28	Litho.	Perf. 14		
327	A68	10p Spinning	.25	.25
328	A68	13p Camping	.25	.25
329	A68	15p Kayaking	.35	.35
330	A68	26p Duke of Edinburgh	.55	.55
	Nos. 327-330 (4)		1.40	1.40

The Holy Virgin, by Guido Reni (1575-1642) — A69

Christmas: 3p, Adoration of the Holy Child, 16th cent. Dutch. 13p, Holy Family in an Italian Landscape, 17th cent. Italian.

1981, Nov. 9	Litho.	Perf. 14		
331	A69	3p multicolored	.25	.25
332	A69	13p multicolored	.50	.50
333	A69	26p multicolored	.75	.75
	Nos. 331-333 (3)		1.50	1.50

This set was issued Nov. 2 in London by the Crown Agents.

Rock Cod — A70

Designs: Shelf fish — 5p, Falkland herring, horiz. 15p, Patagonian hake, horiz. 25p, Southern blue whiting, horiz. 26p, Gray-tailed skate.

1981, Dec. 7				
334	A70	5p multicolored	.25	.25
335	A70	13p shown	.30	.35
336	A70	15p multicolored	.35	.40
337	A70	25p multicolored	.55	.75
338	A70	26p multicolored	.55	.75
	Nos. 334-338 (5)		2.00	2.50

Shipwrecks A71

Designs: 5p, Lady Elizabeth, 1913. 13p, Capricorn, 1882. 15p, Jhelum, 1870. 25p, Snowsquall, 1864. 26p, St. Mary, 1890.

1982, Feb. 15	Wmk. 373	Perf. 14½		
339	A71	5p multicolored	.35	.35
340	A71	13p multicolored	.45	.45
341	A71	15p multicolored	.50	.50
342	A71	25p multicolored	.70	.70
343	A71	26p multicolored	.70	.70
	Nos. 339-343 (5)		2.70	2.70

Sesquicentennial of Charles Darwin's Visit — A72

1982, Apr. 19	Litho.	Perf. 14		
344	A72	5p Darwin	.45	.45
345	A72	17p Microscope	.55	.55
346	A72	25p Warrah	.85	.85
347	A72	34p Beagle	1.10	1.10
	Nos. 344-347 (4)		2.95	2.95

Princess Diana Issue
Common Design Type

1982, July 5	Wmk. 373	Perf. 13		
348	CD333	5p Arms	.30	.30
349	CD333	17p Diana	.60	.60
350	CD333	37p Wedding	.90	.90
351	CD333	50p Portrait	1.15	1.15
	Nos. 348-351 (4)		2.95	2.95

Nos. 264, 271 Overprinted

1982, Oct. 7	Litho.	Perf. 14		
352	A55	5p multicolored	.25	.30
353	A55	25p multicolored	.50	1.00

12th Commonwealth Games, Brisbane, Australia, Sept. 30-Oct. 9.

Tussock Bird — A73

Designs: 10p, Black-chinned siskin. 13p, Grass wren. 17p, Black-throated finch. 25p, Falkland-correndera pipit. 34p, Dark-faced ground-tyrant.

1982, Dec. 6		Perf. 15x14½		
354	A73	5p shown	.40	.40
355	A73	10p multicolored	.50	.50
356	A73	13p multicolored	.50	.50
357	A73	17p multicolored	.50	.50
358	A73	25p multicolored	.60	.60
359	A73	34p multicolored	.70	.70
	Nos. 354-359 (6)		3.20	3.20

British Occupation Sesquicentennial — A74

1p, Raising the Standard, Port Louis, 1833. 2p, Chelsea pensioners & barracks, 1849. 5p, Wool trade, 1874. 10p, Ship repairing trade, 1850-90. 15p, Government House, early 20th cent. 20p, Battle of the Falkland Islands, 1914. 25p, Whalebone Arch centenary, 1933. 40p, Contribution to World War II effort, 1939-45. 50p, Visit of Duke of Edinburgh, 1957. £1, Royal Marines, 1933, 1983, vert. £2, Queen Elizabeth II.

1983, Jan. 1	Litho.	Perf. 14		
360	A74	1p multi, vert.	.35	.35
361	A74	2p multi	.40	.40
362	A74	5p multi, vert.	.40	.40
363	A74	10p multi	.55	.70
364	A74	15p multi	.55	.80
365	A74	20p multi, vert.	.75	1.25
366	A74	25p multi	.75	1.25
367	A74	40p multi, vert.	.80	1.25
368	A74	50p multi	.95	1.25
369	A74	£1 multi	1.25	1.75
370	A74	£2 multi, vert.	2.50	3.00
	Nos. 360-370 (11)		9.25	12.40

For surcharges see Nos. 402-403.

A75

1983, Mar. 14				
371	A75	5p No. 69	.25	.25
372	A75	17p No. 65	.45	.45
373	A75	34p No. 75, vert.	.70	1.00
374	A75	50p No. 370, vert.	.90	1.00
	Nos. 371-374 (4)		2.30	2.70

Commonwealth Day.

First Anniv. of Liberation — A76

1983, June 14	Wmk. 373	Perf. 14		
375	A76	5p Army	.30	.30
376	A76	13p Merchant Navy	.40	.40
377	A76	17p Royal Air Force	.60	.60
378	A76	50p Royal Navy	1.20	1.75
a.	Souvenir sheet of 4, #375-378		2.50	2.75
	Nos. 375-378 (4)		2.50	3.05

Local Fruit — A77

1983, Oct. 10	Litho.	Perf. 14		
379	A77	5p Diddle dee	.25	.25
380	A77	17p Tea berries	.35	.40
381	A77	25p Mountain berries	.50	.60
382	A77	34p Native strawberries	.70	.80
	Nos. 379-382 (4)		1.80	2.05

Britten-Norman Islander — A78

Designs: 13p, DHC-2 Beaver. 17p, Noorduyn Norseman. 50p, Auster.

1983, Nov. 14	Litho.	Perf. 14		
383	A78	5p shown	.25	.25
384	A78	13p multicolored	.35	.40
385	A78	17p multicolored	.45	.50
386	A78	50p multicolored	1.00	1.25
	Nos. 383-386 (4)		2.05	2.40

Green Spider — A79

Insects and Spiders: 2p, 7p, Ichneumon-Fly. 3p, Brocade Moth. 4p, Black Beetle. 5p, Fritillary. 6p, Green Spider, diff. 8p, Ochre Shoulder. 9p, Clocker Weevil. 10p, Hover Fly. 20p, Weevil. 25p, Metallic Beetle. 50p, Camel Cricket. £1, Beauchene Spider. £3, Southern Painted Lady.

1984, Jan. 1	Litho.	Perf. 14		
387	A79	1p shown	.30	.80
388	A79	2p multicolored	2.75	2.50
a.	Inscribed "1986"		4.00	3.25
389	A79	3p multicolored	.65	.85
390	A79	4p multicolored	.50	.85
391	A79	5p multicolored	.50	.85
392	A79	6p multicolored	.50	.85
393	A79	7p multicolored	.50	.70
394	A79	8p multicolored	.50	.70
395	A79	9p multicolored	.50	.70
396	A79	10p multicolored	.50	.70
397	A79	20p multicolored	2.75	1.10
398	A79	25p multicolored	.65	1.10
399	A79	50p multicolored	1.10	1.75
400	A79	£1 multicolored	1.40	2.50
401	A79	£3 multicolored	4.00	6.50
	Nos. 387-401 (15)		17.10	22.45

Nos. 364, 366 Surcharged

1984, Jan. 3	Litho.	Perf. 14		
402	A74	17p on 15p multi	.65	.90
403	A74	22p on 25p multi	.35	.45

Lloyd's List Issue
Common Design Type

Designs: 6p, Wavertree. 17p, Port Stanley, 1910. 22p, Oravia. 52p, Cunard Countess.

1984, May 7	Wmk. 373	Perf. 14½		
404	CD335	6p multi	.60	.50
405	CD335	17p multi	.90	.65
406	CD335	22p multi	.90	.75
407	CD335	52p multi	1.10	1.75
	Nos. 404-407 (4)		3.50	3.65

Great Grebe — A80

1984, Aug. 6		Perf. 14½x14		
408	A80	17p shown	1.25	1.25
409	A80	22p Silver grebe	1.50	1.50
410	A80	52p Rolland's grebe	2.25	3.25
	Nos. 408-410 (3)		5.00	6.00

See Nos. 450-453.

1984 UPU Congress — A81

1984, June 25	Litho.	Perf. 14		
411	A81	22p Emblem, jet, ship	.60	.75

Wildlife Conservation — A82

FALKLAND ISLANDS 489

1984, Nov. 5   Litho.   Perf. 14½
412	A82	6p Birds	1.00	1.00
413	A82	17p Plants	.90	.70
414	A82	22p Mammals	1.00	.80
415	A82	52p Marine Life	1.60	2.25
a.		Souvenir sheet of 4, #412-415	7.00	7.75
		Nos. 412-415 (4)	4.50	4.75

Camber Railway, 1915-1927 — A83

1985, Feb. 18   Litho.   Perf. 14
416	A83	7p multicolored	.35	.35
417	A83	22p multicolored	.65	.65
418	A83	27p multicolored	.70	.85

Size: 77x26mm
419	A83	54p multicolored	1.40	1.75
		Nos. 416-419 (4)	3.10	3.60

Queen Mother 85th Birthday
Common Design Type

Designs: 7p, Commonwealth Visitor's Reception. 22p, With Prince Charles, Mark Phillips, Princess Anne. 27p, 80th birthday celebration. 54p, Holding Prince Henry. £1, In coach with Princess Diana.

1985, June 7   Litho.   Perf. 14⅛x14   Wmk. 384
420	CD336	7p multicolored	.35	.35
421	CD336	22p multicolored	.90	.70
422	CD336	27p multicolored	1.00	1.00
423	CD336	54p multicolored	1.10	1.60
		Nos. 420-423 (4)	3.35	3.65

Souvenir Sheet
424	CD336	£1 multicolored	4.00	3.00

Mount Pleasant Airport Opening — A84

Designs: 7p, Pioneer camp, docked ship. 22p, Construction site. 27p, Runway layout. 54p, Aircraft landing.

1985, May 12   Litho.   Perf. 14½
425	A84	7p multicolored	.75	.40
426	A84	22p multicolored	1.00	1.00
427	A84	27p multicolored	1.30	1.30
428	A84	54p multicolored	1.75	2.40
		Nos. 425-428 (4)	4.80	5.10

Captain J. McBride, HMS Jason, 1765 — A85

18th-19th century naval explorers: 22p, Commodoro J. Byron, HMS Dolphin and Tamar, 1765. 27p, Vice-Adm. R. Fitzroy, HMS Beagle, 1831. 54p, Adm. Sir B.J. Sulivan, HMS Philomel, 1842.

1985, Sept. 23
429	A85	7p multicolored	.75	.45
430	A85	22p multicolored	1.25	.90
431	A85	27p multicolored	1.35	1.15
432	A85	54p multicolored	2.50	2.25
		Nos. 429-432 (4)	5.85	4.75

Philibert Commerson (1727-1773), Commerson's Dolphin — A86

Naturalists, endangered species: 22p, Rene Primevere Lesson (1794-1849), kelp. 27p, Joseph Paul Gaimard (1796-1858), diving petrel. 54p, Charles Darwin (1803-1882), Calceolaria darwinii.

1985, Nov. 4   Perf. 14½
433	A86	7p multicolored	.85	.30
434	A86	22p multicolored	1.10	1.10
435	A86	27p multicolored	2.00	2.00
436	A86	54p multicolored	2.25	2.25
		Nos. 433-436 (4)	6.20	5.65

Seashells — A87

Designs: 7p, Painted keyhole limpet. 22p, Magellanic volute. 27p, Falkland scallop. 54p, Rough thorn drupe.

1986, Feb. 10   Wmk. 384   Perf. 14½
437	A87	7p multicolored	.95	.95
438	A87	22p multicolored	1.50	1.50
439	A87	27p multicolored	1.60	1.90
440	A87	54p multicolored	2.75	3.25
		Nos. 437-440 (4)	6.80	7.60

Queen Elizabeth II 60th Birthday
Common Design Type

Designs: 10p, With Princess Margaret at St. Paul's, Waldenbury, 1932. 24p, Christmas broadcast from Sandringham, 1958. 29p, Order of the Thistle, St. Giles Cathedral, Edinburgh, 1962. 45p, Royal reception on the Britannia, US visit, 1976. 58p, Visiting Crown Agents' offices, 1983.

1986, Apr. 21   Litho.   Perf. 14x14½
441	CD337	10p scar, blk & sil	.30	.30
442	CD337	24p ultra, blk & sil	.55	.65
443	CD337	29p green & multi	.60	.85
444	CD337	45p violet & multi	1.25	1.40
445	CD337	58p rose vio & multi	1.25	1.75
		Nos. 441-445 (5)	3.95	4.95

AMERIPEX '86 A88

SS Great Britain's arrival in the Falkland Isls.—Cent.: 10p, Maiden voyage, crossing the Atlantic, 1845. 24p, Wreck in Sparrow Cove, 1937. 29p, Refloating wreck, 1970. 58p, Restored vessel, Bristol, 1986.

1986, May 22
446	A88	10p multicolored	.50	.50
447	A88	24p multicolored	.60	.90
448	A88	29p multicolored	.75	1.10
449	A88	58p multicolored	1.10	2.25
a.		Souvenir sheet of 4, #446-449	3.75	3.75
		Nos. 446-449 (4)	2.95	4.75

Bird Type of 1984

Rockhopper Penguins.

1986, Aug. 25   Wmk. 373   Perf. 14½
450	A80	10p Adult	1.00	.75
451	A80	24p Adults swimming	1.90	1.90
452	A80	29p Adults, diff.	2.10	2.10
453	A80	58p Adult and young	3.25	4.25
		Nos. 450-453 (4)	8.25	9.00

Wedding of Prince Andrew and Sarah Ferguson — A90

Various photographs: 17p, Presenting Queen's Polo Cup, Windsor, 1986. 22p, Open carriage, wedding. 29p, Andrew wearing military fatigues.

1986, Nov. 10   Wmk. 384   Perf. 14½
454	A90	17p multicolored	.70	.70
455	A90	22p multicolored	.90	.90
456	A90	29p multicolored	1.25	1.25
		Nos. 454-456 (3)	2.85	2.85

Royal Engineers, 200th Anniv. — A91

10p, Surveying Sapper Hill. 24p, Explosives disposal. 29p, Boxer Bridge, Pt. Stanley. 58p, Postal services, Stanley Airport.

1987, Feb. 9   Litho.   Perf. 14½
457	A91	10p multicolored	1.35	.90
458	A91	24p multicolored	2.40	1.50
459	A91	29p multicolored	2.10	2.50
460	A91	58p multicolored	3.50	4.25
		Nos. 457-460 (4)	9.35	9.15

Seals — A92

Designs: 10p, Southern sea lion. 24p, Falkland fur seal. 29p, Southern elephant seal. 58p, Leopard seal.

1987, Apr. 27
461	A92	10p multicolored	1.25	1.25
462	A92	24p multicolored	2.00	2.00
463	A92	29p multicolored	2.25	2.25
464	A92	58p multicolored	3.00	4.50
		Nos. 461-464 (4)	8.50	10.00

Hospitals — A93

Designs: 10p, Victorian Cottage Home, c. 1912. 24p, King Edward VII Memorial Hospital, c. 1914. 29p, Churchill Wing, 1953. 58p, Prince Andrew Wing, 1987.

1987, Dec. 8   Perf. 14
465	A93	10p multicolored	.65	.50
466	A93	24p multicolored	1.10	.90
467	A93	29p multicolored	1.25	1.00
468	A93	58p multicolored	2.00	1.50
		Nos. 465-468 (4)	5.00	3.90

Fungi — A94

10p, Suillus luteus. 24p, Mycena. 29p, Camarophyllus adonis. 58p, Gerronema schusteri.

1987, Sept. 14   Litho.   Perf. 14½
469	A94	10p multicolored	2.50	1.75
470	A94	24p multicolored	3.50	3.00
471	A94	29p multicolored	4.00	3.50
472	A94	58p multicolored	5.00	5.50
		Nos. 469-472 (4)	15.00	13.75

1940 Morris Truck, Fitzroy — A95

Classic automobiles: 24p, 1929 Citroen Kegresse, San Carlos. 29p, 1933 Ford 1-Ton Truck, Port Stanley. 58p, 1935 Ford Model T Saloon, Darwin.

1988, Apr. 11   Litho.   Perf. 14
473	A95	10p multicolored	.65	.35
474	A95	24p multicolored	1.10	.65
475	A95	29p multicolored	1.25	.75
476	A95	58p multicolored	1.90	1.50
		Nos. 473-476 (4)	4.90	3.25

Geese — A96

1988, July 25
477	A96	10p Kelp	2.50	.60
478	A96	24p Upland	3.25	.90
479	A96	29p Ruddy-headed	3.50	1.10
480	A96	58p Ashy-headed	5.75	2.50
		Nos. 477-480 (4)	15.00	5.10

Lloyds of London, 300th Anniv.
Common Design Type

Designs: 10p, Lloyd's Nelson Collection silver service. 24p, Hydroponic Gardens, horiz. 29p, Supply ship A.E.S., horiz. 58p, Wreck of the Charles Cooper near the Falklands, 1866.

1988, Nov. 14   Litho.   Wmk. 373
481	CD341	10p multicolored	.45	.45
482	CD341	24p multicolored	.85	.85
483	CD341	29p multicolored	1.75	1.05
484	CD341	58p multicolored	2.40	1.50
		Nos. 481-484 (4)	5.45	3.85

Ships of Cape Horn — A97

Designs: 1p, Padua. 2p, Priwall, vert. 3p, Passat. 4p, Archibald Russell, vert. 5p, Pamir, vert. 6p, Mozart. 7p, Pommern. 8p, Preussen. 9p, Fennia. 10p, Cassard. 20p, Lawhill. 25p, Garthpool. 50p, Grace Harwar. £1, Criccieth Castle. £3, Cutty Sark, vert. £5, Flying Cloud.

1989, Feb. 28
485	A97	1p multicolored	1.75	.85
486	A97	2p multicolored	1.40	1.40
a.		Wmk. 384	1.20	1.20
487	A97	3p multicolored	1.40	1.40
a.		Wmk. 384	1.20	1.20
488	A97	4p multicolored	2.40	.85
489	A97	5p multicolored	2.40	.85
490	A97	6p multicolored	1.90	1.90
a.		Wmk. 384	1.90	1.90
491	A97	7p multicolored	2.40	.95
492	A97	8p multicolored	2.40	.95
493	A97	9p multicolored	1.90	1.90
a.		Wmk. 384	2.50	2.50
494	A97	10p multicolored	2.40	.95
495	A97	20p multicolored	3.50	1.90
496	A97	25p multicolored	3.75	1.90
497	A97	50p multicolored	4.25	3.00
498	A97	£1 multicolored	5.00	4.75
a.		Wmk. 384	6.00	6.00
499	A97	£3 multicolored	15.00	10.00
500	A97	£5 multicolored	27.50	11.50
		Nos. 485-500 (16)	79.35	45.05

Nos. 486a, 487a, 490a, 493a, 498a are dated "1991."

Whales A98

1989, May 15   Wmk. 384   Perf. 14
501	A98	10p Southern right	1.50	.85
502	A98	24p Minke	2.50	1.25
503	A98	29p Humpback	3.25	2.00
504	A98	58p Blue	4.75	3.00
		Nos. 501-504 (4)	12.00	7.10

Sports Assoc. Activities — A99

Children's drawings.

1989, Sept. 16
505	A99	5p Gymkhana	.30	.30
506	A99	10p Steer Riding	.35	.35
507	A99	17p Sheep shearing	.55	.55
508	A99	24p Dog trial	.70	.70
509	A99	29p Horse racing	.95	.95
510	A99	45p Sack race	1.25	1.25
		Nos. 505-510 (6)	4.10	4.10

Battles — A100

Commanders, ships and ship crests: 10p, Vice-Adm. Sturdee, HMS Invincible. 24p, Vice-Adm. Von Spee, SMS Scharnhorst. 29p, Commodore Harwood, HMS Ajax. 58p, Capt. Langsdorff, Admiral Graff Spee.

1989, Dec. 8   Perf. 14x13½
511	A100	10p multicolored	1.35	.35
512	A100	24p multicolored	2.25	.80
513	A100	29p multicolored	2.25	1.00
514	A100	58p multicolored	3.25	2.50
		Nos. 511-514 (4)	9.10	4.65

Battle of the Falklands, 75th anniv. (10p, 24p); Battle of the River Plate, 50th anniv. (29p, 58p).

Emblems and Presentation Spitfires, 1940 — A101

FALKLAND ISLANDS

Designs: 12p, No. 92 Squadron, whole plane. 26p, No. 611 Squadron. 31p, No. 92 Squadron, close up of cockpit. 62p, Spitfires scramble. £1, Battle of Britain.

1990, May 3	Wmk. 373	Perf. 14		
515	A101	12p multicolored	1.00	1.00
516	A101	26p multicolored	1.40	1.40
517	A101	31p multicolored	1.75	1.75
518	A101	62p multicolored	3.00	3.00
	Nos. 515-518 (4)		7.15	7.15

Souvenir Sheet

519	A101	£1 multicolored	7.00	7.00

Stamp World London '90.
For souvenir sheet similar to No. 519, see No. 530.

A102

1990, Apr. 1	Wmk. 384	Perf. 14½		
520	A102	12p Kidney Is.	.80	.55
521	A102	26p Beauchene Is.	1.25	.55
522	A102	31p Bird Is.	1.75	1.25
523	A102	62p Elephant Jason Is.	2.25	2.75
	Nos. 520-523 (4)		5.80	5.10

Nature reserves and bird sanctuaries.

Queen Mother, 90th Birthday
Common Design Types

26p, Queen Mother in Dover. £1, Steering the "Queen Elizabeth," 1946.

1990, Aug. 4	Wmk. 384	Perf. 14x15		
524	CD343	26p multicolored	1.00	1.00

Perf. 14½			
525	CD344	£1 multicolored	3.75 3.75

A103

Designs: 12p, Black browed albatross. 26p, Adult bird. 31p, Adult, chick. 62p, Bird in flight.

Wmk. 384

1990, Oct. 3	Litho.	Perf. 14		
526	A103	12p multicolored	1.00	.75
527	A103	26p multicolored	1.90	1.25
528	A103	31p multicolored	2.25	1.50
529	A103	62p multicolored	3.50	3.50
	Nos. 526-529 (4)		8.65	7.00

Battle of Britain Type of 1990
inscribed "SECOND VISIT OF / HRH THE DUKE OF EDINBURGH"
Souvenir Sheet

1991, Mar. 7				
530	A101	£1 multicolored	13.00	13.00

Orchids — A104

Designs: 12p, Gavilea australis. 26p, Codonorchis lessonii. 31p, Chlorea gaudichaudii. 62p, Gavilea littoralis.

1991, Mar. 18		Wmk. 373		
531	A104	12p multi	1.60	1.00
532	A104	26p multi	1.90	1.50
533	A104	31p multi	2.25	1.75
534	A104	62p multi	3.50	4.00
	Nos. 531-534 (4)		9.25	8.25

King Penguin — A105

2p, Two adults crossing bills. 6p, Two adults, one brooding. 12p, Adult with two young. 20p, Adult swimming. 31p, Adult feeding young. 62p, Two adults, diff.

1991, Aug. 26		Wmk. 384		
535	A105	2p multi	1.10	1.10
536	A105	6p multi	1.60	1.60
537	A105	12p multi	2.00	2.00
538	A105	20p multi	2.25	2.25
539	A105	31p multi	2.25	2.25
540	A105	62p multi	3.25	3.25
	Nos. 535-540 (6)		12.45	12.45

World Wildlife Fund.

Falkland Islands Bisects, Cent. — A106

1991, Sept. 10	Wmk. 384	Perf. 14½		
541	A106	12p #9, #15	1.00	.90
542	A106	26p On cover	1.90	1.50
543	A106	31p Unsevered pair	1.50	1.50
544	A106	62p S.S. Isis	2.50	3.25
	Nos. 541-544 (4)		6.90	7.15

Discovery of America, 500th Anniv. (in 1992) — A107

Sailing ships: 14p, STV Eye of the Wind. 29p, STV Soren Larsen. 34p, Nina, Santa Maria, Pinta. 68p, Columbus and Santa Maria.

1991, Dec. 12	Wmk. 373	Perf. 14		
545	A107	14p multicolored	.90	.90
546	A107	29p multicolored	2.00	1.75
547	A107	34p multicolored	2.25	2.00
548	A107	68p multicolored	3.50	4.25
	Nos. 545-548 (4)		8.65	8.70

World Columbian Stamp Expo '92, Chicago and Genoa '92 Intl. Philatelic Exhibitions.

Queen Elizabeth II's Accession to the Throne, 40th Anniv.
Common Design Type

1992, Feb. 6				
549	CD349	7p multicolored	.65	.50
550	CD349	14p multicolored	.90	.90
551	CD349	29p multicolored	1.00	1.10
552	CD349	34p multicolored	1.40	1.40
553	CD349	68p multicolored	2.00	2.00
	Nos. 549-553 (5)		5.95	5.90

Christ Church Cathedral, Cent. — A108

Designs: 14p, Laying foundation stone. 29p, Interior, 1920. 34p, Bishop's chair. 68p, Without tower c. 1900, horiz.

1992, Feb. 21	Wmk. 384	Perf. 14½		
554	A108	14p multicolored	1.00	.75
555	A108	29p multicolored	2.00	1.25
556	A108	34p multicolored	2.25	1.50
557	A108	68p multicolored	3.00	2.75
	Nos. 554-557 (4)		8.25	6.25

A109

Designs: 22p, Capt. John Davis using backstaff. 29p, Capt. Davis working on chart. 34p, Queen Elizabeth I, Queen Elizabeth II. 68p, The Desire sights Falkland Islands.

1992, Aug. 14	Wmk. 373			
558	A109	22p multicolored	1.60	1.10
559	A109	29p multicolored	2.00	1.50
560	A109	34p multicolored	2.10	1.90
561	A109	68p multicolored	3.50	5.00
	Nos. 558-561 (4)		9.20	9.50

First sighting of Falkland Islands by Capt. John Davis, 400th anniv.

Falkland Islands Defense Force and West Yorkshire Regiment — A110

7p, Private, Falkland Islands Volunteers, 1892. 14p, Officer, Falkland Islands Defense Corps, 1914. 22p, Officer, Falkland Islands Defense Force, 1920. 29p, Private, Falkland Islands Defense Force, 1939-45. 34p, Officer, West Yorkshire Regiment, 1942. 68p, Private, West Yorkshire Regiment, 1942.

1992, Oct. 1		Perf. 14		
562	A110	7p multicolored	.60	.60
563	A110	14p multicolored	.90	.90
564	A110	22p multicolored	1.25	.90
565	A110	29p multicolored	1.50	1.25
566	A110	34p multicolored	1.90	1.60
567	A110	68p multicolored	3.00	3.75
	Nos. 562-567 (6)		9.15	9.00

Gulls and Terns — A111

Designs: 15p, South American tern. 31p, Pink breasted gull. 36p, Dolphin gull. 72p, Dominican gull.

	Perf. 14x14½			
1993, Jan. 2	Litho.	Wmk. 384		
568	A111	15p multicolored	1.40	1.00
569	A111	31p multicolored	1.90	1.50
570	A111	36p multicolored	2.50	2.25
571	A111	72p multicolored	3.50	5.50
	Nos. 568-571 (4)		9.30	10.25

Souvenir Sheet

Visit of Liner QE II to Falkland Islands A112

	Wmk. 373			
1993, Jan. 22	Litho.	Perf. 14		
572	A112	£2 multicolored	10.00	10.00

Royal Air Force, 75th Anniv.
Common Designs Type

Designs: No. 573, Lockheed Tristar. No. 574, Lockheed Hercules. No. 575, Boeing Vertol Chinook. No. 576, Avro Vulcan. No. 577a, Hawker Siddeley Andover. b, Westland Wessex. c, Panavia Tornado F3. d, McDonnell Douglas Phantom.

	Wmk. 373			
1993, Apr. 3	Litho.	Perf. 14		
573	CD350	15p multicolored	1.15	1.15
574	CD350	15p multicolored	1.15	1.15
575	CD350	15p multicolored	1.15	1.15
576	CD350	15p multicolored	1.15	1.15
	Nos. 573-576 (4)		4.60	4.60

Souvenir Sheet of 4

577	CD350	36p #a.-d.	6.25	6.25

Fisheries A113

Designs: 15p, Short-finned squid. 31p, Stern haul of whiptailed hake. 36p, Fishery Patrol Vessel Falklands Protector. 72p, Aerial surveillance by Britten-Norman Islander.

	Wmk. 384			
1993, July 1	Litho.	Perf. 14		
578	A113	15p multicolored	.85	.85
579	A113	31p multicolored	1.75	1.75
580	A113	36p multicolored	2.10	2.10
581	A113	72p multicolored	3.25	5.00
	Nos. 578-581 (4)		7.95	9.70

Launch of SS Great Britain, 150th Anniv. — A114

	Perf. 14x13½			
1993, July 19	Litho.	Wmk. 384		
582	A114	8p In drydock, Bristol	.80	.50
583	A114	£1 At sea	4.25	5.50

Cruise Ships and Penguins A115

16p, Explorer. 34p, Rockhopper penguins. 39p, World Discoverer. 78p, Columbus Caravelle.

	Wmk. 373			
1993, Oct. 1	Litho.	Perf. 14		
584	A115	16p multicolored	1.60	.80
585	A115	34p multicolored	2.50	1.60
586	A115	39p multicolored	2.75	2.00
587	A115	78p multicolored	3.75	7.50
	Nos. 584-587 (4)		10.60	11.90

Pets — A116

	Perf. 14x14½			
1993, Dec. 1	Litho.	Wmk. 384		
588	A116	8p Pony	.90	.90
589	A116	16p Lamb	1.10	1.00
590	A116	34p Puppy, kitten	2.25	1.50

	Perf. 14½x14			
591	A116	39p Kitten, vert.	2.75	2.75
592	A116	78p Collie, vert.	3.75	5.75
	Nos. 588-592 (5)		10.75	11.25

Ovptd. with Hong Kong '94 Emblem

1994, Feb. 18				
593	A116	8p on #588	1.00	1.25
594	A116	16p on #589	1.25	1.50
595	A116	34p on #590	2.75	3.00
596	A116	39p on #591	3.00	4.00
597	A116	78p on #592	4.00	6.50
	Nos. 593-597 (5)		12.00	16.25

Inshore Marine Life — A117

Designs: 1p, Goose barnacles, vert. 2p, Painted shrimp. 8p, Common limpet. 9p, Mullet. 10p, Sea anemones. 20p, Rock eel. 25p, Spider crab. 50p, Lobster krill, vert. 80p, Falkland skate. £1, Centollon crab. £3, Rock cod. £5, Octopus, vert.

	Wmk. 384			
1994, Apr. 4	Litho.	Perf. 14		
598	A117	1p multicolored	1.00	.75
599	A117	2p multicolored	1.75	.75
600	A117	8p multicolored	2.00	1.00
601	A117	9p multicolored	2.00	1.00
602	A117	10p multicolored	2.00	.75
603	A117	20p multicolored	2.75	1.00
604	A117	25p multicolored	2.75	1.00
605	A117	50p multicolored	2.75	2.75
606	A117	80p multicolored	2.75	2.75
607	A117	£1 multicolored	2.75	3.00
a.	Souv. sheet of 1, wmk. 373		6.75	6.75
608	A117	£3 multicolored	12.00	8.00
609	A117	£5 multicolored	18.00	14.00
	Nos. 598-609 (12)		52.50	36.75

No. 607a for return of Hong Kong to China. Issued 7/1/97.
See No. 671.

FALKLAND ISLANDS

Founding of Stanley, 150th Anniv. — A118

9p, Blacksmith's shop, dockyard, Sir James Clark Ross, explorer. 17p, James Leith Mody, 1st colonial chaplain, home at 21 Fitzroy Road. 30p, Stanley cottage, Dr. Henry J. Hamblin, 1st colonial surgeon. 35p, Pioneer row, Sergeant Major Henry Felton. 40p, Government House, Governor R. C. Moody R.E. 65p, View of Stanley, Edward Stanley, 14th Earl of Derby, Secretary of State for Colonies.

Wmk. 373

1994, July 1	Litho.		Perf. 14
610 A118 9p multicolored		.85	.75
611 A118 17p multicolored		1.25	1.00
612 A118 30p multicolored		2.00	1.25
613 A118 35p multicolored		2.25	1.75
614 A118 40p multicolored		2.50	2.00
615 A118 65p multicolored		3.00	3.50
Nos. 610-615 (6)		11.85	10.25

Methods of Transportation A119

17p, Tristar over Gypsy Cove. 35p, Cruise ship, Sea Lion Island. 40p, FIGAS Islander, Pebble Island Beach. 65p, Land Rover, Volunteer Beach.

Wmk. 384

1994, Oct. 24	Litho.		Perf. 14
616 A119 17p multicolored		1.10	.75
617 A119 35p multicolored		2.10	1.50
618 A119 40p multicolored		2.75	2.75
619 A119 65p multicolored		3.25	4.25
Nos. 616-619 (4)		9.20	9.25

South American Missionary Society, 150th Anniv. — A120

Designs: 5p, Mission House, Keppel Island. 17p, Thomas Bridges, compiler of Yahgan dictionary. 40p, Fuegian Indians. 65p, Schooner Allen Gardiner, Capt. Allen Gardiner.

1994, Dec. 1

620 A120 5p multicolored	.30	.30
621 A120 17p multicolored	.85	.85
622 A120 40p multicolored	1.75	1.75
623 A120 65p multicolored	2.75	3.50
Nos. 620-623 (4)	5.65	6.40

Flowering Shrubs — A121

Designs: 9p, Lupinus arboreus. 17p, Boxwood. 30p, Fuchsia magellanica. 35p, Berberis ilicifolia. 40p, Gorse. 65p, Veronica.

Perf. 14½x14

1995, Jan. 3	Litho.		Wmk. 384
624 A121 9p multicolored		.90	.65
625 A121 17p multicolored		1.10	1.00
626 A121 30p multicolored		1.45	1.45
627 A121 35p multicolored		1.75	1.45
628 A121 40p multicolored		1.90	1.60
629 A121 65p multicolored		3.25	4.25
Nos. 624-629 (6)		10.35	10.20

Shore Birds — A122

Designs: 17p, Magellanic oystercatcher. 35p, Rufous chested dotterel. 40p, Black oystercatcher. 65p, Two banded plover.

Wmk. 373

1995, Mar. 1	Litho.		Perf. 13½
630 A122 17p multicolored		1.75	.90
631 A122 35p multicolored		2.50	1.50
632 A122 40p multicolored		2.75	1.75
633 A122 65p multicolored		4.00	7.00
Nos. 630-633 (4)		11.00	11.15

End of World War II, 50th Anniv.
Common Design Types

17p, Falkland Islands Victory Parade contingent. 35p, Governor Sir Alan Wolsey Cardinall on Bren gun carrier. 40p, HMAS Esperance Bay, 1942. 65p, HMS Exeter, 1939. £1, Reverse of War Medal 1939-45.

Wmk. 373

1995, May 8	Litho.		Perf. 14
634 CD351 17p multicolored		1.50	.90
635 CD351 35p multicolored		2.40	1.50
636 CD351 40p multicolored		2.75	2.00
637 CD351 65p multicolored		4.75	5.50
Nos. 634-637 (4)		11.40	9.90

Souvenir Sheet

638 CD352 £1 multicolored	7.25	7.25

Transporting Peat — A123

Wmk. 384

1995, Aug. 1	Litho.		Perf. 14
639 A123 17p Ox, cart		.80	.80
640 A123 35p Horse, cart		1.75	1.25
641 A123 40p Tractor, sledge		2.00	1.60
642 A123 65p Truck, peat bank		3.50	4.00
Nos. 639-642 (4)		8.05	7.55

Miniature Sheet of 6

Wildlife — A124

Designs: a, Kelp geese. b, Albatross. c, Cormorants. d, Magellanic penguins. e, Fur seals. f, Rockhopper penguins.

1995, Sept. 11

643 A124 35p #a.-f.	19.00	19.00

No. 643 is a continuous design.

Wild Animals — A125

1995, Nov. 6 **Wmk. 373**

644 A125 9p Rabbit	1.00	.90
645 A125 17p Hare	1.60	1.10
646 A125 35p Guanaco	2.50	1.75
647 A125 40p Fox	3.00	2.00
648 A125 65p Otter	4.00	5.00
Nos. 644-648 (5)	12.10	10.75

Visit by Princess Anne — A126

Princess Anne and: 9p, Government House. 19p, San Carlos Cemetery. 30p, Christ Church Cathedral. 73p, Goose Green.

1996, Jan. 30 **Perf. 14½**

649 A126 9p multicolored	1.00	.60
650 A126 19p multicolored	1.35	1.00
651 A126 30p multicolored	1.75	1.50
652 A126 73p multicolored	6.00	7.50
Nos. 649-652 (4)	10.10	10.60

Queen Elizabeth II, 70th Birthday
Common Design Type

Various portraits of Queen, scenes from Falkland Islands: 17p, Steeple Jason. 40p, Ship, KV Tamar. 45p, New Island with shipwreck on beach. 65p, Community School. £1, Queen in formal dress at Sandringham Ball.

1996, Apr. 21 **Perf. 13½**

653 CD354 17p multicolored	.90	.70
654 CD354 40p multicolored	2.25	1.35
655 CD354 45p multicolored	2.40	1.90
656 CD354 65p multicolored	3.00	2.25
Nos. 653-656 (4)	8.55	6.20

Souvenir Sheet

657 CD354 £1 multicolored	5.00	5.00

CAPEX '96 — A127

Mail delivery: 9p, Horseback, 1890. 40p, Norseman floatplane. 45p, Inter-island ship. 76p, Beaver floatplane. £1, LMS Jubilee Class 4-6-0 locomotive.

1996, June 8 **Wmk. 384** **Perf. 14**

658 A127 9p multicolored	.90	.65
659 A127 40p multicolored	2.40	1.50
660 A127 45p multicolored	2.50	1.60
661 A127 76p multicolored	3.50	4.00
Nos. 658-661 (4)	9.30	7.75

Souvenir Sheet

662 A127 £1 multicolored	4.25	4.25

No. 662 contains one 48x32mm stamp.

Beaked Whales A128

Designs: 9p, Southern bottlenose whale. 30p, Cuvier's beaked whale. 35p, Straptoothed beaked whale. 75p, Gray's beaked whale.

Wmk. 373

1996, Sept. 2	Litho.		Perf. 14
663 A128 9p multicolored		.80	.60
664 A128 30p multicolored		1.60	1.50
665 A128 35p multicolored		1.90	1.75
666 A128 75p multicolored		4.00	4.00
Nos. 663-666 (4)		8.30	7.85

Magellanic Penguins A129

Designs: 17p, Two adults. 35p, Young in nest. 40p, Chick, adult. 65p, Swimming.

Wmk. 373

1997, Jan. 2	Litho.		Perf. 14
667 A129 17p multicolored		2.00	.75
668 A129 35p multicolored		3.00	1.25
669 A129 40p multicolored		3.25	1.50
670 A129 65p multicolored		4.50	3.25
Nos. 667-670 (4)		12.75	6.75

Fish Type of 1994
Souvenir Sheet
Wmk. 373

1997, Feb. 3	Litho.		Perf. 14
671 A117 £1 Smelt		5.50	5.50

Hong Kong '97.

Ferns — A130

Perf. 14½x14

1997, Mar. 3	Litho.		Wmk. 373
672 A130 17p Coral		1.75	.60
673 A130 35p Adder's tongue		2.50	1.25
674 A130 40p Fuegian tall		2.50	1.50
675 A130 65p Small fern		3.50	3.00
Nos. 672-675 (4)		10.25	6.35

Lighthouses A131

Designs: 9p, Bull Point. 30p, Cape Pembroke. £1, Cape Meredith.

Wmk. 373

1997, July 1	Litho.		Perf. 14
676 A131 9p multi		3.25	1.00
677 A131 30p multi		4.50	2.00
678 A131 £1 multi		10.50	5.00
Nos. 676-678 (3)		18.25	8.00

Queen Elizabeth II and Prince Philip, 50th Wedding Anniv. A132

No. 679, Queen holding flowers. No. 680, Prince with horse. No. 681, Queen riding in open carriage. No. 682, Prince in uniform. No. 683, Queen in red coat & hat, Prince. No. 684, Princes William and Harry on horseback. £1.50, Queen, Prince riding in open carriage.

1997 **Wmk. 384** **Perf. 14½x14**

679	9p multicolored	1.00	.75
680	9p multicolored	1.00	.75
a. A132 Pair, #679-680		2.75	2.75
681	17p multicolored	1.75	1.00
682	17p multicolored	1.75	1.00
a. A132 Pair, #681-682		4.00	4.00
683	40p multicolored	3.00	1.50
684	40p multicolored	3.00	1.50
a. A132 Pair, #683-684		8.00	8.00
Nos. 679-684 (6)		11.50	6.50

Souvenir Sheet

685 A132 £1.50 multicolored	9.00	9.00

Endangered Species A133

Designs: 17p, Phalcoboenus australis. 19p, Otaria flavescens. 40p, Calandrinia feltonii. 73p, Aplochiton zebra.

Wmk. 373

1997, Oct. 16	Litho.		Perf. 14½
686 A133 17p multicolored		3.75	1.75
687 A133 19p multicolored		2.75	2.25
688 A133 40p multicolored		4.50	3.00
689 A133 73p multicolored		7.50	8.50
Nos. 686-689 (4)		18.50	15.50

Fire Service in Falkland Islands, Cent. — A134

Equipment, manufacturer: 9p, Greenwich Gem, Merryweather & Son. 17p, Hatfield trailer pump, Merryweather & Son. 40p, Godiva trailer pump, Coventry Climax. 65p, Water tender type B, Carmichael Bedford.

Wmk. 384

1998, Feb. 26	Litho.		Perf. 14½
690 A134 9p multicolored		3.25	1.50
691 A134 17p multicolored		3.75	1.50
692 A134 40p multicolored		6.00	3.00
693 A134 65p multicolored		8.00	9.25
Nos. 690-693 (4)		21.00	15.25

Diana, Princess of Wales (1961-97)
Common Design Type

Portraits: a, Looking left. b, In red dress. c, Hand on cheek. d, Investigating land mines.

Perf. 14½x14

1998, Mar. 31		Wmk. 373
694 CD355 30p Sheet of 4, #a-d	5.00	5.00

No. 694 sold for £1.20 + 20p, with surtax from international sales being donated to the Princess Diana Memorial Fund and surtax

FALKLAND ISLANDS

from national sales being donated to designated local charity.

Birds — A135

1p, Tawny-throated dotterel. 2p, Hudsonian godwit. 5p, Eared dove. No. 698, Great grebe. No. 699, Roseate spoonbill. 10p, Southern lapwing. 16p, Buff-necked ibis. 17p, Astral parakeet. 30p, Ashy-headed goose. 35p, American kestrel. 65p, Red-legged shag. 88p, Red shoveler. £1, Red-fronted coot. £3, Chilean flamingo. £5, Fork-tailed flycatcher.

Wmk. 373
1998, July 14   Litho.   Perf. 14

695	A135	1p multicolored	1.00	1.25
696	A135	2p multicolored	1.00	1.25
697	A135	5p multicolored	1.00	1.25
698	A135	9p multicolored	1.50	1.00
699	A135	9p multicolored	6.00	9.50
700	A135	10p multicolored	2.25	1.00
701	A135	16p multicolored	2.25	2.25
702	A135	17p multicolored	1.25	2.25
a.		Booklet pane, 2 #699, 8 #702 + 2 labels	22.00	
		Complete booklet, #702a	22.00	
703	A135	30p multicolored	2.50	1.75
704	A135	35p multicolored	3.00	4.00
		Complete booklet, 6 #704	18.00	
705	A135	65p multicolored	4.00	2.50
706	A135	88p multicolored	4.25	6.25
707	A135	£1 multicolored	4.50	4.50
708	A135	£3 multicolored	11.00	15.00
709	A135	£5 multicolored	15.00	22.50
		Nos. 695-709 (15)	60.50	76.25

Boats — A136

Boat, country flag, year: 17p, Penelope, Germany, 1926. 35p, Ilen, Italy, 1926. 40p, Weddell, Chile, 1940. 65p, Lively, Scotland, 1940.

Wmk. 373
1998, Sept. 30   Litho.   Perf. 14

710	A136	17p multicolored	2.50	1.00
711	A136	35p multicolored	3.50	2.00
712	A136	40p multicolored	3.75	2.25

Size: 29x18mm

713	A136	65p multicolored	5.50	6.00
		Nos. 710-713 (4)	15.25	11.25

FIGAS (First Medivac Air Ambulance Service), 50th Anniv. — A137

17p, Man carrying patient, airplane. £1, Airplane, map of Islands, float plane.

Wmk. 373
1998, Dec. 1   Litho.   Perf. 14

714	A137	17p multicolored	3.00	1.25
715	A137	£1 multicolored	12.50	12.50

Military Uniforms — A138

Uniform, background location: 17p, Marine Private, 1776, The Block House at Port Egmont, Saunders Island. 30p, Marine Officer, 1833, Port Louis, East Falkland. 35p, Royal Marine Corporal, 1914, HMS Kent. 65p, Royal Marine Bugler, 1976, Government House.

Wmk. 373
1998, Dec. 8   Litho.   Perf. 14½

716	A138	17p multicolored	3.00	1.00
717	A138	30p multicolored	4.00	2.50
718	A138	35p multicolored	4.25	2.50
719	A138	65p multicolored	6.50	9.50
		Nos. 716-719 (4)	17.75	15.50

St. Mary's Church, Cent. — A139

Designs: 17p, Inside view. 40p, Outside view. 75p, Laying cornerstone, 1899.

Wmk. 373
1999, Feb. 12   Litho.   Perf. 14

720	A139	17p multi	2.40	.90
721	A139	40p multi	3.75	3.00
722	A139	75p multi	7.75	2.75
		Nos. 720-722 (3)	13.90	6.65

Australia '99, World Stamp Expo — A140

25p, HMS Beagle. 35p, HMAS Australia. 40p, SS Canberra. No. 726, SS Great Britain. No. 727, All-England Eleven visit Australia, 1861-62.

1999, Mar. 5   Wmk. 384

723	A140	25p multicolored	3.25	2.00
724	A140	35p multicolored	3.50	2.50
725	A140	40p multicolored	4.75	2.75
726	A140	40p multicolored	4.50	7.00
727	A140	50p multicolored	4.50	7.00
a.		Pair, #726-727	9.00	14.00
		Nos. 723-727 (5)	20.50	21.25

1999 Visit of HRH Prince of Wales — A141

Perf. 14x13½
1999, Mar. 13   Litho.   Wmk. 384

728	A141	£2 multicolored	16.00	16.00

Wedding of Prince Edward and Sophie Rhys-Jones
Common Design Type

Perf. 13¾x14
1999, June 15   Litho.   Wmk. 384

729	CD356	80p Separate portraits	6.00	6.00
730	CD356	£1.20 Couple	8.00	8.00

PhilexFrance '99, World Philatelic Exhibition — A142

Designs: 35p, French cruiser, Jeanne d'Arc, Port Stanley, 1931. 40p, CAMS 37/11 Flying Boat's first flight. £1, CAMS 37 Flying Boat over Port Stanley, 1931.

Wmk. 373
1999, June 21   Wmk. 373   Perf. 14

731	A142	35p multicolored	5.25	5.25
732	A142	40p multicolored	5.75	5.75

Souvenir Sheet

733	A142	£1 multicolored	13.00	14.00

No. 733 contains one 48x31mm stamp.

Queen Mother's Century
Common Design Type

Queen Mother: 9p, With King George VI at Port of London. 20p, With Queen Elizabeth at Women's Institute, Sandringham. 30p, With Princes Charles, William and Harry at Clarence House, 95th birthday. 67p, As Colonel-in-Chief of the Queen's Royal Hussars. £1.40, With Ernest Shackleton, Robert F. Scott and Edward A. Wilson.

1999, Aug. 18   Litho.   Perf. 13½

734	CD358	9p multi	2.00	1.00
735	CD358	20p multi	3.00	1.50
736	CD358	30p multi	3.50	1.75
737	CD358	67p multi	5.50	8.00
		Nos. 734-737 (4)	14.00	12.25

Souvenir Sheet

738	CD358	£1.40 multi	16.00	16.00

For overprint see No. 767.

Waterfowl — A143

Perf. 14¼x14½
1999, Sept. 9   Litho.   Wmk. 384

739	A143	9p Chiloe wigeon	2.50	1.75
740	A143	17p Crested duck	3.25	2.00
741	A143	30p Brown pintail	4.00	3.25
742	A143	35p Silver teal	4.25	3.00
743	A143	40p Yellow billed teal	4.75	4.00
744	A143	65p Flightless steamer duck	7.00	9.50
		Nos. 739-744 (6)	25.75	24.00

California Gold Rush — A144

Designs: 9p, Vicar of Bray, 1999. 35p, Gold panning, 1849. 40p, Gold rocking cradle, 1849. 80p, Vicar of Bray, 1849. £1, Vicar of Bray in San Francisco Harbor, 1849.

Wmk. 373
1999, Nov. 3   Litho.   Perf. 14

745	A144	9p multicolored	1.10	1.10
746	A144	35p multicolored	4.25	4.25
747	A144	40p multicolored	4.75	4.75
748	A144	80p multicolored	10.00	12.00
		Nos. 745-748 (4)	20.10	22.10

Souvenir Sheet
Perf. 13¾

749	A144	£1 multicolored	15.00	15.00

No. 749 contains one 48x31mm stamp.

Millennium — A145

Designs: No. 750, Kelp gull. No. 751, Upland goose. No. 752, Christchurch Cathedral. No. 753, Night heron. No. 754, King penguin. No. 755, Christmas at home.

1999, Dec. 6   Perf. 14x14½

750	A145	9p multicolored	2.75	2.75
751	A145	9p multicolored	2.75	2.75
752	A145	9p multicolored	2.75	2.75
753	A145	30p multicolored	4.75	4.75
754	A145	30p multicolored	4.75	4.75
755	A145	30p multicolored	4.75	4.75
		Nos. 750-755 (6)	22.50	22.50

Visit of Princess Alexandra A146

Designs: 9p, Princess in patterned dress, trees. £1, Princess in blue dress, trees.

Perf. 13¼x13¾
2000, Feb. 1   Litho.   Wmk. 373

756	A146	9p multicolored	2.00	2.00
757	A146	£1 multicolored	9.50	9.50

Sir Ernest Shackleton (1874-1922), Polar Explorer — A147

17p, Ship Endurance, discovery of the Caird Coast. 45p, Endurance trapped in pack ice. 75p, Shackleton, Chilean tugboat Yelcho.

2000, Feb. 10   Wmk. 373   Perf. 14

758	A147	17p multicolored	5.00	2.00
759	A147	45p multicolored	8.50	4.50
760	A147	75p multicolored	12.50	14.00
		Nos. 758-760 (3)	26.00	20.50

See British Antarctic Territory Nos. 285-287, South Georgia and South Sandwich Islands Nos. 254-256.

British Monarchs — A148

a, Elizabeth I. b, James II. c, George I. d, William IV. e, Edward VIII. f, Elizabeth II.

2000, Feb. 29   Wmk. 373   Perf. 14

761	A148	40p Sheet of 6, #a.-f.	17.00	17.00

The Stamp Show 2000, London.

Prince William, 18th Birthday
Common Design Type

William: 10p, As toddler with fireman's helmet, vert. 20p, In checked suit and in navy suit, vert. 37p, With blue shirt. 43p, In gray suit and in navy suit holding flowers. 50p, As child with dog.

Perf. 13¾x14¼, 14¼x13¾
2000, June 21   Litho.   Wmk. 373
Stamps with White Border

762	CD359	10p multi	1.50	1.25
763	CD359	20p multi	2.10	1.50
764	CD359	37p multi	3.00	2.75
765	CD359	43p multi	4.00	3.00
		Nos. 762-765 (4)	10.60	8.50

Souvenir Sheet
Stamps Without White Border
Perf. 14¼

766		Sheet of 5	14.00	14.00
a.		CD359 10p multi	1.00	1.00
b.		CD359 20p multi	1.50	1.50
c.		CD359 37p multi	2.50	2.50
d.		CD359 43p multi	3.00	3.00
e.		CD359 50p multi	5.00	5.00

No. 738 Ovptd. in Gold

Wmk. 384
2000, Aug. 4   Litho.   Perf. 13½

767	CD358	£1.40 multi	17.00	17.00

Bridges — A149

Bridges over: 20p, Malo River. 37p, Bodie Creek. 43p, Fitzroy River.

2000, Oct. 16   Perf. 14¼x14½

768-770	A149	Set of 3	17.00	17.00

Christmas — A150

Designs: 10p, Shepherd, sheep. 20p, Shepherds, sheep, angel. 33p, Holy family, shepherds, Magus, donkey, sheep. 43p, Angel, two Magi. 78p, Camel.

FALKLAND ISLANDS

493

2000, Nov. 1			Wmk. 373	
771-775	A150	Set of 5	15.50	15.50
775a		Souvenir sheet, #771-775	17.50	17.50

Sunrises and Sunsets — A151

Various photos: 10p, 20p, 37p, 43p.

2001, Jan. 10			Perf. 14½x14¼	
776-779	A151	Set of 4	15.00	15.00

Souvenir Sheet

New Year 2001 (Year of the Snake) — A152

Birds: a, Striated caracara. b, Mountain hawk eagle.

	Perf. 14½x14¼	Wmk. 373	
2001, Feb. 1	Litho.		
780 A152	37p Sheet of 2, #a-b	10.50	12.00

Hong Kong 2001 Stamp Exhibition.

Age of Victoria — A153

Designs: 3p, Falkland Islands #1. 10p, S.S. Great Britain, horiz. 20p, Stanley Harbor, 1888, horiz. 43p, Cape Pembroke Lighthouse, telephones, 1897. 93p, Royal Marines, 1900. £1.50, Queen Victoria, by Franz Xavier Winterhalter, 1859. £1, Funeral procession for Queen Victoria.

2001, May 24			Perf. 14	
781-786	A153	Set of 6	24.50	24.50

Souvenir Sheet

| 787 | A153 | £1 multi | 10.50 | 10.50 |

Royal Navy Connections to Falkland Islands — A154

Designs: 10p, Welfare, ship that made first recorded landing, 1690. 17p, HMS Invincible, ship in Battle of the Falklands, 1914. 20p, HMS Exeter, ship in Battle of the River Plate, 1939. 37p, SN.D6 Hovercraft, 1967. 43p, Antarctic patrol ship HMS Protector and Wasp helicopter, 1955. 68p, Desire, ship that made first sighting, 1592.

2001, July 24				
788-793	A154	Set of 6	27.50	27.50

Carcass Island and Its Flora and Fauna — A155

No. 794, 37p: a, Yellow violet. b, Tussac bird.
No. 795, 43p: a, Carcass Island settlement. b, Black-crowned night heron.

	Wmk. 373		
2001, Sept. 28	Litho.	Perf. 13¾	
	Pairs, #a-b		
794-795	A155	Set of 2	19.00	19.00

Gentoo Penguins — A156

Designs: 10p, Birds flapping wings. 33p, Feeding young. 37p, Bird with beak open. 43p, Four birds walking.

2001, Oct. 26		Perf. 14½x14¼	
796-799	A156	Set of 4	10.00	10.00

Falkland Islands Company, 150th Anniv. — A157

Designs: 10p, Company coat of arms, and gathering of cattle. 20p, Company flag, and ship Amelia. 43p, Manager F. E. Cobb, and company buildings. £1, Sheep farmer William Wickham Bertrand, sheep dip.

	Wmk. 373		
2002, Jan. 10	Litho.	Perf. 14	
800-803	A157	Set of 4	16.00	16.00

Reign Of Queen Elizabeth II, 50th Anniv. Issue
Common Design Type

Designs: Nos. 804, 808a, 20p, Princess Elizabeth reading, 1945. Nos. 805, 808b, 37p, In 1977. Nos. 806, 808c, 43p, Holding Prince Charles, 1949. Nos. 807, 808d, 50p, At Garter ceremony, 1994. No. 808e, 50p, 1955 portrait by Annigoni (38x50mm).

	Perf. 14¼x14½, 13¾ (#808e)		
2002, Feb. 6	Litho.	Wmk. 373	
	With Gold Frames		
804 CD360	20p multicolored	1.75	1.00
805 CD360	37p multicolored	2.25	2.00
806 CD360	43p multicolored	3.50	3.50
807 CD360	50p multicolored	4.00	4.00
	Nos. 804-807 (4)	11.50	10.50

Souvenir Sheet
Without Gold Frames

| 808 CD360 | Sheet of 5, #a-e | 11.50 | 11.50 |

Falkland Islands War, 20th Anniv. — A158

No. 809, 22p: a, HMS Hermes, 1982. b, Fishery patrol vessel, 2002.
No. 810, 40p: a, Troops landing, 1982. b, Mine clearing, 2002.
No. 811, 45p: a, RAF Harrier on HMS Hermes, 1982. b, RAF Tristar, 2002.

	Wmk. 373		
2002, June 14	Litho.	Perf. 14	
	Horiz. pairs, #a-b		
809-811	A158	Set of 3	20.00	20.00

Queen Mother Elizabeth (1900-2002)
Common Design Type

Designs: 22p, Wearing hat and scarf (black and white photograph). 25p, Wearing blue hat with polka dots. Nos. 814, 816a, 95p, Wearing feathered hat (black and white photograph). Nos. 815, 816b, £1.20, Wearing light blue hat.

	Wmk. 373		
2002, Aug. 5	Litho.	Perf. 14¼	
	With Purple Frames		
812 CD361	22p multicolored	1.00	1.00
813 CD361	25p multicolored	1.25	1.25
814 CD361	95p multicolored	5.00	5.00
815 CD361	£1.20 multicolored	6.75	6.75
	Nos. 812-815 (4)	14.00	14.00

Souvenir Sheet
Without Purple Frames
	Perf. 14½x14¼		
816 CD361	Sheet of 2, #a-b	14.50	14.50

Worldwide Fund for Nature (WWF) — A159

Penguins: 36p, Rockhopper. 40p, Magellanic. 45p, Gentoo. 70p, Macaroni.

	Wmk. 373		
2002, Aug. 30	Litho.	Perf. 14¼	
817-820	A159	Set of 4	11.50	11.50
a.	Horiz. strip of 4, #817-820	13.00	13.00

West Point Island and its Flora and Fauna — A160

No. 821, 40p: a, Felton's flower. b, Black-browed albatross.
No. 822, 45p: a, Rockhopper penguin. b, Island settlement.

	Perf. 14¼x14½		
2002, Oct. 31	Litho.	Wmk. 373	
	Horiz. Pairs, #a-b		
821-822	A160	Set of 2	15.00	15.00

Visit of Prince Andrew — A161

No. 823: a, 22p, In uniform. b, £1.52, In suit and tie.

2002, Nov. 11		Perf. 13¼x13½	
823 A161	Horiz. pair, #a-b	14.50	14.50

Shepherds' Houses — A162

Designs: 10p, Gun Hill shanty, Little Chartres. 22p, Paragon House, Lafonia. 45p, Dos Lomas, Lafonia. £1, Old House, Shallow Bay Farm.

	Wmk. 373		
2003, Mar. 31	Litho.	Perf. 14	
824-827	A162	Set of 4	12.00	12.00

Head of Queen Elizabeth II
Common Design Type

	Wmk. 373		
2003, June 2	Litho.	Perf. 13¾	
828 CD362	£2 multi	9.00	9.00

Prince William, 21st Birthday
Common Design Type

Color photographs: a, In suit at right. b, With Prince Harry at left.

	Wmk. 373		
2003, June 21	Litho.	Perf. 14¼	
829	Horiz. pair	13.50	13.50
a.-b.	CD364 95p Either single	5.50	5.50

Birds — A163

Designs: 1p, Chiloe widgeon. 2p, Dolphin gull, vert. 5p, Falkland flightless steamer duck. 10p, Black-throated finch, vert. 22p, White-tufted grebe. 25p, Rufous-chested dotterel, vert. 45p, Upland goose. 50p, Dark-faced ground-tyrant, vert. 95p, Black-crowned night heron. £1, Red-backed hawk, vert. £3, Black-necked swan. £5, Short-eared owl, vert.

	Perf. 13x13¼, 13¼x13		
2003, July 21		Wmk. 373	
830 A163	1p multi	.60	1.25
831 A163	2p multi	.90	1.50
832 A163	5p multi	1.25	1.50
833 A163	10p multi	1.50	1.50
834 A163	22p multi	1.75	1.25
835 A163	25p multi	2.00	1.25
836 A163	45p multi	2.50	2.00
837 A163	50p multi	3.00	3.00
838 A163	95p multi	4.25	5.25
839 A163	£1 multi	4.50	5.25
840 A163	£3 multi	12.00	13.00
841 A163	£5 multi	18.00	20.00
	Nos. 830-841,C1 (13)	54.75	59.25

See Nos. 917-919, C1.

Bird Life International — A164

Black-browed albatross: No. 842, Adult on nest, facing right. No. 843, Chick. 40p, Heads of two adults, vert. £1, Adult on nest, facing left, vert.
16p, In flight.

	Perf. 14¼x13¾, 13¾x14¼		
2003, Sept. 26			
842 A164	22p multi	1.75	1.75
a.	Perf. 14¼x14½	1.75	1.75
843 A164	22p multi	1.75	1.75
a.	Perf. 14¼x14½	1.75	1.75
844 A164	40p multi	2.75	2.75
a.	Perf. 14¼x14¼	2.75	2.75
845 A164	£1 multi	7.25	7.25
a.	Perf. 14¼x14½	7.25	7.25
	Nos. 842-845 (4)	13.50	13.50

Souvenir Sheet
| 846 | Sheet, #842a-846a | 16.50 | 16.50 |
| a. | A164 16p multi, perf. 14¼x14½ | 1.40 | 1.40 |

New Island and its Flora and Fauna — A165

No. 847, 40p: a, Striated caracara. b, Lady's slipper.
No. 848, 45p: a, Stone Cottage. b, King penguin.

	Wmk. 373		
2003, Oct. 24	Litho.	Perf. 13¾	
	Pairs, #a-b		
847-848	A165	Set of 2	18.00	18.00

Christmas — A166

Various depictions of Pale maiden flower: 16p, 30p, 40p, 95p.

2003, Nov. 3		Perf. 14x14¼	
849-852	A166	Set of 4	16.50	16.50

Sheep Farming — A167

Designs: 19p, Traditional hand shearing. 22p, Driving the sheep. 45p, Big House, Hill Cove. 70p, The early years. £1, Wool collection, SS Fitzroy.

	Unwmk.		
2004, Apr. 30	Litho.	Perf. 14	
853-857	A167	Set of 5	22.50	22.50

Wildlife Conservation in Falkland Islands, 25th Anniv. — A168

FALKLAND ISLANDS

Designs: 20p, Man planting tussac grass. 24p, People cleaning beach. 50p, Satellite tracking of rockhopper penguins. £1, Weighing of albatross chick.

2004, June 17	Litho.	Perf. 14
858-861 A168	Set of 4	18.00 18.00

Sir Rowland Hill (1795-1879) and Falkland Islands Postage Stamps — A169

Hill and: 24p, #20. 50p, #74. 75p, #94. £1, #151a.

2004, Aug. 31	Litho.	Perf. 13¼
862-865 A169	Set of 4	19.00 19.00

Sea Lion Island and its Flora and Fauna — A170

No. 866, 42p: a, King cormorant. b, Dog orchid.
No. 867, 50p: a, Magellanic penguin. b, Sea Lion Lodge.

2004, Sept. 15		Perf. 13¾
	Pairs, #a-b	
866-867 A170	Set of 2	19.50 19.50
866c	As #866a, dated "2005"	2.25
866d	As #866b, dated "2005"	2.25
866e	Pair, #866c-866d	7.00

Owls — A171

Designs: 18p, Head of short-eared owl. 45p, Short-eared owl. 50p, Barn owl in flight. £1.50, Barn owl.
£2, Barn owl in flight, horiz.

2004, Oct. 25
868-871 A171	Set of 4	18.00 18.00
Souvenir Sheet		
872 A171	£2 multi	12.00 12.00

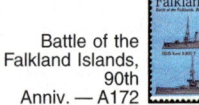

Battle of the Falkland Islands, 90th Anniv. — A172

No. 873: a, HMS Kent, HMS Inflexible, half of HMS Carnarvon, half of HMS Cornwall. b, British Navy flag, HMS Glasgow, half of HMS Carnarvon, half of HMS Cornwall, half of HMS Invincible. c, Medals, half of HMS Invincible.
No. 874: a, Medals, half of SMS Scharnhorst. b, German imperial war ensign, SMS Dresden, half of SMS Scharnhorst, half of SMS Leipzig. c, SMS Nürnberg, SMS Gneisenau, half of SMS Leipzig.

2004, Dec. 8	Litho.	Perf. 14
873	Horiz. strip of 3	9.50 9.50
a.-c.	A172 24p Any single	2.40 1.90
874	Horiz. strip of 3	17.50 17.50
a.-c.	A172 50p Any single	4.25 3.25

Camber Railway, 90th Anniv. — A173

Designs: 3p, Old track bed. 24p, Kerr Stuart Wren Class locomotive at Camber Depot, horiz. 50p, Kerr Stuart Wren Class locomotive

Falkland Islands Express, horiz. £2, Camber sailing wagon.

2005, Feb. 28		Perf. 13¾
875-878 A173	Set of 4	17.00 17.00

Wedding of Prince Charles and Camilla Parker Bowles — A174

Designs: 24p, Couple. 50p, Couple in formal wear, vert.
£2, Couple, Windsor Castle.

2005, Apr. 29		Perf. 14
879-880 A174	Set of 2	5.00 5.00
Souvenir Sheet		
881 A174	£2 multi	10.50 10.50

End of World War II, 60th Anniv. — A175

No. 882, 24p: a, Walrus reconnaissance seaplane. b, Presentation Spitfire X4616.
No. 883, 80p: a, HMS Exeter at Port Stanley. b, Governor, King Edward Memorial Hospital staff, Rear Admiral Harwood and Capt. Bell.
No. 884, £1: a, Fitzroy. b, HMS William Scoresby.

	Perf. 13¼x13½	
2005, June 29		Litho.
	Horiz. Pairs, #a-b	
882-884 A175	Set of 3	28.00 28.00

Maritime Heritage — A176

Designs: 24p, Snow Squall escaping CSS Tuscaloosa, 1863. No. 886, 55p, Jhelum, 1870. No. 887, 55p, Charles Cooper, 1866. £1.20, SS Imo colliding with the Mont Blanc, Halifax Harbor, 1917.

2005, Aug. 29	Litho.	Perf. 14
885-888 A176	Set of 4	13.00 13.00

Pebble Island and its Flora and Fauna — A177

No. 889, 45p: a, Gentoo penguin. b, Falkland lavender.
No. 890, 55p: a, Pebble Island Lodge. b, Black-necked swan.

2005, Sept. 12		Perf. 13¾
	Pairs, #a-b	
889-890 A177	Set of 2	14.00 14.00

Souvenir Sheet

The Fall of Nelson, Battle of Trafalgar, 21 October 1805, by Denis Dighton — A178

2005, Oct. 21
891 A178	£2 multi	12.00 12.00

Battle of Trafalgar, bicent.

Hans Christian Andersen (1805-75), Author — A179

Stories: 18p, The Little Mermaid. 30p, The Snowman. 45p, The Ugly Duckling. £1, Thumbelina.

2005, Oct. 28		Perf. 14
892-895 A179	Set of 4	11.50 11.50

Stanley Infant and Junior School, 50th anniv.

Black-crowned Night Heron — A180

Designs: 24p, Head. 55p, Bird on one leg. 80p, Juvenile standing. £1, Head of juvenile.

2006, Feb. 10	Litho.	Perf. 13¾
896-899 A180	Set of 4	13.00 13.00

Queen Elizabeth II, 80th Birthday — A181

Queen wearing: 24p, Yellow hat. 55p, Green hat. 80p, Blue hat. £1, Red hat.
£2, Tiara and white hat, horiz.

2006, Apr. 21		Perf. 14
900-903 A181	Set of 4	13.00 13.00
Souvenir Sheet		
904 A181	£2 multi	11.00 11.00

SS Great Britain — A182

View of: 24p, Bow. 55p, Stern. £1.50, Deck and masts.

2006, May 19		Perf. 13¾x13¼
905-907 A182	Set of 3	13.00 13.00

Birds — A183

Designs: No. 908, 25p, Gentoo penguin chicks. No. 909, 25p, King cormorants. No. 910, 60p, King penguin. No. 911, 60p, Wandering albatross.

2006, Aug. 30	Litho.	Perf. 14¼x14
908-911 A183	Set of 4	11.00 11.00

Bleaker Island and its Flora and Fauna — A184

No. 912, 50p: a, Woolly Falkland ragwort. b, Macaroni penguin.
No. 913, 60p: a, The Outlook and sheep. b, Long-tailed meadowlark.

2006, Sept. 18		Perf. 13¼x13
	Pairs, #a-b	
912-913 A184	Set of 2	15.00 15.00

Victoria Cross, 150th Anniv. — A185

Designs: Nos. 914, 916a, 60p, Lt. Col. H. Jones. Nos. 915, 916b, 60p, Sgt. Ian McKay. No. 916c, £1, Victoria Cross.

2006, Nov. 11		Perf. 13¼
	Stamps With White Frames	
914-915 A185	Set of 2	7.00 7.00
Souvenir Sheet		
Stamps Without White Frames		
916 A185	Sheet of 3, #a-c	7.00 7.00

Bird Type of 2003

Designs: 20p, Black-browed albatross, vert. 25p, Rufous-chested dotterel, vert. £5, Short-eared owl, vert.

	Perf. 13¼x13	
2006, Nov. 15	Litho.	Unwmk.
917 A163	20p multi	2.50 2.00
918 A163	25p multi	2.75 2.50
919 A163	£5 multi	22.50 24.00
Nos. 917-919 (3)		27.75 28.50

Nos. 918-919 differ from Nos. 835 and 841 by having less color around the Queen's head. Nos. 917-919 are dated "2006."

Worldwide Fund for Nature (WWF) — A186

Striated caracara: 25p, Heads of two birds. 50p, Bird in flight. 60p, Bird standing. 85p, Bird eating shellfish.

2006, Dec. 20	Litho.	Perf. 13¾
920-923 A186	Set of 4	10.00 10.00
923a	Miniature sheet, 4 each #920-923	47.50 47.50

Fisheries, 20th Anniv. — A187

Designs: 3p, Fishermen at sea. 11p, Fishing boat at night. 25p, Fishermen leaving boat. 30p, Japanese jigger. 60p, Fishery protection boat Dorada. £1.05, Trawler transferring fish to a freezer container ship.

2007, Feb. 24		Perf. 14¼
924-929 A187	Set of 6	13.50 13.50

HMS Plymouth — A188

HMS Plymouth: 25p, Joining Falkland Islands Task Force. 40p, Supporting SBS. 60p, Under attack by Argentine fighters. £1.05, Docked at Port Stanley.

2007, Mar. 27		
930-933 A188	Set of 4	17.50 17.50

Souvenir Sheet

Falkland Islands War, 25th Anniv. A189

No. 934: a, Avro Vulcan prototype VX770. b, Avro Vulcan XM597. c, Avro Vulcan XM607. d, Vulcan in the Sky Project.

2007, May 25	Litho.	Perf. 13¼
934 A189	60p Sheet of 4, #a-d	14.00 14.00

FALKLAND ISLANDS 495

Miniature Sheets

British and Falkland Islander Casualties of the Falkland Islands War — A190

No. 935, 25p — Casualties beginning with: a, Doreen Bonner. b, G. W. J. Batt. c, J. R. Carlyle. d, S. J. Dixon. e, I. R. Farrell. f, G. C. Grace. g, R. R. Heath. h, A. S. James.
No. 936, 60p: a, D. Lee. b, P. B. McKay. c, G. T. Nelson. d, J. B. Pashley. e, M. Sambles. f, D. A. Strickland. g, R. G. Thomas. h, P. A. West.

2007, June 14   Litho.   Perf. 14¼
Sheets of 8, #a-h
935-936   A190   Set of 2   30.00   30.00

Scouting, Cent. — A191

Designs: 10p, Scouts on ladder of RRS Discovery. 20p, Dignitaries on ship's deck. 25p, Dignitaries, diff. £2, RRS Discovery.

2007, July 23   Litho.   Perf. 13½x13¼
937-940   A191   Set of 4   12.00   12.00
Voyage of RRS Discovery from Falkland Islands for presentation to British Scout Association, 70th anniv.

Princess Diana (1961-97) — A192

2007, Aug. 31   Perf. 14
941   A192   60p multi   3.75   3.75
Printed in sheets of 8 stamps + 2 labels.

Saunders Island and its Flora and Fauna — A193

No. 942, 50p: a, Rockhopper penguin. b, Dusty miller.
No. 943, 55p: a, Crested caracara. b, Earliest British settlement at Port Egmont.

2007, Sept. 28   Litho.   Perf. 13¾
Pairs, #a-b
942-943   A193   Set of 2   15.00   15.00

A194

2007, Nov. 20   Litho.   Perf. 14
944   A194   £1 multi   6.00   6.00
Wedding of Queen Elizabeth II and Prince Philip, 60th Anniv.

Polar Explorers and Their Ships — A195

Explorers and ships: 4p, James Weddell (1787-1834), and Jane. 25p, James Clark Ross (1800-62), and HMS Erebus. 85p, William Spiers Bruce (1867-1921), and Scotia. £1.61, James Marr (1902-65), and Discovery II.

2008, Apr. 7
945-948   A195   Set of 4   13.00   13.00

Southern Elephant Seals — A196

Designs: 27p, Seal pup. 55p, Male and female. 65p, Seals play fighting. £1.10, Seal and tussock bird.

2008, July 15   Litho.   Perf. 14
949-952   A196   Set of 4   14.00   14.00

Aircraft — A197

Designs: 1p, Taylorcraft Auster Mk 5. 2p, Boeing 747-300. 5p, De Havilland Canada DHC-6 Twin Otter. 10p, Lockheed C-130 Hercules. 27p, De Havilland Canada DHC-2 Beaver. 55p, Airbus A320. 65p, Lockheed L-1011-385-3 Tristar C2. 90p, Avro Vulcan B2. £1, Britten-Norman BN-2 Islander. £2, Panavia Tornado F3. £3, De Havilland Canada DHC-7-110 Dash 7. £5, BAE Sea Harrier.

2008, Aug. 1   Litho.   Perf. 14
953	A197	1p multi	.40	.75
954	A197	2p multi	.40	.75
955	A197	5p multi	.75	.85
956	A197	10p multi	.90	.90
957	A197	27p multi	1.75	1.75
958	A197	55p multi	2.25	2.25
959	A197	65p multi	2.75	2.75
960	A197	90p multi	3.50	3.50
961	A197	£1 multi	4.00	4.00
962	A197	£2 multi	7.25	8.00
963	A197	£3 multi	10.00	11.00
964	A197	£5 multi	16.00	18.00

Nos. 953-964 (12)   49.95   54.50

Souvenir Sheet
Stamps With Royal Air Force 90th Anniv. Emblem Added
965   Sheet of 4   14.50   14.50
   a. A197 10p Like #956   .40   .40
   b. A197 65p Like #959   2.60   2.60
   c. A197 90p Like #960   3.50   3.50
   d. A197 £2 Like #962   8.00   8.00

Port Louis, 175th Anniv. — A198

Designs: 27p, Sailor raising British flag. 65p, Royal Marines, British flag. £2, Capt. Onslow of HMS Clio, British flag.

2008, Sept. 22   Litho.   Perf. 14
966-967   A198   Set of 2   4.75   4.75
Souvenir Sheet
968   A198   £2 multi   9.00   9.00

Islands and Rocks — A199

Designs: 22p, The Slipper. 40p, Kidney Island. 60p, Stephens Bluff and Castle Rock. £1, The Colliers.

2008, Oct. 1   Litho.   Perf. 13¾
969-972   A199   Set of 4   10.00   10.00
See Nos. 986-989, 1025-1028.

Retirement of Queen Elizabeth 2 as Ocean Liner — A200

Designs: 23p, Launch of Queen Elizabeth 2. 27p, Service of Queen Elizabeth 2 as troop ship in Falkland Islands War. 65p, Queen Elizabeth 2, Palm Jumeirah, Dubai. £2, Queen Elizabeth 2 (70x34mm).

2008, Nov. 21   Litho.   Perf. 13¼
973-976   A200   Set of 4   13.00   13.00

Charles Darwin (1809-82), Naturalist A201

Designs: 4p, Darwin seated. 27p, Warrah. 65p, HMS Beagle in Berkeley Sound, 1834. £1.10, Darwin encountering a Magellanic penguin.

2009, Apr. 23   Litho.   Perf. 14
977-980   A201   Set of 4   8.00   8.00

Naval Aviation, Cent. — A202

Royal Navy aircraft and ships: 30p, Westland/Aerospatiale Gazelle AH1 helicopter. 50p, Westland Lynx HAS2 helicopter. 65p, Westland Wessex HU5 helicopter. £1.10, Westland Sea King HAS5 helicopter. £2, BAe Sea Harrier, HMS Hermes.

2009, May 7   Litho.   Perf. 14
981-984   A202   Set of 4   11.00   11.00
Souvenir Sheet
985   A202   £2 multi   7.50   7.50

Islands and Rocks Type of 2008

Designs: 27p, Seal Rocks. 40p, Beauchene Island. 65p, Jason East Cay, Steeple Jason. £1.50, Horse Block.

2009, Aug. 14   Litho.   Perf. 13¾
986-989   A199   Set of 4   11.50   11.50

Albatrosses A203

Designs: 22p, Black-browed albatross. 27p, Gray-headed albatross. 60p, Light-mantled sooty albatross. 90p, Wandering albatross.

2009, Oct. 19   Litho.   Perf. 13¾
990-993   A203   Set of 4   8.50   8.50

Cobb's Wren — A204

Designs: Nos. 994, 998a, 27p, Wren on cowood. Nos. 995, 998b, 65p, Wrens at nest. Nos. 996, 998c, 90p, Wren on rock. Nos. 997, 998d, £1.10, Two wrens.

2009, Nov. 10   Perf. 13¾
Stamps With WWF Emblem
994-997   A204   Set of 4   10.00   10.00
997a   Sheet of 16, 4 each #994-997   52.50   52.50
Souvenir Sheet
Stamps With Falklands Conservation Emblem
998   A204   Sheet of 4, #a-d   10.00   10.00

Ships Named HMS Exeter — A205

Ship used from: 4p, 1931-42. 20p, 1931-42, with helicopter. 30p, 1980-2009, with helicopter. £1.66, 1980-2009, with helicopter, diff.

2009, Dec. 8   Litho.   Perf. 14
999-1002   A205   Set of 4   7.50   7.50

Skies in Four Seasons — A206

Designs: 27p, Carcass Island in spring. 55p, Beach on New Island in summer. 65p, Rainbow over Stanley in autumn. £1.10, Islands in winter.

2010, Jan. 25   Litho.   Perf. 13
1003-1006   A206   Set of 4   8.00   8.00

Restoration of the SS Great Britain — A207

SS Great Britain: 27p, On pontoon near jetty in Stanley. 50p, Beached at Sparrow Cove. 65p, Bow. £1.10, Mast and rigging.

2010, Apr. 12   Perf. 13¼
1007-1010   A207   Set of 4   8.00   8.00

Miniature Sheet

Battle of Britain, 70th Anniv. A208

No. 1011 — Airplanes: a, Hawker Hurricane P2961. b, Supermarine Spitfire P9398. c, Hawker Hurricane P3854. d, Supermarine Spitfire P7350. e, Hawker Hurricane V6665. f, Supermarine Spitfire L1035. g, Hawker Hurricane P3576. h, Supermarine Spitfire X4620.

2010, May 7   Litho.   Perf. 14x14¼
1011   A208   65p Sheet of 8, #a-h   15.00   15.00
London 2010 Festival of Stamps.

Birds — A209

Designs: Nos. 1012, 1016a, 27p, Sooty shearwater. Nos. 1013, 1016b, 70p, White-chinned petrel. Nos. 1014, 1016c, 95p, Southern giant petrel. Nos. 1015, 1016d, £1.15, Greater shearwater.

2010, July 8   Litho.   Perf. 13¾
Stamps With White Frames
1012-1015   A209   Set of 4   9.50   9.50
Souvenir Sheet
Stamps Without White Frames
1016   A209   Sheet of 4, #a-d   11.50   11.50

FALKLAND ISLANDS

Flowering Shrubs — A210

Designs: 27p, Fuchsia. 70p, Boxwood. 95p, Gorse. £1.15, Honeysuckle.

2010, Oct. 27	Litho.	Perf. 13¼x13
1017-1020 A210	Set of 4	10.00 10.00

Royal Air Force Search and Rescue Force, 70th Anniv. A211

Anniversary emblem and: 27p, Helicopter on ground. 70p, Helicopter in flight. 95p, Crew in helicopter cockpit. £1.15, Helicopter in flight with open door.

2011, Mar. 9		Perf. 13¼
1021-1024 A211	Set of 4	10.00 10.00

Islands and Rocks Type of 2008

Designs: 3p, Bird Island. 27p, Eddystone Rock. 70p, Round Island and Sail Rock. £1.71, Direction Island.

2011, Apr. 11		Perf. 13¼x13
1025-1028 A199	Set of 4	8.50 8.50

Wedding of Prince William and Catherine Middleton A212

2011, Apr. 29		Perf. 13¼
1029 A212	£2 multi	6.75 6.75

Worldwide Fund for Nature (WWF) — A213

Southern sea lions: 27p, Males and females on beach. 40p, Pod in water. 70p, Males on beach. £1.15, Head.

2011, May 30		Perf. 13¾
1030-1033 A213	Set of 4	8.75 8.75
1033a	Miniature sheet of 16, 4 each #1030-1033	35.00 35.00

Queen Elizabeth II, 85th Birthday — A214

Queen Elizabeth II wearing: 27p, Red violet hat with flower. 30p, Fur hat. 70p, White hat with pink and white ribbons. £1.50, White hat with feather.

2011, June 11		Perf. 13¾
1034-1037 A214	Set of 4	8.50 8.50

Souvenir Sheet

Queen Elizabeth II A215

2011, Aug. 8	Litho.	Perf. 14¼x15
1038 A215	£2 multi	6.75 6.75

Commonwealth Parliamentary Association, cent.

Wildlife — A216

Designs: 27p, Gentoo penguins. 70p, Leopard seal. 95p, Gonatus squid. £1.15, Gentoo penguins, diff.

2011, Nov. 16		Perf. 13¾
1039-1042 A216	Set of 4	10.00 10.00

Marine Life — A217

Designs: 27p, Sea anemone. 50p, Jellyfish. 70p, Starfish. £1.15, Nudibranch.

2012, Apr. 11		Perf. 13¼x13½
1043-1046 A217	Set of 4	8.00 8.00

Reign of Queen Elizabeth II, 60th Anniv. — A218

Photograph of Queen Elizabeth II in: 27p, 1952. 30p, 1977. 70p, 2002. £1.71, 2012. £3, Queen Elizabeth II wearing tiara, 1955.

2012, May 10		Perf. 13½x13¼
1047-1050 A218	Set of 4	9.00 9.00

Souvenir Sheet
Perf. 13¼

1051 A218	£3 multi	9.00 9.00

No. 1051 contains one 30x48mm stamp.

Liberation of the Falkland Islands, 30th Anniv. — A219

Designs: No. 1052, 30p, Ferry MV Concordia Bay. No. 1053, 30p, Liberation Monument, Stanley. No. 1054, 75p, School, Stanley. No. 1055, 75p, Wind turbines. £1, Sign and houses near Stanley Harbor. £1.20, Children and penguins.

2012, June 14		Perf. 14
1052-1057 A219	Set of 6	12.50 12.50

Coastal Landscapes A220

Designs: 30p, Surf Bay, East Falkland Island. 75p, Cliffs, New Island. £1, Mountain, Steeple Jason Island. £1.20, Deaths Head and Grave Cove, West Falkland Island.

2012, July 12		Perf. 13
1058-1061 A220	Set of 4	9.25 9.25

Sinking of the P.S.N.C. Oravia, Cent. — A221

Designs: 30p, Oravia at sea. 75p, Passengers and crew wearing life vests. £1, Passengers filling lifeboats. £1.20 Oravia and the Samson.

2012, Aug. 28		Perf. 14
1062-1065 A221	Set of 4	12.00 12.00

Sinking of the Titanic, Cent. A222

2012, Aug. 28		Perf. 14x14¾
1066 A222	£2 multi	9.00 9.00

Dolphins and Whales A223

Designs: 1p, Southern right whale dolphins. 2p, Minke whale. 5p, Peale's dolphin. 10p, Dusky dolphin. 30p, Southern right whale. 50p, Fin whale. 75p, Hourglass dolphin. £1, Long-finned pilot whale. £1.20, Killer whales. £2, Sperm whale. £3.50, Commerson's dolphin. £5, Sei whale.

2012, Nov. 9		Perf. 13¼
1067 A223	1p multi	.25 .25
1068 A223	2p multi	.25 .25
1069 A223	5p multi	.25 .25
1070 A223	10p multi	.30 .30
1071 A223	30p multi	.95 .95
1072 A223	50p multi	1.60 1.60
1073 A223	75p multi	2.40 2.40
1074 A223	£1 multi	3.25 3.25
1075 A223	£1.20 multi	4.00 4.00
1076 A223	£2 multi	6.50 6.50
1077 A223	£3.50 multi	11.00 11.00
1078 A223	£5 multi	14.00 14.00
Nos. 1067-1078 (12)		44.75 44.75

See No. 1172.

Color in Nature A224

No. 1079: a, Night heron. b, Diddle-dee berries.
No. 1080: a, Short-eared owl. b, Scurvy grass flowers.

2012, Dec. 14		Perf. 13
1079	Pair	2.00 2.00
a.-b.	A224 30p Either single	1.00 1.00
1080	Pair	4.50 4.50
a.-b.	A224 75p Either single	2.25 2.25

See Nos. 1108-1109, 1122-1123, 1136-1137.

2013 Referendum on Political Status — A225

Map, of Falkland Island, hand and ballot box with denomination color of: 3p, Deep blue. 40p, Red violet. 75p, Green. £1.76, Red brown. £3, Purple.

2013, Feb. 15		
1081-1084 A225	Set of 4	8.75 8.75

Souvenir Sheet
Perf. 13½x13¼

| 1085 A225 | £3 multi | 9.00 9.00 |

No. 1085 contains one 56x45mm stamp.

Wildlife — A226

Designs: 30p, Johnny rook. 75p, Rockhopper penguins. £1, Rockhopper penguin swimming. £1.20, Lobster krill.

2013, Mar. 28		Perf. 13¾
1086-1089 A226	Set of 4	10.00 10.00

Lady Margaret Thatcher (1925-2013), British Prime Minister — A227

Lady Thatcher: 30p, And husband, Denis arriving at 10 Downing Street, 1979. 75p, Inspecting Falkland Islands minefield, 1983. £1, With flag at celebration of 10th anniversary of Falkland Islands liberation, 1992. £1.20, Holding Falkland Islands coin commemorating 25th anniversary of the liberation, 2007.

2013, May 16		Perf. 13¾
1090-1093 A227	Set of 4	10.00 10.00

Sir Rex Hunt (1926-2012), Governor of Falkland Islands — A228

Falkland Islands coat of arms and Hunt: 30p, As Civil Commissioner, 1982. 75p, In uniform next to Governor's car. £1, With flag of Falkland Islands, 1992. £1.20, Talking to Queen Elizabeth II, 2000.

2013, June 11		Perf. 14
1094-1097 A228	Set of 4	10.00 10.00

Coronation of Queen Elizabeth II, 60th Anniv. — A229

Queen Elizabeth II: 30p, Wearing coronation gown. 75p, With crown and orb. £1, Waving. £1.20, With Prince Philip.

2013, July 22		Perf. 13½x13¼
1098-1101 A229	Set of 4	10.00 10.00

Shallow Marine Surveys Group — A230

Marine life: Nos. 1102, 1106a, 30p, Saffron sea cucumber. Nos. 1103, 1106b, 75p, Stalked jellyfish. Nos. 1104, 1106c, £1, Scythe-edged serolis. Nos. 1105, 1106d, £1.20, Naked sea urchin.
No. 1107a, £1, Painted shrimp, vert.

2013, Aug. 29		Perf. 13¼x13½
Stamps With White Frames		
1102-1105 A230	Set of 4	10.50 10.50
Stamps Without White Frames		
1106 A230	Strip of 4, #a-d	10.50 10.50

Souvenir Sheet
Perf. 13½x13¼

| 1107 A230 | Sheet of 3 (see footnote) | 9.75 9.75 |
| a. | A230 £1 multi | 3.25 3.25 |

No. 1107 contains No. 1107a, Ascension No. 1104a and South Georgia and South Sandwich Islands No. 485a. This sheet was sold in Ascension, Falkland Islands and South Georgia and South Sandwich Islands.

Color in Nature Type of 2012

No. 1108: a, Macaroni penguin. b, Purple cap fungi.
No. 1109: a, Crested duck. b, Southern painted lady butterfly.

2013, Oct. 3		Perf. 13¼
1108	Pair	1.90 1.90
a.-b.	A224 30p Either single	.95 .95
1109	Pair	4.80 4.80
a.-b.	A224 75p Either single	2.40 2.40

Wildlife — A231

FALKLAND ISLANDS

Designs: 30p, King penguin and chick. 75p, Gaptooth lanternfish. £1, Southern sea lion. £1.20, King penguins, diff.

2014, Mar. 25	Litho.	Perf. 13¼
1110-1113 A231	Set of 4	11.00 11.00

Mushrooms — A232

Designs: 30p, False chanterelle. 75p, Red wax cap. £1, Clustered domecap. £1.20, Shaggy inkcap.

2014, Apr. 15	Litho.	Perf. 13¼
1114-1117 A232	Set of 4	10.00 10.00

Royal Christenings — A233

Photograph from christening of: 30p, Queen Elizabeth II. 75p, Prince Charles. £1, Prince William. £1.20, Prince George.

2014, May 21	Litho.	Perf. 13¼
1118-1121 A233	Set of 4	10.00 10.00

Color in Nature Type of 2012

No. 1122: a, King penguins. b, Marsh marigolds.
No. 1123: a, Black oystercatcher. b, Vanilla daisies.

2014, Sept. 16	Litho.	Perf. 13¼
1122	Pair	2.00 2.00
a.-b.	A224 30p Either single	1.00 1.00
1123	Pair	5.00 5.00
a.-b.	A224 75p Either single	2.50 2.50

Battle of the Falkland Islands, Cent. — A234

Designs: 30p, SMS Scharnhorst. 75p, HMS Invincible. £1, British and German flags, poppies. £1.20, Sailor, Battle of the Falkland Islands Monument.

2014, Dec. 8	Litho.	Perf. 13¾
1124-1127 A234	Set of 4	10.00 10.00

Type 42 Destroyers A235

Designs: 30p, HMS Sheffield. 75p, HMS Exeter. £1, HMS Liverpool. £1.20, HMS Edinburgh.

2014, Dec. 22	Litho.	Perf. 14
1128-1131 A235	Set of 4	9.00 9.00

Birds — A236

Adult and chicks: 30p, Pied oystercatchers. 75p, Gentoo penguins. £1, Black-browed albatrosses. £1.20, Falkland skuas.

2015, Feb. 11	Litho.	Perf. 13¾
1132-1135 A236	Set of 4	10.00 10.00

Color in Nature Type of 2012

No. 1136: a, Black-throated finch. b, Fuegian ferns.
No. 1137: a, Dolphin gulls. b, Yellow daisies.

2015, May 12	Litho.	Perf. 13¼
1136	Pair	1.90 1.90
a.-b.	A224 30p Either single	.95 .95
1137	Pair	4.50 4.50
a.-b.	A224 75p Either single	2.25 2.25

Magna Carta, 800th Anniv. — A237

Designs: 30p, King John, Magna Carta and barons. 75p, Courtroom. £1, Gilbert House, Stanley. £1.20, King John, arms of Falkland Islands.

2015, June 15	Litho.	Perf. 14
1138-1141 A237	Set of 4	10.50 10.50

Wildlife — A238

Designs: 30p, Magellanic penguin. 75p, Falkland sprats. £1, Falkland skua. £1.20, Heads of two magellanic penguins.

2015, Aug. 21	Litho.	Perf. 13¾
1142-1145 A238	Set of 4	10.00 10.00

Queen Elizabeth II, Longest-Reigning British Monarch — A239

Queen Elizabeth II and events during her reign: 30p, Publications reporting on her coronation, 1953. 75p, Arrival of first Land Rovers in the Falkland Islands, 1950s. £1, Coach used for Golden Jubilee, 2012. £1.25, Falkland Islands referendum, 2013.

2015, Sept. 9	Litho.	Perf. 14
1146-1149 A239	Set of 4	10.00 10.00

Elephant Seal Research Group, 20th Anniv. — A240

No. 1150, 30p: a, Seal in water. b, Researcher with equipment near seal.
No. 1151, 75p: a, Pod of seals on beach. b, Researcher approaching seal.
No. 1152, £1: a, Seal and penguins. b, Researcher holding measuring stick above seal.

2015, Nov. 30	Litho.	Perf. 13
Horiz. Pairs, #a-b		
1150-1152 A240	Set of 3	12.50 12.50

Clouds A241

Designs: 31p, Asperitas. 76p, Altocumulus. £1.01, Altocumulus lenticularis. £1.22, Cumulonimbus and Stratocumulus.

2015, Dec. 9	Litho.	Perf. 13¼
1153-1156 A241	Set of 4	9.75 9.75

Birds of Prey — A242

Designs: No. 1157, 31p, Barn owl. No. 1158, 31p, Short-eared owl. No. 1159, 76p, Red-backed buzzard. No. 1160, 76p, Crested caracara. £1.01, Peregrine falcon. £1.22, Striated caracara.

2016, Jan. 13	Litho.	Perf. 13¾
1157-1162 A242	Set of 6	13.00 13.00

Items at Historic Dockyard Museum — A243

Designs: 31p, Traditional horse gear. 76p, Peat-burning stove. £1.01, Warrah skull. £1.22, Antarctic exploration hut.

2016, Mar. 30	Litho.	Perf. 13¾
1163-1166 A243	Set of 4	9.50 9.50

Queen Elizabeth II, 90th Birthday — A244

Photographs of Queen Elizabeth from: 31p, 1977. 76p, 1982. £1.01, 1953. £1.22, 2014. £3, Queen Elizabeth II in 1962.

2016, Apr. 21	Litho.	Perf. 14
1167-1170 A244	Set of 4	9.75 9.75

Souvenir Sheet

1171 A244 £3 multi	9.00 9.00

Dolphins and Whales Type of 2012

2016, Aug. 1	Litho.	Perf. 13¼
1172 A223 31p Southern right whale		.85 .85

Endemic Plants — A245

Designs: No. 1173, 31p, Falkland rockcress. No. 1174, 31p, Lady's slipper. No. 1175, 76p, False-plantain. No. 1176, 76p, Silvery buttercup. No. 1177, £1.01, Snakeplant. No. 1178, £1.01, Falkland nassauvia.
No. 1179, 66p: a, Like No. 1173. b, Like No. 1174. c, Like No. 1175. d, Like No. 1176. e, Like No. 1177. f, Like No. 1178.

2016, Nov. 21	Litho.	Perf. 13¾
1173-1178 A245	Set of 6	11.00 11.00

Miniature Sheet

1179 A245 66p Sheet of 6, #a	10.00 10.00

No. 1179 has cream colored margins around the stamps.

Shipwrecks A246

Designs: 31p, Actaeon. 76p, Charles Cooper. £1.01, Afterglow. £1.22, Capricorn.

2017, Mar. 27	Litho.	Perf. 13
1180-1183 A246	Set of 4	8.25 8.25

See Nos. 1213-1216, 1244-1247, 1264-1267.

Falkland Islands Journal, 50th Anniv. — A247

Journal cover from: 31p, 2010. 76p, 2013r. £1.01, 2014. £1.22, 2016.

2017, July 5	Litho.	Perf. 13½x13¼
1184-1187 A247	Set of 4	8.50 8.50

A248   Birds — A249

Designs: 1p, Tussacbird. 2p, Long-tailed meadowlark. 5p, Black-chinned siskin. 10p, Falkland pipit, above white flowers. 20p, Cobb's wren. 50p, White-bridled finch. 76p, Falkland thrush. £1, Two-banded plover. £1.20, Falkland grass wren. £2, Dark-faced ground tyrant. £3.50, Rufous-chested dotterel. £5, Magellanic snipe.
(31p), Falkland pipit, above red flowers.

2017, Aug. 14	Litho.	Perf. 13
1188 A248	1p multi	.25 .25
1189 A248	2p multi	.25 .25
1190 A248	5p multi	.25 .25
1191 A248	10p multi	.30 .30
1192 A248	20p multi	.55 .55
1193 A248	50p multi	1.40 1.40
1194 A248	76p multi	2.00 2.00
1195 A248	£1 multi	2.75 2.75
1196 A248	£1.20 multi	3.25 3.25
1197 A248	£2 multi	5.25 5.25
1198 A248	£3.50 multi	9.25 9.25
1199 A248	£5 multi	13.50 13.50
Nos. 1188-1199 (12)		39.00 39.00

Booklet Stamp
Self-Adhesive
Serpentine Die Cut 13

1200 A249 (31p) multi	.85 .85
a. Booklet pane of 10	8.50
b. Dated "2019"	.80 .80
c. Booklet pane of 10 #1200b	8.00

Issued: No. 1200b, 8/6/19. No. 1200b sold for 32p on day of issue.

Falkland Islands Fisheries, 30th Anniv. — A250

Designs: 31p, Toothfish and CFL Hunter. 76p, FPV Protegat and fishery RIB. £1.01, Argos Vigo and Frank Wild. £1.22, Robin M. Lee and Falkland calamari.

2017, Oct. 23	Litho.	Perf. 13½x13¼
1201-1204 A250	Set of 4	8.75 8.75

70th Wedding Anniversary of Queen Elizabeth II and Prince Philip — A251

Photograph of Queen Elizabeth II and Prince Philip from: 31p, 1952. 76p, 1961. £1.22, 1972. £1.78, 2016.

2017, Nov. 20	Litho.	Perf. 13¼x13
1205-1208 A251	Set of 4	11.00 11.00

Christ Church Cathedral, Stanley, 125th Anniv. — A252

Various views of Cathedral: 31p, 76p, £1.01, £1.22.

2017, Dec. 18	Litho.	Perf. 13¼x13
1209-1212 A252	Set of 4	9.00 9.00

Shipwrecks Type of 2017

Designs: 31p, Glengowan. 76p, Jhelum. £1.01, Golden Chance. £1.22, Lady Elizabeth.

2018, Mar. 2	Litho.	Perf. 13
1213-1216 A246	Set of 4	9.25 9.25

497

FALKLAND ISLANDS

Wildlife — A253

Designs: 31p, Macaroni penguin on nest. 76p, Euphausiid krill. £1.01, Southern sea lion. £1.22, Two Macaroni penguins.

2018, Apr. 18	Litho.		Perf. 13	
1217-1220	A253	Set of 4	9.00	9.00

Royal Air Force, Cent. — A254

Designs: 31p, Hawker Siddeley Nimrod MR2. 76p, McDonnell Douglas F-4 Phantom. £1.22, Hawker Siddeley Harrier GR.3. £1.92, Eurofighter Typhoon.

2018, July 2	Litho.		Perf. 13¼x13½	
1221-1224	A254	Set of 4	11.00	11.00

Wedding of Prince Harry and Meghan Markle — A255

Designs: 31p, Engagement photograph. 75p, Couple at ANZAC Day service. £1.10, Couple at altar on wedding day. £1.22, Couple leaving wedding. £3, Couple kissing, vert.

		Perf. 13¼x13½		
2018, Aug. 14		Litho.		
1225-1228	A255	Set of 4	8.25	8.25

Souvenir Sheet
Perf. 13½x13¼

| 1229 | A255 | £3 multi | 7.75 | 7.75 |

Migratory Birds — A256

No. 1230 — Southern rockhopper penguin and map of: a, 31p, South America and Northern Patagonian Shelf. b, 76p, Southern tip of South America and the Falkland Islands.
No. 1231 — Sooty shearwater and map of: a, £1.01, North America, Europe and Northern Africa. b, £1.22, South America, Falkland Islands and Southern Africa.

2018, Oct. 18	Litho.	Perf. 13¼x13½		
1230	A256	Vert. pair, #a-b	2.75	2.75
1231	A256	Vert. pair, #a-b	5.75	5.75

Old Fox Bay Post Office, Cent. — A257

Fox Bay cancel and: 31p, 1940s photograph of Post Office. 76p, Old post office scales. £1.01, Princess Anne mailing postcard, old postmark box. £1.22, Old Post Office and Museum.

Perf. 13¼x13½

2018, Nov. 28		Litho.		
1232-1235	A257	Set of 4	8.50	8.50

Falkland Islands Government Air Service, 70th Anniv. — A258

Airplanes: 31p, Auster 4. 76p, Norseman V. £1.01, DHC-2 Beaver. £1.22, BN-2B-26 Islander.

Perf. 13¼x13½

2018, Dec. 19		Litho.		
1236-1239	A258	Set of 4	8.50	8.50

Landscapes — A259

Photographs: 31p, Quarry Point, Fox Bay, by Carli Sudder. 76p, New Island, by Georgina Strange. £1.01, Road to Nowhere, Port Howard, by Maria Forman. £1.22, Towards Albemarle, by Ben Cockwell.

2018, Dec. 28	Litho.		Perf. 13¼	
1240-1243	A259	Set of 4	8.50	8.50

Shipwrecks Type of 2017

Designs: 31p, Lily. 76p, Plym. £1.01, Philomel. £1.22, Protector.

2019, Mar. 4	Litho.		Perf. 13	
1244-1247	A246	Set of 4	8.75	8.75

D-Day, 75th Anniv. — A260

Designs: 32p, Troops looking at graffiti on side of their glider. 78p, Airplanes for invasion on runway in England. £1.04, Soldiers landing on Utah Beach. £1.26, Tank in water after leaving landing craft.

2019, June 6	Litho.		Perf. 13¼x13½	
1248-1251	A260	Set of 4	8.75	8.75

Feathers — A261

Feathers of: No. 1252, 32p, Striated caracara. No. 1253, 32p, Black-browed albatross. No. 1254, 78p, Yellow-billed teal. No. 1255, 78p, Barn owl. No. 1256, £1.26, Black-crowned night heron. No. 1257, £1.26, King penguin.

2019, Aug. 5	Litho.		Perf. 13¼x13½	
1252-1257	A261	Set of 6	11.50	11.50

Cancer Support and Awareness Fund Emblem and Peter Collins A262

Stephen Jaffray Memorial Medical Emergency Assistance Fund Emblem and Stephen Jaffray (1970-92) A263

2019, Dec. 6	Litho.		Perf. 13	
1258	A262	78p multi	2.10	2.10
1259	A263	78p multi	2.10	2.10

Land Rovers — A264

Designs: 32p, Series I 88-inch. 78p, Series I hard top. £1.26, Series IIA roadless traction forest rover. £1.96, Series IIB forward control.

2019, Dec. 20	Litho.		Perf. 13	
1260-1263	A264	Set of 4	11.50	11.50

Shipwrecks Type of 2017

Designs: 32p, Samson. 78p, St. Mary. £1.04, Weddell. £1.26, Garland.

2020, Mar. 16	Litho.		Perf. 13	
1264-1267	A246	Set of 4	8.50	8.50

Penguins Depicted on Falkland Islands 50-Pence Coins — A265

Designs: 32p, Rockhopper penguin. 68p, King penguin. 78p, Magellanic penguin. £1.04, Gentoo penguin. £1.26, Macaroni penguin.

Perf. 13¼x13½

2020, Aug. 10		Litho.		
1268-1272	A265	Set of 5	11.00	11.00

Falkland Islands Philatelic Study Group, 50th Anniv. — A266

Designs: 32p, Falkland Islands #21, Stanley Post Office and Philatelic Bureau. 78p, Falkland Islands #74, Jane Cameron National Archives. £1.04, Falkland Islands #94a, publications of Falkland Islands Philatelic Study Group. £1.26, Falkland Islands #151a, 1875 cover sent from Falkland Islands to Tobago.

2020, Sept. 7	Litho.		Perf. 13¼x13½	
1273-1276	A266	Set of 4	8.75	8.75

Paintings of Birds by Mike Peake (1939-2005) A267

Painting of: 32p, Black-necked swan. 40p, Black-crowned night heron. 78p, Upland geese. £1.04, Belcher's gull. £1.26, Variable hawk. £1.35, Upland geese and seal.

2020, Oct. 1	Litho.		Perf. 13	
1277-1282	A267	Set of 6	13.50	13.50

Falkland Islands Mine Clearance Program — A268

Designs: 32p, Discovered mines. 49p, Manual demining. £1.10, Penguin watchers. £1.96, Mechanical demining.

Perf. 13¼x13½

2020, Nov. 14		Litho.		
1283-1286	A268	Set of 4	10.50	10.50

Christmas — A269

Children's art by: 32p, Rylee Molkernbuhr. 78p, Tessa Blake. £1.04, Laura Blake. £1.26, Neve Stanworth.

2020, Nov. 20	Litho.		Perf. 13¼x13	
1287-1290	A269	Set of 4	9.25	9.25

Queen Elizabeth II, 95th Birthday — A270

Designs: 32p, Princess Elizabeth as child in ballet costume. 49p, Queen Elizabeth II at her coronation. 78p, Queen Elizabeth II with Prince Philip, 2007. £1.04, Queen Elizabeth II holding camera, 1982. £1.10, Queen Elizabeth II at Trooping the Color ceremony. £1.26, Queen Elizabeth II, 2017.

2021, Apr. 21		Litho.	Perf. 13¼	
1291-1296	A270	Set of 6	14.00	14.00

See Isle of Man No. 2150a.

Paintings of Settlements by Mike Peake (1939-2005) A271

Painting of: 27p, Port Howard. 32p, Stanley. 68p, Goose Green. 78p, Port Louis. £1.82, Egg Harbour. £1.96, Horseshoe Bay.

2021, July 14	Litho.		Perf. 13	
1297-1302	A271	Set of 6	16.50	16.50

Prince Philip (1921-2021) A272

Designs: 32p, Prince Philip reviewing troops in Falkland Islands, 1957. 78p, Prince Philip on horse. £1.04, Prince Philip facing right. £1.26, Prince Philip, cabinet with glass door in background.

2021, Aug. 30	Litho.		Perf. 13¼x13	
1303-1306	A272	Set of 4	9.50	9.50

Winning Photographs in Tourism Recovery Incentive Program Stamp Design Contest — A273

Photograph of: 32p, Sea Lion Island cliff, by Adam Yould. 68p, Southern elephant seal, by Yould. 78p, Steamer duck and ducklings, by Chris Gilbert. £1.04, Falkland Islands Government Air Service plane and Sea Lion Island Lodge, by Gilbert. £1.26, Magellanic snipe, by Jesse Ross. £1.35, Wreck of the Protector 2, by Jody Aldridge.

2021, Oct. 22	Litho.		Perf. 13	
1307-1312	A273	Set of 6	15.00	15.00

Black-browed Albatrosses A274

Designs: 32p, Heads of two albatrosses. 78p, Adult albatross feeding chicks. £1.04, Albatross in flight. £1.26, Head of albatross.

2021, Nov. 17	Litho.		Perf. 13	
1313-1316	A274	Set of 4	9.50	9.50

Souvenir Sheet

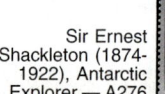

Arrival of RRS Sir David Attenborough in the Falkland Islands — A275

2021, Dec. 11	Litho.		Perf. 13¼x13	
1317	A275	£3 multi	8.25	8.25

Sir Ernest Shackleton (1874-1922), Antarctic Explorer — A276

Designs: 32p, Shackleton as child. 78p, Shackleton, Tom Crean, Captain Ingvar Thom, and Capt. Frank Worsley in Stanley, 1916. £1.10, Shackleton and his ice-bound ship,

FALKLAND ISLANDS

Nimrod. £1.26, Shackleton's Cairn, Grytviken, South Georgia.

2022, Jan. 5   Litho.   Perf. 13¼x13
1318-1321 A276 Set of 4   9.50 9.50

Reign of Queen Elizabeth II, 70th Anniv. — A277

Photograph of Queen Elizabeth II wearing: No. 1322, £2, Diadem, 1957. No. 1323, £2, Hat, 2021.
£3.50, Queen Elizabeth II wearing diadem, vert.

2022, Mar. 24   Litho.   Perf. 13¼x13
1322-1323 A277 Set of 2   10.50 10.50
Souvenir Sheet
Perf. 13x13¼
1324 A277 £3.50 multi   9.25 9.25
No. 1324 contains one 29x48mm stamp.

A278

Designs: £1.30, Royal Mail Aircraft Hudson. £2.05, A330 Voyager.

2022, June 2   Litho.   Perf. 13¼x13¾
1325-1326 A278 Set of 2   8.50 8.50
First direct airmail flight from Great Britain to the Falkland Islands, 70th anniv.

Liberation of the Falkland Islands, 40th Anniv. — A279

Designs: 33p, Stylized "40" with flag of Great Britain. 80p, Fishing boat CFA Hunter. £1.07, Tourist ship and penguins. £1.30, Sheep at pasture.

Perf. 13¼x13¾
2022, June 14   Litho.
1327-1330 A279 Set of 4   8.50 8.50

Designation of Stanley as a Jubilee City — A280

Designs: 33p, Christ Church Cathedral and Centennial Monument. 80p, Secretariat Building and 1982 Liberation Memorial. £1.13, Government House. £1.30, Residential houses.

2022, Aug. 5   Litho.   Perf. 13¼x13½
1331-1334 A280 Set of 4   8.75 8.75

Lighthouse Seafarer's Mission 25th Anniv. — A281

Designs: 33p, Mission building. 80p, Mission building, anchor, dog and car. £1.10, Mission building and dog. £1.45, Aerial view of Mission building and boats in harbor.

Perf. 13¼x13½
2022, Sept. 20   Litho.
1335-1338 A281 Set of 4   8.25 8.25

A282

Rural Heritage — A283

Designs: 1p, Vehicle crossing San Carlos River at Rudd's Pass. 2p, Shipwreck of the St. Mary. 5p, Hillside House. 10p, Ferguson's Lookout. 54p, Mission station, Keppel Island. 77p, Farm caravan. 80p, Little Chartres Bridge. £1, Bull's House. £2, Whaling station, New Island. £2.05, Stone corral. £3.60, Sheep dip. £5, Standing man (stone cairn), Weddell Island.
(33p), Farm cart.

2022, Oct. 10   Litho.   Perf. 11½
1339	A282	1p multi	.30	.30
1340	A282	2p multi	.30	.30
1341	A282	5p multi	.30	.30
1342	A282	10p multi	.30	.30
1343	A282	54p multi	1.25	1.25
1344	A282	77p multi	1.75	1.75
1345	A282	80p multi	1.90	1.90
1346	A282	£1 multi	2.25	2.25
1347	A282	£2 multi	4.50	4.50
1348	A282	£2.05 multi	4.75	4.75
1349	A282	£3.60 multi	8.00	8.00
1350	A282	£5 multi	11.00	11.00
Nos. 1339-1350 (12)   36.60 36.60

Booklet Stamp
Self-Adhesive
Serpentine Die Cut 12¾
1351 A283 (33p) multi   .75 .75
 a. Booklet pane of 10   7.50

Queen Elizabeth II (1926-2022) — A284

Photograph of Queen Elizabeth II from: No. 1352, £3, 1952 (denomination at UR). No. 1353, £3, 2014 (denomination at UL).

2023, Feb. 15   Litho.   Perf. 13x13¼
1352-1353 A284 Set of 2   14.50 14.50
1353a Souvenir sheet of 2, #1352-1353   14.50 14.50

Paintings of Falkland Islands Buildings and Scenery by Mike Peake (1939-2005) A285

Painting of: 20p, House, Seal Bay. 33p, Creek. 80p, Shipwreck of Jhelum. £1.07, Stanley. £1.30, Shepherd's House. £1.90, Paragon House, Lafonia.

2023, Mar. 6   Litho.   Perf. 13¼x13
1354-1359 A285 Set of 6   14.00 14.00

Coronation of King Charles III — A286

Designs: 35p, King Charles III in Diamond Jubilee State Coach. 80p, Placement of crown on head of King Charles III. £1.09, King Charles III in Gold State Coach. £1.40, King Charles III and Queen Consort Camilla waving.
£3, King Charles III holding orb and scepter, vert.

Perf. 13¼x13½
2023, Aug. 21   Litho.
1360-1363 A286 Set of 4   9.25 9.25
Souvenir Sheet
Perf. 13½x13¼
1364 A286 £3 multi   7.50 7.50

SEMI-POSTAL STAMPS

Catalogue values for unused stamps in this section are for Never Hinged items.

Rebuilding after Conflict with Argentina — SP1

Wmk. 373
1982, Sept. 13   Litho.   Perf. 11
B1 SP1 £1 + £1 Battle sites   3.00 3.00

Liberation of Falkland Islands, 10th Anniv. — SP2

Designs: 14p+6p, San Carlos Cemetery. 29p+11p, 1982 War Memorial, Port Stanley. 34p+16p, South Atlantic Medal. 68p+32p, Government House, Port Stanley.

Wmk. 373
1992, June 14   Litho.   Perf. 14
B2	SP2	14p + 6p multicolored	1.00	1.60
B3	SP2	29p + 11p multicolored	1.75	2.00
B4	SP2	34p + 16p multicolored	2.00	2.25
B5	SP2	68p + 32p multicolored	2.75	3.50
 a. Souvenir sheet of 4, #B2-B5   8.50 8.50
Nos. B2-B5 (4)   7.50 9.35

Surtax for Soldiers', Sailors' and Airmen's Families Association.

AIR POST STAMPS

Bird Type of 2003
Design: Rockhopper penguins, vert.
Booklet Stamp
Serpentine Die Cut 6x6½ Syncopated
2003, Sept. 19   Litho.
Self-Adhesive
C1 A163 (40p) multi   2.50 2.50
 a. Booklet pane of 8   20.00

Penguins — AP1

Designs: No. C2, (55p), King penguin. No. C3, (55p), Macaroni penguin. No. C4, (55p), Magellanic penguin. No. C5, (55p), Rockhopper penguin. No. C6, (55p), Gentoo penguin. No. C7, (55p), Albino rockhopper penguin.

2008, Dec. 1   Litho.   Perf. 13¼
C2-C7 AP1 Set of 6   19.00 19.00
C7a Souvenir sheet, #C2-C7   19.00 19.00

Penguins — AP2

Designs: Nos. C8, C14a, (70p), King penguin. Nos. C9, C14b, (70p), Macaroni penguin. Nos. C10, C14c, (70p), Rockhopper penguins. Nos. C11, C14d, (70p), Albino and normal rockhopper penguins. Nos. C12, C14e, (70p), Magellanic penguin. Nos. C13, C14f, (70p), Gentoo penguins.

2010, Sept. 29   Litho.   Perf. 13¾
Stamps With White Frames
C8-C13 AP2 Set of 6   13.50 13.50
Stamps Without White Frames
C14 AP2 (70p) Sheet of 6, #a-f   13.50 13.50

Albino and Normal Rockhopper Penguins AP3

Gentoo Penguins AP4

Magellanic Penguin AP5

Rockhopper Penguins AP6

King Penguins AP7

Macaroni Penguins AP8

2013, Nov. 21   Litho.   Perf. 13¼
Stamps With White Frames
C15	AP3	(65p) multi	2.10	2.10
C16	AP4	(65p) multi	2.10	2.10
C17	AP5	(65p) multi	2.10	2.10
C18	AP6	(65p) multi	2.10	2.10
C19	AP7	(65p) multi	2.10	2.10
C20	AP8	(65p) multi	2.10	2.10
Nos. C15-C20 (6)   12.60 12.60

Souvenir Sheet
Stamps Without White Frames
C21 Sheet of 6   14.00 16.00
 a. AP3 (65p) multi   2.25 2.60
 b. AP4 (65p) multi   2.25 2.60
 c. AP5 (65p) multi   2.25 2.60
 d. AP6 (65p) multi   2.25 2.60
 e. AP7 (65p) multi   2.25 2.60
 f. AP8 (65p) multi   2.25 2.60

AP9

AP10

AP11

King Penguins — AP12

2023, Oct. 3   Litho.   Perf. 13½x13¼
C22	AP9	(74p) multi	1.75	1.75
C23	AP10	(74p) multi	1.75	1.75
C24	AP11	(80p) multi	2.00	2.00
C25	AP12	(£1.40) multi	3.50	3.50
Nos. C22-C25 (4)   9.00 9.00

POSTAGE DUE STAMPS

Catalogue values for unused stamps in this section are for never hinged items.

FALKLAND ISLANDS

Penguin — D1

Perf. 14½x14
1991, Jan. 7   Litho.   Wmk. 373
J1	D1	1p lilac rose & lake	.25	.60
J2	D1	2p buff & brown org	.25	.60
J3	D1	3p yel & orange yel	.25	.60
J4	D1	4p lt bl grn & dk bl grn	.25	.60
J5	D1	5p sky blue & Prus bl	.25	.60
J6	D1	10p lt blue & dk blue	.35	.70
J7	D1	20p lt violet & dk vio	.90	1.50
J8	D1	50p brt yel grn & dk yel green	2.00	3.00
		Nos. J1-J8 (8)	4.50	8.20

Penguins — D2

Various penguins.

2005, Dec. 2   Litho.   Perf. 13¾
J9	D2	1p multi	.25	.25
J10	D2	3p multi	.25	.25
J11	D2	5p multi	.25	.25
J12	D2	10p multi	.45	.45
J13	D2	20p multi	.85	.85
J14	D2	50p multi	1.90	1.90
J15	D2	£1 multi	3.75	3.75
J16	D2	£2 multi	7.50	7.50
J17	D2	£3 multi	11.00	11.00
J18	D2	£5 multi	17.00	17.00
		Nos. J9-J18 (10)	43.20	43.20

WAR TAX STAMPS

Regular Issue of 1912-14 Overprinted

1918-20   Wmk. 3   Perf. 14
MR1	A7	½p dp ol grn	.55	7.25
MR2	A7	1p org ver ('19)	.55	4.00
a.		Double overprint	4,250.	
MR3	A7	1sh bis brn	6.50	52.50
a.		Pair, one without overprint	18,000.	
b.		Double ovpt., one albino	2,250.	
c.		1sh brn, thick grayish paper ('20)	6.00	50.00
d.		As "c," double ovpt., one albino	2,000.	
		Nos. MR1-MR3 (3)	7.60	63.75

No. MR3a probably is caused by a foldover and is not constant.

FALKLAND ISLANDS DEPENDENCIES

Catalogue values for unused stamps in this section are for Never Hinged items.

Map of Falkland Islands — A1

Engr., Center Litho. in Black
1946, Feb. 1   Wmk. 4   Perf. 12
1L1	A1	½p yellow green	1.10	3.50
1L2	A1	1p blue violet	1.30	2.00
1L3	A1	2p deep carmine	1.30	2.60
1L4	A1	3p ultramarine	1.90	5.25
1L5	A1	4p deep plum	2.40	5.00
1L6	A1	6p orange yellow	3.75	5.25
1L7	A1	9p brown	2.25	4.00
1L8	A1	1sh rose violet	3.00	4.50
		Nos. 1L1-1L8 (8)	17.00	32.10

Nos. 1L1-1L8 were reissued in 1948, printed on more opaque paper with the lines of the map finer and clearer. Value for set, unused or used $130.
See No. 1L13.

Common Design Types
pictured following the introduction.

Peace Issue
Common Design Type
1946, Oct. 4   Perf. 13½x14
1L9	CD303	1p purple	.50	.50
1L10	CD303	3p deep blue	.80	.50

Silver Wedding Issue
Common Design Types
1948, Dec. 6   Photo.   Perf. 14x14½
| 1L11 | CD304 | 2½p brt ultra | 1.75 | 3.25 |

Perf. 11½x11   Engr.
| 1L12 | CD305 | 1sh blue violet | 2.50 | 2.75 |

Type of 1946
1949, Mar. 6   Perf. 12
Center Litho. in Black
| 1L13 | A1 | 2½p deep blue | 9.00 | 4.25 |

UPU Issue
Common Design Types
Engr.; Name Typo. on 2p, 3p
1949, Oct. 10   Perf. 13½, 11x11½
1L14	CD306	1p violet	1.10	4.00
1L15	CD307	2p deep carmine	5.00	4.00
1L16	CD308	3p indigo	3.75	2.25
1L17	CD309	6p red orange	4.75	4.25
		Nos. 1L14-1L17 (4)	14.60	14.50

Coronation Issue
Common Design Type
1953, June 4   Perf. 13½x13
| 1L18 | CD312 | 1p purple & black | 1.80 | 1.40 |

John Biscoe — A2

Trepassey — A3

Ships: 1½p, Wyatt Earp. 2p, Eagle. 2½p, Penola. 3p, Discovery II. 4p, William Scoresby. 6p, Discovery. 9p, Endurance. 1sh, Deutschland. 2sh, Pourquoi-pas? 2sh6p, Français. 5sh, Scotia. 10sh, Antarctic. £1, Belgica.

1954, Feb. 1   Engr.   Perf. 12½
Center in Black
1L19	A2	½p blue green	.25	2.00
1L20	A3	1p sepia	1.75	1.50
1L21	A3	1½p olive	2.00	1.75
1L22	A3	2p rose red	1.25	2.50
1L23	A3	2½p yellow	1.25	.35
1L24	A3	3p ultra	1.25	.35
1L25	A3	4p red violet	3.00	1.75
1L26	A3	6p rose violet	3.50	1.75
1L27	A2	9p black	3.50	2.00
1L28	A3	1sh org brown	3.50	2.00
1L29	A3	2sh lilac rose	18.00	10.00
1L30	A2	2sh6p blue gray	19.00	7.00
1L31	A2	5sh violet	40.00	7.50
1L32	A3	10sh brt blue	55.00	18.00
1L33	A2	£1 black	85.00	47.50
		Nos. 1L19-1L33 (15)	238.25	105.95

Nos. 20, 23-24, 26 Ovptd. in Black

1956, Jan 30   Center in Black
1L34	A3	1p sepia	.30	.30
1L35	A3	2½p yellow	.55	.55
1L36	A3	3p ultramarine	.65	.65
1L37	A2	6p rose violet	.75	.75
		Nos. 1L34-1L37 (4)	2.25	2.25

Trans-Antarctic Expedition, 1955-1958.

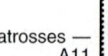
A4

1p, Map of Dependencies. 2p, Shag Rocks. 3p, Bird and Willis Islands. 4p, Gulbrandsen Lake. 5p, King Edward Point. 6p, Shackleton's Memorial Cross. 7p, Shackleton's grave. 8p, Grytviken Church. 9p, Coaling Hulk "Louise". 10p, Clerke Rocks. 20p, Candlemas Island. 25p, Twitcher Rock, Cook Island. 50p, "John Biscoe". £1, "Bransfield". £3, "Endurance".

1980, May 5   Litho.   Perf. 13½
1L38	A4	1p multicolored	.25	.25
1L39	A4	2p multicolored	.25	.25
1L40	A4	3p multicolored	.25	.25
1L41	A4	4p multicolored	.25	.25
1L42	A4	5p multicolored	.25	.25
1L43	A4	6p multicolored	.25	.25
1L44	A4	7p multicolored	.25	.25
1L45	A4	8p multicolored	.25	.25
1L46	A4	9p multicolored	.25	.30
1L47	A4	10p multicolored	.25	.30
1L48	A4	20p multicolored	.45	.55
1L49	A4	25p multicolored	.60	.70
1L50	A4	50p multicolored	1.10	1.25
1L51	A4	£1 multicolored	2.25	2.75
1L52	A4	£3 multicolored	5.50	7.00
		Nos. 1L38-1L52 (15)	12.40	14.85

Nos. 38-50 exist dated 1984; issued May 3, 1984. Value, set $16.

1985, Nov. 18   Wmk. 384
1L48a	A4	20p	3.25	4.50
1L49a	A4	25p	3.25	4.50
1L50a	A4	50p	3.25	4.50
1L51a	A4	£1	3.25	4.50
1L52a	A4	£3	7.50	6.50
		Nos. 1L48a-1L52a (5)	20.50	24.50

Magellanic Clubmoss — A5

Designs: 6p, Alpine cat's-tail. 7p, Greater burnet. 11p, Antarctic bedstraw. 15p, Brown rush. 25p, Antarctic hair grass.

Wmk. 373
1981, Feb. 5   Litho.   Perf. 14
1L53	A5	3p shown	.25	.25
1L54	A5	6p multicolored	.25	.25
1L55	A5	11p multicolored	.25	.25
1L56	A5	11p multicolored	.35	.35
1L57	A5	15p multicolored	.45	.45
a.		Brown missing	3,750.	
1L58	A5	25p multicolored	.65	.65
		Nos. 1L53-1L58 (6)	2.20	2.20

Royal Wedding Issue
Common Design Type
Wmk. 373
1981, July 22   Litho.   Perf. 14
1L59	CD331	10p Bouquet	.25	.25
1L60	CD331	13p Charles	.35	.35
1L61	CD331	52p Couple	.85	.85
		Nos. 1L59-1L61 (3)	1.45	1.45

Reindeer in Spring — A6

Wmk. 373
1982, Jan. 29   Litho.   Perf. 14
1L62	A6	5p shown	.25	.60
1L63	A6	12p Autumn	.35	.75
1L64	A6	25p Winter	.45	1.00
1L65	A6	26p Late winter	.50	1.00
		Nos. 1L62-1L65 (4)	1.55	3.35

Gamasellus Racovitzai — A7

10p, Alaskozetes antarcticus. 13p, Cryptopygus antarcticus. 15p, Notiomaso australis. 25p, Hydromedion sparsutum. 26p, Parochlus steinenii.

Wmk. 373
1982, Mar. 16   Litho.   Perf. 14
1L66	A7	5p shown	.25	.25
1L67	A7	10p multicolored	.25	.35
1L68	A7	13p multicolored	.30	.40
1L69	A7	15p multicolored	.35	.40
1L70	A7	25p multicolored	.40	.50
1L71	A7	26p multicolored	.45	.50
		Nos. 1L66-1L71 (6)	2.00	2.40

Princess Diana Issue
Common Design Type
Perf. 13½x14
1982, July 1   Litho.   Wmk. 373
1L72	CD333	5p Arms	.25	.25
1L73	CD333	17p Diana	.35	.45
a.		Perf. 13.5	2.50	2.75
1L74	CD333	37p Wedding	.90	.90
1L75	CD333	50p Portrait	1.00	1.00
		Nos. 1L72-1L75 (4)	2.50	2.60

Crustacea — A8

5p, Euphausia superba. 17p, Glyptonotus antarcticus. 25p, Epimeria monodon. 34p, Serolis pagenstecheri.

Perf. 14½x14
1984, Mar. 23   Wmk. 373
1L76	A8	5p multicolored	.30	.30
1L77	A8	17p multicolored	.40	.40
1L78	A8	25p multicolored	.70	.70
1L79	A8	34p multicolored	1.10	1.10
		Nos. 1L76-1L79 (4)	2.50	2.50

Manned Flight Bicentenary — A9

Designs: 5p, Westland Whirlwind. 13p, Westland Wasp. 17p, Saunders-Roe Walrus. 50p, Auster.

Wmk. 373
1983, Dec. 23   Litho.   Perf. 14
1L80	A9	5p multicolored	.25	.25
1L81	A9	13p multicolored	.45	.45
1L82	A9	17p multicolored	.55	.55
1L83	A9	50p multicolored	1.75	1.75
		Nos. 1L80-1L83 (4)	3.00	3.00

South Sandwich Islds. Volcanoes — A10

6p, Zavodovski Island. 17p, Mt. Michael, Saunders Island. 22p, Bellingshausen Island. 52p, Bristol Island.

1984, Nov. 8   Wmk. 373   Perf. 14½
1L84	A10	6p multicolored	.60	.60
1L85	A10	17p multicolored	1.40	1.40
1L86	A10	22p multicolored	2.00	2.00
1L87	A10	52p multicolored	3.50	3.50
		Nos. 1L84-1L87 (4)	7.50	7.50

Albatrosses — A11

7p, Diomedea chrysostoma. 22p, Diomedea melanophris. 27p, Diomedea exulans. 54p, Phoebetria palpebrata.

1985, May 5   Wmk. 384   Perf. 14½
1L88	A11	7p multicolored	.80	.80
1L89	A11	22p multicolored	2.25	2.25
1L90	A11	27p multicolored	2.50	2.50
1L91	A11	54p multicolored	4.75	4.75
		Nos. 1L88-1L91 (4)	10.30	10.30

Queen Mother 85th Birthday
Common Design Type

Designs: 7p, 14th birthday celebration. 22p, With Princess Anne, Lady Sarah Armstrong-Jones, Prince Edward. 27p, Queen Mother. 54p, Holding Prince Henry. £1, On the Britannia.

FALKLAND ISLANDS — FAR EASTERN REPUBLIC

Perf. 14½x14

1985, June 23   Wmk. 384
1L92	CD336	7p multicolored	.25	.25
1L93	CD336	22p multicolored	.75	.75
1L94	CD336	27p multicolored	1.00	1.00
1L95	CD336	54p multicolored	2.00	2.00
		Nos. 1L92-1L95 (4)	4.00	4.00

Souvenir Sheet
1L96	CD336	£1 multicolored	4.00	4.00

Falkland Islands Naturalists Type of 1985

Naturalists, endangered species: 7p, Dumont d'Urville (1790-1842), kelp. 22p, Johann Reinhold Forster (1729-1798), king penguin. 27p, Johann Georg Adam Forster (1754-1794), tussock grass. 54p, Sir Joseph Banks (1743-1820), dove prion.

Perf. 13½x14

1985, Nov. 4   Wmk. 373
1L97	A86	7p multicolored	.75	.75
1L98	A86	22p multicolored	1.60	1.60
1L99	A86	27p multicolored	2.00	2.00
1L100	A86	54p multicolored	3.75	3.75
		Nos. 1L97-1L100 (4)	8.10	8.10

SEMI-POSTAL STAMP

Rebuilding Type of Falkland Islands
Wmk. 373

1982, Sept. 13   Litho.   Perf. 11
1LB1	SP1	£1 Map of So. Georgia	2.75	2.75

ISSUES FOR THE SEPARATE ISLANDS

Graham Land

Nos. 84, 85B, 86A, 87A, 88-91 Overprinted in Red

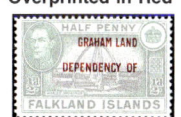

1944, Feb. 12   Wmk. 4   Perf. 12
2L1	A22	½p green & black	.45	2.25
2L2	A22	1p dk vio & black	.45	1.10
2L3	A22	2p rose car & blk	.55	1.10
2L4	A22	3p deep bl & blk	.55	1.10
2L5	A22	4p rose vio & blk	1.90	1.75
2L6	A22	6p brown & black	19.00	2.75
2L7	A22	9p slate bl & blk	1.25	1.50
2L8	A22	1sh dull blue	1.25	1.50
		Nos. 2L1-2L8 (8)	25.40	13.05

South Georgia

1944, Apr. 3   Wmk. 4   Perf. 12
3L1	A22	½p green & black	.35	2.25
3L2	A22	1p dark vio & blk	.35	1.10
3L3	A22	2p rose car & blk	.55	1.10
3L4	A22	3p deep bl & blk	.55	1.10
3L5	A22	4p rose vio & blk	1.90	1.75
3L6	A22	6p brown & black	19.00	2.50
3L7	A22	9p slate bl & blk	1.25	1.50
3L8	A22	1sh dull blue	1.25	1.50
		Nos. 3L1-3L8 (8)	25.20	12.80

South Orkneys

1944, Feb. 21   Wmk. 4   Perf. 12
4L1	A22	½p green & black	.45	2.25
4L2	A22	1p dark vio & blk	.45	1.10
4L3	A22	2p rose car & blk	.75	1.10
4L4	A22	3p deep bl & blk	.75	1.10
4L5	A22	4p rose vio & blk	1.75	1.75
4L6	A22	6p brown & black	19.00	2.50
4L7	A22	9p slate bl & blk	1.25	1.50
4L8	A22	1sh dull blue	1.25	1.50
		Nos. 4L1-4L8 (8)	25.65	12.80

South Shetlands

1944   Wmk. 4   Perf. 12
5L1	A22	½p green & black	.45	2.25
5L2	A22	1p dark vio & blk	.45	1.10
5L3	A22	2p rose car & blk	.55	1.10
5L4	A22	3p deep bl & blk	.55	1.10
5L5	A22	4p rose vio & blk	1.25	1.75
5L6	A22	6p brown & black	19.00	2.50
5L7	A22	9p slate bl & blk	1.25	1.50
5L8	A22	1sh dull blue	1.25	1.50
		Nos. 5L1-5L8 (8)	24.75	12.80

FAR EASTERN REPUBLIC

ˈfär ˈē-stərn ri-ˈpə-blik

LOCATION — In Siberia east of Lake Baikal
GOVT. — Republic
AREA — 900,745 sq. mi.
POP. — 1,560,000 (approx. 1920)
CAPITAL — Chita

A short-lived independent government was established here in 1920.

100 Kopecks = 1 Ruble

Watermark

Wmk. 171 — Diamonds

Vladivostok Issue
Russian Stamps Surcharged or Overprinted

a   b

c

On Stamps of 1909-17
Perf. 14, 14½x15, 13½

1920   Unwmk.
2	A14(a)	2k green	10.00	15.00
3	A14(a)	3k red	10.00	10.00
4	A11(b)	3k on 35k red brn & grn	40.00	50.00
5	A15(a)	4k carmine	10.00	12.00
6	A11(b)	4k on 70k brn & org	10.00	15.00
8	A11(b)	7k on 15k red brn & bl	2.00	2.00
a.		Inverted surcharge		
b.		Pair, one ovptd. "DBP" only		100.00
9	A15(a)	10k dark blue	100.00	75.00
a.		Overprint on back	125.00	
10	A12(c)	10k on 3½r mar & lt grn	25.00	25.00
11	A11(a)	14k blue & rose	50.00	35.00
12	A11(a)	15k red brn & bl	35.00	25.00
13	A8(a)	20k blue & car	150.00	100.00
14	A11(b)	20k on 14k bl & rose	10.00	8.00
a.		Surcharge on back	30.00	
15	A11(a)	25k green & vio	25.00	20.00
16	A11(a)	35k red brn & grn	75.00	50.00
17	A8(a)	50k brn vio & grn	10.00	12.00
18	A9(a)	1r pale brn, dk brn & org	700.00	700.00

On Stamps of 1917
Imperf
21	A14(a)	1k orange	25.00	10.00
22	A14(a)	2k gray grn	20.00	10.00
23	A14(a)	3k red	20.00	10.00
25	A11(b)	7k on 15k red brn & dp bl	2.00	5.00
a.		Pair, one without surcharge	100.00	
b.		Pair, one ovptd. "DBP" only	100.00	
26	A12(c)	10k on 3½r mar & lt grn	30.00	15.00
27	A9(a)	1r pale brn, brn & red org	50.00	20.00

On Stamps of Siberia 1919
Perf. 14, 14½x15
30	A14(a)	35k on 2k green	5.00	8.00
a.		"DBP" on back	25.00	50.00

Imperf
31	A14(a)	35k on 2k green	35.00	25.00
32	A14(a)	70k on 1k orange	6.00	6.00

Counterfeit surcharges and overprints abound, including digital forgeries.

On Russia Nos. AR2, AR3

Perf. 14½x15 Wmk. 171
35	PF1	1k on 5k green, buff	30.00	25.00
36	PF1	2k on 10k brown, buff	40.00	30.00

The letters on these stamps resembling "DBP," are the Russian initials of "Dalne Vostochnaya Respublika" (Far Eastern Republic).

Chita Issue

A2   A2a

1921   Unwmk.   Typo.   *Imperf.*
38	A2	2k gray green	1.50	1.50
39	A2a	4k rose	3.00	3.00
40	A2	5k claret	3.00	3.00
41	A2a	10k blue	2.50	2.50
		Nos. 38-41 (4)	10.00	10.00

For overprints see Nos. 62-65.

Blagoveshchensk Issue

A3

1921   Litho.   *Imperf.*
42	A3	2r red	3.00	2.00
43	A3	3r dark green	3.00	2.00
44	A3	5r dark blue	3.00	2.00
a.		Tête bêche pair	50.00	15.00
45	A3	15r dark brown	3.00	2.00
46	A3	30r dark violet	3.00	2.00
a.		Tête bêche pair	35.00	15.00
		Nos. 42-46 (5)	15.00	10.00

Remainders of Nos. 42-46 were canceled in colored crayon or by typographed bars. These sell for half of foregoing values.

Chita Issue

A4   A5

1922   Litho.   *Imperf.*
49	A4	1k orange	1.00	.85
50	A4	3k dull red	.40	.45
51	A5	4k dp rose & buff	.40	.45
52	A4	5k orange brown	.80	.45
53	A4	7k light blue	1.50	1.50
a.		Perf. 11½	2.00	2.50
b.		Rouletted 9	3.00	3.00
c.		Perf. 11½x11½ rouletted	6.50	6.50
54	A5	10k dk blue & red	.60	.65
55	A4	15k dull rose	.80	1.10
56	A5	20k blue & red	.80	1.10
57	A5	30k green & red org	1.25	1.10
58	A5	50k black & red org	3.00	2.25
		Nos. 49-58 (10)	10.55	9.90

The 4k exists with "4" omitted. Value $100.

Vladivostok Issue

Stamps of 1921 Overprinted in Red

1922   A2   *Imperf.*
62	A2	2k gray green	35.00	25.00
a.		Inverted overprint	250.00	
63	A2a	4k rose	35.00	25.00
a.		Inverted overprint	250.00	
b.		Double overprint	250.00	
64	A2	5k claret	35.00	35.00
a.		Inverted overprint	100.00	
b.		Double overprint	350.00	
65	A2a	10k blue	35.00	35.00
		Nos. 62-65 (4)	140.00	120.00

Russian revolution of Nov. 1917, 5th anniv. Once in the setting the figures "22" of 1922 have the bottom stroke curved instead of straight. Value, each $75.
No. 63 exists in a block with overprints missing on some stamps.

Vladivostok Issue

Russian Stamps of 1922-23 Surcharged in Black or Red

1923   *Imperf.*
66	A50	1k on 100r red	.40	1.00
a.		Inverted surcharge	60.00	
67	A50	2k on 70r violet	.40	.75
68	A49	5k on 10r blue (R)	.40	.75
69	A50	10k on 50r brown	.90	1.25
a.		Inverted surcharge	250.00	

Perf. 14½x15
70	A50	1k on 100r red	.90	1.25
		Nos. 66-70 (5)	3.00	5.00

OCCUPATION STAMPS

Issued under Occupation of General Semenov
Chita Issue
Russian Stamps of 1909-12 Surcharged

a   b

c

1920   Unwmk.   Perf. 14, 14½x15
N1	A15	1r on 4k car	150.00	100.00
N2	A8 (b)	2r50k on 20k bl & car	40.00	30.00
N3	A14 (c)	5r on 5k clar	25.00	50.00
a.		Double surcharge	200.00	
N4	A11 (a)	10r on 70k brn & org	20.00	25.00
		Nos. N1-N4 (4)	235.00	205.00

501

FAROE ISLANDS

'far-,ü 'ī-lənds

(The Faroes)

LOCATION — North Atlantic Ocean
GOVT. — Self-governing part of Kingdom of Denmark
AREA — 540 sq. mi.
POP. — 41,059 (1999 est.)
CAPITAL — Thorshavn

100 Ore = 1 Krone

> Catalogue values for unused stamps in this country are for Never Hinged items, beginning with Scott 7.

Denmark No. 97 Handstamp Surcharged

1919, Jan.   Typo.   Perf. 14x14½
1	A16	2o on 5o green		1,400. 475.00

Counterfeits of surcharge exist.
Denmark No. 88a, the bisect, was used with Denmark No. 97 in Faroe Islands Jan. 3-23, 1919.

Denmark Nos. 220, 224, 238A, 224C Surcharged in Blue or Black

Nos. 2, 5-6   No. 3

No. 4

1940-41   Engr.   Perf. 13
2	A32	20o on 1o ('41)	40.00	110.00
3	A32	20o on 5o ('41)	40.00	35.00
4	A30	20o on 15o (Bk)	60.00	92.50
5	A32	50o on 60o (Bk)	275.00	90.00
6	A32	60o on 60o (Bk)	125.00	250.00
	Nos. 2-6 (5)		540.00	507.50
	Set, never hinged		1,150.	

Issued during British administration.

> Catalogue values for unused stamps in this section, from this point to the end of the section, are for Never Hinged items.

Map of Islands, 1673 — A1   Map of North Atlantic, 1573 — A2

West Coast, Sandoy — A3   Vidoy and Svinoy, by Eyvindur Mohr — A4

Designs: 200o, like 70o. 250o, 300o, View of Streymoy and Vagar. 450o, Houses, Nes, by Ruth Smith. 500o, View of Hvitanes and Skalafjordur, by S. Joensen-Mikines.

Unwmk.
1975, Jan. 30   Engr.   Perf. 13
7	A1	5o sepia	.25	.25
8	A2	10o emer & dark blue	.25	.25
9	A1	50o graysh green	.25	.25
10	A2	60o brown & dark blue	.80	.80
11	A3	70o vio bl & slate grn	.80	.80
12	A2	80o ocher & dark blue	.45	.45
13	A1	90o red brown	.80	.80
14	A2	120o brt bl & dark bl	.60	.40
15	A3	200o vio bl & slate grn	.60	.60
16	A3	250o multicolored	.60	.60
17	A3	300o multicolored	5.00	1.60

Photo.   Perf. 12½x13
18	A4	350o multicolored	.80	.80
19	A4	450o multicolored	.80	.80
20	A4	500o multicolored	1.00	1.00
	Nos. 7-20 (14)		13.00	9.40

Faroe Boat — A5   Faroe Flag — A6

Faroe Mailman — A7

Perf. 12½x13, 12 (A6)
1976, Apr. 1   Engr.; Litho. (A6)
21	A5	125o copper red	1.60	1.25
22	A6	160o multicolored	.45	.45
23	A7	800o olive	1.75	1.25
	Nos. 21-23 (3)		3.80	2.95

Faroe Islands independent postal service, Apr. 1, 1976.

Motor Fishing Boat — A8

Faroese Fishing Vessels and Map of Islands: 125o, Inland fishing cutter. 160o, Modern seine fishing vessel. 600o, Deep-sea fishing trawler.

1977, Apr. 28   Photo.   Perf. 14½x14
24	A8	100o green & black	4.50	3.75
25	A8	125o carmine & black	.65	.65
26	A8	160o blue & black	.90	.65
27	A8	600o brown & black	1.60	1.10
	Nos. 24-27 (4)		7.65	6.15

Common Snipe — A9

Photogravure & Engraved
1977, Sept. 29   Perf. 14½x14
28	A9	70o shown	.25	.25
29	A9	180o Oystercatcher	.55	.55
30	A9	250o Whimbrel	.65	.65
	Nos. 28-30 (3)		1.45	1.45

North Coast, Puffins A10   Mykines Village A11

Mykines Island: 140o, Coast. 150o, Aerial view. 180o, Map.

Perf. 13x13½, 13½x13
1978, Jan. 26   Photo.
Size: 21x28mm, 28x21mm
31	A10	100o multicolored	.25	.25
32	A11	130o multicolored	.45	.45
33	A11	140o multicolored	.55	.55
34	A10	150o multicolored	.55	.55

Size: 37x26mm
Perf. 14½x14
35	A11	180o multicolored	.55	.55
	Nos. 31-35 (5)		2.35	2.35

Sea Birds — A12

Lithographed and Engraved
1978, Apr. 13   Perf. 12x12½
36	A12	140o Gannets	.45	.45
37	A12	180o Puffins	.55	.55
38	A12	400o Guillemots	1.40	1.10
	Nos. 36-38 (3)		2.40	2.10

Old Library — A13

1978, Dec. 7   Perf. 13
39	A13	140o shown	.45	.45
40	A13	180o New library	.55	.55

Completion of New Library Building.

Girl Guide, Tent and Fire — A14

1978, Dec. 7   Photo.   Perf. 13½
41	A14	140o multicolored	.45	.45

Faroese Girl Guides, 50th anniversary.

Ram — A15

Lithographed and Engraved
1979, Mar. 19   Perf. 12
42	A15	25k multicolored	6.00	6.00

Denmark No. 88a — A16

Europa: 180o, Faroe Islands No. 1.

1979, May 7   Perf. 12½
43	A16	140o yellow & blue	.45	.45
44	A16	180o rose, grn & blk	.55	.55

Girl Wearing Festive Costume — A17

Children's Drawings and IYC Emblem: 150o, Fisherman. 200o, Two friends.

1979, Oct. 1   Perf. 12
45	A17	110o multicolored	.45	.45
46	A17	150o multicolored	.45	.45
47	A17	200o multicolored	.55	.55
	Nos. 45-47 (3)		1.45	1.45

International Year of the Child.

Sea Plantain — A18

1980, Mar. 17   Photo.   Perf. 12x11½
48	A18	90o shown	.25	.25
49	A18	110o Glacier buttercup	.45	.45
50	A18	150o Purple saxifrage	.55	.55
51	A18	200o Starry saxifrage	.55	.55
52	A18	400o Lady's mantle	.90	.90
	Nos. 48-52 (5)		2.70	2.70

Europa — A19

Europa: 150o, Jakob Jakobsen (1864-1918), linguist. 200o, Venceslas Ulricus Hammershaimb (1819-1909), theologian, linguist and folklorist.

1980, Oct. 6   Engr.   Perf. 11½
53	A19	150o dull green	.40	.40
54	A19	200o dull red brown	.60	.60

Perf. 13 bicolored examples of Nos. 53-54 are rejected stamps never put on sale that were to have been burned, but which escaped destruction.

Coat of Arms, Virgin and Child, Gothic Pew Gable — A20

Kirkjubour Pew Gables, 15th Century: 140o, Norwegian coat of arms, John the Baptist. 150o, Christ's head, St. Peter. 200o, Hand in halo, Apostle Paul.

Photo. & Engr.
1980, Oct. 6   Perf. 13½
55	A20	110o multicolored	.45	.45
56	A20	140o multicolored	.45	.45
57	A20	150o multicolored	.45	.45
58	A20	200o multicolored	.55	.55
	Nos. 55-58 (4)		1.90	1.90

See Nos. 102-105, 389-392

A21

Sketches of Old Torshavn by Ingalzur Reyni.

1981, Mar. 2   Engr.
59	A21	110o dark green	.45	.45
60	A21	140o black	.45	.45
61	A21	150o dark brown	.45	.45
62	A21	200o dark blue	.55	.55
	Nos. 59-62 (4)		1.90	1.90

The Ring Dance — A22

Europa: 200o, The garter dance.

1981, June 1   Engr.   Perf. 13x14
63	A22	200o pale rose & grn	.35	.35
64	A22	200o pale yel grn & dk brn	.55	.55

Rune Stones, 800-1000 AD — A23

Historic Writings: 1k, Folksong, 1846. 3k, Sheep Letter excerpt, 1298. 6k, Seal and text,

FAROE ISLANDS

1533, 10k, Titlepage from Faeroae et Faeroa, by Lucas Jacobson Debes, library.

Photo. & Engr.
1981, Oct. 19   *Perf. 11½*
65	A23	10o multicolored	.25	.25
66	A23	1k multicolored	.25	.25
67	A23	3k multicolored	1.00	.65
68	A23	6k multicolored	1.60	1.25
69	A23	10k multicolored	2.75	2.75
		Nos. 65-69 (5)	5.85	5.15

Nos. 70-80 not assigned.

Europa 1982 — A24

1.50k, Viking North Atlantic routes. 2k, Viking house foundation.

1982, Mar. 15   Engr.   *Perf. 13½*
| 81 | A24 | 1.50k dk blue & blue | .45 | .45 |
| 82 | A24 | 2k gray & blk | .55 | .55 |

View of Gjogv, by Ingalvur av Reyni — A25

1982, June 7   Litho.   *Perf. 12½x13*
83	A25	180o shown	.45	.45
84	A25	220o Hvalvik	1.00	.75
85	A25	250o Kvivik	.65	.65
		Nos. 83-85 (3)	2.10	1.85

Ballad of Harra Paetur and Elinborg — A26

Scenes from the medieval ballad of chivalry.

1982, Sept. 27   Litho.
86	A26	220o multicolored	.65	.65
87	A26	250o multicolored	.75	.75
88	A26	350o multicolored	1.00	1.00
89	A26	450o multicolored	1.20	1.20
		Nos. 86-89 (4)	3.60	3.60

Cargo Ships — A27

1983, Feb. 21   Litho.   *Perf. 14x14½*
90	A27	220o Arcturus, 1856	.65	.65
91	A27	250o Laura, 1882	.90	.90
92	A27	700o Thyra, 1866	2.00	2.00
		Nos. 90-92 (3)	3.55	3.55

Chessmen, by Pol í Duni (1791-1857) — A28

1983, May 2   Engr.   *Perf. 13 Vert.*
Booklet Stamps
93	250o King	2.25	2.25
94	250o Queen	2.25	2.25
a.	Bklt. pane of 6, 3 each #93-94	16.00	
b.	A28 Pair, #93-94	5.50	5.50

Europa 1983 — A29

Nobel Prizewinners in Medicine: 250o, Niels R. Finsen (1860-1903), ultraviolet radiation pioneer. 400o, Alexander Fleming (1881-1955), discoverer of penicillin.

1983, June 6   Engr.   *Perf. 12x11½*
| 95 | A29 | 250o dark blue | .65 | .65 |
| 96 | A29 | 400o red brown | 1.10 | 1.10 |

A30

1983, Sept. 19   Litho.   *Perf. 12½x13*
97	A30	250o Tusk	.65	.65
98	A30	280o Haddock	.85	.85
99	A30	500o Halibut	1.60	1.60
100	A30	900o Catfish	2.50	2.50
		Nos. 97-100 (4)	5.60	5.60

Souvenir Sheet

Traditional Costumes — A31

Various national costumes.

1983, Nov. 4   Litho.   *Perf. 12*
| 101 | A31 | Sheet of 3 | 10.00 | 11.00 |
| a.-c. | | 250o multicolored | 2.75 | 2.75 |

Nordic House Cultural Center opening. Margin shows Scandinavian flags.

Pew Gables Type of 1980

Designs: 250o, John, shield with three crowns. 300o, St. Jacob, shield with crossed keys. 350o, Thomas, shield with crossbeam. 400o, Judas Taddeus, Toulouse cross halo.

Photo. & Engr.
1984, Jan. 30   *Perf. 14x13½*
102	A20	250o lil, pur & dk brn	.75	.75
103	A20	300o red brn, dk buff & dk brn	.85	.85
104	A20	350o blk, lt gray & dk brn	1.00	1.00
105	A20	400o ol grn, pale yel & dk brn	1.10	1.10
		Nos. 102-105 (4)	3.70	3.70

Europa (1959-84) — A33

1984, Apr. 2   Engr.   *Perf. 13½*
| 106 | A33 | 250o red | .60 | .60 |
| 107 | A33 | 500o dark blue | 1.40 | 1.40 |

Sverri Patursson (1871-1960), Writer — A34

Poets: 2.50k, Joannes Patursson (1866-1946). 3k, J. H. O. Djurhuus (1881-1948). 4.50k, H.A. Djurhuus (1883-1951).

1984, May 28   Engr.   *Perf. 13½*
108	A34	2k olive green	.55	.55
109	A34	2.50k red	.65	.65
110	A34	3k dark blue	.85	.85
111	A34	4.50k violet	1.25	1.25
		Nos. 108-111 (4)	3.30	3.30

Faroese Smack (Fishing Boat) — A35

Designs: 300o, Fishermen, vert. 12k, Helmsman, vert.

Perf. 12½x13, 13x12½
1984, Sept. 10   Engr.
112	A35	280o dark blue	.75	.75
113	A35	300o brown	.85	.85
114	A35	12k deep grn	3.75	3.75
		Nos. 112-114 (3)	5.35	5.35

Fairytale Illustrations by Elinborg Lutzen — A36

Designs: No. 115, Beauty of the Veils. No. 116, Veils, diff. No. 117, Girl Shy Prince. No. 118, The Glass Sword. No. 119, Little Elin. No. 120, The Boy and the Ox.

1984, Oct. 29   Litho.   *Perf. 13 Vert.*
Booklet Stamps
115	A36	140o multicolored	5.00	5.00
116	A36	280o multicolored	5.00	5.00
117	A36	280o multicolored	5.00	5.00
118	A36	280o multicolored	5.00	5.00
119	A36	280o multicolored	5.00	5.00
120	A36	280o multicolored	5.00	5.00
a.	Booklet pane of 6, #115-120	30.00	

View of Torshavn and the Forts, by Edward Dayes — A37

Dayes' Landscapes, 1789: 280o, Skaeling. 550o, View Towards the North Seen from the Hills Near Torshavn in Stremoy, Faroes. 800o, The Moving Stones in Eysturoy, Faroes.

Litho. & Engr.
1985, Feb. 4   *Perf. 13*
121	A37	250o multicolored	.65	.65
122	A37	280o multicolored	.85	.85
123	A37	550o multicolored	2.00	2.00
124	A37	800o multicolored	2.50	2.50
		Nos. 121-124 (4)	6.00	6.00

Europa 1985 — A38

Children taking music lessons.

1985, Apr. 1   Litho.   *Perf. 13½x14½*
| 125 | A38 | 280o multicolored | .85 | .85 |
| 126 | A38 | 550o multicolored | 1.90 | 1.90 |

Paintings, Faroese Museum of Art — A39

Designs: 280o, The Garden, Hoyvik, 1970, by Thomas Arge (1942-78). 450o, Self-Portrait, 1952, by Ruth Smith (1913-58), vert. 550o, Winter's Day in Nolsoy, 1959, by Steffan Danielsen (1922-76).

Litho. & Engr.
1985, June 3   *Perf. 12½*
127	A39	280o multicolored	1.25	1.25
128	A39	450o multicolored	1.75	1.75
129	A39	550o multicolored	2.50	2.50
		Nos. 127-129 (3)	5.50	5.50

Lighthouses — A40

1985, Sept. 23   Litho.   *Perf. 13½x14*
130	A40	270o Nolsoy, 1893	.85	.85
131	A40	320o Thorshavn, 1909	1.25	1.25
132	A40	350o Mykines, 1909	1.25	1.25
133	A40	470o Map of locations	1.60	1.60
		Nos. 130-133 (4)	4.95	4.95

Passenger Aviation in the Faroes, 22nd Anniv. — A41

Designs: No. 134, Douglas DC-3. No. 135, Fokker Friendship. No. 136, Boeing 737. No. 137, Interisland LM-IKB. No. 138, Helicopter Snipan.

Perf. 13½ Horiz.
1985, Oct. 28   Photo.
Booklet Stamps
134	A41	300o multicolored	2.75	2.75
135	A41	300o multicolored	2.75	2.75
136	A41	300o multicolored	2.75	2.75
137	A41	300o multicolored	2.75	2.75
138	A41	300o multicolored	2.75	2.75
a.	Booklet pane of 5, #134-138	14.00	14.00

Skrimsla, Ancient Folk Ballad — A42

Designs: No. 139, Peasant in woods. No. 140, Meets Giant. No. 141, Giant loses game. No. 142, Giant grants Peasant's wish.

1986, Feb. 3   Litho.   *Perf. 12½x13*
139	A42	300o multicolored	.80	.80
140	A42	420o multicolored	1.20	1.20
141	A42	550o multicolored	1.40	1.40
142	A42	650o multicolored	1.60	1.60
		Nos. 139-142 (4)	5.00	5.00

Europa 1986 — A43

1986, Apr. 7   Litho.   *Perf. 13½*
| 143 | A43 | 3k shown | 1.60 | 1.60 |
| 144 | A43 | 5.50k Sea pollution | 2.25 | 2.25 |

Amnesty Intl., 25th Anniv. — A44

Winning design competition artwork.

1986, June 2   *Perf. 14x13½*
145	A44	3k Olivur vid Neyst	1.25	1.25
146	A44	4.70k Eli Smith	1.90	1.90
147	A44	5.50k Ranna Kunoy	2.40	2.40
		Nos. 145-147 (3)	5.55	5.55

Nos. 145-146 horiz.

Souvenir Sheet

HAFNIA '87, Copenhagen — A45

Design: East Bay of Torshavn, watercolor, 1782, by Christian Rosenmeyer (1728-1802).

1986, Aug. 29   Litho.   *Perf. 13x13½*
148	Sheet of 3	8.75	8.75
a.	3k multicolored	2.75	2.75
b.	4.70k multicolored	2.75	2.75
c.	6.50k multicolored	2.75	2.75

Sold for 20k.

Old Stone Bridges — A46

2.70k, Glyvrar on Eysturoy. 3k, Leypanagjogv on Vagar, vert. 13k, Skaelinger on Streymoy.

Perf. 13½x14½, 14½x13½
1986, Oct. 13   Engr.
149	A46	2.70k dp brown vio	1.75	1.75
150	A46	3k bluish blk	1.40	1.40
151	A46	13k gray green	3.00	3.00
		Nos. 149-151 (3)	6.15	6.15

FAROE ISLANDS

Farmhouses A47

Traditional architecture: 300o, Depil on Borooy, 1814. 420o, Depil, diff. 470o, Frammi vio Gjonna on Streymoy, c. 1814. 650o, Frammi, diff.

1987, Feb. 9	Engr.	Perf. 13x14½
152 A47 300o pale blue & blue	.90	.90
153 A47 420o buff & brown	1.40	1.40
154 A47 470o pale grn & dp grn	1.75	1.75
155 A47 650o pale gray & black	2.25	2.25
Nos. 152-155 (4)	6.30	6.30

Europa 1987 — A48

Nordic House.

1987, Apr. 6		Perf. 13x14
156 A48 300o Exterior	.85	.85
157 A48 550o Interior	1.90	1.60

Fishing Trawlers — A49

Designs: 3k, Joannes Patursson. 5.50k, Magnus Heinason. 8k, Sjurdarberg.

1987, June 1	Litho.	Perf. 14x13½
158 A49 3k multi	.90	.90
159 A49 5.50k multi	1.90	1.90
160 A49 8k multi	4.00	4.00
Nos. 158-160 (3)	6.80	6.80

Hestur (Horse) Island — A50

1987, Sept. 7	Litho. & Engr.	Perf. 13
161 A50 270o Map	.80	.80
162 A50 300o Seaport	.75	.75
163 A50 420o Bird cliff	1.60	1.60
164 A50 470o Pasture, sheep	1.75	1.75
165 A50 550o Seashore	1.75	1.75
Nos. 161-165 (5)	6.65	6.65

Nos. 161, 163 and 165 vert.

Collages by Zacharias Heinesen — A51

West Bay of Torshavn, Watercolor by Rosenmeyer — A52

1987, Oct. 16	Litho.	Perf. 13½x14
166 A51 4.70k Eystaravag	1.25	1.25
167 A51 6.50k Vestarvag	1.75	1.75

Souvenir Sheet
Perf. 13½x13

| 168 A52 3k multicolored | 3.50 | 3.50 |

HAFNIA '87. Sold for 4k.

Flowers — A53

Designs: 2.70k, Bellis perennis. 3k, Dactylorchis maculata. 4.70k, Potentilla erecta. 9k, Pinguicula vulgaris.

1988, Feb. 8	Litho.	Perf. 11½
Granite Paper		
169 A53 2.70k multicolored	1.10	1.10
170 A53 3k multicolored	.65	.65
171 A53 4.70k multicolored	1.75	1.75
172 A53 9k multicolored	2.50	2.50
Nos. 169-172 (4)	6.00	6.00

Europa — A54

Communication and transport: 3k, Satellite dish, satellite. 5.50k, Fork lift, crane, ship.

1988, Apr. 11	Photo.	Perf. 11½
173 A54 3k multicolored	.90	.90
174 A54 5.50k multicolored	1.50	1.50

A55

Writers: 270o, Jorgen-Frantz Jacobsen (1900-38). 300o, Christian Matras (b. 1900). 470o, William Heinesen (b. 1900). 650o, Hedin Bru (1901-87).

1988, June 6	Engr.	Perf. 13½
175 A55 270o myrtle green	1.40	1.40
176 A55 300o rose lake	.85	.85
177 A55 470o dark blue	2.00	2.00
178 A55 650o brown black	2.25	2.25
Nos. 175-178 (4)	6.50	6.50

A56

Text, illustrations and cameo portraits of organizers: 3k, Announcement and Djoni Geil, Enok Baerentsen and H.H. Jacobsen. 3.20k, Meeting, Rasmus Effersoe, C.L. Johannesen and Samal Krakusteini. 12k, Oystercatcher and lyrics of Now the Hour Has Come, by poet Sverri Patursson (1871-1960), Just A. Husum, Joannes Patursson and Jens Olsen.

Granite Paper

1988, Sept. 5	Photo.	Perf. 12
179 A56 3k multicolored	.80	.80
180 A56 3.20k multicolored	1.20	1.20
181 A56 12k multicolored	4.50	4.50
Nos. 179-181 (3)	6.50	6.50

1888 Christmas meeting to preserve cultural traditions and the natl. language, cent.

Kirkjubour Cathedral Ruins — A57

270o, Exterior. 300o, Arch. 470o, Crucifixion, bas-relief. 550o, Interior.

1988, Oct. 17	Engr.	Perf. 13
182 A57 270o dark green	1.40	1.40
183 A57 300o dark bl, vert.	1.10	1.10
184 A57 470o dark brn, vert.	1.60	1.60
185 A57 550o dark violet	1.60	1.60
Nos. 182-185 (4)	5.70	5.70

Havnar Church, Torshavn, 200th Anniv. — A58

Designs: 350o, Church exterior. 500o, Crypt, vert. 15k, Bell, vert.

1989, Feb. 6	Engr.	Perf. 13
186 A58 350o dark green	1.00	1.00
187 A58 500o dark brown	1.75	1.75
188 A58 15k deep blue	3.50	3.50
Nos. 186-188 (3)	6.25	6.25

Folk Costumes — A59

Photo. & Engr.

1989, Apr. 10		Perf. 13½
189 A59 350o Man	1.00	1.00
190 A59 600o Woman	2.00	2.00

Europa 1989 — A60

Wooden children's toys.

1989, Apr. 10	Photo.	Perf. 12x11½
Granite Paper		
191 A60 3.50k Boat	1.00	1.00
192 A60 6k Horse	1.50	1.50

Island Games, July 5-13 — A61

1989, June 5	Photo.	Perf. 12½
Granite Paper		
193 A61 200o Rowing	.75	.75
194 A61 350o Handball	1.25	1.25
195 A61 600o Soccer	1.75	1.75
196 A61 700o Swimming	2.25	2.25
Nos. 193-196 (4)	6.00	6.00

A62

Bird cliffs of Suduroy.

1989, Oct. 2	Engr.	Perf. 14x13½
197 A62 320o Tvoran	1.00	1.00
198 A62 350o Skuvanes	1.40	1.40
199 A62 500o Beinisvord	1.75	1.75
200 A62 600o Asmundarstakkur	2.00	2.00
Nos. 197-200 (4)	6.15	6.15

A63

Modern fish factory (filleting station): 3.50k, Unloading fish. 3.70k, Cleaning and sorting. 5k, Filleting. 7k, Packaged frozen fish.

1990, Feb. 5	Litho.	Perf. 14x13½
201 A63 3.50k multi	1.00	1.00
202 A63 3.70k multi	1.00	1.00
203 A63 5k multi	1.25	1.25
204 A63 7k multi	2.00	2.00
Nos. 201-204 (4)	5.25	5.25

Europa 1990 — A64

Post offices.

1990, Apr. 9	Litho.	Perf. 13½x14
205 A64 3.50k Gjogv	1.00	1.00
206 A64 6k Klaksvik	1.75	1.75

Souvenir Sheet

Recognition of the Merkid, Flag of the Faroes, by the British, 50th Anniv. — A65

Designs: a, Flag. b, Fishing trawler Nyggjaberg, disappeared, 1942. c, Sloop Saana, sunk by the Germans, 1942.

1990, Apr. 9	Photo.	Perf. 12
Granite Paper		
207 A65 Sheet of 3	4.50	4.50
a.-c. 3.50k any single	1.60	1.60

Whales — A66

Designs: 320o, Mesoplodon bidens. 350o, Balaena mysticetus. 600o, Eubalaena glacialis. 700o, Hyperoodon ampullatus.

1990, June 6	Photo.	Perf. 11½
Granite Paper		
208 A66 320o multi	1.25	1.25
209 A66 350o multi	1.50	1.50
210 A66 600o multi	2.25	2.25
211 A66 700o multi	2.50	2.50
Nos. 208-211 (4)	7.50	7.50

Nolsoy Island by Steffan Danielsen — A67

1990, Oct. 8	Photo.	Perf. 11½
Granite Paper		
212 A67 50o shown	.25	.25
213 A67 350o Coastline	1.10	1.10
214 A67 500o Town	1.50	1.50
215 A67 1000o Coastline, cliffs	3.00	3.00
Nos. 212-215 (4)	5.85	5.85

Flora and Fauna — A68

3.70k, Plantago lanceolata. 4k, Rumex longifolius. 4.50k, Amara aulica. 6.50k, Lumbricus terrestris.

1991, Feb. 4	Litho.	Perf. 13
216 A68 3.70k multi	1.00	1.00
217 A68 4k multi	1.20	1.20
218 A68 4.50k multi	1.50	1.50
219 A68 6.50k multi	2.00	2.00
Nos. 216-219 (4)	5.70	5.70

Europa — A69

Designs: 3.70k, Weather satellite. 6.50k, Celestial navigation.

1991, Apr. 4   Litho.   Perf. 13
220	A69	3.70k multicolored	1.00	1.00
221	A69	6.50k multicolored	1.75	1.75

Town of Torshavn, 125th Anniv. — A70

1991, Apr. 4   Perf. 14x13½
222	A70	3.70k Town Hall	1.25	1.25
223	A70	3.70k View of town	1.25	1.25

Birds — A71

1991, June 3   Litho.   Perf. 13½
224	A71	3.70k Rissa tridactyla	1.20	1.20
225	A71	3.70k Sterna paradisaea	1.20	1.20
a.		Bklt. pane, 3 each #224-225	9.00	

Village of Saksun — A72

Design: 650o, Cliffs of Vestmanna.

1991, June 3
226	A72	370o shown	1.00	1.00
227	A72	650o multicolored	1.75	1.75

Samal Joensen-Mikines (1906-1979), Painter — A73

Designs: 340o, Funeral Procession. 370o, The Farewell. 550o, Handanagarthur. 1300o, Winter morning.

1991, Oct. 7   Litho.   Perf. 13½
228	A73	340o multi	1.00	1.00
229	A73	370o multi	1.10	1.10
230	A73	550o multi	1.60	1.60
231	A73	1300o multi	3.75	3.75
		Nos. 228-231 (4)	7.45	7.45

Mail Boats — A74

1992, Feb. 10   Litho.   Perf. 13½x14
232	A74	200o Ruth	.70	.70
233	A74	370o Ritan	1.00	1.00
234	A74	550o Sigmundur	1.50	1.50
235	A74	800o Masin	2.50	2.50
		Nos. 232-235 (4)	5.70	5.70

Europa — A75

Designs: 3.70k, Map of North Atlantic, Viking ship. 6.50k, Map of Central Atlantic region, one of Columbus's ships.

1992, Apr. 6   Litho.   Perf. 13½x14
236	A75	3.70k multicolored	1.10	1.10
237	A75	6.50k multicolored	2.00	2.00

Souvenir Sheet
238	A75	Sheet of 2, #236-237	8.50	8.50

First landing in the Americas by Leif Erikson (No. 236). Discovery of America by Christopher Columbus, 500th anniv. (No. 237).
See Iceland Nos. 749-751.

Seals — A76

Designs: No. 239, Halichoerus grypus. No. 240, Phoca vitulina.

1992, June 9   Litho.   Perf. 14x13½
239	A76	3.70k multi	1.40	1.40
240	A76	3.70k multi	1.40	1.40
a.		Bklt. pane, 3 #239, 3 #240	17.50	

Minerals — A77

1992, June 9   Photo.   Perf. 12
Granite Paper
241	A77	370o Stilbite	1.25	1.25
242	A77	650o Mesolite	2.25	2.25

Traditional Houses — A78

1992, Oct. 5   Litho.   Perf. 13½
243	A78	3.40k Hja Glyvra Hanusi	1.00	1.00
244	A78	3.70k I Nordragotu	1.10	1.10
245	A78	6.50k Blasastova	2.00	2.00
246	A78	8k Jakupsstova	2.40	2.40
		Nos. 243-246 (4)	6.50	6.50

Nordic House Entertainers A79

1993, Feb. 8   Litho.   Perf. 13½
247	A79	400o Dancers	1.10	1.10
248	A79	400o Pianist	1.10	1.10
249	A79	400o Trio	1.10	1.10
a.		Souv. sheet, #247-249, perf 12½	4.00	4.00
		Nos. 247-249 (3)	3.30	3.30

Village of Gjogv — A80

1993, Apr. 5
250	A80	4k View toward sea	1.50	1.50
251	A80	4k Ravino, village	1.50	1.50
a.		Booklet pane, 3 each #250-251	9.00	

Europa — A81

Sculptures by Hans Pauli Olsen: 4k, Movement. 7k, Reflection.

1993, Apr. 5
252	A81	4k multicolored	1.50	1.50
253	A81	7k multicolored	2.00	2.00

Horses — A82

Perf. 13½x13, 13x13½
1993, June 7   Engr.
254	A82	400o shown	1.10	1.10
255	A82	20k Mare, foal, horiz.	5.50	5.50

Butterflies — A83

1993, Oct. 4   Litho.   Perf. 14½
256	A83	350o Apamea zeta	1.10	1.10
257	A83	400o Hepialus humuli	1.25	1.25
258	A83	700o Vanessa atalanta	2.10	2.10
259	A83	900o Perizoma albulata	2.75	2.75
		Nos. 256-259 (4)	7.20	7.20

Fish — A84

Designs: 10o, Gasterosteus aculeatus. 4k, Neocyttus helgae. 7k, Salmo trutta fario. 10k, Hoplostethus atlanticus.

1994, Feb. 7   Litho.   Perf. 14½
260	A84	10o multi	.25	.25
261	A84	4k multi	1.25	1.25
262	A84	7k multi	2.25	2.25
263	A84	10k multi	3.00	3.00
		Nos. 260-263 (4)	6.75	6.75

Voyages of St. Brendan (484-577) — A85

Europa: 4k, St. Brendan on island with sheep, Irish monks in boat. 7k, St. Brendan, monks sailing past volcano.

1994, Apr. 18   Litho.   Perf. 14½x14
264	A85	4k multicolored	1.25	1.25
265	A85	7k multicolored	2.40	2.00
a.		Miniature sheet of 2, #264-265	4.50	4.50

Nos. 264-265 have designers name below the design. Stamps in No. 265a do not.
See Iceland Nos. 780-781; Ireland Nos. 923-924.

Sheepdogs — A86

Design: No. 267, Dog watching over sheep.

1994, June 6   Litho.   Perf. 13½
266	A86	4k multicolored	1.40	1.40

Size: 39x25mm
267	A86	4k multicolored	1.40	1.40
a.		Booklet pane, 3 each #266-267	8.50	
		Complete booklet, #267a	9.50	

School of Navigation — A87

Designs: 3.50k, Man using sextant, schooner. 7k, Ship, man at computer.

1994, June 6
268	A87	3.50k multicolored	1.00	1.00
269	A87	7k multicolored	2.50	2.50

Brusajokil's Lay — A88

Scenes, verses of the ballad: 1k, Ship at sea. 4k, Asbjorn entering Brusajokil's cave. 6k, Ormar with cat, trolls. 7k, Ormar pulling Brusajokil's beard.

1994, Sept. 19   Litho.   Perf. 14
270	A88	1k multicolored	.35	.35
271	A88	4k multicolored	1.40	1.40
272	A88	6k multicolored	1.75	1.75
273	A88	7k multicolored	2.25	2.25
		Nos. 270-273 (4)	5.75	5.75

Twelve Days of Christmas — A89

No. 274, Goats, men, deer, hides. No. 275, Ducks, cattle, sheep, horses, banners, barrels.

1994, Oct. 31   Litho.   Perf. 14x13
274	A89	4k multicolored	1.10	1.10
275	A89	4k multicolored	1.10	1.10
a.		Bklt. pane, 3 each #274-275	7.00	
		Complete booklet, #275a	7.00	

Leafhoppers — A90

Designs: 50o, Ulopa reticulata. 4k, Streptanus sordidus. 5k, Anoscopus flavostriatus. 13k, Macrosteles alpinus.

1995, Feb. 6   Litho.   Perf. 14
276	A90	50o multicolored	.25	.25
277	A90	4k multicolored	1.60	1.60
278	A90	5k multicolored	1.60	1.60
279	A90	13k multicolored	4.50	4.50
		Nos. 276-279 (4)	7.95	7.95

Tourism — A91

1995, Apr. 10   Litho.   Perf. 13½x14
280	A91	4k Village of Famjin	1.50	1.50
281	A91	4k Vatnsdalur valley	1.50	1.50

Peace & Freedom — A92

Europa: 4k, Island couple, "Vidar, vali og baldur." 7k, Couple looking toward sun, "Liv og livtrasir."

1995, Apr. 10   Perf. 13x14
282	A92	4k multicolored	1.20	1.20
283	A92	7k multicolored	2.50	2.50

Nordic Art — A93

Designs: 2k, Museum of Art, Torshavn. 4k, Woman, by Frimod Joensen, vert. 5.50k, Self-portrait, by Joensen, vert.

Perf. 13½x14, 14x13½
1995, June 12   Litho.
284	A93	2k multicolored	.65	.65
285	A93	4k multicolored	1.40	1.40
286	A93	5.50k multicolored	1.90	1.90
		Nos. 284-286 (3)	3.95	3.95

Corvus Corax — A94

Designs: No. 287, Black raven. No. 288, White-speckled raven.

FAROE ISLANDS

1995, June 12		Perf. 13½x14	
287	A94 4k multicolored	1.40	1.40
288	A94 4k multicolored	1.40	1.40
a.	Booklet pane, 5 each #287-288	14.00	
	Complete booklet, #288a	14.00	

Saint Olaf (955?-1030), Patron Saint of Faroe Islands — A95

Litho. & Engr.

1995, Sept. 12		Perf. 13½x13	
289	A95 4k multicolored	1.60	1.60

See Aland Islands No. 119.

Early Folk Life — A95a

4k, Dairy maids carrying buckets. 6k, Peasants fleecing sheep. 15k, Schooners, saltfish being brought ashore, vert.

1995, Sept. 12	Engr.	Perf. 12½	
290	A95a 4k dark green	1.50	1.50
291	A95a 6k pur brn, vert.	2.25	2.25
292	A95a 15k ultra	5.00	5.00
	Nos. 290-292 (3)	8.75	8.75

Church of Mary Catholic Church — A96

Designs: No. 293, Stained glass window. No. 294, Exterior view of church.

1995, Nov. 9	Litho.	Perf. 13½	
293	A96 4k multicolored	1.40	1.40
294	A96 4k multicolored	1.40	1.40
a.	Booklet pane, 5 ea #293-294	14.00	
	Complete booklet, #294a	14.00	

Rocky Coastline — A97

1996, Jan. 1	Litho.	Perf. 14	
295	A97 4.50k multicolored	1.40	1.40

Seaweed — A98

4k, Ptilota plumosa. 5.50k, Fucus spiralis. 6k, Ascophyllum nodosum. 9k, Laminaria hyperborea.

1996, Feb. 12		Perf. 15	
296	A98 4k multicolored	1.10	1.10
297	A98 5.50k multicolored	1.40	1.40
298	A98 6k multicolored	1.60	1.60
299	A98 9k multicolored	2.75	2.75
	Nos. 296-299 (4)	6.85	6.85

Birds — A99

Designs: No. 300, Laxia curvirostra. No. 301, Bombycilla garrulus.

1996, Apr. 15	Litho.	Perf. 14x15	
300	A99 4.50k multicolored	1.40	1.40
301	A99 4.50k multicolored	1.40	1.40
a.	Booklet pane, 5 each #300-301	14.00	
	Complete booklet, #301a	14.00	

See Nos. 313-314.

A100

Europa (Wives of Faroese Seamen): 4.50k, Woman standing beside sea coast. 7.50k, Portrait of a woman, vert.

1996, Apr. 15	Perf. 15x14½, 14½x15		
302	A100 4.50k multicolored	1.50	1.50
303	A100 7.50k multicolored	2.00	2.00

A101

Nordatlantex '96 (Children's drawings): a, Boy playing with hoop, stick, by Bugvi. b, Two girls on steet, road sign, by Gudrid. c, Girl on bicycle, car on street, by Herborg.

1996, June 7	Litho.	Perf. 14½	
	Souvenir Sheet of 3		
304	A101 4.50k #a.-c.	3.50	3.50

A102

Sea bed off the Faroes.

Litho. & Engr.

1996, June 7		Perf. 13	
305	A102 10k violet & multi	2.50	2.50
306	A102 16k green & multi	4.00	4.00

See Nos. 319-320, 343, 377-378.

Janus Kamban (b. 1913), Sculptor, Graphic Artist — A103

Works of art: 4.50k, Flock of Sheep. 6.50k, Fisherman on the Way Home. 7.50k, View from Tórshavn's Old Quarter.

1996, Sept. 16	Litho.	Perf. 14	
307	A103 4.50k multicolored	1.40	1.40
308	A103 6.50k multicolored	1.60	1.60
309	A103 7.50k multicolored	2.25	2.25
	Nos. 307-309 (3)	5.25	5.25

A104

Christian's Church, Klaksvík — A105

Designs: No. 310, Exterior. No. 311, Interior, altar fresco.

1996, Nov. 4	Litho.	Perf. 14x15	
310	A104 4.50k multi	1.40	1.40
311	A105 4.50k multi	1.40	1.40
a.	Booklet pane, 6 #310, 4 #311	14.00	
	Complete booklet, #311a	14.00	

Christmas.

Souvenir Sheet

Reign of Queen Margaret II, 25th Anniv. — A106

1997, Jan. 14	Litho.	Perf. 14½	
312	A106 4.50k multicolored	1.25	1.25

Bird Type of 1996

Designs: No. 313, Pyrrhula pyrrhula. No. 314, Carduelis flammea.

1997, Feb. 17	Litho.	Perf. 14x15	
313	A99 4.50k multi	1.25	1.25
314	A99 4.50k multi	1.25	1.25
a.	Booklet pane, 5 each #313-314	12.50	
	Complete booklet, #314a	12.50	

Mushrooms — A107

Designs: 4.50k, Hygrocybe helobia. 6k, Hygrocybe chlorophana. 6.50k, Hygrocybe virginea. 7.50k, Hygrocybe psittacina.

1997, Feb. 17		Perf. 14½	
315	A107 4.50k multicolored	1.10	1.10
316	A107 6k multicolored	1.60	1.60
317	A107 6.50k multicolored	1.60	1.60
318	A107 7.50k multicolored	2.00	2.00
	Nos. 315-318 (4)	6.30	6.30

Map Type of 1996
Litho. & Engr.

1997, May 20		Perf. 13	
319	A102 11k red & multi	2.90	2.90
320	A102 18k claret & multi	4.50	4.50

Europa — A108

Legends illustrated by William Heinesen: 4.50k, The Temptations of Saint Anthony. 7.50k, The Merman sitting at bottom of sea eating fish bait.

1997, May 20	Litho.	Perf. 14½	
321	A108 4.50k multicolored	1.40	1.40
322	A108 7.50k multicolored	2.25	2.25

Kalmar Union, 600th Anniv. — A109

1997, May 20	Engr.	Perf. 12½	
323	A109 4.50k deep blue violet	1.50	1.50

A110

Barbara, Film Shot in Faroe Islands (Scenes from film): 4.50k, Danish theologian Poul Aggerso arriving at Faroe Islands. 6.50k, Barbara and Poul. 7.50k, Barbara with men on boat. 9k, Barbara in row boat, sailing ship.

1997, Sept. 15	Litho.	Perf. 14	
324	A110 4.50k multicolored	1.25	1.25
325	A110 6.50k multicolored	1.60	1.60
326	A110 7.50k multicolored	2.00	2.00
327	A110 9k multicolored	2.25	2.25
	Nos. 324-327 (4)	7.10	7.10

A111

Hvalvik church.

1997, Sept. 15			
328	A111 4.50k Interior	1.25	1.25
329	A111 4.50k Exterior	1.25	1.25
a.	Booklet pane, 5 each #328-329	12.50	
	Complete booklet, #329a	12.50	

Birds — A112

1998, Feb. 23	Litho.	Perf. 14x14½	
330	A112 4.50k Sturnus vulgaris	1.25	1.25
331	A112 4.50k Turdus merula	1.25	1.25
a.	Bklt. pane, 5 each #330-331	12.50	
	Complete booklet, #331a	12.50	

A113

Scenes from the Sigurd poem "Brynhild's Ballad": 4.50k, King Buole, daughter Brynhild. 6.50k, Sigurd riding through wall of fire on horseback. 7.50k, Sigurd, Brynhild together. 10k, Guthrun alone leading horse.

1998, Feb. 23		Perf. 14	
332	A113 4.50k multicolored	1.25	1.25
333	A113 6.50k multicolored	1.60	1.60
334	A113 7.50k multicolored	1.90	1.90
335	A113 10k multicolored	2.50	2.50
	Nos. 332-335 (4)	7.25	7.25

Europa — A114

1998, May 18	Litho.	Perf. 14	
336	A114 4.50k Parade	1.25	1.25
337	A114 7.50k Processional	1.25	1.25

Olavsoka, Natl. Festival of Faroe Islands.

A115

1998, May 18		Perf. 14½	
338	A115 7.50k multicolored	1.90	1.90

UN Declaration of Human Rights, 50th anniv.

Intl. Year of the Ocean — A116

Toothed whales: 4k, Lagenorhynchus acutus. 4.50k, Orcinus orca. 7k, Tursiops truncatus. 9k, Delphinapterus leucas.

1998, May 18		Perf. 14½x14	
339	A116 4k multicolored	1.00	1.00
340	A116 4.50k multicolored	1.10	1.10
341	A116 7k multicolored	1.75	1.75
342	A116 9k multicolored	2.25	2.25
	Nos. 339-342 (4)	6.10	6.10

FAROE ISLANDS

Map Type of 1996
Litho. & Engr.
1998, Sept. 14   **Perf. 13**
343 A102 14k multicolored   3.75 3.75

Frederickschurch — A117

Designs: No. 344, Exterior, coastline. No. 345, Interior.

1998, Sept. 14   **Litho.**   **Perf. 14**
344 A117 4.50k multi   1.25 1.25
345 A117 4.50k multi   1.25 1.25
   a. Bklt. pane, 5 each #344-345   12.50
     Complete booklet, #345a   12.50

A118

Paintings by Hans Hansen (1920-70): 4.50k, Fell-field, 1966. 5.50k, Village Interior, 1965. 6.50k, Portrait of Farmer Ólavur í Útistovu from Mikladalur, 1968. 8k, Self-portrait, 1968.

Perf. 13½x14, 14x13½
1998, Sept. 14
346 A118 4.50k multi   1.25 1.25
347 A118 5.50k multi   1.50 1.50
348 A118 6.50k multi, vert.   1.60 1.60
349 A118 8k multi, vert.   2.25 2.25
   Nos. 346-349 (4)   6.60 6.60

Birds — A119

Designs: No. 350, Passer domesticus. No. 351, Troglodytes troglodytes.

1999, Feb. 22   **Litho.**   **Perf. 13½**
350 A119 4.50k multi   1.25 1.25
351 A119 4.50k multi   1.25 1.25
   a. Bklt. pane, 5 each #350-351   12.50
     Complete booklet, #351a   12.50

Ships Named "Smyril" — A120

1999, Feb. 22   **Perf. 14½x14**
352 A120 4.50k 1895   1.25 1.25
353 A120 5k 1932   1.40 1.40
354 A120 8k 1967   2.25 2.25
355 A120 13k 1975   3.50 3.50
   Nos. 352-355 (4)   8.40 8.40

Northern Islands — A121

1999, May 25   **Litho.**   **Perf. 13½**
356 A121 50o Kalsoy   .25 .25
357 A121 100o Vithoy   .25 .25
358 A121 400o Svinoy   1.10 1.10
359 A121 450o Fugloy   1.25 1.25
360 A121 600o Kunoy   1.60 1.60
361 A121 800o Borthoy   2.10 2.10
   Nos. 356-361 (6)   6.55 6.55

See Nos. 383-386.

Waterfalls — A122

Europa: 6k, Svartifossur. 8k, Foldarafossur.

1999, May 25   **Perf. 14x14½**
362 A122 6k multicolored   1.60 1.60
363 A122 8k multicolored   2.25 2.25

Abstract Paintings of Ingálvur av Reyni — A123

1999, Sept. 27   **Litho.**   **Perf. 12½**
364 A123 4.50k Bygd   1.25 1.25
365 A123 6k Húsavík   1.60 1.60
366 A123 8k Reytt regn   2.10 2.10
367 A123 20k Genta   5.25 5.25
   Nos. 364-367 (4)   10.20 10.20

Bible Stories — A124

1999, Sept. 27   **Perf. 14½x14**
368 A124 4.50o John 1:1 5   1.25 1.25
   a. Booklet pane of 6   7.50
     Complete booklet, #368a   7.50
369 A124 600o Luke 1:26-28   1.60 1.60
   a. Booklet pane of 6   10.00
     Complete booklet, #369a   10.00

See Nos. 387-388, 407-408.

A125

Christianity in the Faroes, 1000th Anniv.: 4.50k, Man on rocks in ocean. 5.50k, Monk with cross, man with sword. 8k, People, flags. 16k, Cross in sky.

Perf. 13½x13¼
2000, Feb. 21   **Litho.**
370 A125 4.50k multi   1.25 1.25
371 A125 5.50k multi   1.40 1.40
372 A125 8k multi   2.10 2.10
373 A125 16k multi   4.25 4.25
   Nos. 370-373 (4)   9.00 9.00

A126

School and: No. 374, Sanna av Skarthi, Anna Suffia Rasmussen, wives of founders. No. 375, Rasmus Rasmussen (1871-1962), Símun av Skarthi (1872-1942), school founders.

2000, Feb. 21
374 A126 4.50k multi   1.25 1.25
375 A126 4.50k multi   1.25 1.25
   a. Bklt. pane, 4 ea #374-375   10.00
     Complete booklet, #375a   10.00

Faroese Folk High School, cent.

Europa, 2000
Common Design Type
2000, May 9   **Litho.**   **Perf. 13¼x13**
376 CD17 8k multi   2.40 2.40

Map Type of 1996
Litho. & Engr.
2000, May 22   **Perf. 13¼x13**
377 A102 15k multi   3.75 3.75
378 A102 22k multi   5.75 5.75

Stampin' The Future Children's Stamp Design Contest Winners — A127

Art by: 4k, Katrin Mortensen. 4.50k, Sigga Andreassen. 6k, Steingrímur Joensen. 8k, Dion Dam Frandsen.

2000, May 22   **Litho.**   **Perf. 13x13½**
379 A127 4k multi   1.10 1.10
380 A127 4.50k multi   1.25 1.25
381 A127 6k multi   1.60 1.60
382 A127 8k multi   2.25 2.25
   Nos. 379-382 (4)   6.20 6.20

Island Type of 1999
2000, Sept. 18   **Litho.**   **Perf. 13½**
383 A121 200o Skúvoy   .65 .65
384 A121 650o Hestoy   1.60 1.60
385 A121 750o Koltur   1.90 1.90
386 A121 1000o Nólsoy   2.50 2.50
   Nos. 383-386 (4)   6.65 6.65

Bible Story Type of 1999
2000, Sept. 18   **Litho.**   **Perf. 13x13¼**
387 A124 4.50k Micah 5:1   1.25 1.25
   a. Booklet pane of 6   7.50
     Booklet, #387a   7.50
388 A124 6k John 1:14   1.60 1.60
   a. Booklet pane of 6   10.00
     Booklet, #388a   10.00

Pew Gables Type of 1980
Kirkjubour pew gables: 430o, St. Andrew with cross. 650o, St. Bartholomew. 800o, Unknown apostle. 18k, Unknown apostle, diff.

Photo. & Engr.
2001, Feb. 12   **Perf. 12¾x12½**
389 A20 450o multi   1.25 1.25
390 A20 650o multi   1.60 1.60
391 A20 800o multi   2.10 2.10
392 A20 18k multi   4.50 4.50
   Nos. 389-392 (4)   9.45 9.45

Faroese Red Cross, 75th Anniv. — A128

Designs: 4.50k, Old person. 6k, Relief worker.

2001, Feb. 12   **Litho.**   **Perf. 14½x14**
393 A128 4.50k multi   1.25 1.25
   a. Booklet pane of 6   7.50
     Booklet, #393a   7.50
394 A128 6k multi   1.60 1.60
   a. Booklet pane of 6   10.00
     Booklet, #394a   10.00

Souvenir Sheet

Faroe Islands Postal Service, 25th Anniv. A129

No. 395: a, Boat for interisland mail transport, 19th cent. b, Tórshavn post office, 1906. c, Simon Pauli Poulson (Morkabóndin), mail carrier.

Photo. & Engr.
2001, Apr. 1   **Perf. 13x13¼**
395 A129 4.50k Sheet of 3, #a-c   5.00 5.00

Nordic Myths and Legends About Light and Darkness — A130

No. 396: a, The Death of Hogni. b, The Tree of the Year. c, The Harp. d, Gram and Grane. e, The Ballad of Nornagest. f, Gudrun's Evil Magic.

Litho. with Foil Application
2001, Apr. 1   **Perf. 13½x13¼**
396 A130 6k Sheet of 6, #a-f   10.00 10.00

Hafnia 2001 Philatelic Exhibition, Copenhagen.

Paintings by Zacharias Heinesen — A131

Designs: 4k, The Artist's Mother, 1992. 4.50k, Úti á Reyni, 1974. 10k, Ur Vágunum, 2000. 15k, Sunrise, 1975.

2001, June 11   **Litho.**   **Perf. 13¼x13**
397 A131 4k multi   1.10 1.10
398 A131 4.50k multi   1.25 1.25
399 A131 10k multi   2.75 2.75
400 A131 15k multi   4.00 4.00
   Nos. 397-400 (4)   9.10 9.10

Europa — A132

Hydroelectric power stations: 6k, Fossáverkith. 8k, Eithisverkith.

2001, June 11   **Perf. 13x13½**
401 A132 6k multi   1.60 1.60
402 A132 8k multi   2.25 2.25

Whales — A133

Designs: 4.50k, Physeter macrocephalus. 6.50k, Balaenoptera physalus. 9k, Balaenoptera musculus. 20k, Balaenoptera borealis.

Perf. 13¾x13¼
2001, Sept. 17   **Litho.**
403 A133 4.50k multi   1.25 1.25
404 A133 6.50k multi   1.60 1.60
405 A133 9k multi   2.25 2.25
406 A133 20k multi   5.50 5.50
   Nos. 403-406 (4)   10.60 10.60

Bible Stories Type of 1999
2001, Sept. 17   **Perf. 13**
407 A124 5k Luke 2.34-35   1.40 1.40
   a. Booklet pane of 6   8.50
     Booklet, #407a   8.50
408 A124 6.50k Matthew 2:18   1.60 1.60
   a. Booklet pane of 6   10.00
     Booklet, #408a   10.00

Mollusks — A134

Designs: 5k, Sepiola atlantica. 7k, Modiolus modiolus. 7.50k, Polycera faeroensis. 18k, Buccinum undatum.

2002, Feb. 11   **Litho.**   **Perf. 13**
409 A134 5k multi   1.40 1.40
410 A134 7k multi   1.75 1.75
411 A134 7.50k multi   1.90 1.90
412 A134 18k multi   4.50 4.50
   Nos. 409-412 (4)   9.55 9.55

Portions of the designs were applied by a thermographic process producing a shiny, raised effect.

Souvenir Sheet

Viking Voyages A135

508 FAROE ISLANDS

No. 413: a, Navigation tool. b, Viking sailor on boat. c, Viking boat.

Litho. & Engr.
2002, Feb. 11 — Perf. 13
413 A135 6.50k Sheet of 3, #a-c 5.00 5.00

Europa — A136

Designs: 6.50k, Clowns. 8k, Various circus performers.

2002, Apr. 8 Litho. Perf. 13¼x13½
414 A136 6.50k multi 1.60 1.60
415 A136 8k multi 2.10 2.10

Art by Tróndur Patursson A137

Designs: 5k, Bládypi. 6.50k, Kosmiska Rúmith.

2002, Apr. 8
416 A137 5k multi 1.40 1.40
417 A137 6.50k multi 1.60 1.60
  a. Booklet pane of 8, 4 each #416-417 13.00 —
    Booklet, #417a 13.00

Eggs and Chicks — A138

Designs: 5k, Numenius phaeopus. 7.50k, Gallinago gallinago. 12k, Haematopus ostralegus. 20k, Pluvialis apricaria.

2002, June 17 — Perf. 14x14½
418 A138 5k multi 1.40 1.40
419 A138 7.50k multi 1.90 1.90
420 A138 12k multi 3.00 3.00
421 A138 20k multi 5.25 5.25
  Nos. 418-421 (4) 11.55 11.55

Souvenir Sheet

Faroese Representative Council, 150th Anniv. — A139

Designs: 5k, Royal book and seal. 6.50k, Royal book, Protocol of 1852.

2002, June 17 — Perf. 14
422 A139 Sheet of 2, #a-b 4.00 4.00

Falco Columbarius Subaesalon A140

Litho. & Embossed
2002, Sept. 23 — Perf. 13¼
423 A140 30k multi 8.25 8.25

Gota Church — A141

2002, Sept. 23 Litho. Perf. 12¼
424 A141 5k Exterior 1.40 1.40
425 A141 6.50k Interior 1.60 1.60
  a. Booklet pane, 5 each #424-425 15.00 —
    Booklet, #425a 15.00

Souvenir Sheet

Intl. Council for the Exploration of the Sea, Cent. — A142

No. 426: a, Micromesistius poutassou and island. b, Exploration ship Magnus Heinason and fish.

Litho. & Engr.
2002, Sept. 23 — Perf. 13
426 A142 8k Sheet of 2, #a-b 4.50 4.50
See Denmark Nos. 1237-1238, Greenland Nos. 401-402.

Opening of Vagár-Streymoy Tunnel, Nov. 2002 — A143

Designs: No. 427, Wheeled tunneling machine at right. No. 428, Workers in red uniforms at left.

2003, Feb. 24 Litho. Perf. 13¼x13
427 A143 5k multi 1.40 1.40
428 A143 5k multi 1.40 1.40
  a. Booklet pane, 5 each #427-428 14.00
    Complete booklet, #428a 14.00

Voluspá, Ancient Norse Poem A144

No. 429: a, Seeress Heid holding staff. b, Heid sees animal and man in vision. c, Nude man and woman. d, Scribe and horseman. e, Battle between group with swords and man with hammer. f, Horseman and warriors. g, Men, large sword. h, Longboat. i, Attack on man holding spear, fire. j, Two figures with staffs, winged serpent.

2003, Feb. 24 — Perf. 14
429 A144 Sheet of 10 17.50 17.50
  a.-j. 6.50k Any single 1.60 1.60

Europa — A145

Poster art for Nordic House: 6.50k, Fish Tree, by Astrid Andreasen, 1991. 8k, Ceramics by Guthrith Poulsen, 1997.

2003, Apr. 14 — Perf. 13½x13¼
430 A145 6.50k multi 1.60 1.60
431 A145 8k multi 2.10 2.10

Children's Songs — A146

No. 432: a, Woman playing hopscotch (26x44mm). b, Boy on rocks, moon (26x44mm). c, Girl with missing teeth (26x26mm). d, Boy with toy sailboat (26x26mm). e, Cat, horse and girl (26x26mm). f, Butterfly and fly (26x26mm). g, Girl in bed, boy with stars (44x26mm). h, Cat on stairs, mouse (26x36mm). i, Man playing drums (26x26mm). j, King and queen in longboat (44x26mm).

Perf. 13¼, 13¼x13¼x13¼x14 (#432g, 432j), 13¼x14 (#432h)
2003, Apr. 14
432 A146 Sheet of 10 14.00 14.00
  a.-j. 5k Any single 1.25 1.25

Small Towns — A147

2003, June 10 Litho. Perf. 13x13¼
433 A147 5k Bour 1.40 1.40
434 A147 5k Gásadalur 1.40 1.40

Communities With Post Offices 100 Years Old — A148

No. 435: a, Fuglafjorthur. b, Strendur. c, Sandur. d, Eithi. e, Vestmanna. f, Vágur. g, Mithvágur. h, Hvalba.

2003, June 10 — Perf. 13¼x13
435 A148 Sheet of 8 11.00 11.00
  a.-h. 5k Any single 1.25 1.25

Theologians — A149

Designs: 5k, Jesper Rasmussen Brochmand (1585-1652). 6.50k, Thomas Kingo (1634-1703).

2003, Sept. 22 — Perf. 13x13¼
436 A149 5k multi 1.40 1.40
437 A149 6.50k multi 1.60 1.60
  a. Booklet pane, 5 each #436-437 15.00 —
    Complete booklet, #437a 15.00

Souvenir Sheet

Dancing in the Inn's Smoking Room, by Emil Krause A150

Litho. & Engr.
2003, Sept. 22 — Perf. 12¼
438 A150 25k multi 7.50 7.50
100th Faroese stamp engraved by Czeslaw Slania.

Islands Type of 1999
2004, Jan. 26 Litho. Perf. 13½
439 A121 550o Stóra Dímun 1.40 1.40
440 A121 700o Lítla Dímun 1.90 1.90

Suthuroy Island A151

No. 441: a, Sigmundargjogv, Sandvik. b, Fiskieithi, Hvalba. c, A Hamri, Frothba. d, Tjaldavíksholmur, Oravík. e, Fossurin Stóri, Fámjin. f, Hovsfjorthur, Hov. g, I Eystrum, Porkeri. h, A Okrum. i, I Horg, Sumba. j, I Akrabergi.

2004, Jan. 26 — Perf. 13x13¼
441 A151 5k Sheet of 10, #a-j 14.00 14.00

1854 Cruise of Yacht "Maria" A152

No. 442: a, Gáshólmur and Tindhólmur. b, Framvith "Diamantunum." c, Hús av tí betra slagnum. d, Mylingur sunnanífrá. e, Mylingur northanífrá. f, Kalsoyggin northanífrá. g, Raetha teir infoddu. h, Sunnari endi av Kunoynni.

2004, Mar. 26 Litho. Perf. 13
442 A152 6.50k Sheet of 8, #a.-h. 14.00 14.00

Souvenir Sheet

Norse Gods A153

No. 443: a, Thor, in boat, fighting Midgard serpent. b, Ran in fishing net.

2004, Mar. 26
443 A153 6.50k Sheet of 2, #a.-b. 4.50 4.50

Souvenir Sheet

Wedding of Crown Prince Frederik and Mary Donaldson — A154

Litho. & Photo.
2004, May 14 — Perf. 13¼
444 A154 Sheet of 2 + central label 4.00 4.00
  a. 5k Couple facing right 1.60 1.60
  b. 6.50k Couple facing left 2.25 2.25
See Denmark No. 1275 and Greenland Nos. 429-430.

Soccer Organization Centenaries — A155

FAROE ISLANDS

Soccer players and emblems of: 5k, Klaksvík and Tórshavn teams. 6.50k, FIFA (Fédération Internationale de Football Association).

2004, May 24   Litho.   Perf. 13¼x13
445	A155	5k multi	1.40	1.40
446	A155	6.50k multi	1.60	1.60
a.	Booklet pane, 4 each #445-446		12.00	
	Complete booklet, #446a		12.00	

Europa — A156

Designs: 6.50k, Tourists in gorge, Hestur. 8k, Tourists at shore, Stóra Dímun.

2004, May 24   Perf. 13x13¼
447	A156	6.50k multi	1.60	1.60
448	A156	8k multi	2.25	2.25

Churches — A157

2004, Sept. 20   Litho.   Perf. 13¼x13
449	A157	5.50k Vágur	1.40	1.40
450	A157	7.50k Tvoroyri	2.00	2.00
a.	Booklet pane, 4 each #449-450		14.00	
	Complete booklet, #450a		14.00	

Poems by Janus Djurhuus (1881-1948) — A158

No. 451: a, Atlantis. b, Grímur Kamban. c, Gandkvaethi Tróndar. d, Til Foroya I-III. e, Mín sorg. f, Loki. g, I búri og Slatur. h, Heimferth Nólsoyar Páls. i, Móses á Sinai fjalli. j, Cello.

2004, Sept. 20   Perf. 13
451	A158	Sheet of 10	20.00	20.00
a.-j.	7.50k Any single		2.00	2.00

Souvenir Sheet

Life of the Vikings A159

No. 452: a, Men tending sheep. b, Men with farm implements. c, Women weaving and woman milking cow.

Litho. & Engr.

2005, Feb. 7   Perf. 13
452	A159	Sheet of 3	6.00	6.00
a.-c.	7.50k Any single		2.00	2.00

Miniature Sheet

Vágar Island A160

No. 453: a, Víkar. b, Gásadalur. c, Bour. d, Slaettanes. e, Kvígandalsá. f, Sorvágur. g, Sandavágur. h, Vatnsoyrar. i, Fjallavatn. j, Mithvágur.

2005, Feb. 7   Litho.   Perf. 13x13¼
453	A160	Sheet of 10	15.00	15.00
a.-j.	5.50k Any single		1.50	1.50

Lepus Timidus — A161

2005, Apr. 18   Perf. 13¼x13½
454	A161	5.50k shown	1.60	1.60
455	A161	5.50k Brown fur	1.60	1.60
a.	Booklet pane, 4 each #454-455		13.00	
	Complete booklet, #455a		13.00	

Europa A162

Various traditional foods with: 7.50k, Brown panel. 10k, Green panel.

2005, Apr. 18   Perf. 13¼x13
456	A162	7.50k multi	2.00	2.00
457	A162	10k multi	2.75	2.75

Worldwide Fund for Nature (WWF) — A163

Petrels: 8.50k, Oceanodroma leucorhoa. 9k, Hydrobates pelagicus. 12k, Oceanodroma leucorhoa on ground. 20k, Hydrobates pelagicus on ground.

2005, June 6   Perf. 13
458	A163	8.50k multi	1.60	1.60
459	A163	9k multi	2.75	2.75
460	A163	12k multi	3.25	3.25
461	A163	20k multi	5.50	5.50
	Nos. 458-461 (4)		13.10	13.10

Miniature Sheet

Landscapes by Jógvan Waagstein (1879-1949) — A164

No. 462: a, Path and wall at LL, denomination in red, year date in black in grass. b, Path and wall at LL, denomination in white, year date in black on wall. c, Stone hut at left, denomination in red, year date in black. d, Path at right, denomination in red, year date in black. e, Two large rocks at right, denomination in red, year date in black. f, Rocks at LL, denomination in red, year date in white. g, Path at center, denomination in white, year date in black on path. h, Buildings at LL, denomination in red, year date in black in path. i, Churches, denomination in white, year date in black in water.

2005, Sept. 19   Litho.   Perf. 14x14¼
462	A164	Sheet of 9	17.00	17.00
a.-i.	7.50k Any single		1.90	1.90

End of British Occupation In World War II, 60th Anniv. — A165

Soldiers with: 5.50k, Arms. 9k, Children.

2005, Sept. 19   Perf. 14
463	A165	5.50k pale blue & blk	1.40	1.40
464	A165	9k pale yel & blk	2.40	2.40

Christmas — A166

Ballads: 5.50k, Jólavísan. 7.50k, Rudisar Vísa.

2005, Nov. 7   Perf. 13½x13¼
465	A166	5.50k multi	1.40	1.40
466	A166	7.50k multi	2.00	2.00
a.	Booklet pane, 5 each #465-466		17.00	
	Complete booklet, #466a		17.00	

Villages — A167

2006, Feb. 13   Litho.   Perf. 13¾
467	A167	7k Sythrugota	1.90	1.90
468	A167	12k Fuglafjorthur	2.50	2.50
469	A167	20k Leirvik	5.00	5.00
	Nos. 467-469 (3)		9.40	9.40

Miniature Sheet

Fish A168

No. 470: a, Himantolophus groenlandicus. b, Gonostoma elongatum. c, Sebastes mentella. d, Neoraja caerulea. e, Rhinochimaera atlantica. f, Linophryne lucifer. g, Ceratias holboelli. h, Lampris guttatus. i, Argyropelecus olfersi. j, Lophius piscatorius.

2006, Feb. 13   Perf. 14
470	A168	Sheet of 10	15.00	15.00
a.-j.	5.50k Any single		1.40	1.40

Souvenir Sheet

Norse Folklore A169

No. 471: a, Norns surrounding sleeping child. b, Sea ghost.

2006, Mar. 29   Perf. 13
471	A169	7.50k Sheet of 2, #a-b	4.00	4.00

Miniature Sheet

Ballad of the Long Serpent, by Jens Christian Djurhuus A170

No. 472: a, Building of ship. b, Launch of ship. c, King on throne. d, King's fleet at sea (brown ship at LL, blue ship at LR). e, King and sailors on shore. f, King pointing. g, Ship with red sail at R. h, Battle scene (injured men falling into water). i, Battle scene (men with shields jumping from ship to ship). j, Dead men on ship's deck.

2006, Mar. 29   Perf. 13¼x13
472	A170	Sheet of 10	15.00	15.00
a.-j.	5.50k Any single		1.40	1.40

Opening of Northoy Tunnel — A171

Tunnel and: No. 473, Fish. No. 474, Canoe.

2006, June 12   Perf. 13¼
473	A171	5.50k multi	1.40	1.40
474	A171	5.50k multi	1.40	1.40
a.	Booklet pane, 4 each #473-474		11.00	
	Complete booklet, #474a		11.00	

Europa — A172

2006, June 12   Perf. 13¾
475	A172	7.50k shown	2.00	2.00
476	A172	10k Hands, diff.	2.75	2.75

Miniature Sheet

Sandoy Island A173

No. 477: a, Sunnan fyri Skopun. b, Dalur. c, Coltuvík. d, Skálavík. e, Skopun. f, Sandur. g, Skarvanes. h, Húsavík.

2006, Sept. 18   Litho.   Perf. 13x13¼
477	A173	Sheet of 8	16.00	16.00
a.-h.	7.50k Any single		1.90	1.90

Sandur Church — A174

Designs: 5.50k, Building exterior, steeple cross. 7.50k, Interior.

2006, Sept. 18   Perf. 14
478	A174	5.50k multi	1.40	1.40
479	A174	7.50k multi	2.00	2.00
a.	Booklet pane, 4 each #478-479		14.00	
	Complete booklet, #479a		14.00	

FAROE ISLANDS

Wave Energy — A175

2007, Feb. 12   Litho.   Perf. 12½x13
480 A175 7.50k multi   2.00 2.00

Art From 1838 La Recherche Expedition A176

Art by Barthélemy Lauvergne: 5.50k, La Recherche off Nólsoy. 7.50k, Skaelingsfjall.

2007, Feb. 12
481 A176 5.50k multi   1.40 1.40
482 A176 7.50k multi   2.00 2.00
 a.   Booklet pane, 4 each #481-482 12.00   —
      Complete booklet, #482a   12.00

Miniature Sheet

Legend of the Seal Woman A177

No. 483: a, Man, head of white seal. b, Woman and seals in ring. c, Man, nude woman, seals. d, Man and nude woman seated on chest. e, Ship and two seals. f, Children, seal woman nursing child. g, Seal woman and man. h, Sleeping man and seal woman with hands open. i, Man and dead seals. j, Seal woman.

2007, Feb. 12   Perf. 14
483 A177 Sheet of 10   15.00 15.00
 a.-j.   5.50k Any single   1.50 1.50

Miniature Sheet

The Old Man and His Sons, Novel by Hethin Brú A178

No. 484: a, Ketil cutting whale's throat. b, Men carrying injured Klávus on log. c, Kálvur and fiancee, Klávusardóttir with pot and kettle. d, Ketil and Kálvur in fishing boat. e, Ketil's wife arguing with daughter-in-law. f, Ketil catching flying northern fulmars. g, Kálvur and stone fence. h, Ketil, Kálvur and cow.

2007, Apr. 10   Litho.   Perf. 13x12½
484 A178 Sheet of 8   16.00 16.00
 a.-h.   7.50k Any single   2.00 2.00

Europa — A179

Design: 5.50k, Scout holding bird. 10k, Tent.

2007, Apr. 10
485 A179 5.50k multi   1.40 1.40
486 A179 10k multi   2.75 2.75
      Scouting, cent.

Souvenir Sheet

Bible Translators — A180

No. 487: a, Jákup Dahl (1878-1944). b, Kristian O. Videro (1906-91). c, Victor Danielsen (1894-1961).

2007, June 11   Litho.   Perf. 13x12½
487 A180 Sheet of 3   5.00 5.00
 a.-c.   5.50k Any single   1.60 1.60

Domesticated Birds — A181

Designs: 9k, Chickens and rooster. 20k, Ducks. 25k, Geese.

2007, June 11   Perf. 12½x13
488 A181 9k multi   2.40 2.40
489 A181 20k multi   5.00 5.00
490 A181 25k multi   6.50 6.50
      Nos. 488-490 (3)   13.90 13.90

Hoyvík A182

2007, Oct. 1   Perf. 13½
491 A182 7.50k multi   2.00 2.00

Wooden Religious Statues of Kirkjubour Cathedral — A183

2007, Oct. 1   Perf. 13x12½
492 A183 5.50k Jesus   1.40 1.40
493 A183 7.50k Mary   2.00 2.00
 a.   Booklet pane, 4 each #492-493 14.00   —
      Complete booklet, #493a   14.00

Miniature Sheet

Stone Fence and Wildlife A184

No. 494: a, Bird, worm. b, Two red beetles, fern. c, Mouse, purple flowers. d, Mosquito, pink flowers. e, Large black and white bird, dandelions. f, Bird with black wings, buttercups. g, Earwigs, grass. h, Bird and eggs.

2007, Oct. 1   Perf. 13½x14¼
494 A184 Sheet of 8   12.00 12.00
 a.-h.   5.50k Any single   1.40 1.40

Klaksvík, Cent. — A185

Litho. & Embossed
2008, Feb. 11   Perf. 14
495 A185 5.50k multi   1.40 1.40

Tinganes — A186

2008, Feb. 11   Litho.   Perf. 13¼
496 A186 14k multi   3.50 3.50

Hoydalar Tuberculosis Sanatorium, Cent. — A187

Lungs and: 5.50k, Patients, buildings. 9k, Dr. Vilhelm Magnussen examining patient, child.

2008, Feb. 11   Perf. 12½x13
497 A187 5.50k multi   1.40 1.40
498 A187 9k multi   2.50 2.50
 a.   Booklet pane, 4 each #497-498 16.00
      Complete booklet, #498a   16.00

Miniature Sheet

Prints by Elinborg Lützens A188

No. 499: a, Houses below mountain. b, Milk maids (30x30mm). c, Houses. d, Underwater scene. e, Chicken (30x30mm). f, Person and bird near wooden bucket.

2008, Feb. 11   Perf. 13¼
499 A188 Sheet of 6   16.00 16.00
 a.-f.   10k Any single   2.60 2.60

Souvenir Sheet

Mythical Places A189

No. 500: a, Alvheyggur. b, Klovningasteinur.

2008, Mar. 27   Litho.   Perf. 12½x13
500 A189 Sheet of 2   4.00 4.00
 a.-b.   7.50k Either single   2.00 2.00

Caltha Palustris — A190

2008, May 19   Perf. 13¼
501 A190 30k multi   8.00 8.00

Europa — A191

Designs: 550o, Heart and "Teg." 750o, Posthorn with "@" symbol and "Hey."

2008, May 19   Perf. 13¼x13
502 A191 550o multi   1.40 1.40
503 A191 750o multi   2.00 2.00

Miniature Sheet

Famous People A192

No. 504: a, Niels Winther (1822-92), politician and newspaper publisher. b, Súsanna Helena Patursson (1864-1916), writer and newspaper publisher. c, Rasmus C. Effersoe (1857-1916), writer and newspaper editor. d, Jógvan Poulsen (1854-1941), religious and school book writer. e, Frithrikur Petersen (1853-1917), poet. f, Andreas Christian Evensen (1874-1917), magazine publisher and school book writer.

2008, May 19   Perf. 13½x13½
504 A192 Sheet of 6   9.00 9.00
 a.-f.   5.50k Any single   1.40 1.40

Miniature Sheet

Ferns A193

No. 505: a, Gymnocarpium dryopteris. b, Polypodium vulgare. c, Dryopteris dilatata. d, Asplenium adiantum-nigrum. e, Athyrium filix-femina. f, Dryopteris filix-mas. g, Cystopteris fragilis. h, Phegopteris connectilis. i, Polystichum lonchitis. j, Asplenium trichomanes.

2008, Sept. 22   Litho.   Perf. 13x13½
505 A193 Sheet of 10   25.00 25.00
 a.-j.   800o Any single   2.40 2.40

Christmas — A194

2008, Sept. 22   Perf. 13x12½
506 A194 6k shown   1.60 1.60
507 A194 10k Wooden cross   2.75 2.75
 a.   Booklet pane of 8, 4 each
      #506-507   17.00   —
      Complete booklet, #507a   17.00

Global Warming — A195

Designs: 6k, Earth and "No entry" sign. 8k, Earth in shape of water droplet.

2009, Feb. 23   Litho.   Perf. 13¾x14
508 A195 6k multi   1.60 1.60
509 A195 8k multi   2.10 2.10
 a.   Souvenir sheet, #508-509   3.75 3.75

Portions of the designs were applied by a thermographic process producing a shiny raised effect.

FAROE ISLANDS

Miniature Sheet

Scenes From *The Lost Musicians,* by William Heinesen — A196

No. 510: a, People, stylized harp. b, Ring of silhouetted dancers. c, Woman on roof of house, kneeling people and standing woman near house. d, Silhouetted man approaching woman on park bench. e, Women and seated cellist. f, Violinist and two silhoutted men. g, Man in bed. h, People in rowboat.

2009, Feb. 23			Perf. 13½	
510	A196	Sheet of 8	19.00	19.00
a.-h.	8k Any single		2.25	2.25

Europa — A197

Designs: 10k, Trollhovdi Island and Saturn. 12k, Heygadrangur Island, Jupiter and one of its moons, Europa.

2009, May 25		Litho.	Perf. 13x12½	
511	A197	10k multi	2.75	2.75
512	A197	12k multi	3.25	3.25

Intl. Year of Astronomy.

Miniature Sheet

Geological Formation of the Faroe Islands — A198

No. 513: a, Large volcano spewing lava, trees. b, Smaller volcano spewing ash, dead tree, lava on landscape. c, Map of area 60 million years ago. d, Map of area 15 million years ago. e, Map of Faroe Isands, map of Faroe Islands and area nearby. f, Glacier, rock pinnacles.

2009, May 25			Perf. 12½x13	
513	A198	Sheet of 6	18.00	18.00
a.-f.	10k Any single		3.00	3.00

Thorshavn Gymnastics Club, Cent. — A199

Gymnasts: 6k, Male lifting female. 10k, Female doing handstand. 26k, Male on rings.

2009, May 25			Perf. 14	
514	A199	6k multi	1.75	1.75
515	A199	10k multi	3.00	3.00
516	A199	26k multi	7.75	7.75
	Nos. 514-516 (3)		12.50	12.50

Serpentine Die Cut 14
Booklet Stamps
Self-Adhesive

517	A199	6k multi	2.00	2.00
518	A199	10k multi	3.00	3.00
a.	Booklet pane of 8, 4 each #517-518		20.00	

Leynar A200

2009, Sept. 16			Perf. 12¾	
519	A200	10k multi	3.00	3.00

Rock Pigeons — A201

Designs: 14k, Two pigeons on rocks. 36k, Head of pigeon, two pigeons in flights.

2009, Sept. 16			Perf. 13	
520	A201	14k multi	4.00	4.00
521	A201	36k multi	11.00	11.00

Altarpiece at Vestmanna Church A202

Altarpiece at Hattarvik Church A203

2009, Sept. 16			Perf. 13¾x13¼	
522	A202	6k multi	1.75	1.75
a.	Perf. 13¾ vert.		1.75	1.75
523	A203	10k multi	3.25	3.25
a.	Perf. 14¼x13¾ on 3 sides		3.25	3.25
b.	Booklet pane of 8, 4 each #522a, 523a		20.00	
	Complete booklet, #523b		20.00	

Christmas.

Globicephala Melas — A204

2010, Feb. 22		Litho.	Perf. 14¾	
524	A204	50k multi	15.00	15.00

Marine Flora and Fauna — A205

Various photographs.

2010, Feb. 22			Perf. 13¼x13½	
525	A205	1k multi	.35	.35
526	A205	6k multi	1.75	1.75
527	A205	8k multi	2.50	2.50
528	A205	12k multi	3.50	3.50
	Nos. 525-528 (4)		8.10	8.10

Butterflies and Moths — A206

Designs: 6k, Inachis io. 8k, Vanessa cardui. 14k, Agrius convolvuli. 16k, Acherontia atropos.

2010, Feb. 22			Perf. 13x12¾	
529	A206	6k multicolored	1.75	1.75
530	A206	8k multicolored	2.50	2.50
531	A206	14k multicolored	4.25	4.25
532	A206	16k multicolored	5.00	5.00
	Nos. 529-532 (4)		13.50	13.50

Souvenir Sheet

Aquaculture — A207

No. 533: a, Fish, net. b, Fisherman holding net.

2010, Mar. 24			Perf. 14¼x14½ Litho.	
533	A207	Sheet of 2	6.00	6.00
a.-b.	10k Either single		3.00	3.00

Paintings by Eli Smith — A208

Various paintings.

2010, Apr. 26			Perf. 14½	
534	A208	18k multicolored	5.50	5.50
535	A208	24k multicolored	7.50	7.50

Europa — A209

Scenes from children's books: 10k, A Dog, A Cat and A Mouse, by Bárthur Oskarsson. 12k, Moss Mollis's Journey, by Janus á Húsagarthi.

2010, Apr. 26			Perf. 13¾	
536	A209	10k multicolored	3.00	3.00
537	A209	12k multicolored	3.50	3.50

Booklet Stamps
Self-Adhesive
Serpentine Die Cut 14

538	A209	10k multicolored	3.00	3.00
539	A209	12k multicolored	3.50	3.50
a.	Booklet pane of 8, 4 each #538-539		26.00	26.00

Jens Christian Svabo (1746-1824), Writer and Lexicographer A210

Writings of Svabo and Svabo: 6k, Holding walking stick. 12k, At desk. 14k, Holding book. 22k, With sheaf of papers, pen and inkwell.

2010, Sept. 20			Perf. 13¼x13¾ Litho. & Engr.	
540	A210	6k multicolored	1.75	1.75
541	A210	12k multicolored	3.75	3.75
542	A210	14k multicolored	4.50	4.50
543	A210	22k multicolored	7.00	7.00
	Nos. 540-543 (4)		17.00	17.00

Vegetables — A211

2010, Sept. 20		Litho.	Perf. 13x13¼	
544	A211	6k Potatoes	1.75	1.75
545	A211	8k Turnips	2.50	2.50

Christmas — A212

Carols: 6k, My Little Sweet Brownie (Lítla Fitta Nissa Mín). 10k, In My Early Childhood (A Barnaárum Ungu).

2010, Sept. 20			Perf. 13x12½	
546	A212	6k multicolored	1.75	1.75
547	A212	10k multicolored	3.25	3.25
a.	Booklet pane of 8, 4 each #546-547		20.00	—
	Complete booklet, #547a		20.00	

See Nos. 570-571, 592-593.

Intl. Women's Day, Cent. — A213

2011, Feb. 21		Litho.	Perf. 14	
548	A213	10k multicolored	3.00	3.00

Traditional Women's Professions A214

Designs: 6k, Nurses with patient and child. 16k, Midwives holding babies.

2011, Feb. 21			Perf. 13x13¼	
549	A214	6k multicolored	1.75	1.75
550	A214	16k multicolored	5.00	5.00

Cats — A215

Color of cat: 6k, Black and white. 10k, Brown and white.

2011, Feb. 21			Perf. 13¾	
551	A215	6k multicolored	1.75	1.75
552	A215	10k multicolored	3.25	3.25

Booklet Stamps
Self-Adhesive
Serpentine Die Cut 14

553	A215	6k multicolored	1.75	1.75
554	A215	10k multicolored	3.25	3.25
a.	Booklet pane of 8, 4 each #553-554		20.00	

Souvenir Sheet

Legend of Annika od Dímun A216

No. 555 — Annika: a, With chalice. b, With guards. c, With bound hands in water.

2011, Feb. 21			Perf. 14¾	
555	A216	Sheet of 3	9.00	9.00
a.-c.	10k Any single		3.00	3.00

Paintings by Bergithe Johannessen (1905-95) A217

Designs: 2k, Skerjut Strond (Glowing Beach). 24k, Ur Nólsoy (From Nólsoy).

FAROE ISLANDS

2011, Apr. 26   *Perf. 12½x13*
556 A217 2k multicolored .65 .65
557 A217 24k multicolored 7.50 7.50

Paintings by Frida Zachariassen (1912-92) — A218

Designs: 6k, Urtagardhur (The Garden). 26k, Kona (Woman).

2011, Apr. 26   *Perf. 13*
558 A218 6k multicolored 1.75 1.75
559 A218 26k multicolored 7.50 7.50

Europa — A219

Tree plantations on: 10k, Tórshavn. 12k, Kunoy, vert.

2011, Apr. 26   *Perf. 12½*
560 A219 10k multicolored 3.25 3.25
561 A219 12k multicolored 3.75 3.75

Intl. Year of Forests.

Flowers — A220

Designs: 14k, Silene dioica. 20k, Geranium sylvaticum.

2011, Apr. 26   *Perf. 13¼*
562 A220 14k multicolored 4.50 4.50
563 A220 20k multicolored 6.00 6.00

Berries — A221

Designs: 50o, Juniperus communis subsp. alpina. 6.50k, Empetrum nigrum. subsp. hermaphroditum.

2011, Sept. 1   *Litho.*   *Perf. 12¾x13½*
564 A221 50o multicolored .25 .25
565 A221 6.50k multicolored 2.00 2.00

Stóridrangur — A222

2011, Sept. 28   *Perf. 12½x13*
566 A222 10.50k multicolored 3.25 3.25

Old Motor Vehicles — A223

Designs: No. 567, Black Ford TT truck, first vehicle on Faroe Islands. No. 568, Red Morris bus. No. 569, White De Luxe Model, automobile built on Faroe Islands.

2011, Sept. 28   *Perf. 13½x12¾*
567 A223 13k multicolored 4.00 4.00
568 A223 13k multicolored 4.00 4.00
569 A223 13k multicolored 4.00 4.00
  a. Souvenir sheet of 3, #567-569 12.50 12.50
  Nos. 567-569 (3) 12.00 12.00

Christmas Type of 2010

Carols: 6.50k, I Can't Wait for Christmas to Come (Eg Eri So Spent Til Jóla). 10.50k, I Rejoice Every Christmas Eve (Eg Gledist So Hvort Jólakvold).

2011, Sept. 28   *Perf. 13x12½*
570 A212 6.50k multi 2.00 2.00
571 A212 10.50k multi 3.25 3.25
  a. Booklet pane of 8, 4 each #570-571 21.00
  Complete booklet, #571a 21.00

Reign of Queen Margrethe II, 40th Anniv. — A224

Litho. & Engr.
2012, Jan. 4   *Perf. 13¼*
572 A224 10.50k multicolored 3.00 3.00
  a. Souvenir sheet of 1 3.00 3.00

Extinct Animals — A225

Designs: 13k, Pinguinis impennis. 21k, Dímun sheep (Ovis aries), horiz.

2012, Feb. 20   *Litho.*   *Perf. 13¼x13*
573 A225 13k multicolored 4.00 4.00
   Perf. 13x13¼
574 A225 21k multicolored 6.00 6.00

Sea Anemones — A226

Various sea anemones.

2012, Feb. 20   *Perf. 14*
575 A226 3k multi .90 .90
576 A226 6.50k multi 2.00 2.00
577 A226 8.50k multi 2.40 2.40
578 A226 10.50k multi 3.00 3.00
  Nos. 575-578 (4) 8.30 8.30

Booklet Stamps
Self-Adhesive
Serpentine Die Cut 14
579 A226 6.50k multi 2.00 2.00
580 A226 10.50k multi 3.00 3.00
  a. Booklet pane of 8, 4 each #579-580 20.00

Sea Rescue A227

No. 581: a, Helicopter. b, Life raft.

2012, Mar. 21   *Perf. 14¼x13½*
581 A227 Sheet of 2 6.00 6.00
  a.-b. 10.50k Either single 3.00 3.00

Europa A228

Designs: 6.50k, Tourists on boat near Suthuroy Island cliffs. 10.50k, Hikers on rocks.

2012, Apr. 30   *Perf. 12½x13*
582 A228 6.50k multi 2.00 2.00
583 A228 10.50k multi 3.00 3.00

Monsters — A229

Designs: 6.50k, Gryla. 11k, Marra. 17k, Nithagrisur. 19k, Fjorutroll.

2012, Apr. 30   *Perf. 13*
584 A229 6.50k multi 2.00 2.00
585 A229 11k multi 3.25 3.25
586 A229 17k multi 4.75 4.75
587 A229 19k multi 5.50 5.50
  Nos. 584-587 (4) 15.50 15.50

Old Pharmacy, Klaksvík — A230

2012, Sept. 24   *Perf. 12½x13*
588 A230 8.50k multi 2.40 2.40

Contemporary Art — A231

Designs: 13k, Mr. Walker on the Faroes, by Jan Hafström. 21k, Egg Procession, by Edward Fuglo.

2012, Sept. 24   *Perf. 13*
589 A231 13k multicolored 3.50 3.50
590 A231 21k multicolored 5.75 5.75

Miniature Sheet

Legend of Regin the Blacksmith — A232

No. 591: a, Hjordis attends to dying husband, Sigmund, on battlefield. b, Sigurd on horse. c, Regin hammering sword. d, Sigurd on horseback encounters Odin. e, Sigurd attacks serpent. f, Birds watching Sigurd cooking serpent's heart.

Litho., Litho & Embossed (#591e)
2012, Sept. 24   *Perf. 13¼x13*
591 A232 Sheet of 6 20.00 20.00
  a.-f. 11k Any single 3.25 3.25

Christmas Type of 2010

Carols: 6.50k, Why is Everything So Cozy Tonight? (Hví Man Tadh Vera?) 12.50k, Silent Night (Gledhilig Jól).

2012, Sept. 24   *Litho.*   *Perf. 13x12½*
592 A212 6.50k multi 2.00 2.00
593 A212 12.50k multi 4.00 4.00
  a. Booklet pane of 8, 4 each #592-593 24.00 24.00
  Complete booklet, #593a 24.00 24.00

Lambs A233

2013, Feb. 25   *Perf. 13¼x13¾*
594 A233 12.50k multi 4.00 4.00

Crustaceans A234

Designs: 7k, Cancer pagurus. 9k, Chaceon affinis. 23k, Pandalus borealis. 34k, Nephrops norvegicus.

2013, Feb. 25   *Perf. 12½x13*
595 A234 7k multi 2.50 2.50
596 A234 9k multi 3.25 3.25
597 A234 23k multi 8.00 8.00
598 A234 34k multi 12.00 12.00
  Nos. 595-598 (4) 25.75 25.75

Miniature Sheet

Traditional Faroese Rowboat — A235

No. 599: a, Tollur og homluband (oarlock and strap, 26x23mm). b, Arar (oars, 66x23mm). c, Rodhur og rodhurarmur (rudder, 26x23mm). d, Kumpass (compass, 26x23mm). e, Seksmannafar (hull of six-man boat, 66x23mm). f, Kaggi (barrel, 26x23mm). g, Eyskar (bailing scoop, 26x23mm). h, Mastur og vrá vidh segli (mast and sail, 66x23mm). i, Nogla og togendi (bung and rope, 26x23mm).

Litho. & Engr.
2013, Feb. 25   *Perf. 13¼*
599 A235 Sheet of 9 20.00 20.00
  a.-i. 7k Any single 2.00 2.00

Soren Kierkegaard (1813-55), Philosopher A266

2013, Mar. 4   *Perf. 12¼*
600 A266 35k multi 11.00 11.00

Europa — A267

Designs: 7k, Postal van. 12.50k, Postal truck.

2013, Apr. 29   *Litho.*   *Perf. 14*
601 A267 7k multi 2.25 2.25
602 A267 12.50k multi 4.00 4.00

Booklet Stamps
Self-Adhesive
Serpentine Die Cut 14
603 A267 7k multi 2.25 2.25
604 A267 12.50k multi 4.00 4.00
  a. Booklet pane of 8, 4 each #603-604 27.00

Rodents — A268

Designs: 11k, Rattus norvegicus. 12.50k, Mus domesticus.

2013, Apr. 29   *Perf. 13¾x13¼*
605 A268 11k multi 3.50 3.50
606 A268 12.50k multi 4.00 4.00

Paintings by Olivur Vith Neyst — A269

Designs: 19k, Sólskin (Sunshine). 38k, Vestaravág (West Harbor).

2013, Sept. 23   *Perf. 12½*
607 A269 19k multi 5.50 5.50
608 A269 38k multi 11.00 11.00

FAROE ISLANDS

Souvenir Sheet

Nordafar Fishery, Foroyinghavn, Greenland — A270

No. 609: a, Fishing boat, white building in background. b, Fishermen on dock. c, Fishing boats, red buildings in background.

Perf. 13¼x13¾
2013, Sept. 23   Litho. & Engr.
609   A270   Sheet of 3   8.50   8.50
   a.-c.   9k Any single   2.75   2.75

See Greenland No. 652.

Christmas — A271

Designs: 7k, Manger. 12.50k, Holy Family.

2013, Sept. 23   Litho.   **Perf. 12¾**
610   A271   7k multi   2.25   2.25
611   A271   12.50k multi   3.75   3.75
   a.   Booklet pane of 8, 4 each
     #610-611   24.00
     Complete booklet, #611a   24.00

See Nos. 632-633, 651-652.

Rosa Mollis A272

2014, Feb. 26   Litho.   **Perf. 12½x13**
612   A272   14.50k multi   4.75   4.75

Jellyfish — A273

Designs: 8k, Aurelia aurita. 15.50k, Cyanea capillata. 18.50k, Pelagia noctiluca. 26k, Beroe cucumis.

2014, Feb. 26   Litho.   **Perf. 13**
613   A273   8k multi   2.50   2.50
614   A273   15.50k multi   4.75   4.75
615   A273   18.50k multi   5.75   5.75
616   A273   26k multi   7.60   7.60
   Nos. 613-616 (4)   20.50   20.50

Souvenir Sheet

Legend of the Lady of Husavik A274

No. 617: a, Woman holding horn of Viking chief. b, Woman and nykur (mythical beast). c, Woman on throne.

2014, Feb. 26   Litho.   **Perf. 13x13½**
617   A274   Sheet of 3   10.00   10.00
   a.-c.   10k Any single   3.25   3.25

Souvenir Sheet

Ferry MS Norröna A275

No. 618: a, Ship's stern. b, Ship's bow.

2014, Mar. 17   Litho.   **Perf. 13x13¼**
618   A275   Sheet of 2   9.00   9.00
   a.-b.   14.50k Either single   4.25   4.25

Europa — A276

Designs: 14.50k, Faroese Symphony Orchestra. 19.50k, Bass players, vert.

2014, Apr. 28   Litho.   **Perf. 13¼x13¼**
619   A276   14.50k multi   4.50   4.50

Perf. 13¼x13
620   A276   19.50k multi   6.00   6.00

Lighthouses A277

Designs: 14.50k, Akraberg Lighthouse. 15.50k, Dimun Lighthouse. 17k, Toftir Lighthouse.

2014, Apr. 28   Litho.   **Perf. 14**
621   A277   14.50k multi   4.50   4.50
622   A277   15.50k multi   4.75   4.75
623   A277   17k multi   5.25   5.25
   Nos. 621-623 (3)   14.50   14.50

Booklet Stamps
Self-Adhesive
Serpentine Die Cut 14

624   A277   14.50k multi   4.50   4.50
625   A277   15.50k multi   4.75   4.75
626   A277   17k multi   5.25   5.25
   a.   Booklet pane of 6, 2 each
     #624-626   29.00
   Nos. 624-626 (3)   14.50   14.50

Prince Henrik, 80th Birthday — A278

Perf. 13½x13¼
2014, June 11   Litho.
627   A278   14.50k multi   4.50   4.50

Booklet Stamp
Self-Adhesive
Die Cut Perf. 13½x13¼

628   A278   14.50k multi   4.50   4.50
   a.   Booklet pane of 4   18.00

Roger Casement, Boats, Congolese Natives, and Daniel J. Danielsen A279

Perf. 13¼x13½
2014, Sept. 24   Litho.
629   A279   25k multi   7.50   7.50

Danielsen (1871-1916), missionary to the Congo, and documenter of human rights abuses reported on in Casement's 1904 report to the British Government.

Captain Vilhelm Reinert-Joensen (1891-1949), Ships Used in D-Day Invasion — A280

Perf. 13¼x13½
2014, Sept. 24   Litho.
630   A280   26k multi   7.50   7.50

D-Day, 70th anniv.

Miniature Sheet

World War I, Cent. A281

No. 631: a, Newspaper headlines, map of Europe, man in rowboat. b, Children, ration coupons, national leaders of the World War I combatants. c, Faroese boat attacked by German submarine, map of Faroe islands and British Isles. d, Map of Vimy Ridge, Faroese-Canadian soldier Christian L. Petersen, soldiers.

Perf. 13¼x13½
2014, Sept. 24   Litho.
631   A281   Sheet of 4   10.00   10.00
   a.-d.   8k Any single   2.50   2.50
   e.   Like #631, with "In Memoriam" and poppies added in red in sheet margin   9.00   9.00

Issued: No. 631e, 5/13/15.

Christmas Type of 2013

2014, Sept. 24   Litho.   **Perf. 12¾**
632   A271   8k multi   2.50   2.50
633   A271   14.50k multi   4.50   4.50
   a.   Booklet pane of 8, 4 each
     #632-633   28.00   —
     Complete booklet, #633a   28.00

Magna Carta, 800th Anniv. — A282

2015, Feb. 23   Litho.   **Perf. 13½**
634   A282   24k multi   7.00   7.00

Woman Suffrage, Cent. — A283

2015, Feb. 23   Litho.   **Perf. 13x13¼**
635   A283   36k multi   11.00   11.00

Opening of New Terminal at Vagar Airport — A284

Designs: 8.50k, Airplanes on ground. 15k, New terminal.

2015, Feb. 23   Litho.   **Perf. 13x13¼**
636   A284   8.50k multi   2.60   2.60
637   A284   15k multi   4.50   4.50
   a.   Booklet pane of 8, 4 each
     #636-637   28.50
     Complete booklet, #637a   28.50

Miniature Sheet

1833 Expedition of George Clayton Atkinson to Faroe Islands — A285

No. 638 — Paintings by Thomas Miles Richarson of: a, Vatnmylla (watermill). b, Tórshavn. c, Waterfall on Vágar, Koltur and Hestur Islands. d, Trollkonufingur.

2015, Feb. 23   Litho.   **Perf. 13x13¼**
638   A285   Sheet of 4   10.50   10.50
   a.-d.   8.50k Any single   2.60   2.60

March 20, 2015 Total Solar Eclipse — A286

Eclipse at: 17k, Right. 19k, Left.

2015, Mar. 11   Litho.   **Perf. 12**
639   A286   17k multi   5.00   5.00
640   A286   19k multi   5.75   5.75
   a.   Souvenir sheet of 2, #639-640   11.00   11.00

Booklet Stamps
Self-Adhesive
Die Cut Perf. 11½

641   A286   17k multi   5.00   5.00
   a.   Booklet pane of 4   20.00
642   A286   19k multi   5.75   5.75
   a.   Booklet pane of 4   23.00

Faroe Islands Flag, 75th Anniv. — A287

Designs: 11k, Arne Vatnhamar holding Faroe Islands flag on Mt. Everest. 12k, Map and flag of Faroe Islands.

2015, Apr. 14   Litho.   **Perf. 13½**
643   A287   11k multi   3.50   3.50
644   A287   12k multi   3.75   3.75

Europa — A288

Old toys: 17k, Rag doll. 22k, Hoop made of ram's horn.

2015, Apr. 14   Litho.   **Perf. 13½**
645   A288   17k multi   5.25   5.25
646   A288   22k multi   6.75   6.75

Knitted Art by Randi Samsonsen A289

2015, Sept. 28   Litho.   **Perf. 13x12¾**
647   A289   17k multi   5.25   5.25

H. N. Jacobsen's Bookstore, 150th Anniv. — A290

Designs: 17k, Bookstore exterior. 26k, Bookstore interior, book covers, bindery machinery.

2015, Sept. 28   Litho.   **Perf. 12½**
648   A290   17k multi   5.25   5.25
649   A290   26k multi   8.00   8.00

Souvenir Sheet

Christian Artifacts of the Viking Era A291

FAROE ISLANDS

No. 650 — Inscriptions: a, Krossteinur úr Olansgardhi í Skúvoy (stone with crucifix from Olansgardhi). b, Botnur úr laggadhum traeílati (cross on wooden bucket bottom). c, Vadhsteinur vidh ihogdum St. Hanskrossi (stone fishing sinkers with St. Hans crucifix).

2015, Sept. 28 — Litho. & Engr. — Perf. 12¾x13
| 650 | A291 | Sheet of 3 | 11.50 | 11.50 |
| a.-c. | | 12k Any single | 3.75 | 3.75 |

Christmas Type of 2013

Designs: 8.50k, Magi on camels. 17k, Holy Family fleeing to Egypt.

2015, Sept. 28 — Litho. — Perf. 12¾
651	A271	8.50k multi	2.60	2.60
652	A271	17k multi	5.25	5.25
a.		Booklet pane of 8, 4 each #651-652	32.00	—
		Complete booklet, #652a	32.00	

Oystercatchers in Flight — A292

2016, Feb. 22 — Perf. 13¼x13¾ — Litho.
| 653 | A292 | 17k multi | 5.25 | 5.25 |

Grounding of the Westerbeek off Lopra, 274th Anniv. — A293

Designs: 17k, Chest and the Westerbeek. 19k, Grounding of the Westerbeek.

2016, Feb. 22 — Perf. 13¾x13½ — Litho.
654	A293	17k multi	5.25	5.25
655	A293	19k multi	5.75	5.75
a.		Souvenir sheet of 2, #654-655	11.00	11.00

Fire Fighting Equipment A294

Designs: 1k, Fire pump, 1776. 15k, 1948 Bedford K fire truck. 19k, 1937 Triangle fire truck.

2016, Feb. 22 — Litho. — Perf. 13
656	A294	1k multi	.30	.30
657	A294	15k multi	4.75	4.75
658	A294	19k multi	5.75	5.75
		Nos. 656-658 (3)	10.80	10.80

Booklet Stamps
Self-Adhesive
Serpentine Die Cut 13¼
659	A294	1k multi	.30	.30
660	A294	15k multi	4.75	4.75
661	A294	19k multi	5.75	5.75
a.		Booklet pane of 6, 2 each #659-661	22.00	
		Nos. 659-661 (3)	10.80	10.80

Faroe Islands Mailboxes — A295

Designs: 9k, Blue Postverk Foroya mailbox used 1976-present. 17k, Red Danish Postal Service mailbox used until 1976.

2016, Apr. 1 — Litho. — Perf. 14¼
| 662 | A295 | 9k multi | 2.75 | 2.75 |

Souvenir Sheet
| 663 | | Sheet of 2, #662, 663a | 8.00 | 8.00 |
| a. | | A295 17k multi | 5.25 | 5.25 |

Postverdi Foroya (Faroe Islands Postal Service), 40th anniv.

Foods in Faroese Drying Shed A296

2016, Apr. 26 — Litho. — Perf. 13½
| 664 | A296 | 9k multi | 2.75 | 2.75 |

Nólsoyar Páll (1766-1808 or 1809), National Hero — A297

2016, Apr. 26 — Litho. & Engr. — Perf. 13
| 665 | A297 | 24k blk & brn lake | 7.50 | 7.50 |

Europa — A299

2016, May 9 — Litho. — Perf. 13½x13
| 666 | A298 | 9k green | 2.75 | 2.75 |
| 667 | A299 | 17k multi | 5.25 | 5.25 |

Booklet Stamps
Self-Adhesive
Serpentine Die Cut 13¾
667A	A298	9k green	2.75	2.75
667B	A299	17k multi	5.25	5.25
c.		Booklet pane of 6, 3 each #667A-667B	24.00	

Think Green Issue.

Cod — A300

Litho. & Engr.
2016, Sept. 26 — Perf. 13x13¼
| 668 | A300 | 50k multi | 15.00 | 15.00 |

A square of tanned cod skin with engraved text is affixed to No. 668. The square of cod skin has a fish odor and may detach from the stamp if soaked.

Traditional Woman's Blouse A301 — Traditional Men's Waistcoat A302

2016, Sept. 26 — Litho. — Perf. 13x13½
| 669 | A301 | 17k multi | 5.25 | 5.25 |
| 670 | A302 | 20k multi | 6.00 | 6.00 |

Booklet Stamps
Self-Adhesive
Serpentine Die Cut 14x13¾
670A	A301	17k multi	5.25	5.25
670B	A302	20k multi	6.00	6.00
c.		Booklet pane of 6, 3 each #670A-670B	34.00	

Miniature Sheet

Life of Jesus A303

No. 671 — Wood carvings by Edward Fuglo depicting: a, Annunciation. b, Adoration of the Shepherds. c, Jesus as child in temple. d, Baptism of Jesus. e, Jesus feeding the multitude. f, Jesus healing lepers. g, Jesus calming storm at sea. h, Entry into Jerusalem. i, Jesus carrying cross. j, Resurrection.

2016, Sept. 26 — Litho. — Perf. 13x12½
| 671 | A303 | Sheet of 10 | 27.50 | 27.50 |
| a.-j. | | 9k Any single | 2.75 | 2.75 |

House Near Skorá River Waterfall — A304

2017, Feb. 27 — Litho. — Perf. 13
| 672 | A304 | 9.50k multi | 2.75 | 2.75 |

Leitisvatn Lake A305

Lakeside: 17k, Cliffs. 19k, Buildings.

Perf. 13½x13¼
2017, Feb. 27 — Litho.
| 673 | A305 | 17k multi | 5.00 | 5.00 |
| 674 | A305 | 19k multi | 5.50 | 5.50 |

Booklet Stamps
Self-Adhesive
Serpentine Die Cut 9
674A	A305	17k multi	5.00	5.00
674B	A305	19k multi	5.50	5.50
c.		Booklet pane of 6, 3 each #674A-674B	32.00	

Somateria Mollissima Faeroensis A306

Eider facing: 18k, Right. 27k, Left.

Perf. 13½x13¾
2017, Feb. 27 — Litho.
| 675 | A306 | 18k multi | 5.25 | 5.25 |
| 676 | A306 | 27k multi | 7.75 | 7.75 |

Miniature Sheet

Natural Dyes A307

No. 677: a, Trifolium repens. b, Erica cinerea. c, Ochrolechia tartarea. d, Parmelia saxatilis. e, Narthecium ossifragum. f, Filipendula ulmaria.

2017, Feb. 27 — Litho. — Perf. 13x12½
| 677 | A307 | Sheet of 6 | 16.50 | 16.50 |
| a.-f. | | 9.50k Any single | 2.75 | 2.75 |

Europa — A308

Legend of the Princess of Nólsoy: 9.50k, Ship and castle. 17k, Ship, Princess and her husband.

2017, May 15 — Litho. — Perf. 14
| 678 | A308 | 9.50k multi | 3.00 | 3.00 |
| 679 | A308 | 17k multi | 5.25 | 5.25 |

Booklet Stamps
Self-Adhesive
Serpentine Die Cut 13½
680	A308	9.50k multi	3.00	3.00
681	A308	17k multi	5.25	5.25
a.		Booklet pane of 6, 3 each #680-681	25.00	

Items From 1817 Visit to Faroe Islands of Hans Christian Lyngbye (1782-1837), Botanist — A309

Designs: 9.50k, Carex lyngbyei. 13k, Illustrations of seaweeds from Lyngbye's book, *Tentamen Hydrophytologiae Danicae*, horiz. 19k, Illustrations by Lyngbye of Faroese baptismal fonts and rocking stones, horiz. 22k, Seaweed from Lyngbye's herbarium, horiz.

2017, May 15 — Litho. — Perf. 13¼x13
| 682 | A309 | 9.50k multi | 3.00 | 3.00 |

Perf. 13x13¼
683	A309	13k multi	4.00	4.00
684	A309	19k multi	5.75	5.75
685	A309	22k multi	6.75	6.75
		Nos. 682-685 (4)	19.50	19.50

Souvenir Sheet

Queen Margrethe II and Prince Henrik, 50th Wedding Anniversary — A310

2017, May 15 — Litho. — Perf. 13½
| 686 | A310 | 50k gold & multi | 15.00 | 15.00 |

See Denmark No. 1777, Greenland No. 754.

Legend of the Seven Swans — A311

Designs: 9.50k, Men turning into swans. 19k, Woman near stake.

Perf. 13¾x13¼
2017, Sept. 8 — Litho. & Engr.
687	A311	9.50k multi	3.00	3.00
688	A311	19k multi	6.00	6.00
a.		Souvenir sheet of 2, #687-688	9.00	9.00

Traditional Clothing — A312

Designs: 9.50k, Women's dress, apron and shoes. 17k, Men's breeches, stockings and shoes.

2017, Oct. 2 — Litho. — Perf. 12¾x13½
| 689 | A312 | 9.50k multi | 3.00 | 3.00 |
| 690 | A312 | 17k multi | 5.50 | 5.50 |

Booklet Stamps
Self-Adhesive
Serpentine Die Cut 13¾
691	A312	9.50k multi	3.00	3.00
692	A312	17k multi	5.50	5.50
a.		Booklet pane of 6, 3 each #691-692	26.00	

FAROE ISLANDS

Martin Luther Nailing 95 Theses to Church Door — A313

2017, Oct. 2   Litho.   Perf. 13¼x13
693   A313   18k multi   5.75   5.75
   a.   Souvenir sheet of 1   5.75   5.75
Protestant Reformation, 500th anniv.

Faroese Knives and Sheaths A314

Litho. & Embossed With Foil Application
2017, Oct. 2   Perf. 13¼x13
Inscribed "sepac"
694   A314   19k gold & multi   6.00   6.00

Souvenir Sheet
Without "sepac" Inscription
695   A314   19k gold & multi   6.00   6.00

Hans C. Müller (1818-97), First Postal Agent for Denmark in the Faroe Islands — A315

2018, Feb. 26   Litho.   Perf. 13½
696   A315   18k multi   6.00   6.00

Seabird Fowling — A316

Designs: 10k, Man carrying fowling net. 44k, Men fowling in boat.

2018, Feb. 26   Engr.   Perf. 12¾x13
697   A316   10k deep claret   3.25   3.25
698   A316   44k dp vio blue   14.50   14.50

Lakes A317

Designs: 10k, Sandsvatn Lake. 20k, Toftavatn Lake.

Perf. 13½x13¾
2018, Feb. 26   Litho.
699   A317   10k multi   3.25   3.25
700   A317   20k multi   6.50   6.50

Booklet Stamps
Self-Adhesive
Serpentine Die Cut 9
701   A317   10k multi   3.25   3.25
702   A317   20k multi   6.50   6.50
   a.   Booklet pane of 6, 3 each #701-702   29.50

Miniature Sheet

Flies A318

No. 703: a, Protophormia terraenovae. b, Bibio pomonae. c, Scatophaga stercoraria. d, Musca domestica.

Perf. 13½x13¼
2018, Feb. 26   Litho.
703   A318   Sheet of 4   16.00   16.00
   a.-d.   12k Any single   4.00   4.00

Scomber Scombrus A319

2018, Apr. 23   Litho.   Perf. 13¾x13¼
704   A319   18k multi   6.00   6.00

Recreational Vehicles and Large Wave Near Torshavn — A320

2018, Apr. 23   Litho.   Perf. 13½x13¼
705   A320   20k multi   6.50   6.50

Celtic Quaternary Knot — A321

Gate to the World, Sculpture by 7-9-13 Art Group — A322

2018, Apr. 23   Litho.   Perf. 13¼x13
706   A321   14k multi   4.50   4.50

Perf. 13x13¼
707   A322   22k multi   7.25   7.25
Town of Fuglafjordhur, cent.

Europa — A323

Designs: 10k, Streymin Bridge. 18k, Sandá River Bridge.

2018, Apr. 23   Litho.   Perf. 13x13¼
708   A323   10k multi   3.25   3.25
709   A323   18k multi   6.00   6.00

Booklet Stamps
Self-Adhesive
Die Cut Perf. 13x12½
710   A323   10k multi   3.25   3.25
711   A323   18k multi   6.00   6.00
   a.   Booklet pane of 6, 3 each #710-711   28.00

Souvenir Sheet

Tórshavn Actors' Association, Cent. — A324

No. 712 — Masks and: a, Three actors. b, Five actors.

2018, Apr. 23   Litho.   Perf. 14
712   A324   Sheet of 2   12.50   12.50
   a.-b.   19k Either single   6.25   6.25

Miniature Sheet

End of World War I, Cent. A325

No. 713: a, Soldiers and map of battle lines of 100 Day Offensive in France. b, Airplanes, ambulance, wounded soldier and Red Cross nurses. c, Dove and soldiers. d, Dove, soldier, woman at cemetery.

Perf. 13¼x13¾
2018, Sept. 24   Litho.
713   A325   Sheet of 4   13.00   13.00
   a.-d.   10k Any single   3.25   3.25

Regin Dahl (1918-2007), Poet and Musician A326

2018, Sept. 24   Litho.   Perf. 13x12¾
714   A326   28k multi   8.75   8.75

Traditional Clothing — A327

Designs: 18k, Woman wearing bonnet. 20k, Man wearing hat.

Perf. 12¾x13½
2018, Sept. 24   Litho.
715   A327   18k multi   5.75   5.75
716   A327   20k multi   6.25   6.25

Booklet Stamps
Self-Adhesive
Serpentine Die Cut 14x13¾
717   A327   18k multi   5.75   5.75
718   A327   20k multi   6.25   6.25
   a.   Booklet pane of 6, 3 each #717-718   36.00

Christmas — A328

Icon of: 10k, Angel and gannet. 18k, Madonna and Child.

Litho. & Embossed
2018, Sept. 24   Perf. 13
719   A328   10k gold & multi   3.25   3.25
720   A328   18k gold & multi   5.75   5.75

Souvenir Sheet

1919 Provisional Stamp, Cent. — A329

No. 721: a, Surcharging device (21x28mm). b, Essays of handwritten surcharge (63x28mm).

2019, Jan. 11   Litho.   Perf. 13¼x13½
721   A329   Sheet of 2   7.00   7.00
   a.-b.   11k Either single   3.50   3.50

Old Farmhouse, Kirkjubour — A330

Litho. & Silk-Screened
2019, Feb. 25   Perf. 13
722   A330   19k multi   5.75   5.75

Detail From 1539 Nautical Map by Olaus Magnus (1490-1557) — A331

Various map details.

2019, Feb. 25   Litho.   Perf. 13
723   A331   11k multi   3.50   3.50
724   A331   17k multi   5.25   5.25
725   A331   27k multi   8.25   8.25
   a.   Souvenir sheet of 3, #723-725, perf. 13 on 3 sides   17.00   17.00
   Nos. 723-725 (3)   17.00   17.00

Lakes A332

Designs: Nos. 726, 728, Lake Leynar. No. 727, 729, Lake Eidhi.

Perf. 13½x13¼
2019, Feb. 25   Litho.
726   A332   19k multi   5.75   5.75
727   A332   19k multi   5.75   5.75

Booklet Stamp
Self-Adhesive
Serpentine Die Cut 9
728   A332   19k multi   5.75   5.75
729   A332   19k multi   5.75   5.75
   a.   Booklet pane of 6, 3 each #728-729   34.50

First Man on the Moon, 50th Anniv. — A333

2019, Apr. 29   Litho.   Perf. 13¾
730   A333   17k multi   5.25   5.25

1896 Drawings of Water Mills by Daniel Bruun (1856-1931) — A334

Mill in: 11k, Sandágerdhi. 35k, Frodhba.

Perf. 13½x13¾
2019, Apr. 29   Litho. & Engr.
731   A334   11k multi   3.50   3.50
732   A334   35k multi   10.50   10.50

Europa — A335

Cepphus grylle taeroeensis: 19k, Two on rock. 26k, One in water.

2019, Apr. 29   Litho.   Perf. 13
733   A335   19k multi   5.75   5.75
734   A335   26k multi   7.75   7.75

Booklet Stamp
Self-Adhesive
Die Cut Perf. 13x12¾
735   A335   19k multi   5.75   5.75
   a.   Booklet pane of 6   34.50

FAROE ISLANDS

Souvenir Sheet

Venceslaus Ulricus Hammershaimb (1819-1909), Theologian, Linguist, and Folklorist — A336

No. 736: a, Faroese Anthology, by Hammershaimb. b, Hammershaimb. c, The Native Tongue, sculpture by Janus Karnban, and alphabet of Hammershaimb's orthography.

2019, Apr. 29   Litho.   *Perf. 13¼x13¼*
736 A336   Sheet of 3   14.50   14.50
   a.   11k multi   3.50   3.50
   b.   17k multi   5.25   5.25
   c.   19k multi   5.75   5.75

Souvenir Sheet

Labels Created for Fatherless Children's Fund — A337

No. 737: a, Flag of Faroe Islands. b, Mother and child.

2019, June 3   Litho.   *Perf. 13¼*
737 A337   Sheet of 2   14.00   14.00
   a.   11k multi   3.50   3.50
   b.   35k multi   10.50   10.50

Children's Aid Foundation, 77th anniv.; flag of the Faroe Islands, cent.

Smacks Johanna and Westward Ho — A338

2019, Sept. 23   Litho.   *Perf. 13¼*
738 A338   11k multi   3.25   3.25

Sculpture of Elinborg Lützen, by Pauli Olsen — A339

2019, Sept. 23   Litho.   *Perf. 13¼x13*
739 A339   55k multi   16.00   16.00

Lützen (1919-95), graphic artist.

Chasubles — A340

Chasuble from church in: 11k, Sandvík. 19k, Funning.

2019, Sept. 23   Litho.   *Perf. 13¼x13*
740 A340   11k multi   3.25   3.25
741 A340   19k multi   5.50   5.50

Booklet Stamps
Self-Adhesive
Die Cut Perf. 12¾x13
742 A340   11k multi   3.25   3.25
743 A340   19k multi   5.50   5.50
   a.   Booklet pane of 6, 3 each #742-743   36.00

See Nos. 765-766.

Vatndalsvatn Lake — A341

No. 744: a, Aerial view of lake. b, Aerial view of lake, text and location marker.

2020, Feb. 14   Litho.   *Perf. 14½*
744 A341   Horiz. pair, #a-b   6.00   6.00
   a.   8k multi   2.40   2.40
   b.   12k multi   3.50   3.50

St. Valentine's Day.

Seal Pup — A342

2020, Feb. 24   Litho.   *Perf. 13x13¼*
745 A342   20k multi   6.00   6.00

Booklet Stamp
Self-Adhesive
Die Cut Perf. 13x12¾
746 A342   20k multi   6.00   6.00
   a.   Booklet pane of 6   36.00

Volleyball, 125th Anniv. — A343

Designs: 12k, Male player. 17k, Female player.

2020, Feb. 24   Litho.   *Perf. 13¼*
747 A343   12k multi   3.50   3.50
748 A343   17k multi   5.25   5.25

Mother Teresa at Eidhi — A344

Bread Which Satiates Hunger — A345

2020, Feb. 24   Litho.   *Perf. 13¼*
749 A344   12k multi   3.50   3.50
750 A345   27k multi   8.00   8.00

Paintings by Sigrun Gunnarsdóttir.

Souvenir Sheet

Mikkjal Dánjalsson á Ryggi (1879-1956), Writer — A346

No. 751: a, Profile portrait. b, Full-face portrait.

2020, Feb. 24   Litho.   *Perf. 13*
751 A346   Sheet of 2   13.00   13.00
   a.   17k multi   5.25   5.25
   b.   26k multi   7.75   7.75

Souvenir Sheet

Bird Song and Animal Language She Was Able to Understand, by Edward Fuglo — A347

Litho. With Foil Application
2020, Apr. 16   *Perf. 13*
752 A347   50k multi   15.00   15.00

Queen Margrethe II, 80th birthday.

Moon Pigeons, by Díthrikur á Skarvanesi (1802-65) — A348

2020, Apr. 27   Litho.   *Perf. 13x13¼*
753 A348   20k multi   6.00   6.00

British World War II Field Post Offices in the Faroe Islands — A349

Military Post Office in: 20k, Midvágur. 35k, Tórshavn.

2020, Apr. 27   Litho.   *Perf. 13¼x13*
754 A349   20k multi   6.00   6.00
   a.   Souvenir sheet of 1   6.00   6.00
755 A349   35k multi   10.50   10.50

Europa A350

Map of postal route and: 17k, Postmen in snowstorm on mountain. 20k, Mailboat Olavur and dinghy.

2020, Apr. 27   Litho.   *Perf. 13¼*
756 A350   17k multi   5.00   5.00
757 A350   20k multi   6.00   6.00

Booklet Stamps
Self-Adhesive
Die Cut Perf. 11¾
758 A350   17k multi   5.00   5.00
759 A350   20k multi   6.00   6.00
   a.   Booklet pane of 6, 3 each #758-759   33.00

Souvenir Sheet

Ludwig van Beethoven (1770-1827), Composer — A351

2020, Sept. 21   Litho.   *Perf. 13¼x13*
760 A351   44k multi   14.00   14.00

A352

Scenes from Faroese motion pictures: 12k, Bye Bye Blue Bird, 1999. 26k, Ludo, 2014.

2020, Sept. 21   Litho.   *Perf. 13*
761 A352   12k multi   3.75   3.75
762 A352   26k multi   8.25   8.25

First screening of motion pictures to audience, 125th anniv.

Chess — A353

Designs: 17k, Standard chessboard, rook, silhouettes of other pieces. 27k, Four-player chessboard, king, queen, bishop and knight.

2020, Sept. 21   Litho.   *Perf. 13¼*
763 A353   17k multi   5.50   5.50
764 A353   27k multi   8.50   8.50

Chasubles Type of 2019

Chasuble from church in: 12k, Vithareithi. 20k, Kvívík, horiz.

2020, Sept. 21   Litho.   *Perf. 13¼x13¼*
765 A340   12k multi   3.75   3.75
          Perf. 13x13¼
766 A340   20k multi   6.50   6.50

Booklet Stamps
Self-Adhesive
Die Cut Perf. 12¾x13
767 A340   12k multi   3.75   3.75
Die Cut Perf. 13x12¾
768 A340   20k multi   6.50   6.50
   a.   Booklet pane of 6, 3 each #767-768   39.00

Souvenir Sheet

Postal History of the Faroe Islands, 150th Anniv. A354

No. 769: a, Postal knapsack. b, Postmen carrying mail. c, Sketch of boat drawn by Czeslaw Slania (1921-2005), stamp engraver.

2021, Jan. 7   Litho.   *Perf. 13¼x13¾*
769 A354   Sheet of 3   16.50   16.50
   a.-c.   17k Any single   5.50   5.50

Postal Services Act of 1871, 150th anniv., and establishment of Postverk Faroya (Faroe Islands Postal Service), 45th anniv.

Miniature Sheet

Wood Sculptures by Joel Cole — A355

No. 770: a, Torn. b, Casual Alien. c, Round My Edges. d, In My Father's Footsteps. e, Floral Fireworks. f, Full Circle.

Perf. 13¾x13¼
2021, Feb. 19   Litho.
770 A355   Sheet of 6   21.50   21.50
   a.-c.   5k Any single   1.60   1.60
   d.-f.   17k Any single   5.50   5.50

Car and Eysturoy Tunnel Traffic Circle — A356

Eysturoy Tunnel — A357

FAROE ISLANDS

2021, Feb. 19 Litho. Perf. 13x13¼
| 771 | A356 | 10k multi | 3.25 | 3.25 |
| 772 | A357 | 17k multi | 5.50 | 5.50 |

Opening of the Eysturoy Tunnel.

Kirkja — A358

Hattarvík — A359

2021, Feb. 19 Litho. Perf. 13x13½
| 773 | A358 | 17k multi | 5.50 | 5.50 |
| 774 | A359 | 27k multi | 8.75 | 8.75 |

Booklet Stamps
Self-Adhesive
Die Cut Perf. 13x12¾
775	A358	17k multi	5.50	5.50
776	A359	27k multi	8.75	8.75
a.	Booklet pane of 6, 4 #775, 2 #776		40.00	

Andrea Arting (1891-1988), Trade Union Leader — A360

2021, Mar. 8 Litho. Perf. 13½x13
| 777 | A360 | 39k multi | 12.50 | 12.50 |

Souvenir Sheet

1578 Map of the Faroe Islands by Sebastian Münster (1488-1552) — A361

Perf. 14¼x14½ on 3 Sides
2021, Apr. 26 Litho.
| 778 | A361 | 27k multi | 8.75 | 8.75 |

Cattle Farming in the Faroe Islands — A362

Designs: 7k, Head of cow, manure, pail of milk, hay bale and grain. 10k, Woman milking cow. 17k, Cows in field.

2021, Apr. 26 Litho. Perf. 13x13¼
779	A362	7k multi	2.25	2.25
780	A362	10k multi	3.25	3.25
781	A362	17k multi	5.50	5.50
	Nos. 779-781 (3)		11.00	11.00

Visit of King Christian X to Faroe Islands, Cent. — A363

Designs: 17k, King Christian X and Queen Alexandrine and sailors in rowboat. 27k, Tórshavn dignitaries welcoming King on his arrival.

2021, Apr. 26 Litho. Perf. 13
| 782 | A363 | 17k multi | 5.50 | 5.50 |
| 783 | A363 | 27k multi | 8.75 | 8.75 |

Fratercula Arctica — A364

Endangerd animals: 17k, Head of puffin. 27k, Three puffins on rock.

2021, Apr. 26 Litho. Perf. 13¼x13
| 784 | A364 | 17k multi | 5.50 | 5.50 |
| 785 | A364 | 27k multi | 8.75 | 8.75 |

Booklet Stamps
Self-Adhesive
Die Cut Perf. 12¾x13
786	A364	17k multi	5.50	5.50
787	A364	27k multi	8.75	8.75
a.	Booklet pane of 6, $ #786, 2 #787		39.50	

Europa.

Souvenir Sheet

Czeslaw Slania (1921-2005), Engraver of Postage Stamps — A365

Litho. & Engr.
2021, Aug. 12 Perf. 13¼x13
| 788 | A365 | 39k multi | 12.50 | 12.50 |

See Denmark No. 1879, Greenland No. 874.

Souvenir Sheet

Diseases A366

No. 789: a, Salmon, infectious salmon anemia virus. b, COVID-19 viruses, Petri dish and cotton swab.

2021, Sept. 20 Litho. Perf. 12½
789	A366	Sheet of 2	14.00	14.00
a.	20k multi		6.25	6.25
b.	25k multi		7.75	7.75

Tinganoc, Painting by Ingálvur av Reyni (1920-2005) A367

Through Tima and Spaces, Painting by Reyni A368

2021, Sept. 20 Litho. Perf. 14½
| 790 | A367 | 17k multi | 5.50 | 5.50 |
| 791 | A368 | 39k multi | 12.50 | 12.50 |

Bishop's Cope — A369

Designs: 17k, White cope with cross. 27k, Gold cope with floral trim.

2021, Sept. 20 Litho. Perf. 13¼x13
| 792 | A369 | 17k multi | 5.50 | 5.50 |
| 793 | A369 | 27k multi | 8.50 | 8.50 |

Booklet Stamps
Self-Adhesive
Die Cut Perf. 12¾x13
794	A369	17k multi	5.50	5.50
795	A369	27k multi	8.50	8.50
a.	Booklet pane of 6, 3 each #794-795		42.00	

Souvenir Sheet

Reign of Queen Margrethe II, 50th Anniv. — A370

Litho. & Engr. With Foil Application
2022, Jan. 14 Perf. 13
| 796 | A370 | 50k multi | 15.00 | 15.00 |

Kalsoy Island, Filming Location for 2021 Movie, *No Time to Die* A372

A371

Perf. 13½x13¼
2022, Feb. 28 Litho.
| 797 | A371 | 19k multi | 5.75 | 5.75 |
| 798 | A372 | 29k multi | 8.75 | 8.75 |

Booklet Stamps
Self-Adhesive
Die Cut Perf. 11¾
799	A371	19k multi	5.75	5.75
800	A372	29k multi	8.75	8.75
a.	Booklet pane of 6, 3 each #799-800		43.50	

A373

Aurora Borealis — A374

2022, Feb. 28 Litho. Perf. 13x13¼
| 801 | A373 | 19k multi | 5.75 | 5.75 |
| 802 | A374 | 43k multi | 13.00 | 13.00 |

Souvenir Sheet

Map of Voyage from Scotland to Faroe Islands and Iceland A375

2022, Feb. 28 Litho. Perf. 12
| 803 | A375 | 61k multi | 18.50 | 18.50 |

Trip to Faroe Islands by William Morris (1834-96), fabric designer, 150th anniv.

Simon Hansen (1863-1935), Founder of Föroya Bjór Brewery, Glass of Beer and Ram Emblem — A376

2022, May 16 Litho. Perf. 12
| 804 | A376 | 29k multi | 8.50 | 8.50 |

Babyboom, Fabric Art by Astrid Andreasen A377

Embroidery by Jórunn D. Poulsen A378

Roots, Rope and Fabric Art by Tita Vinther (1941-2019) A379

A Year's Work, Art by Andreasen A380

Fabric Art by Poulsen A381

Sea Anemones, Horsehair and Fabric Art by Vinther A382

2022, May 16 Litho. Perf. 13¾x13½
805	A377	19k multi	5.50	5.50
806	A378	19k multi	5.50	5.50
807	A379	19k multi	5.50	5.50
808	A380	29k multi	8.50	8.50
809	A381	29k multi	8.50	8.50
810	A382	29k multi	8.50	8.50
	Nos. 805-810 (6)		42.00	42.00

Europa — A383

Designs: 19k, Legend of Svinoy, Island of pigs. 29k, Legend of floating islands.

2022, May 10 Litho. Perf. 12
| 811 | A383 | 19k multi | 5.50 | 5.50 |
| 812 | A383 | 29k multi | 8.50 | 8.50 |

Booklet Stamps
Self-Adhesive
Die Cut Perf. 10½x10¾
813	A383	19k multi	5.50	5.50
814	A383	29k multi	8.50	8.50
a.	Booklet pane of 6, 3 each #813-814		42.00	

Souvenir Sheet

Printing of First Book in the Faroe Islands, 200th Anniv. A384

FAROE ISLANDS

No. 815: a, Dragon, dancers and sheet music. b, Title page of *Faroese Heroic Ballads of Sigurd, the Slayer of the Dragon Fafnir and His Kindred*, by H. C. Lyngbe.

2022, May 16   Litho.   *Perf. 12½*
815 A384 Sheet of 2   21.00   21.00
   a. 29k multi   8.50   8.50
   b. 43k multi   12.50   12.50

Souvenir Sheet

Minerals A385

No. 816: a, Calcite. b, Copper.

2022, Oct. 24   Litho.   *Perf. 12*
816 A385 Sheet of 2   19.50   19.50
   a. 29k multi   7.75   7.75
   b. 43k multi   11.50   11.50

Christmas — A386

Candles on: 19k, Wreath. 29k, Christmas tree.

2022, Oct. 24   Litho.   *Perf. 12*
817 A386 19k multi   5.25   5.25
818 A386 29k multi   7.75   7.75

Booklet Stamps
Self-Adhesive
Die Cut Perf. 10¾x10½
819 A386 19k multi   5.25   5.25
820 A386 29k multi   7.75   7.75
   a. Booklet pane of 6, 3 each #819-820   39.00

Paintings by Arnold Vegghamar — A387

Designs: 21k, Skyming (Twilight). 47k, Bygd (Village).

2023, Feb. 20   Litho.   *Perf. 13¼x13*
821 A387 21k multi   6.00   6.00
822 A387 47k multi   13.50   13.50

Skálhovdi Promontory A388

View From Skálhovdi — A389

2023, Feb. 20   Litho.   *Perf. 12*
823 A388 21k multi   6.00   6.00
824 A389 31k multi   9.00   9.00

Booklet Stamps
Self-Adhesive
Die Cut Perf. 10½
825 A388 21k multi   6.00   6.00
826 A389 31k multi   9.00   9.00
   a. Booklet pane of 6, 3 each #825-826   45.00

A390

Sornfelli Radar Base, 60th Anniv. A391

2023, Feb. 20   Litho.   *Perf. 12*
827 A390 31k multi   9.00   9.00

Souvenir Sheet
828 A391 61k multi   17.50   17.50

Europa — A392

2023, May 9   Litho.   *Perf. 12*
829 A392 31k multi   9.00   9.00

Booklet Stamp
Self-Adhesive
Die Cut Perf. 10½
830 A392 31k multi   9.00   9.00
   a. Booklet pane of 6   54.00

A Hymn for Peace, Painting by Edward Fuglo — A393

2023, May 9   Litho.   *Perf. 12*
831 A393 47k multi   13.50   13.50

Souvenir Sheets

Spring A394

Summer A395

Autumn A396

Winter A397

Litho. With Foil Application
2023, June 23   *Die Cut Perf. 9¾*
832 A394 100k multi   29.50   29.50
833 A395 100k multi   29.50   29.50
834 A396 100k multi   29.50   29.50
835 A397 100k multi   29.50   29.50
   Nos. 832-835 (4)   118.00   118.00

Crypto stamps.

Souvenir Sheet

The Cairn, Painting by Edward Fuglo A398

Litho. & Engr.
2023, Aug. 10   *Perf. 13x13¼*
836 A398 100k multi   29.50   29.50

Parts of the design are coated with a gritty substance.

Souvenir Sheet

Flight of Danish Astronaut Andreas Mogensen to International Space Station — A399

Perf. 13¼ on 3 Sides
2023, Aug. 11   Litho.
837 A399 31k multi   9.25   9.25

See Greenland No. 932.

Souvenir Sheet

Returning From Fishing, Painting by Emil Krause (1871-1945) — A400

Litho. & Engr.
2023, Aug. 11   *Perf. 13¼x13*
838 A400 50k multi   15.00   15.00

Thousandth stamp design engraved by Martin Mörck.

Fish Market at Tórshavn — A401

2023, Aug. 11   Litho.   *Perf. 13¼*
839 A401 31k multi   9.25   9.25

White Water Lily — A402

2023, Oct. 23   Litho.   *Perf. 12*
840 A402 21k multi   6.00   6.00

Post Europ, 30th anniv.

Souvenir Sheet

Sound Art Live Theatre, Suthuroy A403

No. 841: a, Interior. b, Exterior.

2023, Oct. 23   Litho.   *Perf. 12*
841 A403 Sheet of 2   23.50   23.50
   a. 21k multi   6.00   6.00
   b. 61k multi   17.50   17.50

Christmas — A404

Angel with: 21k, Small head. 31k, Large head.

2023, Oct. 23   Litho.   *Perf. 12*
842 A404 21k multi   6.00   6.00
843 A404 31k multi   9.00   9.00

FERNANDO PO

fər-'nan-ˌdō 'pō

LOCATION — An island in the Gulf of Guinea off west Africa.
GOVT. — Former province of Spain
AREA — 800 sq. mi.
POP. — 62,612 (1960)
CAPITAL — Santa Isabel

Together with the islands of Elobey, Annobon and Corisco, Fernando Po came under the administration of Spanish Guinea. Postage stamps of Spanish Guinea were used until 1960.

The provinces of Fernando Po and Rio Muni united Oct. 12, 1968, to form the Republic of Equatorial Guinea.

100 Centimos = 1 Escudo = 2.50 Pesetas

100 Centimos = 1 Peseta

1000 Milesimas = 100 Centavos = 1 Peso (1882)

Catalogue values for unused stamps in this country are for Never Hinged items, beginning with Scott 181 in the regular postage section and Scott B1 in the semi-postal section.

 Isabella II — A1

1868		Unwmk.	Typo.	Perf. 14	
1	A1	20c brown		350.00	140.00
a.		20c red brown		525.00	140.00

No. 1 is valued in the grade of fine, as illustrated. Examples with very fine centering are uncommon and sell for more.
Forgeries exist.

 Alfonso XII — A2

1879		Centimos de Peseta		
2	A2	5c green	52.50	15.00
3	A2	10c rose	40.00	15.00
4	A2	50c blue	90.00	15.00
		Nos. 2-4 (3)	182.50	45.00

1882-89		Centavos de Peso		
5	A2	1c green	9.50	6.25
6	A2	2c rose	18.00	8.75
7	A2	5c gray blue	60.00	12.00
8	A2	10c dk brown ('89)	82.50	6.75
		Nos. 5-8 (4)	170.00	33.00

Nos. 5-7 Handstamp Surcharged in Blue, Black or Violet — a

1884-95				
9	A2	50c on 1c green ('95)	120.00	19.00
11	A2	50c on 2c rose	22.00	6.00
12	A2	50c on 5c blue ('87)	150.00	25.00
		Nos. 9-12 (3)	302.50	50.00

Values above are for examples surcharged in black. Stamps surcharged in violet or blue are worth about 25% more.
Inverted and double surcharges exist. No. 12 exists overprinted in carmine. Value $100.

 King Alfonso XIII — A4

1894-97			Perf. 14	
13	A4	⅛c slate ('96)	22.00	3.00
14	A4	2c rose ('96)	15.50	2.50
15	A4	5c blue grn ('97)	16.00	2.50
16	A4	6c dk violet ('96)	13.00	3.00
17	A4	10c blk vio ('94)	450.00	115.00
17A	A4	10c dark brown ('94)	30.00	5.00
18	A4	10c lake ('95)	50.00	8.75
19	A4	10c org brn ('96)	10.50	2.50
20	A4	12½c dk brown ('96)	11.50	3.00
21	A4	20c slate bl ('96)	11.50	3.00
22	A4	25c claret ('96)	23.00	3.00
		Nos. 13-22 (11)	653.00	151.25

Most exist imperf. Value, set, pairs Nos. 13-16 and Nos. 18-22, $2,500.

Stamps of 1894-97 Handstamped in Blue, Black or Red

 b   c

Type "b" Surcharge

1896-98				
22A	A4	5c on ⅛c slate (Bl)	100.00	27.50
23	A4	5c on 2c rose (Bl)	50.00	16.50
23A	A4	5c on 6c dk vio (Bl)	180.00	45.00
24	A4	5c on 10c brn vio (Bl)	180.00	45.00
24A	A4	5c on 10c org brn (Bl)	180.00	45.00
24B	A4	5c on 10c dk brn (Bk)	67.50	27.50
25	A4	5c on 12½c brn (Bl)	37.50	13.00
a.		Black surcharge	37.50	13.00
25B	A4	5c on 20c sl bl (R)	180.00	45.00
25C	A4	5c on 25c claret (Bk)	180.00	35.00
		Nos. 22A-25C (9)	1,155.	299.50

Type "c" Surcharge

26	A4	5c on ⅛c slate (Bk)	32.50	6.75
27	A4	5c on 2c rose (Bl)	32.50	6.75
a.		Black surcharge	32.50	6.75
28	A4	5c on 5c green (R)	160.00	22.00
29	A4	5c on 6c dk vio (R)	23.00	14.00
a.		Violet surcharge	24.00	15.50
30	A4	5c on 10c org brn (Bk)	210.00	27.50
30A	A4	5c on 10c dk brn (Bk)	160.00	26.00
30B	A4	5c on 10c lake (Bl)	400.00	110.00
31	A4	5c on 12½c brn (R)	70.00	11.00
32	A4	5c on 20c sl bl (R)	40.00	10.50
33	A4	5c on 25c claret (Bk)	37.50	11.00
a.		Blue surcharge	37.50	13.50
		Nos. 26-33 (10)	1,166.	245.50

Exist surcharged in other colors.

Type "a" Srch. in Blue or Black

1898-99				
34	A4	50c on 2c rose	92.50	11.50
35	A4	50c on 10c brn vio	220.00	33.00
36	A4	50c on 10c lake	230.00	33.00
37	A4	50c on 10c org brn	220.00	33.00
38	A4	50c on 12½c brn (Bk)	190.00	22.00

The "a" surch. also exists on ⅛c, 5c & 25c. Values, $325, $225 and $210, respectively.

Revenue Stamps Privately Handstamped in Blue

 A5   A6

Arms

1897-98			Imperf.	
39	A5	5c on 10c rose	28.00	12.50
40	A6	10c rose	24.00	11.00

Revenue Stamps Handstamped in Black or Red

 A7

 A8

 Arms — A9a

1899			Imperf.	
41	A7	15c on 10c grn	45.00	23.00
a.		Blue surcharge, vert.	39.00	21.00
42	A8	10c on 25c grn	120.00	65.00
43	A9	15c on 25c grn	190.00	120.00
43A	A9a	15c on 25c grn (R)	1,800.	1,100.
b.		Black surcharge	1,800.	1,100.

Surcharge on No. 41 is either horizontal, inverted or vertical.
On No. 42 "CORREOS" is ovptd. in red.
On Nos. 43A and 43Ab, the signature is always in black.

 King Alfonso XIII — A10

Double-lined shaded letters at sides.

1899			Perf. 14	
44	A10	1m orange brn	2.40	.45
45	A10	2m orange brn	2.40	.45
46	A10	3m orange brn	2.40	.45
47	A10	4m orange brn	2.40	.45
48	A10	5m orange brn	2.40	.45
49	A10	1c black vio	2.40	.45
50	A10	2c dk blue grn	2.40	.45
51	A10	3c dk brown	2.40	.45
52	A10	4c orange	13.00	1.10
53	A10	6c carmine rose	2.50	.45
54	A10	6c dark blue	2.50	.45
55	A10	8c gray brn	8.00	.45
56	A10	10c vermilion	5.25	.45
57	A10	15c slate grn	5.25	.45
58	A10	20c maroon	14.50	1.10
59	A10	40c violet	100.00	19.00
60	A10	60c black	100.00	19.00
61	A10	80c red brown	100.00	19.00
62	A10	1p yellow grn	325.00	92.50
63	A10	2p slate blue	325.00	95.00
		Nos. 44-63 (20)	1,020.	252.55

Nos. 44-63 exist imperf. Value for set, $3,500.
See Nos. 66-85. For surcharges see Nos. 64, 65, 88, 88B.

1900		Surcharged type "a"		
64	A10	50c on 20c maroon	16.00	2.50
a.		Blue surcharge	32.00	4.75

Surcharged type "b"

| 64B | A10 | 5c on 20c maroon | 300.00 | 40.00 |

Surcharged type "c"

| 65 | A10 | 5c on 20c maroon | 9.50 | 2.40 |
| | | Nos. 64-65 (3) | 325.50 | 44.90 |

| 1900 | | Dated "1900" | | |

Solid letters at sides.

66	A10	1m black	3.00	.50
67	A10	2m black	3.00	.50
68	A10	3m black	3.00	.50
69	A10	4m black	3.00	.50
70	A10	5m black	3.00	.50
71	A10	1c green	3.00	.50
72	A10	2c violet	3.00	.50
73	A10	3c rose	3.00	.50
74	A10	4c black brn	3.00	.50
75	A10	5c blue	3.00	.50
76	A10	6c orange	3.00	.50
77	A10	8c bronze grn	3.00	.50
78	A10	10c claret	3.00	.50
79	A10	15c dk violet	3.00	.50
80	A10	20c olive brn	3.00	.50
81	A10	40c brown	7.75	2.25
82	A10	60c green	16.50	2.50
83	A10	80c dark blue	17.50	3.75
84	A10	1p red brown	110.00	30.00
85	A10	2p orange	190.00	62.50
		Nos. 66-85 (20)	386.75	108.50
		Set, never hinged	750.00	

Nos. 66-85 exist imperf. Value, set $3,500.

Revenue Stamps Overprinted or Surcharged with Handstamp in Red or Black

 A11   A12

1900			Imperf.	
86	A11	10c blue (R)	37.50	17.50
87	A12	5c on 10c blue	100.00	40.00
		Set, never hinged	175.00	

Nos. 52 and 80 Surcharged type "a" in Violet or Black

1900				
88	A10	50c on 4c orange (V)	14.00	4.00
a.		Green surcharge	22.50	12.00
88B	A10	50c on 20c ol brn	14.00	3.50
		Set, never hinged	37.50	

Dated "1901"

 A13

1901			Perf. 14	
89	A13	1c black	2.60	.90
90	A13	2c orange brn	2.60	.90
91	A13	3c dk violet	2.60	.90
92	A13	4c lt violet	2.60	.90
93	A13	5c orange red	1.60	.90
94	A13	10c violet brn	1.60	.90
95	A13	25c dp blue	1.75	.90
96	A13	50c claret	2.60	.90
97	A13	75c dk brown	2.00	.90
98	A13	1p blue grn	60.00	7.50
99	A13	2p red brown	40.00	10.00
100	A13	3p olive grn	400.00	14.00
101	A13	4p dull red	40.00	14.00
102	A13	5p dk green	47.50	14.00
103	A13	10p buff	115.00	40.00
		Nos. 89-103 (15)	722.45	107.60
		Set, never hinged	850.00	

Dated "1902"

1902		Control Numbers on Back		
104	A13	5c dk green	2.60	.45
105	A13	10c slate	2.90	.50
106	A13	25c claret	6.25	1.00
107	A13	50c violet brn	15.00	3.25
108	A13	75c lt violet	15.00	3.25
109	A13	1p car rose	18.50	4.00
110	A13	2p olive grn	40.00	9.50
111	A13	5p orange red	57.50	20.00
		Nos. 104-111 (8)	157.75	41.95
		Set, never hinged	250.00	

Exist imperf. Value for set, $1,500.

 A14

Dated "1903"

1903			Perf. 14	
		Control Numbers on Back		
112	A14	¼c dk violet	.45	.25
113	A14	½c black	.45	.25
114	A14	1c scarlet	.45	.25
115	A14	2c dk green	.45	.30
116	A14	3c blue grn	.45	.30
117	A14	4c violet	.45	.30
118	A14	5c rose lake	.50	.30
119	A14	10c orange buff	.60	.45
120	A14	15c blue green	2.50	1.00
121	A14	25c red brown	2.75	1.25
122	A14	50c black brn	4.50	2.00
123	A14	75c carmine	16.50	3.50
124	A14	1p dk brown	25.00	6.00
125	A14	2p dk olive grn	32.50	7.50
126	A14	3p claret	32.50	7.50
127	A14	4p dark blue	40.00	12.50
128	A14	5p dp dull blue	60.00	16.00
129	A14	10p dull red	130.00	27.50
		Nos. 112-129 (18)	350.05	87.15
		Set, never hinged	600.00	

Dated "1905"

1905		Control Numbers on Back		
136	A14	1c dp violet	.40	.30
137	A14	2c black	.40	.30
138	A14	3c vermilion	.40	.30
139	A14	4c dp green	.40	.30
140	A14	5c blue grn	.45	.35
141	A14	10c violet	1.60	.75
142	A14	15c car lake	1.60	.75

FERNANDO PO

143	A14	25c orange buff	12.50	2.25
144	A14	50c green	8.00	2.75
145	A14	75c red brown	11.00	7.50
146	A14	1p dp gray brn	12.50	7.50
147	A14	2p carmine	20.00	12.50
148	A14	3p deep brown	32.50	14.00
149	A14	4p bronze grn	40.00	18.00
150	A14	5p claret	62.50	25.00
151	A14	10p deep blue	90.00	35.00
		Nos. 136-151 (16)	294.25	127.55
		Set, never hinged	600.00	

King Alfonso XIII — A15

1907   Control Numbers on Back

152	A15	1c blue black	.30	.25
153	A15	2c car rose	.30	.25
154	A15	3c dp violet	.40	.25
155	A15	4c black	.40	.25
156	A15	5c orange buff	.40	.25
157	A15	10c maroon	2.00	.80
158	A15	15c bronze grn	.55	
159	A15	25c dk brown	65.00	15.00
160	A15	50c blue green	.45	.30
161	A15	75c vermilion	.45	.30
162	A15	1p dull blue	3.00	.60
163	A15	2p brown	11.00	4.00
164	A15	3p lake	11.00	4.00
165	A15	4p violet	11.00	4.00
166	A15	5p black brn	11.00	4.00
167	A15	10p orange brn	11.00	4.00
		Nos. 152-167 (16)	128.25	38.60
		Set, never hinged	350.00	

No. 157 Handstamp Surcharged in Black, Blue or Red

1908

168	A15	5c on 10c mar (Bk)	2.75	2.00
a.		Blue surcharge	10.00	5.50
b.		Red surcharge	30.00	10.00
169	A15	25c on 10c mar (Bk)	60.00	20.00
		Set, never hinged	77.50	

The surcharge on Nos. 168-169 exist inverted, double, etc. The surcharge also exists on other stamps.

Seville-Barcelona Issue of Spain, 1929, Overprinted in Blue or Red

1929   Perf. 11

170	A52	5c rose lake	.25	.25
171	A53	10c green (R)	.25	.25
a.		Perf. 14	.65	.65
172	A50	15c Prus bl (R)	.25	.25
173	A51	20c purple (R)	.25	.25
174	A50	25c brt rose	.25	.25
175	A52	30c black brn	.25	.25
176	A53	40c dk blue (R)	.45	.45
177	A51	50c dp orange	1.00	1.00
178	A52	1p blue blk (R)	3.75	3.75
179	A53	4p deep rose	20.00	20.00
180	A53	10p brown	25.00	25.00
		Nos. 170-180 (11)	51.70	51.70
		Set, never hinged	100.00	

Catalogue values for unused stamps in this section, from this point to the end of the section, are for Never Hinged items.

Virgin Mary — A16

1960   Unwmk.   Photo.   Perf. 13x12½

181	A16	25c dull gray vio	.40	.25
182	A16	50c brown olive	.40	.25
183	A16	75c violet brn	.40	.25
184	A16	1p orange ver	.40	.25
185	A16	1.50p lt blue grn	.40	.25
186	A16	2p red lilac	.40	.25
187	A16	3p dark blue	4.00	.80
188	A16	5p lt red brn	.65	.25
189	A16	10p lt olive grn	.80	.30
		Nos. 181-189 (9)	7.85	2.85

Tricorn and Windmill from "The Three-Cornered Hat" by Falla — A17

Manuel de Falla — A18

1960   Perf. 13x12½, 12½x13

190	A17	35c slate green	.60	.60
191	A18	80c Prus green	.70	.70

Issued to honor Manuel de Falla (1876-1946), Spanish composer. See Nos. B1-B2.

Map of Fernando Po — A19

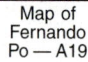

General Franco — A20

Designs: 70c, Santa Isabel Cathedral.

Perf. 13x12½, 12½x13
1961, Oct. 1   Photo.   Unwmk.

192	A19	25c gray violet	.35	.35
193	A20	50c olive brown	.35	.35
194	A19	70c brt green	.40	.40
195	A20	1p red orange	.45	.45
		Nos. 192-195 (4)	1.55	1.55

25th anniv. of the nomination of Gen. Francisco Franco as Chief of State.

Ocean Liner — A21

Design: 50c, S.S. San Francisco.

1962, July 10   Perf. 12½x13

196	A21	25c dull violet	.30	.30
197	A21	50c gray olive	.35	.35
198	A21	1p orange brn	.35	.35
		Nos. 196-198 (3)	1.00	1.00

Mailman A22

Mail Transport Symbols A23

Perf. 13x12½, 12½x13
1962, Nov. 23   Unwmk.

199	A22	15c dark green	.30	.30
200	A23	35c lilac rose	.35	.35
201	A22	1p brown	.35	.35
		Nos. 199-201 (3)	1.00	1.00

Issued for Stamp Day.

1963, Jan. 29   Perf. 13x12½

202	A24	50c olive gray	.30	.30
203	A24	1p deep magenta	.35	.35

Issued to help victims of the Seville flood.

Nuns — A25

Design: 50c, Nun and child, vert.

Perf. 12½x13, 13x12½
1963, July 6   Photo.   Unwmk.

204	A25	25c bright lilac	.30	.30
205	A25	50c dull green	.35	.35
206	A25	1p red orange	.35	.35
		Nos. 204-206 (3)	1.00	1.00

Issued for child welfare.

Child and Arms — A26

1963, July 12   Perf. 12½x13

207	A26	50c brown olive	.30	.30
208	A26	1p carmine rose	.35	.35

Issued for Barcelona flood relief.

Governor Chacon A27

Orange Blossoms A28

1964, Mar. 6   Perf. 12½x13, 13x12½

209	A27	25c violet black	.30	.30
210	A28	50c dark olive	.35	.35
211	A27	1p brown red	.35	.35
		Nos. 209-211 (3)	1.00	1.00

Issued for Stamp Day 1963.

Men in Dugout Canoe — A29

Design: 50c, Pineapple.

1964, June 1   Photo.   Perf. 13x12½

212	A29	25c purple	.30	.30
213	A28	50c dull olive	.35	.35
214	A29	1p deep claret	.35	.35
		Nos. 212-214 (3)	1.00	1.00

Issued for child welfare.

Ring-necked Francolin — A30

Designs: 15c, 70c, 3p, Ring-necked francolin. 25c, 1p, 5p, Two mallards. 50c, 1.50p, 10p, Head of great blue touraco.

1964, July 1

215	A30	15c chestnut	.30	.30
216	A30	25c dull violet	.30	.30
217	A30	50c dk olive grn	.30	.30
218	A30	70c green	.30	.30
219	A30	1p brown orange	.35	.30
220	A30	1.50p grnsh blue	.40	.35
221	A30	3p violet blue	.65	.35
222	A30	5p dull purple	1.60	.40
223	A30	10p bright green	2.40	1.00
		Nos. 215-223 (9)	6.60	3.60

The Three Kings — A31

Designs: 50c, 1.50p, Caspar, vert.

Perf. 13x12½, 12½x13
1964, Nov. 23   Unwmk.

224	A31	50c green	.35	.35
225	A31	1p orange ver	.40	.35
226	A31	1.50p deep green	.45	.35
227	A31	3p ultra	1.75	1.40
		Nos. 224-227 (4)	2.95	2.45

Issued for Stamp Day, 1964.

Boy A32

Woman Fruit Picker A33

1.50p, Girl learning to write, and church.

1964, Mar. 1   Photo.   Perf. 13x12½

228	A32	50c indigo	.30	.30
229	A33	1p dark red	.35	.30
230	A33	1.50p grnsh blue	.40	.35
		Nos. 228-230 (3)	1.05	.95

Issued to commemorate 25 years of peace.

Plectrocnemia Cruciata — A34

Design: 1p, Metopodontus savagei, horiz.

Perf. 13x12½, 12½x13
1965, June 1   Photo.   Unwmk.

231	A34	50c slate green	.45	.35
232	A34	1p rose red	.45	.35
233	A34	1.50p Prus blue	.45	.35
		Nos. 231-233 (3)	1.35	1.05

Issued for child welfare.

Pole Vault — A35

Arms of Fernando Po — A36

Perf. 12½x13, 13x12½
1965, Nov. 23   Photo.   Unwmk.

234	A35	50c yellow green	.30	.30
235	A36	1p brt org brn	.35	.30
236	A35	1.50p brt blue	.40	.35
		Nos. 234-236 (3)	1.05	.95

Issued for Stamp Day, 1965.

Children Reading — A37

1.50p, St. Elizabeth of Hungary, vert.

Perf. 12½x13, 13x12½
1966, June 1   Photo.   Unwmk.

237	A37	50c dark green	.30	.30
238	A37	1p brown red	.35	.30
239	A37	1.50p dark blue	.35	.30
		Nos. 237-239 (3)	1.00	.95

Issued for child welfare.

Fetish — A24

FERNANDO PO — FIJI

White-nosed Monkey — A38

Stamp Day: 40c, 4p, Head of moustached monkey, vert.

1966, Nov. 23   Photo.   Perf. 13
240	A38	10c dk blue & yel	.35	.30
241	A38	40c lt brn, bl & blk	.40	.30
242	A38	1.50p ol bis, brn org & blk	.45	.40
243	A38	4p sl grn, brn org & blk	.55	.45

Nos. 240-243 (4)   1.75   1.45

Flowers — A39

Designs: 40c, 4p, Six flowers.

1967, June 1   Photo.   Perf. 13
244	A39	10c brt car & pale grn	.30	.30
245	A39	40c red brn & org	.35	.30
246	A39	1.50p red lil & lt red brn	.40	.40
247	A39	4p dk blue & lt grn	.45	.40

Nos. 244-247 (4)   1.50   1.35

Issued for child welfare.

Linsang — A40

Stamp Day: 1.50p, Needle-clawed galago, vert. 3.50p, Fraser's scaly-tailed flying squirrel.

1967, Nov. 23   Photo.   Perf. 13
248	A40	1p black & bister	.35	.30
249	A40	1.50p brown & olive	.40	.30
250	A40	3.50p rose lake & dl grn	.50	.40

Nos. 248-250 (3)   1.25   1.05

Stamp of 1868, No. 1, and Arms of San Carlos — A41

Fernando Po No. 1 and: 1.50p, Arms of Santa Isabel. 2.50p, Arms of Fernando Po.

1968, Feb. 4   Photo.   Perf. 13
251	A41	1p brt plum & brn org	.30	.30
252	A41	1.50p dp blue & brn org	.40	.30
253	A41	2.50p brn & brn org	.50	.40

Nos. 251-253 (3)   1.20   1.00

Centenary of the first postage stamp.

Signs of the Zodiac — A42

1968, Apr. 25   Photo.   Perf. 13
254	A42	1p Libra	.30	.30
255	A42	1.50p Leo	.40	.35
256	A42	2.50p Aquarius	.50	.40

Nos. 254-256 (3)   1.20   1.05

Issued for child welfare.

SEMI-POSTAL STAMPS

Catalogue values for unused stamps in this section are for Never Hinged items.

Types of Regular Issue, 1960

Designs: 10c+5c, Manuel de Falla. 15c+5c, Dancers from "Love, the Magician."

Perf. 12½x13, 13x12½
1960   Photo.   Unwmk.
B1	A18	10c + 5c maroon	.35	.30
B2	A17	15c + 5c dk brn & bister	.35	.35

The surtax was for child welfare.

Whale — SP1

Design: Nos. B4, B6, Harpooning whale.

1961   Perf. 12½x13
B3	SP1	10c + 5c rose brown	.35	.30
B4	SP1	20c + 5c dk slate grn	.35	.30
B5	SP1	30c + 10c olive brn	.40	.30
B6	SP1	50c + 20c dark brn	.45	.30

Nos. B3-B6 (4)   1.55   1.20

Issued for Stamp Day, 1960.

Hand Blessing Woman — SP2

Design: 25c+10c, Boy making sign of the cross, and crucifix.

1961, June 21   Perf. 13x12½
B7	SP2	10c + 5c rose brn	.40	.30
B8	SP2	25c + 10c gray vio	.40	.30
B9	SP2	80c + 20c dk grn	.50	.35

Nos. B7-B9 (3)   1.30   .95

The surtax was for child welfare.

Ethiopian Tortoise — SP3

Stamp Day: 25c+10c, 1p+10c, Native carriers, palms and shore.

1961, Nov. 23   Perf. 12½x13
B10	SP3	10c + 5c rose red	.35	.30
B11	SP3	25c + 10c dk pur	.40	.30
B12	SP3	30c + 10c vio brn	.40	.30
B13	SP3	1p + 10c red org	.50	.40

Nos. B10-B13 (4)   1.65   1.30

FIJI

'fē-,jē

LOCATION — Group of 332 islands (106 inhabited) in the South Pacific Ocean east of Vanuatu
GOVT. — Independent nation in British Commonwealth
AREA — 7,078 sq. mi.
POP. — 896,000 (2020 est.)
CAPITAL — Suva

A British colony since 1874, Fiji became fully independent in 1970.

12 Pence = 1 Shilling
20 Shillings = 1 Pound
100 Cents = 1 Dollar (1872-74, 1969)

Syncopated Perforations
Type A (1st stamp #873): On shorter sides, the seventh hole from the larger side is an oval hole equal in width to three holes.

> Catalogue values for unused stamps in this country are for Never Hinged items, beginning with Scott 137 in the regular postage section and Scott B1 in the semi-postal section.

Values for unused stamps are for examples with original gum as defined in the catalogue introduction except for Nos. 1-10 which are valued without gum. Additionally, Nos. 1-10 are valued with roulettes showing on two or more sides, but expect small faults that do not detract from the appearance of the stamps. Very few examples of Nos. 1-10 will be found free of faults, and these will command substantial premiums.

Watermark

Wmk. 17 — FIJI POSTAGE Across Center Row of Sheet

A1

1870   Unwmk. Typeset   *Rouletted*
Thin Quadrille Paper
1	A1	1p black, *pink*	4,500.	4,750.
2	A1	3p black, *pink*	5,500.	5,000.
a.		Comma after "EXPRESS"	8,000.	8,000.
3	A1	6p black, *pink*	3,000.	3,000.
4	A1	1sh black, *pink*	2,250.	2,500.

1871   **Thin Vertically Laid Paper**
6	A1	1p black, *pink*	1,250.	2,100.
7	A1	3p black, *pink*	1,900.	3,400.
8	A1	6p black, *pink*	1,600.	2,100.
9	A1	9p black, *pink*	3,400.	4,000.
10	A1	1sh black, *pink*	1,900.	1,900.

This service was established by the *Fiji Times*, a weekly newspaper, for the delivery of the newspaper. Since there was no postal service to the other islands, delivery of letters to agents of the newspaper on the islands was offered to the public.
Nos. 1-5 were printed in the same sheet, one horizontal row of 6 of each (6p, 1sh, 1p, 3p). Nos. 6-10 were printed from the same plate with three 9p replacing three 3p.
Most used examples have pen cancels.
Up to three sets of imitations exist. One on pink laid paper, pin-perforated, measuring 22½x16mm. Originals measure 22½x18½mm. A later printing was made on pink wove paper.
Forgeries also exist plus fake cancellations.

Crown and "CR" (Cakobau Rex)
A2   A3

A4

1871   Typo.   Wmk. 17   Perf. 12½
Wove Paper
15	A2	1p blue	62.50	140.00
16	A3	3p green	125.00	400.00
17	A4	6p rose	170.00	325.00

Nos. 15-17 (3)   357.50   865.00

Sheets of 50 (10x5).
For overprints and surcharges see Nos. 18-39.
Forgeries exist.

Stamps of 1871 Surcharged in Black

1872, Jan. 13
18	A2	2c on 1p blue	60.00	65.00
19	A3	6c on 3p green	90.00	90.00
20	A4	12c on 6p rose	125.00	90.00

Nos. 18-20 (3)   275.00   245.00

Nos. 18-20 with Additional Overprint in Black

b   c

1874, Oct. 10
21	A2(b)	2c on 1p blue	1,250.	340.00
a.		No period after "R"	3,250.	1,150.
22	A2(c)	2c on 1p blue	1,150.	300.00
a.		Invtd. "A" instead of "V"	3,250.	1,500.
b.		Period after "R" is a Maltese Cross	3,250.	1,500.
c.		No period after "R"	3,250.	1,500.
d.		Round raised period after "V"	3,250.	1,500.
e.		Round raised period after "V" and "R"	3,250.	1,500.
23	A3(b)	6c on 3p green	3,250.	1,000.
a.		No period after "R"	5,500.	2,000.
24	A3(c)	6c on 3p green	2,750.	750.00
a.		Period after "R" is a Maltese Cross	5,250.	2,000.
b.		No period after "R"	5,500.	2,000.
c.		Round raised period after "V"	5,500.	2,000.
d.		Round raised period after "V" and "R"	5,500.	2,000.
25	A4(b)	12c on 6p rose	1,050.	275.00
a.		"V.R." inverted	7,500.	
b.		No period after "R"	3,000.	1,150.
26	A4(c)	12c on 6p rose	1,000.	250.00
a.		Inverted "A"	3,000.	1,200.
b.		Period after "R" is a Maltese Cross	3,000.	1,200.
c.		"V.R." inverted	—	6,250.
d.		No period after "R"	3,000.	1,225.
e.		Round raised period after "V"	3,000.	1,225.
f.		Round raised period after "V" and "R"	3,000.	1,225.

Forged overprints exist on both forged stamps and on genuine stamps.
Types "b" and "c" were in the same sheet.

Nos. 23-26 with Additional Surcharge in Black or Red

1875
27	A3(b)	2p on 6c on 3p	2,750.	800.00
a.		Period btwn. "2" and "d"	4,750.	1,600.
b.		"V.R." double	5,500.	4,500.
c.		No period after "R"	4,750.	1,600.
28	A3(b)	2p on 6c on 3p (R)	900.00	325.00
a.		Period btwn. "2" and "d"	2,250.	860.00
b.		No period after "R"	2,250.	900.00
29	A3(c)	2p on 6c on 3p	1,900.	600.00
a.		Inverted "A"	4,750.	1,600.
b.		Period after "R" is a Maltese Cross	4,750.	1,000.
c.		No period after "2d"	4,750.	1,600.
d.		No period after "R"	4,750.	1,600.
e.		Round raised period after "V"	4,750.	1,600.
f.		Round raised period after "V" and "R"	4,750.	1,600.
30	A3(c)	2p on 6c on 3p (R)	750.00	250.00
a.		Inverted "A"	2,400.	850.00
b.		Period after "R" is a Maltese Cross	2,400.	875.00
c.		No period after "2d"	2,400.	875.00
d.		No period after "R"	2,400.	875.00
e.		Round raised period after "V"	2,400.	875.00
f.		Round raised period after "V" and "R"	2,400.	875.00
31	A4(b)	2p on 12c on 6p	3,250.	1,000.
a.		Period btwn. "2" and "d"		
b.		No period after "R"		
c.		"2d, VR" double		5,500.
32	A4(c)	2p on 12c on 6p	3,000.	900.00
a.		Inverted "A"	4,500.	1,400.
b.		No period after "R"	—	2,250.
c.		"2d, VR" double		5,500.

FIJI

d.	Round raised period after "R"	—	1,250.
f.	As "a," with raised period after "V"	3,000.	1,000.

Forged overprints exist on both forged stamps and on genuine stamps.

Types of 1871 Overprinted or Surcharged in Black

e   f

1876, Jan. 31 Wove Paper Unwmk.

33	A2(e)	1p ultramarine	60.00	60.00
a.		Inverted surcharge		1,000.
b.		Dbl. impression of stamp	1,000.	
c.		Horiz. pair, imperf vert.	1,000.	
34	A3(e+f)	2p on 3p dk grn	60.00	65.00
a.		Dbl. surch. "Two Pence"		
35	A4(e)	6p rose	70.00	65.00
b.		Surcharge inverted		
c.		Dbl. impression of stamp	2,750.	
		Nos. 33-35 (3)	190.00	190.00

1877 Laid Paper

36	A2(e)	1p ultramarine	32.50	50.00
a.		Horiz. pair, imperf. vert.	1,000.	
37	A3(e+f)	2p on 3p dk grn	80.00	85.00
b.		Perf 10	400.00	
c.		Perf 11	375.00	
d.		Horiz. pair, imperf. vert.	1,100.	
e.		Horiz. pair, imperf. between	1,000.	
38	A3(e+f)	4p on 3p lilac	110.00	27.50
a.		Horiz. pair, imperf. vert.	1,000.	
39	A4(e)	6p rose	60.00	40.00
a.		Horiz. pair, imperf. vert.	800.00	
		Nos. 36-39 (4)	282.50	202.50

Many of the preceding stamps are known imperforate. They are printer's waste and were never issued.

A12   A13

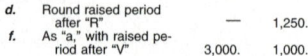
Queen Victoria
A14   A15

Perf. 10-13½ & Compound
1878-01 Wove Paper Typo.

40	A12	1p ultra ('79), perf. 12½	20.00	20.00
a.		1p blue	65.00	6.50
41	A12	2p green, perf. 12½ ('79)	45.00	1.75
b.		2p ultramarine (error), perf. 12½	40,000.	
42	A12	4p brt vio, perf. 11x11¾ ('96)	16.00	9.00
a.		4p mauve, perf. 11 ('96)	47.50	12.00
43	A13	6p brt rose, 11x11¾ ('01)	16.00	4.75
a.		6p dull rose, perf. 11 ('96)	55.00	60.00
e.		As "a," printed on both sides	2,500.	2,000.
44	A14	1sh pale yel brn, perf. 11x11¾ ('99)	60.00	12.50
a.		1sh deep brown	75.00	50.00

Litho. & Typo.

45	A15	5sh blk & red brn, perf. 10 ('82)	75.00	50.00
		Nos. 40-45 (6)	232.00	98.00

No. 41b was not put on sale. All examples were supposed to be destroyed.

A quantity of No. 45 was sold as remainders, canceled-to-order with the following Suva dates: 15.DEC.00; 22.DE.1900; 28.DEC.1900; 12.DEC.01; 15.DEC.01; 16.DE.1901; 21.JUN.02; 15.DEC.02; 15. DE. 1902; and 21.DE.1902. Examples so canceled are worth less than normally used examples.

Nos. 44 and 45 imperf was sold only as a remainder, canceled "Suva, 15.DEC.00."

A late printing of the 5sh, made from an electrotyped plate, exists in gray black and red orange, perf 10, differing from No. 45 in many details. It was also sold only as a remainder, canceled "Suva, 15.DEC.00." It is scarce.

For surcharges see Nos. 46-52.

Nos. 40-45 exist with sheetmaker's watermark. Watermarked stamps are scarcer than unwatermarked.

1881-90 Perf. 10

40d	A12	1p ultramarine	32.50	3.00
40e	A12	1p blue	65.00	3.25
41d	A12	2p yellow green	45.00	1.00
41e	A12	2p blue green	55.00	6.00
42d	A12	4p mauve	85.00	75.00
43d	A13	6p bright rose	30.00	32.50
43e	A13	6p pale rose	75.00	32.50
44d	A14	1sh pale yel brown	100.00	32.50
44e	A14	1sh deep brown	100.00	32.50

Surcharged type "f" in Black
1878-90 Typo.

46	A12	2p on 3p green	12.00	42.50
47	A12	4p on 1p vio ('90)	75.00	60.00
48	A12	4p on 2p lilac ('83)	100.00	16.00
		Nos. 46-48 (3)	187.00	118.50

Nos. 40-43 Surcharged in Black

g   h

j   k

1891-92 Perf. 10

49	A12(g)	½p on 1p ('92)	62.50	80.00
50	A12(h)	2½p on 2p	52.50	55.00
a.		Wider space (2mm) between "2" and "½"	140.00	150.00
51	A12(j)	5p on 4p ('92)	62.50	80.00
52	A13(k)	5p on 6p ('92)	67.50	75.00
a.		"FIVE" and "PENCE" 3mm apart	75.00	85.00
		Nos. 49-52 (4)	245.00	290.00

No. 50a resulted from loose type, sometimes printing narrow, sometimes wide. Intermediate spacing is known.

A18   A20

Fijian Canoe — A19

1891-96 Perf. 10-12 & Compound

53	A18	½p grnsh blk, perf. 11 ('96)	2.75	7.00
a.		½p gray, perf. 11	3.75	7.00
54	A19	1p black, perf. 11x10 ('93)	22.50	7.50
55	A19	1p lilac rose, perf. 11 ('96)	22.50	1.10
56	A19	2p green, perf. 11 ('93)	9.00	.85
a.		Perf. 10x11¾ ('94)	800.00	425.00
57	A20	2½ red brown, perf. 11x11¾ ('97)	9.00	6.50
58	A19	5p ultra, perf. 11x10 ('93)	25.00	8.00
		Nos. 53-58 (6)	90.75	30.95

Perf. 10

53d	A18	½p slate gray	6.75	10.00
54d	A19	1p black	30.00	6.00
56d	A19	2p green	145.00	22.50
57d	A20	2½p brown	60.00	30.00
58d	A19	5p ultramarine	125.00	65.00

Edward VII — A22

1903, Feb. 1 Wmk. 2 Perf. 14

59	A22	½p gray grn & pale grn	3.25	2.25
60	A22	1p vio & blk, red	20.00	.65
61	A22	2p vio & orange	4.50	1.40
62	A22	2½ vio & ultra, bl	15.00	1.75
63	A22	3p vio & red vio	1.60	4.00
64	A22	4p violet & blk	1.60	2.75
65	A22	5p vio & green	1.60	2.50
66	A22	6p vio & car rose	1.60	2.00
67	A22	1sh grn & car rose	18.50	85.00
68	A22	5sh green & blk	85.00	170.00
69	A22	£1 vio & blk & ultra	400.00	500.00
		Revenue cancel		75.00
		Nos. 59-68 (10)	152.65	272.30

Numerals of 2p, 4p, 6p and 5sh of type A22 are in color on plain tablet.

1904-12 Ordinary Paper Wmk. 3

70	A22	½p grn & pale grn ('04)	18.50	3.25
70A	A22	½p green ('08)	15.00	3.50
71	A22	1p vio & blk, red ('04)	40.00	.25
72	A22	1p carmine ('06)	25.00	.25
73	A22	2½p ultra ('10)	7.50	10.00

Chalky Paper

74	A22	6p violet ('10)	30.00	50.00
75	A22	1sh grn & car rose ('09)	32.50	42.50
76	A22	1sh blk, grn ('11)	11.00	16.00
77	A22	5sh grn & scar, yel ('11)	75.00	105.00
78	A22	£1 vio & blk, red ('12)	360.00	300.00
		Nos. 70-77 (9)	254.50	230.75

George V — A23

Die I

For description of Dies I and II see "Dies of British Colonial Stamps" in Table of Contents.

1912-23 Ordinary Paper

79	A23	¼p brown ('16)	2.75	.40
80	A23	½p green	4.50	1.10
81	A23	1p scarlet	3.75	.50
a.		1p carmine ('16)	2.25	.75
82	A23	2p gray ('14)	2.00	.25
83	A23	2½p ultra ('14)	3.50	3.75
84	A23	3p violet, yel	4.50	12.50
a.		Die II ('21)	3.25	30.00
85	A23	4p blk & red, lem ('21)	24.00	22.50
a.		Die II ('23)	3.25	35.00

Chalky Paper

86	A23	5p dl vio & ol grn ('14)	5.50	12.50
87	A23	6p dl vio & red vio ('14)	2.40	6.00
88	A23	1sh black, green	1.30	14.50
a.		1sh black, blue green, ol back	3.25	11.00
b.		1sh black, emerald ('21)	5.50	67.50
c.		Die II ('22)	3.25	37.50
89	A23	2sh 6p blk & red, blue	37.50	35.00
90	A23	5sh grn & scar, yellow	37.50	45.00
91	A23	£1 vio & blk, red	300.00	325.00
a.		Die II ('21)	300.00	325.00
		Revenue cancel		52.50

Surface-colored Paper

92	A23	1sh black, green	1.25	14.50
		Nos. 79-90,92 (13)	130.45	168.50

Numerals of ¼p, 1½p, 2p, 4p, 6p, 2sh, 2sh6p and 5sh of type A23 are in color on plain tablet.

For overprints see Nos. MR1-MR2.

Die II

1922-27 Wmk. 4 Ordinary Paper

93	A23	¼p dark brown	3.75	27.50
94	A23	½p green	1.10	1.50
95	A23	1p rose red	6.00	1.00
96	A23	1p violet ('27)	1.40	.25
97	A23	1½p rose red ('27)	4.50	1.50
98	A23	2p gray	1.40	.25
a.		"2d" and value tablet omitted	27,500.	
99	A23	3p ultra ('23)	3.00	1.20
100	A23	4p blk & red, yel	16.00	7.00
101	A23	5p dl vio & ol grn	1.75	2.25
102	A23	6p dl vio & red violet	2.40	1.50

Chalky Paper

103	A23	1sh blk, emerald	14.00	2.75
104	A23	2sh vio & ultra, bl	30.00	72.50
105	A23	2sh6p blk & red, bl	12.50	35.00
106	A23	5sh grn & scar, yellow	55.00	90.00
		Nos. 93-106 (14)	152.80	244.20

The only known example of No. 98a is the center stamp of an unused block of nine.

Common Design Types pictured following the introduction.

Silver Jubilee Issue
Common Design Type

1935, May 6 Perf. 13½x14

110	CD301	1½p car & blue	1.00	10.00
111	CD301	2p gray blk & ultra	1.50	.50
112	CD301	3p blue & brown	2.75	5.50
113	CD301	1sh brt vio & indigo	15.00	18.00
		Nos. 110-113 (4)	20.25	34.00
	Set, never hinged		30.00	

Coronation Issue
Common Design Type

1937, May 12 Perf. 11x11½

114	CD302	1p dark violet	.45	1.25
115	CD302	2p gray black	.45	2.25
116	CD302	3p indigo	.45	2.25
		Nos. 114-116 (3)	1.35	5.75
	Set, never hinged		2.00	

Outrigger Canoe A24   Fijian Village A25

Outrigger Canoe — A26   Map of Fiji Islands — A27

Government Buildings — A27a   Canoe and Arms of Fiji — A28

(caption continued)

Sugar Cane — A29   Spear Fishing at Night — A30

Arms of Fiji — A31   Suva Harbor — A32

River Scene — A33   Fijian House — A34

Papaya Tree — A35   Bugler — A36

8p, 1sh5p, 1sh6p, Arms of Fiji.

Perf. 13½, 12½ (1p)

1938-55	Engr.	Wmk. 4		
117	A24	½p green	.25	1.00
c.		Perf. 14 ('41)	16.00	6.75
d.		Perf. 12 ('48)	.80	3.00
118	A25	1p blue & brn	.40	.25
119	A26	1½p rose car (empty canoe)	12.00	.50

FIJI

120	A27	2p grn & org brn (no "180 degree")	40.00	.50
121	A27a	2p mag & grn	.45	.80
a.		Perf. 12 ('46)	1.25	.90

Perf. 12½, 13x12 (6p), 13¾x14 (8p)

122	A28	3p dp ultra	.80	.40
123	A29	5p rose red & blue	32.50	13.00
124	A29	5p rose red & yel grn	.25	.40
125	A27	6p blk (no "180 degree")	45.00	16.00
126	A31	8p rose car	1.40	3.50
a.		Perf. 13¼ ('50)	1.25	3.50
127	A30	1sh black & yel	1.50	.90

Perf. 14

128	A31	1sh5p car & blk	.25	.25
128A	A31	1sh6p ultra	2.75	3.50
b.		Perf. 13 ('55)	1.10	20.00

Perf. 12½

129	A32	2sh vio & org	2.25	.55
130	A33	2sh6p brn & grn	4.00	2.00
131	A34	5sh dk vio & grn	4.00	2.50
131A	A35	10sh emer & brn org	27.50	52.50
131B	A36	£1 car & ultra	37.50	65.00
		Nos. 117-131B (18)	212.80	163.55

Issued: 1sh5p, 6/13/40; 5p, 10/1/40; No. 121, 5/19/42; 8p, 11/15/48; 10sh, £1, 3/13/50; 1sh6p, 8/1/50; others, 4/5/38.

Types of 1938-40 Redrawn

Man in Canoe — A36a

180 Degree Added to the Lower Right Hand Corner of the Design — A36b

Perf. 13½ (1½p, 2p, 6p), 14 (2½p)

1940-49   **Wmk. 4**

132	A36a	1½p rose carmine	1.00	3.00
a.		Perf. 12 ('49)	.80	1.60
b.		Perf. 14 ('42)	14.50	22.50
133	A36b	2p grn & org brn ("180 degree")	12.50	17.50
134	A36b	2½p grn & org brn	.50	1.25
a.		Perf. 12 ('48)	.80	.60
b.		Perf. 13½ ('42)	.55	1.00
135	A36b	6p blk ("180 degree")	2.50	2.00
a.		Perf. 12 ('47)	1.40	1.50
		Nos. 132-135 (4)	16.50	23.75

Issued: 2½p, Jan. 6, 1942; others Oct. 1, 1940.

No. 133 Surcharged in Black

1941, Feb. 10   **Perf. 13½**

136	A36b	2½p on 2p grn & org brn	1.50	1.00
		Never hinged		2.50

Catalogue values for unused stamps in this section, from this point to the end of the section, are for Never Hinged items.

Peace Issue
Common Design Type

1946, Aug. 17   **Perf. 13½**

137	CD303	2½p bright green	.25	1.50
138	CD303	3p deep blue	.50	.25

Silver Wedding Issue
Common Design Types

1948, Dec. 17 Photo.   Perf. 14x14½

139	CD304	2½p dark green	.70	2.50

Engr.; Name Typo.
Perf. 11½x11

140	CD305	5sh blue violet	17.50	9.00

UPU Issue
Common Design Types
Engr.; Name Typo. on 3p, 8p
Perf. 13½, 11x11½

1949, Oct. 10   **Wmk. 4**

141	CD306	2p red violet	.35	.75
142	CD307	3p indigo	2.25	7.50
143	CD308	8p dp carmine	.35	4.50
144	CD309	1sh6p blue	.40	3.00
		Nos. 141-144 (4)	3.35	15.75

Coronation Issue
Common Design Type

1953, June 2   **Perf. 13½x13**

145	CD312	2½p dk green & blk	1.00	.60
		Nos. 145 (1)	1.00	.60

Type of 1938-40 with Portrait of Queen Elizabeth II Inscribed: "Royal Visit 1953"

1953, Dec. 16   **Perf. 13**

146	A31	8p carmine lake	.65	.35

Visit of Queen Elizabeth II and the Duke of Edinburgh, 1953.

Types of 1938-50 with Portrait of Queen Elizabeth II, and

A39   Loading Copra — A40

Designs: 1sh6p, Sugar cane train. 2sh, Bananas for export. 5sh, Gold industry.

Perf. 11½ (A24, A27, A39); 11½x11 (A40); 12 (A27, 2p); 12½ (A30, A33, A35, A36); 13 (A31)

1954-56   **Engr.**

147	A24	½p green	1.00	1.60
148	A39	1p grnsh blue	1.90	.25
149	A39	1½p brown	3.00	.70
150	A27a	2p mag & green	1.35	.40
151	A39	2½p blue vio	3.25	.25
152	A40	3p purple & brn	5.00	.25
153	A27	6p black	2.75	.90
154	A27	6p black	2.75	.90
155	A31	8p carmine lake	8.50	1.90
156	A30	1sh black & yel	3.25	.25
157	A40	1sh6p grn & dp ultra	17.00	1.05
158	A40	2sh brt car & blk	5.00	.65
159	A33	2sh6p brn & bl grn	1.90	.25
160	A40	5sh dp ultra & yel	8.50	1.30
161	A35	10sh emer & brn org	8.00	15.00
162	A36	£1 car & ultra	35.00	11.00
		Nos. 147-162 (15)	105.40	35.75

Issued: 2p, 1sh, 2sh6p, 2/1/54; ½p, 6p, 8p, 10sh, £1, 7/1/54; 1p, 6/1/56; 1½p, 2½p, 3p, 1sh6p, 2sh, 5sh, 10/1/56.

Types of 1954-56 and

Nautilus Shells A41   Hibiscus A42

Kandavu Parrot — A43

½p, 2p, 2½p, Queen Elizabeth II (A39). 1p, Queen, turtles in bottom panels. 6p, Fijian beating drum (lali). 10p, Yaqona ceremony. 1sh, South Pacific map. 2sh6p, Nadi Airport. 10sh, Cutting sugar cane. £1, Arms of Fiji.

Perf. 11½ (A39, A41); 11½x11 (A40); 14½x14 (A42); 14x14½ (A43)
Engr. (A39, A40, A41); others Photo.

1959-63   **Wmk. 4**

163	A39	½p green ('61)	.25	2.60
164	A41	1p dk blue ('62)	3.75	2.60
165	A41	1½p dk brown ('62)	3.75	2.60
166	A39	2p crim rose ('61)	1.60	.25
167	A39	2½p brown org ('62)	3.25	5.00
168	A40	6p blk & car rose ('61)	1.90	.25
169	A42	8p gray, red, yel & grn ('61)	.55	.30
170	A40	10p car & brn ('63)	2.60	.65
171	A40	1sh dk bl & bl ('61)	1.60	.25
172	A40	2sh6p pur & blk ('61)	9.50	.25
173	A43	4sh dk grn, red, bl & emer	3.00	1.30
174	A40	10sh sep & emer ('61)	2.75	1.30
175	A40	£1 org & blk ('61)	5.75	3.75
		Nos. 163-175 (13)	40.25	21.10

Issued: 4sh, 7/13; 8p, 8/1; ½p, 2p, 6p, 1sh, 2sh6p, 10sh, £1, 11/14; 1p, 1½p, 2½p, 12/3; 10p, 4/1.

For type overprinted see No. 205.

Types of 1954-63 and

Elizabeth II — A44

1sh6p, 180th meridian and Intl. Date Line. 2sh, White orchids. 5sh, Orange dove.

Perf. 11½ (A41); 12½ (A44); 11½x11 (A40); 14x14½ (A43)
Engr. (A39, A40, A41); others Photo.

1962-67   **Wmk. 314**

176	A41	1p dark blue ('64)	1.00	3.75
177	A39	2p crim rose ('65)	.50	.25
178	A44	3p rose cl & multi	.25	.25
179	A40	6p blk & car rose ('64)	1.50	.25
180	A42	9p ultra, red, yel & grn ('63)	.90	.65
181	A40	10p car & brn ('64)	.60	.50
182	A40	1sh dk bl & bl ('66)	2.25	.45
183	A43	1sh6p dk bl & multi	1.50	.60
184	A42	2sh gold, yel grn & grn	10.00	3.50
185	A40	2sh6p pur & blk ('65)	5.50	1.25
186	A43	4sh grn & multi, wmk. sideways ('67)	4.25	1.00
a.		As #186, wmk. upright ('64)	7.50	2.00
b.		4sh dark green & multi ('66)	6.00	2.50
187	A43	5sh dk gray, yel & red	10.00	.35
188	A40	10sh sep & emer ('64)	7.50	2.50
189	A40	£1 org & blk ('64)	14.00	7.00
		Nos. 176-189 (14)	59.75	22.30

Issued: 3p, 1sh6p, 2sh, 5sh, 12/3; 9p, No. 186a, 4/1; 1p, 10p, 10sh, 1/14; 6p, £1, 6/9; 2p, 2sh6p, 8/3; No. 186b, 3/1; No. 186, 2/16.

Nos. 178 and 171 Overprinted

1963, Feb. 1

196	A44	3p multicolored	.50	.35
197	A40	1sh dark blue & blue	.65	.35

Visit of Elizabeth II & Prince Philip, Feb. 3.

Freedom from Hunger Issue
Common Design Type

1963, June 4 Photo.   Perf. 14x14½

198	CD314	2sh ultramarine	3.50	2.25

Running — A45

9p, Throwing the discus, vert. 1sh, Field hockey, vert. 2sh6p, Women's high jump.

Perf. 14½x14, 14x14½

1963, Aug. 6   **Wmk. 314**

199	A45	3p yel, blk & brn	.45	.25
200	A45	9p violet, blk & brn	.45	1.00
201	A45	1sh green, blk & brn	.45	.45
202	A45	2sh6p blue, blk & brn	1.10	.95
		Nos. 199-202 (4)	2.45	2.45

1st So. Pacific Games, Suva, 8/29-9/7.

Red Cross Centenary Issue
Common Design Type

1963, Sept. 2 Litho.   Perf. 13

203	CD315	2p black & red	1.00	.30
204	CD315	2sh ultra & red	2.25	2.50

Type of 1959-63 Overprinted

1963, Dec. 2   Engr.   Perf. 11½x11

205	A40	1sh dark blue & blue	1.00	.35

Opening of the Commonwealth Pacific (telephone) Cable service, COMPAC.

Fiji Scout Badge A46   Scouts of India, Fiji and Europe Tying Knot A47

1964, Aug. 3   Photo.   Perf. 12½

206	A46	3p multicolored	.50	.50
207	A47	1sh ocher & purple	.65	.65

50th anniv. of the founding of the Fiji Boy Scouts.

Amphibian "Aotearoa," 1939 — A48   Map of Fiji and Tonga Islands and Plane — A49

Design: 9p, Heron plane.

1964, Oct. 24   **Perf. 12½, 14½**

208	A48	3p brt red & black	.50	.35
209	A48	6p ultra & red	.85	.85
210	A49	1sh grnsh blue & black	.85	.85
		Nos. 208-210 (3)	2.20	2.05

Fiji-Tonga airmail service, 25th anniv.

ITU Issue
Common Design Type
Perf. 11x11½

1965, May 17   Litho.   Wmk. 314

211	CD317	3p blue & rose red	.50	.30
212	CD317	2sh yel & bister	1.50	.75

Intl. Cooperation Year Issue
Common Design Type

1965, Oct. 25   **Perf. 14½**

213	CD318	2p blue grn & claret	.35	.25
214	CD318	2sh6p lt vio & grn	1.60	1.00

Churchill Memorial Issue
Common Design Type

1966, Jan. 24   Photo.   Perf. 14
Design in Black, Gold and Carmine Rose

215	CD319	3p brt blue	.75	.25
216	CD319	9p green	1.10	1.25
217	CD319	1sh brown	1.10	.25
218	CD319	2sh6p violet	1.45	1.25
		Nos. 215-218 (4)	4.40	3.00

World Cup Soccer Issue
Common Design Type

1966, July 1   Litho.   Perf. 14

219	CD321	2p multicolored	.30	.25
220	CD321	2sh multicolored	1.40	.35

FIJI

H.M.S. Pandora and Split Island, Rotuma — A50

Designs: 10p, Rotuma chiefs, Pandora, and Rotuma's position in Pacific. 1sh6p, Rotuma islanders welcoming Pandora.

1966, Aug. 29	Photo.		Perf. 14x13
221	A50	3p multicolored	.40 .25
222	A50	10p multicolored	.40 .25
223	A50	1sh6p multicolored	.65 .95
	Nos. 221-223 (3)		1.45 1.45

175th anniv. of the discovery of Rotuma, a group of eight islands forming part of the colony of Fiji.

WHO Headquarters Issue
Common Design Type

1966, Sept. 20	Litho.		Perf. 14
224	CD322	6p multicolored	1.45 .30
225	CD322	2sh6p multicolored	3.25 3.00
	Nos. 224-225 (2)		4.70 3.30

Woman Runner — A51

Designs: 9p, Shot put, vert. 1sh, Diver.

1966, Dec. 8	Photo.		Perf. 14x14½
226	A51	3p ol, black & lt brn	.25 .25
227	A51	9p brt blue, blk & brn	.35 .35
228	A51	1sh blue green & multi	.40 .40
	Nos. 226-228 (3)		1.00 1.00

2nd South Pacific Games, Noumea, New Caledonia, Dec. 8-18.

Military Band — A52

Intl. Tourist Year: 9p, Reef diving. 1sh, Beqa fire walkers. 2sh, Liner Oriana and Mt. Rama volcano.

1967, Oct. 20			Perf. 14x13
229	A52	3p multi & gold	.60 .25
230	A52	9p multi & silver	.30 .25
231	A52	1sh multi & gold	.30 .25
232	A52	2sh multi & silver	.60 .30
	Nos. 229-232 (4)		1.80 1.05

Admiral Bligh, H.M.S. Providence and Old Map of "Feejee" — A53

Designs: 1sh, Bligh's longboat being chased by double canoe and map of Fiji Islands. 2sh6p, Bligh's tomb, St. Mary's Cemetery, Lambeth, London.

Perf. 15x14, 12½x13 (1sh)

1967, Dec. 7	Photo.		Wmk. 314
	Size: 35x21mm		
233	A53	4p emer, blk & yel	.25 .25
	Size: 54x20mm		
234	A53	1sh brt bl, brn org & blk	40 .25
	Size: 35x21mm		
235	A53	2sh6p sepia & multi	.40 .30
	Nos. 233-235 (3)		1.05 .80

150th anniv. of the death of Adm. William Bligh (1754-1817), captain of the Bounty and principal discoverer of the Fiji Islands.

Simmonds "Spartan" Seaplane — A54

Designs: 6p, Fiji Airways Hawker-Siddeley H748 and emblems of various airlines. 1sh, Fokker "Southern Cross," Capt. Charles Kingsford-Smith, his crew and Southern Cross constellation. 2sh, Lockheed Altair "Lady Southern Cross."

Perf. 14x14½

1968, June 5			Wmk. 314
236	A54	2p green & black	.25 .25
237	A54	6p brt blue, car & blk	.25 .25
238	A54	1sh dp violet & green	.30 .25
239	A54	2sh org brn & dk blue	.50 .25
	Nos. 236-239 (4)		1.30 1.00

40th anniv. of the first Trans-Pacific Flight through Fiji under Capt. Charles Kingsford-Smith.

Fijian Bures A55   Eastern Reef Heron A56

1p, Passion fruit flowers. 2p, Nautilus pompilius shell. 4p, Hawk moth. 6p, Reef butterflyfish. 9p, Bamboo raft (bilibili). 10p, Tiger moth. 1sh, Black marlin. 1sh6p, Orange-breasted honey eaters. 2sh, Ringed sea snake, horiz. 2sh6p, Outrigger canoes (takia), horiz. 3sh, Golden cowrie shell. 4sh, Emperor gold mine and gold ore. 5sh, Bamboo orchids, horiz. 10sh, Tabua (ceremonial whale's tooth). £1, Coat of Arms and Queen Elizabeth II, horiz.

Perf. 13½ (A55), 14 (A56)

1968, July 15	Photo.		Wmk. 314
240	A55	½p multicolored	.25 .25
241	A55	1p multicolored	.25 .25
242	A55	2p multicolored	.25 .25
243	A56	3p multicolored	.45 .25
244	A55	4p multicolored	.95 1.60
245	A55	6p multicolored	.30 .25
246	A55	9p multicolored	.25 1.60
247	A55	10p multicolored	1.50 .25
248	A56	1sh multicolored	.25 .25
249	A56	1sh6p multicolored	5.50 4.50
250	A56	2sh multicolored	.90 1.60
251	A56	2sh6p multicolored	.90 .30
252	A56	3sh multicolored	1.90 4.75
253	A56	4sh multicolored	4.25 2.25
254	A56	5sh multicolored	2.40 1.25
255	A56	10sh multicolored	1.25 2.40
256	A56	£1 red & multi	1.50 2.40
	Nos. 240-256 (17)		23.05 24.40

See Nos. 260-276.

WHO Emblem, Map of Fiji and Nurses — A57

WHO Emblem and: 9p, Medical team loading patient on stretcher on dinghy and medical ship "Vuniwai." 3sh, People playing on beach.

1968, Dec. 9	Litho.		Perf. 14
257	A57	3p blue green & multi	.25 .25
258	A57	9p brt blue & multi	.40 .40
259	A57	3sh dk blue & multi	.60 .60
	Nos. 257-259 (3)		1.25 1.25

WHO, 20th anniv.

Types of 1968
Values in Cents and Dollars

Designs: 1c, Passion fruit flowers. 2c, Nautilus pompilius shell. 3c, Reef heron. 4c, Hawk moth. 5c, Reef butterflyfish. 6c, Fijian bures. 8c, Bamboo raft. 9c, Tiger moth. 10c, Black marlin. 15c, Orange-breasted honey-eater. 20c, Ringed sea snake, horiz. 25c, Outrigger canoes (takia), horiz. 30c, Golden cowrie shell. 40c Emperor gold mine and gold ore. 50c, Bamboo orchids, horiz. $1, Tabua (ceremonial whale's tooth). $2, Coat of Arms and Queen Elizabeth II, horiz.

Perf. 13½ (A55), 14 (A56)

1969, Jan. 13	Photo.		Wmk. 314
260	A55	1c multicolored	.25 .25
261	A55	2c multicolored	.25 .25
262	A56	3c multicolored	1.25 1.00
263	A55	4c multicolored	1.50 1.00
264	A55	5c multicolored	.25 .25
265	A55	6c multicolored	.25 .25
266	A55	8c multicolored	.25 .25
267	A55	9c multicolored	1.50 2.25
268	A56	10c multicolored	.25 .25
269	A56	15c multicolored	6.50 6.00
270	A56	20c multicolored	1.25 .80
271	A56	25c multicolored	1.00 .25
272	A55	30c multicolored	3.50 1.50
273	A56	40c multicolored	7.50 4.00
274	A56	50c multicolored	2.00 .25
275	A56	$1 multicolored	1.50 .40
276	A56	$2 red & multi	3.00 1.50
	Nos. 260-276 (17)		32.00 20.45

For overprints & surcharges see Nos. 286-288, B5-B6.

Nos. 274 and 275 exist on glazed paper. Values, set: $15 unused, $5 used.

Fiji Soldiers and Map of Solomon Islands — A58

Designs: 10c, Flags of Fiji Military Force, soldiers in full and battle dress. 25c, Cpl. Sefanaia Sukanaivalu and Victoria Cross.

1969, June 23		Wmk. 314	Perf. 14
277	A58	3c emerald & multi	.50 .25
278	A58	10c red & multi	.55 .25
279	A58	25c black & multi	.85 .45
	Nos. 277-279 (3)		1.90 .95

25th anniv. of the Fiji Military Forces campaign in the Solomon Islands and of the posthumous award of the Victoria Cross to Cpl. Sefanaia Sukanaivalu.

Yachting — A59

Designs: 4c, Javelin. 20c, Winners and South Pacific Games medal.

1969, Aug. 18	Photo.		Perf. 14½x14
280	A59	4c red, brown & blk	.30 .30
281	A59	8c blue & black	.40 .40
282	A59	20c ol grn, blk & ocher	.50 .50
	Nos. 280-282 (3)		1.20 1.20

3rd South Pacific Games, Port Moresby, Papua New Guinea, Aug. 13-23.

Students in Laboratory A60

2c, Map of South Pacific and mortarboard. 8c, Site of University at Royal New Zealand Air Force Seaplane Station, Laucala Bay, RNZAF badge and Sunderland flying boat.

1969, Nov. 10			Perf. 14x14½
283	A60	2c multicolored	.25 .25
284	A60	8c red & multi	.35 .35
285	A60	25c dk green & multi	.80 .75
	Nos. 283-285 (3)		1.40 1.35

Inauguration of the University of the South Pacific, Laucala Bay, Suva.

Nos. 261, 268 and 271 Overprinted

1970, Mar. 4			Perf. 13½, 14
286	A55	2c multicolored	.30 .40
287	A56	10c multicolored	.40 .30
288	A55	25c multicolored	.80 .80
	Nos. 286-288 (3)		1.50 1.50

Visit of Queen Elizabeth II, Prince Philip and Princess Anne, Mar. 4-5.

Nuns Sitting under Chaulmoogra Tree, and Chaulmoogra Fruit — A61

Designs: 10c, Paintings by Semisi Maya (former patient). No. 291, Cascade, vert. No. 291, Sea urchins, vert. 30c, Aerial view of Makogai Hospital.

Perf. 14x14½, 14½x14

1970, May 25	Photo.		Wmk. 314
289	A61	2c brt pink & multi	.25 .55
290	A61	10c gray green & blk	.50 .55
291	A61	10c blue, car & blk	.50 .55
a.	Pair, #290-291		1.00 1.10
292	A61	30c orange & multi	1.00 .60
	Nos. 289-292 (4)		2.25 2.25

Closing of the Leprosy Hospital on Makogai Island in 1969.

Abel Tasman and Ship's Log, 1643 — A62

3c, Capt. James Cook & "Endeavour." 8c, Capt. William Bligh & longboat, 1789. 25c, Man of Fiji & Fijian ocean-going canoe.

1970, Aug. 18	Litho.		Perf. 13x12½
293	A62	2c blue green & multi	.75 .55
294	A62	3c gray green & multi	1.25 .55
295	A62	8c multicolored	1.25 .45
296	A62	25c dull lilac & multi	.75 .45
	Nos. 293-296 (4)		4.00 2.00

Discoverers and explorers of Fiji Islands.

King Cakobau and Cession Stone at Lavuka — A63

Designs: 3c, Chinese, Fijian, Indian and European children. 10c, Prime Minister Ratu Sir Kamisese Mara and flag of Fiji. 25c, Fijian male dancer and Indian female dancer.

1970, Oct. 10		Wmk. 314	Perf. 14
297	A63	2c multicolored	.25 .25
298	A63	3c multicolored	.25 .25
299	A63	10c multicolored	1.10 .25
300	A63	25c multicolored	.30 .30
	Nos. 297-300 (4)		1.90 1.05

Fijian independence.

Fiji Nos. 1 and 3 — A64

15c, Fiji #15, 44, 59, 81, 127, 166. 20c, Fiji Times Office, Levuka, & G. P. O., Suva.

1970, Nov. 2	Photo.		Perf. 14½x14
	Size: 35x21mm		
301	A64	4c multicolored	.30 .25
	Size: 60x21½mm		
302	A64	15c multicolored	.75 .30
	Size: 35x21mm		
303	A64	20c multicolored	.75 .30
	Nos. 301-303 (3)		1.80 .85

Centenary of first postage stamps of Fiji.

Gray-backed White Eyes — A65

Yellow-breasted Musk Parrots — A66

Designs: 1c, Cirrhopetalum umbellatum. 2c, Cardinal honey eaters. 3c, Calanthe furcata.4c, Bulbophyllum. 6c, Phaius tancarvilliae. 8c, Blue-crested broadbills. 10c, Acanthephippiumvitiense. 15c, Dendrobium tokai. 20c, Slaty flycatchers. 25c, Kandavu honey eaters. 30c, Dendrobium gordonii. 50c, White-throated pigeon. $1, Collared lories (kula). $2, Dendrobium platygastrium. (Orchids shown on 1c, 3c, 4c, 6c, 10c, 15c, 30c, $2.)

FIJI

Wmk. 314 Upright
1971-72 Litho. Perf. 13½x14

305	A65	1c blk & multi ('72)	.25	.30
306	A65	2c carmine & multi	.45	.25
307	A65	3c multi ('72)	.85	.25
308	A65	4c blk & multi ('72)	.65	1.75
309	A65	5c brown & multi	.35	.25
310	A65	6c lt bl & multi ('72)	4.75	6.00
311	A65	8c black & multi	.35	.25
312	A65	10c multi ('72)	.35	.25
313	A65	15c multi ('72)	4.75	1.00
314	A65	20c gray & multi	1.35	.30

Perf. 14

315	A66	25c sepia & multi	3.75	.25
316	A66	30c grn & multi ('72)	8.75	.85
317	A66	40c blue & multi	4.00	.45
318	A66	50c gray & multi	2.60	.45
319	A66	$1 red & multi	3.50	.85
320	A66	$2 multi ('72)	2.75	8.00
		Nos. 305-320 (16)	39.45	21.45

Issued: 5c, 20c, 40c, 50c, 8/6; 2c, 8c, 25c, $1, 11/22; 1c, 10c, 30c, $2, 1/4; 3c, 4c, 6c, 15c, 6/23.

1972-74 Wmk. 314 Sideways

306c	A65	2c ('73)	.40	9.00
307c	A65	3c ('73)	2.25	.50
308c	A65	4c ('73)	5.50	.85
309c	A65	5c ('73)	7.75	3.75
310c	A65	6c ('73)	9.75	1.40
311c	A65	8c ('73)	3.50	.80
313c	A65	15c ('73)	5.00	2.50
314c	A65	20c	13.50	2.10
315c	A66	25c ('73)	1.75	.95
317c	A66	40c ('74)	2.75	9.50
318c	A66	50c ('74)	2.75	4.00
319c	A66	$1	2.75	4.50
320c	A66	$2	2.75	4.50
		Nos. 306c-320a (13)	60.40	44.35

Issued: 20c, $1, $2, 11/17; 3c, 5c, 3/8; 4c, 6c, 8c, 15c, 25c, 4/11; 2c, 12/12; 40c, 50c, 3/15.

1975-77 Wmk. 373

305b	A65	1c	1.00	4.50
306b	A65	2c	.80	4.50
307b	A65	3c	.45	4.50
308b	A65	4c ('76)	3.50	.25
309b	A65	5c	1.30	4.75
310b	A65	6c ('76)	2.90	.25
311b	A65	8c ('76)	.35	.25
312b	A65	10c	.40	2.50
313b	A65	15c ('76)	2.60	.50
314b	A65	20c ('77)	3.75	.65
316b	A66	30c ('76)	5.00	1.10
317b	A66	40c ('76)	4.50	.65
318b	A66	50c ('76)	3.00	.65
319b	A66	$1 ('76)	3.00	1.05
320b	A66	$2	1.45	1.05
		Nos. 305b-320b (15)	34.00	27.10

Issued: 1c, 2c, 3c, 5c, 10c, 4/9; 20c, 7/15; others, 9/3.

Women's Basketball — A67

1971, Sept. 6 Wmk. 314 Perf. 14

321	A67	8c shown	.25	.25
322	A67	10c Running	.50	.50
323	A67	25c Weight lifting	1.00	.95
		Nos. 321-323 (3)	1.75	1.70

4th South Pacific Games, Papeete, French Polynesia, Sept. 8-19.

Community Education — A68

Designs: 4c, Public health. 50c, Economic growth (farm scenes).

1972, Feb. 7

324	A68	2c bright rose & multi	.25	.25
325	A68	4c gray & multi	.25	.25
326	A68	50c bright blue & multi	1.05	1.05
		Nos. 324-326 (3)	1.55	1.55

South Pacific Commission, 25th anniv.

Arts Festival Emblem — A69

1972, Apr. 10

| 327 | A69 | 10c blue, org & black | .40 | .40 |

South Pacific Festival of Arts, May 6-20.

Silver Wedding Issue, 1972
Common Design Type

Queen Elizabeth II, Prince Philip, flowers, shells.

1972, Nov. 20 Photo. Perf. 14x14½

328	CD324	10c slate grn & multi	.25	.25
329	CD324	25c red lilac & multi	.45	.45
a.		Blue omitted	550.00	

On No. 329a, Prince Philip's coat is brown instead of blue.

Rugby — A70

1973, Mar. 9 Litho. Perf. 14

330	A70	2c shown	.40	.40
331	A70	8c Tackle	.80	.80
332	A70	25c Kicking ball	1.05	1.05
		Nos. 330-332 (3)	2.25	2.25

60th anniversary of Fiji Rugby Union.

Forestry Development A71

Development projects: 8c, Irrigation of rice field. 10c, Low income housing. 25c, Highway construction.

1973, July 23 Perf. 14

333	A71	5c multicolored	.25	.15
334	A71	8c multicolored	.35	.25
335	A71	10c multicolored	.40	.25
336	A71	25c multicolored	.70	.75
		Nos. 333-336 (4)	1.70	1.70

Holy Family — A72

Festivals: 10c, Diwali (Candles; Indian New Year). 20c, Id-Ul-Fitar (Friendly greeting and mosque; Moslem, Ramadan). 25c, Chinese New Year (dragon dance).

1973, Oct. 26 Perf. 14x14½

337	A72	3c blue & multi	.30	.25
338	A72	10c purple & multi	.30	.25
339	A72	20c emerald & multi	.55	.60
340	A72	25c red & multi	.55	.60
		Nos. 337-340 (4)	1.70	1.70

Festivals celebrated by various groups in Fiji.

Runners — A73

1974, Jan. 7

341	A73	3c shown	.40	.25
342	A73	8c Boxing	.40	.25
343	A73	50c Lawn bowling	1.20	1.50
		Nos. 341-343 (3)	2.00	2.00

10th British Commonwealth Games, Christchurch, N.Z., Jan. 24-Feb. 2.

Centenary of Cricket in Fiji — A74

Designs: 3c, Bowler. 25c, Batsman and wicketkeeper. 40c, Fielder, horiz.

Perf. 14x14½, 14½x14
1974, Feb. 21 Litho.

344	A74	3c multicolored	1.10	.25
345	A74	25c multicolored	1.35	.25
346	A74	40c multicolored	1.60	2.25
		Nos. 344-346 (3)	4.05	2.75

Mailman and UPU Emblem — A75

UPU Emblem and: 8c, Loading mail on ship. 30c, Post office and truck. 50c, Jet.

1974, May 22 Wmk. 314 Perf. 14

347	A75	3c orange & multi	.25	.25
348	A75	8c multicolored	.30	.25
349	A75	30c lt blue & multi	.45	.40
350	A75	50c multicolored	.90	1.00
		Nos. 347-350 (4)	1.90	1.90

Centenary of the Universal Postal Union.

Cub Scouts — A76

Designs: 10c, Boy Scouts reading map. 40c, Scouts and Fiji flag, vert.

1974, Aug. 30

351	A76	3c multicolored	.25	.25
352	A76	10c multicolored	.50	.25
353	A76	40c multicolored	1.25	1.80
		Nos. 351-353 (3)	2.00	2.30

First National Boy Scout Jamboree, Lautoka, Viti Levu Island.

Cakobau Club and Flag — A77

King Cakobau, Queen Victoria — A78

Designs: 50c, Signing ceremony at Levuka.

1974, Oct. 9 Litho. Perf. 13½x13

354	A77	3c multicolored	.25	.25
355	A78	8c multicolored	.25	.25
356	A78	50c multicolored	.60	.60
		Nos. 354-356 (3)	1.10	1.10

Deed of Cession, cent. and 4th anniv. of independence.

Diwali, Hindu Festival of Lights — A79

Designs: 15c, Id-Ul-Fitar (women exchanging greetings under moon). 25c, Chinese New Year (girl twirling streamer, and fireworks). 30c, Christmas (man and woman singing hymns, and star).

1975, Oct. 31 Wmk. 373 Perf. 14

357	A79	3c black & multi	.25	.25
358	A79	15c black & multi	.45	.25
359	A79	25c black & multi	.85	.25
360	A79	30c black & multi	1.10	1.90
a.		Souvenir sheet of 4, #357-360	4.50	4.50
		Nos. 357-360 (4)	2.65	2.65

Festivals celebrated by various groups in Fiji.

Steam Locomotive No. 21 — A80

Sugar mill trains: 15c, Diesel locomotive No. 8. 20c, Diesel locomotive No. 1. 30c, Free passenger train.

1976, Jan. 26 Litho. Perf. 14½

361	A80	4c yellow & multi	.45	.25
362	A80	15c salmon & multi	.85	.40
363	A80	20c multicolored	.95	1.00
364	A80	30c blue & multi	1.20	1.80
		Nos. 361-364 (4)	3.45	3.45

Fiji Blind Society and Rotary Emblems — A81

Rotary Intl. of Fiji, 40th Anniv.: 25c, Ambulance and Rotary emblems.

Perf. 13x13½
1976, Mar. 26 Wmk. 373

365	A81	10c lt green, brn, ultra	.25	.25
366	A81	25c multicolored	.65	.65

De Havilland Drover A82

Planes: 15c, BAC One-Eleven. 25c, Hawker-Siddeley 748. 30c, Britten Norman Trislander.

1976, Sept. 1 Litho. Perf. 14

367	A82	4c multicolored	.60	.25
368	A82	15c multicolored	1.10	1.10
369	A82	25c multicolored	1.25	1.25
370	A82	30c multicolored	1.40	1.75
		Nos. 367-370 (4)	4.35	4.35

Fiji air service, 25th anniversary.

Queen's Visit, 1970 — A83

Designs: 25c, King Edward's Chair. 30c, Queen wearing cloth-of-gold supertunica.

1977, Feb. 7 Litho. Perf. 14x13½

371	A83	10c silver & multi	.25	.25
372	A83	25c silver & multi	.30	.25
373	A83	30c silver & multi	.40	.30
		Nos. 371-373 (3)	.95	.80

25th anniv. of reign of Elizabeth II.

World Map, Sinusoidal Projection A84

Design: 30c, Map showing Fiji Islands.

Wmk. 373
1977, Apr. 12 Litho. Perf. 14½

374	A84	4c multicolored	.25	.25
375	A84	30c multicolored	.60	.60

First Joint Council of Ministers Conference of the European Economic Community (EEC)

FIJI

and of African, Caribbean and Pacific States (ACP).

Hibiscus — A85

1977, Aug. 27	Wmk. 373		Perf. 14	
376	A85	4c red	.25	.25
377	A85	15c orange	.25	.25
378	A85	30c pink	.45	.30
379	A85	35c yellow	.75	.90
	Nos. 376-379 (4)		1.70	1.70

Fiji Hibiscus Festival, 21st anniversary.

Drua, Double Canoe — A86

Canoes: 15c, Tabilai. 25c, Takia, dugout outrigger canoe. 40c, Camakau.

1977, Nov. 7	Litho.		Perf. 14½	
380	A86	4c multicolored	.25	.25
381	A86	15c multicolored	.35	.30
382	A86	25c multicolored	.50	.45
383	A86	40c multicolored	.60	.70
	Nos. 380-383 (4)		1.70	1.70

Elizabeth II Coronation Anniversary Issue
Common Design Types
Souvenir Sheet
Unwmk.

1978, Apr. 21	Litho.		Perf. 15	
384	Sheet of 6		1.75	1.75
a.	CD326 25c White hart of Richard II		.25	.25
b.	CD327 25c Elizabeth II		.25	.25
c.	CD328 25c Banded iguana		.25	.25

No. 384 contains 2 se-tenant strips of Nos. 348a-348c, separated by horizontal gutter.

Southern Cross on Naselai Beach — A87

4c, Fiji Defence Force surrounding Southern Cross. 25c, Wright Flyer. 30c, Bristol F2B.

1978, June 26	Wmk. 373		Perf. 14½	
385	A87	4c multicolored	.25	.25
386	A87	15c multicolored	.40	.30
387	A87	25c multicolored	.75	.60
388	A87	30c multicolored	1.10	.75
	Nos. 385-388 (4)		2.50	1.90

50th anniv. of Kingsford-Smith's Trans-Pacific flight, May 31-June 10, 1928 (4c, 15c); 75th anniv. of Wright brothers' first powered flight, Dec. 17, 1903 (25c); 60th anniv. of Royal Air Force, Apr. 1, 1918 (30c).

Necklace of Sperm Whale Teeth — A88

Fiji artifacts: 4c, Wooden oil dish in shape of man, vert. 25c, Twin water bottles. 30c, Carved throwing club (Ula), vert.

1978, Aug. 14	Litho.		Perf. 14	
389	A88	4c multicolored	.25	.25
390	A88	15c multicolored	.25	.25
391	A88	25c multicolored	.30	.30
392	A88	30c multicolored	.45	.45
	Nos. 389-392 (4)		1.25	1.25

Christmas Wreath and Candles — A89

Festivals: 15c, Diwali (oil lamps). 25c, Id-Ul-Fitr (fruit, coffeepot and cups). 40c, Chinese New Year (paper dragon).

1978, Oct. 30			Perf. 14	
393	A89	4c multicolored	.25	.25
394	A89	15c multicolored	.25	.25
395	A89	25c multicolored	.35	.35
396	A89	40c multicolored	.55	.55
	Nos. 393-396 (4)		1.40	1.40

Banded Iguana — A90

Endangered species and Wildlife Fund emblem: 15c, Tree frog. 25c, Long-legged warbler. 30c, Pink-billed parrot finch.

1979, Mar. 19	Litho.		Wmk. 373	
397	A90	4c multicolored	1.25	.50
398	A90	15c multicolored	2.00	1.00
399	A90	25c multicolored	8.75	1.50
400	A90	30c multicolored	8.75	5.00
	Nos. 397-400 (4)		20.75	8.00

Indian Women Making Music — A91

15c, Indian men sitting around kava bowl. 30c, Indian sugar cane, houses. 40c, Sailing ship Leonidas, map of South Pacific.

1979, May 11	Wmk. 373		Perf. 14	
401	A91	4c multicolored	.25	.25
402	A91	15c multicolored	.25	.25
403	A91	30c multicolored	.35	.35
404	A91	40c multicolored	.50	.50
	Nos. 401-404 (4)		1.35	1.35

Arrival of Indians as indentured laborers, cent.

Soccer — A92

Games Emblem and: 15c, Rugby. 30c, Tennis. 40c, Weight lifting.

1979, July 2	Litho.		Perf. 14	
405	A92	4c multicolored	.30	.25
406	A92	15c multicolored	.40	.30
407	A92	30c multicolored	.80	.65
408	A92	40c multicolored	.95	1.25
	Nos. 405-408 (4)		2.45	2.45

6th South Pacific Games.

Old Town Hall, Suva — A93

2c, Dudley Church, Suva. 3c, Telecommunications building, Suva. 4c, 5c, Lautoka Mosque. 6c, GPO, Suva. 8c, 12c, Levuka Public School. 10c, Visitors' Bureau, Suva. 15c, Colonial War Memorial Hospital Suva. 18c, Labasa Sugar Mill. 20c, Rewa Bridge, Nausori. 30c Sacred Heart Cathedral, Suva. 35c Grand Pacific Hotel, Suva. 45c, Shiva Temple, Suva. 50c Serua Island Village. $1, Solo Lighthouse. $2, Baker memorial Hall, Nausori. $5, Government House.

Without Inscribed Date, except #411B (1991)
Chalky Paper (#409-411, 414, 416, 418-419, 425)
Ordinary Paper (#412-413, 415, 417, 420-424)

1979-94	Wmk. 373		Perf. 14	
409	A93	1c multicolored	.30	.60
a.	Ordinary paper		1.75	2.00
b.	Inscribed "1994"		2.00	3.00
410	A93	2c multicolored	.90	.75
a.	Ordinary paper		1.75	2.00
b.	Inscribed "1983"		1.00	.50
c.	Inscribed "1986"		1.50	.25
d.	Inscribed "1991"		.75	.75
e.	Inscribed "1993"		3.50	3.50
f.	Inscribed "1994"		1.00	1.50
411	A93	3c multicolored	.75	.75
a.	Ordinary paper		2.00	2.00
b.	Inscribed "1993"		4.50	4.50
411B	A93	4c multicolored	1.50	1.50
a.	Inscribed "1993"		6.00	6.00
b.	Inscribed "1994"		3.50	5.50
412	A93	5c multicolored	.25	.25
a.	Inscribed "1983"		.60	.25
413	A93	6c multicolored	.25	.75
a.	Inscribed "1983"		.30	.25
414	A93	10c multicolored	.40	.25
a.	Ordinary paper		2.00	1.75
b.	Inscribed "1991"		2.75	3.00
415	A93	12c multicolored	.40	2.75
a.	Inscribed "1993"		3.50	4.00
b.	Inscribed "1994"		2.00	3.50
416	A93	15c multicolored	.75	1.75
a.	Ordinary paper		1.75	1.75
b.	Inscribed "1991"		3.50	3.50
417	A93	18c multicolored	.30	.25
418	A93	20c multicolored	1.00	.25
a.	Ordinary paper		2.50	2.00
b.	Inscribed "1993"		3.75	3.75
c.	Inscribed "1994"		3.50	3.50
419	A93	30c multi, vert.	1.25	.60
a.	Ordinary paper		.60	1.75
420	A93	35c multicolored	.60	1.50
421	A93	45c multicolored	.45	.45
422	A93	50c multicolored	.60	.40
a.	Inscribed "1994"		3.50	4.00

Perf. 14x13½, 13½x14
Size: 45x29mm, 29x45mm (#423)

423	A93	$1 multi, vert.	1.50	2.50
424	A93	$2 multicolored	1.50	1.75
425	A93	$5 multicolored	2.50	2.75
	Nos. 409-425 (18)		15.20	18.60

Issued: 5c, 6c, 12c, 18c, 35c-$2, 12/22/80; No. 411B, 11/1991; others, 11/11/79.

1986-92			Wmk. 384	
With Date Inscription				
1986				
410g	A93	2c multicolored	1.25	1.25
413B	A93	8c multicolored	4.50	4.50
1988				
410h	A93	2c multicolored	1.00	1.00
411h	A93	3c multicolored	1.00	1.00
411Bh	A93	4c multicolored	1.00	1.00
418h	A93	20c multicolored	2.00	2.00
1990				
414i	A93	10c multicolored	1.50	1.50
418i	A93	20c multicolored	2.00	2.00
1991				
409j	A93	1c multicolored	1.75	3.50
410j	A93	2c multicolored	1.00	1.00
411j	A93	3c multicolored	1.75	1.75
411Bj	A93	4c multicolored	1.00	1.00
414j	A93	10c multicolored	2.00	2.00
416j	A93	15c multicolored	1.00	1.00
420j	A93	35c multicolored	2.75	2.75
422j	A93	50c multicolored	3.75	3.75
423j	A93	$1 multi, vert.	9.00	9.00
1992				
409k	A93	1c multicolored	2.00	2.00
411k	A93	3c multicolored	3.75	3.75
411Bk	A93	4c multicolored	3.75	3.75
416k	A93	15c multicolored	2.75	2.75
418k	A93	20c multicolored	5.50	5.50
420k	A93	35c multicolored	5.50	5.50
422k	A93	50c multicolored	5.50	5.50
423k	A93	$1 multi, vert.	11.00	11.00

Southern Cross, 1873, London 1980 Emblem — A94

1980, Apr. 28	Wmk. 373		Perf. 13½	
426	A94	6c shown	.25	.25
427	A94	20c Levuka, 1910	.35	.25
428	A94	45c Matua, 1936	.70	.50
429	A94	50c Oronsay, 1951	.70	1.00
	Nos. 426-429 (4)		2.00	2.00

London 80 Intl. Stamp Exhib., May 6-14.

Sovi Bay — A95

Designs: 20c, Yanuca Island, evening scene. 45c, Dravuni Beach. 50c, Wakaya Island.

1980, Aug. 18			Perf. 13½x14	
430	A95	6c shown	.25	.25
431	A95	20c multicolored	.25	.25
432	A95	45c multicolored	.40	.40
433	A95	50c multicolored	.40	.40
	Nos. 430-433 (4)		1.30	1.30

Opening of Parliament, 1979 — A96

1980, Oct. 6	Litho.		Perf. 13	
434	A96	6c shown	.25	.25
435	A96	20c Coat of arms, vert.	.35	.25
436	A96	45c Fiji flag	.50	.50
437	A96	50c Elizabeth II, vert.	.60	.65
	Nos. 434-437 (4)		1.70	1.65

Independence, 10th anniversary.

Coastal Scene, by Semisi Maya — A97

Intl. Year of the Disabled: Paintings and portrait of disabled artist Semisi Maya.

1981, Apr. 21	Wmk. 373		Perf. 14	
438	A97	6c shown	.25	.25
439	A97	35c Underwater Scene	.35	.35
440	A97	50c Maya Painting, vert.	.45	.45
441	A97	60c Peacock, vert.	.50	.50
	Nos. 438-441 (4)		1.55	1.55

Royal Wedding Issue
Common Design Type

1981, July 22	Wmk. 373		Perf. 14	
442	CD331	6c Bouquet	.25	.25
443	CD331	45c Charles	.40	.25
444	CD331	$1 Couple	.70	.85
	Nos. 442-444 (3)		1.35	1.35

Operator Assistance Center — A98

35c, Microwave station, map. 50c, Satellite earth station. 60c, Cableship Retriever.

1981, Aug. 7	Litho.		Perf. 14	
445	A98	6c shown	.25	.25
446	A98	35c multicolored	.50	.50
447	A98	50c multicolored	.60	.60
448	A98	60c multicolored	.75	.75
	Nos. 445-448 (4)		2.10	2.10

World Food Day — A99

1981, Sept. 21	Litho.		Perf. 14½x14	
449	A99	20c multicolored	.45	.25

Ratu Sir Lala Sukuna, First Legislative Council Speaker — A100

Designs: 35c, Mace, flag. 50c, Suva Civic Center. 60c, Emblem, participants' flags.

1981, Oct. 19	Litho.		Perf. 14	
450	A100	6c shown	.25	.25
451	A100	35c multicolored	.40	.25
452	A100	50c multicolored	.60	.60
	Nos. 450-452 (3)		1.25	1.25

Souvenir Sheet

453	A100	60c multicolored	1.10	1.10

27th Commonwealth Parliamentary Assoc. Conf., Suva.

World War II Aircraft — A101

6c, Bell P-39 Aircobra. 18c, Consolidated PBY-5 Catalina. 35c, Curtiss P-40 Warhawk. 60c, Short Singapore.

1981, Dec. 7	Litho.		Perf. 14	
454	A101	6c multi	1.50	.25
455	A101	18c multi	2.40	.30
456	A101	35c multi	3.25	.65
457	A101	60c multi	3.50	5.00
	Nos. 454-457 (4)		10.65	6.20

FIJI

Scouting Year — A102

1982, Feb. 22   Litho.   Perf. 14½
458	A102	6c Building	.35	.25
459	A102	20c Sailing, vert.	.60	.35
460	A102	45c Campfire	.75	.50
461	A102	60c Baden-Powell, vert.	1.00	1.00
		Nos. 458-461 (4)	2.70	2.10

Disciplined Forces — A103

Designs: 12c, UN checkpoint. 30c, Construction project. 40c, Police, car. 70c, Navy ship.

1982, May 10   Wmk. 373   Perf. 14
462	A103	12c multicolored	.60	.25
463	A103	30c multicolored	.70	.55
464	A103	40c multicolored	2.00	1.00
465	A103	70c multicolored	2.00	3.50
		Nos. 462-465 (4)	5.30	5.30

1982 World Cup — A104

Designs: 6c, Fiji Soccer Assoc. emblem. 18c, Flag, ball. 50c, Stadium. 90c, Emblem.

1982, June 15   Litho.   Perf. 14
466	A104	6c multicolored	.25	.25
467	A104	18c multicolored	.35	.25
468	A104	50c multicolored	.85	.50
469	A104	90c multicolored	1.25	1.60
		Nos. 466-469 (4)	2.70	2.60

Princess Diana Issue
Common Design Type

1982, July 1   Perf. 14½x14
470	CD333	20c Arms	.35	.35
471	CD333	35c Diana	.50	.35
472	CD333	45c Wedding	.65	.50
473	CD333	$1 Portrait	1.75	1.75
		Nos. 470-473 (4)	3.25	2.95

October Royal Visit — A105

1982, Nov. 1   Litho.   Perf. 14
474	A105	6c Duke of Edinburgh	.30	.30
475	A105	45c Elizabeth II	1.10	1.10

Souvenir Sheet
476		Sheet of 3	3.50	3.50
c.	A105	$1 Britannia	1.00	1.00

No. 476 contains Nos. 474-475 and 476c.

Christmas — A106

Designs: 6c, Holy Family. 20c, Adoration of the Kings. 35c, Carolers. $1, Faith, from The Three Virtues, by Raphael.

1982, Nov. 22   Perf. 14x14½
477	A106	6c multi	.25	.25
478	A106	20c multi	.40	.40
479	A106	35c multi	.70	.70
		Nos. 477-479 (3)	1.35	1.35

Souvenir Sheet
480	A106	$1 multi	2.00	2.00

Red-throated Lory — A107

Parrots: 40c, Blue-crowned lory. 55c, Sulphur-breasted musk parrot. 70c, Red-breasted musk parrot.

1983, Feb. 14   Litho.   Perf. 14
481	A107	20c shown	2.00	.30
482	A107	40c multicolored	2.50	.60
483	A107	55c multicolored	3.00	1.75
484	A107	70c multicolored	3.25	5.25
		Nos. 481-484 (4)	10.75	7.90

A108

Designs: 8c, Traditional house. 25c, Barefoot firewalkers. 50c, Sugar cane crop. 80c, Kava Yagona ceremony.

1983, Mar. 14
485	A108	8c multicolored	.25	.25
486	A108	25c multicolored	.30	.30
487	A108	50c multicolored	.50	.50
488	A108	80c multicolored	.65	.65
		Nos. 485-488 (4)	1.70	1.70

Commonwealth Day.

Manned Flight Bicentenary A109

1983, July 18   Wmk. 373   Perf. 14
489	A109	8c Montgolfiere, 1783	.45	.25
490	A109	20c Wright Flyer	.55	.35
491	A109	25c DC-3	.65	.40
492	A109	40c DeHavilland Comet	1.00	.70
493	A109	50c Boeing 747	1.15	.85
494	A109	58c Columbia space shuttle	1.35	1.00
		Nos. 489-494 (6)	5.15	3.55

Cordia Subcordata — A110

Flowers: 25c, Gmelina vitiensis. 40c, Carruthersia scandens. $1, Amylotheca insularum.

1983, Sept. 26   Litho.   Perf. 14
495	A110	8c shown	.25	.25
496	A110	25c multicolored	.45	.30
497	A110	40c multicolored	.55	.45
498	A110	$1 multicolored	.90	1.15
		Nos. 495-498 (4)	2.15	2.15

See Nos. 505-508.

Earth Satellite Station, Fijian Playing Lali — A111

Perf. 14x13½
1983, Nov. 7   Wmk. 373
499	A111	50c multicolored	.75	.75

Dacryopinax Spathularia — A112

Various fungi: 15c, Podoscypha involuta. 40c, Lentinus squarrosulus. 50c, Scleroderma flavidum. $1, Phillipsia domingensis.

1984, Jan. 9   Perf. 14x13½, 13½x14
500	A112	8c shown	1.25	.25
501	A112	15c multicolored	1.50	.45
502	A112	40c multicolored	2.50	1.10
503	A112	50c multicolored	2.50	1.50
504	A112	$1 multicolored	3.75	3.50
		Nos. 500-504 (5)	11.50	6.80

Flower Type of 1983

Designs: 15c, Pseuderanthemum laxiflorum. 20c, Storkiella vitiensis. 50c, Paphia vitiensis. 70c, Elaeocarpus storkii.

1984   Litho.   Perf. 14x14½
505	A110	15c multicolored	.40	.25
506	A110	20c multicolored	.50	.30
507	A110	50c multicolored	.70	.80
508	A110	70c multicolored	.80	1.05
		Nos. 505-508 (4)	2.40	2.40

Lloyd's List Issue
Common Design Type
Perf. 14½x14

1984, May 7   Wmk. 373
509	CD335	8c Tui Lau on reef	.80	.25
510	CD335	40c Tofua	1.50	.90
511	CD335	55c Canberra	1.50	1.50
512	CD335	60c Suva Wharf	1.50	2.25
		Nos. 509-512 (4)	5.30	4.90

Souvenir Sheet

1984 UPU Congress — A113

1984, June 14   Litho.   Perf. 14½
513	A113	25c Map	2.50	2.50

Ausipex '84 — A114

Designs: 8c, Yalavou cattle. 25c, Wailoa Power Station, vert. 40c, Boeing 737. $1, Cargo ship Fua Kavenga.

1984, Sept. 17   Wmk. 373
514	A114	8c multicolored	.25	.25
515	A114	25c multicolored	.50	.55
516	A114	40c multicolored	1.90	.95
517	A114	$1 multicolored	1.60	2.40
		Nos. 514-517 (4)	4.15	4.15

No. 515 is perf. 14½x14

Christmas A115

Designs: 8c, Church on hill. 20c, Sailing. 25c, Santa, children, tree. 40c, Going to church. $1, Family, tree, vert.

1984, Nov. 5   Litho.   Perf. 14
518	A115	8c multicolored	.25	.25
519	A115	20c multicolored	.50	.25
520	A115	25c multicolored	.50	.25
521	A115	40c multicolored	.50	.60
522	A115	$1 multicolored	.95	1.35
		Nos. 518-522 (5)	2.70	2.70

Butterflies A116

Designs: 8c, Monarch. 25c, Common eggfly. 40c, Long-tailed blue, vert. $1, Meadow argus, vert.

1985, Feb. 4   Perf. 14
523	A116	8c multicolored	2.00	.25
524	A116	25c multicolored	3.25	.80
525	A116	40c multicolored	4.00	1.40
526	A116	$1 multicolored	5.75	6.50
		Nos. 523-526 (4)	15.00	8.95

EXPO '85, Tsukuba, Japan — A117

Designs: 20c, Outrigger canoe, Toberua Island. 25c, Wainivula Falls. 50c, Mana Island. $1, Sawa-I-Lau Caves.

1985, Mar. 18   Litho.   Perf. 14
527	A117	20c multi	.90	.40
528	A117	25c multicolored	1.20	.50
529	A117	50c multicolored	1.35	1.25
530	A117	$1 multicolored	1.60	2.50
		Nos. 527-530 (4)	5.05	4.65

Queen Mother 85th Birthday Issue
Common Design Type

Designs: 8c, Holding Prince Andrew. 25c, With Prince Charles. 40c, On Oaks Day, Epsom Races. 50c, Holding Prince Henry. $1, In Royal Wedding Cavalcade, 1981.

Perf. 14½x14
1985, June 7   Wmk. 384
531	CD336	8c multicolored	.25	.25
532	CD336	25c multicolored	.40	.40
533	CD336	40c multicolored	1.00	.80
534	CD336	50c multicolored	1.00	1.20
		Nos. 531-534 (4)	2.65	2.65

Souvenir Sheet
535	CD336	$1 multicolored	3.50	3.50

Shallow Water Fish — A118

Designs: 40c, Horned squirrel fish. 50c, Yellow-banded goatfish. 55c, Fairy cod. $1, Peacock rock cod.

1985, Sept. 23   Perf. 14½
536	A118	40c multicolored	1.50	.75
537	A118	50c multicolored	1.75	1.00
538	A118	55c multicolored	2.00	1.50
539	A118	$1 multicolored	2.75	4.50
		Nos. 536-539 (4)	8.00	7.75

Sea Birds — A119

Designs: 15c, Collared petrel. 20c, Lesser frigate bird. 50c, Brown booby. $1, Crested tern.

1985, Nov. 4   Perf. 14
540	A119	15c multi	2.50	.45
541	A119	20c multi	2.50	.50
542	A119	50c multi	4.75	4.00
543	A119	$1 multi	7.25	8.00
		Nos. 540-543 (4)	17.00	12.95

Queen Elizabeth II 60th Birthday Issue
Common Design Type

20c, With the Duke of York at the Royal Tournament, 1936. 25c, On Buckingham Palace balcony, wedding of Princess Margaret and Anthony Armstrong-Jones, 1960. 40c, Inspecting the Guard of Honor, Suva, 1982.

FIJI

50c, State visit to Luxembourg, 1976. $1, Visiting Crown Agents' offices, 1983.

1986, Apr. 21   *Perf. 14x14½*   *Wmk. 384*
544	CD337	20c scar, blk & sil	.40	.30
545	CD337	25c ultra & multi	.40	.30
546	CD337	40c green & multi	.65	.50
547	CD337	50c violet & multi	.75	.75
548	CD337	$1 rose vio & multi	.80	1.15
	Nos. 544-548 (5)		3.00	3.00

Intl. Peace Year — A120

1986, June 23   *Wmk. 373*   *Perf. 14½*
549	A120	8c shown	.50	.25
550	A120	40c Dove	.85	1.10

Halley's Comet — A121

Designs: 25c, Newton's reflector telescope. 40c, Comet over Lomaiviti. $1, Comet nucleus, Giotto probe.

1986, July 7   *Perf. 13½*
551	A121	25c multicolored	2.00	.55
552	A121	40c multicolored	2.25	.95
553	A121	$1 multicolored	2.75	5.50
	Nos. 551-553 (3)		7.00	7.00

Reptiles and Amphibians A122

1986, Aug. 1   *Perf. 14½*
554	A122	8c Ground frog	1.05	.25
555	A122	20c Burrowing snake	1.50	.30
556	A122	25c Spotted gecko	1.50	.35
557	A122	40c Crested iguana	1.60	.85
558	A122	50c Blotched skink	1.60	2.50
559	A122	$1 Speckled skink	2.00	5.50
	Nos. 554-559 (6)		9.25	9.75

Ancient War Clubs — A123

1986, Nov. 10   *Wmk. 384*   *Perf. 14*
560	A123	25c Gatawaka	.95	.35
561	A123	40c Siriti	1.25	.60
562	A123	50c Bulibuli	1.40	1.60
563	A123	$1 Culacula	2.50	3.00
	Nos. 560-563 (4)		6.10	5.55

Cone Shells — A124

1987, Feb. 26   *Litho.*   *Perf. 14x14½*
564	A124	15c Weasel	1.25	.25
565	A124	20c Pertusus	1.25	.30
566	A124	25c Admiral	1.40	.30
567	A124	40c Leaden	1.50	1.00
568	A124	50c Imperial	1.75	2.25
569	A124	$1 Geography	2.00	5.00
	Nos. 564-569 (6)		9.15	9.10

Souvenir Sheet

Tagimoucia Flower — A125

1987, Apr. 23   *Wmk. 373*   *Perf. 14½*
570	A125	$1 multicolored	4.75	3.75

No. 570 Overprinted

1987, June 13
571	A125	$1 multicolored	40.00	40.00

Intl. Year of Shelter for the Homeless A126

Designs: 55c, Hut. 70c, Government housing.

1987, July 20   *Perf. 14*
572	A126	55c multicolored	.65	.65
573	A126	70c multicolored	.85	.85

Beetles A127

Designs: 20c, Bulbogaster ctenostomoides. 25c, Paracupta flaviventris. 40c, Cerambyrhynchus schoenherri. 50c, Rhinoscapha lagopyga. $1, Xixuthrus heros.

1987, Sept. 7   *Wmk. 384*
574	A127	20c multicolored	2.50	.45
575	A127	25c multicolored	2.50	.55
576	A127	40c multicolored	3.00	1.75
577	A127	50c multicolored	3.25	3.50
578	A127	$1 multicolored	4.00	8.50
	Nos. 574-578 (5)		15.25	14.75

Christmas A128

Designs: 8c, Holy Family, vert. 40c, Shepherds see star. 50c, Three Kings follow star. $1, Adoration of the Magi.

1987, Nov. 19
579	A128	8c multicolored	1.00	.25
580	A128	40c multicolored	2.25	.65
581	A128	50c multicolored	2.75	1.50
582	A128	$1 multicolored	3.75	5.00
	Nos. 579-582 (4)		9.75	7.40

World Expo '88, Apr. 30-Oct. 30, Brisbane, Australia — A129

1988, Apr. 27   *Litho.*   *Perf. 14*
583	A129	30c Windsurfing	1.60	1.60

Intl. Council of Women, Cent. — A130

1988, June 14
584	A130	45c Fiji Nouna	1.30	1.30

Pottery — A131

Designs: 9c, Lapita (bowl). 23c, Kuro (cooking pot). 58c, Saqa (Priest drinking vessel). 63c, Saqa, diff. 69c, Ramarama (oil lamp). 75c, Tall Kuro, vert.

Wmk. 384, 373 (69c)
1988, Aug. 29   *Litho.*   *Perf. 13½*
585	A131	9c multicolored	.25	.25
586	A131	23c multicolored	.40	.25
587	A131	58c multicolored	.80	.80
588	A131	63c multicolored	.90	.90
589	A131	69c multicolored	.95	1.00
590	A131	75c multicolored	1.10	1.20
	Nos. 585-590 (6)		4.40	4.40

Fiji Tree Frog — A132

1988, Oct. 3   *Wmk. 384*   *Perf. 14*
591	A132	18c multi	4.50	3.00
592	A132	23c multi, diff.	5.00	3.00
593	A132	30c multi, diff.	5.75	5.75
594	A132	45c multi, diff.	6.50	10.00
	Nos. 591-594 (4)		21.75	21.75

World Wildlife Fund.

Indigenous Flowering Plants — A133

Designs: 9c, Dendrobium mohlianum. 30c, Dendrobium cattilare. 45c, Degenaria vitiensis. $1, Degenaria roseiflora.

1988, Nov. 21   *Wmk. 373*
595	A133	9c multicolored	.85	.25
596	A133	30c multicolored	1.25	.45
597	A133	45c multicolored	.95	1.35
598	A133	$1 multicolored	1.75	2.75
	Nos. 595-598 (4)		4.80	4.80

Intl. Red Cross and Red Crescent Orgs., 125th Anniv. — A134

Designs: 58c, Battle of Solferino, 1859. 63c, Jean-Henri Dunant, vert. 69c, Medicine. $1, Anniv. emblem, vert.

1989, Feb. 6   *Wmk. 384*
599	A134	58c multicolored	1.75	1.00
600	A134	63c multicolored	1.75	1.10
601	A134	69c multicolored	2.25	1.40
602	A134	$1 multicolored	2.75	1.90
	Nos. 599-602 (4)		8.50	5.40

Epic Voyage of William Bligh — A135

Designs: 45c, Plans (line drawing) of the Bounty's launch. 58c, Diary and inscription on artifacts "The cup I eat my miserable allowance out of." 80c, Silhouette, lightning, quote "O Almighty God, relieve us. . ." $1, Map of Bligh's Islands, launch and compass rose.

1989, Apr. 28   *Perf. 14½*
603	A135	45c multicolored	2.10	.70
604	A135	58c multicolored	2.25	1.50
605	A135	80c multicolored	3.50	3.25
606	A135	$1 multicolored	4.75	3.50
	Nos. 603-606 (4)		12.60	8.95

Coral — A136

Designs: 46c, Platygyra daedalea. 60c, Caulastrea furcata. 75c, Acropora echinata. 90c, Acropora humilis.

1989, Aug. 21   *Wmk. 373*   *Perf. 14*
607	A136	46c multicolored	2.00	1.00
608	A136	60c multicolored	2.50	2.00
609	A136	75c multicolored	3.00	2.50
610	A136	90c multicolored	3.75	3.00
	Nos. 607-610 (4)		11.25	8.50

Nos. 609-610 vert.

1990 World Cup Soccer Championships, Italy — A137

Various Fijian soccer players.

1989, Sept. 25   *Wmk. 384*   *Perf. 14½*
611	A137	35c shown	1.35	.75
612	A137	63c multi, diff.	2.40	2.40
613	A137	70c multi, diff.	2.60	2.60
614	A137	85c multi, diff.	2.90	3.00
	Nos. 611-614 (4)		9.25	8.75

Christmas — A138

Designs: 9c, Church service. 45c, Delonix regia tree. $1, Holy family. $1.40, Tree, Fijian children.

1989, Nov. 1   *Wmk. 373*
615	A138	9c multicolored	.40	.25
616	A138	45c multicolored	1.00	.25
617	A138	$1 multicolored	2.00	2.10
618	A138	$1.40 multicolored	2.25	3.00
	Nos. 615-618 (4)		5.65	5.60

Fish — A139

Designs: 50c, Mangrove jack. 70c, Orange-spotted therapon perch. 85c, Spotted scat. $1, Flagtail.

1990, Apr. 23   *Litho.*   *Wmk. 384*
619	A139	50c multicolored	2.60	1.00
620	A139	70c multicolored	3.50	3.50
621	A139	85c multicolored	3.75	3.75
622	A139	$1 multicolored	4.25	4.25
	Nos. 619-622 (4)		14.10	12.50

Souvenir Sheet

Stamp World London '90 A140

1990, May 1
623	A140	Sheet of 2	12.50	9.50
a.		$1 No. 243	3.75	2.60
b.		$2 No. 249	8.00	6.00

FIJI

Soil Conservation A141

50c, Vertiver grass contours. 70c, Mulching. 90c, Contour cultivation. $1, Proper land use.

1990, July 23   Litho.   Wmk. 373
625	A141	50c multi	1.25	.65
626	A141	70c multi	1.75	1.75
627	A141	90c multi	1.90	2.25
628	A141	$1 multi, vert.	2.00	2.50
		Nos. 625-628 (4)	6.90	7.15

Trees — A142

25c, Dacrydium nidulum. 35c, Decussocarpus vitiensis. $1, Agathis vitiensis. $1.55, Santalum yasi.

1990, Oct. 2
629	A142	25c multi	.90	.25
630	A142	35c multi	1.00	.35
631	A142	$1 multi	3.00	3.00
632	A142	$1.55 multi	4.25	5.50
		Nos. 629-632 (4)	9.15	9.10

Christmas A143

Christmas carols: 10c, Hark! The Herald Angels Sing. 35c, Silent Night. 65c, Joy to the World! $1, The Race that Long in Darkness Pined.

1990, Nov. 26   Wmk. 373   Perf. 14
633	A143	10c multicolored	.40	.25
634	A143	35c multicolored	1.00	.35
635	A143	65c multicolored	1.60	1.75
636	A143	$1 multicolored	2.50	2.75
		Nos. 633-636 (4)	5.50	5.10

Scenic Views — A144

Designs: 35c, Sigatoka sand dunes. 50c, Monu, Monuriki Islands. 65c, Ravilevu Nature Reserve. $1, Colo-I-Suva Forest Park.

1991, Feb. 25   Wmk. 384
637	A144	35c multicolored	1.35	.35
638	A144	50c multicolored	2.25	1.25
639	A144	65c multicolored	2.60	2.75
640	A144	$1 multicolored	4.00	4.50
		Nos. 637-640 (4)	10.20	8.85

Discovery of Rotuma Island, Bicent. — A145

Designs: 54c, HMS Pandora. 70c, Map of Rotuma Island. 75c, Natives. $1, Mt. Solroroa, Uea Island.

1991, Aug. 8   Wmk. 373   Perf. 14
641	A145	54c multicolored	2.75	1.25
642	A145	70c multicolored	3.00	3.00
643	A145	75c multicolored	3.00	3.00
644	A145	$1 multicolored	4.75	4.75
		Nos. 641-644 (4)	13.50	12.00

Crabs — A146

Designs: 38c, Scylla serrata. 54c, Metopograpsus messor. 96c, Parasesarma erythrodactyla. $1.65, Cardisoma carnifex.

1991, Sept. 26   Perf. 14½x14
645	A146	38c multicolored	1.15	.45
646	A146	54c multicolored	1.75	.75
647	A146	96c multicolored	2.90	2.75
648	A146	$1.65 multicolored	4.00	5.50
		Nos. 645-648 (4)	9.80	9.45

Christmas — A147

Designs: 11c, Mary, Joseph travelling to Bethlehem. 75c, Manger scene. 96c, Jesus being baptized at temple in Jerusalem. $1, Baby Jesus.

1991, Oct. 31   Wmk. 384   Perf. 14
649	A147	11c multicolored	.65	.25
650	A147	75c multicolroed	2.00	.75
651	A147	96c multicolored	2.10	2.50
652	A147	$1 multicolored	2.25	2.50
		Nos. 649-652 (4)	7.00	6.00

No. 649 exists with wmk. 373.

Air Pacific, 40th Anniv. — A148

Airplanes: 54c, Dragon Rapide, Harold Gatty, founder. 75c, Douglas DC3. 96c, ATR 42. $1.40, Boeing 767.

1991, Nov. 18   Perf. 14½
653	A148	54c multicolored	2.40	1.25
654	A148	75c multicolored	3.25	2.50
655	A148	96c multicolored	3.50	3.50
656	A148	$1.40 multicolored	4.75	5.00
		Nos. 653-656 (4)	13.90	12.25

Expo '92, Seville A149

Designs: 27c, Traditional dance and costumes. 75c, Faces of people. 96c, Train and gold bars. $1.40, Cruise ship in port.

Perf. 14½x14
1992, Mar. 23   Litho.   Wmk. 373
657	A149	27c multicolored	.75	.50
658	A149	75c multicolored	1.75	1.75
659	A149	96c multicolored	8.25	5.50
660	A149	$1.40 multicolored	8.75	8.25
		Nos. 657-660 (4)	19.50	16.00

Inter-Islands Shipping A150

1992, June 22   Perf. 14
661	A150	38c Tabusoro	2.75	.75
662	A150	54c Degei II	3.25	1.50
663	A150	$1.40 Dausoko	5.50	4.50
664	A150	$1.65 Nivanga	5.50	4.50
		Nos. 661-664 (4)	17.00	11.25

1992 Summer Olympics, Barcelona — A151

1992, July 30   Perf. 13½
665	A151	20c Running	1.00	1.00
666	A151	86c Yachting	3.00	2.50
667	A151	$1.34 Swimming	3.50	4.00
668	A151	$1.50 Judo	3.50	4.00
		Nos. 665-668 (4)	11.00	10.75

Levuka — A152

30c, European War Memorial. 42c, Map. 59c, Beach Street. 77c, Sacred Heart Church, vert. $2, Deed of Cession Site, vert.

1992, Sept. 21   Perf. 14½
669	A152	30c multicolored	.45	.30
670	A152	42c multicolored	.65	.50
671	A152	59c multicolored	.95	.95
672	A152	77c multicolored	1.20	1.25
673	A152	$2 multicolored	2.50	2.75
		Nos. 669-673 (5)	5.75	5.75

Intl. Planned Parenthood Federation, 40th Anniv. — A153

1992, Nov. 2   Perf. 15x14½
674	A153	77c Globe	1.35	1.00
675	A153	$2 Family	3.50	3.50

Christmas A154

Bible interpretations: 12c, "God so loved the world..." 77c, "We love because God first loved us." 83c, "It is more blessed to give..." $2, "Every good gift..."

1992, Nov. 17
676	A154	12c multicolored	.75	.25
677	A154	77c multicolored	2.25	1.75
678	A154	83c multicolored	2.50	2.00
679	A154	$2 multicolored	4.00	5.50
		Nos. 676-679 (4)	9.50	9.50

Peace Corps in Fiji, 25th Anniv. — A155

Designs: 59c, Voluntary service. 77c, Fiji/US friendship. $1, Education. $2, Income generating business through volunteer help.

Wmk. 373
1993, Feb. 22   Litho.   Perf. 14½
680	A155	59c multicolored	1.40	.75
681	A155	77c multicolored	1.90	1.00
682	A155	$1 multicolored	2.00	1.50
683	A155	$2 multicolored	3.50	5.00
		Nos. 680-683 (4)	8.80	8.25

Hong Kong Rugby Sevens — A156

Designs: 77c, Players performing traditional Cibi Dance. $1.06, Two players, map of Fiji, Hong Kong, and Australia. $2, Stadium, players in scrum.

Perf. 14x15
1993, Mar. 26   Litho.   Wmk. 384
684	A156	77c multicolored	1.75	1.50
685	A156	$1.06 multicolored	4.00	2.50
686	A156	$2 multicolored	4.25	5.50
		Nos. 684-686 (3)	10.00	9.50

Royal Air Force, 75th Anniv.
Common Design Type

Designs: 59c, Gloster Gauntlet. 77c, Armstrong Whitworth Whitley. 83c, Bristol F2b. $2, Hawker Tempest.

No. 691: a, Vickers Vildebeest. b, Handley Page Hampden. c, Vickers Vimy. d, British Aerospace Hawk.

1993, Apr. 1   Perf. 14
687	CD350	59c multicolored	1.50	.75
688	CD350	77c multicolored	1.75	1.40
689	CD350	83c multicolored	2.25	1.75
690	CD350	$2 multicolored	3.50	4.75
		Nos. 687-690 (4)	9.00	8.65

Souvenir Sheet of 4
691	CD350	$1 #a.-d.	8.75	8.75
e.		Overprinted in sheet margin	9.75	9.75

Overprint on No. 691e is exhibition emblem for Hong Kong '94.

Nudibranchs A157

12c, Chromodoris fidelis. 42c, Halgerda carlsoni. 53c, Chromodoris lochi. 83c, Glaucus atlanticus. $1, Phyllidia bourguini. $2, Hexabranchus sanguineus.

Wmk. 373
1993, July 27   Litho.   Perf. 14
692	A157	12c multicolored	.80	.25
693	A157	42c multicolored	1.60	.50
694	A157	53c multicolored	1.75	1.00
695	A157	83c multicolored	2.50	2.25
696	A157	$1 multicolored	2.90	2.25
697	A157	$2 multicolored	4.00	6.50
		Nos. 692-697 (6)	13.55	12.75

Tropical Fruit — A158

Wmk. 373
1993, Oct. 25   Litho.   Perf. 13½
698	A158	30c Mango	1.90	.50
699	A158	42c Guava	2.10	1.00
700	A158	$1 Lemon	3.75	3.00
701	A158	$2 Soursop	6.00	8.00
		Nos. 698-701 (4)	13.75	12.50

Souvenir Sheet

Hong Kong '94 A159

Butterflies: a, Caper white. b, Blue branded king crow. c, Vagrant. d, Glasswing

Perf. 14½x13
1994, Feb. 18   Litho.   Wmk. 373
702	A159	$1 Sheet of 4, #a.-d.	9.00	9.00

Easter A160

59c, The Last Supper. 77c, The Crucifixion. $1, The Resurrection. $2, Jesus showing his wounds to his disciples.

Perf. 14x15, 15x14
1994, Mar. 31   Litho.   Wmk. 373
703	A160	59c multi	1.35	.50
704	A160	77c multi, vert.	1.75	.75
705	A160	$1 multi	2.00	1.75
706	A160	$2 multi, vert.	3.75	5.25
		Nos. 703-706 (4)	8.85	8.25

Edible Seaweeds — A161

42c, Codium bulbopilum. 83c, Coulerpa racemosa. $1, Hypnea pannosa. $2, Graciliaria.

Wmk. 384

1994, June 6		Litho.	*Perf. 14*	
707	A161	42c multicolored	1.10	.40
708	A161	83c multicolored	2.25	1.60
709	A161	$1 multicolored	2.75	1.90
710	A161	$2 multicolored	4.00	6.25
	Nos. 707-710 (4)		10.10	10.15

Souvenir Sheet

White-Collared Kingfisher — A162

Designs: a, On branch. b, In flight.

Wmk. 373

1994, Aug.			Litho.	*Perf. 13½*	
711	A162	$1.50 Sheet of 2,		11.50	11.50
		#a.-b.		11.50	11.50
c.	Overprinted in sheet margin			11.50	11.50

Overprint on No. 711c consists of exhibition emblem and "JAKARTA '95."
Issued: #711, 8/16; #711c, 8/19.

Souvenir Sheet

Singpex '94 A163

Neoveitchia storckii: a, Complete tree. b, Fruits, inflorescence.

1994, Aug. 31		Wmk. 384	*Perf. 14*	
712	A163	$1.50 Sheet of 2, #a.-b.	9.00	9.00

First Catholic Missionaries in Fiji, 150th Anniv. — A164

Designs: 23c, Father Ioane Batita. 31c, Local catechist. 44c, Sacred Heart Cathedral. 63c, Lomary Church. 81c, Pope Gregory XVI. $2, Pope John Paul II.

Wmk. 373

1994, Dec. 16		Litho.	*Perf. 14*	
713	A164	23c multicolored	.50	.25
714	A164	31c multicolored	.60	.25
715	A164	44c multicolored	.80	.60
716	A164	63c multicolored	1.10	1.00
717	A164	81c multicolored	1.50	1.50
718	A164	$2 multicolored	4.00	4.75
	Nos. 713-718 (6)		8.50	8.35

Souvenir Sheet

Ecotourism in Fiji — A165

Designs: a, Waterfalls, banded iguana. b, Mountain trekking, Fiji tree frog. c, Bilibili River trip, kingfisher. d, Historic sites, flying fox.

Wmk. 373

1995, Mar. 27		Litho.	*Perf. 14*	
719	A165	81c Sheet of 4, #a.-d.	8.25	8.25

End of World War II, 50th Anniv. Common Design Types

Designs: 13c, Fijian regiment guarding crashed Japanese Zero Fighter. 63c, Kameli Airstrip, Solomon Islands, built by Fijian regiment. 87c, Corp. Sukanaivalu VC, Victoria Cross. $1.12, HMS Fiji.
$2, Reverse side of War Medal 1939-45.

Wmk. 373

1995, May 8		Litho.	*Perf. 13½*	
720	CD351	13c multicolored	1.25	.25
721	CD351	63c multicolored	2.75	1.75
722	CD351	87c multicolored	3.25	2.75
723	CD351	$1.12 multicolored	3.75	3.25
	Nos. 720-723 (4)		11.00	8.00

Souvenir Sheet
Perf. 14

724	CD352	$2 multicolored	6.50	6.50

Birds — A166

1c, Red-headed parrotfinch. 2c, Golden whistler. 3c, Ogea flycatcher. 4c, Peale's pigeon. 6c, Blue-crested broadbill. 13c, Island thrush. 23c, Many-colored fruit dove. 31c, Mangrove heron. 44c, Purple swamphen. 63c, Fiji goshawk. 81c, Kadavu fantail. 87c, Collared lory. $1, Scarlet robin. $2, Peregrine falcon. $3, Barn owl. $5, Yellow-breasted musk parrot.

1995		Litho.	Wmk. 373	*Perf. 13*	
725	A166	1c multi		1.00	1.75
726	A166	2c multi		1.00	1.75
727	A166	3c multi		1.00	1.75
728	A166	4c multi		1.00	1.75
729	A166	6c multi		1.00	1.75
730	A166	13c multi		.75	.25
731	A166	23c multi		.75	.30
732	A166	31c multi		.85	.35
733	A166	44c multi		1.00	.40
734	A166	63c multi		1.50	.50
735	A166	81c multi		1.75	.65
736	A166	87c multi		2.00	.75
737	A166	$1 multi		2.00	.85
738	A166	$2 multi		3.00	1.75
739	A166	$3 multi		4.25	3.75
739A	A166	$5 multi		4.50	5.50
	Nos. 725-739A (16)			27.35	23.80

Issued: 13c, 23c, 31c, 44c, 63c, 81c, $2, $3, 7/25; 1c, 2c, 3c, 4c, 6c, 87c, $1, $5, 11/7.
For surcharges, see Nos. 1149-1160, 1191-1197C, 1214-1223A, 1249-1254G, 1314-1317, 1346-1347, 1353-1356, 1370-1371, 1407A-1407B, 1466-1477.

Souvenir Sheet

Singapore '95 — A167

Orchids: a, Arundina graminifolia. b, Phaius tankervilliae.

Wmk. 373

1995, Sept. 1		Litho.	*Perf. 14*	
740	A167	$1 Sheet of 2, #a.-b.	7.50	7.50

Independence, 25th Anniv. — A168

Designs: 81c, Pres. Kamisese Mara, Parliament Building. 87c, Fijian youth. $1.06, Playing rugby. $2, Air Pacific Boeing 747.

Wmk. 373

1995, Oct. 4		Litho.	*Perf. 14*	
741	A168	81c multicolored	1.50	1.10
742	A168	87c multicolored	1.35	1.35
743	A168	$1.06 multicolored	2.10	2.25
744	A168	$2 multicolored	4.25	4.50
	Nos. 741-744 (4)		9.20	9.20

Christmas — A169

Paintings: 10c, Praying Madonna with the Crown of Stars, from Correggio Workshop. 63c, Madonna and Child with Crowns on porcelain. 87c, The Holy Virgin with the Holy Child and St. John, after Titian. $2, The Holy Family and St. John, from Rubens Workshop.

Wmk. 373

1995, Nov. 22		Litho.	*Perf. 13*	
745	A169	10c multicolored	.30	.25
746	A169	63c multicolored	1.20	1.00
747	A169	87c multicolored	1.60	1.50
748	A169	$2 multicolored	3.50	3.75
	Nos. 745-748 (4)		6.60	6.50

Arrival of Banabans in Fiji, 50th Anniv. — A170

Perf. 14x14½, 14½x14

1996, Jan. 24		Litho.	Wmk. 373	
749	A170	81c Trolling lure	2.25	1.25
750	A170	87c Canoes	2.50	1.25
751	A170	$1.12 Warrior, vert.	2.75	2.00
752	A170	$2 Frigate bird, vert.	5.25	7.00
	Nos. 749-752 (4)		12.75	11.50

A171

Radio, Cent.: 44c, L2B portable tape recorder. 63c, Fiji Broadcasting Center. 81c, Communications satellite in orbit. $3, Marconi.

Wmk. 373

1996, Mar. 11		Litho.	*Perf. 14½*	
753	A171	44c multicolored	.90	.50
754	A171	63c multicolored	1.25	.75
755	A171	81c multicolored	1.60	1.20
756	A171	$3 multicolored	5.25	6.50
	Nos. 753-756 (4)		9.00	9.00

A172

Ancient Chinese artifacts: 63c, Bronze monster mask and ring, c. 450 BC. 81c, Archer, 210 BC. $1, Plate, Hsuan Te Period, 1426-35. $2, Central Asian horseman, dated 706. 30c, Yan Deng Mountain.

Wmk. 384

1996, Apr. 25		Litho.	*Perf. 13½*	
757	A172	63c multicolored	1.25	.50
758	A172	81c multicolored	1.60	1.00
759	A172	$1 multicolored	2.00	1.50
760	A172	$2 multicolored	3.50	4.25
	Nos. 757-760 (4)		8.35	7.25

Souvenir Sheet
Perf. 13½x13

761	A172	30c multicolored	2.50	2.50

No. 761 contains one 48x76mm stamp.
CHINA '96, 9th Asian Intl. Philatelic Exhibition.

A173

Wmk. 373

1996, June 18		Litho.	*Perf. 14*	
762	A173	31c Hurdling	.65	.25
763	A173	63c Judo	1.50	1.00
764	A173	87c Sailboarding	2.10	1.75
765	A173	$1.12 Swimming	2.40	2.50
	Nos. 762-765 (4)		6.65	5.50

Souvenir Sheet

766	A173	$2 Athlete, 1896	3.75	3.75

Modern Olympic Games, cent.

A174

31c, Computerized telephone exchange, horiz. 44c, Mail being unloaded, horiz. 81c, Manual switchboard operator. $1, Mail delivery.
No. 771: a, #117. b, #527.

1996, July 1				
767	A174	31c multicolored	.60	.35
768	A174	44c multicolored	.85	.75
769	A174	81c multicolored	1.20	1.50
770	A174	$1 multicolored	2.10	2.10
	Nos. 767-770 (4)		4.75	4.70

Souvenir Sheet of 2

771	A174	$1.50 #a.-b.	8.25	8.25

Creation of independent Postal, Telecommunications Companies.

UNICEF, 50th Anniv. — A175

Designs: 81c, "Our children, our future." 87c, Village scene. $1, "Living in harmony the world over." $2, "Their future."

Wmk. 384

1996, Aug. 13		Litho.	*Perf. 14*	
772	A175	81c multicolored	2.00	1.50
773	A175	87c multicolored	2.00	1.50
774	A175	$1 multicolored	2.10	1.60
775	A175	$2 multicolored	3.25	4.75
	Nos. 772-775 (4)		9.35	9.35

Nadi Intl. Airport, 50th Anniv. — A176

Designs: 31c, First airplane in Fiji, 1921. 44c, Nadi Airport commences Commercial Operations, 1946. 63c, First jet in Fiji, 1959. 87c, Airport entrance. $1, Control tower, 1996. $2, Global positioning system, first commercial use, 1994.

Wmk. 373

1996, Oct. 1		Litho.	*Perf. 14*	
776	A176	31c multicolored	.80	.35
777	A176	44c multicolored	1.00	.50
778	A176	63c multicolored	1.60	1.15
779	A176	87c multicolored	1.75	1.60
780	A176	$1 multicolored	2.10	1.90
781	A176	$2 multicolored	3.50	5.00
	Nos. 776-781 (6)		10.75	10.50

Christmas A177

Scene from the Christmas story and native story or scene: 13c, Angel Gabriel & Mary, beating of Lali. 81c, Shepherds with sheep, Fijian canoe. $1, Wise men on camels, multiracial Fiji. $3, Mary, Christ Child in stable, blowing of conch shell.

1996, Nov. 20			Wmk. 373	
782	A177	13c multicolored	.50	.25
783	A177	81c multicolored	1.90	1.00
784	A177	$1 multicolored	2.10	1.50
785	A177	$3 multicolored	6.25	7.25
	Nos. 782-785 (4)		10.75	10.00

FIJI

Hong Kong '97 — A178

Cattle: a, Brahman. b, Freisian (Holstein). c, Hereford. d, Fiji draught bullock.

1997, Feb. 12
786 A178 $1 Sheet of 4, #a.-d.   8.50 8.50

Souvenir Sheet

Black-Faced Shrikebill — A179

1997, Feb. 21   *Perf. 14x15*
787 A179 $2 multicolored   4.25 4.25

Singpex '97.

 Orchids — A180

Designs: 81c, Dendrobium biflorum. 87c, Dendrobium dactylodes. $1.06, Spathoglottis pacifica. $2, Dendrobium macropus.

1997, Apr. 22   Wmk. 384   Litho.   *Perf. 14*
788 A180 81c multicolored   2.40 1.50
789 A180 87c multicolored   2.40 1.50

   Wmk. 373
790 A180 $1.06 multicolored   2.75 2.50
791 A180 $2 multicolored   4.50 4.50
   Nos. 788-791 (4)   12.05 10.00

Souvenir Sheet

Hawksbill Turtle — A181

Designs: a, 63c, Female laying eggs. b, 81c, Baby turtles emerging from nest. c, $1.06 Young turtles in water. d, $2, One adult in water, coral.

1997, May 26   Wmk. 373
792 A181 Sheet of 4, #a.-d.   10.00 10.00

Coral — A182

Designs: 63c, Branching hard coral. 87c, Massive hard coral. $1, Soft coral, sinularia. $3, Soft coral, dendronephthya.

1997, July 16   Wmk. 373   Litho.   *Perf. 14*
793 A182 63c multicolored   1.25 .50
794 A182 87c multicolored   1.90 1.00
795 A182 $1 multicolored   2.10 1.50
796 A182 $3 multicolored   5.25 7.50
   Nos. 793-796 (4)   10.50 10.50

Fijian Monkey-faced Bat — A183

63c, With nose pointed downward. 81c, Hanging below flower. $2, Between leaves on tree branch.

   Perf. 13½
1997, Oct. 15   Litho.   Unwmk.
797 A183 44c multicolored   1.00 .50
798 A183 63c multicolored   1.40 .75
799 A183 81c multicolored   1.75 1.15
800 A183 $2 multicolored   3.50 4.50
   a. Sheet, 2 each #797-800   15.50 15.50
   Nos. 797-800 (4)   7.65 6.90

World Wildlife Fund.

Christmas — A184

Designs: 13c, Angel, shepherd. 31c, Birth of Jesus. 87c, Magi. $3, Madonna and Child.

   Perf. 14x14½
1997, Nov. 18   Wmk. 373
801 A184 13c multicolored   .35 .25
802 A184 31c multicolored   .75 .25
803 A184 87c multicolored   1.75 .85
804 A184 $3 multicolored   4.25 5.75
   Nos. 801-804 (4)   7.10 7.10

 A185

1997 Rugby World Cup Sevens Champions: a, 50c, Waisale Serevi, captain, highest point scorer. b, 50c, Taniela Qauqau. c, 50c, Jope Tuikabe. d, 50c, Leveni Duvuduvukula. e, 50c, Inoke Maraiwai. f, 50c, Aminiasi Naituyaga. g, 60o, Lomeki Koroi. h, 50c, Marika Vunibaka, highest try scorer. i, 50c, Luke Erenavula. j, 50c, Manasa Bari. k, $1, Entire team.

1997, Oct. 30   Wmk. 373   Litho.   *Perf. 14*
805 A185 Sheet of 11, #a.-k.   14.50 14.50
   No. 805k is 53x39mm.

 A186

1998, Jan. 20   Wmk. 373   Litho.   *Perf. 14*
806 A186 81c multicolored   1.25 .75
807 A186 87c multicolored   1.25 1.00
808 A186 $1.12 multicolored   1.50 1.50
809 A186 $2 multicolored   2.75 3.50
   Nos. 806-809 (4)   6.75 6.75

Asian and Pacific Decade of Disabled Persons, 1993-2000 A187

63c, Mastering modern technology. 87c, Assisting the will to overcome. $1, Using natural born skills. $2, Competing to win.

   Wmk. 373
1998, Mar. 18   Litho.   *Perf. 13*
810 A187 63c multicolored   1.25 .60
811 A187 87c multicolored   1.50 .75
812 A187 $1 multicolored   1.50 1.40
813 A187 $2 multicolored   2.75 4.25
   Nos. 810-813 (4)   7.00 7.00

Royal Air Force, 80th Anniv.
Common Design Type of 1993 Re-Inscribed

Designs: 44c, R34 Airship. 63c, Handley Page Heyford. 87c, Supermarine Swift FR.5. $2, Westland Whirlwind.
No. 818: a, Sopwith Dolphin. b, Avro 504K. c, Vickers Warwick V. d, Shorts Belfast.

1998, Apr. 1   *Perf. 13½x14*
814 CD350 44c multicolored   1.00 .50
815 CD350 63c multicolored   1.25 .75
816 CD350 87c multicolored   1.75 1.50
817 CD350 $2 multicolored   3.00 3.00
   Nos. 814-817 (4)   7.00 5.75

Souvenir Sheet of 4

818 CD350 $1 #a.-d.   7.00 7.00

Diana, Princess of Wales (1961-97)
Common Design Type

Design: No. 819, Wearing plaid jacket. No. 820: a, Wearing blue jacket. b, In high-collared blouse. c, Holding flowers.

1998, Mar. 31   Litho.   *Perf. 14x14½*
819 CD355 81c multicolored   1.00 1.00
820 CD355 81c Sheet of 4, #819,
   a.-c.   4.25 4.25

No. 820 sold for $3.24 + 50c, with surtax from international sales being donated to the Princess Diana Memorial Fund and surtax from national sales being donated to designated local charity.

Sperm Whale A188

Designs: 81c, Adult, calf. 87c, Breaching. $2, Sperm whale tooth.

   Wmk. 373
1998, June 22   Litho.   *Perf. 14*
821 A188 63c shown   1.75 .75
822 A188 81c multi   1.90 1.00
823 A188 87c multi   2.25 1.25
824 A188 $2 multi   3.00 4.00
   a. Souvenir sheet   5.50 5.50
   Nos. 821-824 (4)   8.90 7.00

16th Commonwealth Games, Kuala Lumpur, Malaysia — A189

Designs: 44c, Athletics. 63c, Lawn bowls. 81c, Javelin. $1.12, Weight lifting. $2, Waisale Serevi, rugby sevens.

   Wmk. 384
1998, Sept. 11   Litho.   *Perf. 14*
825 A189 44c multi   .85 .35
826 A189 63c multi   1.00 .50
827 A189 81c multi   1.40 1.15
828 A189 $1.12 multi   1.75 2.50
   Nos. 825-828 (4)   6.00 4.60

Souvenir Sheet
829 A189 $2 multi   4.25 4.25

Maritime Heritage A190

Designs: 13c, Takia, hollowed-out log with outrigger. 44c, Camakau, sailing canoe. 87c, Drua, twin-hulled sailing canoe. $3, MV Pioneer motor yacht. $1.50, Camakau, map of Fiji.

   Wmk. 384
1998, Oct. 26   Litho.   *Perf. 13½*
830 A190 13c multicolored   .45 .25
831 A190 44c multicolored   .75 .35
832 A190 87c multicolored   1.40 1.00
833 A190 $3 multicolored   5.00 6.00
   Nos. 830-833 (4)   7.60 7.60

Souvenir Sheet
834 A190 $1.50 multicolored   3.75 3.75
Australia '99, World Stamp Expo (#834). See Nos. 843-847.

Christmas A191

Children's drawings: 13c, "Jesus in a Manger." 50c, "A Time for Family and Friends." $1, "What Christmas Means to Me," vert. $2, "The Joy of Christmas," vert.

1998, Nov. 23   Wmk. 373
835 A191 13c multicolored   .50 .25
836 A191 50c multicolored   1.20 .45
837 A191 $1 multicolored   2.00 1.10
838 A191 $2 multicolored   2.60 4.50
   Nos. 835-838 (4)   6.30 6.30

Traditional Dances — A192

Designs: 13c, Vakamalolo (women's sitting dance). 81c, Mekeiwau (club dance). 87c, Seasea (women's fan dance). $3, Meke ni yaqona (Kava serving dance).

   Wmk. 373
1999, Jan. 20   Litho.   *Perf. 14½*
839 A192 13c multicolored   .75 .25
840 A192 81c multicolored   1.75 1.25
841 A192 87c multicolored   1.75 1.25
842 A192 $3 multicolored   5.25 6.75
   Nos. 839-842 (4)   9.50 9.50

Maritime Heritage Type of 1998

Designs: 63c, SS Toufua, 1920-30's. 81c, MF Adi Beti, 1920-30's. $1, SS Niagara, 1920-30's. $2, MV Royal Viking Sun, 1990's. $1.50, SS. Makatea, 1920's.

1999, Mar. 19   Wmk. 384   *Perf. 13½*
843 A190 63c multicolored   1.60 .50
844 A190 81c multicolored   1.75 .75
845 A190 $1 multicolored   1.90 1.50
846 A190 $2 multicolored   3.00 4.00
   Nos. 843-846 (4)   8.25 6.75

Souvenir Sheet
847 A190 $1.50 multicolored   4.00 4.00
Australia '99, World Stamp Exhibition (#847).

Souvenir Sheet

Ducks A193

a, Wandering whistling. b, Pacific black.

1999, Apr. 27   Wmk. 373
848 A193 $2 Sheet of 2, #a.-b.   6.25 6.25
IBRA '99, Intl. Philatelic Exhibition, Nuremberg.

Orchids — A194

532 FIJI

Designs: 44c, Calanthe ventilabrum. 63c, Dendrobium prasinum. 81c, Dendrobium macrophyllum. $3, Dendrobium tokai.

1999, June 28

849	A194	44c multicolored	1.00	.50
850	A194	63c multicolored	1.25	.90
851	A194	81c multicolored	1.75	1.00
852	A194	$3 multicolored	4.00	5.00
		Nos. 849-852 (4)	8.00	7.40

1st Manned Moon Landing, 30th Anniv.
Common Design Type

13c, Astronaut waves goodbye. 87c, Stage 3 fires towards moon. $1, Aldrin walks on lunar surface. $2, Command module fires towards earth.

$2, Looking at earth from moon.

Perf. 14x13¾

1999, July 20 — Wmk. 384

853	CD357	13c multicolored	.60	.25
854	CD357	87c multicolored	1.35	1.10
855	CD357	$1 multicolored	1.45	1.25
856	CD357	$2 multicolored	2.60	2.60
		Nos. 853-856 (4)	6.00	5.20

Souvenir Sheet
Perf. 14

| 857 | CD357 | $2 multicolored | 3.25 | 3.25 |

No. 857 contains one circular stamp 40mm in diameter.

Queen Mother's Century
Common Design Type

Queen Mother: 13c, Visiting Hull to see bomb damage. 63c, With Prince Charles. 81c, As Colonel-in-Chief of Light Infantry. $3, With Prince Charles at Clarence House.

$2, With crowd on Armistice Day.

Wmk. 384

1999, Aug. 18 Litho. *Perf. 13½*

858	CD358	13c multicolored	.80	.50
859	CD358	63c multicolored	1.25	.75
860	CD358	81c multicolored	2.00	1.75
861	CD358	$3 multicolored	4.00	5.50
		Nos. 858-861 (4)	8.05	8.50

Souvenir Sheet

| 862 | CD358 | $2 multicolored | 4.75 | 4.75 |

UPU, 125th Anniv. A195

Sugar Mills rolling stock: 50c, Diesel locomotive. 87c, Steam locomotive. $1, Diesel locomotive, diff. $2, Free passenger train.

Wmk. 373

1999, Oct. 26 Litho. *Perf. 13¾*

863	A195	50c multicolored	.85	.40
864	A195	87c multicolored	1.25	.75
865	A195	$1 multicolored	1.40	1.10
866	A195	$2 multicolored	2.50	3.75
		Nos. 863-866 (4)	6.00	6.00

Christmas A196

Designs: 13c, Giving gifts. 31c, Angels and star. 63c, Bible, Magi, Holy family. 87c, Joseph, mary, donkey, vert. $1, Mary, Jesus, animals, vert. $2, Children, Santa, vert.

Perf. 13¼x13

1999, Nov. 29 Litho. Wmk. 373

867	A196	13c multicolored	.25	.25
868	A196	31c multicolored	.60	.35
869	A196	63c multicolored	.95	.50
870	A196	87c multicolored	1.15	.75
871	A196	$1 multicolored	1.30	.85
872	A196	$2 multicolored	2.25	3.50
		Nos. 867-872 (6)	6.50	6.20

Millennium — A197

Designs: No. 873, Outstretched hands, islands (arch at top). No. 874, Map, flag (arch at right). No. 875, Globe, warrior beating lali,

temple (arch at bottom). No. 876, Globe, drua, red line (arch at left).

No. 877: a, Fiji petrel (arch at top). b, Crested iguana, islands (arch at top). c, Red prawns (arch at bottom). d, Tagimaucia (arch at bottom).

Perf. 13¼ Syncopated Type A
Litho. with Foil Application

2000, Jan. 1 Unwmk.

873	A197	$5 gold & multi	7.00	7.00
874	A197	$5 gold & multi	7.00	7.00
875	A197	$5 gold & multi	7.00	7.00
876	A197	$5 gold & multi	7.00	7.00
		Nos. 873-876 (4)	28.00	28.00

Souvenir Sheet

| 877 | A197 | $10 Sheet of 4, #a-d | 60.00 | 60.00 |

Beetles A198

Designs: 15c, Paracupta sulcata. 87c, Agrilus sp. $1.06, Cyphogastra abdominalis. $2, Paracupta sp.

Perf. 13¾x14

2000, Mar. 14 Litho. Wmk. 373

878	A198	15c multi	.40	.25
879	A198	87c multi	1.20	.75
880	A198	$1.06 multi	1.45	1.50
881	A198	$2 multi	2.40	3.00
		Nos. 878-881 (4)	5.45	5.50

Sesame Street A199

No. 882: a, Big Bird. b, Oscar the Grouch. c, Cookie Monster. d, Grover. e, Elmo. f, Ernie. g, Zoe. h, The Count. i, Bert.
No. 883, Big Bird, Elmo and Ernie, horiz. No. 884, Cookie Monster, Bert and Ernie, horiz.

Perf. 14½x14¾

2000, Apr. 20 50c Sheet of 9, #a-i | 7.75 | 7.75

Souvenir Sheets
Perf. 14¾x14½

| 883 | A199 | $2 multi | 3.25 | 3.25 |
| 884 | A199 | $2 multi | 3.25 | 3.25 |

The Stamp Show 2000, London (#882).

Pres. Ratu Sir Kamisese Mara, 80th Birthday — A200

President with: 15c, Lumberjack, timber truck. 81c, Women. $1, Workers in cane field. $3, Ships.

2000, May 13 *Perf. 14x13¾*

885	A200	15c multi	.35	.25
886	A200	81c multi	.95	.65
887	A200	$1 multi	1.05	.75
888	A200	$3 multi	4.50	5.00
		Nos. 885-888 (4)	6.85	6.65

Prince William, 18th Birthday
Common Design Type

William: Nos. 889, 893a, As child, wearing fireman's helmet, vert. Nos. 890, 893b, Wearing navy suit, vert. Nos. 891, 893c, Wearing

scarf. Nos. 892, 893d, Wearing suit and wearing blue shirt. No. 893e, As child, wearing camouflage and beret.

Perf. 13¾x14¼, 14¼x13¾

2000, June 21 Wmk. 373
Stamps With White Border

889	CD359	$1 multi	1.35	1.35
890	CD359	$1 multi	1.35	1.35
891	CD359	$1 multi	1.35	1.35
892	CD359	$1 multi	1.35	1.35
		Nos. 889-892 (4)	5.40	5.40

Souvenir Sheet
Stamps Without White Border
Perf. 14¼

| 893 | CD359 | $1 Sheet of 5, #a-e | 7.50 | 7.50 |

2000 Summer Olympics, Sydney A201

Wmk. 373

2000, Aug. 8 Litho. *Perf. 13¾*

894	A201	44c Swimming, vert.	.75	.50
895	A201	87c Judo, vert.	1.15	.75
896	A201	$1 Running	1.25	1.25
897	A201	$2 Windsurfing	2.25	2.90
		Nos. 894-897 (4)	5.40	5.40

Souvenir Sheet

Alsmithia Longipes A202

No. 898: a, Red frond at R. b, Red frond at L. c, Yellow frond. d, Fruit.

Wmk. 373

2000, Sept. 12 Litho. *Perf. 13½*

| 898 | A202 | $1 Sheet of 4, #a-d | 6.50 | 6.50 |

Lapita Pottery Shards and Discovery Sites — A203

44c, Yanuca Island. 63c, Mago Island. $1, Ugaga Island. $2, Sigatoka sand dunes.

2000, Oct. 24 *Perf. 13¾*

| 899-902 | A203 | Set of 4 | 5.75 | 5.75 |

Christmas — A204

Designs: 15c, Jungle. 81c, Cliffside trail. 87c, Coastal village. $3, Outrigger canoe.

2000, Nov. 21

| 903-906 | A204 | Set of 4 | 6.25 | 6.25 |

Souvenir Sheet

Taveuni Rain Forest A205

Designs: a, Orange dove. b, Xixuthrus heyrovskyi.

Perf. 13¾x13½

2001, Feb. 1 Litho. Unwmk.

| 907 | A205 | $2 Sheet of 2, #a-b | 6.00 | 6.00 |

Moths — A206

Designs: 17c, Macroglossum hirundo vitiensis. 48c, Hippotion celerio. 69c, Gnathothlibus erotus eras. 89c, Theretra pinastrina intersecta. $1.17, Deilephila placida torenia. $2, Psilogramma jordana.

2001, Mar. 20 *Perf. 13¼x13¾*

| 908-913 | A206 | Set of 6 | 6.75 | 6.75 |

Souvenir Sheet

Gallus Gallus A207

Designs: a, Hen. b, Rooster.

2001, May 22 *Perf. 13¾x14*

| 914 | A207 | $2 Sheet of 2, #a-b | 7.00 | 7.00 |

Society for Prevention of Cruelty — A208

Designs: 34c, Girl, cat. 96c, Boy, dogs. $1.23, Girl, cat, diff. $2, Boy, dog.

Perf. 14x13¾

2001, June 26 Litho. Unwmk.

| 915-918 | A208 | Set of 4 | 6.50 | 6.50 |

Pigeons A209

Designs: 69c, White-throated. 89c, Pacific, vert. $1.23, Peal's, vert. $2, Rock.

2001, July 20 *Perf. 14x13¾, 13¾x14*

| 919-922 | A209 | Set of 4 | 7.25 | 7.25 |

Westpac Pacific Bank, 100th Anniv. in Fiji — A210

Bank office in: 48c, 1901. 96c, 1916. $1, 1934. $2, 2001.

2001, Aug. 10 *Perf. 13¼x13¾*

| 923-926 | A210 | Set of 4 | 5.00 | 5.00 |

Fish — A211

Designs: 50c, Yellowfin tuna. 96c, Wahoo. $1.17, Dolphin fish. $2, Pacific blue marlin.

2001, Aug. 23

| 927-930 | A211 | Set of 4 | 5.50 | 5.50 |

FIJI

Christmas — A212

Designs: 17c, Angel appears to Mary. 34c Nativity. 48c, Adoration of the shepherds. 69c, Adoration of the Magi. 89c, Flight to Egypt. $2, Fijian Christ child.

2001, Oct. 29   Litho.   Perf. 13¾x13¼
931-936 A212   Set of 6   6.75 6.75

Colonial Financial Services Group, 125th Anniv. in Fiji — A213

Designs: 17c, Bank office. 48c, Women using automatic teller machine. $1, Suva Private Hospital. $3, Hoisting of British flag.

2001, Nov. 16   Litho.   Perf. 13¼
937-940 A213   Set of 4   6.75 6.75

Air Pacific, 50th Anniv. — A214

No. 941: a, De Havilland Drover. b, Hawker Siddley HS-748. c, Douglas DC-10-30. d, Boeing 747-200.

2001, Nov. 30   Litho.   Perf. 13
941   Horiz. strip of 4   7.50 7.50
  a. A214 89c multi   1.50 1.50
  b. A214 96c multi   1.75 1.75
  c. A214 $1 multi   1.75 1.75
  d. A214 $2 multi   2.25 2.25

Spices — A215

Designs: 69c, Pepper. 89c, Nutmeg. $1, Vanilla. $2, Cinnamon.

2002, Mar. 12   Litho.   Perf. 13¼
942-945 A215   Set of 4   6.25 6.25

Souvenir Sheet

Balaka Palm A216

Palm and: a, Bird, butterfly, beetle. b, Lizard, butterfly

2002, Apr. 29
946 A216 $2 Sheet of 2, #a-b   6.75 6.75

Freshwater Fish — A217

Designs: 48c, Redigobius sp. 96c, Spotted flagtail. $1.23, Silverstripe mudskipper. $2, Snakehead gudgeon.

2002, May 13
947-950 A217   Set of 4   6.50 6.50

Fruit — A218

Designs: 25c, Breadfruit. 34c, Wi. $1, Jakfruit. $3, Avocado.

2002, July 25   Litho.   Perf. 13¾x13¼
951-954 A218   Set of 4   6.25 6.25

Murex Shells — A219

Designs: 69c, Saul's murex. 96c, Caltrop murex. $1, Purple Pacific drupe. $2, Ramose murex.

2002, Aug. 20   Perf. 13¾
955-958 A219   Set of 4   7.00 7.00

Fiji Goshawk — A220

Designs: 48c, Goshawk and eggs. 89c, Chicks in nest. $1, Juvenile on branch. $3, Adult.

2002, Sept. 10
959-962 A220   Set of 4   8.25 8.25

2002 Operation Open Heart Visit to Fiji — A221

Designs: 34c, Doctors performing operation, vert. 69c, Doctor listening to patient's heart with stethoscope. $1.17, Technician administering echocardiogram. $2, Administration of anesthesia to patient, vert.

2002, Oct. 30   Perf. 13¼
963-966 A221   Set of 4   7.25 7.25

Fiji Natural Artesian Water — A222

Designs: 25c, Bottle of water, flowers, vert. 48c, Bottling plant. $1, Delivery truck. $3, Children with bottled water, vert.

2002, Nov. 5
967-970 A222   Set of 4   7.50 7.50

Christmas — A223

Designs: 17c, Christian church. 89c, Mosque. $1, Hindu temple. $3, Christian church, diff.

2002, Nov. 20
971-974 A223   Set of 4   7.50 7.50

Post Fiji, Ltd. Improvements A224

Designs: 48c, General Post Office. 96c, Post Fiji Mail Center. $1, Post Fiji Logistics Center. $2, Smart Mail.

2003, Mar. 19   Litho.   Perf. 13¼
975-978 A224   Set of 4   6.75 6.75

Souvenir Sheet

Intl. Year of Fresh Water A225

No. 979: a, Top of waterfall, flowers. b, Base of waterfall, butterfly.

2003, Apr. 22
979 A225 $2 Sheet of 2, #a-b   7.25 7.25

2003 South Pacific Games, Suva — A226

Designs: 10c, Track athlete with arms raised. 14c, Baseball. 20c, Netball. No. 983, $5, Shot put.
No. 984, $5, Flags of participating nations, venues, volleyball players.

2003   Perf. 13¼
980-983 A226   Set of 4   7.25 7.25
Size: 120x85mm
Imperf
984 A226 $5 multi   6.75 6.75
Issued: Nos. 980-983, 5/26; No. 984, 6/28.

Fish — A227

Siganus uspi: 58c, Fish, crab and coral. 83c, Two fish and coral. $1.15, Two fish, coral, and other fish species. $3, Fish and coral.

2003, Aug. 12   Perf. 13¼
985-988 A227   Set of 4   8.50 8.50

Bird Life International — A228

Designs: 41c, Long-legged warbler. 60c, Silktail. $1.07, Red-throated lorikeet. $3, Pink-billed parrot finch.

2003, Sept. 16
989-992 A228   Set of 4   13.00 13.00

Geckos A229

Designs: 83c, Pacific slender-toed gecko. $1.07, Indopacific tree gecko. $1.15, Mann's gecko. $2, Voracious gecko.

2003, Oct. 21   Litho.   Perf. 13¼
993-996 A229   Set of 4   9.75 9.75

Christmas A230

Children's art: 18c, Children, Christmas tree. 41c, Children, flag of Fiji. 58c, Children, Santa Claus, reindeer pulling sleighs, vert. 83c, Santa Claus on chimney, gifts, children, Christmas tree, vert. $1.07, Children with candles, Christmas tree, vert. $1.15, Santa Claus, children, bell, rainbow, vert. $1.41, Handshake.

2003, Nov. 26   Litho.   Perf. 13¼
997-1002 A230   Set of 6   7.25 7.25
Souvenir Sheet
1003 A230 $1.41 multi   3.50 3.50

Tagimoucia A231

2003, Dec. 1   Litho.   Perf. 14½x14
1004 A231 50c multi + label   5.00 5.00
Sold in sheets of 10 stamps + 10 labels that could be personalized for $15 per sheet.

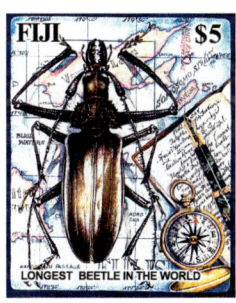

Xixuthrus Heyrovskyi, Longest Beetle in the World   A232

2003, Feb. 27   Imperf.
1005 A232 $5 multi   7.50 7.50

Miniature Sheet

Worldwide Fund for Nature (WWF) — A233

No. 1006: a, 58c, Skipjack tuna. b, 83c, Albacore tuna. c, $1.07, Yellowfin tuna. d, $3, Bigeye tuna.

2004, Apr. 7   Perf. 13¼
1006 A233   Sheet of 4, #a-d   8.50 8.50
  e. Like #1006, with artist's name at LL of each stamp   8.50 8.50

Land Snails A234

534 FIJI

Designs: 18c, Malleated placostyle. 41c, Kandavu placostyle. $1.15, Fragile orpiella. $3, Thin Fijian placostyle.

2004, May 28
1007-1010 A234 Set of 4 7.25 7.25

Bird Type of 1995 and

No. 1011A

Perf. 13¼x13
2004, June 26 Unwmk.
1011 A166 18c Island thrush 1.90 1.90
1011A A166 4c on 18c #1011 250.00 250.00

No. 1011A issued Aug. 2008. Surcharge on No. 1011A exists only inverted. Values are for stamps with surcharge at top, as shown. Value, with surcharge centered $400.

Coral Reef Shrimp — A235

Designs: 58c, Boxer shrimp. 83c, Bumblebee shrimp. $1.07, Mantis shrimp. $3, Anemone shrimp.

2004, June 30 Perf. 13¼
1012-1015 A235 Set of 4 7.25 7.25

Birds — A236

Designs: 41c, Wandering tattler. 58c, Whimbrel. $1.15, Pacific golden plover. $3, Bristle-thighed curlew.

2004, July 28
1016-1019 A236 Set of 4 10.00 10.00

2004 Summer Olympics, Athens — A237

Designs: 41c, Swimming. 58c, Judo, vert. $1.40, Weight lifting, vert. $2, Makelesi Bulikiobo, runner.

2004, Aug. 12
1020-1023 A237 Set of 4 7.25 7.25

Musket Cove to Port Vila Yacht Race, 25th Anniv. A238

Various yachts: 83c, $1.07, $1.15, $2. $1.07 and $2 are vert.

2004, Sept. 18 Perf. 14¼
1024-1027 A238 Set of 4 8.00 8.00
1027a Souvenir sheet of 1 4.25 4.25

Joint issue between Fiji and Vanuatu. See Vanuatu Nos. 858-861.

Souvenir Sheet

Coconut Crab A239

2004, Oct. 20 Litho. Perf. 14
1028 A239 $5 multi 7.50 7.50

Papilio Schmeltzii A240

Designs: 58c, Newly-emerged adult, vert. 83c, Larva. $1.41, Adult. $3, Pupa, vert.

Perf. 14x14½, 14½x14
2004, Nov. 10
1029-1032 A240 Set of 4 9.50 9.50

Christmas — A241

Designs: 18c, Annunciation. 58c, Infant in manger. $1.07, Madonna and child. $3, Adoration of the Shepherds.

2004, Dec. 1 Litho. Perf. 13¼
1033-1036 A241 Set of 4 9.00 9.00

Birds — A242

No. 1037: a, Little heron. b, Great white egret. c, White-faced heron. d, Pacific reef heron.

2005, Jan. 26
1037 Horiz. strip of 4 9.25 9.25
a.-d. A242 $1 Any single 2.25 2.25

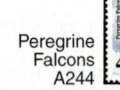

Flowers For Perfume — A243

Designs: 58c, Cananga odorata. $1.15, Euodia hortensis. $1.41, Pandanus tecorius. $2, Santalum yasi.

2005, Feb. 20 Perf. 14x14½
1038-1041 A243 Set of 4 7.50 7.50

Peregrine Falcons A244

Designs: 41c, Head of falcon. 83c, Adult at nest. $1.07, Chicks. $3, Adult on rock.

2005, Mar. 14 Litho. Perf. 14½x14
1042-1045 A244 Set of 4 9.50 9.50

Triggerfish A245

Designs: 58c, Whitebanded triggerfish. 83c, Yellow-spotted triggerfish. $1.15, Orange-lined triggerfish. $2, Clown triggerfish.

2005, Apr. 27
1046-1049 A245 Set of 4 8.00 8.00

European Philatelic Cooperation, 50th Anniv. (in 2006) — A246

Color of arches: 58c, Red. 83c, Blue green. $1.41, Purple. $4, Yellow bister.

2005, June 1 Perf. 13¾
1050-1053 A246 Set of 4 10.00 10.00
1053a Souvenir sheet, #1050-1053 10.00 10.00

Europa stamps, 50th anniv. (in 2006).

Miniature Sheet

End of World War II, 60th Anniv. A247

No. 1054: a, HMNZS Achilles. b, Japanese Yokosuka E14Y "Glen" over Suva Harbor. c, Fijian South Pacific Scouts in Solomon Islands. d, USS Chicago. e, Patrol vessel HMS Viti. f, British Prime Minister Winston Churchill. g, HMS Hood. h, Dambusters Raid. i, German King Tiger tank in Ardennes. j, Gen. Dwight D. Eisenhower.

2005, June 27 Litho. Perf. 13¾
1054 A247 83c Sheet of 10, #a-j 12.75 12.75

Game Fish — A248

Designs: 41c, Great barracuda. 58c, Narrow-barred Spanish mackerel. $1.07, Giant trevally. $3, Indo-Pacific sailfish.

2005, July 27 Litho. Perf. 14½x14
1055-1058 A248 Set of 4 8.75 8.75

Pope John Paul II (1920-2005) — A249

2005, Aug. 18 Perf. 14
1059 A249 $1 multi 2.50 2.50

Dragonflies A250

Designs: 83c, Yellow-striped flutterer. $1.07, Agrionoptera insignis. $1.15, Green skimmer. $2, Common percher.

2005, Aug. 30 Litho. Perf. 13¼
1060-1063 A250 Set of 4 7.50 7.50

Albert Einstein (1879-1955), Physicist — A251

Einstein: 83c, As a child. $1.07, In 1905. $1.15, And blackboard. $2, And galaxies.

2005, Sept. 27 Litho. Perf. 14¼x14
1064-1067 A251 Set of 4 9.25 9.25

Intl. Year of Physics.

Root Crops — A252

Designs: 41c, Manihot utilissima. 83c, Ipomoea satatas. $1.41, Colocasia esculenta. $2, Dioscorea sativa.

2005, Oct. 13 Perf. 13¼
1068-1071 A252 Set of 4 7.25 7.25

Tall Ships — A253

Designs: 83c, Eliza of Province. $1.15, Elbe. $1.41, HMS Rosario. $2, L'Astrolabe.

2005, Nov. 21 Litho. Perf. 14x14¼
1072-1075 A253 Set of 4 9.00 9.00

Barn Owls — A254

Owl: 18c, And eggs. $1.15, Juvenile. $1.41, With prey. $2, Perched.

2006, Jan. 10 Litho. Perf. 14¼x14
1076-1079 A254 Set of 4 9.75 9.75

Platymantis Vitianus A255

Various depictions: 50c, 83c, $1.15, $2.

2006, Feb. 8 Litho. Perf. 14x14¼
1080-1083 A255 Set of 4 8.00 8.00

Skinks — A256

Designs: 18c, Pygmy snake-eyed skink. 58c, Brown-tailed copper striped skink. $1.15, Pacific black skink. $3, Pacific blue-tailed skink.

2006, Mar. 22
1084-1087 A256 Set of 4 7.50 7.50

Queen Elizabeth II, 80th Birthday — A257

FIJI

Designs: 50c, As child. 65c, Wearing tiara. 90c, Wearing blue hat. $3, Wearing blue hat, diff.
No. 1092: a, Like 65c. b, Like 90c.

2006, Apr. 21   Litho.   Perf. 14
With White Frames
1088-1091 A257 Set of 4   7.00 7.00
Souvenir Sheet
Without White Frames
1092 A257 $2 Sheet of 2, #a-b   5.75 5.75

Miniature Sheet

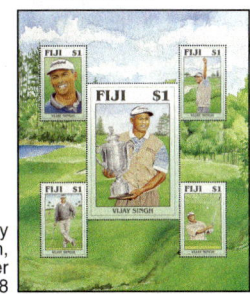

Vijay Singh, Golfer A258

No. 1097 — Singh: a, Head. b, With arm raised. c, Leaning on golf club. d, Hitting ball from sand trap. e, Holding trophy (60x87mm).

Perf. 14x14¼
2006, May 26   Litho.   Unwmk.
1097 A258 $1 Sheet of 5, #a-e   8.50 8.50

2006 World Cup Soccer Championships, Germany — A259

Various players: 65c, 90c, $1.20, $2.

2006, June 9   Perf. 14¼x14
1098-1101 A259 Set of 4   7.50 7.50

Souvenir Sheet

Purple Swamphen — A260

No. 1102: a, Swamphen and flowers. b, Swamphen on nest.

2006, July 20   Perf. 14½x14
1102 A260 $2 Sheet of 2, #a-b   6.50 6.50

Extinct Species A261

Designs: 50c, Brachylophus vitiensis. $1.10, Natunaornis gigoura, vert. $1.20, Vitirallus watlingi, vert. $1.50, Platymantis megabotoniviti.

Perf. 14x14¼, 14¼x14
2006, Aug. 15   Litho.
1103-1106 A261 Set of 4   7.00 7.00

Phasmids A262

Designs: 10c, Hermarchus apollonius. $1.10, Cotylosoma dipneusticum. $1.20, Chitoniscus feejeeanus. $2, Graeffea crouanii.

2006, Sept. 7   Perf. 14½x14
1107-1110 A262 Set of 4   7.00 7.00

Honey Production — A263

Designs: 18c, Bees and honeycomb. 40c, Apiarist examining honeycomb, horiz. $1, Woman and beehives, horiz. $3, Man and bottle of honey.

2006, Oct. 16   Perf. 14x14½, 14½x14
1111-1114 A263 Set of 4   7.50 7.50

Christmas — A264

Flowering plants: 18c, Decaspermum vitiense. 65c, Quisqualis indica. 90c, Mussaenda raiateensis. $3, Delonix regia.

2006, Dec. 5   Perf. 14x14½
1115-1118 A264 Set of 4   7.50 7.50

Anemonefish A265

Designs: 18c, Spine-cheek anemonefish. 60c, Pink anemonefish. 90c, Orange-fin anemonefish. $3, Dusky anemonefish.

Perf. 14½x14, 14x14½
2006, Nov. 7   Litho.
1119-1122 A265 Set of 4   7.50 7.50

Souvenir Sheet

Thalassina Anomala — A266

2007, Jan. 24   Perf. 13½
1123 A266 $4 multi   5.50 5.50

Traditional Architecture A267

Designs: 20c, Coastal dwelling. 65c, Inland dwelling. $1.10, Temple, Bau. $3, Lauan-style house.

2007, Mar. 20   Litho.   Perf. 13¼
1124-1127 A267 Set of 4   7.25 7.25

Freshwater Gobies A268

Designs: 20c, Sicyopterus lagocephalus. $1.10, Stiphodon rutilaureus. $1.20, Sicyopus zosterophorum. $2, Stiphodon sp.

2007, Apr. 5   Litho.   Perf. 13¼
1128-1131 A268 Set of 4   6.25 6.25

Birds Introduced to Fiji — A269

Designs: 50c, Red-vented bulbul. 65c, Spotted dove, horiz. $1.50, Australian magpie, horiz. $2, Java sparrow.

2007, May 22
1132-1135 A269 Set of 4   7.50 7.50

Scouting, Cent. — A270

Designs: 50c, Scout in kayak, hand holding compass. 90c, Three Scouts wearing helmets, hands tying knot. No. 1138, $1.50, Scout in harness climbing, Scout saluting. $2, Scout writing observation notes, hands tying neckerchief.
No. 1140, $1.50, vert.: a, Scout emblem. b, Lord Robert Baden-Powell.

2007, July 9   Perf. 13¾
1136-1139 A270 Set of 4   7.00 7.00
Souvenir Sheet
1140 A270 $1.50 Sheet of 2, #a-b   4.75 4.75

Snails — A271

Designs: 40c, Clithon diadema. 90c, Neritina variegata. $1.20, Fijidoma maculata. $2, Neritina squamaepicta.

2007, Aug. 18   Perf. 14x14¼
1141-1144 A271 Set of 4   6.50 6.50

Orchids — A272

Designs: 20c, Liparis layardii. 65c, Dendrobium catillare, horiz. $1.10, Dendrobium mohlianum, horiz. $3, Glomera montana.

Perf. 14¼x14, 14x14¼
2007, Aug. 21
1145-1148 A272 Set of 4   7.25 7.25

Nos. 725 and 729 Surcharged

No. 1149   No. 1150

Methods, Types and Watermarks As Before
2006-08
1149 A166 1c on 6c #729   1.50 1.50
1150 A166 1c on 6c #729   7.00 7.00

No. 1149 exists with inverted surcharge. Value, $90. No. 1149 also exists with double surcharge, one inverted. Value, $150. No. 1149 also exists with normal surcharge shifted 75% upward. Value, $50. No. 1149 exists with "c" omitted from surcharge.

No. 1151   No. 1152

No. 1152c

1151 A166 2c on 1c #725   4.50 4.50
1152 A166 2c on 1c #725,
           larger font   2.50 2.50
  c.   1½mm gap between "2" and
       "c" (position 67)   60.00 60.00

No. 1152 exists with normal surcharge shifted 50% upward. Value, $50.

No. 1152A   No. 1152Ab

No. 1152Ac

1152A A166 2c on 1c #725,
           4mm between "c"
           and obliterator   200.00 200.00
  b.   5mm between "c" and
       obliterator   200.00 200.00
  c.   3mm between "c" and
       obliterator   —

No. 1152Ab exists with inverted surcharge. Value, $375.

No. 1153   No. 1153a

No. 1153c

1153 A166 2c on 6c #729,
           4mm between
           "c" and obliterator   1.25 1.25
  a.   5mm between "c" and oblit-
       erator   1.25 1.25
  c.   1½mm gap between "2" and
       "c" (position 57)   60.00 60.00

No. 1153a exists with inverted surcharge. Value, $110. No. 1153a also exists with double surcharge, one inverted. Value, $150.

No. 1153B   No. 1154

No. 1154A

1153B A166 2c on 6c #729   550.00 550.00
1154 A166 3c on 1c #725   1.25 1.25
1154A A166 3c on 1c #725,
           larger font   650.00 650.00

No. 1154 exists with inverted surcharge. Value, $275. No. 1154 exists with double surcharge, one inverted. Value, $225.

FIJI

No. 1155

No. 1156

1155 A166 4c on 1c #725   1.50   1.50
  a. 1½mm gap between "4" and "c" (position 57)   60.00   60.00

No.
1155a

No.
1156a

1156 A166 4c on 6c #729, 4mm between "c" an obliterator   1.25   1.25
  a. 5mm between "c" and obliterator   1.25   1.25

No. 1156a exists with inverted surcharge. Value, $110. No. 1156a also exists with double surcharge, one inverted. Value, $150. No. 1156a also exists with normal surcharge shifted 75% upward and 50% upward. Values, each $50.

No. 1156B   No. 1157

1156B A166 6c on 6c #729   650.00   650.00
1157 A166 18c on 6c #729, 4mm between "c" and obliterator   6.50   6.50

No. 1157 exists with double surcharge, one with normal 4mm between "c" and obliterator and the other with 2½mm between "c" and obliterator. One surcharge is shifted 75% upward. Half of the errors have the normal separation between "c" and obliterator at top and half have it at bottom. Each error variety is equally scarce. Value, each $130. No. 1157 exists with double surcharge, both with 4mm between "c" and obliterator. Value, $150. No. 1157 also exists with normal surcharge shifted 75% upward but with no second surcharge. Value, $50.

No. 1158   No. 1158a

1158 A166 18c on 6c #729, 2½mm between "c" and obliterator   11.00   11.00
  a. 4mm between "c" and obliterator   22.00   22.00

No. 1158 exists with double surcharge. Value, $150. No. 1158 also exists with double surcharge, both inverted. Value, $225.

No. 1159   No. 1159a

1159 A166 20c on 6c #729, 2½mm between "c" and obliterator   6.50   6.50
  a. 4mm between "c" and obliterator   14.50   14.50

No. 1159 exists with inverted surcharge. Value, $110.

No. 1160   No. 1160a

No. 1160b

1160 A166 20c on 6c #729, 4mm between "c" and obliterator   30.00   30.00
  a. 1½mm between "c" and obliterator   60.00   60.00
  b. No gap between "c" and obliterator   475.00   475.00
  Nos. 1149-1160 (16)   2,125.   2,125.

No. 1160a exists with double surcharge. Value, $150.

Issued: No. 1149, 5/30/07; No. 1150, 9/19/07; No. 1151, 4/3; No. 1152, 11/13; No. 1152A, July 2007, No. 1152Ab, 8/20/08; No. 1153, 1153B 2/19/07; No. 1153a, 2/27/07; No. 1154, 3/13; No. 1155, 6/27; No. 1156, 6/6/07; No. 1156a, 2/19/08; No. 1156B, Feb. 2007; No. 1157, 6/8; No. 1158, 9/8; No. 1158a, Aug. 2007; No. 1159, 1/19/07; No. 1159a, Jan. 2007; No. 1160, 3/8/07; No. 1160a, 4/12/08.

Fish — A273

Designs: 50c, Coronation trout. 90c, Roving coral trout. $1.50, Squaretail coral trout. $2, Chinese footballer.

2007, Oct. 15   Litho.   *Perf. 13¼*
1161-1164 A273   Set of 4   7.75   7.75

Butterflies — A274

Designs: 20c, Polyura caphontis. $1.10, Hypolimnas bolina, horiz. $1.20, Doleschallia bisaltide, horiz. $2, Danaus hamata.

2007, Nov. 20   Litho.   *Perf. 13¼*
1165-1168 A274   Set of 4   6.00   6.00

Souvenir Sheet

Barred-winged Rail — A275

No. 1169: a, Head of adult. b, Chick.

2007, Dec. 3
1169 A275 $2 Sheet of 2, #a-b   5.50   5.50

National Medals — A276

Designs: 50c, Medal of the Order of Fiji. 65c, Member of the Order of Fiji. $1.20, Officer of the Order of Fiji. $2, Companion of the Order of Fiji.

2008, Feb. 20   Litho.   *Perf. 13¼*
1170-1173 A276   Set of 4   6.25   6.25

Souvenir Sheet

Spiny Lobster A277

2008, Apr. 22   Litho.   *Perf. 14x14½*
1174 A277 $4 multi   5.25   5.25

First Trans-Pacific Flight of the Southern Cross, 80th Anniv. A278

Southern Cross: 20c, Over Fiji. 90c, In Albert Park, Suva. $1.50, Surrounded by police guard. $2, With crew.

2008, June 13   *Perf. 13½*
1175-1178 A278   Set of 4   5.75   5.75

2008 Summer Olympics, Beijing — A279

Designs: 20c, Bamboo, Running. 65c, Dragon, Judo. 90c, Lanterns, Shooting. $1.50, Carp, Swimming.

2008, May 5   Litho.   *Perf. 13¼*
1179-1182 A279   Set of 4   4.25   4.25

Red-breasted Musk Parrot Varieties — A280

Prosopeia tabuensis: 65c, Koroensis. 90c, Atrogularis, horiz. $1.50, Taviunensis, horiz. $2, Splendens.

2008, Mar. 25   Litho.   *Perf. 13½*
1183-1186 A280   Set of 4   6.75   6.75

Humpback Whales A281

Humpback whale: 20c, Pair underwater. 50c, Breaching water's surface. $1.10, Reentering water. $3, Flukes.

2008, July 17   Litho.   *Perf. 14½x14*
1187-1190 A281   Set of 4   6.00   6.00

Nos. 729-731 Surcharged Like Nos. 1149-1160

No. 1191   No. 1191A

No. 1191Ab

Methods, Perfs and Watermarks As Before

2007-09
1191 A166 1c on 13c #730, 5mm between "c" and obliterator   1.50   1.50
  b. 4mm between "c" and obliterator (positions 3 and 89)   50.00   50.00
1191A A166 1c on 23c #731, 4mm between "c" and obliterator   1.00   1.00
  b. 5mm between "c" and obliterator   1.00   1.00
  c. Pair, Nos. 1191Ab and 1191A (positions 3 and 89)   50.00   50.00

No. 1191 exists with double surcharge, one inverted. Value, $150. No. 1191 exists with double surcharge: one upright with "XX" obliterator, the other inverted with "xxx" obliterator. Value, $175. No. 1191A exists with inverted surcharge. Value, $160. No. 1191A exists with a "2c" surcharge having a 1½mm gap between the "2" and the "c" (position 57). Value, $100. No. 1191Ab exists with inverted surcharge. Value, $160. No. 1191Ab also exists with double surcharge, one inverted. Value, $175.

No. 1191C   No. 1192

1191C A166 2c on 6c #729   175.00   175.00
  d. 1½mm gap between "2" and "c" (position 57)   —   —
1192 A166 2c on 6c #729   175.00   175.00
  c. 2½mm gap between pair of double bars of obliterator   400.00   400.00
  d. 4mm between "c" and obliterator   325.00   325.00

No. 1192 exists with obliterator of three double bars and with obliterator of four double bars. Value, each $500. No. 1192 exists with obliterator of two double bars and a single bar. Value, $400. No. 1192 exists with obliterator omitted. Value, $750.

No. 1192A   No. 1192Ab

No. 1193   No. 1193a

No. 1193B   No. 1193C

1192A A166 2c on 6c #729   175.00   175.00
  b. Short obliterator   250.00   250.00
  e. 4½mm obliterator   250.00   250.00
  f. 12½mm obliterator   250.00   250.00
1193 A166 2c on 13c #730, 5 mm between "c" and obliterator   1.50   1.50
  a. 4mm between "c" and obliterator (positions 3 and 89)   50.00   50.00

FIJI 537

1193B A166 2c on 23c #731, 5 mm between "c" and obliterator 125.00 125.00
   a. 4mm between "c" and obliterator (positions 3 and 89) 200.00 200.00
1193C A166 3c on 13c #730 175.00 175.00

No. 1192A has an 8mm obliterator. Two lines comprise the obliterator on No. 1192Ab: one long, one short. The obliterator on No. 1192Af extends into the right margin and must be collected with right selvage attached to show the entire obliterator.

No. 1193 exists with double surcharge, one inverted. Value, $150. No. 1193 exists with double surcharge: one upright with "XX" obliterator, the other inverted with "xxx" obliterator. Value, $175. No. 1193 exists with a period after the "2c." Value, $500.

No. 1194

No. 1195

No. 1195A

No. 1196

No. 1197

No. 1197a

1194 A166 4c on 13c #730, 5mm between "c" and obliterator 1.50 1.50
   a. 4mm between "c" and obliterator (positions 3 and 89) 50.00 50.00
   b. 1½mm gap between "4" and "c" 225.00 225.00
1195 A166 20c on 6c #729 100.00 100.00
   b. No gap between "c" and obliterator 550.00 550.00

No. 1194 exists with double surcharge, one inverted at top of stamp. Value, $200. No. 1194 exists with double surcharge, one inverted in center of stamp. Value, $200.

1195A A166 20c on 23c #731
   c. 3½mm between "c" and obliterator 400.00 400.00

No. 1195A exists with normal surcharge shifted 75% upward. Value, $300. No. 1195A also exists with inverted surcharge. Value, $350. No. 1195A also exists with "c" of surcharge omitted. Value, $400.

1196 A166 20c on 23c #731 2.00 2.00
   a. No gap between "c" and obliterator (position 70) 35.00 35.00

No. 1196 exists with inverted surcharge. Value, $90. No. 1196 also exists with double surcharge and with double surcharge, one inverted. Value, each $150. No. 1196 also exists surcharged on gum side only; the surcharge is always inverted. Value, $200. No. 1196 also exists surcharged on both sides. Value, $180.

No. 1197d

No. 1197e

No. 1197f

1197 A166 20c on 23c #731, 1½mm between "c" and obliterator 200.00 200.00
   a. 2½mm between "c" and obliterator 90.00 90.00
   d. 3mm between "c" and obliterator 100.00 100.00
   e. 4mm between "c" and obliterator 90.00 90.00
   f. 5mm between "c" and obliterator 175.00 175.00
   g. Pair, #1191A, 1197

No. 1197 exists with surcharge shifted 75% upward. Value, $175. No. 1197d exists with inverted surcharge. Value, $150.

No. 1197B

No. 1197C

1197B A166 20c on 23c #731 35.00 35.00
   a. No gap between "c" and obliterator (positions 70 and 79) 100.00 100.00
   c. 3mm between "c" and obliterator 70.00 70.00
1197C A166 20c on 23c #731 175.00 175.00
   a. No gap between "c" and obliterator 450.00 450.00
Nos. 1191-1197C (15) 1,743. 1,743.

No. 1197B exists with inverted surcharge. Value, $150. No. 1197C exists with inverted surcharge. Value, $350. No 1197C exists with obliterator of two double bars with a dash between them. Value, $450.

Issued: No. 1191, 8/22/08; No. 1191A, 12/18/08; No. 1191Ab, 1/23/09; No. 1191C, 1192, 1192A, 2/19/07; Nos. 1193, 1194, 8/20/08; No. 1195, 4/28/08; No. 1195A, Apr. 2008; Nos. 1196, 4/12/08; Nos. 1197, 1197a, 1197d, 1197e, 1197f. Apr. 2008; 1197B, 4/12/08; 1197C, Apr. 2008.

Bananas — A282

Various banana varieties: 65c, $1.10, $1.20, $2.

2008, Sept. 23   Litho.   Perf. 14x14½
1198-1201 A282   Set of 4   5.50 5.50

Eels — A283

Designs: 50c, Anguilla obscura. 90c, Anguilla marmorata. $1.50, Anguilla obscura, diff. $2, Gymnothorax polyuranodon.

2008, Oct. 15   Perf. 14½x14
1202-1205 A283   Set of 4   5.50 5.50

Christmas A284

Various choirs: 20c, 50c, 65c, $3.

2008, Dec. 10   Litho.   Perf. 14½x14
1206-1209 A284   Set of 4   4.50 4.50

Fruit Doves — A285

Designs: 50c, Many-colored fruit dove. 65c, Crimson-crowned fruit dove. 90c, Whistling dove. $3, Orange dove.

2009, Feb. 17   Litho.   Perf. 14x14½
1210-1213 A285   Set of 4   5.50 5.50

Nos. 729-731 Surcharged Like Nos. 1149-1160

No. 1214

No. 1214B

No. 1215

No. 1215A

Methods, Perfs and Watermarks As Before

2009-12
1214 A166 1c on 13c #730 45.00 45.00
   a. 2½mm gap between "c" and obliterator (positions 3 and 89) 120.00 120.00
1214B A166 1c on 13c #730, small font 90.00 90.00
1215 A166 1c on 23c #731 1.25 1.25
   b. 2½mm gap between "c" and obliterator (positions 3 and 89) 50.00 50.00
1215A A166 1c on 23c #731, small font 1.00 1.00

No. 1215 exists with inverted surcharge. Value, $90. No. 1215A exists with inverted surcharge. Value, $90. No. 1215A also exists with "xx" obliterator (position 70). Value, $300.

No. 1216

No. 1216A

No. 1216B

No. 1216D

1216 A166 2c on 6c #729 100.00 100.00
   a. 2½mm gap between "c" and obliterator (positions 3 and 89) 175.00 175.00
1216A A166 2c on 13c #730 45.00 45.00
   c. 2½mm gap between "c" and obliterator (positions 3 and 89) 120.00 120.00
1216B A166 2c on 23c #731 175.00 175.00
1216D A166 2c on 13c #730, small font 175.00 175.00

No. 1216D has a 2½mm gap between "c" and obliterator.

No. 1217

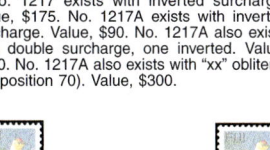
No. 1217A

1217 A166 2c on 23c #731 20.00 20.00
   b. 2½mm between "c" and obliterator (positions 3 and 89) 50.00 50.00
1217A A166 2c on 23c #731, small font 1.00 1.00

No. 1217 exists with inverted surcharge. Value, $175. No. 1217A exists with inverted surcharge. Value, $90. No. 1217A also exists with double surcharge, one inverted. Value, $120. No. 1217A also exists with "xx" obliterator (position 70). Value, $300.

No. 1218

No. 1218A

1218 A166 3c on 23c #731 45.00 45.00
   b. 2½mm between "c" and obliterator (positions 3 and 89) 140.00 140.00
1218A A166 3c on 23c #731, small font 1.00 1.00

No. 1218 exists with "3" of surcharge omitted. Most of the known singles have irregular perforations from being roughly removed from sheets. Value thus, $100. Errors with intact perforations are extremely scarce. Value, $300. Value of single error in pair with normal stamp, $350.

No. 1218A exists with double surcharge. Value, $150. No. 1218A exists with inverted surcharge. Value, $100. No. 1218A exists with double surcharge, one inverted. Value, $130. No. 1218A exists with "xx" obliterator (position 70). Value, $300.

No. 1219

No. 1219B

No. 1220

No. 1220B

No. 1220C

No. 1220D

1219 A166 4c on 6c #729 70.00 70.00
   a. 2½mm between "c" and obliterator (positions 3 and 89) 100.00 100.00
1219B A166 40c on 6c #729 100.00 100.00
   a. No gap between "c" and obliterator (position 70) 200.00 200.00
1219C A166 4c on 6c #729, small font 85.00 85.00
1220 A166 4c on 13c #730 45.00 45.00
   a. 2½mm between "c" and obliterator (positions 3 and 89) 120.00 120.00
1220B A166 5c on 13c #730 160.00 130.00
1220C A166 4c on 13c #730, small font 90.00 90.00
1220D A166 40c on 13c #730 400.00 400.00
   a. No gap between "c" and obliterator (position 70) —

Nos. 1219 and 1219a exist with inverted surcharge. Value, each $200. No. 1219C exists with inverted surcharge. Value, $175. No. 1219C also exists with double surcharge, one inverted. Value, $225. No. 1220C exists with inverted surcharge. Value, $100.

538 FIJI

No. 1221

No. 1222

No. 1222A — No. 1222C

1221	A166	4c on 23c #731	90.00	90.00
a.		4mm between "c" and obliterator (positions 3 and 89)	250.00	250.00
1222	A166	4c on 23c #731	1.50	1.50
b.		2½mm between "c" and obliterator (positions 3 and 89)	50.00	50.00
1222A	A166	4c on 23c #731, small font	1.00	1.00
1222C	A166	50c on 23c #731	300.00	300.00
a.		No gap between "c" and obliterator (position 70)	1,000.	

No. 1221 exists with inverted surcharge. Value, $150.

No. 1222 exists with inverted surcharge. Value, $90. No. 1222 exists with double surcharge, one inverted. Value, $130. No. 1222 exists with double surcharge, one with normal 4mm between "c" and obliterator and the other with 2½mm between "c" and obliterator. Value, $150.

No. 1222A exists with inverted surcharge. Value, $100. No. 1222A exists with double surcharge, one inverted. Value, $120. No. 1222A exists with double surcharge. Value, $150.

No. 1223

No. 1223c — No. 1223A

1223	A166	5c on 23c #731, 4mm between "c" and obliterator	1.50	1.50
b.		2½mm between "c" and obliterator (positions 3 and 89)	50.00	50.00
c.		No obliterator	325.00	325.00
1223A	A166	5c on 23c #731, small font	1.00	1.00
		Nos. 1214-1223A (23)	1,644.	1,614.

No. 1223 exists with surcharge shifted 50% upward. Value, $60. No. 1223 also exists with inverted surcharge and with double surcharge, one inverted. Values, $100 and $150, respectively. No. 1223A exists with inverted surcharge. Value, $90.

On Nos. 1215, 1217, 1218, 1219, 1222 and 1223, the "c" and the obliterator are 4mm apart.

Issued: Nos. 1214, 1215, 1215b, Mar. 10; Nos. 1215A, 1217A, 1218A, 8/5/10; No. 1216A, Mar. 30; Nos. 1216, 1216B, Mar.; No. 1217, 1217b, Mar. 30; No. 1218, Aug. 27; No. 1219, 1220, 1221, 1222, Mar. 10; No. 1222A, 8/3/10; No. 1223, July 8; No. 1223A, 8/6/10.

Weddings in Fiji — A286

Designs: 20c, Chinese wedding. 40c, Muslim wedding. $1.50, Indian wedding. $3, Fijian wedding, vert.

Perf. 14½x14, 14x14½
2009, Aug. 17 Litho. Unwmk.
1224-1227 A286 Set of 4 6.00 6.00

Passion Fruit — A287

Designs: 20c, Passiflora foetida. 65c, Passiflora edulis (yellow green). $1.20, Passiflora maliformis. $2, Passiflora edulis (purple).

2009, Sept. 29 Perf. 14x14¼
1228-1231 A287 Set of 4 6.00 6.00

Souvenir Sheet

People's Republic of China, 60th Anniv. A288

2009, Oct. 1 Perf. 13¼
1232 A288 $5 multi 6.00 6.00

Ferns — A289

Designs: 20c, Cyathea lunulata. 40c, Asplenium australasicum. $1.50, Diplazium proliferum. $3, Nephrolepis biserrata.

2009, Dec. 15 Perf. 14x14½
1233-1236 A289 Set of 4 6.00 6.00

Snakes A290

Designs: 20c, Yellow-bellied sea snake. 90c, Fiji burrowing snake. $1.10, Banded sea krait. $2, Pacific boa.

2010, Mar. 30 Litho. Perf. 14½x14
1237-1240 A290 Set of 4 4.50 4.50

Peonies A291

No. 1241: a, 20c, Pink peony. b, 40c, Red peony.

2010, Apr. 8 Litho. Perf. 13¼
1241 A291 Horiz. pair, #a-b 13.00 13.00

Raiateana Knowlesi — A292

No. 1242: a, 20c, Newly-emerged insect. b, $1.50, Mature insect.

Perf. 14x14½
2010, June 30 Unwmk.
1242 A292 Vert. pair, #a-b 2.00 2.00

A293

A294

A295

Worldwide Fund for Nature (WWF) — A296

2010, Oct. 27 Perf. 14¼x14
1243		Horiz. strip of 4	9.00	9.00
a.	A293	$2 multi	2.25	2.25
b.	A294	$2 multi	2.25	2.25
c.	A295	$2 multi	2.25	2.25
d.	A296	$2 multi	2.25	2.25

Fruit — A297

Designs: 20c, Citrus maxima. 40c, Barringtinia edulis. 65c, Pometia pinnata. $1.20, Musa troglogytarum. $10, Syzygium malacensis.

2010, Dec. 2 Perf. 14¼
1244-1248 A297 Set of 5 14.50 14.50

No. 1249

No. 1249A

No. 1249Ab

No. 1252

No. 1254

No. 1254C

No. 1251

No. 1253

No. 1254a

No. 1254G

Methods, Perfs and Watermarks As Before

2011-14
1249	A166	1c on 31c #732	1.00	1.00
c.		3½mm between "c" and obliterator	75.00	75.00
d.		1½mm between "c" and obliterator	125.00	125.00
e.		4mm between "c" and obliterator, larger font	50.00	50.00
f.		2¼mm between "c" and obliterator	100.00	100.00
g.		2½mm between "c" and obliterator	75.00	75.00
1249A	A166	1c on 31c #732	80.00	80.00
b.		Extra large "XX" (position 51)	275.00	275.00
1250	A166	2c on 31c #732	1.00	1.00
a.		4mm between "c" and obliterator	95.00	95.00
b.		3mm between "c" and obliterator (positions 3 and 89)	185.00	185.00
1251	A166	3c on 31c #732	1.00	1.00
1252	A166	4c on 31c #732	1.00	1.00
a.		4mm between "c" and obliterator	95.00	95.00
b.		3mm between "c" and obliterator (positions 3 and 89)	185.00	185.00
1253	A166	5c on 31c #732	1.00	1.00
a.		3½mm between "c" and obliterator	75.00	75.00
b.		1½mm between "c" and obliterator	100.00	100.00
c.		2¼mm between "c" and obliterator	100.00	100.00
1254	A166	20c on 31c #732	2.00	2.00
a.		Larger font	50.00	50.00
b.		As "a," 2½mm between "c" and obliterator	100.00	100.00
d.		As No. 1254, no gap between "c" and obliterator (position 70)	35.00	35.00
f.		As "a," no gap between "c" and obliterator	250.00	300.00
h.		3¾mm btwn "c" and obliterator	180.00	180.00
1254C	A166	20c on 31c #732	125.00	125.00
1254E	A166	40c on 31c #732	3.00	3.00
a.		No gap between "c" and obliterator	50.00	50.00
1254G	A166	20c on 31c #732	180.00	180.00
a.		No gap between "c" and obliterator	225.00	225.00
		Nos. 1249A-1254G (10)	395.00	395.00

Nos. 1249-1253 have 2½mm between "c" and obliterator. No. 1249A has 3½mm spacing. Nos. 1249Ab, 1254, 1254a, 1254E and 1254G have 1½mm spacing.

No. 1249 exists with inverted surcharge. Value, $90. No. 1249 exists with double surcharge. Value, $120; and with double surcharge, one inverted, value, $130. No. 1249A exists with denomination omitted (position 77). Value, $500.

No. 1250 exists with inverted surcharge. Value, $90. No. 1250 exists with double surcharge. Value, $120. No. 1250 exists with double surcharge, one inverted. Value, $130. No. 1250a exists with double surcharge. Value, $200.

No. 1251 exists with inverted surcharge. Value, $100. No. 1251 exists with double surcharge. Value, $120. No. 1251 exists with

FIJI

double surcharge, one inverted. Value, $130. No. 1251 exists with surcharge shifted 50% upward. Value, $50. No. 1252 exists with inverted surcharge. Value, $90. No. 1252 exists with double surcharge. Value, $120. No. 1252 with double surcharge, one inverted. Value, $130.
No. 1253 exists with inverted surcharge. Value, $90. No. 1253 exists with double surcharge, with double surcharge, one shifted 50% upward, and with double surcharge, one inverted, value, each $130. No. 1253 exists with surcharge shifted 50% upward. Value, $50.
No. 1254 exists with inverted surcharge. Value, $100. No. 1254 exists with double surcharge. Value, $65. No. 1254 exists with double surcharge, one with large "20," the other with small "20." Value, $175. No. 1254 exists with double surcharge, one inverted: one with large "20," the other with small "20." Value, $175. No. 1254 exists with double surcharge, one inverted (top surcharge inverted, bottom shifted 50% upward). Value, $110. No. 1254 exists with surcharge shifted 50% upward. Value, $50. No. 1254 exists with double surcharge, one shifted 50% upward. Value, $100. No. 1254 exists with double surcharge, one shifted 50% upward; both with no gap between "c" and obliterator. Value, $300. No. 1254a exists with surcharge shifted 50% upward. Value, $80. No. 1254a exists with surcharge inverted and shifted 50% upward. Value, $130. No. 1254f exists with surcharge shifted 50% upward. Value, $250.
No. 1254E exists with inverted surcharge. Value, $90. No. 1254E exists with double surcharge, one inverted. Value, $120. No. 1254E exists with double surcharge, one inverted. Value, $130. No. 1254E exists with surcharge shifted 45% upward. Value, $50.
No. 1254G exists with inverted surcharge. Value, $225. No. 1254G also exists with "c" of "20c" omitted. Value, $325.
Issued: No. 1249, 6/6; No. 1249A, 7/30/14; Nos. 1250, 1253, 3/24; No. 1250a, 3/2014; No. 1251, 7/8; No. 1252, 5/20; No. 1252a, 2/2014; No. 1254, 5/4; Nos. 1254a, 1254b, 2011; No. 1254d, 5/4; Nos. 1254E, 1254Ea, 12/7/12.

Souvenir Sheet

Wedding of Prince William and Catherine Middleton — A298

Perf. 14¾x14¼
2011, Apr. 29 Litho. Wmk. 406
1255 A298 $10 multi   11.50 11.50

Campaign Against AIDS — A299

People, UNAIDS emblem and slogan: 20c, Protect youth from HIV infection. 40c, Zero new HIV infections, vert. 65c, Stop mothers & babies from being infected with HIV, vert. $5, Zero discrimination.

Perf. 14½x14, 14x14½
2011, June 22   Unwmk.
1256-1259 A299 Set of 4   7.25 7.25

Frangipani Flowers A300

Designs: 50c, Plumeria rubra bud. 90c, Plumeria rubra f. rubra flower. $1.50, Plumeria rubra f. lutea. $3, Plumeria obtusa.

2011, July 12   **Perf. 14½x14**
1260-1263 A300 Set of 4   6.75 6.75

Pomegranate Tree Branches and Birds — A301

No. 1264: a, 65c, Bird on branch. b, $1.20, Bird in flight near branch.

2011, Aug. 15   **Perf. 13¼x13¾**
1264 A301 Horiz. pair, #a-b   2.25 2.25

No. 1264 was printed in sheets containing three pairs.

War Clubs A302

Designs: 20c, Saulaki vividrasa. 65c, Cali. $1.20, Totokia. $10, I ula tavatava.

2011, Aug. 15   **Perf. 14½x14**
1265-1268 A302 Set of 4   14.00 14.00

Intl. Year of Volunteers A303

Volunteers for: 40c, St. John Ambulance Association. 90c, Suva City Council, vert. $1.10, Red Cross, vert. $10, National Blood Bank.

Perf. 14½x14, 14x14½
2011, Nov. 25
1269-1272 A303 Set of 4   14.50 14.50

Christmas A304

Designs: 20c, Fijian with gift box. 65c, Fijian with pottery. $1.20, Fijian with necklace. $2, Holy Family.

2011, Dec. 16   **Perf. 14½x14**
1273-1276 A304 Set of 4   4.50 4.50

New Year 2012 (Year of the Dragon) — A305

2012, Jan. 23   **Perf. 14¼**
1277 A305 $3 multi   3.50 3.50

No. 1277 was printed in sheets of 4.

Endangered Flora — A306

Designs: 20c, Fijian acmopyle. 65c, Lau fan palm. $1.20, Cycad. $2, Fiji magnolia.

2012, Apr. 26   **Perf. 14½x14**
1278-1281 A306 Set of 4   4.50 4.50

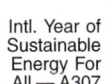

Intl. Year of Sustainable Energy For All — A307

Designs: 20c, Water power. 50c, Biomass. $1.20, Wind energy. $3, Solar power.

2012, June 25
1282-1285 A307 Set of 4   5.50 5.50

A308

A309

A310

Worldwide Fund for Nature (WWF) — A311

2012, July 11   **Perf. 14¼x14**
1286   Horiz. strip of 4   0.00 0.00
  a. A308 $2 multi   2.25 2.25
  b. A309 $2 multi   2.25 2.25
  c. A310 $2 multi   2.25 2.25
  d. A311 $2 multi   2.25 2.25

Christmas A312

Designs: 20c, Journey to Bethlehem. 40c, Holy Family. 65c, Adoration of the Shepherds. $1.20, Adoration of the Shepherds, diff. $5, Adoration of the Magi.

2012, Dec. 14   Litho.   **Perf. 14½x14**
1287-1291 A312 Set of 5   8.50 8.50

Birth of Prince George of Cambridge — A313

Prince George and: 40c, Duke and Duchess of Cambridge. 65c, Duchess of Cambridge. $1.20, Duke and Duchess of Cambridge, diff. $5, Duke of Cambridge.

2013, Aug. 28   Litho.   **Perf. 13½**
1292-1295 A313 Set of 4   7.75 7.75

Mangrove Protection A314

Designs: 50c, Mangroves. 65c, Mangrove, jellyfish, starfish. $1.20, Fish and underwater root system of mangrove. $10, People planting mangroves.

2013, Oct. 30   Litho.   **Perf. 13½**
1296-1299 A314 Set of 4   13.50 13.50

Christmas — A315

Bell-shaped Christmas ornament with: 40c, Cathedral. 65c, Flowers. $1.20, Fijian family

walking on beach. $3, Fijian children with Christmas gifts.

2013, Dec. 2   Litho.   **Perf. 13½**
1300-1303 A315 Set of 4   5.75 5.75

Submarine Cable Between Fiji and Vanuatu — A316

No. 1304: a, Workers, ship and cable with floats. b, Diver examining cable. c, Electronic cables plugged into machine.

Litho. With Foil Application
2014, Jan. 15   **Perf. 14½x14**
1304   Horiz. strip of 6 + central label, #1304a-1304c, Vanuatu #1070a-1070c   14.50 14.50
  a. A316 65c multi   .70 .70
  b. A316 $1.20 multi   1.25 1.25
  c. A316 $6 multi   6.50 6.50

No. 1304 sold for $13.30 in Fiji and 750v in Vanuatu. See Vanuatu No. 1070.

Sharks — A317

Designs: 50c, Blacktip reef shark. 90c, Silky shark. $1.20, Oceanic whitetip shark. $5, Bigeye thresher shark.

2014, July 28   Litho.   **Perf. 13¾x13¼**
1305-1308 A317 Set of 4   8.25 8.25

Grand Pacific Hotel, Cent. — A318

Designs: 40c, Hotel driveway and entrance. 65c, Sofas and tables. 90c, Swimming pool. $1.20, Dining area. $5, Entrance, diff.

2014, Aug. 8   Litho.   **Perf. 13¾x13¼**
1309-1313 A318 Set of 5   8.75 8.75

Nos. 732-733 Surcharged

No. 1313A

No. 1314

No. 1014b

No. 1013D

No. 1313E

40c xxx
No. 1315

No. 1315B

No. 1316

540 FIJI

No. 1317

Methods, Perfs and Watermarks As Before

2014-15
1313A	A166	1c on 44c #733	4.00	4.00
b.		2¼mm between "c" and obliterator	50.00	50.00
c.		4¼mm between "c" and obliterator	40.00	40.00
1314	A166	20c on 44c #733	1.50	1.50
a.		No gap between "c" and obliterator (position 70)	50.00	50.00
b.		Large "20"	30.00	30.00
c.		As "b," no gap between "c" and obliterator (positions 70 and 79)	75.00	75.00
d.		As "b," 3mm between "c" and obliterator (positions 31, 41, 61, 71, 81 and 91)	50.00	50.00
e.		3¾mm between "c" and obliterator (position 3)	175.00	175.00
1313D	A166	1c on 44c #733, Capital "XX"	—	—
1313E	A166	1c on 44c #733, Lower case "xx"	—	—
1315	A166	40c on 44c #733	2.00	2.00
a.		No gap between "c" and obliterator (position 70)	60.00	60.00
1315B	A166	50c on 3c #727	450.00	450.00
c.		No gap between "c" and obliterator (position 70)	—	—
1316	A166	50c on 31c #732	6.00	6.00
a.		No gap between "c" and obliterator (position 70)	50.00	50.00
1317	A166	50c on 44c #733	3.00	3.00
a.		No gap between "c" and obliterator (position 70)	65.00	65.00
		Nos. 1313A-1317 (6)	466.50	466.50

No. 1313A exists with double surcharge. Value, $120. No. 1313A also exists with inverted surcharge. Value, $110.
No. 1314 exists with surcharge shifted 50% upward. Value, $25. No. 1314 exists with surcharge inverted. Value, $60. No. 1314a exists with surcharge shifted 50% upward. Value, $75. No. 1314b exists with surcharge inverted. Value, $100. No. 1314b exists with double surcharge. Value, $120.
No. 1315 exists with surcharge shifted 50% upward. Value, $25. No. 1315a exists with surcharge shifted 50% upward. Value, $80.
No. 1316 exists with double surcharge. Value, $70. Nos. 1316 and 1316a exist with inverted surcharge. Value, both $120.
No. 1317 exists with surcharge shifted 50% upward. Value, $30. No. 1317a exists with surcharge shifted 50% upward. Value, $90.
Issued: No. 1313A, 8/28/15; No. 1314, 6/11; No. 1314b, 7/31; Nos. 1315, 1317, 6/10. No. 1316, 3/5.

Christmas — A319

Houses of worship: 40c, The Church of Jesus Christ of Latter-day Saints, Suva. 65c, Holy Redeemer Anglican Church, Levuka. $3, Baker Memorial Methodist Church, Nausori. $10, St. Francis Xavier Church, Navunibitu.

Perf. 13½
2014, Dec. 4 Litho. Unwmk.
1320-1323 A319 Set of 4 14.00 14.00

Souvenir Sheet

Blue Coral A320

No. 1324 — Heliopora coerulea: a, 65c. b, $5.

Perf. 13½x13¼
2015, Feb. 23 Litho.
1324 A320 Sheet of 2, #a-b 5.50 5.50

Fiji Flying Fox — A321

Fiji flying fox: 40c, Head. 65c, In flight, horiz. 90c, Head, horiz. $10, Hanging from tree.

Perf. 13¼x13¾, 13¾x13¼
2015, Apr. 30 Litho.
1325-1328 A321 Set of 4 13.50 13.50

Levuka UNESCO World Heritage Site — A322

Designs: 50c, Fiji Times Building, Beach Street, c. 1894. 65c, Sacred Heart Church, c. 1902, vert. 90c, Levuka Public School, c. 1884, vert. $5, Public Office, Nasova, c. 1877-82.

2015, June 16 Litho. Perf. 13½
1329-1332 A322 Set of 4 6.75 6.75

Voyages of Uto Ni Yalo Outrigger Canoe — A323

Uto Ni Yalo: 40c, Near shore with white and black sails. 65c, Near Sydney Harbour Bridge and Sydney Opera House. $1.50, Near Golden Gate Bridge. $10, Near shore with red and black sails.

Perf. 13¾x13¼
2015, Aug. 31 Litho.
1333-1336 A323 Set of 4 11.50 11.50

Medicinal Plants — A324

Designs: 40c, Scaevola sericea. 65c, Vigna marina. 90c, Ipomoea pes-caprae subsp. brasiliensis. $1.20, Clerodendrum inerme. $5, Morinda citrifolia.

2015, Oct. 21 Litho. Perf. 13¾x13¼
1337-1341 A324 Set of 5 7.75 7.75

Christmas — A325

Archangels: 40c, St. Uriel. 65c, St. Gabriel. 90c, St. Raphael. $10, St. Michael.

2015, Dec. 7 Litho. Perf. 13¼x13¾
1342-1345 A325 Set of 4 11.50 11.50

Nos. 735 Surcharged

Nos. 734 Surcharged

No. 1347d

Methods, Perfs. and Watermarks As Before

2015-16
1346	A166	1c on 81c #735	7.50	10.00
a.		2¼mm between and obliterator (positions 1 and 2)	125.00	125.00
b.		4¼mm between "c" and obliterator (position 51)	175.00	175.00
1347	A166	20c on 63c #734	20.00	20.00
a.		No gap between "c" and obliterator (position 70)	120.00	120.00
b.		3¼mm between "c" and obliterator (position 3)	120.00	120.00
c.		Large "20"	120.00	120.00
d.		2½mm between "c" and obliterator ('23)	—	—

No. 1346 has 3¼mm between "c" and obliterator. No. 1347 has 1½mm between "c" and obliterator.
Issued: No. 1346, 1/29/16; No. 1347, 12/31; No. 1347d, 2023.

New Year 2016 (Year of the Monkey) — A326

No. 1348: a, Macaca arctoides, bananas. b, Rhinopithecus, peonies. c, Rhesus macaque, coconut palm trees. d, White-headed langur, hibiscus flowers.

Perf. 13½x13¼
2016, Mar. 30 Litho. Unwmk.
1348		Horiz. strip of 4 + central label	11.50	11.50
a.	A326	38c multi	.40	.40
b.	A326	47c multi	.45	.45
c.	A326	85c multi	.85	.85
d.	A326	$10 multi	9.75	9.75

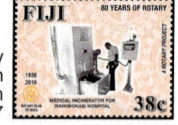

Rotary International in Fiji, 80th Anniv. — A327

Designs: 38c, Medical incinerator for Wainibokasi Hospital. 62c, Dialysis machine for Kidney Foundation of Fiji, vert. $1.04, Emergency Response Kit label, vert. $5, Braille machine for Fiji Society for the Blind.

Perf. 13½x13¼, 13¼x13½
2016, May 19 Litho. Unwmk.
1349-1352 A327 Set of 4 6.75 6.75

No. 733 Surcharged

No. 1353

No. 1354

No. 1355

No. 1356

No. 1356A

Methods, Perfs. and Watermarks As Before

2016-21 ?
1353	A166	3c on 44c #733	3.00	3.00
1354	A166	4c on 44c #733	3.00	3.00
1355	A166	5c on 44c #733	3.00	3.00
1356	A166	23c on 44c #733	4.50	4.50
1356A	A166	23c on 44c #733, "xxx" obliterator	—	—
b.		"xxxx" obliterator	—	—
		Nos. 1353-1356 (4)	13.50	13.50

No. 1355 exists with double surcharge. Value, $800.

Issued: No. 1353, 6/13; No. 1354, 6/15; No. 1355, 8/26; No. 1356, 10/25.

Thatched Structures at Navala Village — A328

Designs: 38c, Dwelling. 47c, Home for the elderly. 85c, Meeting house. $10, Chief's home.

Perf. 13½x13¼
2016, July 27 Litho. Unwmk.
1357-1360 A328 Set of 4 11.50 11.50

Flowers — A329

Designs: 47c, Pink Hibiscus rosa-sinensis. 58c, Abelmoschus esculentus (okra). 85c, Red Hibiscus rosa-sinensis. $1.04, Thespesia populnea. $15, Hibiscus tiliaceus.

Perf. 13¼x13½
2016, Aug. 12 Litho. Unwmk.
1361-1365 A329 Set of 5 17.50 17.50

Christmas — A330

Designs: 40c, Carolers. 90c, People preparing lovo for feast. $1.20, Family going to church. $10, Exchanging gifts.

Perf. 13½x13¼
2016, Dec. 5 Litho. Unwmk.
1366-1369 A330 Set of 4 12.00 12.00

No. 733 Surcharged

No. 1370   No. 1371

Methods, Perfs. and Watermarks As Before

2016-17
1370	A166	2c on 44c #733	3.00	3.00
a.		1½mm btwn "c" and obliterator	75.00	75.00
1371	A166	50c on 44c #733	24.00	24.00

Issued: No. 1370, 2016; No. 1371, 2017. Compare No. 1371 with No. 1317.
No. 1370 has a standard gap of 2¼mm between the "c" and the obliterator.

New Year 2017 (Year of the Rooster) — A331

Designs: 85c, Rooster and red hibiscus flower. $1.20, Hen and yellow frangipani flower. $3, Rooster and palm trees. $15, Rooster and tree blossoms.

Perf. 13¼x13½
2017, Feb. 10 Litho. Unwmk.
1372-1375 A331 Set of 4 19.50 19.50

Great Sea Reef — A332

FIJI

Designs: 62c, Branching coral. 85c, Boulders. $1.04, Soft coral. $15, Plate coral.

Perf. 13½x13¼
2017, May 19 Litho. Unwmk.
1376-1379 A332 Set of 4 17.00 17.00

National Women's Expo — A333

Women and: 40c, Pottery. 62c, Boxes, baskets and handbags. $1.14, Pottery, baskets and textiles. $10, Textiles, bowls and kitchen utensils.

Perf. 13½x13¼
2017, June 14 Litho. Unwmk.
1380-1383 A333 Set of 4 12.00 12.00

Sigatoka Sand Dunes — A334

Designs: 40c, Vegetation surrounding the dunes. 85c, People trekking through the dunes. $1.14, Dunes overlooking the Pacific Ocean. $5, Team training at the dunes.

Perf. 13½x13¼
2017, Sept. 28 Litho. Unwmk.
1384-1387 A334 Set of 4 7.25 7.25

2017 United Nations Climate Change Conference, Bonn — A335

Designs: 40c, Drua. 62c, People planting mangroves. $1.40, Traditional Fijian houses. $10, Workers in sugar cane field.

Perf. 13½
2018, Feb. 5 Litho. Unwmk.
1388-1391 A335 Set of 4 12.50 12.50

New Year 2018 (Year of the Dog) — A336

Various dogs: 38c, 50c, $1.04, $10.

2018, Feb. 28 Litho. Perf. 14½
1392-1395 A336 Set of 4 12.00 12.00

Peace Corps in Fiji, 50th Anniv. — A337

Various Peace Corps workers and Fijians: 40c, $1.14, $2, $10.

2018, Mar. 28 Litho. Perf. 14½
1396-1399 A337 Set of 4 13.50 13.50

Reptiles — A338

Designs: 38c, Giant forest gecko. 40c, Fiji barred tree skink. $1.63, Gau banded iguana. $5, Ono I Lau skink.

2018, July 13 Litho. Perf. 13½
1400-1403 A338 Set of 4 7.25 7.25

Mohandas K. Gandhi (1869-1948), Indian Nationalist Leader — A339

Gandhi and: 38c, Manil Doctor (1881-1956), Indian barrister assisting Indians in Fiji, Charles Freer Andrews (1871-1940), social reformer in India, and Totaram Sanadhya (1876-1947), indentured Indian laborer working in Fiji. 50c, Devanagari script and pencil. 90c, Doves. $15, Drua.

Perf. 13½
2018, Dec. 20 Litho. Unwmk.
1404-1407 A339 Set of 4 16.00 16.00

Nos. 729 and 733 Surcharged

No. 1407A   No. 1407B

Methods, Perfs. and Watermarks As Before
2018-19 ?
1407A A166 3c on 6c #729 425.00 425.00
1407B A166 40c on 44c #733 30.00 30.00
  c. 1¼mm btwn "c" and "XX," 125.00 125.00

Issued: No. 1407A, 2019 ?; No. 1407B, Sept. 2018. Compare No. 1407B with No. 1315.
The issue date of No. 1407A is uncertain and may have been as early as 2007.

New Year 2019 (Year of the Pig) — A340

Designs: 38c, Flower, bananas and orange and red pig. 40c, Flowers and blue pig. $1.20, Dove, trees and red pig. $10, Trees and green pig.

Perf. 14½
2019, Feb. 2 Litho. Unwmk.
1408-1411 A340 Set of 4 11.50 11.50

International Labor Organization, Cent. A341

Designs: 40c, Five workers. 90c, Worker wearing face mask. $1.15, Child playing with blocks. $10, People on arrows surrounding globe.

Perf. 14¼
2019, May Litho. Unwmk.
1412-1415 A341 Set of 4 11.50 11.50

Morris Hedstrom Ltd., 150th Anniv. in Fiji — A342

Designs: Inscribed: 50c, The Voyage — MH Copra Boat. 65c, They Way We Were. 85c, Steeped in History. $1.50, Way Back When. $5, The Birth of a Legacy.

Perf. 14x13½
2019, July Litho. Unwmk.
1416-1420 A342 Set of 5 8.00 8.00

No. 733 Surcharged

6c xxx

Method, Perf. and Watermark As Before
2020, Aug.
1421 A166 6c on 44c #733 — —

Fish — A343

Designs: 40c, Brown marbled grouper. 90c, Squaretail coral grouper. $1.10, Leopard coral grouper. $15, Camouflage grouper.

2019, Sept. 16 Litho. Perf. 14½x14
1422-1425 A343 Set of 4 16.00 16.00

Religious Festivals A344

Designs: 38c, Chinese New Year. $1.20, Eid ul-Fitr. $3, Diwali. $5, Christmas.

2019, Dec. 4 Litho. Perf. 14½x14
1426-1429 A344 Set of 4 9.00 9.00

New Year 2020 (Year of the Rat) — A345

Designs: 40c, Rat and split pineapple. 90c, Rats and mangos. $1.10, Rats and split coconut. $15, Rats on bamboo.

2020, Jan. 17 Litho. Perf. 14½
1430-1433 A345 Set of 4 16.00 16.00

Independence, 50th Anniv. — A346

Perf. 13½x13¼
2020, Sept. 29 Litho.
1434 A346 38c multi — —

Diplomatic Relations Between Fiji and People's Republic of China, 45th Anniv. A347

Designs: 38c, Rugby players. $1.38, Table tennis players. $2.30, Fijian woman. $5, Chinese woman.

2020, Nov. 5 Litho. Perf. 14½x14
1435-1438 A347 Set of 4 — —

Dorjo Chang Buddha III, Religious Leader — A348

2021, Feb. 26 Litho. Perf. 12x11½
1439 A348 $3 multi 3.00 3.00

New Year 2021 (Year of the Ox) — A349

Designs: 38c, Ox and palm trees. $1.04, Ox and mountains. $2.38, Ox and Fijian houses. $10, Ox plowing field.

2021, Feb. 9 Litho. Perf. 14x14½
1440-1443 A349 Set of 4 — —

Swami Pranavanandaji Maharaj (1896-1941), Founder of Bharat Sevashram Sangha — A350

Designs: 38c, Girl at summer camp. $1.38, Members of Nar-Narayan Seva walking in water. $2, Nationwide Ganesh Utsav. $5, Swami Pranavanandaji Mahara.

2021, Mar. 1 Litho. Perf. 13½x13¼
1444-1447 A350 Set of 4 — —

Nos. 730, 732 and 734 Surcharged

 1c xxx
No. 1466

 1c xxx
No. 1466a

 1c xxx
No. 1466b

 2c xxx
No. 1467

 2c xxx
No. 1467a

 3c xxx
No. 1468

 4c xxx
No. 1469

 5c xxx
No. 1470

 5c xxx
No. 1470a

 6c xxx
No. 1471

 6c xxx
No. 1471a

 23c xxx
No. 1472

 23c xxx
No. 1472a

 23c xxx
No. 1473

 23c xxx
No. 1473a

 40c xxx
No. 1474

 40cxxx
No. 1474a

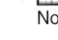 40c XX
No. 1475

542 FIJI — FINLAND

No. 1475a

No. 1476

No. 1477

Method, Perf. and Watermark As Before

2022-23
1466	A166	1c on 63c #734, 3½mm between "c" and "xxx"	— —
a.		2½mm between "c" and "xxx"	— —
b.		1½mm between "c" and "xxx"	— —
1467	A166	2c on 63c #734, 2½mm between "c" and "xxx"	— —
a.		1½mm between "c" and "xxx"	— —
1468	A166	3c on 63c #734, 1½mm between "c" and "xxx"	— —
1469	A166	4c on 63c #734, 2½mm between "c" and "xxx"	— —
a.		1½mm between "c" and "xxx"	— —
1470	A166	5c on 63c #734, 2½mm between "c" and "xxx"	— —
a.		1½mm between "c" and "xxx"	— —
1471	A166	6c on 63c #734, 2½mm between "c" and "xxx"	— —
a.		1½mm between "c" and "xxx"	— —
1472	A166	23c on 31c #732, 1½mm between "c" and "xxx," "xxx" same height as "c"	— —
a.		1½mm between "c" and "xxx," "xxx" taller than "c"	— —
1473	A166	23c on 63c #734, 1½mm between "c" and "xxx," "xxx" same height as "c"	— —
a.		1½mm between "c" and "xxx," "xxx" taller than "c"	— —
1474	A166	40c on 63c #734, 1½mm between "c" and "xxx"	— —
a.		No gap between "c" and "xxx"	— —
1475	A166	40c on 63c #734, 2½mm between "c" and "XX"	— —
a.		1½mm between "c" and "XX"	— —
1476	A166	50c on 13c #730, 1½mm between "c" and "XX" ('22)	— —
1477	A166	50c on 63c #734, 1½mm between "c" and "XX"	— —

SEMI-POSTAL STAMPS

Catalogue values for unused stamps in this section are for Never Hinged items.

Children at Play SP1

Rugby Player SP2

Perf. 13x13½
1951, Sept. 17   Engr.   Wmk. 4
B1 SP1 1p + 1p brown   .30 1.60
B2 SP2 2p + 1p deep green   .55 1.10

Bamboo River Raft — SP3

Design: 2½p+½p, Cross of Lorraine.

1954, Apr. 1   Perf. 11x11½
B3 SP3 1½p + ½p green & brn   .25 1.10
B4 SP3 2½p + ½p black & org   .30   .30

Nos. 269 and 272 Surcharged

1972, Dec. 4   Photo.   Perf. 14, 13½
B5 A56 15c + 5c multi   .40   .35
B6 A55 30c + 10c multi   1.10 .35

Indian Boy, Map of Fiji — SP4

Map of Fiji and: 15c+2c, European girl. 30c+3c, Chinese girl. 40c+4c, Fijian boy.

Wmk. 373
1979, Sept. 17   Litho.   Perf. 14½
B7   SP4 4c + 1c multicolored   .25 .25
B8   SP4 15c + 2c multicolored   .25 .25
B9   SP4 30c + 3c multicolored   .40 .40
B10 SP4 40c + 4c multicolored   .60 .60
     Nos. B7-B10 (4)   1.50 1.50

The surtax was for IYC fund.

Iliesa Delana, Gold Medalist at 2012 Paralympic Games — SP5

Delana: 40c+10c, High jumping. 65c+10c, Standing and waving flag of Fiji, vert. $1.20+10c, Wearing gold medal, vert. $2+10c, Going around track waving flag of Fiji.

2013, Mar. 7   Perf. 14½x14, 14x14½
B11-B14 SP5 Set of 4   5.25 5.25

Surtax for Fiji Paralympic Committee.

POSTAGE DUE STAMPS

D1

D2

D3

1917   Unwmk.   Typeset   Perf. 11
Laid Papers; Without Gum
J1 D1 ½p black   1,450. 500.00
J2 D2 ½p black   550. 300.00
a.   Narrow setting   500. 150.00
J3 D3 1p black   575. 150.00
a.   Narrow setting   350. 150.00
J4 D3 2p black   325.   80.00
a.   Narrow setting 1,350. 650.00
J5 D3 3p black   675. 125.00
J6 D3 4p black   1,600. 575.00
a.   Strip of 8, 3 #J3, 1 ea. #J1 and #J6, and 3 #J5   19,000.
     Nos. J1-J6 (6)   5,175. 1,730.

There were two printings of this issue. In the first printing, the 2d was printed in sheets of 84 (7x12), and the other four values were printed together in sheets of 96 (8x12), with each row consisting of three 1p, one ½p, one 4p and three 3p values. Setenant multiples exist. Sheets were not perforated on the margins, so that marginal stamps were not perforated on the outer edge. Examples from the first printing are 25mm wide (including margins).
In the second printing, the ½p, 1p and 2p were printed in separate sheets of 84 (7x12). The clichés were set a little closer, so that examples of this printing are 23mm wide.

D4

Perf. 14
1918, June 1   Typo.   Wmk. 3
J7   D4 ½p black   3.25   30.00
J8   D4 1p black   3.75   5.50
J9   D4 2p black   3.50   8.00
J10 D4 3p black   3.50   60.00
J11 D4 4p black   6.50   30.00
     Nos. J7-J11 (5) 20.50 133.50

D5

1940   Wmk. 4   Perf. 12½
J12 D5 1p bright green   9.00   72.50
J13 D5 2p bright green   17.50   72.50
J14 D5 3p bright green   20.00   80.00
J15 D5 4p bright green   20.00   85.00
J16 D5 5p bright green   24.00   90.00
J17 D5 6p bright green   25.00   90.00
J18 D5 1sh dk carmine   25.00 115.00
J19 D5 1sh6p dk carmine   25.00 175.00
     Nos. J12-J19 (8)   165.50 780.00
     Set, never hinged   295.00

WAR TAX STAMPS

Regular Issue of 1912-16 Overprinted

Die I
1916   Wmk. 3   Perf. 14
MR1 A23 ½p green   1.90   7.50
a.   Inverted overprint   700.00
b.   Double overprint
MR2 A23 1p scarlet   4.00   .80
a.   1p carmine   42.50 27.50
b.   Pair, one without ovpt. 8,000.
c.   Inverted overprint   800.00

Most examples of No. MR2b are within horiz. strips of 12.

FINLAND

ˈfin-lənd

(Suomi)

LOCATION — Northern Europe bordering on the Gulfs of Bothnia and Finland
GOVT. — Republic
AREA — 130,119 sq. mi.
POP. — 5,540,000 (2020 est.)
CAPITAL — Helsinki

Finland was a Grand Duchy of the Russian Empire from 1809 until December 1917, when it declared its independence.

100 Kopecks = 1 Ruble
100 Pennia = 1 Markka (1866)
100 Cents = 1 Euro (2002)

Catalogue values for unused stamps in this country are for Never Hinged items, beginning with Scott 220 in the regular postage section, Scott B39 in the semipostal section, Scott C2 in the airpost section, Scott M1 in the military stamp section, and Scott Q6 in the parcel post section.

Unused stamps are valued with original gum as defined in the catalogue introduction except for Nos. 1-3B which are valued without gum. Used values for Nos. 1-3B are for pen-cancelled examples. Very fine examples of the serpentine rouletted issues, Nos. 4-13B, will have roulettes cutting the design slightly on one or more sides and will have all "teeth" complete and intact. Stamps with roulettes clear of the design on all four sides are extremely scarce and sell for substantial premiums. Stamps with teeth entirely missing or with several short roulettes are worth much less. See *Scott Classic Specialized Catalogue* for values for used stamps with one or two short roulettes.

Watermarks

Wmk. 121 — Multiple Swastika

Wmk. 208 — Post Horn

Wmk. 168 — Wavy Lines and Letters

Wmk. 273 — Roses

Wmk. 363 — Tree Stump

Syncopated Perforations

Type A (1st stamp #1065): On one longer side, groups of five holes are separated by an oval hole equal in width to eight holes.

Type B (1st stamp, #1142): On the top groups of 3 holes at left and right and a middle group of 4 holes separated by rectangular perforations equal in width to 4 holes.

Issues under Russian Empire

Coat of Arms — A1

FINLAND

1856-58   Unwmk.   Typo.   Imperf.
Small Pearls in Post Horns
Wove Paper

1	A1	5k blue	5,000.	1,200.
		Pen and town cancellation		1,580.
		Town cancellation		2,500.
a.		Tête bêche pair	55,000.	50,000.
		Pen and town cancellation		75,000.
2	A1	10k rose	7,500.	350.
		Pen and town cancellation		450.
		On cover		1,850.
		Town cancellation		700.
		On cover		2,850.
a.		Tête bêche pair	60,000.	50,000.
		Pen and town cancellation		55,000.

Cut to shape

1	A1	5k blue		150.
		Pen and town cancellation		200.
		Town cancellation		250.
2	A1	10k rose		65.
		Pen and town cancellation		60.
		Town cancellation		100.

Wide Vertically Laid Paper

2C	A1	10k rose ('58)	—	1,200.
		Pen and town cancellation		1,600.
		Town cancellation		2,000.
d.		Tête bêche pair		2,500.

Cut to shape

2C	A1	10k rose		500.
		Pen and town cancellation		650.
		Town cancellation		300.

Narrow Vertically Laid Paper

2C	A1	10k carmine		625.
		Pen and town cancellation		800.
		Town cancellation		900.

The wide vertically laid paper has 13-14 distinct lines per 2 centimeters. The narrow laid paper has lines that sometimes are indistinct.

A 5k blue with small pearls exists on narrow vertically laid paper. It is rare. Value $16,250 used.

Stamps on diagonally laid paper are envelope cut squares. Envelope cut squares also exist on unwatermarked wove paper.

Large Pearls in Post Horns
1858   Wove Paper

3	A1	5k blue	7,500.	1,200.
		Pen and town cancellation		1,400.
		Town cancellation		2,000.
a.		Tête bêche pair		45,000.
		Pen and town cancellation		50,000.

Cut to shape

3	A1	5k blue		90.
		Pen and town cancellation		120.
		Town cancellation		150.

1859   Wide Vertically Laid Paper

3B	A1	5k blue	—	15,000.
		Pen and town cancellation		20,000.

Cut to shape

3B	A1	5k blue		2,000.
		Pen and town cancellation		2,500.

Reprints of Nos. 2 and 3, made in 1862, are on brownish paper, on vertically laid paper, and in tête bêche pairs on normal and vertically laid paper. Reprints of 1871, 1881 and 1893 are on yellowish or white paper. Value for least costly of each, $40.

In 1956, Nos. 2 and 3 were reprinted for the Centenary with post horn watermark and gum. Value, $50 each.

Values for rouletted stamps with one or two short teeth are considerably less than the values shown, which are for stamps with all teeth full and intact. See the *Scott Classic Specialized Catalogue* for greater detail. Stamps with several short teeth or teeth entirely missing sell for very small percentages of the values shown.

Coat of Arms — A2

I — Depth 1-1 1/4mm
II — Depth 1 1/2-1 3/4mm
III — Depth 2-2 1/4mm

IV — Shovel-shaped teeth. Depth 1 1/4-1 1/2mm

Wove Paper
1860   Serpentine Roulette 7 1/2, 8

4	A2	5k blue, *bluish*, I	800.00	175.00
a.		Roulette II	800.00	190.00
b.		Perf. vert.		
5	A2	10k rose, *pale rose*, I	550.00	47.50
a.		Roulette II	1,100.	140.00

A3

A4

1866-74   Serpentine Roulette

6	A3	5p pur brn, *lil*, I ('73)	300.00	150.00
a.		Roulette II		3,500.
b.		5p red brn, *lil*, III ('71)	275.00	160.00
7	A3	8p blk, *grn*, III ('67)	275.00	160.00
a.		Ribbed paper, III ('72)	1,000.	750.00
b.		Roulette II ('74)	300.00	240.00
c.		As "b", ribbed paper ('74)	340.00	200.00
d.		Roulette I ('73)	450.00	280.00
e.		As "d," ribbed paper	900.00	350.00
f.		Serpentine roulette 10 1/2 ('67)		12,500.
8	A3	10p blk, *yel*, III ('70)	600.00	300.00
a.		10p blk, *buff*, II	700.00	400.00
b.		10p blk, *buff*, I ('73)	650.00	325.00
9	A3	20p bl, *bl*, III	500.00	50.00
a.		Roulette II	550.00	90.00
b.		Roulette I ('73)	600.00	100.00
c.		Roulette IV ('73)		1,000.
d.		Perf. horiz.		
e.		Printed on both sides (40p blue on back)		10,500.
10	A3	40p rose, *lil rose*, III	450.00	60.00
a.		Ribbed paper, III ('73)	500.00	140.00
b.		Roulette II	450.00	75.00
c.		As "b," ribbed paper ('73)	500.00	125.00
d.		Roulette I	650.00	150.00
e.		As "d," ribbed paper	600.00	100.00
f.		Roulette IV		2,000.
g.		As "f," ribbed paper		
h.		Serpentine roulette 10 1/2		
11	A4	1m yel brn, III ('67)	2,000.	750.00
a.		Roulette II	2,500.	1,500.

Nos. 7f and 10h are private roulettes and are also known in compound serpentine roulette 10 1/2 and 7 1/2.

Nos. 4-11 were reprinted in 1893 on thick wove paper. Colors differ from originals. Roulette type IV. Value for Nos. 4-5, each $40; Nos. 6-10, each $50. Value for No. 11, $55.

Thin or Thick Laid Paper

12	A3	5p red brn, *lil*, III	290.00	130.00
a.		Roulette II	350.00	275.00
b.		Roulette I	290.00	275.00
d.		5p blk, *buff*, roul. III (error)		20,000.
		Tête bêche pair		17,500.
13	A3	10p black, *buff*, III	600.00	250.00
a.		10p black, *yel*, II	750.00	250.00
b.		10p black, *buff*, I	1,000.	650.00
c.		10p red brown, *lil*, III (error)	7,000.	6,250.

Forgeries of No. 13c exist.

A5

1875   Perf. 14x13 1/2

16	A5	32p lake	2,000.	400.00

Forgeries exist of No. 16 that have been created by perforating cut squares.

1875-82   Perf. 11

17	A5	2p gray	45.00	50.00
18	A5	5p orange	100.00	10.00
a.		5p yellow org	100.00	10.00
19	A5	8p blue green	225.00	65.00
a.		8p yellow green	200.00	50.00
20	A5	10p brown ('81)	500.00	50.00
21	A5	20p ultra	125.00	3.00
a.		20p blue	125.00	4.50
b.		20p Prussian blue	300.00	32.50
c.		Tête bêche pair		2,500.
22	A5	25p car ('79)	200.00	15.00
a.		25p rose ('82)	275.00	65.00
23	A5	32p carmine	300.00	30.00
a.		32p rose	325.00	32.50
24	A5	1m violet ('77)	750.00	120.00
		Nos. 17-24 (8)	2,245.	343.00

A souvenir card issued in 1974 for NORDIA 1975 reproduced a block of four of the unissued "1 MARKKAA" design.

Nos. 19, 23 were reprinted in 1892-93, perf. 12 1/2. Value $20 each. They exist imperf.

1881-83   Perf. 12 1/2

25	A5	2p gray	15.00	14.00
a.		Imperf., pair	425.00	350.00
26	A5	5p orange	45.00	5.00
a.		Tête bêche pair	6,250.	3,500.
b.		Imperf. vert., pair		600.00
c.		Imperf. horiz., pair		800.00
27	A5	10p brown	75.00	17.50
28	A5	20p ultra	75.00	15.00
a.		20p blue	47.50	1.50
b.		Tête bêche pair		1,750.
c.		Imperf., pair	—	
29	A5	25p rose ('82)	40.00	8.50
a.		25p carmine	40.00	15.00
b.		Tête bêche pair		15,000.
30	A5	1m violet ('82)	350.00	40.00
		Nos. 25-30 (6)	600.00	100.00

Nos. 27-29 were reprinted in 1893 in deeper shades, perf. 12 1/2. Value $30 each.

Most examples of No. 28c are from printer's waste.

1881   Perf. 11x12 1/2

26d	A5	5p orange	400.00	80.00
27d	A5	10p brown	800.00	200.00
28d	A5	20p ultra	550.00	40.00
28e	A5	20p blue	500.00	37.50
29c	A5	25p rose	600.00	160.00
29d	A5	25p carmine	500.00	100.00
30a	A5	1m violet		1,250.

1881   Perf. 12 1/2x11

26e	A5	5p orange	400.00	80.00
27b	A5	10p brown		275.00
28f	A5	20p ultra	500.00	37.50
28g	A5	20p blue	500.00	37.50
29e	A5	25p rose	—	250.00
29f	A5	25p carmine	500.00	100.00

1885   Perf. 12 1/2

31	A5	5p emerald	15.00	.50
a.		5p yellow green	17.50	1.00
b.		Tête bêche pair	10,000.	8,000.
32	A5	10p carmine	22.50	2.50
a.		10p rose	35.00	4.00
33	A5	20p orange	25.00	.40
a.		20p yellow	32.50	5.00
b.		Tête bêche pair	—	2,500.
34	A5	25p ultra	55.00	3.00
a.		25p blue	50.00	2.50
35	A5	1m gray & rose	27.50	10.00
36	A5	5m grn & rose	350.00	350.00
37	A5	10m brn & rose	450.00	550.00

Denomination on No. 35 is spelled "MARKKA." Denomination on Nos. 36-37 is spelled "MARKKAA."

A6

1889-92   Perf. 12 1/2

38	A6	2p slate ('90)	.50	.80
39	A6	5p green ('90)	25.00	.40
40	A6	10p carmine ('90)	50.00	.40
a.		10p rose ('90)	75.00	.40
b.		Imperf.	80.00	
41	A6	20p orange ('92)	60.00	.30
a.		20p yellow ('89)	60.00	.90
42	A6	25p ultra ('91)	60.00	.70
a.		25p blue	60.00	.70
43	A6	1m slate & rose ('92)	3.50	3.00
a.		1m brnsh gray & rose ('90)	20.00	3.00
44	A6	5m grn & rose ('90)	20.00	60.00
45	A6	10m brn & rose ('90)	30.00	80.00
		Nos. 38-45 (8)	249.00	145.60

The 2p slate, perf. 14x13, is believed to be an essay.

See Nos. 60-63.

See Russia for types similar to A7-A18. Finnish stamps have "dot in circle" devices or are inscribed "Markka," "Markkaa," "Pen." or "Pennia."

Imperial Arms of Russia
A7   A8   A9

A10   A11

Laid Paper
1891-92   Wmk. 168   Perf. 14 1/2x15

46	A7	1k org yel	5.00	9.00
47	A7	2k green	5.00	9.00
48	A7	3k carmine	11.00	18.00
49	A8	4k rose	10.00	14.00
50	A7	7k dark blue	6.00	2.25
51	A8	10k dark blue	13.00	14.00
52	A9	14k blue & rose	16.00	22.50
53	A8	20k blue & car	15.00	18.00
54	A8	35k vio & grn	20.00	45.00
55	A8	50k vio & grn	25.00	32.50

Perf. 13 1/2

56	A10	1r brn & org	70.00	70.00
57	A11	3 1/2r blk & gray	240.00	400.00
		3 1/2r black & yellow (error)	11,000.	13,500.
58	A11	7r blk & yel	180.00	250.00
		Nos. 46-58 (13)	616.00	904.25

Forgeries of Nos. 57, 57a, 58 exist.

Type of 1889-90
Wove Paper
1895-96   Unwmk.   Perf. 14x13

60	A6	5p green	.60	.40
61	A6	10p carmine	.60	.50
62	A6	20p orange	.60	.40
b.		Imperf.	120.00	
63	A6	25p ultra	.70	.60
a.		25p blue	1.75	.60
b.		Imperf.	90.00	
		Nos. 60-63 (4)	2.50	1.90

A12   A13

A14   A15

1901   Litho.   Perf. 14 1/2x15
Chalky Paper

64	A12	2p yellow	4.50	6.00
65	A12	5p green	9.00	1.20
66	A13	10p carmine	20.00	2.00
67	A12	20p dark blue	50.00	1.00
68	A14	1m violet & grn	250.00	7.50

Perf. 13 1/2

69	A15	10m black & gray	240.00	260.00
		Nos. 64-69 (6)	573.50	277.70

Imperf sheets of 10p and 20p, stolen during production, were privately perforated 11 1/2 to defraud the P.O. Uncanceled imperfs. of Nos. 65-68 are believed to be proofs.

See Nos. 70-75, 82.

FINLAND

Types of 1901 Redrawn

No. 64

No. 70

2p. On No. 64, the "2" below "II" is shifted slightly leftward. On No. 70, the "2" is centered below "II."

No. 65

No. 71

5p. On No. 65, the frame lines are very close. On No. 71, a clear white space separates them.

Nos. 66, 67

Nos. 72, 73

10p, 20p. On Nos. 66-67, the horizontal central background lines are faint and broken. On Nos. 72-73, they are clear and solid, though still thin.

20p. On No. 67, "H" close to "2" with period midway. On No. 73 they are slightly separated with period close to "H."

No. 68

Nos. 74, 74a

1m. On No. 68, the "1" following "MARKKA" lacks serif at base. On Nos. 74-74a, this "1" has serif.

No. 69

No. 75

10m. On No. 69, the serifs of "M" and "A" in top and bottom panels do not touch. On No. 75, the serifs join.

Perf. 14¼x14¾, 14¼x14

		1901-14	Typo.	Ordinary Paper	
70	A12	2p orange		.50	1.20
		Never hinged		1.50	
71	A12	5p green		1.50	.60
a.		Perf 14¼x14 ('06)		1.50	.75
		Never hinged		3.50	
72	A13	10p carmine		10.00	.50
a.		Perf 14¼x14 ('07)		65.00	.70
		Never hinged		110.00	
b.		Background inverted, perf 14¼x14¾		12.50	2.00
c.		Background inverted, perf 14¼x14		70.00	2.00
73	A12	20p dark blue		7.50	.50
a.		Perf 14¼x14 ('06)		60.00	.80
		Never hinged		100.00	
74	A14	1m lil & grn, perf. 14¼x14 ('14)		1.20	.80
a.		1m violet & blue green, perf. 14¼x14¾ ('02)		7.50	.80
		Never hinged		25.00	
		Nos. 70-74 (5)		20.70	3.60
		Set, never hinged		90.00	

Perf. 13½

75	A15	10m blk & drab ('03)	120.00	45.00
		Never hinged	240.00	

Imperf Pairs

70a	A12	2p	280.00	400.00
71b	A12	5p	75.00	150.00
72d	A13	10p	85.00	180.00
73b	A12	20p	150.00	180.00
74b	A14	1m	140.00	160.00
		Nos. 70a-74b (5)	730.00	1,070.

A16   A17   A18

		1911-16		Perf. 14, 14¼x14¾	
77	A16	2p orange		.25	.80
78	A16	5p green		.25	.40
a.		Imperf.			
b.		Perf. 14¼x14¾		1,000.	100.00
		Never hinged		2,200.	
79	A17	10p rose ('15)		.25	.50
a.		Imperf. pair		80.00	120.00
b.		Perf. 14¼x14¾ ('16)		2.50	9.00
		Never hinged		6.50	
80	A16	20p deep blue		.25	.50
a.		Imperf.		140.00	110.00
b.		Perf. 14¼x14¾		20.00	2.50
		Never hinged		45.00	
81	A18	40p violet & blue		.30	.40
a.		Perf. 14¼x14¾		4,500.	3,000.
		Nos. 77-81 (5)		1.30	2.60
		Set, never hinged		2.70	

There are three minor types of No. 79. Values are for the least expensive type.

Perf. 14½

82	A15	10m blk & grnsh gray ('16)	120.00	160.00
		Never hinged	270.00	
a.		Horiz. pair, imperf. vert.	2,800.	

Republic
Helsinki Issue

Arms of the Republic — A19

Type I

Type II

Two types of the 40p.
Type I — Thin figures of value.
Type II — Thick figures of value.

Perf. 14, 14¼x14¾

		1917-30		Unwmk.	
83	A19	5p green		.30	.25
84	A19	5p gray ('19)		.30	.30
85	A19	10p rose		.30	.40
a.		Imperf., pair		180.00	300.00
86	A19	10p green ('19)		1.10	.80
a.		Perf. 14¼x14¾			2,200.
87	A19	10p brt blue ('21)		.30	.40
88	A19	20p buff		.30	.40
89	A19	20p rose ('20)		.30	.40
90	A19	20p brown ('24)		.60	.70
a.		Perf. 14¼x14¾		.50	22.50
		Never hinged		1.20	
91	A19	25p blue		.30	.40
92	A19	25p lt brn ('19)		.30	.25
93	A19	30p green ('23)		.40	.50
94	A19	40p violet (I)		.30	.25
a.		Perf. 14¼x14¾		300.00	20.00
		Never hinged		650.00	
95	A19	40p bl grn (II) ('29)		.40	2.50
a.		Type I ('24)		10.00	4.50
		Never hinged		25.00	
b.		Perf. 14¼x14¾		1.00	18.00
		Never hinged		2.00	
96	A19	50p orange brn		.40	.40
97	A19	50p dp blue ('19)		3.00	.50
a.		Perf. 14¼x14¾			1,600.
98	A19	50p green ('21)		3.50	.40
a.		Perf. 14¼x14¾		.30	1.20
		Never hinged		1.00	
99	A19	60p red vio ('21)		.70	.40
a.		Imperf., pair		—	
100	A19	75p yellow ('21)		.30	.60
101	A19	1m dull rose & blk		10.00	.25
102	A19	1m red org ('25)		6.50	20.00
a.		Perf. 14 ('30)		20.00	450.00
		Never hinged		.80	
103	A19	1½m bl grn & red vio ('29)		.30	1.50
a.		Perf. 14¼x14¾		.40	1.00
		Never hinged		.90	
104	A19	2m green & blk ('21)		2.50	.70
105	A19	2m dk blue & ind ('22)		2.00	.40
a.		Perf. 14¼x14¾		.50	3.50
		Never hinged		1.20	
106	A19	3m blue & blk ('21)		50.00	.90
107	A19	5m red vio & blk		12.50	.40
108	A19	10m brn & gray blk, perf. 14		.80	1.00
a.		10m light brown & black, perf. 14¼x14¾ ('29)		3.00	380.00
		Never hinged		5.50	
110	A19	25m dull red & yel ('21)		.80	24.00
		Nos. 83-108,110 (27)		98.50	59.00
		Set, never hinged		205.90	

Examples of a 2½p gray of this type exist. They are proofs from the original die which were distributed through the UPU. No plate was made for this denomination.

See Nos. 127-140, 143-152. For surcharge and overprints see Nos. 119-126, 153-154.

Vasa Issue

Arms of the Republic — A20

		1918	Litho.	Perf. 11½	
111	A20	5p green		.40	1.00
112	A20	10p red		.40	1.00
113	A20	30p slate		.70	2.50
114	A20	40p brown vio		.40	1.00
115	A20	50p orange brn		.40	4.00
116	A20	70p gray brown		1.50	18.00
117	A20	1m red & gray		.40	1.40
118	A20	5m red violet & gray		35.00	85.00
		Nos. 111-118 (8)		39.20	113.90
		Set, never hinged		80.00	

Nos. 111-118 exist imperforate but were not regularly issued in that condition.
Sheet margin examples, perf. on 3 sides, imperf. on margin side, were sold by post office.

Stamps and Type of 1917-29 Surcharged

		1919		Perf. 14	
119	A19	10p on 5p green		.40	.70
120	A19	20p on 10p rose		.40	.70
121	A19	50p on 25p blue		.80	.70
122	A19	75p on 20p orange		.40	.70
		Nos. 119-122 (4)		2.00	2.80
		Set, never hinged		4.95	

Stamps and Type of 1917-29 Surcharged

Nos. 123-125

No. 126

		1921			
123	A19	30p on 10p green		.70	.90
124	A19	60p on 40p red violet		3.00	1.20
125	A19	90p on 20p rose		.30	.40
126	A19	1½m on 50p blue		1.10	.60
a.		Thin "2" in "½"		9.00	6.00
b.		Imperf., pair		200.00	350.00
		Nos. 123-126 (4)		5.10	3.10
		Set, never hinged		12.40	

Arms Type of 1917-29
Perf. 14, 14¼x14¾

		1925-29		Wmk. 121	
127	A19	10p ultra ('27)		.40	2.00
128	A19	20p brown		.40	1.50
129	A19	25p brn org ('29)		.70	75.00
130	A19	30p yel green		.30	.70
a.		Perf. 14¼x14¾		.30	
		Never hinged		.50	
131	A19	40p blue grn (I) ('26)		2.50	1.20
a.		Perf. 14¼x14¾ ('26)		5.00	1.00
		Never hinged		15.00	
b.		Type II ('28)		100.00	60.00
		Never hinged		240.00	
c.		As "b," perf. 14¼x14¾ ('28)		7.00	1.00
		Never hinged		20.00	
132	A19	50p gray grn ('26)		.90	.60
a.		Perf. 14¼x14¾ ('26)		.40	.40
		Never hinged		1.20	
133	A19	60p red violet		.30	.70
134	A19	1m dp orange		5.00	.40
a.		Perf. 14¼x14¾		80.00	.90
		Never hinged		200.00	

Perf. 14¼x14¾

135	A19	1½m blue grn & red vio ('26)		4.00	.40
a.		Perf. 14 ('26)		60.00	.50
		Never hinged		130.00	
136	A19	2m dk blue & indigo ('27)		.70	.40
a.		Perf. 14		.80	.40
		Never hinged		2.00	
137	A19	3m chlky blue & blk ('26)		.80	.40
138	A19	5m red violet & blk ('27)		1.00	.40
a.		Perf. 14		2.50	
139	A19	10m lt brn & blk ('27)		3.00	25.00
140	A19	25m dp org & yel ('27)		15.00	300.00
		Nos. 127-140 (14)		34.40	408.70
		Set, never hinged		95.55	

No. 130a is not known cancelled during the period in which it was valid for postal use.

A21

Wmk. 208

		1927, Dec. 6	Typo.	Perf. 14	
141	A21	1½m deep violet		.30	.40
142	A21	2m deep blue		.30	1.80

10th anniv. of Finnish independence.

Arms Type of 1917-29
Perf. 14, 14¼x14¾

		1927-29		Wmk. 208	
143	A19	20p lt brown ('29)		1.50	3.00
144	A19	40p bl grn (II) ('28)		.40	1.00
145	A19	50p gray grn ('28)		.40	.75
146	A19	1m dp orange		.40	1.00
a.		Imperf., pair		100.00	180.00
b.		Perf. 14		.90	.90
147	A19	1½m bl grn & red vio ('28)		3.00	1.00
a.		Perf. 14		800.00	20.00
148	A19	2m dk bl & ind ('28)		.40	1.00
149	A19	3m chlky bl & blk		.40	1.00
a.		Perf. 14		4.00	10.00
150	A19	5m red vio & blk ('28)		.40	1.60
151	A19	10m lt brown & blk		1.10	35.00
152	A19	25m brown org & yel		1.50	180.00
		Nos. 143-152 (10)		9.50	225.35
		Set, never hinged		23.75	

Nos. 146-147 Overprinted

		1928, Nov. 10	Litho.	Wmk. 208	
153	A19	1m deep orange		6.00	16.00
154	A19	1½m bl grn & red vio		6.00	16.00
		Set, never hinged		28.00	

Nos. 153 and 154 were sold exclusively at the Helsinki Philatelic Exhibition, Nov. 10-18, 1928, and were valid only during that period.

S. S. "Bore" Leaving Turku
A23

Turku Cathedral
A24

Turku Castle — A25

Wmk. 208

		1929, May 22	Typo.	Perf. 14	
155	A23	1m olive green		1.50	4.50
156	A24	1½m chocolate		4.00	4.50
157	A25	2m dark gray		1.50	4.50
		Nos. 155-157 (3)		7.00	13.50
		Set, never hinged		20.00	

Founding of the city of Turku (Åbo), 700th anniv.

A26

		1930-46		Unwmk.	Perf. 14
158	A26	5p chocolate		.30	.40
159	A26	10p dull violet		.30	.30
160	A26	20p yel grn		.30	.40
161	A26	25p yel brn		.30	.30
162	A26	40p blue grn		1.50	.25
163	A26	50p yellow		.40	.25
164	A26	50p blue grn ('32)		.30	.30
b.		Imperf., pair		110.00	150.00

FINLAND

165	A26	60p dark gray	.40	.60
165A	A26	75p dp org ('42)	.30	.40
166	A26	1m red org	.40	.25
166B	A26	1m yel grn	.30	.25
167	A26	1.20m crimson	.40	1.00
168	A26	1.25m yel ('32)	.30	.25
169	A26	1½m red vio	1.60	.25
170	A26	1½m car ('32)	.30	.25
170A	A26	1½m sl ('40)	.30	.25
170B	A26	1.75m org yel ('40)	.50	.50
171	A26	2m indigo	.30	.25
172	A26	2m dp vio ('32)	4.50	.40
173	A26	2m car ('36)	.30	.25
		Complete booklet, panes of 4 #161, 164, 166, 168, 173	5.00	
173B	A26	2m yel org ('42)	.30	.25
173C	A26	2m blue grn	.30	.25
174	A26	2½m brt blue ('32)	2.50	.40
174A	A26	2½m car ('42)	.30	.25
174B	A26	2.75m rose vio ('40)	.30	.25
175	A26	3m olive blk	20.00	.40
175B	A26	3m car ('45)	.30	.25
175C	A26	3m yel ('45)	.30	.60
176	A26	3½m brt bl ('36)	7.00	.25
176A	A26	3½m olive ('42)	.30	.25
176B	A26	4m olive ('45)	.40	.25
176C	A20	4½m saph ('42)	.30	.25
176D	A26	5m saph	.40	.25
176E	A26	5m pur ('45)	.40	.40
j.		Imperf., pair	120.00	150.00
176F	A26	5m yel ('46)	.50	.25
k.		Imperf., pair	120.00	150.00
176G	A26	6m car ('45)	.40	.40
m.		Imperf., pair	150.00	200.00
176H	A26	8m pur ('46)	.30	.25
176I	A26	10m saph ('45)	.80	.25
		Nos. 158-176I (38)	48.40	12.55

See Nos. 257-262, 270-274, 291-296, 302-304. For surcharges and overprints see Nos. 195-196, 212, 221-222, 243, 250, 275, M2-M3.

Stamps of types A26-A29 overprinted "ITA KARJALA" are listed under Karelia, Nos. N1-N15.

Castle in Savonlinna
A27

Lake Saima
A28

Woodchopper — A29

1930 — Engr.
177	A27	5m blue	.50	.40
178	A28	10m gray lilac	40.00	4.00
179	A29	25m black brown	.80	4.00
		Nos. 177-179 (3)	41.00	4.00
		Set, never hinged	113.70	

See Nos. 205, 305. For overprint see No. C1.

Elias Lönnrot
A30

Seal of Finnish Literary Society
A31

1931, Jan. 1 — Typo.
180	A30	1m olive brown	2.00	5.00
181	A31	1½m dull blue	10.00	5.00
		Never hinged	30.00	

Centenary of Finnish Literary Society.

A32

1931, Feb. 28
182	A32	1½m red	2.20	8.00
		Never hinged	5.00	
183	A32	2m blue	2.20	10.00
		Never hinged	5.00	

1st use of postage stamps in Finland, 75th anniv.

Nos. 162-163 Surcharged

1931, Dec.
195	A26	50p on 40p blue grn	1.20	1.00
		Never hinged	4.00	
196	A26	1.25m on 50p yellow	3.00	1.80
		Never hinged	10.00	

Svinhufvud — A33

1931, Dec. 15
197	A33	2m gray blue & blk	1.00	3.00
		Never hinged	3.00	

Pres. Pehr Eyvind Svinhufvud, 70th birthday.

Lake Saima Type of 1930
1932-43 — Re-engraved
205	A28	10m red violet ('43)	.50	.40
		Never hinged	1.20	
a.		10m dark violet	15.00	.60
		Never hinged	30.00	

On Nos. 205 and 205a the lines of the islands, the clouds and the foliage are much deeper and stronger than on No. 178.

Alexis Kivi — A34

1934, Oct. 10 — Typo.
206	A34	2m red violet	1.20	4.00
		Never hinged	4.00	

Alexis Kivi, Finnish poet (1834-1872).

Bards Reciting the "Kalevala"
A35

Goddess Louhi, As Eagle Seizing Magic Mill
A36

Kullervo — A37

1935, Feb. 28 — Engr.
207	A35	1¼m brown lake	1.00	1.80
		Never hinged	3.00	
208	A36	2m black	2.50	1.80
		Never hinged	9.00	
209	A37	2½m blue	2.20	1.80
		Never hinged	7.00	
		Nos. 207-209 (3)	5.70	5.40
		Set, never hinged	19.00	

Cent. of the publication of the "Kalevala" (Finnish National Epic).

No. 170 Surcharged in Black

1937, Feb.
212	A26	2m on 1½m car	4.00	1.20
		Never hinged	11.00	

Gustaf Mannerheim — A38

1937, June 4 — Photo. — Perf. 14
213	A38	2m ultra	.50	1.80
		Never hinged	2.00	

70th birthday of Field Marshal Baron Carl Gustaf Mannerheim, June 4th, 1937.

Swede-Finn Co-operation in Colonization — A39

1938, June 1
214	A39	3½m dark brown	.80	2.50
		Never hinged	3.50	

Tercentenary of the colonization of Delaware by Swedes and Finns.

Early Post Office — A40

Designs: 1¼m, Mail delivery in 1700. 2m, Modern mail plane. 3½m, Helsinki post office.

1938, Sept. 6 — Photo. — Perf. 14
215	A40	50p green	.30	.80
		Never hinged	.80	
216	A40	1¼m dk blue	1.00	2.50
		Never hinged	3.50	
217	A40	2m scarlet	1.00	1.50
		Never hinged	5.00	
218	A40	3½m slate black	3.00	8.00
		Never hinged	9.00	
		Nos. 215-218 (4)	5.30	12.80
		Set, never hinged	18.30	

300th anniv. of the Finnish Postal System. Margin strips of each denomination (3 of No. 215, 2 each of Nos. 216, 217, 218) were pasted on to advertising sheets and stapled into a booklet. Value, $90.

Post Office, Helsinki — A44

1939-42 — Photo.
219	A44	4m brown black	.40	.40
		Never hinged	.80	

Engr.
219A	A44	7m black brn ('42)	.50	.40
		Never hinged	1.20	
219D	A44	9m rose lake ('42)	.50	.40
		Never hinged	1.20	
		Nos. 219-219B (3)	1.40	1.20
		Set, never hinged	3.20	

See No. 248.

Catalogue values for unused stamps in this section, from this point to the end of the section, are for Never Hinged items.

University of Helsinki — A45

1940, May 1 — Photo.
220	A45	2m dp blue & blue	.80	.80

300th anniv. of the founding of the University of Helsinki.

Nos. 168 and 173 Surcharged in Black

1940, June 16 — Typo.
221	A26	1.75m on 1.25m yel	2.20	3.00
222	A26	2.75m on 2m carmine	6.50	1.00

President Kallio Reviewing Military Band — A46

1941, May 24 — Engr.
223	A46	2.75m black	.80	.90

Pres. Kyösti Kallio (1873-1940).

Castle at Viborg — A47

1941, Aug. 30 — Typo.
224	A47	1.75m yellow orange	.80	.80
225	A47	2.75m rose violet	.80	.80
226	A47	3.50m blue	1.80	1.80

Field Marshal Mannerheim — A48

1941, Dec. 31 — Engr. — Wmk. 273
227	A48	50p dull green	.90	1.50
228	A48	1.75m deep brown	.90	1.50
229	A48	2m dark red	.90	1.50
230	A48	2.75m dull vio brn	.90	2.00
231	A48	3.50m deep blue	.90	1.50
232	A48	5m slate blue	1.20	1.50
		Nos. 227-232 (6)	5.70	9.50

Pres. Risto Ryti — A49

233	A49	50p dull green	1.00	2.00
234	A49	1.75m deep brown	1.00	2.00
235	A49	2m dark red	2.00	2.00
236	A49	2.75m dull vio brn	2.00	2.00
237	A49	3.50m deep blue	1.00	1.50
238	A49	5m slate blue	1.00	1.50
		Nos. 233-238 (6)	8.00	11.00

Types A48-A49 overprinted "ITA KARJALA" are listed under Karelia, Nos. N16-N27.

Häme Bridge, Tampere — A50

South Harbor, Helsinki — A51

1942 — Unwmk.
239	A50	50m dull brown vio	2.50	.40
240	A51	100m indigo	4.00	.40

See No. 350.

Altar and Open Bible
A52

17th Century Printer
A53

1942, Oct. 10
241	A52	2.75m dk brown	.50	1.00
242	A53	3.50m violet blue	.80	2.50

300th anniv. of the printing of the 1st Bible in Finnish.

No. 174B Surcharged in Black

FINLAND

1943, Feb. 1
243 A26 3.50m on 2.75m rose vio .40 .40

Minna Canth (1844-96), Author and Playwright — A54

1944, Mar. 20
244 A54 3.50m dk olive grn .25 .80

Pres. P. E. Svinhufvud — A55

1944, Aug. 1
245 A55 3.50m black .40 1.20
Death of President Svinhufvud (1861-1944).

K. J. Stahlberg — A56

1945, May 16 Engr. Perf. 14
246 A56 3.50m brown vio .40 .50
80th birthday of Dr. K. J. Stahlberg.

Castle in Savonlinna — A57

1945, Sept. 4
247 A57 15m lilac rose 2.00 .40
248 A44 20m sepia 2.00 .40
See Nos. 219-219B. For a 35m of type A57, see No. 280.

Jean Sibelius — A58

1945, Dec. 8
249 A58 5m dk slate green .50 .50
Jean Sibelius (1865-1957), composer.

No. 176E Surcharged in Black

1946, Mar. 16
250 A26 8(m) on 5m purple .50 .40

Victorious Athletes — A59

1946, June 1 Engr. Perf. 13½
251 A59 8m brown violet .40 .50
3rd Sports Festival, Helsinki, June 27-30, 1946.

Lighthouse at Uto — A60

1946, Sept. 19
252 A60 8m deep violet .40 .50
250th anniv. of the Finnish Department of Pilots and Lighthouses.

Post Bus — A61

1946-47 Unwmk. Perf. 14
253 A61 16m gray black .60 .80
253A A61 30m gray black ('47) 2.00 .40
Issue dates: 16m, Oct. 16, 30m, Feb. 10.

Old Town Hall, Porvoo A62 | Cathedral, Porvoo A63

1946, Dec. 3
254 A62 5m gray black .40 .50
255 A63 8m deep claret .40 .50
600th anniv. of the founding of the city of Porvoo (Borga).

Waterfront, Tammisaari — A64

1946, Dec. 14
256 A64 8m grnsh black .60 .75
400th anniv. of the founding of the town of Tammisaari (Ekenas).

Lion Type of 1930
1947 Typo. Perf. 14
257 A26 2½m dark green .50 .40
258 A26 3m slate gray .40 .25
259 A26 6m deep orange 1.50 .40
260 A26 7m carmine .80 .25
261 A26 10m purple 2.50 .25
262 A26 12m deep blue 2.20 .25
Nos. 257-262 (6) 7.90 1.80
Issued: 3m, 6/9; 7m, 12m, 2/10; others, 1/20.

Pres. Juho K. Paasikivi — A65

1947, Mar. 15 Engr.
263 A65 10m gray black .50 .40

Postal Savings Emblem — A66

1947, Apr. 1
264 A66 10m brown violet .40 .40
60th anniv. of the foundation of the Finnish Postal Savings Bank.

Ilmarinen, the Plowman — A67

1947, June 2
265 A67 10m gray black .40 .40
2nd year of peace following WW II.

Girl and Boy Athletes — A68

1947, June 2
266 A68 10m bright blue .40 .50
Finnish Athletic Festival, Helsinki, June 29-July 3, 1947.

Wheat and Savings Bank Assoc. Emblem — A69

1947, Aug. 21
267 A69 10m red brown .40 .60
Finnish Savings Bank Assoc., 125th anniv.

Sower — A70

1947, Nov. 1
268 A70 10m gray black .50 .50
150th anniv. of Finnish Agricultural Societies.

Koli Mountain and Lake Pielisjärvi — A71

1947, Nov. 1
269 A71 10m indigo .50 .60
60th anniv. of the Finnish Touring Assoc.

Lion Type of 1930
1948 Typo. Perf. 14
270 A26 3m dark green 2.50 .25
271 A26 6m yellow green 1.00 .50
272 A26 9m carmine 1.00 .25
273 A26 15m dark blue 4.00 .40
274 A26 24m brown lake 1.50 .25
Nos. 270-274 (5) 10.00 1.65
Issued: 3m, 2/9; 24m, 4/26; others, 9/13.

No. 261 Surcharged in Black

1948, Feb. 9
275 A26 12(m) on 10m purple 1.20 .40

Statue of Michael Agricola — A72

12m, Agricola translating New Testament.

1948, Oct. 2 Engr. Perf. 14
276 A72 7m rose violet 1.00 1.70
277 A72 12m gray blue 1.00 1.70
400th anniv. of publication of the Finnish translation of the New Testament, by Michael Agricola.

Sveaborg Fortress — A73

1948, Oct. 15
278 A73 12m deep green 1.50 2.00
200th anniv. of the construction of Sveaborg Fortress on the Gulf of Finland.

Post Rider — A74

1948, Oct. 27
279 A74 12m green 7.00 18.00
Helsinki Philatelic Exhibition. Sold only at exhibition for 62m, of which 50m was entrance fee.

Castle Type of 1945
1949
280 A57 35m violet 7.00 .40
See Nos. 219-219B, 248-249.

Sawmill and Cellulose Plant — A75 | Pine Tree and Globe — A76

1949, June 15
281 A75 9m brown 2.00 3.00
282 A76 15m dull green 2.50 3.00
Issued to publicize the Third World Forestry Congress, Helsinki, July 10-20, 1949.

Woman with Torch — A77

1949, July 16 Engr. Perf. 14
283 A77 5m dull green 4.00 7.50
284 A77 15m red (Worker) 4.50 8.00
50th anniv. of the Finnish labor movement.

Harbor of Lappeenranta (Willmanstrand) A78 | Raahe (Brahestad) A79

1949
285 A78 5m dk blue grn 1.50 1.00
286 A79 9m brown carmine 1.50 1.50
287 A78 15m brt blue (Kristi-inan-kaupunki) 2.00 3.00
Nos. 285-287 (3) 5.00 5.50
300th anniv. of the founding of Willmanstrand, Brahestad and Kristinestad (Kristiinan-kaupunki).
Issued: 5m, 8/6; 9m, 8/13; 15m, 7/30.

FINLAND

Technical High School Badge — A80

1949, Sept. 13
288 A80 15m ultra 1.00 1.20
Founding of the technical school, cent.

Hannes Gebhard — A81

1949, Oct. 2
289 A81 15m dull green 1.00 1.20
Establishment of Finnish cooperatives, 50th anniv.

Finnish Lake Country — A82

1949, Oct. 8
290 A82 15m blue 1.20 1.50
75th anniv. of the UPU.

Lion Type of 1930

1950, Jan. 9 Typo. Perf. 14
291 A26 8m brt green 1.50 1.00
292 A26 9m red orange 1.80 .40
293 A26 10m violet brown 5.00 .25
294 A26 12m scarlet 1.00 .40
295 A26 15m plum 13.00 .25
296 A26 20m deep blue 6.00 .25
 Nos. 291-296 (6) 28.30 2.55

Forsell's Map of Old Helsinki — A83

J. A. Ehrenstrom and C. L. Engel — A84

City Hall — A85

1950, June 11 Engr.
297 A83 5m emerald .50 .70
298 A84 9m brown 1.00 1.20
299 A85 15m deep blue .80 .80
 Nos. 297-299 (3) 2.30 2.70
400th anniv. of the founding of Helsinki.

J. K. Paasikivi — A86

1950, Nov. 27
300 A86 20m deep ultra .80 .40
80th birthday of Pres. J. K. Paasikivi.

View of Kajaani — A87

1951, July 7 Unwmk. Perf. 14
301 A87 20m red brown .80 .70
Tercentenary of Kajaani.

Lion and Chopper Types of 1930

1952, Jan. 18 Typo.
302 A26 10m emerald 3.00 .25
303 A26 15m red 3.00 .25
304 A26 25m blue 4.00 .25
  Engr.
305 A29 40m black brown 3.50 .40
 Nos. 302-305 (4) 13.50 1.15

Arms of Pietarsaari — A88

1952, June 19 Unwmk. Perf. 14
306 A88 25m blue 1.00 1.00
300th anniv. of the founding of Pietarsaari (Jacobstad).

Rooftops of Vaasa — A89

1952, Aug. 3
307 A89 25m brown 1.00 1.00
Centenary of the burning of Vaasa.

Chess Symbols — A90

1952, Aug. 10
308 A90 25m gray 2.00 2.50
10th Chess Olympics, Helsinki, 8/10-31/52.

Torch Bearers — A91

1953, Jan. 27
309 A91 25m blue 1.20 1.00
Temperance movement in Finland, cent.

Air View of Hamina (Fredrikshamn) — A92

1953, June 20
310 A92 25m dk gray green .90 .90
Tercentenary of Hamina.

Ivar Wilskman — A93

1954, Feb. 26
311 A93 25m blue .80 .80
Centenary of the birth of Prof. Ivar Wilskman, "father of gymnastics in Finland."

Arms of Finland — A94

1954-59 Perf. 11½
312 A94 1m red brown ('55) .25 .25
313 A94 2m green ('55) .25 .25
314 A94 3m deep orange .25 .25
314A A94 4m gray ('58) .60 .50
315 A94 5m violet blue .70 .25
316 A94 10m blue green 1.20 .25
 a. Bklt. pane of 5 (vert. strip) 15.00 15.00
   Complete booklet, #316a 17.50
317 A94 15m rose red 3.50 .25
318 A94 15m yellow org ('57) 7.00 .25
319 A94 20m rose lilac 12.00 .25
320 A94 20m rose red ('56) 2.50 .25
321 A94 25m deep blue 4.50 .25
322 A94 25m rose lilac ('59) 10.00 .25
323 A94 30m lt ultra ('56) 2.50 .25
 Nos. 312-323 (13) 45.25 3.50
See Nos. 398, 400-405A, 457-459A, 461A-462, 464-464B.

"In the Outer Archipelago" — A95

1954, July 21 Perf. 14
324 A95 25m black .80 .80
Cent. of the birth of Albert Edelfelt, painter.

J. J. Nervander — A96

1955, Feb. 23
325 A96 25m blue 1.00 1.00
150th anniv. of the birth of J. J. Nervander, astronomer and poet.

Composite of Finnish Public Buildings — A97

1955, Mar. 30 Engr. Perf. 14
326 A97 25m gray 9.00 18.00
Sold for 125m, which included the price of admission to the Natl. Postage Stamp Exhibition, Helsinki, Mar. 30-Apr. 3, 1955.

Bishop Henrik with Foot on Lalli, his Murderer — A98

25m, Arrival of Bishop Henrik and monks.

1955, May 19
327 A98 15m rose brown 1.20 .80
328 A98 25m green 1.50 .80
Adoption of Christianity in Finland, 800th anniv.

Conference Hall Helsinki — A99

1955, Aug. 25
329 A99 25m bluish green 1.50 1.80
44th conf. of the Interparliamentarian Union, Helsinki, Aug. 25-31, 1955.

Sailing Vessel and Merchant — A100

1955, Sept. 2
330 A100 25m sepia 1.50 1.80
350th anniv. of founding of Oulu.

Town Hall, Lahti — A101

1955, Nov. 1 Perf. 14x13½
331 A101 25m violet blue 1.50 2.00
50th anniversary of founding of Lahti.

Radio Sender, Map of Finland — A102

Designs: 15m, Otto Nyberg. 25m, Telegraph wires and pines under snow.

Inscribed: Lennatin 1855-1955 Telegrafen

1955, Dec. 10 Perf. 14
332 A102 10m green 1.50 1.50
333 A102 15m dull violet 1.50 .80
334 A102 25m lt ultra 1.80 1.20
 Nos. 332-334 (3) 4.80 3.50
Cent. of the telegraph in Finland.

A103

1956, Jan. 26 Unwmk. Perf. 14
335 A103 25m Lighthouse, Porkkala Peninsula .80 1.00
Return of the Porkkala Region to Finland by Russia, Jan. 1956.

A104

30m, 50m, Church at Lammi. 40m, House of Parliament. 60m, Fortress of Olavinlinna (Olofsborg).

1956-57 Perf. 11½
336 A104 30m gray olive 1.00 .40
337 A104 40m dull purple 3.50 .25
338 A104 50m gray ol ('57) 7.00 .25
338A A104 60m pale pur ('57) 13.00 .25
 Nos. 336-338A (4) 24.50 1.15
Issued: 30m, 3/4; 40m, 3/11; 50m, 3/3; 60m, 4/7. See Nos. 406-408A.

Johan V. Snellman — A105

1956, May 12 Engr. Perf. 14
339 A105 25m violet brn .80 .80
Johan V. Snellman (1806-81), statesman.

Gymnast and Athletes — A106

1956, June 28
340 A106 30m violet blue 1.20 1.00
Finnish Gymnastic and Sports Games, Helsinki, June 28-July 1, 1956.

547

FINLAND

A107

Wmk. 208

1956, July 7 **Typo.** **Rouletted**
341 A107 30m deep ultra 3.50 6.50
  a. Tête bêche pair 7.00 12.00
  b. Pane of 10 42.50 75.00

Issued to publicize the FINLANDIA Philatelic Exhibition, Helsinki, July 7-15, 1956.
Printed in sheets containing four 2x5 panes, with white margins around each group. The stamps in each double row are printed tete-beche, making the position of the watermark differ in the vertical row of each pane of ten.
Sold for 155m, price including entrance ticket to exhibition.

Town Hall at Vasa — A108

Unwmk.
1956, Oct. 2 **Engr.** **Perf. 14**
342 A108 30m bright blue 1.20 1.00

350th anniversary of Vasa.

Northern Countries Issue

Whooper Swans — A108a

1956, Oct. 30 **Perf. 12½**
343 A108a 20m rose red 2.00 1.50
344 A108a 30m ultra 6.00 1.20

See footnote after Denmark No. 362.

University Clinic, Helsinki — A109

1956, Dec. 17 **Perf. 11½**
345 A109 30m dull green 1.50 1.00

Public health service in Finland, bicent.

Scout Sign, Emblem and Globe — A110

1957, Feb. 22 **Perf. 14**
346 A110 30m ultra 1.90 1.20

50th anniversary of Boy Scouts.

Arms Holding Hammers and Laurel — A111

Design: 20m, Factories and cogwheel.

1957 **Engr.** **Perf. 13½**
347 A111 20m dark blue .80 .80
348 A111 30m carmine 1.00 1.00

50th anniv.: Central Fed. of Finnish Employers (20m, issued 9/27); Finnish Trade Union Movement (30m, issued 4/15).

"Lex" from Seal of Parliament — A112

1957, May 23 **Perf. 14**
349 A112 30m olive gray 1.20 1.20

50th anniv. of the Finnish parliament.

Harbor Type of 1942
1957 **Unwmk.** **Perf. 14**
350 A51 100m grnsh blue 10.00 .25

Ida Aalberg — A114

1957, Dec. 4 **Perf. 14**
351 A114 30m vio gray & mar .90 1.00

Birth cent. of Ida Aalberg, Finnish actress.

Arms of Finland — A115

1957, Dec. 6 **Perf. 11½**
352 A115 30m blue 1.00 1.20

40th anniv. of Finland's independence.

Jean Sibelius — A116

1957, Dec. 8 **Perf. 14**
353 A116 30m black 1.50 1.00

Jean Sibelius (1865-1957), composer.

Ski Jump — A117

Design: 30m, Skier, vert.

1958, Feb. 1 **Engr.** **Perf. 11½**
354 A117 20m slate green 1.20 1.00
355 A117 30m blue 1.20 .80

Nordic championships of the Intl. Ski Federation, Lahti.

"March of the Bjorneborgienses," by Edelfelt — A118

1958, Mar. 8
356 A118 30m violet gray .90 .90

400th anniv. of the founding of Pori (Bjorneborg).

South Harbor, Helsinki — A119

1958, June 2 **Unwmk.** **Perf. 11½**
357 A119 100m bluish green 20.00 .25

See No. 410.

Seal of Jyväskylä Lyceum — A120

1958, Oct. 1 **Perf. 11½**
358 A120 30m rose carmine 1.50 1.20

Cent. of the founding of the 1st Finnish secondary school.

Chrismon and Globe — A121

1959, Jan. 19
359 A121 30m dull violet .70 .60

Finnish Missionary Society, cent.

Diet at Porvoo, 1809 — A122

1959, Mar. 22 **Perf. 11½**
360 A122 30m dk blue gray .70 .60

150th anniv. of the inauguration of the Diet at Porvoo.

Saw Cutting Log — A123

1959, May 13 **Engr.**
361 A123 10m shown .70 .70
362 A123 30m Forest .70 .70

No. 361 for the cent. of the establishment of the 1st steam saw-mill in Finland; No. 362, the cent. of the Dept. of Forestry.

Pyhakoski Power Station — A124

1959, May 24
363 A124 75m gray 4.50 .40

See No. 409.

Oil Lamp — A125

1959, Dec. 19
364 A125 30m blue .80 .70

Cent. of the liberation of the country trade.

Woman Gymnast — A126

1959, Nov. 14 **Unwmk.**
365 A126 30m rose lilac 1.00 .80

Finnish women's gymnastics and the cent. of the birth of Elin Oihonna Kallio, pioneer of Finnish women's physical education.

Arms of Six New Towns — A127

1960, Jan. 2 **Perf. 14**
366 A127 30m light violet .90 .90

Issued to commemorate the founding of new towns in Finland: Hyvinkaa, Kouvola, Riihimaki, Rovaniemi, Salo and Seinajoki.

Type of 1860 Issue — A128

1960, Mar. 25 **Typo.** **Rouletted 4½**
367 A128 30m blue & gray 4.00 7.00

Cent. of Finland's serpentine roulette stamps, and in connection with HELSINKI 1960, 40th anniv. exhib. of the Federation of Philatelic Societies of Finland, Mar. 25-31. Sold only at the exhibition for 150m including entrance ticket.

Mother and Child, Waiting Crowd and Uprooted Oak Emblem — A129

1960, Apr. 7 **Engr.** **Perf. 11½**
368 A129 30m rose claret .80 .60
369 A129 40m dark blue 1.00 .60

World Refugee Year, 7/1/59-6/30/60.

Johan Gadolin — A130

1960, June 4 **Perf. 11½**
370 A130 30m dark brown .80 .70

Bicent. of the birth of Gadolin, chemist.

Hj. Nortamo — A131

1960, June 13 **Unwmk.**
371 A131 30m gray green .80 .70

Cent. of the birth of Hj. Nortamo (Hjalmar Nordberg), writer.

Symbolic Tree and Cuckoo — A132

1960, June 18
372 A132 30m vermilion .80 .70

Karelian Natl. Festival, Helsinki, June 18-19.

Geodetic Instrument — A133

Design: 30m, Aurora borealis and globe.

1960, July 26 **Unwmk.** **Perf. 13½**
373 A133 10m blue & pale brn .80 .60
374 A133 30m ver & rose car 1.00 .60

12th General Assembly of the Intl. Union of Geodesy and Geophysics, Helsinki.

FINLAND

 Urho Kekkonen — A134

1960, Sept. 3   **Engr.**   **Perf. 11½**
375 A134 30m violet blue   .90   .40
Issued to honor President Urho Kekkonen on his 60th birthday.

Common Design Types
pictured following the introduction.

Europa Issue, 1960
Common Design Type
1960, Sept. 19   **Perf. 13½**
Size: 30½x21mm.
376 CD3 30m dk bl & Prus bl   .80   .70
377 CD3 40m dk brn & plum   1.00   .70
A 30m gray similar to No. 376 was printed with simulated perforations in a non-valid souvenir sheet privately released in London for STAMPEX 1961.

 Uno Cygnaeus — A135

1960, Oct. 13   **Perf. 11½**
378 A135 30m dull violet   .70   .70
150th anniv. of the birth of Pastor Uno Cygnaeus, founder of elementary schools.

 "Pommern" and Arms of Mariehamn — A136

1961, Feb. 21   **Perf. 11½**
379 A136 30m grnsh blue   2.50   1.80
Centenary of the founding of Mariehamn.

 Lake and Rowboat A137   Turku Castle A138

1961   **Engr.**   **Unwmk.**
380 A137 5m green   .25   .25
381 A138 125m slate green   20.00   .35
See Nos. 399, 411.

 Postal Savings Bank Emblem — A139

1961, May 24
382 A139 30m Prus green   .70   .40
75th anniv. of Finland's Postal Savings Bank.

 Symbol of Standardization A140

1961, June 5   **Litho.**   **Perf. 14x13½**
383 A140 30m dk sl grn & org   .70   .50
Meeting of the Intl. Organization for Standardization (ISO), Helsinki, June 5.

 Juhani Aho — A141

Perf. 11½
1961, Sept. 11   **Unwmk.**   **Engr.**
384 A141 30m red brown   .70   .70
Juhani Aho (1861-1921), writer.

 Various Buildings — A142

1961, Oct. 16   **Perf. 11½**
385 A142 30m slate   .70   .70
150 years of the Central Board of Buildings.

 Arvid Jarnefelt — A143

1961, Nov. 16
386 A143 30m deep claret   .70   .60
Cent. of the birth of Arvid Jarnefelt, writer

 Bank of Finland — A144

1961, Dec. 12   **Engr.**   **Perf. 11½**
387 A144 30m brown violet   .70   .70
150th anniversary of Bank of Finland.

 First Finnish Locomotive — A145

30m, Steam locomotive & timber car. 40m, Diesel locomotive & passenger train.
1962, Jan. 31   **Unwmk.**   **Perf. 11½**
388 A145 10m gray green   1.00   .60
389 A145 30m violet blue   1.50   .60
390 A145 40m dull red brown   4.00   .60
Nos. 388-390 (3)   6.50   1.80
Centenary of the Finnish State Railways.

 Mora Stone — A146

1962, Feb. 15
391 A146 30m gray brown   .70   .80
Issued to commemorate 600 years of political rights of the Finnish people.

 Senate Place, Helsinki — A147

1962, Apr. 8   **Unwmk.**   **Perf. 11½**
392 A147 30m violet brown   .70   .80
Sesquicentennial of the proclamation of Helsinki as capital of Finland.

 Customs Emblem — A148

1962, Apr. 11
393 A148 30m red   .70   .80
Finnish Board of Customs, sesquicentennial.

 Staff of Mercury — A149

1962, May 21   **Engr.**
394 A149 30m bluish green   .70   .70
Cent. of the 1st commercial bank in Finland.

 Santeri Alkio — A150

1962, June 17   **Unwmk.**   **Perf. 11½**
395 A150 30m brown carmine   .80   .80
Cent. of the birth of Santeri Alkio, writer and pioneer of the young people's societies in Finland.

 Finnish Labor Emblem and Conveyor Belt — A151

1962, Oct. 19
396 A151 30m chocolate   .70   .40
National production progress.

 Survey Plane and Compass — A152

1962, Nov. 14
397 A152 30m yellow green   .90   .70
Finnish Land Survey Board, 150th anniv.

Types of 1954-61 and

 House of Parliament — A152a   Church at Lammi — A152b

 Fortress of Olavinlinna — A152c   Log Floating — A153

 Parainen Bridge — A154   Farm on Lake Shore — A155

 Aerial View of Punkaharju — A155a   A155b

 Ristikallio in Kuusamo — A156

1963-67		**Engr.**	**Perf. 11½**	
398	A94	5p vio blue	.80	.25
a.		Booklet pane of 2 (vert. pair)	22.50	20.00
b.		Bklt. pane of 2 (horiz. pair)	12.00	10.00
399	A137	5p green	.25	.25
400	A94	10p blue grn	2.50	.25
a.		Booklet pane of 2 (vert. pair)	22.50	20.00
401	A94	15p yel org	1.50	.25
402	A94	20p rose red	2.50	.25
a.		Booklet pane of 1	24.00	
		Complete booklet, #398a, 400a, 402a	85.00	
b.		Bklt. pane, 2 #400, 1 #402 + label; horiz. strip	45.00	35.00
		Complete booklet, #398b, 402b	100.00	
c.		Bklt. pane, 2 #398, 2 #400, 1 #402; horiz. strip	3.50	3.50
		Complete booklet, #402c	5.00	
403	A94	25p rose lilac	2.50	.25
404	A94	30p lt ultra	4.00	.25
404A	A94	30p blue gray ('65)	7.00	.25
405	A94	35p blue	1.50	.25
405A	A94	40p ultra ('67)	1.50	.40
406	A152a	40p dull pur	7.00	.40
407	A152b	50p gray olive	4.50	.40
408	A152c	60p pale pur	12.00	.40
408A	A152c	65p pale pur ('67)	1.50	.25
409	A124	75p gray	2.50	.40
410	A119	1m bluish grn	1.50	.25
411	A138	1.25m slate grn	2.50	.40
412	A153	1.50m dk grnsh gray	1.50	.40
413	A154	1.75m blue	2.00	.40
414	A155	2m grn ('64)	18.00	.25
414A	A155a	2.50m ultra & yel grn ('67)	15.00	.50
414B	A155b	2.50m ultra, dk grn & yel grn ('69)	2.50	.40
415	A156	5m dk slate grn ('64)	20.00	.40
		Nos. 398-415 (23)	114.55	7.50

Pennia denominations expressed: "0.05," "0.10," etc.
Four stamps of type A94 (5p, 10p, 20p, 25p) come in two types: I. Four vertical lines in "O" of SUOMI. II. Three lines in "O."
For similar designs see Nos. 457-470A.

 Mother and Child — A157

1963, Mar. 21   **Unwmk.**   **Perf. 11½**
416 A157 40p red brown   .55   .40
FAO "Freedom from Hunger" campaign.

 "Christ Today" — A158

Design: 10p, Crown of thorns and medieval cross of consecration.

1963, July 30   **Engr.**   **Perf. 11½**
417 A158 10p maroon   .50   .45
418 A158 30p dark green   .50   .45
4th assembly of the Lutheran World Federation, Helsinki, July 30-Aug. 8.

Europa Issue, 1963
Common Design Type
1963, Sept. 16   Size: 30x20mm
419 CD6 40p red lilac   1.25   .55

 Assembly Building, Helsinki — A159

1963, Sept. 18
420 A159 30p violet blue   .70   .40
Representative Assembly of Finland, cent.

FINLAND

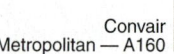

Convair Metropolitan — A160

Design: 40p, Caravelle jetliner.

1963, Nov. 1
421 A160 35p slate green   1.00   .60
422 A160 40p brt ultra   1.10   .50

40th anniversary of Finnish air traffic.

M. A. Castrén — A161

1963, Dec. 2   **Unwmk.**
423 A161 35p violet blue   .70   .45

Matthias Alexander Castrén (1813-52), ethnologist and philologist.

Stone Elk's Head, 2000 B.C. — A162

1964, Feb. 5   **Litho.**   **Perf. 14**
424 A162 35p ocher & slate grn   .70   .45

Cent. of the Finnish Artists' Association. The soapstone sculpture was found at Huittinen.

Emil Nestor Setälä — A163

1964, Feb. 27   **Engr.**   **Perf. 11½**
425 A163 35p dk red brown   .80   .50

Emil Nestor Setälä (1864-1946), philologist, minister of education and foreign affairs and chancellor of Abo University.

Staff of Aesculapius — A164

1964, June 13   **Unwmk.**   **Perf. 11½**
426 A164 40p slate green   1.10   .45

18th General Assembly of the World Medical Association, Helsinki, June 13-19, 1964.

Ice Hockey — A165

1965, Jan. 4   **Engr.**
427 A165 35p dark blue   1.10   .60

World Ice Hockey Championships, Finland, March 3-14, 1965.

Design from Centenary Medal — A166

1965, Feb. 6   **Unwmk.**   **Perf. 11½**
428 A166 35p olive gray   .70   .40

Centenary of communal self-government in Finland.

K. J. Stahlberg and "Lex" by W. Runeberg — A167

1965, Mar. 22   **Engr.**
429 A167 35p brown   .70   .40

Kaarlo Juho Stahlberg (1865-1952), 1st Pres. of Finland.

International Cooperation Year Emblem — A168

1965, Apr. 2   **Litho.**   **Perf. 14**
430 A168 40p bis, dull red, blk & grn   .70   .40

UN International Cooperation Year.

"Fratricide" by Gallen-Kallela — A169

35p, Girl's Head by Akseli Gallen-Kallela.

1965, Apr. 26   **Perf. 13½x14**
431 A169 25p multicolored   1.20   .65
432 A169 35p multicolored   1.20   .65

Centenary of the birth of the painter Aksell Gallen-Kallela.

Sibelius, Piano and Score — A170

Design: 35p, Musical score and bird.

1965, May 15   **Engr.**   **Perf. 11½**
433 A170 25p violet   1.00   .60
434 A170 35p dull green   1.00   .40

Jean Sibelius (1865-1957), composer.

Antenna for Satellite Telecommunication A171

1965, May 17
435 A171 35p blue   .70   .50

Cent. of the ITU.

"Winter Day" by Pekka Halonen — A172

Perf. 14x13½
1965, Sept. 23   **Litho.**   **Unwmk.**
436 A172 35p gold & multi   .70   .70

Centenary of the birth of the painter Pekka Halonen.

Europa Issue, 1965
Common Design Type
Engraved and Lithographed

1965, Sept. 27   **Perf. 13½x14**
437 CD8 40p bister, red brn, dk bl & grn   1.25   .55

"Growth" — A173

1966, May 11   **Litho.**   **Perf. 14**
438 A173 35p vio blue & blue   .70   .40

Centenary of the promulgation of the Elementary School Decree.

Old Post Office — A174

1966, June 11   **Litho.**   **Perf. 14**
439 A174 35p ocher, yel, dk bl & blk   4.00   7.00

Cent. of the 1st postage stamps in Finnish currency, and in connection with the NORDIA Stamp Exhibition, Helsinki, June 11-15. The stamp was sold only to buyers of a 1.25m exhibition entrance ticket.

UNESCO Emblem and World Map — A175

Lithographed and Engraved
1966, Oct. 9   **Perf. 14**
440 A175 40p grn, yel, blk & brn org   .65   .30

20th anniv. of UNESCO.

Finnish Police Emblem — A176

1966, Oct. 15
441 A176 35p dp ultra, blk & sil   .65   .30

Issued to honor the Finnish police.

Insurance Sesquicentennial Medal — A177

1966, Oct. 28   **Engr. & Photo.**
442 A177 35p mar, ol & blk   .65   .30

150th anniv. of the Finnish insurance system.

UNICEF Emblem — A178

1966, Nov. 14
443 A178 15p lt ultra, pur & grn   .50   .40

Activities of UNICEF.

"FINEFTA," Finnish Flag and Circle — A179

1967, Feb. 15   **Engr.**   **Perf. 14**
444 A179 40p ultra   .65   .30

European Free Trade Association, EFTA. See note after Denmark No. 431.

Windmill and Arms of Uusikaupunki — A180

Lithographed and Engraved
1967, Apr. 19   **Perf. 14**
445 A180 40p multicolored   .65   .30

350th anniv. of Uusikaupunki (Nystad).

Mannerheim Monument by Aimo Tukiainen — A181

1967, June 4   **Perf. 14**
446 A181 40p violet & multi   .65   .30

Cent. of the birth of Field Marshal Carl Gustav Emil Mannerheim.

Double Mortise Corner — A182

1967, June 16   **Litho. & Photo.**
447 A182 40p multicolored   .65   .30

Issued to honor Finnish settlers in Sweden.

Watermark of Thomasböle Paper Mill — A183

1967, Sept. 6   **Perf. 14**
448 A183 40p olive & black   .65   .30

300th anniv. of the Finnish paper industry.

Martin Luther, by Lucas Cranach — A184

Photogravure and Engraved
1967, Nov. 4   **Perf. 14**
449 A184 40p bister & brown   .65   .30

450th anniversary of the Reformation.

"Wood and Water" Globe and Flag — A185

Designs (Globe, Flag and): 25p, Flying swan. 40p, Ear of wheat.

1967, Dec. 5   **Perf. 11½**
450 A185 20p green & blue   .80   .30
451 A185 25p ultra & blue   .80   .30
452 A185 40p magenta & bl   .80   .30
    Nos. 450-452 (3)   2.40   .90

50th anniv. of Finland's independence.

Zachris Topelius and Blue Bird — A186

1968, Jan. 14   **Litho.**   **Perf. 14**
453 A186 25p blue & multi   1.10   .50

Topelius (1818-98), writer and educator.

Skiers and Ski Lift — A187

1968, Feb. 19   **Photo.**   **Perf. 14**
454 A187 25p multicolored   .85   .70

Winter Tourism in Finland.

FINLAND

Paper Making, by
Hannes Autere — A188

1968, Mar. 12   Litho.   Wmk. 363
455 A188 45p dk red, brn & org   .70   .45
Finnish paper industry and 150th anniv. of the oldest Finnish paper mill, Tervakoski, whose own watermark was used for this stamp.

World Health
Organization
Emblem — A189

Lithographed and Photogravure
1968, Apr. 6   Unwmk.   Perf. 14
456 A189 40p red org, dk blue & gold   .65   .30
To honor World Health Organization.

Lion Type of 1954-58 and

Market Place and
Mermaid
Fountain, Helsinki
A190

Keuru Wooden Church,
1758
A191

Häme Bridge,
Tampere
A192

Finnish Arms from Grave
of King Gustav Vasa,
1581
A194

A194a

25p, Post bus. 30p, Aquarium-Planetarium, Tampere. No. 463, P.O., Tampere. No. 465, National Museum, Helsinki, vert. No. 467A, like 70p. 1.30m, Helsinki railroad station.

Engr. (type A94, except #459A):
Litho. (#459A, 465 & type A190);
Engr. & Litho. (others)
Perf. 11½; 12½ (#466, 467A); 13
(#465); 13½ (#470); 14 (#463, 470A)
1968-78
457 A94   1p lt red brn   .25   .40
458 A94   2p gray green   .25   .40
459 A94   4p gray   .60   .50
459A A94   5p violet blue   1.80   2.50
460 A192 25p multi ('71)   .80   .25
461 A191 80p multi ('71)   2.00   .25
461A A94   35p dull org
                ('74)   .60   .40
  b.   Bklt. pane of 4, #459A,
       461A, 400, 464A + label   2.50   2.50
       Complete booklet #461b   3.50
462 A94   40p org ('73)   .80   .50
  a.   Bklt. pane of 3, #462, 2
       #404A + 2 labels   6.00   8.00
       Complete booklet #462a   8.00
463 A192 40p multi ('73)   1.20   .25
464 A94   50p lt ultra
                ('70)
                                  2.50   .25
  c.   Bklt. pane of 5, #401, 403,
       464, 2 #459A + 5 labels 13.00 14.50
       Complete booklet #464c   14.00
464A A94   50p rose lake
                ('74)   1.00   .25
  d.   Bklt. pane of 4, #400,
       464A, 2 #402 + label   1.75   1.75
       Complete booklet #464Ad   2.00

464B A94   60p blue ('73)   .80   .25
465 A191 60p multi ('73)   1.20   .25
466 A190 70p multi ('73)   2.00   .40
467 A191 80p multi ('70)   6.00   .40
467A A190 80p multi ('76)   1.00   .40
468 A192 90p multi   1.50   .40
469 A191 1.30m multi ('71)   .80   .40
470 A194 10m multi ('74)   6.00   .25
470A A194a 20m multi ('78)   10.00   1.00
       Nos. 457-470A (20)   41.10   9.70
Issued: 5p, 6/72.

Infantry Monument,
Vaasa — A195

Designs: 25p, War Memorial (cross), Hietaniemi Cemetery. 40p, Soldier, 1968.

1968, June 4   Photo.   Perf. 14
471 A195 20p lt violet & multi 1.00   .40
472 A195 25p lt blue & multi   1.00   .40
473 A195 40p orange & multi   1.00   .40
       Nos. 471-473 (3)   3.00   1.20
To honor Finnish national defense.

Camping
Ground — A196

1968, June 10   Litho.
474 A196 25p multicolored   .80   .70
Issued to publicize Finland for summer vacations.

Paper, Pulp and
Pine — A197

Lithographed and Embossed
1968, July 2   Unwmk.   Perf. 14
475 A197 40p multicolored   .70   .40
Finnish wood industry.

Mustola Lock, Saima
Canal — A198

1968, Aug. 5   Litho.   Perf. 11
476 A198 40p multicolored   .70   .40
Opening of the Saima Canal.

Oskar Merikanto and
Pipe Organ — A199

1968, Aug. 5   Unwmk.
477 A199 40p vio, silver & lt brn 1.10 .40
Centenary of the birth of Oskar Merikanto, composer.

Ships in Harbor and
Emblem of Central
Chamber of
Commerce — A200

1968, Sept. 13   Litho.   Perf. 14
478 A200 40p lt bl, brt bl & blk .70   .40
Publicizing economic development and for the 50th anniv. of the Central Chamber of Commerce of Finland.

Welder — A201

1968, Oct. 11   Litho.   Perf. 14
479 A201 40p blue & multi   .70   .40
Finnish metal industry.

Lyre, Students'
Emblem — A202

Lithographed and Engraved
1968, Nov. 24   Perf. 14
480 A202 40p ultra, vio bl & gold .70   .40
Issued to publicize the work of the student unions in Finnish social life.

Nordic Cooperation Issue

Five Ancient
Ships — A203

1969, Feb. 28   Engr.   Perf. 11½
481 A203 40p lt ultra   2.00   .40
50th anniv. of the Nordic Society and centenary of postal cooperation among the northern countries. The design is taken from a coin found at the site of Birka, an ancient Swedish town. See also Denmark Nos. 454-455, Iceland Nos. 404-405, Norway Nos. 523-524 and Sweden Nos. 808-810.

Town Hall and Arms
of Kemi — A203a

1969, Mar. 5   Photo.   Perf. 14
482 A203a 40p multicolored   .70   .40
Centenary of the town of Kemi.

Europa Issue, 1969
Common Design Type
1969, Apr. 28   Photo.   Perf. 14
Size: 30x20mm
483 CD12 40p dl rose, vio bl & dk bl 2.50 .60

ILO Emblem — A204

Lithographed and Engraved
1969, June 2   Perf. 11½
484 A204 40p dp rose & vio blue .70   .40
50th anniv. of the ILO.

Armas Järnefelt — A205

1969, Aug. 14   Photo.   Perf. 14
485 A205 40p multicolored   1.00   .40
Järnefelt (1869-1958), composer and conductor. Portrait on stamp by Vilho Sjöström.

Emblems and
Flag — A206

1969, Sept. 19   Photo.   Perf. 14
486 A206 40p lt bl, blk, grn & lil .70   .40
Publicizing the importance of National and International Fairs in Finnish economy.

Johannes
Linnankoski — A207

1969, Oct. 18   Litho.
487 A207 40p dk brn red & multi .70   .40
Linnankoski (1869-1913), writer.

Educational
Symbols — A208

Lithographed and Engraved
1969, Nov. 24   Perf. 11½
488 A208 40p gray, vio & grn   .70   .40
Centenary of the Central School Board.

DC-8-62 CF Plane
and Helsinki
Airport — A209

1969, Dec. 22   Photo.   Perf. 14
489 A209 25p sky blue & multi 1.10   .75

Golden
Eagle — A210

1970, Feb. 10   Litho.   Perf. 14
490 A210 30p multicolored   2.00   .50
Year of Nature Conservation, 1970.

Swatches in Shape
of Factories — A211

1970, Mar. 9   Litho.   Perf. 14
491 A211 50p multicolored   .85   .40
Finnish textile industry.

Molecule Diagram
and
Factories — A212

1970, Mar. 26   Photo.   Perf. 14
492 A212 60p multicolored   .65   .40
Finnish chemical industry.

UNESCO
Emblem
and Lenin
A213

Atom
Diagram
and Laurel
A214

FINLAND

UN Emblem and Globe — A215

1970   Litho. and Engr.
493 A213 30p gold & multi .70 .40
494 A214 30p red & multi .70 .40
Photogravure and Gold Embossed
495 A215 30p bl, vio bl & gold .70 .40
    Nos. 493-495 (3) 2.10 1.20

25th anniv. of the UN. No. 493 also publicizes the UNESCO-sponsored Lenin Symposium, Tampere, Apr. 6-10. No. 494 also publicizes the Nuclear Data Conf. of the Atomic Energy Commission, Otaniemi (Helsinki), June 15-19.
Issued: No. 493, 4/6; No. 494, 6/15; No. 495, 10/24.

Handicapped Volleyball Player — A216

1970, June 27   Litho.   Perf. 14
496 A216 50p orange, red & blk 1.00 .40

Issued to publicize the position of handicapped civilians and war veterans in society and their potential contributions to it.

Meeting of Auroraseura Society — A217

1970, Aug. 15   Photo.   Perf. 14
497 A217 50p multicolored .70 .40

200th anniv. of the Auroraseura Soc., dedicated to the study of Finnish history, geography, economy and language. The design of the stamp is after a painting by Eero Jarnefelt.

Uusikaarlepyy Arms, Church and 17th Cent. Building — A218

Design: No. 499, Arms of Kokkola, harbor, Sports Palace and 17th century building.
1970   Perf. 14
498 A218 50p multicolored .70 .40
499 A218 50p multicolored .70 .40

Towns of Uusikaarlepyy and Kokkola, 350th anniv.
Issued: No. 498, Aug. 21; No. 499, Sept. 17.

Urho Kekkonen, Medal by Aimo Tukiainen — A219

1970, Sept. 3   Litho. & Engr.
500 A219 50p ultra, sil & blk .70 .40

70th birthday of Pres. Urho Kekkonen.

Globe, Maps of US, Finland, USSR — A220

Lithographed and Gold Embossed
1970, Nov. 2
501 A220 50p blk, bl, pink & gold .70 .40

Strategic Arms Limitation Talks (SALT) between the US & USSR, Helsinki, 11/2-12/18.

Pres. Paasikivi by Essi Renavall — A221

1970, Nov. 27   Photo.   Perf. 14
502 A221 50p gold, brt bl & slate .70 .40

Centenary of the birth of Juho Kusti Paasikivi (1870-1956), President of Finland.

Cogwheels — A222

1971, Jan. 28   Litho.   Perf. 14
503 A222 50p multicolored .70 .40

Finnish industry.

Europa Issue, 1971
Common Design Type
1971, May 3   Litho.   Perf. 14
Size: 30x20mm
504 CD14 50p dp rose, yel & blk 2.50 .50

Tornio Church — A223

1971, May 12   Litho.   Perf. 14
505 A223 50p multicolored 1.00 .40

350th anniversary of the town of Tornio.

Front Page, January 15, 1771 — A224

1971, June 1   Litho.   Perf. 14
506 A224 50p multicolored .70 .40

Bicentenary of the Finnish press.

Athletes in Helsinki Stadium — A225

50p, Running & javelin in Helsinki Stadium.
1971, July 5   Litho.   Perf. 14
507 A225 30p multicolored 1.00 .50
508 A225 50p multicolored 2.00 .50

European Athletic Championships.

Sailboats — A226

1971, July 14
509 A226 50p multicolored 1.25 .60

International Lightning Class Championships, Helsinki, July 14-Aug. 1.

Silver Tea Pot, Guild's Emblem, Tools — A227

1971, Aug. 6
510 A227 50p lilac & multi .70 .40

600th anniv. of Finnish goldsmiths' art.

"Plastic Buttons and Houses" — A228

Photogravure and Embossed
1971, Oct. 20   Perf. 14
511 A228 50p multicolored .70 .40

Finnish plastics industry.

Europa Issue 1972
Common Design Type
1972, May 2   Litho.   Perf. 14
Size: 20x30mm
512 CD15 30p dk red & multi 1.50 .50
513 CD15 50p lt brn & multi 2.50 .50

Finnish National Theater — A229

1972, May 22.   Litho.   Perf. 14
514 A229 50p lt violet & multi .70 .40

Centenary of the Finnish National Theater, founded by Kaarlo and Emilie Bergbom.

Globe, US and USSR Flags — A230

1972, June 2
515 A230 50p multicolored 1.00 .40

Strategic Arms Limitation Talks (SALT), final meeting, Helsinki, Mar. 28-May 26; treaty signed, Moscow, May 26.

Map and Arms of Aland — A231

1972, June 9
516 A231 50p multicolored 1.50 .50

1st Provincial Meeting of Aland, 50th anniv.

Training Ship Suomen Joutsen — A232

1972, June 19
517 A232 50p orange & multi 1.00 .40

Tall Ships' Race 1972, Helsinki, Aug. 20.

Costume from Perni, 12th Cent. — A233

No. 519, Couple, Tenhola, 18th cent. No. 520, Girl, Nastola, 19th cent. No. 521, Man, Voyni, 19th cent. No. 522, Lapps, Inari, 19th cent.

1972, Nov. 19   Litho.   Perf. 13
518 A233 50p shown 2.00 .40
519 A233 50p multicolored 2.00 .40
520 A233 50p multicolored 2.00 .40
521 A233 50p multicolored 2.00 .40
522 A233 50p multicolored 2.00 .40
   a. Strip of 5, #518-522 10.00 14.50
     Complete booklet, 2 each
     #518-522 20.00

Regional costumes.
See Nos. 533-537.

Circle Surrounding Map of Europe — A234

1972, Dec. 11   Perf. 14x13½
523 A234 50p multicolored 2.00 .50

Preparatory Conference on European Security and Cooperation.

Book, Finnish and Soviet Colors — A235

Litho.; Gold Embossed
1973, Apr. 6   Perf. 14
524 A235 60p gold & multi .70 .40

Soviet-Finnish Treaty of Friendship, 25th anniv.

Kyösti Kallio (1873-1940), Pres. of Finland — A236

1973, Apr. 10   Litho.   Perf. 13
525 A236 60p multicolored .70 .40

Europa Issue 1973
Common Design Type
1973, Apr. 30   Photo.   Perf. 14
Size: 31x21mm
526 CD16 60p bl, brt bl & emer 1.25 .55

Nordic Cooperation Issue

Nordic House, Reykjavik — A236a

1973, June 26   Engr.   Perf. 12½
527 A236a 60p multicolored 1.00 .40
528 A236a 70p multicolored 1.00 .40

A century of postal cooperation among Denmark, Finland, Iceland, Norway and Sweden, and in connection with the Nordic Postal Conference, Reykjavik.

Map of Europe, "EUROPA" as a Maze — A237

Litho. & Embossed
1973, July 3   Perf. 13
529 A237 70p multicolored .75 .40

Conference for European Security and Cooperation, Helsinki, July 1973.

Paddling — A238

1973, July 18   Litho.   Perf. 14
530 A238 60p multicolored .75 .40

Canoeing World Championships, Tampere, July 26-29.

FINLAND

Radiosonde, WMO Emblem — A239

1973, Aug. 6   **Litho.**   *Perf. 14*
531   A239   60p multicolored   .70   .40
Cent. of intl. meteorological cooperation.

Eliel Saarinen and Design for Parliament, Helsinki — A240

1973, Aug. 20   *Perf. 12½x13*
532   A240   60p multicolored   .70   .40
Eliel Saarinen (1873-1950), architect.

Costume Type of 1972
Designs: No. 533, Woman, Kaukola. 534, Woman, Jaaski. No. 535, Married couple, Koivisto. No. 536, Mother and son, Sakyla. No. 537, Girl, Hainavesi.

1973, Oct. 10   **Litho.**   *Perf. 13*
533   A233   60p multicolored   2.50   .40
534   A233   60p multicolored   2.50   .40
535   A233   60p multicolored   2.50   .40
536   A233   60p multicolored   2.50   .40
537   A233   60p multicolored   2.50   .40
  a.   Strip of 5, #533-537   12.50   19.00
Regional costumes.

DC10-30 Jet — A241

1973, Nov. 1   **Litho.**   *Perf. 14*
538   A241   60p multicolored   .80   .40
50th anniv. of regular air service, Finnair.

Santa Claus in Reindeer Sleigh — A242

1973, Nov. 15   **Litho.**   *Perf. 14*
539   A242   30p multicolored   .95   .40
Christmas 1973.

"The Barber of Seville" — A243

1973, Nov. 21
540   A243   60p multicolored   .70   .40
Centenary of opera in Finland.

Production of Porcelain Jug — A244

1973, Nov. 23
541   A244   60p blue & multi   .70   .40
Finnish porcelain.

Nurmi, by Waino Aaltonen — A245

1973, Dec. 11
542   A245   60p multicolored   .85   .40
Paavo Nurmi (1897-1973), runner, Olympic winner, 1920-1924-1928.

Arms, Map and Harbor of Hanko — A246

1974, Jan. 10   **Litho.**   *Perf. 14*
543   A246   60p blue & multi   .75   .40
Centenary of the town of Hanko.

Ice Hockey — A247

1974, Mar. 5   **Litho.**   *Perf. 14*
544   A247   60p multicolored   .70   .40
European and World Ice Hockey Championships, held in Finland.

Seagulls (7 Baltic States) — A248

1974, Mar. 18   *Perf. 12½*
545   A248   60p multicolored   1.00   .40
Protection of marine environment of the Baltic Sea.

Goddess of Freedom, by Waino Aaltonen — A249

1974, Apr. 29   **Litho.**   *Perf. 13x12½*
546   A249   70p sil & multi   1.50   .50
Europa.

Ilmari Kianto and Old Pine — A250

1974, May 7   *Perf. 13*
547   A250   60p multicolored   .70   .40
Ilmari Kianto (1874-1970), writer.

Society Emblem, Symbol — A251

Lithographed and Embossed
1974, June 12   *Perf. 13½x14*
548   A251   60p gold & multi   .70   .40
Centenary of Adult Education.

Grid — A252

1974, June 14   **Litho.**   *Perf. 14x13½*
549   A252   60p multicolored   .70   .40
Rationalization Year in Finland, dedicated to economic and business improvements.

UPU Emblem — A253

1974, Oct. 10   **Litho.**   *Perf. 13½x14*
550   A253   60p multicolored   .70   .40
551   A253   70p multicolored   .70   .40
Centenary of Universal Postal Union.

Elves Distributing Gifts — A254

1974, Nov. 16   **Litho.**   *Perf. 14x13½*
552   A254   35p multicolored   1.00   .25
Christmas 1974.

Concrete Bridge and Granite Bridge, Aunessilta — A255

1974, Dec. 17   **Litho. & Engr.**   *Perf. 14*
553   A255   60p multicolored   .70   .50
Royal Finnish Directorate of Roads and Waterways, 175th anniversary.

Coat of Arms, 1581 A256

Chimneyless Log Sauna A256a

Cheese Frames A257

Carved Wooden Distaffs A258

Kirvu Weather Vane — A258a

1.50m, Wood-carved high drinking bowl, 1542.

Perf. 11½; 14 (2m, 5m)
1975-90   Engr.
555   A256   10p red lil ('78)   .25   .40
  a.   Bklt. pane of 4 (#555, 2 #556, #558) + label   2.25   2.25
    Complete booklet, #555a   2.50
  b.   Bklt. pane of 5 (2 #555, #557, #563, #564)   2.50   2.25
    Complete booklet, #555b   5.00
  c.   As "a," no label   2.50   2.50
    Complete booklet, #555c   3.00
  d.   Perf. 13x12½   .35   .25
556   A256   20p olive ('77)   .25   .40
  a.   20p yellow bister ('85)   1.10   1.40
  b.   As "a," perf. 13x12½   .50   .50
557   A256   30p car ('77)   1.20   1.10
557A   A256   30p car, litho.   2.40   1.50
558   A256   40p orange   .25   .25
  a.   Perf. 13x12½   .70   .70
559   A256   50p green ('76)   .25   .25
  a.   Perf. 13x12½   .80   .80
560   A256   60p blue   .40   .40
  a.   Perf. 13x12½   .60   .60
561   A256   70p sepia   .40   .25
562   A256   80p dl red & bl grn ('76)   .40   .40
  a.   Perf. 13x12½   3.25   3.25
563   A256   90p vio bl ('77)   .40   .40
564   A256   1.10m yellow ('79)   .40   .40
565   A256   1.20m dk blue ('79)   .40   .50
566   A258   1.50m multi ('76)   .80   .25

Litho.
567   A256a   2m multi ('77)   1.00   .25
Lithographed and Engraved
568   A257   2.50m multi ('76)   .90   .40
  a.   Perf. 14   1.20   .80
569   A258   4.50m multi ('76)   1.60   .40
  a.   Perf. 14   2.00   2.00
570   A258a   5m multi ('77)   6.00   .25
  Nos. 555-570 (17)   17.30   7.65

Some denominations of design A256 exist in up to three engraving types.
Nos. 560a and 562a was only issued within the booklet panes Nos. 713a and 715a.
Issued: No. 557A, 6/3/80; No. 560a, 7/25/88; No. 555d, 7/25/89; No. 562a, 3/1/90; No. 558a, 8/18/94; No. 568a, 12/28/88; No. 569a, 9/26/88; No. 556b, 4/3/98.
See Nos. 629, 631-633, 711-715, 861.

Finland No. 16 — A259

Lithographed and Typographed
1975, Apr. 26   *Perf. 13*
571   A259   70p multicolored   3.00   1.00
Nordia 75 Philatelic Exhibition, Helsinki, Apr. 26-May 1. Sold only at exhibition for 3m including entrance ticket.

Girl Combing Hair, by Magnus Enckell — A260

Europa: 90p, The Washerwomen, by Tyko Sallinen (1879-1955).

1975, Apr. 28   **Litho.**   *Perf. 13x12½*
572   A260   70p gray & multi   1.00   .40
573   A260   90p tan & multi   1.50   .40

Balance of Justice, Sword of Legality — A261

1975, May 7   *Perf. 14*
574   A261   70p vio blue & multi   .70   .40
Sesquicentennial of State Economy Comptroller's Office.

Rescue Boat and Sinking Ship — A262

1975, June 2   **Litho.**   *Perf. 14*
575   A262   70p multicolored   .85   .40
12th Intl. Salvage Conf., Finland, stressing importance of coordinating sea, air and communications resources in salvage operations.

Safe and Unsafe Levels of Drugs — A263

1975, July 21   **Litho.**   *Perf. 14*
576   A263   70p multicolored   .70   .40
Importance of pharmacological studies and for the 6th Intl. Pharmacology Cong., Helsinki.

FINLAND

Olavinlinna Castle — A264

1975, July 29
577 A264 70p multicolored   .70   .40
500th anniversary of Olavinlinna Castle.

Swallows over Finlandia Hall — A265

1975, July 30
578 A265 90p multicolored   .70   .40
European Security and Cooperation Conference, Helsinki, July 30-Aug. 1. (The swallows of the design represent freedom, mobility and continuity.) See No. 709.

"Men and Women Working for Peace" — A266

1975, Oct. 24   *Litho.*   *Perf. 13x12½*
579 A266 70p multicolored   .70   .40
International Women's Year 1975.

"Continuity and Growth" — A267

1975, Oct. 29   *Perf. 13*
580 A267 70p brown & multi   .70   .40
Industrial Art and for the centenary of the Finnish Society of Industrial Art.

Boys as Three Kings and Herod — A268

1975, Nov. 8   *Perf. 14*
581 A268 40p blue & multi   1.10 .35
Christmas 1975.

Top Border of State Debenture — A269

Lithographed and Engraved
1976, Jan. 9   *Perf. 11½*
582 A269 80p multicolored   .70   .40
Centenary of State Treasury.

Glider over Lake Region — A270

1976, Jan. 13   *Litho.*   *Perf. 14*
583 A270 80p multicolored   .90   .40
15th World Glider Championships, Ryskala, June 13-27.

Prof. Heikki Klemetti (1876-1953), Musician & Writer — A271

1976, Feb. 14   *Litho.*   *Perf. 13*
584 A271 80p green & multi   .70   .40

Map with Areas of Different Dialects — A272

1976, Mar. 10   *Litho.*   *Perf. 13*
585 A272 80p multicolored   .70   .40
Finnish Language Society, centenary.

Aino Ackté, by Albert Edelfelt — A273

1976, Apr. 23
586 A273 70p yellow & multi .70   .40
Aino Ackté (1876-1944), opera singer.

Europa Issue

Knife from Voyri, Sheath and Belt — A274

1976, May 3   *Litho.*   *Perf. 13*
587 A274 80p violet bl & multi 1.50 .50

Radio and Television — A275

1976, Sept. 9   *Litho.*   *Perf. 13*
588 A275 80p multicolored   .70   .40
Radio broadcasting in Finland, 50th anniv.

Christmas Morning Ride to Church — A276

1976, Oct. 23   *Litho.*   *Perf. 14*
589 A276 50p multicolored   .90   .40
Christmas 1976.

Turku Chapter Seal (Virgin and Child) — A277

1976, Nov. 1   *Litho.*   *Perf. 12½*
590 A277 80p buff, brn & red .70   .40
Cathedral Chapter of Turku, 700th anniv.

Alvar Aalto, Finlandia Hall, Helsinki — A278

1976, Nov. 4
591 A278 80p multicolored   .70   .40
Hugo Alvar Henrik Aalto (1898-1976), architect.

Ice Dancers — A280

1977, Jan. 25   *Litho.*   *Perf. 13*
592 A280 90p multicolored   .70   .40
European Figure Skating Championships, Finland, Jan. 25-29.

Five Water Lilies — A281

Photogravure and Engraved
1977, Feb. 2   *Perf. 12½*
593 A281 90p brt green & multi .70 .40
594 A281 1m ultra & multi   .70   .40
Nordic countries cooperation for protection of the environment and 25th Session of Nordic Council, Helsinki, Feb. 19.

Icebreaker Rescuing Merchantman A282

1977, Mar. 2   *Litho.*   *Perf. 13*
595 A282 90p multicolored   .80   .40
Winter navigation between Finland and Sweden, centenary.

Nuclear Reactor — A283

1977, Mar. 3   *Perf. 12½x13*
596 A283 90p multicolored   .70   .40
Opening of nuclear power station on Hästholmen Island.

Europa Issue

Autumn Landscape, Northern Finland — A284

1977, May 2   *Litho.*   *Perf. 12½x13*
597 A284 90p multicolored   1.50 .45

Tree, Birds and Nest — A285

1977, May 4   *Perf. 13x12½*
598 A285 90p multicolored   .70   .40
75th anniversary of cooperative banks.

Orthodox Church, Valamo Cloister — A286

1977, May 31   *Litho.*   *Perf. 14*
599 A286 90p multicolored   .70   .40
Consecration festival of new Orthodox Church at Valamo Cloister, Heinävesi; 800th anniversary of introduction of orthodoxy in Karelia and of founding of Valamo Cloister.

Paavo Ruotsalainen (1777-1852), Lay Leader of Pietists in Finland — A287

1977, July 8   *Litho.*   *Perf. 13*
600 A287 90p multicolored   .70   .40

People Fleeing Fire and Water — A288

1977, Sept. 14   *Litho.*   *Perf. 14*
601 A288 90p multicolored   .70   .40
Civil defense for security.

Volleyball — A289

1977, Sept. 15
602 A289 90p multicolored   .70   .40
European Women's Volleyball Championships, Finland, Sept. 29-Oct. 2.

Children Bringing Water for Sauna — A290

1977, Oct. 25
603 A290 50p multicolored   1.10 .40
Christmas 1977.

Finnish Flag — A291

1977, Dec. 5   *Litho.*   *Perf. 14*
Size: 31x21mm
604 A291 80p multicolored   .70   .40
Size: 37x25mm
Perf. 13
605 A291 1m multicolored   1.20 .40
Finland's declaration of independence, 60th anniv.

Wall Telephone, 1880, New Telephone — A292

1977, Dec. 9   *Perf. 14*
606 A292 1m multicolored   .70   .40
Centenary of first telephone in Finland.

FINLAND

Harbor, Sunila Factory, Kotka Arms — A293

1978, Jan. 2   Litho.   *Perf. 14*
607 A293 1m multicolored   .70   .40
Centenary of founding of Kotka.

Paimio Sanitarium by Alvar Aalto — A294

Europa: 1.20m, Hvittrask studio house, 1902, horiz.

1978, May 2   Litho.   *Perf. 13*
608 A294   1m multicolored   4.00   .50
609 A294   1.20m multicolored   5.00   6.00

Rural Bus Service — A295

1978, June 8   Litho.   *Perf. 14*
610 A295 1m multicolored   .70   .40

Eino Leino and Eagle — A296

1978, July 6   Litho.   *Perf. 13*
611 A296 1m multicolored   .70   .40
Eino Leino (1878-1926), poet.

Function Theory and Rhythmical Lines — A297

1978, Aug. 15   Litho.   *Perf. 14*
612 A297 1m multicolored   .70   .40
ICM 78, International Congress of Mathematicians, Helsinki, Aug. 15-23.

Child Feeding Birds — A298

1978, Oct. 23   Litho.   *Perf. 14*
613 A298 50p multicolored   .90   .40
Christmas 1978.

A299

1979, Jan. 2   Litho.   *Perf. 13*
614 A299 1.10m multicolored   .75   .40
International Year of the Child.

Runner — A300

1979, Feb. 7   Litho.   *Perf. 14*
615 A300 1.10m multicolored   .70   .40
8th Orienteering World Championships, Finland, Sept. 1-4.

Old School, Hamina, Academy Flag — A301

1979, Mar. 20   Litho.   *Perf. 14*
616 A301 1.10m multicolored   .70   .40
200th anniv. of Finnish Military Academy.

A302

Design: Turku Cathedral and Castle, Prinkkala house, Brahe statue.

1979, Mar. 31
617 A302 1.10m multicolored   .70   .40

Streetcar, Helsinki — A303

1979, May 2   Litho.   *Perf. 14*
618 A303 1.10m multi   .70   .30
Non-polluting urban transportation.

View of Tampere, 1779 — A304

1979, May 2
619 A304 90p multicolored   .70   .40

View of Tampere, 1979 — A305

1979, Oct. 1   Litho.   *Perf. 13*
620 A305 1.10m multicolored   .70   .40
Bicentenary of founding of Tampere.

Optical Telegraph, 1796, Map of Islands — A306

Europa: 1.10m, Letter of Queen Christina to Per Brahe, 1638, establishing postal service.

1979, May 2   *Perf. 13*
621 A306 1.10m multi   1.50   .40
622 A306 1.30m multi, horiz.   2.50   1.00

Shops and Merchants' Signs — A307

1979, Sept. 26   *Perf. 14*
623 A307 1.10m multicolored   .70   .40
Business and industry regulation centenary.

Old and New Cars, Street Crossing — A308

1979, Oct. 1
624 A308 1.10m multicolored   .70   .40
Road safety.

Elves Feeding Horse — A309

1979, Oct. 24
625 A309 60p multicolored   .90   .40
Christmas 1979.

Korppi House, Lapinjarvi — A310

Farm houses, First Row: Syrjala House, Tammela, 2 stamps in continuous design; Murtovaara House, Valtimo; Antila House, Lapua. Second row: Lofts, Pohjanmaa; Courtyard gate, Kanajarvi House, Kalvola; Main door, Havuselka House, Kauhajoki; Maki-Rasinpera House and dinner bell tower; Gable and eaves, Rasula Kuortane granary.

1979, Oct. 27   *Perf. 13*
626   Booklet pane of 10   6.00   4.00
  a.-j. A310 1.10m single stamp   .60   .35
     Complete booklet, #626   6.00
See design A349a.

Type of 1975 and

Kauhaneva Swamp A315

Hame Castle, Hameenlinna A316

Windmill, Harrstrom A318

Multiharju Forest, Seitseminen Natl. Park A319

Bridal Rug, Teisko, 1815 A324

Iron-forged Door, Hollola Church A325

Iron Fish Spear c. 1100 — A326

Design: 1.80m, Eastern Gulf natl. park.

Litho. & Engr., Litho., Engr.
1979-98   *Perf. 14, 11½ (A256, A318)*
627 A315   70p multicolored   .40   .40
628 A316   90p brown red   .40   .40
629 A256   1m red brown   .40   .40
  a.   Perf. 13x12½ ('98)   1.25   1.25
630 A318   1m bl & red brn   .40   .40
631 A256   1.30m dk green   .60   .60
631A A256 1.30m dk green, litho.   .50   .60
  b.   Booklet pane, #555-556, 557-560, 631A   3.00   3.00
     Complete booklet, #631Ab   6.00
632 A256   1.40m purple   .50   .60
633 A256   1.50m grnsh blue   .60   .60
634 A319   1.60m multicolored   .50   .40
635 A315   1.80m multicolored   1.00   .40
636 A322   3m multicolored   1.50   .40
637 A323   6m multicolored   2.50   .25
638 A324   7m multicolored   2.50   .40
639 A325   8m multicolored   3.50   .50
640 A326   9m blk & dk bl   3.00   .70
     Nos. 627-640 (15)   18.30   7.05

Coil Stamps
Perf. 11½ Vert.
641 A316 90p brown red   .40   .40
Perf. 12½ Horiz.
642 A318 1m blue & red brn   .40   .60

Issued: 3m, 10/27/79; 6m, 4/9/80; No. 629, 1/2/81; 70p, 1/12/81; 90p, 9/1/82; 1.60m, 2/8/82; 7m, 2/15/82; No. 631, 1/3/83; Nos. 630, 642, 1/12/83; 1.80m, 8m, 2/10/83; 1.40m, 9m, 1/2/84; 1.50m, 1/2/85; No. 631A, 11/1/85.

Maria Jotuni (1880-1943), Writer — A327

1980, Apr. 9   Litho.
643 A327 1.10m multicolored   .55   .40

Frans Eemil Sillanpaa (1888-1964), Writer — A328

Europa: 1.30m, Artturi Ilmari Virtanen (1895-1973), chemist, vert.

1980, Apr. 28   *Perf. 13*
644 A328 1.10m multicolored   1.00   .40
645 A328 1.30m multicolored   1.50   1.00

Pres. Urho Kekkonen, 80th Birthday — A329

1980, Sept. 3   Litho.   *Perf. 13*
646 A329 1.10m multicolored   .55   .40

Nordic Cooperation Issue

Back-piece Harness, 19th century — A330

FINLAND

1980, Sept. 9   Perf. 14
647 A330 1.10m shown .55 .40
648 A330 1.30m Collar harness, vert. .55 .40

Biathlon — A331

1980, Oct. 17   Litho.   Perf. 14
649 A331 1.10m multicolored .55 .40

World Biathlon Championship, Lahti, Feb. 10-15, 1981.

Pull the Roller, Weighing out the Salt — A332

Christmas 1980 (Traditional Games): 1.10m, Putting out the shoemaker's eye.

1980, Oct. 27
650 A332 60p multicolored .60 .40
651 A332 1.10m multicolored .60 .40

Boxing Match — A333

1981, Feb. 28   Litho.   Perf. 14
652 A333 1.10m multicolored .60 .40

European Boxing Championships, Tampere, May 2-10.

Glass Blowing — A334

1981, Mar. 12
653 A334 1.10m multicolored .60 .40

Glass industry, 300th anniversary.

Mail Boat Furst Menschikoff, 1836 — A335

    Litho. & Engr.
1981, May 6   Perf. 13
654 A335 1.10m brown & tan 2.50 3.00

Nordia '81 Stamp Exhibition, Helsinki, May 6-10. Sold only at exhibition for 3m including entrance ticket.

Europa Issue

Rowing to Church — A336

Design: 1.50m, Midsummer's Eve dance.

1981, May 18   Litho.   Perf. 13
655 A336 1.10m shown .80 .40
656 A336 1.50m multicolored 1.20 .60

Traffic Conference Emblem — A337

1981, May 26   Litho.   Perf. 14
657 A337 1.10m multicolored .60 .40

European Conference of Ministers of Transport, May 25-28.

Boy and Girl Riding Pegasus — A338

1981, June 11
658 A338 1m multicolored .60 .40

Youth associations centenary.

Intl. Year of the Disabled — A339

1981, Sept. 2   Litho.   Perf. 13
659 A339 1.10m multicolored .60 .40

Christmas 1981 — A340

70p, Children, Christmas tree. 1.10m, Decorating tree, vert.

1981, Oct. 27   Litho.   Perf. 14
660 A340 70p multicolored .60 .40
661 A340 1.10m multicolored .80 .40

"Om Konsten att Ratt Behaga" First Issue (Periodicals Bicentenary) — A341

1982, Jan. 15
662 A341 1.20m multicolored .60 .40

Kuopio Bicentenary — A343

1982, Mar. 4   Litho.   Perf. 14
664 A343 1.20m multicolored .60 .40

Score, String Instrument Neck — A344

1982, Mar. 11   Perf. 13
665 A344 1.20m multicolored .80 .45

Centenaries of Sibelius Academy of Music and Helsinki Orchestra.

Electric Power Plant Centenary — A345

1982, Mar. 15   Perf. 14
666 A345 1.20m multicolored .60 .40

Gardening — A346

1982, Apr. 16   Litho.   Perf. 14
667 A346 1.10m multicolored .60 .40

Europa — A347

1.20m, Publication of Abckiria (1st Finnish book), 1543 (Sculpture of Mikael Agricola, translator, by Oskari Jauhiainen, 1951). 1.50m, Turku Academy, 1st Finnish university (Turku Academy Inaugural Procession, 1640, after Albert Edelfelt).

1982, Apr. 29   Litho.   Perf. 13x12½
668 A347 1.20m multicolored 1.00 .40

    Size: 47x31mm
    Perf. 12½
669 A347 1.50m multicolored 1.50 .60

Intl. Monetary Fund and World Bank Emblems — A348

1982, May 12   Perf. 14
670 A348 1.60m multicolored .60 .40

IMF Interim Committee and IMF-WB Joint Development Committee Meeting, Helsinki, May 12-14.

75th Anniv. of Unicameral Parliament — A349

2.40m, Future, by Waino Aaltonen, Parliament.

1982, May 25
671 A349 2.40m ultra & blk .85 .50

Manor Houses — A349a

1st Row: a, Kuitia, Parainen, 1490. b, Louhisaari, Askainen, 1655. c, Frugard, Joroinen, 1780. d, Jokioinen, 1798. e, Moisio, Elimaki, 1820.
2nd Row: f, Sjundby, Siuntio, 1560. g, Fagervik, Inkoo, 1773. h, Mustio, Karjaa, 1792. i, Fiskars, Pohja, 1818. j, Kotkaniemi, Vihti, 1836.

1982, June 14   Litho.   Perf. 13x13½
672   Booklet pane of 10   8.00   8.00
   a.-j. A349a 1.20m single stamp .80 .40
     Complete booklet, #672 8.00 8.00

See design A310.

Christmas 1982 — A350

Designs: 90p, Feeding forest animals. 1.20m, Children eating porridge.

1982, Oct. 25
673 A350 90p multi .70 .40
674 A350 1.20m multi .70 .40

Nordic Cooperation — A351

1.20m, Panning for gold. 1.30m, Kitkajoki River rapids.

1983, Mar. 24   Litho.   Perf. 14
675 A351 1.20m multi .55 .40
676 A351 1.30m multi .55 .40

World Communications Year — A352

1.30m, Postal services. 1.70m, Sound waves, optical cables.

1983, Apr. 9   Litho.   Perf. 13
677 A352 1.30m multi .55 .40
678 A352 1.70m multi .65 .45

Europa 1983 — A353

1.30m, Flash smelting method. 1.70m, Temppeliaukio Church.

1983, May 2   Litho.   Perf. 12½x13
679 A353 1.30m multicolored 1.00 .45
680 A353 1.70m multicolored 3.00 .90

Pres. Lauri Kristian Relander (1883-1942) — A354

1983, May 31   Litho.   Perf. 14
681 A354 1.30m multicolored .60 .40

Running — A355

1983, June 6
682 A355 1.20m Javelin, horiz. .60 .40
683 A355 1.30m shown .60 .40

First World Athletic Championships, Helsinki, Aug. 7-14.

Toivo Kuula (1883-1918) Composer — A356

1983, July 7   Perf. 14
684 A356 1.30m multicolored .55 .40

Christmas 1983 — A357

Childrens drawings: 1m, Santa, reindeer, sled and gifts by Eija Myllyviita. 1.30m, Two candles by Camilla Lindberg.

    Engr., Litho.
1983, Nov. 4   Perf. 12, 14
685 A357 1m dark blue .85 .40
686 A357 1.30m multi, vert. .85 .40

A358

1983, Nov. 25   Litho.   Perf. 14
687 A358 1.30m brt blue & blk .60 .40

President Mauno Henrik Koivisto, 60th birthday.

FINLAND

A360

1.10m, Letters (2nd class rate). 1.40m, Automated sorting (1st class rate), vert.

1984, Mar. 1   Engr.   Perf. 12
689 A360 1.10m multicolored .60 .40

Photo. & Engr.
690 A360 1.40m multicolored .60 .40

Inauguration of Nordic postal rates.

Museum Pieces A361   Work and Skill A362

Designs: No. 691, Pottery, 3200 B.C.; Silver chalice, 1416; Crossbow, 16th cent. No. 692, Kaplan hydraulic turbine.

1984, Apr. 30   Litho.   Perf. 13½
691 A361 1.40m multicolored .50 .40
692 A362 1.40m multicolored .50 .40

Europa (1959-84) A363

1984, May 7   Perf. 12½x13
693 A363 1.40m multicolored 1.50 .40
694 A363 2m multicolored 3.00 1.00

Dentistry — A364

1984, Aug. 27   Litho.   Perf. 14
695 A364 1.40m Dentist, teeth .80 .50

Astronomy — A365

Design: Observatory, planets, sun.

1984, Sept. 12
696 A365 1.10m multicolored 1.00 .55

Aleksis Kivi (1934-72), Writer — A366

Design: Song of my Heart.

1984, Oct. 10   Litho.   Perf. 14
697 A366 1.40m blk & dull mauve .60 .40

Christmas 1984 — A367

Design: Father Christmas, brownie.

Litho. & Engr.
1984, Nov. 30   Perf. 12
698 A367 1.10m multicolored .80 .40

Common Law of 1734 — A368

1984, Dec. 6   Perf. 14
699 A368 2m Statute Book .70 .70

25th Anniv. of EFTA — A369

1985, Feb. 2   Litho.
700 A369 1.20m multicolored .50 .40

100th Anniv. of Society of Swedish Literature in Finland — A370

Design: Johan Ludvig Runeberg.

1985, Feb. 5   Litho.
701 A370 1.50m multicolored .50 .35

Icon — A371

1985, Feb. 18   Litho.   Perf. 11½x12
702 A371 1.50m multicolored .50 .40

Order of St. Sergei and St. Herman, 100th anniv.

150th Anniv. of Kalevala — A372

Designs: 1.50m, Pedri Shemeikka. 2.10m, Larin Paraske.

Litho. & Engr.
1985, Feb. 28   Perf. 13x12½
703 A372 1.50m multicolored .50 .40
704 A372 2.10m multicolored .70 .60

Mermaid and Sea Lions — A373

Litho. & Engr.
1985, May 15   Perf. 13
705 A373 1.50m multicolored 3.00 4.00

NORDIA 1985 philatelic exhibition, May 15-19. Sold for 10m which included admission ticket.

A374

Finnish Banknote Cent.: banknotes of 1886, 1909, 1922, 1945 and 1955.

Photo. & Engr.
1985, May 18   Perf. 11½
706 A374 Booklet pane of 8 6.00 6.00
a.-h. 1.50m any single .80 .60
Complete booklet, #706 6.00

A375

Europa: 1.50m, Children playing the recorder. 2.10m, Excerpt "Ramus Virens Olivarum" from the "Piae Cantiones," 1582.

1985, June 17   Litho.   Perf. 13
707 A375 1.50m multicolored 1.50 .40
708 A375 2.10m multicolored 4.00 1.00

Security Conference Type of 1975
1985, June 19   Litho.
709 A265 2.10m multicolored .75 .60

European Security and Cooperation Conference, 10th Anniv.

Provincial Arms, Count's Seal — A376

1985, Sept. 5   Litho.   Perf. 14
710 A376 1.50m multicolored .80 .35

Provincial Administration Established by Count Per Brahe, 350th Anniv.

Arms Type of 1975 and

Kerimaki Church A376a   Urho Kekkonen Natl. Park A376b

Tulip Damask Table Cloth, 18th Cent. A377   Postal Service A377a

Brown Bear — A377b

Perf. 11½, 13x12½ (2m)
1985-90   Engr.
711 A256 1.60m vermilion .60 .60
712 A256 1.70m black .60 .60
   a. Bklt. pane, #558, 560, 2 each #555, 556a, 712 + 2 labels 9.00 11.00
   Complete booklet, #712a 10.00
713 A256 1.80m ol grn .70 .60
   a. Bklt. pane, 2 ea #555d, 560a, 713b 3.50 3.00
   Complete booklet, #713a 3.50
   b. Perf. 13x12½ 1.00 .90
714 A256 1.90m brt orange .70 .25
715 A256 2m blue grn, bklt. stamp 1.50 .70
   a. Bklt. pane, #562a, 2 ea #715, 555d 7.00 7.00
   Complete booklet, #715a 7.00

Litho.   **Perf. 14**
716 A376a 2.20m multi .80 .25
717 A376b 2.40m multi .90 .40
718 A377 12m multi 4.00 .50

Litho. & Engr.
Perf. 13x12½
719 A377b 50m blk, grn & lt red brn 15.00 5.50
Nos. 711-719 (9) 24.80 9.40

No. 712a contains two labels inscribed to publicize FINLANDIA '88.

Issued: 12m, 9/13/85; 1.60m, 1/2/86; 1.70m, 1/2/87; No. 712a, 8/10/87; 1.80m, 1/4/88; 2.20m, 2.40m, 1/20/88; No. 713b, 7/25/88; 1.90m, 1/2/89; 2m, 1/19/90; 50m, 8/30/89.

Booklet Stamps

No. 720, Telephone, mailbox. No. 721, Postal truck, transport plane. No. 722, Transport plane, fork lift. No. 723, Postman delivering letter. No. 724, Woman accepting letter.

Perf. 12½ on 3 Sides
1988, Feb. 1   Litho.
720 A377a 1.80m multi .80 .40
721 A377a 1.80m multi .60 .40
722 A377a 1.80m multi .60 .40
723 A377a 1.80m multi .60 .40
724 A377a 1.80m multi .60 .40
   a. Bklt. pane, 2 each #720-724 7.00 7.00
   Complete booklet, #724a 7.00
   Nos. 720-724 (5) 3.20 2.00

Nos. 721-722 and 723-724 printed se-tenant in continuous designs. No. 724c sold for 14m to households on mainland Finland. Each household entitled to buy 2 booklets at discount price from Feb. 1 to May 31, with coupon.

Miniature Sheet

Postal Map, 1698 — A378

Designs: a, Postman on foot. b, Postal Map, 1698. c, Sailing vessel, diff. d, Postrider, vert.

FINLAND

Litho. & Engr.
1985, Oct. 16   Perf. 14
728   A378   Sheet of 4   10.00   12.00
   a.-d.   1.50m any single   2.50   3.00
FINLANDIA '88, 350th anniv. of Finnish Postal Service, founded in 1638 by Gov.-Gen. Per Brahe. Sheet sold for 8m.

Intl. Youth Year — A379

1985, Nov. 1   Litho.   Perf. 13
729   A379   1.50m multicolored   .50   .35

Christmas — A380

No. 730, Bird, tulips. No. 731, Cross of St. Thomas, hyacinths.

1985, Nov. 29   Perf. 14
730   A380   1.20m multicolored   1.10   .40
731   A380   1.20m multicolored   1.10   .40

Natl. Geological Society, Cent. — A390

1986, Feb. 8   Litho.   Perf. 14
732   A390   1.30m Orbicular granite   .60   .40
733   A390   1.60m Rapaviki   .70   .40
734   A390   2.10m Veined gneiss   .90   .60
   Nos. 732-734 (3)   2.20   1.40

Europa 1986 — A391

1.60m, Saimaa ringed seal. 2.20m, Environmental conservation.

1986, Apr. 10   Perf. 12½x13
735   A391   1.60m multicolored   1.50   .40
736   A391   2.20m multicolored   4.00   .80

Natl. Construction Year — A392

a, Conference Palace, Baghdad, 1982. b, Lahti Theater, 1983. c, Kuusamo Municipal Offices, 1978. d, Hamina Court Building, 1983. e, Finnish Embassy, New Delhi, 1986. f, Western Sakyla Daycare Center, 1980.

1986, Apr. 19   Perf. 14
737   A392   Booklet pane of 6   4.00   4.00
   a.-f.   1.60m, any single   .70   .60
   Complete booklet, #737   4.00

Nordic Cooperation Issue 1986 — A393

Sister towns.

1986, May 27   Litho.   Perf. 14
738   A393   1.60m Joensuu   .50   .40
739   A393   2.20m Jyvaskyla   .70   .75

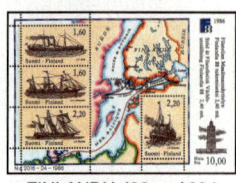
Souvenir Sheet

FINLANDIA '88 — A394

Postal ships: a, Iron paddle steamer Aura, Stockholm-St. Petersburg, 1858. b, Screw vessel Alexander, Helsinki-Tallinn-Lubeck, 1859. c, Steamship Nicolai, Helsinki-Tallinn-St. Petersburg, 1858. d, 1st Ice steamship Express II, Helsinki-Stockholm, 1877-98, vert.

Litho. & Engr.   Perf. 13
1986, Aug. 29
740   A394   Sheet of 4   10.00   10.00
   a.-b.   1.60m, any single   2.50   2.50
   c.-d.   2.20m, any single   2.50   2.50
   Sold for 10k.

Pierre-Louis Moreau de Maupertuis (1698-1759) A395

1986, Sept. 5   Litho.   Perf. 12½x13
741   A395   1.60m multicolored   .70   .40
Lapland Expedition, 250th anniv., proved Earth's poles are flattened. See France No. 2016.

Urho Kaleva Kekkonen (1900-86), Pres. — A396

1986, Sept. 30   Engr.   Perf. 14
742   A396   5m black   1.60   1.00

Intl. Peace Year — A397

1986, Oct. 13   Litho.   Perf. 13
743   A397   1.60m multicolored   .50   .40

A398

Christmas — A399

Photo. & Engr.
1986, Oct. 31   Perf. 12
744   1.30m Denomination at L   .70   .45
745   1.30m Denomination at R   1.20   .40
   a.   A398 Pair, #744-745   2.00   2.00
746   A399   1.60m Elves   .80   .40
   Nos. 744-746 (3)   2.70   1.25

No. 745a has a continuous design.

Postal Savings Bank, Cent. — A400

1987, Jan. 2   Litho.   Perf. 14
747   A400   1.70m multicolored   .50   .40

Natl. Tourism, Cent. — A401

1987, Feb. 4   Litho.   Perf. 14
748   A401   1.70m Winter   .50   .40
749   A401   2.30m Summer   .70   .70

A402

1987, Feb. 4   Perf. 14
750   A402   1.40m multicolored   .50   .40
Metric system in Finland, cent.

A403

1987, Feb. 17   Litho.   Perf. 14
751   A403   2.10m multicolored   1.10   .50
Leevi Madetoja (1887-1947), composer.

European Wrestling Championships — A404

1987, Feb. 17
752   A404   1.70m multicolored   .60   .40

1987 World Bowling Championships — A405

1987, Apr. 13
753   A405   1.70m multicolored   .60   .40

Mental Health — A406

1987, Apr. 13
754   A406   1.70m multicolored   .50   .40

Souvenir Sheet

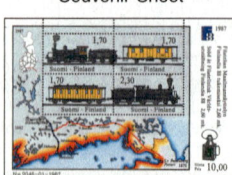
FINLANDIA '88 — A407

Locomotives and mail cars: a, Steam locomotive, 6-wheeled tender. b, 4-window mail car. c, 7-window mail car.

Litho. & Engr.
1987, May 8   Perf. 12½x13
755   A407   Sheet of 4   10.00   12.00
   a.-c.   1.70m any single   2.50   3.00
   d.   2.30m multicolored   2.50   3.00
   Sold for 10m.

Europa 1987 — A408

Modern architecture: 1.70m, Tampere Main Library, 1986, designed by Raili and Reima Pietila. 2.30m, Stoa Monument, Helsinki, c. 1981, by sculptor Hannu Siren.

1987, May 15   Litho.   Perf. 13
756   A408   1.70m multicolored   1.50   .40
757   A408   2.30m multicolored   4.00   1.00

Natl. Art Museum, Ateneum, Cent. — A409

Paintings: a, Strawberry Girl, by Nils Schillmark (1745-1804). b, Still-life on a Lady's Work Table, by Ferdinand von Wright (1822-1906). c, Old Woman with Basket, by Albert Edelfelt (1854-1906). d, Boy and Crow, by Akseli Gallen-Kallela (1865-1931). e, Late Winter, by Tyko Sallinen (1879-1955).

1987, May 15
758   Booklet pane of 5   6.00   6.00
   a.-e.   A409 1.70m any single   1.20   .70
   Complete booklet, #758   6.00

A410

1987, Aug. 12   Perf. 14
759   A410   1.70m multicolored   .50   .40
European Physics Soc. 7th gen. conf., Helsinki, Aug. 10-14.

A411

1987, Oct. 12
760   A411   1.70m ultra, sil & pale lt gray   .60   .40
   Size: 30x41mm
761   A411   10m dark ultra, lt blue & sil   3.50   1.20
Natl. independence, 70th anniv.

Ylppo, Child and Lastenlinna Children's Hospital — A412

1987, Oct. 27
762   A412   1.70m multicolored   .50   .40
Arvo Ylppo (b. 1887), pediatrics pioneer.

Christmas — A413

Design: 1.40m, Santa Claus, youths, horiz.

1987, Oct. 30
763   A413   1.40m multi   1.00   .40
764   A413   1.70m shown   1.00   .40

Finnish News Agency (STT), Cent. — A414

1987, Nov. 1
765   A414   2.30m multicolored   .80   .80

FINLAND

A415

1988, Jan. 5   **Litho.**   *Perf. 14*
766   A415   1.80m blk, chalky blue & brt blue   .70   .40

Lauri "Tahko" Pihkala (1888-1981), promulgator of sports and physical education.

A416

1988, Mar. 14   **Litho.**
767   A416   1.40m multicolored   .50   .40

Meteorological Institute, 150th anniv.

Settlement of New Sweden in America, 350th Anniv. — A417

Design: 17th Century European settlers negotiating with 3 American Indians, map of New Sweden, the Swedish ships Kalmar Nyckel and Fogel Grip, based on an 18th cent. illustration from a Swedish book about the American Colonies.

Litho. & Engr.
1988, Mar. 29   *Perf. 13*
768   A417   3m multicolored   1.25   .80

See US No. C117 and Sweden No. 1672.

FINLANDIA '88, June 1-12, Helsinki Fair Center — A418

Agathon Faberge (1876-1951), famed philatelist, & rarities from his collection.

Booklet Stamp
1988, May 2   **Litho.**   *Perf. 13*
769   A418   5m Pane of 1+2 labels   10.00   12.00
   Complete booklet, #769   10.00

350th Anniv. of the Finnish Postal Service. No. 769 sold for 30m to include the price of adult admission to the exhibition.

Achievements of Finnish Athletes at the 1988 Winter Olympics, Calgary — A419

Design: Matti Nykanen, gold medalist in all 3 ski jumping events at the '88 Games.

1988, Apr. 6   *Perf. 14*
770   A419   1.80m multicolored   .60   .40

Europa 1988 — A420

Communication and transport: 2.40m, Horse-drawn tram, 1890.

1988, May 23   **Litho.**   *Perf. 13*
771   A420   1.80m shown   1.50   .40
772   A420   2.40m multicolored   4.00   1.00

Souvenir Sheet

FINLANDIA '88 — A421

1st airmail flights: a, Finnish air force Breguet 14 biplane transporting mail from Helsinki to Tallinn, Feb. 12, 1920. b, AERO Junkers F-13 making 1st airmail night flight from Helsinki to Copenhagen, May 15, 1930. c, AERO Douglas DC-3, 1st intl. route, Helsinki-Norrkoping-Copenhagen-Amsterdam, 1947. d, Douglas DC 10-30, 1975-88, inauguration of Helsinki-Beijing route, June 2, 1988.

Litho. & Engr.
1988, June 2   *Perf. 13½*
773   A421   Sheet of 4   10.00   12.00
  a.-c.   1.80m any single   2.50   3.00
  d.   2.40m multicolored   2.50   3.00
   Sold for 11m.

Turku Fire Brigade, 150th Anniv. — A422

Design: 1902 Horse-drawn, steam-driven fire pump, preserved at the brigade.

1988, Aug. 15   **Litho.**   *Perf. 14*
774   A422   2.20m multicolored   .70   .55

A423

Missale Aboense, the 1st printed book in Finland, 500th anniv.

1988, Aug. 17
775   A423   1.80m multicolored   .60   .40

A424

Finnish Postal Service, 350th Anniv.: No. 776, Postal tariff issued by Queen Christina of Sweden, Sept. 8, 1638. No. 777, Postal cart, c. 1880. #778, Leyland Sherpa 185 mail van, 1976. No. 779, Malmi P.O. interior. #780, Skier using mobile telephone, c. 1970. No. 781, Telecommunications satellite in orbit.

Booklet Stamps
1988, Sept. 6   **Litho.**   *Perf. 13*
776   A424   1.80m multicolored   .80   .60
777   A424   1.80m multicolored   .80   .60
778   A424   1.80m multicolored   .80   .60
779   A424   1.80m multicolored   .80   .60
780   A424   1.80m multicolored   .80   .60
781   A424   1.80m multicolored   .80   .60
  a.   Booklet pane of 6, #776-781   4.50   4.50
   Complete booklet #781a   4.50

Children's Playgroups (Preschool) — A425

1988, Oct. 10   *Perf. 14*
782   A425   1.80m multicolored   .60   .40

Christmas — A426

1988, Nov. 4   **Litho.**
783   A426   1.40m multicolored   .80   .40
784   A426   1.80m multicolored   1.00   .40

Hameenlinna Township, 350th Anniv. — A427

Design: Market square, coat of arms and 17th century plan of the town.

1989, Jan. 19   **Litho.**
785   A427   1.90m multicolored   .80   .40

1989 Nordic Ski Championships, Lahti, Feb. 17-26 — A428

1989, Jan. 25
786   A428   1.90m multicolored   .80   .40

Salvation Army in Finland, Cent. — A429

1989, Feb. 6   **Litho.**
787   A429   1.90m multicolored   .80   .40

Photography, 150th Anniv. — A430

1.50m, Photographer, box camera, c.1900.

1989, Feb. 6
788   A430   1.50m brn, buff, cream   .60   .55

31st Intl. Physiology Congress, Basel, July 9-14 — A431

Design: Congress emblem, silhouettes of Robert Tigerstedt and Ragnar Granit, eye, flowmeter measuring flow of blood through heart, color-sensitive retinal cells and microelectrode.

1989, Mar. 2
789   A431   1.90m multicolored   .80   .40

Sports — A432

1989, Mar. 10   **Booklet Stamps**
790   A432   1.90m Skiing   .80   .40
791   A432   1.90m Jogging   .80   .40
792   A432   1.90m Cycling   .80   .40
793   A432   1.90m Canoeing   .80   .40
  a.   Booklet pane of 4, #790-793   3.20   3.20
   Complete booklet, #793a   3.20

Souvenir Sheet

Finnish Kennel Club, Cent. A433

Dogs: a, Lapponian herder. b, Finnish spitz. c, Karelian bear dog. d, Finnish hound.

1989, Mar. 17   *Perf. 14*
794   A433   Sheet of 4   3.50   3.50
  a.-d.   1.90m any single   .90   .60

Europa — A434

1989, Mar. 31   *Perf. 13*
795   A434   1.90m Hopscotch   1.50   .40
796   A434   2.50m Sledding   2.50   .65

A435

Nordic Cooperation Year: Folk Costumes.

1989, Apr. 20   *Perf. 14*
797   A435   1.90m Sakyla (man)   1.10   .45
798   A435   2.50m Veteli (woman)   1.10   .65

Finnish Pharmacies, 300th Anniv. — A436

Foxglove, distilling apparatus, mortar, flask.

1989, June 2   **Litho.**
799   A436   1.90m multicolored   .70   .35

A437

1989, June 2
800   A437   1.90m multicolored   .70   .35

Savonlinna Municipal Charter, 350th anniv.

Helsinki Zoo, Cent. — A438

No. 801, Panthera uncia. No. 802, Capra falconeri

1989, June 12
801   A438   1.90m multi   .70   .45
802   A438   2.50m multi   .80   .70

Vocational Training, 150th Anniv. — A439

Interparliamentary Union, Cent. — A440

Council of Europe, 40th Anniv. — A441

1989, Sept. 4   **Litho.**   *Perf. 14*
803   A439   1.50m multicolored   .60   .70
804   A440   1.90m multicolored   .70   .35
805   A441   2.50m multicolored   .90   .70
   Nos. 803-805 (3)   2.20   1.75

Admission of Finland to the Council of Europe (2.50m).

FINLAND

A442

1989, Oct. 9   Litho.
806   A442   1.90m multicolored   .70   .35
Hannes Kolehmainen (1889-1966) winning the 5000-meter race at the Stockholm Olympics, 1912.

A443

1989, Oct. 20
807   A443   1.90m multicolored   .70   .35
Continuing Education in Finland, cent.

A444

Christmas: 1.90m, Sodankyla Church, Siberian jays in snow.

1989, Nov. 3
808   A444   1.50m shown   1.10   .40
809   A444   1.90m multicolored   1.10   .40

A445

1990, Jan. 19   Litho.   Perf. 13x13½
810   A445   1.90m multicolored   .80   .80
811   A445   2.50m multicolored   .90   .40
Incorporation of the State Posts and Telecommunications Services.
Emblem of the corporation was produced by holography. Soaking may affect the design.

Musical Soc. of Turku and Finnish Orchestras, 200th Anniv. — A446

1990, Jan. 26   Perf. 14
812   A446   1.90m multicolored   1.10   .40

Disabled Veteran's Assoc., 50th Anniv. — A447

1990, Mar. 13   Litho.
813   A447   2m multicolored   .70   .35

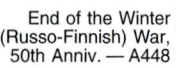
End of the Winter (Russo-Finnish) War, 50th Anniv. — A448

1990, Mar. 13
814   A448   2m blue   .70   .35

University of Helsinki, 350th Anniv. — A449

University crest and: 2m, Queen Christina on horseback. 3.20m, Degree ceremony procession in front of the main university building.

1990, Mar. 26   Litho.   Perf. 13
815   A449   2m multicolored   .70   .40
816   A449   3.20m multicolored   1.00   .70

Europa 1990 — A450

Post Offices: 2m, Lapp man, P.O. at Nuvvus, Mt. Nuvvus Ailigas. 2.70m, Turku main P.O.

1990, Mar. 26   Perf. 12½x13
817   A450   2m multicolored   2.00   .40
818   A450   2.70m multicolored   4.00   1.00

Rural Postal Service and Address Reform, Cent. — A451

1990, Apr. 19   Litho.   Perf. 13
819   A451   2m multicolored   .70   .35

"Ali Baba and the Forty Thieves" A452

"Story of the Great Musician" A453

"Story of the Giants, the Witches and the Daughter of the Sun" A454

"The Golden Bird, the Golden Horse and the Princess" A455

"Lamb Brother" A456

"The Snow Queen" A457

Fairy tale illustrations by Rudolf Koivu.

Booklet Stamps
Perf. 14 on 3 sides
1990, Aug. 29   Litho.
820   A452   2m multicolored   1.60   .65
821   A453   2m multicolored   1.60   .65
822   A454   2m multicolored   1.60   .65
823   A455   2m multicolored   1.60   .65
824   A456   2m multicolored   1.60   .65
825   A457   2m multicolored   1.60   .65
   a.   Booklet pane of 6, #820-825   10.00   8.00
      Complete booklet, #825a   10.00

Souvenir Sheet

Horse Care A458

a, Feeding. b, Riding. c, Watering. d, Currying.

1990, Oct. 10   Litho.   Perf. 14
826   A458   Sheet of 4   3.50   3.50
  a.-d.   2m any single   .90   .60

Christmas — A459

1990, Nov. 2
827   A459   1.70m Santa's elves   1.00   .40
828   A459   2m Santa, reindeer   1.00   .40

Provincial Flowers

A460

A460a

A460b

A460c

A460d

A460e

A460f   A460g

A460h   A460i

A460j   A460k

2m, Wood anemone. 2.10m, Rowan. 2.70m, Heather. 2.90m, Sea buckthorn. 3.50m, Oak. No. 834, Globeflower. No. 835, Hepatica. No. 836, Iris. No. 838, Rosebay willowherb. No. 839, Labrador tea. No. 840, Karelian rose. No. 841, Daisy. No. 842, Water lily. No. 843, Bird cherry. No. 844, Harebell. No. 845, Cowslip.

1990-99   Perf. 13x12½
829   A460   2m multi   1.10   .25
830   A460   2.10m multi   .80   .25
831   A460   2.70m multi   1.40   .40
832   A460   2.90m multi   1.00   .40
833   A460   3.50m multi   1.20   .40
834   A460a   2.50   .50
835   A460b   1 multi   3.00   .25
   Nos. 829-835 (7)   11.00   2.45

Self-Adhesive
Die Cut
836   A460c   2 multi   2.50   .50
   a.   Booklet pane of 20   25.00   25.00
837   A460   2.10m like #830   .80   .40
838   A460d   1 multi   2.50   .35
839   A460e   1 multi   3.00   .40
   a.   Booklet pane of 10   30.00   15.00
840   A460f   1 multi   3.00   .25
841   A460g   1 multi   3.00   .25
842   A460h   1 multi   3.00   .25
843   A460i   1 multi   3.00   .25
844   A460j   1 multi   3.00   .25
845   A460k   1 multi   3.00   .40
   Nos. 836-845 (10)   26.80   3.30

Issued: 2m, 2.70m, 1/19/90; No. 830, 2.90m, 3.50m, 2/5/90; 2.10m, 1991; Nos. 834-835, 3/2/92; No. 838, 10/9/92; No. 836, 3/1/93; No. 839, 6/14/93; No. 840, 5/5/94; No. 841, 3/15/95; No. 842, 6/3/96; No. 843, 3/18/97; No. 844, 3/12/98; No. 845, 4/28/99.
No. 834 sold for 1.60m, No. 836 sold for 1.90m, Nos. 835, 838 for 2.10m, Nos. 839-840 for 2.30m, Nos. 841-844 sold for 2.80m, No. 845 sold for 3m at time of release.
Nos. 837-838, 840-845 issued in sheets of 10. Nos. 836a and 839a were issued as complete booklets. The peelable backing serves as a booklet cover.
The numbers on the stamps represent the class of mail for which each was intended at time of release.

A461

1991, Mar. 1   Perf. 14
846   A461   2.10m multicolored   .70   .40
World Hockey Championships, Turku.

A462

1991, Mar. 1
847   A462   2.10m Cooking class   .60   .40
Home economics teacher education, cent.

Sauna Type of 1977 and

Birds — A463

No. 848, Great tit. No. 849, Wagtail. No. 850, Aegolius funereus. No. 850A, Phoenicurus phoenicurus. No. 851, Chaffinches. No. 852, Robin. No. 856, Bullfinch. No. 857, Waxwing. No. 859, Dendrocopos leucotos.

Perf. 13x12½, 14 (#861)
1991-99   Litho.
Booklet Stamps (#848-859)
848   A463   10p multi   .40   .25
849   A463   10p multi   .25   .25
850   A463   10p multi   .90   .40
850A   A463   20p multi   3.00   2.00
851   A463   60p multi   3.00   .50
852   A463   60p multi   2.50   1.00
856   A463   2.10m multi   .70   .25
   a.   Bklt. pane of #851, 2 each #848, 856   4.00   4.00
     Complete booklet, #856a   4.00
857   A463   2.10m multi   .80   .25
   a.   Bklt. pane of #852, 2 each #849, 857   4.00   4.00
     Complete booklet, #857a   4.00
859   A463   2.30m multi   .80   .40
   a.   Booklet pane of #850A, 2 each #850, #859 + 1 label   6.00   6.00
     Complete booklet, #859a   6.00

Sheet Stamp
861   A256a   4.80m multi   2.50   1.00
   Nos. 848-861 (10)   14.85   6.30

Issued: Nos. 848, 851, 856, 3/20/91; Nos. 849, 852, 857, 4/22/92; Nos. 850, 850A, 859, 6/4/93. 861, 7/1/99.
"SUOMI" is in upper left on Nos. 849, 852, 857.

Fishing — A464

Designs: a, Fly fisherman, trout. b, Perch, bobber. c, Crayfish, trap. d, Trawling for herring. e, Stocking powan.

1991, Mar. 20   Perf. 14
863   Booklet pane of 5   5.00   5.00
  a.-e.   A464 2.10m any single   1.00   .40
     Complete booklet, #863   5.00

Tourism — A465

2.10m, Seurasaari Island. 2.90m, Steamship, Lake Saimaa.

1991, June 4   Litho.   Perf. 14
864   A465   2.10m multi   .80   .25
865   A465   2.90m multi   1.10   .70

FINLAND

 Europa — A466

European map and: 2.10m, Human figures. 2.90m, Satellites, dish antennae.

1991, June 7   Litho.   Perf. 12½x13
866 A466 2.10m multicolored   2.00   .40
867 A466 2.90m multicolored   4.00 1.00

Alfred W. Finch (1854-1930) — A467

Designs: 2.10m, Iris, ceramic vase. 2.90m, Painting, The English Coast at Dover.

1991, Sept. 7   Litho.   Perf. 13
868 A467 2.10m multicolored   1.10   .40
869 A467 2.90m multicolored   2.00 1.20

See Belgium No. 1410.

 Finnish Candy Industry, Cent. — A468

1991, Sept. 17   Photo.   Perf. 11½
870 A468 2.10m multicolored   .70   .50

Souvenir Sheets

Children's Stamp Designs — A469

a, Sun. b, Rainbow. c, Cows grazing.

1991, Sept. 17   Litho.   Perf. 13½
871 A469 Sheet of 3   2.40 2.40
a.-c.   2.10m any single   .80   .60

Skiing A470

Color of skisuit: a, red. b, green. c, yellow. d, blue.

1991, Oct. 4   Perf. 14
872 A470 Sheet of 4   2.80 2.80
a.-d.   2.10m any single   .70   .50

Town Status for Iisalmi, Cent. — A471

1991, Oct. 18   Litho.   Perf. 14
873 A471 2.10m multicolored   .70   .50

Christmas — A472

1.80m, Santa, animals carrying candles. 2.10m, Reindeer pulling Santa's sleigh.

1991, Nov. 1   Litho.   Perf. 14
874 A472 1.80m multi   1.00   .45
875 A472 2.10m multi, vert.   1.00   .45

Chemists' Club, Finnish Chemists' Society, Cent. — A473

1991, Nov. 1
876 A473 2.10m multi   .70   .40
877 A473 2.10m multi, diff.   .70   .40
a.   Pair, #876-877 + label   2.00 2.00

Second and third vertical branches merge while second and third branches below almost touch in the upper left part of camphor molecular structure on No. 877. Nos. 876-877 are designed to produce a three dimensional effect when viewed together.

1992 Olympic Games — A474

Designs: No. 878, Skier, Albertville. No. 879, Swimmer, Barcelona.

1992, Feb. 4   Litho.   Perf. 14
878 A474 2.10m multicolored   1.00   .40
879 A474 2.90m multicolored   1.20   .50

Expo '92, Seville — A475

1992, Mar. 20   Litho.   Perf. 14
880 A475 3.40m multicolored   1.20   .75

Conference on Security and Cooperation in Europe, Helsinki — A476

1992, Mar. 20   Perf. 14½x15
881 A476 16m multicolored   5.00 3.50

Town of Rauma, 550th Anniv. — A477

1992, Mar. 27   Perf. 14
882 A477 2.10m multicolored   1.20   .40

Healthy Brains — A478

1992, Mar. 27
883 A478 3.50m multicolored   1.10   .80

Discovery of America, 500th Anniv. — A479

Designs: No. 884, Santa Maria, map. No. 885, Map, Columbus.

1992, May 8   Litho.   Perf. 12½x13
884 A479 2.10m multicolored   1.50   .40
885 A479 2.10m multicolored   1.50   .40
a.   Pair, #884-885   3.50 3.50

Europa.

Finnish Technology — A480

Hologram of trees and: 2.10m, Drawing of blowing machine. 2.90m, Schematic of electronic circuits. 3.40m, Triangles and grid.

1992, May 8   Litho.   Perf. 13x12½
886 A480 2.10m multicolored   1.10   .60
887 A480 2.90m multicolored   1.20   .75
888 A480 3.40m multicolored   1.50 1.00
     Nos. 886-888 (3)   3.80 2.35

First Finnish patent granted, sesqui. (No. 886), Finnish chairmanship of Eureka (No. 887), Government Technology Research Center, 50th anniv. (No. 888).

Nos. 886-888 have holographic images. Soaking in water may affect the hologram.

Natl. Board of Agriculture, Cent. — A481

Design: Currant harvesting.

1992, June 4   Litho.   Perf. 14
889 A481 2.10m multicolored   .70   .40

Finnish Women — A482

No. 890, Aurora Karamzin (1808-1902), founder of Deaconesses' Institution of Helsinki. No. 891, Baroness Sophie Mannerheim (1863-1928), reformer of nursing education. No. 892, Laimi Leidenius (1877-1938), physician and educator. No. 893, Miina Sillanpaa (1866-1952), Minister for social affairs. No. 894, Edith Sodergran (1892-1923), poet. No. 895, Kreeta Haapasalo (1813-1893), folk singer.

Litho. & Engr.
1992, June 8   Perf. 14
Booklet Stamps
890 A482 2.10m multicolored   .80   .50
891 A482 2.10m multicolored   .80   .50
892 A482 2.10m multicolored   .80   .50
893 A482 2.10m multicolored   .80   .50
894 A482 2.10m multicolored   .80   .50
895 A482 2.10m multicolored   .80   .50
a.   Booklet pane of 6, #890-895 4.50 4.50
      Complete booklet, #895a   4.50

Child's Painting — A483

Independence, 75th Anniv. — A484

1992, Oct. 5   Litho.   Perf. 13
896 A483 2.10m multicolored   .70   .40

Souvenir Sheet
Perf. 13½
897 A484 2.10m multicolored   .70   .50

Nordia '93 — A485

Illustrations depicting "Moomin" characters, by Tove Jansson: No. 898, Winter scene, ice covered bridges. No. 899, Winter scene in forest. No. 900, Boats in water. No. 901, Characters on beach.

Perf. 13 on 3 Sides
1992, Oct. 9   Litho.
Booklet Stamps
898 A485 2.10m multicolored   2.00   .50
899 A485 2.10m multicolored   2.00   .50
900 A485 2.10m multicolored   2.00   .50
901 A485 2.10m multicolored   2.00   .50
a.   Booklet pane of 4, #898-901 8.00 8.00
      Complete booklet, #901a   8.00

A486

1992, Oct. 20   Litho.   Perf. 13
902 A486 2.10m multicolored   .70   .40

Printing in Finland, 350th anniv.

Christmas — A487

Designs: 1.80m, Church of St. Lawrence, Vantaa. 2.10m, Stained glass window of nativity scene, Karkkila Church, vert.

1992, Oct. 30   Litho.   Perf. 14
903 A487 1.80m multicolored   1.00   .45
904 A487 2.10m multicolored   1.00   .45

Central Chamber of Commerce, 75th Anniv. — A488

1993, Feb. 8   Litho.   Perf. 14
905 A488 1.60m multicolored   .50   .40

Friendship — A489

1993, Feb. 8   Litho.   Perf. 14
906 A489 1 multicolored   3.00   .40
a.   Booklet pane of 5 + label 14.00 7.50
      Complete booklet, 2 #906a 30.00

No. 906 sold for 2m at time of release. See note following No. 845.
See Estonia No. 237.

Alopex Lagopus A490

a, Adult with winter white coat. b, Face, full view, winter white coat. c, Mother, kits, summer coat. d, Two on rock, summer coat.

1993, Mar. 19   Litho.   Perf. 12½x13
907 A490 Block of 4   4.00 4.00
a.-d.   2.30m Any single   1.00   .40

World Wildlife Fund.

Sculptures — A491

Europa: 2m, Rumba, by Martti Aiha. 2.90m, Complete Works, by Kari Caven.

1993, Apr. 26   Perf. 13
908 A491 2m multicolored   1.00   .40
909 A491 2.90m multicolored   2.50 1.00

Organized Philately in Finland, Cent. — A492

Design: Rosa pimpinellifolia.

1993, May 6   Perf. 13x12½
910 A492 2.30m multicolored   1.10   .70

FINLAND

Vyborg Castle, 700th Anniv. — A493

1993, May 6   Perf. 13½
911 A493 2.30m multicolored   .70   .25

Tourism — A494

1993, May 7   Perf. 13x12½
912 A494 2.30m Naantali   .80   .25
913 A494 2.90m Imatra   1.00 .50
550th anniv. of Naantali (No. 912).

A495

Independent Finland Defense Forces, 75th Anniv.: 2.30m, Finnish landscape in form of soldier's silhouette. 3.40m, UN checkpoint of Finnish battalion, Middle East.

1993, June 4   Litho.   Perf. 14
914 A495 2.30m multicolored   .70   .25
915 A495 3.40m multicolored   1.10 .80

A496

Art by Martta Wendelin (1893-1986): No. 916, Boy on skis, 1936. No. 917, Mother, daughter knitting, 1931. No. 918, Children building snowman, 1931. No. 919, Mother, children at fence, 1935. #920, Girl with lamb, 1936.

Booklet Stamps
1993, June 14   Litho.   Perf. 12½x13
916 A496 2.30m multicolored   1.30   .40
917 A496 2.30m multicolored   1.30   .40
918 A496 2.30m multicolored   1.30   .40
919 A496 2.30m multicolored   1.30   .40
920 A496 2.30m multicolored   1.30   .40
  a. Booklet pane of 5, #916-920   6.50 6.50
      Complete booklet, #920a   6.50

Water Birds A497

No. 921, Flock of gavia arctica. No. 922, Pair of gavia arctica. No. 923, Mergus merganser. No. 924, Anas platyrhynchos. No. 925, Mergus serrator.

Perf. 12½x13 on 3 or 4 Sides
1993, Sept. 20   Litho.
Booklet Stamps
921 A497 2.30m multicolored   1.00   .70
922 A497 2.30m multicolored   1.00   .70
   Size: 26x40mm
923 A497 2.30m multicolored   1.00   .70
924 A497 2.30m multicolored   1.00   .70
925 A497 2.30m multicolored   1.00   .70
  a. Booklet pane of 5, #921-925   5.00 5.00
      Complete booklet, #925a   5.00

Physical Education in Finnish Schools, 150th Anniv. — A498

1993, Oct. 8   Perf. 14
926 A498 2.30m multicolored   .80   .25

Souvenir Sheet

New Opera House, Helsinki — A499

Operas and ballet: a, 2.30m, Ostrobothnians, by Leevi Madetoja. b, 2.30m, The Faun (four dancers), by Claude Debussy. c, 2.90m, Giselle, by Adolphe Adam. d, 3.40m, The Magic Flute, by Wolfgang Amadeus Mozart.

1993, Oct. 8   Perf. 13
927   A499   Sheet of 4   5.00 5.00
 a.-b.   2.30m Either single 1.00 .80
 c.   2.90m multi   1.50 1.50
 d.   3.40m multi   1.50 2.00

Christmas — A500

Designs: 1.80m, Christmas tree, elves. 2.30m, Three angels.

1993, Nov. 5   Litho.   Perf. 14
928 A500 1.80m multi   1.00   .40
  a. Booklet pane of 10   12.00 12.00
      Complete booklet, #928a   12.00
929 A500 2.30m multi   1.00   .40

Pres. Mauno Koivisto, 70th Birthday — A501

1993, Nov. 25
930 A501 2.30m multicolored   .70   .40

Friendship — A502

Moomin characters: No. 931, Two standing. No. 932, Seven running.

1994, Jan. 27   Litho.   Perf. 12½x13
Booklet Stamps
931 A502 1 multicolored   3.00   .25
932 A502 1 multicolored   3.00   .25
  a. Bklt. pane, 4 each #931-932 24.00 12.00
      Complete booklet, #932a   24.00

Nos. 931-932 each sold for 2.30m at time of release. See note following No. 845.

Souvenir Sheet

Intl. Olympic Committee, Cent. — A503

Winter Olympics medalists from Finland: a, Marja-Liisa Kirvesniemi, Marjo Matikainen, cross-country skiing. b, Clas Thunberg, speed skating. c, Veikko Kankkonen, ski jumping. d, Veikko Hakulinen, cross-country skiing.

1994, Jan. 27   Perf. 13
933 A503 4.20m Sheet of 4, #a-d   6.00 6.00
See No. 939.

A504

Waino Aaltonen (1894-1966), Sculptor — A505

1994, Mar. 8
934 A504 2m "Peace"   .80   .40
935 A505 2m "Muse"   .80   .40
  a. Pair, #934-935   1.60 1.60

Postal Service Civil Servants' Federation, Cent. — A506

1994, Mar. 11
936 A506 2.30m multicolored   .70   .45

Finnish Technology A507

Europa: 2.30m, Paper roll, nitrogen fixation, safety lock, ice breaker MS Fennica. 4.20m, Radiosonde, fishing lure, mobile phone, wind power plant.

1994, Mar. 18
937 A507 2.30m multicolored   2.00   .40
938 A507 4.20m multicolored   2.50   1.20

Olympic Athlete Type of 1994
Souvenir Sheet

Finnish athletes: a, Riitta Salin, Pirjo Haggman, runners. b, Lasse Viren, runner. c, Tiina Lillak, javelin thrower. d, Pentti Nikula, pole vaulter.

1994, May 5   Litho.   Perf. 13
939 A503 4.20m Sheet of 4, #a-d   6.00 6.00
European Track & Field Championships, Finlandia '95.

Finlandia '95, Helsinki A508

Coccinella septempunctata.

1994, May 10   Perf. 13½x13
940 A508 16m multicolored   8.00 8.00
See Nos. 962, 1009.

Miniature Sheet

Wildflowers — A509

Designs: a, Hypericum perforatum (b). b, Lychnis viscaria. c, Campanula rotundifolia. d, Campanula glomerata. e, Geranium sanguineum (d). f, Fragaria vesca. g, Veronica chamaedrys (f, h). h, Saxifraga granulata (c, i). i, Viola tricolor (j). j, Potentilla anserina.

1994, June 1   Perf. 12
941   A509 1 Sheet of 10   30.00 15.00
 a.-j.   Any single   3.00   .40
No. 941 sold for 23m at time of release. See note following No. 845.

Finland-Sweden Track and Field Meet — A510

No. 942, Seppo Raty, Finland, javelin. No. 943, Patrick Sjoberg, Sweden, high jump.

1994, Aug. 26   Litho.   Perf. 12½
Booklet Stamps
942 A510 2.40m multicolored   1.50   .50
943 A510 2.40m multicolored   1.50   .50
  a. Booklet pane, 2 each #942-943 6.00 6.00
      Complete booklet, #943a   6.00
See Sweden Nos. 2091-2092.

Population Registers, 450th Anniv. — A511

1994, Sept. 1
944 A511 2.40m multicolored   1.20   .80

Intl. Year of the Family — A512

1994, Sept. 1
945 A512 3.40m multicolored   1.20   .80

Souvenir Sheet

Letter Writing Day A513

Dog Hill Kids in the Post Office: a, At Post Office window. b, Standing in doorway, mail cart. c, Blowing horn, pig. d, Putting letters in mailbox.

1994, Oct. 7   Litho.   Perf. 14
946 A513 2.80m Sheet of 4, #a-d   6.00 6.00

Christmas — A514

2.10m, Reindeer, bullfinches on antlers. 2.80m, Elves among snow-covered trees.

1994, Nov. 4
947 A514 2.10m multi   .80   .25
  a. Booklet pane of 10   15.00 15.00
      Complete booklet, #947a   15.00
948 A514 2.80m multi, vert.   1.00   .40

Greetings — A515

"Dog Hill Kids," sending/receiving greetings: No. 949, Delivering mail to Moon, spaceman. No. 950, Cat writing letter, clown. No. 951, Receiving mail from postman, baby. No. 952, Writing in bed, friend. No. 953, Winter scene at mailbox, characters at beach. No. 954, On bus, girl friend. No. 955, Standing at microphone with guitar, fan. No. 956, Baby in play pen, teddy bear.

FINLAND

Perf. 13 on 3 Sides
1995, Jan. 30   Litho.
Booklet Stamps

949	A515	2.80m multicolored	1.50	.60
950	A515	2.80m multicolored	1.50	.60
951	A515	2.80m multicolored	1.50	.60
952	A515	2.80m multicolored	1.50	.60
953	A515	2.80m multicolored	1.50	.60
954	A515	2.80m multicolored	1.50	.60
955	A515	2.80m multicolored	1.50	.60
956	A515	2.80m multicolored	1.50	.60
a.	Booklet pane, #949-956		12.00	12.00
	Complete booklet, 956a		12.00	

Nos. 949-952 are printed tete beche with Nos. 953-956. Soaking in water may affect the holographic images on Nos. 949-956.

Souvenir Sheet

Team Sports — A516

a, Paivi Ikola, pesapallo. b, Jari Kurri, ice hockey. c, Jari Litmanen, soccer. d, Lea Hakala, basketball.

1995, Jan. 30   Perf. 13
957 A516 3.40m Sheet of 4, #a-d   6.00   6.00

See No. 961.

Membership in European Union — A517

1995, Jan. 30   Perf. 14
958 A517 3.50m multicolored   1.20   .70

Peace & Liberty — A518

Europa: 2.90m, Stylized parachutists.

1995, Mar. 1   Litho.   Perf. 14
959 A518 2.90m multicolored   2.50   .60

Endangered Species — A519

Designs: a, Felis lynx. b, Lake, forest. c, Rocks, lake. d, Puoa hiopida.

1995, Mar. 1   Perf. 13
960   Block of 4   4.75   4.75
a.-d. A519 2.90m Any single   1.20   .90

Nos. 960a-960b, 960c-960d are continuous designs. See Russia No. 6249.

Athlete Type of 1995
Souvenir Sheet

Motor sports drivers in cars, on motorcycles.
a, Timo Makinen. b, Juha Kankkunen. c, Tommi Ahvala. d, Heikki Mikkola.

1995, May 10   Litho.   Perf. 13
961 A516 3.50m Sheet of 4, #a.-d   8.00   8.00

Insect Type of 1994
1995, May 11
962 A508 19m Geotrupes stercorarius   9.00   9.00

Tourism — A520

Designs: 2.80m, Linnanmaki amusement park, Helsinki. 2.90m, Town of Mantyharju.

1995, May 12
963 A520 2.80m multicolored   1.00   .50
964 A520 2.90m multicolored   1.20   .70

Town of Loviisa, 250th Anniv. — A521

1995, June 30   Litho.   Perf. 14
965 A521 3.20m multicolored   1.20   1.00

Intl. Union of Forestry Research Organizations, 20th World Congress, Tampere — A522

Designs: No. 966, Betula pendula. No. 967, Pinus sylvestris. No. 968, Picea abies. No. 969, Research, tree grown from needle.

Perf. 14 on 2 or 3 Sides
1995, Aug. 8   Litho.
Booklet Stamps

966	A522	2.80m multicolored	2.50	.50
967	A522	2.80m multicolored	2.50	.50
968	A522	2.80m multicolored	2.50	.50
969	A522	2.80m multicolored	1.25	.50
a.	Booklet pane of 4, #966-969		10.00	10.00
	Complete booklet, #969a		10.00	

Wilhelm Roentgen (1845-1923), Discovery of the X-Ray, Cent. — A523

1995, Aug. 8   Perf. 14
970 A523 4.30m multicolored   1.50   1.00

Cats — A525

Designs: No. 972, Somali. No. 973, Siamese. No. 974, Norwegian forest. No. 975, Persian. No. 976, European domestic female. No. 977, Three kittens, frog.

1995, Oct. 9   Litho.   Perf. 13½
972	A525	2.80m multi	1.50	.60
973	A525	2.80m multi	1.50	.60
974	A525	2.80m multi	1.50	.60
975	A525	2.80m multi	1.50	.60

Size: 59x35mm
976	A525	2.80m multi	1.50	.60
977	A525	2.80m multi	1.50	.60
a	Booklet pane of 6, #972-977		9.00	
	Complete booklet, #977a		9.00	

UN, 50th Anniv. — A526

1995, Oct. 20   Perf. 14
978 A526 3.40m multicolored   1.20   .60

A527

Christmas — A528

1995, Nov. 3   Litho.   Perf. 14
979 A527 2m Santa on skates   1.10   .25
980 A528 2.80m Poinsettias   1.10   .60

Letter Stamps — A529

1996, Feb 2   Litho.   Perf. 13½x14
Booklet Stamps

981	A529	1m "M"	.50	.50
982	A529	1m "O"	.50	.50
983	A529	1m "I"	.50	.50
984	A529	1m "H"	.50	.50
985	A529	1m "E"	.50	.50
986	A529	1m "J"	.50	.50
987	A529	1m "A"	.50	.50
988	A529	1m "N"	.50	.50
989	A529	1m "T"	.50	.50
990	A529	1m "P"	.50	.50
991	A529	1m "U"	.50	.50
992	A529	1m "S"	.50	.50
a.	Booklet pane of 12, #981-992		6.00	6.00
	Complete booklet, No. 992a		6.00	

UNICEF, 50th Anniv. — A530

1996, Feb. 2   Perf. 14
993 A530 2.80m multicolored   .90   .55

Women's Gymnastics in Finland, Cent. — A531

1996, Feb. 26   Litho.   Perf. 13
994 A531 2.80m multicolored   .90   .55

Woman Suffrage, 90th Anniv. — A532

Litho. & Engr.
1996, Mar. 8   Perf. 13
995 A532 3.20m multicolored   2.50   .75

Europa.

Cinema, Cent. — A533

Finnish films: No. 996, "Juha," 1937. No. 997, "Laveata Tieta," 1931. No. 998, "Tuntematon Sotilas," 1935. No. 999, Oldest known photo of a motion picture show, 1896. No. 1000, "Jäniksen Vuosi," 1977. No. 1001, "Valkoinen Poura," 1952. No. 1002, "Kaikki Rakastavat," 1935. No. 1003, "Varjoja Paratiisissa," 1986.

1996, Apr. 1   Litho.   Perf. 14x13½
Booklet Stamps

996	A533	2.80m multicolored	1.50	.60
997	A533	2.80m multicolored	1.50	.60
998	A533	2.80m multicolored	1.50	.60
999	A533	2.80m multicolored	1.50	.60
1000	A533	2.80m multicolored	1.50	.60
1001	A533	2.80m multicolored	1.50	.60
1002	A533	2.80m multicolored	1.50	.60
1003	A533	2.80m multicolored	1.50	.60
a.	Bklt. pane of 8, #996-1003		12.00	10.00
	Complete booklet, #1003a		12.00	

Radio, Cent. — A534

1996, Apr. 25   Perf. 14
1004 A534 4.30m multicolored   1.40   1.10

1996 Summer Olympic Games, Atlanta — A535

1996, June 3   Litho.   Perf. 12 Vert.
Booklet Stamps

1005	A535	3.40m Kayaking	1.50	1.00
1006	A535	3.40m Sailing	1.50	1.00
1007	A535	3.40m Rowing	1.50	1.00
1008	A535	3.40m Swimming	1.50	1.00
a.	Booklet pane of 4, #1005-1008		6.00	6.00
	Complete booklet, #1008a		6.00	

Insect Type of 1994
1996, July 1   Litho.   Perf. 13
1009 A508 19m Dytiscus marginalis   9.00   9.00

Shore Birds — A536

No. 1010, Gallinago gallinago. No. 1011, Haematopus ostralegus. No. 1012, Scolopax rusticola. No. 1013, Vanellus vanellus. No. 1014, Numenius arquata.

Perf. 13½ on 3 Sides
1996, Sept. 6   Litho. & Engr.
1010	A536	2.80m multicolored	1.50	.80
1011	A536	2.80m multicolored	1.50	.80
1012	A536	2.80m multicolored	1.50	.80
1013	A536	2.80m multicolored	1.50	.80

Size: 30x52mm
1014	A536	2.80m multicolored	1.50	.80
a.	Sheet of 5, #1010-1014		6.00	6.00

Finnish Comic Strips — A537

No. 1015, "Professor Itikainen" examining plant with magnifying glass, by Ilmari Vainio. No. 1016, "Pekka Puupää (Peter Blockhead)" taking letter from mailbox, by Ola Fogelborg. No. 1017, "Joonas" holding drawing pencil, by Veikko Savolainen. No. 1018, "Mämmilä" wearing helmet, by Tarmo Koivisto. No. 1019, "Rymy-Eetu" smoking pipe, by Erkki Tanttu. No. 1020, "Kieku" writing letter, by Asmo Alho. No. 1021, "Pikku Risunen" with animal, by Riitta Uusitalo. No. 1022, "Kiti" holding up pencil, by Kati Kovács.

1996, Oct. 9   Litho.   Perf. 13½
Booklet Stamps

1015	A537	2.80m black & red	1.50	1.00
1016	A537	2.80m black & red	1.50	1.00
1017	A537	2.80m red & black	1.50	1.00
1018	A537	2.80m black & red	1.50	1.00
1019	A537	2.80m black & red	1.50	1.00
1020	A537	2.80m red & black	1.50	1.00
1021	A537	2.80m red & black	1.50	1.00
1022	A537	2.80m red & black	1.50	1.00
a.	Bklt. pane of 8, #1015-1022		12.00	12.00
	Complete booklet, #1022a		12.00	

Christmas — A538

2m, Snowman, Santa, gnome playing musical instruments. 2.80m, Rabbit, reindeer watching northern lights. 3.20m, Santa reading letters.

1996, Nov. 1   Litho.   Perf. 14
1023	A538	2m multi	1.00	.40
1024	A538	2.80m multi	1.00	.40
1025	A538	3.20m multi, vert.	1.50	1.00
	Nos. 1023-1025 (3)		3.50	1.80

FINLAND

Greetings Stamps — A539

Sticker designs from end of 19th cent.: No. 1026, Two angels. No. 1027, Flowers in basket. No. 1028, Hand reaching through garland, bluebird. No. 1029, Boy, girl dancing. No. 1030, Boy, envelope, shamrocks. No. 1031, Clasping hands through heart-shaped garlands. No. 1032, Roses. No. 1033, Angel.

Perf. 13x12½ on 3 Sides
1997, Jan. 30   Litho.
Booklet Stamps

1026	A539	1 multicolored	3.00	1.00
1027	A539	1 multicolored	3.00	1.00
1028	A539	1 multicolored	3.00	1.00
1029	A539	1 multicolored	3.00	1.00
1030	A539	1 multicolored	3.00	1.00
1031	A539	1 multicolored	3.00	1.00
1032	A539	1 multicolored	3.00	1.00
1033	A539	1 multicolored	3.00	1.00
a.		Bklt. pane of 8, #1026-1033	24.00	12.00
		Complete booklet, #1033a	24.00	

Nos. 1026-1033 sold for 2.80m on day of issue.
Number on stamp represents class of mail.

Mail Order Sales in Finland, Cent. — A540

1997, Jan. 30   Perf. 13½x14
1034   A540   2.80m multicolored   .90   .40

1997 Ice Hockey World Championships, Helsinki — A541

1997, Jan. 30
1035   A541   2.80m multicolored   .90   .40

On each stamp from the right vertical row of the sheet, No. 1035 exists without the thin, curved black line at the center right edge of the stamp. Value, single stamp $3.00.

Lepus Timidus — A542

1997, Mar. 4   Litho.   Perf. 14
1036   A542   2.80m multicolored   .90   .40

Saami Folktale, "Girl Who Turned into a Golden Merganser" A543

Europa: 3.20m, Duck, girl, prince. 3.40m, Girl falling into crevice.

1997, Mar. 4   Perf. 13
1037   A543   3.20m multicolored   2.00   .50
1038   A543   3.40m multicolored   3.00   1.00

Paavo Nurmi (1897-1973), Winner of 9 Olympic Gold Medals — A544

1997, Mar. 18   Perf. 14
1039   A544   3.40m multicolored   1.20   .60

Southwest Archipelago Natl. Park — A545

Litho. & Engr.
1997, Apr. 25   Perf. 14
1040   A545   4.30m multicolored   1.75   .70

Tango — A546

1997, May 19   Litho.
1041   A546   1 multicolored   3.00   .40
     Complete booklet of 5   12.50

No. 1041 sold for 2.80m on day of release. Number on stamp represents class of mail.

A547

Sailing Ships: No. 1042, Astrid. No. 1043, Jacobstads Wapen. No. 1044, Tradewind. No. 1045, Merikokko. No. 1046, Suomen Joutsen. No. 1047, Sigyn.

Booklet Stamps
1997, May 19   Perf. 13½

1042	A547	2.80m multicolored	1.50	1.00
1043	A547	2.80m multicolored	1.50	1.00
1044	A547	2.80m multicolored	1.50	1.00
1045	A547	2.80m multicolored	1.50	1.00

Size: 48x25½mm
1046	A547	2.80m multicolored	1.50	1.00
1047	A547	2.80m multicolored	1.50	1.00
a.		Booklet pane of 6, #1042-1047	9.00	
		Complete booklet, #1047a	9.00	

Pres. Martti Ahtisaari, 60th Birthday — A548

1997, June 23   Litho.   Perf. 14
1048   A548   2.80m multicolored   .90   .40

Independence, 80th Anniv. — A549

Four seasons: No. 1049, Spring, lily-of-the-valley (natl. flower). No. 1050, Summer, white clouds. No. 1051, Fall, colorful leaves. No. 1052, Winter, snow crystals.

Perf. 13x12½ on 2 or 3 Sides
1997, June 23   Booklet Stamps

1049	A549	2.80m multicolored	1.50	1.00
1050	A549	2.80m multicolored	1.50	1.00
1051	A549	2.80m multicolored	1.50	1.00
1052	A549	2.80m multicolored	1.50	1.00
a.		Booklet pane, #1049-1052	6.00	6.00
		Complete booklet, #1052a	6.00	

Souvenir Sheet

A550

Grus Grus (Cranes): a, With young. b, With frog. c, Performing mating dance. d, In flight.

1997, Aug. 19   Litho.   Perf. 14
1053   A550   2.80m Sheet of 4, #a.-d.   6.00   6.00

A551

Finnish Writers Assoc. (Covers from books): No. 1054, "Seven Brothers," by Aleksis Kivi. No. 1055, "Sinuhe the Egyptian," by Mika Waltari. No. 1056, "Täällä Pohjantähden alla I," by Väinö Linna. No. 1057, "Hyvästi Iijoki," by Kalle Päätalo. No. 1058, "Haukka, minum rakkaani," by Kaari Utrio. No. 1059, "Juhannustanssit," by Hannu Salama. No. 1060, "Manillaköysi," by Veijo Meri. No. 1061, "Uppo-Nalle ja Kumma," by Elina Karjalainen.

Booklet Stamps
1997, Oct. 9   Litho.   Perf. 14¼, 14½

1054	A551	2.80m multicolored	1.50	.60
1055	A551	2.80m multicolored	1.50	.60
1056	A551	2.80m multicolored	1.50	.60
1057	A551	2.80m multicolored	1.50	.60
1058	A551	2.80m multicolored	1.50	.60
1059	A551	2.80m multicolored	1.50	.60
1060	A551	2.80m multicolored	1.50	.60
1061	A551	2.80m multicolored	1.50	.60
a.		Booklet pane, #1054-1061	12.00	8.00
		Complete booklet, #1061a	12.00	

No. 1056 exists perf 14½x14¼. The other values also should exist thus. The editors would like to examine such stamps.

Christmas — A552

Designs: 2m, Village. 2.80m, Candelabra, vert. 3.20m, Church, vert.

1997, Oct. 31
1062	A552	2m multi	1.00	.40
1063	A552	2.80m multi	1.00	1.00
1064	A552	3.20m multi	1.25	1.80
		Nos. 1062-1064 (3)	3.25	3.20

Wildlife — A553

2nd, Stizostedion lucioperca. 1st, Turdus merula.

Die Cut Perf. 10 Horiz. Syncopated
1998, Jan. 15   Litho.
Self-Adhesive Coil Stamps
1065   A553   2 multicolored   2.50   .60
1066   A553   1 multicolored   3.00   .40

Nos. 1065-1066 were valued at 2.40m and 2.80m, respectively, on date of issue. Number on stamp represents class of mail.
See Nos. 1099-1100.

A554

Moomin Cartoon Characters, by Tove Jansson: No. 1067, Boy Moomin drawing with pad and pencil. No. 1068, Girl Moomin in sunshine. No. 1069, Organ grinder. No. 1070, Boy Moomin giving flower to girl Moomin.

1998, Jan. 15   Perf. 13 on 3 Sides
Booklet Stamps

1067	A554	1 multicolored	2.90	.60
1068	A554	1 multicolored	2.90	.60
1069	A554	1 multicolored	2.90	.60
1070	A554	1 multicolored	2.90	.60
a.		Booklet pane, #1067-1070	8.00	8.00
		Complete booklet, #1070a	12.00	

Nos. 1067-1070 each sold for 2.80m on day of issue. Number on stamp represents class of mail.
See No. 1127.

A555

1998, Feb. 3   Perf. 14
1071   A555   2.80m multicolored   .90   .40
Finnish Federation of Nurses, cent.

A556

Valentine's Day Surprise Stamps. (Designs beneath scratch-off heart): a, Musical notes, two dogs. b, Elephant, mouse and flowers. c, Puppy, sealed envelope. d, Kittens, kittens hugging. e, Dog with nose in air, bouquet of flowers. f, Flowers, two rodents.

1998, Feb. 3   Perf. 12
1072   1 Sheet of 6   18.00   9.00
a.-f.   A556   Any single, unscratched   3.00   .70

Nos. 1072a-1072f were each valued at 2.80m on day of issue. Number on stamp represents class of mail. Unused values are for singles with attached selvage. Inscriptions are shown in selvage above or below each stamp. Each stamp bears a heart-shaped, golden scratch-off overlay. Values are for unscratched examples. Scratched stamps, with hearts partially or fully removed, sell for about 20 percent less.

Tussilago Farfara — A557

1998, Mar. 27   Litho.   Perf. 14
1073   A557   2.80m multi   .90   .40

National Festivals — A558

Europa: 3.20m, Boy and girl, balloons, "Vappu" (May Day). 3.40m, Boy and girl in a dream floating over water, Midsummer Festival.

1998, Mar. 27   Perf. 14x14½
1074   A558   3.20m multicolored   1.50   .80
1075   A558   3.40m multicolored   2.00   1.50

Finnish Marine Research Institute, 80th Anniv. — A559

Designs: 2.80m, Research vessel, "Aranda." 3.20m, "Vega," chart showing route of Nils Adolf Erik Nordenskjold's expedition.

Litho. & Engr.
1998, May 7   Perf. 14x13
1076   A559   2.80m multicolored   1.00   .70
1077   A559   3.20m multicolored   1.50   1.00

First Performance of National Anthem, 150th Anniv. — A560

1998, May 7   Perf. 13
1078   A560   5m multicolored   2.00   1.00

Puppies — A561

No. 1079, Bernese Mountain dog. No. 1080, Puli. No. 1081, Boxer. No. 1082, Bichon Frisé. No. 1083, Finnish lapphound. No. 1084, Wire-haired dachshund. No. 1085, Scottish cairn terrier. No. 1086, Labrador retriever.

FINLAND

Perf. 13½x13 on 2 or 3 Sides
1998, June 4   Litho.
Booklet Stamps
1079	A561	1 multicolored	3.00	.50
1080	A561	1 multicolored	3.00	.50
1081	A561	1 multicolored	3.00	.50
1082	A561	1 multicolored	3.00	.50
1083	A561	1 multicolored	3.00	.50
1084	A561	1 multicolored	3.00	.50
1085	A561	1 multicolored	3.00	.50
1086	A561	1 multicolored	3.00	.50
a.	Booklet pane, #1079-1086		24.00	12.00
	Complete booklet, #1086a		24.00	

Nos. 1079-1086 each sold for 2.80m on day of issue. Number on stamp represents class of mail.

Owls — A562

Designs: a, Bubo bubo. b, Wing of bubo bubo. c, Bubo bubo, aegolius funereus. d, Strix nebulosa. e, Nyctea scandiaca.

1998, Sept. 4   Litho.   Perf. 13½
1087	A562	Sheet of 5 + label	7.50	7.50
a.-e.		3m any single	1.50	.80

No. 1087b is 52x27mm; Nos. 1087c-1087d, 26x44mm; No. 1087e, 30x44mm.
See No. 1113.

Cycling — A563

1998, Sept. 4   Perf. 14
| 1088 | A563 | 3m multicolored | 1.00 | .40 |

Finnish Design — A564

No. 1089, Savoy vases, by Alvar Aalto. No. 1090, Karuselli chair, by Yrjö Kukkapuro. No. 1091, Tasaraita knitwear, designed by Annika Rimala for Marimekko. No. 1092, Kilta tableware set, by Kaj Franck. No. 1093, Cast iron pot, by Timo Sarpaneva. No. 1094, Carelia cutlery set, by Bertel Gardberg.

Perf. 13½ on 3 Sides
1998, Oct. 9   Litho.
Booklet Stamps
1089	A564	3m multicolored	1.50	.80
1090	A564	3m multicolored	1.50	.80
1091	A564	3m multicolored	1.50	.80
1092	A564	3m multicolored	1.50	.80
1093	A564	3m multicolored	1.50	.80
1094	A564	3m multicolored	1.50	.80
a.	Booklet pane, #1089-1094		7.50	7.50
	Complete booklet, #1094a		7.50	

Nos. 1090-1091, 1093-1094 are 29x34mm.

Christmas — A565

Designs: 2m, Christmas tree, children, vert. 3m, Children, dog riding sled. 3.20m, Winter scene of cottage in center of island.

1998, Oct. 30   Perf. 14
1095	A565	2m multicolored	1.00	.40
1096	A565	3m multicolored	1.00	.50
1097	A565	3.20m multicolored	1.20	.70
	Nos. 1095-1097 (3)		3.20	1.60

Souvenir Sheet

Mika Häkkinen, Formula 1 Driving Champion — A566

1999, Jan. 15   Perf. 13½
| 1098 | A566 | 3m multicolored | 1.50 | 1.50 |

Native Wildlife Type of 1998
2, Salmo salar. 1, Luscinia svecica.

Coil Stamps
Die Cut Perf. 10 Horiz. Syncopated
1999, Jan. 27   Litho.
| 1099 | A553 | 2 multi | 2.50 | .40 |

Die Cut Perf. 10 Vert. Syncopated
| 1100 | A553 | 1 multi, vert. | 3.00 | .40 |

Nos. 1099-1100 were valued at 2.40m and 3m, respectively, on day of issue. Number on stamp represents class of mail.

Friendship — A567

Animals' tails: No. 1101, Zebra, lion. No. 1102, Dog, cat.

Booklet Stamps
Serpentine Die Cut Perf. 13 Horiz.
1999, Jan. 27   Self-Adhesive
1101	A567	3m multicolored	1.20	.50
1102	A567	3m multicolored	1.20	.50
a.	Bklt. pane, 3 each #1101-1102		7.25	7.25

No. 1102a is a complete booklet.

Finnish Labor Movement, Cent. — A568

1999, Jan. 27   Perf. 13½
| 1103 | A568 | 4.50m multicolored | 1.50 | 1.00 |

Finland's Roads — A569

No. 1104, Snow-covered landscape, Arctic Ocean Road. No. 1105, Freeway interchanges, Jyväsjtkä Lakeshore Road. No. 1106, Raippaluoto Bridge. No. 1107, Wooded drive, Kitee.

1999, Feb. 15   Litho.   Perf. 14 Horiz.
Booklet Stamps
1104	A569	3m multicolored	1.50	1.00
a.	Perf. 12¾ horiz.		50.00	10.00
1105	A569	3m multicolored	1.50	1.00
a.	Perf. 12¾ horiz.		50.00	10.00
1106	A569	3m multicolored	1.50	1.00
a.	Perf. 12¾ horiz.		50.00	10.00
1107	A569	3m multicolored	1.50	1.00
a.	Booklet pane, #1104-1107		6.00	
	Complete booklet, #1107a		6.00	
b.	Perf. 12¾ horiz.			10.00
c.	Booklet pane, #1104a, 1105a, 1106a, 1107b		200.00	200.00
	Complete booklet, #1107c		200.00	

A570

Women's Kalevala-style brooches: a, Horse clasp. b, Bird clasp. c, Virusmäki clasp.

1999, Feb. 15   Perf. 13½x14
1108	Sheet of 3		4.50	4.50
a.-c.	A570 3m any single		1.50	.80

1st Publication of Legend of the Kalevala, 150th Anniv.

Crocus Vernus — A571

1999, Mar. 15   Perf. 13x13½
| 1109 | A571 | 3m multi | .90 | .50 |

Martha Organization, Cent. — A572

1999, Mar. 15   Perf. 13½x13
| 1110 | A572 | 3m multicolored | 1.00 | .50 |

Europa — A573

Designs: 2.70m, Esplanade Park. 3.20m, Ruissalo Park.

1999, Mar. 15   Perf. 13½x14
1111	A573	2.70m multi	1.50	1.20
1112	A573	3.20m multi	2.50	1.50

Bird Type of 1998
Designs: a, Luscinia luscinia. b, Cuculus canorus. c, Botaurus stellaris. d, Caprimulgus europaeus. e, Crex crex.

1999, May 18   Perf. 13½
1113	Sheet of 5 + label	6.00	6.00
a.-e.	A562 3m any single	1.20	.75

No. 1113b is 25x43mm. No. 1113c is 45x30mm. No. 1113d-1113e are 26x37mm.

Finland's Presidency of European Union — A574

1999, July 1   Litho.   Perf. 13¾x13½
| 1114 | A574 | 3.50m multicolored | 1.10 | .60 |

Finnish Entertainers — A575

a, Harmony Sisters, Vera (1914-97), Maire (1916-95) & Raija (1918-97) Valtonen. b, Olavi Virta (1915-72), singer. c, Georg Malmstén (1902-81), composer, conductor. d, Topi Kärki (1915-22), composer, and Reino (Repe) Helismaa (1913-65), lyricist. e, Tapio Rautavaara (1915-79), singer. f, Esa Parkarinen (1911-89), musician, actor.

Perf. 13¼ on 3 Sides
1999, Sept. 6   Litho.
1115	A575	Booklet pane of 6	9.00	
a.-f.		3.50m any single	1.50	1.00
		Complete booklet, #1115	9.00	

Nos. 1115a, 1115d are each 60x34mm.

Finnish Commercial Product Design — A576

a, Fiskars cutting tools. b, Zoel/Versoul guitars. c, Ergo II/Silenta hearing protectors. d,

---

Ponsse Cobra HS 10 tree harvester. e, Suunto compass. f, Exel Avanti QLS ski pole.

Perf. 13¼ on 3 Sides
1999, Oct 8   Litho.
1116	A576	Booklet pane of 6	7.00	
a.-f.		3.50m any single	1.20	1.00
		Complete booklet, #1116	7.00	

Size of b, c, e, f: 30x35mm.

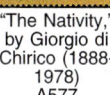

"The Nativity," by Giorgio di Chirico (1888-1978) A577   Rabbits, Birds A578

Design: 2.50m, Santa Claus, vert.

1999, Nov. 5   Perf. 14
1117	A578	2.50m multicolored	.90	.40
1118	A577	3m multicolored	1.20	1.20
1119	A578	3.50m multicolored	1.60	.60
	Nos. 1117-1119 (3)		3.70	2.20

Christmas. See Italy Nos. 2314-2315.

Sveaborg Fortress — A579

2000, Jan. 12   Litho.   Perf. 13¾x13½
| 1120 | A579 | 7.20m multi | 3.00 | 1.50 |

Helsinki, 450th Anniv. — A580

Designs: No. 1121, Baltic herring market (designer's name at UL).
No. 1122: a, Museum of Contemporary Art (blue building), vert. b, Cathedral, Senate Square (green building). c, Finlandia Hall (orange building). d, Glass Palace Film and Media Center (red building), vert.
No. 1123: a, Quest for the Lost Crown, Sveaborg Fortress (children and arch), vert. b, Like No. 1121, no designer's name. c, Forces of Light City Festival. d, Cellist at outdoor concert, Kaivopuisto Park.

2000, Jan. 12   Perf. 14
| 1121 | A580 | 3.50m multi | 1.10 | .60 |

Perf. 14½x14¾ (vert. stamps), 14¾x14½
1122		Booklet pane of 4	8.00	8.00
a.-d.	A580	3.50m Any single	2.00	2.00
1123		Booklet pane of 4	8.00	8.00
a.-d.	A580	3.50m Any single	2.00	2.00
		Complete booklet, #1122-1123	10.00	

Valentine's Day — A581

Designs: a, Earth as basketball. b, Painters on ladder. c, Birds in balloon. d, Alien with magnet. e, Boy with heart-shaped balloon. f, Polar bear and igloo.

Perf. 13x12¾ on 3 sides
2000, Jan. 12
1124		Bklt. pane of 6 + 4 labels	9.00	
a.-f.	A581	3.50m Any single	1.50	1.00
		Complete booklet, #1124	9.00	

Souvenir Sheet of 2
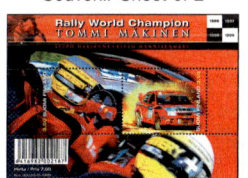
Tommi Mäkinen, 1999 Rally World Champion — A582

566   **FINLAND**

a, Mäkinen behind wheel. b, Race car.

2000, Mar. 3   *Perf. 13x13¼*
1125   A582   3.50m   #a.-b.   3.00   3.00

Caltha Palustris — A583

2000, Mar. 15   *Perf. 13¾x13¼*
1126   A583   3.50m multi   1.10   .60
     Easter.

Moomin Type of 1998

a, Rat with broom looking at Moomins. b, Moomin with uniform, figures sprouting from ground. c, Moomin with hat in forest. d, Moomin with hat, children, in front of stove.

Perf. 13x12¾ on 3 Sides
2000, Mar. 15
1127   Booklet pane of 4   24.00   24.00
   a.-d.   A554 1 Any single   6.00   1.00
     Complete booklet, #1127   30.00   12.00
   e.   As #1127, perf. 13¼ on 3 sides   12.00
   f.-i.   As #a-d, perf. 13¼ on 3 sides   3.00   .70
     Booklet, #1127e   12.50

Nos. 1127a-1127d sold for 3.50m on day of issue. Number on stamp represents class of mail.
Issued: No. 1127e, 7/10/00.

Jubilee Year — A584

Turku Cathedral: a, Nave. b, Woman, votive candles. c, Christ on the Mount of Transfiguration, alterpiece. d, Infant baptism.

2000, Mar. 15   *Litho.*   *Perf. 14 Vert.*
1128   Booklet pane of 4   6.00   3.50
   a.-d.   A584 3.50m Any single   1.50   .60
     Complete booklet, #1128   6.00

Europa, 2000
Common Design Type
2000, May 9   *Perf. 13¼x13*
1129   CD17   3.50m multi   2.00   .60

Provincial Flowers

Spring Anemone   Blue Cornflower
A585   A586

Pulsatilla Patens — A587

Die Cut Perf. 13x12½
2000-01   *Litho.*
Booklet Stamps
Self-Adhesive
1130   A585 1 multi   3.00   .40
   a.   Booklet pane of 10   16.00

Die Cut Perf. 14¾x13½
1131   A586 1 multi   3.00   .40
1132   A587 1 multi   3.00   .40
   a.   Booklet pane, 5 each #1131-1132   30.00

Number on stamp represents class of mail. No. 1130 sold for 3.50m at time of release. Nos. 1131-1132 each sold for 3.60m on day of issue. No. 1132a was issued in two printings. The white box containing the stamps on the original printing is 114mm wide and on the 2003 printing, the box is 110mm wide.
Issued: No. 1130, 5/9. Nos. 1131-1132, 5/16/01.

Souvenir Sheet

Science A595

Designs: a, Children, molecular model (triangular stamp). b, Man's face, DNA strand (rhomboid stamp). c, Man's face, Sierpinski triangles (square stamp).

2000, May 30   *Perf. 14¼*
1140   A595   3.50m Sheet of 3, #a.-c.   4.50   3.60

No. 1140 has holographic image. Soaking in water may affect the hologram.

Finnish Design A596

No. 1141: a, Rug, by Akseli Gallen-Kallela (1865-1931). b, Pearl Bird, by Birger Kaipiainen (1915-88). c, Pot, by Kyllikki Salmenhaara (1915-81). d, Leaf, by Tapio Wirkkala (1915-85). e, Detail from damask, by Dora Jung (1906-80). f, Glass vase, by Valter Jung (1879-1946).

Perf. 13¼ on 3 Sides
2000, Sept. 5   *Litho.*
1141   Booklet pane of 6   9.00   6.00
   a.-f.   A596 3.50m Any single   1.50   1.00
     Booklet, #1141   9.00

Size of b, c, e, f: 30x35mm.

Coregonus   Lagopus
Lavaretus   Lagopus
A597   A598

Coil Stamps
Die Cut Perf. 10 Horiz. Syncopated
2000, Sept. 5   Self-Adhesive
1142   A597 2 multi   2.50   .40
1143   A598 1 multi   3.00   .40

Nos. 1142-1143 sold for 3m and 3.50m respectively on day of sale.

On modern stamps bearing the "denominations" "1" or "2," the number represents the class of mail.

Christmas — A599

2.50m, Costumed Tiernapojat carol singers. 3.50m, Bullfinch on door ornament, vert.

Serpentine Die Cut 14¼
2000, Nov. 3   Photo.
Self-Adhesive
1144-1145   A599 Set of 2   2.20   1.00
Litho.
Serpentine Die Cut 13¾
1146   A599 3.50m multi + label   8.00   8.00

No. 1146 issued in sheets of 20 that sold for 120m, together with a separate sheet of stickers that could be affixed on the label. The labels attached to the stamps are separated by a row of interrupted serpentine die cutting. Labels could be personalized with photographs taken at some sale sites.

European Year of Languages — A600

2001, Jan. 17   *Litho.*   *Perf. 13¼*
1147   A600 1 multi   3.00   .60

No. 1147 sold for 3.50m on day of sale.

World Ski Championships, Lahti — A601

No. 1148: a, Ski jumper Janne Ahonen (yellow helmet). b, Skier Mika Myllylä.

2001, Jan. 17
1148   A601 3.50m Horiz. pair, #a-b   3.00   1.40

Valentine's Day — A602

No. 1149: a, Oval wreath. b, Basket of flowers, letter. c, Heart-shaped wreath. d, Bouquet of flowers, letter. e, Flowers, tea set. f, Flowers, heart-shaped pastry.

Serpentine Die Cut 11½x11¾ on 3 Sides
2001, Jan. 17   Photo.
Self-Adhesive
1149   Booklet pane of 6   18.00   4.20
   a.-f.   A602 1 Any single   3.00   1.00
     Booklet, #1149   18.00

Nos. 1149a-1149f each sold for 3.50m on day of issue.

Souvenir Sheet
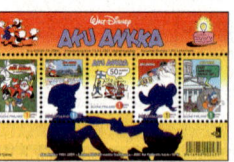

Donald Duck Comics in Finland, 50th Anniv. A603

No. 1150: a, Mickey Mouse, Donald Duck, Santa Claus, Goofy. b, First comics, silhouette of boy. c, Tin soldier with Finnish flag, Chip and Dale (25x30mm). d, Finnish epic hero Väinämöinien, silhouette of Donald Duck. e, Helsinki Cathedral, Donald Duck.

Perf. 7¾ on 3 or 4 Sides
2001, Mar. 13   *Litho.*
1150   A603 1 Sheet of 5, #a-e   10.00   7.50

Nos. 1150a-1150e sold for 3.50m each on day of issue.

Santa Claus and Sleigh — A604

Serpentine Die Cut 14½x14
2001-04   Self-Adhesive
1151   A604 1 multi   3.00   .60
   a.   Serpentine die cut 13¾x13½ ('04)   3.00   1.20

No. 1151 sold for 3.60m on day of issue. No. 1151a sold for 65c on day of issue. No. 1151, 4/2/01. No. 1151a, 12/04.

Europa — A605

2001, Apr. 2   *Perf. 13x13½*
1152   A605 5.40m multi   3.50   1.00

Easter A606

No. 1153: a, Chick. b, Decorated egg.

2001, Apr. 2   *Perf. 13¼*
1153   A606 3.60m Horiz. pair, #a-b   5.00   5.00

Souvenir Sheet

Verla Mill, UNESCO World Heritage Site — A607

Denominations in: a, UL. b, UR. c, LL. d, LR.

2001, Apr. 2
1154   A607 3.60m Sheet of 4, #a-d   6.00   6.00

Orienteering World Championships, Tampere — A608

2001, May 16
1155   A608 3.60m multi   1.40   .60

Values are for stamps with surrounding selvage.

Souvenir Sheet

Woodpeckers — A609

No. 1156: a, Dendrocopos minor (32x36mm). b, Picoides tridactylus (29x36mm). c, Dendrocopos leucotos (32x42mm). d, Dendrocopos major (29x42mm). e, Picus canus (32x41mm). f, Dryocopus martius (29x41mm).

Perf. 14½x14¼ on 2, 3 or 4 Sides
2001, May 16
1156   A609 3.60m Sheet of 6, #a-f   9.00   9.00

Marine Life — A610

No. 1157: a, Lampetra fluviatilis. b, Aspius aspius. c, Coregonus albula.

FINLAND

Die Cut Perf. 10 Horiz. Syncopated
2001, Sept. 6   Photo.
Self-Adhesive
Coil Stamps

1157	Horiz. strip of 3	7.50	4.50
a.-c.	A610 2 Any single	2.50	1.50

Nos. 1157a-1157c were sold in boxes of 100 stamps that sold at a discount price of 270m on day of sale. The franking value on the day of sale for each stamp was 3m.

Birds — A611

No. 1158: a, Parus caeruleus. b, Motacilla alba. c, Oriolus oriolus.

Die Cut Perf. 10 Horiz. Syncopated
2001, Sept. 6   Photo.
Self-Adhesive
Coil Stamps

1158	Horiz. strip of 3	9.00	1.20
a.-c.	A611 1 Any single	3.00	.40

Nos. 1158a-1158c were sold in boxes of 100 stamps that sold at a discount price of 330m on day of sale. The franking value on the day of sale for each stamp was 3.60m.

History of Gulf of Finland — A612

No. 1159: a, Utö Lighthouse. b, Wreck of the St. Mikael. c, Diver exploring St. Mikael. d, Opossum shrimp, isopod. e, Ship's cabin and nautical chart (32x55mm).

Perf. 13¼x13¾ on 2 or 3 Sides
2001, Sept. 6   Litho.

1159	Booklet pane of 5	15.00	5.00
a.-e.	A612 1 Any single	3.00	1.00
	Booklet, #1159		

Nos. 1159a-1159e each sold for 3.60m on day of sale.
See No. 1177.

Christmas — A613

Designs: 2.50m, Elf reading Santa's book, candle. 3.60m, Elf delivering package on sled, horiz.

Serpentine Die Cut 14¼
2001, Oct. 26   Photo.
Self-Adhesive

1160	A613 2.50m multi	1.10	.40
1161	A613 3.60m multi	1.20	.65

Slightly larger examples of Nos. 1160-1161 serpentine die cut 14 are known on first day and other covers produced by the postal service. They were not sold unused to the public.

100 Cents = 1 Euro (€)

Flowers A614   National Symbols A615

Heraldic Lion — A616

Type A614 — No. 1162, Myosotis scorpioides: a, Forty-one flowers. b, Four flowers, five buds. c, One flower, four buds. d, Entire plant. e, Five flowers.
No. 1163, Convallaria majalis: a, Leaf, stem with five flowers. b, Two leaves, stem with eight flowers. c, Two flowers. d, Two leaves, stem with five flowers. e, Entire plants.
Type A615: 50c, Swan, vert. 60c, Birch. 1, Flag and bird. 90c, Kymintehtaalta, by Victor Westerholm. €1.30, Granite cliff. €2.50, Spruce. €3.50, Pine.

Die Cut Perf. 15
2002, Jan. 1   Photo.
Self-Adhesive

1162	Vert. strip of 5	.90	.40
a.-e.	A614 5c Any single	.25	.25
f.	As #1162, die cut perf 14	.80	
g.-k.	A614 5c Any single, die cut perf 14	.25	.25

Die Cut Perf. 14

1163	Vert. strip of 5	1.00	1.20
a.-e.	A614 10c Any single	.35	.25
1164	A615 50c multi	.90	.40
1165	A615 60c multi	1.70	.40

Die Cut Perf. 13¾

1166	A615 1 multi	3.00	1.00
a.	Booklet pane of 10	30.00	
	Booklet, #1166a	30.00	

Die Cut Perf. 14¾x15

| 1167 | A615 90c multi | 1.80 | .65 |

Die Cut Perf. 12 Syncopated

| 1168 | A616 €1 blue & multi | 1.80 | 1.00 |

Die Cut Perf. 14¾x15

1169	A615 €1.30 multi	2.40	1.00
a.	Die cut perf 14 ('04)	2.40	1.00

Die Cut Perf. 14

1170	A615 €2.50 multi	5.00	1.00
1171	A615 €3.50 multi	7.00	1.50

Die Cut Perf. 12 Syncopated

1172	A616 €5 red & multi	10.00	3.00
	Nos. 1162-1172 (11)	35.50	10.95

No. 1166 sold for 60c on day of issue.
Die cut porf 14 oxamplo of No. 1107 exist on first day and other covers produced by the postal service. They were not sold unused to the public.
No. 1169a issued 7/04. No. 1169a has a duller blue panel and a duller black denomination than that found on No. 1169, and a die cut perf. 14 version of No. 1169 that was available only on first day covers with 1/1/02 cancels, and which was not made available to the public unused. Nos. 1169 and 1169a were produced by different printers.
Nos. 1162f-1162k were printed and put on first day and other covers in 2002 but were not sold to the public until 2006.
See Nos. 1179-1180, 1383-1384.

Easter — A617

Die Cut Perf. 14
2002, Mar. 6   Photo.
Self-Adhesive

| 1173 | A617 60c multi | 1.20 | .50 |

Souvenir Sheet

Elias Lönnrot (1802-84), Botanist, Linguist — A618

No. 1174: a, Plantain. b, Opening lines of "Kalevala" (denomination at UL). c, Closing lines of "Kalevala" (denomination at UR). d, Portrait.

Perf. 13¼ on 3 or 4 Sides
2002, Mar. 6   Litho.

| 1174 | A618 60c Sheet of 4, #a-d | 4.75 | 4.75 |

Souvenir Sheet

Old Rauma, UNESCO World Heritage Site — A619

Denominations at: a, UL. b, UR. c, LL. d, LR.

2002, Mar. 6   Perf. 13½

| 1175 | A619 60c Sheet of 4, #a-d | 4.75 | 4.75 |

Europa — A620

2002, Apr. 15   Perf. 13

| 1176 | A620 60c multi | 1.00 | .50 |

Gulf of Finland Type of 2001

No. 1177: a, Birds, fish. b, Sailboat, plankton. c, Flounder on sea bed. d, Shrimp, herring. e, Tvärminne Zoological Station, ship, isopod, oceanographic equipment, mussels (32x55mm).

Perf. 13¼x13¾ on 2 or 3 Sides
2002, Apr. 15

1177	Booklet pane of 5	15.00	5.00
a.-e.	A612 1 Any single	3.00	1.00
	Booklet, #1177	15.00	

Nos. 1177a-1177e each sold for 60c on day of issue.

Sibelius Monument, Helsinki, by Eila Hiltunen — A621

2002, May 3   Perf. 13

| 1178 | A621 60c multi | 1.20 | .50 |

National Symbols Type of 2002 Without Finland Post Emblem

Designs: 60c, Juniperus communis. 1, Reindeer in Lapland.

Die Cut Perf. 14
2002, Oct. 9   Photo.
Self-Adhesive

1179	A615 60c multicolored	1.20	.50
1180	A615 1 multicolored	3.00	1.00

No. 1180 sold for 60c on day of issue.

Christmas — A622

Designs: 45c, Horse-drawn sleigh. 60c, Angel with trumpet, vert.

Serpentine Die Cut 14¼
2002, Nov. 1   Self-Adhesive

| 1181-1182 | A622 Set of 2 | 2.20 | 1.20 |

Fish — A623

No. 1183: a, Abramis brama. b, Salmo trutta lacustris. c, Esox lucius.

Syncopated Die Cut Perf. 10 Horiz.
2003, Jan. 15   Self-Adhesive
Coil Stamps

1183	Horiz. strip of 3	7.50	4.50
a.-c.	A623 2 Any single	2.50	1.50

Nos. 1183a-1183c were sold in boxes of 100 that sold at a discount price of €47 on day of issue. The franking value on the day of issue for each stamp was 50c.

Birds — A624

No. 1184: a, Cuculus canorus. b, Alauda arvensis. c, Perisoreus infaustus.

Syncopated Die Cut Perf. 10 Horiz.
2003, Jan. 15   Self-Adhesive
Coil Stamps

1184	Horiz. strip of 3	3.00	1.50
a.-c.	A624 1 Any single	1.00	.50

Nos. 1184a-1184c were sold in boxes of 100 that sold at a discount price of €57 on day of issue. The franking value on the day of issue for each stamp was 60c.

Viivi and Wagner, by Jussi Tuomola — A625

No. 1185: a, Viivi and Wagner running. b, Viivi and Wagner dancing. c, Viivi writing love letter. d, Wagner and Viivi in bed. e, Viivi and Wagner kissing. f, Wagner reading love letter.

Serpentine Die Cut 11½x11¾ on 3 Sides
2003, Jan. 15   Self-Adhesive

1185	Booklet pane of 6	18.00	
a.-f.	A625 1 Any single	3.00	1.00
	Booklet, #1185	18.00	

Nos. 1185a-1185f each sold for 60c on day of issue.

Ice Hockey World Championships A626

2003, Mar. 3   Litho.   Perf. 13¼x13¾

| 1186 | A626 65c multi | 1.20 | .75 |

St. Bridget (1303-73) — A627

2003, Mar. 3   Perf. 13

| 1187 | A627 65c multi | 1.20 | .75 |

Viola Wittrockiana — A628

Die Cut Perf. 13¾x14
2003, Mar. 3   Photo.
Self-Adhesive

| 1188 | A628 65c multi | 1.20 | .60 |

Fighting Wood Grouses, by Ferdinand von Wright — A629

Die Cut Perf. 13¾
2003, Mar. 3   Self-Adhesive

| 1189 | A629 90c multi | 1.50 | 1.00 |

568　FINLAND

Airplanes — A630

No. 1190: a, Super Caravelle. b, Airbus 320. c, Junkers Ju 52/3m. d, Douglas DC-3.

Perf. 14x14½ on 3 Sides
2003, Mar. 3
1190		Booklet pane of 4 + 4 etiquettes	4.80	—
a.-d.	A630	65c Any single	1.20	.80
		Complete booklet, #1190	4.80	

Finnair, 80th anniv.; Powered flight, cent.

Europa — A631

No. 1191 — Posters by Lasse Hietala: a, Woman with newspaper. b, Hearts.

2003, May 7　Litho.　Perf. 13¾x13¼
1191	A631	Pair	3.00	3.00
a.-b.		65c Either single	1.50	1.20

Souvenir Sheet

Flora and Fauna Seen in Summer A632

No. 1192: a, Moth, flowers (35x29mm). b, Dragonfly, grasshopper (44x35mm). c, Grasshopper, caterpillar, thistle (35x25mm). d, Frog, flowers, butterfly, insects (44x36mm). e, Magpie, snail, flowers (35x46mm). f, Hedgehog, bee, ant, spider, flowers (44x29mm).

Perf. 14½ on 2 or 3 Sides
2003, May 7
1192	A632	Sheet of 6	7.00	7.00
a.-f.		65c Any single	1.20	1.00

Moomins — A633

No. 1193: a, Moomin ancestors. b, Moomins around stove. c, Moomin standing on hands in water. d, Moomin and fox. e, Moomin looking at film negative. f, Moomin with hat, flowers.

Serpentine Die Cut 11½x11¾ on 3 Sides
2003, May 7　Photo.
Self-Adhesive
1193		Booklet pane of 6	18.00	—
a.-f.	A633	1 Any single	3.00	.70
		Complete booklet, #1193	18.00	

Nos. 1193a-1193f each sold for 65c on day of issue.

Cupid — A634

Serpentine Die Cut 11½ Syncopated
2003, May 14　Litho.
Self-Adhesive
1194	A634	1 multi	3.00	1.20

No. 1194 could be personalized. It sold for 65c on day of issue.

Lingonberries — A635

Serpentine Die Cut 14
2003, Sept. 10　Photo.
Self-Adhesive
1195	A635	65c multi	1.20	.60

Philanthropists A636

No. 1196: a, Juho (1852-1913) and Maria (1858-1923) Lallukka. b, Emil Aaltonen (1869-1949), vert. c, Heikki Huhtamäki (1900-70), vert. d, Antti (1883-1962) and Jenny Wihuri. e, Alfred Kordelin (1868-1917), vert. f, Amos Anderson (1878-1961), vert.

Perf. 13¼x13¾, 13¾x13¼ on 3 Sides
2003, Sept. 10　Litho.
1196		Booklet pane of 6	7.25	7.25
a.-f.	A636	65c Any single	1.20	1.20
		Complete booklet, #1196	7.50	

Lighthouses — A637

No. 1197: a, Bengtskär. b, Russarö. c, Rönnskär. d, Harmaja Grahara. e, Söderskär.

2003, Sept. 10　Perf. 13¼x13¾
1197	A637	Sheet of 5	15.00	7.50
a.-e.		1 Any single	3.00	.70

Nos. 1197a-1197e sold for 65c on day of issue. Size of No. 1197a, 28x45mm; Nos. 1197b-1197e, 21x36mm.

Christmas — A638

Designs: 45c, Elf mailing letter. 65c, Elf with ginger biscuit on baking pan, vert.

Serpentine Die Cut 14x14¼, 14¼x14
2003, Oct. 31　Photo.
Self-Adhesive
1198-1199	A638	Set of 2	1.90	1.30

Slightly larger versions of No. 1198 with a serpentine die cutting of 13¼x13¾ and of No. 1199 with a serpentine die cutting of 13¾x13¼ exist only on first day and other covers produced by the postal service. They were not sold unused to the public.

Apples — A639

Serpentine Die Cut 11½ Syncopated
2003, Oct. 31　Litho.
Self-Adhesive
1200	A639	1 multi	3.00	1.20

No. 1200 could be personalized. It sold for 65c on day of issue.

Pres. Tarja Halonen, 60th Birthday — A640

2003, Dec. 1　Litho.　Perf. 13
1201	A640	65c multi	1.20	.60

Linnaea Borealis — A641

Die Cut Perf. 14
2004, Jan. 14　Photo.
Self-Adhesive
1202	A641	30c multi	.70	.70

Souvenir Sheet

Johan Ludvig Runeberg (1804-77), Poet — A642

No. 1203: a, Title page of Tales of Ensign Stahl. b, Sven Dufva with gun. c, Illustration for "Our Country." d, Sculpture of Runeberg.

Perf. 13½x13¼ on 3 or 4 Sides
2004, Jan. 14　Litho.
1203	A642	65c Sheet of 4, #a-d	4.80	4.80

Jean Sibelius (1865-1957), Composer — A643

No. 1204: a, Satu, and Sibelius, paintings by Akseli Gallen-Kallela. b, Hands of Sibelius on piano keyboard. c, Swans, musical score by Sibelius.
No. 1205: a, Sibelius' house, Ainola. b, Sibelius and wife, Aino. c, Score of "Voces Intimae."

Die Cut Perf. 10 Horiz. Syncopated
2004, Jan. 14　Photo.
Coil Stamps
Self-Adhesive
1204		Horiz. strip of 3	7.50	—
a.-c.	A643	2 Any single	2.50	.50
1205		Horiz. strip of 3	9.00	—
a.-c.	A643	1 Any single	3.00	.50

Nos. 1204a-1204c each sold for 55c on day of issue and have two short syncopations; Nos. 1205a-1205c each sold for 65c on day of issue, and have one large syncopation.

Love — A644

Text and: a, Rose. b, Man kissing. c, Woman's eye. d, Man and woman embracing. e, Elderly woman. f, Hand pulling petal from daisy.

Serpentine Die Cut 11½x11¾ on 3 Sides
2004, Jan. 14　Self-Adhesive
1206		Booklet pane of 6	18.00	—
a.-f.	A644	1 Any single	3.00	.75

Nos. 1206a-1206f each sold for 65c on day of issue.

Ursus Arctos — A645

2004, Mar. 1　Die Cut Perf. 14
Self-Adhesive
1207	A645	2 multi	2.50	.80
a.		Pale yellow background, animal name 8mm long	2.50	.80

No. 1207 sold for 55c on day of issue. No. 1207 has a pale pink background and animal name is 6mm long.
Issued: No. 1207a, 2009.

Rose — A646

2004, Mar. 1　Booklet Stamp
Self-Adhesive
1208	A646	1 multi	3.00	.40
a.		Booklet pane of 10	30.00	

No. 1208 sold for 65c on day of issue. Booklet pane was sold folded.

Easter Flowers — A647

Die Cut Perf. 14
2004, Mar. 1　Self-Adhesive　Litho.
1209	A647	65c multi	1.20	.60

Heraldic Lion Type of 2002
Die Cut Perf. 12 Syncopated
2004, Mar. 1　Self-Adhesive
1210	A616	€3 multi	6.50	2.50

Swallows — A648

Orchid — A649

Serpentine Die Cut 11½ Syncopated
2004, Mar. 26　Self-Adhesive
1211	A648	1 multi	3.00	1.50
1212	A649	1 multi	3.00	1.50

Nos. 1211-1212 each sold for 65c on day of issue, and they could be personalized.

Souvenir Sheet

Norse Gods A650

No. 1213: a, Head of Luonnotar (33x30mm). b, Luonnotar with arms extended (22x42mm).

Perf. 14¼x14½ (#1213a), 14½x14 (#1213b)
2004, Mar. 26
1213	A650	65c Sheet of 2, #a-b	3.00	3.00

FINLAND

Forest Animals — A651

No. 1214: a, Red squirrel (40x40mm). b, Raven (40x31mm). c, Variable hare (40x34mm). d, Stoat (40x37mm). e, Lizard (40x34mm). f, Red fox (40x40mm).

Perf. 13¼x14 on 2 or 3 Sides
2004, Apr. 28
1214 A651 Sheet of 6   7.00 7.00
a.-f. 65c Any single   1.20 1.00

Fragaria Vesca — A652

Die Cut Perf. 14
2004, Apr. 28 Photo.
Self-Adhesive
1215 A652 65c multi   1.20 .60

Luxembourg Gardens, by Albert Edelfelt (1854-1905) A653

2004, Apr. 28 Self-Adhesive
1216 A653 1 multi   3.00 .50
No. 1216 sold for 65c on day of issue.

Europa A654

No. 1217: a, People around campfire. b, Family in rowboat.

2004, Apr. 28 Litho. Perf. 13
1217 A654 65c Horiz. pair, #a-b   4.00 3.00

Snufkin and Moomintroll A655

Litho. & Embossed
2004, Sept. 8 Perf. 13
Flocked Paper
1218 A655 1 multi   5.00 1.00
No. 1218 sold for 65c on day of issue.

Shipwreck Treasures — A656

No. 1219: a, Tankard. b, Fabric seal. c, Gold watch. d, Powder keg. e, Figurehead (23x40mm).

Perf. 14¼x13 on 3 or 4 Sides
2004, Sept. 8
1219 Booklet pane of 5   15.00 6.00
a.-e. A656 1 Any single   3.00 1.20
Complete booklet, #1219   15.00

Souvenir Sheet

Sammallahdenmäki, UNESCO World Heritage Site — A657

No. 1220: a, Stone wall and trees. b, Lichen-covered rocks.

2004, Sept. 8 Litho. Perf. 14¾x14¼
1220 A657 65c Sheet of 2, #a-b   3.00 3.00

Rights of the Child A658

No. 1221: a, Two girls. b, Boy painting.

2004, Oct. 29 Perf. 13
1221 A658 65c Horiz. pair, #a-b   3.00 2.40

Christmas — A659

Designs: 45c, Boy writing Santa Claus. 65c, Christmas tree branch, candle, ornaments, vert.

Serpentine Die Cut 13¼x13¾, 13¾x13¼
2004, Oct. 29 Photo.
Self-Adhesive
1222-1223 A659 Set of 2   2.20 1.20

Rotary International, Cent. — A660

2005, Jan. 14 Litho. Perf. 13
1224 A660 65c blue & gold   1.50 .80

Lahti, Cent. A661

No. 1225: a, Sibelius Concert Hall. b, Illuminated radio towers.

2005, Jan. 14
1225 A661 65c Pair, #a-b   3.00 2.40

Oulu, 400th Anniv. A662

No. 1226: a, Child with pail and shovel. b, Woman riding bicycle.

2005, Jan. 14
1226 A662 65c Horiz. pair, #a-b   3.00 2.40

Publishing of First Finnish Almanac, 300th Anniv. — A663

Die Cut Perf. 14
2005, Jan. 14 Photo.
Self-Adhesive
1227 A663 65c multi   1.50 .60

Children's Toys — A664

No. 1228: a, Stuffed lion and tiger. b, Stuffed elephant and dog. c, Airplane, train and car. d, Stuffed bear and rabbit.

Serpentine Die Cut 9¼x8½ on 3 Sides
2005, Jan. 14 Self-Adhesive
1228 Booklet pane of 4   12.00 —
a.-d. A664 1 Any single   3.00 1.00
Stamps sold for 65c each on day of issue.

End of Winter War, 65th Anniv. — A665

2005, Mar. 2 Litho. Perf. 13
1229 A665 65c multi   1.50 .80

Easter — A666

2005, Mar. 2 Serpentine Die Cut 14
Self-Adhesive
1230 A666 65c multi   1.50 .70

Apple Blossom — A667

Die Cut Perf. 14
2005, Mar. 2 Photo.
Booklet Stamp
Self-Adhesive
1231 A667 1 multi   3.00 .50
a. Booklet pane of 10   30.00
No. 1231 sold for 65c on day of issue.

Door Decoration, by Eliel Saarinen — A668

Copper Stove Door — A669

Chair Back A670

Stained Glass Window, by Olga Gummerus-Ehrström A671

Dining Room — A672

Exterior of Hvittränsk — A673

Die Cut Perf. 10 Horiz. Syncopated
2005, Mar. 2 Litho.
Self-Adhesive
Coil Stamps
1232 Horiz. strip of 3   7.50
a. A668 2 multi   2.50 .50
b. A669 2 multi   2.50 .50
c. A670 2 multi   2.50 .50
1233 Horiz. strip of 3   9.00
a. A671 1 multi   3.00 .50
b. A672 1 multi   3.00 .50
c. A673 1 multi   3.00 .50

Hvittränsk, home and studio of architects Eliel Saarinen, Armas Lindgren and Herman Gesellius. Nos. 1232a-1232c each sold for 55c on day of issue and have two short syncopations. Nos. 1233a-1233c each sold for 65c on day of issue and have one large syncopation.

Miniature Schnauzer — A674

Serpentine Die Cut 11½ Syncopated
2005, Apr. 6
1234 A674 1 multi   3.00 1.50
Sold for 65c on day of issue. Sheets could be personalized.

Europa A675

No. 1235 — Plates with: a, Whitefish and beetroot tartare on lettuce. b, Sauteed reindeer and grouse breast.

2005, May 11 Perf. 13
1235 A675 65c Pair, #a-b   3.00 2.40

Souvenir Sheet

Golf A676

No. 1236: a, Man driving ball (44x31mm). b, Boy holding flag, vert. (30x44mm). c, Boy putting, vert. (33x44mm). d, Putter and golf ball (44x32mm).

Perf. 13¼ on 3 or 4 Sides
2005, May 11
1236 A676 65c Sheet of 4, #a-d   6.00 6.00

World Track Championships, Helsinki — A677

Serpentine Die Cut 12½
2005, May 11 Self-Adhesive
1237 A677 65c multi   1.50 .70

Buses in Finland, Cent. — A678

Die Cut Perf. 14
2005, May 11 Photo.
Self-Adhesive
1238 A678 65c brown & black   1.50 .60

FINLAND

Horses — A679

No. 1239: a, Icelandic horse with saddle. b, White Welsh Mountain pony. c, New Forest pony with blanket. d, Shetland Pony.

Serpentine Die Cut 9¼x8½ on 3 Sides
2005, May 11   Self-Adhesive
1239   Booklet pane of 4   12.00
   a.-d. A679 1 Any single   3.00   .80
Stamps sold for 65c each on day of issue.

Cloudberries — A680

Die Cut Perf. 14
2005, Sept. 7   Photo.
   Self-Adhesive
1240   A680 1 multi   3.00   .50
Sold for 65c on day of issue.

Fruits I, by Kari Huhtamo — A681

Die Cut Perf. 11½ Syncopated
2005, Sept. 7   Litho.
   Self-Adhesive
1241   A681 90c multi   3.50   2.50
Sheets could be personalized.

Souvenir Sheet

Petäjävesi Church, UNESCO World Heritage Site — A682

No. 1242: a, Bell tower (26x47mm). b, Church (34x39mm). c, Angel (26x39mm). d, Chandelier (27x39mm).

2005, Sept. 7   Litho.   Perf. 13
1242   A682 65c Sheet of 4, #a-d   6.00   6.00

Icebreakers — A683

No. 1243: a, Urho, 1975. b, Otso, 1986. c, Fennica, 1993. d, Botnica, 1998.

2005, Sept. 7   Perf. 13¼ Horiz.
1243   Booklet pane of 4   12.00
   a.-d. A683 1 Any single   3.00   1.20
Each stamp sold for 65c on day of issue.

Souvenir Sheet

Imperial Winter Egg, by Carl Fabergé A684

No. 684: a, Flowers in egg. b, Frost detail of egg.

Litho. & Embossed with Foil Application
2005, Oct. 28   Perf. 13
1244   A684   €3.50 Sheet of 2, #a-b   15.00   15.00
A limited quantity of 2,500 numbered sheets, which sold for €30, exist. Value, $100.

Christmas — A685

Designs: 50c, Santa Claus reading letters. 1, Santa Claus and wife dancing, horiz.

Serpentine Die Cut 13¾x13¼, 13¼x13¾
2005, Oct. 28   Photo.
   Self-Adhesive
1245-1246   A685   Set of 2   4.00   1.00
No. 1246 sold for 65c on day of issue.

Postal Employees Union, Cent. — A686

2006, Jan. 11   Litho.   Perf. 13
1247   A686 65c multi   1.50   .75

Heart — A687

2006, Jan. 11   Die Cut
   Self-Adhesive
1248   A687 65c bright pink   1.50   .60

Renaming of Helsinki University Library as National Library of Finland — A688

2006, Jan. 11   Die Cut Perf. 14x13¾
   Self-Adhesive
1249   A688 1 multi   3.00   .50
Sold for 65c on day of issue.

Forest in Winter — A689

2006, Jan. 11   Photo.
   Self-Adhesive
1250   A689 1 multi   3.00   .50
Sold for 65c on day of issue.

Taxis, Cent. — A690

No. 1251: a, Women passengers in taxi, 1906. b, Driver standing in front of 1929 Chevrolet taxi. c, Driver leaning on 1957 Pobeda taxi. d, Driver on phone at taxi stand next to Mercedes-Benz taxi.

Serpentine Die Cut 11¼ Vert.
2006, Jan. 11   Litho.
   Self-Adhesive
1251   Booklet pane of 4   6.00
   a.-d. A690 65c Any single   1.50   1.00

Souvenir Sheet

Johan Vilhelm Snellman (1806-81), Philosopher — A691

No. 1252: a, Caricature of Snellman, masthead of his newspaper "Saima." b, Snellman's portrait on 1940 five thousand mark note. c, Snellman and European railway map. d, Ilmarinen, first Finnish locomotive, and European railway map.

2006, Jan. 11   Perf. 13¼x13¾
1252   A691 65c Sheet of 4, #a-d   4.75   4.75

Parliament, Cent. — A692

Serpentine Die Cut 14
2006, Feb. 3   Litho.
   Self-Adhesive
1253   A692 1 multi   3.00   .70
Sold for 65c on day of sale.

Flag — A693

2006, Mar. 1   Self-Adhesive
1254   A693 1 multi   3.00   .50
Sold for 65c on day of sale.

Lilacs — A694

Die Cut Perf. 13¾x14
2006, Mar. 1   Photo.
   Self-Adhesive
1255   A694 1 multi   3.00   .50
Sold for 65c on day of sale.

Easter — A695

2006, Mar. 1   Litho.   Die Cut
   Self-Adhesive
1256   A695 65c multi   1.50   .70

Fortune Teller, by Helene Schjerfbeck — A696

Die Cut Perf. 13¾x14
2006, Mar. 1   Photo.
   Self-Adhesive
1257   A696 95c multi   2.00   1.50

Bil-Bol Poster — A697   Errotaja 2 Poster — A698

Concert Finnois Poster A699   Madonna A700

Self-Portrait A701   Home of Artist Akseli Gallen-Kallela, Tarvaspää A702

Die Cut Perf. 10 Horiz. Syncopated
2006, Mar. 1   Self-Adhesive
   Coil Stamps
1258   Horiz. strip of 3   7.50   —
   a. A697 2 multi   2.50   1.50
   b. A698 2 multi   2.50   1.50
   c. A699 2 multi   2.50   1.50

Die Cut Perf. 10 Vert. Syncopated
1259   Vert. strip of 3   9.00   —
   a. A700 1 multi   3.00   .50
   b. A701 1 multi   3.00   .50
   c. A702 1 multi   3.00   .50

Akseli Gallen-Kallela (1865-1931), artist. Nos. 1258a-1258c each sold for 55c and Nos. 1259a-1259c each sold for 65c on day of issue.

Souvenir Sheet

Norse Mythology — A703

No. 1260 — Fairy tale book cover illustrations by Rudolf Koivu: a, Fairy. b, Fairy dancing with Santa Claus, vert.

Perf. 13½x13¼, 13¼x13½ (#1260b)
2006, Mar. 29   Litho.
1260   A703 65c Sheet of 2, #a-b   3.00   3.00

Europa — A704

2006, May 4   Perf. 13
1261   A704 65c multi   1.50   .80

FINLAND

Vaasa, 400th Anniv. — A705

2006, May 4
1262 A705 1 multi   3.00 .80
Sold for 65c on day of issue.

 A706

Serpentine Die Cut 10 Syncopated
2006, May 4   **Booklet Stamp**
Self-Adhesive
1263 A706 1 multi   3.00 1.50
   a. Booklet pane of 8   24.00

No. 1263 sold for 65c on day of issue. Design portion of stamp could be personalized.

Summer Activities — A707

No. 1264: a, Woman fishing. b, Children making flower garlands. c, Man making sauna whisk. d, Woman weeding flower garden.

Serpentine Die Cut 11¼ Vert.
2006, May 4   **Self-Adhesive**
1264   Booklet pane of 4   12.00
   a.-d. A707 1 Any single   3.00 .80

Nos. 1264a-1264d each sold for 65c on day of issue.

Cats — A708

No. 1265: a, Striped house cat. b, British shorthair (gray cat). c, Ragdoll cat (brown and white). d, Chocolate Persian cat.

2006, May 4   **Self-Adhesive**
1265   Booklet pane of 4   12.00
   a.-d. A708 1 Any single   3.00 1.00

Nos. 1265a-1265d each sold for 65c on day of issue.

Suomenlinna (Sveaborg) Fortress, Helsinki — A709

No. 1266: a, Ship without oars. b, Ship with oars facing fortress. c, Ship with oars, windmill.

Litho. & Engr.
2006, May 4   **Perf. 13x12¾**
1266 A709 Booklet pane of 3   9.00 —
   a.-c. 1 Any single   3.00 1.20

Nos. 1266a-1266c each sold for 65c on day of issue. See Sweden No. 2530.

Blueberries and Blueberry Pie — A710

Die Cut Perf. 14
2006, Aug. 24   Photo.
Self-Adhesive
1267 A710 1 multi   3.00 .70
Sold for 70c on day of issue.

Miniature Sheet

Family Life A711

No. 1268: a, Family watching television. b, Woman writing letter to husband.

2006, Aug. 24   Die Cut
Self-Adhesive
1268 A711 1 Sheet of 2, #a-b   6.00 2.00

Nos. 1268a-1268b each sold for 70c on day of issue.

Newspaper Journalism — A712

Die Cut Perf. 14
2006, Sept. 22   Litho.
Self-Adhesive
1269 A712 70c multi   1.50 .80

Points, Textile Art by Ritva Puotila — A713

Serpentine Die Cut 11½ Syncopated
2006, Sept. 22   **Self-Adhesive**
1270 A713 1 multi   3.00 1.50
Sold for 70c on day of issue.

Dryas Octopetala — A714

Serpentine Die Cut 14
2006, Sept. 22   Photo.
Self-Adhesive
1271 A714 1 multi   3.00 .60
Sold for 70c on day of issue.

Art of Snow and Ice — A715

No. 1272: a, Horse. b, Kemi Snow Castle. c, Wall of ice tiles. d, Snowball lantern.

Serpentine Die Cut 11¾ Vert.
2006, Sept. 22   **Self-Adhesive**
1272   Booklet pane of 4   12.00
   a.-d. A715 1 Any single   3.00 1.00

Nos. 1272a-1272d each sold for 70c on day of issue. Denominations are printed in thermographic ink that changes color when warmed.

Miniature Sheet

Finnish Postage Stamps, 150th Anniv. A716

No. 1273: a, 70c, Heraldic lion and fleurons in white. b, 95c, Part of vignette of type A1. c, €1.40, Heraldic lion in gold, fleurons in red.

Litho. & Embossed With Foil Application
2006, Oct. 27   **Perf. 13½x13**
1273 A716 Sheet of 3, #a-c   6.00 6.00

 A717

Christmas — A718

Serpentine Die Cut 13¼x13¾
2006, Oct. 27   Photo.
Self-Adhesive
1274 A717 50c multi   .70 .70

Serpentine Die Cut 13¾x13¼
1275 A718 1 multi   3.00 .70
No. 1275 sold for 70c on day of issue.

Television Broadcasting in Finland, 50th Anniv. — A719

Die Cut Perf. 14
2007, Jan. 24   Litho.
Self-Adhesive
1276 A719 70c multi   1.50 .60

Faces — A720

2007, Jan. 24   **Self-Adhesive**
1277 A720 70c multi   1.50 .60

Winter Landscape, Haminalahti, by Ferdinand von Wright — A721

2007, Jan. 24   Photo.
Booklet Stamp
Self-Adhesive
1278 A721 1 multi   3.00 .80
   a. Booklet pane of 10   30.00
Sold for 70c on day of issue.

Sun Setting Over Flower Field — A722

2007, Jan. 24   Litho.
Self-Adhesive
1279 A722 €1.40 multi   2.00 1.00

Souvenir Sheet

Intl. Polar Year A723

No. 1280: a, Snowflake. b, Aurora borealis.

Perf. 13 Syncopated (#1280a), 13 (#1280b)
Litho. With Hologram Affixed
2007, Jan. 24
1280 A723 70c Sheet of 2, #a-b + label   3.00 3.00

Truck Transport A724

No. 1281: a, Log truck. b, Milk truck. c, Dump truck. d, Tractor trailer.

Serpentine Die Cut 12¼ Horiz.
2007, Jan. 24   Litho.
Self-Adhesive
1281   Booklet pane of 4   6.00 4.00
   a.-d. A724 70c Any single   1.50 1.00

Central Organization of Finnish Trade Unions — A725

2007, Mar. 7   **Perf. 13**
1282 A725 70c multi   1.50 .60

Soccer Association of Finland, Cent. — A726

2007, Mar. 7   Die Cut
Self-Adhesive
1283 A726 70c multi   1.50 .60

Easter — A727

2007, Mar. 7   Die Cut Perf. 14
Self-Adhesive
1284 A727 1 multi   3.00 .80

Sold for 70c on day of issue. Portions of design were applied by a thermographic process producing a shiny, raised effect.

Lilium Enchantment — A728

FINLAND

2007, Mar. 7   *Litho.*
Booklet Stamp
SELF-ADHESIVE
1285 A728 1 multi   3.00   .80
  a. Booklet pane of 10   30.00
No. 1285 sold for 70c on day of issue.

Souvenir Sheet

Bishop Michael Agricola (1509-57) — A729

No. 1286: a, Text and open book. b, Agricola preaching.

2007, Mar. 7   *Perf. 13½*
1286 A729 70c Sheet of 2, #a-b   3.00   3.00

Tampere Cathedral, Cent. — A730

2007, May 9   *Perf. 13¼*
1287 A730 70c multi   1.50   .80

Europa A731

No. 1288: a, Scouts on sailboat. b, Scouts around campfire.

2007, May 9   *Perf. 12½x13*
1288 A731 Horiz. pair   2.40   2.40
  a.-b. 70c Either single   1.20   1.20
  Scouting, cent.

Helsinki Public Transportation — A732

No. 1289: a, Commuter train in station. b, Tram on street. c, Subway train on bridge. d, People in Kamppi Bus Station.

Serpentine Die Cut 12¼ Horiz.
2007, May 9   **SELF-ADHESIVE**
1289 Booklet pane of 4   8.00   4.75
  a.-d. A732 1 Any single   2.00   1.25
Nos. 1289a-1289d each sold for 70c on day of issue.

Moomins — A733

No. 1290: a, Little My in water. b, Moomintroll running across rocks. c, Moominpappa at typewriter. d, Snork Maiden picking flowers. e, Moominmamma making pancakes. f, Snufkin amid flowers.

Serpentine Die Cut 11¾ Vert.
2007, May 9   *Photo.*
SELF-ADHESIVE
1290 Booklet pane of 6   12.00
  a.-f. A733 1 Any single   2.00   1.00
Nos. 1290a-1290f each sold for 70c on day of issue.

Souvenir Sheet

2007 Eurovision Song Contest, Helsinki — A734

No. 1291: a, Eurovision Song Contest emblem. b, Finnish singers Laila Kinnunen, Marion Rung, Kirka Babitzin and Katri Helena. c, 2006 Finnish contest-winning band, Lordi. d, Lead singer of Lordi.

Litho. With Foil Application
2007, May 9   *Die Cut*
SELF-ADHESIVE
1291 A734 70c Sheet of 4, #a-d   4.75   4.75

A735

Serpentine Die Cut 11½ Syncopated
2007, Aug. 24   *Litho.*
SELF-ADHESIVE
1292 A735 1 multi   3.00   1.00
No. 1292 sold for 70c on day of issue. Design portion of stamp could be personalized.

Home Furnishings — A736

No. 1293 — Picture frame and: a, Empire-style chair, "Porvoo Garland" wallpaper, 19th cent. (country name at LR). b, Paimio chair, "2+3" wallpaper, 20th cent. (country name at LL).

Die Cut Perf. 14
2007, Aug. 24   *Litho.*
SELF-ADHESIVE
1293 Pair   6.00   1.20
  a.-b. A736 1 Either single   3.00   .60
Nos. 1293a-1293b each sold for 70c on day of issue.

Raspberries and Raspberry Cake — A737

Die Cut Perf. 14
2007, Aug. 24   *Photo.*
SELF-ADHESIVE
Booklet Stamp
1294 A737 1 multi   3.00   .60
No. 1294 sold for 70c on day of issue.

Finnish Olympic Committee, Cent. — A738

2007, Aug. 24   *Litho.*
SELF-ADHESIVE
Booklet Stamp
1295 A738 1 multi   3.00   .60
No. 1295 sold for 70c on day of issue.

Butterflies — A739

No. 1296: a, Apatura iris. b, Scolitantides orion. c, Colias palaeno.

Die Cut Perf. 10 Vert., Syncopated at Right
2007, Aug. 24   **SELF-ADHESIVE**
Coil Stamps
1296 Vert. strip of 3   9.00
  a.-c. A739 1 Any single   3.00   .60
Nos. 1296a-1296c had a franking value of 70c on day of issue. A roll of 100 stamps sold for €68.

Miniature Sheet

Independence, 90th Anniv. — A740

No. 1297 — Photographs of people at work and play: a, Man and horse hauling wood. b, Girl blowing horn. c, Four boys with skis. d, People at coffee break. e, People near bonfire. f, Boy ski jumping. g, Boy diving. h, Ice fisherman. Nos. 1297a-1297d are black and white photos.

2007, Nov. 2   *Perf. 13¼*
1297 A740 Sheet of 8   11.00   11.00
  a.-h. 70c Any single   1.30   1.00

Souvenir Sheet

Woodwork — A741

No. 1298: a, Zitan armchair with dragon design, China (denomination at left). b, Modern Finnish bowls (denomination at right).

2007, Nov. 2   *Perf. 13¼x14¼*
1298 A741 Sheet of 2   2.50   2.50
  a.-b. 70c Either single   1.30   1.00
See Hong Kong Nos. 1298-1299.

A742

Christmas — A743

Serpentine Die Cut 13¼x13¾
2007, Nov. 2   *Photo.*
SELF-ADHESIVE
1299 A742 55c multi   .70   .25
Serpentine Die Cut 13¾x13¼
1300 A743 1 multi   3.00   .50
No. 1300 sold for 70c on day of issue.

A744   A745

Water — A746

A747   A748

Islands — A749

2008, Jan. 24   *Photo.*   *Die Cut*
SELF-ADHESIVE
1301 Horiz. strip of 3   .45
  a. A744 5c multi   .25   .25
  b. A745 5c multi   .25   .25
  c. A746 5c multi   .25   .25
1302 Horiz. strip of 3   .90
  a. A747 10c multi   .30   .30
  b. A748 10c multi   .30   .30
  c. A749 10c multi   .30   .30

Souvenir Sheet

Helsinki University of Technology, Cent. — A750

No. 1303: a, Robot. b, University building.

2008, Jan. 24   *Litho.*   *Perf. 13½x13¼*
1303 A750 Sheet of 2   6.00   2.50
  a.-b. 1 Any single   3.00   1.00
Nos. 1303a-1303b each sold for 70c on day of issue.

Miniature Sheet

Love A751

No. 1304: a, Airplane pulling heart banner. b, Carrier pigeon with envelope. c, Heart-shaped smoke signals. d, Heart and cell phone. e, Bottle with hearts.

2008, Jan. 24   *Die Cut*
SELF-ADHESIVE
1304 A751 Sheet of 5   15.00   6.00
  a.-e. 1 Any single   3.00   1.00
Nos. 1304a-1304e each sold for 70c on day of issue.

FINLAND

Miniature Sheet

Snow Sports A752

No. 1305: a, Matti Räty in yellow ski suit. b, Antti Autti (snowboarder) in air in red ski suit. c, Tapio Saarimaki in red ski suit. d, Tanja Poutiainen in white and green ski suit.

Litho. With Three-Dimensional Plastic Affixed
Serpentine Die Cut 9 Syncopated
2008, Jan. 24 Self-Adhesive
1305 A752 Sheet of 4 12.00 4.75
a.-d. 1 Any single
Nos. 1305a-1305d each sold for 70c on day of issue.

Clock and Lamp on Desk — A753

Die Cut Perf. 13¾
2008, Feb. 27 Litho.
Booklet Stamp
Self-Adhesive
1306 A753 1.05 multi 2.25 1.50
a. Booklet pane of 10 22.50

Finnish Book Publishers Association, 150th Anniv. — A754

Serpentine Die Cut 13¼
2008, Feb. 27 Self-Adhesive
1307 A754 1 multi 3.00 .60
No. 1307 sold for 70c on day of issue.

Lathyrus Odoratus — A755

Die Cut Perf. 13¾
2008, Feb. 27 Photo.
Self-Adhesive
1308 A755 1 multi 3.00 .60
No. 1308 sold for 70c on day of issue and has Braille dots applied by a thermographic process.

Easter — A756

Litho. With Foil Application
Serpentine Die Cut 13¾
2008, Feb. 27 Self-Adhesive
1309 A756 1 multi 3.00 .60
No. 1309 sold for 70c on day of issue.

Fauna Associated With Weather Forecasting Folk Beliefs — A757

No. 1310: a, Perch. b, Lambs. c, Frogs. d, Swallows. e, Snail.

Serpentine Die Cut 12¼ Horiz.
2008, Feb. 27 Litho.
Self-Adhesive
1310 Booklet pane of 5 15.00 5.00
a.-e. A757 1 Any single 3.00 1.00
Nos. 1310a-1310e each sold for 70c on day of issue.

Souvenir Sheet

Mythical Places A758

No. 1311: a, Cliff resembling human face, Astuvansalmi. b, Amber carving of head found at Astuvansalmi.

2008, Mar. 27 Perf. 13½
1311 A758 Sheet of 2 2.50 2.50
a.-b. 70c Either single 1.25 1.00

Europa A759

No. 1312 — Handwritten letters and portraits by Pekka Halonen of: a, Himself. b, His wife, Maija.

2008, May 9 Perf. 13
1312 A759 Horiz. pair 2.40 2.40
a.-b. 70c Either single 1.20 1.00

Kvarken Archipelago UNESCO World Heritage Site — A760

Serpentine Die Cut 13¾
2008, May 9 Self-Adhesive
1313 A760 €1.50 blk & red 3.00 1.80

Moths — A761

No. 1314: a, Arctia caja. b, Aglia tau. c, Deilephila elpenor.

Die Cut Perf. 10 Syncopated
2008, May 9 Photo.
Coil Stamps
Self-Adhesive
1314 Vert. strip of 3 6.00 3.00
a.-c. A761 1 Any single 3.00 1.00
Nos. 1314a-1314c each sold for 70c on day of issue.

Psychedelic Art — A762

No. 1315: a, Melting mushrooms and teardrops. b, Guitars. c, Flying fish. d, Flowers and woman's legs in high heels. e, Six balloons.

Serpentine Die Cut 12½ Horiz.
2008, May 9 Litho.
Self-Adhesive
1315 Booklet pane of 5 15.00
a.-e. A762 1 Any single 3.00 1.00
Nos. 1315a-1315e each sold for 70c on day of issue.

Modern Art — A763

No. 1316: a, Sinistä ja Punaista, by Sam Vanni. b, Merirosvolaiva, by Kimmo Kaivanto. c, Hiljaisuuden Kuuntelija, by Juhani Linnovaara. d, Odotan Kevään Tuloa, by Göran Augustson. e, Minä, by Carolus Enckell. f, Pöytä, by Reino Hietanen.

Serpentine Die Cut 11¾ Vert.
2008, May 9 Self-Adhesive
1316 Booklet pane of 6 18.00 4.75
a.-f. A763 1 Any single 3.00 .75
Nos. 1316a-1316f each sold for 70c on day of issue.

Personalized Stamp — A764

Serpentine Die Cut 10
2008, Sept. 5 Litho.
Self-Adhesive
1317 A764 1 multi 3.00 1.00
No. 1317 sold for 80c on day of issue. The generic design portion of the stamp shown could be personalized.

Dogs — A765

No. 1318: a, Spitz with open mouth, facing forward. b, Rough collie, with open mouth, facing right. c, Boxer, facing left. d, Finnish hound, facing left. e, Cavalier King Charles spaniel, facing right. f, Jack Russell terrier, looking over shoulder.

Serpentine Die Cut 11¾ Vert.
2008, Sept. 5 Self-Adhesive
1318 Booklet pane of 6 18.00 6.00
a.-f. A765 1 Any single 3.00 1.00
Nos. 1318a-1318f each sold for 80c on day of issue.

Souvenir Sheet

Mika Waltari (1908-79), Writer — A766

No. 1319: a, Waltari. b, Cover of Waltari's book, Komisario Palmun Erehdys.

2008, Sept. 5 Perf. 14x13½
1319 A766 Sheet of 2 3.00 3.00
a.-b. 80c Either single 1.50 1.20

Souvenir Sheet

Kimi Räikkönen, 2007 Formula 1 Racing Champion — A767

No. 1320: a, Räikkönen (24x30mm). b, Räikkönen's Ferrari Formula 1 race car (74x30mm).

Die Cut Perf. 11x11½ on 2 Sides (#1320a), 11½ Vert. (#1320b)
2008, Sept. 5 Self-Adhesive
1320 A767 Sheet of 2 6.00 3.00
a.-b. 1 Either single 3.00 1.00
Nos. 1320a-1320b each sold for 80c on day of issue.

Souvenir Sheet

Adolf Erik Nordenskiöld (1832-1901), Arctic Explorer — A768

No. 1321: a, Nordenskiöld (29x34mm). b, Ship Sofia (58x34mm).

2008, Oct. 20 Litho. & Engr. Perf. 13x13¼
1321 A768 Sheet of 2 6.00 3.00
a.-b. 1 Either single 3.00 1.20
Nos. 1321a-1321b each sold for 80c on day of issue. See Greenland Nos. 527-528.

A769   A770

Christmas — A771

Die Cut Perf. 14
2008, Nov. 6 Litho.
Self-Adhesive
1322 A769 60c multi .70 .25
Serpentine Die Cut 13¼x13¾
Photo.
1323 A770 1 multi 2.00 .50
Printed On Plastic
Die Cut Perf. 13¾
1324 A771 1 multi 3.00 1.00
Nos. 1322-1324 (3) 5.70 1.75
On day of issue, Nos. 1323 and 1324 each sold for 80c.

Pres. Martti Ahtisaari, 2008 Nobel Peace Laureate — A772

2008, Dec. 10 Litho. Perf. 13
1325 A772 80c light blue 1.50 1.25

Hospital Work — A773

2009, Jan. 22 Litho. Perf. 13
1326 A773 80c multi 1.50 1.20

Pallas-Yllästunturi National Park — A774

2009, Jan. 22 Die Cut Perf. 14
Self-Adhesive
1327 A774 1 multi 3.00 1.20
No. 1327 sold for 80c on day of issue and has Braille dots applied in varnish.

Peony — A775

FINLAND

Die Cut Perf. 14
2009, Jan. 22   Photo.
Self-Adhesive
1328   A775   €1.10 multi   2.50   1.75

Children's Dream Occupations — A776

No. 1329 — Child dressed as: a, Policeman. b, Doctor. c, Firefighter. d, Skier. e, Construction worker.

Serpentine Die Cut 12¼ Vert.
2009, Jan. 22   Litho.
Self-Adhesive
1329   Booklet pane of 5   15.00   6.00
  a.-e.   A776 1 Any single   3.00   1.20

Nos. 1329a-1329e each sold for 80c on day of issue.

Miniature Sheet

Finland as Grand Duchy of Russia, 200th Anniv. — A777

No. 1330: a, Tsar Alexander I (1777-1825), facing left with blue sash. b, Count Georg Magnus Sprengtporten (1740-1819), with red sash and gold epaulets. c, Count Carl Erik Mannerheim (1759-1837), without epaulets. d, Count Gustaf Mauritz Armfelt (1757-1814), facing right, with blue sash. Names are on sheet margin.

Litho. & Embossed With Foil Application
2009, Jan. 22   Perf. 13¾
1330   A777 80c Sheet of 4, #a-d   6.00   6.00

Miniature Sheet

St. Valentine's Day — A778

No. 1331: a, Birthday cake and candle. b, Cupid. c, Three people, flower. d, Swans. e, Teddy bear hugging heart.

2009, Jan. 22   Litho.   Die Cut
Self-Adhesive
1331   A778 1 Sheet of 5, #a-e   15.00   7.50

Nos. 1331a-1331e each sold for 80c on day of issue.

Rose — A779

Die Cut Perf. 14
2009, Mar. 18   Litho.
Self-Adhesive
1332   A779 1 multi   2.00   1.20

No. 1332 sold for 80c on day of issue.

Easter — A780

2009, Mar. 18   **Self-Adhesive**
1333   A780 1 multi   3.00   1.00

No. 1333 sold for 80c on day of issue.

Souvenir Sheet

Preservation of Polar Regions and Glaciers — A781

No. 1334: a, Sky, blue emblem. b, Sea and ice, silver emblem.

Litho. With Foil Application
2009, Mar. 18   Perf.
1334   A781   Sheet of 2   6.00   3.00
  a.-b.   1 Either single   3.00   1.50

Nos. 1334a-1334b each sold for 80c on day of issue.

Greetings — A782

No. 1335: a, Gift and tulips. b, Chocolate-covered strawberries, cake. c, Flowers. d, Coffee cup, letter and rose. e, Dove and apples.

Serpentine Die Cut 10¼ Horiz.
2009, Mar. 18   Litho.
Self-Adhesive
1335   Booklet pane of 5 + 5 labels   15.00   5.00
  a.-e.   A782 1 Any single   3.00   1.00

Nos. 1335a-1335e each sold for 80c on day of issue.

Europa — A783

No. 1336: a, Lake, birds, Moon, stars and other heavenly bodies. b, Lake, comet, Saturn, stars and other heavenly bodies.

2009, May 6   Perf. 13
1336   A783   Horiz. pair   3.00   3.00
  a.-b.   80c Either single   1.50   1.00

Intl. Year of Astronomy.

Sauna A784

No. 1337: a, Towels, scrubber, bucket of birch branches (55x23mm). b, People in sauna (55x23mm). c, Waterside sauna (55x23mm). d, Birch whisk (27x45mm). e, Water tubs and window (27x45mm).

Serpentine Die Cut 11¾ Horiz.
2009, May 6   **Self-Adhesive**
1337   Booklet pane of 5   15.00   6.00
  a.-e.   A784 1 Any single   3.00   1.00

Nos. 1337a-1337e each sold for 80c on day of issue. No. 1337d is impregnated with a birch scent.

Moomins — A785

No. 1338: a, Moomin carrying purse. b, Moominpappa with hat holding paper. c, Little My holding large pair of glasses. d, Moomin at mirror. e, Moomin and Snufkin fishing. f, Moominpappa slipping down hill.

Serpentine Die Cut 11¾ Horiz.
2009, May 6   **Self-Adhesive**
1338   Booklet pane of 6   18.00   6.00
  a.-f.   A785 1 Any single   3.00   1.00

Nos. 1338a-1338f each sold for 80c on day of issue.

Miniature Sheet

Women's Fashion A786

No. 1339: a, Dress by Anna and Tuomas Laitinen (30x45mm). b, Dress by Jasmin Santanen (30x45mm). c, Handbag by Lumi (30x35mm). d, Red shoes by Minna Parikka (30x25mm). e, Shoes by Julia Lundsten (30x30mm).

Serpentine Die Cut 14¼x13¾
2009, May 6   **Self-Adhesive**
1339   A786   Sheet of 5   15.00   7.50
  a.-e.   1 Any single   3.00   1.00

Nos. 1339a-1339e each sold for 80c on day of issue.

Gustavian Style Clock, Table and Candle Holder — A787

Die Cut Perf. 13¾
2009, Sept. 9   Litho.
Self-Adhesive
1340   A787 1 multi   3.00   1.00
  a.   Booklet pane of 10   30.00

No. 1340 sold for 80c on day of issue.

Aurora Borealis — A788

No. 1341 — Various pictures of Aurora Borealis taken at: a, 65 degrees, 1 minute, 17.03 seconds north; 25 degrees, 39 minutes, 31.26 seconds east. b, 65 degrees, 57.16 seconds north; 25 degrees, 39 minutes, 41.01 seconds east. c, 67 degrees, 45 minutes, 2.44 seconds north; 23 degrees, 36 minutes, 41.53 seconds east.

Die Cut Perf. 10 Vert., Syncopated at Right
2009, Sept. 9   **Self-Adhesive**
Coil Stamps
1341   Vert. strip of 3   9.00   3.00
  a.-c.   A788 1 Any single   3.00   1.00

Nos. 1341a-1341c each sold for 80c on day of issue.

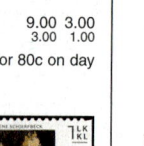

Paintings of Flowers — A789

No. 1342: a, Snapdragons, by Helene Schjerfbeck. b, Blooming Irises, by Wäinö Aaltonen. c, Burnet Roses, by Eero Järnefelt. d, Lone Calla, by Ester Helenius. e, Amaryllis, by Birger Carlstedt. f, Still Life with Carnations, by Tuomas von Boehm.

Serpentine Die Cut 11¾ Horiz.
2009, Sept. 9   **Self-Adhesive**
1342   Booklet pane of 6   18.00   6.00
  a.-f.   A789 1 Any single   3.00   1.00

Nos. 1342a-1342f each sold for 80c on day of issue.

Wreath A790   Girl and Basket of Apples A791

Amaryllis — A792

Personalized Stamp — A793

Die Cut Perf. 14
2009, Nov. 6   Litho.
Self-Adhesive
1343   Horiz. pair   1.40
  a.   A790 60c multi   .70   .25
  b.   A791 60c multi   .70   .25
1344   A792 1 multi   3.00   1.20

Serpentine Die Cut 11½x11¾ Syncopated
1345   A793 1 multi   3.00   1.00

Nos. 1344 and 1345 each sold for 80c on day of issue. The generic design portion of No. 1345, shown, could be personalized.

Antennaria Dioica — A794

Die Cut Perf. 11 Syncopated
2010, Jan. 25   Litho.
Self-Adhesive
1346   A794 1 multi   3.00   1.00

No. 1346 sold for 80c on day of issue.

Miniature Sheet

Fairies A795

No. 1347 — Fairy: a, Holding flowers. b, Holding heart. c, On swing. d, Holding violin. e, With stars.

Serpentine Die Cut 14½x14
Litho. & Silk-screened
2010, Jan. 25   **Self-Adhesive**
1347   A795   Sheet of 5   15.00   7.50
  a.-e.   1 Any single   3.00   1.00

Nos. 1347a-1347e each sold for 80c on day of issue.

FINLAND

Rock Stars — A796

No. 1348: a, Eppu Normaali (45x33mm). b, Yö (41x31mm). c, Popeda (40x28mm). d, Dingo (44x33mm). e, Maarit (34x41mm). f, Mamba (38x36mm).

Die Cut Perf. 8½
2010, Jan. 25   Litho.
Self-Adhesive
1348   Booklet pane of 6   18.00   6.00
   a.-f.   A796 1 Any single   3.00   1.20
Nos. 1348a-1348f each sold for 80c on day of issue.

A797   Easter — A798

Serpentine Die Cut 12½
2010, Mar. 8   **Litho. & Embossed**
Self-Adhesive
1349   A797 1 multi   3.00   1.00
Litho.
Die Cut Perf. 14
1350   A798 1 multi   3.00   1.00
Nos. 1349 and 1350 each sold for 80c on day of issue.

Rural Life A799

No. 1351: a, Mussels, children lifting caught fish. b, Children on swing, strawberries, flowers, horse in meadow. c, Farmer on tractor, farmhouses. d, Milk cans, girl milking cow. e, Musicians and dancers.

Serpentine Die Cut 10¼ Horiz.
2010, Mar. 8   Litho.
Self-Adhesive
1351   Booklet pane of 5   15.00   5.00
   a.-e.   A799 1 Any single   3.00   1.00
Nos. 1351a-1351e each sold for 80c on day of issue.

Famous Women A800

No. 1352: a, Ritva-Liisa Pohjalainen, jewelry and clothing designer. b, Elina Haavio-Mannila, sociologist. c, Aira Samulin, dance instructor. d, Maria-Liisa Nevala, director of National Theater. e, Laila Hirvisaari, writer. f, Leena Palotie (1952-2010), geneticist.

Serpentine Die Cut 11 Horiz. Syncopated
Litho. & Silk-screened
2010, Mar. 8   **Self-Adhesive**
1352   Booklet pane of 6   18.00   6.00
   a.-f.   A800 1 Any single   3.00   1.00
Nos. 1352a-1352f each sold for 80c on day of issue.

Vegetables A801

No. 1353: a, Tomato (38x33mm). b, Onions (47x34mm). c, Pumpkin (34x36mm). d, Cucumber (27x43mm). e, Eggplant (42x41mm). f, Carrot (29x44mm). g, Broccoli (43x35mm). h, Potato (40x30mm).

2010, Mar. 8   Litho.   *Die Cut*
Self-Adhesive
1353   Booklet pane of 8   24.00   8.00
   a.-h.   A801 1 Any single   3.00   1.00
Nos. 1353a-1353h each sold for 80c on day of issue.

Souvenir Sheet

Kotka Harbor A802

No. 1354: a, Vellamo Maritime Center, museum ship Tarmo, crane. b, Sailboat, Wooden Boat Center, vert.

2010, Mar. 24   *Perf. 13¾*
1354   A802   Sheet of 2   6.00   3.00
   a.-b.   1 Either single   3.00   1.50
Nos. 1354a-1354b each sold for 80c on day of issue.

Europa A803

No. 1355 — Children, books, characters and background in: a, Orange. b, Blue green.

2010, May 4   *Perf. 14x13¼*
1355   A803   Horiz. pair   3.00   3.00
   a.-b.   80c Either single   1.50   1.00

Personalized Stamp — A804

Serpentine Die Cut 11¾ Syncopated
2010, May 4   **Self-Adhesive**
1356   A804 1 multi   3.00   1.00
No. 1356 sold for 80c on day of issue. The generic design part of the stamp shown could be personalized.

Sculpture — A805

No. 1357: a, Hymy, by Kain Tapper (28x33mm). b, Hefaistos, by Laila Pullinen (28x33mm). c, Cyclist, by Pekka Aarnio (28x33mm). d, Construction, by Kari Huhtamo (28x33mm). e, Salvos, by Mauno Hartman, horiz. (56x29mm). f, Joy, by Miina Akkijyrkka, horiz. (56x29mm).

Serpentine Die Cut 11¾ Horiz.
2010, May 4   **Self-Adhesive**
1357   Booklet pane of 6   18.00   6.00
   a.-f.   A805 1 Any single   3.00   1.00
Nos. 1357a-1357f each sold for 80c on day of issue.

Souvenir Sheet

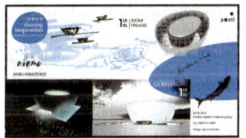

Finnish Pavilion, Expo 2010, Shanghai — A806

No. 1358: a, Aerial view of model and drawing. b, Side view of model.

Serpentine Die Cut 4½ At Bottom
2010, May 4   **Self-Adhesive**
1358   A806   Sheet of 2   6.00   3.00
   a.-b.   1 Either single   3.00   1.50
Nos. 1358a-1358b each sold for 80c on day of issue.

Miniature Sheet

People Jumping A807

No. 1359 — Jumpers in: a, Purple. b, Red. c, Yellow. d, Blue. e, Green.

2010, May 4   *Serpentine Die Cut 5*
Self-Adhesive
1359   A807   Sheet of 5   15.00   5.00
   a.-e.   1 Any single   3.00   1.00
Nos. 1359a-1359e each sold for 80c on day of issue.

Torronsuo National Park — A808

Die Cut Perf. 14
2010, Sept. 13   Litho.
Self-Adhesive
1360   A808 1 multi   3.00   1.20
No. 1360 sold for 75c on day of issue.

1960s-1970s Era Room Furnishings — A809

2010, Sept. 13   **Booklet Stamp**
Self-Adhesive
1361   A809 1 multi   3.00   1.20
   a.   Booklet pane of 10   30.00
No. 1361 sold for 75c on day of issue.

Souvenir Sheet

Autumn A810

No. 1362 — Forest and: a, Crayfish. b, Ducks. c, Elk.

Serpentine Die Cut 12¾x13¼ Syncopated
Litho. & Silk-screened
2010, Sept. 13   **Self-Adhesive**
1362   A810   Sheet of 3   9.00   4.50
   a.-c.   1 Any single   3.00   1.20
On day of issue, Nos. 1362a-1362c each sold for 75c.

Santa Claus A811   Reindeer and Moon A812

Sleigh of Santa Claus Over Lapland — A813

No. 1365: a, Star and Santa Claus with sack. b, Poinsettias, ribbon and bell. c, Sleigh of Santa Claus over church. d, Heart-shaped wreath. e, Reindeer and Aurora Borealis.

Die Cut Perf. 14
2010, Nov. 5   Litho.
Self-Adhesive
1363   Horiz. pair   2.00   1.00
   a.   A811 55c multi   1.00   .50
   b.   A812 55c multi   1.00   .50
1364   A813 1 multi   3.00   1.20
Souvenir Sheet
1365   Sheet of 5   5.00   5.00
   a.   A811 55c multi   1.00   .80
   b.   A811 55c multi   1.00   .80
   c.   A813 55c multi   1.00   .80
   d.   A811 55c multi   1.00   .80
   e.   A811 55c multi   1.00   .80
Christmas. No. 1364 sold for 75c on day of issue. See Japan No. 3209.

Birch Bud A814   Birch Leaves A815

2011, Jan. 24   Litho.   *Die Cut*
Self-Adhesive
1366   A814 20c multi   .40   .25
1367   A815 30c multi   .50   .25

Flag of Finland — A816

2011, Jan. 24   **Litho. & Embossed**
Self-Adhesive
1368   A816 2 gray & blue   2.50   .50
No. 1368 sold for 60c on day of issue.

Birds and Flowers A817

No. 1369: a, Bird on branch, country name in red circle. b, Bird in flight, country name in blue circle. c, Flowers, country name in red circle. d, Bird on branch, country name in blue circle. e, Bird in flight, country name in red circle.

Serpentine Die Cut 10¼ Horiz.
2011, Jan. 24   Litho.
Self-Adhesive
1369   Booklet pane of 5   12.50   6.00
   a.-e.   A817 2 Any single   2.50   1.00
Nos. 1369a-1369e each sold for 60c on day of issue.

Mailboxes — A818

No. 1370: a, Mailbox mounted on tire. b, Snow-covered mailbox. c, Child opening

576 FINLAND

mailbox. d, Mailbox next to sauna. e, Mailbox with posthorn and Finnish lion.

Die Cut Perf. 10 Vert. Syncopated at Right
2011, Jan. 24   *Self-Adhesive*
Coil Stamps

1370		Strip of 5	12.50	4.00
a.-e.	A818	2 Any single	2.50	.80

Nos. 1370a-1370e each sold for 60c on day of issue.

Miniature Sheet

Finnish National Opera, Cent. A819

No. 1371: a, Male and female performers dancing, men in helmets. b, Man with hat and red ribbon, vert. c, Male and female performers in embrace. d, Woman in red dress in water, vert.

Serpentine Die Cut 15½ Horiz.
2011, Jan. 24   *Self-Adhesive*

1371	A819	Sheet of 4	10.00	4.75
a.-d.		2 Any single	2.50	1.00

Nos. 1371a-1371d each sold for 60c on day of issue.

Miniature Sheet

Birds in Trees A820

No. 1372 — Various stylized birds with tree leaves in: a, Green (53x24mm). b, Blue (64x32mm). c, Orange (70x20mm). d, Yellow brown (89x39mm). e, Red violet (78x31mm).

2011, Jan. 24   *Die Cut*
Self-Adhesive

1372	A820	Sheet of 5	12.50	6.00
a.-e.		2 Any single	2.50	1.00

Nos. 1372a-1372e each sold for 60c on day of issue.

Tulips — A821

2011, Apr. 1   *Die Cut Perf. 13¾*
Self-Adhesive

1373	A821	2 multi	2.50	.80

No. 1373 sold for 60c on day of issue.

Dahlias — A822

2011, Apr. 1   *Die Cut*
Self-Adhesive
Color of Country Name

1374	A822	1 red violet	3.00	.50
1375	A822	1 gray green	3.00	.50
a.		Horiz. pair, #1374-1375	6.00	

Nos. 1374-1375 each sold for 75c on day of issue.

Miniature Sheet

Kitchen A823

No. 1376: a, Lamp, counter, pitcher, stove with pots (32x22mm, serpentine die cut 10x10¾). b, Bottles with stoppers (19x46mm, serpentine die cut 9¾x10). c, Hand dropping seasonings into bowl (24x32mm, serpentine die cut 10x10¼). d, Cup, saucer, bowl with lid (22x32mm, serpentine die cut 9½x10¼). e, Cup, eggs in bowl (24x32mm, serpentine die cut 9¾x10).

2011, Apr. 1   *Serpentine Die Cut*
Self-Adhesive

1376	A823	Sheet of 5	12.50	6.00
a.-e.		2 Any single	2.50	1.00

Nos. 1376a-1376e each sold for 60c on day of issue.

Government Buildings — A824

No. 1377: a, House of the Estates, Helsinki, 1890. b, Finnish Embassy, New Delhi, India, 1985. c, Helsinki Music Center, 2011. d, Government Palace, Helsinki, 1828. e, Malmi Airport, Helsinki, 1938. f, Finnish Forest Research Institute Research Center, Joensuu, 2004.

2011, Apr. 1   *Die Cut Perf. 13¼*
Self-Adhesive

1377		Booklet pane of 6	15.00	6.00
a.-f.	A824	2 Any single	2.50	1.00

Nos. 1377a-1377f each sold for 60c on day of issue.

National Council of Women, Cent. — A825

No. 1378 — Comic strip characters Maisa and Kaarina, by Tiina Paju and Sari Luhtanen: a, Holding star-tipped wands. b, Knitting blanket with stars. c, Playing tennis. d, Posing and taking picture. e, Wearing stars on dresses. f, Placing star on cake.

2011, Apr. 1   *Serpentine Die Cut 11*
Self-Adhesive

1378		Booklet pane of 6	15.00	6.00
a.-f.	A825	2 Any single	2.50	1.00

Nos. 1378a-1378f each sold for 60c on day of issue.

Europa A826

No. 1379 — Trees in: a, Spring and summer. b, Autumn and winter.

2011, May 6   *Perf. 12¾x13¼*
Self-Adhesive

1379	A826	Horiz. pair	5.00	2.40
a.-b.		2 Either single	2.50	1.00

Intl. Year of Forests. Nos. 1379a-1379b each sold for 60c on day of issue.

Moomin A827

Mymble A828

Little My A829

Moominmamma and Moomin A830

Hemulen A831

Hattifatteners A832

2011, May 6   *Die Cut*
Self-Adhesive

1380		Booklet pane of 6	15.00	6.00
a.	A827	2 multi	2.50	1.00
b.	A828	2 multi	2.50	1.00
c.	A829	2 multi	2.50	1.00
d.	A830	2 multi	2.50	1.00
e.	A831	2 multi	2.50	1.00
f.	A832	2 multi	2.50	1.00

Nos. 1380a-1380f each sold for 60c on day of issue.

Souvenir Sheet

Struve Geodetic Arc A833

No. 1381: a, Land, water, geodetic arc triangulations. b, Map of Finland with path of triangulations.

2011, May 6   *Die Cut*
Self-Adhesive

1381	A833	Sheet of 2	5.00	2.40
a.-b.		2 Either single	2.50	1.20

Nos. 1381a-1381b each sold for 60c on day of issue.

Miniature Sheet

Tree of Happiness — A834

No. 1382: a, Balloons and gifts (32mm diameter). b, Birds on branch (32mm diameter). c, Cake with Finnish flags (34x29mm oval). d, Bird in birdhouse (34x29mm oval). e, Boy and girl on branch (32mm diameter).

2011, May 6   *Die Cut*
Self-Adhesive

1382	A834	Sheet of 5	12.50	5.00
a.-e.		2 single	2.50	1.00

Nos. 1382a-1382e each sold for 60c on day of issue.

Heraldic Lion Type of 2002
Die Cut Perf. 12 Syncopated
2011, Sept. 5   *Litho.*
Self-Adhesive

1383	A616	€2 green & multi	4.00	2.00
1384	A616	€4 pur & multi	8.00	4.00

Souvenir Sheet

Juhani Aho (1861-1921), Writer — A835

No. 1385: a, Stack of paper, trees. b, Aho on skis.

Litho. & Embossed
2011, Sept. 5   *Perf. 13½*
Self-Adhesive

1385	A835	Sheet of 2	5.00	2.40
a.-b.		2 Either single	2.50	1.20

Nos. 1385a-1385b each sold for 60c on day of issue.

Miniature Sheet

Finnish Comics, Cent. A836

No. 1386: a, Kili ja Possu, by Olavi Vikainen, 1950s. b, Unto Uneksija, by Joonas (Veikko Savolainen), 1960s. c, Herra Kerhonen, by Gösta Thilén, 1930s. d, Antti Puuhaara, by Aarne Nopsanen, 1940s. e, Janne Ankkanen, by Ola Fogelberg, 1910s. f, Olli Pirteä, by Hjalmar Löfving, 1920s.

Die Cut Perf. 8½
2011, Sept. 5   *Litho.*
Self-Adhesive

1386	A836	Sheet of 6	15.00	6.00
a.-f.		2 Any single	2.50	1.00

Nos. 1386a-1386f each sold for 60c on day of issue.

Houses with Snow-covered Roofs — A837

2011, Nov. 7   *Die Cut Perf. 14*
Booklet Stamp
Self-Adhesive

1387	A837	1 multi	3.00	1.00
a.		Booklet pane of 10 + 10 etiquettes		30.00

No. 1387 sold for 75c on day of issue.

Personalized Stamp — A838

FINLAND

Serpentine Die Cut 11¾ Syncopated
2011, Nov. 7 — Self-Adhesive
| 1388 | A838 | 2 multi | 2.50 | 1.00 |

No. 1388 sold for 60c on day of issue. The generic design part of the stamp shown could be personalized.

Christmas — A840

Die Cut Perf. 14
2011, Nov. 7 — Self-Adhesive
| 1389 | A839 | 55c multi | 1.00 | .50 |
| 1390 | A840 | 2 multi | 2.50 | .50 |

No. 1390 sold for 60c on day of issue.

Miniature Sheet

A841

No. 1391: a, Birds on wire. b, Girl with watering can. c, Hearts. d, Girl and dog. e, Woman blowing heart-shaped bubbles. f, Heart-shaped door and key.

2012, Jan. 23 — Die Cut Perf. 13¼x13 Self-Adhesive
| 1391 | A841 | Sheet of 6 | 15.00 | 6.00 |
| a.-f. | | 2 Any single | 2.50 | 1.00 |

Nos. 1391a-1391f each sold for 60c on day of issue.

Miniature Sheet

Sami Culture A842

No. 1392: a, Stick-figure man holding forked stick. b, Stick figure of woman. c, Reindeer at sides of rectangle. d, Three daughters of Sami's mother god and reindeer. Stamps are of various sizes.

2012, Jan. 23 — Die Cut Self-Adhesive
| 1392 | A842 | Sheet of 4 | 12.00 | 4.75 |
| a.-d. | | 1 Any single | 3.00 | 1.20 |

Nos. 1392a-1392d each sold for 75c on day of issue.

The School Girl II — A843

Green Apples and Champagne Glass — A844

Self-Portrait on Black — A845 Silk Shoes — A846

Die Cut Perf. 13, 12¾x13¼ (#1393b), 13¼ (#1393c)
2012, Jan. 23 — Self-Adhesive
1393		Booklet pane of 4	12.00	3.25
a.	A843	1 multi	3.00	.75
b.	A844	1 multi	3.00	.75
c.	A845	1 multi	3.00	.75
d.	A846	1 multi	3.00	.75

Paintings by Helene Schjerfbeck (1862-1946). Nos. 1393a-1393d each sold for 75c on day of issue.

Winning Designs in Future City Stamp Design Contest A847

Designs: No. 1394, Hands, by Varpu Kangas. No. 1395, Shapes and dots, by Kangas. No. 1396, Future City is Diversity, by Chloé Chapeaublanc. No. 1397, Buildings, balloons, and inverted umbrella on tree branch, by Sini Henttonen. No. 1398, Children's drawing in red, blue, and black, by Daniel Kallström, vert. No. 1399, Children's drawing of animal under sun, by Elias Ollila, vert. No. 1400, Rabbits, by Katja Hynninen. No. 1401, Cat's head and heavy man on bicycle, by Ville Korhonen.

Booklet Stamps
Serpentine Die Cut 8¾x9 (#1394, 1400), Rectangle and Arc Die Cut (#1395-1396), Arc Die Cut 12¾ (#1397, 1401), Sawtooth Die Cut 15½x15¼ (#1398-1399)
2012, Jan. 23 — Self-Adhesive
1394	A847	1 multi	3.00	1.50
1395	A847	1 multi	3.00	1.50
a.		Booklet pane of 2, #1394-1395	6.00	3.00
1396	A847	1 multi	3.00	1.50
1397	A847	1 multi	3.00	1.50
a.		Booklet pane of 2, #1396-1397	6.00	3.00
1398	A847	1 multi	3.00	1.50
1399	A847	1 multi	3.00	1.50
a.		Booklet pane of 2, #1398-1399	6.00	3.00
1400	A847	1 multi	3.00	1.50
1401	A847	1 multi	3.00	1.50
a.		Booklet pane of 2, #1400-1401	6.00	3.00
		Complete booklet, #1395a, 1397a, 1399a, 1401a	24.00	16.00
		Nos. 1394-1401 (8)	24.00	12.00

Nos. 1394-1401 each sold for 75c on day of issue.

Wedding Rings — A848

Die Cut Perf. 14
2012, Mar. 5 — Litho. & Engr. Self-Adhesive
| 1402 | A848 | 1 multi | 3.00 | 1.00 |

No. 1402 sold for 75c on day of issue.

Easter — A849

Serpentine Die Cut 8¼ Vert.
2012, Mar. 5 — Litho. Self-Adhesive
| 1403 | A849 | 1 multi | 3.00 | 1.00 |

No. 1403 sold for 75c on day of issue.

Souvenir Sheet

Flowers A850

No. 1404: a, Hepatica triloba (three small yellow flowers at L, large yellow flower at R, denomination at LL). b, Orobus virnus (six yellow and white flowers on stem, denomination at UR), vert. c, Gagea minima (two partially opened buds, denomination at UL). d, Pulmonaria officinalis (four purple flowers, denomination at LR), vert. e, Caltha palustris (yellow flowers, denomination at UR), vert. f, Corydalis solida (cluster of purple flowers, denomination at LL), vert.

2012, Mar. 5 — Die Cut Perf. 10 Self-Adhesive
| 1404 | A850 | Sheet of 6 | 18.00 | 6.00 |
| a.-f. | | 1 Any single | 3.00 | 1.00 |

Nos. 1404a-1404f each sold for 75c on day of issue.

Intl. Women's Day — A851

No. 1405: a, Woman and hearts. b, Women's hands with glasses of fruit, vert. c, Women's legs and shoes, vert. d, Women and musical notes.

2012, Mar. 5 — Die Cut Perf. 12½ Self-Adhesive
| 1405 | | Booklet pane of 4 | 10.00 | 3.25 |
| a.-d. | A851 | 1 Any single | 2.50 | .75 |

Nos. 1405a-1405d each sold for 75c on day of issue.

Railroads in Finland, 150th Anniv. A852

No. 1406: a, Train engineer, steam locomotive. b, Train, ticket. c, Railroad warning sign, train in snow. d, Passenger car and passengers at platform, clock. e, Railway worker, modern train. f, Train, lake, statue.

Serpentine Die Cut 9½ Horiz.
2012, Mar. 5 — Self-Adhesive
| 1406 | | Booklet pane of 6 | 15.00 | 6.00 |
| a.-f. | A852 | 1 Any single | 2.50 | 1.00 |

Nos. 1406a-1406f each sold for 75c on day of issue.

2012 Men's Ice Hockey World Cup Tournament, Finland and Sweden — A853

2012, Mar. 21 — Die Cut Perf. 14 Self-Adhesive
| 1407 | A853 | 1 multi | 3.00 | 1.00 |

No. 1407 sold for 75c on day of issue.

Souvenir Sheet

Rescue Boats A854

No. 1408: a, Jenny Wihuri (red and white boat). b, Merikarhu (green, orange and white boat).

2012, Mar. 21 — Perf. 13½x13 Self-Adhesive
| 1408 | A854 | Sheet of 2 | 6.00 | 3.00 |
| a.-b. | | 1 Either single | 3.00 | 1.50 |

Nos. 1408a-1408b each sold for 75c on day of issue.

Europa — A855

No. 1409: a, Ship on lake. b, People at beach.

2012, May 7 — Perf. 13¼x12¾ Self-Adhesive
| 1409 | A855 | 1 Vert. pair, #a-b | 6.00 | 2.00 |

Nos. 1409a-1409b each sold for 75c on day of issue.

Bothnian Sea National Park — A856

2012, May 7 — Die Cut Perf. 14 Self-Adhesive
| 1410 | A856 | 1 multi | 3.00 | 1.00 |

No. 1410 sold for 75c on day of issue.

Sunflowers — A858

A857

2012, May 7 — Die Cut Perf. 17 Self-Adhesive
| 1411 | A857 | 1 multi | 2.50 | 1.00 |
| 1412 | A858 | 1 multi | 2.50 | 1.00 |

Nos. 1411-1412 each sold for 75c on day of issue.

A859

A860

Clouds — A861

FINLAND

Die Cut Perf. 10 Horiz., Syncopated at Bottom
2012, May 7   Self-Adhesive
Coil Stamps

1413	Horiz. strip of 3	7.50	7.00
a.	A859 1 multi	2.50	1.00
b.	A860 1 multi	2.50	1.00
c.	A861 1 multi	2.50	1.00

Nos. 1413a-1413c each sold for 75c on day of issue.

Souvenir Sheet

Disabled Athletes — A862

No. 1414: a, Leo-Pekka Tahti, cyclist. b, Saana-Maria Sinisalo, archer.

Die Cut Perf. 11¼x11½
Litho. & Silk-screened
2012, May 7   Self-Adhesive

| 1414 | A862 1 Sheet of 2, #a-b | 6.00 | 3.00 |

Nos. 1414a-1414b each sold for 75c on day of issue.

Miniature Sheet

Autumn Dreams — A863

No. 1415: a, Hot-air balloon (36x46mm). b, Moon, lanterns in tree (37x39mm). c, Flying geese (28x36mm). d, Scarecrow and hay rolls (29x46mm). e, Girl feeding carrots to horse (44x34mm).

Serpentine Die Cut 4 to 7
2012, Sept. 3   Litho.
Self-Adhesive

1415	A863	Sheet of 5	12.50	5.00
a.-e.		1 Any single	2.50	1.00

On day of issue, Nos. 1415a-1415e each sold for 80c.

Recording Stars of the 1990s — A864

No. 1416: a, Kaija Koo. b, Jari Sillanpää. c, Laura Voutilainen. d, Yölintu. e, Agents. f, Anna Eriksson.

2012, Sept. 3   *Die Cut Perf. 8½*
Self-Adhesive

1416	Booklet pane of 6	15.00	6.00
a.-f.	A864 1 Any single	2.50	1.00

On day of issue, Nos. 1416a-1416f each sold for 80c.

Pets — A865

No. 1417: a, Cat, inscriptions in red. b, White rabbit facing left. c, Gray rabbit facing right. d, Dachshund puppy, year date at LR. e, Jack Russell terrier puppy, year date at LL. f, Kitten, inscriptions in green.

Serpentine Die Cut 11¾ Horiz.
2012, Sept. 3   Self-Adhesive

| 1417 | Booklet pane of 6 | 15.00 | 6.00 |
| a.-f. | A865 1 Any single | 2.50 | 1.00 |

On day of issue, Nos. 1417a-1417f each sold for 80c.

Christmas Tree A866   Stable Lantern A867

2012, Nov. 5   *Serpentine Die Cut 9½*
Self-Adhesive

| 1418 | A866 60c multi | 1.00 | .50 |

Serpentine Die Cut 10

| 1419 | A867 1 multi | 3.00 | .50 |

Christmas. No. 1419 sold for 80c on day of issue.

Sledders — A868

Self-Adhesive
2013, Jan. 21   *Die Cut Perf. 14*

| 1420 | A868 1 multi | 3.00 | 1.00 |

No. 1420 sold for 80c on day of issue.

Coilostylis Parkinsoniana A869

Self-Adhesive
2013, Jan. 21   *Die Cut Perf. 14*

| 1421 | A869 €1.10 multi | 2.00 | 1.00 |

See No. 1442.

Miniature Sheet

St. Valentine's Day — A870

No. 1422: a, Polar bears. b, Whale. c, Parrots. d, Elephants. e, Chameleon. f, Monkey.

2013, Jan. 21   *Die Cut*
Self-Adhesive

1422	A870	Sheet of 6 + 4 labels	18.00	6.00
a.-f.		1 Any single	3.00	1.00

Nos. 1422a-1422f each sold for 80c on day of issue.

Actors and Actresses A871

No. 1427: a, Ritva Valkama. b, Esko Salminen. c, Outi Mäenpää. d, Martti Suosalo. e, Krista Kosonen. f, Aku Hirviniemi.

Die Cut Perf. 6¾ Vert. Syncopated
2013, Mar. 4   Self-Adhesive

| 1423 | Booklet pane of 6 | 18.00 | 6.00 |
| a.-f. | A871 1 Any single | 3.00 | 1.00 |

Finnish Actors Federation, cent. On day of issue, Nos. 1423a-1423f each sold for 80c.

Easter Rooster — A872

2013, Mar. 8   *Die Cut Perf. 14*
Self-Adhesive

| 1424 | A872 1 multi | 3.00 | 1.00 |

No. 1424 sold for 80c on day of issue.

Roses — A873

2013, Mar. 8   Self-Adhesive

| 1425 | A873 1 multi | 3.00 | 1.00 |

No. 1425 sold for 80c on day of issue.

Blackberries A874   Gooseberry A875

Red Currants — A876

Die Cut Perf. 10 Horiz. Syncopated
2013, Mar. 8   Self-Adhesive
Coil Stamps

1426	Horiz. strip of 3	9.00	3.00
a.	A874 1 multi	3.00	1.00
b.	A875 1 multi	3.00	1.00
c.	A876 1 multi	3.00	1.00

On day of issue, Nos. 1426a-1426c each sold for 80c.

A877   A878

A879   Outhouses — A880

2013, Mar. 8   *Die Cut Perf. 12*
Self-Adhesive

1427	Booklet pane of 4	10.00	4.00
a.	A877 2 multi	2.50	1.00
b.	A878 2 multi	2.50	1.00
c.	A879 2 multi	2.50	1.00
d.	A880 2 multi	2.50	1.00

On day of issue, Nos. 1527a-1527d sold for 70c.

Flower Bouquet — A881

2013, May 6   *Die Cut Perf. 14*
Self-Adhesive

| 1428 | A881 1 multi | 3.00 | 1.00 |

No. 1428 sold for 80c on day of issue.

Nuuksio Natl. Park — A882

2013, May 6   Litho.
Self-Adhesive

| 1429 | A882 1 multi | 3.00 | 1.00 |

No. 1429 sold for 80c on day of issue.

2012 Ford Transit Connect Mail Van — A883

1933 Volvo LV-70 Mail Truck — A884

2013, May 6   *Die Cut Perf. 12½x13¼*
Self-Adhesive

1430	Horiz. pair	6.00	2.00
a.	A883 1 multi	3.00	1.00
b.	A884 1 multi	3.00	1.00

Europa. On day of issue, Nos. 1430a-1430b each sold for 80c.

Miniature Sheet

Odd Finnish Sports and Activities A885

No. 1431: a, Man carrying wife. b, Boot throwing. c, Air guitarist. d, Woman pushing man in milk cart. e, Man sitting on ant hill. f, Swamp soccer.

2013, May 6   *Die Cut Perf. 10*
Self-Adhesive

1431	A885	Sheet of 6 + 6 etiquettes	18.00	6.00
a.-f.		1 Any single	3.00	1.00

On day of issue, Nos. 1431a-1431f each sold for 80c.

Moomins — A886

No. 1432: a, Moominpappa holding drink (red background, 30x34mm). b, Moomintroll jumping (blue background, 33x31mm). c, Moominmamma with purse (green background, 33x34mm). d, Little My with basket on head (yellow orange background, 32x33mm). e, Snorkmaiden and piece of paper (red violet background, 30x35mm). f, Snufkin (brown orange background, 32x36mm).

2013, May 6   *Die Cut*
Self-Adhesive

| 1432 | Booklet pane of 6 + 6 etiquettes | 18.00 | 6.00 |
| a.-f. | A886 1 Any single | 3.00 | 1.00 |

On day of issue, Nos. 1432a-1432f each sold for 80c.

Personalized Stamp — A891

FINLAND

Serpentine Die Cut 11¾ Syncopated
2013, Aug. 12   Litho.
Self-Adhesive
1437   A891   1 black   4.50   4.50

No. 1437 had a franking value of 85c on the day of issue. The vignette shown for No. 1437 is a generic image depicting a Volvo PV 444 police vehicle and is one of ten different police vehicles depicted in the image portion of stamps in a sheet of ten stamps having the same common "frame" that sold for €16.50. Customers purchasing sheets of No. 1437 could also download vignette images from an online library of images on the stamp creation website or use their own downloaded images.

Pres. Sauli Niinistö, 65th Birthday — A895

Die Cut Perf. 12 Syncopated
2013, Aug. 23   Litho.
Self-Adhesive
1441   A895   1 blk & gray   2.75   1.40

No. 1441 sold for 85c on day of issue.

Coilostylis Parkinsoniana Type of 2013
Die Cut Perf. 14
2013, Aug. 23   Litho.
Self-Adhesive
1442   A869   €1.20 multi   2.00   1.00

Souvenir Sheet

Paintings by Eero Järnefelt (1863-1937) — A896

No. 1443: a, Metsämaisema (Forest Scene) (34x49mm). b, Raatajat Rahanalaiset (Under the Yoke - Burning the Brushwood) (44x40mm).

Serpentine Die Cut 14½
2013, Sept. 9   Litho.
Self-Adhesive
1443   A896   Sheet of 2   6.00   3.00
  a.-b.   1 Either single   3.00   1.50

On day of issue, Nos. 1443a-1443b each sold for 85c.

Postcrossing — A897

No. 1444 — Stylized postal card and: a, Hand holding pencil. b, Blackboard. c, Heart-shaped Earth. d, Open mouth.

Serpentine Die Cut 12¼
2013, Sept. 9   Litho.
Self-Adhesive
1444   Booklet pane of 4 + 4 etiquettes   12.00
  a.-d.   A897 1 Any single   3.00   .75

On day of issue Nos. 1444a-1444d each sold for 85c.

Miniature Sheet

Autumn Scenes — A898

No. 1445: a, Boy with umbrella, falling leaves. b, Lakeside sauna, geese in flight, buoy, horiz. c, Rowboat and ducks, horiz. d, Apples in basket, house, falling leaves. e, Park bench, falling leaves, horiz.

Serpentine Die Cut 14x14¼, 14¼x14
2013, Sept. 9   Litho.
Self-Adhesive
1445   A898   Sheet of 5   15.00   5.00
  a.-e.   1 Any single   3.00   1.00

On day of issue, Nos. 1445a-1445e each sold for 85c.

Miniature Sheet

Angry Birds Characters — A899

No. 1446: a, Red Bird. b, Pink Bird, vert. c, Black Bird, vert. d, Yellow Bird. e, Blue Birds, vert. f, King Pig, vert.

Die Cut Perf. 8¼
2013, Sept. 9   Litho.
Self-Adhesive
1446   A899   Sheet of 6 + 6 etiquettes   18.00   4.75
  a.-f.   1 Any single   3.00   .75

On day of issue, Nos. 1446a-1446f each sold for 85c.

Finnish Parliament, 150th Anniv. — A900

Die Cut Perf. 14
2013, Sept. 17   Litho.
Self-Adhesive
1447   A900   1 multi   3.00   1.00

No. 1447 sold for 85c on day of issue.

Finnish School System — A901

No. 1448: a, Girl receiving school lunch, apple, lettuce, pitcher and plate. b, Boy receiving medical examination, posture diagrams. c, Girl practicing writing on blackboard, letters in Finnish alphabet. d, Uno Cygnaeus (1810-88), founder of Finnish school system, map of Finland. e, Children in physical education class, children skiing. f, Teacher watching boys writing at desk, orrery, sun and planet.

Die Cut Perf. 6¾ Horiz. At Top
2013, Nov. 14   Litho.
Self-Adhesive
1448   Booklet pane of 6   18.00   4.75
  a.-f.   A901 1 Any single   3.00   .75

On day of issue, Nos. 1448a-1448f each sold for 85c.

Children Hugging — A902   Angel — A903

Boy with Christmas Trees — A904

Die Cut Perf. 14
2013, Nov. 4   Litho.
Self-Adhesive
1449   A902   65c multi   1.00   .75
1450   A903   2 multi   2.50   1.00
1451   A904   1 multi   3.00   .75
  Nos. 1449-1451 (3)   6.50   2.50

Christmas. On day of issue, No. 1450 sold for 75c; No. 1451, 85c.

Snowmen — A905

Serpentine Die Cut 10¼
2014, Jan. 20   Litho.
Self-Adhesive
1452   A905   1 multi   3.00   1.00

No. 1452 sold for €1 on day of issue.

Miniature Sheet

Teddy Bears — A906

No. 1453: a, Teddy bear writing with quill pen. b, Teddy bear pushing another on sled, horiz. c, Two teddy bears and flower. d, Two Teddy bears dancing. e, Teddy bear sleeping in slipper, horiz. f, Two Teddy bears playing musical instruments.

Serpentine Die Cut 16
2014, Jan. 20   Litho.
Self-Adhesive
1453   A906   Sheet of 6 + 4 stickers   18.00   6.00
  a.-f.   1 Any single   3.00   1.00

Nos. 1453a-1453f each sold for €1 on day of issue.

Castles — A907

No. 1454: a, Turun Linna (Turku Castle) (34x50mm). b, Hämeen Linna (Häme Castle) (34x50mm). c, Raaseporin Linna (Raseborg Castle) (34x50mm). d, Suomenlinna (Sveaborg Fortress) (34x58mm). e, Olavinlinna (Olavinlinna Castle) (34x50mm). f, Kastelholma (Kastelholma Castle) (50x34mm).

Die Cut Perf. 7½
2014, Jan. 20   Litho.
Self-Adhesive
1454   Booklet pane of 6   18.00   4.75
  a.-f.   A907 1 Any single   3.00   .75

Nos. 1454a-1454f each sold for €1 on day of issue.

Souvenir Sheet

Tove Jansson (1914-2001), Creator of Moomins Characters — A908

No. 1456: a, Jansson with telescope. b, Silhouette of Jansson and Moomin character, Sniff.

Die Cut Perf. 12½
2014, Jan. 31   Litho.
Self-Adhesive
1455   A908   Sheet of 2   6.00   3.00
  a.b.   1 Either single   3.00   1.50

Nos. 1455a-1455b each sold for €1 on day of issue.

Easter — A909

Die Cut Perf. 9¾ Horiz.
2014, Mar. 3   Litho.
Self-Adhesive
1456   A909   1 multi   3.00   1.00

No. 1456 sold for €1 on day of issue.

Sami Jauhojärvi and Iivo Niskanen, 2014 Winter Olympic Cross-Country Team Sprint Gold Medalists — A909a

Serpentine Die Cut 11¾ Syncopated
2014, Mar. 3   Litho.
Self-Adhesive
1456A   A909a   1 multi   3.50   3.00

No. 1456A was printed in sheets of 10 that sold for €18. No. 1456 had a franking value of €1 on day of issue.

Fruits and Blossoms — A910

No. 1457: a, Pears (light green background). b, Apples (yellow background). c, Cherries (pink background).

Die Cut Perf. 10 Vert. Syncopated
2014, Mar. 3   Litho.
Coil Stamps
Self-Adhesive
1457   Vert. strip of 3   7.50
  a.-c.   A910 2 Any single   2.50   1.00

Nos. 1457a-1457c each sold for 90c on day of issue.

A911

FINLAND

Congratulations
A912

No. 1458: a, Cat, cake with strawberries. b, Butterflies and flower. c, Squirrel and flowers. d, Strawberries, blueberries and flower. e, Basket of flowers.

Serpentine Die Cut 13¾x13½ (A911), 14½x15¼ (A912)
2014, Mar. 3   Litho.
Self-Adhesive

1458	Booklet pane of 5	15.00	5.00
a.-b.	A911 1 Either single	3.00	1.00
c.-e.	A912 1 Any single	3.00	1.00

Nos. 1458a-1458e each sold for €1 on day of issue.

Souvenir Sheet

Finnjet Ferry
A913

No. 1459 — Ferry with posthorn at: a, Left. b, Right.

Serpentine Die Cut 13½
2014, Mar. 17   Litho.
Self-Adhesive

1459	A913	Sheet of 2	6.00	3.00
a.-b.		1 Either single	3.00	1.50

Nos. 1459a-1459b each sold for €1 on day of issue.

Violas — A914

2014, May 5   Litho.   *Die Cut Perf. 14*
Self-Adhesive

| 1460 | A914 | 1 multi | 3.00 | 1.00 |

No. 1460 sold for €1 on day of issue.

Linnansaari National Park — A915

2014, May 5   Litho.   *Die Cut Perf. 14*
Self-Adhesive

| 1461 | A915 | 1 multi | 3.00 | 1.00 |

No. 1461 sold for €1 on day of issue.

Europa — A916

No. 1462: a, Man playing accordion. b, Woman playing kantele.

Irregular Serpentine Die Cut
2014, May 5   Litho.
Self-Adhesive

1462	Horiz. pair	6.00	2.00
a.-b.	A916 1 Either single	3.00	1.00

Nos. 1462a-1462b each sold for €1 on day of issue.

A917

A918

A919

A920

A921

A922

Die Cut Perf. 13½
2014, May 5   Litho.
Self-Adhesive

1463	Booklet pane of 6	18.00	4.75
a.	A917 1 multi	3.00	.75
b.	A918 1 multi	3.00	.75
c.	A919 1 multi	3.00	.75
d.	A920 1 multi	3.00	.75
e.	A921 1 multi	3.00	.75
f.	A922 1 multi	3.00	.75

Nos. 1463a-1463f each sold for €1 on day of issue.

Miniature Sheet

Caricatures of Dudesons Television Show Cast Members — A923

No. 1464 — Dudeson: a, On snowboard. b, With red cap. c, Wearing shirt with target. d, Running naked, holding book.

Crenellated Die Cut 5
2014, Sept. 1   Litho.
Self-Adhesive

1464	A923	Sheet of 4	12.00	3.25
a.-d.		1 Any single	3.00	.75

Nos. 1464a-1464d each sold for €1 on day of issue.

A924

A925

A926

A927

Watercolors of Yards and Gardens by Urpo Martikainen

Die Cut Perf. 13
2014, Sept. 8   Litho.
Self-Adhesive

1465	Booklet pane of 4	12.00	3.25
a.	A924 1 multi	3.00	.75
b.	A925 1 multi	3.00	.75
c.	A926 1 multi	3.00	.75
d.	A927 1 multi	3.00	.75

Nos. 1465a-1465d each sold for €1 on day of issue.

Celestial and Meteorological Objects — A928

No. 1466: a, Saturn (45x40mm). b, Moon (36x36mm). c, Sun (40x38mm). d, Cloud and lightning bolt (40x51mm). e, Earth and Moon (35x41mm). f, Comet (40x45mm). g, Cloud (48x42mm). h, Rainbow (40x38mm).

Serpentine Die Cut 9¼ on 1 or 2 Sides
2014, Sept. 8   Litho.
Self-Adhesive

1466	Booklet pane of 8	24.00	.50
a.-h.	A928 1 Any single	3.00	.80

Nos. 1466a-1466h each sold for €1 on day of issue.

Souvenir Sheet

Art by Tom of Finland (Touko Laaksonen) (1920-91)
A929

No. 1467: a, Man wearing police cap smoking cigarette (43x32mm). b, Man's head between legs of another man (45x33mm). c, Man's head and buttocks (36x33mm).

Die Cut Perf. 5½
2014, Sept. 8   Litho.
Self-Adhesive

1467	Sheet of 3	9.00	3.00
a.-c.	A929 1 Any single	3.00	1.00

Nos. 1467a-1467c each sold for €1 on day of issue.

A930

A931

A932

A933

A934

A935

A936

A937

A938

Bridges — A939

Die Cut Perf. 8½ Horiz.
2014, Oct. 23   Litho.
Coil Stamps
Self-Adhesive

1468	A930	1 multi + etiquette	3.00	.80
1469	A931	1 multi + etiquette	3.00	.80
1470	A932	1 multi + etiquette	3.00	.80
1471	A933	1 multi + etiquette	3.00	.80
1472	A934	1 multi + etiquette	3.00	.80
1473	A935	1 multi + etiquette	3.00	.80
1474	A936	1 multi + etiquette	3.00	.80
1475	A937	1 multi + etiquette	3.00	.80
1476	A938	1 multi + etiquette	3.00	.80
1477	A939	1 multi + etiquette	3.00	.80
a.		Horiz. strip of 10, #1468-1477, + 10 etiquettes		30.00
	Nos. 1468-1477 (10)		30.00	8.00

On day of issue, Nos. 1468-1477 had a franking value of €1. A complete roll of 100 stamps sold for €97.50 on the day of issue.

Changes in Everyday Items
A940

No. 1478: a, Computer keyboard, computer storage disks, computer, dial telephone, computer chip, television, computer mouse, compact disk and video cassette tapes (54x30mm). b, Potatoes, olives, cookies, cracker, sushi, shrimp, fish, pizza slice (54x30mm). c, Satellite, vacuum cleaner, chest freezer, coffee maker, stove, refrigerator, toaster, washing machine (54x30mm). d, Hay bales, cattle, tractor, storage shed, boarded windows, apartment house, automobiles, house (54x30mm). e, Radio, phonograph record, cassette tape player and headphones, mirrored ball, aerosol cans, electronic piano, dresses, make-up (54x30mm). f, Automobiles, rowboat, bus, scooter, sled, bicycle, cart, train (44x35mm).

2014, Oct. 23   Litho.   *Die Cut*
Self-Adhesive

1478	Booklet pane of 6	18.00	4.75
a.-f.	A940 1 Any single	3.00	.75

Nos. 1478a-1478f each sold for €1 on day of issue.

A941

Christmas — A942

Die Cut Perf. 13
2014, Oct. 23   Litho.
Self-Adhesive

1479	A941	75c multi	2.00	.75
1480	A942	1 multi	3.00	.75

No. 1480 sold for €1 on day of issue.

FINLAND

Christmas — A942a

Serpentine Die Cut 11½ Syncopated
2014, Nov. 17   Litho.
Self-Adhesive
1480A A942a 1 multi   3.00 2.50
No. 1480A had a franking value of €1 on day of issue and was printed in sheets of 10 that sold for €18.

Marigold IceUnity Synchronized Skating Team — A943

Die Cut Perf. 14
2015, Jan. 19   Litho.
Self-Adhesive
Textured Paper
1481 A943 1 multi   3.00 .75
No. 1481 sold for €1 on day of issue.

Miniature Sheet

St. Valentine's Day — A944

No. 1482 — Smiling: a, Snowflakes. b, Trees, snowflakes and bird. c, Mouse and snow angel. d, Birds in nest. e, Berry plants. f, Fox and rabbit.

Serpentine Die Cut 7
2015, Jan. 19   Litho.
Self-Adhesive
1482 A944 Sheet of 6 + 6 etiquettes   18.00 4.75
a.-f.   1 Any single   3.00 .75
Nos. 1482a-1482f each sold for €1 on day of issue.

Artists' Association of Finland, 150th Anniv. — A945

No. 1483: a, Line Form, by Anneli Hilli (36x36mm). b, Point, by Mika Natri (36x36mm). c, Artist's Rollercoaster, by Marjo Suikkanen (36x40mm). d, Dance from the Bride, by Mayumi Niiranen-Hisatomi (32x40mm oval). e, Flight, by Laura Konttinen (36x30mm). f, You Will Know Them By Their Fruits, by Kalevi Karlsson (36x30mm).

Serpentine Die Cut 10¼
2015, Jan. 19   Litho.
Self-Adhesive
1483   Booklet pane of 6 + 6 etiquettes   18.00 4.75
a.-f. A945 1 Any single   3.00 .75
Nos. 1483a-1483f each sold for €1 on day of issue.

Flowers — A946

Die Cut Perf. 13¾
2015, Mar. 2   Litho.
Self-Adhesive
1484 A946 1 multi   3.00 .75
No. 1484 sold for €1.10 on day of issue.

Easter — A947

Serpentine Die Cut 8¾
2015, Mar. 2   Litho.
Self-Adhesive
1485 A947 1 multi   3.00 .75
No. 1485 sold for €1.10 on day of issue.

Student's Cap — A948

Die Cut Perf. 14¼
2015, Mar. 2   Litho.
Self-Adhesive
1486 A948 1 multi   3.00 .75
No. 1486 sold for €1.10 on day of issue.

A949   A950

A951   International Women's Day — A952

2015, Mar. 2   Litho.   Die Cut
Self-Adhesive
1487   Booklet pane of 4   12.00 3.25
a. A949 1 multi   3.00 .75
b. A950 1 multi   3.00 .75
c. A951 1 multi   3.00 .75
d. A952 1 multi   3.00 .75
Nos. 1487a-1487d each sold for €1.10 on day of issue.

Souvenir Sheet

Toivo Kärki (1915-92), Composer — A953

No. 1488 — Kärki and: a, Record album (44mm diameter). b, Score (45x32mm). c, Accordion, silhouette of man and woman (45x32mm).

Die Cut (#1488a), Die Cut Perf. 9¾
2015, Mar. 2   Litho.
Self-Adhesive
1488 A953 Sheet of 3   9.00 2.50
a.-c.   1 Any single   3.00 .75
Nos. 1488a-1488c each sold for €1.10 on day of issue.

Rugosa Roses — A954   Orchids — A955

Die Cut Perf. 13¾
2015, May 8   Litho.
Self-Adhesive
1489   Horiz. pair   5.00 2.00
a. A954 2 multi   2.50 1.00
b. A955 2 multi   2.50 1.00
Nos. 1489a-1489b each sold for €1 on day of issue.

Swan — A956

Litho. With Foil Application
2015, May 8   Die Cut Perf. 13½
Self-Adhesive
1490 A956 1 multi   3.00 .75

A957

Moomin Toys — A958

Serpentine Die Cut 9¾
2015, May 8   Self-Adhesive   Litho.
1491   Horiz. pair   6.00 2.00
a. A957 1 multi   3.00 1.00
b. A958 1 multi   3.00 1.00
Europa. Nos. 1491a-1491b each sold for €1.10 on day of issue.

Miniature Sheet

Sights of Summer A959

No. 1492: a, Strawberry, ladybug and ant (22x30mm). b, Man and woman in rowboat (62x30mm). c, Bicycle (41x30mm). d, Woman with ice cream cone (30x50mm). e, Woman diving into water (30x45mm).

Serpentine Die Cut 9¼x11 (#1492a), 7½x6¼ (#1492b), 8x8¼ (#1492c), 7x6½ (#1492d), 7x7¼ (#1492e)
2015, May 8   Self-Adhesive   Litho.
1492 A959 Sheet of 5   15.00 7.50
a.-e.   1 Any single   3.00 1.00
Nos. 1492a-1492e each sold for €1.10 on day of issue.

Man Pushing Lawnmower — A959a

Serpentine Die Cut 11½ Syncopated
2016, Mar. 30   Litho.
Self-Adhesive
1492F A959a 1 multi   — —
No. 1492F had a franking value of €1.20 on day of issue and was printed in sheets of 10 that sold for €15.

Miniature Sheet

Scenes From Imaginary Town — A960

No. 1493: a, Woman riding giraffe (20x33mm). b, Woman with shopping bag (38x21mm). c, Sailboat and swan (30mm diameter). d, House and horse (41x24mm). e, Rabbits in front of building with clock (34x21mm). f, Birds and flowers in pots (18x35mm).

Serpentine Die Cut 7¾ on 2 Opposite Sides, Die Cut (#1493c, 1493d)
2015, Sept. 11   Litho.
Self-Adhesive
1493 A960 Sheet of 6   15.00
a.-f.   1 Any single   2.50 2.50
Nos. 1493a-1493f each sold for €1.10 on day of issue.

Miniature Sheet

Art A961

No. 1494: a, Horse running. b, Head and arm of woman. c, Woman unzipping dress. d, Woman's legs with high-heeled shoes.

Litho. With Foil Application
Serpentine Die Cut 6¾
2015, Sept. 11   Self-Adhesive
1494 A961 Sheet of 4   10.00
a.-d.   1 Any single   2.50 2.50
Nos. 1494a-1494d each sold for €1.10 on day of issue.

A962   A963

Jean Sibelius (1865-1957), Composer — A964

Serpentine Die Cut 10¼
2015, Sept. 11   Litho.
Self-Adhesive
1495   Booklet pane of 3 + 3 etiquettes   7.50
a. A962 1 multi   2.50 2.50
b. A963 1 multi   2.50 2.50
c. A964 1 multi   2.50 2.50
Nos. 1495a-1495c each sold for €1.10 on day of issue.

FINLAND

The Rasmus
A965

HIM
A966

Apocalyptica
A967

Children of Bodom
A968

Hanoi Rocks
A969

Nightwish
A970

Serpentine Die Cut 10¼x10 (#1496a-1496b), 9¾x10 (#1496c), 10¼x9½ (#1496d), 9½x10 (#1496e), 10¼x9¼ (#1496f)

2015, Sept. 11			Litho.
	Self-Adhesive		
1496	Booklet pane of 6 + 6 etiquettes		15.00
a.	A965 1 multi	2.50	2.50
b.	A966 1 multi	2.50	2.50
c.	A967 1 multi	2.50	2.50
d.	A968 1 multi	2.50	2.50
e.	A969 1 multi	2.50	2.50
f.	A970 1 multi	2.50	2.50

Rock bands. Nos. 1496a-1496f each sold for €1.10 on day of issue.

Finnish Design — A971

No. 1497: a, Marimekko Kukkuluuruu fabric design, by Sanna Annukka (28x45mm). b, Ultima Thule drinking glass, by Tapio Wirkkala (27x27mm). c, Block lamp, by Harri Koskinen (32x27mm). d, Paratiisi plate, by Birger Kaipiainen (27x33mm). e, Mademoiselle lounge chair, by Ilmari Tapiovaara (28x45mm). f, Solifer moped, by Richard Lindh (36x27mm).

Die Cut Perf. 13¼

2015, Sept. 11			Litho.
1497	Booklet pane of 6		15.00
a.-f.	A971 1 Any single	2.50	2.50

Nos. 1497a-1497f each sold for €1.10 on day of issue.

Pertti Kurikan Nimipäivät
A972

Die Cut Perf. 11½ Syncopated

2015, Apr. 28			Litho.
	Self-Adhesive		
1498	A972 1 multi	2.50	2.50

Eurovision Song Contest. No. 1498 sold for €1.10 on day of issue.

Tomatoes
A973

Basil
A974

Peppers — A975

Die Cut Perf. 9¾ Vert. Syncopated

2015, Nov. 6			Litho.
	Coil Stamps		
	Self-Adhesive		
1499	A973 1 multi + etiquette	2.50	2.50
1500	A974 1 multi + etiquette	2.50	2.50
1501	A975 1 multi + etiquette	2.50	2.50
a.	Vert. strip of 3, #1499-1501, + 3 etiquettes		7.50
	Nos. 1499-1501 (3)	7.50	7.50

Nos. 1499-1501 each sold for €1.10 on day of issue.

Miniature Sheet

Craft Items
A976

No. 1502: a, Purse made of tree bark (40x36mm). b, Crocheted square (35x35mm). c, Socks (32x50mm). d, Dancing shoes (38x35mm). e, Mushroom-shaped wooden stool (37x34mm).

Various Die Cuts

2015, Nov. 6			Litho.
	Self-Adhesive		
1502	A976 Sheet of 5		12.50
a.-e.	1 Any single	2.50	2.50

On day of issue, Nos. 1502a-1502e each sold for €1.10.

Father and Son Dragging Christmas Tree Past Church
A977

Child Looking at Christmas Ornament
A978

Die Cut Perf. 11 Syncopated

2015, Nov. 6			Litho.
	Self-Adhesive		
1503	A977 1 multi	2.50	2.50

Booklet Stamp

1504	A978 80c multi	1.90	1.90
a.	Booklet pane of 20		38.00

No. 1503 sold for €1.10 on day of issue and was printed in sheets of 10 + 10 etiquettes.

Victory of Finnish Team in World Junior Ice Hockey Championships
A979

Die Cut Perf. 11½ Syncopated

2016, Jan. 15			Litho.
	Self-Adhesive		
1505	A979 1 multi	2.40	2.40

No. 1505 sold for €1.10 on day of issue.

Snowflake
A980

Litho. With Holographic Foil
Die Cut Perf. 9¾ Horiz.

2016, Jan. 22		Self-Adhesive	
1506	A980 1 multi + etiquette	2.40	2.40

No. 1506 sold for €1.10 on day of issue.

Karelian Pasties
A981

Serpentine Die Cut 8 Syncopated

2016, Jan. 22			Litho.
	Self-Adhesive		
1507	A981 1 multi + etiquette	2.40	2.40

No. 1507 sold for €1.10 on day of issue.

Deer and Bird — A982

Birds — A983

Horse and Dog — A984

Bird and Butterfly
A985

Cat and Dog — A986

Serpentine Die Cut 6½

2016, Jan. 22			Litho.
	Self-Adhesive		
1508	Booklet pane of 5 + 5 etiquettes		12.00
a.	A982 1 multi	2.40	2.40
b.	A983 1 multi	2.40	2.40
c.	A984 1 multi	2.40	2.40
d.	A985 1 multi	2.40	2.40
e.	A986 1 multi	2.40	2.40

On day of issue, Nos. 1508a-1508e each sold for €1.10.

Rabbit and Easter Basket — A987

Die Cut Perf. 13¾

2016, Feb. 26			Litho.
	Self-Adhesive		
1509	A987 1 multi + etiquette	2.60	2.60

No. 1509 sold for €1.20 on day of issue.

Siberian Iris — A988

Die Cut Perf. 13¾

2016, Feb. 26			Litho.
	Self-Adhesive		
1510	A988 1 multi	2.60	2.60

No. 1510 sold for €1.20 on day of issue.

Nuuksio National Park — A989

Birch Tree — A990

Die Cut Perf. 11 Horiz.

2016, Feb. 26			Litho.
	Self-Adhesive		
1511	A989 €1.30 multi + etiquette	3.00	3.00
1512	A990 €1.30 multi + etiquette	3.00	3.00
a.	Horiz. pair, #1511-1512, + 2 etiquettes		6.00

Wings of Thoughts — A991

Die Cut Perf. 13¾

2016, Feb. 26			Litho.
	Self-Adhesive		
1513	A991 €1.80 multi	4.00	4.00

See Nos. 1537, 1554.

Package With Legs — A992

Bird Carrying Letter — A993

Angel Blowing Trumpet — A994

Birthday Cake — A995

Boot and Flowers — A996

2016, Feb. 26	Litho.	Die Cut
	Self-Adhesive	
1514	Booklet pane of 5 + 5 etiquettes and 5 stickers	13.00
a.	A992 1 multi	2.60 2.60
b.	A993 1 multi	2.60 2.60
c.	A994 1 multi	2.60 2.60
d.	A995 1 multi	2.60 2.60
e.	A996 1 multi	2.60 2.60

On day of issue, Nos, 1514a-1514e each sold for €1.20.

FINLAND

This stamp and many other stamps having the same gray panel at bottom were released on Apr. 8, 2016. The stamps, each with a coat of arms of a region or city of Finland, were printed using the Finland Post apparatus used to create personalized stamps. Apparently only coats of arms were printed in the vignette area and no personalized stamps could be created by customers using other vignette images and this gray panel. Even though Finland Post sold these items as "regional stamps," there is no indication that the stamps were sold only in the region of the coat of arms on each stamp, or that the stamps were valid only in those regions. Each stamp was printed in sheets of ten that sold for €15. The coat of arms of the city of Vaasa is shown in the image above.

Feather — A997

Die Cut Perf. 13¾
2016, May 6   Litho.
Self-Adhesive

| 1515 | A997 | 50c multi | 1.10 | 1.10 |

Europa — A998

Serpentine Die Cut 12¼ Syncopated
2016, May 6   Litho.
Self-Adhesive

| 1516 | A998 | 1 multi + etiquette | 2.75 | 2.75 |

Think Green Issue.
No. 1516 sold for €1.20 on day of issue.

Vacation Scenes — A999

No. 1517: a, Woman's crossed feet in sandals, women in park. b, Feet of skateboarder, buildings and cranes. c, Men and women, umbrella and bicycle. d, People at beach. e, Woman at market stall.

2016, May 6   Litho.   **Die Cut Perf. 13**
Self-Adhesive

| 1517 | | Booklet pane of 5 + 5 etiquettes | 14.00 | |
| | a.-e. | A999 1 Any single | 2.75 | 2.75 |

Nos. 1517a-1517e each sold for €1.20 on day of issue.

A1000

A1001

A1002

A1003

Barns — A1004

Die Cut Perf. 9¼ Syncopated
2016, May 6   Litho.
Self-Adhesive

1518		Booklet pane of 5 + 5 etiquettes	14.00	
	a.	A1000 1 multi	2.75	2.75
	b.	A1001 1 multi	2.75	2.75
	c.	A1002 1 multi	2.75	2.75
	d.	A1003 1 multi	2.75	2.75
	e.	A1004 1 multi	2.75	2.75

Nos. 1518a-1518e each sold for €1.20 on day of issue.

Worldwide Fund for Nature (WWF) — A1005

Serpentine Die Cut 4¼ at Top
2016, Sept. 9   Litho.
Self-Adhesive

| 1519 | | Vert. strip of 3 + 3 etiquettes | 8.25 | |
| | a.-c. | A1005 1 Any single + etiquette | 2.75 | 2.75 |

Nos. 1519a-1519c each sold for €1.20 on day of issue.

No. 1519: a, Pusa hispida saimensis. b, Nehalennia speciosa. c, Anser erythropus.

Mushrooms — A1006

No. 1520: a, Russula paludosa. b, Tricholoma matsutake. c, Craterellus cornucopioides. d, Cantharellus cibarius. e, Lactarius deterrimus.

Serpentine Die Cut 14¼x13¾
2016, Sept. 9   Litho.
Self-Adhesive

| 1520 | | Booklet pane of 5 + 5 etiquettes | 14.00 | |
| | a.-e. | A1006 1 Any single | 2.75 | 2.75 |

Nos. 1520a-1520e each sold for €1.20 on day of issue.

People Enjoying Nature — A1007

No. 1521: a, Flower picking. b, Ice fishing. c, Berry harvesting. d, Boating. e, Camping. f, Skiing.

Die Cut Perf. 8¾ on 1 Side
2016, Sept. 9   Litho.
Self-Adhesive

| 1521 | | Booklet pane of 6 + 6 etiquettes | 16.50 | |
| | a.-f. | A1007 1 Any single | 2.75 | 2.75 |

Nos. 1521a-1521f each sold for €1.20 on day of issue.

Miniature Sheet

Art by Ville Andersson and Eeva-Riitta Eerola — A1008

Various unnamed works, as shown.

Serpentine Die Cut 6¾
2016, Sept. 9   Litho.
Self-Adhesive

| 1522 | A1008 | Sheet of 4 | 11.00 | |
| | a.-d. | 1 Any single | 2.75 | 2.75 |

Nos. 1522a-1522d each sold for €1.20 on day of issue.

Kirkonvarkaus Bridge — A1009

Serpentine Die Cut 11½ Syncopated
2016, Sept. 19   Litho.
Self-Adhesive

| 1523 | A1009 | 1 multi | — | — |

No. 1523 had a franking value of €1.20 and was printed in sheets of 10 that sold for €20.

Flag of Finland and Candles — A1010

Serpentine Die Cut 11½ Syncopated
2016, Nov. 4   Litho.
Self-Adhesive

| 1524 | A1010 | (€1.20) multi | | |

No. 1524 was printed in sheets of 10 that sold for €15.

Church, Soini A1011

Wooden Pauper Statue, Soini A1012

Wooden Pauper Statue, Alajärvi — A1013

Church, Alajärvi A1014

Church, Hauho — A1015

Wooden Pauper Statue, Hauho — A1016

Sawtooth Die Cut 6
2016, Nov. 10   Litho.
Self-Adhesive

1525		Booklet pane of 6	16.00	
	a.	A1011 (€1.20) multi	2.60	2.60
	b.	A1012 (€1.20) multi	2.60	2.60
	c.	A1013 (€1.20) multi	2.60	2.60
	d.	A1014 (€1.20) multi	2.60	2.60
	e.	A1015 (€1.20) multi	2.60	2.60
	f.	A1016 (€1.20) multi	2.60	2.60

Reindeer A1017

Girl and Squirrel With Cookies A1018

Snow-covered House — A1019

Die Cut Perf. 7¾
2016, Nov. 10   Litho.
Self-Adhesive

| 1526 | A1017 | (90c) multi | 1.90 | 1.90 |

Die Cut Perf. 7¾x7½

| 1527 | A1018 | (€1.20) multi | 2.60 | 2.60 |

Die Cut Perf. 14

| 1528 | A1019 | (€1.30) multi | 2.75 | 2.75 |
| | | Nos. 1526-1528 (3) | 7.25 | 7.25 |

Etiquettes are found to the sides of No. 1528 in the sheet margin.

Flag of Finland — A1020

Die Cut Perf. 5¾ Horiz.
2017, Jan. 20   Litho.
Self-Adhesive

| 1529 | A1020 | (€1.20) multi | 2.60 | 2.60 |

Snow Castle — A1021

Die Cut Perf. 8¾ Horiz.
2017, Jan. 20   Litho.
Self-Adhesive

| 1530 | A1021 | (€1.20) multi | 2.60 | 2.60 |

Europa.

Hearts — A1022

No. 1531: a, One heart. b, Four hearts. c, 39 hearts. d, Two hearts upright. e, Two hearts sideways.

FINLAND

Die Cut Perf. 9½ Vert.
2017, Jan. 20   Litho.
Self-Adhesive
1531		Booklet pane of 5	13.00	
a.-e.	A1022	(€1.20) Any single	2.60	2.60

Souvenir Sheet

Lions Clubs International, Cent. — A1023

No. 1532 — Various Lions pins and Lions International emblem, with map of Finland at: a, LL. b, UL.

Die Cut Perf. 12¾x12¼
2017, Jan. 20   Litho.
Self-Adhesive
1532	A1023	Sheet of 2	5.25	
a.-b.		(€1.20) Either single	2.60	2.60

Flowers in Cup — A1024

Die Cut Perf. 12½
2017, Feb. 24   Litho.
Self-Adhesive
1533	A1024	(€1.20) multi	2.60	2.60

Pussy Willows — A1025

Die Cut Perf. 8½x8¼
2017, Feb. 24   Litho.
Self-Adhesive
1534	A1025	(€1.20) multi	2.60	2.60

Carousel — A1026

Die Cut Perf. 8½x8¼
2017, Feb. 24   Litho.
Self-Adhesive
1535	A1026	(€1.20) multi	2.60	2.60

Fishermen in Boat — A1027

Reflection of Clouds in Lake — A1028

Swans — A1029

Die Cut Perf. Horiz.
2017, Feb. 24   Litho.
Self-Adhesive
1536		Vert. strip of 3 + 3 etiquettes	8.25	
a.	A1027	(€1.30) multi + etiquette	2.75	2.75
b.	A1028	(€1.30) multi + etiquette	2.75	2.75
c.	A1029	(€1.30) multi + etiquette	2.75	2.75

Wings of Thoughts Type of 2016
Die Cut Perf. 13¾
2017, Mar. 11   Litho.
Self-Adhesive
1537	A991	€2 multi	—	—

Miniature Sheet

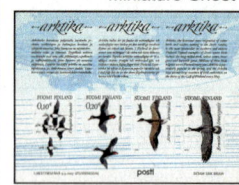

Arctic Birds A1030

No. 1538: a, Clangula hyemalis (27x27mm). b, Melanitta fusca (27x27mm). c, Branta bernicla (27x39mm). d, Branta leucopsis (27x39mm).

Die Cut Perf. 13¼
2017, May 9   Litho.
Self-Adhesive
1538	A1030	Sheet of 4	6.75	
a.		10c multi	.25	.25
b.		20c multi	.45	.45
c.-d.		(€1.30) Either single	3.00	3.00

Nos. 1538a and 1538b were each printed in sheets of 15.

Faces of People Making Up Map of Finland A1031

No. 1539 — Approximate areas of map of Finland: a, Northwestern Lappi Province. b, Northeastern Lappi Province, vert. c, Southwestern Lappi Province and upper Gulf of Bothnia, vert. d, Southeastern Lappi Province and northeastern Oulu Province, vert. e, Southwestern Oulu Province and northern Vaasa Province. f, Eastern Oulu Province. g, Southern Vaasa Province and northern Turku ja Pori Province. h, Mikkeli Province and southern Kuopio and Pohjois-Karjala Provinces. i, Aland Islands and Southern Turku ja Pori Province. j, Uusimaa and Kymi Provinces.

2017, May 9   Litho.   Die Cut Perf. 13
Self-Adhesive
1539	A1031	Booklet pane of 10	30.00	
a.-j.		(€1.30) Any single	3.00	3.00

Independence, cent.

Sauna A1032

Sauna A1033

Sauna A1034

Sauna A1035

Sauna Bucket and Birch Branch Whisk A1036

Die Cut Perf. 6 Horiz.
2017, May 24   Litho.
Self-Adhesive
1540		Booklet pane of 5	15.00	
a.	A1032	(€1.30) multi	3.00	3.00
b.	A1033	(€1.30) multi	3.00	3.00
c.	A1034	(€1.30) multi	3.00	3.00
d.	A1035	(€1.30) multi	3.00	3.00
e.	A1036	(€1.30) multi	3.00	3.00

See Aland Islands Nos. 396-397.

A1037

A1038

A1039

A1040

Moomin Characters A1041

Die Cut Perf. 7 Horiz.
2017, May 24   Litho.
Self-Adhesive
1541		Booklet pane of 5 + 5 etiquettes	16.50	
a.	A1037	(€1.40) multi	3.25	3.25
b.	A1038	(€1.40) multi	3.25	3.25
c.	A1039	(€1.40) multi	3.25	3.25
d.	A1040	(€1.40) multi	3.25	3.25
e.	A1041	(€1.40) multi	3.25	3.25

Souvenir Sheets

A1042

Coat of Arms A1043

Die Cut Perf. 10
2017, May 24   Litho.
Self-Adhesive
1542	A1042	Sheet of 2	6.00	
a.		(€1.30) green	3.00	3.00
b.		(€1.30) blue	3.00	3.00

Souvenir Sheet
Embossed With Foil Application
Die Cut Perf. 13¼
1543	A1043	€10 gold	22.50	22.50

Independence, cent. Finlandia 2017 Stamp Exhibition, Tampere (No. 1542).

Children's Art — A1044

Serpentine Die Cut 11½ Syncopated
2017, May 24   Litho.
Self-Adhesive
1544	A1044	(€1.30) multi	—	—

Pres. Mauno Koivisto (1923-2017) A1045

Die Cut Perf. 13¾
2017, June 9   Litho.
Self-Adhesive
1545	A1045	(€1.30) multi	3.00	3.00

2017 Tall Ship Races, Turku — A1046

Serpentine Die Cut 11½ Syncopated
2017, July 20   Litho.
Self-Adhesive
1546	A1046	(€1.30) multi	—	—

A1047

A1048

Figurines A1049

Die Cut Perf. 8½
2017, Sept. 6   Litho.
Self-Adhesive
1547		Strip of 3	9.75	
a.	A1047	(€1.30) multi	3.25	3.25
b.	A1048	(€1.30) multi	3.25	3.25
c.	A1049	(€1.30) multi	3.25	3.25

FINLAND

 City Parks — A1050

No. 1548 — Park in: a, Porvoo. b, Hämeenlinna. c, Turku.

Die Cut Perf. 10¼
2017, Sept. 6   Litho.
Self-Adhesive
| 1548 | Strip of 3 | 9.75 | |
| a.-c. | A1050 (€1.30) Any single | 3.25 | 3.25 |

 Flower in Spring A1051   Boat on Shore in Summer A1052

 Lake in Autumn A1053   Ice in Winter A1054

Die Cut Perf. 9½ Horiz.
2017, Sept. 6   Litho.
Coil Stamps
Self-Adhesive
1549	A1051	(€1.30) multi	3.25	3.25
1550	A1052	(€1.30) multi	3.25	3.25
1551	A1053	(€1.30) multi	3.25	3.25
1552	A1054	(€1.30) multi	3.25	3.25
a.	Horiz. strip of 4, #1549-1552		13.00	
	Nos. 1549-1552 (4)		13.00	13.00

 Baron Carl Gustaf Emil Mannerheim (1867-1951), President of Finland — A1055

Serpentine Die Cut 11½ Syncopated
2017, Sept. 6   Litho.
Self-Adhesive
| 1553 | A1055 (€1.30) multi | 2.00 | 1.00 |

Wings of ThoughtsType of 2016
Die Cut Perf. 13¾
2017, Oct. 2   Litho.
Self-Adhesive
| 1554 | A991 | €2.10 multi | — | — |

 Presidential Palace, Helsinki A1056

 President Sauli Niinistö, His Three Predecessors and Their Spouses A1057

 Woman in Dressing Room — A1058

 Pres. Niinistö Shaking Hands A1059

 Formal Ball — A1060

 Children Watching Pres. Niinistö Shaking Hands A1061

Serpentine Die Cut 9 Syncopated
2017, Nov. 3   Litho.
Self-Adhesive
1555	Booklet pane of 6	21.00	
a.	A1056 (€1.40) multi	3.50	3.50
b.	A1057 (€1.40) multi	3.50	3.50
c.	A1058 (€1.40) multi	3.50	3.50
d.	A1059 (€1.40) multi	3.50	3.50
e.	A1060 (€1.40) multi	3.50	3.50
f.	A1061 (€1.40) multi	3.50	3.50

Independence of Finland, cent.

 Snow Queen — A1062

Die Cut Perf. 14¾x14
2017, Nov. 3   Litho.
Self-Adhesive
| 1556 | A1062 (€1.40) multi | 3.50 | 3.50 |

 Candles in Christmas Tree A1063

 Man and Squirrels Holding Candles A1064

Die Cut Perf. 14½x14¾
2017, Nov. 3   Litho.
Self-Adhesive
| 1557 | A1063 (95c) multi | 2.25 | 2.25 |

Die Cut Perf. 14¾x14
| 1558 | A1064 (€1.40) multi | 3.50 | 3.50 |

Christmas.

Souvenir Sheet

 Zacharias Topelius (1818-98), Writer A1065

No. 1559: a, Portrait of Topelius by Albert Edelfelt (39x36mm). b, Cradle and Angel Guardians, painting by Rudolf Koivu (39x29mm).

Die Cut Perf. 6½
2018, Jan. 24   Litho.
Self-Adhesive
| 1559 | A1065 Sheet of 2 | 7.00 | |
| a.-b. | (€1.40) Either single | 3.50 | 3.50 |

 A1066

 A1067

 A1068

 A1069

 St. Valentine's Day — A1070

Die Cut Perf. 13x12¾
2018, Jan. 24   Litho.
Self-Adhesive
1560	Booklet pane of 5	17.50	
a.	A1066 (€1.40) multi	3.50	3.50
b.	A1067 (€1.40) multi	3.50	3.50
c.	A1068 (€1.40) multi	3.50	3.50
d.	A1069 (€1.40) multi	3.50	3.50
e.	A1070 (€1.40) multi	3.50	3.50

 Aurora Borealis A1071

 Reindeer A1072

Die Cut Perf. 8½ Horiz.
2018, Jan. 24   Litho.
Self-Adhesive
1561	Horiz. pair	7.50	
a.	A1071 (€1.50) multi + etiquette	3.75	3.75
b.	A1072 (€1.50) multi + etiquette	3.75	3.75

 Worldwide Fund for Nature (WWF) — A1073

No. 1562: a, Vulpes lagopus. b, Bubo scandiacus. c, Salmo salar.

Die Cut Perf. 8½ Horiz.
2018, Feb. 28   Litho.
Self-Adhesive
| 1562 | Vert. strip of 3 | 10.50 | |
| a.-c. | A1073 (€1.40) Any single | 3.50 | 3.50 |

 A1074

 A1075

Easter — A1076

Die Cut Perf. 12½
2018, Feb. 28   Litho.
Self-Adhesive
1563	Vert. strip of 3	10.50	
a.	A1074 (€1.40) multi	3.50	3.50
b.	A1075 (€1.40) multi	3.50	3.50
c.	A1076 (€1.40) multi	3.50	3.50

 Wooden Bridge, Humppila A1077

 Wooden Bridge, Suomussalmi A1078

Serpentine Die Cut 7 Horiz.
2018, May 9   Litho.
Self-Adhesive
1564	Horiz. pair	7.00	
a.	A1077 (€1.50) multi	3.50	3.50
b.	A1078 (€1.50) multi	3.50	3.50

Europa.

 Gerbera Daisies — A1079

 Daisies and Harebells A1080

 Peonies — A1081

 Hydrangeas A1082

 Poppies — A1083

Die Cut Perf. 15¼x14¾
2018, May 9   Litho.
Self-Adhesive
1565	Horiz. strip of 5	17.50	
a.	A1079 (€1.50) multi	3.50	3.50
b.	A1080 (€1.50) multi	3.50	3.50
c.	A1081 (€1.50) multi	3.50	3.50
d.	A1082 (€1.50) multi	3.50	3.50
e.	A1083 (€1.50) multi	3.50	3.50

 1918 Airplane A1084

 2018 Airplane A1085

 1918 Soldier A1086

FINLAND

2018 Soldier A1087

1918 Ship A1088

2018 Ship A1089

Die Cut Perf. 8¼ Horiz.
2018, June 4   Litho.
Self-Adhesive
1566   Booklet pane of 6   21.00
    a.   A1084 (€1.50) multi   3.50   3.50
    b.   A1085 (€1.50) multi   3.50   3.50
    c.   A1086 (€1.50) multi   3.50   3.50
    d.   A1087 (€1.50) multi   3.50   3.50
    e.   A1088 (€1.50) multi   3.50   3.50
    f.   A1089 (€1.50) multi   3.50   3.50
Finnish Defense Forces, cent.

Fish — A1090

No. 1567: a, Sander lucioperca. b, Coregonus albula.

Die Cut Perf. 12½ Horiz. at Bottom
2018, June 6   Litho.
Self-Adhesive
1567   Horiz. pair   7.00
    a.-b.   A1090 (€1.50) Either single   3.50   3.50

A1091

A1092

A1093

A1094

A1095

Popular Foods and Beverages A1096

Sawtooth Die Cut 9¾
2018, June 6   Litho.
Self-Adhesive
1568   Booklet pane of 6   21.00
    a.   A1091 (€1.50) multi   3.50   3.50
    b.   A1092 (€1.50) multi   3.50   3.50
    c.   A1093 (€1.50) multi   3.50   3.50
    d.   A1094 (€1.50) multi   3.50   3.50
    e.   A1095 (€1.50) multi   3.50   3.50
    f.   A1096 (€1.50) multi   3.50   3.50

Miniature Sheet

Traditional Costumes — A1097

No. 1569: a, Woman wearing bonnet (37x25mm). b, Brooch (25x30mm). c, Tasseled scarf and jacket (25x30mm). d, Skirt with horizontal stripes (37x25mm). e, Skirt with vertical stripes (37x25mm). f, Bottom of skirt, stockings and shoes (25x30mm).

Sawtooth Die Cut 5¾x6, 6x6½
2018, June 6   Litho.
Self-Adhesive
1569   A1097   Sheet of 6   21.00
    a.-f.   (€1.50) Any single   3.50   3.50

Grafitti by EGS on Building, Melbourne, Australia A1098

Grafitti by EGS on Truck, St. Petersburg, Russia A1099

Serpentine Die Cut 6¾ Horiz.
2018, Sept. 12   Litho.
Self-Adhesive
1570   Horiz. pair   7.00
    a.   A1098 (€1.50) multi   3.50   3.50
    b.   A1099 (€1.50) multi   3.50   3.50

Seven-spot Ladybug A1100

Whooper Swans A1101

Brown Bears — A1102

Lily of the Valley — A1103

Finnish Spitz — A1104

Die Cut Perf. 9½ Horiz.
2018, Sept. 12   Litho.
Coil Stamps
Self-Adhesive
1571   Horiz. strip of 5   17.50
    a.   A1100 (€1.50) multi   3.50   3.50
    b.   A1101 (€1.50) multi   3.50   3.50
    c.   A1102 (€1.50) multi   3.50   3.50
    d.   A1103 (€1.50) multi   3.50   3.50
    e.   A1104 (€1.50) multi   3.50   3.50
Finnish national flora and fauna.

Park in Pori — A1105

Park in Hanko — A1106

Park in Kotka — A1107

Die Cut Perf. 10¼
2018, Sept. 12   Litho.
Self-Adhesive
1572   Vert. strip of 3   10.50
    a.   A1105 (€1.50) multi   3.50   3.50
    b.   A1106 (€1.50) multi   3.50   3.50
    c.   A1107 (€1.50) multi   3.50   3.50

Souvenir Sheet

Climate Change A1108

No. 1573 — Silhouette of: a, Cloud and snowflakes. b, Arrows and map of Finalnd. c, Bird.

Litho. & Silk-Screened
2018, Sept. 12   **Sawtooth Die Cut 4**
Self-Adhesive
1573   A1108   Sheet of 3   10.50
    a.-c.   (€1.50) Any single   3.50   3.50
Parts of the designs of Nos. 1573a-1573c were printed with thermographic ink, which changes color when warmed.

Rowanberries in Snow A1109

Die Cut Perf. 8½ Horiz.
2018, Nov. 7   Litho.
Self-Adhesive
1574   A1109 (€1.50) multi   3.50   3.50

Ice Skates — A1110

Die Cut Perf. 13x13½
2018, Nov. 7   Litho.
Self-Adhesive
1575   A1110 (€1.60) multi   3.75   3.75

Ornament on Christmas Tree Branch A1111

Candles A1112

Die Cut Perf. 13½x13¼
2018, Nov. 7   Litho.
Self-Adhesive
1576   A1111 (€1.05) multi   2.40   2.40
Die Cut Perf. 13¼x13½
1577   A1112 (€1.50) multi   3.50   3.50
Christmas.

Ice Fishing A1113

Swimming in Ice Water — A1114

Die Cut Perf. 8¾ Horiz.
2019, Jan. 23   Litho.
Self-Adhesive
1578   Horiz. pair   7.00
    a.   A1113 (€1.50) multi   3.50   3.50
    b.   A1114 (€1.50) multi   3.50   3.50

Sharing of Joy — A1115

No. 1579: a, Woman writing post card, white cat. b, Two women walking dogs. c, Two women swimming. d, Two women having tea. e, Woman and child on sled. f, Man giving flower to woman.

2019, Jan. 23   Litho.   **Die Cut**
Self-Adhesive
1579   Booklet pane of 6   21.00
    a.-f.   A1115 (€1.50) Any single   3.50   3.50

Miniature Sheet

Layette Items A1116

No. 1580: a, Striped baby onesie with snaps, socks. b, Two pairs of pants. c, Long sleeve baby onesie, hair brush. d, Children's book, bib. e, Storage box. f, Long sleeve baby onesie with animal print, bonnet.

Sawtooth Die Cut 17½
2019, Jan. 23   Litho.
Self-Adhesive
1580   A1116   Sheet of 6   21.00
    a.-f.   (€1.50) Any single   3.50   3.50

A1117

Easter — A1118

Reversed Die Cut Perf. 4¾ Horiz.
2019, Mar. 13   Litho.
Self-Adhesive
1581   Horiz. pair   7.00
    a.   A1117 (€1.50) multi   3.50   3.50
    b.   A1118 (€1.50) multi   3.50   3.50

Girl Singing Karaoke A1119

Boy Eating Sushi — A1120

Die Cut Perf. 11x11¼
2019, Mar. 13   Litho.
Self-Adhesive
1582   Horiz. pair   7.50
    a.   A1119 (€1.60) multi   3.75   3.75
    b.   A1120 (€1.60) multi   3.75   3.75

Dog With Floral Headdress A1121

Jewelry With Flowers — A1122

FINLAND

Floral Wreath — A1123

Die Cut Perf. 11½ Horiz.
2019, Mar. 13   Litho.
Self-Adhesive

1583	Vert. strip of 3	10.50	
a.	A1121 (€1.50) multi	3.50	3.50
b.	A1122 (€1.50) multi	3.50	3.50
c.	A1123 (€1.50) multi	3.50	3.50
d.	Booklet pane of 15, 5 each #1583a-1583c	52.50	

Miniature Sheet

Helsinki Central Railroad Station A1124

No. 1584: a, Lamps on statues on exterior wall. b, Main entrance, horiz. c, Aerial view of station, horiz. d, Clock tower.

Die Cut Perf. 7 Syncopated
2019, Mar. 13   Litho.
Self-Adhesive

1584	A1124	Sheet of 4	14.00	
a.-d.	(€1.50) Any single		3.50	3.50

Cygnus Cygnus A1125   A1126

Die Cut Perf. 13¼
2019, May 8   Litho.
Self-Adhesive

1585	Vert. pair	7.50	
a.	A1125 (€1.50) multi	3.50	3.50
b.	A1126 (€1.50) multi	3.50	3.50

Europa

Calligraphy by Marja-Liisa Neuvonen A1127

Calligraphy by Taru Tarvainen A1128

Parasta postia pitkään aikaan
Calligraphy by Taru Tarvainen A1128

Calligraphy by Taru Tarvainen A1129   Calligraphy by Maarit Ali-Marttila-Olkkola A1130

Calligraphy by Iiris Lyra — A1131

Serpentine Die Cut 4 Horiz.
2019, May 8   Litho.
Self-Adhesive

1586	Booklet pane of 5	17.50	
a.	A1127 (€1.50) multi	3.50	3.50
b.	A1128 (€1.50) multi	3.50	3.50
c.	A1129 (€1.50) multi	3.50	3.50
d.	A1130 (€1.50) multi	3.50	3.50
e.	A1131 (€1.50) multi	3.50	3.50

Rose on Letter — A1132

Flowers in Wagon — A1133

Sunflower on Typewriter A1134

Tulips in Watering Can — A1135

Roses in Tea Cup — A1136

Rose on Books — A1137

Die Cut Perf. 12¼
2019, May 8   Litho.
Self-Adhesive

1587	Booklet pane of 6	21.00	
a.	A1132 (€1.50) multi	3.50	3.50
b.	A1133 (€1.50) multi	3.50	3.50
c.	A1134 (€1.50) multi	3.50	3.50
d.	A1135 (€1.50) multi	3.50	3.50
e.	A1136 (€1.50) multi	3.50	3.50
f.	A1137 (€1.50) multi	3.50	3.50

Rantapuisto Park and Siltasaari Island, Heinola A1138

Park Along Loimijoki River, Forssa A1139

Kuopio Cathedral — A1140

Die Cut Perf. 10¼
2019, June 5   Litho.
Self-Adhesive

1588	Vert. strip of 3	10.50	
a.	A1138 (€1.50) multi	3.50	3.50
b.	A1139 (€1.50) multi	3.50	3.50
c.	A1140 (€1.50) multi	3.50	3.50
d.	Booklet pane of 15, 5 each #1588a-1588c	52.50	

 A1141
 A1142
 A1143
 A1144
 A1145

Moomin Characters A1146

Die Cut Perf. 5¼ Horiz.
2019, June 5   Litho.
Self-Adhesive

1589	Booklet pane of 6	21.00	
a.	A1141 (€1.50) multi	3.50	3.50
b.	A1142 (€1.50) multi	3.50	3.50
c.	A1143 (€1.50) multi	3.50	3.50
d.	A1144 (€1.50) multi	3.50	3.50
e.	A1145 (€1.50) multi	3.50	3.50
f.	A1146 (€1.50) multi	3.50	3.50

Holly Blue Butterfly A1147

Finnhorse A1148

European Perch — A1149

Silver Birch Trees — A1150

Granite Stones — A1151

Die Cut Perf. 9½ Horiz. (horiz. stamps), Die Cut Perf. 9½ Vert. (vert. stamps)
2019, June 5   Litho.
Coil Stamps
Self-Adhesive

1590	A1147 (€1.50) multi	3.50	3.50
1591	A1148 (€1.50) multi	3.50	3.50
1592	A1149 (€1.50) multi	3.50	3.50
1593	A1150 (€1.50) multi	3.50	3.50
1594	A1151 (€1.50) multi	3.50	3.50
a.	Coil strip of 5, #1590-1594	17.50	
	Nos. 1590-1594 (5)	17.50	17.50

House of Kalle Päätalo (1919-2000), Writer A1152

Die Cut Perf. 8½ Horiz.
2019, Sept. 11   Litho.
Self-Adhesive

| 1595 | A1152 (€1.60) multi | 3.50 | 3.50 |

Calla Lily — A1153

Die Cut Perf. 14
2019, Sept. 11   Litho.
Self-Adhesive

| 1596 | A1153 (€1.60) multi | 3.50 | 3.50 |

A1154

Women's Clothing Designed by Mert Otsamo — A1155

Litho. With Foil Application
Die Cut Perf. 13x13½
2019, Sept. 11   Self-Adhesive

1597	Vert. pair	7.00	
a.	A1154 (€1.60) multi	3.50	3.50
b.	A1155 (€1.60) multi	3.50	3.50

Boy and Puppies — A1156

Girl and Puppy — A1157

Serpentine Die Cut 9½ Horiz.
2019, Sept. 11   Litho.
Self-Adhesive

1598	Pair	7.00	
a.	A1156 (€1.60) multi	3.50	3.50
b.	A1157 (€1.60) multi	3.50	3.50
c.	Booklet pane of 2, #1598a-1598b	7.00	

Snowflakes and Trees — A1158

Litho. With Foil Application
2019, Nov. 6   **Die Cut Perf. 4 Horiz.**
Self-Adhesive

| 1599 | A1158 (€1.60) multi | 3.50 | 3.50 |

Elves A1159

Carolers, Dog and Cat A1160

FINLAND

 Snowman and Rabbits — A1161

Die Cut Perf. 13½x13¼
2019, Nov. 6   Litho.
1600	A1159	(€1.10) multi	2.50	2.50

Die Cut Perf. 13
1601	A1160	(€1.60) multi	3.50	3.50
a.	Booklet pane of 5		17.50	

Die Cut Perf. 13¼
1602	A1161	(€1.70) multi	3.75	3.75
	Nos. 1600-1602 (3)		9.75	9.75

 A1162

 Children's Art — A1163

Litho. With Foil Application
Die Cut Perf. 13¼x13½
2020, Jan. 22   Self-Adhesive
1603	Pair		7.00	
a.	A1162 (€1.60) silver & multi		3.50	3.50
b.	A1163 (€1.60) silver & multi		3.50	3.50

Mannerheim League for Child Welfare, cent.

 People Near Campfire A1164

 Women With Ice Cream Cones A1165

 Woman Blowing Bubbles A1166

 People at Rock Concert A1167

 Men on Carousel Horses A1168

Woman and Child on Swings A1169

Die Cut Perf. 7½ Syncopated
2020, Jan. 22   Litho.
Self-Adhesive
1604	Booklet pane of 6		21.00	
a.	A1164 (€1.60) multi		3.50	3.50
b.	A1165 (€1.60) multi		3.50	3.50
c.	A1166 (€1.60) multi		3.50	3.50
d.	A1167 (€1.60) multi		3.50	3.50
e.	A1168 (€1.60) multi		3.50	3.50
f.	A1169 (€1.60) multi		3.50	3.50

 Moomin in Rowboat A1170

 Moomin and Seahorse in Water — A1171

 Snufkin Fishing — A1172

 Moomin, Pearl and Shell — A1173

 Whale Lifting Moomin's Rowboat A1174

 Mymble in Pot Floating in Water — A1175

Serpentine Die Cut 5¼ Horiz.
2020, Jan. 22   Litho.
Self-Adhesive
1605	Booklet pane of 6		21.00	
a.	A1170 (€1.60) multi		3.50	3.50
b.	A1171 (€1.60) multi		3.50	3.50
c.	A1172 (€1.60) multi		3.50	3.50
d.	A1173 (€1.60) multi		3.50	3.50
e.	A1174 (€1.60) multi		3.50	3.50
f.	A1175 (€1.60) multi		3.50	3.50

 Two Hearts A1176

Serpentine Die Cut 5
2020, Mar. 11   Litho.
Self-Adhesive
1606	A1176	(€1.60) gold & red	3.50	3.50

 Chicken, Chicks and Chick in Egg — A1177

 Birds on Tree — A1178

2020, Mar. 11   Litho.   Die Cut
Self-Adhesive
1607	Pair		7.00	
a.	A1177 (€1.60) multi		3.50	3.50
b.	A1178 (€1.60) multi		3.50	3.50

Easter.

Souvenir Sheet

 Birds A1179

No. 1608: a, Bird on branch. b, Birds in flight. c, Bird on ground facing right. d, Bird on ground facing left.

Serpentine Die Cut 11½x11¾
2020, Mar. 11   Litho.
Self-Adhesive
1608	A1179	Sheet of 4	14.00	
a.-d.	(€1.60) Any single		3.50	3.50

 Flag of Finland and Reflection A1180

Die Cut Perf. 8 Vert. Syncopated
2020, May 6   Litho.
Self-Adhesive
1609	A1180	(€1.60) multi	3.75	3.75

 Owl — A1181

 Stylized Tree — A1182

Die Cut Perf. 13½x13
2020, May 6   Litho.
Self-Adhesive
1610	Horiz. pair		7.50	
a.	A1181 (€1.60) gold & multi		3.75	3.75
b.	A1182 (€1.60) silver & multi		3.75	3.75

 Sleigh of Santa Claus in Flight A1183

Serpentine Die Cut 7¼ Horiz.
Litho. With Foil Application
2020, May 6
Self-Adhesive
1611	A1183	(€1.70) multi	3.75	3.75

Europa.

 Squirrel A1184

 Hedgehog A1185

Die Cut Perf. 8¾ Horiz.
2020, June 3   Litho.
Self-Adhesive
1612	Horiz. pair		7.50	
a.	A1184 (€1.60) multi		3.75	3.75
b.	A1185 (€1.60) multi		3.75	3.75

 Heart Rate Monitor, 1975 A1186

 Xylitol, 1974 A1187

 Wobbler Fishing Lure, 1936 A1188

 Abloy Parking Meter Locks, 1907 A1189

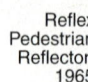 Reflex Pedestrian Reflector, 1965 A1190

 Snow Tire, 1934 A1191

Die Cut Perf. 11¾ Horiz.
2020, June 3   Litho.
Self-Adhesive
1613	Booklet pane of 6		22.50	
a.	A1186 (€1.60) multi		3.75	3.75
b.	A1187 (€1.60) multi		3.75	3.75
c.	A1188 (€1.60) multi		3.75	3.75
d.	A1189 (€1.60) multi		3.75	3.75
e.	A1190 (€1.60) multi		3.75	3.75
f.	A1191 (€1.60) multi		3.75	3.75

Items created in Finland.

 A1192 A1193

 A1194 A1195

 A1196 A1197

 A1198

 Flowers — A1199

Serpentine Die Cut 7½ Horiz.
2020, June 3   Litho.
Coil Stamps
Self-Adhesive
1614	A1192	(€1.60) multi	3.75	3.75
1615	A1193	(€1.60) multi	3.75	3.75
1616	A1194	(€1.60) multi	3.75	3.75
1617	A1195	(€1.60) multi	3.75	3.75
1618	A1196	(€1.60) multi	3.75	3.75
1619	A1197	(€1.60) multi	3.75	3.75
1620	A1198	(€1.60) multi	3.75	3.75
1621	A1199	(€1.60) multi	3.75	3.75
a.	Horiz. coil strip of 8, #1614-1621		30.00	
	Nos. 1614-1621 (8)		30.00	30.00

 Girl Wearing Adult Woman's Shoes — A1200

Die Cut Perf. 10¾ Vert.
2020, Sept. 2   Litho.
Self-Adhesive
1622	A1200	(€1.75) multi	4.25	4.25

 In the Duet, Art by Janne Laine — A1201

FINLAND

The Afterglow, Art by Laine — A1202

Die Cut Perf. 13½
2020, Sept. 2   Litho.
Self-Adhesive

1623		Horiz. pair	8.50	
a.	A1201	(€1.75) multi	4.25	4.25
b.	A1202	(€1.75) multi	4.25	4.25

Miniature Sheet

International Literacy Day — A1203

No. 1624 — Various faces made from letters and symbols with background colors of: a, Light green. b, Pink. c, Pale yellow green. d, Light blue.

Sawtooth Die Cut 11¼ Horiz.
2020, Sept. 2   Litho.
Self-Adhesive

1624	A1203	Sheet of 4	17.00	
a.-d.		(€1.75) Any single	4.25	4.25

Children's Book Characters Tatu and Patu — A1204

No. 1625: a, Patu repairing rip with tape (40x31mm). b, Tatu with pencil (40x41mm). c, Patu peeling back edge of stamp design (40x33mm). d, Tatu and Patu shaking hands (51x37mm). e, Tatu looking through circle (38x33mm). f, Tatu using scissors (40x31mm).

2020, Sept. 2   Litho.   **Die Cut Perf. 7**
Self-Adhesive

1625	A1204	Booklet pane of 6	25.50	
a.-f.		(€1.75) Any single	4.25	4.25

In the vignettes of Nos. 1625a, 1625e and 1625f, small areas enclosed by die cutting may adhere to the backing when the stamps are removed.

Christmas — A1205

A1206   A1207

Christmas — A1208

Die Cut Perf. 12¼x13
2020, Nov. 4   Litho.
Self-Adhesive

| 1626 | A1205 | (€1.20) multi | 3.00 | 3.00 |

Die Cut Perf. 13x12¼
| 1627 | A1206 | (€1.75) multi | 4.25 | 4.25 |

Die Cut Perf. 8¾ Horiz.
| 1628 | A1207 | (€1.75) multi | 4.25 | 4.25 |

Die Cut
| 1629 | A1208 | (€1.85) multi + etiquette | 4.50 | 4.50 |
| | | Nos. 1626-1629 (4) | 16.00 | 16.00 |

Union of Journalists in Finland, Cent. — A1209

Die Cut Perf. 14½
2021, Jan. 20   Litho.
Self-Adhesive

| 1630 | A1209 | (€1.75) black & multi | 4.25 | 4.25 |

Columbines A1210   Day Lily A1211

Die Cut Perf. 13x12½
2021, Jan. 20   Litho.
Self-Adhesive

1631		Horiz. pair	8.50	
a.	A1210	(€1.75) multi	4.25	4.25
b.	A1211	(€1.75) multi	4.25	4.25
c.		Souvenir sheet of 2, #1631a-1631b	8.50	

A1212

A1213

A1214

A1215

A1216

Flora and Fauna — A1217

Serpentine Die Cut 9¾ Horiz.
2021, Jan. 20   Litho.
Self-Adhesive

1632		Booklet pane of 6	25.50	
a.	A1212	(€1.75) multi	4.25	4.25
b.	A1213	(€1.75) multi	4.25	4.25
c.	A1214	(€1.75) multi	4.25	4.25
d.	A1215	(€1.75) multi	4.25	4.25
e.	A1216	(€1.75) multi	4.25	4.25
f.	A1217	(€1.75) multi	4.25	4.25

A1218

Flowers — A1219

Die Cut Perf. 9½ Horiz.
2021, Jan. 20   Litho.
Self-Adhesive

1633		Horiz. pair	8.50	
a.	A1218	(€1.75) pink & multi	4.25	4.25
b.	A1219	(€1.75) yellow & multi	4.25	4.25

Champagne Flutes — A1220

Serpentine Die Cut 5 Syncopated
2021, Apr. 28   Litho.
Self-Adhesive

| 1634 | A1220 | (€1.75) multi | 4.25 | 4.25 |

Health Care Volunteer of Lotta Svärd Foundation A1221

Food Supply Volunteers of Lotta Svärd Foundation A1222

Die Cut Perf. 7¼ Horiz.
2021, Apr. 28   Litho.
Self-Adhesive

1635		Horiz. pair	8.50	
a.	A1221	(€1.75) multi	4.25	4.25
b.	A1222	(€1.75) multi	4.25	4.25

Endangered Animals — A1223

No. 1030. a, Alcedo atthis. b, Parnassius apollo. c, Pteromys volans.

Die Cut Perf. 8½ Horiz. Syncopated
2021, Apr. 28   Litho.
Self-Adhesive

1636		Vert. strip of 3	13.00	
a.-c.		A1223 (€1.75) Any single	4.25	4.25

Europa and Worldwide Fund for Nature (WWF).

First Finnish Post Card, 1871 A1224

Post Card Depicting Farmer and Flag of Finland — A1225   Post Card Depicting Soldier Writing Home — A1226

Post Card Depicting Elf and Princess A1227

Post Card Depicting Porvoo A1228

Post Card With Sender's Photograph A1229

Die Cut Perf. 8¾x8½ Syncopated
2021, Apr. 28   Litho.
Self-Adhesive

1637		Booklet pane of 6	25.50	
a.	A1224	(€1.75) multi	4.25	4.25
b.	A1225	(€1.75) multi	4.25	4.25
c.	A1226	(€1.75) multi	4.25	4.25
d.	A1227	(€1.75) multi	4.25	4.25
e.	A1228	(€1.75) multi	4.25	4.25
f.	A1229	(€1.75) multi	4.25	4.25

Finnish post cards, 150th anniv.

Cactus Pigga, Blown Glass by Alma Jantunen A1230   Fruit Bottles, Blown Glass by Alma Jantunon A1231

Die Cut Perf. 13x13½
2021, Sept. 8   Litho.
Self-Adhesive

1638		Vert. pair	8.50	
a.	A1230	(€1.85) multi	4.25	4.25
b.	A1231	(€1.85) multi	4.25	4.25

Dinner Plate, Fork and Knife — A1232   Running Legs — A1233

Sleeping Snowman A1234   Stylized Recycling Emblem A1235

Shower Head and Water — A1236   Earth — A1237

Die Cut Perf. 9¾ Horiz.
2021, Sept. 8   Litho.
Self-Adhesive

1639		Booklet pane of 6	25.50	
a.	A1232	(€1.85) multi	4.25	4.25
b.	A1233	(€1.85) multi	4.25	4.25
c.	A1234	(€1.85) multi	4.25	4.25
d.	A1235	(€1.85) multi	4.25	4.25
e.	A1236	(€1.85) multi	4.25	4.25
f.	A1237	(€1.85) multi	4.25	4.25

Sustainable living.

FINLAND

Miniature Sheet

Autumnal Landscapes — A1238

No. 1640: a, Sun over wheat field (60x26mm). b, Moon over red house (60x26mm). c, Birch trees along dirt road (60x26mm). d, Lake and boat ramp (26x43mm). e, Forest with sun near horizon (26x43mm).

Die Cut Perf. 10¾
2021, Sept. 8 — Litho.
Self-Adhesive

1640	A1238	Sheet of 5	21.50	
a.-e.	(€1.85) Any single		4.25	4.25

Echo, Painting by Ellen Thesleff (1869-1954) A1239

Boys Playing on the Shore, Painting by Albert Edelfelt (1854-1905) A1240

Skaters Near the Shore of Kalela, Painting by Akseli Gallen-Kallela (1865-1931) A1241

The Convalescent, Painting by Helene Schjerfbeck (1862-1946) A1242

Landscape from Koli, Painting by Eero Järnefelt (1863-1937) A1243

Winter Fishing, Painting by Juho Rissanen (1873-1950) A1244

Sheep Girl, Painting by Hugo Simberg (1873-1917) A1245

The Fighting Capercaillies, Painting by Ferdinand von Wright (1822-1906) — A1246

Die Cut Perf. 13¼x13½ (#1641, 1643, 1647), Die Cut Perf. 13½x13¼ (others)
2021, Sept. 8 — Litho.
Coil Stamps
Self-Adhesive

1641	A1239	(€1.85) multi	4.25	4.25
1642	A1240	(€1.85) multi	4.25	4.25
1643	A1241	(€1.85) multi	4.25	4.25
1644	A1242	(€1.85) multi	4.25	4.25
1645	A1243	(€1.85) multi	4.25	4.25
1646	A1244	(€1.85) multi	4.25	4.25
1647	A1245	(€1.85) multi	4.25	4.25
1648	A1246	(€1.85) multi	4.25	4.25
a.		Strip of 8, #1641-1648	34.00	
		Nos. 1641-1648 (8)	34.00	34.00

Eurasian Bullfinch A1247

Christmas Tree A1248

Dog Catching Snow on Tongue A1249

Snowman A1250

Aurora Borealis — A1251

Serpentine Die Cut 6½
2021, Nov. 3 — Litho.
Self-Adhesive

1649	A1247	(€1.30) sil & multi	3.00	3.00
1650	A1248	(€1.85) multi	4.25	4.25
		Die Cut		
1651		Horiz. pair	8.50	
a.		A1249 (€1.85) multi	4.25	4.25
b.		A1250 (€1.85) multi	4.25	4.25
		Serpentine Die Cut 6½		
1652	A1251	(€1.95) multi	4.50	4.50

Christmas.

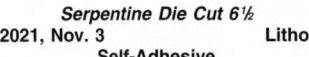

Fazer Blue Chocolate Bar, Cent. — A1252

Serpentine Die Cut 4½ at Bottom
2022, Jan. 19 — Litho.
Self-Adhesive

1653	A1252	(€1.85) multi	4.25	4.25

Cat and Bird on Swing — A1253

Clothesline and Trees — A1254

Serpentine Die Cut 13½ Horiz.
2022, Jan. 19 — Litho.
Self-Adhesive

1654		Horiz. pair	8.50	
a.		A1253 (€1.85) multi	4.25	4.25
b.		A1254 (€1.85) multi	4.25	4.25

Women and Floor Lamp — A1255

Hand Touching Heart — A1256

Rollerskaters A1257

Perfume Bottle — A1258

Women Holding Coffee Cups — A1259

Serpentine Die Cut 7¼ Horiz.
2022, Jan. 19 — Litho.
Booklet Stamps
Self-Adhesive

1655	A1255	(€1.85) multi	4.25	4.25
1656	A1256	(€1.85) multi	4.25	4.25
1657	A1257	(€1.85) multi	4.25	4.25
1658	A1258	(€1.85) multi	4.25	4.25
1659	A1259	(€1.85) multi	4.25	4.25
a.		Booklet pane of 10, 2 each #1655-1659	42.50	
		Nos. 1655-1659 (5)	21.25	21.25

Goddess Päivätär A1260

Goddess Kuutar A1261

Serpentine Die Cut 7 Syncopated
2022, Apr. 27 — Litho.
Self-Adhesive

1660		Vert. pair	9.00	
a.		A1260 (€2.05) sil & multi	4.50	4.50
b.		A1261 (€2.05) multi	4.50	4.50

Europa.

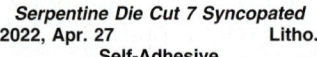

Women Outside the Church at Ruokolahti, Painting by Albert Edelfelt (1854-1905) A1262

The Washerwomen, Painting by Tyko Sallinen (1879-1955) A1263

Dancing Shoes, Painting by Helene Schjerfbeck (1862-1946) A1264

The Luxembourg Gardens, Paris, Painting by Edelfelt A1265

Boy and a Crow, Painting by Akseli Gallen-Kallela (1865-1931) A1266

Maidens at the Headlands, Painting by Pekka Halonen (1865-1933) A1267

Girl with Cats in a Summer Landscape, Painting by Elin Danielson (1861-1919) A1268

Reading Time, Painting by Ellen Thesleff (1869-1954) A1269

Die Cut Perf. 13x13½, 13½x13
2022, Apr. 27 — Litho.
Coil Stamps
Self-Adhesive

1661	A1262	(€1.95) multi	4.25	4.25
1662	A1263	(€1.95) multi	4.25	4.25
1663	A1264	(€1.95) multi	4.25	4.25
1664	A1265	(€1.95) multi	4.25	4.25
1665	A1266	(€1.95) multi	4.25	4.25
1666	A1267	(€1.95) multi	4.25	4.25
1667	A1268	(€1.95) multi	4.25	4.25
1668	A1269	(€1.95) multi	4.25	4.25
a.		Coil strip of 8, #1661-1668	34.00	
		Nos. 1661-1668 (8)	34.00	34.00

Together, by Jenni Tuominen and Jukka Pylväs — A1270

Just Add Water, by Nelli Ahosola A1271

A Bouquet for You, by Anna Kesäniemi A1272

Coffee and Cake, by Tuomas Ikonen A1273

Flower Delivery, by Noora Katto — A1274

Die Cut Perf. 8½x9
2022, Apr. 27 — Litho.
Booklet Stamps
Self-Adhesive

1669	A1270	(€1.95) multi	4.25	4.25
		Serpentine Die Cut 5 Horiz.		
1670	A1271	(€1.95) multi	4.25	4.25
1671	A1272	(€1.95) multi	4.25	4.25
		Serpentine Die Cut 6		
1672	A1273	(€1.95) multi	4.25	4.25
		Die Cut		
1673	A1274	(€1.95) multi	4.25	4.25
a.		Booklet pane of 10, 2 each #1669-1673	42.50	
		Nos. 1669-1673 (5)	21.25	21.25

Winning entries in stamp design contest.

FINLAND

Miniature Sheet

Finnish Baseball, Cent. A1275

No. 1674: a, Players and umpire with bat (30x30mm). b, Batter (40x20mm). c, Pitcher throwing ball (30x30mm). d, Fielder catching ball and runner sliding into base (40x20mm).

Serpentine Die Cut 6 Vert.
2022, Apr. 27 Litho.
Self-Adhesive
1674 A1275 Sheet of 4 17.00
a.-d. (€1.95) Any single 4.25 4.25

Bubblegum Girl, Sculpture by Kim Simonsson A1276

Sleeping Reading Moss Girl, Sculpture by Simonsson A1277

Die Cut Perf. 8¼ Vert.
2022, Sept. 7 Litho.
Self-Adhesive
1675 Vert. pair 8.00
a. A1276 (€1.95) multi 4.00 4.00
b. A1277 (€1.95) multi 4.00 4.00

Moomin Characters and Letters of the Alphabet A1278

No. 1676 — Various Moomin characters and: a, "A." b, "B." c, "C." d, "D." e, "E." f, "F."

Die Cut Perf. 5¼ Horiz.
2022, Sept. 7 Litho.
Self-Adhesive
1676 Booklet pane of 6 24.00
a.-f. A1278 (€1.95) Any single 4.00 4.00

Kristiina Halttu Performing in *Canth* — A1279

Miao Miao Liu Dancing in *COW* — A1280

Various Actors in Lifeboat in Performance of *The Eleventh Moment* — A1281

Michal Krcmár and Zhiyao Chen Dancing in *The Nutcracker and the Mouse King* — A1282

Hannu-Pekka Björkman Performing in *Death of a Salesman* A1283

Xiaoyu He Dancing in *The Sleeping Beauty* — A1284

Minka Kuustonen, Jukka Puotila and Paula Simes Performing in *Exit the King* — A1285

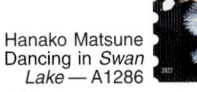
Hanako Matsune Dancing in *Swan Lake* — A1286

Finnish National Theater — A1287

Sergei Popov and Tiina Myllymäki Dancing in *The Little Mermaid* A1288

Die Cut Perf. 3¾ Vert.
2022, Sept. 7 Litho.
Self-Adhesive
1677 Booklet pane of 10 40.00
a. A1279 (€1.95) multi 4.00 4.00
b. A1280 (€1.95) multi 4.00 4.00
c. A1281 (€1.95) multi 4.00 4.00
d. A1282 (€1.95) multi 4.00 4.00
e. A1283 (€1.95) multi 4.00 4.00
f. A1284 (€1.95) multi 4.00 4.00
g. A1285 (€1.95) multi 4.00 4.00
h. A1286 (€1.95) multi 4.00 4.00
i. A1287 (€1.95) multi 4.00 4.00
j. A1288 (€1.95) multi 4.00 4.00

Finnish National Theater, 150th anniv.; Finnish National Ballet, cent.

A1290   A1291

A1292

Christmas — A1293

Reversed Serpentine Die Cut 10¾x10¼ (#1679, 1691), Die Cut Perf. 10¾ (#1680)
2022, Nov. 9 Litho.
Self-Adhesive
1679 A1290 (€2.10) multi 4.50 4.50
1680 Horiz. pair 9.00
a. A1291 (€2.10) multi 4.50 4.50
b. A1292 (€2.10) multi 4.50 4.50

Litho. With Foil Application
1681 A1293 (€2.25) multi + etiquette 4.75 4.75

Gift Box and Ribbon — A1294

Sawtooth Die Cut 4½x4¾
2023, Jan. 18 Litho.
Self-Adhesive
1682 A1294 (€2.10) multi 4.75 4.75

A1295

Arabia Tableware, 150th Anniv. A1296

Die Cut Perf. 9¼ Horiz.
2023, Jan. 18 Litho.
Self-Adhesive
1683 Horiz. pair 9.50
a. A1295 (€2.10) multi 4.75 4.75
b. A1296 (€2.10) multi 4.75 4.75

A1297

Flowers A1298

Reverse Serpentine Die Cut 11½
2023, Jan. 18 Litho.
1684 Horiz. pair 9.50
a. A1297 (€2.10) multi 4.75 4.75
b. A1298 (€2.10) multi 4.75 4.75

Cats and Butterflies A1299

Swans — A1300

Squirrels and Flowers A1301

Puppies A1302

Deer, Rabbit and Flowers A1303

Reverse Serpentine Die Cut 10¾
2023, Jan. 18 Litho.
1685 A1299 (€2.10) multi 4.75 4.75
1686 A1300 (€2.10) multi 4.75 4.75
1687 A1301 (€2.10) multi 4.75 4.75
1688 A1302 (€2.10) multi 4.75 4.75
1689 A1303 (€2.10) multi 4.75 4.75
a. Booklet pane of 10, 2 each #1685-1689 47.50
Nos. 1685-1689 (5) 23.75 23.75

Europa — A1304

Die Cut Perf. 8¾
2023, May 9 Litho.
1690 A1304 (€2.30) multi 5.00 5.00

A1305

A1306

A1307

A1308

Fairies and Flowers A1309

Die Cut Perf. 8½
2023, May 9 Litho.
1691 A1305 (€2.30) multi 5.00 5.00
1692 A1306 (€2.30) multi 5.00 5.00
1693 A1307 (€2.30) multi 5.00 5.00
1694 A1308 (€2.30) multi 5.00 5.00
1695 A1309 (€2.30) multi 5.00 5.00
a. Booklet pane of 10, 2 each #1691-1695 50.00
Nos. 1691-1695 (5) 25.00 25.00

SEMI-POSTAL STAMPS

Arms — SP1

Unwmk.
1922, May 15 Typo. Perf. 14
B1 SP1 1m + 50p gray & red .90 10.00
Never hinged 2.00
a. Perf. 13x13½ 9.00
Never hinged 18.00

Red Cross Standard SP2

Symbolic SP3

FINLAND

Ship of Mercy — SP4

1930, Feb. 6
B2	SP2	1m + 10p red org & red	1.50	10.00
		Never hinged	3.50	
B3	SP3	1½m + 15p grysh grn & red	1.00	10.00
		Never hinged	2.50	
B4	SP4	2m + 20p dk bl & red	2.50	45.00
		Never hinged	5.50	
		Nos. B2-B4 (3)	5.00	65.00
		Set, never hinged	11.50	

The surtax on this and subsequent similar issues was for the benefit of the Red Cross Society of Finland.

Church in Hattula — SP5

Designs: 1½p+15p, Castle of Hameenlinna. 2m+20p, Fortress of Viipuri.

1931, Jan. 1 Cross in Red Engr.
B5	SP5	1m + 10p gray grn	1.50	11.00
		Never hinged	4.00	
B6	SP5	1½m + 15p lil brn	9.00	13.00
		Never hinged	27.50	
B7	SP5	2m + 20p dull bl	1.50	30.00
		Never hinged	4.00	
		Nos. B5-B7 (3)	12.00	54.00
		Set, never hinged	35.50	

SP8

1931, Oct. 15 Typo. Rouletted 4, 5
B8	SP8	1m + 4m black	8.00	45.00
		Never hinged	22.50	

The surtax was to assist the Postal Museum of Finland in purchasing the Richard Granberg collection of entire envelopes.

Helsinki University Library SP9

Nikolai Church at Helsinki SP10

2½m+25p, Parliament Building, Helsinki.

1932, Jan. 1 Perf. 14
B9	SP9	1¼m + 10p ol bis & red	1.50	12.50
		Never hinged	4.00	
B10	SP10	2m + 20p dp vio & red	1.00	8.00
		Never hinged	3.00	
B11	SP9	2½m + 25p lt blue & red	1.80	30.00
		Never hinged	4.50	
		Nos. B9-B11 (3)	4.30	50.50
		Set, never hinged	11.50	

Bishop Magnus Tawast SP12

Michael Agricola SP13

Design: 2½m+25p, Isacus Rothovius.

1933, Jan. 20 Engr.
B12	SP12	1¼m + 10p blk brn & red	3.25	9.00
		Never hinged	9.00	
B13	SP13	2m + 20p brn vio & red	.70	4.00
		Never hinged	2.50	
B14	SP13	2½m + 25p indigo & red	.70	7.00
		Never hinged	2.50	
		Nos. B12-B14 (3)	4.65	20.00
		Set, never hinged	14.00	

Evert Horn — SP15

Designs: 2m+20p, Torsten Stalhandske. 2½m+25p, Jakob (Lazy Jake) de la Gardie.

1934, Jan. 20 Cross in Red
B15	SP15	1¼m + 10p brown	.80	3.00
		Never hinged	2.50	
B16	SP15	2m + 20p gray lil	1.20	5.50
		Never hinged	6.50	
B17	SP15	2½m + 25p gray	.90	4.50
		Never hinged	3.00	
		Nos. B15-B17 (3)	2.90	13.00
		Set, never hinged	12.00	

Mathias Calonius — SP18

Designs: 2m+20p, Henrik C. Porthan. 2½m+25p, Anders Chydenius.

1935, Jan. 1 Cross in Red
B18	SP18	1¼m + 15p brown	.80	2.50
		Never hinged	2.50	
B19	SP18	2m + 20p gray lil	2.00	4.50
		Never hinged	6.00	
B20	SP18	2½m + 25p gray bl	1.00	3.00
		Never hinged	3.00	
		Nos. B18-B20 (3)	3.80	10.00
		Set, never hinged	11.50	

Robert Henrik Rehbinder — SP21

2m+20p, Count Gustaf Mauritz Armfelt. 2½m+25p, Count Arvid Bernard Horn.

1936, Jan. 1 Cross in Red
B21	SP21	1¼m + 15p dk brn	.75	3.50
		Never hinged	2.50	
B22	SP21	2m + 20p vio brn	2.50	5.00
		Never hinged	7.00	
B23	SP21	2½m + 25p blue	.75	3.50
		Never hinged	2.50	
		Nos. B21-B23 (3)	4.00	12.00
		Set, never hinged	12.00	

Type "Uusimaa" SP24

Type "Turunmaa" SP25

Design: 3½m+35p, Type "Hameenmaa."

1937, Jan. 1 Cross in Red
B24	SP24	1¼m + 15p brown	.60	3.00
		Never hinged	1.75	
B25	SP25	2m + 20p brn lake	11.00	7.50
		Never hinged	37.50	
B26	SP24	3½m + 35p indigo	.75	3.00
		Never hinged	2.50	
		Nos. B24-B26 (3)	12.35	13.50
		Set, never hinged	41.25	

Aukuste Makipeska — SP27

Designs: 1¼m+15p, Robert Isidor Orn. 2m+20p, Edward Bergenheim. 3½m+35p, Johan Mauritz Nordenstam.

1938, Jan. 5 Cross in Red Engr.
B27	SP27	50p + 5p dk grn	.40	1.80
		Never hinged	.95	
B28	SP27	1¼m + 15p dk brn	.70	3.00
		Never hinged	2.00	
B29	SP27	2m + 20p rose lake	6.00	7.00
		Never hinged	14.00	
B30	SP27	3½m + 35p dk blue	.55	3.00
		Never hinged	2.00	
		Nos. B27-B30 (4)	7.65	14.80
		Set, never hinged	18.95	

Skiing — SP31

Designs: 2m+1m, Ski jumper. 3.50m+1.50m, Skier.

1938, Jan. 18
B31	SP31	1.25m + 75p sl grn	2.50	11.50
		Never hinged	6.50	
B32	SP31	2m + 1m dk car	2.50	11.50
		Never hinged	6.50	
B33	SP31	3.50m + 1.50m dk blue	2.50	11.50
		Never hinged	6.50	
		Nos. B31-B33 (3)	7.50	34.50
		Set, never hinged	19.50	

Ski championships held at Lahti.

Soldier — SP34

1938, May 16
B34	SP34	2m + ½m blue	1.20	4.00
		Never hinged	3.50	

Victory of the White Army over the Red Guards. The surtax was for the benefit of the members of the Union of the Finnish Front.

Battlefield at Solferino — SP35

1939, Jan. 2 Cross in Scarlet
B35	SP35	50p + 5p dk grn	.60	1.50
		Never hinged	1.25	
B36	SP35	1¼m + 15p dk brn	.70	2.50
		Never hinged	1.25	
B37	SP35	2m + 20p lake	10.00	4.00
		Never hinged	27.50	
B38	SP35	3½m + 35p dk bl	.60	2.50
		Never hinged	1.00	
		Nos. B35-B38 (4)	11.90	10.50
		Set, never hinged	31.00	

Intl. Red Cross Soc., 75th anniv.

> Catalogue values for unused stamps in this section, from this point to the end of the section, are for Never Hinged items.

Soldiers with Crossbows — SP36

1¼m+15p, Cavalryman. 2m+20p, Soldier of Charles XII of Sweden. 3½m+35p, Officer and soldier of War with Russia, 1808-1809.

1940, Jan. 26 Cross in Red
B39	SP36	50p + 5p dk grn	1.80	1.75
B40	SP36	1¼m + 15p dk brn	2.50	2.50
B41	SP36	2m + 20p lake	4.00	3.50
B42	SP36	3½m + 35p dp ultra	1.75	3.50
		Nos. B39-B42 (4)	10.05	11.25

The surtax aided the Finnish Red Cross.

Arms of Finland — SP40

1940, Feb. 15 Litho.
B43	SP40	2m +2m indigo	.80	1.50

The surtax was given to a fund for the preservation of neutrality.

Mason — SP41

1.75m+15p, Farmer plowing. 2.75m+25p, Mother and child. 3.50m+35p, Finnish flag.

1941, Jan. 1 Cross in Red Engr.
B44	SP41	50p + 5p green	.80	.80
B45	SP41	1.75m + 15p brown	1.75	2.40
B46	SP41	2.75m + 25p brn car	11.00	8.00
B47	SP41	3.50m + 35p dp ultra	1.75	2.50
		Nos. B44-B47 (4)	15.30	13.70

See Nos. B65-B68.

Soldier's Emblem — SP45

1941, May 24 Unwmk.
B48	SP45	2.75m + 25p brt ultra	.80	1.00

The surtax was for the aid of the soldiers who fought in the Russo-Finnish War.

Aland Arms — SP46

Coats of Arms: 1.75m+15p, Nyland. 2.75m+25p, Finland's first arms. 3.50m+35p, Karelia. 4.75m+45p, Satakunta.

1942, Jan. 2 Perf. 14
Cross in Red
B49	SP46	50p + 5p green	1.00	1.00
B50	SP46	1.75m + 15p brown	1.50	2.50
B51	SP46	2.75m + 25p dark red	2.00	2.50
B52	SP46	3.50m + 35p deep ultra	1.50	4.00
B53	SP46	4.75m + 45p dk sl grn	1.00	3.00
		Nos. B49-B53 (5)	7.00	13.00

The surtax aided the Finnish Red Cross.

Lapland Arms — SP51

Coats of Arms: 2m+20p, Hame. 3.50m+35p, Eastern Bothnia. 4.50m+45p, Savo.

Cross in Red
1943, Jan. 2 Inscribed "1943"
B54	SP51	50p + 5p green	.80	1.20
B55	SP51	2m + 20p brown	1.20	2.00
B56	SP51	3.50m + 35p dark red	1.20	2.00
B57	SP51	4.50m + 45p brt ultra	3.00	11.00
		Nos. B54-B57 (4)	6.20	16.20

The surtax aided the Finnish Red Cross.

FINLAND

Soldier's Helmet and Sword
SP55

Mother and Children
SP56

1943, Feb. 1
B58	SP55	2m + 50p dk brown	.50	1.00
B59	SP56	3.50m + 1m brown red	.80	1.00

The surtax was for national welfare.

Red Cross Train — SP57

2m+50p, Ambulance. 3.50m+75p, Red Cross Hospital, Helsinki. 4.50m+1m, Hospital plane.

1944, Jan. 2   Cross in Red   Perf. 14
B60	SP57	50p + 25p green	.25	.40
B61	SP57	2m + 50p sepia	.50	1.20
B62	SP57	3.50m + 75p ver	.50	1.00
B63	SP57	4.50m + 1m brt ultra	1.00	5.00
		Nos. B60-B63 (4)	2.25	7.60

The surtax aided the Finnish Red Cross.

Symbols of Peace — SP61

1944, Dec. 1
B64	SP61	3.50m + 1.50m dk red brn	.40	.80

The surtax was for national welfare.

Type of 1941 Inscribed "1945"
1945, May 2   Photo. & Engr.
Cross in Red
B65	SP41	1m + 25p green	.25	.40
B66	SP41	2m + 50p brown	.25	.80
B67	SP41	3.50m + 75p brn car	.25	.60
B68	SP41	4.50m + 1m dp ultra	.60	2.40
		Nos. B65-B68 (4)	1.35	4.20

The surtax was for the Finnish Red Cross.

Wrestling — SP62

2m+1m, Gymnast. 3.50m+1.75m, Runner. 4.50m+2.25m, Skier. 7m+3.50m, Javelin thrower.

1945, Apr. 16   Engr.   Perf. 13½
B69	SP62	1m + 50p bluish grn	.25	.90
B70	SP62	2m + 1m dp red	.25	.90
B71	SP62	3.50m + 1.75m dull vio	.25	.90
B72	SP62	4.50m + 2.25m ultra	.50	1.20
B73	SP62	7m + 3.50m dull brn	1.00	2.00
		Nos. B69-B73 (5)	2.05	5.90

Fishing — SP67

Designs: 3m+75p, Churning. 5m+1.25m, Reaping. 10m+2.50m, Logging.

Engraved; Cross Typo. in Red
1946, Jan. 7
B74	SP67	1m + 25p dull grn	.40	.50
B75	SP67	3m + 75p lil brn	.25	.40
B76	SP67	5m + 1.25m rose red	.40	.50
a.		Red cross omitted	650.00	650.00

B77	SP67	10m + 2.50m ultra	.50	1.00
		Nos. B74-B77 (4)	1.55	2.40

The surtax was for the Finnish Red Cross.

Nurse and Children — SP71

Design: 8m+2m, Doctor examining infant.

1946, Sept. 2   Engr.
B78	SP71	5m + 1m green	.25	.60
B79	SP71	8m + 2m brown vio	.25	.60

The surtax was for the prevention of tuberculosis.

Nos. B78 and B79 Surcharged with New Values in Black
1947, Apr. 1
B80	SP71	6m + 1m on 5m + 1m	.40	.70
B81	SP71	10m + 2m on 8m + 2m	.40	.70

The surtax was for the prevention of tuberculosis.

SP73

Medical Examination of Infants — SP74

Designs: 10m+2.50m, Infant held by the feet. 12m+3m, Mme. Alli Paasikivi and a child. 20m+5m, Infant standing.

1947, Sept. 15   Engr.
B82	SP73	2.50m + 1m green	.80	1.00
B83	SP74	6m + 1.50m dk red	.80	1.50
B84	SP74	10m + 2.50m red brn	.80	1.50
B85	SP73	12m + 3m dp blue	1.50	2.00
B86	SP74	20m + 5m dk red vio	1.50	3.50
		Nos. B82-B86 (5)	5.40	9.50

The surtax was for the prevention of tuberculosis.
For surcharges see Nos. B91-B93.

Zachris Topelius — SP78

7m+2m, Fredrik Pacius. 12m+3m, Johan L. Runeberg. 20m+5m, Fredrik Cygnaeus.

Engraved; Cross Typo. in Red
1948, May 10   Unwmk.   Perf. 14
B87	SP78	3m + 1m green	.80	1.00
B88	SP78	7m + 2m rose red	.80	1.50
B89	SP78	12m + 3m brt blue	.75	1.50
B90	SP78	20m + 5m dk vio	1.50	2.50
		Nos. B87-B90 (4)	3.85	6.50

The surtax was for the Finnish Red Cross.

Nos. B83, B84 and B86 Surcharged with New Values and Bars in Black
1948, Sept. 13   Engr.   Perf. 13½
B91	SP74	7m + 2m on #B83	1.50	3.00
B92	SP74	15m + 3m on #B84	1.50	3.00
B93	SP74	24m + 6m on #B86	2.50	4.50
		Nos. B91-B93 (3)	5.50	10.50

Tying Birch Boughs — SP79

9m+3m, Bathers in Sauna house. 15m+5m, Rural bath house. 30m+10m, Cold plunge in lake.

Engraved; Cross Typo. in Red
1949, May 5   Perf. 13½x14
B94	SP79	5m + 2m dull grn	.90	1.20
B95	SP79	9m + 3m dk car	.90	1.20
B96	SP79	15m + 5m dp blue	.90	4.00
B97	SP79	30m + 10m dk vio brn	2.00	7.20
		Nos. B94-B97 (4)	4.70	13.60

The surtax was for the Finnish Red Cross.

Wood Anemone — SP83

1949, June 2   Engr.
Inscribed: "1949"
B98	SP83	5m + 2m shown	.90	1.00
B99	SP83	9m + 3m Wild rose	1.20	1.50
B100	SP83	15m + 5m Coltsfoot	1.20	1.50
		Nos. B98-B100 (3)	3.30	4.00

The surtax was for the prevention of tuberculosis.

Similar to Type of 1949
Designs: 5m+2m, Water lily. 9m+3m, Pasqueflower. 15m+5m, Bell flower cluster.

1950, Apr. 1   Inscribed: "1950"
B101	SP83	5m + 2m emer	2.70	2.20
B102	SP83	9m + 3m rose car	2.20	1.50
B103	SP83	15m + 5m blue	2.20	1.50
		Nos. B101-B103 (3)	7.10	5.20

The surtax was for the prevention of tuberculosis.

Hospital Entrance, Helsinki SP84

Blood Donor's Medal SP86

Design: 12m+3m, Giving blood.

Engraved; Cross Typo. in Red
1951, Mar. 17   Unwmk.   Perf. 14
B104	SP84	7m + 2m chocolate	2.50	2.00
B105	SP84	12m + 3m bl vio	2.50	2.00
B106	SP86	20m + 5m car	2.50	3.00
		Nos. B104-B106 (3)	7.50	7.00

The surtax was for the Finnish Red Cross.

Capercaillie — SP87

Designs: 10m+9m, European... 20m+5m, Caspian terns.

1951, Oct. 26   Engr.
B107	SP87	7m + 2m dk grn	2.75	2.75
B108	SP87	12m + 3m rose brn	2.75	2.75
B109	SP87	20m + 5m blue	2.75	2.75
		Nos. B107-B109 (3)	8.25	8.25

The surtax was for the prevention of tuberculosis.

Diver SP88

Soccer Players SP89

No. B112, Stadium, Helsinki. No. B113, Runners.

1951-52
B110	SP88	12m + 2m rose car	1.50	1.50
B111	SP89	15m + 2m grn ('52)	1.75	1.75
B112	SP88	20m + 3m deep blue	1.50	1.50
B113	SP89	25m + 4m brn ('52)	2.00	2.25
		Nos. B110-B113 (4)	6.75	7.00

XV Olympic Games, Helsinki, 1952. The surtax was to help finance the games.
Issued: B110, B112, 11/16; B111, B113, 2/15/52.
Margin blocks of four of each denomination were cut from regular or perf-through-margin sheets and pasted by the selvage, overlapping, in a printed folder to create a kind of souvenir booklet. Value $45.

Field Marshal Mannerheim — SP90

Engraved; Cross Typo. in Red
1952, Mar. 4
B114	SP90	10m + 2m gray	2.50	2.00
B115	SP90	15m + 3m rose vio	2.50	2.00
B116	SP90	25m + 5m blue	2.50	2.00
		Nos. B114-B116 (3)	7.50	6.00

The surtax was for the Red Cross.

Great Titmouse — SP91

Designs: 15m+3m, Spotted flycatchers and nest. 25m+5m, Swift.

1952, Dec. 4   Engr.
B117	SP91	10m + 2m green	2.50	2.50
B118	SP91	15m + 3m plum	2.50	2.50
B119	SP91	25m + 5m dp blue	2.50	2.50
		Nos. B117-B119 (3)	7.50	7.50

The surtax was for the prevention of tuberculosis.
See Nos. B148-B150.

European Red Squirrel — SP92

No. B121, Brown bear. No. B122, European elk.

Unwmk.
1953, Nov. 16   Engr.   Perf. 14
B120	SP92	10m + 2m red brn	2.75	3.00
B121	SP92	15m + 3m violet	2.75	3.00
B122	SP92	25m + 5m dk grn	2.75	3.00
		Nos. B120-B122 (3)	8.25	9.00

Surtax for the prevention of tuberculosis.

Children Receiving Parcel from Welfare Worker — SP93

Designs: 15m+3m, Aged woman knitting. 25m+5m, Blind basket-maker and dog.

FINLAND

Engraved; Cross Typo. in Red
1954, Mar. 8   Perf. 11½
B123 SP93 10m + 2m dk ol grn   2.50   1.75
B124 SP93 15m + 3m dk blue   2.50   1.75
B125 SP93 25m + 5m dk brown   2.50   1.75
Nos. B123-B125 (3)   7.50   5.25

The surtax was for the Finnish Red Cross.

Bumblebees, Dandelions — SP94

15m+3m, Butterfly. 25m+5m, Dragonfly.

Engraved; Cross Typo. in Red
1954, Dec. 7   Perf. 14
B126 SP94 10m + 2m brown   2.00   1.50
B127 SP94 15m + 3m carmine   2.50   2.00
B128 SP94 25m + 5m blue   2.50   2.00
Nos. B126-B128 (3)   7.00   5.50

The surtax was for the prevention of tuberculosis.

European Perch — SP95

Designs: 15m+3m, Northern pike. 25m+5m, Atlantic salmon.

Engraved; Cross Typo. in Red
1955, Sept. 26   Perf. 14
B129 SP95 10m + 2m dl grn   1.50   1.75
B130 SP95 15m + 3m vio brn   2.00   1.75
B131 SP95 25m + 5m dk bl   2.50   1.75
Nos. B129-B131 (3)   6.00   5.25

Surtax for the Anti-Tuberculosis Society.

Gen. von Dobeln in Battle of Juthas, 1808 — SP96

Illustrations by Albert Edelfelter from J. L. Runeberg's "Tales of Ensign Stal": 15m+3m, Col. J. Z. Duncker holding flag. 25m+5m, Son of fallen Soldier.

Engraved; Cross Typo. in Red
1955, Nov. 24
B132 SP96 10m + 2m dp ultra   2.00   1.75
B133 SP96 15m + 3m dk red brn   2.00   1.75
B134 SP96 25m + 5m green   2.00   1.75
Nos. B132-B134 (3)   6.00   5.25

The surtax was for the Red Cross.

Waxwing — SP97

Birds: 20m+3m, Eagle owl. 30m+5m, Mute swan.

Engraved; Cross Typo. in Red
1956, Sept. 25   Perf. 11½
B135 SP97 10m + 2m dl red brn   1.60   1.25
B136 SP97 20m + 3m bl grn   2.25   1.75
B137 SP97 30m + 5m blue   2.75   1.75
Nos. B135-B137 (3)   6.60   4.75

Surtax for the Anti-Tuberculosis Society.

Pekka Aulin — SP98

Portraits: 10m+2m, Leonard von Pfaler. 20m+3m, Gustaf Johansson. 30m+5m, Viktor Magnus von Born.

Engraved; Cross Typo. in Red
1956, Nov. 26   Unwmk.
B138 SP98 5m + 1m grysh grn   1.50   1.00
B139 SP98 10m + 2m brown   1.50   1.25
B140 SP98 20m + 3m mag   1.75   1.75
B141 SP98 30m + 5m lt ultra   1.75   1.75
Nos. B138-B141 (4)   6.50   5.75

The surtax was for the Red Cross.

Wolverine (Glutton) — SP99

20m+3m, Lynx. 30m+5m, Reindeer.

Engraved; Cross Typo. in Red
1957, Sept. 5   Perf. 11½
B142 SP99 10m + 2m dull purple   1.50   1.25
B143 SP99 20m + 3m sepia   2.40   1.75
B144 SP99 30m + 5m dark blue   2.40   1.75
Nos. B142-B144 (3)   6.30   4.75

The surtax was for the Anti-Tuberculosis Society. See Nos. B160-B165.

Red Cross Flag — SP100

1957, Nov. 25   Engr. Cross in Red   Perf. 14
B145 SP100 10m + 2m ol grn   1.75   1.75
B146 SP100 20m + 3m maroon   1.75   2.50
B147 SP100 30m + 5m dull blue   2.25   2.50
Nos. B145-B147 (3)   5.75   6.75

80th anniv. of the Finnish Red Cross.

Type of 1952

Flowers: 10m+2m, Lily of the Valley. 20m+3m, Red clover. 30m+5m, Hepatica.

Engraved; Cross Typo. in Red
1958, May 5   Unwmk.   Perf. 14
B148 SP91 10m + 2m green   1.75   1.25
B149 SP91 20m + 3m lilac rose   2.00   2.00
B150 SP91 30m + 5m ultra   2.25   2.00
Nos. B148-B150 (3)   6.00   5.25

Surtax for the Anti-Tuberculosis Society.

Raspberry — SP101

20m+3m, Cowberry. 30m+5m, Blueberry.

Engraved; Cross Typo. in Red
1958, Nov. 20   Perf. 11½
B151 SP101 10m + 2m orange   1.75   1.40
B152 SP101 20m + 3m red   2.25   1.75
B153 SP101 30m + 5m dk blue   2.25   1.75
Nos. B151-B153 (3)   6.25   4.90

The surtax was for the Red Cross.

Daisy — SP102

20m+5m, Primrose. 30m+5m, Cornflower.

Engraved; Cross Typo. in Red
1959, Sept. 7   Unwmk.
B154 SP102 10m + 2m green   2.00   1.50
B155 SP102 20m + 3m lt brown   3.00   2.50
B156 SP102 30m + 5m blue   3.00   2.50
Nos. B154-B156 (3)   8.00   6.50

Surtax for the Anti-Tuberculosis Society.

Reindeer — SP103

No. B158, Lapp & lasso. No. B159, Mountains.

Engraved; Cross Typo. in Red
1960, Nov. 24   Perf. 11½
B157 SP103 10m + 2m dk gray   1.25   1.25
B158 SP103 20m + 3m gray vio   1.75   1.75
B159 SP103 30m + 5m rose vio   1.75   1.75
Nos. B157-B159 (3)   4.75   4.75

The surtax was for the Red Cross.

Animal Type of 1957

Designs: 10m+2m, Muskrat. 20m+3m, Otter. 30m+5m, Seal.

Engr.; Cross at right, Typo. in Red
1961, Sept. 4
B160 SP99 10m + 2m brn car   1.40   1.00
B161 SP99 20m + 3m slate bl   2.00   1.50
B162 SP99 30m + 5m bl grn   2.00   1.50
Nos. B160-B162 (3)   5.40   4.00

Surtax for the Anti-Tuberculosis Society.

Animal Type of 1957

Designs: 10m+2m, Hare. 20m+3m, Pine marten. 30m+5m, Ermine.

Engraved; Cross Typo. in Red
1962, Oct. 1
B163 SP99 10m + 2m gray   1.50   1.50
B164 SP99 20m + 3m dl red brn   2.00   1.75
B165 SP99 30m + 5m vio bl   2.00   1.75
Nos. B163-B165 (3)   5.50   5.00

The surtax was for the Anti-Tuberculosis Society.

Cross and Outstretched Hands — SP104

Engraved; Cross Typo. in Red
1963, May 8   Perf. 11½
B166 SP104 10p + 2p red brn   .50   .75
B167 SP104 20p + 3p violet   1.00   1.20
B168 SP104 30p + 5p green   1.00   1.20
Nos. B166-B168 (3)   2.50   3.15

The surtax was for the Red Cross.

Attending the Wounded — SP105

Red Cross Activities: 25p+4p, Hospital ship. 35p+5p, Prisoner-of-war health examination. 40p+7p, Gift parcel distribution.

Engraved; Cross Typo. in Red
1964, May 26   Perf. 11½
B169 SP105 15p + 3p vio bl   1.00   .60
B170 SP105 25p + 4p green   1.25   .90
B171 SP105 35p + 5p vio brn   1.25   .90
B172 SP105 40p + 7p dk ol grn   1.25   .90
Nos. B169-B172 (4)   4.75   3.30

The surtax was for the Red Cross.

Finnish Spitz — SP106

Designs: 25p+4p, Karelian bear dog. 35p+5p, Finnish hunting dog.

Engraved; Cross Typo. in Red
1965, May 10   Perf. 11½
B173 SP106 15p + 3p org brn   1.00   1.00
B174 SP106 25p + 4p black   1.50   1.50
B175 SP106 35p + 5p gray brn   1.50   1.50
Nos. B173-B175 (3)   4.00   4.00

Surtax for Anti-Tuberculosis Society.

Artificial Respiration — SP107

First Aid: 25p+4p, Skin diver rescuing occupants of submerged car. 35p+5p, Helicopter rescue in winter.

1966, May 7   Litho.   Perf. 14
B176 SP107 15p + 3p multi   1.10   1.00
B177 SP107 25p + 4p multi   1.25   1.25
B178 SP107 35p + 5p multi   1.25   1.25
Nos. B176-B178 (3)   3.60   3.50

The surtax was for the Red Cross.

Birch — SP108

Trees: 25p+4p, Pine. 40p+7p, Spruce.

1967, May 12   Litho.   Perf. 14
B179 SP108 20p + 3p multi   .75   .75
B180 SP108 25p + 4p multi   1.00   1.00
B181 SP108 40p + 7p multi   1.00   1.00
Nos. B179-B181 (3)   2.75   2.75

Surtax for Anti-Tuberculosis Society. See Nos. B185-B187.

Horse-drawn Ambulance — SP109

25p+4p, Ambulance, 1967. 40p+7p, Red Cross.

Cross in Red
1967, Nov. 24   Litho.   Perf. 14
B182 SP109 20p + 3p dl yel, grn & blk   .90   .90
B183 SP109 25p + 4p vio & blk   1.25   1.25
B184 SP109 40p + 7p dk grn, blk & dk ol   1.25   1.25
Nos. B182-B184 (3)   3.40   3.40

The surtax was for the Red Cross.

Tree Type of 1967

Trees: 20p+3p, Juniper. 25+4p, Aspen. 40p+7p, Chokecherry.

1969, May 12   Litho.   Perf. 14
B185 SP108 20p + 3p multi   .80   .80
B186 SP108 25p + 4p multi   1.20   1.20
B187 SP108 40p + 7p multi   1.20   1.20
Nos. B185-B187 (3)   3.20   3.20

Surtax for Anti-Tuberculosis Society.

"On the Lapp's Magic Rock" — SP110

Designs: 30p+6p, Juhani blowing horn on Impivaara Rock, vert. 50p+10p, The Pale Maiden. The designs are from illustrations by Askeli Gallen-Kallelas for "The Seven Brothers" by Aleksis Kivi.

1970, May 8   Litho.   Perf. 14
B188 SP110 25p + 5p multi   .70   .70
B189 SP110 30p + 6p multi   1.20   1.20
B190 SP110 50p + 10p multi   1.20   1.20
Nos. B188-B190 (3)   3.10   3.10

The surtax was for the Red Cross.

Cutting and Loading Timber — SP111

Designs: 30p+6p, Floating logs downstream. 50p+10p, Sorting logs at sawmill.

FINLAND

1971, Apr. 25 Litho. *Perf. 14*
B191 SP111 25p + 5p multi .90 .80
B192 SP111 30p + 6p multi .90 .80
B193 SP111 50p + 10p multi 1.20 .80
Nos. B191-B193 (3) 3.00 2.40

Surtax for Anti-Tuberculosis Society.

Blood Donor and Nurse — SP112

30p+6p, Blood research (microscope, slides), vert. 50p+10p, Blood transfusion.

1972, Oct. 25
B194 SP112 25p + 5p multi .70 .85
B195 SP112 30p + 6p multi 1.10 .90
B196 SP112 50p + 10p multi 1.10 .90
Nos. B194-B196 (3) 2.90 2.65

Surtax was for the Red Cross.

Girl with Lamb, by Hugo Simberg — SP113

Paintings: 40p+10p, Summer Evening, by Vilho Sjöström. 60p+15p, Woman at Mountain Fountain, by Juho Rissanen.

1973, Sept. 12 Litho. *Perf. 13x12½*
B197 SP113 30p + 5p multi 1.00 1.00
B198 SP113 40p + 10p multi 1.40 1.40
B199 SP113 60p + 15p multi 1.40 1.40
Nos. B197-B199 (3) 3.80 3.80

Surtax for the Finnish Anti-Tuberculosis Assoc. Birth centenaries of featured artists.

Morel — SP114

Mushrooms: 50p+10p, Chanterelle. 60p+15p, Boletus edulis.

1974, Sept. 24 Litho. *Perf. 12½x13*
B200 SP114 35p + 5p multi 1.00 1.00
B201 SP114 40p + 10p multi 1.50 1.50
B202 SP114 60p + 15p multi 1.50 1.50
Nos. B200-B202 (3) 4.00 4.00

Finnish Red Cross.

Echo, by Ellen Thesleff (1869-1954) — SP115

Paintings: 60p+15p, Hilda Wiik, by Maria Wiik (1853-1928). 70p+20p, At Home (old woman in chair), by Helene Schjerfbeck (1862-1946).

1975, Sept. 30 Litho. *Perf. 13x12½*
B203 SP115 40p + 10p multi .90 .90
B204 SP115 60p + 15p multi 1.25 1.00
B205 SP115 70p + 20p multi 1.25 1.25
Nos. B203-B205 (3) 3.40 3.15

Finnish Red Cross. In honor of International Women's Year paintings by women artists were chosen.

Disabled Veterans' Emblem — SP116

Lithographed and Photogravure
1976, Jan. 15 *Perf. 14*
B206 SP116 70p + 30p multi .80 .60

The surtax was for hospitals for disabled war veterans.

Wedding Procession SP117

Designs: 70p+15p, Wedding dance, vert. 80p+20p, Bride, groom, matron and pastor at wedding dinner.

1976, Sept. 15 Litho. *Perf. 13*
B207 SP117 50p + 10p multi .85 .85
B208 SP117 70p + 15p multi 1.10 .90
B209 SP117 80p + 20p multi 1.10 1.10
Nos. B207-B209 (3) 3.05 2.85

Surtax for Anti-Tuberculosis Society.

Disaster Relief — SP118

Designs: 80p+15p, Community work. 90p+20p, Blood transfusion service.

1977, Jan. 19 Litho. *Perf. 14*
B210 SP118 50p + 10p multi .80 .80
B211 SP118 80p + 15p multi 1.20 .80
B212 SP118 90p + 20p multi 1.20 1.20
Nos. B210-B212 (3) 3.20 2.80

Finnish Red Cross centenary.

Long-distance Skiing — SP119

Design: 1m+50p, Ski jump.

1977, Oct. 5 Litho. *Perf. 13*
B213 SP119 80p + 40p multi 2.00 2.00
B214 SP119 1m + 50p multi 1.50 1.50

Surtax was for World Ski Championships, Lahti, Feb. 17-26, 1978.

Saffron Milkcap — SP120

Edible Mushrooms: 80p+15p, Parasol, vert. 1m+20p, Gypsy.

1978, Sept. 13 Litho. *Perf. 13*
B215 SP120 50p + 10p multi 1.00 1.00
B216 SP120 80p + 15p multi 1.50 1.20
B217 SP120 1m + 20p multi 1.50 1.50
Nos. B215-B217 (3) 4.00 3.70

Surtax was for Red Cross. See Nos. B221-B223.

Pehr Kalm, 1716-1779 SP121

Finnish Scientists: 90p+15p, Title page of Pehr Adrian Gadd's (1727-97) book, vert. 1.10m+20p, Petter Forsskal (1732-63).

Perf. 12½x13, 13x12½
1979, Sept. 26 Litho.
B218 SP121 60p + 10p multi .80 .80
B219 SP121 90p + 15p multi 1.20 .80
B220 SP121 1.10m + 20p multi 1.20 1.20
Nos. B218-B220 (3) 3.20 2.80

Surtax for Finnish Anti-Tuberculosis Assoc.

Mushroom Type of 1978

Edible Mushrooms: 60p+10p, Woolly milkcap. 90p+15p, Orange-cap boletus, vert. 1.10m+20p, Russula paludosa.

1980, Apr. 19 Litho. *Perf. 13*
B221 SP120 60p + 10p multi .80 .80
B222 SP120 90p + 15p multi 1.00 1.50
B223 SP120 1.10m + 20p multi 1.50 1.50
Nos. B221-B223 (3) 3.30 3.80

Surtax was for Red Cross.

Fuchsia — SP122

No. B225, African violet. No. B226, Geranium.

1981, Aug. 24 Litho. *Perf. 13*
B224 SP122 70p + 10p shown .80 .80
B225 SP122 1m + 15p multi .90 1.00
B226 SP122 1.10m + 20p multi 1.20 1.20
Nos. B224-B226 (3) 2.90 3.00

Surtax for Finnish Anti-Tuberculosis Assoc.

Garden Dormouse SP123

No. B228, Flying squirrels. No. B229, European minks.

1982, Aug. 16 Litho. *Perf. 13*
B227 SP123 90p + 10p shown .90 .80
B228 SP123 1.10m + 15p multi .90 1.20
B229 SP123 1.20m + 20p multi 1.20 1.20
Nos. B227-B229 (3) 3.00 3.20

Surtax was for Red Cross. No. B228 vert.

Forest and Wetland Plants — SP124

1m+20p, Chickweed wintergreen. 1.20m+25p, Marsh violet. 1.30m+30p, Marsh marigold.

1983, July 7 Litho. *Perf. 13*
B230 SP124 1m + 20p multi .80 .80
B231 SP124 1.20m + 25p multi .80 1.20
B232 SP124 1.30m + 30p multi 1.20 1.20
Nos. B230-B232 (3) 2.80 3.20

Surtax for Finnish Anti-Tuberculosis Assoc.

Globe Puzzle — SP125

2m+40p, Symbolic world communication.

1984, May 28 Litho. *Perf. 13*
B233 SP125 1.40m + 35p multi .60 .60
B234 SP125 2m + 40p multi 1.00 1.00

Surtax for Red Cross.

Butterflies — SP126

No. B235, Anthocharis cardamines. No. B236, Nymphalis antiopa. No. B237, Parnassius apollo.

1986, May 22 Litho. *Perf. 13*
B235 SP126 1.60m + 40p multi 1.00 .60
B236 SP126 2.10m + 45p multi 1.50 1.20
B237 SP126 5m + 50p multi 3.00 3.00
Nos. B235-B237 (3) 5.50 4.80

Surtax for Red Cross.

Festivals — SP127

Designs: No. B238, Christmas. No. B239, Easter. No. B240, Midsummer.

1988, Mar. 14 Litho. *Perf. 13*
B238 SP127 1.40m +40p multi .90 .60
B239 SP127 1.80m +45p multi 1.25 1.20
B240 SP127 2.40m +50p multi 1.25 1.50
Nos. B238-B240 (3) 3.40 3.30

Surtax for the Red Cross.

Heodes virgaureae on Goldrod Plant — SP128

Butterflies and plants: No. B242, Agrodiaetus amandus on meadow vetchling. No. B243, Inachis io on tufted vetch.

1990, Apr. 6 Photo. *Perf. 12x11½*
B241 SP128 1.50m +40p multi .70 .70
B242 SP128 2m +45p multi 1.25 1.25
B243 SP128 2.70m +60p multi 1.50 1.50
Nos. B241-B243 (3) 3.45 3.45

Surtax for the natl. Red Cross Soc.

Paintings by Helene Schjerfbeck — SP129

Designs: No. B244a, The Little Convalescent. No. B244b, Green Still-Life.

1991, Mar. 8 Litho. *Perf. 13*
B244 SP129 Pair 2.00 2.00
a.-b. 2.10m +50p any single 1.00 1.00

Surtax for philately.

Butterflies — SP130

No. B245, Xestia brunneopicta. No. B246, Acerbia alpina. No. B247, Baptria tibiale.

Litho. & Embossed
1992, Apr. 22 *Perf. 13*
B245 SP130 1.60m +40p multi .70 .70
B246 SP130 2.10m +50p multi .90 .90
B247 SP130 5m +60p multi 2.00 2.00
Nos. B245-B247 (3) 3.60 3.60

Surtax for Finnish Red Cross. Embossed "Arla 100" in braille for Arla Institute, training center for the blind. cent.

Autumn Landscape of Lake Pielisjarvi, by Eero Jarnefelt — SP131

a, Tree-covered hill. b, Lake shoreline.

1993, Mar. 19 Litho. *Perf. 13*
B248 SP131 2.30m + 70p Pair, #a.-b. 2.00 2.00

Surtax for philately.

Finnhorses SP132

Designs: No. B249, Draft horses. No. B250, Trotter. No. B251, War horses, vert.

1994, Mar. 11 Litho. *Perf. 13*
B249 SP132 2m +40p multi .80 .80
B250 SP132 2.30m +50p multi 1.20 1.20
B251 SP132 4.20m +60p multi 1.75 1.75
Nos. B249-B251 (3) 3.75 3.75

Surtax for Finnish Red Cross.

FINLAND

Paintings, by Albert Edelfelt (1854-1905) — SP133

No. B252, Playing Boys on the Shore. No. B253, Queen Blanche.

1995, Mar. 1	Litho.		Perf. 13½	
B252	2.40m +60p multi		1.50	1.00
	Size: 22x31mm			
B253	2.40m +60p multi		1.50	1.00
a.	SP133 Pair, #B252-B253		3.00	3.00

Surtax for philately.

Chickens — SP134

Designs: No. B254, Chicks. No. B255, Hens. No. B256, Rooster, vert.

1996, Mar. 18	Litho.	Perf. 13	
B254	SP134 2.80m +60p multi	1.50	1.20
B255	SP134 3.20m +70p multi	2.00	2.00
B256	SP134 3.40m +70p multi	4.00	3.00
	Nos. B254-B256 (3)	7.50	6.20

Surtax for Finnish Red Cross.

The Aino Myth, by Akseli Gallen-Kallela (1865-1931) — SP135

Designs: No. B257, Väinämöinen proposing marriage to Aino in forest. No. B258, Aino jumping into water to escape Väinämöinen. No. B259, Aino at shore for bath.

1997, Sept. 5	Litho.	Perf. 13½x13	
	Booklet Stamps		
B257	SP135 2.80m +60p multi	1.50	1.50
B258	SP135 2.80m +60p multi	1.50	1.50
B259	SP135 2.80m +60p multi	1.50	1.50
a.	Booklet pane, #B257-B259	4.50	4.50
	Complete booklet, #B259a	4.50	

No. B258 is 33x46mm.
Surtax for philately.

Pigs — SP136

2.80m+60p, Sow, piglets. 3.20m+70p, Three piglets. 3.40m+70p, Pig's head.

1998, Mar. 12	Litho.	Perf. 13	
B260	SP136 2.80m +60p multi	1.50	1.50
B261	SP136 3.20m +70p multi	2.00	1.50
B262	SP136 3.40m +70p multi	3.50	2.50
	Nos. B260-B262 (3)	7.00	5.50

Surtax for Finnish Red Cross.

Paintings by Hugo Simberg (1873-1917) SP137

a, Garden of Death. b, Wounded Angel.

Perf. 13¼x13¾
1999, Sept. 24		Litho.	
B263	Booklet pane of 2	4.00	3.00
a.-b.	SP137 3.50m +50p any single	2.00	1.50
	Complete booklet, #B263	4.00	

Surtax for philately.

Cow and Calf — SP138

Perf. 13¾x13¼
2000, Mar. 15		Litho.	
B264	SP138 3.50m +70p Bull, vert.	2.00	1.50

Perf. 13¼x13¾
| B265 | SP138 4.80m +80p shown | 3.00 | 2.50 |

Surtax for Finnish Red Cross.

Post Horn — SP139

2010, May 4	Litho.	Perf. 14½x14¼	
B266	SP139 1 +5c multi	3.00	1.20

No. B266 had a franking value of 80c on day of issue. Surtax for construction of Finland's first solar energy plant.

No. 769 Surcharged in Silver and Black

Methods and Perfs. As Before

2017, May 24			
B267	A418 (€1.30) on 5m + (€28.70) booklet pane of 1 + 2 labels	60.00	60.00
	Complete booklet, #B267	60.00	

No. B267 had a franking value of €1.30. The surtax was for Finlandia 2017 International Philatelic Exhibition, as it does not appear that the purchase of the booklet for €30 included the price of admission to the exhibition, as was the case with No. 789 in 1988. The booklet was sold in a numbered envelope that included a postcard.

AIR POST STAMPS

No. 178 Overprinted in Red

1930, Sept. 24	Unwmk.	Perf. 14	
C1	A28 10m gray lilac	100.00	220.00
a.	1830 for 1930	1,800.	8,500.

Overprinted expressly for use on mail carried in "Graf Zeppelin" on return flight from Finland to Germany on Sept. 24, 1930, after which trip the stamps ceased to be valid for postage. Forgeries are almost always on No. 205, rather than No. 178.

Catalogue values for unused stamps in this section, from this point to the end of the section, are for Never Hinged items.

Douglas DC-2 — AP1

1944		Engr.	
C2	AP1 3.50m dark brown	.50	1.00

Air Transport Service anniv., 1923-43.

Douglas DC-6 Over Winter Landscape — AP2

1950, Feb. 13			
C3	AP2 300m blue	18.00	7.50

Available also for ordinary postage.

Redrawn

1958, Jan. 20		Perf. 11½	
C4	AP2 300(m) blue	30.00	1.00

On No. C4 "mk" is omitted.
See Nos. C9-C9a.

Convair 440 over Lakes — AP3

1958, Oct. 31	Unwmk.	Perf. 11½	
C5	AP3 34m blue	1.80	.90

No. C5 Surcharged

1959, Apr. 5			
C6	AP3 45m on 34m blue	2.50	2.25

C7   C8

1959, Nov. 2			
C7	AP3 45m blue	2.50	1.50

1963, Feb. 15			
C8	AP3 45p blue	1.80	.40

On No. C7 the denomination is "45." On No. C8 it is "0.45."

DC-6 Type, Comma After "3" — AP5

Type I — 16 lines in numeral "0"
Type II — 13 lines in numeral "0"

1963, Oct. 10			
C9	AP5 3m blue, Type II ('73)	2.50	.50
a.	Type I	25.00	.40

Convair Type of 1958

1970, July 15			
C10	AP3 57p ultra	2.50	1.25

MILITARY STAMPS

Catalogue values for unused stamps in this section are for Never Hinged items.

M1

1941, Nov. 1	Unwmk.	Typo.	Imperf.	
M1	M1 (4m) blk, dk org		.40	.70

#M1 has simulated roulette printed in black.

Type of 1930-46 Overprinted in Black

1943, Oct. 16		Perf. 14	
M2	A26 2m deep orange	.25	.70
M3	A26 3½m greenish blue	.25	.70

Post Horn and Sword — M2

1943, July 1		Size: 29½x19½mm	
M4	M2 (2m) green	.50	.50
M5	M2 (3m) rose violet	.70	.50

1944, Feb. 16		Size: 20x16mm	
M6	M2 (2m) green	.50	.40
M7	M2 (3m) rose violet	.40	.40

Post Horns and Arms of Finland — M3

1963, Sept. 26	Litho.	Perf. 14	
M8	M3 violet blue	80.00	80.00

Used during maneuvers Sept. 30-Oct. 5, 1963. Valid from Sept. 26.

No. M8 Overprinted "1983"

1983, Apr. 20			
M9	M3 violet blue	180.00	100.00

Used during maneuvers Apr. 24-30.

PARCEL POST STAMPS

PP1

Wmk. Rose & Triangles Multiple
Rouletted 6 on 2 or 3 Sides

1949-50			Typo.	
Q1	PP1	1m brt grn & blk	.50	3.50
Q2	PP1	5m red & blk	7.50	17.50
Q3	PP1	20m org & blk	15.00	30.00
Q4	PP1	50m bl & blk ('50)	6.00	12.00
Q5	PP1	100m brn & blk ('50)	6.00	12.00
	Nos. Q1-Q5 (5)		35.00	75.00
	Set, never hinged		75.00	

Catalogue values for unused stamps in this section, from this point to the end of the section, are for Never Hinged items.

Mail Bus — PP2

1952-58		Unwmk.	Engr.	Perf. 14	
Q6	PP2	5m car rose		3.00	3.00
Q7	PP2	20m orange		10.00	5.50
Q8	PP2	50m blue ('54)		15.00	12.00
Q9	PP2	100m brn ('58)		25.00	20.00
	Nos. Q6-Q9 (4)			53.00	40.50

Mail Bus — PP3

FINLAND — ALAND ISLANDS

1963   *Perf. 12*

Q10	PP3	5p red & blk	2.00	2.50
Q11	PP3	20p org & blk	2.00	2.50
Q12	PP3	50p blue & blk	3.00	3.00
Q13	PP3	1m brn & blk	1.50	1.50
	Nos. Q10-Q13 (4)		8.50	9.50

Nos. Q1-Q13 were issued only in booklets: panes of 6 for Nos. Q1-Q5, 10 for Nos. Q6-Q9 and 5 for Nos. Q10-Q13.

Used values are for regular postal or mail-bus cancels. Pen strokes, cutting or other cancels sell for half as much.

1981 SISU Bus — PP4

1981, Dec. 7   *Photo. & Engr.*   *Perf. 12 Horiz.*

Q14	PP4	50p dk bl & blk	1.00	4.50
Q15	PP4	1m dk brn & blk	1.50	4.50
Q16	PP4	5m grn & blk	3.50	8.00
Q17	PP4	10m red & blk	5.50	18.00
	Nos. Q14-Q17 (4)		11.50	35.00

Parcel post stamps invalid after Jan. 9, 1985.

ALAND ISLANDS

LOCATION — A group of 6,554 islands at the mouth of the Gulf of Bothnia, between Finland and Sweden.
GOVT. — Province of Finland
AREA — 590 sq. mi.
POP. — 28,354 (2020)
CAPITAL — Mariehamn

The province of Aland was awarded to Finland in 1921 by the League of Nations. The Swedish language is spoken and the province has a considerable amount of self-determination.

> Catalogue values for unused stamps in this country are for Never Hinged items.
> Most Aland Island issues exist favor canceled, and used values are for such cancellations. Postally used examples are worth 30 to 40% more than the values shown.

Gaff-rigged Sloop A1

Aland Flag A2

Midsummer Pole — A3

Landscapes A4

Map of Scandinavia A5

Seal of St. Olaf and Aland Province, 1326 — A6

Artifacts — A7

Sea Birds — A8

Gothic Tower, Jomala Church, 12th Cent. — A9

Mariehamn Town Hall, Designed by Architect Lars Sonck — A9a

Designs: 1.50m, Statue of Frans Petter von Knorring, vicar from 1834 to 1875, and St. Michael's Church, Finstrom, 12th cent. 1.60m, Burial site, clay hands. 1.70m, Somateria mollissima. 2.20m, Bronze Staff of Finby, apostolic decoration. 2.30m, Aythya fuligula. 5m, Outer Aland Archipelago. 8m, Farm and windmill. 12m, Melantha fusca. 20m, Ancient court site, contemporary monument.

1984-90   *Engr.*   *Unwmk.*   *Perf. 12*

1	A1	10p magenta	.25	.25
2	A1	20p brown olive	.25	.25
3	A1	50p bright green	.25	.25
4	A1	1.10m deep blue	.40	.40
5	A1	1.20m black	.40	.40
6	A1	1.30m dark green	.40	.50

Litho.   *Perf. 14, 13x14 (#8)*

7	A2	1.40m multi	.40	.40
8	A9	1.40m multi	1.00	1.20
9	A3	1.50m multi, I	1.00	1.00
9A	A3	1.50m multi, II	.70	.90
10	A9	1.50m multi	1.00	1.25

Perf. 13, 14 (#13)

11	A7	1.60m multi, vert.	1.00	1.00
12	A8	1.70m multi	4.00	6.00
13	A9a	1.90m multi	.80	1.00
14	A4	2m multi	1.00	1.00
15	A7	2.20m multi, vert.	1.00	.80
16	A8	2.30m multi	2.00	2.00
17	A5	3m multi	.90	.80
18	A4	5m multi, horiz.	1.50	1.40
19	A4	8m multi, horiz.	2.50	2.50

Litho. & Engr.

20	A6	10m multi	3.00	2.50

Litho.

21	A8	12m multi	4.00	4.00
22	A7	20m multi	6.00	6.00
	Nos. 1-22 (23)		33.75	35.80

On No. 9A (type II) "Aland" is 10½mm long, figure support is 2mm wide, pole supports are thinner, diagonal black highlighting lines in pole greenery and horizontal black line on support under the man removed.

Issued: Nos. 2-4, 7, 17, 20, 3/1/84; Nos. 1, 5, 6, 9, 1/2/85; Nos. 14, 18-19, 9/16/85; Nos. 11, 15, 22, 4/4/86; Nos. 12, 16, 21, 1/2/87; No. 8, 8/26/88; No. 13, 1/2/89; No. 10, 9/4/89; No. 9A, 5/21/90.

See Nos. 39-42, 87-92, 178-179, 195-196.

A10

Bark Pommern and car ferries, Mariehamn West Harbor

1984, Mar. 1   *Litho.*   *Perf. 14*

23	A10	2m multicolored	1.00	1.20

A11

1986, Jan. 2   *Litho.*   *Perf. 14*

24	A11	1.60m multicolored	1.00	1.20

1986 Nordic Orienteering Championships, Aug. 30-31.

Onningeby Artists' Colony, Cent. — A12

Design: Pallette, pen and ink drawing of Onningeby landscape, 1891, by Victor Westerholm (1860-1919), founder.

1986, Sept. 1   *Litho.*

25	A12	3.70m multicolored	1.00	1.50

Mariehamn Volunteer Fire Brigade, Cent. — A13

1987, Apr. 27   *Litho.*   *Perf. 14*

26	A13	7m multicolored	5.00	7.00

Farjsund Bridge, 50th Anniv., Rebuilt in 1980 — A14

1987, Apr. 27   *Engr.*   *Perf. 13x13½*

27	A14	1m greenish black	.40	.40

Municipal Meeting, Finstrom, 1917 — A15

1987, Aug. 20   *Litho.*   *Perf. 14*

28	A15	1.70m multicolored	1.00	1.20

Movement for reunification with Sweden, 70th anniv.

Loading of Mail Barrels on Sailboat, Post Office, Eckero — A16

1988, Jan. 4   *Litho.*   *Perf. 14*

29	A16	1.80m multicolored	1.00	1.20

Postal Service, 350th anniv. From Feb. I to May 31, Alanders were entitled to buy 20 stamps for 28m with a discount coupon.

New Aland Farm School, Horse-Drawn Plow — A17

1988, Mar. 29   *Litho.*   *Perf. 14*

30	A17	2.20m multicolored	1.20	1.50

Haga Farm School, cent.; Aland Farm School, 75th anniv.; 50th anniv. of experimental farming on Aland.

Sailing Ships — A18

Designs: 1.80m, Albanus, 1904, vert. 2.40m, Ingrid, c. 1900. 11m, Pamir, c. 1900.

1988, June 4   *Litho.*   *Perf. 13*

31	A18	1.80m multi	1.00	1.50
32	A18	2.40m multi	2.00	2.50
33	A18	11m multi	5.00	7.00
	Nos. 31-33 (3)		8.00	11.00

Type of 1988 and

Orchids A19   Fish A20

Handicrafts A21

Fresco, St. Anna's Church of Kumlinge A22

Mammals — A23

Geological Formations A24   A25

Designs: 10p, Boulder field, Geta. No. 35, Dactylorhiza sambucina. No. 36, Clupea harengus membras. No. 37, Erinaceus europauus. No. 38, Drumlin, Finstrom. 1.70m, St. Andrew Church, Lumparland. No. 40, Vardo Church. No. 41, Hammarland Church. No. 42, Sottunga Church. No. 43, Esox lucius. No. 45, Diabase dike, Sottunga, Basskar. 2.10m, Sciurus vulgaris. 2.50m, Cephalanthera longifolia. No. 48, Platichthys flesus. No. 49, Pillow lava, Kumlinge, western Varpskar. No. 50, Capreolus capreolus. No. 51, Rouche Moutonne, Roda Kon, Lumparn. 6m, Folded gneiss, Sottunga, Gloskar. 13m, Tapestry, 1793. 14m, Cypripedium calceolus.

Perf. 13, 14 (Nos. 39-42, 44, 53), 15x14½ (10p, Nos. 38, 45, 49, 51-52)

1989-94   *Litho.*

34	A25	10p multicolored	.25	.25
35	A19	1.50m multicolored	1.00	1.50
36	A23	1.50m multicolored	1.00	1.20
37	A23	1.60m multicolored	1.00	1.20
38	A25	1.60m multicolored	.60	.70
39	A9	1.70m multicolored	1.00	1.20
40	A9	1.80m multicolored	1.00	1.00
41	A9	1.80m multicolored	1.00	1.25
42	A9	1.80m multicolored	1.00	1.25
43	A20	2m multicolored	1.00	1.00
44	A22	2m multicolored	.70	1.00
45	A24	2m multicolored	.70	.60
46	A23	2.10m multicolored	1.00	1.20
47	A19	2.50m multicolored	1.50	1.50
48	A20	2.70m multicolored	1.00	1.20
49	A24	2.70m multicolored	.90	.80
50	A23	2.90m multicolored	1.20	1.40
51	A25	2.90m multicolored	1.00	1.00
52	A24	6m multicolored	1.50	2.00
53	A21	13m multicolored	3.00	4.00
54	A19	14m multicolored	7.00	8.00
	Nos. 34-54 (21)		28.35	33.45

Issued: 2.50m, 14m, No. 35, 4/10/89; 2.70m, No. 36, 43, 3/1/90; 13m, 4/19/90; 1.70m, No. 44, 9/10/90; 1.60m, 2.10m, No. 50, 3/3/91; No. 40, 9/9/91; No. 41 10/5/92; Nos. 45, 49, 52, 9/3/93; No. 42, 10/8/93; 10p, Nos. 38, 51, 2/1/94.

See Nos. 96, 102, 105.

Educational System of the Province, 350th Anniv. — A33

1989, May 31   *Litho.*   *Perf. 14*

57	A33	1.90m multicolored	1.00	1.20

Souvenir Sheet

1991 Aland Island Games A34

598   FINLAND — ALAND ISLANDS

a, Volleyball. b, Shooting. c, Soccer. d, Running.

1991, Apr. 5   Litho.   *Perf. 13x12½*
58   A34   2.10m Sheet of 4, #a.-d.   4.00   4.00

Autonomy of Aland, 70th Anniv. — A35

1991, June 4   *Perf. 13*
59   A35   16m multicolored   4.00   5.00

Kayaking — A36

1991, June 4   *Perf. 14*
60   A36   2.10m shown   .70   1.00
61   A36   2.90m Cycling   1.00   1.25

Rev. Frans Peter Von Knorring (1792-1875), Educator — A37

Cape Horn Congress, Mariehamn, June 8-11 — A38

1992, Mar. 2   Litho.   *Perf. 13*
62   A37   2 multicolored   1.20   1.10

Litho. & Engr.   *Perf. 13½x14*
63   A38   1 multicolored   1.00   1.40

No. 62 sold for 1.60m, No. 63 for 2.10m.

On stamps bearing the "denominations" "1" or "2," the number represents the class of mail.

Lighthouses — A39

1992, May 8   Litho.   *Perf. 13*
Booklet Stamps
64   A39   2.10m Ranno   5.00   5.00
65   A39   2.10m Salskar   5.00   5.00
66   A39   2.10m Lagskar   5.00   5.00
67   A39   2.10m Market   5.00   5.00
   a.   Booklet pane of 4, #64-67   20.00   20.00

First Aland Provincial Parliament, 70th Anniv. — A40

1992, June 8   Litho.   *Perf. 13*
68   A40   3.40m multicolored   1.20   1.40

Joel Pettersson (1892-1937), Painter — A41

Designs: 2.90m, Landscape from Lemland. 16m, Self-Portrait.

1992, June 8
69   A41   2.90m multicolored   1.00   1.40
70   A41   16m multicolored   5.50   5.50

Arms of Aland — A42

1993, Mar. 1   Litho.   *Perf. 14*
71   A42   1.60m gray, sepia & blue   .80   1.00

Autonomy Act, Jan. 1.

Souvenir Sheet

Autonomous Postal Administration — A43

Designs: a, Inscriptions from old letter canceled in Kastelholm, vert. b, Mariehamn post office. c, Ferry, mail truck. d, New post office emblem, vert.

Perf. 12½x13, 14 (#b.-c.)
1993, Mar. 1   Litho., Engr. (#b.-c.)
72   A43   1.90m Sheet of 4, #a.-d.   3.25   4.00

Fiddler, Jan Karlsgarden Museum — A44

2.30m, Boat Shed, Jan Karlsgarden Museum.

Perf. 13x12½, 12½x13
1993, May 7   Litho.
73   A44   2m multicolored   .80   1.00
74   A44   2.30m multi, horiz.   .80   1.00

Folk Dresses — A45

Clothing from: 1.90m, Saltvik. 3.50m, Brando, Eckero, Mariehamn. 17m, Finstrom.

1993, June 1   *Perf. 12½*
75   A45   1.90m multicolored   1.00   1.20
76   A45   3.50m multicolored   1.20   1.50
77   A45   17m multicolored   5.00   6.50
   Nos. 75-77 (3)   7.20   9.20

Butterflies — A46

No. 78, Melitaea cinxia. No. 79, Quercusia quercus. No. 80, Parnassius mnemosyne. No. 81, Hesperia comma.

Perf. 14 on 3 Sides
1994, Mar. 1   Litho.
Booklet Stamps
78   A46   2.30m multicolored   1.00   1.00
79   A46   2.30m multicolored   1.00   1.00
80   A46   2.30m multicolored   1.00   1.00
81   A46   2.30m multicolored   1.00   1.00
   a.   Booklet pane, 2 each #78-81   8.00
   Nos. 78-81 (4)   4.00   4.00

A47

Europa, Inventions and Discoveries: 2.30m, Diagram showing transmission of von Willebrand's Disease, discovered by E. A. von Willebrand. 2.90m, Purification of heparin, by Erik Jorpes.

1994, May 5   Litho.   *Perf. 13*
82   A47   2.30m multicolored   2.00   2.00
83   A47   2.90m multicolored   2.00   2.00

Types of 1989-93 and

Ice Age Survivors A48

Fossils A49

Sea Birds — A50

Bronze Age — A51

Stone Age — A52

Ships — A53

Lichens A54

Primula Veris A55

30p, Saduria entomon, mysis relicta. 40p, Trilobita asaphus. 1.80m, Sterna paradisaea. No. 87, Church of Mariehamn. No. 88, Church of Eckerö. No. 89, St. Bridget's Church, Lemland. No. 90, Church of St. John the Baptist, Sund. No. 91, St. George Church, Geta. No. 92, Church of Brando. No. 93, Bronze sword, bronze dagger. No. 94, Ship tumulus grave. No. 95, Larus canus. 2.30m, Pitcher of Kallskar. No. 97, Pottery. No. 98, Myoxocephalus quadricornis. 2.60m, Larus marinus. No. 100, Stone tools. No. 101, SS Thornbury. 3.40m, Erratic boulders. 3.50m, SS Osmo. 4.30m, Phoca hispida. 7m, Potholes. 9m, Gastropoda euomophalus. 18m, Settlement. 2, Hypogmnia physodes. 1, Xanthoria parietina.

Perf. 13 (A48, A50, A52, A54), 15x14½ (No. 89), 14½x15 (Nos. 101-103, 105), 14½ (40p, Nos. 88, 93-94, 96), 14 (Nos. 87, 90-92), 15 (No. 106)
1994-2000   Engr.
84   A48   30p multi   .25   .25
85   A49   40p multi   .25   .40
86   A50   1.80m multi   .60   .70
87   A9   1.90m multi   1.00   1.00
88   A9   1.90m multi   1.00   1.20
89   A9   1.90m multi   1.00   1.00
90   A9   2m multi   1.00   1.00
91   A9   2m multi   1.00   1.00
92   A9   2m multi   1.00   .80
93   A51   2m multi   .70   .90
94   A51   2.20m multi, vert.   .80   1.00
95   A50   2.20m multi, vert.   .70   .70
96   A24   2.30m multi   .70   .80
97   A52   2.40m vio brn, vert.   1.20   1.50
98   A48   2.40m multi   1.00   .90
99   A50   2.60m multi   .90   .90
100   A52   2.80m bluish blk, vert.   1.00   1.20
101   A53   2.80m multi   1.00   1.20
102   A24   3.40m multi, horiz.   1.10   1.20
103   A53   3.50m multi   1.40   1.50
104   A48   4.30m multi   1.40   1.40
105   A24   7m multi, horiz.   2.20   2.20
106   A49   9m multi   2.70   3.00
107   A52   18m dk grn   6.00   6.00

Perf. 13
107A   A54   2 multi   1.50   1.20
107B   A54   1 multi   2.00   1.40

Self-Adhesive
Serpentine Die Cut Perf. 10
108   A55   2.40m multi   .90   .90
   Nos. 84-108 (27)   34.30   35.25

No. 108 was issued in sheets of 10.
Nos. 107A-107B sold for 2m and 2.40m, respectively, on day of issue.
Issued: Nos. 97, 100, 18m, 8/16/94; No. 90, 10/7/94; 2.30m, 3.40m, 7m, 1/2/95; No. 91, 9/15/95; 40p, No. 92, 9m, 10/9/96; 30p, No. 98, 4.30m, 2/3/97; Nos. 101, 103, 9/8/97; No. 87, 10/9/97; No. 88, 10/9/98; Nos. 93-94, 2/1/99; No. 108, 4/28/99; Nos. 107A-107B, 9/25/99; No. 89, 10/8/99; 1.80m, No. 95, 2.60m, 1/3/00.

Cargo Vessels — A58

Perf. 14 on 3 Sides
1995, Mar. 1   Litho.
Booklet Stamps
109   A58   2.30m Skuta   .80   .70
110   A58   2.30m Sump   .80   .70
111   A58   2.30m Storbat   .80   .70
112   A58   2.30m Jakt   .80   .70
   a.   Booklet pane, 2 each #109-112   8.00   11.00
       Complete booklet, #112a   8.00
   Nos. 109-112 (4)   3.20   2.80

Entry into European Union — A59

1995, Mar. 1   Litho.   *Perf. 13x14*
113   A59   2.90m multicolored   1.00   1.40

Europa — A60

Design: 2.90m, Dove, island in sea.

1995, May 5   Litho.   *Perf. 13x14*
114   A60   2.80m shown   1.20   1.50
115   A60   2.90m multicolored   1.20   1.50

Tourism — A61

1995, May 12
116   A61   2 Golf   1.50   1.50
117   A61   1 Fishing   2.00   1.00

Nos. 116-117 sold for value 2m and 2.30m, respectively.

Optimist Dinghy World Championships A62

1995, June 2   Litho.   *Perf. 13½x14*
118   A62   3.40m multicolored   1.10   1.50

St. Olaf (995?-1030), Patron Saint of Aland — A63

Litho. & Engr.
1995, Sept. 15   *Perf. 13½x13*
119   A63   4.30m multicolored   1.50   1.70
See Faroe Islands No. 289

A64

Greeting Stamps (stylized designs): No. 120, Fish with natl. flag, "Hälsningar fran

FINLAND — ALAND ISLANDS

Aland." No. 121, Yellow bird with flower, "Grattis."

1996, Feb. 14   Litho.   **Perf. 13x14**
| 120 | A64 | 1 multicolored | 2.00 | 1.00 |
| 121 | A64 | 1 multicolored | 2.00 | .80 |

Nos. 120-121 had a face value of 2.30m on day of issue.

A65

Eagle owl (bubo bubo): No. 122, Landing on tree branch over lake. No. 123, Perched on branch over lake. No. 124, Male, darker feathers. No. 125, Female, lighter feathers.

Booklet Stamps
1996, Mar. 1   **Perf. 14 on 3 Sides**
122	A65	2.40m multicolored	.80	1.00
123	A65	2.40m multicolored	.80	1.00
124	A65	2.40m multicolored	.80	1.00
125	A65	2.40m multicolored	.80	1.00
a.	Booklet pane, 2 ea #122-125	8.00	10.00
	Complete booklet, No. 125a	8.00	
	Nos. 122-125 (4)	3.20	4.00

World Wildlife Fund.

Famous Women — A66

Europa: 2.80m, Sally Salminen (1906-76), writer. 2.90m, Fanny Sundström (1883-1944), politician.

1996, May 6   Litho.   **Perf. 14x13**
| 126 | A66 | 2.80m multicolored | 1.00 | 1.50 |
| 127 | A66 | 2.90m multicolored | 1.00 | 1.50 |

A67

1996, June 7   Litho.   **Perf. 13½x14**
| 128 | A67 | 2.40m multicolored | .80 | 1.00 |

Aland '96 Song and Music Festival.

A68

"Haircut," by Karl Emanuel Jansson (1846-74).

1996, June 7   **Perf. 13**
| 129 | A68 | 18m multicolored | 4.50 | 5.00 |

Spring Flowers — A69

Designs: No. 130, Tussilago farfara. No. 131, Hepatica nobilis. No. 132, Anemone nemorosa. No. 133, Anemone ranunculoides.

1997, Feb. 3   Litho.   **Perf. 14**
Booklet Stamps
130	A69	2.40m multicolored	.80	1.00
131	A69	2.40m multicolored	.80	1.00
132	A69	2.40m multicolored	.80	1.00
133	A69	2.40m multicolored	.80	1.00
a.	Booklet pane, 2 each #130-133	8.00	10.00
	Complete booklet, #133a	8.00	

A70

1997, May 3   Litho.   **Perf. 14x13½**
| 134 | A70 | 3.40m multicolored | 1.00 | 1.00 |

1st Floorball World Championships, Aland.

Europa — A71

Devil's Dance with Clergyman's Wife.

1997, May 9   **Perf. 13x14**
| 135 | A71 | 2.90m multicolored | 1.40 | 1.00 |

Kalmar Union, 600th Anniv. — A72

Design: Kastelholm Castle, arms of Lord High Chancellor Bo Jonsson Grip.

1997, May 30   Litho.   **Perf. 14x13**
| 136 | A72 | 2.40m multicolored | .90 | 1.10 |

Souvenir Sheet

Autonomy, 75th Anniv. — A73

1997, June 9   **Perf. 13**
| 137 | A73 | 20m multicolored | 7.50 | 8.00 |

No. 137 contains a holographic image. Soaking in water may affect the hologram.

Horticulture — A74

1998, Feb. 2   Litho.   **Perf. 14½x15**
| 138 | A74 | 2m Apples | .60 | .90 |
| 139 | A74 | 2.40m Cucumbers | 1.00 | 1.00 |

Youth Activities — A75

No. 140, Riding moped. No. 141, Computer. No. 142, Listening to music. No. 143, Aerobics.

1998, Mar. 28   **Perf. 14 on 3 Sides**
Booklet Stamps
140	A75	2.40m multicolored	.80	1.00
141	A75	2.40m multicolored	.80	1.00
142	A75	2.40m multicolored	.80	1.00
143	A75	2.40m multicolored	.80	1.00
a.	Booklet pane, 2 each #140-143	7.50	10.00
	Complete booklet, #143a	8.00	

Midsummer Celebration in Aland — A76

1998, Apr. 27   Litho.   **Perf. 14**
| 144 | A76 | 4.20m multicolored | 1.50 | 1.50 |

Europa.

Passenger Ferry — A77

1998, May 8   **Perf. 14½**
| 145 | A77 | 2.40m multicolored | 1.00 | 1.20 |

Intl. Year of the Ocean — A78

1998, May 8
| 146 | A78 | 6.30m multicolored | 1.50 | 2.00 |

ATP Senior Tour of Champions Tennis Tournament, Mariehamn — A79

Serpentine Die Cut
1998, June 25   Litho.
Self-Adhesive
| 147 | A79 | 2.40m multicolored | .80 | .90 |

Issued in sheets of 10.

Scouting — A80

1998, Aug. 1   **Perf. 14**
| 148 | A80 | 2.80m multicolored | 1.00 | 1.20 |

Foyers — A81

Homesteads: 1.60m, Seffers. 2m, Labbas. 2.90m, Abras.

1998, Sept. 11   Litho.   **Perf. 14½**
149	A81	1.60m multicolored	.70	1.00
150	A81	2m multicolored	.70	1.00
151	A81	2.90m multicolored	1.00	1.20
	Nos. 149-151 (3)	2.40	3.20

18th Century Furniture Ornamentation A82

Perf. 14 on 3 Sides
1999, Feb. 1   Litho.
Booklet Stamps
152	A82	2.40m Wardrobe	.80	1.00
153	A82	2.40m Distaff	.80	1.00
154	A82	2.40m Chest	.80	1.00
155	A82	2.40m Spinning wheel	.80	1.00
a.	Booklet pane, 2 each #152-155	7.50	
	Complete booklet, #155a	8.00	

Passage of Cape Horn by Grain Ships Pamir & Passat, 50th Anniv. — A83

1999, Mar. 19   Litho.   **Perf. 14½**
| 156 | A83 | 3.40m multicolored | 1.20 | 1.20 |

Beginning with No. 157, denominations are indicated on many stamps in both Markkas and Euros. The value shown is in Markkas.

Nature Reserve, Kökar — A84

1999, Apr. 28   Litho.   **Perf. 13**
| 157 | A84 | 2.90m multicolored | 1.25 | 1.20 |

Europa.

Match Sailboat Racing — A85

1999, Aug. 5   Litho.   **Perf. 14½x15**
| 158 | A85 | 2.70m multicolored | 1.20 | 1.20 |

UPU, 125th Anniv. — A86

1999, Sept. 25
| 159 | A86 | 2.90m multicolored | 1.20 | 1.20 |

Finnish Cross-Country Championships, Mariehamn — A87

1999, Oct. 9   Litho.   **Perf. 14¾x14½**
| 160 | A87 | 3.50m multicolored | 1.00 | 1.20 |

Souvenir Sheet

Peace Symbol, Aland Flag A88

Background colors: a, Yellow. b, Red. c, Blue. d, White.

Litho. & Embossed
2000, Jan. 3   **Perf. 13**
| 161 | A88 | 3.40m Sheet of 4, #a.-d. | 4.50 | 4.75 |

Elk — A89

Elk in: No. 162, Spring. No. 163, Summer. No. 164, Autumn. No. 165, Winter.

Perf. 11¾ on 3 sides
2000, Mar. 1   Litho.
Booklet Stamps
162	A89	2.60m multicolored	.90	1.00
163	A89	2.60m multicolored	.90	1.00
164	A89	2.60m multicolored	.90	1.00
165	A89	2.60m multicolored	.90	1.00
a.	Block of 4, #162-165	3.60	4.00
b.	Booklet pane, 2 #165a	6.75	10.50
	Complete booklet, #165b	7.25	

Europa, 2000
Common Design Type
2000, May 9   **Perf. 13**
| 166 | CD17 | 3m multicolored | 1.10 | 1.20 |

A90

600   FINLAND — ALAND ISLANDS

Self-Adhesive Coil Stamp
2000, June 9   Die Cut Perf. 13x13¼
167   A90   2.60m multicolored   .90   1.00
Gymnastics Festival, Mariehamn.

2000, July 21   Litho.   Perf. 13½x13¼
168   A91   3.40m multicolored   1.00   1.20
Cutty Sark Tall Ships race to Mariehamn.

Vikings From Aland — A92

2000, July 28
169   A92   4.50m multicolored   1.00   1.20
Recreation of Viking market, Saltvik.

Architecture by Hilda Hongell (1867-1952) — A93

2000, Aug. 25   Perf. 13¼x13¾
170   A93   3.80m shown   1.00   1.00
171   A93   10m House, diff.   2.50   3.00

Christianity, 2000th Anniv. — A94

2000, Oct. 9   Perf. 13
172   A94   3m multicolored   1.00   1.20

Church Type of 1984-90 and

Swamp Plants — A95

Swamp plants: 1.90m, Equisetum fluviatile. 2.80m, Lycopodium annotinum. 3.50m, Polypodium vulgare.
Churches: No. 179, Föglö Church, Föglö. 2m, Kökar Church, Kökar.

Perf. 13x13¼, 13 (#178)
2000-01   Litho.
177   A95   1.90m multicolored   .70   .80
178   A9   2m multicolored   .80   .80
179   A9   2m multicolored   .70   .80
180   A95   2.80m multicolored   .90   1.00
182   A95   3.50m multicolored   1.20   1.30
     Nos. 177-182 (5)   4.30   4.70

These stamps are part of an ongoing definitive set. Numbers have been reserved for additional stamps.
Issued: 2m, 10/9; 1.90m, 2.80m, 3.50m, 1/2/01; No. 179, 10/9/01.

Worldwide Fund for Nature (WWF) A100

Polysticta stelleri: a, Pair in flight. b, Pair on rock. c, Pair in water. d, Male in water.

Perf. 13¼ on 3 sides
2001, Jan. 2   Litho.
Booklet Stamps
185   A100   Block of 4   3.60   3.60
   a.-d.   2.70m any single   .90   .90
   e.   Booklet pane, 2 #185   7.00   11.00
     Booklet, #185e   8.00

Valentine's Day — A101

2001, Feb. 14   Perf. 14½x14¾
186   A101   3.20m multicolored   1.00   1.20

Europa — A102

2001, May 9   Litho.   Perf. 14½x14¾
187   A102   3.20m multi   1.00   1.20

Windmills — A103

Windmill types: 3m, Archipelago. 7m, Timbered, horiz. 20m, Nest, horiz.

Perf. 13¾x14¼, 14¼x13¾
2001, June 8
188-190   A103   Set of 3   7.50   7.50

Puppies — A104

Designs: 2, Golden retriever. 1, Wire-haired dachshund.

2001, Sept. 3   Perf. 13¼
191-192   A104   Set of 2   5.50   2.00
Nos. 191-192 sold for 2.30m and 2.70m respectively on day of issue.

100 Cents = 1 Euro (€)
Church Type of 1998 with Euro Denominations and

Fauna — A105

Post Terminal A106

Mushrooms — A107

Designs: 5c, Coronella austriaca. 10c, Chanterelle mushroom. 35c, Saltviks Church. 40c, Kumlinge Church. 50c, King Bolete mushroom. 70c, Triturus cristatus. €1, Post Terminal. €2.50, Parasol mushroom.

Perf. 12½, 13 (#193, 196), 13¼ (#198), 14¾x14 (#195)
2002-03   Litho.
193   A105   5c multi   .25   .25
194   A107   10c multi   .25   .25
195   A9   35c multi   .70   .80
196   A9   40c multi   .80   .80
197   A105   50c multi   1.00   1.00
198   A105   70c multi   1.20   1.20
199   A106   €1 multi   2.00   2.20
200   A107   €2.50 multi   4.50   4.00
     Nos. 193-200 (8)   10.70   10.50

Issue dates: 5c, 70c, 1/2/02; €1, 2/28/02; 35c, 10/9/02; 10c, 50c, €2.50, 1/2/03. No. 196, 10/9/03.

Introduction of the Euro — A108

2002, Jan. 2   Litho.   Perf. 12½
201   A108   60c multi   1.20   1.20

St. Canute's Day — A109

2002, Jan. 2
202   A109   €2 multi   4.00   3.50

Cuisine A110

Flavors and: a, Gravlax, boiled potatoes. b, Fried herring, beets, mashed potatoes. c, Black bread, cheese, butter. d, Pancake with prune sauce and whipped cream, coffee.

Perf. 13½x13¼ on 3 Sides
2002, Feb. 28   Litho.
203   A110   Block of 4   12.00   4.00
   a.-d.   1 Any single   3.00   1.00
   e.   Booklet pane, 2 #203   12.00
     Booklet, #203e   24.00

Nos. 203a-203d each sold for 55c on day of issue.

Europa — A111

2002, May 3   Perf. 13¼
204   A111   40c multi   .80   .80

Radar II, Sculpture by Stefan Lindfors — A112

2002, May 3   Perf. 13
205   A112   €3 multi   6.00   5.00

"My Aland," by Lill Lindfors — A113

2002, Aug. 12   Litho.   Perf. 13¼
206   A113   90c multi   2.00   1.50

Iron Age Artifacts — A114

Designs: No. 207, 2, Buckle found in Persby. No. 208, 1, Ornamental pin found in Syllöda.

2002, Sept. 2   Perf. 13x13¼
207-208   A114   Set of 2   5.50   2.00
Nos. 207-208 sold for 45c and 55c respectively on day of issue.

Janne Holmén, Marathon Gold Medalist in European Track and Field Championships A115

2002, Nov. 1   Perf. 12½
209   A115   1 multi   3.00   1.20
Sold for 55c on day of issue.

House Cats — A116

2003, Mar. 14   Litho.   Perf. 13¼
210   A116   2 Tovis   2.50   1.00
211   A116   1 Randi, horiz.   3.00   1.10

Nos. 210-211 sold for 45c and 55c respectively on day of issue.

Landscape in Summer, by Elin Danielson-Gambogi (1861-1919) — A117

No. 212: a, Woman at fence. b, Tree without leaves. c, Sun. d, Boat.

2003, Mar. 28   Perf. 14 Vert.
Booklet Stamps
212   A117   Horiz. strip of 4   12.00   4.75
   a.-d.   1 Any single   3.00   1.20
   e.   Booklet pane, 2 #212   12.50   12.50
     Complete booklet, #212e   24.00

Nos. 212a-212d each sold for 55c on day of issue.

Europa — A118

2003, May 9   Perf. 13¼
213   A118   45c multi   1.00   1.00

Museum Ship "Pommern," Cent. — A119

2003, June 6   Die Cut Perf. 9¼x9½
Booklet Stamp
Self-Adhesive
214   A119   55c multi   1.20   1.20
   a.   Booklet pane of 4   5.00   5.00
     Complete booklet, 2 #214a   9.75

FINLAND — ALAND ISLANDS

Mark and Stephen Levengood on Beach — A120

2003, June 18   *Perf. 12½*
215   A120   55c multi   1.00   1.00

Aland Folk Music Association, 50th Anniv. — A121

2003, Aug. 1   *Perf. 14¼*
216   A121   €1.10 buff & black   2.00   1.50

St. Lucia's Day Celebrations A122

2003, Oct. 9   Litho.   *Perf. 12½*
217   A122   60c multi   1.20   1.00

Mammals — A123

Designs: 20c, Mustela erminea. 60c, Vulpes vulpes. €3, Martes martes.

2004, Feb. 2   Litho.   *Perf. 14½x14¼*
218   A123   20c multi   .40   .40
219   A123   60c multi   1.20   1.00
220   A123   €3 multi   5.50   5.00
    Nos. 218-220 (3)   7.10   6.40

Souvenir Sheet

Norse Gods Fenja and Menja A124

2004, Mar. 26   *Perf. 14¼x14¾*
221   A124   55c multi   2.50   2.50

Aland Flag, 50th Anniv. — A125

Serpentine Die Cut 12½
2004, Apr. 23   Booklet Stamp
   Self-Adhesive
222   A125   1 multi   3.00   1.00
  a.   Booklet pane of 4   12.00   10.00
     Complete booklet, 2 #222a   24.00

No. 222a was reprinted in 2007 with a hole for a pegboard hook. See No. 296.

Finnish Pres. Mauno Koivisto and Guests on Boat — A126

2004, Apr. 23   *Perf. 12½*
223   A126   90c multi   1.80   2.00

Europa — A127

2004, May 10   *Perf. 13¾x14¼*
224   A127   75c multi   1.50   1.20

Destruction of Bomarsund Fortress, 150th Anniv. — A128

No. 225: a, Fortress, six ships in harbor. b, Fortress, three ships in harbor. c, Three soldiers in foreground. d, Six soldiers in foreground.

2004, June 9   *Perf. 13*
225   Booklet pane of 4   6.00   4.00
  a.-d.   A128 75c Any single   1.50   1.00
     Complete booklet, 2 #225   12.00

2004 Summer Olympics, Athens — A183

2004, Aug. 13   Litho.   *Perf. 14¼*
226   A183   80c multi   1.50   1.50

Landscapes A184

Designs: 2, Storklynkan, Brändö. 1, Prästgardsnäset Nature Reserve, Finström.

2004, Aug. 13   *Perf. 12½*
227-228   A184   Set of 2   5.50   2.20

Nos. 227-228 sold for 50c and 60c respectively on day of issue.
See Nos. 252-253, 260.

Christmas — A185

2004, Oct. 8   *Perf. 14½x14¾*
229   A185   45c multi   1.00   .75

Birds — A186

Designs: 15c, Phalacrocorax carbo sinensis. 65c, Cygnus cygnus. €4, Ardea cinerea, vert.

2005, Jan. 14   Litho.   *Perf. 13¼*
230   A186   15c multi   .40   .40
231   A186   65c multi   1.25   1.00
232   A186   €4 multi   8.00   5.00
    Nos. 230-232 (3)   9.65   6.40

Automobiles A187

No. 233: a, 1928 Oakland Sport Cabriolet. b, 1939 Ford V8. c, 1957 Buick Super 4D HT. d, 1964 Volkswagen 1200.

2005, Mar. 4   *Perf. 13¼ Horiz.*
   Booklet Stamps
233   Vert. strip of 4   12.00   4.75
  a.-d.   A187 1 Any single   3.00   1.20
  e.   Booklet pane, 2 #233   24.00
     Complete booklet, #233e   24.00

Stamps sold for 60c each on day of issue.

Europa — A188

2005, Apr. 29   *Perf. 13¼*
234   A188   90c multi   1.20   1.50

Walpurgis Night Bonfire — A189

Serpentine Die Cut 12½
2005, Apr. 29   Booklet Stamp
   Self-Adhesive
235   A189   2 multi   2.50   1.00
  a.   Booklet pane of 4   9.00
    Complete booklet, 2 #235a   20.00

Stamp sold for 50c on day of issue.

Tennis Player Bjorn Borg — A190

2005, May 26   *Perf. 12½*
236   A190   55c multi   1.10   1.00

Mr. Black and Mr. Smith at Bomarsund, by Fritz von Dardel — A191

2005, Aug. 12   Litho.   *Perf. 13¾*
237   A191   €1.30 multi   2.50   2.00

Schooner Linden — A192

2005, Aug. 26   *Perf. 13¼*
238   A192   60c multi   1.30   1.00

Landscapes Type of 2004
Designs: 70c, Pine tree on Sandö Island. 80c, Cliffs, Gröndal.

2005, Aug. 26   *Perf. 12½*
239-240   A184   Set of 2   3.40   2.20

Christmas — A193

Litho. with Hologram Applied
2005, Oct. 10   *Perf. 13*
241   A193   45c multi   .90   .90

Stars in hologram differ on each stamp.

Beetles — A194

Designs: 40c, Potosia cuprea. 65c, Coccinella septempunctata. €2, Oryctes nasicornis.

Litho. & Embossed
2006, Jan. 2   *Perf. 13½*
242   A194   40c multi   .80   .80
243   A194   65c multi   1.30   1.00
244   A194   €2 multi   4.00   3.00
    Nos. 242-244 (3)   6.10   4.80

Woman Suffrage in Finland, Cent. — A195

2006, Mar. 8   Litho.   *Perf. 12½*
245   A195   85c multi   1.90   1.20

Demilitarization of Aland, 150th Anniv. — A196

2006, Mar. 29   *Perf. 13¾*
246   A196   €1.50 multi   3.00   2.00

Souvenir Sheet

Lettesgubbe, Mythological Being — A197

2006, Mar. 29   *Perf. 12½x13*
247   A197   85c multi   2.50   2.50

Europa — A198

2006, May 4
248   A198   €1.30 multi   2.50   1.50

A199

Serpentine Die Cut 10 Syncopated
2006, May 26
249   A199   1 multi   2.00   1.40
  a.   Booklet pane of 8   11.25   11.25

No. 249 sold for 65c on day of issue. Design portion of stamp could be personalized at €10.40 per booklet with a minimum purchase of three booklets. The label design shown is a generic vignette. Other generic vignettes were created for sale at stamp shows beginning in 2008.

FINLAND — ALAND ISLANDS

Tattoos
A200

Tattoos
A200

No. 250: a, Tribal tattoo on man's biceps. b, Sailor's tattoo on man's forearm. c, Flower tattoo, on woman's torso.

2006, Sept. 7   **Perf. 14 Vert.**
Booklet Stamps
250	Horiz. strip of 3	3.50	3.50
a.-c.	A200 65c Any single	1.25	1.25
d.	Booklet pane, 3 #250	10.75	
	Complete booklet, #250d	10.75	

Fishing Boat From Television Film Directed by Ake Lindman — A201

2006, Aug. 4   **Litho.**   **Perf. 12½**
251	A201 75c multi	1.60	1.20

Landscapes Type of 2004

Designs: 55c, Foggy grove, windmill and houses, Söderby, Lemland. €1.20, Rocks, Norra Essvik, Sottunga.

2006, Aug. 4
252-253	A184	Set of 2	3.75	2.50

Christmas — A202

Litho. With Holograms Affixed
2006, Oct. 9   **Perf. 13**
254	A202 (50c) multi	.90	.60

Flowers — A203

Designs: 80c, Tripolium vulgare. 90c, Lythrum salicaria. €5, Angelica archangelica.

2007, Feb. 1   **Litho.**   **Perf. 12½x13**
255	A203 80c multi	1.75	1.75
256	A203 90c multi	2.00	1.25
257	A203 €5 multi	9.50	8.00
	Nos. 255-257 (3)	13.25	11.00

Mail Planes — A204

Designs: 2, Junkers F13. 1, Saab 340.

2007, Mar. 1   **Perf. 12½**
258-259	A204	Set of 2	5.50	2.25

No. 258 sold for 55c, and No. 259 sold for 70c on day of issue.

Landscapes Type of 2004
2007, Mar. 13
260	A184 2 Skaftö, Kumlinge	2.50	1.00

Sold for 55c on day of issue.

Untitled Painting by Tove Jansson — A205

2007, Apr. 18   **Perf. 13¼x13¾**
261	A205 85c multi	1.75	1.25

Europa — A206

2007, May 9   **Perf. 12½x13¼**
262	A206 70c multi	1.40	1.25

Scouting, cent.

Contemporary Crafts — A207

Designs: No. 263, Bridal crown, by Titti Sundblom. No. 264, Floral textile design, by Maria Korpi-Gordon and Adam Gordon. No. 265, Cups, bowl and plate, by Judy Kuyitunen.

2007, May 18   **Perf. 13 Horiz.**
Booklet Stamps
263	A207 1 multi	3.00	1.20
264	A207 1 multi	3.00	1.20
265	A207 1 multi	3.00	1.20
a.	Booklet pane, 3 each #263-265	27.00	27.50
	Complete booklet, #265a	27.00	

Nos. 263-265 each sold for 70c on day of issue.

A208

Serpentine Die Cut 10 Syncopated
2007, June 7   **Booklet Stamp**
Self-Adhesive
266	A208 1 multi	3.00	1.25
a.	Booklet pane of 8	24.00	20.00
	Complete booklet, #266a	24.00	

No. 266 sold for 70c on day of issue. Design portion of stamp could be personalized at €10.40 per booklet with a minimum purchase of three booklets.

Emigration to America — A209

2007, Aug. 9   **Litho.**   **Perf. 13¼x12½**
267	A209 75c multi	1.40	1.20

Kjusan, Hammarland A210

2007, Oct. 1   **Perf. 12½**
268	A210 1 multi	3.00	.80

No. 268 sold for 70c on day of issue.

Christmas — A211

2007, Oct. 9   **Perf. 14**
269	A211 (50c) multi	.90	.50

Fish — A212

Designs: 45c, Perca fluviatilis. €4.50, Sander lucioperca.

2008, Feb. 1   **Litho.**   **Perf. 13¼x13**
270	A212 45c multi	1.00	.70
271	A212 €4.50 multi	8.50	6.50

Souvenir Sheet

Mythical Princess Signhild at Drottningkleven — A213

Perf. 12½x13¼
2008, Mar. 27   **Litho.**
272	A213 (85c) multi	3.00	2.50

Badhusberget, Mariehamn A214   Langvikshagen, Lumparland A215

2008, Apr. 15   **Perf. 13x12½**
273	A214 (70c) multi	2.00	1.00
274	A215 (70c) multi	2.00	1.00

2008 Summer Olympics, Beijing — A216

2008, May 9   **Perf. 13¾**
275	A216 (90c) multi	1.80	1.20

Europa — A217

2008, May 9   **Perf. 13¼x13**
276	A217 €1 multi	2.00	1.20

Lighthouses — A218

No. 277: a, Marhällan Lighthouse. b, Gustaf Dalén Lighthouse. c, Kökarsören Lighthouse. d, Bogskär Lighthouse.

Litho., Litho & Engr (#277c-277d)
2008, June 6   **Perf. 12¾ on 3 Sides**
Booklet Stamps
277	Block or strip of 4	8.00	4.75
a.-d.	A218 (75c) Any single	2.00	1.25
e.	Booklet pane, 2 #277	16.00	
	Complete booklet, #277e	16.00	

Within the booklet pane, stamps in one row are tete-beche in relation to stamps in the adjacent row.

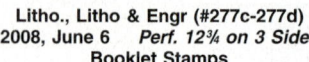

Gravel Road and Profiles of Marcus Grönholm, Rally Driver, and Christoph Treier, Trainer — A219

2008, July 26   **Litho.**   **Perf. 13½**
278	A219 (90c) multi	2.00	1.20

Particles of granite were applied to portions of the design using a thermographic process.

Aland Peasant Bride, by Karl Emanuel Jansson — A220

2008, Aug. 15   **Perf. 13x13¼**
279	A220 €1.50 multi	2.50	2.00

Christmas — A221

Litho. With Hologram Applied
2008, Oct. 9   **Perf. 13¾x13¼**
280	A221 (55c) multi	.90	.70

Personalized Stamp — A222

Serpentine Die Cut 10 Syncopated
2008, Oct. 9   **Litho.**
Booklet Stamp
Self-Adhesive
281	A222 (75c) multi	1.50	1.25
a.	Booklet pane of 8	12.00	10.50
	Complete booklet, #281a	12.00	

The generic design portion of the stamp shown could be personalized. Other generic vignettes were created for sale at stamp shows in 2009 and 2010.

1810 Boundary Post — A223

Litho. & Embossed With Foil Application
2009, Jan. 22   **Perf. 14¼**
282	A223 (80c) multi	2.00	1.20

Souvenir Sheet

Electricity on Aland Islands, Cent. — A224

FINLAND — ALAND ISLANDS

Litho. & Embossed
2009, Jan. 22   Perf. 12½x13¼
283 A224 €2 black   4.00 4.00

Writers — A225

No. 284: a, Ulla-Lena Lundberg and ship. b, Anni Blomqvist (1909-90), sailboat and dockside shack. c, Valdemar Nyman (1904-98), flowers, cattle.

2009, Mar. 21   Litho.   Perf. 13 Horiz.
Booklet Stamps
284   Vert. strip of 3   6.00 3.50
a.-c.   A225 (80c) Any single   2.00 1.25
d.   Booklet pane, 3 #284   18.00
    Complete booklet, #284d   18.00

Movie Theaters in Aland, Cent. — A226

2009, Apr. 6   Perf. 12½x13¼
285 A226 €1.60 multi   3.50 2.50

Divers at Plus Shipwreck — A227

2009, May 8
286 A227 (75c) multi   2.00 1.20

Europa — A228

2009, May 8   Perf. 13
287 A228 (80c) multi   2.00 1.20

Intl. Year of Astronomy. Star-shaped holes are die cut in stamp.

Passenger Ferries — A229

Designs: (75c), SS Viking. (80c), New Viking Line ferry, 2009.

2009, June 1   Litho.   Perf. 13
288-289 A229 Set of 2   4.00 2.25

See Nos. 301-302, 311-312, 325-326, 339, 347, 351-352.

Personalized Stamp — A230

Booklet Stamp
Serpentine Die Cut 10 Syncopated
2009, June 27   Self-Adhesive
290 A230 (90c) multi   2.00 2.00
a.   Booklet pane of 8   16.00
    Complete booklet, #290a   16.00

The generic design portion of the stamp shown could be personalized.

Cliffs, Föglö — A231

Islets, Saltvik — A232

2009, Sept. 16   Perf. 12½
291 A231 (75c) multi   2.00 1.00
292 A232 (80c) multi   2.00 1.00

Honeymoon Cabin of Finland President Martti Ahtisaari — A233

2009, Sept. 29   Perf. 13x12½
293 A233 (90c) multi   2.00 1.50

Christmas — A234

Poinsettia and: (60c), Man and woman. (90c), Woman with scroll.

2009, Oct. 9   Perf. 13¾
294-295 A234 Set of 2   3.00 2.25

Flag Type of 2004 Inscribed "Inrikes"
Serpentine Die Cut 12½
2009, July 1   Litho.
Booklet Stamp
Self-Adhesive
296 A125 (75c) multi   2.00 1.50
a.   Booklet pane of 4   8.00
    Complete booklet, 2 #296a   16.00

Mail Jetty at Eckerö, Painting by Victor Westerholm — A235

2010, Jan. 4   Perf. 13
297 A235 (80c) multi   2.00 1.20

Jesus Christ, Painting by Warner Sallman — A236

Litho. With Foil Application
2010, Mar. 24   Perf. 14x14¼
298 A236 (90c) multi   2.00 1.20

Souvenir Sheet

Kobba Klintar Pilot Station — A237

2010, Mar. 24   Litho.   Perf. 12½
299 A237 (90c) multi   2.00 2.00

Europa — A238

2010, Apr. 19   Perf. 12½x13
300 A238 (85c) multi   2.50 1.50

Ferries Type of 2009
Designs: 75c, MS Skandia. €3.50, MS Prinsessan.

2010, May 3   Litho.   Perf. 13
301-302 A229 Set of 2   9.50 3.25

Plastic Toys Made By Plasto — A239

No. 303: a, Scooter. b, Dump truck. c, Ducks.

2010, May 10   Perf. 13¾ Horiz.
Booklet Stamps
303   Vert. strip of 3   6.00 3.50
a.-c.   A239 (85c) Any single   2.00 1.20
d.   Booklet pane, 3 #303   18.00 18.00
    Complete booklet, #303d   18.00

Farmhand Delivering Mail — A240

2010, June 12   Perf. 12½x13¼
304 A240 (75c) multi   2.00 1.00

Personalized Stamp — A241

2010, June 12   Perf. 12½
305 A241 (85c) black   2.00 2.00

No. 305 was printed in sheets of 8. The generic design portion of the stamp shown could be personalized for an extra fee.

Stained-Glass Windows — A242

Stained-glass window from church in Jomala: 80c, St. Olaf. €1.60, St. Olaf and other figures, horiz.

2010, Aug. 30   Litho.   Perf. 13
306 A242 80c multi   3.00 3.00

Souvenir Sheet
307 A242 €1.60 multi   3.00 3.00

See Macao Nos. 1317-1318.

Shoreline, Eckerö — A243   Cliffs, Bund — A244

2010, Sept. 16   Perf. 12½
308 A243 80c multi   2.00 1.20
309 A244 (85c) multi   2.00 1.30

Christmas — A245

2010, Oct. 8   Perf. 13
310 A245 (65c) multi   2.00 1.20

Ferries Type of 2009
Designs: 80c, MS Alandia. €1.50, MS Apollo.

2011, Feb. 1   Litho.   Perf. 13
311-312 A229 Set of 2   5.00 2.50

Souvenir Sheet

Princess Maria Alexandrovna of Russia (1824-80) — A246

2011, Feb. 21   Perf.
313 A246 €1 multi   2.00 1.50

City of Mariehamn, 150th anniv. A limited edition of No. 313 with gold embossing sold for €15. Value, $30. See Russia No. 7255.

Georg August Wallin (1811-52), Explorer of Arabia — A247

2011, Apr. 1   Perf. 14x14¼
314 A247 (90c) multi   2.00 1.20

Europa — A248

2011, May 9   Perf. 13
315 A248 (85c) multi   2.00 1.20

Intl. Year of Forests.

Comic Book Superheroes Created by Paul Gustafson (1916-77) — A249

No. 316: a, The Arrow. b, Fantom of the Fair. c, Alias the Spider.

2011, May 9   Perf. 13
Booklet Stamps
316   Horiz. strip of 3   6.00 3.50
a.-c.   A249 (90c) Any single   2.00 1.20
d.   Tete-beche block of 6   15.00 15.00
e.   Booklet pane of 3 #316   18.00 17.50
    Complete booklet, #316e   18.00

Champagne Bottles From 1840s Shipwreck — A250

2011, June 3   Litho.   Perf. 13½
317 A250 (90c) multi   1.75 1.00

Chips Ab Potato Chips — A251

2011, June 7   Perf. 13¾
318 A251 85c multi   1.75 1.20

604 FINLAND — ALAND ISLANDS

Strömma Apples — A252

2011, June 7   Litho.
319 A252 5c shown .25 .25
320 A252 €4 Apples, diff. 7.50 1.50

Personalized Stamp — A253

2011, Aug. 16   Perf. 13¾x14¼
321 A253 (95c) blk & grn 2.00 1.50

No. 321 was printed in sheets of 8. The generic design portion of the stamp shown could be personalized for an extra fee.

Kökar — A254   Jomala — A255

2011, Sept. 28   Litho.   Perf. 12½
322 A254 (85c) multi 2.00 1.00
323 A255 (90c) multi 2.00 1.20

Christmas — A256

2011, Oct. 7   Perf. 14½
324 A256 (55c) multi 1.20 .80

Ferries Type of 2009
Designs: 55c, SS Birger Jarl. (75c), MS Sally Albatross.

2012, Feb. 1   Perf. 13¼
325-326 A229 Set of 2 3.00 2.00

No. 326 is inscribed "Lokalpost."

Souvenir Sheet

Fishermen at Sea — A257

2012, Mar. 21   Perf. 13¼x13
327 A257 (€1) multi 2.00 2.00

Sinking of the Titanic, Cent. — A258

2012, Apr. 16   Perf. 12¾x13¼
328 A258 €1.80 multi 3.50 1.50

See Belgium No. 2562.

The Man at the Wheel, Sculpture by Emil Cedercreutz — A259

Litho. & Engr.
2012, Apr. 26   Perf. 13¼x13
329 A259 €3 multi 6.00 3.00

Europa — A260

2012, May 9   Litho.   Perf. 13¾
330 A260 (95c) multi 2.00 1.20

Personalized Stamp — A261

2012, June 4   Perf. 14¼x13¾
331 A261 (95c) multi 2.00 1.00

Printed in sheets of 8. The design portion of this stamp could be personalized. The design shown is a generic vignette. Other generic vignettes were created for sale at stamp shows beginning in 2013.

Dragonflies A262

Designs: (75c), Aeshna cyanea. (95c), Sympetrum sanguineum.

2012, June 4   Perf. 14¼
332-333 A262 Set of 2 4.00 2.25

No. 332 is inscribed "Lokalpost;" No. 333, "Europa."

Architecture A263

No. 334: a, Miramar. b, Societetshusen. c, Badhotellet.

2012, Aug. 23   Perf. 13¾ Horiz.
Booklet Stamps
334 Vert. strip of 3 6.00 3.50
a.-c. A263 (€1) Any single 2.00 1.20
d. Booklet pane of 9, 3 each
  #334a-334c 18.00
  Complete booklet, #334d 18.00

Nos. 334a-334c are each inscribed "Världen."

Public Transportation A264

Designs: No. 335, (95c) 1954 Volvo L224 bus. No. 336, (95c) 1924 Ford TT bus.

2012, Sept. 19   Perf. 13¾x13½
335-336 A264 Set of 2 4.00 2.25

No. 335 is inscribed "Inrikes." No. 336 is inscribed "Europa."

Christmas — A265

2012, Oct. 9   Perf. 13
337 A265 (60c) multi 1.20 .80

Yearning, Painting by Guy Frisk — A266

2013, Jan. 15   Perf. 13¾x13¼
338 A266 (€1.10) multi 2.00 1.20

Aland Art Museum, 50th anniv.

Ferries Type of 2009
Design: (80c), SS Alandsfärjan.

2013, Feb. 19   Perf. 13
339 A229 (80c) multi 2.00 1.00

Worldwide Fund for Nature (WWF) — A267

No. 340: a, Gavia arctica. b, Gavia stellata. c, Podiceps auritus. d, Podiceps cristatus.

2013, Apr. 5   Perf. 12½x12¾
Booklet Stamps
340 A267 Block of 4 8.00 4.75
a.-d. (€1) Any single 2.00 1.20
e. Booklet pane of 8, 2 each
  #340a-340d 16.00 17.50
  Complete booklet, #340e 16.00

Europa — A268

2013, May 6   Perf. 13¾x13¼
341 A268 (€1) multi 2.00 1.20

Personalized Stamp — A269

2013, May 6   Perf. 12½
342 A269 (€1.10) ol grn & blk 2.00 1.50

No. 342 was printed in sheets of 8. The generic design portion of the stamp shown could be personalized for an extra fee. Other generic vignettes were created for sale at stamp shows beginning in 2014.

Water Lilies — A270

Designs: (€1), Nymphaea alba. €2.50, Nuphar lutea.

2013, June 4   Perf. 13x13¼
343-344 A270 Set of 2 6.50 3.00

Crowd at Rockoff Music Festival A271

Woman at Island in the Sun Music Festival A272

2013, July 12   Litho.   Perf. 13¾
345 A271 (80c) multi 2.00 1.00
346 A272 (€1.10) multi 2.00 1.20

Ferries Type of 2009
Design: €2, MS Princess Anastasia.

2013, Aug. 5   Litho.   Perf. 13
347 A229 €2 multi 4.00 1.75

See Russia No. 7468.

Inachis Io — A273

2013, Aug. 20   Litho.   Perf. 13¾
348 A273 (€1.10) multi 2.00 1.20

Christmas — A274

Paintings by Pinturicchio: No. 349, Adoration of the Magi. No. 350, Nativity.

2013, Nov. 8   Litho.   Perf. 13¼x13¾
349 A274 (65c) multi 1.40 1.00
350 A274 65c multi 1.40 1.00

No. 350 was printed in sheets of 8 + central label. Value, $11. See Vatican City Nos. 1549-1550.

Ferries Type of 2009
Designs: No. 351, MS Birka Princess. No. 352, MS Viking Grace.

2014, Feb. 7   Litho.   Perf. 13¾
351 A229 (€1.10) multi 2.00 1.00
352 A229 (€1.10) multi 2.00 1.20

No. 351 is inscribed "Inrikes"; No. 352, "Europa."

Mariehamn Theater Society, Cent. — A275

2014, Feb. 7   Litho.   Perf. 13¼
353 A275 €1.50 multi 3.00 2.00

Souvenir Sheet

Bridge of a Freighter and Horizon A276

2014, Mar. 17   Litho.   Perf. 13¼
354 A276 €3 multi 5.50 3.50

Grand Piano of Alie Lindberg (1849-1933), Concert Pianist — A277

2014, May 8   Litho.   Perf. 13¼x13
355 A277 (€1.10) multi 2.00 1.50

Europa.

FINLAND — ALAND ISLANDS

Campanula Trachelium — A278

2014, May 8　Litho.　Perf. 12½
356　A278　(€1.10) multi　　2.00　1.50

Kenta Sandvik, Weight Lifter — A279

2014, May 31　Litho.　Perf. 13x13¼
357　A279　(90c) multi　　1.40　1.00

Personalized Stamp — A280

2014, May 31　Litho.　Perf. 12½
358　A280　(€1.10) multi　　2.00　2.00

No. 358 was printed in sheets of 8. The generic design portion of the stamp shown could be personalized for an extra fee. Other generic vignettes were created for sale at stamp shows beginning in 2015.

Robert Helenius, Professional Boxer, and Family on Aland Island — A281

2014, June 9　Litho.　Perf. 13x13¼
359　A281　€2.30 multi　　4.00　2.00

Musical Groups of the 1960s — A282

No. 360: a, Hitch Hikers. b, Stockdoves. c, Anacondas.

2014, Aug. 25　Litho.　Perf. 13x12¼
Booklet Stamps
360　　Vert. strip of 3　　4.25　3.00
a.-c.　A282 (90c) Any single　1.40　1.00
d.　Booklet pane of 9, 3 each
　　#360a-360c　　16.00
　　Complete booklet, #360d　16.00

Christmas — A283

Litho. With Foil Application
2014, Oct. 9　Perf. 13¾x13¼
361　A283　(70c) multi　　1.20　.60

New Year 2015 (Year of the Ram) — A284

No. 362: a, Ram, ewe and lamb. b, Ram's head.

Litho. & Engr.
2014, Nov. 5　Perf. 13x12¾
362　A284　Pair　　6.25　6.25
a.-b.　80c Either single　1.50　1.50

Printed in sheets containing two pairs.

Ships — A285

Designs: 85c, Schooner Lemland. (€1.20), Barquentine Leo.

2015, Feb. 2　Litho.　Perf. 13x13¼
363-364　A285　Set of 2　　3.50　3.50

See Nos. 377-378.

Campanula Persicifolia — A286

2015, Apr. 10　Litho.　Perf. 14¼
365　A286　85c multi　　1.70　1.70

Midvinterblot, Painting by Carl Larsson (1853-1919) — A287

2015, Apr. 10　Litho.　Perf. 14x14¼
366　A287　€3 multi　　6.00　6.00

Race Horse Indian Silver — A288

2015, May 1　Litho.　Perf. 14
367　A288　(95c) multi　　1.40　1.00

Europa — A289

2015, May 8　Litho.　Perf. 14¼
368　A289　(€1.20) multi　　2.00　2.00

Personalized Stamp — A290

2015, May 8　Litho.　Perf. 12½
369　A290　(€1.20) multi　　2.00　2.00

Printed in sheets of 8. The design portion of this stamp could be personalized. The design shown is a generic vignette.

Julius Sundblom (1865-1945), Politician — A291

2015, June 22　Litho.　Perf. 13
370　A291　(€1.20) multi　　2.00　2.00

Silver Jewelry — A292

Designs: (€1.20), Buckle from Aland Islands. €2, Brooch from Bern, Switzerland.

Litho. & Embossed
2015, Sept. 3　Perf. 13
371　A292　(€1.20) multi　　2.50　2.00
372　A292　€2 multi　　3.50　1.50

See Switzerland Nos. 1568-1569.

Dogs — A293

No. 373: a, Finnish hound (Finsk stövare). b, Gray Norwegian elkhound (Norsk älghund gra). c, Wire-haired dachshund (Strävharig tax).

2015, Sept. 3　Litho.　Perf. 13
Booklet Stamps
373　　Horiz. strip of 3　　6.00　4.50
a.-c.　A293 (€1.20) Any single　2.00　1.50
d.　Booklet pane of 9, 3 each
　　#373a-373c　　20.00
　　Complete booklet, #373d　20.00

A294

Christmas — A295

2015, Oct. 9　Litho.　Perf. 13
374　A294　(70c) multi　　2.00　1.00
375　A295　(€1.20) multi　　2.50　2.00

Aland Sea Rescue Society, 50th Anniv. — A296

2015, Oct. 30　Litho.　Perf. 13
376　A296　(95c) multi　　2.00　1.00

Ships Type of 2015

Designs: 10c, Brig Altai. €10, Barque Pehr Brahe.

2016, Feb. 2　Litho.　Perf. 13x13¼
377-378　A285　Set of 2　　18.00　7.50

Buckthorn Dessert Made by Chef Michael Björklund — A297

2016, Mar. 18　Litho.　Perf. 14¼
379　A297　(€1.30) multi　　3.00　3.00

Witch Trials, 350th Anniv. — A298

2016, Apr. 8　Litho.　Perf. 13
380　A298　(€1.30) multi　　3.00　3.00

A299　　Europa — A300

2016, May 9　Litho.　Perf. 13
381　A299　(€1.30) multi　　3.00　3.00
382　A300　(€1.30) multi　　3.00　3.00

Think Green Issue.

Medicinal Plants A301

No. 383: a, Hyoscyamus niger. b, Digitalis purpurea. c, Tanacetum vulgare.

2016, May 9　Litho.　Perf. 12 Horiz.
Booklet Stamps
383　　Vert. strip of 3　　9.00　9.00
a.-c.　A301 (€1.30) Any single　3.00　3.00
d.　Booklet pane of 9, 3 each
　　#383a-383c　　27.00
　　Complete booklet, #383d　27.00

Lilla Aland Chair Designed by Carl Malmsten — A302

2016, May 27　Litho.　Perf. 11½
384　A302　€2.50 multi　　5.75　5.75

House and Brudhäll Harbor, by Björn Ulvaeus — A303

2016, July 8　Litho.　Perf. 11½
385　A303　(€1.30) multi　　3.00　3.00

Apple and Blossom — A304

2016, Aug. 12　Litho.　Perf. 12½
386　A304　(€1.30) multi　　3.00　3.00

Elves Decorating Christmas Tree A305

Elf, Reindeer and Gifts A306

2016, Oct. 10　Litho.　Perf. 13
387　A305　(70c) multi　　1.60　1.60
388　A306　(€1.30) multi　　3.00　3.00

Christmas.

Souvenir Sheet

New Year 2017 (Year of the Rooster) A307

No. 389 — Rooster and: a, Flower. b, Rowboat.

FINLAND — ALAND ISLANDS

2016, Nov. 11	Litho.		Perf. 13
389 A307	Sheet of 2		9.00 9.00
a.-b.	€2 Either single		4.50 4.50

Mermerus A308

Mariehamn A309

2017, Feb. 2	Litho.		Perf. 13x13¼
390 A308	20c multi		.45 .45
391 A309	(€1.10) multi		2.40 2.40

Personalized Stamp — A310

2017, Mar. 14	Litho.		Perf. 12½
392 A310	(€1.30) multi		3.00 3.00

No. 392 was printed in sheets of 8. The generic design portion of the stamp shown could be personalized for an extra fee.

Pinus Sylvestris and Salvadora Oleoides — A311

2017, Mar. 14	Litho.		Perf. 13x13¼
393 A311	(€1.30) multi		3.00 3.00

Cultural Diversity.

Kastelholm Castle — A312

2017, May 9	Litho.		Perf. 13x13¼
394 A312	(€1.40) multi		3.25 3.25

Europa.

Independence of Finland, Cent. — A313

Litho. & Embossed With Foil Application

2017, May 24		Perf. 13x13¼
395 A313	€5 multi	11.50 11.50

Sauna Bench, Bucket and Whisk — A314

Exterior of Sauna — A315

2017, May 24	Litho.		Perf. 13¼x13½
396 A314	(€1.40) multi		3.25 3.25
397 A315	(€1.40) multi		3.25 3.25
a.	Souvenir sheet of 2, #396-397		6.50 6.50

See Finland No. 1540.

Handcrafted Jewelry Made From Recycled Items — A316

2017, Aug. 17	Litho.		Perf. 13x13¼
398 A316	€1 multi		2.40 2.40

Mammals — A317

No. 399: a, Lepus timidus. b, Mustela nivalis. c, Nyctereutes procyonoides.

Perf. 14¼x14½

2017, Sept. 15		Litho.
399	Horiz. strip of 3	8.00 8.00
a.-c.	A317 (€1.10) Any single	2.60 2.60
d.	Booklet pane of 9, 3 each #399a-399c	24.00 —
	Complete booklet, #399d	24.00

A318   Gingerbread Houses — A319

2017, Oct. 9	Litho.		Perf. 13¼
400 A318	(70c) multi		1.60 1.60
401 A319	(€1.40) multi		3.25 3.25

Christmas.

Souvenir Sheet

New Year 2018 (Year of the Dog) A320

No. 402 — China dog at: a, Right. b, Left.

2017, Nov. 10	Litho.		Perf. 13¼x13
402 A320	€1 Sheet of 2, #a-b		4.75 4.75

Clipper Ship Albania — A321

Schooner Atlas — A322

2018, Feb. 1	Litho.		Perf. 12
403 A321	(€1.30) multi		3.25 3.25
404 A322	€3 multi		7.50 7.50

Salmo Salar — A323

2018, Mar. 13	Litho.		Perf. 11½
405 A323	(€1.50) sil & multi		3.75 3.75

Bomarsund Bridge A324

2018, May 9	Litho.		Perf. 12
406 A324	(€1.50) multi		3.50 3.50

Europa.

Spray of Wave Hitting Rocks — A325

2018, May 9	Litho.		Perf. 12
407 A325	(€1.50) multi		3.50 3.50

Apis Mellifera — A326

2018, May 28	Litho.		Perf. 13¼
408 A326	(€1.50) gold & multi		3.50 3.50

Motorcycles — A327

No. 409: a, 2011 Victory Cross Country. b, 1919 Harley-Davidson F1000CC. c, 1944 Indian Chief. d, 1980 Harley-Davidson Chopper.

2018, May 28	Litho.		Perf. 13¼
	Booklet Stamps		
409 A327	Block of 4		14.00 14.00
a.-d.	(€1.50) Any single		3.50 3.50
e.	Booklet pane of 8, 2 each #409a-409d		28.00 —
	Complete booklet, #409e		28.00

A328

Fireworks — A329

2018, Sept. 18	Litho.		Perf. 13
410 A328	(€1.50) multi		3.50 3.50
411 A329	€4 multi		9.25 9.25

Christmas
A330   A331

Litho. With Hologram Affixed

2018, Oct. 9		Perf. 13¼
412 A330	(80c) red & multi	1.90 1.90
413 A331	(€1.50) gold & multi	3.50 3.50

Souvenir Sheet

New Year 2019 (Year of the Pig) A332

No. 414 — Apples and: a, Entire pig. b, Head of sow.

2018, Nov. 1	Litho.		Perf. 12
414 A332	Sheet of 2		9.00 9.00
a.-b.	€2 Either single		4.50 4.50

Ships — A333

Designs: €1.40, Schooner Vineta. €1.60, Barque Parma.

2019, Feb. 1	Litho.		Perf. 12
415-416 A333	Set of 2		7.00 7.00

Ice Skaters A334

2019, Mar. 8	Litho.		Perf. 12
417 A334	€1.20 multi		2.75 2.75

Small Boat Transatlantic Voyage Captained by Uno Ekblom (1905-55), 80th Anniv. — A335

2019, Mar. 8	Litho.		Perf. 12
418 A335	€1.60 multi		3.75 3.75

Aurora Borealis and Notvik Tower — A336

2019, Mar. 8	Litho.		Perf. 14
419 A336	€1.70 multi		4.00 4.00

Haliaeetus Albicilla — A337

2019, May 9	Litho.		Perf. 13
420 A337	(€1.40) multi		3.25 3.25

Europa.

Jonesas Farmhouse, Onningeby A338

2019, May 9	Litho.		Perf. 14x14¼
421 A338	(€1.70) multi		4.00 4.00

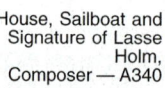
Postcrossing A339

2019, June 7	Litho.		Perf. 13¾
422 A339	(€1.80) multi		4.25 4.25

Values are for stamps with surrounding selvage.

House, Sailboat and Signature of Lasse Holm, Composer — A340

2019, June 7	Litho.		Perf. 13
423 A340	€6 multi		14.00 14.00

Harvest Festival A341

FINLAND — ALAND ISLANDS

No. 424: a, Two girls in hay. b, Person feeding apple to cow. c, Apple in woman's hands.

Perf. 13. Horiz.

2019, Sept. 20   Litho.

Booklet Stamps

424	Vert. strip of 3	10.50	10.50
a.-c.	A341 (€1.60) Any single	3.50	3.50
d.	Booklet pane of 9, 3 each #424a-424c	31.50	—
	Complete booklet, #424d	31.50	

Nos. 424a-424c are each inscribed "Inrikes."

Christmas
A342   A343

2019, Oct. 24   Litho.   *Perf. 13¼*
| 425 | A342 | (90c) multi | 2.00 | 4.00 |
| 426 | A343 | (€1.80) multi | 4.00 | 4.00 |

Souvenir Sheet

New Year 2020 (Year of the Rat) A344

No. 427: a, Two mice. b, Three mice.

2019, Oct. 24   Litho.   *Perf. 13*
| 427 | A344 | Sheet of 2 | 2.80 | 2.80 |
| a.-b. | | 60c Either single | 1.40 | 1.40 |

Ships — A345

Designs: €1.30, Barquentine Mozart. €1.80, Four-masted barque Viking.

2020, Feb. 3   Litho.   *Perf. 13x13¼*
| 428-429 | A345 | Set of 2 | 7.00 | 7.00 |

Sabina Triptych, by Henrik Nylund (1945-82) — A346

2020, Mar. 5   Litho.   *Perf. 13¼x13*
| 430 | A346 | €1.40 multi | 3.00 | 3.00 |

Europa A347

2020, May 8   Litho.   *Perf. 14½x14*
| 431 | A347 | (€2) multi | 4.50 | 4.50 |

Ancient postal routes.

Personalized Stamp — A348

2020, May 8   Litho.   *Perf. 12½*
| 432 | A348 | (€1.80) multi | 4.00 | 4.00 |

No. 432 was printed in sheets of 8. The generic design portion of the stamp shown could be personalized for an extra fee.

Bats and Library Clock — A349

2020, June 5   Litho.   *Perf. 13*
| 433 | A349 | €1 multi | 2.25 | 2.25 |

Tubing Made by Optinova Group — A350

2020, June 5   Litho.   *Perf. 13¼*
| 434 | A350 | (€1.70) multi | 4.00 | 4.00 |

Aland Police Van — A351

2020, Sept. 4   Litho.   *Perf. 14x14¼*
| 435 | A351 | €1.50 multi | 3.50 | 3.50 |

Mariehamn Esplanade in Autumn A352   Mariehamn Esplanade in Winter A353

Mariehamn Esplanade in Spring A354   Mariehamn Esplanade in Summer A355

2020, Sept. 4   Litho.   *Perf. 13*

Booklet Stamps

436	Block of 4	14.00	14.00
a.	A352 (€1.50) multi	3.50	3.50
b.	A353 (€1.50) multi	3.50	3.50
c.	A354 (€1.50) multi	3.50	3.50
d.	A355 (€1.50) multi	3.50	3.50
e.	Booklet pane of 8, 2 each #436a-436d	28.00	—
	Complete booklet, #436e	28.00	

Glogg, Cookie and Nuts — A356   Toffee — A357

2020, Oct. 23   Litho.   *Perf. 13¼x12¾*
| 437 | A356 | (€1) multi | 2.40 | 2.40 |
| 438 | A357 | (€2) multi | 4.75 | 4.75 |

Christmas.

Souvenir Sheet

New Year 2021 (Year of the Ox) A358

No. 439: a, Team of oxen. b, Team of oxen, farmers and plow, horiz.

2020, Oct. 23   Litho.   *Perf. 13*
| 439 | A358 | Sheet of 2 | 4.80 | 4.80 |
| a.-b. | | €1 Either single | 2.40 | 2.40 |

Tractors — A359

Designs: €1.60, 1924 Fordson F tractor. €3, Cletrac tractor, c. 1919.

2021, Feb. 2   Litho.   *Perf. 13x13¼*
| 440-441 | A359 | Set of 2 | 11.00 | 11.00 |

Verner E. Suomi NPP Weather Satellite — A360

Perf. 14¼x13¾

2021, Mar. 25   Litho.
| 442 | A360 | (€2.20) multi | 5.25 | 5.25 |

1747 Nautical Chart of Rödhamn — A361

2021, Mar. 25   Litho.   *Perf. 13*
| 443 | A361 | €4 multi | 9.50 | 9.50 |

Great Northern War, 300th Anniv. — A362

2021, May 7   Litho.   *Perf. 13*
| 444 | A362 | (€1.80) multi | 4.50 | 4.50 |

Rana Arvalis — A363

2021, May 7   Litho.   *Perf. 14*
| 445 | A363 | €2 multi | 5.00 | 5.00 |

Europa.

Autonomy of Aland Islands, Cent. — A364

2021, June 9   Litho.   *Perf. 14*
| 446 | A364 | (€1.70) multi | 4.00 | 4.00 |

Female Premiers of Aland A365

No. 447: a, Veronica Thörnroos. b, Camilla Gunell. c, Viveka Eriksson. d, Katrin Sjögren.

2021, June 9   Litho.   *Perf. 13¾*

Booklet Stamps

447	A365	Block of 4	19.00	19.00
a.-d.		€2 Any single	4.75	4.75
e.		Booklet pane of 8, 2 each #447a-447d	38.00	—
		Complete booklet, #447e	38.00	

A366

2021 Tall Ships Races A367

2021, July 23   Litho.   *Perf. 13*
| 448 | A366 | (€2.20) multi | 5.25 | 5.25 |

Souvenir Sheet
Litho. With Foil Application
| 449 | A367 | €5 multi | 12.00 | 12.00 |

The 2021 Tall Ships Races were canceled because of the COVID-19 pandemic.

Christmas
A368   A369

2021, Oct. 20   Litho.   *Perf. 13¼*
| 450 | A368 | (€1) multi | 2.40 | 2.40 |
| 451 | A369 | (€2.20) multi | 5.25 | 5.25 |

Souvenir Sheet

New Year 2022 (Year of the Tiger) A370

2021, Oct. 20   Litho.   *Perf. 13¼*
| 452 | A370 | €3 multi | 7.00 | 7.00 |

Early 1940s Ford Tractor — A371

1956 Valmet 20 Tractor — A372

2022, Feb. 1   Litho.   *Perf. 13x13¼*
| 453 | A371 | (€1.90) multi | 4.25 | 4.25 |
| 454 | A372 | €3.50 multi | 8.00 | 8.00 |

Aland Yacht Club Pavilion, Cent. — A373

2022, Mar. 25   Litho.   *Perf. 13x13¼*
| 455 | A373 | €2.10 multi | 4.75 | 4.75 |

Disc Golf — A374

2022, Mar. 25   Litho.   *Perf. 13*
| 456 | A374 | (€2.40) multi | 5.50 | 5.50 |

Sjöra (Water Sprite) — A375

2022, May 9   Litho.   *Perf. 13¼*
| 457 | A375 | €2.30 multi | 5.00 | 5.00 |

Europa.

FINLAND — ALAND ISLANDS — FIUME

Contemporary Art — A376

No. 458: a, Aland Originals, photograph by Tiina Tahvanainen (62x41mm). b, Japanese Lantern, engraving by Gunnar Sjöblom (31x29mm). c, Augur I, painting by Kurt Simons (31x29mm). d, #sniffigaround3, painting by Minna Oberg (31x40mm). e, Sacrificial Cardigan, fabric art by Barbro Eriksson (31x40mm). f, All Over the Place, painting by Erica Signell (31x40mm). g, Rooster, sculpture by Johan Karlsson (31x40mm).

		Perf. 13¼ on 2 or 3 Sides		
2022, June 9		Litho.		
458	A376	Booklet pane of 7	47.50	—
a.-g.		€3.20 Any single	6.75	6.75
		Complete booklet, #458	47.50	

Souvenir Sheet

Autonomy of Aland Islands, Cent. — A377

2022, June 9		Litho.	Perf. 14½	
459	A377	€5 multi	10.50	10.50

A similar sheet with country name and denomination in blue sold for €13.

Sea Buckthorn Berries and Bottles of Sea Buckthorn Juice — A378

2022, Sept. 6		Litho.	Perf. 14½x14¼	
460	A378	€1.90 multi	3.75	3.75

Ixodes Ricinus, Borrelia Burgdorferi, and Tick-Borne Disease Researcher — A379

2022, Sept. 6		Litho.	Perf. 13¼x13	
461	A379	€2.70 multi	5.25	5.25

A380

Christmas — A381

2022, Oct. 20		Litho.	Perf. 13¼	
462	A380	(€1.20) multi	2.40	2.40
463	A381	(€2.60) multi	5.25	5.25

Souvenir Sheet

New Year 2023 (Year of the Rabbit) A382

2022, Oct. 20		Litho.	Perf. 14	
464	A382	€3.60 multi	7.25	7.25

Tractors — A383

Designs: €1.80, 1955 Ferguson. €2.90, 1960 Fordson Super Major.

2023, Jan. 4		Litho.	Perf. 13x13½	
465-466	A383	Set of 2	10.50	10.50

Carl Björkman (1873-1948), First Premier of Aland Islands — A384

2023, Feb. 15		Litho.	Perf. 14¾	
467	A384	€4 multi	8.50	8.50

Loxia Pytopsittacus — A385

2023, Mar. 15		Litho.	Perf. 13½x13	
468	A385	(€2.10) multi	4.75	4.75

Clinker Boat — A386

2023, May 9		Litho.	Perf. 13x13½	
469	A386	€1.40 multi	3.00	3.00

Interlocking Hands — A387 | Peace Symbol and Flowers — A388

2023, May 9		Litho.	Perf. 13¼	
470	A387	(€2.80) multi	6.00	6.00
471	A388	(€2.80) multi	6.00	6.00

Europa.

Summer Cottage, Eckerö A389

Summer Cottage, Föglö Archipelago A390

Summer Cottage, Eckerö A391

Booklet Stamps

2023, June 9		Litho.	Perf. 14 Horiz.	
472		Vert. strip of 3	16.50	16.50
a.		A389 (€2.50) multi	5.50	5.50
b.		A390 (€2.50) multi	5.50	5.50
c.		A391 (€2.50) multi	5.50	5.50
d.		Booklet pane of 6, 2 each #472a-472c	33.00	—
		Complete booklet, #472d	33.00	

Raft in Jar, Photograph by Christoffer Relander — A392

2023, June 9		Litho.	Perf. 13½x13	
473	A392	(€3) multi	6.50	6.50

SEMI-POSTAL STAMPS

Campaign Against Breast Cancer — SP1

2012, Oct. 1		Litho.	Perf. 13½x13¾	
B1	SP1	€1+20c multi	2.25	1.50

Surtax for Aland Cancer Society.

Sculpture of Gnome by Hakan Sandberg — SP2

2013, Sept. 2		Litho.	Perf. 13¾x13½	
B2	SP2	€1+20c multi	2.00	1.50

Surtax for Aland Cancer Society.

Zero Tolerance Program Against Drug Abuse SP3

Litho. & Embossed

2014, Apr. 11			Perf. 14¾	
B3	SP3	€1.10 +20c black	2.50	1.50

FIUME

ˈfyü-ˌmā

LOCATION — A city and surrounding territory on the Adriatic Sea
GOVT. — Formerly a part of Italy
AREA — 8 sq. mi.
POP. — 44,956 (estimated 1924)

Fiume was under Hapsburg rule after 1466 and was transferred to Hungarian control after 1870. Of mixed Italian and Croatian population and strategically important, it was Hungary's only international seaport. Following World War I, Fiume was disputed between Italy and the newly created Kingdom of the Serbs, Croats and Slovenes (later Yugoslavia). A force of Allied troops occupied the city in Nov. 1918, while its future status was negotiated at the Paris Peace Conference.

In Sept. 1919, the Italian nationalist poet Gabriele d'Annunzio organized his legionnaires and seized Fiume, together with the islands of Arbe, Carnaro and Veglia, in the name of Italy. D'Annunzio established an autonomous administration, which soon came into conflict with the Italian government. There followed several years of instability, with three Italian interventions after 1920. In Jan. 1924, the Treaty of Rome between Italy and Yugoslavia established formal Italian sovereignty over Fiume, and Fiume stamps were replaced by those of Italy after March 31, 1924.

100 Filler = 1 Korona
100 Centesimi = 1 Corona (1919)
100 Centesimi = 1 Lira

See note on FIUME-KUPA Zone, Italian Occupation, after Yugoslavia No. NJ22.

The overprints on Nos. 1-23a have been extensively forged. Even the inexpensive values are difficult to find with genuine overprints. Forgeries of many later issues also exist, most created for the packet trade in the 1920s. Values are for genuine stamps. Collectors should be aware that stamps sold "as is" are likely to be forgeries, and unexpertized collections should be assumed to consist of mostly forged stamps. Education plus working with knowledgeable dealers is mandatory in this collecting area. More valuable stamps should be expertized.

Hungarian Stamps of 1916-18 Typograph Overprinted, Bold Sans Serif Letters

1918, Dec. 2 Wmk. 137 Perf. 15
On Stamps of 1916
Colored Numerals

1A	A9	20f gray brown	5,500.	3,000.

Hungarian Stamps of 1916-18 Typograph Overprinted

On Stamps of 1916
White Numerals

1	A8	10f rose	7,250.	7,250.
b.		Handstamped overprint	75.00	35.00
2	A8	15f violet	40.00	30.00

Value for No. 1a is for handstamped overprint. Value for No. 2 is for typographed overprint.

On Stamps of 1916-18
Colored Numerals

3	A9	2f brown orange	4.00	2.40
4	A9	3f red violet	4.00	2.40
5	A9	5f green	4.00	2.40
6	A9	6f grnsh blue	4.00	2.40
7a	A9	10f rose red, from	50.00	20.00
8	A9	15f violet	4.00	2.40
9	A9	20f gray brown	3.00	1.50
10	A9	25f deep blue	12.00	3.00
11	A9	35f brown	7.50	4.00
12a	A9	40f olive green, from	30.00	17.50

White Numerals

13	A10	50f red vio & lil	5.00	3.00
14	A10	75f brt bl & pale bl	10.00	4.00
15	A10	80f grn & pale grn	10.00	3.00
16	A10	1k red brn & claret	30.00	7.50
17	A10	2k ol brn & bis	5.00	3.00
18	A10	3k dk vio & ind	40.00	20.00
19	A10	5k dk brn & lt brn	145.00	40.00
20a	A10	10k vio brn & vio, from	400.00	175.00

Inverted or double overprints exist on most of Nos. 4-15.

On Stamps of 1918

21	A11	10f scarlet	3.00	3.00
22	A11	20f dark brown	2.50	2.00
23a	A12	40f olive green	17.50	17.50

The overprint on Nos. 3-23a was applied by 2 printing plates and 6 handstamps. Values are for the less costly. Values of Nos. 7a, 12a,

FIUME

20a and 23a are for handstamps. See the *Scott Specialized Catalogue of Stamps and Covers* for detailed listings.

Postage Due Stamps of Hungary, 1915-20 Ovptd. & Surcharged in Black

1919, Jan.

24	D1	45f on 6f green & red	15.00	10.00
25	D1	45f on 20f green & red	40.00	10.00
		Set, never hinged	138.00	

Hungarian Savings Bank Stamp Surcharged in Black

A2

1919, Jan. 29

26	A2	15f on 10f dk violet	22.00	17.00
		Never hinged	55.00	

Overprints on Nos. 24-26 are typographed. No. 26 also exists with double surcharge, one black and one red, and with one violet and one black.

"Italy" — A3

Italian Flag on Clock-Tower in Fiume — A4

"Revolution" A5

Sailor Raising Italian Flag at Fiume (1918) A6

Nos. 30-43 exist on three types of paper: (A) grayish, porous paper, printed in sheets of 70 stamps (Jan, Feb. printings); (B) translucent or semi-translucent good quality white paper, printed in sheets of 70 stamps (March printing); and (C) good quality medium white paper, plain and opaque, sometimes grayish or yellowish, printed in sheets of 100 (April printing). Values are for the least expensive variety. See the *Scott Specialized Catalogue of Stamps and Covers* for detailed listings.

Perf. 11½

1919, April   Unwmk.   Litho.

27	A3	2c dull blue	1.50	1.50
28	A3	3c gray brown	1.50	1.50
29	A3	5c yellow green	1.50	1.50
30a	A4	10c rose	17.50	9.00
31	A4	15c violet	1.50	1.50
32a	A4	20c emerald green	2.50	3.00
33	A5	25c dark blue	2.25	1.50
34	A6	30c deep violet	2.25	1.50
35	A5	40c brown	2.25	2.25
36	A5	45c orange	2.25	2.25
37	A6	50c yellow green	2.25	1.50
38	A6	60c claret	2.25	1.50
39	A6	1cor brown orange	3.75	2.25
40	A6	2cor brt blue	3.75	2.25
41	A6	3cor orange red	4.50	2.25
42	A6	5cor deep brown	22.00	22.00
43a	A6	10cor olive green	45.00	75.00
		Nos. 27-43a (17)	118.50	132.25

The earlier printings of Jan. and Feb. are on thin grayish paper, the Mar. printing is on semi-transparent white paper, all in sheets of 70. An Apr. printing is on white paper of medium thickness in sheets of 100. Part-perf. examples of most of this series are known.
For surcharges see Nos. 58, 60, 64, 66-69.

A7

A8

A9

A10

1919, July 28   Perf. 11½

46	A7	5c yellow green	2.00	2.00
47	A8	10c rose	2.00	2.00
48	A9	30c violet	7.75	2.50
49	A10	40c yellow brown	2.00	2.00
50	A9	45c orange	8.00	5.50
51	A9	50c yellow green	8.00	5.50
52	A9	60c claret	7.75	5.40
a.		Perf. 13x12½	140.00	
		Never hinged	200.00	
b.		Perf. 10½	320.00	
		Never hinged	825.00	
53	A9	10cor olive green	8.00	15.00
a.		Perf. 13x12½	50.00	72.50
		Never hinged	125.00	
b.		Perf. 10½	320.00	225.00
		Never hinged	825.00	
		Nos. 46-53 (8)	45.50	39.90
		Set, never hinged	115.00	

Five other denominations (25c, 1cor, 2cor, 3cor and 5cor) were not officially issued. Some examples of the 25c are known canceled.
For surcharges see Nos. 60, 61 63, 65, 70.

Stamps and Types of 1919 Handstamp Surcharged

1919-20

58	A4	5c on 20c grn ('20)	2.00	2.00
59	A9	5c on 25c blue	2.00	2.00
60	A5	10c on 45c orange	2.50	2.00
61	A9	15c on 30c vio ('20)	2.00	2.00
62	A10	15c on 45c orange	2.00	2.00
63	A9	15c on 60c cl ('20)	2.00	2.00
64	A6	25c on 50c yel grn ('20)	9.75	24.00
65	A9	25c on 50c yel grn ('20)	2.00	2.00
66	A6	55c on 1cor brn org	30.00	30.00
67	A6	55c on 2cor brt bl	5.00	7.00
68	A6	55c on 3cor org red	5.00	6.00
69	A6	55c on 5cor dp brn	5.00	6.00
70	A6	55c on 10cor ol grn	24.00	27.50
		Nos. 58-70 (13)	93.25	114.50
		Set, never hinged	235.00	

Semi-Postal Stamps of 1919 Surcharged

a   b

First Setting
Surcharge letters thin and small.

1919-20

73	SP6(a)	5c on 5c grn	2.00	2.00
74	SP6(a)	10c on 10c rose	2.00	2.00
75	SP6(a)	15c on 15c gray	2.00	2.00
76	SP6(a)	20c on 20c org	2.00	2.00
78	SP7(b)	45c on 45c ol grn	2.50	2.50
79	SP7(b)	60c on 60c rose	2.50	2.50
80	SP7(b)	80c on 80c vio	4.00	4.00
81	SP7(b)	1cor on 1cor sl	4.00	4.00
82	SP8(a)	2cor on 2cor red brn	4.00	4.00
83	SP8(a)	3cor on 3cor blk brn	5.00	5.00
84	SP8(a)	5cor on 5cor yel brn	6.00	6.00

Second Setting
Surcharge letters bold, 2.5mm between "Cent." and figures of value, 5c-25c; overprint larger, 45c-10cor.

1920, Feb.5

73A	SP6(a)	5c on 5c grn	2.00	2.00
74A	SP6(a)	10c on 10c rose	24.00	5.00
75A	SP6(a)	15c on 15c gray	2.00	2.00
76A	SP6(a)	20c on 20c org	2.00	2.00
77	SP9(a)	25c on 25c bl ('20)	2.00	2.00
78A	SP7(b)	45c on 45c ol grn	2.50	2.50
79A	SP7(b)	60c on 60c rose	2.50	2.50
80A	SP7(b)	80c on 80c lil	2.00	2.00
81A	SP7(b)	1cor on 1cor sl	2.50	2.50
82A	SP8(a)	2cor on 2cor red brn	17.00	20.00
83A	SP8(a)	3cor on 3cor blk brn	35.00	22.00
84A	SP8(a)	5cor on 5cor yel brn	24.00	50.00
85	SP8(a)	10cor on 10cor dk vio ('20)	2.50	2.50

Third Setting, Milano Printing (new plates)
5c and 10c: 2mm spacing between "Cent." and denominations; 15c: new color; 45c: surcharge with bold letters.

1920, Apr. 5

73B	SP6(a)	5c on 5c grn	2.00	2.00
74B	SP6(a)	10c on 10c rose	2.00	2.00
75B	SP6(a)	15c on 15c brown gray	4.00	4.00

Gabriele d'Annunzio — A11

1920, Sept. 12   Typo.   Perf. 11½
Pale Buff Background

86	A11	5c green	3.00	3.00
87	A11	10c carmine	3.00	3.00
88	A11	15c dark gray	3.00	3.00
89	A11	20c orange	3.00	3.00
90	A11	25c dark blue	3.00	3.00
91	A11	30c red brown	3.00	3.00
92	A11	45c olive gray	5.00	5.00
93	A11	50c lilac	5.00	5.00
94	A11	55c bister	5.00	5.00
95	A11	1 l black	17.50	25.00
96	A11	2 l red violet	17.50	25.00
97	A11	3 l dark green	17.50	25.00
98	A11	5 l brown	65.00	45.00
99	A11	10 l gray violet	17.50	25.00
		Nos. 86-99 (14)	168.00	178.00
		Set, never hinged	415.00	

The background print, pale buff, also exists doubly printed or shifted on several denominations.
Counterfeits of Nos. 86 to 99 are plentiful.
For overprints see Nos. 134-148.

Severing the Gordian Knot — A12

Designs: 10c, Ancient emblem of Fiume. 20c, Head of "Fiume." 25c, Hands holding daggers.

1920, Sept. 12

100	A12	5c green	35.00	25.00
a.		Imperf.	135.00	
b.		Horiz. pair, imperf. between	400.00	
101	A12	10c deep red	22.50	22.50
a.		Imperf.	87.50	
102	A12	20c brown orange	35.00	22.50
103	A12	25c blue	22.50	47.50
a.		Imperf.	155.00	
b.		Double impression, imperf.	1,225.	
c.		Horiz. pair, imperf. between	550.00	
d.		25c blue	80.00	80.00
e.		As "d," imperf.	340.00	
f.		As "d," horiz. pair, imperf. between	1,200.	
		Nos. 100-103 (4)	115.00	117.50
		Set, never hinged	280.00	

Anniv. of the occupation of Fiume by d'Annunzio. They were available for franking the correspondence of the legionnaires on the day of issue only, Sept. 12, 1920.
Counterfeits of Nos. 100-103 are plentiful. Genuine stamps have a slight projection on the right side of the second vertical stroke of the "U" of "FIUME", and the basal serif of the "I" of "FIUME" projects more on the left than the right.
For overprints and surcharges see Nos. 104-133, E4-E9.

Nos. 100-103 Overprinted or Surcharged in Black or Red

1920, Nov. 20

104	A12	1c on 5c green	2.40	2.40
a.		Inverted overprint	55.00	55.00
b.		Double overprint	200.00	
105	A12	2c on 25c indigo (R)	2.40	2.40
a.		Inverted overprint	55.00	55.00
b.		Double overprint	72.50	72.50
c.		2c on 25c blue (R)	80.00	80.00
106	A12	5c green	20.00	2.40
a.		Inverted overprint	47.50	47.50
b.		Double overprint	72.50	72.50
107	A12	10c rose	20.00	2.40
a.		Inverted overprint	55.00	55.00
b.		Double overprint	72.50	72.50
108	A12	15c on 10c rose	2.40	2.40
a.		Inverted overprint	65.00	65.00
b.		Double overprint	72.50	72.50
109	A12	15c on 20c brn org	2.40	2.40
a.		Inverted overprint	65.00	65.00
b.		Double overprint	72.50	72.50
110	A12	15c on 25c indigo (R)	2.40	2.40
a.		Inverted overprint	65.00	65.00
b.		Double overprint	72.50	72.50
c.		15c on 25c blue (R)	225.00	225.00
111	A12	20c brn org	2.40	2.40
a.		Inverted overprint	27.50	27.50
b.		Double overprint	125.00	125.00
112	A12	25c indigo (R)	2.40	2.40
a.		Inverted overprint	24.00	24.00
b.		25c blue (R)	8.00	8.00
113	A12	25c indigo (Bk)	175.00	175.00
a.		Inverted overprint	450.00	350.00
b.		25c blue (Bk)	240.00	240.00
c.		As "b," inverted overprint	725.00	
114	A12	25c on 10c rose	2.40	4.75
a.		Double overprint	72.50	72.50
115	A12	50c on 20c brn org	5.00	2.40
a.		Double overprint	72.50	72.50
116	A12	55c on 5c green	21.00	4.75
a.		Inverted overprint	95.00	95.00
b.		Double overprint	72.50	72.50
117	A12	1 l on 10c rose	47.50	40.00
a.		Inverted overprint	275.00	275.00
b.		Double overprint	275.00	
118	A12	1 l on 25c indigo (R)	100.00	100.00
a.		1 l on 25c blue (R)	600.00	600.00
b.		As "a," inverted overprint	875.00	725.00
119	A12	2 l on 5c green	47.50	40.00
a.		Inverted overprint	325.00	
b.		Double overprint	200.00	
120	A12	5 l on 10c rose	225.00	240.00
a.		Inverted overprint	725.00	725.00
b.		Double overprint	725.00	
121	A12	10 l on 20c brn org	700.00	550.00
a.		Inverted overprint	1,600.	800.00
b.		Double overprint	1,600.	800.00
		Nos. 104-121 (18)	1,380.	1,179.
		Set, never hinged	3,050.	

The Fiume Legionnaires of d'Annunzio occupied the islands of Arbe and Veglia in the Gulf of Carnaro Nov. 13, 1920-Jan. 5, 1921.
Varieties of overprint or surcharge exist for most of Nos. 104-121.
Nos. 113, 117-121, 125, 131 have a backprint.

Nos. 106-107, 111, 113, 115-116 Overprinted or Surcharged at top

1920, Nov. 28

122	A12	5c green	35.00	24.00
123	A12	10c rose	45.00	52.50
124	A12	20c brown org	87.50	52.50
125	A12	25c deep blue	52.50	52.50
126	A12	50c on 20c brn org	95.00	52.50
127	A12	55c on 5c green	95.00	52.50
		Nos. 122-127 (6)	410.00	286.50
		Set, never hinged	1,000.	

The overprint on Nos. 122-125 comes in two widths: 11mm and 14mm. Values are for the 11mm width.

FIUME

Nos. 106-107, 111, 113, 115-116 Overprinted or Surcharged at top

1920, Nov. 28

128	A12 5c green	35.00	24.00
129	A12 10c rose	45.00	52.50
130	A12 20c brown orange	87.50	52.50
131	A12 25c deep blue	52.50	52.50
132	A12 50c on 20c brn org	95.00	52.50
133	A12 55c on 5c green	95.00	52.50
	Nos. 128-133 (6)	410.00	286.50
	Set, never hinged	1,000.	

Nos. 86-99 Overprinted

1921, Feb. 2
"Provvisorio" 20mm wide
Space between lines 3mm
Pale Buff Background

134	A11 5c green	2.40	2.40
a.	Inverted overprint	27.50	27.50
b.	Double overprint	52.50	52.50
135	A11 10c carmine	2.40	2.40
a.	Inverted overprint	27.50	27.50
b.	Double overprint	52.50	52.50
136	A11 15c dark gray	2.40	2.40
a.	Inverted overprint	27.50	27.50
b.	Double overprint	52.50	52.50
137	A11 20c orange	4.00	4.00
a.	Inverted overprint	27.50	27.50
b.	Double overprint	27.50	27.50
138	A11 25c dark blue	4.00	4.00
a.	Inverted overprint	27.50	27.50
b.	Double overprint	52.50	52.50
139	A11 30c red brown	4.00	4.00
a.	Inverted overprint	27.50	27.50
b.	Double overprint	27.50	27.50
140	A11 45c olive gray	2.40	2.40
a.	Inverted overprint	55.00	55.00
b.	Double overprint	40.00	40.00
141	A11 50c lilac	4.00	4.00
a.	Inverted overprint	27.50	27.50
142	A11 55c bister	4.00	4.00
a.	Inverted overprint	16.00	16.00
143	A11 1 l black	145.00	180.00
a.	Inverted overprint	350.00	350.00
144	A11 2 l red violet	95.00	95.00
145	A11 3 l dark green	95.00	95.00
146	A11 5 l brown	95.00	95.00
147	A11 10 l gray violet	95.00	95.00

With Additional Surcharge

148	A11 1 l on 30c red brown	2.50	2.50
a.	Inverted overprint	27.50	27.50
b.	Double overprint	55.00	55.00
	Nos. 134-148 (15)	557.10	592.10
	Set, never hinged	1,400.	

Most of Nos. 134-143, 148 and E10-E11 exist with inverted or double overprint. See Nos. E10-E11.

Second Printing, Milan
"Provvisorio" 21mm wide
Space between overprint lines 4mm

1921, Dec. 18

148A	A11 5c yellow green	50.00	57.50
	Never hinged	125.00	
	On cover		300.00
148B	A11 10c carmine	135.00	40.00
	Never hinged	340.00	
	On cover		300.00
c.	Vert. pair, imperf. between	650.00	

First Constituent Assembly

Nos. B4-B15 Overprinted

1921, Apr. 24

149	SP6 5c blue green	6.50	4.75
150	SP6 10c rose	6.50	4.75
a.	Inverted overprint	65.00	65.00
151	SP6 15c gray	6.50	4.75
152	SP6 20c orange	6.50	4.75
153	SP7 45c olive green	17.50	12.00
154	SP7 60c car rose	17.50	12.00
a.	Inverted overprint	47.50	47.50
155	SP7 80c brt violet	27.50	24.00

With Additional Overprint "L"

156	SP7 1 l on 1cor dk slate	32.50	35.00
a.	Inverted overprint	80.00	80.00
157	SP8 2 l on 2cor red brn	120.00	4.25
a.	Inverted overprint	325.00	160.00
158	SP8 3 l on 3cor black brn	120.00	130.00
159	SP8 5 l on 5cor yel brn	120.00	4.25
160	SP8 10 l on 10cor dk vio	175.00	175.00
a.	Inverted overprint	475.00	400.00
	Nos. 149-160 (12)	656.00	415.50
	Set, never hinged	1,625.	

The overprint exists inverted on several denominations.

Second Constituent Assembly
"Constitution" Issue of 1921 With Additional Overprint "1922"

1922

161	SP6 5c blue green	4.75	3.25
a.	Inverted overprint	24.00	24.00
162	SP6 10c rose	2.40	2.40
a.	Inverted overprint	24.00	24.00
b.	Double overprint, one inverted	40.00	40.00
163	SP6 15c gray	20.00	12.00
164	SP6 20c orange	2.40	2.40
a.	Inverted overprint	32.50	32.50
b.	Double overprint	40.00	40.00
c.	Double overprint, one inverted		
165	SP7 45c olive grn	13.00	12.00
a.	Double overprint	40.00	40.00
166	SP7 60c car rose	2.40	3.25
167	SP7 80c brt violet	2.40	3.25
168	SP7 1 l on 1cor dk slate	2.40	2.40
a.	Inverted overprint	55.00	55.00
b.	Double overprint	40.00	40.00
169	SP8 2 l on 2cor red brn	20.00	16.00
170	SP8 3 l on 3cor blk brn	2.50	3.25
171	SP8 5 l on 5cor yel brn	2.50	3.25
	Nos. 161-171 (11)	74.75	63.45
	Set, never hinged	170.00	

Nos. 161-171 have the overprint in heavier type than Nos. 149-160 and "IV" in Roman instead of sans-serif numerals.
The overprint exists inverted or double on almost all values.

Venetian Ship — A16

St. Vitus A18

Roman Arch — A17

Rostral Column A19

1923, Mar. 23   Perf. 11½
Pale Buff Background

172	A16 5c blue green	2.40	2.40
173	A16 10c violet	2.40	2.40
174	A16 15c brown	2.40	2.40
175	A17 20c orange red	2.40	2.40
176	A17 25c dark gray	2.40	2.40
177	A17 30c dark green	2.40	2.40
178	A18 50c dull blue	2.40	2.40
179	A18 60c rose	4.00	4.00
180	A18 1 l dark blue	4.00	4.00
181	A19 2 l violet brown	65.00	20.00
182	A19 3 l olive bister	55.00	45.00
183	A19 5 l yellow brown	55.00	52.50
	Nos. 172-183 (12)	199.80	142.30
	Set, never hinged	465.00	

Nos. 172-183 Overprinted

1924, Feb. 22
Pale Buff Background

184	A16 5c blue green	2.40	12.00
a.	Inverted overprint	20.00	40.00
b.	Double overprint	130.00	
185	A16 10c violet	2.40	12.00
a.	Inverted overprint	16.00	40.00
186	A16 15c brown	2.40	12.00
a.	Inverted overprint	17.00	40.00
187	A17 20c orange red	2.40	12.00
a.	Inverted overprint	21.00	40.00
b.	Double overprint	260.00	
188	A17 25c dk gray	2.40	12.00
189	A17 30c dk green	2.40	12.00
a.	Inverted overprint	42.50	
190	A18 50c dull blue	2.40	12.00
a.	Inverted overprint	42.50	42.50
191	A18 60c red	2.40	12.00
a.	Inverted overprint	87.50	
192	A18 1 l dark blue	2.40	12.00
a.	Inverted overprint	21.00	40.00
193	A19 2 l violet brown	4.00	32.50
a.	Inverted overprint	130.00	160.00
194	A19 3 l olive	6.00	40.00
195	A19 5 l yellow brown	6.00	40.00
	Nos. 184-195 (12)	37.60	220.50
	Set, never hinged	80.00	

The overprint exists inverted on almost all values.

Nos. 172-183 Overprinted

1924, Mar. 1
Pale Buff Background

196	A16 5c blue green	2.40	20.00
197	A16 10c violet	2.40	20.00
198	A16 15c brown	2.40	20.00
199	A17 20c orange red	2.40	20.00
200	A17 25c dark gray	2.40	20.00
201	A17 30c dark green	2.40	20.00
202	A18 50c dull blue	2.40	20.00
203	A18 60c red	2.40	20.00
204	A18 1 l dark blue	2.40	20.00
205	A19 2 l violet brown	4.00	27.50
206	A19 3 l olive	4.00	27.50
207	A19 5 l yellow brown	4.00	27.50
	Nos. 196-207 (12)	33.60	262.50
	Set, never hinged	62.50	

Postage stamps of Fiume were superseded by stamps of Italy.

SEMI-POSTAL STAMPS

Semi-Postal Stamps of Hungary, 1916-17 Overprinted

1918, Dec. 2   Wmk. 137   Perf. 15

B1	SP3 10f + 2f rose	8.00	8.00
a.	Inverted overprint	72.50	40.00
b.	Double overprint	240.00	120.00
B2	SP4 15f + 2f dl vio	8.00	8.00
a.	Inverted overprint	145.00	40.00
b.	Double overprint	145.00	47.50
B3	SP5 40f + 2f brn car	14.50	8.00
a.	Inverted overprint	87.50	37.50
	Nos. B1-B3 (3)	30.50	24.00
	Set, never hinged	72.50	

Examples of Nos. B1-B3 with overprint handstamped sell for higher prices.

Statue of Romulus and Remus Being Suckled by Wolf — SP6

Venetian Galley SP7

Church of St. Mark's, Venice SP8

Perf. 11½

1919, May 18   Unwmk.   Typo.

B4	SP6 5c +5 l bl grn	47.50	32.50
B5	SP6 10c +5 l rose	47.50	32.50
B6	SP6 15c +5 l dk gray	47.50	32.50
B7	SP6 20c +5 l orange	47.50	32.50
B8	SP7 45c +5 l ol grn	47.50	32.50
B9	SP7 60c +5 l car rose	47.50	32.50
B10	SP7 80c +5 l lilac	47.50	32.50
B11	SP7 1cor +5 l dk slate	47.50	32.50
B12	SP8 2cor +5 l red brn	47.50	32.50
B13	SP8 3cor +5 l blk brn	47.50	32.50
B14	SP8 5cor +5 l yel brn	47.50	32.50
B15	SP8 10cor +5 l dk vio	47.50	32.50
	Nos. B4-B15 (12)	570.00	390.00
	Set, never hinged	1,450.	

200th day of peace. The surtax aided Fiume students in Italy. "Posta di Fiume" is printed on the back of Nos. B4-B16.
The surtax is shown on the stamps as "LIRE 5" but actually was 5cor.
For surcharges and overprints see Nos. 73-76, 78-85, 149-171, J15-J26.

Dr. Antonio Grossich — SP9

1919, Sept. 20

B16	SP9 25c + 2 l blue	3.25	3.25
	Never hinged	8.00	

Surtax for the Dr. Grossich Foundation.
For overprint and surcharge, see No. 77.

SPECIAL DELIVERY STAMPS

1916 Special Delivery Stamp of Hungary Overprinted

1918, Dec. 2   Wmk. 137   Perf. 15
Typographed Overprint

E1	SD1 2f gray green & red	4.75	4.75
	Never hinged	12.00	
a.	Double overprint	190.00	175.00

Handstamped overprints sell for more.

SD3

Perf. 11½

1920, Sept. 12   Unwmk.   Typo.

E2	SD3 30c slate blue	25.00	25.00
E3	SD3 50c rose	25.00	25.00
	Set, never hinged	125.00	

For overprints see Nos. E10-E11.

Nos. 102 and 100 Surcharged

1920, Nov.

E4	A12 30c on 20c brn org	190.00	175.00
a.	Inverted overprint	625.00	
b.	Double overprint	625.00	
E5	A12 50c on 5c green	290.00	125.00
a.	Inverted overprint	1,000.	
b.	Double overprint	1,000.	
c.	Double overprint, one inverted	1,100.	

Nos. E4-E5 have a backprint.

Same Surcharge as on Nos. 124, 122

E6	A12 30c on 20c brn org	275.00	180.00
E7	A12 50c on 5c green	210.00	180.00
a.	Double overprint		950.00

Overprint on Nos. E6-E7 is 11mm wide.

FIUME — FRANCE

Same Surcharge as on Nos. 130, 128

E8	A12	30c on 20c brn org	275.00	180.00
E9	A12	50c on 5c green	210.00	180.00
a.		Double overprint	950.00	950.00
		Nos. E4-E9 (6)	1,450.	1,020.
		Set, never hinged	2,900.	

Overprint on Nos. E8-E9 is 17mm wide.

Nos. E2 and E3 Overprinted

1921, Feb. 2

E10	SD3	30c slate blue	11.00	12.00
a.		Inverted overprint	120.00	120.00
b.		Double overprint	40.00	40.00
E11	SD3	50c rose	15.00	12.00
a.		Inverted overprint	27.50	27.50
b.		Double overprint	105.00	105.00
		Set, never hinged	62.50	

Fiume in 16th Century — SD4

1923, Mar. 23   Perf. 11, 11½

E12	SD4	60c rose & buff	24.00	24.00
E13	SD4	2 l dk bl & buff	24.00	24.00
		Set, never hinged	120.00	

Nos. E12-E13 Overprinted

1924, Feb. 22

E14	SD4	60c rose & buff	3.25	20.00
E15	SD4	2 l dk bl & buff	3.25	20.00
a.		Inverted overprint	130.00	160.00
		Set, never hinged	16.00	

Nos. E12-E13 Overprinted

1924, Mar. 1

E16	SD4	60c car & buff	4.00	80.00
E17	SD4	2 l dk bl & buff	4.00	80.00
		Set, never hinged	20.00	

POSTAGE DUE STAMPS

Postage Due Stamps of Hungary, 1915-1916, Overprinted

1918, Dec.   Wmk. 137   Perf. 15

J1c	D1	6f green & black	190.00	105.00
d.		Double overprint	—	1,450.
J2c	D1	12f green & black	180.00	72.50
d.		Double overprint		1,450.
J3c	D1	50c green & black	65.00	35.00
d.		Double overprint		1,450.
J4c	D1	1f green & red	40.00	24.00
d.		Inverted overprint		425.00
e.		Double overprint	525.00	190.00
J5	D1	2f green & red	6.50	6.50
a.		Inverted overprint	52.50	45.00
b.		Double overprint	175.00	
J6c	D1	5f green & red	40.00	47.50
d.		Inverted overprint	320.00	440.00
e.		Double overprint	525.00	525.00
J7	D1	6f green & red	6.50	6.50
a.		Inverted overprint	25.00	25.00
b.		Double overprint	27.50	
J8c	D1	10f green & red	32.50	32.50
d.		Inverted overprint	475.00	475.00
J9	D1	12f green & red	6.50	6.50
J10c	D1	15f green & red	32.50	32.50
d.		Inverted overprint		800.00
e.		Double overprint	440.00	440.00
J11	D1	20f green & red	6.50	6.50
a.		Inverted overprint	45.00	32.50
J12c	D1	30f green & red	32.50	32.50
d.		Inverted overprint		900.00
e.		Double overprint	950.00	950.00
		Nos. J1c-J12 (12)	638.50	407.50
		Set, never hinged	1,275.	

Overprint was applied by press or handstamp. Six minor varieties of the handstamp exist. Some are sought by specialists at much higher values. Excellent forgeries exist. For more detailed listings, see *Scott Classic Specialized Catalogue of Stamps and Covers 1840-1940.*

Eagle — D2

Perf. 11½

1919, July 28   Unwmk.   Typo.

J13	D2	2c brown	2.40	2.40
J14	D2	5c brown	2.40	2.40
		Set, never hinged	12.00	

Semi-Postal Stamps of 1919 Overprinted and Surcharged

1921, Mar. 21

J15	SP6	2c on 15c gray	6.50	6.50
J16	SP6	4c on 10c rose	4.75	4.75
J17	SP9	5c on 25c blue	4.75	4.75
J18	SP6	6c on 20c orange	4.75	4.75
J19	SP6	10c on 20c orange	6.50	6.50

Nos. B8-B11 Surcharged

J20	SP7	20c on 45c ol grn	2.40	4.75
J21	SP7	30c on 1cor dk slate	12.00	12.00
J22	SP7	40c on 80c violet	4.75	6.50
J23	SP7	50c on 60c car	4.75	6.50
J24	SP7	60c on 45c ol grn	2.40	4.75
J25	SP7	80c on 45c ol grn	2.40	4.75

Surcharged like Nos. J15-J19

J26	SP8	1 l on 2cor red brown	24.00	24.00
		Nos. J15-J26 (12)	79.95	90.50
		Set, never hinged	190.00	

See note below No. 85 regarding settings of "Valore Globale" overprint.

NEWSPAPER STAMPS

Newspaper Stamp of Hungary, 1914, Overprinted like Nos. 1-23

1918, Dec. 2   Wmk. 137   Impert.

P1	N5	(2f) orange	4.75	3.25
		Never hinged	15.00	
a.		Inverted overprint	55.00	52.50
b.		Double overprint	210.00	190.00

Handstamped overprints sell for more.

Eagle — N1

1919   Unwmk.   Perf. 11½

P2	N1	2c deep buff	9.50	14.50

Re-engraved

P3	N1	2c deep buff	9.50	14.50
		Set, never hinged	48.00	

In the re-engraved stamp the top of the "2" is rounder and broader, the feet of the eagle show clearly and the diamond at bottom has six lines instead of five.

Steamer N2

1920, Sept. 12

P4	N2	1c gray green	4.00	3.25
		Never hinged	10.00	
a.		Imperf	24.00	24.00

FRANCE

'fran̗t̩s

LOCATION — Western Europe
GOVT. — Republic
AREA — 210,033 sq. mi.
POP. — 65,270,000 (2020 est.)
CAPITAL — Paris

100 Centimes = 1 Franc
100 Cents = 1 Euro (2002)

Catalogue values for unused stamps in this country are for Never Hinged items, beginning with Scott 299 in the regular postage section, Scott B42 in the semipostal section, Scott C18 in the airpost section, Scott CB1 in the airpost semi-postal section, Scott J69 in the postage due section, Scott M10 in the military stamps section, Scott 101 in the section for official stamps for the Council of Europe, Scott 2O1 for the section for UNESCO, Scott S1 for franchise stamps, Scott N27 for occupation stamps, and Scott 2N1 for AMG stamps.

Watermarks

Wmk. 407

Ceres — A1

FORTY CENTIMES

Type I

Type II

1849-50   Typo.   Unwmk.   Imperf.

1	A1	10c bis, yelsh	1,500.	210.00
		('50)		
a.		10c dark bister, yelsh	1,825.	240.00
b.		10c greenish bister	2,350.	600.00
d.		As #1, tête bêche pair	85,000.	18,000.
2	A1	15c grn, grnsh	21,500.	800.00
a.		15c yellow green, grnsh	20,000.	700.00
c.		Tête bêche pair		
3	A1	20c blk, yelsh	340.00	34.00
a.		20c black	375.00	50.00
b.		20c black, buff	1,100.	135.00
c.		Tête bêche pair	9,250.	6,500.
4	A1	20c dark blue	2,400.	
a.		20c blue, bluish		2,050.
b.		20c blue, yelsh		2,750.
c.		Tête bêche pair		60,000.
6	A1	25c lt bl, bluish	5,400.	30.00
a.		25c blue, bluish		30.00
		('50)		
b.		25c blue, yelsh	6,250.	40.00
c.		Tête bêche pair	155,000.	12,500.
7	A1	40c org, yelsh (I)	2,950.	360.00
		('50)		
a.		40c org ver, yelsh (I)	3,500.	475.00
b.		40c orange, yelsh (II)	20,750.	5,250.
c.		Pair, types I and II	31,000.	12,500.
g.		Vertical half used as 20c on cover		260,000.
8	A1	1fr ver, yelsh	92,500.	13,750.
a.		1fr dull orange red	95,000.	17,000.
c.		1fr pale ver ("Vervelle")	20,000.	
d.		As "c," tête bêche pair	450,000.	
9	A1	1fr lt car	8,750.	650.00
a.		Tête bêche pair	200,000.	23,250.
b.		1fr brown carmine	10,000.	800.00
c.		1fr dark carmine, yelsh	12,250.	1,075.

No. 4 was printed but not yet gummed when the rate change to 25c made them unnecessary. An essay with a red "25" surcharge on No. 4 was rejected.

An ungummed sheet of No. 8c was found in 1895 among the effects of Anatole A. Hulot, the printer. It was sold to Ernest Vervelle, a Parisian dealer, by whose name the stamps are known.

See Nos. 329-329e, 612-613, 624.

Nos. 1, 4a, 6a, 7 and 13 are of similar designs and colors to French Colonies Nos. 9, 11, 12, 14, and 8. There are numerous shades of each. Identification by those who are not experts can be difficult, though cancellations can be used as a guide for used stamps.

Because of the date of issue the Colonies stamps are similar in shades and papers to the perforated French stamps, Nos. 23a, 54, 57-59, and are not as clearly printed. Except for No. 13, unused, the French Colonies stamps sell for much less than the values shown here for properly identified French versions.

Expertization of these stamps is recommended.

FRANCE & COLONIES

From Classics to Modern
Top Quality at Realistic Prices
FREE FRANCE PRICE LIST
1923 to 1957
NH & H Singles & Sets
Year Sets Available Starting 1958

Price Lists Also Available for:
FSAT, Fr. Andorra, Fr. Polynesia
Monaco, St. Pierre & Miquelon

WANT LISTS INVITED
for all other French Colonies
Free French Imports Price List!
Ballon Monté Covers Available!

WE BUY!
Especially needed: NH 1920-1950, 2000-date. Sets, Collections & More! Sell to a knowledgeable specialist!

www.hgitner.com
1-800-94-STAMP
(1-800-947-8267)

Henry Gitner
Philatelists, Inc.

P.O. Box 3077-S, Middletown, NY 10940
Tel: 845-343-5151   Fax: 845-343-0068
Toll Free: 1-800-947-8267
E-mail: hgitner@hgitner.com

PHILATELY-THE QUIET EXCITEMENT!

612 FRANCE

1862 Re-issue
1g	A1	10c bister		435.
2d	A1	15c yellow green		560.
3d	A1	20c black, *yellowish*		375.
4d	A1	20c blue		340.
6d	A1	25c blue		400.
7d	A1	40c orange (I)		575.
7e	A1	40c orange (II)		11,000.
h.		Pair, types I and II		15,000.
9d	A1	1fr pale lake		600.

The re-issues are fine impressions in lighter colors and on whiter paper than the originals. An official imitation of the essay, 25c on 20c blue, also in a lighter shade and on whiter paper, was made at the same time as the re-issues.

President Louis Napoleon — A2

Inscribed: "REPUB FRANC"

1852
10	A2	10c pale bister, *yelsh*	30,000.	450.00
a.		10c dark bister, *yelsh*	30,000.	525.00
11	A2	25c blue, *bluish*	2,450.	32.50
b.		25c dark blue, *bluish*	2,900.	50.00

1862 Re-issue
10b	A2	10c bister		525.00
11a	A2	25c blue		350.00

The re-issues are in lighter colors and on whiter paper than the originals.

Emperor Napoleon III — A3

Die I. The curl above the forehead directly below "R" of "EMPIRE" is made up of two lines very close together, often appearing to form a single thick line. There is no shading across the neck.

Die II. The curl is made of two distinct, more widely separated lines. There are lines of shading across the upper neck.

Inscribed: "EMPIRE FRANC"

1853-60 Imperf.
12	A3	1c ol grn, *pale bl* ('60)	165.00	62.50
a.		1c bronze grn, *pale bluish*	155.00	67.50
13	A3	5c grn, *grnsh* (I) ('54)	630.00	62.50
14	A3	10c bis, *yelsh* (I)	360.00	6.50
a.		10c yellow, *yelsh* (I)	1,200.	27.50
b.		10c bister brn, *yelsh* (I)	450.00	18.50
c.		10c bister, *yelsh* (II) ('60)	450.00	19.00
15	A3	20c bl, *bluish* (I)	150.00	1.35
a.		20c dark bl, *bluish* (I)	220.00	1.35
b.		20c milky blue (I)	225.00	10.00
c.		20c blue, *lilac* (I)	4,250.	62.50
d.		20c blue, *bluish* (II) ('60)	285.00	4.00
e.		Half used as 10c on cover		16,000.
f.		Tête bêche pair	155,000.	
16	A3	20c bl, *grnsh* (II)	5,250.	150.00
a.		20c blue, *greenish* (II)	4,250.	100.00
17	A3	25c bl, *bluish* (I)	2,050.	165.00
18	A3	40c org, *yelsh* (I)	2,000.	10.00
a.		40c org ver, *yellowish*	2,850.	16.00
b.		Half used as 20c on cover		110,000.
19	A3	80c lake, *yelsh* (I) ('54)	2,800.	40.00
a.		Tête bêche pair	340,000.	22,000.
b.		Half used as 40c on cover		50,000.
20	A3	80c rose, *pnksh* (I) ('60)	1,875.	42.50
a.		Tête-bêche pair	49,500.	10,000.
21	A3	1fr lake, *yelsh* (I)	7,450.	2,475.
a.		Tête bêche pair	300,000.	135,000.

Most values of the 1853-60 issue are known privately rouletted, pin-perf., perf. 7 and percé en scie.

1862 Re-issue
17c	A3	25c blue (I)		450.
19c	A3	80c lake (I)		1,800.
21c	A3	1fr lake (I)		1,500.
d.		Tête bêche pair		27,500.

The re-issues are in lighter colors and on whiter paper than the originals.

1862-71 Perf. 14x13½
22	A3	1c ol grn, *pale bl* (II)	140.00	30.00
a.		1c bronze grn, *pale bl* (II)	140.00	35.00
		On cover		175.00
		On cover, single franking		325.00

23	A3	5c yel grn, *grnsh* (I)	190.00	10.00
a.		5c deep green, *grnsh* (I)	225.00	12.50
24	A3	5c grn, *pale bl* ('71) (I)	1,800.	110.00
25	A3	10c bis, *yelsh* (II)	1,350.	3.75
a.		10c yel brn, *yelsh* (II)	1,750.	8.50
26	A3	20c bl, *bluish* (II)	200.00	1.25
a.		Tête bêche pair (II)	4,000.	1,000.
27	A3	40c org, *yelsh* (II)	1,200.	6.50
28	A3	80c rose, *pnksh* (I)	1,100.	30.00
a.		80c bright rose, *pinkish* (I)	1,300.	35.00
c.		Tête bêche pair (I)	17,500.	7,750.

No. 26a imperf is from a trial printing.

A4 A5

Napoleon III — A6

1863-70 Perf. 14x13½
29	A4	1c brnz grn, *pale bl* ('70)	37.50	16.00
a.		1c olive green, *pale blue*	37.50	16.00
30	A4	2c red brn, *yelsh*	105.00	25.00
b.		Half used as 1c on cover		36,000.
31	A4	4c gray	165.00	37.50
a.		Tete beche pair	17,500.	11,000.
d.		Half used as 2c on cover		50,000.
32	A5	10c bis, *yelsh* ('67)	215.00	5.00
c.		Half used as 5c on cover with other stamps		3,750.
33	A5	20c bl, *bluish* ('67)	175.00	1.55
c.		Half used as 10c on cover		62,500.
e.		20c dark blue ('67)	275.00	3.25
		No gum	140.00	
		On cover, single franking		4.00
34	A5	30c brn, *yelsh* ('67)	625.00	12.50
a.		30c dk brn, *yellowish*	1,000.	30.00
35	A5	40c pale org, *yelsh* ('68)	700.00	8.00
a.		40c org, *yelsh*	700.00	8.00
c.		Half used as 20c on cover		35,000.
36	A5	80c rose, *pnksh* ('68)	800.00	20.00
a.		80c carmine, *yellowish*	950.00	24.00
d.		Half used as 40c on cover		42,500.
e.		Quarter used as 20c on cover		50,000.
37	A6	5fr vio gray, *pnksh* ('69)	6,000.	750.00

Values for blocks of 4 Original Issue Imperfs
31c	A4	4c gray	270.00 —
32a	A5	10c bis, *yelsh*	360.00 —
33b	A5	20c bl, *bluish*	270.00 —
36c	A5	80c rose, *pnksh*	— —
37b	A6	5fr gray ill, *lav*	7,800. —

Imperfs, "Rothschild" Re-issue Paper Colors are the Same
29b	A4	1c olive green	1,050.	
30a	A4	2c pale red brown	200.00	
31b	A4	4c pale gray	185.00	
32a	A5	10c pale bister	160.00	
33a	A5	20c pale blue	250.00	
34c	A5	30c pale brown	190.00	
35b	A5	40c pale orange	225.00	
36b	A5	80c rose	400.00	

The re-issues constitute the "Rothschild Issue." These stamps were authorized exclusively for the banker to use on his correspondence. Used examples exist.

Ceres

A7 A8

A9 A10

A11

Bordeaux Issue

On the lithographed stamps, except for type I of the 20c, the shading on the cheek and neck is in lines or dashes, not in dots. On the typographed stamps the shading is in dots. The 2c, 5c, 10c and 20c (types II and III) occur in two or more types. The most easily distinguishable are:

2c — Type A. To the left of and within the top of the left "2" are lines of shading composed of dots.
2c — Type B. These lines of dots are replaced by solid lines.
5c — Type A. The head and hairline merge with the background of the medallion, without a distinct separation.
5c — Type B. A white line separates the contour of the head and hairline from the background of the medallion.
10c — Type A. The inner frame lines are of the same thickness as all other frame lines.
10c — Type B. The inner frame lines are much thicker than the others.

Three Types of the 20c.

A9 — The inscriptions in the upper and lower labels are small and there is quite a space between the upper label and the circle containing the head. There is also very little shading under the eye and in the neck.
A10 — The inscriptions in the labels are similar to those of the first type, the shading under the eye and in the neck is heavier and the upper label and circle almost touch.
A11 — The inscriptions in the labels are much larger than those of the two preceding types, and are similar to those of the other values of the same type in the set.

1870-71 Litho. Imperf.
38	A7	1c ol grn, *pale bl*	125.00	155.00
a.		1c bronze green, *pale blue*	160.00	155.00
39	A7	2c red brn, *yelsh* (B)	225.00	225.00
a.		2c brick red, *yelsh* (B)	800.00	700.00
b.		2c chestnut, *yelsh* (B)	1,350.	700.00
c.		2c chocolate, *yelsh* (A)	750.00	700.00
40	A7	4c gray	250.00	200.00
41	A8	5c yel grn, *grnsh* (B)	250.00	160.00
a.		5c grn, *grnsh* (B)	325.00	175.00
b.		5c emerald, *greenish* (B)	3,500.	1,250.
c.		5c yellowish green, *greenish* (A)	2,400.	3,250.
42	A8	10c bis, *yelsh* (A)	825.00	60.00
a.		10c bister, *yellowish* (B)	825.00	90.00
43	A9	20c bl, *bluish*	21,500.	550.00
a.		20c dark blue, *bluish*	25,000.	725.00
44	A10	20c bl, *bluish*	950.00	45.00
a.		20c dark blue, *bluish*	1,150.	85.00
b.		20c ultra, *bluish*	20,000.	3,100.
45	A11	20c bl, *bluish* ('71)	825.00	16.00
a.		20c ultra, *bluish*	2,200.	675.00
46	A8	30c brn, *yelsh*	325.00	200.00
a.		30c blk brn, *yelsh*	1,750.	675.00
47	A8	40c org, *yelsh*	425.00	100.00
a.		40c yel orange, *yelsh*	1,250.	225.00
b.		40c red orange, *yelsh*	625.00	190.00
c.		40c scarlet, *yelsh*	1,250.	675.00
48	A8	80c rose, *pinkish*	600.00	250.00
a.		80c dull rose, *pinkish*	600.00	275.00

All values of the 1870 issue are known privately rouletted, pin-perf and perf. 14. See Nos. 50-53.

A12

Dark Blue Surcharge

1871 Typo. Perf. 14x13½
49	A12	10c on 10c bister	1,400.	
a.		Pale blue surcharge	1,900.	

No. 49 was never placed in use. Counterfeits exist.

A13

Two types of the 40c as in the 1849-50 issue.

1870-73 Typo. Perf. 14x13½
50	A7	1c ol grn, *pale bl*	40.00	11.50
a.		1c bronze grn, *pale bl* ('72)	47.50	14.00
51	A7	2c red brn, *yelsh* ('70)	80.00	13.50
52	A7	4c gray ('70)	250.00	40.00
53	A7	5c yel grn, *pale bl* ('72)	150.00	7.50
a.		5c green	150.00	7.50

54	A13	10c bis, *yelsh*	540.00	55.00
a.		Tête beche pair	5,500.	2,250.
b.		Half used as 5c on cover		4,500.
55	A13	10c bis, *rose* ('73)	265.00	9.50
a.		Tête beche pair	3,750.	1,750.
56	A13	15c bis, *yelsh* ('71)	300.00	4.50
a.		Tête beche pair	37,500.	12,000.
57	A13	20c dl bl, *bluish*	225.00	6.75
a.		20c bright blue, *bluish*	350.00	8.00
b.		Tête beche pair	3,750.	1,450.
c.		Half used as 10c on cover		55,000.
d.		Quarter used as 5c on cover		52,500.
58	A13	25c bl, *bluish* ('71)	110.00	1.10
a.		25c dk bl, *bluish*	135.00	1.10
b.		Tête beche pair	6,750.	3,000.
59	A13	40c org, *yelsh* (I)	475.00	6.00
a.		40c orange yel, *yelsh* (I)	575.00	9.00
b.		40c orange, *yelsh* (II)	3,150.	130.00
c.		40c orange yel, *yelsh* (II)	3,150.	130.00
d.		Pair, types I and II	6,500.	525.00
f.		Half used as 20c on circular		20,000.
g.		Half used as 20c on cover		40,000.

No. 58 exists in three main plate varieties, differing in one or another of the flower-like corner ornaments.
Margins on this issue are extremely small. Nos. 54, 57 and 58 were reprinted imperf. in 1887. See note after No. 37.

Imperf.
50b	A7	1c	270.00
51a	A7	2c	350.00
52a	A7	4c	450.00
53b	A7	5c yel grn, *pale bl*	260.00
55b	A13	10c	350.00
56b	A13	15c	375.00

A14

1872-75 Perf. 14x13½
Larger Numerals
60	A14	10c bis, *rose* ('75)	325.00	11.00
a.		Cliché of 15c in plate of 10c	3,750.	4,250.
b.		Pair, #60, 60a	6,750.	8,500.
61	A14	15c bister ('73)	320.00	3.25
62	A14	30c brn, *yelsh*	550.00	5.25
63	A14	80c rose, *pnksh*	640.00	11.50

Imperf.
62a	A14	30c	475.00
63a	A14	80c	650.00

Peace and Commerce ("Type Sage") — A15

Type I. The "N" of "INV" is under the "B" of "REPUBLIQUE."
Type II. The "N" of "INV" is under the "U" of "REPUBLIQUE."

Type I

1876-78 Perf. 14x13½
64	A15	1c grn, *grnsh*	125.00	70.00
65	A15	2c grn, *grnsh*	1,425.	240.00
66	A15	4c grn, *grnsh*	145.00	55.00
67	A15	5c grn, *grnsh*	650.00	45.00
68	A15	10c grn, *grnsh*	800.00	21.00
69	A15	15c gray ill, *grysh*	800.00	17.50
70	A15	20c red brn, *straw*	575.00	17.50
71	A15	20c bl, *bluish*	27,500.	
72	A15	25c ultra, *bluish*	7,750.	55.00
73	A15	30c brn, *yelsh*	425.00	8.25
74	A15	40c red, *straw* ('78)	600.00	35.00
75	A15	75c car, *rose*	950.00	12.50
76	A15	1fr brnz grn, *straw*	925.00	10.00

No. 71 was never put into use.
The reprints of No. 71 are type II. They are imperforate or with forged perforation.
For overprints and surcharges see Offices in China Nos. 1-17, J7-J10, J20-J22, Offices in Egypt, Alexandria 1-15, Port Said 1-17, Offices in Turkish Empire 1-7, Cavalle 1-8, Dedeagh 1-8, Port Lagos 1-5, Vathy 1-9, Offices in Zanzibar 1-33, 50-54, French Morocco 1-8, and Madagascar 14-27.

Imperf.
64a	A15	1c	150.00
65a	A15	2c	1,000.
66a	A15	4c	160.00
67a	A15	5c	525.00
68a	A15	10c	575.00
69a	A15	15c	575.00
70a	A15	20c	375.00
73a	A15	30c	275.00
74a	A15	40c	250.00
75a	A15	75c	550.00
76a	A15	1fr	400.00

Beware of French Colonies Nos. 24-29.

Type II

1876-77 Perf. 14x13½
77	A15	2c grn, *grnsh*	115.00	19.00
78	A15	5c grn, *grnsh*	25.00	.60
a.		Imperf.	175.00	

FRANCE

79	A15	10c grn, *grnsh*	1,100.	240.00	
80	A15	15c gray lil, *grysh*	675.00	1.90	
81	A15	25c ultra, *bluish*	425.00	1.00	
a.		25c blue, *bluish*	475.00	1.50	
b.		Pair, types I & II	60,000.	17,500.	
c.		Imperf.	325.00		
82	A15	30c yel brn, *yelsh*	82.50	1.40	
a.		30c brown, *yellowish*	90.00	1.40	
b.		Imperf.	525.00		
83	A15	75c car, *rose* ('77)	1,775.	110.00	
84	A15	1fr brnz grn, *straw* ('77)	145.00	7.50	
a.		Imperf.	1,100.		

Beware of French Colonies Nos. 31, 35.

1877-80

86	A15	1c blk, *lil bl*	3.75	1.65	
a.		1c black, *gray blue*	3.75	1.65	
b.		Imperf.	75.00		
87	A15	1c blk, *Prus bl* ('80)	11,000.	4,350.	

Values for No. 87 are for examples with the perfs touching the design on at least one side.

88	A15	2c brn, *straw*	4.50	1.90	
a.		2c brown, *yellow*	4.50	1.90	
b.		Imperf.	210.00		
89	A15	3c yel, *straw* ('78)	200.00	42.50	
a.		Imperf.	150.00		
90	A15	4c claret, *lav*	5.00	1.90	
a.		4c vio brown, *lavender*	8.25	4.50	
b.		Imperf.	60.00		
91	A15	10c blk, *lavender*	35.00	1.00	
a.		10c black, *rose lilac*	37.50	1.00	
b.		10c black, *lilac*	37.50	1.00	
c.		Imperf.	70.00		
92	A15	15c blue ('78)	22.50	.60	
a.		Imperf.	95.00		
b.		15c blue, *bluish*	435.00	15.00	
93	A15	25c blk, *red* ('78)	1,075.	25.00	
a.		Imperf.	675.00		
94	A15	35c blk, *yel org* ('78)	525.00	35.00	
a.		35c blk, *yel org*	525.00	35.00	
b.		Imperf.	250.00		
95	A15	40c red, *straw* ('00)	90.00	2.10	
a.		Imperf.	240.00		
96	A15	5fr vio, *lav*	440.00	70.00	
a.		As #96, imperf.	750.00		
b.		5fr red lilac, *lavender*	650.00	100.00	

Beware of French Colonies Nos. 38-40, 42, 44.

1879-90

97	A15	3c gray, *grysh* ('80)	3.00	1.65	
a.		Imperf.	67.50		
98	A15	20c red, *yel grn*	37.50	4.25	
a.		20c red, *deep green* ('84)	72.50	6.00	
b.		Imperf.	100.00		
99	A15	25c yel, *straw*	340.00	5.00	
a.		Imperf.	250.00		
100	A15	25c blk, *pale rose* ('86)	72.50	1.00	
a.		Imperf.	155.00		
101	A15	50c rose, *rose* ('90)	210.00	2.65	
a.		50c carmine, *rose*	225.00	3.50	
102	A15	75c dp vio, *org* ('90)	215.00	35.00	
a.		75c deep violet, *yellow*	265.00	45.00	
		Nos. 97-102 (6)	878.00	49.55	

Beware of French Colonies No. 43.

1892   Quadrille Paper

103	A15	15c blue	12.50	.35	
a.		Imperf.	175.00		

1898-1900   Ordinary Paper

104	A15	5c yel grn	16.00	1.30	
a.		Imperf.	82.50		

Type I

105	A15	5c yel grn	14.00	1.30	
a.		Imperf.	575.00		
106	A15	10c blk, *lavender*	21.00	2.50	
a.		Imperf.	275.00		
107	A15	50c car, *rose*	200.00	30.00	
108	A15	2fr brn, *azure* ('00)	110.00	40.00	
b.		Imperf.	2,250.		
		Nos. 104-108 (5)	361.00	75.10	

See No. 22B

Reprints of A15, type II, were made in 1887 and left imperf. See note after No. 37. Value for set of 27, $4,000.

Stamps of types A16, A18, A20, A22 and D2 were printed in 1916-20 on paper of poor quality, usually grayish and containing bits of fiber. This is called G. C. (Grande Consommation) paper. These wartime printings are noted (GC) in the descriptions.

Liberty, Equality, Fraternity

"The Rights of Man" A17

Liberty and Peace A18

1900-29   Perf. 14x13½

109	A16	1c gray	.55	.40	
b.		Grayish paper (GC) ('16)	.65	.50	
110	A16	2c violet brn	.70	.25	
b.		Grayish (GC) paper ('17)	1.60	.25	
111	A16	3c orange	.45	.25	
a.		3c red	19.00	7.50	
b.		Grayish (GC) paper ('17)	.55	.50	
112	A16	4c yellow brn	3.00	1.60	
113	A16	5c green	2.00	.35	
b.		Booklet pane of 10	330.00		
114	A16	7½c lilac ('26)	.60	.45	
115	A16	10c lilac ('29)	4.00	.60	
116	A17	10c carmine	25.00	1.50	
a.		Numerals printed separately	24.00	10.00	
117	A17	15c orange	8.00	.60	
118	A17	20c brown vio	55.00	9.25	
119	A17	25c blue	125.00	1.65	
a.		Numerals printed separately	115.00	9.25	
120	A17	30c violet	70.00	6.00	
121	A18	40c red & pale bl	15.00	.85	
a.		Grayish (GC) paper ('16)	25.00	1.20	
122	A18	45c grn & bl ('06)	29.00	2.10	
a.		Grayish (GC) paper ('16)	45.00	4.00	
123	A18	50c bis brn & gray	100.00	1.65	
b.		Grayish paper (GC) ('16)	200.00	2.00	
124	A18	60c vio & ultra ('20)	1.00	1.15	
125	A18	1fr claret & ol grn	26.50	.85	
b.		Grayish paper (GC) ('16)	52.50	.95	
126	A18	2fr gray vio & yel	625.00	75.00	
127	A18	2fr org & pale bl ('20)	42.50	.60	
128	A18	3fr vio & bl ('25)	27.50	7.50	
129	A18	3fr brt vio & rose ('27)	55.00	2.80	
130	A18	5fr dk bl & buff	85.00	5.00	
131	A18	10fr grn & red ('26)	125.00	17.00	
132	A18	2fr mag & grn ('26)	200.00	37.50	
		Nos. 109-132 (24)	1,626.	175.10	

In the 10c and 25c values, the first printings show the numerals to have been impressed by a second operation, whereas, in later printings, the numerals were inserted in the plates. Two operations were used for all 20c and 30c, and one operation for the 15c.

No. 114 was issued precanceled only. Values for precanceled stamps in first column are for those which have not been through the post and have original gum. Values in the second column are for postally used, gumless stamps.

See Offices in China Nos. 34, 40-44, Offices in Crete 1-5, 10-15, Offices in Egypt, Alexandria 16-20, 26-30, 77, 84-86, Port Said 18-22, 28-32, 83, 90-92, Offices in Turkish Empire 21-26, 31-33, Cavalle 9, Dedeagh 9.

For overprints and surcharge see Nos. 197, 246, C1-C2, M1, P7. Offices in China 57, 62-65, 71, 73, 75, 83-85, J14, J27, Offices in Crete 17-20, Offices in Egypt, Alexandria 31-32, 34-35, 40-48, 57-64, 66, 71-73, Port Said 33, 35-40, 43, 46-57, 59, 65-71, 73, 78-80, Offices in Turkish Empire 35-38, 47-49, Cavalle 13-15, Dedeagh 16-18, Offices in Zanzibar 39, 45-49, 55, Offices in Morocco 11-15, 20-22, 26-29, 35-41, 49-54, 72-76, 84-85, 87-89, B6.

Imperf.

109a	A16	1c	55.00		
110a	A16	2c	67.50	60.00	
111b	A16	3c	55.00		
112a	A16	4c	150.00		
113a	A16	5c	75.00		
116b	A17	10c #116 or 116a	235.00	135.00	
117a	A17	15c	190.00	165.00	
119b	A17	25c #119 or 119a	500.00		
121a	A18	40c	190.00	155.00	
122a	A18	45c	260.00		
123a	A18	50c	375.00	275.00	
124a	A18	60c	525.00		
125a	A18	1fr	250.00	225.00	
126a	A18	2fr No gum	1,300.		
127a	A18	2fr	475.00		
128a	A18	3fr	725.00	500.00	
129a	A18	3fr	425.00		
130a	A18	5fr	950.00		

Flat Plate & Rotary Press

The following stamps were printed by both flat plate and rotary press: Nos. 109-113, 144-146, 163, 166, 168, 170, 175, 177-178, 185, 192 and P7.

"Rights of Man" — A19

1902   Perf. 14x13½

133	A19	10c rose red	32.50	.90	
134	A19	15c pale red	11.00	.60	
135	A19	20c brown violet	82.50	14.00	
136	A19	25c blue	100.00	2.25	
137	A19	30c lilac	250.00	14.50	
		Nos. 133-137 (5)	476.00	32.25	

Imperf.

133a	A19	10c rose red	450.00	275.00	
134a	A19	15c pale red	450.00	325.00	
135a	A19	20c brown violet	800.00	475.00	
136a	A19	25c blue	950.00	625.00	
137a	A19	30c lilac	1,100.	675.00	

See Offices in China Nos. 35-39, Offices in Crete 6-10, Offices in Egypt, Alexandria 21-25, 81-82, Port Said 23-27, 87-88, Offices in Turkish Empire 26-30, Cavalle 10-11, Dedeagh 10-11.

For overprints and surcharges see Nos. M2, Offices in China 45, 58-61, 66-70, 76-82, J15-J16, J28-J30, Offices in Crete 16, Offices in Egypt, Alexandria 33, 36-39, 49-50, 52-56, 65, 67-70, B1-B4, Port Said 34, 41-42, 44-45, 57, 60-64, 77, 74-77, B1-B4, Offices in Turkish Empire 34, 39, Cavalle 12, Dedeagh 15, Offices in Zanzibar 40-44, 56-59, Offices in Morocco 16-19, 30-34, 42-48, 77-83, 86, B1-B5, B7, B9.

Sower — A20

1903-38   Perf. 14x13½

138	A20	10c rose	8.00	.40	
139	A20	15c slate grn	4.00	.25	
b.		Booklet pane of 10	450.00		
c.		Grayish (GC) paper ('16)	4.50	.25	
140	A20	20c violet brn	67.50	1.90	
141	A20	25c dull blue	75.00	1.40	
142	A20	30c violet	175.00	5.25	
143	A20	45c lt violet ('26)	6.00	1.90	
144	A20	50c dull black ('21)	27.50	1.40	
145	A20	50c gray grn ('26)	6.25	1.25	
146	A20	50c vermilion	1.25	.25	
a.		Booklet pane of 10	40.00		
147	A20	50c grnsh bl ('38)	1.00	.35	
148	A20	60c lt vio ('24)	6.25	2.10	
149	A20	65c rose ('24)	3.00	1.75	
150	A20	65c gray grn ('27)	6.50	2.10	
151	A20	75c rose lil ('26)	5.25	.60	
152	A20	80c ver ('25)	26.50	9.50	
153	A20	85c ver ('24)	13.50	3.25	
154	A20	1fr dull blue ('26)	6.00	.75	
		Nos. 138-154 (17)	438.50	34.40	
		Set, never hinged	940.00		

See Nos. 941, 942A. For surcharges and overprints see Nos. 229-230, 232-233, 236, 256, B25, B29, B32, B36, B40, M3-M4, M6, Offices in Turkish Empire 46, 54.

Imperf.

138a	A20	10c	175.00		
139a	A20	15c	140.00	55.00	
140a	A20	20c	300.00	160.00	
141a	A20	25c	350.00		
142a	A20	30c	625.00		
144a	A20	50c	140.00		
145a	A20	50c	125.00		
146b	A20	50c No gum	70.00		
147a	A20	50c	67.50		
149a	A20	65c	300.00		
151a	A20	75c	450.00		
154a	A20	1fr	1,000.		

Ground — A21

1906, Apr. 13   Perf. 14x13½

With Ground Under Feet of Figure

155	A21	10c red	2.50	1.75	
a.		Imperf, pair, no gum	275.00	225.00	
		As "a," with gum	450.00		

No Ground — A22

TEN AND THIRTY-FIVE CENTIMES
Type I — Numerals and letters of the inscriptions thin.
Type II — Numerals and letters thicker.

No Ground Under the Feet

1906-37   Perf. 14x13½

156	A22	1c olive bis ('33)	.25	.30	
157	A22	2c dk grn ('33)	.25	.30	
158	A22	3c ver ('33)	.25	.30	
159	A22	5c green ('07)	1.50	.25	
a.		Imperf., pair	40.00	30.00	
b.		Booklet pane of 10	100.00		
c.		Grayish (GC) paper ('16)	2.75	.35	
160	A22	5c orange ('21)	1.25	.30	
a.		Booklet pane of 10	72.50		
161	A22	5c cerise ('34)	.25	.25	
162	A22	10c red (II) ('07)	1.50	.25	
a.		Imperf., pair	37.50	115.00	
b.		10c red (I) ('06)	8.25	1.00	
c.		As #162b, imperf., pair	37.50	115.00	
d.		Booklet pane of 10 (I)	125.00		
e.		Booklet pane of 10 (II)	75.00		
f.		Booklet pane of 6 (II)	240.00		
g.		Grayish (GC) paper ('16)	12.00	2.10	
163	A22	10c grn (II) ('21)	1.00	.55	
a.		10c green (I) ('27)	32.50	37.50	
b.		Booklet pane of 10 (I, "Phena")	350.00		
c.		Booklet pane of 10 (I, "Mineraline")	3,200.		
164	A22	10c ultra ('32)	1.40	.25	
165	A22	15c red brn ('26)	.25	.25	
a.		Imperf., pair	27.50		
166	A22	20c brown	3.00	.65	
a.		Imperf., pair	82.50	100.00	
b.		20c black brown	6.00	2.00	
c.		Grayish (GC) paper ('17)	6.50	.80	
167	A22	20c red vio ('26)	.25	.25	
a.		Booklet pane of 10	7.50		
168	A22	25c blue	2.40	.25	
a.		Booklet pane of 10	37.50		
b.		Imperf, pair (dark blue)	45.00	60.00	
c.		Grayish (GC) paper ('17)	4.00	1.20	
169	A22	25c yel brn ('26)	.25	.25	
a.		25c red brown	.30	.25	
170	A22	30c orange	13.50	1.40	
a.		Imperf., pair	200.00	175.00	
b.		Grayish (GC) paper ('16)	15.00	1.75	
171	A22	30c red ('21)	6.50	2.25	
172	A22	30c cerise ('25)	1.25	.80	
a.		Booklet pane of 10	13.50		
b.		Imperf, pair	575.00		
173	A22	30c lt blue ('25)	3.75	.60	
a.		Booklet pane of 10	35.00		
b.		Imperf, pair	2,200.		
174	A22	30c cop red ('37)	.25	.30	
a.		Booklet pane of 10	9.00		
175	A22	35c vio (II) ('07)	8.25	.90	
a.		Imperf., pair	150.00	120.00	
b.		35c violet (I) ('06)	150.00	7.50	
c.		As "b," Imperf, pair, no gum	575.00		
176	A22	35c grn ('37)	.50	.55	
a.		Imperf., pair	750.00		
177	A22	40c olive ('25)	1.40	.55	
b.		Booklet pane of 10	30.00		
178	A22	40c ver ('26)	2.50	.80	
a.		Booklet pane of 10	25.00		
179	A22	40c violet ('27)	2.00	.90	
180	A22	40c lt ultra ('28)	1.25	.30	
181	A22	1.05fr ver ('25)	9.50	5.25	
182	A22	1.10fr cerise ('27)	11.50	2.50	
183	A22	1.40fr cerise ('26)	20.00	22.50	
184	A22	2fr Prus grn ('31)	14.00	1.75	
		Nos. 156-184 (29)	109.95	45.95	
		Set, never hinged	225.00		

The 10c and 35c, type I, were slightly retouched by adding thin white outlines to the

France, Belgium, Austria & Worldwide

Extensive Stock of Mint & Used

Request our free 68-page price list

ALMAZ CO. Dept. VF
P.O. Box 100-812 • Vanderveer Station
Brooklyn, NY 11210
Phone/Fax (718) 241-6360
AlmazStamps@aol.com

FRANCE

sack of grain, the underside of the right arm and the back of the skirt. It is difficult to distinguish the retouches except on clearly-printed copies. The white outlines were made stronger on the stamps of type II.

Stamps of types A16, A18, A20 and A22 were printed in 1916-20 on paper of poor quality, usually grayish and containing bits of fiber. This is called G. C. (Grande Consommation) paper.

Nos. 160, 162b, 163, 175b and 176 also exist imperf.

See Nos. 241-241b. For surcharges and overprint see Nos. 227-228, 234, 238, 240, 400, B1, B24, B28, B31, B35, B37, B39, B41, M5, P8, Offices in Turkish Empire 40-45, 52, 55.

Louis Pasteur — A23

1923-26

185	A23	10c green	.55	.30
a.		Booklet pane of 10	15.00	
186	A23	15c green ('24)	1.40	.30
187	A23	20c green ('26)	2.75	.90
188	A23	30c red	.90	1.50
189	A23	30c green ('26)	.55	.50
190	A23	45c red ('24)	1.90	2.10
191	A23	50c blue	4.50	.50
192	A23	75c blue ('24)	3.75	1.00
a.		Imperf., pair	250.00	
193	A23	90c red ('26)	11.00	3.50
194	A23	1fr blue ('25)	21.00	.50
195	A23	1.25fr blue ('26)	25.00	8.00
196	A23	1.50fr blue ('26)	5.25	.50
		Nos. 185-196 (12)	78.55	19.60
		Set, never hinged	150.00	

Nos. 185, 188 and 191 were issued to commemorate the cent. of the birth of Pasteur.

For surcharges and overprint see Nos. 231, 235, 257, B26, B30, B33, C4.

No. 125 Overprinted in Blue

1923, June 15

197	A18	1fr claret & ol grn	440.00	500.00
		Never hinged	825.00	

Allegory of Olympic Games at Paris — A24

The Trophy A25 — Milo of Crotona A26

Victorious Athlete — A27

1924, Apr. 1   Perf. 14x13½, 13½x14

198	A24	10c gray grn & yel grn	2.25	1.25
199	A25	25c rose & dk rose	3.00	.80
200	A26	30c brn red & blk	9.50	11.00
201	A27	50c ultra & dk bl	26.00	5.75
		Nos. 198-201 (4)	40.75	18.80
		Set, never hinged	125.00	

Imperf Singles

198a	A24	10c	1,000.	
199a	A25	25c	1,000.	725.
200a	A26	30c	1,000.	
201a	A27	50c	1,000.	1,000.

8th Olympic Games, Paris.

Pierre de Ronsard (1524-85), Poet — A28

1924, Oct. 6   Perf. 14x13½
219	A28	75c blue, *bluish*	1.90	1.40
		Never hinged	2.75	

"Light and Liberty" Allegory A29 — Majolica Vase A30

Potter Decorating Vase — A31

Terrace of Château — A32

1924-25   Perf. 14x13½, 13½x14

220	A29	10c dk grn & yel ('25)	.55	.75
221	A30	15c ind & grn ('25)	.55	.85
a.		Imperf.	400.00	
		Never hinged	640.00	
222	A31	25c vio brn & garnet	.80	.50
223	A32	25c gray bl & vio ('25)	1.60	.65
a.		Imperf.	450.00	150.00
		Never hinged	700.00	
224	A31	75c indigo & ultra	3.50	2.25
225	A29	75c dk bl & lt bl ('25)	18.00	6.50
a.		Imperf.	375.00	
		Never hinged	650.00	
		Nos. 220-225 (6)	25.00	11.50
		Set, never hinged	52.50	

Intl. Exhibition of Decorative Modern Arts at Paris, 1925.

Philatelic Exhibition Issue
Souvenir Sheet

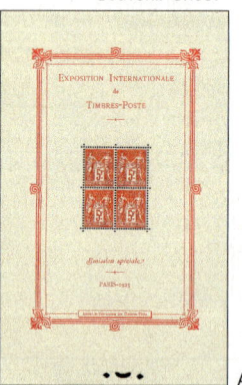

A32a

1925, May 2   Perf. 14x13½

226	A32a	Sheet of 4, A15 II	1,100.	1,100.
		Never hinged	3,750.	
a.		Imperf. sheet	5,000.	1,750.
		Never hinged	7,750.	
b.		5fr carmine, perf.	125.00	140.00
		Never hinged	225.00	
c.		5fr carmine, imperf.	900.00	
		Never hinged	1,325.	

These were on sale only at the Intl. Phil. Exhib., Paris, May, 1925. Size: 140x220mm.

Nos. 148-149, 152-153, 173, 175, 181, 183, 192, 195 Surcharged

1926-27

227	A22	25c on 30c lt bl	.25	.50
a.		Pair, one without surcharge	1,050.	925.00
228	A22	25c on 35c vio	.25	.50
a.		Double surcharge	525.00	350.00
b.		Pair, one without surcharge	550.00	925.00
229	A20	50c on 60c lt vio ('27)	1.40	1.10
a.		Pair, one without surcharge	525.00	925.00
230	A20	50c on 65c rose ('27)	.75	.55
a.		Inverted surcharge	1,225.	1,400.
b.		Pair, one without surcharge	675.00	925.00
231	A23	50c on 75c blue	3.25	1.50
232	A20	50c on 80c ver ('27)	1.25	1.10
a.		Pair, one without surcharge	475.00	925.00
233	A20	50c on 85c ver ('27)	2.25	1.00
234	A22	50c on 1.05fr ver	1.25	.75
a.		Pair, one without surcharge	475.00	925.00
235	A23	50c on 1.25fr blue	2.75	2.25
a.		Pair, one without surcharge	525.00	925.00
236	A20	55c on 60c lt vio	125.00	52.50
238	A22	90c on 1.05fr ver ('27)	2.25	2.75
a.		Pair, one without surcharge	1,000.	925.00
240	A22	1.10fr on 1.40fr cer	1.00	1.10
a.		Pair, one without surcharge	575.00	925.00
		Nos. 227-240 (12)	141.65	65.60
		Set, never hinged	275.00	

Issue dates: Nos. 229-230, 232-234, 1927.

No. 236 is known only precanceled. See second note after No. 132.

Nos. 229, 230, 234, 238 and 240 have three bars instead of two. The 55c surcharge has thinner, larger numerals and a rounded "c". Width, including bars, is 17mm, instead of 13mm.

The 55c was used only precanceled at the Magasins du Louvre department store in Paris, August 1926.

Strasbourg Exhibition Issue
Souvenir Sheet

A32b

1927, June 4

241	A32b	Sheet of 2	1,000.	1,000.
		Never hinged	2,300.	
a.		5fr light ultra (A22)	250.00	250.00
		Never hinged	400.00	
b.		10fr carmine rose (A22)	250.00	250.00
		Never hinged	400.00	

Sold at the Strasbourg Philatelic Exhibition as souvenirs. Size: 111x140mm.

Marcelin Berthelot (1827-1907), Chemist and Statesman — A33

1927, Sept. 7
242	A33	90c dull rose	1.90	.60
		Never hinged	3.00	

For surcharge see No. C3.

Lafayette, Washington, S. S. Paris and Airplane "Spirit of St. Louis" — A34

1927, Sept. 15
243	A34	90c dull red	1.25	1.75
a.		Value omitted	2,000.	1,725.
244	A34	1.50fr deep blue	4.00	2.50
a.		Value omitted	1,450.	
		Set, never hinged	10.00	

Visit of American Legionnaires to France, September, 1927. Exist imperf.

Joan of Arc — A35

1929, Mar.
245	A35	50c dull blue	1.90	.25
		Never hinged	2.75	
a.		Booklet pane of 10	50.00	
b.		Imperf.	140.00	

500th anniv. of the relief of Orleans by the French forces led by Joan of Arc.

No. 127 Overprinted in Blue

1929, May 18
246	A18	2fr org & pale bl	600.00	600.00
		Never hinged	1,325.	

Sold exclusively at the Intl. Phil. Exhib., Le Havre, May, 1929, for 7fr, which included a 5fr admission ticket.

Excellent counterfeits of No. 246 exist.

Reims Cathedral — A37

Die I, II, III   Die IV

Die I   Die II   Die III

Die I — The window of the 1st turret on the left is made of 2 lines. The horizontal line of the frame surrounding 3F is continuous.
Die II — Same as Die I but the line under 3F is not continuous.
Die III — Same as Die II but there is a deeply cut line separating 3 and F.
Die IV — Same as Die III but the window of the first turret on the left is made of three lines.

Mont-Saint-Michel A38

Die I   Die II

Die I — The line at the top of the spire is broken.
Die II — The line is unbroken.

Port of La Rochelle — A39

Dies I & II   Die III

FRANCE

Die I — The top of the "E" of "POSTES" has a serif. The oval of shading inside the "0" of "10 fr" and the outer oval are broken at their bases.
Die II — The same top has no serif. Interior and exterior of "0" broken as in Die I.
Die III — Top of "E" has no serif. Interior and exterior of "0" complete.

Pont du Gard, Nimes — A40

Dies I & II

Die III

Die I — Shading of the first complete arch in the left middle tier is made of horizontal lines. Size 36x20¾mm. Perf. 13½.
Die II — Same, size 35½x21mm. Perf. 11.
Die III — Shading of same arch is made of three diagonal lines. Thin paper. Perf. 13.

1929-33		Engr.	Perf. 11, 13, 13½	
247	A37	3fr dk gray ('30) (I)	62.50	2.40
		Never hinged	115.00	
247A	A37	3fr dk gray ('30) (II)	125.00	3.50
		Never hinged	200.00	
247B	A37	3fr dk gray ('30) (III)	375.00	24.00
		Never hinged	600.00	
248	A37	3fr bluish sl ('31) (IV)	60.00	2.40
		Never hinged	115.00	
249	A38	5fr brn ('30) (I)	24.00	4.25
			40.00	
250	A38	5fr brn ('31) (II)	21.00	.75
		Never hinged	32.50	
251	A39	10fr lt ultra (I)	95.00	15.00
			160.00	
251A	A39	10fr ultra (II)	140.00	26.00
			225.00	
252	A39	10fr dk ultra ('31) (III)	70.00	6.50
			140.00	
253	A40	20fr red brn (I)	275.00	40.00
			500.00	
254	A40	20fr brt red brn ('30) (II)	1,000.	350.00
			1,650.	
254A	A40	20fr org brn ('31) (III)	250.00	35.00
		Never hinged	450.00	
	Nos. 247-254A (12)		2,498.	509.80

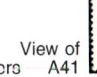

View of Algiers — A41

1929, Jan. 1   Typo.
255   A41   50c blue & rose red   2.40   .50
    Never hinged   5.50

Cent. of the 1st French settlement in Algeria.

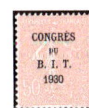

Nos. 146 and 196 Overprinted

1930, Apr. 23   Perf. 14x13½
256   A20   50c vermilion   3.00   3.25
257   A23   1.50fr blue   20.00   14.50
    Set, never hinged   47.50

Intl. Labor Bureau, 48th Congress, Paris.

Colonial Exposition Issue

Fachi Woman A42   French Colonials A43

1930-31		Typo.	Perf. 14x13½	
258	A42	15c gray black	1.10	.30
259	A42	40c dark brown	2.40	.30
260	A42	50c dark red	.65	.25
a.		Booklet pane of 10	12.50	
261	A42	1.50fr deep blue	9.00	.65

Perf. 13½
Photo.
262   A43   1.50fr dp blue ('31)   45.00   2.75
    Nos. 258-262 (5)   58.15   4.25
    Set, never hinged   125.00

No. 260 has two types: type 1 shows four short downward hairlines near top of head, type 2 has no lines. Booklet stamps are type 2.

Arc de Triomphe — A44

1931   Engr.   Perf. 13
263   A44   2fr red brown   40.00   1.25
    Never hinged   80.00

Peace with Olive Branch — A45

1932-39		Typo.	Perf. 14x13½	
264	A45	30c dp green	1.00	.55
265	A45	40c brt violet	.30	.30
266	A45	45c yellow brown	1.75	1.00
267	A45	50c rose red	.25	.25
a.		Imperf., pair	140.00	
b.		Booklet pane of 10	5.50	
268	A45	55c dull vio ('37)	.60	.25
269	A45	60c ocher ('37)	.30	.25
270	A45	65c violet brown	.50	.50
271	A45	65c brt ultra ('37)	.25	.25
a.		Booklet pane of 10	7.00	
272	A45	75c olive green	.25	.30
273	A45	80c orange ('38)	.25	.25
274	A45	90c dk red	32.50	2.00
275	A45	90c brt green ('38)	.25	.25
276	A45	90c ultra ('38)	.90	.25
a.		Booklet pane of 10	8.50	
277	A45	1fr orange	3.25	.25
278	A45	1fr rose pink ('38)	3.25	.50
279	A45	1.25fr brown ol	75.00	4.75
280	A45	1.25fr rose car ('39)	1.90	2.25
281	A45	1.40fr brt red vio ('39)	5.75	5.25
282	A45	1.50fr deep blue	.30	.30
283	A45	1.75fr magenta	4.00	.50
	Nos. 264-283 (20)		132.55	20.20
	Set, never hinged		275.00	

The 50c is found in 4 types, differing in the lines below belt and size of "c".

See Nos. 6344-6345. For surcharges and overprints see Nos. 298, 333, 401-403, 405-409, M7-M9, S1.

Le Puy-en-Velay A46

1933   Engr.   Perf. 13
290   A46   90c rose   3.00   1.10
    Never hinged   5.75

Aristide Briand A47   Paul Doumer A48

Victor Hugo — A49

1933, Dec. 11   Typo.   Perf. 14x13½
291   A47   30c blue green   17.00   8.00
292   A48   75c red violet   27.50   1.90
293   A49   1.25fr claret   6.00   2.00
    Nos. 291-293 (3)   50.50   12.15
    Set, never hinged   110.00

Dove and Olive Branch — A50

1934, Feb. 20
294   A50   1.50fr ultra   50.00   15.00
    Never hinged   95.00

Joseph Marie Jacquard — A51

1934, Mar. 14   Engr.   Perf. 14x13
295   A51   40c blue   3.00   1.10
    Never hinged   4.50

Jacquard (1752-1834), inventor of an improved loom for figured weaving.

Jacques Cartier — A52

1934, July 18   Perf. 13
296   A52   75c rose lilac   30.00   2.25
297   A52   1.50fr blue   50.00   4.25
    Set, never hinged   210.00

Cartier's discovery of Canada, 400th anniv.

No. 279 Surcharged

1934, Nov.   Perf. 14x13½
298   A45   50c on 1.25fr brn ol   3.75   .65
    Never hinged   7.00

Catalogue values for unused stamps in this section, from this point to the end of the section, are for Never Hinged items.

Breton River Scene — A53

1935, Feb.   Engr.   Perf. 13
299   A53   2fr blue green   70.00   1.00
    Hinged   32.50

S. S. Normandie — A54

1935, Apr.
300   A54   1.50fr dark blue   29.00   2.00
    Hinged   14.00
a.   1.50fr pale blue ('36)   145.00   19.00
    Hinged   55.00
b.   1.50fr blue green ('36)   30,000.   12,500.
    Hinged   19,000.
c.   1.50fr turquoise ('36)   400.00   40.00
    Hinged   275.00

Maiden voyage of the transatlantic steamship, the "Normandie."

Benjamin Delessert — A55

1935, May 20
301   A55   75c blue green   47.50   1.75
    Hinged   17.50

Opening of the International Savings Bank Congress, May 20, 1935.

View of St. Trophime at Arles — A56

1935, May 3
302   A56   3.50fr dark brown   70.00   4.25
    Hinged   27.50

Victor Hugo (1802-85) — A57

1935, May 30   Perf. 14x13
303   A57   1.25fr magenta   8.25   2.00
    Hinged   4.00

FRANCE

Cardinal Richelieu — A58

1935, June 12   *Perf. 13*
304 A58 1.50fr deep rose   70.00   1.75
     Hinged   20.00

Tercentenary of the founding of the French Academy by Cardinal Richelieu.

Jacques Callot — A59

1935, Nov.   *Perf. 14x13*
305 A59 75c red   19.00   .75
     Hinged   10.00

300th anniv. of the death of Jacques Callot, engraver.

André Marie Ampère (1775-1836), Scientist, by Louis Boilly — A60

1936, Feb. 27   *Perf. 13*
306 A60 75c brown   37.50   2.00
     Hinged   17.50

Windmill at Fontvielle, Immortalized by Daudet — A61

1936, Apr. 27
307 A61 2fr ultra   5.75   .40
     Hinged   3.00

Publication, in 1866, of Alphonse Daudet's "Lettres de mon Moulin," 75th anniv.

Pilâtre de Rozier and his Balloon — A62

1936, June 4
308 A62 75c Prus blue   37.50   2.75
     Hinged   19.00

150th anniversary of the death of Jean Francois Pilâtre de Rozier, balloonist.

Rouget de Lisle A63

"La Marseillaise" A64

1936, June 27
309 A63 20c Prus green   5.75   2.00
     Hinged   3.25
310 A64 40c dark brown   11.50   3.25
     Hinged   5.50

Cent. of the death of Claude Joseph Rouget de Lisle, composer of "La Marseillaise."

Canadian War Memorial at Vimy Ridge — A65

1936, July 26
311 A65 75c henna brown   25.00   2.00
     Hinged   9.50
312 A65 1.50fr dull blue   32.50   9.50
     Hinged   16.00

Unveiling of the Canadian War Memorial at Vimy Ridge, July 26, 1936.

A66

Jean Léon Jaurès — A67

1936, July 30
313 A66 40c red brown   5.75   1.40
     Hinged   4.00
314 A67 1.50fr ultra   32.50   3.75
     Hinged   13.00

Assassination of Jean Léon Jaurès (1859-1914), socialist and politician.

Herald A68

Allegory of Exposition A69

1936, Sept. 15   *Typo.*   *Perf. 14x13½*
315 A68 20c brt violet   1.00   .50
     Hinged   .30
316 A68 30c Prus green   4.00   1.75
     Hinged   2.40
317 A68 40c ultra   2.50   .50
     Hinged   1.00
318 A68 50c red orange   2.25   .25
     Hinged   1.00
319 A69 90c carmine   25.00   7.50
     Hinged   11.00
320 A69 1.50fr ultra   67.50   4.00
     Hinged   30.00
   Nos. 315-320 (6)   102.25   14.50

Publicity for the 1937 Paris Exposition.

"Peace" — A70

1936, Oct. 1   *Engr.*   *Perf. 13*
321 A70 1.50fr blue   27.50   4.00
     Hinged   12.50

Skiing — A71

1937, Jan. 18
322 A71 1.50fr dark blue   14.00   1.75
     Hinged   7.00

Intl. Ski Meet at Chamonix-Mont Blanc.

Pierre Corneille, Portrait by Charles Le Brun — A72

1937, Feb. 15
323 A72 75c brown carmine   3.75   1.40
     Hinged   1.90

300th anniv. of the publication of "Le Cid."

Paris Exposition Issue

Exposition Allegory — A73

1937, Mar. 15
324 A73 1.50fr turq blue   4.00   1.25
     Hinged   2.25

Jean Mermoz (1901-36), Aviator A74

Memorial to Mermoz A75

1937, Apr. 22
325 A74 30c dk slate green   1.00   .55
     Hinged   .50
326 A75 3fr dark violet   13.50   3.75
     Hinged   6.25
  a.   3fr violet   15.00   4.50
     Hinged   6.75

Electric Train — A76

Streamlined Locomotive A77

1937, May 31
327 A76 30c dk green   1.40   1.75
     Hinged   1.00
328 A77 1.50fr dk ultra   15.00   8.25
     Hinged   7.25

13th International Railroad Congress.

Intl. Philatelic Exhibition Issue
Souvenir Sheet

Ceres Type A1 of 1849-50 A77a

1937, June 18   *Typo.*   *Perf. 14x13½*
329 A77a Sheet of 4   700.00   300.00
     Lightly hinged in margins   360.00
  a.   5c ultra & dark brown   90.00   47.50
  b.   15c red & rose red   90.00   47.50
  c.   30c ultra & rose red   90.00   47.50
  d.   50c red & dark brown   90.00   47.50
  e.   Sheet of 4, imperf   3,000.
     Lightly hinged in margins   2,350.

Issued in sheets measuring 150x220mm. The sheets were sold only at the exhibition in Paris, a ticket of admission being required for each sheet purchased.

René Descartes, by Frans Hals — A78

1937, June   *Engr.*   *Perf. 13*
Inscribed "Discours sur la Méthode"
330 A78 90c copper red   3.25   1.40
     Hinged   1.90
Inscribed "Discours de la Méthode"
331 A78 90c copper red   11.00   1.75
     Hinged   5.50

3rd centenary of the publication of "Discours de la Méthode" by René Descartes.

France Congratulating USA — A79

1937, Sept. 17
332 A79 1.75fr ultra   4.50   2.00
     Hinged   2.50

150th anniv. of the US Constitution.

No. 277 Surcharged in Red

1937, Oct.   *Perf. 14x13½*
333 A45 80c on 1fr orange   1.90   .85
     Hinged   .80
  a.   Inverted surcharge   1,225.
     Hinged   825.00

Mountain Road at Iseran — A80

1937, Oct. 4   *Engr.*   *Perf. 13*
334 A80 90c dark green   3.75   .30
     Hinged   1.90

Issued in commemoration of the opening of the mountain road at Iseran, Savoy.

Ceres — A81

1938-40   *Typo.*   *Perf. 14x13½*
335 A81 1.75fr dk ultra   1.40   .55
     Hinged   .55
336 A81 2fr car rose ('39)   .30   .30
     Hinged   .25
337 A81 2.25fr ultra ('39)   15.00   1.10
     Hinged   8.00
338 A81 2.50fr green ('39)   3.00   .50
     Hinged   1.25
339 A81 2.50fr vio blue ('40)   1.25   .75
     Hinged   .65
340 A81 3fr rose lilac ('39)   1.25   .50
     Hinged   .55
   Nos. 335-340 (6)   22.20   3.70

For surcharges see Nos. 397-399.

Léon Gambetta (1838-82), Lawyer and Statesman — A82

1938, Apr. 2   *Engr.*   *Perf. 13*
341 A82 55c dark violet   .55   .40
     Hinged   .35

Arc de Triomphe of Orange A82a

Miners A83

Keep and Gate of Vincennes A86

Palace of the Popes, Avignon A84

FRANCE

Medieval Walls of Carcassonne A85

Port of St. Malo — A87

1938

342	A82a	2fr brown black	1.75	1.25
	Hinged		.55	
343	A83	2.15fr violet brn	9.50	1.00
	Hinged		4.75	
344	A84	3fr car brown	26.50	5.00
	Hinged		12.50	
345	A85	5fr deep ultra	1.50	.40
	Hinged		.75	
346	A86	10fr brown, *blue*	3.25	1.90
	Hinged		1.50	
347	A87	20fr dk blue grn	80.00	19.00
	Hinged		37.50	
	Nos. 342-347 (6)		122.50	28.55

For surcharges see Nos. 410-413.

Clément Ader, Air Pioneer — A88

1938, June 16

348	A88	50fr ultra (thin paper)	150.00	65.00
	Hinged		95.00	
a.		50fr dark ultra (thick paper)	175.00	77.50
	Hinged		100.00	

For surcharge, see No. 414.

Soccer Players — A89

1938, June 1

349	A89	1.75fr dark ultra	29.00	13.50
	Hinged		13.50	

World Cup Soccer Championship.

Costume of Champagne Region — A90

1938, June 13

350	A90	1.75fr dark ultra	7.50	4.50
	Hinged		3.75	

Tercentenary of the birth of Dom Pierre Pérignon, discoverer of the champagne process.

Jean de La Fontaine — A91

1938, July 8

351	A91	55c dk blue green	1.00	.80
	Hinged		.65	

Jean de La Fontaine (1621-1695) the fabulist.

Seal of Friendship and Peace, Victoria Tower and Arc de Triomphe — A92

1938, July 19

352	A92	1.75fr ultra	1.25	.80
	Hinged		.65	

Visit of King George VI and Queen Elizabeth of Great Britain to France.

Mercury — A93

1938-42		Typo.	Perf. 14x13½	
353	A93	1c dark brn ('39)	.25	.25
	Hinged		.25	
354	A93	2c slate grn ('39)	.25	.25
	Hinged		.25	
355	A93	5c rose	.25	.25
	Hinged		.25	
356	A93	10c ultra	.25	.25
	Hinged		.25	
357	A93	15c red orange	.25	.25
	Hinged		.25	
358	A93	15c org brn ('39)	1.00	.50
	Hinged		.55	
359	A93	20c red violet	.25	.25
	Hinged		.25	
360	A93	25c blue green	.25	.25
	Hinged		.25	
361	A93	30c rose red ('39)	.25	.25
	Hinged		.25	
362	A93	40c dk violet ('39)	.25	.25
	Hinged		.25	
363	A93	45c lt green ('39)	.80	.50
	Hinged		.50	
364	A93	50c deep blue ('39)	4.00	.40
	Hinged		2.25	
365	A93	50c dk green ('41)	.55	.35
	Hinged		.30	
366	A93	50c grnsh blue ('42)	.25	.25
	Hinged		.25	
367	A93	60c red org ('39)	.25	.25
	Hinged		.25	
368	A93	70c magenta ('39)	.25	.25
	Hinged		.25	
369	A93	75c dk org brn ('39)	7.50	2.50
	Hinged		3.75	
	Nos. 353-369 (17)		16.85	7.25

No. 366 exists imperforate. See Nos. 455-458. For overprints and surcharge see Nos. 404, 499-502.

Self-portrait — A95

1939, Mar. 15 Engr. Perf. 13

370	A95	2.25fr Prussian blue	8.25	3.50
	Hinged		3.50	

Paul Cézanne (1839-1906), painter.

Georges Clemenceau and Battleship Clemenceau A96

1939, Apr. 18

371	A96	90c ultra	1.00	.75
	Hinged		.50	

Laying of the keel of the warship "Clemenceau," Jan. 17, 1939.

Statue of Liberty, French Pavilion, Trylon and Perisphere — A97

1939-40

372	A97	2.25fr ultra	17.00	6.50
	Hinged		8.00	
373	A97	2.50fr ultra ('40)	22.50	9.50
	Hinged		8.50	

New York World's Fair.

A98

Design: Joseph Nicéphore Niepce and Louis Jacques Mandé Daguerre.

1939, Apr. 24

374	A98	2.25fr dark blue	16.00	7.00
	Hinged		7.00	

Centenary of photography.

Iris — A99

1939-44		Typo.	Perf. 14x13½	
375	A99	80c red brown ('40)	.25	.25
	Hinged		.25	
376	A99	80c yellow grn ('44)	.25	.25
	Hinged		.25	
377	A99	1fr green	1.00	.25
	Hinged		.55	
378	A99	1fr crimson ('40)	.40	.35
	Hinged		.25	
a.		Booklet pane of 10	7.50	
379	A99	1fr grnsh blue ('44)	.25	.25
	Hinged		.25	
380	A99	1.20fr violet ('44)	.25	.25
	Hinged		.25	
381	A99	1.30fr ultra ('40)	.25	.25
	Hinged		.25	
382	A99	1.50fr red org ('41)	.25	.25
	Hinged		.25	
383	A99	1.50fr henna brn ('44)	.25	.25
	Hinged		.25	
384	A99	2fr violet brn ('44)	.25	.25
	Hinged		.25	
385	A99	2.40fr car rose ('44)	.25	.25
	Hinged		.25	
386	A99	3fr orange ('44)	.25	.25
	Hinged		.25	
387	A99	4fr ultra ('44)	.25	.25
	Hinged		.25	
	Nos. 375-387 (13)		4.15	3.35

Pumping Station at Marly — A100

1939 Engr. Perf. 13

388	A100	2.25fr brt ultra	25.00	5.00
	Hinged		11.00	

France's participation in the International Water Exposition at Liège.

St. Gregory of Tours — A101

1939, June 10

389	A101	90c red	.90	.55
	Hinged		.50	

14th centenary of the birth of St. Gregory of Tours, historian and bishop.

"The Oath of the Tennis Court" by Jacques David A102

1939, June 20

390	A102	90c deep slate green	3.50	1.90
	Hinged		1.90	

150th anniversary of French Revolution.

Cathedral of Strasbourg — A103

1939, June 23

391	A103	70c brown carmine	1.50	1.00
	Hinged		.75	

500th anniv. of the completion of Strasbourg Cathedral.

Porte Chaussée, Verdun — A104

1939, June 23

392	A104	90c black brown	1.00	.80
	Hinged		.80	

23rd anniv. of the Battle of Verdun.

View of Pau — A105

1939, Aug. 25

393	A105	90c brt rose, *gray bl*	1.25	1.25
	Hinged		.80	

Maid of Languedoc A106

Bridge at Lyons — A107

1939

394	A106	70c black, *blue*	.50	.40
	Hinged		.40	
395	A107	90c dull brown vio	1.00	*1.25*
	Hinged		.90	

FRANCE

Imperforates
Nearly all French stamps issued from 1940 onward exist imperforate. Officially 20 sheets, ranging from 25 to 100 subjects, were left imperforate.

Georges Guynemer (1894-1917), World War I Ace — A108

1940, Nov. 7
396	A108	50fr ultra	16.00	9.00
		Hinged	8.00	

Stamps of 1938-39 Surcharged in Carmine

1940-41   Perf. 14x13½
397	A81	1fr on 1.75fr dk ultra	.30	.30
		Hinged	.25	
398	A81	1fr on 2.25fr ultra ('41)	.30	.30
		Hinged	.25	
399	A81	1fr on 2.50fr grn ('41)	1.40	1.40
		Hinged	.65	
		Nos. 397-399 (3)	2.00	2.00

Stamps of 1932-39 Surcharged in Carmine, Red (#408) or Black (#407)

1940-41   Perf. 13, 14x13½
400	A22	30c on 35c grn ('41)	.30	.30
		Hinged	.25	
401	A45	50c on 55c dl vio ('41)	.30	.30
		Hinged	.25	
a.		Inverted surcharge	1,000.	
402	A45	50c on 65c brt ultra ('41)	.30	.30
		Hinged	.25	
403	A45	50c on 75c ol grn ('41)	.30	.30
		Hinged	.25	
404	A93	50c on 75c dk org brn ('41)	.30	.30
		Hinged	.25	
405	A45	50c on 80c org ('41)	.30	.30
		Hinged	.25	
406	A45	50c on 90c ultra ('41)	.30	.30
		Hinged	.25	
a.		Inverted surcharge	550.00	
b.		"05" instead of "50"	9,000.	6,400.
407	A45	1fr on 1.25fr rose car (Bk) ('41)	.30	.30
		Hinged	.25	
408	A45	1fr on 1.40fr brt red vio (R) ('41)	.40	.40
		Hinged	.25	
a.		Double surcharge	1,600.	
409	A45	1fr on 1.50fr dk bl ('41)	1.40	1.40
410	A83	1fr on 2.15fr vio brn	.40	.40
		Hinged	.25	
411	A85	2.50fr on 5fr dp ultra ('41)	.40	.40
		Hinged	.25	
a.		Double surcharge	350.00	190.00
412	A86	5fr on 10fr brn, bl ('41)	1.90	1.90
		Hinged	1.00	
413	A87	10fr on 20fr dk bl grn ('41)	1.60	1.60
		Hinged	1.00	
414	A88	20fr on 50fr dk ultra (#348a) ('41)	70.00	37.50
		Hinged	29.00	
a.		20fr on 50fr ultra, thin paper (#348)	75.00	50.00
		Nos. 400-414 (15)	78.50	46.00

Issued: No. 410, 1940; others, 1941

Marshal Pétain — A109

1941   Perf. 13
415	A109	40c red brown	.40	.25
416	A109	80c turq blue	.45	.40
417	A109	1fr red	.25	.25
418	A109	2.50fr deep ultra	1.40	1.10
		Nos. 415-418 (4)	2.50	2.00

For No. 417 with surcharge, see No. B111.

Frédéric Mistral — A110

1941, Feb. 20   Perf. 14x13
419	A110	1fr brown lake	.25	.25

Issued in honor of Frédéric Mistral, poet and Nobel prize winner for literature in 1904.

Beaune Hospital — A111

View of Angers — A112

Ramparts of St. Louis, Aiguesmortes A113

1941
420	A111	5fr brown black	.35	.25
421	A112	10fr dark violet	.60	.45
422	A113	20fr brown black	1.10	.80
		Nos. 420-422 (3)	2.05	1.50

Inscribed "Postes Francaises"

1942

Imprint: "FELTESSE" at right
423	A111	15fr brown lake	.60	.40

A114

A115

A116

A117

Marshal Pétain — A118

1941-42   Typo.   Perf. 14x13½
427	A114	20c lilac ('42)	.25	.25
428	A114	30c rose red	.25	.25
429	A114	40c ultra	.25	.25
431	A115	50c dp green	.25	.25
432	A115	60c violet ('42)	.25	.25
433	A115	70c saph ('42)	.25	.25
434	A115	70c orange ('42)	.25	.25
435	A115	80c brown	.25	.25
436	A115	80c emerald ('42)	.25	.25
437	A115	1fr rose red	.25	.25
438	A115	1.20fr red brn ('42)	.25	.25
439	A116	1.50fr rose	.25	.25
440	A116	1.50fr dl red brn ('42)	.25	.25
a.		Booklet pane of 10	2.75	
441	A116	2fr blue grn ('42)	.25	.25
443	A116	2.40fr rose red ('42)	.25	.25
444	A116	2.50fr ultra	.25	.55
445	A116	3fr orange	.25	.25
446	A115	4fr ultra ('42)	.25	.25
447	A115	4.50fr dk green ('42)	.25	.25

Engr.   **Perf. 14x13**
448	A115	4fr brt ultra ('42)	.25	.25
449	A115	4.50fr dark green ('42)	.25	.25
450	A117	5fr Prus green ('42)	.25	.25

Perf. 13
451	A118	50fr black ('42)	3.00	3.00
		Nos. 427-451 (23)	8.50	8.80

Nos. 431 to 438 measure 16½x20½mm. Nos. 448 and 449 measure 18x21½mm.

No. 440 was forged by the French Underground ("Defense de la France") and used to frank clandestine journals, etc., from Feb. to June, 1944. The forgeries were ungummed, both perf. 11½ and imperf., with a back handstamp covering six stamps and including the words: "Atelier des Faux."

For surcharge see No. B134.

Jules Massenet — A119

1942, June 22   Perf. 14x13
452	A119	4fr Prus green	.25	.25

Jules Massenet (1842-1912), composer.

Stendhal (Marie Henri Beyle) — A120

1942, Sept. 14   Perf. 13
453	A120	4fr blk brn & org red	.40	.40

Stendhal (1783-1842), writer.

André Blondel — A121

1942, Sept. 14
454	A121	4fr dull blue	.40	.40

André Eugène Blondel (1863-1938), physicist.

Mercury Type of 1938-42
Inscribed "Postes Françaises"

1942   Perf. 14x13½
455	A93	10c ultra	.25	.25
456	A93	30c rose red	.25	.25
457	A93	40c dark violet	.25	.25
458	A93	50c turq blue	.25	.25
		Nos. 455-458 (4)	1.00	1.00

Town-Hall Belfry, Arras — A122

1942, Dec. 8   Engr.   Perf. 13
459	A122	10fr green	.25	.25

Coats of Arms

Lyon — A123

1943   Typo.   Perf. 14x13½
460	A123	5fr shown	.30	.30
461	A123	10fr Brittany	.40	.40
462	A123	15fr Provence	1.75	1.10
463	A123	20fr Ile de France	1.40	1.20
		Nos. 460-463 (4)	3.85	3.00

Antoine Lavoisier (1743-94), French Scientist — A127

1943, July 5   Engr.   Perf. 14x13
464	A127	4fr ultra	.25	.25

Lake Lerie and Meije Dauphiné Alps — A128

1943, July 5   Perf. 13
465	A128	20fr dull gray grn	.75	.75

Nicolas Rolin, Guigone de Salins and Hospital of Beaune — A129

1943, July 21
466	A129	4fr blue	.25	.25

500th anniv. of the founding of the Hospital of Beaune.

Arms of Flanders — A130

1944, Mar. 27   Typo.   Perf. 14x13½
467	A130	5fr shown	.25	.25
468	A130	10fr Languedoc	.25	.25
469	A130	15fr Orleans	.60	.55
470	A130	20fr Normandy	1.00	.85
		Nos. 467-470 (4)	2.10	1.90

Edouard Branly — A134

1944, Feb. 21   Engr.   Perf. 14x13
471	A134	4fr ultra	.25	.25

Cent. of the birth of Edouard Branly, electrical inventor.

Early Postal Car — A135

1944, June 10   Perf. 13
472	A135	1.50fr dark blue green	.55	.45

Cent. of France's traveling postal service.

Chateau de Chenonceaux A136

1944, June 10
473	A136	15fr lilac brown	.60	.45
a.		15fr black brown	10.50	3.00
b.		15fr black	100.00	55.00

See No. 496.

FRANCE

Claude Chappe — A137

1944, Aug. 14   **Perf. 14x13**
474 A137 4fr dark ultra .25 .25

150th anniv. of the invention of an optical telegraph by Claude Chappe (1763-1805).

Arc de Triomphe — OS2

		Unwmk.		
1944, Oct. 9   **Litho.**   **Perf. 11**
475 OS2 5c brt red violet .25 .25
476 OS2 10c lt gray .25 .25
476A OS2 25c brown .25 .25
476B OS2 50c olive bis .25 .25
476C OS2 1fr pck green .25 .25
476D OS2 1.50fr rose pink .25 .25
476E OS2 2.50fr purple .25 .25
476F OS2 4fr ultra .25 .25
476G OS2 5fr black .25 .25
476H OS2 10fr yellow org 27.50 21.00
    Nos. 475-476H (10) 29.75 23.25

Nos 475-476H were printed by the U.S. Bureau of Engraving and Printing and were intended to be used by an Allied Military government, which was expected to administer the liberated areas of France. Instead, the Allies recognized the authority of Gen. de Gaulle's Provisional Government over these territories, and these stamps were transferred to the Free French in July, 1944. They were put on sale in liberated areas as the Allied armies advanced, and on Oct. 9, they were officially issued in Paris.
See Nos. 523A-523J.

Gallic Cock A138   Marianne A139

1944   **Litho.**   **Perf. 12**
477 A138 10c yellow grn .25 .25
478 A138 30c dk rose vio .30 .35
479 A138 40c blue .25 .25
480 A138 50c dark red .25 .25
481 A139 60c olive brown .25 .25
482 A139 70c rose lilac .25 .25
483 A139 80c yellow grn .90 .90
484 A139 1fr violet .25 .25
485 A139 1.20fr dp carmine .25 .25
486 A139 1.50fr deep blue .25 .25
487 A139 2fr indigo .25 .25
488 A139 2.40fr red orange 1.10 1.10
489 A139 3fr dp bluo grn .25 .25
490 A139 4fr grnsh blue .25 .25
491 A139 4.50fr black .25 .25
492 A139 5fr violet blue 3.75 3.75
493 A138 10fr violet 1.60 1.25
494 A138 15fr olive brown 4.25 4.25
495 A138 20fr dk slate grn 3.75 3.75
    Nos. 477-495 (19) 21.55 21.35

Nos. 477-495 were issued first in Corsica after the Allied landing, and released in Paris Nov. 15, 1944.

Chateau Type Inscribed "RF"

1944, Oct. 30   **Engr.**   **Perf. 13**
496 A136 25fr black .75 .65

Thomas Robert Bugeaud — A141

1944, Nov. 20
497 A141 4fr dp blue grn .25 .25

Battle of Isly, Aug. 14th, 1844.

Church of St. Denis — A142

1944, Nov. 20
498 A142 2.40fr brown carmine .30 .30

800th anniv. of the Church of St. Denis.

Type of 1938-42, Overprinted in Black

Inscribed "Postes Francaises"

1944   **Perf. 14x13½**
499 A93 10c ultra .25 .25
500 A93 30c rose red .25 .25
501 A93 40c dark violet .25 .25
502 A93 50c grnsh blue .25 .25
    Nos. 499-502 (4) 1.00 1.00

The overprint "RF" in various forms, with or without Lorraine Cross, was also applied to stamps of the French State at Lyon and fourteen other cities.

French Forces of the Interior and Symbol of Liberation — A143

1945, Jan.
503 A143 4fr dark ultra .30 .30

Issued to commemorate the Liberation.

Marianne — A144

Perf. 11½x12½
				Unwmk.
1944-45   **Engr.**
504 A144 10c ultra .25 .25
505 A144 30c bister .25 .25
506 A144 40c indigo .25 .25
507 A144 50c red orange .25 .25
508 A144 60c chalky blue .25 .25
509 A144 70c sepia .25 .25
510 A144 80c deep green .25 .25
511 A144 1fr lilac .25 .25
512 A144 1.20fr dk ol grn .25 .25
513 A144 1.50fr rose ('44) .25 .25
514 A144 2fr dk brown .25 .25
515 A144 2.40fr red .25 .25
516 A144 3fr brt ol grn .25 .25
517 A144 4fr brt ultra .25 .25
518 A144 4.50fr slate gray .25 .25
519 A144 5fr brt orange .25 .25
520 A144 10fr yellow grn .25 .25
521 A144 15fr lake .25 .25
522 A144 20fr brown org 1.10 1.10
523 A144 50fr deep purple 2.90 2.40
    Nos. 504-523 (20) 8.50 8.00

The 2.40fr exists imperf. in a miniature sheet of 4 which was not issued. Value: never hinged $6,500; unused $4,500.
Compare with type A1759. See Nos. 4905, 4909.

Arc de Triomphe Type of 1944

1945, Feb. 12   **Litho.**   **Perf. 11**
Denominations in Black
523A OS2 30c orange .25 .25
523B OS2 40c pale gray .25 .25
523C OS2 50c olive bis .25 .25
523D OS2 60c violet .25 .25
523E OS2 80c emerald .25 .25
523F OS2 1.20fr brown .25 .25
523G OS2 1.50fr vermilion .25 .25
523H OS2 2fr yellow .25 .25
523I OS2 2.40fr dark rose .25 .25
523J OS2 3fr brt red violet .25 .25
    Nos. 523A-523J (10) 2.50 2.50

Coat of Arms A145

Ceres A146

Marianne — A147

1945-47   **Typo.**   **Perf. 14x13½**
524 A145 10c brown black .25 .25
525 A145 30c dk blue grn .25 .25
526 A145 40c lilac rose .25 .25
527 A145 50c violet blue .25 .25
528 A146 60c brt ultra .25 .25
530 A146 80c brt green .25 .25
531 A146 90c dull grn ('46) .65 .55
532 A146 1fr rose red .25 .25
533 A146 1.20fr brown black .25 .25
534 A146 1.50fr rose lilac .25 .25
535 A147 1.50fr rose pink .25 .25
536 A147 2fr myrtle green .25 .25
536A A146 2fr lt bl grn ('46) .25 .25
537 A147 2.40fr scarlet .30 .30
538 A146 2.50fr brown ('46) .25 .25
539 A147 3fr sepia .25 .25
540 A147 3fr dp rose ('46) .25 .25
541 A147 4fr ultra .25 .25
541A A147 4fr violet ('46) .25 .25
541B A147 4.50fr ultra ('47) .25 .25
542 A147 5fr lt green .25 .25
542A A147 5fr rose pink ('47) .25 .25
543 A147 6fr brt ultra .35 .25
544 A147 6fr crim rose ('46) 1.60 1.60
545 A147 10fr red orange .45 .30
546 A147 10fr ultra ('46) 1.20 .75
547 A147 15fr brt red vio 3.00 1.60
    Nos. 524-547 (27) 12.55 6.65

No. 531 is known only precanceled. See second note after No. 132.
Due to a reduction of the domestic postage rate, No. 542A was sold for 4.50fr.
Compare with types A1814 and A3213. See Nos. 576-580, 594-602, 614, 615, 650-654, 4906, 4908. For surcharges see Nos. 589, 610, 706, Reunion 270-276, 278, 285, 290, 291, 293, 295.

1945-46   **Engr.**   **Perf. 14x13**
548 A147 4fr dark blue .25 .25
549 A147 10fr dp blue ('46) 1.10 .55
550 A147 15fr brt red vio ('46) 6.75 1.75
551 A147 20fr blue grn ('46) 1.00 .55
552 A147 25fr red ('46) 6.75 1.50
    Nos. 548-552 (5) 15.85 4.60

Nos. 548-552 have "GANDON" at lower right in design, and no inscription below design.

Marianne — A148

1945   **Engr.**   **Perf. 13**
553 A148 20fr dark green 1.00 .90
554 A148 25fr violet 1.10 1.10
555 A148 50fr red brown 1.50 1.50
556 A148 100fr brt rose car 10.00 5.50
    Nos. 553-556 (4) 13.60 9.00

CFA

French stamps inscribed or surcharged "CFA" and new value are listed under Réunion at the end of the French listings.

Arms of Metz A149

Arms of Strasbourg A150

1945, Mar. 3   **Perf. 14x13**
557 A149 2.40fr dull blue .25 .25
558 A150 4fr black brown .25 .25

Liberation of Metz and Strasbourg.

A151

Design: Costumes of Alsace and Lorraine and Cathedrals of Strasbourg and Metz.

1945, May 16   **Perf. 13**
559 A151 4fr henna brown .25 .25

Liberation of Alsace and Lorraine. See No. 4907.

World Map Showing French Possessions A152

1945, Sept. 17
560 A152 2fr Prussian blue .25 .25

No. B193 Surcharged in Black

1946   **Perf. 14x13½**
561 SP147 3fr on 2fr+1fr red org .25 .25

Arms of Corsica — A153

1946   **Unwmk.**   **Typo.**   **Perf. 14x13½**
562 A153 10c shown .25 .25
563 A153 30c Alsace .25 .25
564 A153 50c Lorraine .25 .25
565 A153 60c County of Nice .25 .25
    Nos. 562-565 (4) 1.00 1.00

For surcharges see Reunion Nos. 268-269.

Reaching for "Peace" A157

Holding the Dove of Peace A158

1946, July 29   **Engr.**   **Perf. 13**
566 A157 3fr Prussian green .25 .25
567 A158 10fr blue .25 .25

Peace Conference of Paris, 1946.

Vézelay — A159

620 FRANCE

Luxembourg Palace A160

Rocamadour A161

Pointe du Raz, Finistère — A162

1946	Unwmk.		Perf. 13	
568	A159	5fr rose violet	.25	.25
569	A160	10fr dark blue	.25	.25
570	A161	15fr dk violet brn	3.50	.55
571	A162	20fr slate gray	1.00	.25
	Nos. 568-571 (4)		5.00	1.30

See Nos. 591-592. For surcharges see Reunion Nos. 277, 279.

Globe and Wreath — A163

1946, Nov.
572 A163 10fr dark blue .25 .25

Gen. conf. of UNESCO, Paris, 1946.

Cannes — A164

Stanislas Square, Nancy — A165

1946-48	Engr.		Perf. 13	
573	A164	6fr rose red	1.10	.40
574	A165	25fr black brown	3.00	.25
575	A165	25fr dark blue ('48)	10.00	.90
	Nos. 573-575 (3)		14.10	1.55

For surcharges see Reunion Nos. 280-281.

Ceres & Marianne Types of 1945

1947	Unwmk.	Typo.	Perf. 14x13½	
576	A146	1.30fr dull blue	.25	.25
577	A147	3fr green	1.50	.25
578	A147	3.50fr brown red	.60	.30
579	A147	5fr blue	.25	.25
580	A147	6fr carmine	.25	.25
	Nos. 576-580 (5)		2.85	1.30

Colonnade of the Louvre — A166

La Conciergerie, Paris Prison — A167

La Cité, Oldest Section of Paris — A168

Place de la Concorde — A169

1947, May 7	Engr.	Perf. 13	
581	A166	3.50fr chocolate	.30	.30
582	A167	4.50fr dk slate gray	.30	.30
583	A168	6fr red	.85	.85
584	A169	10fr bright ultra	.85	.85
	Nos. 581-584 (4)		2.30	2.30

12th UPU Cong., Paris, May 7-July 7. See No. 5035a.

Auguste Pavie — A170

1947, May 30
585 A170 4.50fr sepia .30 .25

Cent. of the birth of Auguste Pavie, French pioneer in Laos.

Francois Fénelon — A171

1947, July 12
586 A171 4.50fr chocolate .30 .25

Issued to honor Francois de Salignac de la Mothe-Fénelon, prelate and writer.

Fleur-de-Lis and Double Carrick Bend — A172

1947, Aug. 2 Unwmk.
587 A172 5fr brown .30 .25

6th World Boy Scout Jamboree held at Moisson, Aug. 9th-18th, 1947.

Captured Patriot — A173

1947, Nov. 10 Engr. Perf. 13
588 A173 5fr sepia .40 .35

No. 576 Surcharged in Carmine

1947, Nov. Typo. Perf. 14x13½
589 A146 1fr on 1.30fr dull blue .25 .25

View of Conques — A174

1947, Dec. 18 Engr. Perf. 13
590 A174 15fr henna brown 3.50 .70

For surcharge see Reunion No. 282.

Types of 1946-47
1948 Re-engraved
591 A160 12fr rose carmine 2.50 .45
592 A160 15fr bright red .60 .40
593 A174 18fr dark blue 3.50 .40
Nos. 591-593 (3) 6.60 1.25

"FRANCE" substituted for inscriptions "RF" and "REPUBLIQUE FRANCAISE."

Marianne Type of 1945

1948-49	Typo.	Perf. 14x13½	
594	A147	2.50fr brown	2.75	1.25
595	A147	3fr lilac rose	.25	.25
596	A147	4fr lt blue grn	.25	.25
597	A147	4fr brown org	2.50	.90
598	A147	5fr lt blue grn	.60	.25
599	A147	8fr blue	.30	.25
600	A147	10fr brt violet	.25	.25
601	A147	12fr ultra ('49)	2.50	.25
602	A147	15fr crim rose ('49)	.85	.25
a.	Booklet pane of 10		150.00	
	Nos. 594-602 (9)		10.25	3.90

No. 594 known only precanceled. See second note after No. 132.

François René de Chateaubriand A175

1948, July 3 Engr. Perf. 13
603 A175 18fr dark blue .30 .25

Vicomte de Chateaubriand (1768-1848).

Philippe François M. de Hautecloque (Gen. Jacques Leclerc) — A176

1948, July 3
604 A176 6fr gray black .30 .25

See Nos. 692-692A.

Chaillot Palace — A177

A178

1948, Sept. 21
605 A177 12fr carmine rose .35 .30
606 A178 18fr indigo .35 .30

Meeting of the UN General Assembly, Paris, 1948.

Genissiat Dam — A179

1948, Sept. 21
607 A179 12fr carmine rose .85 .75

Paul Langevin — A180

1948, Nov. 17 Perf. 14x13
608 A180 5fr shown .50 .25
609 A180 8fr Jean Perrin .50 .25

Placing of the ashes of physicists Langevin (1872-1946) and Perrin (1870-1942) in the Pantheon.

No. 580 Surcharged with New Value and Bars in Black

1949, Jan. Perf. 14x13½
610 A147 5fr on 6fr carmine .25 .25

Arctic Scene — A181

1949, May 2 Perf. 13
611 A181 15fr indigo .30 .25

French polar explorations.

Types of 1849 and 1945
1949, May 9 Engr. Imperf.
612 A1 15fr red 3.00 3.00
613 A1 25fr deep blue 3.00 3.00

Perf. 14x13
614 A147 15fr red 3.00 3.00
615 A147 25fr deep blue 3.00 3.00
a. Strip of 4, #612-615 + label 14.00 12.00
Nos. 612-615 (4) 12.00 12.00

Cent. of the 1st French postage stamps.

Arms of Burgundy — A182

Arms: 50c, Guyenne (Aquitania). 1fr, Savoy. 2fr, Auvergne. 4fr, Anjou.

1949, May 11 Typo. Perf. 14x13½
616 A182 10c blue, red & yel .25 .25
617 A182 50c blue, red & yel .25 .25
618 A182 1fr brown & red .40 .25
619 A182 2fr green, yel & red .40 .25
620 A182 4fr blue, red & yel .25 .25
Nos. 616-620 (5) 1.60 1.25

See Nos. 659-663, 694-699, 733-739, 782-785. For surcharges see Reunion Nos. 283-284, 288-289, 297, 301, 305, 311.

Collegiate Church of St. Barnard and Dauphiné Arms — A183

1949, May 14 Engr. Perf. 13
621 A183 12fr red brown .30 .25

600th anniv. of France's acquisition of the Dauphiné region.

US and French Flags, Plane and Steamship A184

1949, May 14
622 A184 25fr blue & carmine .45 .35

Franco-American friendship.

Cloister of St. Wandrille Abbey — A185

1949, May 18
623 A185 25fr deep ultra .30 .25

See No. 649. For surcharge see Reunion No. 287.

FRANCE

Type of 1849 Inscribed "1849-1949" in Lower Margin

1949, June 1
624	A1	10fr brown orange	55.00	40.00
a.		Sheet of 10	700.00	450.00

Cent. of the 1st French postage stamp.
No. 624 has wide margins, 40x52mm from perforation to perforation. Sold for 110fr, which included cost of admission to the Centenary Intl. Exhib., Paris, June 1949.

Claude Chappe — A186

15fr, François Arago & André M. Ampère. 25fr, Emile Baudot. 50fr, Gen. Gustave A. Ferrié.

Inscribed: "C.I.T.T. PARIS 1949"

1949, June 13   Unwmk.   Perf. 13
625	A186	10fr vermilion	.75	.70
626	A186	15fr sepia	.75	.70
627	A186	25fr deep claret	1.90	1.90
628	A186	50fr deep blue	3.75	2.75
		Nos. 625-628 (4)	7.15	6.05

International Telegraph and Telephone Conference, Paris, May-July 1949.

Jean Racine — A187

1949
629	A187	12fr sepia	.30	.25

Death of Jean Racine, dramatist, 250th anniv.

Abbey of St. Bertrand de Comminges A188

Meuse Valley, Ardennes — A189

Mt. Gerbier de Jonc, Vivarais — A190

1949   Engr.
630	A188	20fr dark red	.26	.26
631	A189	40fr Prus green	12.50	.25
632	A190	50fr sepia	2.10	.25
		Nos. 630-632 (3)	14.85	.75

For surcharge see Reunion No. 286.

A191

1949, Oct. 18
633	A191	15fr deep carmine	.25	.25

50th anniv. of the Assembly of Presidents of Chambers of Commerce of the French Union.

UPU Allegory — A192

1949, Nov. 7
634	A192	5fr dark green	.25	.25
635	A192	15fr deep carmine	.30	.25
636	A192	25fr deep blue	1.00	.90
		Nos. 634-636 (3)	1.55	1.40

UPU, 75th anniversary.

Raymond Poincaré — A193

1950, May 27   Unwmk.   Perf. 13
637	A193	15fr indigo	.30	.25

Charles Péguy and Cathedral at Chartres A194

François Rabelais A195

1950, June
638	A194	12fr dk brown	.30	.25
639	A195	12fr red brown	.60	.45

Chateau of Chateaudun A196

1950, Nov. 25
640	A196	8fr choc & bis brn	.55	.40

Madame Récamier A197

Marie de Sévigné A198

1950
641	A197	12fr dark green	.45	.40
642	A198	15fr ultra	.45	.40

See footnote after No. 4042.

Palace of Fontainebleau A199

1951, Jan. 20
643	A199	12fr dark brown	.75	.60

Jules Ferry — A200

1951, Mar. 17
644	A200	15fr bright red	.40	.40

Hands Holding Shuttle — A201

1951, Apr. 9
645	A201	25fr deep ultra	.75	.45

Intl. Textile Exposition, Lille, April-May, 1951.

Jean-Baptiste de la Salle — A202

1951, Apr. 28
646	A202	15fr chocolate	.45	.35

300th anniv. of the birth of Jean-Baptiste de la Salle, educator and saint.

Map and Anchor — A203

1951, May 12
647	A203	15fr deep ultra	.60	.30

50th anniv. of the creation of the French colonial troops.

Vincent d'Indy — A204

1951, May 15
648	A204	25fr deep green	1.50	1.50

Vincent d'Indy, composer, birth cent.

Abbey Type of 1949

1951
649	A185	30fr bright blue	4.00	3.25

Marianne Type of 1945-47

1951   Typo.   Perf. 14x13½
650	A147	5fr dull violet	.30	.25
651	A147	6fr green	4.75	.45
652	A147	12fr red orange	.70	.25
653	A147	15fr ultra	.25	.25
a.		Booklet pane of 10	60.00	
654	A147	18fr cerise	15.00	1.20
		Nos. 650-654 (5)	21.00	2.40

A205

Design: Professors Nocard, Bouley and Chauveau; gate at Lyons school.

1951, June 8   Engr.   Perf. 13
655	A205	12fr red violet	.60	.40

Issued to honor Veterinary Medicine.

A206

Design: Gen. Picqué, Cols. Roussin and Villemin; Val de Grace Dome.

1951, June 17   Unwmk.
656	A206	15fr red brown	.75	.40

Issued to honor Military Medicine.

St. Nicholas, by Jean Didier — A207

1951, June 23
657	A207	15fr ind, dp claret & org	1.00	.75

Chateau Bontemps, Arbois — A208

1951, June 23
658	A208	30fr indigo	.75	.25

For surcharge see Reunion No. 296.

Arms Type of 1949

Arms of: 10c, Artois. 50c, Limousin. 1fr, Béarn. 2fr, Touraine. 3fr, Franche-Comté.

1951, June   Typo.   Perf. 14x13½
659	A182	10c red, vio bl & yel	.25	.25
660	A182	50c green, red & blk	.25	.25
661	A182	1fr blue, red & yel	.25	.25
662	A182	2fr vio bl, red & yel	.60	.25
663	A182	3fr red, vio bl & yel	.45	.30
		Nos. 659-663 (5)	1.80	1.00

Seal of Paris — A209

Unwmk.
1951, July 7   Engr.   Perf. 13
664	A209	15fr dp bl, dk brn & red	.55	.30

2,000th anniv. of the founding of Paris.

Maurice Noguès and Globe — A210

1951, Oct. 13
665	A210	12fr indigo & blue	.70	.60

Maurice Nogues, aviation pioneer.

Charles Baudelaire A211

Poets: 12fr, Paul Verlaine. 15fr, Arthur Rimbaud.

1951, Oct. 27
666	A211	8fr purple	.70	.45
667	A211	12fr gray	.70	.45
668	A211	15fr dp green	.70	.45
		Nos. 666-668 (3)	2.10	1.35

Georges Clemenceau, Birth Cent. — A212

1951, Nov. 11
669	A212	15fr black brown	.55	.35

622 FRANCE

Chateau du Clos, Vougeot — A213

1951, Nov. 17
670 A213 30fr blk brn & brn   5.25 1.75

Chaillot Palace and Eiffel Tower — A214

1951, Nov. 6
671 A214 18fr red   .90   .60
672 A214 30fr deep ultra   1.50 1.50

Opening of the Geneva Assembly of the United Nations, Paris, Nov. 6, 1951.

Observatory, Pic du Midi — A215

Abbaye aux Hommes, Caen — A216

1951, Dec. 22
673 A215 40fr violet   4.50   .25
674 A216 50fr black brown   4.00   .25

For surcharge see Reunion No. 294.

Marshal Jean de Lattre de Tassigny, 1890-1952 A217

1952, May 8   Unwmk.   Perf. 13
675 A217 15fr violet brown   .75   .45

See No. 717.

Gate of France, Vaucouleurs — A218

1952, May 11
676 A218 12fr brown black   1.00   .75

Flags and Monument at Narvik, Norway — A219

1952, May 28
677 A219 30fr violet blue   2.50 1.75

Battle of Narvik, May 27, 1940.

Chateau de Chambord A220

1952, May 30
678 A220 20fr dark purple   .45   .25

For surcharge see Reunion No. 292.

Assembly Hall, Strasbourg A221

1952, May 31
679 A221 30fr dark green   6.50 4.50

Issued to honor the Council of Europe.

Monument, Bir-Hacheim Cemetery — A222

1952, June 14
680 A222 30fr rose lake   3.00 1.75

10th anniv. of the defense of Bir-Hacheim.

Abbey of the Holy Cross, Poitiers — A223

1952, June 21
681 A223 15fr bright red   .40   .40

14th cent. of the foundation of the Abbey of the Holy Cross at Poitiers.

A224

1952, July 9
682 A224 30fr deep ultra   7.00 5.25

Design: Leonardo da Vinci, Amboise Chateau and La Signoria, Florence.

Leonardo da Vinci, 500th birth anniv.

Garabit Viaduct — A225

1952, July 5
683 A225 15fr dark blue   .45   .45

Sword and Military Medals, 1852-1952 — A226

1952, July 5
684 A226 15fr choc, grn & yel .45   .40

Cent. of the creation of the Military Medal.

Dr. René Laennec — A227

1952, Nov. 7
685 A227 12fr dark green   .60   .45

Versailles Gate, Painted by Utrillo — A228

1952, Dec. 20
686 A228 18fr violet brown   2.25 1.50

Publicity for the restoration of Versailles Palace. See No. 728.

Mannequin — A229

1953, Apr. 24   Unwmk.   Perf. 13
687 A229 30fr blue blk & rose vio .75 .30

Dressmaking industry of France.

Gargantua of François Rabelais A230

Célimène from The Misanthrope A231

Figaro, from the Barber of Seville A232

Hernani of Victor Hugo A233

1953
688 A230 6fr dp plum & car   .25   .25
689 A231 8fr indigo & ultra   .25   .25
690 A232 12fr vio brn & dk grn .25   .25
691 A233 18fr vio brn & blk brn .50 .25
       Nos. 688-691 (4)   1.25 1.00

For surcharge see Reunion No. 298.

Type of 1948
Inscribed "Général Leclerc Maréchal de France"

1953-54
692   A176 8fr red brown   .75   .60
692A A176 12fr dk grn & gray grn ('54) 2.25 1.50

Issued to honor the memory of General Jacques Leclerc.

Map and Cyclists, 1903-1953 A234

1953, July 26
693 A234 12fr red brn, ultra & blk 1.75 1.10

50th anniv. of the Bicycle Tour de France.

Arms Type of 1949
50c, Picardy. 70c, Gascony. 80c, Berri. 1fr, Poitou. 2fr, Champagne. 3fr, Dauphiné.

1953   Typo.   Perf. 14x13½
694 A182 50c blue, yel & red   .25   .25
695 A182 70c red, blue & yel   .25   .25
696 A182 80c blue, red & yel   .25   .25
697 A182 1fr black, red & yel .25   .25
698 A182 2fr brown, bl & yel   .30   .25
699 A182 3fr red, blue & yel   .45   .25
       Nos. 694-699 (6)   1.75 1.50

Swimming A235

1953, Nov. 28   Engr.   Perf. 13
700 A235 20fr shown   1.90   .25
701 A235 25fr Track   10.50   .25
702 A235 30fr Fencing   1.90   .25
703 A235 40fr Canoe racing   11.00   .25
704 A235 50fr Rowing   6.00   .25
705 A235 75fr Equestrian   30.00 11.00
       Nos. 700-705 (6)   61.30 12.25

For surcharges see Reunion Nos. 299-300.

No. 654 Surcharged with New Value and Bars in Black

1954   Perf. 14x13½
706 A147 15fr on 18fr cerise   .40   .25

Farm Woman A236

Gallic Cock A237

1954   Typo.
707 A236 4fr blue   .25   .25
708 A236 8fr brown red   4.75 1.00
709 A237 12fr cerise   3.00   .55
710 A237 24fr blue green   16.00 3.25
       Nos. 707-710 (4)   24.00 5.05

Nos. 707-710 are known only precanceled. See second note after No. 132.
See Nos. 833-834, 840-844, 910-913, 939, 952-955. For surcharges see Reunion Nos. 324, 326-327.

Tapestry and Gobelin Workshop — A238

Designs: 30fr, Book manufacture. 40fr, Porcelain and glassware. 50fr, Jewelry and metalsmith's work. 75fr, Flowers and perfumes.

1954, May 6   Engr.   Perf. 13
711 A238 25fr red brn car & blk brn 9.50 .45
712 A238 30fr dk grn & lil gray 1.10 .25
713 A238 40fr dk brn, vio brn & org brn 3.50 .25
714 A238 50fr brt ultra, dl grn & org brn 1.10 .25
715 A238 75fr dp car & magenta 11.00 1.10
       Nos. 711-715 (5)   26.20 2.30

For surcharges see Reunion Nos. 303-304.

Entrance to Exhibition Park — A239

1954, May 22
716 A239 15fr blue & dk car   .30   .25

Founding of the Fair of Paris, 50th anniv.

De Lattre Type of 1952
1954, June 5
717 A217 12fr vio bl & indigo 1.50   .75

FRANCE

Allied Landings — A240

1954, June 5
718 A240 15fr scarlet & ultra   1.75   .90
The 10th anniversary of the liberation.

View of Lourdes A241   Street Corner, Quimper A242

Views: 8fr, Seine valley, Les Andelys. 10fr, Beach at Royan. 18fr, Cheverny Chateau. 20fr, Beach, Gulf of Ajaccio.

1954
719 A241 6fr ultra, ind & dk grn   .30   .25
720 A241 8fr brt blue & dk grn   .30   .25
721 A241 10fr aqua & org brn   .25   .25
722 A242 12fr rose vio & dk vio   .30   .25
723 A241 18fr bl, dk grn & ind   2.50   .50
724 A241 20fr blk brn, bl grn & red brn 2.25 1.00
  Nos. 719-724 (6)   5.90 1.75

See No. 873. For surcharges see Reunion Nos. 302, 306-310. See footnote after No. 4642.

Abbey Ruins, Jumièges — A243

1954, June 13
725 A243 12fr vio bl, ind & dk grn   1.50   .75
13th centenary of Abbey of Jumièges.

St. Philibert Abbey, Tournus — A244

1954, June 10
726 A244 30fr indigo & blue   4.00 3.00
1st conf. of the Intl. Center of Romance Studies.

View of Stenay — A245

1954, June 26
727 A245 15fr dk brn & org brn   .70   .30
Acquisition of Stenay by France, 300th anniv.

Versailles Type of 1952

1954, July 10
728 A228 18fr dp bl, ind & vio brn   7.50 4.50

Villandry Chateau — A246

1954, July 17
729 A246 18fr dk bl & dk bl grn   4.00 3.00

Napoleon Awarding Legion of Honor Decoration A247

1954, Aug. 14
730 A247 12fr scarlet   1.20   .75
150th anniv. of the 1st Legion of Honor awards at Camp de Boulogne.

Cadets Marching Through Gateway — A248

1954, Aug. 1
731 A248 15fr vio gray, dk bl & car   1.00 1.00
150th anniversary of the founding of the Military School of Saint-Cyr.

Allegory — A249

1954, Oct. 4
732 A249 30fr indigo & choc   4.00 3.00
Issued to publicize the fact that the metric system was first introduced in France.

Arms Type of 1949

Arms: 50c, Maine. 70c, Navarre. 80c, Nivernais. 1fr, Bourbonnais. 2fr, Angoumois. 3fr, Aunis. 5fr, Saintonge.

1954   Typo.   Perf. 14x13½
733 A182 50c multicolored   .25   .25
734 A182 70c green, red & yel .25   .25
735 A182 80c blue, red & yel   .25   .25
736 A182 1fr red, blue & yel   .25   .25
737 A182 2fr black, red & yel .25   .25
738 A182 3fr brown, red & yel .25   .25
739 A182 5fr blue & yellow   .25   .25
  Nos. 733-739 (7)   1.75 1.75

Duke de Saint-Simon — A250

1955, Feb. 5   Engr.   Perf. 13
740 A250 12fr dk brn & vio brn   .45   .30
Louis de Rouvroy, Duke de Saint-Simon (1675-1755).

Allegory and Rotary Emblem — A251

1955, Feb. 23
741 A251 30fr vio bl, bl & org   2.00   .75
50th anniv. of Rotary International.

Marianne — A252

1955-59   Typo.   Perf. 14x13½
751 A252 6fr fawn   2.00 1.40
752 A252 12fr green   2.40 1.10
  a. Bklt. pane of 10 + 2 labels   30.00
753 A252 15fr carmine   .25   .25
  a. Booklet pane of 10   10.00
754 A252 18fr green ('58)   .25   .25
755 A252 20fr ultra ('57)   .30   .25
756 A252 25fr rose red ('59)   1.00   .25
  a. Booklet pane of 8   40.00
  b. Booklet pane of 10   30.00
  Nos. 751-756 (6)   6.20 3.50

No. 751 was issued in coils of 1,000.

No. 752 was issued in panes of 10 stamps and two labels with marginal instructions for folding to form a booklet.

Nos. 754-755 are found in two types, distinguished by the numerals. On the 18fr there is no serif at left of base of the "1" on the 1st type. The 2nd type has a shorter "1" with no serifs at base. On the 20fr the 2nd type has a well formed "2" and the horiz. lines of the "F" of the denomination are longer and of equal length.

No. 756 also in two types, distinguished by border width. On the 1st type, the border is thicker than the width of the letters. On the 2nd type, the border is thinner than the width of the letters.

For surcharges see Reunion Nos. 330-331.

Philippe Lebon, Inventor of Illuminating Gas — A253

Inventors: 10fr, Barthélemy Thimonnier, sewing machine. 12fr, Nicolas Appert, canned foods. 18fr, Dr. E. H. St. Claire Deville, aluminum. 25fr, Pierre Martin, steel making. 30fr, Bernigaud de Chardonnet, rayon.

1955, Mar. 5   Engr.   Perf. 13
757 A253 5fr dk vio bl & bl   .70   .60
758 A253 10fr dk brn & org brn   .70   .60
759 A253 12fr dk green   .90   .70
760 A253 18fr dk vio bl & ind   2.25 1.40
761 A253 25fr dk brnsh pur & vio 2.50 1.50
762 A253 30fr rose car & scar   2.50 1.50
  Nos. 757-762 (6)   9.55 6.30

St. Stephen Bridge, Limoges — A254

1955, Mar. 26   Unwmk.   Perf. 13
763 A254 12fr yel brn & dk vio brn   1.20 1.00

Gloved Model in Place de la Concorde — A255

1955, Mar. 26
764 A255 25fr blk brn, vio bl & blk   .75   .25
French glove manufacturing. See footnote after No. 4642.

Jean Pierre Claris de Florian — A256

1955, Apr. 2
765 A256 12fr blue green   .60   .40
200th anniv. of the birth of Jean Pierre Claris de Florian, fabulist.

Eiffel Tower and Television Antennas — A257

1955, Apr. 16
766 A257 15fr indigo & ultra   .75   .70
French advancement in television.

Wire Fence and Guard Tower — A258

1955, Apr. 23
767 A258 12fr dk gray bl & brn blk   .75   .60
10th anniv. of the liberation of concentration camps.

Electric Train — A259

1955, May 11
768 A259 12fr blk brn & slate bl   1.60 1.10
Issued to publicize the electrification of the Valenciennes-Thionville railroad line.

Jacquemart of Moulins — A260

1955, May 28
769 A260 12fr black brown   1.40 1.00

Jules Verne and Nautilus — A261

1955, June 3
770 A261 30fr indigo   6.00 3.75
50th anniv. of the death of Jules Verne.

Auguste and Louis Lumière and Motion Picture Projector — A262

1955, June 12
771 A262 30fr rose brown   5.25 3.25
Invention of motion pictures, 60th anniv.

Jacques Coeur and His Mansion at Bourges — A263

1955, June 18
772 A263 12fr violet   1.90 1.20
5th centenary of the death of Jacques Coeur (1395?-1456), French merchant.

Corvette "La Capricieuse" A264

1955, July 9
773 A264 30fr aqua & dk blue   3.75 3.25
Centenary of the voyage of La Capricieuse to Canada.

Bordeaux — A265

Designs: 8fr, Marseille. 10fr, Nice. 12fr, Valentre bridge, Cahors. 18fr, Uzerche. 25fr, Fortifications, Brouage.

FRANCE

1955, Oct. 15

774	A265	6fr carmine lake	.25	.25
775	A265	8fr indigo	.45	.25
776	A265	10fr dp ultra	.25	.25
777	A265	12fr violet & brn	.25	.25
778	A265	18fr bluish grn & ind	.60	.25
779	A265	25fr org brn & red brn	.75	.25
		Nos. 774-779 (6)	2.55	1.50

See Nos. 838-839. For surcharges see Reunion Nos. 312-317, 323.

Mount Pelée, Martinique A266

1955, Nov. 1

780 A266 20fr dk & lt purple 2.40 .25

Gérard de Nerval — A267

1955, Nov. 11

781 A267 12fr lake & sepia .40 .25

Centenary of the death of Gérard de Nerval (Labrunie), author.

Arms Type of 1949

Arms of: 50c, County of Foix. 70c, Marche. 80c, Roussillon. 1fr, Comtat Venaissin.

Perf. 14x13½

1955, Nov. 19   Typo.   Unwmk.

782	A182	50c multicolored	.25	.25
783	A182	70c red, blue & yel	.25	.25
784	A182	80c brown, yel & red	.25	.25
785	A182	1fr blue, red & yel	.25	.25
		Nos. 782-785 (4)	1.00	1.00

Concentration Camp Victim and Monument — A268

1956, Jan. 14   Engr.   Perf. 13

786 A268 15fr brn blk & red brn .45 .40

Natl. memorial for Nazi deportation victims erected at the Natzwiller Struthof concentration camp in Alsace.

Belfry at Douai — A269

1956, Feb. 11

787 A269 15fr ultra & indigo .40 .40

Col. Emil Driant — A270

1956, Feb. 21

788 A270 15fr dark blue .30 .25

40th anniv. of the death of Col. Emil Driant during the battle of Verdun.

Trench Fighting — A271

1956, Mar. 3

789 A271 30fr indigo & dk olive 1.50 1.25

40th anniversary of Battle of Verdun.

A272

A272a

A272b

A272c

Scientists: 12fr, Jean Henri Fabre, Entomology. 15fr, Charles Tellier, Refrigeration. 18fr, Camille Flammarion, Popular Astronomy. 30fr, Paul Sabatier, Catalytic Chemistry.

1956, Apr. 7

790	A272	12fr vio brn & org brn	.75	.40
791	A272a	15fr vio bl & int blk	.75	.40
792	A272b	18fr brt ultra	1.40	1.25
793	A272c	30fr Prus grn & dk grn	3.50	2.00
		Nos. 790-793 (4)	6.40	4.05

Grand Trianon, Versailles — A273

1956, Apr. 14

794 A273 12fr vio brn & gray grn 1.10 .75

For similar stamp with euro denominations, see No. 5449a.

Symbols of Latin American and French Culture — A274

1956, Apr. 21

795 A274 30fr brown & red brn 1.60 1.40

Issued in recognition of the friendship between France and Latin America.

"The Smile of Reims" and Botticelli's "Spring" — A275

1956, May 5

796 A275 12fr black & green .60 .40

Issued to emphasize the cultural and artistic kinship of Reims and Florence.

Leprosarium and Maltese Cross — A276

1956, May 12

797 A276 12fr sepia, red brn & red .40 .35

Issued in honor of the Knights of Malta.

St. Yves de Treguier — A277

1956, May 19

798 A277 15fr bluish gray & blk .35 .25

St. Yves, patron saint of lawyers.

Marshal Franchet d'Esperey — A278

1956, May 26

799 A278 30fr deep claret 2.25 1.40

Centenary of the birth of Marshal Louis Franchet d'Esperey.

Miners Monument — A279

1956, June 2

800 A279 12fr violet brown .45 .40

Town Montceau-les-Mines, 100th anniv.

Basketball — A280

Sports: 40fr, Pelota (Jai alai). 50fr, Rugby. 75fr, Mountain climbing.

1956, July 7

801	A280	30fr gray vio & blk	1.10	.25
802	A280	40fr brown & vio brn	4.00	.25
803	A280	50fr rose vio & vio	1.50	.25
804	A280	75fr indigo, grn & bl	9.00	1.75
		Nos. 801-804 (4)	15.60	2.50

For surcharges see Reunion Nos. 318-321.

Europa Issue

"Rebuilding Europe" — A281

Perf. 13½x14

1956, Sept. 15   Typo.   Unwmk.

805 A281 15fr rose & rose lake .75 .25

Perf. 13

Engr.

806 A281 30fr lt blue & vio bl 4.50 .75

Issued to symbolize the cooperation among the six countries comprising the Coal and Steel Community.

No. 805 measures 21x35½mm, No. 806 measures 22x35½mm.

Dam at Donzère-Mondragon A282

Cable Railway to Pic du Midi A283

Rhine Port of Strasbourg A284

1956, Oct. 6   Engr.   Perf. 13

807	A282	12fr gray vio & vio brn	1.10	.90
808	A283	18fr indigo	2.25	1.50
809	A284	30fr indigo & dk blue	9.50	4.50
		Nos. 807-809 (3)	12.85	6.90

French technical achievements.

Antoine-Augustin Parmentier A285

1956, Oct. 27

810 A285 12fr brn red & brn .65 .45

Parmentier, nutrition chemist, who popularized the potato in France.

Petrarch — A286

Portraits: 12fr, J. B. Lully. 15fr, J. J. Rousseau. 18fr, Benjamin Franklin. 20fr, Frederic Chopin. 30fr, Vincent van Gogh.

1956, Nov. 10

811	A286	8fr green	.60	.45
812	A286	12fr claret	.60	.45
813	A286	15fr dark red	.90	.45
814	A286	18fr ultra	1.90	1.50
815	A286	20fr brt violet	2.40	1.50
816	A286	30fr brt grnsh blue	4.75	2.25
		Nos. 811-816 (6)	11.15	6.60

Famous men who lived in France.

Pierre de Coubertin and Olympic Stadium — A287

1956, Nov. 24

817 A287 30fr dk blue gray & pur 1.50 .90

Issued in honor of Baron Pierre de Coubertin, founder of the modern Olympic Games.

Homing Pigeon — A288

1957, Jan. 12

818 A288 15fr dp ultra, ind & red brn .40 .25

FRANCE

Victor Schoelcher — A289

1957, Feb. 16   Engr.
819   A289   18fr lilac rose   .45   .40

Issued in honor of Victor Schoelcher, who freed the slaves in the French Colonies.

Sèvres Porcelain — A290

1957, Mar. 23   Unwmk.   Perf. 13
820   A290   30fr ultra & vio blue   .60   .40

Bicentenary of the porcelain works at Sèvres (in 1956).

Gaston Planté and Storage Battery — A291

Designs: 12fr, Antoine Béclère and X-ray apparatus. 18fr, Octave Terrillon, autoclave, microscope and surgical instruments. 30fr, Etienne Oemichen and early helicopter.

1957, Apr. 13
821   A291   8fr gray blk & dp cl   .30   .25
822   A291   12fr dk bl, blk & emer   .35   .25
823   A291   18fr rose red & mag   1.00   .90
824   A291   30fr green & slate grn   2.10   1.60
    Nos. 821-824 (4)   3.75   3.00

Uzès Chateau — A292

1957, Apr. 27
825   A292   12fr slate bl & bis brn   .40   .40

Jean Moulin — A293

Portraits: 10fr, Honoré d'Estienne d'Orves. 12fr, Robert Keller. 18fr, Pierre Brossolette. 20fr, Jean-Baptiste Lebas.

1957, May 18
826   A293   8fr violet brown   .90   .30
827   A293   10fr black & vio bl   .90   .30
828   A293   12fr brown & sl grn   1.00   .35
829   A293   18fr purple & blk   1.40   1.10
830   A293   20fr Prus bl & dk bl   1.10   .90
    Nos. 826-830 (5)   5.60   2.95

Issued in honor of the heroes of the French Underground of World War II.
See Nos. 879-882, 915-919, 959-963, 990-999.

Le Quesnoy — A294

1957, June 1
831   A294   8fr dk slate green   .25   .25
    See No. 837.

Symbols of Justice — A295

1957, June 1
832   A295   12fr sepia & ultra   .25   .25

French Cour des Comptes, 150th anniv.

Farm Woman Type of 1954

1957-59   Perf. 14x13½
833   A236   6fr orange   .25   .25
833A   A236   10fr brt green ('59)   .40   .25
834   A236   12fr red lilac   .25   .25
    Nos. 833-834 (3)   .90   .75

Nos. 833-834 issued without precancellation.

Symbols of Public Works — A296

1957, June 20   Engr.   Perf. 13
835   A296   30fr sl grn, brn & ocher   1.50   1.00

Brest — A297

1957, July 6
836   A297   12fr gray grn & brn ol   .90   .75

Scenic Types of 1955, 1957

Designs: 15fr, Le Quesnoy. 35fr, Bordeaux. 70fr, Valentre bridge, Cahors.

1957, July 19   Unwmk.
837   A294   15fr dk bl grn & sep   .25   .25
838   A265   35fr dk bl grn & sl grn   2.90   .90
839   A265   70fr black & dull grn   16.00   1.60
    Nos. 837-839 (3)   19.15   2.75

For surcharge see Reunion No. 322.

Gallic Cock Type of 1954

1957   Typo.   Perf. 14x13½
840   A237   5fr olive bister   .25   .25
841   A237   10fr bright blue   1.50   .25
842   A237   15fr plum   1.25   .50
843   A237   30fr bright red   9.00   2.10
844   A237   45fr green   19.00   9.00
    Nos. 840-844 (5)   31.00   12.10

Nos. 840-844 are known only precanceled. See second note after No. 132.

Leo Lagrange and Stadium — A298

1957, Aug. 31   Engr.   Perf. 13
845   A298   18fr lilac gray & blk   .40   .40

Intl. University Games, Paris, 8/31-9/8.

"United Europe" — A299

1957, Sept. 16
846   A299   20fr red brown & green   .40   .30
847   A299   35fr dk brown & blue   .90   .75

A united Europe for peace and prosperity.

Auguste Comte — A300

1957, Sept. 14
848   A300   35fr brown red & sepia   .40   .25

Centenary of the death of Auguste Comte, mathematician and philosopher.

Roman Amphitheater, Lyon — A301

1957, Oct. 5   Perf. 13
849   A301   20fr brn org & brn vio   .40   .25

2,000th anniv. of the founding of Lyon.

Sens River, Guadeloupe A302

Beynac-Cazenac, Dordogne A303

Designs: 10fr, Elysee Palace. 25fr, Chateau de Valencay, Indre. 35fr, Rouen Cathedral. 50fr, Roman Ruins, Saint-Remy. 65fr, Evian-les-Bains.

1957, Oct. 19
850   A302   8fr green & lt brn   .25   .25
851   A302   10fr dk ol bis & vio brn   .25   .25
852   A303   18fr indigo & dk brn   .25   .25
853   A302   25fr bl gray & vio brn   .55   .25
854   A303   35fr car rose & lake   .25   .25
855   A302   50fr ol grn & ol bister   .35   .25
856   A302   65fr dk blue & indigo   .60   .30
    Nos. 850-856 (7)   2.50   1.80

See Nos. 907-909. See footnote after No. 4642. For overprint and surcharges see No. 101, Reunion Nos. 325, 328-329, 332-334.

Nicolaus Copernicus — A304

Portraits: 10fr, Michelangelo. 12fr, Miguel de Cervantes. 15fr, Rembrandt. 18fr, Isaac Newton. 25fr, Mozart. 35fr, Johann Wolfgang von Goethe.

1957, Nov. 9   Engr.   Perf. 13
857   A304   8fr dark brown   .65   .30
858   A304   10fr dark green   .65   .45
859   A304   12fr dark purple   .65   .45
860   A304   15fr brown & org brn   .80   .60
861   A304   18fr deep blue   1.10   .80
862   A304   25fr lilac & claret   1.25   .90
863   A304   35fr blue   1.50   1.00
    Nos. 857-863 (7)   6.60   4.50

Louis Jacques Thénard — A305

1957, Nov. 30   Unwmk.
864   A305   15fr ol bis & grnsh blk   .40   .30

Centenary of the death of L. J. Thenard, chemist, and the founding of the Charitable Society of the Friends of Science.

Dr. Philippe Pinel — A306

French Physicians: 12fr, Fernand Widal. 15fr, Charles Nicolle. 35fr, René Leriche.

1958, Jan. 25
865   A306   8fr brown olive   .65   .45
866   A306   12fr brt vio blue   .65   .45
867   A306   15fr deep blue   1.00   .50
868   A306   35fr black   1.40   .80
    Nos. 865-868 (4)   3.70   2.20

Joseph Louis Lagrange — A307

French Scientists: 12fr, Urbain Jean Joseph Leverrier. 15fr, Jean Bernard Leon Foucault. 35fr, Claude Louis Berthollet.

1958, Feb. 15   Perf. 13
869   A307   8fr grnsh bl & vio bl   .65   .35
870   A307   12fr sepia & gray   .75   .35
871   A307   15fr slate grn & grn   1.40   .60
872   A307   35fr maroon & cop red   1.75   .90
    Nos. 869-872 (4)   4.55   2.20

Lourdes Type of 1954

1958
873   A241   20fr grnsh bl & ol   .30   .25

Le Havre A308

Maubeuge A309

Designs: 18fr, Saint-Die. 25fr, Sete.

1958, Mar. 29   Engr.   Perf. 13
874   A308   12fr ol grn & car rose   .55   .35
875   A308   15fr brt purple & brn   .60   .35
876   A309   18fr ultra & indigo   .90   .65
877   A308   25fr dk bl, bl grn & brn   1.25   .65
    Nos. 874-877 (4)   3.30   2.00

Reconstruction of war-damaged cities.

French Pavilion, Brussels — A310

1958, Apr. 12
878   A310   35fr brn, dk grn & bl   .30   .25

Issued for the Universal and International Exposition at Brussels.

Heroes Type of 1957

8fr, Jean Cavaillès. 12fr, Fred Scamaroni. 15fr, Simone Michel-Levy. 20fr, Jacques Bingen.

1958, Apr. 19
879   A293   8fr violet & black   .60   .45
880   A293   12fr ultra & green   .60   .45
881   A293   15fr brown & gray   1.50   .85
882   A293   20fr olive & ultra   1.25   .85
    Nos. 879-882 (4)   3.95   2.60

Issued in honor of the heroes of the French Underground in World War II.

Bowling — A311

Sports: 15fr, Naval joust. 18fr, Archery, vert. 25fr, Breton wrestling, vert.

626 FRANCE

1958, Apr. 26
883	A311	12fr rose & brown	.75	.75
884	A311	15fr bl, ol gray & grn	1.00	.75
885	A311	18fr green & brown	1.75	1.00
886	A311	25fr brown & indigo	2.50	1.75
		Nos. 883-886 (4)	6.00	4.25

Senlis Cathedral — A312

1958, May 17
887 A312 15fr ultra & indigo .40 .25

Bayeux Tapestry Horsemen A313

1958, June 21
888 A313 15fr blue & carmine .35 .25

Common Design Types pictured following the introduction.

Europa Issue, 1958
Common Design Type
1958, Sept. 13   Engr.   Perf. 13
Size: 22x36mm
| 889 | CD1 | 20fr rose red | .40 | .25 |
| 890 | CD1 | 35fr ultra | 1.25 | .30 |

Foix Chateau — A314

1958, Oct. 11
891 A314 15fr ultra, grn & ol brn .40 .25

City Halls, Paris and Rome — A315

1958, Oct. 11
892 A315 35fr gray, grnsh bl & rose red .40 .25

Issued to publicize the cultural ties between Rome and Paris and the need for European unity.

UNESCO Building, Paris — A316

Design: 35fr, Different view of building.

1958, Nov. 1   Perf. 13
| 893 | A316 | 20fr grnsh blue & ol bis | .25 | .25 |
| 894 | A316 | 35fr dk sl grn & red org | .25 | .25 |

UNESCO Headquarters in Paris opening, Nov. 3.

Soldier's Grave in Wheat Field — A317

1958, Nov. 11
895 A317 15fr dp green & ultra .30 .25
40th anniv. of the World War I armistice.

Arms of Marseille — A318

Cities: 70c, Lyon. 80c, Toulouse. 1fr, Bordeaux. 2fr, Nice. 3fr, Nantes. 5fr, Lille. 15fr, Algiers.

1958-59   Typo.   Perf. 14x13½
896	A318	50c dk blue & ultra	.25	.25
897	A318	70c multicolored	.25	.25
898	A318	80c red, blue & yel	.25	.25
899	A318	1fr dk bl, yel & red	.25	.25
900	A318	2fr dk bl, red & grn	.25	.25
901	A318	3fr multicolored	.25	.25
902	A318	5fr dk brown & red	.25	.25
903	A318	15fr multi ('59)	.25	.25
		Nos. 896-903 (8)	2.00	2.00

See Nos. 938, 940, 973, 1040-1042, 1091-1095, 1142-1144. For surcharges see Reunion Nos. 336, 345-346, 350-351, 353.

Arc de Triomphe and Flowers — A319

1959, Jan. 17   Engr.   Perf. 13
904 A319 15fr brn, bl, grn, cl & red .40 .30
Paris Flower Festival.

Symbols of Learning and Medal — A320

1959, Jan. 24   Perf. 13
905 A320 20fr lake, blk & vio .25 .25
Sesquicentennial of the Palm Leaf Medal of the French Academy.

Charles de Foucauld — A321

1959, Jan. 31
906 A321 50fr dp brn, bl & mar .40 .30
Issued to honor Father Charles de Foucauld, explorer and missionary of the Sahara.

Type of 1957

Designs: 30fr, Elysee Palace. 85fr, Evian-les Bains, 100fr, Sens River, Guadeloupe.

1959, Feb. 10
907	A302	30fr dk slate green	2.00	.25
908	A302	85fr deep claret	3.00	.30
909	A302	100fr deep violet	25.00	.30
		Nos. 907-909 (3)	30.00	.85

Gallic Cock Type of 1954

1959   Typo.   Perf. 14x13½
910	A237	8fr violet	.40	.25
911	A237	20fr yellow grn	1.50	.50
912	A237	40fr henna brn	3.25	1.60
913	A237	55fr emerald	15.00	6.00
		Nos. 910-913 (4)	20.15	8.35

Nos. 910-913 were issued with precancellation. See second note after No. 132. See Nos. 952-955.

Miners' Tools and School — A322

1959, Apr. 11   Engr.   Perf. 13
914 A322 20fr red, blk & blue .25 .25
175th anniv. of the National Mining School.

Heroes Type of 1957

Portraits: No. 915, The five martyrs of the Buffon school. No. 916, Yvonne Le Roux. No. 917, Médéric-Védy. No. 918, Louis Martin-Bret. 30fr, Gaston Moutardier.

1959, Apr. 25   Engr.   Perf. 13
915	A293	15fr black & vio	.30	.25
916	A293	15fr mag & rose vio	.30	.30
917	A293	20fr green & grnsh bl	.30	.25
918	A293	20fr org brn & brn	.45	.30
919	A293	30fr magenta & vio	.50	.40
		Nos. 915-919 (5)	1.85	1.50

Dam at Foum el Gherza A323

Marcoule Atomic Center A324

Designs: 30fr, Oil field at Hassi Messaoud, Sahara. 50fr, C. N. I. T. Building (Centre National des Industries et des Techniques).

1959, May 23
920	A323	15fr olive & grnsh bl	.30	.25
921	A324	20fr brt car & red brn	.40	.40
922	A324	30fr dk blue, brn & grn	.40	.40
923	A323	50fr ol grn & sl blue	.65	.45
		Nos. 920-923 (4)	1.75	1.50

French technical achievements.

Marceline Desbordes-Valmore — A325

1959, June 20
924 A325 30fr blue, brn & grn .25 .25
Centenary of the death of Marceline Desbordes-Valmore, poet.

Pilots Goujon and Rozanoff — A326

1959, June 13
925 A326 20fr lt blue & lake brn .40 .40
Issued in honor of Charles Goujon and Col. Constantin Rozanoff, test pilots.

Tancarville Bridge — A327

1959, Aug. 1   Engr.   Perf. 13
926 A327 30fr dk blue, brn & ol .40 .25

Marianne and Ship of State — A328

1959, July   Typo.   Perf. 14x13½
927 A328 25fr black & red .30 .25
See Nos. 942, 3521, 4410a, 4513. For surcharge see No. B336.

Jean Jaures — A329

1959, Sept. 12   Engr.   Perf. 13
928 A329 50fr chocolate .40 .25
Jean Jaures, socialist leader, birth cent.

Europa Issue, 1959
Common Design Type
1959, Sept. 19
Size: 22x36mm
| 929 | CD2 | 25fr bright green | .30 | .25 |
| 930 | CD2 | 50fr bright violet | 1.10 | .55 |

Blood Donors — A330

1959, Oct. 17   Engr.
931 A330 20fr magenta & gray .25 .25

French-Spanish Handshake A331

1959, Oct. 24   Perf. 13
932 A331 50fr blue, rose car & org .45 .30
300th anniv. of the signing of the Treaty of the Pyrenees.

Polio Victim Holding Crutches — A332

1959, Oct. 31
933 A332 20fr dark blue .25 .25
Vaccination against poliomyelitis.

Henri Bergson — A333

1959, Nov. 7
934 A333 50fr lt red brown .35 .25
Henri Bergson, philosopher, birth cent.

Avesnes-sur-Helpe — A334

Design: 30fr, Perpignan.

1959, Nov. 14
| 935 | A334 | 20fr sepia & blue | .40 | .25 |
| 936 | A334 | 30fr brn, dp claret & bl | .40 | .25 |

New NATO Headquarters, Paris — A335

1959, Dec. 12
937 A335 50fr green, brn & ultra .45 .30
10th anniv. of the NATO.

Types of 1958-59 and

Farm Woman A336

Sower A337

Designs: 5c, Arms of Lille. 15c, Arms of Algiers. 25c, Marianne and Ship of State.

FRANCE

Victor Schoelcher — A289

1957, Feb. 16   Engr.
819   A289   18fr lilac rose   .45   .40

Issued in honor of Victor Schoelcher, who freed the slaves in the French Colonies.

Sèvres Porcelain — A290

1957, Mar. 23   Unwmk.   Perf. 13
820   A290   30fr ultra & vio blue   .60   .40

Bicentenary of the porcelain works at Sèvres (in 1956).

Gaston Planté and Storage Battery — A291

Designs: 12fr, Antoine Béclère and X-ray apparatus. 18fr, Octave Terrillon, autoclave, microscope and surgical instruments. 30fr, Etienne Oemichen and early helicopter.

1957, Apr. 13
821   A291   8fr gray blk & dp cl   .30   .25
822   A291   12fr dk bl, blk & emer   .35   .25
823   A291   18fr rose red & mag   1.00   .90
824   A291   30fr green & slate grn   2.10   1.60
    Nos. 821-824 (4)   3.75   3.00

Uzès Chateau — A292

1957, Apr. 27
825   A292   12fr slate bl & bis brn   .40   .40

Jean Moulin — A293

Portraits: 10fr, Honoré d'Estienne d'Orves. 12fr, Robert Keller. 18fr, Pierre Brossolette. 20fr, Jean-Baptiste Lebas.

1957, May 18
826   A293   8fr violet brown   .90   .30
827   A293   10fr black & vio bl   .90   .30
828   A293   12fr brown & sl grn   1.00   .35
829   A293   18fr purple & blk   1.40   1.10
830   A293   20fr Prus bl & dk bl   1.40   .90
    Nos. 826-830 (5)   5.60   2.95

Issued in honor of the heroes of the French Underground of World War II.
See Nos. 879-882, 915-919, 959-963, 990-994.

Le Quesnoy — A294

1957, June 1
831   A294   8fr dk slate green   .25   .25
    See No. 837.

Symbols of Justice — A295

1957, June 1
832   A295   12fr sepia & ultra   .25   .25
French Cour des Comptes, 150th anniv.

Farm Woman Type of 1954
1957-59   Perf. 14x13½
833   A236   6fr orange   .25   .25
833A   A236   10fr brt green ('59)   .40   .25
834   A236   12fr red lilac   .25   .25
    Nos. 833-834 (3)   .90   .75

Nos. 833-834 issued without precancellation.

Symbols of Public Works — A296

1957, June 20   Engr.   Perf. 13
835   A296   30fr sl grn, brn & ocher   1.50   1.00

Brest — A297

1957, July 6
836   A297   12fr gray grn & brn ol   .90   .75

Scenic Types of 1955, 1957

Designs: 15fr, Le Quesnoy. 35fr, Bordeaux. 70fr, Valentre bridge, Cahors.

1957, July 19   Unwmk.
837   A294   15fr dk bl grn & sep   .25   .25
838   A265   35fr dk bl grn & sl grn   2.90   .90
839   A265   70fr black & dull grn   16.00   1.60
    Nos. 837-839 (3)   19.15   2.75

For surcharge see Reunion No. 322.

Gallic Cock Type of 1954

1957   Typo.   Perf. 14x13½
840   A237   5fr olive bister   .25   .25
841   A237   10fr bright blue   1.50   .25
842   A237   15fr plum   1.25   .50
843   A237   30fr bright red   9.00   2.10
844   A237   45fr green   19.00   9.00
    Nos. 840-844 (5)   31.00   12.10

Nos. 840-844 are known only precanceled. See second note after No. 132.

Leo Lagrange and Stadium — A298

1957, Aug. 31   Engr.   Perf. 13
845   A298   18fr lilac gray & blk   .40   .40

Intl. University Games, Paris, 8/31-9/8.

"United Europe" — A299

1957, Sept. 16
846   A299   20fr red brown & green   .40   .30
847   A299   35fr dk brown & blue   .90   .75

A united Europe for peace and prosperity.

Auguste Comte — A300

1957, Sept. 14
848   A300   35fr brown red & sepia   .40   .25

Centenary of the death of Auguste Comte, mathematician and philosopher.

Roman Amphitheater, Lyon — A301

1957, Oct. 5   Perf. 13
849   A301   20fr brn org & brn vio   .40   .25

2,000th anniv. of the founding of Lyon.

Sens River, Guadeloupe A302   Beynac-Cazenac, Dordogne A303

Designs: 10fr, Elysee Palace. 25fr, Chateau de Valencay, Indre. 35fr, Rouen Cathedral. 50fr, Roman Ruins, Saint-Remy. 65fr, Evian-les-Bains.

1957, Oct. 19
850   A302   8fr green & lt brn   .25   .25
851   A302   10fr dk ol bis & vio brn   .25   .25
852   A303   18fr indigo & dk brn   .25   .25
853   A303   25fr bl gray & vio brn   .55   .25
854   A303   35fr car rose & lake   .25   .25
855   A302   50fr ol grn & ol bister   .35   .25
856   A302   65fr dk blue & indigo   .60   .30
    Nos. 850-856 (7)   2.50   1.80

See Nos. 907-909. See footnote after No. 4642. For overprint and surcharges see No. 101, Reunion Nos. 325, 328-329, 332-334.

Nicolaus Copernicus — A304

Portraits: 10fr, Michelangelo. 12fr, Miguel de Cervantes. 15fr, Rembrandt. 18fr, Isaac Newton. 25fr, Mozart. 35fr, Johann Wolfgang von Goethe.

1957, Nov. 9   Engr.   Perf. 13
857   A304   8fr dark brown   .65   .30
858   A304   10fr dark green   .65   .45
859   A304   12fr dark purple   .65   .45
860   A304   15fr brown & org brn   .80   .60
861   A304   18fr deep blue   1.10   .80
862   A304   25fr lilac & claret   1.25   .90
863   A304   35fr blue   1.50   1.00
    Nos. 857-863 (7)   6.60   4.50

Louis Jacques Thénard — A305

1957, Nov. 30   Unwmk.
864   A305   15fr ol bis & grnsh blk   .40   .30

Centenary of the death of L. J. Thenard, chemist, and the founding of the Charitable Society of the Friends of Science.

Dr. Philippe Pinel — A306

French Physicians: 12fr, Fernand Widal. 15fr, Charles Nicolle. 35fr, René Leriche.

1958, Jan. 25
865   A306   8fr brown olive   .65   .45
866   A306   12fr brt vio blue   .65   .45
867   A306   15fr deep blue   1.00   .50
868   A306   35fr black   1.40   .80
    Nos. 865-868 (4)   3.70   2.20

Joseph Louis Lagrange — A307

French Scientists: 12fr, Urbain Jean Joseph Leverrier. 15fr, Jean Bernard Leon Foucault. 35fr, Claude Louis Berthollet.

1958, Feb. 15   Perf. 13
869   A307   8fr grnsh bl & vio bl   .65   .35
870   A307   12fr sepia & gray   .75   .35
871   A307   15fr slate grn & grn   1.40   .60
872   A307   35fr maroon & cop red   1.75   .90
    Nos. 869-872 (4)   4.55   2.20

Lourdes Type of 1954

1958
873   A241   20fr grnsh bl & ol   .30   .25

Le Havre A308   Maubeuge A309

Designs: 18fr, Saint-Die. 25fr, Sete.

1958, Mar. 29   Engr.   Perf. 13
874   A308   12fr ol grn & car rose   .55   .35
875   A309   15fr brt purple & brn   .60   .35
876   A309   18fr ultra & indigo   .90   .65
877   A308   25fr dk bl, bl grn & brn   1.25   .65
    Nos. 874-877 (4)   3.30   2.00

Reconstruction of war-damaged cities.

French Pavilion, Brussels — A310

1958, Apr. 12
878   A310   35fr brn, dk grn & bl   .30   .25

Issued for the Universal and International Exposition at Brussels.

Heroes Type of 1957

8fr, Jean Cavaillès. 12fr, Fred Scamaroni. 15fr, Simone Michel-Levy. 20fr, Jacques Bingen.

1958, Apr. 19
879   A293   8fr violet & black   .60   .45
880   A293   12fr ultra & green   .60   .45
881   A293   15fr brown & gray   1.50   .85
882   A293   20fr olive & ultra   1.25   .85
    Nos. 879-882 (4)   3.95   2.60

Issued in honor of the heroes of the French Underground in World War II.

Bowling — A311

Sports: 15fr, Naval joust. 18fr, Archery, vert. 25fr, Breton wrestling, vert.

FRANCE

1958, Apr. 26

883	A311	12fr rose & brown	.75	.75
884	A311	15fr bl, ol gray & grn	1.00	.75
885	A311	18fr green & brown	1.75	1.00
886	A311	25fr brown & indigo	2.50	1.75
		Nos. 883-886 (4)	6.00	4.25

Senlis Cathedral — A312

1958, May 17

887 A312 15fr ultra & indigo .40 .25

Bayeux Tapestry Horsemen A313

1958, June 21

888 A313 15fr blue & carmine .35 .25

Common Design Types pictured following the introduction.

Europa Issue, 1958
Common Design Type
1958, Sept. 13 Engr. Perf. 13
Size: 22x36mm

| 889 | CD1 | 20fr rose red | .40 | .25 |
| 890 | CD1 | 35fr ultra | 1.25 | .30 |

Foix Chateau — A314

1958, Oct. 11

891 A314 15fr ultra, grn & ol brn .40 .25

City Halls, Paris and Rome — A315

1958, Oct. 11

892 A315 35fr gray, grnsh bl & rose red .40 .25

Issued to publicize the cultural ties between Rome and Paris and the need for European unity.

UNESCO Building, Paris — A316

Design: 35fr, Different view of building.

1958, Nov. 1 Perf. 13

| 893 | A316 | 20fr grnsh blue & ol bis | .25 | .25 |
| 894 | A316 | 35fr dk sl grn & red org | .25 | .25 |

UNESCO Headquarters in Paris opening, Nov. 3.

Soldier's Grave in Wheat Field — A317

1958, Nov. 11

895 A317 15fr dp green & ultra .30 .25

40th anniv. of the World War I armistice.

Arms of Marseille — A318

Cities: 70c, Lyon. 80c, Toulouse. 1fr, Bordeaux. 2fr, Nice. 3fr, Nantes. 5fr, Lille. 15fr, Algiers.

1958-59 Typo. Perf. 14x13½

896	A318	50c dk blue & ultra	.25	.25
897	A318	70c multicolored	.25	.25
898	A318	80c red, blue & yel	.25	.25
899	A318	1fr dk bl, yel & red	.25	.25
900	A318	2fr dk bl, red & grn	.25	.25
901	A318	3fr multicolored	.25	.25
902	A318	5fr dk brown & red	.25	.25
903	A318	15fr multi ('59)	.25	.25
		Nos. 896-903 (8)	2.00	2.00

See Nos. 938, 940, 973, 1040-1042, 1091-1095, 1142-1144. For surcharges see Reunion Nos. 336, 345-346, 350-351, 353.

Arc de Triomphe and Flowers — A319

1959, Jan. 17 Engr. Perf. 13

904 A319 15fr brn, bl, grn, cl & red .40 .30

Paris Flower Festival.

Symbols of Learning and Medal — A320

1959, Jan. 24 Perf. 13

905 A320 20fr lake, blk & vio .25 .25

Sesquicentennial of the Palm Leaf Medal of the French Academy.

Charles de Foucauld — A321

1959, Jan. 31

906 A321 50fr dp brn, bl & mar .40 .30

Issued to honor Father Charles de Foucauld, explorer and missionary of the Sahara.

Type of 1957

Designs: 30fr, Elysee Palace. 85fr, Evian-les Bains. 100fr, Sens River, Guadeloupe.

1959, Feb. 10

907	A302	30fr dk slate green	2.00	.25
908	A302	85fr deep claret	3.00	.30
909	A302	100fr deep violet	25.00	.30
		Nos. 907-909 (3)	30.00	.85

Gallic Cock Type of 1954

1959 Typo. Perf. 14x13½

910	A237	8fr violet	.40	.25
911	A237	20fr yellow grn	1.50	.50
912	A237	40fr henna brn	3.25	1.60
913	A237	55fr emerald	15.00	6.00
		Nos. 910-913 (4)	20.15	8.35

Nos. 910-913 were issued with precancellation. See second note after No. 132. See Nos. 952-955.

Miners' Tools and School — A322

1959, Apr. 11 Engr. Perf. 13

914 A322 20fr red, blk & blue .25 .25

175th anniv. of the National Mining School.

Heroes Type of 1957

Portraits: No. 915, The five martyrs of the Buffon school. No. 916, Yvonne Le Roux. No. 917, Médéric-Védy. No. 918, Louis Martin-Bret. 30fr, Gaston Moutardier.

1959, Apr. 25 Engr. Perf. 13

915	A293	15fr black & vio	.30	.25
916	A293	15fr mag & rose vio	.30	.30
917	A293	20fr green & grnsh bl	.30	.25
918	A293	20fr org brn & brn	.45	.30
919	A293	30fr magenta & vio	.50	.40
		Nos. 915-919 (5)	1.85	1.50

Dam at Foum el Gherza A323

Marcoule Atomic Center A324

Designs: 30fr, Oil field at Hassi Messaoud, Sahara. 50fr, C. N. I. T. Building (Centre National des Industries et des Techniques).

1959, May 23

920	A323	15fr olive & grnsh bl	.30	.25
921	A324	20fr brt car & red brn	.40	.40
922	A324	30fr dk blue, brn & grn	.40	.40
923	A323	50fr ol grn & sl blue	.65	.45
		Nos. 920-923 (4)	1.75	1.50

French technical achievements.

Marceline Desbordes-Valmore — A325

1959, June 20

924 A325 30fr blue, brn & grn .25 .25

Centenary of the death of Marceline Desbordes-Valmore, poet.

Pilots Goujon and Rozanoff — A326

1959, June 13

925 A326 20fr lt blue & lake brn .40 .40

Issued in honor of Charles Goujon and Col. Constantin Rozanoff, test pilots.

Tancarville Bridge — A327

1959, Aug. 1 Engr. Perf. 13

926 A327 30fr dk blue, brn & ol .40 .25

Marianne and Ship of State — A328

1959, July Typo. Perf. 14x13½

927 A328 25fr black & red .30 .25

See Nos. 942, 3521, 4410a, 4513. For surcharge see No. B336.

Jean Jaures — A329

1959, Sept. 12 Engr. Perf. 13

928 A329 50fr chocolate .40 .25

Jean Jaures, socialist leader, birth cent.

Europa Issue, 1959
Common Design Type
1959, Sept. 19
Size: 22x36mm

| 929 | CD2 | 25fr bright green | .30 | .25 |
| 930 | CD2 | 50fr bright violet | 1.10 | .55 |

Blood Donors — A330

1959, Oct. 17 Engr.

931 A330 20fr magenta & gray .25 .25

French-Spanish Handshake A331

1959, Oct. 24 Perf. 13

932 A331 50fr blue, rose car & org .45 .30

300th anniv. of the signing of the Treaty of the Pyrenees.

Polio Victim Holding Crutches — A332

1959, Oct. 31

933 A332 20fr dark blue .25 .25

Vaccination against poliomyelitis.

Henri Bergson — A333

1959, Nov. 7

934 A333 50fr lt red brown .35 .25

Henri Bergson, philosopher, birth cent.

Avesnes-sur-Helpe — A334

Design: 30fr, Perpignan.

1959, Nov. 14

| 935 | A334 | 20fr sepia & blue | .40 | .25 |
| 936 | A334 | 30fr brn, dp claret & bl | .40 | .25 |

New NATO Headquarters, Paris — A335

1959, Dec. 12

937 A335 50fr green, brn & ultra .45 .30

10th anniv. of the NATO.

Types of 1958-59 and

Farm Woman A336

Sower A337

Designs: 5c, Arms of Lille. 15c, Arms of Algiers. 25c, Marianne and Ship of State.

FRANCE

Perf. 14x13½

1960-61		Unwmk.	Typo.	
938	A318	5c dk brown & red	2.60	.25
939	A336	10c brt green	.25	.25
940	A318	15c red, ultra, yel & grn	.50	.25
941	A337	20c grnsh bl & car rose	.25	.25
942	A328	25c ver & ultra	1.60	.25
b.		Booklet pane of 8	27.50	
c.		Booklet pane of 10	32.50	
942A	A337	30c gray & ultra ('61)	1.10	.30
		Nos. 938-942A (6)	6.30	1.55

See Nos. 707-708, 833-834 for the Farm Woman type (A336), but with no decimals in denominations.

For surcharges see Reunion Nos. 337-338, 341. For overprint see Algeria No. 286.

Laon Cathedral A338

Kerrata Gorge A339

Designs: 30c, Fougères Chateau. 50c, Mosque, Tlemcen. 65c, Sioule Valley. 85c, Chaumont Viaduct. 1fr, Cilaos Church, Reunion.

1960, Jan. 16   Engr.   Perf. 13

943	A338	15c blue & indigo	.25	.25
944	A338	30c blue, sepia & grn	1.75	.25
945	A339	45c brt vio & ol gray	.60	.25
946	A339	50c sl grn & lt cl	1.20	.25
947	A338	65c sl grn, bl & blk brn	1.10	.25
948	A338	85c blue, sep & grn	1.75	.25
949	A339	1fr vio bl, bl & grn	2.50	.25
		Nos. 943-949 (7)	9.15	1.75

For surcharges see Reunion Nos. 335, 340, 342. For overprint see Algeria Nos. 288-289.

Pierre de Nolhac — A340

1960, Feb. 13

950 A340 20c black & gray   .45 .30

Centenary of the birth of Pierre de Nolhac, curator of Versailles and historian.

Museum of Art and Industry, Saint Etienne A341

1960, Feb. 20

951 A341 30c brn, car & slate   .45 .30

Gallic Cock Type of 1954

1960		Typo.	Perf. 14x13½	
952	A237	8c violet	.40	.25
953	A237	20c yellow grn	1.90	.30
954	A237	40c henna brn	7.50	1.75
955	A237	55c emerald	24.00	11.00
		Nos. 952-955 (4)	33.80	13.30

Nos. 952-955 were issued only precanceled. See second note after No. 132. See Nos. 910-913.

View of Cannes — A342

1960, Mar. 5   Engr.   Perf. 13

956 A342 50c red brn & lt grn   .45 .40

Meeting of European municipal administrators, Cannes, Mar., 1960.

Woman of Savoy and Alps — A343

Woman of Nice and Shore — A344

1960   Unwmk.   Perf. 13

957	A343	30c slate green	.50	.40
958	A344	50c brn, yel & rose	.50	.30

Cent. of the annexation of Nice and Savoy.

Heroes Type of 1957

Portraits: No. 959, Edmund Debeaumarché. No. 960, Pierre Massé. No. 961, Maurice Ripoche. No. 962, Leonce Vieljeux. 50c, Abbé René Bonpain.

1960, Mar. 26

959	A293	20c bister & blk	1.10	.90
960	A293	20c pink & rose cl	1.10	.90
961	A293	30c vio & brt vio	1.50	.90
962	A293	30c sl bl & brt bl	2.10	1.75
963	A293	50c sl grn & red brn	2.40	2.10
		Nos. 959-963 (5)	8.20	6.55

Issued in honor of the heroes of the French Underground of World War II.

"Education" and Children — A345

1960, May 21   Engr.   Perf. 13

964 A345 20c rose lilac, pur & blk   .25 .25

1st secondary school in Strasbourg, 150th anniv.

Blois Chateau — A346

View of La Bourboule A347

1960, May

965	A346	30c dk bl, sep & grn	.60	.45
966	A347	50c ol brown, car & grn	.60	.35

Lorraine Cross — A348

1960, June 18

967 A348 20c red brn, dk brn & yel grn   .45 .25

20th anniv. of the French Resistance Movement in World War II.

Marianne — A349

1960, June 18   Typo.   Perf. 14x13½

968	A349	25c lake & gray	.25	.25
a.		Booklet pane of 8	4.50	
b.		Booklet pane of 10	3.50	

See Nos. 3522, 4410b, 4514. For surcharge see Reunion No. 339. For overprint see Algeria No. 287.

Jean Bouin and Stadium — A350

1960, July 9   Engr.   Perf. 13

969 A350 20c blue, mag & ol gray   .35 .25

17th Olympic Games, Rome, 8/25-9/11.

Europa Issue, 1960
Common Design Type

1960, Sept. 17   Perf. 13
Size: 36x22mm

970	CD3	25c green & bluish grn	.25	.25
971	CD3	50c maroon & red lilac	.25	.25

Lisieux Basilica — A351

1960, Sept. 24   Perf. 13

972 A351 15c blue, gray & blk   .25 .25

Arms Type of 1958-59

Design: Arms of Oran.

1960, Oct. 15   Typo.   Perf. 14x13½

973 A318 5c red, bl, yel & emer   .25 .25

Madame de Stael by François Gerard — A352

1960, Oct. 22   Engr.   Perf. 13

974 A352 30c dull claret & brn   .35 .25

Madame de Stael (1766-1817), writer

Gen. J. B. E. Estienne — A353

1960, Nov. 5

975 A353 15c lt lilac & black   .35 .25

Centenary of the birth of Gen. Jean Baptiste Eugene Estienne.

Marc Sangnier and Youth Hostel at Bierville — A354

1960, Nov. 5

976 A354 20c blue, blk & lilac   .25 .25

Issued to honor Marc Sangnier, founder of the French League for Youth Hostels.

Badge of Order of Liberation — A355

1960, Nov. 14   Engr.   Perf. 13

977 A355 20c black & brt green   .40 .25

Order of Liberation, 20th anniversary.

Lapwings — A356

Birds: 30c, Puffin. 45c, European teal. 50c, European bee-eaters.

1960, Nov. 12

978	A356	20c multicolored	.25	.25
979	A356	30c multicolored	.25	.25
980	A356	45c multicolored	.60	.45
981	A356	50c multicolored	.55	.40
		Nos. 978-981 (4)	1.65	1.35

Issued to publicize wildlife protection.

André Honnorat — A357

1960, Nov. 19

982 A357 30c blue, blk & green   .30 .25

Honnorat, statesman, fighter against tuberculosis and founder of the University City of Paris, an intl. students' community.

St. Barbara and Medieval View of School — A358

1960, Dec. 3   Engr.

983 A358 30c red, bl & ol brn   .30 .25

St. Barbara School, Paris, 500th anniv.

"Mediterranean" by Aristide Maillol — A359

1961, Feb. 18   Unwmk.   Perf. 13

984 A359 20c carmine & indigo   .25 .25

Aristide Maillol, sculptor, birth cent.

Marianne by Cocteau — A360

1961, Feb. 23

985 A300 20c blue & carmine   .25 .25

A second type has an extra inverted V-shaped mark (a blue flag top) at right of hair tip. Value unused $2.25, used 35 cents.
See Nos. 3523, 4410c, 4515.
For surcharge see Reunion No. 357.

Paris Airport, Orly — A361

1961, Feb. 25

986 A361 50c blk, dk bl, & bluish grn   .45 .25

Inauguration of new facilities at Orly airport.

George Méliès and Motion Picture Screen — A362

1961, Mar. 11

987 A362 50c pur, indigo & ol bis   .50 .35

Cent. of the birth of George Méliès, motion picture pioneer.

Jean Baptiste Henri Lacordaire — A363

1961, Mar. 25   Perf. 13

988 A363 30c lt brown & black   .30 .25

Cent. of the death of the Dominican monk Lacordaire, orator and liberal Catholic leader.

FRANCE

A364

1961, Mar. 25
989 A364 30c grn, red brn & red .25 .25
Introduction of tobacco use into France, fourth centenary. By error stamp portrays Jan Nicquet instead of Jean Nicot.

Heroes Type of 1957
Portraits: No. 990, Jacques Renouvin. No. 991, Lionel Dubray. No. 992, Paul Gateaud. No. 993, Mère Elisabeth.

1961, Apr. 22
990	A293 20c blue & lilac	.75	.35
991	A293 20c gray grn & blue	.75	.35
992	A293 30c brown org & blk	1.40	.65
993	A293 30c violet & blk	.90	.80
	Nos. 990-993 (4)	3.80	2.15

Bagnoles-de-l'Orne — A365

1961, May 6
994 A365 20c olive, ocher, bl & grn .25 .25

Dove, Olive Branch and Federation Emblem — A366

1961, May 6
995 A366 50c brt bl, grn & mar .30 .25
World Federation of Ex-Service Men.

Deauville in 19th Century — A367

1961, May 13 Engr.
996 A367 50c rose claret 1.25 .90
Centenary of Deauville.

La Champmeslé — A368

French actors: No. 998, Talma. No. 999, Rachel. No. 1000, Gérard Philipe. No. 1001, Raimu.

1961, June 10 Unwmk. Perf. 13
Dark Carmine Frame
997	A368 20c choc & yel grn	.60	.25
998	A368 30c brown & crimson	.60	.35
999	A368 30c yel grn & sl grn	.65	.35
1000	A368 50c olive & choc	1.10	.45
1001	A368 50c bl grn & red brn	1.10	.45
	Nos. 997-1001 (5)	4.05	1.85

Issued to honor great French actors and in connection with the Fifth World Congress of the International Federation of Actors.

Mont-Dore, Snowflake and Cable Car — A369

1961, July 1
1002 A369 20c orange & rose lilac .25 .25

Pierre Fauchard — A370

1961, July 1
1003 A370 50c dk green & blk .40 .30
Bicentenary of the death of Pierre Fauchard, 1st surgeon dentist.

St. Theobald's Church, Thann — A371

1961, July 1
1004 A371 20c dk grn, pur & red brn .45 .25
800th anniversary of Thann.

Europa Issue, 1961
Common Design Type
1961, Sept. 16 Perf. 13
Size: 35x22mm
1005	CD4 25c vermilion	.25	.25
1006	CD4 50c ultramarine	.25	.25

Beach and Sailboats, Arcachon — A372

Designs: 15c, Saint-Paul, Maritime Alps. 45c, Sully-sur-Loire Chateau. 50c, View of Cognac. 65c, Rance Valley and Dinan. 85c, City hall and Rodin's Burghers, Calais. 1fr, Roman gates of Lodi, Medea, Algeria.

1961, Oct. 9 Engr. Perf. 13
1007	A372 15c blue & purple	.25	.25
1008	A372 30c ultra, sl grn & lt brn	.25	.25
1009	A372 45c vio bl, red brn & grn	.25	.25
1010	A372 50c grn, Prus bl & sl	.75	.25
1011	A372 65c red brn, sl grn & bl	.25	.25
1012	A372 85c sl grn, sl & red brn	.35	.25
1013	A372 1fr dk bl, sl & bis	3.50	.25
	Nos. 1007-1013 (7)	5.60	1.75

For surcharges see Reunion Nos. 347-348.
For overprint see Algeria No. 290.

Blue Nudes, by Matisse A373

Paintings: 50c, "The Messenger," by Braque. 85c, "The Cardplayers," by Cézanne. 1fr, "The 14th July," by Roger de La Fresnaye.

1961, Nov. 10 Perf. 13x12
1014	A373 50c dk brn, bl, blk & gray	2.25	1.20
1015	A373 65c grn, vio, & ultra	3.75	1.90
1016	A373 85c blk, brn, red & ol	1.50	1.10
1017	A373 1fr multicolored	3.00	1.90
	Nos. 1014-1017 (4)	10.50	6.10

Liner France — A374

1962, Jan. 11 Engr. Perf. 13
1018 A374 30c dk blue, blk & car .60 .35
New French liner France.

Skier Going Downhill — A375

1962, Jan. 27 Perf. 13
1019	A375 30c shown	.25	.25
1020	A375 50c Slalom	.35	.25

Issued to publicize the World Ski Championships, Chamonix, Feb. 1962.

Maurice Bourdet — A376

1962, Feb. 17
1021 A376 30c slate .30 .25
60th anniv. of the birth of Maurice Bourdet, radio commentator and resistance hero.

Pierre-Fidele Bretonneau A377

1962, Feb. 17
1022 A377 50c brt lilac & blue .35 .25
Centenary of the death of Pierre-Fidele Bretonneau, physician.

Chateau and Bridge, Laval, Mayenne — A378

1962, Feb. 24
1023 A378 20c bis brn & slate grn .25 .25

Gallic Cock — A379

1962-65 Perf. 13
1024	A379 25c ultra, car & brn	.25	.25
a.	Bklt. pane of 4 (horiz. strip)	2.50	
1024B	A379 30c gray grn, red & brn ('65)	.85	.25
c.	Booklet pane of 5	5.00	
d.	Booklet pane of 10	10.00	

No. 1024 was also issued on experimental luminescent paper in 1963. Value $750.
See Nos. 3524, 4410d, 4516.

Ramparts of Vannes A380

Dunkirk A381

Paris Beach, Le Touquet — A381a

1962 Engr. Perf. 13
1025	A380 30c dark blue	.60	.50
1026	A381 95c grn, bis & red lil	.75	.40
1027	A381a 1fr grn, red brn & bl	.40	.25
	Nos. 1025-1027 (3)	1.75	1.15

No. 1026 for the 300th anniv. of Dunkirk.

Stage Setting and Globe — A382

1962, Mar. 24 Unwmk.
1028 A382 50c sl grn, ocher & mag .40 .25
International Day of the Theater, Mar. 27.

Memorial to Fighting France, Mont Valerien A383

Resistance Heroes' Monument, Vercors A384

Design: 50c, Ile de Sein monument.

1962, Apr. 7
1029	A383 20c olive & slate grn	.50	.40
1030	A384 30c bluish black	.60	.45
1031	A384 50c blue & indigo	.75	.60
	Nos. 1029-1031 (3)	1.85	1.45

Issued to publicize memorials for the French Underground in World War II.

Malaria Eradication Emblem and Swamp — A385

1962, Apr. 14 Engr.
1032 A385 50c dk blue & dk red .35 .25
WHO drive to eradicate malaria.

Nurses with Child and Hospital — A386

1962, May 5 Unwmk. Perf. 13
1033 A386 30c bl grn, gray & red brn .25 .25
National Hospital Week, May 5-12.

Glider — A387

20c, Planes showing development of aviation.

1962, May 12
1034	A387 15c orange red & brn	.30	.25
1035	A387 20c lil rose & rose cl	.35	.25

Issued to publicize sports aviation.

School Emblem — A388

1962, May 19 Engr.
1036 A388 50c mar, ocher & dk vio .40 .25
Watchmaker's School at Besançon, cent.

FRANCE

Louis XIV and Workers Showing Modern Gobelin — A389

1962, May 26   Unwmk.   Perf. 13
1037 A389 50c ol, sl grn & car   .40   .25
Gobelin tapestry works, Paris, 300th anniv.

Blaise Pascal — A390

1962, May 26
1038 A390 50c slate grn & dp org   .40   .25
Blaise Pascal (1623-1662), mathematician, scientist and philosopher.

Palace of Justice, Rennes — A391

1962, June 12
1039 A391 30c blk, grysh bl & grn   1.00   .75

Arms Type of 1958-59
5c, Amiens. 10c, Troyes. 15c, Nevers.

1962-63   Typo.   Perf. 14x13½
1040 A318 5c ver, ultra & yel   .25   .25
1041 A318 10c red, ultra & yel ('63)   .25   .25
1042 A318 15c ver, ultra & yel   .25   .25
  Nos. 1040-1042 (3)   .75   .75

Phosphor Tagging
In 1970 France began to experiment with luminescence. Phosphor bands have been added to Nos. 1041, 1143, 1231, 1231C, 1292A-1294B, 1494-1498, 1560-1579B, etc.

Rose — A392

Design: 30c, Old-fashioned rose.

1962, Sept. 8   Engr.   Perf. 13
1043 A392 20c ol, grn & brt car   .45   .30
1044 A392 30c dk sl grn, ol & car   .55   .40

Europa Issue, 1962
Common Design Type

1962, Sept. 15
Size: 36x22mm
1045 CD5 25c violet   .25   .25
1046 CD5 50c henna brown   .35   .25

Space Communications Center, Pleumeur-Bodou, France — A394

Telstar, Earth and Television Set — A395

1962, Sept. 29   Engr.   Perf. 13
1047 A394 25c gray, yel & grn   .25   .25
1048 A395 50c dk bl, grn & ultra   .40   .30
First television connection of the US and France through Telstar satellite, July 11-12.
For surcharges see Reunion Nos. 343-344.

"Bonjour Monsieur Courbet" by Gustave Courbet A396

Paintings: 65c, "Madame Manet on Blue Sofa," by Edouard Manet. 1fr, "Guards officer on horseback," by Theodore Géricault, vert.

1962, Nov. 9   Perf. 13x12, 12x13
1049 A396 50c multicolored   2.25   1.50
1050 A396 65c multicolored   2.25   1.40
1051 A396 1fr multicolored   4.50   2.00
  Nos. 1049-1051 (3)   9.00   4.90

Bathyscaph "Archimede" A397

1963, Jan. 26   Unwmk.   Perf. 13
1052 A397 30c dk blue & blk   .25   .25
French deep-sea explorations.

Flowers and Nantes Chateau — A398

1963, Feb. 11
1053 A398 30c vio bl, car & sl grn   .25   .25
Nantes flower festival.

St. Peter, Window at St. Foy de Conches — A399

50c, Jacob Wrestling with the Angel, by Delacroix.

1963, Mar. 2   Perf. 12x13
1054 A399 50c multicolored   2.40   1.50
1055 A399 1fr multicolored   3.25   2.25
See Nos. 1076-1077.

Hungry Woman and Wheat Emblem — A400

1963, Mar. 21   Engr.   Perf. 13
1056 A400 50c slate grn & brn   .40   .25
FAO "Freedom from Hunger" campaign.

Cemetery and Memorial, Glières — A401

Design: 50c, Memorial, Ile de la Cité, Paris.

1963, Mar. 23   Unwmk.   Perf. 13
1057 A401 30c dk brown & olive   .40   .30
1058 A401 50c indigo   .40   .30
Heroes of the resistance against the Nazis.

Beethoven, Birthplace at Bonn and Rhine — A402

No. 1060, Emile Verhaeren, memorial at Roisin & residence. No. 1061, Giuseppe Mazzini, Marcus Aurelius statue & Via Appia, Rome. No. 1062, Emile Mayrisch, Colpach Chateau & blast furnace, Esch. No. 1063, Hugo de Groot, Palace of Peace, The Hague & St. Agatha Church, Delft.

1963, Apr. 27   Unwmk.   Perf. 13
1059 A402 20c ocher, sl & brt grn   .30   .25
1060 A402 20c purple, blk & mar   .30   .25
1061 A402 20c maroon, sl & ol   .30   .25
1062 A402 20c mar, dk brn & ocher   .30   .25
1063 A402 30c dk brn, vio & ocher   .30   .25
  Nos. 1059-1063 (5)   1.50   1.25
Issued to honor famous men of the European Common Market countries.

Hotel des Postes and Stagecoach, 1863 — A403

1963, May 4
1064 A403 50c grayish black   .35   .25
1st Intl. Postal Conference, Paris, 1863.

Lycée Louis-le-Grand, Belvédère, Panthéon and St. Etienne du Mont Church — A404

1963, May 18
1065 A404 30c slate green   .30   .25
400th anniversary of the Jesuit Clermont secondary school, named after Louis XIV.

St. Peter's Church and Ramparts, Caen — A405

1963, June 1   Unwmk.   Perf. 13
1066 A405 30c gray blue & brn   .25   .25

Radio Telescope, Nançay A406

1963, June 8   Engr.
1067 A406 50c dk bl & dk brn   .45   .35

Amboise Chateau A407

Saint-Flour A408

Designs: 50c, Côte d'Azur Varoise. 85c, Vittel. 95c, Moissac.

1963, June 15
1068 A407 30c slate, grn & bis   .25   .25
1069 A407 50c dk grn, dk hl & hn brn   .30   .25
1070 A408 60c ultra, dk grn & hn brn   .40   .25
1071 A407 85c dk grn, yel grn & brn   1.00   .25
1072 A408 95c brnsh black   .60   .25
  Nos. 1068-1072 (5)   2.55   1.25
For surcharge see Reunion No. 355.

Water Skiing Slalom — A409

1963, Aug. 31   Unwmk.   Perf. 13
1073 A409 30c sl grn, blk & car   .30   .25
World Water Skiing Championships, Vichy.

Europa Issue, 1963
Common Design Type

1963, Sept. 14
Size: 36x22mm
1074 CD6 25c red brown   .25   .25
1075 CD6 50c green   .35   .25

Art Type of 1963
Designs: 85c, "The Married Couple of the Eiffel Tower," by Marc Chagall. 95c, "The Fur Merchants," window, Chartres Cathedral.

1963, Nov. 9   Engr.   Perf. 12x13
1076 A399 85c multicolored   1.10   .90
1077 A399 95c multicolored   .50   .40

Philatec Issue
Common Design Type

1963, Dec. 14   Unwmk.   Perf. 13
1078 CD118 25c dk gray, sl grn & dk car   .25   .25
For surcharge see Reunion No. 349.

Radio and Television Center, Paris — A411

1963, Dec. 15   Engr.
1079 A411 20c org brn, slate & ol   .25   .25

A412

Design: Fire Brigade Insignia, Symbols of Fire, Water and Civilian Defense.

1964, Feb. 8   Engr.   Perf. 13
1082 A412 30c bl, org & red   .40   .25
Issued to honor the fire brigades and civilian defense corps.

Handicapped Laboratory Technician — A413

1964, Feb. 22   Unwmk.   Perf. 13
1083 A413 30c blue grn, org brn & brn   .25   .25
Rehabilitation of the handicapped.

John II the Good (1319-64) by Girard d'Orleans A414

1964, Apr. 25   Perf. 12x13
1084 A414 1fr multicolored   1.10   .75

FRANCE

Stamp of 1900 — A415

Mechanized Mail Handling — A416

Designs: No. 1086, Stamp of 1900, Type A17. No. 1088, Telecommunications.

1964, May 9			Perf. 13	
1085	A415	25c bister & dk car	.25	.25
1086	A415	25c bister & blue	.25	.25
1087	A416	30c blk, bl & org brn	.25	.25
1088	A416	30c blk, car rose & bluish grn	.25	.25
a.		Strip of 4, #1085-1088 + label	1.10	1.00

Printed in sheets of 20 stamps, containing five No. 1088a. The label shows the Philatec emblem in green.

Plane Landing at Night With "25e ANNIVERSAIRE" Added — A417a — A41a7

1964, May 9
1089 A417a 25c multicolored   .25 .25

25th anniversary, night airmail service. Compare with No. B329.

Madonna and Child from Rose Window of Notre Dame — A417

1964, May 23			Perf. 12x13	
1090	A417	60c multicolored	.50	.40

Notre Dame Cathedral, Paris, 800th anniv. See No. 5933c.

Arms Type of 1958-59

Arms: 1c, Niort. 2c, Guéret. 12c, Agen. 18c, Saint-Denis. Réunion. 30c, Paris.

1964-65		Typo.	Perf. 14x13½	
1091	A318	1c vio blue & yel	.25	.25
1092	A318	2c emer, vio bl & yel	.25	.25
1093	A318	12c black, red & yel	.25	.25
1094	A318	18c multicolored	.25	.25
1095	A318	30c vio bl & red ('65)	.30	.25
a.		Booklet pane of 10	15.00	
		Nos. 1091-1095 (5)	1.30	1.25

Gallic Coin — A418

Perf. 13½x14

1964-66		Typo.	Unwmk.	
1096	A418	10c emer & bister	.75	.25
1097	A418	15c org & bister ('66)	.30	.25
1098	A418	25c lilac & brn	.45	.25
1099	A418	50c brt blue & brn	.85	.75
		Nos. 1096-1099 (4)	2.35	1.50

Nos. 1096-1099 are known only precanceled. See second note after No. 132. See Nos. 1240-1242, 1315-1318, 1421-1424.

Postrider, Rocket and Radar Equipment — A419

1964, June 5		Engr.		Perf. 13
1100	A419	1fr brn, dk red & dk bl	17.50	13.50

Sold for 4fr, including 3fr admission to PHI-LATEC. Issued in sheets of 8 stamps and 8 labels (2x8 subjects with labels in horizontal rows 1, 4, 5, 8; stamps in rows 2, 3, 6, 7). Commemorative inscriptions on side margins. Value $150.

Caesar's Tower, Provins — A420

Chapel of Notre Dame du Haut, Ronchamp — A421

1964-65

1101	A421	40c sl grn, dk brn & brn ('65)	.25	.25
1102	A420	70c slate, grn & car	.30	.25
1103	A421	1.25fr brt bl, sl grn & ol	.70	.25
		Nos. 1101-1103 (3)	1.25	.75

The 40c was issued in vertical coils in 1971. Every 10th coil stamp has a red control number printed twice on the back.
For surcharges see Reunion Nos. 352, 361.

Mandel — A422

1964, July 4		Unwmk.	Perf. 13	
1104	A422	30c violet brown	.25	.25

Georges Mandel (1885-1944), Cabinet minister, executed by the Nazis.

Judo — A423

1964, July 4
1105 A423 50c dk blue & vio brn   .25 .25

18th Olympic Games, Tokyo, 10/10-25/64.

Champlevé Enamel from Limoges, 12th Century — A424

Design: No. 1107, The Lady (Claude Le Viste?) with the Unicorn, 15th cent. tapestry.

1964			Perf. 12x13	
1106	A424	1fr multicolored	.75	.50
1107	A424	1fr multicolored	.40	.30

No. 1106 shows part of an enamel sepulchral plate portraying Geoffrey IV, Count of Anjou and Le Maine (1113-1151), who was called Geoffrey Plantagenet.
Issue dates: No. 1106, July 4. No. 1107, Oct. 31.

Paris Taxis Carrying Soldiers to Front, 1914 — A425

1964, Sept. 5		Unwmk.	Perf. 13	
1108	A425	30c black, blue & red	.25	.25

50th anniversary of Battle of the Marne.

Europa Issue, 1964
Common Design Type

1964, Sept. 12			Engr.	
		Size: 22x36mm		
1109	CD7	25c dk car, dp ocher & grn	.25	.25
1110	CD7	50c vio, yel grn & dk car	.25	.25

Cooperation Issue
Common Design Type

1964, Nov. 6		Unwmk.	Perf. 13	
1111	CD119	25c red brn, dk brn & dk bl	.25	.25

Joux Chateau — A427

1965, Feb. 6			Engr.	
1112	A427	1.30fr redsh brn, brn red & dk brn	.90	.25

"The English Girl from the Star" by Toulouse-Lautrec — A428

St. Paul on the Damascus Road, Window, Cathedral of Sens — A429

Leaving for the Hunt — A430

Apocalypse Tapestry, 14th Century — A431

"The Red Violin" by Raoul Dufy — A432

Designs: No. 1115, "August" miniature of Book of Hours of Jean de France, Duc de Berry ("Les Très Riches Heures du Duc de Berry"), painted by Flemish brothers, Pol, Hermant and Jannequin Limbourg, 1411-16. No. 1116, Scene from oldest existing set of French tapestries, showing the Winepress of the Wrath of God (Revelations 14: 19-20).

1965			Perf. 12x13, 13x12	
1113	A428	1fr multicolored	.40	.30
1114	A429	1fr multicolored	.40	.30
1115	A430	1fr multicolored	.30	.30
1116	A431	1fr multicolored	.30	.30
1117	A432	1fr blk, pink & car	.30	.30
		Nos. 1113-1117 (5)	1.70	1.50

No. 1114 issued to commemorate the 800th anniversary of the Cathedral of Sens.
Issued: No. 1113, 3/12; No. 1114, 6/5; No. 1115, 9/25; No. 1116, 10/30; No. 1117, 11/6.

Returning Deportees, 1945 — A433

1965, Apr. 1		Unwmk.	Perf. 13	
1118	A433	40c Prussian green	.45	.25

20th anniv. of the return of people deported during World War II.

House of Youth and Culture, Troyes — A434

1965, Apr. 10			Engr.	
1119	A434	25c ind, brn & dk grn	.25	.25

20th anniv. of the establishment of recreational cultural centers for young people.

Woman Carrying Flowers — A435

1965, Apr. 24		Unwmk.	Perf. 13	
1120	A435	60c dk grn & ver	.30	.25

Tourist Campaign of Welcome & Amiability.

Flags of France, US, USSR and Great Britain Crushing Swastika — A436

1965, May 8
1121 A436 40c black, car & blue   .30 .25

20th anniv. of victory in World War II.

Telegraph Key, Syncom Satellite and Pleumeur-Bodou Station — A437

1965, May 17
1122 A437 60c dk blue, brn & blk   .30 .25

Centenary of the ITU.

Croix de Guerre — A438

1965, May 22			Engr.	
1123	A438	40c red, brn & brt grn	.35	.25

50th anniv. of the Croix de Guerre medal.

Cathedral of Bourges — A439

Moustiers-Sainte Marie — A440

Views: 30c, Road and tunnel, Mont 60c, Aix-les-Bains, sailboat. 75c, Tarn Lozère mountains. 95c, Vendée Rive

FRANCE

poling boat, and windmill. 1fr, Prehistoric stone monuments, Carnac.

1965

1124	A439	30c bl, vio bl & brn vio	.25	.25
1125	A439	40c gray bl & redsh brn	.25	.25
1126	A440	50c grn, bl gray & bis	.25	.25
1127	A439	60c blue & red brn	.45	.25
1128	A439	75c brown, bl & grn	.75	.60
1129	A440	95c brown, grn & bl	4.50	.75
1130	A440	1fr gray, grn & brn	.75	.25
	Nos. 1124-1130 (7)		7.20	2.60

No. 1124 for the opening of the Mont Blanc Tunnel. No. 1125 (Bourges Cathedral) was issued in connection with the French Philatelic Societies Federation Congress, held at Bourges.

Issued: 40c, June 5; 50c, June 19; 30c, 60c, July 17; others, July 10.

For surcharges see Reunion Nos. 354, 362, 365.

Europa Issue, 1965
Common Design Type

1965, Sept. 25   *Perf. 13*
Size: 36x22mm

1131	CD8	30c red	.25	.30
1132	CD8	60c gray	.45	.25

Planting Seedling — A441

1965, Oct. 2
1133	A441	25c slate grn, yel grn & red brn	.25	.25

National reforestation campaign.

Etienne Régnault, "Le Taureau" and Coast of Reunion — A442

1965, Oct. 2
1134	A442	30c indigo & dk car	.25	.25

Tercentenary of settlement of Reunion.

Atomic Reactor and Diagram, Symbols of Industry, Agriculture and Medicine — A443

1965, Oct. 9
1135	A443	60c brt blue & blk	.50	.30

Atomic Energy Commission, 20th anniv.

Air Academy and Emblem — A444

1965, Nov. 6   *Perf. 13*
1136	A444	25c dk blue & green	.35	.30

Air Academy, Salon-de-Provence, 50th anniv.

French Satellite A-1 Issue
Common Design Type

Design: 60c, A-1 satellite.

1965, Nov. 30   *Engr.*   *Perf. 13*
1137	CD121	30c Prus bl, brt bl & blk	.25	.25
1138	CD121	60c blk, Prus bl & brt bl	.40	.25
a.	Strip of 2, #1137-1138 + label		.65	.65

Launching of France's 1st satellite, 11/26/65.
For surcharges see Reunion Nos. 358-359.

Arms of Auch — A446

Cities: 20c, Saint-Lô. 25c, Mont-de-Marsan.

Typographed, Photogravure (20c)
1966   *Perf. 14x13; 14 (20c)*

1142	A446	5c blue & red	.25	.25
1143	A446	20c vio bl, sil, gold & red	.25	.25
1144	A446	25c red brown & ultra	.30	.25
	Nos. 1142-1144 (3)		.80	.75

The 5c and 20c were issued in sheets and in vertical coils. In the coils, every 10th stamp has a red control number on the back.
For surcharges see Reunion Nos. 360-360A.

French Satellite D-1 Issue
Common Design Type

1966, Feb. 18   *Engr.*   *Perf. 13*
1148	CD122	60c blue blk, grn & cl	.25	.25

Horses from Bronze Vessel of Vix — A448

"The Newborn" by Georges de La Tour — A449

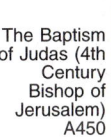

The Baptism of Judas (4th Century Bishop of Jerusalem) A450

"The Moon and the Bull" Tapestry by Jean Lurçat — A451

"Crispin and Scapin" by Honoré Daumier A452

1966   *Perf. 13x12, 12x13*
1149	A110	1fr multicolored	.40	.35
1150	A449	1fr multicolored	.40	.35
1151	A450	1fr multicolored	.40	.35
1152	A451	1fr multicolored	.40	.30
1153	A452	1fr multicolored	.40	.30
	Nos. 1149-1153 (5)		2.00	1.65

The design of No. 1149 is a detail from a 6th century B.C. vessel, found in 1953 in a grave near Vix, Cote d'Or.
The design of No. 1151 is from a stained glass window in the 13th century Sainte-Chapelle, Paris.
No. 1150 exists in an imperf, ungummed souv. sheet with 2 progressive die proofs, issued for benefit of the Postal Museum, and not postally valid. Value $2.
Issued: No. 1149, 3/26; No. 1150, 6/25; No. 1151, 10/22; No. 1152, 11/19; No. 1153, 12/10.

Chessboard, Knight, Emblems for King and Queen — A453

1966, Apr. 2   *Engr.*   *Perf. 13*
1154	A453	60c sepia, gray & dk vio bl	.45	.30

Issued to publicize the Chess Festival.

Rhone Bridge, Pont-Saint-Esprit A454

1966, Apr. 23   *Unwmk.*   *Perf. 13*
1155	A454	25c black & dull blue	.25	.25

St. Michael Slaying the Dragon — A455

1966, Apr. 30   *Litho. & Engr.*
1156	A455	25c multicolored	.25	.25

Millenium of Mont-Saint-Michel.

Stanislas Leszczynski, Lunéville Chateau — A456

1966, May 6   *Engr.*
1157	A456	25c slate, grn & brn	.25	.25

200th anniv. of the reunion of Lorraine and Bar (Barrois) with France.

St. Andrew's and Sèvre River, Niort — A457

1966, May 28   *Engr.*   *Perf. 13*
1158	A457	40c brt bl, indigo & grn	.30	.25

Bernard Le Bovier de Fontenelle and 1666 Meeting Room — A458

1966, June 4
1159	A458	60c dk car rose & brn	.30	.25

300th anniversary, Académie des Sciences.

William the Conqueror, Castle and Norman Ships A459

1966, June 4
1160	A459	60c brown red & dp bl	.40	.30

900th anniversary of Battle of Hastings.

Tracks, Globe and Eiffel Tower — A460

1966, June 11
1161	A460	60c dk brn, car & dull bl	.50	.25

19th International Railroad Congress.

Oléron Bridge — A461

1966, June 20
1162	A461	25c Prus bl, brn & bl	.25	.25

Issued to commemorate the opening of Oléron Bridge, connecting Oléron Island in the Bay of Biscay with the French mainland.

Europa Issue, 1966
Common Design Type

1966, Sept. 24   *Engr.*   *Perf. 13*
Size: 22x36mm

1163	CD9	30c Prussian blue	.25	.25
1164	CD9	60c red	.30	.25

Vercingetorix at Gergovie, 52 B.C. — A462

Bishop Remi Baptizing King Clovis, 496 A.D. — A463

Design: 60c, Charlemagne attending school (page holding book for crowned king).

1966, Nov. 5   *Perf. 13*
1165	A462	40c choc, grn & gray bl	.30	.25
1166	A463	40c dk red brn & blk	.30	.25
1167	A463	60c pur, rose car & brn	.30	.25
	Nos. 1165-1167 (3)		.90	.75

Map of Pneumatic Post and Tube — A464

1966, Nov. 11
1168	A464	1.60fr mar & indigo	.60	.30

Centenary of Paris pneumatic post system.

Val Chateau — A465

1966, Nov. 19   *Engr.*   *Perf. 13*
1169	A465	2.30fr dk bl, ol grn & brn	1.50	.25

Rance Power Station — A466

1966, Dec. 3
1170	A466	60c dk bl, sl grn & brn	.45	.25

Tidal power station in the estuary of the Rance River on the English Channel.

FRANCE

European Broadcasting Union Emblem — A467

1967, Mar. 4   Engr.   Perf. 13
1171 A467 40c dk blue & rose brn   .25   .25
3rd Intl. Congress of the European Broadcasting Union, Paris, Mar. 8-22.

Father Juniet's Gig by Henri Rousseau A468

Francois I by Jean Clouet — A469

The Bather by Jean-Dominique Ingres — A470

St. Eloi, the Goldsmith, at Work A471

1967   Engr.   Perf. 13x12, 12x13
1172 A468 1fr multicolored   .30   .25
1173 A469 1fr multicolored   .30   .25
1174 A470 1fr multicolored   .30   .25
1175 A471 1fr multicolored   .30   .25
   Nos. 1172-1175 (4)   1.20   1.00

The design of No. 1175 is from a 16th century stained glass window in the Church of Sainte Madeleine, Troyes.
Issued: No. 1172, 4/15; No. 1173, 7/1; No. 1174, 9/9; No. 1175, 10/7.

Snow Crystal and Olympic Rings — A472

1967, Apr. 22   Photo.   Perf. 13
1176 A472 60c brt & lt blue & red   .35   .25
Issued to publicize the 10th Winter Olympic Games, Grenoble, Feb. 6-18, 1968.

French Pavilion, EXPO '67 — A473

1967, Apr. 22   Engr.
1177 A473 60c dull bl & bl grn   .35   .30
Intl. Exhibition EXPO '67, Montreal, Apr. 28-Oct. 27, 1967.
For surcharge see Reunion No. 363.

Europa Issue, 1967
Common Design Type
1967, Apr. 29   Size: 22x36mm
1178 CD10 30c blue & gray   .25   .25
1179 CD10 60c brown & lt blue   .30   .25

Great Bridge, Bordeaux — A474

1967, May 8
1180 A474 25c olive, blk & brn   .25   .25

Nungesser, Coli and "L'Oiseau Blanc" — A475

1967, May 8
1181 A475 40c slate, dk & lt brn   .30   .25
40th anniv. of the attempted transatlantic flight of Charles Nungesser and François Coil, French aviators.

Gouin House, Tours — A476

1967, May 13   Engr.   Perf. 13
1182 A476 40c vio bl, red brn & red   .30   .25
Congress of the Federation of French Philatelic Societies in Tours.

Ramon and Alfort Veterinary School — A477

1967, May 27
1183 A477 25c brn, dp bl & yel grn   .25   .25
200th anniv. of the Alfort Veterinary School and to honor Professor Gaston Ramon (1886-1963).

Robert Esnault-Pelterie, Diamant Rocket and A-1 Satellite — A478

1967, May 27
1184 A478 60c slate & vio blue   .30   .25
Issued to honor Robert Esnault-Pelterie (1881-1957), aviation and space expert.

City Hall, Saint-Quentin A479   Saint-Germain-en-Laye A480

Views: 60c, Clock Tower, Vire. 75c, Beach, La Baule, Brittany. 95c, Harbor, Boulogne-sur-Mer. 1fr, Rodez Cathedral. 1.50fr, Morlaix; old houses, grotesque carving, viaduct.

1967
1185 A479 50c bl, sl bl & brn   .25   .25
1186 A479 60c dp bl, sl bl & dk red brn   .30   .25
1187 A480 70c rose car, red brn & bl   .30   .25
1188 A480 75c multicolored   1.10   .60
1189 A480 95c sky bl, lil & sl grn   1.10   .60
1190 A479 1fr indigo & bl gray   .45   .25
1191 A479 1.50fr brt bl, brt grn & red brn   .90   .35
   Nos. 1185-1191 (7)   4.40   2.55
Issued: 1fr, 1.50fr, June 10; 70c, June 17; 50c, 60c, 95c, July 8; 75c, July 24.

Orchids — A481

1967, July 29   Engr.   Perf. 13
1192 A481 40c dp car, brt pink & pur   .50   .40
Orleans flower festival.

Scales of Justice, City and Harbor — A482

1967, Sept. 4
1193 A482 60c dk plum, dl bl & ocher   .50   .30
9th Intl. Accountancy Cong., Paris, 9/6-12.

Cross of Lorraine, Soldiers and Sailors — A483

1967, Oct. 7   Engr.   Perf. 13
1194 A483 25c brn, dp ultra & bl   .25   .25
25th anniv. of the Battle of Bir Hacheim.

Marie Curie, Bowl Glowing with Radium — A484

1967, Oct. 23   Engr.   Perf. 13
1195 A484 60c dk blue & ultra   .30   .25
Marie Curie (1867-1934), scientist who discovered radium and polonium, Nobel prize winner for physics and chemistry.

Lions Emblem — A485

1967, Oct. 28
1196 A485 40c dk car & vio bl   .70   .40
50th anniversary of Lions International.
For surcharge see Reunion No. 364.

Marianne (by Cheffer) — A486

1967, Nov. 4   Engr.
1197 A486 25c dark blue   .25   .25
1198 A486 30c bright lilac   .25   .25
   a. Booklet pane of 5   6.00
   b. Booklet pane of 10   12.00
Coils (vertical) of Nos. 1197 and 1231 show a red number on the back of every 10th stamp.
See Nos. 1230-1231C, 3525, 4410e, 4517.
For surcharges see Reunion Nos. 367-368, 389.
Stamps of various colors and printing methods with denomination of €1 were limited printings sold in 2010. See footnote after No.3478.
A €1.16 stamp of type A486 with an attached label was included in a limited-edition booklet issued Nov. 4, 2020.

King Philip II (Philip Augustus) at Battle of Bouvines — A487

Designs: No. 1200, Election of Hugh Capet as King, horiz. 60c, King Louis IX (St. Louis) holding audience for the poor.

1967, Nov. 13   Engr.   Perf. 13
1199 A487 40c bl gray, blk & dk blue   .30   .25
1200 A487 40c dp bluish grn & blue   .30   .25
1201 A487 60c dp grn & dk red brn   .40   .25
   Nos. 1199-1201 (3)   1.00   .75

Commemorative Medal — A488

1968, Jan. 6   Engr.   Perf. 13
1202 A488 40c dk slate grn & bis   .25   .25
50th anniversary of postal checking service.

Various Road Signs — A489

1968, Feb. 24
1203 A489 25c lil, red & dk bl grn   .25   .25
Issued to publicize road safety.

Prehistoric Paintings, Lascaux Cave A490

Arearea (Merriment) by Paul Gauguin A491

The Dance by Emile Antoine Bourdelle — A492

Portrait of the Model by Auguste Renoir — A493

FRANCE

1968   Engr.   Perf. 13x12, 12x13
1204	A490	1fr multicolored	.50	.30
1205	A491	1fr multicolored	.50	.30
1206	A492	1fr car & gray olive	.50	.30
1207	A493	1fr multicolored	.50	.30
		Nos. 1204-1207 (4)	2.00	1.20

Issued: No. 1204, 4/13; No. 1205, 9/21; No. 1206, 10/26; No. 1207, 11/9.

Audio-visual Institute, Royan — A494

1968, Apr. 13   Perf. 13
1208	A494	40c slate grn, brn & Prus bl	.25	.25

5th Conference for World Cooperation with the theme of teaching living languages by audio-visual means.

Europa Issue, 1968
Common Design Type
1968, Apr. 27   Size: 36x22mm
1209	CD11	30c brt red lil & ocher	.25	.25
1210	CD11	60c brown & lake	.60	.30

Alain René Le Sage — A495

1968, May 4
1211	A495	40c blue & rose vio	.25	.25

Alain René Le Sage (1668-1747), novelist and playwright.

Chateau de Langeais — A496

1968, May 4
1212	A496	60c slate bl, grn & red brn	.65	.30

Pierre Larousse — A497

1968, May 11   Engr.   Perf. 13
1213	A497	40c rose vio & brown	.25	.25

Pierre Larousse (1817-75), grammarian, lexicographer and encyclopedist.

Gnarled Trunk and Fir Tree — A498

1968, May 18   Engr.   Perf. 13
1214	A498	25c grnsh bl, brn & grn	.25	.25

Twinning of Rambouillet Forest in France and the Black Forest in Germany.

Map of Papal Enclave, Valréas, and John XXII Receiving Homage — A499

1968, May 25
1215	A499	60c brn, bis brn & pur	.40	.25

Papal enclave at Valréas, 650th anniv.

Louis XIV, Arms of France and Flanders — A500

1968, June 29
1216	A500	40c rose car, gray & lemon	.25	.25

300th anniv. of the Treaty of Aachen which reunited Flanders with France.

Martrou Bridge, Rochefort — A501

1968, July 20
1217	A501	25c sky bl, blk & dk red brn	.25	.25

Letord Lorraine Bimotor Plane over Map of France — A502

1968, Aug. 17   Engr.   Perf. 13
1218	A502	25c brt blue, indigo & red	.40	.25

1st regularly scheduled air mail route in France from Paris to St. Nazaire, 50th anniv.

Tower de Constance, Aigues-Mortes — A503

1968, Aug. 31
1219	A503	25c red brn, sky bl & olive bister	.25	.25

Bicentenary of the release of Huguenot prisoners from the Tower de Constance, Aigues-Mortes.

Cathedral and Pont Vieux, Beziers — A504

1968, Sept. 7   Engr.   Perf. 13
1220	A504	40c ind, bis & grn	.95	.30

"Victory" over White Tower of Salonika — A505

1968, Sept. 28
1221	A505	40c red lilac & plum	.25	.25

50th anniv. of the armistice on the eastern front in World War I, Sept. 29, 1918.

Louis XV, Arms of France and Corsica — A506

1968, Oct. 5   Perf. 13
1222	A506	25c ultra, grn & blk	.25	.25

Return of Corsica to France, 200th anniv.

Relay Race — A507

1968, Oct. 12
1223	A507	40c ultra, brt grn & ol brn	.40	.25

19th Olympic Games, Mexico City, 10/12-27.

A508

Design: Polar camp with helicopter, plane and Snocat tractor.

1968, Oct. 19
1224	A508	40c Prus bl, lt grnsh bl & brn red	.30	.25

20 years of French Polar expeditions. For surcharge see Reunion No. 366.

Leon Bailby, Paris Opera Staircase and Hospital Beds — A509

1968, Oct. 26
1225	A509	40c ocher & maroon	.25	.25

50th anniv. of the "Little White Beds" children's hospital fund.

"Victory" over Arc de Triomphe and Eternal Flame — A510

1968, Nov. 9   Engr.   Perf. 13
1226	A510	25c dk car rose & dp blue	.25	.25

50th anniv. of the armistice which ended World War I.

Death of Bertrand Du Guesclin at Chateauneuf-de-Randon, 1380 — A511

No. 1228, King Philip IV (the Fair) and first States-General assembly, 1302, horiz. 60c. Joan of Arc leaving Vaucouleurs, 1429.

1968, Nov. 16
1227	A511	40c green, ultra & brn	.30	.25
1228	A511	40c cop red, grn & gray	.40	.25
1229	A511	60c vio bl, sl bl & bis	.40	.30
		Nos. 1227-1229 (3)	1.00	.80

See No. 1260.

Marianne Type of 1967
1969-70   Engr.   Perf. 13
1230	A486	30c green	.35	.25
a.		Booklet pane of 10	8.50	
1231	A486	40c deep carmine	.45	.25
a.		Booklet pane of 5 (horiz. strip)	7.50	
b.		Booklet pane of 10	8.50	
d.		With label ('70)	.50	.25

     Typo.   Perf. 14x13
1231C	A486	30c blue green	.25	.25
		Nos. 1230-1231C (3)	1.05	.75

No. 1231d was issued in sheets of 50 with alternating labels showing coat of arms of Perigueux, arranged checkerwise, to commemorate the inauguration of the Perigueux stamp printing plant.
The 40c coil is noted after No. 1198.

Church of Brou, Bourg-en-Bresse A512

Views: 80c, Vouglans Dam, Jura. 85c, Chateau de Chantilly. 1.15fr, Sailboats in La Trinité-sur-Mer harbor.

1969   Engr.   Perf. 13
1232	A512	45c olive, bl & red brn	.25	.25
1233	A512	80c ol bis, brn red & dk brn	.40	.25
1234	A512	85c sl grn, dl bl & gray	.75	.50
1235	A512	1.15fr brt bl, gray grn & brn	.75	.50
		Nos. 1232-1235 (4)	2.15	1.50

"February" Bas-relief from Amiens Cathedral A513

Philip the Good, by Roger van der Weyden — A514

Sts. Savin and Cyprian before Ladicius, Mural, St. Savin, Vienne A515

The Circus, by Georges Seurat — A515a

1969   Perf. 12x13
1236	A513	1fr dk green & brn	.40	.25
1237	A514	1fr multicolored	.40	.25
1238	A515	1fr multicolored	.40	.25
1239	A515a	1fr multicolored	.40	.25
		Nos. 1236-1239 (4)	1.60	1.00

Issue dates: No. 1236, Feb. 22; No. 1237, May 3; No. 1238, June 28; No. 1239, Nov. 8.

Gallic Coin Type of 1964-66
1969   Typo.   Perf. 13½x14
1240	A418	22c brt green & vio	.30	.25
1241	A418	25c red & ultra	.85	.40
1242	A418	70c ultra & red brn	3.75	1.75
		Nos. 1240-1242 (3)	4.90	2.40

Nos. 1240-1242 are known only precanceled. See note after No. 132.

Hautefort Chateau — A516

1969, Apr. 5   Engr.   Perf. 13
1243	A516	70c blue, slate & bister	.40	.25

FRANCE

Irises — A517

1969, Apr. 12   Photo.
1244 A517 45c multicolored   .35   .25
3rd Intl. Flower Show, Paris, 4/23-10/5.

Europa Issue, 1969
Common Design Type
1969, Apr. 26   Engr.   Perf. 13
Size: 36x22mm
1245 CD12 40c carmine rose   .25   .25
1246 CD12 70c Prussian blue   .30   .25

Albert Thomas and Thomas Memorial, Geneva — A518

1969, May 10   Engr.   Perf. 13
1247 A518 70c mar, lt brn & ind   .40   .25
ILO, 50th anniv., and honoring Thomas (1878-1932), director of the ILO (1920-32).

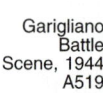
Garigliano Battle Scene, 1944 A519

1969, May 10
1248 A519 45c black & violet   .40   .30
25th anniv. of the Battle of the Garigliano against the Germans.

Chateau du Marché, Chalons-sur-Marne A520

1969, May 24
1249 A520 45c bis, dull bl & grn   .40   .30
Federation of French Philatelic Societies, 42nd congress.

Parachutists over Normandy Beach — A521

1969, May 31
1250 A521 45c inidgo & dk ultra   .85   .40
Landing of Special Air Service and Free French commandos in Normandy, June 6, 1944, 25th anniv.

Monument of the French Resistance, Mt. Mouchet — A522

1969, June 7
1251 A522 45c dk grn, slate & ind   .60   .45
25th anniv. of the battle of Mt. Mouchet between French resistance fighters and the Germans, June 2 and 10, 1944.

French Troops Landing in Provence A523

1969, Aug. 23   Engr.   Perf. 13
1252 A523 45c slate & blk brn   .75   .25
25th anniv. of the landing of French and American forces in Provence, Aug. 15, 1944.

Russian and French Aviators A524

1969, Oct. 18   Engr.   Perf. 13
1253 A524 45c slate, dp bl & car   .75   .45
Issued to honor the French aviators of the Normandy-Neman Squadron who fought on the Russian Front, 1942-45.

Kayak on Isère River — A525

1969, Aug. 2   Engr.   Perf. 13
1254 A525 70c org brn, ol & dk bl   .40   .25
Intl. Canoe and Kayak Championships, Bourg-Saint-Maurice, Savoy, July 31-Aug. 6.

A526

Design: Napoleon as young officer and his birthplace, Ajaccio.

1969, Aug. 16
1255 A526 70c brt grnsh bl, ol & rose vio   .40   .25
Napoleon Bonaparte (1769-1821). For surcharge see Reunion No. 370.

Drops of Water and Diamond — A527

1969, Sept. 27
1256 A527 70c blk, dp bl & brt grn   .40   .25
European Water Charter.

Mediterranean Mouflon — A528

1969, Oct. 11
1257 A528 45c ol, blk & org brn   .60   .50
Issued to publicize wildlife protection.

Central School of Arts and Crafts — A529

1969, Oct. 18
1258 A529 70c dk grn, yel grn & org   .40   .25
Inauguration of the Central School of Arts and Crafts at Chatenay-Malabry.

Nuclear Submarine "Le Redoutable" A530

1969, Oct. 25
1259 A530 70c dp bl, grn & sl grn   .40   .25

Type of 1968 and

Henri IV and Edict of Nantes A531

Designs: No. 1260, Pierre Terrail de Bayard wounded at Battle of Brescia (after a painting in Versailles). No. 1262, Louis XI, Charles the Bold and map of France.

1969, Nov. 8   Engr.   Perf. 13
1260 A511 80c brn, bister & blk   .45   .25
1261 A531 80c blk & vio bl   .45   .25
1262 A531 80c ol, dp grn & dk red brn   .45   .25
Nos. 1260-1262 (3)   1.35   .75

"Firecrest" and Alain Gerbault — A532

1970, Jan. 10   Engr.   Perf. 13
1263 A532 70c ind, brt bl & gray   .45   .30
Completion of Alain Gerbault's trip around the world aboard the "Firecrest," 1923-29, 40th anniv.

A533

Design: Gendarmery emblem, mountain climber, helicopter, motorcyclists and motorboat.

1970, Jan. 31
1264 A533 45c sl grn, dk bl & brn   .80   .40
National Gendarmery, founded 1791.

Field Ball Player — A534

1970, Feb. 21   Engr.   Perf. 13
1265 A534 80c slate green   .45   .40
7th Intl. Field Ball Games, Feb. 26-Mar. 8.

Alphonse Juin and Church of the Invalides A535

1970, Feb. 28
1266 A535 45c gray bl & dk brn   .35   .25
Issued to honor Marshal Alphonse Pierre Juin (1888-1967), military leader.

Aerotrain — A536

1970, Mar. 7
1267 A536 80c purple & gray   .45   .40
Introduction of the aerotrain, which reaches a speed of 320 miles per hour.

A537

Design: Pierre Joseph Pelletier, Joseph Bienaimé Caventou, Quinine formula and cell.

1970, Mar. 21   Engr.   Perf. 13
1268 A537 50c slate grn, sky bl & dp car   .35   .25
Discovery of quinine, 150th anniversary.

Pink Flamingos — A538

1970, Mar. 21
1269 A538 45c olive, gray & pink   .35   .25
European Nature Conservation Year, 1970.

Diamant B Rocket and Radar — A539

1970, Mar. 28
1270 A539 45c bright green   .50   .25
Space center in Guyana and the launching of the Diamant B rocket, Mar. 10, 1970.

Europa Issue, 1970
Common Design Type
1970, May 2   Engr.   Perf. 13
1271 CD13 40c deep carmine   .25   .25
1272 CD13 80c sky blue   .40   .25

Annunication, by Primitive Painter of Savoy, 1480 — A540

The Triumph of Flora, by Jean Baptiste Carpeaux A541

Diana Returning from the Hunt, by François Boucher A542

FRANCE

Dancer with Bouquet, by Edgar Degas — A543

1970   *Perf. 12x13, 13x12*
1273	A540	1fr multicolored	.50	.35
1274	A541	1fr red brown	.50	.35
1275	A542	1fr multicolored	.50	.35
1276	A543	1fr multicolored	.50	.35
		Nos. 1273-1276 (4)	2.00	1.40

Issued: No. 1273, 5/9; No. 1274, 7/4; No. 1275, 10/10; No. 1276, 11/14.

Arms of Lens, Miner's Lamp and Pit Head — A544

1970, May 16   *Engr.*   *Perf. 13*
1277	A544	40c scarlet	.25	.25

43rd Natl. Congress of the Federation of French Philatelic Societies, Lens, May 14-21.

Diamond Rock, Martinique A545

Haute Provence Observatory and Spiral Nebula A546

Designs: 95c, Chancelade Abbey, Dordogne. 1fr, Gosier Islet, Guadeloupe.

1970, June 20   *Engr.*   *Perf. 13*
1278	A545	50c sl grn, brt bl & plum	.30	.25
1279	A545	95c lt ol, car & brn	.80	.80
1280	A545	1fr sl grn, brt bl & dk car rose	.90	.25
1281	A546	1.30fr dk bl, vio bl & dk grn	1.10	.90
		Nos. 1278-1281 (4)	3.10	2.20

Hand Reaching for Freedom — A547

1970, June 27
1282	A547	45c vio bl, bl & bister	.40	.25

Liberation of concentration camps, 25th anniv.

Handicapped Javelin Thrower — A548

1970, June 27
1283	A548	45c rose car, ultra & emer	.40	.25

Issued to publicize the International Games of the Handicapped, St. Etienne, June 1970.

Pole Vault — A549

1970, Sept. 11   *Engr.*   *Perf. 13*
1284	A549	45c car, bl & indigo	.45	.25

First European Junior Athletic Championships, Colombes, Sept. 11-13.

Royal Salt Works, Arc-et-Senans A550

1970, Sept. 26
1285	A550	80c bl, brn & dk grn	.70	.65

Restoration of the 18th cent. Royal Salt Works buildings, by Claude Nicolas Ledoux (1736-1806) at Arc-et-Senans, for use as a center for studies of all aspects of future human life.

Armand Jean du Plessis, Duc de Richelieu A551

Designs: No. 1287, Battle of Fontenoy, 1745. No. 1288, Louis XIV and Versailles.

1970, Oct. 17   *Engr.*   *Perf. 13*
1286	A551	45c blk, sl & car rose	.50	.30
1287	A551	45c org, brn & indigo	.50	.30
1288	A551	45c sl grn, lem & org brn	.50	.30
		Nos. 1286-1288 (3)	1.50	.90

UN Headquarters in New York and Geneva — A552

1970, Oct. 24   *Engr.*   *Perf. 13*
1289	A552	80c ol, dp ultra & dk pur	.40	.25

25th anniversary of the United Nations.

View of Bordeaux and France No. 43 — A553

1970, Nov. 7
1290	A553	80c vio bl & gray bl	.40	.25

Centenary of the Bordeaux issue.

Col. Denfert-Rochereau and Lion of Belfort, by Frederic A. Bartholdi — A554

1970, Nov. 14
1291	A554	45c dk bl, ol & red brn	.40	.25

Centenary of the siege of Belfort during Franco-Prussian War.

Marianne (by Bequet) — A555

1971-74   *Typo.*   *Perf. 14x13*
1292	A555	45c sky blue	.30	.25
1292A	A555	60c green ('74)	.50	.25

For surcharges see Reunion Nos. 371, 397-398.

     Engr.   *Perf. 13*
1293	A555	50c rose carmine	.30	.25
a.		Bklt. pane of 5 (horiz. strip)	5.00	
b.		Booklet pane of 10	10.00	
1294	A555	60c green ('74)	4.00	.25
a.		Booklet pane of 10	65.00	
1294B	A555	80c car rose ('74)	.50	.25
c.		Booklet pane of 5	9.00	
d.		Booklet pane of 10	12.00	
		Nos. 1293-1294B (3)	4.80	.75

Nos. 1294 and 1294B issued also in vertical coils with control number on back of every 10th stamp.

No. 1293 issued only in booklets and in vertical coils with red control number on back of every 10th stamp.

See Nos. 1494-1498, 3526, 4410f, 4518, 6130-6133.

St. Matthew, Sculpture from Strasbourg Cathedral — A556

Winnower, by François Millet — A557

The Dreamer, by Georges Rouault — A558

1971   *Engr.*   *Perf. 12x13*
1295	A556	1fr dark red brown	.50	.40
1296	A557	1fr multicolored	.50	.40
1297	A558	1fr multicolored	.50	.40
		Nos. 1295-1297 (3)	1.50	1.20

Issued: No. 1295, 1/23; No. 1296, 4/3; No. 1297, 6/5.

Figure Skating Pair — A560

1971, Feb. 20   *Engr.*   *Perf. 13*
1299	A560	80c vio bl, sl & aqua	.50	.30

World Figure Skating Championships, Lyons, Feb. 23-28.

Underwater Exploration — A561

1971, Mar. 6
1300	A561	80c blue blk & bl grn	.45	.25

International Exhibition of Ocean Exploration, Bordeaux, Mar. 9-14.

Cape Horn Clipper "Antoinette" and Solidor Castle, Saint-Malo A562

1971, Apr. 10   *Engr.*   *Perf. 13*
1301	A562	80c blue, pur & slate	.80	.45

For surcharge see Reunion No. 372.

Pyrenean Chamois — A563

1971, Apr. 24   *Engr.*   *Perf. 13*
1302	A563	65c bl, dk brn & brn ol	.50	.30

National Park of Western Pyrenees.

Europa Issue, 1971
Common Design Type and

Santa Maria della Salute, Venice — A564

1971, May 8   *Engr.*   *Perf. 13*
1303	A564	50c blue gray & ol bis	.30	.25

Size: 36x22mm
1304	CD14	80c rose lilac	.45	.40

Cardinal, Nobleman and Lawyer A565

Storming of the Bastille A566

Design: No. 1306, Battle of Valmy.

1971
1305	A565	45c bl, rose red & pur	.45	.30
1306	A565	45c bl, ol bis & brn red	.50	.30
1307	A566	65c dk brn, gray bl & mag	.65	.45
		Nos. 1305-1307 (3)	1.60	1.05

No. 1305 commemorates the opening of the Estates General, May 5, 1789; No. 1306, Battle of Valmy (Sept. 20, 1792) between French and Prussian armies; 65c, Storming of the Bastille, Paris, July 14, 1789.

Issued: No. 1305, 5/8; No. 1306, 9/18; 65c, 7/10.

Grenoble — A568

1971, May 29   *Engr.*   *Perf. 13*
1308	A568	50c ocher, lil & rose red	.35	.25

44th Natl. Cong. of the Federation of French Philatelic Societies, Grenoble, May 30-31.

"Rural Family Aid" Shedding Light on Village — A569

1971, June 5
1309	A569	40c vio, bl & grn	.25	.25

Aid for rural families.

FRANCE

For surcharge see Reunion No. 373.

Chateau and Fort de Sedan A570

Pont d'Arc, Ardèche Gorge A571

Views: 60c, Sainte Chapelle, Riom. 65c, Fountain and tower, Dole. 90c, Tower and street, Riquewihr.

1971		Engr.		Perf. 13	
1310	A571	60c black, grn & bl		.30	.25
1311	A571	65c lil, ocher & blk		.55	.25
1312	A571	90c grn, vio brn & red brn		.55	.25
1313	A570	1.10fr sl grn, Prus bl & brn		.65	.45
1314	A571	1.40fr sl grn, bl & dk brn		.75	.45
		Nos. 1310-1314 (5)		2.80	1.45

Issued: 60c, 6/19; 65c, 90c, 7/3; 1.10fr, 1.40fr, 6/12.
For surcharges see Reunion Nos. 374, 381.

Gallic Coin Type of 1964-66

1971, July 1		Typo.		Perf. 13½x14	
1315	A418	26c lilac & brn		.30	.25
1316	A418	30c lt brown & brn		.35	.25
1317	A418	45c dull green & brn		1.20	.40
1318	A418	90c red & brown		1.50	.75
		Nos. 1315-1318 (4)		3.35	1.65

Nos. 1315-1318 are known only precanceled. See second paragraph after No. 132.

Bourbon Palace — A572

1971, Aug. 28 Engr. Perf. 13
1319 A572 90c violet blue .50 .35
59th Conf. of the Interparliamentary Union.

Embroidery and Tool Making — A573

1971, Oct. 16
1320 A573 90c brn red, brt lil & cl .50 .30
40th anniv. of the first assembly of presidents of artisans' guilds.
For surcharge see Reunion No. 375.

Reunion Chameleon A574

1971, Nov. 6 Photo. Perf. 13
1321 A574 60c brn, yel, grn & blk .65 .45
Nature protection.

De Gaulle Issue
Common Design Type and

De Gaulle in Brazzaville, 1944 — A576

Designs: No. 1324, De Gaulle entering Paris, 1944. No. 1325, Pres. de Gaulle, 1970.

1971, Nov. 9 Engr.
1322 CD134 50c black .65 .45
1323 A576 50c ultra .65 .45
1324 A576 50c rose red .65 .45
1325 CD134 50c black .65 .45
   a. Strip of 4, #1322-1325 + label 3.00 2.50
    Nos. 1325a (1) 3.00 2.50

1st anniv. of the death of Charles de Gaulle. See Nos. 5947Bd, 5947Bf, Reunion Nos. 377, 380.

Antoine Portal and first Session of Academy A577

1971, Nov. 13
1326 A577 45c dk purple & mag .40 .25
Sesquicentennial of the founding of the National Academy of Medicine; Baron Antoine Portal was first president.

L'Etude, by Jean Honoré Fragonard A578

Women in Garden, by Claude Monet — A579

St. Peter Presenting Pierre de Bourbon, by Maitre de Moulins — A580

Boats, by André Derain A581

1972 Engr. Perf. 12x13, 13x12
1327 A578 1fr black & multi .50 .40
1328 A579 1fr slate grn & multi 1.00 .50
1329 A580 2fr dk brown & multi 1.25 1.00
1330 A581 2fr yellow & multi 1.25 1.00
    Nos. 1327-1330 (4) 4.00 2.90

Issued: No. 1327, 1/22; No. 1328, 6/17; No. 1329, 10/14; No. 1330, 12/16.

Map of South Indian Ocean, Penguin and Ships — A582

1972, Jan. 29 Perf. 13
1331 A582 90c black, bl & ocher .50 .30
Bicentenary of discovery of the Crozet and Kerguelen Islands.

Slalom and Olympic Emblems — A583

1972, Feb. 7
1332 A583 90c dk olive & dp car .50 .30
11th Winter Olympic Games, Sapporo, Japan, Feb. 3-13.

Hearts, UN Emblem, Caduceus and Pacemaker A584

1972, Apr. 8 Engr. Perf. 13
1333 A584 45c dk car, org & gray .35 .25
"Your heart is your health," world health month.

Red Deer, Sologne Plateau A585

Charlieu Abbey A585a

Bazoches-du-Morvand Chateau — A586

Saint-Just Cathedral, Narbonne A587

1972 Perf. 13
1334 A585 1fr ocher & red brn .50 .25
1335 A585a 1.20fr sl & dull brn .65 .25
1336 A586 2fr sl grn, blk & red brn 1.00 .25
1337 A587 3.50fr bl, gray ol & car rose 1.50 .45
    Nos. 1334-1337 (4) 3.65 1.20

Issued: 1fr, 9/10; 1.20fr, 4/29; 2fr, 9/9; 3.50fr, 4/8.
For surcharge see Reunion No. 388.

Eagle Owl — A588

Nature protection: 60c, Salmon, horiz.

1972
1338 A588 60c grn, ind & brt bl 1.50 .60
1339 A588 65c sl, ol brn & sep .80 .50
Issue dates: 60c, May 27; 65c, Apr. 15.

Europa Issue
Common Design Type and

Aix-la-Chapelle Cathedral — A589

1972, Apr. 22 Engr. Perf. 13
1340 A589 50c yel, vio brn & dk ol .25 .25

Photo. Size: 22x36mm
1341 CD15 90c red org & multi .50 .35
    Nos. 1341 (1) .50 .35

Bouquet Made of Hearts and Blood Donors' Emblem — A590

1972, May 5 Engr.
1342 A590 40c red .30 .25
20th anniv. of the Blood Donors Association of Post and Telecommunications Employees.
For surcharge see Reunion No. 383.

Newfoundlander "Côte d'Emeraude" — A591

1972, May 6
1343 A591 90c org, vio bl & sl grn .75 .55

Cathedral, Saint-Brieuc A592

1972, May 20
1344 A592 50c lilac rose .35 .25
45th Congress of the Federation of French Philatelic Societies, Saint-Brieuc, May 21-22.

Hand Holding Symbol of Postal Code — A593

1972, June 3 Typo. Perf. 14x13
1345 A593 30c green, blk & car .25 .25
1346 A593 50c car, blk & yel .30 .25
Introduction of postal code system.
For surcharges see Reunion Nos. 384-385.

Old and New Communications — A594

1972, July 1 Engr. Perf. 13
1347 A594 45c slate & vio blue .40 .25
21st Intl. Congress of P.T.T. (Post, Telegraph & Telephone) Employees, Paris, 7/1-7.

Hurdler and Olympic Rings — A595

1972, July 8
1348 A595 1fr deep olive .50 .25
20th Olympic Games, Munich, 8/26-9/11.

FRANCE

Hikers and Mt. Aigoual — A596

1972, July 15   **Photo.**   **Perf. 13**
1349 A596 40c brt rose & multi   .75   .30

Intl. Year of Tourism and 25th anniv. of the Natl. Hikers Association.

Bicyclist — A597

1972, July 22   **Engr.**
1350 A597 1fr gray, brn & lil   1.20   .60

World Bicycling Championships, Marseille, July 29-Aug. 2.

"Incroyables and Merveilleuses," 1794 — A598

French History: 60c, Bonaparte at the Arcole Bridge. 65c, Egyptian expedition (soldiers and scientists finding antiquities; pyramids in background).

1972   **Engr.**   **Perf. 13**
1351 A598 45c ol, dk grn & car rose   .40   .30
1352 A598 60c red, blk & ind   .65   .35
1353 A598 65c ocher, ultra & choc   .65   .35
  Nos. 1351-1353 (3)   1.70   1.00

Issued: 45c, Oct. 7; 60c, 65c, Nov. 11.

Champollion, Rosetta Stone with Key Inscription — A599

1972, Oct. 11
1354 A599 90c vio bl, brn red & blk   .50   .30

Sesquicentennial of the deciphering of hieroglyphs by Jean-François Champollion.

St. Teresa, Portal of Notre Dame of Alençon — A600

1973, Jan. 6   **Engr.**   **Perf. 13**
1355 A600 1fr Prus blue & indigo   .50   .30

Centenary of the birth of St. Teresa of Lisieux, the Little Flower (Thérèse Martin, 1873-1897), Carmelite nun.

Anthurium (Martinique) — A601

1973, Jan. 20   **Photo.**
1356 A601 50c gray & multi   .35   .25

Colors of France and Germany Interlaced A602

1973, Jan. 22
1357 A602 50c multicolored   .40   .25

10th anniv. of the Franco-German Cooperation Treaty. See Germany No. 1101.

Polish Immigrants A603

1973, Feb. 3   **Engr.**   **Perf. 13**
1358 A603 40c slate grn, dp car & brn   .40   .25

50th anniversary of Polish immigration into France, 1921-1923.

Last Supper, St. Austremoine Church, Issoire — A604

Kneeling Woman, by Charles Le Brun — A605

Angel, Wood, Moutier-D'Ahun A606

Lady Playing Archlute, by Antoine Watteau — A607

1973   **Engr.**   **Perf. 12x10**
1359 A604 2fr brown & multi   1.25   .75
1360 A605 2fr dk red & yel   1.25   .75
1361 A606 2fr ol brn & vio brn   1.25   .75
1362 A607 2fr black & multi   1.25   .75
  Nos. 1359-1362 (4)   5.00   3.00

Issued: No. 1359, 2/10, No. 1360, 4/28, No. 1361, 5/26; No. 1362, 9/22.

Tuileries Palace, Telephone Relays — A608

Oil Tanker, Francis I Lock — A609

Airbus A300-B — A610

1973
1363 A608 45c ultra, sl grn & bis   .30   .25
1364 A609 90c plum, blk & bl   .55   .25
1365 A610 3fr dk brn, bl & blk   1.25   .65
  Nos. 1363-1365 (3)   2.10   1.15

French technical achievements.
Issued: 45c, 5/15; 90c, 10/27; 3fr, 4/7.

Europa Issue 1973
Common Design Type and

City Hall, Brussels, CEPT Emblem — A611

1973, Apr. 14   **Engr.**   **Perf. 13**
1366 A611 50c brt pink & choc   .40   .25

Photo.
Size: 36x22mm
1367 CD16 90c slate grn & multi   1.25   .75

Masonic Lodge Emblem — A612

1973, May 12   **Engr.**   **Perf. 13**
1368 A612 90c magenta & vio bl   .50   .30

Bicentenary of the Free Masons of France.

Guadeloupe Raccoon — A613

White Storks — A614

1973
1369 A613 40c lilac, sepia & olive   .35   .25
1370 A614 60c blk, aqua & org red   .50   .25

Nature protection.
Issue dates: 40c, June 23; 60c, May 12.

Tourist Issue

Doubs Waterfall A615

Clos-Lucé, Amboise A617

Palace of Dukes of Burgundy, Dijon — A616

Design: 90c, Gien Chateau.

1973   **Engr.**   **Perf. 13**
1371 A615 60c multicolored   .30   .25
1372 A616 65c red & purple   .30   .25
1373 A616 90c Prus bl, ind & brn   .40   .25
1374 A617 1fr ocher, bl & sl grn   .45   .25
  Nos. 1371-1374 (4)   1.45   1.00

Issued: 60c, 9/8; 65c, 5/19; 90c, 8/18; 1fr, 6/23.
For surcharge see Reunion No. 387.

Academy Emblem — A618

1973, May 26
1375 A618 1fr lil, slate grn & red   .50   .30

Academy of Overseas Sciences, 50th anniv.

Racing Car and Clocks — A619

1973, June 2
1376 A619 60c dk brown & blue   .50   .30

24-hour automobile race at Le Mans, 50th anniv.

Five-master France II — A620

1973, June 9
1377 A620 90c ultra, Prus bl & ind   .90   .45

For surcharge see Reunion No. 386.

Tower and Square, Toulouse — A621

1973, June 9
1378 A621 50c purple & red brn   .30   .25

46th Congress of the Federation of French Philatelic Societies, Toulouse, June 9-12.

Dr. Armauer G. Hansen — A622

1973, Sept. 29   **Engr.**   **Perf. 13**
1379 A622 45c grn, dk ol & ocher   .30   .25

Centenary of the discovery of the Hansen bacillus, the cause of leprosy.

Ducretet and his Transmission Diagram — A623

1973, Oct. 6
1380 A623 1fr yel grn & magenta   .40   .30

75th anniversary of the first transmission of radio signals from the Eiffel Tower to the Pantheon by Eugene Ducretet (1844-1915).

FRANCE

Molière as Sganarelle — A624

1973, Oct. 20
1381 A624 1fr dk red & olive brn .45 .30
Molière (Jean-Baptiste Poquelin; 1622-1673), playwright and actor.

Pierre Bourgoin and Philippe Kieffer — A625

1973, Oct. 27
1382 A625 1fr red, rose cl & vio bl .45 .30
Pierre Bourgoin (1907-70), and Philippe Kieffer (1899-1963), heroes of the Free French forces in World War II.

Napoleon, Jean Portalis and Palace of Justice, Paris A626

Exhibition Halls A627

The Coronation of Napoleon, by Jean Louis David — A628

1973   Engr.   Perf. 13
1383 A626 45c blue, choc & gray .40 .30
1384 A627 60c ol, sl grn & brn .40 .40
1385 A628 1fr sl grn, ol & claret .55 .40
   Nos. 1383-1385 (3) 1.35 1.10
History of France. 45c, for the preparation of the Code Napoleon; 60c, Napoleon's encouragement of industry; 1fr, his coronation.
Issued: 45c, 11/3; 60c, 11/24; 1fr, 11/12.

Eternal Flame, Arc de Triomphe — A629

1973, Nov. 10
1386 A629 40c pur, vio bl & red .40 .30
50th anniv. of the Eternal Flame at the Arc de Triomphe, Paris.

Weather Vane — A630

1973, Dec. 1
1387 A630 65c ultra, blk & grn .40 .30
50th anniv. of the Dept. of Agriculture.

Human Rights Flame and Man — A631

1973, Dec. 8   Engr.   Perf. 13
1388 A631 45c car, org & blk .30 .25
25th anniversary of the Universal Declaration of Human Rights.

Postal Museum — A632

1973, Dec. 19
1389 A632 50c maroon & bister .30 .25
Opening of new post and philately museum, Paris.

ARPHILA 75 Emblem — A633

1974, Jan. 19   Engr.   Perf. 13
1390 A633 50c brn, bl & brt lil .30 .25
ARPHILA 75 Philatelic Exhibition, Paris, June 1975.
For surcharge see Reunion No. 390.

Concorde over Charles de Gaulle Airport — A634

Turbotrain T.G.V. 001 — A635

Phenix Nuclear Power Station — A636

1974   Engr.   Perf. 13
1391 A634 60c pur & ol gray .40 .30
1392 A635 60c multicolored .85 .40
1393 A636 65c multicolored .40 .30
   Nos. 1391-1393 (3) 1.65 1.00
French technical achievements.
Issued: No. 1391, 3/18; No. 1392, 8/31; 65c, 9/21.

Cardinal Richelieu, by Philippe de Champaigne A637

Painting by Joan Miró — A638

Canal du Loing, by Alfred Sisley A639

"In Honor of Nicolas Fouquet," Tapestry by Georges Mathieu — A640

Engr., Photo. (#1395, 1397)
1974   Perf. 12x13, 13x12
1394 A637 2fr multicolored 1.25 1.00
1395 A638 2fr multicolored 1.25 1.00
1396 A639 2fr multicolored 1.25 1.00
1397 A640 2fr multicolored 1.25 1.00
   Nos. 1394-1397 (4) 5.00 4.00
Nos. 1394-1397 are printed in sheets of 25 with alternating labels publicizing "ARPHILA 75," Paris, June 6-16, 1975.
Issued: No. 1394, 3/23; No. 1395, 9/14; No. 1396, 11/9; No. 1397, 11/16.
For surcharges see Reunion Nos. 391-394.

French Alps and Gentian — A641

1974, Mar. 30   Engr.   Perf. 13
1398 A641 65c vio blue & gray .40 .25
Centenary of the French Alpine Club.

Europa Issue 1974

"Age of Bronze," by Auguste Rodin A642

"Air," by Aristide Maillol A643

1974, Apr. 20   Perf. 13
1399 A642 50c brt rose lil & blk .30 .25
1400 A643 90c olive & brown .55 .40

Sea Rescue A644

1974, Apr. 27
1401 A644 90c multicolored .50 .30
Reorganized sea rescue organization.
For surcharge see Reunion No. 395.

Council Building, View of Strasbourg and Emblem A645

1974, May 4   Engr.   Perf. 13
1402 A645 45c indigo, bister & bl .30 .25
25th anniversary of the Council of Europe.

Tourist Issue

View of Salers A646

Basilica of St. Nicolas de Porte A647

Seashell over Corsica — A648

Design: 1.10fr, View of Lot Valley.

1974   Engr.   Perf. 13
1403 A646 65c yel grn & choc .25 .25
1404 A646 1.10fr choc & sl grn .45 .30
1405 A647 2fr gray & lilac .80 .35
1406 A648 3fr multicolored 1.00 .40
   Nos. 1403-1406 (4) 2.50 1.25
Issued: 65c, 6/22; 1.10fr, 9/7; 2fr, 10/12; 3fr, 5/11.

Bison — A649

Giant Armadillo of Guyana — A650

1974
1407 A649 40c bis, choc & bl .35 .25
1408 A650 65c slate, olive & grn .35 .25
Nature protection.
Issued: No. 1407, 5/25; No. 1408, 10/19.

Americans Landing in Normandy and Arms of Normandy A651

General Marie-Pierre Koenig — A652

Order of the French Resistance A653

1974
1409 A651 45c grn, rose & ind .80 .50
1410 A652 1fr multicolored .50 .35
1411 A653 1fr multicolored .65 .50
   Nos. 1409-1411 (3) 1.95 1.35
30th anniversary of the liberation of France from the Nazis. Design of No. 1410 includes diagram of battle of Bir-Hakeim and Free French and Bir-Hakeim memorials.
Issued: 45c, 6/8; No. 1410, 5/25; No. 1411, 11/23.
See No. B478.

FRANCE

Pfister House, 16th Century, Colmar — A654

1974, June 1
1412 A654 50c multicolored .25 .25
47th Congress of the Federation of French Philatelic Societies, Colmar, May 30-June 4.

Chess — A655

1974, June 8
1413 A655 1fr dk brown & multi .50 .30
21st Chess Olympiad, Nice, June 6-30.

Facade with Statue of Louis XIV, and 1675 Medal — A656

1974, June 15
1414 A656 40c indigo, bl & brn .30 .25
300th anniversary of the founding of the Hotel des Invalides (Home for poor and sick officers and soldiers).

Peacocks Holding Letter, and Globe A657

1974, Oct. 5 Engr. Perf. 13
1415 A657 1.20fr ultra, dp grn & dk car .50 .30
Centenary of Universal Postal Union.
For surcharge see Reunion No. 396.

Copernicus and Heliocentric System A658

1974, Oct. 12
1416 A658 1.20fr multicolored .50 .25
500th anniversary of the birth of Nicolaus Copernicus (1473-1543), Polish astronomer.

Tourist Issue

Palace of Justice, Rouen A659

Saint-Pol-de-Leon A660

Chateau de Rochechouart A661

1975 Engr. Perf. 13
1417 A659 85c multicolored .50 .30
1418 A660 1.20fr bl, bis & choc .50 .30
1419 A661 1.40fr brn, ind & grn .60 .30
Nos. 1417-1419 (3) 1.60 .90
Issued: 85c, 1/25; 1.20fr, 1/18; 1.40fr, 1/11.

Snowy Egret — A662

1975, Feb. 15 Engr. Perf. 13
1420 A662 70c brt blue & bister .40 .30
Nature protection.

Gallic Coin — A663

1975, Feb. 16 Typo. Perf. 13½x14
1421 A663 42c orange & mag .90 .45
1422 A663 48c lt bl & red brn 1.00 .70
1423 A663 70c brt pink & red 1.75 1.00
1424 A663 1.35fr lt green & brn 2.40 1.25
Nos. 1421-1424 (4) 6.05 3.40
Nos. 1421-1424 are known only precanceled. See second note after No. 132. See Nos. 1460-1463, 1487-1490.

The Eye — A664

Ionic Capital — A665

Graphic Art — A666

Ceres — A667

1975 Engr. Perf. 13
1425 A664 1fr red, pur & org .45 .30
1426 A665 2fr grn, sl grn & mag .80 .55
1427 A666 3fr dk car & ol grn 1.25 .90
1428 A667 4fr red, sl grn & bis 1.60 1.25
Nos. 1425-1428 (4) 4.10 3.00

Souvenir Sheet
1429 Sheet of 4 7.50 7.50
a. A664 2fr dp car & slate blue 1.00 1.00
b. A665 3fr brt bl, sl bl & dp car 1.40 1.40
c. A666 4fr slate blue, brt bl & plum 2.00 2.00
d. A667 6fr brt bl, sl bl & plum 2.50 2.50
ARPHILA 75, Intl. Philatelic Exhibition, Paris, 6/6-16. Issued: 1fr, 3/1; 2fr, 3/22; 3fr, 4/19; 4fr, 5/17; No. 1429, 4/2.

Pres. Georges Pompidou — A668

1975, Apr. 3 Engr. Perf. 13
1430 A668 80c black & gray .40 .25
Georges Pompidou (1911-74), President of France, 1969-74.

Paul as Harlequin, by Picasso — A669

Europa; 1.20fr, Woman on Balcony, by Kees van Dongen

1975, Apr. 26 Photo. Perf. 13
1431 A669 80c multi .45 .35
1432 A669 1.20fr multi, horiz. .80 .70

Machines, Globe, Emblem — A670

1975, May 3 Engr.
1433 A670 1.20fr blue, blk & red .50 .30
World Machine Tool Exhib., Paris, 6/7-26.

Senate Assembly Hall — A671

1975, May 24 Engr. Perf. 13
1434 A671 1.20fr olive & dk car .50 .30
Centenary of the Senate of the Republic.

Meter Convention Document, Atom Diagram and Waves A672

1975, May 31
1435 A672 1fr multicolored .50 .30
Cent. of Intl. Meter Convention, Paris, 1875.

Metro Regional Train — A673

"Gazelle" Helicopter — A674

1975
1436 A673 1fr blue & brt bl .55 .30
1437 A674 1.30fr vio bl & grn .60 .40
French technical achievements.
Issue dates: 1fr, June 21; 1.30fr, May 31.

Youth and Flasks, Symbols of Study and Growth — A675

1975, June 21
1438 A675 70c red pur & blk .30 .25
Student Health Foundation.

People's Theater, Bussang, and Maurice Pottecher — A676

1975, Aug. 9 Engr. Perf. 13
1439 A676 85c multicolored .35 .25
80th anniversary of the People's Theater at Bussang, founded by Maurice Pottecher.

Regions of France

Central France — A677

Aquitaine A678

Limousin A679

Picardy A680

Loire A682

Auvergne A684

Burgundy A681

Guyana A683

Poitou-Charentes A685

Southern Pyrenees — A686

Pas-de-Calais A687

1975-76 Engr. Perf. 13
1440 A677 25c blue & yel grn .25 .25
1441 A678 60c multicolored .25 .25
1442 A679 70c multicolored .50 .35
1443 A680 85c bl, grn & org .70 .35
1444 A681 1fr red, yel & mar .70 .35

640 FRANCE

1445	A682	1.15fr bl, bis & grn	.70	.35
1446	A683	1.25fr multicolored	.65	.50
1447	A684	1.30fr dk bl & red	.85	.50
1448	A685	1.90fr sl, ol & Prus bl	1.00	.50
1449	A686	2.20fr multicolored	1.10	1.00
1450	A687	2.80fr car, bl & blk	1.40	1.00
		Nos. 1440-1450 (11)	8.10	5.40

Issued: 85c, 11/15; 1fr, 10/25; 1.15fr, 9/6; 1.30fr, 10/4/75; 1.90fr, 12/6; 2.80fr, 12/13; 25c, 1/31/76; 2.20fr, 1/10/76; 60c, 5/22/76; 70c, 5/29/76; 1.25fr, 10/16/76.

A690

French Flag, F.-H. Manhes, Jean Verneau, Pierre Kaan

1975, Sept. 27
1453 A690 1fr multicolored .60 .30

Liberation of concentration camps, 30th anniversary. F.-H. Manhes (1889-1959), Jean Verneau (1890-1944) and Pierre Kaan (1903-1945) were French resistance leaders, imprisoned in concentration camps.

A691

Monument, by Joseph Riviere.

1975, Oct. 11
1454 A691 70c multicolored .45 .30

Land Mine Demolition Service, 30th anniversary. Monument was erected in Alsace to honor land mine victims.

Symbols of Suburban Living — A692

1975, Oct. 18
1455 A692 1.70fr brown, bl & grn .75 .50

Creation of new towns.

Women and Rainbow — A693

1975, Nov. 8 Photo.
1456 A693 1.20fr silver & multi .50 .40

International Women's Year 1975.

Saint-Nazaire Bridge — A694

1975, Nov. 8 Engr.
1457 A694 1.40fr bl, ind & grn .60 .30

French and Russian Flags — A695

1975, Nov. 22
1458 A695 1.20fr bl, red & ocher .50 .30

Franco-Soviet diplomatic relations, 50th anniv.

Frigate Melpomene — A696

1975, Dec. 6
1459 A696 90c multicolored 1.00 .50

Gallic Coin Type of 1975

1976, Jan. 1		Typo.	Perf. 13½x14	
1460	A663	50c lt green & brn	1.00	.65
1461	A663	60c lilac & brn	1.60	.95
1462	A663	90c orange & brn	2.00	1.25
1463	A663	1.60fr violet & brn	3.75	1.90
		Nos. 1460-1463 (4)	8.35	4.75

Nos. 1460-1463 are known only precanceled. See second note after No. 132.

Lintel, St. Genis des Fontaines Church — A697

Venus of Brassempouy (Paleolithic) A698

"The Joy of Life," by Robert Delaunay — A699

Ramses II, from Abu Simbel Temple, Egypt A700

Still Life, by Maurice de Vlaminck A701

1976		Engr.	Perf. 13	
1464	A697	2fr blue & slate bl	1.10	.60
1465	A698	2fr dk brn & yel	1.10	.60
		Photo.	Perf. 12½x13	
1466	A699	2fr multicolored	1.10	.60
		Engr.	Perf. 13x12½	
1467	A700	2fr multicolored	.80	.50
		Perf. 13		
1468	A701	2fr multicolored	.80	.50
		Nos. 1464-1468 (5)	4.90	2.80

Issued: No. 1464, 1/24; No. 1465, 3/6; No. 1466, 7/24; No. 1467, 9/4; No. 1468, 12/18.

Tourist Issue

Chateau Fort de Bonaguil A702 — Lodève Cathedral A703

Biarritz A704 — Thiers A705

Ussel A706 — Chateau de Malmaison A707

1976		Engr.	Perf. 13	
1469	A702	1fr multicolored	.35	.25
1470	A703	1.10fr violet blue	.40	.25
1471	A704	1.40fr multicolored	.60	.25
1472	A705	1.70fr multicolored	.60	.25
1473	A706	2fr multicolored	.90	.25
1474	A707	3fr multicolored	1.10	.25
		Nos. 1469-1474 (6)	3.95	1.50

Issued: 1fr, 2fr, 7/10; 1.10fr, 11/13; 1.40fr, 9/25; 1.70fr, 10/9; 3fr, 4/10.

Destroyers, Association Emblem — A708

1976, Apr. 24
1475 A708 1fr vio bl, mag & lem .50 .30

Naval Reserve Officers Assoc., 50th anniv.

Gate, Rouen — A709

1976, Apr. 24
1476 A709 80c olive gray & sal .35 .25

49th Congress of the Federation of French Philatelic Societies, Rouen, Apr. 23-May 2.

Young Person — A710

1976, Apr. 27
1477 A710 60c bl grn, ind & car .35 .25

JUVAROUEN 76, International Youth Philatelic Exhibition, Rouen, Apr. 25-May 2.

Europa Issue

Ceramic Pitcher, Strasbourg, 18th Century — A711

1.20fr, Sevres porcelain plate & CEPT emblem.

1976, May 8		Photo.	Perf. 13	
1478	A711	80c multicolored	.30	.30
1479	A711	1.20fr multicolored	.65	.55

Count de Vergennes and Benjamin Franklin A712

1976, May 15 Engr. Perf. 13
1480 A712 1.20fr multicolored .50 .30

American Bicentennial.

Battle of Verdun Memorial — A713

1976, June 12 Engr.
1481 A713 1fr multicolored .45 .25

Battle of Verdun, 60th anniversary.

Communication — A714

1976, June 12 Photo.
1482 A714 1.20fr multicolored .50 .40

Troncais Forest — A715

1976, June 19 Engr.
1483 A715 70c green & multi .35 .25

Protection of the environment.

FRANCE

Cross of Lorraine — A716

1976, June 19
1484 A716 1fr multicolored .50 .25
Association of Free French, 30th anniv.

Symphonie Communications Satellite — A717

1976, June 26 Photo.
1485 A717 1.40fr multicolored .65 .50

Gallic Coin Type of 1975

1976, July 1 Typo. *Perf. 13½x14*
1487 A663 52c ver & dk brn .40 .30
1488 A663 62c vio & dk brn 1.00 .70
1489 A663 95c tan & dk brn 1.00 .90
1490 A663 1.70fr dk bl & dk brn 2.75 1.40
  Nos. 1487-1490 (4) 5.15 3.30

Nos. 1487-1490 are known only precanceled. See second note after No. 132.

Paris Summer Festival — A719

1976, July 10 Engr.
1491 A719 1fr multicolored .50 .30
Summer festival in Tuileries Gardens, Paris.

Emblem and Soldiers — A720

1976, July 8
1492 A720 1fr blk, dp bl & mag .50 .25
Officers Reserve Corps, centenary.

Sailing — A721

1976, July 17
1493 A721 1.20fr blue, blk & vio .50 .25
21st Olympic Games, Montreal, Canada, July 17-Aug. 1.

Marianne Type of 1971-74

1976 Typo. *Perf. 14x13*
1494 A555 80c green .40 .25

  Engr. *Perf. 13*
1495 A555 80c green 1.25 .50
  a. Booklet pane of 10 15.00
1496 A555 1fr carmine rose .50 .25
  a. Booklet pane of 5 4.00
  b. Booklet pane of 10 9.00
  Nos. 1495-1496 (2) 1.75 .75

No. 1495 issued in booklets only. "POSTES" 6mm long on Nos. 1292A and 1494; 4mm on others.
Nos. 1494, 1496 were issued untagged in 1977.

Coil Stamps

1976, Aug. 1 Engr. *Perf. 13 Horiz.*
1497 A555 80c green .80 .55
1498 A555 1fr carmine rose .80 .55

Red control number on back of every 10th stamp.

Woman's Head, by Jean Carzou A722

1976, Sept. 18 Engr. *Perf. 13x12½*
1499 A722 2fr multicolored .90 .65

Old and New Telephones A723

1976, Sept. 25 Engr. *Perf. 13*
1500 A723 1fr multicolored .50 .25
Centenary of first telephone call by Alexander Graham Bell, Mar. 10, 1876.

Festival Emblem and Trophy, Pyrenees, Hercules and Pyrène — A724

1976, Oct. 2
1501 A724 1.40fr multicolored .65 .40
10th Intl. Tourist Film Festival, Tarbes, 10/4-10.

Police Emblem — A725

1976, Oct. 9 Engr. *Perf. 13*
1502 A725 1.10fr ultra, red & ol .50 .30
National Police, help and protection.

Atomic Particle Accelerator, Diagram — A726

1976, Oct. 22 Photo.
1503 A726 1.40fr multicolored .75 .45
European Center for Nuclear Research (CERN).

"Exhibitions" — A727

1976, Nov. 20 Engr. *Perf. 13*
1504 A727 1.50fr multicolored .75 .50

Trade Fairs and Exhibitions

Abstract Design — A728

1976, Nov. 27 Photo.
1505 A728 1.10fr multicolored .50 .30
Customs Service.

Atlantic Museum, Port Louis A729

1976, Dec. 4 Engr.
1506 A729 1.45fr grnsh bl & olive .60 .50

Regions of France

Réunion A730

Martinique A731

Franche-Comté A732

Brittany A733

Languedoc-Roussillon A734

Rhône-Alps A735

Champagne-Ardennes A736

Alsace A737

Photo. (1.45fr, 1.50fr, 2.50fr); Engr.
1977 *Perf. 13*
1507 A730 1.45fr grn & lil rose .65 .40
1508 A731 1.50fr multicolored .65 .60
1509 A732 2.10fr multicolored .90 .65
1510 A733 2.40fr multicolored 1.10 .35
1511 A734 2.50fr multicolored 1.10 .85
1512 A735 2.75fr Prus blue 1.40 .90
1513 A736 3.20fr multicolored 1.40 .80
1514 A737 3.90fr multicolored 2.50 1.50
  Nos. 1507-1514 (8) 9.70 5.95

Issued: 1.45fr, 2/5; 1.50fr, 1/29; 2.10fr, 1/8; 2.40fr, 2/19; 2.50fr, 1/15; 2.75fr, 1/22; 3.20fr, 4/16; 3.90fr, 2/26.

Pompidou Cultural Center A738

1977, Feb. 5 Engr. *Perf. 13*
1515 A738 1fr multicolored .35 .25
Inauguration of the Georges Pompidou National Center for Art and Culture, Paris.

Dunkirk Harbor — A739

1977, Feb. 12
1516 A739 50c multicolored .25 .25
Expansion of Dunkirk harbor facilities.

Bridge at Mantes, by Corot A740

Virgin and Child, by Rubens — A741

Tridimensional Design, by Victor Vasarely — A742

Head and Eagle, by Pierre-Yves Tremois — A743

1977 Engr. *Perf. 13x12½*
1517 A740 2fr multicolored .95 .75
  Perf. 12x13
1518 A741 2fr multicolored 1.10 .75
  Perf. 12½x13
1519 A742 3fr sl grn & pale lil 1.25 .75
  Photo.
1520 A743 3fr dark red & blk 1.40 1.25
  Nos. 1517-1520 (4) 4.70 3.50

Issue dates: No. 1517, Feb. 12; No. 1518, Nov. 5; No. 1519, Apr. 7; No. 1520, Sept. 17.

Hand Holding Torch and Sword — A744

1977, Mar. 5 Engr. *Perf. 13*
1521 A744 80c ultra & multi .45 .30
"France remembers its dead."

Pisces — A745

Zodiac Signs: 58c, Cancer. 61c, Sagittarius. 68c, Taurus. 73c, Aries. 78c, Libra. 1.05fr, Scorpio. 1.15fr, Capricorn. 1.05fr, Leo. 1.05fr, Aquarius. 2fr, Virgo. 2.10fr, Gemini.

1977-78 Engr. *Perf. 13*
1522 A745 54c violet blue .65 .30
1523 A745 58c emerald 1.00 .40
1524 A745 61c brt blue .55 .30
1525 A745 68c deep brown .85 .35
1526 A745 73c rose carmine 1.50 .80
1527 A745 78c vermilion .65 .35
1528 A745 1.05fr brt lilac 1.50 .75
1529 A745 1.15fr orange 2.25 1.40
1530 A745 1.25fr lt olive grn 1.25 .60
1531 A745 1.85fr slate grn 2.75 1.25
1532 A745 2fr blue green 3.00 1.75
1533 A745 2.10fr lilac rose 1.65 1.00
  Nos. 1522-1533 (12) 17.60 9.25

Issued: 54c, 68c, 1.05fr, 1.85fr, 4/1/77; others, 1978.

FRANCE

Nos. 1522-1533 are known only precanceled. See second note after No. 132.

Village in Provence — A746

Europa: 1.40fr, Brittany port.

1977, Apr. 23
| 1534 | A746 | 1fr multicolored | .45 | .25 |
| 1535 | A746 | 1.40fr multicolored | 1.00 | .35 |

Flowers and Gardening A747

1977, Apr. 23 Engr. Perf. 13
1536 A747 1.70fr multicolored .80 .50

National Horticulture Society, centenary.

Symbolic Flower — A748

1977, May 7
1537 A748 1.40fr multicolored .65 .40

Intl. Flower Show, Nantes, May 12-23.

Battle of Cambray — A749

1977, May 14
1538 A749 80c multicolored .40 .30

Capture of Cambray and the incorporation of Cambresis District into France, 300th anniv.

Carmes Church, School, Map of France — A750

1977, May 14
1539 A750 1.10fr multicolored .50 .30

Catholic Institutes in France.

Modern Constructions — A751

1977, May 21
1540 A751 1.10fr multicolored .50 .30

European Federation of the Construction Industry.

Annecy Castle — A752

1977, May 28
1541 A752 1fr multicolored .50 .30

Congress of the Federation of French Philatelic Societies, Annecy, May 28-30.

Tourist Issue

Abbey, Pont-à-Mousson A753

Abbey Tower, Saint-Amand-les-Eaux A754

Collegiate Church of Dorat A755

Fontenay Abbey A756

Bayeux Cathedral A757

Chateau de Vitré A758

1977 Engr. Perf. 13
1542	A753	1.25fr multicolored	.50	.30
1543	A754	1.40fr multicolored	.50	.30
1544	A755	1.45fr multicolored	.55	.35
1545	A756	1.50fr multicolored	.55	.30
1546	A757	1.90fr black & yel	.75	.30
1547	A758	2.40fr black & yel	.80	.30
		Nos. 1542-1547 (6)	3.65	1.80

Issued: 1.25fr, 10/1; 1.40fr, 9/17; 1.45fr, 7/16; 1.50fr, 6/4; 1.90fr, 7/9; 2.40fr, 9/24.

Polytechnic School and "X" — A759

1977, June 4 Engr. Perf. 13
1548 A759 1.70fr multicolored .70 .30

Relocation at Palaiseau of Polytechnic School, founded 1794.

Soccer and Cup A760

1977, June 11
1549 A760 80c multicolored .60 .40

Soccer Cup of France, 60th anniversary.

De Gaulle Memorial — A761

Photo. & Embossed

1977, June 18
1550 A761 1fr gold & multi 1.00 .40

5th anniversary of dedication of De Gaulle memorial at Colombey-les-Deux-Eglises.
A €1.16 stamp of type A761 was included in a limited-edition booklet issued Nov. 4, 2020.

Stylized Map of France — A762

1977, June 18 Engr. Perf. 13
1551 A762 1.10fr ultra & red .50 .30

French Junior Chamber of Commerce.

Battle of Nancy — A763

1977, June 25
1552 A763 1.10fr blue & slate .60 .40

Battle of Nancy between the Dukes of Burgundy and Lorraine, 500th anniversary.

Arms of Burgundy — A764

1977, July 2
1553 A764 1.25fr ol brn & slate grn .55 .25

Annexation of Burgundy by the French Crown, 500th anniversary.

Association Emblem — A765

1977, July 8
1554 A765 1.40fr ultra, olive & red .65 .25

French-speaking Parliamentary Association.

Red Cicada — A766

1977, Sept. 10 Photo. Perf. 13
1555 A766 80c multicolored .40 .30

Nature protection.

French Handicrafts A767

1977, Oct. 1 Engr. Perf. 13
1556 A767 1.40fr multicolored .40 .45

French craftsmen.

Industry and Agriculture — A768

1977, Oct. 22
1557 A768 80c brown & olive .30 .25

Economic & Social Council, 30th anniv.

Table Tennis — A769

1977, Dec. 17 Engr. Perf. 13
1558 A769 1.10fr multicolored 1.25 .75

French Table Tennis Federation, 50th anniv., and French team, gold medal winner, Birmingham.

Abstract, by Roger Excoffon A770

1977, Dec. 17 Perf. 13x12½
1559 A770 3fr multicolored 1.40 1.00

Sabine, after David — A771

1977-78 Engr. Perf. 13
1560	A771	1c slate	.25	.25
1561	A771	2c brt violet	.25	.25
1562	A771	5c slate green	.25	.25
1563	A771	10c red brown	.25	.25
1564	A771	15c Prus blue	.25	.25
1565	A771	20c brt green	.25	.25
1566	A771	30c orange	.25	.25
1567	A771	50c red lilac	.25	.25
1568	A771	80c green	.50	.25
a.		Booklet pane of 10	10.00	
1569	A771	80c olive	.50	.25
1570	A771	1fr red	.60	.25
a.		Booklet pane of 5	7.00	
b.		Booklet pane of 10	10.00	
1571	A771	1fr green	.50	.25
a.		Booklet pane of 5	7.00	
1572	A771	1.20fr red	.55	.25
a.		Booklet pane of 5	5.00	
b.		Booklet pane of 10	8.50	
1573	A771	1.40fr brt blue	1.00	.25
1574	A771	1.70fr grnsh blue	.75	.25
1575	A771	2fr emerald	.90	.25
1576	A771	2.10fr lilac rose	1.00	.25
1577	A771	3fr dark brown	1.25	.25
		Nos. 1560-1577 (18)	9.55	4.50

Issued: Nos. 1560-1567, 1573, 1575, 1577, 4/3/78; Nos. 1568, 1570, 12/19/77; Nos. 1569, 1571, 1572, 1574, 1576, 6/5/78.

Coil Stamps

1978 Perf. 13 Horiz.
1578	A771	80c bright green	1.10	.90
1579	A771	1fr bright green	1.50	.90
1579A	A771	1fr bright red	1.10	.90
1579B	A771	1.20fr bright red	1.10	.90
		Nos. 1578-1579B (4)	4.80	3.60

See Nos. 1658-1677, 3527, 4410g, 4520, 5336-5343.
For similar design inscribed "REPUBLIQUE FRANCAISE" see type A900.

Percheron, by Jacques Birr A772

Osprey A773

FRANCE

1978 Photo. Perf. 13
1580 A772 1.70fr multicolored 1.00 .80
Engr.
1581 A773 1.80fr multicolored .90 .50
Nature protection.
Issue dates: 1.70fr, Jan. 7; 1.80fr, Oct. 14.

Tournament, 1662, Etching — A774

Institut de France and Pont des Arts, Paris, by Bernard Buffet A776

Horses, by Yves Brayer A777

1978 Engr. Perf. 12x13
1582 A774 2fr black 1.00 .80
Perf. 13x12
1584 A776 3fr multicolored 1.40 1.25
1585 A777 3fr multicolored 1.40 1.25
Nos. 1582-1585 (3) 3.80 3.30
Issued: 2fr, 1/14; No. 1584, 2/4; No. 1585, 12/9.

Communications School and Tower — A778

1978, Jan. 19 Engr. Perf. 13
1586 A778 80c Prussian blue .40 .25
Natl. Telecommunications School, cent.

Swedish and French Flags, Map of Saint Barthelemy A779

1978, Jan. 19
1587 A779 1.10fr multicolored .55 .25
Centenary of the reunion with France of Saint Barthelemy Island, West Indies.

Regions of France

Ile de France A780
Tanker, Refinery, Flower, Upper Normandy A781

Lower Normandy A782

1978 Photo. Perf. 13
1588 A780 1fr red, blue & blk .45 .25
Engr.
1589 A781 1.40fr multicolored .60 .30
Photo.
1590 A782 1.70fr multicolored .80 .30
Nos. 1588-1590 (3) 1.85 .85
Issued: 1fr, 3/4; 1.40fr, 1/21; 1.70fr, 3/31.

Stylized Map of France — A788

1978, Feb. 11 Engr. Perf. 13
1596 A788 1.10fr dp ultra & green .45 .25
Program of administrative changes, 15th anniv.

Young Stamp Collector — A789

1978, Feb. 25
1597 A789 80c multicolored .35 .25
JUVEXNIORT, Youth Philatelic Exhibition, Niort, Feb. 25-March 5.

Tourist Issue

Verdon Gorge A790

Saint-Saturnin Church A792

Pont Neuf, Paris — A791

Our Lady of Bec-Hellouin Abbey — A793

Chateau D'Esquelbecq A794

Aubazine Abbey — A795

Fontevraud Abbey — A796

1978 Engr. Perf. 13
1598 A790 50c multicolored .25 .25
1599 A791 80c multicolored .35 .25
1600 A792 1fr black .45 .25
1601 A793 1.10fr multicolored .50 .25
1602 A794 1.10fr multicolored .50 .25
1603 A795 1.25fr carmine & brn .60 .30
1604 A796 1.70fr multicolored .80 .30
Nos. 1598-1604 (7) 3.45 1.85
Issued: 1.25fr, 2/18; 50c, 3/6; No. 1601, 3/26; 80c, 5/27; 1fr, 6/10; 1.70fr, 6/3; No. 1602, 6/17.

See No. 5035b.

Fish and Corals — A797

1978, Apr. 15 Photo. Perf. 13
1605 A797 1.25fr multicolored .80 .70
Port Cros National Park, 15th anniversary.

Flowers, Butterflies and Houses — A798

1978, Apr. 22 Engr. Perf. 13
1606 A798 1.70fr multicolored 1.25 .50
Beautification of France campaign, 50th anniv.

Hands Shielding Source of Heat and Light — A799

1978, Apr. 22
1607 A799 1fr multicolored .50 .25
Energy conservation.

World War I Memorial near Lens — A800

1978, May 6
1608 A800 2fr lemon & magenta .50 .30
Colline Notre Dame de Lorette memorial of World War I.

Fountain of the Innocents, Paris — A801

Europa: 1.40fr, Flower Park Fountain, Paris.

1978, May 6
1609 A801 1fr multicolored .40 .25
1610 A801 1.40fr multicolored .75 .30

Maurois Palace, Troyes — A802

1978, May 13
1611 A802 1fr multicolored .45 .25
51st Congress of the Federation of French Philatelic Societies, Troyes, May 13-15.

Roland Garros Tennis Court and Player A803

1978, May 27
1612 A803 1fr multicolored 1.00 .40
Roland Garros Tennis Court, 50th anniv.

Hand and Plant — A804

1978, Sept. 9 Engr. Perf. 13
1613 A804 1.30fr brown, red & grn .50 .25
Encouragement of handicrafts.

Printing Office Emblem — A805

1978, Sept. 23
1614 A805 1fr multicolored .50 .25
National Printing Office, established 1538.

Fortress, Besançon, and Collegiate Church, Dole A806

Valenciennes and Maubeuge A807

1978
1615 A806 1.20fr multicolored .55 .25
1616 A807 1.20fr multicolored .55 .25
Reunion of Franche-Comté and Valenciennes and Maubeuge with France, 300th anniversary.
Issued: No. 1615, 9/23; No. 1616, 9/30.

Sower Type of 1906-1937 and Academy Emblem — A808

1978, Oct. 7
1617 A808 1fr multicolored .40 .30
Academy of Philately, 50th anniversary.

Gymnasts, Strasbourg Cathedral, Storks — A809

1978, Oct. 21
1618 A809 1fr multicolored .50 .30
19th World Gymnastics Championships, Strasbourg, Oct. 23-26.

FRANCE

Various Sports — A810

1978, Oct. 21
1619 A810 1fr multicolored .50 .30
Sports for all.

Polish Veterans' Monument — A811

1978, Nov. 11
1620 A811 1.70fr multicolored .75 .45
Polish veterans of World War II.

Railroad Car and Monument, Compiègne Forest, Rethondes A812

1978, Nov. 11 Engr. Perf. 13
1621 A812 1.20fr indigo .60 .30
60th anniversary of World War I armistice.

Handicapped People — A813

1978, Nov. 18
1622 A813 1fr multicolored .45 .25
Rehabilitation of the handicapped.

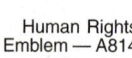
Human Rights Emblem — A814

1978, Dec. 9 Engr. Perf. 13
1623 A814 1.70fr dk brown & blue .80 .40
30th anniversary of Universal Declaration of Human Rights.

Child and IYC Emblem — A815

1979, Jan. 6 Engr. Perf. 13
1624 A815 1.70fr multicolored 1.25 .80
International Year of the Child.

"Music," 15th Century Miniature A816

1979, Jan. 13 Perf. 13x12½
1625 A816 2fr multicolored 1.00 .80

Diana Taking a Bath, d'Ecouen Castle — A817

Church at Auvers-on-Oise, by Vincent Van Gogh — A818

Head of Marianne, by Salvador Dali — A819

Fire Dancer from The Magic Flute, by Chaplain Midy — A820

1979		Photo.	Perf. 12½x13
1626	A817	2fr multicolored	1.00 .80
1627	A818	2fr multicolored	1.50 .80
1628	A819	3fr multicolored	1.50 1.00
1629	A820	3fr multicolored	1.50 1.00
		Nos. 1626-1629 (4)	5.50 3.60

Issued: No. 1626, 9/22; No. 1627, 10/27; No. 1628, 11/19; No. 1629, 11/26.

Orange Agaric — A821

Mushrooms: 83c, Death trumpet. 1.30fr, Olive wood pleurotus. 2.25fr, Cauliflower claveria.

1979, Jan. 15 Engr. Perf. 13
1630	A821	64c orange	.40 .25
1631	A821	83c brown	.40 .25
1632	A821	1.30fr yellow bister	.85 .40
1633	A821	2.25fr brown purple	1.25 .85
		Nos. 1630-1633 (4)	2.90 1.75

Nos. 1630-1633 are known only precanceled. See second note after No. 132.

Victor Segalen — A822

1979, Jan. 20
1634 A822 1.50fr multicolored .60 .30
Physician, explorer and writer (1878-1919).

Hibiscus and Palms — A823

1979, Feb. 3
1635 A823 35c multicolored .25 .25
International Flower Festival, Martinique.

Buddha, Stupas, Temple of Borobudur A824

1979, Feb. 24
1636 A824 1.80fr ol & slate grn .85 .40
Save the Temple of Borobudur, Java, campaign.

Boy, by Francisque Poulbot (1879-1946) — A825

1979, Mar. 24 Photo.
1637 A825 1.30fr multicolored .60 .25

Tourist Issue

Chateau de Maisons, Laffitte A826

Bernay and St. Pierre sur Dives Abbeys A827

View of Auray A827a

Steenvorde Windmill A828

Wall Painting, Niaux Cave — A829

Royal Palace, Perpignan A830

1979		Engr.	Perf. 13
1638	A826	45c multicolored	.45 .25
1639	A827	1fr multicolored	.45 .25
1640	A827a	1fr multicolored	.55 .25
1641	A828	1.20fr multicolored	.65 .25
1642	A829	1.50fr multicolored	.70 .40
1643	A830	1.70fr multicolored	.75 .60
		Nos. 1638-1643 (6)	3.55 2.00

Issued: 45c, 10/6; No. 1639, 6/16; No. 1640, 6/30; 1.20fr, 6/12; 1.50fr, 7/9; 1.70fr, 4/21.

Honey Bee — A831

1979, Mar. 31 Engr. Perf. 13
1644 A831 1fr multicolored .50 .30
Nature protection.

St. Germain des Prés Abbey — A832

1979, Apr. 21
1645 A832 1.40fr multicolored .60 .30

Simoun Mail Monoplanes, 1935, and Map of Mail Routes — A833

Europa: 1.70fr, Floating spheres used on Seine during siege of Paris, 1870.

1979, Apr. 28
1646 A833 1.20fr multicolored .75 .35
1647 A833 1.70fr multicolored 1.00 .50

Ship and View of Nantes — A834

1979, May 5 Engr. Perf. 13
1648 A834 1.20fr multicolored .55 .30
52nd National Congress of French Philatelic Societies, Nantes, May 5-7.

Royal Palace, 1789 — A835

1979, May 19
1649 A835 1fr car rose & pur .45 .25

European Elections — A836

1979, May 19 Photo. Perf. 13
1650 A836 1.20fr multicolored .55 .25
European Parliament, 1st direct elections, June 10.

Joan of Arc Monument A837

1979, May 24 Engr.
1651 A837 1.70fr brt lilac rose .70 .40
Joan of Arc, the Maid of Orleans (1412-1431).

Felix Guyon and Catheters — A840

1979, June 23
1652 A840 1.80fr sepia & blue .80 .35
Felix Guyon (1831-1920), urologist.

FRANCE

Lantern Tower, La Rochelle — A841

Towers: 88c, Chartres Cathedral. 1.40fr, Bourges Cathedral. 2.35fr, Amiens Cathedral.

1979, Aug. 13		Engr.	Perf. 13	
1653	A841	68c vio brn & blk	.35	.25
1654	A841	88c ultra & blk	.40	.25
1655	A841	1.40fr gray grn & blk	.65	.50
1656	A841	2.35fr dull brn & blk	1.10	.60
	Nos. 1653-1656 (4)		2.50	1.60

Nos. 1653-1656 are known only precanceled. See second note after No. 132. See Nos. 1684-1687, 1719-1722, 1814-1817.

Telecom '79 — A842

1979, Sept. 22				
1657	A842	1.10fr multicolored	.45	.25

3rd World Telecommunications Exhibition.

Sabine Type of 1977-78

1979-81		Engr.	Perf. 13	
1658	A771	40c brown ('81)	.25	.25
1659	A771	60c red brn ('81)	.25	.25
1660	A771	70c violet blue	.35	.25
1661	A771	90c brt lilac ('81)	.45	.30
1662	A771	1fr gray olive	.45	.25
1663	A771	1.10fr green	.50	.25
1664	A771	1.20fr green ('80)	.40	.25
1665	A771	1.30fr rose red	.55	.25
1666	A771	1.40fr rose red ('80)	.60	.25
1667	A771	1.60fr purple	.75	.30
1668	A771	1.80fr ocher	.80	.50
1669	A771	3.50fr lt ol grn ('81)	1.40	.60
1670	A771	4fr brt car ('81)	1.60	.40
1671	A771	5fr brt grnsh bl ('81)	2.00	.30
	Nos. 1658-1671 (14)		10.35	4.40

Coil Stamps

1979-80		Perf. 13 Horiz.		
1674	A771	1.10fr green	1.25	.60
1675	A771	1.20fr green ('80)	.70	.50
1676	A771	1.30fr rose red	1.25	.60
1677	A771	1.40fr rose red ('80)	.45	.40
	Nos. 1674-1677 (4)		3.65	2.10

Lorraine Region — A845

1979, Nov. 10				
1678	A845	2.30fr multicolored	1.00	.30

Gears — A847

1979, Nov. 17		Perf. 13		
1680	A847	1.80fr multicolored	.90	.70

Central Technical School of Paris, 150th anniv.

Judo Throw — A848

1979, Nov. 24		Engr.		
1681	A848	1.60fr multicolored	.75	.40

World Judo Championships, Paris, Dec.

Violins — A849

1979, Dec. 10				
1682	A849	1.30fr multicolored	.60	.35

Eurovision A850

1980, Jan. 12		Engr.	Perf. 13x13½	
1683	A850	1.80fr multicolored	.90	.70

Tower Type of 1979

Designs: 76c, Chateau d'Angers. 99c, Chateau de Kerjean. 1.60fr, Chateau de Pierrefonds. 2.65fr, Chateau de Tarascon.

1980, Jan. 21		Engr.		
1684	A841	76c grnsh bl & blk	.35	.30
1685	A841	99c slate grn & blk	.45	.30
1686	A841	1.60fr red & blk	.75	.55
1687	A841	2.65fr brn org & blk	1.25	.65
	Nos. 1684-1687 (4)		2.80	1.80

Nos. 1684-1687 are known only precanceled. See second note after No. 132.

Self-portrait, by Albrecht Dürer, Philexfrance '82 Emblem — A051

Woman Holding Fan, by Ossip Zadkine — A852

Abstract, by Raoul Ubak — A853

Hommage to J.S. Bach, by Jean Picart Le Doux — A854

Peasant, by Louis Le Nain — A855

Woman with Blue Eyes, by Modigliani A856

Abstract, by Hans Hartung — A857

Engraved, Photogravure (#1691, 1694)

1980		Perf. 12½x13, 13x12½		
1688	A851	2fr multicolored	1.00	.80
1689	A852	3fr multicolored	1.40	1.00
1690	A853	3fr multicolored	1.40	1.00
1691	A854	3fr multicolored	1.40	1.00
1692	A855	3fr multicolored	1.40	1.00
1693	A856	4fr multicolored	1.75	1.25
1694	A857	4fr ultra & black	1.75	1.25
	Nos. 1688-1694 (7)		10.10	7.30

Issued: No. 1688, 6/7; No. 1689, 1/19; No. 1690, 2/2; No. 1691, 9/20; No. 1693, 10/26; No. 1692, 11/10; No. 1694, 12/20.

Giants of the North Festival — A858

1980, Feb. 16			Perf. 13	
1695	A858	1.60fr multicolored	.75	.30

French Cuisine — A859

1980, Feb. 23				
1696	A859	90c red & lt brown	.60	.40

Woman Embroidering — A860

Photogravure and Engraved

1980, Mar. 29			Perf. 13	
1697	A860	1.10fr multicolored	.50	.30

Fight Against Cigarette Smoking — A861

1980, Apr. 5		Photo.	Perf. 13	
1698	A861	1.30fr multicolored	.50	.25

Aristide Briand — A862

Europa: 1.80fr, St. Benedict.

1980, Apr. 26		Engr.	Perf. 13	
1699	A862	1.30fr multicolored	.60	.30
1700	A862	1.80fr red & red brown	.85	.50

Aristide Briand (1862-1932), prime minister, 1909-1911, 1921-1922; St. Benedict, patron saint of Europe.

Liancourt, College, Map of Northwestern France — A863

1980, May 19		Engr.	Perf. 13	
1701	A863	2fr dk green & pur	.80	.30

National College of Arts and Handicrafts (founded by Larochefoucauld Liancourt) bicentenary.

Cranes, Town Hall Tower, Dunkirk — A864

1980, May 24				
1702	A864	1.30fr multicolored	.60	.25

53rd Natl. Congress of French Federation of Philatelic Societies, Dunkirk, May 24-26.

Tourist Issue

Chateau de Maintenon A866

Cordes A865

Montauban A867

St. Peter's Abbey, Solesmes A868

Puy Cathedral — A869

1980		Engr.	Perf. 13	
1703	A865	1.50fr multicolored	.55	.30
1704	A866	2fr multicolored	.80	.30
1705	A867	2.30fr multicolored	1.00	.30
1706	A868	2.50fr multicolored	1.25	.30
1707	A869	3.20fr multicolored	1.40	.50
	Nos. 1703-1707 (5)		5.00	1.70

Issued: No. 1703, 4/5; No. 1704, 6/7; No. 1705, 5/7; No. 1706, 9/20; No. 1707, 5/12.

FRANCE

Graellsia
Isabellae — A870

1980, May 31   Photo.
1708 A870 1.10fr multicolored   .70   .30

Association
Emblem — A871

1980, June 10   Photo.
1709 A871 1.30fr red & blue   .55   .25
Intl. Public Relations Assoc., 25th anniv.

Marianne, French
Architecture
A872

1980, June 21   Engr.
1710 A872 1.50fr bluish & gray blk   .70   .30
Heritage Year.

Earth
Sciences — A873

1980, July 5
1711 A873 1.60fr dk brown & red   .70   .50
International Geological Congress.

Rochambeau's
Landing — A874

1980, July 15
1712 A874 2.50fr multicolored   1.10   .50
Rochambeau's landing at Newport, R.I. (American Revolution), bicentenary.

Message of
Peace, by
Yaacov
Agam — A875

1980, Oct. 4   Photo.   Perf. 11½x13
1713 A875 4fr multicolored   1.75   1.00

French Golf
Federation
A876

1980, Oct. 18   Engr.
1714 A876 1.40fr multicolored   .60   .30

Comedie
Francaise, 300th
Anniversary
A877

1980, Oct. 18
1715 A877 2fr multicolored   .75   .40

Charles de
Gaulle
A878

1980, Nov. 10   Photo.   Perf. 13
1716 A878 1.40fr multicolored   .90   .50
40th anniversary of De Gaulle's appeal of June 18, and 10th anniversary of his death.

Guardsman — A879

1980, Nov. 24   Engr.   Perf. 13
1717 A879 1.70fr multicolored   .80   .45

Rambouillet
Chateau — A880

1980, Dec. 6   Engr.   Perf. 13
1718 A880 2.20fr multicolored   1.00   .35

Tower Type of 1979

Designs: 88c, Imperial Chapel, Ajaccio. 1.14fr, Astronomical Clock, Besancon. 1.84fr, Coucy Castle ruins. 3.05fr, Font-de-Gaume cave drawing, Les Eyzies de Tayac.

1981, Jan. 11   Engr.   Perf. 13
1719 A841   88c dp mag & blk   .40   .25
1720 A841 1.14fr ultra & blk   .55   .30
1721 A841 1.84fr dk green & blk   .85   .50
1722 A841 3.05fr brn red & blk   1.40   .80
     Nos. 1719-1722 (4)   3.20   1.85

Nos. 1719-1722 are known only precanceled. See second note after No. 132.

Microelectronics
A881

1981   Photo.
1723 A881 1.20fr shown   .55   .30
1724 A881 1.20fr Biology   .55   .30
1725 A881 1.40fr Energy   .65   .30
1726 A881 1.80fr Marine exploration   .85   .50
1727 A881 2fr Telemetry   .90   .65
     Nos. 1723-1727 (5)   3.50   2.05
Issue dates: No. 1723, 2/5; others, 3/28.

Abstract, by
Albert
Gleizes — A882

1981, Feb. 28   Perf. 12½x13
1728 A882 4fr multicolored   1.75   .90

The
Footpath by
Camille
Pissaro
A883

1981, Apr. 18   Engr.   Perf. 13x12½
1729 A883 2fr multicolored   1.00   .80

Child Watering Smiling
Map of France — A884

1981, Mar. 14   Engr.   Perf. 13
1730 A884 1.40fr multicolored   .65   .25

Sully Chateau,
Rosny-sur-Seine
A885

1981, Mar. 21
1731 A885 2.50fr multicolored   1.10   .40

Tourist Issue

Roman Temple,
Nimes — A886

1981, Apr. 11   Engr.   Perf. 13
1732 A886 1.70fr multicolored   .85   .30

Church of   St. Anne
St. Jean,   d'Auray
Lyon   Basilica
A887   A888

1981
1733 A887 1.40fr dk red & dk brn   .65   .30
1734 A888 2.20fr blue & black   1.00   .40
Issue dates: 1.40fr, May 30; 2.20fr, July 4.

Vaucelles
Abbey — A889

Notre Dame of
Louviers — A890

1981
1735 A889   2fr red & black   .90   .40
1736 A890 2.20fr red brn & dk brn   1.00   .50
     Nos. 1732-1736 (5)   4.40   1.90
Issue dates: 2fr, Sept. 19; 2.20fr, Sept. 26.

Europa Issue

Folkdances
A891

1981, May 4   Perf. 13
1737 A891 1.40fr Bouree   .65   .30
1738 A891   2fr Sardane   1.00   .40

Bookbinding — A892

1981, Apr. 4   Perf. 13
1739 A892 1.50fr olive & car rose   .70   .40

Cadets — A893

1981, May 16
1740 A893 2.50fr multicolored   1.00   .30
Military College at St. Maixent centenary.

Man
Drawing
Geometric
Diagram
A894

1981, May 23   Photo.
1741 A894 2fr shown   1.00   .75
1742 A894 2fr Faces   1.00   .75
   a. Pair, #1741-1742 + label   2.50   2.00
PHILEXFRANCE '82 Stamp Exhibition, Paris, June 11-21, 1982.

Theophraste Renaudot
and Émile de
Girardin — A895

1981, May 30   Engr.
1743 A895 2.20fr black & red   1.00   .30
350th anniversary of La Gazette (founded by Renaudot), and death centenary of founder of Le Journal (de Girardin).

Public Gardens,
Vichy — A896

1981, June 6
1744 A896 1.40fr multicolored   .65   .30
54th National Congress of French Federation of Philatelic Societies, Vichy.

Higher National College for
Commercial Studies Centenary
A897

1981, June 20   Perf. 13
1745 A897 1.40fr multicolored   .65   .30

FRANCE

647

Sea Shore Conservation A898

1981, June 20
1746 A898 1.60fr multicolored .75 .55

 World Fencing Championship, Clermont-Ferrand, July 2-13 — A899

1981, June 27
1747 A899 1.80fr multicolored .85 .45

 Sabine, after David — A900

1981, Sept. 1 Engr.
1755 A900 1.40fr green .70 .25
1756 A900 1.60fr red .80 .25
1757 A900 2.00fr blue 1.40 .65
Nos. 1755-1757 (3) 2.90 1.35

Coil Stamps
1981 Engr. Perf. 13 Horiz.
1758 A900 1.40fr green .75 .50
1759 A900 1.60fr red .75 .50

 Highway Safety ("Drink or Drive") — A901

1981, Sept. 5 Perf. 13
1768 A901 1.60fr multicolored .75 .30

 45th Intl. PEN Club Congress — A902

1981, Sept. 19 Perf. 13
1769 A902 2fr multicolored 1.00 .35

 Jules Ferry, Statesman — A903

1981, Sept. 26 Perf. 12½x13
1770 A903 1.60fr multicolored .75 .35
Free compulsory public school centenary.

 Natl. Savings Bank Centenary A904

1981, Sept. 21 Photo. Perf. 13
1771 A904 1.40fr multicolored .65 .25
1772 A904 1.60fr multicolored .75 .25

 The Divers, by Edouard Pignon A905

1981, Oct. 3 Perf. 13x12½
1773 A905 4fr multicolored 1.75 .90

 Alleluia, by Alfred Manessier A906

1981, Dec. 19 Photo. Perf. 12x13
1774 A906 4fr multicolored 1.75 .90

Tourist Issue

 Saint-Emilion A907

 Crest A908

1981 Engr. Perf. 13x12½
1775 A907 2.60fr dk red & lt ol grn 1.10 .25
Perf. 13
1776 A908 2.90fr dk green 1.20 .25
Issued: No. 1775, 10/10; No. 1776, 11/28.

 150th Anniv. of Naval Academy — A909

1981, Oct. 17 Perf. 13
1777 A909 1.40fr multicolored .65 .30

 A910

St. Hubert Kneeling before the Stag, 15th cent. sculpture.

1981, Oct. 24
1778 A910 1.60fr multicolored .75 .30
Museum of hunting and nature.

 A911

V. Schoelcher, J. Jaures, J. Moulin, the Pantheon.

1981, Nov. 2
1779 A911 1.60fr blue & dull pur .75 .30

 Intl. Year of the Disabled — A912

1981, Nov. 7
1780 A912 1.60fr multicolored .75 .25

 Men Leading Cattle, 2nd Cent. Roman Mosaic A913

1981, Nov. 14 Perf. 13x12
1781 A913 2fr multicolored 1.00 .75
Virgil's birth bimillennium.

 Martyrs of Chateaubriant — A914

1981, Dec. 12 Engr. Perf. 13
1782 A914 1.40fr multicolored .70 .25

 Liberty, after Delacroix — A915

1982 Engr. Perf. 13
1783 A915 5c dk green .25 .25
1784 A915 10c dull red .25 .25
1785 A915 15c brt rose lilac .35 .35
1786 A915 20c brt green .25 .25
1787 A915 30c orange .25 .25
1788 A915 40c brown .25 .25
a. Bklt. pane of 5, 4 No. 1784, No. 1788 ('87) 1.00
1789 A915 50c lilac .25 .25
1790 A915 60c lt red brn .30 .25
1791 A915 70c ultra .35 .25
1792 A915 80c lt olive grn .35 .25
1793 A915 90c brt lilac .40 .25
1794 A915 1fr olive green .30 .25
1795 A915 1.40fr green .65 .25
1796 A915 1.60fr green .75 .25
1797 A915 1.60fr red .75 .25
1798 A915 1.80fr red .85 .25
1799 A915 2fr brt yel grn .85 .25
1800 A915 2.30fr blue 1.50 1.25
1801 A915 2.60fr blue 1.25 1.00
1802 A915 3fr chocolate 1.40 .30
1803 A915 4fr brt carmine 1.75 .30
1804 A915 5fr gray blue 2.25 .25
Nos. 1783-1804 (22) 15.55 7.45

Coil Stamps
Perf. 13 Horiz.
1805 A915 1.40fr green 1.25 .90
1806 A915 1.60fr red 1.25 .90
1807 A915 1.60fr green .85 .50
1807A A915 1.80fr red .90 .50
Nos. 1805-1807A (4) 4.25 2.80

Issued: 5c-50c, 1fr-1.40fr, 2fr, 2.30fr, 5fr, No. 1797, 1/2; 1.80fr, 2.60fr, No. 1796, 6/1; 60c-90c, 3fr, 4fr, 11/3.
See Nos. 1878-1897A, 2077-2080, 3528, 4410h, 4521, 6346-6349. For surcharge see No. 2115.

Tourist Issue

 St. Pierre and Miquelon A916

 Corsica A917

Renaissance Fountain, Aix-en Provence — A918

 Collonges-la-Rouge — A919

 Castle of Henry IV, Pau — A920

 Lille — A921

 Chateau Ripaille, Haute-Savoie A921a

1982 Engr. Perf. 12½
1808 A916 1.60fr dk blue & blk 1.25 .30
1809 A917 1.90fr blue & red .90 .25
Perf. 13
1810 A918 2fr multicolored .90 .40
1811 A919 3fr multicolored 1.25 .40
1812 A920 3fr ultra & dk bl 1.25 .40
Issued: 1.60fr, 1.90fr, Jan. 9; 2fr, June 21, No. 1811, July 5, No. 1812, May 15.
Perf. 13x12½
1813 A921 1.80fr dull red & ol .85 .25
1813A A921a 2.90fr multicolored 1.40 .80
Nos. 1808-1813A (7) 7.80 2.80
Issue dates: 1.80fr, Oct. 16; 2.90fr, Sept. 4.

Tower Type of 1979
97c, Tanlay Castle, Yonne. 1.25fr, Salses Fort, Pyrenees-Orientales. 2.03fr, Montlhery Tower, Essonne. 3.36fr, Chateau d'If Bouches-du-Rhone.

1982, Jan. 11 Engr. Perf. 13
1814 A841 97c olive grn & blk .45 .25
1815 A841 1.25fr red & blk .55 .25
1816 A841 2.03fr sepia & blk .95 .25
1817 A841 3.36fr ultra & blk 1.50 .80
Nos. 1814-1817 (4) 3.45 1.80
Nos. 1814-1817 are known only precanceled. See second note after No. 132.

 800th Birth Anniv. of St. Francis of Assisi — A922

1982, Feb. 6 Photo. & Engr.
1818 A922 2fr black & blue .90 .40

 Posts and Mankind A923

 Posts and Technology A924

1982, Feb. 13 Photo.
1819 A923 2fr multicolored 1.50 1.25
1820 A924 2fr multicolored 1.50 1.25
a. Pair, #1819-1820 + label 3.50 3.00
PHILEXFRANCE '82 Stamp Exhibition, Paris, June 11-21.

Souvenir Sheet

Marianne, by Jean Cocteau — A925

FRANCE

1982, June 11
1821	A925	Sheet of 2	10.00	9.00
a.		4fr red & blue	4.00	3.50
b.		6fr blue & red	5.00	4.50

Sold only with 20fr show admission ticket.

Scouting Year — A926

1982, Feb. 20   Engr.
1822 A926 2.30fr yel grn & blk   1.00   .30

31st Natl. Census — A927

1982, Feb. 27   Photo.
1823 A927 1.60fr multicolored   .75   .25

Bale-Mulhouse Airport Opening — A928

1982, Mar. 15   Engr.   Perf. 13
1824 A928 1.90fr multicolored   .90   .50

Fight Against Racism — A929

1982, Mar. 20
1825 A929 2.30fr brn & red org   1.00   .50

Blacksmith — A930

1982, Apr. 17
1826 A930 1.40fr multicolored   .65   .40

Europa 1982 — A931

1982, Apr. 24
1827 A931 1.60fr Treaty of Rome, 1957   .90   .30
1828 A931 2.30fr Treaty of Verdun, 843   1.20   .40

1982 World Cup — A932

1982, Apr. 28
1829 A932 1.80fr multicolored   .90   .30

Young Greek Soldier, Hellenic Sculpture, Agde — A933

1982, May 15   Perf. 12½x13
1830 A933 4fr multicolored   1.90 1.00

Embarkation for Ostia, by Claude Gellee A934

The Lacemaker, by Vermeer — A935

Turkish Chamber, by Balthus A936

1982   Photo.   Perf. 13x12½, 12½x13
1831 A934 4fr multicolored   1.90 1.00
1832 A935 4fr multicolored   1.90 1.00
1833 A936 4fr multicolored   1.90 1.00
    Nos. 1831-1833 (3)   5.70 3.00

Issued: No. 1831, 6/19; No. 1832, 9/4; No. 1833, 11/6.

35th Intl. Film Festival, Cannes — A937

1982, May 15   Photo.   Perf. 13
1834 A937 2.30fr multicolored   1.00   .75

Natl. Space Studies Center, 20th Anniv. — A938

1982, May 15   Engr.
1835 A938 2.60fr multicolored   1.20   .50

A939

1982, June 4   Photo.
1836 A939 2.60fr multicolored   1.20   .50

Industrialized Countries' Summit Meeting, Versailles, June 4-6.

A940

1982, June 4   Engr.   Perf. 13
1837 A940 1.60fr ol grn & dk grn   .75   .25

Jules Valles (1832-1885), writer.

Frederic and Irene Curie, Radiation Diagrams — A941

1982, June 26
1838 A941 1.80fr multicolored   .85   .30

Electric Street Lighting Centenary A942

1982, July 10
1839 A942 1.80fr dk blue & vio   .90   .30

The Family, by Marc Boyan — A943

Photogravure and Engraved

1982, Sept. 18   Perf. 12½x13
1840 A943 4fr multicolored   1.75 1.00

Natl. Fed. of Firemen, Cent. — A944

1982, Sept. 18   Engr.   Perf. 13
1841 A944 3.30fr red & sepia   1.60   .40

Marionettes — A945

1982, Sept. 25
1842 A945 1.80fr multicolored   .90   .30

Rugby — A946

1982, Oct. 9
1843 A946 1.60fr multicolored   1.50   .30

Higher Education A947

1982, Oct. 16
1844 A947 1.80fr red & black   .90   .30

TB Bacillus Centenary A948

1982, Nov. 13
1845 A948 2.60fr red & black   1.10   .40

St. Teresa of Avila (1515-82) — A949

1982, Nov. 20
1846 A949 2.10fr multicolored   1.00   .45

Leon Blum (1872-1950), Politician — A950

1982, Dec. 18   Engr.   Perf. 13
1847 A950 1.80fr dk brn & brn   .85   .25

Cavelier de la Salle (1643-1687), Explorer — A951

1982, Dec. 18   Perf. 13x12½
1848 A951 3.25fr multicolored   1.25   .50

Spring — A952

1983, Jan. 17   Engr.   Perf. 13
1849 A952 1.05fr shown   .45   .25
1850 A952 1.35fr Summer   .50   .30
1851 A952 2.19fr Autumn   1.00   .75
1852 A952 3.63fr Winter   1.40 1.10
    Nos. 1849-1852 (4)   3.35 2.40

Nos. 1849-1852 known only precanceled. See second note after No. 132.

Provence-Alpes-Cote d'Azur — A953

Brantome (Perigord) A954

Concarneau A955

Noirlac Abbey — A956

1983   Photo.   Perf. 13
1853 A953 1fr multicolored   .45   .25
    Engr.
    Perf. 13x12½
1854 A954 1.80fr multicolored   .85   .25
    Perf. 13
1855 A955 3fr multicolored   1.25   .60
    Perf. 13x12½
1856 A956 3.60fr multicolored   1.60   .30

Issued: 1fr, 1/8; 1.80fr, 2/5; 3fr, 6/11; 3.60fr, 7/2.

Jarnac — A957

FRANCE

Charleville-Mezieres — A958

1983   *Perf. 13x12½*
1857 A957 2fr multicolored .90 .35
1858 A958 3.10fr multicolored 1.40 .85
    Nos. 1853-1858 (6) 6.45 2.60
    Issued: 2fr, Oct. 8; 3.10fr, Sept. 17.

Martin Luther (1483-1546) — A959

1983, Feb. 12   *Engr.*   *Perf. 13*
1859 A959 3.30fr dk brn & tan 1.40 .55

Alliance Francaise Centenary A960

1983, Feb. 19
1860 A960 1.80fr multicolored .85 .30

Danielle Casanova (d. 1942), Resistance Leader — A961

1983, Mar. 8
1861 A961 3fr blk & red brn 1.25 .30

World Communications Year — A962

1983, Mar. 12   *Photo.*
1862 A962 2.60fr multicolored 1.10 .65

Manned Flight Bicentenary A963

1983, Mar. 19   *Photo.*   *Perf. 13*
1863   2fr Hot air balloon .80 .55
1864   3fr Hydrogen balloon 1.25 .70
   a. A963 Pair, #1863-1864 + label 2.25 2.25

Female Nude, by Raphael — A964

Aurora-Set, by Dewasne A965

1983   *Engr.*   *Perf. 13*
1865 A964 4fr multicolored 1.75 1.00
     Photo.
1866 A965 4fr multicolored 1.75 1.00
    Issued: No. 1866, 3/19; No. 1865, 4/9.

Illustration from Perrault's Folk Tales, by Gustave Dore — A966

1983, June 18   *Engr.*   *Perf. 13*
1867 A966 4fr red & black 1.75 1.00

Homage to Jean Effel — A967

1983, Oct. 15
1868 A967 4fr multicolored 1.75 1.00

Le Lapin Agile, by Utrillo A968

1983, Dec. 3   *Perf. 13x12½*
1869 A968 4fr multicolored 1.75 1.00

Thistle — A969

1983, Apr. 23   *Engr.*   *Perf. 12½x12*
1870 A969 1fr shown .35 .30
1871 A969 2fr Martagon lily .80 .30
1872 A969 3fr Aster 1.25 .30
1873 A969 4fr Aconite 1.75 .60
    Nos. 1870-1873 (4) 4.15 1.80

Europa 1983 — A970

1.80fr, Symbolic shutter. 2.60fr, Lens-to-screen diagram.

1983, Apr. 29   *Perf. 13*
1874 A970 1.80fr multi 1.00 .40
1875 A970 2.60fr multi 1.25 .75

Centenary of Paris Convention for the Protection of Industrial Property — A971

1983, May 14   *Photo.*   *Perf. 13*
1876 A971 2fr multicolored .85 .30

French Philatelic Societies Congress, Marseille — A972

1983, May 21   *Engr.*   *Perf. 13*
1877 A972 1.80fr multicolored .85 .35

Liberty Type of 1982

1983-87   *Engr.*   *Perf. 13*
1878 A915 1.70fr green .75 .25
1879 A915 1.80fr green .80 .25
1880 A915 1.90fr green 1.25 .25
1881 A915 2fr red .90 .25
1882 A915 2fr green .90 .25
1883 A915 2.10fr red .95 .25
1884 A915 2.20fr red 2.00 .25
  a. Booklet pane of 10 20.00
  b. Bklt. pane, #1788, 4 #1884 8.50
  c. With label ('87) 1.00 .25
1885 A915 2.80fr blue 1.25 .90
1886 A915 3fr blue 1.25 .50
1887 A915 3.20fr blue 1.50 .90
1888 A915 3.40fr blue 1.60 .75
1889 A915 3.60fr blue 1.60 .65
1890 A915 10fr purple 4.50 .25
1891 A915 (1.90fr) green .90 .25
1892 A915 (2fr) green .90 .25
    Nos. 1878-1892 (15) 21.05 6.20

Coil Stamps
    Engr.   *Perf. 13 Horiz.*
1893 A915 1.70fr green .90 .80
1894 A915 1.80fr green 1.00 .50
1895 A915 1.90fr green 1.25 .30
1896 A915 2fr red 1.00 .30
1897 A915 2.10fr red 1.10 .60
1897A A915 2.20fr red 1.00 .50
    Nos. 1893-1897A (6) 6.25 3.00

  No. 1891 is inscribed "A," No. 1892 "B."
  No. 1884c was issued in sheets of 50 plus 50 alternating labels picturing the PHILEX-FRANCE '89 emblem to publicize the international philatelic exhibition.
  Issued: 2.80fr, 10fr, No. 1881, 6/1; 1.70fr, 2.10fr, 3fr, 7/1/84; 1.80fr, 2.20fr, 3.20fr, 8/1/85; 3.40fr, No. 1891, 8/1/86; 1.00fr, 0/13/00; No. 1882, 10/15/87; 3.60fr, No. 1892, 8/1/87.
  For surcharge see No. 2115.

50th Anniv. of Air France — A973

1983, June 18
1898 A973 3.45fr multicolored 1.50 .85

Treaties of Versailles and Paris Bicentenary A974

1983, Sept. 2   *Perf. 13x12½*
1899 A974 2.80fr multicolored 1.40 .60

Jewelry Making — A975

1983, Sept. 10   *Photo.*   *Perf. 13*
1900 A975 2.20fr multicolored .90 .35

30th Anniv. of Customs Cooperation Council — A976

1983, Sept. 22   *Engr.*   *Perf. 13x12½*
1901 A976 2.30fr multicolored 1.00 .40

Michaux's Bicycle — A977

1983, Oct. 1   *Engr.*   *Perf. 13*
1902 A977 1.60fr multicolored 1.10 .30

Natl. Weather Forecasting — A978

1983, Oct. 22   *Engr.*   *Perf. 12½x13*
1903 A978 1.50fr multicolored .70 .25

Berthie Albrecht (1893-1943) A979

1983, Nov. 5
1904 A979 1.60fr dk brown & olive .75 .30
1905 A979 1.60fr Rene Levy (1906-1943) .75 .30
  Resistance heroines.

A980

1983, Dec. 16
1906 A980 2fr dk gray & red .80 .25
  Pierre Mendes France (1907-1982), Premier.

Union Leader Waldeck-Rousseau A981

1984, Mar. 22   *Perf. 13*
1907 A981 3.60fr multi 1.60 .30
  Trade Union centenary.

Homage to the Cinema, by Cesar A982

1984, Feb. 4   *Engr.*   *Perf. 12½x13*
1908 A982 4fr multicolored 1.75 1.00

Four Corners of the Sky, by Jean Messagier A983

1984, Mar. 31   *Photo.*   *Perf. 13x12½*
1909 A983 4fr multicolored 1.75 1.00

Dining Room Corner, at Cannet, by Pierre Bonnard A984

Photogravure and Engraved
1984, Apr. 14   *Perf. 12½x12*
1910 A984 4fr multicolored 1.75 1.00

FRANCE

Pythia, by Andre Masson — A985

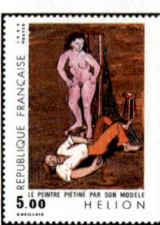

Painter at the Feet of His Model, by Helion — A986

1984		Photo.	Perf. 12x13
1911	A985 5fr multicolored	2.25	1.00
1912	A986 5fr multicolored	2.25	1.00

Issue dates: No. 1911, 10/13; No. 1912, 12/1.

Guadeloupe A987

Design: Map, West Indian dancers.

1984, Feb. 25			Perf. 13
1913	A987 2.30fr multicolored	1.00	.30

Vauban Citadel, Belle Ile-en-Mer A988

Cordouan Lighthouse A989

1984		Engr.	Perf. 13
1914	A988 2.50fr multicolored	1.10	.35
1915	A989 3.50fr multicolored	1.60	.40

Issued: No. 1914, 5/26; No. 1915, 6/23.

La Grande Chartreuse Monastery, 900th Anniv. — A990

Palais Ideal, Hauterives-Drome A991

Montsegur Chateau — A992

1984

1916	A990 1.70fr multicolored	.80	.40
1917	A991 2.10fr multicolored	.95	.30
1917A	A992 3.70fr multicolored	1.60	.40
	Nos. 1914-1917A (5)	6.05	1.85

Issued: 1.70fr, 7/7; 2.10fr, 6/30; 3.70fr, 9/15.

Flora Tristan (1803-44), Feminist — A992a

1984, Mar. 8			
1918	A992a 2.80fr multicolored	1.25	.50

Playing Card Suits — A993

1984, Apr. 11		Engr.	
1919	A993 1.14fr Hearts	.50	.45
1920	A993 1.47fr Spades	.65	.55
1921	A993 2.38fr Diamonds	1.00	.75
1922	A993 3.95fr Clubs	1.60	1.25
	Nos. 1919-1922 (4)	3.75	3.00

Nos. 1919-1922 known only precanceled. See second note after No. 132.

450th Anniv. of Cartier's Landing in Quebec — A994

1984, Apr. 20		Photo. & Engr.	
1923	A994 2fr multicolored	.90	.25

See Canada No. 1011.

Philex '84, Dunkirk — A995

1984, Apr. 21			Perf. 13x12½
1924	A995 1.60fr multicolored	.75	.35

Europa (1959-84) — A996

1984, Apr. 28		Engr.	Perf. 13
1925	A996 2fr red brown	.80	.30
1926	A996 2.80fr blue	1.25	.50

2nd European Parliament Election — A997

1984, Mar. 24		Photo.	Perf. 13
1927	A997 2fr multicolored	.90	.25

Foreign Legion — A998

1984, Apr. 30		Engr.	Perf. 13x12½
1928	A998 3.10fr multicolored	1.40	.50

40th Anniv. of Liberation — A999

Photogravure and Engraved

1984, May 8			Perf. 12½x13
1929	A999 2fr Resistance	.85	.50
1930	A999 3fr Landing	1.25	.60
a.	Pair, #1929-1930 + label	2.50	2.00

Olympic Events A1000

1984, June 1			Perf. 13
1931	A1000 4fr multicolored	1.75	1.00

Intl. Olympic Committee, 90th anniv. and 1984 Summer Olympics.

Engraving — A1001

1984, June 8			Engr.
1932	A1001 2fr multicolored	.90	.25

See No. 5864.

Bordeaux A1002

1984, June 9			Perf. 13x12½
1933	A1002 2fr red	.85	.25

French Philatelic Societies Congress, Bordeaux.

Natl. Telecommunications College, 40th Anniv. — A1003

Design: Satellite, phone, keyboard.

1984, June 16		Photo.	Perf. 13
1934	A1003 3fr multicolored	1.25	.30

25th Intl. Geography Congress, Paris — A1004

1984, Aug. 25		Engr.	Perf. 13x12½
1935	A1004 3fr Alps	1.25	.45

Telecom I Satellite — A1005

1984, Sept. 1		Photo.	Perf. 13
1936	A1005 3.20fr multicolored	1.50	.50

High-speed Train Mail Transport A1006

Design: Electric train, Paris-Lyon.

1984, Sept. 8			
1937	A1006 2.10fr multicolroed	1.00	.25

Local Birds — A1007

Design: 1fr, Gypaetus barbatus. 2fr, Circaetus gallicus. 3fr, Accipiter nisus. 5fr, Peregrine falcon.

Photogravure and Engraved

1984, Sept. 22			Perf. 12½x12
1938	A1007 1fr multi	.45	.25
1939	A1007 2fr multi	.90	.25
1940	A1007 3fr multi	1.40	.75
1941	A1007 5fr multi	2.25	.55
	Nos. 1938-1941 (4)	5.00	1.80

Marx Dormoy (1888-1941) — A1008

1984, Sept. 22		Engr.	Perf. 13
1942	A1008 2.40fr multicolored	1.00	.30

A1009

1984, Oct. 6		Engr.	Perf. 12½x13
1943	A1009 3fr Automobile plans	1.40	.30

100th anniv. of the automobile.

A1010

1984, Nov. 3			
1944	A1010 2.10fr multicolored	.95	.30

Pres. Vincent Auriol (1884-1966).

9th 5-Year Plan — A1011

1984, Dec. 8		Photo.	Perf. 13
1945	A1011 2.10fr dk blue & scar	.95	.25

French Language Promotion — A1012

1985, Jan. 15		Engr.	Perf. 12½x13
1946	A1012 3fr multicolored	1.25	.30

Tourism Issue

View of Vienne — A1013

Cathedral at Montpelier A1014

St. Michel de Cuxa (Codalet) Abbey A1015

Talmont Church, Saintonge Romane — A1016

Solutre — A1017

FRANCE

1985   *Perf. 13x12½*
1947	A1013	1.70fr ol blk & dk grn	.75 .25
1948	A1014	2.10fr sepia & org	.90 .25
1949	A1015	2.20fr multicolored	.90 .35
1950	A1016	3fr multicolored	1.25 .55
1951	A1017	3.90fr multicolored	1.50 .40
		Nos. 1947-1951 (5)	5.30 1.80

Issue dates: 1.70fr, Jan. 19; 2.10fr, Mar. 30; 2.20fr, July 6; 3fr, June 15; 3.90fr, Sept. 28.

French TV, 50th Anniv. — A1018

1985, Jan. 26   *Photo.*   *Perf. 13*
1952	A1018	2.50fr multicolored	1.10 .50

Months of the Year — A1019

1985, Feb. 11   *Engr.*
1953	A1019	1.22fr January	.60 .35
1954	A1019	1.57fr February	.70 .40
1955	A1019	2.55fr March	1.25 .90
1956	A1019	4.23fr April	2.00 1.25

1986, Feb. 10   *Engr.*   *Perf. 13*
1957	A1019	1.28fr May	.65 .35
1958	A1019	1.65fr June	.75 .40
1959	A1019	2.67fr July	1.25 1.00
1960	A1019	4.44fr August	2.25 1.60

1987, Feb. 16   *Engr.*
1961	A1019	1.31fr September	.70 .30
1962	A1019	1.69fr October	.75 .40
1963	A1019	2.74fr November	1.25 1.00
1964	A1019	4.56fr December	2.25 1.75
		Nos. 1953-1964 (12)	14.40 9.75

Nos. 1953-1964 are known only precanceled. See second note after No. 132.

St. Valentine, by Raymond Peynet — A1020

1985, Feb. 14   *Photo.*   *Perf. 13x12½*
1965	A1020	2.10fr multicolored	.95 .25

Pauline Kergomard (1838-1925) A1021

1985, Mar. 8   *Engr.*   *Perf. 13x12½*
1966	A1021	1.70fr int bl & cop red	.75 .25

Stained Glass Window, Strasbourg Cathedral A1022

Still-life with Candle, Nicolas de Stael A1023

1985   *Engraved*   *Perf. 12x13*
1967	A1022	5fr multicolored	2.25 1.25

Photo.   *Perf. 13x12*
1968	A1023	5fr multicolored	2.25 1.00

Issue dates: No. 1967, 4/13; No. 1968, 6/1.

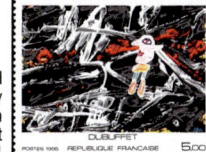

Untitled Abstract by Jean Dubuffet A1024

Octopus Overlaid on Manuscript, by Pierre Alechinsky A1025

Photogravure; Engraved (#1970)
1985   *Perf. 13x12½*
1969	A1024	5fr multicolored	2.25 1.00
1970	A1025	5fr multicolored	2.25 1.00

Issued: No. 1969, 10/14; No. 1970, 10/12.

The Dog, Abstract by Alberto Giacometti (1901-1966) A1026

1985, Dec. 7   *Engr.*   *Perf. 13x12½*
1971	A1026	5fr grnsh blk & lt lem	2.25 1.00

Housing in Givors — A1027

Contemporary architecture by Jean Renaude.

1985, Apr. 20   *Engr.*   *Perf. 13*
1972	A1027	2.40fr blk, yel org & ol grn	1.00 .50

Landevennec Abbey, 1500th Anniv. — A1028

1985, Apr. 20   *Engr.*   *Perf. 13x12½*
1973	A1028	1.70fr green & brn vio	.75 .25

A1029

Europa: 2.10fr, Adam de la Halle (1240-1285), composer. 3fr, Darius Milhaud (1892-1974), composer.

1985, Apr. 27   *Perf. 12½x13*
1974	A1029	2.10fr dr bl, blk, & brt bl	.95 .30
1975	A1029	3fr dk bl, brt bl & blk	1.40 .50

A1030

1985, May 8   *Perf. 13x12½*
1976	A1030	2fr Return of peace	.75 .50
1977	A1030	3fr Return of liberty	1.25 .50
a.		Pair, #1976-1977 + label	2.25 2.00

Liberation of France from German occupation forces, 40th anniv.

Natl. Philatelic Congress, Tours — A1031

Design: Tours Cathedral.

1985, May 25   *Perf. 12½x13*
1978	A1031	2.10fr multicolored	.95 .30

Rabies Vaccine Cent. — A1032

Design: Pasteur inoculating patient.

1985, June 1   *Perf. 13x12½*
1979	A1032	1.50fr multicolored	.70 .30

Mystere Falcon-900 A1033

1985, June 1   *Perf. 13*
1980	A1033	10fr blue	4.50 2.00

Lake Geneva Life-Saving Society Cent. — A1034

1985, June 15
1981	A1034	2.50fr blk, red & brt ultra	1.00 .40

UN, 40th Anniv. — A1035

1985, June 26   *Perf. 13x12½*
1982	A1035	3fr multicolored	1.10 .30

Huguenot Cross — A1036

1985, Aug. 31   *Engr.*   *Perf. 12½x13*
1983	A1036	2.50fr dp vio, dk red brn & dk red	1.00 .30

King Louis XIV revoked the Edict of Nantes on Oct. 18, 1685, dispossessing French Protestants of religious and civil liberty.

A1037

Trees, leaves and fruit of the beech, elm, oak and spruce varieties: 2fr, Ulmus montana. 3fr, Quercus pedunculata. 5fr, Picea abies.

1985, Sept. 21   *Engr.*   *Perf. 12½*
1984	A1037	1fr shown	.45 .25
1985	A1037	2fr multicolored	.90 .25
1986	A1037	3fr multicolored	1.25 .60
1987	A1037	5fr multicolored	2.25 .30
		Nos. 1984-1987 (4)	4.85 1.40

La France Mourning the Dead, Eternal Flame.

1985, Nov. 2   *Engr.*   *Perf. 12½x13*
1988	A1038	1.80fr brn blk, org & lake	.85 .25

Memorial Day.

A1039

1985, Nov. 9   *Engr.*
1989	A1039	3.20fr black & blue	1.25 .40

Charles Dullin, 1885-1949, impresario, theater.

A1040

1985, Nov. 16   *Engr.*   *Perf. 13x12½*
1990	A1040	2.20fr red & black	.90 .25

National information system.

Thai Ambassadors at the Court of King Louis XIV, Painting — A1041

1986, Jan. 25   *Engr.*   *Perf. 13*
1991	A1041	3.20fr rose lake & blk	1.25 .65

Normalization of diplomatic relations with Thailand, 300th anniv.

Leisure, by Fernand Leger — A1042

1986, Feb. 1   *Photo.*   *Perf. 13*
1992	A1042	2.20fr multicolored	.90 .25

1936 Popular Front, 50th anniv.

Venice Carnival, Paris — A1043

1986, Feb. 12   *Perf. 12½x13*
1993	A1043	2.20fr multicolored	.90 .25

FRANCE

La Marianne, Typograph by Raymond Gid — A1044

Photogravure & Engraved
1986, Mar. 3   Perf. 12½x13½
1994 A1044 5fr black & dk red   2.25 1.00

Tourism Issue

Filitosa, South Corsica — A1045

Loches Chateau — A1046

Norman Manor, St. Germain de Livet — A1047

Notre-Dame-en-Vaux Monastery, Marne — A1048

Market Square, Bastide de Monpazier, Dordogne — A1049

1986		Engr.		Perf. 13
1995	A1045	1.80fr multicolored	.85	.25
1996	A1046	2fr int blue & blk	.90	.50
1997	A1047	2.20fr grnsh bl, brn & grn	1.00	.35
1998	A1048	2.50fr henna brn & sepia	1.10	.40

Perf. 13x12½
1999 A1049 3.90fr blk & yel org   1.75 .90
Nos. 1995-1999 (5)   5.60 2.40
Issued: 2.20fr, 3/3; 2fr, 6/14; 2.50fr, 6/9; 1.80fr, 3.90fr, 7/5.

Louise Michel (1830-1905), Anarchist A1050

1986, Mar. 10   Engr.
2000 A1050 1.80fr dk red & gray blk   .80 .25

City of Science and Industry, La Villette A1051

1986, Mar. 17
2001 A1051 3.90fr multicolored   1.60 .50

Center for Modern Asia-Africa Studies — A1052

1986, Apr. 12   Photo.   Perf. 13
2002 A1052 3.20fr Map   1.25 .25

Skibet, Abstract by Maurice Esteve A1053

Virginia, Abstract by Alberto Magnelli A1054

Abstract, by Pierre Soulages A1055

The Dancer, by Jean Arp — A1056

Isabelle d'Este, by Leonardo da Vinci — A1057

Perf. 12½x13, 13x12½ (#2005, 2006)
1986   Photo., Engr. (#2005, 2007)
2003 A1053 5fr multicolored   2.25 1.00
2004 A1054 5fr multicolored   2.25 1.00
2005 A1055 5fr brt vio, blk & brn gray   2.25 1.00
2006 A1056 5fr multicolored   2.25 1.00
2007 A1057 5fr blk, red brn & grnsh yel   2.25 1.00
Nos. 2003-2007 (5)   11.25 5.00
Issued: No. 2003, 4/14; No. 2004, 6/25; No. 2005, 6/22; Nos. 2006, 2007, 11/10.

Victor Basch (1863-1944), IPY Emblem — A1058

1986, Apr. 28   Engr.   Perf. 13
2008 A1058 2.50fr black & yel grn   1.10 .25
International Peace Year.

Europa 1986 — A1059

1986, Apr. 28   Perf. 13x12½
2009 A1059 2.20fr Civet cat   1.00 .30
2010 A1059 3.20fr Bat   1.40 .60

St. Jean-Marie Vianney, Curé of Ars — A1060

1986, May 3   Engr.   Perf. 13x12½
2011 A1060 1.80fr sepia, brn org & brn   .80 .25

Philatelic Societies Federation Congress, Nancy — A1061

1986, May 17   Perf. 13
2012 A1061 2.20fr Exposition Center   .90 .25

Mens World Volleyball Championship — A1062

1986, May 24   Engr.   Perf. 13
2013 A1062 2.20fr dk vio, brn vio & scar   .90 .30

Statue of Liberty, Cent. — A1063

1986, July 4   Perf. 13
2014 A1063 2.20fr scar & dk blue 1.00 .30
See US No. 2224.

1st Ascent of Mt. Blanc, 1786 — A1064

1986, Aug. 8   Engr.   Perf. 13x12½
2015 A1064 2fr J. Balmat, M.G. Paccard   .90 .50

Pierre-Louis Moreau de Maupertuis (1698-1759), La Condamine and Sextant — A1065

1986, Sept. 5
2016 A1065 3fr multicolored   1.25 .55
Lapland Expedition, 250th anniv., proved Earth's poles are flattened.
See Finland No. 741.

Marcassite — A1066

1986, Sept. 13   Perf. 12½
2017 A1066 2fr shown   .90 .25
2018 A1066 3fr Quartz   1.40 .25
2019 A1066 4fr Calcite   1.75 .70
2020 A1066 5fr Fluorite   2.25 .70
Nos. 2017-2020 (4)   6.30 1.90

Souvenir Sheet

Natl. Film Industry, 50th Anniv. — A1067

Personalities and film scenes: a, Louis Feuillade, The Vampires. b, Max Linder. c, Sacha Guitry, Romance of the Trickster. d, Jean Renoir, The Grand Illusion. e, Marcel Pagnol, The Baker's Woman. f, Jean Epstein, The Three-Sided Mirror. g, Rene Clair, Women of the Night. h, Jean Gremillon, Talk of Love. i, Jacques Becker, Helmet of Gold. j, Francois Truffaut, The Young Savage.

1986, Sept. 20   Photo.   Perf. 13x12½
2021 A1067 Sheet of 10   10.00 10.00
a.-j.   2.20fr any single   1.00 1.00

Scene from Le Grand Meaulnes, by Henry Alain-Fournier (b. 1886), Novelist — A1068

1986, Oct. 4   Engr.   Perf. 12½x13
2022 A1068 2.20fr black & dk red   .90 .25

Professional Education, Cent. — A1069

1986, Oct. 4
2023 A1069 1.90fr brt vio & dp lil rose   .85 .25

World Energy Conf., Cannes — A1070

1986, Oct. 5   Photo.   Perf. 13
2024 A1070 3.40fr multicolored   1.50 .50

Mulhouse Technical Museum — A1071

1986, Dec. 1   Engr.
2025 A1071 2.20fr int blue, dk red & blk   1.00 .50

Museum at Orsay, Opening A1072

1986, Dec. 10   Photo.
2026 A1072 3.70fr bluish blk & pck bl   1.60 .60

FRANCE

Fulgence Bienvenue (1852-1934), and the Metro — A1073

1987, Jan. 17 Engr. Perf. 13
2027 A1073 2.50fr vio brn, brn & dk grn 1.10 .30

A1074

1987, Jan. 24
2028 A1074 1.90fr grn & grnsh blk .85 .25

Raoul Follereau (1903-1977), care for lepers.

A1075

1987, Mar. 7 Engr. Perf. 12½x13
2029 A1075 1.90fr black & red .85 .25
Cutlery industry, Thiers.

Tourist Issue

Redon, Ille et Vilaine — A1076

Azay-le-Rideau Chateau — A1077

Meuse District A1078

Etretat — A1079

Les Baux-de-Provence — A1080

1987 Engr. Perf. 13
2030 A1076 2.20fr dp rose lil, blk & brn ol 1.00 .25
2031 A1077 2.50fr Prus blue & olive grn 1.25 .55
  Perf. 12½
2032 A1078 3.70fr multicolored 1.75 1.40
  Photo. Perf. 13
2033 A1079 2.20fr multicolored 1.00 .25
  Engr.
2034 A1080 3fr dk ol bis & dp vio 1.25 .40
  Nos. 2030-2034 (5) 6.25 2.85

Issued: No. 2030, 3/7; No. 2033, 6/12; 2.50fr, 5/9; 3fr, 6/27; 3.70fr, 5/30.

Charles Edouard Jenneret (Le Corbusier) (1887-1965), Architect A1081

1987, Apr. 11 Photo. Perf. 13x12½
2035 A1081 3.70fr Abstract 1.60 .50

Europa 1987 — A1082

Modern architecture: 2.20fr, Metal factory at Boulogne-Billancourt, by architect Claude Vasconi. 3.40fr, Rue Mallet-Stevens housing, by Robert Mallet-Stevens.

1987, Apr. 25 Engr. Perf. 13x12½
2036 A1082 2.20fr dk blue & grn 1.00 .50
2037 A1082 3.40fr brn & dk grn 1.50 .65

Abstract Painting, by Bram van Velde A1083

Woman under Parasol, by Eugene Boudin (1824-1898) A1084

Precambrien, by Camille Bryen — A1085

World, Bronze Sculpture by Antoine Pevsner A1086

Perf. 12½x13, 13x12½ (Nos. 2039, 2041)
Photo., Engr. (Nos. 2039, 2041)
1987
2038 A1083 5fr multicolored 2.25 1.00
2039 A1084 5fr multicolored 2.25 1.00
2040 A1085 5fr multicolored 2.25 1.00
2041 A1086 5fr bister & blk 2.25 1.00
  Nos. 2038-2041 (4) 9.00 4.00

Issue dates: No. 2038, 4/25; No. 2039, 5/23; No. 2040, 9/12; No. 2041, 11/14.

Gaspard de Montagnes, from a Manuscript Illustration — A1087

1987, May 9 Engr. Perf. 13
2042 A1087 1.90fr dp grn & sepia .85 .25
Henri Pourrat (1887-1959), novelist.

Natl. Philatelic Societies Congress, Lens — A1088

1987, June 6 Perf. 13x13½
2043 A1088 2.20fr choc & red .90 .30

Involvement of U.S. Forces in WW I, 70th Anniv. — A1089

Design: Stars and Stripes, troops, Gen. John J. Pershing (1860-1948), American army commander.

1987, June 13 Perf. 13
2044 A1089 3.40fr olive grn, saph & ver 1.50 .70

A1090

1987, June 17 Photo.
2045 A1090 2fr multicolored .90 .50
6th Intl. Cable Car Transport Congress, Grenoble.

A1091

1987, June 20 Litho.
2046 A1091 1.90fr pale chalky blue & blk .90 .50

Accession of Hugh Capet (c.938-996), 1st king of France, millenary.

A1092

1987, June 20 Engr. Perf. 12½x13
2047 A1092 2.20fr multicolored .90 .30
La Fleche Natl. Military School.

A1093

1987, June 27 Photo. Perf. 13
2048 A1093 1.90fr multicolored .90 .55

World Assembly of Expatriate Algerians, Nice. A 97c stamp of type A1091 was included in a limited-edition booklet issued Nov. 4, 2020.

World Wrestling Championships A1094

1987, Aug. 21 Engr.
2049 A1094 3fr brt pur, vio gray & brt olive grn 1.25 .60

Mushrooms — A1095

2fr, Gyroporus cyanescens. 3fr, Gomphus clavatus. 4fr, Morchella conica. 5fr, Russula virescens.

1987, Sept. 5 Perf. 12½
2050 A1095 2fr multicolored .90 .25
2051 A1095 3fr multicolored 1.25 .30
2052 A1095 4fr multicolored 1.75 .60
2053 A1095 5fr multicolored 2.25 .60
  Nos. 2050-2053 (4) 6.15 1.75

William the Conqueror (c. 1027-1087) — A1096

1987, Sept. 5 Perf. 13
2054 A1096 2fr Bayeux Tapestry detail .90 .30

Montbenoit Le Saugeais A1097

Design: Abbey of Medieval Knights, cloisters, winter scene.

1987, Sept. 19
2055 A1097 2.50fr saph, blk & scar 1.10 .55

Pasteur Institute, Cent. — A1098

1987, Oct. 3
2056 A1098 2.20fr dp blue & dk red .85 .25

Blaise Cendrars (1887-1961), Poet and Novelist — A1099

Pen and ink portrait by Modigliani.

1987, Nov. 6 Perf. 12½
2057 A1099 2fr brt grn, buff & blk .90 .35

Treaty of Andelot, 1400th Anniv. — A1100

1987, Nov. 28 Perf. 12½x13
2058 A1100 3.70fr multicolored 1.60 .55

Gen. Leclerc (1902-1947), Marshal of France — A1101

1987, Nov. 28 Perf. 13x12½
2059 A1101 2.20fr multicolored .90 .25

654 FRANCE

Liberty Type of 1982

1987-90   Perf. 13
2077 A915 3.70fr brt lilac rose 1.75 .30
2078 A915 (2.10fr) green ('90) .95 .25
2079 A915 (2.30fr) red ('90) 1.00 .25
    Nos. 2077-2079 (3) 3.70 .80

Coil Stamp
Engr.   Perf. 13 Horiz.
2080 A915 2fr emerald green .90 .30
Issued: 2fr, 8/1; 3.70fr, 11/16; Nos. 2078-2079, 1/2.
Nos. 2078-2079 are inscribed "C."

Franco-German Cooperation Treaty, 25th Anniv. — A1102

1988, Jan. 15   Perf. 13
2086 A1102 2.20fr Adenauer, De Gaulle 1.00 .30
See Fed. Rep. of Germany No. 1546.

Marcel Dassault (1892-1986), Aircraft Designer A1103

1988, Jan. 23   Photo.
2087 A1103 3.60fr brt ultra, gray blk & dk red 1.60 .70

Communications A1104

Angouleme Festival prize-winning cartoons.

1988, Jan. 29   Photo.   Perf. 13½x13
Booklet Stamps
2088 A1104 2.20fr Pellos 1.00 .40
2089 A1104 2.20fr Reiser 1.00 .40
2090 A1104 2.20fr Marijac 1.00 .40
2091 A1104 2.20fr Fred 1.00 .40
2092 A1104 2.20fr Moebius 1.00 .40
2093 A1104 2.20fr Gillon 1.00 .40
2094 A1104 2.20fr Bretecher 1.00 .40
2095 A1104 2.20fr Forest 1.00 .40
2096 A1104 2.20fr Mezieres 1.00 .40
2097 A1104 2.20fr Tardi 1.00 .40
2098 A1104 2.20fr Lob 1.00 .40
2099 A1104 2.20fr Bilal 1.00 .40
   a. Bklt. pane of 12, #2088-2099 12.00 8.50

Great Synagogue, Rue Victoire, Paris — A1105

1988, Feb. 7   Litho.   Perf. 13
2100 A1105 2fr black & gold .90 .25

The Four Elements — A1106

1988, Feb. 1   Engr.   Perf. 13
2101 A1106 1.36fr Air .65 .40
2102 A1106 1.75fr Water .80 .40
2103 A1106 2.83fr Fire 1.25 1.00
2104 A1106 4.75fr Earth 2.25 1.75
   Nos. 2101-2104 (4) 4.95 3.55
Nos. 2101-2104 known only precanceled. See second note after No. 132.

PHILEXFRANCE '89 — A1107

1988, Mar. 4
2105 A1107 2.20fr #1885, emblem 1.00 .25

Postal Training College, Cent. — A1108

1988, Mar. 29
2106 A1108 3.60fr multicolored 1.60 .40

Philex-Jeunes '88, Youth Stamp Show — A1109

1988, Apr. 8   Perf. 13x12½
2107 A1109 2fr multicolored .90 .25

Blood Donation — A1110

1988, Apr. 9   Photo.   Perf. 13½x13
2108 A1110 2.50fr multicolored 1.10 .40

Europa 1988 — A1111

Communication and transportation.

1988, Apr. 30   Engr.   Perf. 13
2109 A1111 2.20fr Cables, satellites 1.00 .30
2110 A1111 3.60fr Rail cars 1.75 .40

Jean Monnet (1888-1979), Economist — A1112

1988, May 10   Perf. 12½x13
2111 A1112 2.20fr black & brn ol 1.00 .25

Philatelic Congress, Valence — A1113

1988, May 21   Perf. 13x12½
2112 A1113 2.20fr multicolored 1.00 .35

Intl. Medical Assistance A1114

1988, May 28   Photo.   Perf. 13
2113 A1114 3.60fr multicolored 1.60 .50

Aid to the Handicapped A1115

1988, May 28
2114 A1115 3.70fr multicolored 1.60 .50

No. 1884 Surcharged in European Currency Units

1988, Apr. 16   Engr.
2115 A915 2.20fr red 1.00 .25

Tourist Issue

Hermes Dicephalus (Roman Empire), Frejus — A1116

1988, June 12   Engr.   Perf. 13x12½
2116 A1116 3.70fr multicolored 1.75 .80

Ship Museum, Douarnenez A1117

Chateau Sedieres, Correze A1118

Cirque de Gavarnie A1119

1988   Perf. 13, 12½x13 (#2118)
2117 A1117 2fr multicolored .90 .25
2118 A1118 2.20fr multicolored 1.00 .35
2119 A1119 3fr multicolored 1.25 .40
Issued: 2.20fr, 7/2; 2fr, 7/4; 3fr, 7/23.

View of Perouges, Ain — A1120

1988, Sept. 10   Perf. 13x12½
2120 A1120 2.20fr multicolored 1.00 .25
   Nos. 2116-2120 (5) 5.90 2.05

French Revolution, Bicent. A1121

1988, June 18   Engr.
2121 A1121 3fr multicolored 1.25 1.00
2122 A1121 4fr multicolored 1.75 1.00
   a. Pair, #2121-2122 + label 3.50 3.00
PHILEXFRANCE '89.

Designs: 3fr, Assembly of the Three Estates, Vizille. 4fr, Day of the Tiles (Barricades), Grenoble.

Buffon's Natural History — A1122

1988, June 18   Perf. 12½
2123 A1122 2fr Otters .90 .25
2124 A1122 3fr Stag 1.25 .30
2125 A1122 4fr Fox 1.75 .70
2126 A1122 5fr Badger 2.25 .60
   Nos. 2123-2126 (4) 6.15 1.85

Alpine Troops, Cent. — A1123

1988, June 25   Perf. 13
2127 A1123 2.50fr multicolored 1.10 .60

A1124

Design: Roland Garros (1888-1918), 1st pilot to fly across the Mediterranean, Sept. 23, 1913.

1988, July 2   Engr.   Perf. 13x12½
2128 A1124 2fr brt grn bl & olive .90 .25

A1125

1988, Sept. 10   Engr.   Perf. 13
2129 A1125 2.20fr brt blue, gray & blk 1.00 .25
Nov. 11, 1918 Armistice Ending World War I, 70th anniv.

Homage to Leon Degand, Sculpture by Robert Jacobsen A1126

1988, Sept. 22   Perf. 12½x13
2130 A1126 5fr blk & dp claret 2.25 1.00
French-Danish cultural exchange program, 10th anniv. See Denmark No. 860.

Strasbourg, 2000th Anniv. — A1127

1988, Sept. 24   Perf. 13
2131 A1127 2.20fr Municipal arms 1.00 .25

St. Mihiel Sepulcher, by Ligier Richier (c. 1500-1567), Sculptor A1128

Composition, 1954, by Serge Poliakoff (1906-1969) — A1129

FRANCE

La Pieta de Villeneuve-les-Avignon, by Enguerrand Quarton (1444-1466) — A1130

Anthropometry of the Blue Period, by Yves Klein — A1131

1988-89		Engr.	Perf. 13x12½
2132	A1128	5fr black brown	2.25 1.00
		Photo.	
2133	A1129	5fr multicolored	2.25 1.00
2134	A1130	5fr multicolored	2.25 1.00
2135	A1131	5fr multi ('89)	2.25 1.00
	Nos. 2132-2135 (4)		9.00 4.00

Issue dates: No. 2132, 10/15; No. 2133, 10/22; No. 2134, 12/10; No. 2135, 1/21.

Thermal Springs — A1132

1988, Nov. 21		Engr.	Perf. 13x12½
2136	A1132	2.20fr multicolored	1.00 .25

Metamecanique, by Jean Tinguely — A1133

1988, Nov. 25			Photo.
2137	A1133	5fr multicolored	2.25 1.00

See Switzerland No. 828.

UN Declaration of Human Rights, 40th Anniv. — A1134

1988, Dec. 12		Litho.	Perf. 13
2138	A1134	2.20fr dk bl & grnsh bl	1.00 .25

French Revolution, Bicent. A1135

1989, Jan. 1		Photo.	Perf. 13x12½
2139	A1135	2.20fr red & vio blue	1.00 .25

A1136

Design: Valentin Hauy (1745-1822), founder of the school for the blind, Paris, 1791.

Photo. & Embossed

1989, Jan. 28			
2140	A1136	2.20fr multicolored	1.00 .40

A 97c stamp of type A1136 was included in a limited-edition booklet issued Nov. 4, 2020.

Estienne School, Cent. — A1137

1989, Feb. 4		Engr.	Perf. 12½
2141	A1137	2.20fr gray, black & red	1.00 .25

European Parliament Elections A1138

1989, Mar. 4		Litho.	Perf. 13
2142	A1138	2.20fr multicolored	1.00 .25

A1139

1989		Engr.	Perf. 12½x13
2143	A1130	2.20fr Liberty	1.00 .25
2144	A1139	2.20fr Equality	1.00 .25
2145	A1139	2.20fr Fraternity	1.00 .25
a.	Strip of 3, #2143-2145 + label		3.00 2.50

Bicent. of the French revolution and the Declaration of Rights of Man and the Citizen. No. 2145a contains inscribed label picturing PHILEXFRANCE '89 emblem.

Issue dates: No. 2143, 3/18; No. 2144, 4/22; No. 2145, 5/27; No. 2145a, 7/14.

French-Soviet Joint Space Flight — A1140

1989, Mar. 4		Litho.	Perf. 13
2146	A1140	3.60fr multicolored	1.60 .50

Historic Sights, Paris — A1141

Designs: No. 2147, Arche de la Defense. No. 2148, Eiffel Tower. No. 2149, Grand Louvre. No. 2150, Notre Dame Cathedral. No. 2151, Bastille Monument and Opera de la Bastille. No. 2151a has a continuous design.

1989, Apr. 21		Engr.	Perf. 13x12½
2147	A1141	2.20fr multicolored	1.00 .75
2148	A1141	2.20fr multicolored	1.00 .75
2149	A1141	2.20fr multicolored	1.00 .75
2150	A1141	2.20fr multicolored	1.00 .75
2151	A1141	2.20fr multicolored	1.00 .75
a.	Strip of 5, #2147-2151		5.00 5.00

Europa 1989 — A1142

Children's games.

1989, Apr. 29			Perf. 13
2152	A1142	2.20fr Hopscotch	1.00 .30
2153	A1142	3.60fr Catch (ball)	1.60 .60

ITU Plenipotentiaries Conference, Nice — A1143

1989, May 23			Litho.
2154	A1143	3.70fr dk bl, dl org & red	1.60 .40

Tourist Issue

Fontainebleau Forest — A1144

Vaux le Vicomte A1145

La Brenne A1146

1989, May 20		Engr.	Perf. 13
2155	A1144	2.20fr multicolored	.90 .30
			Perf. 13x12½
2156	A1145	3.70fr ol bis & blk	1.60 .75
2157	A1146	4fr violet blue	1.60 .75
	Nos. 2155-2157 (3)		4.10 1.80

Issued: 2.20fr, 5/20; 3.70fr, 7/14; 4fr, 8/25.

World Cycling Championships, Chambery A1147

1989, June 3		Litho.	Perf. 13
2158	A1147	2.20fr multi	1.00 .25

Jehan de Malestroit, Dept. of Morbihan — A1148

1989, June 10		Engr.	Perf. 12½x13
2159	A1148	3.70fr multicolored	1.60 .55

Preliminary Sketch (Detail) for *Oath of the Tennis Court,* by David A1149

Regatta with Wind Astern, by Charles Lapicque A1150

1989, June 19		Photo.	Perf. 13x12½
2160	A1149	5fr multicolored	2.25 1.00
			Perf. 12½
2161	A1150	5fr multicolored	2.25 1.00

No. 2160 for French revolution bicent. Issued: No. 2160, 6/19; No. 2161, 9/23.

Souvenir Sheet

Revolution Bicentennial — A1151

Revolutionaries: a, Madame Roland (1754-1793). b, Camille Desmoulins (1760-1794). c, Condorcet (1743-1794). d, Kellermann (1735-1820).

1989, June 26		Engr.	Perf. 13
2162	A1151	Sheet of 4	4.00 3.50
a.-d.	2.20fr any single		1.00 .60

A1152

2.20fr, 15th Summit of the Arch Meeting of Leaders from Industrial Nations, July 14-16.

1989, July 14			Photo.
2163	A1152	2.20fr multicolored	1.00 .35

Declaration of the Rights of Man and the Citizen, Versailles, Aug. 26, 1789 — A1153

Details of an anonymous 18th-19th cent. painting in Carnavalet Museum: No. 2168a, Preamble, Article I. No. 2168b, Articles VII-XI. No. 2168c, Articles II-VI. No. 2168d, Articles XII-XVII.

		Litho. & Engr.	
1989, Aug. 26			**Perf. 13x11½**
2164	A1153	2.50fr Preamble, Article I	1.00 .80
2165	A1153	2.50fr Art. II-VI	1.00 .80
2166	A1153	2.50fr Art. VII-XI	1.00 .80
2167	A1153	2.50fr Art. XII-XVII	1.00 .80
a.	Strip, #2164-2167 + label		4.50 3.25

Souvenir Sheet

			Perf. 13x12½
2168	A1153	Sheet of 4	10.00 10.00
a.-d.	5fr any single		2.25 2.00

No. 2168 contains 4 52x41mm stamps. Sold for 60fr, including admission fee to PHILEXFRANCE '89.

Value of No. 2168 is for examples on plain paper. Examples on fluorescent paper seem to have been distributed in North America, and may not have been distributed widely or made available in Europe. Value $400.

Musical Instruments — A1154

1989		Litho.	Perf. 12x12½
2169	A1154	1.39fr Harp	.65 .50
2170	A1154	1.79fr Piano	.80 .50
2171	A1154	2.90fr Trumpet	1.25 1.00
2172	A1154	4.84fr Violin	2.25 1.75
	Nos. 2169-2172 (4)		4.95 3.75

Nos. 2169-2172 are known only precanceled. See second note after No. 132.

FRANCE

See Nos. 2233-2239, 2273-2283, 2303-2306, 2368-2371.

TGV Atlantic — A1155

1989, Sept. 23   *Photo.*   *Perf. 13*
2173 A1155 2.50fr dk bl, sil & red   1.10   .50

Clermont-Ferrand Tramway, Cent. — A1156

1989, Oct. 28   *Engr.*
2174 A1156 3.70fr blk & dk ol bis   1.75   .40

Villers-Cotterêts Ordinance, 450th Anniv. — A1157

1989, Oct. 28   *Engr.*
2175 A1157 2.20fr blk, dp cl & red   1.00   .25

Baron Augustin-Louis Cauchy (1789-1857), Mathematician A1158

1989, Nov. 10   *Perf. 13x12½*
2176 A1158 3.60fr red, blk & bl grn   1.60   .50

Marshal Jean de Lattre de Tassigny (1889-1952) A1159

1989, Nov. 18   *Perf. 13*
2177 A1159 2.20fr bl, blk & red   1.00   .25

Harki Soldiers of France — A1160

1989, Dec. 9   *Photo.*
2178 A1160 2.20fr multicolored   1.00   .30

Marianne — A1161

1990-92   *Engr.*   *Perf. 13*
2179	A1161	10c brn blk	.25	.25
a.		Bklt. pane, #2180, 4 #2179	1.00	
2180	A1161	20c lt green	.25	.25
2181	A1161	50c brt violet	.25	.25
2182	A1161	1fr orange	.45	.25
2183	A1161	2fr apple grn	.90	.25
2184	A1161	2.10fr dark grn	.95	.25
2185	A1161	2.20fr dark grn	1.00	.25
2186	A1161	2.20fr emerald	1.00	.25
2187	A1161	2.30fr red	1.00	.25
a.		Bklt. pane, #2180, 4 #2187	5.00	
2188	A1161	2.50fr red	1.10	.25
2189	A1161	3.20fr blue	1.50	.75
2190	A1161	3.40fr blue	1.60	.40
2191	A1161	3.80fr lilac rose	1.75	.30
2192	A1161	4fr lilac rose	1.90	.25
2193	A1161	4.20fr lilac rose	1.90	.25
2194	A1161	5fr greenish blue	2.25	.25
2195	A1161	10fr violet	4.50	.25
2196	A1161	(2.20fr) dk grn	1.00	.25
2197	A1161	(2.50fr) red	1.10	.25
		Nos. 2179-2197 (19)	24.65	5.45

Coil Stamps
Perf. 13 Horiz.
2198	A1161	2.10fr dk grn	1.00	.25
2199	A1161	2.20fr dk grn	1.00	.60
2200	A1161	2.30fr red	1.00	.25
2201	A1161	2.50fr red	1.10	.25
		Nos. 2198-2201 (4)	4.10	1.35

Die Cut
Self-Adhesive
2202	A1161	2.30fr red	1.00	.25
a.		Booklet pane of 10	10.00	
2203	A1161	2.50fr red	1.10	.25
a.		Booklet pane of 10	11.00	
b.		Booklet pane of 5	5.50	
2204	A1161	(2.50fr) red	1.10	.25
a.		Booklet pane of 10	11.00	
		Nos. 2202-2204 (3)	3.20	.75

Issued: No. 2187, 1/2; No. 2198, 1/1; 10c, 20c, 50c, 3.20fr, 3.80fr, 3/26; No. 2202, 1/29; Nos. 2182-2183, 2194-2195, 5/21; Nos. 2196-2197, 8/19/91; 2.20fr, 2.50fr, 3.40fr, 4fr, 9/30/91; Nos. 2179a, 2187a, 2199, 2201, 1991; 4.20fr, 9/24/92; Nos. 2203-2204, 1992; 2.10fr, 1993.

Peelable paper backing serves as booklet cover for Nos. 2202, 2203. No. 2203b has separate backing with no printing.

A €1.16 stamp of type A11161 was included in a limited-edition booklet issued Nov. 4, 2020.

Nos. 2196-2197, 2204 inscribed "D."
See Nos. 2333-2348, 3529, 4410i, 4522.

Lace Work — A1162

1990, Feb. 3   *Engr.*   *Perf. 13x12½*
2205 A1162 2.50fr red   1.00   .40

1992 Winter Olympics, Albertville — A1163

1990, Feb. 9   *Photo.*   *Perf. 13*
2206 A1163 2.50fr multicolored   1.00   .25

Charles de Gaulle (1890-1970) — A1164

1990, Feb. 24   *Engr.*   *Perf. 12½x13*
2207 A1164 2.30fr brt vio, vio bl & blk   1.00   .25

See No. 5947Be.

Max Hymans (1900-1961), Planes and ACC Emblem — A1165

1990, Mar. 3   *Perf. 13*
2208 A1165 2.30fr brt vio, brt bl & dk ol grn   1.00   .25

Profile of a Woman, by Odilon Redon — A1166

Head of Christ, Wissembourg A1167

Cambodian Dancer by Auguste Rodin — A1168

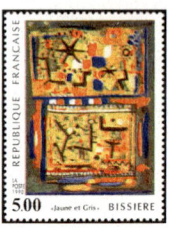
Jaune et Gris by Roger Bissière — A1169

1990   *Litho.*   *Perf. 13½x14*
2209 A1166 5fr multicolored   2.25   1.00

Perf. 12½x13
Engr.
2210 A1167 5fr multicolored   2.25   1.00
2211 A1168 5fr multicolored   2.25   1.00

Photo.
2212 A1169 5fr multicolored   2.25   1.00
    Nos. 2209-2212 (4)   9.00   4.00

Issue dates: No. 2209, Mar. 3; No. 2210, June 16; No. 2211, June 9; No. 2212, Dec. 8.

Jean Guéhenno (1890-1978) — A1170

Litho. & Engr.
1990, Mar. 24   *Perf. 13*
2213 A1170 3.20fr buff & red brn   1.50   .40

Tourism Series

Flaran Abbey, Gers — A1171

1990, Apr. 21   *Engr.*   *Perf. 13*
2214 A1171 3.80fr sepia & blk   1.75   .50

Cluny — A1172

Pont Canal de Briare — A1173

Cap Canaille, Cassis — A1174

1990
2215	A1172	2.30fr multicolored	1.00	.25
2216	A1173	2.30fr multicolored	1.00	.25
2217	A1174	3.80fr multicolored	1.75	.50
		Nos. 2215-2217 (3)	3.75	1.00

Issued: No. 2215, 6/23; No. 2216, 7/7; 3.80fr, 7/14.

Europa 1990 — A1175

Post offices.

1990, Apr. 28   *Engr.*   *Perf. 13*
2218 A1175 2.30fr Macon   1.00   .30
2219 A1175 3.20fr Cerizay   1.50   .60

Arab World Institute — A1176

1990, May 5   *Perf. 12½x13*
2220 A1176 3.80fr brt bl, dk red & dp bl   1.75   .40

Labor Day, Cent. — A1177

1990, May 1   *Photo.*   *Perf. 13*
2221 A1177 2.30fr multicolored   1.00   .25

Villefranche-sur-Saone — A1178

1990, June 2   *Engr.*   *Perf. 13x12½*
2222 A1178 2.30fr multicolored   1.00   .25

National philatelic congress.

A1179

1990, June 6   *Perf. 13x12½*
2223 A1179 2.30fr La Poste   1.00   .25

Whitbread trans-global yacht race.

A1181

1990, June 17   *Perf. 12½x13*
2225 A1181 2.30fr multicolored   1.00   .25

De Gaulle's Call for French Resistance, 50th anniv.

Franco-Brazilian House, Rio de Janeiro — A1182

1990, July 14   *Perf. 13*
2226 A1182 3.20fr multicolored   1.50   .70

See Brazil No. 2255.

FRANCE

 A1183

1990, Oct. 6   Engr.   Perf. 12½
2227 A1183 2fr Rutilus rutilus   .90 .25
2228 A1183 3fr Perca fluviatilis   1.25 .25
2229 A1183 4fr Salmo salar   1.75 .40
2230 A1183 5fr Esox lucius   2.25 .40
    Nos. 2227-2230 (4)   6.15 1.30

 A1184

1990, Sept. 29   Photo.   Perf. 12½x13
2231 A1184 2.30fr multicolored   1.00 .30
Natl. Institute of Geography, 50th anniv.

Souvenir Sheet

French Revolution, Bicentennial — A1185

Designs: a, Gaspard Monge. b, Abbe Gregoire. c, Creation of the Tricolor. d, Creation of the French departments.

1990, Oct. 15   Engr.   Perf. 13
2232 A1185 Sheet of 4   4.50 4.00
  a.-d.   2.50fr any single   1.10 .80

Musical Instrument Type of 1989

Designs: 1.46fr, Accordion. 1.89fr, Breton bagpipe. 3.06fr, Tambourin. 5.10fr, Hurdy-gurdy.

1990, Sept. 1   Litho.   Perf. 13
2233 A1154 1.46fr multi   .65 .40
2234 A1154 1.89fr multi   .75 .60
2235 A1154 3.06fr multi   1.50 1.50
2236 A1154 5.10fr multi   2.50 2.40
    Nos. 2233-2236 (4)   5.40 4.90

1990, Nov.   Litho.   Perf. 13
2237 A1154 1.93fr like #2169   1.00 .60
2238 A1154 2.39fr like #2170   1.10 .80
2239 A1154 2.74fr like #2172   1.25 1.25
    Nos. 2237-2239 (3)   3.35 2.65

Nos. 2233-2239 are known only precanceled. See second note after No. 132.

Maurice Genevoix (1890-1980), Novelist — A1186

1990, Nov. 12   Engr.   Perf. 13
2240 A1186 2.30fr lt green & blk   1.00 .25

 A1187

1990, Dec. 15   Litho.
2241 A1187 3.20fr dk & lt blue   1.50 .70
Organization for Economic Cooperation and Development, 30th Anniv.

"The Swing" by Auguste Renoir (1841-1919) A1188

1991, Feb. 23   Engr.   Perf. 12½x13
2242 A1188 5fr multicolored   2.25 1.00

Youth Philatelic Exhibition, Cholet — A1189

1991, Mar. 30   Litho.   Perf. 13
2243 A1189 2.50fr multicolored   1.10 .40

Art Series

Le Noeud Noir by Georges Seurat (1859-1891) A1190

Apres Nous La Maternite, by Max Ernst (1891-1976) A1191

Volte Faccia by Francois Rouan — A1192

O Tableau Noir by Roberto Matta (b. 1911) A1193

1991   Engr.   Perf. 12½x13
2244 A1190 5fr pale yellow & blk   2.25 1.00

    Photo.   Perf. 13
2245 A1191 2.50fr multicolored   1.00 .70

    Engr.   Perf. 12½x13
2246 A1192 5fr black   2.25 1.00

    Photo.   Perf. 13x12½
2247 A1193 5fr multicolored   2.25 1.00
    Nos. 2244-2247 (4)   7.75 3.70

Issued: No. 2244, 4/13; No. 2245, 10/10; No. 2246, 11/9; No. 2247, 11/30.

Wolfgang Amadeus Mozart (1756-1791), Composer A1194

1991, Apr. 9   Photo.   Perf. 13
2248 A1194 2.50fr bl, blk & red   1.10 .60

National Printing Office, 350th Anniv. — A1195

1991, Apr. 13
2249 A1195 4fr multicolored   1.75 .75

Tourism Series

Chevire Bridge, Nantes A1196

Carennac Castle A1197

Pipe Organ, Wasquehal A1198

Valley of Munster — A1199

1991   Engr.   Perf. 13
2250 A1196 2.50fr multicolored   1.10 .25
    Perf. 12x13
2251 A1197 2.50fr multicolored   1.10 .30
    Perf. 12
2252 A1198 4fr black & buff   1.75 .55
    Perf. 13x12½
2253 A1199 4fr violet   1.75 .55
    Nos. 2250-2253 (4)   5.70 1.65

Issue dates: No. 2250, Apr. 27; Nos. 2251, 2253, July 6; No. 2252, June 22.

Europa — A1200

2.50fr, Ariane launch site, French Guiana.
3.50fr, Television satellite.

1991, Apr. 27   Perf 12½x13
2254 A1200 2.50fr multi   1.10 .25
2255 A1200 3.50fr multi   1.60 .55

Compare with No. 2483.

Concours Lepine, 90th Anniv. — A1201

1991, Apr. 27   Perf. 13
2256 A1201 4fr multicolored   1.75 .75
French Assoc. of Small Manufacturers and Inventors.

Philatelic Society Congress, Perpignan A1202

1991, May 18
2257 A1202 2.50fr multicolored   1.10 .25

French Open Tennis Championships, Cent. — A1203

1991, May 24   Engr.   Perf. 13
2258 A1203 3.50fr multicolored   1.60 .50

Souvenir Sheet

French Revolution, Bicent. — A1204

Designs: a, Theophile Malo Corret, La Tour d'Auvergne (1743-1800). b, Liberty Tree. c, National police, bicent. d, Louis Antoine-Leon de St. Just (1767-1794).

1991, June 1   Perf. 13
2259 A1204 Sheet of 4   4.50 3.50
  a.-d.   2.50fr any single   1.10 .80

A1205

1991, June 13   Photo.   Perf. 13
2260 A1205 2.50fr multicolored   1.10 .40
Gaston III de Foix (Febus) (1331-1391), general.

Wildlife — A1206

Designs: 2fr, Ursus arctos. 3fr, Testudo hermanni. 4fr, Castor fiber. 5fr, Alcedo atthis.

1991, Sept. 14   Engr.   Perf. 12½
2261 A1206 2fr multi   .90 .30
2262 A1206 3fr multi   1.25 .30
2263 A1206 4fr multi   1.75 .70
2264 A1206 5fr multi   2.25 .70
    Nos. 2261-2264 (4)   6.15 2.00

FRANCE

10th World Forestry Congress A1207

1991, Sept. 22   **Engr.**   **Perf. 13x12½**
2265 A1207 2.50fr multicolored   1.10   .25

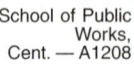
School of Public Works, Cent. — A1208

1991, Oct. 5   **Litho. & Engr.**   **Perf. 13**
2266 A1208 2.50fr multicolored   1.10   .30

A €1.16 stamp of type A1208 was included in a limited-edition booklet issued Nov. 4, 2020.

Marcel Cerdan (1916-1949), Middleweight Boxing Champion A1209

1991, Oct. 19   **Photo.**   **Perf. 13**
2267 A1209 2.50fr black & red   1.00   .30

Amnesty International, 30th Anniv. — A1210

1991, Oct. 19
2268 A1210 3.40fr multicolored   1.50   .60

1992 Winter Olympics, Albertville — A1211

1991, Nov. 14   **Engr.**   **Perf. 13**
2269 A1211 2.50fr Olympic flame   1.10   .25

Fifth Handicapped Olympics — A1212

1991, Dec. 7   **Perf. 13**
2270 A1212 2.50fr dk & lt blue   1.10   .25

A1213

1991, Dec. 21   **Engr.**
2271 A1213 2.50fr multicolored   1.10   .25

Voluntary attachment of Mayotte to France, sesquicentennial.

French Pavilion, Expo '92, Seville — A1214

Litho. & Engr.
1992, Jan. 18   **Perf. 13**
2272 A1214 2.50fr multicolored   1.10   .25

Musical Instruments Type of 1989
1992, Jan. 31   **Litho.**   **Perf. 13**
2273 A1154 1.60fr Guitar   60.00   25.00
2274 A1154 1.98fr like #2233   3.00   2.25
2275 A1154 2.08fr Saxophone   1.25   1.00
2276 A1154 2.46fr like #2234   1.25   1.00
2277 A1154 2.98fr Banjo   1.50   1.50
2278 A1154 3.08fr like #2235   6.00   4.00
2279 A1154 3.14fr like #2236   2.00   1.50
2280 A1154 3.19fr like #2169   7.00   4.00
2281 A1154 5.28fr Xylophone   3.00   1.50
2282 A1154 5.30fr like #2170   3.00   1.50
2283 A1154 5.32fr like #2172   3.00   1.50
Nos. 2273-2283 (11)   91.00   44.75

Perf. 12
2273a A1154 1.60fr Guitar   7.50   4.50
2274a A1154 1.98fr like #2233   150.00   140.00
2275a A1154 2.08fr Saxophone   40.00   30.00
2276a A1154 2.46fr like #2234   12.00   7.50
2278a A1154 3.08fr like #2235   12.00   7.50
2279a A1154 3.14fr like #2236   60.00   50.00
2280a A1154 3.19fr like #2169   8.00   5.00
2281a A1154 5.28fr Xylophone   30.00   20.00
2282a A1154 5.30fr like #2170   75.00   60.00
2283a A1154 5.32fr like #2172   25.00   20.00
Nos. 2273a-2283a (10)   419.50   344.50

Nos. 2273-2283 are known only precanceled. See 2nd note after No. 132. See Nos. 2303-2306.

1992 Summer Olympics, Barcelona A1215

1992, Apr. 3   **Photo.**   **Perf. 13**
2284 A1215 2.50fr multicolored   1.10   .25
See Greece No. 1730.

Marguerite d'Angouleme (1492-1549) — A1216

1992, Apr. 11   **Litho.**   **Perf. 13**
2285 A1216 3.40fr multicolored   1.60   .75

Founding of Ajaccio, 500th Anniv. — A1217

Virgin and Child Beneath a Garland by Botticelli.

1992, Apr. 30   **Photo.**   **Perf. 13**
2286 A1217 4fr multicolored   1.75   .60

Europa — A1218

Discovery of America, 500th Anniv.: 2.50fr, Map, navigation instruments. 3.40fr, Sailing ship, map.

1992, May 9   **Engr.**   **Perf. 13x12½**
2287 A1218 2.50fr multicolored   1.25   .30
2288 A1218 3.40fr multicolored   1.75   .60

Intl. Bread and Cereal Congress — A1219

1992, May 30   **Litho.**   **Perf. 13**
2289 A1219 3.40fr multicolored   1.60   .70

Tourism Series

Ourcq Canal — A1220

1992, May 30   **Engr.**   **Perf. 13**
2290 A1220 4fr black, blue & grn   1.75   .40

Mt. Aiguille — A1221

1992, June 27   **Engr.**   **Perf. 13**
2291 A1221 3.40fr multicolored   1.60   .70
First ascension of Mt. Aiguille, 500th anniv.

Lorient — A1222

1992, July 4   **Engr.**   **Perf. 13**
2292 A1222 4fr multicolored   1.25   .25

Biron Castle — A1223

1992, July 4   **Perf. 12½x13**
2293 A1223 2.50fr multicolored   1.75   .40

Natl. Philatelic Societies Congress, Niort — A1224

1992, June 6   **Photo.**   **Perf. 13**
2294 A1224 2.50fr multicolored   1.10   .25
Natl. Art Festival.

1992 Olympic Games, Albertville and Barcelona A1225

1992, June 19   **Perf. 12½x13½**
2295 A1225 2.50fr multicolored   1.10   .30

Tautavel Man — A1226

1992, June 20   **Photo.**   **Perf. 13**
2296 A1226 3.40fr multicolored   1.60   .60

Portrait of Claude Deruet (1588-1660), by Jacques Callot (1592-1635) A1227

1992, June 27   **Engr.**   **Perf. 12x13**
2297 A1227 5fr buff & brown   2.25   1.00

Flowers — A1228

2fr, Pancratium maritimum. 3fr, Drosera rotundifolia. 4fr, Orchis palustris. 5fr, Nuphar luteum.

1992, Sept. 12   **Engr.**   **Perf. 12½**
2298 A1228 2fr multicolored   .90   .30
2299 A1228 3fr multicolored   1.25   .30
2300 A1228 4fr multicolored   1.75   .60
2301 A1228 5fr multicolored   2.25   .60
Nos. 2298-2301 (4)   6.15   1.80

First French Republic, Bicent. — A1229

1992, Sept. 26   **Perf. 13**
2302 A1229 2.50fr multicolored   1.10   .25

Musical Instruments Type of 1989
1992, Oct.   **Litho.**   **Perf. 13**
2303 A1154 1.73fr like #2273   .80   .25
2304 A1154 2.25fr like #2275   1.00   .50
2305 A1154 3.51fr like #2277   2.00   1.00
2306 A1154 5.40fr like #2281   2.75   1.75
Nos. 2303-2306 (4)   6.55   3.50

Nos. 2303-2306 are known only precancelled. See second note after No. 132.

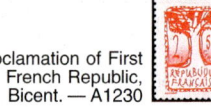
Proclamation of First French Republic, Bicent. — A1230

Paintings or drawings by contemporary artists: No. 2307, Tree of Freedom, by Pierre Alechinsky. No. 2308, Portrait of a Young Man, by Martial Raysse. No. 2309, Marianne with Body and Head of Rooster, by Gerard Garouste. No. 2310, "Republique Francaise," by Jean-Charles Blais.

1992, Sept. 26   **Engr.**   **Perf. 13**
2307 A1230 2.50fr red   1.10   .25
2308 A1230 2.50fr red   1.10   .25
2309 A1230 2.50fr red   1.10   .25
2310 A1230 2.50fr red   1.10   .25
Nos. 2307-2310 (4)   4.40   1.00

Single European Market — A1231

1992, Nov. 6   **Photo.**   **Perf. 12½x13½**
2311 A1231 2.50fr multicolored   1.10   .30

First Mail Flight from Nancy to Luneville, 80th Anniv. — A1232

1992, Nov. 12   **Perf. 13**
2312 A1232 2.50fr multicolored   1.10   .40

Marcel Paul (1900-1982), Minister of Industrial Production — A1233

1992, Nov. 13   **Engr.**
2313 A1233 4.20fr claret & blue   1.90   .50

FRANCE 659

Contemporary Art — A1234

No. 2314, Le Rendezvous d'Ephese, by Paul Delvaux, Belgium. No. 2315, Abstract painting, by Alberto Burri, Italy. No. 2316, Abstract painting, by Antoni Tapies, Spain. No. 2317, Portrait of John Edwards, by Francis Bacon, Great Britain.

1992		Photo.	Perf. 13x12½
2314	A1234	5fr multicolored	2.25 1.00
2315	A1234	5fr multicolored	2.25 1.00
2316	A1234	5fr multicolored	2.25 1.00
2317	A1234	5fr multicolored	2.25 1.00
		Nos. 2314-2317 (4)	9.00 4.00

Issued: No. 2314, 11/20; Nos. 2315-2317, 11/21.
See Nos. 2379-2390.

Gypsy Culture — A1235

1992, Dec. 5		Photo.	Perf. 13
2318	A1235	2.50fr multicolored	1.10 .25

Yacht "La Poste," Entrant in Whitbread Trans-Global Race — A1236

1993, Feb. 6		Engr.	Perf. 12
2319	A1236	2.50fr multicolored	1.10 .30

See No. 2375.

Water Birds — A1237

1993, Feb. 6			Perf. 12½x12
2320	A1237	2fr Harle piette	.90 .30
2321	A1237	3fr Fuligule nyroca	1.25 .30
2322	A1237	4fr Tadorne de belon	1.75 .60
2323	A1237	5fr Harle huppe	2.25 .70
		Nos. 2320-2323 (4)	6.15 1.90

Memorial to Indochina War, Frejus — A1238

1993, Feb. 16		Litho. & Engr.	Perf. 13x13½
2324	A1238	4fr multicolored	1.75 .60

Stamp Day — A1239

1993, Mar. 6		Photo.	Perf. 13
2325	A1239	2.50fr red & multi	1.50 .80
2326	A1239	2.50fr +60c red & multi	1.25 1.00
a.		Bklt. pane of 4 #2325, 3 #2326 + label	10.00

Mediterranean Youth Games, Agde — A1240

1993, Mar. 13		Photo.	Perf. 13
2327	A1240	2.50fr multicolored	1.10 .25

Human Rights, Intl. Mixed Masonic Order, Cent. — A1241

1993, Apr. 3		Engr.	Perf. 13
2328	A1241	3.40fr blue & black	1.60 .50

Contemporary Art — A1242

Europa: 2.50fr, Painting, Rouge Rythme Bleu, by Olivier Debre. 3.40fr, Sculpture, Le Griffu, by Germaine Richier, vert.

		Perf. 13x12½, 12½x13	
1993, Apr. 17			Litho.
2329	A1242	2.50fr multicolored	1.10 .30
2330	A1242	3.40fr multicolored	1.60 .80

Marianne Type of 1990

1993-96		Engr.	Perf. 13
2333	A1161	2fr blue	1.00 .25
2334	A1161	2.40fr emerald	1.25 .25
2335	A1161	2.70fr emerald	1.40 .25
2336	A1161	3.50fr apple green	1.60 .30
2337	A1161	3.80fr blue	1.75 .50
2338	A1161	4.40fr blue	2.00 .40
2339	A1161	4.50fr mag	2.00 .40
2340	A1161	(2.50fr) red	1.75 .25
		Complete booklet, 10 #2340	17.50
		Nos. 2333-2340 (8)	12.75 2.60

Perf. 13 Horiz.
Coil Stamps

2341	A1161	2.40fr emerald	1.10 .60
2342	A1161	2.70fr emerald	1.60 .25
2343	A1161	(2.80fr) red	1.75 .25

Self-Adhesive
Die Cut

| 2344 | A1161 | 70c brown | 13.00 9.00 |

Serpentine Die Cut Vert.

2345	A1161	70c brown	13.00 9.00
2346	A1161	1fr orange	4.25 2.50
a.		Booklet pane, 8 #2348, 1 #2346	9.00
		Complete bklt., 2 #2346a	20.00

Die Cut

2347	A1161	(2.50fr) red	1.75 .25
a.		Booklet pane of 10 (see footnote)	17.50
b.		Bklt. pane of 4 + label	7.00
c.		Booklet pane, #2344, 3 #2347 + label	30.00
d.		Booklet pane of 10 (see footnote)	15.00

Serpentine Die Cut 6¾ Vert.

2348	A1161	(2.80fr) red	1.75 .25
a.		Bklt. pane of 4 + label	7.00
b.		Booklet pane of 10 (see footnote)	17.50
c.		Booklet pane, #2345, 3 #2348 + label	19.00
d.		Booklet pane of 10 (see footnote)	17.50
e.		Booklet pane of 10 (see footnote)	17.50
f.		Booklet pane of 10 (see footnote)	—

Nos. 2340, 2347 pay postage for the first class letter rate and sold for 2.50fr when first released. They have no denomination or letter inscription. Nos. 2343 and 2348 had a face value of 2.80fr when released.
No. 2347a has all stamps adjoining and has selvage covering backing paper (booklet cover), No. 2347d is comprised of two strips of 5 stamps each with yellow backing paper showing.
No. 2348b has the same format as No. 2347a. No. 2348d has a format similar to No. 2347d except there is a narrow selvage strip between the left six stamps and the right four stamps. No. 2348e is like No. 2347b but lacks the selvage strip. No. 2348f has a format similar to No. 2347a except it has a wide selvage strip between the left four stamps and the right six stamps.
Backing paper of Nos. 2347b and 2347c may have cuts along fold and were sold in a booklet for 20fr.
Issued: #2340, 2347, 4/19/93; 70c, July; 2fr, 7/31/94; Nos. 2341-2343, 4/1/94; Nos. 2345, 2348, 2/14/94; 1fr, 2.70fr, 3.80fr, 4.50fr, 3/18/96.

Tourism Series

Chinon A1243

1993, Apr. 24		Engr.	Perf. 13x12½
2355	A1243	4.20fr dk grn, ol grn & brn	2.00 .80

Village of Minerve — A1244

1993, July 17			Perf. 13
2356	A1244	4.20fr red brown & yel grn	2.00 .50

Chaise-Dieu Abbey — A1245

Montbeliard A1246

1993			
2357	A1245	2.80fr multicolored	1.25 .30
2358	A1246	4.40fr multicolored	2.00 .60
		Nos. 2355-2358 (4)	7.25 2.20

Issued: No. 2357, 9/4; No. 2358, 9/11.

Ninth European Conference on Protection of Human Rights — A1247

1993, May 8		Engr.	Perf. 12½x13
2359	A1247	2.50fr multicolored	1.10 .30

Django Reinhardt (1910-1953), Musician A1248

1993, May 14		Litho.	Perf. 13
2360	A1248	4.20fr multicolored	1.90 .50

Louise Weiss (1893-1983), Suffragist — A1249

1993, May 15		Engr.	Perf. 13x12½
2361	A1249	2.50fr blk, buff & red	1.10 .30

Philatelic Society Congress, Lille — A1250

1993, May 29		Engr.	Perf. 13x12½
2362	A1250	2.50fr bl, dk bl & lil	1.10 .40

Natural History Museum, Bicent. — A1251

1993, June 5		Litho. & Engr.	Perf. 13
2363	A1251	2.50fr multicolored	1.10 .30

Martyrs and Heroes of the Resistance A1252

1993, June 18		Photo.	Perf. 13
2364		2.50fr red, black & gray	1.10 .60
2365		4.20fr red, black & gray	1.90 1.00
a.		A1252 Pair, #2364-2365	3.00 2.50

A1254

1993, July 10		Engr.	Perf. 13x12½
2366	A1254	2.50fr multicolored	1.10 .30

Claude Chappe's Semaphore Telegraph, bicent.

A1255

1993, July 10		Engr.	Perf. 12½x13
2367	A1255	3.40fr bl, grn & red	1.50 .70

Train to Lake Artouste, Laruns, highest train ride in Europe.

Musical Instruments Type of 1989

1993, July 1		Litho.	Perf. 13
2368	A1154	1.82fr like #2171	.80 .25
2369	A1154	2.34fr like #2235	1.10 .60
2370	A1154	3.86fr like #2236	1.75 .90
2371	A1154	5.93fr like #2281	2.75 1.75
		Nos. 2368-2371 (4)	6.40 3.50

Nos. 2368-2371 are known only precanceled. See note after No. 132.

Liberation of Corsica, 50th Anniv. — A1256

1993, Sept. 9		Engr.	Perf. 13
2372	A1256	2.80fr lake, bl & blk	1.25 .30

Saint Thomas, by Georges de la Tour (1593-1652) A1257

1993, Sept. 9		Photo.	Perf. 12½x13
2373	A1257	5fr multicolored	2.25 1.00

660 FRANCE

Service as Military Hospital of Val de Grace Monastery, Bicent. — A1258

1993, Sept. 25   Engr.   Perf. 13
2374 A1258 3.70fr multicolored   1.60   .30

Whitbread Trans-Global Race Type
1993, Sept. 27   Engr.   Perf. 12
2375 A1236 2.80fr multicolored   1.25   .40

The Muses, by Maurice Denis (1870-1943) A1259

1993, Oct. 2   Photo.   Perf. 12½x13
2376 A1259 5fr multicolored   2.25 1.00

The Clowns, by Albert Gleizes (1881-1953) — A1260

1993, Oct. 2   Photo.   Perf. 13½x12½
2377 A1260 2.80fr multicolored   1.25   .30

Natl. Circus Center, Chalons-sur-Marne.

Clock Tower Bellringer Statues of Lambesc — A1261

1993, Oct. 9   Engr.   Perf. 13x12½
2378 A1261 4.40fr multicolored   2.00   .60

European Contemporary Art Type
Designs: No. 2379, Abstract, by Takis. No. 2380, Abstract, by Maria Helena Vieira da Silva. No. 2381, Abstract Squares, by Sean Scully. No. 2382, Abstract, by Georg Baselitz, Germany.

1993-94   Photo.   Perf. 13x12½
2379 A1234 5fr blk & ver   2.25 1.00
2380 A1234 5fr multicolored   2.25 1.00
2381 A1234 6.70fr multicolored 3.00 1.00

Perf. 13
2382 A1234 6.70fr multicolored 3.00 1.00
       Nos. 2379-2382 (4)   10.50 4.00

Issued: No. 2379, 10/9/93; No. 2380, 12/11/93; No. 2381, 1/29/94; No. 2382, 11/19/94.

Greetings — A1266

Greeting, artist: No. 2383, Happy Birthday, Claire Wendling. No. 2384, Happy Birthday, Bernard Olivie. No. 2385, Happy Anniversary, Stephane Colman. No. 2386, Happy Anniversary, Guillaume Sorel. No. 2387, With Love, Jean-Michel Thiriet. No. 2388, Please Write, Etienne Davodeau. No. 2389, Congratulations, Johan de Moor. No. 2390, Good luck, "Mezzo," No. 2391, Best Wishes, Nicolas de Crecy. No. 2392, Best Wishes, Florence Magnin. No. 2393, Merry Christmas, Thierry Robin. No. 2394, Merry Christmas, Patrick Prugne.

1993, Oct. 21   Photo.   Perf. 13½x13
Booklet Stamps
2383 A1266 2.80fr multicolored 1.25 .30
2384 A1266 2.80fr multicolored 1.25 .30
2385 A1266 2.80fr multicolored 1.25 .30
2386 A1266 2.80fr multicolored 1.25 .30
2387 A1266 2.80fr multicolored 1.25 .30
2388 A1266 2.80fr multicolored 1.25 .30
2389 A1266 2.80fr multicolored 1.25 .30
2390 A1266 2.80fr multicolored 1.25 .30
2391 A1266 2.80fr multicolored 1.25 .30
2392 A1266 2.80fr multicolored 1.25 .30
2393 A1266 2.80fr multicolored 1.25 .30
2394 A1266 2.80fr multicolored 1.25 .30
   a. Bklt. pane, #2383-2394   15.00

Perf. 12½
2383a A1266 2.80fr   1.25 .30
2384a A1266 2.80fr   1.25 .30
2385a A1266 2.80fr   1.25 .30
2386a A1266 2.80fr   1.25 .30
2387a A1266 2.80fr   1.25 .30
2388a A1266 2.80fr   1.25 .30
2389a A1266 2.80fr   1.25 .30
2390a A1266 2.80fr   1.25 .30
2391a A1266 2.80fr   1.25 .30
2392a A1266 2.80fr   1.25 .30
2393a A1266 2.80fr   1.25 .30
2394b A1266 2.80fr   1.25 .30
   c. Booklet pane of 12,
      #2383a-2393a, 2394b   16.50

Souvenir Sheet

European Stamp Exhibition, Salon du Timbre — A1267

a, Rhododendrons. b, Flowers in park, Paris.

1993, Nov. 10   Perf. 13
2395 A1267 2.40fr #a.-b.+ 2
             labels   12.00 10.00
       Sold for 15fr.

Louvre Museum, Bicent. — A1268

1993, Nov. 20
2396 A1268 2.80fr Louvre, 1793 1.25 1.00
2397 A1268 4.40fr Louvre, 1993 2.00 1.25
   a. Pair, #2396-2397   3.50 2.50

Glassware, 1901 A1269

Cast Iron, c. 1900 A1270

Furniture, c. 1902 A1271

Stoneware, c. 1898 A1272

Decorative arts by: No. 2398, Emile Galle (1846-1904). No. 2399, Hector Guimard (1867-1942). No. 2400, Louis Majorelle (1859-1926). No. 2401, Pierre-Adrien Dalpayrat (1844-1910).

Perf. 13½x12½
1994, Jan. 22   Photo.
2398 A1269 2.80fr multicolored 1.25 .35
2399 A1270 2.80fr multicolored 1.25 .35
2400 A1271 4.40fr multicolored 2.00 .65
2401 A1272 4.40fr multicolored 2.00 .65
       Nos. 2398-2401 (4)   6.50 2.00

Stained Glass Window, St. Julian's Cathedral, Le Mans — A1273

1994, Feb. 12   Engr.   Perf. 12½x13
2402 A1273 6.70fr multicolored 3.00 1.00

City of Bastia — A1274

1994, Feb. 19   Perf. 13x12½
2403 A1274 4.40fr blue & brown 2.00 .60

Tourism Series

Argentat A1275

1994, June 18   Engr.   Perf. 12x12½
2404 A1275 4.40fr red brn & rose
             car   2.00 .60

European Parliamentary Elections A1276

1994, Feb. 26   Litho.   Perf. 13
2405 A1276 2.80fr multicolored 1.25 .25

Laurent Mourguet (1769-1844), Creator of Puppet, Guignol — A1277

1994, Mar. 4   Photo.   Perf. 13
2406 A1277 2.80fr multicolored 1.25 .30

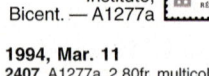

French Polytechnic Institute, Bicent. — A1277a

1994, Mar. 11
2407 A1277a 2.80fr multicolored 1.25 .30

Stamp Day — A1278

1994, Mar. 12   Engr.   Perf. 13
2408 A1278 2.80fr blue & red   2.00 1.60
2409 A1278 2.80fr +60c blue &
             red   1.40 1.25
   a. Booklet pane of 4 #2408, 3
      #2409 + 1 label   25.00

No. 2408 issued only in booklets.

Swedish Ballet Costume — A1279

Banquet for Gustavus III at the Trianon, 1784, by Lafrensen A1280

French-Swedish cultural relations: No. 2411, Tuxedo costume for Swedish ballet. No. 2412, Viking ships. No. 2413, Viking ship. No. 2415, Swedish, French flags.

1994, Mar. 18   Engr.   Perf. 13
2410 A1279 2.80fr multicolored 1.25 1.00
2411 A1279 2.80fr multicolored 1.25 1.00
2412 A1279 2.80fr multicolored 1.25 1.00
2413 A1279 2.80fr multicolored 1.25 1.00
2414 A1280 3.70fr multicolored 3.00 2.00
2415 A1280 3.70fr multicolored 3.00 2.00
   a. Booklet pane of #2410-2415 16.00

See Sweden Nos. 2065-2070.

Pres. Georges Pompidou (1911-1974) — A1281

1994, Apr. 9   Engr.   Perf. 13
2416 A1281 2.80fr olive brown   1.25 .30

Resistance of the Maquis, 50th Anniv. — A1282

1994, Apr. 9
2417 A1282 2.80fr multicolored 1.25 .30

Philexjeunes '94, Grenoble A1283

1994, Apr. 22   Photo.
2418 A1283 2.80fr multicolored 1.25 .30

Europa — A1284

Discoveries: 2.80fr, AIDS virus, by scientists of Pasteur Institute. 3.70fr, Formula for wave properties of matter, developed by Louis de Brogile.

1994, Apr. 30   Photo. & Engr.
2419 A1284 2.80fr multicolored 1.25 .30
   a. With label   1.25 .75
2420 A1284 3.70fr multicolored 1.75 .85

No. 2419a issued Dec. 1, 1994.

Opening of Channel Tunnel A1285

Designs: Nos. 2421, 2423, British lion, French rooster, meeting over Channel. Nos. 2422, 2424, Joined hands above speeding train.

1994, May 3   Photo.   Perf. 13
2421 A1285 2.80fr dk blue & mul-
             ti   1.25 .30
2422 A1285 2.80fr dk blue & mul-
             ti   1.25 .30
   a. Pair #2421-2422   2.75 1.50
2423 A1285 4.30fr lt blue & multi 2.00 .90
2424 A1285 4.30fr multicolored 2.00 .90
   a. Pair #2423-2424   4.50 2.25
       Nos. 2421-2424 (4)   6.50 2.40

See Great Britain Nos. 1558-1561.

FRANCE

Asian Development Bank, Board of Governors Meeting, Nice — A1286

1994, May 3   *Photo.*   *Perf. 13*
2425   A1286   2.80fr multicolored   1.25   .30

Federation of French Philatelic Societies, 67th Congress, Martigues — A1287

1994, May 20   *Engr.*   *Perf. 12x12½*
2426   A1287   2.80fr multicolored   1.25   .30

Court of Cassation — A1288

   Litho. & Engr.
1994, June 3   *Perf. 13*
2427   A1288   2.80fr multicolored   1.25   .30

D-Day, 50th Anniv. — A1289

No. 2429, Tank, crowd waving Allied flags.

1994, June 4   *Engr.*
2428   A1289   4.30fr multicolored   2.00   .50
2429   A1289   4.30fr multicolored   2.00   .50
Liberation of Paris, 50th anniv. (No. 2429).

Mount St. Victoire, by Paul Cezanne (1839-1906) — A1290

1994, June 18   *Photo.*   *Perf. 13*
2430   A1290   2.80fr multicolored   1.25   .30

Intl. Olympic Committee, Cent. — A1291

1994, June 23   *Litho.*   *Perf. 13*
2431   A1291   2.80fr multicolored   1.25   .25

Saulx River Bridge, Rupt aux Nonains — A1292

1994, July 2   *Engr.*
2432   A1292   2.80fr blackish blue   1.25   .25

Organ, Poitiers Cathedral — A1293

1994, July 2   *Perf. 13x12½*
2433   A1293   4.40fr multicolored   2.00   .55

Allied Landings in Provence, 50th Anniv. — A1294

1994, Aug. 13   *Engr.*   *Perf. 13*
2434   A1294   2.80fr multicolored   1.25   .30

Moses and the Daughters of Jethro, by Nicolas Poussin (1594-1665) — A1295

1994, Sept. 10
2435   A1295   4.40fr yel brn & blk   1.90   .90

Natl. Conservatory of Arts and Crafts, Bicent. — A1296

1994, Sept. 24   *Perf. 13x12½*
2436   A1296   2.80fr Foucault's pendulum   1.25   .25

The Great Cascade, St. Cloud Park — A1297

1994, Sept. 24   *Perf. 12½x13*
2437   A1297   3.70fr multicolored   1.75   .60

Leaves — A1298

1994   *Litho.*   *Perf. 13*
2438   A1298   1.91fr Oak   .85   .40
2439   A1298   2.46fr Sycamore   1.10   .70
2440   A1298   4.24fr Chestnut   2.00   1.00
2441   A1298   6.51fr Holly   3.00   1.75
   Nos. 2438-2441 (4)   6.95   3.85
Nos. 2438-2441 are known only precanceled. See second note after No. 132. See Nos. 2517-2520.

Ecole Normale Superieure (Teachers' School), Bicent. — A1299

1994, Oct. 8   *Engr.*   *Perf. 13*
2442   A1299   2.80fr red & dk bl   1.25   .25

Georges Simenon (1903-89), Writer — A1300

   Litho. & Engr.
1994, Oct. 15   *Perf. 13*
2443   A1300   2.80fr multicolored   1.25   .25
See Belgium No. 1567, Switzerland No. 948.

Souvenir Sheet

European Stamp Exhibition — A1301

a, Flowers in park, Paris. b, Dalhias, vert.

1994, Oct. 15   *Photo.*   *Perf. 13*
2444   A1301   2.80fr Sheet of 2, #a.-b.   10.00   9.00
No. 2444 sold for 16fr.

Natl. Drug Addiction Prevention Day — A1302

1994, Oct. 15
2445   A1302   2.80fr multicolored   1.25   .25

Grand Lodge of France, Cent. — A1303

1994, Nov. 5   *Engr.*
2446   A1303   2.80fr multicolored   1.25   .25

Alain Colas (1943-78), Sailor — A1304

1994, Nov. 19
2447   A1304   3.70fr green & black   1.60   .60

French Natl. Press Federation, 50th Anniv. — A1305

1994, Dec. 9   *Photo.*   *Perf. 13*
2448   A1305   2.80fr multicolored   1.25   .30

Champs Elysees — A1306

1994, Dec. 31
2449   A1306   4.40fr multi + label   2.00   .75
See No. 5762D

Souvenir Sheet

Motion Pictures, Cent. A1307

Faces on screen and: a, Projector at right. b, Projector facing away from screen. c, Projector facing screen. d, Reels of film.

1995, Jan. 14   *Photo.*   *Perf. 13*
2450   A1307   Sheet of 4   5.00   5.00
   a.-d.   2.80fr any single   1.00   1.00

Normandy Bridge — A1308

1995, Jan. 20   *Engr.*   *Perf. 13*
2451   A1308   4.40fr multicolored   2.00   .75

European Notaries Public — A1309

1995, Jan. 21   *Perf. 13x12*
2452   A1309   2.80fr multicolored   1.25   .30

Louis Pasteur (1822-95) — A1310

1995, Feb. 18   *Photo.*   *Perf. 13*
2453   A1310   3.70fr multicolored   1.60   1.00

Art Series

St. Taurin's Reliquary, Evreaux A1311

Study for the Dream of Happiness, by Pierre Prud'hon (1758-1823) A1312

Abstract, by Zao Wou-ki A1313

Abstract, by Per Kirkeby, Denmark A1314

1995   *Photo. & Engr.*   *Perf. 12x13*
2454   A1311   6.70fr multicolored   3.00   1.10
   Engr.
   Perf. 13x12
2455   A1312   6.70fr slate & blue   3.00   1.10
   Litho.
   Perf. 14
2456   A1313   6.70fr multicolored   3.00   1.10
   Photo.
   Perf. 13
2457   A1314   6.70fr multicolored   3.00   1.10
   Nos. 2454-2457 (4)   12.00   4.40
Issued: No. 2454, 2/25; No. 2455, 5/12; No. 2456, 6/10; No. 2457, 9/23.

FRANCE

Tourism Series

Stenay Malt Works — A1315

Remiremont, Vosges — A1316

Nyons Bridge, Drome — A1317

Barbizon, Home of Landscape Artists — A1318

1995	Engr.		Perf. 13x12½
2458	A1315 2.80fr ol & dk grn	1.25	.30
2459	A1316 2.80fr brn, grn & bl	1.25	.30

Perf. 12½x13
2460 A1317 4.40fr multicolored   2.00   .75

Photo. Perf. 13½
2461 A1318 4.40fr multicolored   2.00   .75
      Nos. 2458-2461 (4)   6.50 2.10

Issued: No. 2458, 2/25; No. 2459, 5/13; No. 2460, 5/20; No. 2461, 9/30.

A1319

John J. Audubon (1785-1851) — A1320

Designs: No. 2462, Snowy egret. No. 2463, Band-tailed pigeon. 4.30fr, Common tern. 4.40fr, Brown-colored rough-legged buzzard.

1995, Feb. 25   Photo.   Perf. 12½x12
2462	A1319 2.80fr multicolored	1.25	.40
2463	A1320 2.80fr multicolored	1.25	.40
2464	A1319 4.30fr multicolored	2.00	.75
2465	A1320 4.40fr multicolored	2.00	.75
a.	Souvenir sheet of 4, #2462-2465, perf. 13	7.00	7.00
	Nos. 2462-2465 (4)	6.50	2.30

Stamp Day — A1321

1995, Mar. 4   Engr.   Perf. 13
2466	A1321 2.80fr multicolored	2.00	1.00
2467	A1321 2.80fr +60c multi	1.50	1.25
a.	Booklet pane, 4 #2466, 3 #2467+label	15.00	
	Complete booklet, #2467	16.00	

No. 2466 issued only in booklets.

Work Councils, 50th Anniv. — A1322

1995, Mar. 7   Engr.   Perf. 13
2468 A1322 2.80fr dk bl, brn & sky bl   1.25   .30

Advanced Institute of Electricity, Cent. — A1323

1995, Mar. 11   Photo.
2469 A1323 3.70fr multicolored   1.75   .60

Institute of Oriental Languages, Bicent. — A1324

1995, Mar. 25   Photo.   Perf. 13
2470 A1324 2.80fr multicolored   1.25   .30

Jean Giono (1895-1970), Writer — A1325

1995, Mar. 25   Engr.
2471 A1325 3.70fr multicolored   1.75   .60

Iron and Steel Industry in Lorraine — A1326

1995, Apr. 1   Perf. 13x12
2472 A1326 2.80fr multicolored   1.25   .30

End of World War II, 50th Anniv. — A1327

Europa: 2.80fr, Barbed wire, laurel wreath. 3.70fr, Broken sword, emblem of European Union.

1995, Apr. 29   Photo.   Perf. 13
| 2473 | A1327 2.80fr multicolored | 1.25 | .40 |
| 2474 | A1327 3.70fr multicolored | 1.75 | 1.00 |

Forestry Profession, Ardennes — A1328

1995, May 2   Engr.   Perf. 12½x13
2475 A1328 4.40fr multicolored   2.00   .60

End of World War II, 50th Anniv. — A1329

1995, May 8   Photo.   Perf. 13
2476 A1329 2.80fr multicolored   1.25   .30

Natl. Assembly A1330

1995, May 13   Photo.   Perf. 13x12½
2477 A1330 2.80fr multicolored   1.25   .60

French's People's Relief Assoc., 50th Anniv. — A1331

1995, May 20   Engr.   Perf. 12½x13
2478 A1331 2.80fr multicolored   1.25   .30

Scenes of France — A1332

No. 2479, Forest, Vosges. No. 2480, Massif, Brittany. No. 2481, Wetlands, cattle, Camargue. No. 2482, Volcanoes, Auvergne.

1995, May 27   Perf. 13
2479	A1332 2.40fr green	1.10	.25
2480	A1332 2.40fr green	1.10	.25
2481	A1332 2.80fr red	1.25	.30
2482	A1332 2.80fr red	1.25	.30
	Nos. 2479-2482 (4)	4.70	1.10

Ariane Rocket on Launch Pad, French Guiana — A1333

1995, March 28   Engr.   Perf. 12½x13
2483 A1333 2.80fr bl, grn & red   1.25   .30

Compare with No. 2254.

A1334

1995, June 2   Engr.   Perf. 13
2484 A1334 2.80fr multicolored   1.25   .30

68th Congress of French Federation of Philatelic Organizations, Orleans.

Town of Correze — A1335

1995, June 3
2485 A1335 4.40fr multi   2.00   .60

A1336

Fables of Jean de la Fontaine (1621-95): No. 2486, The Grasshopper and The Ant. No. 2487, The Frog Who Could Make Himself Larger than an Ox. No. 2488, The Wolf and the Lamb. No. 2489, The Crow and the Fox. No. 2490, The Cat, the Weasel, and the Small Rabbit. No. 2491, The Tortoise and the Hare.

1995, June 24   Photo.   Perf. 13
2486	A1336 2.80fr multicolored	1.40	.50
2487	A1336 2.80fr multicolored	1.40	.50
2488	A1336 2.80fr multicolored	1.40	.50
2489	A1336 2.80fr multicolored	1.40	.50
2490	A1336 2.80fr multicolored	1.40	.50
2491	A1336 2.80fr multicolored	1.40	.50
a.	Strip, #2486-2491 + 2 labels	9.00	8.00

Velodrome d'Hiver Raid — A1337

1995, July 9   Photo.   Perf. 13
2492 A1337 2.80fr multicolored   1.25   .30

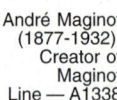
André Maginot (1877-1932), Creator of Maginot Line — A1338

1995, Sept. 9   Engr.   Perf. 13
2493 A1338 2.80fr multicolored   1.25   .30

Women's Grand Masonic Lodge of France, 50th Anniv. — A1339

1995, Sept. 16   Perf. 13x12½
2494 A1339 2.80fr multicolored   1.25   .30

Hospital Pharmacies, 500th Anniv. — A1340

1995, Sept. 23   Perf. 12½x13
2495 A1340 2.80fr multicolored   1.25   .30

Natl. School of Administration, 50th Anniv. — A1341

1995, Oct. 5   Photo.   Perf. 13
2496 A1341 2.80fr multicolored   1.25   .30

The Cradle, by Berthe Morisot (1841-95) A1342

1995, Oct. 7   Litho.   Perf. 13½x14
2497 A1342 6.70fr multicolored   3.00 1.00

The French Institute, Bicent. — A1343

1995, Oct. 14   Engr.   Perf. 12½x13
2498 A1343 2.80fr blk, grn & red   1.25   .30

Automobile Club of France, Cent. — A1344

1995, Nov. 4   Engr.   Perf. 13x12½
2499 A1344 4.40fr blk, bl & red   2.00   .60

FRANCE 663

UN, 50th Anniv. — A1345

1995, Nov. 16   Photo.   Perf. 13
2500 A1345 4.30fr multicolored   2.00 .60

Francis Jammes (1868-1938), Poet — A1346

1995, Dec. 2   Engr.   Perf. 13
2501 A1346 3.70fr black & blue   1.60 .60

A1347

1995, Dec. 9   Litho. & Engr.
2502 A1347 2.80fr Evry Cathedral   1.25 .30

A1348

1995, Dec. 12   Photo.   Perf. 13
2503 A1348 2.80fr multicolored   1.25 .30
1998 World Cup Soccer Championships, France.

Art Series

Abstract, by Lucien Wercollier A1349

Design: No. 2505, The Netherlands (Horizon), abstract photograph, by Jan Dibbets.

1996   Perf. 13x12½
2504 A1349 6.70fr multicolored   3.00 1.00
2505 A1349 6.70fr multicolored   3.00 1.00
Issued: No. 2504, 1/20; No. 2505, 2/10.

Arawak Civilization, Saint Martin — A1350

Design: 2.80fr Dog figurine, 550 B.C.

1996, Feb. 10   Engr.   Perf. 13
2506 A1350 2.80fr multicolored   1.25 .30

The Augustus Bridge over the Nera River, by Camille Corot (1796-1875) A1351

1996, Mar. 2   Litho.   Perf. 13
2507 A1351 6.70fr multicolored   3.00 1.00

St. Patrick — A1352

1996, Mar. 16   Photo.   Perf. 13
2508 A1352 2.80fr multicolored   1.25 .30

The Sower, 1903 — A1353

1996, Mar. 16   Litho. & Engr.
2509 A1353 2.80fr multicolored   2.00 1.50
2510 A1353 2.80fr +60c multi   1.50 1.25
  a. Booklet pane, 4 #2509, 3 #2510 + label   13.00
     Complete booklet, #2510a   15.00
Stamp Day.

Jacques Rueff (1896-1978), Economist A1354

1996, Mar. 23   Engr.   Perf. 13x12½
2511 A1354 2.80fr multicolored   1.25 .30

René Descartes (1596-1650) — A1355

1996, Mar. 30   Engr.   Perf. 12½x13
2512 A1355 4.40fr red   2.00 .75

Gas & Electric Industries, 50th Anniv. — A1356

1996, Apr. 6   Photo.   Perf. 13
2513 A1356 3fr multicolored   1.25 .30

Natl. Parks — A1357

1996, Apr. 20
2514 A1357 3fr Cévennes   1.25 .40
2515 A1357 4.40fr Vanoise   2.00 .75
2516 A1357 4.40fr Mercantour   2.00 .75
  Nos. 2514-2516 (3)   5.25 1.90
See Nos. 2569-2572.

Leaf Type of 1994

1996, Mar.   Litho.   Perf. 13
2517 A1298 1.87fr Ash   .95 .25
2518 A1298 2.18fr Beech   1.00 .50
2519 A1298 4.66fr Walnut   2.10 1.00
2520 A1298 7.11fr Elm   3.00 1.75
  Nos. 2517-2520 (4)   6.95 3.50

Nos. 2517-2520 are known only precanceled. Values for precanceled stamps in first column are for those which have not been through the post and have original gum. Values in second column are for postally used, gumless stamps.

Madame Marie de Sévigné (1626-96), Writer — A1358

1996, Apr. 27   Photo.   Perf. 13
2521 A1358 3fr multicolored   1.25 .40
Europa.

Natl. Institute of Agronomy Research, 50th Anniv. — A1359

1996, May 4   Photo.   Perf. 13
2522 A1359 3.80fr multicolored   1.75 .60

Joan of Arc's House, Domremy-La-Pucelle — A1360

1996, May 11
2523 A1360 4.50fr multicolored   2.10 .75

RAMOGE Agreement Between France, Italy, Monaco, 20th Anniv. — A1361

1996, May 14   Photo. & Engr.
2524 A1361 3fr multicolored   1.25 .30
See Monaco No. 1998, Italy No. 2077.

69th Congress of Federation of Philatelic Assoc., Clermont-Ferrand A1362

1996, May 24   Engr.   Perf. 13
2525 A1362 3fr brn, red & grn   1.25 .30

Tourism Series

Bitche, Moselle — A1363

Iles Sanguinaires, Ajaccio, Southern Corsica — A1364

Thoronet Abbey, Var — A1365

Chambéry Cathedral, Savoie — A1366

1996   Engr.   Perf. 12½x13
2526 A1363 3fr multicolored   1.25 .30
2527 A1364 3fr multicolored   1.25 .30
     Perf. 13x12½
2528 A1365 3.80fr brn & claret   1.75 .60
     Photo.   Perf. 13
2529 A1366 4.50fr multicolored   2.00 .75
  Nos. 2526-2529 (4)   6.25 1.95
Issued: No. 2526, 5/25; No. 2527, 6/1; 3.80fr, 7/6; 4.50fr, 6/8.

1998 World Cup Soccer Championships, France — A1367

Various stylized soccer plays, name of host city in France.

1996, June 1   Photo.   Perf. 13
2530 A1367 3fr Lens   1.25 .30
2531 A1367 3fr Toulouse   1.25 .30
2532 A1367 3fr Saint-Etienne   1.25 .30
2533 A1367 3fr Montpellier   1.25 .30
  Nos. 2530-2533 (4)   5.00 1.20
See Nos. 2584-2587, 2623-2624, sheet of 10, No. 2624a.

Art Series

Gallo-Roman Bronze Statue of Horse, Neuvy-en-Sullias, Loiret — A1368

Imprints of Cello Fragments, by Arman A1369

1996   Engr.   Perf. 13
2534 A1368 6.70fr multicolored   3.00 1.00
       Photo.
2535 A1369 6.70fr multicolored   3.00 1.00
Issued: No. 2534, 6/8; No. 2535, 9/21.

Modern Olympic Games, Cent. — A1371

1996, June 15   Photo.   Perf. 13
2537 A1371 3fr multicolored   1.25 .30

A1372

1996, June 15   Engr.   Perf. 12½x13
2538 A1372 4.40fr deep purple   2.00 .70
Jacques Marette (1922-84), Member of Parliament.

A1373

1996, June 29   Photo.   Perf. 13
2539 A1373 3fr multicolored   1.25 .30
Train between Ajaccio and Vizzavona, cent.

664 FRANCE

A1374

1996, Sept. 6   Engr.   *Perf. 13x12½*
2540 A1374 3fr dark blue & yel   1.25   .30
Notre Dame de Fourvière Basilica, Lyon, cent.

Baptism of Clovis, 1500th Anniv. — A1375

1996, Sept. 14   *Perf. 13*
2541 A1375 3fr multicolored   1.25   .30

Henri IV High School, Bicent. — A1376

1996, Oct. 12   Engr.   *Perf. 12½x13*
2542 A1376 4.50fr brown & blue   2.00   .80

UNICEF, 50th Anniv. — A1377

1996, Oct. 19   Photo.   *Perf. 13*
2543 A1377 4.50fr multicolored   2.00   .80

Economic and Social Council, 50th Anniv. — A1378

1996, Oct. 26   Engr.   *Perf. 13*
2544 A1378 3fr red, black & blue   1.25   .30

UNESCO, 50th Anniv. — A1379

1996, Nov. 2   Litho.   *Perf. 13*
2545 A1379 3.80fr multicolored   1.75   .60

Autumn Stamp Show, 50th Anniv. — A1380

1996, Nov. 7   Photo.   *Perf. 13*
2546 A1380 3fr multicolored   1.25   .30

A1381

1996, Nov. 16
2547 A1381 3fr multicolored   1.25   .30
Creation of French Overseas Departments, 50th anniv.

André Malraux (1901-76), Writer — A1382

1996, Nov. 23   Engr.   *Perf. 13*
2548 A1382 3fr deep green black   1.25   .30

French School in Athens, 150th Anniv. — A1383

1996, Nov. 23   Photo.
2549 A1383 3fr multicolored   1.25   .30

Cannes Film Festival, 50th Anniv. — A1384

1996, Nov. 30
2550 A1384 3fr multicolored   1.25   .30

New National Library of France — A1385

1996, Dec. 14
2551 A1385 3fr multicolored   1.25   .30

Francois Mitterrand (1916-96) — A1386

1997, Jan. 4
2552 A1386 3fr multicolored   1.25   .30

Participatory Innovation — A1387

1997, Jan. 24   Photo.   *Perf. 13*
2553 A1387 3fr multicolored   1.25   .30

A1388

1997, Jan. 31   Engr.   *Perf. 12½x13*
2554 A1388 3fr multicolored   1.25   .30
Georges Pompidou Natl. Center of Art and Culture, 20th Anniv.

Happy Holiday — A1389

1997, Feb. 8   Photo.   *Perf. 13*
2555 A1389 3fr shown   1.25   .30
2556 A1389 3fr Happy birthday   1.25   .30

A1390

1997, Feb. 14   Photo. & Engr.   *Perf. 12½x13*
2557 A1390 3fr multicolored   1.25   .30
Natl. School of Bridges and Highways, 250th Anniv.

Saint-Laurent-du-Maroni, French Guiana — A1391

1997, Feb. 22   Photo. & Engr.   *Perf. 12½x13*
2558 A1391 3fr multicolored   1.25   .30

Art Series

Church Fresco, Tavant — A1392

Painting by Bernard Moninot A1393

The Thumb, Polished Bronze, by César — A1394

Grapes and Pomegranates, by Jean Baptiste Chardin — A1395

1997   Engr.   *Perf. 13*
2559 A1392 6.70fr multicolored   3.00   1.00
    Photo.
2560 A1393 6.70fr multicolored   3.00   1.00
2561 A1394 6.70fr multicolored   3.00   1.00
2562 A1395 6.70fr multicolored   3.00   1.00
    Nos. 2559-2562 (4)   12.00   4.00

Issued: No. 2559, 3/1; No. 2560, 3/29; No. 2561, 9/13; No. 2562, 9/27.

Tourism Series

Millau   Guimiliau Church
A1396   Close
      A1398

Fresco, Saint Eutrope des Salles-Lavauguyon — A1397

Sablé-Sur-Sarthe A1399

1997   Engr.   *Perf. 12½x13*
2563 A1396   3fr grn & dk bl
       grn   1.25   .30
    Perf. 13
2564 A1397 4.50fr multicolored   2.10   .75
2565 A1398 3fr multicolored   1.25   .30
    Perf. 12½x13
2566 A1399 3fr multicolored   1.25   .30
    Nos. 2563-2566 (4)   5.85   1.65

Issued: No. 2563, 3/15; No. 2564, 6/14; No. 2565, 7/12; No. 2566, 9/20.

Vignette of Type A17 — A1400

1997, Mar. 15   Litho. & Engr.   *Perf. 13½x13*
2567 A1400 3fr multicolored   2.50   1.50
2568 A1400 3fr +60c multi   1.50   1.25
   a. Booklet pane, 4 #2567, 3
      #2568 + label   15.00
      Complete booklet, #2568a   16.00

Stamp Day.
No. 2567 issued only in booklets.

National Parks Type of 1996

No. 2569, Parc des Ecrins. No. 2570, Guadeloupe Park. No. 2571, Parc des Pyrénées. No. 2572, Port-Cros Park.

1997, Apr. 12   Photo.   *Perf. 13*
2569 A1357 3fr multi   1.25   .40
2570 A1357 3fr multi   1.25   .40
2571 A1357 4.50fr multi   2.00   .70
2572 A1357 4.50fr multi   2.00   .70
    Nos. 2569-2572 (4)   6.50   2.20

Puss-in-Boots — A1401

1997, Apr. 26   Engr.   *Perf. 13*
2573 A1401 3fr blue   1.25   .30
Europa.

Philexjeunes '97, Nantes — A1402

1997, May 2   Litho.   *Perf. 13*
2574 A1402 3fr multicolored   1.25   .30

FRANCE

Cartoon Journey of a Letter — A1403

"Envelope": No. 2575, Writing letter. No. 2576, Climbing ladder to go into letter box. No. 2577, On wheels. No. 2578, Following postman carrying another "Envelope." No. 2579, Held by girl. No. 2580, At feet of girl reading long letter.

1997, May 8   Photo.   Perf. 13
2575	A1403	3fr multicolored	1.25	1.00
2576	A1403	3fr multicolored	1.25	1.00
2577	A1403	3fr multicolored	1.25	1.00
2578	A1403	3fr multicolored	1.25	1.00
2579	A1403	3fr multicolored	1.25	1.00
2580	A1403	3fr multicolored	1.25	1.00
a.	Strip of 6, #2575-2580 + label		8.00	8.00

Self-Adhesive
Serpentine Die Cut 11
2580B	A1403	3fr like #2575	1.25	1.00
2580C	A1403	3fr like #2576	1.25	1.00
2580D	A1403	3fr like #2577	1.25	1.00
2580E	A1403	3fr like #2578	1.25	1.00
2580F	A1403	3fr like #2579	1.25	1.00
2580G	A1403	3fr like #2580	1.25	1.00
h.	Booklet pane, 2 each #2580B-2580G		15.00	15.00

By its nature No. 2580h is a complete booklet. The peelable paper backing serves as a booklet cover.
See Nos. 2648-2659.

Honoring French Soldiers in North Africa (1952-62) A1404

1997, May 10   Litho.   Perf. 13
2581	A1404	3fr multicolored	1.25	.30

French Federation of Philatelic Associations, 70th Congress, Versailles — A1405

1997, May 17   Photo.   Perf. 13
2582	A1405	3fr multicolored	1.25	.40

Printed with se-tenant label.

Château de Plessis-Bourré, Maine and Loire Rivers — A1406

1997, May 24   Litho. & Engr.
2583	A1406	4.40fr multicolored	2.00	1.25

1998 World Cup Soccer Championships Type

Stylized action scenes, name of host city in France.

1997, May 31   Photo.   Perf. 13½
2584	A1367	3fr Lyon	1.25	.30
2585	A1367	3fr Marseilles	1.25	.30
2586	A1367	3fr Nantes	1.25	.30
2587	A1367	3fr Paris	1.25	.30
	Nos. 2584-2587 (4)		5.00	1.20

Saint Martin of Tours (316-97) Apostle of the Gauls — A1408

1997, July 5   Engr.   Perf. 13
2588	A1408	4.50fr multicolored	2.00	.75

Marianne — A1409

1997, July 14   Engr.   Perf. 13
2589	A1409	10c brown	.25	.25
2590	A1409	20c brt blue grn	.25	.25
2591	A1409	50c purple	.25	.25
2592	A1409	1fr bright grn	.45	.25
2593	A1409	2fr bright blue	1.00	.25
2594	A1409	2.70fr bright grn	1.25	.25
2595	A1409	(3fr) red	1.90	.25
2596	A1409	3.50fr apple grn	1.60	.25
2597	A1409	3.80fr blue	1.75	.25
2598	A1409	4.20fr dark org	1.90	.30
2599	A1409	4.40fr blue	2.00	.30
2600	A1409	4.50fr bright pink	2.10	.30
2601	A1409	5fr brt grn blue	5.25	.30
2602	A1409	6.70fr dark grn	3.00	.30
a.	Souvenir sheet, #2594-2600, 2602		14.00	14.00
2603	A1409	10fr violet	4.50	.35
a.	Souvenir sheet, #2589-2593, 2601, 2603		12.00	12.00
	Nos. 2589-2603 (15)		27.45	4.15

Self-Adhesive
Booklet Stamps
Die Cut x Serpentine Die Cut 7
2603B	A1409	1fr brt org	2.25	.50
c.	Booklet pane, #2603B, 3 #2604		7.75	
	Booklet, 2 #2603Bc		16.00	
2604	A1409	(3fr) red	1.40	.25
a.	Booklet pane of 10		14.00	

Coil Stamps
Perf. 13 Horiz.
2604B	A1409	2.70fr bright grn	1.25	.50
2605	A1409	(3fr) red	1.75	.25

Nos. 2595, 2604-2605 were valued at 3fr on day of issue.
Issued: Nos. 2602a, 2603a, 11/12/01. No. 2603B, 9/1/97.
See Nos. 2835-2835C, 2921-2922, 3530, 4410j, 4523.

1997 World Rowing Championships, Savoie — A1410

1997, Aug. 30   Engr.   Perf. 13x12½
2606	A1410	3fr blue & magenta	1.25	.30

Basque Corsairs A1411

1997, Sept. 13   Perf. 13
2607	A1411	3fr multicolored	1.25	.30

Saint-Maurice Basilica, Epinal — A1412

1997, Sept. 20   Perf. 13x12½
2608	A1412	3fr multicolored	1.25	.30

Fresh Fish Merchants, Port of Boulogne A1413

1997, Sept. 26   Perf. 13
2609	A1413	3fr multicolored	1.25	.30

Japan Year — A1414

1997, Oct. 4   Engr.   Perf. 13
2610	A1414	4.90fr multicolored	1.00	1.25

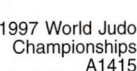

1997 World Judo Championships A1415

1997, Oct. 9   Photo.   Perf. 13
2611	A1415	3fr multicolored	1.25	.30

Sceaux Estate, Hauts-de-Seine A1416

1997, Oct. 11
2612	A1416	3fr multicolored	1.25	.30

Saar-Lorraine-Luxembourg Summit — A1417

1997, Oct. 16   Photo.   Perf. 13
2613	A1417	3fr multicolored	1.25	.30

See Germany No. 1982, Luxembourg No. 972.

College of France — A1418

1997, Oct. 18   Engr.
2614	A1418	4.40fr multicolored	2.00	.70

Quality — A1419

1997, Oct. 18   Photo.
2615	A1419	4.50fr multicolored	2.00	.80

A1420   Season's Greetings — A1421

1997   Photo.   Perf. 13
2616	A1420	3fr Cat & mouse	1.50	.30

Photo. & Embossed
2617	A1421	3fr Mailman	1.25	.30

Issued: No. 2616, 11/8; No. 2617, 11/22.

Protection of Abused Children — A1422

1997, Nov. 20   Photo.
2618	A1422	3fr multicolored	1.25	.30

A1423

Design: Marshal Jacques Leclerc (Philippe de Haute Cloque) (1902-47).

1997, Nov. 28   Photo.   Perf. 13
2619	A1423	3fr multicolored	1.25	.30

Philexfrance '99, World Stamp Exposition A1424

1997, Dec. 6   Engr.
2620	A1424	3fr red & blue	1.25	.30

Abbey of Moutier D'Ahun, Creuse — A1425

1997, Dec. 13
2621	A1425	4.40fr multicolored	2.00	.70

Michel Debré (1912-96), Politician A1426

1998, Jan. 15   Photo.
2622	A1426	3fr multicolored	1.25	.30

1998 World Cup Soccer Championships Type

Stylized action scenes, name of host city in France.

1998, Jan. 24   Perf. 13½
2623	A1367	3fr Saint-Denis	1.25	.30
2624	A1367	3fr Bordeaux	1.25	.30
a.	Sheet of 10, #2530-2533, #2584-2587, #2623-2624 + label		14.00	14.00

National Assembly, Bicent. — A1427

1998, Jan. 24   Perf. 13
2625	A1427	3fr multicolored	1.25	.30

Valentine's Day — A1428

1998, Jan. 31
2626	A1428	3fr multicolored	1.25	.30

Office of Mediator of the Republic, 25th Anniv. — A1429

1998, Feb. 5
2627	A1429	3fr multicolored	1.25	.30

A1430

1998, Feb. 28   Photo.   Perf. 12½
2628	A1430	3fr multicolored	1.25	.30

Self-Adhesive
Serpentine Die Cut
2629	A1430	3fr like #2628	1.25	.30
a.	Booklet pane of 10		14.00	14.00
b.	Sheet of 1 + 7 labels		17.00	16.00

1998 World Cup Soccer Championships, France.
The peelable paper backing of No. 2629a serves as a booklet cover.

666 FRANCE

A €1.16 stamp of type A1430 was included in a limited-edition booklet issued Nov. 4, 2020. See No. 2665.

 A1431

1998, Feb. 21 Engr. Perf. 13½x13
2630 A1431 3fr Detail of design A16 3.00 1.60
2631 A1431 3fr +60c like #2630 1.50 1.40
  a. Booklet pane, 4 #2630, 3 #2631 + label 14.00
    Complete booklet, #2631a 15.00

Stamp Day. No. 2630 issued only in booklets.

 A1432

1998, Feb. 28 Engr. Perf. 13
2632 A1432 4.50fr blue 2.00 .75

Father Franz Stock (1904-48), prison chaplain.

 Happy Birthday — A1433

1998, Mar. 13 Photo. Perf. 13x13½
2633 A1433 3fr multicolored 1.25 .30

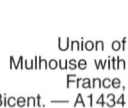 Union of Mulhouse with France, Bicent. — A1434

1998, Mar. 14
2634 A1434 3fr multicolored 1.25 .30

 Citeaux Abbey, 900th Anniv. — A1435

1998, Mar. 14 Engr. Perf. 13
2635 A1435 3fr multicolored 1.25 .30

 Sous-Préfecture Hotel, Saint-Pierre, Réunion — A1436

1998, Apr. 4 Engr. Perf. 13
2636 A1436 3fr multicolored 1.25 .30

Réunion's architectural heritage.

 "The Return," by René Magritte A1437

1998, Apr. 18 Photo.
2637 A1437 3fr multicolored 1.40 .50

See Belgium No. 1691.

 Edict of Nantes, 400th Anniv. — A1438

1998, Apr. 18 Litho.
2638 A1438 4.50fr Henry IV 2.00 .75

Art Series

 Detail from "Entry of the Crusaders into Constantinople," by Delacroix (1798-1863) A1439

 Le Printemps, by Pablo Picasso (1881-1973) A1440

 Neuf Moules Malic, by Marcel Duchamp (1887-1968) A1441

 Vision After the Sermon, by Paul Gauguin (1848-1903) A1442

1998 Engr. Perf. 12x13
2639 A1439 6.70fr multicolored 3.00 1.00
Litho. Perf. 13
2640 A1440 6.70fr multicolored 3.00 1.00
Photo.
2641 A1441 6.70fr multicolored 3.00 1.00
2642 A1442 6.70fr multicolored 3.00 1.00

Issued: No. 2639, 4/25; No. 2640, 5/15; No. 2641, 10/17; No. 2642, 12/5.

 Abolition of Slavery, 150th Anniv. — A1443

1998, Apr. 25 Litho. Perf. 13
2643 A1443 3fr multicolored 1.25 .30

Tourism Series

 Le Gois Causeway, Island of Noirmoutier, Vendée A1444

 Bay of Somme, Picardy A1445

 Château de Crussol, Ardèche A1446

 Collegiate Church of Mantes A1447

1998, May 2 Photo.
2644 A1444 3fr multicolored 1.25 .30
2645 A1445 3fr multicolored 1.25 .30
Engr.
2646 A1446 3fr multicolored 1.25 .30
2647 A1447 4.40fr multicolored 2.00 .70
  Nos. 2644-2647 (4) 5.75 1.60

Issued: No. 2644, 5/2; No. 2645, 6/27; No. 2646, 7/4; No. 2647, 9/19.

Journey of a Letter Type

Historic "letters:" No. 2648, Dove carrying letter, Noah's Ark. No. 2649, Egyptian writing letter on papyrus. No. 2650, Soldier running to Athens with letter to victory at Marathon. No. 2651, Knight carrying letter on horseback. No. 2652, Writing letters with quill and ink. No. 2653, Astronaut carrrying letter in space from earth to the moon.

1998, May 9 Photo. Perf. 13x13½
2648 A1403 3fr multicolored 1.25 1.00
2649 A1403 3fr multicolored 1.25 1.00
2650 A1403 3fr multicolored 1.25 1.00
2651 A1403 3fr multicolored 1.25 1.00
2652 A1403 3fr multicolored 1.25 1.00
2653 A1403 3fr multicolored 1.25 1.00
  a. Strip, #2648-2653 + label 8.00 6.50

Booklet Stamps
Self-Adhesive
Serpentine Die Cut 11

2654 A1403 3fr like #2648 1.25 1.00
2655 A1403 3fr like #2649 1.25 1.00
2656 A1403 3fr like #2650 1.25 1.00
2657 A1403 3fr like #2651 1.25 1.00
2658 A1403 3fr like #2652 1.25 1.00
2659 A1403 3fr like #2653 1.25 1.00
  a. Bklt. pane, 2 ea #2654-2659 16.00 14.00

By its nature No. 2659a is a complete booklet. The peelable paper backing serves as a booklet cover.

 League of Human Rights, Cent. — A1448

1998, May 9 Perf. 13
2660 A1448 4.40fr multicolored 2.00 .70

 Henri Collet (1885-1951), Composer A1449

1998, May 15 Engr. Perf. 12x13
2661 A1449 4.50fr black, gray & buff 2.00 .80

 French Federation of Philatelic Assoc., 71st Congress, Dunkirk — A1450

Photo. & Engr.
1998, May 29 Perf. 13
2662 A1450 3fr multicolored 1.25 .30

 Mont-Saint-Michel A1451

1998, June 6 Photo. Perf. 13
2663 A1451 3fr multicolored 1.40 .30

 Natl. Music Festival — A1452

1998, June 13
2664 A1452 3fr multicolored 1.25 .50

Europa.

1998 World Cup Soccer Championships Type with Added Inscription, "Champion du Monde"

1998, July 12 Photo. Perf. 12½
2665 A1430 3fr multicolored 1.25 .30

 Stéphane Mallarmé (1842-98), Poet — A1453

Photo. & Engr.
1998, Sept. 5 Perf. 13
2666 A1453 4.40fr multicolored 2.00 .70

 Flowers — A1453a

1.87fr, Liseron. 2.18fr, Coquelicot. 4.66fr, Violette. 7.11fr, Bouton d'or.

1998, Sept. 9 Litho. Perf. 13
2666A A1453a 1.87fr multi .85 .25
2666B A1453a 2.18fr multi 1.00 .50
2666C A1453a 4.66fr multi 2.10 1.00
2666D A1453a 7.11fr multi 3.00 1.75
  Nos. 2666A-2666D (4) 6.95 3.50

Nos. 2666A-2666D are known only precanceled. See second note after No. 132.

 Aéro Club of France, Cent. — A1454

1998, Sept. 12 Photo.
2667 A1454 3fr multicolored 1.25 .30

 A1455

"The Little Prince," by Antoine de Saint-Exupéry (1900-44): a, Standing in uniform with sword, horiz. b, Seated on wall. c, "The Little Prince on Asteroid B-612." d, Pouring water from sprinkling can. e, Walking along cliff, fox, horiz.

1998, Oct. 23 Photo. Perf. 13
2668 Strip of 5 + 2 labels 6.50 4.00
  a.-e. A1455 3fr any single 1.25 .70
  f. Souv. sheet, #2668a-2668e 8.00 8.00

Philexfrance '99. No. 2668f was released 9/12 and sold for 25fr.

FRANCE

Hall of Heavenly Peace, Imperial Palace, Beijing, China — A1456

1998, Sept. 12 Photo. Perf. 13x13½
2669 A1456 3fr shown 1.25 .40
2670 A1456 4.90fr The Louvre, France 2.40 1.25
See People's Republic of China Nos. 2895-2896.

Garnier Palace, Home of the Paris Opera — A1457

1998, Sept. 19 Photo. Perf. 13
2671 A1457 4.50fr multicolored 2.00 .70

Horses — A1458

1998, Sept. 27
2672 A1458 2.70fr Camargue 1.10 .30
2673 A1458 3fr Pottok 1.25 .40
2674 A1458 3fr French trotter 1.25 .40
2675 A1458 4.50fr Ardennais 2.10 .80
Nos. 2672-2675 (4) 5.70 1.90

Paris Auto Show, Cent. — A1459

1998, Oct. 1 Perf. 12
2676 A1459 3fr multicolored 1.25 .30

5th Republic, 40th Anniv. — A1460

1998, Oct. 3 Photo. Perf. 13
2677 A1460 3fr blue, gray & red 1.25 .30

Saint-Dié, Capital of Vosges Mountain Region — A1461

1998, Oct. 3 Engr. Perf. 13
2678 A1461 3fr Tower of Liberty 1.25 .30

End of World War I, 80th Anniv. — A1462

1998, Oct. 17 Photo. Perf. 13x13½
2679 A1462 3fr multicolored 1.25 .30

Intl. Union for the Conservation of Nature and Natural Resources, 50th Anniv. — A1463

1998, Nov. 3 Litho.
2680 A1463 3fr multicolored 1.25 .40

New Year A1464   Christmas A1465

1998, Nov. 7 Photo. Perf. 13
Background Colors
2681 A1464 3fr deep blue 1.60 .70
2682 A1465 3fr green 1.60 .70
2683 A1464 3fr yellow 1.60 .70
2684 A1465 3fr red 1.60 .70
2685 A1464 3fr green 1.60 .70
a. Strip of 5, #2681-2685 8.00 3.50
Issued in sheets of 10 stamps. Location of "Bonne Annee" and "Meilleurs Voeux" varies.

Doctors Without Borders — A1466

1998, Nov. 21 Perf. 13x13½
2686 A1466 3fr multicolored 1.25 .30

European Parliament, Strasbourg A1467

1998, Dec. 5 Photo. Perf. 13
2687 A1467 3fr multicolored 1.25 .30

Universal Declaration of Human Rights, 50th Anniv. — A1468

No. 2688, Faces of people of various races, globe. No. 2689, René Cassin (1887-1976), principal author of Declaration, Eleanor Roosevelt (1884-1962), Chaillot Palace, Paris.

1998, Dec. 10 Litho. Perf. 13
2688 A1468 3fr multicolored 1.25 .40
2689 A1468 3fr multicolored 1.25 .40

Discovery of Radium, Cent., ZOE Reactor, 50th Anniv. — A1469

1998, Dec. 15 Photo. Perf. 13
2690 A1469 3fr multicolored 1.25 .30

Introduction of the Euro — A1470

1999 Engr. Perf. 13
2691 A1470 3fr red & blue 1.25 .25

Booklet Stamps
Self-Adhesive
Die Cut x Serpentine Die Cut 7
2691A A1470 3fr red & blue 1.25 .25
b. Booklet pane of 10 12.50
Issued: No. 2691, 1/1/99. No. 2691A, 2/15/99. Values are shown in both Francs and Euros on Nos. 2691-2691A. No. 2691Ab is a complete booklet.
Euro currency did not circulate until 2002.

French Postage Stamps, 150th Anniv. — A1471

1999, Jan. 1 Photo. Perf. 13
Booklet Stamps
2692 A1471 3fr black & red 7.00 6.00
2693 A1471 3fr red & black 1.25 1.00
a. Booklet pane, #2692, 4 #2693 + label 13.00
Complete booklet, #2693a 14.00
No. 2692 has black denomination; No. 2693 has red denomination.
Stamp Day.

Public Assistance Hospital, Paris, 150th Anniv. — A1472

1999, Jan. 9
2694 A1472 3fr multicolored 1.25 .30

Diplomatic Relations with Israel, 50th Anniv. — A1473

1999, Jan. 24
2695 A1473 4.40fr multicolored 2.00 .75

Festival Stamps — A1474

1999, Feb. 6 Photo. Perf. 13
2696 A1474 3fr Stars, "Je t'aime" 1.25 .30
2697 A1474 3fr Rose 1.25 .30

Booklet Stamps
Self-Adhesive
Die Cut Perf. 10
2698 A1474 3fr like #2696 1.25 .30
2699 A1474 3fr like #2697 1.25 .30
a. Bklt. pane, 5 ea #2698-2699 14.00
No. 2699a is a complete booklet.
A €1.16 stamp of type A1474 was included in a limited-edition booklet issued Nov. 4, 2020.

Art Series

St. Luke the Evangelist, Sculpture by Jean Goujon (1510-66) A1475

Painting, "Waterlillies in Moonlight," by Claude Monet (1840-1926) A1476

Stained Glass, Cathedral of Auch, by Arnauld de Moles, 16th Cent. — A1477

Charles I, King of England, by Sir Anthony Van Dyck — A1478

1999 Engr. Perf. 13
2700 A1475 6.70fr multicolored 3.00 1.00
Litho.
2701 A1476 6.70fr multicolored 3.00 1.00
Engr.
2702 A1477 6.70fr multicolored 3.00 1.00
Photo. Perf. 13¼x13
2703 A1478 6.70fr multicolored 3.00 1.00
Nos. 2700-2703 (4) 12.00 4.00
Issued: No. 2700, 2/13; No. 2701, 5/29; No. 2702, 6/19; No. 2703, 11/11.

National Census — A1479

1999, Feb. 20 Photo. Perf. 13½
2704 A1479 3fr multicolored 1.25 .30

Cultural Heritage of Lebanon A1480

Mosaic illustrating transformation of Zeus into bull, Natl. Museum of Beirut.

1999, Feb. 27 Perf. 12½
2705 A1480 4.40fr multicolored 2.00 .70

Asterix, by Albert Uderzo and Rene Goscinny — A1481

1999, Mar. 6 Photo. Perf. 13¼
2706 A1481 3fr multicolored 1.25 .30
a. Perf. 13¼x12¾ 1.40 1.20

Booklet Stamp
Perf. 13¼x12¾
2707 A1481 3fr +60c like #2706 3.00 1.50
b. Booklet pane, 4 #2706a, 3 #2707 + label 14.00
Complete booklet, #2707b 15.00

Souvenir Sheet
2707A A1481 3fr +60c like #2706 2.50 2.00
Stamp Day. Stamp design in No. 2707A continues into the margins.

Council of Europe, 50th Anniv. — A1482

1999, Mar. 19
2708 A1482 3fr multicolored 1.25 .30

A1483

668   FRANCE

Announcements
A1483a

No. 2709, Marriage (Oui). No. 2710, It's a boy (C'est un garcon). No. 2711, It's a girl (C'est une fille). No. 2712, Thank you.

1999, Mar. 20			Perf. 13	
2709	A1483	3fr multi	1.25	.30
2710	A1483	3fr multi	1.25	.30
2711	A1483	3fr multi	1.25	.30
2712	A1483a	3fr multi	1.25	.30
	Nos. 2709-2712 (4)		5.00	1.20

See Nos. 2721-2722.

Souvenir Sheet

PhilexFrance '99 — A1484

Works of art: a, Venus de Milo. b, Mona Lisa, by Da Vinci. c, Liberty Guiding the People, by Delacroix.

Litho. & Engr.

1999, Mar. 26			Perf. 13¼	
2713	A1484	Sheet of 3	80.00	60.00
a.-b.		5fr each	17.50	12.50
c.		10fr multicolored	37.50	30.00

No. 2713 sold for 50fr, with 30fr serving as a donation to the Assoc. for the Development of Philately.

Elections to the European Parliament A1485

1999, Mar. 27	Photo.		Perf. 13	
2714	A1485	3fr multicolored	1.25	.30

Richard I, the Lion-Hearted (1157-1199), King of England — A1486

1999, Apr. 10	Engr.		Perf. 13x12½	
2715	A1486	3fr multicolored	1.25	.35

Tourism Series

Dieppe — A1487

Haut-Koenigsbourg Castle, Bas-Rhin — A1488

 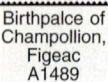

Birthpalce of Champollion, Figeac A1489   Chateau, Arnac-Pompadour A1490

1999	Engr.		Perf. 13½	
2716	A1487	3fr multicolored	1.25	.30

Litho. & Engr.
Perf. 13

2717	A1488	3fr multicolored	1.40	.50
2718	A1489	3fr multicolored	1.25	.30

Engr.

2719	A1490	3fr multicolored	1.25	.30
	Nos. 2716-2719 (4)		5.15	1.40

Issued: No. 2716, 4/17; No. 2717, 5/15; No. 2718, 6/26; No. 2719, 7/10.

The Camargue Nature Preserve A1491

1999, Apr. 24	Photo.		Perf. 13x13½	
2720	A1491	3fr multicolored	1.25	.30

Europa.

Announcements Type of 1999 and

A1492

No. 2721, Nice Holiday (bonnes vacances). No. 2722, Happy Birthday (joyeux anniversaire). No. 2723, Long Live Vacations (Vive les vacances).

1999, May 13	Photo.		Perf. 13	
2721	A1483	3fr multi	1.25	.30
2722	A1483	3fr multi	1.25	.30
2723	A1492	3fr multi	1.25	.30
	Nos. 2721-2723 (3)		3.75	.90

Saint Pierre, Martinique A1493

1999, May 15				
2724	A1493	3fr multi	1.25	.30

Detail of "Noctuelles" Dish, by Émile Gallé, School of Nancy Museum A1494

1999, May 22				
2725	A1494	3fr multi	1.25	.30

Souvenir Sheet

World Old Roses Competition, Lyon — A1495

a, 4.50fr, Mme. Caroline Testout. b, 3fr, Mme. Alfred Carrière. c, 4.50fr, La France.

1999, May 28			Perf. 13½x13	
2726	A1495	Sheet of 3, #a.-c.	5.50	4.50

Court of Saint-Emilion, 800th Anniv. — A1496

1999, May 29	Engr.		Perf. 13¼x13	
2727	A1496	3.80fr multicolored	1.75	.60

Hotel de la Monnaie, French Mint Headquarters A1497

1999, June 5	Engr.		Perf. 13	
2728	A1497	4.50fr brn org & bl	2.00	.75

A1498

1999, June 12	Photo.		Perf. 13¼	
2729	A1498	3fr multicolored	1.25	.30

Countess of Segur (1799-1874), children's storyteller.

Loving Welcome — A1499

1999, June 19			Perf. 13	
2730	A1499	3fr multicolored	1.25	.30

René Caillié (1799-1838), Explorer of Africa — A1500

1999, June 26	Engr.		Perf. 13¼	
2731	A1500	4.50fr multicolored	2.00	.75

1st French Postage Stamps, 150th Anniv. — A1501

1999, July 2	Photo.		Perf. 11¾x13	
2732	A1501	6.70fr multicolored	3.00	1.00

PhilexFrance '99, World Philatelic Exhibition. No. 2732 was printed with a se-tenant label and contains a holographic image. Soaking in water may affect the hologram.

Celebrating the Year 2000 — A1502

1999, July 5	Photo.		Perf. 13	
2733	A1502	3fr multicolored	1.25	.30

Year 2000 Stamp Design Contest Winner A1503

1999, July 6

2734	A1503	3fr multicolored	1.25	.30

Total Solar Eclipse, Aug. 11, 1999 — A1504

1999, July 8			Perf. 12x12¼	
2735	A1504	3fr multicolored	1.25	.30

Gathering of Tall Ships, Rouen, July 9-18 — A1505

Sailing ships: a, Simón Bolivar. b, Iskra. c, Statsraad Lehmkuhl. d, Asgard II. e, Belle Poule. f, Belem. g, Amerigo Vespucci. h, Sagres. i, Europa. j, Cuauhtemoc.

1999, July 10	Photo.		Perf. 13	
2736		1fr Sheet of 10	6.50	6.50
a.-j.	A1505	any single	.60	.50

1999 Rugby World Cup, Cardiff, Wales — A1506

1999, Sept. 11	Photo.		Perf. 13¼	
2737	A1506	3fr multicolored	1.25	.40
a.		Miniature sheet of 10		12.50

Value is for stamp with surrounding selvage. One stamp in No. 2737a has a missing "F" in the printer's mark.

Frédéric Ozanam (1813-53), Historian — A1507

1999, Sept. 11	Engr.		Perf. 13	
2738	A1507	4.50fr multicolored	2.00	.75

Emmaus Movement, 50th Anniv. — A1508

1999, Sept. 26	Photo.		Perf. 13	
2739	A1508	3fr multicolored	1.25	.30

Cats and Dogs — A1509

Designs: No. 2740, Chartreux cat. No. 2741, European cat. No. 2742, Pyrenean Mountain dog. No. 2743, Brittany spaniel.

1999, Oct. 2	Photo.		Perf. 13¼	
2740	A1509	2.70fr multi	1.25	.30
2741	A1509	3fr multi	1.25	.30
2742	A1509	3fr multi	1.25	.30
2743	A1509	4.50fr multi	2.00	.75
	Nos. 2740-2743 (4)		5.75	1.65

Frédéric Chopin (1810-49), Composer A1510

1999, Oct. 17	Engr.		Perf. 13¼	
2744	A1510	3.80fr multicolored	1.75	.70

See Poland No. 3484.

FRANCE

A1511

Best Wishes for Year 2000 — A1512

1999, Nov. 20   Photo.   Perf. 13x13¼
2745 A1511 3fr multi   1.25 .30
2746 A1512 3fr multi   1.25 .30
No. 2746 was printed with se-tenant label.

Paris Metro, Cent. — A1513

1999, Dec. 4   Photo.   Perf. 13
2747 A1513 3fr multi   1.25 .30

Council of State, Bicent. — A1514

1999, Dec. 11
2748 A1514 3fr multi   1.25 .30

Reconstruction of Lighthouses — A1515

2000, Jan. 1   Photo.   Perf. 13x12¾
2749 A1515 3fr multi   1.25 .30
Reconstruction of San Juan de Salvamento Lighthouse, Argentina and replication of its design at La Rochelle, France.

Hearts — A1516

2000, Jan. 8   Photo.   Perf. 13
2750 A1516 3fr Snakes   1.25 .30
2751 A1516 3fr Face   1.25 .30
 a. Souvenir sheet, 3 #2750, 2 #2751   8.00 6.50

Self-Adhesive Booklet Stamps
Serpentine Die-Cut
2752 A1516 3fr Like #2750 1.25 .30
2753 A1516 3fr Like #2751 1.25 .30
 a. Bkt. pane, 5 ea #2752-2753 12.50
Values for Nos. 2750-2751 are for stamps with surrounding selvage. No. 2753a is a complete booklet.

Bank of France, Bicent. — A1517

2000, Jan. 15   Litho.   Perf. 13
2754 A1517 3fr multi   1.25 .30

Prefectorial Corps, Bicent. — A1518

2000, Feb. 17   Photo.   Perf. 13x12¼
2755 A1518 3fr multi   1.25 .30

Art Series

Venus and the Graces Offering Gifts to a Young Girl, by Sandro Botticelli (1445-1510) A1519

The Waltz, by Camille Claudel — A1520

Visage Rouge, by Gaston Chaissac A1521

Carolingian Mosaic, Germigny-des-Prés — A1522

2000   Photo.   Perf. 13¼x13
2756 A1519 6.70fr multi 3.00 1.00
2757 A1520 0.70fr multi 0.60 0.60
2758 A1521 6.70fr multi 3.00 1.00
2759 A1522 6.70fr multi 3.00 1.00
Issued: No. 2756, 2/25; No. 2757, 4/8; No. 2758, 9/23; 10/21.

Tourism Series

Carcassonne — A1523

Saint-Guilhem-Le-Désert — A1524

Gérardmer — A1525

Abbey Church of Ottmarsheim A1526

2000   Photo.   Perf. 13
2760 A1523 3fr multi   1.25 .30
Engr.
Perf. 13¼
2761 A1524 3fr multi   1.25 .30
2762 A1525 3fr multi   1.25 .30
Perf. 12¼x13
2763 A1526 3fr multi   1.25 .30
Nos. 2760-2763 (4) 5.00 1.20
Issued: No. 2760, 3/3; No. 2761, 4/8; No. 2762, 4/17; No. 2763, 6/17.

Tintin — A1527

2000, Mar. 11   Photo.   Perf. 13¼
2764 A1527 3fr multi   1.25 .30
 a. Perf. 13½x13   1.40 1.20
2765 A1527 3fr + 60c multi 2.50 2.00
 a. Booklet pane, 4 #2764a, 3 #2765 + label   14.00
     Complete booklet, #2765a 15.00
 b. Souvenir sheet of 1 2.50 2.00
Stamp Day.

Bretagne Parliament Building Restoration A1528

2000, Mar. 25   Photo.   Perf. 13¼
2766 A1528 3fr multi   1.25 .30

Madagascar Periwinkles A1529

2000, Mar. 25   Litho.   Perf. 13x13¼
2767 A1529 4.50fr multi 2.00 .80

Felicitations A1530

2000, Apr. 7   Photo.   Perf. 13x13¼
2768 A1530 3fr multi   1.25 .30

The 20th Century A1531

No. 2769: a, France as World Cup soccer champions, 1998, vert. b, Marcel Cerdan wins middleweight boxing title, 1948. c, Charles Lindbergh flies solo across Atlantic, 1927. d, Jean-Claude Killy wins three Winter Olympics gold medals, 1968, vert. e, Carl Lewis wins four Olympic gold medals, 1984, vert.

Perf. 13¼x13 (vert. stamps), 13x13¼
2000, Apr. 15
2769 A1531 Sheet, 2 ea #a-e 14.00 14.00
 a.-e. 3fr any single   1.40 .75
Top part of No. 2769 contains Nos. 2769a-2769e and is separated from bottom part of sheet by a row of rouletting.
See No. 2787, 2804, 2837, 2881, 2915.

Automobiles — A1532

No. 2770: a, Bugatti 35. b, Citroen Traction. c, Renault 4CV. d, Simca Chambord. e, Hispano-Suiza K6. f, Volkswagen Beetle. g, 1962 Cadillac. h, Peugeot 203. i, Citroen DS19. j, Ferrari 250 GTO.

2000, May 5   Perf. 13¼x13
2770 A1532 Sheet of 10, #a.-j. 7.50 7.50
 a.-e. 1fr any single   .45 .35
 f.-j. 2fr any single   .90 .60

Europa, 2000
Common Design Type
2000, May 9   Photo.   Perf. 13¼
2771 CD17 3fr multi   1.25 .40

Henry-Louis Duhamel du Monceau (1700-82), Agronomist A1533

2000, May 13   Engr.   Perf. 13
2772 A1533 4.50fr multi 2.00 .80

French Federation of Philatelic Associations, 73rd Congress, Nevers — A1534

2000, May 19   Engr.   Perf. 13¼
2773 A1534 3fr multi   1.25 .30

Happy Vacation — A1535

2000, June 1   Photo.   Perf. 13¼x13
2774 A1535 3fr multi   1.25 .30

A1536

2000, June 3   Engr.   Perf. 13x12¼
2775 A1536 3fr multi   1.25 .30
First Ascent of Annapurna, 50th anniv.

670 FRANCE

Nature — A1537

2.70fr, Agrias sardanapalus butterfly. No. 2777, Giraffe. No. 2778, Allosaurus. 4.50fr, Tulipa lutea.

2000, June 17   Photo.   Perf. 13¼
2776	A1537	2.70fr multi	1.25	.30
2777	A1537	3fr multi, vert.	1.25	.30
2778	A1537	3fr multi	1.25	.30
2779	A1537	4.50fr multi, vert	2.00	.75
a.		Souvenir sheet, #2776-2779	6.00	6.00
		Nos. 2776-2779 (4)	5.75	1.65

Antoine de Saint-Exupéry (1900-44), Aviator, Writer — A1538

2000, June 24   Photo.   Perf. 13¼x13
| 2780 | A1538 | 3fr multi | 1.25 | .30 |

Yellow Train of Cerdagne, Cent. — A1539

2000, July 14   Perf. 13x13¼
| 2781 | A1539 | 3fr multi | 1.25 | .30 |

Folklore — A1540

2000, Aug. 12   Photo.   Perf. 13
| 2782 | A1540 | 4.50fr multi | 2.00 | .80 |

2000 Summer Olympics, Sydney — A1541

Designs: No. 2783, Cycling, fencing, relay racer. No. 2784, Relay racer, judo, diving.

2000, Sept. 9
2783	A1541	3fr multi	1.40	.30
2784	A1541	3fr multi	1.40	.30
a.		Pair, #2783-2784	3.00	2.00
b.		Sheet, 5 #2784a + label	15.00	15.00

Olymphilex 2000, Sydney (No. 2784b).

Brother Alfred Stanke (1904-75) A1542

2000, Sept. 23   Engr.
| 2785 | A1542 | 4.40fr multi | 2.00 | .70 |

S.O.S. Amitié, 40th Anniv. — A1543

2000, Sept. 30   Litho.   Perf. 13
| 2786 | A1543 | 3fr multi | 1.40 | .30 |

20th Century Type

No. 2787: a, Man on the Moon, 1969, vert. b, Paid vacations, 1936. c, Invention of washing machine, 1901, vert. d, Woman suffrage, 1944, vert. e, Universal Declaration of Human Rights, 1948.

Perf. 13¼x13 (vert. stamps), 13x13¼
2000, Sept. 30   Photo.
| 2787 | A1531 | Sheet, 2 each | 14.00 | 14.00 |
| a.-e. | | 3fr Any single | 1.40 | .50 |

The top and bottom parts of No. 2787 contains Nos. 2787a-2787e and are separated by a row of rouletting.

2001, Start of New Millennium A1544

2000, Oct. 14   Litho.   Perf. 13
| 2788 | A1544 | 3fr multi | 1.40 | .30 |

The Lovers' Kiosk, by Peynet — A1545

2000, Nov. 4   Engr.   Perf. 13¼x13
| 2789 | A1545 | 3fr multi | 1.40 | .50 |

Endangered Birds — A1546

2000, Nov. 4   Photo.   Perf. 13¼
| 2790 | A1546 | 3fr Kiwi | 1.40 | .40 |
| 2791 | A1546 | 5.20fr Falcon | 2.50 | 1.50 |

See New Zealand Nos. 1688, 1694.

Start of the 3rd Millennium — A1547

2000, Nov. 9   Photo.   Perf. 13x13¼
| 2792 | A1547 | 3fr multi + label | 1.40 | .30 |

Issued in sheets of 10 stamps + 10 labels, which could be personalized for an extra fee.

Holiday Greetings A1548

2000, Nov. 11   Perf. 12¼x13
| 2793 | A1548 | 3fr Meilleurs voeux | 1.40 | .30 |

Perf. 13¼
| 2794 | A1548 | 3fr Bonne année | 1.40 | .30 |

Union of Metallurgical & Mining Industries, Cent. — A1549

Engr. with Foil Application
2000, Dec. 9   Perf. 13x13¼
| 2795 | A1549 | 4.50fr multi | 2.10 | .90 |

World Handball Championships A1550

2001, Jan. 20   Photo.   Perf. 13¼
| 2796 | A1550 | 3fr multi | 1.40 | .30 |

Heart — A1551

2001, Jan. 27
| 2797 | A1551 | 3fr multi | 1.40 | .30 |
| a. | | Souvenir sheet of 5 | 10.00 | 10.00 |

Value of No. 2797 is for stamp with surrounding selvage.

Art Series

The Peasant Dance, by Pieter Breughel, the Elder A1552

Hotel des Chevaliers de Saint-Jean-de-Jérusalem — A1553

Yvette Guilbert Singing "Linger, Longer, Loo," by Henri de Toulouse-Lautrec (1864-1901) A1554

Honfleur at Low Tide, by Johan Barthold Jongkind A1555

Engr., Photo (#2800), Litho (#2801)
2001   Perf. 13x13¼, 13¼x13 (#2800)
2798	A1552	6.70fr multi	3.00	1.00
2799	A1553	6.70fr multi	3.00	1.00
2800	A1554	6.70fr multi	3.00	1.00
2801	A1555	6.70fr multi	3.00	1.00
		Nos. 2798-2801 (4)	12.00	4.00

Issued: No. 2798, 2/3; No. 2799, 4/21; No. 2800, 9/8; No. 2801, 10/27.

Gaston Lagaffe, by André Franquin — A1556

2001, Feb. 24   Photo.   Perf. 13¼
| 2802 | A1556 | 3fr multi | 1.40 | .30 |
| a. | | Perf. 13¼x13 | 1.40 | 1.20 |

Perf. 13¼x13
2803	A1556	3fr +60c multi	3.00	1.50
a.		Souvenir sheet of 1	6.00	3.50
b.		Booklet pane, 5 #2802a, 3 #2803	18.00	
		Booklet, #2803b	19.00	

Stamp Day.

20th Century Type of 2000

No. 2804 — Communications: a, Television. b, Compact disc. c, Advertisements, vert. d, Radio, vert. e, Portable telephone, vert.

Perf. 13¼x13 (vert. stamps), 13x13¼
2001, Mar. 17   Photo.
| 2804 | A1531 | Sheet, 2 each | 14.00 | 14.00 |
| a.-e. | | 3fr Any single | 1.40 | .75 |

Top part of No. 2804 contains Nos. 2804a-2804e and is separated from bottom part by a row of rouletting.

Announcements A1557

Designs: No. 2805, It's a girl. No. 2806, It's a boy. No. 2807, Thank you. 4.50fr, Yes (marriage).

2001   Frame Color   Perf. 13
2805	A1557	3fr brt pink	1.40	.30
a.		Litho., stamp + label	6.50	6.50
2806	A1557	3fr brt blue	1.40	.30
a.		Litho., stamp + label	6.50	6.50
2807	A1557	3fr brt yel grn	1.40	.30
a.		Litho., stamp + label	6.50	6.50
2808	A1557	4.50fr orange	2.10	.75
		Nos. 2805-2808 (4)	6.30	1.65

Issued: Nos. 2805-2808, 3/23; Nos. 2805a-2807a, 11/8.

Nos. 2805a-2807a were issued in sheets of 10 stamps and 10 labels that sold for 60fr on day of issue. The labels could be personalized. Frames on Nos. 2805 and 2806 look splotchy, while those on Nos. 2805a and 2806a have a distinct dot structure. The frame on No. 2807 has tightly spaced small dots, while on No. 2807a, the dots are more widely spaced.

Wildlife — A1558

2001, Apr. 21   Photo.   Perf. 13¼
2809	A1558	2.70fr Squirrel	1.25	.40
2810	A1558	3fr Roe deer	1.40	.40
2811	A1558	3fr Hedgehog, horiz.	1.40	.40
2812	A1558	4.50fr Ermine	2.10	.75
a.		Souvenir sheet, #2809-2812	7.00	6.50
		Nos. 2809-2812 (4)	6.15	1.95

Tourism Issue

Nogent-le-Rotrou A1559

Besançon A1560

Calais — A1561

Château de Grignan A1562

FRANCE

Engr., Litho & Engr. (#2813)
2001   Perf. 13¼x13 (#2813), 13

2813	A1559	3fr multi	1.40	.40
2814	A1560	3fr multi	1.40	.30
2815	A1561	3fr multi	1.40	.30
2816	A1562	3fr multi	1.40	.30
		Nos. 2813-2816 (4)	5.60	1.30

Issued: No. 2813, 4/28; No. 2814, 5/5; No. 2815, 6/16; No. 2816, 7/7.

Europa — A1563

2001, May 8   Photo.   Perf. 13
2817   A1563   3fr multi   1.40   .35

Gardens of Versailles — A1564

2001, May 12
2818   A1564   4.40fr multi   2.00   .80

Singers — A1565

Designs: No. 2819, Claude François (1939-78). No. 2820, Lóo Forró (1016-93). No. 2821, Serge Gainsbourg (1928-91). No. 2822, Dalida (1933-87). No. 2823, Michel Berger (1947-92). No. 2824, Barbara (1930-97).

2001, May 19   Photo.   Perf. 13

2819	A1565	3fr multi	1.40	.75
2820	A1565	3fr multi	1.40	.75
2821	A1565	3fr multi	1.40	.75
2822	A1565	3fr multi	1.40	.75
2823	A1565	3fr multi	1.40	.75
2824	A1565	3fr multi	1.40	.75
a.		Souvenir sheet, #2819-2824	12.00	12.00
		Nos. 2819-2824 (6)	8.40	4.50

No. 2824a sold for 28fr with the Red Cross receiving 10fr of that.

Old Lyon — A1566

2001, May 19   Engr.   Perf. 13¼
2825   A1566   3fr multi   1.40   .30

French Federation of Philatelic Associations 74th Congress, Tours — A1567

2001, June 1
2826   A1567   3fr multi   1.40   .30

Jean Vilar (1912-71), Actor — A1568

Litho. & Engr.
2001, June 7   Perf. 13
2827   A1568   3fr multi   1.40   .40

Vacation A1569

2001, June 10   Litho.   Perf. 13
2828   A1569   3fr multi   1.40   .30

Booklet Stamp
Self-Adhesive
2829   A1569   3fr multi   1.40   .30
   a.   Booklet of 10   14.00

1 Euro Coin — A1570

2001, June 23   Photo.   Perf. 12½
2830   A1570   3fr multi   1.40   .30

Value is for copy with surrounding selvage.

Albert Caquot (1881-1976), Engineer A1571

2001, June 30   Engr.   Perf. 13¼
2831   A1571   4.50fr multi   2.00   .75

Law Guaranteeing Freedom of Association, Cent. — A1572

2001, July 1   Photo.   Perf. 13
2832   A1572   3fr multi   1.40   .30

Trains A1573

No. 2833: a, Eurostar. b, American 220. c, Crocodile. d, Crampton. e, Garratt 59. f, Pacific Chapelon. g, Mallard. h, Capitole. i, Autorail Panoramique. j, 230 Class P8.

2001, July 6   Photo.   Perf. 13¼
2833   A1573   Sheet of 10   10.00   8.00
   a.-j.   1.50fr Any single   .90   .65

Geneva Convention on Refugees, UN High Commisioner for Refugees, 50th Anniv. — A1574

2001, July 28   Perf. 13
2834   A1574   4.50fr multi   2.00   .75

Marianne Type of 1997 Inscribed "RF" at Lower Left Instead of "La Poste"
2001   Engr.   Perf. 13
2835   A1409   (3fr) red   1.40   .25
   d.   Sheet of 15 + 15 labels   60.00   —

Serpentine Die Cut 6¾ Vert.
Self-Adhesive
2835A   A1409   (3fr) red   1.40   .25
   b.   Booklet of 10   15.00
   e.   No. 2835 with attached label   6.00

No. 2835Ae is from a sheet having either small or large-sized labels that could be personalized.

2001, Aug. 1   Engr.   Perf. 13 Horiz.
Coil Stamp
Water-Activated Gum
2835C   A1409   (3fr) red   1.40   .25

Issued: Nos. 2835, 2835C, 8/1; No. 2835A, 9/24. No. 2835Ae, 2004.
No. 2835d sold for €10.03. Labels could be personalized for an additional price.

Pierre de Fermat (1601-65), Mathematician A1575

2001, Aug. 19   Engr.   Perf. 13¼x13
2836   A1575   4.50fr multi   2.00   .75

20th Century Type of 2000
No. 2837 — Science: a, First man in space. b, DNA. c, Chip cards. d, Laser. e, Penicillin.

Perf. 13¼x13 (vert. stamps), 13
2001, Sept. 22   Photo.
2837   A1531   Sheet, 2 each #a-e   14.00   14.00
   a.-e.   3fr Any single   1.40   .70

Top part of No. 2837 contains Nos. 2837a-2837e and is separated from bottom part of sheet by a row of rouletting.

Astrolabe Sculpture, Val-de-Reuil A1576

2001, Sept. 29   Perf. 13
2838   A1576   3fr multi   1.40   .30

Halloween A1577

2001, Oct. 20
2839   A1577   3fr multi   1.40   .30
   a.   Souvenir sheet of 5 + 4 labels   8.00   8.00

Jean Pierre-Bloch (1905-99), Human Rights Advocate — A1578

2001, Nov. 8   Engr.   Perf. 13
2840   A1578   4.50fr multi   2.00   .75

Albert Decaris (1901-88), Artist — A1579

2001, Nov. 9   Engr.   Perf. 13¼x13
2841   A1579   3fr multi   1.40   .40

Jacques Chaban-Delmas (1915-2000), Politician — A1580

2001, Nov. 10   Engr.   Perf. 13x13¼
2842   A1580   3fr multi   1.40   .40

Holiday Greetings A1581

Designs: Nos. 2843, 2845 Bonne Année (Happy New Year). Nos. 2844, 2846 Meilleurs Voeux (Best wishes).

2001, Nov. 9   Litho.   Perf. 13
2843   A1581   3fr multi   1.40   .30
2844   A1581   3fr multi   1.40   .30

Serpentine Die Cut 11
Self-Adhesive
Booklet Stamps
2845   A1581   3fr multi   1.40   .30
2846   A1581   3fr multi   1.40   .30
   a.   Booklet, 5 each # 2845-2846   14.00

Fountains — A1582

Designs: 3fr, Nejjarine Fountain, Fez, Morocco. 3.80fr, Wallace Fountain, Paris.

2001, Dec. 14   Photo.   Perf. 13¼
2847   A1582   3fr multi   1.40   .40
2848   A1582   3.80fr multi   1.75   1.00

See Morocco Nos. 914-915.

100 Cents = 1 Euro (€)

Marianne (With Euro Denominations) — A1583

2002, Jan. 1   Engr.   Perf. 13

2849	A1583	1c yellow	.25	.25
2850	A1583	2c brown	.25	.25
2851	A1583	5c brt bl grn	.25	.25
2852	A1583	10c purple	.25	.25
2853	A1583	20c brt org	.60	.30
2854	A1583	41c brt green	1.20	.25
2855	A1583	50c dk blue	1.50	.25
2856	A1583	53c apple grn	1.60	.40
2857	A1583	58c blue	1.75	.50
2858	A1583	64c dark org	1.90	.50
2859	A1583	67c brt blue	2.00	.50
a.		67c deep blue	2.00	.50
2860	A1583	69c brt pink	2.10	.60
2861	A1583	€1 Prus blue	3.00	.80
2862	A1583	€1.02 dk green	3.00	.90
a.		Souvenir sheet, #2835, 2854, 2856, 2858, 2860a, 2860, 2862	15.00	15.00
2863	A1583	€2 violet	6.00	1.50
a.		Souvenir sheet, #2849-2853, 2855, 2861, 2863	12.00	12.00
		Nos. 2849-2863 (15)	25.65	7.50

Coil Stamp
Perf. 13 Horiz.
2864   A1583   41c brt green   1.50   .30

See Nos. 2952-2957, 3043, 3043P-3043Q.

Orchids — A1584

Designs: 29c, Orchis insularis. 33c, Ophrys fuciflora.

2002, Jan. 2   Litho.   Perf. 13
2865   A1584   29c multi   1.00   .30
2866   A1584   33c multi   1.50   .40

Nos. 2865-2866 are known only precanceled. See second note after No. 132.
See Nos. 2958-2959, 3046, 3168.

672　　　　　　　　　　　　　　　　　　　　　　　　　FRANCE

Heart of Voh, Photograph by Yann Arthurs-Bertrand A1585

2002, Jan. 18		Photo.	Perf. 13¼
2867	A1585 46c multi	1.40	.40
a.	Souvenir sheet of 5	7.00	7.00

Value of No. 2867 is for stamp with surrounding selvage.

2002 Winter Olympics, Salt Lake City — A1586

2002, Jan. 26			Perf. 13
2868	A1586 46c multi	1.40	.30

Art Series

Sphere Concorde, by Jesús Rafael Soto — A1587

The Kiss, by Gustav Klimt — A1588

The Dancers, by Fernando Botero — A1589

Self-Portrait, by Elisabeth Vigée-Lebrun A1590

2002		Photo.	Perf. 13¼x13
2869	A1587 75c multi	2.25	1.00
2870	A1588 €1.02 multi	3.00	1.00
2871	A1589 €1.02 multi	3.00	1.00
		Engr.	
2872	A1590 €1.02 multi	3.00	1.00
	Nos. 2869-2872 (4)	11.25	4.00

Issued: No. 2869, 11/11. No. 2870, 2/8; No. 2871, 4/27. No. 2872, 10/12.

Alain Bosquet (1919-98), Poet — A1591

2002, Feb. 16		Engr.	Perf. 13
2873	A1591 58c multi	1.75	.80

It's A Girl — A1592

It's A Boy — A1593

Yes — A1594

2002, Feb. 23			Photo.
2874	A1592 46c multi	1.40	.30
2875	A1593 46c multi	1.40	.30
2876	A1594 69c multi	2.00	.80
	Nos. 2874-2876 (3)	4.80	1.40

Europa — A1595

2002, Mar. 2			Perf. 13¼
2877	A1595 46c multi	1.40	.30

Boule and Bill, by Jean Roba — A1596

Designs: 46c, Boule, Bill, bird. 46c+9c, Boule, Bill, ball.

2002, Mar. 16			Perf. 13¼
2878	A1596 46c multi	1.40	.50
a.	Perf. 13¼x13	1.40	1.20
		Perf. 13¼x13	
2879	A1596 46c +9c multi	3.00	1.50
a.	Souvenir sheet of 1	3.00	2.50
b.	Booklet pane, 5 #2878a, 3 #2879	18.00	—
	Booklet, #2879b	19.00	

Stamp Day. No. 2879 surtax for Red Cross. Stamp on No. 2879a has continuous design.

Nimes Amphitheater — A1597

		Litho. & Engr.	
2002, Mar. 22			Perf. 13
2880	A1597 46c multi	1.40	.30

20th Century Type of 2000

No. 2881 — Transportation: a, Concorde supersonic airplane. b, TGV train. c, Ocean liner France, vert. d, Mobylette motor scooter, vert. e, Citroen 2 CV automobile, vert.

	Perf. 13, 13¼x13 (vert. stamps)		
2002, Mar. 23			Photo.
2881	A1531 Sheet, 2 each #a-e	14.00	14.00
a.-e.	46c Any single	1.40	.75

Top part of No. 2881 contains Nos. 2881a-2881e and is separated from bottom part of sheet by a row of roulletting.

Encounter of Matthew Flinders and Nicolas Boudin, Bicent. — A1598

Map of Australia, portrait and ship of: 46c, Flinders. 79c, Boudin.

2002, Apr. 4			Perf. 13¼
2882	A1598 46c multi	1.40	.40
2883	A1598 79c multi	2.25	1.50

See Australia Nos. 2053-2054.

Tourism Series

La Charité-sur-Loire A1599

Collioure A1600

Locronan A1601

Neufchateau A1602

	Engraved (#2884, 2886), Photo. (#2885)		
2002			Perf. 13¼
2884	A1599 46c multi	1.40	.30
2885	A1600 46c multi	1.40	.30
2886	A1601 46c multi	1.40	.30
2887	A1602 46c multi	1.40	.30
	Nos. 2884-2887 (4)	5.60	1.20

Issue dates: No. 2884, 4/6; No. 2885, 6/22; No. 2886, 7/13; No. 2887, 10/12/02.
Numbers have been reserved for additional stamps in this set.

Birthday Greetings A1603

Invitation — A1604

2002, Apr. 6		Photo.	Perf. 13
2888	A1603 46c multi	1.40	.30
a.	Litho., stamp + label	6.00	6.00
2889	A1604 46c multi	1.40	.30
a.	Litho., stamp + label	6.00	6.00

Issued: Nos. 2888a, 2889a, 11/7. Nos. 2888a and 2889a were issued in sheets of 10 stamps and 10 labels that sold for €6.19 on day of issue. The labels could be personalized.
No. 2888a has a duller blue in "Anniversaire" than No. 2888, but is otherwise quite similar in appearance. The gold ink on No. 2889a has a more coppery look than that on No. 2889.

100th Paris-Roubaix Bicycle Race — A1605

2002, Mar. 13			
2890	A1605 46c multi	1.40	.30

2002 World Cup Soccer Championships, Japan and Korea — A1606

No. 2891: a, Flags, soccer ball and field (32mm diameter). b, Soccer player, year of French championship.

2002, Apr. 27			Perf. 12¾
2891	A1606 Horiz. pair	2.75	2.50
a.-b.	46c Any single	1.40	.30
c.	Sheet, 5 #2891	15.00	15.00

Issued: No. 2891c, 5/18.
See Argentina No. 2184, Brazil No. 2840, Germany No. 2163, Italy No. 2526 and Uruguay No. 1946.

Marine Life — A1607

Designs: 41c, Sea turtle (tortue luth), vert. No. 2893, Killer whale (orque). No. 2894, Dolphin (grand dauphin). 69c, Seal (phoque veau marin).

2002, May 4			Perf. 13¼
2892	A1607 41c multi	1.25	.30
2893	A1607 46c multi	1.25	.30
2894	A1607 46c multi	1.25	.30
2895	A1607 69c multi	2.00	.75
a.	Souvenir sheet, #2892-2895	6.50	6.50
	Nos. 2892-2895 (4)	5.75	1.65

Worldwide Fund for Nature (No. 2895a).

French Federation of Philatelic Associations 75th Congress, Marseilles — A1608

2002, May 17		Engr.	Perf. 13
2896	A1608 46c multi	1.40	.30

Legion of Honor, Bicent. — A1609

2002, May 18			Photo.
2897	A1609 46c multi	1.40	.30

Rocamadour — A1610

2002, May 25			Perf. 13¼
2898	A1610 46c multi	1.40	.30

Louis Delgrés (1766-1802), Soldier — A1611

2002, May 25			
2899	A1611 46c multi	1.40	.30

Vacation — A1612

2002, June 8		Litho.	Perf. 13
2900	A1612 46c multi	1.40	.30

Self-Adhesive
Serpentine Die Cut 11

2901	A1612 46c multi	1.40	.30
a.	Booklet pane of 10	14.00	

FRANCE 673

World Disabled Athletics Championships A1613

2002, June 15 Photo. Perf. 13¼
2902 A1613 46c multi 1.40 .30

Saint-Ser Chapel — A1614

2002, June 22 Engr. Perf. 13x13¼
2903 A1614 46c multi 1.40 .30

Metz Cathedral Stained Glass — A1615

2002, July 6 Engr. Perf. 13¼x13
2904 A1615 46c multi 1.40 .40

Jazz Musicians — A1616

Designs: No. 2905, Louis Armstrong (1901-71). No. 2906, Ella Fitzgerald (1918-96). No. 2907, Duke Ellington (1899-1974). No. 2908, Stéphane Grappelli (1908-97). No. 2909, Michel Petrucciani (1962-99), horiz. No. 2910, Sidney Bechet (1897-1959), horiz.

2002, July 13 Photo. Perf. 13
2905 A1616 46c multi 1.40 .75
2906 A1616 46c multi 1.40 .75
2907 A1616 46c multi 1.40 .75
2908 A1616 46c multi 1.40 .75
2909 A1616 46c multi 1.40 .75
2910 A1616 46c multi 1.40 .75
  a. Souvenir sheet, #2905-2910 12.00 12.00
  Nos. 2905-2910 (6) 8.40 4.50

No. 2910a sold for €4.36, with the Red Cross receiving €1.60 of that.

Pilgrimages to Notre Dame de la Salette, 150th Anniv. — A1617

2002, Aug. 15 Engr. Perf. 13¼x13
2911 A1617 46c multi 1.40 .30

Choreography — A1618

2002, Sept. 13 Photo. Perf. 13x13¼
2912 A1618 53c multi 1.60 .70

Motorcycles — A1619

No. 2913: a, Honda 750 four. b, Terrot 500 RGST. c, Majestic. d, Norton Commando 750. e, Voxan 1000 Café Racer. f, BMW R90S. g, Harley Davidson Hydra Glide. h, Triumph Bonneville 650. i, Ducati 916. j, Yamaha 500 XT.

2002, Sept. 14 Perf. 13¼x13
2913 A1619 Sheet of 10 12.00 12.00
  a.-e. 16c any single .75 .60
  f.-j. 30c any single .90 .75

Georges Perec (1936-82), Writer — A1620

2002, Sept. 21 Engr. Perf. 13¼
2914 A1620 46c multi 1.40 .30

20th Century Type of 2000

No. 2915 — Photographs of everyday life: a, Family on motor scooter, 1955, vert. b, Man, horse and wagon, 1947. c, Woman ironing, 1950. d, Boy at fountain, 1950, vert. e, Girl in classroom, 1965, vert.

Perf. 13¼x13 (vert. stamps), 13
2002, Sept. 28 Photo.
2915 A1531 Sheet, 2 each #a-e 14.00 14.00
  a.-e. 46c any single 1.40 .75

Top part of No. 2915 contains Nos. 2915a-2915e and is separated from bottom part of sheet by a row of rouletting.

Emile Zola (1840-1902), Novelist — A1621

2002, Oct. 5 Perf. 13
2916 A1621 46c multi 1.40 .30

Souvenir Sheet

European Capitals — A1622

Attractions in Rome: a, Trevi Fountain. b, Coliseum, horiz. c, Trinità de Monti Church and Spanish Steps. d, St. Peter's Basilica, horiz.

2002, Nov. 7 Perf. 13¼x13, 13x13¼
2917 A1622 Sheet of 4 6.00 6.00
  a.-d. 46c Any single 1.40 .90

See Nos. 2985, 3052, 3138, 3223, 3340, 3535, 3728, 3908, 3986, 4183, 4365.

Globe and Microcircuits A1623

2002, Nov. 8 Photo. Perf. 13
2918 A1623 46c multi 1.40 .30
  a. Litho., stamp + label 6.00 6.00

Issued: No. 2918a, 11/7. No. 2918a was issued in sheets of 10 stamps and 10 labels that sold for €6.19 on day of issue. The labels could be personalized.
No. 2918a has a hairline at top, above "RF" that No. 2918 does not have, but is otherwise quite similar in appearance.

Holiday Greetings A1624

2002, Nov. 8 Photo. Perf. 13
2919 A1624 46c multi 1.40 .30
  a. Litho., stamp + label 6.00 6.00

Booklet Stamp
Self-Adhesive
Serpentine Die Cut 11
2920 A1624 46c multi 1.40 .30
  a. Booklet pane of 10 14.00

Issued: No. 2919a, 11/7. No. 2919a was issued in sheets of 10 stamps and 10 labels that sold for €6.19 on day of issue. The labels could be personalized.
No. 2919a has a finer dot structure, which is most noticeable in the chimney smoke, than No. 2919.

Marianne Type of 1997 Inscribed "RF" at Lower Left
2002, Nov. 9 Engr. Perf. 13
2921 A1409 (41c) bright green 1.20 .25

Coil Stamp
Perf. 13 Horiz.
2922 A1409 (41c) bright green 1.20 .25

Alexandre Dumas (Father) (1802-70), Writer — A1625

2002, Nov. 30 Photo. Perf. 13
2924 A1625 46c multi 1.40 .30

Léopold Sédar Senghor (1906-2001), President of Senegal, Poet — A1626

2002, Dec. 20
2925 A1626 46c multi 1.40 .30

Hearts — A1627

2003, Jan. 11 Perf. 13¼
2926 A1627 46c Four hearts 1.40 .30
  a. Souvenir sheet of 5 7.00 7.00
2927 A1627 69c Roses 2.00 .75

Values for Nos. 2926-2927 are for examples with surrounding salvage.

Thank You — A1628

Birth — A1629

2003, Jan. 11 Perf. 13
2928 A1628 46c multi 1.40 .30
2929 A1629 46c brt org & brt bl 1.40 .30

Franco-German Cooperation Treaty, 40th Anniv. — A1630

2003, Jan. 16 Perf. 13¼
2930 A1630 46c multi 1.40 .40

A1631

2003, Feb. 8 Photo. Perf. 13
2931 A1631 46c multi 1.40 .30

Delegation for Land-use Planning and Regional Action, 40th Anniv.

Geneviève de Gaulle Anthonioz (1920-2002), World War II Resistance Fighter — A1632

2003, Feb. 11
2932 A1632 46c blk & ol brn 1.40 .30

Paris Chamber of Commerce and Industry, Bicent. — A1633

2003, Feb. 22 Perf. 13¼
2933 A1633 46c multi 1.40 .30

Lucky Luke, by Morris (Maurice De Bevere) — A1634

Lucky Luke and Jolly Jumper: 46c, Skipping rope on ball on high wire. 46c+9c, Following Joy, Rantanplan.

2003, Mar. 15 Photo. Perf. 13¼
2934 A1634 46c multi 1.40 .65
  a. Perf. 13¼x13 1.40 .65

Perf. 13¼x13
2935 A1634 46c +9c multi 3.50 2.00
  a. Souvenir sheet of 1 3.00 2.50
  b. Booklet pane, 5 #2934a, 3 #2935 17.50 —
  Complete booklet, #2935b 18.00

Stamp Day

Birds — A1635

Designs: 41c, Colibri à tete bleue (Cyanophaia bicolor). No. 2037, Toucan ariel (Ramphastos vitellinus). No. 2938, Colibri grenat (Eulampis jugularis), vert. 69c, Terpsiphone de Bourbon (Terpsiphone bourbonnensis).

2003, Mar. 22 Photo. Perf. 13¼
2936 A1635 41c multi 1.20 .30
2937 A1635 46c multi 1.40 .30
2938 A1635 46c multi 1.40 .30
2939 A1635 69c multi 2.00 .75
  a. Souvenir sheet, #2936-2939 7.00 7.00
  Nos. 2936-2939 (4) 6.00 1.65

Nantes — A1636

2003, Apr. 4   Engr.
2940 A1636 46c multi   1.40 .30

Pierre Bérégovoy (1925-93), Prime Minister — A1637

2003, Apr. 30   Engr.   Perf. 13x13¼
2941 A1637 46c multi   1.40 .30

Milan Stefanik (1880-1919), Czechoslovakian General — A1638

2003, May 3   Perf. 13¼
2942 A1638 50c multi   1.50 .40

See Slovakia No. 428.

Europa — A1639

2003, May 8   Photo.
2943 A1639 50c multi   1.50 .40

Charter of Fundamental Rights of the European Union — A1640

2003, May 8
2944 A1640 50c multi   1.50 .30

Aircraft Carrier "Charles de Gaulle" — A1641

2003, May 8   Engr.
2945 A1641 50c multi   1.50 .30

Aspects of Life in the French Regions — A1642

No. 2946: a, Beach cabins. b, Fishing net. c, Vineyards of Champagne. d, Camembert cheese, vert. e, Foie gras, vert. f, Petanque. g, Puppet show (Guignol). vert. h, Crepe, vert. i, Cassoulet. j, Limoges porcelain.

2003, May 24   Photo.   Perf. 13
2946   Sheet of 10   16.00 16.00
a.-j. A1642 50c Any single   1.50 1.30

No. 2946 has three vertical rows of rouletting, separating sheet into quarters.

Nos. 2946a-2946j were also issued in large booklets containing panes of 1 of each stamp. The booklet sold for €19.

See Nos. 2978, 3007, 3047, 3106, 3139, 3192, 3234, 3299, 3300-3301, 3357, 3427, 3505.

Art Series

"The Dying Slave" and "The Rebel Slave," by Michelangelo A1643

The Red Buoy, by Paul Signac — A1644

Untitled Abstract by Vassily Kandinsky A1645

Marilyn, by Andy Warhol — A1646

2003   Engr.   Perf. 13¼x13
2947 A1643 75c multi   2.50 1.25
    Photo.
2948 A1644 75c multi   2.50 1.25
    Litho.
2949 A1645 €1.11 multi   3.50 1.25
2950 A1646 €1.11 multi   3.50 1.40
    Nos. 2947-2950 (4)   12.00 5.15

Issued: No. 2947, 5/24. Nos. 2948, 2949, 7/5. No. 2950, 11/8.
A sheet containing 3 No. 2949 and 12 imperforate color progressive proofs was bound in a book that sold for €60.

Happy Birthday — A1647

2003, May 31   Photo.   Perf. 13¼
2951 A1647 50c multi   1.50 .35
a.   Souvenir sheet of 5   7.50 7.50
b.   Litho., stamp + label   1.75 1.50

Issued: No. 2951b, 2004. No. 2951b was issued in sheets of 10 stamps + 10 labels that sold for €6.67 on day of issue. The labels could be personalized. The background on No. 2951 looks splotchy while that of No. 2951b has a dot structure.

Marianne With Euro Denominations Type of 2002

2003, June 1   Engr.   Perf. 13
2952 A1583 58c apple grn   1.75 .40
2953 A1583 70c yellow grn   2.00 .50
2954 A1583 75c bright blue   2.25 .25
2955 A1583 90c dark blue   2.60 1.00
2956 A1583 €1.11 red lilac   3.25 .25
2957 A1583 €1.90 vio brn   5.75 .40
a.   Souvenir sheet, #2835,
    2921, 2952-2957   22.00 22.00
    Nos. 2952-2957 (6)   17.60 2.80

No. 2957a issued 2/28/04.

Orchids Type of 2002

Designs: 30c, Platanthera chlorantha. 35c, Dactylorhiza savogiensis.

2003, June 1   Litho.   Perf. 13
2958 A1584 30c multi   1.00 .30
2959 A1584 35c multi   1.50 .40

Nos. 2958-2959 are known only precanceled. See second note after No. 132.

French Federation of Philatelic Associations 76th Congress, Mulhouse — A1648

2003, June 6   Engr.   Perf. 13¼
2960 A1648 50c multi   1.50 .30

Vacation — A1649

    Perf. 12¾x13¼
2003, June 14   Litho.
2961 A1649 50c multi   1.50 .30

Self-Adhesive Booklet Stamp
    Serpentine Die Cut 11
2962 A1649 50c multi   1.50 .30
a.   Booklet pane of 10   15.00

Tourism Issue

Notre Dame de l'Epine Basilica A1650

Tulle A1651

Arras A1652

Pontarlier — A1653

    Perf. 13x13¼, 13 (#2965)
2003, June 21   Engr.
2963 A1650 50c multi   1.50 .30
2964 A1651 50c multi   1.50 .30
2965 A1652 50c multi   1.50 .30
2966 A1653 50c multi   1.50 .30
    Nos. 2963-2966 (4)   6.00 1.20

Issued: Nos. 2963, 2964, 6/21. No. 2965, 9/20. No. 2966, 10/11.

French Freemasonry, 275th Anniv. — A1654

2003, June 28   Engr.   Perf. 13¼x13
2967 A1654 50c multi   1.50 .30

Tour de France Bicycle Race, Cent. — A1655

2003, June 28   Photo.   Perf. 13
2968 A1655   Vert. pair   3.00 2.00
a.-b.   50c Either single   1.50 .30

Values are for stamps with surrounding selvage.

No. 2968: a, Maurice Garin, winner of 1903 race. b, Cyclist with arms raised.

Saint-Père Church, Yonne — A1656

2003, July 12   Engr.   Perf. 13¼
2969 A1656 50c multi   1.50 .30

World Track and Field Championships, Paris — A1657

2003, July 19   Photo.   Perf. 13
2970 A1657 50c multi   1.50 .30

Characters From French Literature — A1658

Designs: No. 2971, Eugène-François Vidocq (1775-1857), convict and police official. No. 2972, Esmerelda, from *Notre-Dame de Paris*, by Victor Hugo. No. 2973, Claudine, from *Claudine* novels, by Colette. No. 2974, Nana, from *Rougon-Macquart*, by Emile Zola. No. 2975, La Comte de Monte-Cristo, from *La Comte de Monte-Cristo*, by Alexandre Dumas (pere). No. 2976, Gavroche, from *Les Miserables*, by Hugo.

2003, Aug. 30   Photo.   Perf. 13
2971 A1658 50c multi   1.50 .75
2972 A1658 50c multi   1.50 .75
2973 A1658 50c multi   1.50 .75
2974 A1658 50c multi   1.50 .75
2975 A1658 50c multi   1.50 .75
2976 A1658 50c multi   1.50 .75
a.   Souvenir sheet, #2971-
    2976   14.00 14.00
    Nos. 2971-2976 (6)   9.00 4.50

No. 2976a sold for €4.60, with the Red Cross receiving €1.60 of that.

Ahmad Shah Massoud (1953-2001), Afghan Northern Alliance Leader — A1659

2003, Sept. 9
2977 A1659 50c multi   1.50 .30

Aspects of Life in French Regions Type of 2003

No. 2978: a, Chateau de Chenonceau. b, House, Alsace. c, Roof, Bourgogne. d, Genoese Tower, Corsica, vert. e, Arc de Triomphe,

FRANCE

vert. f, Farm house, Provence. g, Pointe du Raz, vert. h, Mont Blanc, vert. i, Basque house. j, Pont du Gard.

2003, Sept. 20   **Photo.**   **Perf. 13**
2978   Sheet of 10   15.00   15.00
   a.-j.   A1642 50c Any single   1.50   1.25

No. 2978 has three vertical rows of rouletting, separating sheet into quarters.
Nos. 2978a-2978j were also issued in large booklets containing panes of 1 of each stamp. The booklet sold for €19.

Gardens and Parks — A1660

No. 2979: a, Buttes-Chaumont Park. b, Jardin du Luxembourg.

2003, Sept. 27   **Perf. 13¼x13**
2979   Sheet of 2   12.00   12.00
   a.-b.   A1660 €1.90 Either single   6.00   6.00

Salon du Timbre 2004. No. 2979 has four vertical rows of rouletting, separating sheet into fifths, with the two stamps in the central fifth.
See Nos. 3029, 3118, 3201, 3316, 3429.

Motor Vehicles A1661

No. 2980: a, 1964 Icobloc 648 DP 102 bus (Autocar). b, 1950 SFV 302 Tractor. c, 1938 Delahaye fire truck with mechanical aerial ladder. d, Renault Kangaroo Express postal van. e, 1932 Renault TN6 Paris city bus. f, 1910 Berliet 22hp Type M delivery truck. g, 1957 Berliet T100 heavy-duty truck. h, Citroen police van. i, Citroen DS ambulance. j, 1964 Hotchkiss fire truck.

2003, Oct. 24   **Photo.**   **Perf. 13¼**
2980   A1661   Sheet of 10   9.00   9.00
   a.-e.   20c Any single   .55   .45
   f.-j.   30c Any single   1.00   .75

Philexjeunes 2003 Philatelic Exhibition, Dunkerque.

Holiday Greetings A1663

2003, Nov. 6   **Photo.**   **Perf. 13**
2981   A1662   50c multi   1.50   .35
   a.   Litho., stamp + label   6.00   6.00

Litho.
2982   A1663   50c multi   1.50   .35
   a.   Sheet of 10 + 10 labels   60.00   60.00

Booklet Stamp
Self-Adhesive
Serpentine Die Cut 11¼
2983   A1663   50c multi   1.50   .35
   a.   Booklet pane of 10   16.00

Nos. 2981a, 2982a, 2004. Nos. 2981a and 2982 were issued in sheets of 10 stamps + 10 labels that sold for €6.67 each on day of issue. The labels could be personalized. The background on No. 2981 looks splotchy while that of No. 2981a has a dot structure.
A souvenir sheet containing No. 2982 was sold for €6 by mail order only. It was not available through standing order subscriptions and was not offered in the philatelic bureau's sales catalog. 50,000 copies of this sheet were printed. Value $100.

Sower Type of 1903, Cent. — A1664

Serpentine Die Cut 6¾ Vert.
2003, Nov. 6   **Engr.**
Booklet Stamp
2984   A1664   50c red   3.50   2.00
   a.   Booklet pane, 5 each # 2984, 2835A   25.00

See Nos. 4727b, 6147.

European Capitals Type of 2002
No. 2985 — Attractions in Luxembourg: a, Citadelle Saint-Esprit. b, Notre Dame Cathedral, horiz. c, Adolphe Bridge, horiz. d, Grand Duke's Palace.

Perf. 13¼x13, 13x13¼
2003, Nov. 7   **Photo.**
2985   A1622   Sheet of 4   7.50   7.50
   a.-d.   50c Any single   1.50   1.00

Indian and French Artisan's Work — A1665

Designs: 50c, Illumination depicting rooster, France, 15th cent. 90c, Jewelry design, India, 19th cent.

2003, Nov. 29   **Engr.**   **Perf. 13¼x13**
2986   A1665   50c multi   1.50   .45
2987   A1665   90c multi   2.60   1.50

See India No. 2040.

Launch of the Queen Mary 2 — A1666

2003, Dec. 12   **Photo.**   **Perf. 13¼**
2988   A1666   50c multi   1.50   .30

Greetings A1667

Holes punched through dots in "i's."
2004, Jan. 9   **Photo.**   **Perf. 13**
2989   A1667   50c shown   1.50   .30
2990   A1667   50c Un grand merci   1.50   .30

No Holes Punched Through Dots of "i's"
Stamp + Label
2991   A1667   50c Like No. 2989   6.00   6.00
2992   A1667   50c Like No. 2990   6.00   6.00

Nos. 2991-2992 were issued in sheets of 10 stamps + 10 labels that sold for €6.67 on day of issue. The labels could be personalized.
Compare with Types A2203 and SP411. See Nos. 3096-3097D, 3569A-3569B.

It's a Boy — A1668

It's a Girl — A1669

2004   **Litho.**   **Perf. 13**
Stamp + Label
2993   A1668   50c multi   6.00   6.00
2994   A1669   50c multi   6.00   6.00

Booklet Stamps
Self-Adhesive
Serpentine Die Cut 11
2995   A1668   50c multi   1.50   .35
   a.   Booklet pane of 10   15.00
2996   A1669   50c multi   1.50   .35
   a.   Booklet pane of 10   15.00

Nos. 2993-2994 were issued in sheets of 10 stamps + 10 labels that sold for €6.67 on day of issue. The labels could be personalized.
Nos. 2995-2996 issued 1/9/04.

Hearts — A1670

Designs: 50c, Chanel No. 5 perfume bottle. 75c, Woman, Eiffel Tower.

2004, Jan. 9   **Photo.**   **Perf. 13**
2997   A1670   50c multi   1.50   .35
   a.   Souvenir sheet of 5   7.50   7.50
   b.   Litho., stamp + label, perf. 13¼   6.00   6.00
2998   A1670   75c multi   2.25   .75
   a.   Litho., stamp + label, perf. 13¼   6.00   6.00

Nos. 2997b and 2998a were each printed in sheets of 10 stamps + 10 labels that could be personalized and sold for €6.69 and €10 respectively. On No. 2997b, there are large brown dots arranged in circles in the shading on the green rectangles, while on No. 2997 the brown dots are small and arranged in rows. On No. 2998a, the dots in the sky are larger and father apart than the tiny dots found on No. 2998.
Values are for stamps with surrounding selvage.
See Nos. 3133, 3135.

Tourism Issue

Lille, 2004 European Cultural Capital — A1671

2004, Jan. 10   **Photo.**   **Perf. 13**
2999   A1671   50c multi   1.50   .35

Art Series

Statue of Liberty, Sculpted by Frederic Auguste Bartholdi (1834-1904) A1672

2004, Feb. 21   **Engr.**   **Perf. 13¼x13**
3000   A1672   90c multi   2.60   1.50

Queen Eleanor of Aquitaine (c. 1122-1204) — A1673

2004, Feb. 28   **Perf. 13x13¼**
3001   A1673   50c multi   1.50   .35

Stamp Day — A1674

Characters of Walt Disney: 45c, Donald Duck. 50c, Mickey Mouse. 75c, Minnie Mouse.

2004, Mar. 6   **Photo.**   **Perf. 13¼**
3002   A1674   50c multi   1.50   .35
   a.   Perf. 13¼x13 (from booklet pane)   1.50   .35

Booklet Stamps
Perf. 13¼x13
3003   A1674   45c multi   2.25   1.00
3004   A1674   75c multi   2.25   .75
   a.   Booklet pane, 2 #3003, 4 each #3002a, 3004   23.00   —
     Complete booklet, #3004a   24.00

Civil Code, Bicent. — A1675

2004, Mar. 12   **Engr.**   **Perf. 13¼x13**
3005   A1675   50c multi   1.50   .35

George Sand (1804-76), Writer — A1676

2004, Mar. 20   **Engr.**   **Perf. 13¼x13**
3006   A1676   50c multi   1.50   .35

Aspects of Life in French Regions Type of 2003
No. 3007: a, Cutlery. b, Produce of Provence, vert. c, Beaujolais grapes, vert. d, Bread. e, Woman wearing coif, vert. f, Oysters, vert. g, Quiche Lorraine. h, Bullfighting. i, Clafoutis. j, Bagpipers.

2004, Mar. 26   **Photo.**   **Perf. 13**
3007   Sheet of 10   15.00   15.00
   a.-j.   A1642 50c Any single   1.50   1.25

No. 3007 has three vertical rows of rouletting, separating sheet into quarters.

Clermont-Ferrand A1677

2004, Mar. 26   **Engr.**   **Perf. 13¼**
3008   A1677   50c multi   1.50   .30

Entente Cordiale, Cent. — A1678

Designs: 50c, Coccinelle, by Sonia Delaunay. 75c, Lace 1 (trial proof) 1968, by Sir Terry Frost.

2004, Apr. 6   **Photo.**   **Perf. 13¼**
3009   A1678   50c multi   1.50   .35
3010   A1678   75c multi   2.25   .85

See Great Britain Nos. 2200-2201.

676 FRANCE

Road Safety — A1679

2004, Apr. 7
3011 A1679 50c multi 1.50 .30
See United Nations Offices in Geneva No. 424.

Art Series

La Méridienne d'Après Millet, by Vincent van Gogh A1680

2004, July 2 Photo. Perf. 13x13¼
3012 A1680 75c multi 2.50 .95

Art Series

Un Combat de Coqs, by Jean-Léon Gérôme A1681

Galatée aux Sphères, by Salvador Dali — A1682

2004 Photo. Perf. 13x13¼
3013 A1681 €1.11 multi 3.50 1.25
3014 A1682 €1.11 multi 3.50 1.25
Issued: No. 3013, 4/17; No. 3014, 6/19.

Tourism Issue

Bordeaux — A1683

Vaux-sur-Mer A1684

Notre Dame de l'Assomption Cathedral, Luçon A1685

2004 Litho. & Engr. Perf. 13
3015 A1683 50c multi 1.50 .30
  Engr.
  Perf. 13¼
3016 A1684 50c multi 1.50 .30
3017 A1685 50c multi 1.50 .30
Issued: No. 3015, 4/26; No. 3016, 7/17; No. 3017, 10/2.

Farm Animals A1686

2004, Apr. 26 Photo. Perf. 13¼
3018 A1686 45c Rabbit 1.25 .30
3019 A1686 50c Cow, vert. 1.50 .30
3020 A1686 50c Chicken 1.50 .30
3021 A1686 75c Burro, vert. 2.25 .90
  a. Souvenir sheet, #3018-3021 7.00 7.00

Expansion of the European Union — A1687

2004, May 1 Photo. Perf. 13¼
3022 A1687 50c multi 1.50 .30

Battle of Dien Bien Phu, 50th Anniv. — A1688

2004, May 7 Perf. 13¼x13
3023 A1688 50c multi 1.50 .30

Europa — A1689

2004 Photo. Perf. 13x13¼
3024 A1689 50c multi 1.50 .30
  Litho.
  Booklet Stamp
  Self-Adhesive
  Serpentine Die Cut 11
3025 A1689 50c multi 1.50 .30
  a. Booklet pane of 10 15.00
Issued: No. 3024, 5/9; No. 3025, 6/4.

Blake and Mortimer, Comic Book Characters by Edgar P. Jacobs — A1690

2004, May 15 Photo. Perf. 13¼
3026 A1690 50c multi 1.50 .30
3027 A1690 €1 multi 3.00 1.25
See Belgium No. 2020.

Blake and Mortimer and: 50c, Brick wall, vert. €1, Blue background.

FIFA (Fédération Internationale de Football Association), Cent. — A1691

2004, May 20 Perf. 13¼x13
3028 A1691 50c multi 1.50 .30

Gardens and Parks Type of 2003
No. 3029: a, Jardin des Tuileries. b, Parc Floral de Paris.

2004, June 4 Perf. 13¼x13
3029 Sheet of 2 12.00 12.00
  a.-b. A1660 €1.90 Either single 5.75 5.00
  c. Souvenir sheet, #2979a-2979b, 3029a-3029b 35.00 35.00
Salon du Timbre 2004. No. 3029 has four vertical rows of rouletting, separating sheet into fifths, with the two stamps in the central fifth.

D-Day Invasion of France, 60th Anniv. — A1692

2004, June 5 Perf. 13
3030 A1692 50c multi 1.50 .30

Organ Donation — A1693

2004, June 22 Perf. 13¼
3031 A1693 50c multi 1.50 .30

Pierre Dugua de Mons, Leader of First French Settlement in Acadia, and Ship — A1694

  Litho. & Engr.
2004, June 26 Perf. 13
3032 A1694 90c multi 2.75 1.00
See Canada No. 2044.

Napoleon I and the Imperial Guard — A1695

Designs: No. 3033, Light cavalry (Chasseur à cheval). No. 3034, Artilleryman and cannon (Artilleur à pied), horiz. No. 3035, Dragoon. No. 3036, Mameluke. No. 3037, Napoleon I. No. 3038, Grenadier (Grenadier à pied).

2004, June 26 Photo.
3033 A1695 50c multi 1.50 .75
3034 A1695 50c multi 1.50 .75
3035 A1695 50c multi 1.50 .75
3036 A1695 50c multi 1.50 .75
3037 A1695 50c multi 1.50 .75
3038 A1695 50c multi 1.50 .75
  a. Souvenir sheet, #3033-3038 12.50 12.50
  Nos. 3033-3038 (6) 9.00 4.50
No. 3038a sold for €4.60, with the Red Cross receiving €1.60 of that.

French Federation of Philatelic Associations 77th Congress, Paris — A1696

  Litho. & Engr.
2004, June 27 Perf. 13¼x13
3039 A1696 50c multi 1.50 .30

2004 Summer Olympics, Athens A1697

2004, June 28 Photo. Perf. 13¼
3040 50c Modern athletes 1.50 .75
3041 50c Ancient athletes 1.50 .75
  a. A1697 Pair, #3040-3041 3.25 2.25
Printed in sheets containing five of each stamp.
A souvenir sheet containing No. 3041 was issued Aug. 2 and sold for €2.51. Value $20.

Happy Birthday — A1698

2004, June 30 Photo. Perf. 13¼
3042 A1698 50c multi 1.50 .30
  a. Souvenir sheet of 5 7.50 7.50
  b. Litho. stamp + label 6.00 6.00
No. 3042b printed in sheets of 10 stamps + 10 labels that could be personalized that sold for €8. No. 3042b has a dark green inscription at left with a distinct dot pattern. No. 3042 has a lighter green inscription.

Marianne Type of 1997 Inscribed "RF" at Lower Left and Type of 2002 With Euro Denominations

2004 Litho. Perf. 13
3043 Sheet of 15 + 15 labels 60.00 60.00
  a. A1583 1c orange yellow .25 .25
  b. A1583 2c brown .25 .25
  c. A1583 5c brt bl green .25 .25
  d. A1583 10c purple .30 .30
  e. A1583 20c orange .60 .60
  f. A1583 58c apple green 1.75 1.75
  g. A1583 70c olive 2.10 2.10
  h. A1583 75c sky blue 2.25 2.25
  i. A1583 90c dark blue 2.75 2.75
  j. A1583 €1 Prussian blue 3.00 3.00
  k. A1583 €1.11 red lilac 3.25 3.25
  l. A1583 €1.90 violet brown 5.75 5.75
  m. A1583 €2 violet 6.00 6.00
  n. A1409 (45c) green 1.40 1.40
  o. A1409 (50c) red 1.50 1.50

  Engr.
  Serpentine Die Cut 6¾ Vert
  Self-Adhesive
3043P A1583 75c brt blue + label 8.75 8.75
3043Q A1583 €1.11 purple + label 10.50 10.50
3043R A1583 €1.11 chocolate + label — —

No. 3043 sold for €10.03. Stamps have a glossy varnish.
Labels on Nos. 3043P-3043R could be personalized.

Marianne and Emblem of World Fund to Combat AIDS, Tuberculosis and Smoking A1699

2004, July 1 Engr. Perf. 13
3044 A1699 (50c) red 1.50 .35

Extreme Sports A1700

No. 3045: a, Skateboarding. b, Parachuting. c, Sailboarding. d, Surfing. e, Luge. f, BMX bicycling. g, Paragliding. h, Jetskiing. i, Snowboarding. j, Rollerblading.

FRANCE

2004, July 3 Photo. Perf. 13¼x13
3045 A1700 Sheet of 10 7.50 7.50
 a.-e. 20c Any single .60 .50
 f.-j. 30c Any single .90 .75

Orchid Type of 2002
Design: 39c, Orchis insularis.

2004, Sept. 1 Litho. Perf. 13
3046 A1584 39c multi 1.50 .75

No. 3046 known only precanceled. See second note after No. 132.

Aspects of Life in the French Regions Type of 2003

No. 3047: a, House, Normandy. b, Chambord Chateau. c, Gorges, Tarn, vert. d, Notre Dame Cathedral, Paris, vert. e, Windmill, vert. f, Cave dwellings. g, Creek, Cassis, vert. h, Cap-Ferret Lighthouse, vert. i, Castle ruins. j, Alpine chalet.

2004, Sept. 18 Photo. Perf. 13
3047 Sheet of 10 15.00 15.00
 a.-j. A1642 50c Any single 1.50 1.25

No. 3047 has three vertical rows of rouletting separating sheet into quarters.
Each stamp exists in booklet pane of 1 from booklet that sold for €19.

Halloween — A1701

2004, Oct. 9 Litho. Perf. 13
3048 A1701 50c multi 1.50 .30

Félix Eboué (1884-1944), Colonial Governor — A1702

2004, Oct. 16 Photo.
3049 A1702 50c multi 1.50 .30

Ouistreham Lighthouse — A1703

2004, Oct. 30 Perf. 13¼
3050 A1703 50c multi 1.50 .30

Marianne — A1704

Serpentine Die Cut 6¾ Vert.

2004, Nov. 10 Engr.
Booklet Stamp
Self-Adhesive
3051 A1704 50c multi 3.00 2.00
 a. Booklet pane, 5 each #2835A, 3051 22.50

European Capitals Type of 2002

No. 3052 — Attractions in Athens: a, Greek Academy. b, Parthenon. c, Odeon of Herodes Atticus. d, Church of the Holy Apostles, vert.

Perf. 13x13¼, 13¼x13
2004, Nov. 11 Photo.
3052 A1622 Sheet of 4 7.50 7.50
 a.-d. 50c Any single 1.50 .90

A1705

A1706

A1707

A1708

A1709

Holiday Greetings A1710

2004, Nov. 12 Photo. Perf. 13
3053 A1705 50c multi 1.50 .30
Litho.
3054 A1706 50c multi + label 6.00 6.00
3055 A1707 50c multi + label 6.00 6.00
3056 A1708 50c multi + label 6.00 6.00
3057 A1709 50c multi + label 6.00 6.00
3058 A1710 50c multi + label 6.00 6.00
 a. Vert. strip of 5, #3054-3059 + 5 labels 30.00 30.00
  Miniature sheet, 2 #3058a + 10 labels 70.00 70.00

Booklet Stamps
Self-Adhesive
Serpentine Die Cut 11¼x11
3059 A1706 50c multi 1.50 .30
3060 A1707 50c multi 1.50 .30
3061 A1708 50c multi 1.50 .30
3062 A1709 50c multi 1.50 .30
3063 A1710 50c multi 1.50 .30
 a. Booklet pane, 2 each #3059-3063 15.00
 Nos. 3053-3063 (11) 39.00 31.80

Miniature sheet containing Nos. 3054-3058 sold for €6.69. Labels could be personalized. No. 3055 exists in a souvenir sheet of 1 stamp without label that sold for €3. Value $35.

Henri Wallon (1812-1904), Historian and Politician — A1711

2004, Nov. 13 Photo. Perf. 13
3064 A1711 50c multi 1.50 .30

Opening of Millau Viaduct A1712

2004, Dec. 14 Photo. Perf. 13
3065 A1712 50c multi 2.50 1.00

Marianne — A1713

Inscribed "ITVF" at Bottom
2005-07 Engr. Perf. 13
3066 A1713 1c yellow .25 .25
 a. Inscribed "Phil@poste" at bottom .25 .25
3067 A1713 5c brn blk .25 .25
 a. Inscribed "Phil@poste" at bottom .25 .25
3068 A1713 10c violet .25 .25
3069 A1713 (45c) green 1.60 .25
 a. Inscribed "Phil@poste" at bottom 1.60 .25
3070 A1713 (50c) red 3.00 .25
 a. Sheet of 15 + 15 labels 70.00 70.00
 b. Inscribed "Phil@poste" at bottom 2.00 .25
3071 A1713 55c dark blue 1.60 .50
3072 A1713 58c olive green 1.75 .40
3073 A1713 64c dark green 1.90 .40
3074 A1713 70c dark green 2.10 .50
3075 A1713 75c light blue 2.25 .25
3076 A1713 82c fawn 4.00 .50
3077 A1713 90c dark blue 2.75 .80
3078 A1713 €1 orange 3.00 .25
 a. Inscribed "Phil@poste" at bottom 3.25 .75
3079 A1713 €1.11 red violet 3.25 .25
3080 A1713 €1.22 red violet 3.00 .30
3081 A1713 €1.90 chocolate 5.75 .30
3082 A1713 €1.98 chocolate 6.00 1.25
 Nos. 3066-3082 (17) 42.70 6.95

Self-Adhesive (#3083-3085)
Serpentine Die Cut 6¾ Vert.
3083 A1713 (50c) red 1.50 .25
 a. Booklet pane of 10 (see footnote) 15.00
 b. Booklet pane of 10 (see footnote) 15.00
 c. Booklet pane of 20 30.00
 d. As #3083, with "Phil@poste" inscription 1.50 .25
 e. Booklet pane, 10 #3083d 15.00
 f. Booklet pane of 12 #3083d 17.00
 g. No. 3083 with attached label 7.50
3084 A1713 82c fawn + label 12.00 12.00
3085 A1713 €1.22 red violet 15.00 15.00

Coil Stamps
Perf. 13 Horiz.
3086 A1713 (45c) green 2.00 .30
 a. Inscribed "Phil@poste" at bottom 1.40 .25
3087 A1713 (50c) red 2.00 .25
 c. Inscribed "Phil@poste" at bottom — —
3087A A1713 55c dark blue 2.50 1.25
 b. Inscribed "Phil@poste" at bottom 1.60 .25
 Nos. 3083-3087A (6) 35.00 29.05

Issued: Nos. 1c, 10c, (45c), (50c), 58c, 70c, 75c, 90c, €1, €1.11, €1.90, 1/8. 5c, No. 3071, 64c, 82c, €1.22, €1.98, 3/1. No. 3087A, 7/15. Nos. 3083d, 3083e, 10/1/06. Nos. 3066a, 3067a, 3069a, 3070b, 2006. No. 3083f, Jan. 2007. Nos. 3083g, 3084-3085, Apr. 2007. No. 3086a was issued in 2008 and sold for 50c. No. 3087b was issued in 2008 and sold for 55c.

Face values shown for Nos. 3069, 3070, 3083, 3086 and 3087 are those the stamps sold for on the day of issue. On day of issue, No. 3069a sold for 49c; No. 3070b for 54c.

No. 3070a sold for €10.03 and the labels could be personalized for an additional fee.

No. 3083a has a narrow strip of selvage separating the four stamps at left, from the six stamps, at right, and is on a white backing paper. No. 3083b is comprised of two horizontal strips of five stamps on a yellow backing paper. No. 3083d sold for 54c on day of issue. No. 3083g was printed in sheets containing 15 stamps + 15 small or large-sized labels that could be personalized. Nos. 3084 and 3085 were each printed in sheets of 30 stamps + 30 large-sized labels that could be personalized.

A sheet of 10 litho. stamps similar to No. 3068 + 10 labels exists, but was not sold.

See Nos. 3211, 3211N, 3212, 3247-3255E, 3302, 3302N, 3383-3388A, 3389, 3531, 4410k, 4524.

Rabbi Shlomo Yitshaqi (Rashi) (1040-1105) A1714

2005, Jan. 16 Engr. Perf. 13¼
3088 A1714 50c multi 1.75 .30

Hearts — A1715

Designs: 53c, Polka dots. 82c, Bird and flowers.

2005, Jan. 29 Photo. Perf. 13¼
3089 A1715 53c multi 1.50 .30
 a. Souvenir sheet of 5 7.50 7.50
 b. Litho. stamp + label 6.00 6.00
3090 A1715 82c multi 2.50 1.00
 b. Litho. stamp + label 6.00 6.00

Values are for stamps with surrounding selvage.
Sheets of 10 of No. 3089b sold for €6.86, and sheets of 10 of No. 3090a sold for €8.78.

Labels could be personalized for an additional fee.
See Nos. 3134, 3136.

New Year 2005 (Year of the Rooster) — A1716

Photo. & Embossed
2005, Jan. 29 Perf. 13½x13
3091 A1716 (50c) multi 1.75 .30

See No. 4969a.

Rotary International, Cent. — A1717

2005, Feb. 19 Photo. Perf. 13¼
3092 A1717 53c multi 1.50 .30

See No. 3227A.

Titeuf A1718

Nadia A1719

Manu — A1720

2005, Feb. 28 Photo. Perf. 13¼
3093 A1718 (50c) red & multi 1.50 .30
 a. Perf. 13¼x13 (booklet stamp) 1.50 .30

Booklet Stamps
3094 A1719 (45c) green & multi 3.00 .60
3095 A1720 (90c) blue & multi 2.50 1.00
 a. Booklet pane, 2 #3094, 4 each #3093a, 3095 22.00 —
  Complete booklet, #0005a 23.00

Characters from Titeuf, comic strip by Zep. Stamp Day.

Greetings Type of 2004 Inscribed "Lettre 20g"

Designs: Nos. 3096, 3097A, "Ceci est une invitation." Nos. 3097, 3097B, "Un grand merci."
No. 3097C, "Ceci est une invitation." No. 3097D, "Un grand merci."

2005-06 Photo. Perf. 13
Holes Punched Through Dots of "i's"
3096 A1667 (53c) brt lil rose & yel 2.00 .30
3097 A1667 (53c) brt yel grn & red lil 2.00 .30

Litho.
No Holes Punched Through Dots of "i's"
Stamp + Label
3097A A1667 (53c) brt lil rose & yel 5.00
3097B A1667 (53c) brt yel grn & red lil 5.00

678 FRANCE

Self-Adhesive
No Holes Punched Through Dots of "i's"
Serpentine Die Cut 11¼x11
Stamp + Label

3097C	A1667	(53c) brt lil rose & yel	5.00	5.00
3097D	A1667	(53c) brt yel grn & rrd lil	5.00	5.00

Nos. 3097A-3097B were issued in sheets of 10 stamps + 10 labels that sold for €8 on day of issue. The labels could be personalized.
Nos. 3097C-3097D were each issued in sheets of 10 stamps + 10 labels that sold for €8.61. Labels could be personalized.
Issued: Nos. 2096-3097B, 3/1/05. Nos. 3097C-3097D, 2006.

Art Series

The Guitarist, by Jean-Baptiste Greuze (1725-1805) A1721

White Bear, Sculpture by François Pompon A1722

Sicile, by Nicolas de Stael A1723

2005		Photo.	Perf. 13x13¼	
3098	A1721	82c multi	2.50	.50
3099	A1722	90c multi	3.00	1.25
3100	A1723	€1.22 multi	3.75	1.25

Issued: €1.22, 3/5. 90c, 7/2. 82c, 9/24.

Orchids — A1725

Designs: No. 3102, Cypripedium calceolus. No. 3103, Paphiopedilum Mabel Sanders. 55c, Oncidium papilio. 82c, Paphinia cristata, horiz.

2005, Mar. 11		Photo.	Perf. 13¼	
3102	A1725	53c multi	1.60	.30
3103	A1725	53c multi	1.60	.30
3104	A1725	55c multi	1.60	.30
3105	A1725	82c multi	2.50	.60
a.		Souvenir sheet, #3102-3105	7.50	7.50
		Nos. 3102-3105 (4)	7.30	1.50

Aspects of Life in French Regions Type of 2003

No. 3106: a, Nautical jousting. b, Clocks of Franche-Comte, vert. c, Cantal cheese and bread, vert. d, Dancers and accordion player. e, Bouillabaisse. f, P'tit Quinquin statue, vert. g, Rillettes (chopped pork). h, Sauerkraut and sausage, beer stein. i, Pelota, vert. j, Sugar cane, vert.

2005, Mar. 19		Photo.	Perf. 13	
3106		Sheet of 10	16.00	16.00
a.-j.	A1642	53c Any single	1.50	1.25

No. 3106 has three vertical rows of roulet- ting, separating sheet into quarters.
Each stamp exists in a booklet pane of 1 from a booklet that sold for €19. Value $50.

Tourism Issue

Aix-en-Provence A1726

Gulf of Morbihan A1727

Villefranche-sur-Mer — A1728

La Roque-Gageac A1729

2005		Engr.	Perf. 13¼, 13 (#3108)	
3107	A1726	53c multi	1.60	.30
		Photo.		
3108	A1727	53c multi	1.60	.30
3109	A1728	53c multi	1.60	.30
		Engr.		
3110	A1729	53c multi	1.60	.30

Issued: No. 3107, 4/1; No. 3108, 5/5; No. 3109, 6/4; No. 3110, 7/23.

Happy Birthday — A1730

2005, Apr. 2		Photo.	Perf. 13	
3111	A1730	(53c) multi	2.00	.30
a.		Souvenir sheet of 5	10.00	9.00
b.		Litho., stamp + label	8.00	8.00

Litho.
Serpentine Die Cut 11
Self-Adhesive

| 3111C | A1730 | (53c) multi + label | — | — |

Sheets of 10 and 10 labels of No. 3111b and 3111C each sold for €6.86. Labels could be personalized for an additional fee.

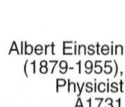

Albert Einstein (1879-1955), Physicist A1731

2005, Apr. 16			Perf. 13¼	
3112	A1731	53c multi	1.60	.30

Alexis de Tocqueville (1805-59), Writer — A1732

2005, Apr. 23		Engr.	Perf. 13x13¼	
3113	A1732	90c multi	2.75	1.00

Liberation of Concentration Camp Internees, 60th Anniv. — A1733

2005, Apr. 24		Photo.	Perf. 13¼	
3114	A1733	53c multi	1.60	.30

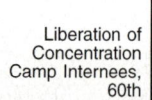

Battle of Austerlitz, Bicent. — A1734

2005, May 4		Litho. & Engr.	Perf. 13¼	
3115	A1734	55c multi	1.60	.45

See Czech Republic No. 3273.

French Federation of Philatelic Associations, 78th Congress, Nancy — A1735

2005, May 5		Engr.	Perf. 13	
3116	A1735	53c multi + label	1.60	.30

A souvenir sheet of one stamp without label exists. Value $12.

Europa — A1736

2005, May 8		Photo.	Perf. 13¼	
3117	A1736	53c multi	1.60	.30

Gardens and Parks Type of 2003
Souvenir Sheet

No. 3118 — Sculptures in Jardin de la Fon- taine, Nimes: a, Denomination in green. b, Denomination in white.

2005, May 15			Perf. 13¼x13	
3118		Sheet of 2	12.00	12.00
a.-b.	A1660	€1.98 Either single	6.00	6.00

Salon du Timbre 2005. No. 3118 has four vertical rows of rouletting, separating sheet into fifths, with the two stamps in the central fifth.

Vacation — A1737

Serpentine Die Cut 11
2005, May 23 *Litho.*
Booklet Stamp
Self-Adhesive

| 3119 | A1737 | (53c) multi | 2.00 | .25 |
| a. | | Booklet pane of 10 | 20.00 | |

Stories by Jules Verne (1828-1905) — A1738

Designs: No. 3120, Five Weeks in a Balloon (Cinq Semaines en Ballon). No. 3121, From the Earth to the Moon (De la Terre à la Lune). No. 3122, Journey to the Center of the Earth (Voyage au Centre de la Terre), horiz. No. 3123, Michael Strogoff, horiz. No. 3124, Around the World in Eighty Days (Le Tour du Monde en Quatre-vingts Jours). No. 3125, 20,000 Leagues Under the Sea (Vingt Mille Lieues Sous les Mers).

2005, May 28		Photo.	Perf. 13	
3120	A1738	53c multi	1.60	.75
3121	A1738	53c multi	1.60	.75
3122	A1738	53c multi	1.60	.75
3123	A1738	53c multi	1.60	.75
3124	A1738	53c multi	1.60	.75
3125	A1738	53c multi	1.60	.75
a.		Souvenir sheet, #3120-3125	12.00	12.00
		Nos. 3120-3125 (6)	9.60	4.50

No. 3125a sold for €4.80 with the Red Cross receiving €1.62 of that.

Miniature Sheet

Gordon Bennett Cup, Cent. A1739

No. 3126 — Inscriptions: a, La Coupe Gordon Bennett (Car No. 1 facing right). b, La Coupe Gordon Bennett (Car No. 1 facing left). c, La Formule 1, vert. d, Le Rallye-Raid, vert. e, Les Rallyes. f, La Course d'endurance.

2005, June 2		Photo.	Perf.	
3126	A1739	Sheet of 10, #a-b, 2 each #c-f	19.00	19.00
a.-f.		53c Any single	1.75	.85

A souvenir sheet containing No. 3126a sold for €3. Value $100.

Environmental Charter — A1740

2005, June 5		Litho.	Perf. 13	
3127	A1740	53c multi, lt green	1.60	.30

Enactment of Handicapped Persons Rights Law — A1741

2005, June 18		Photo.	Perf. 13¼	
3128	A1741	53c multi	1.60	.30

It's a Boy — A1742

It's a Girl — A1743

2005		Litho.	Perf. 13x13¼	
3129	A1742	(53c) multi + label	5.00	5.00
3130	A1743	(53c) multi + label	5.00	5.00

Booklet Stamps
Self-Adhesive
Serpentine Die Cut 11¼x11

3131	A1742	(53c) multi	2.00	.30
a.		Booklet pane of 10	20.00	
b.		Sheet of 10 + 10 labels	50.00	
3132	A1743	(53c) multi	2.00	.30
a.		Booklet pane of 10	20.00	
b.		Sheet of 10 + 10 labels	50.00	

Sheets of 10 stamps and 10 labels of Nos. 3129 and 3130 each sold for €6.86. Nos. 3131b and 3132b each sold for €8.61. Labels could be personalized for an additional fee.

Hearts Types of 2004-05
Serpentine Die Cut
2005, July 15 *Photo.*
Self-Adhesive

3133	A1670	50c Like #2997	4.00	2.50
3134	A1715	53c Like #3089	4.00	3.00
3135	A1670	75c Like #2998	6.00	3.50
3136	A1715	82c Like #3090	6.00	4.00
		Nos. 3133-3136 (4)	20.00	13.00

Haras du Pin Natl. Stud Farm — A1744

2005, July 16			Perf. 13	
3137	A1744	53c multi	1.60	.30

FRANCE

European Capitals Type of 2002

No. 3138 — Attractions in Berlin: a, Brandenburg Gate. b, Kaiser Wilhelm Memorial Church, vert. c, Philharmonic Hall. d, Reichstag.

Perf. 13x13¼, 13¼x13
2005, Aug. 27   **Photo.**
3138 A1622   Sheet of 4   7.00   7.00
a.-d.   53c Any single   1.75   1.00

Aspects of Life in the French Regions Type of 2003

No. 3139: a, Lake Annecy. b, Etretat Cliffs, vert. c, Pigeon house, vert. d, Wash house (lavoir). e, Banks of the Seine. f, Carnac megaliths. g, House, Sologne. h, Pilat Sand Dune. i, Stiff Lighthouse, vert. j, Stone hut (borie), vert.

2005, Sept. 17   **Perf. 13**
3139   Sheet of 10   17.00 17.00
a.-j.   A1642 53c Any single   1.60   1.25

No. 3139 has three vertical rows of rouletting, separating sheet into quarters.
Nos. 3139a-3139j were also issued in large booklets containing panes of 1 of each stamp. The booklet sold for €19. Value $60.

Art Series

Les Halles Centrales, Designed by Victor Baltard (1805-74) — A1745

2005, Sept. 17   **Engr.**   **Perf. 13x13¼**
3140 A1745 €1.22 multi   3.75 1.10

Breast Cancer Awareness — A1746

2005, Oct. 1   **Photo.**   **Perf. 13¼**
3141 A1746 53c multi   1.60   .30

 A1747

 A1748

 A1749

 A1750

 A1751

 A1752

 A1753

 A1754

 A1755

Cat, Comics by Philippe Geluck — A1756

Serpentine Die Cut 11¼x11
2005, Oct. 1   **Litho.**
Booklet Stamps
Self-Adhesive

3142	A1747 (53c) multi	2.00	.30
3143	A1748 (53c) multi	2.00	.30
3144	A1749 (53c) multi	2.00	.30
3145	A1750 (53c) multi	2.00	.30
3146	A1751 (53c) multi	2.00	.30
3147	A1752 (53c) multi	2.00	.30
3148	A1753 (53c) multi	2.00	.30
3149	A1754 (53c) multi	2.00	.30
3150	A1755 (53c) multi	2.00	.30
3151	A1756 (53c) multi	2.00	.30
a.	Booklet pane of 10, #3142-3151	20.00	

Raymond Aron (1905-83), Philosopher — A1757

2005, Oct. 7   **Engr.**   **Perf. 13¼x13**
3152 A1757 53c multi   1.60   .30

Souvenir Sheet

The Annunciation, by Raphael — A1758

No. 3153: a, Drawing of Angel, painting of Virgin Mary. b, Painting of Angel, drawing of Virgin Mary.

Litho. & Engr.
2005, Nov. 10   **Perf. 13x13¼**
3153 A1758   Sheet of 2   4.00 4.00
a.   53c multi   1.60 1.60
b.   55c multi   1.75 1.75

See Vatican City Nos. 1312-1314.

Marianne — A1759

Serpentine Die Cut 6¾ Vert.
2005, Nov. 11   **Engr.**
Booklet Stamp
Self-Adhesive

3154 A1759 53c red   0.50 0.00
a.   Booklet pane, 5 each #3083, 3154   25.00

See No. 4911.

Video Game Characters — A1760

No. 3155: a, Link. b, Pac-Man. c, Prince of Persia. d, Spyro. e, Donkey Kong. f, Mario. g, Adibou. h, Rayman. i, Lara Croft. j, The Sims.

2005, Nov. 11   **Photo.**   **Perf. 13¼x13**
3155 A1760   Sheet of 10   9.00 9.00
a.-e.   20c Any single   .60 .50
f.-j.   33c Any single   1.00 .75

Avicenna (980-1037), Scientist — A1761

2005, Nov. 12   **Engr.**   **Perf. 13¼x13**
3156 A1761 53c multi   1.60   .30

Holiday Greetings A1762

Designs: Nos. 3157, 3162, Bear, three penguins and sled. Nos. 3158, 3163, Two penguins, reindeer and sled. Nos. 3159, 3164, Two penguins, bear and sled. Nos. 3160, 3165, Three penguins. Nos. 3161, 3166, Two penguins, reindeer and snowman.

2005, Nov. 12   **Litho.**   **Perf. 13**
3157	A1762 (53c) multi + label	6.00	4.00
3158	A1762 (53c) multi + label	6.00	4.00
3159	A1762 (53c) multi + label	6.00	4.00
3160	A1762 (53c) multi + label	6.00	4.00
3161	A1762 (53c) multi + label	6.00	4.00
a.	Vert. strip of 5, #3157-3161, + 5 labels	30.00	30.00
	Miniature sheet, 2 #3161a	60.00	60.00

Booklet Stamps
Self-Adhesive
Serpentine Die Cut 11¼x11

3162	A1762 (53c) multi	2.00	.30
3163	A1762 (53c) multi	2.00	.30
3164	A1762 (53c) multi	2.00	.30
3165	A1762 (53c) multi	2.00	.30
3166	A1762 (53c) multi	2.00	.30
a.	Booklet pane, 2 each #3162-3166	16.00	
	Nos. 3157-3166 (10)	40.00	21.50

Miniature sheet containing Nos. 3157-3161 sold for €6.86. Labels could be personalized.
No. 3161 exists in a souvenir sheet of one stamp without label, that sold for €6. Value $30.

Jacob Kaplan (1895-1994), Grand Rabbi of France — A1763

2005, Nov. 14   **Engr.**   **Perf. 13**
3167 A1763 53c multi   1.60   .30

Orchid Type of 2002

Design: Orchis insularis.

2005   **Litho.**   **Perf. 13**
3168 A1584 42c multi   2.50   .75

No. 3168 is known only precanceled. See second note after No. 132.

Law Separating Church and State, Cent. — A1764

2005, Dec. 3   **Photo.**   **Perf. 13¼x13**
3169 A1764 53c multi   1.60   .30

Hearts — A1765

Designs: (53c), Hearts, octagons and diamonds. (82c), Heart and stripes.

2006, Jan. 7   **Photo.**   **Perf. 13¼**
3170 A1765 (53c) multi   1.60   .30
a.   Souvenir sheet of 5   10.00 8.00
b.   Litho., stamp + label   5.00 5.00
3171 A1765 (82c) multi   3.00 1.00
a.   Litho., stamp + label   12.00 12.00

Self-Adhesive
Serpentine Die Cut

3172 A1765 (53c) Like #3170   4.00 3.00
a.   Sheet of 10 + 10 labels   40.00
3173 A1765 (82c) Like #3171   6.00 4.50
a.   Sheet of 10 + 10 labels   60.00

Values are for stamps with surrounding selvage. Sheets of 10 of No. 3170b sold for €6.86, and sheets of No. 3172a sold for €8.61; No. 3173a for €11.54. Labels could be personalized for an additional fee.

New Year 2006 (Year of the Dog) — A1766

2006, Jan. 21   **Photo.**   **Perf. 13¼x13**
3174 A1766 (53c) multi   1.60   .30

A souvenir sheet containing No. 3174 sold for €3. Value $8.
See No. 4969b.

Impressionist Paintings — A1767

Designs: Nos. 3175a, 3176, Portraits from the Country, by Gustave Caillebotte. Nos. 3175b, 3183, Dancers, by Edgar Degas. Nos. 3175c, 3181, Marguerite Gachet in the Garden, by Vincent Van Gogh. Nos. 3175d, 3179, Two Young Girls at the Piano, by Auguste Renoir. Nos. 3175e, 3177, The Butterfly Hunt, by Berthe Morisot. Nos. 3175f, 3184, Luncheon on the Grass, by Edouard Manet. Nos. 3175g, 3182, Evening Air, by Henri-Edmond Cross. Nos. 3175h, 3180, The Shepherdess (Young Peasant Girl with a Stick), by Camille Pissarro. Nos. 3175i, 3178, Mother and Child, by Mary Cassatt. Nos. 3175j, 3185, Women of Tahiti on the Beach, by Paul Gauguin.

2006   **Litho.**   **Perf. 13¼**
3175   Sheet of 10 +10 labels   60.00 60.00
a.-j.   A1767 (53c) Any single + label   5.00 5.00

Booklet Stamps
Self-Adhesive
Serpentine Die Cut 11¼x11

3176 A1767 (53c) multi   2.00   .30
3177 A1767 (53c) multi   2.00   .30
3178 A1767 (53c) multi   2.00   .30
3179 A1767 (53c) multi   2.00   .30

680 FRANCE

3180	A1767	(53c) multi	2.00	.30
3181	A1767	(53c) multi	2.00	.30
3182	A1767	(53c) multi	2.00	.30
3183	A1767	(53c) multi	2.00	.30
3184	A1767	(53c) multi	2.00	.30
3185	A1767	(53c) multi	2.00	.30
a.	Booklet pane of 10, #3176-3185,			20.00
b.	Sheet of 10, #3176-3185, + 10 labels			110.00

Issued: No. 3175, 6/1; Nos. 3176-3185, 1/21. No. 3175 sold for €6.86. No. 3185b sold for €8.61. Labels could be personalized.

2006 Winter Olympics, Turin — A1768

2006, Feb. 4   *Photo.*   *Perf. 13*
3186   A1768   53c multi   1.60   .30

Spirou A1769   Fantasio, Spip and Spirou A1770

Fantasio — A1771

2006, Feb. 25   *Perf. 13¼*
3187   A1769   (53c) multi   2.00   .30
   a.   Perf. 13¼x13 (booklet stamp)   1.25   .30

Booklet Stamps
Perf. 13¼x13
3188   A1770   (48c) multi   2.50   1.00
3189   A1771   (90c) multi   3.00   .75
   a.   Booklet pane, 4 each #3187a, 3188, 2 #3189   23.00
      Complete booklet, #3189a   24.00

Characters from Spirou, by Robert Velter. Stamp Day.

Courrières Coal Mine Disaster, Cent. — A1772

2006, Feb. 25   *Perf. 13¼*
3190   A1772   53c multi   1.60   .30

Douaumont Ossuary A1773

2006, Mar. 4   *Engr.*
3191   A1773   53c multi   1.60   .30

Aspects of Life in the French Regions Type of 2003

No. 3192: a, Yellow plums (mirabelle). b, Salt marsh (marais salants). c, Butter (beurre). d, Roquefort cheese, vert. e, Olive oil, vert. f, Carnival, vert. g, Grape harvests (vendanges), vert. h, Waiter at café, vert. i, Transhumance of livestock. j, Marshland gardens (hortilonages).

2006, Mar. 25   *Photo.*   *Perf. 13*
3192   Sheet of 10   16.00   16.00
   a.-i.   A1642 53c Any single   1.60   1.25

No. 3192 has three vertical rows of rouletting, separating sheet into quarters.

Nos. 3192a-3192j were also issued in large booklets containing panes of 1 of each stamp. The booklet sold for €19. Value $35.

Tourism Issue

Yvoire — A1774

Dijon — A1775

Antibes Juan-les-Pins A1776

Thionville A1777

2006   *Photo.*   *Perf. 13*
3193   A1774   53c multi   1.60   .30
     Engr.
     Perf. 13¼
3194   A1775   53c multi   1.60   .30
     Litho. & Engr.
     Perf. 13x13¼
3195   A1776   53c multi   1.60   .30
     Engraved
3196   A1777   54c multi   1.60   .40
     Nos. 3193-3196 (4)   6.40   1.30

Issued: No. 3193, 3/25; No. 3194, 4/7. No. 3195, 7/15. No. 3196, 9/16.

Art Series

Prehistoric Drawings in Rouffignac Cave A1778

Bathers, by Paul Cézanne A1779

Untitled Painting by Claude Viallat — A1780

Beggars Receiving Alms at the Door of a House, by Rembrandt A1781

Engr., Photo (#3198, 3199)
2006   *Perf. 13x13¼*
3197   A1778   55c multi   2.25   .75
3198   A1779   82c multi   2.50   1.00

Perf. 13¼x13
3199   A1780   €1.22 brt pink & bl grn   3.75   1.25
3200   A1781   €1.30 multi   4.75   1.25
     Nos. 3197-3200 (4)   13.25   4.25

Issued: 82c, 4/8; 55c, 5/27; No. 3199, 6/3. No. 3200, 11/10.

Gardens and Parks Type of 2003
Souvenir Sheet

No. 3201: a, Vallée-aux-Loups Park. b, Albert Kahn Gardens.

2006, Apr. 22   *Photo.*   *Perf. 13¼x13*
3201   Sheet of 2   13.00   13.00
   a.-b.   A1660 €1.98 Either single   6.00   6.00
   c.   Souvenir sheet, #3118a, 3118b, 3201a, 3201b   50.00   50.00

Salon du Timbre 2006. No. 3201 has four vertical rows of rouletting, separating sheet into fifths, with the two stamps in the central fifth.

No. 3201c issued 6/16.

Young Animals — A1782

Designs: No. 3202, Puppy. No. 3203, Kitten. 55c, Foal, horiz. 82c, Lamb, horiz..

2006, Apr. 22   *Perf. 13¼*
3202   A1782   53c multi   1.60   .30
3203   A1782   53c multi   1.60   .30
3204   A1782   55c multi   1.60   .30
3205   A1782   82c multi   2.40   .75
   a.   Souvenir sheet, #3202-3205   7.50   7.50
     Nos. 3202-3205 (4)   7.20   1.65

Europa — A1783

2006, Apr. 30
3206   A1783   53c multi   1.60   .30

Pierre Bayle (1647-1706), Philiosopher — A1784

2006, May 2   *Engr.*   *Perf. 13x13¼*
3207   A1784   53c blk & brn   1.60   .30

Remembrance of Slavery Day, 5th Anniv. — A1785

2006, May 10   *Photo.*   *Perf. 13¼*
3208   A1785   53c multi   1.60   .30

Vacation — A1786

Serpentine Die Cut 11¼x11
Booklet Stamp
Self-Adhesive
2006, May 27   *Litho.*
3209   A1786   (53c) multi   2.00   .25
   a.   Booklet pane of 10   20.00

Miniature Sheet

2006 World Cup Soccer Championships, Germany — A1787

No. 3210: a, Replacement players (39x25mm). b, Fans (39x25mm). c, Player with ball near chest (32mm diameter). d, Player kicking ball (32mm diameter). e, Goalie throwing ball (32mm diameter). f, Player making scissor kick (32mm diameter). g, Two players (32mm diameter). h, Referee (25x39mm). i, Coach (39x25mm). j, Cameramen (39x25mm).

2006, May 27   *Photo.*   *Perf. 12¾*
3210   A1787   Sheet of 10   16.00   16.00
   a.-j.   53c Any single   1.60   1.25

Marianne Type of 2005
2006   *Litho.*   *Perf. 13*
3211   Sheet of 15, #a-k, 2 each #l-m, + 15 labels   70.00   70.00
   a.   A1713 1c yellow orange   .35   .35
   b.   A1713 5c dark brown   .35   .35
   c.   A1713 10c violet   .55   .55
   d.   A1713 55c blue   2.75   2.75
   e.   A1713 64c olive green   3.25   3.25
   f.   A1713 75c light blue   3.50   3.50
   g.   A1713 82c fawn   4.25   4.25
   h.   A1713 90c dark blue   4.50   4.50
   i.   A1713 €1 dull orange   5.00   5.00
   j.   A1713 €1.22 red violet   6.00   6.00
   k.   A1713 €1.98 brown   9.50   9.50
   l.   A1713 (48c) green   2.50   2.50
   m.   A1713 (53c) red   2.60   2.60

Serpentine Die Cut 11¼
Self-Adhesive
3211N   Sheet of 15, #3211No-3211Ny, 2 each #3211Nz, 3211Naa, + 15 labels   250.00
   o.   A1713 1c yellow orange   .75   .75
   p.   A1713 5c dark brown   .75   .75
   q.   A1713 10c violet   1.25   1.25
   r.   A1713 55c blue   6.75   6.75
   s.   A1713 64c olive green   7.50   7.50
   t.   A1713 75c light blue   8.75   8.75
   u.   A1713 82c fawn   9.50   9.50
   v.   A1713 90c dark blue   11.00   11.00
   w.   A1713 €1 dull orange   12.00   12.00
   x.   A1713 €1.22 red violet   15.00   15.00
   y.   A1713 €1.98 brown   20.00   20.00
   z.   A1713 (48c) green   5.50   5.50
   aa.   A1713 (53c) red   6.25   6.25

Etched on Foil
Die Cut Perf. 13
3212   A1713   €5 silver   17.50   12.50

Nos. 3211a-3211m, 3211No-3211Naa and 3212 have "Phil@poste" inscription at bottom. Nos. 3211 and 3211N have stamps with a glossy varnish. No. 3211 sold for €12.04 and labels could be personalized. No. 3211N sold for €15.05 and labels could be personalized. No. 3212 was sold in a protective package.

Costumes From Operas by Wolfgang Amadeus Mozart — A1788

Designs: No. 3213, The Magic Flute. No. 3214, Don Giovanni. No. 3215, The Marriage of Figaro. No. 3216, The Clemency of Titus. No. 3217, The Abduction from the Seraglio (L'enlèvement au Sérail). No. 3218, Cosi Fan Tutte.

2006, June 17   *Photo.*   *Perf. 13*
3213   A1788   53c multi   1.60   .75
3214   A1788   53c multi   1.60   .75
3215   A1788   53c multi   1.60   .75
3216   A1788   53c multi   1.60   .75
3217   A1788   53c multi   1.60   .75
3218   A1788   53c multi   1.60   .75
   a.   Souvenir sheet, #3213-3218   12.00   12.00
     Nos. 3213-3218 (6)   9.60   4.50

Nos. 3213-3218 were each printed in souvenir sheets containing one stamp that sold as a set for €15, and in booklet panes containing one stamp in a large book that sold for €19. Value: set of 6 sheets $40; set of 6 panes in book $50. No. 3218a sold for €4.80, with the Red Cross receiving €1.62 of that.

FRANCE

681

UNESCO World Heritage Sites — A1789

Designs: 53c, Provins. 90c, Mont Saint-Michel.

2006, June 17   Photo.   Perf. 13¼
3219   A1789   53c multi   1.60   .30
3220   A1789   90c multi   2.75   1.20

See United Nations Offices in Geneva Nos. 459-461.

Garnier Opera House, Paris A1790

2006, June 18   Engr.   Perf. 13x13¼
3221   A1790   53c multi + label   1.60   .40

French Federation of Philatelic Associations 79th Congress, Paris. No. 3221 exists in a souvenir sheet of 1 (without label), issued in 2007 that sold for €3. Value, $12. See No. 5762b.

Happy Birthday — A1791

2006, June 19   Photo.   Perf. 13
3222   A1791   (53c) multi   2.00   .30
  a.   Souvenir sheet of 5   10.00   10.00
  b.   Litho. stamp + label   6.00   6.00

Serpentine Die Cut 11
Self-Adhesive
3222C   A1791   (53c) multi + label   15.00   15.00

Sheets of 10 of No. 3222b sold for €6.86. No. 3222C was printed in sheets of 10 stamps + 10 labels that sold for €8.61. Labels could be personalized for an additional fee.

European Capitals Type of 2002
Souvenir Sheet

No. 3223 — Attractions in Nicosia, Cyprus: a, Chrysaliniotissa Church. b, Archaeological Museum. c, Famagusta Gate. d, Archbishop's residence (Archeveché).

2006, June 20   Photo.   Perf. 13x13¼
3223   A1622   Sheet of 4   7.00   7.00
  a.-d.   53c Any single   1.60   1.00

Tango Dancing — A1792

2006, June 21   Photo.   Perf. 12¼
3224   A1792   53c Dancers   1.60   .30
3225   A1792   90c Musician   2.75   1.20

See Argentina Nos. 2395-2396.

La Poste's Business Foundation, 10th Anniv. — A1793

2006, June 22   Litho.   Perf. 13
3226   A1793   (53c) multi, *tan*   2.00   .30

French Open Golf Championship, Cent. — A1794

Photo. & Embossed
2006, June 24   Perf. 13
3227   A1794   53c multi   1.60   .30

A souvenir sheet containing No. 3227 sold for €3. Value $8.

Rotary International Type of 2005
Serpentine Die Cut 11
2006, July 1   Photo.
Self-Adhesive
3227A   A1717   53c multi   5.00   4.00

French Soccer Team's Second-Place Showing in 2006 World Cup — A1795

2006, July 5   Photo.   Perf. 13¼
Size: 35x26mm
3228   A1795   53c multi.   1.60   .40
Litho.
Size: 35x22mm
Perf. 13
3229   A1795   53c multi + label   5.00   4.00
Serpentine Die Cut 11¼x11
Self-Adhesive
3229A   A1795   53c multi + label   13.00   13.00

No. 3229 was printed in sheets of 10 stamps and 10 labels that sold for €6.94. Value $55. No. 3229A was printed in sheets of 10 stamps + 10 labels that sold for €8.61. Value $150. Labels could be personalized.

Quai Branly Museum A1796

2006, July 8   Photo.   Perf. 13x13¼
3230   A1796   53c multi   1.60   .40

Reinstatement of Capt. Alfred Dreyfus, Cent. — A1797

2006, July 12   Engr.
3231   A1797   53c multi   1.60   .30

Claude-Joseph Rouget de Lisle (1760-1836), Composer of "La Marseillaise" A1798

2006, July 13   Photo.   Perf. 13¼
3232   A1798   53c multi   1.60   .30

Pablo Casals (1876-1973), Cellist — A1799

2006, July 29
3233   A1799   53c multi   1.60   .30

Aspects of Life in French Regions Type of 2003

No. 3234: a, Catalan Towers. b, La Croisette, Cannes. c, Brocéliande Forest. d, Volcanic craters, Auvergne, vert. e, Les Invalides, Paris, vert. f, Chateau de Chaumont, Chaumont-sur-Loire. g, Ardèche Gorges, vert. h, Flour mill, Valmy, vert. i, Grotto of Messabielle, Lourdes. j, Calanches de Piana, Corsica.

2006, Sept. 2   Photo.   Perf. 13
3234   Sheet of 10   16.00   16.00
  a.-j.   A1642 54c Any single   1.60   1.25

No. 3234 has three vertical rows of rouletting, separating sheet into quarters.
Nos. 3234a-3234j were also issued in large booklets containing panes of 1 of each stamp. The booklet sold for €19. Value $35.

A1800

A1801

A1802

A1803

A1804

A1805

A1806

A1807

A1808

Cubitus, Comics by Michel Rodrigue and Pierre Aucaigne A1809

Serpentine Die Cut 11¼x11
2006, Sept. 20   Litho.
Self-Adhesive
Booklet Stamps
3235   A1800   (54c) multi   2.00   .30
3236   A1801   (54c) multi   2.00   .30
3237   A1802   (54c) multi   2.00   .30
3238   A1803   (54c) multi   2.00   .30
3239   A1804   (54c) multi   2.00   .30
3240   A1805   (54c) multi   2.00   .30
3241   A1806   (54c) multi   2.00   .30
3242   A1807   (54c) multi   2.00   .30
3243   A1808   (54c) multi   2.00   .30
3244   A1809   (54c) multi   2.00   .30
  a.   Booklet pane of 10, #3235-3244   20.00

Sculptures by Constantin Brancusi (1876-1957) A1810

Designs: 54c, Sleeping Muse. 85c, Sleep.

2006, Sept. 25   Photo.   Perf. 13¼
3245   A1810   54c multi   1.60   .30
3246   A1810   85c multi   2.75   .90

See Romania Nos. 4878-4879.

Marianne Type of 2005
2006   Engr.   Perf. 13
Inscribed "Phil@poste" at Bottom
3247   A1713   10c gray   .30   .25
3248   A1713   60c dark blue   1.75   .40
3249   A1713   70c yel green   2.10   .40
3250   A1713   85c purple   2.75   .50
3251   A1713   86c fawn   2.75   .50
3252   A1713   €1.15 blue   3.50   .75
3253   A1713   €1.30 red violet   4.00   1.00
3254   A1713   €2.11 chocolate   6.25   .50
  Nos. 3247-3254 (8)   23.40   4.30

Coil Stamp
Perf. 13 Horiz.
3255   A1713   60c dark blue   2.00   .75

Serpentine Die Cut 11¼
Self-Adhesive
3255A   A1713   (54c) red + label   12.00   12.00
  f.   Inscribed "ITVF" at bottom + label   —   —

Inscribed "Phila@poste" at Bottom
3255B   A1713   55c dk blue + label   —   —
3255C   A1713   60c dark blue + label   13.00   13.00
3255D   A1713   82c fawn + label   15.00   15.00
3255E   A1713   86c fawn + label   13.00   13.00
  Nos. 3255A-3255E (4)   53.00   53.00

Issued: Nos. 3247-3255, 10/1, others, 2006. Nos. 3255A, 3255Af, 3255C and 3255E were printed in sheets of 15 stamps + 15 labels that could be personalized. Nos. 3255B and 3255D were printed in sheets containing 10 stamps + 10 large labels or 15 stamps and 15 small labels. Labels could be personalized. Sheets of Nos. 3255A and 3255Af each sold for €13.29; No. 3255C, €14.04; No. 3255D, €17.31. For Nos. 3255A, 3255C, 3255D and 3255E, adjacent labels came in large and small sizes.

Aviation Without Borders — A1811

2006, Oct. 7   Photo.   Perf. 13
3256   A1811   54c multi   1.60   .30

Henri Moissan (1852-1907), 1906 Nobel Chemistry Laureate A1812

2006, Oct. 14   Engr.   Perf. 13¼x13
3257   A1812   54c multi   1.60   .30

"Shared Memories," Intl. Conference on Veterans, Paris — A1813

2006, Oct. 26   Photo.   Perf. 13¼
3258   A1813   54c multi   1.60   .30

Marianne — A1814

Serpentine Die Cut 6¾ Vert.
2006, Nov. 8   Engr.
Self-Adhesive
Booklet Stamp
3259   A1814   54c red   4.00   3.00
  a.   Booklet pane, 5 each #3083d, 3259   30.00

Compare with types A147 and A3213. See No. 4910.

FRANCE

Miniature Sheet

Flying Machines — A1815

No. 3260: a, Gustave Ponton d'Amécourt's helicopter. b, Alberto Santos-Dumont's monoplane, "Demoiselle," horiz. c, Jean Marie Le Bris's bird-shaped glider, horiz. d, Clément Ader's "Avion III," horiz. e, Henri Fabré's seaplane, horiz. f, Jean-Pierre Blanchard's balloon.

Litho. & Engr.

2006, Nov. 9			Perf. 13	
3260	A1815	Sheet of 6	10.00	10.00
a.-f.		54c Any single	1.60	1.40

Inauguration of Aulnay-sous-Bois to Bondy Tram-Train Line — A1816

2006, Nov. 18	Photo.	Perf. 13x13¼	
3261	A1816 54c multi	1.60	.30

Holiday Greetings A1817

Designs: No. 3262, Reindeer, sleigh, four penguins. No. 3263, Reindeer with fishing pole, three penguins. No. 3264, Reindeer, Christmas tree, two penguins. No. 3265, Reindeer skating, three penguins. No. 3266, Reindeer with gift boxes, three penguins.

2006, Nov. 25   Litho.   Perf. 13¼

3261A	A1817	(54c) multi + label	2.00	.30
3261B	A1817	(54c) multi + label	2.00	.30
3261C	A1817	(54c) multi + label	2.00	.30
3261D	A1817	(54c) multi + label	2.00	.30
3261E	A1817	(54c) multi + label	2.00	.30
f.		Vert. strip of 5, #3261A-3261E, + 5 labels	12.00	12.00
		Miniature sheet, 2 #3261Ef	30.00	30.00

Self-Adhesive
Booklet Stamps
Serpentine Die Cut 11¼x11

3262	A1817 (54c) multi	2.00	.30
3263	A1817 (54c) multi	2.00	.30
3264	A1817 (54c) multi	2.00	.30
3265	A1817 (54c) multi	2.00	.30
3266	A1817 (54c) multi	2.00	.30
a.	Booklet pane, 2 each #3262-3266	20.00	
	Nos. 3262-3266 (5)	10.00	1.50

Miniature sheet containing Nos. 3261A-3261E sold for €6.94. Value $60. Labels could be personalized. Value $60.
A souvenir sheet containing a perf. 13 example of No. 3266 sold for €3. Value $17.50. A sheet containing 5 No. 3261A + 5 labels exists, but was not sold.

Grand Masonic Lodge of France — A1818

2006, Dec. 1	Photo.	Perf. 13x13¼	
3267	A1818 54c multi	1.60	.30

Alain Poher (1909-96), Politician, and Senate Building A1819

2006, Dec. 2	Engr.	Perf. 13¼	
3268	A1819 54c multi	1.60	.30

Opening of New Paris Tramway A1820

2006, Dec. 16	Photo.	Perf. 13¼	
3269	A1820 54c multi	1.75	.30

Orchids Type of 2002

Designs: 31c, Platanthera chlorantha. 36c, Dactylorhiza savogiensis. 43c, Orchis insularis.

2007, Jan. 2   Litho.   Perf. 13

3270	A1584 31c multi	1.50	.50
3271	A1584 36c multi	1.50	.60
3272	A1584 43c multi	2.50	.75
	Nos. 3270-3272 (3)	5.50	1.85

Nos. 3270-3272 are known only precanceled. See second note after No. 132.

Hearts — A1821

"Givenchy" in: (54c), Black and white. (86c), Red.

2007, Jan. 6   Photo.   Perf. 13¼
Inscribed "Lettre 20 g"

3273	A1821 (54c) red & black	2.00	.30
a.	Souvenir sheet of 5	10.00	10.00

Inscribed "Lettre 50 g"

3274	A1821 (86c) black & red	3.00	1.00

Values are for stamps with surrounding selvage.

Serpentine Die Cut
Self-Adhesive

3275	A1821 (54c) Like #3273	16.00	13.00

Inscribed "Lettre 50 g"

3276	A1821 (86c) Like #3274	16.00	13.00

New Year 2007 (Year of the Pig) — A1822

2007, Jan. 27   Photo.   Perf. 13¼x13

3277	A1822 (54c) multi	2.00	.30
a.	Litho., stamp + label	8.00	8.00

Serpentine Die Cut 11
Self-Adhesive

3277B	A1822 (54c) multi + label	15.00	15.00

No. 3277 has a somewhat blurrier image than No. 3277a. Sheets of 5 #3277a + 5 labels sold for €3.51. Value $15. Labels could be personalized. No. 3277 exists in a souvenir sheet of 1 that sold for €3. Value $12.
No. 3277B was printed in sheets of 10 + 10 labels that sold for €8.86. Value $150. Labels could be personalized.
See No. 4969c.

Egyptian Hippopotamus Figurine — A1823

Head of Aphrodite A1824

Winged Victory of Samothrace A1825

Fresco, Pompeii — A1826

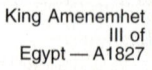

King Amenemhet III of Egypt — A1827

Statue of Juno — A1828

Egyptian Harpist — A1829

Etruscan Sarcophagus of Husband and Wife — A1830

Egyptian Statue of Seated Scribe — A1831

Head of Pericles — A1832

Serpentine Die Cut 11¼x11
2007, Jan. 27   Litho.
Booklet Stamps
Self-Adhesive

3279	A1823 (54c) multi	2.00	.30
3280	A1824 (54c) multi	2.00	.30
3281	A1825 (54c) multi	2.00	.30
3282	A1826 (54c) multi	2.00	.30
3283	A1827 (54c) multi	2.00	.30
3284	A1828 (54c) multi	2.00	.30
3285	A1829 (54c) multi	2.00	.30
3286	A1830 (54c) multi	2.00	.30
3287	A1831 (54c) multi	2.00	.30
3288	A1832 (54c) multi	2.00	.30
a.	Booklet pane of 10, #3279-3288	20.00	

Tourism Issue

Valenciennes A1833

2007	Engr.	Perf. 13¼	
3289	A1833 54c red & blue	1.50	.30

Issued: No. 3289, 2/3.

Tourism Issue

Limoges A1834

2007	Engr.	Perf. 13¼	
3290	A1834 54c multi	2.25	.30

Issued: No. 3290, 3/23.

Tourism Issue

Arcachon A1835

2007, May 19	Photo.	Perf. 13¼	
3291	A1835 54c multi	2.25	.30

Tourism Issue

Castres — A1836

2007, July 20	Engr.	Perf. 13¼	
3292	A1836 54c multi	1.60	.30

Tourism Issue

Firminy — A1837

2007, Sept. 15	Engr.	Perf. 13¼	
3293	A1837 54c multi	1.75	.30

Rights of France — A1838

2007, Feb. 5	Photo.	Perf. 13¼	
3294	A1838 54c multi	2.00	.30

Art Issue

Book Illumination from Sélestat Library — A1839

Galerie des Glaces, Versailles Palace A1840

La Barrière Fleurie, by Paul Sérusier A1841

Gallic Boar Ensign A1842

FRANCE

Perf. 12¼x13, 13¼x13 (#3297), 13x13¼ (#3296, 3298)
Engraved, Photo. (#3296, 3297, 3298A)

2007-08
3295	A1839	60c multi	1.75	.60
3296	A1840	85c multi	3.50	1.00
3297	A1841	86c multi	3.00	1.00
3298	A1842	€1.30 multi	4.50	1.25
	Nos. 3295-3298 (4)		12.75	3.85

Self-Adhesive
Serpentine Die Cut 11

3298A	A1840	85c multi	20.00	12.00

Issued: No. 3295, 2/10. No. 3297, 10/13. No. 3298, 6/2. No. 3296, 11/10. No. 3298A, 2008.

Aspects of Life in the French Regions Type of 2003

No. 3299: a, Baux-de-Provence. b, Banks of the Loire. c, Grande-Chartreuse Massif. d, Saint-Tropez. e, Doubs Waterfall, vert. f, Fontainebleau Forest, vert. g, Chantilly Castle. h, Saint-Malo. i, Ballon d'Alsace, vert. j, Midi Canal, vert.

2007, Feb. 24   Photo.   Perf. 13
3299		Sheet of 10	16.00	16.00
a.-j.	A1642	54c Any single	1.50	1.25

No. 3299 has three vertical rows of rouletting, separating sheet into quarters.

Nos. 3299a-3299j were also issued in large booklets containing panes of 1 of each stamp. The booklet sold for €19.

Aspects of Life in French Regions Type of 2003 Inscribed "Lettre Prioritaire 20g"

Designs: Nos. 3300-3301, Arc de Triomphe, vert.

2007, Feb.   Photo.   Perf. 13
3300	A1642	(54c) multi + label	8.00	8.00

Serpentine Die Cut 11x11¼
3301	A1642	(54c) multi + label	45.00	45.00

Nos. 3300-3301 each were printed in sheets of 10 stamps + 10 different labels that sold for €6.85. Value of sheets: No. 3300, $80; No. 3301, $450.

Marianne Type of 2005
2007   Litho.   Perf. 13
Stamps Inscribed "Phil@poste"
Without Varnish

3302		Sheet of 15, #a-k, 2 each #l-m, + 15 labels	250.00	250.00
a.	A1713	1c yellow orange	1.25	1.25
b.	A1713	5c brown	1.65	1.65
c.	A1713	10c gray	3.00	3.00
d.	A1713	60c blue	11.50	11.50
e.	A1713	70c lt yellow green	13.50	13.50
f.	A1713	85c purple	16.00	16.00
g.	A1713	86c pink	17.00	17.00
h.	A1713	€1 orange	21.00	21.00
i.	A1713	€1.15 light blue	23.00	23.00
j.	A1713	€1.30 red violet	25.00	25.00
k.	A1713	€2.11 maroon	37.50	37.50
l.	A1713	(49c) blue green	10.00	10.00
m.	A1713	(54c) red	11.50	11.50

Litho.
Serpentine Die Cut 11¼
Self-Adhesive
Stamps Inscribed "Phil@poste"
Without Varnish

3302N		Sheet of 15, #3302No-3302Ny, 2 each #3302Nz, 3302Naa, + 15 labels	—	
o.	A1713	1c yellow orange	—	—
p.	A1713	5c brown	—	—
q.	A1713	10c gray	—	—
r.	A1713	60c blue	—	—
s.	A1713	70c lt yellow green	—	—
t.	A1713	85c purple	—	—
u.	A1713	86c pink	—	—
v.	A1713	€1 orange	—	—
w.	A1713	€1.15 light blue	—	—
x.	A1713	€1.30 red violet	—	—
y.	A1713	€2.11 maroon	—	—
z.	A1713	(49c) blue green	—	—
aa.	A1713	(54c) red	—	—

Nos. 3302 and 3302N each sold for €14.40 and have personalizable labels.

Harry Potter — A1843

Designs: (49c), Ron Weasley. (85c), Hermione Granger.

2007, Mar. 12   Photo.   Perf. 13¼
3303	A1843	(54c) red & multi	2.00	.30
a.		Souvenir sheet of 1	2.50	2.00
b.		Perf. 13¼x13 (booklet stamp)	2.00	.30

Booklet Stamps
Perf. 13¼x13

3304	A1843	(49c) grn & multi	2.50	1.00
3305	A1843	(85c) blue & multi	3.00	.60
a.		Booklet pane of 10, 4 #3303b, 3 each #3304-3305	22.50	
		Complete booklet, #3305a	22.50	

Stamp Day. Sheets of five serpentine die cut 11 self-adhesive stamps of each denomination and five labels that could not be personalized exist. Each sheet sold for €6.50. Value, set, $150.

Albert Londres (1884-1932), Journalist A1844

2007, Mar. 16   Engr.   Perf. 13x13¼
3306	A1844	54c multi	1.60	.30

Six different souvenir sheets containing one No. 3306 exist. The set sold for €15. Value, set $45.

Audit Office, Bicent. — A1845

2007   Perf. 13¼x13
3307	A1845	54c multi	2.00	.30

Serpentine Die Cut 11
Self-Adhesive
3307A	A1845	54c multi	5.00	4.00

Issued: No. 3307, 3/17; No. 3307A, 7/20.

Treaty of Rome, 50th Anniv. — A1846

2007, Mar. 23   Photo.   Perf. 13¼
3308	A1846	54c multi	1.50	.30

Sébastien Le Prestre de Vauban (1633-1707), Military Engineer A1847

2007, Mar. 30   Engr.
3309	A1847	54c multi	1.50	.30

2007 Rugby World Cup — A1848

2007, Apr. 14   Photo.   Perf. 13¼
3310	A1848	54c multi	1.50	.30
a.		Perf. 13¼x13 + label	5.00	5.00

Serpentine Die Cut 11¼
Self-Adhesive
3311	A1848	54c multi + label	12.50	12.50

No. 3310a was printed in sheets of 5 stamps and 5 labels that could be personalized that sold for €4.20. Value $60.

No. 3311 was printed in sheets of 10 + 10 labels that could be personalized. Sheets sold for €10.60. Value, sheet $125.

Endangered Animals in Overseas Departments — A1849

Designs: No. 3312, Antillean iguana. No. 3313, Raccoon, horiz. 60c. Jaguar, horiz. 86c. Barau's petrel, horiz..

2007, Apr. 28   Photo.   Perf. 13¼
3312	A1849	54c multi	1.50	.30
3313	A1849	54c multi	1.50	.30
3314	A1849	60c multi	1.75	.60
3315	A1849	86c multi	2.40	.60
a.		Souvenir sheet, #3312-3315	7.25	7.25
		Nos. 3312-3315 (4)	7.15	1.80

Gardens and Parks Type of 2003
Souvenir Sheet

No. 3316 — Parc de la Tete d'Or, Lyon: a, Red flowers. b, White flowers.

2007, Apr. 28   Perf. 13¼x13
3316		Sheet of 2	12.00	12.00
a.-b.	A1660	€2.11 Either single	6.00	5.00

Salon du Timbre. No. 3316 has four vertical rows of rouletting, separating sheet into fifths, with the two stamps in the central fifth.

Vacations A1850

Designs: No. 3317, Wooden fence and red hollyhocks. No. 3318, Angelfish. No. 3319, Blue flowers. No. 3320, Blueberries. No. 3321, Canoes. No. 3322, Dyed wool hanging on rods. No. 3323, Glacier. No. 3324, Palm tree. No. 3325, Beach umbrellas and woman. No. 3326, Boxes of color pigments.

Serpentine Die Cut 11¼x11
2007, Apr. 20   Litho.
Booklet Stamps
Self-Adhesive

3317	A1850	(54c) multi	1.75	.30
3318	A1850	(54c) multi	1.75	.30
3319	A1850	(54c) multi	1.75	.30
3320	A1850	(54c) multi	1.75	.30
3321	A1850	(54c) multi	1.75	.30
3322	A1850	(54c) multi	1.75	.30
3323	A1850	(54c) multi	1.75	.30
3324	A1850	(54c) multi	1.75	.30
3325	A1850	(54c) multi	1.75	.30
3326	A1850	(54c) multi	1.75	.30
a.		Booklet pane of 10, #3317-3326	17.50	

Europa — A1851

2007, May 1   Photo.   Perf. 13¼
3327	A1851	60c multi	1.50	.40

Scouting, cent.

Intl. Sailing Federation, Cent. — A1852

2007, May 4   Perf. 13
3328	A1852	85c multi	2.25	.80

A souvenir sheet containing No. 3328 sold for €3. Value, $12.

Tintin and Snowy — A1853

Characters from Tintin comic strips and books, by Hergé: No. 3330, Professor Calculus (Tournesol). No. 3331, Captain Haddock. No. 3332, Thomson and Thompson (Dupondt). No. 3333, Bianca Castafiore. No. 3334, Chang (Tchang).

2007, May 12
3329	A1853	54c multi	1.50	.50
3330	A1853	54c multi	1.50	.50
3331	A1853	54c multi	1.50	.50
3332	A1853	54c multi	1.50	.50
3333	A1853	54c multi	1.50	.50
3334	A1853	54c multi	1.50	.50
a.		Souvenir sheet, #3329-3334	13.50	13.50

No. 3334a sold for €5, with the Red Cross receiving €1.76 of that.

Religious Art — A1854

Designs: 54c, Nativity, 15th cent. miniature, from Armenia. 85c, The Smile of Reims.

2007, May 22   Perf. 13¼
3335	A1854	54c multi	1.60	.30
3336	A1854	85c multi	2.50	1.00

See Armenia Nos. 749-750.

Inauguration of Eastern France TGV Train Service — A1855

2007, June 9   Perf. 13
3337	A1855	54c multi	1.50	.30

French Federation of Philatelic Associations 80th Congress, Poitiers — A1856

2007, June 15   Engr.   Perf. 13x13¼
3338	A1856	54c multi + label	1.75	.30

Miniature Sheet

2007 Rugby World Cup, France A1857

No. 3339 — Inscriptions: a, Touche (Throw-in, 30x39mm elliptical). b, Melée (scrum). c, Attaque (player running with ball). d, Essai (try). e, Transformation (kick, 30x39mm elliptical). f, Passe (pass). g, Raffut (stiff-arm). h, Haka (dance). i, Plaquage (tackle). j, Supporteurs (fans).

2007, June 23   Perf. 13x13¼
3339	A1857	Sheet of 10	17.00	17.00
a.-j.		54c Any single	1.50	1.25

European Capitals Type of 2002
Souvenir Sheet

No. 3340 — Attractions in Brussels: a, Maison du Roi (Royal Palace). b, Hotel du Ville (City Hall), vert. c, Mannekin Pis, vert. d, Atomium.

FRANCE

Perf. 13x13¼, 13¼x13 (vert. stamps)
2007, June 30
3340 A1622 Sheet of 4 7.50 7.50
a.-d. 54c Any single 1.60 .90

Association of French Mayors, Cent. — A1858

2007, July 5 Photo. Perf. 13¼
3341 A1858 54c multi 1.50 .30

Pierre Pfimlin (1907-2000), Mayor of Strasbourg — A1859

2007, July 7 Photo. Perf. 13¼
3342 A1859 60c multi 1.75 .60

2007 Rugby World Cup, France — A1860

Litho. With Three-Dimensional Plastic Affixed
2007, Sept. 5 Serpentine Die Cut 11
Self-Adhesive
3343 A1860 €3 multi 10.00 6.00

Happy Birthday — A1861

2007, Sept. 8 Photo. Perf. 13x13¼
3344 A1861 (54c) multi 5.00 .30
a. Litho., with attached label 2.40 2.40

No. 3344 was printed in a sheet of 5; No. 3344a was printed in a sheet of 5 + 5 labels that sold for €4.20.

Gift Boxes — A1862

Boxes and: Nos. 3345a, 3346, Butterflies. Nos. 3345b, 3348, Flowers. Nos. 3345c, 3347, Hearts. Nos. 3345d, 3350, Musical notes. Nos. 3345e, 3349, Bubbles.

2007, Sept. 8 Litho. Perf. 13¼
3345 Sheet of 5 + 5 labels 12.00 12.00
a.-e. A1862 (54c) Any single + label 2.40 2.40

Self-Adhesive
Booklet Stamps
Serpentine Die Cut 11
3346 A1862 (54c) multi 1.60 .55
3347 A1862 (54c) multi 1.60 .55
3348 A1862 (54c) multi 1.60 .55
3349 A1862 (54c) multi 1.60 .55
3350 A1862 (54c) multi 1.60 .55
a. Booklet pane of 5 #3346-3350 8.00

No. 3345 sold for €4.20.

Sully Prudhomme (1839-1907), Poet — A1863

2007, Sept. 15 Engr. Perf. 13¼
3351 A1863 €1.30 multi 3.75 1.25

A1864

A1865

A1866

A1867

A1868

Cows — A1868

Serpentine Die Cut 11
2007, Sept. 20 Litho.
Self-Adhesive
Booklet Stamps
3352 A1864 (54c) multi 1.60 .55
3353 A1865 (54c) multi 1.60 .55
3354 A1866 (54c) multi 1.60 .55
3355 A1867 (54c) multi 1.60 .55
3356 A1868 (54c) multi 1.60 .55
a. Booklet pane, 2 each #3352-3356 16.00
Nos. 3352-3356 (5) 8.00 2.75

Aspects of Life in French Regions Type of 2003

No. 3357: a, Sèvres porcelain. b, Grasse perfume. c, Christmas market. d, Marseille soap. e, Giants, vert. f, Basque beret, vert. g, Aubusson tapestries. h, Lyonnaise tavern. i, Slipper, vert. j, Canteloupe, vert.

2007, Sept. 29 Photo. Perf. 13
3357 Sheet of 10 16.00 16.00
a.-j. A1642 54c Any single 1.60 .55

No. 3357 has three vertical rows of rouletting separating sheet into quarters.
Nos. 3357a-3357j were also issued in large booklets containing panes of 1 of each stamp. The booklet sold for €19. Value $55.

Space Age, 50th Anniv. A1869

2007, Oct. 4 Perf. 13x12½
3358 A1869 85c multi 2.40 1.00

Medical Research Foundation, 60th Anniv. — A1870

2007, Oct. 20 Perf. 13¼
3359 A1870 54c multi 1.60 .30

Guy Moquet (1924-41), World War II Resistance Fighter — A1871

2007, Oct. 22 Engr.
3360 A1871 54c multi 1.60 .30

Dole — A1872

2007, Nov. 2
3361 A1872 54c multi 1.60 .30

Personalized Stamp With Country Name on Short Side — A1873

Personalized Stamp With Country Name on Long Side — A1874

Serpentine Die Cut 11¼ Syncopated
2007, Nov. Litho.
Self-Adhesive
Inscribed: "Lettre Prioritaire 20 g"
3362 A1873 (54c) multi 6.00 6.00
3363 A1874 (54c) multi 6.00 6.00
Inscribed: "Monde 20 g"
3364 A1873 (85c) multi 6.00 6.00
3365 A1874 (85c) multi 6.00 6.00
Inscribed: "Lettre Prioritaire 50 g"
3366 A1873 (86c) multi 6.00 6.00
3367 A1874 (86c) multi 6.00 6.00
Nos. 3362-3367 (6) 36.00 36.00

Nos. 3362-3367 were each printed in sheets of ten, having vignettes that could be personalized or chosen from a library of stock designs, two of which are shown on the illustrated stamps. Sheets of Nos. 3362 and 3363 each sold for €10.03, and sheets of Nos. 3364-3367 each sold for €13.38. Sheets were made available with different frame colors. Starting in 2008, numerous sheets containing a varying number of stamps with these frames and having various pre-selected vignettes were produced and sold by La Poste for various prices per sheet, each well above the franking value of the stamps at the time of issue. Any stamp with a vignette and/or frame color differing from the items shown is an equivalent item to those shown. Also starting in 2008, stamps were created having dozens of different rate inscriptions other than "Lettre Prioritaire 20g," "Monde 20g," and "Lettre Prioritaire 50g" inscriptions listed here. In 2019, a round stamp with similar features was produced in a souvenir sheet of 1.

Jean-Baptiste Charcot (1867-1936), Polar Explorer — A1875

Ship Pourquoi-Pas? — A1876

2007, Nov. 8 Engr. Perf. 13x12¾
3368 A1875 54c multi 1.60 .55
3369 A1876 60c multi 1.75 .60
a. Horiz. pair, #3368-3369 3.50 1.25

See Greenland No. 505. A sheet containing Nos. 3368-3369 sold for €4 in 2008.

Marianne — A1877

Serpentine Die Cut 6¾ Vert.
2007, Nov. 8 Engr.
Self-Adhesive
Booklet Stamp
3370 A1877 54c red 3.00 2.00
a. Booklet pane, 6 each #3083d, 3370 27.50

Miniature Sheet

Lighthouses — A1878

No. 3371: a, Cap Fréhel Lighthouse. b, Espiguette Lighthouse. c, D'ar-Men Lighthouse. d, Grand-Léjon Lighthouse. e, Porquerolles Lighthouse, horiz. f, Chassiron Lighthouse, horiz.

Litho. & Engr.
2007, Nov. 9 Perf. 13
3371 A1878 Sheet of 6 9.75 9.75
a.-f. 54c Any single 1.60 .30

2007 Women's World Handball Championships, France — A1879

2007, Nov. 10 Photo. Perf. 13¼
3372 A1879 54c multi 1.60 .30

Holiday Greetings A1880

No. 3377: a, Squirrel with stocking cap. b, Bird with party hat. c, Hedgehog with party cap. d, Dog with stocking cap. e, Deer with stocking cap.
No. 3378, Squirrel with stocking cap. No. 3379, Bird with party hat. No. 3380, Deer with stocking cap. No. 3381, Hedgehog with party hat. No. 3382, Dog with stocking cap.

2007, Nov. 24 Litho. Perf. 13¼
3377 Sheet of 5 + 5 labels 20.00 20.00
a.-e. A1880 (54c) Any single + label 2.50 2.50

Booklet Stamps
Self-Adhesive
Serpentine Die Cut 11
3378 A1880 (54c) multi 2.00 .30
3379 A1880 (54c) multi 2.00 .30
3380 A1880 (54c) multi 2.00 .30
3381 A1880 (54c) multi 2.00 .30
3382 A1880 (54c) multi 2.00 .30
a. Booklet pane, 2 each #3378-3382 20.00

No. 3377 sold for €4.20 and had labels that could not be personalized.
A souvenir sheet of 1 of No. 3381 sold for €3. Value, $12.

Marianne Type of 2005
2008 Engr. Perf. 13
3383 A1713 (65c) dk blue 2.50 .40
3384 A1713 72c yel green 2.25 .40
3385 A1713 88c fawn 2.75 .50
3386 A1713 €1.25 blue 4.00 .80
3387 A1713 €1.33 red vio 4.25 .85
3388 A1713 €2.18 choc 6.50 1.40
Nos. 3383-3388 (6) 22.25 4.35

FRANCE

Coil Stamp
Perf. 13 Horiz.

3388A A1713 (65c) dk blue 3.00 .40
Issued: Nos. 3383-3388A, 3/1.

Marianne Type of 2005
Serpentine Die Cut 6¾ Vert.

2008	Self-Adhesive Booklet Stamp	Engr.

3389 A1713 (60c) blue 2.50 .50
 a. Booklet pane of 12 30.00
Issued: No. 3389, 1/2.

Hearts — A1881

Designs: (54c), Face. (86c), (88c), Plant with heart-shaped leaves.

2008, Jan. 5   Photo.   Perf. 13¼
3390 A1881 (54c) multi 1.60 .30
 a. Souvenir sheet of 5 8.00 8.00
 b. Sheet of 10 + 10 labels 20.00 —
3391 A1881 (86c) multi 2.60 1.00

Self-Adhesive
Serpentine Die Cut
3392 A1881 (54c) multi 16.00 12.00
3392A A1881 (88c) multi 16.00 12.00

Values are for stamps with surrounding selvage.
Nos. 3390, 3390a, 3390b, 3391-3392 issued 1/5/08. No. 3390b was sold for €6.86. Labels could not be personalized.

New Year 2008 (Year of the Rat) — A1882

2008, Jan. 26   Photo.   Perf. 13¼x13
3393 A1882 (54c) multi 1.60 .30

Printed in sheets of 5. A souvenir sheet of one No. 3393 sold for €3.
See No. 4969d.

Paintings — A1883

Designs: No. 3394, Legend of St. Francis: Sermon to the Birds, by Giotto di Bondone. No. 3395, Seaport at Sunset, by Claude Lorrain. No. 3396, The Birth of Venus, by Sandro Botticelli. No. 3397, Napoleon Bonaparte Crossing the Alps, by Jacques-Louis David. No. 3398, La Belle Jardinière (Madonna and Child with St. John the Baptist), by Raphael, vert. No. 3399, Head of a Girl in a Turban, by Jan Vermeer, vert. No. 3400, Summer, by Giuseppe Arcimboldo, vert. No. 3401, Mona Lisa, by Leonardo da Vinci, vert. No. 3402, Infant Maria Marguerita, by Diego Velásquez, vert. No. 3403, Money Changer with Wife, by Quentin Massys (Metsys), vert.

Serpentine Die Cut 11
2008, Jan. 26   Litho.
Booklet Stamps
Self-Adhesive

3394 A1883 (54c) multi 1.60 .55
3395 A1883 (54c) multi 1.60 .55
3396 A1883 (54c) multi 1.60 .55
3397 A1883 (54c) multi 1.60 .55
3398 A1883 (54c) multi 1.60 .55
3399 A1883 (54c) multi 1.60 .55
3400 A1883 (54c) multi 1.60 .55
3401 A1883 (54c) multi 1.60 .55
3402 A1883 (54c) multi 1.60 .55
3403 A1883 (54c) multi 1.60 .55
 a. Booklet pane of 10, #3394-3403 16.00

France Stadium, 10th Anniv. — A1884

2008, Jan. 28   Photo.   Perf. 13¼
3404 A1884 54c multi 1.60 .30

Tourism Issue

Vendôme A1885

La Rochelle A1886

Toulon — A1887

Richelieu A1888

Le Havre A1889

2008   Engr.   Perf. 13¼
3405 A1885 54c multi 1.60 .30

Perf. 13
3406 A1886 55c multi 1.50 .30
3407 A1887 55c multi 1.50 .30
3408 A1888 55c multi 1.50 .30
3409 A1889 55c multi 1.50 .30
 Nos. 3405-3409 (5) 7.60 1.50

Issued: No. 3405, 2/2; No. 3406, 4/5; Nos. 3407-3408, 7/5; No. 3409, 9/13. A souvenir sheet of one of No. 3406 sold for €3.

Art Issue

Globes of Vincenzo Coronelli A1890

Young Girl Warming Her Hands at a Large Stove, by Jean-Jacques Henner — A1891

Untitled Work by Gérard Garouste A1892

A Theater Box Office, by Honoré Daumier A1893

Litho. & Engr., Photo (A1891-A1892), Engr. (A1893)
2008   Perf. 13¼x13
3410 A1890 85c multi 3.00 1.25
3411 A1891 88c multi 3.00 .60
3412 A1892 €1.33 multi 4.00 1.25
3413 A1893 €1.33 choc & bl gray 4.50 1.00
 Nos. 3410-3413 (4) 14.50 4.10

Self-Adhesive
Serpentine Die Cut 11
3413A A1891 88c multi 6.00 4.00
3413B A1892 €1.33 multi 120.00 50.00
3413C A1893 €1.33 choc & bl gray 200.00 75.00
 Nos. 3413A-3413C (3) 326.00 129.00

Issued: No. 3410, 2/11; No. 3412, 6/19; No. 3411, 10/18; No. 3413, 11/7.
A souvenir sheet containing No. 3410 sold for €3.

Emir Abdelkader (1808-83), Algerian Leader — A1894

2008, Feb. 20   Engr.   Perf. 13¼
3414 A1894 54c multi 1.75 .30

Droopy Dog — A1895

Red-haired Woman — A1896

The Wolf — A1897

Design: €2.18, Droopy Dog, diff.

2008, Mar. 1   Photo.   Perf. 13¼
3415 A1895 (55c) multi 1.75 .30
3416 A1896 (55c) multi 1.75 .30
3417 A1897 (55c) multi 1.75 .30
 a. Strip of 3, #3415-3417 5.25 1.90

Souvenir Sheet
Perf. 13x13¼
3418 A1895 €2.18 multi 6.75 6.75

Booklet Stamps
Self-Adhesive
Serpentine Die Cut 11
3419 A1895 (55c) multi 1.75 .30
3420 A1896 (55c) multi 1.75 .30
3421 A1897 (55c) multi 1.75 .30
 a. Booklet pane of 10, 4 #3419, 3 each #3420-3421 17.50

Cartoon characters created by Tex Avery; Stamp Day. No. 3418 contains one 35x27mm stamp that has thermographic ink (on cartoon balloon) that when warmed, changes color allowing a message below the ink to appear Nos. 3419-3421 exist in three sheets, each containing 5 of each stamp + 5 non-personalizable labels. Each sheet sold for €6.50. Value, each $40.

Sound Recording Libraries A1898

2008, Mar. 15   Photo.   Perf. 13¼
3422 A1898 55c multi 1.75 .30

Flowers — A1899

Designs: 37c, Aquilegia. 38c, Tulipa sp. 44c, Bellis perennis. 45c, Primula veris.

2008, Mar. 1   Litho.   Perf. 13
3423 A1899 37c multi 1.25 .60
3424 A1899 38c multi 1.25 .60
3425 A1899 44c multi 1.75 .70
3426 A1899 45c multi 1.75 .70
 Nos. 3423-3426 (4) 6.00 2.60

Nos. 3423-3426 are known only precanceled. See second note after No. 132. Compare with types A2174-A2177.

Aspects of Life in French Regions Type of 2003

No. 3427: a, Chateau d'Ussé, Rigny-Ussé. b, Vézelay. c, Place des Vosges, Le Marais district, Paris. d, Le Marais Poitevin (Poitevin Marsh). e, Cugarel Windmill, Castelnaudary, vert. f, Red granite coastal rocks, vert. g, Honfleur. h, La Petite France district, Strasbourg. i, La Boétie House, Sarlat-la-Canéda, vert. j, Marfate Cirque, Reunion, vert.

2008, Mar. 29   Photo.   Perf. 13
3427 Sheet of 10 17.50 17.50
 a.-j. A1642 55c Any single 1.75 1.25

No. 3427 has three vertical rows of rouletting, separating sheet into quarters. Nos. 3427a-3427j were also issued in a large booklet containing panes of 1 of each stamp. The booklet sold for €19.

Lyon A1900

Litho. & Engr.
2008, Apr. 4   Perf. 13
3428 A1900 55c multi 1.75 .30

Gardens and Parks Type of 2003

No. 3429: a, Parc Longchamp, Marseille. b, Parc Borely, Marseille.

2008   Photo.   Perf. 13¼x13
3429 Sheet of 2 13.50 13.50
 a.-b. A1660 €2.18 Either single 6.75 3.50
 c. Miniature sheet of 4, #3316a, 3316b, 3429a, 3429b 50.00 50.00

Salon du Timbre. No. 3429 has four vertical rows of rouletting, separating sheet into fifths, with the two stamps in the central fifth.
Issued: No. 3429, 4/12; No. 3429c, 6/14.

Prehistoric Animals — A1901

Designs: No. 3430, Phorusrhacos. No. 3431, Smilodon. 65c, Megaloceros, horiz. 88c, Mammoth, horiz.

2008, Apr. 19   Perf. 13¼
3430 A1901 55c multi 1.75 .30
3431 A1901 55c multi 1.75 .30
3432 A1901 65c multi 2.00 .50
3433 A1901 88c multi 2.75 1.00
 a. Miniature sheet, #3430-3433 8.25 8.25
 Nos. 3430-3433 (4) 8.25 2.10

686 FRANCE

First Heart Transplant in Europe, 40th Anniv. — A1902

2008, Apr. 24   *Perf. 13¼x13*
3434 A1902 55c red & black   1.60 .30

Valentré Bridge, Cahors — A1903

2008, Apr. 26   *Engr.*   *Perf. 13x13¼*
3435 A1903 55c multi   1.60 .30

Europa — A1904

2008, May 4   *Photo.*   *Perf. 13x13¼*
3436 A1904 55c multi   1.75 .30

Self-Adhesive
Serpentine Die Cut 11
3436A A1904 55c multi   3.00 3.00

Quebec City, Canada, 400th Anniv. — A1905

2008, May 16   *Engr.*   *Perf. 13*
3437 A1905 85c multi   2.75 1.00

See Canada No. 2269.
A souvenir sheet containing No. 3437 and Canada No. 2269 sold for $4.99 in Canada and was sold in France for €15 as part of a set additionally containing six different souvenir sheets containing only No. 3437.

Happy Birthday — A1906

2008, May 28   *Photo.*
3438 A1906 (55c) multi   1.75 .30

Printed in sheets of 5.

It's a Boy — A1907

It's a Girl — A1908

2008, May 28   *Serpentine Die Cut 11*
Booklet Stamps
Self-Adhesive
3439 A1907 (55c) multi, un-scratched panel   2.00 2.00
   a. Scratched panel   .60
   b. Booklet pane of 10 #3439   20.00

3440 A1908 (55c) multi, un-scratched panel   2.00 2.00
   a. Scratched panel   .60
   b. Booklet pane of 10 #3440   20.00

Scratch-off panels on Nos. 3439-3440 cover pictures and text for baby boy and girl, respectively.

Vacations A1909

Designs: No. 3441, Ferns. No. 3442, Butterfly on leaf. No. 3443, Hands holding plant's leaves. No. 3444, Coconut palm tree. No. 3445, Path beside forest lake. No. 3446, Golf ball, putter and hole. No. 3447, Water lily and lily pads. No. 3448, Watering cans and foliage. No. 3449, Sliced kiwi fruit. No. 3450, Shelled and unshelled peas.

Serpentine Die Cut 11
2008, May 28   *Litho.*
Booklet Stamps
Self-Adhesive
3441 A1909 (55c) multi   1.75 .60
3442 A1909 (55c) multi   1.75 .60
3443 A1909 (55c) multi   1.75 .60
3444 A1909 (55c) multi   1.75 .60
3445 A1909 (55c) multi   1.75 .60
3446 A1909 (55c) multi   1.75 .60
3447 A1909 (55c) multi   1.75 .60
3448 A1909 (55c) multi   1.75 .60
3449 A1909 (55c) multi   1.75 .60
3450 A1909 (55c) multi   1.75 .60
   a. Booklet pane of 10, #3441-3450   17.50

Evreux Belfry — A1910

2008, May 31   *Engr.*   *Perf. 13*
3451 A1910 55c multi   1.60 .60

Grand Palais, Paris A1911

2008, June 14   *Perf. 13x13¼*
3452 A1911 55c multi + label   1.60 .60

French Federation of Philatelic Associations 81st Congress, Paris. See No. 5762a.

Marianne and Stars A1912

Hand Depositing Ballot A1913

Tree in Hand A1914

Dove A1915

2008		Engr.	Perf. 13
3453	A1912	1c yellow	.25 .25
3454	A1912	5c gray brown	.25 .25
3455	A1912	10c gray	.30 .25
3456	A1912	(50c) green	1.60 .25
3457	A1912	(55c) red	1.75 .40
3458	A1912	(65c) dark blue	2.10 .50
3459	A1912	72c olive green	2.25 .60
3460	A1912	85c purple	2.75 .70
3461	A1912	88c fawn	2.75 .70
3462	A1912	€1 orange	3.25 .80
3463	A1912	€1.25 blue	4.00 1.00
3464	A1912	€1.33 red violet	4.25 1.10
3465	A1912	€2.18 chocolate	7.00 2.40

Self-Adhesive (#3466)
Etched on Foil
Die Cut Perf. 13
3466 A1912 €5 silver   16.00 16.00
   Nos. 3453-3466 (14)   48.50 25.20

Litho.
Perf. 13
3467 Sheet of 15, #3467a-3467k, 2 each #3467l-3467m, + 15 labels   40.00 40.00
   a. A1912 1c yellow   .25 .25
   b. A1912 5c brown   .25 .25
   c. A1912 10c gray   .35 .35
   d. A1912 (65c) dark blue   2.40 2.40
   e. A1912 72c olive green   2.60 2.60
   f. A1912 85c purple   3.00 3.00
   g. A1912 88c fawn   3.25 3.25
   h. A1912 €1 orange   3.50 3.50
   i. A1912 €1.25 blue   4.50 4.50
   j. A1912 €1.33 red violet   4.75 4.75
   k. A1912 €2.18 brn violet   7.75 7.75
   l. A1912 (50c) green   1.75 1.75
   m. A1912 (55c) red   2.00 2.00

Coil Stamps
Perf. 13 Horiz.
Engr.
3468 A1912 (50c) green   3.50 2.00
3469 A1912 (55c) red   4.00 2.00
3470 A1912 (65c) dark blue   4.50 2.00

Booklet Stamps (Types A1913-A1915)
Self-Adhesive
Serpentine Die Cut 6¾ Vert.
3471 A1912 (55c) red   2.50 1.00
   a. Booklet pane of 20   50.00
   b. Booklet pane of 10   25.00
   c. Booklet pane of 12   30.00
3472 A1913 55c red   2.50 1.00
3473 A1914 55c red   2.50 1.00
3474 A1915 55c red   2.50 1.00
   a. Booklet pane of 12, 6 #3471, 2 each #3472-3474   30.00
3475 A1912 (65c) dark blue   2.50 1.00
   a. Booklet pane of 12   30.00
3476 A1913 65c dark blue   2.50 1.00
3477 A1914 65c dark blue   2.50 1.00
3478 A1915 65c dark blue   2.50 1.00
   a. Booklet pane of 12, 6 #3475, 2 each #3476-3478   30.00
   Nos. 3471-3478 (8)   20.00 8.00

Issued: No. 3457, 6/17; No. 3741c, 9/8; No. 3466, 7/1; No. 3475a, 2009; others, 6/14. On day of issue, No. 3467 sold for €12.54. Labels on No. 3467 could not be personalized.
No. 3471b is comprised of two horizontal strips of five stamps on a yellow backing paper. Nos. 3471 and 3475 were also printed in sheets of 100 later in 2008.
See Nos. 3532, 3551-3566, 3612-3616E, 3730, 3871-3882, 4410l, 4525.
Typographed, engraved and silk-screened perf. 13 stamps of types A486 and A1912 with denomination of €1 in red were produced in pairs with 2 labels and photogravure perf. 13 stamps of these types with denominations of €1 in blue, green and multicolored were printed in blocks of 8 + 8 labels. These items were created in very limited quantities in 2010.

Ecology — A1916

Designs: No. 3479, Tree. No. 3480, Bicycle. No. 3481, World map. No. 3482, Computer. No. 3483, Water droplets. No. 3484, Sun. No. 3485, Two plastic bottles. No. 3486, Three plastic bottles. No. 3487, Apple core. No. 3488, Strawberry.

Serpentine Die Cut 11
2008, June 14   *Photo.*
Booklet Stamps
Self-Adhesive
3479 A1916 (55c) multi   1.75 .50
3480 A1916 (55c) multi   1.75 .50
3481 A1916 (55c) multi   1.75 .50
3482 A1916 (55c) multi   1.75 .50
3483 A1916 (55c) multi   1.75 .50
3484 A1916 (55c) multi   1.75 .50
3485 A1916 (55c) multi   1.75 .50
3486 A1916 (55c) multi   1.75 .50
3487 A1916 (55c) multi   1.75 .50
3488 A1916 (55c) multi   1.75 .50
   a. Booklet pane of 10, #3479-3488   17.50

Trapeze Artist A1917

Bareback Rider A1918

Clown A1919   Lion Tamer A1920

Clown A1921   Juggler A1922

2008, June 15   *Photo.*   *Perf. 13*
3489 A1917 55c multi   1.75 .60
3490 A1918 55c multi   1.75 .60
3491 A1919 55c multi   1.75 .60
3492 A1920 55c multi   1.75 .60
3493 A1921 55c multi   1.75 .60
3494 A1922 55c multi   1.75 .60
   a. Souvenir sheet, #3489-3494   16.50 16.50
   Nos. 3489-3494 (6)   10.50 3.60

No. 3494a sold for €5.10, with the Red Cross receiving €1.80 of that.

2008 Summer Olympics, Beijing — A1923

Designs: No. 3495, Equestrian, cycling. No. 3496, Swimming, rowing, horiz. No. 3497, Judo, fencing, horiz. No. 3498, Tennis, running.

Perf. 13¼x13, 13x13¼
2008, June 16
3495 A1923 55c multi   1.75 .60
3496 A1923 55c multi   1.75 .60
3497 A1923 55c multi   1.75 .60
   a. Pair, #3496-3497   3.50 1.75
3498 A1923 55c multi   1.75 .60
   a. Vert. pair, #3495, 3498   3.50 1.75
   Nos. 3495-3498 (4)   7.00 2.40

Nos. 3495-3498 were printed in a sheet of 10 containing 2 each #3495 and 3498 and 3 each #3496-3497.

Charles de Gaulle Memorial, Paris — A1924

2008, June 18   *Engr.*   *Perf. 13¼*
3499 A1924 55c multi   1.75 .60

Miniature Sheet

European Projects — A1925

No. 3500: a, Map of Europe, 1-euro coin. b, Flags of France and European Union, horiz (French Presidency of European Union). c, Earth and Galileo satellite, horiz. d, Students

FRANCE 687

and flags (Erasmus higher education program).

2008, June 19		Photo.		Perf. 13
3500	A1925	Sheet of 4	7.00	7.00
a.-d.	55c Any single		1.75	.60

Miniature Sheet

Famous Ships — A1926

No. 3501: a, Confiance. b, Grande Hermine, horiz. c, Boudeuse, horiz. d, Astrolabe, horiz. e, Hermione, horiz. f, Boussole.

2008, June 20				
3501	A1926	Sheet of 6	10.50	10.50
a.-f.	55c Any single		1.75	.60

French and Brazilian Landscapes — A1927

Designs: 55c, Amazonian forest, Brazil. 85c, Glacier, France.

2008, July 13				
3502	A1927	55c multi	1.75	.60
3503	A1927	85c multi	2.75	.90
a.	Horiz. pair, #3502-3503		4.50	2.25

See Brazil No. 3052.

Mediterranean Summit, Paris — A1928

2008, July 13		Perf. 13¼
3504	A1928 55c multi	1.75 .60

Aspects of Life in French Regions Type of 2003

No. 3505: a, Espadrilles. b, Stew (pot au feu). c, Chestnuts (chataigne). d, Fireworks (feu d'artifice). e, Epinal prints (l'image d'Epinal), vert. f, Lentils (lentille), vert. g, Reblochon cheese. h, Calissons (candy). i, Stilt walker (les échasses), vert. j, Mustard (moutarde), vert.

2008, Sept. 6		Photo.	Perf. 13
3505	Sheet of 10	15.00	15.00
a.-j.	A1642 55c Any single	1.50	.50

No. 3505 has three vertical rows of rouletting, separating sheet into quarters.
Nos. 3505a-3505j also were issued in large booklets containing panes of 1 of each stamp. The booklet sold for €19.

Josselin — A1929

2008, Sept. 20		Engr.	Perf. 13¼
3506	A1929 55c multi		1.75 .50

A1930

A1931

A1932

A1933

A1934

A1935

A1936

A1937

A1938

Garfield, Comic Strip by Jim Davis — A1939

Serpentine Die Cut 11¼x11
2008, Sept. 18   Photo.

Booklet Stamps
Self-Adhesive

3507	A1930	(55c) multi	1.75	.50
3508	A1931	(55c) multi	1.75	.50
3509	A1932	(55c) multi	1.75	.50
3510	A1933	(55c) multi	1.75	.50
3511	A1934	(55c) multi	1.75	.50
3512	A1935	(55c) multi	1.75	.50
3513	A1936	(55c) multi	1.75	.50
3514	A1937	(55c) multi	1.75	.50
3515	A1938	(55c) multi	1.75	.50
3516	A1939	(55c) multi	1.75	.50
a.	Booklet pane of 10, #3507-3516		17.50	
	Nos. 3507-3516 (10)		17.50	5.00

"I Am Sport" — A1940

2008, Oct. 2		Photo.	Perf. 12½
3517	A1940 55c multi		1.50 .50

Values are for stamps with surrounding selvage.

Fifth Republic, 50th Anniv. — A1941

2008, Oct. 4			Perf. 13¼
3518	A1941 55c multi		1.50 .50

Seascapes of Viet Nam and France — A1942

Designs: 55c, Along Bay, Viet Nam. 85c, Strait of Bonifacio, France.

2008, Oct. 15		Photo.	Perf. 13x12¾
3519	A1942 55c multi		1.40 .45
3520	A1942 85c multi		2.25 .75

See Viet Nam Nos. 3340-3341.

Types of 1959-2008
Serpentine Die Cut 6¾ Vert.
2008, Nov. 6   Photo.

Booklet Stamps
Self-Adhesive

3521	A328	55c multi	1.40	.45
3522	A349	55c multi	1.40	.45
3523	A360	55c multi	1.40	.45
3524	A379	55c multi	1.40	.45
3525	A486	55c dark red	1.40	.45
3526	A555	55c rose carmine	1.40	.45
3527	A771	55c bright red	1.40	.45
3528	A915	55c red	1.40	.45
3529	A1161	55c red	1.40	.45
3530	A1409	55c red	1.40	.45
3531	A1713	55c red	1.40	.45
3532	A1912	55c red	1.40	.45
a.	Booklet pane of 12, #3521-3532		17.00	
	Nos. 3521-3532 (12)		16.80	5.40

Landmarks of France and Israel — A1943

Airplane, stamped first flight cover and: 55c, Haifa waterfront, Israel. 85c, Eiffel Tower, Paris.

2008, Nov. 6		Photo.	Perf. 13
3533	A1943 55c multi		1.40 .45
3534	A1943 85c multi		2.25 .75

First flight between France and Israel, 60th anniv. See Israel Nos. 1750-1751.

European Capitals Type of 2002

No. 3535 — Attractions in Prague: a, Tour du Petit Coté (Charles Bridge and Tower), vert. b, Hotel de ville horloge astronomique et calandrier (City Hall astronomical clock), vert. c, Eglise Notre-Dame-de-Tyn (Tyn Cathedral), vert. d, Le Chateau (Hradcany Castle).

Perf. 13¼x13, 13x13¼ (#3535d)
2008, Nov. 7   Photo.

3535	A1022	Sheet of 4	5.75	5.75
a.-d.	55c Any single		1.40	.45

A1944   A1945

A1946   A1947

A1948   A1949

A1950

A1951

A1952

A1953

A1954

A1955

A1956

Happy Holidays — A1957

Serpentine Die Cut 11¼x11
2008, Nov. 8   Photo.

Booklet Stamps
Self-Adhesive

3536	A1944	(55c) multi	1.40	.45
3537	A1945	(55c) multi	1.40	.45
3538	A1946	(55c) multi	1.40	.45
3539	A1947	(55c) multi	1.40	.45
3540	A1948	(55c) multi	1.40	.45
3541	A1949	(55c) multi	1.40	.45

Serpentine Die Cut 11x11¼

3542	A1950	(55c) multi	1.40	.45
3543	A1951	(55c) multi	1.40	.45
3544	A1952	(55c) multi	1.40	.45
3545	A1953	(55c) multi	1.40	.45
3546	A1954	(55c) multi	1.40	.45
3547	A1955	(55c) multi	1.40	.45
3548	A1956	(55c) multi	1.40	.45
3549	A1957	(55c) multi	1.40	.45
a.	Booklet pane of 14, #3536-3549		20.00	
	Nos. 3536-3549 (14)		19.60	6.30

A souvenir sheet containing one perf. 13x13¼ stamp like No. 3543 with water-activated gum sold for €3.

End of World War I, 90th Anniv. — A1958

2008, Nov. 11		Engr.	Perf. 13¼
3550	A1958 55c multi		1.40 .45

Marianne and Stars Type of 2008
Serpentine Die Cut 6¾ Vert.

2008	Engr.		Self-Adhesive
3551	A1912	1c yellow	.25 .25
3552	A1912	5c gray brown	.25 .25
3553	A1912	10c gray	.30 .30
3554	A1912	(50c) green	1.40 1.40
3555	A1912	72c olive green	2.00 2.00
3556	A1912	85c purple	2.40 2.40
3557	A1912	88c fawn	2.50 2.50
3558	A1912	€1 orange	2.75 2.75
3559	A1912	€1.25 blue	3.50 3.50
3560	A1912	€1.33 red violet	3.75 3.75
3561	A1912	€2.18 chocolate	6.00 6.00
	Nos. 3551-3561 (11)		25.10 25.10

688 FRANCE

Serpentine Die Cut 6¾ Horiz.
Coil Stamps

3564	A1912	(50c)	green	1.40	1.40
3565	A1912	(55c)	red	1.50	1.50
3566	A1912	(65c)	dark blue	1.90	1.90

Nos. 3564-3566 (3) 4.80 4.80

Nos. 3551-3561 each were printed in sheets of 100.

Flowers — A1959

Designs: 31c, Helianthus annuus. 33c, Magnolia.

2008, Nov. 12   Litho.   Perf. 13

3567	A1959	31c multi	.80	.25
3568	A1959	33c multi	.85	.25

Nos. 3567-3568 are known only precanceled. See note under No. 132.

Trees and Map of Mediterranean Area — A1960

2008, Nov. 20   Photo.   Perf. 13x12¾

3569	A1960	85c multi	2.50	.75

See Lebanon No. 645.

Greetings Type of 2004 Inscribed "Lettre Prioritaire 20g"

Designs: No. 3569A, "Ceci est une invitation." No. 3569B, "Un grand merci."

2008   Photo.   Serpentine Die Cut 11
Self-Adhesive

3569A	A1667	(55c)	brt lil rose & yel	1.60	1.60
3569B	A1667	(55c)	brt yel grn & red lil	1.60	1.60

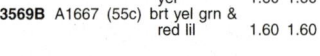

Louis Braille (1809-52), Educator of the Blind — A1961

Engr. & Embossed

2009, Jan. 4   Perf. 13x12¾

| 3570 | A1961 | 55c blk & violet | 1.50 | .50 |

New Year 2009 (Year of the Ox) — A1962

2009, Jan. 10   Photo.   Perf. 13¼x13

| 3571 | A1962 | (55c) multi | 1.50 | .50 |

No. 3571 was printed in sheets of 5. A souvenir sheet of 1 sold for €3. Value, $8. See No. 4970a.

Decorated Glasses, Nancy Museum — A1963 | Decorated Clock, Louvre Museum — A1964

Marquetry, Valençay Chateau — A1965 | Quimper Faience, Sèvres Museum — A1966

Enamelwork, Apt Cathedral A1967 | Tapestry, Malmaison Chateau A1968

Stained Glass, St. Joan of Arc Church, Rouen — A1969 | Cabinetwork, Louvre Museum — A1970

Wrought Iron, Army Museum, Paris A1971 | Mosaic, Palace of Versailles A1972

Jewelry, Malmaison Chateau A1973 | Crystal, Clichy Glassworks A1974

Booklet Stamps
Serpentine Die Cut 11

2009, Jan. 10   Self-Adhesive

3572	A1963	(55c) multi	1.50	.50
3573	A1964	(55c) multi	1.50	.50
3574	A1965	(55c) multi	1.50	.50
3575	A1966	(55c) multi	1.50	.50
3576	A1967	(55c) multi	1.50	.50
3577	A1968	(55c) multi	1.50	.50
3578	A1969	(55c) multi	1.50	.50
3579	A1970	(55c) multi	1.50	.50
3580	A1971	(55c) multi	1.50	.50
3581	A1972	(55c) multi	1.50	.50
3582	A1973	(55c) multi	1.50	.50
3583	A1974	(55c) multi	1.50	.50
a.		Booklet pane of 12, #3572-3583	18.00	

Nos. 3572-3583 (12) 18.00 6.00

René I, Duke of Anjou (1409-80) — A1975

2009, Jan. 16   Engr.   Perf. 13¼

| 3584 | A1975 | 55c multi | 1.50 | .50 |

Hearts — A1976

Flowers and: (55c), One parrot. (88c), Two parrots.

2009, Jan. 17   Photo.   Perf. 13¼

3585	A1976	(55c) multi	1.50	.50
a.		Souvenir sheet of 5	7.50	7.50
3586	A1976	(88c) multi	2.40	1.25

Self-Adhesive
Serpentine Die Cut

3587	A1976	(55c) multi	1.50	.50
3588	A1976	(88c) multi	2.40	1.25
a.		Booklet pane of 12	29.00	

Nos. 3585-3588 (4) 7.80 3.50

Tourism Issue

Les Sables D'Olonne A1977 | Menton A1978

Chaumont A1979

Château de la Bâtie d'Urfé — A1980

Bordeaux — A1981

Abbey of Royaumont A1982

Photo., Engr. (#3590, 3592-3594)
2009   Perf. 13¼, 13 (#3593)

3589	A1977	55c multi	1.40	.45
3590	A1978	56c multi	1.40	.45
3591	A1979	56c multi	1.60	.55
3592	A1980	56c multi	1.60	.55

Perf. 13

3593	A1981	56c multi	1.60	.55
3594	A1982	56c multi	1.75	.60

Nos. 3589-3594 (6) 9.35 3.15

Self-Adhesive
Serpentine Die Cut 11

| 3594A | A1981 | 56c multi | 1.60 | 1.60 |

Issued: No. 3589, 1/31; No. 3590, 2/21; No. 3591, 5/16. No. 3592, 6/6; Nos. 3593, 3594A, 6/20. No. 3594, 9/26.

Miniature Sheet

World Alpine Skiing Championships, Val d'Isère — A1983

No. 3595: a, Super combined skier. b, Slalom skier. c, Downhill (Descente) skier. d, Giant slalom skier. e, Skiers at Val d'Isère.

2009, Jan. 31   Photo.   Perf. 13x13¼

3595	A1983	Sheet of 5	7.00	7.00
a.-e.		55c Any single	1.40	.45

France Foundation, 40th Anniv. — A1984

2009, Feb. 5   Photo.   Perf. 13¼

| 3596 | A1984 | 55c multi | 1.40 | .45 |

Art Series

Angel, St. Cecilia Cathedral, Albi — A1985

La Promenade, by Hansi (Jean-Jacques Waltz) — A1986

Wrapping of Pont-Neuf, by Christo and Jeanne-Claude A1987

Paintings by Pierre-Auguste Renoir — A1988

No. 3600: a, Monsieur et Madame Bernheim de Villers. b, Gabrielle à la Rose.

Perf. 13, 13x13¼ (#3598), 13¼x13 (#3599)
2009   Litho. (#3597), Photo.

3597	A1985	85c multi	2.25	1.10
3598	A1986	90c multi	2.75	1.40
3599	A1987	€1.35 multi	3.75	1.90

Nos. 3597-3599 (3) 8.75 4.40

Souvenir Sheet
Perf. 13¼

3600	A1988	Sheet of 2	6.50	6.50
a.		85c multi	2.50	1.25
b.		€1.35 multi	4.00	2.00

Self-Adhesive
Serpentine Die Cut 11

3601	A1985	85c multi	2.50	2.50
3602	A1986	90c multi	2.75	2.75
3603	A1987	€1.35 multi	3.75	3.75

Issued: No. 3597, 2/7; No. 3598, 10/24; Nos. 3599, 3603, 6/13 No. 3600, 11/5. A souvenir sheet of 1 of No. 3597 sold for €3.

Road Runner and Wile E. Coyote — A1989

Sylvester and Tweety Bird — A1990

Daffy Duck and Bugs Bunny — A1991

Design: €1, Yosemite Sam, Wile E. Coyote, Sylvester, Tasmanian Devil, Bugs Bunny, Daffy Duck, Road Runner, Marvin the Martian and Tweety Bird.

FRANCE

2009, Feb. 28   Photo.   Perf. 13x13¼

3605	A1989	56c multi	1.40	.45
3606	A1990	56c multi	1.40	.45
3607	A1991	56c multi	1.40	.45
a.	Strip of 3, #3605-3607		4.25	1.40
	Nos. 3605-3607 (3)		4.20	1.35

Souvenir Sheet
3608	A1989	€1 multi	2.60	1.25

Booklet Stamps
Self-Adhesive
Litho.
Serpentine Die Cut 11

3609	A1989	(56c) multi	1.40	.45
3610	A1991	(56c) multi	1.40	.45
3611	A1990	(56c) multi	1.40	.45
a.	Booklet pane of 12, 4 each #3609-3611		17.00	
	Nos. 3609-3611 (3)		4.20	1.35

Stamp Day. No. 3608 contains one 80x26mm stamp. Sheets of five serpentine die cut 11 self-adhesive stamps like Nos. 3605-3607 and 5 labels each sold for €6.50.

Marianne and Stars Type of 2008
2009, Feb. 28   Engr.   Perf. 13

3612	A1912	73c ol grn	1.90	.50
3613	A1912	90c fawn	2.25	.55
3614	A1912	€1.30 blue	3.25	.85
3615	A1912	€1.35 red vio	3.50	.90
3616	A1912	€2.22 choc	5.75	1.40
	Nos. 3612-3616 (5)		16.65	4.20

Serpentine Die Cut 6¾ Vert.
Self-Adhesive

3616A	A1912	73c ol grn	1.90	1.90
3616B	A1912	90c fawn	2.25	2.25
3616C	A1912	€1.30 blue	3.25	3.25
3616D	A1912	€1.35 red vio	3.50	3.50
3616E	A1912	€2.22 choc	5.75	5.75
	Nos. 3616A-3616E (5)		16.65	16.65

Constitutional Council — A1992

2009, Mar. 5   Photo.   Perf. 13¼

| 3617 | A1992 | 56c multi | 1.40 | .45 |

Self-Adhesive
Serpentine Die Cut 11

| 3617A | A1992 | 56c multi | 1.60 | 1.60 |

Papal Palace, Avignon — A1993

2009, Mar. 7   Engr.   Perf. 13x12¾

| 3618 | A1993 | 70c multi | 1.90 | .65 |

Portraits of Women by Titouan Lamazou — A1994

Designs: No. 3619, Helena, United States. No. 3620, Dayu, Indonesia. No. 3621, Deborah, France. No. 3622, Kabari, Bangladesh. No. 3623, Mel Mel, China. No. 3624, Malika, Morocco. No. 3625, Dayan, Colombia. No. 3626, Francine, Rwanda. No. 3627, Blessing, Nigeria. No. 3628, Nandita, India. No. 3629, Elmas, Turkey. No. 3630, Nadia, Brazil.

Serpentine Die Cut 11
2009, Mar. 9   Booklet Stamps   Litho.
Self-Adhesive

3619	A1994	(56c) multi	1.50	.50
3620	A1994	(56c) multi	1.50	.50
3621	A1994	(56c) multi	1.50	.50
3622	A1994	(56c) multi	1.50	.50
3623	A1994	(56c) multi	1.50	.50
3624	A1994	(56c) multi	1.50	.50
3625	A1994	(56c) multi	1.50	.50
3626	A1994	(56c) multi	1.50	.50
3627	A1994	(56c) multi	1.50	.50
3628	A1994	(56c) multi	1.50	.50
3629	A1994	(56c) multi	1.50	.50
3630	A1994	(56c) multi	1.50	.50
a.	Booklet pane of 12, #3619-3630		18.00	
	Nos. 3619-3630 (12)		18.00	6.00

Mâcon — A1995

2009, Mar. 27   Engr.   Perf. 13x12¾

| 3631 | A1995 | 56c multi | 1.50 | .50 |

Souvenir Sheet

Protection of Polar Regions — A1996

No. 3632: a, Iceberg and bird. b, Emperor penguins, vert.

Perf. 13x13¼, 13¼x13 (85c)
2009, Mar. 28   Litho. & Engr.

3632	A1996	Sheet of 2	4.00	4.00
a.	56c multi		1.50	.50
b.	85c multi		2.50	.85

Aimé Césaire (1913-2008), Martinique Politician — A1997

2009, Apr. 17   Photo.   Perf. 13¼x13

| 3633 | A1997 | 56c multi | 1.50 | .50 |

Flora of the French Regions — A1998

Designs: No. 3634, Plum (quetsche), Alsace. No. 3635, Plum (mirabelle), Lorraine. No. 3636, Birch tree, Centre. No. 3637, Bee orchid, Champagne-Ardenne. No. 3638, Lily, Paris. No. 3639, Bluebells, Ile de France. No. 3640, Gorse, Bretagne. No. 3641, Lily-of-the-valley, Pays de la Loire. No. 3642, Apples, Basse-Normandie. No. 3643, Beech leaves, Haute-Normandie. No. 3644, Rose, Picardie. No. 3645, Potatoes, Nord-Pas de Calais. No. 3646, Olives, Provence-Alpes-Côte d'Azur. No. 3647, Chestnut, Corse. No. 3648, Wild thyme, Languedoc-Roussillon. No. 3649, Yellow gentian, Auvergne. No. 3650, Boletus mushroom, Limousin. No. 3651, Saltwort, Poitou-Charentes. No. 3652, Maritime pine, Aquitaine. No. 3653, Norway spruce, Franche-Comté. No. 3654, Awara palm, French Guiana. No. 3655, Toulouse violet, Midi-Pyrénées. No. 3656, Blueberries, Rhône-Alpes. No. 3657, Black currants, Bourgogne.

Serpentine Die Cut 11
2009, Apr. 25   Photo.
Booklet Stamps
Self-Adhesive

3634	A1998	(56c) multi	1.50	.50
3635	A1998	(56c) multi	1.50	.50
a.	Booklet pane of 2, #3634-3635		3.00	
3636	A1998	(56c) multi	1.50	.50
3637	A1998	(56c) multi	1.50	.50
a.	Booklet pane of 2, #3636-3637		3.00	
3638	A1998	(56c) multi	1.50	.50
3639	A1998	(56c) multi	1.50	.50
a.	Booklet pane of 2, #3638-3639		3.00	
3640	A1998	(56c) multi	1.50	.50
3641	A1998	(56c) multi	1.50	.50
a.	Booklet pane of 2, #3640-3641		3.00	
3642	A1998	(56c) multi	1.50	.50
3643	A1998	(56c) multi	1.50	.50
a.	Booklet pane of 2, #3642-3643		3.00	
3644	A1998	(56c) multi	1.50	.50
3645	A1998	(56c) multi	1.50	.50
a.	Booklet pane of 2, #3644-3645		3.00	
	Complete booklet, #3635a, 3637a, 3639a, 3641a, 3643a, 3645a		18.00	
3646	A1998	(56c) multi	1.50	.50
3647	A1998	(56c) multi	1.50	.50
a.	Booklet pane of 2, #3646-3647		3.00	
3648	A1998	(56c) multi	1.50	.50
3649	A1998	(56c) multi	1.50	.50
a.	Booklet pane of 2, #3648-3649		3.00	
3650	A1998	(56c) multi	1.50	.50
3651	A1998	(56c) multi	1.50	.50
a.	Booklet pane of 2, #3650-3651		3.00	
3652	A1998	(56c) multi	1.50	.50
3653	A1998	(56c) multi	1.50	.50
a.	Booklet pane of 2, #3652-3653		3.00	
3654	A1998	(56c) multi	1.50	.50
3655	A1998	(56c) multi	1.50	.50
a.	Booklet pane of 2, #3654-3655		3.00	
3656	A1998	(56c) multi	1.50	.50
3657	A1998	(56c) multi	1.50	.50
a.	Booklet pane of 2, #3656-3657		3.00	
	Complete booklet, #3647a, 3649a, 3651a, 3653a, 3655a, 3657a		18.00	
	Nos. 3634-3657 (24)		36.00	12.00

Souvenir Sheet

Europa — A1999

No. 3658: a, Saturn. b, Exoplanet.

2009, May 3   Litho.   Perf. 13¼x13

3658	A1999	Sheet of 2	4.00	4.00
a.-b.	70c Either single		2.00	.65

Intl. Year of Astronomy.

A2000   Vacations — A2001

Designs: No. 3659, Tennis ball on red clay court. No. 3660, Red-striped director's chair. No. 3661, Red turban. No. 3662, Ladybug. No. 3663, Red air mattress. No. 3664, Cherry tomatoes. No. 3665, Rooster. No. 3666, Poppy. No. 3667, License plate of Bonaire, Netherlands Antilles. No. 3668, Monarch butterfly. No. 3669, Raspberries. No. 3670, Doorknocker on red door. No. 3671, Flowers near house number. No. 3672, Red boat, rope and cleat.

Serpentine Die Cut 11
2009, May 13   Litho.
Booklet Stamps
Self-Adhesive

3659	A2000	(56c) multi	1.60	.55
3660	A2000	(56c) multi	1.60	.55
3661	A2000	(56c) multi	1.60	.55
3662	A2000	(56c) multi	1.60	.55
3663	A2000	(56c) multi	1.60	.55
3664	A2000	(56c) multi	1.60	.55
3665	A2001	(56c) multi	1.60	.55
3666	A2001	(56c) multi	1.60	.55
3667	A2001	(56c) multi	1.60	.55
3668	A2001	(56c) multi	1.60	.55
3669	A2001	(56c) multi	1.60	.55
3670	A2001	(56c) multi	1.60	.55
3671	A2001	(56c) multi	1.60	.55
3672	A2001	(56c) multi	1.60	.55
a.	Booklet pane of 14, #3659-3672		22.50	
	Nos. 3659-3672 (14)		22.40	7.70

Timber-frame Houses, Alsace — A2002

Azay-le-Rideau Chateau — A2003

Notre Dame Cathedral, Paris — A2004

Vineyards, Bordeaux A2005

Nice — A2006

Mont-Saint-Michel A2007

Eiffel Tower — A2008

Provence A2009

Serpentine Die Cut 11
2009, May 13   Litho.
Booklet Stamps
Self-Adhesive

3673	A2002	(85c) multi	2.40	.80
3674	A2003	(85c) multi	2.40	.80
3675	A2004	(85c) multi	2.40	.80
3676	A2005	(85c) multi	2.40	.80
3677	A2006	(85c) multi	2.40	.80
3678	A2007	(85c) multi	2.40	.80
3679	A2008	(85c) multi	2.40	.80
3680	A2009	(85c) multi	2.40	.80
a.	Booklet pane of 8, #3673-3680		19.50	
	Nos. 3673-3680 (8)		19.20	6.40

Nos. 3678 and 3679 each were printed in sheets of 50 in 2010.

John Calvin (1509-64), Theologian and Religious Reformer A2010

2009, May 22   Engr.   Perf. 13¼

| 3681 | A2010 | 56c multi | 1.60 | .55 |

Miniature Sheet

Chocolate — A2011

No. 3682: a, Cacao leaves, pods and beans. b, Aztec Indian. c, Spanish soldier. d, Castle. e, Map of French Atlantic coast. f, European man and woman of 16th cent. g, Production of chocolate. h, Chocolate bar. i, Cocoa service. j, Person eating chocolate bar.

2009, May 23   Photo.   Perf. 13

3682	A2011	Sheet of 10	16.00	16.00
a.-j.	56c Any single		1.60	.55

No. 3682 is impregnated with a chocolate scent. €1.16 stamps having the designs Nos. 3682a-3682d, 3682f-3682k was included in a limited-edition booklet issued Nov. 4, 2020.

French Federation Of Philatelic Associations 82nd Congress, Tarbes — A2012

2009, June 12   Engr.   Perf. 13x13¼

| 3683 | A2012 | 56c multi + label | 1.60 | .55 |

690 FRANCE

Jean Moulin Memorial, Rhône — A2013

2009, June 20   Engr.   Perf. 13¼
3684 A2013 56c multi   1.60   .55

Serpentine Die Cut 11
Self-Adhesive
3685 A2013 56c multi   1.60 1.60

Endangered Animals — A2014

Designs: No. 3686, Giant panda. No. 3687, Rhinoceros. 70c, Aurochs, horiz. 90c, California condor, horiz.

2009, June 20   Photo.   Perf. 13¼
3686 A2014 56c multi   1.60   .55
3687 A2014 56c multi   1.60   .55
3688 A2014 70c multi   2.00   .65
3689 A2014 90c multi   2.50   .85
 a. Souvenir sheet of 4, #3686-3689   7.75 7.75
Nos. 3686-3689 (4)   7.70 2.60

Gordon Bennett Aviation Cup, Cent. — A2015

2009, June 27   Engr.   Perf. 13¼
3690 A2015 56c blk & brn   1.60   .55

Etienne Dolet (1509-46), Printer and Translator — A2016

2009, July 4   Engr.   Perf. 13x13¼
3691 A2016 56c multi   1.60   .55

Miniature Sheet

Fair Attractions — A2017

Designs: a, Parachute jump. b, Ferris wheel. c, Roller coaster. d, Carousel. e, Candy apple. f, Fishing arcade game.

2009, Sept. 5   Photo.   Perf. 13
3692 A2017 Sheet of 6   10.50 10.50
 a.-f. 56c Any single   1.75   .60

A2018

Invitation — A2019

Designs: No. 3693, Yellow background, man with red violet pants and shoes. No. 3694, Red background, woman wearing dress. No. 3695, Red violet background, woman scattering papers. No. 3696, Light blue background, cow with flowers. No. 3697, Blue background, man with red violet pants and blue shoes. No. 3698, Brown black background, birthday cake with slice on cake server. No. 3699, Yellow green background, woman with brown pants and green shoes. No. 3700, Green background, man with blue pants and shoes. No. 3701, Brown background, cut birthday cake. No. 3702, Red violet background, woman with red violet pants and shoes. No. 3703, Pink background, woman with balloons. No. 3704, Red background, bird. No. 3705, Yellow green background, woman with green skirt and shoes. No. 3706, Orange background, woman scattering papers.

Serpentine Die Cut 11
2009, Sept. 5   Litho.
Booklet Stamps
Self-Adhesive
3693 A2018 (56c) multi   1.75   .60
3694 A2018 (56c) multi   1.75   .60
3695 A2018 (56c) multi   1.75   .60
3696 A2018 (56c) multi   1.75   .60
3697 A2018 (56c) multi   1.75   .60
3698 A2018 (56c) multi   1.75   .60
3699 A2018 (56c) multi   1.75   .60
3700 A2018 (56c) multi   1.75   .60
3701 A2019 (56c) multi   1.75   .60
3702 A2019 (56c) multi   1.75   .60
3703 A2019 (56c) multi   1.75   .60
3704 A2019 (56c) multi   1.75   .60
3705 A2019 (56c) multi   1.75   .60
3706 A2019 (56c) multi   1.75   .60
 a. Booklet pane of 14, #3693-3706   24.50
Nos. 3693-3706 (14)   24.50 8.40

Eugène Vaillé (1875-1959), First Conservator of the Postal Museum A2020

2009, Sept. 19   Engr.   Perf. 13¼
3707 A2020 56c multi   1.75   .60

Self-Adhesive
Serpentine Die Cut 11
3708 A2020 56c multi   1.75 1.75

Souvenir Sheet

Jardin des Plantes, Paris A2021

No. 3709: a, Gazebo. b, Mexican Hothouse.

2009, Sept. 19   Photo.   Perf. 13¼x13
3709 A2021 Sheet of 2   13.00 13.00
 a.-b. €2.22 Either single   6.50 3.25
Salon du Timbre.

A2022

Le Petit Nicolas, by René Goscinny — A2023

Designs: No. 3710, Nicolas, wearing striped shirt, holding envelope and book bag. No. 3711, Geoffroy. No. 3712, Eudes. No. 3713, Nicolas, wearing scarf, holding envelope and book bag. No. 3714, Nicolas writing. No. 3715, Joachim. No. 3716, "Chouette, des nouvelles!" No. 3717, Character at typewriter. No. 3718, "Vous me ferez cent lignes!" No. 3719, "Chère Maman. . ." No. 3720, "C'est toi la plus jolie!", vert. No. 3721, "J'ai fait le bonheur de tout le monde.", vert. No. 3722, "Moi, je veux pas grand chose réellement. . .", vert. No. 3723, "C'est pout toi, Maman!", vert.

Serpentine Die Cut 11
2009, Sept. 19   Litho.
Booklet Stamps
Self-Adhesive
3710 A2022 (56c) multi   1.75   .60
3711 A2022 (56c) multi   1.75   .60
3712 A2022 (56c) multi   1.75   .60
3713 A2022 (56c) multi   1.75   .60
3714 A2022 (56c) multi   1.75   .60
3715 A2022 (56c) multi   1.75   .60
3716 A2023 (56c) multi   1.75   .60
3717 A2023 (56c) multi   1.75   .60
3718 A2023 (56c) multi   1.75   .60
3719 A2023 (56c) multi   1.75   .60
3720 A2023 (56c) multi   1.75   .60
3721 A2023 (56c) multi   1.75   .60
3722 A2023 (56c) multi   1.75   .60
3723 A2023 (56c) multi   1.75   .60
 a. Booklet pane of 14, #3710-3723   24.50
Nos. 3710-3723 (14)   24.50 8.40

René de Saint-Marceaux (1845-1915), Sculptor of UPU Monument A2024

2009, Oct. 9   Litho. & Engr.   Perf. 13x13¼
3724 A2024 70c multi   2.10   .70
See Switzerland No. 9022.

Miniature Sheet

Dolls A2025

No. 3725: a, Porcelain doll. b, GéGé doll, horiz. c, Rag doll, horiz. d, Bella doll, horiz. e, Baigneur Petitcollin, horiz. f, Unglazed porcelain doll (poupée en biscuit).

2009, Oct. 17   Perf. 13
3725 A2025 Sheet of 6   10.50 10.50
 a.-f. 56c Any single   1.75   .60

Juliette Dodu (1848-1909), Spy — A2026

2009, Oct. 28   Engr.   Perf. 13¼
3726 A2026 56c multi   1.75   .60

Self-Adhesive
Serpentine Die Cut 11
3727 A2026 56c multi   1.75 1.75

European Capitals Type of 2002
Miniature Sheet

No. 3728 — Attractions in Lisbon: a, Hieronymites Monastery. b, Bairro Alto Quarter, vert. c, Belém Tower. d, Monument to the Discoveries.

Perf. 13x13¼, 13¼x13 (#3728b)
2009, Nov. 5   Photo.
3728 A1622 Sheet of 4   7.00 7.00
 a.-d. 56c Any single   1.75   .60

Francisco de Miranda (1750-1816), Revolutionist in France and Venezuela A2027

2009, Nov. 6   Photo.   Perf. 13¼
3729 A2027 85c multi   2.60   .90
See Venezuela No. 1693.

Marianne and Stars Type of 2008
Miniature Sheet
Photo., Engr. (#3456-3458)
2009, Nov. 6   Perf. 13
3730   Sheet of 13, #3456-3458, 3730a-3730j
        + label   31.00 31.00
 a. A1912 1c yellow   .25   .25
 b. A1912 5c gray brown   .25   .25
 c. A1912 10c gray   .30   .30
 d. A1912 73c olive green   2.25 2.25
 e. A1912 85c purple   2.60 2.60
 f. A1912 90c fawn   2.75 2.75
 g. A1912 €1 orange   3.00 3.00
 h. A1912 €1.30 blue   4.00 4.00
 i. A1912 €1.35 red violet 4.00 4.00
 j. A1912 €2.22 chocolate   6.50 6.50

Euromed Postal Conference A2028

2009, Nov. 7   Engr.   Perf. 13¼
3731 A2028 56c multi   1.75   .60

A2029   A2030

A2031   A2032

A2033   A2034

A2035   A2036

A2037   A2038

A2039   A2040

A2041   A2042

Serpentine Die Cut 11
2009, Nov. 7   Photo.
Booklet Stamps
Self-Adhesive
3732 A2029 (56c) multi   1.75   .60
3733 A2030 (56c) multi   1.75   .60
3734 A2031 (56c) multi   1.75   .60
3735 A2032 (56c) multi   1.75   .60
3736 A2033 (56c) multi   1.75   .60
3737 A2034 (56c) multi   1.75   .60
3738 A2035 (56c) multi   1.75   .60
3739 A2036 (56c) multi   1.75   .60
3740 A2037 (56c) multi   1.75   .60
3741 A2038 (56c) multi   1.75   .60
3742 A2039 (56c) multi   1.75   .60
3743 A2040 (56c) multi   1.75   .60
3744 A2041 (56c) multi   1.75   .60

FRANCE

691

3745	A2042	(56c) multi	1.75	.60
a.	Booklet pane of 14, #3732-3745		24.50	
	Nos. 3732-3745 (14)		24.50	8.40

A souvenir sheet containing one No. 3743 sold for €3.

Helicopter Carrier Jeanne d'Arc — A2043

Sailors of the Jeanne d'Arc — A2044

2009, Nov. 21   Engr.   Perf. 13x12¾

3746	A2043	56c multi	1.75	.60
3747	A2044	56c multi	1.75	.60
a.	Horiz. pair, #3746-3747		3.50	1.20

A souvenir sheet containing Nos. 3746-3747 sold for €3.

Asterix, Comic Strip by René Goscinny and Albert Uderzo — A2045

No. 3749: a, Assurancetorix on rope (40x30mm). b, Eight characters, horiz. (80x26mm). c, Falbala with basket (30x40mm). d, Idefix and bone, horiz. (22x19mm). e, Obelix carrying rock (50x100mm).

2009, Dec. 2   Photo.   Perf. 13

3748	A2045	56c multi		1.75	.60
3749	Sheet of 6, #3748, 3749a-3749e			15.50	15.50
a.	A2045 56c multi, perf. 13x13¼			2.50	2.50
b.	A2045 56c multi, perf. 13			2.50	2.50
c.	A2045 56c multi, perf. 13¼x13			2.50	2.50
d.	A2045 56c multi, perf. 13¼x12½			2.50	2.50
e.	A2045 56c multi, perf. 13¼x12¼			2.50	2.50

No. 3749 sold for €5.20, with the Red Cross receiving €1.84 of that. No. 3749e has a gritty substance affixed to the rock.

A2046   Hearts — A2047

Type I — Bow ties extend to perforations.
Type II — Bow ties do not touch perforations (red frame all around).

2010, Jan. 8   Photo.   Perf. 13¼

3750	A2046	56c multi, type I	1.60	.55

Perf.

| 3751 | A2046 | 56c multi, type II | 1.60 | .55 |

Perf. 13¼

| 3752 | A2047 | 90c multi | 2.50 | 1.25 |
| | Nos. 3750-3752 (3) | | 5.70 | 2.35 |

**Self-Adhesive
Serpentine Die Cut**

| 3753 | A2046 | 56c multi, type I | 1.60 | 1.60 |
| 3754 | A2047 | 90c multi | 2.50 | 2.50 |

Values for Nos. 3750, 3752 are for stamps with surrounding selvage. No. 3751 was printed in sheets of 5.

New Year 2010 (Year of the Tiger) — A2048

2010, Jan. 15   Photo.   Perf. 13¼x13

| 3755 | A2048 | 56c multi | 1.60 | .55 |

No. 3755 was printed in sheets of 5. A souvenir sheet of 1 sold for €3. See No. 4970b.

Abbé Pierre (1912-2007), Founder of Emmaus Movement — A2049

2010, Jan. 22   Engr.   Perf. 13¼

| 3756 | A2049 | 56c multi | 1.60 | .55 |

**Self-Adhesive
Serpentine Die Cut 11**

| 3757 | A2049 | 56c multi | 1.60 | 1.60 |

A souvenir sheet containing No. 3756 was printed in 2011 and sold for €3.

Musical Instruments in Art — A2050

Designs: No. 3758, Lyre, by Gustave Moreau. No. 3759, Harp (Harpe), by François André Vincent. No. 3760, Violincello (Violincelle), by Karl Gustav Klingstedt. No. 3761, Guitar (Guitare), by Camille Roqueplan. No. 3762, Horn (Cor), by Daniel Rabel. No. 3763, Saxophone, by Marthe and Juliette Vesque. No. 3764, Organ (Orgue), by François Garas. No. 3765, Bugle (Clairon), by Auguste Mayer. No. 3766, Clavecin, by Louis Carrogis Carmontelle. No. 3767, Piano, by Pierre-Désiré Lamy. No. 3768, Tambourine (Tambourin), by Théodore Chassériau. No. 3769, Drums (Tambour), by Jacques-Antoine Delaistre.

**Serpentine Die Cut 11
2010, Jan. 30   Photo.
Booklet Stamps
Self-Adhesive**

3758	A2050	(56c) multi	1.60	.55
3759	A2050	(56c) multi	1.60	.55
3760	A2050	(56c) multi	1.60	.55
3761	A2050	(56c) multi	1.60	.55
3762	A2050	(56c) multi	1.60	.55
3763	A2050	(56c) multi	1.60	.55
3764	A2050	(56c) multi	1.60	.55
3765	A2050	(56c) multi	1.60	.55
3766	A2050	(56c) multi	1.60	.55
3767	A2050	(56c) multi	1.60	.55
3768	A2050	(56c) multi	1.60	.55
3769	A2050	(56c) multi	1.60	.55
a.	Booklet pane of 12, #3758-3769		19.50	
	Nos. 3758-3769 (12)		19.20	6.60

See Nos. 3882A-3882B.

2010 Winter Olympics, Vancouver A2051

2010, Feb. 6   Perf. 13x13¼

3770	A2051	85c Figure skaters	2.40	1.25
3771	A2051	85c Skier	2.40	1.25
a.	Horiz. pair, #3770-3771		4.80	2.50
b.	Tete-beche block of 4, 2 #3771a		9.60	5.00

Art Issue

Museum of Art and Industry (La Piscine), Roubaix A2052

The Beach at Calais at Ebb Tide, by Joseph Mallord William Turner A2053

Maman, by Louise Bourgeois A2054

Allegory of Spring, by Sandro Botticelli A2055

No. 3775: a, Flora, Zephyrus and Chloris. b, The Three Graces.

2010   Photo.   Perf. 13x13¼

3772	A2052	85c multi	2.10	1.10
3773	A2053	€1.35 multi	3.75	1.90
3774	A2054	€1.35 multi	3.50	1.75
	Nos. 3772-3774 (3)		9.35	4.75

Perf. 13¼x13

3775	A2055	Sheet of 2	6.25	6.25
a.	87c multi		2.40	1.25
b.	€1.40 multi		3.75	1.90

**Self-Adhesive
Serpentine Die Cut 11
Photo.**

3776	A2052	85c multi	2.10	2.10
3776A	A2055	87c Like #3775b	2.40	2.40
3777	A2053	€1.35 multi	3.75	3.75
3778	A2054	€1.35 multi	3.50	3.50
3779	A2055	€1.40 Like #3775a	3.75	3.75
	Nos. 3776-3779 (5)		15.50	15.50

Issued: Nos. 3772, 3776, 5/15; Nos. 3773, 3777, 2/19; Nos. 3774, 3778, 6/17; No. 3775, 11/8/10; Nos. 3776A, 3779, 11/18/10

A2056

Stamp Day A2057

2010, Feb. 27   Engr.   Perf. 13

| 3780 | A2056 | 56c blue & red | 1.60 | .55 |

**Souvenir Sheet
Litho. & Embossed
Perf. 13¼x13**

| 3781 | A2057 | €2 multi | 5.50 | 2.75 |

Protection of Water — A2058

Inscriptions: No. 3782, Grands mammifères marins (large marine mammals). No. 3783,

Marée noire (black tide). No. 3784, Irrigation. No. 3785, Plaisir de l'eau (pleasure of water). No. 3786, Inondation (flood). No. 3787, Source. No. 3788, Aigues vertes (green water). No. 3789, Secheresse (drought). No. 3790, Hydro-électricité (hydroelectricity). No. 3791, Géothermie (geothermal energy). No. 3792, Pluies acides (acid rain). No. 3793, Fonte des glaciers (melting of glaciers).

**Serpentine Die Cut 11
2010, Feb. 27   Photo.
Booklet Stamps
Self-Adhesive**

3782	A2058	(56c) multi	1.60	.55
3783	A2058	(56c) multi	1.60	.55
3784	A2058	(56c) multi	1.60	.55
3785	A2058	(56c) multi	1.60	.55
3786	A2058	(56c) multi	1.60	.55
3787	A2058	(56c) multi	1.60	.55
3788	A2058	(56c) multi	1.60	.55
3789	A2058	(56c) multi	1.60	.55
3790	A2058	(56c) multi	1.60	.55
3791	A2058	(56c) multi	1.60	.55
3792	A2058	(56c) multi	1.60	.55
3793	A2058	(56c) multi	1.60	.55
a.	Booklet pane of 12, #3782-3793		19.50	
	Nos. 3782-3793 (12)		19.20	6.60

Savoy as Part of France, 150th Anniv — A2059

2010, Mar. 27   Engr.   Perf. 13¼x13

| 3794 | A2059 | 56c multi | 1.60 | .55 |

**Self-Adhesive
Serpentine Die Cut 11**

| 3795 | A2059 | 56c multi | 1.60 | 1.60 |

Tourism Issue

Villeneuve lez Avignon A2060

Orcival Basilica A2061

Pornic A2062

Arcueil-Cachan Aqueduct Bridge — A2063

2010   Engr.   Perf. 13¼

| 3796 | A2060 | 56c multi | 1.50 | .50 |
| 3797 | A2061 | 56c multi | 1.40 | .45 |

Perf. 13

| 3798 | A2062 | 56c multi | 1.40 | .45 |

Perf. 13¼

| 3799 | A2063 | 58c multi | 1.60 | .55 |
| | Nos. 3796-3799 (4) | | 5.90 | 1.95 |

**Self-Adhesive
Engr.
Serpentine Die Cut 11**

| 3800 | A2060 | 56c multi | 1.50 | 1.50 |

Issued: Nos. 3796, 3800, 4/17; No. 3797, 5/13; No. 3798, 5/25; No. 3799, 9/24.

A2064

A2065

FRANCE

A2066

A2067   A2068

A2069   A2070

A2071   A2072

A2073   A2074

Campaign Against Violence Toward Women — A2075

Serpentine Die Cut 11
2010, Apr. 20 Litho.
Booklet Stamps
Self-Adhesive

3801	A2064	(56c) multi	1.50	.50
3802	A2065	(56c) multi	1.50	.50
3803	A2066	(56c) multi	1.50	.50
3804	A2067	(56c) multi	1.50	.50
3805	A2068	(56c) multi	1.50	.50
3806	A2069	(56c) multi	1.50	.50
3807	A2070	(56c) multi	1.50	.50
3808	A2071	(56c) multi	1.50	.50
3809	A2072	(56c) multi	1.50	.50
3810	A2073	(56c) multi	1.50	.50
3811	A2074	(56c) multi	1.50	.50
3812	A2075	(56c) multi	1.50	.50
a.	Booklet pane of 12, #3801-3812		18.00	

Nos. 3801-3812 (12) 18.00 6.00

Colmar — A2076

2010, Apr. 23 Engr. Perf. 13¼
3813 A2076 56c multi 1.50 .50
Self-Adhesive
Serpentine Die Cut 11
3814 A2076 56c multi 1.50 1.50

National Sheepcote, Rambouillet A2077

2010, May 1 Perf. 13¼
3815 A2077 90c multi 2.40 1.25

Europa — A2078

2010, May 9 Photo.
3816 A2078 70c multi 1.75 .60

Miniature Sheet

Stamp Bourse in Paris, 150th Anniv. A2079

No. 3817 — Famous philatelists: a, Pres. Franklin Delano Roosevelt (1882-1945). b, Lucien Berthelot (1903-85), President of International Philatelic Federation. c, Louis Yvert (1866-1950), stamp catalogue publisher, horiz. d, Arthur Maury (1844-1907), stamp catalogue publisher, horiz. e, Alberto Bolaffi (1874-1944), stamp catalogue publisher.

2010, May 13 Engr. Perf. 13
3817 A2079 Sheet of 5 7.00 7.00
a.-e. 56c Any single 1.40 .45

Deauville, 150th Anniv. — A2080

2010, May 14 Photo. Perf. 13¼
3818 A2080 85c multi 2.10 1.10

Mother Teresa (1910-97), Humanitarian A2081

2010, May 27 Engr. Perf. 13¼x13
3819 A2081 85c multi 2.10 1.10
Self-Adhesive
Serpentine Die Cut 11
3820 A2081 85c multi 2.10 2.10

Institute of Human Paleontology, Paris, Cent. — A2082

2010, June 1 Perf. 13x12¾
3821 A2082 56c multi 1.40 .45
See Monaco No. 2597.

Nice as Part of France, 150th Anniv. — A2083

2010, June 11 Photo. Perf. 13¼
3822 A2083 56c multi 1.40 .45
Self-Adhesive
Serpentine Die Cut 11
3823 A2083 56c multi 1.40 1.40

Front Side of No. 3824

Rear Side of No. 3824 A2084

A2085

2010 World Cup Soccer Championships, South Africa — A2086

No. 3825: a, Soccer player and ball. b, Soccer players, vert. c, South African building, vert. d, Aerial view of Cape Town.

2010 Photo. Perf. 13x12¾
3824 A2084 56c multi 2.75 .50
Perf. 13x13¼, 13¼x13
3825 A2085 Sheet of 4 8.50 8.50
a.-d. 85c Any single 2.10 1.10

Embossed and Etched on Silver
Die Cut Perf. 12¾
Self-Adhesive
3826 A2086 €5 silver 12.50 12.50

Issued: Nos. 3824, 3825, 6/13; No. 3826, 6/11. No. 3824 is gummed on both sides and sold for €1.12. Both sides of the stamp could be used. Values for used examples of No. 3824 are for stamps canceled on either or both sides.

Launch of Soyuz Space Flights From French Guiana — A2087

2010, June 12 Photo. Perf. 13¼
3827 A2087 85c multi 2.25 1.10
Self-Adhesive
Serpentine Die Cut 11
3828 A2087 85c multi 2.25 2.25

Souvenir Sheet

Jardins de Giverny, by Claude Monet A2088

No. 3829: a, Bridge. b, Pond.

2010, June 12 Perf. 13¼x13
3829 A2088 Sheet of 2 11.50 11.50
a.-b. €2.22 Either single 5.75 3.00
c. Souvenir sheet, #3709a, 3709b, 3829a, 3829b 22.50 22.50
2010 Salon du Timbre (No. 3829c).

Regional Cuisine — A2089

Designs: No. 3830, Eclade (grilled mussels), Poitou-Charentes. No. 3831, Baeckaoffe (stew), Alsace. No. 3832, Tomme des Pyrénées cheese, Midi-Pyrénées. No. 3833, Tarte aux mirabelles (plum tart), Lorraine. No. 3834, Potage aux cresson (watercress soup), Ile-de-France. No. 3835, Flamiche (leek pie), Picardy. No. 3836, Pont l'Evêque cheese, Basse-Normandie. No. 3837, Blanc-manger (blancmange), Antilles. No. 3838, Caviar, Aquitaine. No. 3839, Chapon (capon), Franche-Comté. No. 3840, Fourme d'Ambert cheese, Auvergne. No. 3841, Tarte tatin (upside-down apple tart), Centre. No. 3842, Quenelles (dumplings), Rhône-Alpes. No. 3843, Escalope normande (veal cutlet), Haute-Normandie. No. 3844, Maroilles cheese, Nord-Pas-de-Calais. No. 3845, Clafoutis (baked fruit and batter), Limousin. No. 3846, Gougères (cheese pastry), Bourgogne. No. 3847, Tian (baked vegetables), Provence-Alpes-Côte d'Azur. No. 3848, Brocciu cheese, Corsica. No. 3849, Abricots rouges au miel (apricots in honey), Languedoc-Roussillon. No. 3850, Homard breton (lobster), Bretagne. No. 3851, Brochet au beurre blanc (pike with white butter), Pays de la Loire. No. 3852, Chaource cheese, Champagne-Ardennes. No. 3853, Paris-Brest (butter cream-filled pastry), Paris.

Serpentine Die Cut 11
2010, June 12 Photo.
Booklet Stamps
Self-Adhesive

3830	A2089	(56c) multi	1.40	.45
3831	A2089	(56c) multi	1.40	.45
3832	A2089	(56c) multi	1.40	.45
3833	A2089	(56c) multi	1.40	.45
a.	Booklet pane of 4, #3830-3833		5.60	
3834	A2089	(56c) multi	1.40	.45
3835	A2089	(56c) multi	1.40	.45
3836	A2089	(56c) multi	1.40	.45
3837	A2089	(56c) multi	1.40	.45
a.	Booklet pane of 4, #3834-3837		5.60	
3838	A2089	(56c) multi	1.40	.45
3839	A2089	(56c) multi	1.40	.45
3840	A2089	(56c) multi	1.40	.45
3841	A2089	(56c) multi	1.40	.45
a.	Booklet pane of 4, #3838-3841		5.60	
	Complete booklet, #3833a, 3837a, 3841a		17.00	
3842	A2089	(56c) multi	1.40	.45
3843	A2089	(56c) multi	1.40	.45
3844	A2089	(56c) multi	1.40	.45
3845	A2089	(56c) multi	1.40	.45
a.	Booklet pane of 4, #3842-3845		5.60	
3846	A2089	(56c) multi	1.40	.45
3847	A2089	(56c) multi	1.40	.45
3848	A2089	(56c) multi	1.40	.45
3849	A2089	(56c) multi	1.40	.45
a.	Booklet pane of 4, #3846-3849		5.60	
3850	A2089	(56c) multi	1.40	.45
3851	A2089	(56c) multi	1.40	.45
3852	A2089	(56c) multi	1.40	.45
3853	A2089	(56c) multi	1.40	.45
a.	Booklet pane of 4, #3850-3853		5.60	
	Complete booklet, #3845a, 3849a, 3853a		17.00	

Nos. 3830-3853 (24) 33.60 10.80

Romanesque Art — A2090

Designs: No. 3854, Bas-relief, Tournus. No. 3855, Interior of Cistercian Abbey, Léoncel. No. 3856, Painting, St. Sever. No. 3857, Serrabone Priory, Boule d'Amont. No. 3858, Sculpture, L'Ile-Bouchard. No. 3859, Painting, Citeaux Abbey. No. 3860, Fresco from St. Martin's Church, Nohant-Vic. No. 3861, Bas-relief, Clermont-Ferrand. No. 3862, Fresco, St. Jacques-des-Guérets. No. 3863, Bas-relief, Angouleme. No. 3864, Painting of the Consecration of the third Abbey Church, Cluny. No. 3865, Bas-reliefs, tympanum of Saint-Foy Abbey Church, Conques.

Serpentine Die Cut 11
2010, June 14 Photo.
Booklet Stamps
Self-Adhesive

3854	A2090	(56c) multi	1.40	.45
3855	A2090	(56c) multi	1.40	.45
3856	A2090	(56c) multi	1.40	.45
3857	A2090	(56c) multi	1.40	.45
3858	A2090	(56c) multi	1.40	.45
3859	A2090	(56c) multi	1.40	.45
3860	A2090	(56c) multi	1.40	.45
3861	A2090	(56c) multi	1.40	.45
3862	A2090	(56c) multi	1.40	.45
3863	A2090	(56c) multi	1.40	.45
3864	A2090	(56c) multi	1.40	.45
3865	A2090	(56c) multi	1.40	.45
a.	Booklet pane of 12, #3854-3865		17.00	

Nos. 3854-3865 (12) 16.80 5.40

See Nos. 3870A-3870B.

FRANCE 693

Miniature Sheet

Mills
A2091

No. 3866: a, Windmill, Montbrun-Lauragais. b, Windmill, Cassel. c, Aigremonts Windmill, Bléré, horiz. d, Daudet Windmill, Fontvieille, horiz. e, Flour mill, Villeneuve-d'Ascq. f, Birlot Watermill, Ile-de-Bréhat, horiz.

Litho. & Engr.
2010, June 15 — Perf. 13
3866 A2091 Sheet of 6 — 8.50 8.50
a.-f. 56c Any single — 1.40 .45

2010 Youth Olympics, Singapore — A2092

2010, June 16 Photo. Perf. 13¼
3867 A2092 85c multi — 2.25 1.10

Souvenir Sheet

Charles de Gaulle's Appeal of June 18 Speech, 70th Anniv.
A2093

2010, June 18 Engr. Perf. 13x13¼
3868 A2093 56c multi — 1.40 .45
See No. 5947Bc.

Conciergerie, Paris — A2094

2010, June 19
3869 A2094 56c multi + label — 1.40 .45
French Federation of Philatelic Associations, 83rd Congress, Paris.

French Pavilion, Expo 2010, Shanghai A2095

2010, June 20 Photo. Perf. 13¼
3870 A2095 85c multi — 2.25 1.10

Romanesque Art Type of 2010
Designs: No. 3870A, Like #3855. No. 3870B, Like #3858.

Serpentine Die Cut 11
2010, June 21 Litho.
Self-Adhesive
3870A A2090 (56c) multi — 1.40 1.40
3870B A2090 (56c) multi — 1.40 1.40
Nos. 3870A-3870B each were printed in sheets of 50. The red panels of Nos. 3855 and 3858 are splotchy, typical of photogravure printings. Under magnification black dots can be seen in the red panels on Nos. 3870A-3870B.

Marianne and Stars Type of 2008
2010, July 1 Engr. Perf. 13
3871 A1912 75c olive green — 1.90 .50
3872 A1912 87c purple — 2.25 .55
3873 A1912 95c fawn — 2.40 .60
3874 A1912 €1.35 blue — 3.50 .90
3875 A1912 €1.40 red violet — 3.50 .90
3876 A1912 €2.30 chocolate — 5.75 1.50
Nos. 3871-3876 (6) — 19.30 4.95

Self-Adhesive
Serpentine Die Cut 6¾ Vert.
3877 A1912 75c olive green — 1.90 1.90
3878 A1912 87c purple — 2.25 2.25
3879 A1912 95c fawn — 2.40 2.40
3880 A1912 €1.35 blue — 3.50 3.50
3881 A1912 €1.40 red violet — 3.50 3.50
3882 A1912 €2.30 chocolate — 5.75 5.75
Nos. 3877-3882 (6) — 19.30 19.30

Musical Instruments Type of 2010
Designs: No. 3882A, Like #3761. No. 3882B, Like #3767.

Serpentine Die Cut 11
2010, July 1 Litho.
Self-Adhesive
3882A A2050 (58c) multi — 1.50 1.50
3882B A2050 (58c) multi — 1.50 1.50
Nos. 3882A-3882B were each printed in sheets of 50. The gray blue portions of Nos. 3761 and 3767 are splotchy, typical of photogravure printings, and not splotchy on Nos. 3882A and 3882B.

Independence of French Colonies in Africa, 50th Anniv. — A2096

2010, July 15 Photo. Perf. 13¼
3883 A2096 87c multi — 2.25 1.10

Self-Adhesive
Serpentine Die Cut 11
3884 A2096 87c multi — 2.25 2.25

Butterflies A2097

Designs: Nos. 3885, 3886b, Morpho menelaus. No. 3886a, Cerura vinula caterpillar. 75c, Thersamolycaena dispar, vert. 95c, Callophrys rubi.

Litho. (#3885, 3886a), Litho. & Embossed
2010, Sept. 3 Perf. 13¼
3885 A2097 58c multi — 1.50 .50
3886 Sheet of 4 — 7.50 7.50
a. A2097 58c multi — 1.50 .50
b. A2097 58c multi — 1.50 .50
c. A2097 75c multi — 2.00 .65
d. A2097 95c multi — 2.50 .85

Universal Israelite Alliance, 150th Anniv. — A2098

Litho. & Engr.
2010, Sept. 7 Perf. 13¼
3887 A2098 58c multi — 1.50 .50

A2099

A2100

A2101

A2102

A2103

A2104

A2105

A2106

A2107

A2108

A2109

Cartoons With Letters — A2110

Serpentine Die Cut 11
2010, Oct. 11 Photo.
Booklet Stamps
Self-Adhesive
3888 A2099 (58c) multi — 1.75 .60
3889 A2100 (58c) multi — 1.75 .60
3890 A2101 (58c) multi — 1.75 .60
3891 A2102 (58c) multi — 1.75 .60
3892 A2103 (58c) multi — 1.75 .60
3893 A2104 (58c) multi — 1.75 .60
3894 A2105 (58c) multi — 1.75 .60
3895 A2106 (58c) multi — 1.75 .60
3896 A2107 (58c) multi — 1.75 .60
3897 A2108 (58c) multi — 1.75 .60
3898 A2109 (58c) multi — 1.75 .60
3899 A2110 (58c) multi — 1.75 .60
a. Booklet pane of 12, #3888-3899 — 21.00
Nos. 3888-3899 (12) — 21.00 7.20

Aviation Pioneers — A2111

Designs: Nos. 3900, 3902, Elise Deroche (1882-1919).
No. 3901: a, Hubert Latham (1883-1912). b, Orville (1871-1948) and Wilbur Wright (1867-1912). c, Henry Farman (1874-1958). d, Jules Védrines (1881-1919). e, Léon Delagrange (1872-1910).

2010, Oct. 15 Photo. Perf. 13
3900 A2111 58c multi — 1.75 .60
3901 Sheet of 6, #3900, 3901a-3901e — 15.00 15.00
a.-e. A2111 58c Any single — 2.50 2.50

Self-Adhesive
Serpentine Die Cut 11
3902 A2111 58c multi — 1.75 1.75
No. 3901 sold for € 5.40, with the Red Cross receiving €1.92 of that.

World Fencing Championships, Paris — A2112

Designs: 58c, Wheelchair fencing. 87c, Fencing.

2010, Oct. 22 Engr. Perf. 13x13¼
3903 A2112 58c multi — 1.75 .60
3904 A2112 87c multi — 2.50 .85
a. Horiz. pair, #3903-3904 + central label — 4.25 1.50

Paris Bar Association, Bicent. — A2113

2010, Oct. 28 Photo. Perf. 13¼
3905 A2113 58c black & lt blue — 1.75 .60

Self-Adhesive
Serpentine Die Cut 11
3906 A2113 58c black & lt blue — 1.75 1.75

Villeneuve-sur-Lot — A2114

2010, Oct. 30 Engr. Perf. 13¼
3907 A2114 58c multi — 1.75 .60

European Capitals Type of 2002
Miniature Sheet
No. 3908 — Attractions in Paris: a, Arc de Triomphe de l'Etoile. b, Notre Dame Cathedral. c, Garnier Opera House. d, Eiffel Tower, vert.

Perf. 13x13¼, 13¼x13 (#3908d)
2010, Nov. 4 Photo.
3908 A1622 Sheet of 4 — 7.00 7.00
a.-d. 58c Any single — 1.75 .60

A2115

A2116

A2117

A2118

A2119

A2120

A2121

A2122

694 FRANCE

A2123

A2124

A2125

A2126

A2127

"Best Wishes" — A2128

Serpentine Die Cut 11
2010, Nov. 5 Photo.
Booklet Stamps
Self-Adhesive

3909	A2115	(58c) multi	1.75	.60
3910	A2116	(58c) multi	1.75	.60
3911	A2117	(58c) multi	1.75	.60
3912	A2118	(58c) multi	1.75	.60
3913	A2119	(58c) multi	1.75	.60
3914	A2120	(58c) multi	1.75	.60
3915	A2121	(58c) multi	1.75	.60
3916	A2122	(58c) multi	1.75	.60
3917	A2123	(58c) multi	1.75	.60
3918	A2124	(58c) multi	1.75	.60
3919	A2125	(58c) multi	1.75	.60
3920	A2126	(58c) multi	1.75	.60
3921	A2127	(58c) multi	1.75	.60
3922	A2128	(58c) multi	1.75	.60

a. Booklet pane of 14, #3909-3922, + 14 stickers   24.50
Nos. 3909-3922 (14)   24.50   8.40

A souvenir sheet containing one perf. 13x13¼ example of No. 3915 with water-activated gum sold for €3.

First French Revenue Stamp, 150th Anniv. — A2129

Serpentine Die Cut 6¾ Vert.
2010, Nov. 6 Engr.
Booklet Stamp
Self-Adhesive

3923	A2129	(58c) brown	1.60	.40
a.	Booklet pane of 12, 6 each #3471, 3923		19.50	

Souvenir Sheet

Primitive Flemish Paintings A2130

2010, Nov. 6 Photo. Perf. 13
3924	A2130	Sheet of 2	10.00	10.00
a.-b.	€1.80 Either single		5.00	2.50

No. 3924: a, Madonna and Child, by Roger de la Pasture. b, Portrait of Laurent Froimont, by Rogier van der Weyden.

See Belgium No. 2478.

Independence Movements of Latin America and the Caribbean, Bicent. — A2131

2010, Nov. 27 Perf. 13¼
| 3925 | A2131 | 87c multi | 2.40 | .80 |

Hearts — A2132

Designs: 58c, Multicolored outlines of hearts. 95c, Red heart.

Photo., Photo. With Foil Application (95c)
2011, Jan. 7 Perf. 13
3926	A2132	58c multi	1.60	.55
a.	Sheet of 5		8.00	8.00
3927	A2132	95c black & red	2.60	.85

Self-Adhesive
Serpentine Die Cut
| 3928 | A2132 | 58c multi | 1.60 | 1.60 |
| 3929 | A2132 | 95c black & red | 2.60 | 2.60 |

New Year 2011 (Year of the Rabbit) — A2133

2011, Jan. 14 Photo. Perf. 13¼x13
| 3930 | A2133 | 58c multi | 1.60 | .55 |

No. 3930 was printed in sheets of 5. A souvenir sheet of 1 sold for €3.
See No. 4970c.

Mulhouse Tram-Train A2134

2011, Jan. 14 Engr. Perf. 13¼
| 3931 | A2134 | 58c multi | 1.60 | .55 |

Fabric Designs — A2135

Fabric designs from: Nos. 3932, 3936, French Polynesia. Nos. 3933, 3942, Japan. No. 3934, France, from 1780. No. 3935, Ivory Coast. No. 3937, Italy. No. 3938, Iran. No. 3939, Egypt. No. 3940, India. No. 3941, China. No. 3943, Peru. No. 3944, Morocco. No. 3945, France, from First Empire period.

Serpentine Die Cut 11
2011, Jan. 21 Photo.
Self-Adhesive
With Faint Blue Dots Behind Type in Area Below Vignette

| 3932 | A2135 | (58c) multi | 1.60 | 1.60 |
| 3933 | A2135 | (58c) multi | 1.60 | 1.60 |

Booklet Stamps
Without Dots Behind Type In Area Below Vignette

3934	A2135	(58c) multi	1.60	.55
3935	A2135	(58c) multi	1.60	.55
3936	A2135	(58c) multi	1.60	.55
3937	A2135	(58c) multi	1.60	.55
3938	A2135	(58c) multi	1.60	.55
3939	A2135	(58c) multi	1.60	.55
3940	A2135	(58c) multi	1.60	.55
3941	A2135	(58c) multi	1.60	.55
3942	A2135	(58c) multi	1.60	.55
3943	A2135	(58c) multi	1.60	.55
3944	A2135	(58c) multi	1.60	.55
3945	A2135	(58c) multi	1.60	.55
a.	Booklet pane of 12, #3934-3945		19.50	

Nos. 3934-3945 (12)   19.20   6.60

Marie Curie (1867-1934), Chemist — A2136

2011, Jan. 27 Engr. Perf. 13¼
| 3946 | A2136 | 87c red & dk blue | 2.40 | .80 |

Self-Adhesive
Serpentine Die Cut 11
| 3947 | A2136 | 87c red & dk blue | 2.40 | 2.40 |

Intl. Year of Chemistry.

Art Issue

Plongée, by Jean Bazaine A2137

Le Kiosque des Noctambules, Sculpture by Jean-Michel Othoniel A2138

Buddha, by Odilon Redon — A2139

Dying Centaur, Sculpture, by Antoine Bourdelle (1861-1929) A2140

The Three Nymphs, Sculpture by Aristide Maillol (1861-1944) — A2140a

2011 Photo. Perf. 13x13¼
| 3948 | A2137 | 87c multi | 2.50 | 1.25 |

Perf. 13¼x13
3949	A2138	€1.40 multi	3.75	1.90
3950	A2139	€1.40 multi	3.75	1.90
Nos. 3948-3950 (3)			10.00	5.05

Souvenir Sheet
Engr.
3951		Sheet of 2	6.50	6.50
a.	A2140	89c multi	2.50	1.25
b.	A2140a	€1.45 multi	4.00	2.00

Self-Adhesive
Serpentine Die Cut 11
3952	A2137	87c multi	2.50	2.50
3953	A2138	€1.40 multi	3.75	3.75
3954	A2139	€1.40 multi	3.75	3.75
3955	A2140	89c multi	2.50	2.50
3955A	A2140a	€1.45 multi	4.00	4.00
Nos. 3952-3955A (5)			16.50	16.50

Issued: Nos. 3948, 3952, 3/18; Nos. 3949, 3953, 2/11; Nos. 3950, 3954, 4/1; Nos. 3951, 3955, 3955A, 11/4.

Strawberry and Strawberry Plant — A2142

2011, Feb. 26 Engr. Perf. 13
| 3956 | A2141 | 58c multi | 1.75 | .60 |

Souvenir Sheet
Photo. & Engr.
Perf. 13¼x13
| 3957 | A2142 | €2 multi | 5.75 | 3.00 |

Stamp Day. No. 3957 has printing and a strawberry-scented scratch-and-sniff panel on the reverse.

Marianne and Hand Planting Seedling A2141

Hand Planting Seedling A2143

Leaf on Edge of Cliff — A2144

Flora and Earth — A2145

Hedgehog and Plants — A2146

Field — A2147

Tree With Various Fruits — A2148

Man Carrying Earth in Wheelbarrow A2149

Heart-shaped Plants in Flower Pots — A2150

Hands Holding Potatoes A2151

Man Watering Tree on Earth — A2152

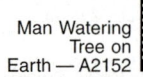
Earth on Plant — A2153

Farmer's Field and House — A2154

FRANCE 695

Serpentine Die Cut 11
2011, Feb. 26   Photo.

Self-Adhesive
Smooth, Glossy Paper

3958	A2143	(58c) multi	1.75	1.75
3959	A2144	(58c) multi	1.75	1.75
3960	A2145	(58c) multi	1.75	1.75
	Nos. 3958-3960 (3)		5.25	5.25

Booklet Stamps
Rough, Textured Paper

3961	A2143	(58c) multi	1.75	.60
3962	A2144	(58c) multi	1.75	.60
3963	A2146	(58c) multi	1.75	.60
3964	A2147	(58c) multi	1.75	.60
3965	A2148	(58c) multi	1.75	.60
3966	A2149	(58c) multi	1.75	.60
3967	A2150	(58c) multi	1.75	.60
3968	A2151	(58c) multi	1.75	.60
3969	A2152	(58c) multi	1.75	.60
3970	A2153	(58c) multi	1.75	.60
3971	A2154	(58c) multi	1.75	.60
3972	A2145	(58c) multi	1.75	.60
a.	Booklet pane of 12, #3961-3972		21.00	
	Nos. 3961-3972 (12)		21.00	7.20

Stamp Day.

Tristan Corbière (1845-75), Poet — A2155

2011, Mar. 4   Engr.   Perf. 13
3973	A2155	75c multi	2.10	.70

Art of Miss.Tic (Radhia de Ruiter) — A2156

Woman and text: No. 3974, Femme de lêtre. No. 3975, Je suis la votelle du mot voyou. No. 3976, Femme de tête mais l'esprit de corps. No. 3977, Tout achevor cauf lo désir. No. 3978, Soyons heureuses en attendant le bonneur. No. 3979, Je crois on l'éternel féminin. No. 3980, L'homme et le passé de la femme. No. 3981, Le masculin l'emporte mais où? No. 3982, Je ne me suis pas laissé défaire. No. 3983, Mieux que rien c'est pas assez. No. 3984, Il fait un temps de chienne. No. 3985, Cueillir l'éros de la vie.

Serpentine Die Cut 11
2011, Mar. 8   Photo.
Booklet Stamps
Self-Adhesive

3974	A2156	(58c) black & red	1.75	.60
3975	A2156	(58c) black & red	1.75	.60
3976	A2156	(58c) black & red	1.75	.60
3977	A2156	(58c) black & red	1.75	.60
3978	A2156	(58c) black & red	1.75	.60
3979	A2156	(58c) black & red	1.75	.60
3980	A2156	(58c) black & red	1.75	.60
3981	A2156	(58c) black & red	1.75	.60
3982	A2156	(58c) black & red	1.75	.60
3983	A2156	(58c) black & red	1.75	.60
3984	A2156	(58c) black & red	1.75	.60
3985	A2156	(58c) black & red	1.75	.60
a.	Booklet pane of 12, #3974-3985		21.00	
	Nos. 3974-3985 (12)		21.00	7.20

Intl. Women's Day.

European Capitals Type of 2002
Miniature Sheet

No. 3986 — Attractions in Budapest: a, Parliament. b, Pont des Chaînes (Chain Bridge). c, Royal Palace. d, Bains Széchenyi (Szechenyi Baths), vert.

Perf. 13x13¼, 13¼x13 (#3986d)
2011, Mar. 25   Photo.
3986	A1622	Sheet of 4	7.00	7.00
a.-d.	(58c) Any single		1.75	.60

Tourism Issue

Angers — A2157

Wooden Bridge, Crest — A2158

Autun A2159

Varengeville-sur-Mer A2160

Notre Dame Church, Royan A2161

2011   Engr.   Perf. 13¼
3987	A2157	58c multi	1.75	.60
3988	A2158	58c multi	1.75	.60

Perf. 13
3989	A2159	58c multi	1.75	.60

Perf. 13¼
3990	A2160	50c multi	1.75	.60
3991	A2161	60c multi	1.75	.60
	Nos. 3987-3991 (5)		8.75	3.00

Issued: No. 3990, 6/24. No. 3991, 10/23.

Gothic Houses of Worship — A2162

Designs: Nos. 3992, 4001, Notre Dame Cathedral, Strasbourg. Nos. 3993, 4002, Notre Dame Cathedral, Amiens. Nos. 3994, 4005, Sainte-Chapelle, Paris. No. 3995, St. Etienne Cathedral, Sens. No. 3996, Notre Dame Cathedral, Chartres. No. 3997, Notre Dame Cathedral, Laon. No. 3998, St. Etienne Cathedral, Metz. No. 3999, St. Pierre Cathedral, Beauvais. No. 4000, St. Etienne Cathedral, Bourges. No. 4003, Notre Dame Cathedral, Bayeux. No. 4004, Notre Dame Cathedral, Rouen. No. 4006, St. Denis Basilica, Saint-Denis.

Serpentine Die Cut 11
2011, Apr. 15   Litho.
3992	A2162	(58c) multi	1.75	1.75
3993	A2162	(58c) multi	1.75	1.75
3994	A2162	(58c) multi	1.75	1.75
	Nos. 3992-3994 (3)		5.25	5.25

Photo.
Booklet Stamps

3995	A2162	(58c) multi	1.75	.60
3996	A2162	(58c) multi	1.75	.60
3997	A2162	(58c) multi	1.75	.60
3998	A2162	(58c) multi	1.75	.60
3999	A2162	(58c) multi	1.75	.60
4000	A2162	(58c) multi	1.75	.60
4001	A2162	(58c) multi	1.75	.60
4002	A2162	(58c) multi	1.75	.60
4003	A2162	(58c) multi	1.75	.60
4004	A2162	(58c) multi	1.75	.60
4005	A2162	(58c) multi	1.75	.60
4006	A2162	(58c) multi	1.75	.60
a.	Booklet pane of 12, #3995-4006		21.00	
	Nos. 3995-4006 (12)		21.00	7.20

On lithographed stamps, "Phil@poste" is sharp and crisp, while on photogravure stamps it is muddy and unclear.

Dogs — A2163

Designs: No. 4007, Labrador retriever. No. 4008a, Berger allemand (German shepherd), vert. 75c, Caniche (poodle). 95c, Yorkshire terrier, vert.

Perf. 13¼, 13¼x13¼x12¾x13¼ (#4008b)
2011, Apr. 28   Photo.
4007	A2163	58c multi	1.75	.60
4008	Sheet of 4, #4008a-4008c, 4007		8.50	8.50
a.	A2163 58c multi		1.75	.60
b.	A2163 75c multi		2.25	.75
c.	A2163 95c multi		2.75	.90

Souvenir Sheet

Reims Cathedral, 800th Anniv. — A2164

No. 4009 — Stained-glass window depicting: a, King. b, Saint and man.

2011, May 6   Engr.   Perf.
4009	A2164	Sheet of 2	4.25	4.25
a.	58c multi		1.75	.60
b.	87c multi		2.50	.85

A souvenir sheet containing Nos. 4009a-4009b with a different sheet margin sold for €3.

Europa — A2165

2011, May 8   Photo.   Perf. 13¼
4010	A2165	75c multi	2.10	.70

Self-Adhesive
Serpentine Die Cut 11
4011	A2165	75c multi	2.10	2.10

Intl. Year of Forests.

Claude Bourgelat (1712-79), Founder of World's First Veterinary School — A2166

2011, May 14   Engr.   Perf. 13¼
4012	A2166	58c dark blue	1.75	.60

Self-Adhesive
Serpentine Die Cut 11
4013	A2166	58c dark blue	1.75	1.75

Regional Festivals and Traditions A2167

Inscriptions and location: Nos. 4014, 4018, La Braderie, Lille. Nos. 4015, 4033, La Saint-Vincent Tournante, Bourgogne. No. 4016, Lo Théâtre des Cabotans, Amiens. No. 4017, Le Feu d'Artifices du 14 Juillet, Paris. No. 4019, Les Médiévales, Provins. No. 4020, La Bénédiction de la Mer, Port-en-Bessin-Huppain. No. 4021, La Fête du Hareng, Haute-Normandie. No. 4022, La Fête des Brodeuses, Pont-l'Abbé. No. 4023, La Fête des Chalands Fleuris, Saint-André-des-Eaux. No. 4024, La Force Basque, Biarritz, Hendaye and Esplette. No. 4025, Les Nuits Romanes, Poitou-Charentes. No. 4026, La Sardane, Céret. No. 4027, La Fête de la Transhumance, Midi-Pyrénées. No. 4028, La Saint Nicolas, Lorraine. No. 4029, Le Mariage de l'Ami Fritz, Marlenheim. No. 4030, Les Fêtes Johanniques, Reims. No. 4031, Les Soufflaculs, Saint-Claude. No. 4032, La Fête de l'Estive, allanche. No. 4034, La Foire aux Potirons, Tranzault. No. 4035, La Frairie des Petits Ventres, Limoges. No. 4036, La Fête du Citron, Menton. No. 4037, La Fête des Lumières, Lyon. No. 4038, L'Abolition de l'Esclavage, Réunion. No. 4039, Les Chants Corses, Corsica.

2011   Litho.   Serpentine Die Cut 11
Self-Adhesive
4014	A2167	(58c) multi	1.75	1.75
4015	A2167	(58c) multi	1.75	1.75

Photo.
Booklet Stamps

4016	A2167	(58c) multi	1.75	.60
4017	A2167	(58c) multi	1.75	.60
4018	A2167	(58c) multi	1.75	.60
4019	A2167	(58c) multi	1.75	.60
a.	Booklet pane of 4, #4016-4019		7.00	
4020	A2167	(58c) multi	1.75	.60
4021	A2167	(58c) multi	1.75	.60
4022	A2167	(58c) multi	1.75	.60
4023	A2167	(58c) multi	1.75	.60
a.	Booklet pane of 4, #4020-4023		7.00	
4024	A2167	(58c) multi	1.75	.60
4025	A2167	(58c) multi	1.75	.60
4026	A2167	(58c) multi	1.75	.60
4027	A2167	(58c) multi	1.75	.60
a.	Booklet pane of 4, #4024-4027		7.00	
	Complete booklet, #4019a, 4023a, 4027a		21.00	
4028	A2167	(58c) multi	1.75	.60
4029	A2167	(58c) multi	1.75	.60
4030	A2167	(58c) multi	1.75	.60
4031	A2167	(58c) multi	1.75	.60
a.	Booklet pane of 4, #4028-4031		7.00	
4032	A2167	(58c) multi	1.75	.60
4033	A2167	(58c) multi	1.75	.60
4034	A2167	(58c) multi	1.75	.60
4035	A2167	(58c) multi	1.75	.60
a.	Booklet pane of 4, #4032-4035		7.00	
4036	A2167	(58c) multi	1.75	.60
4037	A2167	(58c) multi	1.75	.60
4038	A2167	(58c) multi	1.76	.60
4039	A2167	(58c) multi	1.75	.60
a.	Booklet pane of 4, #4036-4039		7.00	
	Complete booklet, #4031a, 4035a, 4039a		21.00	
	Nos. 4016-4039 (24)		42.00	14.40

The black text on No. 4014 is sharper than that on No. 4018. The black text on No. 4015 is sharper than that on No. 4033.
Issued: No. 4014, 6/30. Nos. 4016-4039, 5/28.

French Federation of Philatelic Associations 84th Congress, Metz — A2168

2011, June 10   Engr.   Perf. 13x13¼
4040	A2168	58c multi + label	1.75	.60

A souvenir sheet containing No. 4040 was issued in 2012 and sold fro €3.

Miniature Sheet

Bicycles A2169

No. 4041 — Inscriptions: a, Bicyclette à Pneumatiques. b, Draisenne, horiz. c, Vélocipède à Pédales, horiz. d, Vélo de Ville, horiz. e, Bicyclette à Chaine, horiz. f, Grand Bi.

Litho. & Engr.
2011, June 17   Perf. 13
4041	A2169	Sheet of 6	10.50	10.50
a.-f.	58c Any single		1.75	.60

Pres. Georges Pompidou (1911-74), and Pompidou Center, Paris — A2170

2011, June 22   Engr.   Perf. 13¼
4042	A2170	58c gray grn & brt bl	1.75	.60

Train des Pignes, Provence, Cent. — A2171

2011, June 24
4043	A2171	58c multi	1.75	.60

696 FRANCE

Organization for Economic Cooperation and Development, 50th Anniv. — A2172

2011, June 24			Photo.
4044	A2172	87c multi	2.50 .85

World Judo Championships, Paris — A2173

2011, July 1			Perf. 13x12¾
4045	A2173	89c multi	2.50 .85

Aquilegia A2174

Tulipa Sp. A2175

Bellis Perennis A2176

Primula Veris A2177

2011, July 1	Litho.		Perf. 13
4046	A2174	(38c) multi	1.10 .25
4047	A2175	(39c) multi	1.10 .25
4048	A2176	(46c) multi	1.40 .30
4049	A2177	(47c) multi	1.40 .30
	Nos. 4046-4049 (4)		5.00 1.10

Nos. 4046-4049 are known only precanceled. See note after No. 132. Compare with Nos. 3423-3426.

"Ecopli 20g" A2178

"Lettre Prioritaire 20g" A2179

"Europe 20g" A2180

"Monde 20g" A2181

"Lettre Prioritaire 50g" A2182

"Lettre Prioritaire 100g" A2183

"Lettre Prioritaire 250g" — A2184

Engr., Litho. (#4057a-4057d)

2011			Perf. 13
4050	A2178	(55c) gray	1.60 .25
4051	A2179	(60c) red	1.75 .40
4052	A2180	(77c) dark blue	2.25 .60
4053	A2181	(89c) purple	2.50 .65
4054	A2182	(€1) fawn	3.00 .75
4055	A2183	(€1.45) red violet	4.25 1.10
4056	A2184	(€2.40) chocolate	6.75 2.40
	Nos. 4050-4056 (7)		22.10 6.15

Souvenir Sheet

4057		Sheet of 7, #4050-4052, 4057a-4057d, + label	21.50 21.50
a.	A2181	(89c) purple, litho.	2.50 2.50
b.	A2182	(€1) fawn, litho.	2.75 2.75
c.	A2183	(€1.45) red violet, litho.	4.00 4.00
d.	A2184	(€2.40) chocolate, litho.	6.75 6.75

Coil Stamps
Perf. 13 Horiz.

| 4058 | A2179 | (60c) red | 1.75 .40 |
| 4059 | A2180 | (77c) blue | 2.25 .60 |

Self-Adhesive
Serpentine Die Cut 6¾ Vert.

4060	A2178	(55c) gray	1.60 1.60
4061	A2179	(60c) red	1.75 1.75
a.	Booklet pane of 12		21.00
b.	Booklet pane of 20		35.00
c.	Booklet pane of 10		17.50
4062	A2180	(77c) blue	2.25 2.25
a.	Booklet pane of 12		27.00
4063	A2181	(89c) purple	2.50 2.50
4064	A2182	(€1) fawn	3.00 3.00
4065	A2183	(€1.45) red violet	4.25 4.25
4066	A2184	(€2.40) chocolate	6.75 6.75
	Nos. 4060-4066 (7)		22.10 22.10

Issued: Nos. 4050-4056, Nos. 4060-4066, 7/1; No. 4057, 11/3; Nos. 4058-4059, 7/6; No. 4061a, 7/1; Nos. 4061b-4061c, 4/16/12; No. 4062a, 8/16. See Nos. 4089-4090.

G20 and G8 Summits, Cannes and Deauville A2185

2011, July 8			Photo.	Perf. 12¼
4067	A2185	89c multi		2.50 .85

Self-Adhesive
Serpentine Die Cut 11

| 4068 | A2185 | 89c multi | 2.50 2.50 |

2011 Rugby World Cup, New Zealand — A2186

No. 4069: a, Player with ball behind scrum. b, Player carrying ball, vert. c, Auckland skyline, vert. d, Lake and mountains, New Zealand. €5, Two players.

Perf. 13¼x13, 13x13¼

2011, July 8			Photo.
4069	A2186	Sheet of 4	10.00 10.00
a.-d.		89c Any single	2.50 .85

Embossed and Etched on Silver
Self-Adhesive
Die Cut Perf. 12¾

| 4070 | A2187 | €5 silver | 14.00 14.00 |

Protection of Water Type of 2010
Serpentine Die Cut 11

2011, Sept. 9			Litho.
4071	A2058	(60c) Like #3782	1.75 1.75
4072	A2058	(60c) Like #3787	1.75 1.75

Nos. 4071-4072 have a dot structure not found on Nos. 3782 and 3787, which are printed by photogravure.

Souvenir Sheet

Gardens A2188

No. 4073: a, Cheverny Gardens. b, Villandry Gardens.

2011, Sept. 16	Photo.		Perf. 13¼x13
4073	A2188	Sheet of 2	13.00 13.00
a.-b.		€2.40 Either single	6.50 3.25

Salon du Timbre 2012.

Firefighters of Paris, Bicent. — A2189

No. 4074: a, Horse-drawn fire wagon (38x38mm). b, Fireman holding hose (26x40mm). c, Firemen attending to victim on gurney, ambulance (26x40mm). d, Fireman with rescue dog (30x40mm). e, Firefighter's badge (26x40mm). f, Firemen in truck holding flag, Arc de Triomphe (26x40mm). g, Fireman wearing helmet without visor (30x40mm). h, Firemen in antique fire truck (40x26mm). i, Fireman and modern ladder truck (40x26mm). j, j, Fireman wearing helmet with visor (30x40mm).

Perf. 13, 13¼ (#4074a), 13¼x13 (#4074d, 4074g, 4074j)

2011, Sept. 16			
4074	A2189	Sheet of 10	17.50 17.50
a.-j.		60c Any single	1.75 .60

Self-Adhesive
Serpentine Die Cut 11

| 4075 | A2189 | 60c Like #4074b | 1.75 1.75 |
| 4076 | A2189 | 60c Like #4074i | 1.75 1.75 |

A set of six souvenir sheets, each containing one example of Nos. 4074a, 4074b, 4074f, 4074h, 4074i, and 4074j, sold for €15.

TGV Train Service, 30th Anniv. — A2190

2011, Sept. 27			Perf. 13¼
4077	A2190	60c multi	1.75 .60

Self-Adhesive
Serpentine Die Cut 11

| 4078 | A2190 | 60c multi | 1.75 1.75 |

A2191 A2192

Marianne, Stars and Leaf

A2193 A2194

2011, Sept. 30			Engr.	Perf. 13
4079	A2191	(57c) green		1.60 .25
4080	A2192	(95c) yellow green		2.60 .55
4081	A2193	(€1.40) blue green		4.00 .80
4082	A2194	(€2.30) dk bl green		6.25 1.25
	Nos. 4079-4082 (4)			14.45 2.85

Coil Stamp
Perf. 13 Horiz.

| 4083 | A2191 | (57c) green | 1.60 .25 |

Self-Adhesive
Serpentine Die Cut 6¾ Vert.

4084	A2191	(57c) green	1.60 1.60
a.	Booklet pane of 10		16.00
b.	Booklet pane of 12		19.50
c.	Booklet pane of 20		32.00
4085	A2192	(95c) yellow green	2.60 2.60
4086	A2193	(€1.40) blue green	4.00 4.00
4087	A2194	(€2.30) dk bl green	6.25 6.25

Serpentine Die Cut 6¾ Horiz.

| 4088 | A2191 | (57c) green | 1.60 .40 |
| | Nos. 4084-4088 (5) | | 16.05 14.85 |

Marianne and Stars Types of 2011
Serpentine Die Cut 6¾ Horiz.

2011, Oct. 1			Engr.
	Coil Stamps		
	Self-Adhesive		
4089	A2179	(60c) red	1.75 .40
4090	A2180	(77c) dark blue	2.10 .60

Souvenir Sheet

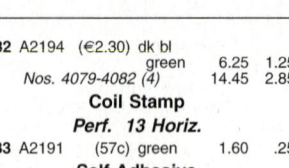

World Weight Lifting Championships, Paris — A2195

No. 4091: a, Male weight lifter (43mm diameter). b, Female weight lifter (49mm diameter).

2011, Oct. 7			Photo.	Perf.
4091	A2195	Sheet of 2		4.25 4.25
a.		60c multi		1.75 .60
b.		89c multi		2.50 .85

Souvenir Sheets

Chantilly Lace A2196

Lace of Puy-en-Velay Region — A2197

Alençon Lace A2198

Calais Lace A2199

Litho. with Lace Affixed

2011, Oct. 8			
4092	A2196	€2.50 multi	7.00 7.00
4093	A2197	€2.50 multi	7.00 7.00
4094	A2198	€2.50 multi	7.00 7.00
4095	A2199	€2.50 multi	7.00 7.00
	Nos. 4092-4095 (4)		28.00 28.00

FRANCE

National Center for Space Studies, 50th Anniv. — A2200

2011, Oct. 12	Engr.	Perf. 13¼
4096	A2200 60c multi	1.75 .60

Discovery of Clipperton Island, 200th Anniv. — A2201

2011, Oct. 21		
4097	A2201 €1 multi	2.75 .90

Second-Place Finish of French Team in 2011 Rugby World Cup Championships A2202

2011, Oct. 23		Photo.
4098	A2202 60c multi	1.75 .60

Values are for stamp with surrounding selvage.

Words of Ben — A2203

"Ben" (artist Benjamin Vautier) and inscription: No. 4099, Je suis timbré. No. 4100, J'aime écrire. No. 4101, Les mots c'est la vie. No. 4102, Entre nous. . . No. 4103, Cette idée. . . voyage. No. 4104, Pour l'instant tout va bien. No. 4105, Enfin de l'art. No. 4106, J'ai quelque chose à dire. No. 4107, Mots d'amour. No. 4108, Ceci est un lettre. No. 4109, Garderem lo moral. No. 4110, Vous êtes formidables!

Serpentine Die Cut 11
2011, Oct. 24 — Photo.
Booklet Stamps
Self-Adhesive

4099	A2203 (60c) multi	1.75 .60
4100	A2203 (60c) multi	1.75 .60
4101	A2203 (60c) multi	1.75 .60
4102	A2203 (60c) multi	1.75 .60
4103	A2203 (60c) multi	1.75 .60
4104	A2203 (60c) multi	1.75 .60
4105	A2203 (60c) multi	1.75 .60
4106	A2203 (60c) multi	1.75 .60
4107	A2203 (60c) multi	1.75 .60
4108	A2203 (60c) multi	1.75 .60
4109	A2203 (60c) multi	1.75 .60
4110	A2203 (60c) multi	1.75 .60
a.	Booklet pane of 12, #4099-4110	21.00
	Nos. 4099-4110 (12)	21.00 7.20

Compare with types A1667 and SP411.

Gaston Monnerville (1897-1991), Senate President — A2204

2011, Nov. 7	Engr.	Perf. 13¼
4111	A2204 60c multi	1.75 .60

Henri Mouhot (1826-61), Explorer of Southeast Asia — A2205

2011, Nov. 7		
4112	A2205 89c multi	2.50 .85

Christmas — A2206

Paintings: No. 4113, Adoration of the Shepherds, by Robert Campin, Master of Flémalle. No. 4114, Adoration of the Shepherds, by Mathias Stormer. No. 4115, The Newborn, by Georges de La Tour. No. 4116, Adoration of the Magi, by Italian School artist. No. 4117, Adoration of the Magi, by Francisco de Zurbaran. No. 4118, Nativity, by Jean Fouquet. No. 4119, Nativity, by the Master of the Nativity in the Louvre. No. 4120, Triptych of the Adoration of the Magi, by the Master of 1518. No. 4121, Adoration of the Magi, by Peter Paul Rubens. No. 4122, Adoration of the Infant Jesus, by the Master of Moulins. No. 4123, Adoration of the Child, by the Master of the St. Bartholomew Altarpiece. No. 4124, Scenes from the Life of Christ — Nativity, by Mariotto di Nardo.

Serpentine Die Cut 11
2011, Nov. 7 — Photo.
Booklet Stamps
Self-Adhesive

4113	A2206 (60c) multi	1.75 .60
4114	A2206 (60c) multi	1.75 .60
4115	A2206 (60c) multi	1.75 .60
4116	A2206 (60c) multi	1.75 .60
4117	A2206 (60c) multi	1.75 .60
4118	A2206 (60c) multi	1.75 .60
4119	A2206 (60c) multi	1.75 .60
4120	A2206 (60c) multi	1.75 .60
4121	A2206 (60c) multi	1.75 .60
4122	A2206 (60c) multi	1.75 .60
4123	A2206 (60c) multi	1.75 .60
4124	A2206 (60c) multi	1.75 .60
a.	Booklet pane of 12, #4113-4124	21.00
	Nos. 4113-4124 (12)	21.00 7.20

A souvenir sheet containing one perf. 13x13¼ example of No. 4115 with water-activated gum sold for €3.

Discovery of Insulin, 90th Anniv. — A2207

2011, Nov. 17	Photo.	Perf. 13¼
4125	A2207 60c multi	1.75 .60

Serpentine Die Cut 11
Self-Adhesive

4126	A2207 60c multi	1.75 .60

Year of Overseas Territories A2208

Drawings of: No. 4127, Carved rocks, Guadeloupe. No. 4128, Harbor, Cayenne, French Guiana. No. 4129, Beach scene, New Caledonia. No. 4130, Tattoo designs of tiki and compass rose, French Polynesia. No. 4131, Tree blossoms, St. Martin. No. 4132, Buildings, St. Pierre and Miquelon. No. 4133, House, Martinique. No. 4134, Man on path near Morne Langevin, Reunion. No. 4135, Pirogue, near Mt. Choungi, Mayotte. No. 4136, Building, Saint-Barthélemy. No. 4137, Kava bowl and building, Wallis and Futuna Islands. No. 4138, Penguins, French Southern and Antarctic Territories (T.A.A.F.).

Serpentine Die Cut 11
2011, Nov. 25 — Photo.
Booklet Stamps
Self-Adhesive

4127	A2208 (60c) multi	1.75 .60
4128	A2208 (60c) multi	1.75 .60
4129	A2208 (60c) multi	1.75 .60
4130	A2208 (60c) multi	1.75 .60
4131	A2208 (60c) multi	1.75 .60
4132	A2208 (60c) multi	1.75 .60
4133	A2208 (60c) multi	1.75 .60
4134	A2208 (60c) multi	1.75 .60
4135	A2208 (60c) multi	1.75 .60
4136	A2208 (60c) multi	1.75 .60
4137	A2208 (60c) multi	1.75 .60
4138	A2208 (60c) multi	1.75 .60
a.	Booklet pane of 12, #4127-4138	21.00
	Nos. 4127-4138 (12)	21.00 7.20

New Year 2012 (Year of the Dragon) — A2209

2012, Jan. 6		Perf. 13¼x13
4139	A2209 60c multi	1.60 .55

No. 4139 was printed in sheets of 5. A souvenir sheet of one sold for €3. See No. 4970d.

Hearts — A2211

2012, Jan. 13	Photo.	Perf. 13
4140	A2210 €1 red & black	2.75 .95

Self-Adhesive
Serpentine Die Cut

4141	A2210 €1 red & black	2.75 2.75

On Plastic

4142	A2211 60c red & black	1.60 1.60
a.	Souvenir sheet of 5	8.00

Brass Relief, France, 18th Cent. — A2212

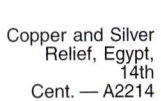

Bronze Relief, China, 2nd Cent. — A2213

Copper and Silver Relief, Egypt, 14th Cent. — A2214

Marble Relief, Andalusia, 11th Cent. — A2215

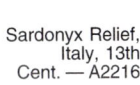

Sardonyx Relief, Italy, 13th Cent. — A2216

Stone Relief, Egypt, 1440 B.C. — A2217

Litho., Engr. (olive gray stamps)
Serpentine Die Cut 11
2012, Jan. 20 — **Self-Adhesive**
Booklet Stamps

4143	A2212 (60c) multi	1.60 .55
4144	A2212 (60c) olive gray	1.60 .55
4145	A2213 (60c) multi	1.60 .55
4146	A2213 (60c) olive gray	1.60 .55
4147	A2214 (60c) multi	1.60 .55
4148	A2214 (60c) olive gray	1.60 .55
4149	A2215 (60c) multi	1.60 .55
4150	A2215 (60c) olive gray	1.60 .55
4151	A2216 (60c) multi	1.60 .55
4152	A2216 (60c) olive gray	1.60 .55
4153	A2217 (60c) multi	1.60 .55
4154	A2217 (60c) olive gray	1.60 .55
a.	Booklet pane of 12, #4143-4154	19.50
	Nos. 4143-4154 (12)	19.20 6.60

Art Issue

Morning Sun, by Edward Hopper A2218

2012, Feb. 3	Photo.	Perf. 13x13¼
4155	A2218 €1.45 multi	4.00 2.00

Self-Adhesive
Serpentine Die Cut 11

4156	A2218 €1.45 multi	4.00 4.00

Flowers — A2219

Designs: No. 4157, Arums. No. 4158, Tulips. No. 4159, Roses. No. 4160, Violets. No. 4161, Pansies (Pensée). No. 4162, Lily of the valley (Muguet). No. 4163, Irises. No. 4164, Dahlias. No. 4165, Poppies (Coquelicot). No. 4166, Peonies (Pivoine). No. 4167, Daisies (Marguerite). No. 4168, Pinks (Oeillet).

Serpentine Die Cut 11
2012, Feb. 10 — **Self-Adhesive**
Booklet Stamps

4157	A2219 (60c) multi	1.60 .55
4158	A2219 (60c) multi	1.60 .55
4159	A2219 (60c) multi	1.60 .55
4160	A2219 (60c) multi	1.60 .55
4161	A2219 (60c) multi	1.60 .55
4162	A2219 (60c) multi	1.60 .55
4163	A2219 (60c) multi	1.60 .55
4164	A2219 (60c) multi	1.60 .55
4165	A2219 (60c) multi	1.60 .55
4166	A2219 (60c) multi	1.60 .55
4167	A2219 (60c) multi	1.60 .55
4168	A2219 (60c) multi	1.60 .55
a.	Booklet pane of 12, #4157-4168	19.50
	Nos. 4157-4168 (12)	19.20 6.60

Grand Mosque of Paris, 90th Anniv. — A2220

2012, Feb. 11	Engr.	Perf. 13¼
4169	A2220 60c multi	1.60 .55

Henri Queuille (1884-1970), Prime Minister — A2221

2012, Feb. 17		
4170	A2221 €1 black & brown	2.75 .95

Portraits of Women — A2222

Details of paintings: No. 4171, Young Woman in a Ball Gown, by Berthe Morisot. No. 4172, Portrait of Lydia Cassat, by Mary Cassatt. No. 4173, Biskra Woman, by Marie Caire. No. 4174, Woman with Turban, by Marie Laurencin. No. 4175, Madame Molé-Raymond, by Elisabeth Vigée-Lebrun. No. 4176, Portrait of

698   FRANCE

a Young Woman, by Edgar Degas. No. 4177, Mandy, by Edouard Barnard Lintott. No. 4178, Orphan Girl at the Cemetery, by Eugène Delacroix. No. 4179, Woman with a Mirror, by Titian. No. 4180, Madeleine Bernard, by Paul Gauguin. No. 4181, Young Woman, by Hippolyte Flandrin. No. 4182, Portrait of Berthe Morisot with a Bouquet of Violets, by Edouard Manet.

Serpentine Die Cut 11
2012, Mar. 8   *Photo.*
Booklet Stamps
Self-Adhesive

4171	A2222	(60c) multi	1.60	.55
4172	A2222	(60c) multi	1.60	.55
4173	A2222	(60c) multi	1.60	.55
4174	A2222	(60c) multi	1.60	.55
4175	A2222	(60c) multi	1.60	.55
4176	A2222	(60c) multi	1.60	.55
4177	A2222	(60c) multi	1.60	.55
4178	A2222	(60c) multi	1.60	.55
4179	A2222	(60c) multi	1.60	.55
4180	A2222	(60c) multi	1.60	.55
4181	A2222	(60c) multi	1.60	.55
4182	A2222	(60c) multi	1.60	.55
a.	Booklet pane of 12, #4171-4182		19.50	
	Nos. 4171-4182 (12)		19.20	6.60

European Capitals Type of 2002
Miniature Sheet

No. 4183 — Attractions in Copenhagen, Denmark: a, The Little Mermaid statue. b, Amalienborg Palace, horiz. c, Rosenborg Castle. d, Nyhavn, horiz.

Perf. 13¼x13, 13x13¼ (horiz. stamps)
2012, Mar. 23   *Photo.*

4183	A1622	Sheet of 4	6.50	6.50
a.-d.	60c Any single		1.60	.55

Tourism Issue

Moulins A2223

2012, Mar. 23   *Engr.*   *Perf. 13x12¾*

4184	A2223	60c multi	1.60	.55

Miniature Sheet

Way of St. James A2224

No. 4185: a, Via Turonensis in Paris. b, Via Lemovicensis in Vézelay, horiz. c, Via Podiensis in Puy-en Velay, horiz. d, Via Tolosana in Arles.

Litho. & Engr.
2012, Mar. 30   *Perf. 13*

4185	A2224	Sheet of 4	8.50	8.50
a.-d.	77c Any single		2.10	.70

Fruits — A2225

Designs: No. 4186, Pineapple (Ananas). No. 4187, Melon. No. 4188, White grapes (Raisins blancs). No. 4189, Hazel nuts (Noisettes). No. 4190, Kiwis. No. 4191, Gooseberries (Groseilles à maquereaux). No. 4192, Green papayas (Papayes vertes). No. 4193, Dates (Dattes). No. 4194, Bananas (Bananes vertes). No. 4195, Mangos (Mangues). No. 4196, Pippin apples (Pommes "Reinette grise"). No. 4197, Pear (Poire William).

Serpentine Die Cut 11
2012, Mar. 30   *Photo.*
Booklet Stamps
Self-Adhesive

4186	A2225	(57c) multi	1.50	.50
4187	A2225	(57c) multi	1.50	.50
4188	A2225	(57c) multi	1.50	.50
4189	A2225	(57c) multi	1.50	.50
4190	A2225	(57c) multi	1.50	.50
4191	A2225	(57c) multi	1.50	.50
4192	A2225	(57c) multi	1.50	.50
4193	A2225	(57c) multi	1.50	.50
4194	A2225	(57c) multi	1.50	.50
4195	A2225	(57c) multi	1.50	.50
4196	A2225	(57c) multi	1.50	.50
4197	A2225	(57c) multi	1.50	.50
a.	Booklet pane of 12, #4186-4197		18.00	
	Nos. 4186-4197 (12)		18.00	6.00

Tourism Issue

Epernay A2226

2012, Apr. 13   *Engr.*   *Perf. 13¼*

4198	A2226	60c multi	1.60	.55

Tropical Fish — A2227

Designs: No. 4199, Amphiprion ocellaris. No. 4200a, Phycodurus eques, hoirz. No. 4200b, Heniochus acuminatus, horiz. No. 4200c, Pomacanthus imperator.

2012, Apr. 20   *Photo.*   *Perf. 13¼*

4199	A2227	60c multi	1.60	.55
4200		Sheet of 4, #4199, 4200a-4200c	8.00	8.00
a.	A2227	60c multi	1.60	.55
b.	A2227	77c multi	2.10	.70
c.	A2227	€1 multi	2.60	.90

Art — A2228

Designs: No. 4201, Douglas Castle, painting by unknown Chinese artist. No. 4202, Crab, sculpture by Cheung Yee. Nos. 4203, 4205, The Racecourse — Amateur Jockeys Close to a Carriage, painting by Edgar Degas. No. 4204, The Horse, sculpture by Raymnond Duchamp-Villon.

2012, May 3   *Photo.*   *Perf. 13¼*

4201	A2228	60c multi	1.60	.55
4202	A2228	60c multi	1.60	.55
4203	A2228	89c multi	2.40	.80
4204	A2228	89c multi	2.40	.80
	Nos. 4201-4204 (4)		8.00	2.70

Self-Adhesive
Serpentine Die Cut 11

4205	A2228	89c multi	2.40	2.40

See Hong Kong Nos. 1490-1493.

Cubist Art — A2229

Designs: No. 4206, La Table Louis-Philippe, by Roger de La Fresnaye. No. 4207, Three Figures Under a Tree, by Pablo Picasso. No. 4208, The Three Poets, by Louis Marcoussis, vert. No. 4209, Still Life with a Red Ball, by Auguste Herbin, vert. No. 4210, The Blue Bird, by Jean Metzinger, vert. No. 4211, The 14th of July, by Fernand Léger, vert. No. 4212, Music, by Frantisek Kupka. No. 4213, Rugby, by André Lhote. No. 4214, The War Song, Portrait of Florent Schmitt, by Albert Gleizes, vert. No. 4215, The Book, by Juan Gris, vert. No. 4216, Compotier et Cartes, by Georges Braque, vert. No. 4217, Marine, by Lyonel Feininger, vert.

2012, May 10   *Serpentine Die Cut 11*
Booklet Stamps
Self-Adhesive

4206	A2229	(60c) multi	1.50	.50
4207	A2229	(60c) multi	1.50	.50
4208	A2229	(60c) multi	1.50	.50
4209	A2229	(60c) multi	1.50	.50
4210	A2229	(60c) multi	1.50	.50
4211	A2229	(60c) multi	1.50	.50
4212	A2229	(60c) multi	1.50	.50
4213	A2229	(60c) multi	1.50	.50
4214	A2229	(60c) multi	1.50	.50
4215	A2229	(60c) multi	1.50	.50
4216	A2229	(60c) multi	1.50	.50
4217	A2229	(60c) multi	1.50	.50
a.	Booklet pane of 12, #4206-4217		18.00	
	Nos. 4206-4217 (12)		18.00	6.00

Pacific 231 K8 Locomotive, Cent. — A2230

2012, May 11   *Engr.*   *Perf. 13¼*

4218	A2230	60c multi	1.50	.50

Self-Adhesive
Serpentine Die Cut 11

4219	A2230	60c multi	1.50	1.50

A souvenir sheet of one of No. 4218 sold for €3.

St. Joan of Arc (c. 1412-31) — A2231

Photo. & Engr.
2012, May 11   *Perf. 13*

4220	A2231	77c multi	2.00	.65

See Vatican City No. 1499.

Souvenir Sheet

Battle of Denain, 300th Anniv. A2232

2012, May 12   *Photo.*   *Perf. 13¼*

4221	A2232	77c multi	2.00	.65

Birds — A2233

Designs: No. 4222a, Little bustard (Outarde canepetière). No. 4222b, Bluethroat (Gorgebleue à miroir), horiz. No. 4222c, Osprey (Balbuzard pêcheur). Nos. 4222d, 4223, Atlantic puffin (Macareux moine).

Perf. 13¼x13, 13x13¼ (#4222b)
2012, May 12

4222		Sheet of 4	6.00	6.00
a.-d.	A2233 57c Any single		1.50	.50

Self-Adhesive
Serpentine Die Cut 11

4223	A2233	57c multi	1.50	1.50

Bird Protection League, cent.

Europa A2234

2012, May 20   *Engr.*   *Perf. 13*

4224	A2234	77c multi	2.00	.65

Self-Adhesive
Serpentine Die Cut 11

4225	A2234	77c multi	2.00	2.00

Tourism Issue

Chateau de Suscinio A2235

2012, May 26   *Perf. 13¼*

4226	A2235	60c multi	1.50	.50

Souvenir Sheet

Saint-Cloud Park, Paris — A2236

No. 4227: a, Cascade. b, Reflecting ponds,

2012, June 9   *Photo.*   *Perf. 13x13¼*

4227	A2236	Sheet of 2	12.00	12.00
a.-b.	€2.40 Either single		6.00	3.00
c.	Souvenir sheet of 4, #4073a, 4073b, 4227a, 4227b		24.00	24.00

2012 Salon du Timbre, Paris.

Historic Residences A2237

Designs: Nos. 4228, 4245, Palais du Luxembourg, Paris. No. 4229, Château Guillaume-le-Conquérant, Falaise. No. 4230, Château des Comtes de Foix. No. 4231, Château de Boulogne sur Mer. No. 4232, Château de Saumur. No. 4233, Château d' Anjony, Tournemire. No. 4234, Château de Pompadour. No. 4235, Citadelle de Corte. No. 4236, Forteresse de Salses. No. 4237, Château d'If. No. 4238, Hôtel de Mauroy, Troyes. No. 4239, Maison Pfister, Colmar. No. 4240, Château du Taureau, Baie de Morlaix. No. 4241, Palais Ducal de Nevers. No. 4242, Château d'Azay-le-Rideau. No. 4243, Château de Puyguilhem. No. 4244, Château de Crazannes. No. 4246, Château de Vaux-le-Vicomte. No. 4247, Château de Brémontier-Merval. No. 4248, Château de Lesdiguières, Vixille. No. 4249, Château de Pierrefonds. No. 4250, Villa Palladienne de Syam. No. 4251, Maison Souques-Pagès, Pointe-à-Pitre. No. 4252, Villa Majorelle, Nancy.

Serpentine Die Cut 11
2012, June 9   *Litho.*
Self-Adhesive

4228	A2237	(60c) multi	1.50	1.50

Photo.
Booklet Stamps

4229	A2237	(60c) multi	1.50	.50
4230	A2237	(60c) multi	1.50	.50
4231	A2237	(60c) multi	1.50	.50
4232	A2237	(60c) multi	1.50	.50
a.	Booklet pane of 4, #4229-4232		6.00	
4233	A2237	(60c) multi	1.50	.50
4234	A2237	(60c) multi	1.50	.50
4235	A2237	(60c) multi	1.50	.50
4236	A2237	(60c) multi	1.50	.50
a.	Booklet pane of 4, #4233-4236		6.00	
4237	A2237	(60c) multi	1.50	.50
4238	A2237	(60c) multi	1.50	.50
4239	A2237	(60c) multi	1.50	.50
4240	A2237	(60c) multi	1.50	.50
a.	Booklet pane of 4, #4237-4240		6.00	
	Complete booklet, #4232a, 4236a, 4240a		18.00	
4241	A2237	(60c) multi	1.50	.50
4242	A2237	(60c) multi	1.50	.50
4243	A2237	(60c) multi	1.50	.50
4244	A2237	(60c) multi	1.50	.50
a.	Booklet pane of 4, #4241-4244		6.00	
4245	A2237	(60c) multi	1.50	.50
4246	A2237	(60c) multi	1.50	.50
4247	A2237	(60c) multi	1.50	.50
4248	A2237	(60c) multi	1.50	.50
a.	Booklet pane of 4, #4245-4248		6.00	

FRANCE

4249	A2237	(60c) multi	1.50	.50
4250	A2237	(60c) multi	1.50	.50
4251	A2237	(60c) multi	1.50	.50
4252	A2237	(60c) multi	1.50	.50
a.	Booklet pane of 4, #4249-4252		6.00	
	Complete booklet, #4244a, 4248a, 4252a		18.00	
	Nos. 4229-4252 (24)		36.00	12.00

Lettering, most evident in the "Phil@poste" inscription at bottom, is sharp on No. 4228 and fuzzy on No. 4245.

Miniature Sheet

Soldiers — A2238

No. 4253: a, Croisé (crusader), 12th cent. b, Vercingetorix (c. 82-46 B.C.), Gallic chieftain, horiz. c, Fantassin (foot soldier), 16th cent. d, Tambour (drummer), 18th cent. e, Grognard (member of Napoleon's Old Guard). f, Fantassin (foot soldier), 1914.

2012, June 10 — Litho. & Engr. — Perf. 13
4253	A2238	Sheet of 6	9.00	9.00
a.-f.		60c Any single	1.50	.50

A set of six souvenir sheets, each containing one example of Nos. 4253a-4253f, sold for €15.

Handball — A2239

Embossed and Etched on Silver
2012, June 11 — Die Cut Perf. 12¾
Self-Adhesive
| 4254 | A2239 | €5 silver | 12.50 | 12.50 |

2012 Summer Olympics, London — A2240

2012, June 12 — Photo. — Perf. 13
| 4255 | A2240 | 89c multi | 2.25 | .75 |

Miles Davis (1926-91), Jazz Trumpet Player A2241

Edith Piaf (1915-63), Singer A2242

2012, June 12 — Perf. 13
4256	A2241	60c multi	1.50	.50
4257	A2242	89c multi	2.25	.75
a.		Horiz. pair, #4256-4257	3.75	1.25

See United States Nos. 4692-4693.

Vegetables A2243

Designs: No. 4258, Peas (petits pois). No. 4259, Salad greens (salades). Nos. 4260, Pimentos (piments). No. 4261, Green beans (haricots verts). No. 4262, Broccoli (chou brocoli). No. 4263, Zucchini (courgettes). No. 4264, Snap beans (haricots mange-tout). No. 4265, Leeks (poireaux). No. 4266, Green peppers (poivron "Lamuyo"). No. 4267, Artichoke (artichaut "Gros Camus"). No. 4268, Squashes (potirons vers). No. 4269, Cabbage (chou cabus).

Serpentine Die Cut 11
2012, June 13 — Self-Adhesive
Booklet Stamps
4258	A2243	(57c) multi	1.40	.45
4259	A2243	(57c) multi	1.40	.45
4260	A2243	(57c) multi	1.40	.45
4261	A2243	(57c) multi	1.40	.45
4262	A2243	(57c) multi	1.40	.45
4263	A2243	(57c) multi	1.40	.45
4264	A2243	(57c) multi	1.40	.45
4265	A2243	(57c) multi	1.40	.45
4266	A2243	(57c) multi	1.40	.45
4267	A2243	(57c) multi	1.40	.45
4268	A2243	(57c) multi	1.40	.45
4269	A2243	(57c) multi	1.40	.45
a.	Booklet pane of 12, #4258-4269		17.00	
	Nos. 4258-4269 (12)		16.80	5.40

First Heart-Lung Transplant in Europe, 30th Anniv. — A2244

2012, June 14 — Perf. 13¼
| 4270 | A2244 | 60c multi | 1.50 | .50 |

Issenheim Altarpiece, 500th Anniv. — A2245

Sheet with Altarpiece Doors Closed (Covering Stamps)

No. 4271: a, St. Augustine, "Le Retable d'Issenheim" at right (19x56mm). b, St. Hieronymus, "Le Retable d'Issenheim" at left (19x50mm). c, St. Anthony (34x65mm).

Perf. 13¼x13, 13 (#4271c)
2012, June 15 — Litho.
4271	A2245	Sheet of 3	12.50	12.50
a.-b.		€1.50 Either single	3.75	1.25
c.		€2 multi	5.00	1.75

Card stock doors printed on both sides that depict artwork on the two alterpiece doors, are pasted on top of each other at the left and right of the stamps. Values for the sheet are for examples with all four doors affixed.

Musée d'Orsay, Paris — A2246

2012, June 16 — Engr. — Perf. 13x13¼
| 4272 | A2246 | 60c multi + label | 1.50 | .50 |

French Federation of Philatelic Associations, 85th Congress, Paris.

Tourism Issue

Pointe Saint-Mathieu A2247

2012, June 22 — Perf. 13¼
| 4273 | A2247 | 57c multi | 1.40 | .45 |

Souvenir Sheet

2012 World Karate Championships, Paris — A2248

No. 4274: a, Karateka kicking. b, Eiffel Tower. c, Karateka kicking, horiz.

Perf. 13¼x13, 13x13¼ (#4274c)
2012, Sept. 7 — Photo.
| 4274 | A2248 | Sheet of 3 | 7.25 | 7.25 |
| a.-c. | | 89c Any single | 2.40 | .80 |

2012 World Pétanque Championships, Marseille — A2249

Photo. & Embossed
2012, Sept. 14 — Perf. 13x13¼
| 4275 | A2249 | 89c multi | 2.40 | .80 |

Art Issue

Figures Representing Seven Continents, by Jaume Plensa, Place Masséna, Nice — A2250

2012, Sept. 14 — Photo.
| 4276 | A2250 | €1.45 multi | 3.75 | 1.90 |

Camp des Milles, World War II Internment Camp — A2251

2012, Sept. 21 — Engr.
| 4277 | A2251 | 60c multi | 1.60 | .55 |

Tourism Issue

Verneuil-sur-Avre A2252

2012, Sept. 21 — Perf. 13¼
| 4278 | A2252 | 60c multi | 1.60 | .55 |

Marianne and Stars — A2253

2012, Oct. 1 — Perf. 13
| 4279 | Souvenir sheet of 3, #4051, 4079, 4279a | | 5.00 | 5.00 |
| a. | A2253 60c orange | | 1.60 | .55 |

Torch, Marianne and Stars — A2254

The Temptation of St. Anthony, by Hieronymus Bosch — A2255

Items on Fire — A2256

Designs: No. 4282, Lava (La lave). No. 4283, Welder (la soudure). No. 4284, Glassblowing (Le travail du verre). No. 4285, Flame of the Unknown Soldier, Paris (La flamme du soldat inconnu). No. 4286, Halloween jack o'lantern. No. 4287, People around Midsummer's Eve bonfire (Feu de la Saint-Jean). No. 4288, Fire fighters and fire (Les pompiers). No. 4289, Charcoal fire (Les braises). No. 4290, Candles (bougies). No. 4291, Light show (Spectacle). No. 4292, Sunset (Coucher de soleil). No. 4293, Birthday candles on cake (Bougies d'anniversaire).

2012, Oct. 13 — Engr. — Perf. 13
| 4280 | A2254 | 60c orange & red | 1.60 | .55 |

Souvenir Sheet
Litho. & Engr.
Perf. 13x13¼
| 4281 | A2255 | €2 multi | 5.25 | 2.60 |

Photo.
Booklet Stamps
Self-Adhesive
4282	A2256	(60c) multi	1.60	.55
4283	A2256	(60c) multi	1.60	.55
4284	A2256	(60c) multi	1.60	.55
4285	A2256	(60c) multi	1.60	.55
4286	A2256	(60c) multi	1.60	.55
4287	A2256	(60c) multi	1.60	.55
4288	A2256	(60c) multi	1.60	.55
4289	A2256	(60c) multi	1.60	.55
4290	A2256	(60c) multi	1.60	.55
4291	A2256	(60c) multi	1.60	.55
4292	A2256	(60c) multi	1.60	.55
4293	A2256	(60c) multi	1.60	.55
a.	Booklet pane of 12, #4282-4293		19.50	
	Nos. 4282-4293 (12)		19.20	6.60

Stamp Day. An illustration and a bar code is found on the reverse of the sheet margin of No. 4281.

Historic Residences Type of 2012
Design: (60c), Chaâteau d'If.

Serpentine Die Cut 11
2012, Oct. 29 — Litho.
Self-Adhesive
| 4294 | A2237 | (60c) multi | 1.60 | 1.60 |

Lettering, most evident in the "Phil@poste" inscription at bottom, is sharp on No. 4294 and fuzzy on No. 4237.

Court House, Lyon A2257

2012, Oct. 26 — Engr. — Perf. 13
| 4295 | A2257 | 60c multi | 1.60 | .55 |

FRANCE

Lion of Belfort Statue, by Frédéric Auguste Bartholdi — A2258

2012, Nov. 2   Perf. 13x13¼
4296   A2258   60c multi + label   1.60   .55

Timbres Passion 2012 Stamp Exhibition, Belfort. A souvenir sheet containing No. 4296 was issued in 2013 and sold for €3.

King Henri IV of France (1553-1610), Co-Prince of Andorra — A2259

2012, Nov. 8
4297   A2259   60c multi   1.60   .55
   a.   Sheet of 10, 5 each #4297, French Andorra #710   16.00   16.00

See French Andorra No. 710.

Souvenir Sheet

The Masked Ball, Opera by Daniel Auber — A2260

No. 4298: a, Auber (1782-1871). b, King Gustav III of Sweden (1746-92), main character in opera.

Litho. & Engr.
2012, Nov. 9   Perf. 13¼
4298   A2260   Sheet of 2   3.75   3.75
   a.   60c multi   1.60   .55
   b.   77c multi   2.00   .65

See Sweden No. 2697.

Souvenir Sheet

Organ from Church of St. Jacques, Lunéville — A2261

No. 4299 — Various details of organ's ornamentation: a, 89c. b, €1.45, vert.

Perf. 13x13¼, 13¼x13
2012, Nov. 10   Engr.
4299   A2261   Sheet of 2   6.25   6.25
   a.   89c multi   2.40   .80
   b.   €1.45 multi   3.75   1.25

Laurent Bonnevay (1870-1957), Politician, and Apartment Building — A2262

2012, Nov. 12   Engr.   Perf. 13¼
4300   A2262   57c multi   1.50   .50

Bonnevay Law on rent-controlled housing, cent.

Souvenir Sheet

French History — A2263

No. 4301: a, Intercession by St. Geneviève on behalf of Paris, c. 480. b, Clovis at Battle of Vouillé, 507, horiz.

Perf. 13¼x13, 13x13¼
2012, Nov. 12
4301   A2263   Sheet of 2   7.00   7.00
   a.-b.   €1.35 Either single   3.50   1.10

A2264   A2265

A2266   A2267

A2268   A2269

A2270   A2271

A2272   A2273

A2274   Greetings Stamps — A2275

Booklet Stamps
Serpentine Die Cut 11

2012, Nov. 12   Photo.
Self-Adhesive
4302   A2264   (57c) multi   1.50   .50
4303   A2265   (57c) multi   1.50   .50
4304   A2266   (57c) multi   1.50   .50
4305   A2267   (57c) multi   1.50   .50
4306   A2268   (57c) multi   1.50   .50
4307   A2269   (57c) multi   1.50   .50
4308   A2270   (57c) multi   1.50   .50
4309   A2271   (57c) multi   1.50   .50
4310   A2272   (57c) multi   1.50   .50
4311   A2273   (57c) multi   1.50   .50
4312   A2274   (57c) multi   1.50   .50
4313   A2275   (57c) multi   1.50   .50
   a.   Booklet pane of 12, #4302-4313   18.00
   Nos. 4302-4313 (12)   18.00   6.00

A souvenir sheet containing one perf. 13x13¼ example of No. 4309 with water-activated gum sold for €3. See No. 4329.

Elysée Treaty, 50th Anniv. — A2276

2013, Jan. 2   Litho.   Perf. 13
4314   A2276   80c multi   2.25   .75

See Germany No. 2703.

New Year 2013 (Year of the Snake) — A2277

2013, Jan. 4   Photo.   Perf. 13¼x13
4315   A2277   63c multi   1.75   .60

No. 4315 was printed in sheets of 5. A souvenir sheet of one sold for €3. See No. 4971a.

Bronze Sculpture of Goat — A2278   Terra Cotta Figurine of Rabbit, From Studio of Bernard Palissy — A2279

Bronze Sculpture of Buffalo — A2280   Brass Sculpture of Rooster — A2281

Bronze Sculpture of Tiger, by Antoine Louis Barye — A2282   Porcelain Figurine of Rats and Egg — A2283

Glazed Clay Figurine of Pig — A2284

 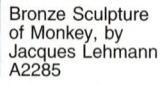

Bronze Sculpture of Monkey, by Jacques Lehmann A2285

Enameled Stone Sculpture of Dog — A2286   Earthenware Figurine of Dragon — A2287

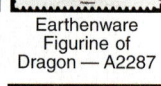

Gold Sculpture of Snake — A2288

Bronze Sculpture of Horse, by Edgar Degas — A2289

2013, Jan. 4   *Serpentine Die Cut 11*
Booklet Stamps
Self-Adhesive
4316   A2278   (58c) multi   1.60   .55
4317   A2279   (58c) multi   1.60   .55
4318   A2280   (58c) multi   1.60   .55
4319   A2281   (58c) multi   1.60   .55
4320   A2282   (58c) multi   1.60   .55
4321   A2283   (58c) multi   1.60   .55
4322   A2284   (58c) multi   1.60   .55
4323   A2285   (58c) multi   1.60   .55
4324   A2286   (58c) multi   1.60   .55
4325   A2287   (58c) multi   1.60   .55
4326   A2288   (58c) multi   1.60   .55
4327   A2289   (58c) multi   1.60   .55
   a.   Booklet pane of 12, #4316-4327   19.50
   Nos. 4316-4327 (12)   19.20   6.60

Marseille, 2013 European Capital of Culture — A2290

2013, Jan. 12   Photo.   Perf. 13¼
4328   A2290   80c multi   2.25   .75

Greetings Type of 2012
Serpentine Die Cut 11
2013, Jan. 14   Litho.
Self-Adhesive
4329   A2265   (58c) multi   1.60   1.60

Lettering, most evident in the "Phil@poste" inscription at bottom, is sharp on No. 4329 and fuzzy on No. 4303.

Souvenir Sheet

Notre Dame Cathedral, Paris, 850th Anniv. — A2291

No. 4330 — Stained-glass window depicting: a, Peasant with scythe (44x44mm). b, Madonna and Child (42mm diameter).

Litho., Sheet Margin Litho. & Engr.
2013, Jan. 19   Perf.
4330   A2291   Sheet of 2   7.25   7.25
   a.   €1.05 multi   3.00   1.00
   b.   €1.55 multi   4.25   1.40
   c.   Sheet of 2, #4330a, 4330b, lithographed sheet margin   13.50   13.50

No. 4330c has a different margin design and sold for €5.

A €1.16 stamp having the design of No. 4330a was included in a limited-edition booklet issued Nov. 4, 2020.

Art Issue

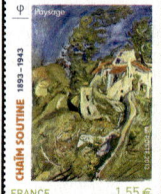

Landscape, by Chaim Soutine (1893-1943) — A2292

2013, Jan. 25   Photo.   Perf. 13¼x13
4331   A2292   €1.55 multi   4.25   2.10

A2293   A2294

Hearts A2295

No. 4334: a, Two white hearts embellished with flowers. b, Bird with long tail. c, Swan facing left. d, Swan facing right.

2013, Jan. 25   Perf. 13¼
4332   A2293   58c multi   1.60   .55
4333   A2294   97c multi   2.75   .90

FRANCE 701

Souvenir Sheet
Perf.

| 4334 | A2295 | Sheet of 5, #4332, 4334a-4334d | 8.00 | 8.00 |
| a.-d. | | 58c Any single | 1.60 | .55 |

Self-Adhesive
Serpentine Die Cut

| 4335 | A2293 | 58c multi | 1.60 | 1.60 |
| 4336 | A2294 | 97c multi | 2.75 | 2.75 |

Values for Nos. 4332-4333 are for stamps with surrounding selvage.

Art Issue

85.8 Degree Arc x 16, Sculpture, by Bernar Venet A2296

2013, Feb. 1   Perf. 13x13¼
4337 A2296 €1.55 multi   4.25 2.10

Animal Proverbs and Idioms — A2297

Designs: No. 4000, Qui vole un oeuf vole un boeuf ("Who steals an egg steals an ox"). No. 4339, Etre serrés come des sardines ("Be packed like sardines"). No. 4340, Etre heureux comme un poisson dans l'eau ("Be happy as a fish in water"). No. 4341, Pleurer des larmes de crocodile ("Cry crocodile tears"). No. 4342, Quand les poules auront des dents ("When chickens have teeth" or "When pigs fly"). No. 4343, Avaler des couleuvres ("To swallow snakes" or "To endure affronts"). No. 4344, Le chat parti, les souris dansent ("The cat's away, the mice will play"). No. 4345, Sauter du coq à l'âne ("Jump from the rooster to the donkey" or "Jump from one thing to another"). No. 4346, Se regarder en chiens de faïence ("To stare like clay dogs" or "To stare menacingly at each other"). No. 4347, Ménager la chèvre et le chou ("To take care of the goat and the cabbage" or "To run with the hares and hunt with the hounds"). No. 4348, Cela ne se trouve pas sous les sabots d'un cheval ("That is not under the hooves of a horse"). No. 4349, Pratique la politique de l'autruche ("Practice the policy of an ostrich" or "Bury one's head in the sand like an ostrich").

2013, Feb. 4   *Serpentine Die Cut 11*
Booklet Stamps
Self-Adhesive

4338	A2297	(58c) multi	1.60	.55
4339	A2297	(58c) multi	1.60	.55
4340	A2297	(58c) multi	1.60	.55
4341	A2297	(58c) multi	1.60	.55
4342	A2297	(58c) multi	1.60	.55
4343	A2297	(58c) multi	1.60	.55
4344	A2297	(58c) multi	1.60	.55
4345	A2297	(58c) multi	1.60	.55
4346	A2297	(58c) multi	1.60	.55
4347	A2297	(58c) multi	1.60	.55
4348	A2297	(58c) multi	1.60	.55
4349	A2297	(58c) multi	1.60	.55
a.		Booklet pane of 12, #4338-4349	19.50	
		Nos. 4338-4349 (12)	19.20	6.60

Compare types A2297 and A2498.

Raphael Elizé (1891-1945), First Black Mayor in France — A2298

2013, Feb. 15   Engr.   Perf. 13¼
4350 A2298 63c multi   1.75 .60

Miniature Sheet

Way of St. James A2299

No. 4351: a, Via Lemovicensis in Neuvy-Saint-Sépulchre. b, Via Turonensis in Aulnay. c, Via Tolosana in Saint-Gilles, horiz. d, Via Podiensis in Conques, horiz.

Litho. & Engr.
2013, Feb. 22   *Perf. 13*
4351 A2299 Sheet of 4   8.50 8.50
a.-d. 80c Any single   2.10 .70

50th International Agricultural Show, Paris — A2300

2013, Feb. 25   Photo.   Perf. 13¼
4352 A2300 95c multi   2.50 .85

Intl. Women's Day — A2301

Qualities of women in Aicha des Gazelles Rally, Morocco: No. 4353, Courage. No. 4354, Partage (sharing). No. 4355, Dépassement de soi (surpassing oneself). No. 4356, Entraide (mutual aid). No. 4357, Enthusiasme (enthusiasm). No. 4358, Solidarité (solidarity). No. 4359, Esprit d'équipe (team spirit). No. 4360, Engagement. No. 4361, Emotion. No. 4362, Performance. No. 4363, Confiance (confidence). No. 4364, Respect.

2013, Mar. 8   *Serpentine Die Cut 11*
Booklet Stamps
Self-Adhesive

4353	A2301	(58c) multi	1.50	.50
4354	A2301	(58c) multi	1.50	.50
4355	A2301	(58c) multi	1.50	.50
4356	A2301	(58c) multi	1.50	.50
4357	A2301	(58c) multi	1.50	.50
4358	A2301	(58c) multi	1.50	.50
4359	A2301	(58c) multi	1.50	.50
4360	A2301	(58c) multi	1.50	.50
4361	A2301	(58c) multi	1.50	.50
4362	A2301	(58c) multi	1.50	.50
4363	A2301	(58c) multi	1.50	.50
4364	A2301	(58c) multi	1.50	.50
a.		Booklet pane of 12, #4353-4364	18.00	
		Nos. 4353-4364 (12)	18.00	6.00

See No. 4406.

European Capitals Type of 2002
Miniature Sheet

No. 4365 — Attractions in Madrid, Spain: a, Plaza Mayor. b, Almudena Cathedral, horiz. c, Palace of Communication (Cibeles Palace), horiz. d, Royal Palace, horiz.

Perf. 13¼x13 (#4365a), 13x13¼
2013, Mar. 15
4365 A1622 Sheet of 4   6.50 6.50
a.-d. 63c Any single   1.60 .55

Opening of Jacques Chaban-Delmas Vertical Lift Bridge, Bordeaux A2302

2013, Mar. 16   Perf. 13¼
4366 A2302 58c multi   1.50 .50

Water Towers, Designed by Philolaos Tloupas, Valence — A2303

2013, Mar. 22   Engr.
4367 A2303 58c multi   1.50 .50

Spring Philatelic Show, Mâcon — A2304

2013, Apr. 5   Perf. 13¼
4368 A2304 63c multi   1.75 .60

Horses — A2305

Horse breeds and horses at work: No. 4369, Breton horse. No. 4370, Norman Cob horse. No. 4371, Boulonnais horse. No. 4372, Trait du Nord horse. No. 4373, Ardennais horse. No. 4374, Comtois horse. No. 4375, Poitevin Mulsassier horse. No. 4376, Horse pulling wagon (Attelage en roulotte). No. 4377, Percheron horse. No. 4378, Horse working in vineyard (Travail de la vigne). No. 4379, Auxois horse. No. 4380, Horse pulling logs in forest (Débardage en forêt).

Serpentine Die Cut 11
2013, Apr. 5   Photo.
Booklet Stamps
Self-Adhesive

4369	A2305	(58c) multi	1.50	.50
4370	A2305	(58c) multi	1.50	.50
4371	A2305	(58c) multi	1.50	.50
4372	A2305	(58c) multi	1.50	.50
4373	A2305	(58c) multi	1.50	.50
4374	A2305	(58c) multi	1.50	.50
4375	A2305	(58c) multi	1.50	.50
4376	A2305	(58c) multi	1.50	.50
4377	A2305	(58c) multi	1.50	.50
4378	A2305	(58c) multi	1.50	.50
4379	A2305	(58c) multi	1.50	.50
4380	A2305	(58c) multi	1.50	.50
a.		Booklet pane of 12, #4369-4380	18.00	
		Nos. 4369-4380 (12)	18.00	6.00

Champs-Elysées Theater, Paris, Cent. — A2306

2013, Apr. 8   Engr.   Perf. 13¼
4381 A2306 €1.05 multi   2.75 .90

Chateau des Vaux, Home of Apprentices of Auteuil — A2307

2013, Apr. 12
4382 A2307 58c multi   1.50 .50

Bats — A2308

Designs: No. 4383, Rhinolophus ferrumequinum. No. 4384: a, Pteropus seychellensis comorensis, vert. b, Plecotus macrobullaris, vert. c, Myotis nattereri.

2013, Apr. 19   Photo.
4383 A2308 58c multi   1.50 .50

Miniature Sheet

4384		Sheet of 4, #4383, 4384a-4384c	8.00	8.00
a.	A2308	58c multi	1.50	.50
b.	A2308	80c multi	2.10	.70
c.	A2308	€1.05 multi	2.75	.90

Notre Dame de Melun Collegiate Church, 1000th Anniv. — A2309

2013, Apr. 20   Engr.
4385 A2309 63c multi   1.75 .60

Impressionist Paintings Depicting Water — A2310

Designs: No. 4386, L'Ile de la Grande Jatte, Neuilly-sur-Seine, by Alfred Sisley. No. 4387, L'Estaque - Vue du Golfe de Marseille (Gulf of Marseille as Seen from L'Estaque), by Paul Cézanne. No. 4388, Sur la Plage (On the Beach), by Edouard Manet. No. 4389, L'Anse des Pilotes au Havre, Haute Mer Après Midi, Soleil, by Camille Pissarro. No. 4390, Régates à Argenteuil (Regatta at Argenteuil), by Claude Monet. No. 4391, Alphonsine Fournaise, by Pierre-Auguste Renoir. No. 4392, La Rivière Blanche (Breton Boy by the Aven River), by Paul Gauguin. No. 4393, L'Homme à la Barre (Man at the Helm), by Théo van Rysselberghe. No. 4394, Les Pecheurs à la Ligne, Étude pour la Grande Jatte (Fishermen), by Georges Seurat. No. 4395, Dans le Port de Rouen (In the Port of Rouen), by Albert Lebourg. No. 4396, La Nuit Etoilée, Arles (Starry Night Over the Rhone), by Vincent van Gogh. No. 4397, La Jetée de Deauville (The Jetty at Deauville), by Louis-Eugène Boudin.

Serpentine Die Cut 11
2013, Apr. 29   Photo.
Booklet Stamps
Self-Adhesive

4386	A2310	(58c) multi	1.50	.50
4387	A2310	(58c) multi	1.50	.50
4388	A2310	(58c) multi	1.50	.50
4389	A2310	(58c) multi	1.60	.60
4390	A2310	(58c) multi	1.50	.50
4391	A2310	(58c) multi	1.50	.50
4392	A2310	(58c) multi	1.50	.50
4393	A2310	(58c) multi	1.50	.50
4394	A2310	(58c) multi	1.50	.50
4395	A2310	(58c) multi	1.50	.50
4396	A2310	(58c) multi	1.50	.50
4397	A2310	(58c) multi	1.50	.50
a.		Booklet pane of 12, #4386-4397	18.00	
		Nos. 4386-4397 (12)	18.00	6.00

See Nos. 4449-4452.

Rixheim A2311

2013, May 3   Litho. & Engr.   Perf. 13
4398 A2311 63c multi   1.75 .60

A souvenir sheet of one No. 4398 sold for €3.

Charles Gonzaga (1580 1637), Duke of Mantua and Monferrat, Founder of Charleville — A2312

2013, May 6   Engr.   Perf. 13¼
4399 A2312 80c red & black   2.25 .75

World Table Tennis Championships, Paris — A2313

Designs: 63c, Female player (blue shirt). 95c, Male player (red shirt).

2013, May 13   Perf. 13x13¼
4400 A2313 63c multi   1.75 .60
4401 A2313 95c multi   2.50 .80
a.   Horiz. pair, #4400-4401, + central label   4.25 1.40

FRANCE

Cathedral and Jules Verne Circus,
Amiens — A2314

2013, May 17
4402 A2314 63c multi + label 1.75 .60

French Federation of Philatelic Associations, 86th Congress, Amiens. A souvenir sheet containing No. 4402 was issued in 2014 and sold for €3.20.

Europa
A2315

Designs: No. 4403, Mail coach, 1840. No. 4404, Renault Kangoo ZE mail van.

2013, May 19 Photo.
4403 80c multi 2.25 .75
4404 80c multi 2.25 .75
  a. A2315 Horiz. pair, #4403-4404 4.50 1.50

Souvenir Sheet

Works of André Le Nôtre (1613-1700),
Landscape Architect for King Louis
XVI — A2316

No. 4405 — Fountains and gardens at: a, Versailles. b, Chantilly.

2013, May 31 Perf. 13x13¼
4405 A2316 Sheet of 2 14.00 14.00
  a.-b. €2.55 Either single 7.00 2.50
  c. Sheet of 2, #4405a-4405b, different sheet margin 24.00 24.00

No. 4405c sold for €9.

Intl. Women's Day Type of 2013
Serpentine Die Cut 11

2013, June 1 Litho.
Self-Adhesive
4406 A2301 (58c) Like #4359 1.60 1.60

No. 4406 has a dot structure not found on No. 4359, which is printed by photogravure.

Abbaye-aux-Dames, Saintes — A2317

2013, June 14 Engr. Perf. 13¼
4407 A2317 63c multi 1.75 .60

Jacques Baumel
(1918-2006),
Politician
A2318

2013, June 15
4408 A2318 €1.05 multi 3.00 1.00

Miniature Sheet
100th
Tour de
France
Bicycle
Race
A2319

No. 4409: a, Rider wearing yellow jersey, Annecy in background (40x30mm). b, Rider wearing polka-dot jersey near Bagnères-de-Bigorre (26x40mm). c, Rider wearing light blue and dark blue jersey near Mont Ventoux (26x40mm). d, Peloton going along Alpe d'Huez mountain road (40x40mm). e, Rider wearing green jersey in foreground, Calvi in background (40x26mm). f, Rider wearing white jersey, Versailles Palace in background (40x30mm). g, Rider wearing yellow jersey winning race, Arc de Triomphe, Paris (30x40mm). h, Rider in red and black jersey, Mont-Saint-Michel (40x30mm).

Perf. 13x13¼ (#4409a, 4409f),
13¼x13 (#4409g), 13

2013, June 29 Photo.
4409 A2319 Sheet of 8 15.50 15.50
  a.-d. 58c Any single 1.50 .50
  e.-f. 80c Either single 2.10 .70
  g.-h. 95c Either single 2.50 .85

A souvenir sheet containing Nos. 4409e and 4409g sold for €4.

Types of 1959-2008
Miniature Sheet

2013 Engr. Perf. 13
4410 Sheet of 12 21.00 21.00
  a. A328 63c black 1.75 .60
  b. A349 63c black 1.75 .60
  c. A360 63c black 1.75 .60
  d. A379 63c black 1.75 .60
  e. A486 63c black 1.75 .60
  f. A555 63c black 1.75 .60
  g. A771 63c black 1.75 .60
  h. A915 63c black 1.75 .60
  i. A1161 63c black 1.75 .60
  j. A1409 63c black 1.75 .60
  k. A1713 63c black 1.75 .60
  l. A1912 63c black 1.75 .60
  m. Booklet pane of 12, #4410a-4410l 21.00 —

No. 4410 was only sold together with No. 4437a.

Issued: No. 4410, 7/15; No. 4410m, 11/6

Marianne and Children
A2320

Marianne and Children
"Ecopli"
A2321

Marianne and Children
"Lettre Prioritaire"
A2322

Marianne and Children
"Europe"
A2323

Marianne and Children
"Monde" — A2324

Type A2322 gram limits (at LL): Nos. 4415, 4422, 4428, 4435, 20g. Nos. 4419, 4432, 50g. Nos. 4420, 4433, 100g. Nos. 4421, 4434, 250g.

2013, July 15 Engr. Perf. 13
4411 A2320 1c yellow .25 .25
4412 A2320 5c dk brown .25 .25
4413 A2320 10c brown .25 .25
4414 A2321 (56c) dk gray 1.50 .30
4415 A2322 (63c) red 1.75 .35
  a. As No. 4415, engraved, glossy paper (#4437g) 1.75 1.75
  b. As No. 4415, photogravure, glossy paper (#4437g) 1.75 1.75
  c. As No. 4415, litho., glossy paper (#4437g) 1.75 1.75
  d. As No. 4415, typo., glossy paper (#4437g) 1.75 1.75
  e. As No. 4415, silk-screened, glossy paper (#4437g) 1.75 1.75
  f. No. 4415a with overprint "Marianne 1944-2014" (#4437o) 1.75 1.75
  g. No. 4415b with overprint "Marianne 1944-2014" (#4437o) 1.75 1.75
  h. No. 4415c with overprint "Marianne 1944-2014" (#4437o) 1.75 1.75
  i. No. 4415d with overprint "Marianne 1944-2014" (#4437o) 1.75 1.75
  j. No. 4415e with overprint "Marianne 1944-2014" (#4437o) 1.75 1.75
4416 A2323 (80c) blue 2.10 .45
4417 A2324 (95c) purple 2.50 .65
4418 A2320 €1 orange 2.60 .65
4419 A2322 (€1.05) fawn 2.75 .70
4420 A2322 (€1.55) red violet 4.00 1.00
4421 A2322 (€2.55) chocolate 6.75 2.40
Nos. 4411-4421 (11) 24.70 7.25

Coil Stamps
Perf. 13 Horiz.

4422 A2322 (63c) red 1.75 .35
4423 A2323 (80c) blue 2.10 .45

Self-Adhesive
Serpentine Die Cut 6¾ Vert.

4424 A2320 1c yellow .25 .25
4425 A2320 5c dk brown .25 .25
4426 A2320 10c brown .25 .25
4427 A2321 (56c) dk gray 1.50 1.50
4428 A2322 (63c) red 1.75 .35
  a. Booklet pane of 10 17.50
  b. Booklet pane of 12 21.00
  c. Booklet pane of 20 35.00
4429 A2323 (80c) blue 2.10 .45
  a. Booklet pane of 12 25.50
4430 A2324 (95c) purple 2.50 2.50
4431 A2320 €1 orange 2.60 2.60
4432 A2322 (€1.05) fawn 2.75 2.75
4433 A2322 (€1.55) red violet 4.00 4.00
4434 A2322 (€2.55) chocolate 6.75 6.75
Nos. 4424-4434 (11) 24.70 21.65

Coil Stamps
Serpentine Die Cut 6¾ Horiz.

4435 A2322 (63c) red 1.75 .35
4436 A2323 (80c) blue 2.10 .45

Issued: Nos. 4415a-4415e, 11/6; Nos. 4415f-4415j, 11/6/14. No. 4415e uses an ink that is shinier than that used on No. 4415a that causes the small lettering at the base of the stamp to be indistinct. Nos. 4415f-4415j had a franking value of 66c on day of issue. Compare with types A2534, A2536. See No. 4519. For overprint, see No. 5447.

Marianne and Tree "Lettre
Verte" — A2325

Type A2325 gram limits (at LL): Nos. 4437, 4441, 4442, 4446, 20g. Nos. 4438, 4443, 50g. Nos. 4439, 4444, 100g. Nos. 4440, 4445, 250g.

2013, July 15 Engr. Perf. 13
4437 A2325 (58c) green 1.50 .25
  a. Souvenir sheet of 2, #4415, 4437 3.25 3.25
  b. As No. 4437, engraved, glossy paper (#4437g) 1.60 1.60
  c. As No. 4437, photogravure, glossy paper (#4437g) 1.60 1.60
  d. As No. 4437, litho., glossy paper (#4437g) 1.60 1.60
  e. As No. 4437, typo., glossy paper (#4437g) 1.60 1.60
  f. As No. 4437, silk-screened, glossy paper (#4437g) 1.60 1.60
  g. Sheet of 40, 8 each #4415a, 4437b, 4 each #4415b, 4415e, 4437d, 4437e, 2 each #4415c, 4415d, 4437c, 4437f, + label 67.00 67.00
  h. Booklet pane of 2, #4415, 4437 3.50 —
  Complete booklet, #4410m, 4437h 24.50
  i. Booklet pane of 2, #4079, 4437 3.00 —
  j. No. 4437b with overprint "Marianne 1944-2014" (#4437o) 1.60 1.60
  k. No. 4437c with overprint "Marianne 1944-2014" (#4437o) 1.60 1.60
  l. No. 4437d with overprint "Marianne 1944-2014" (#4437o) 1.60 1.60
  m. No. 4437e with overprint "Marianne 1944-2014" (#4437o) 1.60 1.60
  n. No. 4437f with overprint "Marianne 1944-2014" (#4437o) 1.60 1.60
  o. Sheet of 40, 8 each #4415f, 4437j, 4 each #4415g, 4415j, 4437l, 4437m, 2 each #4415h, 4415i, 4437k, 4437n, + label 67.00 67.00

4438 A2325 (97c) yel grn 2.60 .55
4439 A2325 (€1.45) dk bl grn 3.75 .80
4440 A2325 (€2.35) dk bl grn 6.25 1.25
Nos. 4437-4440 (4) 14.10 2.85

Coil Stamp
Perf. 13 Horiz.

4441 A2325 (58c) green 1.50 .25

Self-Adhesive
Serpentine Die Cut 6¾ Vert.

4442 A2325 (58c) green 1.50 .25
  a. Booklet pane of 10 15.00
  b. Booklet pane of 12 18.00
4443 A2325 (97c) yel grn 2.60 2.60
4444 A2325 (€1.45) dk bl grn 3.75 3.75
4445 A2325 (€2.35) dk bl grn 6.25 6.25
Nos. 4442-4445 (4) 14.10 12.85

Coil Stamp
Serpentine Die Cut 6¾ Horiz.

4446 A2325 (58c) green 1.50 .25

Issued: Nos. 4437b-4437h, 11/6, No. 4437i-4437o, 11/6/14. No. 4437a was only sold together with No. 4410. No. 4437a is 144x106mm. A 209x103mm sheet similar to No. 4473a was sold with a folder for €4. No. 4437f uses an ink that is shinier than that used on No. 4437b that causes the small lettering at the base of the stamp to be indistinct. Nos. 4437j-4437n each had a franking value of 61c on day of issue. The 80x52mm label on No. 4437g depicting an enlarged example of Type A2325 is not valid for postage. The 80x52mm label on No. 4437o was also overprinted "Marianne 1944-2014" but is not valid for postage. Compare with type A2535.
See No. 4512. For overprint, see No. 5448.

Gaston Doumergue
(1863-1937),
Politician
A2326

2013, Aug. 1 Engr. Perf. 13¼
4447 A2326 58c dark blue 1.60 .55

Pierre-Georges
Latécoère (1883-1943), Aircraft
Manufacturer
A2327

2013, Aug. 15 Photo.
4448 A2327 €1.05 multi 3.00 1.00

Impressionist Paintings Type of 2013

Designs: No. 4449, Like #4387. No. 4450, Like #4389. No. 4451, Like #4390. No. 4452, Like #4396.

Serpentine Die Cut 11

2013, Aug. 26 Litho.
Self-Adhesive
4449 A2310 (58c) multi 1.60 1.60
4450 A2310 (58c) multi 1.60 1.60
4451 A2310 (58c) multi 1.60 1.60
4452 A2310 (58c) multi 1.60 1.60
Nos. 4449-4452 (4) 6.40 6.40

Nos. 4449-4452 each have a dot structure in the colored panels at right that is not found on the photogravure stamps. The appearance of "France" on Nos. 4449-4452 appears lighter and grayer than that found on the photogravure stamps.

Patronage Law, 10th
Anniv. — A2328

2013, Sept. 5 Photo. Perf. 13¼
4453 A2328 63c multi 1.75 .60

FRANCE

Sculpture of Virgin Mary and Infant Jesus A2329

Keystone, Sainte-Chapelle de Vincennes A2330

Mirror With Ivory Carving of Chess Players A2331

Annunciation of the Virgin, Reims Cathedral A2332

Carving of Rooster, St. Pierre's Cathedral, Poitiers — A2333

Decorated Mirror of Louis d'Anjou — A2334

Marriage of the Virgin, Notre Dame Cathedral, Paris — A2335

Angel From Canopy of King Charles VII — A2336

Illumination From Les Très Riches Heures du Duc de Berry A2337

Reliquary Medallion A2338

Illumination from Heures de François de Guise — A2339

Bas-relief of Man Presenting Flower to Woman — A2340

Serpentine Die Cut 11
2013, Sept. 6   Photo.
Booklet Stamps
Self-Adhesive

4454	A2329	(63c)	multi	1.75	.60
4455	A2330	(63c)	multi	1.75	.60
4456	A2331	(63c)	multi	1.75	.60
4457	A2332	(63c)	multi	1.75	.60
4458	A2333	(63c)	multi	1.75	.60
4459	A2334	(63c)	multi	1.75	.60
4460	A2335	(63c)	multi	1.75	.60
4461	A2336	(63c)	multi	1.75	.60
4462	A2337	(63c)	multi	1.75	.60
4463	A2338	(63c)	multi	1.75	.60
4464	A2339	(63c)	multi	1.75	.60
4465	A2340	(63c)	multi	1.75	.60
a.	Booklet pane of 12, #4454-4465			21.00	

Nos. 4454-4465 (12)   21.00   7.20

Gothic art.

French Heritage — A2341

Designs: No. 4466, House of the Lumière Brothers, Lyon. No. 4467, Buffon Museum, Montbard. No. 4468, House of George Sand, Nohant. No. 4469, House of Georges Clemenceau, Saint-Vincent-sur-Jard. No. 4470, Château de La Motte-Tilly, La Motte-Tilly. No. 4471, Castle and ramparts, Carcassonne. No. 4472, Château de Carrouges, Carrouges. No. 4473, Château de Champs-sur-Marne, Champs-sur-Marne. No. 4474, Aligned stones of Carnac. No. 4475, Roman structures (Mausoleum of the Julii, Triumphal arch of Glanum, Saint-Rémy-de-Provence. No. 4476, Mosaics at Montcaret archaeological site. No. 4477, Gallo-Roman Villa, Montmaurin.

Serpentine Die Cut 11
2013, Sept. 6   Photo.
Booklet Stamps
Self-Adhesive

4466	A2341	(58c)	multi	1.60	.55
4467	A2341	(58c)	multi	1.60	.55
4468	A2341	(58c)	multi	1.60	.55
4469	A2341	(58c)	multi	1.60	.55
a.	Booklet pane of 4, #4466-4469			6.50	
4470	A2341	(58c)	multi	1.60	.55
4471	A2341	(58c)	multi	1.60	.55
4472	A2341	(58c)	multi	1.60	.55
4473	A2341	(58c)	multi	1.60	.55
a.	Booklet pane of 4, #4470-4473			6.50	
4474	A2341	(58c)	multi	1.60	.55
4475	A2341	(58c)	multi	1.60	.55
4476	A2341	(58c)	multi	1.60	.55
4477	A2341	(58c)	multi	1.60	.55
a.	Booklet pane of 4, #4474-4477			6.50	
	Complete booklet, #4469a, 4473a, 4477a			19.50	

Nos. 4466-4477 (12)   19.20   6.60

Judicial Police of Paris, Cent. — A2342

2013, Sept. 13   Photo.   *Perf. 13¼*
| 4478 | A2342 | 63c | multi | 1.75 | .60 |

Art Issue

Faience Vase, by Théodore Deck (1823-91) A2343

2013, Sept. 20   Photo.   *Perf. 13¼x13*
| 4479 | A2343 | €1.55 | multi | 4.25 | 2.10 |

Alexandre Yersin (1863-1943), Bacteriologist A2344

Yersin a: 63c, Older man. b: 95c, Young man.

2013, Sept. 20   Engr.   *Perf. 13x13¼*
| 4480 | A2344 | 63c | multi | 1.75 | .60 |
| 4481 | A2344 | 95c | multi | 2.60 | .85 |

See Viet Nam Nos. 3488-3489.

Art Issue
Souvenir Sheet

Paintings by Georges Braque (1882-1963) — A2345

No. 4482: a, Le Guéridon. b, Le Salon.

2013, Sept. 27   Photo.   *Perf. 13x13¼*
| 4482 | A2345 | Sheet of 2 | | 8.50 | 8.50 |
| a.-b. | €1.55 Either single | | | 4.25 | 2.10 |

St. Bernard of Clairvaux (1090-1153), Abbot, and His Birthplace, Fontaine-lès-Dijon — A2346

2013, Oct. 4   Engr.   *Perf. 13¼*
| 4483 | A2346 | 58c | multi | 1.60 | .55 |

Miniature Sheet

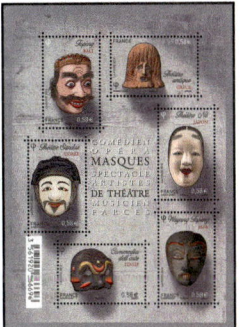
Theatrical Masks — A2347

No. 4484: a, Balinese Topeng. b, Greek theater mask, horiz. c, Korean Sandae mask. d, Japanese Noh theater mask. e, Italian Commedia dell'arte mask, horiz. f, Javanese shadow theater mask.

2013, Oct. 4   Litho. & Engr.   *Perf. 13*
| 4484 | A2347 | Sheet of 6 | | 9.75 | 9.75 |
| a.-f. | 58c Any single | | | 1.60 | .55 |

A set of six souvenir sheets, each containing one each of Nos. 4484a-4484f, sold for €15.

Marianne and Balloon — A2348

Balloons and Paraglider — A2349

Man Blowing on Fire — A2350

Bottle of Air in Water — A2351

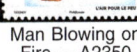
Man Pumping Air Into Tire — A2352

Paramedics Tending to Man Wearing Oxygen Mask — A2353

Hang Glider — A2354

Sailboat — A2355

Birds — A2356

Hummingbird and Flowers — A2357

Horn Player — A2358

Runner — A2359

Polynesian Canoe — A2360

Wind Turbine — A2361

2013, Oct. 12   Engr.   *Perf. 13*
| 4485 | A2348 | 58c | multi | 1.60 | .55 |

Photo. & Embossed
Souvenir Sheet
Perf. 13¼x13
| 4486 | A2349 | €2.35 | multi | 6.50 | 3.25 |

Photo.
Booklet Stamps
Self-Adhesive
Serpentine Die Cut 11

4487	A2350	(63c)	multi	1.75	.60
4488	A2351	(63c)	multi	1.75	.60
4489	A2352	(63c)	multi	1.75	.60
4490	A2353	(63c)	multi	1.75	.60
4491	A2354	(63c)	multi	1.75	.60
4492	A2355	(63c)	multi	1.75	.60
4493	A2356	(63c)	multi	1.75	.60
4494	A2357	(63c)	multi	1.75	.60
4495	A2358	(63c)	multi	1.75	.60
4496	A2359	(63c)	multi	1.75	.60
4497	A2360	(63c)	multi	1.75	.60
4498	A2361	(63c)	multi	1.75	.60
a.	Booklet pane of 12, #4487-4498			21.00	

Nos. 4487-4498 (12)   21.00   7.20

Stamp Day. See Nos. 4535-4536.

Miniature Sheet

Television Personalities — A2362

No. 4499: a, Pierre Sabbagh (1918-94), news reporter and producer. b, Léon Zitrone (1914-95), news and sports reporter. c, Catherine Langeais (1923-98), show host. d, Denise Glaser (1920-83), show host and producer. e, Jacqueline Joubert (1921-2005), show host and producer, horiz. f, Pierre Desgraupes (1918-93), news reporter, horiz.

2013, Oct. 18   Photo.   *Perf. 13*
| 4499 | A2362 | Sheet of 6 | | 9.75 | 9.75 |
| a.-f. | 58c Any single | | | 1.60 | .55 |

Little Pleasures — A2363

Designs: No. 4500, People and tea set (Thé partagé). No. 4501, Tree of life (Arbre de vie). No. 4502, Peacock holding letter (Paon messager). No. 4503, Carousel (Carrousel). No. 4504, Tree and falling coins (Pluie d'écus). No. 4505, Robin (Le rouge-gorge). No. 4506, Child and dove (Enfant de paix). No. 4507, Flying horse and rider (Cheval porte-bonheur). No. 4508, Cookies, pastries and snacks (Gourmandises). No. 4509, Citrus fruit and blossoms (Magie d'agrumes). No. 4510, Mother, child and flowers (Bienveillance). No. 4511, Shoe filled with gifts (L'escarpin).

Serpentine Die Cut 11
2013, Oct. 25   Photo.
Booklet Stamps
Self-Adhesive

4500	A2363	(58c)	multi	1.60	.55
4501	A2363	(58c)	multi	1.60	.55
4502	A2363	(58c)	multi	1.60	.55
4503	A2363	(58c)	multi	1.60	.55
4504	A2363	(58c)	multi	1.60	.55

704 — FRANCE

Scott#	Type	Denom	Color	Unused	Used
4505	A2363	(58c)	multi	1.60	.55
4506	A2363	(58c)	multi	1.60	.55
4507	A2363	(58c)	multi	1.60	.55
4508	A2363	(58c)	multi	1.60	.55
4509	A2363	(58c)	multi	1.60	.55
4510	A2363	(58c)	multi	1.60	.55
4511	A2363	(58c)	multi	1.60	.55
a.	Booklet pane of 12, #4500-4511			19.50	
	Nos. 4500-4511 (12)			19.20	6.60

A souvenir sheet containing a perf. 12¾ example of No. 4510 with water-activated gum sold for €3.

Types of 1959-2013
Serpentine Die Cut 11
2013, Nov. 6   Engr.
Booklet Stamps
Self-Adhesive

4512	A2325	(58c) green	1.60	.35
4513	A328	63c black	1.75	.60
4514	A349	63c black	1.75	.60
4515	A360	63c black	1.75	.60
4516	A379	63c black	1.75	.60
4517	A486	63c black	1.75	.60
4518	A555	63c black	1.75	.60
4519	A2322	(63c) red	1.75	.60
4520	A771	63c black	1.75	.60
4521	A915	63c black	1.75	.60
4522	A1161	63c black	1.75	.60
4523	A1409	63c black	1.75	.60
4524	A1713	63c black	1.75	.60
4525	A1912	63c black	1.75	.60
a.	Booklet pane of 14, #4512-4525		24.50	
	Nos. 4512-4525 (14)		24.35	8.15

Trade Treaty Between France and Denmark, 350th Anniv. — A2364

Map and compass rose with ship at: 63c, Right. 80c, Left.

2013, Nov. 7   Engr.   Perf. 13
4526	A2364	63c multi	1.75	.60
4527	A2364	80c multi	2.25	.75

See Denmark Nos. 1663-1664.

Fashion — A2365

Designs: No. 4528, Finished dresses on three dress forms. No. 4529, Flower, three women wearing white dresses. No. 4530, Three dress forms. No. 4531, Three women wearing white dresses.

2013, Nov. 8   Photo.   Perf. 13¼
4528	A2365	63c multi	1.75	.60
4529	A2365	63c multi	1.75	.60
4530	A2365	95c multi	2.60	.85
4531	A2365	95c multi	2.60	.85
	Nos. 4528-4531 (4)		8.70	2.90

See Singapore Nos. 1640-1643.

Souvenir Sheet

French History A2366

No. 4532: a, Battle of Muret, 1213. b, Capture of Tournoel, 1212.

2013, Nov. 8   Engr.   Perf. 13x13¼
4532	A2366	Sheet of 2	8.00	8.00
a.-b.	€1.45 Either single		4.00	1.40

National Order of Merit, 50th Anniv. — A2367

2013, Nov. 9   Engr.   Perf. 13¼
| 4533 | A2367 | 63c blue | 1.75 | .60 |

2013 French Kickboxing World Championships, Clermont-Ferrand A2368

2013, Nov. 16   Photo.   Perf. 13
| 4534 | A2368 | 95c multi | 2.60 | .85 |

Sailboat and Horn Player Types of 2013
Serpentine Die Cut 11
2013, Nov. 18   Litho.
Self-Adhesive

4535	A2355	(63c) multi	1.75	1.75
4536	A2358	(63c) multi	1.75	1.75

"Phil@poste" is sharper on Nos. 4535-4536 than on Nos. 4492 and 4495.

Items with Spirals — A2369

Spirals in: No. 4537, Solarium shell (Coquillage solarium). No. 4538, Pottery design from Iznik, Turkey (Céramique Iznik). No. 4539, Spirograph. No. 4540, Red rose (Rose rouge). No. 4541, Ammonite fossil (Fossile d'ammonite). No. 4542, Chinese highway interchange (Echangeur Shanghai Nanpu). No. 4543, Kite (Cerf-volant). No. 4544, Cyclone Ingrid. No. 4545, Tree rings (Sapin-coupe transversale). No. 4546, Basket (Vannerie). No. 4547, Lighthouse staircase (Phare de la Coubre). No. 4548, School of barracudas (Banc des barracudas).

Serpentine Die Cut 11
2014, Jan. 4   Photo.
Booklet Stamps
Self-Adhesive

4537	A2369	(66c) multi	1.75	.60
4538	A2369	(66c) multi	1.75	.60
4539	A2369	(66c) multi	1.75	.60
4540	A2369	(66c) multi	1.75	.60
4541	A2369	(66c) multi	1.75	.60
4542	A2369	(66c) multi	1.75	.60
4543	A2369	(66c) multi	1.75	.60
4544	A2369	(66c) multi	1.75	.60
4545	A2369	(66c) multi	1.75	.60
4546	A2369	(66c) multi	1.75	.60
4547	A2369	(66c) multi	1.75	.60
4548	A2369	(66c) multi	1.75	.60
a.	Booklet pane of 12, #4537-4548		21.00	
	Nos. 4537-4548 (12)		21.00	7.20

See Nos. 4566-4567, 4698.

Hearts — A2370

"Baccarat" and: 61c, Chandelier. €1.02, Goblet.

Silk-Screened, Engraved & Embossed
2014, Jan. 7   Perf. 13
4549	A2370	61c multi	1.75	.60
a.	Souvenir sheet of 5		8.75	8.75
4550	A2370	€1.02 multi	2.75	.90

Silk-Screened & Engraved
Serpentine Die Cut
Self-Adhesive

4551	A2370	61c multi	1.75	1.75
4552	A2370	€1.02 multi	2.75	2.75

See No. 4651.

Anne, Duchess of Brittany (1477-1514) A2371

Litho. & Engr.
2014, Jan. 11   Perf. 13
| 4553 | A2371 | 66c multi | 1.75 | .60 |

A souvenir sheet of one sold for €3.20.

Signs of the Zodiac — A2372

Designs: No. 4554, Aries (Bélier). No. 4555, Taurus (Taureau). No. 4556, Gemini (Gémeaux). No. 4557, Cancer. No. 4558, Leo (Lion). No. 4559, Virgo (Vierge). No. 4560, Libra (Balance). No. 4561, Scorpio (Scorpion). No. 4562, Sagittarius (Sagittaire). No. 4563, Capricorn (Capricorne). No. 4564, Aquarius (Verseau). No. 4565, Pisces (Poissons).

Serpentine Die Cut 11
2014, Jan. 20   Photo.
Booklet Stamps
Self-Adhesive

4554	A2372	(61c) multi	1.75	.60
4555	A2372	(61c) multi	1.75	.60
4556	A2372	(61c) multi	1.75	.60
4557	A2372	(61c) multi	1.75	.60
4558	A2372	(61c) multi	1.75	.60
4559	A2372	(61c) multi	1.75	.60
4560	A2372	(61c) multi	1.75	.60
4561	A2372	(61c) multi	1.75	.60
4562	A2372	(61c) multi	1.75	.60
4563	A2372	(61c) multi	1.75	.60
4564	A2372	(61c) multi	1.75	.60
4565	A2372	(61c) multi	1.75	.60
a.	Booklet pane of 12, #4554-4565		21.00	
	Nos. 4554-4565 (12)		21.00	7.20

Items With Spirals Type of 2014
Designs: No. 4566, Like #4542. No. 4567, Like #4543.

Serpentine Die Cut 11
2014, Jan. 27   Litho.
Self-Adhesive

4566	A2369	(66c) multi	1.75	1.75
4567	A2369	(66c) multi	1.75	1.75

"Phil@poste" is sharper on Nos. 4566-4567 than on Nos. 4542-4543.

New Year 2014 (Year of the Horse) — A2373

2014, Jan. 31   Photo.   Perf. 13¼x13
| 4568 | A2373 | 66c multi | 1.75 | .60 |

No. 4568 was printed in sheets of 5. A souvenir sheet of one sold for €3.20. See No. 4971b.

Art Issue

Bust of Julius Caesar — A2374

2014, Feb. 14   Engr.   Perf. 13¼x13
| 4569 | A2374 | €1.65 multi | 4.50 | 2.25 |

Cattle Breeds — A2375

Inscriptions: No. 4570, La Bretonne Pie Noir. No. 4571, L'Armoricaine. No. 4572, La Béarnaise. No. 4573, La Maraîchine. No. 4574, La Mirandaise. No. 4575, La Villard de Lans. No. 4576, La Saosnoise. No. 4577, La Nantaise. No. 4578, La Bordelaise. No. 4579, La Lourdaise. No. 4580, La Casta. No. 4581, La Ferrandaise.

Serpentine Die Cut 11
2014, Feb. 22   Photo.
Booklet Stamps
Self-Adhesive

4570	A2375	(61c) multi	1.75	.60
4571	A2375	(61c) multi	1.75	.60
4572	A2375	(61c) multi	1.75	.60
4573	A2375	(61c) multi	1.75	.60
4574	A2375	(61c) multi	1.75	.60
4575	A2375	(61c) multi	1.75	.60
4576	A2375	(61c) multi	1.75	.60
4577	A2375	(61c) multi	1.75	.60
4578	A2375	(61c) multi	1.75	.60
4579	A2375	(61c) multi	1.75	.60
4580	A2375	(61c) multi	1.75	.60
4581	A2375	(61c) multi	1.75	.60
a.	Booklet pane of 12, #4570-4581		21.00	
	Nos. 4570-4581 (12)		21.00	7.20

Art Issue

Tokyo 04, Photograph by Maxime Bruno A2376

2014, Feb. 28   Litho.   Perf. 13x13¼
| 4582 | A2376 | €1.65 multi | 4.50 | 2.25 |

Miniature Sheet

Way of St. James A2377

No. 4583: a, Via Lemovicensis in Bazas. b, Via Podiensis in Moissac. c, Via Tolosana in Auch. d, Via Turonensis in Pons.

Litho. & Engr.
2014, Mar. 14   Perf. 13
4583	A2377	Sheet of 4	9.00	9.00
a.-d.	83c Any single		2.25	.75

Alexandre Glais-Bizoin (1800-77), Politician A2378

2014, Mar. 15   Engr.   Perf. 13x13¼
| 4584 | A2378 | 66c multi | 1.90 | .65 |

Bears — A2379

Designs: No. 4585, Giant panda (Panda géant). No. 4586: a, Spectacled bear (Ours andin). b, Kermode bear (Ours Kermode). c, Polar bear (Ours polaire).

2014, Mar. 21   Photo.   Perf. 13¼
| 4585 | A2379 | 61c multi | 1.75 | .60 |

Miniature Sheet

4586	Sheet of 4, #4585, 4586a-4586c	7.00	7.00
a.-c.	A2379 61c Any single	1.75	.60

FRANCE

Diplomatic Relations Between France and People's Republic of China, 50th Anniv. A2380

Designs: 66c, Qinhuai River, Nanjing. 98c, Seine River, Paris.

2014, Mar. 27 Engr. Perf. 13x13¼
4587 A2380 66c multi   1.90 .65
4588 A2380 98c multi   2.75 .90

See No. 5933b and People's Republic of China Nos. 4172-4173.

Art Issue

Painting by Joan Mitchell (1925-92) A2381

2014, Mar. 28 Litho. Perf. 13¼x13
4589 A2381 €1.65 multi   4.50 2.25

Sell and Buy Used Items A2382 — Turn Off Appliances A2383

Fruits and Vegetables A2384 — Fix Leaks Quickly A2385

Sort and Recycle Paper A2386 — Control Indoor Temperatures A2387

Conserve Water — A2388 — People in Carpool — A2389

Use Public Transportation A2390 — Save Energy A2391

Drive Ecologically Friendly Automobiles A2392 — Recycle Waste Products A2393

Serpentine Die Cut 11
2014, Apr. 3   Photo.
Booklet Stamps
Self-Adhesive
4590 A2382 (61c) multi   1.75 .60
4591 A2383 (61c) multi   1.75 .60
4592 A2384 (61c) multi   1.75 .60
4593 A2385 (61c) multi   1.75 .60
4594 A2386 (61c) multi   1.75 .60
4595 A2387 (61c) multi   1.75 .60
4596 A2388 (61c) multi   1.75 .60
4597 A2389 (61c) multi   1.75 .60
4598 A2390 (61c) multi   1.75 .60
4599 A2391 (61c) multi   1.75 .60
4600 A2392 (61c) multi   1.75 .60
4601 A2393 (61c) multi   1.75 .60
  a. Booklet pane of 12, #4590-4601   21.00
Nos. 4590-4601 (12)   21.00 7.20

Opera Theater, Clermont-Ferrand A2394

2014, Apr. 4 Engr. Perf. 13¼
4602 A2394 61c multi   1.75 .60

Spring Philatelic Show, Clermont-Ferrand.

Marguerite Duras (1914-96), Writer and Film Director — A2395

2014, Apr. 4 Engr. Perf. 13¼
4603 A2395 €1.10 multi   3.00 1.00

Arrest and Deportation of Jews at Izieu Orphanage, 70th Anniv. — A2396

Litho. & Engr.
2014, Apr. 6 Perf. 13x13¼
4604 A2396 61c multi   1.75 .60

Miniature Sheet

European Capitals — A2397

No. 4605 — Attractions in Vienna: a, Secession Building. b, Belvedere Palace, horiz. c, Karlskirche (St. Charles' Church). d, Hofburg Palace, horiz.

Perf. 13¼x13, 13x13¼
2014, Apr. 18   Photo.
4605 A2397 Sheet of 4 + 2 labels   7.75 7.75
  a.-d. 66c Any single   1.90 .65

Souvenir Sheet

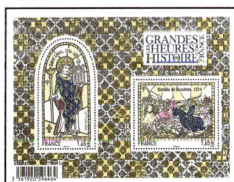

French History A2398

No. 4606: a, St. Louis (1214-70) (35x66mm). b, Battle of Bouvines, 1214 (52x41mm).

2014, Apr. 25 Engr. Perf. 13x13¼
4606 A2398 Sheet of 2   9.50 9.50
  a.-b. €1.65 Either single 4.75 2.25
  c. Souvenir sheet of 4, #4532a, 4532b, 4606a, 4606b   17.00 17.00

Salon du Timbre 2014 (No. 4606c). Issued: No. 4606c, 6/23/14.

Palace of Poitiers A2399

2014, May 1 Engr. Perf. 13x13¼
4607 A2399 61c multi + label 1.75 .60

Vacation — A2400

Designs: No. 4608, Dog with sunglasses eating ice cream bar. No. 4609, Snail with trailer for shell. No. 4610, Crab building sand castle. No. 4611, Cats dancing. No. 4612, Turtle playing luto, turtle dancing. No. 4613, Lobster holding beach gear. No. 4614, Chicken and egg wearing headphones. No. 4615, Fish surfing. No. 4616, Ram with backpack and mountain climbing gear. No. 4617, Rabbits on tandem bicycle. No. 4618, Frogs with umbrellas in swan boat. No. 4619, Geese, tent, snails on picnic plate.

Serpentine Die Cut 11
2014, May 3   Photo.
Booklet Stamps
Self-Adhesive
4608 A2400 (61c) multi   1.75 .60
4609 A2400 (61c) multi   1.75 .60
4610 A2400 (61c) multi   1.75 .60
4611 A2400 (61c) multi   1.75 .60
4612 A2400 (61c) multi   1.75 .60
4613 A2400 (61c) multi   1.75 .60
4614 A2400 (61c) multi   1.75 .60
4615 A2400 (61c) multi   1.75 .60
4616 A2400 (61c) multi   1.75 .60
4617 A2400 (61c) multi   1.75 .60
4618 A2400 (61c) multi   1.75 .60
4619 A2400 (61c) multi   1.75 .60
  a. Booklet pane of 12, #4608-4619   21.00
Nos. 4608-4619 (12)   21.00 7.20

Harp Created by Jean Henri Naderman, 1787 — A2401

2014, May 4 Photo. Perf. 13¼x13
4620 A2401 83c multi   2.25 .75

Europa.

Opening of English Channel Tunnel, 20th Anniv — A2402

2014, May 6 Engr. Perf. 13¼
4621 A2402 66c multi   1.90 .65

Tourism Series

Boulogne-sur-Mer — A2403

2014, May 9 Engr. Perf. 13x12¾
4622 A2403 61c multi   1.75 .60

D-Day, 70th Anniv. A2404

2014, June 5 Photo. Perf. 13x12¾
4623 A2404 66c multi   1.90 .65

Two souvenir sheets of one, issued in 2014 and in 2015, each sold for €3.20.

Tourism Issue

Pontigny Abbey, Yonne — A2405

2014, June 7 Engr. Perf. 13¼
4624 A2405 61c multi   1.75 .60

Massacre of Tulle, 70th Anniv. — A2406

2014, June 9 Photo. Perf. 13¼
4625 A2406 66c multi   1.90 .65

Souvenir Sheet

Benjamin Rabier (1864-1939), Comic Book Illustrator — A2407

No. 4626: a, Duckling hatching, ring with rabbits, chick and chicken (41x41mm). b, Rabier, chicken, rabbit and duck (30x41mm).

2014, June 14 Engr. Perf. 13¼
4626 A2407 Sheet of 2   5.00 5.00
  a. 66c multi   1.90 .65
  b. €1.10 multi   3.00 1.00

A 200x95mm sheet containing Nos. 4626a and 4626b, but having a different margin design sold for €6.
See Nos. 4676, 4680.

Trains — A2408

Designs: No. 4627, Buddicom No. 33, Haute-Normandie. No. 4628, Z 209, Vallée de Chamonix. No. 4629, Pacific Chapelon Nord 3.1192, Paris, Gare du Nord. No. 4630, Micheline XM 5005, Haute-Marne. No. 4631, Mikado 141 R 1187, Côte Vermeille. No. 4632, BB 12125, Moselle. No. 4633, Z 6181, Ile-de-France. No. 4634, BB 66001, Les Cévennes. No. 4635, BB 9004, Les Landes. No. 4636, RTG T 2057, Gare de Boulogne-Aroglisseurs. No. 4637, CC 6572, Limoges, Gare des Bénédictins. No. 4638, TGV Duplex, Gare de Belfort-Montbéliard TGV.

Serpentine Die Cut 11
2014, June 14   Photo.
Booklet Stamps
Self-Adhesive
4627 A2408 (66c) multi   1.90 .65
4628 A2408 (66c) multi   1.90 .65
4629 A2408 (66c) multi   1.90 .65
4630 A2408 (66c) multi   1.90 .65
  a. Booklet pane of 4, #4627-4630   7.60
4631 A2408 (66c) multi   1.90 .65
4632 A2408 (66c) multi   1.90 .65
4633 A2408 (66c) multi   1.90 .65
4634 A2408 (66c) multi   1.90 .65
  a. Booklet pane of 4, #4631-4634   7.60
4635 A2408 (66c) multi   1.90 .65
4636 A2408 (66c) multi   1.90 .65
4637 A2408 (66c) multi   1.90 .65

706 FRANCE

4638	A2408	(66c) multi	1.90	.65
a.		Booklet pane of 4, #4635-4638	7.60	
		Complete booklet, #4630a, 4634a, 4638a	23.00	
		Nos. 4627-4638 (12)	22.80	7.80

Paris Zoo, 80th Anniv. — A2409

2014, June 15   *Photo.*   *Perf. 13*

4639	A2409	98c multi	2.75	.95

A souvenir sheet containing No. 4639 sold for €3.20.

Jean Jaurès (1859-1914), Assassinated Socialist Party Leader — A2410

Jaurès: 61c, Without hat. €1.02, With hat.

2014, June 17   *Engr.*   *Perf. 13¼*

4640	A2410	61c blue	1.75	.60
4641	A2410	€1.02 red	2.75	.95
a.		Horiz. pair, #4640-4641	4.50	2.25

See Nos. 4675, 4679.

Miniature Sheet

The 1950s — A2411

No. 4642: a, Automobile. b, Electricity advertisement, vert. c, People packing for vacation, vert. d, Vendor in movie theater. e, Musicians. f, Two women modeling fashions, veret.

2014, June 18   *Photo.*   *Perf. 13*

4642	A2411	Sheet of 6	11.50	11.50
a.-f.		66c Any single	1.90	.65

See Nos. 4677, 4678.

A set of 10 miniature sheets containing reproductions of old French stamps (Nos. 641, 722, 764, 850, B34, B92, B97, B172, B248 and C22) with denominations was produced in limited quantities and offered only as a complete set. Each sheet contained five reproductions of one of the ten stamps in different colors, one with a €2.20 denomination and four with €2.45 denominations. **Similar sets were produced in limited quantities in subsequent years with reproductions of different stamps having different new denominations of more than €1.40.**

Ceres — A2412

2014, June 18   *Engr.*   *Imperf.*
With Printer's Inscription at Base of Stamp

4643	A2412	€1 rose carmine	2.75	1.40
4644	A2412	€1 red	2.75	1.40

Typo.

4645	A2412	€1 vermilion	2.75	1.40
a.		With printer information at top of stamp	2.75	1.40
4646	A2412	€1 rose	2.75	1.40
a.		With printer information at top of stamp	2.75	1.40
		Nos. 4643-4646 (4)	11.00	5.60

Printed in sheets of 20 containing Nos. 4645a, 4646a, 5 each Nos. 4643-4644, 4 each Nos. 4645-4646. See No. 4727a.

Tourism Issue

Coareze — A2413

Locmariaquer — A2414

2014   *Engr.*   *Perf. 13¼*

4647	A2413	61c multi	1.75	.60
4648	A2414	61c multi	1.75	.60

Issued: No. 4647, 6/19; No. 4648, 6/20. See Nos. 4673, 4674.

French Institute, Paris — A2415

2014, June 21   *Engr.*   *Perf. 13x13¼*

4649	A2415	61c multi + label	1.75	.60

French Federation of Philatelic Associations, 87th Congress, Paris. See Nos. 4672, 5762c.

Art Issue

The Seine at Pont du Carrousel, by Jean Dufy (1888-1964) — A2416

2014, June 22   *Litho.*   *Perf. 13x13¼*

4650	A2416	€1.65 multi	4.50	2.25

See No. 4681.

Baccarat Hearts Type of 2014
Silk-Screened & Engraved

2014, June 23   *Perf.*

4651	A2370	€3 multi	8.25	4.25

No. 4651 was printed in sheets of 5.

National Institute of Health and Medical Research, 50th Anniv. — A2417

2014, July 3   *Photo.*   *Perf. 13¼*

4652	A2417	66c multi	1.75	.60

Jeanne Antoinette Poisson, Marquise de Pompadour (1721-64), Patron of the Arts — A2418

2014, July 4   *Engr.*   *Perf. 13¼*

4653	A2418	66c multi	1.75	.60

Art Issue

Les Boîtes de Conserve, by Jean Fautrier (1898-1964) — A2419

2014, July 11   *Engr.*   *Perf. 13x13¼*

4654	A2419	€1.65 multi	4.50	2.25

General Mobilization of World War I Troops, Cent. — A2420

2014, Aug. 2   *Engr.*   *Perf. 13x13¼*

4655	A2420	66c blue & red	1.75	.60

Miniature Sheet

2014 World Equestrian Games, Normandy — A2421

No. 4656: a, Dressage (40x30mm). b, Endurance (40x30mm). c, Concours complet d'équitation (40x40mm). d, Para-dressage (30x40mm). e, Voltige (30x40mm). f, Attelage (40x40mm). g, Saut d'obstacles (40x30mm). h, Reining (40x30mm).

2014, Aug. 23   *Photo.*   *Perf. 13x13¼*

4656	A2421	Sheet of 8	17.50	8.75
a.-d.		61c Any single	1.60	.55
e.-h.		€1.02 Any single	2.75	.90

A souvenir sheet containing examples of Nos. 4656e and 4656f with different perforations, sold for €6.

Charles Péguy (1873-1914), Writer — A2422

2014, Sept. 5   *Engr.*   *Perf. 13¼*

4657	A2422	€1.55 multi	4.00	1.40

Renaissance Objets d'Art — A2423

Designs: No. 4658, Gardens of Château de Villandry. No. 4659, Clock, Rouen. No. 4660, Stairway sculpture, by Jean Goujon. No. 4661, Sculpture of salamander, Château de Fontainbleau. No. 4662, Buckle of King Charles IX. No. 4663, Detail of tapestry depicting Jupiter and Latona. No. 4664, Portrait of King Francis I, by Jean Clouet. No. 4665, Stainedd-glass window depicting angel playing flute, Sainte-Etienne Cathedral, Sens. No. 4666, Enamel painting of Ulysses, by Léonard Limousin. No. 4667, Book cover by Etienne Roffet. No. 4668, Armor of King Henri II. No. 4669, Stained-glass emblem of Queen Anne of Brittany depicting ermine and crown.

Serpentine Die Cut 11
2014, Sept. 6   *Photo.*
Booklet Stamps
Self-Adhesive

4658	A2423	(61c) multi	1.60	.55
4659	A2423	(61c) multi	1.60	.55
4660	A2423	(61c) multi	1.60	.55
4661	A2423	(61c) multi	1.60	.55
4662	A2423	(61c) multi	1.60	.55
4663	A2423	(61c) multi	1.60	.55
4664	A2423	(61c) multi	1.60	.55
4665	A2423	(61c) multi	1.60	.55
4666	A2423	(61c) multi	1.60	.55
4667	A2423	(61c) multi	1.60	.55
4668	A2423	(61c) multi	1.60	.55
4669	A2423	(61c) multi	1.60	.55
a.		Booklet pane of 12, #4658-4669	19.50	
		Nos. 4658-4669 (12)	19.20	6.60

Souvenir Sheet

First Battle of the Marne, Cent. — A2424

No. 4670: a, Troops and automobile. b, Troops on horseback.

Photo. & Litho.
2014, Sept. 12   *Perf. 13¼*

4670	A2424	Sheet of 2	4.25	2.10
a.		66c multi	1.75	.60
b.		98c multi	2.50	.85

A souvenir sheet containing Nos. 4670a and 4670b but with as different margin sold for €5.

Art Issue

Mural on Necker Hospital Staircase, by Keith Haring (1958-90) — A2425

2014, Sept. 19   *Photo.*   *Perf. 12¼x13*

4671	A2425	€2.65 multi	6.75	3.50

Types of 2014
Serpentine Die Cut 11
2014, Sept. 25   *Photo.*
Booklet Stamps
Self-Adhesive

4672	A2415	61c Like #4649 + label (22x16mm)	1.60	.55
4673	A2413	61c Like #4647 (22x16mm)	1.60	.55
4674	A2414	61c Like #4648 (21x16mm)	1.60	.55
4675	A2410	61c Like #4640 (15x22mm)	1.60	.55
4676	A2407	66c Like #4626a (21x22mm)	1.75	.60
4677	A2411	66c Like #4642e (30x22mm)	1.75	.60
4678	A2411	66c Like #4642a (30x22mm)	1.75	.60
4679	A2410	€1.02 Like #4641 (15x22mm)	2.60	.85
4680	A2407	€1.10 Like #4626b (15x22mm)	2.75	.90
4681	A2416	€1.65 Like #4650 (46x38mm)	4.25	1.40
a.		Booklet pane of 10, #4672-4681 + label	21.50	
		Nos. 4672-4681 (10)	21.25	7.15

Sense of Smell — A2426

Designs: No. 4682, Man and woman in love. No. 4683, Dog with magnifying glass. No. 4684, Coffee pot and cup. No. 4685, Skunks. No. 4686, Perfume atomizer. No. 4687, Athletic shoe and flowers. No. 4688, Fish with clothespin on nose. No. 4689, Cheese and foxes. No. 4690, Roast chicken. No. 4691, Woman smelling rose. No. 4692, Mother and baby. No. 4693, Face, herbs and spices.

Serpentine Die Cut 11
2014, Oct. 1   *Photo.*
Booklet Stamps
Self-Adhesive

4682	A2426	(61c) multi	1.60	.55
4683	A2426	(61c) multi	1.60	.55
4684	A2426	(61c) multi	1.60	.55
4685	A2426	(61c) multi	1.60	.55
4686	A2426	(61c) multi	1.60	.55
4687	A2426	(61c) multi	1.60	.55
4688	A2426	(61c) multi	1.60	.55

FRANCE

4689	A2426	(61c) multi	1.60	.55
4690	A2426	(61c) multi	1.60	.55
4691	A2426	(61c) multi	1.60	.55
4692	A2426	(61c) multi	1.60	.55
4693	A2426	(61c) multi	1.60	.55
a.	Booklet pane of 12, #4682-4693		19.50	
	Nos. 4682-4693 (12)		19.20	6.60

Douai Court House 300th Anniv. — A2427

2014, Oct. 3   Engr.   Perf. 13¼
4694   A2427   83c multi   2.10   .70

Green Turtle — A2428

2014, Oct. 9   Litho.   Perf. 13x13¼
4695   A2428   98c multi   2.50   .85

See Comoro Islands No. , French Southern & Antarctic Territories No. 511, Malagasy Republic No. 1637, Mauritius No. 1144, Seychelles No. 904.

Salsa Dancers — A2429

Break Dancers A2430

2014, Oct. 11   Engr.   Perf. 13¼
4696   A2429   61c multi   1.50   .50

Souvenir Sheet
Litho.
Perf. 13¼x13
4697   A2430   €2.45 multi   6.25   2.10
Stamp Day.

Items With Spirals Type of 2014
Serpentine Die Cut 11
2014, Oct. 15   Litho.
Self-Adhesive
4698   A2369   (66c) Like #4540   1.75   1.75

"Phil@poste" is sharper on No. 4698 than on No. 4540.

Maximilien Vox (1894-1974), Creator of Typographical Classification System — A2431

2014, Oct. 17   Engr.   Perf. 13¼
4699   A2431   €1.10 multi   2.75   .90

Miniature Sheet

Cameras — A2432

No. 4700: a, 1865 Derogy four-lens camera. b, 1902 Girard Le Reve folding camera. c, 1930 Kodak Beau Brownie camera. d, 1898 Bazin & Leroy Stereocycle camera. e, 1910 folding camera, horiz. f, 1935 Gaumont Spido Reportage camera.

Litho. & Engr.   Perf. 13
2014, Oct. 24
4700   A2432   Sheet of 6   10.50   5.25
a.-f.   66c Any single   1.75   .60

A set of six souvenir sheets containing one example of Nos. 4700a-4700f sold as a set for €16.

A2433   A2434

A2435   A2436

A2437   A2438

A2439   A2440

A2441   A2442

A2443   A2444

Serpentine Die Cut 11
2014, Oct. 24   Photo.
Booklet Stamps
Self-Adhesive

4701	A2433	(61c) multi	1.50	.50
4702	A2434	(61c) multi	1.50	.50
4703	A2435	(61c) multi	1.50	.50
4704	A2436	(61c) multi	1.50	.50
4705	A2437	(61c) multi	1.50	.50
4706	A2438	(61c) multi	1.50	.50
4707	A2439	(61c) multi	1.50	.50
4708	A2440	(61c) multi	1.50	.50
4709	A2441	(61c) multi	1.50	.50
4710	A2442	(61c) multi	1.50	.50
4711	A2443	(61c) multi	1.50	.50
4712	A2444	(61c) multi	1.50	.50
a.	Booklet pane of 12, #4701-4712		18.00	
	Nos. 4701-4712 (12)		18.00	6.00

A souvenir sheet containing one perf. 13¼ example of a stamp like No. 4706 sold for €3.20.

New French Industries A2445

Serpentine Die Cut 11
2014, Oct. 27   Photo.
Self-Adhesive
4713   A2445   (98c) multi   —   —

New French Industries A2446

Inscriptions: No. 4714, Usine du futur. No. 4715, Transition numérique. No. 4716, Développement durable. No. 4717, Patrimoine. No. 4718, Gastronomie. No. 4719, Transition énergétique. No. 4720, Elégance. No. 4721, Economi sociale et solidaire. No. 4722, Electromobilité. No. 4723, Exportations. No. 4724, Métiers d'art. No. 4725, Innovation 2030.

Serpentine Die Cut 11
2014, Oct. 27   Photo.
Booklet Stamps
Self-Adhesive

4714	A2446	(61c) multi	1.50	.50
4715	A2446	(61c) multi	1.50	.50
4716	A2446	(61c) multi	1.50	.50
4717	A2446	(61c) multi	1.50	.50
4718	A2446	(61c) multi	1.50	.50
4719	A2446	(61c) multi	1.50	.50
4720	A2446	(61c) multi	1.50	.50
4721	A2446	(61c) multi	1.50	.50
4722	A2446	(61c) multi	1.50	.50
4723	A2446	(61c) multi	1.50	.50
4724	A2446	(61c) multi	1.50	.50
4725	A2446	(61c) multi	1.50	.50
a.	Booklet pane of 12, #4714-4725		18.00	
	Nos. 4714-4725 (12)		18.00	6.00

Public Sale of Blue Cornflowers Made by World War I Veterans, 80th Anniv. — A2447

2014, Nov. 6   Photo.   Perf. 13¼
4726   A2447   €1.10 multi   2.75   .90

Types of 2003-14
2014, Nov. 6   Engr.   Perf. 13
4727   Sheet of 4, #4079, 4437, 4727a, 4727b   6.00   3.00
a.   A2412 61c green (20x26mm)   1.50   .50
b.   A1664 61c green   1.50   .50
c.   Booklet pane of 12, 6 each #4727a-4727b   18.00   —
   Complete booklet, #4437b, 4727c   21.00

Evariste de Parny (1753-1814), Poet — A2448

2014, Nov. 7   Engr.   Perf. 13¼
4728   A2448   83c multi   2.10   .70

Republican Security Companies (Riot Control Forces), 70th Anniv. — A2449

2014, Dec. 8   Photo.   Perf. 13x12¾
4729   A2449   €1.10 multi   2.75   .90

Handicrafts A2450

Inscriptions: Nos. 4730, 4742, Pierres précieuses (jewelery making). No. 4731, Bois (sanding wood). No. 4732, Verre (glass making). No. 4733, Métal (blacksmithing). No. 4734, Tissu (embroidery). No. 4735, Terre (pottery making). No. 4736, Papier (paper making). No. 4737, Tissu (weaving). No. 4738, Cuir (leather work). No. 4739, Bois (barrel making). No. 4740, Pierre (sculpting). No. 4741, Végétal (flower arranging).

2015   Litho.   Serpentine Die Cut 11
Self-Adhesive
4730   A2450   (76c) multi   1.75   1.75

Photo.
Booklet Stamps

4731	A2450	(76c) multi	1.75	.60
4732	A2450	(76c) multi	1.75	.60
4733	A2450	(76c) multi	1.75	.60
4734	A2450	(76c) multi	1.75	.60
4735	A2450	(76c) multi	1.75	.60
4736	A2450	(76c) multi	1.75	.60
4737	A2450	(76c) multi	1.75	.60
4738	A2450	(76c) multi	1.75	.60
4739	A2450	(76c) multi	1.75	.60
4740	A2450	(76c) multi	1.75	.60
4741	A2450	(76c) multi	1.75	.60
4742	A2450	(76c) multi	1.75	.60
a.	Booklet pane of 12, #4731-4742		21.00	
	Nos. 4731-4742 (12)		21.00	7.20

No. 4730 has a visible dot pattern in the upper right part of the vignette and a sharper "Phil@poste" than No. 4742. Issued: Nos. 4730, 1/5; others 1/3.

Marianne and Children "Lettre Suivie" — A2450a

2015-16   Litho.   Die Cut
Self-Adhesive
4742B   A2450a (€1.08) red lilac + label, background dots close together   —   —
c.   red lilac, background dots farther apart   —   —
d.   €1.10 As "c," magenta   —   —
e.   lt magenta, finer background dots   —   —
f.   As "e," dots and circles in background, coarse portrait with jagged curved lines   —   —

Issued: No. 4742B, 1/1. No. 4742Bd, 1/1/16. Sheet margins differ. No. 4742B has a green panel at left and destination and date lines over green background. No. 4742Bc is like No. 4742B, but with destination and date lines over a white background. No. 4742Bd has a magenta panel at left with "Indemnisation**" and "€" at lower left. Nos. 4742Be and 4742Bf are like No. 4742Bd, but with "Epaisseur 3cm max" at lower left.

Art Issue

The Great Wave, by Katsushika Hokusai (1760-1849) A2451

2015, Jan. 16   Photo.   Perf. 13x13¼
4743   A2451   €1.90 multi   4.50   2.25

Hearts — A2452

"JC de Castelbajac," people kissing and: 68c, Hearts. €1.15, Flowers.

2015, Jan. 23   Photo.   Perf.
With White Frame Around Stamp
4744   A2452   68c multi   1.60   .55

708 FRANCE

Without White Frame Around Stamp
Perf. 13

| 4745 | A2452 | 68c multi | 1.60 | .55 |
| 4746 | A2452 | €1.15 multi | 2.60 | .85 |

Self-Adhesive
Serpentine Die Cut

| 4747 | A2452 | 68c multi | 1.60 | 1.60 |
| 4748 | A2452 | €1.15 multi | 2.60 | 2.60 |

No. 4744 was printed in sheets of 5. Values for Nos. 4745-4748 are for examples with surrounding selvage. Designs on Nos. 4745-4748 continue onto the surrounding selvage.

New Year 2015 (Year of the Goat) — A2453

2015, Jan. 30 Photo. *Perf. 13¼x13*
| 4749 | A2453 | 76c multi | 1.75 | .60 |

No. 4749 was printed in sheets of 5. A souvenir sheet of one sold for €3.20. See No. 4971c.

Drawings of Hands — A2454

Drawing by: No. 4750, Alphonse Legros. No. 4751, Unknown 18th century Italian School artist. No. 4752, Paul Delaroche. No. 4753, Gustave Moreau. No. 4754, Eugène Carrière. No. 4755, Pablo Picasso. No. 4756, Annibale Carrache. No. 4757, Unknown 17th century Italian School artist (four hands holding handles). No. 4758, Louis Tocque (one hand). No. 4759, Pierre Mignard. No. 4760, Tocque (two hands holding hoop with flowers). No. 4761, Unknown 17th Italian School artist (hand, water drop and goblet).

Serpentine Die Cut 11
2015, Jan. 30 Litho.
Booklet Stamps
Self-Adhesive

4750	A2454	(68c) multi	1.60	.55
4751	A2454	(68c) multi	1.60	.55
4752	A2454	(68c) multi	1.60	.55
4753	A2454	(68c) multi	1.60	.55
4754	A2454	(68c) multi	1.60	.55
4755	A2454	(68c) multi	1.60	.55
4756	A2454	(68c) multi	1.60	.55
4757	A2454	(68c) multi	1.60	.55
4758	A2454	(68c) multi	1.60	.55
4759	A2454	(68c) multi	1.60	.55
4760	A2454	(68c) multi	1.60	.55
4761	A2454	(68c) multi	1.60	.55
a.	Booklet pane of 12, #4750-4761		19.50	
Nos. 4750-4761 (12)			19.20	6.60

Landmine Removal Service, 70th Anniv. — A2455

2015, Feb. 20 Photo. *Perf. 13¼*
| 4762 | A2455 | €1.20 multi | 2.75 | .90 |

Goat Breeds — A2456

Inscriptions: No. 4763, La Créole. No. 4764, La Poitevine. No. 4765, L'Alpine. No. 4766, La Chèvre du Massif Central. No. 4767, La Lorraine. No. 4768, La Rove. No. 4769, La Chèvre des Fossés. No. 4770, La Saanen. No. 4771, La Pyrénéenne. No. 4772, L'Angora. No. 4773, La Provençale. No. 4774, La Corse.

Serpentine Die Cut 11
2015, Feb. 21 Photo.
Booklet Stamps
Self-Adhesive

4763	A2456	(68c) multi	1.50	.50
4764	A2456	(68c) multi	1.50	.50
4765	A2456	(68c) multi	1.50	.50
4766	A2456	(68c) multi	1.50	.50
4767	A2456	(68c) multi	1.50	.50
4768	A2456	(68c) multi	1.50	.50
4769	A2456	(68c) multi	1.50	.50
4770	A2456	(68c) multi	1.50	.50
4771	A2456	(68c) multi	1.50	.50
4772	A2456	(68c) multi	1.50	.50
4773	A2456	(68c) multi	1.50	.50
4774	A2456	(68c) multi	1.50	.50
a.	Booklet pane of 12, #4763-4774		18.00	
Nos. 4763-4774 (12)			18.00	6.00

Souvenir Sheet

Enamel Art of Léonard Limosin (c. 1505-77) — A2457

No. 4775: a, The Judgment of Paris. b, Eritrean Sibyl (Sybila Richea), vert.

Perf. 13x13¼, 13¼x13
2015, Feb. 27 Photo.
4775	A2457	Sheet of 2	8.50	8.50
a.-b.	€1.90 Either single		4.25	1.40
c.	Souvenir sheet of 2, #4775a-4775b, #4775a at right		14.00	14.00

No. 4775c sold for €6.20.

Souvenir Sheet

Basilica of Saint-Denis — A2458

No. 4776: a, Tombs (41x30mm). b, Stained-glass window (41x41mm).

2015, Mar. 14 Engr. *Perf. 13¼*
4776	A2458	Sheet of 2	4.50	4.50
a.	76c multi		1.75	.60
b.	€1.25 multi		2.75	.90

A souvenir sheet of 2, containing Nos. 4776a-4776b, with No. 4776a at left sold for €6.20.

Spring Philatelic Show, Paris A2459

2015, Mar. 19 Engr. *Perf. 13x12¾*
| 4777 | A2459 | 68c multi | 1.50 | .50 |

Belgian Government in Exile in Sainte-Adresse, Cent. — A2460

Mailboxes, Belgian government officials in exile and: 76c, French and Belgian flags, building. 95c, Ministerial residence.

2015, Mar. 19 Photo. *Perf. 13¼*
4778	A2460	76c multi	1.75	.60
4779	A2460	95c multi	2.10	.70
a.	Souvenir sheet of 2, #4778-4779		7.00	7.00

No. 4779a sold for €3.20. See Belgium No. 2748.

Art Issue

L'O, Light Sculpture by Yann Kersalé — A2461

2015, Mar. 20 Photo. *Perf. 13¼*
| 4780 | A2461 | €1.90 multi | 4.25 | 2.10 |

Nicole Mangin (1878-1919), World War I Physician — A2462

2015, Mar. 21 Engr. *Perf. 13x13¼*
| 4781 | A2462 | 68c multi | 1.50 | .50 |

Renaissance Architecture A2463

Designs: No. 4782, Château d'Amboise. No. 4783, Château de Valençay. No. 4784, Palais Ducal de Nevers. No. 4785, Château de Villandry. No. 4786, Château d'Ancy-le-Franc. No. 4787, Palais du Louvre. No. 4788, Château de Chambord. No. 4789, Château d'Ecouen. No. 4790, Château d'Azay-le-Rideau. No. 4791, Château de Chenonceau. No. 4792, Château d'Anet. No. 4793, Château de Blois.

Serpentine Die Cut 11
2015, Mar. 27 Litho.
Booklet Stamps
Self-Adhesive

4782	A2463	(68c) multi	1.50	.50
4783	A2463	(68c) multi	1.50	.50
4784	A2463	(68c) multi	1.50	.50
4785	A2463	(68c) multi	1.50	.50
4786	A2463	(68c) multi	1.50	.50
4787	A2463	(68c) multi	1.50	.50
4788	A2463	(68c) multi	1.50	.50
4789	A2463	(68c) multi	1.50	.50
4790	A2463	(68c) multi	1.50	.50
4791	A2463	(68c) multi	1.50	.50
4792	A2463	(68c) multi	1.50	.50
4793	A2463	(68c) multi	1.50	.50
a.	Booklet pane of 12, #4782-4793		18.00	
Nos. 4782-4793 (12)			18.00	6.00

Saintes-Maries-de-la-Mer Religious Procession, 700th Anniv. — A2464

2015, Mar. 29 Engr. *Perf. 13¼*
| 4794 | A2464 | 68c multi | 1.50 | .50 |

Miniature Sheet

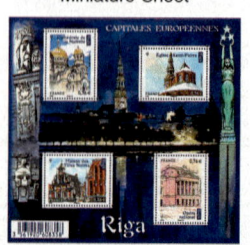

European Capitals — A2465

No. 4795 — Attractions in Riga, Latvia: a, Nativity Cathedral. b, St. Peter's Church, horiz. c, House of the Blackheads, horiz. d, National Opera.

Perf. 13¼x13, 13x13¼
2015, Apr. 3 Photo.
| 4795 | A2465 | Sheet of 4 | 7.00 | 7.00 |
| a.-d. | 76c Any single | | 1.75 | .60 |

Croix de Guerre, Cent. — A2466

2015, Apr. 8 Engr. *Perf. 13¼*
| 4796 | A2466 | 76c multi | 1.75 | .60 |

Souvenir Sheet

French History A2467

No. 4797: a, Coronation of Charlemagne, 768. b, Educational reforms of Charlemagne, 789, horiz.

Perf. 13¼x13, 13x13¼
2015, Apr. 10 Engr.
| 4797 | A2467 | Sheet of 2 | 8.50 | 8.50 |
| a.-b. | €1.90 Either single | | 4.25 | 1.40 |

French and Indian Cooperation in Space, 50th Anniv. — A2468

Designs: 76c, Saral satellite. €1.20, Megha-Tropiques satellite.

2015, Apr. 10 Photo. *Perf. 13¼*
| 4798 | A2468 | 76c multi | 1.75 | .60 |
| 4799 | A2468 | €1.20 multi | 2.75 | .90 |

See India Nos. 2725-2726.

Chalon-sur-Saône A2469

2015, Apr. 17 Engr. *Perf. 13¼*
| 4800 | A2469 | 68c multi | 1.60 | .55 |

Liberation of Concentration Camps, 70th Anniv. — A2470

2015, Apr. 24 Photo. *Perf. 13¼*
| 4801 | A2470 | 76c multi | 1.75 | .60 |

Miniature Sheet

Way of St. James A2471

No. 4802 — Sites in: a, Oloron-Sainte-Marie. b, Aire-sur l'Adour, vert. c, Saint-Jean-Pied-de Port. d, Blaye.

Litho. & Engr.
2015, Apr. 24 *Perf. 13*
| 4802 | A2471 | Sheet of 4 | 9.00 | 9.00 |
| a.-d. | 95c Any single | | 2.25 | .75 |

FRANCE

Europa — A2472

2015, May 2   **Photo.**   **Perf. 13¼**
4803   A2472   95c multi   2.25   .75

Paintings of Flowers — A2473

Designs: No. 4804, Irises and Red Geraniums, by Paul Cézanne. No. 4805, Peonies, by Paul Gauguin. No. 4806, Carnations, by Jeanne Magnin. No. 4807, Wisteria, by Pierre Bracquemond. No. 4808, Daisies and Hydrangea, by Emile Boutin. No. 4809, Roses and Anémones, by Vincent van Gogh. No. 4810, Gladioluses, by Auguste Renoir. No. 4811, Wildflowers by Odilon Redon. No. 4812, Peonies, by Edouard Manet. No. 4813, Roses, by Gustave Caillebotte. No. 4814, Queens Daisies, by Marie Duhem. No. 4815, Roses, by Henri Fantin-Latour.

Serpentine Die Cut 11
2015, May 2   **Litho.**
Booklet Stamps
Self-Adhesive
4804   A2473   (68c) multi   1.60   .55
4805   A2473   (68c) multi   1.60   .55
4806   A2473   (68c) multi   1.60   .55
4807   A2473   (68c) multi   1.60   .55
4808   A2473   (68c) multi   1.60   .55
4809   A2473   (68c) multi   1.60   .55
4810   A2473   (68c) multi   1.60   .55
4811   A2473   (68c) multi   1.60   .55
4812   A2473   (68c) multi   1.60   .55
4813   A2473   (68c) multi   1.60   .55
4814   A2473   (68c) multi   1.60   .55
4815   A2473   (68c) multi   1.60   .55
   a.   Booklet pane of 12, #4804-4815   19.50
   Nos. 4804-4815 (12)   19.20   6.60

Victory in World War II, 70th Anniv. — A2474

2015, May 7   **Photo.**   **Perf. 13¼**
4816   A2474   68c multi   1.50   .50

Marshal Jacques II de Chabannes, Lord of La Palice (1470-1525) — A2475

2015, May 15   **Engr.**   **Perf. 13¼**
4817   A2475   76c multi   1.75   .60

Mâcon A2476

2015, May 22   **Engr.**   **Perf. 13x13¼**
4818   A2476   68c multi + label   1.50   .50
French Federation of Philatelic Associations, 88th Congress, Mâcon.

17th World Convention of Rose Societies, Lyon — A2477

Designs: 76c, Red and pink roses. €1.20, Pink and yellow roses.

2015, May 29   **Photo.**   **Perf. 13¼**
4819   A2477   76c multi   1.75   .60
4820   A2477   €1.20 multi   2.75   .90
   a.   Horiz. pair, #4819-4820   4.50   2.25

A souvenir sheet containing Nos. 4819-4820 sold for €6.20.

Service Central d'Etat Civil, 50th Anniv. — A2478

2015, June 6   **Engr.**   **Perf. 13¼**
4821   A2478   €1.25 multi   2.75   .90

The 1960's A2479

No. 4822: a, Radio France Headquarters. b, Men and women dancing, vert. c, Movie poster for *Les Demoiselles de Rochefort*, vert. d, 1961 Peugeot 404 convertible. e, Ocean liner SS France. f, Women wearing short dresses, vert.

2015, June 12   **Photo.**   **Perf. 13**
4822   A2479   Sheet of 6   10.50   10.50
   a.-f.   76c Any single   1.75   .60

Hartmannswillerkopf National Monument — A2480

2015, June 19   **Engr.**   **Perf. 13¼**
4823   A2480   95c multi   2.10   .70

Saint-Martial Church, Lestards A2481

2015, June 24   **Engr.**   **Perf. 13¼**
4824   A2481   68c multi   1.50   .50

A2482   A2483

A2484

A2485

A2486   A2487

A2488

A2489

A2490

A2491

A2492

Vacations A2493

Serpentine Die Cut 11
2015, June 29   **Photo.**
Booklet Stamps
Self-Adhesive
4825   A2482   (68c) multi   1.50   .50
4826   A2483   (68c) multi   1.50   .50
4827   A2484   (68c) multi   1.50   .50
4828   A2485   (68c) multi   1.50   .50
4829   A2486   (68c) multi   1.50   .50
4830   A2487   (68c) multi   1.50   .50
4831   A2488   (68c) multi   1.50   .50
4832   A2489   (68c) multi   1.50   .50
4833   A2490   (68c) multi   1.50   .50
4834   A2491   (68c) multi   1.50   .50
4835   A2492   (68c) multi   1.50   .50
4836   A2493   (68c) multi   1.50   .50
   a.   Booklet pane of 12, #4825-4836   18.00
   Nos. 4825-4836 (12)   18.00   6.00

Haguenau, 900th Anniv. — A2494

2015, July 3   **Engr.**   **Perf. 13¼**
4837   A2494   68c multi   1.50   .50

Martin Nadaud (1815-98), Mason and Politician A2495

2015, July 3   **Engr.**   **Perf. 13¼**
4838   A2495   68c multi   1.50   .50

Gilberto Bosques (1892-1995), Mexican Diplomat Who Saved Jews In World War II — A2496

Bosques and: 76c, Notre Dame de la Garde Basilica, Marseilles, and signed travel visa. €1.20, Embassy, Mexican consular handstamp.

2015, July 16   **Litho.**   **Perf. 13**
4839   A2496   76c multi   1.75   .60
4840   A2496   €1.20 multi   2.75   .90
   a.   Horiz. pair, #4839-4840   4.50   2.25

See Mexico Nos. 2940-2941.

Animal Eyes — A2497

Eye of: No. 4841, Requin à aileron blanc du lagon (whitetip reef shark). No. 4842, Petit-duc du Grant (southern white-faced owl). No. 4843, Rainette à yeux rouges (red-eyed tree frog). No. 4844, Toucan. No. 4845, Coq de race Brahma (Brahma chicken). No. 4846, Agame (agama lizard). No. 4847, Ara hyacinthe (hyacinth macaw). No. 4848, Iguane des Fidji (Fiji banded iguana). No. 4849, Tarente géante (giant wall gecko). No. 4850, Serpentaire (serpent eagle). No. 4851, Poisson-lime gribouillé (scrawled filefish). No. 4852, Gypaète barbu (bearded vulture).

Serpentine Die Cut 11
2015, July 31   **Photo.**
Booklet Stamps
Self-Adhesive
4841   A2497   (76c) multi   1.75   .60
4842   A2497   (76c) multi   1.75   .60
4843   A2497   (76c) multi   1.75   .60
4844   A2497   (76c) multi   1.75   .60
4845   A2497   (76c) multi   1.75   .60
4846   A2497   (76c) multi   1.75   .60
4847   A2497   (76c) multi   1.75   .60
4848   A2497   (76c) multi   1.75   .60
4849   A2497   (76c) multi   1.75   .60
4850   A2497   (76c) multi   1.75   .60
4851   A2497   (76c) multi   1.75   .60
4852   A2497   (76c) multi   1.75   .60
   a.   Booklet pane of 12, #4841-4852   21.00
   Nos. 4841-4852 (12)   21.00   7.20

Animal Proverbs and Idioms — A2498

Designs: No. 4853, Un froid de canard ("Freezing cold"). No. 4854, Rire comme une baleine ("Laughing like a whale"). No. 4855, Comme un chien dans un jeu de quilles ("Like a bull in a China shop"). No. 4856, Prendre le taureau par les cornes ("Take the bull by the horns"). No. 4857, Fier comme un paon ("Proud as a peacock"). No. 4858, Donner de la confiture aux cochons ("Cast pearls before swine"). No. 4859, Avoir un appétit d'oiseau ("Have the appetite of a bird"). No. 4860, Donner sa langue au chat ("Cat got your tongue?"). No. 4861, Etre le bouc émissaire ("Be the scapegoat"). No. 4862, Faire le pied de grue ("To cool one's heels"). No. 4863, Araignée du soir espoir ("A spider in the evening, hope"). No. 4864, Poser un lapin ("To stand someone up").

Serpentine Die Cut 11
2015, Aug. 28   **Photo.**
Booklet Stamps
Self-Adhesive
4853   A2498   (68c) multi   1.60   .55
4854   A2498   (68c) multi   1.60   .55
4855   A2498   (68c) multi   1.60   .55
4856   A2498   (68c) multi   1.60   .55
4857   A2498   (68c) multi   1.60   .55
4858   A2498   (68c) multi   1.60   .55
4859   A2498   (68c) multi   1.60   .55
4860   A2498   (68c) multi   1.60   .55
4861   A2498   (68c) multi   1.60   .55
4862   A2498   (68c) multi   1.60   .55
4863   A2498   (68c) multi   1.60   .55
4864   A2498   (68c) multi   1.60   .55
   a.   Booklet pane of 12, #4853-4864   19.50
   Nos. 4853-4864 (12)   19.20   6.60

Compare types A2498 and A2297.

710 FRANCE

Souvenir Sheet

Battle of Huningue, 200th Anniv. — A2499

2015, Aug. 29	Photo.	Perf. 13¼
4865 A2499 €1.25 multi		3.00 1.00

2015 World Rowing Championships, Aiguebelette — A2500

Boat with: 76c, Two female rowers. €1.20, Male rowers (35x26mm).

2015, Aug. 30	Photo.	Perf. 13x13¼
4866 A2500 76c multi		1.75 .60
4867 A2500 €1.20 multi		2.75 .90
a. Horiz. pair, #4866-4867		4.50 2.25

Marianne and Children "Europe" With Data Matrix Code — A2501

Marianne and Children "Monde" With Data Matrix Code — A2502

2015, Sept. 4	Engr.	Perf. 13
4868 A2501 (95c) blue		2.25 .75
4869 A2502 (€1.20) purple		2.75 .90

Self-Adhesive
Serpentine Die Cut 6¾ Vert.

4870 A2501 (95c) blue	2.25 .75
a. Booklet pane of 6	13.50
4871 A2502 (€1.20) purple	2.75 .90

The Data Matrix codes on types A2501 and A2502 differ, but all examples of stamps of either type have identical codes. Compare with Types A2538-A2539.

Art Issue

Woman with White Stockings, by Suzanne Valadon (1865-1938) A2503

2015, Sept. 18	Photo.	Perf. 13¼x13
4872 A2503 €1.90 multi		4.25 2.10

Freedom, Equality, Fraternity, Painting by Jonone in National Assembly — A2504

2015, Sept. 19	Photo.	Perf. 13¼
4873 A2504 76c multi		1.75 .60

Landing of French on Mauritius, 300th Anniv. — A2505

2015, Sept. 25	Photo.	Perf. 13¼
4874 A2505 76c multi		1.75 .60

See Mauritius No. 1147.

Sense of Sight — A2506

Designs: No. 4875, Room with a window (Chambre avec vue). No. 4876, Eye chart (A ma vue). No. 4877, Land in sight (Terre en vue). No. 4878, Eye (A vue d'oeil). No. 4879, Sun on horizon (Déjà vue). No. 4880, Women viewed through binoculars (Jumelles en vue). No. 4881, Planets (Vue imprenable). No. 4882, Nose and butterfly (A vue de nez). No. 4883, Diver and pool (Vue plongeante). No. 4884, Clouds (A perte de vue). No. 4885, Woman wearing mask (Ni vue, ni connue). No. 4886, Ghost and pink flying elephant (Vue de l'esprit).

Serpentine Die Cut 11

2015, Sept. 25		Photo.

Booklet Stamps
Self-Adhesive

4875 A2506 (68c) multi	1.60 .55
4876 A2506 (68c) multi	1.60 .55
4877 A2506 (68c) multi	1.60 .55
4878 A2506 (68c) multi	1.60 .55
4879 A2506 (68c) multi	1.60 .55
4880 A2506 (68c) multi	1.60 .55
4881 A2506 (68c) multi	1.60 .55
4882 A2506 (68c) multi	1.60 .55
4883 A2506 (68c) multi	1.60 .55
4884 A2506 (68c) multi	1.60 .55
4885 A2506 (68c) multi	1.60 .55
4886 A2506 (68c) multi	1.60 .55
a. Booklet pane of 12, #4875-4886	19.50
Nos. 4875-4886 (12)	19.20 6.60

Jean-Henri Fabre (1823-1915), Entomologist — A2507

2015, Oct. 2	Litho.	Perf. 13¼
4887 A2507 €2.60 multi		6.00 2.00

A souvenir sheet of one of No. 4887 sold for €6.20.

A2508

Design: Pierre Laroque (1907-97), Director of Social Security, and Ambroise Croizat (1901-51), Politician.

2015, Oct. 6	Photo.	Perf. 13x13¼
4888 A2508 68c multi		1.50 .50

French Social Security System, 70th anniv.

Tango Dancers — A2509

Ballet Preljocaj A2510

2015, Oct. 10	Litho. & Engr.	Perf. 13¼
4889 A2509 68c multi		1.50 .50

Photo.
Souvenir Sheet

4890 A2510 €1.15 multi	2.60 .85

Stamp Day. A souvenir sheet of one No. 4889 was produced in 2016 and sold for €3.20.

Saint-Gobain Corporation, 350th Anniv. — A2511

2015, Oct. 14	Litho. & Engr.	Perf. 13¼
4891 A2511 68c multi		1.50 .50

Laure Diebold-Mutschler (1915-65), Resistance Leader in World War II — A2512

2015, Oct. 16	Engr.	Perf. 13¼
4892 A2512 68c multi		1.50 .50

A2513   A2514

A2515   A2516

A2517   A2518

A2519   A2520

A2521   A2522

A2523   Happy New Year — A2524

Serpentine Die Cut 11

2015, Oct. 30		Photo.

Booklet Stamps
Self-Adhesive

4893 A2513 (68c) multi	1.50 .50
4894 A2514 (68c) multi	1.50 .50
4895 A2515 (68c) multi	1.50 .50
4896 A2516 (68c) multi	1.50 .50
4897 A2517 (68c) multi	1.50 .50
4898 A2518 (68c) multi	1.50 .50
4899 A2519 (68c) multi	1.50 .50
4900 A2520 (68c) multi	1.50 .50
4901 A2521 (68c) multi	1.50 .50
4902 A2522 (68c) multi	1.50 .50
4903 A2523 (68c) multi	1.50 .50
4904 A2524 (68c) multi	1.50 .50
a. Booklet pane of 12, #4893-4904	18.00
Nos. 4893-4904 (12)	18.00 6.00

A souvenir sheet containing one perf. 12¾ example of a stamp like No. 4902 sold for €3.20.

Types of 1944-45 with Denominations in Euro Currency and Types of 2005-06

2015, Nov. 5	Engr.	Perf. 13x12¾
4905 A144 €1 dark blue		2.10 .70

Perf. 12¾x13

4906 A147 €1 dark blue	2.10 .70

Perf. 13

4907 A151 €4 dark blue	8.50 2.60
Nos. 4905-4907 (3)	12.70 4.00

Booklet Stamps

4908 A147 76c red, 15x19mm design	1.60 .55
4909 A144 76c red, 15x19mm design	1.60 .55
a. Booklet pane of 2, #4908-4909	3.25 —
4910 A1814 76c red	1.60 .55
4911 A1759 76c red	1.60 .55
a. Booklet pane of 12, 6 each #4910-4911	19.50 —
Complete booklet, #4909a, 4911a	23.00
Nos. 4908-4911 (4)	6.40 2.20

Nos. 4905-4907 were printed in sheets of 14 containing 6 each Nos. 4905-4906 and 2 No. 4907.

Tapestry Depicting the Sacrifice of Abraham A2525

Unicorn Hide, Tapetry by Nicolas Buffe A2526

2015, Nov. 6	Litho.	Perf. 13

Flocked Paper

4912 A2525 76c multi	1.60 .55
4913 A2526 €1.20 multi	2.60 .85
a. Horiz. pair, #4912-4913, + central label	4.25 1.40

Aubusson, International City of Tapestries.

FRANCE

Miniature Sheet

Music Boxes A2527

No. 4914 — Inscriptions: a, La pendule à orgues. b, La leçon de chant. c, L'automate magicien. d, Boîte à musique danseuse. e, L'oiseau chanteur, horiz. f, La joueuse de typanon.

Litho. & Engr.
2015, Nov. 6   Perf. 13
4914 A2527 Sheet of 6   9.00   9.00
  a.-f. 68c Any single   1.50   .50

Nos. 4914a-4914f were each printed in souvenir sheets containing one stamp that sold as a set for €16.

Souvenir Sheet

Roland Barthes (1915-80), Semiotician — A2528

2015, Nov. 12   Engr.   Perf. 13¼
4915 A2528 €1.15 multi   2.50   .85

Roosters — A2529

Designs: No. 4916, Coq gaulois. No. 4917: a, Coq de Houdan. b, Coq meusien. c, Coq de Marans.

2015, Nov. 13   Photo.   Perf. 13¼
4916 A2529 68c multi   1.50   .50
4917   Sheet of 4, #4916, 4917a-4917c   6.00   6.00
  a.-c. A2529 68c Any single   1.50   .50

Two souvenir sheets, one containing Nos. 4916 and 4917b, and the other containing Nos. 4917a and 4917c, sold as a set for €6.20.

National Forestry Office, 50th Anniv. — A2530

2015, Nov. 20   Photo.   Perf. 13¼
4918 A2530 68c multi   1.50   .50

COP21 Climate Conference, Paris — A2531

2015, Nov. 24   Photo.   Perf. 13¼
4919 A2531 (€1.20) multi   2.60   .85

Values are for stamps with surrounding selvage.

Launch of Astérix Satellite, 50th Anniv. A2532

2015, Nov. 26   Photo.   Perf. 13¼
4920 A2532 68c multi   1.50   .50
  a. Tete-beche pair   3.00   1.00

A €1.16 stamp of type A2532 was included in a limited-edition booklet issued Nov. 4, 2020.

City Halls — A2533

City Hall in: No. 4921, La Pernelle. No. 4922, Brunstatt. No. 4923, Chambourcy. No. 4924, Châteaugiron. No. 4925, Sennecey-le-Grand. No. 4926, Saint-Nicolas-de-la-Grave. No. 4927, Caudebec-en-Caux. No. 4928, Cercy-la-Tour. No. 4929, Clamart. No. 4930, Créteil. No. 4931, Toul. No. 4932, Le Pêchereau.

Serpentine Die Cut 11
2015, Dec. 10   Photo.
Booklet Stamps
Self-Adhesive
4921 A2533 (70c) multi   1.60   .55
4922 A2533 (70c) multi   1.60   .55
4923 A2533 (70c) multi   1.60   .55
4924 A2533 (70c) multi   1.60   .55
4925 A2533 (70c) multi   1.60   .55
4926 A2533 (70c) multi   1.60   .55
4927 A2533 (70c) multi   1.60   .55
4928 A2533 (70c) multi   1.60   .55
4929 A2533 (70c) multi   1.60   .55
4930 A2533 (70c) multi   1.60   .55
4931 A2533 (70c) multi   1.60   .55
4932 A2533 (70c) multi   1.60   .55
  a. Booklet pane of 12, #4921-4932   19.50
Nos. 4921-4932 (12)   19.20   6.60

Marianne and Children, "Ecopli" Without Gram Limit Inscription A2534

Marianne and Tree, "Lettre Vorto" Without Gram Limit Inscription A2535

Marianne and Children, "Lettre Prioritaire" Without Gram Limit Inscription — A2536

2016, Jan. 1   Engr.   Perf. 13
4933 A2534 (68c) gray black   1.50   .30
4934 A2535 (70c) emerald   1.60   .35
4935 A2536 (80c) red   1.75   .45
Nos. 4933-4935 (3)   4.85   1.10

Coil Stamps
Perf. 13 Horiz.
4936 A2535 (70c) green   1.60   .35
4937 A2536 (80c) red   1.75   .45

Self-Adhesive
Serpentine Die Cut 6¾ Vert.
4938 A2534 (68c) gray black   1.50   .30
4939 A2535 (70c) emerald   1.60   .35
  a. Booklet pane of 10   16.00
  b. Booklet pane of 12   19.50
4940 A2536 (80c) scarlet   1.75   .45
  a. Booklet pane of 10   17.50
  b. Booklet pane of 12   21.00
  c. Booklet pane of 20   35.00
Nos. 4938-4940 (3)   4.85   1.10

Compare with types A2321, A2322 and A2325. See No. B775.

Marianne and Children "Europe" With Data Matrix Code Without Gram Limit Inscription A2538

Marianne and Children "Monde" With Data Matrix Code Without Gram Limit Inscription A2539

2016, Jan. 1   Engr.   Perf. 13
4942 A2538 (€1) blue   2.25   .75
4943 A2539 (€1.25) purple   2.75   .90

Self-Adhesive
Serpentine Die Cut 6¾ Vert.
4944 A2538 (€1) multi   2.25   .75
  a. Booklet pane of 6   —
4945 A2539 (€1.25) dp reddish vio   2.75   .90

Compare with types A2501-A2502. Data Matrix codes differ on types A2501 and A2538, and on types A2502 and A2539.

Minerals — A2540

Designs: No. 4946, Gold (or). No. 4947, Labradorite. No. 4948, Topaz (topaze). No. 4949, Amethyst (amethyste). No. 4950, Olivine. No. 4951, Quartz. No. 4952, Turquoise. No. 4953, Fluorite. No. 4954, Sulfur (soufre). No. 4955, Ruby (rubis). No. 4956, Silver (argent). No. 4957, Copper (cuivre).

Serpentine Die Cut 11
2016, Jan. 7   Photo.
Booklet Stamps
Self-Adhesive
4946 A2540 (80c) multi   1.75   .60
4947 A2540 (80c) multi   1.75   .60
4948 A2540 (80c) multi   1.75   .60
4949 A2540 (80c) multi   1.75   .60
4950 A2540 (80c) multi   1.75   .60
4951 A2540 (80c) multi   1.75   .60
4952 A2540 (80c) multi   1.75   .60
4953 A2540 (80c) multi   1.75   .60
4954 A2540 (80c) multi   1.75   .60
4955 A2540 (80c) multi   1.75   .60
4956 A2540 (80c) multi   1.75   .60
4957 A2540 (80c) multi   1.75   .60
  a. Booklet pane of 12, #4946-4957   21.00
Nos. 4946-4957 (12)   21.00   7.20

Winning Designs in Children's Stamp Design Contest — A2543

A2541   A2542

2016, Jan. 11   Photo.   Perf. 13¼
4958 A2541 70c multi   1.60   .55
4959 A2542 70c multi   1.60   .55
4960 A2543 70c multi   1.60   .55
  a. Horiz. strip of 3, #4958-4960   5.00   1.75
Nos. 4958-4960 (3)   4.80   1.65

Hearts — A2544

"Courrèges" and: Nos. 4961, 4965, Light blue heart, bright pink denomination. No. 4962, No. 4966, White heart, slate denomination.

No. 4963 — "Courrèges," light blue heart and denomination in: a, Pale yellow. b, Light blue. c, Dark blue. d, Bright orange.
No. 4964 — "Courrèges," and heart in: a, Bright pink. b, Bright green. c, Bright yellow. d, Dark blue. e, Bright orange.

Photo., Litho. (#4964)
2016   Perf. 13
4961 A2544 70c multi   1.60   .55
4962 A2544 €1.40 multi   3.25   1.10
Perf.
4963   Sheet of 5, #4961, 4963a-4963d   8.00   8.00
  a.-d. A2544 70c Any single   1.60   .55
4964   Sheet of 5   34.00   34.00
  a.-e. A2544 €3 Any single   6.75   3.50
Self-Adhesive
Serpentine Die Cut
4965 A2544 70c multi   1.60   .55
4966 A2544 €1.40 multi   3.25   1.10

Issued: Nos. 4964, 5/19; others, 1/15. Values for Nos. 4961-4962 are for stamps with surrounding selvage.

Art Issue

Black, Red Over Black on Red, by Mark Rothko (1903-70) A2545

2016, Jan. 22   Photo.   Perf. 13¼x13
4967 A2545 €1.60 multi   3.50   1.75

New Year Types of 2005-15 and

New Year 2016 (Year of the Monkey) — A2546

2016, Jan. 29   Photo.   Perf. 13¼x13
4968 A2546 80c multi   1.75   .60
4969   Sheet of 4   8.75   8.75
  a. A1716 80c multi   2.10   2.10
  b. A1766 80c multi   2.10   2.10
  c. A1822 80c multi   2.10   2.10
  d. A1882 80c multi   2.10   2.10
4970   Sheet of 4   8.75   8.75
  a. A1962 80c multi   2.10   2.10
  b. A2040 80c multi   2.10   2.10
  c. A2133 80c multi   2.10   2.10
  d. A2209 80c multi   2.10   2.10
4971   Sheet of 4, #4968, 4971a-4971c   8.75   8.75
  a. A2277 80c multi   2.10   2.10
  b. A2373 80c multi   2.10   2.10
  c. A2453 80c multi   2.10   2.10
Nos. 4969-4971 (3)   26.25   26.25

No. 4900 was printed in sheets of 5. A souvenir sheet of 1 #4968 sold for €3.20. Nos. 4969-4971 sold as a set for €12.

Sense of Hearing — A2549

Ear, playback buttons and: No. 4972, Cricket. No. 4973, Various insects. No. 4974, Man's head and singing angels. No. 4975, Marbles rolling down stairs. No. 4976, Pinball game. No. 4977, Water drip. No. 4978, Bird. No. 4979, Lion. No. 4980, Musicians. No. 4981, Sea shell. No. 4982, Harp, lyre, hands, butterflies and flowers. No. 4983, Children.

Serpentine Die Cut 11
2016, Jan. 30   Litho.
Booklet Stamps
Self-Adhesive
4972 A2549 (70c) multi   1.60   .55
4973 A2549 (70c) multi   1.60   .55
4974 A2549 (70c) multi   1.60   .55
4975 A2549 (70c) multi   1.60   .55
4976 A2549 (70c) multi   1.60   .55
4977 A2549 (70c) multi   1.60   .55
4978 A2549 (70c) multi   1.60   .55
4979 A2549 (70c) multi   1.60   .55
4980 A2549 (70c) multi   1.60   .55
4981 A2549 (70c) multi   1.60   .55
4982 A2549 (70c) multi   1.60   .55

FRANCE

4983	A2549	(70c) multi	1.60	.55
a.	Booklet pane of 12, #4972-4983		19.50	
	Nos. 4972-4983 (12)		19.20	6.60

Marguerite Long (1874-1966), Pianist — A2550

2016, Feb. 12   Engr.   Perf. 13¼
| 4984 | A2550 | 70c multi | 1.50 | .50 |

Art Issue

Annie Hall, by Jan Toorop (1858-1928) A2551

2016, Feb. 19   Litho.   Perf. 13
| 4985 | A2551 | €2.80 multi | 6.25 | 3.25 |

Georges Charpak (1924-2010), 1992 Nobel Laureate in Physics — A2552

2016, Feb. 26   Engr.   Perf. 13¼
| 4986 | A2552 | 70c gold & multi | 1.50 | .50 |

Roosters — A2557

Inscriptions: No. 4987, Coq Barbezieux. No. 4988, Coq Bourbonnais. No. 4989, Coq Gaulois. No. 4990, Coq Gournay. No. 4991, Coc Coucou de Rennes. No. 4992, Coq Faverolles. No. 4993, Coq d'Alsace. No. 4994, Coq Bresse. No. 4995, Coq Meusien. No. 4996, Coq Marans. No. 4997, Coq Gâtinais. No. 4998, Coq La Flèche.

Serpentine Die Cut 11
2016, Feb. 27   Photo.
Booklet Stamps
Self-Adhesive
4987	A2557	(70c) multi	1.50	.50
4988	A2557	(70c) multi	1.50	.50
4989	A2557	(70c) multi	1.50	.50
4990	A2557	(70c) multi	1.50	.50
4991	A2557	(70c) multi	1.50	.50
4992	A2557	(70c) multi	1.50	.50
4993	A2557	(70c) multi	1.50	.50
4994	A2557	(70c) multi	1.50	.50
4995	A2557	(70c) multi	1.50	.50
4996	A2557	(70c) multi	1.50	.50
4997	A2557	(70c) multi	1.50	.50
4998	A2557	(70c) multi	1.50	.50
a.	Booklet pane of 12, #4987-4998		18.00	
	Nos. 4987-4998 (12)		18.00	6.00

Pierre Messmer (1916-2007), Prime Minister — A2558

2016, Mar. 11   Engr.   Perf. 13¼
| 4999 | A2558 | 80c multi | 1.90 | .65 |

Sophie Germain (1776-1831), Mathematician A2559

2016, Mar. 18   Engr.   Perf. 13¼
| 5000 | A2559 | 70c multi | 1.60 | .55 |

Notre-Dame-des-Missions Church, Epinay-sur-Seine — A2560

2016, Mar. 18   Engr.   Perf. 13¼
| 5001 | A2560 | 70c multi | 1.60 | .55 |

Auteuil Apprentices, 150th Anniv. — A2561

2016, Mar. 18   Photo.   Perf. 13¼
| 5002 | A2561 | 70c multi | 1.60 | .55 |

2016 European Soccer Championships, France — A2562

2016   Photo.   Perf. 13
5003	A2562	€1 multi	2.25	.75
a.	Souvenir sheet of 5	11.50	11.50
5004	A2562	€2 multi	4.50	2.25

Issued: No. 5003, 3/26; No. 5004, 5/19. Values are for stamps with surrounding selvage. No. 5004 was printed in sheets of 5 and has varnish covering the trophy in the design.

Sculptor A2563

2016, Mar. 31   Engr.   Perf. 12¼
| 5005 | A2563 | 70c multi | 1.60 | .55 |

Spring Philatelic Show, Belfort A2564

2016, Apr. 1   Engr.   Perf. 13x12¾
| 5006 | A2564 | 70c multi | 1.60 | .55 |

Portraits — A2565

Designs: No. 5007, Portrait of a Young Boy, by Paul Gauguin. No. 5008, Portrait of the Artist's Son, by Paul Cézanne. No. 5009, Young Woman Wearing a Black Hat, by Pierre-Auguste Renoir. No. 5010, Young Woman with a Low-cut Dress and Flower in Hair, by Berthe Morisot. No. 5011, Margot Lux with a Wide Hat, by Mary Cassatt. No. 5012, Portrait of Irma Brunner, La Viennoise, by Edouard Manet. No. 5013, Portrait of Léon Bonnat, by Edgar Degas. No. 5014, Self-portrait, by Gustave Caillebotte. No. 5015, Portrait of a Young Girl, by Armand Guillaumin. No. 5016, Self-portrait, by Vincent van Gogh. No. 5017, Portrait of Blanche Hoschedé, by Claude Monet. No. 5018, Woman with a Green Scarf, by Camille Pissarro.

Serpentine Die Cut 11
2016, Apr. 2   Litho.
Booklet Stamps
Self-Adhesive
5007	A2565	(70c) multi	1.60	.55
5008	A2565	(70c) multi	1.60	.55
5009	A2565	(70c) multi	1.60	.55
5010	A2565	(70c) multi	1.60	.55
5011	A2565	(70c) multi	1.60	.55
5012	A2565	(70c) multi	1.60	.55
5013	A2565	(70c) multi	1.60	.55
5014	A2565	(70c) multi	1.60	.55
5015	A2565	(70c) multi	1.60	.55
5016	A2565	(70c) multi	1.60	.55
5017	A2565	(70c) multi	1.60	.55
5018	A2565	(70c) multi	1.60	.55
a.	Booklet pane of 12, #5007-5018		19.50	
	Nos. 5007-5018 (12)		19.20	6.60

National Center of Costume and Scenography, Moulins — A2566

Litho. & Engr.
2016, Apr. 8   Perf. 13x13¼
| 5019 | A2566 | 80c multi | 1.90 | .65 |

A souvenir sheet containing No. 5019 sold for €3.20.

Edmond Locard (1877-1966), Forensic Scientist — A2567

2016, Apr. 15   Engr.   Perf. 13¼
| 5020 | A2567 | 70c multi | 1.60 | .55 |

Marquis de Jouffroy d'Abbans (1751-1832) and Steamboat A2568

2016, Apr. 22   Engr.   Perf. 13¼
| 5021 | A2568 | €1.25 red & blue | 3.00 | 1.00 |

Steamboat navigation on the Seine, 200th anniv.

Deposits and Consignments Fund, 200th Anniv. — A2569

Engr. & Embossed
2016, Apr. 28   Perf. 13¼
| 5022 | A2569 | 80c black & red | 1.90 | .60 |

A self-adhesive version of this stamp on a cream-colored paper was printed in sheets of 4 that were produced in limited quantities.

Europa — A2570

2016, May 8   Photo.   Perf. 13¼
| 5023 | A2570 | €1 multi | 2.25 | .75 |

Think Green Issue.

Saint-Brevin-les-Pins — A2571

2016, May 13   Photo.   Perf. 13¼
| 5024 | A2571 | 70c multi | 1.60 | .55 |

Soccer Plays — A2572

Inscriptions: No. 5025, Frappe (kick). No. 5026, Coup du sombrero (heading ball). No. 5027, Amorti poitrine (chest stop). No. 5028, Coup franc laucarne (corner kick). No. 5029, Reprise de volée (volley). No. 5030, Aile de pigeon (pigeon wing). No. 5031, Arrêt gardien (goalie's save). No. 5032, Coup du foulard (behind-the-planted-leg kick). No. 5033, Coup de pied retourné (bicycle kick). No. 5034, Joueuse qui gagne (winning player).

Serpentine Die Cut 11
2016, May 19   Litho.
Booklet Stamps
Self-Adhesive
5025	A2572	(70c) multi	1.60	.55
5026	A2572	(70c) multi	1.60	.55
5027	A2572	(70c) multi	1.60	.55
5028	A2572	(70c) multi	1.60	.55
5029	A2572	(70c) multi	1.60	.55
5030	A2572	(70c) multi	1.60	.55
5031	A2572	(70c) multi	1.60	.55
5032	A2572	(70c) multi	1.60	.55
5033	A2572	(70c) multi	1.60	.55
5034	A2572	(70c) multi	1.60	.55
a.	Booklet pane of 10, #5025-5034		16.00	
	Nos. 5025-5034 (10)		16.00	5.50

Types of 1947-78
Souvenir Sheet
Engr., Sheet Margin Photo. & Embossed With Foil Application
2016, May 19   Perf. 13
5035	Sheet of 3	13.50	13.50
a.	A169 €2 blue	4.50	2.25
b.	A791 €2 gray & dull brown	4.50	2.25
c.	SP171 €2 gray black	4.50	2.25

2016 Paris-Philex Stamp Show.

Bees — A2573

Inscriptions: No. 5036, Collète. No. 5037: a, Osmie, vert. b, Anthophore. c, Mégachile, vert.

2016, May 20   Photo.   Perf. 13¼
5036	A2573	70c multi	1.60	.55
5037	Sheet of 4, #5036, 5037a-5073c	6.50	6.50
a.-c.	A2573 70c Any single	1.60	.55

Two souvenir sheets, one containing Nos. 5036 and 5037a, and the other containing Nos. 5037b and 5037c, sold as a set for €6.20.

Place des Vosges, Paris A2574

2016, May 21   Engr.   Perf. 13x13¼
| 5038 | A2574 | 70c multi + label | 1.60 | .55 |

French Federation of Philatelic Associations, 89th Congress, Paris.

FRANCE

Miniature Sheet

The 1970's A2575

No. 5039: a, Renault 5 automobile. b, Women's fashions, vert. c, Skiers, chair lift and resort, vert. d, L'île aux Enfants children's televison show. e, Parc des Princes Stadium, Paris. f, People dancing at discotheque, vert.

2016, May 21 Photo. Perf. 13
5039 A2575 Sheet of 6   11.50 11.50
  a.-f.   80c Any single   1.90 .60

Louise Labé (c. 1524-1566), Poet — A2576

2016, May 22 Engr. Perf. 13x13¼
5040 A2576 €1.40 multi   3.25 1.10

Battle of Verdun, Cent. A2577

Litho. & Engr.
2016, May 29 Perf. 13x12¾
5041 A2577 70c multi   1.60 .55

A souvenir sheet containing No. 5041 sold for €3.20. A souvenir sheet issued in 2017 containing No. 5041, a denominated proof of No. 5041 with black, brown and yellow inks, and a non-denominated proof of No. 5041 with red, yellow and blue inks sold for €6.20.

Saint-Etienne School of Mines, 200th Anniv. — A2578

2016, June 3 Engr. Perf. 13¼
5042 A2578 70c multi   1.60 .55

Diplomatic Relations Between France and South Korea, 130th Anniv. — A2579

Designs: 80c, Korean Celadon incense burner, 12th cent. €1.25, French reliquary.

2016, June 3 Photo. Perf. 13¼
5043 A2579 80c multi   1.90 .60
5044 A2579 €1.25 multi   2.75 .90

See South Korea No. 2469.

French History A2580

No. 5045: a, Catherine de Medici (1519-89), Queen of France. b, 1520 meeting of King Henry VIII of England and King François I of France at Field of the Cloth of Gold, horiz.

Perf. 13¼x13, 13x13¼
2016, June 3 Engr.
5045 A2580 Sheet of 2   6.50 6.50
  a.-b.   €1.40 Either single   3.25 1.60

A 200x95mm sheet containing Nos. 5045a and 5045b, but with a different margin design sold for €6.20.

First Women in French Government, 80th Anniv. — A2581

2016, June 4 Photo. Perf. 13
5046 A2581 70c red & black   1.60 .55

Cécile Brunschvicg (1877-1946), Undersecretary of State for National Education; Irène Joliot-Curie (1897-1956), Undersecretary of State for Scientific Research; Suzanne Lacore (1875-1975), Undersecretary of State for Public Health.

Art Issue

Lost Illusions, by Charles Gleyre (1806-74) A2582

2016, June 5 Engr. Perf. 13x13¼
5047 A2582 €1.60 multi   3.75 1.90

Holy Cross Abbey, Quimperlé A2583

2016, June 17 Engr. Perf. 13¼
5048 A2583 70c multi   1.60 .55

League of Education, 150th Anniv. — A2584

2016, June 23 Photo. Perf. 13¼
5049 A2584 €1 multi   2.25 .75

Pierre Mauroy (1928-2013), Prime Minister — A2585

2016, June 24 Engr. Perf. 13¼
5050 A2585 80c multi   1.90 .60

Academy of Sciences, 350th Anniv. — A2586

2016, June 28 Photo. Perf. 13¼
5051 A2586 €2.50 multi   5.75 1.90

Souvenir Sheet

Battle of the Somme, Cent. A2587

No. 5052: a, Soldiers shaking hands, castle and British tank. b, Damaged Albert Cathedral, Theipval Memorial, Visitor's Center.

2016, July 1 Photo. Perf. 13¼
5052 A2587 Sheet of 2   4.25 4.25
  a.   80c multi   1.90 .60
  b.   €1 multi   2.25 .75

A 200x95mm sheet containing Nos. 5052a and 5052b, but with a different margin design sold for €6.20.

 A2588

 A2589   A2590

 A2591

 A2592   A2593

 A2594   A2595

 A2596

A2597

A2598

Summer Vacation — A2599

Serpentine Die Cut 11
2016, July 2 Photo.
Booklet Stamps
Self-Adhesive
5053 A2588 (70c) multi   1.60 .55
5054 A2589 (70c) multi   1.60 .55
5055 A2590 (70c) multi   1.60 .55
5056 A2591 (70c) multi   1.60 .55
5057 A2592 (70c) multi   1.60 .55
5058 A2593 (70c) multi   1.60 .55
5059 A2594 (70c) multi   1.60 .55
5060 A2595 (70c) multi   1.60 .55
5061 A2596 (70c) multi   1.60 .55
5062 A2597 (70c) multi   1.60 .55
5063 A2598 (70c) multi   1.60 .55
5064 A2599 (70c) multi   1.60 .55
  a.   Booklet pane of 12, #5053-5064   19.50
     Nos. 5053-5064 (12)   19.20 6.60

Mediterranean Sea Fish — A2600

2016, July 9 Photo. Perf. 13x12½
5065 A2600 €1 multi   2.25 .75

Flowers — A2601

Inscriptions: No. 5066, Oiseau de paradis (bird-of-paradise flower). No. 5067, Coquelicot (poppy). No. 5068, Muguet (lily-of-the-valley). No. 5069, Balisier (heliconia). No. 5070, Lys rouge (red lily). No. 5071, Iris. No. 5072, Rose. No. 5073, Tournesol (sunflower). No. 5074, Jonquille (jonquil). No. 5075, Marguerite (daisy). No. 5076, Belle-de-nuit (four o'clock flower). No. 5077, Passiflore (passionflower).

Serpentine Die Cut 11
2016, July 30 Photo.
Booklet Stamp
Self-Adhesive
5066 A2601 (80c) multi   1.75 .60
5067 A2601 (80c) multi   1.75 .60
5068 A2601 (80c) multi   1.75 .60
5069 A2601 (80c) multi   1.75 .60
5070 A2601 (80c) multi   1.75 .60
5071 A2601 (80c) multi   1.75 .60
5072 A2601 (80c) multi   1.75 .60
5073 A2601 (80c) multi   1.75 .60
5074 A2601 (80c) multi   1.75 .60
5075 A2601 (80c) multi   1.75 .60
5076 A2601 (80c) multi   1.75 .60
5077 A2601 (80c) multi   1.75 .60
  a.   Booklet pane of 12, #5066-5077   21.00
     Nos. 5066-5077 (12)   21.00 7.20

Eagle Dam, Soursac, and World War II Resistance Fighters — A2602

2016, Sept. 2 Engr. Perf. 13x12¾
5078 A2602 €3.20 multi   7.25 2.40

Animal Proverbs and Idioms — A2603

Designs: No. 5079, Courir plusieurs lièvres à la fois ("to try to do more than one thing at once"). No. 5080, Quand on parle du loup on en voit la queue ("speak of the devil and he appears"). No. 5081, Avoir des oursins dans le porte-monnaie ("to be stingy"). No. 5082, Avoir une mémoire d'éléphant ("have the memory of an elephant"). No. 5083, Muet comme une carpe ("silent like a carp"). No. 5084, La part du lion ("the lion's share"). No. 5085, Dormir comme un loir ("to sleep like a log"). No. 5086, Etre le dindon de la farce ("being the butt of the joke"). No. 5087, Peigner la girafe ("to do nothing effective"). No. 5088, C'est le serpent qui se mord la queue ("to be in a vicious cycle"). No. 5089, Monter sur ses grands chevaux ("to get carried away"). No. 5090, Bayer aux corneilles ("to stand and gape").

Serpentine Die Cut 11
2016, Sept. 3 Photo.
Booklet Stamps
Self-Adhesive
5079 A2603 (70c) multi   1.60 .55
5080 A2603 (70c) multi   1.60 .55
5081 A2603 (70c) multi   1.60 .55
5082 A2603 (70c) multi   1.60 .55
5083 A2603 (70c) multi   1.60 .55
5084 A2603 (70c) multi   1.60 .55
5085 A2603 (70c) multi   1.60 .55
5086 A2603 (70c) multi   1.60 .55
5087 A2603 (70c) multi   1.60 .55
5088 A2603 (70c) multi   1.60 .55
5089 A2603 (70c) multi   1.60 .55
5090 A2603 (70c) multi   1.60 .55
  a.   Booklet pane of 12, #5079-5090   19.50
     Nos. 5079-5090 (12)   19.20 6.60

714 FRANCE

Léo Ferré (1916-93), Musician A2604

2016, Sept. 8   Photo.   *Perf. 12¼*
5091   A2604   €1.40 multi   3.25   1.10

Françoise Giroud (1916-2003), Minister of Culture — A2605

2016, Sept. 9   Engr.   *Perf. 13x13¼*
5092   A2605   80c lt blue & maroon   1.75   .60

Characters From *Les Legendaires*, Cartoons by Patrick Sobral — A2606

Designs: No. 5093, Danael. No. 5094, Jadina and Shimy.

2016, Sept. 16   Photo.   *Perf. 13¼*
5093   A2606   70c multi   1.60   .55
5094   A2606   70c multi   1.60   .55
  a.   Horiz. pair, #5093-5094, + 2 alternating labels   3.20   1.10

 A2607   A2608

 A2609   A2610

A2611   A2612

 A2613   A2614

 A2615   A2616

A2617

Stars and Heavenly Bodies — A2618

Serpentine Die Cut 11
2016, Oct. 1   Photo.
Booklet Stamps
Self-Adhesive
5095   A2607   (70c) multi   1.60   .55
5096   A2608   (70c) multi   1.60   .55
5097   A2609   (70c) multi   1.60   .55
5098   A2610   (70c) multi   1.60   .55
5099   A2611   (70c) multi   1.60   .55
5100   A2612   (70c) multi   1.60   .55
5101   A2613   (70c) multi   1.60   .55
5102   A2614   (70c) multi   1.60   .55
5103   A2615   (70c) multi   1.60   .55
5104   A2616   (70c) multi   1.60   .55
5105   A2617   (70c) multi   1.60   .55
5106   A2618   (70c) multi   1.60   .55
  a.   Booklet pane of 12, #5095-5106   19.50
  Nos. 5095-5106 (12)   19.20   6.60

Charleston Dancers — A2619

Ballet Dancer in *Swan Lake* A2620

2016, Oct. 8   Engr.   *Perf. 13¼*
5107   A2619   70c multi   1.60   .55
Souvenir Sheet
Photo. & Embossed
Perf. 13¼x13
5108   A2620   €1.40 multi   3.25   1.10
Stamp Day.

Eclair Airplane Propellers, Cent. — A2621

2016, Oct. 13   Photo.   *Perf. 13¼*
5109   A2621   70c multi   1.60   .55

St. Étienne Cathedral, Toul — A2622

2016, Oct. 21   Engr.   *Perf. 13x13¼*
5110   A2622   70c multi + label   1.60   .55

Architecture of Paris and Lisbon A2623

Designs: 80c, Rua Augusta Arch, Lisbon. €1, Buildings along Rue Royale, Paris.

2016, Oct. 21   Engr.   *Perf. 13x12½*
5111   A2623   80c multi   1.75   .60
5112   A2623   €1 multi   2.25   .75
See Portugal Nos. 3847-3848.

Pres. François Mitterrand (1916-96) — A2624

2016, Oct. 26   Engr.   *Perf. 13¼*
5113   A2624   80c multi   1.75   .60

Miniature Sheet

European Capitals — A2625

No. 5114 — Attractions in Amsterdam, Netherlands: a, Begijnhof (Le Béguinage). b, Rijksmuseum. c, Westerkerk, vert. d, Canals and buildings.

Perf. 13¼x13½, 13½x13¼
2016, Nov. 3   Photo.
5114   A2625   Sheet of 4   7.00   7.00
  a.-d.   80c Any single   1.75   .60

 A2626   A2626a

Peace and Commerce ("Type Sage") With Denominations in Euro Currency).
Type I: The "N" of "INV" is under the "B" of "REPUBLIQUE."
Type II: The "N" of "INV" is under the "U" of "REPUBLIQUE."

2016, Nov. 3   Engr.   *Perf. 12¾x13¼*
Type I
5115   A2626   €1 dark green   2.25   .75
Type II
5116   A2626   €1 dark green   2.25   .75
  a.   Pair, #5115-5116   4.50   1.50
Booklet Stamps
Type I
Design Size: 15x19mm
Perf. 12¾x13
5117   A2626   80c red   1.75   .45
5118   A2626a   80c black   1.75   .45
  a.   Booklet pane of 2, #5117-5118   3.50   —
  b.   Booklet pane of 12, 6 each #5117-5118   21.00   —
    Complete booklet, #5118a, 5118b   24.50

Nos. 5115-5116 were printed in sheets containing 10 of each stamp.

Brive-la-Gaillarde — A2627

2016, Nov. 4   Engr.   *Perf. 13x12¾*
5119   A2627   70c multi   1.50   .50

Miniature Sheet

Pens A2628

No. 5120: a, Person dipping Sergent-Major pen into ink, 19th cent. b, Calames (ancient reed pen). c, Monk with quill pen, 12th cent. d, Metallic pen nibs, 19th cent. e, Cat, writer with fountain pen, horiz. f, Voltaire writing with quill pen, 1775.

Litho. & Engr.
2016, Nov. 4   *Perf. 13*
5120   A2628   Sheet of 6   9.00   9.00
  a.-f.   70c Any single   1.50   .50
  g.   Souvenir sheet of 3, #5120a, 5120d, 5120e   6.75   6.75
  h.   Souvenir sheet of 3, #5120b, 5120c, 5120f   6.75   6.75

Nos. 5120g and 5120h were sold as a set for €6.20.

Restoration and Reopening of Bièvre River — A2629

2016, Nov. 5   Photo.   *Perf. 13¼*
5121   A2629   70c multi   1.50   .50

Art Issue
Souvenir Sheet

Paintings by Marie Laurencin (1883-1956) — A2630

No. 5122: a, Portrait of Baroness Gourgaud in Black Mantilla, 1923. b, Young Girl with Guitar, 1940.

2016, Nov. 6   Photo.   *Perf. 13¼x13*
5122   A2630   Sheet of 2   7.00   7.00
  a.-b.   €1.60 Either single   3.50   1.75

National Office of Veterans and War Victims, Cent. — A2631

2016, Nov. 9   Photo.   *Perf. 13¼*
5123   A2631   70c multi   1.50   .50

Jewelry Making — A2632

2016, Nov. 10   Engr.   *Perf. 12¼*
5124   A2632   €1 multi   2.25   .75

FRANCE

A2633   A2634

A2635   A2636

A2637   A2638

A2639   A2640

A2641   A2642

A2643

Contest Stamps With Scratch-off Panel — A2644

Serpentine Die Cut 11
2016, Nov. 14   Photo.

Booklet Stamps Self-Adhesive Unscratched Panels

5125	A2633	(70c) multi	1.50	.50
	a.	Scratched panel		.35
5126	A2634	(70c) multi	1.50	.50
	a.	Scratched panel		.35
5127	A2635	(70c) multi	1.50	.50
	a.	Scratched panel		.35
5128	A2636	(70c) multi	1.50	.50
	a.	Scratched panel		.35
5129	A2637	(70c) multi	1.50	.50
	a.	Scratched panel		.35
5130	A2638	(70c) multi	1.50	.50
	a.	Scratched panel		.35
5131	A2639	(70c) multi	1.50	.50
	a.	Scratched panel		.35
5132	A2640	(70c) multi	1.50	.50
	a.	Scratched panel		.35
5133	A2641	(70c) multi	1.50	.50
	a.	Scratched panel		.35
5134	A2642	(70c) multi	1.50	.50
	a.	Scratched panel		.35
5135	A2643	(70c) multi	1.50	.50
	a.	Scratched panel		.35
5136	A2644	(70c) multi	1.50	.50
	a.	Scratched panel		.35
	b.	Booklet pane of 12, #5125-5136	18.00	
		Nos. 5125-5136 (12)	18.00	6.00

Gold scratch-off panels on Nos. 5125-5136 hide codes that could be entered at the contest website for a chance to win various prizes.

Stained-Glass Windows — A2645

Window from: No. 5137, Notre Dame Cathedral, Coutances. No. 5138, Saint-Denis Chapel, Paris. No. 5139, Notre Dame Cathedral, Chartres. No. 5140, Saint-Nazaire Basilica, Carcassonne. No. 5141, Notre Dame Cathedral, Strasbourg. No. 5142, Saint-Savin-de-Gartempe Abbey, Saint-Savin. No. 5143, Saint-Etienne Cathedral, Bourges. No. 5144, Saint-Julien Cathedral, Le Mans. No. 5145, Saint-Denis Basilica, Saint-Denis. No. 5146, Notre Dame Cathedral, Bayeux. No. 5147, Saint-Pierre Cathedral, Beauvais. No. 5148, Notre Dame Cathedral, Paris.

Serpentine Die Cut 11
2016, Nov. 26   Photo.

Booklet Stamps Self-Adhesive

5137	A2645	(70c) multi	1.50	.50
5138	A2645	(70c) multi	1.50	.50
5139	A2645	(70c) multi	1.50	.50
5140	A2645	(70c) multi	1.50	.50
5141	A2645	(70c) multi	1.50	.50
5142	A2645	(70c) multi	1.50	.50
5143	A2645	(70c) multi	1.50	.50
5144	A2645	(70c) multi	1.50	.50
5145	A2645	(70c) multi	1.50	.50
5146	A2645	(70c) multi	1.50	.50
5147	A2645	(70c) multi	1.50	.50
5148	A2645	(70c) multi	1.50	.50
	a.	Booklet pane of 12, #5137-5148	18.00	
		Nos. 5137-5148 (12)	18.00	6.00

French Academy in Rome, 350th Anniv. — A2646

2016, Nov. 30   Photo.   Perf. 13¼
| 5149 | A2646 | €1 chestnut & red | 2.25 | .75 |

A souvenir sheet of one sold for €3.50. See Italy No. 3433.

Landscape Reflections A2647

Designs: No. 5150, Nusa Dua, Bali, Indonesia. No. 5151, Siwa Oasis, Egypt. No. 5152, Mont Blanc, France. No. 5153, Laguna Colorada, Bolivia. No. 5154, Mount Shompole, Tanzania. No. 5155, Moremi Game Reserve, Botswana. No. 5156, Mount Fuji, Japan. No. 5157, Dolomites, Italy. No. 5158, Avenue of Baobabs, Madagascar. No. 5159, Mountains, Sermersooq Municipality, Greenland. No. 5160, Everglades, United States. No. 5161, Mountains, Ultima Esperanza Province, Chile.

Serpentine Die Cut 11
2017, Jan. 7   Photo.

Booklet Stamps Self-Adhesive

5150	A2647	(85c) multi	1.90	.65
5151	A2647	(85c) multi	1.90	.65
5152	A2647	(85c) multi	1.90	.65
5153	A2647	(85c) multi	1.90	.65
5154	A2647	(85c) multi	1.90	.65
5155	A2647	(85c) multi	1.90	.65
5156	A2647	(85c) multi	1.90	.65
5157	A2647	(85c) multi	1.90	.65
5158	A2647	(85c) multi	1.90	.65
5159	A2647	(85c) multi	1.90	.65
5160	A2647	(85c) multi	1.90	.65
5161	A2647	(85c) multi	1.90	.65
	a.	Booklet pane of 12, #5150-5161	23.00	
		Nos. 5150-5161 (12)	22.80	7.80

Art Issue
Souvenir Sheet

Art by Marc Chagall (1887-1985) — A2648

No. 5162: a, Peace (stained-glass window), 1976. b, Paradise (painting), 1961.

2017, Jan. 13   Photo.   Perf. 13¼
| 5162 | A2648 | Sheet of 2 | 7.50 | 4.00 |
| | a.-b. | €1.70 Either single | 3.75 | 1.90 |

A2649   Hearts — A2650

2017, Jan. 20   Photo.   Perf. 13¼
5163	A2649	73c multi	1.60	.55
	a.	Souvenir sheet of 5	8.00	8.00
5164	A2650	€1.46 multi	3.25	1.10

Self-Adhesive
Serpentine Die Cut
| 5165 | A2649 | 73c multi | 1.60 | .55 |
| 5166 | A2650 | €1.46 multi | 3.25 | 1.10 |

Values for Nos. 5163-5164 are for stamps with surrounding selvage.

Tourism Issue

Chateau de Pailly — A2651

2017, Jan. 28   Engr.   Perf. 13¼
| 5167 | A2651 | 73c multi | 1.60 | .55 |

Rat — A2652   Ox — A2653

Tiger — A2654   Rabbit — A2655

Dragon A2656   Snake A2657

Horse — A2658   Goat — A2659

Monkey A2660   Rooster A2661

Dog — A2662   Pig — A2663

Serpentine Die Cut 11
2017, Jan. 28   Photo.

Booklet Stamps Self-Adhesive

5168	A2652	(73c) multi	1.60	.55
5169	A2653	(73c) multi	1.60	.55
5170	A2654	(73c) multi	1.60	.55
5171	A2655	(73c) multi	1.60	.55
5172	A2656	(73c) multi	1.60	.55
5173	A2657	(73c) multi	1.60	.55
5174	A2658	(73c) multi	1.60	.55
5175	A2659	(73c) multi	1.60	.55
5176	A2660	(73c) multi	1.60	.55
5177	A2661	(73c) multi	1.60	.55
5178	A2662	(73c) multi	1.60	.55
5179	A2663	(73c) multi	1.60	.55
	a.	Booklet pane of 12, #5168-5179	19.50	
		Nos. 5168-5179 (12)	19.20	6.60

New Year 2017 (Year of the Rooster).

Women and Lucien Neuwirth (1924-2013), Politician — A2664

2017, Feb. 9   Photo.   Perf. 13¼
| 5180 | A2664 | 85c multi | 1.90 | .65 |

Passage of Neuwirth Law legalizing birth control, 50th anniv.

Art Issue

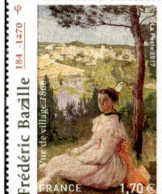
La Vue de Village, by Frédéric Bazille (1841-70) A2665

2017, Feb. 17   Photo.   Perf. 13¼x13
| 5181 | A2665 | €1.70 multi | 3.75 | 1.90 |

Farm Animals — A2666

Designs: No. 5182, Bélier (ram). No. 5183, Lapereau (rabbit). No. 5184, Anesse (female donkey). No. 5185, Dindon (turkey). No. 5186, Oie (goose). No. 5187, Veau (calf). No. 5188, Porcelet (piglet). No. 5189, Anon (male donkey). No. 5190, Canard (duck). No. 5191, Brebis (ewe). No. 5192, Vache (cow). No. 5193, Poule (hen).

Serpentine Die Cut 11
2017, Feb. 24   Photo.

Booklet Stamps Self-Adhesive

5182	A2666	(73c) multi	1.60	.55
5183	A2666	(73c) multi	1.60	.55
5184	A2666	(73c) multi	1.60	.55

FRANCE

5185	A2666	(73c) multi	1.60	.55
5186	A2666	(73c) multi	1.60	.55
5187	A2666	(73c) multi	1.60	.55
5188	A2666	(73c) multi	1.60	.55
5189	A2666	(73c) multi	1.60	.55
5190	A2666	(73c) multi	1.60	.55
5191	A2666	(73c) multi	1.60	.55
5192	A2666	(73c) multi	1.60	.55
5193	A2666	(73c) multi	1.60	.55

a. Booklet pane of 12, #5182-5193 ... 19.50
Nos. 5182-5193 (12) ... 19.20 6.60

Anne Morgan (1873-1952), Philanthropist and Provider of War Relief — A2667

2017, Feb. 24   Engr.   Perf. 13¼
5194   A2667   85c multi   1.90   .65

Montmartre — A2668

2017, Mar. 9   Engr.   Perf. 13x12¾
5195   A2668   73c multi   1.60   .55

Spring Philatelic Show, Paris.

Miniature Sheet

European Capitals — A2669

No. 5196 — Attractions in Valletta, Malta: a, Palais des Grand Maîtres (Grandmaster's Palace). b, Gallarija (building balconies). c, St. John's Co-cathedral, vert. d, Fort Saint Elmo (canals and buildings).

Perf. 13x13¼, 13¼x13
2017, Mar. 10   Photo.
5196   A2669   Sheet of 4   7.75   7.75
a.-d.   85c Any single   1.90   .65

Germaine Ribière (1917-99), Resistance Fighter Who Saved Jews in World War II — A2670

2017, Mar. 10   Engr.   Perf. 13¼
5197   A2670   €1.10 multi   2.40   .80

Waltzers — A2671

The Star, by Edgar Degas (1834-1917) — A2672

2017, Mar. 11   Engr.   Perf. 13¼
5198   A2671   73c multi   1.60   .55

Souvenir Sheet
Photo.
Perf. 13¼x13
5199   A2672   €1.46 multi   3.25   1.10

Stamp Day. A souvenir sheet containing No. 5198 was issued in 2018 and sold for €4.

Law on Commercial And Industrial Credit, Cent. — A2673

2017, Mar. 13   Photo.   Perf. 13¼
5200   A2673   85c multi   1.90   .65

French-Algerian War Ceasefire, 55th Anniv. — A2674

2017, Mar. 15   Photo.   Perf. 13¼
5201   A2674   €1.30 multi   2.75   .90

Maurice Faure (1922-2014), Politician — A2675

2017, Mar. 25   Engr.   Perf. 13¼
5202   A2675   85c multi   1.90   .65

Photographs of Items Looking Like Masks, by Michelangelo Durazzo — A2676

Mask number: No. 5203, 7. No. 5204, 13. No. 5205, 12. No. 5206, 9. No. 5207, 32. No. 5208, 29. No. 5209, 26. No. 5210, 35. No. 5211, 3. No. 5212, 17. No. 5213, 21. No. 5214, 44.

Serpentine Die Cut 11
2017, Mar. 31   Photo.
Booklet Stamps
Self-Adhesive

5203	A2676	(73c) multi	1.60	.55
5204	A2676	(73c) multi	1.60	.55
5205	A2676	(73c) multi	1.60	.55
5206	A2676	(73c) multi	1.60	.55
5207	A2676	(73c) multi	1.60	.55
5208	A2676	(73c) multi	1.60	.55
5209	A2676	(73c) multi	1.60	.55
5210	A2676	(73c) multi	1.60	.55
5211	A2676	(73c) multi	1.60	.55
5212	A2676	(73c) multi	1.60	.55
5213	A2676	(73c) multi	1.60	.55
5214	A2676	(73c) multi	1.60	.55

a. Booklet pane of 12, #5203-5214 ... 19.50
Nos. 5203-5214 (12) ... 19.20 6.60

Ironwork — A2677

2017, Mar. 31   Engr.   Perf. 12¼
5215   A2677   73c multi   1.60   .55

Souvenir Sheet

Battle of Vimy Ridge, Cent. — A2678

No. 5216: a, Pillars and statue. b, Statue of weeping woman.

2017, Apr. 7   Engr.   Perf. 13¼
5216   A2678   Sheet of 2   5.00   5.00
a.   85c multi   1.90   .65
b.   €1.30 multi   3.00   1.00

See Canada Nos. 2981-2982.

Souvenir Sheet

Second Battle of Chemin des Dames, Cent. — A2679

No. 5217: a, Seven Senegalese soldiers. b, Eight soldiers in Dragon Cavern.

2017, Apr. 14   Photo.   Perf. 13¼
5217   A2679   Sheet of 2   5.00   5.00
a.-b.   €1.10 Either single   2.40   .80

A 200x95mm sheet containing Nos. 5217a and 5217b, but with a different margin design sold for €6.20.

Jean-Baptiste Charcot (1867-1936), Polar Explorer, and Ship Pourquoi-Pas? — A2680

2017, Apr. 22   Engr.   Perf. 13x12¾
5218   A2680   €1.30 multi   3.00   1.00

A souvenir sheet containing No. 5218 sold for €3.20.

Concours Lépine Inventor's Show — A2681

2017, Apr. 27   Photo.   Perf. 13¼
5219   A2681   €1.30 multi   3.00   1.00

Flowers in Objets d'Art — A2682

Inscription: No. 5220, Cristal pierres & or (crystal stones and gold). No. 5221, Bois peint & doré (painted and gilded wood). No. 5222, Argent travaillé (worked silver). No. 5223, Faience & glaçure, peinte (glazed and painted faience). No. 5224, Bronze doré (gilded bronze). No. 5225, Mosaique, pierres dures (stone mosaic). No. 5226, Porcelaine tendre (soft porcelain). No. 5227, Bois sculpté (sculpted wood). No. 5228, Laine & soie (wool and silk). No. 5229, Bois gravé (engraved wood). No. 5230, Perles, diamants, or & argent (pearls, diamonds, gold and silver). No. 5231, Coton & fil de soie, broderie (cotton and silk thread embroidery).

Serpentine Die Cut 11
2017, Apr. 28   Photo.
Booklet Stamps
Self-Adhesive

5220	A2682	(73c) multi	1.60	.55
5221	A2682	(73c) multi	1.60	.55
5222	A2682	(73c) multi	1.60	.55
5223	A2682	(73c) multi	1.60	.55
5224	A2682	(73c) multi	1.60	.55
5225	A2682	(73c) multi	1.60	.55
5226	A2682	(73c) multi	1.60	.55
5227	A2682	(73c) multi	1.60	.55
5228	A2682	(73c) multi	1.60	.55
5229	A2682	(73c) multi	1.60	.55
5230	A2682	(73c) multi	1.60	.55
5231	A2682	(73c) multi	1.60	.55

a. Booklet pane of 12, #5220-5231 ... 19.50
Nos. 5220-5231 (12) ... 19.20 6.60

Cholet — A2683

2017, Apr. 28   Engr.   Perf. 13x13¼
5232   A2683   73c multi + label   1.60   .55

French Federation of Philatelic Associations, 90th Congress, Cholet.

Bid of Paris to Host 2024 Summer Olympics and Paralympics — A2684

2017, May 13   Photo.   Perf. 13x13¼
5233   A2684   73c multi + label   1.75   .60

For overprint, see No. 5303.

Chambord, Azay-le-Rideau and Chenonceau Chateaux — A2685

2017, May 14   Photo.   Perf. 13x12¾
5234   A2685   €1.10 multi   2.50   .85

Europa.

Coupe de France Soccer Tournament, Cent. — A2686

2017, May 19   Photo.   Perf. 13¼
5235   A2686   73c multi   1.75   .60

Saint-Benoît-sur-Loire Abbey — A2687

2017, May 19   Engr.   Perf. 13¼
5236   A2687   73c multi   1.75   .60

Insects — A2688

Designs: No. 5237, Coccinelle (ladybug). No. 5238: a, Demoiselle (banded damselfly). b, Hanneton (cockchafer), vert. c, Carabe (beetle), vert.

2017, May 19   Photo.   Perf. 13¼
5237   A2688   73c multi   1.75   .60
5238   Sheet of 4, #5237, 5238a-5238c   7.00   7.00
a.-c.   A2688   73c Any single   1.75   .60

Two souvenir sheets, one containing Nos. 5237 and 5238c, and the other containing Nos. 5238a and 5238b, sold as a set for €6.20.

National Sea Rescue Society, 50th Anniv. — A2689

2017, May 23   Photo.   Perf. 13¼
5239   A2689   85c multi   1.90   .65

FRANCE

Lions Clubs International, Cent. — A2690

2017, May 27	Photo.		Perf. 13¼	
5240	A2690	85c multi	1.90	.65

Haunted House Ride — A2691

Bumper Cars — A2692

Cotton Candy — A2693

Carousel — A2694

Candy Apples — A2695

Duck Hooking Game — A2696

Stuffed Animal Prizes — A2697

Ferris Wheel — A2698

Roller Coaster — A2699

Bowling — A2700

Swing Ride — A2701

Slide — A2702

Serpentine Die Cut 11
2017, June 2   Photo.
Booklet Stamps
Self-Adhesive

5241	A2691	(73c) multi	1.75	.60
5242	A2692	(73c) multi	1.75	.60
5243	A2693	(73c) multi	1.75	.60
5244	A2694	(73c) multi	1.75	.60
5245	A2695	(73c) multi	1.75	.60
5246	A2696	(73c) multi	1.75	.60
5247	A2697	(73c) multi	1.75	.60
5248	A2698	(73c) multi	1.75	.60
5249	A2699	(73c) multi	1.75	.60
5250	A2700	(73c) multi	1.75	.60
5251	A2701	(73c) multi	1.75	.60
5252	A2702	(73c) multi	1.75	.60
a.	Booklet pane of 12, #5241-5252		21.00	
Nos. 5241-5252 (12)			21.00	7.20

Louis Vicat (1786-1861), Buildings and Bridge — A2703

2017, June 2	Photo.		Perf. 13¼	
5253	A2703	€1.30 multi	3.00	1.00

Invention of artificial cement by Vicat. 200th anniv.

Art Issue

Woman, Sculpture by Jeanne Bardey (1872-1954) A2704

2017, June 2	Engr.		Perf. 13¼x13	
5254	A2704	€1.70 multi	4.00	2.00

Rochefort-en-Terre — A2705

2017, June 14	Engr.		Perf. 13¼	
5255	A2705	73c multi	1.75	.60

Arrival of American Troops in World War I, Cont. — A2706

2017, June 23	Engr.		Perf. 13¼	
5256	A2706	€1.30 multi	3.00	1.00

Joachim Murat (1767-1815), French Marshal and Admiral and King of Naples — A2707

2017, June 23	Engr.		Perf. 13¼	
5257	A2707	85c multi	2.00	.70

Harness Race at Rambouillet Hippodrome A2708

2017, June 24	Photo.		Perf. 13¼	
5258	A2708	73c multi	1.75	.60

Diplomatic Relations Between France and the Philippines, 70th Anniv. — A2709

Unnamed painting by: 85c, Philippino painter Macario Vitalis (1898-1989). €1.30, French painter Jacques Villon (1875-1963).

2017, June 26	Photo.		Perf. 13¼	
5259	A2709	85c multi	2.00	.70
5260	A2709	€1.30 multi	3.00	1.00
a.	Souvenir sheet of 2, #5259-5260		7.50	7.50

No. 5260a sold for €3.20. See Philippines No. 3732.

Souvenir Sheet

French History A2710

No. 5261: a, Anne of France (1461-1522), Duchess of Beaujeu (41x53mm oval stamp). b, Treaty of Picquigny, 1475 (53x42mm).

Perf., Perf. 13x13¼ (#5261b)
2017, June 30			Engr.	
5261	A2710	Sheet of 2	7.00	7.00
a.-b.	€1.46 Either single		3.50	1.25

A 200x95mm sheet containing Nos. 5261a and 5261b, but with a different margin design sold for €6.50.

Grains — A2711

Designs: No. 5262, Avoine (oats). No. 5263, Blé dur (durum wheat). No. 5264, Maïs (corn). No. 5265, Millet. No. 5266, Riz (rice). No. 5267, Seigle (rye). No. 5268, Blé tendre (soft wheat). No. 5269, Epeautre (spelt). No. 5270, Orge (barley). No. 5271, Petit épautre (einkorn wheat). No. 5272, Sorgho (sorghum). No. 5273, Triticale.

Serpentine Die Cut 11
2017, June 30   Photo.
Booklet Stamps
Self-Adhesive

5262	A2711	(85c) multi	2.00	.70
5263	A2711	(85c) multi	2.00	.70
5264	A2711	(85c) multi	2.00	.70
5265	A2711	(85c) multi	2.00	.70
5266	A2711	(85c) multi	2.00	.70
5267	A2711	(85c) multi	2.00	.70
5268	A2711	(85c) multi	2.00	.70
5269	A2711	(85c) multi	2.00	.70
5270	A2711	(85c) multi	2.00	.70
5271	A2711	(85c) multi	2.00	.70
5272	A2711	(85c) multi	2.00	.70
5273	A2711	(85c) multi	2.00	.70
a.	Booklet pane of 12, #5262-5273		24.00	
Nos. 5262-5273 (12)			24.00	8.40

Cherbourg-en-Cotentin — A2712

2017, July 7	Engr.		Perf. 13¼	
5274	A2712	73c multi	1.75	.60

Trees of the Mediterranean Area — A2713

2017, July 10	Photo.		Perf. 13¼	
5275	A2713	€1.10 multi	2.60	.90

2017 World Wrestling Championships, Paris — A2714

2017, July 22	Photo.		Perf. 13x12¾	
5276	A2714	€1.30 multi	3.25	1.10

Espelette Pepper A2715

Woman Holding Strawberry A2716

Loaf of Bread, Croissant and Roll — A2717

Chocolate Bar Elephant — A2718

Beans — A2719

Lobster — A2720

Woman Drinking Citrus Juice — A2721

Cows and Cheese — A2722

Tomato and Olive Salad — A2723

Toucan With Cup of Coffee — A2724

Toast With Flavored Honey — A2725

People Drinking Mint Tea — A2726

Serpentine Die Cut 11
2017, Aug. 5   Photo.
Booklet Stamps
Self-Adhesive

5277	A2715	(73c) multi	1.75	.60
5278	A2716	(73c) multi	1.75	.60
5279	A2717	(73c) multi	1.75	.60
5280	A2718	(73c) multi	1.75	.60
5281	A2719	(73c) multi	1.75	.60
5282	A2720	(73c) multi	1.75	.60
5283	A2721	(73c) multi	1.75	.60
5284	A2722	(73c) multi	1.75	.60
5285	A2723	(73c) multi	1.75	.60
5286	A2724	(73c) multi	1.75	.60
5287	A2725	(73c) multi	1.75	.60
5288	A2726	(73c) multi	1.75	.60
a.	Booklet pane of 12, #5277-5288		21.00	
Nos. 5277-5288 (12)			21.00	7.20

Sense of taste.

Le Havre, 500th Anniv. — A2727

2017, Aug. 31	Engr.		Perf. 13¼	
5289	A2727	85c multi	2.10	.70

Bridges — A2728

Designs: No. 5290, Pont du Gard, Vers-Pont-du-Gard, France. No. 5291, Pont du Diable, Saint-Jean-de-Fos, France. No. 5292, Morlaix Viaduct, Morlaix, France. No. 5293, Digoin Canal Bridge, Digoin, France. No. 5294, Garabit Viaduct, Ruynes-en-Margeride, France. No. 5295, Tower Bridge, London. No. 5296, Pont Valentré, Cahors, France. No. 5297, Ponte Vecchio, Florence. No. 5298, U Bein Bridge, Amarapura, Myanmar. No. 5299, Manhattan and Brooklyn Bridges, New York City. No. 5300, Pont Alexandre III and Pont de la Concorde, Paris. No. 5301, Rochefort-Martrou Transporter Bridge, Rochefort, France.

Serpentine Die Cut 11
2017, Sept. 1   Photo.
Booklet Stamps
Self-Adhesive

5290	A2728	(73c) multi	1.75	.60
5291	A2728	(73c) multi	1.75	.60
5292	A2728	(73c) multi	1.75	.60
5293	A2728	(73c) multi	1.75	.60
5294	A2728	(73c) multi	1.75	.60
5295	A2728	(73c) multi	1.75	.60
5296	A2728	(73c) multi	1.75	.60
5297	A2728	(73c) multi	1.75	.60
5298	A2728	(73c) multi	1.75	.60
5299	A2728	(73c) multi	1.75	.60
5300	A2728	(73c) multi	1.75	.60

718 FRANCE

5301	A2728 (73c) multi	1.75	.60
a.	Booklet pane of 12, #5290-5301	21.00	
	Nos. 5290-5301 (12)	21.00	7.20

Normandie-Niemen Air Regiment, 75th Anniv. — A2729

2017, Sept. 1   Engr.   Perf. 13x12¾
| 5302 | A2729 €1.30 multi | 3.25 | 1.10 |

A souvenir sheet containing No. 5302, a denominated example of No. 5302 with black and red inks only, and a non-denominated example of No. 5302 without the black and red inks sold for €6.20. See Russia No. 7843.

No. 5233 Overprinted in Dark Blue

Method and Perf. As Before
2017, Sept. 13
| 5303 | A2684 73c multi + label | 1.75 | .60 |

Selection of Paris as host city of 2024 Summer Olympics.

Art Issue

The Kiss, Sculpture by Auguste Rodin (1840-1917) A2730

2017, Sept. 15   Engr.   Perf. 13¼x13
| 5304 | A2730 €1.30 multi | 3.25 | 1.60 |

A souvenir sheet containing No. 5304 sold for €3.20.

Nadia Boulanger (1887-1979), Conductor and Teacher — A2731

2017, Sept. 16   Engr.   Perf. 13¼x13
| 5305 | A2731 85c multi | 2.00 | .70 |

Jeanne Lanvin (1867-1946), Fashion Designer A2732

2017, Sept. 23   Photo.   Perf. 13¼x13
| 5306 | A2732 €1.46 multi | 3.50 | 1.25 |

A souvenir sheet containing No. 5306 sold for €3.20.

Characters Maestro, Nabot and Globus From *Hello Maestro!* Animated Television Series — A2733

2017, Sept. 23   Photo.   Perf. 13¼
| 5307 | A2733 73c multi | 1.75 | .60 |
| a. | Miniature sheet of 10 | | |

Woman in Hoop A2734

Rabbit in Magician's Hat A2736

Mime A2737

Lion Tamer A2738

Human Tower A2740

Ringmaster A2742

Trick Rider on Horse A2744

Elephant Act A2735

Acrobat A2739

Clown Playing Guitar A2741

Unicyclist A2743

Aerial Contortionist A2745

Serpentine Die Cut 11
2017, Sept. 29   Photo.
Booklet Stamps
Self-Adhesive
5308	A2734 (73c) multi	1.75	.60
5309	A2735 (73c) multi	1.75	.60
5310	A2736 (73c) multi	1.75	.60
5311	A2737 (73c) multi	1.75	.60
5312	A2738 (73c) multi	1.75	.60
5313	A2739 (73c) multi	1.75	.60
5314	A2740 (73c) multi	1.75	.60
5315	A2741 (73c) multi	1.75	.60
5316	A2742 (73c) multi	1.75	.60
5317	A2743 (73c) multi	1.75	.60
5318	A2744 (73c) multi	1.75	.60
5319	A2745 (73c) multi	1.75	.60
a.	Booklet pane of 12, #5308-5319	21.00	
	Nos. 5308-5319 (12)	21.00	7.20

Circus acts.

Electronic Military Transmissions, 150th Anniv. — A2746

2017, Sept. 29   Photo.   Perf. 13¼
| 5320 | A2746 €1.46 multi | 3.50 | 1.25 |

Father Victor Dillard (1897-1945), Minister to Deported French Slaves of Germany in World War II — A2747

2017, Oct. 6   Engr.   Perf. 13¼
| 5321 | A2747 73c multi | 1.75 | .60 |

Miniature Sheet

Actors and Actresses — A2748

No. 5322: a, Magali Noel (1931-2015). b, Bruno Crémer (1929-2010). c, Odile Versois (1930-80). d, Jean-Claude Brialy (1933-2007).

2017, Oct. 13   Photo.   Perf. 13¼
| 5322 | A2748 Sheet of 4 | 8.00 | 8.00 |
| a.-d. | 85c Any single | 2.00 | .70 |

Joseph Peyré (1892-1968), Writer — A2749

2017, Oct. 20   Engr.   Perf. 13¼
| 5323 | A2749 €1.10 multi | 2.60 | .90 |

A2750

A2751

A2752

A2753

A2754

A2755

A2756

A2757

A2758

A2759

A2760

Contest Stamps With Scratch-off Panel — A2761

Serpentine Die Cut 11
2017, Nov. 6   Photo.
Booklet Stamps
Self-Adhesive
5324	A2750 (73c) gold & multi	1.75	.60
a.	Scratched panel		.40
5325	A2751 (73c) gold & multi	1.75	.60
a.	Scratched panel		.40
5326	A2752 (73c) gold & multi	1.75	.60
a.	Scratched panel		.40
5327	A2753 (73c) gold & multi	1.75	.60
a.	Scratched panel		.40
5328	A2754 (73c) gold & multi	1.75	.60
a.	Scratched panel		.40
5329	A2755 (73c) gold & multi	1.75	.60
a.	Scratched panel		.40
5330	A2756 (73c) gold & multi	1.75	.60
a.	Scratched panel		.40
5331	A2757 (73c) gold & multi	1.75	.60
a.	Scratched panel		.40
5332	A2758 (73c) gold & multi	1.75	.60
a.	Scratched panel		.40
5333	A2759 (73c) gold & multi	1.75	.60
a.	Scratched panel		.40
5334	A2760 (73c) gold & multi	1.75	.60
a.	Scratched panel		.40
5335	A2761 (73c) gold & multi	1.75	.60
a.	Scratched panel		.40
b.	Booklet pane of 12, #5324-5335	21.00	
	Nos. 5324-5335 (12)	21.00	7.20

Sabine Type of 1977-78 With Denominations in Euros
2017, Nov. 9   Engr.   Perf. 13
5336	A771 €1 red	2.40	.80
5337	A771 €1 green	2.40	.80
a.	Pair, #5336-5337	4.80	1.60

Size: 30x47mm
5338	A771 €5 red	12.00	4.00
5339	A771 €5 green	12.00	4.00
a.	Horiz. pair, #5338-5339	24.00	8.00
	Nos. 5336-5339 (4)	28.80	9.60

Booklet Stamps
5340	A771 73c green	1.75	.60
5341	A771 85c red	2.00	.65
a.	Booklet pane of 12, 6 each #5340-5341	22.50	

Size: 30x47mm
5342	A771 €1.46 green	3.50	1.25
5343	A771 €1.70 red	4.00	1.40
a.	Booklet pane of 2, #5342-5343	7.50	

FRANCE

Complete booklet, #5341a,
5343a ... 30.00
Nos. 5340-5343 (4) ... 11.25 3.90

Nos. 5336-5339 were printed in sheets of 12 containing 5 each Nos. 5336-5337 and 1 each Nos. 5338-5339.

Souvenir Sheet

Tulle Lace A2762

No. 5344: a, Butterfly. b, Rose.

Photo. & Engr.
2017, Nov. 9   Perf. 13¼
5344 A2762 Sheet of 2 ... 4.00 4.00
   a.-b. 85c Either single ... 2.00 .65

Augustin-Alphonse Marty (1862-1940), Reformer of Military Postal System — A2763

2017, Nov. 10   Engr.   Perf. 13¼x13
5345 A2763 73c multi ... 1.75 .60

Art Issue

Spaces and Lights, by Geneviève Asse — A2764

2017, Nov. 10   Photo.   Perf. 13¼x13
5346 A2764 €1.70 multi ... 4.00 2.00

Miniature Sheet

Postal Balances and Scales A2765

No. 5347 — Inscription: a, Balance Romaine. b, Pèse-lettres Type "Roberval," horiz. c, Balance de Guichet. d, Balance à Fléau. e, Balance à Trébuchet, horiz. f, Pèse-lettres de Poche.

Litho. & Engr.
2017, Nov. 11   Perf. 13
5347 A2765 Sheet of 6 ... 10.50 10.50
   a.-f. 73c Any single ... 1.75 .60
   g. Souvenir sheet of 3, #5347a, 5347c, 5347e ... 7.50 7.50
   h. Souvenir sheet of 3, #5347b, 5347d, 5347f ... 7.50 7.50

Nos. 5347g and 5347h were sold together for €6.20.

Cabinetmaking A2766

2017, Nov. 12   Engr.   Perf. 12¼
5348 A2766 €1.10 multi ... 2.60 .85

Photographs of Natural Phenomena A2767

Inscriptions: No. 5357, Détail de marbre (detail of marble, buff panel). No. 5358, Détail de marbre (detail of marble, red panel). No. 5359, Tronc d'arbre (tree trunk). No. 5360, Eau gelée (ice crystals). No. 5361, Sable-traces de crabes (sand balls made by crabs). No. 5362, Bulles d'air dans la glace (air bubbles in ice). No. 5363, Lichen crustacé sur un rocher (lichen covering rock). No. 5364, Roche chargée de fer (iron in rock). No. 5365, Flyschs à helminthoides (worm trails). No. 5366, Concrétions (rock concretions). No. 5367, Début de rouille (beginnings of rust). No. 5368, Mineral de fer sur la roche (Iron ore in rock).

Serpentine Die Cut 11
2018, Jan. 5   Photo.
Booklet Stamps
Self-Adhesive
5357 A2767 (95c) multi ... 2.40 .80
5358 A2767 (95c) multi ... 2.40 .80
5359 A2767 (95c) multi ... 2.40 .80
5360 A2767 (95c) multi ... 2.40 .80
5361 A2767 (95c) multi ... 2.40 .80
5362 A2767 (95c) multi ... 2.40 .80
5363 A2767 (95c) multi ... 2.40 .80
5364 A2767 (95c) multi ... 2.40 .80
5365 A2767 (95c) multi ... 2.40 .80
5366 A2767 (95c) multi ... 2.40 .80
5367 A2767 (95c) multi ... 2.40 .80
5368 A2767 (95c) multi ... 2.40 .80
   a. Booklet pane of 12, #5357-5368 ... 29.00
Nos. 5357-5368 (12) ... 28.80 9.60

Heart and Faces — A2768
Heart and Lips — A2769

2018, Jan. 12   Photo.   Perf. 13¼
5369 A2768 80c blk & red ... 2.00 .65
   a. Souvenir sheet of 5 ... 10.00 10.00
5370 A2769 €1.60 blk & red ... 4.00 1.40

Self-Adhesive
Serpentine Die Cut
5371 A2768 80c blk & red ... 2.00 .65
5372 A2769 €1.60 blk & red ... 4.00 1.40

Values for Nos. 5369-5370 are for stamps with surrounding selvage.

Art Issue

Le Quai aux Fleurs, Notre-Dame, by Léonard Foujita (1886-1968) — A2770

2018, Jan. 26   Photo.   Perf. 13x13¼
5373 A2770 €1.90 multi ... 4.75 2.40

Clermont-Ferrand Short Film Festival, 40th Anniv. — A2771

2018, Feb. 2   Photo.   Perf. 13¼
5374 A2771 €1.30 multi ... 3.25 1.10

Sculptures of Dogs — A2772

Designs: No. 5375, African wooden sculpture of dog. No. 5376, Sculpture of spaniel by Antoine-Louis Barye (1795-1875). No. 5377, Sculpture of Boston terrier by François Pompon (1855-1933). No. 5378, Japanese sculpture of dog on table. No. 5379, Oriental sculptures of two dogs facing left. No. 5380, Egyptian sculpture of dog. No. 5381, Oriental sculpture of dog and bowl. No. 5382, Sculpture of basset hound by Barye. No. 5383, Chinese sculpture of dog. No. 5384, Two European sculptures of spaniels. No. 5385, Sculpture of dog by Louis de Monard (1873-1939). No. 5386, Asian sculpture of dog with ball.

Serpentine Die Cut 11
2018, Feb. 2   Photo.
Booklet Stamp
Self-Adhesive
5375 A2772 (80c) multi ... 2.00 .65
5376 A2772 (80c) multi ... 2.00 .65
5377 A2772 (80c) multi ... 2.00 .65
5378 A2772 (80c) multi ... 2.00 .65
5379 A2772 (80c) multi ... 2.00 .65
5380 A2772 (80c) multi ... 2.00 .65
5381 A2772 (80c) multi ... 2.00 .65
5382 A2772 (80c) multi ... 2.00 .65
5383 A2772 (80c) multi ... 2.00 .65
5384 A2772 (80c) multi ... 2.00 .65
5385 A2772 (80c) multi ... 2.00 .65
5386 A2772 (80c) multi ... 2.00 .65
   a. Booklet pane of 12, #5375-5386 ... 24.00
Nos. 5375-5386 (12) ... 24.00 7.00

Art Issue

Desir, Sculpture by Annette Messager A2773

2018, Feb. 16   Photo.   Perf. 13x13¼
5387 A2773 €1.90 multi ... 4.75 2.40

Suzanne Noel (1878-1954), Plastic Surgeon — A2774

2018, Mar. 2   Photo.   Perf. 13¼
5388 A2774 95c multi ... 2.40 .80

17th Century Tableware A2775

Designs: No. 5389, Cup made in Nevers. No. 5390, Plate made in Lille. No. 5391, Terrine made in Vincennes. No. 5392, Plate made in Moustiers-Sainte-Marie. No. 5393, Decorative cruet made in Strasbourg. No. 5394, Plate made in Limoges. No. 5395, Plate made in Moulins. No. 5396, Dessert service made in Gien. No. 5397, Tureen made in Sceaux. No. 5398, Plates made in Lyon. No. 5399, Plate and ewer made in Sèvres. No. 5400, Pot with lid made in Chantilly.

Serpentine Die Cut 11
2018, Mar. 2   Photo.
Booklet Stamp
Self-Adhesive
5389 A2775 (80c) multi ... 2.00 .65
5390 A2775 (80c) multi ... 2.00 .65
5391 A2775 (80c) multi ... 2.00 .65
5392 A2775 (80c) multi ... 2.00 .65
5393 A2775 (80c) multi ... 2.00 .65
5394 A2775 (80c) multi ... 2.00 .65
5395 A2775 (80c) multi ... 2.00 .65
5396 A2775 (80c) multi ... 2.00 .65
5397 A2775 (80c) multi ... 2.00 .65
5398 A2775 (80c) multi ... 2.00 .65
5399 A2775 (80c) multi ... 2.00 .65
5400 A2775 (80c) multi ... 2.00 .65
   a. Booklet pane of 12, #5389-5400 ... 24.00
Nos. 5389-5400 (12) ... 24.00 7.80

Stamp Day — A2776

Automobiles: 80c, Alpine Renault A110. €1.60, Renault Maxi 5 Turbo.

2018, Mar. 10   Engr.   Perf. 13¼
5401 A2770 80c multi ... 2.00 .65

Souvenir Sheet

Photo.
Perf. 13
5402 A2776 €1.60 multi ... 4.00 1.40

No. 5402 contains one 52x41mm stamp.

Art Issue

Plans Par Couleurs, by Frantisek Kupka (1871-1957) A2777

2018, Mar. 18   Photo.   Perf. 12¼x13
5403 A2777 €1.90 multi ... 4.75 2.40

A souvenir sheet containing a perf. 13¼ example of No. 5403 and three labels sold for €4.

Savings Banks, 200th Anniv. — A2778

2018, Mar. 22   Photo.   Perf. 13¼
5404 A2778 95c multi ... 2.40 .80

Tourist Attractions A2779

Designs: No. 5405, Umbrellas on beach, Deauville. No. 5406, Chaîne des Puys. No. 5407, Dune of Pilat. No. 5408, Eiffel Tower and Tour Montparnasse, Paris. No. 5409, Vineyard, Bourgogne. No. 5410, Mont Blanc massif. No. 5411, Field, Alpes-de-Haute-Provence. No. 5412, Rocks on beach, Belle-Ile-en-Mer.

Serpentine Die Cut 11
2018, Mar. 23   Photo.
Booklet Stamps
Self-Adhesive
5405 A2779 (€1.30) multi ... 3.25 1.10
5406 A2779 (€1.30) multi ... 3.25 1.10
5407 A2779 (€1.30) multi ... 3.25 1.10
5408 A2779 (€1.30) multi ... 3.25 1.10
5409 A2779 (€1.30) multi ... 3.25 1.10
5410 A2779 (€1.30) multi ... 3.25 1.10
5411 A2779 (€1.30) multi ... 3.25 1.10
5412 A2779 (€1.30) multi ... 3.25 1.10
   a. Booklet pane of 8, #5405-5412 ... 26.00
Nos. 5405-5412 (8) ... 26.00 8.80

720 FRANCE

A2780

2018, Mar. 24   Photo.   Perf. 13x13¼
5413 A2780 80c multi + label   2.00   .65
Posts, Telegraphs and Telecommunications Sporting Association, 120th Anniv.

Leatherwork A2781

2018, Mar. 30   Engr.   Perf. 12¼
5414 A2781 €1.30 multi   3.25   1.10

Sorgues A2782

2018, Apr. 6   Engr.   Perf. 13
5415 A2782 95c multi   2.25   .75
Spring Philatelic Show, Sorgues.

Sosthène Mortenol (1859-1930), Naval Hero — A2783

Litho. & Engr.
2018, Apr. 13   Perf. 13x13¼
5416 A2783 €1.20 multi   3.00   1.00

Miniature Sheet

European Capitals — A2784

No. 5417 — Attractions in Tallinn, Estonia: a, Viru Gate. b, Alexander Nexsky Cathedral, vert. c, Toompea Castle, vert. d, Town Hall Square.

Perf. 13x13¼, 13¼x13
2018, Apr. 20   Photo.
5417 A2784 Sheet of 4   12.00   12.00
a.-d. €1.20 Any single   3.00   1.00

Souvenir Sheet

Vrai Guignolet Puppet Theater, Paris, 200th Anniv. — A2785

No. 5418: a, Two puppets with red and green headdresses. b, Two puppets, hot air balloon in background.

2018, May 10   Engr.   Perf. 13
5418 A2785 Sheet of 2   12.00   12.00
a.-b. €2.60 Either single   6.00   2.00

Deux Rives Pedestrian Bridge, Strasbourg A2786

2018, May 18   Photo.   Perf. 13¼
5419 A2786 €1.20 multi   3.00   1.00
Europa.

A2787   A2788

A2789   A2790

A2791   A2792

A2793   A2794

A2795   A2796

A2797   Emojis — A2798

Serpentine Die Cut 11
2018, May 18   Photo.
Booklet Stamps
Self-Adhesive
5420 A2787 (80c) multi   1.90   .65
5421 A2788 (80c) multi   1.90   .65
5422 A2789 (80c) multi   1.90   .65
5423 A2790 (80c) multi   1.90   .65
5424 A2791 (80c) multi   1.90   .65
5425 A2792 (80c) multi   1.90   .65
5426 A2793 (80c) multi   1.90   .65
5427 A2794 (80c) multi   1.90   .65
5428 A2795 (80c) multi   1.90   .65
5429 A2796 (80c) multi   1.90   .65
5430 A2797 (80c) multi   1.90   .65
5431 A2798 (80c) multi   1.90   .65
a. Booklet pane of 12, #5420-5431   23.00
Nos. 5420-5431 (12)   22.80   7.80

Lucie (1912-2007) and Raymond Aubrac (1914-2012), World War II Resistance Leaders — A2799

2018, May 26   Engr.   Perf. 13x13¼
5432 A2799 €1.30 multi   3.00   1.00

United Nations Peacekeepers, 70th Anniv. — A2800

2018, May 29   Photo.   Perf. 13
5433 A2800 €1.30 multi   3.00   1.00

A2801

Photographs of Earth Features Taken By Thomas Pesquet on the International Space Station: No. 5434, Snow and three lines of trees, Russia, taken Feb. 16, 2017. No. 5435, Paris, France, taken Apr. 14, 2017. No. 5436, Betsiboka River, Madagascar, taken May 6, 2017. No. 5437, Bijagos Archipelago, Guinea-Bissau, taken Feb. 4, 2017. No. 5438, Green River, Utah, taken Apr. 14, 2017. No. 5439, Persian Gulf islands, taken Dec. 31, 2016. No. 5440, Irrigated fields in desert, Saudi Arabia, taken Jan. 1, 2017. No. 5441, Fields, Spain, taken Apr. 12, 2017. No. 5442, Road in wilderness, Canada, taken Dec. 26, 2016. No. 5443, Melting ice in Himalayas, People's Republic of China, taken Apr. 27, 2017. No. 5444, Ile de Noirmoutier, France, taken Feb. 16, 2017. No. 5445, Coral reef and volcanic islands, French Polynesia, taken Mar. 16, 2017.

Serpentine Die Cut 11
2018, June 2   Photo.
Self-Adhesive
Booklet Stamps
5434 A2801 (80c) multi   1.90   .65
5435 A2801 (80c) multi   1.90   .65
5436 A2801 (80c) multi   1.90   .65
5437 A2801 (80c) multi   1.90   .65
5438 A2801 (80c) multi   1.90   .65
5439 A2801 (80c) multi   1.90   .65
5440 A2801 (80c) multi   1.90   .65
5441 A2801 (80c) multi   1.90   .65
5442 A2801 (80c) multi   1.90   .65
5443 A2801 (80c) multi   1.90   .65
5444 A2801 (80c) multi   1.90   .65
5445 A2801 (80c) multi   1.90   .65
a. Booklet pane of 12, #5434-5445   23.00
Nos. 5434-5445 (12)   22.80   7.80

Elysée Palace, Paris A2802

2018, June 7   Engr.   Perf. 13
5446 A2802 95c multi + label   2.25   .75
French Federation of Philatelic Associations, 91st Congress, Paris.

Nos. 4413 and 4437 Overprinted in Blue or Red

2018, June 8   Engr.   Perf. 13
5447 A2320 10c brown (Bl)   —   —
5448 A2325 (80c) green (R)   —   —
Nos. 5447-5448 were sold only at the Paris Philex show on the day of issue. The entire 250,000-stamp print run of No. 5448 sold out on the day of issue.

Miniature Sheets

A2803

Paris Philex 2018 Stamp Show A2804

No. 5449 — French stamps depicting Paris landmarks of 1939-56 redrawn: a, Grand Trianon, Versailles (like #794). b, Church of the Invalides, vert. (like #B203). c, Eiffel Tower, vert. (like #B85). d, Alexander III Bridge, Petit Palais (like #C24).

No. 5450 — French Orphan Relief stamps of 1917-19 redrawn: a, Widow at gate, vert. (like #B3). b, War orphans, vert. (like #B4). c, Woman plowing (like #B5). d, Woman plowing (like #B6). e, "Trench of Bayonets" (like #B7). f, Lion of Belfort (like #B8). g, "La Marseillaise" (like #B9). h, "La Marseiillaise" (like #B10).

Engr., Sheet Margin Litho. With Foil Application
2018, June 7   Perf. 13
5449 A2803 Sheet of 4   23.50   23.50
a. €2 brown lake   4.75   4.75
b. €2 brown lake   4.75   4.75
c. €2 brown lake   4.75   4.75
d. €4 brown lake   9.25   9.25

Typo.
5450 A2804 Sheet of 8   71.00   71.00
a. €1 violet brown   2.40   2.40
b. €1 sage green   2.40   2.40
c. €2 sage green   4.75   4.75
d. €2 light blue   4.75   4.75
e. €3 gray grn & lilac   7.00   7.00
f. €3 brn pur & lt brn   7.00   7.00
g. €3 brn rose & maroon   7.00   7.00
h. €15 lt blue & gray grn   35.00   35.00

Art Issue

Self-portrait, by Edouard Vuillard (1868-1940) A2805

2018, June 8   Photo.   Perf. 13x12¾
5451 A2805 €1.30 multi   3.00   1.50
No. 5451 was printed in sheets of 9 + 8 triangular labels.

Souvenir Sheet

French History A2806

No. 5452: a, Treaty of the Pyrenees, 1659. b, Queen Maria Theresa (1638-83).

2018, June 9   Engr.   Perf. 13
5452 A2806 Sheet of 2   12.00   12.00
a.-b. €2.60 Either single   6.00   6.00
c. Souvenir sheet of 2, #5452a-5452b, with different sheet margin   18.50   18.50
No. 5452c sold for €8.

Birds — A2807

Designs: No. 5453, Mésange bleue (European blue tit).
No. 5454: a, Rouge-gorge (European robin). b, Moineau (sparrow). c, Pie (magpie).

2018, June 10   Photo.   Perf. 13¼
5453 A2807 80c multi   1.90   .65

Souvenir Sheet
5454 Sheet of 4, #5453, 5454a-5454c   7.75   7.75
a.-c. A2807 80c Any single   1.90   .95
d. Souvenir sheet of 2, #5454a-5454b   7.00   7.00
e. Souvenir sheet of 2, #5453, 5454c   7.00   7.00
Nos. 5454d-5454e sold together as a set for €6.

Trois-Fontaines Abbey, 900th Anniv. — A2808

2018, June 15   Photo.   Perf. 13¼x13
5455 A2808 95c multi   2.25   .75

FRANCE

Tourism Issue

Kaysersberg — A2809

2018, June 20 Photo. Perf. 13x12¾
5456 A2809 80c multi 1.90 .65

Ploumanc'h Lighthouse, Perros-Guirec A2810

2018, June 22 Photo. Perf. 13¼
5457 A2810 80c multi 1.90 .65

Mickey Mouse and Eiffel Tower — A2811

Mickey Mouse and Mont-Saint-Michel Abbey — A2812

Mickey Mouse and Azay-le-Rideau Chateau — A2813

Mickey Mouse and Pont Saint-Bénézet, Avignon — A2814

Mickey Mouse and Bonifacio, Corsica — A2815

Mickey Mouse and Beach — A2816

Mickey Mouse and Etretat Cliffs — A2817

Mickey Mouse and Auvergne Region Volcano — A2818

Mickey Mouse and Cable Car — A2819

Mickey Mouse and Lumière Monument, Lyon — A2820

Mickey Mouse and Saint-Tropez A2821

Mickey Mouse and Strasbourg Cathedral A2822

Serpentine Die Cut 11
2018, June 29   Photo.
Booklet Stamps
Self-Adhesive

5458	A2811	(80c) multi	1.90	.65
5459	A2812	(80c) multi	1.90	.65
5460	A2813	(80c) multi	1.90	.65
5461	A2814	(80c) multi	1.90	.65
5462	A2815	(80c) multi	1.90	.65
5463	A2816	(80c) multi	1.90	.65
5464	A2817	(80c) multi	1.90	.65
5465	A2818	(80c) multi	1.90	.65
5466	A2819	(80c) multi	1.90	.65
5467	A2820	(80c) multi	1.90	.65
5468	A2821	(80c) multi	1.90	.65
5469	A2822	(80c) multi	1.90	.65

a. Booklet pane of 12, #5458-5869   23.00
Nos. 5458-5469 (12)   22.80 7.80

Ryder Cup, Flags of United States and European Union — A2823

2018   Photo.   Perf. 13x13¼
5470 A2823 €1.30 multi + label   3.00 1.00
  a. Sheet of 4 + 4 labels, sheet margin with white background   12.00 12.00
5470B A2823 €2.60 multi + label   6.00 2.00

42nd Ryder Cup Matches, Guyancourt. Issued: No. 5470, 6/30; No. 5470B, 9/15. No. 5470B was printed in sheets of 4.

Camargue Region House — A2824

2018, July 6   Photo.   Perf. 13¼
5471 A2824 €1.30 multi   3.00 1.00

Viaur Viaduct A2825

2018, July 6   Photo.   Perf. 13x12¾
5472 A2825 95c multi   2.25 .75

Marianne and Denomination A2826

Marianne "Ecopli" A2827

Marianne "Lettre Verte" A2828

Marianne "Lettre Prioritaire" A2829

Marianne "Europe" With Data Matrix Code — A2830

Marianne "Monde" With Data Matrix Code — A2831

2018, July 20   Engr.   Perf. 13
Inscribed "Phil@poste"

5473	A2826	1c yellow	.25	.25
a.	Inscribed "Philaposte" ('22)		.30	.30
5474	A2826	5c dk brown	.25	.25
a.	Inscribed "Philaposte" ('22)		.30	.30
5475	A2826	10c brown	.25	.25
a.	Souvenir sheet of 3, #5473-5475		.60	.60
b.	Inscribed "Philaposte" ('22)		.30	.30
5476	A2827	(78c) dk gray	1.90	.50
a.	Inscribed "Philaposte" ('22)		2.40	1.25
5477	A2828	(80c) emerald	1.90	.50
a.	Inscribed "Philaposte" ('22)		2.50	1.25
5478	A2829	(95c) red	2.25	.55
a.	Souvenir sheet of 2, #5477-5478		6.75	6.75
b.	Booklet pane of 12, 6 each #5477-5478		25.00	—
c.	Tete-beche pair, #5478d (6034b)		4.50	4.50
d.	Inscribed "Philaposte" ('21)		3.00	1.50
5479	A2826	€1 orange	2.40	.60
a.	Souvenir sheet of 2, #5476, 5479		6.75	6.75
b.	Inscribed "Philaposte" ('22)		2.10	1.10
5480	A2830	(€1.20) dull blue	2.75	.70
5481	A2831	(€1.30) purple	3.00	.75
a.	Souvenir sheet of 5, #5476-5478, 5480-5481		12.00	12.00
b.	Souvenir sheet of 2, #5480-5481		9.50	9.50

Nos. 5473-5481 (9)   14.95 4.35

Coil Stamps
Perf. 13 Horiz.
5482	A2828	(80c) emerald	1.90	.50
a.	Inscribed "Philaposte" ('22)		2.50	1.25
5483	A2829	(95c) red	2.25	.55
a.	Inscribed "Philaposte" ('22)		3.00	1.50

Self-Adhesive
Serpentine Die Cut 6¾ Vert.
5484	A2826	1c yellow	.25	.25
a.	Inscribed "Philaposte" ('22)		.30	.30
5485	A2826	5c dk brown	.25	.25
a.	Inscribed "Philaposte" ('22)		.30	.30
5486	A2826	10c brown	.25	.25
a.	Inscribed "Philaposte" ('22)		.30	.30
5487	A2827	(78c) dk gray	1.90	.50
a.	Inscribed "Philaposte" ('22)		2.40	1.25
5488	A2828	(80c) emerald	1.90	.50
a.	Booklet pane of 12		23.00	
b.	Inscribed "Philaposte" ('22)		2.50	1.25
c.	Booklet pane of 12 #5488b		30.00	
d.	Booklet pane of 20 #5488b		50.00	
5489	A2829	(95c) red	2.25	.55
a.	Booklet pane of 10		22.50	
b.	Booklet pane of 12		27.00	
c.	Booklet pane of 20		45.00	
d.	Inscribed "Philaposte" ('22)		3.00	1.50
e.	Booklet pane of 12 #5489d ('22)		36.00	
5490	A2826	€1 orange	2.40	.60
a.	Inscribed "Philaposte" ('22)		2.10	1.10
5491	A2830	(€1.20) dull blue	2.75	.70
5492	A2831	(€1.30) purple	3.00	.75

Nos. 5484-5492 (9)   14.95 4.35

Coil Stamps
Serpentine Die Cut 6¾ Horiz.
5493	A2828	(80c) emerald	1.90	.50
a.	Inscribed "Philaposte" ('22)		2.50	1.25
5494	A2829	(95c) red	2.25	.55
a.	Inscribed "Philaposte" ('22)		3.00	1.50

Issued: No. 5478b, 11/12/18; No. 5478c, 6/17/21. Nos. 5475a, 5478a, 5479a and 5481b sold as a set for €10. On day of issue, Nos. 5476a and 5487a each sold for €1.14, Nos. 5477a, 5482a and 5488b each sold for €1.16, and Nos. 5478d, 5489d and 5494e each sold for €1.43. Compare types A2831 and A2888.
See Nos. 5558-5561, 5756, 6036, 6129. For overprints, see Nos. 5539-5540, 5932, 6351-6352.

Trees — A2832

Designs: No. 5495, Betula papyrifera. No. 5496, Adansonia digitata. No. 5497, Cedrus libani. No. 5498, Carpinus betulus. No. 5499, Quercus robur. No. 5500, Fraxinus excelsior. No. 5501, Acer saccharum. No. 5502, Pinus sylvestris. No. 5503, Sequoiadendron giganteum. No. 5504, Ginkgo biloba. No. 5505, Olea europaea. No. 5506, Fagus sylvatica.

Serpentine Die Cut 11
2018, Aug. 3   Photo.
Booklet Stamps
Self-Adhesive
5495	A2832	(95c) multi	2.25	.75
5496	A2832	(95c) multi	2.25	.75
5497	A2832	(95c) multi	2.25	.75
5498	A2832	(95c) multi	2.25	.75
5499	A2832	(95c) multi	2.25	.75
5500	A2832	(95c) multi	2.25	.75
5501	A2832	(95c) multi	2.25	.75
5502	A2832	(95c) multi	2.25	.75
5503	A2832	(95c) multi	2.25	.75
5504	A2832	(95c) multi	2.25	.75
5505	A2832	(95c) multi	2.25	.75
5506	A2832	(95c) multi	2.25	.75

a. Booklet pane of 12, #5495-5506   27.00
Nos. 5495-5506 (12)   27.00 9.00

Teapot From Jiangsu, China — A2833

Teapot From China — A2834   Teapot From England — A2835

Teapot From Sèvres, France A2836   Teapot From Delft, Netherlands A2837

Teapot From Jingdezhen, China — A2838

Teapot From Sèvres, France — A2839

Teapot From Kyoto, Japan — A2840

Teapot From Paris, France — A2841

Teapot From Moscow, Russia — A2842

Teapot From Venice, Italy — A2843

Teapot From Lille, France — A2844

Serpentine Die Cut 11
2018, Aug. 31   Photo.
Booklet Stamps
Self-Adhesive
5507	A2833	(80c) multi	1.90	.65
5508	A2834	(80c) multi	1.90	.65
5509	A2835	(80c) multi	1.90	.65
5510	A2836	(80c) multi	1.90	.65
5511	A2837	(80c) multi	1.90	.65
5512	A2838	(80c) multi	1.90	.65
5513	A2839	(80c) multi	1.90	.65
5514	A2840	(80c) multi	1.90	.65
5515	A2841	(80c) multi	1.90	.65
5516	A2842	(80c) multi	1.90	.65
5517	A2843	(80c) multi	1.90	.65
5518	A2844	(80c) multi	1.90	.65

a. Booklet pane of 12, #5507-5518   23.00
Nos. 5507-5518 (12)   22.80 7.80

722 FRANCE

Mickey Mouse, 90th Anniv. — A2845

2018, Sept. 5   Photo.   Perf. 13¼x13
5519 A2845 €1.30 multi   3.00 1.00

Miniature Sheet

Stage Actors and Actresses — A2846

No. 5520: a, François-Joseph Talma (1763-1826). b, Rachel Félix (1821-58). c, Sarah Bernhardt (1844-1923). d, Benoît-Constant Coquelin (Coquelin Aîné) (1841-1909).

2018, Sept. 7   Photo.   Perf. 13¼
5520 A2846 Sheet of 4 + 5 labels   11.00 11.00
a.-d. €1.20 Any single   2.75 .90

Ceramics A2847

2018, Sept. 15   Engr.   Perf. 13
5521 A2847 €1.30 multi   3.00 1.00
A souvenir sheet of 1 sold for €4.

Pierre Schoendoerffer (1928-2012), Film Director and War Reporter A2848

2018, Sept. 21   Engr.   Perf. 13¼
5522 A2848 €1.30 multi   3.00 1.00

Louise de Bettignies (1880-1918), World War I Secret Agent — A2849

2018, Sept. 28   Photo.   Perf. 13¼
5523 A2849 80c multi   1.90 .65

Rose Valland (1898-1980), Art Historian and World War II Resistance Leader — A2850

2018, Sept. 28   Photo.   Perf. 13¼
5524 A2850 €1.20 multi   2.75 .90

Françoise Dolto (1908-88), Pediatrician and Psychoanalyst A2851

2018, Oct. 5   Photo.   Perf. 13¼
5525 A2851 95c multi   2.25 .75

A2852   A2853

A2854   A2855

A2856   A2857

A2858   A2859

A2860   A2861

Photographs of Snowflakes
A2862   A2863

Serpentine Die Cut 11
2018, Oct. 5   Photo.
Booklet Stamps
Self-Adhesive
5526 A2852 (80c) multi   1.90 .65
5527 A2853 (80c) multi   1.90 .65
5528 A2854 (80c) multi   1.90 .65
5529 A2855 (80c) multi   1.90 .65
5530 A2856 (80c) multi   1.90 .65
5531 A2857 (80c) multi   1.90 .65
5532 A2858 (80c) multi   1.90 .65
5533 A2859 (80c) multi   1.90 .65
5534 A2860 (80c) multi   1.90 .65
5535 A2861 (80c) multi   1.90 .65
5536 A2862 (80c) multi   1.90 .65
5537 A2863 (80c) multi   1.90 .65
a.   Booklet pane of 12, #5526-5537   23.00
Nos. 5526-5537 (12)   22.80 7.80

Elise (1898-1983) and Célestin (1896-1966) Freinet, Educational Reformers A2864

2018, Oct. 12   Photo.   Perf. 13¼
5538 A2864 95c multi   2.25 .75

Nos. 5480-5481 Overprinted in Red or Blue

Methods and Perfs. As Before
2018, Oct. 15
5539 A2830 (€1.20) dull blue   2.75 1.40
      (R)
5540 A28310 (€1.30) purple (Bl)   3.00 1.50

Art Issue

Photograph of Woman Reading Letter by Sophie Calle A2865

2018, Oct. 19   Photo.   Perf. 13x13¼
5541 A2865 €1.90 multi   4.50 2.25

Périgueux — A2866

2018, Oct. 26   Engr.   Perf. 13x13¼
5542 A2866 80c multi + label   1.90 .65

Postal Checks, Cent. — A2867

2018, Oct. 31   Photo.   Perf. 12¼
5543 A2867 80c multi   1.90 .65

Vases — A2868

Vase by: 95c, Emile Gallé (1846-1904), France. €1.20, Antonija Krasnik (1874-1956), Croatia.

2018, Nov. 8   Photo.   Perf. 12¼
5544 A2868 95c multi   2.25 .75
5545 A2868 €1.20 multi   2.75 .90

See Croatia Nos. 1092-1093.

"Bonne Année"   House and
A2869   Trees
               A2870

Heart and   Reindeer and
Flowers   Flowers
A2871   A2872

"Bonne Année"   Candle,
A2873   Flowers and
                Hearts
                A2874

Christmas   Reindeer
Ornament   A2876
A2875

Gift   "Joyeuses
A2877   Fêtes"
                A2878

"Joie"   Head of
A2879   Reindeer
                A2880

Serpentine Die Cut 11
2018, Nov. 8   Photo.
Booklet Stamps
Self-Adhesive
5546 A2869 (80c) gold & multi   1.90 .65
      Scratched panel   .40
5547 A2870 (80c) gold & multi   1.90 .65
      Scratched panel   .40
5548 A2871 (80c) gold & multi   1.90 .65
      Scratched panel   .40
5549 A2872 (80c) gold & multi   1.90 .65
      Scratched panel   .40
5550 A2873 (80c) gold & multi   1.90 .65
      Scratched panel   .40
5551 A2874 (80c) gold & multi   1.90 .65
      Scratched panel   .40
5552 A2875 (80c) gold & multi   1.90 .65
      Scratched panel   .40
5553 A2876 (80c) gold & multi   1.90 .65
      Scratched panel   .40
5554 A2877 (80c) gold & multi   1.90 .65
      Scratched panel   .40
5555 A2878 (80c) gold & multi   1.90 .65
      Scratched panel   .40
5556 A2879 (80c) gold & multi   1.90 .65
      Scratched panel   .40
5557 A2880 (80c) gold & multi   1.90 .65
      Scratched panel   .40
a.   Booklet pane of 12, #5546-5557   23.00
Nos. 5546-5557 (12)   22.80 7.80

Christmas and New Year's greetings.

Marianne Types of 2018 and

Marianne A2881

2018, Nov. 12   Engr.   Perf. 13
Booklet Stamps
Size: 30x46mm
5558 A2826 €1.60 green   3.75 1.25
5559 A2826 €1.90 red   4.50 1.50
a.   Booklet pane of 2, #5558-5559   8.25 —

FRANCE

Complete booklet, #5478b,
5559a ... 33.50

Self-Adhesive
Design Size: 15x23mm (Nos. 5560-5561)
Photo.
Serpentine Die Cut 11

5560	A2828	(80c) green	1.90	.50
5561	A2829	(95c) red	2.25	.60
5562	A2881	(€3.20) black & gray	7.25	2.40
a.	Bklt. pane of 13, #5562, 6 each #5560-5561		32.50	
	Nos. 5560-5562 (3)		11.40	3.50

Marianne "Lettre Suivie" — A2881a

2018 ? *Litho.* *Die Cut*
Self-Adhesive

| 5563 | A2881a | (€1.28) cerise + label | — | — |

Ivan Turgenev (1818-83), Writer — A2882

2018, Nov. 9 *Photo.* *Perf. 13¼*
| 5565 | A2882 | €1.30 multi | 3.00 | 1.00 |

Miniature Sheet

Hats A2883

No. 5566: a, Capeline. b, Haut de forme (top hat). c, Cloche. d, Mambo (pork pie hat), horiz. e, Toque. f, Chapeau melon (bowler hat), horiz.

Litho. & Engr.
2018, Nov. 9 *Perf. 13*
5566	A2883	Sheet of 6	13.50	13.50
a.-f.		95c Any single	2.25	.75
g.		Souvenir sheet of 3, #5566a, 5566d, 5566f	9.25	9.25
h.		Souvenir sheet of 3, #5566b, 5566c, 5566e	9.25	9.25

Nos. 5566g and 5566h were sold together for €8.

Souvenir Sheet

World War I Armistice, Cent. — A2884

No. 5567: a, Soldiers celebrating. b, Civilians celebrating.

2018, Nov. 11 *Photo.* *Perf. 13¼*
5567	A2884	Sheet of 2	12.00	12.00
a.-b.		€2.60 Either stamp	6.00	2.00
c.		Souvenir sheet of 2, #5567a-5567b, different sheet margin	18.50	18.50

No. 5567c sold for €8.

A2885

General Henri M. Berthelot (1861-1931) A2886

2018, Nov. 27 *Photo.* *Perf. 13¼*
5568	A2885	€1.30 multi	3.00	1.00
5569	A2886	€1.30 multi	3.00	1.00
a.		Souvenir sheet of 2, #5568-5569	9.25	9.25

No. 5569a sold for €4. See Romania Nos. 6201-6202.

Universal Declaration of Human Rights, 70th Anniv. — A2887

2018, Dec. 10 *Photo.* *Perf. 13¼*
| 5570 | A2887 | 88c multi | 2.00 | .65 |

Marianne "International" and Data Matrix Code — A2888

2019, Jan. 1 *Engr.* *Perf. 13*
Inscribed "Phil@poste"
| 5571 | A2888 | (€1.30) purple | 3.00 | .75 |
| a. | | Inscribed "Philaposte" ('22) | 3.50 | 1.75 |

Booklet Stamp
Self-Adhesive
Serpentine Die Cut 6¾ Vert.
5572	A2888	(€1.30) purple	3.00	.75
a.		Booklet pane of 6	19.00	
b.		Inscribed "Philaposte" ('22)	3.50	1.75

On day of issue, Nos. 5571a and 5572b each sold for €1.65.
Compare types A2831 and A2888.

A2889

A2890

A2891

A2892

A2893

A2894

A2895

A2896

A2897

A2898

A2899

African Fabric Patterns — A2900

Serpentine Die Cut 11
2019, Jan. 4 *Photo.*
Booklet Stamps
Self-Adhesive

5573	A2889	(88c) multi	2.10	.70
5574	A2890	(88c) multi	2.10	.70
5575	A2891	(88c) multi	2.10	.70
5576	A2892	(88c) multi	2.10	.70
a.	Larger dots in flowers and background		2.10	.70
5577	A2893	(88c) multi	2.10	.70
5578	A2894	(88c) multi	2.10	.70
5579	A2895	(88c) multi	2.10	.70
5580	A2896	(88c) multi	2.10	.70
5581	A2897	(88c) multi	2.10	.70
5582	A2898	(88c) multi	2.10	.70
5583	A2899	(88c) multi	2.10	.70
5584	A2900	(88c) multi	2.10	.70
a.	Booklet pane of 12, #5573-5584		26.60	
	Nos. 5573-5584 (12)		25.20	8.40

No. 5576a was printed only in sheets of 50.

Emilie du Châtelet (1706-49), Philosopher, Mathematician and Physicist — A2901

2019, Jan. 18 *Photo.* *Perf. 13¼*
| 5585 | A2901 | 88c multi | 2.10 | .70 |

Heart and Vine — A2902   Heart and Vendôme Column, Paris — A2903

2019, Jan. 18 *Photo.* *Perf. 13¼*
5586	A2902	88c multi	2.10	.70
a.	Souvenir sheet of 5		10.50	10.50
5587	A2903	€1.76 multi	4.00	1.40

Self-Adhesive
Serpentine Die Cut
| 5588 | A2902 | 88c multi | 2.10 | .70 |
| 5589 | A2903 | €1.76 multi | 4.00 | 1.40 |

Values for Nos. 5586-5589 are for stamps with surrounding selvage.

New Year 2019 (Year of the Pig) — A2904

Designs: 88c, Pig holding Chinese lantern. €1.30, Three pigs on Chinese lantern.

2019, Jan. 25 *Photo.* *Perf. 13*
5590		Sheet of 5, #5590a, 4 #5590b	10.50	10.50
a.		A2904 88c 33x40mm stamp	2.10	.70
b.		A2904 88c 29x35mm stamp	2.10	.70
5591		Sheet of 5, #5591a, 4 #5591b	15.00	15.00
a.		A2904 €1.30 33x40mm stamp	3.00	1.00
b.		A2904 €1.30 29x35mm stamp	3.00	1.00

Architectural Details of French Buildings — A2905

Designs: No. 5592, Chapelle Sainte-Marie, Nevers. No. 5593, Château de Vitré. No. 5594, Grand Palais, Paris. No. 5595, Château de Chambord. No. 5596, Notre Dame Cathedral, Strasbourg. No. 5597, Pavillon de l'Horloge, Louvre Museum, Paris. No. 5598, Saline Royale (Royal Saltworks), Arc-et-Senans. No. 5599, Museum of Grenoble. No. 5600, Church, Saint-Nectaire. No. 5601, Notre-Dame-des-Champs Church, Avranches. No. 5602, Maison Carrée, Nîmes. No. 5603, Saint-Front Cathedral, Périgueux.

Serpentine Die Cut 11
2019, Feb. 1 *Photo.*
Booklet Stamps
Self-Adhesive

5592	A2905	(€1.05) multi	2.40	.80
5593	A2905	(€1.05) multi	2.40	.80
5594	A2905	(€1.05) multi	2.40	.80
5595	A2905	(€1.05) multi	2.40	.80
a.	Larger and coarser dot structure		2.40	.80
5596	A2905	(€1.05) multi	2.40	.80
a.	Larger and coarser dot structure		2.40	.80
5597	A2905	(€1.05) multi	2.40	.80
5598	A2905	(€1.05) multi	2.40	.80
5599	A2905	(€1.05) multi	2.40	.80
5600	A2905	(€1.05) multi	2.40	.80
5601	A2905	(€1.05) multi	2.40	.80
5602	A2905	(€1.05) multi	2.40	.80
5603	A2905	(€1.05) multi	2.40	.80
a.	Booklet pane of 12, #5592-5603		29.00	
	Nos. 5592-5603 (12)		28.80	9.60

Nos. 5595a and 5596a were both printed in sheets of 50. The larger and coarser dot structure can best be seen in the upper left triangle.

Louise de Vilmorin (1902-69), Writer — A2906

2019, Feb. 8 *Photo.* *Perf. 13¼*
| 5604 | A2906 | €1.05 multi | 2.40 | .80 |

Sister Cities of Dinan, France and Dinant, Belgium A2907

2019, Feb. 15 *Photo.* *Perf. 13x12¾*
| 5605 | A2907 | €1.30 multi | 3.00 | 1.00 |

Saltwater Fish — A2908

Designs: No. 5606, Thunnus thynnus. No. 5607, Scorpaena scrofa. No. 5608, Dicentrarchus labrax. No. 5609, Zeus faber. No. 5610, Sparus aurata. No. 5611, Scophthalmus maximus. No. 5612, Solea solea. No. 5613, Scomber scombrus. No. 5614, Epinephelus marginatus. No. 5615, Ssrdina pilchardus. No. 5616, Raja clavata. No. 5617, Gadus morhua.

Serpentine Die Cut 11
2019, Feb. 22 *Photo.*
Booklet Stamps
Self-Adhesive

5606	A2908	(88c) multi	2.00	.65
5607	A2908	(88c) multi	2.00	.65
5608	A2908	(88c) multi	2.00	.65
5609	A2908	(88c) multi	2.00	.65
5610	A2908	(88c) multi	2.00	.65
5611	A2908	(88c) multi	2.00	.65
5612	A2908	(88c) multi	2.00	.65
5613	A2908	(88c) multi	2.00	.65
5614	A2908	(88c) multi	2.00	.65
5615	A2908	(88c) multi	2.00	.65
5616	A2908	(88c) multi	2.00	.65
5617	A2908	(88c) multi	2.00	.65
a.	Booklet pane of 12, #5606-5617		24.00	
	Nos. 5606-5617 (12)		24.00	7.80

FRANCE

Art Series

Calendula (Marigold), Photograph by Valérie Belin — A2909

2019, Feb. 22 Litho. Perf. 13
5618 A2909 €2.10 multi   4.75 2.40

Citroen Automobiles A2910

Designs: 88c, Citroen Type A 10 HP. €1.76, Citroen Traction.

2019, Mar. 9 Photo. Perf. 13¼
5619 A2910 88c multi   2.00   .65

Souvenir Sheet
Perf. 13x13¼
5620 A2910 €1.76 sil & multi 4.00 1.40

Stamp Day. No. 5620 contains one 52x41mm stamp.

Fontaine Saint-Michel, Paris — A2911

2019, Mar. 14 Engr. Perf. 13
5621 A2911 88c multi   2.00   .65

Spring Philatelic Show, Paris.

Ceres — A2912

Photo. & Typo.
2019, Mar. 14   Imperf.
5622 A2912 20c black   .85   .85
  a. Tête bêche pair   —   —
5623 A2912 88c black   2.00   .65
  a. As #5623, with inverted vignette   —   —
  b. Pair, #5623-5623a   —   —

No. 5622 was printed in sheets of 150 (with one stamp inverted) that sold for €55. No. 5623 was printed in sheets of 20 (with one stamp with inverted vignette). See Nos. 5754-5755.

Crystal Production A2913

2019, Mar. 15 Engr. Perf. 13¼
5624 A2913 €1.30 indigo & slate vio   3.00 1.00

A souvenir sheet containing No. 5624 sold for €4.

Miniature Sheet

European Capitals — A2914

No. 5625 — Attractions in Helsinki, Finland: a, Lutheran Cathedral. b, Kruununhaka. c, Suomenlinna. d, Sibelius Monument.

2019, Mar. 16 Photo. Perf. 13x13¼
5625 A2914 Sheet of 4   12.00 12.00
  a.-d. €1.30 Any single   3.00 1.00

Sculptures of Nude Women — A2915

Designs: No. 5626, Sculpture by Charles Despiau. No. 5627, Sculpture by Antoine Bourdelle. No. 5628, Ancient Egyptian sculpture. No. 5629, Ancient Greek sculpture (Venus de Milo). No. 5630, Sculpture by Edgar Degas. No. 5631, Ancient Oriental sculpture. No. 5632, Sculpture by Jacquio Ponce. No. 5633, Sculpture by Aristide Maillol. No. 5634, Nepalese sculpture. No. 5635, Statue by unknown artist in style of Etienne Maurice Falconet. No. 5636, Statue from Upper Paleolithic era. No. 5637, Sculpture from Ivory Coast (Côte d'Ivoire).

Serpentine Die Cut 11
2019, Mar. 29   Photo.
Booklet Stamps
Self-Adhesive
5626 A2915 (88c) multi   2.00   .65
5627 A2915 (88c) multi   2.00   .65
5628 A2915 (88c) multi   2.00   .65
5629 A2915 (88c) multi   2.00   .65
5630 A2915 (88c) multi   2.00   .65
5631 A2915 (88c) multi   2.00   .65
5632 A2915 (88c) multi   2.00   .65
5633 A2915 (88c) multi   2.00   .65
5634 A2915 (88c) multi   2.00   .65
5635 A2915 (88c) multi   2.00   .65
5636 A2915 (88c) multi   2.00   .65
5637 A2915 (88c) multi   2.00   .65
  a. Booklet pane of 12, #5626-5637   24.00
  Nos. 5626-5637 (12)   24.00 7.80

Souvenir Sheet

Diplomatic Relations Between France and Poland, Cent. — A2916

No. 5638: a, Charles de Gaulle (1890-1970), as army captain (later president of France). b, Józef Haller (1873-1960), Polish lieutenant general.

2019, Apr. 2 Photo. Perf. 13¼
5638 A2916 Sheet of 2   5.00 5.00
  a. 88c multi   2.00   .65
  b. €1.30 multi   3.00 1.00

A souvenir sheet containing Nos. 5638a-5638b with a different sheet margin sold for €6. See Poland No. 4409.

Souvenir Sheet

Mogador Theater, Paris, Cent. A2917

No. 5639: a, Seats in theater. b, Architectural detail depicting ram's head.

2019, Apr. 2 Photo. Perf. 13¼
5639 A2917 Sheet of 2   6.00 6.00
  a.-b. €1.30 Either single   3.00 1.00

A souvenir sheet containing Nos. 5639a-5639b with a different sheet margin sold for €6.

Woman Suffrage in France, 75th Anniv. — A2918

2019, Apr. 19 Photo. Perf. 13¼
5640 A2918 88c multi   2.00   .65

Souvenir Sheet

Paintings A2919

No. 5641: a, The Gulf of Marseille Seen From L'Estaque, by Paul Cézanne (1839-1906). b, Mohammed V Square, Casablanca, by Jacques Majorelle (1886-1962).

2019, Apr. 26 Photo. Perf. 13¼
5641 A2919 Sheet of 2   5.00 5.00
  a. 88c multi   2.00   .65
  b. €1.30 multi   3.00 1.00

See Morocco No. 1269.

Art Issue

Lascaux Cave Drawings A2920

2019, Apr. 26 Engr. Perf. 13x12
5642 A2920 88c multi   2.00 1.00

A souvenir sheet containing a perf. 13x13¼ example of No. 5642 sold for €4.

A2921

A2922

A2923

A2924

A2925

A2926

A2927

A2928

A2929

A2930

A2931

Photographs of Flowers by Jacques du Sordet — A2932

Serpentine Die Cut 11
2019, May 3   Photo.
Booklet Stamps
Self-Adhesive
5643 A2921 (88c) multi   2.00   .65
5644 A2922 (88c) multi   2.00   .65
5645 A2923 (88c) multi   2.00   .65
5646 A2924 (88c) multi   2.00   .65
5647 A2925 (88c) multi   2.00   .65
5648 A2926 (88c) multi   2.00   .65
5649 A2927 (88c) multi   2.00   .65
5650 A2928 (88c) multi   2.00   .65
5651 A2929 (88c) multi   2.00   .65
5652 A2930 (88c) multi   2.00   .65
5653 A2931 (88c) multi   2.00   .65
5654 A2932 (88c) multi   2.00   .65
  a. Booklet pane of 12, #5643-5654   24.00
  Nos. 5643-5654 (12)   24.00 7.80

Lighthouse, Fresnel Lens and Augustin Fresnel (1788-1827), Physicist A2933

2019, May 3 Engr. Perf. 13¼
5655 A2933 €1.05 multi   2.40   .80

Stylized Birds A2934

2019, May 10 Photo. Perf. 13
5656 A2934 €1.30 multi   3.00 1.00

Europa.

Endangered Flora — A2935

Designs: No. 5657, Violette de Rouen. No. 5658: a, Saxifrage oeil-de-bouc. b, Faujasia écailleuse. c, Dracocéphale d'Autriche.

2019, May 17 Photo. Perf. 13¼
5657 A2935 88c multi   2.00   .65

Miniature Sheet
5658 Sheet of 4, #5657, 5658a-5658c   8.00 8.00
  a.-c. A2935 88c Any single   2.00   .65
  d. Souvenir sheet of 2, #5657, 5658b   6.75 6.75
  e. Souvenir sheet of 2, #5658a, 5658c   6.75 6.75

Nos. 5658d and 5658e were sold together for €6.

FRANCE

Miniature Sheet

Sports A2936

No. 5659: a, Volleyball. b, Table tennis, horiz. c, Soccer, horiz. d, Field hockey. e, Kayaking, horiz. f, Wheelchair basketball.

2019, May 18   Litho.   Perf. 13
5659 A2936 Sheet of 6   18.00 18.00
 a.-f. €1.30 Any single   3.00   1.00

Château de Chambord, 500th Anniv. — A2937

2019, May 31   Engr.   Perf. 13x12¾
5660 A2937 88c multi   2.00   .65

A souvenir sheet containing No. 5660 sold for €4.

Characters from Astérix Comic Strips — A2938

Designs: No. 5661, Falbala. No. 5662, Obélix. No. 5663, Panoramix. No. 5664, Ordralfabétix. No. 5665, Abraracourcix. No. 5666, Bonemine. No. 5667, Cétautomatix. No. 5668, Assurancetourix. No. 5669, Agecanonix. No. 5670, Mrs. Agecanonix. No. 5671, Idéfix. No. 5672, Astérix.

Serpentine Die Cut 11
2019, June 6   Photo.
Booklet Stamps
Self-Adhesive
5661 A2938 (88c) multi   2.00   .65
5662 A2938 (88c) multi   2.00   .65
5663 A2938 (88c) multi   2.00   .65
5664 A2938 (88c) multi   2.00   .65
5665 A2938 (88c) multi   2.00   .65
5666 A2938 (88c) multi   2.00   .65
5667 A2938 (88c) multi   2.00   .65
5668 A2938 (88c) multi   2.00   .65
5669 A2938 (88c) multi   2.00   .65
5670 A2938 (88c) multi   2.00   .65
5671 A2938 (88c) multi   2.00   .65
5672 A2938 (88c) multi   2.00   .65
 a. Booklet pane of 12, #5661-5672   24.00
 Nos. 5661-5672 (12)   24.00 7.80

Art Issue

Self-Portrait with a Black Dog, by Gustave Courbet (1819-77) A2939

2019, June 7   Photo.   Perf. 13x13¼
5673 A2939 €2.10 multi   4.75 2.10

Opéra Comédie, Montpellier — A2940

2019, June 7   Engr.   Perf. 13x13¼
5674 A2940 €1.05 multi + label 2.40 .80

French Federation of Philatelic Associations, 92nd Congress, Montpellier.

Saint-Philbert-de-Grand-Lieu Abbey — A2941

2019, June 14   Photo.   Perf. 13¼
5675 A2941 88c multi   2.00   .65

Fountain of the Quatre-Vallées, Tarbes — A2942

2019, June 21   Photo.   Perf. 13¼
5676 A2942 88c multi   2.00   .65

Reuze-Papa and Reuze-Maman Statues, Cassel — A2943

2019, June 27   Photo.   Perf. 13x12¾
5677 A2943 88c multi   2.00   .65

A2944   A2945

A2946   A2947

A2948   A2949

A2950   A2951

A2952   A2953

A2954

Vacation — A2955

Serpentine Die Cut 11
2019, June 28   Photo.
Booklet Stamps
Self-Adhesive
5678 A2944 (88c) multi   2.00   .65
5679 A2945 (88c) multi   2.00   .65
5680 A2946 (88c) multi   2.00   .65
5681 A2947 (88c) multi   2.00   .65
5682 A2948 (88c) multi   2.00   .65
5683 A2949 (88c) multi   2.00   .65
5684 A2950 (88c) multi   2.00   .65
5685 A2951 (88c) multi   2.00   .65
5686 A2952 (88c) multi   2.00   .65
5687 A2953 (88c) multi   2.00   .65
5688 A2954 (88c) multi   2.00   .65
5689 A2955 (88c) multi   2.00   .65
 a. Booklet pane of 12, #5678-5689   24.00
 Nos. 5678-5689 (12)   24.00 7.80

Françoise d'Aubigne, Marquise de Maintenon (1635-1719), Second Wife of King Louis XIV — A2956

2019, June 28   Photo.   Perf. 13
5690 A2956 €1.05 multi   2.40   .80

Values are for stamps with surrounding selvage.

A2957

2019, July 5   Engr.   Perf. 13
5691 A2957 €1.05 multi   2.40   .80

Awarding of Legion of Honor and Croix de Guerre to city of Reims, cent.

Mediterranean Women's Costumes and Euromed Postal Emblem — A2958

2019, July 5   Photo.   Perf. 13¼
5692 A2958 €1.30 multi   3.00 1.00

First Man on the Moon, 50th Anniv. — A2959

2019, July 19   Photo.   Perf. 13x13¼
5693 A2959 €1.30 multi   3.00 1.00

Lighthouses — A2960

Designs: No. 5694, Dunkerque Lighthouse. No. 5695, Goury Lighthouse. No. 5696, Ile Vierge Lighthouse. No. 5697, Kéréon Lighthouse. No. 5698, Ar-Men Lighthouse. No. 5699, Pilier Lighthouse. No. 5700, Chassiron Lighthouse. No. 5701, Cordouan Lighthouse. No. 5702, Biarritz Lighthouse. No. 5703, Cap Béar Lighthouse. No. 5704, Cap Camarat Lighthouse. No. 5705, Lavezzi Lighthouse.

Serpentine Die Cut 11
2019, Aug. 2   Photo.
Booklet Stamps
Self-Adhesive
5694 A2960 (€1.05) multi   2.40   .80
5695 A2960 (€1.05) multi   2.40   .80
5696 A2960 (€1.05) multi   2.40   .80
5697 A2960 (€1.05) multi   2.40   .80
5698 A2960 (€1.05) multi   2.40   .80
5699 A2960 (€1.05) multi   2.40   .80
5700 A2960 (€1.05) multi   2.40   .80
5701 A2960 (€1.05) multi   2.40   .80
5702 A2960 (€1.05) multi   2.40   .80
5703 A2960 (€1.05) multi   2.40   .80
5704 A2960 (€1.05) multi   2.40   .80
5705 A2960 (€1.05) multi   2.40   .80
 a. Booklet pane of 12, #5694-5705   29.00
 Nos. 5694-5705 (12)   28.80 9.60

Liberation of Paris, 75th Anniv. — A2961

2019, Aug. 25   Photo.   Perf. 13x12¾
5706 A2961 €1.30 multi   3.00 1.00

A souvenir sheet containing No. 5706 sold for €4.

Monte Cinto, Corsica — A2962

2019, Sept. 6   Photo.   Perf. 13¼
5707 A2962 88c multi   1.90   .65

Astérix Comic Strips, 60th Anniv. — A2963

2019, Sept. 6   Photo.   Perf. 13x13¼
5708 A2963 88c multi   1.90   .65

No. 5708 was printed in sheets of 5.

Protection of Architectural Treasures A2964

Designs: No. 5709, Notre Dame Church, Rigny. No. 5710, Longuay Abbey, Aubepierre-sur-Aube. No. 5711, Château de Bon Repos, Jarrie. No. 5712, Château de Carneville. No. 5713, Canal du Midi. No. 5714, Grande Forge de Buffon. No. 5715, Fort Cicogne, Glénan Archipelago. No. 5716, Pont du Moulin, Thorame-Haute. No. 5717, Saint-François Convent, Pino. No. 5718, Saint-Léger Church, Barly. No. 5719, Château de Bouteville. No. 5720, Château de Lassay.

Serpentine Die Cut 11
2019, Sept. 12   Photo.
Booklet Stamps
Self-Adhesive
5709 A2964 (88c) multi   1.90   .65
5710 A2964 (88c) multi   1.90   .65
5711 A2964 (88c) multi   1.90   .65
5712 A2964 (88c) multi   1.90   .65
5713 A2964 (88c) multi   1.90   .65
5714 A2964 (88c) multi   1.90   .65
5715 A2964 (88c) multi   1.90   .65
5716 A2964 (88c) multi   1.90   .65
5717 A2964 (88c) multi   1.90   .65
5718 A2964 (88c) multi   1.90   .65
5719 A2964 (88c) multi   1.90   .65
5720 A2964 (88c) multi   1.90   .65
 a. Booklet pane of 12, #5709-5720   23.00
 Nos. 5709-5720 (12)   22.80 7.80

FRANCE

Le Creusot Buildings and Steam Hammer — A2965

2019, Sept. 20   Photo.   *Perf. 13¼*
5721   A2965   88c multi   1.90   .65

Bookbinding — A2966

2019, Sept. 20   Engr.   *Perf. 13x13¼*
5722   A2966   €1.05 multi   2.40   .80

Mohandas K. Gandhi (1869-1948), Indian Nationalist Leader — A2967

2019, Oct. 2   Engr.   *Perf. 13¼*
5723   A2967   €1.30 multi   3.00   1.00

Suez Canal, 150th Anniv. A2968

2019, Oct. 3   Photo.   *Perf. 13x13¼*
5724   A2968   €1.30 multi   3.00   1.00

A souvenir sheet containing No. 5724 sold for €4.

Alexandre Varenne (1870-1947), Founder of *La Montagne* Newspaper — A2969

2019, Oct. 4   Engr.   *Perf. 13*
5725   A2969   88c multi   2.00   .70

Sèvres Plate A2970

Sèvres Plate A2971

Sèvres Plate A2972

Creil & Montereau Plate A2973

Casteldurante Plate A2974

Sèvres Plate A2975

Sienne Plate A2976

Creil & Montereau Plate A2977

Plate by Unknown Manufacturer A2978

Limoges Plate A2979

Sèvres Plate A2980

Sèvres Plate A2981

Serpentine Die Cut 11

2019, Oct. 4   Photo.
Booklet Stamps
Self-Adhesive

5726	A2970	(88c) multi	2.00	.70
5727	A2971	(88c) multi	2.00	.70
5728	A2972	(88c) multi	2.00	.70
5729	A2973	(88c) multi	2.00	.70
5730	A2974	(88c) multi	2.00	.70
5731	A2975	(88c) multi	2.00	.70
5732	A2976	(88c) multi	2.00	.70
5733	A2977	(88c) multi	2.00	.70
5734	A2978	(88c) multi	2.00	.70
5735	A2979	(88c) multi	2.00	.70
5736	A2980	(88c) multi	2.00	.70
5737	A2981	(88c) multi	2.00	.70

a.   Booklet pane of 12, #5726-5737   24.00
Nos. 5726-5737 (12)   24.00   8.40

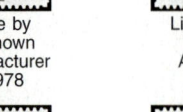

ESCP Europe Business School, Paris, 200th Anniv. — A2982

2019, Oct. 11   Photo.   *Perf. 13¼*
5738   A2982   €1.30 multi   3.00   1.00

Souvenir Sheet

National Opera of Paris, 350th Anniv. A2983

No. 5739: a, Dancer's feet. b, Performer's head.

2019, Oct. 18   Engr.   *Perf. 13¼*
5739   A2983   Sheet of 2   6.00   6.00
a.-b.   €1.30 Either single   3.00   1.00

A souvenir sheet containing Nos. 5739a-5739b with a different sheet margin sold for €6.

Art Issue

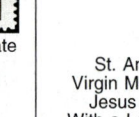

St. Anne, the Virgin Mary and Jesus Playing With a Lamb, by Leonardo da Vinci (1452-1519) A2984

2019, Oct. 25   Photo.   *Perf. 13*
5740   A2984   €2.10 multi   4.75   2.40
a.   Souvenir sheet of 1   9.00   9.00

No. 5740a sold for €4.

Polar Bear A2985

Owl A2986

Fox's Body — A2987

Fox's Tails — A2988

Reindeer's Antlers — A2989

Polar Bear's Head A2990

Reindeer A2991

Owl's Head and Chest A2992

Fox's Head A2993

Fox's Head and Tail — A2994

Reindeer's Head — A2995

Polar Bear's Body — A2996

Serpentine Die Cut 11

2019, Nov. 2   Photo.
Booklet Stamps
Self-Adhesive

5741	A2985	(88c) multi	2.00	.70
5742	A2986	(88c) multi	2.00	.70
5743	A2987	(88c) multi	2.00	.70
5744	A2988	(88c) multi	2.00	.70
5745	A2989	(88c) multi	2.00	.70
5746	A2990	(88c) multi	2.00	.70
5747	A2991	(88c) multi	2.00	.70
5748	A2992	(88c) multi	2.00	.70
5749	A2993	(88c) multi	2.00	.70
5750	A2994	(88c) multi	2.00	.70
5751	A2995	(88c) multi	2.00	.70
5752	A2996	(88c) multi	2.00	.70

a.   Booklet pane of 12, #5741-5752   24.00
Nos. 5741-5752 (12)   24.00   8.40

Paper art by Lila Poppins.

Ceres — A2997

2019, Nov. 7   Engr.   *Imperf.*
5753   A2997   €5 black   11.00   11.00

No. 5753 was printed in sheets of 4.

Ceres and Marianne Types of 2018-19

2019, Nov. 7   Engr.   *Imperf.*
Booklet Stamps
Size: 15x19mm
5754   A2912   €1.05 black   2.40   .80
a.   Booklet pane of 12, 6 each #5478, 5754   28.00   —

Size: 40x53mm
Perf. 13
5755   A2912   €2.10 black   4.75   1.60
5756   A2829   €2.10 red   4.75   1.60
a.   Booklet pane of 2, #5755-5756   9.50   —
   Complete booklet, #5754a, 5756a   37.50

Renovation of Postal Museum, Paris — A2998

2019, Nov. 7   Engr.   *Perf. 13*
5757   A2998   88c mag & dp ultra   2.00   .70

Souvenir Sheet

French History A2999

No. 5758 — Negotiators of the 1529 Treaty of Cambrai (Ladies' Peace): a, Archduchess Margaret of Austria (1480-1530). b, Louise of Savoy (1476-1531).

2019, Nov. 7   Engr.   *Perf. 13*
5758   A2999   Sheet of 2   11.50   11.50
a.-b.   €2.60 Either single   5.75   1.90
c.   Souvenir sheet of 2, #5758a-5758b, different sheet margin   18.00   18.00

No. 5758c sold for €8.

Miniature Sheet

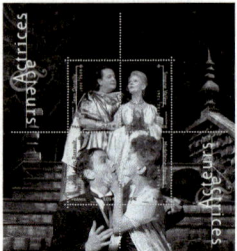

Husband and Wife Actors and Actresses — A3000

No. 5759: a, Jean Desailly (1920-2008). b, Simone Valère (1921-2010). c, Jean-Louis Barrault (1910-94). d, Madeleine Renaud (1900-94).

2019, Nov. 8   Photo.   *Perf. 13¼*
5759   A3000   Sheet of 4   9.75   9.75
a.-d.   €1.05 Any single   2.40   .80

FRANCE

Tromelin Island, French Southern and Antarctic Territories
A3001

2019, Nov. 9   Engr.   Perf. 13x13¼
5760 A3001 €1.30 multi   3.00 1.00

Art Issue

Unnamed Painting by Fabienne Verdier
A3002

2019, Nov. 15   Photo.   Perf. 13
5761 A3002 €2.10 multi   4.75 2.40

Types of 1995-2014
Miniature Sheet

No. 5762 — Sites in Paris: a, Grand Palais. b, Opéra Garnier. c, French Institute. d, Champs Elysées.

Engr., Sheet Margin Litho. & Embossed With Foil Application
Perf. 10x13¼, 13 (#5762d)
2019, Dec. 3
5762 Sheet of 4   22.50 22.50
  a. A1911 €2 sepia   4.50 1.50
  b. A1790 €2 sepia   4.50 1.50
  c. A2415 €2 sepia   4.50 1.50
  d. A1306 €4 sepia   9.00 3.00

Le Carré d'Encre Stamp Shop, Paris, 10th anniv.

Lille, 2020 World Capital of Design — A3003

2020, Jan. 3   Photo.   Perf. 13¼
5763 A3003 97c multi   2.25   .75

Butterfly Wing Details — A3004

Designs: No. 5764, Ornithoptera goliath. No. 5765, Zerynthia rumina. No. 5766, Melitaea phoebe. No. 5767, Agrias claudina. No. 5768, Morpho hecuba. No. 5769, Papilio demoleus. No. 5770, Agatasa calydonia (white area near center). No. 5771, Parnassius nomion. No. 5772, Agatasa calydonia ("L" in "Lettre" over black area). No. 5773, Papilio machaon. No. 5774, Graellsia isabellae. No. 5775, Morpho peleides.

Serpentine Die Cut 11
2020, Jan. 3   Photo.
Booklet Stamps
Self-Adhesive
5764 A3004 (€1.16) multi   2.60   .90
5765 A3004 (€1.16) multi   2.60   .90
5766 A3004 (€1.16) multi   2.60   .90
5767 A3004 (€1.16) multi   2.60   .90
5768 A3004 (€1.16) multi   2.60   .90
5769 A3004 (€1.16) multi   2.60   .90
5770 A3004 (€1.16) multi   2.60   .90
5771 A3004 (€1.16) multi   2.60   .90
5772 A3004 (€1.16) multi   2.60   .90
5773 A3004 (€1.16) multi   2.60   .90
5774 A3004 (€1.16) multi   2.60   .90
5775 A3004 (€1.16) multi   2.60   .90
  a. Booklet pane of 12, #5764-5775   31.50
     Nos. 5764-5775 (12)   31.20 10.80

A3005   Hearts — A3006

2020, Jan. 10   Photo.   Perf. 13½
5776 A3005 97c red, blk & dk blue   2.25   .75
  a. Souvenir sheet of 5   11.50 11.50
5777 A3006 €1.94 blk, red & dk blue   4.25 1.40

Self-Adhesive
Serpentine Die Cut
5778 A3005 97c red, blk & dk blue   2.25   .75
5779 A3006 €1.94 blk, red & dk blue   4.25 1.40

Values for Nos. 5776-5777 are for stamps with surrounding selvage.

New Year 2020 (Year of the Rat) — A3007

Designs: 97c, Rat and flower. €1.40, Rat in robe.

2020, Jan. 17   Photo.   Perf. 13
5780 Sheet of 5, #5780a, 4 #5780b   11.50 11.50
  a. A3007 97c 33x40mm stamp   2.25   .75
  b. A3007 97c 29x35mm stamp   2.25   .75
5781 Sheet of 5, #5781a, 4 #5781b   16.50 16.50
  a. A3007 €1.40 33x40mm stamp 3.25 1.10
  b. A3007 €1.40 29x35mm stamp 3.25 1.10

Art Issue

Portrait Presumed to be Madeleine, by Marie-Guillemine Benoist (1768-1826)
A3008

2020, Feb. 4   Photo.   Perf. 13¼x13
5782 A3008 €2.32 multi   5.25 2.60

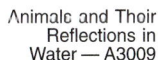

Animals and Their Reflections in Water — A3009

Inscriptions: No. 5783, Zèbres des plaines (Plains zebras). No. 5784, Tigre de Sibérie (Siberian tiger). No. 5785, Couple de lions (Lions) No. 5786, Phoque gris (Gray seal). No. 5787, Ours polaire (Polar bear). No. 5788, Manchots royaux (King penguins). No. 5789, Flamants roses (Greater flamingos). No. 5790, Lama (llama). No. 5791, Grenouilles vertes (Green frogs). No. 5792, Héron crabier (Squacco heron). No. 5793, Goéland argenté (European herring gull). No. 5794, Rorqual à bosse (Humpback whale).

Serpentine Die Cut 11
2020, Feb. 7   Photo.
Booklet Stamps
Self-Adhesive
5783 A3009 (97c) multi   2.25   .75
5784 A3009 (97c) multi   2.25   .75
5785 A3009 (97c) multi   2.25   .75
5786 A3009 (97c) multi   2.25   .75
5787 A3009 (97c) multi   2.25   .75
5788 A3009 (97c) multi   2.25   .75
5789 A3009 (97c) multi   2.25   .75
5790 A3009 (97c) multi   2.25   .75
5791 A3009 (97c) multi   2.25   .75
5792 A3009 (97c) multi   2.25   .75
5793 A3009 (97c) multi   2.25   .75
5794 A3009 (97c) multi   2.25   .75
  a. Booklet pane of 12, #5783-5794   27.00
     Nos. 5783-5794 (12)   27.00 9.00

Jacqueline de Romilly (1913-2010), Writer — A3010

2020, Feb. 7   Engr.   Perf. 13¼
5795 A3010 €1.16 multi   2.60   .90

René Guy Cadou (1920-51), Poet — A3011

2020, Feb. 14   Engr.   Perf. 13¼
5796 A3011 97c black & lt blue   2.25   .75

Organ Building
A3012

2020, Feb. 21   Engr.   Perf. 13x13¼
5797 A3012 €1.40 multi   3.25 1.10

A souvenir sheet containing No. 5797 sold for €4.50.

Boris Vian (1920-59), Writer and Musician
A3013

2020, Mar. 6   Photo.   Perf. 13¼x12¼
5798 A3013 97c multi   2.10   .70

A souvenir sheet containing No. 5798 sold for €4.50. See No. 5845.

Drawing of Tulips   Sundial
A3014   A3015

Nautilus Shell Mounted on Decorative Base
A3016

Indian Painting of Butterfly
A3017

Owl
A3018

Herring Fishing, by Adriaen Van der Kabel (1631-1705)
A3019

Woman in Blue, by Jean-Baptiste-Camille Corot (1796-1875)
A3020

Seashell
A3021

Ewer
A3022

Rhinoceros, by Albrecht Dürer (1471-1528)
A3023

Drawings of Armadillos   Armillary Sphere
A3024   A3025

Serpentine Die Cut 11
2020, Mar. 6   Photo.
Booklet Stamps
Self-Adhesive
5799 A3014 (97c) multi   2.10   .70
5800 A3015 (97c) multi   2.10   .70
5801 A3016 (97c) multi   2.10   .70
5802 A3017 (97c) multi   2.10   .70
5803 A3018 (97c) multi   2.10   .70
5804 A3019 (97c) multi   2.10   .70
5805 A3020 (97c) multi   2.10   .70
5806 A3021 (97c) multi   2.10   .70
5807 A3022 (97c) multi   2.10   .70
5808 A3023 (97c) multi   2.10   .70
5809 A3024 (97c) multi   2.10   .70
5810 A3025 (97c) multi   2.10   .70
  a. Booklet pane of 12, #5799-5810   25.50
     Nos. 5799-5810 (12)   25.20 8.40

Miniature Sheet

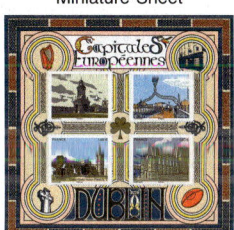

European Capitals — A3026

No. 5811 — Attractions in Dublin, Ireland: a, Trinity College. b, Ha'penny Bridge. c, St. Patrick's Cathedral. d, Dublin Castle.

2020, Mar. 13   Photo.   Perf. 13
5811 A3026 Sheet of 4   12.00 12.00
  a.-d. €1.40 Any single   3.00 1.00

FRANCE

Andrèe Chedid (1920-2011), Writer — A3027

2020, Mar. 20	Photo.	Perf. 13¼		
5812	A3027	€1.40 multi	3.00	1.00

Dole A3028

2020, Mar. 27	Engr.	Perf. 13x12¾		
5813	A3028	97c multi	2.10	.70

Spring Philatelic Show, Dole.

A3029   A3029a

A3030

Félix Nadar (1820-1910), Photographer — A3031

2020, Apr. 3	Photo.	Perf. 13¼x13		
5814		Sheet of 4 + 8 labels	12.00	12.00
a.	A3029	€1.40 multi	3.00	1.00
b.	A3029a	€1.40 multi	3.00	1.00
c.	A3030	€1.40 multi	3.00	1.00
d.	A3031	€1.40 multi	3.00	1.00

Bird Eggs — A3032

Inscriptions: No. 5817, Faucon crécerelle (common kestrel). No. 5818, Corneille noire (carrion crow). No. 5819, Gobemouche gris (spotted flycatcher). No. 5820, Autriche d'Afrique (common ostrich). No. 5821, Hirondelle rustique (barn swallow). No. 5822, Bruant fou (rock bunting). No. 5823, Moineau domestique (house sparrow). No. 5824, Grive musicienne (song thrush). No. 5825, Poule pondeuse rouse (chicken). No. 5826, Dinde (turkey). No. 5827, Vanneau huppé (northern lapwing). No. 5828, Emeu d'Australie (emu).

Serpentine Die Cut 11
2020, Apr. 3   Photo.
Booklet Stamps
Self-Adhesive

5817	A3032	(97c) multi	2.10	.70
5818	A3032	(97c) multi	2.10	.70
5819	A3032	(97c) multi	2.10	.70
5820	A3032	(97c) multi	2.10	.70
5821	A3032	(97c) multi	2.10	.70
5822	A3032	(97c) multi	2.10	.70
5823	A3032	(97c) multi	2.10	.70
5824	A3032	(97c) multi	2.10	.70
5825	A3032	(97c) multi	2.10	.70
5826	A3032	(97c) multi	2.10	.70
5827	A3032	(97c) multi	2.10	.70
5828	A3032	(97c) multi	2.10	.70
a.		Booklet pane of 12, #5817-5828	25.50	
		Nos. 5817-5828 (12)	25.20	8.40

Art Issue

The Virgin of Loretto, by Raphael (1483-1520) A3033

2020, Apr. 17	Engr.	Perf. 13		
5829	A3033	€2.32 multi	5.25	2.60

A souvenir sheet containing No. 5829 sold for €6.50.

A3034   A3035

A3036   A3037

A3038   A3039

A3040   A3041

A3042   A3043

Cosmos Flowers
A3044   A3045

Serpentine Die Cut 11
2020, Apr. 30   Photo.
Booklet Stamps
Self-Adhesive

5830	A3034	(97c) multi	2.10	.70
5831	A3035	(97c) multi	2.10	.70
5832	A3036	(97c) multi	2.10	.70
5833	A3037	(97c) multi	2.10	.70
5834	A3038	(97c) multi	2.10	.70
5835	A3039	(97c) multi	2.10	.70
5836	A3040	(97c) multi	2.10	.70
5837	A3041	(97c) multi	2.10	.70
5838	A3042	(97c) multi	2.10	.70
5839	A3043	(97c) multi	2.10	.70
5840	A3044	(97c) multi	2.10	.70
5841	A3045	(97c) multi	2.10	.70
a.		Booklet pane of 12, #5830-5841	25.50	
		Nos. 5830-5841 (12)	25.20	8.40

Horse-drawn Carriage and Maps of Postal Routes — A3046

2020, May 7	Engr.	Perf. 13¼x13		
5842	A3046	€1.40 multi	3.25	1.10

Europa.

Souvenir Sheet

French Hydrographic Service, 300th Anniv. — A3047

No. 5843: a, Hydrographer on ship with flag taking sounding. b, Ship, compass wheel and star.

2020, May 22	Photo.	Perf. 13¼		
5843	A3047	Sheet of 2	6.50	6.50
a.-b.		€1.40 Either single	3.25	1.10

A souvenir sheet containing Nos. 5843a-5843b having a different sheet margin sold for €6.50.

Frédéric Dard (1921-2000), Writer of Crime Novels — A3048

2020, June 12	Litho.	Perf. 13¼		
5844	A3048	97c multi	2.25	.75

Boris Vian Type of 2020
2020, June 12	Photo.	Perf. 13¼		
5845	A3013	€1.16 multi	2.60	.85
a.		Tete-beche pair	5.25	1.75

No. 5845 was printed in sheets of 6 + 6 labels.

Flowers Used for Perfumes A3049

No. 5846, Rose de Mai.
No. 5847: a, Tubéreuse (tuberose), vert. b, Violette (violet). c, Fleur d'oranger (orange blossoms), vert.

2020, June 12	Photo.	Perf. 13¼		
5846	A3049	97c multi	2.25	.75

Miniature Sheet

5847		Sheet of 4, #5846, 5847a-5847c	9.00	9.00
a.-c.	A3049	97c Any single	2.25	.75
d.		Souvenir sheet of 2, #5846, 5847c	7.25	7.25
e.		Souvenir sheet of 2, #5847a, 5847b	7.25	7.25

Nos. 5847d and 5847e sold as a set for €6.50. Nos. 5847 and 5847d are impregnated with an orange blossom scent.

University of Montpellier Buildings, François de la Peyronie (1678-1747), Surgeon, and Paul Joseph Barthez (1734-1806), Physician — A3050

2020, June 13	Photo.	Perf. 13x12¾		
5848	A3050	€1.16 multi	2.60	.85

University of Montpellier Faculty of Medicine, 800th anniv.

Snacks With Faces A3051   Woman in Hammock A3052

Book Reader, Cloud and Birds — A3053   Woman Pulling Suitcase — A3054

Woman's Feet in Sandals — A3055   Surfer — A3056

Children in Inflatable Pool Toys — A3057   Woman With Shells in Hair — A3058

Flowers and Butterflies A3059   Fisherman in Boat A3060

Vacationers Carrying Gear — A3061   Tandem Bicycle — A3062

Serpentine Die Cut 11
2020, June 19   Photo.
Booklet Stamps
Self-Adhesive

5849	A3051	(97c) multi	2.25	.75
5850	A3052	(97c) multi	2.25	.75
5851	A3053	(97c) multi	2.25	.75
5852	A3054	(97c) multi	2.25	.75
5853	A3055	(97c) multi	2.25	.75
5854	A3056	(97c) multi	2.25	.75
5855	A3057	(97c) multi	2.25	.75
5856	A3058	(97c) multi	2.25	.75
5857	A3059	(97c) multi	2.25	.75
5858	A3060	(97c) multi	2.25	.75
5859	A3061	(97c) multi	2.25	.75
5860	A3062	(97c) multi	2.25	.75
a.		Booklet pane of 12, #5849-5860	27.00	
		Nos. 5849-5860 (12)	27.00	9.00

Tourism Issue

Rodemack — A3063

2020, June 26	Engr.	Perf. 13¼		
5861	A3063	97c multi	2.25	.75

FRANCE

Olympe de Gouges (1748-93), Playwright A3064

2020, June 26   Photo.   *Perf. 13¼x13*
5862   A3064   €2.32 multi   5.25   1.75

Souvenir Sheet

Map of Corsica and GR 20 Hiking Trail A3065

2020, June 26   Photo.   *Perf. 13¼*
5863   A3065   €1.16 multi   2.60   .85

GR 20 Hiking Trail, 50th anniv.

Engraving Type of 1984

2020, June 26   Engr.   *Perf. 13*
5864   A1001   €4 multi   9.00   3.00

No. 5864 was printed in sheets of 6.

Saint-Vaast-la-Hougue — A3066

2020, July 2   Photo.   *Perf. 13x12¾*
5865   A3066   97c multi   2.25   .75

St. Odile of Alsace (c. 662-720) A3067

2020, July 3   Photo.   *Perf. 13¼*
5866   A3067   97c multi   2.25   .75

Bouillabaise Ingredients — A3068

2020, July 10   Litho.   *Perf. 13¼*
5867   A3068   €1.40 multi   3.25   1.10

Luis Mariano (1914-70), Opera Singer — A3069

2020, July 10   Photo.   *Perf. 13*
5868   A3069   €1.16 multi   2.75   .95

Bès-Bédène — A3070

2020, July 17   Engr.   *Perf. 13x12¾*
5869   A3070   97c multi   2.25   .75

Souvenir Sheet

Exterior Decorations of Notre Dame Cathedral, Paris — A3071

2020, July 17   Engr.   *Perf. 13*
5870   A3071   €1.40 multi   3.25   1.10

Amiens Cathedral, 800th Anniv. — A3072

2020, July 27   Engr.   *Perf. 13¼*
5871   A3072   €1.16 black & gold   2.75   .95

Raving Rabbid Behind Stamp A3073

Raving Rabbid With Tape Dispenser A3074

Raving Rabbid on Upside-Down Picture A3075

Raving Rabbid Drawing Stamp A3076

Raving Rabbid in Hole A3077

Raving Rabbid Licking Stamp A3078

Raving Rabbid Painting — A3079   Raving Rabbid Writing — A3080

Stamps Stuck on Raving Rabbid A3081

Raving Rabbids Holding Envelope Upside Down A3082

Raving Rabbid With Magnifying Glass — A3083   Group of Raving Rabbids — A3084

Serpentine Die Cut 11
2020, July 24   Photo.
Booklet Stamps
Self-Adhesive

5872	A3073	(97c) multi	2.25 .75
5873	A3074	(97c) multi	2.25 .75
5874	A3075	(97c) multi	2.25 .75
5875	A3076	(97c) multi	2.25 .75
5876	A3077	(97c) multi	2.25 .75
5877	A3078	(97c) multi	2.25 .75
5878	A3079	(97c) multi	2.25 .75
5879	A3080	(97c) multi	2.25 .75
5880	A3081	(97c) multi	2.25 .75
5881	A3082	(97c) multi	2.25 .75
5882	A3083	(97c) multi	2.25 .75
5883	A3084	(97c) multi	2.25 .75

a.   Booklet pane of 12, #5872-5883   27.00
Nos. 5872-5883 (12)   27.00   9.00

Raving Rabbids video game characters.

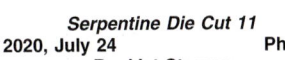

Lighthouses — A3085

Designs: No. 5884, Cayeux Lighthouse. No. 5885, Grand Léjon Lighthouse. No. 5886, Créac'h Lighthouse. No. 5887, Saint Mathieu Lighthouse. No. 5888, La Vieille Lighthouse. No. 5889, Eckmühl Lighthouse. No. 5890, Four du Croisic Lighthouse. No. 5891, Cap Ferret Lighthouse. No. 5892, Espiguette Lighthouse. No. 5893, Sanguinaires Lighthouse. No. 5894, Bel Air Lighthouse. No. 5895, Caravelle Lighthouse.

Serpentine Die Cut 11
2020, Aug. 28   Photo.
Booklet Stamps
Self-Adhesive

5884	A3085	(€1.16) multi	2.75 .95
5885	A3085	(€1.16) multi	2.75 .95
5886	A3085	(€1.16) multi	2.75 .95
5887	A3085	(€1.16) multi	2.75 .95
5888	A3085	(€1.16) multi	2.75 .95
5889	A3085	(€1.16) multi	2.75 .95
5890	A3085	(€1.16) multi	2.75 .95
5891	A3085	(€1.16) multi	2.75 .95
5892	A3085	(€1.16) multi	2.75 .95
5893	A3085	(€1.16) multi	2.75 .95
5894	A3085	(€1.16) multi	2.75 .95
5895	A3085	(€1.16) multi	2.75 .95

a.   Booklet pane of 12, #5884-5895   33.00
Nos. 5884-5895 (12)   33.00   11.40

Raving Rabbids Video Game Characters — A3086

2020, Sept. 4   Photo.   *Perf. 13x12¾*
5896   A3086   97c multi   2.25   .75

Tourism Issue

La Roche-sur-Yon A3087

2020, Sept. 7   Photo.   *Perf. 13¼*
5897   A3087   97c red & black   2.25   .75

Health Care Workers — A3088   Helicopter Pilot and Ambulance Crew — A3089

Postal Worker Delivering Mail — A3090   Post Office Clerk — A3091

Store Cashier — A3092   Bus Driver — A3093

Health Care Workers Cleaning A3094   Health Care Worker and Woman in Wheelchair A3095

Police Officers — A3096   Sanitation Workers — A3097

Truck Driver — A3098   Farm Workers — A3099

Serpentine Die Cut 11
2020, Sept. 11   Photo.
Booklet Stamps
Self-Adhesive

5898	A3088	(97c) multi	2.25 .75
5899	A3089	(97c) multi	2.25 .75
5900	A3090	(97c) multi	2.25 .75
5901	A3091	(97c) multi	2.25 .75
5902	A3092	(97c) multi	2.25 .75
5903	A3093	(97c) multi	2.25 .75
5904	A3094	(97c) multi	2.25 .75
5905	A3095	(97c) multi	2.25 .75
5906	A3096	(97c) multi	2.25 .75
5907	A3097	(97c) multi	2.25 .75
5908	A3098	(97c) multi	2.25 .75
5909	A3099	(97c) multi	2.25 .75

a.   Booklet pane of 12, #5898-5909   27.00
Nos. 5898-5909 (12)   27.00   9.00

Salute to French workers during COVID-19 pandemic.

730 FRANCE

Château of the Dukes of Bourbon, Montluçon — A3100

2020, Sept. 18	Engr.	Perf. 13¼
5910 A3100 €1.16 multi		2.75 .95

Miniature Sheet

Sports A3101

No. 5911: a, Gymnastics. b, Badminton, vert. c, Taekwondo. d, Sailboarding, vert. e, Rowing. f, Pole vault.

	Perf. 13x13¼, 13¼x13	
2020, Sept. 18	Photo.	
5911 A3101 Sheet of 6		19.50 19.50
a.-f. €1.40 Any single		3.25 1.10

Miniature Sheet

Aspects of French Life A3102

No. 5912: a, Education. b, Quality of life, vert. c, Equality, vert. d, Living together.

2020, Sept. 18	Photo.	Perf. 13¼
5912 A3102 Sheet of 4		9.00 9.00
a.-d. 97c Any single		2.25 .75

Pres. Jacques Chirac (1932-2019) — A3103

2020, Sept. 26	Engr.	Perf. 13¼
5913 A3103 97c multi		2.25 .75

Peugeot 204 Cabriolet A3104

Peugeot 404 Berline A3105

2020, Sept. 26	Engr.	Perf. 13x13¼
5914 A3104 97c multi		2.25 .75
5915 A3104 €1.16 multi		2.75 .95

Souvenir Sheet
Litho.

5916 A3105 €1.94 multi	4.50 1.50

Stamp Day. No. 5915 was printed in sheets of 6. Nos. 5914 and 5916 were intended to have been issued on Mar. 28, 2020, but were delayed because of the COVID-19 pandemic.

Art Issue

Zamer, Artwork by Mohamed Bourouissa A3106

2020, Oct. 9	Photo.	Perf. 13¼x13
5917 A3106 €2.32 multi		5.50 2.75

Annexation of Béarn as French Province by King Louis XIII, 400th Anniv. — A3107

2020, Oct. 16	Photo.	Perf. 13¼
5918 A3107 €1.16 multi		2.75 .95

Steam-Powered Vehicle Invented by Nicolas-Joseph Cugnot (1725-1804), 250th Anniv. — A3108

2020, Oct. 16	Engr.	Perf. 13x12¾
5919 A3108 €1.16 ochre & black		2.75 .95

A3109

A3111

A3112

A3113

A3114

A3115

A3116

Owl, Courrier Suivi Emblem, Tracking Number and Encryption — A3117

Serpentine Die Cut 11
2020, Oct. 16		Photo.
Booklet Stamps		
Self-Adhesive		
5920 A3109 (€1.42) multi	3.50	1.75
5921 A3110 (€1.42) multi	3.50	1.75
5922 A3111 (€1.42) multi	3.50	1.75
5923 A3112 (€1.42) multi	3.50	1.75
5924 A3113 (€1.42) multi	3.50	1.75
5925 A3114 (€1.42) multi	3.50	1.75
5926 A3115 (€1.42) multi	3.50	1.75
5927 A3116 (€1.42) multi	3.50	1.75
5928 A3117 (€1.42) multi	3.50	1.75
a. Booklet pane of 9, #5920-5928		31.50
Nos. 5920-5928 (9)	31.50	15.75

On the day of issue, Nos. 5920-5928 paid the 97c lettre verte rate plus the 45c letter tracking fee. Tracking numbers on each stamp are repeated in booklet selvage below that stamp. Letters bearing these stamps could be tracked by entering the tracking number on the La Poste website. The tracking numbers and encryption on each stamp differ.
Compare with types A3391-A3399.

Ludwig van Beethoven (1770-1827), Composer — A3118

2020, Oct. 23	Photo.	Perf. 13¼
5929 A3118 €1.40 multi		3.25 1.10

Hôtel de Mora, Moulins A3119

2020, Oct. 30	Engr.	Perf. 13x13¼
5930 A3119 97c multi + label		2.25 .75

2020 Stamp Passion Youth Philatelic Exhibition. Moulins. For surcharge, see No. 6317.

Emblem of French Tennis Federation, Tennis Ball, and Suzannne Lenglen (1899-1938), Tennis Player — A3120

2020, Oct. 30	Photo.	Perf. 13
5931 A3120 €1.16 reddish org		2.75 .95

French Tennis Federation, cent., naming of new tennis court at Roland Garros Stadium after Lenglen, 25th anniv.

No. 5477 Overprinted

Method and Perf. As Before
2020, Nov. 4	
5932 A2828 (97c) emerald	2.40 .80

A booklet printed in limited quantities was issued on Nov. 4, 2020, containing 97c stamps of types A1091 and A1136, €1.16 stamps of type A486 + label, A761, A1161, A1208, A1430, A1474, and A2532, and €1.16 stamps having the designs of Nos. 3682a-3682d, 3682f-3682k, and 4330a.

Types of 1947-2014 Redrawn With Denominations in Euros
Engr., Sheet Margin Litho. with Foil Application

2020, Nov. 4		Perf. 13¼x13
5933 Sheet of 4		29.00 29.00
a. SP171 €2 dark green, like #B217		4.75 4.75
b. A2380 €2 dark green, like #4588		4.75 4.75

| c. A417 €4 dark green, like #1090 | 9.75 | 9.75 |
| d. AP11 €4 dark green, like #C22 | 9.75 | 9.75 |

Notre Dame Cathedral, Paris.

A3121

A3122

A3123

A3124

A3125

A3126

A3127

A3128

A3129

A3130

A3131

Christmas A3132

Serpentine Die Cut 11
2020, Nov. 4		Photo.
Booklet Stamps		
Self-Adhesive		
5934 A3121 (97c) multi	2.40	.80
5935 A3122 (97c) multi	2.40	.80
5936 A3123 (97c) multi	2.40	.80
5937 A3124 (97c) multi	2.40	.80
5938 A3125 (97c) multi	2.40	.80
5939 A3126 (97c) multi	2.40	.80
5940 A3127 (97c) multi	2.40	.80
5941 A3128 (97c) multi	2.40	.80
5942 A3129 (97c) multi	2.40	.80
5943 A3130 (97c) multi	2.40	.80
5944 A3131 (97c) multi	2.40	.80
5945 A3132 (97c) multi	2.40	.80
a. Booklet pane of 12, #5934-5945		29.00
Nos. 5934-5945 (12)	28.80	9.60

On back of No. 5945a there is a scratch inscribed "Grattez ici" off for a 100% winning game.

Charles de Gaulle (1890-1970), Wearing General's Uniform A3133

FRANCE

De Gaulle (1890-1970), As President of France A3134

2020, Nov. 5	Engr.		Perf. 13¼	
5946	A3133	€1.16 multi	2.75	.90
5947	A3134	€1.16 multi	2.75	.90
a.	Horiz. pair, #5946-5947		5.50	1.90

Charles de Gaulle Types of 1971-2010 Redrawn
Miniature Sheet
Perf. 13x13¼, 13¼x13

2020, Nov. 5			Engr.	
5947B		Sheet of 4	48.00	48.00
a.	A2093 €5 blue		12.00	12.00
b.	A576 €5 black (like #1324)		12.00	12.00
c.	A1164 €5 multi		12.00	12.00
d.	CD134 €5 red violet (like #1325)		12.00	12.00

Ceres — A3135

2020, Nov. 6	Litho.		Imperf.	
Booklet Stamps				
5948	A3135	10c green	.25	.25
5949	A3135	€1.40 red	3.50	1.25
a.	Booklet pane of 12, 6 each #5948-5949		22.50	—

Size: 36x45mm

5950	A3135	€3.50 green	8.40	3.00
5951	A3135	€3.50 red	8.40	3.00
a.	Booklet pane of 2, #5950-5951		17.00	
	Complete booklet, #5949a, 5951a		39.50	

Metal Engraving A3136

2020, Nov. 6	Engr.		Perf. 13	
5952	A3136	€1.40 multi	3.50	1.25

A souvenir sheet containing No. 5952 sold for €4.50.

Palais Galliera, Paris A3137

2020, Nov. 7	Engr.		Perf. 13x13¼	
5953	A3137	€1.16 multi + label	2.75	.90

French Federation of Philatelic Associations, 93rd Congress, Paris.

Souvenir Sheet

French History A3138

No. 5954: a, Matilda of Flanders (c. 1031-83), Queen of England, Duchess of Normandy and wife of William the Conqueror. b, William the Conqueror (c. 1028-87), King of England and Duke of Normandy.

2020, Nov. 7	Engr.		Perf. 13	
5954	A3138	Sheet of 2	13.50	13.50
a.-b.	€2.80 Either single		6.75	6.75
c.	Souvenir sheet of 2, #5954a-5954b, with different sheet margin		20.50	20.50

No. 5954c sold for €8.50.

Order of Liberation, 80th Anniv. — A3139

2020, Nov. 16	Engr.		Perf. 13	
5955	A3139	€1.40 multi	3.50	1.25

For overprint, see No. 6150.

Aerial View of Vineyard, Bas-Rhin Department A3140

Aerial View of Orchard, Loiret Department A3141

Aerial View of Salt Marsh, Bouches-du-Rhône Department A3142

Aerial View of Beach, Corse-du-Sud Department A3143

Aerial View of Pasture, Lozère Department A3144

Aerial View of Basalt Columns, Lozère Department A3145

Aerial View of Coast, Morbihan Department A3146

Aerial View of Oyster Farm, Charente-Maritime Department A3147

Aerial View of Salt Marshes, Vendée Department A3148

Aerial View of Vegetable Fields, Seine-Maritime Department A3149

Aerial View of Salt Meadows, Somme Department A3150

Aerial View of Wheat and Rapeseed Fields, Côte d'Or Department A3151

Serpentine Die Cut 11

2021, Jan. 2			Photo.	
Booklet Stamps				
Self-Adhesive				
5956	A3140	(€1.28) multi	3.25	1.10
5957	A3141	(€1.28) multi	3.25	1.10
5958	A3142	(€1.28) multi	3.25	1.10
5959	A3143	(€1.28) multi	3.25	1.10
5960	A3144	(€1.28) multi	3.25	1.10
5961	A3145	(€1.28) multi	3.25	1.10
5962	A3146	(€1.28) multi	3.25	1.10
5963	A3147	(€1.28) multi	3.25	1.10
5964	A3148	(€1.28) multi	3.25	1.10
5965	A3149	(€1.28) multi	3.25	1.10
5966	A3150	(€1.28) multi	3.25	1.10
5967	A3151	(€1.28) multi	3.25	1.10
a.	Booklet pane of 12, #5956-5967		39.00	
	Nos. 5956-5967 (12)		39.00	13.20

Birds — A3152

Designs: No. 5968, Pinguouin torda (razor-billed auk).
No. 5969: a, Tuit tuit (Reunion cuckooshrike), horiz. b, Oriole de Martinique (Martinique oriole). c, Grive à pattes jaunes (forest thrush).

2021, Jan. 8	Photo.		Perf. 13¼	
5968	A3152	€1.08 multi	2.60	.85
Souvenir Sheet				
5969		Sheet of 4, #5968, 5969a-5969c	10.50	10.50
a.-c.	A3152 €1.08 Any single		2.60	.85
d.	Souvenir sheet of 2, #5968, 5969b		8.00	8.00
e.	Souvenir sheet of 2, #5969a, 5969c		8.00	8.00

Nos. 5969d and 5969e were sold as a set for €6.50.

Madeleine Brès (1842-1921), First French Woman to Obtain Medical Degree — A3153

2021, Jan. 15	Photo.		Perf. 13¼	
5970	A3153	€1.08 multi	2.60	.85

Heart and Bottle of Chanel No. 5 Perfume — A3154

2021, Jan. 22	Photo.		Perf. 13¼	
5971	A3154	€1.08 red & black	2.60	.85
a.	Souvenir sheet of 5		13.00	13.00
5972	A3154	€2.16 pink & black	5.25	1.75

Self-Adhesive
Serpentine Die Cut

5973	A3154	€1.08 red & black	2.60	.85
5974	A3154	€2.16 pink & black	5.25	1.75

Values for Nos. 5971-5972 are for stamps with surrounding selvage.

New Year 2021 (Year of the Ox) — A3155

Designs: €1.08, Man on ox. €1.50, Ox.

2021, Feb. 5	Photo.		Perf. 13¼x13	
5975		Sheet of 5, #5975a, 4 #5975b	13.00	13.00
a.	A3155 €1.08 multi, 33x40mm stamp		2.60	.85
b.	A3155 €1.08 multi, 29x35mm stamp		2.60	.85
5976		Sheet of 5, #5976a, 4 #5976b	19.00	19.00
a.	A3155 €1.50 multi, 33x40mm stamp		3.75	1.25
b.	A3155 €1.50 multi, 29x35mm stamp		3.75	1.25

Art Issue

Untitled (Skull), by Jean-Michel Basquiat (1960-88) A3156

2021, Feb. 5	Photo.		Perf. 13	
5977	A3156	€2.56 multi	6.25	3.25

Stained-Glass Window Craftsmanship A3157

Engr. & Embossed

2021, Feb. 12			Perf. 13	
5978	A3157	€1.50 multi	3.75	1.25

A souvenir sheet containing No. 5978 sold for €4.50.

Camel Tracks — A3158

African Lion Tracks — A3159

Chacma Baboon Tracks — A3160

Mallard Duck Tracks — A3161

Jaguar Tracks — A3162

Grizzly Bear Tracks — A3163

Gentoo Penguin Tracks — A3164

Hedgehog Tracks — A3165

African Elephant Tracks — A3166

Gray Heron Tracks — A3167

Roe Deer Tracks — A3168

Alpine Chamois Tracks — A3169

Serpentine Die Cut 11

2021, Feb. 12			Photo.	
Booklet Stamps				
Self-Adhesive				
5979	A3158	(€1.08) multi	2.60	.85
5980	A3159	(€1.08) multi	2.60	.85
5981	A3160	(€1.08) multi	2.60	.85
5982	A3161	(€1.08) multi	2.60	.85
5983	A3162	(€1.08) multi	2.60	.85
5984	A3163	(€1.08) multi	2.60	.85
5985	A3164	(€1.08) multi	2.60	.85
5986	A3165	(€1.08) multi	2.60	.85
5987	A3166	(€1.08) multi	2.60	.85
5988	A3167	(€1.08) multi	2.60	.85
5989	A3168	(€1.08) multi	2.60	.85

732 FRANCE

5990	A3169	(€1.08) multi	2.60	.85
a.	Booklet pane of 12, #5979-5990		31.50	
	Nos. 5979-5990 (12)		31.20	10.20

National School of Charters, Paris, 200th Anniv. — A3170

2021, Feb. 22   Engr.   Perf. 13
5991 A3170 €2.56 multi   6.25 2.10

The Kid, Motion Picture with Charlie Chaplin and Jackie Coogan, Cent. — A3171

2021, Feb. 26   Engr.   Perf. 12¾x13
5992 A3171 €1.50 blk & gray   3.75 1.25
A souvenir sheet issued in 2022 containing No. 5992 sold for €4.50.

Simone de Beauvoir (1908-86), Feminist Writer — A3172

2021, Mar. 5   Engr.   Perf. 13¼
5993 A3172 €1.28 dp vio & lil   3.00 1.00

Agricultural Order of Merit — A3173

2021, Mar. 12   Photo.   Perf. 13x12¾
5994 A3173 €1.08 multi   2.60 .85

Camille Saint-Saens (1835-1921), Composer — A3174

2021, Mar. 19   Engr.   Perf. 13¼
5995 A3174 €1.28 org brn & grnsh blue   3.00 1.00

Dans le Circle (Entire Painting), by Vassily Kandinsky (1866-1944) — A3175

A3176   A3177

A3178   A3179

A3180   A3181

A3182   A3183

A3184

Dans le Circle (Details) — A3185

Serpentine Die Cut 11
2021, Mar. 26   Photo.
Booklet Stamps
Self-Adhesive

5996	A3175	(€1.08) multi	2.60	.85
5997	A3176	(€1.08) org & multi	2.60	.85
5998	A3177	(€1.08) dk grn & multi	2.60	.85
5999	A3178	(€1.08) dk red brn & multi	2.60	.85
6000	A3179	(€1.08) purple & multi	2.60	.85
6001	A3180	(€1.08) org brn & multi	2.60	.85
6002	A3181	(€1.08) yel brown & multi	2.60	.85
6003	A3182	(€1.08) dark blue & multi	2.60	.85
6004	A3183	(€1.08) choc & multi	2.60	.85
6005	A3184	(€1.08) black & multi	2.60	.85
6006	A3185	(€1.08) Prus. blue & multi	2.60	.85
a.	Booklet pane of 12, #5997-6006, 2 #5996		31.50	
	Nos. 5996-6006 (11)		28.60	9.35

Miniature Sheet

European Capitals — A3186

No. 6007 — Attractions in Stockholm, Sweden: a, Royal Opera House. b, City Hall, vert. c, Royal Palace. d, Buildings in Gamla Stan District.

2021, Mar. 26   Photo.   Perf. 13¼
6007 A3186 Sheet of 4   14.00 14.00
a.-d. €1.50 Any single   3.50 1.25

Tourism Issue

Pont-en-Royans — A3187

2021, Apr. 2   Photo.   Perf. 13x12¾
6008 A3187 €1.28 multi   3.25 1.10

Publication in France of *The Little Prince,* Children's Book by Antoine de Saint-Exupéry (1900-44), 75th Anniv. — A3188

2021, Apr. 9   Photo.   Perf. 13¼
6009 A3188 €1.08 multi   2.60 .85

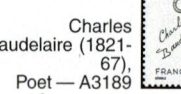

Charles Baudelaire (1821-67), Poet — A3189

2021, Apr. 9   Engr.   Perf. 13¼
6010 A3189 €1.28 multi   3.25 1.10

Bel Group, Cheese Manufacturers, 156th Anniv. — A3190

2021, Apr. 16   Photo.   Perf. 13
6011 A3190 €1.08 multi   2.60 .85
No. 6011 was printed in sheets of 8.

Souvenir Sheet

Napoleon Bonaparte (1769-1821), Emperor — A3191

No. 6012: a, Napoleon and laurels. b, Napoleon on St. Helena looking at ocean, horiz.

Litho., Engr. & Embossed With Foil Application
2021, Apr. 17   Perf. 13
6012 A3191 Sheet of 2   7.50 7.50
a.-b. €1.50 Either single   3.75 1.25
A souvenir sheet containing Nos. 6012a-6012b with a different sheet margin sold for €6.50.

Souvenir Sheet

Stained-Glass Window Depicting Adam and Eve, Notre Dame Cathedral, Paris — A3192

2021, Apr. 23   Engr.   Perf.
6013 A3192 €1.50 multi   3.75 1.25

Tourism Issue

Bibracte Archaelogical Site, Mont Beuvray — A3193

2021, May 6   Photo.   Perf. 13x12¾
6014 A3193 €1.28 multi   3.25 1.10

Gladiolus Fabric Pattern — A3194   Rose and Lily of the Valley Fabric Pattern — A3195

Rose Fabric Pattern — A3196   Hydrangea and Peony Fabric Pattern — A3197

Rose Fabric Pattern — A3198   Iris and Tulip Fabric Pattern — A3199

Lilac Fabric Pattern — A3200   Sunflower and Anemone Fabric Pattern — A3201

Rose and Lilac Fabric Pattern — A3202   Tulip Fabric Pattern — A3203

Hyacinth and Crocus Fabric Pattern — A3204   Poppy Fabric Pattern — A3205

Serpentine Die Cut 11
2021, May 7   Photo.
Booklet Stamps
Self-Adhesive

6015	A3194	(€1.08) multi	2.75	.90
6016	A3195	(€1.08) multi	2.75	.90
6017	A3196	(€1.08) multi	2.75	.90
6018	A3197	(€1.08) multi	2.75	.90
6019	A3198	(€1.08) multi	2.75	.90
6020	A3199	(€1.08) multi	2.75	.90
6021	A3200	(€1.08) multi	2.75	.90
6022	A3201	(€1.08) multi	2.75	.90
6023	A3202	(€1.08) multi	2.75	.90
6024	A3203	(€1.08) multi	2.75	.90
6025	A3204	(€1.08) multi	2.75	.90
6026	A3205	(€1.08) multi	2.75	.90
a.	Booklet pane of 12, #6015-6026		33.00	
	Nos. 6015-6026 (12)		33.00	10.80

Endangered Animals — A3206

2021, May 21   Photo.   Perf. 13¼
6027 A3206 €1.50 blk & grn   3.75 1.25

Europa

FRANCE

Chamonix Guides Company, 200th Anniv. — A3207

2021, May 21	Photo.		Perf. 13¼	
6028	A3207	€1.08 multi	2.75	.90

Art Issue

Untitled (Seated Model in Profile in Evening Dress and Jacket), Photograph by Dora Maar (1907-97) A3208

The Boat, Painting by Sophie Taeuber-Arp (1889-1943) A3209

2021, May 28	Photo.		Perf. 13¼	
6029	A3208	€2.56 multi	6.25	3.25
6030	A3209	€2.56 multi	6.25	3.25

Traffic Laws, Cent. A3210

2021, June 11	Photo.		Perf. 13x12¾	
6031	A3210	€1.08 multi	2.60	.85

Elsa Triolet (1896-1970), Writer — A3211

2021, June 12	Photo.		Perf. 13¼	
6032	A3211	€1.28 multi	3.00	1.00

French Pavilion at Expo 2020, Dubai A3212

2021, June 17	Photo.		Perf. 13	
6033	A3212	€1.50 multi	3.50	1.25

Marianne Type of 2018 and

Marianne — A3213

2021, June 17	Engr.		Perf. 13	
	Booklet Stamps			
6034	A3213	€1.08 emerald	2.60	.85
a.	Tete-beche pair		5.25	5.25
b.	Booklet pane of 12, 6 each #5478d, 6034		29.50	—
	Size: 30x46mm			
6035	A3213	€2.16 emerald	5.25	1.75
6036	A2826	€2.56 red	6.25	2.10
a.	Booklet pane of 2, #6035-6036		11.50	
	Complete booklet, #6034b, 6036a		41.00	

Compare type A3213 with types A147 and A1814.

A3214   A3215

A3216   A3217

A3218   A3219

A3220   A3221

A3222   A3223

Publication in France of *The Little Prince*, by Antoine de Saint-Exupery (1900-44), 75th Anniv.

A3224   A3225

Serpentine Die Cut 11

2021, June 17			Photo.	
	Booklet Stamps			
	Self-Adhesive			
6037	A3214	(€1.08) multi	2.60	.85
6038	A3215	(€1.08) multi	2.60	.85
6039	A3216	(€1.08) multi	2.60	.85
6040	A3217	(€1.08) multi	2.60	.85
6041	A3218	(€1.08) multi	2.60	.85
6042	A3219	(€1.08) multi	2.60	.85
6043	A3220	(€1.08) multi	2.60	.85
6044	A3221	(€1.08) multi	2.60	.85
6045	A3222	(€1.08) multi	2.60	.85
6046	A3223	(€1.08) multi	2.60	.85
6047	A3224	(€1.08) multi	2.60	.85
6048	A3225	(€1.08) multi	2.60	.85
a.	Booklet pane of 12, #6037-6048		31.50	
	Nos. 6037-6048 (12)		31.20	10.20

20th Century Chess Set — A3226

Four 19th Century Chess Pieces — A3227

19th Century Chess Set — A3228

The Chess Game, Painting by Maria Helena Vieira da Silva (1908-92) A3229

Illustration From Treatise on Chess A3230

The Chess Board, Painting by Victor Vasarely (1906-97) A3231

Cavalier, Photomontage by Dora Maar (1907-97) A3232

19th Century Silver and Copper Chess Set A3233

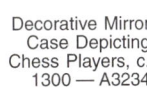

Decorative Mirror Case Depicting Chess Players, c. 1300 — A3234

Chess Set Designed by Jean Puiforcat (1897-1945) A3235

Three 19th Century Chess Pieces — A3236

Porcelain Chess Set Designed by Jean-Jacques Prolongeau (1917-94) A3237

Serpentine Die Cut 11

2021, June 17			Photo.	
	Booklet Stamps			
	Self-Adhesive			
6049	A3226	(€1.08) multi	2.60	.85
6050	A3227	(€1.08) multi	2.60	.85
6051	A3228	(€1.08) multi	2.60	.85
6052	A3229	(€1.08) multi	2.60	.85
6053	A3230	(€1.08) multi	2.60	.85
6054	A3231	(€1.08) multi	2.60	.85
6055	A3232	(€1.08) multi	2.60	.85
6056	A3233	(€1.08) multi	2.60	.85
6057	A3234	(€1.08) multi	2.60	.85
6058	A3235	(€1.08) multi	2.60	.85
6059	A3236	(€1.08) multi	2.60	.85
6060	A3237	(€1.08) multi	2.60	.85
a.	Booklet pane of 12, #6049-6060		31.50	
	Nos. 6049-6060 (12)		31.20	10.20

Miniature Sheet

Sports A3238

No. 6061: a, Breakdancing. b, Wheelchair fencing, horiz. c, Skateboarding. d, Rock climbing. e, Judo, horiz. f, Rugby sevens.

2021, June 18		Photo.	Perf. 13	
6061	A3238	Sheet of 6	21.00	21.00
a.-f.	€1.50 Any single		3.50	1.25

Solar Impulse Experimental Solar-Powered Aircraft — A3239

2021, June 19	Photo.		Perf. 13x12¾	
6062	A3239	€1.08 multi	2.60	.85

Tourism Issue

Hunspach, 2020 Favorite Village in France A3240

2021, July 1	Photo.		Perf. 13	
6063	A3240	€1.08 multi	2.60	.85

Saint-Louis Royal Chapel, Dreux — A3241

Engr. With Foil Application

2021, July 2			Perf. 13	
6064	A3241	€1.28 gold & dk blue	3.00	1.00

A souvenir sheet containing No. 6064 sold for €4.50.

Gien Faience Factory, 200th Anniv. — A3242

2021, July 2	Engr.		Perf. 13	
6065	A3242	€2.56 blue & dk blue	6.25	2.10

A souvenir sheet containing No. 6065 sold for €6.50.

Souvenir Sheet

Jean de La Fontaine (1621-95), Fabulist — A3243

No. 6066: a, Characters from fable "The Frog and the Ox" (53x41mm). b, House of Jean de La Fontaine, Château-Thierry (30x41mm).

734 FRANCE

Perf. 13x13¼ (#6066a), 13¼ (#6066b)
2021, July 8   Engr.
6066 A3243   Sheet of 2   10.50 10.50
  a.-b.   €2.16 Either single   5.25   1.75

Coral Ear Pendant, Maltese Cross, and Coulas Bracelet — A3244

2021, July 9   Photo.   Perf. 13¼x13
6067 A3244   €1.50 multi   3.75   1.25
Traditional Mediterranean jewelry.

Tourist Attractions A3245

Designs: No. 6068, Puy de Sancy Volcano. No. 6069, Rochers des Deux Jumeaux (Twin Rocks). No. 6070, Forêt de Fontainebleau (Fontainebleau Forest). No. 6071, Grand Ballon Mountain. No. 6072, Cascade des Tufs waterfall. No. 6073, Désert de Platé limestone outcropping. No. 6074, Dune du Pilat et Banc d'Arguin sand dune. No. 6075, Pointe du Raz promontory. No. 6076, Terril No. 74A slag heap. No. 6077, Colorado Provençal ocher quarry. No. 6078, Paysage de l'Aubrac plateau grassland. No. 6079, Loire River.

Serpentine Die Cut 11
2021, July 9   Photo.
Booklet Stamps
Self-Adhesive
6068 A3245   (€1.08) multi   2.60   .85
6069 A3245   (€1.08) multi   2.60   .85
6070 A3245   (€1.08) multi   2.60   .85
6071 A3245   (€1.08) multi   2.60   .85
6072 A3245   (€1.08) multi   2.60   .85
6073 A3245   (€1.08) multi   2.60   .85
6074 A3245   (€1.08) multi   2.60   .85
6075 A3245   (€1.08) multi   2.60   .85
6076 A3245   (€1.08) multi   2.60   .85
6077 A3245   (€1.08) multi   2.60   .85
6078 A3245   (€1.08) multi   2.60   .85
6079 A3245   (€1.08) multi   2.60   .85
  a.   Booklet pane of 12, #6068-6079   31.50
  Nos. 6068-6079 (12)   31.20 10.20

Speleologists in Cave — A3246

2021, July 23   Photo.   Perf. 13
6080 A3246   €1.50 multi   3.75   1.25

Children's Stories — A3247

Designs: No. 6081, Le Petit Chaperon Rouge (Little Red Riding Hood). No. 6082, Le Chat Botté (Puss in Boots). No. 6083, Le Petit Poucet (Tom Thumb). No. 6084, Les Musiciens de Brême (The Musicians of Bremen). No. 6085, La Petite Poucette (Thumbelina). No. 6086, Le Vilain Petit Canard (The Ugly Duckling). No. 6087, Aladin (Aladdin). No. 6088, Peau d'Ane (Donkeyskin). No. 6089, La Barbe Bleue (Bluebeard). No. 6090, La Belle au Bois Dormant (Sleeping Beauty). No. 6091, La Princesse au Petit Pois (The Princess and the Pea). No. 6092, Cendrillon (Cinderella).

Serpentine Die Cut 11
2021, Sept. 3   Photo.
Booklet Stamps
Self-Adhesive
6081 A3247   (€1.08) multi   2.50   .85
6082 A3247   (€1.08) multi   2.50   .85
6083 A3247   (€1.08) multi   2.50   .85
6084 A3247   (€1.08) multi   2.50   .85
6085 A3247   (€1.08) multi   2.50   .85
6086 A3247   (€1.08) multi   2.50   .85
6087 A3247   (€1.08) multi   2.50   .85
6088 A3247   (€1.08) multi   2.50   .85
6089 A3247   (€1.08) multi   2.50   .85
6090 A3247   (€1.08) multi   2.50   .85
6091 A3247   (€1.08) multi   2.50   .85
6092 A3247   (€1.08) multi   2.50   .85
  a.   Booklet pane of 12, #6081-6092   30.00
  Nos. 6081-6092 (12)   30.00 10.20

Art Issue

In My Humble Opinion, Drawing by Camille Henrot A3248

2021, Sept. 10   Photo.   Perf. 13x13¼
6093 A3248   €2.56 multi   6.00   3.00

Miniature Sheet

Environmental Protection — A3249

No. 6094: a, Agriculture durable (sustainable agriculture). b, Circuit court (locally produced produce), horiz. c, Consommer durable (sustainable consuming). d, Bien-être et santé (well-being and health), horiz.

2021, Sept. 17   Photo.   Perf. 13¼
6094 A3249   Sheet of 4   10.00 10.00
  a.-d.   €1.08 Any single   2.50   .85

Featherwork A3250

Litho. & Engr.
2021, Sept. 24   Perf. 13
6095 A3250   €1.50 multi   3.50   1.25

Citroen Méhari — A3251

Citroen 2CV A3252

2021, Sept. 25   Engr.   Perf. 13
6096 A3251   €1.08 multi   2.50   .85

Souvenir Sheet
Photo.   Perf. 13x13¼
6097 A3252   €2.16 multi   5.00   5.00
Stamp Day.

Gustave Roussy (1874-1948), Neurologist A3253

2021, Oct. 1   Engr.   Perf. 13¼
6098 A3253   €1.28 multi   3.00   1.00

Valenciennes City Hall — A3254

2021, Oct. 8   Engr.   Perf. 13x13¼
6099 A3254   €1.28 multi + label   3.00   1.00
French Federation of Philatelic Associations 94th Congress, Valenciennes.

National Center for Space Studies (CNES), 60th Anniv. — A3255

2021, Oct. 8   Photo.   Perf. 13¼
6100 A3255   €1.50 multi   3.50   1.25

Mailbox of Japan A3256   Mailbox of France A3257

2021, Oct. 8   Litho.   Perf. 13
6101 A3256   €1.28 red & blue   3.00   1.00
6102 A3257   €1.50 yellow & blue   3.50   1.25
  a.   Pair, #6101-6102   6.50   2.25
Joint issue between France and Japan. See Japan Nos. 4549-4550.
A souvenir sheet containing Nos. 6101-6102 sold for €6.50.

Souvenir Sheet

Goldorak (Grandizer) — A3258

No. 6103 — Scenes from Goldorak (Grandizer) animated television series: a, Goldorak, Koji Kabuto, Blaki. b, Goldorak, Gandal, Duke Fleed, Emperor of Darkness.

2021, Oct. 8   Photo.   Perf. 13¼x13
6103 A3258   Sheet of 2   7.00   2.50
  a.-b.   €1.50 Either single   3.50   1.25

Paintings of Stars and Celestial Objects — A3259

Various paintings with inscriptions of: No. 6104, Tutoyer les étoiles. No. 6105, Naine blanche, Géant rouge ou bleue. No. 6106, Mesurer la distance qui nous sépare. No. 6107, A la lumière de l'infiniti lointain. No. 6108, Interroger le coeur des nébuleuses. No. 6109, Où brillent les jeunes étoiles turbulentes. No. 6110, Nova, Supernova, Pulsar. No. 6111, Chaque étoile porte un nom. No. 6112, Des millions d'étoiles en mouvement. No. 6113, Au fond des galaxies en fuite. No. 6114, Nous sommes poussière d'étoiles. No. 6115, Dans l'univers en expansion infinie.

Serpentine Die Cut 11
2021, Oct. 8   Photo.
Booklet Stamps
Self-Adhesive
6104 A3259   (€1.08) multi   2.50   .85
6105 A3259   (€1.08) multi   2.50   .85
6106 A3259   (€1.08) multi   2.50   .85
6107 A3259   (€1.08) multi   2.50   .85
6108 A3259   (€1.08) multi   2.50   .85
6109 A3259   (€1.08) multi   2.50   .85
6110 A3259   (€1.08) multi   2.50   .85
6111 A3259   (€1.08) multi   2.50   .85
6112 A3259   (€1.08) multi   2.50   .85
6113 A3259   (€1.08) multi   2.50   .85
6114 A3259   (€1.08) multi   2.50   .85
6115 A3259   (€1.08) multi   2.50   .85
  a.   Booklet pane of 12, #6104-6115   30.00
  Nos. 6104-6115 (12)   30.00 10.20

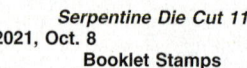

Georges Brassens (1921-81), Singer — A3260

2021, Oct. 22   Photo.   Perf. 13¼
6116 A3260   €1.08 multi   2.50   .85

Deer, Owl and Gift A3261   Fox A3262

Penguins A3263   Fawn A3264

Trees, Star, and Seeds A3265   Snowflakes and Ornaments A3266

Flowers and Stars — A3267   Fawns, Foxes and Trees — A3268

Squirrels, Acorns and Snowflake A3269   Fox and Gifts A3270

Bear Wearing Scarf A3271   Deer and Penguins A3272

Serpentine Die Cut 11
2021, Oct. 29   Photo.
Booklet Stamps
Self-Adhesive
6117 A3261   (€1.08) multi   2.50   .85
6118 A3262   (€1.08) multi   2.50   .85
6119 A3263   (€1.08) multi   2.50   .85
6120 A3264   (€1.08) multi   2.50   .85
6121 A3265   (€1.08) multi   2.50   .85
6122 A3266   (€1.08) multi   2.50   .85
6123 A3267   (€1.08) multi   2.50   .85
6124 A3268   (€1.08) multi   2.50   .85

FRANCE

6125	A3269	(€1.08) multi	2.50	.85
6126	A3270	(€1.08) multi	2.50	.85
6127	A3271	(€1.08) multi	2.50	.85
6128	A3272	(€1.08) multi	2.50	.85
a.	Booklet pane of 12, #6117-6128		30.00	
Nos. 6117-6128 (12)			30.00	10.20

Christmas.

Marianne and Denomination Type of 2018

2021, Nov. 4   Engr.   Perf. 12¾
Size: 25x32mm

6129	A2826	€7 gold	16.00	8.00

No. 6129 was printed in sheets of 4.

Marianne Type of 1971-74 With Euro Denominations

2021, Nov. 4   Engr.   Perf. 13
Booklet Stamps

6130	A555	€1.08 grnsh blue	2.50	.65
6131	A555	€1.28 red	3.00	.75
a.	Booklet pane of 12, 6 each #6130-6131		33.00	

Size: 40x52mm

6132	A555	€1.50 grnsh blue	3.50	.90
6133	A555	€1.50 red	3.50	.90
a.	Booklet pane of 2, #6132-6133		7.00	
	Complete booklet, #6131a, 6133a		40.00	

A3273

A3274

A3275

A3276   A3277

A3278   A3279

A3280   A3281

A3282

A3283

Stamp Boxes — A3284

Serpentine Die Cut
2021, Nov. 4   Photo.
Booklet Stamps
Self-Adhesive

6134	A3273	(€1.08) multi	2.50	.85

Serpentine Die Cut 11

6135	A3274	(€1.08) multi	2.50	.85
6136	A3275	(€1.08) multi	2.50	.85
6137	A3276	(€1.08) multi	2.50	.85
6138	A3277	(€1.08) multi	2.50	.85
6139	A3278	(€1.08) multi	2.50	.85
6140	A3279	(€1.08) multi	2.50	.85
6141	A3280	(€1.08) multi	2.50	.85
6142	A3281	(€1.08) multi	2.50	.85
6143	A3282	(€1.08) multi	2.50	.85
6144	A3283	(€1.08) multi	2.50	.85
6145	A3284	(€1.08) multi	2.50	.85
a.	Booklet pane of 12, #6134-6145		30.00	
Nos. 6134-6145 (12)			30.00	10.20

Souvenir Sheet

Roger North and Jean Farcigny, Founders of Autumn Philatelic Show
A3285

2021, Nov. 4   Engr.   Perf. 13x13¼

6146	A3285	€1.28 multi	3.00	1.00

Autumn Philatelic Show, 75th anniv.

Sower Type of 2003

2021, Nov. 4   Engr.   Perf. 13¼x13

6147		Sheet of 6, 4 #6147a, 2 #6147b	55.00	55.00
a.	A1664	€3 dull purple	6.75	3.00
b.	A1664	€6 grnsh blue	14.00	7.00

Souvenir Sheet

French History
A3286

2021, Nov. 5   Engr.   Perf. 13

6148	A3286	Sheet of 2	13.50	13.50
a.-b.		€3 Either single	6.75	6.75
c.		Souvenir sheet of 2, #6148a-6148b, with different sheet margin	19.50	19.50

No. 6148c sold for €8.50.

Gustave Flaubert (1821-80), Writer — A3287

2021, Nov. 6   Photo.   Perf. 13¼

6149	A3287	€1.28 multi	3.00	1.00

A souvenir sheet containing No. 6149 sold for €4.50.

No. 5955 Overprinted in Red

Method and Perf. As Before
2021, Nov. 15

6150	A3139	€1.40 multi	3.25	1.10

The overprint marks the last issue to be printed in sheets of 30 stamps.

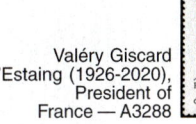

Valéry Giscard d'Estaing (1926-2020), President of France — A3288

2021, Nov. 19   Engr.   Perf. 13¼

6151	A3288	€1.28 multi	3.00	1.00

First Written Mention of a Christmas Tree in Municipal Archives of Sélestat, 500th Anniv. — A3289

Photo. With Foil Application
2021, Nov. 20   Perf. 13¼

6152	A3289	€1.50 gold & multi	3.50	1.25

A souvenir sheet containing No. 6152 sold for €4.50.

Great Barrier Reef, Australia — A3290   Strokkur Geyser, Iceland — A3291

Iceberg in Lake Sassolo, Switzerland A3292   Ice Cliff, Norway A3293

Okavango Delta, Botswana A3294   Iguazú Falls, Brazil and Argentina A3295

Stream and Waterfall, New Zealand — A3296   Atlantic Ocean Waves, France — A3297

Gorges du Chéran, France — A3298   Trappstegsforsen Rapids, Sweden — A3299

Ahé Atoll, French Polynesia A3300   Lake Oum el Ma, Libya A3301

Serpentine Die Cut 11
2022, Jan. 7   Photo.
Booklet Stamps
Self-Adhesive

6153	A3290	(€1.43) multi	3.25	1.10
6154	A3291	(€1.43) multi	3.25	1.10
6155	A3292	(€1.43) multi	3.25	1.10
6156	A3293	(€1.43) multi	3.25	1.10
6157	A3294	(€1.43) multi	3.25	1.10
6158	A3295	(€1.43) multi	3.25	1.10
6159	A3296	(€1.43) multi	3.25	1.10
6160	A3297	(€1.43) multi	3.25	1.10
6161	A3298	(€1.43) multi	3.25	1.10
6162	A3299	(€1.43) multi	3.25	1.10
6163	A3300	(€1.43) multi	3.25	1.10
6164	A3301	(€1.43) multi	3.25	1.10
a.	Booklet pane of 12, #6153-6164		39.00	
Nos. 6153-6164 (12)			39.00	13.20

French Presidency of the Council of the European Union — A3302

Litho. & Engr.
2022, Jan. 10   Perf. 13¼

6165	A3302	€1.65 multi	3.75	1.25

Molière (1622-73), Playwright and Actor A3303

2022, Jan. 14   Engr.   Perf. 13x13¼

6166	A3303	€1.43 black & gold	3.25	1.10

A souvenir sheet containing No. 6166 sold for €4.50.

Daniel Boulanger (1922-2014), Writer and Actor — A3304

2022, Jan. 21   Photo.   Perf. 13¼

6167	A3304	€1.43 multi	3.25	1.10

A3305

New Year 2022 (Year of the Tiger) — A3306

2022, Jan. 22   Photo.   Perf. 13¼x13

6168		Sheet of 5, #6168a, 4 #6168b	13.00	13.00
a.	A3305	€1.16 multi, 33x40mm stamp	2.60	.85
b.	A3305	€1.16 multi, 29x35mm stamp	2.60	.85
6169		Sheet of 5, #6169a, 4 #6169b	19.00	19.00
a.	A3306	€1.65 multi, 33x40mm stamp	3.75	1.25
b.	A3306	€1.65 multi, 29x35mm stamp	3.75	1.25

Heart, Bird and Saint-Louis Crystal Chandelier A3307

2022, Jan. 28   Litho.   Perf. 13¼

6170	A3307	€1.16 sil & multi	2.60	.85
a.		Souvenir sheet of 5	13.00	13.00
6171	A3307	€2.32 multi	5.25	1.75

Self-Adhesive
Serpentine Die Cut

6172	A3307	€1.16 multi	2.60	.85
6173	A3307	€2.32 multi	5.25	1.75

Values for Nos. 6170-6171 are for stamps with surrounding selvage.

FRANCE

Louis Pasteur (1822-95), Microbiologist, and His Birthplace, Dole — A3308

2022, Feb. 4   Engr.   Perf. 13¼
6174 A3308 €1.16 multi   2.60   .85

A souvenir sheet containing No. 6174 sold for €4.50.

Violin Making — A3309

2022, Feb. 11   Engr.   Perf. 13¼
6175 A3309 €1.65 multi   3.75 1.25

A souvenir sheet containing No. 6175 sold for €4.50.

Silhouettes of Animals — A3310

Silhouette of: No. 6176, African elephant. No. 6177, Giant kangaroo. No. 6178, Yellow-crested cockatoo. No. 6179, King penguins. No. 6180, European fallow deer. No. 6181, Baboons. No. 6182, Bottlenose dolphins. No. 6183, Guanacos. No. 6184, Lion. No. 6185, White stork and nest. No. 6186, Leopard. No. 6187, Great egrets and black-headed gull.

Serpentine Die Cut 11
2022, Feb. 11   Photo.
Booklet Stamps
Self-Adhesive
6176 A3310 (€1.16) multi   2.60   .85
6177 A3310 (€1.16) multi   2.60   .85
6178 A3310 (€1.16) multi   2.60   .85
6179 A3310 (€1.16) multi   2.60   .85
6180 A3310 (€1.16) multi   2.60   .85
6181 A3310 (€1.16) multi   2.60   .85
6182 A3310 (€1.16) multi   2.60   .85
6183 A3310 (€1.16) multi   2.60   .85
6184 A3310 (€1.16) multi   2.60   .85
6185 A3310 (€1.16) multi   2.60   .85
6186 A3310 (€1.16) multi   2.60   .85
6187 A3310 (€1.16) multi   2.60   .85
  a. Booklet pane of 12, #6176-6187   31.50
  Nos. 6176-6187 (12)   31.20 10.20

Shells and Crustaceans A3311

Designs: No. 6188, Crevette bouquet (common prawn).
No. 6189: a, Tourteau (brown crab). b, Coquille Saint-Jacques (great scallop). c, Lambi (queen conch).

2022, Feb. 18   Photo.   Perf. 13¼
6188 A3311 €1.16 multi   2.60   .85
Souvenir Sheet
6189   Sheet of 4, #6189a-6189c   10.50 10.50
  a.-c. A3311 €1.16 Any single   2.60   .85
  d. Souvenir sheet of 2, #6188, 6189a   7.25 7.25
  e. Souvenir sheet of 2, #6189b, 6189c   7.25 7.25

Nos. 6189d and 6189e were sold as a set for €6.50.

Art Issue

The Tree of Paradise, Painting by Séraphine Louis (1864-1942) A3312

Portrait of a Lion, Painting by Rosa Bonheur (1822-99) A3313

2022   Photo.   Perf. 13¼x13
6190 A3312 €2.86 multi   6.50 3.25
Litho.
6191 A3313 €2.86 multi   6.50 3.25

Issued: No. 6190, 2/25; No. 6191, 3/4. A souvenir sheet containing No. 6191 sold for €6.50.

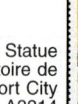

Lion of Belfort Statue and Territoire de Belfort City Hall — A3314

2022, Mar. 11   Photo.   Perf. 13¼
6192 A3314 €1.16 multi   2.60   .85

Departmental status of Territoire de Belfort, cent.

Famous Explorers and Travelers — A3315

Designs: No. 6193, Marco Polo (1254-1324). No. 6194, Ferdinand Magellan (1480-1521). No. 6195, James Cook (1728-79). No. 6196, Jeanne Barret (1740-1807). No. 6197, Gertrude Bell (1868-1926). No. 6198, Isabelle Eberhardt (1877-1904). No. 6199, Christopher Columbus (1451-1506). No. 6200, Jacques Cartier (1491-1557). No. 6201, Roald Amundsen (1872-1928). No. 6202, Nellie Bly (1864-1922). No. 6203, Alexandra David-Néel (1868-1969). No. 6204, Amelia Earhart (1897-1937).

Serpentine Die Cut 11
2022, Mar. 11   Photo.
Booklet Stamps
Self-Adhesive
6193 A3315 (€1.16) multi   2.60   .85
6194 A3315 (€1.16) multi   2.60   .85
6195 A3315 (€1.16) multi   2.60   .85
6196 A3315 (€1.16) multi   2.60   .85
6197 A3315 (€1.16) multi   2.60   .85
6198 A3315 (€1.16) multi   2.60   .85
6199 A3315 (€1.16) multi   2.60   .85
6200 A3315 (€1.16) multi   2.60   .85
6201 A3315 (€1.16) multi   2.60   .85
6202 A3315 (€1.16) multi   2.60   .85
6203 A3315 (€1.16) multi   2.60   .85
6204 A3315 (€1.16) multi   2.60   .85
  a. Booklet pane of 12, #6193-6204   31.50
  Nos. 6193-6204 (12)   31.20 10.20

TER Train — A3316

Hikers A3317

2022, Mar. 12   Engr.   Perf. 13¼
6205 A3316 €1.16 multi   2.50   .85
Souvenir Sheet
Photo.   Perf. 13x13¼
6206 A3317 €2.32 multi   5.25 5.25

Stamp Day.

Château de Villers-Cotterêts A3318

2022, Mar. 19   Engr.   Perf. 13¼
6207 A3318 €1.65 multi   3.75 1.25

Opening of Villers-Cotterêts International City of the French Language Project.

Odeillo Solar Furnace — A3319

2022, Mar. 25   Photo.   Perf. 13¼
6208 A3319 €1.16 multi   2.60   .85

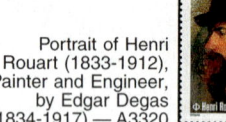

Portrait of Henri Rouart (1833-1912), Painter and Engineer, by Edgar Degas (1834-1917) — A3320

2022, Apr. 8   Photo.   Perf. 13¼
6209 A3320 €1.43 multi   3.00 1.00

Souvenir Sheet

Pipe Organ of Notre Dame Cathedral, Paris — A3321

2022, Apr. 15   Engr.   Perf. 13
6210 A3321 €1.65 multi   3.50 3.50

Miniature Sheet

European Capitals — A3322

No. 6211 — Attractions in Ljubljana, Slovenia: a, Dragon Bridge. b, St. Nicholas's Cathedral, vert. c, Ljubljana Castle. d, Tivoli Park.

Litho. & Engr.
2022, Apr. 22   Perf. 13¼
6211 A3322   Sheet of 4   14.00 14.00
  a.-d.   €1.65 Any single   3.50 1.25

Legend of the Mélusine A3323

2022, May 6   Engr.   Perf. 13¼x13
6212 A3323 €1.65 gold & black   3.50 1.25

Europa.

Poppy and Candy Lozenge A3324

Chestnut Catkins and Candied Chestnut A3325

Acacia Flowers and Gum A3326

Marshmallow Flowers and Marshmallow Candy A3327

Mint and Bêtise de Cambrai Candy A3328

Anise and Anis de Flavigny Candy A3329

Cacao Flowers and Chocolate Candy A3330

Violets and Violet Candy A3331

Bergamot Flower and Bergamote de Nancy Candy A3332

Coconut Flowers and Coconut Ball Candy A3333

FRANCE 737

Licorice Flower and Candy A3334

Almond Blossoms and Dragées A3335

2022, May 6   Photo.
Booklet Stamps Self-Adhesive
Serpentine Die Cut 11

6213	A3324	(€1.16) multi	2.50	.85
6214	A3325	(€1.16) multi	2.50	.85
6215	A3326	(€1.16) multi	2.50	.85
6216	A3327	(€1.16) multi	2.50	.85
6217	A3328	(€1.16) multi	2.50	.85
6218	A3329	(€1.16) multi	2.50	.85
6219	A3330	(€1.16) multi	2.50	.85
6220	A3331	(€1.16) multi	2.50	.85
6221	A3332	(€1.16) multi	2.50	.85
6222	A3333	(€1.16) multi	2.50	.85
6223	A3334	(€1.16) multi	2.50	.85
6224	A3335	(€1.16) multi	2.50	.85
a.	Booklet pane of 12, #6213-6224		30.00	
	Nos. 6213-6224 (12)		30.00	10.20

Solitude (c. 1772-1802), Guadeloupian Slave Executed by French Colonial Forces — A3336

2022, May 13   Litho.   *Perf. 13¼*
6225   A3336   €1.16 multi   2.50 .85

Tourism Issue

Church and Priory Gardens, Souvigny, and Anne of France (1461-1522), Regent for King Charles VIII — A3337

2022, May 13   Engr.   *Perf. 13¼x13*
6226   A3337   €1.43 multi   3.00 1.00

Jeanne Moreau (1928-2017), Actress — A3338

2022, May 20   Photo.   *Perf. 13¼*
6227   A3338   €1.43 multi   3.00 1.00

Emile Erckmann (1822-99), and Alexandre Chatrian (1826-90), Writers — A3339

2022, May 20   Engr.   *Perf. 13x13¼*
6228   A3339   €2.86 multi   6.25 2.10

Balata Garden, Fort-de-France, Martinique — A3340

2022, May 27   Photo.   *Perf. 13¼*
6229   A3340   €1.65 multi   3.50 1.25
A souvenir sheet containing No. 6229 sold for €4.50.

Art Issue

Swallow Stories, Photograph by Sarah Moon A3341

2022, May 27   Photo.   *Perf. 13x13¼*
6230   A3341   €2.86 multi   6.25 3.25

Alain Resnais (1922-2014), Movie Director — A3342

2022, June 3   Photo.   *Perf. 13¼x13*
6231   A3342   €1.16 multi   2.40 .80

Sympathy A3343

Triumph A3345

Desire A3347

Satisfaction A3349

Adoration A3351

Excitement A3344

Romance A3346

Admiration A3348

Joy A3350

Bliss A3352

Calm A3353

Amusement A3354

2022, June 3   Photo.
Booklet Stamps Self-Adhesive
Serpentine Die Cut 11

6232	A3343	(€1.16) multi	2.40	.80
6233	A3344	(€1.16) multi	2.40	.80
6234	A3345	(€1.16) multi	2.40	.80
6235	A3346	(€1.16) multi	2.40	.80
6236	A3347	(€1.16) multi	2.40	.80
6237	A3348	(€1.16) multi	2.40	.80
6238	A3349	(€1.16) multi	2.40	.80
6239	A3350	(€1.16) multi	2.40	.80
6240	A3351	(€1.16) multi	2.40	.80
6241	A3352	(€1.16) multi	2.40	.80
6242	A3353	(€1.16) multi	2.40	.80
6243	A3354	(€1.16) multi	2.40	.80
a.	Booklet pane of 12, #6232-6243		29.00	
	Nos. 6232-6243 (12)		28.80	9.60

Pasteur Type of Semi-Postals of 1936 With Euro Denominations
Miniature Sheet
Engr., Sheet Margin Engr. & Embossed With Foil Application
2022, June 23   *Perf. 13*
6244   Sheet of 4, 2 each #6244a-6244b   25.50 25.50
a. SP22 €2 dark blue   4.25 2.10
b. SP22 €4 dp gray blue   8.50 4.25

Types of 1946-2008
Miniature Sheet

No. 6245 — Palaces in Paris: a, Chaillot Palace. b, Luxembourg Palace. c, Elysée Palace. d, Grand Palace.

Engr., Sheet Margin Litho. With Foil Application
2022, June 23   *Perf. 13*
6245   Sheet of 4   25.00 25.00
a. A178 €3 blue   6.25 3.25
b. A160 €3 blue   6.25 3.25
c. A302 €3 blue   6.25 3.25
d. A1961 €3 blue   6.25 3.25

2022 Paris Philex.

Cité Internationale Universitaire de Paris — A3355

2022, June 23   Engr.   *Perf. 13x13¼*
6246   A3355   €1.43 multi + label   3.00 1.00
French Federation of Philatelic Associations 95th Congress, Paris

Funerary Mask of King Tutankhamun A3356

Photo. With Foil Application
2022, June 23   *Perf. 13¼x13*
6247   A3356   €1.65 gold & multi   3.50 1.25
A souvenir sheet containing No. 6247 sold for €4.50.

Sower With Euro Denominations — A3357

2022, June 23   Typo.   *Perf. 13*
Booklet Stamps

6248	A3357	€1.16 green	2.40	.60
6249	A3357	€1.43 red	3.00	.75
a.	Booklet pane of 12, 6 each #6248-6249		32.50	

Size: 40x52mm

6250	A3357	€2.32 green	5.00	2.50
6251	A3357	€2.86 red	6.00	3.00
a.	Booklet pane of 2, #6250-6251		11.00	—
	Complete booklet, #6249a, 6251a		43.50	

A3358

A3359

A3360

A3361

A3362

A3363

A3364

A3365

A3366

A3367

A3368

738 FRANCE

Illustrations From Old Post Cards — A3369

Serpentine Die Cut 11
2022, June 23   Photo.
Booklet Stamps
Self-Adhesive

6252	A3358	(€1.16) multi	2.40	.80
6253	A3359	(€1.16) multi	2.40	.80
6254	A3360	(€1.16) multi	2.40	.80
6255	A3361	(€1.16) multi	2.40	.80
6256	A3362	(€1.16) multi	2.40	.80
6257	A3363	(€1.16) multi	2.40	.80
6258	A3364	(€1.16) multi	2.40	.80
6259	A3365	(€1.16) multi	2.40	.80
6260	A3366	(€1.16) multi	2.40	.80
6261	A3367	(€1.16) multi	2.40	.80
6262	A3368	(€1.16) multi	2.40	.80
6263	A3369	(€1.16) multi	2.40	.80
a.	Booklet pane of 12, #6252-6263		29.00	
Nos. 6252-6263 (12)			28.80	9.60

French post cards, 150th anniv.

Miniature Sheet

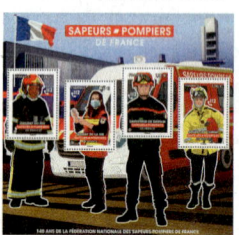

Fire Fighters A3370

No. 6264 — Inscription: a, Soldat du feu (fire soldier). b, Soldat de la vie (soldier of life). c, Sauveteur de demain (lifeguard of tomorrow). d, Soldat du climat (climate soldier).

2022, June 23   Photo.   Perf. 13¼
6264	A3370	Sheet of 4	9.75	9.75
a.-d.	€1.16 Any single		2.40	.80

National Federation of Fire Fighters, 140th anniv.

Miniature Sheet

Sports A3371

No. 6265: a, Boxing. b, Handball. c, Wheelchair tennis. d, Equestrian jumping. e, Diving. f, Archery.

2022, June 23   Photo.   Perf. 13
6265	A3371	Sheet of 6	21.00	21.00
a.-f.	€1.65 Any single		3.50	1.25

Miniature Sheet

Philatelists — A3372

No. 6266: a, Ernest Dole (1872-1947). b, Maurice Langlois (1860-1948). c, Henri Kastler (1863-1957). d, Théodule Tellier (1855-1922). e, Ladislas Varga (1897-1981). f, Leon Boscus (1897-1989).

2022, June 23   Engr.   Perf. 13¼
6266	A3372	Sheet of 6	51.00	51.00
a.-f.	€4 Any single		8.50	8.50

Souvenir Sheet

Ceres A3373

Photo., Sheet Margin Typo.
2022, June 23   Perf. 13x13¼
| 6267 | A3373 | €3.30 pink & brown | 7.00 | 7.00 |

French postal cards, 150th anniv.

Tourism Issue

Sancerre, 2021 Favorite Village in France A3374

2022, June 30   Photo.   Perf. 13
| 6268 | A3374 | €1.16 multi | 2.40 | .80 |

Typical House, Haut-Rhin Department A3375

Typical House, Pyrénées-Atlantiques Department A3376

Typical House, Hérault Department A3377

Typical House, Finistère Department A3378

Typical House, Martinique Overseas Department A3379

Typical House, Loir-et-Cher Department A3380

Typical House, Réunion Overseas Department A3381

Typical House, Calvados Department A3382

Typical House, Saône-et-Loire Department A3383

Typical House, Vaucluse Department A3384

Typical House, Nord Department A3385

Typical House, Savoie Department A3386

Serpentine Die Cut 11
2022, July 1   Photo.
Booklet Stamps
Self-Adhesive

6269	A3375	(€1.16) multi	2.40	.80
6270	A3376	(€1.16) multi	2.40	.80
6271	A3377	(€1.16) multi	2.40	.80
6272	A3378	(€1.16) multi	2.40	.80
6273	A3379	(€1.16) multi	2.40	.80
6274	A3380	(€1.16) multi	2.40	.80
6275	A3381	(€1.16) multi	2.40	.80
6276	A3382	(€1.16) multi	2.40	.80
6277	A3383	(€1.16) multi	2.40	.80
6278	A3384	(€1.16) multi	2.40	.80
6279	A3385	(€1.16) multi	2.40	.80
6280	A3386	(€1.16) multi	2.40	.80
a.	Booklet pane of 12, #6269-6280		29.00	
Nos. 6269-6280 (12)			28.80	9.60

Col du Tourmalet Mountain Pass — A3387

2022, July 8   Photo.   Perf. 13¼
| 6281 | A3387 | €1.16 multi | 2.40 | .80 |

Underwater Archaeology — A3388

2022, July 8   Photo.   Perf. 13¼
| 6282 | A3388 | €1.65 multi | 3.50 | 1.25 |

Château de Commequiers A3389

2022, July 15   Photo.   Perf. 13¼
| 6283 | A3389 | €1.43 multi | 3.00 | 1.00 |

Marcel Proust (1871-1922), Writer — A3390

2022, July 22   Engr.   Perf. 13¼x13
| 6284 | A3390 | €1.65 multi | 3.50 | 1.25 |

A souvenir sheet containing No. 6284 sold for €4.50.

A3391

A3392

A3393

A3394

A3395

A3396

A3397

A3398

Owl, Courrier Suivi Emblem, Tracking Number and Encryption — A3399

Serpentine Die Cut 11
2022, Aug. 19   Photo.
Booklet Stamps
Self-Adhesive

6285	A3391	(€1.66) multi	3.50	1.75
6286	A3392	(€1.66) multi	3.50	1.75
6287	A3393	(€1.66) multi	3.50	1.75
6288	A3394	(€1.66) multi	3.50	1.75
6289	A3395	(€1.66) multi	3.50	1.75
6290	A3396	(€1.66) multi	3.50	1.75
6291	A3397	(€1.66) multi	3.50	1.75
6292	A3398	(€1.66) multi	3.50	1.75
6293	A3399	(€1.66) multi	3.50	1.75
a.	Booklet pane of 9, #6285-6293		31.50	
Nos. 6285-6293 (9)			31.50	15.75

On the day of issue, Nos. 6285-6293 paid the €1.16 lettre verte rate plus the 50c letter tracking fee. Tracking numbers on each stamp are repeated in booklet selvage below that stamp. Letters bearing these stamps could be tracked by entering the tracking number on the La Poste website. The tracking numbers and encryption on each stamp differ.
Compare with types A3109-A3117.

Details From Famous Paintings — A3400

Detail from: No. 6294, Liberty Leading the People, by Eugène Delacroix (1798-1863). No. 6295, Mona Lisa, by Leonardo da Vinci (1452-1519). No. 6296, The Card Players, by Paul Cézanne (1839-1906). No. 6297, La Grande Odalisque, by Jean-Auguste-Dominique Ingres (1780-1867). No. 6298, 1889 Self-portrait, by Vincent van Gogh (1853-90). No. 6299, The Intervention of the Sabine Women, by Jacques-Louis David (1748-1825). No. 6300, Pierrot, by Jean-Antoine Watteau (1684-1721). No. 6301, François I of France, by Jean Clouet (1480-1541). No. 6302, Helena Fourment with Children, by Peter Paul Rubens (1577-1640). No. 6303, Spring, by Giuseppe Arcimboldo (c. 1526-93). No. 6304, Two Young Girls at the Piano, by Pierre-Auguste Renoir (1841-1919). No. 6305, Marquise de Pompadour, by Maurice Quentin de La Tour (1704-88).

Serpentine Die Cut 11
2022, Sept. 2   Photo.
Booklet Stamps
Self-Adhesive

6294	A3400	(€1.16) multi	2.25	.75
6295	A3400	(€1.16) multi	2.25	.75
6296	A3400	(€1.16) multi	2.25	.75
6297	A3400	(€1.16) multi	2.25	.75
6298	A3400	(€1.16) multi	2.25	.75
6299	A3400	(€1.16) multi	2.25	.75
6300	A3400	(€1.16) multi	2.25	.75
6301	A3400	(€1.16) multi	2.25	.75
6302	A3400	(€1.16) multi	2.25	.75
6303	A3400	(€1.16) multi	2.25	.75
6304	A3400	(€1.16) multi	2.25	.75
6305	A3400	(€1.16) multi	2.25	.75
a.	Booklet pane of 12, #6294-6305		27.00	
Nos. 6294-6305 (12)			27.00	9.00

FRANCE

Art Issue

Painting by Françoise Pétrovitch — A3401

2022, Sept. 9		Litho.		Perf. 13¼
6306	A3401	€2.32	multi	4.50 2.25

Petit Louvre, La Pacaudière — A3402

2022, Sept. 9		Photo.		Perf. 13¼
6307	A3402	€1.16	multi	2.25 .75

Tourism Issue

Familistère de Guise Housing Complex — A3403

2022, Sept. 16		Engr.		Perf. 13¼
6308	A3403	€1.65	multi	3.25 1.10

Miniature Sheet

Renewable Energy Sources — A3404

No. 6309: a, Underwater generator. b, Wind generators, girl with pinwheel, horiz. c, People on sand dune with solar panels, horiz. d, Woman holding fruits, leaves and branches.

2022, Sept. 16		Photo.		Perf. 13¼
6309	A3404	Sheet of 4		9.00 9.00
a.-d.		€1.16 Any single		2.25 .75

Blind Man and Guide Dog — A3405

2022, Sept. 23		Photo. & Embossed		Perf. 13¼
6310	A3405	€1.16	black & red	2.25 .75

Coppersmithing A3406

2022, Sept. 30		Engr. & Embossed		Perf. 13
6311	A3406	€1.65	multi	3.25 1.10

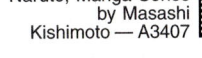

Naruto, Manga Series by Masashi Kishimoto — A3407

2022, Oct. 7		Litho.		Perf. 13¼
6312	A3407	€1.16	multi	2.40 .80

Frédéric Passy (1822-1912), 1901 Nobel Peace Laureate — A3408

2022, Oct. 7		Engr.		Perf. 13¼
6313	A3408	€1.65	multi	3.25 1.10

Ada Lovelace (1815-52), Mathematician A3409

2022, Oct. 11		Photo.		Perf. 13¼
6314	A3409	€1.65	multi	3.25 1.10

A souvenir sheet containing No. 6314 sold for €4.50.

Lakes of the Orient Forest Regional Natural Park — A3410

2022, Oct. 14		Photo.		Perf. 13¼
6315	A3410	€1.16	multi	2.40 .80

Tourism Issue

Notre Dame Bridge, Notre-Dame-et-Saint-Privat Cathedral, and Gévaudan Museum, Mende — A3411

2022, Oct. 21		Engr.		Perf. 13x12¾
6316	A3411	€1.65	multi	3.25 1.10

No. 5930 Surcharged

Method and Perf. As Before
2022, Oct. 28
| 6317 | A3119 | €1.16 on 97c | #5930 | 2.40 .80 |

A3412   A3413

A3414   A3415

A3416   A3417

A3418   A3419

A3420   A3421

A3422

Christmas A3423

Serpentine Die Cut 11

2022, Nov. 2			Booklet Stamps Self-Adhesive	Photo.	
6318	A3412	(€1.16)	multi	2.40	.80
6319	A3413	(€1.16)	multi	2.40	.80
6320	A3414	(€1.16)	multi	2.40	.80
6321	A3415	(€1.16)	multi	2.40	.80
6322	A3416	(€1.16)	multi	2.40	.80
6323	A3417	(€1.16)	multi	2.40	.80
6324	A3418	(€1.16)	multi	2.40	.80
6325	A3419	(€1.16)	multi	2.40	.80
6326	A3420	(€1.16)	multi	2.40	.80
6327	A3421	(€1.16)	multi	2.40	.80
6328	A3422	(€1.16)	multi	2.40	.80
6329	A3423	(€1.16)	multi	2.40	.80
a.		Booklet pane of 12, #6318-6329		29.00	
		Nos. 6318-6329 (12)		28.80	9.60

Raymond Devos (1922-2006), Comedian and Actor — A3424

2022, Nov. 3		Photo.		Perf. 13¼
6330	A3424	€1.16	multi	2.40 .80

Souvenir Sheet

French History A3425

No. 6331: a, Marie Leszczynska (1703-68), Queen Consort of King Louis XV. b, King Louis XV (1710-74).

2022, Nov. 3		Engr.		Perf.
6331	A3425	Sheet of 2		14.00 14.00
a.-b.		€3.30 Either single		7.00 7.00
c.		Souvenir sheet of 2, #6631a-6631b, with different sheet margin		17.50 17.50

No. 6331c sold for €8.50.

1902 Grimaud Playing Cards — A3426

Designs: No. 6332, Queen of Spades. No. 6333, Queen of Hearts. No. 6334, Queen of Diamonds. No. 6335, Queen of Clubs. No. 6336, Ace of Spades. No. 6337, Ace of Hearts. No. 6338, Ace of Diamonds. No. 6339, Ace of Clubs. No. 6340, King of Spades. No. 6341, King of Hearts. No. 6342, King of Diamonds. No. 6343, King of Clubs.

Serpentine Die Cut 11

2022, Nov. 3			Booklet Stamps Self-Adhesive	Photo.	
6332	A3426	(€1.16)	multi	2.40	.80
6333	A3426	(€1.16)	multi	2.40	.80
6334	A3426	(€1.16)	multi	2.40	.80
6335	A3426	(€1.16)	multi	2.40	.80
6336	A3426	(€1.16)	multi	2.40	.80
6337	A3426	(€1.16)	multi	2.40	.80
6338	A3426	(€1.16)	multi	2.40	.80
6339	A3426	(€1.16)	multi	2.40	.80
6340	A3426	(€1.16)	multi	2.40	.80
6341	A3426	(€1.16)	multi	2.40	.80
6342	A3426	(€1.16)	multi	2.40	.80
6343	A3426	(€1.16)	multi	2.40	.80
a.		Booklet pane of 12, #6332-6343		29.00	
		Nos. 6332-6343 (12)		28.80	9.60

Peace with Olive Branch Type of 1932-39 With Euro Denominations

2022, Nov. 3		Typo.		Perf. 13
6344	A45	€3	bluish gray	6.25 6.25
6345	A45	€5	citron	10.50 10.50

Printed in sheets of 6 containing 3 each Nos. 6344-6345.

Liberty After Delacroix Type of 1982 With Euro Denominations

2022, Nov. 3		Engr.		Perf. 13
		Booklet Stamps		
6346	A915	€1.16	emerald	2.40 .80
6347	A915	€1.43	red	3.00 1.00
a.		Booklet pane of 12, 6 each #6346-6347		32.50 —

Design Size: 30x48mm

6348	A915	€2.32	multi	5.00 2.50
6349	A915	€2.86	red	6.00 3.00
a.		Booklet pane of 2, #6348-6349		11.00
		Complete booklet, #6347a, 6349a		43.50

Liberty After Delacroix stamps, 40th anniv.

Molière Type of Semi-Postals of 1944 With Euro Denomination

2022, Nov. 22		Engr.		Perf. 13
6350	SP133	€1.16	rose carmine	2.40 .80

No. 6350 was printed in sheets of 4.

No. 5476a Overprinted in Red

No. 5478d Overprinted

Methods and Perfs As Before
2022, Nov. 3

| 6351 | A2827 | (€1.14) | dk gray (R) | 2.40 1.25 |
| 6352 | A2829 | (€1.43) | red (Bk) | 3.00 1.50 |

A3427

Marianne, "Lettre Services Plus," Data Matrix Code — A3428

2023		Engr.		Perf. 13
6353	A3427	(€2.95)	aqua + small label at right	6.25 3.25
a.		Souvenir sheet of 3 + 3 labels		19.00 19.00

Coil Stamps
Perf. 12½x13 on 3 Sides

| 6354 | A3428 | (€2.95) | aqua + large label at right | 6.25 3.25 |

740 FRANCE

Self-Adhesive
Serpentine Die Cut 6¾ Horiz. and Die Cut Between Stamp and Label

| 6355 | A3428 | (€2.95) | aqua + large label at right | 6.25 | 3.25 |

Booklet Stamp
Serpentine Die Cut 6¾ Vert. Between Stamp and Label at Right

| 6356 | A3427 | (€2.95) | aqua + small label at right | 6.25 | 3.25 |
| a. | Booklet pane of 6 + 6 labels | | | 37.50 | |

Issued: No. 6353a, 3/23; others, 1/1.

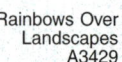

Rainbows Over Landscapes — A3429

Rainbow over landscape in: No. 6357, Zimbabwe. No. 6358, England (Angleterre). No. 6359, France. No. 6360, Canada. No. 6361, South Africa (Afrique du Sud). No. 6362, Thailand (Thailande). No. 6363, Germany (Allemagne). No. 6364, Poland (Pologne). No. 6365, French Polynesia (Polynésie Française). No. 6366, Denmark (Danemark). No. 6367, Italy (Italie). No. 6368, Iceland (Islande).

Serpentine Die Cut 11
2023, Jan. 6   Photo.
Booklet Stamps
Self-Adhesive

6357	A3429	(€1.16)	multi	2.60	.85
6358	A3429	(€1.16)	multi	2.60	.85
6359	A3429	(€1.16)	multi	2.60	.85
6360	A3429	(€1.16)	multi	2.60	.85
6361	A3429	(€1.16)	multi	2.60	.85
6362	A3429	(€1.16)	multi	2.60	.85
6363	A3429	(€1.16)	multi	2.60	.85
6364	A3429	(€1.16)	multi	2.60	.85
6365	A3429	(€1.16)	multi	2.60	.85
6366	A3429	(€1.16)	multi	2.60	.85
6367	A3429	(€1.16)	multi	2.60	.85
6368	A3429	(€1.16)	multi	2.60	.85
a.	Booklet pane of 12, #6357-6368			31.50	
Nos. 6357-6368 (12)				31.20	10.20

New Year 2023 (Year of the Rabbit) — A3430

Rabbit, with Chinese characters at: €1.16, Upper left. €1.80, Upper right.

2023, Jan. 16   Photo.   Perf. 13¼x13

6369	Sheet of 5, #6369a, 4 #6369b			13.00	13.00
a.	A3430 €1.16 multi, 33x40mm stamp			2.60	.85
b.	A3430 €1.16 multi, 29x35mm stamp			2.60	.85
6370	Sheet of 5, #6370a, 4 #6370b			20.00	20.00
a.	A3430 €1.80 multi, 33x40mm stamp			4.00	1.40
b.	A3430 €1.80 multi, 29x35mm stamp			4.00	1.40

Nelson Mandela (1918-2013), President of South Africa — A3431

2023, Jan. 20   Litho. & Engr.   Perf. 13¼

| 6371 | A3431 | €1.80 multi | 4.00 | 1.40 |

A souvenir sheet containing No. 6371 sold for €4.50.

Hearts (Agnès B.) — A3433   A3432

2023, Jan. 27   Litho.   Perf. 13¼

6372	A3432	€1.16 multi	2.60	.85
a.	Souvenir sheet of 5	13.00	13.00
6373	A3433	€2.32 multi	5.00	1.75

Photo.
Serpentine Die Cut
Self-Adhesive

| 6374 | A3432 | €1.16 multi | 2.60 | .85 |
| 6375 | A3433 | €2.32 multi | 5.00 | 1.75 |

Values for Nos. 6372-6373 are for stamps with surrounding selvage.

Mountain Flora — A3434

Designs: No. 6376, Ancolie des Alpes (alpine columbines). No. 6377: a, Saxifrage de Gizia (Gizia saxifrage). b, Jasione crépue d'Auvergne (dwarf sheep's-bit). c, Lis des Pyrénées (Pyrenean lily).

2023, Feb. 3   Photo.   Perf. 13¼

| 6376 | A3434 | €1.16 multi | 2.50 | .85 |

Souvenir Sheet

6377	Sheet of 4, #6376, 6377a-6377c		10.00	10.00
a.-c.	A3434 €1.16 Any single		2.50	.85
d.	Souvenir sheet of 2, #6376, 6377a		7.00	7.00
e.	Souvenir sheet of 2, #6377b, 6377c		7.00	7.00

Nos. 6377d and 6377e were sold as a set for €6.50.

Sheep A3435   Flamingos A3436

European Bee-eaters A3437   Lions A3438

Impalas A3439   Short-tailed Albatrosses A3440

Giraffes — A3441   Hafflinger Horses — A3442

Alpacas — A3443   Cats — A3444

Irish Setters — A3445   Zebras — A3446

Serpentine Die Cut 11
2023, Feb. 3   Photo.
Booklet Stamps
Self-Adhesive

6378	A3435	(€1.16)	multi	2.50	.85
6379	A3436	(€1.16)	multi	2.50	.85
6380	A3437	(€1.16)	multi	2.50	.85
6381	A3438	(€1.16)	multi	2.50	.85
6382	A3439	(€1.16)	multi	2.50	.85
6383	A3440	(€1.16)	multi	2.50	.85
6384	A3441	(€1.16)	multi	2.50	.85
6385	A3442	(€1.16)	multi	2.50	.85
6386	A3443	(€1.16)	multi	2.50	.85
6387	A3444	(€1.16)	multi	2.50	.85
6388	A3445	(€1.16)	multi	2.50	.85
6389	A3446	(€1.16)	multi	2.50	.85
a.	Booklet pane of 12, #6378-6389			30.00	
Nos. 6378-6389 (12)				30.00	10.20

Fan Making — A3447

2023, Feb. 10   Engr.   Perf. 13¼x13

| 6390 | A3447 | €1.80 multi | 4.00 | 1.40 |

A souvenir sheet containing No. 6390 sold for €4.50.

Art Issue

The Hand of Laetitia Casta, Photograph by Dominique Issermann A3448

2023, Feb. 24   Photo.   Perf. 13x13¼

| 6391 | A3448 | €2.32 multi | 5.00 | 2.50 |

Engraver at Work — A3449   Stonecutter at Work — A3450

Foundry Worker Pouring Molten Metal — A3451   Tailor at Work — A3452

Wood Inlayer at Work — A3453   Chef at Work — A3454

Violin Maker at Work — A3455   Roofer at Work — A3456

Jeweler at Work — A3457   Stained-Glass Craftsman at Work — A3458

Farrier at Work — A3459   Watchmaker at Work — A3460

Serpentine Die Cut 11
2023, Mar. 3   Photo.
Booklet Stamps
Self-Adhesive

6392	A3449	(€1.16)	multi	2.60	.85
6393	A3450	(€1.16)	multi	2.60	.85
6394	A3451	(€1.16)	multi	2.60	.85
6395	A3452	(€1.16)	multi	2.60	.85
6396	A3453	(€1.16)	multi	2.60	.85
6397	A3454	(€1.16)	multi	2.60	.85
6398	A3455	(€1.16)	multi	2.60	.85
6399	A3456	(€1.16)	multi	2.60	.85
6400	A3457	(€1.16)	multi	2.60	.85
6401	A3458	(€1.16)	multi	2.60	.85
6402	A3459	(€1.16)	multi	2.60	.85
6403	A3460	(€1.16)	multi	2.60	.85
a.	Booklet pane of 12, #6392-6403			31.50	
Nos. 6392-6403 (12)				31.20	10.20

Electric Bicycle — A3461

Tourists on Bicycles A3462

2023, Mar. 11   Engr.   Perf. 13¼

| 6404 | A3461 | €1.16 multi | 2.60 | .85 |

Souvenir Sheet
Photo.
Perf.

| 6405 | A3462 | €2.32 multi | 5.00 | 5.00 |

Stamp Day.

Marcel Marceau (1923-2007), Mime — A3463

2023, Mar. 17   Engr.   Perf. 13x13¼

| 6406 | A3463 | €1.80 black | 4.00 | 1.40 |

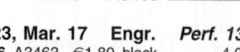

Pif the Dog, Comic Strip Character by José Cabrero Arnal (1909-82), 75th Anniv. — A3464

2023, Mar. 23   Photo.   Perf. 13x12¾

| 6407 | A3464 | €1.16 multi | 2.60 | .85 |

Arnaud Beltrame (1973-2018), Gendarmerie Lieutenant Colonel Killed by Terrorists — A3465

2023, Mar. 23   Engr.   Perf. 13¼

| 6408 | A3465 | €1.16 multi | 2.60 | .85 |

Paris Catacombs A3466

2023, Mar. 23   Engr.   Perf. 13x13¼

| 6409 | A3466 | €1.16 multi | 2.60 | .85 |

Spring Stamp Show, Paris.

Eiffel Tower Type of Semi-postals of 1939 and Gustave Eiffel Type of Semi-postals of 1982 With Euro Denominations

2023, Mar. 23   Engr.   Perf. 13x12¾

6410	Sheet of 6		52.50	52.50
a.	SP44 €4 lilac		8.75	8.75
b.	SP44 €4 olive brown		8.75	8.75
c.	SP44 €4 cerise		8.75	8.75
d.	SP291 €4 lilac		8.75	8.75
e.	SP291 €4 olive brown		8.75	8.75
f.	SP291 €4 cerise		8.75	8.75

FRANCE

Gustave Eiffel (1832-1923), Civil Engineer, and Eiffel Tower Ironwork — A3467

2023, Mar. 23   Engr.   Perf. 13x13¼
6411   A3467 €1.16 multi   4.00   4.00

A souvenir sheet with a different sheet margin than that shown sold for €4.50.

Notre Dame de l'Assomption Church, Fontenay-le-Comte — A3468

2023, Apr. 7   Photo.   Perf. 13¼x13
6412   A3468 €1.16 multi   2.00   .05

Souvenir Sheet

Jacques (1769-1823) and Jeanne Labrosse Garnerin (1775-1847), Parachute Inventors — A3469

2023, Apr. 7   Engr.   Perf. 12¾x13¼
6413   A3469 €2.32 multi   5.25   5.25

Souvenir Sheet

Bell, Notre Dame Cathedral, Paris — A3470

2023, Apr. 17   Engr.   Perf. 13
6414   A3470 €1.80 multi   4.00   4.00

Art Issue

The Sparrow, Painting by Eva Gonzalès (1849-83) — A3471

2023, Apr. 21   Photo.   Perf. 13¼x13
6415   A3471 €2.32 multi   5.25   2.60

Europa — A3472

2023, May 5   Litho.   Perf. 13¼
6416   A3472 €1.80 multi   4.00   1.40

Miniature Sheet

European Capitals — A3473

No. 6417 — Attractions in Bratislava, Slovakia: a, Bratislava Castle. b, Old Town Hall, vert. c, St. Elizabeth's Church, vert. d, St. Michael's Gate, vert.

2023, May 5   Photo.   Perf. 13¼
6417   A3473 Sheet of 4   16.00 16.00
a.-d. €1.80 Any single   4.00   1.40

A3474   A3475

A3476   A3477

A3478   A3479

A3480   A3481

A3482   A3483

A3484

Flower and Butterfly Stencil Designs by Emile-Allain Séguy (1877-1951) — A3485

Serpentine Die Cut 11

2023, May 12   Photo.
Booklet Stamps
Self-Adhesive
6418   A3474   (€1.16) multi   2.50   .85
6419   A3475   (€1.16) multi   2.50   .85
6420   A3476   (€1.16) multi   2.50   .85
6421   A3477   (€1.16) multi   2.50   .85
6422   A3478   (€1.16) multi   2.50   .85
6423   A3479   (€1.16) multi   2.50   .85
6424   A3480   (€1.16) multi   2.50   .85
6425   A3481   (€1.16) multi   2.50   .85
6426   A3482   (€1.16) multi   2.50   .85
6427   A3483   (€1.16) multi   2.50   .85
6428   A3484   (€1.16) multi   2.50   .85
6429   A3485   (€1.16) multi   2.50   .85
  a.   Booklet pane of 12, #6418-
       6429   30.00
       Nos. 6418-6429 (12)   30.00 10.20

Art Issue

Young Girl in Green, Painting by Tamara de Lempicka (1898-1980) — A3486

2023, May 12   Photo.   Perf. 13¼x13
6430   A3486 €2.32 multi   5.00   2.50

Marie-Madeleine Pioche de La Vergne, Comtesse de La Fayette (Madame de La Fayette), (1634-93), Writer — A3487

2023, May 19   Photo.   Perf. 13¼
6431   A3487 €1.16 multi   2.50   .85

Song of the Partisans, 80th Anniv. — A3488

2023, May 26   Engr.   Perf. 13¼
6432   A3488 €1.16 multi   2.50   .85

Nicéphore Niépce Monument, Chalon-sur-Saône — A3489

2023, May 26   Engr.   Perf. 13x13¼
6433   A3489 €1.16 multi + label   2.50   .85

French Federation of Philatelic Associations 96th Congress, Chalon-sur-Saône.

Miniature Sheet

24 Hours of Le Mans Automobile Race, Cent. — A3490

No. 6434: a, Airplanes over race course, cars at start line, starter holding French flag (52x41mm). b, Centenary emblem (42mm diameter). c, Car racing at twilight, starter waving racing flag (52x41mm). d, Starter waving checkered flag at end of race (52x41mm).

Perf. 13x13¼ (rectangular stamps), Perf. (#A3490)
Photo., Sheet Margin Photo. & Embossed

2023, May 26
6434   A3490   Sheet of 4   16.00 16.00
a.-d. €1.80 Any single   4.00   1.40

Fruits — A3491

Designs: No. 6435, Lemons (citrons). No. 6436, Bananas (bananes). No. 6437, Passion fruits (fruits de la passion). No. 6438, Cherries (cerises). No. 6439, Figs (figues). No. 6440, Grapes (raisin). No. 6441, Kiwis. No. 6442, Strawberries (fraises). No. 6443, Apricots (abricots). No. 6444, Blueberries (myrtilles). No. 6445, Apples (pommes). No. 6446, Tangerines (mandarines).

Serpentine Die Cut 11

2023, June 2   Photo.
Booklet Stamps
Self-Adhesive
6435   A3491   (€1.16) multi   2.60   .85
6436   A3491   (€1.16) multi   2.60   .85
6437   A3491   (€1.16) multi   2.60   .85
6438   A3491   (€1.16) multi   2.60   .85
6439   A3491   (€1.16) multi   2.60   .85
6440   A3491   (€1.16) multi   2.60   .85
6441   A3491   (€1.16) multi   2.60   .85
6442   A3491   (€1.16) multi   2.60   .85
6443   A3491   (€1.16) multi   2.60   .85
6444   A3491   (€1.16) multi   2.60   .85
6445   A3491   (€1.16) multi   2.60   .85
6446   A3491   (€1.16) multi   2.60   .85
  a.   Booklet pane of 12, #6435-
       6446   31.50
       Nos. 6435-6446 (12)   31.20 10.20

Pen Tips and Box Picturing Eiffel Tower — A3492

Eiffel Tower Pin — A3493

Eiffel Tower Plate — A3494

Eiffel Tower Pencil Sharpener — A3495

Eiffel Tower on Camembert Cheese Label — A3496

Eiffel Tower on Magic Lantern Slides — A3497

Eiffel Tower Bottle Openers — A3498

Eiffel Tower on Medal — A3499

Serpentine Die Cut 11

2023, June 2   Photo.
Booklet Stamps
Self-Adhesive
6447   A3492   (€1.80) multi   4.00   1.40
6448   A3493   (€1.80) multi   4.00   1.40
6449   A3494   (€1.80) multi   4.00   1.40
6450   A3495   (€1.80) multi   4.00   1.40
6451   A3496   (€1.80) multi   4.00   1.40
6452   A3497   (€1.80) multi   4.00   1.40
6453   A3498   (€1.80) multi   4.00   1.40
6454   A3499   (€1.80) multi   4.00   1.40
  a.   Booklet pane of 8, #6447-
       6454   32.00
       Nos. 6447-6454 (8)   32.00 11.20

FRANCE

Miniature Sheet

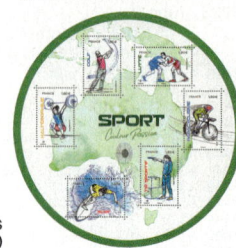

Sports A3500

No. 6455: a, Golf. b, Wrestling, horiz. c, Weight lifting. d, Paracycling. e, Surfing, horiz. f, Shooting.

2023, June 2 Photo. Perf. 13
6455 A3500 Sheet of 6 24.00 24.00
a.-f. €1.80 Any single 4.00 1.40

Pierre Loti (1850-1923), Naval Officer and Writer — A3501

2023, June 9 Photo. Perf. 13¼
6456 A3501 €1.16 multi 2.60 .85

Blaise Pascal (1623-62), Mathematician A3502

Litho. & Engr.
2023, June 16 Perf. 13¼
6457 A3502 €1.16 multi 2.60 .85

Notre Dame Abbey, Sénanque A3503

2023, June 23 Photo. Perf. 13¼
6458 A3503 €1.16 multi 2.60 .85

No. 6458 is impregnated with a lavender scent.

House of Gustave Caillebotte, Yerres — A3504

2023, June 23 Engr. Perf. 13¼
6459 A3504 €1.16 multi 2.60 .85

A souvenir sheet containing No. 6459 sold for €4.50.

Tourism Issue

Bergheim A3505

2023, June 30 Engr. Perf. 13¼
6460 A3505 €1.16 multi 2.60 .85

Alice Guy (1873-1968), Filmmaker A3506

2023, June 30 Photo. Perf. 13¼
6461 A3506 €1.80 multi 4.00 1.40

Arles Photography Festival — A3507

2023, July 7 Litho. Perf. 13¼
6462 A3507 €1.80 multi 4.00 1.40

Paths — A3508

Path in: No. 6463, Aveyron Department. No. 6464, Jura Department. No. 6465, Bas-Rhin Department. No. 6466, Guadeloupe Overseas Department. No. 6467, Alpes-de-Haute-Provence Department. No. 6468, Loire-Atlantique Department. No. 6469, Finistère Department. No. 6470, Corse-du-Sud Department. No. 6471, Guyane Overseas Department. No. 6472, Gironde Department. No. 6473, Calvados Department. No. 6474, Somme Department.

Serpentine Die Cut 11
2023, July 7 Photo.
Booklet Stamps
Self-Adhesive

6463 A3508 (€1.16) multi 2.60 .85
6464 A3508 (€1.16) multi 2.60 .85
6465 A3508 (€1.16) multi 2.60 .85
6466 A3508 (€1.16) multi 2.60 .85
6467 A3508 (€1.16) multi 2.60 .85
6468 A3508 (€1.16) multi 2.60 .85
6469 A3508 (€1.16) multi 2.60 .85
6470 A3508 (€1.16) multi 2.60 .85
6471 A3508 (€1.16) multi 2.60 .85
6472 A3508 (€1.16) multi 2.60 .85
6473 A3508 (€1.16) multi 2.60 .85
6474 A3508 (€1.16) multi 2.60 .85
a. Booklet pane of 12, #6463-6474 31.50
Nos. 6463-6474 (12) 31.20 10.20

Souvenir Sheet

Route Napoléon (Route N85) — A3509

No. 6475: a, Ibexes and Great yellow gentians (41x30mm). b, European bee-eater, lavender and Sisteron (41x41mm). c, Egyptian vulture, sailboat, olives (41x30mm).

2023, July 13 Photo. Perf. 13¼
6475 A3509 Sheet of 3 8.00 8.00
a.-c. €1.16 Any single 2.60 .85
d. Souvenir sheet of 1 #6475a 4.75 4.75
e. Souvenir sheet of 1 #6475b 4.75 4.75
f. Souvenir sheet of 1 #6475c 4.75 4.75

Nos. 6475d-6475f sold together as a set for €6.50.

French Cyclotourism Federation, Cent. — A3510

2023, July 21 Photo. Perf. 13¼
6476 A3510 €1.16 multi 2.60 .85

Immigration of Poles to France, Cent. — A3511

2023, Sept. 1 Photo. Perf. 13¼
6477 A3511 €1.80 multi 4.00 1.40

Jules Isaac (1877-1963), Jewish Historian — A3512

2023, Sept. 1 Engr. Perf. 13¼
6478 A3512 €1.16 multi 2.50 .85

Disney Cartoon Characters A3513

Characters From Disney Animated Films — A3514

Characters: No. 6480, Pocahontas. No. 6481, Lady and the Tramp (La Belle et le Clochard). No. 6482, Cinderella (Cendrillon). No. 6483, Peter Pan. No. 6484, Snow White, from Snow White and the Seven Dwarfs, (Blanche-Neige et les Sept Nains). No. 6485, Belle and the Beast, from Beauty and the Beast (La Belle et la Bête). No. 6486, Simba, from the Lion King (Le Roi Lion). No. 6487, Ariel, from The Little Mermaid (La Petite Sirène). No. 6488, Remy, from Ratatouille. No. 6489, Thomas O'Malley and Duchess, from The Aristocats (Les Aristochats). Nos. 6490, Elsa and Anna, from Frozen (La Reine des Neiges). No. 6491, Mowgli and Baloo, from The Jungle Book (La Livre de la Jungle).

2023 Litho. Perf. 13x12¾
6479 A3513 €1.16 multi 2.50 .85

Booklet Stamps
Self-Adhesive
Serpentine Die Cut 11

6480 A3514 (€1.16) multi 2.50 .85
6481 A3514 (€1.16) multi 2.50 .85
6482 A3514 (€1.16) multi 2.50 .85
6483 A3514 (€1.16) multi 2.50 .85
6484 A3514 (€1.16) multi 2.50 .85
6485 A3514 (€1.16) multi 2.50 .85
6486 A3514 (€1.16) multi 2.50 .85
6487 A3514 (€1.16) multi 2.50 .85
6488 A3514 (€1.16) multi 2.50 .85
6489 A3514 (€1.16) multi 2.50 .85
6490 A3514 (€1.16) multi 2.50 .85
6491 A3514 (€1.16) multi 2.50 .85
a. Booklet pane of 12, #6480-6491 30.00
Nos. 6480-6491 (12) 30.00 10.20

Walt Disney Company, cent. Issued: No. 6479, 10/6; Nos. 6480-6491, 9/1.

Rugby, 200th Anniv. — A3515

2023, Sept. 8 Photo. Perf. 13¼
6492 A3515 €1.80 multi 4.00 1.40

Art Issue

Rêverie, Poster by Alphonse Mucha (1860-1939) A3516

2023, Sept. 15 Photo. Perf. 13¼x13
6493 A3516 €2.32 multi 5.00 2.50

Maison Berger Paris Fragrances, 125th Anniv. — A3517

2023, Sept. 15 Litho. Perf. 13
6494 A3517 €2.32 multi 5.00 1.75

A souvenir sheet containing No. 6494 sold for €6.50.

Souvenir Sheet

Mailbox, Letters, Pencil, Flowers and QR Code A3518

Serpentine Die Cut 11 Syncopated
2023, Sept. 18 Litho.
Self-Adhesive
6495 A3518 €8 multi 17.00 17.00

The lower right corner of the stamp on No. 6495 has microperforations of "NFT" in a hexagon.

Community Garden — A3519

2023, Sept. 22 Photo. Perf. 13¼
6496 A3519 €1.16 multi 2.50 .85

Illuminated Letter — A3520

2023, Sept. 29 Engr. Perf. 13
6497 A3520 €1.80 multi 4.00 1.40

A souvenir sheet containing No. 6497 sold for €4.50.

Souvenir Sheet

Orient Express Train, 140th Anniv. A3521

2023, Sept. 29 Litho. Perf. 13
6498 A3521 €1.80 multi 4.00 4.00

A souvenir sheet containing No. 6497, having a 201x100mm margin lacking any text, sold for €4.50.

FRANCE

Still Life Paintings — A3522

Designs: No. 6499, Basket of Apricots, by Louise Moillon (1610-96). No. 6500, Flower Study, by Eugène Cauchois (1850-1911). No. 6501, Still Life with Basket of Apples, by Vincent van Gogh (1853-90). No. 6502, A Bouquet of Flowers, by Jacqueline Marval (1866-1932). No. 6503, Apples and Oranges, by Paul Cézanne (1839-1906). No. 6504, Chrysanthemums, or The Overturned Basket, by Berthe Morisot (1841-95). No. 6505, Pimientos, by Pierre-Auguste Renoir (1841-1919). No. 6506, Still Life on a Table, by Georges Valmier (1885-1937). No. 6507, A Bunch of Asparagus, by Edouard Manet (1832-83). No. 6508, Dame-Jeanne and Caisse, by Félix Vallotton. No. 6509, Still Life with Artichoke, by Hippolyte Chaignet (1820-65). No. 6510, Still Life with Pot, Skillet and Eggs, by Jean Siméon Chardin (1699-1779).

Serpentine Die Cut 11
2023, Oct. 6   Photo.
Booklet Stamps
Self-Adhesive

6499	A3522	(€1.16)	multi	2.50	.85
6500	A3522	(€1.16)	multi	2.50	.85
6501	A3522	(€1.16)	multi	2.50	.85
6502	A3522	(€1.16)	multi	2.50	.85
6503	A3522	(€1.16)	multi	2.50	.85
6504	A3522	(€1.16)	multi	2.50	.85
6505	A3522	(€1.16)	multi	2.50	.85
6506	A3522	(€1.16)	multi	2.50	.85
6507	A3522	(€1.16)	multi	2.50	.85
6508	A3522	(€1.16)	multi	2.50	.85
6509	A3522	(€1.16)	multi	2.50	.85
6510	A3522	(€1.16)	multi	2.50	.85
a.	Booklet pane of 12, #6499-6510			30.00	
Nos. 6499-6510 (12)				30.00	10.20

Art Issue

Project Phenix, Sculpture by Prune Nourry — A3523

2023, Oct. 12   Photo & Embossed   Perf. 13
| 6511 | A3523 | €2.32 | gray | 5.00 | 2.50 |

Miniature Sheet

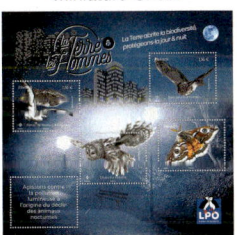

Nocturnal Animals — A3524

No. 6512: a, Pétrel de Barau (Barau's petrel). b, Barbastelle d'Europe (Western barbastelle). c, Chouette hulotte (Tawny owl). d, Petit paon de nuit (Small emperor moth).

2023, Oct. 14   Photo.   Perf. 13x13¼
| 6512 | A3524 | Sheet of 5 + label | | 10.00 | 10.00 |
| a.-d. | €1.16 Any single | | | 2.50 | .85 |

Jules Rimet (1873-1956), Soccer Executive A3525

2023, Oct. 20   Photo.   Perf. 13¼
| 6513 | A3525 | €1.80 | multi | 3.75 | 1.25 |

 A3526   A3527

 A3528   A3529

 A3530   A3531

 A3532   A3533

 A3534   A3535

 A3536

 A3537

Christmas A3537

Serpentine Die Cut 11
2023, Nov. 3   Photo.
Booklet Stamps
Self-Adhesive

6514	A3526	(€1.16)	multi	2.50	.85
6515	A3527	(€1.16)	multi	2.50	.85
6516	A3528	(€1.16)	multi	2.50	.85
6517	A3529	(€1.16)	multi	2.50	.85
6518	A3530	(€1.16)	multi	2.50	.85
6519	A3531	(€1.16)	multi	2.50	.85
6520	A3532	(€1.16)	multi	2.50	.85
6521	A3533	(€1.16)	multi	2.50	.85
6522	A3534	(€1.16)	multi	2.50	.85
6523	A3535	(€1.16)	multi	2.50	.85
6524	A3536	(€1.16)	multi	2.50	.85
6525	A3537	(€1.16)	multi	2.50	.85
a.	Booklet pane of 12, #6514-6525			30.00	
Nos. 6514-6525 (12)				30.00	10.20

SCOTT
France
Album Set 1848-2020

Save when you purchase the complete France Album Set covering 1848-2020 in 682 Scott Specialty Series album pages. Also includes 4 Large Scott 3-Ring, metal hinged Binders with matching slipcases and binder labels.

Item #: 310SET
Retail: $1049.99

$853.49
AA PRICE

Package Components:
- Scott France 1849-1958,
- Scott France 1959-1976,
- Scott France 1977-1987,
- Scott France 1988-1994,
- Scott France 1995-2000,
- Scott France 2001-2015,
- Scott France 2016-2020
- 4 of the Scott Specialty Green 3-Ring Binders - Large,
- 4 of the Scott Specialty Green 3-Ring Binder Slipcases - Large,
- and 4 France labels

FREE SHIPPING on orders $75 or more

Order them individually at
AmosAdvantage.com

Item		Retail	AA
310S021	2021 France Supplement	$39.21	$33.33
310S022	2022 France Supplement	$39.21	$33.33
310S023	2023 France Supplement	$41.99	$35.69
310BLANK	Blank Pages for France (20 pgs)	$24.25	$20.61

AmosAdvantage.com
1-800-572-6885

ORDERING INFORMATION: *AA prices apply to paid subscribers of Amos Media titles, or for orders placed online. Prices, terms and product availability subject to change.
SHIPPING & HANDLING: U.S.: Orders total $0-$10.00 charged $4.99 shipping. U.S. Order total $10.01-$74.99 charged $9.99 shipping. Orders totaling $75+ will ship FREE! Taxes will apply in CA, OH, & IL. Canada: 20% of order total. Minimum charge $19.99 Maximum charge $200.00. Foreign orders are shipped via FedEx Intl. or USPS and billed actual freight.

Subject index of French commemorative Issues

A-1 Satellite 1137-1138
Abbaye-aux-Dames 4407
Abbé Pierre 3756-3757
Abdelkader, Emir of Algeria 3414
Abeland, Peter B516
Abolition of Slavery................. 2643
Abolition of Slavery, Reunion.. 4038
Abricots rouge au miel 3849
Academy of Philately 1617
Academy of Sciences ... 1159, 5051
Accountancy Congress 1193
Aconit 1873
Actors' Federation 997-1001
Ader, Clement 348, CB3
Administration, National
  School of 2496
Administrative Changes 1596
Advanced Institute of
  Electricity 2469
Advertisements.................... 2804c
Aerial Views 5956-5967
Aero Club of France 2667
Aerospace and space
  show C51, C53
Aerotrain 1267
Affre, Dennis A. B231
African Fabric Patterns ...5573-5584
Agam, Yaacov 1713
Agen, arms 1093
Agnes B. (hearts) 6372-6375
Agriculture Department 1387
Agricultural Order of Merit 5994
Ahe Atoll, French Polynesia... 6163
Aid to the Handicapped 2114
AIDS Virus Discovery 2419
Aigle, Caroline C77
Aiguesmortes 422
Air Academy 1136
Air France 1898
Airbus A300, 30th Anniv.
  of first flight........................... C64
Airbus A300-B 1363
Airbus A300-B4 .... C62
Airbus A380 .... C68
Airmail, first route C50
Airmail, night service 1089, B329
Airmen's Fund B130
Aix-en Provence 1810, 3107
Aix-les-Bains 1127
Ajaccio, 500th Anniv. 2286
Ajaccio Gulf 724
Ajaccio-Vizzavona Train 2539
Aladdin 6087
Alain (Emile Chartier) B650
Alain-Fournier, Henry 2022
Albatrosses, Short-tailed 6383
Albert the Workingman B227
Albertville Winter Olympics ... 2206, 2269, 2295, B611, B621-B627, B636-B637
Albi Cathedral B189
Albrecht, Berthie 1904
Alechinsky, Pierre 1970
Alfort Veterinary School 1183
Algeria 255
Algiers, arms 903, 940
Alliance Francaise 1860
Along Bay, Viet Nam 3519
Alpacas 6386
Alpes-Cote d'Azur 1853
Alpes-de-Haute Provence 5411
Alpine Renault A110 5401
Alpine Troops 2127
Alsace 563, 1514
Alsace, liberation 559, 4907
Alsace timber-framed houses... 3673
Amazon Forest 3502
Amboise Chateau 682, 1068
Amboise, Clos-Luce 1374
American Legionnaires ... 243-244
Amethyst 4949
Amiens Cathedral................ 4402
Amiens, arms 1040
Amiens Cathedral 1236, 5871, B187, B530-B531
Amnesty International 2268

Ampere, Andre M. 306, 626
Amsterdam 5114
Amundsen, Roald................ 6201
Amusement Park
  Attractions.................5241-5252
Amyot, Jacques B367
Andelot, Treaty of 2058
Andre, Adeline 4140-4142
Angers 421, 3987
Angers, arms B140
Angers, David d' B333, B374
Angouleme Cathedral ... B185, 3863
Angouleme, Marguerite d' 2285
Angoumois, arms 737
Animal Eyes............... 4841-4852
Animal Proverbs and
  Idioms.......4338-4349, 4853-4864, 5079-5090
Animal Tracks 5979-5990
Anjou, arms 620
Annapurna, First ascent of 2775
Anne, Duchess of Brittany..... 4553
Anne, Duchess of Beaujeu ... 5261a
Annecy Castle 1541
Announcements 2709-2712, 2721-2723, 2805-2808, 2928-2929, 2993-2996
Anthonioz, Genevieve
  de Gaulle 2932
Anthurium 1356
Antibes Juan-les-Pins 3195
Antiquities 3297-3288
Antoinette, Cape Horner 1301
Apocalypse tapestry 1116
Apollinaire, Guillaume B355
Appert, Nicolas 759
Apples 4196, 6445
Apricots 6443
Apricots in honey................. 3849
Aquitaine 1441
Arab World Institute 2220
Arago, Etienne B223
Arago, Francois J. 626, B575
Aragon, Louis B630
Arawak Civilization 2506
Arbois Chateau 658
Arc de Triomphe 263, 3300
Arc de Triomphe, Orange 342
Arcachon 3291
Arcachon beach 1008
Archaeology, Underwater...... 6282
Arche de la Defense 2147
Archery 6265f
"Archimede" bathyscaph 1052
Architectural Details 5592-5603
Arcimboldo, Giuseppe ... 3400, 6303
Arctic exploration 611
Arcueil-Cachan Aqueduct
  Bridge 3799
Ardeche Gorge, Pont d'Arc 1314
Ardennes Forestry 2475
Argenson, Count Marc d' B275
Argentat 2404
Ariane Rocket 2483
Aristocats, The 6489
Arles Photography Festival..... 6462
Armadillos......................... 5809
Arman 2535
Armand, Louis B533
Ar-Men Lighthouse 5698
Armillary sphere 5810
Armistice, World War I 895, 1221, 1226, 1621, 2129, 2679, 3550, 5567, B77
Armstrong, Louis 2905
Army Engineering Corps B82
Army Medical Corps B73
Arnac-Pompadour 2719
Aron, Raymond 3152
Arp, Jean 2006
ARPHILA '75 ..... 1390, 1394-1397, 1425-1429
Arras 2965
Arras, belfry 459
Art and Industry Museum 951
Arthurs-Bertrand, Yann (heart) 2867

Arthus, J. 915
Artichoke 4267
Artois, arms 659
Asian Development Bank 2425
Aspects of French Life.......... 5912
Aspects of Life in the French
  Regions ... 2946, 2978, 3007, 3047, 3106, 3139, 3192, 3234, 3299-3301, 3357, 3427, 3505
Asse, Genevieve................. 5346
Assembly of Expatriate
  Algerians 2048
Assembly of the Three
  Estates 2121
Association of French Mayors 3341
Aster 1872
Asterix Satellite.................... 4920
Asterix the Gaul 2706-2707, 3748-3749, 5661-5672, 5708
Astrolabe (ship)................... 3501d
Atget, Eugene B695
Athens, Greece 3052
Athens, French School 2549
Atlantic mail flights C16-C17
Atlantic Museum 1506
Atlantic Ocean 6160
Atomic Energy Commission . 1135
Aubazine Abbey 1603
Auber, Daniel-Francois 4298a, B445
Aubrac, Lucie and Raymond ... 5432
Aubuisson Tapestries 4912-4913
Auch, arms 1142
Auch Cathedral................... 2702
Audit Office................3307 -3307A
Audubon, J. J., birds ... 2462-2465
Aunis, arms 738
Auray 1640
Auric, Georges B646
Auriol, Jacqueline C65
Auriol, Vincent 1944
Aurochs 3688
Austerlitz, Battle of 3115
Auteuil Apprentices 5002
Automobile, Cent. 1943
Automobile Club of France ... 2499
Automobiles 2770
Auto race, 24-hour 1376
Autumn B246
Autumn Stamp Show ... 2546, 6146
Autun 3989
Auvergne 1446, 2482
Auvergne, arms 619
Auvergne, costume B171
Avanti B529
Avery, Tex (cartoon
  characters)...................3415-3421
Avesnes-sur-Helpe 935
Aviation 1034-1035
Aviation Pioneers.........3900-3902
Aviation Without Borders....... 3256
Avicenna 3156
Avignon, Palace of Popes 344
Azay-le-Rideau Chateau 2031, 3674, 4242

Baccarat (hearts)4549-4552, 4651
Bachelard, Gaston B562
Bacon, Francis 2317
Badger 2126
Baeckaoffe 3831
Bagnoles-de-l'Orne 994
Baillon B557
Baker, Josephine B658
Balata Garden 2905
Balavoine, Daniel................B721e
Bale-Gulhouse Airport 1824
Ballet Preljocaj..................... 4890
Ballons Montes.....................C63
Balmain (hearts) 5163-5166
Baltard, Victor 3140
Balthus 1833
Balzac, Honore de B88, B88A
Bananas 4194, 6436
Bank of France 2754
Bar (Barrois) 1157

Barau's Petrel 3315
Barbara 2824
Barbes, Armand B230
Barbey d'Aurevilly B475
Barbizon 2461
Bardey, Jeanne 5254
Barley 5270
Barnave, A.P.J.M. B606
Barrault, Jean-Louis 5759c
Barrel making 4739
Barres, Maurice B307
Barret, Jeanne 6196
Bart, Jean B322
Barthes, Roland 4915
Bartholdi, Frederic A. B335
Basch, Victor 2008
Baselitz, Georg 2382
Basketball........................... 801
Basque Corsairs................. 2607
Basquiat, Jean-Michel......... 5977
Bastia 2403
Bastie, Maryse C33
Bastille Monument 2151
Bastille, Storming of 1307
Bats 4383-4384
Battle of Austerlitz 3115
Battle of Chemin des Dames,
  2nd 5217
Battle of Denain 4221
Battle of Solferino................B717b
Battle of the Somme 5052
Battle of Verdun.... 392, 789, 1481, 5041
Battle of Vimy Ridge............. 5216
Battle of Vouille 4301b
Baudelaire, Charles P. ... 666, 6010
Baudot, Emile 627
Baudry, J. 915
Baumel, Jacques 4408
Baux-de-Provence 2034
Bayard, Chevalier
  Pierre de 1260, B164
Bayeux Cathedral 1546
Bayeux tapestry 888
Bayle, Pierre 3207
Bazaine, Jean 3948, 3952
Bazille, Frederic 5181
Bazoches-du-Morvand
  Chateau 1336
Beans, Green.................... 4261
Beans, Snap 4264
Bears 2261, 4585-4586
Bearn, Annexation of............. 5918
Bearn, arms 661
Beaumarchais B405
Beaune Hospital 420, 466
Beautification campaign 1606
Beauty and the Beast............ 6485
Beauvais Cathedral B188
Beauvoir, Simone de 5993
Beaver 2263
Becaud, Gilbert B721f
Bec d'Allier B727
Bec-Hellouin Abbey 1601
Bechet, Sidney 2910
Becker, Jacques 2021i
Beclere, Antoine 822
Becquerel, Henri B202
Bee eaters 981, 6380
Bees 5036-5037
Beethoven, Ludwig van 1059, 5929
Bel Air Lighthouse 5894
Bel Group (cheese
  manufacturer) 6011
Belfort 5006, 6192
Belfort, Siege of 1291
Belgian Government in
  Exile 4778-4779
Belin, Edouard B456
Belin, Valerie 5618
Bell, Gertrude 6197
Bell of Notre Dame Cathedral,
  Paris 6414
Bellay, Joachim du B321
Belle-Ile-en-Mer.................. 5412

Beltrame, Arnaud 6408	Borobudur Temple 1636	Brossolette, Pierre 829	Carcassonne Castle and
Ben, Words of............. 4099-4110, B809-B818	Bosch, Hieronymus 4281	Brou Church 1232	Ramparts........................... 4471
	Boscus, Leon 6266f	Brouage, ramparts 779	Carennac Castle 2251
Benediction de la Mer, Port-en-Bessin-Huppain.................. 4020	Bosques, Gilberto.......... 4839-4840	Broussais, Francois B462	Carline 1870
Benoist, Marie-Guillemine 5762	Bosquet, Alain 2873	Bruant, Aristide B615	Carnac monuments 1130
Benoit, P. 915	Bossuet, Jacques B. B286	Bruno, Maxime 4582	Carnot, Lazare N. B251
Bercheny, Marshal de B514	Botero, Fernando 2871	Brunschvicg, Cecile 5046	Carnot, Sadi B287
Beregovoy, Pierre 2941	Botticelli, Sandro 2756, 3396, 3775, 3776A, 3779	Brunstatt City Hall 4922	Carpeaux, Jean Baptiste 1274, B325
Berger, Michel....................... 2823		Brussels, Belgium 3340	
Berges, Aristide B454	Bouchard, L'île 3858, 3870B	Brussels City Hall 1366	Carrache, Annibale 4756
Bergheim 6460	Bouchardon, Edme B360	Brussels Exposition 878	Carriere, Eugene 4754, B291
Bergson, Henri 934	Boucher, Francois 1275	Bryen, Camille 2040	Cartier, Jacques ... 296-297, 1923, 6200
Berlin, Germany 3138	Boucher, Helene C46	Budapest, Hungary 3986	
Berlioz, Hector B50, B56, B552	Boucheron 5586-5589	Bude, Guillaume B303	Cartier-Bresson, Henri............ B694
Bernanos, Georges B506	Boudin, Eugene 2039, 4397	Buffet, Bernard ("Paris") 1584	Cartoon Journey of a Letter 2575-2580, 2580B-2580G, 2648-2659
Bernard, Claude B89, B89A, B510	Boudin, Nicolas 2883	Buffon, Georges de B241	
Bernhardt, Sarah 5520c, B191	Boudouse (ship) 3501c	Buffon martyrs 915	
Berri, arms 696	Bougainville, Louis-Antoine de B597	Buffon Museum 4467	Cartoons With Letters ...3888-3899
Berthelot, Gen. Henri M. ...5568-5569		Buffon's Natural History ... 2123-2126	Casals, Pablo 3233
Berthelot, Lucien 3817b	Bouillabaise ingredients 5867	Bugeaud, Thomas R. 497	Casanova, Danielle 1861
Berthelot, Marcelin 242	Bouin, Jean 969	Bugle 3765	Cascade des Tufs waterfall 6072
Berthollet, Claude L. 872	Boulanger, Daniel 6167	Burgundy 1444	Cassatt, Mary 3175i, 3178, 4172, 5011
Besancon 2814	Boulanger, Nadia 5305	Burgundy, arms 616, 1553	
Bes-Bedene 5869	Boule and Bill 2878-2879	Burgundy, costume B170	
Bettignies, Louise de 5523	Boule d'Amont 3857	Burma, Nestor B675	Cassel 5677
Beyle, Henri 453	Bouley, W. 655	Burri, Alberto 2315	Cassin, Rene 2688, B554
Beziers 1220	Boulogne-sur-Mer 1189, 4622	Burro 3021	Castelbajac, J.C. de (hearts)...................... 4744-4748
Bianca Castafiore 3333	Bourbonnais, arms 736	Butterflies 3885-3886, 5802	
Biarritz 1471	Bourdelle, Antoine ... 1206, 3951a, 3955, 5627, B288	Butterfly wings..........5764-5775	Casterel, Norbert................... D703
Biarritz Lighthouse.................. 5702		Buttes-Chaumont Park......... 2979a	Castres 3292
Bibliotheque Nationale 2551	Bourdet, Maurice 1021		Carnac, Aligned Stones of 4474
Bibracte Archaeological Site 6014	Bourgelat, Claude...........4012-4013	**Cabbage**........................... **4269**	Carzou, Jean 1499
Dichat, M. F. Xavier B334	Bourges Cathedral 1655	Cabinetmaking 5348	Cat Comic Strip 3142-3151
Bicycle Championships 1350	Bourgooic, Louise............ 3774, 3778	Cabinetwork 3570	Catacombs, Paris 6409
Bicycle Tour 693	Bourgoin, Pierre, WW II hero ... 1382	Cable Car Transport Congress 2045	Catholic Institutes 1539
Bicycles 4041, 6404-6405	Bourouissa, Mohamed 5917		Cats 2740-2741, 6387
Bievre River Restoration......... 5121	Boussole (ship) 3501e	Cacharel (hearts) 3089-3090, 3134, 3136	Cattle Breeds............... 4570-4581
Biology 1724	Boutin, Emile 4808		Cauchois, Eugene 6500
Bingen, Jacques 882	Bouvines, Battle of 4606b	Cadets 1740	Cauchy, Augustin-Louis 2176
Bird Eggs 5817-5828	Bouvril B659	Cadou, Rene Guy 5796	Caudebec-en-Caux City Hall 4927
Birds 978-981, 1938-1941, 2320-2323, 2790-2791, 2936-2939, 4222-4223, 5453-5454, 5968-5969	Boxing 6265a	Caen Abbey 674	Caudron, Gaston C78
	Boy Scouts 587	Caen church, ramparts 1066	Cavailles, Jean 879
	Boyan, Marc 1840	Caen ruins B199	Caviar................................... 3838
Bir Hacheim 680, 1194	Boyau, Maurice and Coiffard, Michel............................... C81	Caesar, Julius (bust) 4569	Cayeux Lighthouse 5884
Biron Castle 2293		Cahors bridge 777, 839	Celimene 689
Birr, Jacques ("Percheron") 1580	Bracquemond, Pierre 4807	Caillebotte, Gustave 3175a, 3176, 4813, 5014	Cendrars, Blaise 2057
Birth 2929	Braderie, Lille.............. 4014, 4018		Census 1823, 2704
Birthday Candles 4293	Braille, Louis 3570, B272	Caillebotte House 6459	Center for Modern Asia-Africa Studies 2002
Birthday Greetings................. 2888	Brancusi, Constantin 3245-3246	Caillie, Rene 2731	
Bissiere, Roger 2212	Branly, Edouard 471, B438	Caire, Marie 4173	Central France, Region of 1440
Bitche 2526	Brantome 1854	Calais 2815	Central School of Arts and Crafts 1258
Bizet, Georges B345	Braque, Georges 1014, 4216, 4482, B717c	Calais City Hall 1012	
Blacksmithing...................... 4733		Calcite 2019	Central Technical School 1680
Blake and Mortimer 3026-3027	Brassai (Gyula Halasz)............ B602	Calf 5187	Ceramics 5521
Blanc, Louis B226	Brassens, Georges 6116, B620	California Condor 3689	Cercy-la-Tour City Hall 4928
Blanc-manger 3837	Bratislava, Slovakia 6417	Calle, Sophie 5541	Cerdagne, Yellow Train of 2781
Blériot, Louis B457, C7, C71	Brayer, Yves 1585	Callot, Jacques ... 305, 2297, B48, B55, B318-B319	Cerdan, Marcel 2267, 2769b
Blier, Bernard....................... B688	Bread and Cereal Congress 2289		Ceres 2692-2693, 4643-4646, 5948-5951
Blind Aid B79	Break dancers 4697, 6061a	Calmette, A. Leon B232	
Blois B730	Breast Cancer Awareness 3141	Calvin, John 3681, B383	Cerizay Post Office 2219
Blois Chateau 965	Breguet, Bi-plane C54	Camargue 2481, 2720	Cervantes, Miguel de 859
Blondel, Andre E. 454	Brel, Jacques B619	Camargue Region House 5471	Césaire, Aimé 3033
Blood donation 2108	Drenne 2157	Cambray, Battle of 1538	César 1908, 2561
Blood donors 931, 1342	Bres, Madeleine 5970	Cameras 4700	Cevennes Natl. Park 2514
Bluebeard 6089	Brescia, Battle of 1260	Camp des Milles 4277	Cezanne, Paul 370, 1016, 3198, 4387, 4449, 4804, 5008, 5641a, 6296, 6503
Blueberries 6444	Brest 836	Campaign Against Violence Toward Women 3801-3812	
Blum, Leon 1047	Bretagne Parliament Bldg. restoration 2766		
Bly, Nellie 6202		Campin, Robert 4113	Chaban-Delmas, Jacques 2842
Boegner, Marc B535	Breton, Andre B629	Camus, Albert B407	Chabannes, Marshal Jacques II de 4017
Boethos of Calcedonia ("Child with Goose") B301	Breton River 299	Canal du Midi 5713	
	Bretonneau, Pierre F. 1022	Cancer control B76, B110, B202, B441	Chabrier, Alexis E. B131
Boileau, Nicolas B343	Droughel, Pieter, the Elder 2798		Chagall, Marc 1076, 5162
Bolaffi, Alberto 3817e	Breuguet XIV....................... C60		Chaignet, Hippolyte 6509
Bolland, Adrienne C67	Breuil, Abbe B500	Candes-Saint-Martin B731	Chaillot Palace 605-606, 671-672, 6245a
Bonaquil, Chateau Fort de 1469	Brialy, Jean-Claude 5322d	Candies and Flowers..... 6213-6224	
Bonaparte at Arcole Bridge ... 1352	Briand, Aristide 291, 1699	Candles 4290, 4293	Chaine des Puys 5406
Bonheur, Rosa 6191	Bridges 5290-5301	Cannes 573	Chaise-Dieu Abbey 2357
Bonnard, Pierre 1910	Britanny ... 461, 1510, 1535, 2480, B168	Cannes Film Festival 1834, 2550	Chaissac, Gaston 2758
Bonnevay, Laurent 4300		Canoe-Kayak Meet 1254	Chalon-sur-Saône 4800, 6433
Bonpain, Abbe Rene 963	Brive-la-Gaillarde.................. 5119	Cap Bear Lighthouse 5703	Chalons-sur-Marne 1249
Bookbinding 1739, 5722	Brocciu cheese 3848	Cap Ferret Lighthouse........... 5891	Chambers of Commerce Presidents' Assembly 633
Book manufacturing 712	Broccoli 4262	Cap Canaille, Cassis 2217	
Bordeaux ... 774, 838, 1180, 1933, 3015, 3593, 3594A, C24	Brochet au beurre blanc......... 3851	Cap Camarat Lighthouse 2831	Chambery, arms B135
	Broglie, Louis de 2420	Capet, Hugh 1200, 2046	Chambery Cathedral 2529
Bordeaux, arms 899, B120	Broglie, Maurice de B439	Capon 3839	Chambord Chateau 678
Bordeaux, Great Bridge 1180	Brongniart, Alexandre B255	Captain Fracasse B681	Chambourcy City Hall 4923
Bordeaux Issue 1290	Bronze Horse, Neuvy-en-Sullas 2534	Captain Haddock 3331	Chamonix Guides Company ... 6028
Bordeaux Philatelic Congress ... 197		Caquot, Albert 2831	Chamonix Ski Championships ... 322, 1019-1020
Bordeaux vineyard.................. 3676	Brooklyn Bridge, New York 5299	Caravelle Lighthouse 5895	
	Brosset, Gen. C. D. B446	Carcassonne 345, 2760	Champagne, arms 698
			Champagne process 350

SUBJECT INDEX OF FRENCH COMMEMORATIVE ISSUES

Champagne-Ardennes 1513
Champaign, Philippe de 1394
Champlain, Samuel de B305
Champleve enamel 1106
Champmesle, La 997
Champollion, Jean-Francois 1354
Champollion's Birthplace 2718
Champs Elysees 2449, 5762d
Champs-Elysees Theater 4381
Champtoceaux B733
Chamson, Andre B653
Chancelade Abbey,
  Dordogne 1279
Chanel (hearts) ...2997-2998, 3133, 3135, 5971-5974
Channel Tunnel ... 2421-2424, 4621
Chantarelle Violette 2051
Chantemesse, Andre B543
Chantilly Chateau 1234
Chants Corses, Corsica 4039
Chaource cheese 3852
Chapelle Sainte-Marie,
  Nevers 5592
Chaplin, Charlie 5992
Chapon 3839
Chappe, Claude ... 474, 625, 2366
Char, Rene B633
Charcoal fire 4289
Charcot, Jean-Baptiste 3368, 5218, B68-B69
Charcot, Jean-Martin B344
Chardin, Jean Baptiste 2562
Chardin, Jean Siméon 6510, B205, B306
Chardin, Pierre Teilhard de ... B537
Chardonnet, Bernigaud de 762
Charite-sur-Loire 2884
Charlemagne 1167, 4797
Charles VII B212
"Charles de Gaulle" Aircraft
  Carrier 2945
Charles d'Orleans B389
Charles the Bold, Duke of
  Burgundy 1262
Charleston Dancers 5107
Charleville-Gezieres 1858
Charlieu Abbey 1335
Charpak, Georges 4986
Charpentier, Gustave B362
Charter of Fundamental Rights
  of the European Union 2944
Chartres Cathedral 1077, B186
Chartreuse, La Grande 1916
Chassiron Lighthouse 5700
Chateau d'Amboise 4782
Chateau d'Ancy-le-Franc 4786
Chateau d'Anet 4792
Chateau d'Anjony 4233
Chateau d'Azay-le-Rideau 2031, 3674, 4242, 4790, 5234
Chateau de Blois 4793
Chateau de Bon Repos 5711
Chateau de Boulogne sur
  Mer 4231
Chateau de Bouteville 5719
Chateau de Bremontier-
  Merval 4247
Chateau de Carneville 5712
Chateau de Carrouges 4472
Chateau de Chambord 4788, 5234, 5595, 5660
Chateau de Champs-sur-
  Marne 4473
Chateau de Chenonceau 4791, 5234
Chateau de Commequiers 6283
Chateau de Crazannes 4244
Chateau d'Ecouen 4789
Chateau de Grignan 2816
Chateau de la Batie d'Urfé ... 3592
Chateau de La Motte-Tilly 4470
Chateau de Lassay 5720
Chateau de Lesdiguieres 4248
Chateau de Maintenon 1704
Chateau de Pailly 5167
Chateau de Pierrefonds 4249
Chateau de Plessis-Bourré 2583
Chateau de Pompadour 4234
Chateau de Puyguilhem 4243
Chateau des Comtes de Foix .. 4230

Chateau de Saumur 4232
Chateau de Sedieres 2118
Chateau de Suscinio 4226
Chateau de Valençay 4783
Chateau des Vaux 4382
Chateau de Vaux-le-Vicomte .. 4246
Chateau de Villandry 4785
Chateau de Villers-Cotterets .. 6207
Chateau de Vitre 5593
Chateau d'If 4237, 4294
Chateau du Taureau 4240
Chateau Guillaume-le-
  Conquerant 4229
Chateaubriand, Francois R. de .. 603
Chateaubriant Martyrs 1782
Chateaudun 640
Chateaugiron City Hall 4924
Chateau of the Dukes of
  Bourbon 5810
Chatelet, Emilie du 5585
Chatrian, Alexandre, and
  Erckmann, Emile 6228
Chaumont 3591
Chaumont viaduct 948
Chauveau, J. B. A. 655
Chavannes, Puvis de B86
Chedid, Andree 5812
Chef 6397
Chenier, Andre de B249
Chenonceaux 473, 496
Cherbourg-en-Cotentin 5274
Cherries 6438
Chess 6049-6060
Chess Festival 1154
Chess Olympiad, Nice 1413
Chevalier, Maurice B617
Cheverny Chateau 723
Chevire Bridge 2250
Chicken 3020
Child Welfare B194
Child, Intl. Year of 1624
Children, Protection of
  Abused 2618
Children's Art 4958-4960
Children's Games 2152-2153
Children's Stories 6081-6092
Chinese Zodiac Animal
  Sculptures 4316-4327
Chinon 2355
Chip Cards 2837c
Chirac, Jacques 5913
Chocolate 3682
Cholet 5232
Chomedey, Paul de B455
Choiseul, Etienne F. de B237
Chopin, Frederic 815, 2744
Choreography 2912
Christmas 2681-2685, 4113-4124, 5934-5945, 6117-6128, 6318-6329, 6514-6525, B690
Christmas and
  New Year's 5546-5557
Christmas tree 6152
Christo and Jeanne-Claude 3599, 3603
Cilaos Church 949
Cinderella 6092, 6482
Circus Arts, Natl. Center 2377
Circus Performers 3489-3494, 5308-5319
Cirque de Gavarnie 2119
Citadelle de Corte 4235
Cite (Paris) 583
Cite Internationale Universitaire
  de Paris 6246
Citeaux Abbey 2635, 3859
Citroen Automobile 2881e, 5619-5620, 6096-6097
City Halls 4921-4932
Civil Code 3005
Civil Defense 1082
Civilian war victims B80, B103
Clafoutis 3845
Clair, Rene 2021g
Clamart City Hall 4929
Claudel, Camille 2757
Claudel, Paul B420
Claudine 2973
Clavecin 3766
Clemenceau, Georges 371, 669

Clemenceau, Georges,
  House of 4469
Clermont-Ferrand 2525, 3008
Clermont-Ferrand, Arms B122
Clermont-Ferrand, Bas-relief ... 3861
Clermont-Ferrand Church B214
Clermont-Ferrand Opera
  theater 4602
Clermont-Ferrand Short
  Film Festival 5374
Clermont-Ferrand Tramway 2174
Clipperton Island Discovery ... 4097
Clock, Decorated 3573
Clos Chateau 670
Clostermann, Pierre & Roman,
  Claire C64
Clouet, Francois B162
Clouet, Jean 1173, 6301
Clovis 1166, 2541
Cluny 2215, 3864
CNES 6100
C.N.I.T. Building 923
Coareze 4647, 4673
Cocteau, Jean 1821, B651
Codos, Paul C47
Coeur, Jacques 772
Cognac 1010
Coiffard, Michel and Boyau,
  Maurice C81
Col du Tournalet 6281
Colas, Alain 2447
Colbert, Jean Baptiste B183
Colette, Gabrielle-Sidonie B466
Coligny, Gaspard de B463
College of France 2614
Collegiate Church of Mantes .. 2647
Collet, Henri 2661
Colline Notre Dame de Lorette
  War Memorial 1608
Collioure 2885
Collonges-la-Rouge 1811
Colman, Stephane 2385
Colmar 3813-3814
Colonial Exposition 258-262
Colonial Troops 647
Colorado Provencal quarry 6077
Coluche B661
Columbus, Christopher 6199
Comedie Francaise 1715
Commercial Studies College ... 1745
Communication ... 1482, 2088-2099
Community Garden 6496
Commynes, Philippe de B209
Compact disc 2804b
Comtat Venaissin 785
Comte, Auguste M. 848
Comte de Monte-Cristo 2975
Concarneau 1855
Concentration camps ... 767, 786, 1282, 1453, 3114, 4801
Conciergerie 582, 3869
Concorde ... 2881a, C42, C48, C82
Concours Lepine 2256, 5219
Condorcet, Marquis de 2162c
Confiance (ship) 3501a
Conques 590, 593, 3865
Conservation of Nature 1269
Conservatory of Arts & Crafts .. 2436
Constitutional Council ... 3617-3617A
Contest Stamps 5125-5136, 5324-5335
Cook, James 6195
COP21 Climate Conference ... 4919
Copenhagen, Denmark 4183
Copernicus, Nicolaus ... 857, 1416
Copper 4957
Coppersmithing 6311
Coquelin, Benoit-Constant 5520d
Corbiere, Tristan 3973
Cordes 1703
Cordouan Lighthouse 1915, 5701
Corn 5264
Corneille, Pierre 323, B561
Coronelli globes 3410
Corot, J. B. C. ... 1517, 2507, 5805
Correze 2118, 2485
Corsica 1809
Corsica, arms 562
Corsica, Return of 1222
Cosmos Flowers 5830-5841

Costes, Dieudonne C54
Cote d'Azur 1069
Coty, Rene B382
Coubertin, Pierre de 817
Coulomb, Charles B352
Council of Europe 679, 2708
Council of the European
  Union, 6165
Council of State 2748
Coupe de France Soccer
  Tournament 5235
Couperin, Francois B417
Cour des Comptes 832
Courbet, Gustave 1049, 5673, B324
Courreges (hearts) 4961-4966
Courrieres Coal Mine
  Disaster 3190
Court House, Lyon 4295
Court of Cassation 2427
Court of Saint-Emilion 2727
Courteline, Georges B517
Cousteau, Jacques-Yves B702
Couzinet 70 .... C63
COVID-19 Pandemic,
  Workers in 5898-5909
COVID-19 Report 6317
Cow 3019, 5192
Cows (cartoon) 3352-3356
Craftsmen of France 1556
Cratere de Vix 1149
Creac'h Lighthouse 5886
Cremer, Bruno 5322b
Crest 1776
Crest Wooden Bridge 3988
Creteil City Hall 4930
Croix de Guerre ... 1123, 4796, 5691
Croizat, Ambroise and
  Laroque, Pierre 4888
Cros, Charles B502
Cross, Henri-Edmond ...3175g, 3182
Crozet & Kerguelen Isls. 1331
Crustaceans and Shells .. 6188-6189
Crystal 3583, 5624
Cubitus 3235-3244
Cugnot, Fardier de 5919
Curie, Frederic and Irene 1838
Curie, Marie 1195, 3946-3947
Curie, Pierre and Marie B76
Customs Cooperation 1901
Customs Service 1505
Cutlery Industry 2029
Cuvier, Georges B430
Cyrano de Bergerac B680

D-1 Satellite 1148
D-Day 2428, 3030, 4623
D'Artagnan B679
Dagnaux, Col. Jean CB2
Daguerre, Louis J. 374
Dali, Salvador 3014
Dalida 2822
"Dans le Circle"
  (painting) 5996-6006
Danton, Georges J. B252
Dard, Frederic 5844
Dassault, Marcel 2087
Dates 4193
Daudet, Alphonse 307
Daumesnil, Gen. Pierre B493
Daumier, Honore 1153, 3413, 3413C, B354
Dauphine 621
Dauphine, arms 699
Daurat, Didier C45
David, Jacques L. 390, 2160, 3397, 6299, B250
David-Neel, Alexandra 6203, B699
Davis, Miles 4256
Davodeau, Etienne 2388
Day of the Tiles 2122
Daviel, Jacques B369
Deauville 996, 3818, 5405
Debeaumarche, Edmond 959
Debré, Michel 2622
Debre, Olivier 2329
Debre, Robert B545
Debussy, Claude B87, B87A
Decaris, Albert 2841
Deck, Theodore 4479

SUBJECT INDEX OF French COMMEMORATIVE ISSUES

Declaration of the Rights of Man
 and the Citizen 2143-2145,
 2164-2168
Decorative Arts 2398-2401,
 3572-3583
Decorative Modern Arts
 Exhibition 220-225
De Crecy, Nicolas 2391
Deep-sea explorations 1052
Degas, Edgar 1276, 3175b,
 3183, 4176, 4203, 4205, 5013,
 5199, 5630, B346
De Funés, Louis B687
De Gaulle, Gen.
 Charles 1322-1325,
 1716, 2207, 5638a, 5946-5947,
 5947B
De Gaulle Memorial, Colombey-
 les-Deux Eglises 1550
De Gaulle Memorial, Paris 3499
De Gaulle Appeal of June 18
 Speech 3868
Delacroix, Eugene 1054, 2639,
 4178, 6294, B259
Delagrange, Léon 3901e
Delaroche, Paul 4752
Delaunay, Robert 1466,
 B798-B807
Delegation for Land Use
 Planning 2931
Delessert, Benjamin 301
Delestraint, Gen. C. G. B449
Delgres, Louis 2899
Delorme, Philibert B434
Delvaux, Paul 2314
De Moor, Johan 2389
Denain, Battle of 4221
Denis, Maurice 2376
Departments, Creation of ... 2232d
Deportees 1118
Deposits and Consignments
 Fund 5022
Derain, Andre 1330
Deroche, Elise 3900, 3902
Desailly, Jean 5759a
Desaix de Veygoux,
 Gen. Louis B418
Desbordes-Valmore, Marceline ... 924
Descartes, Rene 330-331, 2512
Desert de Plate 6073
Desgenettes, Nicolas B461
Desgraupes, Pierre 4499f
Desmoulins, Camille 2162b
Despiau, Charles 5626
Despreaux B343
D'Esquelbecq Chateau 1602
Deux Rives Pedestrian Bridge ... 5419
Deville, E. H. St. Claire 760
Devos, Raymond 6330
Dewasne 1866
Dewoitine 338 Airplane C59
Dewoitine D1 Airplane C87
Diamant Rocket ... 1137, 1184, 1270
Diamond Rock, Martinique 1278
Dibbets, Jan 2505
Diderot, Denis B323
Diebold-Mutschler, Laura 4892
Dien Bien Phu, Battle of 3023
Dieppe 2716
Digoin Canal Bridge 5293
Dijon 3194
Dijon, arms D141
Dijon, Bourgogne Palace 1372
Dillard, Victor 5321
Dinan, France and Dinant,
 Belgium 5605
Diplomatic Relations Between
 France and People's Republic of
 China 4587-4588
Diplomatic Relations Between
 France and Philippines 5259-5260
Diplomatic Relations Between
 France and Poland 5638
Diplomatic Relations Between
 France and South
 Korea 5043-5044
Discovery of America,
 500th anniv. 2287-2288
Disney Cartoon
 Characters 6479-6491

Dissay Chapel
 frescoes B443-B444
Dives Abbey 1639
Diving 6265e
DNA 2837b
Doctors Without Borders 2686
Dodu, Juliette 3726-3727
Dogs ... 2742-2743, 4007-4008, 6388
Dogs, Sculptures of 5375-5386
Doisneau, Robert B691
Dole 1311, 3361, 5813
Dole, Ernest 6266a
Dolet, Etienne 3691
Dolls 3725
Dolphin 2894
Dolto, Francoise 5525
Donald Duck 3003
Donkey 5184, 5189
Donkeyskin 6088
Donzere-Mondragon Dam 807
Dorat, Collegiate Church 1544
Dordogne 852, 1999
Dore, Gustave 1867
Dorelac, Francoise B723a
Dorgeles, Roland B570
Dormoy, Marx 1942
Douai belfry 787
Douai Court House 4694
Douarnenez Ship Museum ... 2117
Douaument Ossuary 3191
Doubs waterfall 1371
Douglas Castle 4201
Doumer, Paul 292
Doumergue, Gaston 4447
Dove and olive branch 294
Dressmaking 687
Dreyfus, Capt. Alfred 3231
Driant, Col. Emil 788
Drouet, Jean Baptiste B607
Drouot, Antoine B353
Drug Addiction Prevention
 Day 2445
Drums 3769
Dublin, Ireland 5811
Dubray, Lionel 991
Dubuffet, Jean 1969
Duchamp, Marcel 2641
Duchamp-Villon, Raymond 4204
Ducks 980, 5190
Dufy, Jean 4650, 4681
Dufy, Raoul 1117
Dugua de Mons, Pierre 3032
Duguay-Trouin, Rene B467
Du Guesclin, Bertrand, death 1227
Duhamel du Monceau,
 Henry-Louis 2772
Duhem, Marie 4814
Dukas, Paul B389
Dullin, Charles 1989
Dumas, Alexandre 2924, B437
Dumont d'Urville, Jules B598
Dunant, Jean Henri B328,
 B717a, B808a
Dune of Pilat 5407, 6074
Dunkerque Lighthouse 5694
Dunkirk 1025-1027, 1516,
 B197, 1702
Dunkirk victims B158
Dupleix, Joseph F. B242
Dupondt 3332
Duquesne, Marquis Abraham B593
Duras, Marguerite 4603
Durazzo, Michelangelo 5203-5214
Durer, Albrecht 1688, 5808

Eagle Dam 5078
Earhart, Amelia 6204
Earth Sciences 1711
Eastern France TGV Train
 Service 3337
Eberhardt, Isabelle 6198
Eboue, Felix 3049
Eckmuhl Lighthouse 5889
Eclade 3830
Eclaire Airplane Propellers 5109
Eclosion 5643-5654
Ecole Normale Superieure 2442
Ecology 3479-3488, 3956,
 3958-3972, 4590-4601

Economic & Social Council 1557,
 2544
Edict of Nantes 2638
Effel, Jean 1868
Eggs, Bird 5817-5828
Egyptian expedition 1353
Egyptian sculpture, ancient 5628
Eiffel, Gustave 6410d, 6410e,
 6410f, 6411, B546
Eiffel Tower 2148, 3679, 5408,
 6410a, 6410b, 6410c, B85
Eiffel Tower Souvenirs ... 6447-6454
Einstein, Albert 3112
Eleanor of Aquitaine 3001
Electric Bicycle 6404
Electric Street Lighting 1839
Electricity, Advanced Institute
 of 2469
Electricity & Gas Industries 2513
Electronic Military
 Transmissions 5320
Elize, Raphael 4530
Ellington, Duke 2907
Eluard, Paul B628
Elysee Palace 851, 907, 5448,
 6245c
Elysee Treaty 4314
Embroidering 1697, 4734
Emmaus Movement 2739
Emojis 5420-5431
Enamelwork 3576
Endangered Animals 3312-3315,
 3686-3689, 6027
Endangered Flora 5657-5658
Energy 1725
Energy Conference, Cannes ... 2024
Energy, Renewable 6309
Engraving 1932, 5864, 6392
Entente Cordiale 3009-3010
Environmental Charter 3127
Environmental Protection 6094
Epee, Charles M. de l' B337
Epernay 4198
Ephebe of Agde 1830
Epstein, Jean 2021f
Equality 4959
Equestrian Jumping 6265d
Erckmann, Emile, and
 Chatrian, Alexandre 6228
Ermine 2812
Ernst, Max 2245
Escalope normande 3843
ESCP Europe Business
 School 5738
Esmeralda 2972
Esnault-Pelterie, Robert 1184
Esperey, Franchet d' 799
Espiguette Lighthouse 5892
Estates General 1305
Estaunie, Edouard B363
Esteve, Maurice ("Skibet") 2003
Estienne, Jean B. 975
Estienne School 2141
Eternal Flame 1386, 1988
Etretat 2033
Euro Coin 2830
Euromed Postal Conference 3731
Europa 805-806, 846-847,
 889-890, 929-930, 970-971,
 1005-1006, 1074-1075, 1109-1110,
 1131-1132, 1163-1164, 1178-1179,
 1209-1210, 1245-1246, 1271-1272,
 1303-1304, 1340-1341, 1366-1367,
 1399-1400, 1431-1432, 1478-1479,
 1522-1523, 1534-1535, 1609-1610,
 1646-1647, 1737-1738, 1827-1828,
 1874-1875, 1925-1926, 1974-1975,
 2009-2010, 2036-2037, 2109-2110,
 2152-2153, 2219-2220, 2254-2255,
 2287-2288, 2329-2330, 2419-2420,
 2473-2474, 2521, 2573, 2664, 2720,
 2771, 2817, 2877, 2943, 3024-3025,
 3117, 3206, 3327, 3436-3436A,
 3658, 3816, 4010-4011, 4224-4225,
 4403-4404, 4803, 5023, 5234, 5419,
 5656, 5842, 6027, 6212, 6416
European Bee-eaters 6380
European Broadcasting
 Union 1171
European Capital of Culture 4328

European Capitals 2917, 2985,
 3052, 3138, 3223, 3340, 3535,
 3728, 3908, 3986, 4183, 4365,
 4605, 4795, 5114, 5196, 5417,
 5625, 5811, 6007, 6211, 6417
European Construction
 Federation 1540
European Junior Games 1284
European Parliament
 Elections 1650, 1927, 2142,
 2405, 2714
European Parliament 1650,
 1927, 2687
European Projects 3500
European Soccer
 Championships 5003-5004
European Union Expansion 3022
European Water Charter 1256
Eurovision 1683
Evian-les-Bains 856, 908
Evreux Belfry 3451
Evry Cathedral 2502
Ewe 5191
Ewer 5807
Excoffon, Roger 1559
Expatriate Algerians,
 World Assembly of 2048
Explorers 6193-6204, B593-B598
EXPO '67, Montreal 1177
EXPO '92, Seville 2272
EXPO 2010, Shanghai 3870
EXPO 2020, Dubai 6033
Ex-Servicemen's Federation 995
Extreme Sports 3045
Eyes, Animal 4841-4852

Fabre, Henri B577, C72
Fabre, Jean H. 790, 4887
Fabric Designs 3932-3945,
 5573-5584, 6015-6026
Fair Attractions 3692
Fairs and Exhibitions 1504
Falconet, Etienne M. B256
Familistere de Guise Housing
 Complex 6308
Fan Making 6390
Fantin-Latour, Henri 4815
Fantomas B673
Farcigny, Jean, and North,
 Roger 6146
Farm animals 3018-3021,
 5182-5193
Farman F-60 Goliath C56
Farman, Henri 3901c, B448
Farmer B233
Farrier 6402
Fashion 4528-4531
Fauchard, Pierre 1003
Fautrier, Jean 4654
Faure, Gabriel B397
Faure, Maurice 5202
Featherwork 6095
Febus, Gaston 2260
Federation Internationale de
 Football Association 3028
Feininger, Lyonel 4217
Felicitations 2768
Felix, Rachel 5520b
Fencing Championship 1747,
 3903-3904
Fenelon, Francois 586
Fermat, Pierre de 2836
Fernandel B657
Ferre, Leo 2820, 5091
Ferrie, Gustave A. 628
Ferry, Jules F. 644, 1770
Fete, Paris 1491
Fete de la Transhumance,
 Midi-Pyrenees 4027
Fete de l'Estive, Allanche 4032
Fete des Brodeuses,
 Pont l'Abbe 4022
Fete des Chalands Fleuris,
 Saint-Andre-des-Eaux 4023
Fete des Lumieres, Lyon 4037
Fete du Citron, Menton 4036
Fete du Hareng, Haute-
 Normandie 4021
Fetes Johanniques, Reims 4030

Feu d'Artifices du 14 Juillet, Paris 4017	Fragonard, Jean H. 1327, B92, B365-B366	Gabin, Jean B686	Gogh, Vincent van 816, 3012, 3175c, 3181, 4396, 4452, 4809, 5016, 6298, 6501
Feuillade, Louis 2021a	Frairie des Petits Ventres, Limoges 4035	Gabriel, J.A. B551	
Field Ball Games 1265		Gainsbourg, Serge 2821	
Field Hockey 5659d	France, Anatole B49, B54	Galante, Maurizio (hearts) 3926-3929	Gold 4946
FIFA 3028	France Foundation 3596		Goldorak 6103
Fifth Republic 3518	"France" liner 1018, 2881c	Galerie des Glaces 3296, 3298A	Golf 6455a
Figaro 690	France, Pierre Mendes 1906	Gallic Boar Ensign 3298	Golf Federation 1714
Fight Against Racism 1825	France Stadium 3404	Gallieni, Joseph S. B99	Gonzaga, Charles 4399
Fight Against Smoking 1698	"France II," 5-master 1377	Galois, Evariste B564	Gonzales, Eva 6415
Figs 6439	Franche-Comte 663, 1509-1615	Gambetta, Leon 341	Goose 5186
Film Industry 2021	Franck, Cesar B642	Gandhi, Mohandas K. 5723	Gooseberries 4191
Fire Brigades 1082	Franco-African-Madagascar cooperation 1111	Garabit Viaduct 683, 5294	Gordon Bennett Aviation Cup ... 3690
Fire, Items on 4282-4293		Gardens and Parks 2979, 3029, 3118, 3201, 3327, 3429, 3709, 3829, 4073, 4227	Gordon Bennett Cup 3126
Firefighters 4288, 6264	Franco-American friendship ... 622		Gorges du Cheran 6161
Firefighters of Paris 4074-4076	Franco-Brazilian House 2226		Gosier Islet, Guadeloupe 1280
Firemen Federation 1841	Franco-German Cooperation Treaty 1357, 2086, 2930	Garfield (comic strip) 3507-3516	Gothic Art 4454-4465
Firminy 3293		Gargantua 688	Gothic Houses of Worship 3992-4006
First French Airmail Flight 2312, C74	Franco-Israeli Diplomatic Relations 2695	Garigliano Battle 1248	
		Garnerin, Jacques and Jeanne 6413	Gougères 3846
First French Revenue Stamp ... 3923	Franco-Italian friendship 892		Gouges, Olympe de 5862
First Man in Space 2837a	Franco-Latin American friendship 795	Garnier Opera House 3221, 5762b	Gourmet Cooking 1696
First Republic 2302, 2307-2310		Garnier, Tony B469	Gouin House, Tours 1182
First Women in French Government 5046	Franco-Soviet relations 1458	Garnier Palace 2671	Goujon, Charles 925
	Franco-Swedish relations 2415	Garouste, Gerard 3412, 3413B	Goujon, Jean 2700, B304
Fish ... 2227-2230, 5065, 5506-5617	Francois, Claude 2819	Garros, Roland ... 2128, 2258, C76	Gounod, Charles B174
Fisherman B234	Francois I 1173	Gas & Electricity Industries 2513	Goury Lighthouse 5695
Fish Merchants, Boulogne 2609	Francois of Taxis B302	Gascony, arms 695	Goya B538
Fitzgerald, Ella 2906	Franklin, Benjamin 814	Gaston Lagaffe 2802-2803	GR 20 Hiking Trail, Corsica 5863
Five Year Plan, 9th 1945	Fraternity 4960	Gateaud, Paul 992	Graellsia Isabellae 1708
Flag, Creation of 2232c	Free French Assn. 1484	Gauguin, Paul ... 1205, 2642, 3175j, 3185, 4180, 4392, 4805, 5007	Grains 5262-5273
Flame of the Unknown Solder 4285	Freedom of Association Law ... 2832		Grand Ballon Mountain 6071
Flamiche 3835	Freemasonry 2967	Gautier, Theophile B459	Grand Lejon Lighthouse 5885
Flamingos 6379	Freinet, Elise and Celestin ... 5538	Gavroche 2976	Grand Louvre 2149
Flammarion, Camille 792	Frejus flood victims B336	Gay-Lussac, Joseph L. B260	Grand Masonic Lodge 2446, 3267
Flanders, arms 467, 1216	French Academy 304	Gazelle helicopter 1437	Grand Mosque of Paris 4169
Flanders, reunion 1216	French Academy in Rome 5149	Gellee, Claude 1831	Grand Palais, Paris 3452, 5594, 5762a, 6245d
Flandrin, Hippolyte 4181	French-Algerian War Ceasefire 5201	Genainville B558	
Flaran Abbey, Gers 2214		Gendarmerie, National ... 1264, 2259c	Grande Forge de Buffon 5714
Flaubert, Gustave 6149, B267	French Alpine Club 1398	Geneva Convention on Refugees 2834	Grande Hermine (ship) 3501b
Flinders, Matthew 2882	French Cyclotourism Federation 6476		Grapes 4188, 6440
Flora of French Regions ... 3634-3657		Geneva Conventions B717d	Grappelli, Stephane 2908
Floral Fabric Patterns 6015-6026	French Guiana 4128	Genevoix, Maurice 2240	Grasse, Admiral de B458
Florian, Jean P. de 765	French History ... 4301, 4532, 4606, 4797, 5045, 5261, 5452, 5758, 5954, 6148, 6331	Genissiat Dam 607	Great Barrier Reef 6153
Flower arranging 4741		Geoffrey IV, Plantagenet 1106	Great Synagogue, Paris 2100
Flower Festival ... 904, 1053, 1244, 1537, 1635		Geography Congress, 125th ... 1935	Green Beans 4261
	French Hydrographic Service ... 5843	Geometric Drawing 1741-1742	Green Peppers 4266
Flowering Plants 1870-1873, 2298-2301	French industries, New 4713, 4714-4725	George VI visit 352	Greetings 2383-2394, 2696-2699, 2750-2753, 2768, 2774, 2981-2983, 2989-2992, 3053-3063, 3157-3166, 3261A-3266, 3377-3382, 3536-3549, 3569A-3569B, 4302-4313, 4329, 4701-4712
		Gerardmer 2762	
Flower Park Fountain, Paris ... 1610	French Institute 2498, 4649, 4672, 5762c	Gerbault, Alain 1263	
Flowers 4157-4168, 4804-4815, 5066-5077, 5220-5231, 5643-5654, 5846-5847, B735-B745, B776-B785		Gerbert B384	
	French Kickboxing World Championships 4534	Gericault, Jean 1051	
Fluorite 2020, 4953		Germain, Sophie 5000	Gregoire, Abbe 2232b
Flying Machines 3260	French Language 1946	Germigny-des-Pres mosaic ... 2759	Grelot, P. 915
Foal 3204	French Open Golf Championships 3227	Gerome, Jean-Leon 3013	Gremillon, Jean 2021h
Foch, Ferdinand B98		Gerson, Jean de B211	Grenoble 1308, B139
Foire aux Potirons, Tranzault 4034	French Open Tennis Championships 2258	Giacometti, Alberto 1971	Greuze, J. B. 3098, B292
Foix, arms 782		Giant Panda 3686	Grignard, Victor B447
Foix Chateau 891	French Philatelic Societies, Federation of 1476, 1541, 1611, 1648, 1702, 1744, 1877, 1933, 1978, 2012, 2043, 2112, 2222, 2257, 2294, 2362, 2426, 2484, 2525, 2662, 2773, 2826, 2896, 2960, 3039, 3116, 3338, 3452, 3683, 3869, 4040, 4272, 4402, 4649, 4672, 4818, 5038, 5232, 5446, 5674, 5953, 6099, 6246, 6433	Gid, Raymond ("La Marianne") 1994	Grignon de Montfort B473
Folklore 2782			Gris, Juan 4215
Follereau, Raoul 2028		Gide, Andre B431	Groot, Hugo de 1063
Fontainebleau Forest ... 2155, 6070		Gien Chateau 1373	Guadeloupe 850, 909, 1280, 1913, 4127
Fontainebleau Palace 643		Given Faience Factory 6065	
Fontenay Abbey 1545		Gift Boxes 3345-3350	Guadeloupe Park 2570
Fontennelle, Bernard de 1159		Giono, Jean 2471	Guardsman 1717
Fontenoy, Battle of 1287		Giotto di Bondone 3394	Guehenno, Jean 2213
Fontevraud Abbey 1604		Giraffes 6384	Gueret, arms 1092
Football 349, 3824		Girardin, Emile 1743	Guerlain (hearts) 5776-5779
Force Basque, Biarritz, Hendaye and Esplette 4024		Girardot, Annie B723f	Guesclin, Bertrand Du B350
	French Polynesia 4130	Giraudoux, Jean B476	Guesde, Jules B317
Foreign Legion 1928	French Postal Cards 6267	Giscard d'Estaing, Valery 6151	Guide Dog 6310
Forestry Congress, 10th World 2265	French Republic, First 2302, 2307-2310	Giroud, Francoise 5092	Guienne, arms 617
		Givenchy (hearts) 3273-3276	Guilds 1320
Fort Cicogne 5715	French Republic, Fifth 2677, 3518	Givors 1972	Guillaumet, Henri C47
Forteresse de Salses 4236	French Revolution 390	Glacier 3503	Guillaumin, Armand 5015
Foucauld, Charles de 906	French Revolution Bicentennial 2121-2122, 2139, 2143-2145, 2147-2151, 2162, 2164-2168, 2232, 2259	Glais-Bizoin, Alexandre 4584	Guimillau Church 2565
Foucault, Jean Baptiste 871		Glaser, Denise 4499d	Guitar 3761, 3882A
Fouchet, Max B553		Glassblowing 4284	Guitry, Sacha 2021c
Fougeres Chateau 944		Glassmaking 4732	Gulf of Morbihan 3108
Foujita, Leonard 5373	French Southern and Antarctic Territories 4138	Glasses, Decorated 3572	Gustavus III of Sweden at Trianon 2414
Foum el Gherza Dam 920		Gleizes, Albert 1728, 4214	
Foundry Worker 6394	French-Soviet Space Flight ... 2146	Glen B728	Guy, Alice 6461
Fountain of Innocents, Paris ... 1609	French-speaking Parliamentary Assn. 1554	Gleyre, Charles 5047	Guyana Space Center 1270
Fountains 2847-2848		Glieres memorial 1057	Guynemer, Georges M. ... 396, C80
Fouquet, Jean 4118, B208	French Tennis Federation 5931	Globe and microcircuits 2918	Guyon, Felix 1652
Four du Croisic Lighthouse 5890	Fresnel, Augustin 5655	Glove manufacturing 764	Gymnastics Championships ... 1618
Fourme d'Ambert cheese 3840	Frozen 6490	Goat Breeds 4763-4774	Gypsy Culture 2318
Fournier, Alfred B201, B221	Fruits 4186-4197, 6435-6446	Gobelin tapestry works ... 711, 1037	
Fox 2125	**G20 and G8 Summits ... 4067-4068**	Goethe, Johann W. von 863	**Hachette, Jeanne 6148a**
			Hafflinger Horses 6385

SUBJECT INDEX OF FRENCH COMMEMORATIVE ISSUES

Haguenau 4837
Haiti Earthquake Relief....B718-B719
Hall of Heavenly Peace 2669
Halle, Adam de la 1974
Halles Centrales 3140
Halloween 2839, 3048
Halpern, Bernard B586
Handball 4254, 6265b
Handball Championships 2796
Handball Championships,
  Women's 3372
Handicapped 1083, 1283, 1622
Handicapped Persons
  Rights Law 3128
Handicapped Olympics 2270
Handicrafts 1556, 1613,
  4730-4742
Hands, Drawings of........4750-4761
Hansen bacillus 1379
Hansi 3598, 3602
Happy Birthday 2556, 2633, 2951,
  3042, 3111, 3111C, 3222, 3222C,
  3344, 3438
Happy Holiday 2555
Happy New Year............ 4893-4904
Haras du Pin Stud Farm 3137
Haring, Keith 1671
Harki Soldiers 2178
Harp 3759, 4620
Hartmannswillerkopf National
  Monument 4823
Hartung, Hans 1694
Harry Potter Characters ...3303-3305
Hassi Messaoud oil fields 922
Hastings, Battle of 1160
Hats 5566
Haussmann, Georges E. B271
Haut-Koenigsbourg Castle 2717
Haute Provence Observatory ... 1281
Hautecloque, Philippe F. de ... 604,
  692, 692A
Hautefort Chateau 1243
Hauts-de-Seine 2612
Hauy, Valentin B338, 2140
Hazel nuts 44189
Hearing, Sense of 4972-4983
Heart.....................2797, 2926-2927,
  2997-2998, 3089-3090, 3133-3136,
  3170-3173, 3273-3276, 3390-
  3392A, 3585-3588, 3750-3754,
  3926-3929, 4140-4142, 4332-4336,
  4549-4552, 4651, 4744-4748,
  4961-4966, 5163-5166, 5369-5372,
  5586-5589, 5776-5779, 5971-5974,
  6170-6173, 6372-6375
Heart (Health), World Month ... 1333
Heart of Voh........................... 2867
Heart Transplant, First
  European 3434
Heart-Lung Transplant, First
  European 4270
Hodgehog 2811
Helicopters, Cent.................... C69
Helion 1912
Hello Maestro! 5307
Helsinki, Finland 5625
Hen 5193
Henner, Jean-Jacques....3411, 3413A
Henri IV ... 1261, 1812, 4297, B166
Henri IV School 2542
Henrot, Camille 6093
Herbin, Auguste..................... 4209
Hermes Dicephalus 2116
Hermes (hearts) 4332-4336
Hernani 691
Heroult, Paul B579
Herriot, Edouard B499
Higher Education 1844
Highway Safety 1768
Hikers 6206
Hilsz, Maryse C46
Hoche, Louis L. B254
Hokusai, Katsushika............. 4743
Homard breton 3850
Honegger, Arthur B645
Honey Bee 1644
Honnorat, Andre 982
Hopper, Edward 4155-4156
Horn.................................. 3762

Horses 2672-2675, 4369-4380, 6385
Horticulture Society, National 1536
Hospital of Paris 2694
Hospital Pharmacies 2495
Hospital Week 1033
Hotel de la Monnaie 2728
Hotel de Mauroy 4238
Hotel de Mora........................ 5930
Hotel des Chevaliers de
  Saint-Jean-de Jerusalem 2799
Hotel des Invalides 1414
Houdon, Jean A. B255
Houses 6269-6280
Hugo, Victor 293, 303, 691,
  B51, B57, B571
Huguenot Cross 1983
Human Rights, European
  Conference on 2359
Human Rights, Declaration
  of 1388, 1623
Hunger, Freedom from 1056
Huningue, Battle of.............. 4865
Hunspach 6063
Hymans, Max 2207

Ice Cliff, Norway 6156
Ideal Palace 1917
Iguana, Antillean 3312
Iguazu Falls 6158
Ile Bouchard 3858, 3870B
Ile de Bourbon 1134
Ile-de-France, arms 463, 1588
Ile-de-France, costume D160
Ile de la Cite 1058, C22
Ile de Sein monument 1031
Iles Sanguinaires 2527
Ile Vierge Lighthouse 5696
Illuminated Letter................. 6497
Immigration of Poles 6477
Impalas 6382
Incroyables and Merveilleuse ... 1351
Independence Movements
  of Latin America and the
  Caribbean 3925
Independence of French
  Colonies in Africa 3883-3884
Indian and French Artisan's
  Work 2986-2987
Indigotier 2050
Indochina War Memorial 2324
Indre Chateau 853
Industrial Protection 1876
Industrial Summit 1836
Indy, Vincent d' 648
Infantrymen's Monument B71-B72
Ingrandes-sur-Loire B732
Ingres, Jean-Dominique ... 1174, 6297
Innovation........................... 2553
Insects 5237-5238
Institute of Human
  Paleontology..................... 3821
Insulin, Discovery of 4125-4126
Intellectuals' Fund B42-B43,
  B48-B59, B86-B98A
Intl. Agricultural Show 4352
Intl. Humanitarian Law........... B831
Intl. Labor Organization 1247
Intl. Medical Assistance 2113
Intl. Olympic Committee 2431
Intl. Sailing Federation........... 3328
Intl. Space Station Photographs
  of Earth Features 5434-5445
Intl. Telecommunication
  Union 1122
Intl. Telecommunication Union
  Plenipotentiaries Conference ... 2154
Intl. Union for the Conservation of
  Nature & Natural Resources ... 2680
Intl. Year of the Disabled 1780
Intl. Women's Day ...4353-4364, 4406
Intl. Women's Year 1456
Interparliamentary Union 1319
Invalides Church B203
Invitation....2889, 2989, 2991, 3096,
  3097A, 3097C, 3693-3706
Irish Setters 6388
Ironwork........................... 5215
Isaac, Jules....................... 6478

Isard (Pyrenean chamois) 1302
Iseran mountain road 334
Israel, First Flight between
  France and 3533-3534
Issenheim Altarpiece 4271
Issermann, Dominique 6391
Italian School 4116, 4751, 4757, 4761
It's a boy 2710, 2806, 2875, 3129,
  3131, 3439
It's a girl ... 2711, 2805, 2874, 3130,
  3132, 3440
Ivory carvings B409-B410
Ivory Coast statue 5637
Izieu Orphanage Deportation
  of Jews 4604

Jack o'lantern ... 2839, 3048, 4286
Jacob, Max B491
Jacobsen, Robert 2130
Jacquard, Joseph M. 295
Jacques Chaban-Delmas
  Vertical Lift Bridge 4366
Jaguar 3314
Jammes, Francis 2501
Jamot, Eugene B585
Japan Year........................... 2610
Jardin des Plantes................. 3709
Jardin du Luxembourg 2979b
Jardin du Tuileries 3029a
Jardins de Cheverny............. 4073a
Jardins de Giverny................ 3829
Jardins de Villandry 4073b
Jarnao 1857
Jaures, Jean L. 313-314, 928,
  1779, 4640-4641, 4675, 4679
Javouhey, Sister Anne Marie ... B532
"Jeanne d'Arc" Helicopter
  Carrier 3746
"Jeanne d'Arc" Sailors 3747
Jehan de Malestroit 2159
Jewelry 3582, 6067
Jewelry Industry 714, 1900
Jewelry making............. 4730, 4742,
  5124, 6400
Joan of Arc 245, 1229, 1651,
  4220, B210, B521-B522
Joan of Arc's House 2523
Joffre, Joseph C. B97
John the Good 1084
Joinville, Jean de B312
Joliot-Curie, Irene 5046
Jongkind, Johan Barthold 2810
Jonone 4073
Josselin 3506
Joubert, Jacqueline 4499e
Jouffroy d'Abbans, Marquis de....5021
Jouhaux, Leon B515
Jouvet, Louis B534
Joux Chateau 1112
Judas, Bishop 1151
Judicial Police of Paris 4478
Judo 6061e
Judo, World Championships 1681
Juin, Marshal A. P. 1266
Jumieges Abbey 725
Jungle Book, The 6491
Junior Chamber of
  Commerce 1551
Juvarouen 76 1477
Juvexniort 1597

Kandinsky, Vassily 2949, 5996-6006
Kaplan, Jacob 3167
Kastler, Henri 6266c
Kayaking 5659e
Kayserberg 5456
Keller, Robert 828
Kellermann, Francois 2162d
Kereon Lighthouse 5697
Kergomard, Pauline 1966
Kersalé, Yann 4780
"Kid. The" (movie) 5992
Kieffer, Philippe, WW II hero ... 1382
Killer Whale....................... 2893
Killy, Jean-Claude............... 2769d
Kingfisher 2264
Kirkeby, Per 2457
Kitten 3203

Kiwis 4190, 6441
Klein, Yves 2135
Klimt, Gustav 2870
Knights of Malta 797
Kupka, Frantisek 4212, 5403

La Baule, Beach 1188
Labe, Louise 5040
Labor Day, Cent. 2221
La Bourboule 966
La Bourdonnais, B.F. Mde B596
Labradorite 4947
Labruine, Gerard de 781
"La Capricieuse" corvette ... 773
Lac de Grangent................ B726
Lace 2205, 4092-4095
Lacordaire, J. B. H. 988
Lacore, Suzanne 5046
Lacroix, Christian (heart)........2797
Lady and the Tramp 6481
"Lady with the Unicorn" 1107
Laennec, Rene T. 685
La Fayette, Madame de 6431
Lafayette, Marquis de 243-244, B605
La Feronerie 1826
Laffitte 1638
La Fleche 2047
La Fontaine, Jean de 351, 2486-2491, 6066
La Fresnaye, Roger de ... 1017, 4206
La Gazette 1743
Lagrange, Joseph L. 869
Lagrange, Leo 845
Lakanal, Joseph B361
Lake Artouste, Train to 2367
Lake Geneva 1981
Lake Lerie 465
Lake Oum el Ma, Libya 6164
Lake Sassolo, Switzerland ... 6155
Lakes of the Orient Forest
  Natural Park 6315
Lamartine, Alphonse de B224
Lamazou, Titouan, Portraits
  of Women 3619-3630
Lamb 3205
Lambesc Clock Tower
  Statues 2378
Lamennais, Hugues R. de B315
Land Mine Demolition
  Service 1454, 4762
Landevennec Abbey 1973
Landscape Reflections 5150-5161
Langeais, Catherine 4499o
Langeais Chateau 1212
Langevin, Paul 608
Langlois, Maurice 6266b
Languedoc 394, 468
Languedoc-Roussillon 1511
Lannes, Marshal Jean D429
Lanvin (hearts) 3750-3754
Lanvin, Jeanne 5306
Laon Cathedral 643
La Pernelle City Hall 4921
La Perouse, Jean F. de B129, B595
Lapicque, Charles 2161
La Piscine 3772, 3776
La Place, Pierre S. de B298
Lapland Expedition,
  250th anniv. 2016
La Poste Business Foundation ...3226
Lapwings 978
La Roche-sur-Yon................ 5897
La Rochelle 251-252, 3406
La Rochelle, arms B136
La Rochelle Lighthouse 2749
Laroque, Pierre and Croizat,
  Ambroise 4888
La Roque-Gageac 3110
Larousse, Pierre 1213
Larrey, Dominique B386
Lartique, Jacques............... B693
La Salle, Cavelier de 1848
Lascaux paintings 1204, 5642
Laser 2837d
Latecoere, Pierre-Georges 4448
Latham, Hubert 3901a
La Tour d'Auvergne 2259a
La Tour, Georges de 1150, 2373, 4115

La Tour, Quentin de ... 6305, B265, B314
La Trinite-sur-Mer 1235
Lattre de Tassigny, Jean de ... 675, 717, B442, 2177
Laurencin, Marie........... 4174, 5122
Lava 4282
Laval bridge, chateau 1023
La Vallette, Antoine M. de B284
Lavezzi Lighthouse................ 5705
La Vieille Lighthouse.............. 5888
Lavoisier, Antoine L. 464
Law on Commercial and Industrial Credit 5200
League of Education 5049
League of Human Rights........ 2660
Leather work............... 4738, 5414
Lebanon 3569
Lebanon's Cultural Heritage... 2705
Lebas, Jean-Baptiste 830
Lebon, Philippe 757
Lebourg, Albert..................... 4395
Le Bossu B682
Le Brix, Joseph C54
Le Brun, Charles 1360
Leclerc, Jacques 604, 692, 692A, B432, 2059, 2619
Leconte de Lisle, Charles B508
Le Corbusier 2035
Le Creusot 5721
Ledru-Rollin, Alexandre A. B225
Leeks................................. 4265
Leger, Fernand 1992, 4211
Legion of Honor ... 730, 2897, 5691
Legros, Alphonse 4750
Legros, L. 915
Le Havre ... 874, 3409, 5289, B143
Le Havre Philatelic Exhibition ... 246
Le Mans cathedral B216, 2402
Le Mans, 24 Hours of............. 6434
Le Mennais, Jean-Marie de ... B525
Lemons............................... 6435
Lempicka, Tamara de 6430
Le Nain, Louis B283, B309
Le Notre, Andre ... 1692, 4405, B331
Lenglen, Suzanne.................. 5931
Lens 2043
Léoncel 3855, 3870A
Le Pechereau City Hall 4932
Le Petit Nicolas characters..................... 3710-3723
Le Puy-en-Velay 290
Le Quesnoy 831, 837
Leriche, Rene 868
Le Rond, Jean B332
Le Roux, Yvonne 916
Le Sage, Alain Rene 1211
Les Andelys 720
Les Legendaires Cartoon Characters 5093-5094
Les Sables d'Olonne 3589
"Les Tres Riches Heures" 1115
Leszczynska, Marie 6331a
Le Touquet 1027
Lettre en Ligne...................... 4279a
Le Vau, Louis B435
Leverrier, Jean J. 870
Le Vista, Claude 1107
Levy, Rene 1905
Lewis, Carl.......................... 2769e
L'Hospital, Michel de B341
Lhote, Andre 4213
Liancourt, Laroche Foucauld ... 1710
Liberation 503, 557-558, 559, 718, 1409-1411, 1420, 1929, 1930, 1975, 2429, 4907, B377-B381, B432, B478
Liberation of Corsica 2372
Liberation Order Badge 977
Liberty................................. 4958
Liberty, Equality and Fraternity 2143-2145
Liberty Highway B220
Liberty, Statue of 2014
Liberty Tree 2259b
Life Saving Society 1981
Light Show 4291
Lighthouses......... 3371, 5694-5705, 5884-5895
Lighthouse reconstructions.... 2749
Lille, arms 902, 938, B118

Lille 1813, 2362, 2999, 5763
Limbourg brothers 1115
Limoges............................... 3290
Limoges, arms B142
Limoges bridge 763
Limosin, Léonard 4775
Limousin 660, 1442
Linder, Max 2021b
Lindbergh transatlantic flight......................... 2769c, C49
Lintott, Edouard Banard 4177
Lion King, The 6486
Lion of Belfort Statue ... 4296, 6192
Lions................................... 6381
Lions Clubs International 1196, 5240
Lisbon, Portugal 3728
Lisieux Basilica 972
Little Pleasures 4500-4511
Little Mermaid, The................ 6487
Little Prince, The......... 2668, 6009, 6037-6048
Little Red Riding Hood 6061
Little White Beds 1225
Littre, Emile B559
Ljubljana, Slovenia................ 6210
Lobster 3850
Locard, Edmond................... 5020
Loches Chateau 1996
Locmariaquer 4648, 4674
Locronoan 2886
Lodeve Cathedral 1470
Loire 1445, 6078
Loire River B725-B734
Londres, Albert 3306
Long, Marguerite 4984
Longuay Abbey 5710
Lorient 2292
Lorrain, Claude 3395
Lorraine 1157, 1678
Lorraine, arms 564
Lorraine liberation 559, 4907
Lorraine Iron and Steel Industry 2472
Lot Valley 1404
Loti, Piere 6456, B63
Louis, Seraphine................... 6190
Louis-le-Grand School 1065
Louis II B182
Louis IX 1201, B285
Louis XI 1262, 6148b, B196
Louis XIV ... 1037, 1288, 1991, B184
Louis XV 6331b
Louise of Savoy 5758b
Lourdes 719, 873
Louviers, Notre Dame 1736
Louvois, Francois de B218
Louvre......... 581, 2149, 2396-2397, 2670, 5597, B66-B67
Louvre, Petit 6307
Lovelace, Ada 6314
Lozere Mountains 1128
Lucky Luke 2934-2935
Lully, Jean Baptiste 812
Lumiere, Auguste and Louis ... 771
Lumiere Brothers House......... 4466
Luneville Chateau 1157
Lupin, Arsene B671
Lurcat, Jean 1152
Luther, Martin 1859
Luxembourg Palace 569, 591-592, 4228, 4245, 6245b
Luxembourg, Luxembourg 2985
Lyautey, Hubert G. B281
Lyon................................... 3428
Lyon, aerial view C25
Lyon, arms 460, 897, B124
Lyon bridge 395
Lyon, founding 849
Lyon, Old 2825
Lyon, St. Jean Church 1733
Lyre 3758

Maar, Dora................ 6029, 6055
Machault, Guillaume de B501
Machine Tool Exhibition 1433
Macôn 3631, 4368, 4818
Macôn Post Office 2218
Madame de La Fayette 6431
Madrid, Spain 4365

Magellan, Ferdinand............... 6194
Maginot, Andre 2493
Magnelli, Alberto ("Virginia") ... 2004
Magnin, Florence 2392
Magnin, Jeanne 4806
Magritte, René 2637
Maigret, Commissioner B674
Mail Coach 4403
Mail flight, First 2312, C74
Mailbox of France 6102
Mailbox of Japan 6101
Maillan, Jacqueline............... B723c
Maillol, Aristide 984, 3951b, 3955A, 5633
Maine, arms 733
Maine-et-Loire 2583
Maintenon, Chateau de 1704
Maintenon, Marquise de 5690
Maison Berger Paris Fragrances 6494
Maison Carree, Nimes........... 5602
Maison Pfister 4239
Maison Souques-Pages 4251
Maitre de Moulins 1329, B264
Majorelle, Jacques 5641b
Malaria eradication 1032
Malherbe, Francois de B295
Mallarmé, Stéphane 2666
Mallet-Stevens, Robert 2037
Malmaison Chateau 1474
Malraux, Andre 2548, B519
Mammoth 3433
Mandel, Georges 1104
Mandela, Nelson 6371
Manessier, Alfred 1774
Manet, Edouard 1050, 3175f, 3184, 4182, 4388, 4812, 5012, 6507, B268, B375
Mangin, Nicole 4781
Mangos 4195
Manhattan Bridge, New York... 5299
Manned flight 1863-1864
Mansart, Francois B394
Maquis 2417
Marais de Briere B734
Marais, Jean B723b
Marcassite 2017
Marceau, Gen. Francois B426
Marceau, Marcel 6406
Marche 783
Marcoule atomic center 921
Marcoussis, Louis 4208
Marengo, death of General Desaix B418
Marette, Jacques 2538
Margaret of Austria, Archduchess..................... 5758a
Maria Theresa, Queen 5452b
Mariage de l'Ami Fritz, Marienheim...................... 4029
Marianne and Balloon 4485
Marianne and Environmental Protection 3956
Marianne and World Fund to Combat AIDS, Tuberculosis and Smoking 3044
Marianne, Architecture 1710
Marianne, Typography 1994
Mariano, Luis 5868
Marine Exploration 1726
Marine Life................... 2892-2895
Marionettes 1842
Maritime Postal Service B311
Marivaux, Pierre de B368
Marly Pumping Station 388
Marne, Battle of the ... 1108, 4670
Maroilles cheese................... 3844
Marquetry 3574
Marriage 2709
Marseillaise 309-310
Marseilles 775, 1877, 2896, 4328, C5-C6, C26
Marseilles, arms 896, B123
Martagon 1871
Martigues 2426
Martin, Alexandre B227
Martin, Pierre E. 761
Martin-Bret, Louis 918
Martinique 780, 1278, 1356, 1508, 4133

Marty, Augustin-Alphonse....... 5345
Marval, Jacqueline 6502
Marvingt, Marie C66
Masked Ball, The (opera)...... 4298b
Masks, Items Looking Like 5203-5214
Masks, Theatrical 4484
Masonic Lodge, Women's 2494
Masonic Order "Le Droit Humaine" 2328
Masons in France, Bicent. 1368
Masse, Pierre 960
Massenet, Jules E. 452
Masson, Andre 1911
Massoud, Ahmad Shah 2977
Massys, Quentin 3403
Master of 1518 4120
Master of Moulins................. 4122
Master of the Nativity in the Louvre......................... 4119
Master of the St. Bartholomew Altarpiece 4123
Mathieu, Georges 1397
Matilda of Flanders............... 5954a
Matisse, Henri ("Blue Nudes") 1015
Matta, Roberto 2247
Maubeuge 875, 1616
Maupassant, Guy de B649
Maupertuis, Pierre-Louis Moreau de 2016
Mauriac, Francois B572
Mauritius, Landing of French on 4874
Maurois Palace, Troyes 1611
Mauroy, Pierre 5050
Maury, Arthur 3817d
Mayotte 4135
Mayotte sesquicentennial 2271
Mayrisch, Emile 1062
Mazzini, Giuseppe 1061
Medea, ruins 1013
Mederic-Vedy 917
Mediator of the Republic 2627
Medical Research Foundation 3359
Medici, Catherine de 5045a
Medicine, National Academy 1326
Medievales, Provins 4019
Mediterranean Sea Fish 5065
Mediterranean Summit........... 3504
Mediterranean Women's Costumes 5692
Mediterranean Youth Games ... 2327
Meeting of King Henry VII and King Francois I............. 5045b
Megaloceros 3432
Megha-Tropiques Satellite 4799
Mehul, Etienne N. B371
Meije Dauphine Alps 465
Melies, George 987
Melon................................ 4187
Melpomene, frigate 1459
Melusine 6212
Mende 6316
Mendes France, Pierre 1906
Menton 3590
Mercantour Natl. Park 2516
Mere Elisabeth 993
Merimee, Prosper B436
Mermoz, Jean 325-326, C43
Messager, Andre B550
Messager, Annette................ 5387
Messagier, Jean 1909
Messmer, Pierre.................... 4999
Metal Engraving.................... 5952
Metalworker B236
Metchnikoff, Elie B398
Meteorology 1903
Meter Convention centenary 1435
Metric system 732
Metro, Paris, Centennial......... 2747
Metro Regional train system ... 1436
Metro station 2027
Metz 4040
Metz, arms 557
Metz Cathedral stained glass ... 2904
Metzinger, Jean 4210
Meuse District 2032
Meuse Valley 631

SUBJECT INDEX OF FRENCH COMMEMORATIVE ISSUES

"Mezzo" (Pascal de Mesenburg) 2390
Michaux's Bicycle 1902
Michel, Louise 2000
Michelangelo 858, 2947
Michelet, Edmond B484
Michelet, Jules B280
Michel-Levy, Simone 881
Mickey Mouse 3002, 5519
Mickey Mouse and Tourist Attractions 5458-5489
Microelectronics 1728
Midsummer's Eve Bonfire....... 4287
Mignard, Nico........... B421-B424
Mignard, Pierre 4759
Milhaud, Darius 1975
Military Medal 684
Military School, St. Cyr 731
Millau 2563
Millau Viaduct 3065
Millennium (Year 2000) 2733-2734, 2745-2746, 2788, 2792, B697
Millet (grain) 5265
Millet, Francois ("Winnower") 1296
Mills 3866
Minerals 2017-2020, 4946-4957
Miners 343, B235
Minerve 2356
Minnie Mouse 3004
Mirabeau, Comte de (H.G. Riqueti) B603
Miranda, Francisco de........... 3729
Miro, Joan 1395
Misanthrope 689
Miss.Tic 3974-3985
Mistral, Frederic 419, B526
Mitchell, Joan 4589
Mitterrand, Francois 2552, 5113
Mobilized Men's Fund B94-B95
Mobylette Motor Scooter 2881d
Modigliani 1693
Mogador Theater, Paris 5639
Moillon, Louise 6199
Moissac 1072
Moissan, Henri 3257, B576
Moliere 1381, 6166, 6350, B179
Moncey, Marshal A. J. de B490
Mondor, Henri B542
Monge, Gaspard 2232a, B279
Moninot, Bernard 2560
Monnerville, Gaston 4111
Monnet, Jean 2111, B524
Monod, Jacques B589
Montaigne, Michel de B161
Montand, Yves B660
Montbeliard 2358
Montbenoit Le Saugeais 2055
Montcaret Mosaics........... 4476
Montceau-les-Mines 800
Mont-de-Marsan 1144
Mont-Dore 1002
Monte Cinto 5707
Montesquieu, Charles de la ... B238
Mont Gerbier de Jonc B725
Montmartre............ 5195
Montmaurin Gallo-Roman Villa....4477
Montpellier............ 5674
Montpellier, arms B127
Montpellier Cathedral 1948
Montpellier, University of 5040
Mont-Saint-Michel 249-250, 1156, 2663, 3220, 3678
Montsegur Chateau 1917A
Moon landing............ 2787a, 5693
Moon, Sarah 6230
Moquet, Guy........... 3360
Moreau, Gustave 4753
Moreau, Jeanne 6227
Morgan, Anne 5194
Morillo Conique 2052
Morisot, Berthe 2497, 3175e, 3177, 4171, 5010, 6504
Morlaix 1191
Morlaix Viaduct 5292
Mortenol, Sosthene 5416
Mosaic............ 3581
Mother Teresa............ 3819-3820
Motion Pictures Centenary ... 2450

Motor Vehicles................ 2980
Motorcycles............ 2913
Mouhot, Henri 4112
Moulin, Jean 826, 1779
Moulin, Jean, Memorial....3684-3685
Moulins 4184, 5930
Moulins, Jacquemart 769
Mounet-Sully, Jean B492
Mt. Aiguille 2291
Mt. Blanc 1124, 2015
Mt. Blanc Massif............. 5410
Mt. Gerbier, Vivarais 632
Mt. Mouchet Memorial 1251
Mt. St. Victoire 2430
Mt. Valerien, memorial 1029
Mountain Climbing 804
Mountain Flora 6376-6377
Mourguet, Laurent 2406
Moustiers-Sainte-Marie 1126
Moutardier, Gaston 919
Moutier d'Ahun Abbey 2621
Moutier d'Ahun Angel............. 1361
Movie Industry 2021
Moynier, Gustave................ B808b
Mozart, Wolfgang A. 862, 2248
Mucha, Alphonse 6493
Municipal Administrators' Meeting 956
Mulhouse 2960
Mulhouse Technical Museum ... 2025
Mulhouse Tram-Train 3931
Mulhouse, Union with France ... 2634
Munster, Valley of 2253
Mural, Joachim 5257
Muret, Battle of 4532a
Musee d'Orsay 2026, 4272
Museum of Art and Industry........... 3772, 3776
Museum of Grenoble............ 5599
Mushrooms 2050-2053
Music boxes 4914
Music charities B131
"Music," Miniature 1625
Musical Instruments in Art........3758-3769, 3882A-3882B
Musicians of Bremen, The...... 6084
Musset, Alfred de B258
Mystere Falcon 900 1980

Nadar, Felix................5814, B696
Nadaud, Martin............ 4838
Naderman, Jean Henri........... 4620
Nana 2974
Nancay radio telescope 1067
Nancy 574-575, 2012, 3116, B117
Nancy, Battle of 1552
Nantes 1648, 2940
Nantes, arms 901, B144
Nantes, Edict of 1261
Nantes Flower Festival ... 1053, 1537
Napoleon I 1255, 1383-1385, 6012, B263
Napoleon I and Imperial Guard............ 3033-3038
Narbonne Cathedral 1337
Nardi, Francois B638
Nardo, Mariotto di 4124
Naruto 6312
Narvik, Battle of 677
National Assembly 2477, 2625
National Center for Space Studies............. 1006, 6100
National Center of Costume and Scenography 5019
National College of Arts 1710
National Forestry Office........... 4918
National Information System ... 1000
National Institute of Agronomy Research 2522
National Institute of Geography 2231
National Institute of Health and Medical Research........... 4652
National Library 2551
National Mining School 914
National Music Festival 2664
National Office of Veterans and War Victims 5123
National Order of Merit............. 4533
National Opera of Paris 5739

National Parks 2514-2516
National Police 1502
National Press Federation 2448
National Printing Office ... 1614, 2249
National Relief B104-B107, B112-B113, B129, B132, B134-B146, B149-B157, B161-B172
National Sea Rescue Society.... 5239
National School of Bridges & Highways............ 2557
National School of Charters ... 5991
National Sheepcote................ 3815
National Telecommunications College 1934
Natural History Museum........ 2363
Natural Phenomena........5357-5368
Nature................2776-2779
Nature Protection 1321, 1338-1339, 1369-1370, 1407-1408, 1420, 1555, 1572, 1580-1581
Natzwiller Struthof concentration camp 786
Nautilus shell 5801
Naval Academy 1777
Naval charities B204
Naval Reserve Officers Assn. 1475
Navarre, arms 734
Nejjarine Fountain, Fez, Morocco 2847
Nepalese sculpture............. 5634
Nerval, Gerard de 781
Neufchateau 2887
Neuwirth Law............. 5180
Nevers, arms 1042
Nevers, Ducal Palace of 4784
New Caledonia 4129
Newton, Issac 861
New towns, suburban 1455
New York World's Fair 372-373
New Zealand Stream and Waterfall................ 6159
NFT 6495
Niaux Cave 1642
Nice ... 776, 958, 3677, 3822-3823
Nice, arms 565, 900, B145
Nicolle, Charles J. 867
Nicosia, Cyprus 3223
Nicot, Jean 989
Niepce, Joseph N. 374
Niepce Monument 6433
Nieuport, Edouard C79
Nimes, Amphitheater............. 2880
Nimes, Roman Temple 1732
Nineteen-fifties 4042, 4677, 4678
Nineteen-sixties............ 4822
Nineteen-seventies................ 5039
Niort, arms 1091
Niort, National art festival 2294
Niort, scene 1158
Nivernais, arms 735
Noailles, Anna de B495
Noailles, Louis-Marie de B604
Nocard, Edmond I 655
Nocturnal Animals 6512
Noel, Magali 5322a
Noel, Marie B505
Noel, Suzanne 5388
Nogent-le-Retrou 2813
Nogues, Maurice 665
Nohant-Vic 3860
Noiret, Philippe................ B723e
Noirlac Abbey 1856
Noirmoutier, Isle de............. 2644
Nolhac, Pierre de 950
"Normandie" liner 300
Normandie-Niemen Air Regiment............. 5302
Normandy, arms 470
Normandy, Allied Invasion of 2428
Normandy Bridge 2451
Normandy, Lower 1590
Normandy-Neman Squadron ... 1253
Normandy, Upper 1589
North Atlantic Treaty Organization 937
North Africa (1952-62) 2581
North Festival Giants 1695
North, Roger, and Farcigny, Jean.............. 6146
Notaries Public 2452

Notre Dame Abbey, Senanque 6458
Notre Dame Cathedral, Amiens................ 3993, 4002
Notre Dame Cathedral, Bayeux............ 4003
Notre Dame Cathedral, Chartres................ 3996
Notre Dame Cathedral. Laon.... 3997
Notre Dame Cathedral, Paris 1090, 2150, 3675, 4330, 5035c, 5870, 6013, 6414, B217
Notre Dame Cathedral, Rouen....4004
Notre Dame Cathedral, Strasbourg.......... 3992, 4001, 5596
Notre Dame Church, Rigny 5709
Notre Dame Church, Royan ... 3991
Notre Dame de l'Assomption Cathedral, Fontenay-le-Comte............ 6412
Notre Dame de l'Assomption Cathedral, Lucon............. 3017
Notre Dame des Champs Church, Arranches............. 5601
Notre Dame de Fourviere Basilica............. 2540
Notre Dame de l'Epine Basilica............. 2963
Notre Dame de la Salette Pilgrimages............. 2911
Notre Dame de Melun Collegiate Church............. 4385
Notre Dame des Missions Church............. 5001
Notre Dame du Haut 1101, 1103
Notre-Dame-en-Vaux Monastery 1998
Nougaro, Claude B721d
Nourry, Prune 6511
Nuclear research, European center 1503
Nuclear Submarine 1259
Nude Sculptures............. 5626-5637
Nuits Romanes, Poitou-Charentes............. 4025
Nungesser-Coli flight 1181
Nyons Bridge 2460

Oath of the Tennis Court 390
Oats............. 5262
Ocean Exploration 1300
Odeillo Solar Furnace 6208
Oemichen, Etienne 824
Offenbach, Jacques B536
Officers Reserve Corps 1492
Okavango Delta, Botswana.... 6157
Oleron Bridge 1162
Olivie, Bernard............. 2384
Olivine............. 4950
Olympic Games Centenary 2537
Olympics, Summer 969, 1105, 1223, 1348, 1493, 1931, 2284, 2206, 2783-2784, 3040-3041, 3495-3498, 4255
Olympics, Winter 198-201, 1176, 1332, 2206, 2269, 2295, 2868, 3186, 3770-3771, B411-B415, B611, B621-B627, B636-B637, B639
Olympics, Youth 3867
Opera Costumes 3213-3218
Opera de la Bastille 2151
Oradour B195
Oran, arms 973
Orchids 3102-3105
Orcival Basilica 3797
Order of Liberation 977, 5955, 6150
Organ (musical instrument) 3764
Organ building 5797
Organ, Church of St. Jacques 4299
Organ, Notre Dame Cathedral....6210
Organ Donation 3031
Organization for Economic Cooperation & Development ... 2241, 4044
Orient Express 6498
Oriental Language Institute 2470
Oriental sculpture, ancient 5431
Orleans 2484
Orleans, arms 469, B138

Orleans, Charles d' B390
Orleans Flower Festival 1192
Orleans, Girard d' ("John the
   Good") 1084
Orly Airport 986
Orsay Museum 2026, 4272
Orves, Honore d'Estienne d' 827
Osprey 1581
Othoniel, Jean-Michel ... 3949, 3953
Otters 2123
Ottmarsheim, Abbey
   Church of 2763
Ouistreham Lighthouse 3050
Ourcq Canal 2290
Overseas Departments,
   Creation of 2547
Overseas possessions ... B96, B115
Overseas Sciences,
   Academy of 1375
Owl ...5803, 5920-5928, 6285-6293
Ozanam, Frederic 2738

Pacific 231 K8
   Locomotive 4218-4219
Pagnol, Marcel 2021e, B652
Paid vacations 2787b
Palais du Louvre 4787
Palais du Luxembourg 569,
   591-592, 4228, 4245
Palais Ducal de Nevers ... 4241, 4784
Palais Galliera 5953
Paleolithic statue 5636
Palissy, Bernard B313
Palm Leaf Medal 905
Palomet 2053
Pantheon 1779
Papal Palace, Avignon 3618
Papayas 4192
Paper art 5741-5752
Paper making 4736
Papin, Denis B359
Paracycling 655d
Paralympics 2270
Parachutists, Normandy
   Landing 1250
Parc des Ecrins 2569
Parc des Pyrénées 2571
Parc Borely, Marseille 3429b
Parc Floral de Paris 3029b
Parc Longchamp, Marseille ... 3429a
Pardaillan B678
Pare, Ambroise B163
Paris, arms 1095, B128
Paris Auto Show 2676
Paris Bar Association ... 3905-3906
Paris-Brest pastry 3853
Paris Catacombs 6409
Paris Chamber of Commerce
   & Industry 2933
Paris City Hall 892
Paris Conciergerie 582, 3869
Paris Exposition, 1937 315-320,
   324
Paris Fair 716
Paris Flower Festival 904
Paris, founding 664
Paris, liberation 2429, 5706, B432
Paris Opera 2671
Paris-Orleans Railroad B178
Paris Peace Conference ... 566-567
Paris Philatelic Exhibitions 226,
   329, 1078, 1085-1089, 1100, 1390,
   1394-1397, 1425-1429, 2395,
   5449-5450
Paris Postal Conference 1054
Paris-Roubaix Bicycle Race ... 2890
Paris Stamp Bourse 3817
Paris Tramway 3269
Paris, views 581-584, 3908,
   C8-C15, C22, C27-C28, C86, C88
Paris Zoo 4639
Parmentier, Antoine A. 810
Parny, Evariste de 4728
Pascal, Blaise ... 1038, 6457, B181
Pas-de-Calais 1449
Passion Fruits 6437
Passy, Frederic 6313
Pasteur Institute 2056
"Pasteur" liner B114

Pasteur, Louis 185-196, 2453,
   6174, 6244, B53, B59, B468
Pasture, Roger de la 3924a
Paths 6463-6474
Patronage Law 4453
Pau 393, 1812
Paul, Marcel 2313
Paulhan, Jean B563
Pavie, Auguste 585
Pavilion de l'Horloge 5597
Paysage de l'Aubrac 6078
Peace 322
Peace Conference 566-567
Peace Year, Intl. 2008
Pear 4197
Peas 4258
Pegoud, Adolphe C75
Peguy, Charles P. 638, 4657
Pelota 802
Pen Club 1769
Penicillin 2837e
Pens 5120
People's Theater, Bussang ... 1439
Peppers, Green 4266
Pequet, Henri C73
Perec, Georges 2914
Perfume flowers 5846-5847
Perfume industry 715
Pergaud, Louis B544
Perignon, Dom Pierre 350
Perigueux 5542
Perigueux Cathedral B215
Periwinkles, Madagascar 2767
Perouges 2120
Perpignan 936, 1643, 2257
Perrin, Jean Baptiste 609
Perse, Saint John B527
Pershing, Gen. John J. 2044
Personalized Stamps 3362-3367
Petain, Henri P. 415-418, 451,
   B149-B152, B153-B157
Peter Pan 6483
Petit Louvre 6307
Petrarch, Francesco 811
Petrel, Barau's 3315
Petrovitch, Francoise 6306
Petrucciani, Michel 2909
Peugeot automobiles 5914-5916
Pevsner, Antoine 2041
Peynet, Raymond 1965, 2789
Peyre, Joseph 5323
Pfimlin, Pierre 3342
Pharmacies, Hospital 2495
Philatelic Federation ... 1277, 1308,
   1378, 1412, 2582
Philatelists 1924
Philex '84 Dunkirk 1924
Philexfrance '82 .... 1688, 1741-1742,
   1889-1820
Philexfrance '89 2105
Philexfrance '99 .... 2620, 2668,
   2713, 2732
Philexjeunes '88 2107
Philexjeunes '91 2243
Philexjeunes '94 2418
Philexjeunes '97 2574
Philexjeunes '03 2980
Philip II (Philippe Auguste) ... 1199,
   B294
Philip III (the Good) 1237
Philip IV (the Fair) 1228
Philipe, Gerard 1000
Phorusrhacos 3430
Photography 374
Piaf, Edith 4257, B618
Piano 3767, 3882B
Pic du Midi cable railway 808
Pic du Midi observatory 673
Picardy 1443
Picardy, arms 694
Picardy, costume B167
Picart Le Doux, Jean 1691
Picasso, Pablo 2640, 4207,
   4755, B547
Picque, General 656
Pierre, Abbé 3756-3757
Pierre-Bloch, Jean 2840
Pif the Dog 6407
Pigalle, Jean Baptiste B300
Pigeon 818

Piglet 5188
Pignon, Edouard 1773
Pilier Lighthouse 5699
Pimentos 4260
Pineapple 4186
Pinel, Philippe 865
Pissarro, Camille 1729, 3175h,
   3180, 4389, 4450, 5018
Place de la Concorde 584, 5035a
Place des Vosges, Paris 5038
Plante, Gaston 821
Plates 5726-5737
Playing Cards 6332-6343
Plensa, Jaume 4276
Pleumeur-Bodou space
   center 1047
Ploumanc'h Lighthouse 5457
Pneumatic Post, Paris 1168
Pocahontas 6480
Poher, Alain 3268
Poincare, J. Henri B270
Poincare, Raymond 637
Pointe de Coupain B729
Pointe du Raz 571, 6075
Pointe Saint-Mathieu 4273
Poitiers 3338
Poitiers Abbey 681
Poitiers, arms B137
Poitiers Cathedral Organ ... 2433
Poitiers, Palace of 4607
Poitou, arms 697
Poitou-Charentes 1447
Polar expeditions 611, 1224
Poliakoff, Serge 2133
Poliomyelitis 933
Polish immigration 1358
Polish Veterans, W.W. II ... 1620
Political Refugees' Fund ... B44-B45
Polo, Marco 6193
Polytechnic School 1548, 2407
Pompadour, Marquise de 4653
Pompidou, Georges ... 1430, 2416,
   4042
Pompidou Art Center ... 1515, 2554
Pompon, Francois 3099
Ponce, Jacquio 5632
Ponge, Francis B631
Pont Alexandre III 5300
Pont-a-Mousson 1542
Pontarlier 2966
Pont Canal de Briare 2216
Pont de la Concorde 5300
Pont du Diable 5291
Pont du Gard 253-254A, 5290
Pont du Moulin 5716
Pont-en-Royans 6008
Pontigny Abbey 4624
Pont l'Eveque cheese 3836
Pont Neuf, Paris 1599, 5035b
Pont-Saint-Esprit 1155
Pont Valentre 3435, 5296
Ponte Vecchio, Florernce ... 5297
Poquelin, Jean Baptiste B179
Porcelain industry 713, 820
Pornic 3798
Port Cros National Park ... 1605,
   2572
Portable telephone 2804e
Post Card Illustrations 6252, 6263
Postal Balances and Scales ... 5347
Postal Checking Service 1202
Postal Checks 5543
Postal Code 1345-1346
Postal Employees' Fund ... B60-B62
Postal Ministry Building B83
Postal Museum 1389, 5757,
   B92, B205
Postal Service 472
Postal Training College ... 2106
Postel, Guillame B541
Posts, Telegraphs and
   Telecommunications Sporting
   Association 5413
Potage aux cresson 3834
Potez 25 .... C61
Pottecher, Maurice 1439
Pottery making 4735
Poulbot, Francisque 1637
Poulenc, Francis B474
Pourquoi-Pas? (ship) 3369

Pourrat, Henri 2042
Poussin, Nicolas B388, 2435
Prague, Czech Republic 3535
Prefectorial Corps 2755
Prehistoric Animals 3430-3433
Prevert, Jacques B632
Primitive of Savoy 1273
Princess and the Pea, The 6091
Printemps, Yvonne B656
Professional Education 2023
Protection of Polar Regions ... 3632
Protection of Water ... 3782-3793,
   4071-4072
Proudhon, Pierre J. B228
Proust, Marcel 6284, B396
Provencal Nativity
   Figures B664-B669
Provence, arms 462
Provence, costume B172
Provence Landing, 1944 1252,
   2434
Provence village 1534, 3680
Provins Tower 1102, 3219
Prudhomme, Sully 3351
Prud'hon, Pierre 2455
Prugne, Patrick 2394
P.T.T. Employees Congress ... 1347
Public Health Service B64-B65
Public Relations Assoc. 1709
Public School 1770
Public works 835
Puffin 979
Puget, Pierre B351
Puppy 3202
Puss-in-Boots 2573, 6082
Puy Cathedral 1707
Puy de Sancy volcano 6068
Pyrenees, Southern 1448
Pyrenees Treaty 932

Quai Branly Museum 3230
Quality 2615
Quarton, Enguerrand 2134
Quartz 2018, 4951
Quebec City, Founding of ... 3437
"Queen Mary 2" Ocean Liner ... 2988
Quenelles 3842
Queuille, Henri 4170
Quimper 722
Quimper Faiance 3575
Quimperle 5048
Quinine discovery 1268

Rabbit 3018, 5183
Rabelais, Francois 639, 688
Rabier, Benjamin ... 4626, 4676, 4680
Rabies Vaccine 1979
Raccoon 3313
Rachel 999
Rachi 3088
Racine, Jean Baptiste 629
Radio 2804d
Radio and Television Center ... 1079
Radio transmissions by
   Ducretet 1380
Radium, Discovery of 2690
Railroad Congress ... 327-328, 1161
Raimu 1001
Rainbows 6357-6368
Ram 5182
Rambouillet Chateau 1718
Rambouillet Hippodrome ... 5258
Rambouillet Sheepcote 3815
Rameau, Jean P. B278
RAMOGE Agreement 2524
Ramses II 1467
Rance Power Station 1170
Rance Valley 1011
Raphael 1865, 3153, 3398, 5829
Rashi 3088
Ratatouille 6488
Ravel, Maurice B308
Raving Rabbids 5872-5883, 5896
Recamier, Madame 641

SUBJECT INDEX OF FRENCH COMMEMORATIVE ISSUES

Red Cross ... B11, B81, B255-B256, B264-B265, B273-B283, B291-B292, B300-B301, B309-B310, B318-B319, B327-B335, B337-B339, B341-B349, B356-B375, B382-B386, B443-B444, B452-B453, B471-B472, B479-B480, B503-B504, B512-B513, B521-B522, B530-B531, B539-B540, B548-B549, B557-B558, B566, B574, B583, B592, B601, B610, B614, B638, B648, B655, B662, B663, B676, B690, B697, B704, B705, B706, B707, B708, B710, B711-B712, B713-B714, B715-B716, B717, B720, B721, B722, B723, B724, B725-B734, B735, B736-B745, B748, B749-B756, B757, B758-B765, B766, B767-B774, B775, B776-B785, B786, B787-B796, B797, B798-B807, B808, B809-B818, B819, B820-B829, B830, B831, B832-B841, B842
Redon 2030
Redon, Odilon 2209, 3950, 3954, 4811
Reflections of Animals...5783-5794
Reforestation 1133
Refugee, World Year B340
Reggiani, Serge B721c
Regional Cuisine............3830-3853
Regional Festivals and Traditions..................4014-4039
Regions of France 1440-1450, 1507-1514, 1588-1590, 1678, 1808-1809, 1853, 3634-3657
Reims, arms B126
Reims, awarding of medals to 5691
Reims Cathedral ... 247-248, 4009, B74
Reims-Florence 796
Reinhardt, Django................... 2360
Relief Assn, French People's 2478
Reliefs, Stone and Metal ...4143-4154
Religious Art 3335-3336
Rembrandt 860, 3200, B556
Remembrance of Slavery Day 3208
Remiremont 2459
Renaissance architecture................4782-4793
Renaissance objets d'art....4658-4669
Renan, Ernest B464
Renard, Colette B721a
Renaud, Madeleine 5759d
Renaudot, Theophraste 1743
Renault Kangoo Mail Van 4404
Renault Maxi 5 Turbo 5402
René I, Duke of Anjou............. 3584
Renewable Energy................. 6309
Rennes, arms B125
Rennes Palace of Justice 1039
Renoir, Pierre-Auguste 1207, 2243, 3175d, 3179, 3600, 4391, 4810, 5009, 6304, 6505, B299, B392-B393
Renoir, Jean 2021d
Renouvin, Jacques 990
Repatriation B75
Repopulation campaign B90-B91
Republican Security Companies 4729
Resistance 588, 826-830, 879-882, 915-919, 959-963, 967, 990-993, 2225, B377-B381
Resistance Monuments ... 1020-1001, 1057-1058, 1251, 2364-2365
Resnais, Alain 6231
Reunion ... 949, 1134, 1507, 2636, 4134
Reunion of Bar and Lorraine with France........................... 1157
Revolution, 1848 .... B224-B231
Rhinoceros 3687, 5808
Rhone-Alps 1512
Ribiere, Germaine 5197
Rice 5266
Richard I, the Lion-Hearted 2715
Richelieu 3408
Richelieu, Cardinal 307, 1286, 1394
Richet, Charles B584
Richier, Germaine 2330
Richier, Ligier 2132

Riga, Latvia........................... 4795
Rights of France 3294
Rimbaud, Arthur 668
Rimet, Jules 6513
Riom, Ste. Chapelle 1310
Ripaille Chateau 1813A
Ripoche, Maurice 961
Riquet, Piette Paul de B528
Riquewihr 1312
Rixheim 4398
Road safety 3011
Road signs 1203
Robert-Houdin, J. E. B450
Robespierre, Maximilian de ... B253
Robin, Thierry 2393
Rocamadour 570, 2898
Rocambole B670
Rochambeau's Landing 1712
Rochechouart, Chateau de 1419
Rochefort-Martrou Bridge ... 1217, 5301
Rochefort-en-Terre 5255
Rochefoucauld, Francois de la B387
Rochers des Deux Jumeaux.... 6069
Rock Climbing 6061d
Rodemack 5861
Rodez Cathedral 1190
Rodin, Auguste 2211, 5304, B52, B58
Roe deer 2810
Roland, Madame 2162a
Roland Garros Tennis Court ... 1612
Rolin, Nicolas 466
Rolland, Romain B569
Romains, Jules B567
Roman, Claire & Clostermann, Pierre...........C84
Roman Mosaic 1781
Romance Studies Center Conf. 726
Romanesque Art........3854-3865, 3870A-3870B
Rome, Italy 2917
Romilly, Jacqueline de........... 5795
Ronsard, Pierre de 219
Roofer 6399
Roosevelt, Eleanor 2688
Roosevelt, Franklin D. 3817a
Roosters 4916-4917, 4987-4998
Rose Societies, Convention of 4819-4820
Roses 1043-1044, 2726
Rosny-Sur-Seine 1731
Rossi, Tino B617
Rostand, Jean B588
Rotary 741, 3092, 3227A
Rothko, Mark 4967
Rouan, Francois 2246
Rouart, Henri 6209
Rouault, Georges 1297, B356-B357
Rouen, arms D119
Rouen Cathedral 854
Rouen Gate 1476
Rouen, Palais de Justice 1417
Rouen, ruins B198
Rouen, Tall Ships 2736
Rouffignac Cave Drawings.... 3197
Rouget de Lisle, Claude-Joseph.......309-310, 3232
Rouletabille, Joseph B672
Rousseau, Henri 1172
Rousseau, Jean Jacques 813, B509
Roussel, Albert B428
Roussillon 784
Roussin, Col. Fr. 656
Roussy, Gustave.................. 6098
Route Napoleon 6475
Rouvroy, Louis de 740
Roux, Emile B289
Roux, Paul-Pierre B419
Royal Palace 1649
Royal Saltworks 5598
Royan 721
Royaumont Abbey 3594
Rozanoff, Constantin 925
Rozier, Pilatre de 308
Rua Augusta Arch, Lisbon.... 5111

Rubens, Peter Paul..... 1518, 4121, 6302
Ruby 4955
Rue Royale, Paris 5112
Rueff, Jacques 2511
Rugby 803, 1843, 6492
Rugby Sevens 6061f
Rugby World Cup....2737, 3310-3311, 3339, 3343, 4069-4070, 4098
Rural Family Aid 1309
Rural mailman B416
Ryder Cup 5470, 5470B
Rye 5267
Rykiel, Sonia (hearts).....5369-5372
Rysselberghe, Theo van 4393

Saar-Lorraine-Luxembourg Summit 2613
Sabatier, Paul 793
Sabbagh, Pierre................... 4499a
Sablé-Sur-Sarthe 2566
Sacred Heart Church Window B339-B340
Sage Type of 1876 .... B489
Sainte-Adresse Belgian Government in Exile 4778-4779
Saint-Amand-les-Eaux 1543
St. Anne d' Auray 1734
St. Austremoine Church, Issoire 1359
St. Barbara School 983
Saint Barthelemy 1587, 4136
St. Benedict 1700
Saint-Benoit-sur Loire Abbey ... 5236
St. Bernard of Clairvaux 4483, B276
St. Bertrand Abbey 630
Saint-Beuve, C. A. B427
Saint-Brevin-les-Pins............. 5024
Saint-Brieuc, Cathedral 1344
St. Cecilia Cathedral Angel, Albi 3597, 3601
Saint-Cloud Park 2437, 4227
Saint-Cyr Military School 731
St. Denis Basilica ... 498, 4006, 4776
Saint-Denis, Reunion, arms ... 1094
Saint-Dié 876, 2678
Sainte-Chapelle ... 1151, 3994, 4005
Sainte Madeleine, Church 1175
Saint-Emilion 1775
Saintes 4407
Saint-Etienne, arms B146
Saint-Etienne School of Mines....5042
St. Etienne Cathedral, Bourges 4000
St. Etienne Cathedral, Metz... 3998
St. Etienne Cathedral, Sens ... 3995
St. Etienne Cathedral, Toul..... 5110
Saint-Etienne Museum 951
Saint Eutrope des Salles-Lavauguyon 2564
Saint-Exupery, Antoine de ... 2668, 2700, C43, C85, CB1
St. Florent, Corsica 1406
Saint-Flour 1070
St. Francis of Assisi 1818
Saint Francois Convent 5717
St. Foy Church 1054
St. Francois de Sales B406
Saint-Front Cathedral, Perigueux 5603
St. Genevieve intercession ... 4301a
St. Genis de Fontaines Church, lintel 1464
St. Germain de Livet 1997
St. Germain de Pres Abbey ... 1645
Saint-Germain-en-Laye 1187
Saint-Gobain Corporation 4891
St. Gregory of Tours 389
Saint-Guilhem-le-Desert........ 2761
St. Hubert 1778
St. Jacques-des-Guérets 3862
St. Joan of Arc Church Stained Glass 3578
St. Just, Louis de 2259d
Saint-Laurent-du-Maroni, French Guiana 2558
Saint Laurent, Yves (hearts)....................2750-2753
Saint-Leger Church 5718

St. Louis 4606a
St. Louis Chandelier (hearts)....................6170-6173
Saint-Louis Royal Chapel....... 6064
Saint-Malo port 347
Saint-Malo, ruins B200
Saint-Marceaux, René de....... 3724
Saintes-Maries-de-la-Mer Religious Procession 4794
Saint-Martial Church 4824
St. Martin B347-B348
St. Martin (overseas territory).... 4131
St. Martin of Tours 2588
Saint-Mathieu Lighthouse 5887
Saint-Maurice Basilica, Epinal.....2608
St. Michael 1156
St. Michel de Cuxa Abbey 1949
Saint-Michel Fountain, Paris.... 5621
Saint-Nazaire Bridge 1457
Saint-Nazaire monument B219
Saint-Nectaire Church 5600
St. Nicholas 657
Saint-Nicolas-de-la-Grave City Hall 4926
St. Nicholas de Porte, Basilica 1405
Saint Nicolas, Lorraine 4028
St. Odile of Alsace 5800
Saintonge, arms 739
St. Patrick 2508
St. Paul 1114
Saint-Paul 1007
Saint-Pere Church 2969
St. Peter 1054
Saint-Philbert-de-Grand-Lieu Abbey 5675
St. Pierre Cathedral, Beauvais 3999
St. Pierre Fourier B395
St. Pierre and Miquelon 1808, 4132
St. Pierre, Martinique 2724
Saint-Pol-de-Leon 1418
Saint-Pol-Roux B419
Saint-Quentin, City Hall 1185
Saint-Remy, ruins 855, 4475
Saint-Saens, Camille 5995, B269
Saint-Saturnin Church 1600
Saint-Savin Church Mural, Vienne 1238
Saint-Ser Chapel 2903
St. Sever 3856
Saint-Simon, Louis de 740
Saint-Taurin Reliquary 2454
St. Teresa of Avila 1846
St. Teresa of Lisieux 1355
St. Theobald's Church 1004
St. Trophime 302
Saint-Vaast-la-Hougue 5865
St. Vincent de Paul B327
Saint Vincent Tournante, Bourgogne 4015, 4033
St. Wandrille 623, 649
St. Yves 798
Salad greens...................... 4259
Sale of Blue Cornflowers....... 4726
Salers 1403
Saline Royale...................... 5598
Salins, Guigone de 466
Salle, Jean Baptiste de la......... 646
Salon du Timbre 2444, 2979, 3029, 3118, 3201, 3316, 3429, 3709
Salsa dancers..................... 4696
Salt Works 1285
Salvador, Henri..................B721b
San Juan de Salvamento Lighthouse 2749
Sancerre 6268
Sand, George 3006, B316
Sand, George, House of......... 4468
Sanguier, Marc 976
Sanguinaires Lighthouse 5893
Santos Dumont, Alberto B465
Saral Satellite...................... 4798
Sardane, Ceret 4026
Sartre, Jean-Paul B568
Satie, Erik B643
Saulx River Bridge 2432
Savings Bank, National ... 1771-1772
Savings Banks, Bicent........... 5404
Savoy..................957, 3794-3795

Savoy, arms 618
Saxophone 3763
Scamaroni, Fred 880
Scherrer, Jean-Louis
  (hearts) 3170-3173
Schoelcher, Victor 819, 1779
School of Nancy Museum 2725
School of Public Works 2266
Schmitt, Florent B644
Schneider, Romy B684
Schoendoerffer, Pierre 5522
Schuman, Robert B485
Schweitzer, Albert B483
Scouting, Cent. 3327
Scouting Year 1822
Scully, Sean 2381
Sculpting 4740
Sculptor 5005
Sea Rescue 1401
Sea Turtle 2892
Seal 2895
Seamen's Fund B68-B69, B93,
  B116, B133
Seaplane C55, C57
Seashell 5806
Season's Greetings 2616-2617,
  2793-2794, 2843-2846, 2921-2922
Secondary School 964
Sedan, Chateau Fort de 1313
Segalen, Victor 1634
Seguin, Marc B578
Segur, Countess of 2729
Seguy, Emile-Allain 6418-6429
Seine Valley at Les Andelys 720
Selestat Library Book
  Illumination 3295
Senate centenary 1434
Senghor, Leopold Sedar 2925
Senlis Cathedral 887
Sennecey-le-Grand City Hall ... 4925
Sens Cathedral 1114
Separation of Church and
  State, Law of 3169
Serrault, Michel B723d
Serres, Oliver de B277
Serusier, Paul 3297
Service Central d'Etat 4820
Sete 877
Seurat, Georges ... 1239, 2244, 4394
Sevigne, Marie de 642
Sevres porcelain 820
Shared Memories Conference ... 3258
Sheep 6378
Shells and Crustaceans ... 6188-6189
Ships 3501
Shooting 6455f
Shore Conservation 1746
Siegfried, Andre B487
Sieyes, Emmanuel-Joseph ... B602
Sight, Sense of 4875-4886
Signac, Paul 2948
Signoret, Simone B685
Silhouettes of Animals ... 6176-6187
Silva, Vieira da (stained glass
  window) B583
Silver 4956
Simenon, Georges 2443
Singers 2819-2824
Single European Market 2311
Sinking Fund ... B24-B37, B39-B41
Sioule Valley 947
Sir Lancelot B677
Sisley, Alfred 1396, 4386
Skateboarding 6061c
Skating Championships 1299
Ski Championships 322,
  1019-1020, 3595
Sleeping Beauty 6090
Smell, Sense of 4682-4693
Smiling Map 1730
Smiley Faces 6232-6243
Smilodon 3431
Snap beans 4264
Snow White 6484
Snowflakes 5526-5537
Soccer 349, 1549, 3824,
  5025-5034, 5659c
Social Security System 4888
Solar Eclipse 2735
Solar Impulse (airplane) 6062

Soldiers 4253
Solesmes 1706
Solferino, Battle of B717b
Solitude 6225
Sologne Plateau 1334
Solutre 1951
Somme, Battle of the 5052
Song of the Partisans 6432
Sorbier, Franck (hearts) ... 3390-3392A
Sordet, Jacques du 5643-5654
Sorel, Guillaume 2386
Sorghum 5272
Sorgues 5415
S.O.S. Amitie 2786
Soto, Jesus Rafael 2869
Soufflaculs, Saint-Claude 4031
Soulages, Pierre 2005
Sound Recording Libraries 3422
South Corsica, Filitosa 1995
Soutine, Chaim 4331
Souvenir Francais 1521
Souvigny 6226
Soyuz Space Flights launched
  from French Guiana 3827-3828
Space Age, 50th Anniv. 3358
Space Studies Center 1835
Speleologists 6080
Spelt 5269
Spirals, Items with 4537-4548,
  4566-4567, 4698
Sport, I Am 3517
Sports 700-705, 801-804,
  883-886, 1619, 5659, 5911, 6061,
  6265, 6455, B60-B62
Spring B244
Spring Philatelic Show ... 4368, 4777,
  5006, 5195, 5415, 5813
Squashes 4268
Squirrel 2809
Stael, Madame de 974
Stael, Nicolas de 1968, 3100
Stag 2124
Stained Glass 3578, 5137-5148,
  5978, 6013, 6401
Stamp bourse, Paris 3817
Stamp boxes 6134-6145
Stamp centenary 612-615
Stamp sesquicentennial 2732
Stamp Day 2325-2326, 2408-
  2409, 2466-2467, 2509-2510, 2567-
  2568, 2630-2631, 2692-2693,
  2706-2707, 2764-2765, 2878-2879,
  2934-2935, 3002-3004, 3093-3095,
  3187-3189, 3303-3305, 3415-3421,
  3605-3611, 3780-3781, 3956-3972,
  4280-4293, 4485-4498, 4535-4536,
  4696-4697, 4889-4890, 5401-5402,
  5619-5620, 5914-5916, 6096-6097,
  6205-6206, 6404-6405, B190, B196,
  B206, B218, B223, B237, B248,
  B257, B266, B275, B284, B293,
  B303, B311, B320, B329, B339,
  B349, B358, B370, B376, B391,
  B400, B408, B416, B425, B440,
  B451, B460, B470, B477, B488,
  B498, B511, B520, B529, B538,
  B547, B556, B565, B573, B581-B582,
  B590-B591, B599-B600, B608-B609,
  B612-B613, B634-B635, B640-B641
Stamp Passion Youth Philatelic
  Exhibition 5930
Stanislas Square, Nancy ... 574-575
Stanke, Alfred 2785
Stars and Heavenly
  Bodies 5095-5106, 6104-6115
States-General Assembly 1228
Statue of Liberty 2014, 3000
Steenvorde Windmill 1641
Stefanik, Milan 2942
Stenay 727
Stenay Malt Works 2458
Stendhal 453, B555
Still Life Paintings 6499-6510
Stock, Fr. Franz 2632
Stockholm 6007
Stonecutter 6393
Stormer, Matthias 4114
Strait of Bonifacio 3520
Strasbourg, arms 558
Strasbourg bimillinary 2131

Strasbourg Cathedral 391,
  1618, 1967
Strasbourg Cathedral
  sculpture 1295
Strasbourg liberation B433
Strasbourg Philatelic
  Exhibition 241
Strasbourg port 809
Strawberry 3957, 6442
Strokkur Glacier, Iceland 6154
Student Health Foundation 1438
Student Relief B78
Subway 2027
Suez Canal 5724
Suffren, Pierre Andre de B594
Sulfur 4954
Sully, Maximilien de B165
Sully-sur-Loire Chateau 1009
Summer B245
Summer Olympics, 2024,
  Bid for 5233, 5303
Summit Meeting of Industrial
  Nations 2163
Sundial 5800
Sunset 4292
Surcouf, Robert B261
Surfing 6455e
Swan Lake Ballet 5108
Swedish Ballet 2410-2411
Sylvester II, Pope B384
Symphonie satellite 1485

Tabarly, Eric B698
Table tennis 1558, 5659b
Tableware of the
  17th Century 5389-5400
Taeuber-Arp, Sophie 6030
Tailleferre, Germaine B647
Tailor 6395
Taine, Hippolyte B399
Takis 2379
Tall Ships 2736
Talleyrand, C. M. B262
Tallinn, Estonia 5417
Talma, Francois-Joseph 998,
  5520a
Talmont Church 1949
Tambourine 3768
Tancarville Bridge 926
Tangerines 6446
Tango Dancing 3224-3225, 4889
Tapestry 3577, 4912-4913
Tapestry industry 711, 1037
Tapies, Antoni 2316
Tarbes 3683, 5676
Tarte aux mirabelles 3833
Tarte tatin 3841
Taste, Sense of 5277-5288
Tautavel Man 2296
Tavant 2559
Tazieff, Haroun B700
Tchang 3334
Teapots 5507-5518
Technical achievements .. 1363-1365,
  1391-1393, 1436-1437, 1485, 1503
Telecom I 1936
Telecom '79, 3rd Exhibition ... 1657
Telecommunications, National
  School 1586
Telemetry 1727
Telephone 1500
Telephone and Telegraph
  Conference C28
Television 766, 2804a
Television, French 1952
Television Pioneers 4499
Tellier, Charles A. 791
Tellier, Theodule 6266d
Telstar satellite 1047-1048
TER Train 6205
Terril No. 74A slag heap 6076
Terrillon, Octave 823
Textile Exposition 645
TGV Atlantic 2173
TGV Train 2881b, 4077-4078
Thailand relations 1991
Thank You 2712, 2807, 2928,
  2990, 2992, 3097, 3097B, 3097D
Thann Church 1004
Theater Day 1028

Theatre des Cabotans, Amiens ... 4016
Thenard, Louis J. 864
Thermal Springs 2136
Thibault, Jacques A. B49, B54
Thiers 1472
Thiers, Adolphe B272
Thimonnier, Barthelemy 758
Thionville 3196
Thiriet, Jean-Michel 2387
Thomas, Albert 1247
Thomas, Eugene B486
Thoronet Abbey 2528
Thumbelina 6085
Tian 3847
Tinguely, Jean 2137
Tintin 2764-2765, 3329-3334
Titian 4179
Tlemcen mosque 946
Tocque, Louis 4758, 4760
Tocqueville, Alexis de 3113
Tolstoi, Leo B507
Tom Thumb 6083
Tomme des Pyrénées cheese ... 3832
Toorop, Jan 4985
Topaz 4948
Torch and Marianne 4280
Torrente (hearts) 2926-2927
Toul City Hall 4931
Toulon 3407
Toulouse, arms 898, B121
Toulouse church B213
Toulouse-Lautrec, Henri de 1113,
  2800, B326
Tour de France Bicycle
  Race 2968, 4409
Tour Montparnasse 5408
Touraine, arms 662
Tourism 1120
Tourism Year 1349
Tourist Film Festival 1501
Tournament, 1662 1582
Tournesol 3330
Tournoel, Capture of 4532b
Tournus Abbey 726, 3854
Tours 2826
Tours Cathedral 1978
Tours, Gouin House 1182
Tourville, Adm. Hilarion de B173
Tower Bridge, London 5295
Trade Treaty, Denmark-
  France 4526-4527
Trade Union Cent. 1907
Traffic Laws 6031
Train des Pignes 4043
Train, Mail Transport 1937
Trains 2833, 4627-4638
Tram-Train 3261
Transatlantic Flight,
  1st nonstop C52
Trappstegsforsen Rapids,
  Sweden 6162
Treaty of Andelot 2058
Treaty of Picquigny 5261b
Treaty of Rome 3308
Treaty of the Pyrenees .. 5452a
Trees 1984-1987, 5495-5506
Trees, Mediterranean 5275
Tremois, Pierre-Yves 1520
Tricolor Legion B157
Triolet, Elsa 6032
Tristan, Flora 1918
Triticale 5273
Trois-Fontaines Abbey .. 5455
Tromelin Island 5760
Troncais Forest 1483
Tropical Fish 4199-4200
Troyes, arms 1041
Troyes, Church of
  St. Madeleine 1175
Troyes House of Youth &
  Culture 1119
Truffaut, Francois 2021j
Tsunami Relief B709
Tuberculosis Bacillus 1845
Tuberculosis Fund B193
Tulips 5799
Tulle 2964
Tulle Lace 5344
Tulle, Massacre of 4625
Turenne, Viscount of B342

SUBJECT INDEX OF FRENCH COMMEMORATIVE ISSUES

Turgenev, Ivan.........................5565
Turgot, A. R. J. B243
Turkey (bird) 5185
Turner, Joseph Mallord
  William 3773, 3777
Turquoise 4952
Tutankhamun Funerary Mask ..6247
Turtle 2262, 4695
Twentieth Century........2769, 2787,
  2804, 2837, 2881

U Bein Bridge, Myanmar......5298
Ubak, Raoul 1690
Ugly Duckling, The 6086
Ukrainian Solidarity B830
Underground ....(see Resistance)
Underwater Archaeology........6282
Unemployment Aid B46, B84
Ungaro, Emanuel
  (hearts).....................3585-3588
U.N.E.S.C.O., 20th anniv. 206-208
U.N.E.S.C.O., 50th anniv. 2545
U.N.E.S.C.O. conference 572
U.N.E.S.C.O.
  Headquarters 893-894
U.N.E.S.C.O. World Heritage
  Sites........................3219-3220
U.N. General Assembly ...605-606,
  671-672
U.N. High Commissioner for
  Refugees 2834
U.N.I.C.E.F. 2543
Union of Metallurgical & Mining
  Industries.............................2705
United Nations ... 1289, 1982, 2500
United Nations Peacekeepers 5433
Universal Declaration of Human
  Rights 2138, 2688-2689, 2787e,
  5570
Universal Israelite Alliance......3887
University Games 845
University of Montpellier.........5848
Upper Normandy 1588
U.P.U., 75th anniversary 634-636
U.P.U. Centenary 1415
U.P.U. Congress 581-584, C22
U.S. Bicentennial 1480
U.S. Constitution 332
Ussel 1473
Utrillo 1869
Uzerche 778
Uzes Chateau 825

Vacation 2828-2829, 2900-
  2901, 2961-2962, 3119, 3209,
  3317-3326, 3441-3450, 3659-3672,
  4608-4619, 4825-4836, 5053-5064,
  5678-5689, 5849-5860
Vaillé, Eugène 3707-3708
Val Chateau 1169
Val de Grace Monastery 2374
Val-de-Reuil.........................2838
Valadon, Suzanne..................4872
Valence 2112
Valence Water Towers 4367
Valenciennes 3289
Valenciennes and Maubeuge
  reunion 1616
Valenciennes City Hall 6099
Valenciennes-Thionville
  Railroad 768
Valentine's Day 2626
Valentre Bridge............3435, 5296
Valere, Simone....................5759b
Valery, Paul B290
Valland, Rose 5524
Valles, Jules 1837
Valletta 5196
Valley of Munster 2253
Vallotton, Felix 6508
Valmier, Georges..................6506
Valmy, Battle of 1306
Valreas Papal Enclave 1215
Van de Kabel, Adriaen 5804
Van Dyck, Anthony 2703
Van Loo, L. M. B565
Van Velde, Bram 2038
Vanier, Raymond C45
Vannes ramparts 1025

Vanoise Natl. Park 2515
Varane, Fouquet de la B206
Varengeville-sur-Mer..............3990
Varenne, Alexandre................5725
Varga, Ladislas 6266e
Vasarely, Victor 1519, 6054
Vasconi, Claude 2036
Vases 5544-5545
Vauban Citadel,
  Belle-Ile-en-Mer 1914
Vauban, Sebastien de ... 3309, B296
Vaucelles Abbey 1735
Vaucouleurs 676
Vauquelin, Nicolas L. B372
Vaux le Vicomte 2156
Vaux-sur-Mer.......................3016
Védrines, Jules 3901d
Velasquez, Diego 3402
Velodrome d'Hiver 2492
Vendee River 1129
Vendome 3405
Venereal disease control B201
Venet, Bernar......................4337
Venice Carnival 1993
Ventura, Lino B689
Venus of Brassempouy 1465
Venus de Milo 5629
Vercingetorix 1165
Vercors monument 1030
Verdier, Fabienne 5761
Verdon Gorge 1598
Verdun, Battle of 392, 789,
  1481, 5041
Vergennes, Charles G. de B297
Verhaeren, Emile 1060
Verlaine, Paul 667
Vermeer, Jan 1832, 3399
Verne, Jules 770, 3120-3125,
  B548-B549
Verneuil-sur-Avre 4278
Versailles fountain B273-B274
Versailles gardens................2018
Versailles Gate 686, 728
Versailles, Grand Trianon 794
Versailles Palace 1288, B70
Versailles, Treaty 1899
Versois, Odile......................5322c
Veterinary Medicine 655
Vezelay 568
Viallat, Claude 3199
Vian, Boris 5798, 5845
Vianney, St. Jean-Marie 2011
Viaud, Louis M. B63
Viaur Viaduct 5472
Vicat, Louis 5253
Vichy, Public Gardens 1744
Victor, Paul-Emile B701
Video Game Characters 3155
Vidocq, Eugene-Francois 2971
Vieira da Silva, Maria
  Helena 2380, 6052
Vieljeux, Leonce 962
Vienna, Austria 4606
Vienne, Jean de 1947, B133
Vigee-Lebrun, Madame
  Elisabeth 2872, 4175, B282
Vigny, Alfred de B373
Vikings 2412-2413
Vilar, Jean 2827
Villa Majorelle...................4252
Villa Paladienne de Syam 4250
Villandry Chateau 729
Villayer, Renouard de, arms ... B190
Villefranche-sur-Mer............3109
Villefranche-sur-Saone 2222
Villehardouin, Geoffroi de ...B330
Villemin, Col. Jean A. 656
Villeneuve lez Avignon ... 3796, 3800
Villeneuve-sur-Lot..............3907
Villers-Cotterets Chateau 6207
Villers-Cotterets Ordinance ... 2175
Villette, La, City of Science
  and Industry 2001
Villon, Francois B207
Villon, Jacques 5260
Vilmorin, Louise de 5604
Vimy Ridge 311-312
Vincennes 346
Vincent, Hyacinthe B364

Vinci, Leonardo da 682, 2007,
  3401, 5740, 6295
Vineyard, Bourgogne 5409
Vineyards, Bordeaux 3676
Viollet le Duc, Eugene B523
Violin Making 6175, 6398
Violincello 3760
Violins 1682
Vire, Clock Tower 1186
Virgil 1781
Vitalis, Macario 5259
Vitre Chateaux 1547
Vittel 1071
Vlaminck, Maurice de 1468
Volleyball 2013, 5659a
Voltaire B239
Vosges 2479
Vouglans Dam, Jura 1233
Vox, Maximilien 4699
Vrai Guignolet Puppet Theater....5418
Vuillard, Edouard 5451

Waldeck-Rousseau, Pierre ... 1907
Wallace Fountain 2848
Wallis and Futuna Islands.....4137
Wallon, Henri 3064
Waltzers 5198
War charities B97-B100
War orphans B3-B10
War prisoners B108-B109,
  B159-B160
War veterans B203
War victims B80, B103, B192
Warhol, Andy 2950
Warner Brothers Cartoon
  Characters 3605-3611
Washing machine, Invention
  of 2787c
Washington, George ...243-244
Wasquehal Pipe Organ 2252
Watchmaker 6403
Watchmakers' School,
  Besancon 1036
Water 1730
Water Exposition 388
Water Skiing Championships 1073
Watteau, Antoine 1362, 6300,
  B240, B310
Way of St. James 4185, 4351,
  4583, 4802
Weaving 4737
Weight Lifting 6455c
Weil, Simone B518
Welder 4283
Weiss, Louise 2361
Welcome 2730
Wendling, Claire 2383
Wercollier, Lucien 2504
Western Pyrenees, Natl. Park ... 1302
Weyden, Rogier van der 3924b
Wheat, Durum 5263
Wheat, Einkorn 5271
Wheat, Soft......................5268
Wheelchair Fencing 6061b
Wheelchair Tennis.............6265c
Whitbread Yacht Race........2223,
  2319, 2375
Wibault 283 Monoplane C58
Widal, Fernand I. 866
Wildlife 2261-2264, 2809-2812
Wildlife protection ... 978-981, 1257
William the Conqueror 1160,
  2054, 5954b
Winged Victory B66-B67
Winter B247
Wissembourg Head of Christ 2210
Woman suffrage 2787d, 5640
Women 4171-4182
Wood Inlayer 6396
Wooden Bridge, Crest 3988
Woodworking 4731
Words of Ben 4099-4110
Work Councils 2468
Workers in COVID-19
  Pandemic 5898-5909
World Alpine Skiing
  Championships 3595
World Capital of Design..........5763
World Communications Year ... 1862

World Cooperation
  Conference 1208
World Cup '82 1829
World Cup '98 .... 2503, 2530-2533,
  2584-2587, 2623-2624, 2628-2629,
  2665, 2769a
World Cup '02 2891
World Cup '06 ...3210, 3228-3229,
  3229A
World Cup '10 3824-3826
World Cycling
  Championships 2158
World Disabled Athletics
  Championships 2902
World Equestrian Games........4656
World Forestry Congress 2265
World Judo Championships ... 2611,
  4045
World Karate Championships...4274
World Petanque
  Championships 4275
World Refugee Year B340
World Rowing
  Championships 2606, 4866-4867
World Table Tennis
  Championships 4400-4401
World Track & Field
  Championships 2970
World War I armistice 895, 1221,
  1226, 1626, 2129, 2679, 3550,
  5567, B77
World War I troop mobilization....4655
World War I, entrance of U.S.
  Forces 2044, 5256
World War II victory ... 1121, 4816,
  B442
World War II victory, 50th
  Anniv. 2473-2474, 2476
World Weight Lifting
  Championships 4091
World Wrestling
  Championships 2049, 5276
Wrestling............................6455b
Wright, Orville and Wilbur.....3901b
Wrought Iron....................3580

**Yachting, Round-the-
  world race** 2223, 2319, 2375
Year of Overseas
  Territories.................4127-4138
Year of the Dog...........3174, 4969b
Year of the Dragon......4139, 4970d
Year of the Goat......4749, 4971c
Year of the Horse.......4568, 4971b
Year of the Monkey.............4968
Year of the Ox 3571, 4970a,
  5975-5976
Year of the Pig 3277, 3277B,
  4969c, 5590-5591
Year of the Rabbit......3930, 4970c,
  6369-6370
Year of the Rat...........3393, 4969d,
  5780-5781
Year of the Rooster.....3091, 4969a,
  5168-5179
Year of the Snake 4315, 4971a
Year of the Tiger 3755, 4970b,
  6168-6169
Yee, Cheung 4202
Yersin, Alexandre 4480-4481,
  B587
Yes.......................2808, 2876
Yourcenar, Marguerite..........B664
Yvert, Louis 3817c
Yvoire 3193

Zadkine, Ossip 1689
Zao Wou-ki 2456
Zay, Jean B560
Zebras 6389
Zitrone, Leon 4499b
Zodiac Signs 4554-4565
ZOE Reactor.......................2690
Zola, Emile 2916, B404
Zucchini 4263
Zurbaran, Francisco de 4117

FRANCE

SEMI-POSTAL STAMPS

No. 162 Surcharged in Red

and

SP2

1914   Unwmk.   Typo.   Perf. 14x13½

B1	A22	10c + 5c red	5.00	4.25
	Never hinged		7.00	
B2	SP2	10c + 5c red	32.50	3.25
	Never hinged		90.00	
a.	Booklet pane of 10		600.00	
	Never hinged		800.00	

Issue dates: No. B1, Aug. 11; No. B2, Sept. 10.
See Nos. B746a, B746b.
For overprint see Offices in Morocco No. B8.

Widow at Grave SP3   War Orphans SP4

Woman Plowing SP5   "Trench of Bayonets" SP6

Lion of Belfort — SP7

"La Marseillaise" SP8

1917-19

B3	SP3	2c + 3c vio brn	4.50	5.00
	Never hinged		10.00	
B4	SP4	5c + 5c grn ('19)	21.00	9.50
	Never hinged		60.00	
B5	SP5	15c + 10c gray green	30.00	27.50
	Never hinged		85.00	
B6	SP5	25c + 15c dp bl	80.00	57.50
	Never hinged		175.00	
B7	SP6	35c + 25c slate & vio	135.00	125.00
	Never hinged		350.00	
B8	SP7	50c + 50c pale brn & dk brn	225.00	180.00
	Never hinged		650.00	
B9	SP8	1fr + 1fr cl & mar	425.00	400.00
	Never hinged		1,100.	
B10	SP8	5fr + 5fr dp bl & blk	1,600.	1,550.
	Never hinged		4,000.	
	Nos. B3-B10 (8)		2,521.	2,355.

See No. B20-B23. For surcharges see No. B12-B19. For similar stamps with euro denominations, see No. 5450.

Hospital Ship and Field Hospital — SP9

1918, Aug.

B11	SP9	15c + 5c sl & red	125.00	60.00
	Never hinged		250.00	

See No. B746d.

Semi-Postal Stamps of 1917-19 Surcharged

1922, Sept. 1

B12	SP3	2c + 1c violet brn	.50	.80
	Never hinged		1.00	
B13	SP4	5c + 2½c green	.80	1.25
	Never hinged		1.50	
B14	SP5	15c + 5c gray grn	1.25	1.60
	Never hinged		2.60	
B15	SP5	25c + 5c deep bl	2.30	2.50
	Never hinged		4.75	
B16	SP6	35c + 5c slate & vio	13.00	15.00
	Never hinged		30.00	
B17	SP7	50c + 10c pale brn & dk brn	19.00	24.00
	Never hinged		39.00	
a.	Pair, one without surcharge			
B18	SP8	1fr + 25c cl & mar	32.50	37.50
	Never hinged		60.00	
B19	SP8	5fr + 1fr bl & blk	150.00	155.00
	Never hinged		275.00	
	Nos. B12-B19 (8)		219.35	237.65
	Set, never hinged		415.00	

Style and arrangement of surcharge differs for each denomination.

Types of 1917-19

1926-27

B20	SP3	2c + 1c violet brn	1.50	1.40
	Never hinged		4.00	
B21	SP7	50c + 10c ol brn & dk brn	20.00	12.50
	Never hinged		72.50	
B22	SP8	1fr + 25c dp rose & red brn	55.00	42.50
	Never hinged		150.00	
B23	SP8	5fr + 1fr sl bl & blk	105.00	100.00
	Never hinged		240.00	
	Nos. B20-B23 (4)		181.50	156.40

Sinking Fund Issues

Types of Regular Issues of 1903-07 Surcharged in Red or Blue

1927, Sept. 26

B24	A22	40c + 10c lt blue (R)	5.75	5.75
	Never hinged		10.50	
B25	A20	50c + 25c green (Bl)	8.25	9.00
	Never hinged		14.00	

Surcharge on No. B25 differs from illustration.

Type of Regular Issue of 1923 Surcharged in Black

1928

B26	A23	1.50fr + 50c orange	14.50	14.00
	Never hinged		37.50	
a.	Pair, one without surcharge		2,000.	
	Nos. B24-B26 (3)		28.50	28.75

See Nos. B28-B33, B35-B37, B39-B41.

Industry and Agriculture SP10

1928, May   Engr.   Perf. 13½

B27	SP10	1.50fr + 8.50fr dull blue	140.00	150.00
	Never hinged		225.00	
a.	Blue green		500.00	550.00
	Never hinged		725.00	

Types of 1903-23 Issues Surcharged like Nos. B24-B26

1928, Oct. 1   Perf. 14x13½

B28	A22	40c + 10c gray lil (R)	13.00	14.00
	Never hinged		32.50	
B29	A20	50c + 25c org brn (Bl)	32.50	29.00
	Never hinged		60.00	
B30	A23	1.50fr + 50c rose lilac (Bk)	52.50	42.50
	Never hinged		100.00	
	Nos. B28-B30 (3)		98.00	85.50

Types of 1903-23 Issues Surcharged like Nos. B24-B26

1929, Oct. 1

B31	A22	40c + 10c green	18.00	19.00
	Never hinged		37.50	
B32	A20	50c + 25c lilac rose	30.00	30.00
	Never hinged		60.00	
B33	A23	1.50fr + 50c chestnut	60.00	65.00
	Never hinged		130.00	
	Nos. B31-B33 (3)		108.00	114.00

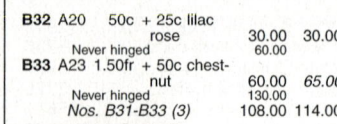

"The Smile of Reims" — SP11

1930, Mar. 15   Engr.   Perf. 13

B34	SP11	1.50fr + 3.50fr red vio	80.00	82.50
	Never hinged		130.00	
a.	Booklet pane of 4		300.00	
	Never hinged		525.00	
b.	Booklet pane of 8		600.00	
	Never hinged		1,050.	
	Complete booklet, #B34b		1,100.	

Booklets containing No. B34 have two panes of 4 (No. B34a) connected by a gutter, the complete piece constituting #B34b, which is stapled into the booklet through the gutter. See footnote after No. 4642.

Types of 1903-07 Issues Surcharged like Nos. B24-B25

1930 Oct. 1   Perf. 14x13½

B35	A22	40c + 10c cerise	20.00	21.00
	Never hinged		70.00	
B36	A20	50c + 25c gray brown	37.50	42.50
	Never hinged		120.00	
B37	A22	1.50fr + 50c violet	65.00	70.00
	Never hinged		190.00	
	Nos. B35-B37 (3)		122.50	133.50

Allegory, French Provinces — SP12

1931, Mar. 1   Perf. 13

B38	SP12	1.50fr + 3.50fr green	125.00	140.00
	Never hinged		300.00	

Types of 1903-07 Issues Surcharged like Nos. B24-B25

1931, Oct. 1   Perf. 14x13½

B39	A22	40c + 10c ol grn	40.00	45.00
	Never hinged		100.00	
B40	A20	50c + 25c gray vio	100.00	110.00
	Never hinged		235.00	
B41	A22	1.50fr + 50c deep red	100.00	110.00
	Never hinged		200.00	
	Nos. B39-B41 (3)		240.00	265.00

Catalogue values for unused stamps in this section, from this point to the end of the section, are for Never Hinged items.

"France" Giving Aid to an Intellectual SP13

Symbolic of Music — SP14

1935, Dec. 9   Engr.   Perf. 13

B42	SP13	50c + 10c ultra	4.00	2.50
	Hinged		2.50	
B43	SP14	50c + 2fr dull red	125.00	45.00
	Hinged		55.00	

The surtax was for the aid of distressed and exiled intellectuals.
For surcharge see No. B47.

Statue of Liberty — SP15

1936-37

B44	SP15	50c + 25c dk blue ('37)	7.50	5.00
	Hinged		4.00	
B45	SP15	75c + 50c violet	20.00	10.00
	Hinged		9.50	

Surtax for the aid of political refugees.
For surcharge see No. B47.

Children of the Unemployed — SP16

1936, May

B46	SP16	50c + 10c copper red	7.50	5.00
	Hinged		4.50	

The surtax was for the aid of children of the unemployed.

No. B43 Surcharged in Black

1936, Nov.

B47	SP14	20c on 50c + 2fr dull red	4.75	3.50
	Hinged		3.25	

Jacques Callot SP17

Anatole France (Jacques Anatole Thibault) SP18

Hector Berlioz — SP19

Victor Hugo — SP20

Auguste Rodin — SP21

Louis Pasteur — SP22

1936-37   Engr.

B48	SP17	20c + 10c brn car	4.50	2.50
	Hinged		2.25	
B49	SP18	30c + 10c emer ('37)	5.00	2.75
	Hinged		2.25	
B50	SP19	40c + 10c emer	4.50	2.75
	Hinged		2.25	
B51	SP20	50c + 10c copper red	8.75	3.75
	Hinged		3.75	
B52	SP21	90c + 10c rose red ('37)	13.00	6.50
	Hinged		6.00	
B53	SP22	1.50fr + 50c deep ultra	40.00	20.00
	Hinged		20.00	
	Nos. B48-B53 (6)		75.75	38.25

The surtax was used for relief of unemployed intellectuals. See No. 6244.

1938

B54	SP18	30c + 10c brn car	3.00	1.75
	Hinged		1.75	

FRANCE

B55	SP17	35c + 10c dull green	3.50	2.40
	Hinged			2.40
B56	SP19	55c + 10c dull vio	10.00	4.00
	Hinged			6.00
B57	SP20	65c + 10c ultra	11.50	4.00
	Hinged			6.00
B58	SP21	1fr + 10c car lake	8.50	4.50
	Hinged			4.75
B59	SP22	1.75fr + 25c dp blue	35.00	17.00
	Hinged			17.00
		Nos. B54-B59 (6)	71.50	33.65

Tug of War — SP23

Foot Race SP24

Hiking SP25

1937, June 16

B60	SP23	20c + 10c brown	3.00	2.25
	Hinged			1.60
B61	SP24	40c + 10c red brn	3.00	2.25
	Hinged			1.60
B62	SP25	50c + 10c black brn	3.00	2.25
	Hinged			1.60
		Nos. B60-B62 (3)	9.00	6.75

The surtax was for the Recreation Fund of the employees of the Post, Telephone and Telegraph.

Pierre Loti (Louis Marie Julien Viaud) — SP26

1937, Aug.

B63	SP26	50c + 20c rose car	7.50	5.00
	Hinged			3.75

The surtax was for the Pierre Loti Monument Fund.

"France" and Infant — SP27

1937-39

B64	SP27	65c + 25c brown vio	5.25	2.75
	Hinged			3.25
B65	SP27	90c + 30c pck bl ('39)	3.50	2.75
	Hinged			2.10

The surtax was used for public health work.

Winged Victory of Samothrace — SP28

1937, Aug.

B66	SP28	30c blue green	175.00	40.00
	Hinged			65.00
B67	SP28	55c red	175.00	40.00
	Hinged			65.00

On sale at the Louvre for 2.50fr. The surtax of 1.65fr was for the benefit of the Louvre Museum.

Jean Baptiste Charcot — SP29

1938-39

B68	SP29	65c + 35c dk bl grn	3.00	3.00
	Hinged			1.60

B69	SP29	90c + 35c brt red vio ('39)	30.00	13.50
	Hinged			11.00

Surtax for the benefit of French seamen.

Palace of Versailles — SP30

1938, May 9

B70	SP30	1.75fr + 75c dp bl	37.50	19.00
	Hinged			19.00

Natl. Exposition of Painting and Sculpture at Versailles.
The surtax was for the benefit of the Versailles Concert Society.

French Soldier — SP31

1938, May 16

B71	SP31	55c + 70c brown vio	8.50	5.25
	Hinged			4.75
B72	SP31	65c + 1.10fr pck bl	8.50	5.25
	Hinged			4.75

The surtax was for a fund to erect a monument to the glory of the French Infantrymen.

Monument — SP32

1938, May 25

B73	SP32	55c + 45c vermilion	22.50	12.50
	Hinged			10.00

The surtax was for a fund to erect a monument in honor of the Army Medical Corps.

Reims Cathedral — SP33

1938, July 10

B74	SP33	65c + 35c ultra	17.50	10.50
	Hinged			8.50

Completion of the reconstruction of Reims Cathedral, July 10, 1938.

"France" Welcoming Her Sons — SP34

1938, Aug. 8

B75	SP34	65c + 60c rose car	8.50	5.75
	Hinged			4.00

The surtax was for the benefit of French volunteers repatriated from Spain.

Curie Issue
Common Design Type

1938, Sept. 1

B76	CD80	1.75fr + 50c dp ultra	21.00	12.50
	Hinged			8.75

Victory Parade Passing Arc de Triomphe — SP36

1938, Oct. 8

B77	SP36	65c + 35c brown car	5.75	4.50
	Hinged			3.25

20th anniversary of the Armistice.

Student and Nurse — SP37

1938, Dec. 1

B78	SP37	65c + 60c pck blue	15.00	8.25
	Hinged			8.00

The surtax was for Student Relief.

Blind Man and Radio — SP38

1938, Dec.

B79	SP38	90c + 25c brown vio	15.00	9.00
	Hinged			8.00

The surtax was used to help provide radios for the blind.

Civilian Facing Firing Squad — SP39

1939, Feb. 1

B80	SP39	90c + 35c black brn	17.00	10.50
	Hinged			8.75

The surtax was used to erect a monument to civilian victims of World War I.

Red Cross Nurse — SP40

1939, Mar. 24

B81	SP40	90c + 35c dk sl grn, turq bl & red	13.00	8.25
	Hinged			6.75

75th anniv. of the Intl. Red Cross Society. See No. B746o.

Army Engineer — SP41

1939, Apr. 3

B82	SP41	70c + 50c vermilion	12.50	8.25
	Hinged			4.25

Army Engineering Corps. The surtax was used to erect a monument to those members who died in World War I.

Ministry of Post, Telegraph and Telephone SP42

1939, Apr. 8

B83	SP42	90c + 35c turq blue	37.50	20.00
	Hinged			19.00

The surtax was used to aid orphans of employees of the postal system. Opening of the new building for the Ministry of Post, Telegraph and Telephones.

Mother and Child — SP43

1939, Apr. 24

B84	SP43	90c + 35c red	3.75	2.50
	Hinged			2.40

The surtax was used to aid children of the unemployed.

50th Anniv. of the Eiffel Tower — SP44

1939, May 5

B85	SP44	90c + 50c red violet	15.00	9.00
	Hinged			8.25

The surtax was used for celebration festivities. For stamps with euro denominations see Nos. 5449c, 6410a-6410c.

Puvis de Chavannes SP45

Claude Debussy SP46

Honoré de Balzac — SP47   Claude Bernard — SP48

1939-40

B86	SP45	40c + 10c ver	1.75	1.00
	Hinged			.80
B87	SP46	70c + 10c brn vio	8.25	2.50
	Hinged			3.50
B87A	SP46	80c + 10c brn vio ('40)	9.00	7.50
	Hinged			4.25
B88	SP47	90c + 10c brt red vio	7.25	2.50
	Hinged			3.25
B88A	SP47	1fr + 10c brt red vio ('40)	9.00	7.50
	Hinged			4.25
B89	SP48	2.25fr + 25c brt ultra	28.00	11.50
	Hinged			14.50
B89A	SP48	2.50fr + 25c brt ultra ('40)	9.00	7.50
	Hinged			4.25
		Nos. B86-B89A (7)	72.25	40.00

The surtax was used to aid unemployed intellectuals.

Mothers and Children
SP49   SP50

1939, June 15

B90	SP49	70c + 80c bl, grn & vio	5.25	4.50
	Hinged			3.25

FRANCE

B91 SP50 90c + 60c dk brn, dl vio & brn   8.50   5.25
Hinged   4.75
The surtax was used to aid France's repopulation campaign.

"The Letter" by Jean Honoré Fragonard — SP51

1939, July 6
B92 SP51 40c + 60c multi   4.25   2.75
Hinged   2.40
The surtax was used for the Postal Museum. See footnote after No. 4642.

Statue of Widow and Children — SP52

1939, July 20
B93 SP52 70c + 30c brown vio   25.00   12.00
Hinged   12.00
Surtax for the benefit of French seamen.

French Soldier — SP53

Colonial Trooper — SP54

1940, Feb. 15
B94 SP53 40c + 60c sepia   3.25   2.75
Hinged   1.50
B95 SP54 1fr + 50c turq blue   3.25   2.75
Hinged   1.50
The surtax was used to assist the families of mobilized men.

World Map Showing French Possessions SP55

1940, Apr. 15
B96 SP55 1fr + 25c scarlet   2.50   1.50
Hinged   1.50

Marshal Joseph J. C. Joffre SP56   Marshal Ferdinand Foch SP57

Gen. Joseph S. Gallieni — SP58

Woman Plowing — SP59

1940, May 1
B97 SP56 80c + 45c choc   6.00   3.75
Hinged   3.00

B98 SP57 1fr + 50c dk vio   4.50   3.00
Hinged   2.50
B99 SP58 1.50fr + 50c brown red   4.50   3.00
Hinged   2.50
B100 SP59 2.50fr + 50c indigo & dl bl   12.00   7.50
Hinged   6.00
Nos. B97-B100 (4)   27.00   17.25
The surtax was used for war charities. See footnote after No. 4642.

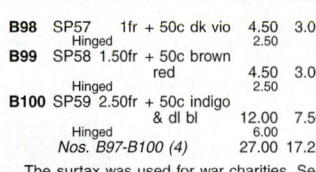
Doctor, Nurse, Soldier and Family — SP60

Nurse and Wounded Soldier — SP61

1940, May 12
B101 SP60 80c + 1fr dk grn & red   7.25   3.50
Hinged   3.50
B102 SP61 1fr + 2fr sep & red   9.00   3.50
Hinged   3.50
The surtax was used for the Red Cross. See Nos. B747a, B747e.

Nurse with Injured Children — SP62

1940, Nov. 12
B103 SP62 1fr + 2fr sepia   1.25   .80
Hinged   .80
The surtax was used for victims of the war.

Wheat Harvest — SP63

Sowing — SP64

Picking Grapes — SP65

Grazing Cattle — SP66

1940, Dec. 2
B104 SP63 80c + 2fr brn blk   3.00   1.50
Hinged   1.40
B105 SP64 1fr + 2fr chestnut   3.00   1.50
Hinged   1.40
B106 SP65 1.50fr + 2fr brt vio   3.00   1.50
Hinged   1.40
B107 SP66 2.50fr + 2fr dp grn   3.25   1.75
Hinged   1.75
Nos. B104-B107 (4)   12.25   6.25
The surtax was used for national relief.

Prisoners of War SP67   SP68

1941, Jan. 1
B108 SP67 80c + 5fr dark grn   1.50   1.50
B109 SP68 1fr + 5fr rose brn   1.50   1.50
The surtax was for prisoners of war.

Science Fighting Cancer — SP69

1941, Feb. 20
B110 SP69 2.50fr + 50c slate blk & brn   1.50   1.25
Surtax used for the control of cancer.

No. 417 Surcharged in Blue

1941, Mar. 4
B111 A109 1fr + 10c crimson   .25   .25

Men Hauling Coal — SP70

"France" Aiding Needy Man — SP71

1941
B112 SP70 1fr + 2fr sepia   2.25   1.00
B113 SP71 2.50fr + 7.50fr dk bl   7.50   2.00
The surtax was for Marshal Pétain's National Relief Fund.

Liner Pasteur — SP72

1941, July 17   Red Surcharge
B114 SP72 1fr + 1fr on 70c dk bl grn   .30   .30

World Map, Mercator Projection SP73

1941
B115 SP73 1fr + 1fr multi   .65   .45

Fisherman — SP74

1941, Oct. 23
B116 SP74 1fr + 9fr dk blue grn   .80   .70
Surtax for benefit of French seamen.

Arms of Various Cities

Nancy SP75   Lille SP76

 Rouen SP77
 Toulouse SP79
 Marseille SP81
 Rennes SP83
 Montpellier SP85

 Bordeaux SP78
 Clermont-Ferrand SP80
 Lyon SP82
 Reims SP84
 Paris SP86

1941   Perf. 14x13
B117 SP75 20c + 30c brn blk   2.75   2.00
B118 SP76 40c + 60c org brn   2.75   2.00
B119 SP77 50c + 70c grnsh blue   2.75   2.00
B120 SP78 70c + 80c rose vio   2.75   2.00
B121 SP79 80c + 1fr dp rose   2.75   2.00
B122 SP80 1fr + 1fr black   2.75   2.00
B123 SP81 1.50fr + 2fr dk bl   2.75   2.00
B124 SP82 2fr + 2fr dk vio   2.75   2.00
B125 SP83 2.50fr + 3fr brt grn   2.75   2.00
B126 SP84 3fr + 5fr org brn   2.75   2.00
B127 SP85 5fr + 6fr brt ultra   2.75   2.00
B128 SP86 10fr + 10fr dk red   2.75   2.00
Nos. B117-B128 (12)   33.00   24.00

Count de La Pérouse — SP87

1942, Mar. 23   Perf. 13
B129 SP87 2.50fr + 7.50fr ultra   1.25   1.40
Jean Francois de Galaup de La Pérouse, (1741-88), French navigator and explorer. The surtax was for National Relief.

Planes over Fields — SP88

1942, Apr. 4
B130 SP88 1.50fr + 3.50fr lt vio   2.40   2.40
The surtax was for the benefit of French airmen and their familes.

FRANCE

Alexis Chabrier — SP89

1942, May 18
B131 SP89 2fr + 3fr sepia   1.25   1.25

Emmanuel Chabrier (1841-1894), composer, birth centenary. The surtax was for works of charity among musicians.

Symbolical of French Colonial Empire — SP90

1942, May 18
B132 SP90 1.50fr + 8.50fr black   1.10   1.10

The surtax was for National Relief.

Jean de Vienne — SP91

1942, June 16
B133 SP91 1.50fr + 8.50fr sepia   1.10   1.10

600th anniv. of the birth of Jean de Vienne, 1st admiral of France. The surtax was for the benefit of French seamen

Type of Regular Issue, 1941 Surcharged in Carmine

1942, Sept. 10   Perf. 14x13½
B134 A116 1.50fr + 50c brt ultra   .25   .25

The surtax was for national relief ("Secours National").

Arms of Various Cities

Chambéry SP92   La Rochelle SP93

Poitiers SP94   Orléans SP95

Grenoble SP96   Angers SP97

Dijon SP98   Limoges SP99

Le Havre SP100   Nantes SP101

 Nice SP102

 St. Etienne SP103

1942, Oct.   Perf. 14x13
         Unwmk.   Engr.
B135 SP92 50c + 60c blk   3.50   3.25
B136 SP93 60c + 70c grnsh blue   3.50   3.25
B137 SP94 80c + 1fr rose   3.50   3.25
B138 SP95 1fr + 1.30fr dk green   3.50   3.25
B139 SP96 1.20fr + 1.50fr rose vio   3.50   3.25
B140 SP97 1.50fr + 1.80fr slate bl   3.50   3.25
B141 SP98 2fr + 2.30fr deep rose   3.50   3.25
B142 SP99 2.40fr + 2.80fr slate grn   3.50   3.25
B143 SP100 3fr + 3.50fr dp violet   3.50   3.25
B144 SP101 4fr + 5fr lt ultra   3.50   3.25
B145 SP102 4.50fr + 6fr red   3.50   3.25
B146 SP103 5fr + 7fr brt red vio   3.50   3.25
Nos. B135-B146 (12)   42.00   39.00

The surtax was for national relief.

 Tricolor Legion — SP104

1942, Oct. 12   Perf. 13
B147 SP104 1.20 + 8.80fr dk blue   10.00   10.00
   a. Vert. pair, #B147, B148 + albino impression   22.50   25.00
B148 SP104 1.20 + 8.80fr crim   10.00   10.00

These stamps were printed in sheets of 20 stamps and 5 albino impressions arranged: 2 horizontal rows of 5 dark blue stamps, 1 row of 5 albino impressions, and 2 rows of 5 crimson stamps.

Marshal Henri Philippe Pétain
SP105   SP106

1943, Feb. 8
B149 SP105 1fr + 10fr rose red   2.75   2.75
B150 SP105 1fr + 10fr blue   2.75   2.75
B151 SP106 2fr + 12fr rose red   2.75   2.75
B152 SP106 2fr + 12fr blue   2.75   2.75
   a. Strip, #B149-B152 + label   12.50   12.50

The surtax was for national relief. Printed in sheets of 20, the 10 blue stamps at left, the 10 rose red at right, separated by a vert. row of 5 white labels bearing a tri-colored battle-ax.

 Marshal Pétain SP107

 "Work" SP108

 "Family" SP109

 "State" SP110

 Marshal Pétain — SP111

1943, June 7
B153 SP107 1.20fr + 1.40fr dull vio   12.00   11.00
B154 SP108 1.50fr + 2.50fr red   12.00   11.00
B155 SP109 2.40fr + 7fr brn   12.00   11.00
B156 SP110 4fr + 10fr dk violet   12.00   11.00
B157 SP111 5fr + 15fr red brn   12.00   11.00
   a. Strip of 5, #B153-B157   100.00   100.00

Pétain's 87th birthday. The surtax was for national relief.

 Civilians Under Air Attack — SP112

1943, Aug. 23
B158 SP112 1.50fr + 3.50fr black   .40   .40

Surtax was for bomb victims at Billancourt, Dunkirk, Lorient, Saint-Nazaire.

 Civilians Doing Farm Work SP113

 Prisoner's Family Doing Farm Work SP114

1943, Sept. 27
B159 SP113 1.50fr + 8.50fr sepia   .75   .75
B160 SP114 2.40fr + 7.60fr dk grn   .80   .80

The surtax was for families of war prisoners.

 Michel de Montaigne — SP115

1.20fr+1.50fr, Francois Clouet. 1.50fr+3fr, Ambrose Paré. 2.40fr+4fr, Chevalier Pierre de Bayard. 4fr+6fr, Duke of Sully. 5fr+10fr, Henri IV.

1943, Oct. 2
B161 SP115 60c + 80c Prus green   1.75   1.75
B162 SP115 1.20fr + 1.50fr black   1.50   1.50
B163 SP115 1.50fr + 3fr deep ultra   1.50   1.50
B164 SP115 2.40fr + 4fr red   1.50   1.50
B165 SP115 4fr + 6fr dull brn red   1.75   1.75
B166 SP115 5fr + 10fr dull green   1.75   1.75
Nos. B161-B166 (6)   9.75   9.75

The surtax was for national relief. Issued to honor famous 16th century Frenchmen.

 Picardy Costume — SP121

Designs: 18th Century Costumes: 1.20fr+2fr, Brittany. 1.50fr+4fr, Ile de France.

2.40+5fr, Burgundy. 4fr+6fr, Auvergne. 5fr+7fr, Provence.

1943, Dec. 27
B167 SP121 60c + 1.30fr sepia   1.60   1.60
B168 SP121 1.20fr + 2fr lt vio   1.60   1.60
B169 SP121 1.50fr + 4fr turq blue   1.60   1.60
B170 SP121 2.40fr + 5fr rose car   1.60   1.60
B171 SP121 4fr + 6fr chlky blue   2.50   2.50
B172 SP121 5fr + 7fr red   2.50   2.50
Nos. B167-B172 (6)   11.40   11.40

The surtax was for national relief. See footnote after No. 4642.

 Admiral Tourville — SP127

1944, Feb. 21
B173 SP127 4fr + 6fr dull red brn   .60   .60

300th anniv. of the birth of Admiral Anne-Hilarion de Cotentin Tourville (1642-1701).

 Charles Gounod — SP128

1944, Mar. 27   Perf. 14x13
B174 SP128 1.50fr + 3.50fr sepia   .75   .60

50th anniv. of the death of Charles Gounod, composer (1818-1893).

 Marshal Pétain — SP129

 Farming — SP130

 Industry — SP131

1944, Apr. 24   Perf. 13
B175 SP129 1.50fr + 3.50fr sepia   3.00   3.00
B176 SP130 2fr + 3fr dp ultra   .50   .45
B177 SP131 4fr + 6fr rose red   .50   .45
Nos. B175-B177 (3)   4.00   3.90

Marshal Henri Pétain's 88th birthday.

 Modern Streamliner, 19th Cent. Train — SP132

1944, Aug. 14
B178 SP132 4fr + 6fr black   1.50   1.50

Centenary of the Paris-Rouen, Paris-Orléans railroad.

FRANCE

Molière (Jean-Baptiste Poquelin) — SP133

Designs: 80c+2.20fr, Jules Hardouin Mansart. 1.20fr+2.80fr, Blaise Pascal. 1.50fr+3.50fr, Louis II of Bourbon. 2fr+4fr, Jean-Baptiste Colbert. 4fr+6fr, Louis XIV.

1944, July 31
B179	SP133	50c + 1.50fr rose car	1.50	1.00
B180	SP133	80c + 2.20fr dk green	1.50	1.00
B181	SP133	1.20fr + 2.80fr black	1.50	1.00
B182	SP133	1.50fr + 3.50fr brt ultra	1.50	1.00
B183	SP133	2fr + 4fr dull brn red	1.50	1.00
B184	SP133	4fr + 6fr red	1.50	1.00
		Nos. B179-B184 (6)	9.00	6.00

Noted 17th century Frenchmen. See No. 6350.

Angoulême SP139   Chartres SP140

Amiens SP141   Beauvais SP142

Albi — SP143

1944, Nov. 20
B185	SP139	50c + 1.50fr black	.60	.40
B186	SP140	80c + 2.20fr rose vio	.60	.40
B187	SP141	1.20fr + 2.80fr brn car	.60	.40
B188	SP142	1.50fr + 3.50fr dp blue	.60	.40
B189	SP143	4fr + 6fr orange red	.60	.40
		Nos. B185-B189 (5)	3.00	2.00

French Cathedrals.

Coat of Arms of Renouard de Villayer — SP144

1944, Dec. 9   **Engr.**
B190 SP144 1.50fr + 3.50fr dp brn   .25   .25
Stamp Day.

Sarah Bernhardt — SP145

1945, May 16   **Unwmk.**   **Perf. 13**
B191 SP145 4fr + 1fr dk violet brn   .30   .25
100th anniv. of the birth of Sarah Bernhardt, actress.

War Victims — SP146

1945, May 16
B192 SP146 4fr + 6fr dk violet brn   .25   .25
The surtax was for war victims of the P.T.T.

Tuberculosis Patient — SP147

1945, May 16   **Typo.**   **Perf. 14x13½**
B193 SP147 2fr + 1fr red orange   .25   .25
Surtax for the aid of tuberculosis victims. For surcharge see No. 561.

Boy and Girl — SP148

1945, July 9   **Engr.**   **Perf. 13**
B194 SP148 4fr + 2fr Prus green   .25   .25
The surtax was used for child welfare.

Burning of Oradour Church — SP149

1945, Oct. 13
B195 SP149 4fr + 2fr sepia   .25   .25
Destruction of Oradour, June, 1944.

Louis XI and Post Rider — SP150

1945, Oct. 13
B196 SP150 2fr + 3fr deep ultra   .35   .25
Stamp Day.
For overprint see French West Africa No. B2.

Ruins of Dunkirk — SP151

Ruins of Rouen — SP152

Ruins of Caen — SP153

Ruins of Saint-Malo SP154

1945, Nov. 5
B197	SP151	1.50fr + 1.50fr red brown	.40	.30
B198	SP152	2fr + 2fr violet	.40	.30
B199	SP153	2.40fr + 2.60fr blue	.40	.30
B200	SP154	4fr + 4fr black	.40	.30
		Nos. B197-B200 (4)	1.60	1.20

The surtax was to aid the suffering residents of Dunkirk, Rouen, Caen and Saint Malo.

Alfred Fournier SP155   Henri Becquerel SP156

1946, Feb. 4   **Engr.**   **Perf. 13**
B201 SP155 2fr + 3fr red brown   .30   .25
B202 SP156 2fr + 3fr violet   .30   .25

Issued to raise funds for the fight against venereal disease (No. B201) and for the struggle against cancer (No. B202).
No. B202 for the 50th anniv. of the discovery of radioactivity by Henri Becquerel.
See No. B221.

Church of the Invalides, Paris — SP157

1946, Mar. 11
B203 SP157 4fr + 6fr red brown   .30   .25
The surtax was to aid disabled war veterans. For stamp with euro denominations, see No. 5449b.

French Warships SP158

1946, Apr. 8
B204 SP158 2fr + 3fr gray black   .75   .40
The surtax was for naval charities.

"The Letter" by Jean Siméon Chardin — SP159

1946, May 25
B205 SP159 2fr + 3fr brown red   .40   .30
The surtax was used for the Postal Museum.

Fouquet de la Varane — SP160

1946, June 29
B206 SP160 3fr + 2fr sepia   .50   .25
Stamp Day.

François Villon — SP161

Designs: 3fr+1fr, Jean Fouquet. 4fr+3fr, Philippe de Commynes. 5fr+4fr, Joan of Arc. 6fr+5fr, Jean de Gerson. 10fr+6fr, Charles VII.

1946, Oct. 28
B207	SP161	2fr + 1fr dk Prus grn	1.25	.90
B208	SP161	3fr + 1fr dk blue vio	1.25	.90
B209	SP161	4fr + 3fr henna brn	1.25	.90
B210	SP161	5fr + 4fr ultra	1.25	.90
B211	SP161	6fr + 5fr sepia	1.25	.90
B212	SP161	10fr + 6fr red	1.25	.90
		Nos. B207-B212 (6)	7.50	5.40

Church of St. Sernin, Toulouse SP167   Notre Dame du Port, Clermont-Ferrand SP168

Cathedral of St. Front, Perigueux SP169

Cathedral of St. Julien, Le Mans SP170   Cathedral of Notre Dame, Paris SP171

1947   **Engr.**
B213	SP167	1fr + 1fr car rose	.85	.60
B214	SP168	3fr + 2fr dk bl vio	2.25	1.40
B215	SP169	4fr + 3fr henna brn	1.10	.90
B216	SP170	6fr + 4fr dp bl	1.10	.90
B217	SP171	10fr + 6fr dk gray grn	2.25	1.60
		Nos. B213-B217 (5)	7.55	5.40

See Nos. 5035c, 5933a.

François Michel le Tellier de Louvois — SP172

1947, Mar. 15
B218 SP172 4.50fr + 5.50fr car rose   1.10   .55
Stamp Day, Mar. 15, 1947.

FRANCE

Submarine Pens, Shipyard and Monument — SP173

1947, Aug. 2
B219 SP173 6fr + 4fr bluish black   .50   .30
British commando raid on the Nazi U-boat base at St. Nazaire, 1942.

Liberty Highway Marker — SP174

1947, Sept. 5
B220 SP174 6fr + 4fr dk green   .75   .55
The surtax was to help defray maintenance costs of the Liberty Highway.

Fournier Type of 1946
1947, Oct. 20
B221 SP155 2fr + 3fr indigo   .30   .25

Louis Braille — SP175

1948, Jan. 19
B222 SP175 6fr + 4fr purple   .30   .25

Etienne Arago — SP176

1948, Mar. 6
B223 SP176 6fr + 4fr black brn   .45   .25
Stamp Day, March 6-7, 1948.

Alphonse de Lamartine — SP177

Designs: 3fr+2fr, Alexandre A. Ledru-Rollin. 4fr+3fr, Louis Blanc. 5fr+4fr, Albert (Alexandre Martin). 6fr+5fr, Pierre J. Proudhon. 10fr+6fr, Louis Auguste Blanqui. 15fr+7fr, Armand Barbès. 20fr+8fr, Dennis A. Affre.

1948, Apr. 5 Engr. Perf. 13
B224 SP177 1fr + 1fr dk grn   1.10   .75
B225 SP177 3fr + 2fr henna brn   1.10   .75
B226 SP177 4fr + 3fr vio brn   1.10   .75
B227 SP177 5fr + 4fr lt bl grn   2.50   1.50
B228 SP177 6fr + 5fr indigo   2.25   1.10
B229 SP177 10fr + 6fr car rose   2.25   1.10
B230 SP177 15fr + 7fr sl blk   2.50   1.50
B231 SP177 20fr + 8fr purple   2.50   1.50
Nos. B224-B231 (8)   15.30   8.95
Centenary of the Revolution of 1848.

Dr. Léon Charles Albert Calmette SP178

1948, June 18
B232 SP178 6fr + 4fr dk grnsh bl   .75   .35
1st Intl. Congress on the Calmette-Guerin bacillus vaccine.

Farmer — SP179

Designs: 5fr+3fr, Fisherman. 8fr+4fr, Miner. 10fr+6fr, Metal worker.

1949, Feb. 14
B233 SP179 3fr + 1fr claret   .65   .45
B234 SP179 5fr + 3fr dk blue   .75   .45
B235 SP179 8fr + 4fr indigo   .75   .45
B236 SP179 10fr + 6fr dk red   .80   .45
Nos. B233-B236 (4)   2.95   1.80

Étienne François de Choiseul and Post Cart — SP180

1949, Mar. 26
B237 SP180 15fr + 5fr dk green   .80   .45
Stamp Day, Mar. 26-27, 1949.

Baron de la Brède et de Montesquieu — SP181

Designs: 8fr+2fr, Voltaire. 10fr+3fr, Antoine Watteau. 12fr+4fr, Georges de Buffon. 15fr+5fr, Joseph F. Dupleix. 25fr+10fr, A. R. J. Turgot.

1949, Nov. 14
B238 SP181 5fr + 1fr dk grn   2.50   1.50
B239 SP181 8fr + 2fr indigo   2.50   1.50
B240 SP181 10fr + 3fr brn red   3.00   1.90
B241 SP181 12fr + 4fr purple   3.50   1.90
B242 SP181 15fr + 5fr rose car   3.75   2.25
B243 SP181 25fr + 10fr ultra   4.50   3.00
Nos. B238-B243 (6)   19.75   12.05

"Spring" — SP182

Designs: 8fr+2fr, Summer. 12fr+3fr, Autumn. 15fr+4fr, Winter.

1949, Dec. 19
B244 SP182 5fr + 1fr green   1.50   .90
B245 SP182 8fr + 2fr yel org   1.90   1.10
B246 SP182 12fr + 3fr purple   1.90   1.50
B247 SP182 15fr + 4fr dp blue   3.50   1.75
Nos. B244-B247 (4)   8.80   5.25

Postman — SP183

1950, Mar. 11
B248 SP183 12fr + 3fr dp bl   3.00   1.75
Stamp Day, Mar. 11-12, 1950. See footnote after No. 4642.

André de Chénier — SP184

8fr+3fr, J. L. David. 10fr+4fr, Lazare Carnot. 12fr+5fr, G. J. Danton. 15fr+6fr, Maximilian Robespierre. 20fr+10fr, Louis Hoche.

1950, July 10 Engr. Perf. 13
Frames in Indigo
B249 SP184 5fr + 2fr brn vio   10.00   5.25
B250 SP184 8fr + 3fr blk brn   10.00   5.50
B251 SP184 10fr + 4fr lake   11.00   5.75
B252 SP184 12fr + 5fr red brn   13.00   6.00
B253 SP184 15fr + 6fr dk grn   14.00   6.00
B254 SP184 20fr + 10fr dk vio bl   14.00   6.00
Nos. B249-B254 (6)   72.00   34.50

Alexandre Brongniart, Bust by Houdon — SP185

15fr+3fr, "L'Amour" by Etienne M. Falconet.

1950, Dec. 22
B255 SP185 8fr + 2fr ind & car   2.00   1.25
B256 SP185 15fr + 3fr red brn & car   2.25   1.25
The surtax was for the Red Cross.

Mail Car Interior — SP186

1951, Mar. 10 Unwmk. Perf. 13
B257 SP186 12fr + 3fr lilac gray   3.00   2.25
Stamp Day, Mar. 10-11, 1951.

Alfred de Musset — SP187

8fr+2fr, Eugène Delacroix. 10fr+3fr, J.-L. Gay-Lussac. 12fr+4fr, Robert Surcouf. 15fr+5fr, C. M. Talloyrand. 30fr+10fr, Napoleon I.

Frames in Dark Brown
1951, June 2
B258 SP187 5fr + 1fr dk grn   5.25   3.00
B259 SP187 8fr + 2fr vio brn   7.50   3.00
B260 SP187 10fr + 3fr grnsh black   6.75   3.00
B261 SP187 12fr + 4fr dk vio brn   6.75   3.75
B262 SP187 15fr + 5fr brn car   6.75   3.75
B263 SP187 30fr + 10fr indigo   12.00   6.00
Nos. B258-B263 (6)   45.00   22.50

Child at Prayer by Le Maître de Moulins SP188

18th Century Child by Quentin de la Tour SP189

1951, Dec. 15 Cross in Red
B264 SP188 12fr + 3fr dk brown   3.00   1.75
B265 SP189 15fr + 5fr dp ultra   3.50   2.00
The surtax was for the Red Cross.

Stagecoach of 1844 — SP190

1952, Mar. 8 Perf. 13
B266 SP190 12fr + 3fr dp green   3.50   2.25
Stamp Day, Mar. 8, 1952.

Gustave Flaubert — SP191

Portraits: 12fr+3fr, Edouard Manet. 15fr+4fr, Camille Saint-Saens. 18fr+5fr, Henri Poincaré. 20fr+6fr, Georges-Eugene Haussmann. 30fr+7fr, Adolphe Thiers.

1952, Oct. 18
Frames in Dark Brown
B267 SP191 8fr + 2fr dk blue   6.75   3.00
B268 SP191 12fr + 3fr vio blue   6.75   3.00
B269 SP191 15fr + 4fr dk grn   0.75   0.00
B270 SP191 18fr + 5fr dk brn   7.50   3.75
B271 SP191 20fr + 6fr car   8.25   4.50
B272 SP191 30fr + 7fr purple   9.00   4.50
Nos. B267-B272 (6)   45.00   21.75

Cupid from Diana Fountain Versailles SP192

15fr+5fr, Similar detail, cupid facing left.

1952, Dec. 13 Cross in Red
B273 SP192 12fr + 3fr dk grn   4.25   2.50
B274 SP192 15fr + 3fr indigo   4.25   2.50
  a. Booklet pane of 10   225.00
      Complete booklet   375.00
The surtax was for the Red Cross.

Count d'Argenson — SP193

1953, Mar. 14
B275 SP193 12fr + 3fr dp blue   2.50   1.50
Day of the Stamp. Surtax for the Red Cross.

St. Bernard — SP194

12fr+3fr, Olivier de Serres. 15fr+4fr, Jean Philippe Rameau. 18fr+5fr, Gaspard Monge. 20fr+6fr, Jules Michelet. 30fr+7fr, Marshal Hubert Lyautey.

1953, July 9
B276 SP194 8fr + 2fr ultra   6.00   3.00
B277 SP194 12fr + 3fr dk grn   6.00   3.00
B278 SP194 15fr + 4fr brn car   9.00   4.50
B279 SP194 18fr + 5fr dk blue   10.00   5.25
B280 SP194 20fr + 6fr dk car   10.00   5.25
B281 SP194 30fr + 7fr brown   10.00   5.25
Nos. B276-B281 (6)   51.00   26.25
The surtax was for the Red Cross.

Madame Vigée-Lebrun and her Daughter — SP195

Design: 15fr+5fr, "The Return from Baptism," by Louis Le Nain.

1953, Dec. 12   **Cross in Red**
B282 SP195 12fr + 3fr red brn   7.50   3.75
    a.   Bklt. pane, 4 each, gutter btwn.   85.00
B283 SP195 18fr + 5fr indigo   10.00   5.25

The surtax was for the Red Cross.

Count Antoine de La Vallette — SP196

1954, Mar. 20   **Engr.**   **Perf. 13**
B284 SP196 12fr + 3fr dp grn & choc   3.75   2.25

Stamp Day, Mar. 20, 1954.

Louis IX — SP197

Portraits: 15fr+5fr, Jacques Benigne Bossuet. 18fr+6fr, Sadi Carnot. 20fr+7fr, Antoine Bourdelle. 25fr+8fr, Dr. Emile Roux. 30fr+10fr, Paul Valéry.

1954, July 10
B285 SP197 12fr + 4fr dp bl   17.50   10.00
B286 SP197 15fr + 5fr pur   21.00   10.00
B287 SP197 18fr + 6fr dk brn   21.00   10.00
B288 SP197 20fr + 7fr crim   26.00   13.00
B289 SP197 25fr + 8fr ind   26.00   13.00
B290 SP197 30fr + 10fr dp claret   26.00   13.00
    Nos. B285-B290 (6)   137.50   69.00

See Nos. B303-B308, B312-B317.

"The Sick Child," by Eugene Carrière — SP198

Design: 15fr+5fr, "Young Girl with Doves," by Jean Baptiste Greuze.

1954, Dec. 18   **Cross in Red**
B291 SP198 12fr + 3fr vio gray & indigo   10.00   4.50
    a.   Bklt. pane, 4 each, gutter btwn.   110.00
B292 SP198 15fr + 5fr dk brn & org brn   10.50   6.00

No. B291a for 90th anniv. of the Red Cross. The surtax was for the Red Cross.

Balloon Post, 1870 — SP199

1955, Mar. 19   **Unwmk.**   **Perf. 13**
B293 SP199 12fr + 3fr multi   3.75   2.25

Stamp Day, Mar. 19-20, 1955.

King Philip II — SP200

Portraits: 15fr+6fr, Francois de Malherbé. 18fr+7fr, Sebastien de Vauban. 25fr+8fr, Charles G. de Vergennes. 30fr+9fr, Pierre S. de Laplace. 50fr+15fr, Pierre Auguste Renoir.

1955, June 11
B294 SP200 12fr + 5fr brt pur   13.50   7.50
B295 SP200 15fr + 6fr dp bl   13.50   7.50
B296 SP200 18fr + 7fr dp green   13.50   7.50
B297 SP200 25fr + 8fr gray   19.00   9.00
B298 SP200 30fr + 9fr rose brn   26.00   10.00
B299 SP200 50fr + 15fr blue grn   26.00   11.00
    Nos. B294-B299 (6)   111.50   52.50

See Nos. B321-B326.

Child with Cage by Pigalle — SP201

Design: 15fr+5fr, Child with Goose, by Boethus of Chalcedon.

1955, Dec. 17   **Cross in Red**
B300 SP201 12fr + 3fr claret   6.50   3.75
B301 SP201 15fr + 5fr dk bl   5.25   3.00
    a.   Booklet pane of 10   150.00
      Complete booklet   300.00

The surtax was for the Red Cross.

Francois of Taxis — SP202

1956, Mar. 17   **Engr.**   **Perf. 13**
B302 SP202 12fr + 3fr ultra, grn & dk brn   2.25   1.10

Stamp Day, Mar. 17-18, 1956.

Portrait Type of 1954

Portraits: No. 303, Guillaume Budé. No. B304, Jean Goujon. No. B305, Samuel de Champlain. No. B306, Jean Simeon Chardin. No. B307, Maurice Barrès. No. B308, Maurice Ravel.

1956, June 9   **Perf. 13**
B303 SP197 12fr + 3fr saph   4.00   3.00
B304 SP197 12fr + 3fr lil gray   4.00   3.00
B305 SP197 12fr + 3fr brt red   5.25   3.00
B306 SP197 15fr + 5fr green   6.75   4.50
B307 SP197 15fr + 5fr vio brn   6.75   4.50
B308 SP197 15fr + 5fr dp vio   9.00   4.50
    Nos. B303-B308 (6)   35.75   22.50

Peasant Boy by Le Nain — SP203

Design: 15fr+5fr, Gilles by Watteau.

1956, Dec. 8   **Unwmk.**   **Cross in Red**
B309 SP203 12fr + 3fr ol gray   2.25   1.10
    a.   Bklt. pane, 4 ea, gutter btwn.   40.00
B310 SP203 15fr + 5fr rose lake   2.50   1.25

The surtax was for the Red Cross.

Genoese Felucca, 1750 — SP204

1957, Mar. 16   **Perf. 13**
B311 SP204 12fr +3fr bluish gray & brn blk   1.60   1.00

Day of the Stamp, Mar. 16, 1957, and honoring the Maritime Postal Service.

Portrait Type of 1954

1957, June 15

Portraits: No. B312, Jean de Joinville. No. B313, Bernard Palissy. No. B314, Quentin de la Tour. No. B315, Hugues Félicité Robert de Lamennais. No. B316, George Sand. No. B317, Jules Guesde.

B312 SP197 12fr + 3fr ol gray & ol grn   1.90   1.10
B313 SP197 12fr + 3fr grnsh blk & grnsh bl   1.90   1.10
B314 SP197 15fr + 5fr cl & brt red   3.00   1.40
B315 SP197 15fr + 5fr ultra & ind   2.75   1.40
B316 SP197 18fr + 7fr grnsh blk & dk grn   3.25   1.60
B317 SP197 18fr + 7fr dk vio brn & red brn   3.25   1.60
    Nos. B312-B317 (6)   16.05   8.20

Blind Man and Beggar, Engraving by Jacques Callot — SP205

Design: 20fr+8fr, Women beggars.

1957, Dec. 7   **Engr.**   **Perf. 13**
B318 SP205 15fr + 7fr ultra & red   3.50   1.75
    a.   Bklt. pane, 4 ea, gutter btwn.   45.00   45.00
B319 SP205 20fr + 8fr dk vio brn & red   4.50   2.40

The surtax was for the Red Cross.

Motorized Mail Distribution SP206

1958, Mar. 15
B320 SP206 15fr + 5fr multi   1.20   .75

Stamp Day, Mar. 15.

Portrait Type of 1955

Portraits: No. B321, Joachim du Bellay. No. B322, Jean Bart. No. B323, Denis Diderot. No. B324, Gustave Courbet. 20fr+8fr, J. B. Carpeaux. 35fr+15fr, Toulouse-Lautrec.

1958, June 7   **Engr.**   **Perf. 13**
B321 SP200 12fr + 4fr yel grn   1.40   .90
B322 SP200 12fr + 4fr dk blue   1.40   .90
B323 SP200 15fr + 5fr dull cl   1.50   1.00
B324 SP200 15fr + 5fr ultra   1.60   1.10
B325 SP200 20fr + 8fr brt red   1.60   1.00
B326 SP200 35fr + 15fr green   2.10   1.10
    Nos. B321-B326 (6)   9.60   6.00

St. Vincent de Paul — SP207

Portrait: 20fr+8fr, J. H. Dunant.

1958, Dec. 6   **Unwmk.**   **Cross in Carmine**
B327 SP207 15fr + 7fr grayish grn   1.00   .45
    a.   Bklt. pane, 4 each, gutter btwn.   20.00
B328 SP207 20fr + 8fr violet   1.00   .45

The surtax was for the Red Cross. See No. B747d.

Plane Landing at Night — SP208

1959, Mar. 21
B329 SP208 20fr + 5fr sl grn, blk & rose   .45   .30

Issued for Stamp Day, Mar. 21, and to publicize night air mail service. The surtax was for the Red Cross. See No. 1089.

Geoffroi de Villehardouin and Ships — SP209

Designs: No. B331, André Le Nôtre and formal garden. No. B332, Jean Le Rond d'Alembert, books and wheel. No. B333, David d'Angers, statue and building. No. B334, M. F. X. Bichat and torch. No. B335, Frédéric Auguste Bartholdi, Statue of Liberty and Lion of Belfort.

1959, June 13   **Engr.**   **Perf. 13**
B330 SP209 15fr + 5fr vio blue   1.00   .60
B331 SP209 15fr + 5fr dk sl grn   1.00   .60
B332 SP209 20fr + 10fr olive bis   .90   .60
B333 SP209 20fr + 10fr dk gray   1.10   .65
B334 SP209 30fr + 10fr dk car rose   1.00   .65
B335 SP209 30fr + 10fr org brn   1.20   .65
    Nos. B330-B335 (6)   6.20   3.75

The surtax was for the Red Cross.

No. 927 Surcharged

1959, Dec.   **Typo.**   **Perf. 14x13½**
B336 A328 25fr + 5fr black & red   .25   .25

Surtax for the flood victims at Frejus.

Charles Michel de l'Épée — SP210

Design: 25fr+10fr, Valentin Hauy.

1959, Dec. 5   **Engr.**   **Perf. 13**
             Cross in Carmine
B337 SP210 20fr + 10fr blk & cl   1.60   1.00
    a.   Bklt. pane, 4 each, gutter btwn.   30.00
B338 SP210 25fr + 10fr dk blue & blk   2.00   1.10

The surtax was for the Red Cross.

Ship Laying Underwater Cable — SP211

1960, Mar. 12
B339 SP211 20c + 5c grnsh bl & dk bl   1.10   .90

Issued for the Day of the Stamp. The surtax went to the Red Cross.

Refugee Girl Amid Ruins — SP212

1960, Apr. 7
B340 SP212 25c + 10c grn, brn & ind   .30   .25

World Refugee Year, July 1, 1959-June 30, 1960. The surtax was for aid to refugees.

Michel de L'Hospital SP213

No. B342, Henri de la Tour D'Auvergne, Viscount of Turenne. No. B343, Nicolas Boileau (Despreaux). No. B344, Jean-Martin Charcot, M.D. No. B345, Georges Bizet. 50c+15c, Edgar Degás.

FRANCE

1960, June 11	Engr.	Perf. 13
B341 SP213 10c + 5c pur & rose car	1.10	.90
B342 SP213 20c + 10c ol & vio brn	1.90	1.60
B343 SP213 20c + 10c Prus grn & dp yel grn	1.50	1.25
B344 SP213 30c + 10c rose car & rose red	2.60	2.25
B345 SP213 30c + 10c dk bl & vio bl	3.00	2.50
B346 SP213 50c + 15c sl bl & gray	3.50	2.75
Nos. B341-B346 (6)	13.60	11.25

The surtax was for the Red Cross. See Nos. B350-B355.

Staff of the Brotherhood of St. Martin — SP214

25c+10c, St. Martin, 16th cent. wood sculpture.

1960, Dec. 3	Unwmk.	Perf. 13
B347 SP214 20c + 10c rose cl & red	2.60	2.25
a. Bklt. pane, 4 each, gutter btwn.	32.50	
B348 SP214 25c + 10c lt ultra & red	2.60	2.25

The surtax was for the Red Cross.

Letter Carrier, Paris 1760 — SP215

1961, Mar. 18		Perf. 13
B349 SP215 20c + 5c sl grn, brn & red	.60	.45

Stamp Day. Surtax for Red Cross.

Famous Men Type of 1960

Designs: 15c+5c, Bertrand Du Guesclin. No. B351, Pierre Puget. No. B352, Charles Coulomb. 30c+10c, Antoine Drouot. 45c+10c, Honoré Daumier. 50c+15c, Guillaume Apollinaire.

1961, May 20		Engr.
B350 SP213 15c + 5c red brn & blk	1.60	1.50
B351 SP213 20c + 10c dk grn & lt bl	1.50	1.50
B352 SP213 20c + 10c ver & rose car	1.75	1.50
B353 SP213 30c + 10c blk & brn org	1.75	1.60
B354 SP213 45c + 10c choc & dk grn	2.60	2.25
B355 SP213 50c + 15c dk car rose & vio	2.60	2.25
Nos. B350-B355 (6)	11.80	10.50

"Love" by Rouault — SP216

Designs from "Miserere" by Georges Rouault: 25c+10c, "The Blind Consoles the Seeing."

1961, Dec. 2		Perf. 13
B356 SP216 20c + 10c brn, blk & red	1.90	1.50
a. Bklt. pane, 4 each, gutter btwn.	30.00	
B357 SP216 25c + 10c brn, blk & red	2.25	1.90

The surtax was for the Red Cross.

Medieval Royal Messenger — SP217

1962, Mar. 17		
B358 SP217 20c + 5c rose red, bl & sepia	.60	.55

Stamp Day. Surtax for Red Cross.

Denis Papin, Scientist — SP218

Portraits: No. B360, Edme Bouchardon, sculptor. No. B361, Joseph Lakanal, educator. 30c+10c, Gustave Charpentier, composer. 45c+15c, Edouard Estaunié, writer. 50c+20c, Hyacinthe Vincent, physician and bacteriologist.

1962, June 2		Engr.
B359 SP218 15c + 5c bluish grn & dk gray	1.50	1.25
B360 SP218 20c + 10c cl brn	1.50	1.25
B361 SP218 20c + 10c grav & sl	1.50	1.25
B362 SP218 30c + 10c brt bl & ind	1.90	1.60
B363 SP218 45c + 15c org brn & choc	2.10	1.75
B364 SP218 50c + 20c grnsh bl & blk	2.00	1.75
Nos. B359-B364 (6)	10.50	8.85

The surtax was for the Red Cross.

Rosalie Fragonard by Fragonard — SP219

Design: 25c+10c, Child dressed as Pierrot.

1962, Dec. 8		Cross in Red
B365 SP219 20c + 10c redsh brown	.90	.75
a. Bklt. pane, 4 ea, gutter btwn.	32.00	
B366 SP219 25c + 10c dull grn	1.50	1.40

The surtax was for the Red Cross. For surcharges see Reunion Nos. B16-B17.

Jacques Amyot, Classical Scholar — SP220

30c+10c, Pierre de Marivaux, playwright. 50c+20c, Jacques Daviel, surgeon.

1963, Feb. 23	Unwmk.	Perf. 13
B367 SP220 20c + 10c mar, gray & pur	.75	.65
B368 SP220 30c + 10c Prus grn & mar	.75	.65
B369 SP220 50c + 20c ultra, ocher & ol	.90	.75
Nos. B367-B369 (3)	2.40	2.05

The surtax was for the Red Cross.

Roman Chariot — SP221

1963, Mar. 16		Engr.
B370 SP221 20c + 5c brn org & vio brn	.25	.25

Stamp Day. Surtax for Red Cross.

Étienne Méhul, Composer SP222

Designs: 30c+10c, Nicolas-Louis Vauquelin, chemist. 50c+20c, Alfred de Vigny, poet.

1963, May 25	Unwmk.	Perf. 13
B371 SP222 20c + 10c dp bl, dk brn & dp org	.90	.75
B372 SP222 30c + 10c mag, gray ol & blk	.75	.65
B373 SP222 50c + 20c sl, blk & brn	1.20	1.00
Nos. B371-B373 (3)	2.85	2.40

The surtax was for the Red Cross.

"Child with Grapes" by David d'Angers and Centenary Emblem — SP223

25c+10c, "The Fifer," by Edouard Manet.

1963, Dec. 9	Unwmk.	Perf. 13
B374 SP223 20c + 10c black & red	.65	.55
a. Bklt. pane, 4 each, gutter btwn.	9.00	9.00
B375 SP223 25c + 10c sl grn & red	.65	.55

Cent. of the Intl. and French Red Cross. Surtax for the Red Cross. For surcharges see Reunion Nos. B18-B19.

Post Rider, 18th Century — SP224

1964, Mar. 14		Engr.
B376 SP224 20c + 5c Prus green	.25	.25

Issued for Stamp Day.

Resistance Memorial by Watkin, Luxembourg Gardens SP225

De Gaulle's 1940 Poster "A Tous les Francais" SP226

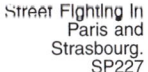

Street Fighting in Paris and Strasbourg. SP227

Designs: 20c+5c, "Déportation, concentration camp with watchtower and barbed wire. No. B379, Allied troops landing in Normandy and Provence.

1964		Engr.	Perf. 13
B377 SP225 20c + 5c slate blk		.45	.40
	Perf. 12x13		
B378 SP226 25c + 5c dk red, bl, red & blk		.75	.60
	Perf. 13		
B379 SP227 30c + 5c blk, bl & org brn		.60	.55
B380 SP227 30c + 5c org brn, cl & blk		.60	.55
B381 SP227 50c + 5c dk bl & brn		.60	.55
Nos. B377-B381 (5)		3.00	2.65

20th anniv. of liberation from the Nazis. Issue dates: Nos. B377, B381, 3/21; No. B378, 6/18; No. B379, 6/6; No. B380, 8/22.

President René Coty — SP229

Portraits: No. B383, John Calvin. No. B384, Pope Sylvester II (Gerbert).

1964	Unwmk.	Perf. 13
B382 SP229 30c + 10c dp cl & blk	.30	.25
B383 SP229 30c + 10c dk grn, blk & brn	.30	.25
B384 SP229 30c + 10c slate & cl	.30	.25
Nos. B382-B384 (3)	.90	.75

The surtax was for the Red Cross. Issued: No. B382, 4/25; No. B383, 5/25; No. B384, 6/1.

Jean Nicolas Corvisart — SP230

Portrait: 25c+10c, Dominique Larrey.

Cross in Carmine

1964, Dec. 12		Engr.
B385 SP230 20c + 10c black	.30	.25
a. Bklt. pane, 4 ea, gutter btwn.	3.50	
B386 SP230 25c + 10c black	.30	.25

Jean Nicolas Corvisart (1755-1821), physician of Napoleon I, and Dominique Larrey (1766-1842), Chief Surgeon of the Imperial Armies. The surtax was for the Red Cross. For surcharges see Reunion Nos. B20-B21.

Paul Dukas, Composer — SP231

No. B387, Duke François de La Rochefoucauld, writer. No. B388, Nicolas Poussin, painter. No. B389, Duke Charles of Orléans, poet.

1965, Feb.	Engr.	Perf. 13
B387 SP231 30c + 10c org brn & dk bl	.30	.25
B388 SP231 30c + 10c car & dk red brn	.30	.25
B389 SP231 40c + 10c dk red brn, dk red & Prus bl	.45	.40
B390 SP231 40c + 10c dk brn & sl bl	.45	.40
Nos. B387-B390 (4)	1.50	1.30

The surtax was for the Red Cross. Issued: Nos. B387, B390 2/13; Nos. B388-B389 2/20.

Packet "La Guienne" — SP232

1965, Mar. 29	Unwmk.	Perf. 13
B391 SP232 25c + 10c multi	.40	.40

Issued for Stamp Day, 1965. "La Guienne" was used for transatlantic mail service. Surtax was for the Red Cross.

Infant with Spoon by Auguste Renoir — SP233

Design: 30c+10c, Coco Writing (Renoir's son Claude).

FRANCE

1965, Dec. 11   Engr.   Perf. 13
Cross in Carmine
B392 SP233 25c + 10c slate .25 .25
   a.   Bklt. pane, 4 ea, gutter btwn. 2.75
B393 SP233 30c + 10c dull red brn .25 .25

The surtax was for the Red Cross.
For surcharges see Reunion Nos. B22-B23.

Francois Mansart and Carnavalet Palace, Paris — SP234

No. B395, St. Pierre Fourier and Basilica of St. Pierre Fourier, Mirecourt. No. B396, Marcel Proust and St. Hilaire Bridge, Illiers. No. B397, Gabriel Fauré, monument and score of "Penelope." No. B398, Elie Metchnikoff, microscope and Pasteur Institute. No. B399, Hippolyte Taine and birthplace.

1966   Engr.   Perf. 13
B394 SP234 30c + 10c dk red brn & grn .25 .25
B395 SP234 30c + 10c blk & gray grn .25 .25
B396 SP234 30c + 10c ind, sep & grn .25 .25
B397 SP234 30c + 10c bis brn & ind .25 .25
B398 SP234 30c + 10c blk & dl brn .25 .25
B399 SP234 30c + 10c grn & ol brn .25 .25
   Nos. B394-B399 (6) 1.50 1.50

The surtax was for the Red Cross.
Issued: Nos. B394-B396, 2/12; others, 6/25.

Engraver Cutting Die and Tools — SP235

1966, Mar. 19   Engr.   Perf. 13
B400 SP235 25c + 10c slate, brn pur & dp org .25 .25

Stamp Day. Surtax for Red Cross.

Angel of Victory, Verdun Fortress, Marching Troops — SP236

1966, May 28   Perf. 13
B401 SP236 30c + 5c Prus bl, ultra & dk grn .25 .25

Victory of Verdun, 50th anniversary.

First Aid on Battlefield, 1859 — SP237

No. B403, Nurse giving first aid to child, 1966.

Cross in Carmine
1966, Dec. 10   Engr.   Perf. 13
B402 SP237 25c + 10c green .25 .25
   a.   Bklt. pane, 4 ea, gutter btwn. 3.50
B403 SP237 30c + 10c slate .30 .25

The surtax was for the Red Cross.
See No. B746e. For surcharges see Reunion Nos. B24-B25.

Emile Zola — SP238

No. B405, Beaumarchais (pen name of Pierre Augustin Caron). No. B406, St. François de Sales (1567-1622). No. B407, Albert Camus (1913-1960).

1967   Engr.   Perf. 13
B404 SP238 30c + 10c sl bl & bl .30 .25
B405 SP238 30c + 10c rose brn & lil .30 .25
B406 SP238 30c + 10c dl vio & pur .30 .25
B407 SP238 30c + 10c brn & dl cl .30 .25
   Nos. B404-B407 (4) 1.20 1.00

The surtax was for the Red Cross.
Issued: Nos. B404-B405, 2/4; others, 6/24.

Letter Carrier, 1865 — SP239

1967, Apr. 8
B408 SP239 25c + 10c indigo, grn & red .30 .25

Issued for Stamp Day.

Ivory Flute Player — SP240

30c+10c, Violin player, ivory carving.

Cross in Carmine
1967, Dec. 16   Engr.   Perf. 13
B409 SP240 25c + 10c dl vio & lt brn .30 .25
   a.   Bklt. pane, 4 ea, gutter btwn. 3.50
B410 SP240 30c + 10c grn & lt brn .35 .25

The surtax was for the Red Cross.
For surcharges see Reunion Nos. B26-B27.

Ski Jump and Long Distance Skiing — SP241

Designs: 40c+10c, Ice hockey. 60c+20c, Olympic flame and snowflakes. 75c+25c, Woman figure skater. 95c+35c, Slalom.

1968, Jan. 27
B411 SP241 30c + 10c ver, gray & brn .30 .30
B412 SP241 40c + 10c lil, lem & brt mag .30 .30
B413 SP241 60c + 20c dk grn, org & brt vio .40 .40
B414 SP241 75c + 25c brt pink, yel grn & blk .50 .50
B415 SP241 95c + 35c bl, brt pink & red brn .60 .50
   Nos. B411-B415 (5) 2.10 2.00

Issued for the 10th Winter Olympic Games, Grenoble, Feb. 6-18.

Rural Mailman, 1830 — SP242

1968, Mar. 16   Engr.   Perf. 13
B416 SP242 25c + 10c multi .25 .25

Issued for Stamp Day.

François Couperin, Composer, and Instruments SP243

Portraits: No. B418, Gen. Louis Desaix de Veygoux (1768-1800) and scene showing his death at the Battle of Marengo, Italy. No. B419, Saint-Pol-Roux (pen name of Paul-Pierre Roux, 1861-1940), Christ on the Cross and ruins of Camaret-sur-Mer. No. B420, Paul Claudel (poet and diplomat, 1868-1955) and Joan of Arc at the stake.

1968   Engr.   Perf. 13
B417 SP243 30c + 10c pur & rose lil .25 .25
B418 SP243 30c + 10c dk grn & brn .25 .25
B419 SP243 30c + 10c cop red & ol bis .25 .25
B420 SP243 30c + 10c dk brn & lil .25 .25
   Nos. B417-B420 (4) 1.00 1.00

Issue dates: Nos. B417-B418, Mar. 23; Nos. B419-B420, July 6.

Spring, by Nicolas Mignard — SP244

Paintings by Nicolas Mignard; 30c+10c, Fall. No. B423, Summer. No. B424, Winter.

1968-69   Engr.   Perf. 13
Cross in Carmine
B421 SP244 25c + 10c pur & dk bl .30 .25
   a.   Bklt. pane, 4 ea #B421-B422 with gutter btwn.) 3.00
B422 SP244 30c + 10c org brn & car red .30 .30
B423 SP244 40c + 15c dk brn & brn ('69) .45 .30
   a.   Bklt. pane, 4 ea #B423, B424 with gutter btwn.) 3.50
B424 SP244 40c + 15c pur & Prus bl ('69) .45 .30
   Nos. B421-B424 (4) 1.50 1.15

The surtax was for the Red Cross.
For surcharges see Reunion Nos. B28-B31.

Mailmen's Omnibus, 1881 — SP245

1969, Mar. 15   Engr.   Perf. 13
B425 SP245 30c + 10c brn, grn & blk .25 .25

Issued for Stamp Day.
For surcharge see Reunion No. B32.

Gen. Francois Marceau — SP246

Portraits: No. B427, Charles Augustin Sainte-Beuve (1804-1869), writer. No. B428, Albert Roussel (1869-1937), musician. No. B429, Marshal Jean Lannes (1769-1809). No. B430, Georges Cuvier (1769-1832), naturalist. No. B431, André Gide, (1869-1951), writer.

1969
B426 SP246 50c + 10c brn red .40 .35
B427 SP246 50c + 10c slate bl .40 .35
B428 SP246 50c + 10c dp vio bl .40 .35
B429 SP246 50c + 10c choc .40 .35
B430 SP246 50c + 10c dp plum .40 .35
B431 SP246 50c + 10c blue grn .40 .35
   Nos. B426-B431 (6) 2.40 2.10

The surtax was for the Red Cross.
Issued: Nos. B426-B428, Mar. 24; No. B429, May 10; No. B430-B431, May 17.

Gen. Jacques Leclerc, La Madeleine and Battle SP247

1969, Aug. 23   Engr.   Perf. 13
B432 SP247 45c + 10c slate & brn .75 .60

Liberation of Paris, 8/25/44, 25th anniv.

Inscribed Liberation de Strasbourg
1969, Nov. 22   Engr.   Perf. 13
B433 SP247 70c + 10c brn, choc & olive 2.75 2.00

25th anniv. of the liberation of Strasbourg.

Philibert Delorme, Architect, and Chateau d'Anet — SP248

Designs: No. B435, Louis Le Vau (1612-1670), architect, and Vaux-le-Vicomte Chateau, Paris. No. B436, Prosper Merimée (1803-1870), writer, and Carmen. No. B437, Alexandre Dumas (1802-1870), writer, and Three Musketeers. No. B438, Edouard Branly (1844-1940), physicist, electric circuit and convent of the Carmes, Paris. No. B439, Maurice de Broglie (1875-1960), physicist, and X-ray spectrograph.

1970   Engr.   Perf. 13
B434 SP248 40c + 10c slate grn .40 .35
B435 SP248 40c + 10c dk car .40 .35
B436 SP248 40c + 10c Prus blue .40 .35
B437 SP248 40c + 10c violet bl .40 .35
B438 SP248 40c + 10c dp brown .40 .35
B439 SP248 40c + 10c dk gray .40 .35
   Nos. B434-B439 (6) 2.40 2.10

The surtax was for the Red Cross.
Issued: No. B434-B436, 2/14; others, 4/11.

City Mailman, 1830 — SP249

1970, Mar. 14
B440 SP249 40c + 10c blk, ultra & dk car rose .30 .25

Issued for Stamp Day.
For surcharge see Reunion No. B33.

"Life and Death" — SP250

1970, Apr. 4
B441 SP250 40c + 10c brt bl, ol & car rose .25 .25

Issued to publicize the fight against cancer in connection with Health Day, Apr. 7.

Marshal de Lattre de Tassigny SP251

1970, May 8   Engr.   Perf. 13
B442 SP251 40c + 10c slate & vio bl .50 .30

25th anniv. of the entry into Berlin of French troops under Marshal Jean de Lattre de Tassigny, May 8, 1945.

FRANCE 765

Lord and Lady, Dissay Chapel Fresco — SP252

No. B444, Angel holding whips, from fresco in Dissay Castle Chapel, Vienne, c. 1500.

1970, Dec. 12   Engr.   Perf. 13
Cross in Carmine
B443   SP252   40c + 15c green   .30   .25
  a.   Bklt. pane, 4 ea, gutter btwn.   12.50
B444   SP252   40c + 15c cop red   .30   .25

The surtax was for the Red Cross.
For surcharges see Reunion Nos. B34-B35.

Daniel-Francois Auber and "Fra Diavolo" Music — SP253

No. B446, Gen. Charles Diego Brosset (1898-1944), Basilica of Fourvière. No. B447, Victor Grignard (1871-1935), chemist, Nobel Prize medal. No. B448, Henri Farman (1874-1958), plane. No. B449, Gen. Charles Georges Delestraint (1879-1945), scroll. No. B450, Jean Eugène Robert-Houdin (1805-71), magician's act.

1971   Engr.   Perf. 13
B445   SP253   50c + 10c brn vio & brn   .50   .30
B446   SP253   50c + 10c dk sl grn & ol gray   .50   .30
B447   SP253   50c + 10c brn red & olive   .50   .30
B448   SP253   50c + 10c vio bl & vio   .50   .30
B449   SP253   50c + 10c pur & cl   .60   .45
B450   SP253   50c + 10c sl grn & bl grn   .60   .45
  Nos. B445-B450 (6)   3.20   2.10

The surtax was for the Red Cross.
Issued: Nos. B445-B446, 3/6; No. B447, 5/8; No. B448, 5/29; Nos. B449-B450, 10/16.

Army Post Office, 1914-1918 SP254

1971, Mar. 27   Engr.   Perf. 13
B451   SP254   50c + 10c ol, brn & bl   .40   .30

Stamp Day, 1971.
For surcharge see Reunion No. B36.

Girl with Dog, by Greuze — SP255

Design: 50c+10c, "The Dead Bird," by Jean-Baptiste Greuze (1725-1805).

1971, Dec. 11   Cross in Carmine
B452   SP255   30c + 10c violet bl   .55   .45
  a.   Bklt. pane, 4 each, gutter btwn.   6.00
B453   SP255   50c + 10c dp car   .55   .45

The surtax was for the Red Cross.
For surcharges see Reunion Nos. B37-B38.

Aristide Bergès (1833-1904) — SP256

No. B455, Paul de Chomedey (1612-76), founder of Montreal, and arms of Neuville-sur-Vanne. No. B456, Edouard Belin (1876-1963), inventor. No. B457, Louis Blériot (1872-1936), aviation pioneer. No. B458, Adm. François Joseph, Count de Grasse (1722-88), hero of the American Revolution. No. B459, Théophile Gautier (1811-72), writer.

1972   Engr.   Perf. 13
B454   SP256   50c + 10c blk & grn   .50   .40
B455   SP256   50c + 10c blk & bl   .50   .40
B456   SP256   50c + 10c blk & lil rose   .50   .40
B457   SP256   50c + 10c red & blk   .50   .40
B458   SP256   50c + 10c org & blk   .50   .40
B459   SP256   50c + 10c blk & brn   .50   .40
  Nos. B454-B459 (6)   3.00   2.40

The surtax was for the Red Cross.
Issued: Nos. B454-B455, 2/19; No. B456, 6/24; No. B457, 7/1; Nos. B458-B459, 9/9.

Rural Mailman, 1894 — SP257

1972, Mar. 18   Engr.   Perf. 13
B460   SP257   50c + 10c bl, yel & ol gray   .50   .40

Stamp Day 1972.
For surcharge see Reunion No. B39.

Nicolas Desgenettes — SP258

Designs: 30c+10c, René Nicolas Dufriche, Baron Desgenettes, M.D. (1762-1837). 50c+10c, François Joseph Broussais, M.D. (1772-1838).

1972, Dec. 16   Engr.   Perf. 13
B461   SP258   30c + 10c sl grn & red   .40   .30
  a.   Bklt. pane, 4 ea, gutter btwn.   7.00
B462   SP258   50c + 10c red   .45   .40

The surtax was for the Red Cross.
See No. B747b. For surcharges see Reunion Nos. B40-B41.

Tony Garnier (1869-1948), architect — SP259

No. B463, Gaspard de Coligny (1519-1572), admiral and Huguenot leader. No. B464, Ernest Renan (1823-1892), philologist and historian. No. B465, Alberto Santos Dumont (1873-1932), Brazilian aviator. No. B466, Gabrielle-Sidonie Colette (1873-1954), writer. No. B467, René Duguay-Trouin (1673-1736), naval commander. No. B468, Louis Pasteur (1822-1895), chemist, bacteriologist. No. B469, Tony Garnier (1869-1948), architect.

1973   Engr.   Perf. 13
B463   SP259   50c + 10c multi   .50   .40
B464   SP259   50c + 10c multi   .50   .40
B465   SP259   50c + 10c multi   .50   .40
B466   SP259   50c + 10c multi   .50   .40
B467   SP259   50c + 10c multi   .50   .40
B468   SP259   50c + 10c multi   .50   .40
B469   SP259   50c + 10c multi   .50   .40
  Nos. B463-B469 (7)   3.50   2.80

Issued: No. B463, 2/17; No. B464, 4/28; No. B465, 5/26; No. B466, 6/2; No. B467, 6/9; No. B468, 10/6; No. B469, 11/17.

Mail Coach, 1835 — SP260

1973, Mar. 24   Engr.   Perf. 13
B470   SP260   50c + 10c grnsh blue   .40   .25

Stamp Day, 1973.
For surcharge see Reunion No. B42.

Mary Magdalene — SP261

50c+10c, Mourning woman. Designs are from 15th cent. Tomb of Tonnerre.

1973, Dec. 1
B471   SP261   30c + 10c sl grn & red   .40   .30
  a.   Bklt. pane, 4 each, gutter btwn.   6.00
B472   SP261   50c + 10c dk gray & red   .45   .40

Surtax was for the Red Cross.
For surcharges see Reunion Nos. B43-B44.

St. Louis-Marie de Montfort — SP262

Portraits: No. B474, Francis Poulenc (1899-1963), composer. No. B475, Jules Barbey d'Aurevilly (1808-1889), writer. No. B476, Jean Giraudoux (1882-1944), writer.

1974, Feb. 23   Engr.   Perf. 13
B473   SP262   50c + 10c multi   .50   .40
B474   SP262   50c + 10c multi   .50   .40
B475   SP262   80c + 15c multi   .60   .50
B476   SP262   80c + 15c multi   .60   .50
  Nos. B473-B476 (4)   2.20   1.80

Issue dates: No. B473, Mar. 9; No. B474, July 20; Nos. B475-B476, Nov. 16.

Automatically Sorted Letters — SP263

1974, Mar. 9   Engr.   Perf. 13
B477   SP263   50c + 10c multi   .30   .25

Stamp Day 1974. Automatic letter sorting center, Orleans-la-Source, opened 1/30/73.
For surcharge see Reunion No. B45.

Order of Liberation and 5 Honored Cities SP264

1974, June 15   Engr.   Perf. 13
B478   SP264   1fr + 10c multi   .55   .30

30th anniv. of liberation from the Nazis.

"Summer" — SP265

Designs: B481, "Spring" (girl on swing). B482, "Fall" (umbrella and rabbits).

1974, Nov. 30   Engr.   Perf. 13
B479   SP265   60c + 15c multi   .45   .40
  a.   Bklt. pane, 4 ea, gutter btwn.   6.00
B480   SP266   80c + 15c multi   .45   .40

For surcharges see Reunion Nos. B46-B47.

"Winter" — SP266

1975, Nov. 29
B481   SP265   60c + 15c multi   .40   .30
  a.   Bklt. pane, 4 ea, gutter btwn.   4.75
B482   SP266   80c + 20c multi   .50   .40

Surtax was for the Red Cross.

Dr. Albert Schweitzer SP267

Edmond Michelet SP268

André Siegfried and Map — SP269

No. B483, Albert Schweitzer (1875-1965), medical missionary. No. B484, Edmond Michelet (1899-1970), Resistance hero, statesman. No. B485, Robert Schuman (1886-1963), promoter of United Europe. No. B486, Eugene Thomas (1903-69), minister of PTT. No. B487, André Siegfried (1875-1959), political science professor, writer.

1975   Engr.   Perf. 13
B483   SP267   80c + 20c multi   .50   .40
B484   SP268   80c + 20c bl & ind   .50   .40
B485   SP268   80c + 20c blk & ind   .50   .40
B486   SP268   80c + 20c blk & sl   .50   .40
B487   SP269   80c + 20c blk & bl   .50   .40
  Nos. B483-B487 (5)   2.50   2.00

Issued: No. B483, 1/11; No. B484, 2/22; No. B485, 5/10; No. B486, 6/28; No. B487, 11/15.

Second Republic Mailman's Badge — SP270

1975, Mar. 8   Photo.
B488   SP270   80c + 20c multi   .45   .35

Stamp Day.

"Sage" type of 1876 — SP271

1976, Mar. 13   Engr.   Perf. 13
B489   SP271   80c + 20c blk & lil   .40   .35

Stamp Day 1976.

Marshal A. J. de Moncey — SP272

No. B491, Max Jacob (1876-1944), Dadaist writer, by Picasso. No. B492, Jean Mounet-Sully (1841-1916), actor. No. B493, Gen. Pierre Daumesnil (1776-1832). No. B494, Eugène Fromentin (1820-1876), painter.

766　　　　　　　　　　　　　　　　　　　　FRANCE

1976		Engr.		Perf. 13
B490	SP272	80c + 20c multi	.40	.30
B491	SP272	80c + 20c red brn & ol	.40	.30
B492	SP272	80c + 20c multi	.40	.30
B493	SP272	1fr + 20c multi	.50	.30
B494	SP272	1fr + 20c multi	.50	.30
Nos. B490-B494 (5)			2.20	1.50

Issued: No. B490, 5/22; No. B491, 7/22; No. B492, 8/28; No. B493, 9/4; No. B494, 9/25.

Anna de Noailles — SP273

1976, Nov. 6		Engr.		Perf. 13
B495	SP273	1fr + 20c multi	.50	.30

Anna de Noailles (1876-1933), writer & poet.

St. Barbara — SP274

Design: 1fr+25c, Cimmerian Sibyl. Sculptures from Brou Cathedral.

1976, Nov. 20		Cross in Carmine		
B496	SP274	80c + 20c violet	.45	.40
a.	Bklt. pane, 4 ea, gutter btwn.		6.00	
B497	SP274	1fr + 25c dk brown	.65	.45

Surtax was for the Red Cross.

Marckolsheim Relay Station Sign — SP275

1977, Mar. 26		Engr.		Perf. 13
B498	SP275	1fr + 20c multi	.40	.25

Stamp Day.

Edouard Herriot, Statesman and Writer — SP276

Designs: No. B500, Abbé Breuil (1877-1961), archaeologist. No. B501, Guillaume de Machault (1305-1377), poet and composer. No. B502, Charles Cross (1842-1888).

1977			Engr.	Perf. 13
B499	SP276	1fr + 20c blk	.40	.30
B500	SP276	1fr + 20c multi	.40	.30
B501	SP276	1fr + 20c multi	.40	.30
B502	SP276	1fr + 20c multi	.40	.30
Nos. B499-B502 (4)			1.60	1.20

Issued: No. B499, 10/8; No. B500, 10/15; No. B501, 11/12; No. B502, 12/3.

Christmas Figurine, Provence — SP277

1fr+25c, Christmas figurine (woman), Provence.

1977, Nov. 26				
B503	SP277	80c + 20c red & ind	.40	.30
a.	Bklt. pane, 4 ea, gutter btwn.		4.50	
B504	SP277	1fr + 25c red & sl grn	.45	.30

Surtax was for the Red Cross.

Marie Noel, Writer — SP278

No. B506, Georges Bernanos (1888-1948), writer. No. B507, Leon Tolstoy (1828-1910), Russian writer. No. B508, Charles Marie Leconte de Lisle (1818-1894), poet. No. B509, Voltaire (1694-1778) and Jean Jacques Rousseau (1712-1778). No. B510, Claude Bernard (1813-1878), physiologist.

1978		Engr.		Perf. 13
B505	SP278	1fr + 20c multi	.40	.30
B506	SP278	1fr + 20c multi	.40	.30
B507	SP278	1fr + 20c multi	.40	.30
B508	SP278	1fr + 20c multi	.40	.30
B509	SP278	1fr + 20c multi	.40	.30
B510	SP278	1fr + 20c multi	.40	.30
Nos. B505-B510 (6)			2.40	1.80

Issued: No. B505, 2/11; No. B506, 2/18; No. B507, 4/15; No. B508, 3/26; No. B509, 7/1; No. B510, 9/16.

Mail Collection, 1900 — SP279

1978, Apr. 8		Engr.		Perf. 13
B511	SP279	1fr + 20c multi	.40	.30

Stamp Day 1978.

SP280

1fr+25c, The Hare & the Tortoise. 1.20fr+30c, The City Mouse & the Country Mouse.

1978, Dec. 2		Engr.		Perf. 13
B512	SP280	1fr + 25c multi	.60	.50
a.	Bklt. pane, 4 ea, gutter btwn.		6.00	
B513	SP280	1.20fr + 30c multi	.65	.55

Surtax was for the Red Cross.

SP281

No. B514, Ladislas Marshal de Berchény (1689-1778). No. B515, Leon Jouhaux (1879-1954), labor leader. No. B516, Peter Abelard (1079-1142), theologian and writer. No. B517, Georges Courteline (1860-1929), humorist. No. B518, Simone Weil (1909-1943), social philosopher. No. B519, André Malraux (1901-1976), novelist.

1979		Engr.		Perf. 13
B514	SP281	1.20fr + 30c multi	.50	.40
B515	SP281	1.20fr + 30c multi	.50	.40
B516	SP281	1.20fr + 30c multi	.50	.40
B517	SP281	1.20fr + 30c multi	.50	.40
B518	SP281	1.30fr + 30c multi	.60	.40
B519	SP281	1.30fr + 30c multi	.60	.40
Nos. B514-B519 (6)			3.20	2.40

Issued: No. B514, 1/13; No. B515, 5/12; No. B516, 6/9; No. B517, 6/25; No. B518, 11/12; No. B519, 11/26.

General Post Office, from 1908 Post Card — SP282

1979, Mar. 10		Engr.		Perf. 13
B520	SP282	1.20fr + 30c multi	.50	.30

Stamp Day 1979.

Woman, Stained-Glass Window — SP283

Stained-glass windows, Church of St. Joan of Arc, Rouen: 1.30fr+30c, Simon the Magician.

1979, Dec. 1		Engr.		Perf. 13
B521	SP283	1.10fr + 30c multi	.50	.40
B522	SP283	1.30fr + 30c multi	.60	.45
a.	Bklt. pane, 4 each #521-522, with gutter btwn., perf. 12½x13		6.00	

Surtax was for the Red Cross.

Eugene Viollet le Duc (1814-1879), Architect SP284

Jean-Marie de Le Mennais (1780-1860), Priest and Educator SP285

Designs: No. B524, Jean Monnet (1888-1979), economist and diplomat. No. B526, Frederic Mistral (1830-1914), poet. No. B527, Saint-John Perse (Alexis Leger, 1887-1975), poet and diplomat. No. B528, Pierre Paul de Riquet (1604-1680), canal builder.

1980		Engr.		Perf. 13
B523	SP284	1.30fr + 30c multi	.60	.55
B524	SP285	1.30fr + 30c multi	.60	.55
B525	SP285	1.40fr + 30c blue	.60	.55
B526	SP285	1.40fr + 30c black	.60	.55
B527	SP285	1.40fr + 30c multi	.60	.55
B528	SP284	1.40fr + 30c multi	.60	.55
Nos. B523-B528 (6)			3.60	3.30

Issued: No. B523, Feb. 16; Nos. B524-B526, Sept. 6; Nos. B527-B528, Oct. 11.

The Letter to Melie, by Avati, Stamp Day, 1980 SP286

1980, Mar. 8			Photo.	
B529	SP286	1.30fr + 30c multi	.50	.40

Filling the Granaries, Choir Stall Detail, Amiens Cathedral — SP287

No. B531, Grapes from the Promised Land.

1980, Dec. 6		Engr.		Perf. 13
B530	SP287	1.20fr + 30c red & dk red brn	.50	.40
B531	SP287	1.40fr + 30c red & dk red brn	.60	.40
a.	Bklt. pane, 4 #B530-B531, with gutter btwn., perf. 12½x13		6.50	

SP288

No. B532, Louis Armand (1905-71), railway engineer. No. B533, Louis Jouvet (1887-1951), theater director. No. B534, Marc Boegner (1881-1970), peace worker. No. B535, Sister Anne-Marie Javouhey (1779-1851), founded congregation of St. Joseph of Cluny. No. B536, Jacques Offenbach (1819-80), composer. No. B537, Pierre Teilhard de Chardin (1881-1955), philosopher.

Nos. B532-B533, B537 vert.

1981		Engr.		Perf. 13
B532	SP288	1.20 + 30c multi	.55	.45
B533	SP288	1.20 + 30c multi	.55	.45
B534	SP288	1.40 + 30c multi	.55	.45
B535	SP288	1.40 + 30c multi	.55	.45
B536	SP288	1.40 + 30c multi	.55	.45
B537	SP288	1.40 + 30c multi	.55	.45
Nos. B532-B537 (6)			3.30	2.70

Issued: No. B532, 5/23; No. B533, 6/13; No. B534, 11/14; No. B535, 2/7; No. B536, 2/14; No. B537, 5/23.

The Love Letter, by Goya SP289

1981, Mar. 7			Perf. 13x12½
B538	SP289	1.40 + 30c multi	.65	.60

Stamp Day 1981.

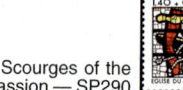

Scourges of the Passion — SP290

Stained-glass Windows, Church of the Sacred Heart, Audincourt: 1.60fr+30c, "Peace."

1981, Dec. 5		Photo.		Perf. 13
B539	SP290	1.40 + 30c multi	.60	.55
B540	SP290	1.60 + 30c multi	.75	.65
a.	Bklt. pane, 4 ea, gutter btwn.		6.00	

Guillaume Postel (1510-1581), Theologian SP291

No. B542, Henri Mondor (1885-1962), physician. No. B543, Andre Chantemesse (1851-1919), Scientist. No. B544, Louis Pergaud (1882-1915), writer. No. B545, Robert Debre (1882-1978), writer. No. B546, Gustave Eiffel (1832-1923), engineer.

1982		Engr.		Perf. 13
B541	SP291	1.40fr + 30c multi	.60	.50
B542	SP291	1.40fr + 30c dk brn & dk bl	.60	.50
B543	SP291	1.60fr + 30c multi	.60	.50
B544	SP291	1.60fr + 40c multi	.60	.50
B545	SP291	1.60fr + 40c dk blue	.65	.60
B546	SP291	1.80fr + 40c sepia	.65	.60
Nos. B541-B546 (6)			3.70	3.20

See Nos. 6410d-6410f for Eiffel stamps with euro denominations.

Woman Reading, by Picasso SP292

1982, Mar. 27			Perf. 13x12½
B547	SP292	1.60 + 40c multi	.75	.60

Stamp Day.

FRANCE

SP293

Jules Verne books: 1.60fr+30c, Five Weeks in a Balloon. 1.80fr+40c, 20,000 Leagues under the Sea.

1982, Nov. 20   **Perf. 13**

B548	SP293	1.60 + 30c multi	.65	.50
B549	SP293	1.80 + 40c multi	.75	.60
a.	Bklt. pane, 4 each #B548-B549, with gutter btwn., perf. 12½x13		8.00	

Surtax was for Red Cross.

SP294

No. B550, Andre Messager (1853-1929). No. B551, J.A. Gabriel (1698-1782), architect. No. B552, Hector Berlioz (1803-69), composer. No. B553, Max Fouchet (1913-80). No. B554, Rene Cassin (1887-1976). No. B555, Stendhal (Marie Henri Beyle, 1783-1842).

1983   **Engr.**   **Perf. 12½x13**

B550	SP294	1.60 + 30c multi	.65	.60
B551	SP294	1.60 + 30c multi	.65	.60
B552	SP294	1.80 + 40c dp lil & blk	.65	.60
B553	SP294	1.80 + 40c multi	.75	.60
B554	SP294	2fr + 40c multi	.80	.65
B555	SP294	2fr + 40c multi	.80	.65
	Nos. B550-B555 (6)		4.30	3.70

Issued: No. B550, 1/15; No. B551, 4/16; No. B552, 1/22; No. B553, 4/30; No. B554, 6/25; No. B555, 11/12.

Man Dictating a Letter, by Rembrandt — SP295

Photo. & Engr.

1983, Feb. 26   **Perf. 13X12½**

B556	SP295	1.80 + 40c multi	.90	.60

Stamp Day.

Virgin with Child, Baillon, 14th Cent. — SP296

Design: No. B558, Virgin with Child, Genainville, 16th Cent.

1983, Nov. 26   **Engr.**   **Perf. 13**

B557	SP296	1.60 + 40c shown	.65	.15
B558	SP296	2fr + 40c multi	.75	.40
a.	Bklt. pane of 4, #B557-B558, with gutter btwn., perf. 12½x13		6.50	

Emile Littre (1801-1881), Physician SP297

No. B560, Jean Zay (1904-44). No. B561, Pierre Corneille (1606-1684). No. B562, Gaston Bachelard (1884-1962). No. B563, Jean Paulhan (1884-1968). No. B564, Evariste Galois (1811-1832).

1984   **Engr.**   **Perf. 13**

B559	SP297	1.60fr + 40c plum & blk	.65	.60
B560	SP297	1.60fr + 40c dk grn & blk	.65	.60
B561	SP297	1.70fr + 40c dp vio & blk	.75	.60
B562	SP297	2fr + 40c gray & blk	.75	.60
B563	SP297	2.10fr + 40c dk brn & blk	.90	.65
B564	SP297	2.10fr + 40c ultra & blk	.90	.65
	Nos. B559-B564 (6)		4.60	3.70

SP298

Diderot Holding a Letter, by L.M. Van Loo.

1984, Mar. 17   **Engr.**   **Perf. 12½x13**

B565	SP298	2fr + 40c multi	.90	.60

SP299

The Rose Basket, by Caly.

1984, Nov. 24   **Photo.**   **Perf. 12½x13**

B566	SP299	2.10fr + 50c pnksh (basket) & multi	.80	.60
a.	Salmon (basket) & multi, perf. 13½x13		.90	.60
b.	As "a," bklt. pane of 10 + 2 labels		9.00	

Surtax was for the Red Cross.

Jules Romains (1885-1972) SP300

Authors: No. B568, Jean-Paul Sartre (1905-1980). No. B569, Romain Rolland (1866-1944). No. B570, Roland Dorgeles (1885-1973). No. B571, Victor Hugo (1802-1885). No. B572, Francois Mauriac (1885-1970).

1985, Feb. 23   **Engr.**   **Perf. 13**

B567	SP300	1.70fr + 40c	1.10	.90
B568	SP300	1.70fr + 40c	1.10	.90
B569	SP300	1.70fr + 40c	1.10	.90
B570	SP300	2.10fr + 50c	1.25	1.00
B571	SP300	2.10fr + 50c	1.25	1.00
B572	SP300	2.10fr + 50c	1.25	1.00
a.	Bklt. pane, 1 each + 2 labels, perf. 15x14½		15.00	
	Nos. B567-B572 (6)		7.05	5.70

SP301

Stamp Day: Canceling apparatus invented by Eugene Daguin (1849-1888).

1985, Mar. 16   **Engr.**   **Perf. 12½x13**

B573	SP301	2.10fr + 50c brn blk & bluish gray	.90	.60

SP302

Issenheim Altarpiece retable.

1985, Nov. 23   **Photo.**

B574	SP302	2.20fr + 50c multi	.80	.60
a.	As "b," bklt. pane of 10		8.00	
b.	Perf. 13½x13		.90	.60

Surtax for the Red Cross.

SP303

Famous men: No. B575, Francois Arago (1786-1853), physician, politician. No. B576, Henri Moissan (1852-1907), chemist. No. B577, Henri Fabre (1882-1984), engineer. No. B578, Marc Seguin (1786-1875), engineer. No. B579, Paul Heroult (1863-1914), chemist.

1986, Feb. 22   **Engr.**   **Perf. 13**

B575	SP303	1.80fr + 40c multi	.75	.65
B576	SP303	1.80fr + 40c multi	.75	.65
B577	SP303	1.80fr + 40c multi	.75	.65
B578	SP303	2.20fr + 50c multi	.80	.65
B579	SP303	2.20fr + 50c multi	.80	.65
a.	Bklt. pane of 5, #B575-B579, + 3 labels		6.00	
	Nos. B575-B579 (5)		3.85	3.25

SP304

1986, Mar. 1   **Engr.**   **Perf. 13x12½**

B580	SP304	2.20fr + 50c brn blk	4.50	4.50

Pierre Cot (1895-1977).

Mail Britzska — SP305

1986, Apr. 5   **Perf. 13**

B581	SP305	2.20fr + 60c pale tan & dk vio brn	.85	.60

Booklet Stamp

B582	SP305	2.20fr + 60c buff & blk	.85	.60
a.	Bklt. pane of 6 + 2 labels		6.00	

Stamp Day. See Nos. B590-B591, B599-B600, B608-B609.

Stained Glass Window (detail), by Vieira da Silva, St. Jacques of Reims Church, Marne — SP306

1986, Nov. 24   **Photo.**   **Perf. 12½x13**

B583	SP306	2.20fr + 60c multi	.85	.60
a.	As "b," bklt. pane of 10		9.00	
b.	Perf. 13½x13		.90	.60

Surtaxed to benefit the natl. Red Cross.

Physicians and Biologists SP307

No. B584, Charles Richet (1850-1935). No. B585, Eugene Jamot (1879-1937). No. B586, Bernard Halpern (1904-1978). No. B587, Alexandre Yersin (1863-1943). No. B588, Jean Hostand (1894-1977). No. B589, Jacques Monod (1910-1976).

1987, Feb. 21   **Engr.**   **Perf. 13**

B584	SP307	1.90fr + 50c deep ultra	.75	.60
B585	SP307	1.90fr + 50c dull lil	.75	.60
B586	SP307	1.90fr + 50c grnsh gray	.75	.60
B587	SP307	2.20fr + 50c grnsh gray	.85	.60
B588	SP307	2.20fr + 50c deep ultra	.85	.60
B589	SP307	2.20fr + 50c dull lil	.85	.65
a.	Bklt. pane of 6, #B584-B589		5.00	
	Nos. B584-B589 (6)		4.80	3.75

Stamp Day Type of 1986

Stamp Day 1987: Berline carriage.

1987, Mar. 14   **Engr.**

B590	SP305	2.20fr + 60c buff & sepia	.85	.60

Booklet Stamp

B591	SP305	2.20fr + 60c pale & dk bl	.85	.60
a.	Bklt. pane of 6 + 2 labels		6.00	

Flight Into Egypt, Retable by Melchior Broederlam — SP308

1987, Nov. 21   **Photo.**   **Perf. 12½x13**

B592	SP308	2.20fr + 60c multi	.85	.60
a.	As "b," bklt. pane of 10 + 2 labels		8.00	
b.	Perf. 13½x13		.90	.60

Surtaxed to benefit the Red Cross.

Explorers SP309

Profiles & maps: No. B593, Marquis Abraham Duquesne (1610-1688), naval commander. No. B594, Pierre Andre de Suffren (1729-1788). No. B595, Jean-Francois de La Perouse (1741-1788). No. B596, Mahe de La Bourdonnais (1699-1753). No. B597, Louis-Antoine de Bougainville (1729-1811). No. B598, Jules Dumont d'Urville (1790-1842).

1988, Feb. 20   **Engr.**   **Perf. 13**

B593	SP309	2fr + 50c multi	.75	.50
B594	SP309	2fr + 50c multi	.75	.50
B595	SP309	2fr + 50c multi	.75	.50
B596	SP309	2.20fr + 50c multi	.85	.60
B597	SP309	2.20fr + 50c multi	.85	.60
B598	SP309	2.20fr + 50c multi	.85	.60
a.	Bklt. pane of 6, #B593-B598		4.50	

Stamp Day Type of 1986

Stamp Day 1988: Postal coach.

1988, Mar. 29   **Engr.**

B599	SP305	2.20fr + 60c dk lilac	.85	.60

Booklet Stamp

B600	SP305	2.20fr + 60c sepia	.85	.60
a.	Bklt. pane of 6 + 2 labels		5.00	

Intl. Red Cross, 125th Anniv. — SP310

1988, Nov. 19   **Engr.**   **Perf. 12½x13**

B601	SP310	2.20fr + 60c multi	.85	.60
a.	As "b," bklt. pane of 10+2 labels		8.00	
b.	Perf. 13½x13		.85	.75

See No. B747c.

Revolution Leaders and Heroes — SP311

No. B602, Emmanuel Joseph Sieyès (1748-1836). No. B603, Honore Gabriel Riqueti, Comte de Mirabeau (1749-91). No. B604, Louis Marie de Noailles (1756-1804). No. B605, Lafayette. No. B606, Antoine Pierre Joseph Marie Barnave (1761-93). No. B607, Jean Baptiste Drouet (1763 1824).

1989, Feb. 25   **Engr.**   **Perf. 13**

B602	SP311	2.20fr + 50c multi	.85	.60
B603	SP311	2.20fr + 50c multi	.85	.60
B604	SP311	2.20fr + 50c multi	.85	.60
B605	SP311	2.20fr + 50c multi	.85	.60
B606	SP311	2.20fr + 50c multi	.85	.60
B607	SP311	2.20fr + 50c multi	.85	.60
a.	Bklt. pane of 6, 1 each + 2 labels		5.00	

French Revolution, bicent.

Stamp Day Type of 1986

Design: Paris-Lyon stagecoach.

768 FRANCE

1989, Apr. 15 Engr. Perf. 13
B608 SP305 2.20fr +60c pale bl & dk bl .85 .60

Booklet Stamp
B609 SP305 2.20fr +60c pale lil & pur .85 .60
a. Bklt. pane of 6 + 2 labels 6.00

Stamp Day 1989.

Bird From a Silk Tapestry, Lyon, 18th Cent. — SP312

1989, Nov. 18 Photo. Perf. 12½x13
B610 SP312 2.30fr +60c multi .85 .60
a. As "b," bklt. pane of 10 9.00
b. Perf. 13½x13 .90 .60

Surtax for the natl. Red Cross.

1992 Winter Olympics, Albertville SP313

1990, Feb. 9 Engr. Perf. 13
B611 SP313 2.30fr +20c red, bl & blk .90 .70

See Nos. B621-B627, B636-B637, B639.

Stamp Day — SP314

1990, Mar. 17 Photo.
B612 SP314 2.30fr +60c ultra, bl & brt yel .90 .70

Booklet Stamp
B613 SP314 2.30fr +60c ultra, grn, yel & brt grn .90 .70
a. Bklt. pane of 6 + 2 labels 6.00

SP315

Quimper or Brittany Ware Faience plate.

1990, May 5 Photo. Perf. 12½x13
B614 SP315 2.30fr +60c multi .90 .70
a. As "b," bklt. pane of 10+2 labels 9.00
b. Perf. 13½x13 .95 .70

Surcharge benefited the Red Cross.

SP316

No. B615, Aristide Bruant. No. B616, Maurice Chevalier. No. B617, Tino Rossi. No. B618, Edith Piaf. No. B619, Jacques Brel. No. B620, Georges Brassens.

1990, June 16 Photo. Perf. 13
B615 SP316 2.30fr +50c multi .90 .70
B616 SP316 2.30fr +50c multi .90 .70
B617 SP316 2.30fr +50c multi .90 .70
B618 SP316 2.30fr +50c multi .90 .70
B619 SP316 2.30fr +50c multi .90 .70
B620 SP316 2.30fr +50c multi .90 .70
a. Bklt. pane, 1 each +2 labels 5.00

Albertville Olympic Type
Designs: No. B621, Ski jumping. No. B622, Speed skiing. No. B623, Slalom skiing. No. B624, Cross-country skiing. No. B625, Ice hockey. No. B626, Luge. No. B627, Curling.

1990-91 Engr. Perf. 13
B621 SP313 2.30fr +20c multi .90 .70
B622 SP313 2.30fr +20c multi .90 .70
B623 SP313 2.30fr +20c multi .90 .70
B624 SP313 2.30fr +20c multi .90 .70
B625 SP313 2.30fr +20c multi .90 .70
B626 SP313 2.50fr +20c multi .90 .70
B627 SP313 2.50fr +20c multi .90 .70
Nos. B621-B627 (7) 6.30 4.90

Issued: No. B621, 12/22/90; No. B622, 12/29/90; No. B623, 1/19/91; No. B624, 2/2/91; No. B625, 2/9/91; No. B626, 3/2/91; No. B627, 4/20/91.

No. B624 inscribed "La Poste 1992."

Paul Eluard (1895-1952) SP317

Poets: No. B629, Andre Breton (1896-1966). No. B630, Louis Aragon (1897-1982). No. B631, Francis Ponge (1899-1988). No. B632, Jacques Prevert (1900-1977). No. B633, Rene Char (1907-1988).

1991, Feb. 23 Engr. Perf. 12½x13
B628 SP317 2.50fr +50c multi 1.00 .75
B629 SP317 2.50fr +50c multi 1.00 .75
B630 SP317 2.50fr +50c multi 1.00 .75
B631 SP317 2.50fr +50c multi 1.00 .75
B632 SP317 2.50fr +50c multi 1.00 .75
B633 SP317 2.50fr +50c multi 1.00 .75
a. Bklt. pane, 1 each +2 labels, perf. 13 6.00

Stamp Day — SP318

Designs: No. B634, Postal sorting with blue machine. No. B635, Postal sorting with purple machine.

1991, Mar. 16 Photo. Perf. 13
B634 SP318 2.50fr +60c multi 1.00 .75
B635 SP318 2.50fr +60c multi 1.00 .75
a. Bklt. pane of 6 + 2 labels 6.00

Winter Olympics Type of 1990
No. B636, Acrobatic skiing. No. B637, Alpine skiing.

1991 Engr. Perf. 13
B636 SP313 2.50fr +20c multi 1.00 .75
B637 SP313 2.50fr +20c multi 1.00 .75

Issued: No. B636, Aug. 3; No. B637, Aug. 17.

Nos. B636-B637 inscribed "La Poste 1992."

The Harbor of Toulon by Francois Nardi — SP319

1991, Dec. 2 Photo. Perf. 13x12½
B638 SP319 2.50fr +60c multi 1.00 .75
a. Perf. 13x13½ 1.10 .75
b. As "a," bklt. pane of 10 + 2 labels 9.00

Surtax for the Red Cross.

Winter Olympics Type of 1990
Miniature Sheet
No. B639: a, like #B611. b, like #B621. c, like #B622. d, like #B623. e, like #B624. f, like #B625.

1992, Feb. 8 Engr. Perf. 13
B639 Sheet of 10 + label 15.00 15.00
a.-f. SP313 2.50fr +20c multi 1.00 .75

No. B639 contains one each B626-B627, B636-B637, B639a-B639f. Central label is litho.

Stamp Day — SP320

Designs: Careers in Post, Welcome — No. B640, gray people. No. B641, red people.

1992, Mar. 7 Litho. Perf. 13
B640 SP320 2.50fr +60c gray people 1.00 .75

Booklet Stamp
Photo.
B641 SP320 2.50fr +60c red people 1.00 .75
a. Bklt. pane of 6 + 2 labels 6.00

SP321

Composers: No. B642, Cesar Franck (1822-1890). No. B643, Erik Satie (1866-1925). No. B644, Florent Schmitt (1870-1958). No. B645, Arthur Honegger (1892-1955). No. B646, Georges Auric (1899-1983). No. B647, Germaine Tailleferre (1892-1983).

1992, Apr. 11 Photo. Perf. 13
B642 SP321 2.50fr +50c multi 1.00 .75
B643 SP321 2.50fr +50c multi 1.00 .75
B644 SP321 2.50fr +50c multi 1.00 .75
B645 SP321 2.50fr +50c multi 1.00 .75
B646 SP321 2.50fr +50c multi 1.00 .75
B647 SP321 2.50fr +50c multi 1.00 .75
a. Bklt. pane of 6, #B642-B647 6.00

SP322

1992, Nov. 28 Photo. Perf. 13½x13
B648 SP322 2.50fr +60c multi 1.00 .70
a. Bklt. pane of 10 + 2 labels 9.00

Mutual Aid, Strasbourg. Surtax for the Red Cross.

Writers — SP323

No. B649, Guy de Maupassant (1850-93). No. B650, Alain (Emile Chartier) (1868-1951). No. B651, Jean Cocteau (1889-1963). No. B652, Marcel Pagnol (1895-1974). No. B653, Andre Chamson (1900-83). No. B654, Marguerite Yourcenar (1903-87).

1993, Apr. 24 Photo. Perf. 13
B649 SP323 2.50fr +50c multi 1.00 .75
B650 SP323 2.50fr +50c multi 1.00 .75
B651 SP323 2.50fr +50c multi 1.00 .75
B652 SP323 2.50fr +50c multi 1.00 .75
B653 SP323 2.50fr +50c multi 1.00 .75
B654 SP323 2.50fr +50c multi 1.00 .75
a. Bklt. pane of 6, #B649-B654 + 2 labels 6.00

When Nos. B650-B654 are normally centered, inscriptions at base of the lower panel are not parallel to the perforations at bottom. On all six stamps the lower panel is not centered between the side perforations.

SP324

St. Nicolas, Image of Metz.

1993, Nov. 27 Engr. Perf. 12½x13
B655 SP324 2.80fr +60c multi 1.10 .75
a. Perf. 13½x13 1.20 .75
b. As "a," Bklt. pane of 10 +2 labels 12.00

Surtax for Red Cross.

SP325

Stage and Screen Personalities: No. B656, Yvonne Printemps (1894-1977). No. B657, Fernandel (1903-71). No. B658, Josephine Baker (1906-75). No. B659, Bourvil (1917-70). No. B660, Yves Montand (1921-91). No. B661, Coluche (1944-86).

1994, Sept. 17 Photo. Perf. 13
B656 SP325 2.80fr +60c multi 1.10 .75
B657 SP325 2.80fr +60c multi 1.10 .75
B658 SP325 2.80fr +60c multi 1.10 .75
B659 SP325 2.80fr +60c multi 1.10 .75
B660 SP325 2.80fr +60c multi 1.10 .75
B661 SP325 2.80fr +60c multi 1.10 .75
a. Bklt. pane, #B656-B661 + 2 labels 6.00

SP326

Designs: No. B662, St. Vaast, Arras Tapestry. No. B663, Brussels tapestry from Reydams workshop, Horse Museum, Saumur.

1994-95 Photo. Perf. 12½x13
B662 SP326 2.80fr +60c multi 1.10 .75
a. Perf. 13½x13 1.20 .75
b. Bklt. pane, 10 #B662a + 2 labels 12.00
Complete booklet, #B662b 13.00
B663 SP326 2.80fr +60c multi 1.10 .75
a. Perf. 13½x13 1.20 .75
b. Bklt. pane, 10 #B663a + 2 labels 12.00
Complete booklet, #B663b 13.00

Surtax for Red Cross.
Issued: No. B662, 11/26/94; No. B663, 5/13/95.

SP327

Provencal Nativity Figures: No. B664, The Shepherd. No. B665, The Miller. No. B666, The Simpleton and the Tambour Player. No. B667, The Fishmonger. No. B668, The Scissor Grinder. No. B669, The Elders.

1995, Nov. 25 Engr. Perf. 13
B664 SP327 2.80fr +60c multi 1.10 .85
B665 SP327 2.80fr +60c multi 1.10 .85
B666 SP327 2.80fr +60c multi 1.10 .85
B667 SP327 2.80fr +60c multi 1.10 .85
B668 SP327 2.80fr +60c multi 1.10 .85
B669 SP327 2.80fr +60c multi 1.10 .85
a. Booklet pane, Nos. B664-B669 + 2 labels 7.50
Complete booklet, No. B669a 11.00

SP328

Famous Fictional Detectives and Criminals: No. B670, Rocambole. No. B671, Arsène Lupin. No. B672, Joseph Rouletabille. No. B673, Fantômas. No. B674, Commissioner Maigret. No. B675, Nestor Burma.

1996, Oct. 5 Photo. Perf. 13
B670 SP328 3fr +60c multi 1.10 .85
B671 SP328 3fr +60c multi 1.10 .85
B672 SP328 3fr +60c multi 1.10 .85
B673 SP328 3fr +60c multi 1.10 .85
B674 SP328 3fr +60c multi 1.10 .85
B675 SP328 3fr +60c multi 1.10 .85
a. Booklet pane, #B670-B675 + 2 labels 7.50
Complete booklet, #B675a 11.00

FRANCE

Christmas — SP329

1996, Nov. 16 Photo. *Perf. 12¾x13*
B676 SP329 3fr +60c multi 1.10 .85
  a. Perf. 13¼x13 1.20 .85
  b. Booklet pane, 10 #B676a + 2 labels 12.00 —
    Complete booklet, #B676b 13.00

Surtax for Red Cross.

Adventure Heroes — SP330

No. B677, Sir Lancelot. No. B678, Pardaillan. No. B679, D'Artagnan. No. B680, Cyrano de Bergerac. No. B681, Captain Fracasse. No. B682, Le Bossu.

1997, Oct. 25 Photo. *Perf. 13*
B677 SP330 3fr +60c multi 1.10 .85
B678 SP330 3fr +60c multi 1.10 .85
B679 SP330 3fr +60c multi 1.10 .85
B680 SP330 3fr +60c multi 1.10 .85
B681 SP330 3fr +60c multi 1.10 .85
B682 SP330 3fr +60c multi 1.10 .85
  a. Booklet pane, #B677-B682 + 2 labels 7.50
    Complete booklet, #B682a 7.50

Christmas, New Year — SP331

1997, Nov. 6 Photo. *Perf. 12¾x13*
B683 SP331 3fr +60c multi 1.10 .90
  a. Perf. 13¼x13 1.20 .95
  b. Booklet pane, 10 #B683a + 2 labels 12.00 —
    Complete booklet, #B683b 13.00

Surtax for the Red Cross.

SP332

Actors of the French Cinema: No. B684, Romy Schneider (1938-82). No. B685, Simone Signoret (1921-85). No. B686, Jean Gabin (1904-76). No. B687, Louis de Funés (1914-83). No. B688, Bernard Blier (1916-89). No. B689, Lino Ventura (1919-87).

1998, Oct. 3 Photo. *Perf. 13*
B684 SP332 3fr +60c multi 1.10 .85
B685 SP332 3fr +60c multi 1.10 .85
B686 SP332 3fr +60c multi 1.10 .85
B687 SP332 3fr +60c multi 1.10 .85
B688 SP332 3fr +60c multi 1.10 .85
B689 SP332 3fr +60c multi 1.10 .85
  a. Booklet pane, #B684-B689 + label 7.50
    Complete booklet, #B689a 8.00

Christmas — SP333

1998, Nov. 5 Photo. *Perf. 12½x13*
B690 SP333 3fr +60c multi 1.10 .85
  a. Perf. 13¼x13 1.20 .85
  b. Booklet pane, 10 #B690a + 2 labels 12.00 —
    Complete booklet, #B690b 13.00

Surtax for Red Cross.

Famous Photographers SP334

Photographs by: No. B691, Robert Doisneau (1912-94). No. B692, Brassai (Gyula Halasz) (1899-1984). No. B693, Jacques Lartigue (1894-1986). No. B694, Henri Cartier-Bresson (1908-2004). No. B695, Eugene Atget (1857-1927). No. B696, Felix Nadar (1820-1910).

1999, July 10 Photo. *Perf. 13*
B691 SP334 3fr +60c multi 1.10 .85
B692 SP334 3fr +60c multi 1.10 .85
B693 SP334 3fr +60c multi 1.10 .85
B694 SP334 3fr +60c multi 1.10 .85
B695 SP334 3fr +60c multi 1.10 .85
B696 SP334 3fr +60c multi 1.10 .85
  a. Booklet pane, #B691-B696 7.50
    Complete booklet, #B696a 8.00

New Year 2000 — SP335

1999, Nov. 10 Photo. *Perf. 12¾x13*
B697 SP335 3fr +60c multi 1.20 .85
  a. Perf. 13¼x13 1.25 .85
  b. Booklet pane, 10 #B697a + 2 labels 9.00 —
    Complete booklet, #B697b 10.00

Surtax for Red Cross.

Adventurers — SP336

No. B698, Eric Tabarly (1931-98), sailor. No. B699, Alexandra David-Néel (1868-1969), opera singer, Asian traveler. No. B700, Haroun Tazieff (1914-98), vulcanologist. No. B701, Paul-Emile Victor (1907-75), ethnologist, polar explorer. No. B702, Jacques-Yves Cousteau (1910-97), oceanographer. No. B703, Norbert Casteret (1897-1987), speleologist.

2000, Sept. 16 Photo. *Perf. 13¼x13*
B698 SP336 3fr +60c multi 1.20 .85
B699 SP336 3fr +60c multi 1.20 .85
B700 SP336 3fr +60c multi 1.20 .85
B701 SP336 3fr +60c multi 1.20 .85
B702 SP336 3fr +60c multi 1.20 .85
B703 SP336 3fr +60c multi 1.20 .85
  a. Booklet pane, #B698-B703 7.00
    Booklet, #B703a 7.50

Toy Airplane — SP337

2000, Nov. 9 Photo. *Perf. 13¼x13*
B704 SP337 3fr +60c multi 1.10 .85
  a. Booklet pane of 10 + 2 labels 12.00 —
    Booklet, #B704a 13.00

Surtax for Red Cross.

Santa Claus and Tree Ornaments — SP338

2001, Nov. 8 Photo. *Perf. 12¾x13*
B705 SP338 3fr +60c multi 1.10 .85
  a. Perf 13½x13 1.20 .85
  b. Booklet pane of 10 11.00 —
    Booklet, #B705a 11.00

Surtax for Red Cross.

Infant Jesus Asleep, by Giovanni Battista Salvi — SP339

2002, Nov. 7 Photo. *Perf. 12¾x13*
B706 SP339 46c +9c multi 1.10 .85
  a. Perf. 13½x13 1.20 .85
  b. As "a," booklet pane of 10 11.00 —
    Booklet, #B706b 11.00

Surtax for Red Cross.

Virgin with Grapes, by Pierre Mignard — SP340

2003, Nov. 6 Photo. *Perf. 13¼x13* **Booklet Stamp**
B707 SP340 50c +(16c) multi 1.50 1.00
  a. Booklet pane of 10 15.00 —
    Complete booklet, #B707a 15.00

Surtax for Red Cross.

Virgin With Child, Attributed to Cretan School — SP341

2004, Nov. 10 Photo. *Perf. 13¼x13* **Booklet Stamp**
B708 SP341 50c +(16c) multi 1.50 1.00
  a. Booklet pane of 10 + 2 labels 15.00 —
    Complete booklet, #B708a 15.00

Surtax for Red Cross.

Dec. 26, 2004 Tsunami Victim Relief — SP342

2005, Jan. 13 Engr. *Perf. 13*
B709 SP342 (50c) +20c red 1.75 .50

Virgin and Child, by Hans Memling — SP343

2005, Nov. 10 Photo. *Perf. 13½x13* **Booklet Stamp**
B710 SP343 53c +(17c) multi 1.50 1.00
  a. Booklet pane of 10 + 2 labels 15.00 —
    Complete booklet, #B710a 15.00

Surtax for Red Cross.

SP344   Children's Art — SP345

2006, Nov. 25 Photo. *Perf. 13½x13* **Booklet Stamps**
B711 SP344 (54c) +(17c) multi 1.90 .85
B712 SP345 (54c) +(17c) multi 1.90 .85
  a. Booklet pane, 5 each #B711-B712, + 2 labels 19.00 —
    Complete booklet, #B712a 19.00

Surtax for Red Cross.

Red Cross
SP346   SP347

Serpentine Die Cut 11
2007, Nov. 24 Photo. **Self-Adhesive Booklet Stamps**
B713 SP346 (54c) +(17c) multi 1.90 .85
B714 SP347 (54c) +(17c) multi 1.90 .85
  a. Booklet pane, 5 each #B713-B714 19.00

Surtax for Red Cross.

Red Cross
SP348   SP349

Serpentine Die Cut 11x11¼
2008, Nov. 8 Photo. **Booklet Stamps Self-Adhesive**
B715 SP348 (55c) +(18c) multi 1.90 .85
B716 SP349 (55c) +(18c) multi 1.90 .85
  a. Booklet pane of 10, 2 each #B715-B716 19.00

Surtax for Red Cross.

Miniature Sheet

Red Cross SP350

No. B717: a, Henri Dunant. b, Battle of Solferino. c, Pélias et Nélée, by Georges Braque, horiz. d, Geneva Conventions. e, Globe and symbols of the International Red Cross and Red Crescent Societies.

2009, Sept. 19 Photo. *Perf. 13*
B717 SP350 Sheet of 5 12.00 12.00
  a.-e. 56c +(40c) Any single 2.50 2.50

Surtax for Red Cross.

Haiti Earthquake Relief — SP351

2010, Jan. 19 Engr. *Perf. 13*
B718 SP351 (56c) +44c red 2.25 1.50

Self-Adhesive Serpentine Die Cut 11
B719 SP351 (56c) +44c red 4.50 4.00

Surtax was for French Red Cross relief efforts in Haiti.

Miniature Sheet

Red Cross SP352

No. B720: a, Woman on telephone. b, Man assisting unconscious woman. c, Red Cross emblem, horiz. d, Woman performing Heimlich maneuver on choking man. e, Cardio-pulmonary resuscitation.

FRANCE

Photo., Photo. & Embossed (#B720c)
2010, Nov. 5   Perf. 13
- B720 SP352 Sheet of 5   12.00   8.00
- a.-e. 58c +(40c) Any single   2.00   1.25

Surtax for Red Cross.

Miniature Sheet

Singers SP353

No. B721: a, Colette Renard (1924-2010). b, Henri Salvador (1917-2008). c, Serge Reggiani (1922-2004). d, Claude Nougaro (1929-2004). e, Daniel Balavoine (1952-86). f, Gilbert Bécaud (1927-2001).

2011, Oct. 14   Photo.   Perf. 13
- B721 SP353 Sheet of 6   12.00   9.00
- a.-f. 60c + (33⅓c) Any single   2.00   1.50

Surtax for Red Cross.

Miniature Sheet

Red Cross SP354

No. B722: a, People carrying person on litter. b, Three hands. c, Red Cross, horiz. d, Red Cross volunteer teaching illiterates. e, Red Cross volunteer giving bottle to infant.

2011, Nov. 4
- B722 SP354 Sheet of 5   10.00   7.50
- a.-e. 60c + (40c) Any single   2.00   1.50

Surtax for Red Cross.

Miniature Sheet

Movie Stars SP355

No. B723: a, Françoise Dorléac (1942-67). b, Jean Marais (1913-98). c, Jacqueline Maillan (1923-92). d, Michel Serrault (1928-2007). e, Philippe Noiret (1930-2006). f, Annie Girardot (1931-2011).

2012, Oct. 19
- B723 SP355 Sheet of 6   12.00   9.00
- a.-f. 60c + (33⅓c) Any single   2.00   1.50

Surtax for Red Cross.

Miniature Sheet

Red Cross SP356

No. B724: a, Heart and hands. b, Man carrying man with injured foot. c, Red Cross, horiz. d, Three parachutists. e, People and dog hugging heart.

2012, Nov. 8
- B724 SP356 Sheet of 5   12.50   12.50
- a.-e. 57c + (40c) Any single   2.50   2.50

Surtax for Red Cross.

Loire River — SP357

The Loire River at: No. B725, Mont Gerbier de Jonc. No. B726, Lac de Grangent. No. B727, Bec d'Allier. No. B728, Gien. No. B729, Pointe de Coupain. No. B730, Blois. No. B731, Candes-Saint-Martin. No. B732, Ingrandes-sur-Loire. No. B733, Champtoceaux. No. B734, Marais de Brière.

2013, June 1   Serpentine Die Cut 11
Booklet Stamps
Self-Adhesive
B725	SP357	(58c+20c)	multi	1.60	.50
B726	SP357	(58c+20c)	multi	1.60	.50
B727	SP357	(58c+20c)	multi	1.60	.50
B728	SP357	(58c+20c)	multi	1.60	.50
B729	SP357	(58c+20c)	multi	1.60	.50
B730	SP357	(58c+20c)	multi	1.60	.50
B731	SP357	(58c+20c)	multi	1.60	.50
B732	SP357	(58c+20c)	multi	1.60	.50
B733	SP357	(58c+20c)	multi	1.60	.50
B734	SP357	(58c+20c)	multi	1.60	.50

a.   Booklet pane of 10, #B725-B734   18.00

Nos. B725-B734 (10)   16.00   5.00

Surtax for the Red Cross.

Red Cross SP358

No. B735: a, One stylized person. b, Two stylized people. c, Red Cross, horiz. d, Three stylized people. e, Four stylized people.

2013, Nov. 7   Photo.   Perf. 13
- B735 SP358 Sheet of 5   10.00   7.50
- a.-e. 58c + (40c) Any single   1.75   1.25

Surtax for Red Cross.

Flowers — SP359

Designs: No. B736, Roses. No. B737, Daisies (Marguerite). No. B738, Tulips (Tulipe). No. B739, Sunflowers (Tournesol). No. B740, Irises. No. B741, Orchids (Orchidée). No. B742, Jonquils (Jonquille). No. B743, Lilies (Lys). No. B744, Carnations (Oeillet). No. B745, Gardenias (Gardénia).

Serpentine Die Cut 11
2014, May 24   Photo.
Booklet Stamps
Self-Adhesive
B736	SP359	(61c) + (20c)	multi	1.75	1.00
B737	SP359	(61c) + (20c)	multi	1.75	1.00
B738	SP359	(61c) + (20c)	multi	1.75	1.00
B739	SP359	(61c) + (20c)	multi	1.75	1.00
B740	SP359	(61c) + (20c)	multi	1.75	1.00
B741	SP359	(61c) + (20c)	multi	1.75	1.00
B742	SP359	(61c) + (20c)	multi	1.75	1.00
B743	SP359	(61c) + (20c)	multi	1.75	1.00
B744	SP359	(61c) + (20c)	multi	1.75	1.00
B745	SP359	(61c) + (20c)	multi	1.75	1.00

a.   Booklet pane of 10, #B736-B745   20.00

Nos. B736-B745 (10)   17.50   10.00

Red Cross, 150th anniv. Surtax for Red Cross.

Semi-Postal Stamps of 1914-88 Redrawn
2014, June 14   Litho.
- B746 Sheet of 5   14.00   14.00
- a. SP2 61c +30c like #B2, perf. 13¼   2.50   2.50
- b. A22 61c +30c like #B1, perf. 13¼   2.50   2.50
- c. SP40 61c +30c like #B81, perf. 13   2.50   2.50
- d. SP9 61c +30c like #B11, perf. 13x13¼   2.50   2.50
- e. SP237 61c +30c like #B403, perf. 13   2.50   2.50
- B747 Sheet of 5   14.00   14.00
- a. SP60 61c +30c like #B101, perf. 13x13¼   2.50   2.50
- b. SP258 61c +30c like #B462, perf. 13   2.50   2.50
- c. SP310 61c +30c like #B601, perf. 13¼x13   2.50   2.50
- d. SP207 61c +30c like #B328, perf. 13¼x13¼   2.50   2.50
- e. SP61 61c +30c like #B102, perf. 13   2.50   2.50

Nos. B746-B747 sold together as a set for €12.

Miniature Sheet

French Red Cross, 150th Anniv. SP360

No. B748: a, Jean-Henri Dunant, 1864. b, White angel with Red Cross arm band treating soldier, 1914. c, Red cross and 150th anniv. emblem, horiz. d, Red Cross worker giving aid to refugee, 1945. e, Red Cross workers in Haiti, 2010.

2014, Nov. 7   Photo.   Perf. 13
- B748 SP360 Sheet of 5   10.00   8.00
- a.-e. 61c+(30c) Any single   2.00   1.25

Surtax for the Red Cross.

SP361

SP362

SP363

SP364

SP365

SP366

SP367

Red Cross Workers in Action — SP368

Serpentine Die Cut 11
2015, May 16   Litho.
Booklet Stamps
Self-Adhesive
B749	SP361	(68c+25c)	multi	2.10	2.10
B750	SP362	(68c+25c)	multi	2.10	2.10
B751	SP363	(68c+25c)	multi	2.10	2.10
B752	SP364	(68c+25c)	multi	2.10	2.10
B753	SP365	(68c+25c)	multi	2.10	2.10
B754	SP366	(68c+25c)	multi	2.10	2.10
B755	SP367	(68c+25c)	multi	2.10	2.10
B756	SP368	(68c+25c)	multi	2.10	2.10

a.   Booklet pane of 8, #B749-B756   17.00

Nos. B749-B756 (8)   16.80   16.80

Surtax for the Red Cross.

Miniature Sheet

Red Cross SP369

No. B757: a, Red cross, heart and arrows. b, Sun, red crosses, ambulance. c, Red cross and text, horiz. d, Red cross and heart. e, Red Cross and text, diff.

2015, Nov. 7   Photo.   Perf. 13
- B757 SP369 Sheet of 5   11.50   11.50
- a.-e. 68c+(40c) Any single   2.25   2.25

Surtax for the Red Cross.

SP370

SP371

SP372

SP373

SP374

SP375

SP376

Red Cross Workers — SP377

Serpentine Die Cut 11
2016, Apr. 30   Litho.
Booklet Stamps
Self-Adhesive
B758	SP370	(70c+25c)	multi	2.25	2.25
B759	SP371	(70c+25c)	multi	2.25	2.25
B760	SP372	(70c+25c)	multi	2.25	2.25
B761	SP373	(70c+25c)	multi	2.25	2.25
B762	SP374	(70c+25c)	multi	2.25	2.25
B763	SP375	(70c+25c)	multi	2.25	2.25
B764	SP376	(70c+25c)	multi	2.25	2.25
B765	SP377	(70c+25c)	multi	2.25	2.25

a.   Booklet pane of 8, #B758-B765   18.00

Nos. B758-B765 (8)   18.00   18.00

Surtax for the Red Cross.

FRANCE

Miniature Sheet

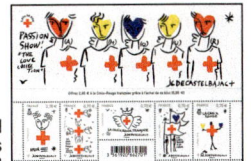

Red Cross SP378

No. B766: a, Head on top of cross. b, Heads and three crosses. c, Cross in winged and crowned heart, horiz. d, Flags with cross and heart. e, Stylized person with cross as torso and arms.

2016, Nov. 5 Photo. Perf. 13
B766 SP378 Sheet of 5 12.00 12.00
a.-e. 70c+(40c) Any single 2.40 2.40

Surtax for the Red Cross.

SP379

SP380

SP381 SP382

SP383

SP384

SP385

Work of the Red Cross — SP386

Serpentine Die Cut 11
2017, May 5 Photo.
Booklet Stamps
Self-Adhesive

B767	SP379	(73c+25c) multi	2.25	2.25
B768	SP380	(73c+25c) multi	2.25	2.25
B769	SP381	(73c+25c) multi	2.25	2.25
B770	SP382	(73c+25c) multi	2.25	2.25
B771	SP383	(73c+25c) multi	2.25	2.25
B772	SP384	(73c+25c) multi	2.25	2.25
B773	SP385	(73c+25c) multi	2.25	2.25
B774	SP386	(73c+25c) multi	2.25	2.25
a.	Booklet pane of 8, #B767-B774		18.00	

Nos. B767-B774 (8) 18.00 18.00

Surtax for Red Cross.

Marianne and Children "Lettre Prioritaire" Without Gram Limit Inscription Type of 2016
2017, Oct. 20 Photo. Perf. 13
B775 A2536 (85c+66c) red 3.50 3.50

No. B775 was printed in sheets of 3 that sold for €4.55, €2 of which was for the Red Cross.

Flowers — SP387

Designs: No. B776, Anemones and shell. No. B777, Asters and daisies (asters et marguerites), keys. No. B778, Dahlias, eglantine roses and peaches. No. B779, Snapdragons and cornflowers (moufliers et bleuets), elephant figurine. No. B780, Peonies (pivoines), cat figurine. No. B781, Ranunculus (renoncules), letter and shell. No. B782, Roses, hourglass. No. B783, Calendulas (soucis) and oranges. No. B784, Sunflowers and blue thistles (tournesols et chardons bleus), teapot and owl figurine. No. B785, Zinnias, snail and butterflies.

Serpentine Die Cut 11
2018, May 4 Photo.
Booklet Stamps
Self-Adhesive

B776	SP387	(80c+20c) multi	2.40	2.40
B777	SP387	(80c+20c) multi	2.40	2.40
B778	SP387	(80c+20c) multi	2.40	2.40
B779	SP387	(80c+20c) multi	2.40	2.40
B780	SP387	(80c+20c) multi	2.40	2.40
B781	SP387	(80c+20c) multi	2.40	2.40
B782	SP387	(80c+20c) multi	2.40	2.40
B783	SP387	(80c+20c) multi	2.40	2.40
B784	SP387	(80c+20c) multi	2.40	2.40
B785	SP387	(80c+20c) multi	2.40	2.40
a.	Booklet pane of 10, #B776-B785		24.00	

Nos. B776-B785 (10) 24.00 24.00

Surtax was for Red Cross.

Marianne and Red Cross — SP388

2018, Oct. 26 Photo. Perf. 13
B786 SP388 (95c+66c) multi 3.75 3.75

No. B786 was printed in sheets of 3 that sold for €4.85, €2 of which was for the Red Cross.

SP389

SP391

SP393

SP395

SP397

SP390

SP392

SP394

SP396

Photographs of People by Christian Guémy — SP398

Serpentine Die Cut 11
2019, May 10 Photo.
Booklet Stamps
Self-Adhesive

B787	SP389	(88c+20c) multi	2.50	2.50
B788	SP390	(88c+20c) multi	2.50	2.50
B789	SP391	(88c+20c) multi	2.50	2.50
B790	SP392	(88c+20c) multi	2.50	2.50
B791	SP393	(88c+20c) multi	2.50	2.50
B792	SP394	(88c+20c) multi	2.50	2.50
B793	SP395	(88c+20c) multi	2.50	2.50
B794	SP396	(88c+20c) multi	2.50	2.50
B795	SP397	(88c+20c) multi	2.50	2.50
B796	SP398	(88c+20c) multi	2.50	2.50
a.	Booklet pane of 10, #B787-B796		25.00	

Nos. B787-B796 (10) 25.00 25.00

Surtax for Red Cross.

Souvenir Sheet

Red Cross Workers SP399

No. B797: a, Red Cross worker in food storeroom. b, Nurse at dispensary. c, Red Cross worker at clothing warehouse.

2019, Oct. 18 Photo. Perf. 13
B797 SP399 Sheet of 3 11.50 11.50
a.-c. €1.05+(66c) Any single 3.75 3.75

No. B786 sold for €5.15, €2 of which was for the Red Cross.

SP400

SP402

SP401

SP403

SP404

SP405

SP406

SP407

SP408

Rhythm, Joy of Life, Painting by Robert Delaunay (1885-1941) SP409

Serpentine Die Cut 11
2020, May 15 Photo.
Booklet Stamps
Self-Adhesive

B798	SP400	(97c+20c) multi	2.60	2.60
B799	SP401	(97c+20c) multi	2.60	2.60
B800	SP402	(97c+20c) multi	2.60	2.60
B801	SP403	(97c+20c) multi	2.60	2.60
B802	SP404	(97c+20c) multi	2.60	2.60
B803	SP405	(97c+20c) multi	2.60	2.60
B804	SP406	(97c+20c) multi	2.60	2.60
B805	SP407	(97c+20c) multi	2.60	2.60
B806	SP408	(97c+20c) multi	2.60	2.60
B807	SP409	(97c+20c) multi	2.60	2.60
a.	Booklet pane of 10, #B798-B807 + sticker		26.00	

Nos. B798-B807 (10) 26.00 26.00

Surtax was for Red Cross.

Souvenir Sheet

SP410

No. B808: a, Henry Dunant (1828-1910), co-founder of Red Cross. b, Gustave Moynier (1826-1910), co-founder of Red Cross. c, Volunteers collecting donations for Red Cross, horiz.

2020, Oct. 2 Photo. Perf. 13¼
B808 SP410 Sheet of 3 13.00 13.00
a.-c. €1.16 +(66c) Any single 4.25 4.25

No. B808 sold for €5.48, of which €2 was for the Red Cross.

Words of Ben — SP411

"Ben" (artist Benjamin Vautier), Red Cross, and inscription: No. B809, Important! No. B810, Chaque instant est unique. No. B811, Il va falloir s'adapter. No. B812, Un grand merci. No. B813, On peut le faire. No. B814, Vous êtes formidables! No. B815, Il faut oser. No. B816, J'aime la vie. No. B817, Nous finirons par vaincre. No. B818, Mots d'amour.

Serpentine Die Cut 11
2021, Apr. 23 Photo.
Booklet Stamps
Self-Adhesive

B809	SP411	(€1.08) +(20c) multi	3.25	3.25
B810	SP411	(€1.08) +(20c) multi	3.25	3.25
B811	SP411	(€1.08) +(20c) multi	3.25	3.25
B812	SP411	(€1.08) +(20c) multi	3.25	3.25
B813	SP411	(€1.08) +(20c) multi	3.25	3.25
B814	SP411	(€1.08) +(20c) multi	3.25	3.25
B815	SP411	(€1.08) +(20c) multi	3.25	3.25
B816	SP411	(€1.08) +(20c) multi	3.25	3.25
B817	SP411	(€1.08) +(20c) multi	3.25	3.25
B818	SP411	(€1.08) +(20c) multi	3.25	3.25
a.	Booklet pane of 10, #B809-B818		32.50	

Nos. B809-B818 (10) 32.50 32.50

Surtax was for Red Cross. Compare with types A1667 and A2203.

772 FRANCE

Souvenir Sheet

SP412

No. B819: a, Food aid worker packing groceries. b, Red Cross workers wearing protective face masks. c, Red Cross worker administering vaccination.

2021, Oct. 22   Photo.   Perf. 13¼
B819   SP412   Sheet of 3   13.50   13.50
  a.-c.   €1.28 +(66c) Any single   4.50   4.50

No. B819 sold for €5.84, of which €2 was for the Red Cross.

 SP413
 SP414
 SP415
 SP416
 SP417
 SP418
 SP419
 SP420
 SP421

Woolen Fabric Designs From the Mulhouse Museum of Printed Textiles — SP422

Serpentine Die Cut 11
2022, Apr. 22   Photo.

Booklet Stamps
Self-Adhesive
B820   SP413   (€1.16) + (20c) multi   3.00   3.00
B821   SP414   (€1.16) + (20c) multi   3.00   3.00
B822   SP415   (€1.16) + (20c) multi   3.00   3.00
B823   SP416   (€1.16) + (20c) multi   3.00   3.00
B824   SP417   (€1.16) + (20c) multi   3.00   3.00
B825   SP418   (€1.16) + (20c) multi   3.00   3.00
B826   SP419   (€1.16) + (20c) multi   3.00   3.00
B827   SP420   (€1.16) + (20c) multi   3.00   3.00
B828   SP421   (€1.16) + (20c) multi   3.00   3.00
B829   SP422   (€1.16) + (20c) multi   3.00   3.00
  a.   Booklet pane of 10, #B820-B829   30.00
Nos. B820-B829 (10)   30.00   30.00

Surtax was for Red Cross.

Solidarity With Ukraine After Russian Invasion — SP423

2022, June 23   Photo.   Perf. 13
B830   SP423   (€1.16) +84c multi   4.25   4.25

Surtax was for Red Cross fund for Ukrainian relief efforts.

Souvenir Sheet

International Humanitarian Law — SP424

No. B831: a, Hands, people and globe stand. b, Refugees, stylized heads and balance scale. c, Face on flags, vert.

2022, Oct. 21   Photo.   Perf. 13¼
B831   SP424   Sheet of 3   11.00   11.00
  a.-c.   €1.16 +(66c) Any single   3.50   3.50

No. B831 sold for €5.48, of which €2 was for the Red Cross.

 SP425   SP426

 SP427   SP428

SP429   SP430

 SP431   SP432

 SP433

Prevention and Education Services of the Red Cross — SP434

Serpentine Die Cut 11
2023, Apr. 21   Photo.

Booklet Stamps
Self-Adhesive
B832   SP425   (€1.16) +20c multi   3.00   3.00
B833   SP426   (€1.16) +20c multi   3.00   3.00
B834   SP427   (€1.16) +20c multi   3.00   3.00
B835   SP428   (€1.16) +20c multi   3.00   3.00
B836   SP429   (€1.16) +20c multi   3.00   3.00
B837   SP430   (€1.16) +20c multi   3.00   3.00
B838   SP431   (€1.16) +20c multi   3.00   3.00
B839   SP432   (€1.16) +20c multi   3.00   3.00
B840   SP433   (€1.16) +20c multi   3.00   3.00
B841   SP434   (€1.16) +20c multi   3.00   3.00
  a.   Booklet pane of 10, #B832-B841   30.00
Nos. B832-B841 (10)   30.00   30.00

Surtax for Red Cross.

Souvenir Sheet

Red Cross Workers SP435

No. B842: a, Françoise, from Morbihan. b, Hélène and Pierre, from Aisne, vert. c, Olivier, from Cantal.

2023, Oct. 20   Photo.   Perf. 13¼
B842   SP435   Sheet of 3   11.50   11.50
  a.-c.   €1.16 + (66c) Any single   3.75   3.75

No. B842 sold for €5.48, €2 of which was for the Red Cross.

AIR POST STAMPS

Nos. 127, 130 Overprinted in Dark Blue or Black

Perf. 14x13½
1927, June 25   Unwmk.
C1   A18   2fr org & bl (DB)   200.00   225.00
  Never hinged   400.00
C2   A18   5fr dk bl & buff   200.00   225.00
  Never hinged   400.00

On sale only at the Intl. Aviation Exhib. at Marseilles, June, 1927. One set could be purchased by each holder of an admission ticket. Excellent counterfeits exist.

Nos. 242, 196 Surcharged

1928, Aug. 23
C3   A33   10fr on 90c   2,400.   1,800.
  Never hinged   3,500.
  a.   Inverted surcharge   16,500.   16,500.
    Never hinged   25,000.
  b.   Space between "10" and bars 6½mm   3,100.   3,100.
    Never hinged   5,100.
C4   A23   10fr on 1.50fr   10,000.   8,250.
  Never hinged   14,000.
  a.   Space between "10" and bars 6½mm   13,000.   13,000.
    Never hinged   20,000.

Nos. C3-C4 received their surcharge in New York by order of the French consul general. They were for use in paying the 10fr fee for letters leaving the liner Ile de France on a catapulted hydroplane when the ship was one day off the coast of France on its eastward voyage.

The normal space between "10" and bars is 4½mm, but on 10 stamps in each pane of 50 the space is 6½mm. Counterfeits exist.

View of Marseille, Church of Notre Dame at Left — AP1

1930-31   Engr.   Perf. 13
C5   AP1   1.50fr dp car   21.00   4.00
  Never hinged   40.00
  a.   With perf. initials "E.I.P.A.30"   2,750.   3,750.
    Never hinged   3,600.
C6   AP1   1.50fr dk bl ('31)   19.00   2.25
  Never hinged   35.00
  a.   1.50fr ultramarine   50.00   21.00
    Never hinged   90.00
  b.   As "a," with perf. initials "E.I.P.A.30"   450.00   350.00
    Never hinged   700.00

Nos. C5a, C6a were sold at the Intl. Air Post Exhib., Paris, Nov. 6-20, 1930, at face value plus 5fr, the price of admission.

Forgeries abound of Nos. C5a and C6b. Certificates from recognized authorities are recommended.

Blériot's Monoplane AP2

1934, Sept. 1   Perf. 13
C7   AP2   2.25fr violet   24.00   6.00
  Never hinged   32.50

1st flight across the English Channel, by Louis Blériot.

Plane over Paris — AP3

1936
C8   AP3   85c deep green   2.25   2.25
  Never hinged   6.50
C9   AP3   1.50fr blue   10.50   5.50
  Never hinged   18.00
C10   AP3   2.25fr violet   18.00   7.00
  Never hinged   35.00
C11   AP3   2.50fr rose   32.50   8.25
  Never hinged   45.00
C12   AP3   3fr ultra   26.00   2.50
  Never hinged   37.50
C13   AP3   3.50fr orange brn   62.50   24.00
  Never hinged   105.00
C14   AP3   50fr emerald   825.00   325.00
  Never hinged   1,450.
  b.   50fr green   850.00   350.00
    Never hinged   1,500.
Nos. C8-C14 (7)   976.75   374.50

Monoplane over Paris — AP4

Paper with Red Network Overprint

1936, July 10   Perf. 12½
C15   AP4   50fr ultra   625.00   310.00
  Never hinged   1,700.

See No. C86.

FRANCE

Airplane and Galleon
AP5

Planes over the Atlantic, New York-Paris
AP24

1936, Aug. 17   Perf. 13
C16 AP5 1.50fr dk ultra   17.50   5.25
    Never hinged   35.00
C17 AP6 10fr Prus green   290.00   130.00
    Never hinged   700.00

100th air mail flight across the South Atlantic.

Catalogue values for unused stamps in this section, from this point to the end of the section, are for Never Hinged items.

Airplane and Globe AP6

1949-50   Unwmk.   Perf. 13
C23 AP12 100fr sepia   1.20   .40
C24 AP12 200fr dk bl grn   11.50   .75
C25 AP12 300fr purple   15.00   9.00
C26 AP12 500fr brt red   55.00   4.75
C27 AP13 1000fr blk, dull gray vio ('50)   130.00   24.00
    Nos. C23-C27 (5)   212.70   38.90

See No. C88. For surcharges see Reunion Nos. C39-C41.

Concorde Issue
Common Design Type
1969, Mar. 2   Engr.   Perf. 13
C42 CD129 1fr indigo & brt bl   .75   .35

The 0.95fr stamp in this design was prepared but not issued. Value $30,000.

Jean Mermoz, Antoine de Saint-Exupéry and Concorde — AP19

1977, June 4   Engr.   Perf. 13
C49 AP24 1.90fr multicolored   .75   .40

1st transatlantic flight by Lindbergh from NY to Paris, 50th anniv., and 1st attempted westbound flight by French aviators Charles Nungesser and Francois Coli.

Plane over Flight Route — AP25

1978, Oct. 14   Engr.   Perf. 13
C50 AP25 1.50fr multicolored   .60   .35

65th anniversary of first airmail route from Villacoublay to Pauillac, Gironde.

Alexander III Bridge and Petit Palais, Paris AP14

1949, June 13
C28 AP14 100fr brown car   5.25   5.25

International Telegraph and Telephone Conference, Paris, May-July 1949. See No. C89 for stamp with euro denomination.

1970, Sept. 19   Engr.   Perf. 13
C43 AP19 20fr blue & indigo   8.00   .55

Jean Mermoz (1901-36) and writer Antoine de Saint-Exupéry (1900-44), aviators and air mail pioneers.

Balloon, Gare d'Austerlitz, Paris — AP20

Centaur and Plane AP7

Iris AP8

Jet Plane, Mystère IV — AP15

Planes: 200fr, Noratlas. 500fr, Miles Magister. 1000fr, Provence.

1954, Jan. 16
C29 AP15 100fr red brn & bl   2.25   .25
C30 AP15 200fr blk brn & vio bl   9.00   .25
C31 AP15 500fr car & org   175.00   10.50
C32 AP15 1000fr vio brn, bl grn & ind   95.00   14.00
    Nos. C29-C32 (4)   281.25   25.00

See No. C37. For surcharges see Reunion Nos. C42-C45, C48.

1971, Jan. 16   Engr.   Perf. 13
C44 AP20 95c bl, vio bl, org & sl grn   .75   .55

Centenary of the balloon post from besieged Paris, 1870-71.

Rocket, Concorde, Exhibition Hall — AP26

1979, June 9   Engr.   Perf. 13
C51 AP26 1.70fr ultra, org & brn   .75   .60

33rd International Aerospace and Space Show, Le Bourget, June 11-15.

Zeus Carrying Hebe — AP9

Maryse Bastié and Plane — AP16

1955, June 4   Unwmk.   Perf. 13
C33 AP16 50fr dp plum & rose pink   5.25   3.75

Issued to honor Maryse Bastié, 1898-1952.

AP21

Design: Didier Daurat, Raymond Vanier and plane landing at night.

1971, Apr. 17   Engr.   Perf. 13
C45 AP21 5fr Prus bl, blk & lt grn   1.75   .25

Didier Daurat (1891-1969) and Raymond Vanier (1895-1965), aviation pioneers.
For surcharge see Reunion No. C52.

First Nonstop Transatlantic Flight, Paris-New York — AP27

1980, Aug. 30   Engr.   Perf. 13
C52 AP27 2.50fr vio brn & ultra   .90   .30

Chariot of the Sun — AP10

1946-47   Engr.   Unwmk.
C18 AP7 40fr dk green   .55   .25
C19 AP8 50fr rose pink   .60   .25
C20 AP9 100fr dk blue ('47)   6.25   3.25
C21 AP10 200fr red   5.25   1.50
    Nos. C18-C21 (4)   12.65   5.25

Issued: 50fr, 200fr, 5/27; 40fr, 7/1; 100fr, Jan.
For surcharges see Reunion Nos. C35-C38.

Morane Saulnier 760 Paris — AP17

Designs: 500fr, Caravelle. 1000fr, Alouette helicopter.

1957-59   Engr.   Perf. 13
C34 AP17 300fr sl grn, grnsh bl & sep ('59)   5.00   2.25
C35 AP17 500fr dp ultra & blk   21.00   3.00
C36 AP17 1000fr lil, ol blk & blk ('58)   45.00   19.00
    Nos. C34-C36 (3)   71.00   24.25

See Nos. C38-C41. For surcharges see Reunion Nos. C46-C47, C49-C51.

Hélène Boucher, Maryse Hilsz and Caudron-Renault and Moth-Morane Planes — AP22

Design: 15fr, Henri Guillaumet, Paul Codos, Latécoère 521, Guillaumet's crashed plane in Andes, skyscrapers.

1972-73   Engr.   Perf. 13
C46 AP22 10fr plum, red & sl   3.50   .40
C47 AP22 15fr dp car, gray & brn ('73)   5.25   .75

Hélène Boucher (1908-34), Maryse Hilsz (1901-46), Henri Guillaumet (1902-40) and Paul Codos (1896-1960), aviation pioneers.
Issue dates: 10fr, June 10; 15fr, Feb. 24.

34th Intl. Space and Aeronautics Exhibition, June 5-14 — AP28

1981, June 6   Engr.   Perf. 13
C53 AP28 2fr multicolored   1.20   .40

Ile de la Cité, Paris, and Gull AP11

1947, May 7
C22 AP11 500fr dk Prus grn   45.00   27.50

UPU 12th Cong., Paris, May 7-July 7. See footnote after No. 4642. See No. 5933d.

Types of 1954-59
Planes: 2fr, Noratlas. 3fr, MS760. Paris. 5fr, Caravelle. 10fr, Alouette helicopter.

1960, Jan. 11
C37 AP15 2fr vio bl & ultra   1.10   .25
   a. 2fr ultramarine   3.00   .75
C38 AP17 3fr sl grn, grnsh bl & sep   1.20   .25
C39 AP17 5fr dp ultra & blk   2.25   .65
C40 AP17 10fr lil, ol blk & blk   10.00   2.00
    Nos. C37-C40 (4)   14.55   3.15

Type of 1957-59
Design: 2fr, Jet plane, Mystère 20.

1965, June 12   Engr.   Perf. 13
C41 AP17 2fr slate bl & indigo   .75   .25

Concorde AP23

1976, Jan. 10   Engr.   Perf. 13
C48 AP23 1.70fr brt bl, red & blk   .75   .40

First flight of supersonic jet Concorde from Paris to Rio de Janeiro, Jan. 21.

Dieudonné Costes and Joseph Le Brix and their Breguet Bi-plane AP29

1981, Sept. 12   Engr.
C54 AP29 10fr dk brown & red   3.50   .40

1st So. Atlantic crossing, Oct. 14-15, 1927.

View of Lille — AP12

Air View of Paris AP13

200fr, Bordeaux. 300fr, Lyon. 500fr, Marseille.

Seaplane Late-300 AP30

1982, Dec. 4   Engr.
C55 AP30 1.60fr multicolored   .75   .40

Farman F-60 Goliath AP31

773

774 FRANCE

Planes: 20fr, CAMS-53 seaplane. 30fr, Wibault 283 Monoplane. 50fr, Dewoitine 338.

1984-87   **Engr.**
C56 AP31 15fr dark blue 5.00 .75
C57 AP31 20fr dp org ('85) 6.50 .75
C58 AP31 30fr brt vio ('86) 10.00 1.50
C59 AP31 50fr green ('87) 15.00 4.50
 Nos. C55-C59 (5) 37.25 7.90
Issued: 15fr, 3/3; 20fr, 3/2; 30fr, 10/11; 50fr, 4/11.

Breguet XIV — AP32

1997, Nov. 15 **Photo.** **Perf. 13x13¼**
C60 AP32 20fr shown 9.00 3.00
 Perf. 13x12½ 6.00 1.50
C61 AP32 30fr Potez 25 12.50 3.50
 Perf. 13x12½ 10.00 2.25
Issued: No. C60 11/15/97; No. C60a, 7/13/98; 30fr, 7/13/98.

Airbus A300-B4 AP33

1999, Apr. 10 **Photo.** **Perf. 13x13¼**
C62 AP33 15fr multicolored 15.00 3.00
a. Perf. 13x12½ 5.25 1.25

Couzinet 70 — AP34

2000, Feb. 12   **Perf. 13¼x13¼**
C63 AP34 50fr multi 17.50 6.00
a. Perf. 13x12½ 22.50 7.50

First Flight of Airbus A300, 30th Anniv. AP35

2002, Oct. 26 **Photo.** **Perf. 13x13¼**
C64 AP35 €3 multi 7.00 1.50
No. C64 was issued both in panes of 40 and 10, same perforation.

Jacqueline Auriol (1917-2000), Pilot, and Jet — AP36

Litho. & Engr.
2003, June 21   **Perf. 13**
C65 AP36 €4 multi 9.00 2.25
a. Miniature sheet of 10 90.00 —

Marie Marvingt (1875-1963), Pilot — AP37

Litho. & Engr.
2004, June 29   **Perf. 13¼x13**
C66 AP37 €5 multi 11.00 3.00
a. Sheet of 10 110.00 —

Adrienne Bolland (1895-1975), Pilot — AP38

Litho. & Engr.
2005, Oct. 22   **Perf. 13**
C67 AP38 €2 multi 4.50 1.50
a. Miniature sheet of 10 45.00 —

Airbus A380 AP39

2006, June 23 **Photo.** **Perf. 13x13¼**
C68 AP39 €3 multi 6.50 1.50
a. Miniature sheet of 10 65.00 —

Helicopters, Cent. AP40

2007, Feb. 19 **Photo.** **Perf. 13x12½**
C69 AP40 €3 multi 6.50 1.50
 Perf. 13x13¼ 9.00 2.25
No. C69 was issued in panes of 40; No. C69a in panes of 10.

French Acrobatic Patrol AP41

Litho. & Engr.
2008, Sept. 13   **Perf. 13**
C70 AP41 €3 multi 6.50 1.50

Louis Blériot (1872-1936) and Blériot XI Airplane AP42

Litho. & Engr.
2009, July 25   **Perf. 13x12¾**
C71 AP42 €2 multi 4.50 1.25
First flight across English Channel, cent.

Henri Fabre (1882-1984) and Le Canard Seaplane AP43

Litho. & Engr.
2010, Mar. 27   **Perf. 13**
C72 AP43 €3 multi 6.50 1.50
First seaplane flight, cent.

Henri Pequet (1888-1974), Pilot for First Official Air Mail Flight in India — AP44

2011, Feb. 18
C73 AP44 €2 multi 4.50 1.25

First French Airmail Flight Between Nancy and Luneville, Cent. AP45

2012, July 30
C74 AP45 €3 multi 6.50 1.50

First Parachute Jump by Adolphe Pégoud (1889-1915), Cent. — AP46

2013, June 13
C75 AP46 €2.55 multi 5.50 1.50
a. Miniature sheet of 10 65.00 65.00

First Trans-Mediterranean Flight by Roland Garros, Cent. — AP47

2013, Sept. 21 **Photo.** **Perf. 13x12¾**
C76 AP47 €3.40 multi 8.00 1.50

Caroline Aigle (1974-2007), First Female Fighter Pilot in French Air Force — AP48

Litho. & Engr.
2014, Apr. 5   **Perf. 13**
C77 AP48 €3.55 multi 8.50 1.50

Gaston Caudron (1882-1915), Pilot and Aircraft Manufacturer — AP49

Litho. & Engr.
2015, June 15   **Perf. 13**
C78 AP49 €4.10 multi 9.00 2.00

Edouard Nieuport (1875-1911), Aviator and Airplane Manufacturer, and Nieuport 11 — AP50

Litho. & Engr.
2016, June 10   **Perf. 13**
C79 AP50 €4.80 multi 11.00 5.50

Georges Guynemer (1894-1917), Ace Fighter Pilot in World War I, and Spad XIII — AP51

Litho. & Engr.
2017, Sept. 8   **Perf. 13**
C80 AP51 €5.10 multi 12.00 6.00
a. Miniature sheet of 10 — —

Michel Coiffard (1892-1918), and Maurice Boyau (1888-1918), World War I Flying Aces AP52

Litho. & Engr.
2018, Nov. 10   **Perf. 13**
C81 AP52 €3.80 multi 8.75 4.50

First Flight of the Concorde, 50th Anniv. AP53

2019, Mar. 1 **Photo.** **Perf. 13**
C82 AP53 €4.20 multi 9.50 4.75

Ballons Montés, 150th Anniv. AP54

Litho. & Engr.
2020, Nov. 5   **Perf. 13**
C83 AP54 €4.64 multi 11.50 5.75
a. Miniature sheet of 10 115.00 —

Pierre Clostermann (1921-2006), and Claire Roman (1906-41), World War II Pilots AP55

Litho. & Engr.
2021, Apr. 4   **Perf. 13**
C84 AP55 €4.71 multi 11.50 5.75
a. Miniature sheet of 10 115.00 —

Antoine de Saint-Exupery Air Post Semi-Postal Type of 1948 Redrawn
Miniature Sheet
Engr., Sheet Margin Engr. With Foil Application
2021, June 17   **Perf. 13**
C85 Sheet of 6, 2 each #C85a-C85c 57.00 57.00
a. SPAP1 €4 violet 9.50 9.50
b. SPAP1 €4 yellow green 9.50 9.50
c. SPAP1 €4 dp bluish grn 9.50 9.50

A sheet containing five redrawn stamps of type SPAP1 (two €1.50, two €7.50 stamps, and a larger €12 stamp) was printed in limited quantities.

Monoplane Over Paris Type of 1936 With Euro Denomination
2022, June 23 **Engr.** **Perf. 13x13¼**
Paper with Pink Network Overprint
C86 AP4 €7 deep ultra 14.50 14.50
No. C86 was printed in sheets of 4.

Dewoitine D1 and Aircraft Carrier Béarn AP56

Litho. & Engr.
2022, Nov. 3   **Perf. 13**
C87 AP56 €5.26 multi 11.00 5.50

FRANCE

Air View of Paris Type of 1950 With Euro Denomination

2022, Nov. 3   Engr.   Perf. 13x13¼
| C88 | AP13 | €7 blk & dl gray vio | 14.50 | 14.50 |

No. C88 was printed in sheets of 4.

Alexander III Bridge and Petit Palais Type of 1949 With Denomination in Euros

2023, Mar. 23   Engr.   Perf. 13x13¼
| C89 | AP14 | €7 brown carmine | 15.50 | 15.50 |

No. C89 was printed in sheets of 4.

AIR POST SEMI-POSTAL STAMPS

Catalogue values for unused stamps in this section are for Never Hinged items.

Antoine de Saint-Exupéry — SPAP1

Col. Jean Dagnaux — SPAP2

1948   Unwmk.   Engr.   Perf. 13
| CB1 | SPAP1 | 50fr + 30fr vio brn | 2.75 | 1.60 |
| CB2 | SPAP2 | 100fr + 70fr dk blue | 3.75 | 2.25 |

See No. C85.

Modern Plane and Ader's "Eole" — SPAP3

1948, Feb.
| CB3 | SPAP3 | 40fr + 10fr dk blue | 1.60 | 1.50 |

50th anniv. of the flight of Clément Ader's plane, the Eole, in 1897.

POSTAGE DUE STAMPS

D1

1859-70   Unwmk.   Litho.   Imperf.
| J1 | D1 | 10c black | 30,500. | 240.00 |
| J2 | D1 | 15c black ('70) | 140.00 | 250.00 |

In the lithographed stamps the central bar of the "E" of "CENTIMES" is very short, and the accent on "a" slants at an angle of 30 degree, for the 10c and 17 degree for the 15c, while on the typographed the central bar of the "E" is almost as wide as the top and bottom bars and the accent on the "a" slants at an angle of 47 degree.

No. J2 is known rouletted unofficially.

1859-78   Typo.
J3	D1	10c black	30.00	17.50
J4	D1	15c black ('63)	35.00	15.00
J5	D1	20c black ('77)	4,100.	
J6	D1	25c black ('71)	150.00	50.00
a.		Double impression	6,000.	
J7	D1	30c black ('78)	225.00	125.00
J8	D1	40c blue ('71)	325.00	425.00
a.		40c ultramarine	6,500.	5,750.
b.		40c Prussian blue	2,600.	
J9	D1	60c bister ('71)	475.00	1,050.
J10	D1	60c blue ('78)	60.00	110.00
a.		60c dark blue	800.00	725.00
J10B	D1	60c black	2,700.	

The 20c & 60c black were not put into use. Nos. J3, J4, J6, J8 and J9 are known rouletted unofficially and Nos. J4, J6, J7 and J10 pin-perf. unofficially.

D2

1882-92   Perf. 14x13½
J11	D2	1c black	2.50	2.50
J12	D2	2c black	30.00	26.00
J13	D2	3c black	30.00	25.00
J14	D2	4c black	60.00	40.00
J15	D2	5c black	130.00	32.50
J16	D2	10c black	110.00	2.50
J17	D2	15c black	77.50	10.50
J18	D2	20c black	350.00	140.00
J19	D2	30c black	210.00	2.50
J20	D2	40c black	140.00	60.00
J21	D2	50c blk ('92)	600.00	175.00
J22	D2	60c blk ('84)	600.00	57.50
J23	D2	1fr black	750.00	350.00
J24	D2	2fr blk ('84)	1,400.	825.00
J25	D2	5fr blk ('84)	3,000.	1,600.

Excellent counterfeits exist of Nos. J23-J25. See Nos. J26-J45A. For overprints and surcharges see Offices in China Nos. J1-J6, J33-J40, Offices in Egypt, Alexandria J1-J5, Port Said J1-J8, Offices in Zanzibar 60-62, J1-J5, Offices in Morocco 9-10, 24-25, J1-J5, J10-J12, J17-J22, J35-J41.

1884
J26	D2	1fr brown	400.00	90.00
J27	D2	2fr brown	190.00	130.00
J28	D2	5fr brown	450.00	325.00

1893-1941
J29	D2	5c blue ('94)	.25	.30
a.		Grayish paper (GC) ('16)	3.50	2.50
J30	D2	10c brown	.25	.30
a.		Grayish paper (GC) ('16)	3.50	.75
J31	D2	15c lt grn ('94)	28.00	1.40
a.		Grayish paper (GC) ('16)	22.50	1.50
J32	D2	20c ol grn ('06)	6.50	.65
a.		Grayish paper (GC) ('16)	11.00	.75
J33	D2	25c rose ('23)	6.50	3.75
J34	D2	30c red ('94)	.25	.25
a.		Grayish paper (GC) ('16)	3.75	.75
J35	D2	30c org red ('94)	475.00	85.00
J36	D2	40c rose ('25)	11.50	4.50
J37	D2	45c grn ('24)	9.00	5.25
J38	D2	50c brn vio ('95)	.50	.30
a.		50c lilac	.50	.30
b.		Grayish paper (GC) ('16)	11.00	.30
J39	D2	60c bl grn ('25)	1.00	.55
J40	D2	1fr rose, straw ('96)	475.00	375.00
J41	D2	1fr red brn, straw ('20)	9.50	.30
J42	D2	1fr red brn ('35)	1.25	.40
J43	D2	2fr red org ('10)	225.00	65.00
J44	D2	1fr brt vio ('26)	.65	.75
J45	D2	3fr magenta ('26)	.65	.75
J45A	D2	5fr red org ('41)	1.40	2.25

D3

1908-25
J46	D3	1c olive grn	1.00	1.25
J47	D3	10c violet	1.10	.30
a.		Imperf. pair	175.00	
J48	D3	20c bister ('19)	40.00	1.25
J49	D3	30c red ('09)	14.00	.40
J50	D3	50c red ('09)	275.00	60.00
J51	D3	60c red ('25)	2.75	3.75
		Nos. J46-J51 (6)	333.85	66.95

"Recouvrements" stamps were used to recover charges due on undelivered or refused mail which was returned to the sender.

For surcharges see Offices in Morocco Nos. J6-J9, J13-J16, J23-J26, J42-J45.

Nos. J49-J50 Surcharged

1917
J52	D3	20c on 30c bister	20.00	4.00
J53	D3	40c on 50c red	10.50	4.00
a.		Double surcharge	475.00	

In Jan. 1917 several values of the current issue of postage stamps were handstamped "T" in a triangle and used as postage due stamps.

Recouvrements Stamps of 1908-25 Surcharged

1926
J54	D3	50c on 10c lilac	3.50	3.25
J55	D3	60c on 1c ol grn	7.00	5.00
J56	D3	1fr on 60c red	18.00	10.00
J57	D3	2fr on 60c red	18.00	10.50
		Nos. J54-J57 (4)	46.50	28.75

D4

1927-31
J58	D4	1c olive grn ('28)	1.00	1.00
J59	D4	10c rose ('31)	1.90	1.40
J60	D4	30c bister	4.50	.50
J61	D4	60c red	4.50	.50
J62	D4	1fr violet	14.00	3.25
J63	D4	1fr Prus grn ('31)	17.00	.55
J64	D4	2fr blue	80.00	42.50
J65	D4	2fr olive brn ('31)	150.00	26.00
		Nos. J58-J65 (8)	272.90	75.70

Nos. J62 to J65 have the numerals of value double-lined.

Nos. J64, J62 Surcharged in Red or Black

1929
| J66 | D4 | 1.20fr on 2fr blue | 42.50 | 11.00 |
| J67 | D4 | 5fr on 1fr vio (Bk) | 65.00 | 15.00 |

No. J61 Surcharged

1931
| J68 | D4 | 1fr on 60c red | 30.00 | 2.75 |

Catalogue values for unused stamps in this section, from this point to the end of the section, are for Never Hinged items.

Sheaves of Wheat — D5

Perf. 14x13½

1943-46   Unwmk.   Typo.
J69	D5	10c sepia	.25	.25
J70	D5	30c brt red vio	.25	.25
J71	D5	50c blue grn	.25	.25
J72	D5	1fr brt ultra	.25	.25
J73	D5	1.50fr rose red	.25	.25
J74	D5	2fr turq blue	.25	.25
J75	D5	3fr brn org	.30	.25
J76	D5	4fr dp vio ('45)	4.50	2.25
J77	D5	5fr brt pink	.40	.25
J78	D5	10fr red org ('45)	2.50	.60
J79	D5	20fr ol bis ('46)	8.00	2.25
		Nos. J69-J79 (11)	17.20	7.10

Type of 1943 Inscribed "Timbre Taxe"

1946-53
J80	D5	10c sepia ('47)	.75	.40
J81	D5	30c brt red vio ('47)	.75	.40
J82	D5	50c blue grn ('47)	19.00	6.50
J83	D5	1fr brt ultra ('47)	.25	.25
J85	D5	2fr turq blue	.25	.25
J86	D5	3fr brown org	.25	.25
J87	D5	4fr deep violet	.25	.25
J88	D5	5fr brt pink ('47)	.25	.25
J89	D5	10fr red org ('47)	.25	.25
J90	D5	20fr olive bis ('47)	1.25	.30
J91	D5	50fr dk green ('50)	19.00	.75
J92	D5	100fr dp green ('53)	65.00	6.00
		Nos. J80-J92 (12)	107.25	15.85

For surcharges see Reunion Nos. J36-J44.

Sheaves of Wheat — D6

1960   Typo.   Perf. 14x13½
J93	D6	5c bright pink	2.75	.40
J94	D6	10c red orange	3.75	.25
J95	D6	20c olive bister	3.50	.75

J96	D6	50c dark green	9.75	.75
J97	D6	1fr deep green	40.00	1.50
		Nos. J93-J97 (5)	59.75	3.65

For surcharges see Reunion Nos. J46-J48. For overprints see Algeria Nos. J49-J53.

D7

Flowers: 5c, Centaury. 10c, Gentian. 15c, Corn poppy. 20c, Violets. 30c, Forget-me-not. 40c, Columbine. 50c, Clover. 1fr, Soldanel.

1964-71   Typo.   Perf. 14x13½
J98	D7	5c car rose, red & grn ('65)	.25	.25
J99	D7	10c car rose, brt bl & grn ('65)	.25	.25
J100	D7	15c brn, grn & red	.25	.25
J101	D7	20c dk grn, grn & vio ('71)	.25	.25
J102	D7	30c brn, ultra & grn	.25	.25
J103	D7	40c dk grn, scar & yel ('71)	.25	.25
J104	D7	50c vio bl, car & grn	.25	.25
J105	D7	1fr vio bl, lil & grn ('65)	.40	.25
		Nos. J98-J105 (8)	2.15	2.00

For surcharges see Reunion Nos. J49-J55.

D8

Designs: 10c, Ampedus Cinnabarinus. 20c, Dorcadion fuliginator. 30c, Leptura cordigera. 40c, Paedarus littoralis. 50c, Pyrochroa coccinea. 1fr, Scarites laevigatus. 2fr, Trichius gallicus. 3fr, Adalia alpina. 4fr, Apoderus coryli. 5fr, Trichodes alvearius.

1982-83   Engr.   Perf. 13
J106	D8	10c multicolored	.25	.25
J107	D8	20c multicolored	.25	.25
J108	D8	30c multicolored	.25	.25
J109	D8	40c multicolored	.25	.25
J110	D8	50c multicolored	.25	.25
J111	D8	1fr multicolored	.40	.25
J112	D8	2fr multicolored	.65	.25
J113	D8	3fr multicolored	1.00	.25
J114	D8	4fr multicolored	1.40	.25
J115	D8	5fr multicolored	1.75	.25
		Nos. J106-J115 (10)	6.45	2.50

Issued: 30c, 40c, 3fr, 5fr, 1/3/83; others, 1/4/82.

MILITARY STAMPS

Regular Issue Overprinted in Black or Red

1901-39   Unwmk.   Perf. 14x13½
M1	A17	15c orange ('01)	65.00	6.00
a.		Inverted overprint	300.00	150.00
b.		Imperf., pair	425.00	
M2	A19	15c pale red ('03)	65.00	6.00
M3	A20	15c orange ('04)	52.50	6.00
a.		No period after "M"	110.00	57.50
b.		Imperf., pair	290.00	
M4	A20	10c rose ('06)	30.00	8.25
a.		No period after "M"	82.50	45.00
b.		Imperf., pair	350.00	
M5	A22	10c red ('07)	1.75	1.00
a.		Inverted overprint	105.00	65.00
b.		Imperf., pair	190.00	
M6	A20	50c vermilion ('29)	4.75	1.00
a.		No period after "M"	32.50	18.00
b.		Period in front of F	32.50	18.00
M7	A45	50c rose red ('34)	2.75	.55
a.		No period after "M"	29.00	16.00
b.		Inverted overprint	150.00	110.00
M8	A45	65c vio ultra (R) ('38)	.30	.30
a.		No period after "M"	29.00	16.00
M9	A45	90c ultra (R) ('39)	.40	.35
		Nos. M1-M9 (9)	222.45	29.45

"F. M." are initials of Franchise Militaire (Military Frank). See No. S1.

Catalogue values for unused stamps in this section, from this point to the end of the section, are for Never Hinged items.

FRANCE

M1

1946-47   Typo.
M10 M1   dark green   1.75   .65
M11 M1   rose red ('47)   .30   .25

Nos. M10-M11 were valid also in the French colonies.

Flag — M2

1964, July 20   Perf. 13x14
M12 M2   multicolored   .30   .35

OFFICIAL STAMPS

FOR THE COUNCIL OF EUROPE

For use only on mail posted in the post office in the Council of Europe Building, Strasbourg.

Catalogue values for unused stamps in this section are for Never Hinged items.

For French stamp inscribed "Conseil de l'Europe" see No. 679.

France No. 854 Overprinted

1958, Jan. 14   Unwmk.   Engr.   Perf. 13
1O1 A303 35fr car rose & lake   .75   2.00

Council of Europe Flag — O1

1958-59   Flag in Ultramarine
1O2 O1   8fr red org & brn vio   .25   .25
1O3 O1   20fr yel & lt brn   .25   .25
1O4 O1   25fr lil rose & sl grn ('59)   .60   .30
1O5 O1   35fr red   .40   .25
1O6 O1   50fr lilac rose ('59)   .75   .75
Nos. 1O2-1O6 (5)   2.25   1.80

1963, Jan. 3   Flag in Ultramarine
1O7 O1   20c yel & lt brn   .90   .65
1O8 O1   25c lil rose & sl grn   1.40   1.10
1O9 O1   50c lilac rose   1.90   1.60
Nos. 1O7-1O9 (3)   4.20   3.35

Centime value stamps shown the denomination as "0,20", etc.

1965-71
Flag in Ultramarine & Yellow
1O10 O1   25c ver, yel & sl grn   .75   .55
1O11 O1   30c ver & yel   .35   .35
1O12 O1   40c ver, yel & gray   .75   .55
1O13 O1   50c red, yel & grn   1.50   1.10
1O14 O1   60c ver, yel & vio   1.10   1.00
1O15 O1   70c ver, yel & dk brn   2.25   2.10
Nos. 1O10-1O15 (6)   6.70   5.65

Issue dates: 25c, 30c, 60c, 1/16/65; 50c, 2/20/71; others, 3/24/69.

Type of 1958 Inscribed "FRANCE"
Flag in Ultramarine & Yellow

1975-76   Engr.   Perf. 13
1O16 O1   60c org, yel & emer   .60   .55
1O17 O1   80c yel & mag   .75   .60

1O18 O1   1fr car, yel & gray ol ('76)   1.50   1.25
1O19 O1   1.20fr org, yel & bl   4.00   2.25
Nos. 1O16-1O19 (4)   6.85   4.65

Issue dates: 1fr, 10/16; others, 11/22.

New Council Headquarters, Strasbourg — O2

1977, Jan. 22   Engr.   Perf. 13
1O20 O2   80c car & multi   .80   .50
1O21 O2   1fr brown & multi   .75   .30
1O22 O2   1.40fr gray & multi   1.50   .75
Nos. 1O20-1O22 (3)   3.05   1.55

Human Rights Emblem in Upper Left Corner

1978, Oct. 14
1O23 O2   1.20fr red lilac & multi   .45   .40
1O24 O2   1.70fr blue & multi   .60   .55

30th anniversary of the Universal Declaration of Human Rights.

Council Headquarters Type of 1977

1980, Nov. 24   Engr.   Perf. 13
1O25 O2   1.40fr olive   .50   .50
1O26 O2   2fr blue gray   .75   .75

New Council Headquarters, Strasbourg — O3

1981-84   Engr.
1O27 O3   1.40fr multicolored   .50   .50
1O28 O3   1.60fr multicolored   .50   .40
1O29 O3   1.70fr emerald   .60   .40
1O30 O3   1.80fr multicolored   .70   .60
1O31 O3   2fr multicolored   .75   .40
1O32 O3   2.10fr red   .75   .60
1O33 O3   2.30fr multicolored   .85   .60
1O34 O3   2.60fr multicolored   .90   .75
1O35 O3   2.80fr multicolored   1.00   .75
1O36 O3   3fr brt blue   1.10   .90
Nos. 1O27-1O36 (10)   7.65   5.90

Issued: 1.40, 1.60, 2.30fr, 11/21; 1.80, 2.60fr, 11/13/82; 2, 2.80fr, 11/21/83; 1.70, 2.10, 3fr, 11/5/84.

Youth's Leg, Sneaker, Shattered Eggshell — O4

1985, Aug. 31   Engr.   Perf. 13
1O37 O4   1.80fr brt green   .70   .60
1O38 O4   2.20fr vermilion   .75   .60
1O39 O4   3.20fr brt blue   1.10   1.00
Nos. 1O37-1O39 (3)   2.55   2.20

New Council Headquarters, Strasbourg — O5

1986-87   Engr.   Perf. 13
1O40 O5   1.90fr green   .70   .60
1O41 O5   2fr brt yel grn   .90   .60
1O42 O5   2.20fr red   .75   .60
1O43 O5   3.40fr blue   1.20   1.00
1O44 O5   3.60fr brt blue   1.40   1.10
Nos. 1O40-1O44 (5)   4.95   3.90

Issued: 1.90, 2.20, 3.40fr, 12/13; 2, 3.60fr, 10/10/87.

Council of Europe, 40th Anniv. — O6

1989, Feb. 4   Litho. & Engr.
1O45 O6   2.20fr multicolored   .90   .70
1O46 O6   3.60fr multicolored   1.40   1.10

Denominations also inscribed in European Currency Units (ECUs).

Map of Europe — O7

1990-91   Litho.   Perf. 13
1O47 O7   2.30fr multicolored   .90   .75
1O48 O7   2.50fr multicolored   .90   .75
1O49 O7   3.20fr multicolored   1.10   1.00
1O50 O7   3.40fr multicolored   1.10   1.00
Nos. 1O47-1O50 (4)   4.00   3.50

Issued: 2.30fr, 3.20fr, 5/26/90; 2.50fr, 3.40fr, 11/23/91.

36 Heads, by Hundertwasser — O8

1994, Jan. 15   Litho.   Perf. 13
1O51 O8   2.80fr multicolored   1.40   .75
1O52 O8   3.70fr multicolored   2.25   1.00

Palace of Human Rights, Strasbourg — O9

1996, June 1   Litho.   Perf. 13
1O53 O9   3fr multicolored   1.50   .75
1O54 O9   3.80fr multicolored   1.75   1.00

Charioteer of Delphi — O10

1999, Sept. 18   Photo.   Perf. 13
1O55 O10   3fr shown   1.40   .75
1O56 O10   3.80fr Nike   1.75   1.00

Girl, Penguin and Boy — O11

2001, Dec. 1   Litho.   Perf. 13
1O57 O11   3fr red & multi   2.00   .70
1O58 O11   3.80fr grn & multi   2.40   1.00

Hiker on Stars — O12

2003, Oct. 18   Litho.   Perf. 13
1O59 O12   50c Hiker facing left   2.00   .70
1O60 O12   75c Hiker facing right   2.50   1.20

O13   O14

2005, Sept. 18   Litho.   Perf. 13
1O61 O13   55c multi   2.00   .75
1O62 O14   75c multi   2.50   1.20

Map of Europe — O15

Sculpture by Mariano González Beltrán — O16

2007, June 23   Litho.   Perf. 13
1O63 O15   60c multi   2.00   .75
1O64 O16   85c multi   2.50   1.25

Council of Europe, 60th Anniv. — O17

European Court of Human Rights, 50th Anniv. — O18

2009, May 16   Litho.   Perf. 13
1O65 O17   56c multi   2.00   .75
1O66 O18   70c multi   2.50   1.25

Tree — O19   Chain — O20

2010, Sept. 17   Litho.   Perf. 13
1O67 O19   75c multi   2.10   .75
1O68 O20   87c multi   2.40   1.25

European Human Rights Convention, 60th anniv. (No. 1O68).

Map of Europe and Flags — O21

2011, Sept. 9   Litho.   Perf. 13
1O69 O21   89c multi   2.50   1.25

European Social Charter, 50th anniv.

European Youth Center, Strasbourg, 40th Anniv. — O22

2012, Sept. 28
1O70 O22   89c multi   2.40   1.25

Balance of Rights and Responsibilties of Citizens in a Democracy O23

2013, Sept. 27   Litho.   Perf. 13
1O71 O23   95c multi   2.60   1.25

FRANCE

European Directorate for the Quality of Medicines and Health Care, 50th Anniv. — O24

European Cultural Cooperation, 60th Anniv. — O25

2014, Oct. 3	Photo.		Perf. 13	
1072	O24	83c multi	2.10	1.00
1073	O25	98c multi	2.50	1.25

European Union Flag, 60th Anniv. — O26

2015, Oct. 2	Litho.		Perf. 13	
1074	O26	95c multi	2.25	1.10

European Social Charter — O27

2016, Oct. 14	Litho.		Perf. 13	
1075	O27	€1 multi	2.25	2.25

Council of Europe Cultural Routes 30th Anniv. — O28

2017, Oct. 13	Litho.		Perf. 13	
1076	O28	€1.10 multi	2.60	2.60

Framework Convention for the Protection of National Minorities, 20th Anniv. — O29

2018, Oct. 12	Litho.		Perf. 13	
1077	O29	€1.20 multi	2.75	2.75

Council of Europe, 70th Anniv. — O30

European Court of Human Rights, 60th Anniv. — O31

2019, May 5	Litho.		Perf. 13¼	
1078	O30	€1.30 multi	3.00	3.00
1079	O31	€1.30 multi	3.00	3.00

European Convention on Human Rights, 70th Anniv. — O32

European Court of Human Rights Building, 25th Anniv. — O33

2020, Sept. 4	Litho.		Perf. 13¼	
1080	O32	€1.40 multi	3.25	3.25
1081	O33	€1.40 dk blue	3.25	3.25

Freedom of Expression — O34

Digital Printing

2021, Sept. 30			Perf. 13¼	
1082	O34	€1.50 multi	3.50	3.50

Gender Equality — O35

Digital Printing

2022, Sept. 2			Perf. 13¼	
1083	O35	€1.65 multi	3.25	3.25

Ukrainian Child — O36

2023, Sept. 8	Photo.		Perf. 13¼	
1084	O36	€1.80 multi	4.00	4.00

Solidarity with Ukraine in war against Russia.

FOR THE UNITED NATIONS EDUCATIONAL, SCIENTIFIC AND CULTURAL ORGANIZATION

For use only on mail posted in the post office in the UNESCO Building, Paris.

Catalogue values for unused stamps in this section are for Never Hinged items.

For French stamps inscribed "UNESCO" see Nos. 572, 893-894, 2545.

Khmer Buddha and Hermes by Praxiteles — O1

1961-65	Unwmk.	Engr.	Perf. 13	
201	O1	20c dk gray, ol bis & bl	.25	.55
202	O1	25c blk, lake & grn	.40	.90
203	O1	30c choc & bis brn ('65)	.90	.60
204	O1	50c blk, red & vio bl	.90	1.75
205	O1	60c grnsh bl, red brn & rose lil ('65)	1.00	1.40
	Nos. 201-205 (5)		3.45	5.20

Book and Globe — O2

1966, Dec. 17				
206	O2	25c gray	.30	.25
207	O2	30c dark red	.45	.35
208	O2	60c green	.75	.65
	Nos. 206-208 (3)		1.50	1.25

20th anniversary of UNESCO.

Human Rights Flame — O3

1969-71	Engr.		Perf. 13	
209	O3	30c sl grn, red & dp brn	.30	.30
2010	O3	40c dk car rose, red & dp brn	.45	.40
2011	O3	50c ultra, car & brn ('71)	.75	.60
2012	O3	70c pur, red & sl	1.50	1.40
	Nos. 209-2012 (4)		3.00	2.70

Universal Declaration of Human Rights.

Type of 1969 Inscribed "FRANCE" — O3a

1975, Nov. 15	Engr.		Perf. 13	
2013	O3a	60c bl grn, red & choc	.60	.55
2014	O3a	80c ocher, red & red brn	.90	.60
2015	O3a	1.20fr ind, red & brn	3.00	2.25
	Nos. 2013-2015 (3)		4.50	3.40

O4

1976-78	Engr.		Perf. 13	
2016	O4	80c multi	.65	.55
2017	O4	1fr multi	.35	.30
2018	O4	1.20fr multi	.50	.40
2019	O4	1.40fr multi	1.25	.90
2020	O4	1.70fr multi	.75	.60
	Nos. 2016-2020 (5)		3.50	2.75

Issued: 1.20, 1.70fr, 10/14/78; others, 10/23/76.

Slave Quarters, Senegal — O5

Designs: 1.40fr, Mohenjo-Daro excavations, Pakistan. 2fr, Sans-Souci Palace, Haiti.

1980, Nov. 17	Engr.		Perf. 13	
2021	O5	1.20fr multi	.50	.50
2022	O5	1.40fr multi	.55	.50
2023	O5	2fr multi	.80	.65
	Nos. 2021-2023 (3)		1.85	1.65

Hue, Vietnam — O7

Designs: 1.40fr, Building, Fez, Morocco. 1.60fr, Seated deity, Sukhotai, Thailand. 2.30fr, Fort St. Elmo, Malta, horiz. 2.60fr, St. Michael Church ruins, Brazil.

1981-82				
2024	O7	1.40fr multi	.50	.35
2025	O7	1.60fr multi	.50	.35
2026	O7	1.80fr shown	.70	.55
2027	O7	2.30fr multi	.60	.50
2028	O7	2.60fr multi	.75	.55
	Nos. 2024-2028 (5)		3.05	2.30

Issued: 1.80fr, 2.60fr, 10/23/82; others, 12/12/81.

Mosque, Chinguetti, Mauritania — O8

Roman Theater and Female Standing Sculpture, Carthage, Tunisia — O8a

Architecture: 1.70fr, Church, Lalibela, Ethiopia. 2.10fr, San'a, Yemen. 2.20fr, Old Town Square and wrought iron latticework, Havana. 2.80fr, Enclosure wall interior, Istanbul. 3fr, Church, Kotor, Yugoslavia. 3.20fr, Temple of Anuradhapura and bas-relief of two women, Sri Lanka.

1983-85			Engr.	
2029	O8	1.70fr multi	.55	.35
2030	O8a	1.80fr multi	.65	.55
2031	O8	2fr multi	.75	.40
2032	O8	2.10fr multi	.75	.60
2033	O8a	2.20fr multi	.75	.60
2034	O8	2.80fr multi	1.00	.60
2035	O8	3fr multi	1.10	.90
2036	O8a	3.20fr multi	1.10	1.00
	Nos. 2029-2036 (8)		6.65	5.00

Issued: 2fr, 2.80fr, 10/10; 1.70fr, 2.10fr, 3fr, 10/22/84; 1.80fr, 2.20fr, 3.20fr, 10/26/85.

Tikal Temple, Guatemala — O9

3.40fr, Bagerhat Mosque, Bangladesh.

1986, Dec. 6	Engr.		Perf. 13	
2037	O9	1.90fr shown	.75	.65
2038	O9	3.40fr multicolored	1.25	1.20

The Parthenon, Athens — O10

3.60fr, Temple of Philae, Egypt.

1987, Dec. 5	Engr.		Perf. 13x12½	
2039	O10	2fr shown	.90	.60
2040	O10	3.60fr multicolored	1.40	1.20

Shibam, Yemen People's Democratic Republic — O11

2.30fr, San Francisco de Lima, Peru, vert.

	Perf. 13x12½, 12½x13			
1990, Apr. 7			Engr.	
2041	O11	2.30fr multicolored	.90	.75
2042	O11	3.20fr shown	1.20	1.00

Bagdaon Temple, Nepal — O12

3.40fr, Citadel of Harat, Afghanistan, horiz.

1991, Nov. 23				
2043	O12	2.50fr choc & dk red	.90	.75
2044	O12	3.40fr grn, brn & ol	1.20	1.00

Tassili N'Ajjer Natl. Park, Algeria — O13

Design: 2.80fr, Angkor Wat Archaeological Park, Cambodia, vert.

1993, Oct. 23	Litho.		Perf. 13	
2045	O13	2.80fr multicolored	1.25	.75
2046	O13	3.70fr multicolored	1.50	1.00

FRANCE

UNESCO, 50th Anniv. — O14

Designs: 3fr, Uluru Natl. Park, Australia. 3.80fr, Los Glaciares Natl. Park, Argentina.

1996, June 1		Litho.		Perf. 13	
2O47	O14	3fr multicolored		1.50	.75
2O48	O14	3.80fr multicolored		2.00	1.00

Detail of Dionysus Fresco, Pompeii O15

Moai Statues, Easter Island O16

1998, Oct. 24		Litho.		Perf. 13	
2O49	O15	3fr multicolored		1.50	.75
2O50	O16	3.80fr multicolored		1.90	1.25

Sphinx and Pyramids, Egypt — O17

Komodo Dragon, Komodo Natl. Park, Indonesia — O18

2001, Dec. 1		Litho.		Perf. 13	
2O51	O17	3fr multi		2.00	.75
2O52	O18	3.80fr multi		2.50	1.00

Reindeer, Lapland O19

Church of the Resurrection, St. Petersburg, Russia O20

2003, Dec. 6		Litho.		Perf. 13	
2O53	O19	50c multi		2.00	.75
2O54	O20	75c multi		2.50	1.40

Bison in Bialowieza Forest, Poland O21

Petra, Jordan O22

2005, Nov. 26		Litho.		Perf. 13	
2O55	O21	55c multi		2.00	.75
2O56	O22	90c multi		2.50	1.40

Siberian Tiger — O23

Luang Prabang, Laos — O24

2006, Dec. 7		Litho.		Perf. 13	
2O57	O23	60c multi		2.00	.75
2O58	O24	85c multi		2.50	1.25

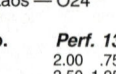

Ksar d'Ait-Ben-Haddou, Morocco — O25

Koala, Australia — O26

2007, Dec. 13		Litho.		Perf. 13	
2O59	O25	60c multi		2.00	.75
2O60	O26	85c multi		2.50	1.40

Gorilla — O27

Machu Picchu, Peru — O28

2008, Dec. 3		Litho.		Perf. 13	
2O61	O27	65c multi		2.00	1.00
2O62	O28	85c multi		2.50	1.25

Polar Bear — O29

Suzhou, China — O30

2009, Dec. 9		Litho.		Perf. 13	
2O63	O29	70c multi		2.10	1.00
2O64	O30	85c multi		2.50	1.25

Alhambra, Spain — O31

Alpaca — O32

2010, Dec. 1		Litho.		Perf. 13	
2O65	O31	75c multi		2.00	1.00
2O66	O32	87c multi		2.40	1.20

Bactrian Camel — O33

Milford Sound, New Zealand — O34

2011, Oct. 19					
2O67	O33	77c multi		2.10	1.00
2O68	O34	89c multi		2.50	1.25

Stonehenge, Great Britain — O35

African Elephants — O36

2012, Nov. 22					
2O69	O35	77c multi		2.00	1.00
2O70	O36	89c multi		2.40	1.20

Japanese Cranes O37

Sigiriya UNESCO World Heritage Site, Sri Lanka O38

2013, Nov. 7		Litho.		Perf. 13	
2O71	O37	58c multi		1.60	.80
2O72	O38	95c multi		2.60	1.25

Trulli of Alberobello UNESCO World Heritage Site, Italy O39

Hyacinth Macaw O40

2014, Nov. 8		Litho.		Perf. 13x13¼	
2O73	O39	83c multi		2.10	1.00
		Perf. 13¼x13			
2O74	O40	98c multi		2.50	1.25

African Gnu O41

Sagrada Familia Basilica, Barcelona O42

2015, Nov. 6		Litho.		Perf. 13	
2O75	O41	95c multi		2.00	2.00
2O76	O42	€1.20 multi		2.60	2.60

UNESCO, 70th anniv.

Florida Panther O43

Ruins, Ephesus, Turkey O44

2016, Sept. 9		Litho.		Perf. 13	
2O77	O43	€1 multi		2.25	2.25
2O78	O44	€1.25 multi		2.75	2.75

Samarkand, Uzbekistan O45

Orangutan O46

2017, June 30		Litho.		Perf. 13	
2O79	O45	€1.10 multi		2.50	2.50
2O80	O46	€1.30 multi		3.00	3.00

UNESCO Man and Biosphere Program — O47

2018, Sept. 7		Photo.		Perf. 12¼	
2O81	O47	€1.30 multi		3.00	3.00

International Year of Indigenous Languages O48

2019, Sept. 13		Litho.		Perf. 13¼	
2O82	O48	€1.30 multi		3.00	3.00

UNESCO, 75th Anniv. — O49

2020, Sept. 11		Litho.		Perf. 13	
2O83	O49	€1.40 multi		3.25	3.25

"United Against Racism and Discrimination" O50

Digital Printing

2021, Sept. 17				Perf. 13	
2O84	O50	€1.50 multi		3.50	3.50

Florence Cathedral — O51

Digital Printing

2022, Sept. 9				Perf. 13¼	
2O85	O51	€1.65 multi		3.25	3.25

Convention Concerning the Protection of the World Cultural and Natural Heritage, 50th anniv.

FRANCE

Zaouli Dancer, Ivory Coast — O52

2023, Sept. 8   Litho.   Perf. 13¼
2O86 O52 €1.80 multi   4.00 4.00
Convention for Safeguarding the Intangible Cultural Heritage, 20th anniv.

NEWSPAPER STAMPS

Coat of Arms — N1

1868   Unwmk.   Typo.   Imperf.
P1 N1 2c lilac   300.00   65.00
P2 N1 2c (+ 2c) blue   600.00 275.00

Perf. 12½
P3 N1 2c lilac   52.50   25.00
P4 N1 2c (+ 4c) rose   250.00 100.00
P5 N1 2c (+ 2c) blue   75.00   35.00
P6 N1 5c lilac   1,250.   550.00

Nos. P2, P4, and P5 were sold for face plus an added fiscal charge indicated in parenthesis. Nos. P1, P3 and P6 were used simply as fiscals.

The 2c rose and 5c lilac imperforate and the 5c rose and 5c blue, both imperforate and perforated, were never put into use.

Nos. P1-P6 were reprinted for the 1913 Ghent Exhibition and the 1937 Paris Exhibition (PEXIP).

No. 109 Surcharged in Red

1919   Perf. 14x13½
P7 A16 ½c on 1c gray   .30   .30
  a.   Inverted surcharge 1,200. 1,150.
  c.   Grayish paper (GC) ('16) .30 .30

No. 156 Surcharged
1933
P8 A22 ½c on 1c olive bister   .30 .30

PARCEL POST STAMPS

Inscribed "I APPORT A LA GARE" — PP1

Perfs As Noted
1892   Unwmk.   Typo.
Q1 PP1 25c brown, yel,
         perf 13½   825.00 290.00
         Never hinged   1,500.
Q2 PP1 25c brown, yel,
         perf 11   30.00   24.00
         Never hinged   46.00
  a.   Printed on both sides 400.00
         Never hinged   650.00

Inscribed "II VALEUR DECLAREE" — PP2

Q3 PP2 10c red, perf 13½ 1,000. 275.00
         Never hinged   1,750.
Q4 PP2 10c red, perf
         10x13½   875.00 325.00
         Never hinged   1,600.

Q5 PP2 10c org red, perf
         11   30.00   14.00
         Never hinged   42.50
Q6 PP2 10c red, imperf   22.50   16.50
         Never hinged   32.50

Inscribed "III LIVRAISON PAR EXPRESS" — PP3

Q7 PP3 25c green, perf
         13½   57.50   32.50
         Never hinged   115.00
Q8 PP3 25c green, perf
         11   45.00   24.00
         Never hinged   70.00

See Nos. Q22-Q26.

Locomotive — PP4

A set of six stamps, in the design above, was prepared in 1901 as postal tax stamps for expedited parcels but were not issued. All are perf 14x13½. Values: 5c gray, $3, never hinged $4; 10c yellow green, $3, never hinged $5; 20c rose, $20, never hinged $29; 50c blue, $7, never hinged $11.50; 1fr brown, $8, never hinged $12; 2fr brown red, $37.50, never hinged $57.50.

PP5

Large Trefoil

Type I: Large Trefoil Under "N" of "MAJORATION"

1918   Perf. 11
Q9   PP5 5c black   1.25   .85
          Never hinged   2.00
Q10 PP5 15c brn lilac   1.25   .85
          Never hinged   2.00

Imperforate
Q11 PP5 5c black   3.25   2.50
          Never hinged   6.25
Q12 PP5 15c brn lilac   9.00   4.25
          Never hinged   14.00
          Nos. Q9-Q12 (4) 14.75   8.45

40c values, perforated 11 and imperf, in orange, were prepared but not issued. Value, perf or imperf, $375.

PP5a

Small Trefoil

Type II: Small Trefoil Under "O" of "MAJORATION"

Q13 PP5a 5c black   140.00 45.00
           Never hinged   275.00
Q14 PP5a 35c red   3.75   2.50
           Never hinged   5.00
Q15 PP5a 50c vio blue   4.50   1.60
           Never hinged   7.00
Q16 PP5a 1fr yellow   4.25   1.60
           Never hinged   7.00

Imperforate
Q17 PP5a 5c black   130.00 45.00
           Never hinged   260.00
Q18 PP5a 15c brn lilac   30.00 16.50
           Never hinged   50.00
Q19 PP5a 35c red   3.25   2.50
           Never hinged   6.75

Q20 PP5a 50c vio blue   24.00 14.00
           Never hinged   40.00
Q21 PP5a 1fr yellow   18.50 12.50
           Never hinged   30.00
           Nos. Q13-Q21 (9) 358.25 141.20

See Nos. Q41-Q44, Q143-Q145.
For surcharges, see Nos. Q28-Q40.

Type of 1892
1918-23   Perf. 10½x11
Q22 PP1 30c brn, yel   37.50 16.50
          Never hinged   55.00
  a.   Imperf   200.00
          Never hinged   290.00
Q23 PP1 60c brn, straw
          ('23)   47.50 30.00
          Never hinged   70.00
  a.   Imperf   190.00
          Never hinged   275.00
Q24 PP2 15c vermilion ('22) 16.00 11.00
          Never hinged   23.00
Q25 PP3 30c green   40.00 21.00
          Never hinged   57.50
  a.   Imperf   240.00
          Never hinged   325.00
Q26 PP3 60c green ('23) 75.00 50.00
          Never hinged   110.00
          Nos. Q22-Q26 (5) 216.00 128.50

PP6

1924, Oct.   Perf. 14
Q27 PP6 15c rose & blue   4.00   3.75
          Never hinged   5.00
  a.   Imperf   550.00
          Never hinged   750.00

No. Q27 is a postal tax stamp, issued to show the collection of a new 15c excise fee on rail parcels. On July 3, 1925, its use was extended to all fiscal categories.

Surcharged in Black or Red (R) on Nos. Q9//Q16 and Types of 1918

1926   Perf. 13
Q28 PP5 20c on 2fr rose   1.90   1.10
          Never hinged   2.75
Q29 PP5 30c on 2fr yellow 1.90   1.10
          Never hinged   2.75
  a.   "0f30" omitted   190.00
          Never hinged   250.00
Q30 PP5 40c on 3fr gray   1.90   1.40
          Never hinged   2.75
Q31 PP5 45c on 3fr orange 1.90   1.40
          Never hinged   2.75
  a.   Period after "f" omitted 19.00 19.00
          Never hinged   30.00
Q32 PP5 95c on 1fr yel   8.00   2.75
          Never hinged   12.50
  a.   Imperf   90.00
          Never hinged   150.00
Q33 PP5 1.35fr on 3fr vio 10.50   4.50
          Never hinged   14.00
          On postal document   70.00
  a.   Imperf   150.00
          Never hinged   225.00
Q34 PP5 1.45fr on 5fr blk
          (R)   1.90   1.00
          Never hinged   2.75
Q35 PP5 1.75fr on 2fr blue 10.50 4.50
          Never hinged   14.00
Q36 PP5 1.85fr on 10c org 1.90   1.20
          Never hinged   2.75
Q37 PP5 1.95fr on 15c brn
          lilac   2.50   1.75
          Never hinged   3.50
  a.   Imperf   110.00
          Never hinged   175.00
Q38 PP5 2.35fr on 25c grn 1.90   1.00
          Never hinged   2.75
  a.   Imperf   110.00
          Never hinged   175.00
Q39 PP5 2.90fr on 35c red 2.50   1.00
          Never hinged   3.50
  a.   Dots before and after "f" 140.00
          Never hinged   200.00
  b.   Imperf   125.00
          Never hinged   190.00
Q40 PP5 3.30fr on 50c blue
          violet (R)   2.50   1.25
          Never hinged   3.50
  a.   Double surcharge 250.00
          Never hinged   375.00
  b.   Imperf   90.00
          Never hinged   140.00
          Nos. Q28-Q40 (13) 49.80 23.95

Type of 1918
1926   Perf. 11
Q41 PP5 10c orange   2.00   1.25
          Never hinged   3.75
  a.   Imperf   4.00
          Never hinged   6.50
Q42 PP5 25c pale green   2.00   1.25
          Never hinged   3.75
  a.   Imperf   4.00
          Never hinged   6.50

Q43 PP5 2fr pale blue   25.00 14.50
          Never hinged   42.50
  a.   Imperf   50.00
          Never hinged   80.00
Q44 PP5 3fr violet   110.00 67.50
          Never hinged   190.00
  a.   Imperf   225.00
          Never hinged   360.00
          Nos. Q41-Q44 (4) 139.00 84.50

No. 51

Inscribed "APPORT A LA GARE" — PP7

1926
Q45 PP7 1fr on 60c brn,
          yel   13.50 10.50
          Never hinged   24.00
  a.   Imperf   190.00
          Never hinged   300.00
Q46 PP7 1fr brn, yel   17.50 13.00
          Never hinged   30.00
Q47 PP7 1.30fr on 1fr brn,
          yel   17.50 12.50
          Never hinged   30.00
Q48 PP7 1.50fr brn, yel 20.00 11.50
          Never hinged   32.50
Q49 PP7 1.65fr brn, yel 15.00 12.50
          Never hinged   24.00
Q50 PP7 1.90fr on 1fr brn,
          yel   17.50 12.50
          Never hinged   30.00
Q51 PP7 2.10fr on 1.65fr
          brn, yel   17.50 12.50
          Never hinged   30.00
          Nos. Q45-Q51 (7) 118.50 85.00

See Nos. Q91-Q95, footnote following No. Q102, Q143-Q145.
For overprints and surcharges, see Nos. Q76-Q78, Q83-Q86, Q91-Q92, boxed note following Q95, Q96-Q99, Q107-QQ109, boxed note following Q159.

PP8

Type I   Type II

Type III

1926-38
Q52 PP8 15c brown, yel,
          type I   7.50   3.00
          Never hinged   11.00
  a.   Imperf   100.00
          Never hinged   275.00
Q53 PP8 15c brown, yel,
          type II ('32)   8.00   4.25
          Never hinged   11.50
  a.   Type III ('33)   210.00
          Never hinged   275.00
  b.   As "a," imperf   240.00
          Never hinged   300.00

Nos. Q52-Q53a were issued for use in Paris only. No. Q53a was prepared but not issued.

Inscribed "VALEUR DECLAREE" — PP9

The additional numerals overprinted on Nos. Q56-Q63 and on Nos. Q72-Q75 indicate the weight category of the parcels being sent.

FRANCE

1926

Cat.	Type	Description	Unused	Used
Q54	PP9	50c on 15c red	3.00	1.60
		Never hinged	5.00	
a.		Imperf	180.00	
		Never hinged	275.00	
Q55	PP9	50c red	750.00	750.00
		Never hinged	1,200.	
a.		Imperf	1,200.	
		Never hinged	1,650.	
Q56	PP9	50c red, ovptd. "1"	4.50	2.00
		Never hinged	7.00	
a.		Imperf	200.00	
		Never hinged	300.00	
b.		Double overprint "1"	300.00	
		Never hinged	400.00	
Q57	PP9	55c on 15c red, ovptd. "1"	6.75	5.00
		Never hinged	11.50	
a.		Imperf	190.00	—
Q58	PP9	55c on 50c red, ovptd. "1"	6.75	5.00
		Never hinged	11.50	
Q59	PP9	65c on 50c red	2.50	2.50
		Never hinged	4.25	
Q60	PP9	65c on 50c red, ovptd. "1"	15.00	8.25
		Never hinged	27.50	
Q61	PP9	1.50fr on 50c red, ovptd. "3"	7.00	5.00
		Never hinged	12.00	
a.		Imperf	275.00	
		Never hinged	375.00	
Q62	PP9	2.00fr on 50c red, ovptd. "4"	8.25	3.75
		Never hinged	14.00	
Q63	PP9	2.50fr on 50c red, ovptd. "5"	15.00	8.25
		Never hinged	26.50	
Nos. Q54-Q63 (10)			818.75	791.35

See Nos. Q79, Q93, Q150-Q152.

For overprints and surcharges, see No. Q87, boxed note following No. Q95, Q100, Q110, Q123-Q124, Q138.

Inscribed "LIVRAISON PAR EXPRESS" — PP10

Q64	PP10	1.00fr on 60c grn	13.50	10.50
		Never hinged	24.00	
a.		Imperf	225.00	
		Never hinged	325.00	
Q65	PP10	1.00fr green	125.00	75.00
		Never hinged	250.00	
Q66	PP10	1.30fr on 1fr grn	16.50	12.50
		Never hinged	29.00	
Q67	PP10	1.50fr green	16.50	15.00
		Never hinged	32.50	
Q68	PP10	1.65fr green	16.50	15.00
		Never hinged	32.50	
Q69	PP10	1.90fr on 1.50fr grn	16.50	12.50
		Never hinged	30.00	
Q70	PP10	2.10fr on 1.65fr grn	30.00	14.00
		Never hinged	50.00	
Nos. Q64-Q70 (7)			234.50	154.50

For overprints and surcharges, see Nos. Q80-Q82, Q88-Q90, Q94, boxed note following Q95, Q101-Q105, Q111-Q113, Q125-Q132, Q139-Q141, Q146-Q149.

Inscribed "INTERETS A LA LIVRAISON" — PP11

No. Q72

No. Q73

Q71	PP11	50c lilac	3.00	1.60
		Never hinged	5.00	
a.		Imperf	225.00	190.00
		Never hinged	325.00	
Q72	PP11	50c lil, ovptd. "1"	6.75	4.25
		Never hinged	10.00	
a.		Imperf	200.00	
		Never hinged	300.00	
Q73	PP11	1.50fr on 50c lil, ovptd. "3"	7.50	5.00
		Never hinged	11.50	
a.		Imperf	200.00	
		Never hinged	300.00	
Q74	PP11	2.00fr on 50c lil, ovptd. "4"	10.00	7.00
		Never hinged	16.00	
Q75	PP11	2.50fr on 50c lil, ovptd. "5"	10.00	7.00
		Never hinged	16.50	
a.		Imperf	210.00	
		Never hinged	310.00	
Nos. Q71-Q75 (5)			37.25	24.85

1926 Issues Overprinted

A

1928

Inscribed "APPORT A LA GARE"

Q76	PP7	1.00fr brn, yel	16.50	14.00
		Never hinged	25.00	
a.		Imperf	190.00	190.00
		Never hinged	300.00	
Q77	PP7	1.50fr brn, yel	16.50	13.00
		Never hinged	25.00	
Q78	PP7	1.65fr brn, yel	16.50	13.00
		Never hinged	25.00	

Inscribed "VALEUR DECLAREE"

Q79	PP9	50c red	5.75	4.25
		Never hinged	8.25	
a.		Imperf	190.00	190.00
		Never hinged	300.00	
b.		Inverted overprint	210.00	
		Never hinged	310.00	

Inscribed "LIVRAISON PAR EXPRESS"

Q80	PP10	1.00fr green	17.00	13.50
		Never hinged	26.00	
Q81	PP10	1.50fr green	17.00	13.50
		Never hinged	26.00	
Q82	PP10	1.65fr green	17.00	13.50
		Never hinged	27.50	
Nos. Q76-Q82 (7)			106.25	84.75

1926 Issues Surcharged

1928

Inscribed "APPORT A LA GARE"

Q83	PP7	1.45fr on 60c brn, yel	7.00	6.75
		Never hinged	10.00	
Q84	PP7	1.45fr on 1fr brn, yel	40.00	32.50
		Never hinged	70.00	
Q85	PP7	2.15fr on 1.50fr brn, yel	62.50	42.50
		Never hinged	105.00	
Q86	PP7	2.35fr on 1.65fr brn, yel	62.50	42.50
		Never hinged	105.00	

Inscribed "VALEUR DECLAREE"

Q87	PP9	75c on 50c red	2.10	1.60
		Never hinged	3.25	
a.		Imperf	210.00	
		Never hinged	400.00	

Inscribed "LIVRAISON PAR EXPRESS"

Q88	PP10	1.45fr on 1fr green	62.50	42.50
		Never hinged	105.00	
Q89	PP10	2.15fr on 1.50fr green	62.50	42.50
		Never hinged	105.00	
Q90	PP10	2.35fr on 1.65fr green	62.50	42.50
		Never hinged	105.00	
Nos. Q83-Q90 (8)			361.60	253.35

Types of 1926

1933

Inscribed "APPORT A LA GARE"

Q91	PP7	1.45fr brn, yel	55.00	25.00
		Never hinged	82.50	
Q92	PP7	2.35fr brn, yel	1,400.	
		Never hinged	1,900.	

A 2.15fr value, brown on yellow paper, was prepared but not issued without overprint or surcharge.

For overprints and surcharges, see Nos. Q96, Q98, Q99, Q107-Q109, Q115, Q116, Q118, Q120-Q122, Q135-Q137.

Inscribed "VALEUR DECLAREE"

Q93	PP9	75c red	18.00	3.25
		Never hinged	22.50	
a.		Imperf		180.00

For overprints and surcharges on No. Q93, see Nos. Q110, Q123, Q124, Q138. A 1.15fr black in this design, imperf, was prepared but not issued. Value, $400.

Inscribed "LIVRAISON PAR EXPRESS"

Q94	PP10	1.45fr yel grn	450.00	300.00
		Never hinged	675.00	

Two other values, 2.15fr and 2.35fr were prepared but not issued without overprint or surcharge.

Inscribed "COLIS ENCOMBRANT"

1934

Q95	PP12	2fr blue	45.00	21.00
		Never hinged	70.00	

For overprints and surcharges, see Nos. Q106, Q114, Q133, Q134, Q142.

Nos. Q46, Q48, Q49, Q55, Q65, Q67 and Q68 overprinted "B" were not issued. Values: 1fr (No. Q46), $95; never hinged $130; 1.50fr (No. Q48), $95, never hinged $130; 1.65fr (No. Q49), $95, never hinged $130; 50c (No. Q55), $95, never hinged $130; 1fr (No. Q65), $92.50, never hinged $140; 1.50fr (No. Q67), $92.50, never hinged $140; 1.65fr (No. Q68), $92.50, never hinged $140.

Stamps and Types of 1926-34 Overprinted

1937

Inscribed "APPORT A LA GARE"

Q96	PP7	1.45fr brn, yel	6.75	6.75
		Never hinged	10.00	
Q97	PP7	2.15fr on 1.50fr brn, yel	37.50	31.00
		Never hinged	57.50	
Q98	PP7	2.15fr brn, yel	25.00	19.00
		Never hinged	37.50	
Q99	PP7	2.35fr brn, yel	25.00	19.00
		Never hinged	37.50	

Inscribed "VALEUR DECLAREE"

Q100	PP9	75c red	17.50	16.50
		Never hinged	25.00	
a.		Imperf	225.00	
		Never hinged	325.00	

Inscribed "LIVRAISON PAR EXPRESS"

Q101	PP10	1.45fr green	17.50	16.50
		Never hinged	25.00	
Q102	PP10	2.15fr on 1.50fr grn	17.50	16.50
		Never hinged	25.00	
Q103	PP10	2.15fr on 1.50fr grn	42.50	30.00
		Never hinged	67.50	
a.		Imperf	210.00	
		Never hinged	315.00	
Q104	PP10	2.35fr on 1.65fr grn	250.00	110.00
		Never hinged	350.00	
Q105	PP10	2.35fr green	17.50	12.50
		Never hinged	26.00	

Inscribed "COLIS ENCOMBRANT"

Q106	PP12	2fr blue	37.50	35.00
		Never hinged	57.50	
Nos. Q96-Q106 (11)			494.25	312.75

For overprints and surcharges, see Nos. Q146-Q149.

Types of 1933-34 Surcharged

1937

Inscribed "APPORT A LA GARE"

Q107	PP7	1.85fr on 1.45fr brn, yel	15.00	12.50
		Never hinged	26.00	
Q108	PP7	2.75fr on 2.15fr brn, yel	26.00	17.50
		Never hinged	45.00	
Q109	PP7	3.05fr on 2.55fr brn, yel	50.00	26.00
		Never hinged	90.00	

Inscribed "VALEUR DECLAREE"

Q110	PP9	.95fr on 75c red	42.50	25.00
		Never hinged	67.50	

Inscribed "LIVRAISON PAR EXPRESS"

Q111	PP10	1.85fr on 1.45fr grn	70.00	45.00
		Never hinged	120.00	
Q112	PP10	2.75fr on 2.15fr grn	70.00	45.00
		Never hinged	120.00	
Q113	PP10	3.05fr on 2.35fr grn	70.00	45.00
		Never hinged	120.00	

Inscribed "COLIS ENCOMBRANT"

Q114	PP12	2.60fr on 2fr bl	17.50	17.50
		Never hinged	26.00	
Nos. Q107-Q114 (8)			361.00	233.50

Stamps and Types of 1926-34 Overprinted

D

1937

Inscribed "APPORT A LA GARE"

Q115	PP7	1.45fr brn, yel	3.00	2.50
		Never hinged	4.50	
Q116	PP7	1.85fr on 1.45fr brn, yel	3.00	2.50
		Never hinged	4.50	
Q117	PP7	2.15fr on 1.50fr brn, yel	2.50	2.50
		Never hinged	4.25	
Q118	PP7	2.15fr brn, yel	42.50	35.00
		Never hinged	62.50	
Q119	PP7	2.35fr on 1.65fr brn, yel	575.00	475.00
		Never hinged	800.00	
Q120	PP7	2.35fr on 2.15fr brn, yel	3.00	2.50
		Never hinged	4.50	
Q121	PP7	2.75fr on 2.15fr brn, yel	3.25	2.50
		Never hinged	5.75	
Q122	PP7	3.05fr on 2.35fr brn, yel	6.50	6.25
		Never hinged	10.00	

Inscribed "VALEUR DECLAREE"

Q123	PP9	75c red	3.75	3.50
		Never hinged	5.50	
a.		Pair, one without overprint	225.00	
		Never hinged	350.00	
Q124	PP9	95c on 75c red	3.00	3.00
		Never hinged	3.75	

Inscribed "LIVRAISON PAR EXPRESS"

Q125	PP10	1.45fr green	4.25	3.25
		Never hinged	6.25	
Q126	PP10	1.85fr on 1.45fr green	5.75	4.25
		Never hinged	8.25	
Q127	PP10	2.15fr on 1.50fr grn	375.00	325.00
		Never hinged	500.00	
Q128	PP10	2.15fr green	18.50	16.50
		Never hinged	27.50	
Q129	PP10	2.35fr on 1.65fr grn	675.00	725.00
		Never hinged	775.00	
Q130	PP10	2.35fr green	11.00	10.50
		Never hinged	15.00	
Q131	PP10	2.75fr on 2.15fr grn	35.00	45.00
		Never hinged	55.00	
Q132	PP10	3.05fr on 2.35fr grn	35.00	45.00
		Never hinged	55.00	

Inscribed "COLIS ENCOMBRANT"

Q133	PP12	2fr blue	3.00	2.10
		Never hinged	4.50	
a.		Pair, imperf between	130.00	
		Never hinged	210.00	
Q134	PP12	2.60fr on 2fr bl	3.25	2.50
		Never hinged	5.50	
Nos. Q115-Q134 (20)			1,811.	1,714.

For additional surcharges, see Nos. Q146-Q149.

1938

Inscribed "APPORT A LA GARE"

Q135	PP7	2.30fr on 1.45fr brn, yel	3.75	3.00
		Never hinged	5.50	
Q136	PP7	3.45fr on 2.15fr brn, yel	3.75	3.00
		Never hinged	5.50	

FRANCE

Q137	PP7	3.85fr on 2.35fr brn, *yel*		3.75	3.00
		Never hinged		5.50	

Inscribed "VALEUR DECLAREE"

Q138	PP9	1.15fr on 75c red	1.60	1.60
		Never hinged	2.50	

Inscribed "LIVRAISON PAR EXPRESS"

Q139	PP10	2.30fr on 1.45fr grn	3.75	3.00
		Never hinged	5.50	
Q140	PP10	3.45fr on 2.15fr grn	3.75	3.00
		Never hinged	5.50	
Q141	PP10	3.85fr on 2.35fr grn	3.75	3.00
		Never hinged	5.50	

Inscribed "COLIS ENCOMBRANT"

Q142	PP12	3.25fr on 2fr bl	1.60	1.60
		Never hinged	2.50	
Nos. Q135-Q142 (8)			25.70	21.20

For Nos. Q135-Q138, Q140-Q142 overprinted "E," see editor's note following No. Q159.

Type of 1918

1938 — 11, Imperf (#Q161)

Q143	PP5	10c gray black	17.50	16.00
		Never hinged	26.00	
a.		Imperf	26.00	
		Never hinged	42.50	
Q144	PP5	20c brown lilac	17.50	16.00
		Never hinged	26.00	
a.		Imperf	42.50	
		Never hinged	62.50	
Q145	PP5	25c green, imperf	50.00	20.00
		Never hinged	80.00	
Nos. Q143-Q145 (3)			85.00	52.00

Two additional values, a 10c rose lilac and a 15c ultramarine, were prepared with this set but not issued. Values, each stamp: $90, never hinged $150. Both stamps also exist imperf. Values, each: $82.50; never hinged $150.

Nos. Q103, Q105, Q112, Q113 Overprinted

1938 — Perf. 11

Q146	PP10	2.30fr on 2.15fr green	62.50	62.50
		Never hinged	80.00	
Q147	PP10	2.30fr on 2.35fr green	62.50	62.50
		Never hinged	80.00	
Q148	PP10	2.30fr on 2.75fr on 2.15fr green	125.00	100.00
		Never hinged	175.00	
Q149	PP10	2.30fr on 3.05fr on 2.35fr green	125.00	100.00
		Never hinged	175.00	
Nos. Q146-Q149 (4)			375.00	325.00

Types of 1926 and

 PP13   PP13a

 PP14   PP15

 PP16

1938-39

Q150	PP9	1fr red ('39)	2.50	2.50
		Never hinged	4.00	
Q151	PP9	1.15fr red	1.25	1.25
		Never hinged	2.10	
		Imperf	140.00	
		Never hinged	225.00	
Q152	PP9	5fr red ('39)	2.50	2.75
		Never hinged	4.00	
Q153	PP13	2.40fr brown, yel	2.50	2.75
		Never hinged	4.00	
Q154	PP13a	3.50fr brown, yel	2.50	2.75
		Never hinged	4.00	
Q155	PP13	3.80fr brown, yel	2.50	2.75
		Never hinged	4.00	
		Imperf	125.00	
		Never hinged	190.00	
Q156	PP14	2.50fr grn yel ('39)	2.50	2.25
		Never hinged	4.00	
Q157	PP14	7.50fr grn yel ('39)	2.75	2.50
		Never hinged	4.25	
Q158	PP15	1fr lilac ('39)	9.50	6.75
		Never hinged	14.00	
Q159	PP16	3.20fr blue	11.00	7.50
		Never hinged	16.00	
Nos. Q150-Q159 (10)			39.50	33.75

Two additional values, 3.45fr and 3.85fr, type PP7, brown on yellow paper, imperforate, were prepared but not issued. Values, each: $140; never hinged, $225.

Nos. Q135-Q138, Q140-Q142 were overprinted "E" in 1939, in anticipation of new rates to take effect April 1, but were not issued. Values: 2.30fr on 1.45fr, $675, never hinged $1,000; 3.45fr on 2.15fr, $875, never hinged $1,300; 3.85fr on 2.35fr, $875, never hinged $1,300; 1.15fr on 75c, $300, never hinged $450; 3.45fr on 2.15fr, $2,800, never hinged $4,000; 3.85fr on 2.35fr, $2,800, never hinged $4,000; 3.25fr on 2fr, $675, never hinged $1,000.

In 1941, two sets were prepared in anticipation of new rate increases on April 1. They were not issued.

Six stamps in a new design, consisting of a 10c greenish gray, 30c blue, 50c brown, 1fr blue violet, 2fr orange and 5fr red. Values: 10c $185, never hinged $275; 30c $240, never hinged $350; 50c $240, never hinged $350; 1fr $185, never hinged $275; 2fr $185, never hinged $275; 5fr $185, never hinged $275.

Nos. Q93, Q153-Q155 and Q159 overprinted "E." Values: 75c; other values $575, never hinged.

PP17

PP18

Without Denominations

1941 — Perf. 12½

Q160	PP17	(2.70fr) brown	5.00	4.00
		Never hinged	8.25	
Q161	PP17	(3.90fr) blue	5.00	4.00
		Never hinged	8.25	
Q162	PP17	(4.20fr) green	5.00	4.00
		Never hinged	8.25	
Q163	PP18	(3.50fr) blue	9.50	8.50
		Never hinged	12.50	
Nos. Q160-Q163 (4)			24.50	20.50

Five stamps in the designs of PP20-PP22 below, but with blank value tablets, were prepared with Nos. Q160-Q163 but were not issued. Values: (1fr) brown, (5fr) red and (2.50fr) blue, each $60, never hinged $80; (7.50fr) green, $260, never hinged $360; (1fr) violet, $110, never hinged $160.

See Nos. Q178-Q181, Q200-Q206.

"Domicile" PP19

"Valeur Declaree" PP20

"Remboursement" PP21

"Interet A La Livraison" PP22

"Encombrant" PP23

1941 — Perf. 12½, 13 (#Q167-171)

Q164	PP19	2.70fr brown	6.00	5.00
		Never hinged	10.00	
Q165	PP19	3.90fr blue	6.00	5.00
		Never hinged	10.00	
Q166	PP19	4.20fr green	6.00	5.00
		Never hinged	10.00	
Q167	PP20	1fr brown	2.40	1.10
		Never hinged	3.75	
Q168	PP20	5fr red	1.20	1.50
		Never hinged	1.90	
Q169	PP21	2.50fr blue	1.20	1.50
		Never hinged	1.90	
Q170	PP21	7.50fr green	3.50	3.00
		Never hinged	5.25	
Q171	PP22	1fr violet	.85	.75
		Never hinged	1.50	
Q172	PP23	3.50fr blue	32.50	16.00
		Never hinged	47.50	
Nos. Q164-Q172 (9)			59.65	38.85

See Nos. Q173-Q177, Q186-Q194, Q200-Q206.

For surcharges, see footnote following No. Q177, Nos. Q182-Q185, Q207-Q210.

Types of 1941 with Bold Numerals

1942, Feb. — Perf. 13

Q173	PP20	1fr brown	1.25	1.10
		Never hinged	1.90	
Q174	PP20	5fr red	4.00	5.00
		Never hinged	6.00	
Q175	PP21	2.50fr blue	1.25	1.10
		Never hinged	1.90	
Q176	PP21	7.50fr green	6.00	6.50
		Never hinged	9.75	
Q177	PP22	1fr violet	60.00	
		Never hinged	95.00	
Nos. Q173-Q177 (5)			72.50	13.70

See Nos. Q173-Q177, Q186-Q194, Q200-Q206. See No. Q194.

Nine stamps from the 1941-42 issues were surcharged "+3F / C.N.S. / Cheminots" to raise funds for a philatelic exhibition organized by railroad employees, which took place in Paris on Dec. 26 and 27, 1942. They were not valid for postage. Value, set: $110; never hinged $150.

Type of 1941 Inscribed in Value Tablets

1943 — Perf. 12½

Q178	PP17	(3fr) brown	2.60	2.60
		Never hinged	4.00	
Q179	PP17	(4.00fr) blue	2.00	2.00
		Never hinged	4.00	
Q180	PP17	(4.70fr) green	2.60	2.60
		Never hinged	4.00	
Q181	PP18	(3.50fr) blue	6.00	6.00
		Never hinged	12.00	
Nos. Q178-Q181 (4)			13.80	13.80

Stamps of 1941 Surcharged in Deep Blue or Red

1943

Q182	PP19	3fr on 2.70fr brn	12.50	12.50
		Never hinged	19.00	
Q183	PP19	4.3fr on 3.90fr blue (R)	2.25	2.60
		Never hinged	4.00	
Q184	PP19	4.7fr on 4.20fr green (R)	3.00	2.60
		Never hinged	4.50	
Q185	PP23	3.9fr on 3.50fr blue (R)	3.00	3.00
		Never hinged	4.50	
Nos. Q182-Q185 (4)			20.75	20.70

Denominations in Black or Red

1943 — Unwmk.

Q186	PP19	3fr brn	5.00	3.75
		Never hinged	5.00	
Q187	PP19	4.3fr blue (R)	9.00	5.25
		Never hinged	11.50	
Q188	PP19	4.7fr green (R)	10.00	2.25
		Never hinged	13.50	
Q189	PP23	3.9fr blue (R)	65.00	52.50
		Never hinged	97.50	
Nos. Q186-Q189 (4)			87.50	63.75

1943 — Wmk. 407

Q190	PP19	3fr brn	11.00	9.75
		Never hinged	19.00	
Q191	PP19	4.3fr blue	19.00	12.00
		Never hinged	30.00	
Q192	PP19	4.7fr green	19.00	12.00
		Never hinged	30.00	
Q193	PP23	3.9fr blue	12.00	12.00
		Never hinged	19.00	
Nos. Q190-Q193 (4)			61.00	45.75

1944

Q194	PP21	20fr orange	4.50	6.00
		Never hinged	6.00	

Hydroelectric Dam — PP24

Electric Train — PP25

782   FRANCE

Power Line — PP26

1944   **Perf. 12½**
Q195	PP24	1fr dk mauve	6.00	6.00
	Never hinged		8.25	
Q196	PP24	5fr red brn	6.00	6.00
	Never hinged		8.25	
Q197	PP25	2.5fr blue	6.00	6.00
	Never hinged		8.25	
Q198	PP25	7.5fr green	6.00	6.00
	Never hinged		8.25	
Q199	PP26	1fr violet	6.00	6.00
	Never hinged		8.25	
	Nos. Q195-Q199 (5)		30.00	30.00

A 20fr orange, design PP25, was prepared but not issued. Values: $1,050; never hinged, $1,600.

Nos. Q195-Q199 exist unwatermarked, but were not issued in this form. Values, each: $275; never hinged $375.

Types of 1941 Inscribed "G" in Value Tablets

1945   **Unwmk.**
Q200	PP17	(5fr) brown	5.00	5.25
	Never hinged		6.50	
Q201	PP17	(7.20fr) blue	5.00	5.25
	Never hinged		6.50	
Q202	PP17	(7.60fr) green	5.00	5.25
	Never hinged		6.50	
Q203	PP18	(6.60fr) blue	5.50	6.00
	Never hinged		8.00	
	Nos. Q200-Q203 (4)		20.50	21.75

Wmk. 407
Q204	PP17	(5fr) brown	15.00	15.00
	Never hinged		21.00	
Q205	PP17	(7.20fr) blue	11.00	11.00
	Never hinged		16.50	
Q206	PP17	(7.60fr) green	11.00	11.00
	Never hinged		16.50	
	Nos. Q204-Q206 (3)		37.00	37.00

Nos. Q190-Q193 Surcharged

1945   **Wmk. 407**
Q207	PP19	5fr on 3fr brown	5.50	5.50
	Never hinged		8.00	
Q208	PP19	7.2fr on 4.30fr blue	5.50	5.50
	Never hinged		8.00	
Q209	PP19	7.8fr on 4.70fr green	5.50	5.50
	Never hinged		8.00	
Q210	PP23	6.6fr on 3.90fr blue	6.75	6.75
	Never hinged		10.00	
	Nos. Q207-Q210 (4)		23.25	23.25

Nos. Q186-Q189 were also surcharged but were not issued. Values, each: $40; never hinged $67.50.

Electric Train PP27   Transformer PP28

1945   **Denominations in Black**
Q211	PP27	5fr mauve	14.00	14.00
	Never hinged		20.00	
Q212	PP27	7.2fr blue	13.50	13.50
	Never hinged		20.00	
Q213	PP27	7.8fr green	13.50	13.50
	Never hinged		20.00	

Denomination in Purple
Q214	PP28	6.6fr blue	6.00	6.00
	Never hinged		8.25	
	Nos. Q211-Q214 (4)		47.00	47.00

Nos. Q211-Q213 without watermark were not issued. Value, set: $45; never hinged, $72.50.

A set of ten stamps in the design of the first three images were prepared in 1945 but were not issued. Value, each: $300; never hinged $475.

Four stamps of types PP27-PP28, inscribed "H" in the value tablet, were prepared but not issued. Value, set: $2,400; never hinged $4,000.

Locomotive — PP29

Nos. Q215-216, Q222-Q223: 16x22mm; Nos. Q217-Q221, Q224-Q228: 18.5x22mm

1944   **Wmk. 407**   **Perf. 13**
Q215	PP29	1fr deep green	3.75	1.10
	Never hinged		7.50	
Q216	PP29	2fr violet	5.25	1.50
	Never hinged		11.00	
Q217	PP29	5fr ultramarine	24.00	1.50
	Never hinged		32.50	
Q218	PP29	10fr red	12.00	1.50
	Never hinged		20.00	
Q219	PP29	20fr olive green	10.00	1.50
	Never hinged		16.00	
Q220	PP29	50fr red orange	19.00	1.50
	Never hinged		26.00	
Q221	PP29	100fr gray black	35.00	1.50
	Never hinged		52.50	
	Nos. Q215-Q221 (7)		109.00	10.10

Unwmk.
Q222	PP29	1fr deep green	9.75	4.75
	Never hinged		15.00	
Q223	PP29	2fr violet	12.50	4.75
	Never hinged		19.00	
Q224	PP29	5fr ultramarine	40.00	4.75
	Never hinged		65.00	
Q225	PP29	10fr red	26.00	4.75
	Never hinged		37.50	
Q226	PP29	20fr olive green	19.00	4.75
	Never hinged		30.00	
Q227	PP29	50fr red orange	37.50	4.75
	Never hinged		55.00	
Q228	PP29	100fr gray black	67.50	5.25
	Never hinged		97.50	
	Nos. Q222-Q228 (7)		212.25	33.75

Nos. Q215-Q234 were issued for use on small packets. Effective January 1, 1946, the parcel and small packet services were unified, and all issued thereafter were valid for both services.

See Nos. Q229-Q254.

Nos. Q229-Q230: 16x22mm; Nos. Q231-Q254: 18.5x22mm

1944-45   **Wmk. 407**
Q229	PP29	3fr gray	6.00	1.50
	Never hinged		11.00	
Q230	PP29	4fr black	9.75	2.25
	Never hinged		15.00	
Q231	PP29	7fr violet	62.50	2.60
	Never hinged		100.00	
Q232	PP29	8fr yel grn	18.00	2.25
	Never hinged		26.00	
Q233	PP29	9fr dk blue	30.00	4.00
	Never hinged		50.00	
Q234	PP29	30fr red brn	82.50	1.50
	Never hinged		125.00	
	Nos. Q229-Q234 (6)		208.75	14.10

1946
Q235	PP29	6fr claret	16.00	1.50
	Never hinged		23.00	
Q236	PP29	40fr yel brn	24.00	1.50
	Never hinged		35.00	
Q237	PP29	60fr lake red	26.00	1.50
	Never hinged		37.50	
Q238	PP29	70fr violet	175.00	26.00
	Never hinged		260.00	
Q239	PP29	80fr yel grn	24.00	2.25
	Never hinged		35.00	
Q240	PP29	90fr dk blue	140.00	25.00
	Never hinged		225.00	
Q241	PP29	200fr emer grn	30.00	2.25
	Never hinged		47.50	
	Nos. Q235-Q241 (7)		435.00	60.00

1947
Q242	PP29	5fr pale blue	19.00	1.90
	Never hinged		30.00	
Q243	PP29	7fr pale vio	250.00	16.00
	Never hinged		400.00	
Q244	PP29	9fr pale bl	190.00	15.00
	Never hinged		290.00	
Q245	PP29	30fr pale gray brn	67.50	1.90
	Never hinged		100.00	
Q246	PP29	70fr pale viol	175.00	6.75
	Never hinged		260.00	
Q247	PP29	90fr pale ultra	130.00	2.25
	Never hinged		200.00	
Q248	PP29	100fr yellow	350.00	2.25
	Never hinged		490.00	
	Nos. Q242-Q248 (7)		1,182.	46.05

1948
Q249	PP29	500fr yel org	80.00	2.25
	Never hinged		120.00	
Q250	PP29	1000fr yel	290.00	16.00
	Never hinged		425.00	

1951-52
Q251	PP29	10fr grn	52.50	7.50
	Never hinged		82.50	
Q252	PP29	20fr vio	52.50	13.50
	Never hinged		82.50	
Q253	PP29	50fr blue	65.00	9.00
	Never hinged		100.00	
Q254	PP29	100fr rose ver	19.00	1.50
	Never hinged		26.00	
	Nos. Q251-Q254 (4)		189.00	31.50

National Railway Company — PP30

1960
Q255	PP30	5c orange	11.50	2.10
	Never hinged		17.50	
Q256	PP30	10c red	10.50	8.25
	Never hinged		16.00	
Q257	PP30	20c dp red	8.75	3.75
	Never hinged		13.50	
Q258	PP30	30c dp red	8.75	3.75
	Never hinged		13.50	
Q259	PP30	40c dp red	8.75	7.50
	Never hinged		13.50	
Q260	PP30	50c dp red	8.75	4.25
	Never hinged		13.50	
Q261	PP30	60c dp red	7.50	4.25
	Never hinged		11.00	
Q262	PP30	70c dp red	7.50	4.25
	Never hinged		11.00	
Q263	PP30	80c dp red	11.50	4.25
	Never hinged		17.50	
Q264	PP30	90c dp red	11.50	4.25
	Never hinged		17.50	
Q265	PP30	1fr blue	13.00	2.25
	Never hinged		20.00	
Q266	PP30	2fr blue	13.00	2.25
	Never hinged		20.00	
Q267	PP30	3fr blue	13.00	2.25
	Never hinged		20.00	
Q268	PP30	4fr blue	13.00	2.25
	Never hinged		20.00	
Q269	PP30	5fr blue	13.00	2.25
	Never hinged		20.00	
Q270	PP30	10fr yellow	15.00	2.50
	Never hinged		22.50	
Q271	PP30	20fr dp grn	20.00	16.00
	Never hinged		30.00	
	Nos. Q255-Q271 (17)		195.00	76.35

1960   **Unwmk.**
Q272	PP30	5c orange	14.00	6.25
	Never hinged		32.50	
Q273	PP30	20c dp red	210.00	55.00
	Never hinged		325.00	
Q274	PP30	30c dp red	150.00	55.00
	Never hinged		325.00	
Q275	PP30	40c dp red	110.00	30.00
	Never hinged		160.00	
Q276	PP30	70c dp red	22.50	7.50
	Never hinged		32.50	
Q277	PP30	80c dp red	22.50	6.50
	Never hinged		32.50	
Q278	PP30	90c dp red	22.50	6.50
	Never hinged		32.50	
Q279	PP30	1fr blue	20.00	3.75
	Never hinged		30.00	
Q280	PP30	2fr blue	20.00	3.75
	Never hinged		30.00	
Q281	PP30	3fr blue	20.00	3.75
	Never hinged		30.00	
Q282	PP30	4fr blue	20.00	3.75
	Never hinged		30.00	
Q283	PP30	5fr blue	20.00	3.75
	Never hinged		30.00	
Q284	PP30	10fr yellow	25.00	6.25
	Never hinged		37.50	
Q285	PP30	20fr dp grn	30.00	21.00
	Never hinged		45.00	
	Nos. Q272-Q285 (14)		706.50	212.75

FRANCHISE STAMPS

No. 276 Overprinted

1939   **Unwmk.**   **Perf. 14x13½**
S1	A45	90c ultramarine	1.90	2.50
	Never hinged		2.75	
a.	Period following "F"		30.00	30.00
	Never hinged		50.00	

No. S1 was for the use of Spanish refugees in France. "F" stands for "Franchise."

OCCUPATION STAMPS

FRANCO-PRUSSIAN WAR
Issued under German Occupation
(Alsace and Lorraine)

OS1

Network Points Up

1870   **Typo.**   **Unwmk.**   **Perf. 13½x14**
Network with Points Up
N1	OS1	1c bronze green	75.00	100.00
a.		1c olive grn	75.00	100.00
N2	OS1	2c dark brown	125.00	175.00
a.		2c red brown	115.00	175.00
N3	OS1	4c gray	135.00	100.00
N4	OS1	5c yel grn	125.00	14.00
N5	OS1	10c bistre brn	110.00	5.75
a.		10c yellow brown	110.00	6.50
b.		Network lemon yellow	135.00	10.00
N6	OS1	20c ultra	115.00	16.50
N7	OS1	25c brown	150.00	100.00
a.		25c black brown	145.00	100.00

There are three varieties of the 4c and two of the 10c, differing in the position of the figures of value, and several other setting varieties.

Network Points Down

Network with Points Down
N8	OS1	1c olive grn	350.00	625.00
N9	OS1	2c red brn	150.00	550.00
N10	OS1	4c gray	150.00	200.00
N11	OS1	5c yel grn	6,500.	650.00
N12	OS1	10c bister	150.00	21.50
a.		Network lemon yellow	225.00	50.00
N13	OS1	20c ultra	225.00	90.00
N14	OS1	25c brown	450.00	300.00

Official imitations have the network with points downward. The "P" of "Postes" is 2½mm from the border in the imitations and 3mm in the originals.

The word "Postes" measures 12¾ to 13mm on the imitations, and from 11 to 12½mm on the originals.

The imitations are perf. 13½x14½; originals, perf. 13½x14¼.

The stamps for Alsace and Lorraine were replaced by stamps of the German Empire on Jan. 1, 1872.

WORLD WAR I
German Stamps of 1905-16 Surcharged

1916   **Wmk. 125**   **Perf. 14, 14½**
N15	A16	3c on 3pf brown	1.25	1.25
N16	A16	5c on 5pf green	1.25	1.25
N17	A22	8c on 7½pf org	2.00	

FRANCE — FRANCE OFFICES ABROAD — Offices in China

N18	A16	10c on 10pf car	2.00	2.00
N19	A22	15c on 15pf yel brn	1.25	1.25
N20	A16	25c on 20pf blue	1.25	1.25
a.		25c on 20pf ultramarine	2.00	2.00
N21	A16	40c on 30pf org & blk, *buff*	2.90	2.75
N22	A16	50c on 40pf lake & blk	2.90	2.75
N23	A16	75c on 80pf mag	12.50	12.50
N24	A16	1fr on 80pf lake & blk, *rose*	12.50	12.50

N25	A17	1fr25c on 1m car	47.50	47.50
a.		Double surcharge		—
N26	A21	2fr50c on 2m gray bl	47.50	47.50
a.		Double surcharge		—
		Nos. N15-N26 (12)	134.80	134.50

These stamps were also used in parts of Belgium occupied by the German forces.

Catalogue values for unused stamps in this section, from this point to the end of the section, are for Never Hinged items.

WORLD WAR II
Alsace
Issued under German Occupation

Stamps of Germany 1933-36 Overprinted in Black

1940   **Wmk. 237**   **Perf. 14**

N27	A64	3pf olive bister	.80	.55
N28	A64	4pf dull blue	.80	.55
N29	A64	5pf brt green	.80	.55
N30	A64	6pf dark green	.80	.55
a.		Inverted overprint	1,500.	
N31	A64	8pf vermilion	.80	.55
a.		Inverted overprint	4,000.	
N32	A64	10pf chocolate	.80	.55
N33	A64	12pf dp carmine	1.00	.55
N34	A64	15pf maroon	1.00	.55
N35	A64	20pf brt blue	1.65	.75
N36	A64	25pf ultra	1.65	.75
N37	A64	30pf olive grn	1.65	.75
N38	A64	40pf red violet	2.90	1.00
N39	A64	50pf dk grn & blk	7.00	3.25
N40	A64	60pf claret & blk	7.00	3.25
N41	A64	80pf dk blue & blk	17.50	7.00
N42	A64	100pf orange & blk	17.50	7.00
		Nos. N27-N42 (16)	63.65	28.15

Lorraine
Issued under German Occupation

Stamps of Germany 1933-36 Overprinted in Black

1940   **Wmk. 237**   **Perf. 14**

N43	A64	3pf olive bister	1.00	.75
N44	A64	4pf dull blue	1.00	.75
N45	A64	5pf brt green	1.00	4.00
N46	A64	6pf dark green	1.00	.75
N47	A64	8pf vermilion	1.00	.75
N48	A64	10pf chocolate	1.50	.85
N49	A64	12pf deep carmine	1.50	.85
N50	A04	15pf maroon	1.50	.75
a.		Inverted surcharge		
N51	A64	20pf brt blue	1.65	1.00
N52	A64	25pf ultra	1.40	1.00
N53	A64	30pf olive grn	2.10	1.00
N54	A64	40pf red violet	2.50	1.25
N55	A64	50pf dk grn & blk	6.00	3.00
N56	A64	60pf claret & blk	6.00	3.00
N57	A64	80pf dk blue & blk	18.00	7.50
N58	A64	100pf orange & blk	18.00	7.50
		Nos. N43-N58 (16)	65.15	34.70

Besetztes Gebiet Nordfrankreich

These three words, in a rectangular frame covering two stamps, were hand-stamped in black on Nos. 267, 367 and 369 and used in the Dunkerque region in July-August, 1940. The German political officer of Dunkerque authorized the overprint. The prevalence of forgeries and later favor overprints make expertization mandatory.

ALLIED MILITARY GOVERNMENT

Stamps formerly listed in this section as Nos. 2N1-2N20 are now listed with regular stamps of France as Nos. 475-476H and 523A-523J.

FRANCE OFFICES ABROAD

OFFICES IN CHINA

Prior to 1923 several of the world powers maintained their own post offices in China for the purpose of sending and receiving overseas mail. French offices were maintained in Canton, Hoi Hao (Hoihow), Kwangchowan (Kouang-tchéou-wan), Mongtseu (Mong-tseu), Packhoi (Paknoi), Tong King (Tchongking), Yunnan Fou (Yunnanfu).

100 Centimes = 1 Franc
100 Cents = 1 Piaster
100 Cents = 1 Dollar

Peace and Commerce Stamps of France Ovptd. in Red, Carmine or Black

1894-1900   **Unwmk.**   **Perf. 14x13½**

1	A15	5c grn, *grnsh* (R)	3.25	3.00
2	A15	5c yel grn, I (R) ('00)	4.25	3.00
a.		type II	47.50	32.50
3	A15	10c blk, *lav*, I (R)	9.25	3.00
a.		Type II	27.50	17.50
4	A15	15c bl (R), quadrillé paper	12.50	4.25
5	A15	20c red, *grn*	7.50	5.00
6	A15	25c blk, *rose* (C)	9.25	2.50
a.		Double overprint	225.00	
b.		Pair, one without overprint	550.00	
d.		Imperf	120.00	45.00
7	A15	30c brn, *bis*	9.25	6.25
8	A15	40c red, *straw*	9.25	7.50
9	A15	50c car, *rose*, I	26.00	17.50
a.		Carmine overprint	62.50	
b.		Type II (Bk)	25.00	16.00
10	A15	75c dp vio, *org* (R)	80.00	60.00
11	A15	1fr brnz grn, *straw*	17.00	8.50
a.		Double overprint	425.00	450.00
12	A15	2fr brn, *az* ('00)	30.00	29.00
12A	A15	5fr red lil, *lav*	75.00	60.00
b.		Red overprint	525.00	
		Nos. 1-12A (13)	292.50	209.50

For surcharges and overprints see Nos. 13-17, J7-J10, J20-J23.

No. 11 Surcharged in Black

13	A15	25c on 1fr brnz grn, *straw*	125.00	75.00

No. 6 Surcharged in Red

1901

14	A15	2c on 25c blk, *rose*	1,100.	340.00
15	A15	4c on 25c blk, *rose*	1,350.	450.00
16	A15	6c on 25c blk, *rose*	1,100.	375.00
17	A15	16c on 25c blk, *rose*	325.00	200.00
a.		Black surcharge		7,250.
		Nos. 14-17 (4)	3,875.	1,365.

Stamps of Indo-China Surcharged in Black

Two types of Nos. 18-33: type I, 13mmx3mm, "C" and "H" wide, "E" with fine serifs; type II, 12½mmx2¾mm, "C" and "H" narrower, "E" with heavy serifs.

1902-04

18a	A3	1c blk, *lil bl*	2.50	2.50
19	A3	2c brn, *buff*	4.25	4.25
20a	A3	4c claret, *lav*	4.25	3.40
21a	A3	5c yellow grn	5.00	3.40
22	A3	10c red	6.75	6.00
23	A3	15c gray	7.50	6.75
24a	A3	20c red, *grn*	9.25	8.50
25a	A3	25c blk, *rose*	12.50	12.50
26	A3	25c blue	10.00	8.50
27a	A3	30c brn, *bis*	9.25	8.50
28a	A3	40c red, *straw*	25.00	21.00
29	A3	50c car, *rose*	67.50	67.50
30	A3	50c brn, *azure*	10.00	9.25
31a	A3	75c vio, *org*	40.00	37.50
32a	A3	1fr brnz grn, *straw*	45.00	42.50
33a	A3	5fr red lil, *lav*	97.50	90.00
		Nos. 18a-33a (16)	356.25	332.05

The Chinese characters surcharged on Nos. 18-33 are the Chinese equivalents of the French values and therefore differ on each denomination. Two printings exist, differing slightly in the size of "CHINE." Values above are for the less expensive variety. See the *Scott Classic Specialized Catalogue of Stamps and Covers* for detailed listings. Many varieties of surcharge exist.

"Liberty, Equality and Fraternity" A3   "Rights of Man" A4

A5

1902-03   **Typo.**

34	A3	5c green	6.00	3.75
35	A4	10c rose red ('03)	3.00	2.10
36	A4	15c pale red	3.00	2.10
37	A4	20c brn vio ('03)	8.50	7.25
38	A4	25c blue ('03)	6.75	3.40
39	A4	30c lilac ('03)	9.25	7.50
40	A5	40c red & pale bl	19.00	16.00
41	A5	50c bis brn & lav	23.00	19.00
42	A5	1fr claret & ol grn	30.00	19.00
43	A5	2fr gray vio & yel	62.50	45.00
44	A5	5fr dk bl & buff	92.50	72.50
		Nos. 34-44 (11)	263.50	197.60

For surcharges and overprints see Nos. 45, 57-85, J14-J16, J27-J30.

1903

45	A4	5c on 15c pale red	17.50	12.00
a.		Inverted surcharge	135.00	75.00

Stamps of Indo-China, 1904-06, Surcharged as Nos. 18-33 in Black

1904-05

46	A4	1c olive grn	2.10	2.10
47	A4	2c vio brn, *buff*	2.10	2.10
47A	A4	4c cl, *bluish*	975.00	800.00
48	A4	5c deep grn	2.10	2.10
49	A4	10c carmine	3.00	3.00
50	A4	15c org brn, *bl* (I)	3.00	3.00
51	A4	20c red, *grn*	11.50	11.00
52	A4	25c deep blue	10.00	6.00
53	A4	40c blk, *bluish*	8.50	6.00
54	A4	1fr pale grn	360.00	300.00
55	A4	2fr brn, *org*	42.50	37.50
56	A4	10fr org brn, *grn*	165.00	155.00
		Nos. 46-56 (12)	1,585.	1,328.

Many varieties of the surcharge exist.

Stamps of 1902-03 Surcharged in Black

1907

57	A3	2c on 5c green	2.50	1.60
58	A4	4c on 10c rose red	2.50	1.75
a.		Pair, one without surcharge	—	
59	A4	6c on 15c pale red	3.40	2.50
60	A4	8c on 20c brn vio	6.00	6.00
a.		"8" inverted	75.00	75.00
61	A4	10c on 25c blue	2.10	1.25
62	A5	20c on 50c bis brn & lav	6.25	3.75
a.		Double surcharge		
b.		Triple surcharge	440.00	440.00
63	A5	40c on 1fr claret & ol grn	22.00	13.50
64	A5	2pi on 5fr dk bl & buff	23.00	13.50
a.		Double surcharge	2,300.	1,900.
		Nos. 57-64 (8)	67.75	43.85

Stamps of 1902-03 Surcharged in Black

1911-22

65	A3	2c on 5c green	2.10	1.50
66	A4	4c on 10c rose red	2.50	1.75
67	A4	6c on 15c org	5.00	2.10
68	A4	8c on 20c brn vio	2.10	1.80
69	A4	10c on 25c bl ('21)	4.25	2.10
70	A4	20c on 50c bl ('22)	55.00	55.00
71	A5	40c on 1fr cl & ol grn	7.50	6.00

No. 44 Surcharged

73	A5	$2 on 5fr bl & buff ('22)	175.00	200.00
		Nos. 65-73 (8)	253.45	270.25

Types of 1902-03 Surcharged like Nos. 65-71

1922

75	A3	1c on 5c org	6.00	6.75
76	A4	2c on 10c grn	6.75	7.50
77	A4	3c on 15c org	9.25	11.00
78	A4	4c on 20c red brn	11.00	13.50
79	A4	5c on 25c dk vio	6.00	6.00
80	A4	6c on 30c red	12.00	11.00
82	A4	10c on 50c blue	14.50	12.00
83	A5	20c on 1fr claret & ol grn	35.00	40.00
84	A5	40c on 2fr org & pale bl	45.00	55.00
85	A5	$1 on 5fr dk bl & buff	150.00	160.00
		Nos. 75-85 (10)	295.50	322.75

POSTAGE DUE STAMPS

Postage Due Stamps of France Handstamped in Red or Black

1901-07   **Unwmk.**   **Perf. 14x13½**

J1	D2	5c lt bl (R)	7.50	1.25
a.		Double overprint	160.00	
J2	D2	10c choc (R)	11.00	6.00
a.		Double overprint	160.00	
J3	D2	15c lt grn (R)	11.00	7.50
a.		Pair, one stamp without ovpt.	275.00	
b.		Imperf, single	160.00	
J4	D2	20c ol grn (R) ('07)	12.50	11.00
J5	D2	30c carmine	17.00	12.00
a.		Double overprint	160.00	
J6	D2	50c lilac	17.00	12.50
a.		Triple overprint	160.00	
b.		Pair, one stamp without overprint	275.00	
		Nos. J1-J6 (6)	76.00	53.25

FRANCE OFFICES ABROAD — Offices in China

Stamps of 1894-1900 Handstamped in Carmine

1903
J7	A15	5c yel grn	—	2,250.
	a.	Purple handstamp		
	b.	5c green, *greenish*		
J8	A15	10c blk, *lavender*	—	—
	a.	Purple handstamp		
J9	A15	15c blue	2,750.	1,250.
	a.	Purple handstamp		
J10	A15	30c brn, *bister*	1,500.	350.00
	a.	Purple handstamp		

Same Handstamp on Stamps of 1902-03 in Carmine

1903
J14	A3	5c green	—	2,000.
	a.	Purple handstamp		
J15	A4	10c rose red	750.	425.00
	a.	Purple handstamp		
J16	A4	15c pale red	750.	325.00
	a.	Purple handstamp		

Stamps of 1894-1900 Handstamped in Carmine

1903
J20	A1	5c yellow green	—	1,100.
	a.	Purple handstamp		
	b.	5c green, *greenish*		
J21	A1	10c blk, *lavender*	—	—
	a.	Purple handstamp		
J22	A1	15c blue	1,250.	350.
	a.	Purple handstamp		
J23	A1	30c brn, *bister*	600.	325.
	a.	Purple handstamp		

Same Handstamp on Stamps of 1902-03 in Carmine or Purple

1903
J27	A3	5c green (C)	—	1,750.
	a.	Purple handstamp		
J28	A4	10c rose red (C)	340.	225.
	a.	Purple handstamp		
J29	A4	15c pale red (C)	675.	225.
	a.	Purple handstamp		
J30	A4	30c lilac (P)		

The handstamps on Nos. J7-J30 are found inverted, double, etc.
The cancellations on these stamps should have dates between Sept. 1, and Nov. 30, 1903, to be genuine.

Postage Due Stamps of France, 1893-1910 Surcharged like Nos. 65-71

1911
J33	D2	2c on 5c blue	3.00	2.50
	a.	Double surcharge	140.00	—
J34	D2	4c on 10c choc	3.00	2.50
	a.	Double surcharge	140.00	
J35	D2	8c on 20c ol grn	3.40	3.00
	a.	Double surcharge	140.00	
J36	D2	20c on 50c lilac	3.40	3.00
		Nos. J33-J36 (4)	12.80	11.00

1922
J37	D2	1c on 5c blue	82.50	95.00
J38	D2	2c on 10c brn	145.00	165.00
J39	D2	4c on 20c ol grn	145.00	165.00
J40	D2	10c on 50c brn vio	125.00	185.00
		Nos. J37-J40 (4)	497.50	610.00

CANTON

Stamps of Indo-China, 1892-1900, Overprinted in Red

1901 Unwmk. Perf. 14x13½
1	A3	1c blk, *lil bl*	2.10	2.10
1A	A3	2c brn, *buff*	2.50	2.50
2	A3	4c claret, *lav*	4.25	4.25
2A	A3	5c grn, *grnsh*	600.00	600.00
3	A3	5c yel grn	3.40	3.40
4	A3	10c blk, *lavender*	7.25	7.25
5	A3	15c blue, quadrille paper	6.75	6.75
6	A3	15c gray	7.50	7.50
	a.	Double overprint	19.00	
7	A3	20c red, *grn*	22.50	22.50
8	A3	25c blk, *rose*	13.50	13.50
9	A3	30c brn, *bister*	32.50	32.50
10	A3	40c red, *straw*	32.50	32.50
11	A3	50c car, *rose*	35.00	35.00
12	A3	75c dp vio, *org*	35.00	35.00
13	A3	1fr brnz grn, *straw*	45.00	45.00
14	A3	5fr red lil, *lav*	250.00	250.00
		Nos. 1-14 (16)	1,100.	1,100.

The Chinese characters in the overprint on Nos. 1-14 read "Canton." On Nos. 15-64, they restate the denomination of the basic stamp.

Surcharged in Black

1903-04
15	A3	1c blk, *lil bl*	4.25	4.25
16	A3	2c brn, *buff*	4.50	4.25
17	A3	4c claret, *lav*	4.50	4.25
18	A3	5c yellow green	4.25	4.25
19	A3	10c rose red	4.50	4.25
20	A3	15c gray	4.50	4.25
21	A3	20c red, *grn*	21.00	17.50
22	A3	25c blue	7.50	7.50
23	A3	25c blk, *rose* ('04)	10.00	8.50
24	A3	30c brn, *bister*	27.50	21.00
25	A3	40c red, *straw*	67.50	55.00
26	A3	50c car, *rose*	340.00	310.00
27	A3	50c brn, *az* ('04)	85.00	72.50
28	A3	75c dp vio, *org*	67.50	67.50
	a.	"INDO-CHINE" inverted	55,000.	
29	A3	1fr brnz grn, *straw*	67.50	67.50
30	A3	5fr red lil, *lav*	67.50	67.50
		Nos. 15-30 (16)	787.50	720.00

Many varieties of the surcharge exist on Nos. 15-30.

Stamps of Indo-China, 1892-1906, Surcharged in Red or Black

A second printing of the 1906 surcharges of Canton, Hoi Hao, Kwangchowan, Mongtseu, Packhoi, Tong King and Yunnan Fou was made in 1908. The inks are grayish instead of full black and vermilion instead of carmine. Values are for the cheaper variety which usually is the second printing.
The 4c and 50c of the 1892 issue of Indo-China are known with this surcharge and similarly surcharged for other cities in China. The surcharges on these two stamps are always inverted. It is stated that they were irregularly produced and never issued.

1906
31	A4	1c ol grn (R)	2.50	2.50
32	A4	2c vio brn, *buff*	2.50	2.50
33	A4	4c cl, *bluish* (R)	2.50	2.50
34	A4	5c dp grn (R)	2.10	2.10
35	A4	10c carmine	3.00	3.00
36	A4	15c org brn, *bl*	22.50	22.50
37	A4	20c red, *grn*	12.50	12.50
38	A4	25c deep blue	5.00	5.00
39	A4	30c pale brn	17.00	17.00
40	A4	35c blk, *yel* (R)	12.50	12.50
41	A4	40c blk, *bluish* (R)	21.00	21.00
42	A4	50c bister brn	14.50	14.50
43	A3	75c dp vio, *org* (R)	67.50	67.50
44	A3	1fr pale grn	30.00	30.00
45	A4	2fr brn, *org* (R)	42.50	42.50
46	A3	5fr red lil, *lav*	92.50	92.50
47	A4	10fr org brn, *grn*	85.00	85.00
		Nos. 31-47 (17)	435.10	435.10

Surcharge exists inverted on 1c, 25c & 1fr.

Stamps of Indo-China, 1907, Srchd. in Red or Blue

Chinese Characters

1908
48	A5	1c ol brn & blk	1.25	1.25
49	A5	2c brn & blk	1.25	1.25
50	A5	4c bl & blk	2.50	1.25
51	A5	5c grn & blk	2.50	2.10
52	A5	10c red & blk (Bl)	3.40	2.50
53	A5	15c vio & blk	4.25	3.40
54	A6	20c vio & blk	5.00	5.00
55	A6	25c bl & blk	5.00	4.25
56	A6	30c brn & blk	8.50	8.50
57	A6	35c ol grn & blk	8.50	8.50
58	A6	40c brn & blk	11.00	8.50
59	A6	50c car & blk (Bl)	11.00	8.50
60	A7	75c ver & blk (Bl)	11.00	10.00
61	A8	1fr car & blk (Bl)	18.00	15.00
62	A9	2fr grn & blk	45.00	37.50
63	A10	5fr bl & blk	62.50	55.00
64	A11	10fr pur & blk	92.50	92.50
		Nos. 48-64 (17)	293.15	265.00

Nos. 48-64 Surcharged with New Values in Cents or Piasters in Black, Red or Blue

1919
65	A5	⅖c on 1c	1.25	1.25
66	A5	⅘c on 2c	1.25	1.25
67	A5	1⅗c on 4c (R)	1.25	1.25
68	A5	2c on 5c	1.60	1.60
69	A5	4c on 10c (Bl)	2.10	2.10
	a.	Chinese "2" instead of "4"	42.50	42.50
70	A6	6c on 15c	2.50	2.10
71	A6	8c on 20c	4.25	2.10
72	A6	10c on 25c	5.00	1.60
73	A6	12c on 30c	2.10	2.10
	a.	Double surcharge	140.00	140.00
74	A6	14c on 35c	2.10	1.60
	a.	Closed "4"	10.00	10.00
75	A6	16c on 40c	2.50	1.60
76	A6	20c on 50c (Bl)	2.50	2.10
77	A7	30c on 75c (Bl)	2.50	2.10
78	A8	40c on 1fr (Bl)	12.50	7.50
79	A9	80c on 2fr (R)	19.00	12.00
80	A10	2pi on 5fr (R)	32.50	32.50
81	A11	4pi on 10fr (R)	32.50	32.50
		Nos. 65-81 (17)	127.40	106.75

HOI HAO

Stamps of Indo-China Overprinted in Red

1901 Unwmk. Perf. 14x13½
1	A3	1c blk, *lil bl*	3.40	3.40
2	A3	2c brn, *buff*	4.25	4.25
3	A3	4c claret, *lav*	4.25	4.25
4	A3	5c yel grn	5.00	5.00
5	A3	10c blk, *lavender*	13.50	12.00
6	A3	15c blue	1,850.	800.00
7	A3	15c gray	7.50	5.00
8	A3	20c red, *grn*	32.50	25.00
9	A3	25c blk, *rose*	17.00	12.50
10	A3	30c brn, *bister*	67.50	67.50
11	A3	40c red, *straw*	67.50	67.50
12	A3	50c car, *rose*	67.50	67.50
13	A3	75c dp vio, *org*	250.00	225.00
14	A3	1fr brnz grn, *straw*	800.00	740.00
15	A3	5fr red lil, *lav*	800.00	675.00
		Nos. 1-15 (15)	3,990.	2,714.

The Chinese characters in the overprint on Nos. 1-15 read "Hoi Hao." On Nos. 16-66, they restate the denomination of the basic stamp.

Surcharged in Black

1903-04
16	A3	1c blk, *lil bl*	2.50	2.50
17	A3	2c brn, *buff*	2.50	2.50
18	A3	4c claret, *lav*	4.25	4.25
19	A3	5c yel grn	4.25	4.25
20	A3	10c red	4.25	4.25
21	A3	15c gray	5.00	5.00
22	A3	20c red, *grn*	7.50	7.50
23	A3	25c blue	5.00	5.00
24	A3	25c blk, *rose* ('04)	8.50	8.50
25	A3	30c brn, *bister*	6.75	6.75
26	A3	40c red, *straw*	32.50	32.50
27	A3	50c car, *rose*	30.00	30.00
28	A3	50c brn, *az* ('04)	170.00	170.00
29	A3	75c dp vio, *org*	50.00	50.00
	a.	"INDO-CHINE" inverted	45,000.	
30	A3	1fr brnz grn, *straw*	67.50	67.50
31	A3	5fr red lil, *lav*	225.00	225.00
		Nos. 16-31 (16)	625.50	625.50

Many varieties of the surcharge exist on Nos. 1-31.

Stamps of Indo-China, 1892-1906, Surcharged in Red or Black

1906
32	A4	1c ol grn (R)	8.50	8.50
33	A4	2c vio brn, *buff*	8.50	8.50
34	A4	4c cl, *bluish* (R)	8.50	8.50
35	A4	5c dp grn (R)	8.50	8.50
36	A4	10c carmine	8.50	8.50
37	A4	15c org brn, *bl*	32.50	32.50
38	A4	20c red, *grn*	13.50	13.50
39	A4	25c deep blue	11.00	11.00
40	A4	30c pale brn	13.50	13.50
41	A4	35c blk, *yel* (R)	21.00	21.00
42	A4	40c blk, *bluish* (R)	21.00	21.00
43	A4	50c gray brn	21.00	21.00
44	A4	75c dp vio, *org* (R)	62.50	62.50

Stamps of Indo-China, 1907, Srchd. in Red or Blue

45	A4	1fr pale grn	62.50	62.50
46	A4	2fr brn, *org* (R)	62.50	62.50
47	A4	5fr red lil, *lav*	135.00	135.00
48	A4	10fr org brn, *grn*	150.00	150.00
		Nos. 32-48 (17)	648.50	648.50

Chinese Characters

1908
49	A5	1c ol brn & blk	1.70	1.70
50	A5	2c brn & blk	1.70	1.70
51	A5	4c bl & blk	1.70	1.70
52	A5	5c grn & blk	3.00	3.00
53	A5	10c red & blk (Bl)	3.00	3.00
54	A5	15c vio & blk	6.75	6.75
55	A6	20c vio & blk	7.50	7.50
56	A6	25c bl & blk	7.50	7.50
57	A6	30c brn & blk	7.50	7.50
58	A6	35c ol grn & blk	7.50	7.50
59	A6	40c brn & blk	8.50	8.50
60	A6	50c car & blk (Bl)	10.00	10.00
61	A7	75c ver & blk (Bl)	10.00	10.00
62	A8	1fr car & blk (Bl)	29.00	29.00
63	A9	2fr grn & blk	42.50	42.50
64	A10	5fr bl & blk	75.00	75.00
65	A11	10fr org brn, *grn*	110.00	110.00
		Nos. 49-66 (17)	332.85	332.85

Nos. 49-66 Surcharged with New Values in Cents or Piasters in Black, Red or Blue

1919
67	A5	⅖c on 1c	1.25	1.25
68	A5	⅘c on 2c	1.25	1.25
69	A5	1⅗c on 4c (R)	2.10	2.10
70	A5	2c on 5c	2.50	2.50
71	A5	4c on 10c (Bl)	3.00	3.00
	a.	Chinese "2" instead of "4"	14.50	14.50
72	A6	6c on 15c	2.50	2.50
73	A6	8c on 20c	4.25	4.25
	a.	"S" of "CENTS" omitted	170.00	170.00
74	A6	10c on 25c	6.75	6.75
75	A6	12c on 30c	4.25	4.25
76	A6	14c on 35c	3.40	3.40
	a.	Closed "4"	42.50	42.50
77	A6	16c on 40c	4.25	4.25
78	A6	20c on 50c (Bl)	3.40	3.40
79	A7	30c on 75c (Bl)	11.00	11.00
80	A8	40c on 1fr (Bl)	22.00	22.00
81	A9	80c on 2fr (R)	62.50	62.50
82	A10	2pi on 5fr (R)	92.50	92.50
83	A11	4pi on 10fr (R)	225.00	225.00
	a.	Triple surch. of new value	750.00	750.00
84	A11	4pi on 10fr (R)	225.00	225.00
		Nos. 67-84 (17)	451.90	451.90

KWANGCHOWAN

A Chinese Territory leased to France, 1898 to 1945.

Stamps of Indo-China, 1892-1906, Surcharged in Red or Black

1906 Unwmk. Perf. 14x13½
1	A4	1c ol grn (R)	8.50	8.50
2	A4	2c vio brn, *buff*	8.50	8.50
3	A4	4c cl, *bluish* (R)	8.50	8.50
4	A4	5c dp grn (R)	8.50	8.50
5	A4	10c carmine	8.50	8.50
6	A4	15c org brn, *bl*	32.50	32.50
7	A4	20c red, *grn*	13.50	13.50
8	A4	25c deep blue	11.00	11.00
9	A4	30c pale brn	13.50	13.50
10	A4	35c blk, *yel* (R)	21.00	21.00
11	A4	40c blk, *bluish* (R)	21.00	21.00
12	A4	50c bister brn	25.00	25.00
13	A3	75c dp vio, *org* (R)	67.50	67.50
14	A4	1fr pale grn	42.50	42.50
15	A4	2fr brn, *org* (R)	55.00	55.00
16	A3	5fr red lil, *lav*	225.00	225.00
17	A4	10fr org brn, *grn*	275.00	275.00
		Nos. 1-17 (17)	845.00	845.00

Various varieties of the surcharge exist on Nos. 2-10.

Stamps of Indo-China, 1907, Srchd. in Red or Blue

Value in Chinese

1908
18	A5	1c ol brn & blk	1.70	1.70
19	A5	2c brn & blk	1.70	1.70
20	A5	4c bl & blk	1.70	1.70
21	A5	5c grn & blk	1.70	1.70

FRANCE OFFICES ABROAD — Offices in China

22	A5	10c red & blk (Bl)	1.70	1.70
23	A5	15c vio & blk	4.25	4.25
24	A6	20c vio & blk	6.75	6.75
25	A6	25c bl & blk	6.75	6.75
26	A6	30c brn & blk	10.00	10.00
27	A6	35c ol grn & blk	14.50	14.50
28	A6	40c brn & blk	14.50	14.50
30	A6	50c car & blk (Bl)	17.00	17.00
31	A7	75c ver & blk (Bl)	17.00	17.00
32	A8	1fr car & blk (Bl)	24.00	24.00
33	A9	2fr grn & blk	32.50	32.50
34	A10	5fr bl & blk	75.00	75.00
35	A11	10fr pur & blk	105.00	105.00
a.		Double surcharge	1,050.	
b.		Triple surcharge	1,050.	
		Nos. 18-35 (17)	335.75	335.75

The Chinese characters overprinted on Nos. 1 to 35 repeat the denomination of the basic stamp.

Nos. 18-35 Srchd. in Cents or Piasters in Black, Red or Blue

1919

36	A5	⅖c on 1c	1.25	.85
37	A5	⅘c on 2c	1.25	.85
38	A5	1⅗c on 4c (R)	1.25	.85
39	A5	2c on 5c	2.10	1.25
a.		"2 CENTS" inverted	97.50	
40	A5	4c on 10c (Bl)	3.75	3.40
41	A5	6c on 15c	2.10	2.10
42	A6	8c on 20c	4.25	4.25
43	A6	10c on 25c	14.50	13.50
44	A6	12c on 30c	3.40	3.40
45	A6	14c on 35c	3.40	3.40
a.		Closed "4"	45.00	
46	A6	16c on 40c	2.10	2.10
48	A6	20c on 50c (Bl)	2.10	2.10
49	A7	30c on 75c (Bl)	11.00	11.00
50	A8	40c on 1fr (Bl)	12.00	12.00
a.		"40 CENTS" inverted		
51	A9	80c on 2fr (R)	20.00	20.00
52	A10	2pi on 5fr (R)	175.00	175.00
53	A11	4pi on 10fr (R)	32.50	32.50
		Nos. 36-53 (17)	291.95	288.55

Stamps of Indo-China, 1922-23, Overprinted in Black, Red or Blue

1923

54	A12	⅒c blk & sal (Bl)	.35	.35
55	A12	⅕c dp bl & blk (R)	.35	.35
a.		Black overprint	135.00	
56	A12	⅖c ol brn & blk (R)	.40	.40
57	A12	⅘c brt rose & blk	.60	.60
58	A12	1c yel brn & blk (Bl)	.60	.60
59	A12	2c gray grn & blk (R)	.95	.95
60	A12	3c vio & blk (R)	1.00	1.00
61	A12	4c org & blk	1.25	1.25
62	A12	5c car & blk	1.25	1.25
63	A13	6c dl red & blk	1.25	1.25
64	A13	7c ol grn & blk	1.70	1.70
65	A13	8c black (R)	2.50	2.50
66	A13	9c yel & blk	2.50	2.50
67	A13	10c bl & blk	2.10	2.10
68	A13	11c vio & blk	2.10	2.10
69	A13	12c brn & blk	2.10	2.10
70	A13	15c org & blk	3.00	3.00
71	A13	20c bl & blk, straw (R)	3.00	3.00
72	A13	40c ver & blk, bluish (Bl)	3.40	3.40
73	A13	1pi bl grn & blk, grnsh	7.50	7.50
74	A13	2pi red & blk, pnksh (Bl)	17.00	17.00
		Nos. 54-74 (21)	54.90	54.90

Accent omitted varieties exist for Nos. 54-74. For detailed listings, see "Scott Classic Specialized Catalogue of Stamps and Covers 1840-1940".

Indo-China Stamps of 1927 Overprinted in Black or Red

1927

75	A14	⅒c ol grn (R)	.35	.35
76	A14	⅕c orange	.35	.35
77	A14	⅖c lt blue	.50	.50
78	A14	⅘c dp brown	.50	.50
79	A14	1c orange	.85	.85
80	A14	2c blue grn	1.25	1.25
81	A14	3c indigo (R)	1.25	1.25
82	A14	4c lilac rose	1.25	1.25
83	A14	5c deep violet	1.25	1.25
84	A15	6c deep red	1.25	1.25
85	A15	7c lt brown	1.25	1.25
86	A15	8c gray grn (R)	1.25	1.25
87	A15	9c red violet	1.70	1.70
88	A15	10c lt bl (R)	1.70	1.70
89	A15	11c orange	1.70	1.70
90	A15	12c myr grn (R)	1.70	1.70
91	A16	15c dl rose & ol brn	3.00	3.00
92	A16	20c vio & sl (R)	2.50	2.50
93	A17	25c org brn & lil rose	2.50	2.50
94	A17	30c dp bl & ol gray (R)	1.70	1.70
95	A18	40c ver & lt bl	1.70	1.70
96	A18	50c lt grn & sl (R)	2.50	2.50
97	A19	1pi dk bl, blk & yel (R)	4.25	4.25
98	A19	2pi red, dp bl & org (R)	6.00	6.00
a.		Double surcharge	160.00	
		Nos. 75-98 (24)	42.25	42.25

Accent omitted varieties exist for Nos. 75-90. For detailed listings, see "Scott Classic Specialized Catalogue of Stamps and Covers 1840-1940".

Stamps of Indo-China, 1931-41, Overprinted in Black or Red

1937-41 Perf. 13, 13½

99	A20	⅒c Prus blue	.25	.25
100	A20	⅕c lake	.25	.25
101	A20	⅖c orange red	.10	.10
102	A20	½c red brown	.35	.35
103	A20	⅘c dk violet	.35	.35
104	A20	1c black brown	.35	.35
105	A20	2c dk green	.35	.35
a.		Inverted overprint	140.00	
106	A21	3c dk green	.75	.75
107	A21	3c yel brn ('41)	.35	.35
108	A21	4c dk blue (R)	1.00	1.00
109	A21	4c dk green ('41)	.35	.35
110	A21	4c yel org ('41)	2.75	2.75
111	A21	5c dp violet	.95	.95
112	A21	5c dp green ('41)	.50	.50
113	A21	6c orange red	.65	.65
114	A21	7c black ('41)	.65	.65
115	A21	8c rose lake	.75	.75
116	A21	9c blk, yel ('41)	.75	.75
d.		Black overprint	9.25	9.25
117	A22	10c dk blue (R)	1.10	1.10
118	A22	10c ultra, pink (R) ('41)	.85	.85
119	A22	15c dk bl (R)	.75	.75
120	A22	18c bl (R) ('41)	.65	.65
121	A22	20c rose	.75	.75
122	A22	21c olive grn	.75	.75
123	A22	22c green ('41)	.60	.60
124	A22	25c dp violet	3.00	3.00
125	A22	25c dk bl (R) ('41)	.85	.85
126	A22	30c orange brn	.85	.85
127	A23	50c dk brown	1.10	1.10
128	A23	60c dl violet	1.10	1.10
129	A23	70c lt bl (R) ('41)	.85	.85
130	A23	1pi yel green	2.10	2.10
131	A23	2pi red	2.25	2.25
		Nos. 99-131 (33)	29.55	29.55

Accent omitted varieties exist for Nos. 99-124 and No. 126. For detailed listings, see "Scott Classic Specialized Catalogue of Stamps and Covers 1840-1940".

Common Design Types pictured following the introduction.

Colonial Arts Exhibition Issue
Common Design Type
Souvenir Sheet

1937 Engr. Imperf.

132	CD79	30c grn & sepia	9.25	11.00

New York World's Fair Issue
Common Design Type

1939 Unwmk. Perf. 12½x12

133	CD82	13c car lake	1.25	1.25
134	CD82	23c ultra	1.25	1.25

Petain Issue
Indo-China Nos. 209-209A Overprinted "KOUANG TCHEOU" in Blue or Red

1941 Engr. Perf. 12½x12

135	A27a	10c car lake (B)	.85	.85
136	A27a	25c blue (R)	.85	.85

Nos. 135-136 were issued by the Vichy government in France, but were not placed on sale in Kwangchowan.

For surcharges, see Nos. B9-B10.

Indo-China Types of 1937-41 without "RF" Overprinted "KOUANG TCHEOU" in Blue or Red

1942-44

137	A20	⅖c orange red	.25	
138	A20	½c red brown	.25	
139	A20	1c black brown	.35	
140	A20	2c dark green	.65	
141	A21	3c yellow brown	.65	
142	A21	4c yellow orange	.35	
143	A21	5c deep green	.50	
144	A21	9c black, yellow	.35	
145	A22	10c ultra, pink (R)	.60	
146	A22	18c blue (R)	190.00	
147	A22	22c green	.60	
148	A22	30c orange brown	.65	
149	A23	50c dark brown	.60	
150	A23	60c dull violet	.65	
151	A23	70c light blue (R)	.85	
152	A23	1pi yellow green	1.30	
153	A23	2pi red	1.40	
		Nos. 137-153 (17)	200.00	

Nos. 137-153 were issued by the Vichy government in France, but were not placed on sale in Kwangchowan.

SEMI-POSTAL STAMPS

French Revolution Issue
Common Design Type

1939 Unwmk. Photo. Perf. 13
Name and Value typo. in Black

B1	CD83	6c + 2c green	9.25	9.25
B2	CD83	7c + 3c brown	9.25	9.25
B3	CD83	9c + 4c red org	9.25	9.25
B4	CD83	13c + 10c rose pink	9.25	9.25
B5	CD83	23c + 20c blue	9.25	9.25
		Nos. B1-B5 (5)	46.25	46.25

Indo-China Nos. B19A and B19C Overprinted "KOUANG-TCHEOU" in Blue or Red, and Common Design Type

1941 Photo. Perf. 13½

B6	SP1	10c + 10c red (B)	.85	.85
B7	CD86	15c + 30c mar & car	.85	.85
B8	SP2	15c + 10c blue (R)	.85	.85
		Nos. B6-B8 (3)	2.55	

Nos. B6-B8 were issued by the Vichy government in France, but were not placed on sale in Kwangchowan.

Indo-China Nos. B21A-B21B Overprinted in Blue or Red

1944 Engr. Perf. 12½x12

B9	A27a	5c + 15c on 25c deep blue (R)	1.00	
B10	A27a	+25c on 10c car lake	1.10	

Colonial Development Fund.

Nos. B9-B10 were issued by the Vichy government in France, but were not placed on sale in Kwangchowan.

AIR POST SEMI-POSTAL STAMPS

Indo-China Nos. CD2-CD4 Overprinted "KOUANG-TCHEOU" in Blue or Red
Methods and Perfs as Before

1942, June 22

CB1	SPAP1	15c + 35c green (R)	.95	
CB2	SPAP2	20c + 80c brown	.95	
CB3	SPAP3	30c + 90c car red	.95	
		Nos. CB1-CB3 (3)	2.85	

Native children's welfare fund.

Nos. CB1-CB3 were issued by the Vichy government in France, but were not placed on sale in Kwangchowan.

Colonial Education Fund
Indo-China No. CB5 Overprinted "KOUANG-TCHEOU" in Blue or Red

Perf. 12½x13½

1942, June 22 Engr.

CB4	CD86a	12c + 18c blue & red	1.00	

No. CB4 was issued by the Vichy government in France, but was not placed on sale in Kwangchowan.

MONGTSEU (MENGTSZ)

Stamps of Indo-China Surcharged in Black

1903-04 Unwmk. Perf. 14x13½

1	A3	1c blk, lil bl	7.50	7.50
2	A3	2c brn, buff	6.75	6.75
3	A3	4c claret, lav	8.50	8.50
4	A3	5c yel grn	6.00	6.00
5	A3	10c red	9.25	9.25
6	A3	15c gray	10.00	10.00
7	A3	20c red, grn	12.50	12.50
7C	A3	25c blk, rose	725.00	725.00
8	A3	25c blue	12.50	12.50
9	A3	30c brn, bister	11.00	11.00
10	A3	40c red, straw	75.00	75.00
11	A3	50c car, rose	440.00	440.00
12	A3	50c brn, az ('04)	150.00	150.00
13	A3	75c dp vio, org	120.00	120.00
		"INDO-CHINE" inverted	67,500.	
14	A3	1fr brnz grn, straw	110.00	110.00
15	A3	5fr red lil, lav	110.00	110.00
		Nos. 1-15 (16)	1,814.	1,814.

Many surcharge varieties exist on Nos. 1-15.

Stamps of Indo-China, 1892-1906, Surcharged in Red or Black

1906

16	A4	1c ol grn (R)	5.00	5.00
17	A4	2c vio brn, buff	5.00	5.00
18	A4	4c cl, bluish (R)	5.00	5.00
19	A4	5c dp grn (R)	6.00	6.00
20	A4	10c carmine	5.00	5.00
21	A4	15c org brn, bl	35.00	35.00
22	A4	20c red, grn	13.50	13.50
23	A4	25c deep blue	10.00	10.00
24	A4	30c pale brn	13.50	13.50
25	A4	35c blk, yel (R)	12.50	12.50
26	A4	40c blk, bluish (R)	20.00	20.00
27	A4	50c bister brn	21.00	21.00
28	A3	75c dp vio, org (R)	67.50	67.50
a.		"INDO-CHINE" inverted	67,500.	
29	A4	1fr pale grn	42.50	42.50
30	A4	2fr brn, org (R)	55.00	55.00
31	A3	5fr red lil, lav	140.00	140.00
32	A4	10fr org brn, grn	150.00	150.00
a.		Chinese characters inverted	1,750.	2,100.
		Nos. 16-32 (17)	606.50	606.50

Inverted varieties of the surcharge exist on Nos. 19, 22 and 32.

Stamps of Indo-China, 1907, Srchd. in Red or Blue

Value in Chinese

1908

33	A5	1c ol brn & blk	1.25	1.25
34	A5	2c brn & blk	1.25	1.25
35	A5	4c bl & blk	1.25	1.25
36	A5	5c grn & blk	1.25	1.25
37	A5	10c red & blk (Bl)	3.00	3.00
38	A5	15c vio & blk	3.00	3.00
39	A6	20c vio & blk	6.00	6.00
40	A6	25c bl & blk	15.00	15.00
41	A6	30c brn & blk	6.75	6.75
42	A6	35c ol grn & blk	7.50	7.50
43	A6	40c brn & blk	5.00	5.00
44	A6	50c car & blk (Bl)	6.75	6.75
45	A7	75c ver & blk (Bl)	14.50	14.50
46				
47	A8	1fr car & blk (Bl)	15.90	15.90
48	A9	2fr grn & blk	19.00	19.00
49	A10	5fr bl & blk	105.00	105.00
50	A11	10fr pur & blk	125.00	125.00
		Nos. 33-50 (17)	335.00	335.00

The Chinese characters overprinted on Nos. 1 to 50 repeat the denomination of the basic stamp.

Nos. 33-50 Srchd. in Cents or Piasters in Black, Red or Blue

1919

51	A5	⅖c on 1c	1.70	1.70
52	A5	⅘c on 2c	1.70	1.70
53	A5	1⅗c on 4c	1.70	1.70
54	A5	2c on 5c	1.70	1.70
55	A5	4c on 10c (Bl)	3.00	3.00
56	A5	6c on 15c		

FRANCE OFFICES ABROAD — Offices in China — Offices in Crete

57	A6	8c on 20c	6.75	6.75
58	A6	10c on 25c	5.00	5.00
59	A6	12c on 30c	5.00	5.00
60	A6	14c on 35c	3.40	3.40
a.		Closed "4"	21.00	21.00
61	A6	16c on 40c	4.25	4.25
63	A6	20c on 50c (Bl)	5.00	5.00
64	A7	30c on 75c (Bl)	9.25	9.25
65	A8	40c on 1fr (Bl)	10.00	10.00
66	A9	80c on 2fr (R)	10.00	10.00
a.		Triple surch., one inverted	550.00	550.00
67	A10	2pi on 5fr (R)	200.00	200.00
a.		Triple surch., one inverted	625.00	625.00
b.		Double surcharge	925.00	925.00
68	A11	4pi on 10fr (R)	30.00	30.00
		Nos. 51-68 (17)	301.45	301.45

PAKHOI

Stamps of Indo-China Surcharged in Black

1903-04		Unwmk.	Perf. 14x13½	
1	A3	1c blk, *lil bl*	6.75	6.75
2	A3	2c brn, *buff*	6.75	6.75
3	A3	4c claret, *lav*	6.75	6.75
4	A3	5c yel grn	5.00	5.00
5	A3	10c red	5.00	5.00
6	A3	15c gray	5.00	5.00
7	A3	20c red, *grn*	11.00	11.00
8	A3	25c blue	9.25	9.25
9	A3	25c blk, *rose*('04)	6.75	6.75
10	A3	30c brn, *bister*	8.50	8.50
11	A3	40c red, *straw*	57.50	57.50
12	A3	50c car, *rose*	340.00	340.00
13	A3	50c brn, *az* ('04)	47.50	47.50
14	A3	75c dp vio, *org*	67.50	67.50
a.		"INDO-CHINE" inverted	47,500.	
15	A3	1fr brnz grn, *straw*	67.50	67.50
16	A3	5fr red lil, *lav*	135.00	135.00
		Nos. 1-16 (16)	785.75	785.75

Many varieties of the surcharge exist.

Stamps of Indo-China 1892-1906, Surcharged in Red or Black

1906				
17	A4	1c ol grn (R)	8.50	8.50
18	A4	2c vio brn, *buff*	8.50	8.50
19	A4	4c cl, *bluish* (R)	8.50	8.50
20	A4	5c dp grn (R)	8.50	8.50
21	A4	10c carmine	8.50	8.50
22	A4	15c org brn, *bl*	32.50	32.50
23	A4	20c red, *grn*	13.50	13.50
24	A4	25c deep blue	11.00	11.00
25	A4	30c pale brn	13.50	13.50
26	A4	35c blk, *yel* (R)	21.00	21.00
27	A4	40c blk, *bluish*(R)	21.00	21.00
28	A4	50c bister brn	21.00	21.00
29	A3	75c dp vio, *org* (R)	67.50	67.50
30	A4	1fr pale grn	42.50	42.50
31	A4	2fr brn, *org*(R)	55.00	55.00
32	A3	5fr red lil, *lav*	140.00	140.00
33	A4	10fr org brn, *grn*	150.00	150.00
		Nos. 17-33 (17)	631.00	631.00

Various surcharge varieties exist on Nos. 17-24.

Stamps of Indo-China, 1907, Surcharged "PAKHOI" and Value in Chinese in Red or Blue

1908				
34	A5	1c ol brn & blk	1.25	1.25
35	A5	2c brn & blk	1.25	1.25
36	A5	4c bl & blk	1.25	1.25
37	A5	5c grn & blk	1.70	1.70
38	A5	10c red & blk (Bl)	1.70	1.70
39	A5	15c vio & blk	2.10	2.10
40	A6	20c vio & blk	2.50	2.50
41	A6	25c bl & blk	3.00	3.00
42	A6	30c brn & blk	3.40	3.40
43	A6	35c ol grn & blk	3.40	3.40
44	A6	40c brn & blk	3.40	3.40
46	A6	50c car & blk (Bl)	3.40	3.40
47	A7	75c ver & blk (Bl)	7.25	7.25
48	A8	1fr car & blk (Bl)	7.50	7.50
49	A9	2fr grn & blk	16.00	16.00
50	A10	5fr bl & blk	85.00	85.00
51	A11	10fr pur & blk	150.00	150.00
		Nos. 34-51 (17)	294.10	294.10

The Chinese characters overprinted on Nos. 1 to 51 repeat the denomination of the basic stamps.

Nos. 34-51 Surcharged with New Values in Cents or Piasters in Black, Red or Blue

1919				
52	A5	⅖c on 1c	1.25	1.25
a.		"PAK-HOI" and Chinese double	170.00	
53	A5	⅘c on 2c	1.25	1.25
54	A5	1⅗c on 4c (R)	1.25	1.25
55	A5	2c on 5c	2.50	2.50
56	A5	4c on 10c (Bl)	3.40	3.40
57	A5	6c on 15c	1.70	1.70
58	A6	8c on 20c	3.40	3.40
59	A6	10c on 25c	5.00	5.00
60	A6	12c on 30c	1.70	1.70
a.		"12 CENTS" double	675.00	
61	A6	14c on 35c	1.25	1.25
a.		Closed "4"	14.50	14.50
62	A6	16c on 40c	3.00	3.00
64	A6	20c on 50c (Bl)	2.10	2.10
65	A7	30c on 75c (Bl)	9.25	9.25
66	A8	40c on 1fr (Bl)	12.50	12.50
67	A9	80c on 2fr (R)	10.00	10.00
68	A10	2pi on 5fr (R)	16.00	16.00
69	A11	4pi on 10fr (R)	35.00	35.00
		Nos. 52-69 (17)	110.55	110.55

TCHONGKING (CHUNGKING)

Stamps of Indo-China Surcharged in Black

1903-04		Unwmk.	Perf. 14x13½	
1	A3	1c blk, *lil bl*	5.00	5.00
2	A3	2c brn, *buff*	5.00	5.00
3	A3	4c claret, *lav*	6.00	6.00
4	A3	5c yel grn	6.00	6.00
5	A3	10c red	6.00	6.00
6	A3	15c gray	6.00	6.00
7	A3	20c red, *grn*	8.50	8.50
8	A3	25c blue	55.00	55.00
9	A3	25c blk, *rose* ('04)	10.00	10.00
10	A3	30c brn, *bister*	15.00	15.00
11	A3	40c red, *straw*	62.50	62.50
12	A3	50c car, *rose*	225.00	225.00
13	A3	50c brn, *az* ('04)	140.00	140.00
14	A3	75c vio, *org*	45.00	45.00
15	A3	1fr brnz grn, *straw*	60.00	60.00
16	A3	5fr red lil, *lav*	105.00	105.00
		Nos. 1-16 (16)	760.00	760.00

Many surcharge varieties exist on Nos. 1-14. Stamps of Indo-China and French China, issued in 1902 with similar overprint, but without Chinese characters, were not officially authorized.

Stamps of Indo-China, 1892-1906, Surcharged in Red or Black

1906				
17	A4	1c ol grn (R)	8.50	8.50
18	A4	2c vio brn, *buff*	8.50	8.50
19	A4	4c cl, *bluish* (R)	8.50	8.50
20	A4	5c dp grn (R)	8.50	8.50
21	A4	10c carmine	8.50	8.50
22	A4	15c org brn, *bl*	32.50	32.50
23	A4	20c red, *grn*	13.50	13.50
24	A4	25c deep blue	11.00	11.00
25	A4	30c pale brn	13.50	13.50
26	A4	35c blk, *yellow* (R)	21.00	21.00
27	A4	40c blk, *bluish* (R)	21.00	21.00
28	A4	50c bis brn	25.00	25.00
29	A3	75c dp vio, *org* (R)	67.50	67.50
30	A4	1fr pale grn	42.50	42.50
31	A4	2fr brn, *org* (R)	55.00	55.00
32	A3	5fr red lil, *lav*	140.00	140.00
33	A4	10fr org brn, *grn*	150.00	150.00
		Nos. 17-33 (17)	635.00	635.00

Variety "T" omitted in surcharge occurs once in each sheet of Nos. 17-33. For detailed listings, see "Scott Classic Specialized Catalogue of Stamps and Values". Other surcharge varieties exist. Inverted surcharge on 1c and 2c are of private origin.

Stamps of Indo-China, 1907, Surcharged "TCHONGKING" and Value in Chinese in Red or Blue

1908				
34	A5	1c ol brn & blk	.85	.85
35	A5	2c brn & blk	.85	.85
36	A5	4c bl & blk	1.25	1.25
37	A5	5c grn & blk	2.10	2.10
38	A5	10c red & blk (Bl)	2.10	2.10
39	A5	15c vio & blk	3.00	3.00
40	A6	20c vio & blk	3.00	3.00
41	A6	25c bl & blk	5.50	5.50
42	A6	30c brn & blk	3.40	3.40
43	A6	35c ol grn & blk	7.50	7.50
44	A6	40c brn & blk	15.00	15.00
45	A6	50c car & blk (Bl)	12.00	12.00
46	A7	75c ver & blk (Bl)	10.00	10.00
47	A8	1fr car & blk (Bl)	13.50	13.50
48	A9	2fr grn & blk	85.00	85.00
49	A10	5fr bl & blk	37.50	37.50
50	A11	10fr pur & blk	225.00	225.00
		Nos. 34-50 (17)	427.55	427.55

The Chinese characters overprinted on Nos. 1 to 50 repeat the denomination of the basic stamp.

Nos. 34-50 Surcharged with New Values in Cents or Piasters in Black, Red or Blue

1919				
51	A5	⅖c on 1c	1.25	1.25
52	A5	⅘c on 2c	1.25	1.25
53	A5	1⅗c on 4c (R)	1.25	1.25
54	A5	2c on 5c	1.70	1.70
55	A5	4c on 10c (Bl)	1.25	1.25
56	A5	6c on 15c	1.70	1.70
57	A6	8c on 20c	3.00	3.00
58	A6	10c on 25c	8.50	8.50
59	A6	12c on 30c	3.00	1.25
60	A6	14c on 35c	2.10	1.70
a.		Closed "4"	35.00	35.00
61	A6	16c on 40c	2.10	1.70
a.		"16 CENTS" double	125.00	125.00
62	A6	20c on 50c (Bl)	11.00	10.00
63	A7	30c on 75c (Bl)	9.25	6.75
64	A8	40c on 1fr (Bl)	9.25	6.75
65	A9	80c on 2fr (R)	9.25	6.75
66	A10	2pi on 5fr (R)	9.25	9.25
67	A11	4pi on 10fr (R)	17.50	17.50
		Nos. 51-67 (17)	92.60	79.80

YUNNAN FOU

(Formerly Yunnan Sen, later known as Kunming)

Stamps of Indo-China Surcharged in Black

1903-04		Unwmk.	Perf. 14x13½	
1	A3	1c blk, *lil bl*	6.75	6.75
2	A3	2c brn, *buff*	6.75	6.75
3	A3	4c claret, *lav*	7.50	7.50
4	A3	5c yel green	6.75	6.75
5	A3	10c red	7.50	7.50
6	A3	15c gray	7.50	7.50
7	A3	20c red, *grn*	12.50	12.50
8	A3	25c blue	7.50	7.50
9	A3	30c brn, *bister*	12.50	12.50
10	A3	40c red, *straw*	75.00	60.00
11	A3	50c car, *rose*	350.00	350.00
12	A3	50c brn, *az* ('04)	180.00	180.00
13	A3	75c dp vio, *org*	67.50	62.50
a.		"INDO-CHINE" inverted	47,500.	
14	A3	1fr brnz grn, *straw*	67.50	62.50
15	A3	5fr red lil, *lav*	125.00	125.00
		Nos. 1-15 (15)	940.25	915.25

The Chinese characters overprinted on Nos. 1 to 15 repeat the denomination of the basic stamp. Many varieties of the surcharge exist.

Stamps of Indo-China, 1892-1906, Surcharged in Red or Black

1906		Unwmk.	Perf. 14x13½	
17	A4	1c ol grn (R)	5.00	5.00
18	A4	2c vio brn, *buff*	5.00	5.00
19	A4	4c cl, *bluish* (R)	5.00	5.00
20	A4	5c dp grn (R)	5.00	5.00
21	A4	10c carmine	5.00	5.00
22	A4	15c org brn, *bl*	35.00	35.00
23	A4	20c red, *grn*	13.50	13.50
24	A4	25c deep blue	11.00	11.00
25	A4	30c pale brn	13.50	13.50
26	A4	35c blk, *yel* (R)	17.00	17.00
27	A4	40c blk, *bluish* (R)	17.00	17.00
28	A4	50c bister brn	21.00	21.00
29	A3	75c dp vio, *org* (R)	67.50	67.50
30	A4	1fr pale grn	42.50	42.50
31	A4	2fr brn, *org* (R)	55.00	55.00
32	A3	5fr red lil, *lav*	140.00	140.00
33	A4	10fr org brn, *grn*	150.00	150.00
		Nos. 17-33 (17)	608.00	608.00

Various surcharge varieties exist on Nos. 18, 20, 21 and 27.

Stamps of Indo-China, 1907, Surcharged "YUNNANFOU," and Value in Chinese in Red or Blue

1908				
34	A5	1c ol brn & blk	1.25	1.25
35	A5	2c brn & blk	1.25	1.25
36	A5	4c bl & blk	2.10	2.10
37	A5	5c grn & blk	3.00	3.00
38	A5	10c red & blk (Bl)	3.00	3.00
39	A5	15c vio & blk	6.75	6.75
40	A6	20c vio & blk	6.25	6.25
41	A6	25c bl & blk	9.25	9.25
42	A6	30c brn & blk	7.50	7.50
43	A6	35c ol grn & blk	7.50	7.50
44	A6	40c brn & blk	8.50	8.50
45	A6	50c car & blk (Bl)	9.25	9.25
46	A7	75c ver & blk (Bl)	11.00	11.00
47	A8	1fr car & blk (Bl)	17.00	17.00
48	A9	2fr grn & blk	29.00	29.00
a.		"YUNANNFOU"	2,500.	2,500.
49	A10	5fr bl & blk	60.00	60.00
a.		"YUNANNFOU"	2,500.	2,500.
50	A11	10fr pur & blk	120.00	120.00
a.		"YUNANNFOU"	2,500.	2,500.
		Nos. 34-50 (17)	302.60	302.60

The Chinese characters overprinted on Nos. 17-50 repeat the denomination of the basic stamp.

Nos. 34-50 Surcharged with New Values in Cents or Piasters in Black, Red or Blue

1919				
51	A5	⅖c on 1c	1.25	1.25
a.		New value double	140.00	
52	A5	⅘c on 2c	1.25	1.25
53	A5	1⅗c on 4c (R)	1.25	1.25
54	A5	2c on 5c	2.10	2.10
a.		Triple surcharge	210.00	
55	A5	4c on 10c (Bl)	1.70	1.70
56	A5	6c on 15c	3.00	3.00
57	A6	8c on 20c	2.10	2.10
58	A6	10c on 25c	3.75	3.75
59	A6	12c on 30c	9.25	9.25
60	A6	14c on 35c	14.50	14.50
a.		Closed "4"	140.00	140.00
61	A6	16c on 40c	9.25	9.25
62	A6	20c on 50c (Bl)	3.00	3.00
63	A7	30c on 75c (Bl)	9.25	9.25
64	A8	40c on 1fr (Bl)	35.00	35.00
65	A9	80c on 2fr (R)	14.50	14.50
a.		Triple surch., one inverted	250.00	
66	A10	2pi on 5fr (R)	67.50	67.50
67	A11	4pi on 10fr (R)	35.00	35.00
		Nos. 51-67 (17)	213.65	213.65

OFFICES IN CRETE

Austria, France, Italy and Great Britain maintained their own post offices in Crete during the period when that country was an autonomous state.

100 Centimes = 1 Franc

Liberty, Equality and Fraternity — A1

"Rights of Man" — A2

Liberty and Peace (Symbolized by Olive Branch) — A3

		Perf. 14x13½		
1902-03		Unwmk.		Typo.
1	A1	1c dark gray	2.35	2.75
a.	A1	1c light gray	2.35	2.75
2	A1	2c violet brown	2.35	2.75
3	A1	3c red orange	2.35	2.75
4	A1	4c yellow brown	2.35	2.75
5	A1	5c green	2.35	2.75
6	A2	10c rose red	2.75	2.75
7	A2	15c pale red ('03)	4.25	3.00
8	A2	20c brown vio ('03)	5.25	4.00
9	A2	25c blue ('03)	6.75	4.50
10	A2	30c lilac ('03)	6.75	4.50
11	A3	40c red & pale bl	13.00	13.00
12	A3	50c bis brn & lav	18.00	15.00
13	A3	1fr claret & ol grn	24.50	22.50
14	A3	2fr gray vio & yel	25.00	37.50
a.		Imperf, pair	675.00	
15	A3	5fr dk blue & buff	62.50	60.00
		Nos. 1-15 (15)	180.50	180.50
		Set, never hinged	375.00	

A4

A5

FRANCE OFFICES ABROAD — Offices in Crete — Offices in Egypt

1903		Black Surcharge		
16	A4	1pi on 25c blue	55.00	47.50
17	A5	2pi on 50c bis brn & lav	75.00	57.50
18	A5	4pi on 1fr claret & ol grn	110.00	100.00
19	A5	8pi on 2fr gray vio & yel	140.00	145.00
20	A5	20pi on 5fr dk bl & buff	235.00	225.00
	Nos. 16-20 (5)		615.00	575.00

OFFICES IN EGYPT

French post offices formerly maintained in Alexandria and Port Said.

100 Centimes = 1 Franc

ALEXANDRIA

Stamps of France Ovptd. in Red, Blue or Black

1899-1900		Unwmk.	Perf. 14x13½	
1	A15	1c blk, *lil bl* (R)	2.10	2.10
a.		Double overprint	150.00	
b.		Triple overprint	180.00	
2	A15	2c brn, *buff* (Bl)	3.25	2.50
3	A15	3c gray, *grysh* (Bl)	3.25	2.50
4	A15	4c cl, *lav* (Bl)	4.25	3.25
5	A15	5c yel grn, (I) (R)	6.00	3.25
a.		Type II (R)	160.00	97.50
6	A15	10c blk, *lav*, (I) (R)	9.25	7.50
a.		Type II (R)	62.50	37.50
7	A15	15c blue (R)	9.25	4.25
8	A15	20c red, *grn*	14.50	7.50
9	A15	25c blk, *rose* (R)	7.50	4.25
a.		Inverted overprint	97.50	
b.		Double ovpt., one invtd.	160.00	
10	A15	30c brn, *bis*	15.00	12.00
11	A15	40c red, *straw*	13.50	13.50
12	A15	50c car, *rose* (II)	35.00	17.50
a.		Type I	150.00	27.50
13	A15	1fr brnz grn, *straw*	32.50	22.50
14	A15	2fr brn, *az* ('00)	82.50	80.00
15	A15	5fr red lil, *lav*	120.00	110.00
	Nos. 1-15 (15)		357.85	292.60

 A2   A3

 A4

1902-13				
16	A2	1c pale gray	.80	.65
17	A2	2c violet brn	.75	.75
18	A2	3c red orange	.75	.75
19	A2	4c yellow brn	1.00	.65
20	A2	5c green	5.00	4.25
21	A3	10c rose red	1.50	.75
22	A3	15c orange ('13)	1.75	1.25
a.		15c pale red ('03)	4.75	1.60
23	A3	20c brn vio ('03)	3.00	1.50
24	A3	25c blue ('03)	1.75	.75
25	A3	30c violet ('03)	7.50	4.25
26	A4	40c red & pale bl	5.00	2.50
27	A4	50c bis brn & lav	11.00	3.00
28	A4	1fr cl & ol grn	10.00	4.25
29	A4	2fr gray vio & yel	24.00	12.00
30	A4	5fr dk bl & buff	29.00	17.00
	Nos. 16-30 (15)		102.80	54.50

The 2c, 5c, 10c, 20c and 25c exist imperf. value, each $55.

See #77-86. For surcharges see #31-73, B1-B4.

Stamps of 1902-03 Surcharged Locally in Black

1921				
31	A2	2m on 5c green	7.50	5.00
32	A2	3m on 3c red org	14.50	12.00
a.		Wider numeral	140.00	125.00
33	A3	4m on 10c rose	6.75	6.00
34	A3	5m on 1c gray	14.50	12.00
35	A3	5m on 4c yel brn	19.00	13.50
36	A3	6m on 15c orange	6.75	6.00
a.		Wider numeral	110.00	110.00
37	A3	8m on 20c brn vio	7.50	6.00
a.		Wider numeral	80.00	60.00

38	A3	10m on 25c blue	4.25	4.25
a.		Inverted surcharge	45.00	45.00
b.		Double surcharge	45.00	45.00
39	A3	12m on 30c vio	17.50	17.50
40	A2	15m on 2c vio brn	14.50	14.50

Nos. 26-30 Surcharged

41	A4	15m on 40c	25.00	19.00
42	A4	15m on 50c (#27a)	12.00	12.00
43	A4	30m on 10c bl	175.00	175.00
44	A4	60m on 2fr	250.00	250.00
a.		Wider numerals	1,050.	1,050.
45	A4	150m on 5fr	350.00	350.00

Port Said Nos. 20 and 19 Surcharged like Nos. 32 and 40

45A	A2	3m on 3c red org	150.00	150.00
46	A2	15m on 2c vio brn	150.00	150.00
	Nos. 31-46 (17)		1,225.	1,203.

Alexandria No. 28 Srchd.

1921
| 46A | A4 | 30m on 15m on 1fr | 1,200. | 1,350. |

The surcharge "15 Mill." was made in error and is canceled by a bar.

The surcharges were lithographed on Nos. 31, 33, 36, 39 and 42 and typographed on the other stamps of the 1921 issue. Nos. 34, 36 and 37 were surcharged by both methods.

Alexandria Stamps of 1902-03 Surcharged in Paris

1921-23				
47	A2	1m on 1c slate	3.25	2.50
48	A2	2m on 5c green	2.25	1.90
49	A3	4m on 10c rose	2.75	2.50
50	A3	4m on 10c green ('23)	2.50	2.50
51	A2	5m on 3c red org ('23)	6.75	5.00
52	A3	6m on 15c orange	2.25	1.90
53	A3	8m on 20c brn vio	2.25	1.25
54	A3	10m on 25c blue	1.40	1.25
55	A3	10m on 30c vio	4.25	3.25
56	A3	15m on 50c bl ('23)	3.25	3.00

Nos. 27-30 and Type of 1902 Surcharged

57	A4	15m on 50c	5.00	3.25
58	A4	30m on 1fr	4.25	3.00
59	A4	60m on 2fr	2,250.	2,400.
60	A4	60m on 2fr org & pale bl ('23)	13.50	13.00
61	A4	150m on 5fr	13.50	8.00
	Nos. 47-58,60-61 (14)		67.15	52.80

Stamps and Types of 1902-03 Surcharged with New Values and Bars in Black

1925				
62	A2	1m on 1c slate	1.25	1.25
63	A2	2m on 5c orange	1.25	1.25
64	A2	2m on 5c green	1.75	1.75
65	A3	4m on 10c green	1.10	.85
66	A2	5m on 3c red org	1.50	1.25
67	A3	6m on 15c orange	1.40	1.25
68	A3	8m on 20c brn vio	1.75	1.40
69	A3	10m on 25c blue	1.10	1.00
70	A3	15m on 50c blue	2.40	1.40
71	A4	30m on 1fr cl & ol grn	3.50	2.90
72	A4	60m on 2fr org & pale bl	4.25	3.50
73	A4	150m on 5fr dk bl & buff	6.00	5.00
	Nos. 62-73 (12)		27.25	22.80

Types of 1902-03 Issue

1927-28				
77	A2	3m orange ('28)	2.50	2.10
81	A3	15m slate blue	2.50	2.10
82	A3	20m rose lil ('28)	6.75	5.00
84	A4	50m org & blue	11.00	9.35
85	A4	100m sl bl & buff	15.00	12.00
86	A4	250m gray grn & red	25.00	16.00
	Nos. 77-86 (6)		62.75	46.55

SEMI-POSTAL STAMPS

Regular Issue of 1902-03 Surcharged in Carmine

1915		Unwmk.		
B1	A3	10c + 5c rose	1.25	1.25

Sinking Fund Issue

Type of 1902-03 Issue Surcharged in Blue or Black

1927-30				
B2	A3	15m + 5m deep org	6.00	6.00
B3	A3	15m + 5m red vio ('28)	9.25	9.25
a.		15m + 5m violet ('30)	15.00	15.00

Type of 1902-03 Issue Surcharged as in 1927-28

1929				
B4	A3	15m + 5m fawn	12.00	12.00

POSTAGE DUE STAMPS

Postage Due Stamps of France, 1893-1920, Surcharged in Paris in Black

1922		Unwmk.	Perf. 14x13½	
J1	D2	2m on 5c blue	2.50	2.50
J2	D2	4m on 10c brown	2.50	2.50
J3	D2	10m on 30c rose red	3.00	3.00
J4	D2	15m on 50c brn vio	3.25	3.25
J5	D2	30m on 1fr red brn, *straw*	4.50	4.50
	Nos. J1-J5 (5)		15.75	15.75

D3

1928			Typo.	
J6	D3	1m slate	1.60	1.60
J7	D3	2m light blue	1.25	1.25
J8	D3	4m lilac rose	1.75	1.75
J9	D3	5m gray green	2.00	2.00
J10	D3	10m light red	2.50	2.50
J11	D3	20m violet brn	2.25	2.25
J12	D3	30m green	5.00	5.00
J13	D3	40m lt violet	6.25	6.25
	Nos. J6-J13 (8)		22.00	22.00

Nos. J6-J13 were also available for use in Port Said.

PORT SAID

Stamps of France Overprinted in Red, Blue or Black

1899-1900		Unwmk.	Perf. 14x13½	
1	A15	1c blk, *lil bl* (R)	2.10	1.70
2	A15	2c brn, *buff* (bl)	2.10	1.70
3	A15	3c gray, *grysh* (Bl)	2.10	2.10
4	A15	4c claret, *lav* (Bl)	1.75	2.10
5	A15	5c yel grn (I) (R)	11.00	5.00
a.		Type II (R)	55.00	25.00
6	A15	10c blk, *lav* (I) (R)	14.00	12.50
a.		Type II (R)	72.50	55.00
7	A15	15c blue (R)	14.00	8.50
8	A15	20c red, *grn*	17.00	11.00
9	A15	25c blk, *rose* (R)	14.00	5.00
a.		Double overprint	300.00	
b.		Inverted overprint	300.00	
10	A15	30c brn, *bister*	17.00	14.00
a.		Inverted overprint	325.00	
11	A15	40c red, *straw*	14.00	14.00
12	A15	50c car, *rose* (II)	20.00	14.00
a.		Type I	300.00	100.00
b.		Double overprint (II)	425.00	
13	A15	1fr brnz grn, *straw*	30.00	17.50
14	A15	2fr brn, *az* ('00)	75.00	65.00
15	A15	5fr red lil, *lav*	120.00	92.50
	Nos. 1-15 (15)		354.05	266.60

Regular Issue Surcharged in Red

1899
16	A15	25c on 10c blk, *lav*	130.00	35.00
a.		Inverted surcharge		250.00

With Additional Surcharge "25c" in Red

17	A15	25c on 10c blk, *lav*	475.00	160.00
a.		"25" inverted	1,500.	
b.		"25" in black		2,600.
c.		As "b," "VINGT CINQ" inverted		3,400.
d.		As "b," "25" vertical		3,400.
e.		As "c" and "d"		3,400.

 A2

 A3

 A4

1902-03			Typo.	
18	A2	1c pale gray ('16)	.65	.65
19	A2	2c violet brn	.75	.75
20	A2	3c red orange	.85	.75
21	A2	4c yellow brown	1.10	.90
22	A2	5c blue green ('04)	1.20	.85
a.		5c yellow green	5.00	3.00
23	A3	10c rose red	1.60	1.10
24	A3	15c pale red ('03)	3.25	2.25
a.		15c orange	5.00	3.00
25	A3	20c brn vio ('03)	3.25	2.25
26	A3	25c blue ('03)	2.50	1.60
27	A3	30c gray violet ('03)	6.75	5.00
28	A4	40c red & pale bl	6.00	4.25
29	A4	50c bis brn & lav	9.25	6.75
30	A4	1fr claret & ol grn	12.00	9.25
31	A4	2fr gray vio & yel	15.00	15.00
32	A4	5fr dk bl & buff	35.00	32.50
	Nos. 18-32 (15)		99.15	83.85

See Nos. 83-92. For surcharges see Nos. 33-80, B1-B4.

Stamps of 1902-03 Surcharged Locally

1921
33	A2	2m on 5c green	10.00	10.00
a.		Inverted surcharge	50.00	50.00
34	A3	4m on 10c rose	9.25	9.25
a.		Inverted surcharge	50.00	50.00
35	A3	5m on 1c slate	14.00	14.00
b.		5m on 1c light gray	26.00	26.00
c.		Surcharged "2 Milliemes" on #35	67.50	67.50
36	A3	5m on 2c	24.00	24.00
a.		Surcharged "2 Milliemes"	75.00	75.00
b.		As "a," inverted	160.00	160.00
37	A3	5m on 3c	15.00	15.00
a.		Inverted surcharge	62.50	62.50
b.		On Alexandria #18	400.00	400.00
38	A3	6m on 4c	11.00	11.00
a.		Inverted surcharge	90.00	90.00
39	A2	10m on 2c	25.00	25.00
40	A2	10m on 4c	35.00	35.00
a.		Inverted surcharge	85.00	85.00
b.		Double surcharge	100.00	105.00
41	A3	10m on 25c	9.25	9.25
a.		Inverted surcharge	85.00	85.00
42	A3	12m on 30c	42.50	42.50
43	A3	15m on 4c	10.00	10.00
a.		Inverted surcharge	85.00	85.00
b.		Double surcharge	92.50	97.50
44	A3	15m on 15c pale red	67.50	67.50
a.		Inverted surcharge	160.00	160.00
45	A3	15m on 20c	67.50	67.50
a.		Inverted surcharge	160.00	160.00
46	A4	30m on 50c	300.00	300.00
47	A4	60m on 20c	350.00	350.00
48	A4	150m on 50c	400.00	400.00

Nos. 46, 47 and 48 have a bar between the numerals and "Milliemes," which is in capital letters.

FRANCE OFFICES ABROAD — Offices in Egypt — Offices in Turkey (Levant)

Same Surcharge on Stamps of French Offices in Turkey, 1902-03

49	A2	2m on 2c vio brn	160.00	160.00
50	A2	5m on 1c gray	150.00	150.00
a.		"5" inverted	7,250.	
		Nos. 33-50 (18)	1,700.	1,700.

Nos. 28-32 Surcharged

51	A4	15m on 40c	60.00	60.00
52	A4	15m on 50c	85.00	85.00
b.		Bar below 15	50.00	50.00
53	A4	30m on 1fr	300.00	300.00
54	A4	60m on 2fr	85.00	92.50
55	A4	150m on 5fr	250.00	275.00
		Nos. 51-55 (5)	780.00	812.50

Overprinted "MILLtEMES"

51a	A4	15m on 40c	425.00	425.00
52a	A4	15m on 50c	500.00	500.00
53a	A4	30m on 1fr	1,400.	1,400.
54a	A4	60m on 2fr	400.00	400.00
55a	A4	150m on 5fr	1,050.	1,050.
		Nos. 51a-55a (5)	3,775.	3,775.

Stamps of 1902-03 Surcharged in Paris

1921-23

56	A2	1m on 1c slate	1.60	1.60
57	A2	2m on 5c green	1.60	1.60
58	A3	4m on 10c rose	2.50	2.50
59	A2	5m on 3c red org	9.25	9.25
60	A3	6m on 15c orange	3.25	3.25
a.		6m on 15c pale red	14.00	14.00
61	A3	8m on 20c brn vio	5.00	5.00
62	A3	10m on 25c blue	2.50	2.50
63	A3	10m on 30c violet	7.50	7.50
64	A3	15m on 50c blue	6.75	6.75

Nos. 29-32 and Type of 1902 Surcharged

65	A4	15m on 50c	6.00	6.00
66	A4	30m on 1fr	9.25	9.25
67	A4	60m on 2fr	130.00	130.00
68	A4	60m on 2fr org & pale blue	12.50	12.50
69	A4	150m on 5fr	20.00	20.00
		Nos. 56-69 (14)	217.70	217.70

Stamps and Types of 1902-03 Surcharged

1925

70	A2	1m on 1c light gray	.75	.75
71	A2	2m on 5c green	1.10	1.10
72	A3	4m on 10c rose red	.90	.90
73	A2	5m on 3c red org	1.10	1.10
74	A3	6m on 15c orange	1.10	1.10
75	A3	8m on 20c brn vio	1.00	1.00
76	A3	10m on 25c blue	1.40	1.40
77	A3	15m on 50c blue	1.60	1.60
78	A4	30m on 1fr cl & ol grn	2.75	2.75
79	A4	60m on 2fr org & pale blue	2.50	2.50
80	A4	150m on 5fr dk bl & buff	4.25	4.25
		Nos. 70-80 (11)	18.45	18.45

Type of 1902-03 Issue and

 A5

1927-28

83	A5	3m orange ('28)	2.10	2.10
87	A3	15m slate bl	2.50	2.50
88	A3	20m rose lil ('28)	2.50	2.50
90	A4	50m org & blue	4.50	4.50
91	A4	100m slate bl & buff	6.00	6.00
92	A4	250m gray grn & red	9.25	9.25
		Nos. 83-92 (6)	26.85	26.85

SEMI-POSTAL STAMPS

Regular Issue of 1902-03 Surcharged in Carmine

1915 Unwmk. Perf. 14x13½

B1	A3	10c + 5c rose	1.60	1.60

Sinking Fund Issue

Type of 1902-03 Issue Surcharged like Alexandria Nos. B2-B3 in Blue or Black

1927-30

B2	A3	15m + 5m dp org (Bl)	5.00	5.00
B3	A3	15m + 5m red vio ('28)	8.50	8.50
b.		15m + 5m violet ('30)	14.00	14.00
B4	A3	15m + 5m fawn ('29)	10.00	10.00
		Nos. B2-B4 (3)	23.50	23.50

POSTAGE DUE STAMPS

Postage Due Stamps of France, 1893-1906, Srchd. Locally in Black

1921 Unwmk. Perf. 14x13½

J1	D2	12m on 10c brown	62.50	67.50
J2	D2	15m on 5c blue	92.50	105.00
J3	D2	30m on 20c ol grn	92.50	105.00
a.		Inverted surcharge	1,100.	1,100.
J4	D2	30m on 50c red vio	3,000.	3,400.

Same Surcharged in Red or Blue

1921

J5	D2	2m on 5c bl (R)	55.00	60.00
a.		Blue surcharge	300.00	300.00
b.		Accent omitted from "è" of "Millièmes"	190.00	200.00
c.		Second "m" of "Millièmes" inverted	190.00	200.00
d.		"S" of "Millièmes" omitted	190.00	250.00
J6	D2	4m on 10c brn (Bl)	55.00	62.50
a.		Surcharged "15 Millièmes"	725.00	725.00
b.		Accent omitted from "è" of "MILLIÈMES"	190.00	200.00
c.		Second "m" of "Millièmes" inverted	190.00	200.00
d.		"S" of "Millièmes" omitted	190.00	225.00
J7	D2	10m on 30c red (Bl)	55.00	60.00
a.		Inverted surcharge	160.00	160.00
b.		Accent omitted from "è" of "Millièmes"	190.00	190.00
c.		Second "M" of "Millièmes" inverted	190.00	190.00
d.		"S" of "Millièmes" inverted	190.00	225.00
e.		"Q" for "O" in surcharge (1Qm)	1,450.	1,500.
J8	D2	15m on 50c brn vio (Bl)	67.50	72.50
a.		Inverted surcharge	160.00	160.00
b.		Accent omitted from "è" of "Millièmes"	190.00	190.00
c.		Second "m" of "Millièmes" inverted	200.00	190.00
d.		"S" of "Millièmes" omitted	210.00	250.00
e.		As "a," accent omitted from è of "Millièmes"	425.00	
		Nos. J5-J8 (4)	232.50	255.00

Alexandria Nos. J6-J13 were also available for use in Port Said.

OFFICES IN TURKEY (LEVANT)

Various powers maintained post offices in the Turkish Empire before World War I by authority of treaties which ended with the signing of the Treaty of Lausanne in 1923. The foreign post offices were closed Oct. 27, 1923.

100 Centimes = 1 Franc
25 Centimes = 40 Paras = 1 Piaster

Stamps of France Surcharged in Black or Red

1885-1901 Unwmk. Perf. 14x13½

1	A15	1pi on 25c yel, straw	550.00	16.00
a.		Inverted surcharge	2,500.	2,400.
2	A15	1pi on 25c blk, rose (R) ('86)	4.25	1.25
		Never hinged	8.00	
a.		Inverted surcharge	400.00	325.00
3	A15	2pi on 50c car, rose (II) ('90)	18.00	3.00
		Never hinged	35.00	
a.		Type I ('01)	375.00	50.00
		Never hinged	725.00	
4	A15	3pi on 75c car, rose	30.00	15.00
		Never hinged	60.00	
5	A15	4pi on 1fr brnz grn, straw	30.00	15.00
		Never hinged	60.00	
6	A15	8pi on 2fr brn, az ('00)	37.50	25.00
		Never hinged	67.50	
7	A15	20pi on 5fr red lil, lav ('90)	110.00	60.00
		Never hinged	225.00	
		Nos. 1-7 (7)	779.75	135.25

 A2   A3

 A4

Nos. 29, 32, 36 and Types of A4 Surcharged

No. 34   No. 35

1902-07 Typo. Perf. 14x13½

21	A2	1c gray	.65	.65
		Never hinged	1.25	
22	A2	2c vio brn	.65	.65
23	A2	3c red org	.65	.65
24	A2	4c yel brn	3.00	1.10
a.		Imperf., pair	90.00	
25	A2	5c lt yel green ('03)	2.00	.80
26	A3	10c rose red	1.00	.65
27	A3	15c pale red ('03)	3.00	1.25
28	A3	20c brn vio ('03)	3.25	2.00
29	A3	25c blue ('07)	45.00	60.00
a.		Imperf., pair	425.00	
30	A3	30c lilac ('03)	6.00	3.00
31	A4	40c red & pale bl	6.00	3.25
32	A4	50c bis brn & lav ('07)	190.00	225.00
a.		Imperf., pair	925.00	
33	A4	1fr claret & ol grn ('07)	425.00	450.00
a.		Imperf., pair	1,100.	

Black Surcharge

34	A3	1pi on 25c bl ('03)	1.20	.65
a.		Second "l" omitted	32.50	25.00
b.		Double surcharge	72.50	60.00
35	A4	2pi on 50c bis brn & lavender	4.25	1.60
36	A4	4pi on 1fr cl & ol grn	5.00	2.10
a.		Imperf., pair	750.00	
37	A4	8pi on 2fr gray vio & yel	20.00	15.00
38	A4	20pi on 5fr dk bl & buff	10.00	6.00
		Nos. 21-38 (18)	726.65	774.35

Nos. 29, 32-33 were used during the early part of 1907 in the French Offices at Harar and Diredawa, Ethiopia. Djibouti and Port Said stamps were also used.

No. 27 Surcharged in Green

1905

39	A3	1pi on 15c pale red	2,100.	325.
a.		"Piastte"	7,000.	1,700.

Stamps of France 1900-21 Surcharged

On A22   On A20

On A18

1921-22

40	A22	30pa on 5c grn	1.00	1.00
41	A22	30pa on 5c org	1.00	.85
42	A22	1pi20pa on 10c red	1.10	1.10
43	A22	1pi20pa on 10c grn	1.10	.85
44	A22	3pi30pa on 25c bl	1.60	1.00
45	A22	4pi20pa on 30c org	1.60	1.10
a.		"4" omitted	1,050.	
46	A20	7pi20pa on 50c bl	1.60	1.25
47	A18	15pi on 1fr car & ol grn	3.00	2.10
48	A18	30pi on 2fr org & pale bl	12.50	10.00
49	A18	75pi on 5fr dk bl & buff	11.00	7.50
		Nos. 40-49 (10)	35.50	26.75

Stamps of France, 1903-07, Handstamped

1923

52	A22	1pi20pa on 10c red	62.50	60.00
54	A20	3pi30pa on 15c gray grn (GC)	25.00	25.00
55	A22	7pi20pa on 35c vio	30.00	30.00
b.		1pi20pa on 35c violet	1,400.	1,400.
		Nos. 52-55 (3)	117.50	115.00

CAVALLE (CAVALLA)

Stamps of France Ovptd. or Srchd. in Carmine, Red, Blue or Black

1893-1900 Unwmk. Perf. 14x13½

1	A15	5c grn, grnsh (R)	25.00	21.00
a.		Type II (C)	25.00	21.00
2	A15	5c yel grn (I) ('00) (R)	21.00	21.00
3	A15	10c blk, lav (II)	26.00	26.00
a.		10c black, lavender (I)	180.00	150.00
4	A15	15c blue (R)	47.50	30.00
a.		15c blue (C)	47.50	30.00
5	A15	1pi on 25c blk, rose	28.00	20.00
6	A15	2pi on 50c car, rose	92.50	65.00
7	A15	4pi on 1fr brnz grn, straw (R)	97.50	87.50
b.		4pi on 1fr brnz grn, straw (C)	95.00	87.50
8	A15	8pi on 2fr brn, az ('00) (Bk)	120.00	120.00
		Nos. 1-8 (8)	457.50	390.50
		Set, never hinged	1,000.	

 A3   A4

A5   A6

1902-03

9	A3	5c green	2.25	1.75
a.		5c yel grn	2.50	2.00
10	A4	10c rose red ('03)	2.25	1.75
11	A4	15c orange	2.25	1.75
a.		15c pale red ('03)	12.50	12.50

Surcharged in Black

12	A5	1pi on 25c bl	4.75	3.00
13	A6	2pi on 50c bis brn & lav	13.00	7.00
14	A6	4pi on 1fr cl & ol grn	16.00	13.00

FRANCE OFFICES ABROAD — Offices in Turkey (Levant) — Offices in Zanzibar

15	A6	8pi on 2fr gray vio & yel	21.00	19.00
		Nos. 9-15 (7)	61.50	47.25

DEDEAGH (DEDEAGATCH)

Stamps of France Ovptd. or Srchd. in Carmine, Red, Blue or Black

1893-1900		Unwmk.	Perf. 14x13½	
1	A15	5c grn, grnsh (II) (R)	18.00	15.00
a.		Type II (C)	18.00	15.00
2	A15	5c yel grn (I) ('00)	14.50	14.00
3	A15	10c blk, lav (II)	27.50	20.00
a.		Type I	47.50	32.50
b.		As "a", double overprint	300.00	
4	A15	15c blue (II) (R)	37.50	30.00
		Type II (C)	37.50	30.00
5	A15	1pi on 25c blk, rose	42.50	37.50
6	A15	2pi on 50c car, rose	70.00	50.00
7	A15	4pi on 1fr brnz grn, straw (R)	82.50	70.00
8	A15	8pi on 2fr brn, az ('00) (Bk)	120.00	95.00
		Nos. 1-8 (8)	412.50	331.50
		Set, never hinged	1,000.	

A3

A4

A5   A6

1902-03				
9	A3	5c green ('03)	3.00	2.50
a.		5c yellow green	3.50	3.00
10	A4	10c rose red ('03)	3.50	2.75
11	A4	15c orange	5.00	3.75
a.		15c rose red ('03)	7.00	6.00
15	A5	1pi on 25c bl ('03)	3.50	2.75
16	A6	2pi on 50c bis brn & lav	11.50	10.00
a.		Double surcharge	300.00	
17	A6	4pi on 1fr cl & ol grn	22.50	18.50
18	A6	8pi on 2fr gray vio & yel	32.50	27.50
		Nos. 9-18 (7)	81.50	67.75
		Set, never hinged	175.00	

PORT LAGOS

Stamps of France Ovptd. or Srchd. in Carmine, Red or Blue

1893		Unwmk.	Perf. 14x13½	
1	A15	5c grn, grnsh (R)	30.00	32.50
a.		5c grn, grnsh (C)	30.00	32.50
2	A15	10c blk, lav	62.50	47.50
3	A15	15c blue (R)	92.50	72.50
a.		15c blue (C)	97.50	77.50
4	A15	1pi on 25c blk, rose	77.50	62.50
5	A15	2pi on 50c car, rose	185.00	97.50
6	A15	4pi on 1fr brnz grn, straw (R)	112.50	97.50
		Nos. 1-6 (6)	500.00	410.00
		Set, never hinged	1,300.	

VATHY (SAMOS)

Stamps of France Ovptd. or Srchd. in Carmine, Red, Blue or Black

1894-1900		Unwmk.	Perf. 14x13½	
1	A15	5c grn, grnsh (R)	8.75	8.00
a.		5c grn, grnsh (II) (C)	10.00	8.75
2	A15	5c yel grn (I) ('00) (R)	8.75	7.50
		Type II	87.50	87.50
3	A15	10c blk, lav (I)	17.50	15.00
a.		Type II	50.00	47.50
4	A15	15c blue (R)	17.50	15.00
5	A15	1pi on 25c blk, rose	17.50	11.50
6	A15	2pi on 50c car, rose	30.00	27.50
7	A15	4pi on 1fr brnz grn, straw (R)	42.50	35.00
8	A15	8pi on 2fr brn, az ('00) (Bk)	75.00	75.00
9	A15	20pi on 5fr lil, lav ('00) (Bk)	110.00	110.00
		Nos. 1-9 (9)	327.50	304.50
		Set, never hinged	600.00	

OFFICES IN ZANZIBAR

Until 1906 France maintained post offices in the Sultanate of Zanzibar, but in that year Great Britain assumed direct control over this protectorate and the French withdrew their postal system.

16 Annas = 1 Rupee

Stamps of France Surcharged in Red, Carmine, Blue or Black

1894-96		Unwmk.	Perf. 14x13½	
1	A15	½a on 5c grn, grnsh	10.00	7.50
2	A15	1a on 10c blk, lav (Bl)	15.00	12.50
3	A15	1½a on 15c bl ('96)	22.50	21.00
a.		"ANNAS"	100.00	92.50
4	A15	2a on 20c red, grn ('96) (Bk)	19.00	15.00
a.		"ANNA"	2,300.	2,300.
5	A15	2½a on 25c blk, rose (Bl)	12.50	9.25
a.		Double surcharge	250.00	250.00
6	A15	3a on 30c brn, bis ('96) (Bk)	21.00	18.00
7	A15	4a on 40c red, straw ('96) (Bk)	29.00	25.00
8	A15	5a on 50c car, rose (Bk)	37.50	32.50
9	A15	7½a on 75c vio, org ('96) (Bk)	500.00	400.00
10	A15	10a on 1fr brnz grn, straw	67.50	55.00
11	A15	50a on 5fr lil, lav ('96)	325.00	260.00
		Nos. 1-11 (11)	1,059.	855.75

1894				
12	A15	½a & 5c on 1c blk, lil bl (R)	200.00	220.00
13	A15	1a & 10c on 3c gray, grysh (R)	180.00	200.00
14	A15	2½a & 25c on 4c cl, lav (Bk)	230.00	275.00
15	A15	5a & 50c on 20c red, grn (Bk)	250.00	275.00
16	A15	10a & 1fr on 40c red, straw	475.00	525.00
		Nos. 12-16 (5)	1,335.	1,495.

There are two distinct types of the figures 5c, four of the 25c and three of each of the others of this series.

Stamps of France Srchd. in Red, Carmine, Blue or Black

1896-1900				
17	A15	½a on 5c grn, grnsh (R)	11.00	8.50
18	A15	½a on 5c yel grn (I) (R)	7.50	6.75
a.		Type II	9.25	7.50
19	A15	1a on 10c blk, lav (II) (Bl)	9.25	7.50
a.		Type I	22.50	19.00
20	A15	1½a on 15c bl (R)	11.00	9.25
21	A15	2a on 20c red, grn	9.25	9.25
a.		"ZANZIBAR" double	210.00	210.00
b.		"ZANZIBAR" triple	210.00	210.00
22	A15	2½a on 25c blk, rose (Bl)	11.00	9.25
a.		Inverted surcharge	275.00	210.00
23	A15	3a on 30c brn, bis	11.00	9.25
24	A15	4a on 40c red, straw	13.50	10.00
25	A15	5a on 50c rose, rose (II) (Bl)	45.00	32.50
a.		Type I	125.00	100.00
26	A15	10a on 1fr brnz grn, straw (R)	29.00	25.00
27	A15	20a on 2fr brn, az	35.00	29.00
a.		"ZANZIBAS"	675.00	750.00
b.		"ZANZIBAR" triple		1,600.
28	A15	50a on 5fr lil, lav	67.50	62.50
a.		"ZANZIBAS"	9,250.	
		Nos. 17-28 (12)	260.00	218.75

For surcharges see Nos. 50-54.

A4   A5

1897				
29	A4	2½a & 25c on ½a on 5c grn, grnsh	1,300.	240.
30	A4	2½a & 25c on 1a on 10c lav	4,500.	1,100.
31	A4	2½a & 25c on 1½a on 15c blue	4,400.	950.
32	A5	5a & 50c on 3a on 30c brn, bis	4,400.	950.
33	A5	5a & 50c on 4a on 40c red, straw	4,500.	1,300.

Printed on the Margins of Sheets of French Stamps

A6   A7

Perf. 14x13½ on one or more sides

1897				
34	A6	2½a & 25c grn, grnsh		1,300.
35	A6	2½a & 25c blk, lav		4,000.
36	A6	2½a & 25c blue		3,000.
37	A7	5a & 50c brn, bis		2,900.
38	A7	5a & 50c red, straw		4,000.

There are 5 varieties of figures in the above surcharges.

Surcharged in Red or Black

A8   A9

A10

1902-03		Perf. 14x13½		
39	A8	½a on 5c grn (R)	6.75	6.00
40	A9	1a on 10c rose red ('03)	7.50	7.50
41	A9	1½a on 15c pale red ('03)	15.00	14.00
42	A9	2a on 20c brn vio ('03)	18.00	15.00
43	A9	2½a on 25c bl ('03)	10.00	15.00
44	A9	3a on 30c lil ('03)	13.00	13.00
a.		5a on 30c (error)	325.00	375.00
45	A10	4a on 40c red & pale bl	30.00	25.00
46	A10	5a on 50c bis brn & lav	25.00	21.00
47	A10	10a on 1fr cl & ol grn	32.50	29.00
48	A10	20a on 2fr gray vio & yel	85.00	75.00
49	A10	50a on 5fr dk bl & buff	100.00	92.50
		Nos. 39-49 (11)	350.75	313.00

For see Reunion Nos. 55-59.

Nos. 23-24 Surcharged in Black

a   b

c

1904				
50	A15	(a) 25c & 2½a on 4a on 40c		1,000.
51	A15	(b) 50c & 5a on 3a on 30c		1,200.
52	A15	(b) 50c & 5a on 4a on 40c	6,500.	1,200.
53	A15	(c) 1fr & 10a on 3a on 30c		2,000.
54	A15	(c) 1fr & 10a on 4a on 40c		2,000.

Nos. 39-40, 44 Surcharged in Red or Black

d   e

f   g

55	A8	(d) 25c & 2a on ½a on 5c (П)	3,100.	140.00
56	A9	(e) 25c & 2½a on 1a on 10c	6,500.	150.00
a.		Inverted surcharge		1,500.
57	A9	(e) 25c & 2½a on 3a on 30c		2,400.
a.		Inverted surcharge		4,100.
b.		Double surch., both invtd.		2,600.
58	A9	(f) 50c & 5a on 3a on 30c		1,250.
59	A9	(g) 1fr & 10a on 3a on 30c		2,000.

No. J1-J3 With Various Surcharges Overprinted:
"Timbre" in Red

| 60 | D1 | ½a on 5c blue | | 450.00 |

Overprinted "Affranchi" in Black

| 61 | D1 | 1a on 10c brn | | 450.00 |

With Red Bars Across "CHIFFRE" and "TAXE"

| 62 | D1 | 1½a on 15c grn | | 1,000. |

The illustrations are not exact reproductions of the new surcharges but are merely intended to show their relative positions and general styles.

POSTAGE DUE STAMPS

Postage Due Stamps of France Ovptd. in Red, Blue or Black Like Nos. 17-28

1897		Unwmk.	Perf. 14x13½	
J1	D2	½a on 5c blue (R)	21.00	12.50
J2	D2	1a on 10c brn (Bl)	21.00	12.50
a.		Inverted surcharge	160.00	190.00
J3	D2	1½a on 15c grn (R)	32.50	12.50
J4	D2	3a on 30c car (Bk)	29.00	21.00
J5	D2	5a on 50c lil (Bl)	32.50	25.00
a.		2½a on 50c lilac (Bl)	1,400.	1,300.
		Nos. J1-J5 (5)	136.00	83.50

For overprints see Nos. 60-62.

REUNION

LOCATION — An island in the Indian Ocean about 400 miles east of Madagascar
GOVT. — Department of France
AREA — 970 sq. mi.
POP. — 490,000 (est. 1974)
CAPITAL — St. Denis

The colony of Réunion became an integral part of the Republic, acquiring the same status as the departments in metropolitan France, under a law effective Jan. 1, 1947.

On Jan. 1, 1975, stamps of France replaced those inscribed or overprinted "CFA."

100 Centimes = 1 Franc

> Catalogue values for unused stamps in this country are for Never Hinged items, beginning with Scott 224 in the regular postage section, Scott B15 in the semipostal section, Scott C18 in the airpost section, and Scott J26 in the postage due section.

For French stamps inscribed "Reunion" see Nos. 949, 1507.

 A1   A2

1852 Unwmk. Typo. Imperf.

1	A1	15c black, *blue*	39,000.	25,000.
2	A2	30c black, *blue*	39,000.	25,000.

Four varieties of each value.
The reprints are printed on a more bluish paper than the originals. They have a frame of a thick and a thin line, instead of one thick and two thin lines. Value, $62.50 each.

Stamps of French Colonies Surcharged or Overprinted in Black

a

Overprint Type "a"

1885

3	A1(a)	5c on 40c org, *yelsh*	450.00	375.00
a.		Inverted surcharge	2,250.	2,100.
b.		Double surcharge	2,250.	2,100.
4	A1(a)	25c on 40c org, *yelsh*	70.00	55.00
a.		Inverted surcharge	1,000.	900.00
b.		Double surcharge	1,000.	900.00
5	A5(a)	5c on 30c brn, *yelsh* (I)	70.00	57.50
a.		"5" inverted	3,500.	3,000.
b.		Double surcharge	1,100.	900.00
c.		Inverted surcharge	1,000.	900.00
6	A4(a)	5c on 40c org, *yelsh* (I)	62.50	45.00
a.		5c on 40c org, *yelsh* (II)	2,500.	2,500.
b.		Inverted surcharge (I)	1,100.	900.00
c.		Double surcharge (I)	1,100.	900.00
7	A8(a)	5c on 30c brn, *yelsh*	22.50	18.00
8	A8(a)	5c on 40c ver, *straw*	135.00	115.00
a.		Inverted surcharge	950.00	850.00
b.		Double surcharge	925.00	850.00
9	A8(a)	10c on 40c ver, *straw*	27.50	22.50
a.		Inverted surcharge	950.00	850.00
b.		Double surcharge	950.00	850.00
10	A8(a)	20c on 30c brn, *yelsh*	90.00	75.00

b

Overprint Type "b"
With or Without Accent on "E"

1891

11	A4	40c org, *yelsh* (I)	575.00	550.00
		40c orange, *yelsh* (II)	6,750.	6,750.
b.		Double overprint	750.00	750.00
12	A7	80c car, *pnksh*	80.00	62.50
13	A8	30c brn, *yelsh*	52.50	52.50
14	A8	40c ver, *straw*	42.50	42.50
15	A8	75c car, *rose*	475.00	475.00
16	A8	1fr brnz grn, *straw*	62.50	52.50

Perf. 14x13½

17	A9	1c blk, *lil bl*	4.75	4.00
a.		Inverted overprint	60.00	60.00
b.		Double overprint	52.50	52.50
18	A9	2c brn, *buff*	6.50	5.00
a.		Inverted overprint	40.00	40.00
19	A9	4c claret, *lav*	10.00	8.00
a.		Inverted overprint	72.50	72.50
20	A9	5c grn, *grnsh*	11.50	9.00
a.		Inverted overprint	60.00	60.00
b.		Double overprint	60.00	57.50
21	A9	10c blk, *lav*	40.00	8.00
a.		Inverted overprint	90.00	80.00
b.		Double overprint	100.00	80.00
22	A9	15c blue	57.50	9.00
a.		Inverted overprint	120.00	110.00
23	A9	20c red, *grn*	45.00	30.00
a.		Inverted overprint	175.00	150.00
b.		Double overprint	175.00	150.00
24	A9	25c blk, *rose*	50.00	7.25
a.		Inverted overprint	125.00	120.00
25	A9	35c dp vio, *yel*	45.00	35.00
a.		Inverted overprint	180.00	175.00
26	A9	40c red, *straw*	72.50	62.50
a.		Inverted overprint	240.00	225.00
27	A9	75c car, *rose*	675.00	575.00
			1,600.	1,400.
28	A9	1fr brnz grn, *straw*	575.00	500.00
a.		Inverted overprint	1,600.	1,500.
b.		Double overprint	1,500.	1,400.

The varieties "RUNION," "RUENION," "REUNIONR," "ERUNION," "EUNION," "REUNIN," "REUNIOU" and "REUNOIN" are found on most stamps of this group. See *Scott Classic Specialized Catalogue of Stamps and Covers* for detailed listings. There are also many broken letters.

For surcharges see Nos. 29-33, 53-55.

No. 23 with Additional Surcharge in Black

c   d

e   f

1891

29	A9(c)	02c on 20c red, *grn*	14.50	14.50
a.		Inverted surcharge	90.00	90.00
b.		No "c" after "02"	57.50	57.50
30	A9(c)	15c on 20c red, *grn*	18.00	18.00
a.		Inverted surcharge	70.00	70.00
31	A9(d)	2c on 20c red, *grn*	5.00	5.00
32	A9(e)	2c on 20c red, *grn*	6.00	5.75
33	A9(f)	2c on 20c red, *grn*	10.00	10.00
		Nos. 29-33 (5)	53.50	53.25

The varieties "RUNION" and "RUENION" appear on several stamps from this set. See *Scott Classic Specialized Catalogue of Stamps and Covers* for listings.

 Navigation and Commerce — A14

1892-1905 Typo. Perf. 14x13½
Name of Colony in Blue or Carmine

34	A14	1c blk, *lil bl*	2.00	1.25
35	A14	2c brn, *buff*	2.00	1.25
36	A14	4c claret, *lav*	3.25	2.25
37	A14	5c grn, *grnsh*	7.25	2.25
38	A14	5c yel grn ('00)	1.75	1.75
39	A14	10c blk, *lav*	9.50	3.50
40	A14	10c red ('00)	4.50	4.50
41	A14	15c bl, quadrille paper	30.00	3.50
42	A14	15c gray ('00)	10.00	3.50
43	A14	20c red, *grn*	20.00	9.00
44	A14	25c blk, *rose*	22.50	3.50
		"Reunion" double	425.00	450.00
45	A14	25c blue ('00)	29.00	27.50
46	A14	30c brn, *bis*	23.00	12.00
47	A14	40c red, *straw*	32.50	19.00
48	A14	50c car, *rose*	80.00	42.50
a.		"Reunion" in red and blue	500.00	
49	A14	50c brn, *az* ("Reunion" in car) ('00)	57.50	50.00
50	A14	50c brn, *az* ("Reunion" in bl) ('05)	57.50	50.00
51	A14	75c dp vio, *org*	62.50	45.00
a.		"Reunion" double	375.00	375.00
52	A14	1fr brnz grn, *straw*	50.00	35.00
a.		"Reunion" double	360.00	375.00
		Nos. 34-52 (19)	504.75	317.25

Perf. 13½x14 stamps are counterfeits.
For surcharges and overprint see Nos. 56-59, 99-106, Q1.

French Colonies No. 52 Surcharged in Black

g   h

j

1893

53	A9(g)	2c on 20c red, *grn*	3.25	3.25
54	A9(h)	2c on 20c red, *grn*	6.00	6.00
55	A9(j)	2c on 20c red, *grn*	22.50	22.50
		Nos. 53-55 (3)	31.75	31.75

Reunion Nos. 47-48, 51-52 Surcharged in Black

1901

56	A14	5c on 40c red, *straw*	7.00	7.00
a.		Inverted surcharge	47.50	47.50
b.		No bar	240.00	240.00
c.		Thin "5"	240.00	—
d.		"5" inverted	1,400.	1,200.
57	A14	5c on 50c car, *rose*	7.75	7.25
a.		Inverted surcharge	47.50	47.50
b.		No bar	240.00	240.00
c.		Thin "5"	—	—
58	A14	15c on 75c vio, *org*	22.50	22.50
a.		Inverted surcharge	57.50	57.50
b.		No bar	240.00	240.00
c.		Thin "5" and small "1"	47.50	47.50
d.		As "c," inverted	800.00	800.00
59	A14	15c on 1fr brnz grn, *straw*	19.00	19.00
a.		Inverted surcharge	57.50	57.50
b.		No bar	240.00	240.00
c.		Thin "5" and small "1"	47.50	47.50
d.		As "c," inverted	—	—
		Nos. 56-59 (4)	56.25	55.75

Map of Réunion — A19

Coat of Arms and View of St. Denis — A20

View of St. Pierre — A21

1907-30 Typo.

60	A19	1c vio & lt rose	.30	.30
61	A19	2c brn & ultra	.30	.30
62	A19	4c ol grn & red	.40	.40
a.		Center double	225.00	
63	A19	5c grn & red	1.35	.40
64	A19	5c org & vio ('22)	.30	.30
65	A19	10c car & grn	2.75	.40
66	A19	10c grn ('22)	.30	.30
67	A19	10c brn red & org red, *bluish*	.70	.70
		('26)		
68	A19	15c blk & ultra ('17)	.55	.40
a.		Center double	250.00	250.00
69	A19	15c gray grn & bl grn ('26)	.40	.40
70	A19	15c bl & lt red ('28)	.55	.45
71	A20	20c gray grn & bl grn	.45	.45
a.		Center omitted	1,100.	1,100.
72	A20	25c dp bl & vio brn	7.00	4.00
73	A20	25c lt brn & bl ('22)	.55	.55
74	A20	30c yel brn & grn	1.50	1.00
75	A20	30c rose & pale rose ('22)	1.50	1.50
76	A20	30c gray & car rose ('26)	.55	.55
77	A20	30c dp grn & yel grn ('28)	1.20	1.20
78	A20	35c ol grn & bl	1.75	1.10
79	A20	40c gray grn & brn ('25)	.70	.70
80	A20	45c vio & car rose	1.90	1.10
81	A20	45c red brn & ver ('25)	.90	.90
82	A20	45c vio & red org ('28)	3.00	2.75
83	A20	50c red brn & ultra	5.00	1.75
84	A20	50c bl & ultra ('22)	1.40	1.40
85	A20	50c yel & vio ('26)	1.10	1.10
86	A20	60c dk bl & yel brn ('25)	1.10	1.10
87	A20	65c vio & lt bl ('28)	1.60	1.40
88	A20	75c red & car rose	.80	.70
89	A20	75c ol brn & red vio ('28)	2.50	2.25
90	A20	90c brn red & brt red ('30)	9.00	8.25
91	A21	1fr ol grn & bl	1.50	1.40
92	A21	1fr blue ('25)	.95	.95
93	A21	1fr yel brn & lav ('28)	1.50	.70
94	A21	1.10fr org brn & rose lil ('28)	1.50	1.40
95	A21	1.50fr dk bl & ultra ('30)	16.00	16.00
96	A21	2fr red & grn	6.75	4.25
97	A21	3fr red vio ('30)	14.50	9.50
98	A21	5fr car & vio brn	11.50	6.75
		Nos. 60-98 (39)	105.60	79.05

For surcharges see Nos. 107-121, 178-180, B1-B3.

Stamps of 1892-1900 Surcharged in Black or Carmine

1912
Spacing between figures of surcharge 1.5mm (5c), 2mm (10c)

99	A14	5c on 2c brn, *buff*	1.60	1.60
100	A14	5c on 15c gray (C)	1.40	1.40
a.		Inverted surcharge	210.00	210.00
101	A14	5c on 20c red, *grn*	2.40	2.40
102	A14	5c on 25c blk, *rose* (C)	1.60	1.60
103	A14	5c on 30c brn, *bis* (C)	1.40	1.40
104	A14	10c on 40c red, *straw*	1.40	1.40
105	A14	10c on 50c brn, *az*	5.75	5.75
106	A14	10c on 75c dp vio, *org*	9.50	9.50
		Nos. 99-106 (8)	25.05	25.05

Two spacings between the surcharged numerals are found on Nos. 99 to 106. For detailed listings, see the *Scott Classic Specialized Catalogue of Stamps and Covers.*

No. 62 Surcharged

1917

107	A19	1c on 4c ol grn & red	2.00	2.00
a.		Inverted surcharge	80.00	80.00
b.		Double surcharge	70.00	70.00
c.		In pair with unsurcharged #62	625.00	625.00

REUNION

Stamps and Types of 1907-30 Surcharged in Black or Red

1922-33

108	A20	40c on 20c grn & yel	.80	.80
a.		Double surcharge, one inverted	175.00	175.00
b.		Center double	175.00	175.00
c.		Surcharge omitted	1,200.	1,200.
109	A20	50c on 45c red brn & ver ('33)	1.20	1.20
109A	A20	50c on 45c vio & red org ('33)	325.00	275.00
b.		Double surcharge	1,750.	
110	A20	50c on 65c vio & lt bl ('33)	1.20	1.20
111	A20	60c on 75c red & rose	.85	.85
a.		Double surcharge	225.00	225.00
112	A19	65c on 15c blk & ultra (R) ('25)	2.00	2.00
113	A19	85c on 15c blk & ultra (R) ('25)	2.00	2.00
114	A20	85c on 75c red & cer ('25)	2.25	2.25
115	A20	90c on 75c brn red & rose red ('27)	2.25	2.25
		Nos. 108-109,110-115 (8)	12.55	12.55

Stamps and Type of 1907-30 Srchd. in Black or Red

1924-27

116	A21	25c on 5fr car & brn	1.10	1.10
a.		Double surcharge	110.00	
117	A21	1.25fr on 1fr bl (R) ('26)	1.10	1.10
a.		Double surcharge	125.00	
118	A21	1.50fr on 1fr ind & ultra, bluish ('27)	1.50	1.50
a.		Double surcharge	140.00	
b.		Surcharge omitted	200.00	
119	A21	3fr on 5fr dl red & lt bl ('27)	4.25	3.00
120	A21	10fr on 5fr bl grn & brn red ('27)	19.50	17.00
121	A21	20fr on 5fr brn & mag ('27)	24.00	19.00
		Nos. 116-121 (6)	51.45	42.70

Common Design Types pictured following the introduction.

Colonial Exposition Issue
Common Design Types

1931   *Engr.*   *Perf. 12½*

Name of Country Typo. in Black

122	CD70	40c dp green	5.50	5.50
123	CD71	50c violet	5.50	5.50
124	CD72	90c red orange	5.50	5.50
125	CD73	1.50fr dull blue	5.50	5.50
		Nos. 122-125 (4)	22.00	22.00

Cascade of Salazie A22

Waterfowl Lake and Anchain Peak A23

Léon Dierx Museum, St. Denis — A24

Perf. 12, 12½ and Compound

1933-40   *Engr.*

126	A22	1c violet	.25	.25
127	A22	2c dark brown	.25	.25
128	A22	3c rose vio ('40)	.25	.25
129	A22	4c olive green	.25	.25
130	A22	5c red orange	.25	.25
131	A22	10c ultramarine	.25	.25
132	A22	15c black	.25	.25
133	A22	20c indigo	.30	.25
134	A22	25c red brown	.40	.30
135	A22	30c dark green	.40	.40
136	A23	35c green ('38)	.55	.55
137	A23	40c ultramarine	.55	.55
138	A23	40c brn blk ('40)	.40	.40
139	A23	45c red violet	1.00	1.00
140	A23	45c green ('40)	.45	.45
141	A23	50c red	.30	.25
142	A23	55c brn org ('38)	1.50	1.00
143	A23	60c dull bl ('40)	.45	.45
144	A23	65c olive green	1.10	.80
145	A23	70c ol grn ('40)	.65	.65
146	A23	75c dark brown	5.00	4.25
147	A23	80c black ('38)	1.00	.80
148	A23	90c carmine	2.50	2.10
149	A23	90c dl rose vio ('39)	1.00	1.00
150	A23	1fr green	2.00	.70
151	A23	1fr dk car ('38)	2.50	.70
152	A23	1fr black ('40)	.70	.70
153	A24	1.25fr orange brown	.70	.55
154	A24	1.25fr brt car rose ('39)	1.00	1.00
155	A22	1.40fr pck bl ('40)	1.00	1.00
156	A24	1.50fr ultramarine	.40	.40
157	A22	1.60fr dk car rose ('40)	1.40	1.40
158	A24	1.75fr olive green	1.00	.65
159	A22	1.75fr dk bl ('38)	1.40	.85
160	A24	2fr vermilion	.55	.55
161	A22	2.25fr brt ultra ('39)	2.00	2.00
162	A22	2.50fr chnt ('40)	1.40	1.40
163	A24	3fr purple	.55	.55
164	A24	5fr magenta	.55	.55
165	A24	10fr dark blue	1.10	1.10
166	A24	20fr red brown	1.50	1.50
		Nos. 126-166 (41)	39.05	32.55

For overprints and surcharges see Nos. 177A, 181-220, 223, C1.
60c, 1fr without "RF," see Nos. 237A-238B.

Paris International Exposition Issue
Common Design Types

1937   *Perf. 13*

167	CD74	20c dp vio	2.25	2.25
168	CD75	30c dk grn	2.25	2.25
169	CD76	40c car rose	2.25	2.25
170	CD77	50c dk brn & blk	2.10	2.10
171	CD78	90c red	2.10	2.10
172	CD79	1.50fr ultra	2.25	2.25
		Nos. 167-172 (6)	13.20	13.20
		Set, never hinged	20.00	

Colonial Arts Exhibition Issue
Souvenir Sheet
Common Design Type

1937   *Imperf.*

173	CD74	3fr ultra	8.50	10.00
		Never hinged	16.00	

New York World's Fair Issue
Common Design Type

1939   *Engr.*   *Perf. 12½x12*

174	CD82	1.25fr car lake	1.40	1.40
175	CD82	2.25fr ultra	1.40	1.40
		Set, never hinged	4.50	

For overprints, see Nos. 221-222.

St. Denis Roadstead and Marshal Pétain — A25

1941   *Unwmk.*   *Perf. 11½x12*

176	A25	1fr brown	.80	
177	A25	2.50fr blue	.80	
		Set, never hinged	2.00	

Nos. 176-177 were issued by the Vichy government in France, but were not placed on sale in Réunion.
For surcharges, see Nos. B13-B14.

No. 144 Surcharged in Carmine

1943

177A		1fr on 65c olive grn	1.10	.65
		Never hinged	1.60	

De Pronis Landing on Reunion — A25a

1943   *Perf. 12½x12*

177B	A25a	60c blk brn & red	.55	
177C	A25a	80c green & blue	.40	
177D	A25a	1.50fr dk brn red	.35	
177E	A25a	4fr ultra & red	.35	
177F	A25a	5fr red brn & black	.55	
177G	A25a	10fr violet & green	.65	
		Nos. 177B-177G,C13A-C13F (12)	5.70	
		Set, never hinged	8.00	

300th Ann. of French settlement on Réunion. Nos. 177B-177G were issued by the Vichy government in France, but were not placed on sale in Réunion.

Stamps of 1907 Overprinted in Blue Violet

q

1943   *Unwmk.*   *Perf. 14x13½*

178	A19(q)	4c ol gray & pale red	6.00	6.00
179	A20(q)	75c red & lil rose	1.75	1.75
180	A21(q)	5fr car & vio brn	60.00	60.00

Stamps of 1933-40 Overprinted in Carmine, Black or Blue Violet

181	A22(r)	1c rose vio (C)	1.00	1.00
182	A22(r)	2c dk brn (C)	1.00	1.00
183	A22(r)	3c rose vio (C)	1.00	1.00
184	A22(r)	4c ol yel (C)	1.00	1.00
185	A22(r)	5c red org (C)	1.00	1.00
186	A22(r)	10c ultra (C)	1.00	1.00
187	A22(r)	15c blk (C)	1.00	1.00
188	A22(r)	20c ind (C)	1.00	1.00
189	A22(r)	25c red brn (BIV)	1.25	1.25
190	A22(r)	30c dk grn (C)	1.40	1.40
191	A23(r)	35c green	1.00	1.00
192	A23(q)	40c dl ultra (C)	1.00	1.00
193	A23(q)	40c brn blk (C)	1.00	1.00
194	A23(q)	45c red vio	1.00	1.00
195	A23(q)	45c green	1.00	1.00
196	A23(q)	50c org red	1.00	1.00
197	A23(q)	55c brn org	1.00	1.00
198	A23(q)	60c dl bl (C)	3.00	3.00
199	A23(q)	65c ol grn	1.00	1.00
200	A23(q)	70c ol grn (C)	2.25	2.25
201	A23(q)	75c dk brn (C)	5.25	5.25
202	A23(q)	80c blk (C)	1.00	1.00
203	A23(q)	90c dl rose vio	1.00	1.00
204	A23(q)	1fr green	1.00	1.00
205	A23(q)	1fr dk car	1.00	1.00
206	A23(q)	1fr blk (C)	3.00	3.00
207	A24(q)	1.25fr org brn (BIV)	1.00	1.00
208	A24(q)	1.25fr brt car rose	3.00	3.00
209	A22(r)	1.40fr pck bl (C)	2.00	2.00
210	A24(q)	1.50fr ultra (C)	1.00	1.00
211	A22(r)	1.60fr dk car rose	2.10	2.10
212	A24(q)	1.75fr ol grn (C)	2.75	2.75
213	A22(q)	1.75fr dk bl (C)	4.50	4.50
214	A24(q)	2fr vermilion	1.00	1.00
215	A22(r)	2.25fr brt ultra (C)	4.50	4.50
216	A22(r)	2.50fr chnt (BIV)	7.50	7.50
217	A24(q)	3fr pur (C)	1.00	1.00
218	A24(q)	5fr brn lake (BIV)	2.10	2.10
219	A24(q)	10fr dk bl (C)	8.50	8.50
220	A24(q)	20fr red brn (BIV)	13.00	13.00

New York World's Fair Issue Overprinted in Black or Carmine

221	CD82(q)	1.25fr car lake	4.00	4.00
222	CD82(q)	2.25fr ultra	4.00	4.00
		Nos. 178-222 (45)	165.85	165.85
		Set, never hinged	235.00	

No. 177A Overprinted

1943   *Unwmk.*   *Perf. 12½*

223	A23	1fr on 65c ol grn	.85	.85

Catalogue values for unused stamps in this section, from this point to the end of the section, are for Never Hinged items.

Produce of Réunion — A26

1943   *Photo.*   *Perf. 14½x14*

224	A26	5c dull brown	.25	.25
225	A26	10c blue & lt blue	.25	.25
226	A26	25c emerald	.25	.25
227	A26	30c dp orange	.25	.25
228	A26	40c dk slate grn	.25	.25
229	A26	80c rose violet	.65	.50
230	A26	1fr red brown	.25	.25
231	A26	1.50fr crimson	.65	.50
232	A26	2fr black	.65	.50
233	A26	2.50fr ultra	1.00	.70
234	A26	4fr dk violet	1.25	.90
235	A26	5fr bister	1.25	.90
236	A26	10fr dark brown	1.75	1.40
237	A26	20fr dark green	2.75	1.75
		Nos. 224-237 (14)	11.45	8.65

For surcharges see Nos. 240-247.

Type of 1933-40 without "RF"

1944   *Engr.*   *Perf. 12½*

237A	A23	60c dull blue	1.40	1.00
237B	A23	1fr black & blue	1.40	1.00

Nos. 237A-237B were issued by the Vichy government in France, but were not placed on sale in Réunion.

Eboue Issue
Common Design Type

1945   *Perf. 13*

238	CD91	2fr black	1.00	1.00
239	CD91	25fr Prussian green	1.40	1.00

Nos. 224, 226 and 233 Surcharged in Carmine or Black

1945   *Perf. 14½x14*

240	A26	50c on 5c dl brn (C)	.30	.25
241	A26	60c on 5c dl brn (C)	.30	.25
242	A26	70c on 5c dl brn (C)	.30	.25
243	A26	1.20fr on 5c dl brn (C)	.70	.50
244	A26	2.40fr on 25c emer	.70	.50
245	A26	3fr on 25c emer	1.25	.90
246	A26	4.50fr on 25c emer	1.25	.90
247	A26	15fr on 2.50fr ultra (C)	1.75	1.10
		Nos. 240-247 (8)	6.55	4.65

Various double and inverted overprints exist for Nos. 240-247.

REUNION

Cliff
A27

Cutting
Sugar Cane
A28

Cascade
A29

Banana
Tree
A30

Mountain
Scene — A31

Ship Approaching
Réunion — A32

1947   Unwmk.   Photo.   Perf. 13½
249	A27	10c org & grnsh blk	.25	.25
250	A27	30c org & brt bl	.25	.25
251	A27	40c org & brn	.25	.25
252	A28	50c bl grn & brn	.25	.25
253	A28	60c dk bl & brn	.25	.25
254	A28	80c brn & ol brn	.55	.45
255	A29	1fr dl bl & vio brn	.55	.45
256	A29	1.20fr bl grn & gray	.80	.65
257	A29	1.50fr org & vio brn	.80	.65
258	A30	2fr gray bl & bl grn	.80	.65
259	A30	3fr vio brn & bl grn	.80	.65
260	A30	3.60fr dl red & rose red	.90	.70
261	A30	4fr gray bl & buff	.80	.70
262	A31	5fr rose lil & brn	1.25	.70
263	A31	6fr bl & brn	1.50	.75
264	A31	10fr org & ultra	3.25	1.50
265	A32	15fr gray bl & vio brn	4.75	2.75
266	A32	20fr bl & org	6.50	4.00
267	A32	25fr rose lil & brn	8.00	4.25
		Nos. 249-267 (19)	32.50	20.10

Nos. 249-267 exist imperf. Value, set $100.

Stamps of France, 1945-49, Surcharged type "a" or "b" in Black or Carmine

On A147

Others

1949   Unwmk.   Perf. 14x13½, 13
268	A153	10c on 30c	.30	.25
269	A153	30c on 50c	.60	.25
270	A146	50c on 1fr	1.40	.90
271	A146	60c on 2fr	8.00	1.40
272	A147	1fr on 3fr	2.00	.70
273	A147	2fr on 4fr	8.00	1.60
274	A147	2.50fr on 5fr	20.00	11.00
275	A147	3fr on 6fr	2.25	1.40
276	A147	4fr on 10fr	2.00	1.60
277	A147	5fr on 20fr (C)	10.00	1.40
278	A147	6fr on 12fr	29.00	2.25
279	A160	7fr on 12fr	9.00	3.00
280	A165	8fr on 25fr (C)	37.50	3.25
281	A165	10fr on 25fr (C)	2.75	1.40
282	A174	11fr on 18fr (C)	16.00	2.25
		Nos. 268-282 (15)	148.80	32.65

The letters "C. F. A." are the initials of "Colonies Francaises d'Afrique," referring to the currency which is expressed in French Africa francs.

The surcharge on Nos. 277, 279, 282 includes two bars.

1950   Perf. 14x13½
283	A182	10c on 50c bl, red & yel	.55	.55
284	A182	1fr on 2fr grn, yel & red (#619)	10.00	3.50
285	A147	2fr on 5fr lt grn	18.00	4.25
		Nos. 283-285 (3)	28.55	8.30

France Nos. 630 & 623 Surcharged

1950-51   Perf. 13
286	A188	5fr on 20fr dk red	10.00	1.75
287	A185	8fr on 25fr dp ultra ('51)	10.00	1.75

Stamps of France, 1951-52, Surcharged in Black or Red

No. 288   No. 292

1951-52   Perf. 14x13½, 13
288	A182	50c on 1fr bl, red & yel	.70	.70
289	A182	1fr on 2fr vio bl, red & yel (#662)	.70	.70
290	A147	2fr on 5fr dl vio	4.25	2.00
291	A147	3fr on 6fr grn	8.00	1.60
292	A220	5fr on 20fr dk pur (R; '52)	3.00	1.75
293	A147	6fr on 12fr red org ('52)	9.00	2.00
294	A215	8fr on 40fr vio (R) ('52)	6.50	.70
295	A147	9fr on 18fr cerise	21.00	4.25
296	A208	15fr on 30fr ind (R)	11.00	2.25
		Nos. 288-296 (9)	64.15	15.95

The surcharge on Nos. 292, 294 and 296 include two bars.

France No. 697 Surcharged in Black

1953   Perf. 14x13½
297	A182	50c on 1fr blk, red & yel	.35	.25

France No. 688 Surcharged Type "c" in Black

Perf. 13
298	A230	3fr on 6fr dp plum & car	1.20	.80

France Nos. 703 and 705 Surcharged in Red or Blue

No. 299

No. 300

1954
299	A235	8fr on 40fr (R)	38.50	7.50
300	A235	20fr on 75fr	80.00	32.50

France Nos. 698, 721, 713, and 715 Surcharged in Black

No. 301

No. 304

301	A182	1fr on 2fr	4.75	2.10
302	A241	4fr on 10fr	4.50	1.25
303	A238	8fr on 40fr	11.00	1.60
304	A238	20fr on 75fr	14.50	1.60

The surcharge on Nos. 303 and 304 includes two bars.

France Nos. 737, 719 and 722-724 Surcharged in Black or Red

a

b

305	A182(b)	1fr on 2fr	.50	.50
306	A241(a)	2fr on 6fr (R)	.80	.50
307	A242(a)	6fr on 12fr	11.00	1.75
308	A241(a)	9fr on 18fr	12.00	5.00
309	A241(a)	10fr on 20fr	8.00	1.40
		Nos. 299-309 (11)	185.55	55.70

The surcharge on Nos. 306-308 includes two bars; on No. 309 three bars.

France No. 720 Surcharged in Red

1955   Perf. 13
310	A241	3fr on 8fr brt bl & dk grn	1.40	1.10

France Nos. 785, 774-779 Surcharged in Black or Red

No. 311

No. 317

Perf. 14x13½, 13

1955-56   Typo., Engr.
311	A182	50c on 1fr	.45	.30
312	A265	2fr on 6fr ('56)	1.20	.70
313	A265	3fr on 8fr	1.00	.50
314	A265	4fr on 10fr	1.25	.50
315	A265	5fr on 12fr (R)	1.30	.50
316	A265	6fr on 18fr (R)	1.00	.50
317	A265	10fr on 25fr	1.75	.50
		Nos. 311-317 (7)	7.95	3.50

The surcharge on Nos. 312-317 includes two bars.

France Nos. 801-804 Surcharged in Black or Red

No. 318

No. 319

No. 320

No. 321

1956   Engr.   Perf. 13
318	A280(a)	8fr on 30fr (R)	5.25	1.10
319	A280(b)	9fr on 40fr	7.75	3.00
320	A280(a)	15fr on 50fr	9.25	1.60
321	A280(a)	20fr on 75fr (R)	8.50	2.25
		Nos. 318-321 (4)	30.75	7.95

The surcharge on Nos. 318, 319 and 321 includes two bars.

France Nos. 837 and 839 Surcharged in Red

1957   Perf. 13
322	A294	7fr on 15fr	1.20	.55
323	A265	17fr on 70fr	6.75	2.10

The surcharge on Nos. 322-323 includes two bars.

No. 322 has three types of "7" in the sheet of 50. There are 34 of the "normal" 7; 10 of a slightly thinner 7, and 6 of a slightly thicker 7.

France Nos. 755-756, 833-834, 851-855, 908, 949 Surcharged in Black or Red Type "a", "b" or

d

Typographed, Engraved

1957-60   Perf. 14x13½, 13
324	A236(b)	2fr on 6fr	.30	.30
325	A302(b)	3fr on 10fr ('58)	.50	.50
326	A236(b)	4fr on 12fr	3.50	.75
327	A236(b)	5fr on 10fr	2.25	1.10
328	A303(b)	6fr on 18fr	1.25	.50
329	A302(a)	9fr on 25fr (R) ('58)	1.25	.65
330	A252(a)	10fr on 20fr (R)	1.75	.30
331	A252(a)	12fr on 25fr	6.75	.50
332	A303(a)	17fr on 35fr	3.75	1.75
333	A302(a)	20fr on 50fr	1.75	.80
334	A302(a)	25fr on 85fr	4.00	1.60
335	A302(d)	50fr on 1fr ('60)	3.00	.75
		Nos. 324-335 (12)	30.05	9.50

The surcharge includes two bars on Nos. 324, 326-327, 329-331, 333 and 335.

France Nos. 973, 939 and 968 Surcharged

e

f

1961-63   Typo.   Perf. 14x13½
336	A318(e)	2fr on 5c multi	.30	.25
a.		Double surcharge	300.00	
b.		Inverted surcharge	1,000.	—
337	A336(e)	5fr on 10c brt grn	1.30	.50
338	A336(b)	5fr on 10c brt grn ('63)	1.60	.75
339	A349(f)	12fr on 25c lake & gray	.30	.30
		Nos. 336-339 (4)	3.50	1.80

The surcharge on No. 337 includes three bars. No. 338 has "b" surcharge and two bars.

RÉUNION

France Nos. 943, 941 and 946 Surcharged in Black or Red

Engraved, Typographed
1961   Unwmk.   Perf. 13, 14x13½
340	A338	7fr on 15c	1.00	.80
341	A337	10fr on 20c	.30	.30
342	A339	20fr on 50c (R)	17.00	4.50
	Nos. 340-342 (3)		18.30	5.60

Surcharge on No. 342 includes 3 bars.

France Nos. 1047-1048 Surcharged

No. 343

No. 344

1963, Jan. 2   Engr.   Perf. 13
343	A394	12fr on 25c	1.00	.95
344	A395	25fr on 50c	1.00	.95

1st television connection of the US and Europe through the Telstar satellite, July 11-12, 1962.

France Nos. 1040-1041, 1007 and 1009 Surcharged

No. 345   No. 346

No. 347

No. 348

Typographed, Engraved
1963   Perf. 14x13½, 13
345	A318	2fr on 5c	.30	.30
346	A318	5fr on 10c	.25	.25
347	A372	7fr on 15c	.60	.50
348	A372	20fr on 45c	1.25	.75
	Nos. 345-348 (4)		2.40	1.80

Two-line surcharge on No. 345; No. 347 has currency expressed in capital "F" and two heavy bars through old value; two thin bars on No. 348.

France No. 1078 Surcharged

1964, Feb. 8   Engr.   Perf. 13
349	CD118	12fr on 25c	1.25	1.25

"PHILATEC," Intl. Philatelic and Postal Techniques Exhib., Paris, June 5-21, 1964.

France Nos. 1092, 1094 and 1102 Surcharged

Typographed, Engraved
1964   Perf. 14x13½, 13
350	A318	1fr on 2c	.25	.25
351	A318	6fr on 18c	.30	.30
352	A420	35fr on 70c	1.50	.95
	Nos. 350-352 (3)		2.05	1.50

Surcharge on No. 352 includes two bars.

France Nos. 1095, 1126, 1070 Surcharged

No. 353

No. 354

No. 355

1965
353	A318	15fr on 30c	.50	.30
354	A440	25fr on 50c	1.00	.95
355	A408	30fr on 60c	1.50	1.00
	Nos. 353-355 (3)		3.00	2.25

Two bars obliterate old denomination on Nos. 354-355.

Etienne Regnault, "Le Taureau" and Coast of Reunion — A33

1965, Oct. 9   Engr.   Perf. 13
356	A33	15fr bluish blk & dk car	1.00	.65

Tercentenary of settlement of Reunion.

France No. 985 Surcharged

1966, Feb. 13   Engr.   Perf. 13
357	A360	10fr on 20c bl & car	1.60	.70

French Satellite A-1 Issue
France Nos. 1137-1138 Surcharged in Red

1966, Mar. 27   Engr.   Perf. 13
358	CD121	15fr on 30c	1.10	1.00
359	CD121	30fr on 60c	1.30	1.10
a.	Strip of 2 + label		3.50	3.00

France Nos. 1142, 1143, 1101 and 1127 Surcharged

No. 360   No. 361

1967-69   Typo.   Perf. 14x13
360	A446	2fr on 5c bl & red	.30	.30

   Photo.   Perf. 13
360A	A446	10fr on 20c multi ('69)	.30	.30

   Engr.
361	A421	20fr on 40c multi	1.10	.95
362	A439	30fr on 60c bl & red brn	1.30	.75

EXPO '67 Issue
France No. 1177 Surcharged

1967, June 12   Engr.   Perf. 13
363	A473	30fr on 60c dl bl & bl grn	2.40	1.75

EXPO '67, Montreal, Apr. 28-Oct. 27.

Lions Issue
France No. 1196 Surcharged in Blue

1967, Oct. 29   Engr.   Perf. 13
364	A485	20fr on 40c	3.00	1.20

50th anniversary of Lions International.

France No. 1130 Surcharged in Violet Blue

1968, Feb. 26   Engr.   Perf. 13
365	A440	50fr on 1fr	2.75	1.60

France No. 1224 Surcharged

1968, Oct. 21   Engr.   Perf. 13
366	A508	20fr on 40c multi	1.50	1.00

20 years of French Polar expeditions.

France Nos. 1230-1231 Surcharged

1969, Apr. 13   Engr.   Perf. 13
367	A486	15fr on 30c green	.65	.50
368	A486	20fr on 40c dp car	.70	.30

France No. 1255 Surcharged

1969, Aug. 18   Engr.   Perf. 13
370	A526	35fr on 70c multi	1.60	1.35

Napoleon Bonaparte (1769-1821).

France No. 1293 Surcharged

1971, Jan. 16   Engr.   Perf. 13
371	A555	25fr on 50c rose car	.90	.30

France No. 1301 Surcharged

1971, Apr. 13   Engr.   Perf. 13
372	A562	40fr on 80c multi	2.00	1.40

France No. 1309 Surcharged

1971, June 5   Engr.   Perf. 13
373	A569	15fr on 40c multi	1.00	.70

Aid for rural families.

France No. 1312 Surcharged

1971, Aug. 30   Engr.   Perf. 13
374	A571	45fr on 90c multi	1.15	.95

France No. 1320 Surcharged

1971, Oct. 18   Engr.   Perf. 13
375	A579	45fr on 90c multi	1.40	1.00

40th anniversary of the first assembly of presidents of artisans' guilds.

Réunion Chameleon — A34

1971, Nov. 8   Photo.   Perf. 13
376	A34	25fr multi	1.40	1.10

Nature protection.

REUNION

Common Design Type and

De Gaulle in Brazzaville, 1944 — A35

Designs: No. 377, Gen. de Gaulle, 1940. No. 379, de Gaulle entering Paris, 1944. No. 380, Pres. de Gaulle, 1970.

1971, Nov. 9 — Engr.
377	CD134	25fr black	1.60	1.60
378	A35	25fr ultra	1.60	1.60
379	A35	25fr rose red	1.60	1.60
380	CD134	25fr black	1.60	1.60
a.		Strip of 4 + label	9.25	8.00

Charles de Gaulle (1890-1970), president of France.
Nos. 377-380 printed se-tenant in sheets of 20 containing 5 strips of 4 plus labels with Cross of Lorraine and inscription. Exists imperf. Value, strip $200.

France No. 1313 Surcharged

1972, Jan. 17 — Engr. — Perf. 13
381	A570	50fr on 1.10fr multi	1.40	1.15

Map of South Indian Ocean, Penguin and Ships — A36

1972, Jan. 31 — Engr. — Perf. 13
382	A36	45fr blk, bl & ocher	2.25	2.25

Bicentenary of the discovery of the Crozet and Kerguelen Islands.

France No. 1342 Surcharged in Red

1972, May 8 — Engr. — Perf. 13
383	A590	15fr on 40c red	1.00	.95

20th anniv. of Blood Donors' Assoc. of Post and Telecommunications Employees.

France Nos. 1345-1346 Surcharged

1972, June 5 — Typo. — Perf. 14x13
384	A593	15fr on 30c multi	.45	.45
385	A593	25fr on 50c multi	.75	.65

Introduction of postal code system.

France No. 1377 Surcharged in Ultramarine

1973, June 12 — Engr. — Perf. 13
386	A620	45fr on 90c multi	2.00	1.35

France No. 1374 Surcharged in Ultramarine

France No. 1336 Srchd. in Red

1973 — Engr. — Perf. 13
387	A617	50fr on 1fr multi (U)	1.15	.95
388	A586	100fr on 2fr multi (R)	2.00	1.10

On No. 388, two bars cover "2.00".
Issue dates: 50fr, June 24; 100fr, Oct. 13.

France No. 1231C Surcharged in Black

1973, Nov. — Typo. — Perf. 14x13
389	A486	15fr on 30c bl grn	5.00	.80

France No. 1390 Surcharged in Red

1974, Jan. 20 — Engr. — Perf. 13
390	A633	25fr on 50c multi	.70	.70

ARPHILA 75 Phil. Exhib., Paris, June 1975.

France Nos. 1394-1397 Surcharged in Black, Ultramarine or Brown

No. 391

No. 394

Engr. (#391, 393), Photo. (#392, 394)
1974 — Perf. 12x13, 13x12
391	A637	100fr on 2fr (Blk)	2.50	2.40
392	A638	100fr on 2fr (U)	3.25	2.40
393	A639	100fr on 2fr (Br)	3.25	2.40
394	A640	100fr on 2fr (U)	3.25	2.40
		Nos. 391-394 (4)	12.25	9.60

Nos. 391-394 printed in sheets of 25 with alternating labels publicizing "ARPHILA 75," Paris June 6-16, 1975.
Two bars obliterate original denomination on Nos. 391-393.

France No. 1401 Surcharged in Red

1974, Apr. 29 — Engr. — Perf. 13
395	A644	45fr on 90c multi	1.90	1.40

Reorganized sea rescue organization.

France No. 1415 Surcharged in Ultramarine

1974, Oct. 6 — Engr. — Perf. 13
396	A657	60fr on 1.20fr multi	1.60	1.35

Centenary of Universal Postal Union.

France Nos. 1292A and 1294B Surcharged in Ultramarine

1974, Oct. 19 — Typo. — Perf. 14x13
397	A555	30fr on 60c grn	1.75	1.60

Engr. — Perf. 13
398	A555	40fr on 80c car rose	2.10	1.75

SEMI-POSTAL STAMPS

No. 65 Surcharged in Black or Red

1915 — Unwmk. — Perf. 14x13½
B1	A19	10c + 5c (Bk)	160.00	120.00
a.		Inverted surcharge	450.00	350.00
B2	A19	10c + 5c (R)	1.75	1.75
a.		Inverted surcharge	77.50	77.50
b.		Double surcharge, both inverted	675.00	675.00

No. 65 Surcharged in Red

1916
B3	A19	10c + 5c	1.90	1.90

Curie Issue
Common Design Type

1938 — Perf. 13
B4	CD80	1.75fr + 50c brt ultra	14.00	14.00
		Never hinged		24.00

French Revolution Issue
Common Design Type

1939 — Photo. — Unwmk.
Name and Value Typo. in Black
B5	CD83	45c + 25c grn	12.50	12.50
B6	CD83	70c + 30c brn	12.50	12.50
B7	CD83	90c + 35c red org	12.50	12.50
B8	CD83	1.25fr + 1fr rose pink	12.50	12.50
B9	CD83	2.25fr + 2fr blue	12.50	12.50
		Nos. B5-B9 (5)	62.50	62.50
		Set, never hinged		110.00

See CB1.

Common Design Type and

Artillery Colonel SP1

Colonial Infantry SP2

1941 — Unwmk. — Perf. 13½
B10	SP1	1fr + 1fr red		1.60
B11	CD86	1.50fr + 3fr claret		1.60
B12	SP2	2.50fr + 1fr blue		1.60
		Nos. B10-B12 (3)		4.80
		Set, never hinged		6.50

Nos. B10-B12 were issued by the Vichy government in France, but were not placed on sale in Reunion. Nos. B10-B12 exist imperf. Value, set $200.

Nos. 176-177 Surcharged in Black or Red

1944 — Engr. — Perf. 12½x12
B13		50c + 1.50fr on 2.50fr deep blue (R)		.80
B14		+ 2.50fr on 1fr yel brn		.80
		Set, never hinged		2.00

Colonial Development Fund.
Nos. B13-B14 were issued by the Vichy government in France, but were not placed on sale in Réunion.

Catalogue values for unused stamps in this section, from this point to the end of the section, are for Never Hinged items.

Red Cross Issue
Common Design Type

1944 — Perf. 14½x14
B15	CD90	5fr + 20fr black	1.60	1.10

The surtax was for the French Red Cross and national relief.

France Nos. B365-B366 Surcharged in Black

1962, Dec. 10 — Engr. — Perf. 13
B16	SP219	10 + 5fr on 20 + 10c	2.50	2.50
B17	SP219	12 + 5fr on 25 + 10c	2.75	2.75

The surtax was for the Red Cross.

France Nos. B374-B375 Surcharged in Red

1963, Dec. 9
B18	SP223	10 + 5fr on 20 + 10c	3.00	3.00
B19	SP223	12 + 5fr on 25 + 10c	3.00	3.00

Centenary of the Intl. Red Cross. The surtax was for the Red Cross.

France Nos. B385-B386 Surcharged in Dark Blue

REUNION

1964, Dec. 13   Unwmk.   Perf. 13
B20 SP230 10 + 5fr on 20 + 10c   1.75 1.75
B21 SP230 12 + 5fr on 25 + 10c   1.90 1.90

Jean Nicolas Corvisart (1755-1821) and Dominique Larrey (1766-1842), physicians. The surtax was for the Red Cross.

France Nos. B392-B393 Surcharged in Black

1965, Dec. 12   Engr.   Perf. 13
B22 SP233 12 + 5fr on 25 + 10c   1.60 1.60
B23 SP233 15 + 5fr on 30 + 10c   1.60 1.60

The surtax was for the Red Cross.

France Nos. B402-B403 Surcharged in Black

1966, Dec. 11   Engr.   Perf. 13
B24 SP237 12 + 5fr on 25 + 10c   1.50 1.50
B25 SP237 15 + 5fr on 30 + 10c   1.50 1.50

The surtax was for the Red Cross.

France Nos. B409-B410 Surcharged in Black

1967, Dec. 17   Engr.   Perf. 13
B26 SP240 12 + 5fr on 25 + 10c   3.00 3.00
B27 SP240 15 + 5fr on 30 + 10c   3.75 3.75

Surtax for the Red Cross.

France Nos. B421-B424 Surcharged in Black

1968-69   Engr.   Perf. 13
B28 SP244 12 + 5fr on 25 + 10c   1.70 1.50
B29 SP244 15 + 5fr on 30 + 10c   1.90 1.50
B30 SP244 20 + 7fr on 40 + 15c   1.60 1.50
B31 SP244 20 + 7fr on 40 + 15c ('69)   1.60 1.50
     Nos. B28-B31 (4)   6.80 6.00

The surtax was for the Red Cross.

France No. B425 Surcharged in Black

1969, Mar. 17   Engr.   Perf. 13
B32 SP245 15fr + 5fr on 30c + 10c   1.40 1.40

Stamp Day.

France No. B440 Surcharged in Black

1970, Mar. 16   Engr.   Perf. 13
B33 SP249 20fr on 40c + 10c   1.10 .95

Stamp day.

France Nos. B443-B444 Surcharged in Black

1970, Dec. 14   Engr.   Perf. 13
B34 SP252 20 + 7fr on 40 + 15c   2.40 2.00
B35 SP252 20 + 7fr on 40 + 15c   2.40 2.40

The surtax was for the Red Cross.

France No. B451 Surcharged in Black

1971, Mar. 29   Engr.   Perf. 13
B36 SP254 25fr + 5fr on 50c + 10c   1.10 .90

Stamp Day.

France Nos. B452-B453 Surcharged in Black

1971, Dec. 13
B37 SP255 15fr + 5fr on 30c + 10c   1.40 1.40
B38 SP255 25fr + 5fr on 50c + 10c   1.40 1.40

The surtax was for the Red Cross.

France No. B460 Surcharged in Black

1972, Mar. 20   Engr.   Perf. 13
B39 SP257 25fr + 5fr on 50c + 10c   1.20 1.20

Stamp Day.

France Nos. B461-B462 Surcharged in Red or Green

1972, Dec. 16   Engr.   Perf. 13
B40 SP258 15 + 5fr on 30c + 10c   1.20 1.20
B41 SP258 25 + 6fr on 50 + 10c (G)   1.40 1.40

Surtax was for the Red Cross.

France No. B470 Surcharged in Red

1973, Mar. 26   Engr.   Perf. 13
B42 SP260 25fr +5fr on 50c +10c   1.40 1.40

Stamp Day.

France Nos. B471-B472 Surcharged in Red

1973, Dec. 3   Engr.   Perf. 13
B43 SP261 15 +5fr on 30c +10c   1.40 1.40
B44 SP261 25 +5fr on 50c +10c   1.40 1.40

Surtax was for the Red Cross.

France No. B477 Surcharged

1974, Mar. 11   Engr.   Perf. 13
B45 SP263 25fr + 5fr on 50c + 10c   1.10 1.10

Stamp Day.

France Nos. B479-B480 Surcharged in Green or Red

1974, Nov. 30   Engr.   Perf. 13
B46 SP265 30 + 7fr on 60 + 15c (G)   1.40 1.40
B47 SP266 40 + 7fr on 80 + 15c (R)   1.40 1.40

Surtax was for the Red Cross.

AIR POST STAMPS

No. 141 Ovptd. in Blue

1937, Jan. 23   Unwmk.   Perf. 12½
C1 A23 50c red   290.00 250.00
  a. Vert. pair, one without overprint   1,800. 1,800.
  b. Inverted overprint   6,000.
  c. As "b," in pair with unoverprinted stamp   26,000.

Flight of the "Roland Garros" from Reunion to France by aviators Laurent, Lenier and Touge in Jan.-Feb., 1937.

Airplane and Landscape — AP2

1938, Mar. 1   Engr.   Perf. 12½
C2 AP2 3.65fr slate blue & car   1.00 .90
C3 AP2 6.65fr brown & org red   1.00 .90
C4 AP2 9.65fr car & ultra   1.00 .90
C5 AP2 12.65fr brown & green   2.00 1.50
  Nos. C2-C5 (4)   5.00 4.20
Set, never hinged   7.00

For overprints see Nos. C14-C17.

Plane and Bridge over East River AP3

Plane and Landscape AP4

1942, Oct. 19   Perf. 12x12½
C6   AP3 50c olive & pur   .35
C7   AP3 1fr dk bl & scar   .35
C8   AP3 2fr brn & blk   .60
C9   AP3 3fr rose lil & grn   1.10
C10 AP3 5fr red org & red brn   1.10

Frame Engr., Center Photo.
C11 AP4 10fr dk grn, red org & vio   1.10
C12 AP4 20fr dk bl, brn vio & red   1.10
C13 AP4 50fr brn car, Prus grn & bl   1.60
  Nos. C6-C13 (8)   7.30
Set, never hinged   9.50

Nos. C6-C13 were issued by the Vichy government in France, but were not placed on sale in Réunion.

De Poivre AP4a

1943   Perf. 12½x12
C13A AP4a 1fr sepia & red   .25
C13B AP4a 2fr green & blue   .35
C13C AP4a 3fr dk brown red   .40
C13D AP4a 5fr ultra & red   .55
C13E AP4a 10fr red brn & blk   .55
C13F AP4a 20fr violet & green   .75
  Nos. C13A-C13F (6)   2.85
Set, never hinged   4.00

300th Ann. of French settlement on Réunion. Nos. C13A-C13F were issued by the Vichy government in France, but were not placed on sale in Réunion.

Nos. C2-C5 Overprinted in Black or Carmine

1943   Unwmk.   Perf. 12½
C14 AP2 3.65fr sl bl & car   5.50 5.50
C15 AP2 6.65fr brn & org red   5.50 5.50
C16 AP2 9.65fr car & ultra (C)   5.50 5.50
C17 AP2 12.65fr brn & grn   5.50 5.50
  Nos. C14-C17 (4)   22.00 22.00
Set, never hinged   32.50

Catalogue values for unused stamps in this section, from this point to the end of the section, are for Never Hinged items.

Common Design Type

1944   Photo.   Perf. 14½x14
C18 CD87 1fr dk org   .50 .30
C19 CD87 1.60fr brt red   .50 .40
C20 CD87 5fr brn red   .70 .45
C21 CD87 10fr black   1.10 .80
C22 CD87 25fr ultra   1.25 .95
C23 CD87 50fr dk grn   1.25 .95
C24 CD87 100fr plum   1.75 1.25
  Nos. C18-C24 (7)   7.05 5.00

Victory Issue
Common Design Type

1946, May 8   Engr.   Perf. 12½
C25 CD92 8fr olive gray   1.10 .90

European victory of the Allied Nations in WWII.

Chad to Rhine Issue
Common Design Types

1946, June 6
C26 CD93 5fr orange   1.40 .85
C27 CD94 10fr sepia   1.40 .85
C28 CD95 15fr grnsh blk   1.40 .85
C29 CD96 20fr lilac rose   1.90 1.25

RÉUNION

C30	CD97	25fr greenish blue	1.90	1.25
C31	CD98	50fr green	2.25	1.50
		Nos. C26-C31 (6)	10.25	6.55

Shadow of Plane — AP5

Plane over Réunion — AP6

Air View of Réunion and Shadow of Plane AP7

Perf. 13x12½

1947, Mar. 24   Photo.   Unwmk.

C32	AP5	50fr ol grn & bl gray	11.00	8.00
C33	AP6	100fr dk brn & org	17.00	12.50
C34	AP7	200fr dk bl & org	21.00	14.00
		Nos. C32-C34 (3)	49.00	34.50

France, Nos. C18-C21 Surcharged in Carmine or Black

1949   Unwmk.   Perf. 13

C35	AP7	20fr on 40fr (C)	3.75	1.25
C36	AP8	25fr on 50fr	4.75	1.40
C37	AP9	50fr on 100fr (C)	11.00	4.25
C38	AP10	100fr on 200fr	55.00	21.00
		Nos. C35-C38 (4)	74.50	27.90

France Nos. C24, C26 and C27 Surcharged in Black

No. C39

No. C40

No. C41

1949-51

C39	AP12	100fr on 200fr		
		('51)	145.00	26.50
C40	AP12	200fr on 500fr	55.00	21.00
C41	AP13	500fr on 1000fr		
		('51)	325.00	210.00
		Nos. C39-C41 (3)	525.00	257.50

France Nos. C29-C32 Surcharged in Blue or Red

No. C42

No. C43

No. C44

No. C45

1954, Feb. 10

C42	AP15	50fr on 100fr	3.50	1.25
C43	AP15	100fr on 200fr (R)	5.50	1.40
C44	AP15	200fr on 500fr	45.00	12.50
C45	AP15	500fr on 1000fr	37.50	12.50
		Nos. C42-C45 (4)	91.50	27.65

France Nos. C35-C36 Surcharged in Red or Black

No. C46

No. C47

1957-58   Engr.   Perf. 13

C46	AP17	200fr on 500fr (R)	25.00	6.75
C47	AP17	500fr on 1000fr		
		('58)	25.00	13.00

France Nos. C37, C39-C40 Surcharged in Red or Black

No. C48

No. C49

No. C50

1961-64

C48	AP15	100fr on 2fr	6.75	1.40
C49	AP17	200fr on 5fr	7.00	3.25
C50	AP17	500fr on 10fr (B;'64)	16.00	6.25
		Nos. C48-C50 (3)	29.75	10.90

France No. C41 Surcharged in Red

1967, Jan. 27   Engr.   Perf. 13

C51	AP17	100fr on 2fr sl bl & ind	2.25	.80

France No. C45 Surcharged in Red

1972, May 14   Engr.   Perf. 13

C52	AP21	200fr on 5fr multi	5.00	1.75

AIR POST SEMI-POSTAL STAMP

French Revolution Issue
Common Design Type

1939   Unwmk.   Perf. 13

Name and Value Typo. in Orange

CB1	CD83	3.65fr + 4fr brn blk	25.00	25.00
		Never hinged		37.50

Felix Guyon Hospital, St. Denis — SPAP1

Perf. 13½x12½

1942, June 22   Engr.

CB2	SPAP1	1.50fr + 3.50fr lt grn	1.00	
CB3	SPAP1	2fr + 6fr yel brn	1.00	
		Set, never hinged		2.50

Native children's welfare fund.
Nos. CB2-CB3 were issued by the Vichy government in France, but were not placed on sale in Réunion.

Colonial Education Fund
Common Design Type

1942, June 22

CB4	CD86a	1.20fr + 1.80fr blue & red	.90
		Never hinged	1.25

No. CB4 was issued by the Vichy government in France, but was not placed on sale in Réunion.

POSTAGE DUE STAMPS

D1

1889-92   Unwmk.   Type-set   Imperf.
Without Gum

J1	D1	5c black	29.00	16.00
J2	D1	10c black	35.00	16.00
J3	D1	15c black ('92)	67.50	42.50
J4	D1	20c black	50.00	27.50
J5	D1	30c black	45.00	27.50
		Nos. J1-J5 (5)	226.50	129.50

Ten varieties of each value.
Nos. J1-J2, J4-J5 issued on yellowish paper in 1889; Nos. J1-J3, J5 on bluish white paper in 1892.
Nos. J1-J5 exist with double impression. Values, each $125-$190.

D2

1907   Typo.   Perf. 14x13½

J6	D2	5c carmine, yel	.90	.90
J7	D2	10c blue, bl	.90	.90
J8	D2	15c black, bluish	1.50	1.50
J9	D2	20c carmine	1.50	1.50
J10	D2	30c green, grnsh	2.25	2.25
J11	D2	50c red, green	2.60	2.60
J12	D2	60c carmine, bl	2.60	2.60
J13	D2	1fr violet	3.00	3.00
		Nos. J6-J13 (8)	15.25	15.25
		Set, never hinged		27.50

Type of 1907 Issue Surcharged

1927

J14	D2	2fr on 1fr org red	12.50	12.50
J15	D2	3fr on 1fr org brn	12.50	12.50
		Set, never hinged		40.00

Arms of Réunion — D3

1933   Engr.   Perf. 13x13½

J16	D3	5c deep violet	.25	.25
J17	D3	10c dark green	.25	.25
J18	D3	15c orange brown	.25	.25
J19	D3	20c light red	.35	.35
J20	D3	30c olive green	.35	.35
J21	D3	50c ultramarine	.80	.80
J22	D3	60c black brown	.80	.80
J23	D3	1fr light violet	.80	.80
J24	D3	2fr deep blue	.80	.80
J25	D3	3fr carmine	1.00	1.00
		Nos. J16-J25 (10)	5.65	5.65
		Set, never hinged		8.75

> **Catalogue values for unused stamps in this section, from this point to the end of the section, are for Never Hinged items.**

Numeral — D4

1947   Unwmk.   Photo.   Perf. 13

J26	D4	10c dark violet	.25	.25
J27	D4	30c brown	.25	.25
J28	D4	50c blue green	.25	.25
J29	D4	1fr orange	.60	.45
J30	D4	2fr red violet	.60	.45
J31	D4	3fr red brown	.85	.65
J32	D4	4fr blue	1.50	1.10
J33	D4	5fr henna brown	2.00	1.40
J34	D4	10fr slate green	2.00	1.40
J35	D4	20fr violet blue	2.00	.90
		Nos. J26-J35 (10)	10.30	7.10

France, Nos. J83-J92 Surcharged in Black

1949-53

J36	D5	10c on 1fr brt ultra	.25	.25
J37	D5	50c on 2fr turq bl	.45	.40
J38	D5	1fr on 3fr brn org	.60	.40
J39	D5	2fr on 4fr dp vio	.60	.40
J40	D5	3fr on 5fr brt pink	6.50	2.75
J41	D5	5fr on 10fr red org	1.10	.70
J42	D5	10fr on 20fr ol bis	2.00	2.00
J43	D5	20fr on 50fr dk grn		
		('50)	12.50	5.50
J44	D5	50fr on 100fr dp grn		
		('53)	30.00	13.00
		Nos. J36-J44 (9)	54.00	25.40

France Nos. J93, J95-J96 Surcharged

1962-63   Typo.   Perf. 14x13½

J46	D6	1fr on 5c brt pink		
		('63)	3.00	1.10
J47	D6	10fr on 20c ol bis ('63)	5.50	2.75
J48	D6	20fr on 50c dk grn	22.00	12.50
		Nos. J46-J48 (3)	30.50	16.35

France Nos. J98-J102, J104-J105 Surcharged

1964-71   Unwmk.   Perf. 14x13½

J49	D7	1fr on 5c	.25	.25
J50	D7	5fr on 10c	.30	.25
J51	D7	7fr on 15c	.50	.45
J52	D7	10fr on 20c ('71)	1.40	.55
J53	D7	15fr on 30c	.65	.45

REUNION — FRENCH COLONIES

J54	D7 20fr on 50c	.80	.55
J55	D7 50fr on 1fr	1.40	1.25
	Nos. J49-J55 (7)	5.30	3.75

PARCEL POST STAMPS

Frame Typographed; Center Handstamped PP1

1890-1903 Unwmk. Typo. Imperf.

Q1	PP1	10c black, yellow, black frame	400.00	200.00
Q2	PP1	10c black, yellow, ultra frame	110.00	100.00
Q3	PP1	10c black, yellow, bl grn frame	30.00	27.50

No. 40 Overprinted

1906 Unwmk. Perf. 14x13½

Q4	A14	10c red	22.50	22.50

Fiscal Stamps Surcharged — PP2

1907-23 Unwmk. Typo. Perf. 14

Q5	PP2	10c blk on grayish brn ('07)	17.50	15.00
Q6	PP2	10c red on gray ('23)	17.50	15.00

FRENCH COLONIES

'french 'kä-lə-nēz

From 1859 to 1906 and from 1943 to 1945 special stamps were issued for use in all French Colonies which did not have stamps of their own.

100 Centimes = 1 Franc

Catalogue values for unused stamps in this country are for Never Hinged items, beginning with Scott B1 in the semi-postal section and Scott J23 in the postage due section.

Perforations: Nos. 1-45 are known variously perforated privately.
Gum: Many of Nos. 1-45 were issued without gum. Some were gummed locally.
Reprints: Nos. 1-7, 9-12, 24, 26-42, 44 and 45 were reprinted officially in 1887. These reprints are ungummed and the colors of both design and paper are deeper or brighter than the originals. Value for Nos. 1-6, $20 each.

Eagle and Crown — A1

1859-65 Unwmk. Typo. Imperf.

1	A1	1c ol grn, pale bl ('62)	24.00	27.50
2	A1	5c yel grn, grnsh ('62)	24.00	16.00
3	A1	10c bister, yel	32.50	8.00
a.	Pair, one sideways		1,000.	525.00
4	A1	20c bl, bluish ('65)	35.00	13.50
5	A1	40c org, yelsh	27.50	13.50
6	A1	80c car rose, pnksh ('65)	110.00	60.00
	Nos. 1-6 (6)		253.00	138.50

For surcharges, see Reunion Nos. 1-4.

Napoleon III A2 A3

Ceres A4

Napoleon III A5

1871-72 Imperf.

7	A2	1c ol grn, pale bl ('72)	80.00	80.00
8	A3	5c yel grn, grnsh ('72)	1,000.	400.00
9	A4	10c bis, yelsh	375.00	130.00
a.	Tête bêche pair		55,000.	22,500.
10	A4	15c bis, yelsh ('72)	325.00	13.00
11	A4	20c blue, bluish	750.00	125.00
a.	Tête bêche pair		—	18,000.
12	A4	25c bl, bluish ('72)	175.00	13.00
13	A5	30c brn, yelsh	175.00	60.00
14	A4	40c org, yelsh (I)	250.00	13.00
a.	Type II		3,500.	650.00
b.	Pair, types I & II		7,250.	1,750.
15	A5	80c rose, pnksh	1,100.	115.00
	Nos. 7-15 (9)		4,230.	949.00

For 40c types I-II see illustrations over France #1.
For surcharges, see Reunion Nos. 5-6.
See note after France No. 9 for additional information on Nos. 8-9, 11-12, 14.

Ceres A6 A7

1872-77 Imperf.

16	A6	1c ol grn, pale bl ('73)	13.00	14.50
17	A6	2c red brn, yelsh ('76)	475.00	750.00
18	A6	4c gray ('76)	11,000.	475.00
19	A6	5c grn, pale bl ('76)	17.50	9.50
20	A7	10c bis, rose ('76)	240.00	13.00
21	A7	15c bister ('77)	525.00	100.00
22	A7	30c brn, yelsh	130.00	21.00
23	A7	80c rose, pnksh ('73)	625.00	140.00

No. 17 was used only in Cochin China, 1876-77. Excellent forgeries of Nos. 17 and 18 exist.
With reference to the stamps of France and French Colonies in the same designs and colors see the note after France No. 9.

Peace and Commerce — A8

1877-78 Type I Imperf.

24	A8	1c grn, grnsh	35.00	45.00
25	A8	4c grn, grnsh	24.00	14.50
26	A8	30c brn, yelsh ('78)	52.50	52.50
27	A8	40c ver, straw	35.00	21.00
28	A8	75c rose, rose ('78)	75.00	100.00
29	A8	1fr brnz grn, straw	40.00	67.50
	Nos. 24-29 (6)		281.50	300.50

Type II

30	A8	2c grn, grnsh	17.50	11.00
31	A8	5c grn, grnsh	24.00	5.50
32	A8	10c grn, grnsh	125.00	24.00
33	A8	15c gray, grnsh	250.00	72.50
34	A8	20c red brn, straw	52.50	9.50
35	A8	25c ultra bluish	52.50	8.75
a.	25c blue, bluish ('78)		4,250.	175.00
36	A8	35c vio blk, org ('78)	67.50	32.50
	Nos. 30-36 (7)		589.00	163.75
	Nos. 24-36 (13)		870.50	464.25

Type II 1878-80

38	A8	1c blk, lil bl	21.00	21.00
39	A8	2c brn, buff	21.00	24.00
40	A8	4c claret, lav	32.50	45.00
41	A8	10c blk, lav ('79)	120.00	27.50
42	A8	15c blue ('79)	35.00	17.50
43	A8	20c red, grn ('79)	87.50	17.50
44	A8	25c blk, red ('79)	600.00	275.00
45	A8	25c yel, straw ('80)	725.00	32.50
	Nos. 38-45 (8)		1,642.	460.00

No. 44 was used only in Mayotte, Nossi-Be and New Caledonia. Forgeries exist.
The 3c yellow, 3c gray, 15c yellow, 20c blue, 25c rose and 5fr lilac were printed together with the reprints, and were never issued.
For stamps of type A8 surcharged and with "SPM" see St. Pierre & Miquelon Nos. 1-8.

Commerce — A9

1881-86 Perf. 14x13½

46	A9	1c blk, lil bl	5.50	4.75
47	A9	2c brn, buff	5.50	4.75
48	A9	4c claret, lav	5.50	5.50
49	A9	5c grn, grnsh	6.50	3.25
50	A9	10c blk, lavender	11.00	4.75
51	A9	15c blue	16.00	3.25
52	A9	20c red, yel grn	52.50	18.00
53	A9	25c yel, straw	17.50	5.50
54	A9	25c blk, rose ('86)	24.00	3.25
55	A9	30c brn, bis	45.00	21.00
56	A9	35c vio blk, yel org	40.00	30.00
a.	35c violet black, yellow	100.00	52.50
57	A9	40c ver, straw	45.00	27.50
58	A9	75c car, rose	120.00	60.00
59	A9	1fr brnz grn, straw	80.00	45.00
	Nos. 46-59 (14)		474.00	236.50

Nos. 46-59 exist imperforate. They are proofs and were not used for postage, except the 10c.
For stamps of type A9 surcharged with numerals see: Cochin China, Diego Suarez, Gabon, Malagasy (Madagascar), Nossi-Be, New Caledonia, Reunion, Senegal, Tahiti.
For stamps of type A9 surcharged with "MQE" see Martinique Nos. 3-4. For stamps of type A9 surcharged and with "SPM" see St. Pierre & Miquelon Nos. 9-11, 15-18.

SEMI-POSTAL STAMPS

Catalogue values for unused stamps in this section are for Never Hinged items.

Resistance Fighters — SP1

1943 Unwmk. Litho. Rouletted

B1	SP1	1.50fr + 98.50fr ind & gray	47.50	65.00
	Without label	21.00	35.00

The surtax was for the benefit of patriots and the French Committee of Liberation.
No. B1 was printed in sheets of 10 (5x2) with adjoining labels showing the Lorraine cross.

Colonies Offering Aid to France — SP2

1943 Perf. 12

B2	SP2	9fr + 41fr redsh pur	3.50	10.50

Surtax for the benefit of French patriots.

Patriots and Map of France — SP3

1943

B3	SP3	50c + 4.50fr yel grn	1.25	10.50
B4	SP3	1.50fr + 8.50fr cerise	1.25	10.50
B5	SP3	3fr + 12fr grnsh bl	1.25	10.50
B6	SP3	5fr + 15fr olive gray	1.25	1.50
	Nos. B3-B6 (4)		5.00	33.00

Surtax for the aid of combatants and patriots.

Refugee Family — SP4

1943

B7	SP4	10fr + 40fr dull blue	5.25	12.50

The surtax was for refugee relief work.

Woman and Child with Wing — SP5

1944

B8	SP5	10fr + 40fr grnsh blk	6.75	21.00

Surtax for the benefit of aviation.
Nos. B1-B8 were prepared for use in the French Colonies, but after the landing of Free French troops in Corsica they were used there and later also in Southern France. They became valid throughout France in Nov. 1944.

POSTAGE DUE STAMPS

D1

1884-85 Unwmk. Typo. Imperf.

J1	D1	1c black	4.00	4.00
J2	D1	2c black	4.00	4.00
J3	D1	3c black	4.00	4.00
J4	D1	4c black	4.75	4.00
J5	D1	5c black	6.50	3.25
J6	D1	10c black	8.75	6.50
J7	D1	15c black	13.00	10.50
J8	D1	20c black	16.00	10.50
J9	D1	30c black	17.50	8.75
J10	D1	40c black	21.00	8.75
J11	D1	60c black	27.50	16.00
J12	D1	1fr brown	35.00	27.50
a.	1fr black		300.00	
J13	D1	2fr brown	35.00	27.50
a.	2fr black		300.00	325.00
J14	D1	5fr brown	110.00	67.50
a.	5fr black		425.00	450.00

Nos. J12a, J13a and J14a were not regularly issued.

1894-1906

J15	D1	5c blue	1.60	1.60
J16	D1	10c brown	1.60	1.60
J17	D1	15c pale green	1.60	1.60
J18	D1	20c olive grn ('06)	1.60	1.00
J19	D1	30c carmine	2.75	1.00
J20	D1	50c lilac	2.75	1.60
J21	D1	60c brown, buff	4.50	2.75
a.	60c dark violet, buff	4.75	2.75
J22	D1	1fr red, buff	7.50	4.50
a.	1fr rose, buff	27.50	19.00
	Nos. J15-J22 (8)		23.90	16.85

For overprints see New Caledonia Nos. J1-J8.

Catalogue values for unused stamps in this section, from this point to the end of the section, are for Never Hinged items.

D2

1945 Litho. Perf. 12

J23	D2	10c slate blue	.45	16.00
J24	D2	15c yel green	.45	16.00
J25	D2	25c deep orange	.45	16.00
J26	D2	50c greenish blk	1.00	16.00

FRENCH COLONIES — FRENCH CONGO

J27	D2	60c copper brn	1.00	16.00
J28	D2	1fr deep red lil	1.00	16.00
J29	D2	2fr red	1.00	16.00
J30	D2	4fr slate gray	4.50	20.00
J31	D2	5fr brt ultra	4.50	20.00
J32	D2	10fr purple	22.50	52.50
J33	D2	20fr dull brown	4.00	20.00
J34	D2	50fr deep green	7.25	27.50
		Nos. J23-J34 (12)	48.10	252.00

FRENCH CONGO

'french 'käṇ‚gō

LOCATION — Central Africa
GOVT. — French possession

French Congo was originally a separate colony, but was joined in 1888 to Gabon and placed under one commissioner-general with a lieutenant-governor presiding in Gabon and another in French Congo. In 1894 the military holdings in Ubangi were attached to French Congo, and in 1900 the Chad military protectorate was added. Postal service was not established in Ubangi or Chad, however, at that time. In 1906 Gabon and Middle Congo were separated and French Congo ceased to exist as such. Chad and Ubangi remained attached to Middle Congo as the joint dependency of "Ubangi-Chari-Chad," and Middle Congo stamps were used there.

Issues of the Republic of the Congo are listed under Congo People's Republic (ex-French).

100 Centimes = 1 Franc

Watermarks

Wmk. 122 Thistle Branch

Wmk. 123 — Rose Branch

Wmk. 124 Olive Branch

Stamps of French Colonies Surcharged Horizontally in Red or Black

1891   **Unwmk.**   **Perf. 14x13½**

1	A9	5c on 1c blk, *lil bl* (R)	6,500.	4,750.
a.		Double surcharge	20,000.	
2	A9	5c on 1c blk, *lil bl*	200.00	110.00
a.		Double surcharge	650.00	425.00
3	A9	5c on 15c blue	350.00	180.00
a.		Double surcharge	725.00	375.00
5	A9	5c on 25c blk, *rose*	130.00	52.50
a.		Inverted surcharge		
b.		Surcharge vertical	275.00	115.00
c.		Double surcharge	600.00	600.00

First "O" of "Congo" is a Capital, "Francais" with Capital "F"

1891-92

6	A9	5c on 20c red, *grn*	1,300.	425.00
7	A9	5c on 25c blk, *rose*	200.00	100.00
a.		Surcharge vertical	250.00	110.00
8	A9	10c on 25c blk, *rose*	240.00	67.50
a.		Inverted surcharge	400.00	160.00
b.		Surcharge vertical	400.00	100.00
d.		Double surcharge	400.00	225.00
9	A9	10c on 40c red, *straw*	2,750.	400.00

10	A9	15c on 25c blk, *rose*	225.00	52.50
a.		Surcharge vertical	260.00	92.50
c.		Double surcharge	400.00	200.00

First "O" of Congo small Surcharge Vert., Down or Up No Period

11	A9	5c on 25c blk, *rose*	300.00	135.00
12	A9	10c on 25c blk, *rose*		—
13	A9	15c on 25c blk, *rose*	425.00	190.00

The listings Nos. 5a and 12 are being re-evaluated. The Catalogue Editors would appreciate any information on these stamps.

Postage Due Stamps of French Colonies Surcharged in Red or Black Reading Down or Up

1892   **Imperf.**

14	D1	5c on 5c blk (R)	200.00	140.00
a.		Double surcharge	1,450.	
15	D1	5c on 20c blk (R)	200.00	140.00
16	D1	5c on 30c blk (R)	260.00	180.00
17	D1	10c on 1fr brown	200.00	140.00
a.		Double surcharge	4,100.	
b.		Surcharge horiz.	2,400.	
c.		"Congo" omitted	475.00	
		Nos. 14-17 (4)	860.00	600.00

Excellent counterfeits of Nos. 1-17 exist.

Navigation and Commerce — A3

1892-1900   **Typo.**   **Perf. 14x13½**
Colony Name in Blue or Carmine

18	A3	1c blk, *lil bl*	1.60	1.60
a.		Name double	225.00	175.00
19	A3	2c brn, *buff*	4.00	3.25
a.		Name double	225.00	175.00
20	A3	4c claret, *lav*	4.00	3.25
a.		Name in blk and in blue	225.00	175.00
21	A3	5c grn, *grnsh*	8.00	8.00
22	A3	10c blk, *lavender*	24.00	20.00
a.		Name double	850.00	600.00
23	A3	10c red ('00)	4.00	4.00
24	A3	15c blue, quadrille paper	55.00	20.00
25	A3	15c gray ('00)	12.00	8.00
26	A3	20c red, *grn*	24.00	20.00
27	A3	25c blk, *rose*	24.00	16.00
28	A3	25c blue ('00)	12.00	12.00
29	A3	30c brn, *bis*	40.00	24.00
30	A3	40c red, *straw*	55.00	32.50
31	A3	50c car, *rose*	55.00	40.00
32	A3	50c brn, *az* ('00)	16.00	16.00
a.		Name double	775.00	775.00
33	A3	75c dp vio, *org*	47.50	40.00
34	A3	1fr brnz grn, *straw*	55.00	40.00
		Nos. 18-34 (17)	441.10	308.60

Perf. 13½x14 stamps are counterfeits.
For surcharges see Nos. 50-51.
No. 21 exists in yellow green on pale green. The stamp was prepared but not issued. Value, $4,000.

Leopard — A4

Type I

Type II

Bakalois Woman A5

Coconut Grove A6

Design A4 exists in two types. Type 1: end of left tusk extends behind and above right tusk. Type 2: end of left tusk does not appear behind right tusk. Type 2 of design A4 appears in position 91 of each pane of 100. For detailed listings, see the *Scott Catalogue Classic Specialized of Stamps & Covers*.

1900-04   **Wmk. 122**   **Perf. 11**

35	A4	1c brn vio & gray lilac (1)	.80	.80
a.		Background inverted	75.00	75.00
36	A4	2c brn & yel (1)	.80	.80
a.		Imperf., pair	80.00	80.00
b.		Pair, imperf between	100.00	110.00
37	A4	4c scar & gray bl	1.60	1.20
a.		Background inverted	95.00	87.50
b.		Type 2	55.00	55.00
38	A4	5c grn & gray grn (1)	2.75	1.60
a.		Imperf., pair	140.00	140.00
39	A4	10c red & rose pink (1)	8.00	3.25
a.		Imperf., pair	140.00	140.00
40	A4	15c dl vio & ol grn (1)	2.40	1.20
a.		Imperf. pair	110.00	

Wmk. 123

41	A5	20c yel grn & org (1)	2.40	2.00
42	A5	25c bl & pale bl	3.50	2.40
43	A5	30c car rose & org	5.50	2.40
44	A5	40c org brn & brt grn	8.00	2.75
a.		Imperf., pair	110.00	110.00
b.		Center and value inverted	200.00	170.00
45	A5	50c gray vio & lil	8.00	6.50
46	A5	75c red vio & org	20.00	11.00
a.		Imperf., pair	110.00	110.00

Wmk. 124

47	A6	1fr gray lil & ol	24.00	20.00
a.		Center and value inverted	300.00	300.00
b.		Imperf., pair	140.00	140.00
48	A6	2fr car & brn	47.50	32.50
a.		Imperf., pair	300.00	300.00
49	A6	5fr brn org & gray	87.50	72.50
a.		5fr ocher & gray	750.00	950.00
b.		Center and value inverted	450.00	450.00
c.		Wmk. 123	500.00	500.00
d.		Imperf., pair	800.00	800.00
		Nos. 35-49 (15)	222.75	160.90

For surcharges see Nos. 52-53.

Nos. 26 and 29 Surcharged in Black

1900   **Unwmk.**   **Perf. 14x13½**

50	A3	5c on 20c red, *grn*	26,000.	6,000.
a.		Double surcharge	18,000.	
51	A3	15c on 30c brn, *bis*	20,000.	2,600.
a.		Double surcharge	6,000.	

Nos. 43 and 48 Surcharged in Black

a

b

1903   **Wmk. 123**   **Perf. 11**

52	A5	5c on 30c	325.00	160.00
a.		Inverted surcharge	2,750.	

Wmk. 124

53	A6	10c on 2fr	375.00	160.00
a.		Inverted surcharge	2,750.	
b.		Double surcharge	3,250.	

Counterfeits of the preceding surcharges are known.

FRENCH EQUATORIAL AFRICA

'french ,ē-kwə-'tōr-ē-əl 'a-fri-kə

LOCATION — North of Belgian Congo and south of Libya
GOVT. — French Colony
AREA — 959,256 square miles
POP. — 4,491,785
CAPITAL — Brazzaville

In 1910 Gabon and Middle Congo, with its military dependencies, were politically united as French Equatorial Africa. The component colonies were granted administrative autonomy. In 1915 Ubangi-Chari-Chad was made an autonomous civilian colony and in 1920 Chad was made a civil colony. In 1934 the four colonies were administratively united as one colony, but this federation was not completed until 1936. Each colony had its own postal administration until 1936. The postal issues of the former colonial subdivisions are listed under the names of those colonies.

In 1958, French Equatorial Africa was divided into four republics: Chad, Congo, Gabon and Central African Republic (formerly Ubangi-Chari).

Stamps other than Nos. 189-192 are inscribed with "Afrique Equatoriale Française" or "AEF" and the name of one of the component colonies are listed under those colonies.

100 Centimes = 1 Franc

> Catalogue values for unused stamps in this country are for Never Hinged items, beginning with Scott 142 in the regular postage section, Scott B8A in the semi-postal section, Scott C17 in the airpost section, and Scott J12 in the postage due section.

Stamps of Gabon, 1932, Overprinted "Afrique Equatoriale Francaise" and Bars Similar to "a" and "b" in Black
Perf. 13x13½, 13½x13

1936 Unwmk.
1	A16	1c brown violet	.40	.80
2	A16	2c black, *rose*	.80	.80
3	A16	4c green	1.20	1.60
4	A16	5c grnsh blue	1.20	1.60
5	A16	10c red, *yel*	1.20	1.60
6	A17	40c brown violet	4.00	3.25
7	A17	50c red brown	3.25	2.40
8	A17	1fr yel grn, *bl*	32.50	16.00
9	A18	1.50fr dull blue	8.00	4.00
10	A18	2fr brown red	20.00	16.00
		Nos. 1-10 (10)	72.55	48.05

Stamps of Middle Congo, 1933 Overprinted in Black

a

b

c

1936
11	A4 (b)	1c lt brown	.40	.50
12	A4 (b)	2c dull blue	.40	.50
13	A4 (b)	4c olive green	1.60	1.60
14	A4 (b)	5c red violet	.80	1.00
15	A4 (b)	10c slate	1.60	1.25
16	A4 (b)	15c dk violet	2.00	1.60
17	A4 (b)	20c red, *pink*	2.00	1.60
18	A4 (b)	25c orange	4.00	2.40
19	A5 (a)	40c orange brn	5.50	2.75
20	A5 (c)	50c black violet	5.50	2.40
21	A5 (c)	75c black, *pink*	5.50	4.75
22	A5 (a)	90c carmine	5.50	4.00
23	A5 (c)	1.50fr dark blue	4.75	2.00
24	A6 (a)	5fr slate blue	55.00	35.00
25	A6 (a)	10fr black	35.00	30.00
26	A6 (a)	20fr dark brown	35.00	32.50
		Nos. 11-26 (16)	164.55	123.85

Other overprints inscribed "Afrique Equatoriale Française" in a different type font on earlier Middle Congo stamps are listed under Middle Congo.

Common Design Types pictured following the introduction.

Paris International Exposition Issue
Common Design Types

1937, Apr. 15 Engr. Perf. 13
27	CD74	20c dark violet	2.40	2.40
28	CD75	30c dark green	2.40	2.40
29	CD76	40c carmine rose	2.40	2.40
30	CD77	50c dk brn & bl	2.40	2.40
31	CD78	90c red	3.25	3.25
32	CD79	1.50fr ultra	3.25	3.25
		Nos. 27-32 (6)	16.10	16.10

Logging on Loême River — A1

People of Chad — A2

Pierre Savorgnan de Brazza — A3

Emile Gentil — A4

Paul Crampel — A5

Governor Victor Liotard — A6

Two types of 25c:
Type I — Wide numerals (4mm).
Type II — Narrow numerals (3½mm).

1937-40 Photo. Perf. 13½x13
33	A1	1c brown & yel	.25	.25
34	A1	2c violet & yel	.25	.25
35	A1	3c blue & yel ('40)	.25	.30
36	A1	4c magenta & bl	.25	.30
37	A1	5c dk & lt green	.25	.30
38	A2	10c magenta & blue	.25	.30
39	A2	15c blue & buff	.25	.30
40	A2	20c brown & yellow	.25	.30
41	A2	25c cop red & bl (I)	.80	.30
a.		Type II	2.75	2.00
42	A3	30c gray grn & grn	.80	.55
43	A3	30c chlky bl, ind & buff ('40)	.40	.50
44	A2	35c dp grn & yel ('38)	.80	.80
45	A3	40c cop red & bl	.40	.30
46	A3	45c dk bl & lt grn	4.75	3.50
47	A3	45c dp grn & red grn ('40)	.40	.80
48	A3	50c brown & yellow	.50	.25
49	A3	55c pur & bl ('38)	.80	.80
50	A3	60c mar & gray bl ('40)	.80	.85
51	A4	65c dk bl & buff	.80	.40
52	A4	70c dp vio & buff ('40)	.80	.95
53	A4	75c ol blk & dl yel	5.50	4.50
54	A4	80c brn & yel ('38)	.40	.80
55	A4	90c copper red & buff	.55	.40
56	A4	1fr dk vio & lt grn	2.40	1.20
57	A3	1fr cer & dl org ('38)	4.00	1.60
58	A4	1fr bl grn & sl grn ('40)	.40	.55
59	A5	1.25fr cop red & buff	2.40	1.20
60	A5	1.40fr dk brn & pale grn ('40)	1.20	1.25
61	A5	1.50fr dk & lt blue	1.60	.80
62	A5	1.60fr dp vio & buff ('40)	1.60	1.25
63	A5	1.75fr brn & yel	2.00	1.20
64	A4	1.75fr bl & lt bl ('38)	.80	.80
65	A	2fr dk & lt green	1.60	.80
66	A6	2.15fr brn, vio & yel ('38)	1.20	.80
67	A6	2.25fr bl & lt bl ('39)	1.60	1.60
68	A6	2.50fr rose lake & buff ('40)	2.00	1.40
69	A6	3fr dk blue & buff	.80	.50
70	A6	5fr dk & lt green	1.60	1.20
71	A6	10fr dk violet & bl	3.25	3.25
72	A6	20fr ol blk & dl yel	4.00	3.50
		Nos. 33-72 (40)	52.95	40.90

For overprints and surcharges see Nos. 80-127, 129-141, B2-B3, B10-B13, B22-B23.

Colonial Arts Exhibition Issue
Souvenir Sheet
Common Design Type

1937 Imperf.
73	CD79	3fr red brown	12.00	16.00
		Never hinged	16.00	

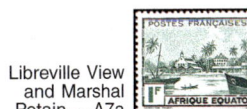
Count Louis Edouard Bouet-Willaumez and His Ship "La Malouine" — A7

1938, Dec. 5 Perf. 13½
74	A7	65c gray brown	1.25	1.25
75	A7	1fr deep rose	1.25	1.25
76	A7	1.75fr blue	1.60	1.60
77	A7	2fr dull violet	2.40	2.40
		Nos. 74-77 (4)	6.50	6.50
		Set, never hinged	8.85	

Centenary of Gabon.

New York World's Fair Issue
Common Design Type

1939, May 10 Engr. Perf. 12½x12
78	CD82	1.25fr car lake	.80	1.60
79	CD82	2.25fr ultra	.80	1.60
		Set, never hinged	2.40	

Libreville View and Marshal Petain — A7a

1941 Engr. Perf. 12½x12
79A	A7a	1fr bluish green		.40
79B	A7a	2.50fr blue		.40
		Set, never hinged	1.60	

Nos. 79A-79B were issued by the Vichy government in France, but were not placed on sale in French Equatorial Africa.
For surcharges, see Nos. B36-B37.

Stamps of 1936-40, Overprinted in Carmine or Black

Nos. 80-82, 84-88, 93

Nos. 83, 89-92, 94-125

1940-41 Perf. 13½x13
80	A1	1c brn & yel (C)	4.00	4.00
81	A1	2c vio & grn (C)	4.00	4.00
82	A1	3c blue & yel (C)	4.00	4.00
83	A4	4c ol grn (No. 13)	24.00	16.00
b.		Inverted overprint	120.00	150.00
84	A1	5c dk grn & lt grn (C)	4.00	4.00
85	A2	10c magenta & bl	4.00	4.00
86	A2	15c blue & buff (C)	4.00	4.00
87	A2	20c brn & yel (C)	4.00	4.00
88	A2	25c cop red & bl	4.00	4.00
89	A3	30c gray grn & grn (C)	16.00	16.00
90	A3	30c gray grn & grn ('41)	16.00	16.00
91	A3	30c chlky bl, ind & buff (C) ('41)	16.00	16.00
92	A3	30c chlky bl, ind & buff ('41)	16.00	16.00
93	A2	35c dp grn & yel (C)	4.00	4.00
94	A3	40c cop red & bl	4.00	4.00
b.		Inverted overprint		100.00
95	A3	45c dp grn & yel grn (C)	4.00	4.00
96	A3	45c dp grn & yel grn ('41)	16.00	16.00
97	A3	50c brn & yel (C)	4.00	4.00
98	A3	50c brn & yel ('41)	8.00	8.00
99	A3	55c pur & bl (C)	4.00	4.00
100	A3	55c pur & bl ('41)	16.00	16.00
101	A3	60c mar & gray bl (C)	4.00	4.00
102	A4	65c dk bl & buff (C)	4.00	4.00
103	A4	70c dp vio & buff	4.00	4.00
104	A4	75c ol blk & dl yel	80.00	80.00
105	A4	80c brown & yellow	4.00	4.00
106	A4	90c cop red & buff	4.00	4.00
107	A4	1fr bl grn & sl grn	8.00	8.00
108	A4	1fr bl grn & sl grn (C) ('41)	20.00	20.00
109	A3	1fr cer & dl org	4.00	4.00
110	A5	1.40fr dk brn & pale grn	4.00	4.00
111	A5	1.50fr dk bl & lt bl	4.00	4.00
112	A5	1.60fr dp vio & buff	4.00	4.00
113	A5	1.75fr brown & yel	4.00	4.00
114	A6	2.15fr brn, vio & yel	4.00	4.00
115	A6	2.25fr bl & lt bl (C)	4.00	4.00
116	A6	2.25fr bl & lt bl ('41)	16.00	16.00
117	A6	2.50fr rose lake & buff	4.00	4.00
118	A6	3fr dk bl & buff (C)	4.00	4.00
119	A6	3fr dk bl & buff ('41)	16.00	16.00
120	A6	5fr dk grn & lt grn (C)	4.00	4.00
121	A6	5fr dk grn & lt grn ('41)	140.00	140.00
122	A6	10fr dk vio & bl (C)	3.25	3.25
123	A6	10fr dk vio & bl ('41)	130.00	130.00
124	A6	20fr ol blk & dl yol (C)	4.00	4.00
125	A6	20fr ol blk & dl yel ('41)	16.00	16.00
		Nos. 80-125 (46)	673.25	665.25

For overprints and surcharges see Nos. 129-132, B12-B13, B22-B23.
For types of Nos. 38//61 without "RF," see Nos. 155A-155D.

Double Overprint
80a	A1	1c	325.00	225.00
81a	A1	2c	32.50	
82a	A1	3c	32.50	
83a	A4	4c	75.00	
84a	A1	5c	32.50	
85a	A2	10c	32.50	40.00
86a	A2	15c	32.50	
87a	A2	20c	32.50	
88a	A2	25c	55.00	
89a	A3	30c	110.00	120.00
90a	A3	30c	47.50	55.00
91a	A3	30c	47.50	47.50
93a	A2	35c	250.00	
94a	A3	40c	47.50	
96a	A3	45c	75.00	
98a	A3	50c	110.00	75.00
100a	A3	55c	75.00	
102a	A4	65c	45.00	
103a	A4	70c	47.50	
104a	A4	75c	175.00	
105a	A4	80c	47.50	
106a	A4	90c	45.00	
b.		one inverted	120.00	
109a	A4	1fr One inverted	120.00	
110a	A5	1.40fr	47.50	
111a	A5	1.50fr	47.50	
114a	A6	2.15fr	40.00	
115a	A6	2.25fr	60.00	
116a	A6	2.25fr	47.50	
117a	A6	2.50fr	47.50	
119a	A6	3fr	60.00	
123a	A6	10fr	60.00	67.50
124a	A6	20fr	60.00	
		Nos. 96a-124a (17)	1,035.	

Nos. 48, 51 Surcharged in Black or Carmine

1940
126	A3	75c on 50c	.80	.80
a.		Double surcharge	40.00	
127	A4	1fr on 65c (C)	.80	.80
a.		Double surcharge	32.50	
		Set, never hinged	3.20	

Middle Congo No. 67 Overprinted in Carmine like No. 80
Perf. 13½
128	A4	4c olive green	65.00	65.00

Stamps of 1940 With Additional Overprint in Black

1940 Perf. 13½x13
129	A4	80c brown & yel	24.00	16.00
a.		Overprint without "2"	150.00	
130	A4	1fr bl grn & sl grn	24.00	20.00
131	A3	1fr cer & dull org	24.00	16.00
132	A5	1.50fr dk bl & lt bl	24.00	16.00
		Nos. 129-132 (4)	96.00	68.00

Arrival of General de Gaulle in Brazzaville, capital of Free France, Oct. 24, 1940.
These stamps were sold affixed to post cards and at a slight increase over face value

FRENCH EQUATORIAL AFRICA

to cover the cost of the cards. Values for unused stamps are for examples without gum.
For surcharges see Nos. B12-B13, B22-B23.

Stamps of 1937-40 Overprinted in Black

1 mm between lines

2 mm between lines

1941
133	A1	1c brown & yel	4.00	4.00
134	A1	2c violet & grn	4.00	4.00
135	A1	3c blue & yel	4.00	4.00
136	A1	5c dk & lt green	4.00	4.00
137	A2	10c magenta & bl	4.00	4.00
138	A2	15c blue & buff	4.00	4.00
139	A2	20c brown & yel	4.00	4.00
140	A2	25c copper red & bl	4.00	4.00
141	A2	35c dp grn & yel	4.00	4.00
a.		Double overprint	120.00	
		Nos. 133-141 (9)	36.00	36.00
		Set, never hinged	55.00	

There are 2 settings of the overprint on Nos. 133-141 & C10. The 1st has 1mm between lines of the overprint (Nos. 133-141), the 2nd has 2mm. Value, set with 2mm spacing $95.

Catalogue values for unused stamps in this section, from this point to the end of the section, are for Never Hinged items.

Phoenix — A8

1941   Photo.   Perf. 14x14½
142	A8	5c brown	.30	.25
143	A8	10c dark blue	.30	.25
a.		Denomination doubled	125.00	
144	A8	25c emerald	.30	.25
145	A8	30c deep orange	.30	.25
146	A8	40c dk slate grn	.55	.30
147	A8	80c red brown	.55	.30
148	A8	1fr deep red lilac	.55	.30
149	A8	1.50fr brt red	.75	.40
150	A8	2fr gray	.75	.40
151	A8	2.50fr brt ultra	.95	.70
152	A8	4fr dull violet	.95	.70
153	A8	5fr yellow bister	.95	.70
154	A8	10fr deep brown	1.40	1.00
155	A8	20fr deep green	1.75	1.25
		Nos. 142-155 (14)	10.35	7.05

For surcharges see #158-165, B14-B21, B24-B35.

Types of 1937-40 without "RF"

1944   Perf. 13½
155A	A2	10c magenta & blue	1.20
155B	A2	15c blue & buff	1.60
155C	A3	60c mar & gray blue	1.60
155D	A5	1.50fr dk & lt blue	2.00
		Nos. 155A-155D (4)	6.40

Nos. 155A-155D were issued by the Vichy government in France, but were not sold in French Equatorial Africa.

Eboue Issue
Common Design Type

1945   Unwmk.   Engr.   Perf. 13
156	CD91	2fr black	.65	.50
157	CD91	25fr Prussian green	1.90	1.50

Nos. 156-157 exist imperforate. Value, set $65.

Nos. 142, 144 and 151 Surcharged with New Values and Bars in Red, Carmine or Black

1946   Perf. 14x14½
158	A8	50c on 5c (R)	.80	.65
159	A8	60c on 5c (R)	.80	.65
160	A8	70c on 5c (R)	.80	.65
161	A8	1.20fr on 5c (C)	.80	.65
162	A8	2.40fr on 25c	1.40	1.00
163	A8	3fr on 25c	1.40	1.00
164	A8	4.50fr on 25c	1.75	1.20
165	A8	15fr on 2.50fr (C)	1.90	1.40
		Nos. 158-165 (8)	9.65	7.20

Black Rhinoceros and Rock Python — A9

Jungle Scene — A10

Mountainous Shore Line — A11

Gabon Forest — A12

Niger Boatman — A13

Young Bacongo Woman — A14

1946   Unwmk.   Engr.   Perf. 12½
166	A9	10c deep blue	.40	.25
167	A9	30c violet blk	.40	.25
168	A9	40c dp orange	.40	.25
169	A10	50c violet bl	.80	.50
170	A10	60c dk carmine	.80	.50
171	A10	80c dk ol grn	.80	.50
172	A11	1fr dp orange	.80	.30
173	A11	1.20fr dp claret	.80	.65
174	A11	1.50fr dk green	1.20	.95
175	A12	2fr dk vio brn	.40	.25
176	A12	3fr rose carmine	.80	.50
177	A12	3.60fr red brown	3.25	2.50
178	A12	4fr deep blue	.80	.30
179	A13	5fr dk brown	.80	.25
180	A13	6fr deep blue	1.25	.30
181	A13	10fr black	2.40	.75
182	A14	15fr brown	2.40	.80
183	A14	20fr dp claret	2.40	.80
184	A14	25fr black	3.25	.80
		Nos. 166-184 (19)	24.15	11.40

Imperforates

Most French Equatorial Africa stamps from 1951 onward exist imperforate in issued and trial colors, and also in small presentation sheets in issued colors.

Pierre Savorgnan de Brazza — A15

1951, Nov. 5   Perf. 13
185	A15	10fr indigo & dk grn	1.60	.40

Cent. of the birth of Pierre Savorgnan de Brazza, explorer.

Military Medal Issue
Common Design Type
Engraved and Typographed

1952, Dec. 1   Perf. 13
186	CD101	15fr multicolored	8.00	5.50

Lt. Gov. Adolphe L. Cureau — A16

1954, Sept. 20   Engr.
187	A16	15fr ol grn & red brn	2.00	.80

Savannah Monitor — A17

1955, May 2   Unwmk.
188	A17	8fr dk grn & claret	2.40	1.25

International Exhibition for Wildlife Protection, Paris, May 1955.

FIDES Issue
Common Design Type

Designs: 5fr, Boali Waterfall and Power Plant, Ubangi-Chari. 10fr, Cotton, Chad. 15fr, Brazzaville Hospital, Middle Congo. 20fr, Libreville Harbor, Gabon.

1956, Apr. 25   Perf. 13x12½
189	CD103	5fr dk brn & claret	.65	.30
190	CD103	10fr blk & bluish grn	.65	.30
191	CD103	15fr ind & gray vio	.80	.40
192	CD103	20fr dk red & red org	1.10	.65
		Nos. 189-192 (4)	3.20	1.65

Coffee Issue

Coffee — A19

1956, Oct.   Engr.   Perf. 13
193	A19	10fr brn vio & vio bl	1.60	.40

Leprosarium at Mayumba and Maltese Cross — A20

1957, Mar. 11
194	A20	15fr grn, bl grn & red	2.00	.80

Issued in honor of the Knights of Malta.

Giant Eland — A21

1957, Nov. 4
195	A21	1fr shown	.80	.40
196	A21	2fr Lions	.80	.40
197	A21	3fr Elephant, vert.	.80	.40
198	A21	4fr Greater kudu, vert.	.90	.40
		Nos. 195-198 (4)	3.30	1.60

WHO Building, Brazzaville — A22

1958, May 19   Engr.   Perf. 13
199	A22	20fr dk green & org brn	1.60	.80

10th anniv. of WHO.

Flower Issue
Common Design Type

1958, July 7   Photo.   Perf. 12x12½
200	CD104	10fr Euadania	1.60	.65
201	CD104	25fr Spathodea	2.00	.95

Human Rights Issue
Common Design Type

1958, Dec. 10   Engr.   Perf. 13
202	CD105	20fr Prus grn & dk bl	2.40	1.25

SEMI-POSTAL STAMPS

Common Design Type

1938, Oct. 24   Engr.
B1	CD80	1.75fr + 50c brt ultra	24.00	24.00
		Never hinged	32.50	

Nos. 51, 64 Surcharged in Black or Red

1938, Nov. 7   Perf. 13x13½
B2	A4	65c + 35c dk bl & lt grn (R)	2.40	2.40
B3	A4	1.75fr + 50c bl & lt bl	4.00	4.00
		Set, never hinged	12.00	

The surtax was for welfare.

French Revolution Issue
Common Design Type
Name and Value Typo. in Black

1939, July 5   Photo.
B4	CD83	45c + 25c green	16.00	16.00
B5	CD83	70c + 30c brown	16.00	16.00
B6	CD83	90c + 35c red org	16.00	16.00
B7	CD83	1.25fr + 1fr rose pink	16.00	16.00
B8	CD83	2.25fr + 2fr blue	16.00	16.00
		Nos. B4-B8 (5)	80.00	80.00
		Set, never hinged	120.00	

Surtax used for the defense of the colonies.

Catalogue values for unused stamps in this section, from this point to the end of the section, are for Never Hinged items.

Common Design Type and

Native Artilleryman SP1

Gabon Infantryman SP2

1941   Photo.   Perf. 13½
B8A	SP1	1fr + 1fr red	3.50
B8B	CD86	1.50fr + 3fr maroon	3.50
B8C	SP2	2.50fr + 1fr blue	3.50
		Nos. B8A-B8C (3)	10.50

Nos. B8A-B8C were issued by the Vichy government in France, but were not placed on sale in French Equatorial Africa.

Brazza and Stanley Pool — SP3

1941   Photo.   Perf. 14½x14
B9	SP3	1fr + 2fr dk brn & red	2.00	1.60

The surtax was for a monument to Pierre Savorgnan de Brazza.

Nos. 67, 71 Srchd. in Red

1943, June 28   Perf. 13½x13
B10	A6	2.25fr + 50fr	47.50	32.50
B11	A6	10fr + 100fr	120.00	80.00

FRENCH EQUATORIAL AFRICA

Nos. 129 and 132 with Add'l. Srch. in Carmine	

1944
| B12 | A4 | 80c + 10fr | 65.00 | 40.00 |
| B13 | A5 | 1.50fr + 15fr | 65.00 | 40.00 |

Surcharged Vertically on Nos. 142-146, 148, 150-151

Perf. 14x14½
B14	A8	5c + 10fr brown	40.00	27.50
B15	A8	10c + 10fr dk bl	40.00	27.50
B16	A8	25c + 10fr emer	40.00	27.50
B17	A8	30c + 10fr dp org	40.00	27.50
B18	A8	40c + 10fr dk sl grn	40.00	27.50
B19	A8	1fr + 10fr dp red lil	40.00	27.50
B20	A8	2fr + 20fr gray	40.00	27.50
B21	A8	2.50fr + 25fr brt ultra	40.00	27.50
		Nos. B12-B21 (10)	450.00	300.00

Nos. 129 and 132 with Add'l. Srch. in Carmine	

1944   **Perf. 13½x13**
| B22 | A4 | 80c + 10fr | 65.00 | 40.00 |
| B23 | A5 | 1.50fr + 15fr | 65.00 | 40.00 |

Surcharged Vertically on Nos. 142-146, 148, 150-155

Perf. 14x14½
B24	A8	5c + 10fr brn	40.00	27.50
B25	A8	10c + 10fr dk bl	40.00	27.50
B26	A8	25c + 10fr emer	40.00	27.50
B27	A8	30c + 10fr dp org	40.00	27.50
B28	A8	40c + 10fr dk sl grn	40.00	27.50
B29	A8	1fr + 10fr dp red lil	40.00	27.50
B30	A8	2fr + 20fr gray	40.00	27.50
B31	A8	2.50fr + 25fr brt ultra	40.00	27.50
B32	A8	4fr + 40fr dl vio	40.00	27.50
B33	A8	5fr + 50fr yel bis	40.00	27.50
B34	A8	10fr + 100fr dp brn	40.00	27.50
B35	A8	20fr + 200fr blue	40.00	27.50
		Nos. B22-B35 (14)	610.00	410.00

Nos. B12 to B35 were issued to raise funds for the Committee to Aid the Fighting Men and Patriots of France.

Nos. 79A-79B Srchd. in Black or Red	

1944   **Engr.**   **Perf. 12½x12**
| B36 | 50c + 1.50fr on 2.50fr deep blue (H) | | .80 |
| B37 | + 2.50fr on 1fr green | | .80 |

Colonial Development Fund.
Nos. B36-B37 were issued by the Vichy government in France but were not placed on sale in French Equatorial Africa.

Red Cross Issue
Common Design Type
1944   **Photo.**   **Perf. 14½x14**
| B38 | CD90 | 5fr + 20fr royal blue | 1.60 | 1.20 |

The surtax was for the French Red Cross and national relief.

Tropical Medicine Issue
Common Design Type
1950, May 15   **Engr.**   **Perf. 13**
| B39 | CD100 | 10fr + 2fr dk bl grn & vio brn | 7.25 | 5.50 |

The surtax was for charitable work.

AIR POST STAMPS

Hydroplane over Pointe-Noire — AP1

Trimotor over Stanley Pool — AP2

1937   **Unwmk.**   **Photo.**   **Perf. 13½**
C1	AP1	1.50fr ol blk & yel	.40	.40
C2	AP1	2fr mag & blue	.55	.55
C3	AP1	2.50fr grn & buff	.55	.55
C4	AP1	3.75fr brn & lt grn	.80	.80
C5	AP2	4.50fr cop red & bl	.90	.90
C6	AP2	6.50fr bl & lt grn	1.60	1.60
C7	AP2	8.50fr red brn & yel	1.60	1.60
C8	AP2	10.75fr vio & lt grn	1.60	1.60
		Nos. C1-C8 (8)	8.00	8.00

For overprints and surcharges see Nos. C9-C16, CB6.

Nos. C1, C3-C7 Overprinted in Black like Nos. 133-141

No. C10

1940-41
C9	AP1	1.50fr ('41)	240.00	240.00
C10	AP1	2.50fr	4.00	4.00
a.	Double overprint	275.00	275.00
b.	Inverted overprint	275.00	275.00
C11	AP1	3.75fr ('41)	240.00	240.00
C12	AP2	4.50fr	4.50	4.50
a.	Double overprint	275.00	275.00
C13	AP2	6.50fr	4.00	4.00
a.	Double overprint	130.00	130.00
C14	AP2	8.50fr	4.00	4.00

No. C8 Surcharged in Carmine

| C15 | AP2 | 50fr on 10.75fr | 12.00 | 12.00 |

No. C3 Surcharged in Black

| C16 | AP1 | 10fr on 2.50fr ('41) | 95.00 | 95.00 |
| | | Nos. C9-C16 (8) | 603.50 | 603.50 |

Counterfeits of Nos. C9 and C11 exist. See note following No. 141.

> Catalogue values for unused stamps in this section, from this point to the end of the section, are for Never Hinged items.

Common Design Type
1941   **Photo.**   **Perf. 14½x14**
C17	CD87	1fr dark orange	.65	.30
C18	CD87	1.50fr brt red	.95	.50
C19	CD87	5fr brown red	1.60	.90
C20	CD87	10fr black	1.75	1.00
C21	CD87	25fr ultra	1.60	1.20
C22	CD87	50fr dark green	1.60	1.20
C23	CD87	100fr plum	2.25	1.25
		Nos. C17-C23 (7)	10.40	6.35

Types of 1937 without "RF" and

Sikorsky 5.43 Seaplane and Canoe — AP2a

Perf. 13½, 13 (#C23M)
1943, Oct. 18-1944   **Unwmk.**
C23A	AP1	1.50fr ol blk & yel	.40
C23B	AP1	2fr mag & blue	.40
C23C	AP1	2.50fr grn & buff	.40
C23D	AP1	3.75fr brn & lt grn	.80
C23E	AP2	4.50fr cop red & bl	.80
C23F	AP2	5fr green	1.20
C23G	AP2	6.50fr bl & lt grn	1.20
C23H	AP2	8.50fr red brn & yel	1.20
C23I	AP2	10fr gray & brn ('44)	1.20
C23J	AP2	10.75fr vio & lt grn	1.20
C23K	AP2	20fr yel & brn red ('44)	1.60
C23L	AP2	50fr gray grn & blk ('44)	2.40
C23M	AP2a	100fr red brn ('44)	1.60
		Nos. C23A-C23M (13)	14.40

Issue dates: Nos. C23I, C23K-L, 4/3/44; C23M, 6/26/44.
Nos. C23A-C23M were issued by the Vichy government in France, but were not sold in French Equatorial Africa.

Victory Issue
Common Design Type
Perf. 12½
1946, May 8   **Unwmk.**   **Engr.**
| C24 | CD92 | 8fr lilac rose | 1.60 | 1.25 |

Chad to Rhine Issue
Common Design Types
1946, June 6
C25	CD93	5fr dk violet	1.60	1.20
C26	CD94	10fr slate green	1.60	1.20
C27	CD95	15fr deep blue	2.75	2.00
C28	CD96	20fr red orange	2.75	2.00
C29	CD97	25fr sepia	2.75	2.00
C30	CD98	50fr brown carmine	3.25	2.40
		Nos. C25-C30 (6)	14.70	10.80

Palms and Village AP3

Village and Waterfront AP4

Bearers in Jungle AP5

1946   **Engr.**   **Perf. 13**
C31	AP3	50fr red brn	3.50	.80
C32	AP4	100fr grnsh blk	5.25	1.25
C33	AP5	200fr deep blue	12.00	2.00
		Nos. C31-C33 (3)	20.75	4.05

UPU Issue
Common Design Type
1949, July 4
| C34 | CD99 | 25fr green | 16.00 | 12.00 |

Brazza Holding Map — AP6

1951, Nov. 5
| C35 | AP6 | 15fr brn, indigo & red | 2.40 | 1.60 |

Cent. of the birth of Pierre Savorgnan de Brazza, explorer.

Archbishop Augouard and St. Anne Cathedral, Brazzaville AP7

1952, Dec. 1
| C36 | AP7 | 15fr ol grn, dk brn & vio brn | 6.50 | 2.40 |

Cent. of the birth of Archbishop Philippe-Prosper Augouard.

Anhingas AP8

1953, Feb. 16
| C37 | AP8 | 500fr grnsh blk, blk & slate | 47.50 | 8.00 |

Liberation Issue
Common Design Type
1954, June 6
| C38 | CD102 | 15fr vio & vio brn | 12.00 | 8.00 |

Log Rafts — AP9

Designs: 100fr, Fishing boats and nets, Lake Chad. 200fr, Age of mechanization.

1955, Jan. 24   **Engr.**
C39	AP9	50fr ind, brn & dk grn	2.40	.80
C40	AP9	100fr aqua, dk grn & blk brn	8.00	1.60
C41	AP9	200fr red & deep plum	12.00	2.40
		Nos. C39-C41 (3)	22.40	4.80

Gov. Gen. Félix Eboué, View of Brazzaville and the Pantheon AP10

1955, Apr. 30   **Unwmk.**   **Perf. 13**
| C42 | AP10 | 15fr sep, brn & slate bl | 6.50 | 2.40 |

Gen. Louis Faidherbe and African Sharpshooter — AP11

1957, July 20
| C43 | AP11 | 15fr sepia & org ver | 3.50 | 2.00 |

Centenary of French African Troops.

AIR POST SEMI-POSTAL STAMPS

French Revolution Issue
Common Design Type
1939   **Unwmk.**   **Photo.**   **Perf. 13**
Name and Value Type in Orange
| CB1 | CD83 | 4.50fr + 4fr brn blk | 40.00 | 40.00 |

SPAP1

FRENCH EQUATORIAL AFRICA — FRENCH GUIANA

SPAP2

SPAP3

1942, June 22   Unwmk.   Engr.   Perf. 13

CB2	SPAP1	1.50fr + 3.50fr green	.80
CB3	SPAP2	2fr + 6fr brown	.80
CB4	SPAP3	3fr + 9fr carmine	.80
	Nos. CB2-CB4 (3)		2.40

Native children's welfare fund.

Nos. CB2-CB4 were issued by the Vichy government in France, but were not placed on sale in French Equatorial Africa.

Colonial Education Fund
Common Design Type

1942, June 22

| CB5 | CD86a | 1.20fr + 1.80fr bl & red | .80 |

No. CB5 was issued by the Vichy government in France, but was not placed on sale in French Equatorial Africa.

No. C8 Surcharged in Red like Nos. B10-B11

1943, June 28   Perf. 13½

| CB6 | AP2 | 10.75fr + 200fr | 400.00 | 240.00 |

Counterfeits exist.

POSTAGE DUE STAMPS

Numeral of Value on Equatorial Butterfly — D1

1937   Unwmk.   Photo.   Perf. 13

J1	D1	5c redsh pur & lt bl	.25	.40
J2	D1	10c cop red & buff	.25	.40
J3	D1	20c dk grn & grn	.30	.50
J4	D1	25c red brn & buff	.30	.50
J5	D1	30c cop red & lt bl	.50	.55
J6	D1	45c mag & yel grn	.75	.80
J7	D1	50c dk ol grn & buff	.80	.95
J8	D1	60c redsh pur & yel	.95	1.10
J9	D1	1fr brown & yel	1.00	1.20
J10	D1	2fr dk bl & buff	1.40	1.50
J11	D1	3fr red brn & lt grn	1.50	1.75
	Nos. J1-J11 (11)		8.00	9.65
	Set, never hinged		12.00	

Catalogue values for unused stamps in this section, from this point to the end of the section, are for Never Hinged items.

D2

1947   Engr.

J12	D2	10c red	.40	.25
J13	D2	30c dp org	.40	.25
J14	D2	50c greenish bl	.50	.30
J15	D2	1fr carmine	.55	.40
J16	D2	2fr emerald	.65	.50
J17	D2	3fr dp red lil	.65	.50
J18	D2	4fr dp ultra	1.60	1.20
J19	D2	5fr red brown	1.60	1.20

J20	D2	10fr peacock blue	2.00	1.60
J21	D2	20fr sepia	2.10	1.90
	Nos. J12-J21 (10)		10.45	8.10

FRENCH GUIANA

'french gē-'a-nə

LOCATION — On the northeast coast of South America bordering on the Atlantic Ocean.
GOVT. — French colony
AREA — 34,740 sq. mi.
POP. — 28,537 (1946)
CAPITAL — Cayenne

French Guiana became an overseas department of France in 1946.

100 Centimes = 1 Franc

Catalogue values for unused stamps in this country are for Never Hinged items, beginning with Scott 171 in the regular postage section, Scott B12 in the semi-postal section, Scott C9 in the airpost section, and Scott J22 in the postage due section.

See France No. 1446 for French stamp inscribed "Guyane."

Stamps of French Colonies Surcharged in Black

1886, Dec.   Unwmk.   Imperf.

1	A8	5c on 2c grn, grnsh, srch 12mm high	750.00	675.00
a.	Double surcharge		1,900.	1,900.
b.	Surcharge 10½mm high		900.00	825.00
c.	No "f" after "O"		950.00	850.00

Perf. 14x13½

2	A9	5c on 2c brn, buff, srch 12mm high	650.00	600.00
a.	No "f" after "O"		525.00	450.00
b.	As "a," double surcharge		1,700.	1,700.

Nos. 1-2 unused are valued without gum.

Stamps of French Colonies Overprinted in Black

"Av" of Date Line Inverted-Reversed

1887, Apr.   Imperf.

4	A8	20c on 35c blk, org	70.00	57.50
a.	Double surcharge		225.00	225.00
b.	No "f" after "O"		150.00	150.00

Date Line Reads "Avril 1887"

5	A8	5c on 2c grn, grnsh	175.00	125.00
a.	Double surcharge		900.00	900.00
b.	No "f" after "O"		375.00	375.00
c.	Pair, one stamp without surcharge		1,500.	
6	A8	20c on 35c blk, org	375.00	375.00
a.	Double surcharge		1,250.	1,250.
b.	No "f" after "O"		850.00	850.00
c.	Vertical pair, #6 + #4		2,200.	
7	A7	25c on 30c brn, yelsh	55.00	47.50
a.	Double surcharge		900.00	900.00
b.	No "f" after "O"		275.00	275.00

Nos. 4-7 unused are valued without gum.

French Colonies Nos. 22 and 26 Surcharged

8	A7	5c on 30c brn, yelsh	155.00	140.00
a.	Double surcharge		800.00	800.00
b.	Inverted surcharge		1,200.	1,200.
c.	Pair, one without surcharge		1,600.	
9	A8	5c on 30c brn, yelsh	1,500.	1,500.

Nos. 8-9 unused are valued without gum.

French Colonies Nos. 22 and 28 Surcharged

1888

10	A7	5c on 30c brn, yelsh	155.00	140.00
b.	Double surcharge		500.00	500.00
c.	Inverted surcharge		600.00	600.00
11	A8	10c on 75c car, rose	400.00	290.00
	No gum		290.00	
a.	Double surcharge		1,100.	1,100.
b.	Pair, one stamp without surcharge		2,500.	

No. 10 unused is valued without gum.

Stamps of French Colonies Overprinted in Black

1892, Feb. 20   Imperf.

12	A8	2c grn, grnsh	850.00	975.00
a.	Inverted overprint		3,500.	
13	A7	30c brn, yelsh	155.00	155.00
a.	Inverted overprint		575.00	575.00
14	A8	35c blk, orange	2,850.	3,000.
15	A8	40c red, straw	175.00	140.00
16	A8	75c car, rose	180.00	140.00
a.	Inverted overprint		625.00	550.00
17	A8	1fr brnz grn, straw	210.00	160.00
a.	Inverted overprint		800.00	800.00
b.	Double overprint		800.00	800.00
c.	Triple overprint		1,800.	1,800.

Nos. 12-14 unused are valued without gum.

1892   Perf. 14x13½

18	A9	1c blk, lil bl	47.50	35.00
19	A9	2c brn, buff	45.00	37.50
20	A9	4c claret, lav	42.50	37.50
21	A9	5c grn, grnsh	47.50	35.00
a.	Inverted overprint		150.00	150.00
b.	Double overprint		150.00	150.00
22	A9	10c blk, lavender	67.50	40.00
a.	Inverted overprint		200.00	200.00
b.	Double overprint		275.00	275.00
23	A9	15c blue	67.50	45.00
a.	Double overprint		275.00	200.00
24	A9	20c red, grn	55.00	42.50
a.	Inverted overprint		225.00	225.00
25	A9	25c blk, rose	75.00	35.00
a.	Double overprint		275.00	275.00
b.	Triple overprint		300.00	300.00
26	A9	30c brn, bis	47.50	40.00
27	A9	35c blk, orange	225.00	225.00
a.	Inverted overprint		575.00	575.00
28	A9	40c red, straw	135.00	135.00
a.	Inverted overprint		300.00	300.00
29	A9	75c car, rose	145.00	125.00
30	A9	1fr brnz grn, straw	250.00	220.00
a.	Double overprint		375.00	
	Nos. 18-30 (13)		1,250.	1,053.

French Colonies No. 51 Surcharged

1892, Dec.

31	A9	5c on 15c blue	70.00	47.50
a.	Double surcharge		300.00	275.00
b.	No "f" after "O"		160.00	135.00
c.	Pair, one stamp without surcharge		1,700.	1,700.

Navigation and Commerce — A12

1892-1904   Typo.   Perf. 14x13½
Name of Colony in Blue or Carmine

32	A12	1c blk, lil bl	2.00	1.75
33	A12	2c brn, buff	1.45	1.45
34	A12	4c claret, lav	2.00	1.90
a.	"GUYANE" double		275.00	
35	A12	5c grn, grnsh	12.50	11.00
36	A12	5c yel grn ('04)	2.40	1.60
37	A12	10c blk, lavender	13.50	8.25
38	A12	10c red ('00)	4.75	1.60
39	A12	15c blue, quadrille paper	42.50	4.00
40	A12	15c gray, lt gray ('00)	122.50	110.00
41	A12	20c red, grn	25.00	18.00
42	A12	25c blk, rose	20.00	5.50
43	A12	25c blue ('00)	22.50	22.50
44	A12	30c brn, bis	24.00	18.00
45	A12	40c red, straw	24.00	16.00
46	A12	50c car, rose	35.00	18.00

47	A12	50c brn, az ('00)	26.00	26.00
48	A12	75c dp vio, org	37.50	27.50
49	A12	1fr brn grn, straw	18.00	14.00
50	A12	2fr vio, rose ('02)	180.00	16.00
	Nos. 32-50 (19)		615.60	323.05

Perf. 13½x14 stamps are counterfeits. For surcharges see Nos. 87-93.

Great Anteater — A13   **Washing Gold** — A14

Palm Grove at Cayenne — A15

1905-28

51	A13	1c black	.40	.40
52	A13	2c blue	.40	.40
a.	Imperf		57.50	
53	A13	4c red brn	.40	.40
54	A13	5c green	1.25	1.10
55	A13	5c org ('22)	.40	.45
56	A13	10c rose	1.50	1.10
57	A13	10c grn ('22)	.65	.40
58	A13	10c red, bluish ('25)	.45	.45
59	A13	15c violet	1.75	1.25
60	A14	20c red brn	.65	.65
61	A14	25c blue	3.00	1.60
62	A14	25c vio ('22)	.60	.50
63	A14	30c black	2.50	1.00
64	A14	30c rose ('22)	.50	.60
65	A14	30c red org ('25)	.45	.45
66	A14	30c dk grn, grnsh ('28)	1.35	1.35
67	A14	35c blk, yel ('06)	.65	.65
68	A14	40c rose	1.50	.85
69	A14	40c black ('22)	.40	.45
70	A14	45c olive ('07)	1.00	.95
71	A14	50c violet	4.25	3.50
72	A14	50c blue ('22)	.55	.65
73	A14	50c gray ('25)	.80	.80
74	A14	60c lil, rose ('25)	.65	.65
75	A14	65c myr grn ('26)	.85	.80
76	A14	75c green	1.60	1.40
77	A14	85c magenta ('26)	.85	.80
78	A15	1fr rose	.90	.85
a.	Imperf		82.50	
79	A15	1fr bl, bluish ('25)	.85	.80
80	A15	1fr bl, yel grn ('28)	2.75	2.75
81	A15	1.10fr lt red ('28)	1.50	1.50
82	A15	2fr blue	1.35	1.35
83	A15	2fr org red, yel ('26)	2.75	2.40
84	A15	5fr black	8.50	6.50
a.	Imperf		82.50	
85	A15	10fr grn, yel ('24)	14.00	14.50
a.	Printed on both sides		140.00	
86	A15	20fr brn lake ('24)	17.50	17.50
	Nos. 51-86 (36)		79.45	71.75

For surcharges see Nos. 94-108, B1-B2.

Issue of 1892 Surcharged in Black or Carmine

1912

Spacing between figures of surcharge 1.5mm (5c), 2mm (10c)

87	A12	5c on 2c brn, buff	1.60	2.00
88	A12	5c on 4c cl, lav (C)	1.20	1.60
89	A12	5c on 20c red, grn	1.75	1.90
90	A12	5c on 25c blk, rose (C)	4.00	4.75
91	A12	5c on 30c brn, bis (C)	1.75	1.90
92	A12	10c on 40c red, straw	1.40	1.90
a.	Pair, one stamp without surcharge		1,250.	
93	A12	10c on 50c car, rose	4.25	5.25
a.	Double surcharge		550.00	
	Nos. 87-93 (7)		15.95	19.30

Two spacings between the surcharged numerals are found on Nos. 87 to 93. For detailed listings, see the *Scott Classic Specialized Catalogue of Stamps and Covers*.

FRENCH GUIANA

No. 59 Surcharged in Various Colors

1922
94	A13	1c on 15c vio (Bk)	.65	.75
a.		Double surcharge	90.00	
95	A13	2c on 15c vio (Bl)	.65	.75
a.		Inverted surcharge	97.50	
b.		In pair with unovptd. stamp	250.00	
c.		No. 95a, in pair with unovptd. stamp	850.00	
96	A13	4c on 15c vio (G)	.65	.75
a.		Double surcharge	90.00	
b.		In pair with unovptd. stamp	275.00	
97	A13	5c on 15c vio (R)	.65	.75
a.		In pair with unovptd. stamp	275.00	
		Nos. 94-97 (4)	2.60	3.00

Type of 1905-28 Srchd. in Blue

1923
98	A15	10fr on 1fr grn, yel	22.50	24.00
99	A15	20fr on 5fr lilac, rose	22.50	24.00

Stamps and Types of 1905-28 Srchd. in Black or Red

1924-27
100	A13	25c on 15c vio ('25)	.85	.95
a.		Triple surcharge	130.00	130.00
b.		In pair with unovptd. stamp	260.00	
101	A14	25c on 2fr bl ('24)	.90	.95
a.		Double surcharge	140.00	
b.		Triple surcharge	150.00	
102	A14	65c on 45c ol (R) ('25)	1.75	1.90
103	A14	85c on 45c ol (R) ('25)	1.75	1.90
104	A14	90c on 75c red ('27)	1.50	1.50
105	A15	1.05fr on 2fr lt yel brn ('27)	1.50	1.50
106	A15	1.25fr on 1fr ultra (R) ('26)	1.60	1.75
107	A15	1.50fr on 1fr lt bl ('27)	1.60	1.75
108	A15	3fr on 5fr vio ('27)	1.75	2.00
a.		No period after "F"	12.00	12.00
		Nos. 100-108 (9)	13.20	14.10

Carib Archer A16

Shooting Rapids, Maroni River A17

Government Building, Cayenne — A18

1929-40 Perf. 13½x14
109	A16	1c gray lil & grnsh bl	.25	.25
a.		Imperf.	35.00	
110	A16	2c dk red & bl grn	.25	.25
a.		Imperf.	35.00	
111	A16	3c gray lil & grnsh bl ('40)	.30	.30
112	A16	4c ol brn & red vio	.30	.30
113	A16	5c Prus bl & red org	.30	.30
114	A16	10c mag & brn	.30	.30
115	A16	15c yel brn & red org	.30	.30
a.		Imperf.	35.00	
116	A16	20c dk bl & ol grn	.30	.30
117	A16	25c dk red & dk brn	.50	.50

Perf. 14x13½
118	A17	30c dl & lt grn	.70	.70
119	A17	30c grn & brn ('40)	.50	.50
120	A17	35c Prus grn & ol grn ('38)	1.10	1.10
121	A17	40c org brn & ol gray	.30	.30
122	A17	45c grn & dk brn	1.20	1.20
123	A17	45c ol grn & lt grn ('40)	.70	.70
124	A17	50c dk bl & ol gray	.40	.40
a.		Imperf.	35.00	
125	A17	55c vio bl & car ('38)	1.50	1.50
126	A17	60c sal & grn ('40)	.75	.75
a.		Imperf.	47.50	
127	A17	65c sal & grn	1.10	1.10
128	A17	70c ind & sl bl ('40)	1.30	1.30
129	A17	75c ind & sl bl	1.15	1.15
130	A17	80c blk & vio bl ('38)	.80	.80
131	A17	90c dk red & ver	1.10	1.10
132	A17	90c red vio & brn ('39)	1.30	1.30
133	A17	1fr lt vio & brn	.70	.70
134	A17	1fr car & lt red ('38)	2.10	2.10
135	A17	1fr blk & vio bl ('40)	.80	.80
136	A18	1.05fr ver & olive	6.25	6.25
137	A18	1.10fr ol brn & red vio	7.25	5.75
138	A18	1.25fr blk brn & bl grn ('33)	.80	.80
139	A18	1.25fr rose & lt red ('39)	1.10	1.10
140	A18	1.40fr ol brn & red vio ('40)	1.30	1.30
141	A18	1.50fr dk bl & lt bl	.40	.40
142	A18	1.60fr ol brn & bl ('39)	1.30	1.30
143	A18	1.75fr brn red & blk brn ('33)	2.25	2.25
144	A18	1.75fr vio bl ('38)	1.75	1.75
145	A18	2fr dk grn & rose red	.65	.65
146	A18	2.25fr vio bl ('39)	1.30	1.30
147	A18	2.50fr cop red & brn ('40)	1.30	1.30
148	A18	3fr brn red & red vio	.75	.75
149	A18	5fr dl vio & yel grn	1.25	1.25
150	A18	10fr ol gray & dp ultra	1.50	1.50
151	A18	20fr indigo & ver	2.50	2.50
		Nos. 109-151 (43)	51.95	50.45

For types A16-A18 without "RF," see Nos. 170C-170E.

Common Design Types pictured following the introduction.

Colonial Exposition Issue
Common Design Types

1931 Engr. Perf. 12½

Name of Country in Black
152	CD70	40c dp green	5.50	5.50
153	CD71	50c violet	5.50	5.50
154	CD72	90c red orange	5.50	5.50
155	CD73	1.50fr dull blue	5.50	5.50
		Nos. 152-155 (4)	22.00	22.00

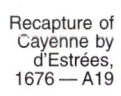

Recapture of Cayenne by d'Estrées, 1676 — A19

Products of French Guiana — A20

1935, Oct. 21 Perf. 13
156	A19	40c gray brn	5.75	5.75
157	A19	50c dull red	10.00	8.00
158	A19	1.50fr ultra	5.75	5.75
159	A20	1.75fr lilac rose	12.50	11.50
160	A20	5fr brown	10.00	9.00
161	A20	10fr blue green	10.50	10.00
		Nos. 156-161 (6)	54.50	50.00

Tercentenary of the founding of French possessions in the West Indies.

Paris International Exposition Issue
Common Design Types

1937, Apr. 15
162	CD74	20c deep violet	1.75	1.75
163	CD75	30c dark green	1.75	1.75
164	CD76	40c car rose	1.75	1.75
165	CD77	50c dark brown	1.75	1.75
166	CD78	90c red	1.75	1.75
167	CD79	1fr 50	2.25	2.25
		Nos. 162-167 (6)	11.00	11.00

Colonial Arts Exhibition Issue
Souvenir Sheet
Common Design Type

1937 Imperf.
168	CD75	3fr violet	11.50	13.50

New York World's Fair Issue
Common Design Type

1939, May 10 Engr. Perf. 12½x12
169	CD82	1.25fr car lake	1.30	1.30
170	CD82	2.25fr ultra	1.30	1.30

View of Cayenne and Marshal Petain — A21a

1941 Engr. Perf. 12½x12
170A	A21a	1fr deep lilac	.80	.80
170B	A21a	2.50fr blue	.80	.80

For surcharges, see Nos. B11A-B11B.

Types of 1929-40 without "RF"

1944 *Methods and Perfs as Before*
170C	A16	15c yel brn & red org		1.10
170D	A17	1fr black & vio blue		1.10
170E	A18	1.50fr dk blue & lt blue		1.40
		Nos. 170C-170E (3)		3.60

Nos. 170C-170E were issued by the Vichy government in France, but were not issued in French Guiana.

Catalogue values for unused stamps in this section, from this point to the end of the section, are for Never Hinged items.

Eboue Issue
Common Design Type

1945 Engr. Perf. 13
171	CD91	2fr black	.95	.80
172	CD91	25fr Prussian green	1.50	1.20

This issue exists imperforate.

Arms of Cayenne — A22

1945 Litho. Perf. 12
173	A22	10c dp gray violet	.30	.25
174	A22	30c brown org	.35	.25
175	A22	40c lt blue	.35	.25
176	A22	50c violet brn	.75	.60
177	A22	60c orange yel	.75	.60
178	A22	70c pale brown	.75	.60
179	A22	80c lt green	.75	.60
180	A22	1fr blue	.35	.25
181	A22	1.20fr brt violet	.75	.60
182	A22	1.50fr dp orange	1.00	.75
183	A22	2fr black	1.10	.85
184	A22	2.40fr red	1.10	.85
185	A22	3fr pink	1.10	.85
186	A22	4fr dp ultra	1.30	1.00
187	A22	4.50fr dp yel grn	1.30	1.00
188	A22	5fr orange brn	1.30	1.00
189	A22	10fr dk violet	1.30	1.00
190	A22	15fr rose carmine	1.30	1.00
191	A22	20fr olive green	1.50	1.25
		Nos. 173-191 (19)	17.40	12.55

Hammock A23

Guiana Girl A26

Maroni River Bank — A24

Inini Scene — A25

Toucans — A27

Parrots — A28

1947, June 2 Unwmk. Perf. 13. Engr.
192	A23	10c dk blue grn	.30	.25
193	A23	30c brt red	.30	.25
194	A23	50c dk vio brn	.30	.25
195	A24	60c grnsh blk	.60	.45
196	A24	1fr red brn	.85	.60
197	A24	1.50fr black brn	.85	.60
198	A25	2fr dp yel grn	1.10	.75
199	A25	2.50fr dp ultra	1.10	.75
200	A25	3fr red brn	1.00	.70
201	A26	4fr black brn	2.50	1.25
202	A26	5fr deep blue	1.75	1.10
203	A26	6fr red brown	1.75	1.10
204	A27	10fr deep ultra	7.25	4.75
205	A27	15fr black brn	7.25	5.00
206	A27	20fr red brn	9.25	5.00
207	A28	25fr brt bl grn	13.00	8.50
208	A28	40fr black brn	11.00	8.00
		Nos. 192-208 (17)	60.15	39.30

SEMI-POSTAL STAMPS

Regular Issue of 1905-28 Surcharged in Red

1915 Unwmk. Perf. 13½x14
B1	A13	10c + 5c rose	17.50	18.00
a.		Inverted surcharge	250.00	250.00
b.		Double surcharge	250.00	250.00

Regular Issue of 1905-28 Surcharged in Rose

B2	A13	10c + 5c rose	1.60	1.60

Curie Issue
Common Design Type

1938 Perf. 13
B3	CD80	1.75fr + 50c brt ultra	13.50	13.50

French Revolution Issue
Common Design Type

1939 Photo.
Name and Value in Black
B4	CD83	45c + 25c green	11.50	11.50
B5	CD83	70c + 3fr brown	11.50	11.50
B6	CD83	90c + 35c red org	11.50	11.50
B7	CD83	1.25fr + 1fr rose pink	11.50	11.50
B8	CD83	2.25fr + 2fr blue	11.50	11.50
		Nos. B4-B8 (5)	57.50	57.50

Common Design Type and

Colonial Infantryman SP1

Colonial Policeman SP2

1941 Photo. Perf. 13½
B9	SP1	1fr + 1fr red		1.30
B10	CD86	1.50fr + 3fr maroon		1.50
B11	SP2	2.50fr + 1fr blue		1.30
		Nos. B9-B11 (3)		4.10

Nos. B9-B11 were issued by the Vichy government in France, but were not placed on sale in French Guiana.

Nos. 170A-170B Srchd. in Black or Red

1944 Engr. Perf. 12½x12
B11A		50c + 1.50fr on 2.50fr deep blue (R)		.80
B11B		+ 2.50fr on 1fr dp lilac		.80

Colonial Development Fund.

FRENCH GUIANA — FRENCH GUINEA

Nos. B11A-B11B were issued by the Vichy government in France, but were not placed on sale in French Guiana.

Catalogue values for unused stamps in this section, from this point to the end of the section, are for Never Hinged items.

Red Cross Issue
Common Design Type

1944			Perf. 14½x14
B12	CD90	5fr + 20fr dk copper brn	1.75 1.25

The surtax was for the French Red Cross and national relief.

AIR POST STAMPS

Cayenne — AP1

		Perf. 13½	
1933, Nov. 20		**Unwmk.**	**Photo.**
C1	AP1	50c orange brn	.30 .30
C2	AP1	1fr yellow grn	.50 .50
C3	AP1	1.50fr dk blue	.70 .70
C4	AP1	2fr orange	.70 .70
C5	AP1	3fr black	.85 .85
C6	AP1	5fr violet	.85 .85
C7	AP1	10fr olive grn	.85 .85
C8	AP1	20fr scarlet	1.25 1.25
		Nos. C1-C8 (8)	6.00 6.00

For No. C1 without "RF," see No. C8A.
A 20fr violet exists, but was not regularly issued. Value, $175.

Catalogue values for unused stamps in this section, from this point to the end of the section, are for Never Hinged items.

Type of 1933 without "RF" and

AP1a   AP1b

		Perf. 13½, 13 (#C8C)	
1941-44		**Photo, Engr.**	**(#C8C)**
C8A	AP1	50c orange brn	1.00
C8B	AP1a	50f bl grn & red brown ('42)	1.40
C8C	AP1b	100f dk blue ('44)	1.60
		Nos. C8A-C8C (3)	4.00

Nos. C8A-C8C were issued by the Vichy government in France, but were not placed on sale in French Guiana.

Common Design Type

1945		Photo.	Perf. 14½x14
C9	CD87	50fr dark green	1.30 1.10
C10	CD87	100fr plum	2.50 2.00

Victory Issue
Common Design Type

1946, May 8		Engr.	Perf. 12½
C11	CD92	8fr black	1.75 1.25

Chad to Rhine Issue
Common Design Types

1946, June 6			
C12	CD93	5fr dk slate bl	1.75 1.50
C13	CD94	10fr lilac rose	1.75 1.50
C14	CD95	15fr dk vio brn	1.75 1.50
C15	CD96	20fr dk slate grn	2.00 1.60
C16	CD97	25fr vio brown	2.40 2.00
C17	CD98	50fr bright lilac	3.00 2.25
		Nos. C12-C17 (6)	12.65 10.35

Eagles — AP2

Tapir — AP3

Toucans — AP4

1947, June 2		Engr.	Perf. 13
C18	AP2	50fr deep green	22.50 17.50
C19	AP3	100fr red brown	15.00 13.00
C20	AP4	200fr dk gray bl	30.00 24.00
		Nos. C18-C20 (3)	67.50 54.50

AIR POST SEMI-POSTAL STAMP

French Revolution Issue
Common Design Type

	Unwmk.		
1939, July 5	**Photo.**		**Perf. 13**
Name & Value Typo. in Orange			
CB1	CD83	5fr + 4fr brn blk	22.00 22.00

Nurse with Mother & Child SPAP1

	Unwmk.		
1942, June 22			**Perf. 13**
CB2	SPAP1	1.50fr + 50c green	1.00
CB3	SPAP1	2fr + 6fr brn & red	1.00

Native children's welfare fund.
Nos. CB2-CB3 were issued by the Vichy government in France, but were not placed on sale in French Guiana.

Colonial Education Fund
Common Design Type

1942, June 22			
CB4	CD86a	1.20fr + 1.80fr blue & red	1.10

No. CB4 was issued by the Vichy government in France, but was not placed on sale in French Guiana.

POSTAGE DUE STAMPS

Postage Due Stamps of France, 1893-1926, Overprinted

1925-27		Unwmk.	Perf. 14x13½
J1	D2	5c light blue	.70 .75
a.	In pair with unovptd. stamp		375.00
J2	D2	10c brown	1.00 1.00
J3	D2	20c olive green	1.10 1.25
J4	D2	50c violet brown	1.50 1.60
J5	D2	3fr magenta ('27)	11.00 12.50

Surcharged in Black

J6	D2	15c on 20c ol grn	1.00 1.10
a.	Blue surcharge		67.50
J7	D2	25c on 5c lt bl	1.30 1.40
a.	In pair with unovptd. stamp		375.00
J8	D2	30c on 20c ol grn	1.50 1.60
J9	D2	45c on 10c brn	1.50 1.60
J10	D2	60c on 5c lt bl	1.50 1.60
J11	D2	1fr on 20c ol grn	2.25 2.40
J12	D2	2fr on 50c vio brn	2.25 2.40
		Nos. J1-J12 (12)	26.60 29.30

Royal Palms — D3

Guiana Girl — D4

1929, Oct. 14		Typo.	Perf. 13½x14
J13	D3	5c indigo & Prus bl	.45 .50
J14	D3	10c bis brn & Prus grn	.45 .50
J15	D3	20c grn & rose red	.45 .50
J16	D3	30c ol brn & rose red	.45 .50
J17	D3	50c vio & ol brn	.95 1.00
J18	D3	60c brn red & ol brn	1.30 1.40
J19	D4	1fr dp bl & org brn	1.75 1.90
J20	D4	2fr brn red & bluish grn	2.00 2.10
J21	D4	3fr violet & blk	4.25 4.50
		Nos. J13-J21 (9)	12.05 12.90

Catalogue values for unused stamps in this section, from this point to the end of the section, are for Never Hinged items.

D5

1947, June 2		Engr.	Perf. 14x13
J22	D5	10c dk car rose	.35 .35
J23	D5	30c dull green	.45 .45
J24	D5	50c black	.45 .45
J25	D5	1fr brt ultra	.55 .55
J26	D5	2fr dk brown red	.55 .55
J27	D5	3fr deep violet	1.00 .80
J28	D5	4fr red	1.30 1.10
J29	D5	5fr brown violet	1.50 1.25
J30	D5	10fr blue green	2.25 1.90
J31	D5	20fr lilac rose	3.00 2.25
		Nos. J22-J31 (10)	11.40 9.65

FRENCH GUINEA

ˈfrench ˈgi-nē

LOCATION — On the coast of West Africa, between Portuguese Guinea and Sierra Leone.
GOVT. — French colony
AREA — 89,436 sq. mi.
POP. — 2,058,442 (est. 1941)
CAPITAL — Conakry

French Guinea stamps were replaced by those of French West Africa around 1944-45. French Guinea became the Republic of Guinea Oct. 2, 1958. See "Guinea" for issues of the republic.

100 Centimes = 1 Franc

See French West Africa No. 66 for additional stamp inscribed "Guinee" and "Afrique Occidentale Francaise."

Navigation and Commerce — A1

		Perf. 14x13½	
1892-1900	**Typo.**		**Unwmk.**
Name of Colony in Blue or Carmine			
1	A1	1c black, *lilac bl*	2.40 1.60
2	A1	2c brown, *buff*	2.40 2.00
3	A1	4c claret, *lav*	3.25 2.00
4	A1	5c green, *grnsh*	8.00 8.00
5	A1	10c blk, *lavender*	8.00 4.75
6	A1	10c red ('00)	45.00 40.00
7	A1	15c blue, quadrille paper	16.00 8.00
8	A1	15c gray, *lt gray* ('00)	100.00 87.50
9	A1	20c red, *grn*	20.00 16.00
10	A1	25c black, *rose*	16.00 8.00
11	A1	25c blue ('00)	24.00 24.00
12	A1	30c brown, *bis*	40.00 32.50
13	A1	40c red, *straw*	40.00 32.50
a.	"GUINEE FRANCAISE" double		475.00 475.00
14	A1	50c car, *rose*	47.50 35.00
15	A1	50c brown, *az* ('00)	40.00 40.00
16	A1	75c dp vio, *org*	65.00 47.50
17	A1	1fr brnz grn, *straw*	50.00 40.00
		Nos. 1-17 (17)	527.55 429.35

Perf. 13½x14 stamps are counterfeits. For surcharges see Nos. 48-54.

Fulah Shepherd — A2

1904			
18	A2	1c black, *yel grn*	1.20 1.20
19	A2	2c vio brn, *buff*	1.20 1.20
20	A2	4c carmine, *bl*	1.60 1.60
21	A2	5c green, *grnsh*	1.60 1.60
22	A2	10c carmine	4.00 2.40
23	A2	15c violet, *rose*	12.00 5.50
24	A2	20c carmine, *grn*	16.00 16.00
25	A2	25c blue	16.00 10.00
26	A2	30c brown	24.00 24.00
27	A2	40c red, *straw*	35.00 24.00
28	A2	50c brown, *az*	32.50 24.00
29	A2	75c green, *org*	32.50 32.50
30	A2	1fr brnz grn, *straw*	47.50 47.50
31	A2	2fr red, *org*	87.50 87.50
32	A2	5fr green, *yel grn*	120.00 120.00
		Nos. 18-32 (15)	432.60 399.00

For surcharges see Nos. 55-62.

Gen. Louis Faidherbé — A3

Oil Palm — A4

Dr. Noel Eugène Ballay — A5

1906-07			
Name of Colony in Red or Blue			
33	A3	1c gray	.80 .80
34	A3	2c brown	1.20 1.20
35	A3	4c brown, *bl*	1.60 1.60
36	A3	5c green	4.00 2.00
37	A3	10c carmine (B)	24.00 1.60
38	A4	20c black, *bl*	8.00 4.00
39	A4	25c blue, *pnksh*	8.00 6.50
40	A4	30c brown, *pnksh*	8.00 4.00
41	A4	35c black, *yellow*	6.50 2.40
42	A4	45c choc, *grnsh gray*	8.00 4.00
43	A4	50c dp violet	16.00 12.00
44	A4	75c blue, *org*	12.00 4.00
45	A5	1fr black, *az*	20.00 24.00
46	A5	2fr blue, *pink*	40.00 45.00
47	A5	5fr car, *straw* (B)	60.00 65.00
		Nos. 33-47 (15)	218.10 178.10

Regular Issues Surcharged in Black or Carmine

1912			
48	A1	5c on 2c brown, *buff*	1.60 2.00
49	A1	5c on 4c cl, *lav* (C)	1.25 1.60
50	A1	5c on 15c blue (C)	1.25 1.60
51	A1	5c on 20c red, *grn*	4.00 5.25
52	A1	5c on 30c brn, *bis* (C)	5.50 6.50
53	A1	10c on 40c red, *straw*	2.40 3.25
54	A1	10c on 75c dp vio, *org*	8.00 9.50
a.	Double surcharge, inverted		325.00

On Issue of 1904

55	A2	5c on 2c vio brn, *buff*	1.20 1.20
a.	Pair, one without surcharge		650.00
b.	Inverted surcharge		210.00
56	A2	5c on 4c car, *blue*	1.20 1.20
57	A2	5c on 15c violet, *rose*	1.20 1.20
58	A2	5c on 20c car, *grn*	1.60 1.20

FRENCH GUINEA

59	A2	5c on 25c blue (C)		1.60	2.00
60	A2	5c on 30c brown (C)		2.00	3.25
61	A2	10c on 40c red, *straw*		2.00	3.25
62	A2	10c on 50c brn, *az* (C)		5.50	6.50
	Nos. 48-62 (15)			40.30	49.90

Two spacings between the surcharged numerals are found on Nos. 48 to 62. For detailed listings, see the *Scott Classic Specialized Catalogue of Stamps and Covers*.

Ford at Kitim — A6

1913-33   Perf. 13½x14

63	A6	1c violet & bl	.25	.25
a.	Imperf.		72.50	
64	A6	2c brn & vio brn	.25	.25
a.	Double impression of vio brn		160.00	
65	A6	4c gray & black	.25	.25
66	A6	5c yel grn & bl grn	1.20	.40
a.	Booklet pane of 4		—	
	Complete booklet, 10 #66a	275.00		
67	A6	5c brn vio & grn ('22)	.40	.25
68	A6	10c red org & rose	1.20	.40
a.	Booklet pane of 4		—	
	Complete booklet, 10 #68a	550.00		
69	A6	10c yel grn & bl grn ('22)	.55	.25
70	A6	10c vio & ver ('25)	.80	.40
a.	Imperf.		45.00	
71	A6	15c vio brn & rose, *chalky paper* ('16)	.80	.40
a.	Booklet pane of 4		—	
	Complete booklet, 10 #71a	1,200.		
72	A6	15c gray grn & yel grn ('25)	.40	.40
73	A6	15c red brn & rose lil ('27)	.40	.30
74	A6	20c brn & vio	.40	.40
75	A6	20c grn & bl grn ('26)	.80	.80
76	A6	20c brn red & brn ('27)	.80	.50
77	A6	25c ultra & blue	2.75	1.60
78	A6	25c black & vio ('22)	.80	.80
79	A6	30c vio brn & grn	1.60	1.20
80	A6	30c red org & rose ('22)	1.20	1.10
81	A6	30c rose red & grn ('25)	.30	.30
82	A6	30c dl grn & bl grn ('28)	1.60	1.60
83	A6	35c blue & rose	.55	.55
84	A6	40c green & gray	1.20	1.20
85	A6	45c brown & red	1.20	1.20
86	A6	50c ultra & black	6.50	4.75
87	A6	50c ultra & bl ('22)	1.60	.80
88	A6	50c yel brn & ol ('25)	.80	.80
89	A6	60c vio, *pnksh* ('25)	.80	.80
90	A6	65c yel brn & sl bl ('26)	2.00	1.20
91	A6	75c red & ultra	1.60	1.60
92	A6	75c indigo & dl bl ('25)	.80	1.20
93	A6	75c mag & yel ('27)	1.60	1.20
94	A6	85c ol grn & red brn ('26)	1.20	1.20
95	A6	90c brn red & rose ('30)	5.50	4.75
96	A6	1fr violet & black	1.60	2.40
97	A6	1.10fr vio & ol brn ('28)	8.00	8.00
98	A6	1.25fr vio & yel brn ('33)	2.40	1.60
99	A6	1.50fr dk bl & lt bl ('30)	6.50	2.40
100	A6	1.75fr ol brn & vio ('33)	1.75	1.60
101	A6	2fr org & vio brn	4.00	4.00
102	A6	3fr red vio ('30)	8.00	5.50
103	A6	5fr black & vio	16.00	16.00
104	A6	5fr dl bl & blk ('27)	4.00	2.40
	Nos. 63-104 (42)		94.35	77.00

For surcharges see Nos. 105-115, B1.
Nos. 66, 68 and 77 pasted on colored cardboard and overprinted "VALEUR D'ECHANGE" were used as emergency currency in 1920.

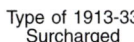

Type of 1913-33 Surcharged

1922

105	A6	60c on 75c violet, *pnksh*	.40	.40

Stamps and Type of 1913-33 Surcharged

1924-27

106	A6	25c on 2fr org & brn (R)	.40	.40
107	A6	25c on 5fr dull bl & blk	.40	.40
108	A6	65c on 75c rose & ultra ('25)	1.60	1.60
109	A6	85c on 75c rose & ultra ('25)	2.40	2.00
110	A6	90c on 75c brn red & cer ('27)	3.25	3.25
111	A6	1.25fr on 1fr dk bl & ultra ('26)	1.20	1.60
112	A6	1.50fr on 1fr dp bl & lt bl ('27)	2.40	2.40
113	A6	3fr on 5fr mag & sl ('27)	4.00	4.00
114	A6	10fr on 5fr bl & bl grn, *bluish* ('27)	8.00	8.00
115	A6	20fr on 5fr rose lil & brn ol, *pnksh* ('27)	20.00	20.00
	Nos. 106-115 (10)		43.65	43.65

Common Design Types pictured following the introduction.

Colonial Exposition Issue
Common Design Types
1931   Engr.   Perf. 12½
Name of Country in Black

116	CD70	40c deep green	4.75	4.75
a.	"GUINÉE FRANÇAISE" omitted		55.00	67.50
117	CD71	50c violet	4.75	4.75
118	CD72	90c red orange	4.75	4.75
a.	"GUINÉE FRANÇAISE" omitted		55.00	70.00
119	CD73	1.50fr dull blue	5.50	5.50
a.	"GUINÉE FRANÇAISE" omitted		55.00	67.50
	Nos. 116-119 (4)		19.75	19.75
	Set, never hinged	32.00		

Paris International Exposition Issue
Common Design Types
1937   Perf. 13

120	CD74	20c deep violet	2.00	2.00
121	CD75	30c dark green	2.00	2.00
122	CD76	40c car rose	2.40	2.40
123	CD77	50c dark brown	1.60	1.60
124	CD78	90c red	1.60	1.60
125	CD79	1.50fr ultra	2.40	2.40
	Nos. 120-125 (6)		12.00	12.00
	Set, never hinged	20.25		

Colonial Arts Exhibition Issue
Souvenir Sheet
Common Design Type

1937   Imperf.

126	CD76	3fr Prussian green	12.00	16.00
	Never hinged	16.00		

Guinea Village — A7

Hausa Basket Workers — A8

Forest Waterfall A9

Guinea Women A10

1938-40   Perf. 13

128	A7	2c vermilion	.25	.25
129	A7	3c ultra	.25	.25
130	A7	4c green	.25	.25
131	A7	5c rose car	.25	.25
132	A7	10c peacock blue	.25	.25
133	A7	15c violet brown	.25	.25
134	A8	20c dk carmine	.30	.25
135	A8	25c pck blue	.40	.25
136	A8	30c ultra	.40	.25
137	A8	35c green	.55	.50
138	A8	40c blk brn ('40)	.40	.40
139	A8	45c dk green ('40)	.40	.40
140	A8	50c red brown	.55	.50
141	A9	55c dk ultra	1.20	.80
142	A9	60c dk ultra ('40)	1.20	.80
143	A9	65c green	1.20	.80
144	A9	70c green ('40)	1.20	1.20
145	A9	80c rose violet	.80	.55
146	A9	90c rose vio ('39)	1.25	1.25
147	A9	1fr orange red	2.40	2.00
148	A9	1fr brn blk ('40)	.40	.40
149	A9	1.25fr org red ('39)	1.40	1.40
150	A9	1.40fr brown ('40)	1.20	1.20
151	A9	1.50fr violet	2.40	2.00
152	A10	1.60fr org red ('40)	1.60	1.60
153	A10	1.75fr ultra	.80	.80
154	A10	2fr magenta	1.20	.80
155	A10	2.25fr brt ultra ('30)	1.75	1.75
156	A10	2.50fr brn blk ('40)	1.60	1.60
157	A10	3fr peacock blue	.95	.40
158	A10	5fr rose violet	.95	.80
159	A10	10fr slate green	1.60	1.60
160	A10	20fr chocolate	2.40	2.40
	Nos. 128-160 (33)		32.00	28.60
	Set, never hinged	45.00		

For surcharges see Nos. B8-B11.

Caillié Issue
Common Design Type
1939   Engr.   Perf. 12½x12

161	CD81	90c org brn & org	.40	.80
162	CD81	2fr brt violet	.40	1.20
163	CD81	2.25fr ultra & dk bl	1.20	3.20
	Nos. 161-163 (3)		1.20	3.20
	Set, never hinged	2.40		

René Caillié, French explorer, death cent.

New York World's Fair Issue
Common Design Type
1939

164	CD82	1.25fr carmine lake	.80	1.60
165	CD82	2.25fr ultra	.80	1.60
	Set, never hinged	2.40		

Ford at Kitim and Marshal Petain — A11

1941   Perf. 12x12½

166	A11	1fr green	.40	—
167	A11	2.50fr deep blue	.40	—
	Set, never hinged	1.60		

For surcharges, see Nos. B15-B16.

Types of 1933-40 without "RF"
1943-44   Perf. 13

168	A7	10c peacock blue	.40	
169	A8	20c dk carmine	.40	
170	A8	30c ultramarine	.40	
171	A8	40c black brown	1.20	
172	A9	60c dk ultramarine	1.20	
173	A9	1.50fr violet	1.20	
174	A10	2fr magenta	1.60	
	Nos. 168-174 (7)		6.40	
	Set, never hinged	9.50		

Nos. 168-174 were issued by the Vichy government in France, but were not placed on sale in French Guinea.

SEMI-POSTAL STAMPS

Regular Issue of 1913 Surcharged in Red

1915   Unwmk.   Perf. 13½x14

B1	A6	10c + 5c org & rose	1.60	1.60

Curie Issue
Common Design Type
1938   Engr.   Perf. 13

B2	CD80	1.75fr + 50c brt ultra	8.75	8.75
	Never hinged		14.00	

French Revolution Issue
Common Design Type
1939   Photo.
Name and Value Typo. in Black

B3	CD83	45c + 25c green	9.50	9.50
B4	CD83	70c + 30c green	9.50	9.50
B5	CD83	90c + 35c red org	9.50	9.50
B6	CD83	1.25fr + 1fr rose pink	9.50	9.50
B7	CD83	2.25fr + 2fr blue	9.50	9.50
	Nos. B3-B7 (5)		47.50	47.50
	Set, never hinged	80.00		

Stamps of 1938, Surcharged in Black

1941   Unwmk.   Perf. 13

B8	A8	50c + 1fr red brn	4.00	4.00
B9	A9	80c + 2fr rose vio	8.00	8.00
B10	A9	1.50fr + 2fr brn	8.00	8.00
B11	A10	2fr + 3fr magenta	8.00	8.00
	Nos. B8-B11 (4)		28.00	28.00
	Set, never hinged	55.00		

Common Design Type and

Senegalese Soldier SP1   Colonial Infantryman SP2

1941   Unwmk.   Perf. 13

B12	SP1	1fr + 1fr red	1.25	
B13	SP2	1.50fr + 3fr maroon	1.40	
B14	SP2	2.50fr + 1fr blue	1.40	
	Nos. B12-B14 (3)		4.05	
	Set, never hinged	6.50		

Nos. B12-B14 were issued by the Vichy government in France, but were not placed on sale in the French Guinea.

Nos. 166-167 Surcharged in Black or Red

1944   Engr.   Perf. 12½x12

B15		50c + 1.50fr on 2.50fr deep blue (R)	.40	
B16		+ 2.50fr on 1fr green	.40	
	Set, never hinged	1.60		

Colonial Development Fund.
Nos. B15-B16 were issued by the Vichy government in France, but were not placed on sale in French Guinea.

FRENCH GUINEA — FRENCH INDIA

AIR POST STAMPS

Common Design Type
1940 Unwmk. Engr. Perf. 12½x12

C1	CD85	1.90fr ultra	.40	.40
C2	CD85	2.90fr dark red	.40	.40
C3	CD85	4.50fr dk gray grn	.80	.80
C4	CD85	4.90fr yellow bis	.80	.80
C5	CD85	6.90fr dp orange	1.60	1.60
	Nos. C1-C5 (5)		4.00	4.00
	Set, never hinged		6.00	

Common Design Types
1942 Engr.

C6	CD88	50c car & blue	.25
C7	CD88	1fr brown & blk	.30
C8	CD88	2fr dk grn & red brn	.30
C9	CD88	3fr dk bl & scar	.50
C10	CD88	5fr vio & brn red	.80

Frame Engraved, Center Typographed

C11	CD89	10fr multicolored	.80
C12	CD89	20fr multicolored	1.20
C13	CD89	50fr multicolored	1.60	—
	Nos. C6-C13 (8)		5.75
	Set, never hinged		12.00

There is doubt whether Nos. C6-C12 were officially placed in use.

AIR POST SEMI-POSTAL STAMPS

Dahomey types SPAP1-SPAP3 inscribed "Guinée Frcaise" or "Guinée"
Perf. 13½x12½, 13 (#CB3)
Photo, Engr. (#CB3)

1942, June 22

CB1	SPAP1	1.50fr + 3.50fr grn	.40 5.50
CB2	SPAP2	2fr + 6fr brown	.40 5.50
CB3	SPAP3	3fr + 9fr car red	.40 5.50
	Nos. CB1-CB3 (3)		1.20 16.50
	Set, never hinged		2.40

Native children's welfare fund.

Colonial Education Fund
Common Design Type
Perf. 12½x13½

1942, June 22 Engr.

CB4	CD86a	1.20fr + 1.80fr blue & red	.40 5.50
	Never hinged		.80

POSTAGE DUE STAMPS

Fulah Woman — D1

1905 Unwmk. Typo. Perf. 14x13½

J1	D1	5c blue	1.60	3.25
J2	D1	10c brown	2.40	3.25
J3	D1	15c green	8.00	6.50
J4	D1	30c rose	8.00	6.50
J5	D1	50c black	12.00	13.00
J6	D1	60c dull orange	12.00	16.00
J7	D1	1fr violet	40.00	47.50
	Nos. J1-J7 (7)		84.00	96.00

Heads and Coast — D2

1906-08

J8	D2	5c grn, *grnsh* ('08)	20.00	13.00
J9	D2	10c violet brn ('08)	8.00	5.50
J10	D2	15c dk blue ('08)	8.00	5.50
J11	D2	20c blk, *yellow*	8.00	5.50
J12	D2	30c red, *straw* ('08)	27.50	26.00
J13	D2	50c violet ('08)	24.00	26.00
J14	D2	60c blk, *buff* ('08)	24.00	21.00
J15	D2	1fr blk, *pnksh* ('08)	16.00	13.50
	Nos. J8-J15 (8)		135.50	116.00

D3

1914

J16	D3	5c green	.40	.55
J17	D3	10c rose	.40	.65
J18	D3	15c gray	.40	.80
J19	D3	20c brown	.80	.80
J20	D3	30c blue	.80	.80
J21	D3	50c black	1.00	1.25
J22	D3	60c orange	2.00	2.40
J23	D3	1fr violet	2.00	2.40
	Nos. J16-J23 (8)		7.80	9.65

Type of 1914 Issue Surcharged

1927

J24	D3	2fr on 1fr lil rose	8.00	8.00
a.		No period after "F"	27.50	32.50
J25	D3	3fr on 1fr org brn	8.00	8.00

D4

1938 Engr.

J26	D4	5c dk violet	.25	.30
J27	D4	10c carmine	.25	.30
J28	D4	15c green	.25	.30
J29	D4	20c red brown	.25	.40
J30	D4	30c rose violet	.25	.40
J31	D4	50c chocolate	.80	.70
J32	D4	60c peacock blue	.80	1.10
J33	D4	1fr vermilion	.80	1.10
J34	D4	2fr ultra	.80	1.10
J35	D4	3fr black	1.60	1.60
	Nos. J26-J35 (10)		6.05	7.30

For No. J27 without "RF," see No. J36.

Type of 1938 without "RF"
1944

J36	D4	10c carmine	.80
	Never hinged		1.20

No. J36 was issued by the Vichy government in France, but was not placed on sale in French Guinea.

FRENCH INDIA

'french 'in-dē-ə

LOCATION — East coast of India bordering on Bay of Bengal.
GOVT. — French Territory
AREA — 196 sq. mi.
POP. — 323,295 (1941)
CAPITAL — Pondichéry

French India was an administrative unit comprising the five settlements of Chandernagor, Karikal, Mahé, Pondichéry and Yanaon. These united with India in 1949 and 1954.

100 Centimes = 1 Franc
24 Caches = 1 Fanon (1923)
8 Fanons = 1 Rupie

Catalogue values for unused stamps in this country are for Never Hinged items, beginning with Scott 210 in the regular postage section, Scott B14 in the semi-postal section, and Scott C7 in the airpost section.

Navigation and Commerce — A1

Perf. 14x13½

1892-1907 Typo. Unwmk.
Colony Name in Blue or Carmine

1	A1	1c blk, *lil bl*	1.40	1.00
2	A1	2c brn, *buff*	2.40	1.50
3	A1	4c claret, *lav*	3.00	2.50
4	A1	5c grn, *grnsh*	6.00	3.75
5	A1	10c blk, *lavender*	13.50	2.75
6	A1	10c red ('00)	5.00	2.40
7	A1	15c blue, quadrille paper	16.00	5.50

8	A1	15c gray, *lt gray* ('00)	30.00	30.00
9	A1	20c red, *grn*	8.00	5.50
10	A1	25c blk, *rose*	5.25	2.75
11	A1	25c blue ('00)	19.00	16.00
12	A1	30c brn, *bis*	57.50	50.00
13	A1	35c blk, *yel* ('06)	19.00	9.00
14	A1	40c red, *straw*	7.50	7.25
15	A1	45c blk, *gray grn* ('07)	5.25	6.00
16	A1	50c car, *rose*	7.25	7.25
17	A1	50c brn, *az* ('00)	16.00	17.50
18	A1	75c dp vio, *org*	9.75	9.50
19	A1	1fr brnz grn, *straw*	14.00	14.50
	Nos. 1-19 (19)		245.80	194.65

Perf. 13½x14 stamps are counterfeits.

Nos. 10 and 16 Surcharged in Carmine or Black

1903

20	A1	5c on 25c blk, *rose*	400.00	240.00
21	A1	10c on 25c blk, *rose*	375.00	225.00
22	A1	15c on 25c blk, *rose*	125.00	115.00
23	A1	40c on 50c car, *rose* (Bk)	525.00	425.00
	Nos. 20-23 (4)		1,425.	1,005.

Counterfeits of Nos. 20-23 abound.

A2

Revenue Stamp Surcharged in Black

1903

24	A2	5c gray blue	30.00	30.00

The bottom of the revenue stamps were cut off.

Brahma A5

Kali Temple near Pondichéry A6

1914-22 Perf. 13½x14, 14x13½

25	A5	1c gray & blk	.30	.30
a.		1c light gray & black	.55	.55
26	A5	2c brn vio & blk	.30	.30
27	A5	2c grn & brn vio ('22)	.45	.45
28	A5	3c brown & blk	.40	.40
29	A5	4c orange & blk	.40	.40
30	A5	5c bl grn & blk	.70	.70
31	A5	5c brn & blk ('22)	.60	.60
32	A5	10c dp rose & blk	1.25	1.25
33	A5	10c grn & blk ('22)	.90	.90
34	A5	15c vio & blk	1.10	1.10
35	A5	20c org red & blk	2.00	2.00
36	A5	25c blue & blk	2.00	2.00
37	A5	25c ultra & fawn ('22)	1.60	1.60
38	A5	30c ultra & blk	4.00	4.00
39	A5	30c rose & blk ('22)	1.75	1.75
40	A6	35c choc & blk	2.25	2.25
41	A6	40c org red & blk	2.25	2.25
42	A6	45c bl grn & blk	2.25	2.25
43	A6	50c dp rose & blk	2.25	2.25
44	A6	50c ultra & bl ('22)	3.00	3.00
45	A6	75c blue & blk	4.50	4.50
46	A6	1fr yellow & blk	4.50	4.50
47	A6	2fr violet & blk	6.75	6.75
48	A6	5fr ultra & blk	3.50	3.50
49	A6	5fr rose & blk ('22)	5.50	5.50
	Nos. 25-49 (25)		54.50	54.50

For surcharges see Nos. 50-79, 113-116, 156A, B1-B5.

No. 34 Surcharged in Various Colors

1922

50	A5	1c on 15c (Bk)	.80	.80
51	A5	2c on 15c (Bl)	.80	.80
53	A5	5c on 15c (Bk)	.80	.80
	Nos. 50-53 (3)		2.40	2.40

Stamps and Types of 1914-22 Surcharged with New Values in Caches, Fanons and Rupies in Black, Red or Blue

No. 55

No. 69

No. 78

1923-28

54	A5	1ca on 1c gray & blk (R)	.30	.30
a.		Imperf.	50.00	50.00
55	A5	2ca on 5c vio brn & blk	.50	.50
a.		Horizontal pair, imperf. between	—	
b.		Imperf.	45.00	45.00
56	A5	3ca on 3c brn & blk	.55	.55
57	A5	4ca on 4c org & blk	.80	.80
58	A5	6ca on 10c grn & blk	.95	.95
a.		Double surcharge	175.00	
59	A6	6ca on 45c bl grn & blk (R)	.95	.95
60	A5	10ca on 20c dp red & bl grn ('28)	2.50	2.50
61	A5	12ca on 15c vio & blk	.95	.95
62	A5	15ca on 20c org & blk	1.50	1.50
63	A6	16ca on 35c lt bl & yel brn ('28)	2.60	2.60
64	A6	18ca on 30c rose & blk	2.40	2.40
65	A6	20ca on 45c grn & dl red ('28)	2.00	1.50
66	A5	1fa on 25c dp grn & rose red ('28)	3.50	3.50
67	A6	1fa3ca on 35c choc & blk (Bl)	1.10	1.10
68	A6	1fa6ca on 40c org & blk (R)	1.50	1.25
69	A6	1fa12ca on 50c ultra & bl (Bl)	1.75	1.50
70	A6	1fa12ca on 75c bl & blk (Bl)	1.25	1.25
a.		Double surcharge	145.00	
71	A6	1fa16ca on 75c brn red & grn ('28)	3.50	3.00
72	A5	2fa9ca on 25c ultra & fawn (Bl)	1.50	1.20
73	A6	2fa12ca on 1fr vio & dk brn ('28)	3.00	3.00
74	A6	3fa3ca on 1fr yel & blk (R)	1.75	1.45
a.		Double surcharge	145.00	
75	A6	6fa6ca on 2fr vio & blk	5.25	4.50
76	A6	1r on 1fr grn & dp bl (R) ('26)	9.50	7.75
77	A6	2r on 5fr rose & blk (R)	7.50	7.00
a.		Double surcharge	145.00	
78	A6	3r on 2fr gray & bl vio (R) ('26)	21.00	19.00
79	A6	5r on 5fr rose & blk, *grnsh* ('26)	27.50	24.00
	Nos. 54-79 (26)		105.60	95.00

Nos. 60, 63, 66 and 73 have the original value obliterated by bars.

A7

A8

1929

80	A7	1ca dk gray & blk	.25	.25
81	A7	2ca vio brn & blk	.25	.25
82	A7	3ca brn & blk	.25	.25
83	A7	4ca org & blk	.30	.30
84	A7	6ca gray grn & grn	.30	.30
85	A7	10ca brn, red & grn	.30	.30
86	A8	12ca grn & lt grn	.75	.70
87	A7	16ca brt bl & blk	.95	.95

FRENCH INDIA

88	A7	18ca brn red & ver	.95	.95
89	A7	20ca dk bl & grn, *bluish*	.75	.75
90	A8	1fa gray grn & rose red	.75	.75
91	A8	1fa6ca red org & blk	.75	.70
92	A8	1fa12ca dp bl & ultra	.75	.70
93	A8	1fa16ca rose red & grn	.95	.95
94	A8	2fa12ca brt vio & brn	1.20	1.00
95	A8	6fa6ca dl vio & blk	1.20	1.00
a.		Imperf.	50.00	
96	A8	1r gray grn & dp bl	1.10	1.00
97	A8	2r rose & blk	1.60	1.20
a.		Imperf.	50.00	
98	A8	3r lt gray & gray lil	3.00	2.25
99	A8	5r rose & blk, *grnsh*	3.00	2.40
		Nos. 80-99 (20)	19.35	16.90

For overprints and surcharges see Nos. 117-134, 157-176, 184-209G.

Common Design Types pictured following the introduction.

Colonial Exposition Issue
Common Design Types

1931			Perf. 12½	
100	CD70	10ca deep green	4.50	4.50
101	CD71	12ca violet	4.50	4.50
102	CD72	18ca red orange	4.50	4.50
103	CD73	1fa12ca dull blue	4.50	4.50
		Nos. 100-103 (4)	18.00	18.00

Paris International Exposition Issue
Common Design Types

1937			Perf. 13	
104	CD74	8ca dp violet	2.00	4.00
105	CD75	12ca dk green	2.25	4.00
106	CD76	16ca car rose	2.25	4.00
107	CD77	20ca dk brown	1.40	4.00
108	CD78	1fa12ca red	1.75	4.00
109	CD79	2fa12ca ultra	2.25	4.00
		Nos. 104-109 (6)	11.90	24.00

For overprints see Nos. 135-139, 177-181.

Colonial Arts Exhibition Issue
Souvenir Sheet
Common Design Type

1937			Imperf.	
110	CD79	5fa red violet	9.25	12.50

For overprint see No. 140.

New York World's Fair Issue
Common Design Types

1939		Engr.	Perf. 12½x12	
111	CD82	1fa12ca car lake	1.25	4.00
112	CD82	2fa12ca ultra	1.75	4.00

For overprints see Nos. 141-142, 182-183.

Temple near Pondichéry and Marshal Pétain — A9

1941		Engr.	Perf. 12½x12	
112A	A9	1fa16ca car & red	.80	
c.		Denomination omitted	55.00	
112B	A9	4fa4ca blue	.80	
d.		Denomination omitted	200.00	

Nos. 112A-112B were issued by the Vichy government in France, but were not placed on sale in French India.
For surcharges, see Nos. B13B-B13C.

Nos. 62, 64, 67, 72 Overprinted in Carmine or Blue (#116)

a   b

1941		Unwmk.	Perf. 13½x14	
113	A5 (a)	15ca on 20c	85.00	85.00
114	A5 (a)	18ca on 30c	16.00	16.00
115	A6 (a)	1fa3ca on 35c	130.00	130.00
a.		Horiz. overprint	125.00	125.00
116	A5 (b)	2fa9ca on 25c	1,600.	1,150.
a.		Overprint "a" (Bl)	1,400.	1,150.
b.		Overprint "b" (C)	2,100.	2,100.

Nos. 81-99 Overprinted Type "a" in Carmine or Blue

1941				
117	A7	2ca (C)	12.50	12.50
118	A7	3ca (C)	4.75	4.75
119	A7	4ca (C)	13.50	13.50
120	A7	6ca (C)	4.75	4.75
121	A7	10ca (Bl)	6.50	6.50
122	A8	12ca (C)	4.75	4.75
123	A8	16ca (C)	4.75	4.75
123A	A7	18ca (Bl)	675.00	675.00
124	A7	20ca (C)	4.75	4.75
125	A8	1fa (Bl)	4.75	4.75
126	A8	1fa6ca (C)	4.75	4.75
127	A8	1fa12ca (C)	6.50	6.50
128	A8	1fa16ca (C)	4.75	4.75
129	A8	2fa12ca (C)	4.75	4.75
130	A8	6fa6ca (C)	4.75	4.75
131	A8	1r (C)	4.75	4.75
132	A8	2r (C)	4.75	4.75
133	A8	3r (C)	6.50	6.50
134	A8	5r (C)	10.50	10.50
		Nos. 117-123, 124-134 (18)	113.00	113.00

Same Overprints on Paris Exposition Issue of 1937

1941			Perf. 13	
135	CD74 (b)	8ca (C)	10.00	10.00
135A	CD74 (b)	8ca (Bl)	275.00	275.00
d.		Blk. overprint	1,000.	1,000.
135B	CD74 (a)	8ca (C)	180.00	180.00
135C	CD74 (a)	8ca (Bl)	250.00	250.00
136	CD75 (a)	12ca (C)	6.00	6.00
137	CD76 (a)	16ca (Bl)	6.00	6.00
a.		Blk. overprint	175.00	175.00
138	CD78 (a)	1fa12ca (Bl)	6.00	6.00
139	CD79 (a)	2fa12ca (C)	6.00	6.00
		Nos. 135-139 (8)	739.00	739.00

Inverted overprints exist.

Souvenir Sheet
No. 110 Overprinted "FRANCE LIBRE" Diagonally in Blue Violet

Two types of overprint:
I — Overprint 37mm. With serifs.
II — Overprint 24mm, as type "a" shown above No. 113. No serifs.

1941		Unwmk.	Imperf.	
140	CD79	5fa red vio (I)	800.00	725.00
a.		Type II	1,000.	1,000.
b.		As No. 140, inverted surcharge	5,000.	2,000.

Overprinted on New York World's Fair Issue, 1939

			Perf. 12½x12	
141	CD82 (a)	1fa12ca (Bl)	4.75	4.75
142	CD82 (a)	2fa12ca (C)	5.50	5.50

Lotus Flowers — A10

1942	Unwmk.	Photo.	Perf. 14x14½	
143	A10	2ca brown	.30	.30
144	A10	3ca dk blue	.30	.30
145	A10	4ca emerald	.30	.30
146	A10	6ca dk orange	.30	.30
147	A10	12ca grnsh blk	.30	.30
148	A10	16ca rose violet	.30	.30
149	A10	20ca dk red brn	.65	.65
150	A10	1fa brt red	.70	.65
151	A10	1fa18ca slate blk	.90	.80
152	A10	6fa6ca brt ultra	1.60	1.50
153	A10	1r dull violet	1.40	1.40
154	A10	2r bister	1.75	1.60
155	A10	3r chocolate	1.75	1.60
156	A10	5r dk green	2.25	2.00
		Nos. 143-156 (14)	12.80	12.00

Stamps of 1923-39 Overprinted in Blue or Carmine

c   d

1942-43		Perf. 13½x14, 14x13½		
Overprinted on No. 64				
156A	A5 (c)	18ca on 30c (B)	300.00	230.00

Overprinted on #81-82, 84, 86-99

157	A7 (c)	2ca (C)	3.75	3.75
a.		"FRANCE LIBRE" in black	250.00	175.00
b.		As No. 157, blk. overprint	375.00	375.00
c.		As No. 157, bl. overprint	500.00	500.00
158	A7 (c)	3ca (C)	2.40	2.40
159	A7 (c)	6ca (Bl)	3.25	3.25
a.		Car. overprint	325.00	
b.		Blk. overprint	725.00	
c.		Bl.-Blk. overprint	50.00	35.00
160	A8 (d)	12ca (Bl)	3.75	3.75
161	A7 (c)	16ca (C)	3.25	3.25
162	A7 (c)	18ca (Bl)	2.40	2.40
163	A7 (c)	20ca (Bl)		
		('43)	7.25	5.50
164	A7 (c)	20ca (C)	2.40	2.40
a.		Double overprint, one bl. one car.	1,350.	475.00
165	A8 (d)	1fa (Bl)	2.40	2.40
166	A8 (d)	1fa6ca (C)	3.25	3.25
a.		Bl. overprint	300.00	225.00
167	A8 (d)	1fa12ca (C)	3.25	3.25
168	A8 (d)	1fa16ca (Bl)	3.25	3.25
169	A8 (d)	2fa12ca (Bl)	100.00	80.00
170	A8 (d)	2fa12ca (C)	3.25	3.25
171	A8 (d)	6fa6ca (C)	4.00	4.00
172	A8 (d)	1r (C)	7.25	7.25
173	A8 (d)	2r (C)	7.25	7.25
174	A8 (d)	3r (C)	7.25	7.25
175	A8 (d)	3r (Bl)		
		('43)	200.00	175.00
176	A8 (d)	5r (C)	7.25	7.25
		Nos. 156A-176 (21)	676.85	560.10

Same Overprints on Paris International Exposition Issue of 1937

			Perf. 13	
177	CD74 (c)	8ca (Bl)	7.25	7.25
178	CD75 (d)	12ca (Bl)	7.25	7.25
179	CD76 (d)	16ca (Bl)	1,300.	1,300.
180	CD78 (d)	1fa12ca (Bl)	7.25	7.25
181	CD79 (d)	2fa12ca (C)	7.25	7.25

Same Overprint on New York World's Fair Issue, 1939

			Perf. 12½x12	
182	CD82 (d)	1fa12ca (Bl)	7.25	7.25
183	CD82 (d)	2fa12ca (C)	7.25	7.25

No. 87 Surcharged in Carmine

1942-43			Perf. 13½x14	
184	A7	1ca on 16ca	75.00	45.00
185	A7	4ca on 16ca ('43)	75.00	45.00
186	A7	10ca on 16ca	55.00	35.00
187	A7	15ca on 16ca	55.00	35.00
188	A7	1fa3ca on 16ca ('43)	72.50	45.00
189	A7	2fa9ca on 16ca ('43)	72.50	45.00
190	A7	3fa3ca on 16ca ('43)	55.00	35.00
		Nos. 184-190 (7)	460.00	285.00

Nos. 95-99 Srchd. in Carmine

1943			Perf. 14x13½	
191	A8	1ca on 6fa6ca	11.00	11.00
192	A8	4ca on 6fa6ca	12.50	12.50
193	A8	10ca on 6fa6ca	11.00	11.00
194	A8	15ca on 6fa6ca	11.00	11.00
195	A8	1fa3ca on 6fa6ca	11.00	11.00
196	A8	2fa9ca on 6fa6ca	12.50	12.50
197	A8	3fa3ca on 6fa6ca	12.50	12.50
198	A8	1ca on 1r	4.75	4.75
199	A8	2ca on 1r	1.60	1.60
200	A8	4ca on 1r	1.60	1.60
201	A8	6ca on 2r	1.60	1.60
202	A8	10ca on 2r	1.75	1.75
203	A8	12ca on 2r	1.60	1.60
204	A8	15ca on 3r	1.60	1.60
205	A8	16ca on 3r	1.60	1.60
206	A8	1fa3ca on 3r	1.60	1.60
207	A8	1fa6ca on 5r	2.00	2.00
208	A8	1fa12ca on 5r	2.40	2.40
209	A8	1fa16ca on 5r	2.40	2.40
		Nos. 191-209 (19)	106.00	106.00

In 1943, 200 each of 27 stamps were overprinted in red or dark blue, "FRANCE TOUJOURS" and a Lorraine Cross within a circle measuring 17½mm in diameter. Overprinted were Nos. 81-99, 104-109, 111-112. Values, set: $25,000 unused; $6,000 used.

No. 95 Surcharged in Carmine

1943		Unwmk.	Perf. 14x13½	
209A	A8	1ca on 6fa6ca	35.00	27.50
209B	A8	4ca on 6fa6ca	35.00	27.50
209C	A8	10ca on 6fa6ca	24.00	16.00
209D	A8	15ca on 6fa6ca	24.00	16.00
209E	A8	1fa3ca on 6fa6ca	32.50	27.50
209F	A8	2fa9ca on 6fa6ca	32.50	27.50
209G	A8	3fa3ca on 6fa6ca	35.00	27.50
		Nos. 209A-209G (7)	218.00	169.50

Catalogue values for unused stamps in this section, from this point to the end of the section, are for Never Hinged items.

Eboué Issue
Common Design Type

1945		Engr.	Perf. 13	
210	CD91	3fa8ca black	.80	.70
211	CD91	5r1fa16ca Prus grn	1.40	1.25

Nos. 210 and 211 exist imperforate.

Apsaras — A11

Designs: 6ca, 8ca, 10ca, Dvarabalagar. 12ca, 15ca, 1fa, Vishnu. 1fa6ca, 2fa, 2fa2ca, Dvarabalagar (foot raised). 2fa12ca, 3fa, 5fa, Temple Guardian. 7fa12ca, 1r2fa, 1r4fa12ca, Tigoupalagar.

1948		Photo.	Perf. 13x13½	
212	A11	1ca dk ol grn	.50	.25
213	A11	2ca orange brn	.50	.25
214	A11	4ca vio, *cr*	.55	.30
215	A11	6ca yellow org	1.50	.65
216	A11	8ca gray blk	1.50	1.10
217	A11	10ca dl yel grn, *pale grn*	1.50	1.10
218	A11	12ca violet brn	1.00	.65
219	A11	15ca Prus grn	1.00	.65
220	A11	1fa vio, *pale rose*	1.50	.80
221	A11	1fa6ca brown red	1.50	.85
222	A11	2fa dk green	1.50	.85
223	A11	2fa2ca blue, *cr*	1.50	1.15
224	A11	2fa12ca brown	1.90	1.15
225	A11	3fa dp orange	3.25	1.25
226	A11	5fa red vio, *rose*	3.00	1.25
227	A11	7fa12ca dk brown	3.25	1.25
228	A11	1r2fa brown blk	6.00	4.50
229	A11	1r4fa12ca olive grn	6.50	5.00
		Nos. 212-229 (18)	37.95	23.00

Brahman Ascetic — A12

1952				
230	A12	18ca rose red	2.75	2.00
231	A12	1fa15ca vio blue	3.75	2.50
232	A12	4fa olive grn	4.25	3.50
		Nos. 230-232 (3)	10.75	8.00

Military Medal Issue
Common Design Type

1952	Engr. and Typo.		Perf. 13	
233	CD101	1fa multi	5.50	7.00

SEMI-POSTAL STAMPS

Regular Issue of 1914 Surcharged in Red

FRENCH INDIA

Two printings: 1st, surcharge at bottom of stamp; 2nd, surcharge centered toward top.

1915   **Unwmk.**   **Perf. 14x13½**
B1   A5   10c + 5c rose & blk
         (1st)   2.10   2.10
   b.   Inverted surcharge   210.00   210.00

There were two printings of this surcharge. In the first, it was placed at the bottom of the stamp; in the second, it was centered toward the top.

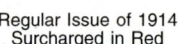

Regular Issue of 1914 Surcharged in Red

1916
B2   A5   10c + 5c rose & blk   21.00   21.00
   a.   Inverted surcharge   210.00   210.00
   b.   Double surcharge   210.00   210.00

No. 32 Surcharged

B3   A5   10c + 5c rose & blk   3.50   3.50

No. 32 Surcharged

B4   A5   10c + 5c rose & blk   1.60   1.60

No. 32 Surcharged

B5   A5   10c + 5c rose & blk   2.25   2.25

Curie Issue
Common Design Type
1938   **Engr.**   **Perf. 13**
B6   CD80   2fa12ca + 20ca brt ultra   10.00   10.00

French Revolution Issue
Common Design Type
1939   **Photo.**
Name and Value Typo. in Black
B7   CD83   18ca + 10ca grn   5.75   6.50
B8   CD83   1fa6ca + 12ca brn   5.75   6.50
B9   CD83   1fa12ca + 16ca red org   5.75   6.50
B10   CD83   1fa16ca + 1fa16ca rose pink   5.75   6.50
B11   CD83   2fa12ca + 3fa blue   5.75   6.50
    Nos. B7-B11 (5)   28.75   32.50

Common Design Type and

Non-Commissioned Officer, Native Guard — SP1

Sepoy — SP2

1941   **Photo.**   **Perf. 13½**
B12   SP1   1fa16ca + 1fa16ca red   1.25
B13   CD86   2fa12ca + 5fa mar   1.25
B13A   SP2   4fa4ca + 1fa16ca bl   1.25
    Nos. B12-B13A (3)   3.75

Nos. B12-B13A were issued by the Vichy government in France, but were not placed on sale in French India.

Nos. 112A-112B Srchd. in Black or Red

1944   **Engr.**   **Perf. 12½x12**
B13B   20ca + 2fa12ca on 4fa4ca deep blue (R)   1.00
B13C   + 4fa4ca on 1fa16ca car & red   1.00

Colonial Development Fund.
Nos. B13B-B13C were issued by the Vichy government in France, but were not placed on sale in French India.

Catalogue values for unused stamps in this section, from this point to the end of the section, are for Never Hinged items.

Red Cross Issue
Common Design Type
1944   **Photo.**   **Perf. 14½x14**
B14   CD90   3fa + 1r4fa dk ol brn   1.50   1.25

The surtax was for the French Red Cross and national relief.

Tropical Medicine Issue
Common Design Type
1950   **Engr.**   **Perf. 13**
B15   CD100   1fa + 10ca ind & dp bl   6.00   4.00

The surtax was for charitable work.

AIR POST STAMPS

Common Design Type
1942   **Unwmk.**   **Photo.**   **Perf. 14½x14**
C1   CD87   4fa dark orange   .90   2.00
C2   CD87   1r bright red   .90   2.00
C3   CD87   2r brown red   1.50   2.00
C4   CD87   5r black   1.50   3.00
C5   CD87   8r ultra   2.25   3.00
C6   CD87   10r dark green   2.25   3.00
    Nos. C1-C6 (6)   9.30   15.00

Catalogue values for unused stamps in this section, from this point to the end of the section, are for Never Hinged items.

Victory Issue
Common Design Type
1946   **Engr.**   **Perf. 12½**
C7   CD92   4fa dk blue green   1.00   4.00

Chad to Rhine Issue
Common Design Types
1946, June 6
C8   CD93   2fa12ca olive bis   1.40   2.00
C9   CD94   5fa dark blue   1.40   2.00
C10   CD95   7fa12ca dk purple   2.25   2.00
C11   CD96   1r2fa green   2.25   3.00
C12   CD97   1r4fa12ca dk car   2.75   3.00
C13   CD98   3r1fa violet brn   2.75   3.00
    Nos. C8-C13 (6)   12.80   15.00

A 3r ultramarine and red, picturing the Temple of Chindambaram, was sold at Paris June 7 to July 8, 1948, but not placed on sale in the colony. Values: $10 never hinged, $7 hinged.

Bas-relief Figure of Goddess AP1

Wing and Temple — AP2

Bird over Palms — AP3

Perf. 12x13, 13x12
1949   **Photo.**   **Unwmk.**
C14   AP1   1r yellow & plum   6.00   10.00
C15   AP2   2r green & dk grn   6.00   10.00
C16   AP3   5r lt bl & vio brn   27.50   30.00
    Nos. C14-C16 (3)   39.50   50.00

UPU Issue
Common Design Type
1949   **Engr.**   **Perf. 13**
C17   CD99   6fa lilac rose   11.50   8.75

Universal Postal Union, 75th anniv.

Liberation Issue
Common Design Type
1954, June 6
C18   CD102   1fa sepia & vio brn   11.00   8.00

AIR POST SEMI-POSTAL STAMPS

Girl's School — SPAP1

Perf. 12½x13½
1942, June 22   **Unwmk.**   **Photo.**
CB1   SPAP1   2fa12ca + 5fa20ca green   .95
CB2   SPAP1   3fa8ca + 1r2fa yel brn   .95

Native children's welfare fund.
Nos. CB1-CB2 were issued by the Vichy government in France, but were not placed on sale in French India.

Colonial Education Fund
Common Design Type
1942, June 22
CB3   CD86a   2fa + 3fa blue & red   .90

No. CB3 was issued by the Vichy government in France, but was not placed on sale in French India.

POSTAGE DUE STAMPS

Postage Due Stamps of France Surcharged like Nos. 54-75 in Black, Blue or Red
1923   **Unwmk.**   **Perf. 14x13½**
J1   D2   6ca on 10c brn   1.25   1.25
J2   D2   12ca on 25c rose (Bk)   1.25   1.25
J3   D2   15ca on 20c ol grn (R)   1.60   1.60
J4   D2   1fa6ca on 30c red   1.60   1.60
J5   D2   1fa12a on 50c brn vio   2.75   2.75
J6   D2   1fa15ca on 5c bl (Bk)   3.00   3.00
J7   D2   3fa3ca on 1fr red brn, straw   3.25   3.25
    Nos. J1-J7 (7)   14.70   14.70

Types of Postage Due Stamps of French Colonies, 1884-85, Surcharged with New Values as in 1923 in Red or Black Bars over Original Values
1928
J8   D1   4ca on 20c gray lil   1.60   1.60
J9   D1   1fa on 30c orange   3.25   3.25
J10   D1   1fa16ca on 5c bl blk (R)   3.25   3.25
J11   D1   3fa on 1fr lt grn   3.75   3.75
    Nos. J8-J11 (4)   11.85   11.85

D3

1929   **Typo.**
J12   D3   4ca deep red   .50   .50
J13   D3   6ca blue   .65   .65
J14   D3   12ca green   .65   .65
J15   D3   1fa brown   1.25   1.25
J16   D3   1fa12ca lilac gray   1.25   1.25
J17   D3   1fa16ca buff   1.75   1.75
J18   D3   3fa lilac   2.10   2.10
    Nos. J12-J18 (7)   8.15   8.15

D4

1948   **Unwmk.**   **Photo.**   **Perf. 13x13½**
J19   D4   1ca dk violet   .30   .30
J20   D4   2ca dk brown   .50   .50
J21   D4   6ca blue green   .50   .50
J22   D4   12ca dp orange   .70   .70
J23   D4   1fa dk car rose   .80   .80
J24   D4   1fa12ca brown   .80   .80
J25   D4   2fa dk slate bl   1.25   1.25
J26   D4   2fa12ca henna brn   1.60   1.60
J27   D4   5fa dk olive grn   2.25   2.25
J28   D4   1r dk blue vio   3.00   3.00
    Nos. J19-J28 (10)   11.70   11.70

FRENCH MOROCCO

'french mə-'rä-ₔkō

LOCATION — Northwest coast of Africa
GOVT. — French Protectorate
AREA — 153,870 sq. mi.
POP. — 8,340,000 (estimated 1954)
CAPITAL — Rabat

French Morocco was a French Protectorate from 1912 until 1956 when it, along with the Spanish and Tangier zones of Morocco, became the independent country, Morocco.

Stamps inscribed "Tanger" were for use in the international zone of Tangier in northern Morocco.

100 Centimos = 1 Peseta
100 Centimes = 1 franc (1917)

Catalogue values for unused stamps in this country are for Never Hinged items, beginning with Scott 177 in the regular postage section, Scott B26 in the semi-postal section, Scott C27 in the airpost section, Scott CB23A in the airpost semi-postal section, and Scott J46 in the postage due section.

French Offices in Morocco

Stamps of France
Surcharged in Red or Black

Type I. The "N" of "INV" is under the "B" of "REPUBLIQUE".
Type II. The "N" of "INV" is under the "U" of "REPUBLIQUE".

		1891-1900	Unwmk.	Perf. 14x13½	
1	A15	5c on 5c grn, grnsh (R)		16.00	4.00
a.		Imperf., pair		175.00	
2	A15	5c on 5c yel grn (II) (R) ('99)		32.50	27.50
a.		Type I		32.50	27.50
3	A15	10c on 10c blk, lav (II) (R)		32.50	4.00
a.		Type I		45.00	20.00
b.		10c on 25c black, rose		1,400.	1,500.
4	A15	20c on 20c red, grn		40.00	32.50
5	A15	25c on 25c blk, rose (R)		32.50	4.00
a.		Double surcharge		225.00	
b.		Imperf., pair		175.00	
6	A15	50c on 50c car, rose (II)		105.00	47.50
a.		Type I		375.00	260.00
7	A15	1p on 1fr brnz grn, straw		120.00	80.00
8	A15	2p on 2fr brn, az (Bk) ('00)		240.00	240.00
		Nos. 1-8 (8)		618.50	439.50

No. 3b was never sent to Morocco.

France Nos. J15-J16
Overprinted in Carmine

1893
9	D2	5c black	3,250.	1,300.
10	D2	10c black	2,900.	900.

Counterfeits exist.

Surcharged in Red or Black

A3   A4

A5

1902-10
11	A3	1c on 1c gray (R) ('08)	2.40	1.20
12	A3	2c on 2c vio brn ('08)	2.40	1.20
13	A3	3c on 3c red org ('08)	3.25	1.60
14	A3	4c on 4c yel brn ('08)	13.00	8.00
15	A3	5c on 5c grn (R)	12.00	4.00
a.		Double surcharge	340.00	340.00
b.		Triple surcharge	340.00	
16	A4	10c on 10c rose red ('03)	8.00	4.00
a.		Surcharge omitted	225.00	
17	A4	20c on 20c brn vio ('03)	40.00	24.00
18	A4	25c on 25c bl ('03)	40.00	4.00
19	A4	35c on 35c vio ('10)	40.00	24.00
20	A5	50c on 50c bis brn & lav	67.50	16.00
21	A5	1p on 1fr cl & ol grn ('03)	120.00	80.00
22	A5	2p on 2fr gray vio & yel ('03)	160.00	120.00
		Nos. 11-22 (12)	508.55	288.00

Nos. 11-14 exist spelled CFNTIMOS or GENTIMOS.
The 25c on 25c with surcharge omitted is listed as No. 81a.
For overprints and surcharges see Nos. 26-37, 72-79, B1, B3.

Postage Due Stamps Nos.
J1-J2 Handstamped

1903
24	D2	5c on 5c light blue	1,500.	1,400.
25	D2	10c on 10c chocolate	2,800.	2,600.

Nos. 24 and 25 were used only on Oct. 10, 1903. Used stamps were not canceled, the overprint serving as a cancellation. Numerous counterfeits exist.

Types of 1902-10 Issue
Surcharged in Red or Blue

1911-17
26	A3	1c on 1c gray (R)	1.20	.90
27	A3	2c on 2c vio brn	1.20	1.20
28	A3	3c on 3c orange	1.20	1.20
29	A3	5c on 5c green (R)	1.20	.80
30	A4	10c on 10c rose	1.20	.80
a.		Imperf., pair	275.00	
31	A4	15c on 15c org ('17)	3.50	2.40
32	A4	20c on 20c brn vio	5.50	4.00
33	A4	25c on 25c blue (R)	2.40	1.60
34	A4	35c on 35c violet (R)	12.00	5.50
35	A5	40c on 40c red & pale bl ('17)	8.00	5.50
36	A5	50c on 50c bis brn & lav (R)	27.50	16.00
37	A5	1p on 1fr cl & ol grn	24.00	12.00
		Nos. 26-37 (12)	88.90	51.90

For surcharges see Nos. B1, B3.

Stamps of this design were issued by the Cherifien posts in 1912-13. The Administration Cherifinne des Postes Telegraphes et Telephones was formed in 1911 under French guidance. See Morocco in *Scott Classic Specialized Catalogue of Stamps & Covers* for listings.

French Protectorate
Issue of 1911-17 Overprinted
"Protectorat Francais"

A6   A7

A8

1914-21
38	A6	1c on 1c lt gray	.40	.50
a.		1c dk gray ('22)	.55	.80
39	A6	2c on 2c vio brn	.80	.50
40	A6	3c on 3c orange	1.20	.65
41	A6	5c on 5c green	1.20	.50
a.		New value omitted	275.00	275.00
42	A7	10c on 10c rose	.80	.30
a.		New value omitted	550.00	550.00
43	A7	15c on 15c org ('17)	.80	.80
a.		New value omitted	120.00	120.00
44	A7	20c on 20c brn vio	4.75	3.50
a.		"Protectorat Francais" double	300.00	300.00
45	A7	25c on 25c blue	3.25	.80
a.		New value omitted	350.00	350.00
46	A7	25c on 25c violet ('21)	1.25	.40
a.		"Protectorat Francais" omitted	80.00	80.00
b.		"Protectorat Francais" double	175.00	175.00
c.		"Protectorat Francais" dbl. (R + Bk)	175.00	175.00
47	A7	30c on 30c vio ('21)	20.00	9.00
48	A7	35c on 35c violet	4.75	1.60
49	A8	40c on 40c red & pale bl	20.00	8.75
a.		New value omitted	375.00	375.00
50	A8	45c on 45c grn & bl ('21)	55.00	40.00
51	A8	50c on 50c bis brn & lav	2.40	.80
a.		"Protectorat Francais" invtd.	200.00	200.00
b.		"Protectorat Francais" double	450.00	450.00
52	A8	1p on 1fr cl & ol grn	5.50	.80
a.		"Protectorat Francais" invtd.	350.00	350.00
b.		New value omitted	200.00	200.00
c.		New value dbl., one invtd.	210.00	210.00
53	A8	2p on 2fr gray vio & yel	8.00	4.00
a.		New value omitted	175.00	175.00
b.		"Protectorat Francais" omitted	110.00	110.00
c.		New value double	225.00	
d.		New value dbl., one invtd.	225.00	
54	A8	5p on 5fr dk bl & buff	15.00	8.00
		Nos. 38-54 (17)	145.10	60.90

For surcharges see Nos. B2, B4-B5.

Tower of Hassan,
Rabat — A9

Mosque of the Andalusians,
Fez — A10

City Gate Chella
A11

Koutoubiah, Marrakesh
A12

Bab Mansour,
Meknes — A13

Roman Ruins,
Volubilis — A14

1917   Engr.   Perf. 13½x14, 14x13½
55	A9	1c grnsh gray	.40	.40
56	A9	2c brown lilac	.40	.40
57	A9	3c orange brn	.80	.80
a.		Imperf., pair	87.50	
58	A10	5c yellow grn	.40	.40
59	A10	10c rose red	.80	.40
60	A10	15c dark gray	.80	.40
a.		Imperf., pair	65.00	
61	A11	20c red brown	4.00	2.40
62	A11	25c dull blue	4.00	1.25
63	A11	30c gray violet	4.75	3.25
64	A12	35c orange	4.75	4.00
65	A12	40c ultra	1.60	1.60
66	A12	45c gray green	32.50	16.00
67	A13	50c dk brown	5.50	4.00
a.		Imperf., pair	65.00	
68	A13	1fr slate	16.00	4.00
a.		Imperf., pair	65.00	
69	A14	2fr black brown	160.00	95.00
70	A14	5fr dk gray grn	47.50	40.00
71	A14	10fr black	47.50	40.00
		Nos. 55-71 (17)	331.30	214.30

See note following No. 115. See Nos. 93-105. For surcharges see Nos. 120-121.

Types of the 1902-10 Issue
Overprinted

1918-24   Perf. 14x13½
72	A3	1c dk gray	.40	.80
73	A3	2c violet brn	.40	.80
74	A3	3c red orange	1.20	1.20
75	A3	5c green	1.20	1.20
76	A3	5c orange ('23)	2.40	2.00
77	A4	10c rose	2.40	1.60
78	A4	10c green ('24)	2.40	1.60
79	A4	15c orange	1.60	1.20
80	A4	20c violet brn	2.40	2.40
81	A4	25c blue	2.40	2.40
a.		"TANGER" omitted	600.00	600.00
82	A4	30c red org ('24)	4.00	2.75
83	A4	35c violet	4.00	2.40
84	A5	40c red & pale bl	4.00	2.40
85	A5	50c bis brn & lav	27.50	16.00
86	A4	50c blue ('24)	24.00	13.50
87	A5	1fr claret & ol grn	16.00	8.00
88	A5	2fr org & pale bl ('24)	80.00	72.50
89	A5	5fr dk bl & buff ('24)	67.50	65.00
		Nos. 72-89 (18)	243.80	197.75

Types of 1917 and

Tower of Hassan, Rabat
A15

Bab Mansour, Meknes
A16

Roman Ruins, Volubilis — A17

1923-27   Photo.   Perf. 13½
90	A15	1c olive green	.25	.25
91	A15	2c brown vio	.25	.25
92	A15	3c yellow brn	.25	.25
93	A10	5c orange	.25	.25
94	A10	10c yellow grn	.25	.25
95	A10	15c dk gray	.25	.25
96	A11	20c red brown	.25	.25
97	A11	20c red vio ('27)	.40	.40
98	A11	25c ultra	.40	.40
99	A11	30c deep red	.40	.40
100	A11	30c turq bl ('27)	1.20	.80
101	A12	35c violet	1.20	.80
102	A12	40c orange red	.25	.25
103	A12	45c deep green	.40	.40
104	A12	50c dull turq	.40	.40
105	A12	50c ol grn ('27)	.40	.40
106	A16	60c lilac	1.20	.80
107	A16	75c red vio ('27)	.80	.40
108	A16	1fr deep brown	.80	.40
109	A16	1.05fr red brn ('27)	1.60	.80
110	A16	1.40fr dull rose ('27)	.80	.80
111	A16	1.50fr red bl ('27)	1.20	.40
112	A17	2fr olive brn	1.60	1.20
113	A17	3fr dp red ('27)	1.60	1.20
114	A17	5fr dk gray grn	4.00	2.75
115	A17	10fr black	12.00	4.75
		Nos. 90-115 (26)	32.80	19.90

Nos. 90-110, 112-115 exist imperf. The stamps of 1917 were line engraved. Those of 1923-27 were printed by photogravure and have in the margin at lower right the imprint "Helio Vaugirard."

See No. B36. For surcharges see Nos. 122-123.

FRENCH MOROCCO

No. 102 Surcharged in Black

1930
120	A12	15c on 40c org red	1.60	1.60
a.		Surcharge bars omitted	72.50	72.50
b.		Pair, one with surcharge omitted	350.00	

Nos. 100, 106 and 110 Surcharged in Blue Similarly to No. 176

1931
121	A11	25c on 30c turq blue	2.50	2.10
a.		Inverted surcharge	140.00	140.00
122	A16	50c on 60c lilac	1.20	.40
a.		Inverted surcharge	150.00	150.00
b.		Double surcharge	150.00	150.00
c.		Surcharge bars omitted	90.00	
123	A16	1fr on 1.40fr rose	3.25	1.60
a.		Inverted surcharge	150.00	150.00
b.		Surcharge bars omitted	90.00	
		Nos. 121-123 (3)	6.95	4.10

Old Treasure House and Tribunal, Tangier — A18

Roadstead at Agadir — A19

Post Office at Casablanca A20

Moulay Idriss of the Zehroun — A21

Kasbah of the Oudayas, Rabat — A22

Court of the Medersa el Attarine at Fez — A23

Kasbah of Si Madani el Glaoui at Ouarzazat A24

Saadiens' Tombs at Marrakesh A25

1933-34 Engr. Perf. 13
124	A18	1c olive blk	.25	.25
125	A18	2c red violet	.25	.25
126	A19	3c dark brown	.25	.25
127	A19	5c brown red	.25	.25
128	A20	10c blue green	.30	.30
129	A20	15c black	.40	.30
130	A20	20c red brown	.40	.30
131	A21	25c dark blue	.40	.30
132	A21	30c emerald	.40	.30
133	A21	40c black brn	.40	.30
134	A22	45c brown vio	.80	.65
135	A22	50c dk blue grn	.80	.30
a.		Booklet pane of 10	—	
b.		Booklet pane of 20	—	
		Complete booklet, #135b	2,000.	
136	A22	65c brown red	.40	.30
a.		Booklet pane of 10	—	
b.		Booklet pane of 20	65.00	
137	A23	75c red violet	.80	.30
138	A23	90c orange red	.40	.30
139	A23	1fr deep brown	1.20	.50
140	A23	1.25fr black ('34)	1.60	1.50
141	A24	1.50fr ultra	.40	.30
142	A24	1.75fr myr grn ('34)	.80	.40
143	A24	2fr yellow brn	4.75	.80
144	A24	3fr car rose	55.00	6.50
145	A25	5fr red brown	12.00	2.50
146	A25	10fr black	10.00	6.50
147	A25	20fr bluish gray	9.50	7.25
		Nos. 124-147 (24)	101.75	30.90

Booklets containing Nos. 135 and 136 each have two panes of 10 (Nos. 135a, 136a) connected by a gutter, the complete piece constituting No. 135b or 136b, which is stapled into the booklet through the gutter.
For surcharges see Nos. 148, 176, B13-B20.

No. 135 Srchd. in Red

1939
| 148 | A22 | 40c on 50c dk bl grn | .95 | .50 |

Mosque of Salé A26

Sefrou A27

Cedars A28

Goatherd A29

Ramparts of Salé — A30

Scimitar-horned Oryxes — A31

Valley of Draa — A32

Fez — A33

1939-42
149	A26	1c rose violet	.25	.25
150	A27	2c emerald	.25	.25
151	A27	3c ultra	.25	.25
152	A26	5c dk bl grn	.25	.25
153	A27	10c brt red vio	.25	.25
154	A28	15c dk green	.25	.25
155	A28	20c black grn	.25	.25
156	A29	30c deep blue	.25	.25
157	A29	40c chocolate	.25	.25
158	A29	45c Prus green	.50	.50
159	A30	50c rose red	1.40	.90
159A	A30	50c Prus grn ('40)	.30	.25
160	A30	60c turq blue	1.25	.75
160A	A30	60c choc ('40)	.30	.25
161	A31	70c dk violet	.25	.25
162	A32	75c grnsh blk	.50	.50
163	A32	80c pck bl ('40)	.30	.25
163A	A32	80c dk grn ('42)	.40	.25
164	A30	90c ultra	.25	.25
165	A28	1fr chocolate	.30	.25
165A	A32	1.20fr rose vio ('42)	.80	.40
166	A32	1.25fr henna brn	1.10	.65
167	A32	1.40fr rose violet	.65	.30
168	A30	1.50fr cop red ('40)	.30	.25
168A	A30	1.50fr rose ('42)	.25	.25
169	A33	2fr Prus green	.25	.25
170	A33	2.25fr dark blue	.65	.50
170A	A26	2.40fr red ('42)	.30	.30
171	A26	2.50fr scarlet	.90	.70
171A	A26	2.50fr dp blue ('40)	1.10	.65
172	A33	3fr black brown	.50	.30
172A	A26	4fr dp ultra ('42)	.40	.40
172B	A32	4.50fr grnsh blk ('42)	.80	.80
173	A31	5fr dark blue	.65	.50
174	A31	10fr red	1.25	.90
174A	A31	15fr Prus grn ('42)	4.75	4.00
175	A31	20fr dk vio brn	2.00	1.75
		Nos. 149-175 (37)	24.70	19.55
		Set, never hinged	32.50	

See Nos. 197-219. For surcharges see Nos. 244, 261-262, B21-B24, B26, B28, B32.

No. 136 Srchd. in Black

1940
176	A22	35c on 65c brown red	1.75	.95
a.		Pair, one without surcharge	3.25	2.40

The surcharge was applied on alternate rows in the sheet, making No. 176a. This was done to make a pair equal 1fr, the new rate.

Catalogue values for unused stamps in this section, from this point to the end of the section, are for Never Hinged items.

One Aim Alone-Victory — A34

1943 Litho. Perf. 12
| 177 | A34 | 1.50fr deep blue | .40 | .25 |

Tower of Hassan, Rabat — A35

1943
178	A35	10c rose lilac	.30	.25
179	A35	30c blue	.30	.25
180	A35	40c lake	.30	.25
181	A35	50c blue green	.30	.25
182	A35	60c dk vio brn	.30	.25
183	A35	70c rose violet	.30	.25
184	A35	80c gray green	.30	.30
185	A35	1fr car lake	.30	.25
186	A35	1.20fr violet	.30	.25
187	A35	1.50fr red	.30	.25
188	A35	2fr lt bl grn	.30	.25
189	A35	2.40fr car rose	.30	.35
190	A35	3fr olive brn	.30	.25
191	A35	4fr dk ultra	.30	.30
192	A35	4.50fr slate blk	.40	.25
193	A35	5fr dull blue	.55	.25
194	A35	10fr orange brn	.55	.40
195	A35	15fr slate grn	1.60	.55
196	A35	20fr deep plum	2.40	.90
		Nos. 178-196 (19)	9.70	6.00

Types of 1939-42
Perf. 13½x14, 14x13½
1945-47 Typo. Unwmk.
197	A27	10c red violet	.40	.25
199	A29	40c chocolate	.40	.25
200	A30	50c Prus grn	.40	.25
203	A28	1fr choc ('46)	.40	.35
204	A32	1.20fr vio brn ('46)	.40	.30
205	A27	1.30fr blue ('47)	.80	.40
206	A30	1.50fr deep red	.40	.25
207	A33	2fr Prus grn	.40	.25
209	A33	3fr black brn	.40	.25
210	A29	3.50fr dk red ('47)	1.20	.80
212	A31	4.50fr magenta ('47)	.80	.40
214	A31	5fr indigo	1.20	.55
215	A32	6fr chlky bl ('46)	.80	.35
216	A31	10fr red	2.00	.80
217	A31	15fr Prus grn	2.40	.80
218	A31	20fr dk vio brn	3.25	1.40
219	A31	25fr black brn	3.25	2.10
		Nos. 197-219 (17)	18.90	9.75

For surcharges see Nos. 261-263, B26, B28, B32.

The Terraces A37

Mountain District A39

Fortress — A38

Marrakesh — A40

Gardens of Fez A41

Ouarzazat District A42

1947 Engr. Unwmk. Perf. 13
221	A37	10c black brn	.40	.25
222	A37	30c brt red	.40	.25
223	A37	50c brt grnsh bl	.40	.25
224	A37	60c brt red vio	.40	.25
225	A38	1fr black	.40	.25
226	A38	1.50fr blue	.40	.25
227	A39	2fr brt green	.80	.40
228	A39	3fr brown red	.40	.25
229	A40	4fr dk bl vio	.40	.25
230	A41	5fr dk green	1.20	.55
231	A40	6fr crimson	.40	.25
232	A41	10fr dp blue	1.20	.40
233	A42	15fr dk grn	1.60	1.20
234	A42	20fr henna brn	1.60	1.20
235	A42	25fr purple	2.40	1.20
		Nos. 221-235 (15)	12.40	6.80

1948-49
236	A37	30c purple	.40	.25
237	A38	2fr vio brn ('49)	.80	.40
238	A40	4fr green	.80	.35
239	A41	8fr org ('49)	1.60	.80
240	A41	10fr blue	1.20	.40
241	A42	10fr car rose	.80	.80
242	A38	12fr red	1.20	.80
243	A42	18fr deep blue	2.40	1.20
		Nos. 236-243 (8)	9.20	5.00

For surcharges see Nos. 263, 293-294.

No. 175 Surcharged with New Value and Wavy Lines in Carmine

1948
| 244 | A31 | 8fr on 20fr dk vio brn | 1.20 | .80 |

Fortified Oasis — A43

Walled City — A44

1949
245	A43	5fr blue green	1.20	.40
246	A44	15fr red	1.60	.80
247	A44	25fr ultra	1.60	2.00
		Nos. 245-247 (3)	4.40	2.00

See No. 300.

FRENCH MOROCCO

Detail, Gate of Oudayas, Rabat A45

Nejjarine Fountain, Fez A46

1951
267	A51	10fr indigo & pur	2.00	1.60
268	A51	15fr Prus grn & red brn	2.00	1.60
269	A51	25fr dk brn & ind	2.40	2.00
		Nos. 267-269 (3)	6.40	5.20

See No. C41.

Todra Valley Type of 1950

1951
270	A49	30fr ultramarine	1.60	.40

Daggers of South Morocco — A59

Designs: 20fr and 25fr, Antique brooches.

1953, Mar. 27   Engr.
285	A59	15fr dk car rose	4.00	3.25
286	A59	20fr violet brn	4.00	3.25
287	A59	25fr dark blue	4.00	3.25
		Nos. 285-287 (3)	12.00	9.75

See No. C46.

Walled City Type of 1949

1954   Engr.   Perf. 13
300	A44	25fr purple	2.40	.80

Marshal Lyautey at Rabat A64

Lyautey, Builder of Cities A65

Designs: 15fr, Marshal Lyautey at Khenifra. 50fr, Hubert Lyautey, Marshal of France.

1954, Nov. 17
301	A64	5fr indigo	2.40	2.00
302	A64	15fr dark green	3.25	2.75
303	A65	30fr rose brown	4.00	3.25
304	A65	50fr dk red brn	4.00	3.25
		Nos. 301-304 (4)	13.65	11.25

Marshal Hubert Lyautey, birth cent.

Garden, Meknes — A47

1949   Perf. 14x13
248	A45	10c black	.40	.25
249	A45	50c rose brn	.40	.25
250	A45	1fr blue vio	.40	.25
251	A46	2fr dk car rose	.40	.25
252	A46	3fr dark blue	.80	.25
253	A46	5fr brt green	1.20	.25
254	A47	8fr dk bl grn	1.60	.80
255	A47	10fr brt red	1.60	.80
		Nos. 248-255 (8)	6.80	3.10

Pigeons at Fountain A52

Karaouine Mosque, Fez A53

Patio, Oudayas A54

Oudayas Point, Rabat A55

Post Rider and Public Letter-writer — A60

1953, May 16
288	A60	15fr violet brown	2.00	1.60

Stamp Day, May 16, 1953.

Postal Administration Building, Meknes A40

1949, Oct.   Perf. 13
256	A40	5fr dark green	2.40	2.00
257	A48	15fr deep carmine	2.40	2.00
258	A48	25fr deep blue	2.75	2.40
		Nos. 256-258 (3)	7.55	6.40

75th anniv. of the UPU.

Patio of Old House — A56

Type I (No. 275)   Type II (No. 276)

Perf. 14x13, 13

1951-53   Engr.   Unwmk.
271	A52	5fr magenta ('52)	.40	.25
272	A53	6fr bl grn ('52)	.40	.40
273	A52	8fr brown ('52)	.40	.40
273A	A53	10fr rose red ('53)	.40	.35
274	A53	12fr dp ultra ('52)	.80	.40
275	A54	15fr red brn (I)	2.75	.25
276	A54	15fr red brn (II)	1.20	.25
277	A55	15fr pur ('52)	1.20	.40
278	A55	18fr red ('52)	2.00	1.20
279	A56	20fr dp grnsh bl ('52)	2.40	.80
		Nos. 271-279 (10)	11.95	4.70

See Nos. 297-299.

Mogador Fortress — A62

Design: 30fr, Moorish knights.

1953, Dec. 4
291	A62	15fr green	2.40	1.60
292	A62	30fr red brown	2.40	1.60

Issued to aid Army Welfare Work.

Franco-Moslem Education A66

Moslem Student at Blackboard A67

Designs: 30fr, Moslem school at Camp Boulhaut. 50fr, Moulay Idriss College at Fez.

1955, Apr. 16   Unwmk.   Perf. 13
305	A66	5fr indigo	2.00	1.60
306	A67	15fr rose lake	2.40	2.00
307	A66	30fr chocolate	2.40	2.00
308	A67	50fr dk blue grn	2.75	2.40
		Nos. 305-308 (4)	9.55	8.00

Franco-Moslem solidarity.

Todra Valley — A49

1950
259	A49	35fr red brown	1.60	.40
260	A49	50fr indigo	1.60	.40

See No. 270.

Nos. 204 and 205 Srchd. in Black or Blue

1950   Perf. 14x13½, 13½x14
261	A32	1fr on 1.20fr vio brn (Bk)	.40	.35
262	A27	1fr on 1.30fr blue (Bl)	.40	.25

The surcharge is transposed and spaced to fit the design on No. 262.

No. 231 Surcharged with New Value and Wavy Lines in Black

1951   Perf. 13
263	A40	5fr on 6fr crimson	.80	.25

Statue of Gen. Jacques Leclerc — A50

1951, Apr. 28   Engr.
264	A50	10fr blue green	2.40	2.00
265	A50	15fr deep carmine	2.75	2.00
266	A50	25fr indigo	2.75	2.00
		Nos. 264-266 (3)	7.90	6.00

Unveiling of a monument to Gen. Leclerc at Casablanca, Apr. 28, 1951. See No. C30.

Loustau Hospital, Oujda — A51

Designs: 15fr, New Hospital, Meknes. 25fr, New Hospital, Rabat.

8th-10th Cent. Capital — A57

Capitals: 20fr, 12th Cent. 25fr, 13th-14th Cent. 50fr, 17th Cent.

1952, Apr. 5   Perf. 13
280	A57	15fr deep blue	3.25	2.40
281	A57	20fr red	3.25	2.40
282	A57	25fr purple	3.25	2.40
283	A57	50fr deep green	3.25	2.40
		Nos. 280-283 (4)	13.00	9.60

Casablanca Monument — A58

1952 Sept. 22   Engr. & Typo.
284	A58	15fr multicolored	3.50	2.40

Creation of the French Military Medal, cent.

Nos. 226 and 243 Surcharged with New Value and Wavy Lines in Black

1954
293	A38	1fr on 1.50fr blue	.40	.25
294	A42	15fr on 18fr dp bl	1.20	.65

Dam Type of 1953

1954, Mar. 8
295	A61	15fr red brn & indigo	1.60	1.20

Bine el Ouidane Dam — A61

1953, Nov. 3   Perf. 13
290	A61	15fr indigo	2.00	1.60

See No. 295.

Station of Rural Automobile Post — A63

1954, Apr. 10
296	A63	15fr dk blue grn	1.40	.80

Stamp Day, April 10, 1954.

Types of 1951-53

1954   Engr.   Perf. 14x13
297	A52	15fr dk blue green	1.20	.40

Typo.
298	A52	5fr magenta	1.20	.40
299	A55	15fr rose violet	1.60	.40
		Nos. 297-299 (3)	4.00	1.20

Map and Rotary Emblem — A68

1955, June 11
309	A68	15fr bl & org brn	2.00	1.20

Rotary Intl., 50th anniv.

Post Office, Mazagan — A69

1955, May 24
310	A69	15fr red	1.20	.80

Stamp Day.

Bab el Chorfa, Fez A70

Mahakma (Courthouse), Casablanca A71

Fortress, Safi — A72

Designs: 50c, 1fr, 2fr, 3fr, Mrissa Gate, Salé. 10fr, 12fr, 15fr, Minaret at Rabat. 30fr,

FRENCH MOROCCO

Menara Garden Marrakesh. 40fr, Tafraout Village. 50fr, Portuguese cistern, Mazagan. 75fr, Garden of Oudaya, Rabat.

1955   Perf. 13½x13, 13x13½, 13
311	A70	50c brn vio	.40	.25
312	A70	1fr blue	.40	.25
313	A70	2fr red lilac	.40	.25
314	A70	3fr bluish blk	.40	.25
315	A70	5fr vermilion	1.60	.40
316	A70	6fr green	.75	.35
317	A70	8fr orange brn	1.20	.40
318	A70	10fr violet brn	1.60	.40
319	A70	12fr greenish bl	.80	.40
320	A70	15fr magenta	1.10	.25
321	A71	18fr dk green	2.00	.80
322	A71	20fr brown lake	1.20	.40
323	A72	25fr brt ultra	2.75	.40
324	A72	30fr green	2.40	.80
325	A72	40fr orange red	2.40	.40
326	A72	50fr black brn	8.00	.80
327	A71	75fr greenish bl	2.40	1.20
		Nos. 311-327 (17)	29.80	8.00

Succeeding issues, released under the Kingdom, are listed under Morocco in Vol. 4.

SEMI-POSTAL STAMPS

French Protectorate

No. 30 Surcharged in Red

1914   Unwmk.   Perf. 14x13½
B1	A4	10c + 5c on 10c	24,000.	28,000.

Known only with inverted red surcharge.

No. 42 Surcharged in Red

B2	A7	10c + 5c on 10c rose	6.50	6.50
a.	Double surcharge		175.00	175.00
b.	Inverted surcharge		225.00	225.00
c.	"c" omitted		110.00	110.00

On Nos. B1 and B2 the cross is set up from pieces of metal (quads), the horizontal bar being made from two long pieces, the vertical bar from two short pieces. Each cross in the setting of twenty-five differs from the others.

No. 30 Handstamp Surcharged in Red

B3	A4	10c + 5c on 10c rose	1,650.	1,400.

No. B3 was issued at Oujda. The surcharge ink is water-soluble.

No. 42 Surcharged in Vermilion or Carmine

B4	A7	10c + 5c on 10c (V)	25.00	25.00
a.	Double surcharge		240.00	240.00
b.	Inverted surcharge		240.00	240.00
c.	Double surch., one invtd.		200.00	200.00
B5	A7	10c + 5c on 10c (C)	475.00	525.00
a.	Inverted surcharge		1,600.	1,600.

On Nos. B4-B5 the horizontal bar of the cross is single and not as thick as on Nos. B1-B2.

No. B5 was sold largely at Casablanca.

Carmine Surcharge SP1

Black Overprint SP2

1915
B6	SP1	5c + 5c green	3.25	2.40
a.	Inverted surcharge		300.00	300.00
B7	SP2	10c + 5c rose	4.75	4.75

No. B6 was not issued without the Red Cross surcharge. No. B7 was used in Tangier.

France No. B2 Overprinted in Black

B8	SP2	10c + 5c red	7.50	7.50

No. 30 Surcharged in Carmine — SP4

1917
B9	SP4	10c + 5c on 10c rose	3.25	3.25

On No. B9 the horizontal bar of the cross is made from a single, thick piece of metal.

Marshal Hubert Lyautey — SP5

1935, May 15   Photo.   Perf. 13x13½
B10	SP5	50c + 50c red	9.50	9.50
B11	SP5	1fr + 1fr dk grn	11.00	11.00
B12	SP5	5fr + 5fr blk brn	45.00	45.00
		Nos. B10-B12 (3)	65.50	65.50
		Set, never hinged	98.00	

Stamps of 1933-34 Surcharged in Blue or Red

1938   Perf. 13
B13	A18	2c + 2c red vio	5.50	5.50
B14	A19	3c + 3c dk brn	5.50	5.50
B15	A20	20c + 20c red brn	5.50	5.50
B16	A21	40c + 40c blk brn (R)	5.50	5.50
B17	A22	65c + 65c brn red	5.50	5.50
B18	A23	1.25fr + 1.25fr blk (R)	5.50	5.50
B19	A24	2fr + 2fr yel brn	5.50	5.50
B20	A25	5fr + 5fr red brn	5.50	5.50
		Nos. B13-B20 (8)	44.00	44.00
		Set, never hinged	64.00	

Stamps of 1939 Srchd. in Black

1942
B21	A29	45c + 2fr Prus grn	6.75	4.75
B22	A30	90c + 4fr ultra	6.75	4.75
B23	A32	1.25fr + 6fr henna brn	8.00	6.50
B24	A26	2.50fr + 8fr scarlet	8.00	6.50
		Nos. B21-B24 (4)	29.50	22.50
		Set, never hinged	40.00	

The arrangement of the surcharge differs slightly on each denomination.

Catalogue values for unused stamps in this section, from this point to the end of the section, are for Never Hinged items.

No. 207 Surcharged in Black

1945   Unwmk.   Perf. 13½x14
B26	A33	2fr + 1fr Prus green	.80	.50

For surcharge see No. B28.

Mausoleum of Marshal Lyautey — SP7

1945   Litho.   Perf. 11½
B27	SP7	2fr + 3fr dark blue	.80	.40

The surtax was for French works of solidarity.

No. B26 Surcharged in Red

1946   Perf. 13½x14
B28	A33	3fr (+ 1fr) on 2fr + 1fr	.40	.25

Statue of Marshal Lyautey — SP8

1946, Dec. 16   Engr.
B29	SP8	2fr + 10fr black	2.40	1.60
B30	SP8	3fr + 15fr cop red	2.40	1.60
B31	SP8	10fr + 20fr brt bl	3.25	2.40
		Nos. B29-B31 (3)	8.05	5.60

The surtax was for works of solidarity.

No. 212 Surcharged in Rose Violet

1947, Mar. 15   Perf. 13½x14
B32	A31	4.50fr + 5.50fr magenta	2.00	1.60

Stamp Day, 1947.

Map and Symbols of Prosperity from Phosphates SP9

1947   Perf. 13
B33	SP9	4.50fr + 5.50fr green	1.60	1.20

25th anniv. of the exploitations of the Cherifien Office of Phosphates.

Power SP10   Health SP11

1948, Feb. 9
B34	SP10	6fr + 9fr red brn	3.25	2.40
B35	SP11	10fr + 20fr dp ultra	3.25	2.40

The surtax was for combined works of Franco-Moroccan solidarity.

Type of Regular Issue of 1923, Inscribed: "Journee du Timbre 1948"

1948, Mar. 6
B36	A16	6fr + 4fr red brown	1.20	.80

Stamp Day, Mar. 6, 1948.

Battleship off Moroccan Coast — SP12

1948, Aug.
B37	SP12	6fr + 9fr purple	2.00	1.60

The surtax was for naval charities.

Wheat Field near Meknes — SP13

Designs: 2fr+5fr, Olive grove, Taroudant. 3fr+7fr, Net and coastal view. 5fr+10fr, Aguedal Gardens, Marrakesh.

1949, Apr. 12   Engr.   Unwmk.
Inscribed: "SOLIDARITÉ 1948"
B38	SP13	1fr + 2fr orange	2.00	1.60
B39	SP13	2fr + 5fr car	2.00	1.60
B40	SP13	3fr + 7fr pck bl	2.00	1.60
B41	SP13	5fr + 10fr dk brn vio	2.00	1.60
a.	Sheet of 4, #B38-B41		27.50	24.00
		Nos. B38-B41,CB31-CB34 (8)	17.60	14.40

Gazelle Hunter, from 1899 Local Stamp — SP14

1949, May 1
B42	SP14	10fr + 5fr choc & car rose	2.00	1.60

Stamp Day and 50th anniversary of Mazagan-Marrakesh local postage stamp.

Moroccan Soldiers, Flag — SP15

1949
B43	SP15	10fr + 10fr bright red	1.60	1.40

The surtax was for Army Welfare Work.

Rug Weaving — SP16

Designs: 2fr+5fr, Pottery making, 3fr+7fr, Bookbinding. 5fr+10fr, Copper work.

Inscribed: "SOLIDARITE 1949"

1950, Apr. 11
B44	SP16	1fr + 2fr dp car	2.75	2.40
B45	SP16	2fr + 5fr dk brnsh bl	2.75	2.40
B46	SP16	3fr + 7fr dk pur	2.75	2.40
B47	SP16	5fr + 10fr red brn	2.75	2.40
a.	Sheet of 4, #B44-B47		32.50	24.00
		Nos. B44-B47,CB36-CB39 (8)	20.60	17.60

Ruins of Sala Colonia at Chella — SP17

1950, Sept. 25   Engr.   Perf. 13
B48	SP17	10fr + 10fr dp mag	2.00	1.60
B49	SP17	15fr + 15fr indigo	2.00	1.60

The surtax was for Army Welfare Work.

FRENCH MOROCCO

AIR POST STAMPS

French Protectorate

Biplane over Casablanca — AP1

1922-27　Photo.　Unwmk.　Perf. 13½

C1	AP1	5c dp org ('27)	.50	.50
C2	AP1	25c dp ultra	1.20	1.20
C3	AP1	50c grnsh blue	.40	.40
C4	AP1	75c dp blue	80.00	16.00
C5	AP1	75c dp green	.80	.40
C6	AP1	80c vio brn ('27)	2.40	.80
C7	AP1	1fr vermilion	1.20	.80
C8	AP1	1.40fr brn lake ('27)	2.40	1.25
C9	AP1	1.90fr dp blue ('27)	2.75	1.60
C10	AP1	2fr black vio	2.40	1.20
a.		2fr deep violet	2.25	1.40
C11	AP1	3fr gray blk	2.75	2.00
		Nos. C1-C11 (11)	96.80	26.15

The 25c, 50c, 75c deep green and 1fr each were printed in two of three types, differing in frameline thickness, or hyphen in "Helio-Vaugirard" imprint. Values are for the more common types.

Imperf., Pairs

C1a	AP1	5c	65.00	65.00
C2a	AP1	25c	72.50	72.50
C3a	AP1	50c	72.50	72.50
C4a	AP1	75c	550.00	550.00
C5a	AP1	75c	72.50	72.50
C6a	AP1	80c	72.50	72.50
C7a	AP1	1fr	90.00	90.00
C10b	AP1	2fr	225.00	225.00

Nos. C8-C9 Srchd. in Blue or Black

1931, Apr. 10

C12	AP1	1fr on 1.40fr (B)	2.40	2.40
a.		Inverted surcharge	310.00	310.00
C13	AP1	1.50fr on 1.90fr (Bk)	2.40	2.40

Rabat and Tower of Hassan — AP2

Casablanca AP3

1933, Jan.　Engr.

C14	AP2	50c dark blue	.80	.80
C15	AP2	80c orange brn	.80	.65
C16	AP2	1.50fr brown red	.80	.80
C17	AP3	2.50fr carmine rose	6.50	1.20
C18	AP3	5fr violet	3.25	1.75
C19	AP3	10fr blue green	1.20	1.20
		Nos. C14-C19 (6)	13.35	6.40

For surcharges see Nos. CB22-CB23.

Storks and Minaret, Chella AP4

Plane and Map of Morocco AP5

1939-40　Perf. 13

C20	AP4	80c Prus green	.25	.25
C21	AP4	1fr dk red	.25	.25
C22	AP5	1.90fr ultra	.40	.30
C23	AP5	2fr red vio ('40)	.40	.30
C24	AP5	3fr chocolate	.50	.25

C25	AP4	5fr violet	1.40	.80
C26	AP5	10fr turq blue	1.25	.55
		Nos. C20-C26 (7)	4.45	2.70

Catalogue values for unused stamps in this section, from this point to the end of the section, are for Never Hinged items.

Plane over Oasis — AP6

1944　Litho.　Perf. 11½

C27	AP6	50c Prus grn	.50	.35
C28	AP6	2fr ultra	.50	.35
C29	AP6	5fr scarlet	.50	.35
C30	AP6	10fr violet	1.40	1.10
C31	AP6	50fr black	2.00	1.60
C32	AP6	100fr dp bl & red	4.00	3.25
		Nos. C27-C32 (6)	8.90	7.00

For surcharge see No. CB24.

Plane — AP7

1945　Engr.　Perf. 13

C33	AP7	50fr sepia	1.20	.95

Moulay Idriss AP8

La Medina AP9

1947-48

C34	AP8	9fr dk rose car	.40	.30
C35	AP8	40fr dark blue	1.20	.80
C36	AP8	50fr dp claret ('47)	1.60	.40
C37	AP9	100fr dp grnsh bl	3.25	1.20
C38	AP9	200fr henna brn	8.00	1.60
		Nos. C34-C38 (5)	14.45	4.30

Leclerc Type of Regular Issue

1951, Apr. 28

C39	A50	50fr purple	3.25	2.75

Unveiling of a monument to Gen. Leclerc at Casablanca, Apr. 28, 1951.

Kasbah of the Oudayas, Rabat — AP11

1951, May 22

C40	AP11	300fr purple	24.00	12.00

Ben Smine Sanatorium AP12

1951, June 4

C41	AP12	50fr pur & Prus grn	3.50	2.75

Fortifications, Chella — AP13

Plane Near Marrakesh AP14

Fort, Anti-Atlas Mountains AP15

View of Fez — AP16

1952, Apr. 19　Unwmk.　Perf. 13

C42	AP13	10fr blue green	1.60	.80
C43	AP14	40fr red	2.40	.80
C44	AP15	100fr brown	5.50	1.60
C45	AP16	200fr purple	10.50	4.00
		Nos. C42-C45 (4)	20.00	7.20

Antique Brooches — AP17

1953, Mar. 27

C46	AP17	50fr dark green	4.00	3.25

"City" of the Agdal, Meknes — AP18

20fr, Yakoub el Mansour, Rabat. 40fr, Ainchock, Casablanca. 50fr, El Aliya, Fedala.

1954, Mar. 8

C47	AP18	10fr olive brown	4.00	2.75
C48	AP18	20fr purple	4.00	2.75
C49	AP18	40fr red brown	4.00	2.75
C50	AP18	50fr deep green	4.00	2.75
		Nos. C47-C50 (4)	16.00	11.00

Franco-Moroccan solidarity.

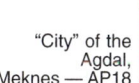

Naval Vessel and Sailboat — AP19

1954, Oct. 18

C51	AP19	15fr dk blue green	2.00	1.60
C52	AP19	30fr violet blue	2.40	2.00

Village in the Anti-Atlas AP20

"Ksar es Souk," Rabat and Plane AP21

200fr, Estuary of Bou Regreg, Rabat and Plane.

1955, July 25　Engr.　Perf. 13

C53	AP20	100fr brt violet	2.75	.80
C54	AP20	200fr brt carmine	6.50	1.20
C55	AP21	500fr grnsh blue	16.00	4.00
		Nos. C53-C55 (3)	25.25	6.00

AIR POST SEMI-POSTAL STAMPS

French Protectorate

Moorish Tribesmen SPAP1

Designs: 25c, Moor plowing with camel and burro. 50c, Caravan nearing Saffi. 75c, Walls, Marrakesh. 80c, Sheep grazing at Azrou. 1fr, Gate at Fez. 1.50fr, Aerial view of Tangier. 2fr, Aerial view of Casablanca. 3fr, Storks on old wall, Rabat. 5fr, Moorish fete.

Perf. 13½

1928, July 26　Photo.　Unwmk.

CB1	SPAP1	5c dp blue	5.25	5.25
CB2	SPAP1	25c brn org	5.25	5.25
CB3	SPAP1	50c red	5.25	5.25
CB4	SPAP1	75c org brn	5.25	5.25
CB5	SPAP1	80c olive grn	5.25	5.25
CB6	SPAP1	1fr orange	5.25	5.25
CB7	SPAP1	1.50fr Prus bl	5.25	5.25
CB8	SPAP1	2fr dp brown	5.25	5.25
CB9	SPAP1	3fr dp violet	5.25	5.25
CB10	SPAP1	5fr brown blk	5.25	5.25
		Nos. CB1-CB10 (10)	52.50	52.50

These stamps were sold in sets only and at double their face value. The money received for the surtax was divided among charitable and social organizations. The stamps were not sold at post offices but solely by subscription to the Moroccan Postal Administration.

Overprinted in Red or Blue (25c, 50c, 75c, 1fr)

1929, Feb. 1

CB11	SPAP1	5c dp blue	5.25	5.25
CB12	SPAP1	25c brown org	5.25	5.25
CB13	SPAP1	50c red	5.25	5.25
CB14	SPAP1	75c org brn	5.25	5.25
CB15	SPAP1	80c olive grn	5.25	5.25
CB16	SPAP1	1fr orange	5.25	5.25
CB17	SPAP1	1.50fr Prus bl	5.25	5.25
CB18	SPAP1	2fr dp brown	5.25	5.25
CB19	SPAP1	3fr dp violet	5.25	5.25
CB20	SPAP1	5fr brown blk	5.25	5.25
		Nos. CB11-CB20 (10)	52.50	52.50

These stamps were sold at double their face values and only in Tangier. The surtax benefited various charities.

Marshal Hubert Lyautey SPAP10

1935, May 15　Perf. 13½

CB21	SPAP10	1.50fr + 1.50fr blue	20.00	20.00

Nos. C14, C19 Surcharged in Red

1938　Perf. 13

CB22	AP2	50c + 50c dk bl	8.00	8.00
CB23	AP3	10fr + 10fr bl grn	5.50	5.50

Catalogue values for unused stamps in this section, from this point to the end of the section, are for Never Hinged items.

Plane over Oasis — SPAP11

1944　Litho.　Perf. 11½

CB23A	SPAP11	1.50fr + 98.50fr	2.40	1.60

The surtax was for charity among the liberated French.

FRENCH MOROCCO

No. C29 Surcharged in Black

1946, June 18   **Perf. 11**
CB24 AP6 5fr + 5fr scarlet   1.60 1.20

6th anniv. of the appeal made by Gen. Charles de Gaulle, June 18, 1940. The surtax was for the Free French Association of Morocco.

Statue of Marshal Lyautey — SPAP12

1946, Dec.   **Engr.**   **Perf. 13**
CB25 SPAP12 10fr +30fr dk grn   6.50 2.75

The surtax was for works of solidarity.

Replenishing Stocks of Food — SPAP13

Agriculture SPAP14

1948, Feb. 9   **Unwmk.**
CB26 SPAP13 9fr +16fr dp grn   2.00 1.60
CB27 SPAP14 20fr +35fr brown   2.00 1.60

The surtax was for combined works of Franco-Moroccan solidarity.

Tomb of Marshal Hubert Lyautey — SPAP15

1948, May 18   **Perf. 13**
CB28 SPAP15 10fr +25fr dk grn   1.60 1.25

Lyautey Exposition, Paris, June, 1948.

P.T.T. Clubhouse SPAP16

1948, June 7   **Engr.**
CB29 SPAP16 6fr + 34fr dk grn   2.40 2.00
CB30 SPAP16 9fr + 51fr red brn   2.40 2.00

The surtax was used for the Moroccan P.T.T. employees vacation colony at Ifrane.

View of Agadir — SPAP17

Designs: 6fr+9fr, Fez. 9fr+16fr, Atlas Mountains. 15fr+25fr, Valley of Draa.

1949, Apr. 12   **Perf. 13**
Inscribed: "SOLIDARITÉ 1948"
CB31 SPAP17 5fr +5fr dk grn   2.40 2.00
CB32 SPAP17 6fr +9fr org red   2.40 2.00
CB33 SPAP17 9fr +16fr blk brn   2.40 2.00

CB34 SPAP17 15fr +25fr ind   2.40 2.00
   a. Sheet of 4, #CB31-CB34   32.50 24.00
   Nos. CB31-CB34 (4)   9.60 8.00

Plane over Globe — SPAP18

1950, Mar. 11   **Engr. & Typo.**
CB35 SPAP18 15fr + 10fr bl grn & car   1.60 1.25

Day of the Stamp, Mar. 11-12, 1950, and 25th anniv. of the 1st post link between Casablanca and Dakar.

Scenes and Map: Northwest Corner — SPAP19

Designs (quarters of map): 6fr+9fr, NE, 9fr+16fr, SW. 15fr+25fr, SE.

1950, Apr. 11   **Engr.**
Inscribed: "SOLIDARITE 1949"
CB36 SPAP19 5fr +5fr dp ultra   2.40 2.00
CB37 SPAP19 6fr +9fr Prus grn   2.40 2.00
CB38 SPAP19 9fr +16fr dk brn   2.40 2.00
CB39 SPAP19 15fr +25fr brn red   2.40 2.00
   a. Sheet of 4, #CB36-CB39   32.50 24.00
   Nos. CB36-CB39 (4)   9.60 8.00

Arch of Triumph of Caracalla at Volubilis SPAP20

1950, Sept. 25   **Unwmk.**
CB40 SPAP20 10fr + 10fr sepia   2.00 1.60
CB41 SPAP20 15fr + 15fr bl grn   2.00 1.60

The surtax was for Army Welfare Work.

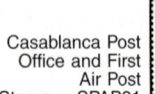

Casablanca Post Office and First Air Post Stamp — SPAP21

1952, Mar. 8   **Perf. 13**
CB42 SPAP21 15fr + 5fr red brn & dp grn   4.75 4.00

Day of the Stamp, Mar. 8, 1952, and 30th anniv. of French Morocco's 1st air post stamp.

POSTAGE DUE STAMPS

French Offices in Morocco

France Postage Due Stamps and Types Surcharged in Red or Black

1896   **Unwmk.**   **Perf. 14x13½**
On Stamps of 1891-93
J1 D2 5c on 5c lt bl (R)   12.00 5.50
J2 D2 10c on 10c choc (R)   16.00 6.50
J3 D2 30c on 30c car   32.50 24.00
   a. Pair, one without surcharge
J4 D2 50c on 50c lilac   32.50 27.50
   a. "S" of "CENTIMOS" omitted   340.00 250.00
J5 D2 1p on 1fr lil brn   350.00 325.00

1909-10   On Stamps of 1908-10
J6 D3 1c on 1c ol grn (R)   4.00 4.00
J7 D3 10c on 10c violet   40.00 32.50
J8 D3 30c on 30c bister   55.00 40.00
J9 D3 50c on 50c red   80.00 72.50
   Nos. J6-J9 (4)   179.00 149.00

Postage Due Stamps of France Surcharged in Red or Blue

1911   On Stamps of 1893-96
J10 D2 5c on 5c blue (R)   4.75 4.75
J11 D2 10c on 10c choc (R)   16.00 16.00
   a. Double surcharge   225.00 260.00
J12 D2 50c on 50c lil (Bl)   20.00 20.00
On Stamps of 1908-10
J13 D3 1c on 1c ol grn (R)   4.00 3.25
J14 D3 10c on 10c vio (R)   8.00 8.00
J15 D3 30c on 30c bis (R)   12.00 12.00
J16 D3 50c on 50c red (Bl)   16.00 16.00
   Nos. J10-J16 (7)   80.75 80.00

For surcharges see Nos. J23-J26.

French Protectorate

France Postage Due Stamps of 1911 Issue Overprinted

1915-17
J17 D4 1c on 1c black   .80 .80
   a. New value double   175.00
J18 D4 5c on 5c blue   3.25 2.00
J19 D4 10c on 10c choc   4.00 2.00
J20 D4 20c on 20c ol grn   4.00 2.00
J21 D4 30c on 30c rose red, grayish   8.00 5.50
J22 D4 50c on 50c vio brn   12.00 10.00
   Nos. J17-J22 (6)   32.05 20.30

Nos. J13 to J16 With Additional Overprint "Protectorat Francais"

1915
J23 D3 1c on 1c ol grn   1.60 1.60
J24 D3 10c on 10c violet   4.00 3.25
J25 D3 30c on 30c bister   4.00 4.00
J26 D3 50c on 50c red   4.00 4.00
   Nos. J23-J26 (4)   13.60 12.85

D5

1917-26   **Typo.**
J27 D5 1c black   .25 .25
J28 D5 5c deep blue   .40 .25
J29 D5 10c brown   .40 .40
J30 D5 20c olive green   2.50 1.60
J31 D5 30c rose   .40 .40
J32 D5 50c lilac brown   .80 .40
J33 D5 1fr red brn, straw ('26)   .85 .80
J34 D5 2fr violet ('26)   2.40 1.60
   Nos. J27-J34 (8)   8.00 5.70

See #J49-J56, Morocco #J1-J4. For surcharges see #J46-J48.

Postage Due Stamps of France, 1882-1906 Overprinted

1918
J35 D2 1c black   1.20 1.20
J36 D2 5c blue   2.40 2.40
J37 D2 10c chocolate   2.00 2.00
J38 D2 15c green, grayish   4.75 4.75
J39 D2 20c olive green   6.50 6.50
J40 D2 30c rose red, grayish   16.00 16.00
J41 D2 50c violet brown   24.00 24.00
   Nos. J35-J41 (7)   56.85 56.85

Postage Due Stamps of France, 1908-19 Overprinted

1918
J42 D3 1c olive green   1.20 1.20
J43 D3 10c violet   2.75 2.75
J44 D3 20c bister, grayish   8.00 8.00
J45 D3 40c red   20.00 20.00
   Nos. J42-J45 (4)   31.95 31.95

Catalogue values for unused stamps in this section, from this point to the end of the section, are for Never Hinged items.

Nos. J31 and J29 Surcharged

1944   **Unwmk.**   **Perf. 14x13½**
J46 D5 50c on 30c rose   3.25 2.40
J47 D5 1fr on 10c brown   5.50 4.00
J48 D5 3fr on 10c brown   13.00 9.50
   Nos. J46-J48 (3)   21.75 15.90

Type of 1917-1926

1945-52   **Typo.**
J49 D5 1fr brn lake ('47)   1.20 .80
J50 D5 2fr rose lake ('47)   1.60 .80
J51 D5 3fr ultra   .80 .35
J52 D5 4fr red orange   .80 .30
J53 D5 5fr green   1.60 .50
J54 D5 10fr yellow brn   2.00 .50
J55 D5 20fr carmine ('50)   2.00 .90
J56 D5 30fr dull brn ('52)   2.75 1.60
   Nos. J49-J56 (8)   12.75 5.75

PARCEL POST STAMPS

French Protectorate

PP1

1917   **Unwmk.**   **Perf. 13½x14**
Q1 PP1 5c green   1.20 .80
Q2 PP1 10c carmine   1.20 .80
Q3 PP1 20c lilac brown   1.20 1.00
Q4 PP1 25c blue   1.60 .80
Q5 PP1 40c dark brown   2.40 1.60
Q6 PP1 50c red orange   4.00 .80
Q7 PP1 75c pale slate   4.00 2.40
Q8 PP1 1fr ultra   5.50 .80
Q9 PP1 2fr gray   12.00 1.60
Q10 PP1 5fr violet   12.00 1.60
Q11 PP1 10fr black   20.00 1.60
   Nos. Q1-Q11 (11)   65.10 13.80

FRENCH POLYNESIA

'french ,pä-lə-'nē-zhə

(French Oceania)

LOCATION — South Pacific Ocean
GOVT. — French Overseas Territory
AREA — 1,522 sq. mi.
POP. — 242,073 (1999 est.)
CAPITAL — Papeete

In 1903 various French Establishments in the South Pacific were united to form a single colony. Most important of the island groups are the Society Islands, Marquesas Islands, the Tuamotu group and the Gambier, Austral, and Rapa Islands. Tahiti, largest of the Society group, ranks first in importance.

100 Centimes = 1 Franc

Catalogue values for unused stamps in this country are for Never Hinged items, beginning with Scott 136 in the regular post-age section, Scott B11 in the semi-postal section, Scott C2 in the air-post section, Scott J18 in the postage due section, and Scott O1 in the officials section.

Navigation and Commerce — A1

Perf. 14x13½
1892-1907   Typo.   Unwmk.
Name of Colony in Blue or Carmine

1	A1	1c black, *lil bl*	1.60	1.60
2	A1	2c brown, *buff*	2.75	2.75
3	A1	4c claret, *lav*	4.50	4.00
4	A1	5c green, *grnsh*	13.50	9.50
5	A1	5c yellow grn ('06)	5.00	2.40
6	A1	10c blk, *lavender*	30.00	12.50
7	A1	10c red ('00)	5.00	2.40
8	A1	15c blue, quadrille paper	35.00	12.00
9	A1	15c gray, *lt gray* ('00)	10.00	7.25
10	A1	20c red, *grn*	17.50	16.00
11	A1	25c black, *rose*	60.00	30.00
12	A1	25c blue ('00)	32.50	16.00
13	A1	30c brown, *bis*	16.00	14.50
14	A1	35c black, *yel* ('06)	11.00	9.50
15	A1	40c red, *straw*	132.50	80.00
16	A1	45c blk, *gray grn* ('07)	6.75	6.75
17	A1	50c car, *pale rose*	10.00	10.00
a.		50c rose, *pale rose*	10.00	9.00
18	A1	75c brown, *az* ('00)	275.00	250.00
19	A1	75c dp vio, *org*	12.00	12.00
20	A1	1fr brnz grn, *straw*	13.50	13.50
		Nos. 1-20 (20)	694.10	512.65

Perf. 13½x14 stamps are counterfeits.
For overprint and surcharge see Nos. 55, B1.

Tahitian Girl A2

Kanakas A3

Fautaua Valley — A4

1913-30

21	A2	1c violet & brn	.25	.25
22	A2	2c brown & blk	.25	.25
23	A2	4c orange & bl	.35	.35
24	A2	5c grn & yel grn	1.60	.90
a.		Double impression of yel grn	500.00	
25	A2	5c bl & blk ('22)	.50	.50
26	A2	10c rose & org	2.25	2.25
27	A2	10c bl grn & yel grn ('22)	1.25	1.25
28	A2	10c org red & brn red, *bluish* ('26)	1.40	1.40
29	A2	15c org & blk ('15)	.85	.65
a.		Imperf., pair	175.00	
30	A2	20c black & vio	1.10	1.00
a.		Imperf., pair	175.00	
31	A2	20c grn & bl grn ('26)	1.00	1.00
32	A2	20c brn red & dk brn ('27)	1.60	1.60
33	A3	25c ultra & blu	1.50	1.25
34	A3	25c vio & rose ('22)	.75	.75
35	A3	30c gray & brown	5.00	4.00
a.		Imperf., pair	325.00	
36	A3	30c rose & red org ('22)	3.25	3.25
37	A3	30c blk & red org ('26)	.75	.75
38	A3	30c slate bl & bl grn ('27)	1.75	1.75
39	A3	35c green & rose	1.25	1.25
40	A3	40c black & green	1.10	1.10
41	A3	45c orange & red	1.10	1.10
42	A3	50c dk brown & blk	17.50	13.50
43	A3	50c ultra & bl ('22)	1.25	1.25
44	A3	50c gray & bl vio ('26)	1.10	1.10
45	A3	60c green & blk ('25)	1.25	1.25
46	A3	65c ol brn & red vio ('27)	3.25	3.25
47	A3	75c vio brn & vio	2.50	2.50
48	A3	90c brn red & rose ('30)	16.50	16.50
a.		Imperf., pair	225.00	
49	A4	1fr rose & black	6.25	4.25
50	A4	1.10fr vio & dk brn ('28)	1.60	1.60
51	A4	1.40fr bis brn & vio ('29)	4.00	4.00
52	A4	1.50fr ind & bl ('30)	16.50	16.50
53	A4	2fr dk brown & grn	6.25	4.25
54	A4	5fr violet & bl	11.00	11.00
a.		Imperf., pair	500.00	
		Nos. 21-54 (34)	117.80	107.55

For surcharges see Nos. 56-71, B2-B4.

No. 7 Overprinted

1915

55	A1	10c red	6.75	6.75
a.		Inverted overprint	225.00	225.00

For surcharge see No. B1.

No. 29 Surcharged

1916
| 56 | A2 | 10c on 15c org & blk | 3.50 | 3.50 |

No. 22 Surcharged

No. 41 Surcharged

No. 29 Surcharged

1921
57	A2	5c on 2c brn & blk	36.00	36.00
58	A3	10c on 45c org & red	36.00	36.00
59	A2	25c on 15c org & blk	9.00	9.00
		Nos. 57-59 (3)	81.00	81.00

On No. 58 the new value and date are set wide apart and without bar.

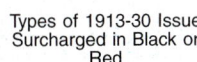

Types of 1913-30 Issue Surcharged in Black or Red

1923-27
60	A3	60c on 75c bl & brn	.75	.75
61	A4	65c on 1fr dk bl & ol (R) ('25)	2.25	2.25
62	A4	85c on 1fr dk bl & ol (R) ('25)	2.25	2.25
63	A3	90c on 75c brn red & cer ('27)	3.00	3.00
		Nos. 60-63 (4)	8.25	8.25

No. 26 Surcharged

1924
64	A2	45c on 10c rose & org	3.00	3.00
a.		Inverted surcharge	2,400.	2,400.

Stamps and Type of 1913-30 Surcharged with New Value and Bars in Black or Red

1924-27
65	A4	25c on 2fr dk brn & grn	1.10	1.10
66	A4	25c on 5fr vio & bl	1.10	1.10
67	A4	1.25fr on 1fr dk bl & ultra (R) ('26)	1.20	1.20
68	A4	1.50fr on 1fr dk bl & lt bl ('27)	4.00	4.00
69	A4	20fr on 5fr org & brt vio ('27)	32.50	26.00
		Nos. 65-69 (5)	39.90	33.40

Surcharged in Black or Red

1926
70	A4	3fr on 5fr gray & blue	3.25	2.50
71	A4	10fr on 5fr grn & blk (R)	7.25	7.25

Papetoai Bay, Moorea — A5

1929, Mar. 25
72	A5	3fr green & dk brn	8.00	8.00
73	A5	5fr lt blue & dk brn	15.00	15.00
74	A5	10fr lt red & dk brn	45.00	45.00
75	A5	20fr lilac & dk brn	57.50	57.50
		Nos. 72-75 (4)	125.50	125.50

For overprints see Nos. 128, 130, 132, 134.

Common Design Types pictured following the introduction.

Colonial Exposition Issue
Common Design Types

1931, Apr. 13   Engr.   Perf. 12½
Name of Country Printed in Black
76	CD70	40c deep green	7.50	7.50
77	CD71	50c violet	7.50	7.50
78	CD72	90c red orange	7.50	7.50
79	CD73	1.50fr dull blue	7.50	7.50
		Nos. 76-79 (4)	30.00	30.00

Spear Fishing — A12

Tahitian Girl — A13

Idols — A14

1934-40   Photo.   Perf. 13½, 13½x13
80	A12	1c gray black	.25	.25
81	A12	2c claret	.35	.35
82	A12	3c lt blue ('40)	.35	.35
83	A12	4c orange	.60	.60
84	A12	5c violet	.90	.90
85	A12	10c dark brown	.40	.40
86	A12	15c green	.60	.60
87	A12	20c red	.60	.60
88	A12	25c gray blue	.90	.90
89	A13	30c yellow green	1.20	1.20
90	A13	30c red orange ('40)	.80	.80
91	A14	35c brt green ('38)	4.00	4.00
92	A13	40c red violet	.60	.60
93	A13	45c brown orange	9.00	9.00
94	A13	45c dk green ('39)	1.60	1.60
95	A13	50c violet	.60	.60
96	A13	55c blue ('38)	6.75	6.75
97	A13	60c black ('39)	.75	.75
98	A13	65c brown	3.25	3.25
99	A13	70c brt pink ('39)	1.40	1.40
100	A13	75c olive green	9.00	9.00
101	A13	80c violet brn ('38)	2.00	2.00
102	A13	90c rose red	.90	.90
103	A14	1fr red brown	.90	.90
104	A14	1.25fr brown violet	8.25	8.25
105	A14	1.25fr rose red ('39)	1.25	1.25
106	A14	1.40fr org yel ('39)	1.25	1.25
107	A14	1.50fr blue	.90	.90
108	A14	1.60fr dull olive ('39)	1.40	1.40
109	A14	1.75fr olive	6.75	6.75
110	A14	2fr red	1.10	1.10
111	A14	2.25fr dp blue ('39)	1.25	1.25
112	A14	2.50fr black ('39)	1.25	1.25
113	A14	3fr brn org ('39)	1.50	1.50
114	A14	5fr red violet ('39)	1.00	1.00
115	A14	10fr dk grn ('39)	3.00	3.00
116	A14	20fr dk brn ('39)	3.50	3.50
		Nos. 80-116 (37)	80.10	80.10

For overprints see Nos. 126-127, 129, 131, 133, 135.

Paris International Exposition Issue
Common Design Types

1937   Engr.   Perf. 13
117	CD74	20c deep violet	3.50	3.50
118	CD75	30c dark green	3.50	3.50
119	CD76	40c carmine rose	3.50	3.50
120	CD77	50c dk brn & blue	4.25	4.25
121	CD78	90c red	4.25	4.25
122	CD79	1.50fr ultra	5.00	5.00
		Nos. 117-122 (6)	24.00	24.00

Colonial Arts Exhibition Issue
Souvenir Sheet
Common Design Type

1937   Imperf.
123	CD78	3fr emerald	36.00	52.50
		Never hinged	55.00	

New York World's Fair Issue
Common Design Type

1939, May 10   Engr.   Perf. 12½x12
124	CD82	1.25fr carmine lake	2.40	2.40
125	CD82	2.25fr ultra	2.40	2.40
		Set, never hinged	8.00	

Fautaua Valley and Marshal Petain — A15

1941   Engr.   Perf. 12½x12
125A	A15	1fr bluish green	1.10	
c.		Denomination ("1F") omitted	80.00	
125B	A15	2.50fr deep blue	1.25	3.25
		Set, never hinged		

Nos. 125A-125B were issued by the Vichy government in France, but were not placed on sale in the French Polynesia.

For surcharges, see Nos. B12B-B12C.

Stamps of 1929-39 Ovptd. in Black or Red

1941   Perf. 14x13½, 13½x13
126	A14	1fr red brn (Bk)	7.00	9.50
a.		Inverted overprint	1,200.	
127	A14	2.50fr black	8.00	11.00
a.		Inverted overprint	1,200.	
128	A5	3fr grn & dk brn	9.00	9.00
129	A14	3fr brn org (Bk)	10.00	12.00
130	A5	5fr lt bl & dk brn	9.00	9.00
131	A14	5fr red vio (Bk)	10.00	10.00

816 FRENCH POLYNESIA

132	A5	10fr lt red & dk brn	25.00	30.00
133	A14	10fr dark green	90.00	110.00
134	A5	20fr lil & dk brn	135.00	135.00
135	A14	10fr dark brown	75.00	95.00
		Nos. 126-135 (10)	378.00	430.50
		Set, never hinged	480.00	

Types of 1934-39 without "RF"

1942-44		Photo.		Perf. 13½
135A	A12	10c brown		.65
135B	A13	30c red orange		.85
135C	A14	1.50fr blue		1.00
135D	A14	10fr dark green		1.75
135E	A14	20fr dark brown		2.50
		Nos. 135A-135E (5)		6.75

Nos. 135A-135E were issued by the Vichy government in France, but were not placed on sale in French Polynesia.

Catalogue values for unused stamps in this section, from this point to the end of the section, are for Never Hinged items.

 Ancient Double Canoe — A16

1942		Photo.	Perf. 14½x14	
136	A16	5c dark brown	.40	.25
137	A16	10c dk gray bl	.40	.25
138	A16	25c emerald	.40	.25
139	A16	30c red orange	.40	.25
140	A16	40c dk slate grn	.40	.25
141	A16	80c red brown	.40	.25
142	A16	1fr rose violet	.50	.35
143	A16	1.50fr brt red	.65	.50
144	A16	2fr gray black	1.00	.75
145	A16	2.50fr brt ultra	2.50	1.75
146	A16	4fr dull violet	1.75	1.25
147	A16	5fr bister	1.75	1.25
148	A16	10fr deep brown	2.50	1.90
149	A16	20fr deep green	3.00	2.10
		Nos. 136-149 (14)	16.05	11.35

For surcharges see Nos. 152-159.

Eboue Issue
Common Design Type

1945		Engr.	Perf. 13	
150	CD91	2fr black	1.00	.75
151	CD91	25fr Prus green	2.60	2.10

Nos. 150 and 151 exist imperforate.

Nos. 136, 138 and 145 Surcharged with New Values and Bars in Carmine or Black

1946			Perf. 14½x14	
152	A16	50c on 5c (C)	.65	.50
153	A16	60c on 5c (C)	.65	.50
154	A16	70c on 5c (C)	.65	.50
155	A16	1.20fr on 5c (C)	.80	.65
156	A16	2.40fr on 25c (Bk)	1.60	1.25
157	A16	3fr on 25c (Bk)	1.00	.75
158	A16	4.50fr on 25c (Bk)	2.00	1.50
159	A16	15fr on 2.50fr (C)	2.40	1.75
		Nos. 152-159 (8)	9.75	7.40

 Coast of Moorèa A17

 Fisherman and Catch A18

 Tahitian Girl — A20

House at Faa — A19

 Island of Borabora — A21

 Island Women — A22

1948		Unwmk.	Engr.	Perf. 13
160	A17	10c brown	.50	.35
161	A17	30c blue green	.50	.35
162	A17	40c deep blue	.50	.35
163	A18	50c red brown	.50	.35
164	A18	60c dk brown ol	.65	.50
165	A18	80c brt blue	.65	.50
166	A19	1fr red brown	.65	.35
167	A19	1.20fr slate	.65	.50
168	A19	1.50fr deep ultra	.65	.50
169	A20	2fr sepia	1.10	.75
170	A20	2.40fr red brown	1.25	1.00
171	A20	3fr purple	11.50	2.50
172	A20	4fr blue black	2.40	1.40
173	A21	5fr sepia	3.75	1.60
174	A21	6fr steel blue	3.75	2.10
175	A21	10fr dk brown ol	4.75	1.75
176	A22	15fr vermilion	7.25	2.75
177	A22	20fr slate	7.25	3.25
178	A22	25fr sepia	9.00	5.00
		Nos. 160-178 (19)	57.25	25.85

Imperforates

Most French Polynesia stamps from 1948 onward exist imperforate in issued and trial colors, and also in small presentation sheets in issued colors.

Military Medal Issue
Common Design Type

1952, Dec. 1		Engr. & Typo.		
179	CD101	3fr multicolored	13.50	10.00

 Girl of Bora Bora — A23

1955, Sept. 26			Engr.	
180	A23	9fr dk brn, blk & red	11.00	7.25

FIDES Issue
Common Design Type

Design: 3fr, Dry dock at Papeete.

1956, Oct. 22		Engr.	Perf. 13x12½	
181	CD103	3fr grnsh blue	4.00	2.00

 Girl Playing Guitar — A24

Designs: 4fr, 7fr, 9fr, Man with headdress. 10fr, 20fr, Girl with shells on beach.

1958, Nov. 3		Unwmk.	Perf. 13	
182	A24	10c grn & redsh brn	.65	.55
183	A24	25c slate grn, cl & car	.80	.60
184	A24	1fr brt bl, brn & red org	1.00	.65
185	A24	2fr brn, vio brn & vio	1.10	.65
186	A24	4fr sl grn & org yel	1.50	1.00
187	A24	7fr red brn, grn & org	3.00	1.60
188	A24	9fr vio brn, grn & org	5.50	2.25
189	A24	10fr dk bl, brn & car	5.00	2.25
190	A24	20fr pur, rose red & brn	9.00	5.00
		Nos. 182-190 (9)	27.55	14.55

See Nos. 304-306.

Human Rights Issue
Common Design Type

1958, Dec. 10				
191	CD105	7fr dk gray & dk bl	13.00	8.75

Flower Issue
Common Design Type

1959, Jan. 3		Photo.	Perf. 12½x12	
192	CD104	4fr Breadfruit	6.50	4.00

Spear Fishing A25

Tahitian Dancers A26

1960, May 16		Engr.	Perf. 13	
193	A25	5fr green, brn & lil	1.25	1.00
194	A26	17fr ultra, brt grn & red brn	6.00	2.50

 Post Office, Papeete — A27

1960, Nov. 19		Unwmk.	Perf. 13	
195	A27	16fr green, bl & claret	5.50	3.25

 Saraca Indica — A28

1962, July 12		Photo.	Perf. 13	
196	A28	15fr shown	15.00	14.00
197	A28	25fr Hibiscus	24.00	16.00

 Map of Australia and South Pacific A29

1962, July 18			Perf. 13x12	
198	A29	20fr multicolored	17.50	7.75

5th South Pacific Conf., Pago Pago, July 1962.

 Spined Squirrelfish A30

Fish: 10fr, One-spot butterflyfish. 30fr, Radiate lionfish. 40fr, Horned boxfish.

1962, Dec. 15		Engr.	Perf. 13	
199	A30	5fr black, mag & bis	4.25	1.90
200	A30	10fr multicolored	6.25	2.75
201	A30	30fr multicolored	12.50	7.75
202	A30	40fr multicolored	15.50	11.50
		Nos. 199-202 (4)	38.50	23.90

 Soccer A30a

Design: 50fr, Throwing the javelin.

1963, Aug. 29		Photo.	Perf. 12½	
203	A30a	20fr brt ultra & brn	9.00	6.25
204	A30a	50fr brt car rose & ultra	16.00	9.25

South Pacific Games, Suva, 8/29-9/7.

Red Cross Centenary Issue
Common Design Type

1963, Sept. 2		Engr.	Perf. 13	
205	CD113	15fr vio brn, gray & car	15.00	12.00

Human Rights Issue
Common Design Type

1963, Dec. 10		Unwmk.	Perf. 13	
206	CD117	7fr green & vio bl	15.00	10.00

Philatec Issue
Common Design Type

1964, Apr. 9		Unwmk.	Perf. 13	
207	CD118	25fr dm, dk sl grn & red	18.00	12.50

 Tahitian Dancer — A31

1964, May 14		Engr.	Perf. 13	
208	A31	1fr multicolored	.40	.40
209	A31	3fr dp claret, blk & org	.90	.90

 Soldiers, Truck and Battle Flag — A32

1964, July 10		Photo.	Perf. 12½	
210	A32	5fr multicolored	11.00	4.25

Issued to honor the Tahitian Volunteers of the Pacific Battalion. See No. C31.

 Tuamotu Scene — A33

Views: 4fr, Borabora. 7fr, Papeete Harbor. 8fr, Paul Gauguin's tomb, Marquesas. 20fr, Mangareva, Gambier Islands.

1964, Dec. 1		Litho.	Perf. 12½x13	
211	A33	2fr multicolored	.90	.50
212	A33	4fr multicolored	1.50	.50
213	A33	7fr multicolored	3.00	1.25
214	A33	8fr multicolored	4.00	1.75
215	A33	20fr multicolored	9.50	2.50
		Nos. 211-215,C32 (6)	28.40	10.50

 Painting from a School Dining Room — A34

1965, Nov. 29		Engr.	Perf. 13	
216	A34	20fr dk brn, sl grn & dk car	20.00	12.00

Publicizing the School Canteen Program. See No. C38.

 Outrigger Canoe on Lagoon — A35

Ships: 11fr, Large cruising yacht. vert. 12fr, Motorboat for sport fishing. 14fr, Outrigger canoes with sails. 19fr, Schooner, vert. 22fr, Modern coaster "Oiseau des Iles II."

1966, Aug. 30		Engr.	Perf. 13	
217	A35	10fr brt ultra, emer & mar	2.75	.90
218	A35	11fr mar, dk bl & sl grn	2.75	1.60
219	A35	12fr emer, dk bl & red lil	3.75	1.75
220	A35	14fr brn, bl & slate grn	5.50	2.00
221	A35	19fr scar, sl grn & dp bl	6.50	2.10
222	A35	22fr multicolored	9.50	4.00
		Nos. 217-222 (6)	30.75	12.35

FRENCH POLYNESIA

High Jump — A36

Designs: 20fr, Pole vault, vert. 40fr, Women's basketball, vert. 60fr, Hurdling.

1966, Dec. 15	Engr.		Perf. 13	
223	A36	10fr dk red, lem & blk	2.25	1.50
224	A36	20fr blue, emer & blk	5.25	2.00
225	A36	40fr emer, brt pink & blk	10.00	5.00
226	A36	60fr dull yel, bl & blk	17.00	8.50
		Nos. 223-226 (4)	34.50	17.00

2nd South Pacific Games, Nouméa, New Caledonia, Dec. 8-18.

Poi Pounder — A37

1967, June 15	Engr.		Perf. 13	
227	A37	50fr orange & blk	17.00	10.00

Society for Oceanic Studies, 50th anniv.

Javelin Throwing — A38

5fr, Spring dance. 15fr, Horse race. 16fr, Fruit carriers' race. 21fr, Canoe race.

1967, July 11				
228	A38	5fr multi, horiz.	1.10	.90
229	A38	13fr multi	4.50	1.50
230	A38	15fr multi, horiz.	4.50	1.60
231	A38	16fr multi	4.50	2.75
232	A38	21fr multi, horiz.	9.50	5.00
		Nos. 228-232 (5)	24.10	11.75

Issued to publicize the July Festival.

Earring — A39

Art of the Marquesas Islands: 10fr, Carved mother-of-pearl. 15fr, Decorated canoe paddle. 23fr, Oil vessel. 25fr, Carved stilt stirrups. 30fr, Fan handles. 35fr, Tattooed man. 50fr, Tikis.

1967-68	Engr.		Perf. 13	
233	A39	10fr dp cl, dl red & ultra	2.25	.65
234	A39	15fr black & emerald	3.00	1.25
235	A39	20fr ol gray, dk car & lt bl	5.25	2.00
236	A39	23fr dk brn, ocher & bl	6.50	4.00
237	A39	25fr dk brn, dk bl & lil	6.50	3.75
238	A39	30fr brown & red lilac	6.25	1.00
239	A39	35fr ultra & dk brn	14.00	6.25
240	A39	50fr brn, sl grn & lt bl	15.00	7.25
		Nos. 233-240 (8)	60.75	29.15

Issued: 20fr, 25fr, 30fr, 50fr, 12/19/67; others 2/28/68.

WHO Anniversary Issue
Common Design Type

1968, May 4	Engr.		Perf. 13	
241	CD126	15fr bl grn, mar & dp vio	11.00	4.75
242	CD126	16fr org, lil & bl grn	11.00	8.00

Human Rights Year Issue
Common Design Type

1968, Aug. 10	Engr.		Perf. 13	
243	CD127	15fr blue, red & brn	12.00	6.00
244	CD127	16fr brn, brt pink & ultra	12.00	8.00

Tiare Apetahi — A40

Flower: 17fr, Tiare Tahiti.

1969, Mar. 27	Photo.		Perf. 12½x13	
245	A40	9fr multicolored	2.10	1.10
246	A40	17fr multicolored	4.25	2.10

3rd South Pacific Games, Port Moresby, Papua and New Guinea, Aug. 13-23 — A41

1969, Aug. 13	Engr.		Perf. 13	
247	A41	9fr Boxer, horiz.	3.25	1.25
248	A41	17fr High jump	7.25	2.00
249	A41	18fr Runner	9.00	3.50
250	A41	22fr Long jump	12.00	7.25
		Nos. 247-250 (4)	31.50	14.00

ILO Issue
Common Design Type

1969, Nov. 24	Engr.		Perf. 13	
251	CD131	17fr org, emer & ol	12.00	5.75
252	CD131	18fr org, dk brn & vio bl	12.00	6.75

Territorial Assembly — A42

Buildings: 14fr, Governor's Residence. 17fr, House of Tourism. 18fr, Maeva Hotel. 24fr, Taharaa Hotel.

1969, Dec. 22	Photo.		Perf. 12½x12	
253	A42	13fr black & multi	2.75	1.25
254	A42	14fr black & multi	4.25	1.50
255	A42	17fr black & multi	7.00	3.50
256	A42	18fr black & multi	7.75	4.00
257	A42	24fr black & multi	13.50	7.00
		Nos. 253-257 (5)	35.25	17.25

Stone Figure with Globe — A43

Designs: 40fr, Globe, plane, map of Polynesia and men holding "PATA" sign, horiz. 60fr, Polynesian carrying globe.

1970, Apr. 7	Engr.		Perf. 13	
258	A43	20fr deep plum, gray & bl	6.75	3.25
259	A43	40fr emer, rose lil & ultra	11.00	5.25
260	A43	60fr red brn, bl & dk brn	19.00	10.00
		Nos. 258-260 (3)	36.75	18.50

Issued to publicize the 1970 Pacific Area Travel Association Congress (PATA).

UPU Headquarters Issue
Common Design Type

1970, May 20	Engr.		Perf. 13	
261	CD133	18fr mar, pur & brn	10.00	4.75
262	CD133	20fr lil rose, ol & ind	10.00	5.25

Night Fishing A44

1971, May 11	Photo.		Perf. 13	
263	A44	10fr multicolored	12.50	5.25
		Nos. 263,C71-C73 (4)	37.50	19.75

Flowers — A45

Designs: Various flowers. 12fr is horiz.

		Perf. 12½x13, 13x12½		
1971, Aug. 27				
264	A45	8fr multicolored	2.25	1.00
265	A45	12fr multicolored	3.50	1.75
266	A45	22fr multicolored	5.75	3.00
		Nos. 264-266 (3)	11.50	5.75

Day of a Thousand Flowers.

Water-skiing Slalom A46

Designs: 20fr, Water-skiing, jump, vert. 40fr, Figure water-skiing.

1971, Oct. 11	Engr.		Perf. 13	
267	A46	10fr grnsh bl, dk red & brn	6.25	2.00
268	A46	20fr car, emer & brn	9.00	4.00
269	A46	40fr brn, grn & lil	20.00	12.00
		Nos. 267-269 (3)	35.25	18.00

World water-skiing championships, Oct. 1971.

De Gaulle Issue
Common Design Type

30fr, As general, 1940. 50fr, As president, 1970.

1971, Nov. 9	Engr.		Perf. 13	
270	CD134	30fr red lilac & blk	22.50	11.00
271	CD134	50fr red lilac & blk	29.00	18.50

Map of Tahiti and Jerusalem Cross — A47

1971, Dec. 18	Photo.		Perf. 13x12½	
272	A47	28fr lt blue & multi	14.00	8.50

2nd rally of French Boy Scouts and Guides, Taravao, French Polynesia.

"Alcoholism" — A48

1972, Mar. 24	Photo.		Perf. 13	
273	A48	20fr brown & multi	11.50	5.75

Fight against alcoholism.

Mother and Child — A49

1973, Sept. 26	Photo.		Perf. 12½x13	
274	A49	28fr pale yellow & multi	9.50	5.00

Day nursery.

A 50fr multicolored stamp for the Second Medical Conference was prepared for release in 1973, but not issued. Between 50 and 75 examples were sold.

Polynesian Golfer — A50

Design: 24fr, Atimaono Golf Course.

1974, Feb. 27	Photo.		Perf. 13	
275	A50	16fr multicolored	8.50	3.25
276	A50	24fr multicolored	10.50	5.25

Atimaono Golf Course.

Hand Throwing Life Preserver to Puppy A51

1974, May 9	Photo.		Perf. 13	
277	A51	21fr brt blue & multi	12.00	5.00

Society for the Protection of Animals.

Around a Fire, on the Beach — A52

Polynesian Views: 2fr, Lagoons and mountains. 6fr, Pebble divers. 10fr, Lonely Mountain and flowers, vert. 15fr, Sailing ship at sunset. 20fr, Lagoon and mountain.

1974, May 22				
278	A52	2fr multicolored	.90	.60
279	A52	5fr multicolored	1.10	.90
280	A52	6fr multicolored	1.90	1.10
281	A52	10fr multicolored	2.10	1.25
282	A52	15fr multicolored	4.25	1.75
283	A52	20fr multicolored	7.00	2.10
		Nos. 278-283 (6)	17.25	7.70

Polynesian Woman and UPU Emblem — A53

1974, Oct. 9	Engr.		Perf. 13	
284	A53	65fr multicolored	12.00	7.75

Centenary of Universal Postal Union.

Lion, Sun and Emblem — A54

1975, June 17			Photo.	
285	A54	26fr multicolored	12.00	5.00

15th anniv. of Lions Intl. in Tahiti.

FRENCH POLYNESIA

Fish and Leaf — A55

1975, July 9   Litho.   *Perf. 12*
286 A55 19fr dp ultra & green   10.00   4.25

Polynesian Association for the Protection of Nature.

Georges Pompidou, Pres. of France — A55a

1976, Feb. 16   Engr.   *Perf. 13*
287 A55a 49fr dk violet & black   11.00   7.00

See France No. 1430.

Alain Gerbault and Sailboat — A56

1976, May 25   Photo.   *Perf. 13*
288 A56 90fr multicolored   13.50   9.00

Alain Gerbault's arrival in Bora Bora, 50th anniv.

Turtle — A57

Design: 42fr, Hand protecting bird.

1976, June 24   Litho.   *Perf. 12½*
289 A57 18fr multicolored   14.00   4.25
290 A57 42fr multicolored   20.00   11.00

World Ecology Day.

A. G. Bell, Telephone, Radar and Satellite A58

1976, Sept. 15   Engr.   *Perf. 13*
291 A58 37fr multicolored   10.00   5.00

Centenary of first telephone call by Alexander Graham Bell, Mar. 10, 1876.

Dugout Canoes A59

1976, Dec. 16   Litho.   *Perf. 13x12½*
292 A59 25fr Marquesas   3.75   2.75
293 A59 30fr Raiatea   4.75   4.75
294 A59 75fr Tahiti   9.50   5.75
295 A59 100fr Tuamotu   12.00   7.00
   Nos. 292-295 (4)   30.00   20.25

Sailing Ship — A60

Designs: Various sailing vessels.

1977, Dec. 22   Litho.   *Perf. 13*
296 A60 20fr multicolored   6.25   2.00
297 A60 50fr multicolored   7.25   2.25
298 A60 85fr multicolored   9.00   3.75
299 A60 120fr multicolored   15.00   5.75
   Nos. 296-299 (4)   37.50   13.75

Hibiscus — A61

Designs: 10fr, Vanda orchids. 16fr, Pua (fagraea berteriana). 22fr, Gardenia.

1978-79   Photo.   *Perf. 12½x13*
300 A61 10fr multicolored   1.10   .50
301 A61 13fr multicolored   2.50   1.00
302 A61 16fr multicolored   2.75   1.75
303 A61 22fr multicolored   1.75   1.00
   Nos. 300-303 (4)   8.10   4.25

Issued: 13fr, 16fr, 8/23; 10fr, 22fr, 1/25/79.

Girl with Shells on Beach — A62

Design A24 with "1958 1978" added: 28fr, Man with headdress. 36fr, Girl playing guitar.

1978, Nov. 3   Engr.   *Perf. 13*
304 A62 20fr multicolored   3.00   .75
305 A62 28fr multicolored   3.75   1.50
306 A62 36fr multicolored   5.75   2.25
   a. Souvenir sheet of 3   27.50   27.50
   Nos. 304-306 (3)   12.50   4.50

20th anniv. of stamps inscribed: Polynesie Francaise. No. 306a contains Nos. 304-306 in changed colors.

Ships — A63

1978, Dec. 29   Litho.   *Perf. 13x12½*
307 A63 15fr Tahiti   1.50   .80
308 A63 30fr Monowai   2.75   1.25
309 A63 75fr Tahitien   4.50   3.25
310 A63 100fr Mariposa   8.50   3.25
   Nos. 307-310 (4)   17.25   8.55

Porites Coral — A64

Design: 37fr, Montipora coral.

1979, Feb. 15   *Perf. 13x12½*
311 A64 32fr multicolored   2.50   1.25
312 A64 37fr multicolored   3.75   2.00

Raiatea — A65

Landscapes: 1fr, Moon over Bora Bora. 2fr, Mountain peaks, Ua Pou. 3fr, Sunset over Motu Tapu. 5fr, Motu. 6fr, Palm and hut, Tuamotu.

1979, Mar. 8   Photo.   *Perf. 13x13½*
313 A65 1fr multicolored   .25   .25
314 A65 2fr multicolored   .25   .25
315 A65 3fr multicolored   .30   .25
316 A65 4fr multicolored   .45   .25
317 A65 5fr multicolored   .80   .35
318 A65 6fr multicolored   1.00   .60
   Nos. 313-318 (6)   3.05   1.95

See Nos. 438-443 for redrawn designs.

Dance Costumes — A66

1979, July 14   Litho.   *Perf. 12½*
319 A66 45fr Fetia   1.75   1.00
320 A66 51fr Teanuanua   2.75   1.25
321 A66 74fr Temaeva   3.75   2.25
   Nos. 319-321 (3)   8.25   4.50

Hill, Great Britain No. 53, Tahiti No. 28 — A67

1979, Aug. 1   Engr.   *Perf. 13*
322 A67 100fr multicolored   5.00   3.00

Sir Rowland Hill (1795-1879), originator of penny postage.

Hastula Strigilata — A68

Shells: 28fr, Scabricola variegata. 35fr, Fusinus undatus.

1979, Aug. 22   Litho.   *Perf. 12½*
323 A68 20fr multicolored   1.50   .50
324 A68 28fr multicolored   2.00   1.00
325 A68 35fr multicolored   2.75   2.00
   Nos. 323-325 (3)   6.25   3.50

Statue Holding Rotary Emblem — A69

1979, Nov. 30   Litho.   *Perf. 13*
326 A69 47fr multicolored   2.75   2.00

Rotary International, 75th anniversary; Papeete Rotary Club, 20th anniversary. For overprint see No. 330.

Myripristis Murdjan — A70

Fish: 8fr, Napoleon. 12fr, Emperor.

1980, Jan. 21   Litho.   *Perf. 12½*
327 A70 7fr multicolored   1.00   1.00
328 A70 8fr multicolored   1.00   .65
329 A70 12fr multicolored   1.65   .95
   Nos. 327-329 (3)   3.65   2.10

No. 326 Overprinted and Surcharged in Gold

1980, Feb. 23   Litho.   *Perf. 13*
330 A69 77fr on 47fr multi   5.75   3.25

Rotary International, 75th anniversary.

CNEXO Fish Hatchery — A71

1980, Mar. 17   Photo.   *Perf. 13x13½*
331 A71 15fr shown   1.75   .90
332 A71 22fr Crayfish   1.75   .90

Papeete Post Office Building Opening — A72

1980, Apr. 30   Photo.   *Perf. 13x12½*
333 A72 50fr multicolored   2.50   1.50

Tiki and Festival Emblem — A73

1980, June 30   Photo.   *Perf. 13½*
334 A73 34fr shown   1.25   .90
335 A73 39fr Drum (pahu)   2.00   1.30
336 A73 49fr Ax (to'i)   2.75   1.75
   a. Souv. sheet of 3, #334-336   13.50   13.00
   Nos. 334-336 (3)   6.00   3.95

South Pacific Arts Festival, Port Moresby, Papua New Guinea.

Titmouse Henparrot — A74

25fr, White sea-swallow, horiz. 45fr, Minor frigate bird, horiz.

Perf. 13x12½, 12½x13
1980, Oct. 20   *Photo.*
337 A74 25fr multi   1.50   .70
338 A74 35fr shown   1.75   .90
339 A74 45fr multi   2.75   1.10
   Nos. 337-339 (3)   6.00   2.70

Charles de Gaulle — A75

1980, Nov. 9   Engr.   *Perf. 12½x13*
340 A75 100fr multicolored   5.00   3.25

FRENCH POLYNESIA

Naso Vlamingi (Karaua) — A76

16fr, Lutjanus vaigensis (toau). 24fr, Plectropomus leopardus (tonu).

1981, Feb. 5   Litho.   Perf. 12½
341	A76	13fr shown	1.00	.50
342	A76	16fr multi	1.10	.60
343	A76	24fr multi	2.25	.75
		Nos. 341-343 (3)	4.35	1.85

Indoor Fish Breeding Tanks, Cnexo Hatchery — A77

1981, May 14   Photo.   Perf. 13x13½
| 344 | A77 | 23fr shown | 1.10 | .80 |
| 345 | A77 | 41fr Mussels | 2.00 | 1.10 |

Folk Dancers — A78

Perf. 13x13½, 13½x13   Litho.
1981, July 10
346	A78	26fr shown	1.25	.65
347	A78	28fr Dancer	1.25	1.10
348	A78	44fr Dancers, vert.	2.10	1.50
		Nos. 346-348 (3)	4.60	3.25

Sterna Bergii A79

53fr, Ptilinopus purpuratus, vert. 65fr, Estrilda astrild, vert.

1981, Sept. 24   Litho.   Perf. 13
349	A79	47fr shown	1.75	1.00
350	A79	53fr multi	1.75	1.20
351	A79	65fr multi	2.25	1.50
		Nos. 349-351 (3)	5.75	3.70

See Nos. 370-372.

Huahine Island — A80

1981, Oct. 22   Litho.   Perf. 12½
352	A80	34fr shown	1.40	.75
353	A80	134fr Maupiti	3.25	2.00
354	A80	136fr Bora-Bora	3.25	2.00
		Nos. 352-354 (3)	7.90	4.75

A81

1982, Feb. 4   Photo.   Perf. 13x13½
355	A81	30fr Parrotfish	1.00	.75
356	A81	31fr Regal angel	1.40	1.00
357	A81	45fr Spotted bass	1.50	1.25
		Nos. 355-357 (3)	3.90	2.75

Pearl Industry — A82

1982, Apr. 22   Photo.   Perf. 13x13½
358	A82	7fr Pearl beds	.85	.45
359	A82	8fr Extracting pearls	.85	.45
360	A82	10fr Pearls	1.20	1.10
		Nos. 358-360 (3)	2.90	2.00

Tahiti "No. 1A," Emblem A83

1982, May 12   Engr.   Perf. 13
| 361 | A83 | 150fr multicolored | 4.75 | 3.50 |
| a. | | Souvenir sheet | 16.00 | 16.00 |

PHILEXFRANCE Stamp Exhibition, Paris, June 11-21. No. 361a contains No. 361 in changed colors.

King Holding Carved Scepter — A84

Designs: Coronation ceremony.

1982, July 12   Photo.   Perf. 13½x13
362	A84	12fr shown	.50	.25
363	A84	13fr King, priest	.50	.25
364	A84	17fr Procession	1.00	.50
		Nos. 362-364 (3)	2.00	1.00

Championship Emblem — A85

1982, Aug. 13   Perf. 13
| 365 | A85 | 90fr multicolored | 2.75 | 2.00 |

4th Hobie-Cat 16 World Catamaran Sailing Championship, Tahiti, Aug. 15-21.

First Colloquium on New Energy Sources — A86

1982, Sept. 29   Litho.
| 366 | A86 | 46fr multicolored | 1.75 | 1.00 |

Motu, Tuamotu Islet — A87

1982, Oct. 12   Litho.   Perf. 13
367	A87	20fr shown	.70	.35
368	A87	33fr Tupai Atoll	.90	.45
369	A87	35fr Gambier Islds.	1.25	.55
		Nos. 367-369 (3)	2.85	1.35

Bird Type of 1981

37fr, Sacred egret. 39fr, Pluvialis dominica, vert. 42fr, Lonchura castaneothorax.

1982, Nov. 17   Litho.   Perf. 13
370	A79	37fr multi	1.40	.55
371	A79	39fr multi	1.40	.60
372	A79	42fr multi	1.75	.90
		Nos. 370-372 (3)	4.55	2.10

Fish — A88

8fr, Acanthurus lineatus. 10fr, Caranx melampygus.   12fr, Carcharhinus melanopterus.

1983, Feb. 9   Litho.   Perf. 13x13½
373	A88	8fr multi	.70	.35
374	A88	10fr multi	.90	.35
375	A88	12fr multi	1.40	.60
		Nos. 373-375 (3)	3.00	1.20

The Way of the Cross, Sculpture by Damien Haturau — A89

1983, Mar. 9   Litho.   Perf. 13
376	A89	7fr shown	.25	.25
377	A89	21fr Virgin and Child	.70	.60
378	A89	23fr Christ	.90	.60
		Nos. 376-378 (3)	1.85	1.45

Traditional Hats — A90

1983, May 24   Litho.   Perf. 13x12½
379	A90	11fr Acacia	.45	.30
380	A90	13fr Niau	.60	.30
381	A90	25fr Ofe	.80	.50
382	A90	35fr Ofe, diff.	1.10	.60
		Nos. 379-382 (4)	2.95	1.70

See Nos. 393-396.

Chieftain in Traditional Costume, Sainte-Christine Isld. — A91

Traditional Costumes, Marquesas Islds.

1983, July 12   Photo.   Perf. 13
383	A91	15fr shown	.70	.30
384	A91	17fr Man	.90	.40
385	A91	28fr Woman	1.10	.50
		Nos. 383-385 (3)	2.70	1.20

See Nos. 397-399, 419-421.

Polynesian Crowns A92

Various flower garlands.

1983, Oct. 19   Litho.   Perf. 13
386	A92	41fr multicolored	1.25	.90
387	A92	44fr multicolored	1.40	.95
388	A92	45fr multicolored	1.50	1.00
		Nos. 386-388 (3)	4.15	2.85

See Nos. 400-402.

Martin Luther (1483-1546) — A93

1983, Nov. 10   Engr.   Perf. 13
| 389 | A93 | 90fr black, brn & lil gray | 2.25 | 1.10 |

Tiki Carvings — A94

Various carvings.

1984, Feb. 8   Litho.   Perf. 12½x13
390	A94	14fr multicolored	.50	.25
391	A94	16fr multicolored	.60	.45
392	A94	19fr multicolored	.75	.45
		Nos. 390-392 (3)	1.85	1.15

Hat Type of 1983

1984, June 20   Litho.   Perf. 13x12½
393	A90	20fr Aeho ope	.50	.35
394	A90	24fr Paeore	.60	.35
395	A90	26fr Ofe fei	.75	.50
396	A90	33fr Hua	.80	.50
		Nos. 393-396 (4)	2.65	1.70

Costume Type of 1983

34fr, Tahitian playing nose flute. 35fr, Priest, Oei-eitia. 39fr, Tahitian adult and child.

1984, July 11   Litho.   Perf. 13
397	A91	34fr multi	.75	.50
398	A91	35fr multi	.90	.50
399	A91	39fr multi	.90	.50
		Nos. 397-399 (3)	2.55	1.50

Garland Type of 1983

1984, Oct. 24   Litho.   Perf. 13x12½
400	A92	46fr Moto'i Lei	.90	.50
401	A92	47fr Pitate Lei	1.00	.60
402	A92	53fr Bougainvillea Lei	1.25	.80
		Nos. 400-402 (3)	3.15	1.90

4th Pacific Arts Festival, Noumea, New Caledonia, Dec. 8-22 — A95

1984, Nov. 20   Litho.   Perf. 13
| 403 | A95 | 150fr Statue, headdress | 3.50 | 2.25 |

See No. C213.

Paysage D'Anaa, by Jean Masson A96

Paintings: 50fr, Sortie Du Culte, by Jacques Boulaire. 75fr, La Fete, by Robert Tatin. 85fr, Tahitiennes Sur La Plage, by Pierre Heyman.

Perf. 12½x13, 13x12½
1984, Dec. 12   Litho.
404	A96	50fr multi, vert.	1.25	.70
405	A96	65fr multicolored	1.40	.90
406	A96	75fr multicolored	1.90	1.00
407	A96	85fr multicolored	2.25	1.75
		Nos. 404-407 (4)	6.80	4.35

Tiki Carvings — A97

1985, Jan. 23   Litho.   Perf. 13½
408	A97	30fr multicolored	.60	.35
409	A97	36fr multicolored	.80	.45
410	A97	40fr multicolored	.90	.75
		Nos. 408-410 (3)	2.30	1.55

FRENCH POLYNESIA

Polynesian Faces — A98

1985, Feb. 20	Photo.		Perf. 12½x13
411	A98	22fr multicolored	.40 .30
412	A98	39fr multicolored	.75 .40
413	A98	44fr multicolored	.95 .70
		Nos. 411-413 (3)	2.10 1.40

Early Tahiti — A99

Designs: 42fr, Entrance to Papeete. 45fr, Girls, vert. 48fr, Papeete market.

	Perf. 13x12½, 12½x13		
1985, Apr. 24			Litho.
414	A99	42fr multicolored	.90 .55
415	A99	45fr multicolored	1.25 .75
416	A99	48fr multicolored	1.40 .85
		Nos. 414-416 (3)	3.55 2.15

5th Intl. Congress on Coral Reefs, Tahiti — A100

Design: Local reef formation.

1985, May 28	Litho.		Perf. 13½
417	A100	140fr multicolored	3.00 2.00

Printed se-tenant with label picturing congress emblem.

National Flag — A101

1985, June 28			
418	A101	9fr Flag, natl. arms	.65 .30

Costume Type of 1983

18th-19th Cent. Prints, Beslu Collection: 38fr, Tahitian dancer. 55fr, Man and woman from Otahiti, 1806. 70fr, Traditional chief.

1985, July 17			Perf. 13
419	A91	38fr multicolored	.95 .65
420	A91	55fr multicolored	1.25 .90
421	A91	70fr multicolored	1.75 1.25
		Nos. 419-421 (3)	3.95 2.80

Local Foods A103

Designs: 25fr, Roasted pig. 35fr, Pit fire. 80fr, Fish in coconut milk. 110fr, Fafaru.

1985-86	Litho.		Perf. 13
422	A103	25fr multi	.85 .60
423	A103	35fr multi	1.10 .65
423A	A103	80fr multi	1.90 1.50
423B	A103	110fr multi	2.40 1.90
		Nos. 422-423B (4)	6.25 4.65

Issued: 25fr, 35fr, 11/14; 80fr, 110fr, 5/20/86. See Nos. 458-459, 474-475.

Catholic Churches A104

90fr, St. Anne's, Otepipi. 100fr, St. Michael's Cathedral, Rikitea. 120fr, Cathedral, exterior.

1985, Dec. 11	Litho.		Perf. 13
424	A104	90fr multi	1.75 1.00
425	A104	100fr multi	1.90 1.00
426	A104	120fr multi	2.25 1.50
		Nos. 424-426 (3)	5.90 3.50

Nos. 424-426 printed se-tenant with labels picturing local religious art.

Crabs — A105

1986, Jan. 22			Perf. 13½
427	A105	18fr Fiddler	.90 .50
428	A105	29fr Hermit	1.40 .65
429	A105	31fr Coconut	2.40 .65
		Nos. 427-429 (3)	4.70 1.80

Faces of Polynesia — A106

1986, Feb. 19	Perf. 12½x13, 13x12½		
430	A106	43fr Boy, fish	1.00 .50
431	A106	49fr Boy, coral	1.25 .50
432	A106	51fr Boy, turtle, vert.	1.40 .60
		Nos. 430-432 (3)	3.65 1.60

Old Tahiti A107

Designs: 52fr, Papeete. 56fr, Harpoon fishing. 57fr, Royal Palace, Papeete.

1986, Mar. 18			Perf. 13x12½
433	A107	52fr multi	1.00 .55
434	A107	56fr multi	1.10 .55
435	A107	57fr multi	1.25 .70
		Nos. 433-435 (3)	3.35 1.80

Tiki Rock Carvings — A108

Designs: 58fr, Atuona, Hiva Oa. 59fr, Ua Huka Hill, Hane Valley.

1986, Apr. 16			
436	A108	58fr multi	1.40 .70
437	A108	59fr multi	1.40 .70

Landscapes Type Redrawn

1986-88	Litho.		Perf. 13½
438	A65	1fr multi, type 2 ('88)	2.50 .35
a.		Type 1 ('86)	4.50 1.25
b.		Type 3 ('91)	18.50 4.50
439	A65	2fr multicolored	.40 .25
440	A65	3fr multicolored	.45 .25
441	A65	4fr multicolored ('87)	1.75 .40
442	A65	5fr multicolored	.75 .30
443	A65	6fr multicolored	.65 .30
		Nos. 438-443 (6)	6.50 1.85

Nos. 438-443 printed in sharper detail, and box containing island name is taller. No. 439-443 margin is inscribed "CARTOR" instead of "DELRIEU."
No. 438 has three types of inscription below design: type 1, photographer's name at left, no inscription at right; type 2, photographer's name at left 9.5mm long, printer's name (Cartor) at right; type 3, photographer's name at left 12.5mm long, Cartor at right.

Traditional Crafts — A109

1986, July 17			Litho.
444	A109	8fr Quilting, vert.	.25 .25
445	A109	10fr Baskets, hats	.25 .25
446	A109	12fr Grass skirts	.80 .30
		Nos. 444-446 (3)	1.30 .80

Building a Pirogue (Canoe) — A110

1986, Oct. 21	Litho.		Perf. 13½
447	A110	46fr Boat-builders	1.00 .65
448	A110	50fr Close-up	1.10 .85

Medicinal Plants — A111

Designs: 40fr, Phymatosorus. 41fr, Barringtonia asiatica. 60fr, Ocimum bacilicum.

1986, Nov. 19			Perf. 13
449	A111	40fr multi	.90 .50
450	A111	41fr multi	1.00 .50
451	A111	60fr multi	1.60 .90
		Nos. 449-451 (3)	3.50 1.90

See Nos. 495-497.

Polynesians — A112

1987, Jan. 21	Litho.		Perf. 13½
452	A112	28fr Old man	.60 .35
453	A112	30fr Mother and child	.75 .50
454	A112	37fr Old woman	1.00 .60
		Nos. 452-454 (3)	2.35 1.45

Crustaceans A113

34fr, Carpilius maculatus. 35fr, Parribacus antarticus. 39fr, Justitia longimana.

1987, Feb. 18			Perf. 12½x13
455	A113	34fr multicolored	2.00 .65
456	A113	35fr multicolored	2.00 .65
457	A113	39fr multicolored	2.50 .65
		Nos. 455-457 (3)	6.50 1.95

Local Foods Type of 1985

1987, Mar. 19	Litho.		Perf. 13
458	A103	33fr Papaya poe	1.10 .70
459	A103	65fr Chicken fafa	2.00 1.00

Polynesian Petroglyphs — A114

1987, May 13			Perf. 12½
460	A114	13fr Tipaerui, Tahiti	.35 .25
461	A114	21fr Turtle, Raiatea Is.	.60 .35

Calling Devices and Musical Instruments, Museum of Tahiti and the Isles — A115

1987, July 1			Perf. 13½
462	A115	20fr Wood horn	.65 .30
463	A115	26fr Triton's conch	.80 .65
464	A115	33fr Nose flutes	1.00 .70
		Nos. 462-464 (3)	2.45 1.65

Medicinal Plants — A116

46fr, Thespesia populnea. 53fr, Ophioglossum reticulatum. 54fr, Dicrocephala latifolia.

1987, Sept. 16			Perf. 12½x13
465	A116	46fr olive green	1.00 .55
466	A116	53fr reddish lilac	1.40 .55
467	A116	54fr dp bluish grn	1.50 .55
		Nos. 465-467 (3)	3.90 1.65

Ancient Weapons and Tools A117

Designs: 25fr, Adze, war club, chisel, flute. 27fr, War clubs, tatooing comb, mallet. 32fr, Headdress, necklaces, nose flute.

1987, Oct. 14		Engr.	Perf. 13
468	A117	25fr lt olive grn & blk	.60 .40
469	A117	27fr Prus grn & int blue	.75 .45
470	A117	32fr brt olive bis & brn blk	.80 .55
		Nos. 468-470 (3)	2.15 1.40

Catholic Missionaries A118

Monsignors: 95fr, Rene Ildefonse Dordillon (1808-1888), bishop of the Marquesas Isls. 105fr, Tepano Jaussen (1815-1891), first bishop of Polynesia. 115fr, Paul Laurent Maze (1885-1976), archbishop of Papeete.

1987, Dec. 9			Litho.
471	A118	95fr multicolored	1.90 1.40
472	A118	105fr multicolored	2.10 1.50
473	A118	115fr multicolored	2.40 1.60
		Nos. 471-473 (3)	6.40 4.50

Local Foods Type of 1985

Designs: 40fr, Crayfish (varo). 75fr, Bananas in coconut milk.

1988, Jan. 12	Litho.		Perf. 13
474	A103	40fr multi	1.90 .55
475	A103	75fr multi	2.75 1.10

Nos. 474-475 are vert.

Authors A119

62fr, James Norman Hall (1887-1951). 85fr, Charles Bernard Nordhoff (1887-1947).

1988, Feb. 10			
476	A119	62fr multicolored	1.40 .75
477	A119	85fr multicolored	1.90 .85

Traditional Housing A120

11fr, Taranpoo Opoa Is., Raiatea. 15fr, Tahaa Village. 17fr, Community meeting house, Tahiti.

FRENCH POLYNESIA

1988, Mar. 16 Litho. Perf. 13x12½
478	A120	11fr multicolored	.50	.30
479	A120	15fr multicolored	.60	.30
480	A120	17fr multicolored	.60	.30
		Nos. 478-480 (3)	1.70	.90

Point Venus Lighthouse, 120th Anniv. — A121

1988, Apr. 21 Litho. Perf. 13
481	A121	400fr multicolored	8.50	5.50

Tapa-cloth Paintings by Paul Engdahl — A122

1988, May 20
482	A122	52fr multicolored	1.25	.75
483	A122	54fr multicolored	1.40	.85
484	A122	64fr multicolored	1.50	1.10
		Nos. 482-484 (3)	4.15	2.70

POLYSAT (Domestic Communications Network) — A123

1988, June 15 Litho. Perf. 12½x12
485	A123	300fr multicolored	6.00	4.75

Tahitian Dolls — A124

Designs: 42fr, Wearing grass skirt and headdress. 45fr, Wearing print dress and straw hat, holding guitar. 48fr, Wearing print dress and straw hat, holding straw bag.

1988, June 27 Perf. 13x12½
486	A124	42fr multicolored	1.00	.60
487	A124	45fr multicolored	1.25	.90
488	A124	48fr multicolored	1.50	.75
		Nos. 486-488 (3)	3.75	1.95

Visiting a Marae at Nuku Hiva, Engraving by J. & E. Verreaux — A125

1988, Aug. 1 Engr. Perf. 13
489	A125	68fr black brown	2.00	1.25

Size: 143x101mm
490	A125	145fr violet brn & grn	5.25	4.00

SYDPEX '88, July 30-Aug. 7, Australia. No. 490 pictures a Russian navy officer (probably Krusenstern) visiting the Marquesas Islanders; denomination LR.

Map Linking South America and South Pacific Islands — A126

1988, Aug. 30 Engr.
491	A126	350fr multicolored	7.50	4.50

Eric de Bisschop (1890-1958), explorer who tried to prove that there was an exchange of peoples between the South Pacific islands and So. America, rather than that the island populations originated from So. America.

Seashells — A127

1988, Sept. 21 Litho. Perf. 13½
492	A127	24fr Kermia barnardi	.60	.35
493	A127	35fr Vexillum suavis	1.00	.50
494	A127	44fr Berthelinia	1.40	.75
		Nos. 492-494 (3)	3.00	1.60

Medicinal Plants Type of 1986

23fr, Davallia solida. 36fr, Rorippa sarmentosa. 49fr, Lindernia crustacea.

1988, Oct. 10 Engr. Perf. 13
495	A111	23fr carmine lake	.75	.30
496	A111	36fr purple brown	1.10	.45
497	A111	49fr deep blue	1.25	.70
		Nos. 495-497 (3)	3.10	1.45

Protestant Missionaries A128

80fr, Henry Nott (1774-1844). 90fr, Papeiha (1800-40). 100fr, Samuel Raapoto (1921-76).

1988, Dec. 7 Litho.
498	A128	80fr multi	1.50	.90
499	A128	90fr multi	2.00	1.25
500	A128	100fr multi	2.25	1.40
		Nos. 498-500 (3)	5.75	3.55

Tahiti Post Office — A129

1989, Jan. 12 Engr.
501	A129	30fr P.O., 1875	.75	.40
502	A129	40fr P.O., 1915	1.00	.55

Center for Arts and Crafts — A130

29fr, Marquesas Is. lidded bowl. 31fr, Mother-of-pearl pendant.

1989, Feb. 15 Litho. Perf. 12½
503	A130	29fr multi	.80	.40
504	A130	31fr multi	.90	.45

Copra Industry

Extracting Coconut Meat From Shell — A131a

Drying Coconut Meat in Sun — A131

1989, Mar. 16 Litho. Perf. 13
505	A131a	55fr multicolored	55.00	40.00
506	A131	70fr multicolored	2.50	2.00

Tapa Art — A132

43fr, Wood statue (pole), Marquesas Islands, vert. 51fr, Hand-painted bark tapestry, Society Is. 56fr, Concentric circles, Tubuai, Austral Islands.

1989, Apr. 18 Litho. Perf. 13½
507	A132	43fr multicolored	.90	.60
508	A132	51fr shown	1.25	.75
509	A132	56fr multicolored	1.50	.90
		Nos. 507-509 (3)	3.65	2.25

Polynesian Environment — A133

Design: 140fr, Diving for seashells.

1989, May 17 Litho. Perf. 13x12½
510	A133	120fr shown	2.25	1.50
511	A133	140fr multicolored	2.75	1.75

Polynesian Folklore — A134

Designs: 47fr, Stone-lifting contest, vert. 61fr, Dancer, vert. 67fr, Folk singers.

Perf. 13x12½, 12½x13
1989, June 28 Litho.
512	A134	47fr multicolored	1.10	.55
513	A134	61fr multicolored	1.40	.70
514	A134	67fr multicolored	1.75	.75
		Nos. 512-514 (3)	4.25	2.00

Bounty Castaways, from an Etching by Robert Dodd A135

1989, July 7 Engr. Perf. 13
515	A135	100fr dp blue & bl grn	2.40	1.50

Souvenir Sheet
Imperf.
516	A135	200fr dk ol grn & dk brn	12.00	12.00

PHILEXFRANCE '89 and 200th anniv. of the mutiny on the Bounty and the French revolution.
No. 515 printed se-tenant with label picturing exhibition emblem.

Reverend-Father Patrick O'Reilly (1900-1988) — A136

1989, Aug. 7 Engr. Perf. 13x13½
517	A136	52fr yel brn & myrtle grn	1.40	.75

Miniature Sheet

Messages A137

a, Get well soon. b, Good luck. c, Happy birthday. d, Keep in touch. e, Congratulations.

1989, Sept. 27 Litho. Perf. 12½
518	A137	42fr Sheet of 5, #a.-e.	12.00	12.00

Sea Shells — A138

1989, Oct. 12 Litho. Perf. 13½
523	A138	60fr Triphoridae	1.60	.80
524	A138	69fr Muricidae favartia	1.75	.90
525	A138	73fr Muricidae morula	2.00	1.00
		Nos. 523-525 (3)	5.35	2.70

Te Faaturama, c. 1892, by Gauguin — A139

1989, Nov. 19 Litho. Perf. 12½x13
526	A139	1000fr multicolored	22.00	12.50

Legends — A140

Designs: 66fr, Maui, birth of the islands, vert. 82fr, Mt. Rotui, the pierced mountain. 88fr, Princess Hina and the eel King of Lake Vaihiria.

1989, Dec. 6 Litho. Perf. 13
527	A140	66fr olive brn & blk	1.40	.90
528	A140	82fr buff & blk	1.90	1.10
529	A140	88fr cream & blk	2.00	1.15
		Nos. 527-529 (3)	5.30	3.15

Vanilla Orchid — A141

1990, Jan. 11 Litho.
530	A141	34fr Flower	1.35	.60
531	A141	35fr Bean pods	1.60	.60

Marine Life — A142

1990, Feb. 9 Litho. Perf. 13½
532	A142	40fr Kuhlia marginata	1.30	.55
533	A142	50fr Macrobrachium	1.50	.70

FRENCH POLYNESIA

Tahiti, Center of Polynesian Triangle — A143

Maohi settlers and maps of island settlements: 58fr, Hawaiian Islands. 59fr, Easter Island. 63fr, New Zealand.

1990, Mar. 14   Engr.   Perf. 13
534	A143	58fr black	1.75	.85
535	A143	59fr bluish gray	45.00	25.00
536	A143	63fr olive green	2.25	.95
537	A143	71fr Prussian blue	2.50	1.10
		Nos. 534-537 (4)	51.50	27.90

See Nos. 544-545.

Papeete Village, Cent. A144

1990, May 16   Litho.
538	A144	150fr New City Hall	3.25	1.75
539	A144	250fr Old Town Hall	4.75	3.00

A145

Designs: Endangered birds.

1990, June 5   Perf. 13½
540	A145	13fr Porzana tabuensis	.75	.25
541	A145	20fr Vini ultramarina	1.75	.35

A146

1990, July 10   Perf. 13
542	A146	39fr multicolored	1.10	.65

Lions Club in Papeete, 30th anniv.

Gen. Charles de Gaulle, Birth Cent. A147

1990, Sept. 2   Litho.
543	A147	200fr multi	4.50	3.25

No. 536 with Different Colors and Inscriptions

1990, Aug. 24   Engr.   Perf. 13
544	A143	125fr Man, map	3.00	2.00

Souvenir Sheet
Imperf
545	A143	230fr like No. 544	6.00	6.00

New Zealand 1990.

Intl. Tourism Day — A148

1990, Sept. 27   Litho.   Perf. 12½
546	A148	8f red & yellow pareo	1.10	.35
547	A148	10fr yellow pareo	1.10	.35
548	A148	12fr blue pareo	1.10	.75
		Nos. 546-548 (3)	3.30	1.45

Polynesian Legends A149

170fr, Legend of the Uru. 290fr, Pipiri-ma, vert. 375fr, Hiro, God of Thieves, vert.

1990, Nov. 7   Litho.   Perf. 13
549	A149	170fr multicolored	4.00	2.50
550	A149	290fr multicolored	7.50	4.00
551	A149	375fr multicolored	11.00	5.00
		Nos. 549-551 (3)	22.50	11.50

Tiare Flower — A150

Designs: 28fr, Flower crown, lei. 30fr, Flowers in bloom. 37fr, Lei.

1990, Dec. 5   Perf. 12½
552	A150	28fr multicolored	.70	.45
553	A150	30fr multicolored	.95	.45
554	A150	37fr multicolored	1.20	.55
		Nos. 552-554 (3)	2.85	1.45

Pineapple — A151

Design: 44fr, Pineapple field.

1991, Jan. 9   Self-adhesive   Die Cut
555	A151	42fr multicolored	1.25	.90
556	A151	44fr multicolored	1.75	1.10

Nos. 555-556 are on paper backing perf. 12½.

Marine Life — A152

1991, Feb. 7   Perf. 12½
557	A152	7fr Nudibranch	.45	.25
558	A152	9fr Galaxaura tenera	.70	.25
559	A152	11fr Adusta cumingii	.70	.25
		Nos. 557-559 (3)	1.85	.75

Maohi Islands — A153

18th Century scenes of: 68fr, Woman of Easter Island, vert. 84fr, Twin-hulled canoe, Hawaii. 94fr, Maori village, New Zealand.

1991, Mar. 13   Engr.   Perf. 13
560	A153	68fr olive	47.50	32.50
561	A153	84fr black	2.50	1.75
562	A153	94fr brown	3.00	1.75
		Nos. 560-562 (3)	53.00	36.00

Basketball, Cent. A154

1991, May 15   Litho.   Perf. 13
563	A154	80fr multicolored	1.75	1.25

Birds — A155

1991, June 5   Perf. 13½
564	A155	17fr Halcyon gambieri	.60	.25
565	A155	21fr Vini kuhlii	.90	.35

Still Life with Oranges in Tahiti by Paul Gauguin A156

1991, June 9   Litho.   Perf. 13
566	A156	700fr multicolored	17.50	9.50

Sculptures of the Marquesas Islands A157

56fr, White Tiki with Club, vert. 102fr, Warriors Carrying Tired Man, vert. 110fr, Native Canoe.

1991, July 17   Litho.   Perf. 13
567	A157	56fr multicolored	1.25	.85
568	A157	102fr multicolored	2.25	1.50
569	A157	110fr multicolored	2.50	1.75
		Nos. 567-569 (3)	6.00	4.10

Wolfgang Amadeus Mozart, Death Bicent. A158

1991, Aug. 28   Engr.   Perf. 13x12½
570	A158	100fr multicolored	3.00	1.75

Stone Fishing A159

25fr, Fishing boats, vert. 57fr, Man hurling stone, vert. 62fr, Trapped fish.

1991, Oct. 9   Litho.   Perf. 13
571	A159	25fr multi	.60	.40
572	A159	57fr multi	1.25	.90
573	A159	62fr multi	1.50	1.25
		Nos. 571-573 (3)	3.35	2.55

Phila Nippon '91 — A160

Designs: 50fr, Drawings of marine life by Jules-Louis Lejeune, vert. 70fr, Sailing ship, La Coquille. 250fr, Contains designs from Nos. 574-575.

Perf. 12½x13, 13x12½
1991, Nov. 16   Engr.
574	A160	50fr multicolored	1.30	.55
575	A160	70fr multicolored	1.75	1.25

Size: 100x75mm
Imperf
576	A160	250fr multicolored	6.00	6.00
		Nos. 574-576 (3)	9.05	7.80

Central Bank for Economic Co-operation, 50th Anniv. — A161

1991, Dec. 2   Litho.   Perf. 13x12½
577	A161	307fr multicolored	7.00	4.50

Christmas A162

Perf. 12½x13, 13x12½
1991, Dec. 11   Litho.
578	A162	55fr Scuba divers	1.25	.75
579	A162	83fr Underwater scene	1.75	1.35
580	A162	86fr Nativity, vert.	1.75	1.35
		Nos. 578-580 (3)	4.75	3.45

Tourism A163

Designs: 2fr, Horses, beach. 3fr, Girl holding fish. 4fr, Waterfalls, vert. 5fr, Sailing. 6fr, Waterfalls, helicopter, vert.

1992, Feb. 12   Perf. 13
581	A163	1fr shown	.25	.25
582	A163	2fr multicolored	.35	.25
583	A163	3fr multicolored	.50	.30
584	A163	4fr multicolored	.60	.35
585	A163	5fr multicolored	.75	.40
586	A163	6fr multicolored	1.00	.45
		Nos. 581-586 (6)	3.45	2.00

Views from Space A164

Designs: 46fr, Tahiti. 72fr, Mataiva. 76fr, Bora Bora. 230fr, Satellite imaging system.

1992, Mar. 18   Litho.   Perf. 13x12½
587	A164	46fr multi	1.75	.90
588	A164	72fr multi	2.00	1.25
589	A164	76fr multi	2.25	1.40

Size: 130x100mm
Imperf
590	A164	230fr multi	6.00	5.75
		Nos. 587-590 (4)	12.00	9.30

International Space Year.

FRENCH POLYNESIA

World Health Day — A165

1992, Apr. 7   **Perf. 13½**
591 A165 136fr multicolored   3.00   2.25

Discovery of America, 500th Anniv. A166

1992, May 22   **Perf. 13**
592 A166 130fr multicolored   3.00   2.25

Size: 140x100mm
Imperf
593 A166 250fr multicolored   6.00   6.00

World Columbian Stamp Expo '92, Chicago.

Traditional Dances A167

Dance from: 95fr, Tahiti. 105fr, Hawaii. 115fr, Tonga.

1992, June 17   **Engr.**   **Perf. 13**
594 A167 95fr brown black   1.90   1.60
595 A167 105fr olive brown   2.10   1.75
596 A167 115fr red brn & olive grn   2.50   1.75
Nos. 594-596 (3)   6.50   5.10

Tattoos — A168

1992, July 8   **Litho.**   **Perf. 12½**
597 A168 61fr Hand   1.90   1.25
598 A168 64fr Man, vert.   2.00   1.25

Children's Games — A169

Designs: 22fr, Outrigger canoe models. 31fr, String game. 45fr, Stilt game, vert.

1992, Aug. 5   **Perf. 13½**
599 A169 22fr multi   .50   .35
600 A169 31fr multi   .75   .45
601 A169 45fr multi   1.25   .70
Nos. 599-601 (3)   2.50   1.50

Herman Melville, 150th Anniv. of Arrival in French Polynesia — A170

1992, Sept. 16   **Perf. 12½**
602 A170 78fr multicolored   4.50   1.25

6th Festival of Pacific Arts, Rarotonga A171

40fr, Men on raft. 65fr, Pirogues, Tahiti.

1992, Oct. 16   **Engr.**   **Perf. 13**
603 A171 40fr lake   1.50   .60
604 A171 65fr blue   2.00   1.00

First French Polynesian Postage Stamps, Cent. A172

1992, Nov. 18   **Photo.**   **Perf. 13**
605 A172 200fr multicolored   4.75   3.25

Paintings — A173

55fr, Two Women Talking, by Erhard Lux. 60fr, Bouquet of Flowers, by Uschi. 75fr, Spearfisherman, by Pierre Kienlen. 85fr, Mother Nursing Child, by Octave Morillot.

1992, Dec. 9   **Perf. 12½x13**
606 A173 55fr multicolored   1.50   .75
607 A173 60fr multicolored   1.75   1.40
608 A173 75fr multicolored   1.90   1.50
609 A173 85fr multicolored   2.50   1.60
Nos. 606-609 (1)   7.65   5.25

Net Thrower — A174

1993, Feb. 10   **Litho.**   **Die Cut**
Self-Adhesive
Size: 26x36mm
610 A174 46fr blue & multi   1.50   1.00
Size: 17x23mm
611 A174 46fr green & multi   1.50   1.00
   a. Booklet pane of 10   15.00

Bonito Fishing — A175

1993, Mar. 10   **Perf. 13½**
612 A175 60fr Line & hook   1.00   1.25
613 A175 84fr Boat, horiz.   1.90   1.50
614 A175 86fr Drying catch   2.10   1.50
Nos. 612-614 (3)   5.60   4.25

Allied Airfield on Bora Bora, 50th Anniv. A176

1993, Apr. 6   **Perf. 10**
615 A176 120fr multicolored   3.00   2.25

Jacques Boullaire, Artist, Birth Cent. A177

Various scenes depicting life on: 32fr, Moorea. 36fr, Tuamotu. 39fr, Rurutu. 51fr, Nuku Hiva.

1993, May 6   **Engr.**
616 A177 32fr brown black   .90   .50
617 A177 36fr brick red   .90   .65
618 A177 39fr violet   1.25   .90
619 A177 51fr light brown   1.50   1.00
Nos. 616-619 (4)   4.55   3.05

Sports Festival — A178

1993, May 15   **Litho.**   **Perf. 12½**
620 A178 30fr multicolored   .85   .50

Australian Mathematics Competition, 15th Anniv. — A179

1993, July 1   **Litho.**   **Perf. 13½**
621 A179 70fr multicolored   1.75   1.10

Intl. Symposium on Inter-Plate Volcanism, French University of the Pacific, Punaauia — A180

1993, Aug. 2   **Litho.**   **Perf. 13**
622 A180 140fr tan, blk & brn   3.50   2.50

Taipei '93 — A181

1993, Aug. 14   **Litho.**   **Perf. 13½**
623 A181 46fr multicolored   1.75   .85

Exists without the Cartor imprint. Value, unused $17.50.

Tourism — A182

14fr, Boat tour. 20fr, Groom preparing for traditional wedding. 29fr, Beachside brunch.

1993, Sept. 27
624 A182 14fr multi, horiz.   .60   .35
625 A182 20fr multi   .65   .35
626 A182 29fr multi, horiz.   .75   .45
Nos. 624-626 (3)   2.00   1.15

Exist without the Cartor imprint. Value, set unused $30.

Arrival of First French Gendarme in Tahiti, 150th Anniv. A183

1993, Oct. 14   **Perf. 13**
627 A183 100fr multicolored   2.50   1.60

Exists without the Cartor imprint. Value, unused $17.50.

Alain Gerbault (1893-1941), Sailor A184

1993, Nov. 17   **Engr.**   **Perf. 13**
628 A184 150fr red, green & blue   4.00   2.75

Paintings A185

Artists: 40fr, Vaea Sylvain. 70fr, A. Marere, vert. 80fr, J. Shelsher. 90fr, P.E. Victor, vert.

1993, Dec. 3   **Photo.**   **Perf. 13**
629 A185 40fr multicolored   1.75   .70
630 A185 70fr multicolored   2.50   1.25
631 A185 80fr multicolored   3.00   1.25
632 A185 90fr multicolored   3.50   1.50
Nos. 629-632 (4)   10.75   4.70

French School of the Pacific, 30th Anniv. — A186

1993, Dec. 7   **Litho.**   **Perf. 12½**
633 A186 200fr multicolored   5.00   3.50

Whales and Dolphins — A187

Designs: 25fr, Whale breeching. 68fr, Dolphins. 72fr, Humpback whales, vert.

1994, Jan. 12   **Litho.**   **Perf. 13½**
634 A187 25fr multi   .75   .45
635 A187 68fr multi   1.75   1.10
636 A187 72fr multi   2.00   1.25
Nos. 634-636 (3)   4.50   2.80

A188

1994, Feb. 18   **Litho.**   **Perf. 13½**
637 A188 51fr multicolored   2.25   .95

Hong Kong '94. New Year 1994 (Year of the Dog).

Sister Germaine Bruel — A189

1994, Mar. 16
638 A189 180fr multicolored   4.00   3.00

Arrival of Nuns from St. Joseph of Cluny, 150th anniv.

A190

1994, Apr. 30   **Litho.**   **Perf. 13½**
639 A190 154fr Tahiti temple   3.50   2.75

Church of Jesus Christ of Latter-day Saints in French Polynesia, 150th Anniv.

FRENCH POLYNESIA

Conservatory of Arts and Crafts, Bicent. — A191

1994, May 25 Photo. Perf. 13
640 A191 316fr multicolored 7.50 5.50
Regional Associated Center of Papeete, 15th anniv.

Internal Self-Government, 10th Anniv. — A192

1994, June 29 Litho. Perf. 13
641 A192 500fr multicolored 12.00 7.50

Tahitian Academy, 20th Anniv. A193

1994, July 2 Engr. Perf. 13
642 A193 136fr multicolored 3.00 2.00

Scenes of Old Tahiti A194

1994, Aug. 10 Litho. Perf. 13
643 A194 22fr Papara .90 .50
644 A194 26fr Mataiea 1.10 .65
645 A194 51fr Taravao, vert. 1.90 .95
 Nos. 643-645 (3) 3.90 2.10
See Nos. 673-675.

Faaturuma, by Paul Gauguin (1848-1903) A195

1994, Sept. 14 Litho. Perf. 13
646 A195 1000fr multicolored 24.00 16.00

Epiphyllum Oxypetalum A196

1994, Oct. 15 Litho. Perf. 13½
647 A196 51fr multicolored 1.75 .95

Hawaiki Nui Va'a '94 (Canoe Race) — A197

Designs: a, 52fr, Yellow canoe, bow paddler. b, 76fr, Paddlers. c, 80fr, Paddlers, blue canoe. d, 94fr, Stern paddler, yellow canoe.

1994, Nov. 10 Litho. Perf. 13½x13
648 A197 Strip of 4, #a.-d. 8.00 4.75
No. 648 is a continuous design.

Paintings of French Polynesia A198

62fr, Young girl, by Michelle Villemin. 78fr, Ocean tide, fish, by Michele Dallet. 102fr, Native carrying bundles of fruit, by Johel Blanchard. 110fr, View of coastline, by Pierre Lacouture.

1994, Dec. 19 Litho. Perf. 13
649 A198 62fr multi, vert. 1.75 .95
650 A198 78fr multi 2.00 1.25
651 A198 102fr multi, vert. 2.25 1.60
652 A198 110fr multi 2.75 1.75
 Nos. 649-652 (4) 8.75 5.55

Don Domingo de Boenechea's Tautira Expedition, 220th Anniv. A199

1995, Jan. 1
653 A199 92fr multicolored 2.25 1.25

South Pacific Tourism Year — A200

1995, Jan. 11 Litho. Perf. 13½
654 A200 92fr multicolored 2.25 1.40

New Year 1995 (Year of the Boar) — A201

1995, Feb. 1 Litho.
655 A201 51fr multicolored 1.75 .80
Portions of the design on No. 655 were applied by a thermographic process producing a shiny, raised effect.
Exists without the Cartor imprint. Value, unused $9.

University Teacher's Training Institute of the Pacific — A202

1995, Mar. 8 Litho. Perf. 13½
656 A202 59fr multicolored 1.50 .95
See New Caledonia No. 710 and Wallis & Futuna No. C182.

Nature Protection A203

1995, May 4 Litho. Perf. 13
657 Strip of 3 + 2 labels 4.25 4.25
 a. A203 22fr Head of turtle .75 .35
 b. A203 29fr Turtle swimming 1.00 .50
 c. A203 91fr Black coral 2.50 1.50

Louis Pasteur (1822-95) A204

1995, May 8
658 A204 290fr dk blue & blue 6.75 4.00

Loti's Marriage, Novel by Julien Viaud (1850-1923) A205

1995, May 19 Photo. Perf. 13
659 A205 66fr multicolored 2.00 1.10

A206

1995, May 24 Litho. Perf. 13½
660 A206 150fr multicolored 3.50 2.25
Tahitian Monoi beauty aid.

Birds — A207

1995, June 7
661 A207 22fr Ptilinopus huttoni .65 .50
662 A207 44fr Ducula galeata 1.40 .75

Tahitian Pearls — A208

1995, June 14
663 A208 66fr shown 1.60 1.10
664 A208 84fr Eight pearls 2.10 1.40
On Nos. 663-664 portions of the design were applied by a thermographic process producing a shiny, raised effect.

Discovery of Marquesas Islands, 400th Anniv. A209

a, Alvaro de Mendana de Neira, sailing ships. b, Pedro Fernandez de Quiros, map of islands.

1995, July 21 Litho. Perf. 13
665 Pair + label 8.00 6.00
 a. A209 161fr multicolored 3.50 2.75
 b. A209 195fr multicolored 4.50 3.25

A210

1995, Aug. 12 Litho. Perf. 13
666 A210 83fr multicolored 2.00 1.40
10th South Pacific Games, Tahiti.

Pandanus Plant — A211

No. 667a, Entire plant. b, Flower. c, Fruit. d, Using dry leaves for weaving.

1995, Sept. 1 Perf. 13½x13
667 Strip of 4 8.50 6.00
 a.-d. A211 91fr any single 2.00 1.50
Singapore '95.

UN, 50th Anniv. A212

1995, Oct. 24 Litho. Perf. 13
668 A212 420fr multicolored 9.50 6.00

Paintings A213

Designs: 57fr, The Paddler with the Yellow Dog, by Philippe Dubois, vert. 76fr, An Afternoon in Vaitape, by Maui Seaman, vert. 79fr, The Mama with the White Hat, by Simone Testeguide. 100fr, In Front of the Kellum House in Moorea, by Christian Deloffre.

1995, Dec. 6 Photo. Perf. 13
669 A213 57fr multicolored 1.50 .90
670 A213 76fr multicolored 1.75 1.25
671 A213 79fr multicolored 1.90 1.25
672 A213 100fr multicolored 2.50 1.60
 Nos. 669-672 (4) 7.65 5.00

Scenes of Old Tahiti Type

Designs: 18fr, Fautaua. 30fr, District of Punaauia. 35fr, Tautira.

1996, Jan. 17 Litho. Perf. 13
673 A194 18fr multi .65 .45
674 A194 30fr multi .80 .50
675 A194 35fr multi .90 .60
 Nos. 673-675 (3) 2.35 1.55

New Year 1996 (Year of the Rat) — A214

1996, Feb. 19 Photo. Perf. 13
676 A214 51fr multicolored 1.75 .80
Portions of the design on No. 676 were applied by a thermographic process producing a shiny, raised effect.

Paul-Emile Victor (1907-95), Explorer, Writer A215

1996, Mar. 7 Litho.
677 A215 500fr multicolored 12.00 8.00

Queen Pomare IV — A216

1996, Mar. 1 Litho. Perf. 13
678 A216 (51fr) multicolored 1.50 .80

FRENCH POLYNESIA

Serpentine Die Cut 7 Vert.
Self-Adhesive
Size: 17x24mm

678A	A216 (51fr) multicolored	2.00	1.15
b.	Booklet pane of 5	10.00	
	Complete booklet, 2 #678b	20.00	

Sea Shells — A217

10fr, Conus pertusus. 15fr, Cypraea alisonae. 25fr, Vexillum roseotinctum.

1996, Apr. 10   Photo.   Perf. 13½x13

679	A217 10fr multicolored	.45	.25
680	A217 15fr multicolored	.50	.25
681	A217 25fr multicolored	.95	.40
	Nos. 679-681 (3)	1.90	.90

Portions of the designs on Nos. 679-681 were applied by a thermographic process producing a shiny, raised effect.

Return of the Pacific Battalion, 50th Anniv. A218

1990, May 5   Litho.   Perf. 13

682	A218 100fr multicolored	3.00	1.60

CHINA '96, 9th Asian Intl. Philatelic Exhibition — A219

Design: 200fr, Chinese School, Tahiti, 1940.

1996, May 18   Perf. 13x13½

683	A219 50fr multicolored	1.25	.80

Souvenir Sheet
Imperf

684	A219 200fr multicolored	4.50	3.40

Birds — A220

1996, June 12   Litho.   Perf. 13x13½

685	A220 66fr Sula sula	1.50	1.10
686	A220 79fr Fregata minor	2.00	1.25
687	A220 84fr Anous stolidus	2.00	1.40
	Nos. 685-687 (3)	5.50	3.75

Musical Instruments A221

Designs: 5fr, Pahu, ukulele, toere. 9fr, Toere. 14fr, Pu, vivo.

1996, July 10   Perf. 13x13½

688	A221 5fr multicolored	.30	.25
689	A221 9fr multicolored	.40	.25
690	A221 14fr multicolored	.50	.25
	Nos. 688-690 (3)	1.20	.75

Raiateana Oulietea — A222

1996, Aug. 7   Litho.   Perf. 13x13½

691	A222 66fr multicolored	1.75	1.10

Ruahatu, God of the Ocean — A223

1996, Sept. 9   Litho.   Perf. 13

692	A223 70fr multicolored	1.75	1.10

7th Pacific Arts Festival.

A224

Stamp Day: Young Tahitian girl (Type A2), Noho Mercier, taken from photo by Henry Lemasson (1870-1956), postal administrator.

1996, Oct. 16   Engr.   Perf. 13

693	A224 92fr black, red & blue	2.50	1.50

First Representative Assembly, 50th Anniv. — A225

1996, Nov. 7   Litho.   Perf. 13

694	A225 85fr multicolored	2.00	1.10

Paintings of Tahitian Women A226

Designs: 70fr, Woman lounging on Bora Bora Beach, by Titi Bécaud. 85fr, "Woman with Crown of Auti leaves," by Maryse Noguier, vert. 92fr, "Dreamy Woman," by Christine de Dinechin, vert. 96fr, Two working women, by Andrée Lang, vert.

1996, Dec. 4   Litho.   Perf. 13

695	A226 70fr multicolored	2.00	.75
696	A226 85fr multicolored	2.25	.90
697	A226 92fr multicolored	2.50	1.00
698	A226 96fr multicolored	3.00	1.00
	Nos. 695-698 (4)	9.75	3.65

A227

1997, Jan. 2   Litho.   Perf. 13

699	A227 55fr brown	1.25	.55

Society of South Sea Studies, 80th anniv.

A228

1997, Feb. 7   Photo.   Perf. 13½x13

700	A228 13fr multicolored	1.00	.30

New Year 1997 (Year of the Ox). Portions of the design were applied by a thermographic process producing a shiny, raised effect.

Arrival of Evangelists in Tahiti, Bicent. A229

Designs: a, Sailing ship, "Duff." b, Painting, "Transfer of the Matavai District to the L.M.S. Missionaries," by Robert Smirke.

1997, Mar. 5   Litho.   Perf. 13

701	A229 43fr Pair, #a.-b. + label	2.00	1.25

Tifaifai (Tahitian Bedspread) A230

Various leaf and floral patterns.

1997, Apr. 16

702	A230 1fr multicolored	.25	.25
703	A230 5fr multicolored	.25	.25
704	A230 70fr multicolored	1.60	.70
	Nos. 702-704 (3)	2.10	1.20

PACIFIC 97 — A231

Sailing ships carrying mail, passengers between Tahiti and San Francisco: No. 705, Tropic Bird, 1897. No. 706, Papeete/Zélee, 1892.

1997, May 29   Litho.   Perf. 13

705	A231 92fr multicolored	3.25	1.60
706	A231 92fr multicolored	3.25	1.60
a.	Pair, #705-706	6.50	6.50
b.	Souvenir sheet, #705-706	65.00	65.00

No. 706b sold for 400fr.

Island Scenes — A232

No. 707, Flower. No. 708, Rowing canoe, sun behind mountain. No. 709, Throwing spears. No. 710, Aerial view of Island. No. 711, Fish. No. 712, Women walking on beach. No. 713, Holding oyster shell with pearls. No. 714, Boat with sail down, sunset across water. No. 715, Snorkeling, sting ray. No. 716, Bananas, pineapples. No. 717, Palm tree, beach. No. 718, Women dancers in costume.

1997, June 25   Litho.   Perf. 13
Booklet Stamps

707	A232 85fr multicolored	14.00	14.00
708	A232 85fr multicolored	14.00	14.00
709	A232 85fr multicolored	14.00	14.00
710	A232 85fr multicolored	14.00	14.00
711	A232 85fr multicolored	14.00	14.00
712	A232 85fr multicolored	14.00	14.00
a.	Bklt. pane of 6, #707-712	90.00	
713	A232 85fr multicolored	14.00	14.00
714	A232 85fr multicolored	14.00	14.00
715	A232 85fr multicolored	14.00	14.00
716	A232 85fr multicolored	14.00	14.00
717	A232 85fr multicolored	14.00	14.00
718	A232 85fr multicolored	14.00	14.00
a.	Bklt. pane of 6, #713-718	90.00	
	Complete booklet, 2 each #712a, #718a	350.00	

Traditional Dance Costumes — A233

Designs: 4fr, Warrior's costume. 9fr, Women's costume. 11fr, Couple.

1997, July 10   Litho.   Perf. 13½x13

719	A233 4fr multicolored	1.00	.30
720	A233 9fr multicolored	1.25	.30
721	A233 11fr multicolored	2.00	.30
	Nos. 719-721 (3)	4.25	.90

Kon-Tiki Expedition, 50th Anniv. A234

1997, Aug. 7   Litho.   Perf. 13

722	A234 88fr multicolored	2.25	.80

Artists in Tahiti A235

Designs: 85fr, Painting, "The Fruit Carrier," by Monique "Mono" Garnier-Bissol. 96fr, "Revival of Our Resources," mother of pearl painting, by Camélia Maraea. 110fr, "Tahitian Spirit," pottery, by Peter Owen, vert. 126fr, "Monoi," surrealist painting, by Elisabeth Stefanovitch.

1997, Oct. 15   Litho.   Perf. 13

723	A235 85fr multicolored	1.90	.80
724	A235 96fr multicolored	2.00	.90
725	A235 110fr multicolored	2.50	1.00
726	A235 126fr multicolored	3.00	1.10
	Nos. 723-726 (4)	9.40	3.80

Te Arii Vahine, by Paul Gauguin (1848-1903) A236

1997, Nov. 6   Litho.   Perf. 13

727	A236 600fr multicolored	13.00	8.00

Christmas A237

1997, Dec. 3   Litho.   Perf. 13

728	A237 118fr multicolored	3.00	1.10

New Year 1998 (Year of the Tiger) — A238

1998, Jan. 28   Photo.   Perf. 13

729	A238 96fr multicolored	2.50	.90

Portions of the design on No. 729 were applied by a thermographic process producing a shiny, raised effect.

FRENCH POLYNESIA

Domestic Airline Network — A239

Designs: a, 70fr, Grumman Widgeon, 1950. b, 85fr, DHC 6 Twin-Otter, 1968. c, 70fr, Fairchild FH 227, 1980. d, 85fr, ATR 42-500, 1998.

1998, Apr. 16   Photo.   Perf. 13
730 A239 Strip of 4, #a.-d. + label   6.50   2.90

Orchids — A240

5fr, Dendrobium "Royal King." 20fr, Oncidium "Ramsey." 50fr, Ascodenca "Laksi." 100fr, Cattleya "hybride."

1998, May 14   Photo.   Perf. 13
731 A240 5fr multi   .25 .25
732 A240 20fr multi, vert.   .50 .25
733 A240 50fr multi, vert.   1.25 .45
734 A240 100fr multi   2.25 .95
Nos. 731-734 (4)   4.25 1.90

On Nos. 731-734 portions of the design were applied by a thermographic process producing a shiny, raised effect.

The Lovers, by Paul Gauguin (1848-1903) A241

1998, June 7   Photo.   Perf. 13x12½
735 A241 1000fr multicolored   22.50 9.00

Printed se-tenant with label.

1998 World Cup Soccer Championships, France — A242

1998, June 10
736 A242 85fr multicolored   2.00 .75

For overprint see No. 742.

Tahiti Festival of Flower and Shell Garlands — A243

Women wearing various garlands of flowers or shells.

1998, July 16   Photo.   Perf. 13½
737 A243 55fr multicolored   1.50 .50
738 A243 65fr multicolored   1.75 .60
739 A243 70fr multicolored   2.00 .65
740 A243 80fr multicolored   2.25 .75
Nos. 737-740 (4)   7.50 2.50

Painting, "Underwater World of Polynesia," by Stanley Haumani — A244

1998, Sept. 10   Photo.   Perf. 12½x13
741 A244 200fr multicolored   4.00 2.00

No. 736 Overprinted in Blue & Black

1998, Oct. 28   Photo.   Perf. 13½
742 A242 85fr multicolored   3.00 1.00

No. 742 has blue, white and red margins and No. 736 has white margins.

Autumn Philatelic Fair, Paris A246

Watercolor paintings of Papeete Bay, by René Gillotin (1814-61), 250fr each: a, Beach at left, people. b, Beach at right, people.

1998, Nov. 5   Perf. 13
743 A246 Pair, #a.-b. + label   12.00 5.00
c. Souvenir sheet, #a.-b., imperf.   12.00 5.00

Life in Tahiti and the Islands — A247

Paintings by André Deymonaz: 70fr, Return to the Market, vert. 100fr, Bonito Fish Stalls, vert. 102fr, Going Fishing. 110fr, Discussion after Church Services.

1998, Dec. 10   Photo.   Perf. 13
744 A247 70fr multicolored   1.50 .80
745 A247 100fr multicolored   2.00 1.00
746 A247 102fr multicolored   2.25 1.00
747 A247 110fr multicolored   2.50 1.10
Nos. 744-747 (4)   8.25 3.90

St. Valentine's Day — A248

1999, Feb. 11   Litho.   Perf. 13
748 A248 96fr multicolored   2.50 .90

New Year 1999 (Year of the Rabbit) — A249

1999, Feb. 16
749 A249 118fr Rabbits, flowers   2.50 1.10

Portions of the design of No. 749 were applied by a thermographic process producing a shiny, raised effect.

Marine Life — A250

Designs: 70fr, Ptérois volitans. 85fr, Hippocampus histrix. 90fr, Antennarius pictus. 120fr, Taenianotus triacanthus.

1999, Mar. 18   Photo.   Perf. 13
750 A250 70fr multicolored   1.50 .65
751 A250 85fr multicolored   1.90 .80
752 A250 90fr multicolored   2.00 .80
753 A250 120fr multicolored   2.75 1.10
Nos. 750-753 (4)   8.15 3.35

Portions of the designs on Nos. 750-753 were applied by a thermographic process producing a shiny, raised effect.

IBRA '99, World Philatelic Exhibition, Nuremberg — A251

Tatooed men of Marquesas Islands, 1804: 90fr, Holding staff, fan. 120fr, Wearing blue cape.

1999, Apr. 27   Photo. & Engr.   Perf. 13¼
754 A251 90fr multicolored   2.00 .90
755 A251 120fr multicolored   2.75 1.25

Mother's Day — A252

1999, May 27   Litho.   Perf. 13¼
756 A252 85fr Children, vert.   1.90 .75
757 A252 120fr shown   2.75 1.00

A253

Island Fruits — A254

No. 758, Breadfruit, vert. 120fr, Coconut. No. 760: a, Papaya. b, Guava (goyave). c, Mombin. d, Rambutan. e, Star apple (pomme-etoile). f, Otaheite gooseberry (seurette). g, Rose apple. h, Star fruit (carambole). i, Spanish lime (quenette). j, Sweetsop (pomme-cannelle). k, Cashew (pomme de cajou). l, Passion fruit.

1999   Litho.   Perf. 13½x13, 13x13½
758 A253 85fr multicolored   1.90 .75
759 A253 120fr multicolored   2.75 1.10

Souvenir Booklet
760   Complete bklt.   32.50
a.-l. A254 85fr Any single   2.00 1.40

Issued: No. 758, 120fr, 7/21; No. 760, 7/21.
No. 760 sold for 1200fr, and contains two booklet panes, containing Nos. 760a-760f, and Nos. 760g-760l. A second variety of No. 760 exists with selling price on cover as 1020fr. Value, complete booklet, $100.

No. 720, 1856 Letter, 1864 Postmark A255

1999, July 2   Litho.   Perf. 13
761 A255 180fr multicolored   4.00 2.25
a. Souvenir sheet of 1   12.00 12.00

150th anniv. of French postage stamps, PhilexFrance 99.
No. 761 issued se-tenant with label. No. 761a sold for 500fr.

Frédéric Chopin (1810-49), Composer A256

1999, July 2   Litho.   Perf. 13
762 A256 250fr multicolored   5.50 2.50

Malardé Medical Research Institute, 50th Anniv. A257

1999, Sept. 27
763 A257 400fr multicolored   8.75 3.75

Nudes — A258

Paintings by: 85fr, J. Sorgniard. 120fr, J. Dubrusk. 180fr, C. Deloffre. 250fr, J. Gandouin.

1999, Oct. 14   Litho.   Perf. 13
764 A258 85fr multi   2.10 .75
765 A258 120fr multi   3.25 1.10
766 A258 180fr multi   4.50 1.60
767 A258 250fr multi   6.00 2.25
Nos. 764-767 (4)   15.85 5.70

Tahiti on the Eve of the Year 2000 — A259

1999, Nov. 10   Litho.   Perf. 13
768 A259 85fr multi   2.50 .75

5th Marquesas Islands Arts Festival — A260

1999, Dec. 10
769 A260 90fr multi   2.00 .80

Year 2000 — A261

85fr, Hands of adult and infant. 120fr, Eye.

FRENCH POLYNESIA

2000, Jan. 3   **Perf. 13¼x13, 13x13¼**
770 A261 85fr multi, vert.   2.50 .75
771 A261 120fr multi   3.25 1.10

New Year 2000 (Year of the Dragon) — A262

2000, Feb. 5   **Litho.**   **Perf. 13x13¼**
772 A262 180fr multi   5.50 1.50

Portions of the design were applied by a thermographic process producing a shiny, raised effect.

Postal Service Emblem and Stamps — A263

2000, Mar. 15   **Litho.**   **Perf. 13x13¼**
773 A263 90fr multi   2.00 .75

First Intl. Tattoo Festival, Raiatea A264

Various tattoos.

2000, Apr. 28   **Perf. 13**
774 A264 85fr multi   1.90 .70
775 A264 120fr multi   2.75 .95
776 A264 130fr multi   2.90 1.00
777 A264 160fr multi   3.50 1.25
  Nos. 774-777 (4)   11.05 3.90

Beautiful Women of French Polynesia A265

2000, May 30
778 A265 300fr multi   7.50 3.00
  a. Souvenir sheet of 1   12.00 12.00
No. 778a sold for 500fr.

Traditional Dresses — A266

Denominations. 85fr, 120fr, 160fr, 250fr.

2000, June 21   **Litho.**   **Perf. 13¼x13**
779-782 A266 Set of 4   13.50 6.00

Mountains A267

Designs: 90fr, Mts. Aorai and Orohena. 180fr, Mts. Orohena and Aorai.

2000, July 10   **Perf. 13x13¼**
783-784 A267 Set of 2   6.00 2.60

Traditional Sports — A268

120fr, Fruit carrying. 250fr, Stone lifting, vert.

Perf. 13x13¼, 13¼x13
2000, Sept. 15
785-786 A268 Set of 2   8.25 3.50

Native Woven Crafts — A269

No. 787, Fans. No. 788, Hat.

2000, Oct. 3   **Litho.**   **Perf. 13x13¼**
787-788 A269 85fr Set of 2   3.75 1.75

Year of Ancient Tahitian Language Reo Ma'ohi — A270

2000, Nov. 9   **Litho.**   **Perf. 13x13¼**
789 A270 120fr multi   2.75 1.20

Portions of the design were applied by a thermographic process producing a shiny, raised effect.

Advent of New Millennium A271

2000, Dec. 28
790 A271 85fr multi   2.50 .90

Central School, Cent. A272

Designs: No. 791, 85fr, Central School. No. 792, 85fr, Paul Gauguin High School.

2001, Jan. 16
791-792 A272 Set of 2   3.75 1.75

New Year 2001 (Year of the Snake) — A273

2001, Jan. 24   **Perf. 13x13¼**
793 A273 120fr multi   2.75 1.20

Portions of the design were applied by a thermographic process producing a shiny, raised effect.

Landscapes — A274

Designs: 35fr, Vaiharuru Waterfall. 50fr, Vahiria Lake, horiz. 90fr, Hakaui Valley.

Perf. 13¼x13, 13x13¼
2001, Feb. 26   **Litho.**
794-796 A274 Set of 3   6.00 1.75

Year of the Polynesian Child — A275

2001, Mar. 28   **Litho.**   **Perf. 13x13¼**
797 A275 55fr multi   1.25 .55

Polynesian Singers — A276

Designs: 85fr, Eddie Lund. 120fr, Charley Mauu. 130fr, Bimbo. 180fr, Marie Mariteragi and Emma Terangi, horiz.

2001, Apr. 12   **Perf. 13¼x13, 13x13¼**
798-801 A276 Set of 4   11.50 5.00

Volunteers of the Pacific Batallion, 60th Anniv. — A277

2001, Apr. 21   **Perf. 13x13¼**
802 A277 85fr multi   2.25 .90

Surfing Waves of Teahupoo A278

2001, May 4
803 A278 120fr multi   2.75 1.20

Internal Autonomy, 17th Anniv. — A279

2001, June 29   **Litho.**   **Perf. 13**
804 A279 250fr multi   5.50 2.50
  a. Souvenir sheet of 1   12.00 12.00
No. 804a sold for 500fr.

Pirogue Racing — A280

Designs: 85fr, Male racers. 120fr, Female racers.

2001, July 12   **Perf. 13¼x13**
805-806 A280 Set of 2   4.50 2.00
  a. Souvenir sheet, #805-806, imperf. 5.50 5.50
No. 806a sold for 250fr.

Hardwood Trees — A281

Designs: 90fr, Tou. 130fr, Ati. 180fr, Miro.

2001, Oct. 23   **Litho.**   **Perf. 13x13½**
807-809 A281 Set of 3   11.00 8.00

AIDS Prevention A282

2001, Sept. 20   **Litho.**   **Perf. 13x13¼**
810 A282 55fr multi   2.75 1.10

Year of Dialogue Among Civilizations — A283

2001, Oct. 9   **Perf. 13**
811 A283 500fr multi   11.50 10.00

Perfume Flowers — A284

Designs: 35fr, Gardenia tahitensis. 50fr, Fagraea berteriana. 85fr, Gardenia jasminoides.

2001, Nov. 8   **Perf. 13¼x13**
812-814 A284 Set of 3   6.00 3.50

Portions of the designs were applied by a thermographic process producing a shiny, raised effect.

Christmas — A285

2001, Dec. 6   **Perf. 13x13¼**
815 A285 120fr multi   2.75 2.40

New Year 2002 (Year of the Horse) — A286

2002, Feb. 12   **Litho.**   **Perf. 13x13¼**
816 A286 130fr multi   3.25 2.60

Portions of the design were applied by a thermographic process producing a shiny, raised effect.

Happy Holidays — A287

Greetings — A288

2002, Feb. 28   **Background Colors**
817 A287 55fr red   1.25 1.10
818 A288 55fr blue   1.25 1.10
819 A287 85fr blue   1.90 1.75
820 A288 85fr green   1.90 1.75
  Nos. 817-820 (4)   6.30 5.70

10th World Outrigger Canoe Championships A289

FRENCH POLYNESIA

Canoe rowers and emblems: 120fr, 180fr.

2002, Mar. 9 Photo. Perf. 13¼
821-822 A289 Set of 2   6.75 6.25

Sea Urchins — A290

Designs: 35fr, Echinometra sp. 50fr, Heterocentrotus trigonarius. 90fr, Echinothrix calamaris. 120fr, Toxopneustes sp.

2002, Apr. 18 Litho. Perf. 13x13¼
823-826 A290 Set of 4   6.50 6.25

Blood Donation — A291

2002, May 3 Litho. Perf. 13¼x13
827 A291 130fr multi   4.00 3.25

2002 World Cup Soccer Championships, Japan and Korea — A292

2002, May 30
828 A292 85fr multi   2.10 1.75

Traditional Sports — A293

Designs: 85fr, Coconut husking. 120fr, Fruit carrying. 250fr, Javelin throwing.

2002, June 27
829-831 A293 Set of 3   10.00 9.00

House of James Norman Hall — A294

2002, July 4 Perf. 13x13¼
832 A294 90fr multi   2.00 1.90

Papeete Market A295

2002, Aug. 30 Litho. Perf. 13
833 A295 400fr multi   8.75 8.00
a.   Souvenir sheet of 1   11.00 11.00

Amphilex 2002 Stamp Exhibition, Amsterdam (No. 833a). No. 833a sold for 500fr.

Pacific Oceanology Center, Vairoa — A296

Designs: 55fr, Research pond, fish, shrimp, oyster, and flasks. 90fr, Aeriel view of center, fish, shrimp and oyster.

2002, Sept. 26 Photo. Perf. 13¼
834-835 A296 Set of 2   3.50 2.40

Taapuna Master 2002 Surfing Competition A297

2002, Oct. 21 Litho. Perf. 13x13¼
836 A297 120fr multi   2.75 2.00

Halophilic Flowers — A298

Designs: 85fr, Hibiscus tiliaceus. 130fr, Scaveola sericea. 180fr, Guettarda speciosa.

2002, Nov. 7
837-839 A298 Set of 3   8.75 6.75

Polynesians at Festivals — A299

Designs: 55fr, Dancers and bus. 120fr, Musicians, vert.

2002, Dec. 5 Perf. 13x13¼, 13¼x13
840-841 A299 Set of 2   3.75 3.00

New Year 2003 (Year of the Ram) — A300

2003, Feb. 1 Litho. Perf. 13¼x13
842 A300 120fr multi   3.00 2.25

Portions of the design was applied by a thermographic process producing a shiny, raised effect.

Polynesian Women — A301

2003, Mar. 8 Litho. Perf. 13¼x13
843 A301 55fr multi   1.25 1.00

Waterfalls A302

2003, Apr. 10 Perf. 13
844 A302 330fr multi   7.25 6.00

Old Papeete — A303

Designs: 55fr, Automobiles and buildings, vert. 85fr, Ship in harbor. 90fr, People with bicycles in front of buildings (50x28mm). 120fr, Tree-lined street (50x28mm).

Perf. 13¼x13, 13x13¼, 13
2003, May 15
845-848 A303 Set of 4   7.75 7.00
848a   Souvenir sheet, #845-848 12.00 12.00

No. 848a sold for 550fr.

Fish — A304

2003, June 12 Litho. Perf. 13
849 A304 460fr multi   9.50 9.50

Portions of the design were applied by a thermographic process producing a shiny, raised effect.

Outrigger Canoes — A305

Designs: No. 850, 85fr, shown. No. 851, 85fr, Three sailors on canoe at sea. No. 852, 85fr, Three sailors on canoe, vert. No. 853, 85fr, Sailor sitting on outrigger, vert.

Perf. 13x13¼, 13¼x13
2003, July 11 Litho.
850-853 A305 Set of 4   7.50 6.50

Firewalkers A306

Orange-banded Cowrie — A307

2003, Aug. 14 Photo. Perf. 13¼
854 A306 130fr multi   2.50 2.50

Perf. 13x13¼
855 A307 420fr multi   8.50 8.50

Are You Jealous? by Paul Gauguin (1848-1903) A308

2003, Sept. 11 Perf. 13x12¼
856 A308 250fr multi   6.50 3.50

Office of Posts and Telecommunications Emblem — A308a

Type I: "Postes 2003" at right.
Type II: "Postes" only at right.

Serpentine Die Cut 6½ Vert.
2003, Oct. 1 Engr.
Booklet Stamp
Self-Adhesive
856A A308a (60fr) blue (type II), 2006 10.00 1.00
b.   Booklet pane of 10   100.00
c.   Type I   40.00 24.00
d.   As "c," booklet pane of 10 400.00
e.   As #856A, inscribed "Phil@poste" 8.00 1.00
f.   Booklet pane of 10 #856Ae 80.00

Issued: No. 856Ac, 10/1/03. No. 856A, 2006. No. 856Ae, 2007.
See Nos. 869, 1070-1070B.

French Polynesian Flag — A309

2003, Oct. 1 Litho. Perf. 13x13¼
857 A309 (60fr) multi   1.50 1.25

Tiki — A310

2003, Oct. 1 Perf. 13¼x13
858 A310 100fr multi   3.00 2.00

Reissued in 2006 on shiny paper with much deeper colors. Values the same.

Flowers — A311

Designs: 90fr, Orchid. 130fr, Rose de porcelain (torch ginger).

2003, Oct. 4 Litho. Perf. 13x13¼
859-860 A311 Set of 2   6.50 4.50

Portions of the designs were applied by a thermographic process producing a shiny, raised effect.

Bora Bora — A312

Designs: No. 861, 60fr, Painting of Bora Bora by A. Van Der Heyde. No. 862, 60fr, Aerial photograph of Bora Bora.

2003, Nov. 6 Litho. Perf. 13x13¼
861-862 A312 Set of 2   5.00 2.75

Tiki — A313

2003, Dec. 6 Perf. 13
863 A313 190fr multi   4.00 4.00

Buildings and Palm Trees — A314

2003, Dec. 19 Perf. 13x13¼
864 A314 90fr multi   3.00 1.90

New Year 2004 (Year of the Monkey) — A315

2004, Jan. 22 Litho. Perf. 13¼x13
865 A315 130fr multi   3.50 3.50

A portion of the design was applied by a thermographic process producing a shiny, raised effect.

FRENCH POLYNESIA

Scenes From Everyday Life — A316

Designs: 60fr, Women working with cloth. 90fr, Street scene, vert.

Perf. 13x13¼, 13¼x13
2004, Feb. 13 Litho.
866-867 A316 Set of 2 3.25 3.25

Polynesian Woman — A317

2004, Mar. 8 **Perf. 13¼x13**
868 A317 90fr multi 4.00 1.90

Post Emblem Type of 2003
Serpentine Die Cut 6¾ Vert.
2004, Apr. 22 Engr.
Booklet Stamp
Self-Adhesive
869 A308a (90fr) red 6.00 2.00
a. Booklet pane of 10 60.00
b. As #869, inscribed "Phil@poste" —
c. Booklet pane of 10 #869b —

No. 869 lacks year date.

Polynesian Economic Development — A318

2004, Apr. 23 Litho. **Perf. 13x12¾**
870 A318 500fr multi 11.00 10.00

Arahurahu Marae, Paea A319

2004, Apr. 23
871 A319 500fr multi 11.00 10.00

Vanilla — A320

2004, May 14 **Perf. 13¼x13**
872 A320 90fr multi 2.10 1.90

No. 872 is impregnated with a vanilla scent.

Mobile Snack Bars A321

2004, May 28 **Perf. 13x12¾**
873 A321 300fr multi 6.50 6.25

Handicrafts A322

Designs: No. 874, 60fr, Artisan braiding fibers. No. 875, 60fr, Mother-of-pearl carving. No. 876, 90fr, Artisan carving statue. No. 877, 90fr, Hat.

2004, June 26 **Perf. 13x13¼**
874-877 A322 Set of 4 10.00 6.25

Portion of the designs were applied by a thermographic process producing a shiny, raised effect.

Involvement in South Pacific Area of Office of Posts and Telecommunications A323

Designs: 100fr, Earth, Sun on horizon. 130fr, Satellite dish, building.

2004, July 23 Photo. **Perf. 13¼**
878-879 A323 Set of 2 5.50 4.75

Information Technology and Communications A324

Designs: No. 880, 190fr, Computer keyboard, "@." No. 881, 190fr, Satellite, satellite dish.

2004, Sept. 23 Litho. **Perf. 13¼x13**
880-881 A324 Set of 2 8.00 8.00

Omai, Polynesian Capt. James Cook Brought to England — A325

2004, Oct. 14 **Perf. 13**
882 A325 250fr multi 5.25 5.25

Shell Collectors A326

2004, Nov. 10 Photo. **Perf. 13¼**
883 A326 60fr multi 1.60 1.40

A souvenir sheet of one sold for 250fr. Value $7.

Adenium Obesum — A327

Alpinia Purpurata A328

Ixora Chinensis A329

Gardenia Taitensis — A330

Heliconia Psittacorum A331

Allamanda Blanchetii A332

Otacanthus Caeruleus A333

Hibiscus Rosa-sinensis A334

Euphorba Milii — A335

Asocenda Hybrid of Vanda x Ascocentrum A336

Mussaenda Erythrophylia A337

Bougainvillea Glabra — A338

2004, Nov. 10 Litho. **Perf. 13x13¼**
884 Booklet pane of 6 17.50 —
a. A327 90fr multi 2.50 2.50
b. A328 90fr multi 2.50 2.50
c. A329 90fr multi 2.50 2.50
d. A330 90fr multi 2.50 2.50
e. A331 90fr multi 2.50 2.50
f. A332 90fr multi 2.50 2.50
885 Booklet pane of 6 17.50 —
a. A333 90fr multi 2.50 2.50
b. A334 90fr multi 2.50 2.50
c. A335 90fr multi 2.50 2.50
d. A336 90fr multi 2.50 2.50
e. A337 90fr multi 2.50 2.50
f. A338 90fr multi 2.50 2.50
Complete booklet, #884-885 30.00
Complete booklet sold for 1200fr.

Christmas A339

2004, Dec. 17
886 A339 60fr multi 1.60 1.40

A portion of the design was applied by a thermographic process producing a shiny, raised effect.

Bamboo — A340

2005, Feb. 9 **Perf. 13¼x13**
887 A340 130fr multi 3.00 3.00

New Year 2005. A portion of the design was applied by a thermographic process producing a shiny, raised effect.

People and Hut — A341

2005, Feb. 25 **Perf. 13x13¼**
888 A341 90fr multi 2.00 2.00

Polynesian Women — A342

Designs: 60fr, Woman wearing lei. 90fr, Woman wearing flower garland on head and robe.

2005, Mar. 8 **Perf. 13¼x13**
889-890 A342 Set of 2 4.00 3.50

Woman Making Tapa Cloth — A343

2005, Apr. 22 **Perf. 13**
891 A343 250fr multi 5.50 5.50

Tifaifai — A344

2005, Mar. 23 Litho. **Perf. 13x13¼**
892 A344 5fr multi .25 .25

Angelfish — A345

Designs: No. 893, 90fr, Centropyge bispinosa. No. 894, 90fr, Centropyge loricula. No. 895, 130fr, Centropyge heraldi. No. 896, 130fr, Centropyge flavissima.

2005, May 27 Litho. **Perf. 13x13¼**
893-896 A345 Set of 4 9.50 9.50
896a Souvenir sheet, #893-896 9.50 9.50

Portions of the designs were applied by a thermographic process producing a shiny, raised effect.

Historic Airplanes — A346

FRENCH POLYNESIA

Designs: No. 897, 60fr, TAI DC-8, first jet in Tahiti, 1961. No. 898, 60fr, Pan American Boeing 707, first foreign flight, 1963. No. 899, 100fr, Air France Boeing 707, first Air France flight to Tahiti, 1973. No. 900, 100fr, Air Tahiti Nui Airbus A340-300, first Tahitian airline, 2000.

2005, June 24
897-900 A346 Set of 4   6.50 6.50

Musical Instruments — A347

Designs: No. 901, 130fr, Drum. No. 902, 130fr, Nose flutes, horiz.

2005, July 22 Perf. 13¼x13, 13x13¼
901-902 A347 Set of 2   5.50 5.50

Polynesian Landscapes A348

2005, Aug. 26   Perf. 13
903 A348 300fr multi   6.25 6.25

Pineapples — A349

Designs: 90fr, Close-up of spines. 130fr, Entire fruit.

2005, Sept. 23 Litho. Perf. 13¼x13
904-905 A349 Set of 2   4.75 4.50
Nos. 904-905 are impregnated with pineapple scent.

Marae A350

Marquesan Tohua A351

2005, Oct. 21   Perf. 13
906 A350 500fr multi   10.00 10.00
907 A351 500fr multi   10.00 10.00

Autonomy, 20th Anniv. (in 2004) — A352

2005, Nov. 10   Perf. 13¼x13
908 A352 60fr multi   4.00 1.75
No. 908 was printed in France and distributed there in June 2004 but was not sold in French Polynesia until 2005, where it was available from the philatelic bureau upon request, and not through standing orders.

O'Parrey Harbor, Tahiti — A353

2005, Nov. 10 Engr. Perf. 13x12½
909 A353 100fr multi   2.00 2.00

Christmas A354

2005, Dec. 16 Litho. Perf. 13x13¼
910 A354 90fr multi   2.00 2.00

Lotus Flower — A355

Litho. & Silk-screened
2006, Jan. 30   Perf. 13x13¼
911 A355 130fr multi   2.60 2.60

A356

Hearts — A357

2006, Feb. 14 Photo. Perf. 13
912 A356 60fr multi   1.25 1.25
913 A357 90fr multi   1.90 1.90
Values are for stamps with surrounding selvage.

Polynesian Women — A358

Woman: 60fr, At water's edge. 90fr, With oil lamp.

2006, Mar. 8 Litho. Perf. 13¼x13
914-915 A358 Set of 2   3.75 3.25

Maupiti A359

2006, Apr. 26 Engr. Perf. 13x13¼
916 A359 500fr multi   11.00 11.00

History of the Marquesas (Washington) Islands — A360

Designs: 60fr, Native man and woman. 130fr, Ships.

2006, May 27 Litho. Perf. 13¼x13
917-918 A360 Set of 2   4.00 4.00
918a   Souvenir sheet, #917-918 4.00 4.00

Diners and Musicians A361

2006, June 6   Perf. 13
919 A361 300fr multi   6.50 6.50

Polynesian Ground Dove — A362

Tuamotu Sandpiper A363

2006, June 21   Perf. 13x13¼
920 A362 250fr multi   5.25 5.25
921 A363 250fr multi   5.25 5.25

Heiva — A364

Designs: 90fr, Canoe race. 130fr, Stone lifting. 190fr, Dancer.

2006, July 19   Perf. 13¼x13
922-924 A364 Set of 3   8.75 8.75

Frangipani Flowers — A365

2006, Aug. 23 Litho. Perf. 13x13½
925 A365 90fr multi   2.25 1.90
No. 925 is impregnated with frangipani scent.

A366

World Tourism Day — A367

Designs: 40fr, Ruins. No. 927, 90fr, Waterfall, woman and child. 130fr, Clothing at open-air market.
No. 929: a, Dancers with yellow skirts. b, Surfer. c, House and palm tree. d, Pearls. e, Fish and coral. f, Islanders in outrigger canoes.
No. 930: a, Woman in hammock. b, Stilt houses. c, Tower and boats. d, Horses and riders. e, Aerial view of island. f, Diver and sting ray.

2006, Sept. 22   Perf. 13¼x13
926-928 A366 Set of 3   6.00 6.00
Booklet Stamps
Perf. 13x13¼
929   Booklet pane of 6   15.00   —
  a.-f.   A367 90fr Any single   2.00 2.00
930   Booklet pane of 6   15.00   —
  a.-f.   A367 90fr Any single   2.00 2.00
           Complete booklet, #929-930 30.00
Complete booklet sold for 1200fr.

Paintings — A368

Designs: 60fr, Javelin Throwing, by Monique Garnier Bissol. 90fr, Market Life, by Albert Luzuy, horiz. 100fr, Island Quay, by Gilbert Chaussoy, horiz. 190fr, Vahine, by Olivier Louzé.

2006, Oct. 25   Perf. 13
931-934 A368 Set of 4   9.50 9.50

Engravings by Paul Gauguin (1848-1903) A369

Engravings depicting: 60fr, Women. 130fr, Cow and man carrying items on stick.

2006, Nov. 8 Engr. Perf. 13¼
935-936 A369 Set of 2   4.25 4.25

Children's Art — A370

2006, Dec. 13 Litho. Perf. 13x13¼
937 A370 90fr multi   2.00 2.00

Beach Gear — A371

Designs: 60fr, Flip-flops. 90fr, Surfboards.

Serpentine Die Cut 11x11¼
2007 Photo. **Self-Adhesive**
938 A371 60fr multicolored   1.25 1.25
  a.   Blue tips of die cutting along left side 1.25 1.25
939 A371 90fr multicolored   2.00 2.00
  a.   Light blue tips of die cutting along bottom 2.00 2.00
Issued: Nos. 938a, 939a, 1/24; Nos. 938-939, Feb. Nos. 938a and 939a are from the original printing, and are from sheets having adjacent stamps and die cutting that does not extend through the backing paper. Nos. 938-939, which were distributed to the philatelic trade, are from sheets with selvage around each stamp, and with rouletting that extends through the backing paper that allows the stamps to be removed from the sheet more easily.

New Year 2007 (Year of the Pig) — A372

2007, Feb. 19 Litho. Perf. 13x13¼
940 A372 130fr multi   3.50 3.50
Portions of the design were applied by a thermographic process producing a shiny, raised effect.

FRENCH POLYNESIA

Painting of Polynesian Woman by Mathius — A373

Photograph of Polynesian Woman by John Stember — A374

2007, Mar. 8		Litho.	Perf. 13¼x13
941	A373	60fr multi	1.50 1.40
		Perf. 13x13¼	
942	A374	90fr multi	2.25 2.00

Audit Office, Bicent. — A375

2007, Mar. 17		Engr.	Perf. 13¼x13
943	A375	90fr multi	2.75 2.00

Shells — A376

Designs: 10fr, Lambis crocata pilsbryi. 60fr, Cypraea thomasi. 90fr, Cyrtulus serotinus. 130fr, Chicoreus laqueatus.

2007, Apr. 25			Litho.	
944-947	A376	Set of 4		6.75 6.75
947a		Souvenir sheet, #944-947		6.75 6.75

Coconut — A377

2007, May 23			Perf. 13x13¼
948	A377	90fr multi	2.25 2.00

No. 948 is impregnated with a coconut scent.

Ships — A378

Designs: No. 949, 250fr, Gunboat Zélée. No. 950, 250fr, Passenger and cargo liner Sagittaire.

2007, June 22			Perf. 13
949-950	A378	Set of 2	12.00 11.50

Heiva Festival — A379

Various women dancers: 65fr, 100fr, 140fr.

2007, July 4			Perf. 13¼x13
951-953	A379	Set of 3	7.50 7.50

Arrival of Kon-Tiki Expedition in Polynesia, 60th Anniv. — A380

Litho. & Silk-screened

2007, Aug. 7			Perf. 13
954	A380	300fr multi	7.00 7.00

Arrival of Ship at Papeete Dock — A381

2007, Aug. 29			Litho.	Perf. 13
955	A381	190fr multi		4.50 4.50

Old and Modern Photos of Papeete — A382

Designs: 65fr, Rue Gauguin, 2007. 100fr, Rue de la Petite-Pologne (now Rue Gauguin), 1907.

2007, Sept. 26				
956-957	A382	Set of 2		4.75 4.00

Old Franc and Centime Notes — A383

Designs: 65fr, 1919 2-franc Chamber of Commerce note. 140fr, 1942 2-franc note. 500fr, 1943 50-centime note.

2007, Oct. 26			Engr.	Perf. 13
958-960	A383	Set of 3		20.00 17.00

Flowers — A384

Designs: 100fr, Hibiscus. 140fr, Bird-of-paradise (Oiseaux de paradis).

Litho. & Silk-screened

2007, Nov. 8			Perf. 13x13¼
961-962	A384	Set of 2	7.50 7.50

Christmas — A385

2007, Dec. 6			Litho.	Perf. 13x13¼
963	A385	100fr multi		2.50 2.50

Marine Life — A386

Designs: 10fr, Himantura fai. 20fr, Tursiops truncatus. 40fr, Megaptera novaeangliae. 65fr, Negaprion acutidens.

2008, Jan. 10				
964-967	A386	Set of 4		4.00 4.00

New Year 2008 (Year of the Rat) — A387

2008, Feb. 7			Photo.	Perf. 13¼x13
968	A387	140fr multi		3.75 3.75

Paintings of Women by Bénilde Menghini — A388

Designs: 65fr, Woman picking mangos. 100fr, Women scaling fish.

2008, Mar. 7			Litho.	
969-970	A388	Set of 2		4.25 4.25

Paintings by Polynesian Artists — A389

Unnamed paintings depicting: No. 971, 100fr, Boat and reef, by Torea Chan. No. 972, 100fr, Polynesian man, by Raymond Vigor. No. 973, 100fr, Fruit bowl, by Teurarea Prokop, horiz.

2008, Apr. 10			Perf. 13x13¼, 13¼x13
971-973	A389	Set of 3	8.00 8.00

Pouvanaa a Oopa (1895-1977), Politician — A390

2008, May 20			Litho.	Perf. 13
974	A390	500fr multi		13.00 13.00

Island Touring Vehicles — A391

Designs: 65fr, Motor scooter. 100fr, Bus, horiz.

Serpentine Die Cut 11
Self-Adhesive

2008, June 12			Photo.
975-976	A391	Set of 2	4.50 4.50

Heiva Festival — A392

Designs: 65fr, Woman with floral headdress. 140fr, Tattooed man. 190fr, Girl dancing.

2008, July 16			Litho.	Perf. 13
977-979	A392	Set of 3		11.00 11.00

Sports — A393

Designs: No. 980, 140fr, Table tennis. No. 981, 140fr, Weight lifting.

2008, Aug. 8			Litho.	Perf. 13¼x13
980-981	A393	Set of 2		7.00 7.00

End of Tahiti Nui Expedition, 50th Anniv. — A394

2008, Aug. 29			Litho.	Perf. 13
982	A394	190fr multi		4.50 4.50

Eric de Bisschop (1890-1958), expedition leader.

Polynesian Scenes — A395

No. 983: a, Woman crouching. b, Woman under shelter. c, Boat in bay near cliffs. d, Orange flowers. e, Red hibiscus flower. f, Island. g, Woman with headdress. h, White flower. i, Woman with headdress and flower garland. j, Pink flower. k, Islands. l, Bay near mountains.

Serpentine Die Cut 11¼x11

2008, Sept. 8		Self-Adhesive	
983		Booklet pane of 12	32.50
a.-d.	A395	65fr Any single	1.50 1.50
e.-h.	A395	100fr Any single	2.40 2.40
i.-l.	A395	140fr Any single	3.25 3.25

Gardenia Taitensis in Bottle of Monoi Oil — A396

2008, Sept. 17			Perf. 13¼x13
984	A396	100fr multi	2.40 2.40

No. 984 is impregnated with a gardenia scent.

Aviation Anniversaries — A397

Designs: No. 985, 250fr, Air service between France and French Polynesia, 50th anniv. No. 986, 250fr, Air Tahiti Nui, 10th anniv.

2008, Oct. 15			Litho.	Perf. 13
985-986	A397	Set of 2		11.00 11.00

French Polynesia Postage Stamps, 50th Anniv. — A398

Designs: 65fr, French Polynesia #185. 100fr, Vignette of French Polynesia #C24. 140fr, French Polynesia #J29.

FRENCH POLYNESIA

2008, Nov. 6   Engr.   Perf. 13
987-989 A398 Set of 3   6.75 6.75
989a   Sheet of 3, #987-989   6.75 6.75

Boater and Dancer — A399

2008, Dec. 5   Litho.   Perf. 13x13¼
990 A399 100fr multi   2.25 2.25

Winning design in children's stamp design contest.

Hypolimnas Bolina — A400

Litho. & Silk-screened
2009, Jan. 16   Perf. 13
991 A400 70fr multi   1.50 1.50

Fire Fighters — A401

Designs: 70fr, Fireman on aerial ladder. 140fr, Fireboat.

2009, Feb. 13   Litho.   Perf. 13
992-993 A401 Set of 2   4.50 4.50

Paintings of Polynesian Women — A402

Designs: 70fr, Woman, by Myriam Stroken. 100fr, Woman with Guitar, by Stanley Haumani.

2009, Mar. 30   Litho.   Perf. 13¼x13
994-995 A402 Set of 2   4.00 4.00

Jacques Brel (1929-78), Singer — A403

Colors: 70fr, Blue. 100fr, Brown.

2009, Apr. 8   Engr.
996-997 A403 Set of 2   4.25 4.25

Pareo Fabric — A404

Pareo in: (70fr), Blue. (100fr), Red. (140fr), Green.

Serpentine Die Cut 11
2009, May 29   Litho.
Self-Adhesive
998-1000 A404 Set of 3   7.25 7.25

Heiva Celebrations of the Past — A405

Various Heiva dancers: 70fr, 100fr, 140fr. 100fr and 140fr are horiz.

Perf. 13¼x13, 13x13¼
2009, June 19
1001-1003 A405 Set of 3   7.50 7.50

First Man on the Moon, 40th Anniv. — A406

2009, July 20   Perf. 13¼
1004 A406 140fr multi   3.50 3.50

Water Activities — A407

Designs: 70fr, Surfing. 100fr, Canoeing (pirogue).

Serpentine Die Cut 11x11¼
2009, Aug. 7   Litho.   Self-Adhesive
1005-1006 A407 Set of 2   4.00 4.00

Passion Fruit — A408

2009, Aug. 14   Perf. 13¼
1007 A408 100fr multi   2.40 2.40

No. 1007 has a scratch-and-sniff coating on the fruit having a passion fruit scent.

Underwater Scenes — A409

Designs: 70fr, Scuba divers. 100fr, Turtles, horiz. 140fr, Whale, horiz.

Litho. & Silk-screened
Perf. 13¼x13, 13x13¼
2009, Sept. 11
1008-1010 A409 Set of 3   7.75 7.75
1010a   Sheet of 3, #1008-1010   7.75 7.75

Fish — A410

No. 1011: a, Chaetodon lunula. b, Chaetodon trichrous. c, Chaetodon ornatissimus. d, Chaetodon pelewensis. e, Pterois antennata. f, Myripristis berndti. g, Priacanthus hamrur. h, Epinephelus polyphekadion. i, Thalassoma lutescens. j, Thalassoma hardwicke. k, Pygoplites diacanthus. l, Coris gaimard.

Serpentine Die Cut 11¼x11
2009, Sept. 11   Self-Adhesive
1011   Booklet pane of 12   31.00
a.-d. A410 70fr Any single   1.75 1.75
e.-h. A410 100fr Any single   2.50 2.50
i.-l. A410 140fr Any single   3.50 3.50

Paintings by Paul Gauguin (1848-1903) — A411

Designs: No. 1012, 250fr, Still Life with a Maori Statuette. No. 1013, 250fr, Still Life with Apples, horiz.

2009, Oct. 16   Litho.   Perf. 13
1012-1013 A411 Set of 2   12.50 12.50

French Polynesia No. 180 — A412

2009, Nov. 5   Engr.
1014 A412 500fr multi   12.50 12.50

Legend of the Coconut Tree — A413

2009, Dec. 11   Litho.   Perf. 13¼x13
1015 A413 190fr multi   4.75 4.75

Papeete Post Office, 150th Anniv. — A414

2010, Jan. 20
1016 A414 70fr multi   1.60 1.60

New Year 2010 (Year of the Tiger) — A415

Litho. & Silk-screened
2010, Feb. 15   Perf. 13¼x13¼
1017 A415 140fr multi   3.25 3.25

Woman and Child — A416

Woman and child: 70fr, Facing forward. 100fr, Facing right.

2010, Mar. 8   Litho.   Perf. 13¼x13
1018-1019 A416 Set of 2   4.00 4.00

Tattoos — A417

Tattooed: No. 1020, 250fr, Woman (green background). No. 1021, 250fr, Man (dark red background).

2010, Apr. 6
1020-1021 A417 Set of 2   11.50 11.50

Tiare Apetahi Flower — A418

Litho. & Silk-screened
2010, Apr. 20   Perf. 13x13¼
1022 A418 70fr multi   1.50 1.50

Captain Frederick William Beechey (1796-1856), Explorer — A419

2010, May 5   Litho.
1023 A419 140fr multi   3.00 3.00

Corals — A420

Various corals: 70fr, 100fr, 140fr. 140fr is vert.

Litho. & Silk-screened
2010, June 4   Perf. 13x13¼, 13¼x13
1024-1026 A420 Set of 3   6.50 6.50
1026a   Sheet of 3, #1024-1026   6.50 6.50

Heiva Festival — A421

Various festival participants: 100fr, 140fr, 190fr.

2010, July 20   Litho.   Perf. 13¼x13
1027-1029 A421 Set of 3   9.50 9.50

Mango — A422

2010, Aug. 8   Perf. 13x13¼
1030 A422 100fr multi   2.25 2.25

No. 1030 has a scratch-and-sniff coating on the fruit having a mango scent.

Phosphate Mining at Makatea, Cent. — A423

Designs: 70fr, Office. 100fr, Train. 140fr, Mining operations.

2010, Aug. 17   Litho.   Perf. 13x13¼
1031-1033 A423 Set of 3   6.75 6.75

Honotua Fiber Optic Submarine Cable Project — A424

FRENCH POLYNESIA

Serpentine Die Cut 11
2010, Sept. 15   Photo.
Self-Adhesive
1034   A424   70fr multi   1.75   1.75

Birds — A425

No. 1035: a, Lori de Kuhl (Kuhl's lorikeet). b, Bécasseau Sanderling (Sanderling). c, Carpophade de la Société (Imperial pigeon). d, Tangara à dos rouge (Crimson-backed tanager). e, Ptilope de Hutton (Rapa fruit dove). f, Sterne huppée (Great crested tern). g, Gygis blanche (White tern). h, Lori Nonnette (Blue lorikeet). i, Chevalier errant (Wandering tattler). j, Martin chasseur des Gambier (Tuamotu kingfisher). k, Fou brun (Brown booby). l, Pluvier fauve (Pacific golden plover).

Litho. & Silk-screened
2010, Sept. 15   Self-Adhesive
1035   Booklet pane of 12   28.00
   a.-l.   A425 100fr Any single   2.25   2.25

Tahiti Faa'a International Airport, 50th Anniv. — A426

2010, Oct. 14   Litho.   Perf. 13
1036   A426   500fr multi   11.50   11.50

Sphinx Moth — A427

2010, Oct. 14   Perf. 13x13½
1037   A427   5fr multi   .25   .25

1948 Air Post Stamps of French Oceania A428

Designs: 70fr, #C17. 100fr, #C18. 140fr, #C19.

2010, Nov. 4   Engr.   Perf. 13
1038-1040   A428   Set of 3   7.25   7.25

Legend of Moua Puta — A429

2010, Dec. 9   Litho.   Perf. 13x13¼
1041   A429   70fr multi   1.60   1.60

Crabs — A430

Designs: 20fr, Atergatopsis cf. germanini. 40fr, Zosimus aeneus. 70fr, Carpilius convexus. 100fr, Carpilius maculatus.

2011, Jan. 18
1042-1045   A430   Set of 4   5.25   5.25
1045a   Souvenir sheet of 4, #1042-1045   5.25   5.25

New Year 2011 (Year of the Rabbit) — A431

Litho. & Silk-screened
2011, Feb. 3   Perf. 13¼x13
1046   A431   140fr multi   3.25   3.25

Images of Polynesia — A432

No. 1047: a, Canoe race. b, Outrigger canoe. c, Aerial view of islands. d, Fish on reef. e, Pearls. f, Flowers.

Serpentine Die Cut 11¼
2011, Mar. 8   Litho.
Self-Adhesive
1047   Booklet pane of 6   14.50
   a.-f.   A432 100fr Any single   2.40   2.40

Intl. Women's Year — A433

Designs: 70fr, Two women weaving. 100fr, Woman standing.

2011, Mar. 8   Perf. 13¼x13
1048-1049   A433   Set of 2   4.00   4.00

Pearl of Tahiti, 50th Anniv. — A434

2011, Apr. 7   Litho.
1050   A434   140fr multi   3.50   3.50

Portions of the design were applied by a thermographic process producing a shiny, raised effect.

Transportation of the Past — A435

Designs: 70fr, Truck, 1939. 100fr, Horse-drawn carriages, 1900.

2011, May 17   Litho.   Perf. 13
1051-1052   A435   Set of 2   4.25   4.25

Fishing — A436

Cartoons: 100fr, Fisherman in boat catching swordfish. 140fr, Spear fisherman and speared fish.

Serpentine Die Cut 11
2011, June 22   Litho.
Self-Adhesive
1053-1054   A436   Set of 2   5.75   5.75

Carved Items — A437

Designs: 70fr, Coral pestle. 140fr, Basalt tiki. 190fr, Oceania rosewood container with lid, hoirz.

2011, July 19   Perf. 13¼x13, 13x13¼
1055-1057   A437   Set of 3   9.75   9.75

Orchid — A438

2011, Aug. 17   Litho.   Perf. 13¼x13
1058   A438   140fr multi   3.25   3.25

No. 1058 is impregnated with an orchid scent.

Islands — A439

Photographs of: 10fr, Rangiroa. 100fr, Ua Pou. 140fr, Bora Bora.

2011, Sept. 27   Perf. 13x13¼
1059-1061   A439   Set of 3   5.75   5.75

Marine Birds and Sea Life — A440

No. 1062: a, Birds. b, Bird and whale. c, Dolphin and fish. d, Red striped fish, black and white striped angelfish. e, Blue and yellow striped fish. f, Lionfish, yellow fish. g, Ray. h, Shark. i, Sea turtle, fish, coral. j, Anemonefish, sea anemones. k, Crab. l, Moray eel, coral.

Serpentine Die Cut 11¼x11
2011, Sept. 27   Self-Adhesive
1062   Booklet pane of 12   29.00
   a.-l.   A440 100fr Any single   2.40   2.40

Filming of *Mutiny on the Bounty* in Tahiti, 50th Anniv. A441

2011, Oct. 19   Perf. 13
1063   A441   500fr multi   11.50   11.50

Fort Collet, Marquesas Islands — A442

No. 1064 — Engraving of Fort from 1854: a, Buildings without flags. b, Buildings with flags.

2011, Nov. 3   Engr.   Perf. 13
1064   A442   250fr Horiz. pair,
     #a-b   11.50   11.50

Ta'aroa, Polynesian God of Creation — A443

2011, Dec. 15   Litho.   Perf. 13¼x13
1065   A443   70fr multi   1.60   1.60

New Year 2012 (Year of the Dragon) — A444

Litho & Silk-screened
2012, Jan. 23   Perf. 13
1066   A444   140fr multi   3.25   3.25

Papeete Maritime Station A445

Ships in Papeete Harbor A446

2012, Jan. 27   Litho.
1067   A445   70fr multi   1.60   1.60
1068   A446   100fr multi   2.25   2.25

Port of Papeete Authority, 50th anniv.

Food Truck Vendors — A447

Serpentine Die Cut 11
2012, Feb. 22   Self-Adhesive
1069   A447   100fr multi   2.25   2.25

Office of Posts and Telecommunications Emblem Type of 2003
Booklet Stamps
Serpentine Die Cut 6¾ Vert.
2012, Feb. 8   Self-Adhesive
1070   A000a   5fr red violet   .25   .25
   c.   Booklet pane of 10 #1070   1.25
1070A   A308a   (75fr) blue, type II   1.75   1.75
   d.   Booklet pane of 10 #1070A   17.50
1070B   A308a   (100fr) rose   2.25   2.25
   e.   Booklet pane of 10 #1070B   22.50
    Nos. 1070-1070B (3)   4.25   4.25

Intl. Women's Day — A448

Designs: 70fr, Woman. 100fr, Woman and child.

2012, Mar. 8   Perf. 13¼x13
1071-1072   A448   Set of 2   3.75   3.75

833

FRENCH POLYNESIA

Flowers — A449

No. 1073: a, Gingembre à abeilles. b, Reine de Malaisie. c, Opuhi alpinia rose. d, Zedoaire. e, Safran indien. f, Opuhi alpinia orchidée.

2012, Mar. 8   **Serpentine Die Cut 11**
Self-Adhesive
1073   Booklet pane of 6   13.50
    a.-f. A449 100fr Any single   2.25   2.25

Nudibranchs
A450

Designs: 75fr, Glossodoris rufomarginata. 100fr, Elysia ornata. 190fr, Cyerce nigricans.

Litho. & Silk-screened
2012, Apr. 26   **Perf. 13x13¼**
1074-1076   A450   Set of 3   8.00   8.00
  1076b   Souvenir sheet of 3, #1074-1076   8.00   8.00

Tiurai (1842-1918),
Healer — A451

2012, June 18   **Litho.**   **Perf. 13¼x13**
1077   A451   75fr multi   1.60   1.60

Tamanu Orange
Picking
Contest — A452

2012, June 27
1078   A452   75fr multi   1.60   1.60

Heiva
Dancer — A453

2012, July 18   **Perf. 13x13¼**
1079   A453   100fr multi   2.10   2.10

Grapefruits
A454

2012, Aug. 22
1080   A454   140fr multi   3.00   3.00

No. 1080 is impregnated with a grapefruit scent.

Airports — A455

Airport at: 5fr, Bora Bora. 75fr, Tikehau. 100fr, Ua Pou.

2012, Sept. 27
1081-1083   A455   Set of 3   4.00   4.00

Landscapes — A456

No. 1084: a, Moorea. b, Mangareva. c, Rurutu. d, Kauehi. e, Hiva Oa. f, Rapa.

Serpentine Die Cut 11
2012, Sept. 27   **Self-Adhesive**
1084   Booklet pane of 6   13.50
   a.-f. A456 100fr Any single   2.25   2.25

Turtles in
Botanical
Gardens,
Papeari — A457

Horses and
Riders,
Marquesas
Islands — A458

2012, Oct. 17   **Perf. 13x13¼**
1085   A457   75fr multi   1.60   1.60
1086   A458   100fr multi   2.25   2.25

First
Stamps of
French
Oceania,
120th Anniv.
A459

No. 1087: a, "Commerce," horse-drawn carriage, people near shore. b, People on rowboat, "Navigation."

2012, Nov. 8   **Engr.**   **Perf. 13xx13¼**
1087   Horiz. pair, #a-b, + central label   11.00   11.00
   a.-b. A459 250fr Either single   5.50   5.50

Season of Matari'i i
Ni'a — A460

2012, Nov. 20   **Litho.**   **Perf. 13**
1088   A460   75fr multi   1.75   1.75

Matavai
Bay — A461

2012, Dec. 13   **Engr.**
1089   A461   500fr blk & gray blue   11.00   11.00

Scenes of
Everyday
Life — A462

Designs: 75fr, Street scene outside of Quinn's Bar, Papeete. 100fr, Street musicians.

2013, Jan. 2   **Litho.**   **Perf. 13x13¼**
1090-1091   A462   Set of 2   4.00   4.00

New Year 2013
(Year of the
Snake) — A463

Litho. & Silk-screened
2013, Feb. 11   **Perf. 13**
1092   A463   140fr multi   3.00   3.00

Queen Pomare IV
(1813-77) — A464

Serpentine Die Cut 11
2013, Feb. 28   **Photo.**
Self-Adhesive
1093   A464   75fr multi   1.75   1.75

Legend of Tahiri
Vahine — A465

Designs: 75fr, Tahiri Vahine (woman with fan). 100fr, Tahiri Vahine with other women.

2013, Mar. 8   **Litho.**   **Perf. 13¼x13**
1094-1095   A465   Set of 2   4.00   4.00
    Intl. Women's Day.

Flora and
Fauna — A466

Designs: 20fr, Lemon (citron). 40fr, Lizard (lézard), horiz. 190fr, Chestnut-breasted mannikin (capuchin).

Litho. & Silk-screened
2013, Apr. 26   **Perf. 13¼x13, 13x13¼**
1096-1098   A466   Set of 3   5.50   5.50
  1098a   Souvenir sheet of 3, #1096-1098   5.50   5.50

Jacques
Brel (1929-
78), Singer
A467

2013, May 10   **Engr.**   **Perf. 13**
1099   A467   500fr multi   11.50   11.50

Fruits — A468

No. 110: a, Pineapples. b, Mangos. c, Bananas. d, Coconuts. e, Papayas. f, Watermelon.

Litho. & Silk-screened
2013, May 10   **Serpentine Die Cut 11**
Self-Adhesive
1100   Booklet pane of 6   13.50
   a.-f. A468 100fr Any single   2.25   2.25

Marine
Life — A469

Designs: 5fr, Starfish. 10fr, Giant clam. 75fr, Sea anemone and clown fish. 100fr, Sea turtle.

Litho. & Silk-screened
2013, June 7   **Perf. 13x13¼**
1101-1104   A469   Set of 4   4.25   4.25
  1104a   Souvenir sheet of 4, #1101-1104   4.25   4.25

Carousel at
Heiva
Fairground
A470

2013, July 16   **Litho.**   **Perf. 13**
1105   A470   100fr multi   2.25   2.25

Jasmine
Flowers — A471

2013, Aug. 22   **Litho.**   **Perf. 13x13¼**
1106   A471   100fr multi   2.25   2.25

No. 1106 is impregnated with a jasmine scent.

FIFA Beach Soccer
World Cup
Tournament,
Tahiti — A472

2013, Sept. 18   **Litho.**   **Perf. 13¼x13**
1107   A472   140fr multi   3.25   3.25

A473   A474

A475   A476

A477   A478

Women
A477   A478

Serpentine Die Cut 11
2013, Sept. 18   **Litho.**
Self-Adhesive
1108   Booklet pane of 6, #1108a-1108f   13.50
  a. A473 100fr multi   2.25   2.25
  b. A474 100fr multi   2.25   2.25
  c. A475 100fr multi   2.25   2.25
  d. A476 100fr multi   2.25   2.25
  e. A477 100fr multi   2.25   2.25
  f. A478 100fr multi   2.25   2.25
  g. A473 100fr Dated "2015"   1.75   1.75
  h. A474 100fr Dated "2015"   1.75   1.75
  i. A475 100fr Dated "2015"   1.75   1.75
  j. A476 100fr Dated "2015"   1.75   1.75
  k. A477 100fr Dated "2015"   1.75   1.75

FRENCH POLYNESIA

l. A478 100fr Dated "2015" 1.75 1.75
m. Booklet pane of 6, #1180g-1108l 10.50

Issued: Nos. 1108g-1108m, 11/5/15.

Canoes — A479

Various canoes: 75fr, 100fr.

2013, Oct. 17		Litho.		Perf. 13
1109-1110	A479	Set of 2	4.00	4.00

Stock Certificates — A480

Stock certificate of: 250fr, Comptoirs Français d'Océanie. 300fr, Compagnie Française de Tahiti.

2013, Nov. 6		Engr.		Perf. 13
1111-1112	A480	Set of 2	12.50	12.50

Old Automobiles — A481

Designs: 75fr, 1915 Ford Model T. 100fr, 1950 Citroen Traction Avant.

2013, Dec. 12		Litho.		Perf. 13
1113-1114	A481	Set of 2	4.00	4.00

New Banknotes — A482

Designs: 10fr, 500-franc banknote. 20fr, 1000-franc banknote. 75fr, 5000-franc banknote. 100fr, 10,000-franc banknote.

Litho. & Silk-Screened

2014, Jan. 20			Perf. 13
1115-1118	A482	Set of 4	4.75 4.75
1118a		Souvenir sheet of 4, #1115-1118	4.75 4.75

Postal Check Center, 50th Anniv. — A483

2014, Jan. 27		Litho.	Perf. 13¼x13
1119	A483	75fr multi	1.75 1.75

New Year 2014 (Year of the Horse) — A484

Litho. & Silk-Screened

2014, Jan. 31			Perf. 13
1120	A484	140fr multi	3.25 3.25

Intl. Year of Family Farming — A485

Designs: 75fr, Woman watering flower garden. 100fr, Farmers, fruits and vegetables.

2014, Feb. 21		Litho.		Perf. 13
1121-1122	A485	Set of 2	4.00	4.00

Intl. Women's Day — A486

Design: 75fr, Head of woman with floral headdress. 100fr, Woman, vert.

Perf. 13x13¼, 13¼x13

2014, Mar. 7		Litho.		
1123-1124	A486	Set of 2	4.00	4.00

Wild Boars — A487

Serpentine Die Cut 11

2014, Apr. 30			Photo.
		Self-Adhesive	
1125	A487	100fr multi	2.40 2.40

 A488
 A489
 A490
 A491
 A492
 A493

Serpentine Die Cut 11

2014, May 16			Litho.
		Self-Adhesive	
1126		Booklet pane of 6	13.50
a.	A488	100fr multi	2.25 2.25
b.	A489	100fr multi	2.25 2.25
c.	A490	100fr multi	2.25 2.25
d.	A491	100fr multi	2.25 2.25
e.	A492	100fr multi	2.25 2.25
f.	A493	100fr multi	2.25 2.25

Graffiti art by Enos.

Sharks — A494

Designs: 10fr, Carcharhinus melanopterus. 40fr, Sphyrna mokarran. 75fr, Carcharhinus albimarginatus. 190fr, Galeocerdo cuvier.

Litho. & Silk-Screened

2014, June 10			Perf. 13
1127-1130	A494	Set of 4	7.25 7.25
1130a		Souvenir sheet of 4, #1127-1130	7.25 7.25

Autonomy, 30th Anniv. — A495

2014, June 27		Litho.	Perf. 13¼x13
1131	A495	75fr multi	1.75 1.75

Woman in Heiva Costume — A496

2014, July 3		Litho.	Perf. 13¼x13
1132	A496	75fr multi	1.75 1.75

Jar of Honey, Honeybee and Honeycomb — A497

2014, Aug. 28		Litho.	Perf. 13x13¼
1133	A497	100fr multi	2.25 2.25

No. 1133 is impregnated with a honey scent.

Bombardment of Papeete, Cent. — A498

Litho. & Engr.

2014, Sept. 30			Perf. 13
1134	A498	300fr multi	6.50 6.50

World War I, cent.

Tiaré Flower — A499

2014, Nov. 6		Litho.	Perf. 13x13¼
1135	A499	2fr multi	.25 .25

Sunset — A500

2014, Nov. 6		Litho.	Perf. 13¼x13
1136	A500	77fr multi	1.60 1.60

Issuance of French Polynesia No. C30, 50th Anniv. — A501

2014, Nov. 6		Litho.	Perf. 13
1137	A501	500fr multi	10.50 10.50

Office of Posts and Telecommunications Emblem — A502

Serpentine Die Cut 6¾ Vert.

2014, Nov. 6			Litho.
		Booklet Stamps	
		Self-Adhesive	
1138	A502	(75fr) deep blue	1.60 1.60
a.		Booklet pane of 10	16.00
1139	A502	(100fr) red	2.10 2.10
a.		Booklet pane of 10	21.00
b.		Dated "2019"	1.90 1.90
c.		Booklet pane of 10 #1139b	19.00

Issued: No. 1139b, 11/4/19.

Legend of Pipiri Ma — A503

2014, Dec. 12		Litho.	Perf. 13
1140	A503	75fr multi	1.50 1.50

Occupations — A504

Designs: 10fr, Underwater spear fisherman. 20fr, Sculptor. 75fr, Masseuse, horiz. 100fr, Seamstress, horiz.

2015, Jan. 29		Litho.	Perf. 13¼x13
1141	A504	10fr multi	.25 .25
1142	A504	20fr multi	.40 .40

Perf. 13x13¼

1143	A504	75fr multi	1.50 1.50
1144	A504	100fr multi	1.90 1.90
	Nos. 1141-1144 (4)		4.05 4.05

New Year 2015 (Year of the Goat) — A505

Litho. & Silk-Screened

2015, Feb. 19			Perf. 13
1145	A505	140fr multi	2.60 2.60

Mama Dolphin at Sea Post Office — A506

2015, Mar. 26		Litho.	Perf. 13x13¼
1146	A506	75fr multi	1.40 1.40

Translation of Bible Into Tahitian by Henry Nott, 180th Anniv. — A507

Discovery of King George Islands by John Byron, 250th Anniv. — A508

Litho. & Engr.

2015, May 13			Perf. 13
1147	A507	140fr multi	2.60 2.60

835

FRENCH POLYNESIA

Litho.

1148	A508 190fr multi		3.50	3.50
a.	Souvenir sheet of 2, #1147-1148		6.25	6.25

Coffee — A509

2015, July 1   Litho.   Perf. 13x13¼

1149	A509 100fr multi	1.90	1.90

No. 1149 is impregnated with a coffee scent.

Children's Art — A510

2015, Aug. 1   Litho.   Perf. 13¼

1150	A510 1fr multi	.25	.25

Orator — A511

2015, Aug. 5   Litho.   Perf. 13x13¼

1151	A511 80fr multi	1.50	1.50

Tropical Architecture A512

Designs: 80fr, Chez Vat Restaurant and Chez Alin Store. 100fr, Houses.

2015, Aug. 14   Litho.   Perf. 13x13¼

1152-1153	A512 Set of 2	3.50	3.50

First Flight Between Tahiti and Santiago, Chile, 50th Anniv. — A513

2015, Aug. 31   Litho.   Perf. 13x13¼

1154	A513 80fr multi	1.50	1.50

1915 Postcard Depicting Papeete A514

2015, Sept. 29   Litho.   Perf. 13¼x13

1155	A514 300fr multi	5.75	5.75

Issuance of Tahiti No. B2, Cent. — A515

Litho. & Engr.

2015, Nov. 5   Perf. 13¼x13

1156	A515 500fr multi	9.00	9.00
a.	Souvenir sheet of 1	9.00	9.00

Sponges — A516

No. 1157: a, Clathrina n. sp. b, Dysidea n. sp. c, Haliclona n. sp. d, Ernstia n. sp. e, Stylissa flabelliformis. f, Darwinella n. sp.

Serpentine Die Cut 11

2015, Nov. 5   Litho.

Self-Adhesive

1157	Booklet pane of 6	10.50	
a.-f.	A516 100fr Any single	1.75	1.75

Papeete Market — A517

Designs: 80fr, Tower and awning. 100fr, Vendors and shoppers, horiz. 140fr, Fish vendors and shoppers, horiz.

2015, Dec. 16   Litho.   Perf. 13

1158-1160	A517 Set of 3	6.00	6.00

Ancient Adornments A518

Designs: 10fr, Pa'e kea and pavahina. 20fr, Hei ku'a. 80fr, Peue kavi'i.

2016, Jan. 29   Litho.   Perf. 13x13¼

1161-1163	A518 Set of 3	2.00	2.00

New Year 2016 (Year of the Monkey) — A519

Litho. & Silk-screened

2016, Feb. 8   Perf. 13

1164	A519 140fr multi	2.60	2.60

Hikers — A520

Serpentine Die Cut 11

2016, Mar. 18   Litho.

Self-Adhesive

1165	A520 100fr multi	1.90	1.90

Ships A521

Designs: 40fr, Queen Elizabeth 2. 80fr, France. 100fr, City of New York.

Litho. & Silk-screened

2016, Apr. 22   Perf. 13

1166-1168	A521 Set of 3	4.25	4.25

Street Art in Papeete by Seth and HTJ — A522

2016, May 27   Litho.   Perf. 13

1169	A522 140fr multi	2.60	2.60

World Stamp Show 2016, New York.

Sandalwood A523

2016, June 17   Litho.   Perf. 13x13¼

1170	A523 100fr multi	1.90	1.90

No. 1170 is impregnated with a sandalwood scent.

Miss Tahiti Pageant Winners — A524

No. 1171: a, Marie Moua, 1965. b, Moea Amiot, 1975. c, Ruth Manea, 1985. d, Timeri Baudry, 1995. e, Mihimana Sachet, 2005. f, Vaimiti Teiefitu, 2015.

Serpentine Die Cut 11

2016, June 24   Litho.

Self-Adhesive

1171	Booklet pane of 6	11.50	
a.-f.	A524 100fr Any single	1.90	1.90

Compare type A524 with type A613. See Nos. 1191, 1211, 1230, 1257, 1266.

Famous People Wearing Heiva Costumes — A525

Designs: 80fr, Gilles Hollande. 100fr, Madeleine Moua (1899-1989).

2016, July 11   Litho.   Perf. 13¼x13

1172-1173	A525 Set of 2	3.50	3.50

Premna Serratifolia — A526

2016, Aug. 12   Engr.   Perf. 13

1174	A526 80fr multi	1.50	1.50

Woman and Plum Blossoms — A527

2016, Oct. 21   Litho.   Perf. 13x13¼

1175	A527 300fr multi	5.75	5.75
a.	Souvenir sheet of 1	5.75	5.75

PhilaTaipei 2016 International Philatelic Exhibition, Taipei.

Francis Ariioehau Sanford (1912-96), Politician — A528

2016, Nov. 3   Engr.   Perf. 13

1176	A528 500fr multi	9.00	9.00

A529   A530

A531   A532

A533

Men — A534

Serpentine Die Cut 11

2016, Nov. 3   Litho.

Self-Adhesive

1177	Booklet pane of 6	10.50	
a.	A529 100fr multi	1.75	1.75
b.	A530 100fr multi	1.75	1.75
c.	A531 100fr multi	1.75	1.75
d.	A532 100fr multi	1.75	1.75
e.	A533 100fr multi	1.75	1.75
f.	A534 100fr multi	1.75	1.75

Birds A535

Designs: 80fr, Striated heron (héron strié). 100fr, Southern Marquesan reed warbler (rousserolle des Marquises).

2016, Dec. 9   Litho.   Perf. 13

1178-1179	A535 Set of 2	3.25	3.25
1179a	Souvenir sheet of 2, #1178-1179	3.25	3.25

Society for Oceania Studies, Cent. — A536

2017, Jan. 2   Litho.   Perf. 13¼x13

1180	A536 100fr multi	1.75	1.75

FRENCH POLYNESIA

Shells — A537

No. 1181: a, Lentigo lentiginosus. b, Mitra papalis. c, Monoplex aquatilis. d, Conus nussatella. e, Oxymeris maculata. f, Drupa clathrata.

Serpentine Die Cut 11
2017, Jan. 3   Litho.
    Self-Adhesive
1181   Booklet pane of 6   10.50
  a.-f. A537 100fr Any single   1.75   1.75

New Year 2017 (Year of the Rooster) — A538

Litho. & Silk-Screened
2017, Jan. 27   Perf. 13
1182   A538   140fr multi   2.60   2.60

Henri Cadousteau (1890-1946), Fighter Pilot, and Salmson 2A2 — A539

Litho. & Silk-Screened
2017, Feb. 17   Perf. 13
1183   A539   80fr multi   1.40   1.40

International Women's Day — A540

Women wearing headdresses: 80fr, 100fr.

2017, Mar. 8   Litho.   Perf. 13¼x13
1184-1185   A540   Set of 2   3.25   3.25

Polynesian Women of the Bounty — A541

2017, Mar. 30   Litho.   Perf. 13
1186   A541   140fr multi   2.50   2.50
See Pitcairn Islands No. 827.

Underwater Scenes — A542

Designs: 10fr, Woman laying on sea floor and ray. 20fr, Diver and school of fish. 80fr, Diver on sea floor and school of fish. 100fr, Woman sitting on sea floor and ray, diff.

2017, May 5   Litho.   Perf. 13x13¼
1187-1190   A542   Set of 4   4.00   4.00
  1190a   Souvenir sheet of 4, #1187-1190   4.00   4.00

Miss Tahiti Pageant Winners Type of 2016

No. 1191: a, Sonia Agnieray, 1966. b, Patricia Servonnat, 1976. c, Loana Bohl, 1986. d, Hinerava Hiro, 1996. e, Tehere Pere, 2006. f, Vaea Ferrand, 2016.

Serpentine Die Cut 11
2017, June 23   Litho.
    Self-Adhesive
1191   Booklet pane of 6   11.50
  a.-f. A524 100fr Any single   1.90   1.90

Oranges — A543

2017, June 23   Litho.   Perf. 13x13¼
1192   A543   100fr multi   1.90   1.90
No. 1192 is impregnated with an orange scent.

Heiva Celebration Dancers — A544

2017, July 13   Litho.   Perf. 13¼x13
1193   A544   80fr multi   1.60   1.60

Lions Clubs International, Cent. — A545

2017, Aug. 25   Litho.   Perf. 13¼x13
1194   A545   190fr multi   3.75   3.75

Cats and Dogs — A546

No. 1195: a, Cat named Kitty. b, Cat named Gribouille. c, Cat named Caramel. d, Dog named Peanuts. e, Dog named Lolly. f, Dog named Sydney.

Serpentine Die Cut 11
2017, Aug. 25   Litho.
    Self-Adhesive
1195   Booklet pane of 6   12.00
  a.-f. A546 100fr Any single   2.00   2.00

Navigators and Boats — A547

Boat and: 40fr, Rodolphe Tuko Harry Williams (1920-86). 100fr, Francis Puara Cowan (1926-2009).

2017, Sept. 27   Engr.   Perf. 13
1196-1197   A547   Set of 2   2.75   2.75

Hina Natua, 2017 Miss Heiva — A548

2017, Oct. 24   Litho.   Perf. 13
1198   A548   300fr multi   6.00   6.00
Brasilia 2017 International Philatelic Exhibition, Brasilia, Brazil.

Halloween — A549

Serpentine Die Cut 11
2017, Oct. 27   Litho.
    Self-Adhesive
1199   A549   80fr multi   1.60   1.60

Fautaua Waterfall — A550

2017, Nov. 9   Engr.   Perf. 13
1200   A550   500fr turq blue & slate grn   10.00   10.00

Souvenir Sheet
Litho.
    Imperf
1200A   A550   500fr multi   10.00   10.00
Pierre Loti (1850-1923), writer.

French Polynesia No. 527 — A551

2017, Dec. 15   Litho.   Perf. 13
1201   A551   80fr multi   1.60   1.60

Air Tahiti, 60th Anniv. — A552

Designs: 10fr, Sunderland Bermuda. 20fr, Douglas DC-4. 40fr, ATR 72-500. 80fr, ATR 72-600.

2018, Jan. 11   Litho.   Perf. 13x13¼
1202-1205   A552   Set of 4   3.25   3.25

New Year 2018 (Year of the Dog) — A553

Litho. & Silk-Screened
2018, Feb. 16   Perf. 13
1206   A553   140fr multi   3.00   3.00
No. 1206 was printed in sheets of 10 + central label.

International Women's Day — A554

2018, Mar. 8   Litho.   Perf. 13¼x13
1207   A554   80fr multi   1.75   1.75

Arrival of Louis-Antoine de Bougainville (1729-1811) in Tahiti, 250th Anniv. — A555

2018, Apr. 6   Engr.   Perf. 12¾x13
1208   A555   250fr mar & dp bluish grn   5.00   5.00

Pointe Vénus Lighthouse, 150th Anniv. — A556

2018, Apr. 23   Litho.   Perf. 13
1209   A556   80fr multi   1.60   1.60

Bird and Kite — A557

Serpentine Die Cut 11
2018, May 25   Litho.
    Self-Adhesive
1210   A557   100fr multi   2.00   2.00

Miss Tahiti Pageant Winners Type of 2016

No. 1211: a, Pageant emblem. b, Timia Terjiero, 1977. c, Meari Manoi, 1987. d, Hinano Teanotoga, 1997. e, Taoahere Richmond, 2007. f, Turouru Temorere, 2017.

Serpentine Die Cut 11
2018, June 1   Litho.
    Self-Adhesive
1211   Booklet pane of 6   12.00
  a.-f. A524 100fr Any single   2.00   2.00

Basil — A558

2018, June 22   Litho.   Perf. 13¼x13
1212   A558   80fr multi   1.60   1.60
No. 1212 is impregnated with a basil scent.

Polynesian Canoes — A559

2018, July 16   Litho.   Perf. 13x13¼
1213   A559   80fr multi   1.60   1.60

FRENCH POLYNESIA

Milan Rastislav Stefánik (1880-1919), Slovak General and His Tahitian Astronomical Observatory A560

2018, Aug. 17   Litho.   Perf. 13
1214   A560   140fr multi   2.75   2.75

Praga 2018 International Philatelic Exhibition, Prague.

Self-portrait with Yellow Christ, by Paul Gauguin (1848-1903) A561

2018, Sept. 21   Litho.   Perf. 13
1215   A561   300fr multi   6.00   6.00
   a.   Souvenir sheet of 1   6.00   6.00

Disappearance of Alain Colas (1943-78), Sailboat Racer, 40th Anniv. — A562

2018, Oct. 26   Litho.   Perf. 13x13¼
1216   A562   100fr multi   1.90   1.90

Babies — A563

No. 1217 — Names at lower right: a, Tahi. b, Hinarani. c, Nainoa. d, Imianau. e, Tevaihereiti. f, Kihani.

Serpentine Die Cut 11
2018, Oct. 26   Litho.
   Booklet Stamps
   Self-Adhesive
1217   Booklet pane of 6   11.50
   a.-f.   A563 100fr Any single   1.90   1.90

French Polynesia No. 184 — A564

2018, Nov. 8   Engr.   Perf. 13
1218   A564   190fr multi   3.75   3.75

First stamps inscribed "Polynésie Française," 60th anniv.

End of World War I, Cent. — A565

2018, Nov. 8   Engr.   Perf. 13
1219   A565   500fr multi   9.50   9.50
   a.   Souvenir sheet of 1   9.50   9.50

Taputapuatea UNESCO World Heritage Site — A566

2018, Dec. 14   Litho.   Perf. 13x13¼
1220   A566   100fr multi   1.90   1.90

Endangered Birds — A567

Designs: 10fr, Pseudobulweria rostrata. 80fr, Pomarea nigra, vert.

   Perf. 13x13¼, 13¼x13
2019, Jan. 25   Litho.
1221-1222   A567   Set of 2   1.75   1.75

New Year 2019 (Year of the Pig) — A568

   Litho. & Silk-Screened
2019, Feb. 5   Perf. 13
1223   A568   140fr multi   2.75   2.75

International Women's Day — A569

Designs: 80fr, Woman and palm trees. 100fr, Woman with flower in hair.

2019, Mar. 8   Litho.   Perf. 13¼x13
1224-1225   A569   Set of 2   3.50   3.50

Tupaia (c. 1725-70), Navigator, Capt. James Cook (1728-79), and Ship, Endeavour A570

2019, Apr. 12   Engr.   Perf. 13
1226   A570   250fr multi   4.75   4.75

Cook's arrival in Tahiti, 250th anniv.

Marine Life in Protected Reserve A571

2019, May 24   Litho.   Perf. 13
1227   A571   100fr multi   1.90   1.90

Campaign Against Obesity — A572

No. 1228: a, Lychee fruit on lollipop stick. b, Mango in ice cream cup. c, Pineapple surrounding soda can. d, Watermelon slice on ice cream stick. e, Peeled banana in candy wrapper. f, Coconut surrounding bottle and straw.

Serpentine Die Cut 11
2019, May 24   Litho.
   Booklet Stamps
   Self-Adhesive
1228   Booklet pane of 6   11.50
   a.-f.   A572 100fr Any single   1.90   1.90

Office of Posts and Telecommunications Emblem — A573

Serpentine Die Cut 6¾ Vert.
2019   Self-Adhesive   Litho.
   Booklet Stamp
1229   A573   (80fr) deep ultra   —   —
   a.   Booklet pane of 10   —   —
   b.   Dated "2020"   —   —
   c.   Booklet pane of 10 #1229b   —   —
   d.   Dated "2021"   —   —
   e.   Booklet pane of 10 #1229d   —   —
   f.   Dated "2022"   —   —
   g.   Booklet pane of 10 #1229f   —   —

Issued: Nos. 1229b, 1229c, 9/21/20; Nos. 1229d, 1229e, 1/3/22. See Nos. 1291-1292.

Miss Tahiti Pageant Winners Type of 2016

No. 1230: a, Viola Teriitahi, 1968. b, Moeata Schmouker, 1978. c, Teumrre Pater, 1988. d, Mareva Galanter, 1998. e, Hinatea Boosie, 2008. f, Vaimalama Chaves, 2018.

Serpentine Die Cut 11
2019, June 7   Litho.
   Self-Adhesive
1230   Booklet pane of 6   11.50
   a.-f.   A524 100fr Any single   1.90   1.90

Cantaloupe A574

2019, June 7   Litho.   Perf. 13x13¼
1231   A574   140fr multi   2.75   2.75

No. 1231 is impregnated with a cantaloupe scent.

Artistic Conservatory of French Polynesia, 40th Anniv. — A575

Serpentine Die Cut 11
2019, July 19   Litho.
   Self-Adhesive
1232   A575   80fr multi   1.50   1.50

André Japy (1904-74), Aviator A576

2019, Aug. 23   Litho.   Perf. 13
1233   A576   100fr multi   1.90   1.90

General Milan Stefánik (1880-1919), Builder of Astronomical Observatory in French Polynesia — A577

2019, Sept. 6   Litho.   Perf. 13
1234   A577   140fr multi   2.60   2.60

Fish — A578

Designs: 40fr, Ruvettus pretiosus. 80fr, Pontinus macrocephalus. 100fr, Etelis carbunculus.

   Litho. & Silk-Screened
2019, Oct. 18   Perf. 13x13¼
1235-1237   A578   Set of 3   4.25   4.25
   1237a   Souvenir sheet of 3, #1235-1237   4.25   4.25

Polynesia, the Sky, by Henri Matisse (1869-1954) A579

Polynesia, the Sea, by Matisse A580

2019, Nov. 7   Litho.   Perf. 13
1238   A579   100fr multi   1.90   1.90
1239   A580   100fr multi   1.90   1.90

Cargo Vessel Hawaiki Nui A581

   Litho. & Engr.
2019, Nov. 7   Perf. 13½x13
1240   A581   500fr multi   9.25   9.25
   a.   Souvenir sheet of 1   9.25   9.25

See St. Pierre & Miquelon No. 1084.

Statue of God A'a — A582

2019, Dec. 13   Litho.   Perf. 13¼x13
1241   A582   80fr multi   1.50   1.50

New Year 2020 (Year of the Rat) — A583

   Litho. & Silk-Screened
2020, Jan. 24   Perf. 13
1242   A583   140fr multi   2.60   2.60

Snails — A584

Designs: 10fr, Partula hyalina. 100fr, Partula nodosa.

2020, Feb. 21   Litho.   Perf. 13x13¼
1243-1244   A584   Set of 2   2.10   2.10
   1244a   Souvenir sheet of 2, #1243-1244   2.10   2.10

FRENCH POLYNESIA

International Women's Day — A585

Designs: 80fr, Maadi Gobrait (1909-80), Nurse for Free French Forces in World War II. 100fr, Tuianu Le Gayic (1922-95), mayor and founder of women's organizations.

2020, Mar. 6   Litho.   Perf. 13¼x13
1245-1246   A585   Set of 2   3.25   3.25

Bearer Certificates A586

Certificate for: 20fr, French-Czechoslovakian Oceanic Islands Society. 80fr, Agricultural Society of Mopélia.

2020, June 26   Litho.   Perf. 13x13¼
1247-1248   A586   Set of 2   1.90   1.90

First day covers of Nos. 1247-1248 have additional cancels with the originally planned day of issue of Apr. 24, 2020, because the issuance of the stamps was delayed because of the coronavirus pandemic.

Island Scenes — A587

Designs: 5fr, Canoe off of Raivavae. 80fr, Horse on Nuku Hiva. 100fr, Bora Bora.

2020, July 31   Litho.   Perf. 13x13¼
1249-1251   A587   Set of 3   3.75   3.75

First day covers of Nos. 1249-1251 have additional cancels with the originally planned day of issue of June 26, 2020, because the issuance of the stamps was delayed because of the coronavirus pandemic.

Women Wearing Protective Face Masks to Prevent Spread of Coronavirus A588

2020, July 31   Litho.   Perf. 13x13¼
1252   A588   80fr multi   1.60   1.60

Bananas — A589

2020, Aug. 20   Litho.   Perf. 13x13¼
1253   A589   100fr multi   2.00   2.00

First day covers of No. 1253 have an additional cancel with the originally planned day of issue of June 26, 2020, because the issuance of the stamps was delayed because of the coronavirus pandemic. No. 1253 is impregnated with a banana scent.

Joe Dassin (1938-80), Singer — A590

2020, Aug. 20   Litho.   Perf. 13
1254   A590   100fr multi   2.00   2.00

Ville d'Amiens, Badge of 1st Free French Division A591

2020, Sept. 2   Litho.   Perf. 13
1255   A591   190fr multi   3.75   3.75

Recognition of Free French Forces by French Polynesian governmental authorities, 80th anniv.

Abandoned Hotel Tahara'a — A592

2020, Oct. 23   Litho.   Perf. 13¼x13
1256   A592   90fr multi   1.75   1.75

Miss Tahiti Pageant Winners Type of 2016

No. 1257: a, Dominique Tepava, 1969. b, Thilda Fuller, 1979. c, Myriam Tuheiava, 1989. d, Manoa Fruge, 1999. e, Puahinano Bonno, 2009. f, Matahari Bousquet, 2019.

Serpentine Die Cut 11
2020, Nov. 4   Litho.
Self-Adhesive
1257   Booklet pane of 6   12.00
a.-f.   A524 100fr Any single   2.00   2.00

Ballons Montes (Letters Sent From Paris by Balloons) of the Franco-Prussian War, 150th Anniv. — A593

Litho. & Engr.
2020, Nov. 4   Perf. 13
1258   A593   500fr multi   10.00   10.00
a.   Souvenir sheet of 1   10.00   10.00

Tutepoganui Mask — A594

2020, Dec. 18   Litho.   Perf. 13¼x13
1259   A594   100fr multi   2.10   2.10

Arrival of Ferdinand Magellan at the Tuamotu Archipelago, 500th Anniv. A595

Litho. & Engr.
2021, Jan. 22   Perf. 13
1260   A595   500fr multi   10.00   10.00
a.   Souvenir sheet of 1   10.00   10.00

New Year 2021 (Year of the Ox) — A596

Litho. & Silk-Screened
2021, Feb. 12   Perf. 13
1261   A596   140fr multi   3.00   3.00

International Women's Day — A597

2021, Mar. 8   Litho.   Perf. 13¼x13
1262   A597   110fr multi   2.25   2.25

Palm Trees — A598

Designs: 10fr, Pelagodoxa henryana. 110fr, Pritchardia mitiaroana.

2021, Apr. 9   Litho.   Perf. 13¼x13
1263-1264   A598   Set of 2   2.50   2.50

Tahiti-Faa'a Airport, 60th Anniv. A599

2021, May 4   Litho.   Perf. 13
1265   A599   100fr multi   2.10   2.10

Miss Tahiti Pageant Winners Type of 2016

No. 1266: a, Teura Teuira, 1960. b, Maire Tehei, 1970. c, Tatiana Teraiamano, 1980. d, Mareva Georges, 1990. e, Vanina Bea, 2000. f, Poehere Hutihuti Wilson, 2010.

Serpentine Die Cut 11
2021, June 4   Litho.
Self-Adhesive
1266   Booklet pane of 6   12.00
a.-f.   A524 100fr Any single   2.00   2.00

Woman and Gardenias — A600

2021, June 25   Litho.   Perf. 13¼x13
1267   A600   100fr multi   2.00   2.00

No. 1267 is impregnated with a gardenia scent.

Fire Walkers — A601

2021, July 16   Litho.   Perf. 13x13¼
1268   A601   110fr multi   2.25   2.25

Statue of God Rao — A602

2021, Aug. 20   Litho.   Perf. 13¼x13
1269   A602   100fr multi   2.00   2.00

Obverse and Reverse of 2021 Coins With New Designs — A603

No. 1270: a, 5-franc coin. b, 10-franc coin. c, 20-franc coin. d, 50-franc coin. e, 100-franc coin. f, 200-franc coin.

Serpentine Die Cut 11
2021, Sept. 1   Litho.
Self-Adhesive
1270   Booklet pane of 6   12.00
a.-f.   A603 100fr Any single   2.00   2.00

Islands — A604

Designs: 30fr, Maupiti. 100fr, Mangareva. 110fr, Fakarava.

2021, Sept. 24   Litho.   Perf. 13x13¼
1271-1273   A604   Set of 3   4.75   4.75

Hotel Maeva Beach — A605

2021, Oct. 22   Litho.   Perf. 13x13¼
1274   A605   110fr multi   2.25   2.25

Three Tahitians, Painting by Paul Gauguin (1848-1903) — A606

Litho. & Silk-Screened
2021, Nov. 4   Perf. 13
1275   A606   500fr multi   9.50   9.50
a.   Souvenir sheet of 1   9.50   9.50

Arrival of Gauguin in Papeete, 130th anniv.

Pomare II (c. 1782-1821), King of Tahiti — A607

2021, Dec. 17   Litho.   Perf. 13¼x13
1276   A607   100fr multi   1.90   1.90

Endangered Plants — A608

Designs: 100fr, Pacifigeron rapensis. 130fr, Erythrina tahitensis.

2022, Jan. 28   Litho.   Perf. 13¼x13
1277-1278   A608   Set of 2   4.50   4.50

New Year 2022 (Year of the Tiger) — A609

FRENCH POLYNESIA

Litho. & Silk-Screened
2022, Feb. 1   Perf. 13
1279   A609   140fr multi   2.75   2.75

International Women's Day — A610

Designs: 20fr, Woman with fishing spear and catch. 130fr, Mother and daughter.

2022, Mar. 8   Litho.   Perf. 13¼x13
1280-1281   A610   Set of 2   2.75   2.75

Charles Darwin (1809-82), Naturalist A611

Litho. & Silk-Screened
2022, Apr. 19   Perf. 13x12¾
1282   A611   500fr multi   9.00   9.00
    a.   Souvenir sheet of 1   9.00   9.00

Polynesian Expedition of Jacob Roggeveen (1659-1729), 300th Anniv. — A612

2022, June 2   Litho.   Perf. 13x13¼
1283   A612   100fr multi   1.90   1.90

Miss Tahiti Pageant Winners — A613

No. 1284: a, Tahia Piehi, 1961. b, Jeanne Burns, 1971. c, Maimiti Kinnander, 1981. d, Hina Sarciaux, 1991. e, Ravanui Teri-itaumihau, 2001. f, Rauata Temauri, 2011. g, Tumateata Buisson, 2021. h, Pageant emblem.

Serpentine Die Cut 11
2022, June 2   Litho.
Self-Adhesive
1284   Booklet pane of 8   15.50
    a.-h. A613 100fr Any single   1.90   1.90
Compare type A613 with type A524.

Battle of Bir Hakeim, 80th Anniv. — A614

2022, June 10   Litho.   Perf. 13x13¼
1285   A614   130fr multi   2.25   2.25

Heiva Dancers — A615

Designs: No. 1286, 130fr, Coco Hotahota (1941-2020). No. 1287, 130fr, Louise Kimitete (1940-2020).

2022, July 8   Litho.   Perf. 13x13¼
1286-1287   A615   Set of 2   4.50   4.50

Lemons — A616

2022, Aug. 26   Litho.   Perf. 13x13¼
1288   A616   130fr multi   2.25   2.25
No. 1288 is impregnated with a lemon scent.

Cetacean Sanctuary, 20th Anniv. — A617

Flag of French Polynesia and: 10fr, Stenella longirostris. 100fr, Megaptera novaeangliae.

2022, Sept. 23   Litho.   Perf. 13x13¼
1289-1290   A617   Set of 2   1.90   1.90

Office of Posts and Telecommunications Emblem Type of 2019
Serpentine Die Cut 6¾ Vert.
2022   Litho.
Self-Adhesive

Office of Posts and Telecommunications Emblem Type of 2019
Serpentine Die Cut 6¾ Vert.
2022, Jan. 3   Litho.
Self-Adhesive
1291   A573   5fr purple   —   —
    a.   Booklet pane of 10
1292   A573   (100fr) red   —   —
    a.   Booklet pane of 10
Nos. 1291-1292 are dated "2021."

Arrival of the Spanish at Tahiti, 250th Anniv. A618

Designs: 100fr, Pomare I (c. 1753-1803), King of Tahiti, black dolerite vessel. 130fr, Domingo Boenechea (1913-75), Spanish explorer of Tahiti, and ship, vert.

2022, Oct. 21   Litho.   Perf. 13
1293-1294   A618   Set of 2   4.00   4.00

Louis Duperrey (1786-1865), Jules Dumont d'Urville (1790-1842), Explorers, and Ship, La Coquille A619

Litho. & Engr.
2022, Nov. 3   Perf. 13
1295   A619   500fr gray & brown   8.75   8.75
    a.   Souvenir sheet of 1   8.75   8.75

Statue of Polynesian God 'Oro — A620

2022, Dec. 16   Litho.   Perf. 13¼x13
1296   A620   130fr multi   2.40   2.40

SEMI-POSTAL STAMPS

Nos. 55 and 26 Surcharged in Red

1915   Unwmk.   Perf. 14x13½
B1   A1   10c + 5c red   32.50   32.50
    a.   "e" instead of "c"   87.50   87.50
    b.   Inverted surcharge   225.00   225.00
    c.   Double surcharge   525.00   525.00
B2   A2   10c + 5c rose & org   12.50   12.50
    a.   "e" instead of "c"   65.00   65.00
    b.   "c" inverted   65.00   65.00
    c.   Inverted surcharge   300.00   300.00
    d.   As "a," inverted surcharge   400.00
    e.   As "b," inverted surcharge   400.00

Surcharged in Carmine

B3   A2   10c + 5c rose & org   5.50   5.50
    a.   "e" instead of "c"   45.00   45.00
    b.   Inverted surcharge   200.00   200.00
    c.   Double surcharge   200.00   200.00
    d.   As "a," inverted surcharge   325.00

Surcharged in Carmine

1916
B4   A2   10c + 5c rose & org   5.50   5.50

Curie Issue
Common Design Type
1938   Engr.   Perf. 13
B5   CD80   1.75fr + 50c brt ultra   20.00   20.00

French Revolution Issue
Common Design Type
1939   Photo.
Name and Value Typo. in Black
B6   CD83   45c + 25c grn   17.50   17.50
B7   CD83   70c + 30c brn   17.50   17.50
B8   CD83   90c + 35c red org   17.50   17.50
B9   CD83   1.25fr + 1fr rose pink   17.50   17.50
B10   CD83   2.25fr + 2fr blue   17.50   17.50
    Nos. B6-B10 (5)   87.50   87.50
    Set, never hinged   145.00

> Catalogue values for unused stamps in this section, from this point to the end of the section, are for Never Hinged items.

Common Design Type and

Marine Officer SP1   "L'Astrolabe" SP2

1941   Photo.   Perf. 13½
B11   SP1   1fr + 1fr red   3.50
B12   CD86   1.50fr + 3fr maroon   3.50
B12A   SP2   2.50fr + 1fr blue   3.50
    Nos. B11-B12A (3)   10.50
Nos. B11-B12A were issued by the Vichy government in France, and were not placed on sale in French Polynesia.

Nos. 125A-125B Srchd. in Black or Red

1944   Engr.   Perf. 12½x12
B12B   50c + 1.50fr on 2.50fr dp blue (R)   1.75
B12C   + 2.50fr on 1fr green   1.75
Colonial Development Fund.
Nos. B12B-B12C were issued by the Vichy government in France, but were not placed on sale in French Polynesia.

Red Cross Issue
Common Design Type
1944   Photo.   Perf. 14½x14
B13   CD90   5fr + 20fr pck blue   2.00   1.60
The surtax was for the French Red Cross and national relief.

Tropical Medicine Issue
Common Design Type
1950, July 17   Engr.   Perf. 13
B14   CD100   10fr + 2fr dk bl grn & dk grn   10.50   8.00
The surtax was for charitable work.

AIR POST STAMPS

Seaplane in Flight — AP1

     Perf. 13½
1934, Nov. 5   Unwmk.   Photo.
C1   AP1   5fr green   1.25   1.25
For overprint see No. C2.
For Type AP1 without "RF," see Nos. C1A-C1D.

Type of 1934 without "RF" and

Beach Scene — AP1a

     Perf. 13½, 13 (#C1E)
1944   Photo., Engr. (#C1E)
C1A   AP1   5fr green   .70
C1B   AP1   10fr black   1.00
C1C   AP1   20fr orange   1.10
C1D   AP1   50fr gray blue   1.50
C1E   AP1a   100fr turquoise blue   2.00
    Nos. C1A-C1E (5)   6.30
Nos. C1A-C1E were issued by the Vichy government in France, but were not placed on sale in French Polynesia.

> Catalogue values for unused stamps in this section, from this point to the end of the section, are for Never Hinged items.

No. C1 Overprinted in Red

1941
C2   AP1   5fr green   7.25   4.75

Common Design Type
1942   Perf. 14½x14
C3   CD87   1fr dark orange   .90   .65
C4   CD87   1.50fr bright red   .95   .70
C5   CD87   5fr brown red   1.25   .95
C6   CD87   10fr black   1.90   1.40
C7   CD87   25fr ultra   2.75   2.10
C8   CD87   50fr dark green   3.00   2.10
C9   CD87   100fr plum   3.00   2.10
    Nos. C3-C9 (7)   13.75   10.00

FRENCH POLYNESIA

Victory Issue
Common Design Type
1946, May 8   Engr.   Perf. 12½
C10   CD92   8fr dark green   2.75   2.00

Chad to Rhine Issue
Common Design Types
1946, June 6
C11   CD93   5fr red orange   2.10   1.60
C12   CD94   10fr dk olive bis   2.10   1.60
C13   CD95   15fr dk yellow grn   2.10   1.60
C14   CD96   20fr carmine   2.75   2.10
C15   CD97   25fr dk rose violet   4.00   3.00
C16   CD98   50fr black   4.50   3.50
    Nos. C11-C16 (6)   17.55   13.40

Shearwater and Moorea Landscape AP2

Fishermen AP3

Shearwater over Maupiti Shoreline AP4

1948, Mar. 1   Unwmk.   Perf. 13
C17   AP2   50fr red brown   30.00   11.00
C18   AP3   100fr purple   24.00   8.00
C19   AP4   200fr blue green   52.50   17.50
    Nos. C17-C19 (3)   106.50   36.50

UPU Issue
Common Design Type
1949
C20   CD99   10fr deep blue   20.00   15.00

Gauguin's "Nafea faaipoipo" — AP5

1953, Sept. 24
C21   AP5   14fr dk brn, dk gray grn & red   80.00   65.00

50th anniv. of the death of Paul Gauguin.

Liberation Issue
Common Design Type
1954, June 6
C22   CD102   3fr dk grnsh bl & bl grn   10.00   8.00

Bahia Peak, Borabora AP6

1955, Sept. 26   Unwmk.   Perf. 13
C23   AP6   13fr indigo & blue   10.00   5.50

Mother-of-Pearl Artist — AP7

Designs: 50fr, "Women of Tahiti," Gauguin, horiz. 100fr, "The White Horse," Gauguin. 200fr, Night fishing at Moorea, horiz.

1958, Nov. 3   Engr.   Perf. 13
C24   AP7   13fr multicolored   13.00   4.50
C25   AP7   50fr multicolored   12.00   4.50
C26   AP7   100fr multicolored   20.00   7.25
C27   AP7   200fr lilac & slate   40.00   21.00
    Nos. C24-C27 (4)   85.00   37.25

Airport, Papeete AP8

1960, Nov. 19
C28   AP8   13fr rose lil, vio, & yel grn   3.50   2.40

Telstar Issue
Common Design Type
1962, Dec. 5   Perf. 13
C29   CD111   50fr red lil, mar & vio bl   11.50   8.00

Tahitian Dancer — AP10

1964, May 14   Photo.   Perf. 13
C30   AP10   15fr multicolored   4.75   2.00

Map of Tahiti and Free French Emblems AP11

1964, July 10   Unwmk.
C31   AP11   16fr multicolored   15.00   9.00

Issued to commemorate the rallying of French Polynesia to the Free French cause.

Moorea Scene AP12

1964, Dec. 1   Litho.   Perf. 13
C32   AP12   23fr multicolored   9.50   4.00

ITU Issue
Common Design Type
1965, May 17   Engr.   Perf. 13
C33   CD120   50fr vio, red brn & bl   80.00   52.50

Paul Gauguin AP13

Design: 25fr, Gauguin Museum (stylized). 40fr, Primitive statues at Gauguin Museum.

1965   Engr.   Perf. 13
C34   AP13   25fr olive green   7.50   4.50
C35   AP13   40fr blue green   15.00   8.00
C36   AP13   75fr brt red brown   20.00   15.00
    Nos. C34-C36 (3)   42.50   27.50

Opening of Gauguin Museum, Papeete. Issued: 25fr, 75fr, 6/13. 40fr, 11/7.

Skin Diver with Spear Gun AP14

1965, Sept. 1   Engr.   Perf. 13
C37   AP14   50fr red brn, dl bl & dk grn   90.00   55.00

World Championships in Underwater Fishing, Tuamotu Archipelago, Sept. 1965.

Painting from a School Dining Room — AP15

1965, Nov. 29
C38   AP15   80fr brn, bl, dl bl & red   22.50   17.50

School Canteen Program.

Radio Tower, Globe and Palm — AP16

1965, Dec. 29   Engr.   Perf. 13
C39   AP16   60fr org, grn & dk brn   19.00   15.00

50th anniversary of the first radio link between Tahiti and France.

French Satellite A-1 Issue
Common Design Type

Designs: 7fr, Diamant Rocket and launching installations. 10fr, A-1 satellite.

1966, Feb. 7
C40   CD121   7fr choc, dp grn & lil   6.75   6.00
C41   CD121   10fr lil, dp grn & dk brn   6.75   6.00
   a.   Pair, #C40-C41 + label   14.00   14.00

French Satellite D-1 Issue
Common Design Type
1966, May 10   Engr.   Perf. 13
C42   CD122   20fr multicolored   7.00   4.75

Papeete Harbor AP17

1966, June 30   Photo.   Perf. 13
C43   AP17   50fr multicolored   15.00   11.00

"Vive Tahiti" by A. Benichou AP18

1966, Nov. 28   Photo.   Perf. 13
C44   AP18   13fr multicolored   11.00   6.50

Explorer's Ship and Canoe AP19

Designs: 60fr, Polynesian costume and ship. 80fr, Louis Antoine de Bougainville, vert.

1968, Apr. 6   Engr.   Perf. 13
C45   AP19   40fr multicolored   8.75   3.25
C46   AP19   60fr multicolored   11.50   6.50
C47   AP19   80fr multicolored   14.50   8.75
   a.   Souv. sheet, #C45-C47   160.00   160.00
    Nos. C45-C47 (3)   34.75   18.50

200th anniv. of the discovery of Tahiti by Louis Antoine de Bougainville. Issued: 40fr, 4/6/68.

The Meal, by Paul Gauguin AP20

1968, July 30   Photo.   Perf. 12x12½
C48   AP20   200fr multicolored   40.00   32.50

See Nos. C63-C67, C78-C82, C89-C93, C98.

Shot Put — AP21

1968, Oct. 12   Engr.   Perf. 13
C49   AP21   35fr dk car rose & brt grn   16.00   9.00

19th Olympic Games, Mexico City, 10/12-27.

Concorde Issue
Common Design Type
1969, Apr. 17
C50   CD129   40fr red brn & car rose   55.00   35.00

PATA 1970 Poster — AP22

1969, July 9   Photo.   Perf. 12½x13
C51   AP22   26fr blue & multi   17.50   7.25

Issued to publicize PATA 1970 (Pacific Area Travel Association Congress), Tahiti.

Underwater Fishing AP23

52fr, Hand holding fish made up of flags, vert.

1969, Aug. 5   Photo.   Perf. 13
C52   AP23   48fr blk, grnsh bl & red lil   35.00   13.50
C53   AP23   52fr bl, blk & red   40.00   22.50

Issued to publicize the World Underwater Fishing Championships.

FRENCH POLYNESIA

Gen. Bonaparte as Commander of the Army in Italy, by Jean Sebastien Rouillard — AP24

1969, Oct. 15   Photo.   Perf. 12½x12
C54 AP24 100fr car & multi   80.00 67.50

Bicentenary of the birth of Napoleon Bonaparte (1769-1821).

Eiffel Tower, Torii and EXPO Emblem — AP25

Design: 30fr, Mount Fuji, Tower of the Sun and EXPO emblem, horiz.

1970, Sept. 15   Photo.   Perf. 13
C55 AP25 30fr multicolored   20.00   8.00
C56 AP25 50fr multicolored   27.50 12.00

EXPO '70 International Exposition, Osaka, Japan, Mar. 15-Sept. 13.

Pearl Diver Descending, and Basket — AP26

Designs: 5fr, Diver collecting oysters. 18fr, Implantation into oyster, horiz. 27fr, Open oyster with pearl. 50fr, Woman with mother of pearl jewelry.

1970, Sept. 30   Engr.   Perf. 13
C57 AP26 2fr slate, grnsh bl & red brn   1.50   .90
C58 AP26 5fr grnsh blue, ultra & org   2.75   1.50
C59 AP26 18fr sl, mag & org   3.75   2.75
C60 AP26 27fr brt pink, brn & dl lil   9.25   4.75
C61 AP26 50fr gray, red brn & org   16.00   7.50
     Nos. C57-C61 (5)   33.25 17.40

Pearl industry of French Polynesia.

The Thinker, by Auguste Rodin and Education Year Emblem AP27

1970, Oct. 15   Engr.   Perf. 13
C62 AP27 50fr bl, ind & fawn   17.00 10.50

International Education Year.

Painting Type of 1968

Paintings by Artists Living in Polynesia: 20fr, Woman on the Beach, by Yves de Saint-Front. 40fr, Abstract, by Frank Fay. 60fr, Woman and Shells, by Jean Guillois. 80fr, Hut under Palms, by Jean Masson. 100fr, Polynesian Girl, by Jean-Charles Bouloc, vert.

Perf. 12x12½, 12½x12
1970, Dec. 14   Photo.
C63 AP20 20fr brn & multi   8.00   4.00
C64 AP20 40fr brn & multi   12.00   7.50
C65 AP20 60fr brn & multi   16.00 11.00
C66 AP20 80fr brn & multi   20.00 16.00
C67 AP20 100fr brn & multi   26.00 22.50
     Nos. C63-C67 (5)   82.00 61.00

South Pacific Games Emblem — AP28

1971, Jan. 26   Perf. 12½
C68 AP28 20fr ultra & multi   8.00   5.00

Publicity for 4th South Pacific Games, held in Papeete, Sept. 8-19, 1971.

Memorial Flame — AP29

1971, Mar. 19   Photo.   Perf. 12½
C69 AP29 5fr multicolored   8.00   5.00

In memory of Charles de Gaulle.

Soldier and Badge AP30

1971, Apr. 21
C70 AP30 25fr multicolored   11.00   6.75

30th anniversary of departure of Tahitian volunteers to serve in World War II.

Water Sports Type

Designs: 15fr, Surfing, vert. 16fr, Skin diving, vert. 20fr, Water-skiing with kite.

1971, May 11   Photo.   Perf. 13
C71 A44 15fr multicolored   6.50   3.50
C72 A44 16fr multicolored   7.50   3.25
C73 A44 20fr multicolored   11.00   7.75
     Nos. C71-C73 (3)   25.00 14.50

Sailing — AP31

1971, Sept. 8   Perf. 12½
C74 AP31 15fr shown   6.50   3.50
C75 AP31 18fr Golf   8.00   4.75
C76 AP31 27fr Archery   12.00   7.25
C77 AP31 53fr Tennis   20.00 13.50
  a. Souv. sheet, #C74-C77 190.00 190.00
     Nos. C74-C77 (4)   46.50 29.00

4th So. Pacific Games, Papeete, Sept. 8-19.

Painting Type of 1968

Paintings by Artists Living in Polynesia: 20fr, Hut and Palms, by Isabelle Wolf. 40fr, Palms on Shore, by André Dobrowolski. 60fr, Polynesian Woman, by Françoise Séli, vert. 80fr, Holy Family, by Pierre Heymann, vert. 100fr, Crowd, by Nicolai Michoutouchkine.

1971, Dec. 15   Photo.   Perf. 13
C78 AP20 20fr multicolored   7.50   4.50
C79 AP20 40fr multicolored 11.00   7.50
C80 AP20 60fr multicolored 13.00 10.00
C81 AP20 80fr multicolored 18.00 12.50
C82 AP20 100fr multicolored 30.00 22.50
     Nos. C78-C82 (5)   79.50 57.00

Papeete Harbor AP32

1972, Jan. 13
C83 AP32 28fr violet & multi 11.00   8.00

Free port of Papeete, 10th anniversary.

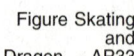

Figure Skating and Dragon — AP33

1972, Jan. 25   Engr.   Perf. 13
C84 AP33 20fr ultra, lake & brt grn   9.00   7.00

11th Winter Olympic Games, Sapporo, Japan, Feb. 3-13.

South Pacific Commission Headquarters, Noumea — AP34

1972, Feb. 5   Photo.   Perf. 13
C85 AP34 21fr blue & multi   11.00   5.25

South Pacific Commission, 25th anniv.

Festival Emblem — AP35

1972, May 9   Engr.   Perf. 13
C86 AP35 36fr orange, bl & grn 8.00   5.25

So. Pacific Festival of Arts, Fiji, May 6-20.

Kon Tiki and Route, Callao to Tahiti AP36

1972, Aug. 18   Photo.   Perf. 13
C87 AP36 16fr dk & lt bl, blk & org 10.00   6.50

25th anniversary of the arrival of the raft Kon Tiki in Tahiti.

Charles de Gaulle and Memorial AP37

1972, Dec. 9   Engr.   Perf. 13
C88 AP37 100fr slate   62.50 42.50

Painting Type of 1968

Paintings by Artists Living in Polynesia: 20fr, Horses, by Georges Bovy. 40fr, Sailboats, by Ruy Juventin, vert. 60fr, Harbor, by André Brooke. 80fr, Farmers, by Daniel Adam, vert. 100fr, Dancers, by Aloysius Pilioko, vert.

1972, Dec. 14   Photo.
C89 AP20 20fr gold & multi   9.75   4.25
C90 AP20 40fr gold & multi 12.00   6.75
C91 AP20 60fr gold & multi 21.00   9.50
C92 AP20 80fr dk grn, buff & dk brn 27.50 13.00
C93 AP20 100fr gold & multi 32.50 25.00
     Nos. C89-C93 (5)   102.75 58.50

St. Teresa and Lisieux Basilica — AP38

1973, Jan. 23   Engr.   Perf. 13
C94 AP38 85fr multicolored   25.00 17.50

Centenary of the birth of St. Teresa of Lisieux (1873-1897), Carmelite nun.

Nicolaus Copernicus AP39

1973, Mar. 7   Engr.   Perf. 13
C95 AP39 100fr brn, vio bl & red lil   30.00 17.50

Copernicus (1473-1543), Polish astronomer.

Plane over Tahiti AP40

1973, Apr. 3   Photo.   Perf. 13
C96 AP40 80fr ultra, gold & lt grn   22.50 16.00

Air France's World Tour via Tahiti.

DC-10 at Papeete Airport AP41

1973, May 18   Engr.   Perf. 13
C97 AP41 20fr bl, ultra & sl grn   16.00   9.00

Start of DC-10 service.

Painting Type of 1968

Design: 200fr, "Ta Matete" (seated women), by Paul Gauguin.

1973, June 7   Photo.   Perf. 13
C98 AP20 200fr multicolored   27.50 20.00

Paul Gauguin (1848-1903), painter.

Pierre Loti and Characters from his Books AP42

1973, July 4   Engr.   Perf. 13
C99 AP42 60fr multicolored   40.00 20.00

Pierre Loti (1850-1923), French naval officer and writer.

Woman with Flowers, by Eliane de Gennes — AP43

Paintings by Artists Living in Polynesia: 20fr, Sun, by Jean Francois Favre. 60fr, Seascape, by Alain Sidet. 80fr, Crowded Bus, by Francois Ravello. 100fr, Stylized Boats, by Jackie Bourdin, horiz.

FRENCH POLYNESIA

1973, Dec. 13   Photo.   Perf. 13
C100	AP43	20fr gold & multi	8.00	2.75
C101	AP43	40fr gold & multi	11.50	6.00
C102	AP43	60fr gold & multi	17.00	10.50
C103	AP43	80fr gold & multi	22.50	17.00
C104	AP43	100fr gold & multi	27.50	20.00
	Nos. C100-C104 (5)		86.50	56.25

Bird, Fish, Flower and Water — AP44

1974, June 12   Photo.   Perf. 13
C105	AP44	12fr blue & multi	7.50	5.25

Nature protection.

Catamaran under Sail — AP45

1974, July 22   Engr.   Perf. 13
C106	AP45	100fr multicolored	27.50	16.00

2nd Catamaran World Championships.

Still-life, by Rosine Temarui-Masson AP46

Paintings by Artists Living in Polynesia: 40fr, Palms and House on Beach, by Marcel Chardon. 60fr, Man, by Marie-Françoise Avril. 80fr, Polynesian Woman, by Henriette Robin. 100fr, Lagoon by Moon-light, by David Farsi, horiz.

1974, Dec. 12   Photo.   Perf. 13
C107	AP46	20fr gold & multi	18.00	8.50
C108	AP46	40fr gold & multi	27.50	9.50
C109	AP46	60fr gold & multi	32.50	12.00
C110	AP46	80fr gold & multi	45.00	16.50
C111	AP46	100fr gold & multi	65.00	27.50
	Nos. C107-C111 (5)		188.00	74.00

See Nos. C122-C126.

Polynesian Gods of Travel AP47

Designs: 75fr, Tourville hydroplane, 1929. 100fr, Passengers leaving plane.

1975, Feb. 7   Engr.   Perf. 13
C112	AP47	50fr sep, pur & brn	11.00	6.00
C113	AP47	75fr grn, bl & red	16.00	8.00
C114	AP47	100fr grn, sep & car	25.00	15.00
	Nos. C112-C114 (3)		52.00	29.00

Fifty years of Tahitian aviation.

French Ceres Stamp and Woman — AP48

1975, May 29   Engr.   Perf. 13
C115	AP48	32fr ver, brn & blk	8.00	5.00

ARPHILA 75 International Philatelic Exhibition, Paris, June 6-16.

Shot Put and Games' Emblem — AP50

Designs: 30fr, Volleyball. 40fr, Women's swimming.

1975, Aug. 1   Photo.   Perf. 13
C117	AP50	25fr shown	4.75	3.00
C118	AP50	30fr multicolored	7.00	3.75
C119	AP50	40fr multicolored	9.25	5.25
	Nos. C117-C119 (3)		21.00	12.00

5th South Pacific Games, Guam, Aug. 1-10.

Flowers, Athlete, View of Montreal — AP51

1975, Oct. 15   Engr.   Perf. 13
C120	AP51	44fr brt bl, ver & blk	11.00	6.50

Pre-Olympic Year 1975.

UPU Emblem, Jet and Letters AP52

1975, Nov. 5   Engr.   Perf. 13
C121	AP52	100fr brn, bl & ol	22.50	13.00

World Universal Postal Union Day

Paintings Type of 1974

Paintings by Artists Living in Polynesia: 20fr, Beach Scene, by R. Marcel Marius, horiz. 40fr, Roofs with TV antennas, by M. Anglade, horiz. 60fr, Street scene with bus, by J. Day, horiz. 80fr, Tropical waters (fish), by J. Steimetz. 100fr, Women, by A. van der Heyde.

1975, Dec. 17   Litho.   Perf. 13
C122	AP46	20fr gold & multi	3.00	1.75
C123	AP46	40fr gold & multi	6.00	3.00
C124	AP46	60fr gold & multi	9.00	4.50
C125	AP46	80fr gold & multi	12.00	7.50
C126	AP46	100fr gold & multi	14.50	12.00
	Nos. C122-C126 (5)		44.50	28.75

Concorde AP53

1976, Jan. 21   Engr.   Perf. 13
C127	AP53	100fr car, bl & ind	19.00	13.00

First commercial flight of supersonic jet Concorde from Paris to Rio, Jan. 21.

Adm. Rodney, Count de la Perouse, "Barfleur" and "Triomphant" in Battle AP54

31fr, Count de Grasse and Lord Graves, "Ville de Paris" & "Le Terible" in Chesapeake Bay Battle.

1976, Apr. 15   Engr.   Perf. 13
C128	AP54	24fr grnsh bl, lt brn & blk	5.00	2.50
C129	AP54	31fr mag, red & lt brn	5.75	3.50

American Bicentennial.

King Pomaré I — AP55

Portraits: 21fr, King Pomaré II. 26fr, Queen Pomaré IV. 30fr, King Pomaré V.

1976, Apr. 28   Litho.   Perf. 12½
C130	AP55	18fr olive & multi	1.75	.75
C131	AP55	21fr multicolored	2.00	1.10
C132	AP55	26fr gray & multi	2.75	1.25
C133	AP55	30fr plum & multi	3.00	1.90
	Nos. C130-C133 (4)		9.50	5.00

Pomaré Dynasty. See Nos. C141-C144.

Running and Maple Leaf AP56

Designs: 34fr, Long jump, vert. 50fr, Olympic flame and flowers.

1976, July 19   Engr.   Perf. 13
C134	AP56	26fr ultra & multi	4.25	2.10
C135	AP56	34fr ultra & multi	6.00	2.75
C136	AP56	50fr ultra & multi	11.50	5.00
a.		Min. sheet, #C134-C136	90.00	90.00
	Nos. C134-C136 (3)		21.75	9.85

21st Olympic Games, Montreal, Canada, July 17-Aug. 1.

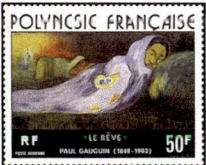

The Dream, by Paul Gauguin AP57

1976, Oct. 17   Photo.   Perf. 13
C137	AP57	50fr multicolored	11.00	7.25

Murex Steeriae — AP58

Sea Shells: 27fr, Conus Gauguini. 35fr, Conus marchionatus.

1977, Mar. 14   Photo.   Perf. 12½x13
C138	AP58	25fr vio bl & multi	4.25	1.25
C139	AP58	27fr ultra & multi	4.25	1.50
C140	AP58	35fr blue & multi	5.00	2.00
	Nos. C138-C140 (3)		13.50	4.75

See Nos. C156-C158.

Royalty Type of 1976

19fr, King Maputeoa, Mangareva. 33fr, King Camatoa V, Raiatea. 39fr, Queen Vaekehu, Marquesas. 43fr, King Teurarii III, Rurutu.

1977, Apr. 19   Litho.   Perf. 12½
C141	AP55	19fr dull red & multi	1.25	.95
C142	AP55	33fr dk blue & multi	1.90	1.25
C143	AP55	39fr ultra & multi	1.90	1.25
C144	AP55	43fr green & multi	2.75	1.90
	Nos. C141-C144 (4)		7.80	5.35

Polynesian rulers.

Pocillopora — AP59

Design: 25fr, Acropora, horiz.

Perf. 13x12½, 12½x13

1977, May 23   Photo.
C145	AP59	25fr multicolored	1.90	1.10
C146	AP59	33fr multicolored	2.75	1.90

3rd Symposium on Coral Reefs, Miami, Fla. See Nos. C162-C163.

De Gaulle Memorial — AP60

Photogravure and Embossed
1977, June 18   Perf. 13
C147	AP60	40fr gold & multi	7.00	5.00

5th anniversary of dedication of De Gaulle memorial at Colombey-les-Deux-Eglises.

Tahitian Dancer — AP61

1977, July 14   Litho.   Perf. 12½
C148	AP61	27fr multicolored	4.00	2.50

Charles A. Lindbergh and Spirit of St. Louis AP62

1977, Aug. 18   Litho.   Perf. 12½
C149	AP62	28fr multicolored	7.00	3.50

Lindbergh's solo transatlantic flight from New York to Paris, 50th anniv.

Mahoe — AP63

1977, Sept. 15   Photo.   Perf. 12½x13
C150	AP63	8fr shown	1.40	.80
C151	AP63	12fr Frangipani	1.75	1.25

FRENCH POLYNESIA

Palms on Shore — AP64

1977, Nov. 8   Photo.   *Perf. 12½x13*
C152   AP64   32fr multicolored   10.00   4.50
Ecology, protection of trees.

Rubens' Son Albert — AP65

1977, Nov. 28   Engr.   *Perf. 13*
C153   AP65   100fr grnsh blk & rose cl   11.00   8.00
Peter Paul Rubens (1577-1640), painter, 400th birth anniversary.

Capt. Cook and "Discovery" AP66

Design: 39fr, Capt. Cook and "Resolution."

1978, Jan. 20   Engr.   *Perf. 13*
C154   AP66   33fr multicolored   2.50   3.00
C155   AP66   39fr multicolored   3.00   3.50
Bicentenary of Capt. James Cook's arrival in Hawaii.
For overprints see Nos. C166-C167.

Shell Type of 1977

Sea Shells: 22fr, Erosaria obvelata. 24fr, Cypraea ventriculus. 31fr, Lambis robusta.

1978, Apr. 13   Photo.   *Perf. 13½x13*
C156   AP58   22fr brt blue & multi   2.25   1.25
C157   AP58   24fr brt blue & multi   2.25   1.50
C158   AP58   31fr brt blue & multi   3.50   2.50
Nos. C156-C158 (3)   8.00   5.25

Tahitian Woman and Boy, by Gauguin — AP67

1978, May 7   *Perf. 13*
C159   AP67   50fr multicolored   8.75   5.25
Paul Gauguin (1848-1903).

Antenna and ITU Emblem — AP68

1978, May 17   Litho.   *Perf. 13*
C160   AP68   80fr gray & multi   6.00   3.25
10th World Telecommunications Day.

Soccer and Argentina '78 Emblem AP69

1978, June 1
C161   AP69   28fr multicolored   3.25   2.10
11th World Cup Soccer Championship, Argentina, June 1-25.

Coral Type of 1977

Designs: 26fr, Fungia, horiz. 34fr, Millepora.

Perf. 13x12½, 12½x13
1978, July 13   Photo.
C162   AP59   26fr multicolored   1.75   1.25
C163   AP59   34fr multicolored   2.25   1.60

Radar Antenna, Polynesian Woman — AP70

1978, Sept. 5   Engr.   *Perf. 13*
C164   AP70   50fr blue & black   3.00   1.75
Papenoo earth station.

Bird and Rainbow over Island AP71

1978, Oct. 5   Photo.
C165   AP71   23fr multicolored   6.00   1.75
Nature protection.

Nos. C154-C155 Overprinted

No. C166

No. C167

1979, Feb. 14   Engr.   *Perf. 13*
C166   AP66   33fr multi   4.00   2.50
C167   AP66   39fr multi (VBI)   5.00   3.50
Bicentenary of Capt. Cook's death. On No. C167 date is last line of overprint.

Children, Toys and IYC Emblem AP72

1979, May 3   Engr.   *Perf. 13*
C168   AP72   150fr multicolored   12.00   7.00
International Year of the Child.

"Do you expect a letter?" by Paul Gauguin AP73

1979, May 20   Photo.   *Perf. 13*
C169   AP73   200fr multicolored   16.00   8.00

Shell and Carved Head AP74

1979, June 30   Engr.   *Perf. 13*
C170   AP74   44fr multicolored   3.50   2.00
Museum of Tahiti and the Islands.

Conference Emblem over Island — AP75

1979, Oct. 6   Photo.   *Perf. 13*
C171   AP75   23fr multicolored   2.25   1.10
19th South Pacific Conf., Tahiti, Oct. 6-12.

Flying Boat "Bermuda" AP76

Planes Used in Polynesia: 40fr, DC-4 over Papeete. 60fr, Britten-Norman "Islander." 80fr, Fairchild F-27A. 120fr, DC-8 over Tahiti.

1979, Dec. 19   Litho.   *Perf. 13*
C172   AP76   24fr multicolored   1.00   .50
C173   AP76   40fr multicolored   1.75   1.00
C174   AP76   60fr multicolored   2.75   1.50
C175   AP76   80fr multicolored   3.50   2.25
C176   AP76   120fr multicolored   6.00   3.00
Nos. C172-C176 (5)   15.00   8.25
See Nos. C180-C183.

Window on Tahiti, by Henri Matisse — AP77

1980, Feb. 18   Photo.
C177   AP77   150fr multicolored   8.00   5.00

Marshi Metua No Tehamana, by Gauguin — AP78

1980, Aug. 24   Photo.   *Perf. 13*
C178   AP78   500fr multicolored   18.00   13.00

Sydpex '80, Philatelic Exhibition, Sydney Town Hall — AP79

1980, Sept. 29   Photo.   *Perf. 13*
C179   AP79   70fr multicolored   8.00   5.25

Aviation Type of 1979

1980, Dec. 15   Litho.   *Perf. 13*
C180   AP76   15fr Catalina   .75   .55
C181   AP76   26fr Twin Otter   1.00   .70
C182   AP76   30fr CAMS 55   1.25   .90
C183   AP76   50fr DC-6   2.00   1.40
Nos. C180-C183 (4)   5.00   3.55

And The Gold of their Bodies, by Gauguin AP80

1981, Mar. 15   Photo.   *Perf. 13*
C184   AP80   100fr multicolored   4.50   2.50

20th Anniv. of Manned Space Flight — AP81

1981, June 15   Litho.   *Perf. 12½*
C185   AP81   300fr multicolored   9.00   7.00

First Intl. Pirogue (6-man Canoe) Championship — AP82

1981, July 25   Litho.   *Perf. 13x12½*
C186   AP82   200fr multicolored   5.50   4.50

Matavai Bay, by William Hodges AP83

Paintings: 60fr, Poedea, by John Weber, vert. 80fr, Omai, by Joshua Reynolds, vert. 120fr, Point Venus, by George Tobin.

1981, Dec. 10   Photo.   *Perf. 13*
C187   AP83   40fr multicolored   1.10   .90
C188   AP83   60fr multicolored   1.75   1.25
C189   AP83   80fr multicolored   2.75   1.75
C190   AP83   120fr multicolored   3.50   2.40
Nos. C187-C190 (4)   9.10   6.30
See Nos. C194-C197, C202-C205.

TB Bacillus Centenary AP84

1982, Mar. 24   Engr.   *Perf. 13*
C191   AP84   200fr multicolored   5.00   3.00

FRENCH POLYNESIA

1982 World Cup — AP85

1982, May 18   Litho.   Perf. 13
C192 AP85 250fr multicolored   6.50   4.50

French Overseas Possessions' Week, Sept. 18-25 — AP86

1982, Sept. 17   Engr.
C193 AP86 110fr multicolored   2.75   1.65

Painting Type of 1981
Designs: 50fr, The Tahitian, by M. Radiguet, vert. 70fr, Souvenir of Tahiti, by C. Giraud. 100fr, Beating Cloth Lengths, by Atlas JL the Younger. 160fr, Papeete Harbor, by C.F. Gordon Cumming.

1982, Dec. 15   Photo.   Perf. 13
C194 AP83 50fr multicolored   1.90   1.00
C195 AP83 70fr multicolored   2.25   1.50
C196 AP83 100fr multicolored   2.75   2.00
C197 AP83 160fr multicolored   4.50   2.75
     Nos. C194-C197 (4)   11.40   7.25

Wood Cutter, by Gauguin — AP87

Photo. & Engr.
1983, May 8   Perf. 12½x13
C198 AP87 600fr multicolored   16.00   8.00

Voyage of Capt. Bligh AP88

1983, June 9   Litho.   Perf. 13
C199 AP88 200fr Map, fruit   6.00   3.00

BRASILIANA '83 Intl. Stamp Exhibition, Rio de Janeiro, July 29-Aug. 7 — AP89

1983, July 29   Litho.   Perf. 13x12½
C200 AP89 100fr multicolored   2.50   1.75
  a.   Souvenir sheet   3.50   3.50

1983, Aug. 4   Litho.   Perf. 13x12½
C201 AP89 110fr Bangkok '83   3.00   2.00
  a.   Souvenir sheet   4.00   4.00

Painting Type of 1981
20th Cent. Paintings: 40fr, View of Moorea, by William Alister MacDonald (1861-1956). 60fr, The Fruit Carrier, by Adrian Herman Gouwe (1875-1965). 80fr, Arrival of the Destroyer Escort, by Nicolas Mordvinoff (1911-1977). 100fr, Women on a Veranda, by Charles Alfred Le Moine (1872-1918).

1983, Dec. 22   Photo.   Perf. 13
C202 AP83 40fr multi   1.00   .75
C203 AP83 60fr multi, vert.   1.50   1.00
C204 AP83 80fr multi, vert.   1.60   1.25
C205 AP83 100fr multi   2.00   1.60
     Nos. C202-C205 (4)   6.10   4.60

ESPAÑA '84 — AP90

Design: Maori canoers.

1984, Apr. 27   Engr.   Perf. 13
C206 AP90 80fr brn red & dk bl   2.25   1.50

Souvenir Sheet
C207 AP90 200fr dk bl & dk red   7.25   7.25

Woman with Mango, by Gauguin — AP91

Photo. & Engr.
1984, May 27   Perf. 12½x13
C208 AP91 400fr multicolored   11.00   6.00

Ausipex '84 — AP92

Details from Human Sacrifice of the Maori in Tahiti, 18th cent. engraving.

1984, Sept. 5   Litho.   Perf. 13x12½
C209 AP92 120fr Worshippers   3.00   2.25
C210 AP92 120fr Preparation   3.00   2.25
  a.   Pair, #C209-C210 + label 7.50   7.50

Souvenir Sheet
C211 AP92 200fr Entire   9.50   9.50

Painting by Gaugin (1848-1903) — AP93

Design: Where have we come from? What are we? Where are we going?

1985, Mar. 17   Litho.   Perf. 13½x13
C212 AP93 550fr multi   14.00   7.50

4th Pacific Arts Festival Type
Design: Islander, tiki, artifacts.

1985, July 3   Litho.   Perf. 13
C213 A95 200fr multicolored   4.50   3.00

Intl. Youth Year AP95

Design: Island youths, frigate bird.

1985, Sept. 18   Litho.
C214 AP95 250fr multi   5.50   3.25

ITALIA '85 — AP96

Designs: Ship sailing into Papeete Harbor, 19th century print.

1985, Oct. 22   Engr.
C215 AP96 130fr multicolored   2.75   2.50

Souvenir Sheet
C216 AP96 240fr multicolored   7.50   7.50

1st Intl. Marlin Fishing Contest, Feb. 27-Mar. 5 — AP97

1986, Feb. 27   Litho.   Perf. 12½
C217 AP97 300fr multicolored   6.50   4.00

Arrival of a Boat, c.1880 AP98

1986, June 24   Engr.   Perf. 13
C218 AP98 400fr intense blue   0.75   5.25

STOCKHOLMIA '86 — AP99

Design: Dr. Karl Solander and Anders Sparrmann, Swedish scientists who accompanied Capt. Cook, and map of Tahiti.

1986, Aug. 28   Engr.   Perf. 13
C219 AP99 150fr multicolored   3.25   2.25

Souvenir Sheet
C220 AP99 210fr multicolored   4.75   4.75

Protestant Churches AP100

1986, Dec. 17   Litho.   Perf. 13
C221 AP100 80fr Tiva, 1955   1.75   .90
C222 AP100 200fr Avera, 1880   4.50   2.10
C223 AP100 300fr Papetoai, 1822 6.50   3.25
     Nos. C221-C223 (3)   12.75   6.25

Broche Barracks, 120th Anniv. AP101

1987, Apr. 21   Litho.   Perf. 12½x12
C224 AP101 350fr multicolored   7.75   5.00

CAPEX '87 AP102

Design: George Vancouver (1757-1798), English navigator and cartographer, chart and excerpt from ship's log.

1987, June 15   Engr.   Perf. 13
C225 AP102 130fr multi   2.90   2.25

Imperf
Size: 143x100mm
C226 AP102 260fr multicolored   5.75   5.75

Soyez Mysterieuses, from a 5-Panel Sculpture by Paul Gauguin, Gauguin Museum — AP103

1987, Nov. 15   Perf. 13
C227 AP103 600fr multicolored 14.00   9.50

AIR POST SEMI-POSTAL STAMPS

Catalogue values for unused stamps in this section are for Never Hinged items.

French Revolution Issue
Common Design Type
Unwmk.
1939, July 5   Photo.   Perf. 13
Name and Value Typo. in Orange
CB1 CD83 5fr + 4fr brn blk   35.00 35.00

Mother & Children on Beach — SPAP1

Perf. 12½x13½
1942, June 22   Engr.
CB2 SPAP1 1.50fr + 3.50fr green 2.00
CB3 SPAP1 2fr + 6fr yel brn   2.00
Native children's welfare fund.
Nos. CB2-CB3 were issued by the Vichy government in France, but were not placed on sale in French Polynesia.

Colonial Education Fund
Common Design Type
1942, June 22
CB4 CD86a 1.20fr + 1.80fr blue & red   2.00
No. CB4 was issued by the Vichy government in France, but was not placed on sale in French Polynesia.

POSTAGE DUE STAMPS

Postage Due Stamps of French Colonies, 1894-1906, Overprinted

1926-27   Unwmk.   Perf. 14x13½
J1 D1 5c light blue   .95   .95
J2 D1 10c brown   .95   .95
J3 D1 20c olive green   1.40 1.40
J4 D1 30c dull red   1.60 1.60
J5 D1 40c rose   3.50 3.50
J6 D1 60c blue green   3.50 3.50
J7 D1 1fr red brown, straw 3.75 3.75

FRENCH POLYNESIA — FRENCH SOUTHERN & ANTARCTIC TERRITORY

J8	D1	3fr magenta ('27)	15.00	15.00

With Additional Surcharge of New Value

J9	D1	2fr on 1fr orange red	4.00	4.75
		Nos. J1-J9 (9)	34.65	35.40

Fautaua Falls, Tahiti — D2

Tahitian Youth — D3

1929 Typo. Perf. 13½x14

J10	D2	5c lt blue & dk brn	.75	.75
J11	D2	10c vermilion & grn	.75	.75
J12	D2	30c dk red	1.75	1.75
J13	D2	50c yel grn & dk brn	1.40	1.40
J14	D2	60c dl vio & yel grn	4.00	4.00
J15	D3	1fr Prus bl & red vio	3.50	3.50
J16	D3	2fr brn red & dk brn	2.00	2.10
J17	D3	3fr bl vio & bl grn	2.10	2.40
		Nos. J10-J17 (8)	16.25	16.65

Catalogue values for unused stamps in this section, from this point to the end of the section, are for Never Hinged items.

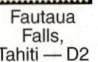

D4

1948 Engr. Perf. 14x13

J18	D4	10c brt blue grn	.40	.25
J19	D4	30c black brown	.40	.25
J20	D4	50c dk car rose	.50	.30
J21	D4	1fr ultra	.65	.50
J22	D4	2fr dk blue green	.95	.70
J23	D4	3fr red	1.90	1.40
J24	D4	4fr violet	2.00	1.60
J25	D4	5fr lilac rose	3.00	2.10
J26	D4	10fr slate	4.00	3.00
J27	D4	20fr red brown	5.50	4.25
		Nos. J18-J27 (10)	19.30	14.35

Polynesian Club — D5

1958 Unwmk. Perf. 14x13

J28	D5	1fr dk brn & grn	.65	.65
J29	D5	3fr bluish blk & hn brn	.90	.90
J30	D5	5fr brown & ultra	1.10	1.10
		Nos. J28-J30 (3)	2.65	2.65

Tahitian Bowl — D6

Designs: 1fr, Mother-of-pearl fish hook, vert. 5fr, Marquesan fan. 10fr, Lamp stand, vert. 20fr, Wood headrest ('87). 50fr, Wood scoop ('87).

1984-87 Litho. Perf. 13

J31	D6	1fr multicolored	.25	.25
J32	D6	3fr shown	.25	.25
J33	D6	5fr multicolored	.30	.30
J34	D6	10fr multicolored	.55	.55
J35	D6	20fr multicolored	.60	.60
J36	D6	50fr multicolored	1.50	1.50
		Nos. J31-J36 (6)	3.45	3.45

Issued: #J31-34, 3/15; #J35-J36, 8/18.

OFFICIAL STAMPS

Catalogue values for unused stamps in this section are for Never Hinged items.

Breadfruit — O1

Polynesian Fruits: 2fr, 3fr, 5fr, like 1fr. 7fr, 8fr, 10fr, 15fr, "Vi Tahiti." 19fr, 20fr, 25fr, 35fr, Avocados. 50fr, 100fr, 200fr, Mangos.

1977, June 9 Litho. Perf. 12½

O1	O1	1fr ultra & multi	.40	.65
O2	O1	2fr ultra & multi	.40	.65
O3	O1	3fr ultra & multi	.40	.65
O4	O1	5fr ultra & multi	.40	.65
O5	O1	7fr red & multi	.65	.95
O6	O1	8fr red & multi	.65	.95
O7	O1	10fr red & multi	.95	1.25
O8	O1	15fr red & multi	1.40	1.60
O9	O1	19fr black & multi	1.60	2.00
O10	O1	20fr black & multi	1.75	2.40
O11	O1	25fr black & multi	2.50	2.75
O12	O1	35fr black & multi	3.25	3.50
O13	O1	50fr black & multi	3.25	3.50
O14	O1	100fr red & multi	7.25	8.00
O15	O1	200fr ultra & multi	14.00	16.00
		Nos. O1-O15 (15)	38.85	45.50

1982-86 Perf. 13

O1a	O1	1fr ultra & multi	.70	1.25
O2a	O1	2fr ultra & multi	.70	1.25
O3a	O1	3fr ultra & multi	.95	1.25
O4a	O1	5fr ultra & multi	2.25	2.40
O5a	O1	7fr red & multi	2.25	2.50
O6a	O1	8fr red & multi	3.25	3.50
O7a	O1	10fr red & multi	3.50	3.50
O8a	O1	15fr red & multi ('84)	3.50	3.50
O10a	O1	20fr black & multi	3.50	3.50
O11a	O1	25fr black & multi ('84)	3.50	3.50
O12a	O1	35fr black & multi ('84)	8.00	10.50
O13a	O1	50fr black & multi ('84)	20.00	22.50
O14a	O1	100fr red & multi ('86)	52.50	60.00
O15a	O1	200fr ultra & multi ('86)	67.50	80.00
		Nos. O1a-O15a (14)	172.10	199.15

Nos. O1-O15 have dull finish (matte) gum. Nos. O1a-O15a have shiny gum.

Stamps and Postmarks — O2

1fr, French Colonies #5. 2fr, French Colonies #27, #12. 3fr, French Colonies #29, 1884 Papeete postmark. 5fr, Newspaper franked with surcharge of Tahiti #2, 1884 Papeete postmark. 9fr, #176. 10fr, #4, 1894 octagonal postmark. 20fr, #6, #8. 46fr, #48. 51fr, #147-148, Vaiteapua-Makatea Island postmark. 70fr, Visit Tahiti postmark on postal card piece. 85fr, #59 with 1921 manuscript cancel, vert. 100fr, #181. 200fr, #C21, 1st day cancel.

Perf. 13¼, 13¼x13 (#O20), 13x13¼ (#O26)

1993-99 Litho.

O16	O2	1fr multicolored	.25	.40
	a.	Perf. 13¼x13 ('98)	8.00	9.50
O17	O2	2fr multicolored	.25	.40
	a.	Perf. 13¼x13 ('97)	1.00	1.25
O18	O2	3fr multicolored	.25	.40
	a.	Perf. 13¼x13 ('98)	8.00	9.50
O19	O2	5fr multicolored	.30	.55
	a.	Perf. 13¼x13 ('97)	1.00	1.25
O20	O2	9fr multicolored	.80	1.25
O21	O2	10fr multicolored	.30	.55
	a.	Perf. 13¼x13 ('99)	1.00	.85
O22	O2	20fr multicolored	.65	.95
	a.	Perf. 13¼x13 ('99)	8.00	9.50
O23	O2	46fr multicolored	1.40	1.60
O24	O2	51fr multicolored	2.50	3.25
O25	O2	70fr multicolored	2.40	2.75
	a.	Perf. 13¼x13 ('97)	4.00	6.50
O26	O2	85fr multicolored	2.50	3.25
O27	O2	100fr multicolored	2.75	3.50
	a.	Perf. 13¼x13 ('99)	2.40	1.90
O28	O2	200fr multicolored	5.25	6.50
		Nos. O16-O28 (13)	19.60	25.35

Issued: 51fr, 4/6/94; 9fr, 85fr, 4/21/97; others, 1/13/93.

FRENCH SOUTHERN & ANTARCTIC TERRITORY

ˈfrench ˈsə-<u>th</u>ərn and ˌant-ärk-tik ˈter-ə-ˈtōr-ēs

POP. — 130 staff

Formerly dependencies of Madagascar, these areas, comprising the Kerguelen Archipelago; St. Paul, Amsterdam and Crozet Islands and Adelie Land in Antarctica achieved territorial status on August 6, 1955.

100 Centimes = 1 Franc
100 Cents = 1 Euro (2002)

Catalogue values for all unused stamps in this country are for Never Hinged items.

Madagascar No. 289 Ovptd. in Red

Unwmk.

1955, Oct. 28 Engr. Perf. 13

1	A25	15fr dk grn & dp ultra	10.00	27.50

Rockhopper Penguins, Crozet Archipelago A1

New Amsterdam A2

Design: 10fr, 15fr, Elephant seal.

1956, Apr. 25 Engr. Perf. 13

2	A1	50c dk blue, sepia & yel	.40	1.00
3	A1	1fr ultra, org & gray	.40	1.00
4	A2	5fr blue & dp ultra	2.40	2.50
5	A2	8fr gray vio & dk brn	14.00	17.50
6	A2	10fr indigo	5.00	5.00
7	A2	15fr indigo & brn vio	6.50	6.50
		Nos. 2-7 (6)	28.70	33.50

Polar Observation — A3

1957, Oct. 11

8	A3	5fr black & violet	2.50	4.25
9	A3	10fr rose red	3.50	5.00
10	A3	15fr dark blue	4.00	6.50
		Nos. 8-10 (3)	10.00	15.75

International Geophysical Year, 1957-58.

Imperforates

Most stamps of this French possession exist imperforate in issued and trial colors, and also in small presentation sheets in issued colors.

Flower Issue
Common Design Type

Design: Pringlea, horiz.

1959 Photo. Perf. 12½x12

11	CD104	10fr sal, grn & yel	8.75	7.50

Common Design Types pictured following the introduction.

Light-mantled Sooty Albatross — A4

Designs: 40c, Skua, horiz. 12fr, King shag.

1959, Sept. 14 Engr. Perf. 13

12	A4	30c blue, grn & red brn	.55	.85
13	A4	40c blk, dl red brn & bl	.55	.85
14	A4	12fr lt blue & blk	10.00	8.00
		Nos. 12-14 (3)	11.10	9.70

Coat of Arms — A5

1959, Sept. 14 Typo. Perf. 13x14

15	A5	20fr ultra, lt bl & yel	13.50	11.00

Sheathbills — A6

4fr, Sea leopard, horiz. 25fr, Weddell seal at Kerguélen, horiz. 85fr, King penguin.

1960, Dec. 15 Perf. 13

16	A6	2fr grnsh bl, gray & choc	2.00	2.50
17	A6	4fr bl, dk brn & dk grn	8.00	7.75
18	A6	25fr sl grn, bis brn & blk	77.50	45.00
19	A6	85fr grnsh bl, org & blk	17.50	17.50
		Nos. 16-19 (4)	105.00	72.75

Yves-Joseph de Kerguélen-Trémarec — A7

1960, Nov. 22

20	A7	25fr red org, dk bl & brn	22.50	21.00

Yves-Joseph de Kerguélen-Trémarec, discoverer of the Kerguélen Archipelago.

Charcot, Compass Rose and "Pourquoi-pas?" A8

1961, Dec. 26 Unwmk. Perf. 13

21	A8	25fr brn, grn & red	24.00	21.00

25th anniv. of the death of Commander Jean Charcot (1867-1936), Antarctic explorer.

Elephant Seals Fighting — A9

1963, Feb. 11 Engr. Perf. 13

22	A9	8fr dk blue, blk & claret	10.00	8.00

See No. C4.

Penguins and Camp on Crozet Island — A10

20fr, Research station & IQSY emblem.

1963, Dec. 16 Unwmk. Perf. 13

23	A10	5fr blk, red brn & Prus bl	55.00	45.00
24	A10	20fr vio, sl & red brn	57.50	52.50

Intl. Quiet Sun Year, 1964-65. See No. C6.

FRENCH SOUTHERN & ANTARCTIC TERRITORY

Great Blue Whale
A11

Black-browed Albatross
A12

10fr, Cape pigeons. 12fr, Phylica trees, Amsterdam Island. 15fr, Killer whale (orca).

1966-69		Engr.		Perf. 13
25	A11	5fr brt bl & indigo	18.50	12.50
26	A12	10fr sl, ind & ol brn	27.50	24.00
27	A11	12fr brt bl, sl grn & lemon	17.50	16.00
27A	A11	15fr ol, dk bl & ind	14.00	9.50
28	A12	20fr slate, ol & org	280.00	225.00
		Nos. 25-28 (5)	357.50	287.00

Issued: 5fr, 12/12; 20fr, 1/3/68; 10fr, 12fr, 1/6/69; 15fr, 12/21/69.

Aurora Australis, Map of Antarctica and Rocket — A13

1967, Mar. 4   Engr.   Perf. 13
29 A13 20fr mag, blue & blk   22.00 20.00

Launching of the 1st space rocket from Adelie Land, Jan., 1967.

Dumont d'Urville — A14

1968, Jan. 20
30 A14 30fr lt ultra, dk bl & dk brn   110.00 75.00

Jules Sébastien César Dumont D'Urville (1790-1842), French naval commander and South Seas explorer.

WHO Anniversary Issue
Common Design Type

1968, May 4   Engr.   Perf. 13
31 CD126 30fr red, yel & bl   62.50 47.50

Human Rights Year Issue
Common Design Type

1968, Aug. 10   Engr.   Perf. 13
32 CD127 30fr grnsh bl, red & brn   55.00 47.50

Polar Camp with Helicopter, Plane and Snocat Tractor
A15

1969, Mar. 17   Engr.   Perf. 13
33 A15 25fr Prus bl, lt grnsh bl & brn red   19.00 11.00

20 years of French Polar expeditions.

ILO Issue
Common Design Type

1970, Jan. 1   Engr.   Perf. 13
35 CD131 20fr org, dk bl & brn   15.00 10.00

UPU Headquarters Issue
Common Design Type

1970, May 20   Engr.   Perf. 13
36 CD133 50fr blue, plum & ol bis   40.00 27.50

Ice Fish — A16

Fish: Nos. 38-43, Antarctic cods, various species. 135fr, Zanchlorhynchus spinifer.

1971		Engr.		Perf. 13
37	A16	5fr brt grn, ind & org	2.50	1.25
38	A16	10fr redsh brn & dp vio	3.50	1.50
39	A16	20fr dp cl, brt grn & org	4.75	2.50
40	A16	22fr pur, brn ol & mag	5.00	3.50
41	A16	25fr grn, ind & org	5.75	3.75
42	A16	30fr sep, gray & bl vio	6.00	4.50
43	A16	35fr sl grn, dk brn & ocher	6.25	3.75
44	A16	135fr Prus bl, dp org & ol grn	10.00	5.75
		Nos. 37-44 (8)	43.75	26.50

Issued: Nos. 37-39, 41-42, 1/1; Nos. 40, 43-44, 12/22.

Map of Antarctica — A17

1971, Dec. 22
45 A17 75fr red   19.00 19.00

Antarctic Treaty pledging peaceful uses of and scientific cooperation in Antarctica, 10th anniv.

Microzetia Mirabilis — A18

Insects: 15fr, Christiansenia dreuxi. 22f, Phtirocoris antarcticus. 30fr, Antarctophytosus atriceps. 40fr, Paractora drenxi. 140fr, Pringleophaga Kerguelenensis.

1972				
46	A18	15fr cl, org & brn	8.50	5.50
47	A18	22fr vio bl, sl grn & yel	12.00	8.50
48	A18	25fr grn, rose lil & pur	5.25	3.50
49	A18	30fr blue & multi	15.00	9.00
50	A18	40fr dk brn, ocher & blk	7.50	4.25
51	A18	140fr bl, emer & brn	11.00	8.00
		Nos. 46-51 (6)	59.25	38.75

Issued: Nos. 40, 50-51, 1/3; Nos. 40-47, 49, 12/16.

De Gaulle Issue
Common Design Type

Designs: 50fr, Gen. de Gaulle, 1940. 100fr, Pres. de Gaulle, 1970.

1972, Feb. 1		Engr.		Perf. 13
52	CD134	50fr brt grn & blk	17.50	13.00
53	CD134	100fr brt grn & blk	22.50	16.50

Kerguelen Cabbage — A19

Designs: 61fr, Azorella selago, horiz. 87fr, Acaena ascendens, horiz.

1972-73				
54	A19	45fr multicolored	8.00	4.75
55	A19	61fr multicolored	3.00	2.50
56	A19	87fr multicolored	5.00	3.50
		Nos. 54-56 (3)	16.00	10.75

Issued: 45fr, 12/18; others, 12/13/73.

Mailship Sapmer and Map of Amsterdam Island
A20

1974, Dec. 31   Engr.   Perf. 13
57 A20 75fr bl, blk & dk brn   6.00 5.00

25th anniversary of postal service.

Antarctic Tern — A21

Designs: 50c, Antarctic petrel. 90c, Sea lioness. 1fr, Weddell seal. 1.20fr, Kerguelen cormorant, vert. 1.40fr, Gentoo penguin, vert.

1976, Jan.		Engr.		Perf. 13
58	A21	40c multicolored	4.00	3.00
59	A21	50c multicolored	4.25	3.00
60	A21	90c multicolored	6.25	4.00
61	A21	1fr multicolored	10.00	9.25
62	A21	1.20fr multicolored	12.00	11.00
63	A21	1.40fr multicolored	13.00	11.50
		Nos. 58-63 (6)	49.50	41.75

Climbing Mount Ross — A22

James Clark Ross — A22a

1976, Dec. 16		Engr.		Perf. 13
64	A22	30c multicolored	3.75	2.75
65	A22a	3fr multicolored	4.00	2.75

First climbing of Mount Ross, Kerguelen Island, Jan. 5, 1975.

James Cook — A23

1976, Dec. 16
66 A23 70c multicolored   10.00 9.00

Bicentenary of Capt. Cook's voyage past Kerguelen Island. See No. C46.

Commerson's Dolphins — A24

1977, Feb. 1		Engr.		Perf. 13
67	A24	1.10fr Blue whale	5.25	3.75
68	A24	1.50fr shown	5.75	4.00

Macrocystis Algae
A25

Salmon Hatchery
A26

Magga Dan — A27

Designs: 70c, Durvillea algae. 90c, Albatross. 1fr, Underwater sampling and scientists, vert. 1.40fr, Thala Dan and penguins.

1977, Dec. 20		Engr.		Perf. 13
69	A25	40c ol brn & bis	1.20	.75
70	A26	50c dk bl & pur	1.25	1.10
71	A25	70c blk, grn & brn	1.40	1.00
72	A26	90c grn, brt bl & brn	1.50	1.10
73	A27	1fr slate	1.25	1.10
74	A27	1.20fr multi	2.50	1.75
75	A27	1.40fr multi	1.75	1.75
		Nos. 69-75 (7)	10.85	8.55

See Nos. 77-79.

A28

Explorer with French and Expedition Flags.

1977, Dec. 21
76 A28 1.90fr multicolored   6.25 5.25

French Polar expeditions, 1947-48.

Types of 1977

40c, Forbin, destroyer. 50c, Jeanne d'Arc, helicopter carrier. 1.40fr, Kerguelen cormoran.

1979, Jan. 1		Engr.		Perf. 13
77	A27	40c black & blue	1.00	1.00
78	A27	50c black & blue	1.25	1.15
79	A26	1.40fr multicolored	1.25	1.25
		Nos. 77-79 (3)	3.50	3.40

French ANTARCTIC

1955 - 2023 FREE PRICE LIST
Mint FSAT sets & Year Sets
Madagascar Forerunner to date!
Buy 1955-2023 Complete and Save 10% off Individual Year Set Prices.
Many FSAT Imperfs, Deluxe Sheets & Proofs Available!

Order Directly from our website
www.hgitner.com
WE BUY!
NH FSAT 1955 to date –
Sets, Collections and More!
Sell to a knowledgeable specialist!
Top Prices Paid!
1-800-94-STAMP

Henry Gitner Philatelists, Inc.
P.O. Box 3077-S, Middletown, NY 10940
Tel: 845-343-5151 Fax: 845-343-0068
Toll Free: 1-800-947-8267
E-mail: hgitner@hgitner.com
PHILATELY - THE QUIET EXCITEMENT!

FRENCH SOUTHERN & ANTARCTIC TERRITORY

Raymond Rallier du Baty — A29

1979, Jan. 1
80 A29 1.20fr citron & indigo   1.10 1.00
See Nos. 97, 100, 111, 117, 129, 135, 188.

French Navigators Monument, Hobart A30

1979, Jan. 1
81 A30 1fr multicolored   .80 .75
French navigators and explorers.

Petrel A31

Design: 70c, Rockhopper penguins, vert.

1979 Engr. Perf. 13
82 A31 70c multi   .90 .90
83 A31 1fr shown   1.10 1.10

Commandant Bourdais — A32

Design: 1.10fr, Doudart de Lagree, vert.

1979
84 A32 1.10fr multicolored   .95 .90
85 A32 1.50fr shown   1.10 1.10

Adm. Antoine d'Entrecasteaux — A33

1979
86 A33 1.20fr multicolored   1.00 1.00

Sebastian de el Cano — A34

Discovery of Amsterdam Island, 1522: 4fr, Victoria, horiz.

1979
87 A34 1.40fr multicolored   .85 .75
88 A34 4fr multicolored   1.75 1.40

Adelie Penguins A35

Adelie Penguin A36

Sea Leopard — A37

1980, Dec. 15 Engr. Perf. 13
89 A35 50c rose violet   1.10 1.00
90 A36 60c multicolored   1.10 1.00
91 A35 1.20fr multicolored   1.75 1.25
92 A37 1.30fr multicolored   1.10 1.00
93 A37 1.80fr multicolored   1.10 1.00
   Nos. 89-93 (5)   6.15 5.25

20th Anniv. of Antarctic Treaty — A38

1981, June 23 Engr. Perf. 13
94 A38 1.80fr multicolored   3.75 3.75

Alouette II — A39

1981-82 Engr. Perf. 13
95 A39 55c brown & multi   .50 .45
96 A39 65c blue & multi   .55 .45

Explorer Type of 1979
1981
97 A29 1.40fr Jean Loranchet   .70 .50

Landing Ship Le Gros Ventre, Kerguelen A41

1983, Jan. 3 Engr. Perf. 13
98 A41 55c multicolored   .80 .60

Our Lady of the Winds Statue and Church, Kerguelen — A42

1983, Jan. 3
99 A42 1.40fr multicolored   .80 .75

Explorer Type of 1979
Design: Martin de Vivies, Navigator.

1983, Jan. 3
100 A29 1.60fr multicolored   .80 .70

Eaton's Ducks — A44

1983, Jan. 3
101 A44 1.50fr multicolored   .75 .55
102 A44 1.80fr multicolored   .80 .75

Trawler Austral A45

1983, Jan. 3
103 A45 2.30fr multicolored   1.25 1.00

Freighter Lady Franklin — A46

1983, Aug. 4 Engr. Perf. 13
104 A46 5fr multicolored   3.50 2.75

Glaciology A47

Design: Scientists examining glacier, base.

1984, Jan. 1 Engr. Perf. 13
105 A47 15c multicolored   .30 .25
106 A47 1.70fr multicolored   .70 .60

Crab-eating Seal — A48

Penguins A49

1984, Jan. 1
107 A48 60c multicolored   .50 .50
108 A49 70c multicolored   .40 .40
109 A49 2fr multicolored   1.10 .90
110 A48 5.90fr multicolored   1.75 1.50
   Nos. 107-110 (4)   3.75 3.30

Explorer Type of 1979
1984, Jan. 1
111 A29 1.80fr Alfred Faure   .80 .65

Biomass A51

1985, Jan. 1 Engr. Perf. 13
112 A51 1.80fr multicolored   .65 .50
113 A51 5.20fr multicolored   1.50 1.25

Emperor Penguins A52

Snowy Petrel A53

1985, Jan. 1 Engr. Perf. 13
114 A52 1.70fr multicolored   .90 .75
115 A53 2.80fr multicolored   1.10 1.00

Port Martin — A54

1985, Jan. 1 Engr. Perf. 13
116 A54 2.20fr multicolored   1.10 .75

Explorer Type of 1979
1985, Jan. 1 Engr. Perf. 13
117 A29 2fr Andre-Frank Liotard   .80 .65

Antarctic Fulmar A56

1986, Jan. 1 Engr. Perf. 13
118 A56 1fr shown   .50 .40
119 A56 1.70fr Giant petrels   .75 .70
   Nos. 118-119,C91 (3)   3.25 2.85

Echinoderms A57

1986, Jan. 1
120 A57 1.90fr shown   .85 .70

Cotula Plumosa — A58

Design: 6.20fr, Lycopodium. saururus.

1986, Jan. 1
121 A58 2.30fr shown   .75 .70
122 A58 6.20fr multicolored   2.00 1.75

Shipping — A59

Designs: 2.10fr, Var research ship. 3fr, Polarbjorn support ship.

1986, Jan. 1
123 A59 2.10fr multicolored   .85 .75
124 A59 3fr multicolored   1.10 1.00

Marine Life — A60

1987, Jan. 1 Engr. Perf. 13½x13
125 A60 50c dk blue & org   .55 .45

Flora — A61

FRENCH SOUTHERN & ANTARCTIC TERRITORY

Designs: 1.80fr, Poa cookii. 6.50fr, Lichen, Neuropogon taylori.

1987, Jan. 1
126 A61 1.80fr multicolored .65 .45
127 A61 6.50fr multicolored 1.90 1.40

Marret Base, Adelie Land — A62

1987, Jan. 1
128 A62 2fr yel brn, dk ultra & lake .80 .65

Explorer Type of 1979

1987, Jan. 1
129 A29 2.20fr Adm. Mouchez .85 .65

Reindeer A64

1987, Jan. 1
130 A64 2.50fr black 1.25 1.00

Transport Ship Eure — A65

1987, Jan. 1
131 A65 3.20fr dk ultra, Prus grn & dk grn 1.25 1.00

Macaroni Penguins A66

1987, Jan. 1 Perf. 13x12½
132 A66 4.80fr multicolored 2.50 1.75

Elephant Grass A67

1900, Jan. 1 Engr. Perf. 13
133 A67 1.70fr Prus grn, emer & olive .75 .60

Rev.-Father Lejay, Explorer — A68

1988, Jan. 1
134 A68 2.20fr vio, ultra & blk .85 .70

Explorer Type of 1979

Design: Robert Gessain (1907-86).

1988, Jan. 1
135 A29 3.40fr gray, dk red & blk 1.25 1.00

Le Gros Ventre, 18th Cent. — A70

1988, Jan. 1
136 A70 3.50fr dp ultra, bl grn & brn 1.25 1.10

Mermaid and B.A.P. Jules Verne, Research Vessel A71

1988, Jan. 1
137 A71 4.90fr gray & dk blue 2.25 1.60

La Fortune, Early 19th Cent. — A72

1988, Jan. 1
138 A72 5fr blk & dull bl grn 2.00 1.60

Wilson's Petrel A73

1988, Jan. 1
139 A73 6.80fr blk, sepia & dl bl grn 2.75 2.00
See Nos. 143-144.

Mt. Ross Campaign (in 1987) A74

Designs: 2.20fr, Volcanic rock cross-sections. 15.10fr, Kerguelen Is.

1988, Jan. 1 Perf. 13x12½
140 A74 2.20fr multi .75 .60
141 A74 15.10fr multi 4.25 3.50
a. Pair, #140-141 + label 6.50 6.50

Darrieus System Wind Vane Electric Generator A75

1988, Jan. 1 Engr. Perf. 13
142 A75 1fr dark blue & blue .50 .30

Fauna Type of 1988

1989, Jan. 1 Engr.
143 A73 1.10fr Lithodes .35 .35
144 A73 3.60fr Blue petrel 1.40 1.10

Fern — A76

Designs: Blechnum penna Marina.

1989, Jan. 1
145 A76 2.00fr multicolored 1.00 .65

Minerals — A77

1989, Jan. 1
146 A77 5.10fr Mesotype 1.90 1.75
147 A77 7.30fr Analcime 2.75 2.75

Henri and Rene Bossiere, Pioneers of the Kerguelen Isls. — A78

1989, Jan. 1
148 A78 2.20fr multicolored 1.10 .65

Kerguelen Is. Sheep A79

1989, Jan. 1 Perf. 13½x13
149 A79 2fr multicolored .80 .60

Scuba Diver, Adelie Coast A80

1989, Jan. 1
150 A80 1.70fr dk olive bis, blue & dk grn .75 .65

Map of Kerguelen Island, Protozoa and Copepod A81

1990, Jan. 1 Engr. Perf. 13
151 A81 1.10fr blk, brt blue & red brn .90 .50
Study of protista, Kerguelan Is.

Cattle on Farm, Sea Birds — A82

1990, Jan. 1
152 A82 1.70fr Prus blue, grn & brn blk .80 .65
Rehabilitation of the environment, Amsterdam Is.

Quoy and *Copendium decollata* — A83

1990, Jan. 1 Perf. 13½x13
153 A83 2.20fr brt blue, blk & red brn .90 .70
Jean Rene C. Quoy (1790-1869), naturalist, navigator.

Dumont d'Urville (1790-1842), Explorer — A84

1990, Jan. 1
154 A84 3.60fr ultra & blk 1.50 1.00

Yellow-billed Albatross A85

1990, Jan. 1 Perf. 13x12½
155 A85 2.80fr multicolored 1.75 1.00

Aragonite — A86

1990, Jan. 1
156 A86 5.10fr deep ultra & dark yel grn 2.75 2.00

Ranunculus pseudo trullifolius — A87

1990, Jan. 1 Perf. 13
157 A87 8.40fr dp bl, org & omor grn 3.00 2.50

Penguin Type of Airpost 1974

1991, Jan. 1
158 AP18 50c blue grn, bl & blk .75 .45
Postal Service at Crozet Island, 30th anniv.

Moss A88

1991, Jan. 1 Perf. 13x12½
159 A88 1.70fr gray, brn & blk .80 .60

Adm. Max Douguet (1903-1989) A89

1991, Jan. 1
160 A89 2.30fr org brn, blk & bl 1.25 .90

Lighter L'Aventure A90

1991, Jan. 1 Engr. Perf. 13
161 A90 3.20fr brn, grn & bl 1.50 1.10

Sea Lions — A91

1991, Jan. 1 Perf. 13
162 A91 3.60fr blue & ol brn 2.25 1.50

FRENCH SOUTHERN & ANTARCTIC TERRITORY

Mordenite — A92

1991, Jan. 1
163 A92 5.20fr blk, grn bl & grn   2.60 1.75

Champsocephalus Gunnari — A93

1991, Jan. 1
164 A93 7.80fr blue & green   3.00 2.50

Antarctic Treaty, 30th Anniv. — A94

1991, Jan. 1
165 A94 9.30fr ol grn & rose red   3.75 3.25

A95

Design: Colobanthus Kerguelensis.

1992, Jan. 1 Engr. Perf. 13
166 A95 1fr bl grn, grn & brn   .85 .40

Globe Challenge Yacht Race — A96

1992, Jan. 1 Litho.
167 A96 2.20fr multicolored   1.75 1.10

Dissostichus Eleginoides A97

1992, Jan. 1 Engr.
168 A97 2.30fr blue, ol grn & red brn   1.60 1.10

Paul Tchernia — A98

1992, Jan. 1 Engr. Perf. 13
169 A98 2.50fr brown & green   .95 .90

Capt. Marion Dufresne (1724-1772) — A99

1992, Jan. 1 Engr. Perf. 13
170 A99 3.70fr red, blk & bl   1.60 1.30

Supply Ship Tottan, 1951 A100

1992, Jan. 1 Engr. Perf. 13
171 A100 14fr blue grn, brn & bl   5.50 4.50

WOCE Program A101

1992, Jan. 1
172 A101 25.40fr multi   11.00 9.50

Coat of Arms — A102

1992-95 Engr. Perf. 13
173 A102 10c black   .25 .25
174 A102 20c greenish blue   .40 .25
175 A102 30c red   .50 .25
176 A102 40c green   .60 .25
177 A102 50c orange   .60 .25
　　Nos. 173-177 (5)   2.35 1.25
Issued: 10c, 1/1/92; 20c, 30c, 1/1/93; 40c, 1/1/94; 50c, 1/2/95.
See Nos. 295-299.

Garnet — A103

1993, Jan. 1 Engr. Perf. 13
183 A103 1fr multicolored   1.40 .35
See Nos. 194, 203, 212, 222, 235, 244, 259, 279, 300, 330.

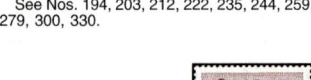
Research Ship Marion Dufresne, 20th Anniv. — A104

1993, Jan. 1
184 A104 2.20fr multicolored   1.25 .70

Lyallia Kerguelensis — A105

1993, Jan. 1
185 A105 2.30fr blue & green   1.25 .70

A106

A107

1993, Jan. 1
186 A106 2.50fr Killer whale   1.25 .80
187 A107 2.50fr Skua   6.50 1.50

A108

Design: 2.50fr, Andre Prudhomme (1930-1959), Meteorologist. 22fr, Weather station, Adelie Land.

1993, Jan. 1 Perf. 12½x13
188　　2.50fr blue, blk & org   1.00 .75
189　　22fr org, blk & bl   7.50 5.25
　a. A108 Pair, #188-189 + label   11.00 11.00
43rd Anniv. of Météo France in French Southern & Antarctic Territory.

Centriscops Obliquus A109

1993, Jan. 1 Perf. 13
190 A109 3.40fr multicolored   1.50 1.00

Freighter Italo Marsano A110

1993, Jan. 1
191 A110 3.70fr multicolored   1.75 .90

ECOPHY Program — A111

1993, Jan. 1
192 A111 14fr black, blue & brn   6.25 3.50

L'Astrolabe on Northeast Route, 1991 — A112

1993, Jan. 1
193 A112 22fr multicolored   9.00 6.25

Mineral Type of 1993
1994, Jan. 1 Engr. Perf. 13
194 A103 1fr Cordierite   1.25 .70

Felis Catus A113

1994, Jan. 1
195 A113 2fr green & black   3.50 1.25

A114

1994, Jan. 1 Engr. Perf. 13
196 A114 2.40fr dk brn, blk & bl   1.50 .65

A115

1994, Jan. 1
197 A115 2.80fr slate blue   1.50 .80

Robert Pommier (1919-61) — A116

1994, Jan. 1
198 A116 2.80fr multicolored   1.50 .85

A117

Designs: 2.80fr, C.A. Vincendon Dumoulin (1811-58), hydrographer. 23fr, Measuring Earth's magnetic field.

1994, Jan. 1 Perf. 12½x13
199　　2.80fr black & blue   1.50 1.00
200　　23fr blue & black   7.25 5.00
　a. A117 Pair, #199-200 + label   10.00 10.00

Rascasse A119

1994, Jan. 1 Perf. 13
201 A119 3.70fr bl grn & red brn   1.40 1.00

Kerguelen of Tremarec A120

1994, Jan. 1
202 A120 4.30fr multicolored   1.75 1.25

Mineral Type of 1993
1995, Jan. 2 Engr. Perf. 13
203 A103 1fr Olivine   1.50 .40

Mancoglosse Antarctique — A121

FRENCH SOUTHERN & ANTARCTIC TERRITORY

1995, Jan. 2
204 A121 2.40fr ol brn, vio & bl grn   1.25 1.00

Andree (1903-90) and Edgar de la Rue (1901-91) — A122

1995, Jan. 2
205 A122 2.80fr bl, red brn & mag   1.40 .90

SODAR Station A123

1995, Jan. 2
206 A123 2.80fr vio, mag & red brn   1.40 1.00

Mont D'Alsace A124

1995, Jan. 2
207 A124 3.70fr dk bl, vio, red brn   1.75 1.10

Balaenoptera Acutorostrata — A125

1995, Jan. 2
208 A125 23fr blue, claret & ind   9.75 6.50

Sailing Ship Tamaris — A126

1995, Jan. 2
209 A126 25.80fr multicolored   10.00 6.75

L'Heroine, Crozet Islands Mission, 1837 — A127

1995, Jan. 2
210 A127 27.30fr blue   11.00 7.25

Creation of the Territories, 40th Anniv. — A128

1995, Aug. 7   Litho.   **Imperf.**
Size: 143x84mm
211 A128 30fr multicolored   15.00 15.00

Mineral Type of 1993
1996, Jan. 1   Engr.   Perf. 13
212 A103 1fr Amazonite   .90 .30

White-chinned Petrel — A129

1996, Jan. 1
213 A129 2.40fr blue black   1.40 .70

Expedition Ship Yves de Kerguelen A130

1996, Jan. 1
214 A130 2.80fr multicolored   1.50 .75

Benedict Point Scientific Research Station, Amsterdam Island — A131

1996, Jan. 1
215 A131 2.80fr multicolored   1.50 .75

Paul-Emile Victor (1907-1995), Polar Explorer — A132

Designs: 2.80fr, Victor crossing Greenland with sled dogs, 1936. 23fr, Victor, penguins, Dumont d'Urville Base, Adélie Land.

1996, Jan. 1
216 A132 2.80fr multicolored   1.40 .85
217 A132 23fr multicolored   11.50 7.50
a. Pair, #216-217 + label   14.00 14.00

Admiral Jacquinot (1796-1879), Antarctic Explorer — A133

1996, Jan. 1
218 A133 3.70fr dark blue & blue   1.50 1.00

Trawler Austral A134

1996, Jan. 1   Photo. & Engr.
219 A134 4.30fr multicolored   2.25 1.25

Lycopodium Magellanicum — A135

1996, Jan. 1   Engr.
220 A135 7.70fr multicolored   3.00 2.25

Search for Micrometeorites, Cape Prudhomme — A136

1996, Jan. 1
221 A136 15fr vio, blk & grn bl   8.00 5.00

Mineral Type of 1993
1997, Jan. 1   Engr.   Perf. 13x12½
222 A103 1fr Amethyst   1.25 .40

Storm Petrel A137

1997, Jan. 1   Perf. 13
223 A137 2.70fr blue & indigo   1.50 .80

Rene Garcia (1915-95), Windmill — A138

1997, Jan. 1
224 A138 3fr multicolored   1.60 .90

Research Ship Marion Dufresne — A139

Photo. & Engr.
1997, Jan. 1   Perf. 13x12½
225 A139 3fr multicolored   1.60 .90

Jean Turquet (1867-1945) — A140

1997, Jan. 1   Engr.   Perf. 13
226 A140 4fr black & brown   1.00 1.10

A141

1997, Jan. 1
227 A141 5.20fr multicolored   2.40 1.50
Church of Our Lady of Birds, Crozet Island.

Army Health Service — A142

1997, Jan. 1
228 A142 8fr multicolored   3.75 2.50

Poa Kerguelensis — A143

1997, Jan. 1
229 A143 29.20fr multi   12.50 8.50

French Polar Expeditions, 50th Anniv. — A144

Designs: No. 230, Greenland Expedition. No. 231, Port Martin, 1950-51, Marret Base, 1952, Adélie Land. No. 232, Dumont D'Urville, 1956, Charcot Station, Magnetic Pole, 1957.

Photo. & Engr.
1997, Feb. 28   Perf. 13x12½
230 1fr multicolored   1.10 .70
231 1fr multicolored   1.10 .70
232 1fr multicolored   1.10 .70
a. A144 Strip of 3, #230-232   8.00 6.00

Yves-Joseph de Kerguelen Trémarec (1734-97) — A145

3fr, Portrait. 24fr, Cook's landing at Kerguelen Island, Dec. 1776.

1997, Mar. 3   Engr.   Perf. 13
233 A145 3fr multicolored   1.25 .90
234 A145 24fr multicolored   9.00 7.00
a. Pair, #233-234 + label   14.00 11.00
No. 234 is 37x37mm.

Mineral Type of 1993
1990, Jan. 2   Engr.   Perf. 13
235 A103 1fr Rock crystal   1.25 .40

Fisheries Management — A146

Designs: No. 236, Fishing boats. No. 237, Examining fish, performing research.

1998, Jan. 2
236 A146 2.60fr multicolored   1.40 .70
237 A146 2.60fr multicolored   1.40 .70
a. Pair, #236-237 + label   3.50 3.50

Gray-headed Albatross — A147

1998, Jan. 2
238 A147 2.70fr multicolored   1.75 .75

FRENCH SOUTHERN & ANTARCTIC TERRITORY

Ecology of St. Paul Island A148

1998, Jan. 2
239 A148 3fr bl, brn & grn   2.25 1.00

Etienne Peau, Antarctic Explorer — A149

1998, Jan. 2   Perf. 13x13½
240 A149 3fr lilac, blue & black   1.75 .85

Georges Laclavere (1906-94), Geographer — A150

1998, Jan. 2
241 A150 4fr lt org, blk & red brn   1.75 1.00

Mole Shark A151

1998, Jan. 2   Perf. 13
242 A151 27fr multicolored   11.00 6.75

"Le Cancalais" A152

1998, Jan. 2
243 A152 29.20fr multicolored   11.50 7.00

Mineral Type of 1993
1999, Jan. 1   Engr.   Perf. 13
244 A103 1fr Epidote, vert.   1.25 .40

Chinstrap Penguin A153

1999, Jan. 1
245 A153 2.70fr brn, blk & bl   1.60 .85

Pierre Sicaud (1911-98), Antarctic Explorer, Commander of Outpost at Kerguelen Islands — A154

1999, Jan. 1
246 A154 3fr black & green   1.25 .80

Penguins of Crozet Islands A155

1999, Jan. 1
247 A155 3fr multicolored   3.00 .85

Jacques-André Martin (1911-49) — A156

1999, Jan. 1
248 A156 4fr multicolored   1.75 1.00

Ray A157

1999, Jan. 1   Perf. 12½
249 A157 5.20fr mag, bl & brn   2.25 2.25
Value is for stamp with surrounding rectangular selvage.

F.S. Floreal A158

1999, Jan. 1   Photo.   Perf. 13
250 A158 5.20fr multicolored   2.25 1.75
No. 250 was printed se-tenant with label. Value is for stamp with label attached.

"Pop Cat" Program, Kerguelen Islands A159

1999, Jan. 1   Engr.
251 A159 8fr multicolored   4.75 3.00

Study of Albatrosses on Artificial Nests — A160

1999, Jan. 1
252 A160 16fr olive, grn & blk   6.50 4.25

Amsterdam Base, Kerguelen Base, 50th Anniv. A161

Designs: 3fr, Amsterdam Base. 24fr, Kerguelen Base.

1999, Jan. 1
253 A161 3fr multi   4.50 1.00
254 A161 24fr multi   8.50 5.00
 a. Pair, #253-254 + label   15.00 12.00

Festuca Contracta — A162

1999, Jan. 1
255 A162 24fr dk grn, ol & bl grn   9.00 6.00

Geoleta Program A163

1999, Jan. 1   Perf. 13x12½
256 A163 29.20fr blk, bl & red brn   11.00 7.00

Voyage of Marion Dufresne II A164

a, Docked, Reunion. b, Passengers in dining salon. c, Penguins, Crozet Island. d, Postal manager of Alfred Faure, Crozet Island, vert. e, Port of France, Kerguelen Island. f, Port Couvreux, Kerguelen Island. g, Offloading stores, Port of France, Kerguelen Island. h, Port Jeanne d'arc, Kerguelen Island. i, St. Paul Island. j, Ruins of lobster cannery, St. Paul Island. k, Martin de Vivies Base, Amsterdam Island. l, Offloading cargo, Amsterdam Island.

1999, May 1   Litho.   Perf. 13
257 A164 Souv. bklt., #a.-l.   90.00
Nos. 257a-257l are all non-denominated. Stamps are valid for 20 gram international letter rate. Each stamp appears on a separate booklet pane showing an enlarged design of the stamp. Booklet sold for 100fr.
See Nos. 294, 329, 359, 390, 420, 482, 573C, 706.

Souvenir Sheet

PhilexFrance '99, World Philatelic Exhibition — A165

Antarctic postmarks on stamps: a, Malagasy Republic #280. b, Malagasy Republic #282. c, Malagasy Republic #C42. d, #21.

1999, July 2   Litho. & Engr.   Perf. 13
258 A165 5.20fr Sheet of 4, #a.-d.   10.00 7.50
Nos. 258b-258c are each 40x52mm.

Mineral Type of 1993
2000, Jan.   Engr.   Perf. 12¾x13
259 A103 1fr Mica, vert.   1.25 .40

Puffin A166

2000, Jan.   Perf. 13x12¾
260 A166 2.70fr multi   2.00 .80

André Beaugé (1913-97) — A167

2000, Jan.   Perf. 12¾x13
261 A167 3fr multi   1.40 .60

Abby Jane Morrell — A168

2000, Jan.   Perf. 13¼x13
262 A168 4fr multi   1.75 .95

Oceanographic Survey — A169

2000, Jan.   Perf. 13x12½
263 A169 4.40fr multi   2.10 1.25

Sled Dog Hobbs — A170

2000, Jan.   Perf. 12¾x13
264 A170 5.20fr multi   2.25 1.25

Sleep Study A171

2000, Jan.   Photo.   Perf. 13x12½
265 A171 8fr multi + label   3.50 2.25

Ship "La Perouse" A172

2000, Jan.   Engr.   Perf. 13x12½
266 A172 16fr multi   7.00 4.25

Lantern Fish A173

2000, Jan.
267 A173 24fr multi   10.50 6.00

Larose Bay — A174

2000, Jan.
268 A174 27fr multi   11.00 7.00

Explorers — A175

No. 269, Yves Joseph de Kerguelen-Trémarec (1734-97). No. 270, Jules Sébastien César Dumont D'Urville (1790-1842). No. 271, Raymond Rallier du Baty (1881-1978). No. 272, Edgar Aubert de La Rüe (1901-91). #273, Paul-Emile Victor (1907-95).

2000, Jan.   Perf. 13
Booklet Stamps
269 A175 3fr multi   1.60 .75
270 A175 3fr multi   1.60 .75
271 A175 3fr multi   1.60 .75
272 A175 3fr multi   1.60 .75

FRENCH SOUTHERN & ANTARCTIC TERRITORY

273	A175	3fr multi	1.60	.75
a.		Bklt. pane, #269-273 + 2 labels	9.00	
		Complete booklet, #273a	10.00	

Souvenir Sheet

The Third Millennium — A176

No. 274: a, Penguins, Crozet Islands. b, Seals, Kerguelen Islands. c, Crustacean, Saint-Paul and Amsterdam Islands. d, Hovering vehicle, Adelie Land.

2000, Jan. Photo. Perf. 13
274 A176 3fr Sheet of 4, #a.-d. 8.50 5.50

Bird Demographic Studies — A177

Designs: 5.20fr, Bird banding. 8fr, Albatross, graph. 16fr, Emperor penguins, graph.

2000, Jan. Perf. 13x13¼
275 A177 5.20fr multi 2.00 1.00

Size: 50x28mm
276 A177 8fr multi 3.00 1.50
277 A177 16fr multi 6.50 4.00
a. Horiz. strip, #275-277 15.00 15.00

Relocation of Headquarters to Reunion — A178

2000, Aug. 6 Litho. Perf. 13
278 A178 27fr multi 12.00 9.00

Mineral Type of 1993

2001, Jan. 1 Engr. Perf. 13x12¾
279 A103 1fr Magnetite 1.25 .40

Diving Petrel A179

2001, Jan. 1 Perf. 13x13¼
280 A179 2.70fr multi 1.50 .60

High Mountain Military Group — A180

2001, Jan. 1 Perf. 13¼x13
281 A180 3fr multi 1.40 .65

Kerguelen Arch A181

2001, Jan. 1 Perf. 13
282 A181 3fr blue gray 2.00 .70

Xavier-Charles Richert (1913-92) — A182

2001, Jan. 1
283 A182 3fr multi 1.40 .65

Jean Coulomb — A183

2001, Jan. 1
284 A183 4fr multi 1.75 .85

Memorial to 1874 Astronomical Observation, St. Paul Island — A184

2001, Jan. 1
285 A184 8fr brn & blk 3.50 1.75

Frigate La Fayette A185

2001, Jan. 1 Perf. 13x13¼
286 A185 16fr multi 7.00 3.50

Squid A186

2001, Jan. 1
287 A186 24fr multi 10.50 5.00

Amateur Radio Link Between Space Station Mir and Crozet Island — A187

2001, Jan. 1 Litho. Perf. 13
288 A187 27fr multi 12.00 5.50

Bryum Laevigatum — A188

2001, Jan. 1 Engr. Perf. 13x12½
289 A188 29.20fr multi 13.00 6.00

Souvenir Sheet

Ships A189

No. 290: a, Carmen. b, Austral. c, Ramuntcho. d, Samper 1.

2001, Jan. 1 Perf. 13x13½
290 A189 5.20fr Sheet of 4, #a-d 9.00 4.50

Souvenir Sheet

Wildlife A190

No. 291: a, Albatrosses. b, Emperor penguins, horiz. c, Sea lions, horiz. d, Whales.

2001, Jan. 1 Litho. Perf. 13
291 A190 3fr Sheet of 4, #a-d 10.50 5.00

Antarctic Treaty, 40th Anniv. — A191

2001, June 23 Engr. Perf. 13x12¾
292 A191 5.20fr dark & sky blue 3.25 1.00

Commission for the Conservation of Antarctic Marine Living Resources, 20th Anniv. A192

2001, Oct. 22 Litho. Perf. 13
293 A192 5.20fr multi 5.00 2.00

Voyage Booklet Type of 1999

Adélie Land: a, Boat in pack ice. b, Dumont d'Urville Base. c, Adélie penguin rookery. d, L'Astrolabe Glacier. e, Pointe Géologie Archipelago. f, Release of meteorological balloon. g, Equipment convoy. h, Helicopter transport of fresh supplies. i, Arrival of emperor penguins. j, Telecommunications center. k, Looking towards the Antarctic. l, Cape Prud'homme. m, Ship L'Astrolabe anchored. n, Dispatch of mail.

2001, Oct. 29 Perf. 13
294 A164 Souvenir booklet, 2 each #a-n 95.00

Nos. 294a-294n are all non-denominated. Stamps are valid for 20 gram international letter rate. Each stamp appears on a separate booklet pane showing an enlarged design of the stamp and on one pane with all of the stamps and four labels found at the center of the booklet. the booklet sold for 196.78fr.

100 Cents = 1 Euro (€)
Arms Type of 1992-95 with Euro Denominations

2002, Jan. 2 Engr. Perf. 13
295	A102	1c black	.25	.25
296	A102	2c greenish blue	.25	.25
297	A102	5c red	.30	.25
298	A102	10c green	.40	.25
299	A102	20c orange	.70	.25
		Nos. 295-299 (5)	1.90	1.25

Mineral Type of 1993 with Euro Denomination

2002, Jan. 2 Engr. Perf. 12¾x13
300 A103 15c Nepheline, vert. 1.00 .40

Albatross — A193

2002, Jan. 2 Perf. 13¼x13
301 A193 41c multi 3.00 .80

Ship "Marion Dufresne" A194

2002, Jan. 2 Perf. 13x13¼
302 A194 46c multi 1.40 .60

1963-83 Telegraph Station, Crozet Island — A195

2002, Jan. 2 Litho. Perf. 13
303 A195 46c multi 1.50 .60

Jacques Dubois (1920-2000) A196

2002, Jan. 2 Engr.
304 A196 61c multi 2.25 .90

Engraved Rock, Saint Paul Island A197

2002, Jan. 2 Perf. 13x13¼
305 A197 79c multi 2.40 1.25

Kerguelen Cabbage — A198

2002, Jan. 2 Perf. 12¼
306 A198 €1.22 multi 3.50 1.75

FRENCH SOUTHERN & ANTARCTIC TERRITORY

Passage of the Ship "Gauss," Cent. A199

2002, Jan. 2		Perf. 13x12¼
307	A199 €2.44 multi	7.25 3.50

Crab A200

2002, Jan. 2		Perf. 13x13¼
308	A200 €3.66 multi	11.00 5.25

Pack Ice Diatoms A201

2002, Jan. 2	Litho.	Perf. 13
309	A201 €4.12 multi	12.50 6.00

French Geographic Society Building, Paris — A202

2002, Jan. 2	Engr.	Perf. 13¼x13
310	A202 €4.45 multi + label	13.50 8.00

Cartoker Program A203

No. 311: a, 46c, Diagram of plate tectonics. b, €3.66, Geological map of Kerguelen Island.

2002, Jan. 2		Perf. 13x12¼
311	A203 Horiz. pair, #a-b, + central label	12.50 12.50

Souvenir Sheet

Olympic Games for Antarctic Animals A204

No. 312: a, Albatrosses flying marathon. b, Langoustines diving, vert. c, Penguins riding bobsled course, vert. d, Killer whales performing synchronized swimming, vert.

2002, Jan. 2	Litho.	Perf. 13
312	A204 46c Sheet of 4, #a-d	6.50 5.50

Souvenir Sheet

Animals and Their Young A205

No. 313: a, Penguins. b, Sea lions. c, Albatrosses. d, Elephant seals.

2002, Jan. 2		
313	A205 79c Sheet of 4, #a-d	10.50 9.50

Introduction of the Euro — A206

2002, Feb. 17		
314	A206 46c blue & black	3.50 .60

Mineral Type of 1993

2003, Jan.	Engr.	Perf. 13¼
315	A103 15c Apatite, vert.	1.25 .40

Lobster Processing Plant, Saint-Paul A207

2003, Jan.		Perf. 13x13¼
316	A207 41c multi	1.25 .65

Luc Marie Bayle (1914-2000), Painter — A208

2003, Jan.	Litho.	Perf. 13
317	A208 46c multi	1.50 .70

Emperor Penguins A209

2003, Jan.		
318	A209 46c multi	2.75 .80

Otice Hydroacoustic Station — A210

2003, Jan.	Engr.	Perf. 13¼
319	A210 61c multi	1.90 1.00

Restoration of Port Jeanne d'Arc A211

2003, Jan.		Perf. 13x12¼
320	A211 79c multi	2.40 1.25

Phylica A212

2003, Jan.		Perf. 13x13¼
321	A212 €1.22 multi	4.50 2.25

Ship "Bougainville" — A213

2003, Jan.		Perf. 13¼x13
322	A213 €2.44 multi	7.25 4.25

Chub A214

2003, Jan.	Engr.	Perf. 13x13¼
323	A214 €3.66 multi	11.00 6.50

Ile aux Pingouins A215

2003, Jan.		Perf. 13x12¼
324	A215 €3.66 black	11.00 6.50

Super Darn Antenna Array A216

2003, Jan.		Perf. 13
325	A216 €4.12 multi	12.50 7.00

Souvenir Sheet

Paintings Revised to Reflect a Less Southerly Antarctica — A217

No. 326: a, Triumph of Venus with fish and lobsters. b, King Louis XV and wife with penguins, vert. c, Jules Dumont d'Urville and wife in a grassy Adélie Land. d, Chevalier Yves de Kerguelin under umbrella, seal in pool, vert.

2003, Jan.		Litho.
326	A217 46c Sheet of 4, #a-d	6.50 6.50

Protective Clothing — A218

Cold-weather outerwear from: a, 1898. b, 1912. c, 2002. d, 1980, e, 1996.

2003, Jan.	Photo.	Perf. 13¼x12
327	Booklet pane of 5	12.00 —
a.-e.	A218 79c Any single	2.40 1.25
	Booklet, #327	12.00

Voyage of the Ship "Français," Cent. — A219

2003, Aug. 31	Engr.	Perf. 13x13¼
328	Horiz. strip of 3	15.00 13.50
a.	A219 79c Capt. J.-B. Charcot	2.50 1.25
b.	A219 €1.22 Ship in ice, horiz.	4.00 2.00
c.	A219 €2.44 Ship in harbor, horiz.	7.50 4.25

Stamp size: Nos. 328b-328c, 49x29mm.

Voyage Booklet Type of 1999

Recipes: a, Truite aus deux citrons (trout and waterfall). b, Veau d'Amsterdam à la savoyarde (cattle). c, Lapin "Volage" à la cannelle (rabbits, penguins). d, Rôti de légine de l'ile de l'est (fish). e, Civet de renne "Volcan du diable," (reindeer). f, Iles antarctiques flottantes. g, Langouste à la mode de Saint-Paul (lobster). h, Gigot de mouflon aux 5 épices et aux pommes (sheep). i, Cabot tropical (fish, ship). j, Tagine d'agneau aux épices de la Réunion (sheep). k, Moules au pastis (mussels). l, Glace à la menthe sauvage d'Amsterdam (mint plant).

2003, Nov. 6	Litho.	Perf. 13
329	A164 Souvenir booklet, #a-l	60.00

Nos. 329a-329l are all non-denominated. Stamps are valid for 20 gram international letter rate. Each stamp appears on a separate booklet pane showing an enlarged design of the stamp. The booklet sold for €17.

Mineral Type of 1993

2004, Jan. 1	Engr.	Perf. 13¼
330	A103 15c Chalcedony, vert.	1.25 .40

A220

2004, Jan. 1	Engr.	Perf. 13x13¼
331	A220 45c multi	1.40 .85

Mario Marret, director of film "Terre Adélie."

Col. Robert Genty (1910-2001) — A221

2004, Jan. 1		
332	A221 50c multi	1.75 .95

FRENCH SOUTHERN & ANTARCTIC TERRITORY

Albert Faure Base, Crozet Island, 40th Anniv. — A222

2004, Jan. 1		Litho. & Engr.
333 A222 50c multi		1.50 .95

Péron's Dolphins — A223

2004, Jan. 1	Litho.	Perf. 13
334 A223 75c multi		3.00 1.50

Twin Otter Flights — A224

2004, Jan. 1	Photo.	Perf. 12¾
335 A224 90c multi		2.75 1.75

Values are for stamps with surrounding selvage.

Iceberg — A225

2004, Jan. 1	Engr.	Perf. 13x13¼
336 A225 €1.30 multi		4.00 2.40

Grave of Sailors from the Volage — A226

2004, Jan. 1		Perf. 13¼x13
337 A226 €2.50 multi		7.50 5.00

Krill — A227

2004, Jan. 1		Perf. 13x13¼
338 A227 €4 multi		12.00 8.00

Ship "Dives" — A228

2004, Jan. 1		
339 A228 €4.50 multi		13.50 9.25

Souvenir Sheet

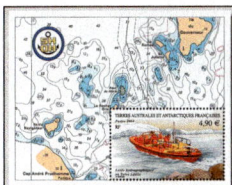
Hydrological Surveys, Adélie Land — A229

2004, Jan. 1	Litho.	Perf. 13
340 A229 €4.90 multi		15.00 10.50

Souvenir Sheet

Imaginary "TAAFland" Theme Park — A230

No. 341: a, Whale statue, pyramidal entrance structure. b, Showgirls, seals, vert. c, Boy and girl with ice cream cones, vert. d, Woman in swimsuit, penguins.

2004, Jan. 1
341 A230 50c Sheet of 4, #a-d   8.00 8.00

Souvenir Sheet

Post Offices — A231

No. 342: a, Amsterdam Island. b, Crozet Island. c, Kerguelen Island. d, Adélie Land.

2004, Jan. 1
342 A231 90c Sheet of 4, #a-d   12.00 12.00

Penguin and Liberty Cap — A232

2004, June 26	Engr.	Perf. 13¼x13
343 A232 €4.50 multi		15.00 7.00

Mineral Type of 1993

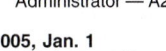

2005, Jan. 1	Engr.	Perf. 13¼
344 A103 15c Agate		.80 .50

Albert Bauer (1916-2003), Glaciologist — A233

2005, Jan. 1		Perf. 13x13¼
345 A233 45c multi		2.00 1.75

Roger Barberot (1915-2002), Administrator — A234

2005, Jan. 1		
346 A234 50c multi		2.00 2.00

Ship "Cap Horn" — A235

2005, Jan. 1		
347 A235 50c multi		2.00 2.00

Seal Pot — A236

2005, Jan. 1	Litho.	Perf. 13
348 A236 50c multi		2.25 2.25

Macgillivray's Prion — A237

2005, Jan. 1	Engr.	Perf. 13x13¼
349 A237 75c multi		2.75 2.75

Studer Valley — A238

2005, Jan. 1		Perf. 13x12½
350 A238 90c multi		3.00 3.00

Peigne des Néréides — A239

2005, Jan. 1		Perf. 12¼
351 A239 €2.50 multi		8.00 7.50

Harpovoluta Charcoti — A240

2005, Jan. 1		Perf. 13x12½
352 A240 €4 multi		14.00 14.00

Murray's Ray — A241

2005, Jan. 1	Litho.	Perf. 13
353 A241 €4.50 multi		14.00 14.00

Elephant Seal and Oceanographic Chart — A242

2005, Jan. 1		Engr.
354 A242 €4.90 multi		16.00 16.00

Concordia Station — A243

2005, Jan. 3	Litho.	Perf. 13
355 A243 50c multi		1.75 1.75

Return of the Ship "Français," Cent. — A244

2005, Mar. 4	Engr.	Perf. 13x13¼
356 A244 €4.50 multi + label		15.00 15.00

Disappearance of Paul-Emile Victor, 10th Anniv. — A245

2005, Mar. 7	Litho.	Perf. 13
357 A245 50c multi		2.50 2.50

50th Anniversary Coat of Arms — A246

2005, Aug. 6		
358 A246 (90c) multi		0.00 0.00
a. Booklet pane of 1		4.00

No. 358a is found in No. 359.

Voyage Booklet Type of 1999

History: a, Discovery of Amsterdam Island, 1522. b, Discovery of Crozet Island, 1772. c, Discovery of Kerguelen Island, 1772, vert. d, Discovery of Adélie Land, 1840. e, Astronomers viewing 1874 transit of Venus on St. Paul Island. f, Wreck of the Strathmore, 1875. g, Port Jeanne d'Arc, 1908. h, Port-Couvreux, 1925. i, Building of Port-Martin, 1950. j, Antarctic Treaty, 1959. k, Building of fourth base, 1963-64.

2005, Aug. 6	Litho.	Perf. 13
359 A164 Souvenir booklet, #a-k, 358a		70.00

Nos. 359a-359k are all non-denominated. Stamps are valid for 90c, the 20 gram international letter rate. Each stamp appears on a separate booklet pane showing an enlarged design of the stamp. The booklet sold for €18.

FRENCH SOUTHERN & ANTARCTIC TERRITORY

Penguins and No. 1 — A247

2005, Nov. 2
360 A247 90c multi 3.25 3.25
French Southern & Antarctic Territories, 50th anniv.

Souvenir Sheet

Maps A248

Maps of: a, Crozet Archipelago. b, Amsterdam and St. Paul Islands. c, Kerguelen Island. d, Adélie Land.

2005, Nov. 10 Litho. & Engr. Perf. 13x13¼
361 A248 50c Sheet of 4, #a-d 6.50 6.50
French Southern & Antarctic Territories, 50th anniv.

Rutile — A249

2006, Jan. 1 Engr. Perf. 13x12½
362 A249 15c multi .80 .80

Charles Vélain (1845-1925), Geologist — A250

2006, Jan. 1 Perf. 13x13¼
363 A250 48c pur & red 1.60 1.60

Albert Seyrolle (1887-1919), Mariner — A251

2006, Jan. 1
364 A251 53c multi 1.60 1.60

Amsterdam Island Garden A252

2006, Jan. 1 Litho. Perf. 13
365 A252 53c multi 1.60 1.60

Ship "Osiris" A253

2006, Jan. 1 Photo. Perf. 13x13¼
366 A253 90c multi 3.00 3.00

Dumont d'Urville Base, 50th Anniv. A254

2006, Jan. 1 Engr. Perf. 13x12½
367 A254 90c multi 2.75 2.75

Virgin of the Seal Hunters — A255

2006, Jan. 1 Perf. 12½x13
368 A255 €2.50 multi 7.50 7.50

Lagenorhynchus Cruciger — A256

2006, Jan. 1 Perf. 13x13¼
369 A256 €4 multi 12.00 12.00

Keguelen Hake A257

2006, Jan. 1
370 A257 €4.53 multi 13.50 13.50

Amsterdam Island Carbon Dioxide Measurements, 25th Anniv. — A258

2006, Jan. 1
371 A258 €4.90 multi 15.00 15.00

Miniature Sheet

Penguins A259

No. 372 — Penguin (background color): a, Emperor penguin (lilac, 22x36mm). b, King penguin (pale yellow green, 22x36mm). c, Gentoo penguin (green, 22x27mm). d, Adélie penguin (pink, 22x27mm). e, Macaroni penguin (orange, 22x27mm). f, Rockhopper penguin (blue, 22x27mm).

2006, Jan. 1 Litho. & Engr. Perf. 13
372 A259 53c Sheet of 6, #a-f 12.00 12.00

Souvenir Sheet

Albatross A260

2006, June 1 Litho. & Engr. Perf. 13
373 A260 €4.53 multi 14.50 14.50

Souvenir Sheet

Albatross A261

2006, Nov. 8 Litho. & Engr. Perf. 13
374 A261 90c multi 3.50 3.50

Corundum — A262

2007, Jan. 1 Engr. Perf. 13¼
375 A262 15c multi 1.25 1.25

A263

2007, Jan. 1 Perf. 13x13¼
376 A263 49c multi 1.50 1.50
Louis-Francois Aleno de Saint Aloüarn (1738-72), explorer who claimed Australia for France.

A264

2007, Jan. 1
377 A264 54c multi 1.60 1.60
Marthe Emmanuel (1901-97), assistant to explorer Jean Charcot.

Cattle, Amsterdam Island A265

2007, Jan. 1 Perf. 13x12½
378 A265 54c multi 1.50 1.50

Ship Tonkinois A266

2007, Jan. 1 Perf. 13x13¼
379 A266 90c multi 2.50 2.50

Ile de la Baleine A267

2007, Jan. 1 Perf. 13x12½
380 A267 90c multi 2.50 2.50

Archaeology on Saint Paul Island — A268

2007, Jan. 1 Perf. 12½x13
381 A268 €2.50 multi 7.00 7.00

Lampris Immaculatus — A269

2007, Jan. 1 Perf. 13x12½
382 A269 €4 multi 11.00 11.00

Astonomy at Concordia A270

2007, Jan. 1 Litho. & Engr. Perf. 13
383 A270 €4.90 multi 14.00 14.00

French Polar Expeditions, 60th Anniv. A271

No. 384: a, Expedition headquarters, Paris, men shaking hands over globe. b, Expedition headquarters.

2007, Jan. 1 Engr. Perf. 13x13¼
384 Horiz. pair + central label 13.50 13.50
 a. A271 54c multi 1.75 1.75
 b. A271 €4 multi 11.00 11.00

Miniature Sheet

Albatrosses — A272

No. 385: a, Amsterdam albatross. b, Great albatross (Grand albatros). c, Black-browed albatross (Albatros à sourcils noir). d, Yellow-

FRENCH SOUTHERN & ANTARCTIC TERRITORY 857

beaked albatross (Albatros à bec jaune). e, Sooty albatross (Albatros fuligineux).

2007, Jan. 1   **Litho. & Engr.**   *Perf. 13*
385 A272 54c Sheet of 5, #a-e   8.00   8.00

Intl. Polar Year A273

No. 386: a, Penguins. b, Map of Antarctica, French Southern & Antarctic Territories #9.

2007, Mar. 1   **Litho.**   *Perf. 13*
386   Horiz. pair + central label   15.00   15.00
   a. A273 90c multi   2.75   2.75
   b. A273 €4 multi   12.00   12.00

Audit Office, Bicent. — A274

2007, Mar. 19   **Engr.**   *Perf. 13¼*
387 A274 90c multi   4.50   4.50

Miniature Sheet

Indian Ocean Islands A275

No. 388: a, Ile Tromelin. b, Iles Glorieuses. c, Ile Juan de Nova. d, Ile Bassas da India. e, Ile Europa.

2007, May 10   **Photo.**   *Perf. 13x13¼*
388 A275 54c Sheet of 5, #a-e   9.00   9.00

Path of Sun on June 21 Over Dumont d'Urville Base A276

2007, June 21
389 A276 90c multi   3.00   3.00

Voyage Booklet Type of 1999

No. 390 — Photographs of land features: a, Apostle Island, Crozet Archipelago. b, Chamonix Lake, Kerguelen Island. c, Phylicia forest, Amsterdam Island. d, Gulf of Morbihan, Kerguelen Islands. e, Mount Cook, Chamonix Lake and glacier, Kerguelen Islands. f, Tourbières Plateau, Amsterdam Island. g, Nuageuses Islands, Kerguelen Islands. h, Caldera, Amsterdam Island. i, Mount Cook, Kerguelen Island. j, Central Plateau, Kerguelen Island. k, Isle of Penguins, Crozet Archipelago. l, Antonelli Crater, Amsterdam Island. m, Lake on Possession Island, Crozet Archipelago. n, Rocks off Apostle Island, Crozet Archipelago. o, Geographic Society Peninsula, Kerguelen Island. p, Ronarch Peninsula, Kerguelen Island.

2007, Nov. 8   **Litho.**   *Perf. 13*
390 A164 (90c) Souvenir booklet, #a-p   70.00

No. 390 sold for €20, and contains four panes, consisting of a block of four stamps of Nos. 390a-390d, 390e-390h, 390i-390l, and 390m-390p.

French Southern and Antarctic Territories Flag — A277

2008, Jan. 1   **Litho.**   *Perf. 13*
Background Color
391 A277 1c black   .25   .25
392 A277 2c blue   .35   .35
393 A277 5c red   .40   .40
394 A277 10c green   .40   .40
395 A277 20c brn orange   .80   .80
   Nos. 391-395 (5)   2.20   2.20

Spinel — A278

2008, Jan. 1   **Engr.**   *Perf. 13¼*
396 A278 15c multi   .80   .45

Samivel (1907-92), Writer — A279

2008, Jan. 1   *Perf. 13x13¼*
397 A279 54c grn & brown   1.60   1.60

St. Paul Island — A280

2008, Jan. 1
398 A280 54c blue & dk blue   1.60   1.60

Construction of Port Jeanne d'Arc, Cent. — A281

2008, Jan. 1   *Perf. 13x12¾*
399 A201 90c multi   2.75   2.75

Rockhopper Penguins A282

2008, Jan. 1   *Perf. 13x12½*
400 A282 90c multi   2.75   2.75

Shipwreck of L'Esperance A283

2008, Jan. 1   **Litho.**   *Perf. 13x12¾*
401 A283 90c multi   2.75   2.75

Macrourus Carinatus A284

2008, Jan. 1   **Engr.**   *Perf. 13x12½*
402 A284 €4 multi   12.00   12.00

Galium Antarcticum — A285

2008, Jan. 1   *Perf. 12½x13*
403 A285 €4.54 multi   13.50   13.50

Adélie Land Coastal Ichthyology Program — A286

2008, Jan. 1   **Litho.**   *Perf. 13*
404 A286 €1.00 multi   14.50   14.50

Souvenir Sheet

Kerguelen Fish Biomass Evaluation Project (POKER) — A287

2008, Jan. 1   **Litho. & Engr.**
405 A287 €2.50 multi   7.50   7.50

Souvenir Sheet

Elephant Seals A288

No. 406: a, Head of adult female. b, Seals initiating combat. c, Juvenile seal. d, Head of adult male.

2008, Jan. 1
406 A288 54c Sheet of 4, #a-d   6.50   6.50

Gérard Mégie (1946-2004), Ozone Researcher — A289

2008, Feb. 15   **Engr.**   *Perf. 13x13¼*
407 A289 54c multi   1.75   1.75

Miniature Sheet

Birds A290

No. 408: a, Sooty tern (Sterne fulgineuse). b, Red-footed booby (Fou a pieds rouges), vert. c, Masked booby (Fou masque), vert. d, Great frigatebird (Fregate du Pacifique), vert. e, Tropicbird (Paille en queue).

Perf. 13¼x13 (#408a, 408e), 13x13¼
2008, June 1   **Litho. & Engr.**
408 A290 54c Sheet of 5, #a-e   8.50   8.50

Earth and Birds A291

2008, June 14   **Photo.**   *Perf. 13*
409 A291 €4.54 multi   14.50   14.50

Ship Marion Dufresne A292

2008, Nov. 6   **Litho.**   *Perf. 13*
410 A292 (55c) multi   1.75   1.75

Compare with type A194.

Pyrite — A293

2009, Jan. 1   **Engr.**   *Perf. 13¼*
411 A293 15c multi   .60   .60

A294

2009, Jan. 1   *Perf. 13x13¼*
412 A294 55c multi   1.60   1.60

Henri Paschal de Rochegude (1741-1834), naval officer.

A295

2009, Jan. 1   *Perf. 13*
413 A295 55c multi   1.60   1.60

Charles Gaston Rouillon (1915-2007), director of French polar scientific expeditions.

Residence de France Seal of Kerguelen Islands, Cent. A296

2009, Jan. 1   **Litho.**
414 A296 90c multi   2.50   2.50

Shark With Dorsal Spines A297

2009, Jan. 1   **Engr.**   *Perf. 13x12½*
415 A297 €2.50 multi   7.00   7.00

FRENCH SOUTHERN & ANTARCTIC TERRITORY

Ship Jeanne d'Arc A298

2009, Jan. 1
416 A298 €4 multi   11.00 11.00

MACARBI Program Scallop Research — A299

2009, Jan. 1
417 A299 €4.55 multi   13.00 13.00

Seaweed A300

No. 418: a, Himantothallus grandifolius and iceberg. b, Laminaria pallida and seals.

2009, Jan. 1 Perf. 13x13¼
418   Horiz. pair + central label   13.50 13.50
  a. A300 90c multi   2.50   2.50
  b. A300 €4 multi   11.00 11.00

Miniature Sheet

Petrels A301

No. 419: a, Soft-plumaged petrel (Petrel soyeux). b, Wilson's petrel (Petrel de Wilson). c, Gray petrel (Petrel gris). d, Diving petrel (Petrel plongeur). e, Snow petrel (Petrel des neiges).

Litho. & Engr.
2009, Jan. 1 Perf. 13¼x13
419 A301 55c Sheet of 5, #a-e   7.75 7.75

Voyage Booklet Type of 1999

No. 420 — Photographs: a, Frigatebirds, Europa Island. b, Beach on north coast of Europa Island. c, Mangroves, Europa Island. d, Flagpole, palm trees, Europa Island. e, Turtle on beach, Juan de Nova Island. f, Sandbanks off Juan de Nova Island. g, Tree, Juan de Nova Island. h, Grounded ship, Juan de Nova Island. i, Brown noddies, Glorioso Islands. j, Flower, Glorioso Islands. k, Pool of water, Glorioso Islands. l, Tree on islet, Glorioso Islands. m, Birds, Tromelin Island. n, Meteorological station, Tromelin Island. o, Coral fossil, Tromelin Island. p, Anchor, Tromelin Island.

2009, Nov. 5 Litho. Perf. 13
420 A164 (90c) Souvenir booklet, #a-p   65.00

No. 420 sold for €21.50, and contains four panes, consisting of a block of four stamps of Nos. 420a-420d, 420e-420h, 420i-4290l, and 420m-420p.

Antarctic Treaty, 50th Anniv. A302

2009, Dec. 1 Engr. Perf. 13x13¼
421 A302 56c multi   1.75   1.75

Tourmaline — A303

2010, Jan. 2 Engr. Perf. 13¼
422 A303 28c multi   .80   .80

Dr. Jean Rivolier (1923-2007), Medical Researcher A304

2010, Jan. 2 Litho. Perf. 13
423 A304 56c multi   1.60   1.60

Birds on Ile du Lys — A305

2010, Jan. 2 Engr. Perf. 13x13¼
424 A305 56c multi   1.60   1.60

Patureau House, Juan de Nova Island A306

2010, Jan. 2
425 A306 56c multi   1.60   1.60

Program Crac-ice A307

2010, Jan. 2
426 A307 90c multi   2.50   2.50

Supply Ship Ile St. Paul A308

2010, Jan. 2
427 A308 €1.35 multi   3.75   3.75

Crozet Orca A309

2010, Jan. 2
428 A309 €2.80 multi   7.75   7.75

Kerguelen Terns A310

2010, Jan. 2
429 A310 €4.30 multi   12.00 12.00

Miniature Sheet
Sea Lions of Amsterdam Island — A311

No. 430: a, Sea lion and ship. b, Two sea lions on rocks, denomination at UR in black, horiz. c, Sea lion, denomination at UL in black, horiz. d, Two sea lions near water, denomination in white at UR, horiz. e, Two sea lions, denomination at LL in black, horiz.

Litho. & Engr.
2010, Jan. 2 Perf. 13
430 A311 56c Sheet of 5, #a-e   7.75 7.75

Miniature Sheet

Polar Transportation — A312

No. 431: a, Team of dogs pulling sled. b, Weasel M29C. c, Sno-cat 743. d, HB40-Castor. e, Challenger 65. f, PB 330.

2010, Jan. 2
431 A312 90c Sheet of 6, #a-f 15.00 15.00

Gabriel Pavilion, Paris A313

2010, May 28 Litho. Perf. 13
432 A313 56c multi   1.40   1.40
Second Elysée Philatelic Club Show, Paris.

Miniature Sheet

Albatross Protection — A314

No. 433: a, Albatross and chick on nest. b, Albatross facing left. c, Albatross facing right. d, Two juvenile albatrosses.

Litho. & Engr.
2010, June 12 Perf. 13
433 A314 56c Sheet of 4, #a-d   5.75 5.75

French Southern & Antarctic Territories Booth at Espace Champerret Stamp Show A315

2010, Nov. 5 Litho. Perf. 13
434 A315 56c multi   3.00   3.00

Self-Adhesive
Serpentine Die Cut 11
435 A315 56c multi   3.00   3.00

Astronomical Observatory, Concordia Base, Antarctica and Southern Cross — A316

Litho. & Engr.
2011, Jan. 2 Perf. 13
436 A316 56c multi   1.50   1.50

Martin de Viviès Base, Amsterdam Island — A317

2011, Jan. 2 Engr. Perf. 13x13¼
437 A317 90c multi   2.40   2.40

Josef Enzensperger (1873-1903), Meteorologist A318

2011, Jan. 2 Perf. 13¼x13
438 A318 90c multi   2.40   2.40

André Chastain (1906-62), Botanist — A319

2011, Jan. 2
439 A319 €1.35 multi   3.75   3.75

Sheathbills A320

2011, Jan. 2 Perf. 13x13¼
440 A320 €1.35 black & purple 3.75 3.75

Artedidraco Orianae A321

2011, Jan. 2
441 A321 €1.35 multi   3.75   3.75

Cruiser Lapérouse A322

2011, Jan. 2
442 A322 €4.30 multi   11.50 11.50

Zircons A323

No. 443: a, Zircons embedded in rock. b, Cut and polished zircon.

Litho. & Engr.
2011, Jan. 2 Perf. 13¼
443 A323 Horiz. pair   1.75   1.75
  a. 28c multi   .75   .75
  b. 34c multi   .90   .90

FRENCH SOUTHERN & ANTARCTIC TERRITORY

December 8, 1929 Mail Plane Crash — A324

No. 444: a, Farman F190 airplane. b, Map of flight. c, Crew and crash covers.

2011, Jan. 2		Perf. 13	
444	Horiz. strip of 3	7.75	7.75
a.	A324 56c multi	1.50	1.50
b.	A324 90c multi	2.40	2.40
c.	A324 €1.35 multi	3.75	3.75

Miniature Sheet

Whales — A325

No. 445: a, Baleine à bosse (humpback whale). b, Baleine franche australe (southern right whale). c, Cachalot (sperm whale). d, Rorqual de Rudolphi (sei whale).

2011, Jan. 2			
445	A325 Sheet of 4, #a-d	6.00	6.00

Patrol Boat Osiris — A326

2011, Apr. 1		Litho.	
446	A326 (60c) multi	1.75	1.75

Gentoo Penguins — A327

2011, June 15	Litho.	Perf. 13	
447	A327 €1 multi + label	3.00	3.00

Orré House (Prefect's Residence), St. Pierre, Reunion — A328

2011, Sept. 19			
448	A328 60c multi	1.75	1.75

Souvenir Sheet

Squadron Escort Forbin — A329

2011, Nov. 3		Litho. & Engr.	
449	A329 €1.10 multi	3.00	3.00

See St. Pierre & Miquelon No. 938.

Adélie Penguins — A330

2011, Dec. 2	Litho.	Perf. 13	
450	A330 60c multi	1.60	1.60

Penguin Breeding Grounds, Baie du Marin, Crozet Island — A331

Views of Baie du Marin in: No. 451, 60c, 1961. No. 452, 60c, 2011.

2011, Dec. 23		Perf. 13x13¼	
451-452	A331 Set of 2	3.25	3.25

Ship Marion Dufresne in Mamoudzou Lagoon — A332

Serpentine Die Cut 11

2011, Dec. 31		Self-Adhesive	
453	A332 60c multi	1.60	1.60

See Mayotte No. 288.

Notodiscus Hookeri — A333

2012, Jan. 2	Engr.	Perf. 13x13¼	
454	A333 60c multi	1.60	1.60

Ship Marius Moutet — A334

2012, Jan. 2			
455	A334 60c multi	1.60	1.60

Weddell Seals — A335

2012, Jan. 2		Perf. 13¼x13	
456	A335 €1 multi	2.60	2.60

Roald Amundsen (1872-1928), Polar Explorer — A336

2012, Jan. 2			
457	A336 €1 multi	2.60	2.60

René-Émile Bossière (1857-1941), Kerguelen Island Business Entrepreneur — A337

2012, Jan. 2			
458	A337 €1.45 multi	3.75	3.75

Lepidonotothen Larseni — A338

Litho. & Silk-screened

2012, Jan. 2		Perf. 13	
459	A338 €2.40 multi	6.25	6.25

Diopside — A339

No. 460: a, Crystals. b, Crystal and cut stone.

2012, Jan. 2			
460	A339 Horiz. pair	1.75	1.75
a.	29c red & green	.80	.80
b.	36c red & green	.95	.95

Point Molloy, Kerguelen Island — A340

No. 461: a, Buildings at Point Molloy. b, Molloy seismological station, 1953-63.

Litho. & Engr.

2012, Jan. 2		Perf. 13x13¼	
461	Horiz. pair	3.25	3.25
a.-b.	A340 60c Either single	1.60	1.60

Military Presence in French Southern & Antarctic Territories — A341

No. 462: a, Second Regiment of Marine Infantry Parachutists on Europa Island. b, Detachment of the Mayotte Foreign Legion on the Glorioso Islands.

Litho. & Silk-screened

2012, Jan. 2		Perf. 13	
462	Horiz. pair	3.25	3.25
a.-b.	A341 60c Either single	1.60	1.60

Miniature Sheet

Derelict Whaling Station, Port-Jeanne d'Arc, Kerguelen Island — A342

No. 463: a, Eight storage tanks. b, Three boilers, vert. c, Two storage silos. d, House, vert.

2012, Jan. 2		Photo.	
463	A342 60c Sheet of 4, #a-d	6.25	6.25

Miniature Sheet

Nature Reserve Flora and Fauna — A343

No. 464: a, Gentoo penguin (manchot papou). b, White-chinned petrel (petrel a menton blanc). c, Lyallia kerguelensis. d, Anatalanta aptera.

2012, Jan. 2		Litho. & Engr.	
464	A343 Sheet of 4	8.50	8.50
a.	20c multi	.55	.55
b.	60c multi	1.60	1.60
c.	€1 multi	2.60	2.60
d.	€1.45 multi	3.75	3.75

Miniature Sheet

Aircraft Used in Polar Regions — A344

No. 465: a, B-24 Liberator. b, DC-4 Skymaster. c, Nord 2501 Noratlas. d, C-130 Hercules. e, DC-3 Basler BT-67. f, DHC-6 Twin Otter.

2012, Jan. 2			
465	A344 €1 Sheet of 6, #a-f	16.00	16.00

Ile Longue, Kerguelen Islands — A345

No. 466: a, 60c, Painting. b, €1, Painting, diff.

2012, Apr. 13	Litho.	Perf. 13x13¼	
466	A345 Pair, #a-b	4.25	4.25

No. 466 was printed in sheets containing two pairs.

Souvenir Sheet

Prince of Monaco Islands — A346

No. 467: a, Giant Antarctic petrel. b, Coastline of Prince of Monaco Islands.

2012, June 9	Litho. & Engr.	Perf. 13¼	
467	A346 €1 Sheet of 2, #a-b	5.00	5.00

See Monaco No. 2680.

National Space Studies Center (CNES) Projects — A347

No. 468: a, Map of Antarctica. b, Penguin with tracking devices. c, Galileo satellite. d, Scientists deploying weather balloon. e, Pleaides satellite.

2012, June 9	Photo.	Perf. 13	
468	Vert. strip of 5 + 5 labels	12.00	12.00
a.-b.	A347 60c Either single + label	1.50	1.50
c.-d.	A347 €1 Either single + label	2.50	2.50
e.	A347 €1.45 multi + label	3.75	3.75

FRENCH SOUTHERN & ANTARCTIC TERRITORY

French Polar Institute, 20th Anniv. A348

2012, July 12   Litho.   *Perf. 13¼x13*
469 A348 60c multi   1.50 1.50

Souvenir Sheet

Bridge for Tracking Adélie Penguins A349

  Litho. & Engr.   *Perf. 13¼x13*
2012, Nov. 2
470 A349 €2 multi   5.25 5.25

Flight of Maryse Hilsz to Juan de Nova Island, 80th Anniv. A350

No. 471: a, Airplane, map of route. b, Hilsz (1901-46) in airplane.

2012, Nov. 8   Litho.   *Perf. 13*
471 A350 Horiz. pair   4.25 4.25
  a. 60c multi   1.60 1.60
  b. €1 multi   2.60 2.60

Prasiola Crispa and Penguins A351

2013, Jan. 1   Engr.   *Perf. 13x13¼*
472 A351 65c multi   1.75 1.75

Charles Petitjean (1914-88), Pilot — A352

2013, Jan. 1   *Perf. 12½x13*
473 A352 65c multi   1.75 1.75

Lepidonothen Squamifrons — A353

2013, Jan. 1   *Perf. 13x13¼*
474 A353 €1 multi   2.75 2.75

Sailboat "Le Mischief" — A354

2013, Jan. 1   *Perf. 12¼*
475 A354 €1 multi   2.75 2.75

Douglas Mawson (1882-1958), Antarctic Explorer, Huts and Penguins — A355

  Litho. & Engr.   *Perf. 13*
2013, Jan. 1
476 A355 €1.45 multi   4.00 4.00

Bernard-Marie Boudin, Chevalier de Tromelin (1735-1816), Explorer and Colonial Administrator A356

2013, Jan. 13   Litho.
477 A356 €2.40 multi   6.50 6.50

Hematite A357

2013, Jan. 1   Engr.   *Perf. 13¼*
478 A357 Horiz. pair   2.75 2.75
  a. 40c Crystals   1.10 1.10
  b. 60c Crystal   1.60 1.60

Miniature Sheet

Eaton's Pintail A358

No. 479: a, Duck in water. b, Heads of two ducks, vert. c, Duck and eggs. d, Head of duck, ducks in flight.

  Litho. & Engr.   *Perf. 13*
2013, Jan. 1
479 A358 Sheet of 4   9.00 9.00
  a. 20c multi   .55 .55
  b. 60c multi   1.60 1.60
  c. €1 multi   2.75 2.75
  d. €1.45 multi   4.00 4.00

Miniature Sheet

Helicopters — A359

No. 480: a, Sud-Ouest Djinn 1221. b, Bell 47 G2. c, Hiller 360. d, Sud-Est Alouette II 3130. e, Ecureuil AS 350. f, Panther AS 565.

2013, Jan. 1
480 A359 €1 Sheet of 6, #a-f   16.00 16.00

Souvenir Sheet

Engravings of Amsterdam and St. Paul Islands — A360

2013, Jan. 1   Litho.
481 A360 €3.40 multi   9.00 9.00

Voyage Booklet Type of 1999

No. 482: a, Ship Astrolabe near Dumont d'Urville Station. b, The Astrolabe, helicopter and Adélie penguins. c, Astrolabe docked near Lion landing strip. d, Four Adélie penguins at Dumont d'Urville station. e, View of Dumont d'Urville Station taken from the Astrolabe. f, Aerial view of Dumont d'Urville Station. g, Aurora Australis. h, Colony of Emperor penguins. i, Five men and plow at Cap Prudhomme Base. j, Aerial view of Cap Prudhomme Base, island at right. k, View of Cap Prudhomme Base, island at center. l, Two penguins. m, Italian, French and European Union flags at Concordia Base. n, Snow vehicle moving containers. o, Astronomical equipment near Concordia Base. p, Steps leading to containers.

2013, Apr. 5   Litho.   *Perf. 13*
482 A164 (€1) Souvenir booklet, #a-p   65.00

No. 482 sold for €25 and contains four panes, consisting of a block of four stamps of Nos. 482a-482d, 482e-482h, 482i-482l, and 482m-482p.

F.S. Floreal A361

2013, Apr. 5   Litho.   *Perf. 13*
483 A361 (63c) multi   1.75 1.75

A362

Silhouettes of Emblems — A363

Designs: 1c, Green turtle. 2c, Helicopter. 3c, Penguin. 4c, Ship "Marion Dufresne." 63c, Green turtle, helicopter, penguin, ship, "TAAF."

2013, Apr. 29   Engr.   *Perf. 13*
484 A362 1c dk bl & bl   .25 .25
485 A362 2c purple   .25 .25
486 A362 3c dk grn & yel grn   .25 .25
487 A362 4c brn org & org   .25 .25

  Litho. & Silk-screened   *Perf. 13¼*
488 A363 63c multi   1.75 1.75
  Nos. 484-488 (5)   2.75 2.75

See Nos. 504-507, 568a.

Souvenir Sheet

Engraver, Map, Penguin — A364

  Engr. (Litho. Margin)
2013, May 17   *Perf. 13*
489 A364 €5 multi   13.50 13.50

Souvenir Sheets

Prélèvement d'une Fusov, by Laurent Tixador — A365

Jours Heureux à l'Ile de la Désolation, by Klavdij Sluban — A366

2013, June 17   Litho.   *Perf. 13*
490 A365 €1 multi   2.75 2.75
491 A366 €1 black   2.75 2.75

Ateliers des Ailleurs art project.

Souvenir Sheet

Whale and Stock Certificate for Kerguelen Fisheries Society — A367

2013, Nov. 6   Litho.   *Perf. 13¼x13*
492 A367 €1 multi   2.75 2.75

Louis Jacquinot (1898-1993), Minister of Overseas France — A368

2014, Jan. 2   Engr.   *Perf. 13¼x13*
493 A368 66c multi   1.90 1.90

Bertrand Imbert (1924-2011), Leader of French Research for International Geophysical Year — A369

2014, Jan. 2   Engr.   *Perf. 12¾x13*
494 A369 66c multi   1.90 1.90

Tromelin Meteorological Station, 60th Anniv. — A370

2014, Jan. 2   Engr.   *Perf. 13x13¼*
495 A370 €1.55 multi   4.25 4.25

FRENCH SOUTHERN & ANTARCTIC TERRITORY

Rock Carvings of Amsterdam Island A371

2014, Jan. 2		Engr.		Perf. 13x13¼
496	A371	€1.55 multi	4.25	4.25

Supply Ship "Le Malin" A372

2014, Jan. 2		Litho.		Perf. 13
497	A372	€1.55 multi	4.25	4.25

Bren Carrier on Kerguelen Island A373

2014, Jan. 2		Engr.		Perf. 13x13¼
498	A373	€2 multi	5.50	5.50

White Tower (Basalt Columns), Crozet Islands — A374

2014, Jan. 2		Litho.		Perf. 13
499	A374	€2 multi	5.50	5.50

Lepidonotothen Mizops — A375

2014, Jan. 2		Engr.		Perf. 13x13¼
500	A375	€2.40 multi	6.50	6.50

Fluorite A376

No. 501: a, Polished stones. b, Crystal.

2014, Jan. 2		Litho.		Perf. 13
501	A376	Horiz. pair	2.75	2.75
a.		37c multi	1.00	1.00
b.		63c multi	1.75	1.75

Miniature Sheet

Mollusks A377

No. 502: a, Moule de Kerguelen (Kerguelen mussel). b, Volute de Challenger (Challenger volute). c, Moule de Magellan (Magellan mussel). d, Buccin antarctique (Antarctic whelk). e, Laternule antarctique (Antarctic clam).

2014, Jan. 2		Litho. & Engr.		Perf. 13
502	A377	63c Sheet of 5, #a-e	8.75	8.75

Miniature Sheet

Birds A378

No. 503: a, Damier du Cap (Cape petrels). b, Manchot royal de Crozet (Crozet Island king penguins). c, Fulmar antarctique (Antarctic fulmars). d, Grand albatros de Crozet (Wandering albatrosses).

2014, Jan. 2		Engr.		Perf. 13x12¾
503	A378	Sheet of 4	11.00	11.00
a.-b.		66c Either single	1.90	1.90
c.		€1.05 multi	2.75	2.75
d.		€1.55 multi	4.25	4.25

Silhouette of Emblems Type of 2013 and

Silhouettes of Emblems — A379

A362 designs as before.
€7, Map of District of Crozet, dolphin, penguin, ship, "TAAF."

2014, Mar. 7		Litho.		Perf. 13
		Dated "2014"		
504	A362	1c dk bl & bl	.25	.25
a.		Litho. & silk-screened (varnish on silhouette), dated "2015"	.25	.25
b.		As "a," dated "2016"	.25	.25
505	A362	2c purple	.25	.25
a.		Litho. & silk-screened (varnish on silhouette), dated "2015"	.25	.25
b.		As "a," dated "2016"	.25	.25
506	A362	3c dk grn & yel grn	.25	.25
a.		Litho. & silk-screened (varnish on silhouette), dated "2015"	.25	.25
b.		As "a," dated "2016"	.25	.25
c.		Pair, #505b-506b	.25	.25
507	A362	4c brn org & org	.25	.25
a.		Litho. & silk-screened (varnish on silhouette), dated "2015"	.25	.25
b.		As "a," dated "2016"	.25	.25
c.		Pair, #504b, 507b	.25	.25

		Litho. & Silk-Screened		
		Perf. 13¼		
508	A379	€7 multi	19.00	19.00
		Nos. 504-508 (5)	20.00	20.00

Issued: Nos. 504a, 505a, 506a, 507a, 3/19; Nos. 504b, 505b, 506b, 507b, 3/30/16. See No. 568b.

Miniature Sheet

Commerson's Dolphins — A380

No. 509: a, 63c, Dolphin sticking head out of water. b, 66c, Three dolphins underwater. c, 66c, Dolphin breaching surface. d, €1.05, Dolphin above water.

		Litho. & Engr.		
2014, June 26				Perf. 13¼x13
509	A380	Sheet of 4, #a-d	8.25	8.25

Map of Madagascar to Tromelin Flight A381

AAC-1 Toucan A382

AAC-1 Toucan and Stamped Cover from Tromelin A383

2014, Sept. 21		Litho.		Perf. 13
510		Horiz. strip of 3	8.50	8.50
a.	A381	66c multi	1.75	1.75
b.	A382	€1.05 multi	2.75	2.75
c.	A383	€1.55 multi	4.00	4.00

First flight between Madagascar and Tromelin, 50th anniv.

Green Turtle — A384

2014, Oct. 9		Litho.		Perf. 13x13¼
511	A384	€1.05 multi	2.60	2.60

See Comoro Islands No. , France No. 4695, Malagasy Republic No. 1637, Mauritius No. 1144, Seychelles No. 904.

Gendarmes A385

No. 512 — Gendarme on: a, Iles Eparses. b, Iles Kerguelen.

		Litho. & Silk-Screened		
2014, Oct. 16				Perf. 13
512		Horiz. pair + central label	3.50	3.50
a.-b	A385	66c Either single	1.75	1.75

Souvenir Sheet

Amateur Radio — A386

No. 513: a, QSL card, radio key, amateur radio antenna on Tromelin Island. b, Radio operator, radio and antenna, vert.

		Perf. 13x13¼, 13¼x13		
2014, Nov. 6		Litho.		
513	A386	Sheet of 2	2.75	2.75
a.		99c multi	1.00	1.00
b.		66c multi	1.75	1.75

Decauville Hopper Cars on Juan de Nova Island A387

2015, Jan. 1		Engr.		Perf. 13x13¼
514	A387	66c multi	1.60	1.60

Euphausia Superba — A388

		Litho. & Engr.		
2015, Jan. 1				Perf. 13¼
515	A388	66c multi	1.60	1.60

Emperor Penguin — A389

2015, Jan. 1		Litho.		Perf. 13
516	A389	€1 multi	2.40	2.40

Leopard Seal in Adélie Land A390

2015, Jan. 1		Engr.		Perf. 13¼x13
517	A390	€1.05 multi	2.60	2.60

Ship Radioleine — A391

2015, Jan. 1		Engr.		Perf. 13x13¼
518	A391	€2.40 multi	5.75	5.75

Antarctic Terns A392

		Litho. & Engr.		
2015, Jan. 1				Perf. 13
519	A392	€4.30 multi	10.50	10.50

Insects — A393

Designs: 66c, Anatopteryx maritima. €2, Ectemnorhinus vanhoeffeanus, horiz.

2015, Jan.1		Litho.		Perf. 13¼
520-521	A393	Set of 2	6.50	6.50

Beryl A394

No. 522: a, Polished gemstones. b, Crystals in matrix.

		Litho. & Engr.		
2015, Jan. 1				Perf. 13
522	A394	Horiz. pair	2.40	2.40
a.		34c multi	.80	.80
b.		66c multi	1.60	1.60

Snowmobile Transport — A395

FRENCH SOUTHERN & ANTARCTIC TERRITORY

No. 523: a, Snowmobile pulling cargo. b, Snowmobile without cargo.

2015, Jan. 1	Litho.		Perf. 13¼
523	Horiz. pair	4.25	4.25
a.	A395 66c multi	1.60	1.60
b.	A395 €1.05 multi	2.60	2.60

Robert Guillard (1919-2013), Polar Explorations Chief of Operations — A396

No. 524 — Guillard and: a, Ship and penguins, Adélie Land. b, Expedition vehicles, Greenland.

2015, Jan. 1	Engr.		Perf. 13x13¼
524	Horiz. pair + central label	4.25	4.25
a.	A396 66c multi	1.60	1.60
b.	A396 €1.05 multi	2.60	2.60

Miniature Sheet

Fish A397

No. 525: a, Chaenodraco wilsoni. b, Chaenodraco myersi. c, Pagetopsis macropterus. d, Pagetopsis maculatus.

2015, Jan. 1	Engr.		Perf. 13
525	A397 Sheet of 4	9.75	9.75
a.-b.	66c Either single	1.60	1.60
c.	€1.05 multi	2.60	2.60
d.	€1.55 multi	3.75	3.75

Paul-Emile Victor (1907-95), Polar Explorer A398

2015, Mar. 7	Engr.		Perf. 13x12½
526	A398 €1 multi	2.25	2.25

Silhouettes of Saint-Paul & Amsterdam District Emblems — A399

Litho. & Silk-Screened

2015, Mar. 19		Perf. 13¼
527 A399 50c multi	1.10	1.10

See No. 568d.

François Tabuteau (1921-2000), Polar Explorer — A400

2015, Apr. 17	Litho.		Perf. 13
528	A400 80c multi	1.90	1.90

French Southern and Antarctic Territories, 60th Anniv. A401

No. 529 — Ship and: a, Airplane, seal, bird, turtle. b, Helicopter, birds, fish, killer whales. c, Penguins and birds in flight.

2015, July 14	Litho.		Perf. 13
529	Horiz. strip of 3	5.25	5.25
a.-c.	A401 80c Any single	1.75	1.75

People Stranded Without Supplies on Saint Paul Island, 1930 A402

2015, Sept. 18	Engr.		Perf. 13
530	A402 €1 multi	2.25	2.25

Ship *Marion Dufresne*, 20th Anniv. A403

2015	Litho. & Engr.		Perf. 13
Denomination Color			
531	A403 80c red	1.90	1.90
532	A403 €1.35 blue	3.00	3.00

Issued: 80c, 10/4; €1.35, 11/5.

Souvenir Sheet

Penguin on Floating Ice A404

Litho. & Embossed

2015, Nov. 5		Perf. 13½x13
533 A404 €1.24 multi	2.75	2.75

Ships — A405

No. 534: a, Croix du Sud I. b, Albius. c, Le Saint-Andre. d, Mascareignes III. e, Ile de la Reunion. f, Cap Horn I. g, Ile Bourbon.

Litho. & Engr.

2015, Dec. 3		Perf. 13
534	Booklet pane of 7	19.50	—
a.-g.	A405 €1.24 Any single	2.75	2.75
	Complete booklet, #534	19.50	

Lozère Waterfall — A406

2016, Jan. 2	Engr.		Perf. 13¼x13
535	A406 50c multi	1.10	1.10

Pringleophaga Crozetensis A407

2016, Jan. 2	Engr.		Perf. 12¼
536	A407 80c black	1.75	1.75

Serge Frolow, Director of Meteorological Service — A408

2016, Jan. 2	Litho.		Perf. 13
537	A408 80c multi	1.75	1.75

Point d'Entrecasteaux — A409

2016, Jan. 2	Engr.		Perf. 13x13¼
538	A409 €1.05 multi	2.40	2.40

Valdivia, Ship From 1898-99 German Deep Sea Expedition A410

2016, Jan. 2	Engr.		Perf. 13x12½
539	A410 €1.24 multi	2.75	2.75

Jean Volot (1921-2012), Polar Expedition Engineer and Priest — A411

2016, Jan. 2	Engr.		Perf. 12½x13
540	A411 €1.35 multi	3.00	3.00

Diatoms — A412

Litho. & Silk-Screened

2016, Jan. 2		Perf. 13
541 A412 €2.80 multi	6.25	6.25

Schooner Rêve and Grave of Raoul Fleurié — A413

2016, Jan. 2	Engr.		Perf. 13x13¼
542	A413 €2.80 multi	6.25	6.25

Sphene A414

No. 543: a, Polished and cut gemstones. b, Crystal.

Litho. & Silk-Screened

2016, Jan. 2		Perf. 13
543	A414 Horiz. pair	2.25	2.25
a.	20c multi	.50	.50
b.	80c multi	1.75	1.75

Kerguelen Island A415

No. 544: a, Whaling. b, Ships from *The Ice Sphinx*, by Jules Verne. c, Cormoran-Vert Hostel, Christmas Harbor.

2016, Jan. 2	Litho.		Perf. 13
544	Horiz. strip of 3	7.50	7.50
a.	A415 80c cream & black	1.75	1.75
b.	A415 €1.24 cream & black	2.75	2.75
c.	A415 €1.35 cream & black	3.00	3.00

Souvenir Sheet

Flyovers of the Kerguelen Islands — A416

No. 545: a, RRS Discovery. b, De Havilland Gipsy Moth seaplane.

2016, Jan. 2	Litho.		Perf. 13
545	A416 Sheet of 2	2.75	2.75
a.	44c multi	1.00	1.00
b.	80c multi	1.75	1.75

Miniature Sheet

Fish A417

No. 546: a, Histiodraco velifer (52x41mm). b, Dolloidraco longedorsalis (60x27mm). c, Pogonophryne phyllopogon (60x27mm). d, Pogonophryne cf. barsukovi (52x31mm).

2016, Jan. 2	Engr.		Perf. 13
546	A417 Sheet of 4	9.00	9.00
a.-b.	80c Either single	1.75	1.75
c.	€1.05 multi	2.40	2.40
d.	€1.35 multi	3.00	3.00

Miniature Sheet

Birds A418

No. 547: a, Fulmar antarctique (Antarctic fulmar). b, Petrel geant (giant petrel), horiz. c, Damier du cap (cape petrel), horiz. d, Skua, horiz.

Litho. & Engr.

2016, Jan. 2		Perf. 13
547	A418 Sheet of 4	9.00	9.00
a.	70c multi	1.50	1.50
b.	80c multi	1.75	1.75
c.	€1.05 multi	2.40	2.40
d.	€1.45 multi	3.25	3.25

Silhouettes of Kerguelen District Emblems — A419

Litho. & Silk-Screened

2016, Mar. 31		Perf. 13¼
548 A419 80c multi	1.90	1.90

See No. 568c.

FRENCH SOUTHERN & ANTARCTIC TERRITORY

No. 2 and Rockhopper Penguin — A420

2016, May 19 *Litho.* *Perf. 13*
549 A420 €2 multi + label 4.50 4.50
Paris Philex 2016.

Souvenir Sheet

Albatrosses — A421

2016, May 21 *Litho.* *Perf. 13¼x13*
550 A421 €1 multi 2.25 2.25

Bernard Duboys de Lavigerie (1934-2008), Ionosphere Researcher — A422

2016, Oct. 1 *Engr.* *Perf. 13¼x13*
551 A422 80c multi 1.90 1.90

Souvenir Sheet

Fillod Prefabricated Buildings In French Southern & Antarctic Territories, 60th Anniv. — A423

No. 552 — Prefabricated building and: a. Penguins. b. Ferdinand Fillod (1891-1956), building manufacturer.

Litho. & Embossed
2016, Nov. 3 *Perf. 13*
552 A423 Sheet of 2 9.25 9.25
 a. €1.60 blue 3.50 3.50
 b. €2.70 blue 5.75 5.75

Cirque du Château, Kerguelen Island A424

2016, Nov. 25 *Litho.* *Perf. 13*
553 A424 50c multi 1.10 1.10

Cabins Near the Mortadella, Kerguelen Island — A425

2017, Jan. 2 *Litho.* *Perf. 13*
554 A425 80c multi 1.75 1.75

Halirythus Amphibius — A426

2017, Jan. 2 *Litho.* *Perf. 13x13¼*
555 A426 80c multi 1.75 1.75

1696 Landing of Willem de Vlamingh on Saint Paul and Amsterdam Islands A427

2017, Jan. 2 *Litho.* *Perf. 13*
556 A427 €1 multi 2.10 2.10

Turborotalita Quinqueloba A428

Photo. & Embossed
2017, Jan. 2 *Perf. 13¼*
557 A428 €1.24 multi 2.60 2.60
Values are for stamps with surrounding selvage.

Challenger 8 Tractor — A429

2017, Jan. 2 *Engr.* *Perf. 13x13¼*
558 A429 €1.24 multi 2.60 2.60

RV Ob, Flagship of 1956 Soviet Antarctic Expedition at Kerguelen Island — A430

2017, Jan. 2 *Engr.* *Perf. 13x13¼*
559 A430 €1.24 multi 2.60 2.60

Amalopteryx Maritima A431

2017, Jan. 2 *Engr.* *Perf. 13x13¼*
560 A431 €1.55 multi 3.25 3.25

Slaves Abandoned on Tromelin Island After 1761 Shipwreck — A432

Litho. & Engr.
2017, Jan. 2 *Perf. 13x13¼*
561 A432 €1.55 multi 3.25 3.25

Pyroxene A433

No. 562: a, Crystal. b, Polished and cut stones.

Litho. & Silk-Screened
2017, Jan. 2 *Perf. 13*
562 A433 Horiz. pair 2.25 2.25
 a. 20c multi .45 .45
 b. 80c multi 1.75 1.75

Founders of French Polar Expeditions A434

Polar Expedition Port-Martin Station, Adélie Land A435

2017, Jan. 2 *Engr.* *Perf. 13x13¼*
563 Horiz. pair + central label 4.50 4.50
 a. A434 80c multi 1.75 1.75
 b. A435 €1.24 multi 2.60 2.60

Souvenir Sheet

CASA CN-235 Over Island A436

2017, Jan. 2 *Litho.* *Perf. 13*
564 A436 €3.90 multi 8.25 8.25

Souvenir Sheet

Tuna Fishing A437

No. 565: a, Albacore tuna. b, Fishing trawler

Litho. & Engr.
2017, Jan. 2 *Perf. 13*
565 A437 Sheet of 2 2.60 2.60
 a. 44c multi .85 .85
 b. 80c multi 1.75 1.75

Miniature Sheet

Gygis Alba A438

No. 566: a, Two terns, blue background, vert. b, Chick, green background. c, Head of tern facing forward, blue background. d, Head of tern facing left, red background.

Litho. & Engr.
2017, Jan. 2 *Perf. 13*
566 A438 Sheet of 4 7.00 7.00
 a.-d. 85c Any single 1.75 1.75

Miniature Sheet

Amphipods — A439

No. 567: a, Epimeria robusta. b, Epimeria inermis. c, Echiniphimedia scotti. d, Anchiphimedia dorsalis.

2017, Jan. 2 *Engr.* *Perf. 13*
567 A439 Sheet of 4 9.50 9.50
 a.-b. 80c Either single 1.75 1.75
 c. €1.24 multi 2.60 2.60
 d. €1.55 multi 3.25 3.25

Silhouettes of Emblems Types of 2013-16

Miniature Sheet
2017, Mar. 9 *Litho.* *Perf. 13*
568 Sheet of 4 16.00 16.00
 a. A363 (€1.24) multi 4.00 4.00
 b. A379 (€1.24) multi 4.00 4.00
 c. A419 (€1.24) multi 4.00 4.00
 d. A399 (€1.24) multi 4.00 4.00

No. 568 sold for €7.50. Nos. 568a-568d are each inscribed "Lettre 20g tarif international."

Ship Marion Dufresne A440

Litho. & Engr.
2017, May 12 *Perf. 13*
569 A440 (€1.24) multi 2.75 2.75

Ship L'Astrolabe — A441

2017, Oct. 9 *Engr.* *Perf. 13x13¼*
570 A441 €1.30 multi 3.00 3.00

Birds of the Arctic and Antarctic A442

Designs: €1.41, Stercorarius maccormicki. €3.63, Aptenodytes forsteri.
No. 573: a, Like No. 571. b, Like No. 572.

Litho. & Engr.
2017, Oct. 27 *Perf. 13x12¾*
Stamps With Gray Frames
571-572 A442 Set of 2 12.00 12.00
Souvenir Sheet
Stamps Without Gray Frames
573 Sheet of 2 + label 6.00 6.00
 a. A442 €1 multi 2.40 2.40
 b. A442 €1.50 multi 3.50 3.50

See Greenland Nos. 763-765.

Voyage Booklet Type of 1999

No. 573C: d, Morne Rouge, Crozet Island. e, Baie Larose, Kerguelen Island. f, Plateau des Tourbières, Amsterdam Island. g, Ile Saint-Paul. h, Diver observing seaweed off Kerguelen Island. i, Scientist measuring lobster. j, Photo-identification chart of orca dorsal fins. k, Photographer on ship near Kerguelen Island. l, Man uprooting invasive non-native plants, Crozet Island. m, Scientist on bird survey, Kerguelen Island. n, Flower and measuring gauge, Kerguelen Island. o, Man inspecting plants, Amsterdam Island. p, Stacks of wooden pathway segments, Crozet Island. q, Freight decontamination at port, Reunion. r, Aerial view of building site, Crozet Island. s, Fence, Kerguelen Island.

2017, Nov. 9 *Litho.* *Perf. 13*
573C A164 (€1.24) Souvenir booklet,
 #d-s 65.00

No. 573C sold for €27 and contains four panes consisting of a block of four of Nos. 573Cd-573Cg, 573Ch-573Ck, 573Cl-573Co and 573Cp-573Cs.

Miniature Sheet

Birds and Reptiles A443

No. 574: a, Phaéton à bec jaune (yellow-billed tropicbird) (44x43mm). b, Scinque aux

FRENCH SOUTHERN & ANTARCTIC TERRITORY

labiales tachetés (skink) (54x54mm diamond). c, Frégate du Pacifique (great frigatebird) (38x38mm). d, Tortue verte (green turtle) (43mm diameter).

Perf. 13, Perf. (#574a, 574d)
2017, Nov. 30   **Litho. & Engr.**
574 A443 Sheet of 4   10.00 10.00
a.-c.   85c Any single   2.10 2.10
d.   €1.45 multi   3.50 3.50

Adélie Penguins A444

Litho. & Silk-screened
2017, Dec. 8   **Perf. 13**
575 A444 €1 multi

Myro Jeanneli — A445

2018, Jan. 2   **Photo.**   **Perf. 13¼**
576 A445 80c brnsh black   2.00 2.00

Cabin in Canyon des Sourcils Noirs, Kerguelen Island — A446

2018, Jan. 2   **Litho.**   **Perf. 13**
577 A446 85c multi   2.10 2.10

Kubota Snow Vehicle A447

2018, Jan. 2   **Litho.**   **Perf. 13**
578 A447 85c multi   2.10 2.10

Dr. Jean Sapin-Jaloustre (1917-99), Polar Expedition Physician — A448

2018, Jan. 2   **Litho.**   **Perf. 13**
579 A448 85c multi   2.10 2.10

Pierre Etienne de Boynes (1718-83), French Secretary of the Navy A449

2018, Jan. 2   **Engr.**   **Perf. 13x12¾**
580 A449 85c multi   2.10 2.10

La Quille Island Near Saint Paul Island A450

2018, Jan. 2   **Engr.**   **Perf. 13x13¼**
581 A450 €1.05 multi   2.60 2.60

Ectemnorhinus Viridis — A451

2018, Jan. 2   **Engr.**   **Perf. 13x13¼**
582 A451 €1.55 multi   3.75 3.75

Transport Ship La Grandière — A452

2018, Jan. 2   **Engr.**   **Perf. 13x13¼**
583 A452 €1.70 multi   4.25 4.25

Ilmenite A453

No. 584: a, Ilmenite in rock. b, Cut and polished ilmenite.

Litho. & Silk-Screened
2018, Jan. 2   **Perf. 13**
584 A453 50c Horiz. pair, #a-b   2.40 2.40

Renker Program, 2011-15 Study of Reindeer on Kerguelen Island A454

No. 585: a, Head of reindeer. b, Herd of reindeer. c, Adult and juvenile reindeer.

2018, Jan. 2   **Litho.**   **Perf. 13**
585   Horiz. strip of 3   6.50 6.50
a.-c. A454 85c Any single   2.10 2.10

Souvenir Sheet

Map of Antarctica — A455

2018, Jan. 2   **Photo.**   **Perf. 13¼**
586 A455 85c multi   2.10 2.10

Madrid Protocol on Envrionmental Protection to the Antarctic Treaty, 20th anniv.

Souvenir Sheet

MacGillivray's Prions — A456

2018, Jan. 2   **Litho.**   **Perf. 13**
587 A456 €1 multi   2.40 2.40

Souvenir Sheet

PBY Catalina, Ship La Pérouse, Map of Forgotten Airfield on Kerguelen Island — A457

2018, Jan. 2   **Litho.**   **Perf. 13¼x13**
588 A457 €3.90 multi   9.50 9.50

Souvenir Sheet

Echinoderms of Adélie Land — A458

No. 589: a, Lophaster gaini (40x40mm). b, Notocidaris platyacantha (52x40mm). c, Promachocrinus kerguelensis (80x53mm).

2018, Jan. 2   **Engr.**   **Perf. 13**
589 A458 Sheet of 3   8.50 8.50
a.   80c multi   2.00 2.00
b.   €1.05 multi   2.60 2.60
c.   €1.55 multi   3.75 3.75

Miniature Sheet

Protected Animals — A459

No. 590: a, Amsterdam albatross. b, Emperor penguin, vert. c, Crozet elephant seal. d, Kerguelen fur seal.

2018, Jan. 2   **Engr.**   **Perf. 13**
590 A459 Sheet of 4   13.00 13.00
a.-b.   85c Either single   2.10 2.10
c.-d.   €1.70 Either single   4.25 4.25

Ship L'Astrolabe A460

2018, Apr. 8   **Litho.**   **Perf. 13**
591 A460 (85c) multi   2.10 2.10

Silhouettes of Adélie Land District Emblems — A461

2018, Apr. 8   **Litho. & Silk-screened**   **Perf. 13¼**
592 A461 €1 multi   2.40 2.40

A stamp similar to No. 592, with an inscription of "lettre - 20g tarif international" was issued on Nov. 7, 2019 in a sheet along with a similarly inscribed stamp similar to No. 617. The franking value of each of these stamps was €1.10, but the sheet sold for €5, along with a folder.

Souvenir Sheet

Symphonie Australe, Musical Composition by Julien Gauthier — A462

2018, Apr. 20   **Litho.**   **Perf. 13¼**
593 A462 €2 multi   5.00 5.00

A463

Penguins A464

Designs: 10c, Rockhopper penguin (gorfou sauteur). 20c, King penguin (manchot royal). 30c, Gentoo penguin (manchot papou). No. 597: a, Emperor penguin (manchot empereur, 40mm diameter). b, King penguin (40x30mm). c, Gentoo penguin (40x30mm). d, Rockhopper penguin (40x30mm).

2018, June 7   **Litho.**   **Perf. 13**
594-596 A463 Set of 3   1.40 1.40
594a   Dated "2019"   .25 .25
595a   Dated "2019"   .45 .45
596a   Dated "2019"   .70 .70

Miniature Sheet
Perf. (#597a), Perf. 13¼ (#597b-597d)
597 A464 Sheet of 4   8.00 8.00
a.-d.   85c Any single   2.00 2.00

Issued: Nos. 594a, 595a, 596a, 3/14/19.

Souvenir Sheet

Alfred Faure (1925-68), Leader of Crozet Island Base — A465

2018, Oct. 17   **Litho.**   **Perf. 13**
598 A465 95c multi   2.25 2.25

Eudyptes Chrysocome Moseleyi — A466

No. 599: a, Head of penguin and Ile Saint-Paul. b, Penguin and volcano cone.

2018, Oct. 26   **Engr.**   **Perf. 13**
599 A466 Horiz. pair + central label   5.50 5.50
a.   95c dp bluish grn & blk lil   2.25 2.25
b.   €1.35 dp bluish grn & blk lil   3.25 3.25

FRENCH SOUTHERN & ANTARCTIC TERRITORY

Souvenir Sheet

Modern Art Exhibition at Dumont d'Urville Station, Antarctica — A467

Photo. & Silk-Screened

2018, Nov. 8			Perf.
600	A467	€2.20 multi	5.00 5.00

Elephant Seal Observation Cabins Near American Bay, Crozet Island A468

2019, Jan. 2	Litho.		Perf. 13
601	A468	95c multi	2.25 2.25

Gygis Alba and Tromelin Island A469

2019, Jan. 2	Engr.		Perf. 13
602	A469	95c multi	2.25 2.25

Yves Vallette (1920-2014), Civil Engineer and Member of 1949-51 French Polar Expeditions — A470

2019, Jan. 2	Engr.		Perf. 12½x13
603	A470	95c multi	2.25 2.25

Mario Zucchelli (1944-2003), Director of Italian Antarctic Program — A471

2019, Jan. 2	Engr.		Perf. 13
604	A471	€1.35 multi	3.25 3.25

Neomaso Antarcticus A472

2019, Jan. 2	Engr.		Perf. 13
605	A472	€1.55 multi	3.50 3.50

Zanclorhynchus Spinifer — A473

2019, Jan. 2	Engr.		Perf. 13
606	A473	€1.70 multi	4.00 4.00

B2M Champlain A474

2019, Jan. 2	Litho.		Perf. 13
607	A474	€1.90 multi	4.50 4.50

Missile Cruiser Colbert A475

2019, Jan. 2	Litho.		Perf. 13
608	A475	€2.80 multi	6.50 6.50

Sapphirines A476

No. 609: a, Raw sapphirine. b, Three cut and polished sapphirines.

Litho. & Silk-Screened

2019, Jan. 2			Perf. 13
609	A476	50c Horiz. pair, #a-b	2.25 2.25

Laboureur, Kerguelen Island — A477

No. 610: a, Mairie Annexe Cabin (40x26mm). b, Laboureur (81x26mm).

2019, Jan. 2	Engr.		Perf. 13
610	Horiz. pair + central label		5.50 5.50
a.	A477	95c multi	2.25 2.25
b.	A477	€1.35 multi	3.25 3.25

Study of Lake Sediment Cores A478

No. 611: a, Workers on barge coring lake sediment. b, Barge on Lac d'Armor. c, Equipment for studying ores.

2019, Jan. 2	Litho.		Perf. 13
611	Horiz. strip of 3		12.00 12.00
a.	A478	95c multi	2.25 2.25
b.	A478	€1.35 multi	3.25 3.25
c.	A478	€2.70 multi	6.25 6.25

Souvenir Sheet

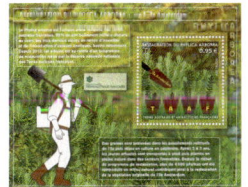

Restoration of Phylica Arborea on Amsterdam Island — A479

2019, Jan. 2	Litho.		Perf. 13
612	A479	95c multi	2.25 2.25

Souvenir Sheet

Flesh-footed Shearwater — A480

2019, Jan. 2	Litho.		Perf. 13
613	A480	€2 multi	4.50 4.50

Souvenir Sheet

Photovoltaic Solar Power Plant on Tromolin Island — A481

No. 614 — Power plant and: a, Bird at UL, sea turtle at LR (40x40mm). b, Bird at UR, sea turtle at LL (40x30mm).

Perf. 13 (#614a), 13x13¼ (#614b)

2019, Jan. 2			Litho.
614	A481	Sheet of 2	4.50 4.50
a.-b.		95c Either single	2.25 2.25

Souvenir Sheet

Shells of Adélie Land A482

No. 615: a, Falsimargarita gemma (40x40mm). b, Trophonella scotiana (52x40mm). c, Trophonella shackletoni (52x40mm).

2019, Jan. 2	Engr.		Perf. 13
615	A482	Sheet of 3	7.25 7.25
a.		70c multi	1.60 1.60
b.		95c multi	2.25 2.25
c.		€1.35 multi	3.25 3.25

Gentoo Penguins A483

2019, Mar. 16	Litho.		Perf. 13
616	A483	€1 multi	2.25 2.25

Silhouettes of Scattered Islands of the Indian Ocean District Emblems — A484

Litho. & Silk-Screened

2019, Mar. 16			Perf. 13¼
617	A484	€1.50 multi	3.50 3.50

A stamp similar to No. 617, with an inscription of "lettre - 20g tarif international" was issued on Nov. 7, 2019 in a sheet along with a similarly inscribed stamp similar to No. 592. The franking value of each of these stamps was €1.10, but the sheet sold for €5, along with a folder.

Oceanographic Ship La Curieuse — A485

2019, June 7	Litho.		Perf. 13
618	A485	€1.35 multi	3.25 3.25

A sheet of two, containing stamps similar to Nos. 592 and 617, but with an inscription of "lettre - 20g tarif international" was issued on Nov. 7, 2019. The franking value of each of these stamps was €1.10, but the sheet sold for €5, along with a folder.

Souvenir Sheet

Aptenodytes Patagonicus — A486

No. 619: a, Three King penguins (40x40mm). b, One King penguin (40x30mm).

Perf. 13 (#619a), 13x13¼ (#619b)

2019, Nov. 28			Litho.
619	A486	Sheet of 2	7.00 7.00
a.-b.		€1.50 Either single	3.50 3.50

Entrecasteaux Cabins, Amsterdam Island — A487

2020, Jan. 2	Litho.		Perf. 13
620	A487	€1.05 multi	2.40 2.40

Channichthys Velifer — A488

2020, Jan. 2	Engr.		Perf. 13x13¼
621	A488	€1.05 multi	2.40 2.40

Bernard Morlet (1932-2010), Geophysicist — A489

2020, Jan. 2	Engr.		Perf. 13¼x13
622	A489	€1.05 multi	2.40 2.40

FRENCH SOUTHERN & ANTARCTIC TERRITORY

Saint Anne's Finger and Larose Bay, Kerguelen Islands A490

2020, Jan. 2		Litho.		Perf. 13
623	A490	€1.45 multi	3.25	3.25

Egretta Dimorpha A491

2020, Jan. 2		Engr.		Perf. 13
624	A491	€1.55 multi	3.50	3.50

Frigate Nivôse A492

2020, Jan. 2		Engr.		Perf. 13
625	A492	€1.55 multi	3.50	3.50

Amethyst A493

No. 626: a, Uncut stone. b, Cut and polished stones.

Litho. & Silk-Screened

2020, Jan. 2			Perf. 13
626	A493	Horiz. pair	2.20 2.20
a.-b.		50c Either single	1.10 1.10

Robert-Guillard Station — A494

No. 627: a, Station and equipment. b, Map showing location of station.

2020, Jan. 2		Litho.		Perf. 13
627	A494	Horiz. pair	8.75	8.75
a.		€1.05 multi	2.40	2.40
b.		€2.80 multi	6.25	6.25

Souvenir Sheet

Great Albatrosses — A495

2020, Jan. 2		Litho.		Perf. 13
628	A495	€1 multi	2.25	2.25

Souvenir Sheet

Penguins and Aurora Australis A496

Litho. & Silk-Screened

2020, Jan. 2				Perf. 13
629	A496	€1.45 multi	3.25	3.25

Souvenir Sheet

Natural Bridge, Crozet Islands A497

2020, Jan. 2		Litho.		Perf. 13x13¼
630	A497	€2.80 multi	6.25	6.25

Souvenir Sheet

Concordia Base Logistics — A498

No. 631: a, DHC-6 Twin Otter over Concordia Base (52x31mm). b, Map showing location of Concordia Base (32x24mm).

Perf. 13 (#631a), 13¼ (#631b)

2020, Jan. 2			Litho.	
631	A498	Sheet of 2	4.80	4.80
a.-b.		€1.05 Either single	2.40	2.40

Souvenir Sheet

Commerson's Dolphins — A499

No. 632: a, Commerson's dolphin near Zodiac boat (40x30mm). b, Commerson's dolphin (40x40mm).

Perf. 13 (#632a), 13x13¼ (#632b)

2020, Jan. 2			Litho.	
632	A499	Sheet of 2	5.50	5.50
a.		€1.05 multi	2.40	2.40
b.		€1.35 multi	3.00	3.00

Souvenir Sheet

Marine Life Management — A500

No. 633: a, Lobster. b, Marker.

Litho. & Silk-Screened

2020, Jan. 2			Perf. 13¼x13	
633	A500	Sheet of 2	7.00	7.00
a.		€1.05 multi	2.40	2.40
b.		€1.95 multi	4.50	4.50

Souvenir Sheet

Cephalopods — A501

No. 634: a, Psychroteuthis glacialis. b, Pareledone turqueti.

2020, Jan. 2		Engr.		Perf. 13
634	A501	Sheet of 2 + label	6.75	6.75
a.		€1.45 multi	3.25	3.25
b.		€1.55 multi	3.50	3.50

Postal Services of the French Southern and Antarctic Territories — A502

No. 635: a, Postage stamps, handstamps and clerk applying cancel. b, Transfer of mail bags.

2020, Oct. 29		Litho.		Perf. 13
635		Horiz. pair + 2 alternating labels	4.75	4.75
a.	A502	95c multi + label	2.25	2.25
b.	A502	€1.05 multi + label	2.50	2.50

Map of Scattered Islands of the Indian Ocean, Palm Tree, Bird, Spider and Crab — A503

Map of St. Paul and Amsterdam Islands, Bird, Plants and Helicopter — A504

Map of Crozet Islands, Birds, Ship, Building, Seal and Helicopter — A505

Map of Kerguelen Islands, Penguin, Ship, Flags and Building — A506

Map of Adélie Land, Penguin, Crab, Starfish, Ship, Buildings and Helicopter — A507

2020, Nov. 1		Photo.		Perf. 13
Stamps With White Frames				
636	A503	€1.05 multi	2.50	2.50
637	A504	€1.05 multi	2.50	2.50
638	A505	€1.05 multi	2.50	2.50
639	A506	€1.05 multi	2.50	2.50
640	A507	€1.05 multi	2.50	2.50
		Nos. 636-640 (5)	12.50	12.50

French Southern & Antarctic Territories, 65th anniv.

French Southern and Antarctic Territories 65th Anniv. Types of 2020
Miniature Sheet

2020, Dec. 1		Litho.		Perf. 13
Stamps Without White Frames				
641		Sheet of 5	19.00	19.00
a.	A503	€1.50 multi	3.75	3.75
b.	A504	€1.50 multi	3.75	3.75
c.	A505	€1.50 multi	3.75	3.75
d.	A506	€1.50 multi	3.75	3.75
e.	A507	€1.50 multi	3.75	3.75

Souvenir Sheet

Paul-Emile Victor (1907-95), Polar Explorer — A508

2020, Nov. 5		Litho.		Perf. 13
642	A508	€1.50 multi	3.75	3.75

Apostle Islets, Crozet Archipelago A509

King Penguins, Larose Bay, Kerguelen Islands A510

Albatross Colony, Cliffs of Entrecasteaux, Amsterdam Island — A511

Pointe des Moines, Possession Island, Crozet Archipelago A512

Birds at Ocean Feeding Zones A513

Penguins on Shoreline Rocks A514

Biodiversity of Fish A515

Aerial View of Shoreline A516

Amsterdam Sea Lions, Amsterdam Island A517

Commerson Dolphins, Morbihan Gulf, Kerguelen Islands A518

FRENCH SOUTHERN & ANTARCTIC TERRITORY 867

Amsterdam Albatrosses, Amsterdam Island — A519

Black-browed Albatrosses, Kerguelen Islands — A520

2020, Nov. 6   Litho.   Perf. 13
643   Souvenir booklet, #643m, 643n, 643o   63.00
   a. A509 (€1.50) multi   5.25   5.25
   b. A510 (€1.50) multi   5.25   5.25
   c. A511 (€1.50) multi   5.25   5.25
   d. A512 (€1.50) multi   5.25   5.25
   e. A513 (€1.50) multi   5.25   5.25
   f. A514 (€1.50) multi   5.25   5.25
   g. A515 (€1.50) multi   5.25   5.25
   h. A516 (€1.50) multi   5.25   5.25
   i. A517 (€1.50) multi   5.25   5.25
   j. A518 (€1.50) multi   5.25   5.25
   k. A519 (€1.50) multi   5.25   5.25
   l. A520 (€1.50) multi   5.25   5.25
   m. Booklet pane of 4, #643e-643h   21.00   —
   n. Booklet pane of 4, #643a-643d   21.00   —
   o. Booklet pane of 4, #643i-643l   21.00   —

French Austral Lands and Seas UNESCO World Heritage Sites. No. 643 sold for €26.

Chalcedony — A521

No. 644: a, Unpolished chalcedony rock. b, Three polished and shaped chalcedony stones.

2021, Jan. 2   Litho.   Perf. 13
644   A521   50c Horiz. pair, #a-b   2.50   2.50

Model of the Marion Dufresne in Bottle — A522

Litho. & Silk-Screened
2021, Jan. 2   Perf. 13x13¼
645   A522   €1.05 multi   2.60   2.60

Pierre-François Péron (1769-1846), Captain Marooned on Amsterdam Island — A523

2021, Jan. 2   Engr.   Perf. 12¾x13¼
646   A523   €1.05 multi   2.60   2.60

Cabins at Pointe Basse, Crozet Archipelago — A524

2021, Jan. 2   Litho.   Perf. 13
647   A524   €1.10 multi   2.75   2.75

Workers Maintining Relay 26, Kerguelen Islands — A525

2021, Jan. 2   Litho.   Perf. 13
648   A525   €1.20 multi   3.00   3.00

André Lebeau (1932-2013), Geophysicist — A526

2021, Jan. 2   Engr.   Perf. 13
649   A526   €1.20 multi   3.00   3.00

Ship La Meurthe at Crozet Archipelago, 1887 — A527

2021, Jan. 2   Engr.   Perf. 13x13¼
650   A527   €1.20 multi   3.00   3.00

Souvenir Sheet

Kerguelen Shag and Crozet Shag — A528

2021, Jan. 2   Litho.   Perf. 13
651   A528   €1 multi   2.50   2.50

Souvenir Sheet

Apostle Islets, Crozet Archipelago — A529

2021, Jan. 2   Litho.   Perf. 13x13¼
652   A529   €1.50 multi   3.75   3.75

Souvenir Sheet

Jellyfish — A530

No. 653: a, 80c, Calycopsis borchgrevinki (40x40mm). b, €1.20, Periphylla periphylla (53x40mm).

Litho. & Engr.
2021, Jan. 2   Perf. 13
653   A530   Sheet of 2, #a-b   5.00   5.00

Souvenir Sheet

Basler BT-67 Airplane — A531

No. 654 — Basler BT-67: a, In flight (82x30mm). b, On ground (52x31mm).

Perf. 13¼ (#654a), 13 (#654b)
2021, Jan. 2   Litho.
654   A531   €1.50 Sheet of 2, #a-b   7.50   7.50

Souvenir Sheet

Coral Reefs of the Glorioso Islands — A532

No. 655 — Various photographs of reef: a, Horizontal stamp. b, Vertical stamp.

Litho. & Engr.
2021, Jan. 2   Perf. 13
655   A532   €2 Sheet of 2, #a-b   10.00   10.00

Miniature Sheet

Amsterdam Sea Lions — A533

No. 656: a, €1.05, Sea lion facing right (52x32mm). b, €1.05, Sea lion facing left (52x32mm). c, €1.45, Sea lion facing right, diff. (31x53mm). d, €1.45, Head of sea lion (41x42mm).

Perf. 13x12¾ (#656a-656b), 12¾x13 (#656c), 13 (#656d)
2021, Jan. 2   Engr.
656   A533   Sheet of 4, #a-d   12.50   12.50

Miniature Sheet

Crabs — A534

No. 657: a, €1.05, Beuroisia duhameli. b, €1.05, Ovalipes trimaculatus. c, €1.45, Chaceon paulensis. d, €1.45, Guinusia chabrus.

2021, Jan. 2   Engr.   Perf. 13
657   A534   Sheet of 4, #a-d   12.50   12.50

Miniature Sheet

Kerguelen Islands Flora — A535

No. 658: a, Pringlea antiscorbutica. b, Lyallia kerguelensis. c, Blechnum penna-marina. d, Acaena magellanica.

2021, Jan. 2   Litho.   Perf. 13¼x13
658   A535   €1.50 Sheet of 4, #a-d   15.00   15.00

Souvenir Sheet

Consultative Meeting on the Antarctic Treaty, Paris — A536

Litho., Sheet Margin Litho. & Embossed
2021, June 11   Perf. 13¼x13
659   A536   €3 multi   7.25   7.25

Wildlife — A537

Designs: 10c, Orca, Crozet Islands. 20c, Australasian gannets, Saint Paul and Amsterdam Islands, vert. No. 662, 40c, Atlantic yellow-nosed albatross and chicks, Kerguelen Islands, vert. No. 663, 40c, Emperor penguins and chicks, Adélie Land, vert. 50c, Great frigatebird, Scattered Islands.
No. 665: a, Like No. 660. b, Like No. 661. c, Like No. 662. d, Like No. 663. e, Like No. 664.

Perf. 13x13¼, 13¼x13
2021, Nov. 4   Photo.
660-664   A537   Set of 5   3.75   3.75
Miniature Sheet
665   A537   Sheet of 5   11.50   11.50
   a.-e. €1 Any single   2.25   2.25

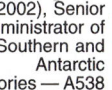

Claude Pieri (1922-2002), Senior Administrator of French Southern and Antarctic Territories — A538

2022, Jan. 2   Engr.   Perf. 13
666   A538   €1.10 multi   2.50   2.50

Sunrise on Ile de l'Est — A539

2022, Jan. 2   Litho.   Perf. 13x13¼
667   A539   €1.10 multi   2.50   2.50

Seabed Near the Scattered Islands — A540

2022, Jan. 2   Litho.   Perf. 13x13¼
668   A540   €1.10 multi   2.50   2.50

Maintenance on Relay 26, Mt. Fernand, Amsterdam Island — A541

2022, Jan. 2   Litho.   Perf. 13
669   A541   €1.20 multi   2.75   2.75

FRENCH SOUTHERN & ANTARCTIC TERRITORY

Shipwreck of Le Meridian Near Amsterdam Island and its Artifacts — A542

2022, Jan. 2	Litho.		Perf. 13x13¼	
670	A542	€1.50 multi	3.50	3.50

Serpentine A543

No. 671: a, One unpolished serpentine rock. b, Three polished serpentine stones.

2022, Jan. 2	Litho.		Perf. 13	
671	A543	50c Horiz. pair, #a-b	2.25	2.25

Souvenir Sheet

Marc-Joseph Marion du Fresne (1724-72), Explorer, Ship, and Ile de la Possession — A544

2022, Jan. 2	Litho. & Engr.		Perf. 13	
672	A544	€1.10 multi	2.50	2.50

Discovery of Crozet Islands by Marion du Fresne, 250th anniv.

Souvenir Sheet

Ship and Kerguelen Island — A545

2022, Jan. 2	Litho. & Engr.		Perf. 13	
673	A545	€1.10 multi	2.50	2.50

Discovery of Kerguelen Islands by Yves-Joseph de Kerguelen-Trémarec, 250th anniv.

Souvenir Sheet

Wheeled Robot at Penguin Colony, Adélie Land A546

2022, Jan. 2	Litho.		Perf. 13	
674	A546	€1.50 multi	3.50	3.50

Souvenir Sheet

Restocking of the Marion Dufresne by Helicopter Off Kerguelen Island — A547

2022, Jan. 2	Litho.		Perf. 13	
675	A547	€1.50 multi	3.50	3.50

Souvenir Sheet

White-chinned Petrel — A548

2022, Jan. 2	Litho.		Perf. 13	
676	A548	€2 multi	4.50	4.50

Souvenir Sheet

Publication of *An Antarctic Mystery*, Novel by Jules Verne (1828-1905), 125th Anniv. — A549

2022, Jan. 2	Litho. & Engr.		Perf. 13	
677	A549	€3 multi	6.75	6.75

Souvenir Sheet

Bénédicte Ardouin (1935-2016), Scientist — A550

2022, Jan. 2	Litho. & Engr.		Perf. 13	
678	A550	€3 multi	6.75	6.75

Souvenir Sheet

Icebreakers — A551

No. 679: a, L'Astrolabe. b, Aurora Australis.

2022, Jan. 2	Litho.		Perf. 13¼x13	
679	A551	Sheet of 2	7.00	7.00
a.-b.		€1.50 Either single	3.50	3.50

Souvenir Sheet

Amsterdam Island and Its Discoverer, Juan Sebastián Elcano (c. 1486-1526) — A552

2022, June 23	Litho.		Perf. 13	
680	A552	€1.50 multi	3.25	3.25

Discovery of Amsterdam Island, 500th anniv.

Antarctic Explorers — A553

Map of Antarctica and: No. 681, Capt. James Cook (1728-79). No. 682, Jules Dumont d'Urville (1790-1842). No. 683, Jean-Baptiste Charcot (1867-1936). No. 684, Roald Amundsen (1872-1928). No. 685, Robert Falcon Scott (1868-1912). No. 686, Douglas Mawson (1882-1958). No. 687, Ernest Shackleton (1874-1922).

2022, June 25   Engr.   Perf. 13
Booklet Stamps

681	A553	€1.50 black	3.25	3.25
682	A553	€1.50 black	3.25	3.25
683	A553	€1.50 black	3.25	3.25
684	A553	€1.50 black	3.25	3.25
685	A553	€1.50 black	3.25	3.25
686	A553	€1.50 black	3.25	3.25
687	A553	€1.50 black	3.25	3.25
a.		Booklet pane of 7, #681-687	23.00	
		Complete booklet, #687a	23.00	
		Nos. 681-687 (7)	22.75	22.75

Souvenir Sheet

Discovery of Tromelin Island By the Crew of the Diane, 300th Anniv. — A554

2022, Nov. 4	Litho. & Engr.		Perf. 13	
688	A554	€2.20 multi	4.75	4.75

Souvenir Sheet

Prince Albert I of Monaco (1848-1922) — A555

No. 689: a, Prince Albert I, map of Antarctica (52x31mm). b, Pourquoi-Pas, ship from the second Charcot expedition to Antarctica (30x40mm).

Perf. 13 (#689a), 13¼x13 (#689b)

2022, Nov. 24			Litho.	
689	A555	Sheet of 2	8.50	8.50
a.-b.		€2 Either single	4.25	4.25

See Monaco No. 3120.

Bougainville-Kerguelen Seaplane, 1939 — A556

2023, Jan. 2	Litho.		Perf. 13	
690	A556	€1.16 multi	2.50	2.50

Galileo Sensor Station, Kerguelen Islands — A557

2023, Jan. 2	Litho.		Perf. 13	
691	A557	€1.16 multi	2.50	2.50

Ile aux Cochons A558

2023, Jan. 2	Litho.		Perf. 13	
692	A558	€1.16 multi	2.50	2.50

Survostral Scientific Program A559

2023, Jan. 2	Litho.		Perf. 13	
693	A559	€1.16 multi	2.50	2.50

RHM Centaure at Amsterdam Island A560

2023, Jan. 2	Engr.		Perf. 13x13¼	
694	A560	€1.16 multi	2.50	2.50

Philibert Commerson (1727-73), Naturalist — A561

2023, Jan. 2	Engr.		Perf. 13	
695	A561	€1.65 black & green	3.50	3.50

Paractora Dreuxi A562

2023, Jan. 2	Engr.		Perf. 13x13¼	
696	A562	€2.32 multi	5.00	5.00

Michel Barré (1919-2005), Leader of 1950-52 French Antarctic Expedition — A563

2023, Jan. 2	Engr.		Perf. 13¼x13	
697	A563	€2.32 black	5.00	5.00

Arfvedsonite A564

No. 698: a, Arfvedsonite crystals embedded in rock. b, Three polished arfvedsonite crystals.

2023, Jan. 2	Litho.		Perf. 13	
698	A564	50c Horiz. pair, #a-b	2.10	2.10

FRENCH SOUTHERN & ANTARCTIC TERRITORY 869

Souvenir Sheet

Restoration of Bird Species on Tromelin Island Through Rat Eradication — A565

2023, Jan. 2		Litho.		Perf. 13
699	A565	€1.65 multi	3.50	3.50

Souvenir Sheet

Light-mantled Albatrosses — A566

2023, Jan. 2		Litho.		Perf. 13
700	A566	€3.30 multi	7.00	7.00

Souvenir Sheet

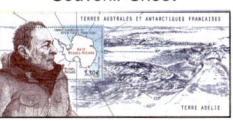

Michel Rocard (1930-2016), Prime Minister of France and Map of Antarctica Showing Bay Named After Him — A567

2023, Jan. 2		Engr.		Perf. 13
701	A567	€3.30 multi	7.00	7.00

Souvenir Sheet

Vehicles Used for Glacial Coring in Adélie Land A568

No. 702: a, Line of snow vehicles towing red shipping containers (80x30mm). b, Snow vehicle and research shelter (52x31mm).

Perf. 13x13¼ (#702a), 13 (#702b)

2023, Jan. 2		Litho.		
702	A568	€1.16 Sheet of 2, #a-b	5.00	5.00

Souvenir Sheet

Marine Life of Adélie Land A569

No. 703: a, Fannyella sp. (52x40mm). b, Cygnodraco mawsoni (60x26mm).

Litho. & Engr.

2023, Jan. 2			Perf. 13
703	A569	€1.65 Sheet of 2, #a-b	7.00 7.00

 A570

 A571

 A572

 A573

Adélie Land Landscapes — A574

2023, Jan. 2		Litho.		Perf. 13
704		Sheet of 5	12.50	12.50
a.	A570	€1.16 multi	2.50	2.50
b.	A571	€1.16 multi	2.50	2.50
c.	A572	€1.16 multi	2.50	2.50
d.	A573	€1.16 multi	2.50	2.50
e.	A574	€1.16 multi	2.50	2.50

Female and Juvenile Elephant Seal A575

Penguins Near Battling Elephant Seals A576

Juvenile Elephant Seals Underwater A577

2023, June 24		Litho.		Perf. 13¼x13
705		Horiz. strip of 3	5.25	5.25
a.	A575	58c multi	1.30	1.30
b.	A576	58c multi	1.30	1.30
c.	A577	€1.16 multi	2.60	2.60

Voyage Booklet Type of 1999

No. 706 — Drawings from voyage on the Marion Dufresne: a, Breeches buoy dangling from helicopter, Tromelin. b, Deck of the Marion Dufresne. c, Life preserver on railing of the Marion Dufresne. d, Helicopter at Marion Dufresne landing pad. e, Helicopter approaching Crozet Island. f, Breeches buoy dangling from helicopter leaving Crozet Island. g, Crane mechanism on the Marion Dufresne near Crozet Island. h, View of the Marion Dufresne from Crozet Island. i, Scientific buildings on Kerguelin Island. j, Helicopters carrying items on cables near Mt. Campbell, Kerguelin Island. k, Dock ramps, Kerguelin Island. l, Road and buildings, Kerguelin Island. m, View from Amsterdam Island of the Marion Dufresne and helicopter. n, View from the Marion Dufresne of helicopter near Amsterdam Island. o, Building and fence, Amsterdam Island. p, Launch from the Marion Dufresne approaching Amsterdam Island. q, Coastal view of Saint Paul Island. r, Passageway and hatch to the bridge of the Marion Dufresne. s, People in lifeboat at side of the Marion Dufresne. t, Helicopter with large rotor blades removed.

Litho. & Photo.

2023, Nov. 8			Perf. 13
706	A164	Souvenir booklet, #a-t	72.00

Nos. 706a-706t are all nondenominated. Stamps are valid for 20 gram international letter rate. The booklet sold for €33 and contains five panes of Nos. 706a-706d, 706e-706h, 706i-706l, 706m-706p, and 706q-706t.

Souvenir Sheet

Scientific Exploration of Kerguelin Island by Etienne Peau (1877-1940) and His Son, Lionel, Cent. — A578

Litho. & Engr.

2023, Nov. 8			Perf. 13
707	A578	€2.32 multi	5.00 5.00

AIR POST STAMPS

Emperor Penguins and Map of Antarctica AP1

		Unwmk.		
1956, Apr. 25		Engr.		Perf. 13
C1	AP1	50fr lt ol grn & dk grn	42.50	29.00
C2	AP1	100fr dl bl & indigo	35.00	25.00

Wandering Albatross AP2

1959, Sept. 14				
C3	AP2	200fr brn red, bl & blk	40.00	27.50

Adélie Penguins AP3

1963, Feb. 11		Unwmk.		Perf. 13
C4	AP3	50fr blk, dk bl & dp cl	42.50	32.50

Telstar Issue
Common Design Type

1962, Dec. 24				
C5	CD111	50fr dp bl, ol & grn	29.00	21.00

Radio Towers, Adelie Penguins and IQSY Emblem — AP4

1963, Dec. 16			Engr.	
C6	AP4	100fr bl, ver & blk	110.00	87.50

International Quiet Sun Year, 1964-65.

Discovery of Adelie Land — AP5

1965, Jan. 20		Engr.		Perf. 13
C7	AP5	50fr blue & indigo	125.00	87.50

125th anniversary of the discovery of Adelie Land by Dumont d'Urville.

ITU Issue
Common Design Type

1965, May 17		Unwmk.		Perf. 13
C8	CD120	30fr multi	200.00	160.00

French Satellite A-1 Issue
Common Design Type

Designs: 25fr, Diamant rocket and launching installations. 30fr, A-1 satellite.

1966, Mar. 2		Engr.		Perf. 13
C9	CD121	25fr dk grn, choc & sl	13.50	10.00
C10	CD121	30fr choc, sl & dk grn	13.50	10.00
a.		Pair, #C9-C10 + label	29.00	24.00

French Satellite D-1 Issue
Common Design Type

1966, Mar. 27				
C11	CD122	50fr dk pur, lil & org	57.50	40.00

Ionospheric Research Pylon, Adelie Land — AP6

1966, Dec. 12				
C12	AP6	25fr plum, bl & dk brn	32.50	17.50

Port aux Français, Emperor Penguin and Explorer AP7

40fr, Aerial view of Saint Paul Island.

1968-69		Engr.		Perf. 13
C13	AP7	40fr brt bl & dk gray	42.50	27.50
C14	AP7	50fr lt ultra, dk grn & blk	175.00	110.00

Issue dates: 50fr, Jan. 21; 40fr, Jan. 5, 1969.

Kerguelen Island and Rocket AP8

Design: 30fr, Adelie Land.

1968, Apr. 22		Engr.		Perf. 13
C15	AP8	25fr sl grn, dk brn & Prus bl	19.00	14.00
C16	AP8	30fr dk brn, sl grn & Prus bl	19.00	14.00
a.		Pair, #C15-C16 + label	40.00	30.00

Space explorations with Dragon rockets, 1967-68.

Eiffel Tower, Antarctic Research Station, Ship from Paris Arms and Albatross — AP9

1969, Jan. 13				
C17	AP9	50fr bright blue	45.00	35.00

5th Consultative Meeting of the Antarctic Treaty Powers, Paris, Nov. 18, 1968.

Concorde Issue
Common Design Type

1969, Apr. 17				
C18	CD129	85fr indigo & blue	55.00	37.50

Prepared but not issued with 87fr denomination. Value $3,000.

FRENCH SOUTHERN & ANTARCTIC TERRITORY

Map of Amsterdam Island — AP10

Map of Kerguelen Island AP11

Coat of Arms — AP12

Designs: 50fr, Possession Island. 200fr, Point Geology Archipelago.

1969-71		Engr.		Perf. 13
C19	AP10	30fr brown	19.00	12.50
C20	AP11	50fr sl grn, bl & dk red	21.00	14.00
C21	AP11	100fr blue & blk	85.00	40.00
C22	AP10	200fr sl grn, brn & Prus bl	70.00	42.50
C23	AP12	500fr pck blue	20.00	15.00
		Nos. C19-C23 (5)	215.00	124.00

30fr for the 20th anniv. of the Amsterdam Island Meteorological Station.
Issued: 100fr, 500fr, 12/21; 30fr, 3/27/70; 50fr, 12/22/70; 200fr, 1/1/71.

Port-aux-Français, 1970 — AP13

Design: 40fr, Port-aux-Français, 1950.

1971, Mar. 9		Engr.		Perf. 13
C24	AP13	40fr bl, ocher & sl grn	19.00	12.00
C25	AP13	50fr bl, grn ol & sl grn	19.00	12.00
a.		Pair, #C24-C25 + label	40.00	27.50

20th anniversary of Port-aux-Français on Kerguelen Island.

Marquis de Castries Taking Possession of Crozet Island, 1772 AP14

250fr, Fleur-de-lis flag raising on Kerguelen Is.

1972		Engr.		Perf. 13
C26	AP14	100fr black	45.00	29.00
C27	AP14	250fr blk & dk brn	100.00	45.00

Bicentenary of the discovery of the Crozet and Kerguelen Islands.
Issue dates: 100fr, Jan. 24; 250fr, Feb. 23.

M. S. Galliéni AP15

1973, Jan. 25		Engr.		Perf. 13
C28	AP15	100fr black & blue	25.00	17.50

Exploration voyages of the Galliéni.

"Le Mascarin," 1772 AP16

Sailing Ships: 145fr, "L'Astrolabe," 1840. 150fr, "Le Rolland," 1774. 185fr, "La Victoire," 1522.

1973, Dec. 13		Engr.		Perf. 13
C29	AP16	120fr brown olive	6.75	4.75
C30	AP16	145fr brt ultra	6.75	4.75
C31	AP16	150fr slate	8.00	8.00
C32	AP16	185fr ocher	10.50	8.00
		Nos. C29-C32 (4)	32.00	25.50

Ships used in exploring Antarctica.
See Nos. C37-C38.

Alfred Faure Base AP17

Design: Nos. C33-C35 show panoramic view of Alfred Faure Base.

1974, Jan. 7		Engr.		Perf. 13
C33	AP17	75fr Prus bl, ultra & brn	8.00	5.25
C34	AP17	110fr Prus bl, ultra & brn	11.00	8.00
C35	AP17	150fr Prus bl, ultra & brn	14.00	8.00
a.		Triptych, Nos. C33-C35	37.50	30.00

Alfred Faure Antarctic Base, 10th anniv.

Penguin, Map of Antarctica, Letters — AP18

1974, Oct. 9		Engr.		Perf. 13
C36	AP18	150fr multicolored	7.00	5.50

Centenary of Universal Postal Union.

Ship Type of 1973

100fr, "Le Français." 200fr, "Pourquoi-pas?"

1974, Dec. 16		Engr.		Perf. 13
C37	AP16	100fr brt blue	5.50	3.00
C38	AP16	200fr dk car rose	9.00	4.50

Ships used in exploring Antarctica.

Rockets over Kerguelen Islands AP19

Design: 90fr, Northern lights over map of northern coast of Russia.

1975, Jan. 26		Engr.		Perf. 13
C39	AP19	45fr purple & multi	7.00	4.00
C40	AP19	90fr purple & multi	9.00	5.25
a.		Pair, #C39-C40 + label	19.00	13.00

Franco-Soviet magnetosphere research.

"La Curieuse" AP20

Ships: 2.70fr, Commandant Charcot. 4fr, Marion-Dufresne.

1976, Jan.		Engr.		Perf. 13
C41	AP20	1.90fr multicolored	3.25	2.00
C42	AP20	2.70fr multicolored	5.00	3.25
C43	AP20	4fr red & multi	9.00	4.25
		Nos. C41-C43 (3)	17.25	9.50

Dumont d'Urville Base, 1956 AP21

4fr, Dumont d'Urville Base, 1976, Adelie Land.

1976, Jan.				
C44	AP21	1.20fr multicolored	9.00	4.00
C45	AP21	4fr multicolored	11.00	7.25
a.		Pair, #C44-C45 + label	24.00	16.00

Dumont d'Urville Antarctic Base, 20th anniv.

Capt. Cook's Ships Passing Kerguelen Island AP22

1976, Dec. 31		Engr.		Perf. 13
C46	AP22	3.50fr slate & blue	13.00	8.00

Bicentenary of Capt. Cook's voyage past Kerguelen Island.

Sea Lion and Cub — AP23

1977-79		Engr.		Perf. 13
C47	AP23	4fr dk blue, grn ('79)	3.00	2.50
C48	AP23	10fr multicolored	10.00	9.00

Satellite Survey, Kerguelen AP24

Designs: 50c, 2.70fr, Satellites, Kerguelen. 70c, Geophysical laboratory. 1.90fr, Satellite and Kerguelen tracking station. 3fr, Satellites, Adelie Land.

1977-79		Engr.		Perf. 13
C49	AP24	50c multi ('79)	.90	.70
C50	AP24	70c multi ('79)	.90	.70
C51	AP24	1.90fr multi ('79)	1.60	1.40
C52	AP24	2.70fr multi ('78)	2.75	2.00
C53	AP24	3fr multicolored	4.25	3.25
		Nos. C49-C53 (5)	10.40	8.05

Elephant Seals — AP25

1979, Jan. 1
C54 AP25 10fr multicolored 5.50 4.50

Challenger AP26

1979, Jan. 1
C55 AP26 2.70fr black & blue 2.25 1.75

Antarctic expeditions to Crozet and Kerguelen Islands, 1872-1876.

La Recherche and L'Esperance AP27

1979
C56 AP27 1.90fr deep blue 1.50 1.10

Arrival of d'Entrecasteaux and Kermadec at Amsterdam Island, Mar. 28, 1792.

Lion Rock AP28

1979
C57 AP28 90c multicolored 1.10 .70

Natural Arch, Kerguelen Island, 1840 AP29

1979
C58 AP29 2.70fr multicolored 1.25 1.10

Phylica Nitida, Amsterdam Island AP30

1979
C59 AP30 10fr multicolored 4.00 3.25

Charles de Gaulle, 10th Anniversary of Death — AP31

1980, Nov. 9		Engr.		Perf. 13
C60	AP31	5.40fr multicolored	11.00	8.00

HB-40 Castor Truck and Trailer AP32

1980, Dec. 15
C61 AP32 2.40fr pur, blue & org 1.25 1.00

Supply Ship Saint Marcouf AP33

FRENCH SOUTHERN & ANTARCTIC TERRITORY

Design: 7.30fr, Icebreaker Norsel.

1980, Dec. 15
C62 AP33 3.50fr shown 1.60 1.10
C63 AP33 7.30fr multicolored 2.50 2.00

Glacial Landscape, Dumont d'Urville Sea — AP34

Chionis AP35

Adele Dumont d'Urville (1798-1842) AP36

Arcad III AP37

25th Anniv. of Charcot Station AP38

Antares AP39

1981 Engr. Perf. 13, 12½x13 (2fr)
C64 AP34 1.30fr multicolored .70 .45
C65 AP35 1.50fr black .70 .50
C66 AP36 2fr black & lt brn .90 .85
C67 AP37 3.85fr multicolored 1.60 1.25
C68 AP38 5fr multicolored 1.75 1.50
C69 AP39 8.40fr multicolored 2.75 2.25
Nos. C64-C69 (6) 8.40 6.80

PHILEXFRANCE '82 Stamp Exhibition, Paris, June 11-21 — AP40

1982, June 11 Engr. Perf. 13
C70 AP40 8fr multicolored 5.50 5.25

French Overseas Possessions Week, Sept. 18-25 AP41

1982, Sept. 17 Engr. Perf. 13
C71 AP41 5fr Commandant Charcot 1.75 1.75

Apostle Islands AP42

1983, Jan. 3 Engr. Perf. 13
C72 AP42 65c multicolored .55 .35

Sputnik I, 25th Anniv. of Intl. Geophysical Year AP43

Orange Bay Base, Cape Horn, 1883, Cent. AP44

5.20fr, Scoresby Sound Base, Greenland, 50th anniv.

1983, Jan. 3
C73 AP43 1.50fr multicolored .60 .60
C74 AP44 3.30fr multicolored 1.75 1.75
C75 AP44 5.20fr multicolored 2.00 2.00
a. Strip of 3, #C73-C75 4.50 4.50

AP45

1983, Jan. 3
C76 AP45 4.55fr dark blue 4.00 3.00

Abstract, by G. Mathieu AP46

1983, Jan. 3 Photo. Perf. 13x13½
C77 AP46 25fr multicolored 10.00 8.00

Erebus off Antarctic Ice Cap, 1842 — AP47

Port of Joan of Arc, 1930 — AP48

1984, Jan. 1 Engr. Perf. 13
C78 AP47 2.60fr ultra & dk blue 1.10 1.00
C79 AP48 4.70fr multicolored 1.75 1.75

Aurora Polaris AP49

1984, Jan. 1 Photo.
C80 AP49 3.50fr multicolored 2.00 1.25

Manned Flight Bicentenary (1983) AP50

Various balloons and airships.

1984, Jan. 1 Engr.
C81 AP50 3.50fr multicolored 1.75 1.75
C82 AP50 7.80fr multicolored 2.75 2.75
a. Pair, #C81-C82 + label 5.00 5.00

Patrol Boat Albatros — AP51

1984, July 2 Engr. Perf. 13
C83 AP51 11.30fr multi 4.25 4.25

NORDPOSTA Exhibition — AP52

Design: Scientific Vessel Gauss.

1984, Nov. 3 Engr. Perf. 13
C84 AP52 9fr multicolored 4.50 3.50
Issued se-tenant with label.

Corsican Sheep AP53

Amsterdam Albatross AP54

Designs: 70c, Mouflons. 3.90fr, Diomedia amsterdamensis.

1985, Jan. 1 Engr. Perf. 13
C85 AP53 70c multicolored .70 .40
C86 AP54 3.90fr multicolored 1.60 1.25

La Novara, Frigate — AP55

Design: La Novara at St. Paul.

1985, Jan. 1 Engr. Perf. 13
C87 AP55 12.80fr multi 5.00 4.50

Explorer and Seal, by Tremois AP56

Design: Explorer, seal, names of territories.

1985, Jan. 1 Photo. Perf. 13x12½
C88 AP56 30fr + label 11.00 8.50

Sailing Ships, Ropes, Flora & Fauna AP57

1985, Aug. 6 Engr. Perf. 13
C89 AP57 2fr blk, brt bl & ol grn .70 .55
C90 AP57 12.80fr blk, ol grn & brt bl 3.75 3.75
a. Pair, #C89-C90 + label 5.50 5.50

French Southern & Antarctic Territories, 30th anniv. No. C90a has continuous design with center label.

Bird Type of 1986

1986, Jan. 1 Engr. Perf. 13½x13
C91 AP56 4.60fr Sea Gulls 2.00 1.75

Antarctic Atmospheric Research, 10th Anniv. AP58

1986, Jan. 1
C92 AP58 14fr blk, dk red & brt org 5.00 4.00

Jean Charcot (1867-1936), Explorer AP59

Designs: 2.10fr, Ship Pourquoi Pas. 14fr, Ship in storm.

1986, Jan. 1
C93 AP59 2.10fr multicolored .90 .60
C94 AP59 14fr multicolored 4.50 4.25
a. Pair, #C93-C94 + label 6.25 6.25

SPOT Satellite over the Antarctic AP60

1986, May 26 Engr. Perf. 13
C95 AP60 8fr dp ultra, sep & dk ol grn 3.25 2.50

J.B. Charcot — AP61

1987, Jan. 1 Engr. Perf. 13x13½
C96 AP61 14.60fr multi 5.00 4.50

Ocean Drilling Program AP62

1987, Jan. 1 Perf. 13½x13
C97 AP62 16.80fr ol bis, ultra & dk blue 5.50 4.50

INMARSAT AP63

1987, Mar. 2 Engr. Perf. 13
C98 AP63 16.80fr multi 8.00 7.50

FRENCH SOUTHERN & ANTARCTIC TERRITORY

French Polar Expeditions, 40th Anniv. AP64

1988, Jan. 1
C99 AP64 20fr lake, ol grn & plum — 8.00 6.75

Views of Penguin Is. — AP65

1988, Jan. 1
C100 AP65 3.90fr dk bl & sep — 1.75 1.50
C101 AP65 15.10fr dp grn, choc brn & dk bl — 5.50 5.00

See Nos. C103, C109.

Founding of Permanent Settlements in the Territories, 40th Anniv. AP66

1989, Jan. 1 Engr. Perf. 13½x13
C102 AP66 15.50fr black — 5.00 4.75

Island View Type

1989, Jan. 1
C103 AP65 8.40fr Apostle Islands — 2.75 2.50

La Curieuse AP68

1989, Jan. 1 Perf. 13x12½
C104 AP68 2.20fr multicolored — .80 .70
C105 AP68 15.50fr multi, diff. — 5.00 5.00
a. Pair, #C104-C105 + label — 6.00 6.00

No. C105a label continues the design.

French Revolution, Bicent. AP69

1989, July 14 Engr. Perf. 13x12½
C106 AP69 5fr pink, dark olive grn & dark blue — 5.50 3.50

Souvenir Sheet
Perf. 13
C107 Sheet of 4 — 10.00 10.00
a. AP69 5fr Prus green, brt ultra & dark red — 2.50 2.50

No. C107 for PHILEXFRANCE '89.

15th Antarctic Treaty Summit Conference AP70

1989, Oct. 9 Engr. Perf. 13
C108 AP70 17.70fr multicolored — 6.00 5.75

Island View Type
1990, Jan. 1 Engr. Perf. 13
C109 AP65 7.30fr Isle of Pigs, Crozet Isls. — 3.00 2.40

L'Astrolabe, Expedition Team AP72

1990, Jan. 1
C110 AP72 15.50fr dk red vio & blk — 5.00 5.00

Discovery of Adelie Land by Dumont D'Urville, 150th anniv.

L'Astrolabe, Commanded by Dumont D'Urville, 1840 AP73

1990, Jan. 1
C111 AP73 2.20fr L'Astrolabe, 1988 — .80 .75
C112 AP73 15.50fr shown — 5.00 5.00
a. Pair, #C111-C112 + label — 6.50 6.50

Bird, by Folon AP74

1990, Jan. 1 Litho. Perf. 12½x13
C113 AP74 30fr multicolored — 10.00 9.50

Albatross, Argos Satellite — AP75

1991, Jan. 1
C114 AP75 2.10fr red brn, bl & brn — 1.50 .95

Climatological Research — AP76

3.60fr, Weather balloons, instruments. 20fr, Research ship.

1991, Jan. 1 Engr. Perf. 13
C115 AP76 3.60fr multi — 1.40 1.40
C116 AP76 20fr multi — 7.75 7.75
a. Pair, #C115-C116 + label — 10.00 10.00

Charles de Gaulle (1890-1970) AP77

1991, Jan. 1
C117 AP77 18.80fr blk, red & bl — 7.75 7.75

Cape Petrel — AP78

1992, Jan. 1 Engr. Perf. 13
C118 AP78 3.40fr multicolored — 2.25 1.40

French Institute of Polar Research and Technology AP79

#C120, Polar bear with man offering flowers.

1991, Dec. 16 Engr. Perf. 13x12
C119 AP79 15fr multicolored — 5.75 5.75
C120 AP79 15fr multicolored — 5.75 5.75
a. Strip, #C119-C120 + label — 12.00 12.00

Christopher Columbus and Discovery of America AP80

1992, Jan. 1
C121 AP80 22fr multicolored — 9.75 9.75

Mapping Satellite Poseidon AP81

1992, Jan. 1 Engr. Perf. 13
C122 AP81 24.50fr multi — 11.00 10.50

Dumont d'Urville Base, Adelie Land AP82

1992, Jan. 1 Litho. Perf. 13x12½
C123 AP82 25.70fr multi — 12.00 10.50

Amateur Radio AP83

1993, Jan. 1 Engr. Perf. 13
C124 AP83 2fr multicolored — 2.00 .75

New Animal Biology Laboratory, Adelie Land AP84

1993, Jan. 1
C125 AP84 25.40fr multicolored — 11.00 6.75

Support Base D10 — AP85

1993, Jan. 1
C126 AP85 25.70fr ol, red & bl — 11.00 7.00

Opening of Adelie Land Airfield AP86

1993, Jan. 1
C127 AP86 30fr multicolored — 13.00 8.75

Krill — AP87

1994, Jan. 1 Engr. Perf. 13
C128 AP87 15fr black — 6.50 4.00

Fishery Management — AP88

1994, Jan. 1
C129 AP88 23fr multicolored — 10.00 6.00

Satellite, Ground Station AP89

Design: 27.30fr, Lidar Station.

1994, Jan. 1
C130 AP89 26.70fr multicolored — 12.00 7.00
C131 AP89 27.30fr multicolored — 12.00 7.25

Arrival of Emperor Penguins AP90

1994, Jan. 1 Perf. 13x12½
C132 AP90 28fr blue & black — 13.00 8.00

Erebus Mission AP91

1995, Jan. 2 Engr. Perf. 13
C133 AP91 4.30fr brt bl, brt redsh pur & gray grn — 2.25 1.50

Moving of Winter Station, Charcot AP92

1995, Jan. 2 Litho.
C134 AP92 15fr multicolored — 6.50 4.25

G. Lesquin (1803-30) — AP93

1995, Jan. 2
C135 AP93 28fr multicolored — 12.00 8.00

Map of East Island AP94

1996, Jan. 1 Engr. Perf. 13
C136 AP94 20fr multicolored — 8.50 6.00

FRENCH SOUTHERN & ANTARCTIC TERRITORY — FRENCH SUDAN

Expedition to Dome/C AP95

1996, Jan. 1
C137 AP95 23fr dark blue   10.00 7.00

Blue Whale, Southern Whale Sanctuary AP96

1996, Jan. 1
C138 AP96 26.70fr multicolored   12.00 8.00

Port-Couvreux — AP97

1996, Jan. 1
C139 AP97 27.30fr multicolored   12.00 8.50

Jasus Paulensis — AP98

1997, Jan. 1   Engr.   Perf. 12½x13
C140 AP98 5.20fr multicolored   3.00 1.75

Racing Yacht Charentes 2 — AP99

1997, Jan. 1   Litho.   Perf. 13
C141 AP99 16fr multicolored   8.00 5.50

John Nunn, Shipwrecked 1825-29, Hope Cottage — AP100

1997, Jan. 1   Engr.
C142 AP100 20fr multicolored   8.75 6.25

ICOTA Program AP101

1997, Jan. 1
C143 AP101 24fr multicolored   10.50 7.50

Harpagifer Spinosus AP102

1997, Jan. 1
C144 AP102 27fr multicolored   12.00 8.50

EPICA Program AP103

1998, Jan. 2   Engr.   Perf. 13
C145 AP103 5.20fr dk brn & lil   2.50 1.40

First Radio Meteorological Station, Port Aux Francais — AP104

1998, Jan. 2
C146 AP104 8fr black, blue & red   4.25 2.25

King Penguin, Argos Satellite — AP105

1998, Jan. 2   Perf. 12½x13
C147 AP105 16fr multicolored   7.00 4.75

Ranunculus Moseleyi — AP106

1998, Jan. 2
C148 AP106 24fr multicolored   10.50 6.50

Intl. Geophysical Year, 40th Anniv. — AP107

1998, Oct.   Engr.   Perf. 13x12½
C149 AP107 5.20fr dk bl, blk & brick red   3.00 1.50

FRENCH SUDAN

'french sü-'dan

LOCATION — In northwest Africa, north of French Guinea and Ivory Coast
GOVT. — French Colony
AREA — 590,966 sq. mi.
POP. — 3,794,270 (1941)
CAPITAL — Bamako

In 1899 French Sudan was abolished as a separate colony and was divided among Dahomey, French Guinea, Ivory Coast, Senegal and Senegambia and Niger. Issues for French Sudan were resumed in 1921.

From 1906 to 1921 a part of this territory was known as Upper Senegal and Niger. A part of Upper Volta was added in 1933. See Mali.

100 Centimes = 1 Franc

See French West Africa No. 70 for stamp inscribed "Soudan Francais" and "Afrique Occidentale Francaise."

French Colonies Nos. 58-59 Srchd. in Black

Perf. 14x13½
1894, Apr. 12   **Unwmk.**
1 A9 15c on 75c car, *rose*   4,600. 2,300.
2 A9 25c on 1fr brnz grn, *straw*   5,000. 1,700.

The imperforate stamp like No. 1 was made privately in Paris from a fragment of the lithographic stone which had been used in the Colony for surcharging No. 1.
Counterfeit surcharges exist.

Navigation and Commerce — A2

1894-1900   Typo.   Perf. 14x13½
Name of colony in Blue or Carmine
3	A2	1c blk, *lil bl*	1.60	2.00
4	A2	2c brn, *buff*	2.40	2.75
5	A2	4c claret, *lav*	8.00	6.50
6	A2	5c grn, *grnsh*	12.00	12.00
7	A2	10c blk, *lav*	24.00	24.00
8	A2	10c red ('00)	8.00	8.00
9	A2	15c blue, quadrille paper	8.00	8.00
10	A2	15c gray, *lt gray* ('00)	8.00	8.00
11	A2	20c red, *grn*	40.00	35.00
12	A2	25c blk, *rose*	32.50	27.50
13	A2	25c blue ('00)	8.00	8.75
14	A2	30c brn, *bister*	40.00	40.00
15	A2	40c red, *straw*	40.00	35.00
16	A2	50c car, *rose*	55.00	65.00
17	A2	50c brn, *az* ('00)	16.00	16.00
18	A2	75c dp vio, *org*	55.00	55.00
19	A2	1fr brnz grn, *straw*	12.00	12.00
		Nos. 3-19 (17)	370.50	365.50

Perf. 13½x14 stamps are counterfeits.
Nos. 8, 10, 13, 17 were issued in error. They were accepted for use in the other colonies.

Stamps and Types of Upper Senegal and Niger, 1914-17, Overprinted

1921-30   **Perf. 13½x14**
21	A4	1c brn vio & vio	.25	.40
22	A4	2c dk gray & ul vio	.30	.50
23	A4	4c blk & blue	.30	.50
24	A4	5c ol brn & dk brn	.30	.40
25	A4	10c yel grn & bl grn	.90	.55
26	A4	10c red vio & bl ('25)	.40	.50
27	A4	15c red brn & org	.50	.55
28	A4	15c yel grn & dp grn ('25)	.40	.40
29	A4	15c org brn & vio ('27)	1.60	1.60
30	A4	20c brn vio & blk	.50	.55
31	A4	25c blk & bl grn	1.25	.80
a.		Booklet pane of 4		
		Complete booklet, 5 #31a	650.00	
		Complete booklet, overprint omitted on one pane	16,000.	
32	A4	30c red org & rose	1.60	1.60
33	A4	30c bl grn & blk ('26)	.80	.70
34	A4	30c dl grn & bl grn ('28)	2.00	2.00
35	A4	35c rose & vio	.40	.55
36	A4	40c gray & rose	1.25	1.25
37	A4	45c bl & ol brn	1.25	1.25
38	A4	50c ultra & bl	1.60	1.25
39	A4	50c red org & bl ('26)	1.25	1.25
40	A4	60c vio, *pnksh* ('26)	1.25	1.25
41	A4	65c bis & pale bl ('28)	1.60	1.60
42	A4	75c org & ol brn	1.60	2.00
43	A4	90c brn red & pink ('30)	5.50	5.50
44	A4	1fr dk brn & dl vio	1.60	2.00
45	A4	1.10fr gray lil & red vio ('28)	3.25	4.00
46	A4	1.50fr dp bl & bl	5.50	5.50
47	A4	2fr grn & bl	2.40	2.75
48	A4	3fr red vio ('30)	12.00	12.00
a.		Double overprint	190.00	
49	A4	5fr vio & blk	8.00	7.25
		Nos. 21-49 (29)	59.55	60.45

Type of 1921 Surcharged

1922, Sept. 28
50 A4 60c on 75c vio, *pnksh*   .80 .80

Stamps and Type of 1921-30 Surcharged

1925-27
51	A4	25c on 45c	.80	.80
52	A4	65c on 75c	2.00	2.40
53	A4	85c on 2fr	2.00	2.40
54	A4	85c on 5fr	2.00	2.40
55	A4	90c on 75c brn red & sal pink ('27)	2.40	2.75
56	A4	1.25fr on 1fr dp bl & lt bl (R) ('26)	1.25	1.60
57	A4	1.50fr on 1fr dp bl & ultra ('27)	1.60	1.60
58	A4	3fr on 5fr dl red & brn org ('27)	6.50	5.50
59	A4	10fr on 5fr brn red & bl grn ('27)	24.00	21.00
60	A4	20fr on 5fr vio & ver ('27)	29.00	29.00
		Nos. 51-60 (10)	71.55	69.85

Sudanese Woman A4

Entrance to the Residency at Djenné A5

Sudanese Boatman — A6

1931-40   Typo.   Perf. 13x14
61	A4	1c dk red & blk	.25	.25
62	A4	2c dp blue & org	.25	.25
63	A4	3c dk red & blk ('40)	.25	.25
64	A4	4c gray lil & rose	.25	.25
65	A4	5c indigo & grn	.25	.25
66	A4	10c ol grn & rose	.25	.25
67	A4	15c blk & brt vio	.40	.30
68	A4	20c hn brn & lt bl	.40	.30
69	A4	25c red vio & lt red	.40	.30
70	A5	30c grn & lt grn	.80	.50
71	A5	30c dk bl & red org ('40)	.30	.30
72	A5	35c ol grn & grn ('38)	.40	.40
73	A5	40c ol grn & pink	.40	.30
74	A5	45c dk bl & red org	1.20	.65
75	A5	45c ol grn & grn ('40)	.50	.50

FRENCH SUDAN — FRENCH WEST AFRICA

76	A5	50c red & black	.40	.30
77	A5	55c ultra & car ('38)	.40	.40
78	A5	60c brt bl & brn ('40)	1.20	1.20
79	A5	65c brt vio & blk	.80	.55
80	A5	70c vio bl & car rose ('40)	.80	.80
81	A5	75c brt bl & ol brn	2.40	2.00
82	A5	80c car & brn ('38)	.80	.80
83	A5	90c dp red & red org	1.60	.80
84	A5	90c brt vio & sl blk ('39)	.90	1.00
85	A5	1fr indigo & grn	8.00	2.40
86	A5	1fr rose red ('38)	5.50	1.60
87	A5	1fr car & brn ('40)	.80	.80
88	A6	1.25fr vio & dl vio ('33)	.80	.80
89	A6	1.25fr red ('39)	.90	1.00
90	A6	1.40fr brt vio & blk ('40)	.90	.90
91	A6	1.50fr dk bl & ultra	.80	.55
92	A6	1.60fr brn & dp bl ('40)	.90	.90
93	A6	1.75fr dk brn & dp bl ('33)	.80	.80
94	A6	1.75fr vio bl ('38)	.80	.80
95	A6	2fr org brn & grn	.80	.55
96	A6	2.25fr vio bl & ultra ('39)	1.00	1.10
97	A6	2.50fr lt brown ('40)	1.60	1.60
98	A6	3fr Prus grn & brn	.80	.40
99	A6	5fr red & blk	2.00	1.20
100	A6	10fr dull bl & grn	2.40	2.00
101	A6	20fr red vio & brn	3.25	2.40
		Nos. 61-101 (41)	47.65	32.70

For surcharges see Nos. B7-B10.
For 10c and 30c, without "RF," see Nos. 120-121.

Common Design Types pictured following the introduction.

Colonial Exposition Issue
Common Design Types

1931, Apr. 13   Engr.   Perf. 12½
Name of Country Printed in Black

102	CD70	40c deep green	4.75	4.75
103	CD71	50c violet	4.75	4.75
104	CD72	90c red orange	4.75	4.75
105	CD73	1.50fr dull blue	4.75	4.75
		Set, never hinged		29.00

Paris International Exposition Issue
Common Design Types

1937, Apr. 15   Perf. 13

106	CD74	20c deep violet	2.00	2.00
107	CD75	30c dark green	2.00	2.00
108	CD76	40c car rose	2.40	2.40
109	CD77	50c dark brown	1.60	1.60
110	CD78	90c red	1.60	1.60
111	CD79	1.50fr ultra	2.40	2.40
		Nos. 106-111 (6)	12.00	12.00
		Set, never hinged		20.25

Colonial Arts Exhibition Issue
Souvenir Sheet
Common Design Type

1937   Engr.   Imperf.

112	CD77	3fr magenta & blk	12.00	16.00
		Never hinged	16.00	

Caillie Issue
Common Design Type

1939, Apr. 5   Perf. 12½x12

113	CD81	90c org brn & org	.40	.80
114	CD81	2fr brt violet	1.20	1.20
115	CD81	2.25fr ultra & dk bl	.40	1.20
		Nos. 113-115 (3)	1.20	3.20
		Set, never hinged		2.40

New York World's Fair Issue
Common Design Type

1939, May 10

116	CD82	1.25fr car lake	.80	1.60
117	CD82	2.25fr ultra	.80	1.60
		Set, never hinged		2.40

Entrance to the Residency at Djenné and Marshal Pétain — A7

1941   Engr.   Perf. 12x12½

118	A7	1fr green	.40	—
119	A7	2.50fr blue	.40	—
		Set, never hinged	1.60	

For surcharges, see Nos. B14-B15.

Types of 1931-40 without "RF"

1943-44   Typo.   Perf. 13½x14

120	A4	10c ol green & rose		.65
121	A5	30c dk bl & red org		.95
		Set, never hinged		2.00

Nos. 120-121 were issued by the Vichy government in France, but were not placed on sale in French Sudan.

Stamps of French Sudan were superseded by those of French West Africa.

SEMI-POSTAL STAMPS

Curie Issue
Common Design Type
Unwmk.

1938, Oct. 24   Engr.   Perf. 13

B1	CD80	1.75fr + 50c brt ultra	12.50	12.50
		Never hinged	21.00	

French Revolution Issue
Common Design Type

1939, July 5   Photo.
Name and Value Typo. in Black

B2	CD83	45c + 25c green	10.00	10.00
B3	CD83	70c + 35c dk brown	10.00	10.00
B4	CD83	90c + 35c red org	10.00	10.00
B5	CD83	1.25fr + 1fr rose pink	10.00	10.00
B6	CD83	2.25fr + 2fr blue	10.00	10.00
		Nos. B2-B6 (5)	50.00	50.00
		Set, never hinged	87.50	

Stamps of 1931-40, Surcharged in Black or Red

1941   Perf. 13x14

B7	A5	50c + 1fr red & blk (R)	4.00	4.00
B8	A5	80c + 2fr car & brn	8.00	8.00
B9	A6	1.50fr + 2fr dk bl & ultra	8.00	8.00
B10	A6	2fr + 3fr org brn & grn	8.00	8.00
		Nos. B7-B10 (4)	28.00	28.00
		Set, never hinged	55.00	

Common Design Type and

Native Officer SP1   Aviation Officer SP2

1941   Photo.   Perf. 13½

B11	SP1	1fr + 1fr red		1.25
B12	CD86	1.50fr + 3fr claret		1.40
B13	SP2	2.50fr + 1fr blue		1.40
		Nos. B11-B13 (3)		4.05
		Set, never hinged		5.50

Surtax for the defense of the colonies. Issued by the Vichy government in France, but not placed on sale in French Sudan.

Petain type of 1941 Surcharged in Black or Red

1944   Engr.   Perf. 12x12½

B14		50c + 1.50fr on 2.50fr deep blue (R)		.40
B15		+ 2.50fr on 1fr green		.40
		Set, never hinged		1.60

Colonial Development Fund.

Nos. B14-B15 were issued by the Vichy government in France, but were not placed on sale in French Sudan.

AIR POST STAMPS

Common Design Type
Perf. 12½x12

1940, Feb. 8   Unwmk.   Engr.

C1	CD85	1.90fr ultra	.40	.40
C2	CD85	2.90fr dark red	.40	.40
C3	CD85	4.50fr dk gray green	.80	.80
C4	CD85	4.90fr yellow bister	.80	.80
C5	CD85	6.90fr deep orange	1.60	1.60
		Nos. C1-C5 (5)	4.00	4.00
		Set, never hinged	5.20	

Common Design Types

1942, Oct. 19

C6	CD88	50c carmine & bl	.40	—
C7	CD88	1fr brown & blk	.40	
C8	CD88	2fr dk grn & red brn	.80	
C9	CD88	3fr dk blue & scar	.80	
C10	CD88	5fr vio & brn red	.80	

Frame Engr., Center Typo.

C11	CD89	10fr ultra, ind & gray blk	1.20	
C12	CD89	20fr rose car, mag & lt vio	1.60	
C13	CD89	50fr yel grn, dl grn & dl bl	2.00	
		Nos. C6-C13 (8)	8.00	
		Set, never hinged	12.00	

There is doubt whether Nos. C7-C12 were officially placed in use.

AIR POST SEMI-POSTAL STAMPS

Maternity Hospital, Dakar SPAP1

Dispensary, Mopti SPAP2

Nurse Weighing Baby SPAP3

Perf. 13½x12½, 13 (#CB3)
Photo, Engr. (#CB3)

1942, June 22

CB1	SPAP1	1.50fr + 3.50fr grn	.40	5.50
CB2	SPAP2	2fr + 6fr brown	.40	5.50
CB3	SPAP3	3fr + 9fr car red	.40	5.50
		Nos. CB1-CB3 (3)	1.20	16.50
		Set, never hinged	2.40	

Native children's welfare fund.

Colonial Education Fund
Common Design Type
Perf. 12½x13½

1942, June 22   Engr.

CB4	CD86a	1.20fr + 1.80fr blue & red	.40	5.50
		Never hinged	.80	

POSTAGE DUE STAMPS

Upper Senegal and Niger Postage Due Stamps Overprinted

Perf. 14x13½

1921, Dec.   Unwmk.   Typo.

J1	D1	5c green	.40	.40
J2	D1	10c rose	.40	.40
J3	D1	15c gray	.40	.80
J4	D1	20c brown	1.20	1.20
J5	D1	30c blue	1.20	1.20
J6	D1	50c black	2.00	2.40
J7	D1	60c orange	2.40	2.40
J8	D1	1fr violet	2.40	3.25
		Nos. J1-J8 (8)	10.40	12.05

Type of 1921 Issue Surcharged

1927, Oct. 10

J9	D1	2fr on 1fr lilac rose	8.00	8.00
J10	D1	3fr on 1fr org brown	8.00	8.00

D2

1931, Mar. 9

J11	D2	5c green	.25	.30
J12	D2	10c rose	.25	.30
J13	D2	15c gray	.25	.50
J14	D2	20c dark brown	.25	.50
J15	D2	30c dark blue	.40	.55
J16	D2	50c black	.40	.55
J17	D2	60c deep orange	.80	.80
J18	D2	1fr violet	1.20	1.20
J19	D2	2fr lilac rose	1.60	1.60
J20	D2	3fr red brown	1.60	1.60
		Nos. J11-J20 (10)	7.00	7.90

FRENCH WEST AFRICA

ˈfrench ˈwest ˈa-fri-kə

LOCATION — Northwestern Africa
GOVT. — French colonial administrative unit
AREA — 1,821,768 sq. mi.
POP. — 18,777,163 (est.)
CAPITAL — Dakar

French West Africa comprised the former colonies of Senegal, French Guinea, Ivory Coast, Dahomey, French Sudan, Mauritania, Niger and Upper Volta.

In 1958, these former colonies became republics, eventually issuing their own stamps. Until the republic issues appeared, stamps of French West Africa continued in use. The Senegal and Sudanese Republics issued stamps jointly as the Federation of Mali, starting in 1959.

> Catalogue values for all unused stamps in this country are for Never Hinged items.

Many stamps other than Nos. 65-72 and 77 are inscribed "Afrique Occidentale Francaise" and the name of one of the former colonies. See listings in these colonies for such stamps.

Senegal No. 156 Surcharged in Red

1943   Unwmk.   Perf. 12½x12

1	A30	1.50fr on 65c dk vio	1.20	.90
2	A30	5.50fr on 65c dk vio	1.60	1.60
3	A30	50fr on 65c dk vio	4.00	2.00

Mauritania No. 91 Surcharged in Red

1943   Perf. 13

4	A7	3.50fr on 65c dp grn	.80	.40
5	A7	4fr on 65c dp grn	.80	.40
6	A7	5fr on 9fr car red	1.60	.80
7	A7	10fr on 65c dp grn	1.60	.80
		Nos. 1-7 (7)	11.60	6.10

FRENCH WEST AFRICA

Senegal No. 143, 148 and 188 Surcharged with New Values in Black and Orange

1944			Perf. 12½x12	
8	A29	1.50fr on 15c blk (O)	.80	.65
9	A29	4.50fr on 15c blk (O)	1.20	.90
10	A29	5.50fr on 2c brn	2.40	1.60
11	A29	10fr on 15c blk (O)	4.00	1.75
12	CD81	20fr on 90c org brn & org	2.40	1.75
13	CD81	50fr on 90c org brn & org	6.50	3.25

Mauritania No. 109 Surcharged in Black

14	CD81	15fr on 90c org brn & org	2.40	1.60
		Nos. 8-14 (7)	19.70	11.50

Common Design Types pictured following the introduction.

Eboue Issue
Common Design Type

1945		Engr.	Perf. 13	
15	CD91	2fr black	.80	.80
16	CD91	25fr Prussian green	1.60	1.60

Nos. 15 and 16 exist imperforate.

Colonial Soldier — A1

1945		Litho.	Perf. 12½x12, 12	
17	A1	10c indigo & buff	.40	.25
18	A1	30c olive & yel	.40	.25
19	A1	40c blue & buff	.40	.25
20	A1	50c red org & gray	.40	.25
21	A1	60c ol brn & bl	.80	.40
22	A1	70c mag & cit	.80	.40
23	A1	80c bl grn & pale lem	.80	.40
24	A1	1fr brn vio & cit	.80	.40
25	A1	1.20fr gray brn & cit	4.00	2.40
26	A1	1.50fr choc & pink	.80	.40
27	A1	2fr ocher and gray	.80	.40
28	A1	2.40fr red & gray	1.25	.40
29	A1	3fr brn red & yelsh	.80	.40
30	A1	4fr ultra & pink	.80	.40
31	A1	4.50fr org brn & yelsh	.80	.40
32	A1	5fr dk pur & yelsh	.80	.40
33	A1	10fr ol grn & pink	1.60	.80
34	A1	15fr orange & yel	2.40	1.20
35	A1	20fr sl grn & grnsh	2.75	2.00
		Nos. 17-35 (19)	21.60	12.20

Rifle Dance, Mauritania — A2

Bamako Dike, French Sudan — A3

Trading Canoe, Niger River — A4

Oasis of Bilma, Niger — A5

Shelling Coconuts, Togo — A6

Kouandé Weaving, Dahomey — A7

Donkey Caravan, Senegal — A8

Crocodile and Hippopotamus, Ivory Coast — A9

Gathering Coconuts, French Guinea — A10

Bamako Fountain, French Sudan — A11

Peul Woman of Dienné — A12

Bamako Market — A13

Dahomey Laborer — A14

Woman of Mauritania — A15

Fula Woman, French Guinea — A16

Djenné Mosque, French Sudan — A17

Monorail Train, Senegal — A18

Agni Woman, Ivory Coast — A19

Azwa Women at Niger River — A20

1947		Engr. Unwmk.	Perf. 12½	
36	A2	10c blue	.40	.25
37	A3	30c red brn	.40	.25
38	A4	40c gray grn	.40	.25
39	A5	50c red brn	.40	.25
40	A6	60c gray blk	.80	.50
41	A7	80c brown vio	.80	.50
42	A8	1fr maroon	.80	.30
43	A9	1.20fr dk blue grn	2.00	1.40
44	A10	1.50fr ultra	2.00	1.10
45	A11	2fr red orange	.80	.25
46	A12	3fr chocolate	.80	.30
47	A13	3.60fr brown red	1.60	1.40
48	A14	4fr deep blue	.80	.30
49	A15	5fr gray green	.40	.25
50	A16	6fr dark blue	.80	.30
51	A17	10fr brn red	.80	.30
52	A18	15fr sepia	2.40	.30
53	A19	20fr chocolate	1.60	.30
54	A20	25fr grnsh blk	2.40	.50
		Nos. 36-54 (19)	20.40	8.95

Types of 1947

1948		Re-engraved		
55	A6	60c brown olive	1.20	.80
56	A12	3fr chocolate	1.20	.55

Nos. 40 and 46 are inscribed "TOGO" in lower margin. Inscription omitted on Nos. 55 and 56.

Imperforates
Most stamps of French West Africa from 1949 onward exist imperforate in issued and trial colors, and also in small presentation sheets in issued colors.

Military Medal Issue
Common Design Type

1952, Dec. 1	Engraved and Typographed	Perf. 13	
57 CD101 15fr multicolored		8.75	6.50

Treich Laplène and Map — A21

1952, Dec. 1		Engr.	
58 A21 40fr brown lake		2.40	.40

Marcel Treich Laplène, a leading contributor to the development of Ivory Coast.

Medical Laboratory — A22

1953, Nov. 18			
59 A22 15fr brn, dk bl grn & blk brn		1.60	.40

Couple Feeding Antelopes — A23

1954, Sept. 20			
60 A23 25fr multicolored		2.00	.40

Gov. Noel Eugène Ballay — A24

1954, Nov. 29			
61 A24 8fr indigo & brown		2.00	.80

Chimpanzee A25

Giant Pangolin A26

1955, May 2	Unwmk.	Perf. 13	
62 A25 5fr dp vio & dk brn		2.00	.80
63 A26 8fr brn & bl grn		2.00	.80

International Exhibition for Wildlife Protection, Paris, May 1955.

Map, Symbols of Industry, Rotary Emblem — A27

1955, July 4			
64 A27 15fr dark blue		2.40	.80

50th anniv. of the founding of Rotary Intl.

FIDES Issue
Common Design Type

Designs: 1fr, Date grove, Mauritania. 2fr, Milo Bridge, French Guinea. 3fr, Mossi Railroad, Upper Volta. 4fr, Cattle raising, Niger. 15fr, Farm machinery and landscape, Senegal. 17fr, Woman and Niger River, French Sudan. 20fr, Palm oil production, Dahomey. 30fr, Road construction, Ivory Coast.

1956		Engr.	Perf. 13x12½	
65	CD103	1fr dk grn & dk grn	1.60	.65
66	CD103	2fr dk bl grn & bl	1.60	.65
67	CD103	3fr dk brn & red brn	1.60	1.00
68	CD103	4fr dk car rose	2.40	1.10
69	CD103	15fr ind & ultra	1.60	.55
70	CD103	17fr dk bl & ind	2.40	.75
71	CD103	20fr rose lake	2.40	.65
72	CD103	30fr dk pur & claret	2.40	1.00
		Nos. 65-72 (8)	16.00	6.35

Coffee — A28a

1956, Oct. 22		Perf. 13	
73 A28a 15fr dk blue green		1.60	.80

Mobile Leprosy Clinic and Maltese Cross — A29

1957, Mar. 11			
74 A29 15fr dk red brn, pur & red		2.40	.80

Issued in honor of the Knights of Malta.

Map of Africa — A30

1958, Feb.	Unwmk.	Perf. 13	
75 A30 20fr multicolored		1.60	.80

6h Intl.Cong. for African Tourism at Dakar.

"Africa" and Communications Symbols — A31

1958, Mar. 15		Engr.	
76 A31 15fr org, ultra & choc		2.00	.80

Stamp Day. See No. 86.

Abidjan Bridge — A32

1958, Mar. 15			
77 A32 20fr dk sl grn & grnsh bl		2.00	.80

Bananas — A33

1958, May 19		Perf. 13	
78 A33 20fr rose lil, dk grn & ol		1.60	.40

FRENCH WEST AFRICA — FUJEIRA

Flower Issue
Common Design Type
10fr, Gloriosa. 25fr, Adenopus. 30fr, Cyrtosperma. 40fr, Cistanche. 65fr, Crinum Moorei.

1958-59		Photo.		Perf. 12x12½	
79	CD104	10fr multicolored		1.20	.40
80	CD104	25fr red, yel & grn		1.60	.80
81	CD104	30fr multicolored		2.00	1.20
82	CD104	40fr blk brn, grn & yel		2.40	1.60
83	CD104	65fr multicolored		3.25	1.60
		Nos. 79-83 (5)		10.45	5.60

Issued: 25fr, 40fr, 1/5/59; others, 7/7/58.

Moro Naba Sagha and Map — A34

1958, Nov. 1		Engr.	Perf. 13	
84	A34	20fr ol brn, car & vio	1.60	.80

10th anniv. of the reestablishment of the Upper Volta territory.

Human Rights Issue
Common Design Type

1958, Dec. 10				
85	CD105	20fr maroon & dk bl	2.40	2.00

Type of 1958 Redrawn

1959, Mar. 21		Engr.	Perf. 13	
86	A31	20fr red, grnsh bl & sl grn	2.75	2.40

Name of country omitted on No. 86; "RF" replaced by "CF," inscribed "Dakar-Abidjan." Stamp Day.

SEMI-POSTAL STAMPS

Red Cross Issue
Common Design Type
Perf. 14½x14

1944, Dec.		Photo.	Unwmk.	
B1	CD90	5fr + 20fr plum	6.50	4.75

The surtax was for the French Red Cross and national relief.

Type of France, 1945, Overprinted in Black

1945, Oct. 13		Engr.	Perf. 13	
B2	SP150	2fr + 3fr orange red	1.20	.80

Tropical Medicine Issue
Common Design Type

1950, May 15			Perf. 13	
B3	CD100	10fr +2fr red brn & sep	9.50	7.25

The surtax was for charitable work.

AIR POST STAMPS

Common Design Type

1945	Photo.	Unwmk.	Perf. 14½x14	
C1	CD87	5.50fr ultra	2.00	1.00
C2	CD87	50fr dark green	3.50	1.40
C3	CD87	100fr plum	4.00	1.50
		Nos. C1-C3 (3)	9.50	3.90

Victory Issue
Common Design Type

1946, May 8		Engr.	Perf. 12½	
C4	CD92	8fr violet	1.60	1.20

Chad to Rhine Issue
Common Design Types

1946, June 6				
C5	CD93	5fr brown car	2.00	1.60
C6	CD94	10fr deep blue	2.00	1.60
C7	CD95	15fr brt violet	2.40	1.60
C8	CD96	20fr dk slate grn	2.40	2.00
C9	CD97	25fr olive brn	3.25	2.40
C10	CD98	50fr brown	4.00	2.75
		Nos. C5-C10 (6)	16.05	11.95

Antoine de Saint-Exupéry, Map and Natives — AP1

Plane over Dakar AP2

Great White Egrets in Flight AP3

Natives and Phantom Plane AP4

1947, Mar. 24			Engr.	
C11	AP1	8fr red brown	1.60	.80
C12	AP2	50fr rose violet	4.00	1.20
C13	AP3	100fr ultra	16.00	4.75
C14	AP4	200fr slate gray	14.00	5.25
		Nos. C11-C14 (4)	35.60	12.00

UPU Issue
Common Design Type

1949, July 4			Perf. 13	
C15	CD99	25fr multicolored	12.00	8.75

Vridi Canal, Abidjan AP5

1951, Nov. 5		Unwmk.	Perf. 13	
C16	AP5	500fr red org, bl grn & dp ultra	32.50	4.75

Liberation Issue
Common Design Type

1954, June 6				
C17	CD102	15fr indigo & ultra	12.00	5.50

Logging AP6

Designs: 100fr, Radiotelephone exchange. 200fr, Baobab trees.

1954, Sept. 20				
C18	AP6	50fr ol grn & org brn	4.00	.80
C19	AP6	100fr ind, dk brn & dk grn	6.50	1.20
C20	AP6	200fr bl grn, grnsh blk & brn lake	17.50	2.75
		Nos. C18-C20 (3)	28.00	4.75

Gen. Louis Faidherbé and African Sharpshooter — AP7

1957, July 20		Unwmk.	Perf. 13	
C21	AP7	15fr indigo & blue	2.00	1.60

Centenary of French African troops.

Gorée Island and Woman AP8

Designs: 20fr, Map with planes and ships. 25fr, Village and modern city. 40fr, Seat of Council of French West Africa. 50fr, Worker, ship and peanut plant. 100fr, Bay of N'Gor.

1958, Mar. 15			Engr.	
C22	AP8	15fr blk brn, grn & vio	1.60	.80
C23	AP8	20fr blk brn, dk bl & red brn	1.60	.80
C24	AP8	25fr blk vio, bis & grn	1.60	1.20
C25	AP8	40fr dk bl, brn & grn	1.60	1.20
C26	AP8	50fr violet, brn & grn	3.25	1.60
C27	AP8	100fr brown, bl & grn	6.50	2.40
a.		Souvenir sheet of 6, #C22-C27	20.00	16.00
		Nos. C22-C27 (6)	16.15	8.00

Centenary of Dakar.

Woman Playing Native Harp — AP9

1958, Dec. 1		Unwmk.	Perf. 13	
C28	AP9	20fr red brn, blk & gray	1.60	.80

Inauguration of Nouakchott as capital of Mauritania.

POSTAGE DUE STAMPS

D1

1947		Engr.	Unwmk.	Perf. 13	
J1	D1	10c red		.40	.25
J2	D1	30c deep orange		.40	.25
J3	D1	50c greenish blk		.40	.25
J4	D1	1fr carmine		.40	.25
J5	D1	2fr emerald		.50	.30
J6	D1	3fr red lilac		.90	.65
J7	D1	4fr deep ultra		1.10	.80
J8	D1	5fr red brown		2.25	1.60
J9	D1	10fr peacock blue		2.90	2.25
J10	D1	20fr sepia		5.25	3.75
		Nos. J1-J10 (10)		14.50	10.35

OFFICIAL STAMPS

Mask — O1

Designs: Various masks.

Perf. 14x13

1958, June 2		Typo.	Unwmk.	
O1	O1	1fr dk brn red	1.10	1.00
O2	O1	3fr brt green	.65	.55
O3	O1	5fr crim rose	.65	.50
O4	O1	10fr light ultra	.80	.65
O5	O1	20fr bright red	1.60	.80
O6	O1	25fr purple	1.60	.80
O7	O1	30fr green	2.75	1.60
O8	O1	45fr gray black	3.25	1.60
O9	O1	50fr dark red	3.25	1.60
O10	O1	65fr brt ultra	4.50	1.60
O11	O1	100fr olive bister	10.50	2.75
O12	O1	200fr deep green	21.00	5.50
		Nos. O1-O12 (12)	51.65	18.95

FUJEIRA

fü-ˈjī-rə

LOCATION — Oman Peninsula, Arabia, on Persian Gulf
GOVT. — Sheikdom under British protection

Fujeira is one of six Persian Gulf sheikdoms to join the United Arab Emirates which proclaimed independence Dec. 2, 1971. See United Arab Emirates.

100 Naye Paise = 1 Rupee

Catalogue values for all unused stamps in this country are for Never Hinged items.

Sheik Hamad bin Mohammed al Sharqi and Grebe — A1

Sheik and: 2np, 50np, Arabian oryx. 3np, 70np, Hoopoe. 4np, 1r, Wild ass. 5np, 1.50r, Herons in flight. 10np, 2r, Arabian horses. 15np, 3r, Leopard. 20np, 5r, Camels. 30np, 10r, Hawks.

1964		Photo. & Litho. Unwmk.	Perf. 14	
		Size: 36x24mm		
1	A1	1np gold & multi	.25	.25
2	A1	2np gold & multi	.25	.25
3	A1	3np gold & multi	.25	.25
4	A1	4np gold & multi	.25	.25
5	A1	5np gold & multi	.25	.25
6	A1	10np gold & multi	.25	.25
7	A1	15np gold & multi	.25	.25
8	A1	20np gold & multi	.25	.25
9	A1	30np gold & multi	.25	.25
		Size: 43x28mm		
10	A1	40np gold & multi	.35	.25
11	A1	50np gold & multi	.40	.25
12	A1	70np gold & multi	.45	.25
13	A1	1r gold & multi	.65	.25
14	A1	1.50r gold & multi	.95	.25
15	A1	2r gold & multi	1.50	.25
		Size: 53½x35mm		
16	A1	3r gold & multi	2.40	.25
17	A1	5r gold & multi	2.25	.35
18	A1	10r gold & multi	7.50	.50
		Nos. 1-18 (18)	18.70	4.85

Issued: 20np, 30np, 70np, 1.50r, 3r, 10r, Nov. 14; others, Sept. 22.
Exist imperf. Value, set $30.

Sheik Hamad and Shot Put — A2

1964, Dec. 6			Perf. 14	
		Size: 43x28mm		
19	A2	25np shown	.25	.25
20	A2	50np Discus	.25	.25
21	A2	75np Fencing	.25	.25
22	A2	1r Boxing	.35	.30
23	A2	1.50r Relay race	.50	.35
24	A2	2r Soccer	.60	.40
		Size: 53½x35mm		
25	A2	3r Pole vaulting	1.15	.50
26	A2	5r Hurdling	3.00	.75
27	A2	7.50r Equestrian	4.25	.90
		Nos. 19-27 (9)	10.60	3.95

18th Olympic Games, Tokyo, 10/10-25/64.
Exist imperf. Value, set $12.

John F. Kennedy — A3

Kennedy: 10np, As sailor in the Pacific. 15np, As naval lieutenant. 20np, On speaker's rostrum. 25np, Sailing with family. 50np, With crowd of people. 1r, With Mrs. Kennedy, Lyndon B. Johnson. 2r, With Eisenhower on White House porch. 3r, With Mrs. Kennedy & Caroline. 5r, Portrait.

FUJEIRA — FUNCHAL

1965, Feb. 23   Photo.   Perf. 13½
Size: 29x44mm
Black Design with Gold Inscriptions

28	A3	5np pale gray	.25	.25
29	A3	10np pale yellow	.25	.25
30	A3	15np pink	.25	.25
31	A3	20np pale greenish gray	.25	.25
32	A3	25np pale blue	.25	.25
33	A3	50np pale rose	.30	.25

Size: 33x51mm

34	A3	1r pale gray	.75	.30
35	A3	2r pale green	1.25	.40
36	A3	3r pale gray	2.50	.50
37	A3	5r pale yellow	3.25	.80
		Nos. 28-37 (10)	9.30	3.50

Pres. John F. Kennedy (1917-1963). A souvenir sheet contains 2 29x44mm stamps similar to Nos. 36-37 with pale blue (3r) and pale rose (5r) backgrounds. Value (unused): perf $7; imperf $9.

Nos. 28-37 exist imperf. Value $14.

AIR POST STAMPS

Wild Ass — AP1

Photo. & Litho.
1965, Aug. 16   Unwmk.   Perf. 13½
Size: 43x28mm

C1	AP1	15np Grebe	.25	.25
C2	AP1	25np Arabian oryx	.25	.25
C3	AP1	35np Hoopoe	.35	.25
C4	AP1	50np Wild ass	.40	.25
C5	AP1	75np Herons in flight	.45	.25
C6	AP1	1r Arabian horses	.60	.25

Size: 53½x35mm

C7	AP1	2r Leopard	1.25	.25
C8	AP1	3r Camels	2.50	.25
C9	AP1	5r Hawks	4.50	.50
		Nos. C1-C9 (9)	10.55	2.50

Exist imperf. Value, set $11.

AIR POST OFFICIAL STAMPS

Type of Air Post Issue, 1965
Photo. & Litho.
1965, Nov. 10   Unwmk.   Perf. 13½
Size: 43x28mm

CO1	AP1	75np Arabian horses	.60	.25

Perf. 13
Size: 53½x35mm

CO2	AP1	2r Leopard	1.50	.40
CO3	AP1	3r Camels	2.50	.60
CO4	AP1	5r Hawks	4.50	1.00
		Nos. CO1-CO4 (4)	9.10	2.25

Exist imperf. Values same as perf.

OFFICIAL STAMPS

Type of Air Post Issue, 1965
Photo. & Litho.
1965, Oct. 14   Unwmk.   Perf. 13½
Size: 43x28mm

O1	AP1	25np Grebe	.25	.25
O2	AP1	40np Arabian oryx	.25	.25
O3	AP1	50np Hoopoe	.35	.25
O4	AP1	75np Wild ass	.55	.25
O5	AP1	1r Herons in flight	1.25	.25
		Nos. O1-O5 (5)	2.65	1.25

Exist imperf. Values same as perf.

FUNCHAL

fün-'shäl

LOCATION — A city and administrative district in the Madeira island group in the Atlantic Ocean northwest of Africa

GOVT. — A part of the Republic of Portugal

POP. — 150,574 (1900)

Postage stamps of Funchal were superseded by those of Portugal.

1000 Reis = 1 Milreis

King Carlos — A1

1892-93   Typo.   Unwmk.
Perf. 11½, 12½, 13½

1	A1	5r yellow	4.25	2.00
2	A1	10r red violet	4.25	2.00
3	A1	15r chocolate	5.50	3.75
4	A1	20r lavender	5.50	3.00
5a	A1	25r dark green	8.00	1.75
6	A1	50r ultramarine	10.25	5.00
7	A1	75r carmine	10.25	6.75
8	A1	80r yellow green	20.00	12.00
9	A1	100r brn, yel ('93)	13.50	5.50
10	A1	150r car, rose ('93)	70.00	31.00
11	A1	200r dk bl, bl ('93)	80.00	15.00
12	A1	300r dk bl, sal ('93)	80.00	55.00
		Nos. 1-12 (12)	311.50	172.75

Nos. 1-12 were printed on both enamel-surfaced and chalky papers. Values are for the most common varieties. For detailed listings, see the Scott Classic Specialized Catalogue.

The reprints of this issue have shiny white gum and clean-cut perforation 13½. The shades differ from those of the originals and the uncolored paper is thin.

King Carlos — A2

Name and Value in Black except Nos. 25 and 34

1897-1905   Perf. 11¾

13	A2	2½r gray	.60	.60
a.		Name and denomination inverted	275.00	
14	A2	5r orange	.60	.60
15	A2	10r light green	.60	.60
16	A2	15r brown	8.00	5.00
17	A2	15r gray grn ('99)	5.50	3.75
18	A2	20r gray vio	2.40	1.20
19	A2	25r sea green	3.75	1.20
20	A2	25r car rose ('99)	2.40	.60
a.		Booklet pane of 6		
21	A2	50r dark blue	9.25	5.00
a.		Perf. 12½	25.00	12.00
22	A2	50r ultra ('05)	2.40	1.20
23	A2	65r slate blue ('98)	1.25	1.20
24	A2	75r rose	2.40	1.20
25	A2	75r brn & red, yel ('05)	3.00	1.40
26	A2	80r violet	2.40	1.75
27	A2	100r dark blue, blue	2.40	1.75
28	A2	115r org brn, pink ('98)	3.50	1.75
29	A2	130r gray brown, buff ('98)	3.50	1.75
30	A2	150r lt brn, buff	4.25	1.75
31	A2	180r sl, pnksh ('98)	3.50	1.75
32	A2	200r red vio, pale lil	4.25	2.40
33	A2	300r blue, rose	4.25	2.40
34	A2	500r blk & red, bl	4.25	2.40
a.		Perf. 12½	17.50	9.00
		Nos. 13-34 (22)	74.45	41.25

Transitioning your stamps to a new album? Do you have duplicate stamps? Scott has a solution for you!

SCOTT ADVANTAGE STOCK PAGES

Scott Advantage Stock sheets provide the protection and durability of crystal acetate pockets. Designed with the collector in mind, the Advantage Stocksheets fit directly in your 3-ring or 2-post binder and match Scott National or Specialty pages in every respect. Perfect for storing new issues, minor varieties and collateral material. Size: 10" x 11 1/2". Sold in Packs of 10

Item#			Retail	AA
AD11	1 Pocket 242mm	National	$22.99	$20.69
AD21	1 Pocket 242mm	Specialty	$22.99	$20.69
AD12	2 Pocket 119mm	National	$22.99	$20.69
AD22	2 Pocket 119mm	Specialty	$22.99	$20.69
AD13	3 Pocket 79mm	National	$22.99	$20.69
AD23	3 Pocket 79mm	Specialty	$22.99	$20.69
AD14	4 Pocket 58mm	National	$22.99	$20.69
AD24	4 Pocket 58mm	Specialty	$22.99	$20.69
AD15	5 Pocket 45mm	National	$22.99	$20.69
AD25	5 Pocket 45mm	Specialty	$22.99	$20.69
AD16	6 Pocket 37mm	National	$22.99	$20.69
AD26	6 Pocket 37mm	Specialty	$22.99	$20.69
AD17	7 Pocket 34mm	National	$22.99	$20.69
AD27	7 Pocket 34mm	Specialty	$22.99	$20.69
AD18	8 Pocket 31mm	National	$22.99	$20.69
AD28	8 Pocket 31mm	Specialty	$22.99	$20.69

PRINZ STOCK PAGES

Prinz stock pages offer convenience and flexibility. Pages are reproduced on thick, archival-quality paper with acetate pockets glued from the bottom of each pocket. Size: 8 1/2" x 11". Sold in Packs of 5

Item#			Retail	AA
S1	1 Pocket 242 mm	Black (Single-Sided)	$11.99	$8.75
S1D	1 Pocket 242 mm	Black (Double-Sided)	$17.99	$13.13
S2	2 Pockets 119mm	Black (Single-Sided)	$11.99	$8.75
S2D	2 Pockets 119mm	Black (Double-Sided)	$17.99	$13.13
S3	3 Pockets 79mm	Black (Single-Sided)	$11.99	$8.75
S3D	3 Pockets 79mm	Black (Double-Sided)	$17.99	$13.13
S4	4 Pockets 58mm	Black (Single-Sided)	$11.99	$8.75
S4D	4 Pockets 58mm	Black (Double-Sided)	$17.99	$13.13
S5	5 Pockets 45mm	Black (Single-Sided)	$11.99	$8.75
S5D	5 Pockets 45mm	Black (Double-Sided)	$17.99	$13.13
S6	6 Pockets 37mm	Black (Single-Sided)	$11.99	$8.75
S6D	6 Pockets 37mm	Black (Double-Sided)	$17.99	$13.13
S7	7 Pockets 31mm	Black (Single-Sided)	$11.99	$8.75
S7D	7 Pockets 31mm	Black (Double-Sided)	$17.99	$13.13
S8	8 Pockets 27mm	Black (Single-Sided)	$11.99	$8.75
S8D	8 Pockets 27mm	Black (Double-Sided)	$17.99	$13.13
S9	3 Pockets 36mm/ 67mm/139mm	Black (Single-Sided)	$11.99	$8.75
S9D	3 Pockets 36mm/ 67mm/139mm	Black (Double-Sided)	$17.99	$13.13

AmosAdvantage.com
1-800-572-6885

ORDERING INFORMATION: *AA prices apply to paid subscribers of Amos Media titles, or for orders placed online. Prices, terms and product availability subject to change. **SHIPPING & HANDLING:** U.S.: Orders total $0-$10.00 charged $4.99 shipping. U.S. Order total $10.01-$74.99 charged $9.99 shipping. Orders totaling $75+ will ship FREE! Taxes will apply in CA, OH, & IL. Canada: 20% of order total. Minimum charge $19.99 Maximum charge $200.00. Foreign orders are shipped via FedEx Intl. or USPS and billed actual freight.

INDEX AND IDENTIFIER

All page numbers shown are those in this Volume 2B.

Postage stamps that do not have English words on them are shown in the Illustrated Identifier.

A & T ovptd. on French Colonies .... Vol. 1A
Aberdeen, Miss. .... Vol. 1A
Abingdon, Va. .... Vol. 1A
Abu Dhabi .... Vol. 1A, Vol. 5A, Vol. 6B
Abyssinia (Ethiopia) 462
A.C.C.P., A.D.C.P. .... Vol. 1B
A Certo ovptd. on stamps of
  Peruc Acores .... Vol. 1B, Vol. 5B
Aden .... Vol. 1A
AEF 799
Aegean Islands (Greek Occupation) .... Vol. 3A
Aegean Islands (Italian Occupation) ... Vol. 3B
Aeroport International de Kandahar
  (Afghanistan #679) .... Vol. 1A
Afars and Issas .... Vol. 1A
AFF EXCEP 463
Afghanistan, Afghan, Afghanes .... Vol. 1A
AFR .... Vol. 5B
Africa, British Offices .... Vol. 3A
Africa, German East .... Vol. 3A
Africa, German South-West .... Vol. 3A
Africa, Italian Offices .... Vol. 3B
Africa Occidental Espanola .... Vol. 6A
Africa Orientale Italiana .... Vol. 3B
Africa, Portuguese .... Vol. 5B
Afrique Equatoriale Francaise 799,
  Vol. 2A, Vol. 4B, Vol. 6B
Afrique Francaise 799
Afrique Occidentale Francaise 874
Agion Oros Athoc (Greece) .... Vol. 3A
Aguera, La .... Vol. 1A
Aguinaldo .... Vol. 5A
AHA (Confed. #44X1) .... Vol. 1A
Aimeliik (Palau #686) .... Vol. 5A
Airai (Palau #686) .... Vol. 5A
Aitutaki .... Vol. 1A
Ajman .... Vol. 1A, Vol. 6B
Aland Islands 596
Alaouites .... Vol. 1A
Albania .... Vol. 1A
Albania, Greek Occupation .... Vol. 3A
Albania, Italian Offices .... Vol. 3B
Albany, Ga. .... Vol. 1A
Alderney .... Vol. 3A
Aleppo .... Vol. 6A
Alerta ovptd. on stamps of Peru .... Vol. 5A
Alexandretta, Alexandrette .... Vol. 1A
Alexandria, Alexandrie, French Offices ... 786
Alexandria, Va. .... Vol. 1A
Alexandroupolis .... Vol. 3A
Algeria, Algerie .... Vol. 1A
Allemagne Duitschland .... Vol. 3A
Allenstein .... Vol. 1B
Allied Military Government (Austria) ... Vol. 1B
Allied Military Gov. (Germany) .... Vol. 3A
Allied Military Government (Italy) .... Vol. 3B
Allied Military Government (Trieste) ... Vol. 3B
Allied Occupation of Azerbaijan .... Vol. 3B
Allied Occupation of Thrace .... Vol. 6B
A L'Ocassion de la Journée Internationale
  de l'Alphabetisation (Afghan. #951) ... Vol. 1A
Alsace 782
Alsace and Lorraine 782
Alwar .... Vol. 3B
A.M.G. .... Vol. 1B, Vol. 3A, Vol. 6B
A.M.G./F.T.T. .... Vol. 3B
A.M.G./V.G. .... Vol. 3B
AM Post .... Vol. 3A
Anatolia .... Vol. 6B
Ancachs .... Vol. 5A
Andalusian Provinces .... Vol. 6A
Anderson Court House, S.C. .... Vol. 1A
Andorra, Andorre .... Vol. 1A
Andorre .... Vol. 1A
Angaur (Palau #686) .... Vol. 5A
Angola .... Vol. 1A
Angra .... Vol. 1A
Anguilla .... Vol. 1A, Vol. 5B
Anhwei .... Vol. 2A
Anjouan .... Vol. 1A
Anna surcharged on France 789
Anna surcharged on Great Britain ..... Vol. 5A
Anna, Annas .... Vol. 3B
Annam .... Vol. 1A
Annam and Tonkin .... Vol. 1A
Annapolis, Md. .... Vol. 1A
Ano do X Aniversario Comunidade
  dos Paises de Lingua Portuguesa
  (Angola 1298-1300) .... Vol. 1A
Antigua .... Vol. 1A, Vol. 5B
Antigua & Barbuda .... Vol. 1A
Antioquia .... Vol. 2A
A.O. ovptd. on Congo .... Vol. 1A
AOF on France 876
A.O.I. ovpt. on Italy .... Vol. 3B
A Payer Te Betalen .... Vol. 1B
A percevoir (see France, French
  colonies, postage due) .... 756, 782, Vol. 3A
Apurimac .... Vol. 5A
A R .... Vol. 4B

A.R. ovptd. on stamps of Colombia ..... Vol. 5A
Arabie Saoudite .... Vol. 6A
Arad .... Vol. 3B
A receber (See Portuguese Colonies) ... Vol. 5B
Arequipa .... Vol. 5A
Argentina .... Vol. 1A
Argyrokastron 420
Arica .... Vol. 5A
Armenia .... Vol. 1A, Vol. 6B
Armenian stamps ovptd. or
  surcharged .... Vol. 3A, Vol. 6B
Army of the North .... Vol. 5B
Army of the Northwest .... Vol. 5B
Aruba .... Vol. 1A
Arwad .... Vol. 1A
Ascension .... Vol. 1A
Assistencia Nacionalaos
  Tuberculosos .... Vol. 5B
Asturias Province .... Vol. 6A
Athens, Ga. .... Vol. 1A
Atlanta, Ga. .... Vol. 1A
Aunus, ovptd. on Finland .... Vol. 5B
Austin, Miss. .... Vol. 1A
Austin, Tex. .... Vol. 1A
Australia .... Vol. 1A
Australia, Occupation of Japan .... Vol. 1A
Australian Antarctic Territory .... Vol. 1A
Australian States .... Vol. 1A
Austria .... Vol. 1B
Austria, Allied Military Govt. .... Vol. 1B
Austria, Adm. of Liechtenstein .... Vol. 4A
Austria, Lombardy-Venetia .... Vol. 4A
Austria-Hungary .... Vol. 1B
Austrian Occupation of Italy .... Vol. 3B
Austrian Occupation of Montenegro ... Vol. 4B
Austrian Occupation of Romania ..... Vol. 5B
Austrian Occupation of Serbia .... Vol. 6A
Austrian Offices Abroad .... Vol. 1B
Austrian stamps surcharged or
  overprinted ... Vol. 1B, Vol. 3B, Vol. 5B, Vol. 6B
Autaugaville, Ala. .... Vol. 1A
Autopaketti, Autorahti 596
Avisporto 165
Ayacucho .... Vol. 5A
Aytonomoe 420
Azerbaijan, Azerbaycan, Azerbaycan,
  Azerbaidjan .... Vol. 1B, Vol. 3B, Vol. 6B
Azirbayedjan .... Vol. 3B
Azores .... Vol. 1B, Vol. 5B

B .... Vol. 1B, Vol. 5A, Vol. 6A
B ovptd. on Straits Settlements .... Vol. 1B
Baden .... Vol. 3A
Baghdad .... Vol. 4B
Bahamas .... Vol. 5A
Bahawalpur .... Vol. 5A
Bahrain .... Vol. 1B, Vol. 5A, Vol. 6B
Baja Cal(ifornia) .... Vol. 4B
Bajar Porto .... Vol. 3B
Baku .... Vol. 1A
Balcony Falls, Va. .... Vol. 1A
Baltimore, Md. .... Vol. 1A
Bamra .... Vol. 3B
Banat, Bacska .... Vol. 3B
Bangkok .... Vol. 1B
Bangladesh .... Vol. 1B
Bani ovptd. on Austria .... Vol. 5B
Bani ovptd. on Hungary .... Vol. 5B
Baranya .... Vol. 3B
Barbados .... Vol. 1B
Barbuda .... Vol. 1B
Barcelona .... Vol. 6A
Barnwell Court House, S.C. .... Vol. 1A
Barranquilla .... Vol. 2A
Barwani .... Vol. 3B
Basel .... Vol. 6A
Bashahr .... Vol. 3B
Basque Provinces .... Vol. 6A
Basutoland .... Vol. 1B
Batavia .... Vol. 5A
Baton Rouge, La. .... Vol. 1A
Batum, Batym (British Occupation) ... Vol. 1B
Bavaria .... Vol. 3A
Bayar Porto .... Vol. 3B
Bayer., Bayern .... Vol. 3A
B.C.A. ovptd. on Rhodesia .... Vol. 1B
B.C.M. .... Vol. 4B
B.C.O.F. .... Vol. 1B
Beaufort, S.C. .... Vol. 1A
Beaumont, Tex. .... Vol. 1A
Bechuanaland .... Vol. 1B
Bechuanaland Protectorate .... Vol. 1B
Beckmann's City Post .... Vol. 1A
Behie .... Vol. 6B
Belarus .... Vol. 1B
Belgian (Belgisch) Congo .... Vol. 1B
Belgian East Africa .... Vol. 5B
Belgian Occ. of German East Africa ... Vol. 3A
Belgian Occupation of Germany ...... Vol. 3A
Belgien .... Vol. 1B
Belgium, Belgique, Belgie .... Vol. 1B
Belgium (German Occupation) .... Vol. 1B
Belize .... Vol. 1B
Belize, Cayes of .... Vol. 1B
Benadir .... Vol. 6A
Bengasi .... Vol. 3B
Beni .... Vol. 5A
Benin .... Vol. 1B
Benin, People's Republic of .... Vol. 1B

Bequia .... Vol. 5B
Bergedorf .... Vol. 3A
Berlin .... Vol. 3A
Berlin-Brandenburg .... Vol. 3A
Bermuda .... Vol. 1B
Besetztes Gebiet Nordfrankreich 782
Besieged ovptd. on Cape of
  Good Hope .... Vol. 2A, Vol. 6B
Beyrouth, French Offices 780
Beyrouth, Russian Offices .... Vol. 5B
B. Guiana .... Vol. 1B
B. Hneipoe 421
Bhopal .... Vol. 3B
Bhor .... Vol. 3B
Bhutan .... Vol. 1B
Biafra .... Vol. 1B
Bijawar .... Vol. 3B
B.I.O.T. ovptd. on Seychelles .... Vol. 1B
Bishop's City Post .... Vol. 1A
Blagoveshchensk 501
Bluefields .... Vol. 5A
Bluffton, S.C. .... Vol. 1A
B.M.A. Eritrea .... Vol. 3A
B.M.A. Malaya .... Vol. 6A
B.M.A. Somalia .... Vol. 3A
B.M.A. Tripolitania .... Vol. 3A
Bocas del Toro .... Vol. 5A
Boer Occupation .... Vol. 2A
Bogota .... Vol. 2A
Bohemia and Moravia 111
Bohmen and Mahren 111
Boletta, Bollettino .... Vol. 3B, Vol. 6A
Bolivar .... Vol. 2A
Bolivia .... Vol. 1B
Bollo .... Vol. 3B
Bollo Postale .... Vol. 6A
Bophuthatswana .... Vol. 6A
Borneo .... Vol. 5A
Boscawen, N.H. .... Vol. 1A
Bosna i Hercegovina .... Vol. 1B, Vol. 6B
Bosnia and Herzegovina .... Vol. 1B, Vol. 6B
Bosnia, Muslim Gov. in Sarajevo ..... Vol. 1B
Bosnia, Croat Administration, Mostar ... Vol. 1B
Bosnia, Serb Administration,
  Banja Luca .... Vol. 1B
Bosnia stamps overprinted or
  surcharged .... Vol. 1B, Vol. 3B, Vol. 6B
Bosnien Herzegowina .... Vol. 1B
Boston, Mass. .... Vol. 1A
Botswana .... Vol. 1B
Boyaca .... Vol. 2A
Brattleboro, Vt. .... Vol. 1A
Braunschweig .... Vol. 3A
Brazil, Brasil .... Vol. 1B
Bremen .... Vol. 3A
Bridgeville, Ala. .... Vol. 1A
British Administration of Bahrain ..... Vol. 1B
British Antarctic Territory .... Vol. 1B
British Bechuanaland .... Vol. 1B
British Central Africa .... Vol. 1B
British Colonies - Dies I & II ..... See table of contents
British Columbia & Vancouver Is. ..... Vol. 2A
British Consular Mail .... Vol. 4B
British Dominion of Samoa .... Vol. 5B
British East Africa .... Vol. 1B
British Forces in Egypt 417
British Guiana .... Vol. 1B
British Honduras .... Vol. 1B
British Indian Ocean Territory .... Vol. 1B
British Levant .... Vol. 3A
British Mandate of Jordan .... Vol. 4A
British New Guinea .... Vol. 5A
British North Borneo .... Vol. 5A
British Occupation (of Batum) .... Vol. 1B
British Occupation of Bushire .... Vol. 1B
British Occupation of Cameroon ..... Vol. 2A
British Occupation of Crete .... Vol. 3A
British Occupation of Faroe Is. 502
British Occ. of German East Africa ... Vol. 3A
British Occ. of Iraq ... Vol. 3B, Vol. 4B
British Occupation of Mesopotamia ... Vol. 4B
British Occ. of Orange River Colony ... Vol. 5A
British Occupation overprint .... Vol. 1B
British Occupation of Palestine .... Vol. 5A
British Occupation of Persia .... Vol. 1B
British Occupation of Togo .... Vol. 6B
British Occ. of Transvaal .... Vol. 6B
British Offices in Africa .... Vol. 3A
British Offices in China .... Vol. 3A
British Offices in Morocco .... Vol. 3A
British Offices in Tangier .... Vol. 3A
British Off. in the Turkish Empire .... Vol. 3A
British Protectorate of Egypt 351
British Samoa .... Vol. 5B
British Solomon Islands .... Vol. 6A
British Somaliland (Somaliland
  Protectorate) .... Vol. 6A
British South Africa (Rhodesia) ...... Vol. 5A
British stamps surcharged .... Vol. 5A
British Vice-Consulate .... Vol. 4B
British Virgin Islands .... Vol. 6B
British Zone (Germany) .... Vol. 3A
Brown & McGill's U.S.P.O. Despatch ... Vol. 1A
Brunei .... Vol. 1B
Brunei (Japanese Occupation) .... Vol. 1B
Brunswick .... Vol. 3A
Buchanan .... Vol. 1A, Vol. 4A
Buenos Aires .... Vol. 1A

Bulgaria, Bulgarie .... Vol. 1B
Bulgarian Occupation of Romania ... Vol. 5B
Bulgarian stamps overprinted or
  surcharged .... Vol. 3A, Vol. 5B, Vol. 6B
Bundi .... Vol. 1B
Bundi stamps overprinted .... Vol. 3B
Bureau International .... Vol. 6A
Burgenland .... Vol. 1B
Burgos .... Vol. 6A
Burkina Faso .... Vol. 1B
Burma .... Vol. 1B
Burma (Japanese Occupation) .... Vol. 1B
Burundi .... Vol. 1B
Bushire .... Vol. 1B
Bussahir .... Vol. 3B
Buu-Chinh .... Vol. 6B
Buu-Bien .... Vol. 6B
Byelorussia .... Vol. 1B

Cabo, Cabo Gracias a Dios .... Vol. 5A
Cabo Juby, Jubi .... Vol. 2A
Cabo Verde .... Vol. 2A
Cadiz .... Vol. 6A
Caicos .... Vol. 6B
Calchi .... Vol. 3B
Cali .... Vol. 2A
Calino, Calimno .... Vol. 3B
Callao .... Vol. 5A
Camb. Aust. Sigillum Nov. .... Vol. 1A
Cambodia, (Int. Com., India) .... Vol. 3B
Cambodia, Cambodge .... Vol. 2A, Vol. 3B
Camden, S.C. .... Vol. 1A
Cameroons (U.K.T.T.) .... Vol. 2A
Cameroun (Republique Federale) ..... Vol. 2A
Campeche .... Vol. 4B
Canada .... Vol. 2A
Canadian Provinces .... Vol. 2A
Canal Zone .... Vol. 2A
Canary Islands, Canarias .... Vol. 6A
Candia .... Vol. 2A
Canouan .... Vol. 5B
Canton, French Offices 784
Canton, Miss. .... Vol. 1A
Cape Juby .... Vol. 2A
Cape of Good Hope .... Vol. 2A
Cape of Good Hope stamps
  surchd. (see Griqualand West) ..... Vol. 3A
Cape Verde .... Vol. 2A
Carchi .... Vol. 3B
Caribbean Netherlands .... Vol. 2A
Caribisch Nederland .... Vol. 2A
Carinthia .... Vol. 1B, Vol. 6B
Carlist .... Vol. 6A
Carolina City, N.C. .... Vol. 1A
Caroline Islands .... Vol. 2A
Carpatho-Ukraine .... Vol. 2A
Carriacou & Petite Martinique .... Vol. 3A
Carriers Stamps .... Vol. 1A
Cartagena .... Vol. 2A
Cartersville, Ga. .... Vol. 1A
Carupano .... Vol. 6B
Caso .... Vol. 3B
Castellorizo, Castelrosso .... Vol. 3B
Catalonia .... Vol. 6A
Cauca .... Vol. 2A
Cavalla (Greek) .... Vol. 3A
Cavalle, Cavalla (French) 788
Cayes of Belize .... Vol. 1B
Cayman Islands .... Vol. 2A
CCCP .... Vol. 5B
C.CH. on French Colonies .... Vol. 2A
C.E.F. ovptd. on Cameroun .... Vol. 2A
C.E.F. ovptd. on India .... Vol. 2A
Cefalonia ovptd. on Greece .... Vol. 3B
Celebes .... Vol. 5A
Cent, cents ..... 782, Vol. 1A, Vol. 4B, Vol. 5A
Centenaire Algerie RF (France No. 255) ... 615
Centenary-1st Postage Stamp
  (Pakistan #63-64) .... Vol. 5A
Centesimi overprinted on Austria
  or Bosnia .... Vol. 3B
Centesimi di corona .... 124, Vol. 1B
Centimes 462, 756
Centimes ovptd. on Austria .... Vol. 1B
Centimes ovptd. on Germany .... Vol. 3A
Centimos (no country name) .... Vol. 6A
Centimos ovptd. on France 809
Central Africa (Centrafricaine) .... Vol. 2A
Central African Republic .... Vol. 2A
Central China .... Vol. 2A
Central Lithuania .... Vol. 2A
Cephalonia .... Vol. 3B
Cerigo .... Vol. 3A, Vol. 6A
Cervantes .... Vol. 6A
Ceska Republica 73
Ceskoslovenska, Ceskoslovensko ... 27
Ceylon .... Vol. 2A
CF 874
CFA 792
C.G.H.S. .... Vol. 6B
Ch .... Vol. 3B, Vol. 4A
Chachapoyas .... Vol. 5A
Chad .... Vol. 2A
Chahar .... Vol. 2A
Chala .... Vol. 5A
Chamba .... Vol. 3B
Channel Islands .... Vol. 3A
Chapel Hill, N.C. .... Vol. 1A
Charkhari .... Vol. 3B

INDEX AND IDENTIFIER

Charleston, S.C. .... Vol. 1A
Charlotte, N.C. .... Vol. 1A
Charlottesville, Va. .... Vol. 1A
Chateau de Beggen
  (Luxembourg #1466) .... Vol. 4A
Chateau de Dommeldange
  (Luxembourg #1467) .... Vol. 4A
Chattanooga, Tenn. .... Vol. 1A
Chekiang .... Vol. 2A
Chemins des Fer 782
Cherifien Posts 792
Chiapas .... Vol. 4B
Chiclayo .... Vol. 5A
Chiffre .... See France and French
  colonies, postage due
Chihuahua .... Vol. 4B
Chile .... Vol. 2A
Chilean Occupation of Peru .... Vol. 5A
Chimarra 421
China, Chinese .... Vol. 2A
China (Japanese Occupation) ...... Vol. 2A
China Expeditionary Force (India) .... Vol. 3B
China, British Offices .... Vol. 3A
China, Formosa .... Vol. 2A, Vol. 4A
China, French Offices 784
China, German Offices .... Vol. 3A
China, Italian Offices .... Vol. 3B
China, Japanese Offices .... Vol. 4A
China, Northeastern Provinces ... Vol. 2A
China, Offices in Manchuria .... Vol. 2A
China, Offices in Tibet .... Vol. 2A
China, People's Republic .... Vol. 2A
China, People's Republic
  Regional Issues .... Vol. 2A
China, People's Republic Hong Kong ... Vol. 3B
China, People's Republic Macao .... Vol. 4B
China, Republic of .... Vol. 2A
China, Russian Offices .... Vol. 5B
China, United States Offices .... Vol. 1A
Chine 784
Chios .... Vol. 3A
Chita 501
Chosen .... Vol. 4A
Christiansburg, Va. .... Vol. 1A
Christmas Island .... Vol. 2A
Chungking 786
C.I.H.S. .... Vol. 6B
Cilicia, Cilicie .... Vol. 2A, Vol. 5A, Vol. 6A
Cincinnati, O. .... Vol. 1A
Cinquan Tenaire .... Vol. 5A
Cirenaica 25
Ciskei .... Vol. 6A
City Despatch Post .... Vol. 1A
City Post .... Vol. 1A
Cleveland, O. .... Vol. 1A
Cluj .... Vol. 3B
c/m 463
C.M.T. .... Vol. 6B
Coamo .... Vol. 1A, Vol. 5B
Cochin .... Vol. 3B
Cochin China .... Vol. 2A
Cochin, Travancore .... Vol. 3B
Co. Ci. ovptd. on Yugoslavia .... Vol. 6B
Cocos Islands .... Vol. 2A
Colaparchee, Ga. .... Vol. 1A
Colis Postaux .... 779, Vol. 1B, Vol. 3B
Colombia .... Vol. 2A
Colombian Dominion of Panama ... 438, Vol. 5A
Colombian States .... Vol. 2A
Colon .... Vol. 5A
Colonie (Coloniali) Italiane .... Vol. 3B
Colonies de l'Empire Francaise 797
Columbia, S.C. .... Vol. 1A
Columbia, Tenn. .... Vol. 1A
Columbus Archipelago 349
Columbus, Ga. .... Vol. 1A
Comayagua .... Vol. 3B
Commando Brief .... Vol. 5A
Common Designs .... See table of contents
Commissioning of Maryan
  Babangida (Nigeria #607) .... Vol. 5A
Communicaciones .... Vol. 6A
Communist China .... Vol. 2A
Comores, Archipel des .... Vol. 2A
Comoro Islands (Comores,
  Comorien) .... Vol. 2A, Vol. 4B
Compania Colombiana .... Vol. 2A
Confederate States .... Vol. 1A
Congo .... Vol. 1B, Vol. 2A
Congo Democratic Republic ..... Vol. 2A, Vol. 6B
Congo People's Republic (ex-French) ... Vol. 2A
Congo, Belgian (Belge) .... Vol. 1B
Congo Francais 798
Congo, Indian U.N. Force .... Vol. 3B
Congo, Portuguese .... Vol. 5B
Congreso .... Vol. 6A
Conseil de l'Europe 776
Constantine, Georgian Offices .... Vol. 3B
Constantinople, Polish Offices .... Vol. 5B
Constantinople, Italian Offices .... Vol. 3B
Constantinople, Romanian Offices ... Vol. 5B
Constantinople, Russian Offices ... Vol. 5B
Constantinople, Turkey .... Vol. 6B
Contribucao Industrial (Macao
  A14, P. Guinea WT1) ...... Vol. 4B, Vol. 5B
Convention States (India) .... Vol. 3B
Coo .... Vol. 3A
Cook Islands .... Vol. 2A
Cook Islands, Niue .... Vol. 5A
Cordoba .... Vol. 1A

Corea, Coree .... Vol. 4A
Corfu .... Vol. 2A, Vol. 3B
Corona .... 124, Vol. 1B
Correio, Correios e Telegraphos ... Vol. 5B
Correo Submarino .... Vol. 6A
Correo, Correos (no name) .... Vol. 1A,
  Vol. 2A, Vol. 5A, Vol. 6A
Corrientes .... Vol. 1A
Cos .... Vol. 3B
Costa Atlantica .... Vol. 5A
Costa Rica .... Vol. 2A
Costantinopoli .... Vol. 3B
Cote d'Ivoire .... Vol. 3B
Cote des Somalis .... Vol. 6A
Council of Europe 776
Cour Permanente de Justice
  Internationale .... Vol. 5A
Courtland, Ala. .... Vol. 1A
Cpbnja .... Vol. 6A
Cracow .... Vol. 5B
Crete .... Vol. 2A, Vol. 3B
Crete, Austrian Offices .... Vol. 1B
Crete, French Offices 786
Crete, Italian Offices .... Vol. 3B
Crimea .... Vol. 5B, Vol. 6A
Croat Administration of Bosnia,
  Mostar .... Vol. 1B
Croatia .... Vol. 2A
Croatia-Slavonia .... Vol. 6B
Croissant Rouge Turc. .... Vol. 6B
C.S.A. Postage .... Vol. 1A
CTOT .... Vol. 1B
Cuautla .... Vol. 4B
Cuthbert, GA .... Vol. 1A
Cuba .... Vol. 1A, Vol. 2A
Cuba stamps overprinted .... Vol. 5B
Cuba, U.S. Administration ... Vol. 1A, Vol. 2A
Cucuta .... Vol. 5A
Cuernavaca .... Vol. 4B
Cundinamarca .... Vol. 2A
Curacao .... Vol. 2A, Vol. 5A
Cuzco .... Vol. 5A
C.X.C. on Bosnia and Herzegovina ... Vol. 6B
Cyprus 1
Cyprus, Turkish Republic of Northern ... Vol. 6B
Cyrenaica .... 24, Vol. 3A, Vol. 4A
Czechoslovakia 27
Czechoslovak Legion Post 111
Czech Rep. 73

D .... Vol. 3B
Dahomey .... 113, Vol. 1B
Dakar-Abidjan 074
Dalmatia 124
Dalton, Ga. .... Vol. 1A
Danish West Indies .... 124, Vol. 1A
Danmark 130
Dansk-Vestindien .... 124, Vol. 1A
Dansk-Vestindiske .... 124, Vol. 1A
Danville, Va. .... Vol. 1A
Danzig 125
Danzig, Polish Offices .... Vol. 5B
Dardanelles .... Vol. 5B
Darlington C.H., S.C. .... Vol. 1A
Datia (Duttia) .... Vol. 3B
D.B.L. ovptd. on Siberia and Russia 501
D.B.P. (Dalni Vostochini Respoublika) ... 501
D. de A. .... Vol. 2A
DDR .... Vol. 3A
Debrecen .... Vol. 3B
Deccan (Hyderabad) .... Vol. 3B
Dedeagatch (Greek) .... Vol. 3A
Dedeagh, Dedeagatch (French) 789
Deficit .... Vol. 5A
Demopolis, Ala. .... Vol. 1A
Denikin .... Vol. 6A
Denmark 130
Denmark stamps surcharged 502
Denver Issue, Mexico .... Vol. 4B
Den Waisen ovptd. on Italy .... Vol. 6B
Despatch (US 1LB, 5LB) .... Vol. 1A
Deutsch-Neu-Guinea .... Vol. 3A
Deutsch-Ostafrika .... Vol. 3A
Deutsch-Sudwest Afrika .... Vol. 3A
Deutsche Bundespost .... Vol. 3A
Deutsche Demokratische Republik ... Vol. 3A
Deutsche Nationalversammlung ... Vol. 3A
Deutsche Post .... Vol. 3A
Deutsche Post Berlin .... Vol. 3A
Deutsche(s) Reich .... Vol. 3A
Deutsche Reich, #21, #16 .... Vol. 3A
Deutschland .... Vol. 3A
Doutcchostrroioh .... Vol. 1B
Dhar .... Vol. 3B
Diego-Suarez 165
Diego-Suarez stamps surcharged ... Vol. 4B
Dienftmarke (Dienstmarke) .... Vol. 3A
Dies I & II, British Colonies ...... See table of
  contents
Diligonoia .... Vol. 6D
Dinar .... Vol. 6B
Dire-Dawa 463, 775
Dispatch (US 1LB) .... Vol. 1A
Distrito ovptd. on Arequipa .... Vol. 5A
DJ ovptd. on Obock .... Vol. 6A
Djibouti (Somali Coast) ...... 166, Vol. 6A
Dobruja District .... Vol. 5B
Dodecanese Islands .... Vol. 3A, Vol. 6A
Dollar, ovptd. on Russia .... Vol. 5B
Dominica 199

Dominican Republic, Dominicana 237
Don Government .... Vol. 6A
Dorpat 461
Drzava SHS .... Vol. 6B
Dubai .... 286, Vol. 5A, Vol. 6B
Duck Stamps (Hunting Permit) .... Vol. 1A
Duitsch Oost Afrika overprinted
  on Congo .... Vol. 3A
Duke de la Torre Regency .... Vol. 6A
Dulce et Decorum est Pro Patria
  Mori (Nepal O1) .... Vol. 5A
Dungarpur .... Vol. 3B
Durazzo .... Vol. 3B
Dutch Guiana (Surinam) .... Vol. 5A
Dutch Indies .... Vol. 5A
Dutch New Guinea .... Vol. 5A
Duttia .... Vol. 3B

EA .... Vol. 1A
E.A.F. overprinted on stamps of
  Great Britain .... Vol. 3A
East Africa (British) .... Vol. 1B
East Africa (German) .... Vol. 3A
East Africa (Italian) .... Vol. 3B
East Africa and Uganda
  Protectorates .... 288, Vol. 4A
East Africa Forces .... Vol. 3A
East China .... Vol. 2A
Eastern Rumelia 289
Eastern Rumelia stamps overprinted .... Vol. 6B
Eastern Silesia 289
Eastern Szechwan .... Vol. 2A
Eastern Thrace .... Vol. 6B
East India .... Vol. 3B
East Saxony .... Vol. 3A
East Timor .... Vol. 1A, Vol. 6B
Eatonton, Ga. .... Vol. 1A
Ecuador 290
E.E.F. .... Vol. 5A
Eesti 438
Egeo .... Vol. 3B
Egiziane (Egypt types A9-A10) 3350
Egypt, Egypte, Egyptiennes .... 350, Vol. 6A
Egypt, French Offices 787
Eire, Eireann (Ireland) .... Vol. 3B
Ekaterinodar .... Vol. 6A
Elobey, Annobon and Corisco 420
El Salvador .... Vol. 5B
Elsas, Elfas 782
Elua Keneta .... Vol. 1A
Emory, Va. .... Vol. 1A
Empire, Franc, Francais 797
En .... Vol. 4A
England .... Vol. 3A
Epirus 420
Equateur (Ecuador #19-21) 290
Equatorial Guinea 422
Eritrea 431
Eritrea (British Military Administration) .... Vol. 3A
Escuelas .... Vol. 6B
Espana, Espanola .... Vol. 6A
Estado da India .... Vol. 5B
Est Africain Allemand overprinted
  on Congo .... Vol. 3A
Estensi .... Vol. 3B
Estero .... Vol. 3B
Estland .... 461, Vol. 5B
Estonia .... 438, Vol. 5B
Etablissments Francais dans l'Inde 806
Ethiopia, Etiopia, Ethiopie,
  Ethiopiennes .... 461, Vol. 3A
Eupen .... Vol. 3A
Europe .... Vol. 3A
Express Letter .... Vol. 2A

15 August 1947 (Pakistan #23) .... Vol. 5A
500 anos, viaje del descubrimiento
  de istmo (Panama #897) .... Vol. 5A
F 782
F. A. F. L. .... Vol. 6A
Falkland Dependencies 500
Falkland Islands 484
Far Eastern Republic 501
Far Eastern Republic surcharged
  or ovptd. .... Vol. 6A
Faridkot .... Vol. 3B
Faroe Islands 502
FCFA ovptd. on France 794
Federacion .... Vol. 6B
Federal Republic (Germany) .... Vol. 3A
Federated Malay States .... Vol. 4B
Fen, Fn. (Manchukuo) .... Vol. 4B
Fernando Po, Fdo. Poo 510
Feudatory States .... Vol. 3B
Fezzan, Fezzan-Ghadames .... Vol. 4A
Fiera Campionaria Tripoli .... Vol. 4A
Fiji 521
Fiji overprinted or surcharged .... Vol. 5A
Filipinas, Filipas. .... Vol. 5A
Fincastle, Va. .... Vol. 1A
Finland 542
Finnish Occupation of Karelia ... Vol. 4A
Finnish Occupation of Russia .... Vol. 4A, Vol. 5B
Fiume 608
Fiume-Kupa Zone (Fiumano Kupa) .... Vol. 6B
Five Cents (Confed. #53X) .... Vol. 1A
Florida .... Vol. 6B
F. M. 775
Foochow, Chinese .... Vol. 2A
Foochow, German .... Vol. 3A

Formosa .... Vol. 2A, Vol. 4A
Foroyar 502
Forsyth, Ga. .... Vol. 1A
Fort Valley, Ga. .... Vol. 1A
Franc 611, 782
Franc ovptd. on Austria .... Vol. 1B
Franca ovptd. on stamps of Peru .... Vol. 5A
Francais, Francaise .... See France
  and French colonies
France 611
France (German occupation) 798
France D'Outre Mer 787
Franco Bollo .... Vol. 3B
Franco Marke .... Vol. 3A
Franco Scrisorei .... Vol. 5B
Franklin, N.C. .... Vol. 1A
Franqueo .... Vol. 5A
Franquicia .... Vol. 6A
Fraziersville, S.C. .... Vol. 1A
Fredericksburg, Va. .... Vol. 1A
Free .... Vol. 1A
Frei Durch Ablosung .... Vol. 3A
Freimarke (No Country Name) ... Vol. 3A
French Administration of Andorra ... Vol. 1A
French Administration of Saar ... Vol. 5B
French Colonies 797
French Colonies surcharged or
  overprinted .... 165, 775, Vol. 1A, Vol. 3A,
  Vol. 3B, Vol. 4B, Vol. 5A, Vol. 6A
French Commemoratives Index ... 744
French Congo 798
French Equatorial Africa ... 799, Vol. 2A,
  Vol. 4B, Vol. 6B
French Guiana 802
French Guinea 804
French India 806
French Levant .... 788, Vol. 6A
French Mandate of Alaouites .... Vol. 1A
French Mandate of Lebanon .... Vol. 4A
French Morocco 809
French Occupation of Cameroun ... Vol. 2A
French Occupation of Castellorizo ... Vol. 2A
French Occupation of Crete ...... Vol. 2A
French Occupation of Germany ... Vol. 3A
French Occupation of Hungary ... Vol. 3B
French Occupation of Libya ...... Vol. 4B
French Occupation of Syria ...... Vol. 6A
French Occupation of Togo ...... Vol. 6B
French Oceania 815
French Offices Abroad 782
French Offices in China 782
French Offices in Crete 786
French Offices in Egypt 787
French Offices in Madagascar ... Vol. 4B
French Offices in Morocco 809
French Offices in Tangier 809, 814
French Offices in Turkish Empire .... Vol. 6A
French Offices in Turkish Empire
  surcharged .... Vol. 6A
French Offices in Zanzibar 789
French Polynesia 815
French Saar .... Vol. 5B
French Southern and Antarctic Territories ... 846
French stamps inscribed CFA 792
French stamps surcharged 786, 794,
  Vol. 4B, Vol. 6A
French Sudan 873
French West Africa 874
French Zone (Germany) .... Vol. 3A
Frimarke, Frmrk (No Country Name) 130,
  Vol. 5A, Vol. 6A
Fujeira .... 876, Vol. 6B
Fukien .... Vol. 2A
Funafuti .... Vol. 6B
Funchal 877

G or GW overprinted on Cape
  of Good Hope .... Vol. 3A
GAB on French Colonies .... Vol. 3A
Gabon, Gabonaise .... Vol. 3A
Gainesville, Ala. .... Vol. 1A
Galapagos Islands 349
Galveston, Tex. .... Vol. 1A
Gambia .... Vol. 1A
Gaston, N.C. .... Vol. 1A
Gaza .... Vol. 3B
G & (et) D overprinted on
  French Colonies .... Vol. 3A
G.E.A. ovptd. .... Vol. 3A, Vol. 6A
General Gouvernement (Poland) ... Vol. 5B
Geneva, Geneve .... Vol. 6A
Georgetown, S.C. .... Vol. 1A
Georgia .... Vol. 3A, Vol. 6D
Georgia, Offices in Turkey .... Vol. 3A
Georgienne, Republique .... Vol. 3A
German Administration of Albania ... Vol. 1A
German Administration of Danzig 128
German Administration of Saar ... Vol. 5B
German Democratic Republic .... Vol. 3A
German Dominion of Cameroun ... Vol. 2A
German Dominion of Caroline Islands ... Vol. 2A
German Dominion of Mariana Is. ... Vol. 4B
German Dominion of Marshall Is. ... Vol. 4B
German Dominion of Samoa ..... Vol. 5B
German Dominion of Togo .... Vol. 6B
German East Africa .... Vol. 3A
German East Africa (Belgian occ.) ... Vol. 3A
German East Africa (British occ.) .... Vol. 3A
German New Guinea .... Vol. 3A
German New Guinea (New Britain) ... Vol. 5A

INDEX AND IDENTIFIER

German Occupation of Belgium ...... Vol. 1B
German Occupation of Estonia 461
German Occupation of France 782
German Occupation of Guernsey ..... Vol. 3A
German Occupation of Ionian Is. ..... Vol. 3A
German Occupation of Jersey .... Vol. 3A
German Occupation of Latvia .... Vol. 4A
German Occupation of Lithuania ..... Vol. 4A
German Occupation of Ljubljana ..... Vol. 6B
German Occupation of Luxembourg ... Vol. 4A
German Occupation of Macedonia ..... Vol. 4B
German Occupation of Montenegro .... Vol. 4B
German Occupation of Poland .... Vol. 5B
German Occupation of Romania .... Vol. 5B
German Occupation of Russia .... Vol. 5B
German Occupation of Serbia .... Vol. 6A
German Occupation of Ukraine .... Vol. 5B
German Occupation of Yugoslavia .... Vol. 6B
German Occupation of Zante .... Vol. 3B
German Offices in China .... Vol. 3A
German Offices in China surcharged ... Vol. 4A
German Offices in Morocco .... Vol. 3A
German Offices in Turkish Empire .... Vol. 3A
German Protectorate of Bohemia
and Moravia 111
German South-West Africa .... Vol. 3A
German stamps surchd. or ovptd. ....Vol. 3A,
Vol. 5B, Vol. 6A
German States .... Vol. 3A
Germany .... Vol. 3A
Germany (Allied Military Govt.) ...... Vol. 3A
Gerusalemme .... Vol. 3B
Ghadames .... Vol. 4A
Ghana .... Vol. 3A
Gibraltar .... Vol. 3A
Gilbert and Ellice Islands .... Vol. 3A
Gilbert Islands .... Vol. 3A
Giumulzina District .... Vol. 6B
Gniezno .... Vol. 5B
Gold Coast .... Vol. 3A
Golfo del Guinea .... Vol. 6A
Goliad, Tex. .... Vol. 1A
Gonzales, Tex. .... Vol. 1A
Gorny Slask .... Vol. 6B
Government (U.S. 1LB) .... Vol. 1A
Governo Militare Alleato .... Vol. 3B
G.P.E. ovptd. on French Colonies .... Vol. 3A
Graham Land 501
Granada .... Vol. 6A
Granadine Confederation, Granadina Vol. 2A
Grand Comoro, Grande Comore .... Vol. 3A
Grand Liban, Gd Liban .... Vol. 4A
Great Britain (see also British) .... Vol. 3A
Great Britain, Gaelic ovpt. .... Vol. 3B
Great Britain, Offices in Africa ..... Vol. 3A
Great Britain, Offices in China ...... Vol. 3A
Great Britain, Offices in Morocco .... Vol. 3A
Great Britain, Offices in
Turkish Empire .... Vol. 3A
Greater Rajasthan Union .... Vol. 3B
Greece .... Vol. 3A
Greek Occupation of Albania, North
Epirus, Dodecanese Islands .... Vol. 3A
Greek Occupation of Epirus 421
Greek Occ. of the Aegean Islands ..... Vol. 3A
Greek Occupation of Thrace .... Vol. 6B
Greek Occupation of Turkey .... Vol. 3A, Vol. 6B
Greek stamps overprinted .... 421, Vol. 6B
Greenland .... Vol. 3A
Greensboro, Ala. .... Vol. 1A
Greensboro, N.C. .... Vol. 1A
Greenville .... Vol. 4A
Greenville, Ala. .... Vol. 1A
Greenville, Tenn. .... Vol. 1A
Greenville Court House, S.C. .... Vol. 1A
Greenwood Depot, Va. .... Vol. 1A
Grenada .... Vol. 3A
Grenadines of Grenada .... Vol. 3A
Grenadines of St. Vincent .... Vol. 5B
Grenville .... Vol. 4A
G.R.I. overprinted on German
New Guinea .... Vol. 5A
G.R.I. overprinted on German Samoa ... Vol. 5B
G.R.I. overprinted on Marshall Is. ... Vol. 5B
Griffin, Ga. .... Vol. 1A
Griqualand West .... Vol. 3A
Grodno District .... Vol. 4A
Gronland .... Vol. 3A
Grossdeutsches Reich
(Germany #529) .... Vol. 3A
Groszy .... Vol. 5B
Grove Hill, Ala. .... Vol. 1A
Gruzija (Georgia) .... Vol. 3A
Guadalajara .... Vol. 4B
Guadeloupe .... Vol. 3A
Guam .... Vol. 1A
Guanacaste .... Vol. 2A
Guatemala .... Vol. 3A
Guayana .... Vol. 6B
Guernsey .... Vol. 3A
Guernsey, German Occupation .... Vol. 3A
Guiana, British .... Vol. 1B
Guiana, Dutch .... Vol. 6A
Guiana, French 802
Guine .... Vol. 3A, Vol. 5B
Guinea .... Vol. 3A, Vol. 6A
Guinea Ecuatorial 422
Guinea, French 804
Guinea, Portuguese .... Vol. 5B
Guinea, Spanish .... Vol. 6A

Guinea-Bissau, Guine-Bissau .... Vol. 3A
Guinee .... 804, Vol. 3A
Guipuzcoa Province .... Vol. 6A
Gultig 9, Armee .... Vol. 5B
Guyana .... Vol. 3A
Guyane, Guy. Franc. 802
G.W. ovptd. on Cape of Good Hope ... Vol. 3A
Gwalior .... Vol. 3B

Habilitado-1/2 (Tlacotalpan #1) ..... Vol. 4B
Habilitado on Stamps of Cuba .... Vol. 1A,
Vol. 2A, Vol. 5A
Habilitado on Telegrafos or
revenues .... Vol. 5A, Vol. 6A
Hadhramaut .... Vol. 1A
Hainan Island .... Vol. 2A
Haiti .... Vol. 1B
Hall, A. D. (Confed. #27XU1) .... Vol. 1A
Hallettsville, Tex. .... Vol. 1A
Hamburg .... Vol. 3A
Hamburgh, S.C. .... Vol. 1A
Hamilton, Bermuda .... Vol. 1B
Hanover, Hannover .... Vol. 3A
Harar 780
Harper .... Vol. 4A
Harrisburgh, Tex. .... Vol. 1A
Hatay .... Vol. 3B
Hatirasi (Turkey Design PT44) .... Vol. 6B
Hatohobei (Palau #686) .... Vol. 5A
Haute Silesie .... Vol. 6B
Haute Volta .... Vol. 1B
Haut Senegal-Niger .... Vol. 6B
Hawaii, Hawaiian .... Vol. 1A
H B A ovptd. on Russia .... Vol. 6A
Hebrew inscriptions .... Vol. 3B
H.E.H. The Nizam's (Hyderabad) ..... Vol. 3B
Heilungkiang .... Vol. 2A
Hejaz .... Vol. 6A
Hejaz-Nejd .... Vol. 6A
Hejaz overprinted .... Vol. 4A, Vol. 6A
Helena, Tex. .... Vol. 1A
Heligoland, Helgoland .... Vol. 3A
Hellas .... Vol. 3A
Helsinki (Helsingfors) 544
Helvetia, Helvetica (Switzerland) .... Vol. 6A
Heraklion .... Vol. 3A
Herceg Bosna .... Vol. 1B
Herzegovina .... Vol. 1B
Herzogth .... Vol. 3A
H.H. Nawabshah Jahanbegam .... Vol. 3B
H.I. Postage .... Vol. 1A
Hillsboro, N.C. .... Vol. 1A
Hoi Hao, French Offices 784
Holkar (Indore) .... Vol. 3B
Holland (Netherlands) .... Vol. 5A
Hollandale, Tex. .... Vol. 1A
Holstein .... Vol. 3A
Honan .... Vol. 2A
Honda .... Vol. 3A
Honduras .... Vol. 3A
Honduras, British .... Vol. 1B
Hong Kong .... Vol. 2A, Vol. 3B
Hong Kong (Japanese Occupation) ..... Vol. 3B
Hong Kong Special Admin. Region ..... Vol. 3B
Hong Kong ovptd. China .... Vol. 3A
Honour's (Hondur's) City .... Vol. 1A
Hopeh .... Vol. 2A
Hopei .... Vol. 2A
Horta .... Vol. 3B
Houston, Tex. .... Vol. 1A
Hrvatska .... Vol. 1B, Vol. 2A, Vol. 6B
Hrzgl. .... Vol. 1B
Huacho .... Vol. 5A
Hunan .... Vol. 2A
Hungary .... Vol. 1B, Vol. 3B
Hungary (French Occupation) .... Vol. 3B
Hungary (Romanian Occupation) .... Vol. 3B
Hungary (Serbian Occupation) .... Vol. 3B
Huntsville, Tex. .... Vol. 1A
Hupeh .... Vol. 2A
Hyderabad (Deccan) .... Vol. 3B

I.B. (West Irian) .... Vol. 3B
Icaria .... Vol. 3A
ICC ovptd. on India .... Vol. 3B
Iceland .... Vol. 3B
Idar .... Vol. 3B
I.E.F. ovptd. on India .... Vol. 3B
I.E.F. 'D' ovptd. on Turkey .... Vol. 4B
Ierusalem .... Vol. 3B
Ifni .... Vol. 3B
Ile Rouad .... Vol. 3B
Imperio Colonial Portugues .... Vol. 5B
Imposto de Selo .... Vol. 5B
Impuesto (Impto) de Guerra .... Vol. 6A
Inde. Fcaise 806
Independence, Tex. .... Vol. 1A
Index of U.S. Issues .... Vol. 1A
India .... Vol. 3B, Vol. 5B
India, China Expeditionary Force .... Vol. 3B
India, Convention States .... Vol. 3B
India, Feudatory States .... Vol. 3B
India, French 806
India, Portuguese .... Vol. 5B
India stamps overprinted .... Vol. 3B,
Vol. 4A, Vol. 5A
India, surcharge and crown .... Vol. 6A
Indian Custodial Unit, Korea .... Vol. 3B
Indian Expeditionary Force .... Vol. 3B
Indian U.N. Force, Congo .... Vol. 3B

Indian U.N. Force, Gaza .... Vol. 3B
Indian Postal Administration of
Bahrain .... Vol. 1B
Indo-China, Indo-chine .... Vol. 3B
Indo-China stamps surcharged .... Vol. 6B
Indo-China, Int. Commission .... Vol. 3B
Indonesia .... Vol. 3B, Vol. 5A
Indore .... Vol. 3B
Industrielle Kriegswirschaft .... Vol. 6A
Inhambane .... Vol. 3B
Inini .... Vol. 3B
Inland (Liberia #21) .... Vol. 4A
Inner Mongolia (Meng Chiang) .... Vol. 2A
Insufficiently prepaid .... Vol. 6B
Instrucao .... Vol. 6B
Instruccion .... Vol. 6B
International Bureau of Education .... Vol. 6A
International Commission in
Indo-China .... Vol. 3B
International Court of Justice .... Vol. 5A
International Labor Bureau .... Vol. 6A
International Olympic Committee ..... Vol. 6A
International Refugee Organization ... Vol. 6A
International Telecommunication
Union .... Vol. 6A
Ionian Islands, IONIKON KPATOE ..... Vol. 3B
I.O.V.R. .... Vol. 5B
Iran, Iraniennes .... Vol. 3B
Iran (Bushire) .... Vol. 1B
Iran, Turkish Occupation .... Vol. 3B
Iran with Rs. 10 denomination
(Pakistan #1101) .... Vol. 5A
Iraq .... Vol. 3B
Iraq (British Occupation) ..... Vol. 3B, Vol. 4B
Ireland .... Vol. 3A
Ireland, Northern .... Vol. 3A
Irian Barat .... Vol. 3B
Isabella, Ga. .... Vol. 1A
Island .... Vol. 3B
Isle of Man .... Vol. 3A
Isole Italiane dell'Egeo .... Vol. 3B
Isole Jonie .... Vol. 3B
Israel .... Vol. 3B
Istria .... Vol. 6B
Itaca ovptd. on Greece .... Vol. 3A
Ita-Karjala .... Vol. 4A
Italia, Italiano, Italiane .... Vol. 3B
Italian Colonies .... Vol. 3B
Italian Dominion of Albania .... Vol. 1A
Italian Dominion of Castellorizo .... Vol. 2A
Italian East Africa .... Vol. 5A
Italian Jubaland .... Vol. 3B
Italian Occ. of Aegean Islands ...... Vol. 3B
Italian Occupation of Austria .... Vol. 1B
Italian Occupation of Corfu .... Vol. 2A
Italian Occupation of Crete .... Vol. 2A
Italian Occupation of Dalmatia 124
Italian Occupation of Ethiopia 484
Italian Occupation of Fiume-Kupa ... Vol. 6B
Italian Occupation of Ionian Islands ... Vol. 6B
Italian Occupation of Ljubljana ...... Vol. 6B
Italian Occupation of Montenegro .... Vol. 4B
Italian Occupation of Yugoslavia .... Vol. 6B
Italian Offices Abroad .... Vol. 3B
Italian Offices in Africa .... Vol. 3B
Italian Offices in Albania .... Vol. 3B
Italian Offices in China .... Vol. 3B
Italian Offices in Constantinople ... Vol. 3B
Italian Offices in Crete .... Vol. 3B
Italian Offices in the Turkish Empire ... Vol. 3B
Italian Social Republic .... Vol. 3B
Italian Somaliland .... Vol. 6A
Italian Somaliland (E.A.F.) .... Vol. 3A
Italian stamps surcharged ..... 124, Vol. 1B,
Vol. 3B
Italian States .... Vol. 3B
Italy (Allied Military Govt.) .... Vol. 3B
Italy (Austrian Occupation) .... Vol. 3B
Italy .... Vol. 3B
Ithaca .... Vol. 3B
Iuka, Miss. .... Vol. 1A
Ivory Coast .... Vol. 3B

J. ovptd. on stamps of Peru .... Vol. 5A
Jackson, Miss. .... Vol. 1A
Jacksonville, Ala. .... Vol. 1A
Jacksonville, Fla. .... Vol. 1A
Jaffa .... Vol. 5B
Jaipur .... Vol. 3B
Jamaica .... Vol. 4A
Jamhuri .... Vol. 6B
Jammu .... Vol. 3B
Jammu and Kashmir .... Vol. 3B
Janina .... Vol. 3B
Japan, Japanese .... Vol. 4A
Japan (Australian Occ.) .... Vol. 1A
Japan (Taiwan) .... Vol. 2A, Vol. 4A
Japanese Offices Abroad .... Vol. 4A
Japan Occupation of Brunei .... Vol. 1B
Japan Occupation of Burma .... Vol. 1B
Japan Occupation of China .... Vol. 2A
Japan Occupation of Dutch Indies .... Vol. 5A
Japan Occupation of Hong Kong .... Vol. 3B
Japan Occupation of Johore .... Vol. 4B
Japan Occupation of Kedah .... Vol. 4B
Japan Occupation of Kelantan .... Vol. 4B
Japan Occupation of Malacca .... Vol. 4B
Japan Occupation of Malaya .... Vol. 4B
Japan Occupation of Negri Sembilan ... Vol. 4B

Japan Occupation of Netherlands
Indies .... Vol. 5A
Japan Occupation of North Borneo ... Vol. 5A
Japan Occupation of Pahang .... Vol. 4B
Japan Occupation of Penang .... Vol. 4B
Japan Occupation of Perak .... Vol. 4B
Japan Occupation of Philippines ..... Vol. 1A,
Vol. 5A
Japan Occupation of Sarawak .... Vol. 6A
Japan Occupation of Selangor .... Vol. 4B
Japan Occupation of
Sts. Settlements .... Vol. 6A
Japan Occ. of Trengganu .... Vol. 6A
Other Japanese Stamps Overprinted ... Vol. 1B,
Vol. 2A, Vol. 4A, Vol. 5A
Jasdan .... Vol. 3B
Java .... Vol. 3B, Vol. 5A
Jedda .... Vol. 6A
Jeend .... Vol. 2A
Jehol .... Vol. 2A
Jersey .... Vol. 3A
Jersey, German Occupation .... Vol. 3A
Jerusalem, Italian Offices .... Vol. 3B
Jerusalem, Russian Offices .... Vol. 5B
Jetersville, Va. .... Vol. 1A
Jhalawar .... Vol. 3B
Jhind, Jind .... Vol. 3B
Johore, Johor .... Vol. 4B
Jonesboro, Tenn. .... Vol. 1A
J. P. Johnson (Confed. #66X1) .... Vol. 1A
Jordan .... Vol. 3B
Jordan (Palestine Occ.) .... Vol. 4A
Journaux 779
Juan Fernandez Islands (Chile) .... Vol. 2A
Jubile de l'Union Postale Universelle
(Switzerland #98) .... Vol. 6A
Jugoslavia, Jugoslavija .... Vol. 3B
Junagarh .... Vol. 3B

K .... Vol. 1A
KA3AKCTAH .... Vol. 4A
Kabul .... Vol. 1A
Kalaallit Nunaat, Kalatdlit Nunat ... Vol. 3A
Kamerun .... Vol. 2A
Kampuchea .... Vol. 2A
Kansu .... Vol. 2A
Karelia, Karjala .... Vol. 4A
Karema ovptd. on Belgian Congo .... Vol. 3A
Karki .... Vol. 3B
Karolinen .... Vol. 2A
Kashmir .... Vol. 3B
Katanga .... Vol. 4A
Kathiri State of Seiyun .... Vol. 1A
Kaunas .... Vol. 4A, Vol. 5B
Kayangel (Palau #686) .... Vol. 5A
Kazakhstan, Kazahstan, Kazakstan .... Vol. 4A
Kedah .... Vol. 4B
Keeling Islands .... Vol. 2A
Kelantan .... Vol. 4B
Kentta Postia 596
Kenya .... Vol. 4A
Kenya and Uganda .... Vol. 4A
Kenya, Uganda, Tanzania .... Vol. 4A
Kenya, Uganda, Tanganyika .... Vol. 4A
Kenya, Uganda, Tanganyika, Zanzibar ... Vol. 4A
Kerassunde .... Vol. 5B
Kermanshah .... Vol. 3B
K.G.C.A. ovptd. on Yugoslavia .... Vol. 6B
K.G.L. .... 130, Vol. 1A
Kharkiv .... Vol. 6B
Khmer Republic .... Vol. 2A
Khor Fakkan .... Vol. 6A
Kiangsi .... Vol. 2A
Kiangsu .... Vol. 2A
Kiauchau, Kiautschou .... Vol. 4A
Kibris .... Vol. 2A
Kibris Cumhuriyeti (Cyprus #198-200) ... 3
Kigoma ovptd. on Belgian Congo ..... Vol. 3A
Kilis .... Vol. 6A
King Edward VII Land
(New Zealand #121a) .... Vol. 5A
Kingman's City Post .... Vol. 1A
Kingston, Ga. .... Vol. 1A
Kionga .... Vol. 4A
Kirghizia .... Vol. 4A
Kiribati .... Vol. 4A
Kirin .... Vol. 2A
Kishangarh, Kishengarh .... Vol. 3B
Kithyra .... Vol. 3A, Vol. 6B
K.K. Post Stempel (or Stampel) ...... Vol. 1B
K.K.T.C. (Turk. Rep. N. Cyprus #RA1) ... Vol. 6B
Klaipeda .... Vol. 4A
Knoxville, Tenn. .... Vol. 1A
Kolomyia .... Vol. 6B
Kolozsvar .... Vol. 6B
Kon ... 542, Vol. 1B, Vol. 4A, Vol. 5B, Vol. 6A
Kongeligt 130
Kop Koh 542
Korca, Korce (Albania) .... Vol. 1A
Korea .... Vol. 4A
Korea, Democratic People's Republic ... Vol. 4A
Korea (Japanese Offices) .... Vol. 4A
Korea, Indian Custodial Unit .... Vol. 3B
Korea, North .... Vol. 4A
Korea, Soviet occupation .... Vol. 4A
Korea, U.S. Military Govt. .... Vol. 4A
Koritsa 420
Koror (Palau #686) .... Vol. 5A
Korytsa (Albania #81) .... Vol. 1A
Kos .... Vol. 3B

INDEX AND IDENTIFIER

Entry	Reference
Kosova	Vol. 4A
Kosovo	Vol. 1A, Vol. 4A
Kotah	Vol. 3B
Kouang Tcheou-Wan	784
KPHTH (Crete)	Vol. 4A
Kr., Kreuzer	Vol. 1B, Vol. 3B
Kraljevstvo, Kraljevina	Vol. 6B
K.S.A.	Vol. 6A
Kuban Government	Vol. 6A
K.U.K., K. und K.	Vol. 1B, Vol. 3B, Vol. 5B
Kunming	786
Kupa Zone	Vol. 6B
Kurdistan	Vol. 6A
Kurland, Kurzeme	Vol. 4A, Vol. 5B
Kurus	Vol. 6B
Kuwait, Koweit	Vol. 4A, Vol. 5A
Kwangchowan	784
Kwangsi	Vol. 2A
Kwangtung	Vol. 2A
Kweichow	Vol. 2A
K. Wurtt. Post	Vol. 3A
Kyiv	Vol. 6B
Kyrgyz Express Post	Vol. 4A
Kyrgyzstan	Vol. 4A
La Aguera	Vol. 1A
Labuan	Vol. 4A
La Canea	Vol. 3B
Lady McLeod	Vol. 6B
La Georgie	Vol. 4A
Lagos	Vol. 4A
La Grange, Tex.	Vol. 1A
Laibach	Vol. 6B
Lake City, Fla.	Vol. 1A
Lanchow	Vol. 2A
Land Post	Vol. 3A
Lao, Laos	Vol. 4A
Laos (Int. Com., India)	Vol. 3B
L.A.R.	Vol. 4A
Las Bela	Vol. 3B
Latakia, Lattaquie	Vol. 4A
Latvia, Latvija	Vol. 4A, Vol. 5B
Laurens Court House, S.C.	Vol. 1A
Lavaca	Vol. 1A
League of Nations	Vol. 6A
Lebanon	Vol. 4A, Vol. 5A, Vol. 6A
Leeward Islands	Vol. 4A
Lefkas	Vol. 3A, Vol. 3B
Lei ovptd. on Austria	Vol. 5B
Lemnos	Vol. 3A
Lenoir, N.C.	Vol. 1A
Lero, Leros	Vol. 3B
Lesbos	Vol. 3A
Lesotho	Vol. 4A
Lesser Sundas	Vol. 5A
Lettland, Lettonia	Vol. 4A
Letzebuerg	Vol. 3A
Levant, British	Vol. 3A
Levant, French	788, Vol. 6A
Levant, Italian	Vol. 3B
Levant, Polish	Vol. 5B
Levant, Romanian	Vol. 5B
Levant, Russian	Vol. 5B
Levant, Syrian (on Lebanon)	Vol. 6A
Lexington, Miss.	Vol. 1A
Lexington, Va.	Vol. 1A
Liaoning	Vol. 2A
Liban, Libanaise	Vol. 4A
Libau ovptd. on German	Vol. 4A
Liberia	Vol. 4A
Liberty, Va.	Vol. 1A
Libya, Libia, Libye	Vol. 4A
Libyan Arab Republic	Vol. 4A
Liechtenstein	Vol. 4A
Lietuva, Lietuvos	Vol. 4A
Lifland	Vol. 5B
Ligne Aeriennes de la France Libre (Syria #MC5)	Vol. 6A
Lima	Vol. 5A
Limestone Springs, S.C.	Vol. 1A
L'Inde	806
Linja-Autorahti Bussfrakt	596
Lipso, Lisso	Vol. 3B
Lithuania	Vol. 4A, Vol. 5B
Lithuania, Central	Vol. 2A
Lithuanian Occupation of Memel	Vol. 4B
Litwa Srodkowa, Litwy Srodkowej	Vol. 2A
Livingston, Ala.	Vol. 1A
Livonia	Vol. 5B
Ljubljana	Vol. 6B
Llanes	Vol. 6A
L McL	Vol. 6B
Local	Vol. 6B
Local Post	Vol. 2A
Lockport, N.Y.	Vol. 1A
Lombardy-Venetia	Vol. 1B
Lorraine	782
Losen	Vol. 6A
Lothringen	782
Louisville, Ky.	Vol. 1A
Lourenco Marques, L. Marques	Vol. 4A
Lower Austria	Vol. 1B
L P overprinted on Russian stamps	Vol. 4A
LTSR on Lithuania	Vol. 4A
Lubeck, Luebeck	Vol. 3A
Lubiana	Vol. 6B
Lublin	Vol. 5B
Luminescence	Vol. 1A
Luxembourg	Vol. 4A
Lviv	Vol. 6B
Lydenburg	Vol. 6B
Lynchburg, Va.	Vol. 1A
Macao, Macau	Vol. 4B
Macedonia	Vol. 4B
Machin Head definitives	Vol. 3A
Macon, Ga.	Vol. 1A
Madagascar, Madagasikara	Vol. 4B
Madagascar (British)	Vol. 4B
Madeira	Vol. 4B, Vol. 5B
Madero Issue (Mexico)	Vol. 4B
Madison, Ga.	Vol. 1A
Madison Court House, Fla.	Vol. 1A
Madrid	Vol. 6A
Madura	Vol. 5A
Mafeking	Vol. 2A
Magdalena	Vol. 2A
Magyar, Magyarorszag	Vol. 3B
Magy. Kir.	Vol. 3B
Majunga	Vol. 4B
Makedonija	Vol. 4B
Malacca	Vol. 4B
Malaga	Vol. 6A
Malagasy Republic	Vol. 4B
Malawi	Vol. 4B
Malaya	Vol. 4B
Malaya (Japanese Occ.)	Vol. 4B, Vol. 5A
Malaya (Thai Occ.)	Vol. 4B
Malaya, Federation of	Vol. 4B
Malaysia	Vol. 4B
Malay States	Vol. 4B
Maldive Islands, Maldives	Vol. 4B
Malgache Republique	Vol. 4B
Mali	Vol. 4D
Malmedy	Vol. 3A
Malta	Vol. 4B
Maluku Selatan (So. Moluccas)	Vol. 6A
Man, Isle of	Vol. 3A
Manchukuo	Vol. 4B
Manchukuo stamps overprinted	Vol. 2A
Manchuria	Vol. 2A
Manizales	Vol. 2A
Mapka, Mapok	543, Vol. 5B
Mariana Islands, Marianen	Vol. 4B
Marienwerder	Vol. 4B
Marietta, Ga.	Vol. 1A
Marion, Va.	Vol. 1A
Markka, Markkaa	543
Maroc, Marocco, Marokko	809, Vol. 3A, Vol. 4B
Marruecos	Vol. 4B, Vol. 6A
Mars Bluff, S.C.	Vol. 1A
Marshall Islands, Marschall-Inseln, Marshall-Inseln	Vol. 4B
Marshall Islands (G.R.I. surch.)	Vol. 5A
Martinique	Vol. 4B
Martin's City Post	Vol. 1A
Mauritania, Mauritanie	Vol. 4B
Mauritania stamps surcharged	874
Mauritius	Vol. 4B
Mayotte	Vol. 4B
Mayreau	Vol. 5B
M.B.D. overprinted	Vol. 3B
McNeel, A.W.	Vol. 1A
Mecca	Vol. 6A
Mecklenburg-Schwerin	Vol. 3A
Mecklenburg-Strelitz	Vol. 3A
Mecklenburg-Vorpommern	Vol. 3A
Mecklenburg-Vorpommern	Vol. 3A
Medellin	Vol. 2A
Medina	Vol. 6A
Medio Real	237
M.E.F. ovptd on Great Britain	Vol. 3A
Mejico	Vol. 4B
Melaka	Vol. 4B
Melekeor (Palau #686)	Vol. 5A
Memel, Memelgebiet	Vol. 4B
Memphis, Tenn.	Vol. 1A
Meng Chiang	Vol. 2A
Menge	Vol. 4B
Mengtsz	785
Merida	Vol. 4B
Meshed	Vol. 3B
Mesopotamia (British Occupation)	Vol. 3A
Metelin	Vol. 5B
Mexico, Mexicano	Vol. 4B
Micanopy, Fla.	Vol. 1A
Micronesia	Vol. 4B
Middle Congo	Vol. 4B
Middle East Forces	Vol. 3A
Mihon	Vol. 4A
Mil	Vol. 6B
Militarpost (Milit. Post)	Vol. 1B
Millbury, Mass.	Vol. 1A
Milledgeville, Ga.	Vol. 1A
Miller, Gen.	Vol. 5B
Milliemes surch. on French Off. in Turkey	788
Milton, N.C.	Vol. 1A
M. Kir.	Vol. 3B
Mn.	Vol. 5A
Mobile, Ala.	Vol. 1A
Mocambique	Vol. 4B
Modena, Modones	Vol. 3B
Moheli	Vol. 4B
Moldavia	Vol. 4B, Vol. 5B
Moldova	Vol. 4B
Moluccas	Vol. 5A
Monaco	Vol. 4B
Monastir	Vol. 6B
Mongolia	Vol. 4B
Mongtseu, Mongtze	785
Monrovia	Vol. 4A
Mont Athos	Vol. 5B
Montenegro	Vol. 4B
Monterrey	Vol. 4B
Montevideo	Vol. 6B
Montgomery, Ala.	Vol. 1A
Montserrat	Vol. 5A
Moquea, Moquegua	Vol. 5A
Morelia	Vol. 4B
Morocco	Vol. 4B
Morocco (British Offices)	Vol. 3A
Morocco (German Offices)	Vol. 3A
Morocco, French	809
Morocco, Spanish	Vol. 6A
Morvi	Vol. 3B
Moschopolis	421
Mosul	Vol. 4B
Mount Athos (Greece)	Vol. 3A
Mount Athos (Turkey)	Vol. 6B
Mount Athos, Russian Offices	Vol. 5B
Mount Lebanon, La.	Vol. 1A
Mount Pleasant, NC	Vol. 1A
Moyen-Congo	Vol. 4B
Mozambique	Vol. 4B
Mozambique Co.	Vol. 4B
MQE ovptd. on French Colonies	Vol. 4B
Muscat and Oman	Vol. 5A
Mustique	Vol. 5B
M.V.iR	Vol. 5B
Myanmar (Burma)	Vol. 1B
Mytilene	Vol. 3A
Nabha	Vol. 3B
Naciones Unidas	Vol. 1A
Nagyvarad	Vol. 3B
Namibia	Vol. 5A, Vol. 6A
Nandgaon	Vol. 3B
Nanking	Vol. 2A
Nanumaga	Vol. 6B
Nanumea	Vol. 6B
Naples, Napoletana	Vol. 3B
Nashville, Tenn.	Vol. 1A
Natal	Vol. 5A
Nations Unies	Vol. 1A, Vol. 6A
Native Feudatory States, India	Vol. 3B
Nauru	Vol. 5A
Navanagar	Vol. 3B
Navarra	Vol. 6A
N.C.E. ovptd on French Colonies	Vol. 5A
Neapolitan Provinces	Vol. 3B
Ncd. (Nederlandse) Antillen	Vol. 5A
Ned. (Nederl, Nederlandse) Indie	Vol. 5A
Nederland	Vol. 5A
Nederlands Nieuw Guinea	Vol. 5A
Negeri Sembilan	Vol. 4B
Negri Sembilan	Vol. 4B
Nejd	Vol. 6A
Nejdi Administration of Hejaz	Vol. 6A
Nepal	Vol. 5A
Netherlands	Vol. 5A
Netherlands Antilles	Vol. 5A
Netherlands Indies	Vol. 5A
Netherlands New Guinea	Vol. 5A
Nevis	Vol. 5A
New Britain	Vol. 5A
New Brunswick	Vol. 2A
New Caledonia	Vol. 5A
New Caledonia stamps overprinted	Vol. 5A
Newfoundland	Vol. 2A
New Granada	Vol. 2A
New Greece	Vol. 3A
New Guinea	Vol. 5A
New Guinea, British	Vol. 5A
New Guinea, German	Vol. 3A
New Haven, Conn.	Vol. 1A
New Hebrides (British)	Vol. 5A
New Hebrides (French)	Vol. 5A
New Orleans, La.	Vol. 1A
New Republic	Vol. 5A
New Smyrna, Fla.	Vol. 1A
New South Wales	Vol. 5A
New York, N.Y.	Vol. 1A
New Zealand	Vol. 5A
Nezavisna	Vol. 2A
N.F. overprinted on Nyasaland Pro.	Vol. 3A
Ngaraard (Palau #686)	Vol. 5A
Ngardmau (Palau #686)	Vol. 5A
Ngaremlengui (Palau #686)	Vol. 5A
Ngchesar (Palau #686)	Vol. 5A
Ngiwal (Palau #686)	Vol. 5A
Nicaragua	Vol. 5A
Nicaria	Vol. 3B, Vol. 6A
Nieuwe Republiek	Vol. 5A
Nieuw Guinea	Vol. 5A
Niger	Vol. 6A
Niger and Senegambia	Vol. 6A
Niger and Upper Senegal	Vol. 6B
Niger Coast Protectorate	Vol. 5A
Nigeria	Vol. 5A
Nikolaevsk	Vol. 6A
Ningsia	Vol. 2A
Nippon	Vol. 4A
Nisiro, Nisiros	Vol. 3B
Niuafo'ou	Vol. 6B
Niue	Vol. 6B
Niutao	Vol. 6B
Nlle. Caledonie	Vol. 5A
No Hay Estampillas	Vol. 2A
N. O. P. O. (Confed. #62XU1)	Vol. 1A
Norddeutscher Postbezirk	Vol. 3A
Noreg (1st stamp #318)	Vol. 5A
Norfolk, Va.	Vol. 1A
Norfolk Island	Vol. 5A
Norge	Vol. 5A
North Borneo	Vol. 5A
North China	Vol. 2A
Northeast China	Vol. 2A
Northeast Postal Service	Vol. 2A
Northeastern Provinces (China)	Vol. 2A
North Epirus (Greek Occupation)	Vol. 3A
Northern Cook Islands	Vol. 5A
Northern Cyprus, Turkish Rep. of	Vol. 6B
Northern Ireland	Vol. 3A
Northern Kiangsu	Vol. 2A
Northern Nigeria	Vol. 5A
Northern Poland	Vol. 5B
Northern Rhodesia	Vol. 5A
Northern Zone, Morocco	Vol. 4B
North German Confederation	Vol. 3A
North Ingermanland	Vol. 3A
North Viet Nam	Vol. 6B
Northwest China	Vol. 2A
North West (N. W.) Pacific Islands	Vol. 5A
Norway	Vol. 5A
Nossi-Be	Vol. 5A
Notopher	Vol. 3A
Nouvelle Caledonie	Vol. 5A
Nouvelle Hebrides	Vol. 5A
Nova Scotia	Vol. 2A
Novocherkassk	Vol. 6A
Nowa	Vol. 1B
Nowa Db ovptd. on Bulgaria	Vol. 5B
Nowanuggur	Vol. 3B
Nowta	Vol. 6A
Nowte	Vol. 5A
Noyta	Vol. 1B, Vol. 3A, Vol. 4A, Vol. 5B, Vol. 6B
NP surcharged on Great Britain	Vol. 5A
Nr. 21, Nr. 16	Vol. 3A
N S B ovptd. on French Colonies	Vol. 5A
N. Sembilan	Vol. 4B
N.S.W.	Vol. 1A
Nueva Granada	Vol. 2A
Nui	Vol. 6B
Nukufetau	Vol. 6B
Nukulaelae	Vol. 6B
Nyasaland (Protectorate)	Vol. 5A
Nyasaland and Rhodesia	Vol. 5A
Nyasaland, overprinted	Vol. 3A
Nyassa	Vol. 5A
N.Z.	Vol. 5A
Oakway, S.C.	Vol. 1A
Oaxaca	Vol. 4B
Obock	Vol. 5A
Ob. Ost ovptd. on Germany (Lithuania)	Vol. 5B
Occupation Francaise	Vol. 3B
Oceania, Oceanie	815
Oesterr. Post, Ofterreich	Vol. 1B
Offentlig Sak, Off. Sak	Vol. 5A
Oil Rivers	Vol. 5A
O K C A (Russia)	Vol. 5B
Oldenburg	Vol. 3A
Olonets	Vol. 5B
Oltre Giuba	Vol. 3A
Oman, Sultanate of	Vol. 5A
ONU (UN Offices in Geneva #384)	Vol. 1A
Oradea	Vol. 3B
Orange River Colony	Vol. 5A
Oranje Vrij Staat	Vol. 5A
Orchha, Orcha	Vol. 3B
Ore surcharged on Denmark	502
Orense	Vol. 6A
Organisation Mondiale de la Sante	Vol. 6A
Oriental	Vol. 6B
Orts-Post	Vol. 6A
O.S.	Vol. 5A
Osten	Vol. 5B
Osterreich	Vol. 1B
Ostland	Vol. 5B
Ottoman, Ottomanes	289, Vol. 6B
Oubangi Chari	Vol. 6B
Outer Mongolia	Vol. 4B
Oviedo	Vol. 6A
O.V.S.	Vol. 5A
Oxford, N.C.	Vol. 1A
O'zbekiston	Vol. 6B
P	501, Vol. 2A, Vol. 4A, Vol. 6A
P on Straits Settlements	Vol. 4B
Pacchi Postali	Vol. 3B, Vol. 6A
Pacific Steam Navigation Co.	Vol. 5A
Packhoi, Pakhoi	785
Pahang	Vol. 4B
Paid (Confed. #35X, etc.)	Vol. 1A
Paid 5 (US #4X1, 7X1, many Confed.)	Vol. 1A
Paid 10 (Confed. #76XU, 101XU, 80XU)	Vol. 1A
Paid 2 Cents (Confed. #2XU)	Vol. 1A
Paid 3 Cents (Confed. #2AXU)	Vol. 1A
Paita	Vol. 5A
Pakistan	Vol. 5A
Pakke-porto	Vol. 3A
Palau	Vol. 5A
Palestine	418, Vol. 5A
Palestine (British Administration)	Vol. 5A
Palestine (Jordan Occ.)	Vol. 4A

881

INDEX AND IDENTIFIER

Palestine overprinted .... Vol. 4A
Palestinian Authority .... Vol. 5A
Panama .... Vol. 5A
Panama (Colombian Dom.) ... Vol. 2A, Vol. 5A
Panama Canal Zone .... Vol. 1A
Papua .... Vol. 5A
Papua New Guinea .... Vol. 5A
Para .... 350, 775, Vol. 6B
Para ovptd. on Austria .... Vol. 1B
Para ovptd. on France 789
Para ovptd. on Germany .... Vol. 3A
Para ovptd. on Italy .... Vol. 3B
Paraguay .... Vol. 5A
Paras .... 350, Vol. 6B
Paras ovpt. on Great Britain .... Vol. 3A
Paras ovpt. on Romania .... Vol. 5B
Paras ovpt. on Russia .... Vol. 5B
Parma, Parm., Parmensi .... Vol. 3B
Pasco .... Vol. 5A
Patiala .... Vol. 3B
Patmo, Patmos .... Vol. 3B
Patterson, N.C. .... Vol. 1A
Patton, N.B. (Confed. #138XU1) .... Vol. 1A
Patzcuaro .... Vol. 4B
Paxos .... Vol. 2A, Vol. 3A, Vol. 3B
PC CP .... Vol. 5B
PD .... Vol. 5B
P.E. (Egypt #4, etc.) 350
Pechino, Peking .... Vol. 3B
Peleliu (Palau #686) .... Vol. 5A
Pen, Penna 543
Penang .... Vol. 4B
Penny Post (US 3LB, 8LB) .... Vol. 1A
Penrhyn Island .... Vol. 5A
Pensacola, Fla. .... Vol. 1A
Penybnnka Cpncka .... Vol. 1B
People's Republic of China .... Vol. 2A
Perak .... Vol. 4B
Perlis .... Vol. 4B
Persekutuan Tanah Melayu
  (Malaya #91) .... Vol. 4B
Persia (British Occupation) .... Vol. 1B
Persia, Persanes .... Vol. 3B
Peru, Peruana .... Vol. 5A
Pesa ovpt. on Germany .... Vol. 3A
Petersburg, Va. .... Vol. 1A
Pfennig, Pfg., Pf. .... 461, Vol. 3A, Vol. 4A
P.G.S. (Perak) .... Vol. 4B
Philadelphia, Pa. .... Vol. 1A
Philippines .... Vol. 2A, Vol. 5A
Philippines (US Admin.) .... Vol. 1A, Vol. 5A
Philippines (Japanese Occ.) ... Vol. 1A, Vol. 5A
Piast., Piaster ovptd. on Austria .... Vol. 1B
Piaster ovptd. on Germany .... Vol. 3A
Piaster ovptd. on Romania .... Vol. 5B
Piastre, Piastra ovptd. on Italy .... Vol. 3B
Piastre .... 350, Vol. 4B, Vol. 6B
Piastre ovptd. on France 788
Piastres ovpt. on Great Britain .... Vol. 3A
Piastres ovpt. on Russia .... Vol. 5B
Pies .... Vol. 2A, Vol. 3B
Pietersburg .... Vol. 6B
Pilgrim Tercentenary (US #548) .... Vol. 1A
Pilipinas .... Vol. 1A, Vol. 5A
Pisco .... Vol. 5A
Piscopi .... Vol. 3B
Pitcairn Islands .... Vol. 5B
Pittsylvania C.H., Va. .... Vol. 1A
Piura .... Vol. 5A
Plains of Dura, Ga. .... Vol. 1A
Pleasant Shade, Va. .... Vol. 1A
Plum Creek, Tex. .... Vol. 1A
P.O. Paid .... Vol. 1A
Pobres (Spain #RA11) .... Vol. 6A
POCCI, POCC R .... Vol. 5B
Poczta, Polska .... 289, Vol. 5B
Pohjois Inkeri .... Vol. 5A
Pokutia .... Vol. 6B
Poland .... Vol. 5B
Poland, exile government in
  Great Britain .... Vol. 5B
Polish Levant .... Vol. 5B
Polish Offices in Danzig .... Vol. 5B
Polish Offices in Turkish Empire .... Vol. 5B
Polska .... Vol. 5B
Polynesia, French (Polynesie) 815
Ponce .... Vol. 1A, Vol. 5B
Ponta Delgada .... Vol. 5B
Р.О.П.иТ .... Vol. 5B
Poonch .... Vol. 3B
Popayan .... Vol. 2A
Port Arthur and Dairen .... Vol. 2A
Porteado .... Vol. 5B
Porte de Conduccion .... Vol. 5A
Porte de Mar .... Vol. 4B
Porte Franco .... Vol. 5A
Port Gibson, Miss. .... Vol. 1A
Port Gdansk .... Vol. 5B
Port Hood, Nova Scotia .... Vol. 2A
Port Lagos 789
Port Lavaca, Tex. .... Vol. 1A
Porto .... Vol. 1A, Vol. 1B, Vol. 6B
Porto Gazetei .... Vol. 5A
Porto Pflichtige .... Vol. 3A
Porto Rico .... Vol. 1A, Vol. 2A, Vol. 5B
Port Said, French Offices 786
Portugal, Portuguesa .... Vol. 5B
Portuguese Africa .... Vol. 5B
Portuguese Congo .... Vol. 5B
Portuguese East Africa (Mozambique) ... Vol. 4B

Portuguese Guinea .... Vol. 5B
Portuguese India .... Vol. 5B
Portuguese India overprinted .... Vol. 6B
Posen (Poznan) .... Vol. 5B
Post .... Vol. 3A, Vol. 3B
Post (Postage) & Receipt .... Vol. 3B
Posta .... Vol. 1A, Vol. 6A
Postage(s) .... Vol. 1A, Vol. 3A, Vol. 3B, Vol. 4B, Vol. 5B
Postage Due .... Vol. 1A, Vol. 3A
Postas le hioc .... Vol. 3B
Poste Locale .... Vol. 6A
Postes .... 782, Vol. 1B, Vol. 4A
Postes Serbes ovptd. on France .... Vol. 6A
Postgebiet Ob. Ost. .... Vol. 5B
Postmarke .... Vol. 3A
Post Office (US #7X, 9X) .... Vol. 1A
Post Stamp .... Vol. 3B
Postzegel .... Vol. 5A
P.P. ovptd. on French postage dues 809
P.P.C. ovptd. on Poland .... Vol. 5B
Pre .... Vol. 6B
Prefecture issues .... Vol. 4A
Preussen .... Vol. 3A
Priamur .... Vol. 6A
Prince Edward Island .... Vol. 2A
Pristina .... Vol. 6B
Province of Canada .... Vol. 2A
Providence (Prov.), R.I. .... Vol. 1A
Prussia .... Vol. 3A
PS .... Vol. 2A, Vol. 3B
P.S.N.C. (Peru) .... Vol. 5A
Puerto Principe .... Vol. 1A, Vol. 2A
Puerto Rico, Pto. Rico .... Vol. 1A, Vol. 2A, Vol. 5B
Puerto Rico (US Admin.) .... Vol. 1A, Vol. 5B
Pul .... Vol. 1A
Pulau Pinang .... Vol. 4B
Puno .... Vol. 5A
Puttialla State .... Vol. 3B

Qatar .... **Vol. 5B**
Qu'aiti State in Hadhramaut .... Vol. 1A
Qu'aiti State of Shihr and Mukalla ...... Vol. 1A
Queensland .... Vol. 1A
Quelimane .... Vol. 5B

R (Armenia) .... **Vol. 1A**
R (Jind, Iran) .... Vol. 3B
R ovptd. on French Colonies 789
Rajasthan .... Vol. 3B
Rajpeepla, Rajpipla .... Vol. 3B
Raleigh, N.C. .... Vol. 1A
Rappen .... Vol. 6A
Rarotonga .... Vol. 2A
Ras al Khaima .... Vol. 5B, Vol. 6B
R.A.U. .... Vol. 6A
Rayon .... Vol. 6A
Recargo .... Vol. 6A
Redonda (Antigua) .... Vol. 1A
Refugee Relief .... Vol. 3B
Regatul .... Vol. 3B
Reichspost .... Vol. 3A
Reis (Portugal) .... Vol. 5B
Repubblica Sociale Italiana .... Vol. 3B
Republic of China .... Vol. 2A
Republique Arab Unie .... Vol. 6A
Republique Democratique du Congo ... Vol. 6B
Reseau d'Etat 779
Resistance overprinted on Syria .... Vol. 6A
Rethymnon, Retymno .... Vol. 2A
Reunion 790
R.F. .... See France or French Colonies
RF - Solidarite Francaise 798
R H .... Vol. 3B
Rheatown, Tenn. .... Vol. 1A
Rheinland-Pfalz .... Vol. 3A
Rhine Palatinate .... Vol. 3A
Rhodes .... Vol. 3B
Rhodesia .... Vol. 5B
Rhodesia (formerly So. Rhodesia) ...... Vol. 5B
Rhodesia and Nyasaland .... Vol. 5B
Rialtar .... Vol. 3B
Riau, Riouw Archipelago .... Vol. 3B
Ricevuta .... Vol. 3B, Vol. 6A
Richmond, Tex. .... Vol. 1A
Rigsbank Skilling 130
Ringgold, Ga. .... Vol. 1A
Rio de Oro .... Vol. 6A
Rio Muni .... Vol. 5B
RIS on Netherlands Indies .... Vol. 3B
Rizeh .... Vol. 1A
Rn. .... Vol. 4A
RNS .... Vol. 3B
R. O. ovptd. on Turkey 289
Robertsport .... Vol. 4A
Rodi .... Vol. 3B
Roepiah .... Vol. 5A
Romagna, Romagne .... Vol. 3B
Romana .... Vol. 3B, Vol. 5B
Romania, Roumania .... Vol. 5B
Romania, Occupation, Offices .... Vol. 5B
Romanian Occupation of Hungary ...... Vol. 3B
Romanian Occupation of
  Western Ukraine .... Vol. 6B
Romania, Offices in the
  Turkish Empire .... Vol. 5B
Roman States .... Vol. 3B
Ross Dependency .... Vol. 5A
Rossija .... Vol. 5B

Rostov .... Vol. 6A
Rouad, Ile .... Vol. 5B
Roumelie Orientale 289
Rpf overprinted on Luxembourg .... Vol. 4A
RSA .... Vol. 6A
R S M (San Marino) .... Vol. 6A
Ruanda ovptd. on Congo .... Vol. 3A
Ruanda-Urundi .... Vol. 5B
Ruffifch-Polen ovptd. on Germany ..... Vol. 5B
Rumania, Roumania .... Vol. 5B
Rumanien on Germany .... Vol. 5B
Rupee on Great Britain .... Vol. 5A
Russia .... Vol. 5B
Russia (Finnish Occupation) Vol. 4A, Vol. 5B
Russia (German Occupation) .... Vol. 5B
Russian Company of Navigation
  & Trade .... Vol. 5B
Russian Dominion of Poland .... Vol. 5B
Russian Empire, Finland 542
Russian Occupation of Crete .... Vol. 2A
Russian Occupation of Germany .... Vol. 3A
Russian Occupation of Korea .... Vol. 1A
Russian Occupation of Latvia .... Vol. 4A
Russian Occupation of Lithuania .... Vol. 4A
Russian Offices .... Vol. 5B
Russian Offices in China .... Vol. 5B
Russian Offices in Turkish Empire ...... Vol. 5B
Russian stamps surch. or ovptd. ... 111, 438, 501, Vol. 1A, Vol. 3A, Vol. 4A, Vol. 5B, Vol. 6A
Russian Turkestan .... Vol. 5B
Rustenburg .... Vol. 6B
Rutherfordton, N.C. .... Vol. 1A
Rwanda, Rwandaise .... Vol. 5B
Ryukyu Islands .... Vol. 1A

S on Straits Settlements .... **Vol. 4B**
S A, S.A.K. (Saudi Arabia) .... Vol. 6A
Saar, Saargebiet, Saar Land .... Vol. 5B
Saba (Caribbean Netherlands #111) ... Vol. 2A
Sabah .... Vol. 4B
Sachsen .... Vol. 3A
Sahara Occidental (Espanol) .... Vol. 6A
St. Christopher .... Vol. 5B
St. Christopher-Nevis-Anguilla .... Vol. 5B
St. Eustatius (Caribbean
  Netherlands #112) .... Vol. 2A
Ste. Marie de Madagascar .... Vol. 1B
St. Georges, Bermuda .... Vol. 1B
St. Helena .... Vol. 5B
S. Thome (Tome) E Principe .... Vol. 5B
St. Kitts .... Vol. 5B
St. Kitts-Nevis .... Vol. 5B
St. Louis, Mo. .... Vol. 1A
St. Lucia .... Vol. 5B
St. Martin .... Vol. 5B
St. Pierre and Miquelon .... Vol. 5B
St. Thomas and Prince Islands .... Vol. 5B
St. Vincent .... Vol. 5B
St. Vincent and the Grenadines .... Vol. 5B
St. Vincent Grenadines .... Vol. 5B
Salamanca Province .... Vol. 6A
Salem, N.C. .... Vol. 1A
Salem, Va. .... Vol. 1A
Salisbury, N.C. .... Vol. 1A
Salonicco, Salonika .... Vol. 3B
Salonika (Turkish) .... Vol. 3B
Salonique .... Vol. 5B, Vol. 6B
Salvador, El .... Vol. 6A
Salzburg .... Vol. 1B
Samoa .... Vol. 5B
Samos .... 779, Vol. 3A
San Antonio, Tex. .... Vol. 1A
San Marino .... Vol. 6A
San Sebastian .... Vol. 6A
Santa Cruz de Tenerife .... Vol. 6A
Santa Maura .... Vol. 3A, Vol. 3B
Santander .... Vol. 2A
Sao Paulo .... Vol. 1B
Sao Tome and Principe .... Vol. 5B
Saorstat .... Vol. 3B
Sarawak .... Vol. 4B, Vol. 6A
Sardinia .... Vol. 3B
Sarre overprinted on Germany
  and Bavaria .... Vol. 5B
Saseno .... Vol. 6A
Saudi Arabia .... Vol. 6A
Saudi Arabia overprinted .... Vol. 4A
Saurashtra .... Vol. 3B
Savannah, Ga. .... Vol. 1A
Saxony .... Vol. 3A
SCADTA .... Vol. 2A
Scarpanto .... Vol. 3B
Schleswig .... Vol. 3A, Vol. 6A
Schleswig-Holstein .... Vol. 3A
Schweizer Reneke .... Vol. 6B
Scinde .... Vol. 3B
Scotland .... Vol. 3A
Scutari, Italian Offices .... Vol. 3B
Segel Porto (on Neth. Indies) .... Vol. 3B
Segnatasse, Segna Tassa .... Vol. 3B
Seiyun .... Vol. 1A
Selangor .... Vol. 4B
Selma, Ala. .... Vol. 1A
Semenov 501
Sen, Sn. .... Vol. 1A, Vol. 4A, Vol. 5B
Senegal .... Vol. 6A
Senegal stamps surcharged 874
Senegambia and Niger .... Vol. 6A
Serb Administration of Bosnia,
  Banja Luca .... Vol. 1B

Serbia, Serbien .... Vol. 6A
Serbia & Montenego .... Vol. 4B, Vol. 6A
Serbian Occupation of Hungary .... Vol. 3B
Service .... Vol. 3B, Vol. 5A
Sevastopol .... Vol. 6A
Seville, Sevilla .... Vol. 6A
Seychelles .... Vol. 6A
S.H. .... Vol. 3A
Shanghai .... Vol. 2A, Vol. 5B
Shanghai (U.S. Offices) .... Vol. 1A
Shanghai and Nanking .... Vol. 2A
Shansi .... Vol. 2A
Shantung .... Vol. 2A
Sharjah .... Vol. 6A
Shensi .... Vol. 2A
Shihr and Mukalla .... Vol. 1A
Shqipenia, Shqiptare, Shqiperija,
  Shqiperise (Albania) .... Vol. 1A
S.H.S. in Bosnia and Herzegovina ...... Vol. 6B
S.H.S. on Hungary .... Vol. 6B
Siam (Thailand) .... Vol. 6B
Siberia .... Vol. 6A
Siberian stamps overprinted or
  surcharged 501
Sicily, Sicilia .... Vol. 3B
Siege de la Ligue Arabe
  (Morocco #44) .... Vol. 4B
Sierra Leone .... Vol. 6A
Sikang .... Vol. 2A
Silesia, Eastern 289
Silesia, Upper .... Vol. 6B
Simi .... Vol. 3B
Sinaloa .... Vol. 4B
Singapore .... Vol. 6A
Sinkiang .... Vol. 2A
Sint Maarten .... Vol. 5B
Sirmoor, Sirmur .... Vol. 3B
Six Cents .... Vol. 1A
Sld. .... Vol. 1B
Slesvig .... Vol. 6A
Slovakia .... 73, Vol. 6A
Slovene Coast .... Vol. 6B
Slovenia, Slovenija .... Vol. 6A
Slovenia, Italian .... Vol. 6B
Slovensko, Slovenska, Slovensky ... 27, Vol. 6A
S. Marino .... Vol. 3B
Smirne, Smyrna .... Vol. 3B
Smyrne .... Vol. 3B
S O ovptd. on Czechoslovakia, Poland 289
Sobreporte .... Vol. 2A
Sociedad Colombo-Alemana .... Vol. 2a
Sociedade de Geographia de Lisboa ... Vol. 5B
Societe des Nations .... Vol. 6A
Soldi .... Vol. 1B
Solomon Islands .... Vol. 6A
Somali, Somalia, Somaliya .... Vol. 6A
Somalia, B.M.A. .... Vol. 3A
Somalia, E.A.F. .... Vol. 3A
Somali Coast (Djibouti) .... Vol. 6A
Somaliland Protectorate .... Vol. 6A
Sonora .... Vol. 4B
Sonsorol (Palau #686) .... Vol. 5A
Soomaaliya, Sooomaliyeed .... Vol. 6A
Soruth, Sorath .... Vol. 3B
Soudan .... 873, Vol. 6A
South Africa .... Vol. 6A
South African Republic (Transvaal) ... Vol. 6B
South Arabia .... Vol. 6A
South Australia .... Vol. 1A
South Bulgaria 289
South Borneo .... Vol. 5A
South China .... Vol. 2A
Southern Nigeria .... Vol. 6A
Southern Poland .... Vol. 5B
Southern Rhodesia .... Vol. 6A
Southern Yemen .... Vol. 6B
South Georgia .... 501, Vol. 6A
South Georgia and South
  Sandwich Islands .... Vol. 6A
South Kasai .... Vol. 6A
South Korea .... Vol. 4A
South Lithuania .... Vol. 4A
South Moluccas .... Vol. 6A
South Orkneys 501
South Russia .... Vol. 5B
South Russian stamps surcharged ...... Vol. 5B
South Shetlands 501
South Sudan .... Vol. 6A
South Viet Nam .... Vol. 6B
South West Africa .... Vol. 6A
Southwest China .... Vol. 2A
Soviet Union (Russia) .... Vol. 5B
Sowjetische Besatzungs Zone .... Vol. 3A
Spain .... Vol. 6A
Spanish Administration of Andorra ... Vol. 1A
Spanish Dominion of Cuba .... Vol. 2A
Spanish Dominion of Mariana Islands ... Vol. 4B
Spanish Dominion of Philippines .... Vol. 5A
Spanish Dominion of Puerto Rico ...... Vol. 5B
Spanish Guinea .... Vol. 6A
Spanish Morocco .... Vol. 6A
Spanish Sahara .... Vol. 6A
Spanish West Africa .... Vol. 6A
Spanish Western Sahara .... Vol. 6A
Sparta, Ga. .... Vol. 1A
Spartanburg, S.C. .... Vol. 1A
SPM ovptd. on French Cols. .... Vol. 5B
Srbija I Crna Gora .... Vol. 6A
Sri Lanka .... Vol. 6A
Srodkowa Litwa .... Vol. 2A

INDEX AND IDENTIFIER

Stamp (Tibet #O1) .... Vol. 6B
Stampalia .... Vol. 3B
Stadt Berlin .... Vol. 3A
Stanyslaviv .... Vol. 6B
Statesville, N.C. .... Vol. 1A
Steinmeyer's City Post .... Vol. 1A
Stellaland .... Vol. 6A
Stempel .... Vol. 1B
Straits Settlements .... Vol. 6A
Straits Settlements overprinted .... Vol. 6A
Strombus gigas Linne
  (Neth. Antilles #1193) .... Vol. 5A
STT Vuja, STT Vujna .... Vol. 1B
Styria .... Vol. 1B
S.U. on Straits Settlements .... Vol. 4B
Submarine mail (Correo Submarino) .... Vol. 6A
Sudan .... Vol. 6A
Sudan, French 873
Suid Afrika .... Vol. 6A
Suidwes-Afrika .... Vol. 6A
Suiyuan .... Vol. 2A
S. Ujong .... Vol. 4B
Sultanate of Oman .... Vol. 5A
Sumatra .... Vol. 3B, Vol. 5A
Sumter, S.C. .... Vol. 1A
Sungei Ujong .... Vol. 4B
Suomi (Finland) 542
Supeh .... Vol. 2A
Surakarta .... Vol. 3B
Surinam, Suriname, Surinaamse ... Vol. 6A
Suvalki .... Vol. 5B
Sverige .... Vol. 6A
S.W.A. .... Vol. 6A
Swaziland, Swazieland .... Vol. 6A
Sweden .... Vol. 6A
Switzerland .... Vol. 6A
Switzerland, Administration of
  Liechtenstein .... Vol. 4A
Syria, Syrie, Syrienne ...... Vol. 5A, Vol. 6A
Syria (Arabian Government) .... Vol. 6A
Syrie .... Vol. 6A
Syrie-Grand Liban .... Vol. 6A
Szechwan .... Vol. 2A
Szeged .... Vol. 3B

T .... 283, Vol. 1B
T ovptd. on stamps of Peru .... Vol. 5A
Tabora ovptd. on Belgian Congo ... Vol. 3A
Tacna .... Vol. 5A
Tadjikistan, Tadzhikistan .... Vol. 6A
Tae Han (Korea) .... Vol. 4A
Tahiti .... Vol. 6A
Taiwan (Republic of China) .... Vol. 2A
Taiwan (Formosa) .... Vol. 2A
Taiwan, Japanese .... Vol. 2A, Vol. 4A
Tajikistan .... Vol. 6A
Takca .... Vol. 1B
Takse .... Vol. 1A
Talbotton, Ga. .... Vol. 1A
Talca .... Vol. 2A
Talladega, Ala. .... Vol. 1A
Tallinn 438
Tanganyika .... Vol. 6A
Tanganyika and Zanzibar .... Vol. 6A
Tanganyika (Tanzania), Kenya,
  Uganda .... Vol. 4A
Tanger .... 809, 814, Vol. 6A
Tangier, British Offices .... Vol. 3A
Tangier, French Offices 809, 814
Tangier, Spanish Offices .... Vol. 6A
Tannu Tuva .... Vol. 6A
Tanzania .... Vol. 6A
Tanzania-Zanzibar .... Vol. 6B
Tartu 461
Tasmania .... Vol. 1A
Tassa Gazzette .... Vol. 3B
Taxa de Guerra .... Vol. 4D, Vol. 5D
Taxyapom 421
Tchad .... Vol. 2A
Tchongking 786
T.C. overprinted on Cochin .... Vol. 3B
T.C., Postalari .... Vol. 6B
Te Betalen .... Vol. 1B, Vol. 5A, Vol. 6A
Tegucigalpa .... Vol. 3B
Teheran .... Vol. 3B
Tellico Plains, Tenn. .... Vol. 1A
Temesvar .... Vol. 3B
Ten Cents .... Vol. 1A
T.E.O. ovptd. on Turkey or France ... Vol. 2A, Vol. 6A
Terres Australes et Antarctiques
  Francaises 846
Territorio Insular Chileno (Chile #1061) ... Vol. 2A
Teruel Province .... Vol. 6A
Tete .... Vol. 6A
Tetuan .... Vol. 6A
Thailand, Thai .... Vol. 4B
Thailand (Occupation of Kedah) ... Vol. 4B
Thailand (Occupation of Kelantan) ... Vol. 4B
Thailand (Occupation of Malaya) ... Vol. 4B
Thailand (Occupation of Perlis) .... Vol. 4B
Thailand (Occupation of Trengganu) ... Vol. 4B
Thessaly .... Vol. 6B
Thomasville, Ga. .... Vol. 1A
Thrace .... Vol. 6A
Three Cents .... Vol. 1A
Thuringia, Thuringen .... Vol. 3A
Thurn and Taxis .... Vol. 3A
Tibet .... Vol. 6B
Tibet (Chinese province) .... Vol. 2A

Tibet, Chinese Offices .... Vol. 2A
Tical .... Vol. 6B
Tientsin (Chinese) .... Vol. 2A
Tientsin (German) .... Vol. 3A
Tientsin (Italian) .... Vol. 3B
Tiflis .... Vol. 3A
Timbre ovptd. on France 809
Timor .... Vol. 6B
Timor-Leste .... Vol. 6B
Timor Lorosae .... Vol. 1A, Vol. 6B
Tin Can Island .... Vol. 6B
Tjedan Solidarnosti
  (Yugoslavia #RA82) .... Vol. 6B
Tjenestefrimerke .... 165, Vol. 5A
Tlacotalpan .... Vol. 4B
Tobago .... Vol. 6B
Toga .... Vol. 6B
Togo, Togolaise .... Vol. 6B
Tokelau Islands .... Vol. 6B
Tolima .... Vol. 2A
Tonga .... Vol. 6B
Tongareva .... Vol. 5A
Tonk .... Vol. 3B
To Pay .... Vol. 3A
Toscano .... Vol. 3B
Tou .... Vol. 3B
Touva, Tovva .... Vol. 6A
Transcaucasian Federated Republics ... Vol. 6B
Trans-Jordan .... Vol. 4A, Vol. 5A
Trans-Jordan (Palestine Occ.) ..... Vol. 4A
Transkei .... Vol. 6A
Transvaal .... Vol. 6B
Transylvania .... Vol. 3B
Trasporto Pacchi .... Vol. 0D
Travancore .... Vol. 6A
Travancore-Cochin, State of .... Vol. 3B
Trebizonde .... Vol. 5B
Trengganu .... Vol. 4B
Trentino .... Vol. 1B
Trieste .... Vol. 1B, Vol. 3B, Vol. 6B
Trinidad .... Vol. 6B
Trinidad and Tobago .... Vol. 6B
Trinidad Society (Trinidad &
  Tobago #B1) .... Vol. 6B
Tripoli di Barberia (Tripoli) .... Vol. 3B
Tripoli, Fiera Campionaria .... Vol. 4A
Tripolitania .... Vol. 4A, Vol. 6B
Tripolitania (B.M.A.) .... Vol. 3A
Tristan da Cunha .... Vol. 6B
Trucial States .... Vol. 6B
Tsinghai .... Vol. 2A
Tsingtau .... Vol. 2A, Vol. 4A
T. Ta. C. .... Vol. 6B
Tullahoma, Tenn. .... Vol. 1A
Tumbes (Peru #129-133) .... Vol. 5A
Tunisia, Tunisie, Tunis, Tunisienne ... Vol. 6B
Turkestan, Russian .... Vol. 5B
Turkey, Turkiye, Turk .... Vol. 6B
Turkey (Greek Occupation) ... Vol. 3A, Vol. 6B
Turkey in Asia .... Vol. 6B
Turk Federe Devleti .... Vol. 6B
Turkish Empire, Austrian Offices ... Vol. 1B
Turkish Empire, British Offices .... Vol. 3A
Turkish Empire, French Offices 789
Turkish Empire, Georgian Offices ... Vol. 3A
Turkish Empire, German Offices ... Vol. 3A
Turkish Empire, Italian Offices .... Vol. 3B
Turkish Empire, Polish Offices .... Vol. 5A
Turkish Empire, Romanian Offices ... Vol. 5B
Turkish Empire, Russian Offices ... Vol. 5B
Turkish Occupation of Iran .... Vol. 3B
Turkish Republic of Northern Cyprus ... Vol. 6B
Turkish stamps surcharged or
  overprinted .... 289, Vol. 3A, Vol. 6A
Turkish Suzerainty of Egypt 350
Turkmenistan, Turkmenpocta ...... Vol. 6B
Turks and Caicos Islands .... Vol. 6B
Turks Islands .... Vol. 6B
Tuscaloosa, Ala. .... Vol. 1A
Tuscany .... Vol. 3B
Tuscumbia, Ala. .... Vol. 1A
Tuva Autonomous Region .... Vol. 6A
Tuvalu .... Vol. 6B
Two Cents (Conted. #53X5) .... Vol. 1A
Two Pence .... Vol. 1A
Two Sicilies .... Vol. 3B
Tyosen (Korea) .... Vol. 4A
Tyrol .... Vol. 1B

UAE ovptd. on Abu Dhabi .... Vol. 6B
U.A.R. .... 356, Vol. 6A, Vol. 6B
Ubangi, Ubangi-Shari .... Vol. 6B
Uganda, U.G. .... Vol. 6B
Uganda, and Kenya .... Vol. 4A
Uganda, Tanganyika, Kenya .... Vol. 4A
Ukraine, Ukraina .... Vol. 6B
Ukraine (German Occupation) .... Vol. 5B
Ukraine stamps surcharged .... Vol. 5B
Ukrainian Soviet Socialist Republic ... Vol. 6B
Ukraine, Western .... Vol. 6B
Uku Leta .... Vol. 1A
Ultramar .... Vol. 6A
Umm al Qiwain .... Vol. 6B
UNEF ovptd. on India .... Vol. 3B
UNESCO 777
U.N. Force in Congo or Gaza (India) ... Vol. 3B
Union Island, St. Vincent .... Vol. 5B
Union Islands .... Vol. 6B
Union of South Africa .... Vol. 6A
Union of Soviet Socialist Republics ... Vol. 5B

Uniontown, Ala. .... Vol. 1A
Unionville, S.C. .... Vol. 1A
United Arab Emirates .... Vol. 6B
United Arab Republic (UAR) .... 356, Vol. 6A, Vol. 6B
United Arab Republic, Egypt 356
United Arab Republic Issues for Syria ... Vol. 6A
United Kingdom .... Vol. 3A
United Nations .... Vol. 6B
United Nations European Office ... Vol. 1A, Vol. 6A
United Nations Offices in Geneva ... Vol. 1A
United Nations Offices in Vienna ... Vol. 1A
United Nations - Kosovo ..... Vol. 1A, Vol. 4A
United Nations - West New Guinea ... Vol. 1A
United State of Saurashtra .... Vol. 3B
United States Adm. of Canal Zone ... Vol. 1A
United States Adm. of Cuba ... Vol. 1A, Vol. 2A
United States Adm. of Guam ...... Vol. 1A
U. S. Adm. of Philippines ... Vol. 1A, Vol. 5A
U. S. Adm. of Puerto Rico .... Vol. 1A, Vol. 5B
U. S. Military Rule of Korea .... Vol. 4A
United States of America .... Vol. 1A
United States of Indonesia .... Vol. 3B
United States of New Granada .... Vol. 2A
United States, Offices in China ... Vol. 1A
Un Real 237
U.S. Zone (Germany) .... Vol. 3A
Universal Postal Union, Intl. Bureau ... Vol. 6A
UNTEA ovptd. on Netherlands
  New Guinea .... Vol. 1A, Vol. 3B
UNTEAT .... Vol. 6B
UPHA ROPA .... Vol. 4B
Upper Austria .... Vol. 1B
Upper Senegal and Niger .... Vol. 6B
Upper Silesia .... Vol. 6B
Upper Volta .... Vol. 1B
Urgente .... Vol. 6A
U.R.I. ovptd. on Yugoslavia .... Vol. 6B
Uruguay .... Vol. 6B
Urundi ovptd. on Congo .... Vol. 3A
Uskup .... Vol. 6B
U.S. Mail .... Vol. 1A
U.S.P.O. .... Vol. 1A
U.S.P.O. Despatch .... Vol. 1A
U.S.S.R. .... Vol. 5B
U. S. T.C. overprinted on Cochin ... Vol. 3B
Uzbekistan .... Vol. 6B

Vaitupu .... Vol. 6B
Valdosta, Ga. .... Vol. 1A
Valencia .... Vol. 6A
Valladolid Province .... Vol. 6A
Valona .... Vol. 3B
Valparaiso .... Vol. 6B
Vancouver Island .... Vol. 2A
Van Diemen's Land (Tasmania) ... Vol. 1A
Vanuatu .... Vol. 6B
Varldspost Kongress (Sweden #197) ... Vol. 6A
Vasa 544
Vathy 789
Vatican City, Vaticane, Vaticano ... Vol. 6B
Venda .... Vol. 6B
Venezia Giulia .... Vol. 1B, Vol. 3B
Venezia Tridentina .... Vol. 1B
Venezuela, Veneza., Venezolana ... Vol. 6B
Venizelist Government .... Vol. 3A
Vereinte Nationen .... Vol. 1A
Vetekeverria .... Vol. 1A
Victoria .... Vol. 1A
Victoria, Tex. .... Vol. 1A
Victoria Land .... Vol. 5A
Vienna .... Vol. 1A, Vol. 1B
Vienna Issues .... Vol. 3B
Viet Minh .... Vol. 6B
Viet Nam .... Vol. 6B
Viet Nam Buu Chinh .... Vol. 6B
Viet Nam Buu Dien .... Vol. 6B
Viet Nam Cong-Hoa .... Vol. 6B
Viet Nam Dan-Chu Cong-Hoa .... Vol. 6B
Viet Nam, Democratic Republic ... Vol. 6B
Viet Nam Doc-Lap .... Vol. 6B
Viet Nam, (Int. Com., India) ...... Vol. 3B
Viet Nam, North .... Vol. 6B
Viet Nam, Republic .... Vol. 6B
Viet Nam, South .... Vol. 6B
Villa Bella (Bolivia #97) .... Vol. 1B
Vilnius .... Vol. 4A, Vol. 5B
Vineta .... Vol. 3A
Virgin Islands .... Vol. 3A
Vladivostok 501
Vojna Uprava .... Vol. 6B
Volksrust .... Vol. 6B
Vom Empfanger .... 129, Vol. 3A
Vorarlberg .... Vol. 1B
V.R. ovptd. on Transvaal .... Vol. 2A, Vol. 6B
Vryburg .... Vol. 2A
Vuja-STT, Vujna-STT .... Vol. 6B

Wadhwan .... Vol. 3B
Walachia .... Vol. 5B
Wales & Monmouthshire .... Vol. 3A
Wallis and Futuna Islands .... Vol. 6B
Walterborough, S.C. .... Vol. 1A
War Board of Trade .... Vol. 6A
Warrenton, Ga. .... Vol. 1A
Warsaw, Warszawa .... Vol. 5B
Washington, Ga. .... Vol. 1A
Watermarks (British Colonies) ...... See table of contents

Weatherford, Tex. .... Vol. 1A
Weihnachten Joos van Cleve-Geburt
  Christi (Austria 2479) .... Vol. 1B
Wenden, Wendensche .... Vol. 5B
Western Army .... Vol. 4A
Western Australia .... Vol. 6A
Western Samoa .... Vol. 5B
Western Szechwan .... Vol. 2A
Western Thrace (Greek Occupation) ... Vol. 6B
Western Turkey .... Vol. 3A
Western Ukraine .... Vol. 6B
West Irian .... Vol. 3B
West New Guinea .... Vol. 1A, Vol. 3B
West Saxony .... Vol. 3A
Wet and dry printings .... Vol. 1A
Wharton's U.S. P.O. Despatch .... Vol. 1A
White Russia .... Vol. 1B
Wiederaufbauspende .... Vol. 3A
Wilayah Persekutuan .... Vol. 4B
Wilkesboro, N.C. .... Vol. 1A
Williams City Post .... Vol. 1A
Winnsborough, S.C. .... Vol. 1A
Wir sind frei 31
Wn. .... Vol. 4A
Wohnungsbau .... Vol. 3A
Wolmaransstad .... Vol. 6B
World Health Organization .... Vol. 6A
World Intellectual Property
  Organization .... Vol. 6A
World Meteorological Organization ... Vol. 6A
Worldwide .... Vol. 3A
Wrangel issues .... Vol. 5B
Wurttemberg .... Vol. 3A
Wytheville, Va. .... Vol. 1A

Xeimappa 420

Yambo .... Vol. 6A
Y.A.R. .... Vol. 6B
Yca .... Vol. 5A
Yemen .... Vol. 6B
Yemen Arab Republic .... Vol. 6B
Yemen People's Republic .... Vol. 6B
Yemen, People's Democratic Rep. ... Vol. 6B
Yen, Yn. .... Vol. 1A, Vol. 4A
Ykp. H.P., Ykpaiha .... Vol. 6B
Yksi Markka 544
Yuan .... Vol. 2A
Yucatan .... Vol. 4B
Yudenich, Gen. .... Vol. 5B
Yugoslavia .... Vol. 6B
Yugoslavia (German Occupation) ... Vol. 6B
Yugoslavia (Italian Occupation) ... Vol. 6B
Yugoslavia (Trieste) .... Vol. 6B
Yugoslavia (Zone B) .... Vol. 6B
Yugoslavia Offices Abroad .... Vol. 6B
Yugoslavia stamps overprinted
  and surcharged .... Vol. 1B
Yunnan (China) .... Vol. 2A
Yunnan Fou, Yunnansen 786

Za Crveni Krst (Yugoslavia #RA2) .... Vol. 6B
Z. Afr. Republiek, Z.A.R. .... Vol. 6B
Zaire .... Vol. 6B
Zambezia .... Vol. 6B
Zambia .... Vol. 6B
Zante .... Vol. 3B
Zanzibar .... Vol. 6B
Zanzibar, French Offices 789
Zanzibar (Kenya, Uganda,
  Tanganyika) .... Vol. 4A
Zanzibar-Tanzania .... Vol. 6B
Z.A.R. ovptd. on Cape of Good Hope ... Vol. 2A
Zelaya .... Vol. 5A
Zentraler Kurierdienst .... Vol. 3A
Zil Eloigne Sesel .... Vol. 6A
Zil Elwagne Sesel .... Vol. 6A
Zil Elwannyen Sesel .... Vol. 6A
Zimbabwe .... Vol. 6B
Zimska Pomoc ovptd. on Italy ..... Vol. 6B
Zone A (Trieste) .... Vol. 3B
Zone B (Istria) .... Vol. 6B
Zone B (Trieste) .... Vol. 6B
Zone Francaise .... Vol. 3A
Zuid Afrika .... Vol. 5A, Vol. 6A
Zuidafrikaansche Republiek .... Vol. 6B
Zuidwest Afrika .... Vol. 6A
Zululand .... Vol. 6D
Zurich .... Vol. 6A

Currency conversion

Country	Dollar	Pound	S Franc	Yen	HK $	Euro	Cdn $	Aus $
Australia	1.4671	1.8673	1.7449	0.0104	0.1879	1.6206	1.1114	—
Canada	1.3201	1.6802	1.5701	0.0094	0.1691	1.4582	—	0.8998
European Union	0.9053	1.1523	1.0767	0.0064	0.1160	—	0.6858	0.6171
Hong Kong	7.8071	9.9370	9.2853	0.0554	—	8.6238	5.9140	5.3215
Japan	140.91	179.35	167.59	—	18.049	155.65	106.74	96.047
Switzerland	0.8408	1.0702	—	0.0060	0.1077	0.9288	0.6369	0.5731
United Kingdom	0.7857	—	0.9344	0.0056	0.1006	0.8679	0.5952	0.5355
United States	—	1.2728	1.1893	0.0071	0.1281	1.1046	0.7575	0.6816

Country	Currency	U.S. $ Equiv.
Cyprus	euro	1.1046
Czech Republic	koruna	.0446
Denmark	krone	.1481
Djibouti	franc	.0056
Dominica	East Caribbean dollar	.3704
Dominican Republic	peso	.0172
Ecuador	US dollar	1.0000
Egypt	pound	.0323
Equatorial Guinea	CFA franc	.0017
Eritrea	nakfa	.0667
Estonia	euro	1.1046
Ethiopia	birr	.0177
Falkland Islands	pound	1.2728
Faroe Islands	krone	.1481
Fiji	dollar	.4547
Finland	euro	1.1046
Aland Islands	euro	1.1046
France	euro	1.1046
French Polynesia	Community of French Pacific (CFP) franc	.0093
French So. & Antarctic Terr.	euro	1.1046

Source: xe.com Jan. 1, 2024. Figures reflect values as of Jan. 1, 2024.

Pronunciation Symbols

ə	....	banana, collide, abut
ˈə, ˌə	....	humdrum, abut
ə	....	immediately preceding \l\, \n\, \m\, \ŋ\, as in battle, mitten, eaten, and sometimes open \ˈō-pᵊm\, lock and key \-ᵊŋ-\; immediately following \l\, \m\, \r\, as often in French table, prisme, titre
ər	....	further, merger, bird
ˈər-, ˈə-r	....	as in two different pronunciations of hurry \ˈhər-ē, ˈhə-rē\
a	....	mat, map, mad, gag, snap, patch
ā	....	day, fade, date, aorta, drape, cape
ä	....	bother, cot, and, with most American speakers, father, cart
ȧ	....	father as pronounced by speakers who do not rhyme it with bother; French patte
au̇	....	now, loud, out
b	....	baby, rib
ch	....	chin, nature \ˈnā-chər\
d	....	did, adder
e	....	bet, bed, peck
ˈē, ˌē	....	beat, nosebleed, evenly, easy
ē	....	easy, mealy
f	....	fifty, cuff
g	....	go, big, gift
h	....	hat, ahead
hw	....	whale as pronounced by those who do not have the same pronunciation for both whale and wail
i	....	tip, banish, active
ī	....	site, side, buy, tripe
j	....	job, gem, edge, join, judge
k	....	kin, cook, ache
ḵ	....	German ich, Buch; one pronunciation of loch
l	....	lily, pool
m	....	murmur, dim, nymph
n	....	no, own
ⁿ	....	indicates that a preceding vowel or diphthong is pronounced with the nasal passages open, as in French un bon vin blanc \œⁿ-bōⁿ-vaⁿ-bläⁿ\
ŋ	....	sing \ˈsiŋ\, singer \ˈsiŋ-ər\, finger \ˈfiŋ-gər\, ink \ˈiŋk\
ō	....	bone, know, beau
ȯ	....	saw, all, gnaw, caught
œ	....	French bœuf, German Hölle
œ̄	....	French feu, German Höhle
ȯi	....	coin, destroy
p	....	pepper, lip
r	....	red, car, rarity
s	....	source, less
sh	....	as in shy, mission, machine, special (actually, this is a single sound, not two); with a hyphen between, two sounds as in grasshopper \ˈgras-ˌhä-pər\
t	....	tie, attack, late, later, latter
th	....	as in thin, ether (actually, this is a single sound, not two); with a hyphen between, two sounds as in knighthood \ˈnīt-ˌhu̇d\
th	....	then, either, this (actually, this is a single sound, not two)
ü	....	rule, youth, union \ˈyün-yən\, few \ˈfyü\
u̇	....	pull, wood, book, curable \ˈkyu̇r-ə-bəl\, fury \ˈfyu̇r-ē\
ue	....	German füllen, hübsch
ṻe	....	French rue, German fühlen
v	....	vivid, give
w	....	we, away
y	....	yard, young, cue \ˈkyü\, mute \ˈmyüt\, union \ˈyün-yən\
ʸ	....	indicates that during the articulation of the sound represented by the preceding character the front of the tongue has substantially the position it has for the articulation of the first sound of yard, as in French digne \dēnʸ\
z	....	zone, raise
zh	....	as in vision, azure \ˈa-zhər\ (actually, this is a single sound, not two); with a hyphen between, two sounds as in hogshead \ˈhȯgz-ˌhed, ˈhägz-\
\	....	slant line used in pairs to mark the beginning and end of a transcription: \ˈpen\
ˈ	....	mark preceding a syllable with primary (strongest) stress: \ˈpen-mən-ˌship\
ˌ	....	mark preceding a syllable with secondary (medium) stress: \ˈpen-mən-ˌship\
-	....	mark of syllable division
( )	....	indicate that what is symbolized between is present in some utterances but not in others: factory \ˈfak-t(ə-)rē\
÷	....	indicates that many regard as unacceptable the pronunciation variant immediately following: cupola \ˈkyü-pə-lə, ÷-ˌlō\

The system of pronunciation is used by permission from Merriam-Webster's Collegiate® Dictionary, Tenth Edition ©1993 by Merriam-Webster Inc., publisher of the Merriam-Webster® dictionaries.

Vols. 2A-2B number additions, deletions and changes

Number in 2024 Catalogue	Number in 2025 Catalogue

Cilicia
83Cc..................83Cd
83dCd.................83Ce

Cyprus
new...................9B
26b..................deleted